W9-BNH-404
3 2109 00920 5999

WORLD TREATY INDEX

Volume 1

INTRODUCTION

MAIN ENTRY SECTION

League of Nations Treaty Series

Volume 2

MAIN ENTRY SECTION

United Nations Treaty Series: Series I, Numbers 1–6485

Volume 3

MAIN ENTRY SECTION

United Nations Treaty Series: Series I, Numbers 6486–10841; Series II, Numbers 1–657

National Treaty Collections

Volume 4

CHRONOLOGICAL SECTION

PARTY SECTION

INTERNATIONAL ORGANIZATION SECTION

UNTS SELF-INDEX SECTION

Volume 5

TOPIC SECTION

WORLD TREATY INDEX

CHRONOLOGICAL SECTION
PARTY SECTION
INTERNATIONAL ORGANIZATION SECTION
UNTS SELF-INDEX SECTION

VOLUME 4

PETER H. ROHN

Associate Professor of Political Science
University of Washington

Santa Barbara, California
Oxford, England

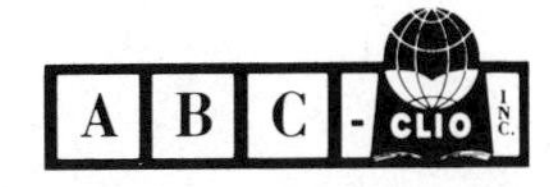

Library of Congress Catalog Card Number 73-83352
ISBN Clothbound 5-Volume Set 0-87436-125-7
ISBN Clothbound 6-Volume Set 0-87436-132-X
ISBN Clothbound Volume 4 0-87436-129-X

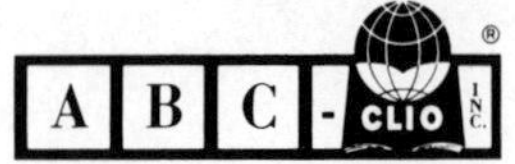

American Bibliographical Center—Clio Press, Inc.
2040 Alameda Padre Serra
Santa Barbara, California

European Bibliographical Center—Clio Press
Woodside House
Hinksey Hill
Oxford OX1 5BE, England

Designed by Barbara Monahan
Composed by Datagraphics Press
Printed and bound by Halliday Lithograph Corporation
in the United States of America

Contents

List of Abbreviations

Accept UN Charter	Unilateral declaration accepting UN Charter obligations
Admin Cooperation	Administrative Cooperation
African Coffee Org	African Coffee Organization
African Devel Bank	African Development Bank
African Insur Org	African Insurance Organization
African Tech Org	African Technical Organization
Afromalagasy Coffee	Afro-Malagasy Coffee Organization
Afromalagasy Org	Afro-Malagasy Organization
AID (Int Devel)	Agency for International Development
Allied Milit Occup	Allied Military Occupation
Anglo-Egypt Sudan	Anglo-Egyptian Sudan
Asian Devel Bank	Asian Development Bank
Asian Productivity	Asian Productivity Organization
Bel-Lux Econ Union	Belgium-Luxembourg Economic Union
BENELUX Econ Union	Belgium-Netherlands-Luxembourg Economic Union
Bnk Int Settlement	Bank for International Settlements
British Occup Germ	British Occupied Germany
Brit Solomon Is	British Solomon Islands
Brit Virgin Is	British Virgin Islands
Central Afri Power	Central African Power Company
Central Afri Rep	Central African Republic
Central Am Bank	Central American Bank
CERN (Nuc Resrch)	European Organization for Nuclear Research
China People's Rep	People's Republic of China
Cmte Industr Devel	Committee for Industrial Development
COMECON (Econ Aid)	Council for Mutual Economic Assistance
Consul/Citizenship	Consular Matters and Citizenship
Customs Coop Coun	Customs Cooperation Council
East Afri Service	East African Common Services Organization
ECSC (Coal/Steel)	European Coal and Steel Community
EEC (Econ Commnty)	European Economic Community
EFTA (Free Trade)	European Free Trade Association
EURATOM	European Atomic Energy Commission
Eur Foot Mouth Dis	European Commission for the Control of Foot and Mouth Disease
EUROCONTROL	European Organization for the Safety of Air Navigation
Eur Plant Protect	European and Mediterranean Plant Protection Organization
Eur Space Research	European Space Research Organization
Eur Space Vehicle	European Space Vehicle Launcher Development Organization
FAO (Food Agri)	Food and Agricultural Organization of the United Nations
Fed Malay States	Federation of Malay States
Fed of Malaya	Federation of Malaya
Fed Rhod/Nyasaland	Federation of Rhodesia and Nyasaland
French Occup Germ	French Occupied Germany
Fr Equatorial Afri	French Equatorial Africa
GATT (Tariff/Trade)	General Agreement on Tariffs and Trade
Gen Communications	General Communications
General HEW	General Health, Education and Welfare

General IGO	General Intergovernmental Organizations
Hague Private IL	The Hague Conference on Private International Law
IAEA (Atom Energy)	International Atomic Energy Agency
IBRD Project	International Bank for Reconstruction and Development Project
IBRD (World Bank)	International Bank for Reconstruction and Development
ICAO (Civil Aviat)	International Civil Aviation Organization
ICJ (Int Court)	International Court of Justice
ICJ Option Clause	International Court of Justice Optional Clause Unilateral declaration accepting ICJ optional clause, or Unilateral declaration regarding UN General Assembly in connection with ICJ optional clause, or Unilateral limited declaration regarding ICJ optional clause
IDA (Devel Assoc)	International Development Association
IFC (Finance Corp)	International Finance Corporation
IGO Establishment	Intergovernmental Organization Establishment
IGO Multilat	Three or more IGO's and no State
IGO Operations	Intergovernmental Organization Operations
IGO Status/Immunit	Intergovernmental Organizational Privileges and Immunities
ILO Labor	International Labour Organization Labor Matters
ILO (Labor Org)	International Labour Organization
IMCO (Maritime Org)	Inter-Governmental Maritime Consultative Organization
IMF (Fund)	International Monetary Fund
Indo-Pac Fish Coun	Indo-Pacific Fisheries Council
Int Bureau Educ	International Bureau of Education
Int Coffee Org	International Coffee Organization
Int Coun Expl Sea	International Council for the Exploration of the Sea
Inter-Allied Com	Inter-Allied Commission
Inter-Am Devel Bnk	Inter-American Development Bank
Inter-Am Nuc Energ	Inter-American Nuclear Energy Commission
Int Exhibit Bureau	International Exhibition Bureau
Intgov Eur Migrat	Intergovernmental Committee for European Migration
Int Org Metrology	International Organization of Legal Metrology
Int Rail Transport	Central Office for International Railway Transport
Int Relief Union	International Relief Union
Int Rice Com	International Rice Commission
Int Sugar Council	International Sugar Council
Int Whaling Com	International Whaling Commission
Int Wheat Coun	International Wheat Council
Int Wine Office	International Vine and Wine Office
IRO (Refugee Org)	International Refugees Organization
It Aegean Colonies	Italian Colonies in the Aegean
ITU (Telecommun)	International Telecommunication Union
LAFTA (Free Trade)	Latin American Free Trade Association
Lat Am Nuclear Arm	Agency for the Prohibition of Nuclear Weapons in Latin America
Medit Fish Council	Mediterranean Fisheries Council
Micronesia (US)	Micronesia (US Trust Territories in the Pacific)
Milit Assistance	Military Assistance
Milit Installation	Military Installations
Milit Occupation	Military Occupation
Milit Servic/Citiz	Military Service and Citizenship
Mostfavored Nation	Most Favored Nation
NATO (North Atlan)	North Atlantic Treaty Organization
NE Atlantic Fish	Northeast Atlantic Fisheries Commission
Netherld Antilles	Netherlands Antilles
New Hebrides Is	New Hebrides Islands
Non-IBRD Project	Non-International Bank for Reconstruction and Development Project
Non-ILO Labor	Non-International Labour Organization Labor Matters
Northern Territ	Northern Territories
NW Atlantic Fish	International Commission for the Northwest Atlantic Fisheries
OAS (Am States)	Organization of American States
OAU (Afri Unity)	Organization of African Unity
OECD (Econ Coop)	Organization for Economic Co-operation and Development
Org Ctrl Am States	Organization of Central American States
Org Rail Collabor	Soviet Railroad Organization
Other HEW	Other Health, Education and Welfare
Other Party Combin	More than one State and more than one IGO, or Other combination of parties

Other Unilat Decla	Other unilateral declaration
Pan Am Health Org	Pan American Health Organization
Patents/Copyrights	Patents and Copyrights
Peace/Disarmament	Peace and Disarmament
Petrol Export Org	Organization of Petroleum Exporting Countries
Portug Colonies	Portuguese Colonies
Portug East Africa	Portuguese East Africa
Portug West Africa	Portuguese West Africa
Privil/Immunities	Privileges and Immunities
Refrigeration Inst	International Institute for Refrigeration
Rhine Navigation	Central Commission for the Navigation of the Rhine
Russ Fed Sov Rep	Russian Federation of Soviet Republics
Scientific Project	Scientific Projects
SEATO (SE Asia)	Southeast Asia Treaty Organization
Serb/Croat/Slovene	The Kingdom of the Serbs, Croats and Slovenes
South Africa	Union of South Africa
South Pacific Com	South Pacific Commission
Spanish Colonies	Spanish Colonies in Africa
Special Decla ICJ	Unilateral special declaration regarding ICJ
Specif Claim/Waive	Specific Claims and Waivers
Specif Goods/Equip	Specific Goods and Equipment
State/IGO Group	One State and mixed group of IGO-State partners, or One State and three or more IGO's, or One State and two IGO's, or Two or more States and one IGO
States Multilat	Three or more military governments and one State, or Three or more States and no IGO, or Three or more States under FAO auspices, or Three or more States under IAEA auspices, or Three or more States under ILO auspices, or Three or more States under UN auspices, or Three or more States under UNESCO auspices, or Three or more States under WHO auspices
Subsahara Tech Com	Commission for Technical Cooperation in Africa South of the Sahara
Tech Assistance	Technical Assistance
Trinidad/Tobago	Trinidad and Tobago
Turk-Caicose Is	Turk-Caicose Islands
UK Great Britain	United Kingdom of Great Britain and Northern Ireland
Ukrainian SSR	Ukrainian Soviet Socialist Republic
UN Charter	United Nations Charter
UN Emergency Fund	United Nations Emergency Fund
UNESCO (Educ/Cult)	United Nations Scientific and Cultural Organization
UN Hi Com Refugees	Office of the United Nations High Commissioner for Refugees
UNICEF (Children)	United Nations Children's Fund
UNIDO (Industrial)	United Nations Industrial Development Organization
United Arab Rep	United Arab Republic
UNKRA (Korean Rec)	United Nations Commission for the Unification and Rehabilitation of Korea
UN Mission Congo	United Nations Mission to the Congo
UN Relief Palestin	United Nations Relief and Works Agency for Palestine Refugees in the Near East
UNRRA (Relief)	United Nations Relief and Rehabilitation Association
UN Special Fund	United Nations Special Fund
UNTAB (Tech Assis)	United Nations Technical Assistance Board
UPU (Postal Union)	Universal Postal Union
US Agri Commod Aid	US Agricultural Commodity Aid
USA (United States)	United States of America
US Occup Germ	United States Occupied Germany
USSR (Soviet Union)	Union of Soviet Socialist Republics
Vatican/Holy See	The Vatican and the Holy See
WEU (West Europe)	Western European Union
WHO (World Health)	World Health Organization
WMO (Meteorology)	World Meteorological Organization
W Pacif Hi Command	West Pacific High Command

CHRONOLOGICAL SECTION

User's Guide

This is one of the five specialized sections of the INDEX. Each specialized section lists treaties in a different order: (1) by date of signature, (2) by party, (3) by international organizations mentioned in the treaty text, (4) by the topical categories of the UNTS Index and (5) by the topical categories of this INDEX.

Within each section there is a standard set of information per treaty: (1) parties, (2) date of signature, (3) topic, (4) citation and (5) treaty number.

In many cases a user will satisfy a query within one of the five specialized sections and will not need to go to the Main Entry Section (Volumes 1–3). It is for limited use of this kind that the present USER'S GUIDE has been designed. However, if the user is unfamiliar with the general format and search techniques of this INDEX, or if the search involves more than one specialized section, it is advisable to consult the Introduction in Volume 1.

Sample of Chronological Section

DATE	PARTY ONE	PARTY TWO	TOPIC	CITATION	NUMBER
1943					
01 Dec	UK Great Britain	USA (United States)	Scientific Project	3UNTS209	100033
1944					
23 Mar	Albania	Yugoslavia	General Military	1UNTS81	100015
1945					
24 Oct	Netherlands	Switzerland	Finance	3UNTS73	100025
06 Nov	Netherlands	Norway	Finance	2UNTS5	100017
07 Nov	Multilateral		IGO Establishment	2UNTS17	100018
15 Nov	Multilateral		Atomic Energy	3UNTS123	100026
30 Nov	Netherlands	Sweden	Finance	2UNTS27	100019

Date. This section is ordered chronologically by date of signature. Other dates (ratification, force, registration, accession, etc.) can be found in the Main Entry Section. Multiple dates of signature are represented only by the most recent date.

Party One. In case of a bilateral treaty this column identifies one of the two parties. In case of a multilateral treaty it shows the word "Multilateral."

Party Two. In case of a bilateral treaty this column identifies the other of the two parties. In a multilateral treaty it remains blank.

Topic. This column identifies the single dominant theme of each treaty. For a full list of INDEX topics see Volume 1, Introduction, Thesaurus, Topic List. The same information is reproduced also in the beginning of Volume 5.

Citation. This column identifies the printed source where the full text of the treaty can be found. For details on abbreviations see Volume 1, Introduction, Thesaurus, Sources and Citations.

Treaty Number. This column identifies the serial number of each treaty under which it is listed in the Main Entry Section. See that location for all further information on any treaty.

League of Nations Treaty Series

DATE	PARTY ONE	PARTY TWO	TOPIC	CITATION	NUMBER
1856					
12 Jun	Austria	Greece	Specif Goods/Equip	2LTS157	300061
1874					
28 Mar	Austria	Greece	Extradition	2LTS169	300063
1886					
09 Sep	Multilateral		Patents/Copyrights	123LTS233	302816
1889					
31 May	Belgium	Netherlands	Extradition	137LTS261	303160
1897					
20 Jan	Germany	Greece	Water Transport	2LTS107	300053
1902					
16 Apr	France	UK Great Britain	Customs	1LTS79	300010
1904					
02 Mar	Cuba	USA (United States)	Territory Boundary	127LTS143	302915
18 Mar	Multilateral		Humanitarian	1LTS83	300011
16 Sep	Austria	Greece	Claims and Debts	2LTS161	300062
21 Dec	Austria-Hungary	Greece	Extradition	2LTS173	300064
1907					
12 Mar	Germany	Greece	Extradition	2LTS111	300054
19 Sep	Canada	France	Customs	1LTS95	300012
1908					
13 Nov	Multilateral		General Ad Hoc	1LTS217	300015
1909					
08 Apr	Brazil	Spain	Dispute Settlement	88LTS86	301987
1910					
20 Aug	Multilateral		Patents/Copyrights	155LTS179	303576
01 Dec	Germany	Greece	Claims and Debts	2LTS123	300055
1911					
02 May	Germany	Sweden	General Economic	2LTS59	300047
22 Jul	Argentina	Venezuela	Dispute Settlement	28LTS287	300715
1912					
12 Jan	Multilateral		Sanitation	4LTS281	300112
23 Jan	Multilateral		Sanitation	8LTS187	300222
07 Apr	Argentina	UK Great Britain	Postal Service	6LTS337	300165
05 Jun	Multilateral		Telecommunications	1LTS135	300013
1913					
10 Apr	Liberia	UK Great Britain	Water Transport	1LTS205	300014
04 Nov	Chile	Netherlands	Consul/Citizenship	84LTS79	301904
18 Dec	Netherlands	USA (United States)	Dispute Settlement	74LTS157	301737
31 Dec	Cuba	Netherlands	Consul/Citizenship	14LTS29	300366

DATE	PARTY ONE	PARTY TWO	TOPIC	CITATION	NUMBER
1914					
20 Mar	Multilateral		Patents/Copyrights	1LTS243	300016
06 Apr	Colombia	USA (United States)	Dispute Settlement	9LTS302	300263
21 Apr	Multilateral		Sanitation	5LTS394	300144
11 Jun	France	Switzerland	General Amity	12LTS361	300329
06 Aug	France	UK Great Britain	Admin Cooperation	10LTS333	300278
15 Sep	Spain	USA (United States)	Dispute Settlement	89LTS427	302030
16 Nov	Chile	Colombia	Extradition	82LTS243	301875
16 Nov	Chile	Colombia	Dispute Settlement	114LTS111	302659
1915					
28 Feb	Paraguay	Uruguay	Admin Cooperation	15LTS195	300393
1917					
25 Jun	Liberia	UK Great Britain	General Ad Hoc	5LTS39	300115
18 Jul	Peru	Uruguay	Dispute Settlement	14LTS359	300384
1918					
11 Apr	Argentina	Uruguay	Territory Boundary	14LTS367	300385
12 Nov	Italy	Switzerland	Land Transport	25LTS369	300625
1919					
06 Mar	Greece	Spain	Claims and Debts	3LTS81	300092
04 Apr	Brazil	UK Great Britain	General Amity	5LTS45	300116
03 Sep	France	Poland	Visas	1LTS337	300028
10 Sep	Multilateral		Admin Cooperation	8LTS25	300202
10 Sep	Multilateral		Health/Educ/Welfare	8LTS11	300201
10 Sep	Multilateral		General Trade	7LTS331	300200
10 Sep	Multilateral		Reparations	2LTS44	300045
10 Sep	Multilateral		General Economic	2LTS35	300044
10 Sep	Multilateral		Reparations	2LTS29	300043
10 Sep	Multilateral		Reparations	2LTS21	300042
30 Sep	France	Italy	ILO Labor	5LTS279	300133
06 Nov	Switzerland	UK Great Britain	Air Transport	1LTS37	300005
12 Nov	Japan	UK Great Britain	Reparations	6LTS333	300164
27 Nov	Bulgaria	Greece	Consul/Citizenship	1LTS67	300009
09 Dec	Multilateral		Territory Boundary	5LTS335	300140
09 Dec	France	Switzerland	Air Transport	1LTS29	300004
1920					
09 Jan	Germany	Poland	Admin Cooperation	9LTS77	300245
09 Jan	Austria	Poland	General Economic	7LTS163	300185
10 Jan	France	UK Great Britain	Telecommunications	5LTS53	300117
10 Jan	France	UK Great Britain	Claims and Debts	1LTS249	300017
18 Jan	Multilateral		Admin Cooperation	12LTS321	300323
22 Jan	Belgium	Portugal	Customs	3LTS149	300096
22 Jan	Romania	UK Great Britain	Commodity Trade	1LTS257	300018
26 Jan	Denmark	Sweden	Water Transport	14LTS273	300379
02 Feb	Estonia	USSR (Soviet Union)	Peace/Disarmament	11LTS29	300289
09 Feb	Multilateral		Territory Boundary	2LTS7	300041

DATE	PARTY ONE	PARTY TWO	TOPIC	CITATION	NUMBER
1920 (Cont.)					
11 Feb	Muscat and Oman	UK Great Britain	Water Transport	5LTS59	300118
12 Feb	UK Great Britain	USSR (Soviet Union)	General Military	1LTS263	300019
19 Feb	France	Italy	Non-ILO Labor	8LTS41	300204
27 Feb	Sweden	USA (United States)	Patents/Copyrights	2LTS147	300059
28 Feb	Switzerland	UK Great Britain	Postal Service	6LTS9	300145
29 Feb	Multilateral		Admin Cooperation	127LTS433	302930
01 Mar	France	Germany	Admin Cooperation	1LTS367	300030
03 Mar	France	Germany	Non-ILO Labor	8LTS45	300205
03 Mar	Sweden	UK Great Britain	Postal Service	5LTS63	300119
08 Mar	Belgium	Netherlands	Telecommunications	1LTS25	300003
15 Mar	Germany	Switzerland	Customs	12LTS19	300303
20 Mar	Czechoslovakia	France	Visas	3LTS139	300095
21 Mar	Persia	UK Great Britain	General Trade	4LTS47	300102
22 Mar	Estonia	Latvia	Dispute Settlement	2LTS187	300066
25 Mar	France	Germany	Claims and Debts	1LTS347	300029
25 Mar	Multilateral		Finance	1LTS45	300006
26 Mar	Argentina	Italy	Non-ILO Labor	15LTS271	300400
26 Mar	Chile	Sweden	Dispute Settlement	4LTS271	300111
05 Apr	Bolivia	UK Great Britain	General Trade	1LTS271	300020
07 Apr	Portugal	UK Great Britain	Non-ILO Labor	5LTS297	300134
13 Apr	Netherlands	UK Great Britain	Extradition	1LTS275	300021
19 Apr	Germany	USSR (Soviet Union)	Reparations	2LTS63	300048
20 Apr	France	Greece	General Aid	3LTS93	300093
20 Apr	Germany	Latvia	Reparations	2LTS71	300049
23 Apr	Belgium	Germany	Admin Cooperation	12LTS29	300305
24 Apr	Multilateral		General Economic	136LTS381	303135
24 Apr	France	UK Great Britain	Specific Resources	1LTS281	300022
26 Apr	China	UK Great Britain	Postal Service	5LTS83	300120
26 Apr	France	UK Great Britain	Admin Cooperation	1LTS287	300023
01 May	Multilateral		Air Transport	11LTS173	300297
05 May	France	Germany	Dispute Settlement	8LTS55	300206
06 May	Portugal	UK Great Britain	Territory Boundary	4LTS93	300103
08 May	Germany	Hungary	Reparations	2LTS79	300050
10 May	Finland	Sweden	Dispute Settlement	2LTS141	300058
11 May	Netherlands	Venezuela	General Amity	7LTS85	300176
11 May	Germany	Netherlands	Loans and Credits	3LTS153	300097
11 May	Multilateral		Finance	1LTS15	300001
19 May	France	Germany	Customs	1LTS383	300031
01 Jun	China	Persia	General Amity	9LTS17	300240
01 Jun	Germany	Hungary	General Economic	7LTS207	300187
04 Jun	Multilateral		Peace/Disarmament	6LTS187	300152
07 Jun	Austria	Czechoslovakia	Consul/Citizenship	3LTS189	300098
08 Jun	France	Portugal	Customs	1LTS393	300032
21 Jun	Multilateral		Health/Educ/Welfare	8LTS65	300207
25 Jun	Germany	UK Great Britain	Admin Cooperation	5LTS303	300135
26 Jun	Denmark	Iceland	Postal Service	12LTS323	300324
29 Jun	Czechoslovakia	Germany	Consul/Citizenship	20LTS85	300509
29 Jun	Czechoslovakia	Germany	General Economic	17LTS139	300431
29 Jun	Czechoslovakia	Germany	General Economic	17LTS69	300430
29 Jun	Sweden	USA (United States)	Consul/Citizenship	2LTS153	300060
30 Jun	France	Germany	Dispute Settlement	8LTS79	300208
30 Jun	Multilateral		Patents/Copyrights	1LTS59	300008
01 Jul	France	Germany	Territory Boundary	8LTS87	300209
01 Jul	Netherlands	UK Great Britain	Dispute Settlement	1LTS291	300024
02 Jul	Switzerland	UK Great Britain	Extradition	1LTS53	300007
05 Jul	Multilateral		Dispute Settlement	2LTS241	300070
06 Jul	Norway	UK Great Britain	Postal Service	5LTS107	300121
07 Jul	Germany	USSR (Soviet Union)	Reparations	2LTS85	300051
08 Jul	Japan	UK Great Britain	Admin Cooperation	1LTS23	300002
09 Jul	Belgium	Germany	Peace/Disarmament	12LTS45	300307
09 Jul	Germany	Switzerland	Commodity Trade	12LTS25	300304
12 Jul	Lithuania	USSR (Soviet Union)	Peace/Disarmament	3LTS106	300094
14 Jul	Finland	Norway	Specific Resources	1LTS317	300027
15 Jul	Germany	Latvia	Dispute Settlement	2LTS91	300052
20 Jul	Estonia	UK Great Britain	Mostfavored Nation	1LTS295	300025

DATE	PARTY ONE	PARTY TWO	TOPIC	CITATION	NUMBER
1920 (Cont.)					
24 Jul	Belgium	France	Reparations	1LTS311	300026
27 Jul	Denmark	Finland	Telecommunications	19LTS71	300484
30 Jul	France	Saar	Extradition	27LTS241	300687
02 Aug	Austria	Czechoslovakia	Finance	32LTS365	300826
03 Aug	Austria	France	Claims and Debts	5LTS355	300141
05 Aug	Multilateral		Territory Boundary	2LTS49	300046
10 Aug	Multilateral		Territory Boundary	28LTS225	300710
10 Aug	Multilateral		Consul/Citizenship	28LTS223	300711
11 Aug	Latvia	USSR (Soviet Union)	Peace/Disarmament	2LTS195	300067
14 Aug	Czechoslovakia	Serb/Croat/Slovene	General Amity	6LTS209	300154
20 Aug	Denmark	UK Great Britain	Postal Service	5LTS129	300122
23 Aug	Austria	Czechoslovakia	Health/Educ/Welfare	3LTS229	300099
27 Aug	France	Italy	Commodity Trade	8LTS95	300210
30 Aug	Denmark	Germany	Telecommunications	14LTS257	300377
01 Sep	Austria	Germany	General Economic	4LTS201	300107
01 Sep	Austria	Germany	Finance	2LTS132	300057
07 Sep	Belgium	France	General Military	2LTS127	300056
12 Sep	France	Italy	Telecommunications	1LTS397	300033
14 Sep	Portugal	USA (United States)	Dispute Settlement	7LTS253	300191
14 Sep	Germany	Switzerland	Air Transport	2LTS331	300087
16 Sep	France	Netherlands	General Transport	12LTS213	300312
20 Sep	Germany	Poland	Admin Cooperation	9LTS103	300246
22 Sep	Austria	UK Great Britain	Admin Cooperation	5LTS309	300136
22 Sep	Greece	UK Great Britain	Admin Cooperation	2LTS367	300090
28 Sep	Latvia	Lithuania	Dispute Settlement	2LTS234	300068
04 Oct	Austria	Belgium	Claims and Debts	5LTS371	300142
05 Oct	Belgium	UK Great Britain	Postal Service	5LTS147	300123
06 Oct	Belgium	Netherlands	Land Transport	18LTS247	300467
07 Oct	Lithuania	Poland	Territory Boundary	8LTS173	300221
11 Oct	Italy	Netherlands	Land Transport	18LTS253	300468
12 Oct	Poland	USSR (Soviet Union)	Peace/Disarmament	4LTS7	300101
14 Oct	Finland	USSR (Soviet Union)	Peace/Disarmament	3LTS5	300091
14 Oct	Norway	Portugal	Water Transport	2LTS237	300069
18 Oct	Czechoslovakia	Serb/Croat/Slovene	General Economic	17LTS19	300424
19 Oct	Estonia	Latvia	Territory Boundary	17LTS189	300437
20 Oct	France	UK Great Britain	Air Transport	2LTS323	300085
31 Oct	Multilateral		Sanitation	164LTS85	303790
02 Nov	Germany	Poland	Reparations	2LTS277	300081
09 Nov	Danzig	Poland	Territory Boundary	6LTS189	300153
10 Nov	Liechtenstein	Switzerland	Postal Service	2LTS305	300084
12 Nov	Italy	Serb/Croat/Slovene	Territory Boundary	18LTS387	300477
13 Nov	Bulgaria	Netherlands	Customs	7LTS107	300178
17 Nov	France	Germany	Peace/Disarmament	8LTS99	300211
22 Nov	Norway	Spain	General Trade	2LTS359	300089
23 Nov	Germany	Poland	Reparations	2LTS295	300082
25 Nov	France	Sweden	General Transport	2LTS183	300065
29 Nov	Lithuania	Poland	Peace/Disarmament	9LTS63	300243
30 Nov	Japan	Paraguay	General Economic	6LTS367	300169
06 Dec	Germany	Switzerland	Finance	2LTS343	300088
08 Dec	Germany	Poland	Consul/Citizenship	7LTS323	300199
09 Dec	Portugal	UK Great Britain	Dispute Settlement	7LTS257	300192
16 Dec	Multilateral		General IGO	6LTS379	300170
16 Dec	Siam	USA (United States)	Admin Cooperation	6LTS291	300161
16 Dec	Germany	Sweden	General Economic	2LTS263	300072
17 Dec	Allied Powers	Germany	Territory Boundary	12LTS39	300306
18 Dec	Spain	Sweden	General Trade	2LTS267	300073
23 Dec	Denmark	UK Great Britain	Air Transport	2LTS249	300071
23 Dec	France	UK Great Britain	Territory Boundary	22LTS353	300564
29 Dec	Multilateral		Telecommunications	13LTS281	300359
31 Dec	Germany	UK Great Britain	Peace/Disarmament	8LTS241	300223
1921					
03 Jan	Belgium	Sweden	Land Transport	2LTS301	300083
10 Jan	Portugal	UK Great Britain	Extradition	7LTS271	300194
10 Jan	Portugal	UK Great Britain	Extradition	7LTS264	300193

DATE	PARTY ONE	PARTY TWO	TOPIC	CITATION	NUMBER
1921 (Cont.)					
18 Jan	Netherlands	UK Great Britain	Telecommunications	5LTS157	300124
19 Jan	Multilateral		Recognition	5LTS9	300113
20 Jan	Germany	Poland	Territory Boundary	6LTS221	300156
24 Jan	Australia	Malay States	Postal Service	23LTS209	300590
25 Jan	Estonia	USSR (Soviet Union)	Postal Service	11LTS73	300290
29 Jan	Canada	France	General Trade	8LTS105	300212
31 Jan	France	Hungary	Claims and Debts	15LTS221	300396
03 Feb	Czechoslovakia	Germany	Territory Boundary	5LTS246	300132
07 Feb	Austria	France	General Military	4LTS251	300108
09 Feb	Belgium	Netherlands	Non-ILO Labor	11LTS333	300299
11 Feb	Muscat and Oman	UK Great Britain	General Economic	8LTS261	300224
11 Feb	Norway	USA (United States)	Postal Service	5LTS217	300130
12 Feb	Germany	Poland	Reparations	9LTS149	300247
14 Feb	Belgium	France	Admin Cooperation	12LTS245	300317
16 Feb	Sweden	UK Great Britain	Air Transport	3LTS233	300100
17 Feb	France	Poland	General Amity	18LTS11	300449
19 Feb	Bulgaria	Germany	Other Economic	6LTS227	300157
24 Feb	Poland	USSR (Soviet Union)	Refugees	4LTS141	300106
25 Feb	Other Unilat Decla	Rhine Navigation	Water Transport	12LTS355	300327
26 Feb	Persia	USSR (Soviet Union)	General Amity	9LTS383	300268
01 Mar	Brazil	UK Great Britain	Postal Service	8LTS265	300225
03 Mar	Poland	Romania	General Amity	7LTS77	300175
10 Mar	Austria	Czechoslovakia	Territory Boundary	9LTS333	300267
13 Mar	Multilateral		Admin Cooperation	8LTS327	300232
15 Mar	Belgium	UK Great Britain	Land Transport	5LTS319	300138
16 Mar	UK Great Britain	USSR (Soviet Union)	General Trade	4LTS127	300104
18 Mar	Poland	USSR (Soviet Union)	Peace/Disarmament	6LTS51	300149
18 Mar	Spain	Sweden	Other Economic	4LTS259	300109
22 Mar	Hungary	Switzerland	General Economic	7LTS235	300189
22 Mar	UK Great Britain	Venezuela	Claims and Debts	5LTS169	300126
23 Mar	Czechoslovakia	Italy	Water Transport	32LTS241	300816
23 Mar	Czechoslovakia	Italy	Finance	32LTS261	300817
23 Mar	Czechoslovakia	Italy	General Trade	32LTS183	300815
23 Mar	Iceland	Sweden	Patents/Copyrights	4LTS137	300105
24 Mar	Netherlands	Spain	General Economic	7LTS115	300179
10 Apr	Germany	Poland	Customs	6LTS233	300158
14 Apr	Bulgaria	Sweden	Mostfavored Nation	5LTS240	300131
16 Apr	France	Netherlands	General Aid	11LTS341	300300
20 Apr	Multilateral		Water Transport	7LTS73	300174
20 Apr	Multilateral		Water Transport	7LTS65	300173
20 Apr	Multilateral		Water Transport	7LTS35	300172
20 Apr	Multilateral		Land Transport	7LTS11	300171
21 Apr	Germany	Poland	General Transport	12LTS61	300308
21 Apr	Romania	UK Great Britain	Peace/Disarmament	8LTS293	300226
21 Apr	Romania	Sweden	Other Economic	4LTS265	300110
22 Apr	Norway	UK Great Britain	Admin Cooperation	5LTS33	300114
23 Apr	Czechoslovakia	Romania	General Economic	15LTS235	300397
23 Apr	France	Norway	Commodity Trade	14LTS375	300386
23 Apr	Czechoslovakia	Romania	General Amity	6LTS215	300155
25 Apr	Estonia	UK Great Britain	General Economic	5LTS173	300127
04 May	Austria	Czechoslovakia	General Economic	15LTS13	300388
05 May	Multilateral		Peace/Disarmament	12LTS419	300338
06 May	Germany	USSR (Soviet Union)	Reparations	12LTS177	300309
06 May	Germany	USSR (Soviet Union)	Reparations	6LTS267	300159
06 May	Portugal	UK Great Britain	Air Transport	5LTS179	300128
13 May	Latvia	Lithuania	Territory Boundary	17LTS211	300438
14 May	Latvia	Lithuania	Consul/Citizenship	17LTS233	300439
20 May	China	Germany	Peace/Disarmament	9LTS271	300261
21 May	Peru	USA (United States)	Claims and Debts	6LTS171	300150
28 May	Sweden	USA (United States)	Water Transport	6LTS41	300147
01 Jun	Italy	UK Great Britain	Reparations	6LTS323	300163
01 Jun	Denmark	UK Great Britain	Admin Cooperation	5LTS161	300125
03 Jun	Germany	Saar	General Ad Hoc	5LTS189	300129
04 Jun	Italy	Sweden	Land Transport	6LTS47	300148
06 Jun	Germany	Poland	Specific Property	34LTS185	300874

DATE	PARTY ONE	PARTY TWO	TOPIC	CITATION	NUMBER
1921 (Cont.)					
08 Jun	Denmark	Sweden	Telecommunications	14LTS195	300374
10 Jun	Finland	UK Great Britain	Sanitation	16LTS133	300403
10 Jun	Multilateral		Customs	8LTS297	300227
18 Jun	Germany	UK Great Britain	Sanitation	16LTS139	300404
19 Jun	Spain	Sweden	Mostfavored Nation	5LTS387	300143
22 Jun	Afghanistan	Persia	General Amity	33LTS285	300853
24 Jun	Netherlands	Spain	General Economic	7LTS121	300180
29 Jun	France	UK Great Britain	Reparations	6LTS23	300146
30 Jun	Norway	USA (United States)	Dispute Settlement	14LTS19	300365
05 Jul	Germany	Netherlands	Territory Boundary	13LTS41	300346
08 Jul	Sweden	UK Great Britain	Claims and Debts	5LTS329	300139
09 Jul	France	UK Great Britain	Non-ILO Labor	6LTS341	300166
12 Jul	Multilateral		Admin Cooperation	37LTS433	300965
12 Jul	Estonia	Latvia	Extradition	37LTS423	300964
12 Jul	Estonia	Lithuania	Extradition	43LTS179	301054
12 Jul	Denmark	Germany	Visas	26LTS163	300646
12 Jul	Multilateral		Postal Service	11LTS111	300293
12 Jul	Estonia	Lithuania	Consul/Citizenship	11LTS99	300292
12 Jul	Estonia	Latvia	Consul/Citizenship	11LTS87	300291
12 Jul	Denmark	UK Great Britain	Admin Cooperation	8LTS397	300238
12 Jul	Latvia	Lithuania	Consul/Citizenship	25LTS299	300619
12 Jul	Latvia	Lithuania	Extradition	25LTS311	300620
12 Jul	Denmark	Germany	Visas	26LTS151	300645
13 Jul	Finland	France	General Trade	29LTS445	300755
14 Jul	Austria	UK Great Britain	Sanitation	16LTS151	300405
14 Jul	Denmark	UK Great Britain	Consul/Citizenship	6LTS181	300151
15 Jul	Norway	UK Great Britain	Air Transport	6LTS307	300162
16 Jul	Finland	Norway	Admin Cooperation	19LTS77	300485
16 Jul	Brazil	UK Great Britain	Admin Cooperation	10LTS407	300279
20 Jul	Bolivia	Germany	General Amity	10LTS301	300275
20 Jul	Belgium	UK Great Britain	Reparations	8LTS301	300228
20 Jul	Multilateral		General Military	8LTS115	300213
21 Jul	Denmark	Norway	Telecommunications	13LTS357	300362
23 Jul	Multilateral		Water Transport	26LTS173	300647
25 Jul	Belgium	Luxembourg	General Economic	9LTS223	300256
27 Jul	Denmark	Norway	Air Transport	9LTS23	300241
27 Jul	Greece	UK Great Britain	Visas	6LTS347	300167
29 Jul	Serb/Croat/Slovene	UK Great Britain	Reparations	10LTS411	300280
29 Jul	Argentina	UK Great Britain	Admin Cooperation	8LTS315	300229
29 Jul	Finland	Sweden	Humanitarian	6LTS353	300168
01 Aug	Brazil	Uruguay	Education	177LTS109	304085
03 Aug	Latvia	Ukrainian SSR	Refugees	17LTS317	300442
03 Aug	Latvia	Ukrainian SSR	Refugees	17LTS295	300441
04 Aug	Czechoslovakia	UK Great Britain	Sanitation	16LTS157	300406
05 Aug	Multilateral		Admin Cooperation	27LTS349	300695
08 Aug	UK Great Britain	Uruguay	Admin Cooperation	8LTS319	300230
11 Aug	Bolivia	UK Great Britain	Admin Cooperation	8LTS323	300231
11 Aug	Austria	Germany	Non-ILO Labor	29LTS429	300753
17 Aug	Austria	Germany	Claims and Debts	19LTS237	300497
24 Aug	Austria	USA (United States)	General Amity	7LTS155	300184
25 Aug	Germany	USA (United States)	Peace/Disarmament	12LTS191	300310
27 Aug	Denmark	Iceland	Postal Service	12LTS345	300325
27 Aug	Greece	UK Great Britain	Other Military	8LTS332	300233
27 Aug	France	Greece	General Military	8LTS137	300214
27 Aug	Peru	UK Great Britain	Specific Resources	7LTS289	300195
29 Aug	Hungary	USA (United States)	General Amity	48LTS191	301161
29 Aug	Sweden	UK Great Britain	Other HEW	6LTS285	300160
02 Sep	Norway	USSR (Soviet Union)	Consul/Citizenship	7LTS293	300196
03 Sep	France	UK Great Britain	Postal Service	8LTS153	300218
03 Sep	Multilateral		Postal Service	8LTS151	300217
03 Sep	Multilateral		Postal Service	8LTS147	300216
03 Sep	France	USA (United States)	Postal Service	8LTS145	300215
03 Sep	Bulgaria	Hungary	Mostfavored Nation	7LTS229	300188
07 Sep	Czechoslovakia	Sweden	Humanitarian	7LTS97	300177
14 Sep	Italy	Serb/Croat/Slovene	Specific Resources	19LTS14	300482

DATE	PARTY ONE	PARTY TWO	TOPIC	CITATION	NUMBER
1921 (Cont.)					
15 Sep	Multilateral		Postal Service	30LTS141	300767
19 Sep	Multilateral		Telecommunications	15LTS191	300392
20 Sep	Portugal	Sweden	Humanitarian	7LTS143	300183
21 Sep	Multilateral		Humanitarian	7LTS127	300181
23 Sep	Austria	Poland	General Economic	7LTS181	300186
24 Sep	Italy	Switzerland	General Transport	12LTS367	300330
26 Sep	China	Mexico	General Amity	13LTS201	300352
27 Sep	Colombia	UK Great Britain	Admin Cooperation	10LTS417	300281
30 Sep	Bulgaria	Sweden	General Economic	7LTS137	300182
04 Oct	Belgium	France	Milit Servic/Citiz	8LTS157	300219
05 Oct	Multilateral		IGO Establishment	51LTS361	301241
05 Oct	UK Great Britain	USA (United States)	General Economic	8LTS371	300235
05 Oct	Multilateral		Admin Cooperation	29LTS73	300734
05 Oct	Multilateral		Admin Cooperation	29LTS79	300735
05 Oct	Multilateral		Admin Cooperation	29LTS67	300733
06 Oct	Multilateral		General Economic	17LTS45	300427
08 Oct	Austria	Hungary	General Economic	16LTS19	300402
08 Oct	Brazil	Italy	Non-ILO Labor	16LTS9	300401
10 Oct	France	UK Great Britain	Air Transport	9LTS181	300250
12 Oct	Japan	Netherlands	Water Transport	12LTS239	300316
13 Oct	Austria	Hungary	Territory Boundary	9LTS203	300254
13 Oct	Iceland	UK Great Britain	Postal Service	8LTS337	300234
15 Oct	Belgium	Netherlands	Postal Service	12LTS233	300315
20 Oct	Latvia	USSR (Soviet Union)	Dispute Settlement	54LTS155	301283
20 Oct	India	Iraq	Postal Service	69LTS139	301601
20 Oct	Multilateral		Peace/Disarmament	9LTS211	300255
21 Oct	UK Great Britain	USA (United States)	Claims and Debts	12LTS425	300339
24 Oct	Danzig	Poland	Recognition	116LTS5	302699
27 Oct	Australia	Nauru	Postal Service	23LTS229	300591
29 Oct	Germany	Switzerland	Finance	13LTS193	300351
29 Oct	Estonia	Finland	Telecommunications	13LTS167	300350
29 Oct	Estonia	Finland	Telecommunications	13LTS159	300349
29 Oct	Estonia	Finland	General Trade	13LTS59	300348
30 Oct	Hungary	UK Great Britain	General Military	8LTS375	300236
06 Nov	Latvia	USSR (Soviet Union)	Refugees	17LTS251	300440
09 Nov	Multilateral		Territory Boundary	12LTS381	300333
09 Nov	France	Sweden	Humanitarian	7LTS303	300197
10 Nov	Greece	UK Great Britain	Sanitation	16LTS165	300407
12 Nov	Other Unilat Decla	Hungary	Admin Cooperation	14LTS385	300387
22 Nov	Afghanistan	UK Great Britain	General Amity	14LTS47	300367
23 Nov	Germany	UK Great Britain	Peace/Disarmament	8LTS381	300237
25 Nov	Estonia	Ukrainian SSR	Consul/Citizenship	11LTS143	300295
25 Nov	Estonia	Ukrainian SSR	Dispute Settlement	11LTS121	300294
25 Nov	Romania	Sweden	General Economic	7LTS247	300190
29 Nov	Sweden	Switzerland	Humanitarian	7LTS313	300198
30 Nov	Belgium	France	Humanitarian	27LTS173	300680
01 Dec	Austria	Netherlands	Extradition	9LTS167	300248
01 Dec	Norway	Spain	General Economic	9LTS69	300244
03 Dec	Germany	Switzerland	Dispute Settlement	12LTS271	300320
06 Dec	UK Great Britain	USSR (Soviet Union)	Telecommunications	31LTS85	300785
06 Dec	Ireland	UK Great Britain	Dispute Settlement	26LTS9	300636
07 Dec	Brazil	Uruguay	Extradition	63LTS223	301492
12 Dec	Iceland	UK Great Britain	Admin Cooperation	12LTS351	300326
13 Dec	Multilateral		Territory Boundary	25LTS184	300607
14 Dec	Finland	USSR (Soviet Union)	Land Transport	16LTS221	300414
16 Dec	Norway	UK Great Britain	Sanitation	16LTS187	300409
16 Dec	Other Unilat Decla	Rhine Navigation	Water Transport	13LTS53	300347
16 Dec	Austria	Czechoslovakia	General Amity	9LTS247	300257
17 Dec	Austria	Czechoslovakia	Finance	22LTS401	300570
20 Dec	Hungary	UK Great Britain	Reparations	10LTS437	300283
20 Dec	Siam	UK Great Britain	Peace/Disarmament	10LTS421	300282
27 Dec	Belgium	Luxembourg	Telecommunications	12LTS253	300318
27 Dec	Poland	Sweden	Humanitarian	8LTS163	300220
29 Dec	Spain	Sweden	Customs	9LTS58	300242
31 Dec	Czechoslovakia	Germany	Taxation	17LTS401	300447

DATE	PARTY ONE	PARTY TWO	TOPIC	CITATION	NUMBER
1921 (Cont.)					
31 Dec	Bolivia	UK Great Britain	Patents/Copyrights	5LTS315	300137
1922					
01 Jan	Sweden	Switzerland	Visas	9LTS11	300239
05 Jan	Netherlands	Spain	General Economic	9LTS257	300259
07 Jan	Estonia	France	General Trade	62LTS9	301452
12 Jan	Costa Rica	UK Great Britain	Claims and Debts	17LTS151	300432
16 Jan	Czechoslovakia	Denmark	Finance	14LTS267	300378
16 Jan	Iraq	UK Great Britain	General Economic	12LTS431	300340
20 Jan	Czechoslovakia	Germany	Admin Cooperation	26LTS201	300648
21 Jan	USA (United States)	Venezuela	Extradition	49LTS435	301196
23 Jan	Palestine	UK Great Britain	General Economic	13LTS9	300342
24 Jan	France	Switzerland	Telecommunications	12LTS371	300331
27 Jan	Multilateral		Visas	9LTS291	300262
30 Jan	France	UK Great Britain	Air Transport	12LTS449	300341
02 Feb	France	UK Great Britain	Admin Cooperation	10LTS448	300284
03 Feb	Greece	UK Great Britain	Reparations	9LTS191	300252
04 Feb	China	Japan	Dispute Settlement	10LTS309	300277
04 Feb	Portugal	UK Great Britain	Health/Educ/Welfare	9LTS187	300251
06 Feb	Multilateral		Customs	38LTS267	300981
06 Feb	Multilateral		General Trade	38LTS277	300982
06 Feb	France	Poland	General Economic	43LTS415	301074
06 Feb	France	Poland	Admin Cooperation	43LTS399	301073
06 Feb	Multilateral		Peace/Disarmament	25LTS201	300609
06 Feb	Multilateral		Admin Cooperation	25LTS195	300608
08 Feb	Austria	Hungary	General Economic	55LTS367	301320
11 Feb	Austria	Czechoslovakia	Taxation	152LTS175	303492
11 Feb	Japan	USA (United States)	Territory Boundary	12LTS201	300311
11 Feb	Muscat and Oman	UK Great Britain	General Economic	10LTS459	300285
18 Feb	Ethiopia	Greece	General Economic	15LTS267	300399
18 Feb	Austria	Czechoslovakia	Taxation	14LTS129	300371
20 Feb	Finland	Germany	Extradition	19LTS81	300486
20 Feb	Netherlands	Romania	General Transport	12LTS219	300313
22 Feb	France	UK Great Britain	Non-ILO Labor	9LTS198	300253
22 Feb	Czechoslovakia	Germany	IGO Operations	26LTS249	300650
22 Feb	Multilateral		Water Transport	26LTS219	300649
24 Feb	Brazil	Paraguay	Extradition	138LTS211	303189
24 Feb	Germany	Poland	Admin Cooperation	26LTS479	300664
24 Feb	Germany	Poland	Admin Cooperation	27LTS15	300665
02 Mar	Peru	UK Great Britain	Specific Resources	10LTS463	300286
03 Mar	Finland	Norway	Specif Goods/Equip	14LTS157	300372
09 Mar	Bulgaria	Netherlands	Customs	9LTS265	300260
17 Mar	Multilateral		Dispute Settlement	11LTS167	300296
18 Mar	Czechoslovakia	Germany	Taxation	17LTS453	300448
20 Mar	France	Switzerland	Customs	12LTS377	300332
23 Mar	Spain	Uruguay	Dispute Settlement	63LTS233	301493
24 Mar	Colombia	Peru	Territory Boundary	74LTS9	301726
28 Mar	China	Japan	Reparations	13LTS213	300353
29 Mar	Norway	Sweden	Telecommunications	13LTS311	300361
30 Mar	Belgium	USA (United States)	General Transport	12LTS259	300319
31 Mar	Multilateral		Humanitarian	9LTS415	300269
01 Apr	Allied Powers	Poland	Reparations	9LTS325	300265
02 Apr	India	Iraq	Postal Service	69LTS157	301602
04 Apr	Norway	Spain	General Economic	9LTS253	300258
05 Apr	Bulgaria	UK Great Britain	Sanitation	16LTS191	300410
06 Apr	Czechoslovakia	Italy	Extradition	55LTS171	301313
06 Apr	Italy	Serb/Croat/Slovene	Privil/Immunities	118LTS207	302725
06 Apr	Italy	Serb/Croat/Slovene	Dispute Settlement	118LTS199	302724
06 Apr	Italy	Serb/Croat/Slovene	Extradition	118LTS221	302726
06 Apr	Czechoslovakia	Italy	Admin Cooperation	55LTS207	301315
06 Apr	Italy	Serb/Croat/Slovene	Admin Cooperation	123LTS289	302819
06 Apr	Czechoslovakia	Italy	Admin Cooperation	55LTS189	301314
06 Apr	Multilateral		Admin Cooperation	123LTS277	302818
06 Apr	Multilateral		Milit Assistance	20LTS11	300501
07 Apr	Denmark	Estonia	Water Transport	14LTS243	300375

DATE	PARTY ONE	PARTY TWO	TOPIC	CITATION	NUMBER
1922 (Cont.)					
10 Apr	Denmark	Germany	Water Transport	44LTS389	301095
10 Apr	Denmark	Germany	Territory Boundary	10LTS73	300274
10 Apr	Denmark	Germany	Territory Boundary	29LTS9	300730
12 Apr	Chile	UK Great Britain	Admin Cooperation	11LTS17	300287
12 Apr	Germany	Poland	Territory Boundary	21LTS327	300548
12 Apr	Czechoslovakia	Germany	Non-ILO Labor	22LTS329	300562
16 Apr	Germany	USSR (Soviet Union)	General Amity	19LTS247	300498
17 Apr	Sweden	USA (United States)	Postal Service	14LTS281	300380
21 Apr	Finland	Germany	General Economic	19LTS87	300487
22 Apr	UK Great Britain	USA (United States)	Postal Service	20LTS415	300530
25 Apr	Denmark	Germany	Air Transport	18LTS227	300466
28 Apr	Afghanistan	France	Consul/Citizenship	105LTS147	302408
29 Apr	Germany	Poland	Admin Cooperation	21LTS391	300549
01 May	Iceland	UK Great Britain	Dispute Settlement	12LTS15	300302
01 May	Denmark	UK Great Britain	Dispute Settlement	12LTS11	300301
04 May	Belgian Colonies	Fr Equatorial Afri	Telecommunications	148LTS61	303403
05 May	Norway	Sweden	Humanitarian	15LTS165	300390
06 May	Lithuania	UK Great Britain	General Economic	13LTS25	300343
06 May	Norway	Spain	General Trade	9LTS329	300266
08 May	Czechoslovakia	Germany	Extradition	23LTS171	300589
10 May	Multilateral		Water Transport	26LTS265	300652
11 May	Italy	UK Great Britain	Other Military	11LTS23	300288
12 May	Italy	Poland	General Trade	59LTS293	301399
12 May	Other Unilat Decla	Lithuania	Admin Cooperation	22LTS393	300569
15 May	UK Great Britain	USA (United States)	Extradition	14LTS89	300369
15 May	Germany	Poland	Visas	10LTS37	300273
15 May	Germany	Poland	Postal Service	10LTS8	300272
17 May	Mexico	UK Great Britain	Admin Cooperation	14LTS83	300368
22 May	Finland	Sweden	Postal Service	14LTS297	300381
22 May	Denmark	Japan	Water Transport	14LTS247	300376
22 May	Estonia	UK Great Britain	Admin Cooperation	13LTS33	300344
22 May	Denmark	Finland	Postal Service	9LTS435	300270
23 May	Finland	Norway	Postal Service	14LTS323	300382
23 May	Austria	Germany	Taxation	26LTS405	300660
28 May	Austria	Germany	Taxation	26LTS445	300661
30 May	Latvia	Vatican/Holy See	General Amity	17LTS365	300443
01 Jun	Finland	USSR (Soviet Union)	Territory Boundary	16LTS319	300415
02 Jun	Netherlands	UK Great Britain	Postal Service	13LTS263	300357
03 Jun	Germany	Poland	Territory Boundary	9LTS465	300271
08 Jun	Denmark	USA (United States)	Postal Service	11LTS311	300298
12 Jun	Norway	Spain	General Economic	10LTS305	300276
13 Jun	Finland	USSR (Soviet Union)	Telecommunications	16LTS349	300416
13 Jun	Belgium	Switzerland	Air Transport	12LTS295	300321
15 Jun	Germany	Poland	Specific Resources	21LTS433	300550
15 Jun	Multilateral		Dispute Settlement	21LTS463	300551
15 Jun	Germany	Poland	Territory Boundary	34LTS201	300875
18 Jun	Germany	Poland	Specific Property	34LTS235	300876
21 Jun	Belgium	UK Great Britain	Admin Cooperation	24LTS91	300597
21 Jun	Germany	Poland	Dispute Settlement	22LTS7	300552
22 Jun	Finland	USSR (Soviet Union)	Postal Service	16LTS361	300417
23 Jun	Germany	Poland	Specific Resources	22LTS25	300553
24 Jun	Latvia	USSR (Soviet Union)	Sanitation	38LTS9	300966
24 Jun	Estonia	Latvia	Sanitation	38LTS57	300967
24 Jun	Germany	Poland	Water Transport	26LTS271	300653
26 Jun	Poland	Switzerland	General Economic	12LTS305	300322
03 Jul	UK Great Britain	USSR (Soviet Union)	General Trade	13LTS37	300345
05 Jul	Multilateral		Reparations	13LTS237	300355
05 Jul	France	Saar	Taxation	27LTS265	300689
07 Jul	Finland	USSR (Soviet Union)	Peace/Disarmament	19LTS99	300488
07 Jul	Latvia	Poland	Sanitation	37LTS317	300958
08 Jul	Belgium	Netherlands	Air Transport	13LTS273	300358
10 Jul	Belgian Colonies	Tanganyika	Telecommunications	148LTS71	303404
11 Jul	Bulgaria	Denmark	Mostfavored Nation	12LTS225	300314
15 Jul	Germany	Poland	General Transport	26LTS353	300654
20 Jul	Chile	Peru	Dispute Settlement	21LTS141	300537

DATE	PARTY ONE	PARTY TWO	TOPIC	CITATION	NUMBER
1922 (Cont.)					
21 Jul	Finland	USA (United States)	Postal Service	13LTS243	300356
01 Aug	Germany	Poland	Specific Property	34LTS253	300877
07 Aug	United Arab Rep	Palestine	Extradition	36LTS343	300933
10 Aug	Germany	USA (United States)	Admin Cooperation	26LTS357	300655
12 Aug	Finland	USSR (Soviet Union)	Refugees	19LTS105	300489
16 Aug	France	Panama	Consul/Citizenship	43LTS423	301075
17 Aug	Iceland	Norway	Postal Service	14LTS9	300363
18 Aug	Multilateral		Telecommunications	13LTS289	300360
25 Aug	Germany	Poland	Non-ILO Labor	22LTS63	300554
26 Aug	Germany	Saar	Admin Cooperation	27LTS249	300688
26 Aug	Germany	Poland	Admin Cooperation	26LTS365	300656
31 Aug	Czechoslovakia	Serb/Croat/Slovene	General Amity	13LTS231	300354
07 Sep	Finland	Norway	Telecommunications	12LTS357	300328
09 Sep	Afghanistan	France	Education	105LTS153	302409
11 Sep	Belgium	Germany	General Amity	41LTS141	301009
14 Sep	Germany	Poland	Admin Cooperation	34LTS265	300878
20 Sep	Finland	USSR (Soviet Union)	Specific Resources	19LTS143	300490
23 Sep	Czechoslovakia	Poland	Scientific Project	50LTS321	301216
25 Sep	Austria	Poland	General Trade	59LTS307	301400
26 Sep	Brazil	Portugal	Patents/Copyrights	25LTS229	300610
02 Oct	Austria	UK Great Britain	Reparations	12LTS413	300337
02 Oct	Other Unilat Decla	Albania	Consul/Citizenship	9LTS173	300249
04 Oct	Other Unilat Decla	Austria	Territory Boundary	12LTS405	300336
04 Oct	Multilateral		Territory Boundary	12LTS391	300335
04 Oct	Multilateral		Territory Boundary	12LTS385	300334
04 Oct	Austria	Sweden	Humanitarian	9LTS317	300264
07 Oct	Czechoslovakia	France	Admin Cooperation	47LTS365	301141
07 Oct	Czechoslovakia	Latvia	General Trade	20LTS379	300528
09 Oct	Denmark	Iceland	Humanitarian	14LTS13	300364
14 Oct	Latvia	USA (United States)	Postal Service	38LTS331	300989
14 Oct	Czechoslovakia	Romania	Admin Cooperation	25LTS163	300604
17 Oct	Latvia	UK Great Britain	Finance	16LTS397	300419
17 Oct	Mexico	Sweden	Humanitarian	15LTS179	300391
19 Oct	UK Great Britain	Uruguay	Sanitation	16LTS201	300411
19 Oct	Estonia	Hungary	General Trade	30LTS347	300774
21 Oct	Finland	USSR (Soviet Union)	Specific Resources	29LTS197	300742
23 Oct	Italy	Serb/Croat/Slovene	Territory Boundary	18LTS461	300481
23 Oct	Italy	Serb/Croat/Slovene	Customs	18LTS441	300480
23 Oct	Italy	Serb/Croat/Slovene	Customs	18LTS413	300479
23 Oct	Italy	Serb/Croat/Slovene	General Economic	18LTS405	300478
25 Oct	Belgium	Sweden	Admin Cooperation	18LTS121	300459
28 Oct	Finland	USSR (Soviet Union)	General Transport	19LTS199	300493
28 Oct	Finland	USSR (Soviet Union)	Water Transport	19LTS183	300492
28 Oct	Finland	USSR (Soviet Union)	Water Transport	19LTS153	300491
28 Oct	Finland	USSR (Soviet Union)	Specific Resources	29LTS211	300743
31 Oct	Spain	UK Great Britain	Water Transport	28LTS339	300719
02 Nov	Multilateral		Peace/Disarmament	149LTS35	303431
05 Nov	Germany	USSR (Soviet Union)	Admin Cooperation	26LTS387	300657
06 Nov	Austria	Netherlands	Consul/Citizenship	17LTS375	300444
07 Nov	Denmark	Sweden	Air Transport	14LTS95	300370
13 Nov	Germany	Saar	Health/Educ/Welfare	27LTS273	300690
16 Nov	Haiti	UK Great Britain	Sanitation	16LTS173	300408
28 Nov	Estonia	Finland	Telecommunications	19LTS213	300494
30 Nov	British Empire	Japan	Water Transport	16LTS207	300412
30 Nov	France	Saar	Customs	27LTS283	300691
01 Dec	China	Japan	Territory Boundary	22LTS179	300559
04 Dec	Albania	Italy	Telecommunications	15LTS213	300395
05 Dec	Denmark	USA (United States)	Taxation	113LTS381	302649
05 Dec	Albania	Italy	Postal Service	15LTS203	300394
05 Dec	China	Japan	Land Transport	22LTS293	300560
07 Dec	Japan	Poland	General Trade	32LTS61	300806
08 Dec	China	Japan	Postal Service	20LTS289	300522
08 Dec	China	Japan	Postal Service	20LTS253	300521
08 Dec	China	Japan	Postal Service	20LTS233	300520
08 Dec	China	Japan	Postal Service	20LTS205	300519

DATE	PARTY ONE	PARTY TWO	TOPIC	CITATION	NUMBER
1922 (Cont.)					
14 Dec	Multilateral		Water Transport	36LTS457	300943
15 Dec	Canada	France	General Trade	21LTS38	300532
18 Dec	Romania	Sweden	General Economic	14LTS353	300383
18 Dec	Germany	Poland	Finance	34LTS283	300879
18 Dec	Germany	Poland	Sanitation	34LTS301	300880
18 Dec	Germany	Poland	Admin Cooperation	26LTS395	300658
19 Dec	Netherlands	Romania	General Economic	14LTS191	300373
26 Dec	France	UK Great Britain	Other Ad Hoc	16LTS213	300413
28 Dec	UK Great Britain	USA (United States)	Postal Service	21LTS9	300531
28 Dec	Estonia	Germany	Water Transport	41LTS147	301010
30 Dec	Multilateral		General Trade	21LTS183	300542
30 Dec	Belgium	Poland	Finance	21LTS201	300543
30 Dec	Siam	USA (United States)	Extradition	25LTS394	300629
1923					
04 Jan	Canada	Italy	General Economic	25LTS375	300626
10 Jan	Czechoslovakia	Greece	General Trade	21LTS217	300544
15 Jan	Germany	Spain	General Economic	26LTS455	300662
17 Jan	Germany	Saar	Land Transport	27LTS290	300692
18 Jan	Austria	Czechoslovakia	Visas	88LTS237	302000
18 Jan	Netherlands	UK Great Britain	Postal Service	18LTS257	300469
19 Jan	Germany	Sweden	Admin Cooperation	41LTS151	301011
23 Jan	Netherlands	UK Great Britain	Postal Service	16LTS425	300420
27 Jan	Germany	Poland	Admin Cooperation	26LTS461	300663
27 Jan	Multilateral		Water Transport	26LTS253	300651
27 Jan	Italy	Switzerland	General Trade	25LTS21	300603
30 Jan	Greece	Turkey	Consul/Citizenship	32LTS75	300807
30 Jan	Greece	Turkey	Consul/Citizenship	36LTS137	300912
31 Jan	Czechoslovakia	UK Great Britain	Customs	20LTS53	300506
05 Feb	Multilateral		Telecommunications	28LTS409	300720
07 Feb	Poland	USSR (Soviet Union)	Sanitation	49LTS285	301186
08 Feb	India	Iraq	Postal Service	85LTS37	301920
11 Feb	Muscat and Oman	UK Great Britain	General Amity	17LTS163	300433
12 Feb	Denmark	Finland	Customs	18LTS71	300454
12 Feb	Denmark	Finland	Extradition	18LTS33	300452
12 Feb	Germany	Iceland	Patents/Copyrights	27LTS405	300700
13 Feb	France	USA (United States)	Territory Boundary	26LTS53	300640
13 Feb	France	USA (United States)	Territory Boundary	26LTS69	300641
21 Feb	Finland	USSR (Soviet Union)	Customs	19LTS219	300495
22 Feb	Norway	UK Great Britain	Air Transport	15LTS159	300389
24 Feb	Sweden	Uruguay	Dispute Settlement	63LTS239	301494
26 Feb	Hungary	Sweden	Admin Cooperation	17LTS35	300426
28 Feb	Uruguay	Venezuela	Admin Cooperation	36LTS451	300942
02 Mar	Canada	USA (United States)	Specific Resources	32LTS93	300809
07 Mar	France	UK Great Britain	Territory Boundary	22LTS363	300565
08 Mar	Czechoslovakia	Hungary	Land Transport	48LTS257	301167
08 Mar	Colombia	UK Great Britain	Sanitation	17LTS167	300434
14 Mar	Peru	Venezuela	Admin Cooperation	20LTS45	300505
15 Mar	Multilateral		Territory Boundary	15LTS259	300398
17 Mar	Czechoslovakia	Serb/Croat/Slovene	Admin Cooperation	30LTS185	300768
20 Mar	Hungary	Serb/Croat/Slovene	Refugees	16LTS447	300422
21 Mar	Germany	Poland	Taxation	34LTS315	300881
24 Mar	Germany	Switzerland	Taxation	27LTS41	300666
25 Mar	Germany	Switzerland	Finance	18LTS273	300470
26 Mar	Portugal	Spain	Postal Service	18LTS373	300476
26 Mar	Portugal	Spain	Postal Service	18LTS349	300475
28 Mar	Austria	UK Great Britain	Customs	17LTS385	300445
28 Mar	Belgium	UK Great Britain	Reparations	16LTS439	300421
29 Mar	Multilateral		Admin Cooperation	20LTS111	300510
29 Mar	Multilateral		Land Transport	23LTS256	300593
29 Mar	Multilateral		Land Transport	23LTS378	300594
29 Mar	Liechtenstein	Switzerland	Customs	21LTS231	300545
31 Mar	Portugal	UK Great Britain	Admin Cooperation	18LTS29	300451
31 Mar	Denmark	Germany	Extradition	17LTS181	300436
03 Apr	Netherlands	USA (United States)	Patents/Copyrights	21LTS175	300541

DATE	PARTY ONE	PARTY TWO	TOPIC	CITATION	NUMBER
1923 (Cont.)					
05 Apr	Germany	UK Great Britain	Reparations	17LTS173	300435
09 Apr	Denmark	Portugal	General Economic	17LTS63	300429
10 Apr	Austria	Hungary	Dispute Settlement	18LTS93	300457
11 Apr	Luxembourg	Sweden	Admin Cooperation	16LTS453	300423
11 Apr	Norway	Portugal	General Trade	16LTS379	300418
21 Apr	Denmark	Finland	Milit Servic/Citiz	17LTS57	300428
21 Apr	Germany	Saar	Non-ILO Labor	27LTS295	300693
23 Apr	Denmark	USSR (Soviet Union)	General Amity	18LTS15	300450
25 Apr	Persia	Russ Fed Sov Rep	Postal Service	110LTS323	302564
25 Apr	Costa Rica	UK Great Britain	General Trade	20LTS19	300502
25 Apr	Denmark	UK Great Britain	Postal Service	22LTS157	300557
27 Apr	Persia	Russ Fed Sov Rep	Telecommunications	110LTS333	302565
28 Apr	Finland	Norway	Admin Cooperation	19LTS225	300496
28 Apr	Multilateral		Patents/Copyrights	33LTS47	300832
28 Apr	Germany	Portugal	General Trade	32LTS385	300827
30 Apr	Netherlands	UK Great Britain	Postal Service	20LTS343	300525
30 Apr	Iraq	UK Great Britain	General Amity	35LTS13	300890
01 May	Japan	Sweden	Admin Cooperation	17LTS391	300446
02 May	Czechoslovakia	Germany	Admin Cooperation	31LTS0	300793
02 May	Germany	Poland	Admin Cooperation	27LTS51	300667
03 May	Multilateral		Customs	33LTS11	300830
03 May	Multilateral		General Trade	33LTS81	300833
03 May	Multilateral		General Amity	33LTS25	300831
04 May	Poland	Serb/Croat/Slovene	Admin Cooperation	85LTS455	301946
07 May	Czechoslovakia	Romania	General Amity	18LTS81	300455
08 May	Denmark	Romania	General Economic	17LTS31	300425
09 May	Poland	Turkey	Sanitation	49LTS315	301187
10 May	Greece	Serb/Croat/Slovene	Land Transport	25LTS441	300635
12 May	France	India	Territory Boundary	25LTS381	300627
23 May	Germany	Netherlands	Customs	25LTS275	300617
24 May	Multilateral		Postal Service	50LTS341	301218
24 May	France	UK Great Britain	Consul/Citizenship	18LTS305	300472
24 May	Romania	UK Great Britain	General Trade	18LTS301	300471
26 May	Norway	Sweden	Air Transport	18LTS155	300462
26 May	Finland	Sweden	Water Transport	18LTS57	300453
30 May	Australia	Netherlands	Postal Service	22LTS129	300556
31 May	Germany	Lithuania	Reparations	51LTS381	301243
01 Jun	Germany	Lithuania	General Economic	51LTS387	301244
03 Jun	Germany	Netherlands	Water Transport	28LTS297	300716
04 Jun	Germany	Poland	Health/Educ/Welfare	34LTS329	300882
05 Jun	Finland	USSR (Soviet Union)	Water Transport	18LTS203	300465
05 Jun	Afghanistan	UK Great Britain	General Trade	21LTS89	300533
14 Jun	Germany	Poland	Admin Cooperation	34LTS343	300883
15 Jun	Netherlands	Serb/Croat/Slovene	Land Transport	20LTS337	300524
21 Jun	Austria	Germany	Admin Cooperation	27LTS57	300668
21 Jun	Austria	Germany	Admin Cooperation	27LTS88	300669
22 Jun	Latvia	UK Great Britain	General Trade	20LTS395	300529
23 Jun	Germany	Poland	Specific Property	67LTS9	301537
23 Jun	UK Great Britain	USA (United States)	Dispute Settlement	23LTS87	300579
27 Jun	Estonia	Germany	General Trade	41LTS161	301013
27 Jun	Estonia	Germany	General Amity	41LTS155	301012
28 Jun	Belgium	Denmark	Air Transport	20LTS59	300507
30 Jun	Austria	Denmark	General Trade	18LTS195	300464
30 Jun	Austria	Denmark	General Trade	18LTS189	300463
02 Jul	France	Netherlands	Air Transport	20LTS131	300512
05 Jul	United Arab Rep	UK Great Britain	Other Ad Hoc	18LTS311	300473
07 Jul	Estonia	Sweden	General Trade	20LTS189	300517
10 Jul	Germany	Poland	General Transport	34LTS349	300884
11 Jul	Multilateral		Admin Cooperation	18LTS85	300456
11 Jul	Netherlands	UK Great Britain	Air Transport	33LTS111	300836
13 Jul	Denmark	Sweden	Admin Cooperation	18LTS143	300461
13 Jul	Denmark	Sweden	Admin Cooperation	18LTS131	300460
13 Jul	Czechoslovakia	Hungary	Claims and Debts	36LTS41	300902
13 Jul	Czechoslovakia	Hungary	Taxation	36LTS53	300903
13 Jul	Czechoslovakia	Hungary	Claims and Debts	35LTS271	300900

1923 (Cont.)

DATE	PARTY ONE	PARTY TWO	TOPIC	CITATION	NUMBER
13 Jul	Czechoslovakia	Hungary	Taxation	35LTS237	300898
13 Jul	Czechoslovakia	Hungary	Claims and Debts	36LTS13	300901
13 Jul	Czechoslovakia	Hungary	Claims and Debts	35LTS253	300899
14 Jul	Belgium	Netherlands	Water Transport	20LTS119	300511
14 Jul	Denmark	Poland	Milit Servic/Citiz	19LTS65	300483
14 Jul	Germany	Poland	Admin Cooperation	26LTS399	300659
14 Jul	Czechoslovakia	UK Great Britain	General Trade	29LTS377	300748
16 Jul	Austria	Italy	General Trade	27LTS383	300699
17 Jul	Belgium	Luxembourg	Humanitarian	27LTS235	300686
18 Jul	Iceland	Lithuania	General Trade	20LTS329	300523
18 Jul	Denmark	Lithuania	General Trade	20LTS197	300518
18 Jul	United Arab Rep	UK Great Britain	Admin Cooperation	18LTS323	300474
19 Jul	France	USA (United States)	Dispute Settlement	25LTS405	300630
23 Jul	Poland	Turkey	General Amity	49LTS323	301188
23 Jul	Poland	Turkey	General Economic	49LTS329	301189
23 Jul	Poland	Turkey	Admin Cooperation	49LTS345	301190
24 Jul	Poland	Romania	Sanitation	18LTS103	300458
24 Jul	Turkey		Sanitation	36LTS157	300915
24 Jul	France	UK Great Britain	Peace/Disarmament	36LTS207	300923
24 Jul	Multilateral		Consul/Citizenship	28LTS221	300709
24 Jul	Multilateral		Taxation	36LTS175	300918
24 Jul	Multilateral		Consul/Citizenship	36LTS167	300917
24 Jul	Turkey		Admin Cooperation	36LTS161	300916
24 Jul	Multilateral		Recognition	36LTS179	300919
24 Jul	Greece		Consul/Citizenship	36LTS153	300914
24 Jul	Multilateral		General Trade	28LTS203	300707
24 Jul	Multilateral		Water Transport	36LTS187	300920
24 Jul	Italy	Turkey	Admin Cooperation	36LTS195	300921
24 Jul	Multilateral		General Amity	36LTS145	300913
24 Jul	Multilateral		Admin Cooperation	36LTS201	300922
24 Jul	Multilateral		Territory Boundary	28LTS215	300708
24 Jul	Multilateral		Peace/Disarmament	28LTS11	300701
24 Jul	Multilateral		Water Transport	28LTS115	300702
24 Jul	Multilateral		General Trade	28LTS171	300705
24 Jul	Multilateral		Admin Cooperation	28LTS283	300714
24 Jul	Multilateral		Territory Boundary	28LTS139	300703
24 Jul	Multilateral		General Trade	28LTS151	300704
24 Jul	Multilateral		Admin Cooperation	28LTS197	300706
27 Jul	Denmark	Estonia	Patents/Copyrights	19LTS259	300500
27 Jul	Denmark	Estonia	Patents/Copyrights	19LTS253	300499
27 Jul	Chile	Norway	Admin Cooperation	33LTS249	300848
28 Jul	Finland	USSR (Soviet Union)	Admin Cooperation	32LTS101	300810
03 Aug	Denmark	Finland	General Trade	21LTS269	300547
06 Aug	Turkey	USA (United States)	Extradition	153LTS71	303509
08 Aug	Belgium	UK Great Britain	Extradition	22LTS375	300566
10 Aug	Iceland	Norway	Postal Service	20LTS363	300527
14 Aug	Italy	UK Great Britain	Admin Cooperation	21LTS127	300534
15 Aug	Czechoslovakia	Germany	Admin Cooperation	27LTS94	300670
22 Aug	Netherlands	Portugal	General Trade	20LTS139	300513
23 Aug	Japan	USA (United States)	Admin Cooperation	30LTS263	300770
30 Aug	UK Great Britain	USA (United States)	Postal Service	24LTS103	300598
05 Sep	Portugal	USA (United States)	Dispute Settlement	50LTS239	301206
05 Sep	Austria	Netherlands	General Trade	20LTS147	300514
06 Sep	Netherlands	UK Great Britain	Postal Service	22LTS433	300572
07 Sep	Estonia	Iceland	General Trade	23LTS131	300584
07 Sep	Denmark	Estonia	General Trade	23LTS73	300577
08 Sep	Austria	USSR (Soviet Union)	Consul/Citizenship	20LTS153	300515
08 Sep	Luxembourg	UK Great Britain	Postal Service	35LTS203	300896
11 Sep	Finland	Sweden	ILO Labor	20LTS79	300508
24 Sep	Multilateral		Dispute Settlement	27LTS157	300678
27 Sep	Other Unilat Decla	Ethiopia	UN Charter	25LTS180	300606
28 Sep	Netherlands	UK Great Britain	Sanitation	23LTS113	300581
29 Sep	France	UK Great Britain	Admin Cooperation	20LTS183	300516
29 Sep	Multilateral		Refugees	20LTS41	300504
29 Sep	Other Unilat Decla	Greece	Refugees	20LTS29	300503

1923 (Cont.)

DATE	PARTY ONE	PARTY TWO	TOPIC	CITATION	NUMBER
29 Sep	France	UK Great Britain	Specific Resources	21LTS137	300536
01 Oct	Mexico	Norway	Admin Cooperation	33LTS255	300849
01 Oct	France	Norway	Admin Cooperation	33LTS237	300847
02 Oct	Czechoslovakia	Norway	General Trade	20LTS355	300526
02 Oct	Netherlands	UK Great Britain	Postal Service	23LTS9	300573
02 Oct	Austria	Japan	General Trade	22LTS349	300563
07 Oct	Norway	Spain	General Trade	59LTS47	301389
10 Oct	France	UK Great Britain	Postal Service	22LTS381	300567
12 Oct	Canada	Irish Free State	Postal Service	56LTS291	301338
12 Oct	Finland	Sweden	Water Transport	21LTS147	300538
16 Oct	Latvia	USA (United States)	Extradition	27LTS371	300698
22 Oct	Italy	Switzerland	Water Transport	65LTS301	301521
23 Oct	Germany	South Africa	Milit Servic/Citiz	28LTS417	300721
27 Oct	Sweden	UK Great Britain	Admin Cooperation	22LTS387	300568
31 Oct	Estonia	Latvia	Water Transport	25LTS321	300621
01 Nov	Estonia	Latvia	Territory Boundary	61LTS315	301443
01 Nov	Estonia	Hungary	General Trade	62LTS47	301453
01 Nov	Estonia	Latvia	Territory Boundary	25LTS345	300623
01 Nov	Estonia	Latvia	Other Economic	25LTS354	300624
01 Nov	Finland	Netherlands	General Trade	23LTS33	300574
01 Nov	Estonia	Latvia	Claims and Debts	25LTS341	300622
01 Nov	Estonia	Latvia	General Amity	23LTS81	300578
03 Nov	Multilateral		Customs	30LTS371	300775
06 Nov	Germany	Hungary	Taxation	45LTS253	301103
06 Nov	Germany	Hungary	Taxation	45LTS279	301104
06 Nov	Japan	Norway	Admin Cooperation	33LTS265	300850
08 Nov	Estonia	USA (United States)	Extradition	43LTS277	301063
10 Nov	Finland	Poland	General Trade	29LTS229	300744
13 Nov	Austria	Poland	Dispute Settlement	34LTS399	300888
13 Nov	France	UK Great Britain	Extradition	21LTS131	300535
15 Nov	Italy	Spain	General Trade	39LTS49	300996
15 Nov	British Empire	USA (United States)	Postal Service	33LTS304	300854
16 Nov	Japan	Serb/Croat/Slovene	General Economic	42LTS99	301035
19 Nov	Hungary	Latvia	General Trade	37LTS341	300959
23 Nov	Multilateral		Claims and Debts	28LTS267	300712
23 Nov	Multilateral		Reparations	28LTS273	300713
23 Nov	Bulgaria	USA (United States)	Consul/Citizenship	25LTS238	300611
26 Nov	Germany	Hungary	Taxation	45LTS309	301105
26 Nov	Poland	UK Great Britain	Water Transport	28LTS428	300722
26 Nov	Norway	USA (United States)	Dispute Settlement	23LTS249	300592
26 Nov	Bulgaria	Serb/Croat/Slovene	Reparations	21LTS153	300539
26 Nov	Bulgaria	Serb/Croat/Slovene	Extradition	26LTS119	300643
26 Nov	Bulgaria	Serb/Croat/Slovene	Reparations	21LTS163	300540
26 Nov	Bulgaria	Serb/Croat/Slovene	Admin Cooperation	26LTS85	300642
26 Nov	Bulgaria	Serb/Croat/Slovene	Humanitarian	26LTS141	300644
27 Nov	Estonia	Sweden	Admin Cooperation	57LTS83	301355
28 Nov	Multilateral		Admin Cooperation	51LTS221	301230
28 Nov	Multilateral		Admin Cooperation	51LTS209	301228
28 Nov	Multilateral		Admin Cooperation	51LTS233	301232
28 Nov	Multilateral		Admin Cooperation	51LTS215	301229
28 Nov	Multilateral		Admin Cooperation	51LTS239	301233
29 Nov	Finland	Sweden	Extradition	23LTS41	300575
30 Nov	Multilateral		Non-ILO Labor	102LTS153	302360
30 Nov	Austria	Czechoslovakia	Non-ILO Labor	126LTS171	302880
30 Nov	Multilateral		Non-ILO Labor	102LTS183	302361
30 Nov	Denmark	Norway	Admin Cooperation	22LTS121	300555
30 Nov	Denmark	Finland	Non-ILO Labor	22LTS427	300571
08 Dec	UK Great Britain	USA (United States)	Postal Service	23LTS93	300580
09 Dec	Multilateral		Water Transport	58LTS284	301379
09 Dec	Multilateral		General Economic	58LTS315	301380
09 Dec	Multilateral		Land Transport	47LTS55	301129
09 Dec	Multilateral		Non-IBRD Project	36LTS76	300905
11 Dec	Hungary	UK Great Britain	Finance	23LTS119	300582
14 Dec	Finland	UK Great Britain	General Trade	29LTS129	300739
14 Dec	Multilateral		General Trade	29LTS37	300732

DATE	PARTY ONE	PARTY TWO	TOPIC	CITATION	NUMBER
1923 (Cont.)					
14 Dec	Finland	UK Great Britain	Non-ILO Labor	23LTS125	300583
18 Dec	Hungary	Turkey	General Amity	43LTS271	301062
18 Dec	Multilateral		Territory Boundary	28LTS541	300729
21 Dec	Lithuania	Norway	General Trade	32LTS55	300805
21 Dec	Nepal	UK Great Britain	General Amity	36LTS357	300934
27 Dec	Hungary	Romania	Dispute Settlement	21LTS263	300546
27 Dec	France	UK Great Britain	Visas	24LTS131	300600
31 Dec	Irish Free State	USA (United States)	Postal Service	56LTS303	301339
31 Dec	Bulgaria	Sweden	General Trade	22LTS323	300561
1924					
03 Jan	Latvia	Poland	Consul/Citizenship	42LTS451	301043
05 Jan	Germany	UK Great Britain	Claims and Debts	36LTS365	300935
07 Jan	China	UK Great Britain	Postal Service	24LTS115	300599
08 Jan	Multilateral		Dispute Settlement	23LTS63	300576
10 Jan	France	Italy	Customs	43LTS431	301076
10 Jan	Estonia	Latvia	Visas	38LTS103	300968
10 Jan	Finland	Sweden	Admin Cooperation	24LTS167	300558
11 Jan	Estonia	Poland	Consul/Citizenship	47LTS129	301132
11 Jan	Germany	Poland	General Economic	41LTS187	301014
12 Jan	Germany	Poland	Specific Resources	65LTS47	301519
21 Jan	France	UK Great Britain	Territory Boundary	28LTS461	300723
21 Jan	Belgium	USA (United States)	Territory Boundary	31LTS137	300791
21 Jan	Japan	UK Great Britain	Admin Cooperation	25LTS11	300601
23 Jan	UK Great Britain	USA (United States)	Sanitation	27LTS181	300681
25 Jan	Multilateral		Sanitation	57LTS135	301360
25 Jan	Czechoslovakia	France	General Amity	23LTS163	300588
27 Jan	Italy	Serb/Croat/Slovene	Admin Cooperation	83LTS87	301886
27 Jan	Italy	Serb/Croat/Slovene	Visas	83LTS139	301887
27 Jan	Italy	Serb/Croat/Slovene	General Amity	24LTS31	300596
28 Jan	Austria	Turkey	Consul/Citizenship	32LTS303	300822
28 Jan	Austria	Turkey	General Trade	32LTS313	300823
28 Jan	Austria	Turkey	General Amity	32LTS297	300821
31 Jan	Czechoslovakia	Denmark	General Trade	23LTS139	300585
07 Feb	Multilateral		Water Transport	25LTS265	300614
07 Feb	France	Netherlands	Gen Communications	25LTS265	300615
09 Feb	Czechoslovakia	Hungary	Postal Service	30LTS325	300772
09 Feb	Czechoslovakia	Hungary	Specific Resources	30LTS335	300773
09 Feb	Spain	UK Great Britain	Admin Cooperation	25LTS17	300602
11 Feb	Muscat and Oman	UK Great Britain	Admin Cooperation	25LTS387	300628
13 Feb	Netherlands	USA (United States)	Admin Cooperation	25LTS269	300616
15 Feb	Netherlands	USA (United States)	Postal Service	31LTS61	300783
16 Feb	France	Spain	Admin Cooperation	25LTS409	300631
17 Feb	Lithuania	Sweden	General Trade	23LTS153	300587
18 Feb	Austria	Germany	Non-ILO Labor	29LTS435	300754
21 Feb	France	Greece	General Economic	43LTS481	301077
23 Feb	Germany	Poland	Territory Boundary	41LTS197	301015
23 Feb	Germany	Poland	Land Transport	49LTS355	301191
24 Feb	Germany	Latvia	Admin Cooperation	41LTS231	301016
27 Feb	Netherlands	Portugal	General Trade	27LTS105	300672
28 Feb	Germany	Siam	General Economic	32LTS399	300828
29 Feb	Albania	Italy	General Trade	44LTS331	301092
29 Feb	Albania	Italy	Consul/Citizenship	44LTS343	301093
01 Mar	Czechoslovakia	Italy	Taxation	36LTS229	300925
01 Mar	Czechoslovakia	Italy	Consul/Citizenship	34LTS55	300867
03 Mar	Germany	Turkey	General Amity	41LTS237	301017
04 Mar	Czechoslovakia	Germany	Land Transport	41LTS243	301018
05 Mar	Germany	Poland	Admin Cooperation	49LTS181	301182
05 Mar	Germany	Poland	Admin Cooperation	49LTS251	301184
05 Mar	Sweden	UK Great Britain	Air Transport	23LTS149	300586
06 Mar	Germany	Nicaragua	General Economic	41LTS264	301019
07 Mar	Germany	Poland	Admin Cooperation	52LTS7	301245
08 Mar	Czechoslovakia	Hungary	Claims and Debts	36LTS61	300904
09 Mar	Japan	Siam	General Trade	31LTS187	300795
12 Mar	Bolivia	Germany	General Amity	73LTS95	301710

DATE	PARTY ONE	PARTY TWO	TOPIC	CITATION	NUMBER
1924 (Cont.)					
12 Mar	Multilateral		General Trade	24LTS17	300595
14 Mar	Multilateral		Finance	25LTS423	300633
14 Mar	Other Unilat Decla	Hungary	Finance	25LTS427	300634
15 Mar	Sweden	USSR (Soviet Union)	General Trade	25LTS251	300613
18 Mar	Estonia	Finland	Admin Cooperation	32LTS119	300811
19 Mar	Austria	Poland	Admin Cooperation	56LTS95	301326
19 Mar	Bulgaria	USA (United States)	Extradition	26LTS27	300638
20 Mar	Sweden	Switzerland	General Trade	25LTS243	300612
21 Mar	Germany	Greece	Patents/Copyrights	30LTS257	300769
22 Mar	Multilateral		Finance	25LTS171	300605
22 Mar	Denmark	Poland	General Trade	31LTS13	300778
22 Mar	Iceland	Poland	General Trade	31LTS35	300779
25 Mar	Iraq	UK Great Britain	Admin Cooperation	35LTS131	300893
25 Mar	Iraq	UK Great Britain	Consul/Citizenship	35LTS35	300891
25 Mar	Iraq	UK Great Britain	Finance	35LTS145	300894
25 Mar	Iraq	UK Great Britain	General Military	35LTS103	300892
27 Mar	Hungary	Italy	Finance	45LTS65	301099
27 Mar	Hungary	Italy	Finance	45LTS229	301101
27 Mar	Hungary	Italy	Finance	45LTS241	301102
27 Mar	Germany	Netherlands	Customs	25LTS289	300618
27 Mar	Hungary	Italy	Finance	45LTS83	301100
27 Mar	Hungary	Italy	Telecommunications	55LTS109	301308
27 Mar	Hungary	Italy	Postal Service	55LTS103	301307
28 Mar	Multilateral		Finance	31LTS46	300780
28 Mar	Multilateral		Finance	31LTS53	300781
29 Mar	Austria	Belgium	Peace/Disarmament	91LTS245	302066
29 Mar	Austria	Poland	Non-ILO Labor	130LTS223	302992
29 Mar	Austria	Serb/Croat/Slovene	Non-ILO Labor	114LTS451	302671
29 Mar	Austria	Czechoslovakia	Non-ILO Labor	94LTS75	302139
29 Mar	Austria	Czechoslovakia	Non-ILO Labor	94LTS103	302140
29 Mar	Austria	Italy	Non-ILO Labor	84LTS293	301910
29 Mar	Austria	Italy	Other HEW	84LTS321	301911
29 Mar	Austria	Serb/Croat/Slovene	Land Transport	114LTS421	302670
29 Mar	Austria	Poland	Non-ILO Labor	130LTS251	302993
31 Mar	Mexico	Spain	Patents/Copyrights	43LTS297	301065
31 Mar	Multilateral		Sanitation	27LTS211	300685
02 Apr	Estonia	Latvia	Land Transport	38LTS113	300969
03 Apr	Denmark	Latvia	General Trade	33LTS393	300860
05 Apr	Poland	Serb/Croat/Slovene	General Economic	49LTS265	301185
09 Apr	Lithuania	USA (United States)	Extradition	51LTS191	301226
10 Apr	France	Italy	General Trade	43LTS485	301078
14 Apr	Hungary	Romania	Specific Resources	46LTS41	301113
15 Apr	Norway	Switzerland	General Economic	27LTS168	300679
16 Apr	Hungary	Romania	General Economic	46LTS95	301114
16 Apr	Hungary	Romania	Admin Cooperation	42LTS165	301039
16 Apr	Hungary	Romania	Finance	45LTS355	301109
16 Apr	Hungary	Romania	Finance	46LTS7	301111
16 Apr	Hungary	Romania	Admin Cooperation	45LTS349	301108
16 Apr	Hungary	Romania	Admin Cooperation	45LTS325	301106
16 Apr	Hungary	Romania	Admin Cooperation	46LTS113	301115
16 Apr	Hungary	Romania	Territory Boundary	46LTS27	301112
16 Apr	Hungary	Romania	Extradition	42LTS145	301038
16 Apr	Hungary	Romania	Finance	45LTS403	301110
16 Apr	Hungary	Romania	Admin Cooperation	45LTS341	301107
19 Apr	Bulgaria	Romania	Extradition	33LTS221	300846
19 Apr	Bulgaria	Romania	Admin Cooperation	33LTS209	300845
24 Apr	Poland	USSR (Soviet Union)	Visas	37LTS33	300947
26 Apr	Switzerland	UK Great Britain	General Economic	27LTS189	300682
28 Apr	Finland	Norway	Visas	30LTS35	300757
28 Apr	Finland	Norway	Territory Boundary	30LTS49	300758
28 Apr	Denmark	Sweden	Customs	27LTS355	300696
30 Apr	Austria	Germany	Admin Cooperation	46LTS175	301119
01 May	Germany	Hungary	Extradition	41LTS282	301021
02 May	Belgium	Netherlands	Admin Cooperation	27LTS113	300673
05 May	Poland	USSR (Soviet Union)	Admin Cooperation	157LTS431	303617

DATE	PARTY ONE	PARTY TWO	TOPIC	CITATION	NUMBER
1924 (Cont.)					
08 May	Czechoslovakia	Iceland	General Economic	46LTS419	301125
08 May	Multilateral		Territory Boundary	29LTS85	300736
19 May	Germany	USA (United States)	Customs	41LTS271	301020
19 May	Italy	UK Great Britain	Territory Boundary	28LTS497	300725
21 May	Estonia	Lithuania	General Transport	62LTS55	301454
21 May	Latvia	Lithuania	Health/Educ/Welfare	37LTS363	300960
22 May	Sweden	USA (United States)	Customs	29LTS421	300752
22 May	Multilateral		General Trade	35LTS175	300895
23 May	China	UK Great Britain	Postal Service	28LTS481	300724
24 May	Norway	USA (United States)	Customs	26LTS43	300639
27 May	Austria	Greece	Patents/Copyrights	27LTS99	300671
28 May	Hungary	Romania	Admin Cooperation	27LTS117	300674
28 May	Finland	Iceland	General Trade	27LTS117	300676
29 May	Denmark	USA (United States)	Sanitation	27LTS361	300697
30 May	Netherlands	Poland	General Trade	34LTS9	300865
30 May	Denmark	Switzerland	General Economic	25LTS415	300632
30 May	Finland	UK Great Britain	Extradition	34LTS79	300868
31 May	China	USSR (Soviet Union)	Land Transport	37LTS193	300956
31 May	Sweden	Turkey	General Amity	38LTS148	300972
31 May	China	USSR (Soviet Union)	General Amity	37LTS175	300955
02 Jun	Sweden	Switzerland	Admin Cooperation	33LTS199	300844
02 Jun	Czechoslovakia	Denmark	Education	57LTS115	301357
05 Jun	Norway	UK Great Britain	Admin Cooperation	27LTS195	300683
06 Jun	Panama	USA (United States)	Commodity Trade	138LTS397	303200
06 Jun	Denmark	Switzerland	Dispute Settlement	34LTS175	300873
06 Jun	Canada	USA (United States)	Customs	43LTS225	301057
07 Jun	Finland	Latvia	Admin Cooperation	58LTS375	301382
07 Jun	Finland	Latvia	Extradition	38LTS343	300990
07 Jun	Finland	Japan	General Economic	58LTS379	301383
10 Jun	Lithuania	Netherlands	General Trade	34LTS373	300885
12 Jun	Dominican Republic	USA (United States)	Admin Cooperation	48LTS91	301153
15 Jun	Austria	Czechoslovakia	Non-ILO Labor	94LTS131	302141
15 Jun	Austria	Czechoslovakia	Non-ILO Labor	94LTS165	302143
15 Jun	Austria	Czechoslovakia	Non-ILO Labor	94LTS149	302142
18 Jun	Austria	Poland	Non-ILO Labor	130LTS309	302996
18 Jun	Austria	Serb/Croat/Slovene	Non-ILO Labor	115LTS9	302673
18 Jun	Austria	Serb/Croat/Slovene	Non-ILO Labor	115LTS25	302674
18 Jun	Austria	Poland	Non-ILO Labor	130LTS293	302995
18 Jun	Austria	Italy	Non-ILO Labor	84LTS349	301912
18 Jun	Austria	Italy	Finance	84LTS381	301914
18 Jun	Austria	Serb/Croat/Slovene	Non-ILO Labor	114LTS481	302672
18 Jun	Austria	Poland	Non-ILO Labor	130LTS279	302994
18 Jun	Austria	Italy	Non-ILO Labor	84LTS367	301913
18 Jun	Finland	USSR (Soviet Union)	Admin Cooperation	47LTS241	301134
18 Jun	Finland	USSR (Soviet Union)	Land Transport	47LTS153	301133
18 Jun	Finland	USSR (Soviet Union)	Telecommunications	29LTS295	300746
18 Jun	Finland	USSR (Soviet Union)	Postal Service	29LTS313	300747
18 Jun	Hungary	Switzerland	Dispute Settlement	34LTS387	300887
18 Jun	Finland	USSR (Soviet Union)	Telecommunications	29LTS265	300745
18 Jun	Denmark	USSR (Soviet Union)	General Trade	27LTS149	300677
20 Jun	Austria	Norway	Admin Cooperation	27LTS123	300675
21 Jun	Ecuador	Peru	Territory Boundary	27LTS345	300694
21 Jun	Finland	UK Great Britain	Water Transport	28LTS511	300726
23 Jun	Brazil	Switzerland	Dispute Settlement	33LTS415	300861
24 Jun	Sweden	USA (United States)	Dispute Settlement	33LTS273	300851
26 Jun	Finland	USA (United States)	Postal Service	30LTS9	300756
27 Jun	Austria	Serb/Croat/Slovene	Non-ILO Labor	115LTS39	302675
27 Jun	Austria	Serb/Croat/Slovene	Non-ILO Labor	115LTS49	302676
27 Jun	Denmark	Finland	Dispute Settlement	33LTS131	300839
27 Jun	Finland	Norway	Dispute Settlement	29LTS403	300751
27 Jun	Denmark	Norway	Dispute Settlement	33LTS173	300842
27 Jun	Denmark	Sweden	Dispute Settlement	33LTS149	300840
27 Jun	Finland	Sweden	Dispute Settlement	29LTS19	300731
27 Jun	Spain	UK Great Britain	General Trade	28LTS523	300727
27 Jun	Norway	Sweden	Dispute Settlement	28LTS309	300717

DATE	PARTY ONE	PARTY TWO	TOPIC	CITATION	NUMBER
1924 (Cont.)					
28 Jun	Finland	Sweden	Land Transport	28LTS327	300718
30 Jun	France	USA (United States)	Admin Cooperation	61LTS415	301451
02 Jul	Latvia	Netherlands	General Trade	37LTS121	300951
03 Jul	Bel-Lux Econ Union	Canada	General Trade	32LTS35	300803
04 Jul	Multilateral		Admin Cooperation	51LTS227	301231
05 Jul	Czechoslovakia	Italy	General Amity	26LTS21	300637
07 Jul	Estonia	Sweden	Water Transport	73LTS27	301702
09 Jul	Denmark	Norway	Territory Boundary	27LTS203	300684
11 Jul	Canada	Netherlands	General Trade	39LTS45	300995
12 Jul	Austria	Czechoslovakia	Finance	50LTS111	301199
12 Jul	Austria	Germany	General Trade	41LTS287	301022
14 Jul	Italy	Serb/Croat/Slovene	Land Transport	82LTS327	301877
14 Jul	Italy	Serb/Croat/Slovene	General Trade	82LTS257	301876
14 Jul	Italy	Serb/Croat/Slovene	Land Transport	82LTS349	301878
14 Jul	Japan	UK Great Britain	General Economic	28LTS537	300728
15 Jul	Italy	UK Great Britain	Territory Boundary	36LTS379	300936
16 Jul	Great Britain	Latvia	Extradition	37LTS369	300961
18 Jul	Japan	Strait Settlements	General Transport	31LTS109	300787
18 Jul	Poland	USSR (Soviet Union)	Consul/Citizenship	49LTS201	301183
22 Jul	Estonia	Netherlands	General Economic	48LTS199	301162
25 Jul	Germany	Spain	General Trade	41LTS363	301023
26 Jul	Austria	Romania	Claims and Debts	85LTS223	301933
26 Jul	Austria	Romania	Finance	85LTS243	301934
26 Jul	Multilateral		Postal Service	30LTS271	300771
26 Jul	Finland	Sweden	Postal Service	29LTS167	300740
29 Jul	Belgium	UK Great Britain	Telecommunications	29LTS389	300749
31 Jul	Denmark	Finland	Postal Service	29LTS183	300741
01 Aug	Finland	USA (United States)	Extradition	34LTS103	300869
07 Aug	Czechoslovakia	Latvia	Sanitation	38LTS123	300970
09 Aug	Austria	Latvia	General Economic	65LTS7	301516
11 Aug	Austria	France	General Trade	44LTS7	301079
12 Aug	Italy	Serb/Croat/Slovene	Sanitation	83LTS19	301884
12 Aug	Italy	Serb/Croat/Slovene	Customs	82LTS391	301880
12 Aug	Italy	Serb/Croat/Slovene	Admin Cooperation	82LTS355	301879
12 Aug	Italy	Serb/Croat/Slovene	Telecommunications	82LTS401	301881
12 Aug	Italy	Serb/Croat/Slovene	Territory Boundary	82LTS423	301882
13 Aug	Poland	UK Great Britain	Air Transport	31LTS213	300796
14 Aug	Latvia	Norway	General Amity	36LTS211	300924
15 Aug	France	Panama	Customs	93LTS425	302130
16 Aug	Netherlands	Turkey	Admin Cooperation	39LTS148	300999
16 Aug	Multilateral		Taxation	41LTS429	301024
18 Aug	Czechoslovakia	France	General Trade	44LTS21	301080
20 Aug	Colombia	Panama	Territory Boundary	33LTS167	300841
21 Aug	Italy	Serb/Croat/Slovene	Consul/Citizenship	82LTS445	301883
21 Aug	Netherlands	USA (United States)	Sanitation	33LTS433	300863
23 Aug	Finland	Latvia	General Trade	37LTS383	300962
25 Aug	Multilateral		Water Transport	120LTS123	302763
25 Aug	Multilateral		Water Transport	120LTS155	302764
25 Aug	France	El Salvador	Admin Cooperation	93LTS365	302124
27 Aug	Netherlands	Portugal	General Trade	31LTS235	300800
28 Aug	Multilateral		Postal Service	41LTS55	301007
28 Aug	Multilateral		Postal Service	41LTS97	301008
28 Aug	Multilateral		Postal Service	40LTS249	301003
28 Aug	Multilateral		Postal Service	40LTS307	301004
28 Aug	Multilateral		Postal Service	40LTS437	301005
28 Aug	Multilateral		Postal Service	41LTS9	301006
28 Aug	Multilateral		Postal Service	40LTS19	301002
29 Aug	Germany	Sweden	Dispute Settlement	42LTS111	301036
30 Aug	Germany	Poland	Consul/Citizenship	32LTS331	300824
30 Aug	Estonia	Sweden	Admin Cooperation	31LTS217	300797
30 Aug	Great Britain	Portugal	Postal Service	38LTS217	300979
30 Aug	Multilateral		Admin Cooperation	30LTS75	300760
30 Aug	Multilateral		General Economic	30LTS63	300759
30 Aug	Multilateral		Reparations	30LTS97	300762
30 Aug	Multilateral		Admin Cooperation	30LTS79	300761

DATE	PARTY ONE	PARTY TWO	TOPIC	CITATION	NUMBER
1924 (Cont.)					
10 Sep	Guatemala	Nicaragua	General Trade	130LTS127	302987
11 Sep	India	Siam	General Economic	31LTS115	300788
12 Sep	Sweden	USSR (Soviet Union)	Postal Service	31LTS75	300784
12 Sep	Germany	Japan	Admin Cooperation	59LTS17	301387
16 Sep	Hungary	Norway	General Trade	33LTS103	300835
19 Sep	Other Unilat Decla	Greece	Refugees	30LTS413	300776
20 Sep	Germany	Saar	Admin Cooperation	30LTS121	300765
20 Sep	Italy	Switzerland	Admin Cooperation	33LTS91	300834
25 Sep	France	Mexico	Claims and Debts	79LTS417	301818
25 Sep	Multilateral		Admin Cooperation	30LTS421	300777
27 Sep	Austria	Italy	Non-ILO Labor	84LTS397	301915
27 Sep	Austria	Italy	Non-ILO Labor	84LTS409	301916
27 Sep	Spain	Turkey	General Amity	43LTS307	301066
29 Sep	Other Unilat Decla	Bulgaria	Consul/Citizenship	29LTS117	300737
29 Sep	Costa Rica	UK Great Britain	Postal Service	31LTS121	300789
29 Sep	Other Unilat Decla	Greece	Consul/Citizenship	29LTS123	300738
30 Sep	Japan	Peru	General Amity	102LTS33	302351
30 Sep	Austria	Hungary	Consul/Citizenship	42LTS177	301040
30 Sep	Multilateral		Mostfavored Nation	30LTS135	300766
30 Sep	Denmark	Iceland	Water Transport	32LTS355	300825
01 Oct	Norway	Romania	General Trade	29LTS397	300750
01 Oct	Czechoslovakia	Romania	Sanitation	51LTS71	301223
02 Oct	Bulgaria	Norway	General Trade	30LTS103	300763
04 Oct	Germany	Guatemala	General Economic	52LTS19	301246
07 Oct	Argentina	Norway	Admin Cooperation	33LTS191	300843
08 Oct	Japan	Mexico	General Amity	36LTS259	300927
09 Oct	Sweden	UK Great Britain	Admin Cooperation	34LTS381	300886
11 Oct	Czechoslovakia	Turkey	General Amity	38LTS317	300987
11 Oct	Finland	Norway	Postal Service	32LTS123	300812
11 Oct	Austria	Switzerland	Dispute Settlement	33LTS423	300862
15 Oct	Germany	Haiti	Finance	52LTS27	301247
17 Oct	Czechoslovakia	Netherlands	General Trade	31LTS93	300786
18 Oct	Latvia	Lithuania	Territory Boundary	56LTS157	301327
20 Oct	Argentina	Belgium	Health/Educ/Welfare	137LTS381	303166
21 Oct	Norway	Portugal	Admin Cooperation	30LTS117	300764
22 Oct	Finland	Italy	General Trade	32LTS149	300814
23 Oct	Multilateral		Land Transport	78LTS17	301779
23 Oct	Multilateral		General Transport	77LTS367	301778
27 Oct	UK Great Britain	USA (United States)	Postal Service	33LTS315	300855
28 Oct	Allied Powers	Germany	General Military	41LTS461	301025
29 Oct	France	Latvia	Extradition	93LTS265	302115
30 Oct	France	Latvia	General Trade	37LTS399	300963
03 Nov	Iceland	Latvia	General Economic	43LTS339	301069
07 Nov	Bel-Lux Econ Union	Guatemala	General Economic	69LTS17	301596
07 Nov	El Salvador	Uruguay	Dispute Settlement	108LTS103	302502
08 Nov	Austria	Hungary	Taxation	44LTS407	301096
08 Nov	Austria	Hungary	Taxation	45LTS21	301097
10 Nov	Austria	Sweden	General Economic	31LTS57	300782
12 Nov	Canada	Irish Free State	Postal Service	56LTS333	301340
14 Nov	Multilateral		Sanitation	86LTS43	301949
14 Nov	Finland	Germany	Postal Service	32LTS137	300813
15 Nov	Czechoslovakia	Italy	Land Transport	92LTS91	302081
15 Nov	Latvia	Sweden	Admin Cooperation	56LTS173	301328
17 Nov	Germany	Switzerland	General Trade	41LTS473	301026
19 Nov	Austria	Switzerland	Water Transport	39LTS26	300994
26 Nov	Multilateral		Finance	48LTS69	301151
26 Nov	China	UK Great Britain	Admin Cooperation	32LTS281	300818
27 Nov	Austria	Czechoslovakia	General Economic	42LTS201	301041
28 Nov	Denmark	Sweden	Water Transport	32LTS41	300804
29 Nov	Multilateral		General IGO	80LTS293	301835
29 Nov	Denmark	Germany	Admin Cooperation	31LTS131	300790
01 Dec	Estonia	Turkey	General Amity	70LTS77	301624
01 Dec	Multilateral		Sanitation	78LTS351	301794
02 Dec	Poland	Sweden	General Amity	36LTS299	300930
03 Dec	Austria	Norway	General Trade	31LTS151	300792

DATE	PARTY ONE	PARTY TWO	TOPIC	CITATION	NUMBER
1924 (Cont.)					
03 Dec	UK Great Britain	USA (United States)	Consul/Citizenship	43LTS41	301046
04 Dec	Latvia	Switzerland	General Trade	34LTS405	300889
05 Dec	Czechoslovakia	USA (United States)	General Economic	56LTS271	301335
06 Dec	Austria	Norway	Consul/Citizenship	31LTS179	300794
09 Dec	Hungary	Netherlands	General Trade	47LTS91	301130
09 Dec	Finland	Turkey	General Amity	59LTS287	301398
09 Dec	France	Poland	General Trade	44LTS127	301081
10 Dec	Greece	UK Great Britain	General Economic	36LTS441	300941
10 Dec	Denmark	Greece	General Economic	31LTS227	300798
10 Dec	Greece	Norway	General Economic	31LTS231	300799
12 Dec	Multilateral		Gen Communications	37LTS113	300950
12 Dec	Finland	UK Great Britain	Postal Service	34LTS123	300870
14 Dec	Hungary	Serb/Croat/Slovene	Admin Cooperation	39LTS91	300997
15 Dec	Czechoslovakia	Germany	Non-ILO Labor	52LTS31	301248
15 Dec	Czechoslovakia	Germany	Non-ILO Labor	52LTS41	301249
16 Dec	Denmark	Poland	Air Transport	32LTS409	300829
18 Dec	Norway	UK Great Britain	Taxation	32LTS9	300801
18 Dec	Denmark	UK Great Britain	Admin Cooperation	32LTS287	300819
18 Dec	Denmark	UK Great Britain	Taxation	32LTS89	300808
19 Dec	Sweden	UK Great Britain	Taxation	32LTS291	300820
22 Dec	Finland	Sweden	Water Transport	73LTS33	301703
22 Dec	Austria	Czechoslovakia	Non-ILO Labor	94LTS179	302144
22 Dec	Norway	Sweden	Admin Cooperation	32LTS13	300802
22 Dec	Latvia	Sweden	General Amity	36LTS283	300928
24 Dec	Belgium	France	Non-ILO Labor	78LTS367	301795
26 Dec	Japan	Switzerland	Dispute Settlement	43LTS393	301072
27 Dec	Bulgaria	Turkey	Admin Cooperation	54LTS135	301281
29 Dec	Germany	Irish Free State	Postal Service	56LTS341	301341
30 Dec	Germany	Poland	Specific Property	52LTS51	301250
31 Dec	China	Germany	Customs	42LTS7	301027
1925					
02 Jan	Estonia	Finland	Extradition	43LTS11	301044
03 Jan	Latvia	Turkey	General Amity	59LTS81	301390
08 Jan	Netherlands	Norway	Air Transport	46LTS279	301122
08 Jan	Canada	USA (United States)	Extradition	43LTS233	301058
09 Jan	Estonia	Germany	Extradition	42LTS13	301028
09 Jan	Netherlands	Norway	Non-ILO Labor	48LTS247	301166
15 Jan	France	Saar	Customs	44LTS181	301082
16 Jan	China	Strait Settlements	Postal Service	36LTS395	300937
17 Jan	Austria	Poland	Non-ILO Labor	130LTS387	302998
17 Jan	Austria	Italy	Non-ILO Labor	84LTS419	301917
17 Jan	Austria	Serb/Croat/Slovene	Health/Educ/Welfare	128LTS453	302949
17 Jan	Austria	Serb/Croat/Slovene	Health/Educ/Welfare	128LTS445	302948
17 Jan	Austria	Italy	Non-ILO Labor	85LTS9	301918
17 Jan	Austria	Czechoslovakia	Non-ILO Labor	94LTS185	302145
17 Jan	Austria	Czechoslovakia	Non-ILO Labor	94LTS245	302146
17 Jan	Austria	Italy	Non-ILO Labor	85LTS19	301919
17 Jan	Austria	Poland	Non-ILO Labor	130LTS327	302997
17 Jan	Multilateral		Dispute Settlement	38LTS357	300991
20 Jan	Japan	USSR (Soviet Union)	General Amity	34LTS31	300866
23 Jan	Netherlands	USA (United States)	Territory Boundary	33LTS445	300864
26 Jan	Denmark	Turkey	General Amity	36LTS317	300931
28 Jan	France	UK Great Britain	Visas	33LTS335	300856
02 Feb	Finland	Germany	Claims and Debts	33LTS127	300838
03 Feb	Austria	Spain	General Economic	43LTS313	301067
06 Feb	Czechoslovakia	Germany	Admin Cooperation	46LTS165	301118
10 Feb	UK Great Britain	USA (United States)	Admin Cooperation	55LTS133	301310
10 Feb	UK Great Britain	USA (United States)	Admin Cooperation	55LTS145	301311
10 Feb	Poland	USA (United States)	General Trade	37LTS141	300953
10 Feb	Germany	Lithuania	Admin Cooperation	42LTS17	301029
10 Feb	UK Great Britain	USA (United States)	Admin Cooperation	55LTS119	301309
11 Feb	Muscat and Oman	UK Great Britain	General Amity	35LTS233	300897
11 Feb	Multilateral		Sanitation	51LTS337	301239
14 Feb	Finland	Norway	Specific Resources	49LTS379	301193

DATE	PARTY ONE	PARTY TWO	TOPIC	CITATION	NUMBER
1925 (Cont.)					
14 Feb	Finland	Norway	Specific Resources	49LTS391	301194
14 Feb	France	Siam	General Amity	43LTS189	301055
18 Feb	Belgium	UK Great Britain	Postal Service	33LTS341	300857
18 Feb	Belgium	UK Great Britain	Postal Service	33LTS361	300858
19 Feb	Multilateral		Admin Cooperation	81LTS317	301845
20 Feb	Bolivia	Germany	General Trade	42LTS43	301030
20 Feb	Finland	USSR (Soviet Union)	Postal Service	34LTS153	300871
24 Feb	Canada	USA (United States)	Territory Boundary	43LTS251	301060
24 Feb	Canada	USA (United States)	Territory Boundary	43LTS239	301059
25 Feb	United Arab Rep	Tanganyika	Postal Service	36LTS409	300938
25 Feb	Denmark	France	Consul/Citizenship	33LTS277	300852
26 Feb	Belgium	UK Great Britain	Telecommunications	71LTS83	301656
27 Feb	Belgium	Portugal	Water Transport	91LTS201	302061
28 Feb	Germany	Saar	Land Transport	33LTS123	300837
02 Mar	Estonia	USA (United States)	General Economic	43LTS289	301064
04 Mar	Austria	France	Admin Cooperation	75LTS97	301755
04 Mar	France	Portugal	General Economic	44LTS197	301083
04 Mar	Austria	France	Admin Cooperation	44LTS205	301084
06 Mar	Albania	Italy	General Economic	44LTS359	301094
06 Mar	Czechoslovakia	Poland	Admin Cooperation	46LTS201	301120
07 Mar	Poland	Switzerland	Dispute Settlement	50LTS261	301209
07 Mar	Finland	Iceland	Patents/Copyrights	34LTS169	300872
09 Mar	Finland	Netherlands	Consul/Citizenship	47LTS431	301148
13 Mar	Estonia	Germany	Consul/Citizenship	51LTS263	301236
14 Mar	Germany	Poland	Territory Boundary	95LTS239	302178
14 Mar	Finland	Germany	Dispute Settlement	43LTS347	301070
16 Mar	UK Great Britain	USA (United States)	Taxation	113LTS105	302639
16 Mar	Germany	Mexico	Reparations	52LTS93	301251
19 Mar	Latvia	USSR (Soviet Union)	Water Transport	38LTS141	300971
20 Mar	Germany	USA (United States)	Taxation	119LTS185	302745
24 Mar	Norway	USA (United States)	Taxation	67LTS417	301563
25 Mar	British Honduras	Mexico	Postal Service	43LTS61	301047
26 Mar	Hungary	Poland	Privil/Immunities	37LTS151	300954
28 Mar	Latvia	Sweden	Dispute Settlement	37LTS131	300952
00 Apr	Multilateral		Water Transport	37LTS21	300945
03 Apr	Germany	UK Great Britain	Reparations	33LTS383	300859
04 Apr	Benelux Econ Union	Germany	General Trade	37LTS203	300957
04 Apr	Bel-Lux Econ Union	France	General Trade	44LTS213	301085
06 Apr	France	Switzerland	Dispute Settlement	147LTS89	303393
07 Apr	Czechoslovakia	Poland	General Trade	56LTS285	301337
08 Apr	Czechoslovakia	Greece	General Trade	38LTS291	300984
11 Apr	Canada	Spain	General Economic	43LTS333	301068
11 Apr	Germany	Norway	Customs	52LTS115	301252
13 Apr	France	Germany	Admin Cooperation	109LTS295	302546
16 Apr	Czechoslovakia	Romania	Territory Boundary	46LTS427	301126
17 Apr	France	UK Great Britain	Postal Service	36LTS429	300939
17 Apr	Greece	Poland	General Trade	38LTS301	300985
18 Apr	Belgium	Germany	Admin Cooperation	42LTS49	301031
18 Apr	Denmark	Germany	Water Transport	37LTS103	300949
18 Apr	Austria	Greece	General Trade	38LTS311	300986
18 Apr	Czechoslovakia	Sweden	General Amity	36LTS289	300929
20 Apr	Estonia	Finland	Telecommunications	51LTS31	301220
23 Apr	Czechoslovakia	Poland	Taxation	44LTS285	301090
23 Apr	Czechoslovakia	Poland	Taxation	44LTS309	301091
23 Apr	Czechoslovakia	Poland	Taxation	44LTS271	301089
23 Apr	Czechoslovakia	Poland	Dispute Settlement	48LTS383	301171
23 Apr	Multilateral		Water Transport	37LTS9	300944
23 Apr	Czechoslovakia	Poland	Admin Cooperation	48LTS287	301170
29 Apr	Bulgaria	Poland	General Economic	60LTS103	301408
30 Apr	Irish Free State	New Zealand	Postal Service	56LTS373	301342
02 May	Finland	USA (United States)	General Economic	47LTS351	301139
04 May	Spain	Sweden	General Trade	36LTS323	300932
05 May	Multilateral		Finance	55LTS225	301318
05 May	Austria	Poland	Air Transport	46LTS269	301121
07 May	Czechoslovakia	Romania	Extradition	54LTS51	301273

DATE	PARTY ONE	PARTY TWO	TOPIC	CITATION	NUMBER
1925 (Cont.)					
07 May	Bulgaria	Great Britain	Postal Service	38LTS153	300973
07 May	Czechoslovakia	Romania	Admin Cooperation	54LTS17	301272
09 May	Finland	Sweden	Territory Boundary	47LTS283	301136
13 May	Norway	UK Great Britain	Admin Cooperation	36LTS435	300940
14 May	Austria	Czechoslovakia	Finance	50LTS39	301198
15 May	Germany	Greece	General Trade	40LTS6	301001
18 May	Netherlands	Switzerland	Air Transport	54LTS365	301299
19 May	Portugal	UK Great Britain	Consul/Citizenship	36LTS125	300910
19 May	Czechoslovakia	Denmark	General Amity	36LTS113	300908
19 May	Austria	Germany	Air Transport	52LTS121	301253
21 May	Germany	USA (United States)	General Economic	52LTS133	301254
21 May	Italy	UK Great Britain	Health/Educ/Welfare	43LTS75	301048
26 May	Czechoslovakia	France	Air Transport	150LTS43	303452
26 May	France	Monaco	Admin Cooperation	44LTS249	301086
29 May	Austria	Czechoslovakia	Non-ILO Labor	98LTS91	302242
29 May	Germany	Sweden	Air Transport	46LTS121	301116
29 May	Estonia	Sweden	Dispute Settlement	46LTS289	301123
30 May	Czechoslovakia	Poland	Territory Boundary	48LTS397	301172
30 May	Czechoslovakia	Poland	General Transport	50LTS243	301207
04 Jun	Denmark	Finland	Water Transport	37LTS24	300946
04 Jun	Denmark	UK Great Britain	Consul/Citizenship	36LTS131	300911
04 Jun	Greece	Hungary	General Trade	39LTS139	300998
04 Jun	Denmark	Hungary	General Amity	36LTS119	300909
08 Jun	Netherlands	Siam	General Economic	56LTS57	301323
09 Jun	Multilateral		Customs	49LTS9	301174
10 Jun	Albania	UK Great Britain	General Economic	43LTS81	301049
10 Jun	Latvia	Norway	Water Transport	36LTS91	300906
11 Jun	Lithuania	Sweden	Dispute Settlement	57LTS191	301364
15 Jun	Italy	UK Great Britain	Water Transport	38LTS189	300976
17 Jun	Multilateral		Peace/Disarmament	94LTS65	302138
17 Jun	Hungary	Spain	General Economic	60LTS69	301406
21 Jun	Germany	Italy	Admin Cooperation	68LTS11	301565
27 Jun	Bel-Lux Econ Union	Japan	Water Transport	36LTS95	300907
29 Jun	Denmark	USSR (Soviet Union)	Water Transport	36LTS251	300926
02 Jul	Czechoslovakia	USA (United States)	Extradition	50LTS143	301200
04 Jul	Japan	Latvia	General Trade	80LTS305	301836
07 Jul	Bel-Lux Econ Union		General Economic	54LTS267	301290
08 Jul	Paraguay	Spain	Patents/Copyrights	138LTS225	303190
12 Jul	Netherlands	UK Great Britain	Admin Cooperation	38LTS207	300977
16 Jul	Germany	Lithuania	General Trade	85LTS357	301939
16 Jul	Finland	Spain	General Trade	47LTS271	301135
19 Jul	Czechoslovakia	Spain	General Economic	60LTS329	301419
20 Jul	Italy	Serb/Croat/Slovene	Consul/Citizenship	83LTS265	301893
20 Jul	Italy	Serb/Croat/Slovene	Land Transport	83LTS247	301890
20 Jul	Italy	Serb/Croat/Slovene	Consul/Citizenship	83LTS271	301894
20 Jul	Italy	Serb/Croat/Slovene	Visas	83LTS253	301891
20 Jul	Italy	Serb/Croat/Slovene	Visas	83LTS287	301896
20 Jul	Italy	Serb/Croat/Slovene	Visas	83LTS277	301895
20 Jul	Italy	Serb/Croat/Slovene	Consul/Citizenship	83LTS159	301888
20 Jul	Italy	Serb/Croat/Slovene	Telecommunications	83LTS295	301897
20 Jul	Italy	Serb/Croat/Slovene	Admin Cooperation	83LTS241	301889
20 Jul	Italy	Serb/Croat/Slovene	Other Ad Hoc	83LTS259	301892
20 Jul	Italy	Serb/Croat/Slovene	General Transport	83LTS33	301885
20 Jul	Hungary	Italy	Admin Cooperation	45LTS39	301098
20 Jul	Colombia	Venezuela	General Transport	39LTS15	300993
22 Jul	Hungary	Poland	Admin Cooperation	48LTS167	301158
22 Jul	Italy	Poland	General Economic	54LTS101	301278
24 Jul	Czechoslovakia	Denmark	Visas	37LTS97	300948
25 Jul	Italy	Latvia	General Economic	60LTS91	301407
28 Jul	Japan	UK Great Britain	Postal Service	49LTS73	301177
30 Jul	Germany	Great Britain	Reparations	38LTS181	300974
30 Jul	Great Britain	Japan	General Economic	65LTS29	301517
03 Aug	France	Spain	General Trade	38LTS371	300992
03 Aug	Siam	Spain	General Economic	55LTS39	301303
09 Aug	Czechoslovakia	Great Britain	Postal Service	38LTS231	300980

DATE	PARTY ONE	PARTY TWO	TOPIC	CITATION	NUMBER
1925 (Cont.)					
10 Aug	Estonia	Germany	Dispute Settlement	63LTS111	301484
13 Aug	Germany	UK Great Britain	General Economic	43LTS89	301050
13 Aug	Germany	Great Britain	Reparations	38LTS185	300975
13 Aug	Great Britain	Latvia	Milit Assistance	56LTS177	301329
14 Aug	France	Germany	Territory Boundary	75LTS103	301756
14 Aug	Portugal	Siam	General Economic	55LTS57	301304
18 Aug	Great Britain	Lithuania	Postal Service	43LTS135	301051
19 Aug	Multilateral		Customs	42LTS73	301033
21 Aug	Norway	Switzerland	Dispute Settlement	51LTS89	301224
28 Aug	Belgium	Netherlands	Dispute Settlement	93LTS431	302131
29 Aug	Great Britain	Portugal	Admin Cooperation	38LTS213	300978
01 Sep	Belgium	Poland	Admin Cooperation	54LTS69	301274
04 Sep	Netherlands	Poland	Air Transport	58LTS179	301371
05 Sep	Czechoslovakia	Poland	Sanitation	58LTS143	301370
06 Sep	Bulgaria	Czechoslovakia	Health/Educ/Welfare	50LTS253	301208
07 Sep	Denmark	Portugal	Water Transport	55LTS215	301316
15 Sep	Siam	UK Great Britain	Admin Cooperation	49LTS29	301175
15 Sep	Siam	UK Great Britain	General Economic	49LTS51	301176
19 Sep	Switzerland	Turkey	General Amity	61LTS395	301449
21 Sep	Greece	Switzerland	Dispute Settlement	87LTS187	301969
25 Sep	Great Britain	USA (United States)	Telecommunications	69LTS179	301603
30 Sep	Czechoslovakia	Switzerland	General Trade	58LTS279	301378
01 Oct	Irish Free State	South Africa	Postal Service	56LTS389	301343
01 Oct	Great Britain	USA (United States)	Telecommunications	69LTS187	301604
01 Oct	Poland	Sweden	Air Transport	54LTS113	301279
03 Oct	Germany	Poland	Admin Cooperation	50LTS189	301201
03 Oct	Belgium	Germany	Visas	38LTS285	300983
03 Oct	Austria	Germany	Customs	52LTS171	301255
12 Oct	Germany	USSR (Soviet Union)	Consul/Citizenship	53LTS163	301258
12 Oct	Germany	USSR (Soviet Union)	Admin Cooperation	53LTS227	301259
12 Oct	Germany	Switzerland	Extradition	53LTS241	301260
12 Oct	Germany	USSR (Soviet Union)	Other Ad Hoc	53LTS7	301257
13 Oct	France	Hungary	General Trade	67LTS255	301553
13 Oct	France	Hungary	General Economic	48LTS9	301150
14 Oct	Estonia	Switzerland	General Economic	49LTS421	301195
16 Oct	Germany	Poland	General Military	54LTS327	301295
16 Oct	Czechoslovakia	Germany	General Military	54LTS341	301296
16 Oct	Bulgaria	Czechoslovakia	General Economic	56LTS265	301334
16 Oct	Belgium	Germany	General Military	54LTS303	301293
16 Oct	Multilateral		Peace/Disarmament	54LTS289	301292
16 Oct	France	Poland	Peace/Disarmament	54LTS353	301297
16 Oct	Czechoslovakia	France	Peace/Disarmament	54LTS359	301298
16 Oct	France	Germany	General Military	54LTS315	301294
17 Oct	Hungary	UK Great Britain	Finance	47LTS373	301142
18 Oct	Bulgaria	Turkey	General Amity	54LTS125	301280
19 Oct	Denmark	France	Mostfavored Nation	38LTS325	300988
19 Oct	Austria	China	General Economic	55LTS9	301301
19 Oct	Denmark	Finland	Taxation	47LTS259	301140
22 Oct	Bulgaria	France	General Trade	44LTS257	301087
23 Oct	Norway	Sweden	Dispute Settlement	39LTS153	301000
28 Oct	Estonia	USA (United States)	Claims and Debts	62LTS63	301455
28 Oct	Estonia	Latvia	Specific Resources	54LTS231	301286
29 Oct	Multilateral		Telecommunications	57LTS201	301365
29 Oct	Multilateral		Land Transport	66LTS147	301529
30 Oct	Czechoslovakia	Japan	General Trade	58LTS263	301377
31 Oct	Germany	Italy	Taxation	53LTS245	301261
31 Oct	Germany	Italy	General Economic	52LTS179	301256
02 Nov	Great Britain	Nejd	Territory Boundary	60LTS419	301423
03 Nov	Portugal	UK Great Britain	Territory Boundary	47LTS379	301143
03 Nov	Poland	Sweden	Dispute Settlement	62LTS263	301466
06 Nov	Multilateral		Other Economic	74LTS341	301746
06 Nov	Multilateral		Patents/Copyrights	74LTS327	301745
06 Nov	Multilateral		Patents/Copyrights	74LTS289	301743
06 Nov	Multilateral		Other Economic	74LTS319	301744
06 Nov	Germany	Switzerland	Customs	53LTS283	301262

DATE	PARTY ONE	PARTY TWO	TOPIC	CITATION	NUMBER
1925 (Cont.)					
10 Nov	Finland	Norway	Dispute Settlement	43LTS381	301071
11 Nov	Estonia	Latvia	Admin Cooperation	42LTS93	301034
12 Nov	Bulgaria	UK Great Britain	General Trade	43LTS165	301052
16 Nov	Hungary	Poland	Dispute Settlement	43LTS265	301061
18 Nov	Finland	Great Britain	Taxation	42LTS445	301042
18 Nov	Belgium	USA (United States)	Extradition	50LTS225	301205
18 Nov	Cuba	USA (United States)	Extradition	61LTS363	301446
18 Nov	Germany	Spain	General Economic	53LTS309	301263
21 Nov	Denmark	Sweden	Water Transport	42LTS55	301032
21 Nov	Denmark	Sweden	General Trade	42LTS139	301037
21 Nov	Netherlands	Sweden	Air Transport	55LTS79	301305
25 Nov	Norway	Sweden	Dispute Settlement	60LTS295	301417
25 Nov	Siam	UK Great Britain	Dispute Settlement	63LTS161	301487
25 Nov	Estonia	Germany	Admin Cooperation	54LTS79	301275
25 Nov	Italy	Spain	Refugees	60LTS59	301405
25 Nov	Hungary	Italy	Taxation	74LTS251	301741
26 Nov	British Empire	Greece	General Trade	63LTS167	301488
26 Nov	Germany	Netherlands	General Economic	57LTS147	301361
26 Nov	Germany	Netherlands	Customs	57LTS159	301362
27 Nov	Multilateral		Water Transport	67LTS63	301539
30 Nov	Greece	UK Great Britain	Reparations	50LTS273	301210
02 Dec	Germany	Poland	Territory Boundary	70LTS427	301649
03 Dec	Great Britain	Irish Free State	Admin Cooperation	44LTS263	301088
05 Dec	Belgium	Hungary	Admin Cooperation	43LTS173	301053
07 Dec	Austria	Czechoslovakia	Admin Cooperation	86LTS7	301947
09 Dec	Belgium	USA (United States)	Other Ad Hoc	72LTS171	301690
10 Dec	Estonia	Finland	Non-ILO Labor	50LTS335	301217
12 Dec	Netherlands	Switzerland	Dispute Settlement	63LTS289	301496
13 Dec	Germany	Turkey	General Economic	53LTS355	301265
14 Dec	Finland	Great Britain	Air Transport	47LTS403	301144
15 Dec	Norway	USSR (Soviet Union)	General Economic	47LTS9	301127
16 Dec	Germany	Poland	Admin Cooperation	46LTS139	301117
17 Dec	Turkey	USSR (Soviet Union)	General Amity	157LTS353	303610
17 Dec	Austria	Norway	Extradition	48LTS77	301152
18 Dec	Canada	Finland	Postal Service	47LTS319	301137
18 Dec	Austria	Portugal	General Economic	54LTS91	301277
19 Dec	Siam	Sweden	General Economic	58LTS429	301386
19 Dec	Austria	Denmark	Education	57LTS121	301358
19 Dec	Finland	Norway	Water Transport	56LTS183	301330
20 Dec	Italy	UK Great Britain	Admin Cooperation	50LTS281	301211
20 Dec	Italy	UK Great Britain	Postal Service	49LTS79	301178
21 Dec	Finland	USA (United States)	Customs	47LTS345	301138
21 Dec	Germany	Saar	Admin Cooperation	55LTS349	301319
23 Dec	Lithuania	USA (United States)	Customs	54LTS377	301300
23 Dec	Estonia	USA (United States)	General Amity	50LTS13	301197
28 Dec	Hungary	UK Great Britain	Postal Service	49LTS125	301179
28 Dec	Bel-Lux Econ Union	Czechoslovakia	General Economic	58LTS189	301372
30 Dec	France	Poland	Extradition	95LTS217	302176
30 Dec	France	Poland	Admin Cooperation	95LTS233	302177
30 Dec	France	Poland	Admin Cooperation	48LTS139	301155
30 Dec	Netherlands	UK Great Britain	Postal Service	61LTS9	301424
30 Dec	France	Poland	Consul/Citizenship	73LTS265	301719
31 Dec	Multilateral		Territory Boundary	79LTS167	301809
31 Dec	Germany	Sweden	Taxation	43LTS219	301056
1926					
02 Jan	Czechoslovakia	Sweden	Dispute Settlement	48LTS173	301159
06 Jan	Austria	Switzerland	General Economic	46LTS299	301124
08 Jan	Austria	Germany	Admin Cooperation	62LTS95	301459
12 Jan	Siam	Strait Settlements	Postal Service	49LTS161	301180
13 Jan	Great Britain	Iraq	Territory Boundary	47LTS419	301147
14 Jan	Denmark	Sweden	Dispute Settlement	51LTS251	301235
15 Jan	Denmark	Norway	Dispute Settlement	60LTS311	301418
16 Jan	France	Luxembourg	Taxation	48LTS149	301156
18 Jan	Estonia	UK Great Britain	General Economic	48LTS209	301163

DATE	PARTY ONE	PARTY TWO	TOPIC	CITATION	NUMBER
1926 (Cont.)					
19 Jan	Netherlands	USA (United States)	Postal Service	50LTS199	301202
19 Jan	Albania	Czechoslovakia	General Trade	64LTS349	301507
20 Jan	Belgium	Paraguay	Extradition	97LTS197	302224
27 Jan	Germany	Poland	Territory Boundary	64LTS113	301504
28 Jan	Multilateral		Water Transport	51LTS9	301219
29 Jan	Italy	UK Great Britain	Extradition	47LTS409	301145
29 Jan	Finland	Sweden	Dispute Settlement	49LTS367	301192
30 Jan	Chile	Turkey	General Amity	59LTS249	301395
30 Jan	Denmark	Finland	Dispute Settlement	51LTS367	301242
01 Feb	Czechoslovakia	UK Great Britain	Customs	49LTS175	301181
01 Feb	Latvia	USA (United States)	General Economic	55LTS33	301302
02 Feb	France	Great Britain	General Amity	56LTS79	301324
02 Feb	Estonia	Latvia	Land Transport	64LTS413	301514
03 Feb	Romania	Switzerland	Dispute Settlement	55LTS91	301306
03 Feb	Finland	Norway	Dispute Settlement	60LTS353	301420
05 Feb	Estonia	Latvia	Specific Resources	64LTS361	301509
10 Feb	Spain	USA (United States)	Admin Cooperation	67LTS131	301543
10 Feb	Liberia	USA (United States)	Dispute Settlement	56LTS279	301336
11 Feb	Great Britain	Muscat and Oman	General Economic	57LTS13	301347
12 Feb	France	Germany	General Economic	48LTS153	301157
26 Feb	Romania	USA (United States)	Mostfavored Nation	51LTS59	301221
01 Mar	Denmark	Siam	General Economic	47LTS103	301131
03 Mar	Afghanistan	Germany	General Amity	62LTS115	301460
03 Mar	Estonia	Latvia	Humanitarian	63LTS13	301476
04 Mar	Cuba	USA (United States)	Admin Cooperation	61LTS369	301447
04 Mar	Estonia	USSR (Soviet Union)	General Transport	62LTS77	301456
05 Mar	Belgium	Netherlands	Postal Service	50LTS213	301203
05 Mar	Austria	Czechoslovakia	General Amity	51LTS349	301240
06 Mar	Austria	Sweden	Admin Cooperation	47LTS39	301128
11 Mar	Cuba	USA (United States)	Admin Cooperation	61LTS383	301448
15 Mar	France	Great Britain	Postal Service	47LTS415	301146
15 Mar	Estonia	UK Great Britain	Telecommunications	50LTS219	301204
20 Mar	Denmark	Germany	Visas	53LTS377	301267
20 Mar	Denmark	Germany	Customs	51LTS317	301237
20 Mar	Denmark	Germany	General Trade	57LTS131	301359
20 Mar	Germany	Portugal	General Economic	53LTS361	301266
20 Mar	India	Indochina	General Trade	57LTS19	301348
22 Mar	Argentina	Austria	Non-ILO Labor	143LTS157	303306
22 Mar	Denmark	Turkey	General Economic	48LTS231	301164
24 Mar	Germany	Netherlands	Telecommunications	51LTS245	301234
26 Mar	Poland	Romania	Peace/Disarmament	60LTS161	301411
27 Mar	Germany	Poland	Land Transport	64LTS249	301506
30 Mar	Hungary	Italy	Finance	54LTS85	301276
00 Apr	Multilateral		Water Transport	57LTS437	301366
04 Apr	India	Irish Free State	Postal Service	56LTS415	301344
09 Apr	Norway	USSR (Soviet Union)	Water Transport	48LTS185	301160
10 Apr	Multilateral		Water Transport	176LTS199	304062
10 Apr	Multilateral		Water Transport	120LTS187	302765
10 Apr	United Arab Rep	Greece	Mostfavored Nation	61LTS305	301441
12 Apr	Denmark	Germany	Customs	48LTS237	301165
13 Apr	Brazil	Venezuela	General Amity	80LTS283	301834
14 Apr	Iceland	Poland	Consul/Citizenship	48LTS279	301169
15 Apr	Czechoslovakia	Poland	Air Transport	67LTS305	301554
16 Apr	Austria	Poland	Dispute Settlement	62LTS329	301471
20 Apr	Finland	Hungary	General Economic	48LTS119	301154
20 Apr	Spain	Switzerland	Dispute Settlement	60LTS23	301403
21 Apr	Czechoslovakia	Poland	Sanitation	58LTS9	301367
22 Apr	Cuba	USA (United States)	Consul/Citizenship	60LTS371	301421
23 Apr	Denmark	Poland	Dispute Settlement	61LTS245	301437
24 Apr	Multilateral		Land Transport	97LTS83	302220
24 Apr	Multilateral		Land Transport	108LTS123	302505
24 Apr	Germany	USSR (Soviet Union)	General Amity	53LTS387	301268
27 Apr	Great Britain	Netherlands	Telecommunications	50LTS295	301212
29 Apr	France	USA (United States)	Claims and Debts	100LTS27	302292
30 Apr	France	San Marino	Extradition	89LTS9	302001

DATE	PARTY ONE	PARTY TWO	TOPIC	CITATION	NUMBER
1926 (Cont.)					
30 Apr	Canada	Norway	Postal Service	51LTS203	301227
30 Apr	Belgium	Sweden	Dispute Settlement	67LTS91	301540
01 May	Denmark	Germany	Visas	107LTS229	302480
02 May	Norway	Turkey	General Amity	56LTS51	301322
03 May	Estonia	UK Great Britain	General Trade	59LTS41	301388
04 May	Czechoslovakia	Italy	Other Economic	61LTS257	301438
05 May	Italy	USA (United States)	Taxation	113LTS21	302631
07 May	Germany	Spain	General Economic	53LTS321	301264
09 May	Italy	Siam	General Economic	61LTS215	301436
10 May	Austria	Hungary	General Trade	56LTS39	301321
10 May	Irish Free State	USA (United States)	Postal Service	56LTS433	301345
11 May	Belgium	UK Great Britain	Postal Service	71LTS97	301657
12 May	Multilateral		Refugees	89LTS47	302004
12 May	Greece	Netherlands	General Trade	61LTS295	301440
14 May	Germany	Sweden	General Economic	51LTS99	301225
15 May	Bulgaria	Czechoslovakia	Admin Cooperation	60LTS203	301413
15 May	Bulgaria	Czechoslovakia	Extradition	60LTS169	301412
17 May	Belgium	UK Great Britain	Territory Boundary	54LTS239	301287
18 May	Lithuania	UK Great Britain	Extradition	61LTS401	301450
20 May	Multilateral		Health/Educ/Welfare	109LTS121	302532
20 May	Germany	Netherlands	Dispute Settlement	66LTS103	301527
20 May	Netherlands	UK Great Britain	Taxation	50LTS309	301214
20 May	Portugal	UK Great Britain	Water Transport	50LTS303	301213
21 May	Austria	Germany	General Economic	53LTS397	301269
22 May	Multilateral		Air Transport	58LTS331	301381
27 May	France	Saar	Non-ILO Labor	55LTS157	301312
28 May	Estonia	Latvia	Taxation	159LTS291	303672
28 May	Austria	Sweden	Dispute Settlement	61LTS193	301434
29 May	Belgium	Germany	Air Transport	127LTS149	302916
29 May	France	Italy	General Trade	62LTS347	301473
29 May	France	Italy	Commodity Trade	62LTS425	301474
30 May	France	Turkey	General Amity	54LTS195	301285
31 May	Australia	Germany	Postal Service	60LTS121	301409
02 Jun	Denmark	UK Great Britain	Non-ILO Labor	61LTS353	301445
02 Jun	Finland	Turkey	General Trade	70LTS329	301644
04 Jun	Iceland	UK Great Britain	Dispute Settlement	61LTS189	301433
04 Jun	Czechoslovakia	UK Great Britain	Extradition	59LTS269	301397
04 Jun	France	Germany	Admin Cooperation	53LTS423	301270
04 Jun	Denmark	UK Great Britain	Dispute Settlement	61LTS185	301432
05 Jun	Denmark	Japan	Water Transport	55LTS219	301317
10 Jun	France	Romania	Dispute Settlement	58LTS233	301374
10 Jun	France	Romania	General Amity	58LTS225	301373
11 Jun	France	Norway	Patents/Copyrights	50LTS315	301215
11 Jun	Czechoslovakia	UK Great Britain	Admin Cooperation	48LTS425	301173
12 Jun	Italy	Latvia	Visas	51LTS65	301222
13 Jun	Romania	Serb/Croat/Slovene	General Military	54LTS257	301289
13 Jun	Czechoslovakia	Romania	General Military	54LTS253	301288
15 Jun	Germany	Norway	Telecommunications	51LTS329	301238
16 Jun	Germany	Poland	Land Transport	65LTS379	301522
18 Jun	Serb/Croat/Slovene	UK Great Britain	General Economic	57LTS23	301349
19 Jun	France	India	Territory Boundary	57LTS35	301350
21 Jun	Multilateral		Sanitation	78LTS229	301793
21 Jun	Germany	Poland	Territory Boundary	72LTS203	301693
22 Jun	Albania	Serb/Croat/Slovene	Consul/Citizenship	91LTS55	302055
22 Jun	Albania	Serb/Croat/Slovene	Extradition	91LTS81	302056
22 Jun	Portugal	South Africa	Territory Boundary	70LTS305	301642
22 Jun	Finland	Greece	General Economic	56LTS197	301331
24 Jun	Belgium	France	Extradition	94LTS349	302153
24 Jun	Estonia	UK Great Britain	Water Transport	57LTS65	301352
24 Jun	Italy	UK Great Britain	Patents/Copyrights	57LTS71	301353
25 Jun	Albania	Greece	Extradition	83LTS305	301898
26 Jun	Finland	Germany	General Economic	56LTS203	301332
28 Jun	Germany	Latvia	General Economic	58LTS403	301385
28 Jun	France	Germany	Extradition	53LTS435	301271
01 Jul	Belgium	Germany	General Transport	62LTS127	301461

DATE	PARTY ONE	PARTY TWO	TOPIC	CITATION	NUMBER
1926 (Cont.)					
01 Jul	Portugal	South Africa	General Ad Hoc	70LTS315	301643
05 Jul	Denmark	France	Dispute Settlement	71LTS455	301684
06 Jul	Czechoslovakia	Latvia	Extradition	62LTS229	301465
09 Jul	Germany	Latvia	Sanitation	63LTS321	301499
12 Jul	Austria	Czechoslovakia	Taxation	86LTS383	301951
12 Jul	Austria	Czechoslovakia	Admin Cooperation	86LTS395	301952
12 Jul	France	UK Great Britain	Reparations	98LTS155	302244
13 Jul	Bel-Lux Econ Union	Siam	General Economic	62LTS287	301468
14 Jul	Austria	Hungary	Visas	61LTS123	301430
14 Jul	Germany	Switzerland	General Trade	59LTS87	301391
14 Jul	Austria	Hungary	Visas	61LTS159	301431
15 Jul	Benelux Econ Union	Germany	Visas	63LTS137	301485
16 Jul	Norway	Siam	General Economic	60LTS35	301404
17 Jul	Czechoslovakia	Estonia	Extradition	63LTS255	301495
17 Jul	Czechoslovakia	Estonia	Admin Cooperation	69LTS385	301620
19 Jul	France	Sweden	Consul/Citizenship	54LTS283	301291
19 Jul	Dominican Republic	USA (United States)	Customs	54LTS145	301282
21 Jul	Sweden	USSR (Soviet Union)	Patents/Copyrights	57LTS9	301346
22 Jul	Albania	UK Great Britain	Admin Cooperation	67LTS165	301545
23 Jul	Denmark	Netherlands	Air Transport	66LTS133	301528
23 Jul	Hungary	UK Great Britain	General Trade	67LTS183	301546
24 Jul	Hungary	Serb/Croat/Slovene	Admin Cooperation	97LTS165	302223
28 Jul	Estonia	Norway	General Economic	43LTS25	301045
29 Jul	Portugal	Spain	Territory Boundary	82LTS95	301863
31 Jul	France	Turkey	General Amity	54LTS177	301284
04 Aug	Austria	Netherlands	Customs	59LTS243	301394
04 Aug	Spain	Switzerland	Admin Cooperation	65LTS39	301518
05 Aug	France	Germany	General Trade	73LTS105	301711
07 Aug	Italy	Spain	General Amity	67LTS365	301558
11 Aug	Netherlands	Turkey	General Economic	48LTS271	301168
11 Aug	Norway	Turkey	General Economic	47LTS441	301149
14 Aug	Netherlands	UK Great Britain	Sanitation	57LTS41	301351
19 Aug	Germany	Poland	Admin Cooperation	64LTS420	301515
24 Aug	Belgium	Luxembourg	Extradition	61LTS311	301442
25 Aug	Denmark	Switzerland	General Amity	69LTS313	301613
27 Aug	France	Switzerland	Admin Cooperation	59LTS231	301392
27 Aug	France	Switzerland	Admin Cooperation	71LTS63	301654
30 Aug	India	Iraq	Postal Service	69LTS193	301605
02 Sep	Italy	Yemen	General Amity	67LTS383	301559
04 Sep	Hungary	USA (United States)	Admin Cooperation	58LTS111	301369
07 Sep	Haiti	Netherlands	General Trade	71LTS219	301665
09 Sep	Bulgaria		Refugees	58LTS245	301375
10 Sep	Other Unilat Decla	Rhine Navigation	Specific Property	62LTS141	301462
10 Sep	Greece	Sweden	General Trade	63LTS37	301479
10 Sep	Great Britain	Italy	Land Transport	57LTS77	301354
10 Sep	Bulgaria	Hungary	General Economic	69LTS333	301615
14 Sep	Multilateral		Non-ILO Labor	77LTS149	301769
15 Sep	Guatemala	Italy	General Trade	70LTS175	301633
16 Sep	Italy	Romania	General Amity	67LTS393	301560
18 Sep	Poland	Serb/Croat/Slovene	Dispute Settlement	78LTS419	301800
18 Sep	Poland	Serb/Croat/Slovene	General Amity	78LTS413	301799
18 Sep	Multilateral		General IGO	59LTS237	301393
19 Sep	Denmark	Turkey	General Economic	56LTS259	301333
21 Sep	Netherlands	Norway	Admin Cooperation	56LTS89	301325
23 Sep	Greece	Spain	Consul/Citizenship	91LTS121	302059
25 Sep	Multilateral		ILO Labor	60LTS253	301414
28 Sep	Bel-Lux Econ Union	Estonia	General Economic	62LTS433	301475
28 Sep	Belgium	Estonia	Water Transport	60LTS9	301401
28 Sep	Lithuania	USSR (Soviet Union)	Peace/Disarmament	60LTS145	301410
30 Sep	Belgium	Hungary	Claims and Debts	97LTS215	302225
30 Sep	Czechoslovakia	Hungary	Territory Boundary	57LTS87	301356
30 Sep	Abyssinia	Netherlands	General Trade	78LTS89	301780
12 Oct	Estonia	Great Britain	Postal Service	60LTS387	301422
13 Oct	Colombia	Costa Rica	Education	95LTS325	302182
13 Oct	Albania	Greece	General Trade	83LTS325	301899

DATE	PARTY ONE	PARTY TWO	TOPIC	CITATION	NUMBER
1926 (Cont.)					
13 Oct	Albania	Greece	Consul/Citizenship	83LTS361	301900
15 Oct	Austria	Estonia	Consul/Citizenship	93LTS137	302106
15 Oct	Austria	Estonia	Extradition	74LTS213	301739
19 Oct	Finland	Turkey	General Economic	58LTS393	301384
19 Oct	Spain	UK Great Britain	Postal Service	61LTS79	301427
19 Oct	Germany	UK Great Britain	Gen Communications	67LTS203	301547
20 Oct	Belgium	Luxembourg	Non-ILO Labor	78LTS375	301796
23 Oct	Denmark	Netherlands	Non-ILO Labor	72LTS13	301686
24 Oct	Greece	Italy	General Trade	63LTS51	301480
25 Oct	Belgium	Denmark	Extradition	58LTS259	301376
27 Oct	Germany	Poland	Admin Cooperation	108LTS275	302513
28 Oct	Denmark	Germany	Milit Servic/Citiz	57LTS185	301363
28 Oct	Liberia	Monaco	Extradition	68LTS241	301588
29 Oct	Estonia	Switzerland	Admin Cooperation	63LTS23	301477
29 Oct	China	Finland	General Amity	67LTS345	301556
30 Oct	Multilateral		Telecommunications	61LTS65	301426
01 Nov	Multilateral		Telecommunications	78LTS109	301782
03 Nov	Germany	Netherlands	Telecommunications	68LTS111	301575
11 Nov	Belgium	Estonia	Extradition	65LTS405	301523
13 Nov	Multilateral		Territory Boundary	77LTS171	301770
13 Nov	Multilateral		Territory Boundary	77LTS199	301771
13 Nov	Multilateral		Territory Boundary	77LTS217	301772
13 Nov	Multilateral		Territory Boundary	77LTS249	301773
14 Nov	Poland	USA (United States)	Finance	58LTS97	301368
16 Nov	Greece	New Zealand	General Trade	85LTS43	301921
17 Nov	Hungary	Romania	Land Transport	61LTS207	301435
19 Nov	Mexico	UK Great Britain	Claims and Debts	85LTS51	301922
23 Nov	Germany	Saar	Admin Cooperation	70LTS105	301627
24 Nov	Greece	Italy	Specific Resources	63LTS91	301481
24 Nov	Austria	Poland	Customs	77LTS359	301777
26 Nov	Switzerland	Uruguay	Extradition	63LTS207	301491
27 Nov	Netherlands	USA (United States)	Taxation	112LTS433	302628
27 Nov	Albania	Italy	General Amity	60LTS15	301402
29 Nov	Greece	Switzerland	General Trade	63LTS27	301478
30 Nov	Estonia	USA (United States)	General Transport	62LTS313	301469
30 Nov	Czechoslovakia	Denmark	Dispute Settlement	67LTS105	301541
01 Dec	Greece	UK Great Britain	Water Transport	61LTS109	301428
10 Dec	Other Unilat Decla	Estonia	Finance	62LTS277	301467
11 Dec	Denmark	Lithuania	Dispute Settlement	67LTS333	301555
11 Dec	Belgium	Latvia	Extradition	63LTS299	301497
15 Dec	Denmark	Norway	Non-ILO Labor	59LTS255	301396
16 Dec	Bel-Lux Econ Union	Serb/Croat/Slovene	General Trade	70LTS371	301647
18 Dec	Italy	Portugal	Finance	93LTS313	302119
18 Dec	Finland	Greece	General Trade	70LTS89	301626
18 Dec	Multilateral		Telecommunications	63LTS185	301489
18 Dec	Denmark	Estonia	Dispute Settlement	63LTS363	301500
20 Dec	Hungary	Turkey	General Trade	72LTS255	301697
20 Dec	Hungary	Turkey	Consul/Citizenship	72LTS245	301696
21 Dec	Czechoslovakia	Switzerland	Admin Cooperation	68LTS393	301594
21 Dec	Czechoslovakia	Switzerland	Admin Cooperation	86LTS443	301956
22 Dec	Germany	Poland	Culture	68LTS263	301590
22 Dec	Bulgaria	Germany	Admin Cooperation	64LTS77	301502
22 Dec	Norway	Poland	General Economic	66LTS359	301530
22 Dec	France	Germany	Territory Boundary	77LTS141	301768
29 Dec	Germany	Italy	Dispute Settlement	78LTS383	301797
31 Dec	Portugal	UK Great Britain	Claims and Debts	61LTS115	301429
1927					
03 Jan	Haiti	Italy	General Trade	71LTS405	301678
04 Jan	Estonia	Greece	General Economic	69LTS33	301598
06 Jan	Bel-Lux Econ Union	Portugal	General Trade	91LTS239	302065
12 Jan	Germany	Turkey	Admin Cooperation	73LTS187	301713
12 Jan	Germany	Turkey	General Trade	73LTS133	301712
20 Jan	Finland	France	Admin Cooperation	66LTS381	301531
22 Jan	Multilateral		Telecommunications	68LTS149	301578

DATE	PARTY ONE	PARTY TWO	TOPIC	CITATION	NUMBER
1927 (Cont.)					
22 Jan	Multilateral		Telecommunications	68LTS129	301576
22 Jan	Czechoslovakia	Germany	Air Transport	89LTS231	302019
22 Jan	Czechoslovakia	Germany	Air Transport	89LTS261	302020
24 Jan	Multilateral		General Ad Hoc	70LTS453	301650
25 Jan	Norway	South Africa	Postal Service	60LTS277	301416
26 Jan	France	Italy	Customs	79LTS49	301804
03 Feb	Denmark	Sweden	Admin Cooperation	109LTS205	302540
05 Feb	Belgium	Switzerland	Dispute Settlement	68LTS45	301567
05 Feb	Austria	Germany	Admin Cooperation	73LTS227	301715
05 Feb	Estonia	Latvia	Customs	62LTS319	301470
05 Feb	Austria	Germany	Territory Boundary	73LTS205	301714
08 Feb	Belgium	Estonia	Consul/Citizenship	74LTS227	301740
08 Feb	Czechoslovakia	Poland	Admin Cooperation	70LTS275	301639
08 Feb	Czechoslovakia	Poland	Admin Cooperation	70LTS299	301641
08 Feb	Czechoslovakia	Poland	Admin Cooperation	70LTS261	301638
08 Feb	Czechoslovakia	Poland	Admin Cooperation	70LTS289	301640
09 Feb	Chile	Norway	General Trade	80LTS325	301837
11 Feb	Muscat and Oman	UK Great Britain	General Amity	64LTS398	301512
15 Feb	Austria	Czechoslovakia	Air Transport	73LTS349	301724
15 Feb	Austria	Czechoslovakia	Air Transport	73LTS381	301725
16 Feb	Czechoslovakia	Switzerland	General Trade	64LTS7	301501
16 Feb	France	Germany	Commodity Trade	62LTS155	301463
16 Feb	Germany	Poland	Territory Boundary	71LTS369	301676
16 Feb	United Arab Rep	Hungary	General Trade	80LTS61	301822
17 Feb	Greece	UK Great Britain	Claims and Debts	90LTS379	302049
19 Feb	Estonia	Poland	General Economic	115LTS177	302686
19 Feb	Denmark	Netherlands	Admin Cooperation	60LTS271	301415
19 Feb	Multilateral		Telecommunications	68LTS139	301577
23 Feb	Denmark	Germany	Dispute Settlement	61LTS325	301444
23 Feb	UK Great Britain	USA (United States)	Admin Cooperation	82LTS17	301856
24 Feb	Multilateral		Telecommunications	68LTS159	301579
24 Feb	Chile	France	Dispute Settlement	69LTS277	301610
25 Feb	Greece	Latvia	General Trade	71LTS25	301652
25 Feb	Multilateral		Telecommunications	78LTS123	301783
26 Feb	Germany	Paraguay	Mostfavored Nation	73LTS235	301716
28 Feb	Belgium	Netherlands	Telecommunications	68LTS169	301580
28 Feb	Bulgaria	Greece	Mostfavored Nation	68LTS59	301568
01 Mar	Austria	Netherlands	Visas	68LTS75	301570
02 Mar	Czechoslovakia	Finland	General Economic	66LTS385	301532
04 Mar	Belgium	Finland	Dispute Settlement	69LTS361	301618
06 Mar	Poland	Serb/Croat/Slovene	Consul/Citizenship	126LTS67	302871
08 Mar	Denmark	Sweden	Visas	63LTS315	301498
08 Mar	Multilateral		Telecommunications	78LTS134	301784
09 Mar	Norway	Sweden	Privil/Immunities	62LTS341	301472
11 Mar	Austria	Hungary	Admin Cooperation	80LTS67	301823
11 Mar	Netherlands	UK Great Britain	Telecommunications	64LTS403	301513
13 Mar	Belgium	Denmark	Dispute Settlement	67LTS117	301542
15 Mar	Austria	Switzerland	Admin Cooperation	87LTS351	301981
15 Mar	Hungary	Italy	Claims and Debts	68LTS221	301585
18 Mar	Multilateral		Telecommunications	68LTS179	301581
19 Mar	Persia	Poland	General Amity	109LTS87	302529
19 Mar	Persia	Poland	General Economic	109LTS53	302528
24 Mar	Belgium	Netherlands	Sanitation	84LTS34	301902
25 Mar	Czechoslovakia	Germany	Land Transport	75LTS353	301758
26 Mar	Germany	Poland	Land Transport	64LTS177	301505
28 Mar	Greece	Romania	Mostfavored Nation	68LTS67	301569
28 Mar	Austria	Portugal	Visas	68LTS81	301571
29 Mar	Finland	USSR (Soviet Union)	General Transport	71LTS11	301651
31 Mar	France	Germany	General Economic	66LTS7	301524
31 Mar	Multilateral		Air Transport	66LTS59	301525
01 Apr	Finland	Sweden	Water Transport	62LTS89	301458
05 Apr	Estonia	Germany	Sanitation	64LTS355	301508
05 Apr	Hungary	Italy	General Amity	67LTS399	301561
07 Apr	Czechoslovakia	Greece	Admin Cooperation	88LTS187	301997
07 Apr	Czechoslovakia	Greece	Admin Cooperation	88LTS211	301998

DATE	PARTY ONE	PARTY TWO	TOPIC	CITATION	NUMBER
1927 (Cont.)					
07 Apr	Czechoslovakia	Greece	Extradition	88LTS219	301999
09 Apr	Greece	UK Great Britain	Claims and Debts	67LTS217	301549
09 Apr	Belgium	UK Great Britain	Telecommunications	67LTS209	301548
11 Apr	Belgium	France	Land Transport	143LTS215	303309
11 Apr	Germany	Poland	Territory Boundary	69LTS419	301621
12 Apr	France	Norway	Commodity Trade	178LTS199	304114
12 Apr	China	Switzerland	Sanitation	66LTS427	301536
14 Apr	Czechoslovakia	Poland	Admin Cooperation	82LTS157	301867
14 Apr	France	Saar	Land Transport	70LTS115	301628
22 Apr	Brazil	UK Great Britain	Territory Boundary	92LTS311	302097
27 Apr	Germany	Norway	Customs	69LTS57	301600
02 May	Multilateral		Telecommunications	68LTS189	301582
02 May	Ceylon (Sri Lanka)	Germany	Postal Service	69LTS203	301606
03 May	Belgium	UK Great Britain	Territory Boundary	140LTS71	303229
04 May	Switzerland	Turkey	General Trade	67LTS141	301544
06 May	Belgium	UK Great Britain	Admin Cooperation	63LTS153	301486
09 May	Denmark	Estonia	Admin Cooperation	72LTS25	301687
10 May	Finland	Sweden	Specific Resources	70LTS201	301634
12 May	Guatemala	Netherlands	General Trade	85LTS323	301937
12 May	Serb/Croat/Slovene	UK Great Britain	General Trade	80LTS165	301825
13 May	Greece	UK Great Britain	General Economic	61LTS15	301425
14 May	Finland	Germany	Visas	66LTS403	301533
14 May	Finland	Latvia	Visas	63LTS97	301482
15 May	United Arab Rep	Serb/Croat/Slovene	General Trade	96LTS367	302213
17 May	Belgium	Lithuania	Extradition	77LTS123	301767
17 May	Estonia	Finland	Visas	66LTS411	301534
17 May	Portugal	Sweden	Admin Cooperation	64LTS373	301510
19 May	Multilateral		Air Transport	68LTS407	301595
19 May	UK Great Britain	USA (United States)	Finance	64LTS101	301503
20 May	British Empire	Hedjaz	General Amity	71LTS131	301658
20 May	Germany	Italy	Air Transport	79LTS179	301810
21 May	Belgium	France	Non-ILO Labor	95LTS283	302180
21 May	Belgium	France	Non-ILO Labor	105LTS125	302407
21 May	Hungary	Italy	Finance	74LTS19	301727
21 May	Hungary	Italy	Finance	74LTS33	301729
21 May	Netherlands	Sweden	Dispute Settlement	79LTS147	301807
21 May	Hungary	Italy	Claims and Debts	74LTS27	301728
23 May	France	UK Great Britain	Telecommunications	67LTS227	301550
25 May	Iceland	USSR (Soviet Union)	General Trade	63LTS105	301483
28 May	Chile	Spain	Dispute Settlement	71LTS329	301673
30 May	Czechoslovakia	Poland	Land Transport	98LTS233	302251
31 May	Czechoslovakia	Turkey	Admin Cooperation	75LTS79	301753
31 May	Czechoslovakia	Turkey	General Trade	71LTS335	301674
31 May	Czechoslovakia	Hungary	General Transport	65LTS61	301520
02 Jun	Latvia	USSR (Soviet Union)	General Economic	68LTS321	301591
03 Jun	Czechoslovakia	France	Consul/Citizenship	131LTS177	303009
03 Jun	Czechoslovakia	Hungary	Admin Cooperation	67LTS31	301538
04 Jun	Romania	Serb/Croat/Slovene	Territory Boundary	158LTS443	303647
11 Jun	Austria	Denmark	Visas	68LTS87	301572
15 Jun	Multilateral		Telecommunications	69LTS375	301619
17 Jun	Bulgaria	UK Great Britain	Dispute Settlement	67LTS239	301551
18 Jun	Finland	Germany	Non-ILO Labor	71LTS361	301675
24 Jun	Latvia	UK Great Britain	Water Transport	67LTS245	301552
24 Jun	Finland	Switzerland	Mostfavored Nation	68LTS103	301574
26 Jun	Argentina	France	Milit Servic/Citiz	62LTS85	301457
28 Jun	Italy	Netherlands	Water Transport	68LTS203	301583
29 Jun	Greece	Norway	General Trade	82LTS187	301869
29 Jun	Germany	UK Great Britain	Air Transport	71LTS165	301659
30 Jun	France	Germany	General Trade	73LTS243	301717
30 Jun	Austria	Latvia	Visas	66LTS97	301526
08 Jul	France	USA (United States)	Taxation	114LTS413	302669
09 Jul	Belgium	Portugal	Dispute Settlement	74LTS39	301730
09 Jul	Belgium	Germany	Admin Cooperation	75LTS367	301759
12 Jul	Multilateral		Direct Aid	135LTS247	303115
14 Jul	Germany	Poland	Non-ILO Labor	73LTS251	301718

DATE	PARTY ONE	PARTY TWO	TOPIC	CITATION	NUMBER
1927 (Cont.)					
14 Jul	Indochina	Siam	Consul/Citizenship	69LTS327	301614
15 Jul	Cuba	Spain	General Trade	120LTS251	302770
18 Jul	Austria	Great Britain	Visas	68LTS97	301573
19 Jul	Belgium	Portugal	Sanitation	71LTS419	301680
19 Jul	Belgium	Czechoslovakia	Extradition	73LTS283	301720
19 Jul	Belgium	Czechoslovakia	Admin Cooperation	73LTS307	301721
19 Jul	Belgium	Spain	Dispute Settlement	80LTS17	301820
20 Jul	Czechoslovakia	Estonia	General Trade	77LTS341	301776
20 Jul	Belgium	Portugal	General Economic	71LTS431	301681
20 Jul	Germany	Japan	General Trade	74LTS107	301736
21 Jul	Austria	Czechoslovakia	General Trade	81LTS7	301842
21 Jul	Germany	Portugal	Admin Cooperation	75LTS375	301760
21 Jul	Belgium	Portugal	Water Transport	71LTS439	301682
21 Jul	Austria	Finland	Visas	66LTS419	301535
22 Jul	Belgium	Portugal	Territory Boundary	71LTS449	301683
22 Jul	Estonia	Latvia	Admin Cooperation	73LTS333	301723
25 Jul	Hungary	Italy	Other Ad Hoc	74LTS77	301733
25 Jul	Hungary	Italy	Water Transport	74LTS53	301731
25 Jul	Hungary	Italy	Customs	74LTS67	301732
28 Jul	Multilateral		Territory Boundary	64LTS379	301511
30 Jul	Spain	UK Great Britain	General Trade	63LTS189	301490
04 Aug	Iraq	Palestine	Postal Service	80LTS211	301826
07 Aug	Switzerland	Turkey	Admin Cooperation	73LTS51	301706
08 Aug	Estonia	USSR (Soviet Union)	Dispute Settlement	70LTS401	301648
08 Aug	Austria	Finland	General Trade	70LTS349	301645
09 Aug	Great Britain	Serb/Croat/Slovene	Reparations	69LTS255	301607
11 Aug	Portugal	Spain	Admin Cooperation	82LTS113	301864
11 Aug	Denmark	Iceland	Taxation	75LTS345	301757
12 Aug	Serb/Croat/Slovene		Claims and Debts	101LTS485	302347
15 Aug	Italy	Spain	Air Transport	94LTS361	302155
16 Aug	Multilateral		Telecommunications	78LTS141	301785
17 Aug	France	Germany	General Trade	76LTS5	301761
20 Aug	Colombia	Switzerland	Dispute Settlement	111LTS229	302589
22 Aug	Latvia	Poland	Mostfavored Nation	115LTS121	302681
27 Aug	Brazil	France	Dispute Settlement	75LTS91	301754
28 Aug	Bel-Lux Econ Union	Turkey	General Trade	82LTS77	301862
29 Aug	France	USA (United States)	Other Military	68LTS253	301589
30 Aug	France	Japan	General Economic	68LTS235	301587
01 Sep	Germany	Italy	Peace/Disarmament	67LTS425	301564
08 Sep	Great Britain	Spain	Patents/Copyrights	69LTS263	301608
10 Sep	Multilateral		Postal Service	75LTS39	301750
10 Sep	Multilateral		Postal Service	75LTS7	301749
12 Sep	Luxembourg	Norway	Visas	68LTS37	301566
12 Sep	Latvia	Norway	Extradition	71LTS303	301671
13 Sep	Colombia	Sweden	Dispute Settlement	132LTS123	303032
14 Sep	France	Great Britain	Admin Cooperation	69LTS269	301609
15 Sep	Greece		Loans and Credits	70LTS9	301622
17 Sep	Italy	Lithuania	Dispute Settlement	72LTS439	301700
17 Sep	Italy	Lithuania	General Trade	73LTS9	301701
24 Sep	Denmark	Turkey	Mostfavored Nation	61LTS287	301439
26 Sep	Multilateral		Dispute Settlement	92LTS301	302096
29 Sep	Denmark	Greece	Mostfavored Nation	62LTS219	301464
30 Sep	Finland	Norway	Customs	67LTS359	301557
01 Oct	Persia	USSR (Soviet Union)	Specific Resources	112LTS297	302621
01 Oct	Persia	USSR (Soviet Union)	Admin Cooperation	112LTS275	302620
05 Oct	France	Germany	Admin Cooperation	77LTS7	301762
06 Oct	Belgium	France	Admin Cooperation	69LTS49	301599
06 Oct	Germany	Serb/Croat/Slovene	General Trade	77LTS19	301763
06 Oct	Portugal	South Africa	Territory Boundary	81LTS359	301846
08 Oct	Sweden	USSR (Soviet Union)	Admin Cooperation	71LTS411	301679
10 Oct	Austria	Belgium	Claims and Debts	91LTS271	302067
10 Oct	Latvia	USSR (Soviet Union)	Dispute Settlement	84LTS47	301903
13 Oct	Germany	Saar	Non-ILO Labor	70LTS121	301629
13 Oct	Denmark	Iceland	Non-ILO Labor	67LTS411	301562
14 Oct	Finland	Switzerland	Visas	71LTS205	301663

DATE	PARTY ONE	PARTY TWO	TOPIC	CITATION	NUMBER
1927 (Cont.)					
15 Oct	Denmark	Japan	Taxation	71LTS75	301655
17 Oct	Belgium	Luxembourg	Dispute Settlement	124LTS203	302834
18 Oct	France	Persia	Scientific Project	112LTS267	302619
20 Oct	France	Luxembourg	Dispute Settlement	106LTS457	302462
24 Oct	Austria	Switzerland	Taxation	85LTS253	301935
25 Oct	Belgium	Netherlands	Extradition	69LTS29	301597
26 Oct	Czechoslovakia	Spain	Extradition	121LTS271	302791
26 Oct	Czechoslovakia	Spain	Privil/Immunities	121LTS287	302792
26 Oct	Czechoslovakia	Spain	Privil/Immunities	121LTS311	302793
26 Oct	Denmark	Italy	Consul/Citizenship	68LTS229	301586
26 Oct	Belgium	Netherlands	Education	89LTS37	302003
27 Oct	Multilateral		Air Transport	148LTS265	303417
29 Oct	Multilateral		Scientific Project	127LTS27	302903
01 Nov	France	Turkey	Visas	92LTS249	302092
02 Nov	Greece	Serb/Croat/Slovene	General Economic	91LTS137	302060
03 Nov	Afghanistan	Poland	General Amity	74LTS83	301734
06 Nov	Portugal	UK Great Britain	Territory Boundary	80LTS219	301827
08 Nov	Multilateral		General Trade	97LTS391	302238
08 Nov	Denmark	Germany	Customs	70LTS83	301625
10 Nov	Chile	Italy	Postal Service	69LTS289	301611
11 Nov	France	Serb/Croat/Slovene	General Amity	68LTS373	301592
11 Nov	France	Serb/Croat/Slovene	Dispute Settlement	68LTS381	301593
11 Nov	Multilateral		Telecommunications	78LTS153	301786
14 Nov	Netherlands	UK Great Britain	Postal Service	71LTS227	301666
16 Nov	Argentina	Denmark	Non-ILO Labor	165LTS177	303809
16 Nov	Great Britain	Latvia	Customs	71LTS185	301660
16 Nov	Finland	Switzerland	Dispute Settlement	77LTS93	301765
19 Nov	Norway	Sweden	Land Transport	68LTS209	301584
21 Nov	Germany	Panama	General Economic	115LTS239	302689
21 Nov	Multilateral		Telecommunications	78LTS163	301787
21 Nov	France	Norway	Education	70LTS167	301632
22 Nov	Poland	USA (United States)	Extradition	92LTS101	302082
22 Nov	Bel-Lux Econ Union	Greece	Milit Assistance	69LTS341	301616
23 Nov	Czechoslovakia	Portugal	Dispute Settlement	123LTS403	302827
23 Nov	Czechoslovakia	Portugal	Extradition	124LTS7	302829
23 Nov	Czechoslovakia	Portugal	Dispute Settlement	123LTS417	302828
24 Nov	Germany	Poland	Non-ILO Labor	92LTS19	302080
25 Nov	Multilateral		Telecommunications	84LTS97	301905
27 Nov	Afghanistan	Persia	General Military	107LTS433	302500
28 Nov	Italy	Spain	Finance	82LTS27	301857
30 Nov	Denmark	Iceland	Postal Service	71LTS43	301653
30 Nov	Norway	Portugal	Water Transport	69LTS355	301617
01 Dec	Greece	Switzerland	Admin Cooperation	84LTS271	301907
07 Dec	Germany	Poland	Specific Property	92LTS203	302088
08 Dec	Multilateral		Loans and Credits	70LTS73	301623
09 Dec	Bulgaria	Greece	Finance	87LTS199	301970
09 Dec	Germany	Spain	Air Transport	79LTS203	301811
10 Dec	Germany	Poland	Specific Resources	120LTS299	302773
10 Dec	Hungary	Italy	Dispute Settlement	78LTS403	301798
13 Dec	Australia	Norway	Non-ILO Labor	69LTS307	301612
14 Dec	Finland	Sweden	General Trade	72LTS29	301688
14 Dec	France	Saar	Dispute Settlement	70LTS155	301630
14 Dec	France	Saar	Admin Cooperation	70LTS163	301631
20 Dec	Germany	Mexico	Claims and Debts	79LTS229	301812
20 Dec	Austria	Sweden	Visas	71LTS293	301670
22 Dec	Austria	Italy	General Economic	91LTS283	302068
23 Dec	Denmark	USSR (Soviet Union)	Patents/Copyrights	70LTS245	301636
24 Dec	Colombia	Panama	Extradition	87LTS409	301985
24 Dec	Netherlands	Sweden	Water Transport	71LTS391	301677
30 Dec	Austria	Italy	General Economic	87LTS109	301964
30 Dec	Netherlands	Sweden	Admin Cooperation	70LTS365	301646
30 Dec	Netherlands	USA (United States)	Finance	72LTS179	301691
1928					
02 Jan	Denmark	Spain	General Trade	71LTS271	301668

DATE	PARTY ONE	PARTY TWO	TOPIC	CITATION	NUMBER
1928 (Cont.)					
07 Jan	El Salvador	UK Great Britain	General Trade	80LTS231	301828
07 Jan	Multilateral		Telecommunications	78LTS187	301789
16 Jan	Norway	USSR (Soviet Union)	Consul/Citizenship	70LTS239	301635
17 Jan	Germany	Norway	Visas	70LTS251	301637
18 Jan	Portugal	Spain	Dispute Settlement	77LTS105	301766
21 Jan	France	Switzerland	General Trade	72LTS275	301698
23 Jan	Belgium	Finland	Extradition	74LTS353	301747
23 Jan	Japan	USSR (Soviet Union)	Specific Resources	80LTS341	301839
23 Jan	Denmark	France	Admin Cooperation	71LTS267	301667
25 Jan	Poland	Sweden	Admin Cooperation	140LTS385	303248
29 Jan	Germany	Lithuania	Dispute Settlement	90LTS233	302042
29 Jan	Germany	Lithuania	Non-ILO Labor	89LTS83	302008
29 Jan	Germany	Lithuania	Territory Boundary	89LTS97	302009
29 Jan	Germany	Lithuania	Specific Resources	89LTS309	302026
29 Jan	Germany	Lithuania	Territory Boundary	89LTS338	302027
01 Feb	Estonia	Serb/Croat/Slovene	General Economic	106LTS139	302441
04 Feb	Germany	Switzerland	Non-ILO Labor	79LTS241	301814
04 Feb	Sweden	Turkey	General Trade	88LTS155	301994
06 Feb	France	USA (United States)	Dispute Settlement	91LTS323	302072
08 Feb	Austria	Norway	Visas	71LTS211	301664
11 Feb	Bulgaria	Estonia	General Trade	79LTS43	301803
12 Feb	Bulgaria	Turkey	General Trade	81LTS383	301848
13 Feb	Haiti	UK Great Britain	Postal Service	85LTS63	301923
14 Feb	Germany	USA (United States)	Admin Cooperation	79LTS235	301813
14 Feb	Denmark	Germany	Taxation	71LTS285	301669
15 Feb	Albania	France	Consul/Citizenship	107LTS307	302487
16 Feb	Afghanistan	Latvia	General Amity	78LTS99	301781
17 Feb	Afghanistan	Switzerland	General Amity	73LTS323	301722
18 Feb	Czechoslovakia	Poland	Specific Resources	119LTS385	302758
18 Feb	Czechoslovakia	Poland	Specific Resources	100LTS273	302301
18 Feb	Multilateral		Patents/Copyrights	132LTS275	303044
20 Feb	Multilateral		Consul/Citizenship	155LTS289	303582
20 Feb	Multilateral		Consul/Citizenship	155LTS259	303581
20 Feb	Multilateral		Air Transport	129LTS223	302963
20 Feb	Multilateral		Admin Cooperation	134LTS45	303082
20 Feb	Multilateral		General Amity	135LTS187	303111
20 Feb	Multilateral		Consul/Citizenship	132LTS323	303046
20 Feb	Multilateral		Privil/Immunities	132LTS301	303045
20 Feb	Multilateral		Other Ad Hoc	86LTS111	301950
21 Feb	Siam	UK Great Britain	Water Transport	87LTS21	301960
22 Feb	Hungary	Serb/Croat/Slovene	Admin Cooperation	181LTS229	304192
22 Feb	Hungary	Serb/Croat/Slovene	Extradition	104LTS151	302385
22 Feb	Hungary	Serb/Croat/Slovene	Taxation	100LTS331	302305
22 Feb	Hungary	Serb/Croat/Slovene	Claims and Debts	100LTS345	302306
22 Feb	Hungary	Serb/Croat/Slovene	Sanitation	113LTS49	302635
22 Feb	Hungary	Serb/Croat/Slovene	Health/Educ/Welfare	110LTS411	302572
22 Feb	Hungary	Serb/Croat/Slovene	Non-ILO Labor	88LTS125	301992
22 Feb	Hungary	Serb/Croat/Slovene	Finance	87LTS331	301979
22 Feb	Hungary	Serb/Croat/Slovene	Consul/Citizenship	87LTS361	301982
22 Feb	Hungary	Serb/Croat/Slovene	Territory Boundary	88LTS111	301991
22 Feb	Guatemala	UK Great Britain	General Economic	97LTS229	302226
23 Feb	France	Germany	General Trade	79LTS247	301815
23 Feb	Bel-Lux Econ Union	France	General Trade	72LTS61	301689
24 Feb	Norway	USSR (Soviet Union)	Admin Cooperation	79LTS9	301801
24 Feb	Austria	Poland	Claims and Debts	81LTS417	301850
25 Feb	Finland	Japan	Visas	71LTS467	301685
25 Feb	Haiti	UK Great Britain	General Trade	85LTS91	301924
29 Feb	Austria	Germany	Non-ILO Labor	79LTS405	301816
03 Mar	Estonia	USSR (Soviet Union)	Patents/Copyrights	80LTS401	301840
03 Mar	France	Sweden	Dispute Settlement	95LTS89	302168
07 Mar	France	Italy	General Trade	72LTS213	301694
08 Mar	Multilateral		Telecommunications	80LTS241	301829
09 Mar	Finland	Sweden	Visas	72LTS429	301699
09 Mar	Colombia	Sweden	General Trade	85LTS443	301944
10 Mar	Multilateral		Telecommunications	132LTS405	303049

DATE	PARTY ONE	PARTY TWO	TOPIC	CITATION	NUMBER
1928 (Cont.)					
10 Mar	France	Netherlands	Dispute Settlement	102LTS109	302356
10 Mar	Iceland	Sweden	Water Transport	71LTS315	301672
12 Mar	Estonia	Turkey	General Trade	86LTS453	301957
14 Mar	Denmark	Spain	Dispute Settlement	74LTS93	301735
15 Mar	Canada	Czechoslovakia	General Trade	82LTS147	301865
16 Mar	France	Germany	Customs	79LTS121	301805
17 Mar	Finland	USSR (Soviet Union)	Water Transport	80LTS151	301824
19 Mar	Multilateral		Telecommunications	78LTS177	301788
20 Mar	Germany	UK Great Britain	Admin Cooperation	90LTS287	302044
21 Mar	Greece	Romania	General Military	108LTS187	302508
22 Mar	Czechoslovakia	Germany	Territory Boundary	93LTS235	302113
22 Mar	France	Spain	Air Transport	73LTS63	301707
23 Mar	Germany	Italy	Admin Cooperation	93LTS165	302108
24 Mar	Germany	Greece	General Economic	90LTS9	302031
25 Mar	Estonia	Latvia	General Economic	72LTS195	301692
26 Mar	Netherlands	UK Great Britain	Territory Boundary	108LTS331	302516
27 Mar	Czechoslovakia	Germany	Visas	90LTS151	302032
28 Mar	Belgium	Portugal	Admin Cooperation	92LTS185	302085
29 Mar	Japan	Norway	Visas	73LTS81	301708
30 Mar	Latvia	Sweden	Water Transport	73LTS39	301704
30 Mar	Austria	Czechoslovakia	Visas	73LTS87	301709
30 Mar	Germany	Nicaragua	Visas	93LTS123	302104
05 Apr	Denmark	Haiti	Dispute Settlement	99LTS19	302264
06 Apr	Austria	Iceland	General Trade	87LTS343	301980
06 Apr	Austria	Denmark	General Trade	85LTS423	301943
07 Apr	Germany	Siam	General Amity	85LTS337	301938
13 Apr	Belgium	Luxembourg	Admin Cooperation	72LTS237	301695
13 Apr	Germany	Latvia	Water Transport	73LTS46	301705
13 Apr	Austria	Great Britain	Patents/Copyrights	80LTS247	301830
16 Apr	Belgium	Netherlands	Admin Cooperation	75LTS61	301751
18 Apr	Chile	Germany	Sanitation	79LTS411	301817
19 Apr	Italy	USA (United States)	Dispute Settlement	113LTS183	302645
20 Apr	Latvia	USA (United States)	General Amity	80LTS35	301821
23 Apr	Multilateral		Telecommunications	78LTS197	301790
25 Apr	Germany	Sweden	Taxation	81LTS281	301844
25 Apr	Greece	USA (United States)	Commodity Trade	91LTS231	302064
25 Apr	Multilateral		Telecommunications	78LTS207	301791
26 Apr	Norway	Poland	General Economic	88LTS179	301996
26 Apr	Belgium	Luxembourg	Admin Cooperation	93LTS159	302107
26 Apr	Czechoslovakia	Finland	Visas	80LTS335	301838
26 Apr	Spain	Sweden	Dispute Settlement	77LTS77	301764
27 Apr	Iceland	UK Great Britain	Taxation	80LTS253	301831
28 Apr	Ecuador	Germany	Visas	90LTS163	302033
28 Apr	Germany	Netherlands	Customs	95LTS333	302183
01 May	Multilateral		Telecommunications	132LTS415	303050
01 May	Austria	Serb/Croat/Slovene	Admin Cooperation	96LTS373	302214
03 May	Argentina	Denmark	Sanitation	168LTS309	303907
05 May	Germany	USA (United States)	Dispute Settlement	90LTS177	302035
05 May	Germany	USA (United States)	Dispute Settlement	90LTS171	302034
05 May	Colombia	Vatican/Holy See	Consul/Citizenship	79LTS157	301808
07 May	Czechoslovakia	France	Extradition	114LTS117	302660
07 May	Czechoslovakia	France	Admin Cooperation	114LTS171	302663
07 May	Finland	Netherlands	Visas	74LTS367	301748
11 May	Austria	Italy	Air Transport	100LTS41	302293
11 May	France	Persia	General Amity	82LTS43	301858
11 May	Czechoslovakia	Germany	Non-ILO Labor	81LTS441	301854
11 May	Austria	Italy	Air Transport	100LTS375	302307
12 May	Hungary	Poland	Taxation	123LTS15	302802
12 May	Hungary	Poland	Taxation	123LTS47	302804
12 May	Finland	Italy	Visas	77LTS334	301775
14 May	Argentina	Sweden	Non-ILO Labor	155LTS109	303573
15 May	Germany	Persia	Privil/Immunities	107LTS389	302495
15 May	Estonia	Latvia	Visas	74LTS281	301742
15 May	Belgium	Persia	General Amity	94LTS447	302160
16 May	France	UK Great Britain	Non-ILO Labor	80LTS257	301832

DATE	PARTY ONE	PARTY TWO	TOPIC	CITATION	NUMBER
1928 (Cont.)					
16 May	Austria	France	General Trade	88LTS21	301986
18 May	Belgium	Luxembourg	Postal Service	89LTS207	302015
18 May	Belgium	Luxembourg	Postal Service	89LTS213	302016
22 May	Multilateral		Telecommunications	85LTS99	301925
22 May	Czechoslovakia	Poland	Water Transport	82LTS171	301868
23 May	Belgium	France	Sanitation	88LTS145	301993
26 May	Czechoslovakia	Hungary	Claims and Debts	101LTS265	302328
28 May	Latvia	Turkey	General Economic	94LTS295	302150
30 May	Belgium	France	Education	95LTS195	302173
30 May	Italy	Turkey	Dispute Settlement	95LTS183	302172
31 May	Persia	USSR (Soviet Union)	Admin Cooperation	110LTS343	302566
31 May	Japan	USA (United States)	Customs	101LTS63	302320
31 May	Finland	Spain	Dispute Settlement	82LTS229	301874
01 Jun	Belgium	Finland	Visas	77LTS327	301774
02 Jun	Albania	Hungary	Water Transport	82LTS201	301870
02 Jun	Germany	Latvia	Visas	75LTS69	301752
05 Jun	Czechoslovakia	Germany	Admin Cooperation	177LTS19	302700
06 Jun	Austria	Serb/Croat/Slovene	Non-ILO Labor	129LTS11	302950
07 Jun	Finland	USA (United States)	Dispute Settlement	87LTS9	301958
07 Jun	Finland	USA (United States)	Dispute Settlement	87LTS15	301959
09 Jun	Mexico	Panama	Consul/Citizenship	141LTS191	303265
09 Jun	Finland	Netherlands	Dispute Settlement	87LTS321	301978
09 Jun	Multilateral		Telecommunications	78LTS219	301792
11 Jun	Austria	Spain	Dispute Settlement	87LTS393	301984
11 Jun	Estonia	Sweden	Admin Cooperation	81LTS277	301843
12 Jun	France	Spain	Territory Boundary	136LTS289	303131
12 Jun	Belgium	Poland	Consul/Citizenship	123LTS25	302803
12 Jun	France	UK Great Britain	Postal Service	85LTS109	301926
14 Jun	Cuba	Germany	Postal Service	124LTS47	302832
14 Jun	Denmark	USA (United States)	Dispute Settlement	88LTS173	301995
14 Jun	Austria	Hungary	General Trade	79LTS17	301802
15 Jun	Persia	Turkey	General Amity	106LTS247	302449
16 Jun	Afghanistan	Belgium	Education	97LTS97	302221
17 Jun	Austria	Persia	Dispute Settlement	112LTS101	302610
19 Jun	Austria	USA (United States)	Consul/Citizenship	118LTS241	302728
20 Jun	Netherlands	Persia	General Amity	81LTS431	301852
21 Jun	Luxembourg	Spain	Dispute Settlement	109LTS137	302533
21 Jun	United Arab Rep	Palestine	General Trade	80LTS277	301833
21 Jun	Latvia	Sweden	Admin Cooperation	88LTS107	301990
22 Jun	Bulgaria	Latvia	General Trade	97LTS379	302236
23 Jun	Estonia	Sweden	Water Transport	87LTS253	301972
25 Jun	Austria	Hungary	Admin Cooperation	100LTS85	302296
26 Jun	Afghanistan	Persia	Admin Cooperation	106LTS321	302453
26 Jun	Belgium	Czechoslovakia	Visas	80LTS9	301819
27 Jun	Netherlands	Portugal	Admin Cooperation	81LTS437	301853
28 Jun	Germany	Luxembourg	Refugees	90LTS183	302036
28 Jun	Greece	Hungary	Water Transport	82LTS209	301871
29 Jun	Cuba	Mexico	Telecommunications	124LTS189	302833
30 Jun	Multilateral		Refugees	89LTS63	302006
30 Jun	Multilateral		Refugees	89LTS53	302005
30 Jun	Belgium	France	IGO Operations	93LTS377	302126
01 Jul	Estonia	Italy	General Economic	87LTS277	301974
02 Jul	Czechoslovakia	France	General Trade	99LTS105	302272
04 Jul	Hungary	Italy	Sanitation	92LTS169	302084
04 Jul	Belgium	France	Visas	85LTS205	301931
04 Jul	Hungary	Italy	General Economic	92LTS117	302083
05 Jul	Germany	Poland	Peace/Disarmament	113LTS189	302646
06 Jul	France	Portugal	Dispute Settlement	126LTS27	302869
06 Jul	Austria	Japan	Visas	81LTS425	301851
09 Jul	Austria	Serb/Croat/Slovene	General Trade	85LTS265	301936
10 Jul	Finland	Sweden	Telecommunications	87LTS131	301966
11 Jul	Persia	USA (United States)	Privil/Immunities	107LTS375	302494
11 Jul	Multilateral		Commodity Trade	95LTS357	302184
11 Jul	Multilateral		Commodity Trade	95LTS373	302185
15 Jul	Multilateral		Patents/Copyrights	79LTS133	301806

DATE	PARTY ONE	PARTY TWO	TOPIC	CITATION	NUMBER
1928 (Cont.)					
16 Jul	Paraguay	UK Great Britain	General Economic	108LTS365	302519
16 Jul	France	Spain	Postal Service	135LTS149	303110
16 Jul	Czechoslovakia	USA (United States)	Consul/Citizenship	96LTS301	302208
17 Jul	Afghanistan	Finland	General Amity	112LTS9	302601
24 Jul	Japan	New Zealand	General Trade	85LTS129	301927
24 Jul	Italy	Persia	General Amity	95LTS269	302179
25 Jul	China	USA (United States)	Customs	107LTS121	302472
25 Jul	Netherlands	Turkey	General Economic	93LTS279	302116
25 Jul	Multilateral		General Amity	87LTS211	301971
26 Jul	Germany	UK Great Britain	Specific Property	85LTS135	301928
02 Aug	Abyssinia	Italy	General Amity	94LTS413	302158
02 Aug	Abyssinia	Italy	Land Transport	94LTS423	302159
09 Aug	Persia	Sweden	General Amity	80LTS407	301841
13 Aug	Czechoslovakia	Spain	Dispute Settlement	121LTS321	302794
15 Aug	Saar	Switzerland	Air Transport	81LTS373	301847
16 Aug	Austria	USA (United States)	Dispute Settlement	88LTS95	301988
16 Aug	Austria	USA (United States)	Dispute Settlement	88LTS101	301989
16 Aug	Czechoslovakia	USA (United States)	Dispute Settlement	89LTS219	302017
16 Aug	Czechoslovakia	USA (United States)	Dispute Settlement	89LTS225	302018
16 Aug	Belgium	Bel-Lux Econ Union	General Trade	81LTS411	301849
16 Aug	Poland	USA (United States)	Dispute Settlement	99LTS409	302286
16 Aug	Poland	USA (United States)	Dispute Settlement	99LTS401	302285
17 Aug	China	Germany	General Trade	91LTS93	302057
17 Aug	Germany	Netherlands	Air Transport	93LTS409	302129
20 Aug	Estonia	Finland	Postal Service	85LTS195	301930
21 Aug	Finland	Italy	Dispute Settlement	89LTS25	302002
21 Aug	Finland	Italy	Admin Cooperation	84LTS265	301906
22 Aug	Denmark	Greece	General Economic	94LTS263	302147
27 Aug	Multilateral		General Military	94LTS57	302137
27 Aug	Germany	Italy	Visas	90LTS191	302037
27 Aug	Netherlands	Switzerland	Admin Cooperation	82LTS153	301866
27 Aug	Multilateral		General Amity	89LTS369	302028
28 Aug	Persia	Switzerland	Privil/Immunities	107LTS397	302496
01 Sep	Germany	South Africa	General Economic	95LTS289	302181
08 Sep	Bulgaria		Loans and Credits	74LTS167	301738
08 Sep	Denmark	Persia	General Amity	82LTS57	301859
11 Sep	Portugal	South Africa	Non-ILO Labor	98LTS9	302239
12 Sep	Belgium	France	Milit Servic/Citiz	123LTS97	302809
12 Sep	Belgium	France	Consul/Citizenship	123LTS91	302808
12 Sep	Multilateral		Telecommunications	104LTS43	302377
17 Sep	Canada	USA (United States)	Taxation	95LTS209	302175
19 Sep	Czechoslovakia	Serb/Croat/Slovene	Admin Cooperation	87LTS309	301976
22 Sep	Poland	Sweden	Admin Cooperation	140LTS391	303249
23 Sep	Greece	Italy	Dispute Settlement	108LTS219	302510
23 Sep	France	UK Great Britain	Postal Service	87LTS29	301961
24 Sep	Sweden	Turkey	General Trade	82LTS9	301855
24 Sep	Finland	USSR (Soviet Union)	Territory Boundary	82LTS63	301860
25 Sep	Panama	UK Great Britain	General Economic	90LTS311	302045
26 Sep	Panama	UK Great Britain	Consul/Citizenship	90LTS327	302046
26 Sep	Multilateral		Dispute Settlement	93LTS343	302123
29 Sep	Czechoslovakia	Serb/Croat/Slovene	Claims and Debts	96LTS421	302215
03 Oct	Italy	Spain	Air Transport	94LTS387	302156
06 Oct	Finland	Lithuania	General Trade	82LTS71	301861
17 Oct	Portugal	Switzerland	Dispute Settlement	96LTS287	302207
19 Oct	Estonia	Latvia	Admin Cooperation	97LTS359	302233
22 Oct	Albania	USA (United States)	Dispute Settlement	92LTS223	302090
22 Oct	Albania	USA (United States)	Dispute Settlement	92LTS217	302089
22 Oct	Austria	Finland	Extradition	89LTS69	302007
23 Oct	Mexico	Panama	Extradition	194LTS137	304518
23 Oct	Hungary	Lithuania	General Trade	84LTS281	301908
23 Oct	Finland	Norway	Water Transport	85LTS211	301932
24 Oct	Mexico	UK Great Britain	Postal Service	87LTS63	301962
25 Oct	Multilateral		Consul/Citizenship	84LTS7	301901
26 Oct	Germany	Uruguay	Visas	90LTS205	302039
27 Oct	Netherlands	Siam	Dispute Settlement	93LTS131	302105

DATE	PARTY ONE	PARTY TWO	TOPIC	CITATION	NUMBER
1928 (Cont.)					
27 Oct	Sweden	USA (United States)	Dispute Settlement	91LTS225	302063
29 Oct	Luxembourg	Poland	Dispute Settlement	111LTS71	302581
29 Oct	Belgium	Norway	Taxation	107LTS75	302469
30 Oct	Multilateral		Non-ILO Labor	130LTS405	302999
30 Oct	Germany	Lithuania	Admin Cooperation	91LTS365	302077
30 Oct	Germany	Lithuania	General Economic	89LTS127	302010
30 Oct	Multilateral		Dispute Settlement	87LTS103	301963
30 Oct	Germany	Lithuania	Consul/Citizenship	90LTS255	302043
07 Nov	Czechoslovakia	Serb/Croat/Slovene	Claims and Debts	95LTS101	302169
07 Nov	Czechoslovakia	Serb/Croat/Slovene	Consul/Citizenship	98LTS297	302252
07 Nov	Lithuania	Poland	Visas	89LTS171	302011
08 Nov	Hungary	Sweden	General Economic	89LTS283	302023
10 Nov	Germany	Romania	Dispute Settlement	91LTS101	302058
10 Nov	France	Mexico	General Trade	86LTS423	301953
12 Nov	France	Saar	Finance	85LTS451	301945
12 Nov	China	Norway	Customs	87LTS381	301983
14 Nov	Czechoslovakia	Hungary	Territory Boundary	110LTS425	302574
14 Nov	Czechoslovakia	Hungary	Water Transport	142LTS227	303295
14 Nov	Lithuania	USA (United States)	Dispute Settlement	100LTS117	302298
14 Nov	Czechoslovakia	Serb/Croat/Slovene	General Economic	97LTS9	302216
14 Nov	Lithuania	USA (United States)	Dispute Settlement	100LTS111	302297
15 Nov	Germany	Great Britain	Visas	90LTS213	302040
15 Nov	Brazil	Colombia	Water Transport	100LTS123	302299
16 Nov	Czechoslovakia	Spain	Dispute Settlement	100LTS313	302303
19 Nov	Hungary	Serb/Croat/Slovene	General Trade	97LTS101	302222
22 Nov	Multilateral		Culture	111LTS343	302598
22 Nov	Bel-Lux Econ Union	China	General Amity	87LTS287	301975
24 Nov	Finland	Norway	Visas	82LTS215	301872
27 Nov	Multilateral		Telecommunications	92LTS321	302098
27 Nov	China	Italy	General Amity	93LTS173	302109
28 Nov	United Arab Rep	Persia	General Amity	93LTS381	302127
29 Nov	Poland	Romania	Admin Cooperation	96LTS15	302188
30 Nov	Hungary	Poland	Dispute Settlement	100LTS67	302294
30 Nov	Multilateral		Telecommunications	87LTS119	301965
30 Nov	Denmark	Norway	Admin Cooperation	82LTS223	301873
01 Dec	Cuba	UK Great Britain	Postal Service	85LTS149	301929
03 Dec	Poland	Spain	Dispute Settlement	101LTS501	302348
07 Dec	Estonia	Germany	General Economic	99LTS259	302273
09 Dec	Switzerland	Turkey	Dispute Settlement	159LTS219	303664
11 Dec	Austria	Estonia	General Trade	92LTS229	302091
12 Dec	Austria	Czechoslovakia	Territory Boundary	108LTS9	302501
12 Dec	Belgium	Denmark	Taxation	107LTS363	302492
12 Dec	China	Denmark	General Amity	91LTS207	302062
12 Dec	Finland	Hungary	Admin Cooperation	96LTS67	302191
12 Dec	Austria	Czechoslovakia	Territory Boundary	107LTS137	302474
13 Dec	Denmark	Sweden	Telecommunications	104LTS55	302378
13 Dec	Czechoslovakia	Spain	General Trade	98LTS65	302240
14 Dec	Germany	Poland	Finance	113LTS367	302648
14 Dec	Multilateral		General Economic	110LTS171	302560
14 Dec	Germany	Poland	Finance	113LTS311	302647
15 Dec	Germany	Serb/Croat/Slovene	Non-ILO Labor	95LTS149	302171
15 Dec	Germany	Serb/Croat/Slovene	Non-ILO Labor	95LTS113	302170
15 Dec	Bel-Lux Econ Union	Spain	General Trade	84LTS287	301909
19 Dec	China	Netherlands	Customs	111LTS161	302585
19 Dec	China	Portugal	General Economic	107LTS93	302471
20 Dec	China	Sweden	Customs	107LTS81	302470
20 Dec	China	Germany	Customs	90LTS337	302047
20 Dec	Multilateral		Specific Resources	86LTS429	301954
21 Dec	Belgium	Iceland	Taxation	107LTS369	302493
21 Dec	Belgium	Great Britain	Admin Cooperation	85LTS415	301942
22 Dec	Multilateral		Telecommunications	104LTS103	302381
23 Dec	China	France	Customs	92LTS267	302095
27 Dec	Costa Rica	UK Great Britain	General Economic	108LTS375	302520
27 Dec	Norway	Spain	Dispute Settlement	97LTS339	302231
31 Dec	Brazil	Peru	Gen Communications	127LTS455	302931

DATE	PARTY ONE	PARTY TWO	TOPIC	CITATION	NUMBER
1928 (Cont.)					
31 Dec	Peru	UK Great Britain	Consul/Citizenship	100LTS431	302312
31 Dec	Germany	Great Britain	Taxation	71LTS193	301661
31 Dec	Great Britain	Portugal	Water Transport	71LTS199	301662
1929					
02 Jan	Spain	Sweden	Admin Cooperation	94LTS353	302154
03 Jan	Portugal	Sweden	Water Transport	87LTS313	301977
04 Jan	Lithuania	Sweden	Admin Cooperation	92LTS191	302086
05 Jan	Multilateral		Telecommunications	132LTS425	303051
05 Jan	Multilateral		Dispute Settlement	130LTS135	302988
05 Jan	Bulgaria	Hungary	Health/Educ/Welfare	118LTS279	302730
05 Jan	Ecuador	UK Great Britain	Consul/Citizenship	90LTS369	302048
05 Jan	Hungary	Turkey	Dispute Settlement	100LTS137	302300
05 Jan	Multilateral		Dispute Settlement	100LTS399	302309
09 Jan	Denmark	Latvia	General Trade	86LTS37	301948
11 Jan	Netherlands	Norway	Taxation	85LTS409	301941
12 Jan	United Arab Rep	Palestine	Dispute Settlement	94LTS9	302132
12 Jan	Latvia	Sweden	Admin Cooperation	85LTS403	301940
12 Jan	Canada	USA (United States)	Telecommunications	102LTS143	302359
14 Jan	Multilateral		Telecommunications	87LTS169	301968
15 Jan	Latvia	Persia	General Amity	162LTS299	303742
15 Jan	Turkey	UK Great Britain	General Economic	108LTS385	302521
15 Jan	France	USA (United States)	Extradition	92LTS259	302093
16 Jan	Multilateral		Telecommunications	87LTS155	301967
18 Jan	Bolivia	UK Great Britain	Postal Service	95LTS9	302161
20 Jan	Dominican Republic	Haiti	Peace/Disarmament	105LTS215	302414
21 Jan	Bulgaria	USA (United States)	Dispute Settlement	93LTS331	302121
21 Jan	Bulgaria	USA (United States)	Dispute Settlement	93LTS337	302122
21 Jan	Dominican Republic	Haiti	Territory Boundary	105LTS193	302413
21 Jan	Denmark	Norway	Telecommunications	104LTS119	302382
21 Jan	Serb/Croat/Slovene	USA (United States)	Dispute Settlement	93LTS301	302117
21 Jan	Serb/Croat/Slovene	USA (United States)	Dispute Settlement	93LTS307	302118
23 Jan	Germany	Norway	Air Transport	93LTS197	302110
23 Jan	Hungary	Japan	General Trade	91LTS317	302071
25 Jan	Germany	USSR (Soviet Union)	Dispute Settlement	90LTS219	302041
25 Jan	Italy	UK Great Britain	Admin Cooperation	95LTS39	302162
26 Jan	Hungary	USA (United States)	Dispute Settlement	96LTS173	302200
26 Jan	Hungary	USA (United States)	Dispute Settlement	96LTS207	302201
26 Jan	Germany	Lithuania	Non-ILO Labor	89LTS181	302012
28 Jan	Belgium	Italy	Extradition	92LTS263	302094
29 Jan	Finland	Serb/Croat/Slovene	General Trade	96LTS77	302192
01 Feb	Hungary	Norway	Customs	86LTS435	301955
02 Feb	Multilateral		Telecommunications	92LTS353	302100
03 Feb	Austria	Czechoslovakia	Non-ILO Labor	101LTS285	302329
03 Feb	Austria	Czechoslovakia	Non-ILO Labor	102LTS191	302362
07 Feb	Norway	Portugal	Water Transport	104LTS137	302383
09 Feb	Germany	Spain	Visas	89LTS369	302038
12 Feb	Latvia	Poland	General Economic	115LTS135	302683
12 Feb	Latvia	Poland	Land Transport	101LTS75	302321
17 Feb	Germany	Persia	General Economic	111LTS263	302591
17 Feb	Germany	Persia	Privil/Immunities	111LTS241	302590
17 Feb	Germany	Persia	General Amity	111LTS19	302576
19 Feb	Belgium	Finland	Taxation	111LTS31	302577
19 Feb	Germany	El Salvador	Visas	99LTS317	302274
19 Feb	Albania	Bel-Lux Econ Union	General Trade	90LTS429	302053
20 Feb	Multilateral		Patents/Copyrights	124LTS357	302840
20 Feb	Norway	USA (United States)	Dispute Settlement	91LTS413	302079
21 Feb	France	Luxembourg	Extradition	123LTS387	302825
21 Feb	Bulgaria	Greece	Extradition	106LTS443	302461
22 Feb	Italy	Sweden	Customs	87LTS265	301973
22 Feb	Austria	Italy	Territory Boundary	89LTS271	302021
25 Feb	Norway	USA (United States)	General Amity	134LTS81	303085
28 Feb	Germany	Romania	Visas	97LTS61	302217
28 Feb	Denmark	Sweden	Telecommunications	104LTS69	302379
28 Feb	Hungary	Spain	General Trade	94LTS313	302151

DATE	PARTY ONE	PARTY TWO	TOPIC	CITATION	NUMBER
1929 (Cont.)					
28 Feb	Multilateral		Telecommunications	97LTS301	302228
01 Mar	Portugal	USA (United States)	Dispute Settlement	99LTS375	302282
06 Mar	Bulgaria	Turkey	Dispute Settlement	114LTS399	302668
06 Mar	France	UK Great Britain	Postal Service	90LTS391	302050
10 Mar	Persia	USSR (Soviet Union)	Customs	107LTS419	302498
10 Mar	France	Italy	Air Transport	93LTS319	302120
11 Mar	France	Greece	General Economic	95LTS401	302187
15 Mar	Estonia	France	General Trade	89LTS381	302029
17 Mar	United Arab Rep	UK Great Britain	Loans and Credits	90LTS413	302051
20 Mar	Belgium	USA (United States)	Dispute Settlement	109LTS261	302542
20 Mar	Czechoslovakia	Germany	Territory Boundary	109LTS219	302541
20 Mar	Belgium	USA (United States)	Dispute Settlement	109LTS267	302543
21 Mar	Romania	USA (United States)	Dispute Settlement	105LTS79	302402
21 Mar	Romania	USA (United States)	Dispute Settlement	105LTS85	302403
22 Mar	Austria	Estonia	Visas	89LTS301	302025
22 Mar	Netherlands	UK Great Britain	Reparations	90LTS421	302052
25 Mar	Colombia	Nicaragua	Extradition	132LTS255	303042
27 Mar	Netherlands	Spain	Admin Cooperation	101LTS479	302346
27 Mar	Belgium	Netherlands	Finance	89LTS201	302014
27 Mar	Greece	Serb/Croat/Slovene	Dispute Settlement	108LTS201	302509
28 Mar	Bel-Lux Econ Union	France	General Trade	96LTS41	302190
28 Mar	Austria	Netherlands	General Economic	109LTS39	302527
30 Mar	Poland	Romania	Land Transport	123LTS147	302812
30 Mar	Japan	Persia	Privil/Immunities	107LTS427	302499
30 Mar	Norway	USA (United States)	Postal Service	91LTS383	302078
02 Apr	UK Great Britain	USA (United States)	Postal Service	94LTS17	302133
06 Apr	UK Great Britain	USA (United States)	Water Transport	99LTS27	302265
06 Apr	Luxembourg	USA (United States)	Dispute Settlement	106LTS475	302464
06 Apr	Luxembourg	USA (United States)	Dispute Settlement	106LTS469	302463
08 Apr	Germany	Portugal	Admin Cooperation	93LTS253	302114
13 Apr	Finland	USSR (Soviet Union)	Customs	96LTS93	302193
16 Apr	Multilateral		Specific Resources	126LTS305	302891
16 Apr	Germany	USSR (Soviet Union)	Water Transport	109LTS327	302547
20 Apr	Multilateral		Admin Cooperation	112LTS395	302624
20 Apr	Multilateral		Admin Cooperation	112LTS371	302623
23 Apr	Estonia	Sweden	Admin Cooperation	89LTS277	302022
23 Apr	Germany	Switzerland	General Trade	96LTS257	302206
25 Apr	France	Germany	Land Transport	109LTS333	302548
26 Apr	Germany	Hedjaz	General Amity	115LTS265	302690
29 Apr	Brazil	Denmark	Admin Cooperation	89LTS295	302024
29 Apr	Belgium	Czechoslovakia	Dispute Settlement	110LTS113	302556
29 Apr	Estonia	Hungary	General Economic	96LTS23	302189
30 Apr	Czechoslovakia	Persia	General Economic	110LTS357	302567
30 Apr	Estonia	Germany	Visas	99LTS325	302275
02 May	Canada	Norway	Taxation	91LTS329	302073
04 May	Netherlands	UK Great Britain	Postal Service	93LTS9	302101
06 May	France	UK Great Britain	Territory Boundary	93LTS27	302102
07 May	United Arab Rep	UK Great Britain	Specific Resources	93LTS43	302103
08 May	Multilateral		Telecommunications	91LTS337	302074
09 May	Bel-Lux Econ Union	Persia	General Economic	110LTS377	302569
09 May	Belgium	Persia	Privil/Immunities	110LTS391	302570
10 May	France	Persia	General Amity	150LTS329	303465
10 May	Norway	Persia	Privil/Immunities	107LTS403	302497
10 May	Persia	Sweden	General Amity	102LTS9	302349
11 May	Norway	Sweden	Water Transport	120LTS263	302771
13 May	Belgium	Sweden	Taxation	111LTS37	302578
15 May	France	UK Great Britain	Postal Service	134LTS263	303097
15 May	Palestine	Switzerland	Postal Service	95LTS395	302186
16 May	Hungary	Lithuania	General Economic	96LTS333	302211
16 May	Germany	Turkey	Dispute Settlement	109LTS451	302549
17 May	Bulgaria	Hungary	Extradition	92LTS197	302087
17 May	Estonia	USSR (Soviet Union)	General Economic	94LTS323	302152
18 May	Belgium	Luxembourg	Customs	119LTS377	302757
21 May	Czechoslovakia	Romania	General Amity	96LTS307	302209
21 May	Romania	Serb/Croat/Slovene	General Amity	98LTS221	302249

DATE	PARTY ONE	PARTY TWO	TOPIC	CITATION	NUMBER
1929 (Cont.)					
21 May	Czechoslovakia	Serb/Croat/Slovene	General Amity	94LTS53	302136
21 May	Multilateral		Dispute Settlement	96LTS311	302210
22 May	Finland	Switzerland	Visas	91LTS311	302070
22 May	Finland	Switzerland	Visas	91LTS305	302069
23 May	Belgium	Persia	General Amity	110LTS369	302568
24 May	Greece	Persia	Mostfavored Nation	121LTS221	302788
24 May	Poland	Romania	Territory Boundary	124LTS333	302836
24 May	Poland	Romania	Territory Boundary	124LTS339	302837
25 May	France	UK Great Britain	Admin Cooperation	95LTS55	302163
25 May	Austria	Uruguay	Visas	93LTS229	302112
27 May	Persia	Sweden	General Amity	105LTS279	302420
28 May	Germany	Turkey	Consul/Citizenship	133LTS257	303069
28 May	Germany	Turkey	Admin Cooperation	133LTS235	303068
28 May	Belgium	Netherlands	Sanitation	89LTS191	302013
28 May	Germany	Switzerland	Territory Boundary	104LTS19	302375
30 May	Bolivia	Netherlands	General Trade	133LTS113	303062
31 May	Multilateral		Water Transport	136LTS81	303127
03 Jun	Chile	Peru	Dispute Settlement	94LTS401	302157
04 Jun	Bulgaria	Germany	Consul/Citizenship	106LTS49	302436
06 Jun	France	India	Admin Cooperation	95LTS61	302164
08 Jun	Czechoslovakia	Greece	General Amity	108LTS255	302512
10 Jun	Greece	USA (United States)	Taxation	98LTS81	302241
10 Jun	Hungary	Spain	Dispute Settlement	101LTS251	302327
10 Jun	Albania	Switzerland	General Trade	104LTS145	302384
10 Jun	Italy	Norway	Dispute Settlement	105LTS161	302410
11 Jun	Romania	Turkey	General Economic	112LTS139	302613
11 Jun	Denmark	Great Britain	Water Transport	93LTS401	302128
14 Jun	Multilateral		Visas	94LTS275	302148
14 Jun	Mexico	Norway	Postal Service	99LTS381	302283
15 Jun	Latvia	Portugal	General Economic	98LTS447	302262
18 Jun	Canada	Denmark	Taxation	95LTS81	302167
19 Jun	Hungary	Persia	Mostfavored Nation	107LTS355	302491
20 Jun	Spain	USA (United States)	Claims and Debts	120LTS401	302776
21 Jun	Colombia	Denmark	General Economic	125LTS113	302850
21 Jun	Greece	UK Great Britain	Finance	94LTS33	302134
21 Jun	Czechoslovakia	Denmark	Visas	91LTS351	302075
25 Jun	Belgium	Greece	Dispute Settlement	113LTS117	302640
25 Jun	Czechoslovakia	Iceland	Visas	91LTS359	302076
27 Jun	Spain	UK Great Britain	Admin Cooperation	101LTS375	302337
28 Jun	Multilateral		Postal Service	103LTS71	302370
28 Jun	Multilateral		Postal Service	103LTS429	302374
28 Jun	Multilateral		Postal Service	103LTS5	302369
28 Jun	Multilateral		Postal Service	103LTS249	302371
28 Jun	Multilateral		Postal Service	103LTS377	302373
28 Jun	Multilateral		Postal Service	102LTS245	302368
28 Jun	Multilateral		Postal Service	103LTS321	302372
01 Jul	Belgium	France	Non-ILO Labor	93LTS371	302125
04 Jul	UK Great Britain	USA (United States)	Postal Service	92LTS329	302099
06 Jul	Germany	Siam	Visas	99LTS333	302276
08 Jul	France	Switzerland	General Economic	114LTS189	302664
09 Jul	Czechoslovakia	Estonia	Dispute Settlement	101LTS423	302341
10 Jul	Finland	Italy	Extradition	111LTS295	302593
11 Jul	UK Great Britain	USA (United States)	Postal Service	98LTS161	302245
13 Jul	Belgium	Germany	Consul/Citizenship	104LTS211	302391
13 Jul	Belgium	Germany	Finance	104LTS201	302390
17 Jul	Germany	UK Great Britain	Postal Service	100LTS439	302313
19 Jul	Colombia	Spain	Dispute Settlement	114LTS105	302658
22 Jul	Bulgaria	Hungary	Dispute Settlement	101LTS41	302317
23 Jul	Norway	USA (United States)	Visas	93LTS223	302111
26 Jul	Norway	Sweden	Admin Cooperation	94LTS287	302149
27 Jul	Multilateral		Other Military	118LTS343	302734
27 Jul	Multilateral		Other Military	118LTS303	302733
31 Jul	Greece	UK Great Britain	Taxation	95LTS67	302165
31 Jul	Japan	Turkey	Mostfavored Nation	111LTS289	302592
02 Aug	France	UK Great Britain	Reparations	100LTS459	302314

DATE	PARTY ONE	PARTY TWO	TOPIC	CITATION	NUMBER
1929 (Cont.)					
02 Aug	Persia	USSR (Soviet Union)	Postal Service	109LTS99	302530
05 Aug	Japan	Spain	Mostfavored Nation	113LTS9	302629
10 Aug	Japan	UK Great Britain	Taxation	95LTS73	302166
11 Aug	Albania	Serb/Croat/Slovene	Territory Boundary	101LTS439	302342
15 Aug	Luxembourg	Portugal	Dispute Settlement	115LTS77	302678
15 Aug	Finland	Italy	Admin Cooperation	99LTS363	302280
20 Aug	Japan	UK Great Britain	Postal Service	107LTS243	302481
20 Aug	Multilateral		Sanitation	98LTS125	302243
22 Aug	Estonia	Portugal	General Trade	98LTS225	302250
23 Aug	Austria	Spain	Visas	97LTS353	302232
24 Aug	Hedjaz	Persia	General Amity	106LTS269	302450
26 Aug	Iceland	Spain	Dispute Settlement	104LTS183	302388
26 Aug	Bel-Lux Econ Union	Switzerland	General Economic	105LTS9	302401
27 Aug	Estonia	USA (United States)	Dispute Settlement	102LTS239	302367
27 Aug	Estonia	USA (United States)	Dispute Settlement	102LTS233	302366
28 Aug	Germany	Poland	Air Transport	146LTS333	303383
29 Aug	France	Turkey	General Economic	123LTS193	302815
30 Aug	Multilateral		Consul/Citizenship	104LTS473	302399
30 Aug	Multilateral		Telecommunications	96LTS129	302195
30 Aug	Multilateral		Telecommunications	96LTS117	302194
30 Aug	Multilateral		General Amity	104LTS487	302400
31 Aug	Belgium	China	Privil/Immunities	123LTS105	302810
05 Sep	Italy	Persia	General Amity	141LTS185	303264
07 Sep	Multilateral		Telecommunications	98LTS345	302255
09 Sep	Italy	Turkey	Consul/Citizenship	129LTS195	302962
09 Sep	Czechoslovakia	Norway	Dispute Settlement	101LTS355	302336
10 Sep	Netherlands	South Africa	Postal Service	98LTS423	302261
11 Sep	Germany	Luxembourg	Dispute Settlement	118LTS97	302715
14 Sep	Multilateral		UN Charter	165LTS353	303822
14 Sep	Estonia	Turkey	General Trade	97LTS365	302234
14 Sep	Czechoslovakia	Netherlands	Dispute Settlement	107LTS201	302477
16 Sep	Estonia	Turkey	General Economic	117LTS377	302704
16 Sep	Italy	Serb/Croat/Slovene	Territory Boundary	101LTS127	302322
16 Sep	Luxembourg	Switzerland	Dispute Settlement	107LTS23	302465
17 Sep	Luxembourg	Netherlands	Dispute Settlement	107LTS35	302466
18 Sep	China	Poland	General Economic	120LTS331	302774
18 Sep	Czechoslovakia	Luxembourg	Dispute Settlement	107LTS49	302467
20 Sep	Czechoslovakia	Switzerland	Dispute Settlement	102LTS123	302357
21 Sep	Germany	Honduras	Visas	133LTS311	303070
21 Sep	Canada	Japan	Taxation	96LTS143	302196
23 Sep	Canada	Netherlands	Taxation	96LTS151	302197
24 Sep	Belgium	Irish Free State	Postal Service	102LTS213	302364
25 Sep	Turkey	UK Great Britain	General Trade	94LTS41	302135
25 Sep	Multilateral		Telecommunications	98LTS361	302256
26 Sep	Bulgaria	Yugoslavia	Territory Boundary	101LTS217	302324
26 Sep	Multilateral		Telecommunications	98LTS395	302259
27 Sep	Serb/Croat/Slovene	Spain	General Economic	98LTS319	302253
29 Sep	Sweden	Turkey	General Economic	119LTS53	302740
30 Sep	China	Greece	General Amity	123LTS127	302811
30 Sep	Canada	Greece	Taxation	96LTS159	302198
30 Sep	Multilateral		Postal Service	99LTS71	302269
30 Sep	Multilateral		Telecommunications	98LTS183	302246
01 Oct	Multilateral		Telecommunications	98LTS197	302247
02 Oct	Czechoslovakia	Finland	Dispute Settlement	115LTS155	302684
04 Oct	Belgium	USA (United States)	Other Military	105LTS189	302412
04 Oct	Poland	UK Great Britain	Postal Service	97LTS261	302227
07 Oct	Belgium	France	Taxation	111LTS43	302579
07 Oct	Finland	USSR (Soviet Union)	Postal Service	96LTS349	302212
07 Oct	Estonia	France	Commodity Trade	104LTS193	302389
08 Oct	Multilateral		Telecommunications	98LTS409	302260
10 Oct	Multilateral		Telecommunications	98LTS375	302257
11 Oct	Czechoslovakia	Norway	Visas	96LTS211	302202
12 Oct	Multilateral		General Transport	137LTS11	303145
12 Oct	Finland	Turkey	General Economic	96LTS239	302205
14 Oct	Denmark	Germany	Water Transport	98LTS211	302248

DATE	PARTY ONE	PARTY TWO	TOPIC	CITATION	NUMBER
1929 (Cont.)					
16 Oct	Italy	Panama	General Economic	138LTS355	303199
18 Oct	Finland	Italy	Visas	97LTS65	302218
18 Oct	Latvia	Serb/Croat/Slovene	General Economic	96LTS229	302204
18 Oct	Greece	Sweden	Admin Cooperation	95LTS201	302174
19 Oct	Sweden	Turkey	General Trade	96LTS221	302203
19 Oct	Chile	Poland	Dispute Settlement	113LTS79	302637
22 Oct	Canada	USA (United States)	Air Transport	97LTS321	302229
23 Oct	Canada	USA (United States)	Sanitation	96LTS167	302199
24 Oct	Poland	Romania	Dispute Settlement	100LTS299	302302
28 Oct	Multilateral		Telecommunications	97LTS71	302219
29 Oct	Irish Free State	Portugal	General Economic	131LTS145	303007
29 Oct	Multilateral		Telecommunications	99LTS85	302270
30 Oct	Poland	Romania	Land Transport	121LTS167	302787
30 Oct	Poland	Romania	Land Transport	121LTS243	302790
31 Oct	Germany	Poland	Claims and Debts	124LTS345	302838
31 Oct	China	UK Great Britain	Admin Cooperation	99LTS441	302289
02 Nov	Germany	Switzerland	Admin Cooperation	109LTS273	302544
06 Nov	Cuba	France	General Economic	114LTS345	302665
07 Nov	Belgium	France	Reparations	134LTS257	303096
07 Nov	Belgium	Germany	Territory Boundary	121LTS327	302795
07 Nov	Brazil	Venezuela	Territory Boundary	99LTS427	302288
09 Nov	Multilateral		Land Transport	125LTS205	302855
09 Nov	China	UK Great Britain	Claims and Debts	99LTS453	302290
09 Nov	Switzerland	UK Great Britain	Non-ILO Labor	100LTS21	302291
11 Nov	Hungary	Yugoslavia	Admin Cooperation	111LTS197	302587
14 Nov	Hungary	Portugal	General Trade	105LTS287	302421
15 Nov	Argentina	UK Great Britain	Non-ILO Labor	160LTS257	303694
18 Nov	Multilateral		Telecommunications	99LTS415	302287
20 Nov	France	Germany	Admin Cooperation	99LTS339	302277
21 Nov	Canada	Sweden	Taxation	97LTS331	302230
21 Nov	Netherlands	Turkey	General Trade	99LTS397	302284
27 Nov	Estonia	Hungary	Dispute Settlement	106LTS331	302454
02 Dec	Colombia	UK Great Britain	Extradition	110LTS401	302571
05 Dec	Belgium	Ecuador	Visas	97LTS385	302237
07 Dec	Poland	Romania	Admin Cooperation	119LTS283	302752
09 Dec	Norway	Poland	Dispute Settlement	101LTS325	302334
10 Dec	Lithuania	UK Great Britain	General Economic	99LTS47	302266
10 Dec	Switzerland	UK Great Britain	Postal Service	99LTS53	302267
11 Dec	Denmark	Italy	Extradition	97LTS373	302235
12 Dec	Denmark	Estonia	Admin Cooperation	98LTS341	302254
17 Dec	Poland	Romania	Consul/Citizenship	119LTS333	302754
17 Dec	Multilateral		Specific Resources	115LTS93	302679
18 Dec	Multilateral		Admin Cooperation	104LTS27	302376
18 Dec	Norway	Sweden	Customs	98LTS389	302258
19 Dec	Poland	Romania	Admin Cooperation	130LTS205	302991
20 Dec	Estonia	Latvia	Telecommunications	106LTS173	302444
21 Dec	France	Hungary	General Trade	132LTS189	303038
21 Dec	Czechoslovakia	Poland	General Amity	115LTS201	302687
21 Dec	UK Great Britain	USSR (Soviet Union)	Consul/Citizenship	99LTS61	302268
21 Dec	Cuba	Japan	Mostfavored Nation	111LTS13	302575
22 Dec	Czechoslovakia	Germany	Customs	110LTS417	302573
23 Dec	Bulgaria	Turkey	Extradition	122LTS17	302796
24 Dec	Czechoslovakia	Latvia	Visas	99LTS9	302263
27 Dec	Austria	Greece	Claims and Debts	100LTS423	302311
28 Dec	Poland	Portugal	General Economic	117LTS363	302703
28 Dec	Germany	UK Great Britain	Admin Cooperation	102LTS49	302352
31 Dec	France	Germany	Reparations	106LTS93	302438
31 Dec	Bulgaria	Poland	Dispute Settlement	113LTS89	302638
31 Dec	Austria	Netherlands	Air Transport	111LTS177	302586
1930					
02 Jan	UK Great Britain	USA (United States)	Territory Boundary	137LTS297	303164
09 Jan	Multilateral		Admin Cooperation	115LTS473	302696
11 Jan	Latvia	Sweden	Land Transport	109LTS193	302539
13 Jan	Lithuania	Persia	General Amity	131LTS221	303013

DATE	PARTY ONE	PARTY TWO	TOPIC	CITATION	NUMBER
1930 (Cont.)					
13 Jan	Netherlands	USA (United States)	Dispute Settlement	107LTS69	302468
14 Jan	Denmark	France	Education	100LTS327	302304
14 Jan	Latvia	USA (United States)	Dispute Settlement	105LTS301	302422
14 Jan	Latvia	USA (United States)	Dispute Settlement	105LTS307	302423
14 Jan	Other Unilat Decla	Greece	Refugees	108LTS349	302518
14 Jan	Multilateral		Telecommunications	99LTS343	302278
16 Jan	Belgium	Germany	Admin Cooperation	104LTS223	302392
17 Jan	Canada	Germany	Reparations	109LTS473	302550
17 Jan	Liberia	UK Great Britain	Territory Boundary	101LTS395	302338
17 Jan	Germany	New Zealand	Reparations	109LTS485	302551
17 Jan	Austria	Germany	Reparations	107LTS325	302488
18 Jan	Austria	Belgium	Admin Cooperation	104LTS231	302393
20 Jan	France	Latvia	Consul/Citizenship	169LTS125	303917
20 Jan	Poland	UK Great Britain	Claims and Debts	126LTS159	302878
20 Jan	Italy	Poland	Claims and Debts	127LTS41	302904
20 Jan	France	Poland	Claims and Debts	126LTS117	302876
20 Jan	Austria	Poland	Claims and Debts	133LTS223	303067
20 Jan	Multilateral		Reparations	104LTS243	302394
20 Jan	Estonia	Sweden	Extradition	106LTS279	302451
20 Jan	Multilateral		Finance	104LTS413	302395
20 Jan	Multilateral		Reparations	112LTS361	302622
20 Jan	Germany	Italy	Peace/Disarmament	106LTS109	302439
20 Jan	France	Yugoslavia	Reparations	104LTS171	302386
20 Jan	Multilateral		Finance	104LTS433	302397
20 Jan	France	Yugoslavia	Claims and Debts	104LTS177	302387
20 Jan	Multilateral		Other Economic	104LTS441	302398
20 Jan	Estonia	USSR (Soviet Union)	Dispute Settlement	102LTS225	302365
20 Jan	Multilateral		Reparations	104LTS421	302396
20 Jan	Multilateral		Reparations	113LTS389	302650
22 Jan	Netherlands	Romania	Dispute Settlement	112LTS121	302611
22 Jan	Luxembourg	Romania	Dispute Settlement	110LTS151	302559
23 Jan	Greece	Spain	Dispute Settlement	139LTS93	303205
24 Jan	Multilateral		Peace/Disarmament	106LTS85	302437
25 Jan	France	Sweden	Taxation	99LTS99	302271
27 Jan	Latvia	Netherlands	Extradition	117LTS343	302701
28 Jan	Greece	Iceland	Mostfavored Nation	118LTS285	302731
30 Jan	Honduras	Nicaragua	General Trade	142LTS241	303297
30 Jan	Latvia	Sweden	Extradition	110LTS139	302558
30 Jan	Austria	USA (United States)	Extradition	106LTS379	302457
30 Jan	Austria	Luxembourg	Admin Cooperation	99LTS357	302279
31 Jan	Czechoslovakia	Germany	Territory Boundary	145LTS51	303345
31 Jan	Belgium	Spain	Taxation	99LTS369	302281
05 Feb	Austria	Germany	Non-ILO Labor	119LTS201	302746
06 Feb	Austria	Italy	Dispute Settlement	105LTS97	302405
08 Feb	Brazil	Italy	Visas	101LTS57	302319
10 Feb	Latvia	Norway	Visas	100LTS79	302295
10 Feb	Netherlands	UK Great Britain	Postal Service	102LTS67	302353
12 Feb	China	Czechoslovakia	General Economic	110LTS285	302561
14 Feb	Netherlands	Spain	Air Transport	137LTS149	303152
14 Feb	Bulgaria	Yugoslavia	Claims and Debts	101LTS135	302323
15 Feb	Austria	Germany	Patents/Copyrights	109LTS501	302552
17 Feb	Multilateral		Dispute Settlement	102LTS87	302354
18 Feb	Portugal	UK Great Britain	General Trade	108LTS393	302522
21 Feb	Brazil	UK Great Britain	Consul/Citizenship	101LTS11	302315
24 Feb	Germany	Persia	Patents/Copyrights	113LTS15	302630
25 Feb	Germany	Italy	Scientific Project	118LTS49	302713
25 Feb	Italy	Romania	Other Economic	106LTS231	302447
25 Feb	Italy	Romania	Peace/Disarmament	106LTS225	302446
25 Feb	Italy	Romania	Sanitation	106LTS423	302459
25 Feb	Multilateral		Telecommunications	101LTS343	302335
25 Feb	Italy	Romania	General Economic	106LTS179	302445
28 Feb	Denmark	Latvia	Dispute Settlement	113LTS27	302632
28 Feb	France	Netherlands	Taxation	101LTS303	302331
28 Feb	Denmark	France	General Economic	101LTS17	302316
01 Mar	Turkey	UK Great Britain	General Economic	108LTS407	302523

DATE	PARTY ONE	PARTY TWO	TOPIC	CITATION	NUMBER
1930 (Cont.)					
05 Mar	Chile	United Arab Rep	Mostfavored Nation	124LTS25	302830
05 Mar	Austria	Panama	Visas	101LTS293	302330
07 Mar	Austria	Luxembourg	Visas	101LTS237	302325
07 Mar	Austria	United Arab Rep	General Economic	100LTS417	302310
08 Mar	Latvia	Spain	Extradition	113LTS135	302641
08 Mar	Finland	Portugal	General Economic	105LTS441	302431
08 Mar	Czechoslovakia	Lithuania	Dispute Settlement	115LTS61	302677
10 Mar	Germany	Haiti	General Trade	119LTS231	302747
12 Mar	Netherlands	Persia	General Amity	111LTS387	302599
13 Mar	United Arab Rep	Yugoslavia	Mostfavored Nation	110LTS133	302557
15 Mar	Multilateral		Finance	113LTS395	302651
16 Mar	Czechoslovakia	United Arab Rep	General Economic	107LTS179	302475
17 Mar	United Arab Rep	Netherlands	Mostfavored Nation	105LTS91	302404
18 Mar	Brazil	UK Great Britain	Territory Boundary	101LTS401	302339
19 Mar	United Arab Rep	Japan	Mostfavored Nation	111LTS223	302588
20 Mar	Siam	UK Great Britain	Postal Service	106LTS363	302456
21 Mar	Costa Rica	Spain	Milit Servic/Citiz	168LTS61	303886
24 Mar	France	UK Great Britain	Telecommunications	105LTS227	302415
24 Mar	Austria	Sweden	Extradition	105LTS313	302424
25 Mar	United Arab Rep	Germany	Mostfavored Nation	115LTS271	302691
25 Mar	Belgium	Yugoslavia	Dispute Settlement	106LTS343	302455
26 Mar	Poland	Romania	Extradition	153LTS87	303510
31 Mar	France	Luxembourg	Privil/Immunities	122LTS29	302797
02 Apr	Romania	UK Great Britain	Postal Service	105LTS235	302416
03 Apr	Estonia	Norway	Extradition	106LTS147	302442
04 Apr	Estonia	Sweden	Patents/Copyrights	101LTS51	302318
07 Apr	Danzig	Norway	Visas	100LTS391	302308
10 Apr	Greece	Poland	General Economic	120LTS369	302775
10 Apr	Greece	Poland	Admin Cooperation	123LTS165	302813
10 Apr	Austria	Poland	Air Transport	108LTS289	302514
10 Apr	Multilateral		Telecommunications	101LTS465	302345
11 Apr	Austria	Hungary	Visas	101LTS309	302332
12 Apr	Multilateral		Milit Servic/Citiz	178LTS227	304117
12 Apr	Multilateral		Admin Cooperation	179LTS89	304137
12 Apr	Multilateral		Admin Cooperation	179LTS115	304138
12 Apr	Austria	Germany	Privil/Immunities	115LTS297	302693
12 Apr	Austria	Germany	Customs	115LTS333	302694
12 Apr	Netherlands	Poland	Dispute Settlement	113LTS65	302636
12 Apr	Austria	Germany	General Transport	115LTS277	302692
16 Apr	United Arab Rep	Romania	Mostfavored Nation	117LTS405	302706
16 Apr	UK Great Britain	USA (United States)	Postal Service	109LTS9	302524
17 Apr	Multilateral		Extradition	126LTS201	302883
17 Apr	Canada	Germany	Taxation	101LTS245	302326
18 Apr	China	UK Great Britain	Recognition	112LTS49	302607
22 Apr	Multilateral		Peace/Disarmament	112LTS65	302608
22 Apr	United Arab Rep	Poland	Mostfavored Nation	118LTS413	302735
26 Apr	Denmark	Sweden	Land Transport	101LTS319	302333
27 Apr	Hungary	Yugoslavia	Dispute Settlement	113LTS153	302642
28 Apr	Finland	France	Dispute Settlement	139LTS381	303222
28 Apr	Multilateral		Claims and Debts	121LTS69	302785
29 Apr	Chile	Peru	Admin Cooperation	112LTS133	302612
02 May	Japan	Lithuania	General Economic	126LTS369	302895
04 May	Hungary	Latvia	Admin Cooperation	101LTS449	302344
05 May	Netherlands	UK Great Britain	Air Transport	105LTS261	302417
05 May	Greece	Hungary	Dispute Settlement	118LTS293	302732
05 May	Colombia	Nicaragua	Territory Boundary	105LTS337	302426
06 May	Afghanistan	UK Great Britain	Admin Cooperation	105LTS265	302418
06 May	China	Japan	Customs	106LTS295	302452
07 May	Denmark	United Arab Rep	General Economic	102LTS137	302358
07 May	Hungary	Italy	Visas	101LTS445	302343
08 May	Norway	Persia	General Economic	134LTS153	303089
09 May	Germany	UK Great Britain	Milit Occupation	105LTS271	302419
09 May	Poland	Romania	Air Transport	112LTS225	302617
09 May	Canada	USA (United States)	Specific Resources	121LTS45	302782
10 May	Irish Free State	Italy	Water Transport	132LTS147	303034

DATE	PARTY ONE	PARTY TWO	TOPIC	CITATION	NUMBER
1930 (Cont.)					
12 May	Germany	Irish Free State	General Economic	131LTS153	303008
12 May	Germany	South Africa	Patents/Copyrights	123LTS301	302821
13 May	Denmark	Estonia	Extradition	106LTS159	302443
14 May	Finland	Norway	Postal Service	105LTS399	302429
14 May	Denmark	Finland	Postal Service	105LTS455	302433
14 May	Finland	Sweden	Postal Service	106LTS9	302434
14 May	Multilateral		Postal Service	105LTS353	302428
15 May	Greece	Irish Free State	General Trade	136LTS33	303122
15 May	Finland	Poland	Visas	111LTS309	302594
16 May	China	France	General Amity	162LTS99	303738
21 May	Hungary	Turkey	Mostfavored Nation	105LTS117	302406
21 May	Hungary	Turkey	General Economic	109LTS153	302534
22 May	UK Great Britain	USSR (Soviet Union)	Specific Resources	102LTS103	302355
23 May	Belgium	France	Telecommunications	119LTS33	302738
27 May	Chile	USA (United States)	Other Economic	133LTS141	303064
27 May	United Arab Rep	Norway	Commodity Trade	105LTS449	302432
27 May	Belgium	Turkey	General Economic	111LTS49	302580
27 May	Germany	Turkey	General Economic	110LTS9	302553
28 May	Netherlands	Yugoslavia	General Economic	129LTS73	302951
30 May	Germany	Norway	Customs	107LTS129	302473
31 May	Iceland	Norway	Non-ILO Labor	108LTS339	302517
31 May	Denmark	Turkey	General Economic	119LTS165	302744
02 Jun	France	Norway	Taxation	102LTS27	302350
03 Jun	France	Italy	Admin Cooperation	153LTS135	303513
03 Jun	Greece	Hungary	General Trade	122LTS37	302798
03 Jun	Netherlands	UK Great Britain	Postal Service	111LTS85	302582
03 Jun	Austria	Hungary	Land Transport	122LTS69	302799
06 Jun	Austria	Italy	Visas	105LTS329	302425
07 Jun	Multilateral		Finance	143LTS257	303313
07 Jun	Multilateral		Finance	143LTS317	303314
07 Jun	Multilateral		Finance	143LTS337	303315
07 Jun	United Arab Rep	UK Great Britain	General Trade	107LTS267	302483
07 Jun	United Arab Rep	Sweden	General Economic	102LTS207	302363
10 Jun	Greece	Turkey	Refugees	108LTS233	302511
10 Jun	Spain	USA (United States)	Taxation	120LTS407	302777
10 Jun	Multilateral		Loans and Credits	112LTS237	302618
12 Jun	United Arab Rep	Hungary	General Economic	106LTS437	302460
13 Jun	United Arab Rep	Finland	Mostfavored Nation	111LTS315	302595
13 Jun	United Arab Rep	France	Health/Educ/Welfare	106LTS39	302435
14 Jun	Portugal	UK Great Britain	Postal Service	107LTS275	302484
16 Jun	France	Italy	Taxation	144LTS115	303323
17 Jun	United Arab Rep	Persia	Mostfavored Nation	107LTS349	302490
18 Jun	Czechoslovakia	Poland	Land Transport	137LTS137	303151
18 Jun	Germany	Romania	Mostfavored Nation	110LTS95	302554
19 Jun	Greece	USA (United States)	Dispute Settlement	136LTS393	303137
19 Jun	Romania	Yugoslavia	Territory Boundary	140LTS229	303238
19 Jun	Greece	USA (United States)	Dispute Settlement	136LTS399	303138
19 Jun	Poland	USA (United States)	Commodity Trade	108LTS223	302515
20 Jun	Czechoslovakia	Romania	Air Transport	150LTS63	303453
20 Jun	Belgium	Germany	Land Transport	110LTS107	302555
20 Jun	Albania	Japan	General Trade	123LTS295	302820
20 Jun	Romania	Spain	Mostfavored Nation	117LTS411	302707
21 Jun	Norway	Romania	General Economic	120LTS113	302762
21 Jun	Denmark	Lithuania	General Economic	114LTS151	302662
21 Jun	Iceland	Lithuania	General Economic	119LTS403	302759
23 Jun	Poland	Romania	General Economic	133LTS163	303066
23 Jun	Germany	USA (United States)	Reparations	106LTS121	302440
24 Jun	Romania	Yugoslavia	Admin Cooperation	140LTS235	303239
26 Jun	Multilateral		Telecommunications	133LTS9	303052
26 Jun	Austria	Greece	Dispute Settlement	119LTS353	302755
27 Jun	Finland	Iceland	Dispute Settlement	167LTS271	303873
27 Jun	China	USA (United States)	Dispute Settlement	140LTS184	303236
27 Jun	Iceland	Sweden	Dispute Settlement	127LTS67	302907
27 Jun	Denmark	Iceland	Dispute Settlement	118LTS121	302717
27 Jun	Portugal	UK Great Britain	Postal Service	107LTS281	302485

DATE	PARTY ONE	PARTY TWO	TOPIC	CITATION	NUMBER
1930 (Cont.)					
27 Jun	Czechoslovakia	Germany	Customs	112LTS169	302614
27 Jun	Czechoslovakia	Romania	General Economic	119LTS73	302742
27 Jun	Iceland	Norway	Dispute Settlement	126LTS417	302900
27 Jun	Romania	Yugoslavia	General Military	107LTS215	302478
30 Jun	Iraq	UK Great Britain	General Military	132LTS363	303048
30 Jun	Denmark	Finland	Land Transport	105LTS179	302411
01 Jul	Multilateral		Claims and Debts	121LTS153	302786
02 Jul	Belgium	Bulgaria	Admin Cooperation	130LTS191	302990
03 Jul	Denmark	Germany	General Transport	105LTS427	302430
08 Jul	France	Italy	Territory Boundary	137LTS93	303148
08 Jul	Belgium	Romania	Dispute Settlement	128LTS403	302944
09 Jul	Netherlands	USA (United States)	Postal Service	125LTS123	302851
12 Jul	Germany	USA (United States)	Extradition	119LTS247	302748
12 Jul	Estonia	Finland	Other Economic	111LTS321	302596
15 Jul	Czechoslovakia	Romania	Territory Boundary	164LTS157	303793
16 Jul	Guatemala	Honduras	Dispute Settlement	137LTS231	303159
17 Jul	Finland	Sweden	Land Transport	105LTS343	302427
17 Jul	Bulgaria	Spain	Extradition	114LTS41	302653
22 Jul	Italy	Poland	Sanitation	121LTS17	302780
24 Jul	Belgium	Shereefian	Non-ILO Labor	138LTS35	303179
24 Jul	Latvia	UK Great Britain	Admin Cooperation	107LTS301	302486
26 Jul	Norway	Portugal	Dispute Settlement	134LTS123	303087
28 Jul	United Arab Rep	Irish Free State	Mostfavored Nation	137LTS421	303172
31 Jul	Italy	Norway	Other Economic	118LTS113	302716
01 Aug	Multilateral		Health/Educ/Welfare	128LTS9	302932
01 Aug	Austria	Germany	Admin Cooperation	115LTS465	302695
01 Aug	Denmark	France	Air Transport	108LTS115	302504
02 Aug	France	Poland	Air Transport	114LTS93	302657
04 Aug	Romania	Yugoslavia	General Economic	107LTS253	302482
06 Aug	Romania	UK Great Britain	General Economic	123LTS307	302822
07 Aug	Italy	Panama	Extradition	140LTS241	303240
10 Aug	Hungary	Romania	General Economic	107LTS185	302476
13 Aug	Hungary	Latvia	Dispute Settlement	117LTS395	302705
16 Aug	Austria	Japan	General Economic	126LTS351	302894
19 Aug	Iraq	UK Great Britain	Finance	118LTS231	302727
20 Aug	Romania	USA (United States)	Mostfavored Nation	115LTS115	302680
22 Aug	Czechoslovakia	Turkey	Admin Cooperation	138LTS311	303195
22 Aug	Czechoslovakia	Turkey	Extradition	138LTS375	303196
23 Aug	Belgium	France	Non-ILO Labor	166LTS11	303825
23 Aug	Italy	Venezuela	Extradition	128LTS377	302943
25 Aug	Romania	Switzerland	Mostfavored Nation	118LTS9	302708
27 Aug	France	Romania	Consul/Citizenship	158LTS379	303644
27 Aug	Poland	Portugal	Water Transport	115LTS127	302682
27 Aug	Hungary	Yugoslavia	Dispute Settlement	113LTS163	302643
28 Aug	Multilateral		Telecommunications	133LTS21	303053
28 Aug	Hungary	Spain	Visas	110LTS307	302562
28 Aug	Finland	Romania	Mostfavored Nation	118LTS193	302723
28 Aug	Sweden	UK Great Britain	Admin Cooperation	114LTS9	302652
28 Aug	Finland	Germany	General Trade	111LTS327	302597
28 Aug	Denmark	Romania	Mostfavored Nation	108LTS165	302506
28 Aug	Italy	UK Great Britain	Postal Service	111LTS91	302583
28 Aug	Bel-Lux Econ Union	Romania	Mostfavored Nation	107LTS221	302479
28 Aug	Denmark	Latvia	Extradition	113LTS169	302644
29 Aug	Netherlands	Romania	Mostfavored Nation	108LTS177	302507
30 Aug	Poland	Sweden	Extradition	129LTS383	302973
30 Aug	Austria	Romania	Mostfavored Nation	118LTS17	302709
30 Aug	Estonia	Romania	Mostfavored Nation	114LTS59	302654
01 Sep	Estonia	Netherlands	Other Economic	111LTS395	302600
02 Sep	Italy	UK Great Britain	Reparations	140LTS19	303225
03 Sep	Germany	Turkey	Extradition	133LTS321	303071
03 Sep	India	Turkey	Mostfavored Nation	109LTS25	302525
03 Sep	Denmark	Sweden	Water Transport	106LTS397	302458
04 Sep	France	UK Great Britain	Finance	109LTS31	302526
05 Sep	El Salvador	USA (United States)	General Amity	134LTS207	303093
05 Sep	Estonia	Latvia	Territory Boundary	112LTS219	302616

DATE	PARTY ONE	PARTY TWO	TOPIC	CITATION	NUMBER
1930 (Cont.)					
12 Sep	Austria	Czechoslovakia	Admin Cooperation	107LTS341	302489
16 Sep	Netherlands	USA (United States)	Postal Service	125LTS173	302853
16 Sep	Netherlands	USA (United States)	Postal Service	125LTS147	302852
16 Sep	Brazil	Netherlands	Mostfavored Nation	125LTS197	302854
16 Sep	UK Great Britain	USSR (Soviet Union)	General Trade	101LTS409	302340
17 Sep	China	UK Great Britain	Admin Cooperation	111LTS153	302584
17 Sep	Lithuania	Turkey	General Amity	125LTS249	302858
17 Sep	Lithuania	USSR (Soviet Union)	General Amity	125LTS255	302859
18 Sep	Chile	Czechoslovakia	General Trade	140LTS161	303233
22 Sep	Panama	Spain	Dispute Settlement	162LTS309	303743
22 Sep	China	UK Great Britain	Reparations	115LTS493	302697
24 Sep	Belgium	Lithuania	Dispute Settlement	129LTS399	302974
27 Sep	Bulgaria	Romania	Mostfavored Nation	118LTS27	302710
01 Oct	Austria	Norway	Extradition	119LTS15	302737
03 Oct	Czechoslovakia	France	Health/Educ/Welfare	125LTS59	302846
16 Oct	Japan	South Africa	Visas	126LTS17	302868
21 Oct	Irish Free State	Norway	Taxation	109LTS177	302536
22 Oct	Japan	Romania	Mostfavored Nation	112LTS15	302602
23 Oct	Multilateral		Water Transport	112LTS21	302603
23 Oct	Multilateral		Water Transport	125LTS95	302849
23 Oct	Latvia	Romania	Mostfavored Nation	118LTS33	302711
29 Oct	Brazil	Switzerland	General Trade	140LTS265	303241
29 Oct	Sweden	USA (United States)	Water Transport	109LTS181	302537
29 Oct	Czechoslovakia	Persia	General Amity	121LTS53	302783
29 Oct	Czechoslovakia	Persia	Privil/Immunities	121LTS59	302784
29 Oct	France	Netherlands	Education	125LTS29	302843
30 Oct	Greece	Turkey	Dispute Settlement	125LTS9	302841
30 Oct	Greece	Turkey	General Economic	125LTS371	302866
31 Oct	Iceland	Sweden	Non-ILO Labor	109LTS171	302535
31 Oct	Multilateral		Dispute Settlement	120LTS9	302760
01 Nov	Norway	USA (United States)	Milit Servic/Citiz	112LTS399	302625
03 Nov	Irish Free State	Switzerland	Non-ILO Labor	132LTS159	303035
03 Nov	Albania	Romania	Mostfavored Nation	118LTS39	302712
06 Nov	Denmark	Norway	Admin Cooperation	109LTS283	302545
08 Nov	Other Unilat Decla	Rhine Navigation	Admin Cooperation	118LTS275	302729
08 Nov	Denmark	Netherlands	Taxation	109LTS115	302531
11 Nov	Finland	Norway	General Trade	130LTS17	302980
14 Nov	Lithuania	Norway	Land Transport	109LTS187	302538
15 Nov	Abyssinia	Japan	General Trade	133LTS135	303063
18 Nov	Norway	UK Great Britain	Recognition	112LTS97	302609
19 Nov	Afghanistan	Japan	General Amity	121LTS237	302789
20 Nov	Finland	Norway	Land Transport	110LTS313	302563
21 Nov	Germany	Poland	Land Transport	139LTS351	303220
24 Nov	Latvia	Lithuania	Dispute Settlement	112LTS405	302626
24 Nov	Latvia	Lithuania	General Economic	112LTS417	302627
27 Nov	Multilateral		Extradition	121LTS39	302781
01 Dec	Austria	Belgium	Admin Cooperation	112LTS43	302606
01 Dec	Austria	Belgium	Extradition	112LTS37	302605
05 Dec	Czechoslovakia	Romania	Claims and Debts	167LTS221	303868
05 Dec	Czechoslovakia	Romania	Claims and Debts	167LTS205	303867
05 Dec	Czechoslovakia	Romania	Claims and Debts	167LTS231	303869
05 Dec	Portugal	Romania	General Economic	114LTS369	302666
05 Dec	Mexico	UK Great Britain	Claims and Debts	119LTS261	302749
05 Dec	Greece	Netherlands	Taxation	117LTS357	302702
06 Dec	Afghanistan	Estonia	General Amity	137LTS445	303174
09 Dec	Afghanistan	Lithuania	General Amity	138LTS29	303178
12 Dec	Belgium	Lithuania	Admin Cooperation	135LTS231	303114
13 Dec	Switzerland	Turkey	General Trade	129LTS267	302964
13 Dec	Switzerland	Turkey	Privil/Immunities	129LTS331	302968
16 Dec	Denmark	India	Postal Service	114LTS73	302656
17 Dec	Italy	UK Great Britain	Admin Cooperation	131LTS79	303004
17 Dec	Sweden	USA (United States)	Dispute Settlement	125LTS233	302856
18 Dec	Belgium	Poland	Health/Educ/Welfare	134LTS177	303090
22 Dec	Czechoslovakia	Romania	Claims and Debts	167LTS263	303872
22 Dec	Czechoslovakia	Romania	Territory Boundary	167LTS243	303870

DATE	PARTY ONE	PARTY TWO	TOPIC	CITATION	NUMBER
1930 (Cont.)					
22 Dec	Czechoslovakia	Romania	Customs	168LTS209	303900
22 Dec	Czechoslovakia	Romania	Territory Boundary	167LTS257	303871
22 Dec	Multilateral		General Trade	126LTS341	302893
22 Dec	Iceland	USA (United States)	Dispute Settlement	108LTS109	302503
1931					
01 Jan	Netherlands	UK Great Britain	Postal Service	115LTS509	302698
15 Jan	Estonia	Lithuania	General Economic	114LTS141	302661
15 Jan	Poland	Romania	Admin Cooperation	115LTS171	302685
16 Jan	Denmark	Estonia	Water Transport	112LTS215	302615
25 Jan	Latvia	Lithuania	Territory Boundary	118LTS143	302719
25 Jan	Latvia	Lithuania	Education	118LTS135	302718
25 Jan	Latvia	Lithuania	Territory Boundary	118LTS175	302722
25 Jan	Latvia	Lithuania	Education	118LTS151	302720
25 Jan	Latvia	Lithuania	Admin Cooperation	118LTS157	302721
26 Jan	Austria	Hungary	General Amity	123LTS171	302814
30 Jan	Norway	UK Great Britain	Privil/Immunities	123LTS343	302823
30 Jan	Albania	Austria	Visas	114LTS65	302655
30 Jan	Hungary	Yugoslavia	Dispute Settlement	120LTS105	302761
31 Jan	Estonia	Norway	Visas	113LTS39	302633
03 Feb	Denmark	Italy	Admin Cooperation	113LTS45	302634
06 Feb	Multilateral		Admin Cooperation	126LTS121	302877
10 Feb	Multilateral		Admin Cooperation	126LTS41	302870
13 Feb	France	Italy	Land Transport	139LTS109	303206
16 Feb	Switzerland	USA (United States)	Dispute Settlement	129LTS465	302978
28 Feb	Estonia	Latvia	Water Transport	114LTS379	302667
04 Mar	Iraq	UK Great Britain	Privil/Immunities	123LTS77	302807
07 Mar	France	India	Postal Service	119LTS269	302750
09 Mar	Belgium	Luxembourg	Taxation	137LTS267	303161
11 Mar	Netherlands	Yugoslavia	Dispute Settlement	129LTS89	302952
16 Mar	Norway	Turkey	General Economic	138LTS41	303180
16 Mar	Finland	Sweden	Taxation	118LTS71	302714
17 Mar	Czechoslovakia	Turkey	Dispute Settlement	133LTS151	303065
19 Mar	Multilateral		Finance	143LTS355	303316
19 Mar	Multilateral		Finance	143LTS407	303317
19 Mar	Multilateral		Admin Cooperation	143LTS7	303301
20 Mar	Finland	Poland	Admin Cooperation	140LTS405	303250
21 Mar	Czechoslovakia	Germany	Non-ILO Labor	143LTS177	303308
21 Mar	Romania	Sweden	General Economic	106LTS237	302448
23 Mar	Ethiopia	Greece	General Amity	153LTS127	303512
27 Mar	Multilateral		ICJ Option Clause	167LTS341	303877
28 Mar	Czechoslovakia	Italy	Culture	125LTS347	302863
28 Mar	Multilateral		Customs	119LTS47	302739
30 Mar	Multilateral		Taxation	138LTS149	303185
30 Mar	Netherlands	Spain	Dispute Settlement	137LTS161	303153
30 Mar	Multilateral		Land Transport	150LTS247	303459
30 Mar	Belgium	France	Non-ILO Labor	126LTS195	302882
30 Mar	Czechoslovakia	Yugoslavia	General Economic	125LTS273	302861
31 Mar	Austria	UK Great Britain	Admin Cooperation	127LTS167	302918
07 Apr	Bulgaria	Poland	Air Transport	127LTS45	302905
09 Apr	Netherlands	UK Great Britain	Education	125LTS41	302844
10 Apr	Luxembourg	Poland	Admin Cooperation	140LTS411	303251
11 Apr	Estonia	Finland	General Economic	124LTS217	302835
13 Apr	Multilateral		Air Transport	119LTS275	302751
15 Apr	Denmark	Spain	Admin Cooperation	115LTS233	302688
15 Apr	Belgium	France	Territory Boundary	119LTS161	302743
17 Apr	Greece	UK Great Britain	Air Transport	129LTS287	302965
20 Apr	Czechoslovakia	Germany	Patents/Copyrights	141LTS307	303271
22 Apr	Greece	Poland	Air Transport	129LTS313	302966
23 Apr	China	Norway	Privil/Immunities	119LTS9	302736
24 Apr	Czechoslovakia	Lithuania	Admin Cooperation	126LTS279	302890
24 Apr	Finland	France	Water Transport	126LTS85	302872
24 Apr	France	Poland	Sanitation	130LTS417	303000
24 Apr	Belgium	Estonia	Customs	119LTS371	302756
24 Apr	Czechoslovakia	Lithuania	Extradition	126LTS261	302889

DATE	PARTY ONE	PARTY TWO	TOPIC	CITATION	NUMBER
1931 (Cont.)					
28 Apr	Italy	Latvia	Dispute Settlement	126LTS399	302898
29 Apr	Czechoslovakia	Germany	Air Transport	133LTS347	303072
29 Apr	Czechoslovakia	Germany	Air Transport	133LTS359	303073
29 Apr	Portugal	South Africa	Territory Boundary	129LTS157	302960
02 May	Poland	Romania	Air Transport	152LTS33	303482
06 May	Greece	USA (United States)	Extradition	138LTS293	303194
06 May	Multilateral		Telecommunications	120LTS217	302767
07 May	Austria	Italy	General Trade	132LTS9	303026
08 May	Iceland	Romania	General Economic	127LTS11	302901
13 May	Belgium	Poland	Extradition	131LTS109	303005
16 May	Belgium	France	Taxation	141LTS333	303274
16 May	Multilateral		Air Transport	136LTS245	303128
16 May	Poland	Sweden	Commodity Trade	120LTS223	302768
16 May	Estonia	Latvia	Taxation	123LTS61	302805
18 May	India	Poland	General Trade	131LTS9	303001
20 May	Estonia	Poland	Admin Cooperation	144LTS327	303336
20 May	Bulgaria	Italy	Patents/Copyrights	129LTS361	302970
20 May	Bulgaria	Italy	Mostfavored Nation	129LTS371	302971
22 May	Chile	France	Customs	124LTS31	302831
23 May	France	Greece	General Trade	125LTS415	302867
23 May	Czechoslovakia	Italy	Admin Cooperation	126LTS185	302881
28 May	Siam	Switzerland	General Trade	125LTS357	302864
30 May	Estonia	Iceland	Water Transport	119LTS69	302741
03 Jun	Estonia	Latvia	Mostfavored Nation	120LTS235	302769
05 Jun	France	Greece	Air Transport	31LTS201	303011
06 Jun	Guatemala	UK Great Britain	Privil/Immunities	132LTS15	303027
08 Jun	Danzig	Finland	Visas	120LTS291	302772
11 Jun	Germany	Poland	Non-ILO Labor	141LTS91	303263
11 Jun	Germany	Netherlands	Land Transport	120LTS413	302778
15 Jun	Poland	USA (United States)	General Amity	139LTS395	303223
23 Jun	Belgium	Bulgaria	Dispute Settlement	137LTS191	303156
23 Jun	Denmark	Germany	Extradition	119LTS321	302753
24 Jun	Germany	USSR (Soviet Union)	Admin Cooperation	157LTS383	303612
24 Jun	Afghanistan	USSR (Soviet Union)	General Amity	157LTS371	303611
26 Jun	Bulgaria	Spain	Dispute Settlement	166LTS341	303850
26 Jun	Hungary	Netherlands	Land Transport	127LTS217	302921
26 Jun	Austria	Netherlands	Land Transport	127LTS225	302922
30 Jun	Multilateral		Scientific Project	149LTS63	303434
30 Jun	Austria	Hungary	General Trade	122LTS123	302800
01 Jul	Italy	Netherlands	General Transport	127LTS235	302923
06 Jul	Sweden	UK Great Britain	Taxation	120LTS211	302766
06 Jul	Austria	Brazil	Visas	123LTS9	302801
09 Jul	Denmark	Finland	Water Transport	123LTS393	302826
11 Jul	Denmark	Iceland	Taxation	141LTS323	303273
11 Jul	Belgium	Italy	Taxation	136LTS9	303120
13 Jul	Multilateral		Other HEW	139LTS301	303219
14 Jul	Austria	UK Great Britain	Dispute Settlement	123LTS383	302824
15 Jul	Germany	Switzerland	Taxation	144LTS389	303341
15 Jul	Netherlands	Yugoslavia	Land Transport	127LTS337	302927
15 Jul	Denmark	Netherlands	Land Transport	127LTS329	302926
15 Jul	Netherlands	Sweden	Land Transport	127LTS321	302925
15 Jul	Netherlands	Norway	Land Transport	127LTS313	302924
16 Jul	Belgium	Germany	Non-ILO Labor	145LTS137	303351
17 Jul	Estonia	Finland	Water Transport	126LTS93	302873
18 Jul	Germany	Hungary	General Trade	150LTS111	303458
20 Jul	Netherlands	Romania	Land Transport	127LTS425	302929
21 Jul	Austria	Yugoslavia	Non-ILO Labor	147LTS123	303397
21 Jul	Belgium	Lithuania	Patents/Copyrights	137LTS225	303158
22 Jul	Austria	Czechoslovakia	General Trade	128LTS59	302938
25 Jul	Czechoslovakia	Germany	Land Transport	187LTS279	304344
29 Jul	Belgium	France	Sanitation	127LTS85	302909
05 Aug	Denmark	Norway	Taxation	121LTS9	302779
05 Aug	Haiti	USA (United States)	Admin Cooperation	125LTS241	302857
08 Aug	Norway	Sweden	Land Transport	123LTS67	302806
09 Aug	Portugal	UK Great Britain	Admin Cooperation	129LTS417	302975
1931 (Cont.)					
11 Aug	Greece	Romania	Health/Educ/Welfare	130LTS79	302983
11 Aug	Greece	Romania	General Economic	130LTS33	302981
11 Aug	Czechoslovakia	Netherlands	Land Transport	127LTS347	302928
11 Aug	Greece	Romania	Recognition	130LTS69	302982
11 Aug	Greece	Romania	Education	130LTS93	302984
12 Aug	Hungary	Romania	General Trade	186LTS325	304321
15 Aug	Greece	Norway	General Economic	123LTS271	302817
17 Aug	Italy	USA (United States)	Water Transport	137LTS175	303154
19 Aug	South Africa	Southern Rhodesia	Customs	129LTS103	302953
19 Aug	South Africa	Swaziland	Customs	129LTS109	302954
21 Aug	Multilateral		Other Ad Hoc	185LTS45	304273
21 Aug	Multilateral		Other Economic	127LTS95	302910
26 Aug	Poland	UK Great Britain	Admin Cooperation	131LTS19	303002
26 Aug	Guatemala	UK Great Britain	Territory Boundary	128LTS427	302946
29 Aug	Poland	Turkey	Consul/Citizenship	144LTS367	303339
07 Sep	Belgium	France	Non-ILO Labor	134LTS65	303083
09 Sep	France	Switzerland	Non-ILO Labor	142LTS205	303293
11 Sep	Brazil	UK Great Britain	Mostfavored Nation	130LTS103	302985
14 Sep	Mexico	Sweden	Postal Service	192LTS195	304472
19 Sep	Hungary	Spain	Visas	124LTS353	302839
22 Sep	Brazil	Netherlands	Territory Boundary	130LTS113	302986
23 Sep	Italy	USA (United States)	General Amity	134LTS191	303091
24 Sep	Multilateral		Specific Resources	155LTS349	303586
25 Sep	France	Hungary	General Trade	132LTS171	303037
28 Sep	Chile	USA (United States)	General Trade	144LTS147	303325
02 Oct	Northern Rhodesia	South Africa	Customs	129LTS115	302955
03 Oct	Estonia	Persia	General Amity	137LTS183	303155
03 Oct	Italy	Netherlands	Air Transport	126LTS109	302875
07 Oct	Czechoslovakia	Denmark	Extradition	127LTS103	302911
07 Oct	Romania	Sweden	General Economic	131LTS51	303003
08 Oct	Irish Free State	Sweden	Taxation	125LTS23	302842
09 Oct	Denmark	Sweden	Specific Resources	126LTS255	302888
14 Oct	Italy	USA (United States)	Air Transport	137LTS209	303157
15 Oct	Multilateral		Water Transport	125LTS83	302847
15 Oct	Chile	UK Great Britain	Mostfavored Nation	128LTS439	302947
15 Oct	Multilateral		Water Transport	125LTS89	302848
16 Oct	Belgium	Netherlands	Admin Cooperation	137LTS411	303171
16 Oct	Brazil	Sweden	Mostfavored Nation	125LTS51	302845
16 Oct	Brazil	Irish Free State	Mostfavored Nation	134LTS75	303084
16 Oct	Lithuania	Sweden	Patents/Copyrights	126LTS233	302885
17 Oct	Switzerland	UK Great Britain	Taxation	131LTS245	303015
22 Oct	Brazil	Germany	General Trade	136LTS443	303143
22 Oct	Belgium	Netherlands	Customs	125LTS367	302865
23 Oct	UK Great Britain	Yugoslavia	Postal Service	126LTS209	302884
26 Oct	Denmark	Poland	Visas	125LTS337	302862
26 Oct	Germany	Hungary	Extradition	133LTS369	303074
28 Oct	Turkey	USA (United States)	Admin Cooperation	138LTS345	303197
03 Nov	Argentina	Finland	Customs	126LTS101	302874
04 Nov	Hungary	Poland	Patents/Copyrights	134LTS199	303092
07 Nov	France	Yugoslavia	Commodity Trade	144LTS281	303331
09 Nov	India	Saudi Arabia	Postal Service	157LTS35	303604
09 Nov	Bolivia	Denmark	General Economic	147LTS27	303387
09 Nov	Bolivia	Iceland	Mostfavored Nation	147LTS43	303388
09 Nov	Germany	Lithuania	Non-ILO Labor	133LTS379	303075
10 Nov	Multilateral		Postal Service	131LTS327	303023
10 Nov	Multilateral		Postal Service	131LTS447	303025
10 Nov	Multilateral		Postal Service	131LTS389	303024
10 Nov	Germany	Greece	Dispute Settlement	133LTS385	303076
13 Nov	Norway	Portugal	General Economic	129LTS455	302977
17 Nov	Belgium	France	Reparations	152LTS121	303490
17 Nov	France	UK Great Britain	Postal Service	134LTS299	303098
17 Nov	Czechoslovakia	Sweden	Extradition	134LTS135	303088
18 Nov	Irish Free State	USA (United States)	Water Transport	131LTS279	303018
19 Nov	Austria	Italy	Extradition	126LTS163	302879
19 Nov	Greece	Sweden	Taxation	126LTS411	302899

DATE	PARTY ONE	PARTY TWO	TOPIC	CITATION	NUMBER
1931 (Cont.)					
20 Nov	Germany	Lithuania	Sanitation	133LTS391	303077
21 Nov	Belgium	Colombia	Extradition	182LTS165	304209
23 Nov	Japan	USSR (Soviet Union)	Postal Service	132LTS133	303033
26 Nov	Bulgaria	Norway	Dispute Settlement	134LTS27	303081
26 Nov	Brazil	Finland	General Trade	126LTS239	302886
27 Nov	Multilateral		Sanitation	177LTS373	304100
27 Nov	Brazil	Czechoslovakia	General Trade	136LTS453	303144
27 Nov	France	UK Great Britain	Postal Service	132LTS25	303028
28 Nov	Turkey	UK Great Britain	Admin Cooperation	141LTS225	303268
28 Nov	France	UK Great Britain	Postal Service	127LTS195	302919
28 Nov	Brazil	Italy	Mostfavored Nation	131LTS273	303017
28 Nov	Brazil	Italy	Extradition	132LTS345	303047
30 Nov	Brazil	Denmark	Customs	128LTS29	302934
30 Nov	Brazil	Iceland	Customs	128LTS369	302942
01 Dec	Germany	Poland	Dispute Settlement	141LTS315	303272
01 Dec	South Africa	USA (United States)	Air Transport	129LTS121	302956
02 Dec	Poland	Yugoslavia	Education	139LTS119	303207
04 Dec	Brazil	Canada	General Trade	139LTS241	303214
04 Dec	Denmark	Norway	Admin Cooperation	128LTS37	302935
04 Dec	Czechoslovakia	Netherlands	Extradition	129LTS343	302969
07 Dec	Brazil	Mexico	General Trade	139LTS247	303215
09 Dec	Brazil	Paraguay	Territory Boundary	136LTS427	303142
10 Dec	Multilateral		Water Transport	129LTS177	302961
11 Dec	Multilateral		Commodity Trade	170LTS251	303941
12 Dec	Italy	Poland	Admin Cooperation	140LTS421	303252
12 Dec	Denmark	Finland	Taxation	112LTS29	302604
14 Dec	Romania	Yugoslavia	Water Transport	135LTS71	303104
14 Dec	Romania	Yugoslavia	Water Transport	135LTS133	303108
14 Dec	Romania	Yugoslavia	Finance	135LTS89	303105
14 Dec	Romania	Yugoslavia	Finance	135LTS99	303106
14 Dec	Romania	Yugoslavia	Water Transport	135LTS31	303103
14 Dec	Romania	Yugoslavia	Water Transport	135LTS143	303109
14 Dec	Romania	Yugoslavia	Water Transport	135LTS117	303107
14 Dec	Bel-Lux Econ Union	Chile	Mostfavored Nation	126LTS247	302887
15 Dec	Germany	Poland	Admin Cooperation	142LTS249	303298
15 Dec	France	UK Great Britain	Admin Cooperation	129LTS445	302976
15 Dec	Latvia	Netherlands	Water Transport	133LTS107	303061
16 Dec	Brazil	Romania	General Trade	139LTS255	303216
16 Dec	Germany	USA (United States)	Water Transport	129LTS129	302957
17 Dec	Chile	Netherlands	Mostfavored Nation	127LTS79	302908
19 Dec	Finland	Poland	Non-ILO Labor	131LTS193	303010
22 Dec	UK Great Britain	USA (United States)	Extradition	163LTS59	303761
22 Dec	Germany	Poland	Visas	144LTS191	303329
22 Dec	Estonia	UK Great Britain	Admin Cooperation	132LTS231	303041
22 Dec	Estonia	UK Great Britain	Claims and Debts	131LTS323	303022
23 Dec	Chile	Denmark	Dispute Settlement	145LTS77	303346
23 Dec	Belgium	France	Taxation	137LTS277	303162
23 Dec	Japan	Norway	Taxation	127LTS21	302902
24 Dec	Brazil	Hungary	Mostfavored Nation	147LTS51	303389
24 Dec	Netherlands	Poland	Admin Cooperation	131LTS269	303016
26 Dec	France	Italy	Patents/Copyrights	133LTS45	303055
28 Dec	France	UK Great Britain	Postal Service	133LTS79	303058
29 Dec	Belgium	Netherlands	General Trade	127LTS163	302917
31 Dec	Brazil	Norway	General Trade	126LTS385	302896
31 Dec	Germany	Lithuania	Privil/Immunities	125LTS265	302860
1932					
02 Jan	Austria	Brazil	Mostfavored Nation	140LTS15	303224
04 Jan	Italy	Turkey	Territory Boundary	138LTS243	303191
04 Jan	Netherlands	UK Great Britain	Postal Service	128LTS307	302939
04 Jan	Netherlands	UK Great Britain	Postal Service	128LTS347	302940
04 Jan	Greece	Poland	Dispute Settlement	131LTS229	303014
05 Jan	Austria	Latvia	Extradition	133LTS59	303056
06 Jan	Denmark	Germany	Admin Cooperation	126LTS333	302892
09 Jan	Iraq	Turkey	Recognition	139LTS263	303217

DATE	PARTY ONE	PARTY TWO	TOPIC	CITATION	NUMBER
1932 (Cont.)					
09 Jan	Iraq	Turkey	Extradition	139LTS273	303218
10 Jan	Iraq	Turkey	Mostfavored Nation	152LTS17	303480
11 Jan	Poland	UK Great Britain	Extradition	148LTS221	303415
14 Jan	Bel-Lux Econ Union	Brazil	Mostfavored Nation	128LTS21	302933
15 Jan	Greece	Italy	Taxation	137LTS397	303169
16 Jan	Iceland	USA (United States)	Water Transport	127LTS135	302914
16 Jan	Denmark	USA (United States)	Water Transport	127LTS127	302913
20 Jan	Multilateral		Extradition	141LTS267	303269
20 Jan	Norway	USA (United States)	Customs	126LTS393	302897
21 Jan	Finland	USSR (Soviet Union)	General Amity	157LTS393	303613
22 Jan	Finland	USSR (Soviet Union)	Dispute Settlement	157LTS401	303614
26 Jan	Austria	Belgium	Extradition	129LTS141	302959
27 Jan	Brazil	Sweden	Admin Cooperation	177LTS119	304086
30 Jan	Denmark	Sweden	Territory Boundary	127LTS57	302906
03 Feb	Brazil	Poland	Mostfavored Nation	147LTS113	303396
04 Feb	Belgium	South Africa	Admin Cooperation	127LTS121	302912
05 Feb	Latvia	USSR (Soviet Union)	General Amity	148LTS113	303408
12 Feb	Luxembourg	Norway	Dispute Settlement	142LTS29	303277
17 Feb	Multilateral		Telecommunications	138LTS61	303181
23 Feb	Denmark	Luxembourg	Admin Cooperation	127LTS211	302920
27 Feb	Belgium	Spain	Air Transport	137LTS111	303149
27 Feb	Belgium	Spain	Air Transport	137LTS129	303150
07 Mar	France	Spain	Military Mission	148LTS385	303424
08 Mar	Denmark	Turkey	Dispute Settlement	143LTS223	303310
08 Mar	France	Latvia	Claims and Debts	128LTS43	302936
09 Mar	Austria	Yugoslavia	General Trade	157LTS145	303609
14 Mar	Belgium	Denmark	Extradition	139LTS39	303202
14 Mar	Multilateral		Territory Boundary	131LTS135	303006
16 Mar	Multilateral		Admin Cooperation	139LTS165	303209
16 Mar	South Africa	Swaziland	Taxation	129LTS377	302972
23 Mar	Japan	Portugal	General Economic	128LTS363	302941
26 Mar	Estonia	France	Claims and Debts	128LTS51	302937
26 Mar	Bel-Lux Econ Union	Hungary	Finance	136LTS405	303139
31 Mar	Argentina	Czechoslovakia	Non-ILO Labor	155LTS379	303589
05 Apr	Albania	USA (United States)	Consul/Citizenship	162LTS31	303732
08 Apr	Spain	Sweden	Air Transport	138LTS135	303184
10 Apr	Poland	USSR (Soviet Union)	Territory Boundary	141LTS349	303275
11 Apr	Brazil	South Africa	Mostfavored Nation	135LTS219	303112
12 Apr	Lithuania	Portugal	General Trade	129LTS135	302958
14 Apr	Turkey	Yugoslavia	Commodity Trade	144LTS291	303332
15 Apr	Italy	Luxembourg	Dispute Settlement	142LTS119	303284
16 Apr	Netherlands	Turkey	Dispute Settlement	143LTS237	303311
19 Apr	Belgium	USA (United States)	Water Transport	134LTS19	303080
20 Apr	Austria	Yugoslavia	Claims and Debts	132LTS217	303040
21 Apr	South Africa	Southern Rhodesia	Taxation	142LTS197	303292
22 Apr	Austria	Poland	Taxation	143LTS45	303304
24 Apr	Sweden	Turkey	Privil/Immunities	129LTS325	302967
25 Apr	Italy	Yugoslavia	General Economic	153LTS305	303526
27 Apr	France	USA (United States)	Taxation	164LTS211	303795
27 Apr	Switzerland	Yugoslavia	Other Economic	131LTS285	303019
28 Apr	Czechoslovakia	Italy	Air Transport	136LTS267	303129
28 Apr	China	UK Great Britain	Postal Service	137LTS319	303165
29 Apr	Finland	Latvia	Water Transport	133LTS71	303057
02 May	Iraq	UK Great Britain	Extradition	141LTS277	303270
04 May	Estonia	USSR (Soviet Union)	General Amity	131LTS297	303020
06 May	Denmark	Sweden	Taxation	130LTS161	302989
09 May	France	India	Admin Cooperation	132LTS37	303029
11 May	Italy	Latvia	Consul/Citizenship	150LTS9	303450
16 May	Brazil	Yugoslavia	Mostfavored Nation	144LTS303	303333
26 May	Spain	UK Great Britain	Water Transport	132LTS43	303030
28 May	Belgium	Monaco	Claims and Debts	136LTS415	303140
30 May	Romania	Vatican/Holy See	Admin Cooperation	201LTS257	304719
31 May	Netherlands	UK Great Britain	Admin Cooperation	140LTS287	303244
31 May	Germany	USA (United States)	Air Transport	133LTS409	303078
31 May	Germany	USA (United States)	Air Transport	133LTS427	303079

DATE	PARTY ONE	PARTY TWO	TOPIC	CITATION	NUMBER
1932 (Cont.)					
01 Jun	Italy	USA (United States)	General Transport	140LTS273	303242
01 Jun	Germany	Sweden	Water Transport	129LTS471	302979
01 Jun	Sweden	USA (United States)	Water Transport	131LTS213	303012
03 Jun	Belgium	Finland	Extradition	132LTS269	303043
04 Jun	Belgium	Bulgaria	Extradition	134LTS241	303094
08 Jun	Czechoslovakia	Yugoslavia	Finance	139LTS45	303203
10 Jun	Hungary	UK Great Britain	Postal Service	132LTS53	303031
16 Jun	Belgium	Lithuania	Extradition	137LTS439	303173
16 Jun	Estonia	USSR (Soviet Union)	Consul/Citizenship	131LTS309	303021
18 Jun	Mexico	USA (United States)	Claims and Debts	158LTS67	303627
18 Jun	Latvia	USSR (Soviet Union)	Dispute Settlement	148LTS129	303409
18 Jun	Belgium	France	Taxation	137LTS289	303163
23 Jun	Estonia	Spain	Admin Cooperation	143LTS31	303303
24 Jun	Bulgaria	Germany	General Economic	147LTS211	303400
28 Jun	Multilateral		Admin Cooperation	140LTS191	303237
29 Jun	Czechoslovakia	Spain	Non-ILO Labor	166LTS355	303851
29 Jun	Netherlands	South Africa	Postal Service	133LTS33	303054
02 Jul	Colombia	Cuba	Extradition	174LTS69	304038
04 Jul	Czechoslovakia	Denmark	Customs	143LTS251	303312
05 Jul	Hungary	Italy	Air Transport	144LTS257	303330
06 Jul	Germany	Spain	Reparations	148LTS391	303425
09 Jul	Hungary	Poland	Admin Cooperation	140LTS429	303253
09 Jul	Hungary	Poland	Admin Cooperation	142LTS239	303296
11 Jul	Sweden	USA (United States)	Postal Service	192LTS205	304473
11 Jul	Greece	Spain	Finance	148LTS397	303426
15 Jul	Multilateral		Direct Aid	135LTS285	303118
16 Jul	Austria	UK Great Britain	Air Transport	144LTS9	303318
21 Jul	Brazil	India	General Trade	133LTS93	303059
23 Jul	Brazil	Switzerland	Extradition	145LTS167	303354
25 Jul	Poland	USSR (Soviet Union)	General Military	136LTS41	303124
26 Jul	Germany	UK Great Britain	Dispute Settlement	133LTS99	303060
27 Jul	Germany	UK Great Britain	Admin Cooperation	134LTS311	303099
29 Jul	France	Yugoslavia	Education	144LTS313	303334
30 Jul	Czechoslovakia	Greece	General Trade	156LTS159	303599
30 Jul	Italy	Spain	Status of Forces	149LTS9	303427
04 Aug	Belgium	Netherlands	Postal Service	134LTS117	303086
05 Aug	Austria	Denmark	Air Transport	132LTS165	303036
05 Aug	Brazil	Denmark	Health/Educ/Welfare	132LTS211	303039
07 Aug	Bel-Lux Econ Union	Yugoslavia	Finance	139LTS223	303212
08 Aug	Denmark	India	Water Transport	140LTS369	303246
13 Aug	Netherlands	UK Great Britain	Postal Service	134LTS317	303100
18 Aug	Latvia	Poland	Admin Cooperation	140LTS443	303254
18 Aug	Bulgaria	USA (United States)	Mostfavored Nation	136LTS73	303126
22 Aug	France	UK Great Britain	Postal Service	136LTS313	303133
24 Aug	Italy	UK Great Britain	Postal Service	136LTS331	303134
02 Sep	Multilateral		Land Transport	154LTS123	303543
03 Sep	Austria	Norway	Finance	137LTS403	303170
14 Sep	Austria	Turkey	Admin Cooperation	135LTS275	303116
14 Sep	El Salvador	UK Great Britain	General Trade	128LTS417	302945
19 Sep	Czechoslovakia	Germany	Health/Educ/Welfare	137LTS453	303175
21 Sep	Brazil	Latvia	General Trade	137LTS61	303146
26 Sep	Northern Rhodesia	South Africa	Visas	135LTS225	303113
30 Sep	Brazil	Estonia	General Trade	134LTS247	303095
30 Sep	Finland	UK Great Britain	Dispute Settlement	135LTS9	303101
01 Oct	France	UK Great Britain	Taxation	135LTS25	303102
03 Oct	France	Italy	Taxation	153LTS55	303507
14 Oct	Austria	Yugoslavia	Air Transport	147LTS173	303398
15 Oct	Brazil	Poland	Admin Cooperation	176LTS373	304074
20 Oct	Argentina	Lithuania	Non-ILO Labor	154LTS113	303542
22 Oct	Belgium	USA (United States)	Air Transport	137LTS389	303167
26 Oct	Austria	Poland	Admin Cooperation	138LTS193	303188
27 Oct	France	Turkey	Land Transport	136LTS23	303121
28 Oct	France	Yugoslavia	General Amity	135LTS281	303117
29 Oct	Germany	UK Great Britain	Postal Service	138LTS69	303182
01 Nov	Brazil	UK Great Britain	Territory Boundary	177LTS127	304087

DATE	PARTY ONE	PARTY TWO	TOPIC	CITATION	NUMBER
1932 (Cont.)					
04 Nov	Belgium	UK Great Britain	Admin Cooperation	153LTS251	303518
12 Nov	Hungary	Italy	Dispute Settlement	142LTS95	303280
12 Nov	Hungary	Italy	Finance	142LTS101	303281
12 Nov	Hungary	Italy	Claims and Debts	142LTS87	303279
12 Nov	Hungary	Italy	Claims and Debts	142LTS115	303283
12 Nov	Hungary	Italy	Claims and Debts	142LTS109	303282
14 Nov	Estonia	Latvia	General Trade	136LTS295	303132
22 Nov	Poland	USSR (Soviet Union)	Dispute Settlement	136LTS55	303125
26 Nov	Italy	UK Great Britain	Admin Cooperation	136LTS385	303136
27 Nov	Austria	Hungary	Culture	162LTS387	303752
27 Nov	Austria	Hungary	Culture	162LTS395	303753
29 Nov	France	USSR (Soviet Union)	General Amity	157LTS411	303615
29 Nov	France	USSR (Soviet Union)	Dispute Settlement	157LTS421	303616
29 Nov	Denmark	UK Great Britain	Admin Cooperation	139LTS9	303201
05 Dec	Bulgaria	Norway	Patents/Copyrights	136LTS281	303130
06 Dec	Portugal	Sweden	Dispute Settlement	145LTS91	303347
06 Dec	Italy	Palestine	Postal Service	139LTS59	303204
07 Dec	Austria	Germany	Extradition	137LTS69	303147
09 Dec	Multilateral		Telecommunications	151LTS5	303479
13 Dec	Multilateral		Territory Boundary	139LTS189	303210
17 Dec	Panama	USA (United States)	Finance	138LTS119	303183
20 Dec	Afghanistan	Iraq	General Amity	155LTS375	303588
21 Dec	Austria	Hungary	General Economic	169LTS161	303919
23 Dec	Denmark	Sweden	Water Transport	136LTS37	303123
28 Dec	Denmark	USA (United States)	Postal Service	140LTS453	303255
28 Dec	France	India	Commodity Trade	140LTS36	303226
29 Dec	Austria	France	Commodity Trade	147LTS101	303394
31 Dec	Denmark	Sweden	Territory Boundary	139LTS205	303211
1933					
03 Jan	Italy	Switzerland	Admin Cooperation	142LTS17	303276
06 Jan	Belgium	Bolivia	Territory Boundary	147LTS59	303390
09 Jan	Germany	Norway	Finance	137LTS395	303168
16 Jan	Norway	Turkey	Dispute Settlement	161LTS173	303710
16 Jan	Romania	Switzerland	General Trade	153LTS359	303532
18 Jan	Austria	Czechoslovakia	Non-ILO Labor	142LTS41	303278
25 Jan	Denmark	Poland	Admin Cooperation	136LTS421	303141
26 Jan	Japan	Netherlands	Taxation	138LTS185	303187
27 Jan	Brazil	Poland	Dispute Settlement	142LTS255	303299
28 Jan	Romania		Tech Assistance	138LTS271	303193
30 Jan	Romania	Yugoslavia	Consul/Citizenship	146LTS173	303369
30 Jan	Romania	Yugoslavia	Extradition	146LTS113	303363
30 Jan	Romania	Yugoslavia	Admin Cooperation	146LTS121	303364
30 Jan	Romania	Yugoslavia	Visas	146LTS179	303370
30 Jan	Romania	Yugoslavia	Taxation	146LTS99	303362
30 Jan	Romania	Yugoslavia	Culture	146LTS183	303371
30 Jan	Romania	Yugoslavia	Territory Boundary	146LTS139	303366
30 Jan	Romania	Yugoslavia	Extradition	146LTS81	303361
30 Jan	Romania	Yugoslavia	Non-ILO Labor	146LTS151	303367
30 Jan	Romania	Yugoslavia	Claims and Debts	146LTS129	303365
30 Jan	Romania	Yugoslavia	Admin Cooperation	146LTS165	303368
31 Jan	Sweden	USA (United States)	Status of Forces	159LTS261	303670
03 Feb	Belgium	Costa Rica	Extradition	166LTS325	303848
10 Feb	Romania	Yugoslavia	Territory Boundary	174LTS115	304042
16 Feb	Multilateral		Admin Cooperation	139LTS233	303213
17 Feb	Czechoslovakia	Poland	Land Transport	143LTS167	303307
20 Feb	Afghanistan	Brazil	General Amity	186LTS385	304322
20 Feb	Belgium	Netherlands	Taxation	164LTS223	303796
20 Feb	Belgium	Netherlands	Non-ILO Labor	165LTS383	303824
21 Feb	Bel-Lux Econ Union	Yugoslavia	Claims and Debts	147LTS203	303399
21 Feb	Belgium	Chile	Extradition	162LTS339	303747
21 Feb	Finland	Netherlands	Extradition	139LTS365	303221
23 Feb	Belgium	Cuba	Admin Cooperation	185LTS279	304294
01 Mar	Albania	USA (United States)	Extradition	166LTS195	303839
03 Mar	Germany	Norway	Visas	138LTS179	303186

DATE	PARTY ONE	PARTY TWO	TOPIC	CITATION	NUMBER
1933 (Cont.)					
03 Mar	France	Hungary	General Trade	140LTS177	303235
04 Mar	France	USA (United States)	Admin Cooperation	138LTS349	303198
08 Mar	Estonia	Netherlands	Extradition	146LTS319	303382
08 Mar	Chile	Sweden	Claims and Debts	142LTS147	303286
10 Mar	Romania	Yugoslavia	Land Transport	146LTS271	303377
10 Mar	Romania	Yugoslavia	Finance	146LTS263	303376
10 Mar	Romania	Yugoslavia	Territory Boundary	146LTS245	303374
10 Mar	Romania	Yugoslavia	Non-ILO Labor	146LTS255	303375
10 Mar	Romania	Yugoslavia	Sanitation	146LTS209	303372
10 Mar	Romania	Yugoslavia	Education	146LTS231	303373
10 Mar	Norway	Sweden	Water Transport	138LTS17	303176
11 Mar	Romania	Yugoslavia	Territory Boundary	146LTS277	303378
11 Mar	Romania	Yugoslavia	Claims and Debts	146LTS285	303379
11 Mar	Multilateral		Water Transport	135LTS301	303119
12 Mar	Netherlands	Yemen	General Amity	146LTS359	303384
13 Mar	France	Sweden	General Trade	142LTS131	303285
13 Mar	Canada	Norway	Postal Service	141LTS211	303266
13 Mar	India	Iraq	Postal Service	140LTS43	303227
14 Mar	Iraq	Norway	Mostfavored Nation	138LTS23	303177
23 Mar	Netherlands	Norway	Dispute Settlement	146LTS291	303380
31 Mar	India	Iraq	Postal Service	140LTS63	303228
05 Apr	Netherlands	Venezuela	Dispute Settlement	144LTS353	303338
07 Apr	France	Hungary	Admin Cooperation	162LTS463	303756
12 Apr	Multilateral		Sanitation	161LTS65	303706
13 Apr	Denmark	Greece	Dispute Settlement	150LTS465	303478
19 Apr	Japan	Netherlands	Dispute Settlement	163LTS351	303778
21 Apr	Greece	UK Great Britain	Visas	140LTS133	303230
24 Apr	Denmark	UK Great Britain	General Trade	139LTS127	303208
27 Apr	Germany	Netherlands	Customs	145LTS155	303353
27 Apr	Estonia	France	General Trade	141LTS43	303260
01 May	Argentina	UK Great Britain	General Trade	143LTS67	303305
03 May	Germany	UK Great Britain	General Trade	140LTS139	303231
06 May	Italy	USSR (Soviet Union)	Customs	158LTS51	303625
15 May	Norway	UK Great Britain	General Trade	145LTS187	303355
15 May	Hungary	Yugoslavia	General Trade	144LTS321	303335
15 May	Sweden	UK Great Britain	General Trade	140LTS317	303245
16 May	Estonia	Finland	Claims and Debts	141LTS19	303257
17 May	Estonia	Lithuania	General Trade	141LTS29	303258
19 May	Iceland	UK Great Britain	General Trade	144LTS33	303319
22 May	Finland	Netherlands	Water Transport	140LTS279	303243
24 May	Ethiopia	Switzerland	General Amity	153LTS63	303508
24 May	Bel-Lux Econ Union	Hungary	Claims and Debts	140LTS169	303234
25 May	Colombia	Peru	Admin Cooperation	138LTS251	303192
29 May	Multilateral		Admin Cooperation	192LTS289	304479
31 May	Belgium	Luxembourg	Consul/Citizenship	141LTS9	303256
01 Jun	Switzerland	Turkey	Admin Cooperation	159LTS187	303662
01 Jun	Switzerland	Turkey	Extradition	159LTS329	303676
01 Jun	Switzerland	Turkey	Dispute Settlement	159LTS229	303665
03 Jun	Poland	USSR (Soviet Union)	Dispute Settlement	142LTS265	303300
06 Jun	Belgium	Ecuador	Extradition	159LTS249	303668
09 Jun	France	Switzerland	Other HEW	181LTS275	304194
10 Jun	Bel-Lux Econ Union	Poland	General Trade	144LTS137	303324
12 Jun	Greece	Romania	Air Transport	150LTS357	303468
14 Jun	Brazil	Germany	Admin Cooperation	178LTS19	304102
16 Jun	Italy	Yugoslavia	General Economic	153LTS317	303527
17 Jun	Dutch Indies	UK Great Britain	Postal Service	144LTS47	303320
17 Jun	Belgium	Honduras	Extradition	167LTS69	303857
19 Jun	Multilateral		Gen Communications	154LTS133	303544
21 Jun	Bel-Lux Econ Union	Bulgaria	Claims and Debts	140LTS375	303247
28 Jun	Austria	Netherlands	Land Transport	152LTS193	303493
28 Jun	Germany	Netherlands	Land Transport	152LTS209	303495
28 Jun	Netherlands	Poland	Land Transport	152LTS201	303494
03 Jul	Multilateral		Peace/Disarmament	147LTS67	303391
04 Jul	Multilateral		Peace/Disarmament	148LTS211	303414
04 Jul	Finland	USSR (Soviet Union)	Territory Boundary	149LTS83	303436

DATE	PARTY ONE	PARTY TWO	TOPIC	CITATION	NUMBER
1933 (Cont.)					
05 Jul	Lithuania	USSR (Soviet Union)	Peace/Disarmament	148LTS79	303405
06 Jul	Italy	Netherlands	Land Transport	152LTS247	303496
06 Jul	Latvia	UK Great Britain	General Trade	142LTS217	303294
07 Jul	Germany	UK Great Britain	Commodity Trade	145LTS237	303356
08 Jul	Denmark	Norway	Water Transport	140LTS149	303232
13 Jul	Belgium	Nicaragua	Extradition	161LTS361	303724
15 Jul	Estonia	UK Great Britain	General Economic	141LTS33	303259
18 Jul	Czechoslovakia	Netherlands	Land Transport	152LTS265	303499
18 Jul	Netherlands	Yugoslavia	Land Transport	152LTS273	303500
18 Jul	Denmark	Netherlands	Land Transport	152LTS253	303497
18 Jul	Netherlands	Norway	Land Transport	152LTS259	303498
19 Jul	Denmark	Germany	Non-ILO Labor	170LTS385	303947
19 Jul	Italy	South Africa	Postal Service	146LTS369	303385
22 Jul	Germany	Hungary	General Economic	171LTS313	303969
22 Jul	Multilateral		Specific Resources	153LTS107	303511
22 Jul	Greece	Yugoslavia	Air Transport	161LTS219	303714
27 Jul	Austria	UK Great Britain	Patents/Copyrights	142LTS157	303287
27 Jul	Estonia	France	General Trade	141LTS65	303261
29 Jul	Germany	Yugoslavia	Mostfavored Nation	149LTS77	303435
29 Jul	Multilateral		Extradition	142LTS165	303288
04 Aug	Belgium	Greece	Extradition	153LTS325	303528
07 Aug	Haiti	USA (United States)	Status of Forces	146LTS305	303381
09 Aug	Austria	Yugoslavia	General Trade	158LTS195	303632
11 Aug	Finland	UK Great Britain	Admin Cooperation	149LTS131	303437
16 Aug	Denmark	Sweden	Consul/Citizenship	164LTS55	303788
22 Aug	Norway	Sweden	Consul/Citizenship	141LTS217	303267
25 Aug	Brazil	Uruguay	General Trade	176LTS381	304075
25 Aug	Multilateral		Commodity Trade	141LTS71	303262
26 Aug	Brazil	Portugal	General Trade	179LTS63	304134
29 Aug	Bulgaria	Czechoslovakia	General Economic	148LTS15	303402
31 Aug	Belgium	El Salvador	Extradition	145LTS129	303350
02 Sep	Italy	USSR (Soviet Union)	General Amity	148LTS319	303418
09 Sep	Sweden	USA (United States)	Air Transport	144LTS153	303326
09 Sep	Sweden	USA (United States)	Air Transport	144LTS183	303328
09 Sep	Sweden	USA (United States)	Air Transport	144LTS171	303327
14 Sep	Greece	Turkey	General Amity	156LTS165	303600
15 Sep	Austria	Greece	General Trade	161LTS251	303717
19 Sep	Australia	Dutch Indies	Postal Service	144LTS335	303337
20 Sep	South Africa	USA (United States)	Air Transport	148LTS203	303413
20 Sep	South Africa	USA (United States)	Air Transport	148LTS189	303412
25 Sep	Romania	UK Great Britain	Consul/Citizenship	149LTS425	303443
26 Sep	Estonia	Poland	Sanitation	150LTS309	303464
29 Sep	Finland	UK Great Britain	General Trade	149LTS167	303438
30 Sep	Multilateral		Extradition	205LTS155	304832
07 Oct	Gold Coast	Togo	Telecommunications	144LTS95	303321
09 Oct	Norway	Sweden	Customs	142LTS171	303289
10 Oct	Argentina	Brazil	Customs	179LTS185	304146
10 Oct	Argentina	Brazil	Education	179LTS165	304144
10 Oct	Argentina	Brazil	Education	179LTS175	304145
10 Oct	Barbados	Curacao	Postal Service	145LTS245	303357
10 Oct	Multilateral		General Amity	163LTS393	303781
11 Oct	Multilateral		Education	155LTS331	303585
11 Oct	Czechoslovakia	Latvia	Dispute Settlement	155LTS195	303577
11 Oct	Multilateral		Consul/Citizenship	150LTS431	303476
13 Oct	Finland	UK Great Britain	Commodity Trade	142LTS187	303291
14 Oct	Portugal	UK Great Britain	General Trade	144LTS107	303322
15 Oct	Finland	USSR (Soviet Union)	Territory Boundary	149LTS243	303439
16 Oct	Norway	USA (United States)	Air Transport	145LTS9	303342
16 Oct	Norway	USA (United States)	Air Transport	145LTS43	303344
16 Oct	Norway	USA (United States)	Air Transport	145LTS31	303343
17 Oct	Romania	Turkey	Dispute Settlement	165LTS273	303814
21 Oct	Poland	Sweden	General Trade	150LTS73	303454
26 Oct	Poland	UK Great Britain	General Economic	158LTS73	303628
27 Oct	New Zealand	Norway	Mostfavored Nation	149LTS429	303444
28 Oct	Multilateral		Refugees	159LTS199	303663

DATE	PARTY ONE	PARTY TWO	TOPIC	CITATION	NUMBER
1933 (Cont.)					
30 Oct	Italy	Poland	Loans and Credits	145LTS103	303348
03 Nov	Iceland	UK Great Britain	Postal Service	145LTS269	303358
04 Nov	Finland	UK Great Britain	Postal Service	149LTS285	303440
07 Nov	Finland	Hungary	Commodity Trade	142LTS179	303290
07 Nov	Multilateral		Finance	155LTS115	303574
08 Nov	Multilateral		Specific Resources	172LTS241	303995
11 Nov	Denmark	USA (United States)	Postal Service	145LTS113	303349
11 Nov	Denmark	Norway	Consul/Citizenship	143LTS25	303302
22 Nov	Italy	UK Great Britain	Territory Boundary	145LTS337	303359
23 Nov	Multilateral		Land Transport	192LTS389	304484
23 Nov	Multilateral		Land Transport	192LTS327	304483
27 Nov	Turkey	Yugoslavia	Dispute Settlement	161LTS229	303715
27 Nov	Czechoslovakia	Italy	General Economic	153LTS351	303531
28 Nov	Turkey	Yugoslavia	Claims and Debts	161LTS245	303716
29 Nov	Netherlands	Sweden	Land Transport	153LTS11	303501
01 Dec	Lithuania	Netherlands	Extradition	150LTS337	303466
01 Dec	Latvia	Lithuania	General Economic	148LTS97	303407
01 Dec	Latvia	Lithuania	Visas	148LTS87	303406
04 Dec	Latvia	USSR (Soviet Union)	General Trade	148LTS145	303410
04 Dec	Latvia	USSR (Soviet Union)	General Economic	148LTS177	303411
05 Dec	Bel-Lux Econ Union	New Zealand	Mostfavored Nation	149LTS435	303445
09 Dec	Canada	USA (United States)	Water Transport	152LTS39	303483
11 Dec	Netherlands	Poland	General Trade	163LTS381	303780
14 Dec	Australia	Belgium	General Trade	147LTS21	303386
15 Dec	Denmark	Germany	Culture	171LTS9	303948
15 Dec	Austria	UK Great Britain	Postal Service	146LTS9	303360
18 Dec	Brazil	Mexico	Education	186LTS395	304323
19 Dec	Finland	Turkey	General Trade	149LTS333	303441
19 Dec	Denmark	Venezuela	Dispute Settlement	158LTS249	303635
20 Dec	Brazil	Uruguay	Visas	181LTS55	304177
20 Dec	Brazil	Uruguay	Admin Cooperation	181LTS91	304179
20 Dec	Brazil	Uruguay	Territory Boundary	181LTS69	304178
20 Dec	Brazil	Uruguay	Culture	181LTS35	304175
20 Dec	Brazil	Uruguay	Customs	181LTS45	304176
21 Dec	Bulgaria	Turkey	General Trade	148LTS9	303401
26 Dec	Multilateral		Extradition	165LTS45	303803
26 Dec	Multilateral		Recognition	165LTS19	303802
29 Dec	Finland	Sweden	General Trade	149LTS23	303429
1934					
11 Jan	France	USSR (Soviet Union)	Customs	167LTS349	303878
12 Jan	Austria	Hungary	Admin Cooperation	162LTS419	303754
13 Jan	Estonia	Lithuania	General Economic	148LTS337	303420
13 Jan	Denmark	Germany	Taxation	144LTS379	303340
16 Jan	Argentina	Bel-Lux Econ Union	Mostfavored Nation	147LTS79	303392
16 Jan	Argentina	Bel-Lux Econ Union	Finance	145LTS145	303352
17 Jan	Denmark	Lithuania	Patents/Copyrights	149LTS43	303432
18 Jan	France	UK Great Britain	Admin Cooperation	171LTS183	303960
25 Jan	Czechoslovakia	Poland	Admin Cooperation	177LTS139	304088
29 Jan	Netherlands	Uruguay	General Economic	166LTS43	303828
31 Jan	Argentina	Netherlands	Mostfavored Nation	148LTS355	303421
31 Jan	Argentina	Netherlands	Finance	148LTS361	303422
03 Feb	Multilateral		Territory Boundary	154LTS349	303560
03 Feb	Poland	Switzerland	General Trade	160LTS83	303685
07 Feb	Belgium	Italy	Consul/Citizenship	147LTS107	303395
09 Feb	Multilateral		General Military	153LTS153	303514
10 Feb	Czechoslovakia	Poland	General Trade	183LTS213	304238
10 Feb	Czechoslovakia	Poland	Admin Cooperation	178LTS159	304111
11 Feb	UK Great Britain	Yemen	General Amity	157LTS63	303605
13 Feb	Finland	USA (United States)	General Amity	152LTS45	303484
16 Feb	UK Great Britain	USSR (Soviet Union)	Mostfavored Nation	149LTS445	303446
17 Feb	Estonia	Latvia	Taxation	159LTS299	303673
17 Feb	Estonia	Latvia	General Amity	150LTS103	303457
17 Feb	Estonia	Latvia	Sanitation	150LTS391	303472
17 Feb	Estonia	Latvia	Education	150LTS299	303463

DATE	PARTY ONE	PARTY TWO	TOPIC	CITATION	NUMBER
1934 (Cont.)					
20 Feb	Denmark	Persia	General Amity	158LTS299	303640
21 Feb	Germany	Hungary	General Economic	171LTS327	303970
01 Mar	Denmark	Germany	General Trade	150LTS31	303451
01 Mar	Italy	Netherlands	General Trade	163LTS367	303779
17 Mar	Austria	Italy	General Economic	154LTS297	303556
17 Mar	Multilateral		General Economic	154LTS287	303555
17 Mar	Multilateral		General Amity	154LTS281	303554
20 Mar	Multilateral		Postal Service	175LTS5	304049
20 Mar	Multilateral		Finance	176LTS9	304053
20 Mar	Multilateral		Postal Service	175LTS269	304051
20 Mar	Multilateral		Postal Service	176LTS55	304054
20 Mar	Multilateral		Postal Service	175LTS363	304052
20 Mar	Multilateral		Postal Service	174LTS171	304048
20 Mar	Multilateral		Postal Service	175LTS73	304050
21 Mar	Romania	Spain	General Trade	159LTS171	303661
24 Mar	Finland	Germany	General Economic	149LTS343	303442
24 Mar	Denmark	USA (United States)	Air Transport	149LTS471	303447
24 Mar	Denmark	USA (United States)	Air Transport	149LTS485	303448
24 Mar	Denmark	USA (United States)	Air Transport	149LTS493	303449
29 Mar	Estonia	Germany	General Trade	148LTS251	303416
04 Apr	Lithuania	USSR (Soviet Union)	Peace/Disarmament	186LTS267	304315
04 Apr	Estonia	USSR (Soviet Union)	General Amity	150LTS87	303455
04 Apr	China	Turkey	Consul/Citizenship	153LTS161	303515
07 Apr	Finland	USSR (Soviet Union)	General Amity	155LTS325	303584
09 Apr	Albania	Czechoslovakia	General Trade	158LTS59	303626
13 Apr	Belgium	UK Great Britain	Dispute Settlement	154LTS361	303561
14 Apr	Albania	Czechoslovakia	Extradition	188LTS255	304362
16 Apr	Multilateral		Water Transport	163LTS185	303767
17 Apr	Poland	USA (United States)	Patents/Copyrights	150LTS403	303473
19 Apr	UK Great Britain	USSR (Soviet Union)	Postal Service	158LTS331	303643
21 Apr	Denmark	Norway	Customs	148LTS331	303419
24 Apr	Lithuania	UK Great Britain	Admin Cooperation	169LTS373	303925
24 Apr	Mexico	USA (United States)	Claims and Debts	149LTS49	303433
24 Apr	Mexico	USA (United States)	Claims and Debts	156LTS81	303593
25 Apr	Persia	Switzerland	Consul/Citizenship	160LTS173	303691
25 Apr	Persia	Switzerland	General Amity	159LTS235	303666
25 Apr	Denmark	Irish Free State	Taxation	149LTS31	303430
26 Apr	Belgium	Guatemala	Extradition	161LTS415	303729
26 Apr	Multilateral		Admin Cooperation	164LTS63	303789
01 May	Denmark	Poland	Customs	154LTS221	303548
02 May	Belgium	UK Great Britain	Admin Cooperation	173LTS291	304020
05 May	Albania	Yugoslavia	General Economic	187LTS179	304337
07 May	Multilateral		Commodity Trade	171LTS203	303961
08 May	France	UK Great Britain	General Economic	154LTS367	303562
08 May	Albania	Yugoslavia	General Economic	159LTS9	303649
10 May	Brazil	USA (United States)	Military Mission	150LTS445	303477
17 May	Finland	USA (United States)	Extradition	152LTS83	303485
17 May	Sweden	USA (United States)	Extradition	150LTS375	303470
17 May	Lithuania	USA (United States)	Extradition	157LTS441	303618
19 May	Spain	Turkey	General Trade	149LTS15	303428
19 May	Austria	USA (United States)	Extradition	153LTS247	303517
22 May	Czechoslovakia	Finland	General Economic	153LTS17	303502
23 May	Peru	USA (United States)	Gen Communications	152LTS99	303487
24 May	Colombia	Peru	General Amity	164LTS21	303786
24 May	Bel-Lux Econ Union	Turkey	Mostfavored Nation	150LTS269	303460
25 May	Finland	USSR (Soviet Union)	Specific Resources	155LTS207	303578
29 May	Cuba	USA (United States)	General Amity	150LTS95	303456
30 May	Australia	France	Postal Service	165LTS81	303804
31 May	Bel-Lux Econ Union	Turkey	General Trade	150LTS289	303462
31 May	Bel-Lux Econ Union	Turkey	Claims and Debts	150LTS277	303461
01 Jun	Chile	Netherlands	Claims and Debts	154LTS325	303559
01 Jun	Multilateral		Territory Boundary	154LTS373	303563
02 Jun	Multilateral		Patents/Copyrights	192LTS17	304459
02 Jun	Multilateral		General Trade	192LTS9	304458
02 Jun	Multilateral		Patents/Copyrights	205LTS179	304834

DATE	PARTY ONE	PARTY TWO	TOPIC	CITATION	NUMBER
1934 (Cont.)					
02 Jun	Finland	France	Commodity Trade	153LTS23	303503
04 Jun	Multilateral		Extradition	184LTS437	304264
06 Jun	Germany	Netherlands	General Trade	174LTS33	304034
06 Jun	Germany	Netherlands	Customs	174LTS44	304035
07 Jun	United Arab Rep	Switzerland	General Amity	159LTS137	303656
07 Jun	Iraq	USA (United States)	Extradition	170LTS267	303942
08 Jun	Czechoslovakia	Hungary	Specific Resources	172LTS61	303979
08 Jun	Australia	United Arab Rep	Postal Service	165LTS95	303805
08 Jun	Bulgaria	USA (United States)	Extradition	161LTS409	303728
09 Jun	France	Sweden	Education	154LTS101	303541
12 Jun	Bulgaria	Hungary	Finance	160LTS73	303684
12 Jun	Multilateral		Milit Installation	155LTS367	303587
13 Jun	China	India	Postal Service	157LTS77	303606
16 Jun	Netherlands	Spain	General Economic	168LTS29	303885
19 Jun	Multilateral		Admin Cooperation	154LTS381	303564
19 Jun	Sweden	Turkey	Claims and Debts	150LTS413	303474
19 Jun	Finland	Lithuania	Patents/Copyrights	153LTS49	303506
20 Jun	Czechoslovakia	Romania	Taxation	168LTS241	303901
20 Jun	Czechoslovakia	Romania	Taxation	168LTS249	303902
20 Jun	Czechoslovakia	Romania	Admin Cooperation	168LTS257	303903
21 Jun	Romania		Finance	168LTS265	303904
21 Jun	Estonia	Japan	General Economic	150LTS423	303475
22 Jun	Australia	Italy	Postal Service	165LTS107	303806
28 Jun	Lithuania	USA (United States)	Postal Service	153LTS295	303525
28 Jun	Latvia	Norway	Visas	152LTS107	303488
30 Jun	Finland	Poland	Customs	153LTS29	303504
03 Jul	Turkey	Yugoslavia	Admin Cooperation	179LTS207	304149
04 Jul	Hungary	Norway	Customs	152LTS115	303489
05 Jul	Estonia	Finland	General Economic	153LTS167	303516
06 Jul	Lithuania	UK Great Britain	General Trade	155LTS9	303565
11 Jul	Estonia	UK Great Britain	General Economic	152LTS131	303491
12 Jul	India	Japan	General Trade	155LTS31	303566
15 Jul	Multilateral		Mostfavored Nation	165LTS9	303801
17 Jul	Latvia	UK Great Britain	General Trade	154LTS25	303536
18 Jul	Germany	Latvia	Extradition	154LTS69	303537
20 Jul	Belgium	Norway	Consul/Citizenship	150LTS369	303469
20 Jul	Multilateral		Territory Boundary	155LTS45	303567
24 Jul	Haiti	USA (United States)	Status of Forces	153LTS285	303523
25 Jul	Multilateral		Other HEW	177LTS59	304080
26 Jul	Poland	USSR (Soviet Union)	General Transport	164LTS301	303799
27 Jul	Belgium	Denmark	Health/Educ/Welfare	150LTS351	303467
27 Jul	Finland	Greece	Claims and Debts	153LTS41	303505
28 Jul	Belgium	France	Visas	152LTS27	303481
30 Jul	Netherlands	UK Great Britain	General Trade	154LTS305	303557
31 Jul	Denmark	France	General Economic	150LTS381	303471
01 Aug	Belgium	Greece	Water Transport	153LTS273	303521
01 Aug	Belgium	Netherlands	Telecommunications	153LTS267	303520
08 Aug	Estonia	Hungary	Extradition	167LTS153	303863
10 Aug	Germany	UK Great Britain	Finance	155LTS53	303568
17 Aug	Chile	USA (United States)	Gen Communications	157LTS15	303602
20 Aug	Other Unilat Decla	USA (United States)	Non-ILO Labor	158LTS45	303624
22 Aug	Chile	Denmark	Patents/Copyrights	154LTS181	303546
24 Aug	Cuba	USA (United States)	General Trade	153LTS369	303533
25 Aug	Martinique	St. Lucia	Postal Service	165LTS183	303810
28 Aug	Belgium	Japan	Health/Educ/Welfare	155LTS395	303591
28 Aug	Germany	Sweden	Claims and Debts	154LTS273	303553
28 Aug	Germany	Sweden	Finance	154LTS249	303551
28 Aug	Germany	Sweden	Finance	154LTS267	303552
03 Sep	Argentina	USA (United States)	Patents/Copyrights	160LTS57	303682
04 Sep	Norway	Portugal	General Trade	161LTS211	303713
05 Sep	Bel-Lux Econ Union	Germany	General Trade	154LTS187	303547
05 Sep	Finland	Sweden	Commodity Trade	154LTS239	303550
06 Sep	Germany	Norway	Finance	161LTS187	303711
07 Sep	Indochina	Malaya	Postal Service	155LTS73	303569
12 Sep	Multilateral		General Amity	154LTS93	303540

DATE	PARTY ONE	PARTY TWO	TOPIC	CITATION	NUMBER
1934 (Cont.)					
17 Sep	UK Great Britain	USA (United States)	Air Transport	153LTS331	303529
17 Sep	Italy	UK Great Britain	Air Transport	155LTS85	303570
18 Sep	Germany	UK Great Britain	Air Transport	155LTS243	303580
20 Sep	Belgium	Lithuania	Water Transport	153LTS289	303524
20 Sep	Italy	Switzerland	Dispute Settlement	158LTS17	303620
22 Sep	Belgium	Sweden	Water Transport	153LTS261	303519
25 Sep	Finland	Germany	General Trade	154LTS9	303534
02 Oct	Finland	Germany	Finance	154LTS17	303535
04 Oct	Dutch Indies	USA (United States)	Postal Service	158LTS395	303646
05 Oct	Poland	USA (United States)	Water Transport	156LTS91	303594
08 Oct	France	USA (United States)	Postal Service	157LTS21	303603
08 Oct	Indochina	Malaya	Postal Service	157LTS95	303607
10 Oct	Estonia	USA (United States)	Extradition	159LTS149	303658
10 Oct	Austria	Romania	Admin Cooperation	158LTS281	303638
10 Oct	San Marino	USA (United States)	Extradition	161LTS149	303708
10 Oct	Latvia	USA (United States)	Extradition	158LTS263	303636
10 Oct	Denmark	Spain	Extradition	153LTS345	303530
13 Oct	Austria	United Arab Rep	Admin Cooperation	153LTS279	303522
19 Oct	Portugal	Sweden	General Trade	154LTS77	303538
20 Oct	Sweden	UK Great Britain	Water Transport	154LTS85	303539
21 Oct	Hungary	Poland	Education	163LTS9	303757
23 Oct	Denmark	Malaya	Postal Service	155LTS141	303575
25 Oct	Turkey	USA (United States)	Claims and Debts	158LTS389	303645
26 Oct	Belgium	Bulgaria	Admin Cooperation	155LTS105	303572
26 Oct	Belgium	Bulgaria	Admin Cooperation	155LTS99	303571
27 Oct	China	UK Great Britain	Taxation	160LTS265	303695
29 Oct	Austria	UK Great Britain	Extradition	165LTS373	303823
30 Oct	Dutch Indies	Malaya	Postal Service	157LTS127	303608
01 Nov	Germany	UK Great Britain	Finance	163LTS79	303762
01 Nov	Denmark	Estonia	Admin Cooperation	154LTS175	303545
05 Nov	Norway	UK Great Britain	Claims and Debts	154LTS231	303549
09 Nov	Norway	USA (United States)	Postal Service	156LTS33	303592
18 Nov	Finland	Persia	Mostfavored Nation	158LTS315	303641
18 Nov	Hungary	Italy	Water Transport	166LTS263	303842
19 Nov	Australia	Belgium	Customs	155LTS385	303590
19 Nov	Multilateral		Admin Cooperation	164LTS243	303797
19 Nov	Bulgaria	Spain	Finance	166LTS277	303843
19 Nov	France	Norway	Commodity Trade	178LTS217	304115
20 Nov	Nicaragua	Spain	Patents/Copyrights	166LTS143	303836
22 Nov	Belgium	UK Great Britain	Specific Resources	190LTS99	304408
22 Nov	Belgium	UK Great Britain	Territory Boundary	190LTS95	304407
01 Dec	Czechoslovakia	Luxembourg	Extradition	168LTS287	303906
05 Dec	Germany	Netherlands	Finance	160LTS109	303686
07 Dec	Multilateral		Air Transport	158LTS91	303629
07 Dec	Estonia	Sweden	Commodity Trade	154LTS319	303558
11 Dec	Malaya	USA (United States)	Postal Service	156LTS101	303595
11 Dec	Germany	Spain	Air Transport	166LTS311	303846
14 Dec	Poland	Spain	General Economic	168LTS315	303908
17 Dec	Turkey	Yugoslavia	Sanitation	178LTS471	304128
19 Dec	Switzerland	UK Great Britain	Extradition	163LTS103	303763
20 Dec	Denmark	Lithuania	Admin Cooperation	155LTS237	303579
20 Dec	Denmark	Lithuania	Admin Cooperation	162LTS347	303748
20 Dec	Latvia	Poland	Non-ILO Labor	162LTS361	303749
21 Dec	Germany	Spain	General Economic	165LTS307	303817
21 Dec	Belgium	Germany	Taxation	162LTS9	303730
22 Dec	Bulgaria	Poland	Consul/Citizenship	159LTS265	303671
22 Dec	Czechoslovakia	Monaco	Extradition	171LTS27	303949
22 Dec	Germany	Sweden	Finance	156LTS127	303596
22 Dec	Multilateral		Admin Cooperation	183LTS153	304231
22 Dec	Multilateral		Visas	183LTS145	304230
22 Dec	Germany	Sweden	Finance	156LTS145	303597
22 Dec	Finland	Germany	General Trade	155LTS317	303583
22 Dec	Germany	Sweden	Claims and Debts	156LTS151	303598
31 Dec	Multilateral		Postal Service	158LTS111	303630

DATE	PARTY ONE	PARTY TWO	TOPIC	CITATION	NUMBER
1935					
02 Jan	Spain	Uruguay	General Trade	164LTS95	303791
07 Jan	Germany	Spain	Air Transport	166LTS363	303852
10 Jan	Switzerland	USA (United States)	Extradition	159LTS243	303667
17 Jan	Greece	Sweden	General Trade	157LTS9	303601
24 Jan	Denmark	Germany	General Trade	160LTS155	303689
28 Jan	Denmark	France	Non-ILO Labor	158LTS11	303619
31 Jan	Hungary	UK Great Britain	Dispute Settlement	160LTS271	303696
31 Jan	France	UK Great Britain	Admin Cooperation	160LTS275	303697
02 Feb	Brazil	USA (United States)	General Trade	166LTS211	303840
11 Feb	France	South Africa	General Trade	189LTS17	304372
14 Feb	Denmark	Latvia	Admin Cooperation	158LTS21	303621
15 Feb	Czechoslovakia	UK Great Britain	Admin Cooperation	161LTS389	303727
16 Feb	Hungary	Italy	Culture	163LTS15	303758
17 Feb	Argentina	Spain	Extradition	166LTS375	303853
20 Feb	Multilateral		Sanitation	193LTS37	304486
20 Feb	Multilateral		Sanitation	193LTS59	304487
20 Feb	Multilateral		Sanitation	186LTS173	304310
20 Feb	Netherlands	South Africa	General Trade	160LTS143	303688
21 Feb	Finland	UK Great Britain	Taxation	158LTS323	303642
23 Feb	Denmark	Norway	Admin Cooperation	158LTS31	303622
26 Feb	Dutch Indies	Malaya	Postal Service	160LTS191	303693
27 Feb	Poland	UK Great Britain	General Trade	162LTS181	303740
27 Feb	Bel-Lux Econ Union	USA (United States)	General Trade	160LTS27	303681
27 Feb	Dominican Republic	Haiti	Territory Boundary	171LTS89	303953
01 Mar	Chile	Finland	Mostfavored Nation	159LTS113	303653
04 Mar	Denmark	Sweden	Admin Cooperation	158LTS39	303623
04 Mar	Austria	Hungary	Education	163LTS33	303759
04 Mar	Czechoslovakia	UK Great Britain	Consul/Citizenship	160LTS283	303698
07 Mar	Germany	USSR (Soviet Union)	Postal Service	169LTS7	303911
09 Mar	Italy	Malaya	Postal Service	163LTS113	303764
13 Mar	Estonia	Turkey	Finance	159LTS87	303650
13 Mar	Argentina	Serb/Croat/Slovene	Non-ILO Labor	158LTS189	303631
13 Mar	Romania	Yugoslavia	Consul/Citizenship	179LTS57	304133
13 Mar	Germany	Sweden	Sanitation	158LTS233	303633
15 Mar	Multilateral		Other Military	170LTS9	303926
18 Mar	Italy	UK Great Britain	General Trade	160LTS289	303699
21 Mar	Netherlands	Sweden	Taxation	148LTS451	303648
22 Mar	Bulgaria	Finland	Mostfavored Nation	159LTS123	303654
22 Mar	Malaya	USA (United States)	Postal Service	161LTS41	303705
22 Mar	France	Sweden	General Trade	158LTS287	303639
23 Mar	Austria	Vatican/Holy See	Visas	167LTS385	303879
25 Mar	Czechoslovakia	USSR (Soviet Union)	General Economic	161LTS257	303718
25 Mar	Czechoslovakia	USSR (Soviet Union)	Patents/Copyrights	161LTS309	303719
26 Mar	Latvia	Sweden	Finance	158LTS269	303637
26 Mar	Estonia	Sweden	Finance	158LTS239	303634
27 Mar	Estonia	Poland	Customs	159LTS97	303651
27 Mar	Brazil	UK Great Britain	Finance	160LTS311	303700
28 Mar	Haiti	USA (United States)	General Trade	161LTS157	303709
29 Mar	Czechoslovakia	USA (United States)	General Trade	159LTS155	303659
30 Mar	China	Malaya	Postal Service	163LTS159	303765
04 Apr	Irish Free State	Spain	General Trade	166LTS391	303855
05 Apr	UK Great Britain	USA (United States)	Air Transport	162LTS59	303734
05 Apr	UK Great Britain	USA (United States)	Air Transport	162LTS39	303733
05 Apr	Poland	USA (United States)	Extradition	170LTS287	303943
06 Apr	Belgium	Netherlands	Water Transport	160LTS137	303687
08 Apr	Bulgaria	Poland	Education	161LTS319	303720
09 Apr	France	UK Great Britain	Taxation	199LTS49	304663
09 Apr	Multilateral		Territory Boundary	163LTS177	303766
10 Apr	Latvia	Lithuania	General Trade	159LTS305	303674
10 Apr	Latvia	Lithuania	Finance	159LTS321	303675
10 Apr	Estonia	Latvia	Finance	159LTS103	303652
15 Apr	Multilateral		Culture	167LTS289	303874
15 Apr	Canada	USA (United States)	Dispute Settlement	162LTS73	303735
23 Apr	Honduras	UK Great Britain	Postal Service	163LTS199	303768
1935 (Cont.)					
24 Apr	Luxembourg	USA (United States)	Extradition	168LTS129	303893
29 Apr	Czechoslovakia	USA (United States)	Extradition	162LTS83	303736
02 May	France	USSR (Soviet Union)	General Amity	167LTS395	303881
03 May	Finland	UK Great Britain	Water Transport	159LTS129	303655
04 May	Belgium	Italy	Air Transport	159LTS165	303660
06 May	Afghanistan	USSR (Soviet Union)	Sanitation	164LTS335	303800
08 May	Estonia	Spain	Finance	159LTS381	303679
08 May	Estonia	Spain	General Trade	159LTS363	303678
09 May	Belgium	France	Territory Boundary	162LTS437	303755
10 May	Belgium	Germany	Territory Boundary	165LTS169	303808
10 May	Belgium	Germany	Territory Boundary	165LTS143	303807
10 May	Belgium	Germany	Territory Boundary	182LTS323	304220
10 May	Belgium	Germany	Territory Boundary	182LTS335	304221
13 May	Norway	Venezuela	Dispute Settlement	167LTS407	303882
14 May	Germany	Sweden	Taxation	163LTS459	303785
14 May	Germany	Sweden	Taxation	163LTS425	303784
16 May	Czechoslovakia	USSR (Soviet Union)	General Amity	159LTS347	303677
17 May	Poland	Romania	Territory Boundary	173LTS363	304027
17 May	Poland	Romania	Territory Boundary	173LTS373	304028
20 May	Estonia	Sweden	Air Transport	162LTS371	303750
21 May	Italy	South Africa	General Trade	189LTS31	304373
22 May	Belgium	Denmark	Admin Cooperation	159LTS255	303669
23 May	Belgium	Luxembourg	Direct Aid	161LTS327	303721
23 May	Belgium	Luxembourg	Taxation	161LTS347	303723
23 May	Belgium	Luxembourg	General Trade	161LTS335	303722
24 May	New Zealand	Sweden	General Economic	159LTS143	303657
25 May	Sweden	USA (United States)	General Trade	161LTS109	303707
25 May	Denmark	Germany	Territory Boundary	159LTS389	303680
25 May	Switzerland	UK Great Britain	Postal Service	163LTS239	303769
29 May	Finland	Germany	Finance	160LTS69	303683
31 May	France	India	Admin Cooperation	163LTS287	303770
03 Jun	Germany	UK Great Britain	General Amity	163LTS415	303782
04 Jun	Turkey	UK Great Britain	General Trade	167LTS91	303860
06 Jun	Netherlands	UK Great Britain	Taxation	169LTS359	303924
06 Jun	Finland	Turkey	General Trade	160LTS165	303690
07 Jun	Germany	UK Great Britain	Water Transport	163LTS293	303771
08 Jun	Hungary	Netherlands	Air Transport	171LTS385	303975
08 Jun	Czechoslovakia	USSR (Soviet Union)	Postal Service	167LTS181	303865
13 Jun	Mexico	USA (United States)	Water Transport	168LTS135	303894
14 Jun	Czechoslovakia	Hungary	General Trade	171LTS401	303976
14 Jun	Romania	UK Great Britain	Consul/Citizenship	163LTS301	303772
15 Jun	El Salvador	Spain	Culture	165LTS321	303818
18 Jun	Germany	UK Great Britain	General Military	161LTS9	303701
18 Jun	Denmark	Portugal	Extradition	163LTS51	303760
18 Jun	Hungary	Switzerland	Air Transport	174LTS7	304033
19 Jun	Bel-Lux Econ Union	Estonia	Finance	170LTS243	303940
20 Jun	Belgium	USA (United States)	Extradition	164LTS205	303794
21 Jun	USA (United States)	Windward Islands	Postal Service	162LTS157	303739
24 Jun	Italy	Sweden	General Trade	161LTS21	303702
24 Jun	Italy	Sweden	Finance	161LTS27	303703
25 Jun	Denmark	Sweden	Sanitation	160LTS185	303692
26 Jun	UK Great Britain	Uruguay	General Trade	176LTS153	304058
26 Jun	Czechoslovakia	Germany	Commodity Trade	173LTS385	304029
02 Jul	Italy	Norway	Finance	162LTS323	303745
02 Jul	Italy	Norway	General Trade	162LTS317	303744
02 Jul	Turkey	USA (United States)	Postal Service	164LTS125	303792
02 Jul	Argentina	Chile	Sanitation	167LTS173	303864
03 Jul	Canada	Poland	General Trade	172LTS69	303980
10 Jul	Bulgaria	USSR (Soviet Union)	Postal Service	168LTS275	303905
15 Jul	USA (United States)	USSR (Soviet Union)	General Trade	162LTS91	303737
16 Jul	Bel-Lux Econ Union	France	Territory Boundary	162LTS19	303731
16 Jul	France	UK Great Britain	Postal Service	168LTS179	303898
18 Jul	Denmark	Finland	Admin Cooperation	161LTS205	303712
19 Jul	Germany	Norway	Land Transport	161LTS375	303726
19 Jul	Germany	Sweden	Loans and Credits	161LTS35	303704

DATE	PARTY ONE	PARTY TWO	TOPIC	CITATION	NUMBER
1935 (Cont.)					
23 Jul	France	Hungary	Air Transport	173LTS243	304016
25 Jul	Iraq	UK Great Britain	Admin Cooperation	176LTS229	304064
26 Jul	Bulgaria	Romania	Land Transport	198LTS9	304621
29 Jul	Italy	Netherlands	Finance	165LTS329	303819
04 Aug	Germany	Iraq	Mostfavored Nation	171LTS65	303951
06 Aug	Belgian Colonies	Ruanda-Urundi	Admin Cooperation	164LTS49	303787
10 Aug	Estonia	Italy	Extradition	185LTS287	304295
14 Aug	Guatemala	Spain	Mass Media	166LTS381	303854
17 Aug	Denmark	Spain	General Trade	163LTS307	303773
23 Aug	Spain	Sweden	General Trade	162LTS331	303746
25 Aug	Belgium	France	Extradition	161LTS369	303725
27 Aug	Iran	USSR (Soviet Union)	General Trade	176LTS299	304069
27 Aug	Iran	USSR (Soviet Union)	Health/Educ/Welfare	176LTS335	304070
27 Aug	Iran	USSR (Soviet Union)	Health/Educ/Welfare	176LTS344	304071
27 Aug	Iran	USSR (Soviet Union)	Sanitation	176LTS349	304072
27 Aug	France	South Africa	General Trade	189LTS41	304374
30 Aug	Belgium	Switzerland	Taxation	162LTS293	303741
31 Aug	France	Malaya	Postal Service	165LTS215	303811
05 Sep	Bel-Lux Econ Union	USSR (Soviet Union)	General Trade	173LTS169	304010
07 Sep	Lithuania	Spain	Visas	163LTS321	303774
13 Sep	Colombia	USA (United States)	General Trade	170LTS293	303944
21 Sep	Denmark	France	Admin Cooperation	162LTS383	303751
23 Sep	Bulgaria	Netherlands	Finance	166LTS51	303829
25 Sep	Finland	Germany	Taxation	173LTS11	304001
25 Sep	Hungary	UK Great Britain	Admin Cooperation	170LTS51	303928
25 Sep	Finland	Germany	Taxation	172LTS359	304000
27 Sep	Czechoslovakia	Germany	Territory Boundary	182LTS267	304217
30 Sep	Colombia	Spain	Education	163LTS337	303776
30 Sep	Germany	Spain	Air Transport	163LTS327	303775
01 Oct	Italy	Spain	Consul/Citizenship	163LTS345	303777
15 Oct	Denmark	UK Great Britain	Extradition	169LTS337	303922
19 Oct	France	Netherlands	Taxation	166LTS67	303830
24 Oct	Portugal	UK Great Britain	Air Transport	167LTS133	303861
28 Oct	Denmark	Sweden	Admin Cooperation	166LTS299	303845
30 Oct	Spain	Switzerland	Patents/Copyrights	166LTS157	303837
30 Oct	Multilateral		Telecommunications	189LTS51	304375
30 Oct	Multilateral		Postal Service	189LTS85	304376
03 Nov	Iraq	Sweden	Mostfavored Nation	163LTS419	303783
05 Nov	Finland	Norway	Territory Boundary	169LTS33	303913
06 Nov	Nicaragua	Spain	Mass Media	166LTS317	303847
07 Nov	Netherlands	UK Great Britain	Water Transport	165LTS337	303820
07 Nov	Turkey	USSR (Soviet Union)	General Amity	179LTS127	304139
08 Nov	Brazil	Chile	Extradition	181LTS297	304197
09 Nov	Bulgaria	Yugoslavia	Territory Boundary	194LTS89	304511
14 Nov	Multilateral		Admin Cooperation	166LTS75	303831
14 Nov	Multilateral		Admin Cooperation	166LTS87	303833
14 Nov	Estonia	Latvia	Admin Cooperation	166LTS83	303832
15 Nov	Canada	USA (United States)	General Trade	168LTS355	303910
16 Nov	Czechoslovakia	USSR (Soviet Union)	Consul/Citizenship	169LTS143	303918
17 Nov	Saudi Arabia	UK Great Britain	Customs	170LTS87	303929
22 Nov	USA (United States)	USSR (Soviet Union)	Admin Cooperation	167LTS303	303875
28 Nov	Dutch Indies	India	Postal Service	168LTS147	303896
02 Dec	Belgium	Italy	Extradition	172LTS209	303992
03 Dec	Finland	Romania	Finance	165LTS287	303815
04 Dec	Germany	Latvia	General Trade	166LTS93	303834
07 Dec	Estonia	Latvia	General Economic	169LTS119	303916
07 Dec	Bulgaria	Denmark	Dispute Settlement	182LTS183	304211
07 Dec	Estonia	Latvia	General Economic	169LTS101	303915
10 Dec	Estonia	Lithuania	Patents/Copyrights	168LTS101	303889
10 Dec	Estonia	Latvia	Territory Boundary	168LTS83	303888
14 Dec	Denmark	Yugoslavia	Dispute Settlement	184LTS99	304245
18 Dec	Honduras	USA (United States)	Customs	167LTS313	303876
18 Dec	Finland	Sweden	Admin Cooperation	165LTS347	303821
18 Dec	Netherlands	UK Great Britain	General Trade	165LTS255	303812
20 Dec	Multilateral		Other Military	167LTS141	303862
20 Dec	Netherlands	USA (United States)	General Trade	178LTS239	304118
21 Dec	France	Spain	General Economic	167LTS9	303856
21 Dec	Estonia	Sweden	Commodity Trade	164LTS293	303798
30 Dec	Czechoslovakia	Germany	Customs	173LTS333	304023
30 Dec	Netherlands	UK Great Britain	Customs	165LTS263	303813
30 Dec	France	USA (United States)	Postal Service	171LTS117	303955
30 Dec	France	Spain	Commodity Trade	172LTS217	303993
30 Dec	Belgium	France	General Trade	166LTS25	303826
31 Dec	Spain	Turkey	General Trade	166LTS163	303838
1936					
04 Jan	France	India	Commodity Trade	170LTS97	303930
06 Jan	Spain	UK Great Britain	Finance	166LTS283	303844
09 Jan	Switzerland	USA (United States)	General Trade	171LTS231	303962
09 Jan	Denmark	Germany	Land Transport	166LTS135	303835
11 Jan	Colombia	USA (United States)	Postal Service	169LTS79	303914
11 Jan	Greece	Sweden	Finance	165LTS299	303816
14 Jan	Irish Free State	Spain	Consul/Citizenship	168LTS201	303899
15 Jan	Sweden	Switzerland	Admin Cooperation	169LTS347	303923
18 Jan	France	Sweden	Customs	167LTS197	303866
21 Jan	Greece	UK Great Britain	Admin Cooperation	168LTS171	303897
27 Jan	Chile	Norway	Dispute Settlement	179LTS433	304169
28 Jan	Czechoslovakia	Finland	General Economic	166LTS259	303841
28 Jan	Belgium	USA (United States)	Taxation	166LTS333	303849
30 Jan	Denmark	Germany	Commodity Trade	174LTS155	304046
31 Jan	Germany	Sweden	Finance	168LTS13	303883
31 Jan	Germany	Sweden	Claims and Debts	168LTS19	303884
07 Feb	Mexico	USA (United States)	Admin Cooperation	178LTS309	304119
07 Feb	Austria	Monaco	Visas	167LTS389	303880
12 Feb	China	Malaya	Postal Service	170LTS19	303927
18 Feb	Chile	Spain	Mass Media	169LTS321	303920
22 Feb	Estonia	France	General Economic	168LTS105	303890
22 Feb	Bel-Lux Econ Union	Latvia	General Trade	171LTS147	303956
24 Feb	Czechoslovakia	Yugoslavia	Taxation	187LTS185	304338
27 Feb	Sweden	Turkey	Finance	167LTS83	303859
27 Feb	Sweden	Turkey	General Trade	167LTS75	303858
27 Feb	Greece	UK Great Britain	Admin Cooperation	185LTS113	304278
27 Feb	UK Great Britain	Yugoslavia	Admin Cooperation	181LTS241	304193
29 Feb	United Arab Rep	Malaya	Postal Service	170LTS103	303931
29 Feb	Belgium	Yugoslavia	Admin Cooperation	184LTS379	304258
02 Mar	Panama	USA (United States)	Specific Property	200LTS17	304686
02 Mar	Panama	USA (United States)	Land Transport	200LTS205	304692
02 Mar	Bel-Lux Econ Union	Poland	General Economic	168LTS67	303887
05 Mar	Peru	Spain	Mass Media	169LTS331	303921
09 Mar	France	USSR (Soviet Union)	Postal Service	179LTS131	304140
11 Mar	Nicaragua	USA (United States)	Customs	173LTS141	304009
13 Mar	Bolivia	Spain	Patents/Copyrights	170LTS179	303933
14 Mar	Norway	Poland	General Trade	171LTS371	303973
19 Mar	Albania	Italy	Finance	173LTS51	304002
19 Mar	Albania	Italy	Finance	173LTS63	304003
19 Mar	Albania	Italy	Loans and Credits	173LTS83	304005
19 Mar	Albania	Italy	Sanitation	173LTS107	304007
19 Mar	Albania	Italy	Loans and Credits	173LTS73	304004
19 Mar	Albania	Italy	General Trade	173LTS131	304008
19 Mar	Albania	Italy	Water Transport	173LTS93	304006
21 Mar	Czechoslovakia	Finland	Admin Cooperation	179LTS295	304156
25 Mar	Multilateral		Peace/Disarmament	184LTS115	304246
26 Mar	Afghanistan	USA (United States)	General Amity	168LTS143	303895
28 Mar	Finland	Latvia	Finance	171LTS155	303957
28 Mar	Greece	Palestine	Postal Service	170LTS145	303932
31 Mar	Poland	USSR (Soviet Union)	Admin Cooperation	186LTS203	304312
31 Mar	Iraq	UK Great Britain	Land Transport	172LTS175	303988
31 Mar	Poland	USSR (Soviet Union)	Water Transport	186LTS211	304313
01 Apr	Luxembourg	Netherlands	Non-ILO Labor	179LTS11	304130
01 Apr	Bel-Lux Econ Union	Bulgaria	Finance	169LTS23	303912

DATE	PARTY ONE	PARTY TWO	TOPIC	CITATION	NUMBER
1936 (Cont.)					
02 Apr	Austria	Czechoslovakia	General Economic	180LTS51	304173
02 Apr	Iraq	Saudi Arabia	General Amity	174LTS131	304044
03 Apr	Finland	Hungary	Visas	172LTS167	303987
03 Apr	Estonia	Finland	General Economic	168LTS111	303891
04 Apr	Norway	Uruguay	General Trade	176LTS115	304055
04 Apr	Bel-Lux Econ Union	Spain	Finance	168LTS339	303909
09 Apr	Netherlands	Poland	Customs	177LTS71	304081
15 Apr	France	UK Great Britain	Admin Cooperation	203LTS123	304755
16 Apr	Estonia	Finland	Telecommunications	171LTS55	303950
23 Apr	France	USA (United States)	Extradition	172LTS197	303990
24 Apr	Hungary	Poland	Consul/Citizenship	185LTS303	304296
24 Apr	Guatemala	USA (United States)	General Trade	170LTS345	303945
24 Apr	Hungary	Poland	Extradition	181LTS115	304183
30 Apr	Sweden	UK Great Britain	Water Transport	168LTS121	303892
01 May	France	India	Postal Service	178LTS57	304107
02 May	Romania	UK Great Britain	Finance	184LTS145	304247
06 May	France	USA (United States)	General Trade	199LTS259	304679
06 May	Denmark	USA (United States)	Extradition	172LTS203	303991
07 May	Finland	Switzerland	Consul/Citizenship	166LTS35	303827
15 May	Belgium	Netherlands	Humanitarian	179LTS41	304131
15 May	Spain	Yugoslavia	General Economic	170LTS185	303934
18 May	Finland	USA (United States)	General Trade	172LTS97	303981
19 May	Germany	Sweden	Admin Cooperation	182LTS395	304224
20 May	Liechtenstein	USA (United States)	Extradition	183LTS181	304235
20 May	Australia	Indochina	Visas	170LTS221	303937
25 May	France	Netherlands	Visas	173LTS187	304011
27 May	Multilateral		Admin Cooperation	203LTS367	304779
27 May	Brazil	USA (United States)	Military Mission	171LTS343	303971
28 May	Germany	Hungary	Culture	178LTS445	304127
08 Jun	Norway	Turkey	General Trade	170LTS227	303938
08 Jun	Norway	Turkey	Finance	170LTS235	303939
12 Jun	Ecuador	USA (United States)	General Trade	170LTS377	303946
13 Jun	Norway	Spain	General Trade	170LTS199	303935
13 Jun	Norway	Spain	Finance	170LTS207	303936
15 Jun	Czechoslovakia	Hungary	General Economic	179LTS73	304135
17 Jun	Denmark	Germany	Admin Cooperation	171LTS163	303958
17 Jun	Hungary	Sweden	Taxation	184LTS11	304239
17 Jun	Hungary	Sweden	Taxation	184LTS25	304240
19 Jun	France	Palestine	Postal Service	172LTS17	303977
19 Jun	United Arab Rep	ILO (Labor Org)	IGO Operations	177LTS343	304096
20 Jun	Finland	Turkey	General Trade	172LTS125	303982
20 Jun	Finland	Turkey	Finance	172LTS135	303983
23 Jun	El Salvador	Sweden	Mostfavored Nation	171LTS291	303966
25 Jun	China	Latvia	General Amity	176LTS275	304066
26 Jun	Multilateral		Other HEW	198LTS299	304648
29 Jun	Denmark	USSR (Soviet Union)	Postal Service	174LTS93	304040
30 Jun	Greece	Italy	Air Transport	185LTS93	304277
03 Jul	Poland	Sweden	General Trade	171LTS307	303968
04 Jul	Multilateral		Refugees	171LTS75	303952
04 Jul	Hungary	Italy	Commodity Trade	181LTS331	304199
06 Jul	Ecuador	Peru	Territory Boundary	173LTS359	304026
06 Jul	Bulgaria	France	Finance	171LTS269	303963
11 Jul	Guatemala	Sweden	Mostfavored Nation	171LTS299	303967
13 Jul	Belgium	Netherlands	Postal Service	177LTS93	304083
16 Jul	Finland	Poland	General Trade	172LTS143	303984
16 Jul	Belgium	France	Admin Cooperation	171LTS287	303965
17 Jul	China	UK Great Britain	Postal Service	173LTS343	304024
20 Jul	Multilateral		Territory Boundary	173LTS213	304015
22 Jul	Brazil	Czechoslovakia	General Trade	188LTS275	304363
23 Jul	Czechoslovakia	Sweden	Non-ILO Labor	171LTS111	303954
23 Jul	Denmark	Japan	Admin Cooperation	171LTS279	303964
25 Jul	Sweden	Switzerland	Non-ILO Labor	171LTS177	303959
27 Jul	Brazil	Norway	General Trade	176LTS125	304056
30 Jul	Multilateral		IGO Status/Immunit	197LTS31	304602
30 Jul	Brazil	Denmark	General Trade	194LTS81	304510

DATE	PARTY ONE	PARTY TWO	TOPIC	CITATION	NUMBER
1936 (Cont.)					
30 Jul	Brazil	Hungary	General Trade	177LTS53	304079
05 Aug	Belgium	Liechtenstein	Extradition	185LTS33	304302
10 Aug	Brazil	UK Great Britain	Mostfavored Nation	172LTS273	303996
10 Aug	Brazil	UK Great Britain	General Economic	172LTS283	303997
11 Aug	France	USSR (Soviet Union)	Admin Cooperation	176LTS365	304073
12 Aug	United Arab Rep	UK Great Britain	Telecommunications	182LTS311	304218
13 Aug	Sweden	Uruguay	General Trade	183LTS161	304232
18 Aug	United Arab Rep	UK Great Britain	General Trade	176LTS177	304059
19 Aug	Australia	Czechoslovakia	General Trade	177LTS245	304093
25 Aug	Italy	Norway	Finance	171LTS377	303974
25 Aug	Finland	Netherlands	General Trade	172LTS151	303985
26 Aug	Austria	Germany	Visas	171LTS357	303972
26 Aug	United Arab Rep	UK Great Britain	Status of Forces	173LTS433	304032
26 Aug	United Arab Rep	UK Great Britain	General Military	173LTS401	304031
27 Aug	Netherlands	UK Great Britain	Air Transport	172LTS53	303978
28 Aug	Netherlands	Romania	Finance	182LTS363	304222
02 Sep	Turkey	UK Great Britain	General Trade	172LTS289	303998
04 Sep	Romania	Turkey	Visas	195LTS429	304564
09 Sep	United Arab Rep	UK Great Britain	Admin Cooperation	182LTS317	304219
12 Sep	Estonia	Finland	Air Transport	172LTS345	303999
14 Sep	Australia	Netherlands	Territory Boundary	173LTS325	304022
15 Sep	Multilateral		Scientific Project	178LTS439	304126
17 Sep	Greece	UK Great Britain	Taxation	176LTS183	304060
18 Sep	Hungary	UK Great Britain	Extradition	181LTS337	304200
20 Sep	Czechoslovakia	Guatemala	General Trade	185LTS269	304293
23 Sep	Multilateral		Gen Communications	186LTS301	304319
28 Sep	Finland	Italy	Finance	172LTS155	303986
02 Oct	Finland	Mexico	General Amity	179LTS303	304157
03 Oct	Australia	Bel-Lux Econ Union	General Trade	177LTS271	304094
04 Oct	France	Switzerland	Admin Cooperation	195LTS287	304550
05 Oct	Greece	Poland	Air Transport	181LTS29	304174
06 Oct	Mexico	USA (United States)	Admin Cooperation	180LTS33	304171
06 Oct	Estonia	Italy	Finance	172LTS189	303989
06 Oct	Estonia	Latvia	Territory Boundary	172LTS221	303994
15 Oct	Netherlands	Switzerland	Air Transport	177LTS101	304084
16 Oct	Peru	USA (United States)	Admin Cooperation	181LTS161	304187
21 Oct	Chile	Sweden	Patents/Copyrights	174LTS109	304041
22 Oct	Canada	Germany	Finance	173LTS311	304021
27 Oct	Bulgaria	Finland	Finance	173LTS201	304013
27 Oct	Bulgaria	Finland	General Trade	179LTS309	304158
30 Oct	Chile	Sweden	General Trade	188LTS283	304364
05 Nov	Bulgaria	Mexico	General Amity	187LTS37	304331
06 Nov	Italy	UK Great Britain	Finance	177LTS183	304090
06 Nov	Italy	UK Great Britain	Customs	177LTS169	304089
06 Nov	Multilateral		General Military	173LTS353	304025
09 Nov	Germany	Greece	Air Transport	182LTS9	304201
10 Nov	Czechoslovakia	Yugoslavia	General Trade	186LTS191	304311
12 Nov	Brazil	USA (United States)	Military Mission	176LTS133	304057
16 Nov	Finland	Romania	Visas	179LTS377	304164
16 Nov	Romania	USA (United States)	Extradition	181LTS178	304188
18 Nov	Norway	UK Great Britain	Water Transport	173LTS193	304012
20 Nov	Denmark	Sweden	Non-ILO Labor	173LTS207	304014
21 Nov	Greece	USA (United States)	Privil/Immunities	183LTS169	304233
21 Nov	Austria	Switzerland	Land Transport	179LTS341	304162
27 Nov	Australia	France	General Trade	177LTS301	304095
27 Nov	UK Great Britain	Yugoslavia	General Trade	181LTS281	304195
27 Nov	Poland	Romania	Other HEW	178LTS191	304113
28 Nov	Costa Rica	USA (United States)	General Trade	181LTS183	304189
01 Dec	Italy	Sweden	Finance	173LTS279	304019
01 Dec	Italy	Sweden	Finance	173LTS269	304018
01 Dec	Italy	Sweden	General Trade	173LTS257	304017
02 Dec	Germany	UK Great Britain	Postal Service	178LTS329	304121
04 Dec	France	Sweden	Taxation	184LTS35	304241
07 Dec	Bulgaria	Sweden	General Trade	173LTS393	304030
07 Dec	Haiti	Jamaica	Postal Service	178LTS65	304108

DATE	PARTY ONE	PARTY TWO	TOPIC	CITATION	NUMBER
1936 (Cont.)					
10 Dec	Norway	Romania	Finance	174LTS59	304037
12 Dec	France	USA (United States)	Customs	176LTS403	304076
14 Dec	Iraq	UK Great Britain	Customs	177LTS221	304091
14 Dec	Sweden	Turkey	Finance	174LTS51	304036
17 Dec	Germany	Malaya	Postal Service	178LTS484	304129
17 Dec	Hungary	Yugoslavia	General Trade	196LTS137	304576
17 Dec	Belgium	Norway	Taxation	178LTS153	304110
17 Dec	Hungary	Yugoslavia	Finance	196LTS143	304577
18 Dec	France	India	Sanitation	178LTS399	304122
18 Dec	Estonia	Finland	Postal Service	178LTS41	304105
21 Dec	Bahamas	USA (United States)	Postal Service	176LTS411	304077
23 Dec	Multilateral		Admin Cooperation	201LTS295	304721
23 Dec	Multilateral		Culture	188LTS125	304355
23 Dec	Multilateral		Dispute Settlement	188LTS53	304352
23 Dec	Multilateral		Land Transport	188LTS99	304354
23 Dec	India	Nepal	Postal Service	178LTS405	304123
23 Dec	Denmark	Germany	Commodity Trade	174LTS165	304047
23 Dec	Multilateral		Peace/Disarmament	188LTS9	304350
23 Dec	Multilateral		General Amity	188LTS31	304351
23 Dec	Germany	Netherlands	Finance	179LTS359	304163
23 Dec	Multilateral		Dispute Settlement	188LTS75	304353
23 Dec	Multilateral		Culture	188LTS151	304356
23 Dec	Multilateral		Dispute Settlement	195LTS229	304548
24 Dec	France	Sweden	Taxation	181LTS315	304198
30 Dec	Chile	Netherlands	General Trade	177LTS87	304082
30 Dec	Latvia	Sweden	Postal Service	174LTS147	304045
30 Dec	Canada	USA (United States)	Taxation	184LTS473	304268
31 Dec	Greece	Sweden	Finance	174LTS87	304039
1937					
01 Jan	Italy	Netherlands	Finance	178LTS415	304124
02 Jan	Italy	UK Great Britain	Water Transport	177LTS241	304092
05 Jan	Gibralter	USA (United States)	Postal Service	177LTS21	304078
13 Jan	Danzig	UK Great Britain	Postal Service	178LTS87	304109
14 Jan	Belgium	Siam	Extradition	179LTS419	304168
15 Jan	Greece	Turkey	Admin Cooperation	202LTS107	304739
15 Jan	Austria	Sweden	Non-ILO Labor	174LTS125	304043
16 Jan	Estonia	Sweden	Postal Service	178LTS49	304106
23 Jan	Multilateral		Extradition	191LTS219	304446
24 Jan	Bulgaria	Yugoslavia	General Amity	176LTS221	304063
27 Jan	Netherlands	Switzerland	Non-ILO Labor	186LTS433	304327
27 Jan	Czechoslovakia	South Africa	General Trade	189LTS97	304377
28 Jan	Estonia	Mexico	General Amity	185LTS39	304272
29 Jan	Canada	USA (United States)	Specific Resources	181LTS209	304190
29 Jan	France	Switzerland	Land Transport	195LTS291	304551
05 Feb	Argentina	Netherlands	Finance	179LTS383	304165
05 Feb	Italy	Latvia	Finance	178LTS25	304103
05 Feb	Italy	Latvia	General Trade	178LTS33	304104
08 Feb	Estonia	Sweden	Commodity Trade	176LTS193	304061
10 Feb	Estonia	Latvia	Admin Cooperation	176LTS287	304067
10 Feb	Multilateral		General Transport	189LTS313	304391
10 Feb	Estonia	Latvia	General Economic	176LTS296	304068
11 Feb	Multilateral		Telecommunications	186LTS55	304303
17 Feb	Netherlands	Turkey	Finance	182LTS221	304213
17 Feb	France	Sweden	General Trade	176LTS267	304065
18 Feb	France	USA (United States)	Customs	184LTS479	304269
19 Feb	El Salvador	USA (United States)	General Trade	179LTS219	304150
19 Feb	Cuba	UK Great Britain	General Trade	192LTS301	304480
22 Feb	Bel-Lux Econ Union	Uruguay	General Trade	196LTS391	304600
27 Feb	Germany	Norway	Finance	178LTS427	304125
03 Mar	Multilateral		Admin Cooperation	182LTS127	304205
06 Mar	Multilateral		Gen Communications	186LTS109	304305
09 Mar	Hungary	Italy	Water Transport	184LTS297	304254
10 Mar	Belgium	Norway	Customs	178LTS12	304101
13 Mar	Chile	Cuba	General Trade	195LTS389	304558

DATE	PARTY ONE	PARTY TWO	TOPIC	CITATION	NUMBER
1937 (Cont.)					
15 Mar	Brazil	Netherlands	General Trade	179LTS395	304166
15 Mar	Brazil	Netherlands	Finance	179LTS405	304167
16 Mar	Malaya	Netherlands	Postal Service	184LTS181	304248
16 Mar	Germany	South Africa	Admin Cooperation	189LTS107	304378
22 Mar	Hungary	UK Great Britain	Air Transport	190LTS59	304405
24 Mar	South Africa	USA (United States)	Visas	189LTS113	304379
24 Mar	Portugal	UK Great Britain	Postal Service	185LTS143	304279
24 Mar	Portugal	UK Great Britain	Postal Service	185LTS151	304280
24 Mar	Portugal	UK Great Britain	Postal Service	185LTS175	304281
24 Mar	Denmark	UK Great Britain	Water Transport	178LTS319	304120
25 Mar	Japan	UK Great Britain	Milit Installation	181LTS289	304196
25 Mar	Japan	USA (United States)	Specific Property	181LTS217	304191
26 Mar	Belgium	Netherlands	Customs	179LTS52	304132
27 Mar	France	Norway	Commodity Trade	178LTS221	304116
30 Mar	Denmark	Sweden	Gen Communications	186LTS117	304306
31 Mar	Italy	Norway	Customs	177LTS349	304097
31 Mar	Czechoslovakia	Italy	General Trade	193LTS165	304492
31 Mar	Siam	UK Great Britain	Admin Cooperation	179LTS257	304153
31 Mar	Italy	Norway	Finance	177LTS367	304099
31 Mar	Italy	Norway	Finance	177LTS355	304098
31 Mar	Multilateral		Commodity Trade	189LTS359	304394
02 Apr	Austria	Netherlands	Customs	179LTS81	304136
03 Apr	France	UK Great Britain	Admin Cooperation	179LTS265	304154
07 Apr	United Arab Rep	Turkey	General Amity	191LTS89	304437
07 Apr	United Arab Rep	Turkey	Privil/Immunities	191LTS95	304438
07 Apr	United Arab Rep	Turkey	Consul/Citizenship	191LTS105	304439
14 Apr	Finland	UK Great Britain	Commodity Trade	179LTS289	304155
17 Apr	Czechoslovakia	Finland	General Economic	179LTS317	304159
23 Apr	Canada	Haiti	General Trade	194LTS59	304507
24 Apr	France	UK Great Britain	Other Military	178LTS186	304112
30 Apr	Germany	Netherlands	Customs	187LTS215	304342
01 May	Belgium	Italy	Visas	198LTS73	304624
05 May	Chile	Netherlands	General Trade	182LTS385	304223
08 May	Multilateral		Privil/Immunities	182LTS37	304202
10 May	Czechoslovakia	Italy	Air Transport	190LTS397	304430
13 May	Romania	Yugoslavia	Consul/Citizenship	197LTS145	304611
13 May	Romania	Yugoslavia	Sanitation	197LTS161	304612
13 May	Romania	Yugoslavia	Territory Boundary	197LTS101	304609
14 May	Sweden	Yugoslavia	General Trade	194LTS21	304504
14 May	Sweden	Yugoslavia	General Trade	179LTS147	304141
20 May	Belgium	United Arab Rep	Taxation	182LTS153	304207
22 May	Bulgaria	Romania	Air Transport	188LTS173	304357
24 May	Poland	Romania	Finance	190LTS361	304428
25 May	Czechoslovakia	Netherlands	Education	180LTS43	304172
26 May	Finland	France	Non-ILO Labor	179LTS327	304160
27 May	Ecuador	Netherlands	General Trade	194LTS179	304521
28 May	Finland	Latvia	Postal Service	179LTS333	304161
28 May	Multilateral		General Trade	180LTS5	304170
01 Jun	Belgium	UK Great Britain	Taxation	196LTS209	304583
02 Jun	Multilateral		Specific Property	184LTS445	304265
06 Jun	Estonia	Turkey	Finance	179LTS159	304143
06 Jun	Estonia	Turkey	General Trade	179LTS151	304142
07 Jun	UK Great Britain	Yugoslavia	Postal Service	184LTS229	304249
07 Jun	UK Great Britain		General Trade	185LTS185	304282
08 Jun	Multilateral		Specific Resources	190LTS79	304406
09 Jun	Belgium	Netherlands	Consul/Citizenship	181LTS153	304186
14 Jun	Norway	Sweden	Taxation	179LTS245	304151
15 Jun	France	Turkey	General Trade	179LTS195	304147
15 Jun	Belgium	Sweden	Visas	198LTS77	304625
18 Jun	Norway	Poland	Customs	190LTS187	304416
18 Jun	Portugal	South Africa	Air Transport	189LTS121	304380
21 Jun	Latvia	USSR (Soviet Union)	General Economic	189LTS131	304381
28 Jun	Argentina	UK Great Britain	Commodity Trade	196LTS263	304588
30 Jun	France	Sweden	Admin Cooperation	179LTS203	304148
30 Jun	Bel-Lux Econ Union	Italy	Finance	182LTS106	304203

DATE	PARTY ONE	PARTY TWO	TOPIC	CITATION	NUMBER
1937 (Cont.)					
30 Jun	Germany	Netherlands	General Trade	189LTS373	304395
30 Jun	Bel-Lux Econ Union	Italy	General Trade	197LTS23	304601
01 Jul	Lithuania	Sweden	Customs	179LTS251	304152
04 Jul	Iran	Iraq	Territory Boundary	190LTS241	304423
07 Jul	Belgium	France	Admin Cooperation	181LTS111	304182
08 Jul	Multilateral		General Amity	190LTS21	304402
13 Jul	Bel-Lux Econ Union	South Africa	General Trade	182LTS247	304214
17 Jul	UK Great Britain	USSR (Soviet Union)	Peace/Disarmament	187LTS93	304333
17 Jul	Germany	UK Great Britain	Peace/Disarmament	187LTS43	304332
18 Jul	Iran	Iraq	General Amity	190LTS259	304424
20 Jul	Bulgaria	Romania	Water Transport	202LTS33	304733
21 Jul	Finland	Norway	General Trade	191LTS75	304435
21 Jul	Multilateral		Admin Cooperation	184LTS271	304250
23 Jul	France	UK Great Britain	Customs	184LTS279	304251
24 Jul	Iran	Iraq	Dispute Settlement	190LTS269	304425
29 Jul	France	UK Great Britain	Privil/Immunities	184LTS351	304257
29 Jul	Denmark	Netherlands	Customs	192LTS137	304467
30 Jul	France	Luxembourg	Admin Cooperation	181LTS107	304181
04 Aug	USA (United States)	USSR (Soviet Union)	General Trade	182LTS113	304204
10 Aug	Romania	USA (United States)	Postal Service	183LTS7	304225
17 Aug	Panama	USA (United States)	Water Transport	182LTS159	304208
21 Aug	China	USSR (Soviet Union)	General Amity	181LTS101	304180
24 Aug	Bel-Lux Econ Union	Romania	Finance	193LTS189	304496
24 Aug	Czechoslovakia	Hungary	Specific Resources	189LTS403	304397
01 Sep	Greece	Luxembourg	Extradition	193LTS151	304491
02 Sep	Estonia	Finland	General Economic	183LTS93	304229
06 Sep	Multilateral		Specific Resources	186LTS419	304326
08 Sep	Iceland	Sweden	Taxation	187LTS405	304346
09 Sep	Belgium	Greece	Visas	197LTS63	304605
10 Sep	Poland	UK Great Britain	Customs	184LTS289	304253
13 Sep	Poland	Sweden	Non-ILO Labor	187LTS431	304348
14 Sep	Multilateral		General Military	181LTS137	304184
15 Sep	Malaya	Siam	Postal Service	191LTS225	304447
15 Sep	Multilateral		Gen Communications	186LTS135	304307
16 Sep	Belgium	Denmark	Visas	197LTS67	304606
16 Sep	Malaya	Siam	Postal Service	191LTS265	304448
17 Sep	Multilateral		Milit Installation	181LTS150	304185
20 Sep	Netherlands	USA (United States)	Postal Service	184LTS319	304256
23 Sep	Multilateral		Postal Service	190LTS299	304427
24 Sep	Mexico	USA (United States)	Admin Cooperation	185LTS23	304270
24 Sep	Germany	Greece	General Economic	190LTS51	304404
28 Sep	Canada	Guatemala	General Trade	194LTS65	304508
28 Sep	Brazil	Lithuania	General Trade	186LTS403	304324
02 Oct	Multilateral		Education	182LTS263	304216
02 Oct	Belgium	France	Water Transport	184LTS65	304242
03 Oct	Germany	Romania	Air Transport	190LTS369	304429
09 Oct	Canada	USA (United States)	Admin Cooperation	185LTS33	304271
11 Oct	Multilateral		Air Transport	182LTS173	304210
11 Oct	France	Greece	Admin Cooperation	185LTS253	304289
12 Oct	France	Yugoslavia	General Amity	182LTS149	304206
13 Oct	France	Switzerland	Taxation	194LTS191	304522
13 Oct	Estonia	Hungary	Education	189LTS433	304400
13 Oct	Afghanistan	Czechoslovakia	General Amity	191LTS9	304431
14 Oct	France	UK Great Britain	General Trade	184LTS457	304266
14 Oct	Poland	UK Great Britain	Customs	191LTS279	304449
16 Oct	Estonia	France	General Trade	183LTS41	304227
16 Oct	Belgium	Czechoslovakia	Visas	184LTS73	304243
16 Oct	Estonia	France	Finance	183LTS37	304226
18 Oct	Lithuania	USA (United States)	Milit Servic/Citiz	191LTS351	304454
21 Oct	Denmark	Haiti	General Trade	190LTS231	304422
21 Oct	United Arab Rep	UK Great Britain	Privil/Immunities	184LTS285	304252
22 Oct	Finland	Hungary	Education	190LTS281	304426
24 Oct	Estonia	Germany	General Economic	182LTS201	304212
24 Oct	Estonia	Germany	Finance	184LTS81	304244
27 Oct	Chile	USA (United States)	Admin Cooperation	186LTS219	304314

DATE	PARTY ONE	PARTY TWO	TOPIC	CITATION	NUMBER
1937 (Cont.)					
31 Oct	Germany	Latvia	Finance	189LTS139	304382
01 Nov	Liberia	USA (United States)	Extradition	201LTS151	304710
04 Nov	Siam	Switzerland	General Amity	190LTS137	304412
04 Nov	Ireland	USA (United States)	Air Transport	185LTS71	304276
05 Nov	Siam	Sweden	Privil/Immunities	182LTS257	304215
05 Nov	Denmark	Siam	General Amity	188LTS187	304358
05 Nov	Bel-Lux Econ Union	Siam	General Amity	190LTS151	304413
05 Nov	Belgium	Siam	Privil/Immunities	190LTS163	304414
08 Nov	Siam	Sweden	General Amity	185LTS337	304298
10 Nov	Germany	UK Great Britain	Taxation	186LTS277	304316
11 Nov	Switzerland	USA (United States)	Milit Servic/Citiz	193LTS183	304494
12 Nov	Hungary	Lithuania	Finance	183LTS197	304236
13 Nov	Siam	USA (United States)	General Amity	192LTS247	304476
15 Nov	Norway	Siam	General Amity	186LTS9	304301
16 Nov	Hungary	Latvia	Finance	183LTS205	304237
16 Nov	Hungary	Norway	Visas	183LTS81	304228
16 Nov	Latvia	Poland	Sanitation	197LTS43	304604
18 Nov	France	Hungary	Admin Cooperation	185LTS257	304290
19 Nov	Chile	France	Admin Cooperation	185LTS261	304291
19 Nov	Poland	Switzerland	Extradition	195LTS297	304552
23 Nov	Siam	UK Great Britain	General Trade	188LTS333	304366
25 Nov	Estonia	Greece	Finance	184LTS427	304263
25 Nov	Greece	Turkey	Land Transport	195LTS137	304543
26 Nov	Chile	UK Great Britain	General Trade	186LTS285	304317
26 Nov	Bel-Lux Econ Union	Yugoslavia	Finance	196LTS19	304567
27 Nov	Denmark	Germany	General Trade	183LTS175	304234
01 Dec	Estonia	Finland	Education	187LTS413	304347
01 Dec	Greece	Lithuania	General Trade	193LTS185	304495
02 Dec	Denmark	Finland	Taxation	187LTS379	304345
02 Dec	Estonia	Hungary	General Trade	184LTS395	304259
03 Dec	Multilateral		Air Transport	186LTS293	304318
03 Dec	Italy	Siam	General Amity	189LTS255	304389
03 Dec	Switzerland	UK Great Britain	Admin Cooperation	194LTS223	304523
03 Dec	France	Switzerland	Admin Cooperation	185LTS265	304292
06 Dec	Romania	UK Great Britain	Admin Cooperation	184LTS467	304267
07 Dec	France	Siam	General Amity	201LTS113	304708
08 Dec	Japan	Siam	General Amity	188LTS375	304367
09 Dec	France	Siam	General Trade	201LTS145	304709
14 Dec	Estonia	UK Great Britain	Postal Service	187LTS223	304343
14 Dec	Italy	UK Great Britain	Air Transport	185LTS199	304283
16 Dec	Italy	USA (United States)	General Trade	187LTS15	304329
16 Dec	Belgium	Monaco	Extradition	187LTS195	304339
17 Dec	Brazil	USA (United States)	Visas	186LTS413	304325
18 Dec	Germany	Netherlands	Finance	190LTS29	304403
18 Dec	Belgium	China	Air Transport	190LTS109	304409
18 Dec	Hungary	Iran	General Trade	189LTS243	304387
21 Dec	China	Estonia	General Amity	194LTS123	304516
23 Dec	Estonia	Germany	Air Transport	189LTS333	304393
23 Dec	Multilateral		Gen Communications	186LTS99	304304
28 Dec	Portugal	UK Great Britain	Territory Boundary	185LTS205	304284
30 Dec	Germany	Siam	General Amity	188LTS401	304368
31 Dec	Sweden	Turkey	Finance	184LTS409	304261
31 Dec	Belgium	Netherlands	Land Transport	189LTS387	304396
31 Dec	Sweden	Turkey	General Trade	184LTS417	304262
31 Dec	Sweden	Turkey	General Trade	184LTS399	304260
31 Dec	Finland	Greece	General Economic	188LTS207	304359
1938					
05 Jan	Bulgaria	USA (United States)	Admin Cooperation	191LTS207	304444
07 Jan	Canada	USA (United States)	Specific Resources	184LTS305	304255
09 Jan	Finland	Sweden	Admin Cooperation	195LTS157	304545
12 Jan	Latvia	Turkey	General Trade	201LTS229	304716
13 Jan	Haiti	USA (United States)	Finance	187LTS201	304340
13 Jan	Bel-Lux Econ Union	Estonia	General Trade	185LTS63	304275
14 Jan	France	USA (United States)	Visas	191LTS213	304445

DATE	PARTY ONE	PARTY TWO	TOPIC	CITATION	NUMBER
1938 (Cont.)					
14 Jan	Estonia	Finland	Admin Cooperation	185LTS53	304274
14 Jan	Netherlands	New Zealand	General Trade	185LTS329	304297
15 Jan	Greece	Latvia	General Trade	195LTS19	304533
19 Jan	Estonia	Hungary	Visas	185LTS363	304300
24 Jan	Canada	USA (United States)	Admin Cooperation	187LTS27	304330
25 Jan	Latvia	Vatican/Holy See	Education	186LTS319	304320
31 Jan	Dominican Republic	Haiti	Territory Boundary	187LTS169	304336
31 Jan	France	Switzerland	Territory Boundary	195LTS313	304553
31 Jan	France	Sweden	General Trade	185LTS223	304286
01 Feb	Chile	USA (United States)	General Trade	190LTS9	304401
01 Feb	Norway	USA (United States)	Extradition	191LTS83	304436
01 Feb	Greece	Sweden	General Trade	185LTS217	304285
01 Feb	Netherlands	Siam	General Amity	193LTS13	304485
07 Feb	Belgium	Netherlands	Admin Cooperation	187LTS9	304328
09 Feb	Poland	Romania	General Economic	197LTS71	304607
09 Feb	Belgium	Turkey	Extradition	198LTS181	304639
10 Feb	Multilateral		Refugees	192LTS59	304461
14 Feb	Finland	Poland	Education	194LTS175	304520
14 Feb	Finland	South Africa	Visas	190LTS211	304419
18 Feb	Hungary	Norway	Visas	185LTS357	304299
18 Feb	Estonia	Sweden	Commodity Trade	185LTS237	304287
18 Feb	Netherlands	USA (United States)	Dispute Settlement	192LTS49	304460
18 Feb	Norway	Venezuela	General Trade	187LTS205	304341
26 Feb	Italy	Netherlands	Air Transport	194LTS75	304509
28 Feb	Greece	Norway	General Trade	186LTS159	304308
28 Feb	Greece	Norway	Finance	186LTS165	304309
01 Mar	India	Indochina	Admin Cooperation	194LTS231	304524
05 Mar	Latvia	Poland	Customs	192LTS283	304478
07 Mar	Czechoslovakia	USA (United States)	General Trade	200LTS87	304687
11 Mar	Greece	Poland	General Economic	194LTS13	304502
15 Mar	Surinam	UK Great Britain	Postal Service	189LTS183	304385
17 Mar	Greece	Mexico	General Amity	198LTS325	304649
18 Mar	Italy	UK Great Britain	General Trade	187LTS139	304334
18 Mar	Italy	UK Great Britain	General Trade	187LTS149	304335
22 Mar	Latvia	Romania	General Trade	187LTS439	304349
24 Mar	Denmark	Netherlands	Taxation	190LTS225	304421
25 Mar	Hungary	Latvia	Visas	188LTS447	304369
30 Mar	Greece	Switzerland	Admin Cooperation	185LTS245	304288
31 Mar	Sweden	USA (United States)	Taxation	189LTS327	304392
06 Apr	Greece	Hungary	Admin Cooperation	188LTS455	304370
09 Apr	El Salvador	Guatemala	Territory Boundary	189LTS275	304390
09 Apr	Multilateral		Admin Cooperation	191LTS165	304442
09 Apr	Multilateral		Admin Cooperation	191LTS119	304441
12 Apr	Finland	Lithuania	Finance	194LTS9	304501
14 Apr	Nicaragua	USA (United States)	Taxation	192LTS275	304477
14 Apr	Germany	Greece	Admin Cooperation	198LTS389	304657
15 Apr	Multilateral		Visas	200LTS285	304698
16 Apr	Italy	UK Great Britain	Peace/Disarmament	195LTS79	304537
16 Apr	Multilateral		Peace/Disarmament	195LTS103	304538
20 Apr	Norway	Sweden	Specific Property	189LTS153	304383
21 Apr	Finland	Norway	Specific Resources	188LTS215	304360
21 Apr	Finland	Norway	Specific Resources	188LTS231	304361
27 Apr	Greece	Turkey	General Amity	193LTS175	304493
27 Apr	Poland	UK Great Britain	Peace/Disarmament	195LTS39	304535
29 Apr	Multilateral		Visas	190LTS115	304410
30 Apr	Belgium	Netherlands	Taxation	190LTS199	304418
05 May	New Zealand	Switzerland	General Trade	189LTS167	304384
11 May	Germany	Greece	Admin Cooperation	197LTS75	304608
11 May	Portugal	UK Great Britain	General Trade	191LTS285	304450
11 May	Multilateral		General Trade	189LTS237	304386
12 May	USA (United States)	Venezuela	General Trade	191LTS35	304433
12 May	Cuba	USA (United States)	Admin Cooperation	191LTS19	304432
14 May	Lithuania	Poland	Water Transport	191LTS373	304456
14 May	Belgium	Switzerland	Extradition	190LTS217	304420
16 May	United Arab Rep	Iraq	General Trade	190LTS177	304415

DATE	PARTY ONE	PARTY TWO	TOPIC	CITATION	NUMBER
1938 (Cont.)					
17 May	Bulgaria	Latvia	General Trade	189LTS249	304388
17 May	Lithuania	Sweden	Postal Service	192LTS237	304474
17 May	Multilateral		Visas	192LTS319	304481
18 May	Czechoslovakia	USA (United States)	Customs	199LTS305	304680
22 May	Lithuania	Poland	Postal Service	191LTS359	304455
25 May	Lithuania	Poland	Land Transport	191LTS391	304457
25 May	Germany	Netherlands	Finance	192LTS143	304468
27 May	Turkey	UK Great Britain	General Trade	190LTS121	304411
27 May	Multilateral		Other Military	188LTS293	304365
27 May	Turkey	UK Great Britain	Milit Assistance	199LTS9	304660
30 May	Multilateral		Visas	191LTS299	304451
02 Jun	Multilateral		Postal Service	192LTS157	304470
10 Jun	Denmark	Sweden	Admin Cooperation	188LTS461	304371
16 Jun	Latvia	Poland	Air Transport	196LTS105	304573
17 Jun	Colombia	Panama	Territory Boundary	193LTS231	304500
20 Jun	USA (United States)	Yugoslavia	Postal Service	195LTS259	304549
20 Jun	Japan	USA (United States)	Postal Service	191LTS43	304434
21 Jun	Italy	Norway	General Trade	190LTS193	304417
21 Jun	France	Morocco	Admin Cooperation	189LTS423	304398
24 Jun	Multilateral		Specific Resources	196LTS131	304575
27 Jun	Multilateral		Visas	191LTS199	304443
27 Jun	Switzerland	Yugoslavia	General Trade	196LTS27	304568
01 Jul	Germany	UK Great Britain	Finance	194LTS245	304526
01 Jul	Germany	UK Great Britain	Finance	194LTS235	304525
01 Jul	Haiti	USA (United States)	Finance	192LTS89	304463
02 Jul	Portugal	Siam	General Amity	200LTS149	304688
05 Jul	Hungary	Norway	Admin Cooperation	189LTS427	304399
15 Jul	Multilateral		Visas	195LTS73	304536
15 Jul	France	Netherlands	Air Transport	192LTS151	304469
19 Jul	Romania	Switzerland	Consul/Citizenship	152LTS89	303486
22 Jul	Belgium	Luxembourg	Territory Boundary	191LTS113	304440
23 Jul	Lithuania	Poland	Land Transport	192LTS83	304462
26 Jul	Switzerland	UK Great Britain	Customs	191LTS307	304452
28 Jul	Canada	USA (United States)	Air Transport	192LTS94	304464
28 Jul	Canada	USA (United States)	Admin Cooperation	192LTS115	304465
28 Jul	Canada	USA (United States)	Admin Cooperation	192LTS125	304466
29 Jul	Belgium	UK Great Britain	Postal Service	201LTS317	304722
31 Jul	Balkan States	Bulgaria	General Amity	196LTS371	304596
06 Aug	Ecuador	USA (United States)	General Trade	193LTS85	304489
08 Aug	Liberia	USA (United States)	General Amity	201LTS163	304711
13 Aug	Germany	UK Great Britain	Finance	194LTS257	304527
15 Aug	Greece	Portugal	General Trade	201LTS201	304707
18 Aug	Multilateral		Admin Cooperation	196LTS113	304574
19 Aug	France	UK Great Britain	Postal Service	192LTS189	304471
29 Aug	Mexico	USA (United States)	Admin Cooperation	195LTS359	304556
02 Sep	Romania	UK Great Britain	Finance	191LTS313	304453
06 Sep	Argentina	Netherlands	Visas	194LTS409	304531
06 Sep	Cuba	Portugal	General Trade	195LTS443	304565
06 Sep	British Guiana	USA (United States)	Postal Service	193LTS117	304490
10 Sep	Germany	UK Great Britain	Recognition	194LTS313	304528
12 Sep	Multilateral		Culture	198LTS111	304630
15 Sep	Canada	USA (United States)	Specific Resources	203LTS207	304763
16 Sep	Bulgaria	Greece	General Trade	195LTS27	304534
21 Sep	Germany	Switzerland	Territory Boundary	196LTS365	304595
22 Sep	Belgium	Mexico	Extradition	198LTS399	304658
30 Sep	Greece	Poland	Air Transport	196LTS387	304599
30 Sep	Burma	United Arab Rep	Postal Service	203LTS373	304780
01 Oct	Germany	Greece	General Economic	197LTS233	304616
05 Oct	Poland	UK Great Britain	Postal Service	194LTS321	304529
07 Oct	Liberia	USA (United States)	Consul/Citizenship	201LTS183	304712
10 Oct	Netherlands	Romania	Finance	195LTS9	304532
25 Oct	Iceland	UK Great Britain	Extradition	198LTS147	304635
25 Oct	Multilateral		Air Transport	192LTS323	304482
26 Oct	France	UK Great Britain	Postal Service	194LTS371	304530
28 Oct	Netherlands	Norway	Visas	193LTS223	304499

DATE	PARTY ONE	PARTY TWO	TOPIC	CITATION	NUMBER
1938 (Cont.)					
28 Oct	Germany	Sweden	Claims and Debts	196LTS91	304571
28 Oct	Germany	Sweden	Claims and Debts	196LTS81	304570
29 Oct	Latvia	Poland	Non-ILO Labor	195LTS169	304547
31 Oct	Iceland	USA (United States)	Postal Service	194LTS149	304519
31 Oct	Multilateral		Sanitation	198LTS205	304642
03 Nov	Aden	United Arab Rep	Postal Service	197LTS241	304617
08 Nov	France	UK Great Britain	Customs	196LTS215	304584
11 Nov	Ecuador	Sweden	Water Transport	195LTS347	304554
11 Nov	Denmark	Germany	General Trade	193LTS79	304488
12 Nov	Brazil	USA (United States)	Military Mission	195LTS375	304557
12 Nov	Estonia	Switzerland	General Trade	194LTS17	304503
15 Nov	Greece	USA (United States)	General Trade	195LTS145	304544
17 Nov	UK Great Britain	USA (United States)	General Trade	200LTS293	304700
17 Nov	Canada	USA (United States)	General Trade	199LTS91	304670
21 Nov	El Salvador	Norway	General Trade	198LTS157	304636
22 Nov	Estonia	Netherlands	General Trade	193LTS209	304497
22 Nov	Australia	Switzerland	General Trade	194LTS35	304505
22 Nov	Estonia	Netherlands	Customs	195LTS133	304542
23 Nov	Colombia	USA (United States)	Military Mission	196LTS147	304578
23 Nov	Colombia	USA (United States)	Military Mission	196LTS157	304579
24 Nov	Bulgaria	UK Great Britain	General Military	195LTS117	304539
03 Dec	Estonia	Lithuania	Taxation	193LTS217	304498
03 Dec	Iraq	USA (United States)	General Trade	203LTS107	304753
03 Dec	Multilateral		Education	200LTS249	304694
06 Dec	Estonia	USA (United States)	Admin Cooperation	198LTS361	304655
08 Dec	Multilateral		Gen Communications	202LTS49	304734
17 Dec	Belgium	Netherlands	Water Transport	198LTS177	304638
19 Dec	France	Greece	Education	196LTS99	304572
20 Dec	Guatemala	Norway	General Trade	198LTS117	304631
20 Dec	Finland	Netherlands	Customs	194LTS55	304506
20 Dec	Canada	USA (United States)	Telecommunications	196LTS171	304580
21 Dec	Norway	UK Great Britain	Taxation	201LTS357	304723
28 Dec	Multilateral		Other Military	196LTS221	304585
30 Dec	Denmark	Norway	General Economic	195LTS121	304540
30 Dec	Denmark	Sweden	General Economic	195LTS413	304561
30 Dec	Colombia	UK Great Britain	General Economic	196LTS231	304586
30 Dec	Norway	Sweden	General Economic	195LTS127	304541
30 Dec	Finland	USA (United States)	Admin Cooperation	195LTS417	304562
1939					
02 Jan	Multilateral		Postal Service	196LTS235	304587
09 Jan	Chile	UK Great Britain	General Trade	196LTS277	304589
10 Jan	Fiji Islands	USA (United States)	Postal Service	196LTS185	304581
11 Jan	Estonia	Latvia	Taxation	194LTS103	304512
15 Jan	Belgium	USA (United States)	Postal Service	199LTS321	304682
20 Jan	Sweden	Turkey	General Trade	194LTS107	304513
20 Jan	Sweden	Turkey	Finance	194LTS113	304514
20 Jan	Sweden	Turkey	General Trade	194LTS119	304515
24 Jan	China	UK Great Britain	Air Transport	199LTS53	304664
25 Jan	Portugal	UK Great Britain	Air Transport	196LTS281	304590
26 Jan	Burma	France	Postal Service	201LTS9	304701
27 Jan	Multilateral		Loans and Credits	196LTS287	304591
27 Jan	Finland	USA (United States)	Milit Servic/Citiz	201LTS187	304713
30 Jan	Estonia	Sweden	Commodity Trade	194LTS131	304517
31 Jan	Bel-Lux Econ Union	Latvia	General Economic	195LTS401	304559
05 Feb	Multilateral		General Amity	196LTS303	304592
07 Feb	Colombia	USA (United States)	Postal Service	196LTS53	304569
10 Feb	Turkey	UK Great Britain	Admin Cooperation	204LTS257	304806
14 Feb	Burma	Siam	Postal Service	197LTS255	304618
15 Feb	Monaco	USA (United States)	Extradition	202LTS61	304735
20 Feb	United Arab Rep	UK Great Britain	Water Transport	195LTS407	304560
20 Feb	Canada	USA (United States)	Gen Communications	197LTS181	304613
24 Feb	Chile	USA (United States)	General Trade	197LTS217	304614
27 Feb	Iceland	Norway	Specific Resources	196LTS377	304598
28 Feb	France	Norway	Admin Cooperation	195LTS165	304546

DATE	PARTY ONE	PARTY TWO	TOPIC	CITATION	NUMBER
1939 (Cont.)					
03 Mar	Germany	Romania	Admin Cooperation	201LTS381	304726
04 Mar	Belgium	Luxembourg	Admin Cooperation	197LTS141	304610
06 Mar	Belgium	France	Non-ILO Labor	195LTS353	304555
07 Mar	Greece	Turkey	Extradition	201LTS239	304717
16 Mar	Germany	USA (United States)	Postal Service	198LTS237	304645
22 Mar	France	India	Commodity Trade	197LTS273	304619
23 Mar	Germany	Romania	Other Economic	199LTS77	304668
23 Mar	Sweden	USA (United States)	Taxation	199LTS17	304661
27 Mar	Finland	Hungary	Visas	195LTS425	304563
28 Mar	Guatemala	USA (United States)	Military Mission	199LTS181	304671
31 Mar	France	Romania	Finance	199LTS219	304677
31 Mar	France	Romania	Education	199LTS213	304676
01 Apr	Turkey	USA (United States)	General Trade	202LTS129	304741
03 Apr	Multilateral		Water Transport	195LTS471	304566
06 Apr	UK Great Britain	USA (United States)	Territory Boundary	196LTS343	304593
08 Apr	Argentina	USA (United States)	Postal Service	198LTS55	304623
15 Apr	Latvia	Sweden	General Trade	196LTS373	304597
18 Apr	France	Sweden	Dispute Settlement	198LTS131	304632
18 Apr	Brazil	South Africa	General Trade	198LTS289	304646
18 Apr	Mexico	USA (United States)	Specific Property	201LTS201	304714
23 Apr	Multilateral		Land Transport	104LTS87	302380
30 Apr	Romania	USA (United States)	Visas	203LTS349	304775
01 May	Greece	Sweden	General Trade	196LTS205	304582
05 May	France	Sweden	Taxation	198LTS201	304641
06 May	Multilateral		Finance	198LTS81	304626
09 May	USA (United States)	Venezuela	General Trade	198LTS135	304633
11 May	Romania	UK Great Britain	General Trade	196LTS351	304594
17 May	Germany	Netherlands	Territory Boundary	199LTS239	304678
22 May	Nicaragua	USA (United States)	Military Mission	199LTS189	304672
23 May	Multilateral		Postal Service	202LTS159	304742
26 May	Estonia	Latvia	General Trade	198LTS99	304628
30 May	Greece	UK Great Britain	Air Transport	202LTS7	304732
31 May	United Arab Rep	South Africa	General Trade	198LTS295	304647
31 May	Denmark	Germany	General Amity	197LTS37	304603
07 Jun	Germany	Latvia	General Amity	198LTS105	304629
07 Jun	Estonia	Germany	General Amity	198LTS49	304622
14 Jun	Liberia	USA (United States)	Air Transport	202LTS93	304737
16 Jun	Germany	UK Great Britain	General Trade	197LTS277	304620
18 Jun	Denmark	Norway	Patents/Copyrights	197LTS227	304615
19 Jun	Belgium	UK Great Britain	Admin Cooperation	198LTS171	304637
22 Jun	Canada	USA (United States)	Other Military	199LTS197	304673
23 Jun	UK Great Britain	USA (United States)	Commodity Trade	198LTS333	304651
30 Jun	Sweden	USA (United States)	Admin Cooperation	199LTS203	304674
01 Jul	Netherlands	Switzerland	Customs	198LTS195	304640
10 Jul	France	Spain	Dispute Settlement	148LTS369	303423
15 Jul	France	USA (United States)	Air Transport	199LTS207	304675
15 Jul	France	USA (United States)	Air Transport	199LTS355	304683
18 Jul	Haiti	USA (United States)	Finance	198LTS329	304650
19 Jul	Australia	Brazil	General Trade	200LTS191	304690
26 Jul	Norway	Spain	General Trade	198LTS87	304627
04 Aug	Netherlands	UK Great Britain	Gen Communications	198LTS349	304653
16 Aug	Mexico	USA (United States)	Extradition	294LTS159	304794
18 Aug	Canada	USA (United States)	Air Transport	199LTS367	304684
21 Aug	Liberia	USA (United States)	Dispute Settlement	204LTS165	304795
21 Aug	Multilateral		Visas	198LTS343	304652
23 Aug	Latvia	UK Great Britain	Admin Cooperation	201LTS37	304702
25 Aug	Poland	UK Great Britain	General Military	199LTS57	304665
25 Aug	Panama	USA (United States)	General Amity	199LTS317	304681
29 Aug	Denmark	Norway	Customs	198LTS231	304644
07 Sep	Multilateral		Loans and Credits	198LTS357	304654
12 Sep	Argentina	USA (United States)	Military Mission	201LTS213	304715
13 Sep	Barbados	USA (United States)	Postal Service	199LTS375	304685
13 Sep	France	UK Great Britain	Telecommunications	201LTS369	304724
14 Sep	Denmark	UK Great Britain	Refugees	198LTS141	304634
22 Sep	Ecuador	USA (United States)	Extradition	204LTS169	304796

DATE	PARTY ONE	PARTY TWO	TOPIC	CITATION	NUMBER
1939 (Cont.)					
28 Sep	Estonia	USSR (Soviet Union)	General Military	198LTS223	304643
05 Oct	Sweden	USA (United States)	Visas	203LTS353	304776
05 Oct	Latvia	USSR (Soviet Union)	General Military	198LTS381	304656
08 Oct	France	UK Great Britain	Admin Cooperation	201LTS59	304703
17 Oct	Argentina	USA (United States)	Admin Cooperation	201LTS273	304720
19 Oct	Hungary	Romania	General Transport	201LTS419	304730
19 Oct	Hungary	Romania	Land Transport	201LTS395	304728
19 Oct	Hungary	Romania	Territory Boundary	201LTS419	304731
19 Oct	Hungary	Romania	Land Transport	201LTS415	304729
19 Oct	Multilateral		General Military	200LTS167	304689
21 Oct	Barbados	Martinique	Postal Service	201LTS65	304704
30 Oct	Germany	Latvia	Refugees	200LTS213	304693
02 Nov	Romania	Switzerland	Finance	200LTS289	304699
06 Nov	USA (United States)	Venezuela	General Trade	203LTS273	304770
13 Nov	United Arab Rep	USA (United States)	Postal Service	198LTS419	304659
22 Nov	Turkey	UK Great Britain	General Trade	201LTS93	304705
25 Nov	Poland	UK Great Britain	General Military	199LTS65	304666
30 Nov	Japan	Thailand	Air Transport	200LTS197	304691
02 Dec	Norway	UK Great Britain	Commodity Trade	201LTS97	304706
16 Dec	Finland	Sweden	Water Transport	199LTS43	304662
18 Dec	Cuba	USA (United States)	General Trade	202LTS71	304736
22 Dec	Denmark	Germany	Commodity Trade	199LTS87	304669
28 Dec	Lithuania	USA (United States)	Postal Service	202LTS381	304743
28 Dec	Finland	Norway	General Economic	199LTS71	304667
30 Dec	Canada	USA (United States)	General Trade	203LTS211	304764
1940					
04 Jan	Panama	USA (United States)	Land Transport	202LTS421	304744
08 Jan	Multilateral		Visas	203LTS133	304756
18 Jan	France	UK Great Britain	Territory Boundary	201LTS375	304725
31 Jan	Switzerland	USA (United States)	Extradition	204LTS175	304797
03 Feb	Turkey	UK Great Britain	General Trade	203LTS399	304781
19 Feb	Nicaragua	USA (United States)	Admin Cooperation	203LTS47	304749
20 Feb	Guatemala	USA (United States)	Extradition	204LTS111	304789
28 Feb	New Zealand	USA (United States)	Admin Cooperation	203LTS11	304746
29 Feb	Sweden	Turkey	General Trade	200LTS267	304695
29 Feb	Sweden	Turkey	Finance	200LTS273	304696
29 Feb	Sweden	Turkey	General Trade	200LTS281	304697
29 Feb	Canada	USA (United States)	Admin Cooperation	203LTS119	304754
04 Mar	Canada	USA (United States)	Admin Cooperation	202LTS429	304745
16 Mar	Dominican Republic	Newfoundland	General Trade	203LTS141	304757
18 Mar	Spain	UK Great Britain	Finance	203LTS157	304759
18 Mar	Spain	UK Great Britain	Loans and Credits	203LTS149	304758
22 Mar	Japan	UK Great Britain	Admin Cooperation	203LTS194	304760
02 Apr	South Africa	USA (United States)	General Amity	204LTS79	304786
11 Apr	Finland	Latvia	Finance	201LTS389	304727
17 Apr	United Arab Rep	UK Great Britain	Claims and Debts	201LTS253	304718
23 Apr	Chile	USA (United States)	Military Mission	203LTS29	304747
06 Jun	Romania	UK Great Britain	Finance	203LTS197	304761
12 Jun	Thailand	UK Great Britain	General Amity	203LTS421	304782
12 Jun	Japan	Thailand	General Amity	204LTS131	304791
18 Jun	Canada	USA (United States)	Finance	203LTS41	304748
24 Jun	Brazil	USA (United States)	Admin Cooperation	203LTS227	304766
29 Jun	Argentina	USA (United States)	Milit Assistance	203LTS57	304750
17 Jul	United Arab Rep	UK Great Britain	Claims and Debts	202LTS97	304738
31 Jul	Peru	USA (United States)	Military Mission	203LTS91	304752
31 Jul	Peru	USA (United States)	Military Mission	203LTS75	304751

DATE	PARTY ONE	PARTY TWO	TOPIC	CITATION	NUMBER
1940 (Cont.)					
03 Aug	United Arab Rep	France	Claims and Debts	202LTS121	304740
25 Aug	Aden	United Arab Rep	Postal Service	204LTS297	304810
28 Aug	Mexico	USA (United States)	Gen Communications	203LTS357	304777
02 Sep	UK Great Britain	USA (United States)	Milit Assistance	203LTS201	304762
06 Sep	Australia	USA (United States)	General Amity	204LTS245	304803
06 Sep	Canada	USA (United States)	General Amity	204LTS249	304804
06 Sep	New Zealand	USA (United States)	General Amity	204LTS253	304805
24 Sep	Dominican Republic	USA (United States)	Customs	204LTS203	304801
27 Sep	Haiti	USA (United States)	Finance	203LTS257	304767
11 Oct	Brazil	USA (United States)	Privil/Immunities	203LTS261	304768
29 Oct	Portugal	UK Great Britain	Territory Boundary	204LTS261	304807
07 Nov	Canada	USA (United States)	Specific Resources	203LTS267	304769
02 Dec	Canada	USA (United States)	Air Transport	203LTS219	304765
09 Dec	UK Great Britain	USA (United States)	General Military	203LTS319	304772
10 Dec	Thailand	UK Great Britain	Territory Boundary	203LTS433	304783
12 Dec	Ecuador	USA (United States)	Military Mission	203LTS305	304771
12 Dec	Honduras	USA (United States)	Admin Cooperation	203LTS341	304774
12 Dec	Ecuador	USA (United States)	Military Mission	203LTS327	304773
1941					
17 Jan	Brazil	USA (United States)	Military Mission	204LTS97	304788
28 Jan	France	India	General Trade	204LTS323	304811
13 Feb	Haiti	USA (United States)	Finance	203LTS363	304778
24 Mar	USA (United States)	Venezuela	Military Mission	204LTS83	304787
27 Mar	UK Great Britain	USA (United States)	Milit Installation	204LTS15	304784
01 Apr	Mexico	USA (United States)	Air Transport	204LTS179	304798
07 Apr	Spain	UK Great Britain	Loans and Credits	204LTS75	304785
09 Apr	Denmark	USA (United States)	General Military	204LTS135	304792
15 Apr	Peru	USA (United States)	Milit Assistance	204LTS117	304790
20 May	Canada	USA (United States)	Specific Resources	204LTS199	304800
22 May	Nicaragua	USA (United States)	Milit Assistance	204LTS283	304809
26 May	United Arab Rep	UK Great Britain	General Trade	204LTS147	304793
27 May	Guatemala	USA (United States)	Milit Assistance	204LTS185	304799
12 Jul	UK Great Britain	USSR (Soviet Union)	General Military	204LTS277	304808
14 Jul	Costa Rica	USA (United States)	Military Mission	204LTS231	304802
1942					
01 Jan	Multilateral		General Military	204LTS381	304817
23 Feb	UK Great Britain	USA (United States)	Milit Assistance	204LTS389	304818
26 Feb	UK Great Britain	Venezuela	Territory Boundary	205LTS131	304830
26 Feb	UK Great Britain	Venezuela	Territory Boundary	205LTS121	304829
23 Apr	Curacao	Trinidad/Tobago	Postal Service	204LTS335	304812
26 May	UK Great Britain	USSR (Soviet Union)	General Military	204LTS353	304813
02 Jun	Multilateral		Patents/Copyrights	205LTS163	304833
04 Jun	Belgium	UK Great Britain	Commodity Trade	204LTS363	304814
17 Jun	Chile	UK Great Britain	General Trade	204LTS371	304815
11 Jul	Norway	USA (United States)	General Military	204LTS415	304821
16 Jul	British Guiana	Curacao	Postal Service	205LTS13	304823
05 Aug	Czechoslovakia	UK Great Britain	General Amity	204LTS377	304816
24 Aug	UK Great Britain	USA (United States)	Patents/Copyrights	204LTS403	304820
03 Sep	UK Great Britain	USA (United States)	Milit Assistance	204LTS395	304819
09 Sep	Multilateral		Commodity Trade	205LTS137	304831
04 Dec	UK Great Britain	USA (United States)	Water Transport	295LTS33	304824
09 Dec	Nigeria	Spanish Colonies	Non-ILO Labor	205LTS41	304825
1943					
11 Jan	China	UK Great Britain	Privil/Immunities	205LTS67	304826
02 Mar	United Arab Rep	USA (United States)	Status of Forces	204LTS425	304822
28 Jun	Chile	UK Great Britain	General Trade	205LTS109	304827
18 Jul	Mexico	UK Great Britain	Milit Servic/Citiz	205LTS115	304828

United Nations Treaty Series
National Treaty Collections

DATE	PARTY ONE	PARTY TWO	TOPIC	CITATION	NUMBER
1919					
28 Nov	Multilateral		ILO Labor	38UNTS93	100589
28 Nov	Multilateral		ILO Labor	38UNTS67	100587
28 Nov	Multilateral		ILO Labor	38UNTS17	100584
28 Nov	Multilateral		ILO Labor	38UNTS41	100585
28 Nov	Multilateral		ILO Labor	38UNTS81	100588
29 Nov	Multilateral		ILO Labor	38UNTS53	100586
1920					
09 Jul	Multilateral		ILO Labor	38UNTS119	100591
09 Jul	Multilateral		ILO Labor	38UNTS109	100590
10 Jul	Multilateral		ILO Labor	38UNTS129	100592
1921					
11 Nov	Multilateral		ILO Labor	38UNTS203	100598
11 Nov	Multilateral		ILO Labor	38UNTS217	100599
12 Nov	Multilateral		ILO Labor	38UNTS153	100594
12 Nov	Multilateral		ILO Labor	38UNTS165	100595
16 Nov	Multilateral		ILO Labor	38UNTS143	100593
17 Nov	Multilateral		ILO Labor	38UNTS187	100597
19 Nov	Multilateral		ILO Labor	38UNTS175	100596
1922					
28 Oct	Finland	USSR (Soviet Union)	Specific Resources	67UNTS157	100874
28 Oct	Finland	USSR (Soviet Union)	Specific Resources	67UNTS153	100873
1925					
05 Jun	Multilateral		ILO Labor	38UNTS257	100602
08 Jun	Multilateral		ILO Labor	38UNTS269	100603
10 Jun	Multilateral		ILO Labor	38UNTS229	100600
10 Jun	Multilateral		ILO Labor	38UNTS243	100601
1926					
05 Jun	Multilateral		ILO Labor	38UNTS281	100604
23 Jun	Multilateral		ILO Labor	38UNTS315	100606
24 Jun	Multilateral		ILO Labor	38UNTS295	100605
1927					
15 Jun	Multilateral		ILO Labor	38UNTS327	100607
15 Jun	Multilateral		ILO Labor	38UNTS343	100608
27 Dec	Argentina	Brazil	Territory Boundary	51UNTS271	200193
1928					
16 Jun	Multilateral		ILO Labor	39UNTS3	100609
26 Jun	Multilateral		ILO Labor	39UNTS15	100610
1929					
21 Jun	Multilateral		ILO Labor	39UNTS27	100611
1930					
28 Jun	Multilateral		ILO Labor	39UNTS55	100612
28 Jun	Multilateral		ILO Labor	39UNTS85	100613
1931					
09 Jan	Greece	Iran	General Amity	166UNTS323	200496
09 Jan	Greece	Iran	General Amity	166UNTS331	200497
1932					
27 Apr	Multilateral		ILO Labor	39UNTS103	100614
30 Apr	Multilateral		ILO Labor	39UNTS133	100615
16 May	Cuba	USA (United States)	Consul/Citizenship	234UNTS283	200537
20 Aug	Canada	Ireland	General Trade	0UNTS0	200645
1933					
17 Jan	Netherlands	USA (United States)	Status of Forces	474UNTS119	106877
12 May	Canada	France	Admin Cooperation	253UNTS285	200545
22 Jun	Multilateral		ILO Labor	78UNTS181	101016
29 Jun	Multilateral		ILO Labor	39UNTS211	100619
29 Jun	Multilateral		ILO Labor	39UNTS259	100621
29 Jun	Multilateral		ILO Labor	39UNTS285	100622
29 Jun	Multilateral		ILO Labor	39UNTS165	100617
29 Jun	Multilateral		ILO Labor	39UNTS235	100620
29 Jun	Multilateral		ILO Labor	39UNTS189	100618
29 Jun	Multilateral		ILO Labor	39UNTS151	100616
1934					
19 Jun	Multilateral		ILO Labor	40UNTS3	100623
21 Jun	Multilateral		ILO Labor	40UNTS33	100625
21 Jun	Multilateral		ILO Labor	40UNTS19	100624
23 Jun	Multilateral		ILO Labor	40UNTS45	100626
1935					
31 Jan	Panama	USA (United States)	Consul/Citizenship	234UNTS277	200536
21 Jun	Multilateral		ILO Labor	40UNTS63	100627
22 Jun	Multilateral		ILO Labor	271UNTS199	103915
22 Jun	Multilateral		ILO Labor	40UNTS73	100628
25 Jun	Multilateral		ILO Labor	40UNTS97	100629
1936					
20 Jun	Multilateral		ILO Labor	40UNTS109	100630
24 Jun	Multilateral		ILO Labor	40UNTS137	100631
25 Jun	Multilateral		Privil/Immunities	161UNTS217	200486
12 Oct	Germany, West	Yugoslavia	Non-ILO Labor	56WGBB9437	425333
12 Oct	Germany, West	Yugoslavia	Non-ILO Labor	69WGBB1473	425336
24 Oct	Multilateral		ILO Labor	40UNTS153	100632
24 Oct	Multilateral		ILO Labor	40UNTS169	100633
24 Oct	Multilateral		ILO Labor	40UNTS187	100634
24 Oct	Multilateral		ILO Labor	40UNTS205	100635

DATE	PARTY ONE	PARTY TWO	TOPIC	CITATION	NUMBER
1937					
22 Jun	Multilateral		ILO Labor	40UNTS217	100636
23 Jun	Multilateral		ILO Labor	40UNTS233	100637
1938					
25 Feb	Bolivia	Brazil	Land Transport	88UNTS379	200254
25 Feb	Bolivia	Brazil	Extradition	54UNTS333	200205
25 Feb	Bolivia	Brazil	Specific Resources	51UNTS245	200192
20 Jun	Multilateral		ILO Labor	40UNTS255	100638
1939					
12 Apr	Netherlands	Yemen	General Amity	79UNTS257	200249
29 May	Luxembourg	UK Great Britain	Extradition	99UNTS301	200284
10 Jun	Canada	USA (United States)	Milit Assistance	149UNTS332	200476
13 Jun	Netherlands	UK Great Britain	Sanitation	5UNTS65	200028
27 Jun	Multilateral		ILO Labor	40UNTS281	100639
27 Jun	Multilateral		ILO Labor	40UNTS311	100640
28 Jun	Multilateral		ILO Labor	209UNTS39	102820
25 Jul	France	USA (United States)	Taxation	125UNTS259	200429
26 Jul	Afghanistan	Netherlands	General Amity	32UNTS381	200177
02 Nov	Anglo-Egypt Sudan	Fr Equatorial Afri	Telecommunications	2UNTS209	200012
1940					
23 Jan	Argentina	Brazil	Admin Cooperation	51UNTS281	200194
27 Jan	Brazil	France	Air Transport	72UNTS77	100929
17 Feb	Multilateral		Privil/Immunities	161UNTS229	200487
15 Mar	Brazil	UK Great Britain	Territory Boundary	5UNTS71	200029
22 Mar	Thailand	UK Great Britain	General Economic	2UNTS215	200013
23 Mar	Panama	USA (United States)	Land Transport	124UNTS195	200420
28 Mar	Norway	USA (United States)	Specif Claim/Waive	88UNTS365	200253
30 Mar	Brazil	Venezuela	Dispute Settlement	51UNTS291	200195
11 May	Taiwan	Dominican Republic	General Amity	10UNTS285	200067
12 May	Multilateral		Scientific Project	101UNTS91	101405
29 May	Canada	USA (United States)	Status of Forces	119UNTS285	200385
14 Jun	Netherlands	UK Great Britain	Finance	2UNTS251	200018
14 Jun	France	Netherlands	Finance	2UNTS263	200019
25 Jul	Netherlands	UK Great Britain	Finance	2UNTS275	200020
30 Jul	Multilateral		Admin Cooperation	161UNTS253	200488
06 Sep	Panama	USA (United States)	Land Transport	124UNTS209	200421
09 Sep	Colombia	USA (United States)	Extradition	125UNTS239	200428
11 Oct	Finland	USSR (Soviet Union)	Territory Boundary	67UNTS139	100872
12 Oct	Multilateral		Specific Resources	161UNTS193	200485
22 Oct	Afghanistan	Sweden	General Amity	191UNTS349	200516
28 Nov	Multilateral		Commodity Trade	139UNTS159	200452
13 Dec	Canada	USA (United States)	General Trade	117UNTS173	200368
1941					
11 Jan	Nicaragua	USA (United States)	Specific Resources	117UNTS253	200374
28 Feb	Honduras	USA (United States)	Specific Resources	117UNTS205	200371
27 Mar	Multilateral		Military Mission	67UNTS231	200222
28 Mar	Panama	USA (United States)	Taxation	103UNTS163	200312
11 Apr	Mexico	USA (United States)	Non-IBRD Project	117UNTS323	200379
14 Apr	Brazil	Paraguay	Commodity Trade	54UNTS269	200199
15 Apr	Argentina	USA (United States)	Visas	103UNTS307	200321
23 May	Haiti	USA (United States)	Military Mission	117UNTS191	200370
05 Jun	Haiti	USA (United States)	Admin Cooperation	101UNTS125	200289
07 Jun	Spain	Vatican/Holy See	Admin Cooperation	53SPBO1911	460267
14 Jun	Brazil	Paraguay	Visas	88UNTS401	200255
14 Jun	Brazil	Paraguay	Culture	54UNTS235	200196
14 Jun	Brazil	Paraguay	Culture	54UNTS249	200197
14 Jun	Brazil	Paraguay	IGO Establishment	54UNTS303	200202
14 Jun	Brazil	Paraguay	Land Transport	54UNTS289	200201
14 Jun	Brazil	Paraguay	Finance	54UNTS313	200203
14 Jun	Brazil	Paraguay	Admin Cooperation	54UNTS279	200200
14 Jun	Brazil	Paraguay	IGO Establishment	54UNTS323	200204
14 Jun	Brazil	Paraguay	Specific Property	54UNTS259	200198
14 Jun	Belgium	Brazil	Extradition	272UNTS157	103936

DATE	PARTY ONE	PARTY TWO	TOPIC	CITATION	NUMBER
1941 (Cont.)					
18 Jun	Costa Rica	USA (United States)	Specific Resources	103UNTS173	200313
18 Jun	Taiwan	UK Great Britain	Territory Boundary	10UNTS227	200064
27 Jun	Canada	USA (United States)	IGO Establishment	103UNTS205	200315
01 Jul	Iceland	USA (United States)	Milit Assistance	12UNTS405	200071
19 Jul	Jordan	UK Great Britain	Territory Boundary	9UNTS381	200054
19 Jul	Jordan	UK Great Britain	Extradition	9UNTS389	200055
02 Aug	USA (United States)	USSR (Soviet Union)	General Trade	102UNTS269	200306
16 Aug	UK Great Britain	USSR (Soviet Union)	Finance	91UNTS341	200269
04 Sep	Bolivia	USA (United States)	Military Mission	8UNTS345	200046
13 Sep	Haiti	USA (United States)	Other Ad Hoc	103UNTS141	200311
14 Oct	Argentina	USA (United States)	General Trade	119UNTS193	200384
17 Oct	Brazil	Canada	General Trade	67UNTS263	200224
10 Nov	Canada	USA (United States)	Specific Resources	23UNTS275	200134
18 Nov	Brazil	Chile	Culture	67UNTS279	200225
19 Nov	Mexico	USA (United States)	Claims and Debts	148UNTS367	200474
19 Nov	Mexico	USA (United States)	Claims and Debts	125UNTS287	200430
21 Nov	Iceland	USA (United States)	Milit Assistance	124UNTS179	200418
27 Nov	El Salvador	USA (United States)	Admin Cooperation	120UNTS161	200389
27 Nov	Canada	USA (United States)	Specific Resources	103UNTS193	200314
23 Dec	Cuba	USA (United States)	General Trade	119UNTS313	200388
1942					
08 Jan	Brazil	Uruguay	Admin Cooperation	54UNTS359	200206
15 Jan	Liberia	USA (United States)	Admin Cooperation	117UNTS227	200372
16 Jan	Costa Rica	USA (United States)	Land Transport	23UNTS285	200135
29 Jan	Multilateral		General Military	93UNTS279	200271
31 Jan	Bolivia	USA (United States)	Admin Cooperation	101UNTS137	200290
13 Feb	El Salvador	USA (United States)	Land Transport	23UNTS293	200136
19 Feb	Haiti	USA (United States)	Customs	105UNTS238	200336
19 Feb	Colombia	USA (United States)	Military Mission	117UNTS185	200369
24 Feb	Ecuador	USA (United States)	Sanitation	26UNTS379	200157
02 Mar	Ecuador	USA (United States)	General Trade	105UNTS195	200332
03 Mar	Brazil	USA (United States)	Tech Assistance	105UNTS91	200324
03 Mar	Brazil	USA (United States)	Tech Assistance	105UNTS99	200325
04 Mar	Canada	USA (United States)	Taxation	124UNTS271	200426
07 Mar	Panama	USA (United States)	Admin Cooperation	101UNTS157	200291
11 Mar	Peru	USA (United States)	Military Mission	117UNTS266	200375
12 Mar	Canada	USA (United States)	Non-ILO Labor	119UNTS295	200386
14 Mar	Brazil	USA (United States)	Sanitation	102UNTS195	200302
16 Mar	Taiwan	Iraq	General Amity	14UNTS335	200091
18 Mar	Canada	USA (United States)	Land Transport	101UNTS205	200294
20 Mar	Canada	USA (United States)	Milit Servic/Citiz	105UNTS169	200330
30 Mar	Germany, West	USA (United States)	Humanitarian	105UNTS219	200334
30 Mar	USA (United States)	Yugoslavia	Milit Servic/Citiz	13UNTS199	200079
31 Mar	Liberia	USA (United States)	General Military	23UNTS302	200137
07 Apr	Haiti	USA (United States)	Sanitation	106UNTS319	200349
08 Apr	Canada	USA (United States)	Milit Servic/Citiz	105UNTS179	200331
08 Apr	Nicaragua	USA (United States)	Milit Installation	132UNTS343	200439
08 Apr	Nicaragua	USA (United States)	Land Transport	24UNTS145	200138
18 Apr	USA (United States)	USSR (Soviet Union)	Milit Assistance	105UNTS285	200339
20 Apr	Saudi Arabia	UK Great Britain	General Trade	10UNTS151	200058
20 Apr	Saudi Arabia	UK Great Britain	Extradition	10UNTS99	200056
20 Apr	Saudi Arabia	UK Great Britain	General Amity	10UNTS117	200057
21 Apr	Peru	USA (United States)	Scientific Project	89UNTS317	200260
22 Apr	Multilateral		Commodity Trade	8UNTS237	200044
30 Apr	Brazil	Portugal	Postal Service	65UNTS183	200210
05 May	El Salvador	USA (United States)	Sanitation	21UNTS215	200124
07 May	Peru	USA (United States)	General Trade	103UNTS219	200316
07 May	Brazil	USA (United States)	Military Mission	6UNTS377	200040
08 May	Honduras	USA (United States)	Sanitation	166UNTS351	200498
09 May	Canada	USA (United States)	Land Transport	101UNTS215	200295
11 May	Peru	USA (United States)	Sanitation	136UNTS353	200447
18 May	Panama	USA (United States)	General Amity	124UNTS221	200422
18 May	Brazil	Uruguay	Telecommunications	54UNTS369	200207
22 May	Nicaragua	USA (United States)	Sanitation	105UNTS141	200328

DATE	PARTY ONE	PARTY TWO	TOPIC	CITATION	NUMBER
1942 (Cont.)					
22 May	Paraguay	USA (United States)	Sanitation	124UNTS243	200423
29 May	Colombia	USA (United States)	Military Mission	8UNTS365	200047
02 Jun	Taiwan	USA (United States)	Milit Assistance	14UNTS343	200092
16 Jun	Belgium	USA (United States)	Milit Assistance	105UNTS159	200329
22 Jun	UK Great Britain	USSR (Soviet Union)	Finance	91UNTS355	200270
27 Jun	Canada	USA (United States)	Other Military	99UNTS223	200276
01 Jul	Poland	USA (United States)	Milit Assistance	103UNTS267	200317
07 Jul	Panama	USA (United States)	Military Mission	9UNTS289	200048
08 Jul	Netherlands	USA (United States)	Milit Assistance	103UNTS277	200318
10 Jul	Netherlands	USSR (Soviet Union)	Consul/Citizenship	241UNTS475	200540
10 Jul	Greece	USA (United States)	Milit Assistance	103UNTS289	200319
11 Jul	Czechoslovakia	USA (United States)	Milit Assistance	90UNTS257	200263
16 Jul	Bolivia	USA (United States)	Sanitation	13UNTS101	200072
17 Jul	Brazil	USA (United States)	Sanitation	102UNTS203	200303
21 Jul	Guatemala	USA (United States)	Military Mission	103UNTS299	200320
21 Jul	USA (United States)	Uruguay	General Trade	120UNTS211	200393
24 Jul	USA (United States)	Yugoslavia	Milit Assistance	34UNTS361	200179
27 Jul	UK Great Britain	USA (United States)	Status of Forces	117UNTS311	200378
04 Aug	Mexico	USA (United States)	Non-ILO Labor	148UNTS379	200475
11 Aug	Bolivia	USA (United States)	Military Mission	9UNTS309	200049
12 Aug	Mexico	USA (United States)	Consul/Citizenship	125UNTS301	200431
15 Aug	Canada	USA (United States)	Other Military	99UNTS233	200277
17 Aug	Iceland	USA (United States)	Admin Cooperation	24UNTS163	200140
24 Aug	Peru	USA (United States)	Education	24UNTS153	200139
28 Aug	Norway	USA (United States)	Other Military	139UNTS361	200461
03 Sep	Brazil	USA (United States)	Non-IBRD Project	13UNTS109	200073
03 Sep	Australia	USA (United States)	Milit Assistance	24UNTS195	200143
03 Sep	France	USA (United States)	Milit Assistance	24UNTS177	200141
03 Sep	New Zealand	USA (United States)	Milit Assistance	24UNTS185	200142
10 Sep	Canada	USA (United States)	Land Transport	101UNTS221	200296
21 Sep	Haiti	USA (United States)	Other Ad Hoc	120UNTS177	200391
30 Sep	UK Great Britain	USA (United States)	Milit Servic/Citiz	13UNTS169	200077
30 Sep	Australia	USA (United States)	Milit Servic/Citiz	13UNTS125	200074
30 Sep	New Zealand	USA (United States)	Milit Servic/Citiz	13UNTS139	200075
30 Sep	Netherlands	USA (United States)	Milit Servic/Citiz	13UNTS151	200076
30 Sep	India	USA (United States)	Milit Servic/Citiz	13UNTS185	200078
30 Sep	Haiti	USA (United States)	Other Ad Hoc	24UNTS205	200144
08 Oct	Brazil	Paraguay	Telecommunications	65UNTS191	200211
13 Oct	USA (United States)	Venezuela	Commodity Trade	138UNTS282	200451
16 Oct	India	USA (United States)	Status of Forces	109UNTS111	200353
16 Oct	Belgium	USA (United States)	Milit Servic/Citiz	13UNTS211	200080
19 Oct	Haiti	USA (United States)	Territory Boundary	120UNTS171	200390
22 Oct	Brazil	Venezuela	Culture	65UNTS203	200212
23 Oct	Colombia	USA (United States)	Sanitation	105UNTS109	200326
24 Oct	Mexico	USA (United States)	Non-IBRD Project	21UNTS189	200123
26 Oct	Honduras	USA (United States)	Land Transport	24UNTS209	200145
27 Oct	Nicaragua	USA (United States)	Scientific Project	99UNTS287	200283
29 Oct	Ecuador	USA (United States)	Scientific Project	89UNTS301	200259
31 Oct	South Africa	USA (United States)	Milit Servic/Citiz	105UNTS269	200338
03 Nov	UK Great Britain	USA (United States)	Admin Cooperation	109UNTS127	200354
04 Nov	Canada	USA (United States)	Non-ILO Labor	24UNTS217	200146
05 Nov	Colombia	USA (United States)	Military Mission	24UNTS227	200147
09 Nov	Canada	USA (United States)	General Trade	101UNTS233	200298
10 Nov	Mexico	USA (United States)	Scientific Project	66UNTS307	200219
12 Nov	Taiwan	Cuba	General Amity	10UNTS243	200065
14 Nov	Dominican Republic	USA (United States)	Customs	24UNTS233	200148
18 Nov	Mexico	USA (United States)	Claims and Debts	120UNTS183	200392
24 Nov	El Salvador	USA (United States)	Military Mission	24UNTS241	200149
28 Nov	Paraguay	USA (United States)	Admin Cooperation	101UNTS173	200292
30 Nov	Canada	USA (United States)	Reparations	119UNTS305	200387
02 Dec	El Salvador	USA (United States)	Scientific Project	122UNTS277	200410
04 Dec	Multilateral		Direct Aid	24UNTS247	200150
07 Dec	Canada	USA (United States)	Land Transport	101UNTS227	200297
09 Dec	Brazil	Dominican Republic	Culture	65UNTS217	200213
10 Dec	Dominican Republic	USA (United States)	Admin Cooperation	24UNTS257	200151

DATE	PARTY ONE	PARTY TWO	TOPIC	CITATION	NUMBER
1942 (Cont.)					
19 Dec	Canada	USA (United States)	Commodity Trade	26UNTS363	200156
23 Dec	Mexico	USA (United States)	Finance	13UNTS231	200081
28 Dec	Canada	USA (United States)	Other Military	99UNTS241	200278
1943					
11 Jan	Taiwan	USA (United States)	Privil/Immunities	10UNTS261	200066
16 Jan	Norway	USA (United States)	Milit Servic/Citiz	13UNTS335	200082
22 Jan	Mexico	USA (United States)	Milit Servic/Citiz	105UNTS259	200337
25 Jan	Dominican Republic	USA (United States)	Military Mission	13UNTS399	200083
27 Jan	Canada	USA (United States)	Milit Installation	101UNTS257	200300
28 Jan	New Zealand	USA (United States)	Admin Cooperation	121UNTS123	200395
30 Jan	Belgium	USA (United States)	Milit Assistance	13UNTS371	200084
01 Feb	Cuba	USA (United States)	Milit Servic/Citiz	13UNTS379	200085
10 Feb	Brazil	USA (United States)	Sanitation	102UNTS217	200304
18 Feb	USA (United States)	Venezuela	Sanitation	21UNTS225	200125
23 Feb	Canada	USA (United States)	Land Transport	101UNTS243	200299
25 Feb	Poland	USA (United States)	Milit Servic/Citiz	13UNTS395	200086
02 Mar	Panama	USA (United States)	Sanitation	107UNTS55	200351
04 Mar	Canada	USA (United States)	Air Transport	13UNTS411	200087
10 Mar	Finland	Sweden	Taxation	198UNTS333	200518
13 Mar	Canada	USA (United States)	Other Military	99UNTS249	200279
16 Mar	Greece	USA (United States)	Milit Servic/Citiz	105UNTS227	200335
25 Mar	El Salvador	USA (United States)	Military Mission	13UNTS419	200088
26 Mar	Multilateral		Specif Goods/Equip	13UNTS427	200089
29 Mar	Colombia	USA (United States)	Milit Installation	124UNTS139	200416
03 Apr	Costa Rica	USA (United States)	Specif Goods/Equip	13UNTS463	200090
08 Apr	Iran	USA (United States)	General Trade	106UNTS155	200340
10 Apr	Canada	USA (United States)	Territory Boundary	21UNTS237	200126
14 Apr	Chile	USA (United States)	Military Mission	9UNTS331	200050
26 Apr	Mexico	USA (United States)	Non-ILO Labor	21UNTS245	200127
29 Apr	Mexico	USA (United States)	Non-ILO Labor	105UNTS119	200327
30 Apr	UK Great Britain	USA (United States)	Specific Resources	28UNTS341	200159
10 May	UK Great Britain	USA (United States)	Postal Service	147UNTS109	200473
11 May	Chile	USA (United States)	Sanitation	139UNTS295	200456
14 May	USA (United States)	Venezuela	Non-IBRD Project	28UNTS359	200160
19 May	Guatemala	USA (United States)	Land Transport	28UNTS377	200161
20 May	Peru	USA (United States)	Non-IBRD Project	100UNTS259	200288
21 May	El Salvador	USA (United States)	Military Mission	9UNTS341	200051
21 May	Taiwan	USA (United States)	Status of Forces	14UNTS353	200093
24 May	Brazil	USA (United States)	Status of Forces	28UNTS385	200162
26 May	Canada	USA (United States)	Privil/Immunities	7UNTS345	200043
31 May	El Salvador	USA (United States)	Milit Servic/Citiz	105UNTS205	200333
07 Jun	Panama	USA (United States)	Specific Property	21UNTS269	200128
08 Jun	Liberia	USA (United States)	Milit Assistance	117UNTS242	200373
10 Jun	Dominican Republic	USA (United States)	Specific Resources	21UNTS277	200129
14 Jun	Netherlands	USA (United States)	General Military	28UNTS397	200163
14 Jun	Mexico	USA (United States)	Scientific Project	66UNTS331	200220
01 Jul	Mexico	USA (United States)	Sanitation	28UNTS407	200164
07 Jul	Dominican Republic	USA (United States)	Sanitation	28UNTS419	200165
17 Jul	Guatemala	USA (United States)	Military Mission	28UNTS431	200166
19 Jul	Canada	USA (United States)	Land Transport	29UNTS289	200167
04 Aug	Belgium	USA (United States)	Status of Forces	109UNTS149	200356
09 Aug	Canada	USA (United States)	Milit Installation	29UNTS295	200168
09 Aug	Ethiopia	USA (United States)	Milit Installation	29UNTS303	200169
13 Aug	Canada	USA (United States)	Admin Cooperation	109UNTS135	200355
19 Aug	UK Great Britain	USA (United States)	Atomic Energy	214UNTS341	200527
20 Aug	Brazil	Taiwan	General Amity	14UNTS365	200094
21 Aug	Iran	USA (United States)	Admin Cooperation	101UNTS189	200293
02 Sep	Argentina	USA (United States)	Military Mission	9UNTS363	200052
13 Sep	Ecuador	USA (United States)	Military Mission	29UNTS349	200171
24 Sep	UK Great Britain	USA (United States)	Admin Cooperation	139UNTS373	200463
25 Sep	France	USA (United States)	Direct Aid	76UNTS183	200245
27 Sep	Iceland	USA (United States)	General Trade	29UNTS317	200170
29 Sep	Mexico	USA (United States)	Claims and Debts	106UNTS265	200345
19 Oct	Dominican Republic	USA (United States)	Non-ILO Labor	21UNTS295	200130

DATE	PARTY ONE	PARTY TWO	TOPIC	CITATION	NUMBER
1943 (Cont.)					
20 Oct	Belgium	Taiwan	Privil/Immunities	14UNTS376	200095
21 Oct	Multilateral		Finance	2UNTS281	200021
21 Oct	Czechoslovakia	USA (United States)	Milit Servic/Citiz	29UNTS369	200172
25 Oct	Nicaragua	USA (United States)	Military Mission	29UNTS383	200173
27 Oct	Paraguay	USA (United States)	Military Mission	29UNTS391	200174
31 Oct	Saudi Arabia	UK Great Britain	General Amity	10UNTS165	200059
01 Nov	USA (United States)	Uruguay	Sanitation	106UNTS311	200348
25 Nov	Brazil	USA (United States)	Sanitation	102UNTS227	200305
27 Nov	Iran	USA (United States)	Military Mission	31UNTS451	200176
01 Dec	UK Great Britain	USA (United States)	Scientific Project	3UNTS209	100033
10 Dec	Paraguay	USA (United States)	Military Mission	21UNTS305	200131
16 Dec	El Salvador	UK Great Britain	General Trade	2UNTS221	200014
20 Dec	Peru	USA (United States)	Military Mission	117UNTS285	200376
21 Dec	Multilateral		Commodity Trade	65UNTS231	200214
31 Dec	Liberia	USA (United States)	Non-IBRD Project	106UNTS199	200341
1944					
13 Jan	USA (United States)	Venezuela	Military Mission	109UNTS171	200358
15 Jan	Multilateral		IGO Establishment	161UNTS281	200489
17 Jan	Canada	USA (United States)	Mass Media	109UNTS199	200360
21 Jan	Australia	New Zealand	General Amity	18UNTS357	200113
27 Jan	Mexico	USA (United States)	IGO Establishment	106UNTS275	200346
03 Feb	Mexico	USA (United States)	Specific Resources	3UNTS313	200025
11 Feb	Dominican Republic	USA (United States)	Milit Assistance	109UNTS251	200363
12 Feb	Colombia	USA (United States)	Milit Servic/Citiz	109UNTS287	200365
16 Feb	Iraq	USA (United States)	Admin Cooperation	109UNTS223	200362
29 Feb	Afghanistan	USA (United States)	Admin Cooperation	106UNTS247	200344
03 Mar	Canada	USA (United States)	Specific Resources	109UNTS191	200359
10 Mar	UK Great Britain	USA (United States)	Patents/Copyrights	5UNTS205	200030
22 Mar	Canada	Taiwan	Milit Assistance	14UNTS397	200096
23 Mar	Canada	USA (United States)	Claims and Debts	125UNTS345	200432
23 Mar	Turkey	UK Great Britain	Specif Claim/Waive	2UNTS227	200015
23 Mar	Albania	Yugoslavia	General Military	1UNTS81	100015
28 Mar	UK Great Britain	USA (United States)	Status of Forces	15UNTS413	200104
31 Mar	Peru	USA (United States)	Military Mission	109UNTS165	200357
04 Apr	Peru	USA (United States)	Scientific Project	89UNTS291	200258
12 Apr	Honduras	USA (United States)	Education	138UNTS271	200450
13 Apr	Guatemala	USA (United States)	Admin Cooperation	106UNTS213	200342
14 Apr	Canada	Taiwan	Privil/Immunities	14UNTS408	200097
15 Apr	Peru	USA (United States)	Education	150UNTS317	200479
19 Apr	Multilateral		Scientific Project	89UNTS279	200257
22 Apr	Turkey	USA (United States)	Customs	109UNTS279	200364
02 May	Peru	USA (United States)	Military Mission	109UNTS211	200361
05 May	Taiwan	Costa Rica	General Amity	14UNTS427	200098
10 May	Australia	USA (United States)	Reparations	106UNTS237	200343
16 May	Netherlands	USA (United States)	Milit Occupation	132UNTS355	200440
16 May	Norway	USA (United States)	Privil/Immunities	67UNTS253	200223
16 May	Belgium	UK Great Britain	Admin Cooperation	90UNTS283	200266
24 May	Brazil	Canada	Culture	65UNTS265	200215
24 May	Brazil	Ecuador	Culture	73UNTS223	200242
27 May	Brazil	UK Great Britain	Milit Servic/Citiz	2UNTS235	200016
29 May	Costa Rica	USA (United States)	Non-ILO Labor	124UNTS155	200417
07 Jun	Canada	USA (United States)	Specific Property	99UNTS259	200280
08 Jun	Canada	USA (United States)	Taxation	124UNTS297	200427
13 Jun	Taiwan	USA (United States)	Status of Forces	107UNTS43	200350
27 Jun	Canada	USA (United States)	Milit Installation	101UNTS273	200301
29 Jun	Ecuador	USA (United States)	Military Mission	80UNTS283	200250
01 Jul	Chile	UK Great Britain	General Trade	2UNTS243	200017
10 Jul	Peru	USA (United States)	Military Mission	117UNTS291	200377
15 Jul	Guatemala	USA (United States)	Scientific Project	106UNTS285	200347
01 Aug	Taiwan	Mexico	General Amity	14UNTS441	200099
02 Aug	Multilateral		Scientific Project	67UNTS221	200221
05 Aug	Canada	USA (United States)	Specific Resources	121UNTS299	200408
11 Aug	Brazil	Paraguay	Land Transport	67UNTS303	200227
13 Aug	Hungary	Yugoslavia	Dispute Settlement	113UNTS233	101553

DATE	PARTY ONE	PARTY TWO	TOPIC	CITATION	NUMBER
1944 (Cont.)					
22 Aug	Belgium	UK Great Britain	Direct Aid	90UNTS295	200267
25 Aug	France	USA (United States)	Milit Occupation	138UNTS247	200449
07 Sep	Bolivia	USA (United States)	Education	162UNTS315	200494
08 Sep	Syria	USA (United States)	Recognition	124UNTS251	200424
08 Sep	Lebanon	USA (United States)	Recognition	124UNTS187	200419
12 Sep	Multilateral		Milit Occupation	227UNTS279	200532
16 Sep	Guatemala	USA (United States)	Education	135UNTS315	200444
23 Sep	UK Great Britain	USSR (Soviet Union)	Telecommunications	10UNTS171	200060
29 Sep	Brazil	USA (United States)	Military Mission	65UNTS271	200216
02 Oct	Netherlands	UK Great Britain	Claims and Debts	231UNTS317	200535
05 Oct	Belgium	UK Great Britain	Finance	5UNTS227	200031
08 Oct	Multilateral		Reparations	45UNTS311	200187
12 Oct	Brazil	UNRRA (Relief)	IGO Establishment	67UNTS321	200228
28 Oct	Multilateral		Peace/Disarmament	123UNTS223	200414
30 Oct	Spain	UK Great Britain	Air Transport	47SPBO2004	460237
14 Nov	Multilateral		Milit Occupation	236UNTS359	200539
14 Nov	Panama	USA (United States)	Education	139UNTS367	200462
22 Nov	Brazil	Uruguay	Specif Goods/Equip	65UNTS289	200217
28 Nov	Portugal	USA (United States)	Milit Assistance	183UNTS311	200508
02 Dec	Spain	USA (United States)	Air Transport	89UNTS345	200262
07 Dec	Multilateral		Air Transport	171UNTS345	200501
07 Dec	Multilateral		Air Transport	171UNTS387	200502
07 Dec	Multilateral		IGO Establishment	15UNTS295	200102
07 Dec	Multilateral		Air Transport	84UNTS389	200252
15 Dec	Multilateral		Sanitation	17UNTS305	200110
15 Dec	Multilateral		Sanitation	16UNTS247	200106
16 Dec	Denmark	USA (United States)	Air Transport	10UNTS213	200063
16 Dec	Sweden	USA (United States)	Air Transport	6UNTS397	200041
16 Dec	Algeria	France	Non-ILO Labor	0UNTS0	110350
16 Dec	Brazil	Uruguay	Admin Cooperation	65UNTS305	200218
19 Dec	Ethiopia	UK Great Britain	General Amity	93UNTS303	200272
1945					
02 Jan	Belgium	Netherlands	Refugees	19UNTS259	200120
05 Jan	Poland	USSR (Soviet Union)	Consul/Citizenship	0SUST169	468305
08 Jan	Haiti	USA (United States)	Specific Resources	121UNTS153	200397
16 Jan	Romania	USSR (Soviet Union)	Reparations	0SUST169	468344
20 Jan	Multilateral		Peace/Disarmament	140UNTS397	200471
22 Jan	Ecuador	USA (United States)	Education	24UNTS273	200152
27 Jan	Iceland	USA (United States)	Air Transport	122UNTS293	200411
31 Jan	Finland	USSR (Soviet Union)	General Trade	0SUST170	468132
03 Feb	Ireland	USA (United States)	Air Transport	122UNTS305	200412
11 Feb	UK Great Britain	USSR (Soviet Union)	Refugees	0SUST173	468424
11 Feb	UK Great Britain	USSR (Soviet Union)	Refugees	0SUST174	468427
11 Feb	UK Great Britain	USSR (Soviet Union)	Refugees	0SUST173	468426
11 Feb	UK Great Britain	USSR (Soviet Union)	Refugees	0SUST173	468425
11 Feb	USA (United States)	USSR (Soviet Union)	Other Military	68UNTS175	200229
13 Feb	Canada	USA (United States)	Status of Forces	200UNTS219	200519
17 Feb	Canada	USA (United States)	Air Transport	122UNTS261	200409
20 Feb	France	USA (United States)	Direct Aid	76UNTS193	200246
20 Feb	France	USA (United States)	IGO Status/Immunit	76UNTS223	200248
21 Feb	Guatemala	USA (United States)	Military Mission	121UNTS133	200396
23 Feb	Turkey	USA (United States)	Direct Aid	121UNTS165	200398
26 Feb	Canada	USA (United States)	Other Military	99UNTS273	200281
28 Feb	France	USA (United States)	IGO Status/Immunit	76UNTS213	200247
01 Mar	Canada	Czechoslovakia	Finance	45UNTS283	200185
06 Mar	Sweden	UK Great Britain	Finance	5UNTS241	200032
06 Mar	Sweden	UK Great Britain	Finance	82UNTS219	101095
08 Mar	Dominican Republic	USSR (Soviet Union)	Consul/Citizenship	0SUST174	468121
08 Mar	Australia	USA (United States)	Claims and Debts	121UNTS205	200400
09 Mar	Romania	USSR (Soviet Union)	Admin Cooperation	0SUST174	468345
13 Mar	Belgium	USSR (Soviet Union)	Refugees	19UNTS235	200117
14 Mar	Bulgaria	USSR (Soviet Union)	General Trade	0SUST175	468028
14 Mar	USSR (Soviet Union)	Venezuela	Consul/Citizenship	0SUST175	468445
20 Mar	Multilateral		General Economic	2UNTS299	200022

DATE	PARTY ONE	PARTY TWO	TOPIC	CITATION	NUMBER
1945 (Cont.)					
22 Mar	Multilateral		General Amity	70UNTS237	200241
27 Mar	France	UK Great Britain	Finance	98UNTS227	200274
30 Mar	Belgium	France	Water Transport	20UNTS297	200122
30 Mar	Belgium	France	Visas	21UNTS325	200132
31 Mar	Czechoslovakia	USSR (Soviet Union)	Claims and Debts	16SUGG61	469880
31 Mar	Czechoslovakia	USSR (Soviet Union)	General Military	16SUGG62	469881
02 Apr	Brazil	USSR (Soviet Union)	Consul/Citizenship	OSUST437	468027
05 Apr	Taiwan	Sweden	Privil/Immunities	OCTRC448	413026
05 Apr	Ecuador	USA (United States)	Milit Servic/Citiz	121UNTS265	200404
07 Apr	Iceland	Sweden	General Trade	45SOFM95	461006
09 Apr	Brazil	Dominican Republic	Culture	67UNTS293	200226
11 Apr	USSR (Soviet Union)	Yugoslavia	General Amity	OSUST175	468459
11 Apr	Iceland	USA (United States)	Air Transport	16UNTS241	200105
12 Apr	Canada	Sweden	Air Transport	45SOFM65	461001
13 Apr	USSR (Soviet Union)	Yugoslavia	General Trade	OSUST175	468460
14 Apr	Czechoslovakia	USSR (Soviet Union)	Milit Installation	16SUGG62	469882
14 Apr	France	Monaco	Finance	45FRJO106	416326
14 Apr	France	Monaco	Finance	45FRJO106	416325
14 Apr	France	Monaco	Admin Cooperation	45FRJO106	416327
16 Apr	Italy	Vatican/Holy See	Territory Boundary	47ITGU169	435335
16 Apr	UK Great Britain	USA (United States)	Taxation	6UNTS359	200039
16 Apr	UK Great Britain	USA (United States)	Taxation	6UNTS189	100076
17 Apr	Colombia	USA (United States)	Customs	139UNTS303	200457
17 Apr	Belgium	USA (United States)	Milit Assistance	139UNTS253	200454
17 Apr	South Africa	USA (United States)	Direct Aid	90UNTS267	200264
17 Apr	South Africa	USA (United States)	Reparations	90UNTS275	200265
18 Apr	Bolivia	USSR (Soviet Union)	Consul/Citizenship	OSUST176	471014
19 Apr	Guatemala	USSR (Soviet Union)	Consul/Citizenship	OSUST176	468171
19 Apr	Belgium	USA (United States)	Milit Installation	139UNTS179	200455
20 Apr	Iceland	Sweden	Air Transport	45SOFM67	461002
21 Apr	Poland	USSR (Soviet Union)	General Military	12UNTS391	200070
28 Apr	Belgium	Luxembourg	Visas	41UNTS265	200181
29 Apr	Austria	USSR (Soviet Union)	Recognition	OSUST176	471015
30 Apr	Netherlands	USA (United States)	Milit Installation	139UNTS319	200459
30 Apr	Netherlands	USA (United States)	Milit Assistance	139UNTS341	200460
04 May	Turkey	UK Great Britain	General Economic	46TURG2301	466095
08 May	Romania	USSR (Soviet Union)	General Trade	OSUST178	468346
08 May	Romania	USSR (Soviet Union)	Finance	OSUST178	468347
08 May	Finland	USSR (Soviet Union)	General Trade	OSUST177	471016
09 May	Argentina	USA (United States)	Commodity Trade	139UNTS227	200453
11 May	USA (United States)	Venezuela	Milit Servic/Citiz	121UNTS273	200405
13 May	Panama	USA (United States)	Visas	89UNTS273	200256
14 May	Belgium	Luxembourg	Refugees	19UNTS243	200118
15 May	Canada	USA (United States)	Peace/Disarmament	125UNTS353	200433
16 May	Denmark	USSR (Soviet Union)	Consul/Citizenship	OSUST178	468115
16 May	Belgium	Czechoslovakia	Refugees	19UNTS251	200119
21 May	Guatemala	USA (United States)	Military Mission	121UNTS185	200399
21 May	Belgium	France	Visas	23UNTS215	200133
24 May	Chile	USA (United States)	Military Mission	121UNTS219	200401
29 May	Taiwan	Netherlands	Privil/Immunities	2UNTS307	200023
29 May	Norway	USA (United States)	Water Transport	34UNTS371	200180
30 May	Belgium	Sweden	General Trade	45SOFM99	461007
30 May	Belgium	Sweden	Finance	45SOFM100	461008
05 Jun	Multilateral		Milit Occupation	68UNTS189	200230
09 Jun	Multilateral		Milit Occupation	139UNTS381	200464
09 Jun	El Salvador	USA (United States)	Education	149UNTS379	200478
11 Jun	Chile	USA (United States)	Milit Servic/Citiz	121UNTS291	200407
12 Jun	Peru	USA (United States)	Milit Servic/Citiz	121UNTS283	200406
15 Jun	Hungary	USSR (Soviet Union)	Reparations	OSUST180	468172
15 Jun	UK Great Britain	USA (United States)	Reparations	89UNTS327	200261
16 Jun	Ecuador	USSR (Soviet Union)	Consul/Citizenship	OSUST180	468122
21 Jun	France	Sweden	Finance	45SOFM107	461010
21 Jun	France	Sweden	General Trade	45SOFM105	461009
25 Jun	Canada	Norway	Finance	45UNTS297	200186
25 Jun	Belgium	UK Great Britain	Reparations	90UNTS307	200268

DATE	PARTY ONE	PARTY TWO	TOPIC	CITATION	NUMBER
1945 (Cont.)					
29 Jun	France	USSR (Soviet Union)	Refugees	OSUST181	468150
29 Jun	Czechoslovakia	USSR (Soviet Union)	Territory Boundary	504UNTS299	200607
01 Jul	Portugal	UK Great Britain	Postal Service	5UNTS263	200034
06 Jul	Poland	USSR (Soviet Union)	Consul/Citizenship	OSUST182	468306
07 Jul	Poland	USSR (Soviet Union)	General Trade	OSUST182	468307
07 Jul	Taiwan	UK Great Britain	Status of Forces	14UNTS455	200100
09 Jul	Poland	Sweden	General Trade	45SOFM115	461011
09 Jul	Multilateral		Milit Occupation	160UNTS359	200484
11 Jul	Poland	USSR (Soviet Union)	Admin Cooperation	OSUST183	468308
17 Jul	Romania	USSR (Soviet Union)	Specific Property	OSUST183	468348
19 Jul	Romania	USSR (Soviet Union)	Specific Property	OSUST183	468349
26 Jul	Multilateral		Milit Occupation	227UNTS297	200533
30 Jul	Chile	USA (United States)	General Trade	6UNTS409	200042
31 Jul	Argentina	Sweden	General Trade	45SOFM119	461012
31 Jul	Iraq	USA (United States)	Milit Assistance	121UNTS239	200402
03 Aug	Switzerland	USA (United States)	Air Transport	51UNTS233	200191
06 Aug	Romania	USSR (Soviet Union)	Consul/Citizenship	OSUST188	468350
06 Aug	Finland	USSR (Soviet Union)	Consul/Citizenship	OSUST188	471017
07 Aug	Denmark	Norway	Telecommunications	10UNTS203	200062
08 Aug	Romania	USSR (Soviet Union)	Specific Property	OSUST189	468351
08 Aug	Multilateral		General Military	82UNTS279	200251
14 Aug	Taiwan	USSR (Soviet Union)	General Amity	10UNTS300	200068
14 Aug	France	USA (United States)	Admin Cooperation	73UNTS237	200243
15 Aug	Romania	USSR (Soviet Union)	Specific Property	OSUST193	468352
16 Aug	Poland	USSR (Soviet Union)	Reparations	OSUST193	468309
16 Aug	Bulgaria	USSR (Soviet Union)	Consul/Citizenship	OSUST193	471018
16 Aug	France	Sweden	Air Transport	45SOFM69	461003
16 Aug	Poland	USSR (Soviet Union)	Territory Boundary	10UNTS193	200061
16 Aug	Denmark	UK Great Britain	Finance	5UNTS251	200033
17 Aug	Finland	Sweden	General Trade	45SOFM124	461013
18 Aug	Taiwan	France	Territory Boundary	14UNTS477	200101
20 Aug	Romania	USSR (Soviet Union)	Consul/Citizenship	OSUST194	468353
20 Aug	Poland	Sweden	General Economic	45SOFM125	461014
24 Aug	Poland	Sweden	Air Transport	45SOFM70	461004
24 Aug	Haiti	USA (United States)	Visas	139UNTS311	200458
29 Aug	France	UK Great Britain	Patents/Copyrights	11UNTS397	200069
31 Aug	France	UK Great Britain	IGO Establishment	98UNTS249	200275
02 Sep	Multilateral		Peace/Disarmament	139UNTS387	200465
06 Sep	Canada	USA (United States)	Other Military	99UNTS281	200282
07 Sep	Netherlands	UK Great Britain	Finance	2UNTS325	200024
12 Sep	Switzerland	Turkey	General Economic	46TURG2301	466090
13 Sep	Romania	USSR (Soviet Union)	Refugees	OSUST197	468359
13 Sep	Romania	USSR (Soviet Union)	Reparations	OSUST197	468355
13 Sep	Romania	USSR (Soviet Union)	Health/Educ/Welfare	OSUST198	468360
13 Sep	Romania	USSR (Soviet Union)	Reparations	OSUST197	468357
13 Sep	Romania	USSR (Soviet Union)	Land Transport	OSUST197	468358
13 Sep	Romania	USSR (Soviet Union)	Reparations	OSUST197	468356
13 Sep	Romania	USSR (Soviet Union)	Commodity Trade	OSUST197	468354
17 Sep	USA (United States)	USSR (Soviet Union)	Milit Occupation	235UNTS346	200538
25 Sep	Hungary	USSR (Soviet Union)	Consul/Citizenship	OSUST98	468173
27 Sep	Multilateral		IGO Establishment	5UNTS327	200035
27 Sep	United Arab Rep	Yemen	General Amity	9UNTS373	200053
02 Oct	UK Great Britain	USSR (Soviet Union)	Milit Occupation	OSUST199	468428
03 Oct	Iran	USSR (Soviet Union)	Sanitation	OSUST199	468224
06 Oct	Norway	USA (United States)	Air Transport	122UNTS319	200413
10 Oct	Denmark	Norway	Visas	104UNTS335	200323
11 Oct	Norway	UK Great Britain	Milit Installation	2NORT430	451149
11 Oct	Greece	UK Great Britain	Reparations	183UNTS329	200509
13 Oct	Dominican Republic	USA (United States)	Education	149UNTS361	200477
15 Oct	USA (United States)	USSR (Soviet Union)	Milit Assistance	278UNTS151	200547
22 Oct	Czechoslovakia	USSR (Soviet Union)	Postal Service	OSUST200	468099
23 Oct	Czechoslovakia	Sweden	Admin Cooperation	46SOFM313	461036
23 Oct	Belgium	Norway	Claims and Debts	183UNTS337	200510
23 Oct	Belgium	Norway	Finance	16UNTS311	200107
24 Oct	Austria	USSR (Soviet Union)	Consul/Citizenship	OSUST200	468050

DATE	PARTY ONE	PARTY TWO	TOPIC	CITATION	NUMBER
1945 (Cont.)					
24 Oct	Netherlands	USSR (Soviet Union)	General Trade	16SUGG62	469883
24 Oct	Denmark	UK Great Britain	Milit Assistance	93UNTS143	101297
24 Oct	Netherlands	Switzerland	Finance	3UNTS73	100025
25 Oct	Belgium	Canada	Finance	230UNTS127	103180
25 Oct	Guatemala	USA (United States)	Postal Service	139UNTS45	101875
26 Oct	Finland	USSR (Soviet Union)	Territory Boundary	0SUST200	468133
26 Oct	South Africa	UK Great Britain	Air Transport	72UNTS41	100927
30 Oct	Belgium	France	Reparations	19UNTS87	100306
01 Nov	Czechoslovakia	UK Great Britain	Finance	5UNTS15	100062
05 Nov	UK Great Britain	USA (United States)	IGO Establishment	138UNTS75	101861
06 Nov	Netherlands	Norway	Finance	2UNTS5	100017
07 Nov	Multilateral		IGO Establishment	2UNTS17	100018
08 Nov	Mexico	USA (United States)	Specific Resources	46MEXD3003	444019
08 Nov	France	USA (United States)	General Trade	76UNTS151	100986
08 Nov	Norway	UK Great Britain	Finance	5UNTS27	100063
10 Nov	Albania	USSR (Soviet Union)	Consul/Citizenship	0SUST201	471019
13 Nov	USSR (Soviet Union)	Yugoslavia	Scientific Project	116UNTS139	101573
15 Nov	Czechoslovakia	Sweden	Air Transport	45SOFM71	461005
15 Nov	Multilateral		Atomic Energy	3UNTS123	100026
16 Nov	Multilateral		IGO Establishment	4UNTS275	100052
17 Nov	Czechoslovakia	Sweden	General Trade	45SOFM137	461015
17 Nov	Czechoslovakia	Sweden	Finance	45SOFM138	461016
23 Nov	Poland	USSR (Soviet Union)	Land Transport	0SUST201	468310
23 Nov	Poland	Yugoslavia	General Economic	115UNTS3	101555
24 Nov	Italy	Sweden	General Trade	45SOFM143	461017
24 Nov	Italy	Sweden	Finance	45SOFM146	461018
26 Nov	Greece	UK Great Britain	Air Transport	35UNTS161	100555
27 Nov	Belgium	USSR (Soviet Union)	Admin Cooperation	0SUST212	468022
27 Nov	Finland	Norway	Finance	17UNTS247	100279
30 Nov	Netherlands	Sweden	General Trade	45SOFM151	461019
30 Nov	Greece	UK Great Britain	Reparations	183UNTS197	102428
30 Nov	USSR (Soviet Union)	Yugoslavia	General Trade	116UNTS153	101574
30 Nov	Netherlands	Sweden	Finance	2UNTS27	100019
03 Dec	Switzerland	Syria	Recognition	11SWRS708	463022
03 Dec	Lebanon	Switzerland	Recognition	11SWRS673	463021
03 Dec	Colombia	USA (United States)	Military Mission	107UNTS3	101462
04 Dec	France	UK Great Britain	Milit Installation	9UNTS121	100129
04 Dec	Multilateral		Telecommunications	9UNTS101	100128
04 Dec	Sweden	USA (United States)	Air Transport	6UNTS273	100080
06 Dec	UK Great Britain	USA (United States)	Finance	126UNTS13	101679
06 Dec	Portugal	UK Great Britain	Air Transport	6UNTS3	100065
06 Dec	Portugal	UK Great Britain·	Air Transport	5UNTS37	100064
06 Dec	Denmark	UK Great Britain	Finance	5UNTS3	100061
06 Dec	Portugal	USA (United States)	Air Transport	3UNTS139	100028
06 Dec	Italy	USA (United States)	General Trade	3UNTS131	100027
08 Dec	Czechoslovakia	France	Education	46UNTS77	100701
10 Dec	UK Great Britain	USA (United States)	Refugees	3UNTS177	100030
10 Dec	Costa Rica	USA (United States)	Military Mission	3UNTS157	100029
13 Dec	Czechoslovakia	Norway	Finance	17UNTS261	100280
15 Dec	Romania	Yugoslavia	General Economic	116UNTS3	101565
20 Dec	Netherlands	UK Great Britain	Milit Assistance	4UNTS303	100053
21 Dec	Canada	UK Great Britain	Air Transport	27UNTS155	100405
26 Dec	Multilateral		Peace/Disarmament	20UNTS259	100319
27 Dec	Multilateral		IGO Establishment	2UNTS39	100020
28 Dec	Honduras	USA (United States)	Military Mission	3UNTS185	100031
29 Dec	France	USSR (Soviet Union)	General Trade	0SUST205	468151
29 Dec	France	USA (United States)	Air Transport	139UNTS105	101878
31 Dec	Finland	USSR (Soviet Union)	Reparations	0SUST205	471020
1946					
01 Jan	Multilateral		Peace/Disarmament	99UNTS131	101375
02 Jan	Poland	Yugoslavia	Visas	115UNTS21	101556
03 Jan	Czechoslovakia	USA (United States)	Air Transport	6UNTS309	100084
04 Jan	Denmark	France	Air Transport	27UNTS169	100406
04 Jan	Multilateral		IGO Establishment	6UNTS35	100066

DATE	PARTY ONE	PARTY TWO	TOPIC	CITATION	NUMBER
1946 (Cont.)					
05 Jan	United Arab Rep	USA (United States)	Status of Forces	160UNTS27	102098
06 Jan	Taiwan	Ecuador	General Amity	7UNTS233	100102
07 Jan	Belgium	Portugal	Finance	19UNTS159	100310
11 Jan	Greece	USA (United States)	General Trade	3UNTS203	100032
14 Jan	Multilateral		Reparations	555UNTS69	108105
15 Jan	Spain	USA (United States)	Air Transport	89UNTS241	101221
18 Jan	Poland	Yugoslavia	General Trade	115UNTS83	101559
21 Jan	Lebanon	USA (United States)	Postal Service	140UNTS73	101884
23 Jan	Taiwan	Thailand	General Amity	161UNTS127	102126
24 Jan	Czechoslovakia	Poland	Air Transport	25UNTS181	100363
24 Jan	Greece	UK Great Britain	Finance	6UNTS45	100067
26 Jan	Spain	Sweden	General Economic	46SOFM169	461020
26 Jan	France	UK Great Britain	Reparations	91UNTS183	101251
30 Jan	Brazil	Venezuela	Consul/Citizenship	65UNTS107	100839
31 Jan	Denmark	Netherlands	Finance	3UNTS3	100021
04 Feb	Costa Rica	Mexico	General Trade	50MEXD1810	444007
05 Feb	USA (United States)	USSR (Soviet Union)	General Ad Hoc	0SUST206	468432
05 Feb	Canada	Netherlands	General Trade	230UNTS199	103184
05 Feb	Canada	Netherlands	Finance	43UNTS3	100658
07 Feb	Canada	Taiwan	Finance	43UNTS23	100659
07 Feb	Mexico	UK Great Britain	Claims and Debts	6UNTS55	100068
07 Feb	France	USA (United States)	Commodity Trade	3UNTS239	100034
07 Feb	Mexico	Netherlands	Specif Claim/Waive	3UNTS13	100022
08 Feb	Poland	USSR (Soviet Union)	Loans and Credits	0SUST206	468311
08 Feb	Canada	Mexico	General Trade	230UNTS183	103183
09 Feb	Netherlands	USA (United States)	Commodity Trade	3UNTS247	100035
11 Feb	UK Great Britain	USA (United States)	Air Transport	3UNTS253	100036
11 Feb	Netherlands	USA (United States)	Claims and Debts	3UNTS37	100023
12 Feb	Syria	Turkey	Air Transport	49TURG1712	466138
12 Feb	Czechoslovakia	Poland	Reparations	25UNTS207	100364
12 Feb	Turkey	USA (United States)	Air Transport	13UNTS3	100196
12 Feb	Turkey	UK Great Britain	Air Transport	6UNTS79	100069
13 Feb	Multilateral		IGO Status/Immunit	1UNTS15	100004
13 Feb	ICJ Option Clause	UK Great Britain	ICJ Option Clause	1UNTS3	100001
15 Feb	Romania	USSR (Soviet Union)	Finance	0SUST206	468361
15 Feb	Romania	USSR (Soviet Union)	Mostfavored Nation	0SUST206	468362
15 Feb	Brazil	USA (United States)	Education	162UNTS21	102130
16 Feb	Poland	Sweden	General Economic	46SOFM183	461021
19 Feb	Colombia	USA (United States)	Sanitation	166UNTS104	102187
21 Feb	Belgium	Norway	General Trade	31UNTS435	100485
21 Feb	Belgium	Norway	Finance	31UNTS199	100479
21 Feb	UK Great Britain	USA (United States)	General Trade	6UNTS137	100073
22 Feb	Belgium	France	Culture	68UNTS157	100892
27 Feb	Turkey	USA (United States)	Loans and Credits	46TURG1005	466117
27 Feb	Mongolia	USSR (Soviet Union)	General Economic	216UNTS221	102938
27 Feb	Mongolia	USSR (Soviet Union)	General Military	48UNTS177	100744
28 Feb	France	UK Great Britain	Air Transport	27UNTS173	100407
28 Feb	Taiwan	France	Milit Occupation	14UNTS151	100217
28 Feb	Taiwan	France	General Amity	14UNTS137	100216
28 Feb	Taiwan	France	Privil/Immunities	14UNTS113	100215
01 Mar	UK Great Britain	USA (United States)	Commodity Trade	3UNTS293	100037
03 Mar	Canada	USA (United States)	Specific Property	6UNTS279	100081
05 Mar	Mexico	USA (United States)	Claims and Debts	120UNTS3	101612
06 Mar	Canada	UK Great Britain	Finance	20UNTS13	100312
06 Mar	Canada	UK Great Britain	Reparations	20UNTS3	100311
06 Mar	France	Norway	Finance	15UNTS13	100227
11 Mar	ILO (Labor Org)	Switzerland	IGO Status/Immunit	15UNTS377	200103
11 Mar	Belgium	UK Great Britain	Status of Forces	26UNTS167	100387
12 Mar	Switzerland	UK Great Britain	Finance	6UNTS107	100070
13 Mar	Netherlands	USA (United States)	Visas	84UNTS3	101113
13 Mar	Taiwan	Switzerland	Consul/Citizenship	14UNTS159	100218
16 Mar	Poland	Yugoslavia	Culture	10UNTS11	100139
18 Mar	Switzerland	USSR (Soviet Union)	Consul/Citizenship	0SUST207	468413
18 Mar	Poland	Yugoslavia	General Military	1UNTS53	100013
20 Mar	Poland	USSR (Soviet Union)	Gen Communications	0SUST207	468312

DATE	PARTY ONE	PARTY TWO	TOPIC	CITATION	NUMBER
1946 (Cont.)					
20 Mar	Romania	USSR (Soviet Union)	Specific Property	0SUST208	468363
21 Mar	Greece	UK Great Britain	Claims and Debts	91UNTS149	101247
21 Mar	Denmark	USA (United States)	Air Transport	3UNTS301	100038
22 Mar	Canada	France	Reparations	230UNTS165	103182
22 Mar	Jordan	UK Great Britain	General Amity	6UNTS143	100074
26 Mar	France	Norway	General Trade	31UNTS69	100468
27 Mar	Brazil	Taiwan	Culture	0CTRC43	413001
27 Mar	France	Netherlands	Visas	247UNTS3	103456
27 Mar	France	USA (United States)	Air Transport	139UNTS114	101879
27 Mar	Greece	USA (United States)	Air Transport	15UNTS233	100239
27 Mar	UK Great Britain	USA (United States)	Patents/Copyrights	4UNTS101	100040
27 Mar	UK Great Britain	USA (United States)	Milit Assistance	4UNTS2	100039
29 Mar	Hungary	USSR (Soviet Union)	Specific Property	0SUST208	468175
29 Mar	Hungary	USSR (Soviet Union)	Specific Property	0SUST208	468174
29 Mar	USA (United States)	Venezuela	Specific Resources	124UNTS57	101666
29 Mar	Iraq	Turkey	Extradition	37UNTS369	100582
29 Mar	Iraq	Turkey	Admin Cooperation	37UNTS333	100581
29 Mar	Iraq	Turkey	General Amity	37UNTS226	100580
30 Mar	Greece	United Arab Rep	Reparations	187UNTS263	102518
30 Mar	Denmark	Norway	General Trade	29UNTS163	100438
30 Mar	Canada	USA (United States)	Milit Installation	7UNTS15	100089
31 Mar	Multilateral		Milit Installation	17UNTS159	100274
01 Apr	Philippines	USA (United States)	Specific Property	1PTS393	465007
05 Apr	Austria	UNRRA (Relief)	Direct Aid	46ABGB116	403205
05 Apr	Multilateral		Specific Resources	231UNTS199	103221
05 Apr	Ireland	UK Great Britain	Air Transport	72UNTS57	100928
05 Apr	Brazil	USA (United States)	Education	12UNTS131	100183
05 Apr	Belgium	USA (United States)	Air Transport	4UNTS125	100041
06 Apr	France	USSR (Soviet Union)	Commodity Trade	0SUST209	471021
08 Apr	Hungary	USSR (Soviet Union)	Specific Property	0SUST209	468177
08 Apr	Hungary	USSR (Soviet Union)	Specific Property	0SUST209	468176
08 Apr	Belgium	Denmark	Claims and Debts	4UNTS429	100059
09 Apr	Canada	France	Finance	43UNTS43	100660
09 Apr	France	Netherlands	Finance	3UNTS57	100024
12 Apr	Poland	USSR (Soviet Union)	General Trade	0SUST210	468313
12 Apr	Czechoslovakia	USSR (Soviet Union)	General Trade	0SUST210	468100
12 Apr	Czechoslovakia	USSR (Soviet Union)	Claims and Debts	0SUST210	468101
12 Apr	Mexico	USA (United States)	Scientific Project	66UNTS293	100861
12 Apr	Netherlands	Portugal	Air Transport	4UNTS317	100054
15 Apr	Romania	USSR (Soviet Union)	Reparations	0SUST210	468364
16 Apr	Portugal	UK Great Britain	Finance	6UNTS119	100071
17 Apr	Belgium	France	Land Transport	49FRJO1509	416276
17 Apr	Italy	USA (United States)	Extradition	206UNTS263	102791
17 Apr	Argentina	UK Great Britain	Air Transport	164UNTS53	102159
17 Apr	Multilateral		Land Transport	27UNTS103	100402
17 Apr	Belgium	UK Great Britain	Health/Educ/Welfare	6UNTS177	100075
18 Apr	USA (United States)	USSR (Soviet Union)	General Ad Hoc	0SUST210	468433
22 Apr	Poland	USA (United States)	Loans and Credits	406UNTS215	105851
23 Apr	USA (United States)	USSR (Soviet Union)	Culture	0SUST210	468434
23 Apr	USA (United States)	Uruguay	Sanitation	160UNTS103	102104
23 Apr	Multilateral		Sanitation	17UNTS3	100265
23 Apr	Multilateral		Sanitation	16UNTS179	100257
24 Apr	Sweden	Turkey	Finance	46SOFM192	461023
24 Apr	Sweden	Turkey	General Trade	45SOFM191	461022
24 Apr	Sweden	Turkey	General Economic	46TURG2312	466088
24 Apr	France	Greece	Finance	91UNTS83	101243
24 Apr	Poland	USA (United States)	General Economic	4UNTS155	100042
26 Apr	USSR (Soviet Union)	Yugoslavia	General Trade	116UNTS163	101575
29 Apr	France	UK Great Britain	Finance	98UNTS123	101360
30 Apr	Finland	USSR (Soviet Union)	Specific Property	0SUST211	468134
30 Apr	France	Portugal	Air Transport	35UNTS197	100556
01 May	Thailand	UK Great Britain	Commodity Trade	99UNTS169	101377
01 May	Thailand	UK Great Britain	Commodity Trade	99UNTS175	101378
03 May	Denmark	Netherlands	General Trade	52NET139	447001
03 May	New Zealand	Norway	Claims and Debts	16UNTS211	100262

DATE	PARTY ONE	PARTY TWO	TOPIC	CITATION	NUMBER
1946 (Cont.)					
04 May	League of Nations	ILO (Labor Org)	IGO Operations	19UNTS187	200114
04 May	USA (United States)	Yemen	General Economic	4UNTS165	100043
06 May	Multilateral		Commodity Trade	157UNTS85	102049
06 May	Thailand	UK Great Britain	Commodity Trade	99UNTS193	101380
06 May	Multilateral		Commodity Trade	99UNTS181	101379
06 May	UK Great Britain	USA (United States)	Admin Cooperation	99UNTS199	101381
07 May	Turkey	USA (United States)	Milit Assistance	6UNTS293	100083
07 May	UK Great Britain	USA (United States)	Water Transport	6UNTS285	100082
09 May	Czechoslovakia	Yugoslavia	General Military	1UNTS67	100014
11 May	Hungary	Yugoslavia	Reparations	129UNTS3	101725
14 May	Haiti	USA (United States)	Finance	4UNTS179	100044
15 May	Finland	Turkey	General Economic	46TURG2312	466052
16 May	Greece	USA (United States)	Direct Aid	184UNTS230	102451
16 May	France	Ireland	Air Transport	44UNTS105	100681
16 May	Belgium	Netherlands	Culture	17UNTS13	100266
16 May	India	USA (United States)	Milit Assistance	4UNTS183	100045
17 May	Portugal	USA (United States)	Commodity Trade	126UNTS3	101678
18 May	Iceland	Sweden	General Trade	46SOFM197	461024
20 May	Taiwan	Denmark	Privil/Immunities	12UNTS59	100180
21 May	Denmark	Luxembourg	Claims and Debts	4UNTS435	100060
24 May	Belgium	Netherlands	Finance	31UNTS169	100477
24 May	USA (United States)	USSR (Soviet Union)	Telecommunications	4UNTS201	100046
28 May	France	USA (United States)	Status of Forces	84UNTS141	101124
28 May	France	USA (United States)	General Trade	84UNTS151	101125
28 May	France	USA (United States)	Mass Media	84UNTS161	101126
28 May	France	USA (United States)	General Economic	84UNTS167	101127
28 May	France	USA (United States)	Reparations	84UNTS93	101121
28 May	France	USA (United States)	Milit Assistance	84UNTS79	101120
28 May	France	USA (United States)	Reparations	84UNTS113	101122
28 May	France	USA (United States)	Milit Assistance	84UNTS59	101119
28 May	France	USA (United States)	Status of Forces	84UNTS121	101123
29 May	Ireland	Sweden	Air Transport	35UNTS231	100557
30 May	Portugal	USA (United States)	Air Transport	174UNTS187	102285
03 Jun	Multilateral		Commodity Trade	7UNTS331	100109
03 Jun	USA (United States)	Venezuela	Military Mission	4UNTS215	100047
05 Jun	Argentina	USSR (Soviet Union)	General Amity	0SUST212	468018
05 Jun	Canada	UK Great Britain	Taxation	86UNTS3	101147
05 Jun	Canada	UK Great Britain	Taxation	27UNTS207	100408
06 Jun	Canada	Norway	Finance	43UNTS67	100661
07 Jun	Bulgaria	Turkey	General Trade	46TURG2112	466048
07 Jun	Australia	USA (United States)	Milit Assistance	4UNTS237	100048
08 Jun	USSR (Soviet Union)	Yugoslavia	General Trade	0SUST213	468461
10 Jun	Bolivia	USA (United States)	Mostfavored Nation	13UNTS19	100197
11 Jun	Ecuador	USA (United States)	Status of Forces	167UNTS135	102203
11 Jun	Australia	Canada	Air Transport	10UNTS47	100142
13 Jun	Afghanistan	USSR (Soviet Union)	Territory Boundary	31UNTS147	100476
14 Jun	Taiwan	USA (United States)	Milit Assistance	4UNTS253	100049
15 Jun	United Arab Rep	USA (United States)	Air Transport	71UNTS157	100917
15 Jun	United Arab Rep	USA (United States)	Air Transport	151UNTS135	101988
18 Jun	France	USA (United States)	Air Transport	42UNTS183	100647
23 Jun	Italy	Sweden	General Trade	46SOFM199	461025
23 Jun	Belgium	Italy	Non-ILO Labor	19UNTS65	100305
24 Jun	Poland	UK Great Britain	Claims and Debts	11UNTS59	100149
25 Jun	Chile	UK Great Britain	General Trade	91UNTS137	101246
26 Jun	Romania	Yugoslavia	Finance	116UNTS21	101566
26 Jun	Sweden	Turkey	Air Transport	14UNTS21	100208
26 Jun	Netherlands	ICJ (Int Court)	IGO Status/Immunit	8UNTS61	100114
27 Jun	Multilateral		ILO Labor	264UNTS163	103792
27 Jun	Multilateral		ILO Labor	164UNTS37	102157
28 Jun	France	Sweden	Finance	46SOFM203	461027
28 Jun	France	Sweden	General Trade	46SOFM201	461026
28 Jun	Multilateral		ILO Labor	442UNTS235	106352
28 Jun	Multilateral		Milit Occupation	138UNTS85	101862
28 Jun	Canada	Czechoslovakia	Finance	43UNTS81	100662
28 Jun	Romania	USA (United States)	Other Military	148UNTS355	101944

DATE	PARTY ONE	PARTY TWO	TOPIC	CITATION	NUMBER
1946 (Cont.)					
28 Jun	Brazil	USA (United States)	Milit Assistance	6UNTS327	100085
28 Jun	Taiwan	USA (United States)	Milit Assistance	34UNTS121	100532
29 Jun	Netherlands	Sweden	General Trade	46SOFM204	461028
29 Jun	France	Switzerland	Refugees	47FRJO2905	416404
29 Jun	Multilateral		ILO Labor	214UNTS233	102901
29 Jun	Multilateral		ILO Labor	94UNTS11	101303
01 Jul	United Nations	Switzerland	Specific Property	1UNTS153	200007
01 Jul	United Nations	Switzerland	IGO Status/Immunit	1UNTS163	200008
01 Jul	Albania	Yugoslavia	Loans and Credits	111UNTS81	101518
01 Jul	Albania	Yugoslavia	General Economic	111UNTS3	101517
03 Jul	Luxembourg	USA (United States)	Mostfavored Nation	32UNTS85	100491
04 Jul	Philippines	USA (United States)	General Trade	43UNTS135	100668
04 Jul	Ethiopia	USA (United States)	Mostfavored Nation	13UNTS27	100198
04 Jul	Philippines	USA (United States)	General Amity	7UNTS3	100088
04 Jul	Philippines	USA (United States)	General Amity	6UNTS335	100086
04 Jul	Iceland	UK Great Britain	Specific Property	6UNTS223	100077
08 Jul	Denmark	USSR (Soviet Union)	General Trade	OSUST214	468116
08 Jul	Norway	USA (United States)	Mostfavored Nation	13UNTS35	100199
08 Jul	Denmark	Norway	Territory Boundary	7UNTS247	100103
09 Jul	UK Great Britain	USSR (Soviet Union)	Telecommunications	OSUST214	468429
10 Jul	Czechoslovakia	USSR (Soviet Union)	Consul/Citizenship	OSUST214	468102
10 Jul	New Zealand	USA (United States)	Milit Assistance	6UNTS341	100087
11 Jul	Spain	USA (United States)	Mostfavored Nation	13UNTS51	100201
11 Jul	Belgium	USA (United States)	Mostfavored Nation	13UNTS43	100200
11 Jul	Albania	Yugoslavia	Air Transport	4UNTS407	100058
13 Jul	Belgium	Canada	Reparations	230UNTS159	103181
13 Jul	Netherlands	Spain	Air Transport	4UNTS351	100055
16 Jul	Austria	USSR (Soviet Union)	Claims and Debts	OSUST215	468049
16 Jul	Spain	Vatican/Holy See	Non-ILO Labor	53SPBO1911	460268
17 Jul	Spain	Switzerland	Air Transport	47SPBO2004	460250
18 Jul	Multilateral		Reparations	125UNTS119	101674
18 Jul	France	USA (United States)	Reparations	125UNTS165	101675
19 Jul	Multilateral		IGO Operations	1UNTS97	200001
19 Jul	League of Nations	United Nations	Specific Property	1UNTS109	200002
20 Jul	Italy	Norway	General Trade	30UNTS177	100456
20 Jul	Italy	Norway	Finance	17UNTS273	100281
22 Jul	Multilateral		IGO Establishment	14UNTS185	100221
22 Jul	Multilateral		IGO Establishment	9UNTS3	100125
25 Jul	Mexico	Venezuela	Culture	48MEXD1011	444043
25 Jul	Czechoslovakia	USSR (Soviet Union)	Air Transport	27UNTS231	100409
26 Jul	Hungary	Sweden	General Trade	46SOFM247	461029
26 Jul	Hungary	Sweden	Finance	46SOFM250	461030
27 Jul	Multilateral		Patents/Copyrights	90UNTS229	101238
29 Jul	Czechoslovakia	Sweden	Finance	46SOFM255	461032
29 Jul	Czechoslovakia	Sweden	General Trade	46SOFM253	461031
29 Jul	Canada	Newfoundland	Air Transport	17UNTS169	100275
30 Jul	Chile	USA (United States)	General Trade	7UNTS41	100090
31 Jul	League of Nations	United Nations	Specific Property	1UNTS119	200003
31 Jul	UK Great Britain	USA (United States)	Air Transport	42UNTS199	100648
01 Aug	France	Switzerland	Customs	12SWRS656	463071
01 Aug	France	Switzerland	Non-ILO Labor	11SWRS615	463015
01 Aug	France	Switzerland	Non-ILO Labor	11SWRS623	463018
01 Aug	France	Switzerland	Non-ILO Labor	11SWRS621	463016
01 Aug	League of Nations	United Nations	Specific Property	1UNTS131	200004
01 Aug	League of Nations	United Nations	Specific Property	1UNTS135	200005
02 Aug	France	Sweden	Air Transport	27UNTS251	100410
02 Aug	Iraq	UK Great Britain	Consul/Citizenship	14UNTS93	100213
03 Aug	Netherlands	Yugoslavia	Finance	52NET25	447002
04 Aug	Philippines	USA (United States)	General Trade	1PTS243	465001
05 Aug	ICJ Option Clause	Netherlands	ICJ Option Clause	1UNTS7	100002
08 Aug	Denmark	USSR (Soviet Union)	Telecommunications	OSUST217	468117
08 Aug	Philippines	USA (United States)	General Trade	1PTS251	465002
08 Aug	Iran	USA (United States)	Military Mission	31UNTS423	100484
09 Aug	Hungary	USA (United States)	Other Military	148UNTS313	101941
11 Aug	Lebanon	USA (United States)	Air Transport	66UNTS211	100856

DATE	PARTY ONE	PARTY TWO	TOPIC	CITATION	NUMBER
1946 (Cont.)					
12 Aug	Ceylon (Sri Lanka)	India	Postal Service	196UNTS209	102626
12 Aug	Hungary	UK Great Britain	Finance	89UNTS219	101220
13 Aug	Netherlands	UK Great Britain	Air Transport	4UNTS367	100056
14 Aug	ICJ Option Clause	USA (United States)	ICJ Option Clause	1UNTS9	100003
15 Aug	United Arab Rep	USA (United States)	Mostfavored Nation	13UNTS59	100202
16 Aug	Norway	Portugal	Commodity Trade	30UNTS215	100459
16 Aug	Denmark	UK Great Britain	Milit Installation	9UNTS163	100130
17 Aug	Denmark	USSR (Soviet Union)	Finance	16SUGG63	469884
17 Aug	Denmark	USSR (Soviet Union)	Dispute Settlement	OSUST217	468118
17 Aug	Denmark	USSR (Soviet Union)	General Economic	8UNTS201	100124
19 Aug	Japan	USSR (Soviet Union)	Refugees	OSUST224	468242
19 Aug	USA (United States)	USSR (Soviet Union)	Admin Cooperation	OSUST218	468435
19 Aug	Finland	USSR (Soviet Union)	Postal Service	OSUST217	468137
19 Aug	Finland	USSR (Soviet Union)	Telecommunications	OSUST217	468135
19 Aug	Peru	USA (United States)	Military Mission	109UNTS15	101485
21 Aug	Italy	Vatican/Holy See	Admin Cooperation	60ITMA422	437336
22 Aug	Philippines	USA (United States)	Reparations	1PTS255	465003
24 Aug	South Africa	UK Great Britain	Telecommunications	51UNTS187	100765
26 Aug	Portugal	USA (United States)	Mostfavored Nation	13UNTS67	100203
27 Aug	Hungary	Norway	General Trade	31UNTS3	100465
28 Aug	Multilateral		IGO Operations	1UNTS139	200006
29 Aug	Poland	USA (United States)	Status of Forces	160UNTS11	102097
29 Aug	Luxembourg	USA (United States)	Reparations	140UNTS101	101885
30 Aug	Norway	Yugoslavia	General Trade	30UNTS187	100457
30 Aug	Norway	Yugoslavia	Finance	15UNTS163	100232
30 Aug	Taiwan	USA (United States)	Direct Aid	12UNTS39	100179
31 Aug	France	Turkey	General Economic	47FRJO310	416467
31 Aug	Norway	UK Great Britain	Air Transport	6UNTS235	100078
03 Sep	Multilateral		Commodity Trade	139UNTS3	101872
05 Sep	Austria	Italy	Peace/Disarmament	47ITGU295	435027
06 Sep	Brazil	USA (United States)	Air Transport	54UNTS197	100805
10 Sep	Denmark	USA (United States)	Mostfavored Nation	13UNTS75	100204
11 Sep	Philippines	USA (United States)	Milit Assistance	43UNTS231	100670
12 Sep	Paraguay	USA (United States)	General Trade	125UNTS179	101677
12 Sep	Luxembourg	USA (United States)	Reparations	149UNTS19	101947
16 Sep	Australia	Sweden	General Trade	10UNTS63	100143
16 Sep	Netherlands	UK Great Britain	Finance	4UNTS401	100057
17 Sep	Argentina	UK Great Britain	General Economic	88UNTS47	101185
17 Sep	Philippines	USA (United States)	IGO Establishment	15UNTS249	100240
17 Sep	Brazil	USA (United States)	Military Mission	7UNTS49	100091
18 Sep	Denmark	New Zealand	Claims and Debts	10UNTS39	100141
19 Sep	Argentina	USA (United States)	Commodity Trade	7UNTS131	100095
24 Sep	Belgium	USA (United States)	Claims and Debts	132UNTS80	101753
24 Sep	Italy	USA (United States)	Other Military	148UNTS323	101942
25 Sep	Monaco	Netherlands	Visas	247UNTS199	103469
26 Sep	Canada	Taiwan	General Trade	14UNTS167	100219
27 Sep	Mexico	UK Great Britain	Consul/Citizenship	91UNTS161	101248
27 Sep	Canada	USA (United States)	Patents/Copyrights	21UNTS3	100320
27 Sep	Norway	UK Great Britain	Milit Installation	6UNTS259	100079
30 Sep	Haiti	USA (United States)	Other Ad Hoc	15UNTS257	100241
30 Sep	Sweden	USA (United States)	Air Transport	42UNTS213	100649
01 Oct	Denmark	USA (United States)	Air Transport	42UNTS219	100650
03 Oct	Spain	Sweden	General Trade	46SOFM257	461033
03 Oct	Albania	Yugoslavia	General Trade	111UNTS227	101537
03 Oct	Albania	Yugoslavia	Loans and Credits	111UNTS87	101519
03 Oct	USA (United States)	Yugoslavia	Mostfavored Nation	13UNTS83	100205
04 Oct	Philippines	USA (United States)	Specif Goods/Equip	1PTS271	465004
07 Oct	Sweden	USSR (Soviet Union)	General Trade	OSUST218	468404
07 Oct	Sweden	USSR (Soviet Union)	General Trade	OSUST219	468406
07 Oct	Sweden	USSR (Soviet Union)	Claims and Debts	OSUST219	468407
07 Oct	Sweden	USSR (Soviet Union)	Loans and Credits	OSUST218	468405
07 Oct	Dominican Republic	USA (United States)	Mostfavored Nation	13UNTS91	100206
07 Oct	Iceland	USA (United States)	Milit Installation	12UNTS163	100184
07 Oct	Peru	USA (United States)	Military Mission	7UNTS71	100092
08 Oct	Greece	USA (United States)	Claims and Debts	180UNTS119	102379

DATE	PARTY ONE	PARTY TWO	TOPIC	CITATION	NUMBER
1946 (Cont.)					
09 Oct	Multilateral		ILO Labor	78UNTS213	101018
09 Oct	Multilateral		ILO Labor	78UNTS198	101017
09 Oct	Multilateral		ILO Labor	78UNTS227	101019
09 Oct	Multilateral		ILO Labor	38UNTS3	100583
09 Oct	Multilateral		IGO Establishment	15UNTS35	100229
12 Oct	Belgium	Netherlands	Claims and Debts	23UNTS179	100347
12 Oct	France	Turkey	Air Transport	14UNTS33	100209
14 Oct	South Africa	UK Great Britain	Taxation	86UNTS51	101152
14 Oct	South Africa	UK Great Britain	Taxation	86UNTS77	101153
14 Oct	Denmark	South Africa	Claims and Debts	10UNTS29	100140
14 Oct	Colombia	USA (United States)	Military Mission	7UNTS97	100093
15 Oct	Multilateral		Refugees	11UNTS73	100150
18 Oct	France	USA (United States)	Taxation	140UNTS23	101882
19 Oct	Philippines	USA (United States)	Telecommunications	43UNTS263	100672
21 Oct	Netherlands	Spain	Finance	46SPBO3010	460208
21 Oct	France	Turkey	General Trade	48TURG2302	466060
21 Oct	Netherlands	Spain	General Trade	46SPBO3010	460207
22 Oct	Czechoslovakia	Sweden	Admin Cooperation	200UNTS31	102692
22 Oct	Mexico	USA (United States)	Non-IBRD Project	21UNTS13	100321
22 Oct	Belgium	Portugal	Air Transport	34UNTS49	100527
25 Oct	Sweden	USSR (Soviet Union)	Air Transport	OSUST220	468408
25 Oct	Sweden	USSR (Soviet Union)	Air Transport	OSUST220	468409
26 Oct	Philippines	Switzerland	General Trade	1PTS319	465005
26 Oct	Poland	Sweden	General Economic	46SOFM311	461035
26 Oct	France	Monaco	Reparations	60FRJO44	416328
26 Oct	ICJ Option Clause	Taiwan	ICJ Option Clause	1UNTS35	100005
29 Oct	Australia	UK Great Britain	Taxation	17UNTS181	100276
30 Oct	Multilateral		IGO Establishment	27UNTS77	100401
30 Oct	Multilateral		IGO Establishment	11UNTS107	100151
31 Oct	Brazil	UK Great Britain	Air Transport	11UNTS115	100152
02 Nov	Syria	UK Great Britain	Dispute Settlement	11UNTS153	100153
04 Nov	Taiwan	USA (United States)	General Amity	25UNTS69	100359
05 Nov	Sweden	USSR (Soviet Union)	Postal Service	OSUST221	468410
12 Nov	Norway	USA (United States)	Air Transport	42UNTS227	100651
14 Nov	India	USA (United States)	Air Transport	22UNTS55	100331
14 Nov	Czechoslovakia	USA (United States)	General Trade	7UNTS119	100094
15 Nov	Int Bureau Educ	Switzerland	IGO Status/Immunit	56SWRO1210	462187
15 Nov	Czechoslovakia	Netherlands	Finance	51NET162	447003
15 Nov	Mexico	USA (United States)	Non-ILO Labor	105UNTS3	101450
15 Nov	Taiwan	Saudi Arabia	General Amity	18UNTS197	100289
15 Nov	Canada	USA (United States)	Specif Claim/Waive	7UNTS141	100096
16 Nov	Philippines	USA (United States)	Dispute Settlement	1PTS321	465006
16 Nov	Philippines	USA (United States)	Air Transport	7UNTS151	100097
16 Nov	ICJ Option Clause	Norway	ICJ Option Clause	1UNTS37	100006
17 Nov	France	Thailand	Admin Cooperation	47FRJO1503	416448
17 Nov	France	Thailand	Reparations	344UNTS59	104943
18 Nov	Denmark	Sweden	Non-ILO Labor	7UNTS251	100104
19 Nov	Mexico	Nicaragua	Telecommunications	51MEXD1105	444031
19 Nov	France	Netherlands	Culture	32UNTS101	100493
19 Nov	Accept UN Charter	Sweden	UN Charter	1UNTS43	100009
19 Nov	Accept UN Charter	Iceland	UN Charter	1UNTS41	100008
19 Nov	Accept UN Charter	Afghanistan	UN Charter	1UNTS39	100007
20 Nov	Czechoslovakia	France	Reparations	48FRJO1501	416436
21 Nov	Netherlands	USA (United States)	General Trade	12UNTS173	100185
22 Nov	Norway	Sweden	Specific Resources	46SOFM307	461034
22 Nov	Switzerland	USA (United States)	Claims and Debts	14SWRS351	463111
22 Nov	Peru	USA (United States)	Non-IBRD Project	100UNTS170	101396
22 Nov	Norway	Sweden	Finance	15UNTS171	100233
27 Nov	Sweden	UK Great Britain	Air Transport	11UNTS229	100162
28 Nov	Albania	Yugoslavia	Land Transport	111UNTS139	101526
28 Nov	Albania	Yugoslavia	Finance	111UNTS171	101530
28 Nov	Albania	Yugoslavia	Non-IBRD Project	111UNTS105	101521
28 Nov	Albania	Yugoslavia	Non-IBRD Project	111UNTS151	101528
28 Nov	Albania	Yugoslavia	Non-IBRD Project	111UNTS123	101524
28 Nov	Albania	Yugoslavia	Non-IBRD Project	111UNTS109	101522

DATE	PARTY ONE	PARTY TWO	TOPIC	CITATION	NUMBER
1946 (Cont.)					
28 Nov	Albania	Yugoslavia	Non-IBRD Project	111UNTS113	101523
28 Nov	Albania	Yugoslavia	Non-IBRD Project	111UNTS93	101520
28 Nov	Albania	Yugoslavia	Non-IBRD Project	111UNTS127	101525
28 Nov	Albania	Yugoslavia	Finance	111UNTS143	101527
28 Nov	Albania	Yugoslavia	Non-ILO Labor	111UNTS163	101529
02 Dec	Multilateral		Specific Resources	161UNTS72	102124
02 Dec	Cuba	UK Great Britain	Admin Cooperation	11UNTS161	100154
02 Dec	UK Great Britain	USA (United States)	Milit Occupation	7UNTS163	100098
03 Dec	France	UK Great Britain	Finance	54UNTS117	100798
03 Dec	France	UK Great Britain	Reparations	54UNTS127	100799
03 Dec	Norway	Poland	Finance	15UNTS203	100234
03 Dec	Australia	USA (United States)	Air Transport	7UNTS201	100100
03 Dec	New Zealand	USA (United States)	Air Transport	7UNTS175	100099
04 Dec	Netherlands	UK Great Britain	Milit Installation	12UNTS241	100187
05 Dec	Finland	USSR (Soviet Union)	General Economic	OSUST222	468136
05 Dec	Bulgaria	Turkey	General Economic	47TURG2802	466049
06 Dec	Brazil	France	Culture	OUNTSO	110228
06 Dec	Canada	USA (United States)	Milit Assistance	149UNTS3	101945
07 Dec	Lebanon	Turkey	Consul/Citizenship	48TURG702	466007
07 Dec	Multilateral		Commodity Trade	157UNTS103	102050
09 Dec	Portugal	Switzerland	Air Transport	310UNTS251	104495
10 Dec	Brazil	Portugal	Air Transport	200UNTS67	102695
10 Dec	United Arab Rep	UK Great Britain	Specif Claim/Waive	105UNTS15	101451
10 Dec	France	USA (United States)	Visas	15UNTS265	100242
10 Dec	ICJ Option Clause	Denmark	ICJ Option Clause	1UNTS45	100010
11 Dec	Multilateral		Sanitation	12UNTS179	100186
11 Dec	Luxembourg	UK Great Britain	Claims and Debts	11UNTS167	100155
12 Dec	Denmark	Sweden	General Trade	47SOFM573	461057
13 Dec	South Africa	USA (United States)	Taxation	167UNTS171	102207
13 Dec	Multilateral		Trusteeship	8UNTS181	100122
13 Dec	Multilateral		Trusteeship	8UNTS165	100121
13 Dec	Multilateral		Trusteeship	8UNTS151	100120
13 Dec	Multilateral		Trusteeship	8UNTS135	100119
13 Dec	Multilateral		Trusteeship	8UNTS119	100118
13 Dec	Multilateral		Trusteeship	8UNTS105	100117
13 Dec	Multilateral		Trusteeship	8UNTS91	100116
13 Dec	Multilateral		Trusteeship	8UNTS71	100115
14 Dec	Taiwan	France	Air Transport	OCTRC160	413002
14 Dec	USA (United States)	Uruguay	Air Transport	532UNTS87	107713
14 Dec	France	UK Great Britain	Taxation	105UNTS27	101452
15 Dec	Multilateral		IGO Establishment	18UNTS3	100283
16 Dec	El Salvador	UK Great Britain	General Trade	6UNTS131	100072
16 Dec	Accept UN Charter	Thailand	UN Charter	1UNTS47	100011
19 Dec	ILO (Labor Org)	United Nations	IGO Operations	1UNTS183	200009
19 Dec	Canada	Nicaragua	General Trade	236UNTS229	103326
20 Dec	Taiwan	USA (United States)	Air Transport	22UNTS87	100332
20 Dec	Denmark	India	Reparations	7UNTS309	100107
23 Dec	Netherlands	Sweden	General Trade	47SOFM1	461037
23 Dec	Austria	UK Great Britain	General Aid	88UNTS93	101186
23 Dec	Hungary	Yugoslavia	Finance	113UNTS125	101549
23 Dec	Romania	Yugoslavia	Loans and Credits	116UNTS33	101567
23 Dec	Multilateral		Commodity Trade	126UNTS47	101681
24 Dec	Lebanon	Turkey	Visas	4UNTS269	100051
27 Dec	Peru	USA (United States)	Air Transport	152UNTS93	102013
27 Dec	Peru	USA (United States)	Air Transport	26UNTS227	100390
27 Dec	Norway	USSR (Soviet Union)	Finance	17UNTS283	100282
27 Dec	France	UK Great Britain	Visas	11UNTS255	100163
30 Dec	Belgium	Sweden	General Trade	47SOFM23	461038
30 Dec	Argentina	Uruguay	Specific Resources	OUNTSO	109540
30 Dec	Canada	Netherlands	Reparations	230UNTS205	103185
30 Dec	Belgium	Sweden	Claims and Debts	23UNTS197	100348
30 Dec	Denmark	Norway	Taxation	8UNTS21	100111
31 Dec	Thailand	USSR (Soviet Union)	Consul/Citizenship	OSUST225	468420

DATE	PARTY ONE	PARTY TWO	TOPIC	CITATION	NUMBER
1947					
01 Jan	Hungary	Yugoslavia	General Trade	113UNTS63	101548
06 Jan	Thailand	UK Great Britain	Reparations	99UNTS149	101376
07 Jan	Finland	USA (United States)	Taxation	15UNTS273	100243
08 Jan	Ecuador	USA (United States)	Air Transport	22UNTS119	100333
09 Jan	Belgium	France	Admin Cooperation	36UNTS145	100568
09 Jan	Canada	USA (United States)	Specific Property	11UNTS341	100173
11 Jan	Jordan	Turkey	General Amity	14UNTS49	100210
15 Jan	Norway	UK Great Britain	Consul/Citizenship	11UNTS187	100156
16 Jan	Italy	UK Great Britain	Non-ILO Labor	48ITGU168	435186
16 Jan	Belgium	UK Great Britain	Milit Installation	54UNTS97	100797
20 Jan	Denmark	UK Great Britain	Telecommunications	118UNTS73	101597
20 Jan	Multilateral		Water Transport	87UNTS247	101176
23 Jan	UK Great Britain	USA (United States)	Status of Forces	15UNTS281	100244
23 Jan	Belgium	USA (United States)	Visas	47UNTS23	100721
24 Jan	Belgium	Spain	Admin Cooperation	19UNTS3	100301
24 Jan	Australia	Netherlands	Finance	10UNTS77	100144
25 Jan	Hungary	Yugoslavia	Reparations	130UNTS3	101726
27 Jan	ICJ Option Clause	Guatemala	ICJ Option Clause	1UNTS49	100012
28 Jan	Netherlands	Norway	General Trade	31UNTS29	100467
28 Jan	Belgium	Denmark	Visas	18UNTS221	100291
29 Jan	Czechoslovakia	Ireland	Air Transport	27UNTS267	100411
30 Jan	Sweden	USSR (Soviet Union)	General Trade	0SUST225	468411
30 Jan	Netherlands	Thailand	General Amity	247UNTS353	103480
03 Feb	Finland	USSR (Soviet Union)	Finance	0SUST225	468138
03 Feb	Finland	USSR (Soviet Union)	Specific Property	0SUST225	468139
03 Feb	Finland	USSR (Soviet Union)	Specific Property	0SUST226	468140
03 Feb	FAO (Food Agri)	United Nations	IGO Operations	1UNTS207	200010
03 Feb	UNESCO (Educ/Cult)	United Nations	IGO Operations	1UNTS233	200011
03 Feb	Finland	USSR (Soviet Union)	Territory Boundary	216UNTS231	102939
03 Feb	Belgium	USA (United States)	Visas	84UNTS255	101134
04 Feb	USSR (Soviet Union)	Yugoslavia	Air Transport	130UNTS235	101731
04 Feb	USSR (Soviet Union)	Yugoslavia	Admin Cooperation	116UNTS171	101576
05 Feb	Belgium	UK Great Britain	Visas	11UNTS261	100164
06 Feb	Multilateral		IGO Establishment	97UNTS227	101352
08 Feb	Multilateral		Patents/Copyrights	14UNTS287	100222
10 Feb	Hungary	USSR (Soviet Union)	Peace/Disarmament	0SUST227	468178
10 Feb	Bulgaria	USSR (Soviet Union)	Peace/Disarmament	0SUST226	468029
10 Feb	Argentina	Taiwan	General Amity	486UNTS143	107077
10 Feb	Multilateral		Reparations	140UNTS111	101886
10 Feb	Multilateral		Peace/Disarmament	41UNTS21	100643
10 Feb	Multilateral		Peace/Disarmament	48UNTS203	100746
10 Feb	Multilateral		Peace/Disarmament	41UNTS135	100644
10 Feb	Multilateral		Peace/Disarmament	42UNTS3	100645
10 Feb	Multilateral		Peace/Disarmament	49UNTS3	100747
11 Feb	Norway	USSR (Soviet Union)	Telecommunications	0SUST228	468292
11 Feb	Norway	USSR (Soviet Union)	Postal Service	0SUST229	468293
11 Feb	Belgium	Chile	Patents/Copyrights	76UNTS107	100983
11 Feb	France	Poland	Reparations	12UNTS287	100189
14 Feb	Philippines	USA (United States)	Non-IBRD Project	16UNTS3	100245
14 Feb	Luxembourg	UK Great Britain	Visas	11UNTS267	100165
18 Feb	ICJ Option Clause	France	ICJ Option Clause	26UNTS91	100378
19 Feb	France	Poland	Scientific Project	47PDZU1044	457001
19 Feb	Norway	USSR (Soviet Union)	General Trade	30UNTS293	100464
19 Feb	Czechoslovakia	UK Great Britain	Milit Installation	9UNTS173	100131
20 Feb	Romania	USSR (Soviet Union)	General Economic	0SUST229	468365
20 Feb	Romania	USSR (Soviet Union)	General Economic	226UNTS79	103110
21 Feb	Greece	UK Great Britain	Air Transport	70UNTS215	100905
25 Feb	Czechoslovakia	Yugoslavia	General Trade	112UNTS3	101539
26 Feb	Italy	Uruguay	General Trade	48ITGU82	435426
26 Feb	Thailand	USA (United States)	Air Transport	16UNTS17	100246
26 Feb	Netherlands	UK Great Britain	Finance	11UNTS279	100167
26 Feb	Norway	UK Great Britain	Visas	11UNTS273	100166
28 Feb	Burma	USA (United States)	Direct Aid	25UNTS27	100355
28 Feb	Paraguay	USA (United States)	Air Transport	44UNTS25	100676

DATE	PARTY ONE	PARTY TWO	TOPIC	CITATION	NUMBER
1947 (Cont.)					
01 Mar	Argentina	Spain	Air Transport	47SPBO2004	460031
03 Mar	Paraguay	USA (United States)	Tech Assistance	135UNTS156	101819
03 Mar	Multilateral		Humanitarian	11UNTS43	100148
04 Mar	France	UK Great Britain	General Amity	9UNTS187	100132
05 Mar	Poland	USSR (Soviet Union)	Specif Goods/Equip	0SUST230	468317
05 Mar	Poland	USSR (Soviet Union)	Tech Assistance	0SUST230	468318
05 Mar	Poland	USSR (Soviet Union)	Milit Assistance	0SUST230	468319
05 Mar	Poland	USSR (Soviet Union)	Finance	0SUST230	468315
05 Mar	Poland	USSR (Soviet Union)	Loans and Credits	0SUST230	468314
05 Mar	Poland	USSR (Soviet Union)	Commodity Trade	0SUST230	468316
05 Mar	Czechoslovakia	Turkey	Air Transport	14UNTS101	100214
06 Mar	Portugal	Sweden	Air Transport	35UNTS243	100558
06 Mar	Canada	USA (United States)	Specific Resources	11UNTS325	100172
06 Mar	Belgium	Czechoslovakia	Culture	34UNTS77	100528
10 Mar	Czechoslovakia	Sweden	General Trade	47SOFM571	461055
10 Mar	Czechoslovakia	Poland	General Military	25UNTS231	100365
10 Mar	Australia	USA (United States)	Air Transport	10UNTS89	100145
11 Mar	France	USA (United States)	Humanitarian	151UNTS159	101991
12 Mar	Belgium	Turkey	Finance	33UNTS43	100513
12 Mar	Belgium	Turkey	General Trade	37UNTS215	100578
12 Mar	Belgium	Turkey	Mostfavored Nation	37UNTS221	100579
14 Mar	France	ICAO (Civil Aviat)	IGO Status/Immunit	94UNTS59	101306
14 Mar	Philippines	USA (United States)	Non-IBRD Project	16UNTS31	100247
14 Mar	Philippines	USA (United States)	Consul/Citizenship	45UNTS23	100690
14 Mar	Philippines	USA (United States)	Milit Installation	43UNTS271	100673
15 Mar	Czechoslovakia	Sweden	Claims and Debts	47SOFM572	461056
15 Mar	Austria	France	Culture	12UNTS109	100182
17 Mar	Mexico	USA (United States)	Sanitation	167UNTS30	102200
18 Mar	Poland	Sweden	Finance	47SOFM137	461039
18 Mar	Canada	USA (United States)	Commodity Trade	117UNTS79	101584
18 Mar	Poland	Sweden	General Economic	12UNTS295	100190
19 Mar	Ireland	Sweden	Visas	553UNTS163	108083
19 Mar	Belgium	Czechoslovakia	Claims and Debts	23UNTS35	100341
19 Mar	Netherlands	Turkey	Air Transport	14UNTS59	100211
19 Mar	Argentina	UK Great Britain	General Trade	11UNTS195	100157
20 Mar	Netherlands	Sweden	Visas	247UNTS145	103463
20 Mar	Czechoslovakia	Norway	General Trade	30UNTS223	100460
20 Mar	Sweden	UK Great Britain	Visas	11UNTS291	100169
20 Mar	Denmark	UK Great Britain	Visas	11UNTS285	100168
20 Mar	Belgium	Sweden	Visas	34UNTS3	100522
21 Mar	Netherlands	UK Great Britain	Visas	52NET64	447004
21 Mar	South Africa	USA (United States)	Milit Assistance	16UNTS47	100248
21 Mar	Netherlands	UK Great Britain	Visas	11UNTS297	100170
21 Mar	Philippines	USA (United States)	Milit Assistance	45UNTS47	100691
24 Mar	Belgium	Poland	Non-ILO Labor	18UNTS279	100297
24 Mar	Australia	Norway	Claims and Debts	18UNTS185	100288
25 Mar	Belgium	Netherlands	Postal Service	18UNTS309	100299
25 Mar	Belgium	Ireland	Visas	18UNTS227	100292
27 Mar	France	USA (United States)	Patents/Copyrights	16UNTS65	100249
28 Mar	Spain	UK Great Britain	Finance	66UNTS91	100849
29 Mar	Italy	Panama	Peace/Disarmament	47ITGU127	435291
31 Mar	Portugal	Spain	Air Transport	47SPBO1107	460228
01 Apr	Greece	Switzerland	Mostfavored Nation	180UNTS115	102378
01 Apr	Taiwan	Portugal	Privil/Immunities	14UNTS177	100220
02 Apr	Mexico	USA (United States)	Non-ILO Labor	148UNTS104	101939
02 Apr	Multilateral		Trusteeship	8UNTS189	100123
04 Apr	Czechoslovakia	Poland	General Economic	85UNTS62	101146
04 Apr	France	USA (United States)	Patents/Copyrights	24UNTS133	100353
05 Apr	Muscat and Oman	UK Great Britain	Air Transport	27UNTS287	100412
05 Apr	ICJ Option Clause	Sweden	ICJ Option Clause	2UNTS3	100016
07 Apr	India	USSR (Soviet Union)	Consul/Citizenship	0SUST231	468209
07 Apr	Greece	UK Great Britain	Territory Boundary	11UNTS201	100158
08 Apr	Greece	Sweden	Air Transport	94UNTS73	101307
10 Apr	South Africa	USA (United States)	Taxation	167UNTS211	102208
11 Apr	League of Nations	United Nations	Specific Property	4UNTS443	200026

DATE	PARTY ONE	PARTY TWO	TOPIC	CITATION	NUMBER
1947 (Cont.)					
11 Apr	Netherlands	USA (United States)	Other Military	148UNTS343	101943
12 Apr	Sweden	Yugoslavia	Finance	47SOFM181	461041
12 Apr	Sweden	Yugoslavia	General Trade	47SOFM161	461040
12 Apr	Italy	Turkey	General Economic	47TURG109	466073
12 Apr	Canada	USA (United States)	Air Transport	122UNTS229	101648
13 Apr	Afghanistan	USSR (Soviet Union)	Telecommunications	0SUST231	468001
14 Apr	League of Nations	United Nations	Specific Property	4UNTS449	200027
14 Apr	Austria	Norway	General Trade	31UNTS21	100466
14 Apr	Iraq	Jordan	General Amity	23UNTS148	100345
14 Apr	Austria	Norway	Finance	15UNTS211	100235
15 Apr	USA (United States)	USSR (Soviet Union)	General Aid	0SUST438	468436
15 Apr	Denmark	Norway	Finance	12UNTS323	100191
16 Apr	Argentina	Italy	Sanitation	61ITMA451	437011
17 Apr	Greece	Netherlands	Air Transport	32UNTS115	100494
17 Apr	Italy	UK Great Britain	Finance	54UNTS149	100801
17 Apr	Italy	UK Great Britain	Claims and Debts	54UNTS169	100802
18 Apr	France	South Africa	Reparations	225UNTS35	103085
18 Apr	Taiwan	Philippines	General Amity	11UNTS361	100175
19 Apr	Italy	Sweden	Non-ILO Labor	48ITGU27	435361
19 Apr	France	USA (United States)	General Trade	132UNTS135	101754
19 Apr	Peru	USA (United States)	Sanitation	136UNTS284	101840
21 Apr	Jordan	United Arab Rep	General Trade	11UNTS3	100146
22 Apr	France	Ireland	Visas	553UNTS51	108068
22 Apr	Denmark	UK Great Britain	Milit Occupation	8UNTS3	100110
24 Apr	Finland	USSR (Soviet Union)	Specific Resources	0SUST231	468141
24 Apr	New Zealand	USA (United States)	Patents/Copyrights	16UNTS79	100250
25 Apr	Canada	Portugal	Air Transport	94UNTS87	101308
25 Apr	Nepal	USA (United States)	Consul/Citizenship	16UNTS97	100251
27 Apr	Czechoslovakia	Yugoslavia	Culture	33UNTS49	100514
28 Apr	Syria	USA (United States)	Air Transport	262UNTS121	103741
28 Apr	Austria	UK Great Britain	Reparations	93UNTS53	101287
28 Apr	Belgium	Netherlands	Visas	37UNTS199	100577
29 Apr	Taiwan	USA (United States)	Milit Assistance	0CTRC719	413029
30 Apr	Poland	USSR (Soviet Union)	Territory Boundary	0SUST232	468321
30 Apr	Austria	Switzerland	Sanitation	48SWRO192	462104
30 Apr	Austria	Switzerland	Land Transport	48SWRO183	462068
30 Apr	Austria	Switzerland	Customs	48SWRO204	462011
30 Apr	Austria	Switzerland	Customs	48SWRO197	462073
30 Apr	Sweden	USA (United States)	Visas	84UNTS33	101116
30 Apr	Switzerland	USA (United States)	Specif Goods/Equip	42UNTS235	100652
31 Apr	Italy	Vatican/Holy See	Territory Boundary	48ITGU190	435337
01 May	Ireland	Netherlands	Visas	247UNTS193	103468
05 May	Canada	France	Reparations	231UNTS81	103208
05 May	France	Greece	Air Transport	76UNTS61	100980
06 May	Poland	USSR (Soviet Union)	Refugees	0SUST232	468320
08 May	Thailand	UK Great Britain	Claims and Debts	100UNTS47	101386
08 May	Thailand	USA (United States)	Air Transport	42UNTS241	100653
09 May	Bulgaria	Denmark	Finance	74UNTS139	100960
09 May	Bulgaria	Denmark	General Trade	74UNTS131	100959
09 May	France	IBRD (World Bank)	IBRD Project	152UNTS111	102014
10 May	Chile	USA (United States)	Air Transport	55UNTS21	100807
11 May	Hungary	Yugoslavia	Direct Aid	130UNTS171	101730
12 May	Honduras	Italy	Peace/Disarmament	47ITGU140	435204
12 May	Netherlands	Uruguay	Air Transport	51NET151	447005
12 May	Philippines	USA (United States)	Scientific Project	16UNTS137	100254
12 May	Philippines	USA (United States)	Scientific Project	16UNTS123	100253
12 May	Philippines	USA (United States)	Scientific Project	16UNTS109	100252
13 May	Denmark	Ireland	Visas	553UNTS37	108066
13 May	Honduras	USA (United States)	Sanitation	166UNTS159	102189
14 May	Czechoslovakia	Denmark	Air Transport	27UNTS297	100413
16 May	Philippines	USA (United States)	Non-ILO Labor	280UNTS177	104057
16 May	Bolivia	USA (United States)	Tech Assistance	168UNTS89	102215
19 May	Canada	USA (United States)	Non-ILO Labor	43UNTS97	100663
19 May	France	Poland	Education	12UNTS95	100181
22 May	ICJ Option Clause	Turkey	ICJ Option Clause	4UNTS265	100050

DATE	PARTY ONE	PARTY TWO	TOPIC	CITATION	NUMBER
1947 (Cont.)					
23 May	South Africa	USA (United States)	Air Transport	66UNTS233	100857
23 May	UK Great Britain	USA (United States)	Specific Property	11UNTS211	100159
24 May	Finland	USSR (Soviet Union)	Specific Property	0SUST232	468142
24 May	Poland	Yugoslavia	General Trade	115UNTS89	101560
24 May	Poland	Yugoslavia	General Trade	115UNTS37	101557
24 May	Poland	Yugoslavia	Finance	115UNTS69	101558
26 May	Panama	USA (United States)	Territory Boundary	138UNTS137	101866
27 May	Multilateral		Air Transport	418UNTS161	106021
27 May	New Zealand	UK Great Britain	Taxation	17UNTS211	100277
28 May	Canada	Taiwan	Direct Aid	0CTRC63	413017
28 May	Netherlands	USA (United States)	General Military	17UNTS29	100267
30 May	Italy	UK Great Britain	Non-ILO Labor	54UNTS131	100800
31 May	Brazil	Ecuador	Consul/Citizenship	72UNTS25	100925
31 May	India	Netherlands	Air Transport	17UNTS65	100268
03 Jun	Netherlands	Norway	Visas	2NORT456	451117
03 Jun	Ireland	USA (United States)	Air Transport	16UNTS151	100255
05 Jun	Norway	UK Great Britain	Milit Occupation	54UNTS181	100803
05 Jun	Greece	UK Great Britain	Status of Forces	9UNTS197	100133
06 Jun	Multilateral		Patents/Copyrights	46UNTS249	100714
09 Jun	Ireland	Switzerland	Visas	553UNTS169	108084
09 Jun	Italy	USA (United States)	Air Transport	104UNTS157	101437
09 Jun	Denmark	USA (United States)	Visas	132UNTS145	101755
10 Jun	Multilateral		Water Transport	208UNTS3	102814
10 Jun	Switzerland	UK Great Britain	Visas	11UNTS217	100160
12 Jun	Romania	USSR (Soviet Union)	Land Transport	0SUST232	468366
12 Jun	Albania	Yugoslavia	IGO Establishment	111UNTS201	101535
12 Jun	Albania	Yugoslavia	Direct Aid	111UNTS177	101531
12 Jun	Albania	Yugoslavia	Dispute Settlement	111UNTS183	101532
12 Jun	Albania	Yugoslavia	Finance	111UNTS195	101534
12 Jun	Albania	Yugoslavia	Loans and Credits	111UNTS189	101533
16 Jun	USA (United States)	USSR (Soviet Union)	Consul/Citizenship	0SUST232	468437
16 Jun	France	Monaco	Consul/Citizenship	47FRJO2106	416329
16 Jun	Czechoslovakia	UK Great Britain	Education	46UNTS61	100700
18 Jun	France	UK Great Britain	Air Transport	9UNTS203	100134
19 Jun	Multilateral		ILO Labor	171UNTS329	102235
20 Jun	Italy	Spain	General Trade	47SPBO2008	460168
20 Jun	Iceland	UK Great Britain	Visas	11UNTS223	100161
20 Jun	Bulgaria	Czechoslovakia	Education	46UNTS15	100698
20 Jun	Greece	USA (United States)	Direct Aid	7UNTS267	100105
21 Jun	Norway	Sweden	Taxation	94UNTS107	101309
21 Jun	Austria	USA (United States)	Reparations	67UNTS89	100868
21 Jun	Austria	USA (United States)	Milit Occupation	67UNTS99	100869
21 Jun	Ecuador	USA (United States)	Sanitation	26UNTS275	100391
22 Jun	Albania	Yugoslavia	General Trade	111UNTS207	101536
24 Jun	Sweden	USA (United States)	General Economic	36UNTS25	100565
25 Jun	Austria	USA (United States)	Direct Aid	22UNTS141	100334
26 Jun	France	Philippines	General Amity	1PTS427	465008
26 Jun	Romania	Yugoslavia	Culture	116UNTS39	101568
26 Jun	United Nations	USA (United States)	IGO Establishment	11UNTS11	100147
27 Jun	League of Nations	United Nations	Specific Property	5UNTS395	200037
27 Jun	League of Nations	United Nations	Specific Property	5UNTS389	200036
27 Jun	Canada	Sweden	Air Transport	27UNTS313	100414
28 Jun	Taiwan	France	Air Transport	0CTRC165	413018
28 Jun	Denmark	Yugoslavia	General Economic	78UNTS242	101020
28 Jun	Bulgaria	Poland	Culture	15UNTS123	100230
30 Jun	Cuba	Italy	Peace/Disarmament	47ITGU300	435099
30 Jun	USA (United States)	Venezuela	Sanitation	166UNTS198	102190
30 Jun	France	Norway	Visas	104UNTS313	101449
30 Jun	Romania	Yugoslavia	Air Transport	116UNTS57	101569
30 Jun	Iraq	Turkey	Air Transport	72UNTS107	100930
30 Jun	United Arab Rep	UK Great Britain	Finance	93UNTS165	101299
30 Jun	Denmark	Turkey	Air Transport	32UNTS301	100504
01 Jul	Belgium	United Arab Rep	Claims and Debts	34UNTS93	100529
02 Jul	Czechoslovakia	Italy	Mostfavored Nation	48ITGU167	435077
02 Jul	France	New Zealand	Commodity Trade	16UNTS219	100263

DATE	PARTY ONE	PARTY TWO	TOPIC	CITATION	NUMBER
1947 (Cont.)					
03 Jul	Belgium	Switzerland	Visas	29UNTS277	100444
04 Jul	Czechoslovakia	Poland	General Economic	50PDZU93	457002
04 Jul	Czechoslovakia	Poland	Culture	25UNTS249	100366
04 Jul	Italy	USA (United States)	Direct Aid	22UNTS173	100336
04 Jul	Haiti	USA (United States)	Other Ad Hoc	22UNTS165	100335
04 Jul	Belgium	South Africa	Claims and Debts	47UNTS9	100720
05 Jul	USSR (Soviet Union)	Yugoslavia	General Economic	0SUST234	468462
05 Jul	USSR (Soviet Union)	Yugoslavia	Finance	0SUST234	468463
05 Jul	Bulgaria	USSR (Soviet Union)	General Economic	0SUST233	468030
05 Jul	India	USA (United States)	Status of Forces	185UNTS293	102476
08 Jul	Greece	USA (United States)	Direct Aid	16UNTS157	100256
09 Jul	Italy	Switzerland	Health/Educ/Welfare	14SWRS526	463145
09 Jul	Italy	Philippines	General Amity	44UNTS3	100674
09 Jul	Denmark	Norway	Territory Boundary	7UNTS321	100108
09 Jul	Albania	Yugoslavia	Culture	33UNTS91	100516
10 Jul	Multilateral		Specific Property	5UNTS401	200038
11 Jul	Multilateral		ILO Labor	218UNTS345	102961
11 Jul	Multilateral		ILO Labor	214UNTS33	102898
11 Jul	Multilateral		ILO Labor	161UNTS113	102125
11 Jul	Multilateral		ILO Labor	54UNTS3	100792
12 Jul	Czechoslovakia	USSR (Soviet Union)	General Trade	0SUST234	468103
12 Jul	Luxembourg	Norway	Visas	90UNTS59	101226
12 Jul	Turkey	USA (United States)	Direct Aid	7UNTS299	100106
12 Jul	ICJ Option Clause	Philippines	ICJ Option Clause	7UNTS229	100101
14 Jul	Canada	Switzerland	Admin Cooperation	43UNTS103	100664
15 Jul	Hungary	USSR (Soviet Union)	General Economic	0SUST234	468179
15 Jul	Australia	USSR (Soviet Union)	Consul/Citizenship	0SUST234	468021
15 Jul	Hungary	USSR (Soviet Union)	General Economic	216UNTS247	102940
15 Jul	UK Great Britain	Uruguay	Finance	71UNTS179	100918
15 Jul	Belgium	Norway	Visas	33UNTS25	100511
15 Jul	France	Norway	Specific Property	15UNTS5	100226
15 Jul	Norway	Switzerland	Finance	12UNTS351	100192
16 Jul	France	India	Air Transport	27UNTS325	100415
16 Jul	Denmark	France	Patents/Copyrights	12UNTS3	100177
17 Jul	Spain	Sweden	General Trade	47SPBO1008	460244
17 Jul	Spain	Sweden	General Economic	47SOFM667	461070
17 Jul	Canada	UK Great Britain	Air Transport	28UNTS3	100416
18 Jul	Netherlands	Thailand	Air Transport	28UNTS27	100417
22 Jul	Greece	Turkey	Air Transport	72UNTS131	100931
22 Jul	Netherlands	South Africa	Air Transport	12UNTS257	100188
23 Jul	Belgium	USA (United States)	Other Military	33UNTS33	100512
23 Jul	Taiwan	UK Great Britain	Air Transport	9UNTS207	100135
24 Jul	Hungary	Yugoslavia	General Trade	114UNTS3	101554
25 Jul	USSR (Soviet Union)	Yugoslavia	Tech Assistance	130UNTS315	101732
25 Jul	Czechoslovakia	USA (United States)	Reparations	90UNTS19	101223
26 Jul	Albania	USSR (Soviet Union)	General Economic	0SUST235	468007
28 Jul	Greece	South Africa	Reparations	185UNTS161	102467
28 Jul	Australia	France	Reparations	97UNTS271	101353
28 Jul	Canada	Greece	Customs	43UNTS111	100665
29 Jul	Norway	USA (United States)	Visas	87UNTS343	101178
30 Jul	Czechoslovakia	Greece	General Trade	185UNTS133	102464
30 Jul	Czechoslovakia	Greece	Reparations	185UNTS149	102466
30 Jul	Czechoslovakia	Greece	Claims and Debts	185UNTS143	102465
30 Jul	Czechoslovakia	Greece	Finance	185UNTS115	102463
30 Jul	Taiwan	Italy	Consul/Citizenship	12UNTS383	100195
30 Jul	Taiwan	Italy	Reparations	12UNTS377	100194
01 Aug	Norway	Switzerland	Visas	90UNTS65	101227
04 Aug	Poland	USSR (Soviet Union)	General Trade	0SUST235	468322
04 Aug	Belgium	India	Reparations	76UNTS23	100976
04 Aug	Multilateral		Air Transport	28UNTS41	100418
05 Aug	Norway	Sweden	General Trade	47SOFM511	461052
07 Aug	Netherlands	IBRD (World Bank)	IBRD Project	152UNTS165	102015
08 Aug	Canada	Ireland	Air Transport	28UNTS47	100419
08 Aug	Czechoslovakia	New Zealand	Claims and Debts	18UNTS161	100285
09 Aug	Poland	Romania	Air Transport	12UNTS363	100193

DATE	PARTY ONE	PARTY TWO	TOPIC	CITATION	NUMBER
1947 (Cont.)					
13 Aug	France	UK Great Britain	Non-ILO Labor	91UNTS169	101249
13 Aug	Iraq	UK Great Britain	Finance	9UNTS259	100136
14 Aug	Multilateral		Reparations	138UNTS111	101863
14 Aug	Italy	USA (United States)	Reparations	36UNTS53	100566
14 Aug	Italy	USA (United States)	Claims and Debts	36UNTS105	100567
14 Aug	India	UK Great Britain	Finance	11UNTS371	100176
19 Aug	El Salvador	USA (United States)	Military Mission	51UNTS57	100752
19 Aug	Denmark	UK Great Britain	Reparations	9UNTS277	100137
20 Aug	Netherlands	USA (United States)	Visas	84UNTS11	101114
20 Aug	Canada	USA (United States)	Telecommunications	27UNTS3	100392
22 Aug	Poland	Yugoslavia	Air Transport	47PDZU293	457003
22 Aug	Denmark	IBRD (World Bank)	IBRD Project	152UNTS223	102016
22 Aug	Bulgaria	Yugoslavia	Finance	111UNTS241	101538
23 Aug	Bulgaria	USSR (Soviet Union)	Loans and Credits	0SUST236	471022
23 Aug	Finland	UNICEF (Children)	IGO Operations	68UNTS224	200233
23 Aug	Bulgaria	UNICEF (Children)	IGO Operations	68UNTS223	200232
23 Aug	USSR (Soviet Union)	Yugoslavia	Reparations	116UNTS281	101577
23 Aug	Poland	UNICEF (Children)	Tech Assistance	65UNTS22	100815
28 Aug	Hungary	UNICEF (Children)	IGO Operations	68UNTS226	200234
28 Aug	Romania	UNICEF (Children)	IGO Operations	68UNTS228	200235
28 Aug	Luxembourg	IBRD (World Bank)	IBRD Project	153UNTS3	102017
28 Aug	Hungary	Poland	Air Transport	15UNTS145	100231
29 Aug	Guatemala	USA (United States)	Status of Forces	27UNTS11	100393
29 Aug	Belgium	Netherlands	Non-ILO Labor	36UNTS349	100573
01 Sep	Czechoslovakia	Netherlands	Air Transport	32UNTS129	100495
02 Sep	Multilateral		General Military	21UNTS77	100324
03 Sep	Italy	USA (United States)	Status of Forces	67UNTS15	100863
03 Sep	Taiwan	USA (United States)	Status of Forces	9UNTS91	100126
04 Sep	Philippines	USA (United States)	Gen Communications	1PTS435	465009
04 Sep	Czechoslovakia	Yugoslavia	Claims and Debts	112UNTS91	101540
05 Sep	Thailand	USA (United States)	Admin Cooperation	73UNTS57	100943
05 Sep	Czechoslovakia	Romania	Education	46UNTS37	100699
08 Sep	Spain	Turkey	Finance	48TURG902	466085
08 Sep	Canada	France	Taxation	253UNTS259	103587
10 Sep	Greece	Lebanon	Dispute Settlement	187UNTS107	102504
10 Sep	Czechoslovakia	Switzerland	Air Transport	35UNTS275	100559
11 Sep	FAO (Food Agri)	ILO (Labor Org)	IGO Operations	18UNTS335	200111
16 Sep	France	USA (United States)	Visas	84UNTS19	101115
16 Sep	Chile	UK Great Britain	Air Transport	133UNTS143	101786
16 Sep	Lebanon	Turkey	Air Transport	44UNTS123	100682
17 Sep	Philippines	USA (United States)	Postal Service	206UNTS249	102790
18 Sep	Turkey	Yugoslavia	General Economic	48TURG2302	466096
19 Sep	Multilateral		Finance	30UNTS269	100462
19 Sep	Multilateral		General Trade	30UNTS249	100461
22 Sep	Hungary	USSR (Soviet Union)	Gen Communications	0SUST236	468180
22 Sep	Bulgaria	Sweden	General Trade	47SOFM499	461050
22 Sep	Bulgaria	Sweden	Finance	47SOFM508	461051
27 Sep	Haiti	USA (United States)	Sanitation	136UNTS258	101839
27 Sep	Philippines	Spain	General Amity	70UNTS133	100902
29 Sep	Ethiopia	UK Great Britain	Territory Boundary	82UNTS191	101092
29 Sep	Multilateral		Peace/Disarmament	45UNTS125	100694
30 Sep	Philippines	USA (United States)	Postal Service	1PTS445	465010
30 Sep	Romania	Yugoslavia	Finance	116UNTS71	101570
30 Sep	Accept UN Charter	Yemen	UN Charter	8UNTS59	100113
30 Sep	Accept UN Charter	Pakistan	UN Charter	8UNTS57	100112
01 Oct	Hungary	USSR (Soviet Union)	Postal Service	0SUST237	468181
01 Oct	Poland	USSR (Soviet Union)	Postal Service	0SUST237	468323
01 Oct	ICAO (Civil Aviat)	United Nations	IGO Operations	8UNTS315	200045
01 Oct	Haiti	USA (United States)	Other Ad Hoc	102UNTS67	101411
01 Oct	France	USA (United States)	Other Military	148UNTS303	101940
02 Oct	Multilateral		Telecommunications	193UNTS188	102616
03 Oct	Czechoslovakia	UNICEF (Children)	Tech Assistance	65UNTS26	100816
05 Oct	Germany, West	Sweden	Finance	47SOFM651	461062
05 Oct	Multilateral		Finance	34UNTS23	100525
06 Oct	Sweden	Yugoslavia	Air Transport	53UNTS107	100775

DATE	PARTY ONE	PARTY TWO	TOPIC	CITATION	NUMBER
1947 (Cont.)					
06 Oct	Iran	USA (United States)	Military Mission	11UNTS303	100171
08 Oct	Netherlands	UK Great Britain	Reparations	252UNTS19	103556
08 Oct	Austria	USA (United States)	Air Transport	25UNTS3	100354
09 Oct	South Africa	UK Great Britain	Finance	17UNTS239	100278
09 Oct	UK Great Britain	USA (United States)	Milit Assistance	34UNTS129	100533
10 Oct	Multilateral		Claims and Debts	54UNTS193	100804
11 Oct	Multilateral		IGO Establishment	77UNTS143	100998
12 Oct	Philippines	USA (United States)	Territory Boundary	1PTS519	465011
13 Oct	UK Great Britain	USA (United States)	Air Transport	66UNTS269	100858
14 Oct	Greece	UNICEF (Children)	Humanitarian	102UNTS39	101409
15 Oct	Canada	USA (United States)	Telecommunications	82UNTS53	101085
15 Oct	Czechoslovakia	Sweden	Air Transport	44UNTS149	100683
15 Oct	Hungary	Yugoslavia	Culture	33UNTS73	100515
16 Oct	Portugal	UK Great Britain	Sanitation	82UNTS203	101093
16 Oct	Colombia	UK Great Britain	Air Transport	160UNTS297	102115
17 Oct	Burma	UK Great Britain	Recognition	70UNTS183	100904
19 Oct	Iceland	Sweden	General Trade	47SOFM480	461047
22 Oct	Netherlands	Spain	Air Transport	48SPBO1108	460209
23 Oct	UK Great Britain	USA (United States)	Territory Boundary	66UNTS277	100859
23 Oct	ICJ Option Clause	Mexico	ICJ Option Clause	9UNTS97	100127
25 Oct	France	USA (United States)	Non-ILO Labor	89UNTS111	101212
27 Oct	Chile	UK Great Britain	Milit Servic/Citiz	82UNTS209	101094
27 Oct	Ecuador	USA (United States)	Air Transport	44UNTS45	100677
27 Oct	Taiwan	USA (United States)	Direct Aid	12UNTS11	100178
28 Oct	Liberia	USA (United States)	Visas	82UNTS23	101081
29 Oct	Ecuador	USA (United States)	Admin Cooperation	21UNTS21	100322
30 Oct	Czechoslovakia	Sweden	Finance	47SOFM494	461049
30 Oct	Czechoslovakia	Sweden	General Trade	47SOFM485	461048
30 Oct	Cuba	USA (United States)	General Economic	119UNTS163	101611
30 Oct	France	USA (United States)	General Economic	125UNTS171	101676
30 Oct	Netherlands	New Zealand	General Economic	76UNTS41	100977
30 Oct	Netherlands	USA (United States)	General Economic	76UNTS47	100978
30 Oct	UK Great Britain	USA (United States)	General Economic	126UNTS39	101680
30 Oct	Belgium	USA (United States)	General Economic	125UNTS103	101672
30 Oct	Multilateral		General Economic	55UNTS188	100814
30 Oct	Canada	USA (United States)	General Economic	27UNTS19	100394
31 Oct	France	Sweden	General Trade	47SOFM455	461045
31 Oct	France	Sweden	Finance	47SOFM480	461046
01 Nov	Multilateral		Trusteeship	10UNTS3	100138
03 Nov	Bolivia	USA (United States)	Air Transport	51UNTS33	100750
04 Nov	Multilateral		Reparations	93UNTS61	101288
06 Nov	Italy	UNICEF (Children)	IGO Operations	68UNTS240	200236
06 Nov	Brazil	Netherlands	Air Transport	53UNTS59	100773
07 Nov	Austria	UNICEF (Children)	IGO Operations	68UNTS252	200237
07 Nov	Poland	Yugoslavia	General Economic	115UNTS137	101561
10 Nov	Taiwan	USA (United States)	Education	0CTRC747	413030
10 Nov	Belgium	USSR (Soviet Union)	Finance	18UNTS299	100298
11 Nov	Ceylon (Sri Lanka)	UK Great Britain	Admin Cooperation	86UNTS31	101150
11 Nov	Ceylon (Sri Lanka)	UK Great Britain	Milit Assistance	86UNTS19	101148
11 Nov	Ceylon (Sri Lanka)	UK Great Britain	Consul/Citizenship	86UNTS25	101149
11 Nov	Norway	Portugal	Air Transport	34UNTS257	100542
12 Nov	Multilateral		Admin Cooperation	46UNTS169	100709
12 Nov	Multilateral		Admin Cooperation	53UNTS13	100770
12 Nov	Multilateral		Admin Cooperation	53UNTS49	100772
12 Nov	Multilateral		Admin Cooperation	53UNTS39	100771
12 Nov	Multilateral		Admin Cooperation	46UNTS201	100710
13 Nov	Multilateral		Visas	251UNTS79	103534
14 Nov	Denmark	Sweden	General Trade	47SOFM513	461054
14 Nov	Brazil	Sweden	Air Transport	94UNTS139	101310
14 Nov	Ecuador	USA (United States)	Education	149UNTS297	101959
14 Nov	Belgium	UK Great Britain	Finance	25UNTS269	100367
14 Nov	Brazil	Denmark	Air Transport	47UNTS39	100722
14 Nov	Brazil	Norway	Air Transport	44UNTS163	100684
14 Nov	Denmark	Greece	Air Transport	35UNTS295	100560
15 Nov	United Nations	WHO (World Health)	IGO Operations	19UNTS193	200115
15 Nov	United Nations	UPU (Postal Union)	IGO Operations	19UNTS219	200116
15 Nov	Finland	Norway	General Trade	29UNTS179	100439
18 Nov	Multilateral		Finance	17UNTS89	100269
18 Nov	Denmark	Ireland	Air Transport	35UNTS309	100561
18 Nov	Burma	Pakistan	Air Transport	35UNTS321	100562
20 Nov	Albania	UNICEF (Children)	IGO Operations	65UNTS163	200208
20 Nov	UNICEF (Children)	Yugoslavia	Tech Assistance	65UNTS28	100817
21 Nov	Ireland	Italy	Air Transport	353UNTS73	105038
21 Nov	Multilateral		IGO Status/Immunit	33UNTS261	100521
22 Nov	France	New Zealand	Visas	15UNTS29	100228
28 Nov	Hungary	Sweden	General Trade	47SOFM575	461058
28 Nov	Czechoslovakia	USSR (Soviet Union)	Sanitation	216UNTS285	102941
29 Nov	France	Italy	Peace/Disarmament	48ITGU38	435110
01 Dec	Czechoslovakia	France	Reparations	50FRJO0	416437
01 Dec	Finland	USSR (Soviet Union)	General Trade	217UNTS3	102942
01 Dec	Denmark	UK Great Britain	Reparations	93UNTS151	101298
02 Dec	France	Netherlands	Finance	63FRRT76	415356
03 Dec	Greece	USA (United States)	Milit Assistance	89UNTS119	101213
06 Dec	Italy	UK Great Britain	Visas	82UNTS243	101097
06 Dec	Taiwan	Netherlands	Air Transport	43UNTS185	100669
07 Dec	Finland	USSR (Soviet Union)	Territory Boundary	0SUST239	468143
08 Dec	Greece	Norway	Loans and Credits	30UNTS171	100455
08 Dec	Taiwan	USA (United States)	Milit Installation	70UNTS3	100895
09 Dec	Hungary	USSR (Soviet Union)	General Economic	0SUST239	468182
09 Dec	Iceland	USA (United States)	Visas	82UNTS31	101082
10 Dec	India	Pakistan	Taxation	51UNTS173	100764
11 Dec	Czechoslovakia	USSR (Soviet Union)	Scientific Project	0SUST240	468104
11 Dec	Czechoslovakia	USSR (Soviet Union)	Loans and Credits	0SUST240	471023
11 Dec	Czechoslovakia	USSR (Soviet Union)	General Economic	0SUST240	471024
11 Dec	Czechoslovakia	USSR (Soviet Union)	General Economic	217UNTS35	102943
15 Dec	USSR (Soviet Union)	Yugoslavia	Education	116UNTS313	101578
15 Dec	Denmark	Portugal	Air Transport	35UNTS329	100563
16 Dec	Multilateral		Reparations	82UNTS237	101096
16 Dec	Sweden	USA (United States)	Admin Cooperation	73UNTS65	100944
17 Dec	Bulgaria	USSR (Soviet Union)	Gen Communications	0SUST241	468031
17 Dec	Bulgaria	USSR (Soviet Union)	Postal Service	0SUST241	468032
17 Dec	Ireland	Norway	Visas	90UNTS71	101228
18 Dec	South Africa	USA (United States)	Extradition	148UNTS85	101938
18 Dec	United Nations	USA (United States)	IGO Status/Immunit	11UNTS347	100174
18 Dec	Norway	USSR (Soviet Union)	Territory Boundary	52UNTS3	100768
19 Dec	Finland	USSR (Soviet Union)	Land Transport	0SUST242	468144
19 Dec	Philippines	USA (United States)	Territory Boundary	1PTS639	465012
19 Dec	Romania	Yugoslavia	General Amity	116UNTS89	101571
19 Dec	Haiti	USA (United States)	Direct Aid	135UNTS130	101818
20 Dec	Hungary	Netherlands	Finance	51NET95	447006
22 Dec	Norway	Sweden	Non-ILO Labor	47SOFM631	461060
22 Dec	Multilateral		Customs	32UNTS143	100496
22 Dec	Norway	Sweden	Non-ILO Labor	22UNTS203	100337
22 Dec	Colombia	USA (United States)	Air Transport	51UNTS45	100751
22 Dec	Peru	UK Great Britain	Air Transport	72UNTS143	100932
23 Dec	Denmark	Sweden	Non-ILO Labor	47SOFM635	461061
23 Dec	Denmark	Sweden	Non-ILO Labor	14UNTS3	100207
24 Dec	Philippines	USA (United States)	Territory Boundary	1PTS645	465013
26 Dec	Canada	USA (United States)	Commodity Trade	27UNTS29	100395
27 Dec	UK Great Britain	USSR (Soviet Union)	Finance	82UNTS251	101098
27 Dec	UK Great Britain	USSR (Soviet Union)	General Economic	91UNTS113	101245
30 Dec	Netherlands	Sweden	General Trade	47SOFM583	461059
30 Dec	Netherlands	Sweden	General Trade	51NET91	447007
31 Dec	Sweden	USSR (Soviet Union)	General Trade	47SOFM511	461053
1948					
01 Jan	Paraguay	USA (United States)	Scientific Project	89UNTS191	101217
01 Jan	Ethiopia	Pakistan	Air Transport	35UNTS3	100547
02 Jan	France	USA (United States)	Direct Aid	31UNTS97	100470
02 Jan	France	Netherlands	Visas	70UNTS105	100899

DATE	PARTY ONE	PARTY TWO	TOPIC	CITATION	NUMBER
1948 (Cont.)					
02 Jan	Austria	USA (United States)	Direct Aid	34UNTS141	100534
03 Jan	Italy	USA (United States)	Direct Aid	31UNTS105	100471
05 Jan	Guatemala	USA (United States)	Education	135UNTS104	101817
05 Jan	United Arab Rep	UK Great Britain	Finance	77UNTS3	100988
07 Jan	Philippines	UK Great Britain	Air Transport	28UNTS63	100420
12 Jan	Taiwan	UK Great Britain	Customs	14UNTS74	100212
12 Jan	Costa Rica	USA (United States)	Consul/Citizenship	70UNTS27	100896
17 Jan	Belgium	France	Non-ILO Labor	36UNTS233	100570
21 Jan	Italy	UK Great Britain	Milit Installation	77UNTS23	100989
21 Jan	Poland	Yugoslavia	Non-IBRD Project	115UNTS155	101562
21 Jan	Denmark	Norway	Non-ILO Labor	14UNTS307	100223
22 Jan	Austria	Netherlands	Air Transport	17UNTS99	100270
22 Jan	Czechoslovakia	New Zealand	Commodity Trade	16UNTS229	100264
24 Jan	Hungary	Romania	General Amity	477UNTS155	106920
24 Jan	France	Lebanon	Finance	173UNTS99	102263
24 Jan	Poland	UK Great Britain	Claims and Debts	87UNTS3	101163
26 Jan	Poland	USSR (Soviet Union)	Loans and Credits	0SUST244	468325
26 Jan	Poland	USSR (Soviet Union)	General Trade	0SUST243	468324
26 Jan	Argentina	Italy	Health/Educ/Welfare	1ITMA82	437012
27 Jan	Cuba	USA (United States)	Scientific Project	67UNTS3	100862
30 Jan	USA (United States)	Venezuela	Military Mission	109UNTS25	101486
31 Jan	Hungary	Poland	Culture	25UNTS283	100368
02 Feb	Hungary	Switzerland	Taxation	49SWRO135	462053
02 Feb	Italy	USA (United States)	General Amity	79UNTS171	101040
02 Feb	ICJ Option Clause	Honduras	ICJ Option Clause	15UNTS217	100236
02 Feb	Brazil	USA (United States)	Status of Forces	67UNTS109	100870
04 Feb	Romania	USSR (Soviet Union)	Territory Boundary	0SUST244	468367
04 Feb	Norway	Poland	General Trade	30UNTS205	100458
04 Feb	Romania	USSR (Soviet Union)	General Military	48UNTS189	100745
06 Feb	Italy	USA (United States)	Air Transport	73UNTS113	100950
09 Feb	Czechoslovakia	USSR (Soviet Union)	General Trade	0SUST244	468105
09 Feb	France	Italy	Education	50FRJO702	416245
09 Feb	Belgium	Italy	Non-ILO Labor	71UNTS143	100915
11 Feb	Haiti	USA (United States)	Specific Resources	149UNTS11	101946
12 Feb	ICJ Option Clause	Brazil	ICJ Option Clause	15UNTS221	100237
12 Feb	Greece	United Nations	Humanitarian	47UNTS223	100732
14 Feb	Italy	USA (United States)	Reparations	67UNTS115	100871
15 Feb	India	UK Great Britain	Finance	134UNTS70	101796
18 Feb	Romania	USSR (Soviet Union)	General Economic	0SUST245	468368
18 Feb	Burma	USSR (Soviet Union)	Consul/Citizenship	0SUST245	468061
18 Feb	Belgium	USSR (Soviet Union)	General Trade	0SUST244	468024
18 Feb	Belgium	USSR (Soviet Union)	Finance	0SUST245	468025
18 Feb	Argentina	Italy	Air Transport	48ITGU179	435013
18 Feb	Hungary	USSR (Soviet Union)	General Military	48UNTS163	100743
19 Feb	France	UNICEF (Children)	IGO Operations	68UNTS75	100885
19 Feb	Norway	UK Great Britain	Culture	34UNTS33	100526
20 Feb	Belgium	Norway	Culture	32UNTS39	100487
21 Feb	Pakistan	UK Great Britain	Finance	134UNTS128	101797
21 Feb	Denmark	Switzerland	Non-ILO Labor	14UNTS321	100224
24 Feb	UK Great Britain	USA (United States)	Milit Installation	73UNTS143	100951
24 Feb	Norway	USA (United States)	Milit Assistance	34UNTS155	100535
25 Feb	ITU (Telecommun)	Switzerland	IGO Status/Immunit	56SWRO1196	462190
25 Feb	Czechoslovakia	Italy	Admin Cooperation	26UNTS103	100380
25 Feb	France	USA (United States)	Milit Servic/Citiz	67UNTS33	100864
25 Feb	Belgium	Turkey	Visas	18UNTS237	100293
26 Feb	Romania	USA (United States)	Admin Cooperation	48UNTS9	100738
27 Feb	France	USA (United States)	Reparations	84UNTS207	101131
27 Feb	Costa Rica	USA (United States)	Direct Aid	135UNTS74	101816
27 Feb	Poland	Romania	Culture	46UNTS143	100707
28 Feb	Denmark	Hungary	Finance	85UNTS35	101144
01 Mar	Hungary	USSR (Soviet Union)	Consul/Citizenship	0SUST438	468184
01 Mar	Czechoslovakia	Romania	Admin Cooperation	26UNTS109	100381
02 Mar	Peru	USA (United States)	Military Mission	109UNTS9	101484
02 Mar	Poland	UK Great Britain	Finance	77UNTS47	100991
02 Mar	France	UK Great Britain	Culture	77UNTS33	100990

DATE	PARTY ONE	PARTY TWO	TOPIC	CITATION	NUMBER
1948 (Cont.)					
03 Mar	United Arab Rep	USSR (Soviet Union)	Mostfavored Nation	0SUST246	468123
04 Mar	Taiwan	Portugal	Finance	0CTRC415	413023
04 Mar	Denmark	Guatemala	General Economic	96UNTS223	101339
04 Mar	Denmark	UK Great Britain	Milit Assistance	77UNTS57	100992
05 Mar	Bulgaria	Czechoslovakia	Admin Cooperation	26UNTS115	100382
06 Mar	Multilateral		Water Transport	289UNTS3	104214
08 Mar	Bulgaria	USA (United States)	Admin Cooperation	29UNTS101	100437
08 Mar	Multilateral		Admin Cooperation	27UNTS117	100403
09 Mar	Hungary	USA (United States)	Admin Cooperation	183UNTS3	102426
10 Mar	France	United Nations	Humanitarian	47UNTS203	100731
11 Mar	Netherlands	UK Great Britain	Reparations	77UNTS69	100993
12 Mar	Canada	New Zealand	Taxation	231UNTS219	103222
12 Mar	Paraguay	USA (United States)	Education	162UNTS30	102131
12 Mar	Hungary	UK Great Britain	Admin Cooperation	104UNTS35	101434
12 Mar	Finland	UK Great Britain	Admin Cooperation	104UNTS29	101433
13 Mar	Bulgaria	UK Great Britain	Postal Service	104UNTS25	101432
13 Mar	Romania	UK Great Britain	Admin Cooperation	104UNTS117	101436
13 Mar	Italy	UK Great Britain	Admin Cooperation	104UNTS41	101435
14 Mar	Czechoslovakia	Yugoslavia	Air Transport	28UNTS81	100421
15 Mar	Canada	Turkey	General Economic	231UNTS63	103205
15 Mar	Norway	USA (United States)	Admin Cooperation	73UNTS81	100946
15 Mar	Jordan	UK Great Britain	General Military	77UNTS77	100994
16 Mar	Finland	USSR (Soviet Union)	Admin Cooperation	0SUST246	468145
16 Mar	Sweden	Switzerland	Non-ILO Labor	197UNTS39	102632
16 Mar	New Zealand	USA (United States)	Taxation	127UNTS133	101703
17 Mar	Switzerland	USSR (Soviet Union)	General Trade	0SUST246	468414
17 Mar	Switzerland	USSR (Soviet Union)	General Trade	217UNTS73	102944
17 Mar	Switzerland	USSR (Soviet Union)	General Trade	217UNTS87	102945
17 Mar	Taiwan	USA (United States)	Reparations	76UNTS157	100987
17 Mar	Multilateral		General Military	19UNTS51	100304
17 Mar	Accept UN Charter	Burma	UN Charter	15UNTS3	100225
18 Mar	Argentina	Norway	Air Transport	2NORT475	451001
18 Mar	Hungary	Yugoslavia	Finance	113UNTS219	101552
18 Mar	Hungary	Yugoslavia	Finance	113UNTS201	101551
18 Mar	Argentina	Denmark	Air Transport	94UNTS175	101311
18 Mar	Hungary	Yugoslavia	General Trade	113UNTS141	101550
18 Mar	Bulgaria	USSR (Soviet Union)	General Military	48UNTS135	100741
19 Mar	France	Poland	Claims and Debts	51FRJO1111	416360
19 Mar	Cuba	UK Great Britain	Air Transport	175UNTS23	102294
23 Mar	United Nations	USA (United States)	Loans and Credits	19UNTS43	100303
23 Mar	Philippines	USA (United States)	Education	43UNTS247	100671
24 Mar	Ecuador	Philippines	General Amity	1PTS695	465014
24 Mar	USA (United States)	Venezuela	Air Transport	44UNTS57	100678
25 Mar	Belgium	Turkey	General Economic	48TURG2906	466044
25 Mar	Belgium	Luxembourg	Taxation	18UNTS323	100300
27 Mar	Belgium	Luxembourg	Culture	178UNTS265	102343
31 Mar	France	Italy	Non-ILO Labor	49ITGU1F7	435111
31 Mar	Canada	USA (United States)	Specific Property	81UNTS235	101077
31 Mar	India	Pakistan	Finance	54UNTS33	100793
01 Apr	Bulgaria	USSR (Soviet Union)	General Trade	0SUST247	471025
01 Apr	Bulgaria	USSR (Soviet Union)	General Economic	217UNTS97	102946
01 Apr	Canada	USA (United States)	Telecommunications	82UNTS99	101086
05 Apr	Czechoslovakia	Poland	Non-ILO Labor	31UNTS355	100482
05 Apr	Czechoslovakia	Poland	Admin Cooperation	31UNTS325	100481
05 Apr	Burma	USA (United States)	Admin Cooperation	73UNTS73	100945
06 Apr	Italy	Luxembourg	Non-ILO Labor	49ITGU166	435261
06 Apr	Finland	USSR (Soviet Union)	General Military	48UNTS149	100742
08 Apr	Poland	USSR (Soviet Union)	Sanitation	26UNTS191	100388
10 Apr	Czechoslovakia	Yugoslavia	General Economic	112UNTS101	101541
12 Apr	Poland	Yugoslavia	General Trade	115UNTS167	101563
13 Apr	Belgium	Netherlands	Customs	32UNTS153	100497
13 Apr	Belgium	France	Territory Boundary	31UNTS409	100483
15 Apr	IMF (Fund)	United Nations	IGO Operations	16UNTS325	200108
15 Apr	IBRD (World Bank)	United Nations	IGO Operations	16UNTS341	200109
16 Apr	Belgium	Ireland	Visas	26UNTS159	100386

DATE	PARTY ONE	PARTY TWO	TOPIC	CITATION	NUMBER
1948 (Cont.)					
17 Apr	Hungary	Yugoslavia	Reparations	130UNTS101	101727
17 Apr	Hungary	Yugoslavia	Reparations	130UNTS111	101728
17 Apr	Hungary	Yugoslavia	Reparations	130UNTS121	101729
19 Apr	Germany, West	Turkey	General Trade	49TURG1902	466065
19 Apr	France	UK Great Britain	Status of Forces	83UNTS201	101109
19 Apr	Iceland	United Nations	Humanitarian	47UNTS251	100733
20 Apr	Philippines	UK Great Britain	Territory Boundary	1PTS705	465015
21 Apr	Denmark	Norway	Finance	18UNTS139	100284
22 Apr	UPU (Postal Union)	Switzerland	IGO Status/Immunit	56SWRO1194	462189
22 Apr	Poland	Sweden	Claims and Debts	49PDZU27	457004
23 Apr	Greece	USA (United States)	Education	74UNTS107	100958
23 Apr	Belgium	France	Territory Boundary	19UNTS95	100307
24 Apr	Italy	Vatican/Holy See	Territory Boundary	50ITGU99	435338
27 Apr	France	Switzerland	Non-ILO Labor	51SWRO1019	462017
28 Apr	Canada	Italy	General Economic	231UNTS69	103206
29 Apr	France	Spain	Air Transport	48SPBO1605	460101
29 Apr	Netherlands	USA (United States)	Taxation	32UNTS167	100498
29 Apr	Norway	Sweden	Commodity Trade	26UNTS41	100376
29 Apr	Norway	Sweden	Commodity Trade	26UNTS33	100375
29 Apr	Norway	Sweden	Finance	26UNTS11	100374
30 Apr	Taiwan	USA (United States)	Direct Aid	0CTRC753	413031
30 Apr	Ceylon (Sri Lanka)	UK Great Britain	Finance	182UNTS2	102421
30 Apr	Multilateral		IGO Establishment	119UNTS3	101609
30 Apr	Multilateral		Dispute Settlement	30UNTS55	100449
30 Apr	Canada	USA (United States)	Sanitation	77UNTS191	100999
30 Apr	Belgium	Italy	Non-ILO Labor	36UNTS305	100571
01 May	Pakistan	USSR (Soviet Union)	Consul/Citizenship	0SUST248	468303
01 May	Italy	South Africa	Admin Cooperation	225UNTS53	103087
03 May	Spain	USA (United States)	Finance	132UNTS155	101756
04 May	India	Pakistan	Dispute Settlement	54UNTS45	100794
05 May	Canada	France	Reparations	231UNTS87	103209
06 May	France	Ireland	General Trade	558UNTS170	108141
06 May	Ireland	Switzerland	Air Transport	334UNTS187	104768
06 May	Pakistan	Sweden	Air Transport	36UNTS3	100564
06 May	Denmark	USA (United States)	Taxation	26UNTS55	100377
07 May	Jordan	Turkey	Air Transport	32UNTS313	100505
10 May	Taiwan	France	Air Transport	0CTRC169	413019
10 May	Multilateral		Culture	289UNTS111	104215
10 May	Multilateral		Reparations	140UNTS129	101887
10 May	Ireland	Netherlands	Air Transport	28UNTS121	100422
11 May	Multilateral		Telecommunications	500UNTS267	107313
13 May	Multilateral		Reparations	140UNTS187	101888
13 May	Hungary	Poland	General Economic	25UNTS301	100369
14 May	Ecuador	USA (United States)	Scientific Project	89UNTS71	101210
14 May	Denmark	Iceland	Non-ILO Labor	23UNTS163	100346
18 May	Israel	USSR (Soviet Union)	Recognition	0SUST248	468236
18 May	Guatemala	USA (United States)	Land Transport	67UNTS161	100875
18 May	Taiwan	UK Great Britain	Milit Assistance	66UNTS113	100850
20 May	Taiwan	Portugal	Customs	0CTRC419	413024
20 May	Finland	United Nations	Humanitarian	47UNTS319	200189
20 May	Philippines	Spain	Consul/Citizenship	70UNTS143	100903
20 May	Norway	Turkey	Air Transport	26UNTS137	100384
21 May	Norway	USSR (Soviet Union)	Claims and Debts	2NORT478	451205
21 May	Taiwan	UNICEF (Children)	Tech Assistance	65UNTS38	100818
21 May	Brazil	UK Great Britain	Finance	66UNTS121	100851
21 May	India	Sweden	Air Transport	34UNTS285	100543
22 May	Indonesia	USSR (Soviet Union)	Consul/Citizenship	0SUST248	468218
24 May	Czechoslovakia	Yugoslavia	Specif Goods/Equip	112UNTS215	101544
24 May	Czechoslovakia	Yugoslavia	Finance	112UNTS225	101545
24 May	Czechoslovakia	Yugoslavia	Finance	112UNTS183	101543
24 May	Czechoslovakia	Yugoslavia	General Trade	112UNTS111	101542
25 May	Portugal	UK Great Britain	Milit Installation	34UNTS311	100544
26 May	Israel	USSR (Soviet Union)	Consul/Citizenship	0SUST248	468237
26 May	Greece	Switzerland	Air Transport	94UNTS217	101312
27 May	Luxembourg	UK Great Britain	Air Transport	53UNTS115	100776

DATE	PARTY ONE	PARTY TWO	TOPIC	CITATION	NUMBER
1948 (Cont.)					
29 May	France	Italy	Patents/Copyrights	49ITGU250	435113
29 May	France	Italy	Patents/Copyrights	49ITGU247	435112
29 May	Bulgaria	Poland	General Military	26UNTS213	100389
30 May	Bulgaria	Poland	General Trade	37UNTS3	100574
02 Jun	France	Netherlands	Education	50FRJO1002	416357
02 Jun	Argentina	Brazil	Air Transport	0UNTS0	109515
02 Jun	France	Netherlands	Non-ILO Labor	204UNTS275	102762
02 Jun	Canada	Netherlands	Air Transport	32UNTS215	100499
03 Jun	Australia	Poland	Direct Aid	16UNTS189	100258
04 Jun	New Zealand	Sweden	Visas	18UNTS171	100286
05 Jun	Belgium	Monaco	Admin Cooperation	18UNTS245	100294
07 Jun	Hungary	USSR (Soviet Union)	Reparations	0SUST249	468185
07 Jun	Romania	USSR (Soviet Union)	Reparations	0SUST249	468369
07 Jun	Sweden	Turkey	General Economic	49TURG1902	466089
07 Jun	Belgium	UK Great Britain	Reparations	20UNTS33	100313
07 Jun	Philippines	USA (United States)	Admin Cooperation	73UNTS89	100947
09 Jun	France	Poland	Non-ILO Labor	32UNTS251	100503
10 Jun	Multilateral		Humanitarian	191UNTS3	102576
10 Jun	Multilateral		Humanitarian	164UNTS113	102163
10 Jun	ICJ Option Clause	Belgium	ICJ Option Clause	16UNTS203	100260
11 Jun	France	Norway	General Trade	31UNTS83	100469
11 Jun	Netherlands	UK Great Britain	General Economic	66UNTS183	100853
11 Jun	France	UK Great Britain	Non-ILO Labor	66UNTS151	100852
12 Jun	Finland	Turkey	Finance	49TURG1902	466053
12 Jun	Finland	Turkey	General Trade	49TURG1902	466054
15 Jun	France	Switzerland	Specific Resources	66FRRT33	415405
16 Jun	Accept UN Charter	Ceylon (Sri Lanka)	UN Charter	223UNTS39	103047
16 Jun	Pakistan	USA (United States)	Air Transport	235UNTS29	103293
16 Jun	Australia	Greece	Claims and Debts	18UNTS211	100290
18 Jun	Hungary	Poland	Culture	25UNTS319	100370
19 Jun	Finland	USSR (Soviet Union)	Dispute Settlement	0SUST249	468146
19 Jun	Multilateral		Air Transport	310UNTS151	104492
21 Jun	Ireland	Norway	Air Transport	34UNTS317	100545
22 Jun	Italy	Switzerland	Non-ILO Labor	48SWRO818	462019
22 Jun	Burma	Pakistan	Postal Service	91UNTS197	101252
22 Jun	ICJ Option Clause	Pakistan	ICJ Option Clause	16UNTS197	100259
23 Jun	Luxembourg	Netherlands	Air Transport	32UNTS229	100500
23 Jun	India	Pakistan	Air Transport	28UNTS143	100423
23 Jun	Spain	UK Great Britain	General Economic	66UNTS193	100854
24 Jun	Czechoslovakia	Netherlands	General Trade	51NET49	447008
24 Jun	Chile	UK Great Britain	Finance	77UNTS113	100995
25 Jun	Greece	Sweden	General Trade	267UNTS337	103849
25 Jun	Italy	UK Great Britain	Air Transport	94UNTS239	101313
26 Jun	Multilateral		Culture	331UNTS217	104757
26 Jun	Norway	Switzerland	General Trade	29UNTS193	100440
28 Jun	New Zealand	Pakistan	Postal Service	91UNTS235	101253
28 Jun	Ireland	USA (United States)	Mostfavored Nation	32UNTS69	100489
28 Jun	France	USA (United States)	Mostfavored Nation	31UNTS115	100472
28 Jun	Italy	USA (United States)	Milit Occupation	25UNTS45	100356
28 Jun	Ireland	USA (United States)	Direct Aid	24UNTS3	100349
28 Jun	Italy	USA (United States)	Direct Aid	20UNTS43	100314
28 Jun	France	USA (United States)	Direct Aid	19UNTS9	100302
29 Jun	Denmark	USA (United States)	Mostfavored Nation	27UNTS35	100396
29 Jun	Denmark	USA (United States)	Direct Aid	22UNTS217	100338
30 Jun	Belgium	USSR (Soviet Union)	Finance	16SUGG64	469885
30 Jun	Iran	USSR (Soviet Union)	Territory Boundary	0IRTB75	433118
30 Jun	Afghanistan	Iran	Territory Boundary	0IRTB1	433001
30 Jun	Peru	USA (United States)	Education	150UNTS45	101962
30 Jun	Brazil	USA (United States)	General Trade	125UNTS111	101673
30 Jun	Paraguay	USA (United States)	Sanitation	124UNTS34	101665
30 Jun	India	Pakistan	Finance	29UNTS199	100441
01 Jul	Australia	Greece	Direct Aid	22UNTS33	100329
01 Jul	Australia	Hungary	Direct Aid	22UNTS3	100325
02 Jul	Netherlands	USSR (Soviet Union)	General Economic	0NET0	447009
02 Jul	Netherlands	USA (United States)	Mostfavored Nation	32UNTS77	100490

DATE	PARTY ONE	PARTY TWO	TOPIC	CITATION	NUMBER
1948 (Cont.)					
02 Jul	Greece	USA (United States)	Mostfavored Nation	31UNTS131	100474
02 Jul	Belgium	USA (United States)	Mostfavored Nation	27UNTS43	100397
02 Jul	Austria	USA (United States)	Milit Occupation	25UNTS53	100357
02 Jul	Greece	USA (United States)	Direct Aid	23UNTS43	100342
02 Jul	Austria	USA (United States)	Direct Aid	21UNTS29	100323
02 Jul	Netherlands	USA (United States)	Direct Aid	20UNTS91	100315
02 Jul	Belgium	USA (United States)	Direct Aid	19UNTS127	100309
03 Jul	Taiwan	USA (United States)	Mostfavored Nation	0CTRC767	413032
03 Jul	Belgium	Czechoslovakia	General Trade	77UNTS137	100997
03 Jul	Sweden	USA (United States)	Milit Occupation	27UNTS69	100400
03 Jul	Norway	USA (United States)	Milit Occupation	27UNTS59	100399
03 Jul	Iceland	USA (United States)	Milit Occupation	27UNTS49	100398
03 Jul	Luxembourg	USA (United States)	Direct Aid	24UNTS35	100350
03 Jul	Sweden	USA (United States)	Direct Aid	23UNTS101	100343
03 Jul	Norway	USA (United States)	Direct Aid	20UNTS185	100317
03 Jul	Iceland	USA (United States)	Direct Aid	20UNTS141	100316
03 Jul	Taiwan	USA (United States)	Direct Aid	17UNTS119	100273
04 Jul	Turkey	USA (United States)	Direct Aid	24UNTS67	100351
04 Jul	Turkey	USA (United States)	Mostfavored Nation	34UNTS185	100536
05 Jul	France	Norway	General Trade	30UNTS281	100463
05 Jul	ICJ Option Clause	Bolivia	ICJ Option Clause	16UNTS207	100261
06 Jul	UK Great Britain	USA (United States)	Milit Occupation	25UNTS61	100358
06 Jul	UK Great Britain	USA (United States)	Direct Aid	22UNTS263	100339
06 Jul	ICJ Option Clause	Switzerland	ICJ Option Clause	17UNTS115	100272
06 Jul	ICJ Option Clause	Switzerland	ICJ Option Clause	17UNTS111	100271
07 Jul	Netherlands	UK Great Britain	Culture	82UNTS259	101099
08 Jul	Poland	USSR (Soviet Union)	Territory Boundary	37UNTS25	100575
08 Jul	Australia	Italy	Direct Aid	22UNTS11	100326
08 Jul	Poland	USSR (Soviet Union)	Dispute Settlement	37UNTS107	100576
09 Jul	Multilateral		ILO Labor	81UNTS147	101070
09 Jul	France	USA (United States)	Mostfavored Nation	32UNTS93	100492
09 Jul	Multilateral		ILO Labor	68UNTS17	100881
09 Jul	Multilateral		ILO Labor	70UNTS85	100898
09 Jul	France	USA (United States)	Direct Aid	24UNTS103	100352
09 Jul	Australia	Yugoslavia	Direct Aid	22UNTS17	100327
10 Jul	ILO (Labor Org)	WHO (World Health)	IGO Operations	19UNTS269	200121
10 Jul	Multilateral		ILO Labor	91UNTS3	101239
12 Jul	France	UK Great Britain	Postal Service	90UNTS83	101230
12 Jul	UK Great Britain	Uruguay	Finance	71UNTS199	100919
14 Jul	Bolivia	USA (United States)	Sanitation	136UNTS238	101838
14 Jul	Multilateral		Mostfavored Nation	31UNTS123	100473
14 Jul	Multilateral		Direct Aid	23UNTS3	100340
15 Jul	UNESCO (Educ/Cult)	WHO (World Health)	IGO Operations	44UNTS323	200184
15 Jul	Netherlands	IBRD (World Bank)	IBRD Project	153UNTS259	102023
15 Jul	Netherlands	IBRD (World Bank)	IBRD Project	153UNTS259	102021
15 Jul	Netherlands	IBRD (World Bank)	IBRD Project	153UNTS259	102022
15 Jul	Netherlands	IBRD (World Bank)	IBRD Project	153UNTS259	102024
15 Jul	Netherlands	IBRD (World Bank)	IBRD Project	153UNTS211	102020
15 Jul	Netherlands	IBRD (World Bank)	IBRD Project	153UNTS259	102025
15 Jul	France	UK Great Britain	Claims and Debts	71UNTS215	100920
16 Jul	Bulgaria	Hungary	General Amity	477UNTS169	106921
16 Jul	Monaco	Norway	Visas	90UNTS77	101229
17 Jul	FAO (Food Agri)	WHO (World Health)	IGO Operations	76UNTS171	200244
18 Jul	Poland	Turkey	General Economic	49TURG1802	466081
19 Jul	USA (United States)	Yugoslavia	Claims and Debts	89UNTS43	101208
19 Jul	Australia	Austria	Direct Aid	22UNTS25	100328
19 Jul	USA (United States)	Yugoslavia	Milit Assistance	34UNTS195	100537
20 Jul	Peru	UK Great Britain	Finance	66UNTS197	100855
24 Jul	Multilateral		Sanitation	66UNTS25	100847
26 Jul	Liberia	USA (United States)	Customs	182UNTS73	102423
28 Jul	Finland	USSR (Soviet Union)	Reparations	16SUGG64	469886
29 Jul	Brazil	USA (United States)	Military Mission	80UNTS111	101047
30 Jul	New Zealand	Switzerland	Visas	18UNTS177	100287
31 Jul	Ireland	UK Great Britain	General Trade	86UNTS37	101151
02 Aug	Australia	Italy	Air Transport	28UNTS165	100424

DATE	PARTY ONE	PARTY TWO	TOPIC	CITATION	NUMBER
1948 (Cont.)					
05 Aug	Taiwan	USA (United States)	IGO Establishment	82UNTS109	101087
06 Aug	Czechoslovakia	France	Taxation	49FRJO2207	416438
06 Aug	Czechoslovakia	France	Claims and Debts	48FRMD1908	417439
09 Aug	Bulgaria	USSR (Soviet Union)	Loans and Credits	0SUST251	468035
10 Aug	Ecuador	Mexico	Culture	52MEXD2810	444015
10 Aug	Brazil	Switzerland	Air Transport	94UNTS269	101314
11 Aug	India	USA (United States)	Visas	224UNTS115	103072
14 Aug	India	Switzerland	General Amity	33UNTS3	100509
17 Aug	France	Poland	Non-ILO Labor	0UNTS0	110700
18 Aug	Multilateral		Water Transport	33UNTS181	100518
20 Aug	Romania	USSR (Soviet Union)	Postal Service	0SUST252	468371
20 Aug	Romania	USSR (Soviet Union)	Gen Communications	0SUST252	468370
23 Aug	FAO (Food Agri)	UNESCO (Educ/Cult)	IGO Operations	18UNTS345	200112
23 Aug	France	Spain	Air Transport	28UNTS173	100425
23 Aug	Philippines	USA (United States)	Patents/Copyrights	82UNTS11	101080
24 Aug	Belgium	Luxembourg	Extradition	117UNTS131	101589
24 Aug	Korea, South	USA (United States)	General Military	79UNTS57	101031
27 Aug	Philippines	USA (United States)	Reparations	44UNTS13	100675
27 Aug	Pakistan	United Nations	Humanitarian	47UNTS269	100734
27 Aug	Canada	United Nations	Humanitarian	47UNTS167	100729
01 Sep	Belgium	Switzerland	Visas	23UNTS139	100344
02 Sep	Ireland	Netherlands	General Trade	558UNTS249	108145
03 Sep	Albania	USSR (Soviet Union)	Loans and Credits	0SUST252	471027
03 Sep	Albania	USSR (Soviet Union)	General Trade	0SUST252	471026
06 Sep	Greece	Lebanon	Air Transport	178UNTS37	102335
06 Sep	Netherlands	UK Great Britain	Finance	32UNTS235	100501
07 Sep	Greece	UK Great Britain	Status of Forces	180UNTS144	102380
10 Sep	Finland	Norway	Specific Resources	32UNTS3	100486
11 Sep	Korea, South	USA (United States)	Milit Assistance	89UNTS155	101216
14 Sep	Multilateral		Milit Occupation	18UNTS267	100296
14 Sep	New Zealand	USA (United States)	General Military	18UNTS251	100295
16 Sep	Czechoslovakia	USA (United States)	Milit Assistance	90UNTS35	101224
16 Sep	Iceland	ICAO (Civil Aviat)	Air Transport	28UNTS267	100429
16 Sep	France	USA (United States)	Culture	84UNTS185	101129
17 Sep	New Zealand	Pakistan	Postal Service	91UNTS275	101254
17 Sep	Multilateral		Telecommunications	97UNTS31	101345
18 Sep	Korea, North	USSR (Soviet Union)	Milit Occupation	0SUST253	468246
20 Sep	Israel	UNICEF (Children)	Direct Aid	71UNTS17	100907
21 Sep	Ecuador	USA (United States)	Military Mission	80UNTS127	101048
21 Sep	Greece	Italy	Culture	77UNTS259	101003
22 Sep	UK Great Britain	USA (United States)	Milit Assistance	71UNTS64	100910
23 Sep	El Salvador	USA (United States)	Sanitation	181UNTS101	102402
24 Sep	Panama	USA (United States)	Education	150UNTS25	101961
25 Sep	Belgium	Netherlands	Taxation	123UNTS81	101655
27 Sep	Switzerland	Yugoslavia	Claims and Debts	48SWRO995	462172
27 Sep	Switzerland	Yugoslavia	General Trade	48SWRO986	462164
27 Sep	Switzerland	Yugoslavia	General Economic	48SWRO990	462165
27 Sep	UNRRA (Relief)	United Nations	IGO Operations	27UNTS349	200158
28 Sep	Portugal	USA (United States)	Mostfavored Nation	31UNTS139	100475
28 Sep	Portugal	USA (United States)	Direct Aid	29UNTS213	100442
29 Sep	Bolivia	USA (United States)	Air Transport	505UNTS139	107370
29 Sep	Italy	USA (United States)	Visas	84UNTS43	101117
30 Sep	UK Great Britain	USA (United States)	Specific Resources	71UNTS241	100922
02 Oct	Hungary	USSR (Soviet Union)	General Economic	0SUST253	468186
05 Oct	United Nations	Thailand	Humanitarian	47UNTS287	100735
06 Oct	Greece	Lebanon	Consul/Citizenship	87UNTS351	101179
06 Oct	Argentina	USA (United States)	Military Mission	80UNTS91	101046
07 Oct	United Nations	San Marino	Humanitarian	47UNTS337	200190
07 Oct	Czechoslovakia	United Nations	Humanitarian	47UNTS185	100730
08 Oct	Guatemala	USA (United States)	Military Mission	121UNTS31	101623
08 Oct	Guatemala	USA (United States)	Military Mission	121UNTS37	101624
08 Oct	Netherlands	Spain	Air Transport	28UNTS209	100426
08 Oct	Australia	Denmark	Claims and Debts	22UNTS43	100330
08 Oct	Multilateral		Education	19UNTS113	100308
09 Oct	Accept UN Charter	Bulgaria	UN Charter	223UNTS31	103045

DATE	PARTY ONE	PARTY TWO	TOPIC	CITATION	NUMBER
1948 (Cont.)					
09 Oct	Belgium	Luxembourg	Taxation	123UNTS29	101652
11 Oct	Belgium	Netherlands	Finance	26UNTS95	100379
12 Oct	Korea, North	USSR (Soviet Union)	General Amity	0SUST253	468247
12 Oct	Czechoslovakia	France	Non-ILO Labor	45UNTS81	100693
12 Oct	Burma	UK Great Britain	Finance	71UNTS255	100923
15 Oct	Trieste	USA (United States)	Direct Aid	29UNTS249	100443
15 Oct	Netherlands	UK Great Britain	Taxation	73UNTS203	100954
15 Oct	Netherlands	UK Great Britain	Taxation	74UNTS3	100955
16 Oct	Sweden	Switzerland	Taxation	197UNTS55	102634
16 Oct	Sweden	Switzerland	Taxation	197UNTS101	102635
16 Oct	Turkey	UK Great Britain	Finance	83UNTS85	101103
18 Oct	Argentina	Spain	Milit Servic/Citiz	48SPBO3110	460032
18 Oct	Argentina	Spain	Culture	48SPBO3110	460033
18 Oct	Argentina	Spain	Health/Educ/Welfare	48SPBO3110	460034
18 Oct	Argentina	Spain	Culture	48SPBO3110	460035
18 Oct	Taiwan	UK Great Britain	Customs	0CTRC645	413028
19 Oct	France	USA (United States)	Air Transport	98UNTS3	101355
19 Oct	Multilateral		Specif Claim/Waive	84UNTS201	101130
21 Oct	Philippines	USA (United States)	Patents/Copyrights	77UNTS197	101000
22 Oct	Peru	ICAO (Civil Aviat)	IGO Status/Immunit	95UNTS3	101315
22 Oct	France	USA (United States)	Education	84UNTS173	101128
22 Oct	Mexico	Portugal	Air Transport	34UNTS329	100546
25 Oct	Greece	USA (United States)	General Trade	185UNTS103	102462
26 Oct	Belgium	USA (United States)	Visas	84UNTS265	101135
28 Oct	Canada	Netherlands	Reparations	231UNTS95	103210
28 Oct	Belgium	USA (United States)	Taxation	173UNTS67	102262
28 Oct	Belgium	France	Visas	25UNTS151	100360
28 Oct	Italy	UK Great Britain	Visas	77UNTS129	100996
29 Oct	Austria	Czechoslovakia	Water Transport	56ABGB74	403022
29 Oct	Argentina	Netherlands	Air Transport	95UNTS21	101316
30 Oct	Poland	USA (United States)	Consul/Citizenship	15UNTS225	100238
01 Nov	Romania	USSR (Soviet Union)	Specific Property	16SUGG64	469887
01 Nov	Greece	USA (United States)	Direct Aid	185UNTS169	102468
05 Nov	Greece	Italy	General Amity	50ITGU265	435195
05 Nov	Greece	Italy	Admin Cooperation	51ITGU205	435196
05 Nov	Panama	USA (United States)	Visas	89UNTS27	101206
09 Nov	Argentina	Norway	Taxation	2NORT488	451002
09 Nov	Austria	Italy	Land Transport	50ITGU44	435028
09 Nov	Austria	Italy	Land Transport	51ITGU71	435029
10 Nov	Italy	Turkey	General Economic	50TURG301	466074
10 Nov	Monaco	UK Great Britain	Visas	81UNTS85	101065
11 Nov	Denmark	UK Great Britain	Finance	25UNTS333	100371
12 Nov	New Zealand	UK Great Britain	Milit Assistance	162UNTS197	102136
12 Nov	Czechoslovakia	Poland	Land Transport	84UNTS347	101141
12 Nov	UK Great Britain	USA (United States)	Visas	84UNTS275	101136
15 Nov	Finland	South Africa	Admin Cooperation	225UNTS59	103088
15 Nov	Multilateral		IGO Establishment	120UNTS59	101615
16 Nov	Hungary	South Africa	Admin Cooperation	225UNTS65	103089
16 Nov	Romania	South Africa	Admin Cooperation	225UNTS71	103090
17 Nov	Canada	Finland	General Trade	231UNTS75	103207
18 Nov	Taiwan	USA (United States)	Direct Aid	198UNTS287	102672
19 Nov	Multilateral		Sanitation	44UNTS277	100688
20 Nov	Argentina	Sweden	Taxation	197UNTS47	102633
20 Nov	Philippines	UNICEF (Children)	Tech Assistance	65UNTS48	100819
23 Nov	Argentina	Sweden	General Economic	49SOFM571	461094
23 Nov	Canada	USA (United States)	Commodity Trade	81UNTS295	101078
26 Nov	Italy	USA (United States)	Direct Aid	79UNTS71	101032
26 Nov	Brazil	USA (United States)	Scientific Project	88UNTS3	101180
27 Nov	Austria	Norway	General Trade	2NORT490	451221
27 Nov	France	USA (United States)	Scientific Project	168UNTS119	102217
29 Nov	Multilateral		IGO Establishment	120UNTS13	101613
29 Nov	Accept UN Charter	Israel	UN Charter	30UNTS53	100448
29 Nov	Austria	Denmark	General Trade	74UNTS243	100967
29 Nov	Austria	Denmark	Finance	74UNTS257	100968
29 Nov	Belgium	Italy	Culture	41UNTS3	100641

DATE	PARTY ONE	PARTY TWO	TOPIC	CITATION	NUMBER
1948 (Cont.)					
01 Dec	Ireland	Luxembourg	Visas	553UNTS111	108075
01 Dec	UK Great Britain	USA (United States)	Direct Aid	81UNTS93	101066
01 Dec	UNICEF (Children)	Thailand	IGO Operations	68UNTS94	100886
02 Dec	Belgium	Turkey	General Economic	50TURG3001	466045
02 Dec	Accept UN Charter	Albania	UN Charter	223UNTS23	103043
04 Dec	Italy	Netherlands	Non-ILO Labor	46UNTS271	100716
06 Dec	Brazil	France	Culture	60FRRT58	415076
06 Dec	South Africa	UK Great Britain	Customs	118UNTS183	101607
08 Dec	Afghanistan	UNESCO (Educ/Cult)	Education	46UNTS3	100697
09 Dec	Finland	USSR (Soviet Union)	Territory Boundary	217UNTS135	102947
09 Dec	Multilateral		Scientific Project	73UNTS39	100942
09 Dec	Australia	Belgium	Claims and Debts	25UNTS159	100361
09 Dec	Multilateral		Scientific Project	20UNTS229	100318
09 Dec	Multilateral		Humanitarian	78UNTS277	101021
10 Dec	Korea, South	USA (United States)	Direct Aid	55UNTS157	100813
11 Dec	Italy	USSR (Soviet Union)	Finance	0SUST255	468241
11 Dec	Italy	USSR (Soviet Union)	Reparations	0SUST255	468240
11 Dec	Italy	USSR (Soviet Union)	General Trade	0SUST255	471028
11 Dec	Italy	USSR (Soviet Union)	General Trade	50ITGU5	435420
11 Dec	Italy	USSR (Soviet Union)	General Trade	0UNTS0	109576
11 Dec	Italy	USSR (Soviet Union)	General Economic	217UNTS181	102948
13 Dec	Denmark	New Zealand	Visas	92UNTS65	101261
14 Dec	Argentina	Chile	Air Transport	635UNTS21	109071
14 Dec	Denmark	Poland	Finance	81UNTS33	101060
14 Dec	Argentina	Denmark	General Economic	74UNTS41	100956
15 Dec	Czechoslovakia	USSR (Soviet Union)	General Economic	0SUST255	468106
15 Dec	Ceylon (Sri Lanka)	Pakistan	Postal Service	91UNTS303	101255
15 Dec	Denmark	Turkey	General Trade	76UNTS17	100975
15 Dec	Argentina	Denmark	Taxation	67UNTS71	100866
15 Dec	Spain	UK Great Britain	Finance	87UNTS49	101165
15 Dec	Denmark	Turkey	Finance	76UNTS3	100974
16 Dec	Multilateral		Direct Aid	79UNTS85	101033
16 Dec	Belgium	Sweden	Visas	26UNTS3	100372
17 Dec	Finland	USSR (Soviet Union)	General Trade	0SUST256	471029
18 Dec	Germany, West	Turkey	General Economic	50TURG1001	466140
18 Dec	Italy	USA (United States)	Education	79UNTS133	101037
18 Dec	Norway	Sweden	Non-ILO Labor	30UNTS117	100450
21 Dec	Ceylon (Sri Lanka)	India	Air Transport	28UNTS223	100427
22 Dec	Philippines	Spain	Dispute Settlement	2PTS93	465016
23 Dec	UK Great Britain	Yugoslavia	Reparations	81UNTS121	101068
23 Dec	UK Great Britain	Yugoslavia	Reparations	81UNTS103	101067
23 Dec	UK Great Britain	Yugoslavia	General Trade	81UNTS133	101069
23 Dec	France	USA (United States)	Direct Aid	67UNTS171	100876
27 Dec	USSR (Soviet Union)	Yugoslavia	General Trade	116UNTS327	101579
27 Dec	Belgium	Greece	General Trade	77UNTS265	101004
27 Dec	Belgium	Greece	Finance	77UNTS293	101005
29 Dec	Belgium	UK Great Britain	Visas	27UNTS135	100404
30 Dec	Brazil	USA (United States)	Sanitation	102UNTS3	101406
30 Dec	Belgium	Denmark	Dispute Settlement	25UNTS173	100362
31 Dec	Romania	Yugoslavia	Visas	116UNTS103	101572
31 Dec	Norway	Poland	General Trade	29UNTS3	100430
1949					
01 Jan	Belgium	Italy	Visas	26UNTS151	100385
03 Jan	Ceylon (Sri Lanka)	Pakistan	Air Transport	28UNTS247	100428
04 Jan	Haiti	USA (United States)	Military Mission	44UNTS69	100679
06 Jan	Mexico	IBRD (World Bank)	IBRD Project	154UNTS3	102027
06 Jan	Mexico	IBRD (World Bank)	IBRD Project	154UNTS81	102028
07 Jan	Australia	Romania	Admin Cooperation	189UNTS263	102550
07 Jan	Australia	Hungary	Admin Cooperation	189UNTS233	102548
07 Jan	Australia	Italy	Admin Cooperation	189UNTS239	102549
07 Jan	Australia	Finland	Admin Cooperation	189UNTS227	102547
08 Jan	Belgium	France	Non-ILO Labor	36UNTS151	100569
12 Jan	WHO (World Health)	Switzerland	IGO Status/Immunit	26UNTS331	200155
14 Jan	Germany, West	Sweden	Finance	49SOFM84	461075

DATE	PARTY ONE	PARTY TWO	TOPIC	CITATION	NUMBER
1949 (Cont.)					
14 Jan	Poland	UK Great Britain	General Economic	83UNTS3	101100
14 Jan	Poland	UK Great Britain	Reparations	83UNTS51	101101
14 Jan	Belgium	Luxembourg	Direct Aid	36UNTS339	100572
15 Jan	Germany, West	Turkey	General Economic	49TURG2812	466066
15 Jan	Argentina	Netherlands	Taxation	46UNTS241	100713
16 Jan	Poland	Yugoslavia	General Trade	115UNTS241	101564
17 Jan	Netherlands	USA (United States)	Direct Aid	32UNTS241	100502
17 Jan	Netherlands	UK Great Britain	Reparations	83UNTS67	101102
19 Jan	Hungary	Sweden	General Trade	49SOFM155	461080
21 Jan	Chile	USA (United States)	Sanitation	160UNTS185	102107
21 Jan	Czechoslovakia	Poland	Admin Cooperation	31UNTS205	100480
22 Jan	Czechoslovakia	Poland	Sanitation	85UNTS3	101142
24 Jan	Romania	USSR (Soviet Union)	Tech Assistance	0SUST257	468372
24 Jan	Romania	USSR (Soviet Union)	General Economic	0SUST257	468373
24 Jan	Germany, East	Sweden	General Trade	49SOFM13	461072
24 Jan	Italy	Lebanon	Air Transport	231UNTS241	103223
25 Jan	Mexico	USA (United States)	IGO Establishment	99UNTS3	101367
26 Jan	Poland	Romania	General Military	85UNTS21	101143
27 Jan	Taiwan	USA (United States)	Direct Aid	0CTRC790	413036
27 Jan	Brazil	IBRD (World Bank)	IBRD Project	153UNTS264	102026
28 Jan	Norway	Sweden	Specific Resources	196UNTS3	102617
28 Jan	Austria	Norway	General Trade	30UNTS145	100452
29 Jan	Greece	USA (United States)	Visas	88UNTS35	101183
31 Jan	Ceylon (Sri Lanka)	USA (United States)	Admin Cooperation	88UNTS21	101181
31 Jan	Canada	USA (United States)	Humanitarian	43UNTS119	100666
01 Feb	Czechoslovakia	Sweden	General Trade	49SOFM63	461073
01 Feb	Czechoslovakia	Sweden	Finance	49SOFM76	461074
03 Feb	France	Italy	Air Transport	53ITGU91	435114
03 Feb	Italy	Yugoslavia	Visas	33UNTS105	100517
04 Feb	Ecuador	USA (United States)	Military Mission	80UNTS137	101049
07 Feb	France	Syria	Finance	50FRJO1003	416423
07 Feb	IRO (Refugee Org)	United Nations	IGO Operations	26UNTS299	200153
07 Feb	France	USA (United States)	Direct Aid	67UNTS189	100877
08 Feb	Denmark	Sweden	General Trade	49SOFM1	461071
08 Feb	Multilateral		Specific Resources	157UNTS157	102053
08 Feb	Denmark	Sweden	Finance	33UNTS227	100519
09 Feb	FAO (Food Agri)	UNESCO (Educ/Cult)	IGO Operations	43UNTS315	200182
09 Feb	France	Norway	General Economic	29UNTS13	100431
09 Feb	Greece	USA (United States)	Direct Aid	79UNTS95	101034
11 Feb	Trieste	USA (United States)	Direct Aid	79UNTS123	101036
11 Feb	Austria	USA (United States)	Direct Aid	79UNTS113	101035
12 Feb	Multilateral		Customs	189UNTS33	102541
14 Feb	Belgium	Sweden	Finance	49SOFM87	461076
14 Feb	Mexico	USA (United States)	Sanitation	160UNTS75	102103
15 Feb	Italy	Lebanon	Admin Cooperation	50ITGU187	435256
15 Feb	Italy	Lebanon	General Amity	51ITGU106	435257
16 Feb	Switzerland	Turkey	Air Transport	72UNTS175	100933
17 Feb	ILO (Labor Org)	United Nations	IGO Operations	26UNTS323	200154
17 Feb	Finland	Sweden	Specific Resources	197UNTS123	102636
17 Feb	Allied Milit Occup	Norway	Milit Occupation	30UNTS137	100451
17 Feb	Korea, South	USA (United States)	Postal Service	74UNTS167	100963
18 Feb	Belgium	France	Claims and Debts	31UNTS173	100478
20 Feb	Romania	USSR (Soviet Union)	Specific Property	16SUGG64	469888
21 Feb	Cuba	USA (United States)	Status of Forces	231UNTS108	103212
21 Feb	Colombia	USA (United States)	Military Mission	92UNTS227	101275
21 Feb	Belgium	Sweden	Air Transport	95UNTS73	101317
21 Feb	Greece	USA (United States)	Status of Forces	88UNTS29	101182
21 Feb	Colombia	USA (United States)	Military Mission	44UNTS83	100680
22 Feb	Multilateral		Sanitation	93UNTS129	101296
22 Feb	South Africa	UK Great Britain	Territory Boundary	93UNTS75	101291
24 Feb	Mongolia	USSR (Soviet Union)	Water Transport	16SUGG65	469889
24 Feb	Mongolia	USSR (Soviet Union)	Specific Resources	0SUST439	468266
24 Feb	Israel	United Arab Rep	Peace/Disarmament	42UNTS251	100654
24 Feb	Norway	Turkey	Finance	30UNTS151	100453
24 Feb	Norway	Turkey	General Trade	29UNTS47	100433

DATE	PARTY ONE	PARTY TWO	TOPIC	CITATION	NUMBER
1949 (Cont.)					
25 Feb	Denmark	Greece	General Trade	78UNTS325	101022
25 Feb	Finland	Netherlands	Air Transport	53UNTS123	100777
25 Feb	Belgium	Luxembourg	Admin Cooperation	47UNTS3	100719
25 Feb	Denmark	Greece	Finance	78UNTS335	101023
26 Feb	Netherlands	Norway	General Economic	29UNTS33	100432
27 Feb	Czechoslovakia	Hungary	Admin Cooperation	26UNTS119	100383
28 Feb	Ceylon (Sri Lanka)	UK Great Britain	Gen Communications	314UNTS269	104551
28 Feb	Canada	Turkey	Visas	231UNTS57	103204
28 Feb	Multilateral		Scientific Project	29UNTS53	100434
01 Mar	Belgium	IBRD (World Bank)	IBRD Project	154UNTS133	102029
01 Mar	Czechoslovakia	Yugoslavia	Finance	112UNTS241	101546
01 Mar	Czechoslovakia	Yugoslavia	General Trade	113UNTS3	101547
01 Mar	Belgium	Portugal	Finance	32UNTS49	100488
02 Mar	Iraq	Pakistan	Visas	141UNTS319	101921
03 Mar	France	Sweden	General Trade	49SOFM97	461077
03 Mar	Czechoslovakia	UK Great Britain	Other Military	83UNTS95	101104
03 Mar	Netherlands	New Zealand	Visas	34UNTS207	100538
04 Mar	Philippines	Spain	Culture	49SPBO1306	460096
04 Mar	Philippines	Spain	Culture	49SPBO1812	460097
07 Mar	Lebanon	Spain	Culture	49SPBO1812	460180
07 Mar	Netherlands	Switzerland	Air Transport	35UNTS69	100551
08 Mar	Belgium	Norway	General Trade	29UNTS83	100435
10 Mar	Accept UN Charter	Hungary	UN Charter	223UNTS55	103051
12 Mar	Mongolia	USSR (Soviet Union)	Specific Property	0SUST439	468267
12 Mar	Greece	Norway	Finance	33UNTS13	100510
12 Mar	Greece	Norway	General Trade	30UNTS161	100454
14 Mar	Ireland	Switzerland	Non-ILO Labor	553UNTS175	108085
14 Mar	New Zealand	USA (United States)	Visas	32UNTS369	100508
14 Mar	Canada	USA (United States)	Reparations	82UNTS3	101079
14 Mar	France	USA (United States)	Claims and Debts	84UNTS237	101133
14 Mar	Argentina	UK Great Britain	Taxation	83UNTS193	101108
14 Mar	France	USA (United States)	Claims and Debts	84UNTS225	101132
16 Mar	Multilateral		Finance	29UNTS95	100436
16 Mar	Germany, West	Greece	General Trade	77UNTS307	101006
16 Mar	Germany, West	Greece	Finance	77UNTS327	101007
17 Mar	Korea, North	USSR (Soviet Union)	General Economic	0SUST257	468248
17 Mar	Korea, North	USSR (Soviet Union)	General Economic	221UNTS3	102999
18 Mar	Finland	Sweden	General Trade	49SOFM137	461078
18 Mar	United Nations	UK Great Britain	Humanitarian	47UNTS305	100736
21 Mar	Belgium	Switzerland	Admin Cooperation	34UNTS17	100524
22 Mar	Denmark	Finland	Finance	33UNTS247	100520
23 Mar	Multilateral		Commodity Trade	203UNTS179	102746
23 Mar	Chile	IBRD (World Bank)	IBRD Project	153UNTS61	102018
23 Mar	Chile	IBRD (World Bank)	IBRD Project	153UNTS141	102019
23 Mar	Austria	USA (United States)	Admin Cooperation	43UNTS127	100667
23 Mar	Israel	Lebanon	Peace/Disarmament	42UNTS287	100655
24 Mar	Chile	Italy	General Amity	1ITMA525	437085
24 Mar	Finland	Greece	Finance	78UNTS13	101009
24 Mar	Finland	Greece	General Trade	78UNTS3	101008
25 Mar	Peru	USA (United States)	Scientific Project	89UNTS15	101205
27 Mar	Taiwan	USA (United States)	Direct Aid	0CTRC770	413033
29 Mar	Finland	USA (United States)	Air Transport	55UNTS59	100808
30 Mar	France	Luxembourg	Milit Servic/Citiz	50FRJO1003	416264
30 Mar	Sweden	UK Great Britain	Taxation	209UNTS129	102826
31 Mar	Multilateral		Reparations	122UNTS57	101636
31 Mar	Panama	USA (United States)	Telecommunications	55UNTS125	100811
31 Mar	United Arab Rep	UK Great Britain	Finance	83UNTS139	101106
31 Mar	Panama	USA (United States)	Air Transport	55UNTS87	100810
31 Mar	France	USA (United States)	Visas	84UNTS283	101137
31 Mar	Panama	USA (United States)	Air Transport	55UNTS141	100812
02 Apr	Sweden	USSR (Soviet Union)	General Trade	49SOFM145	461079
02 Apr	Greece	Turkey	Finance	78UNTS23	101010
03 Apr	Israel	Jordan	Peace/Disarmament	42UNTS303	100656
04 Apr	Multilateral		General Military	34UNTS243	100541
07 Apr	Netherlands	Sweden	General Trade	49SOFM391	461086

DATE	PARTY ONE	PARTY TWO	TOPIC	CITATION	NUMBER
1949 (Cont.)					
08 Apr	France	Sweden	Taxation	197UNTS183	102638
08 Apr	France	Sweden	Taxation	197UNTS177	102637
08 Apr	Multilateral		Milit Occupation	140UNTS196	101889
08 Apr	Denmark	Portugal	Finance	74UNTS221	100965
08 Apr	Denmark	Portugal	General Trade	74UNTS209	100964
09 Apr	Chile	USA (United States)	Customs	122UNTS169	101646
10 Apr	Albania	USSR (Soviet Union)	General Economic	0SUST258	468008
12 Apr	Argentina	Italy	Taxation	52ITGU22	435014
12 Apr	Canada	USA (United States)	Milit Assistance	206UNTS241	102789
12 Apr	Belgium	France	Visas	30UNTS45	100447
13 Apr	Italy	Yugoslavia	Commodity Trade	171UNTS279	102232
14 Apr	Multilateral		Milit Occupation	141UNTS281	101919
14 Apr	Haiti	USA (United States)	Military Mission	80UNTS37	101043
14 Apr	Japan	USA (United States)	Specif Claim/Waive	89UNTS141	101215
14 Apr	Belgium	UK Great Britain	Visas	65UNTS117	100840
15 Apr	Australia	New Zealand	Non-ILO Labor	34UNTS225	100540
16 Apr	Czechoslovakia	Hungary	General Amity	477UNTS183	106922
17 Apr	United Arab Rep	UK Great Britain	Reparations	83UNTS183	101107
22 Apr	Taiwan	Italy	General Amity	0CTRC222	413009
23 Apr	India	Pakistan	Finance	54UNTS51	100795
26 Apr	ITU (Telecommun)	United Nations	IGO Operations	30UNTS315	200175
26 Apr	Luxembourg	Netherlands	Culture	182UNTS187	102425
26 Apr	Finland	Sweden	Air Transport	95UNTS83	101318
26 Apr	Netherlands	USA (United States)	Finance	70UNTS123	100901
26 Apr	Belgium	Bolivia	Finance	34UNTS103	100530
27 Apr	Romania	USSR (Soviet Union)	Mass Media	0SUST258	468374
27 Apr	Romania	USSR (Soviet Union)	Territory Boundary	0SUST263	468375
28 Apr	Multilateral		IGO Establishment	83UNTS105	101105
28 Apr	Multilateral		Dispute Settlement	71UNTS101	100912
30 Apr	Taiwan	France	Air Transport	0CTRC172	413020
04 May	Multilateral		Milit Occupation	138UNTS123	101864
04 May	Multilateral		Admin Cooperation	98UNTS101	101358
04 May	Multilateral		Admin Cooperation	92UNTS19	101257
04 May	Multilateral		Admin Cooperation	30UNTS23	100446
04 May	Multilateral		Admin Cooperation	30UNTS3	100445
04 May	Multilateral		Admin Cooperation	47UNTS159	100728
05 May	Multilateral		IGO Establishment	87UNTS103	101168
09 May	Canada	Netherlands	Reparations	46UNTS263	100715
10 May	India	UNICEF (Children)	IGO Operations	68UNTS96	100887
12 May	Hungary	Turkey	General Economic	49TURG2812	466068
12 May	Austria	Italy	General Trade	51ITGU201	435030
12 May	Denmark	Poland	Claims and Debts	87UNTS179	101172
13 May	Switzerland	USA (United States)	Air Transport	51UNTS129	100761
13 May	Belgium	Netherlands	Customs	65UNTS133	100841
16 May	Bolivia	USA (United States)	Education	162UNTS3	102129
16 May	Bulgaria	Poland	Air Transport	84UNTS313	101140
16 May	Philippines	USA (United States)	Milit Installation	67UNTS199	100878
17 May	Ecuador	USA (United States)	Military Mission	66UNTS3	100845
17 May	Netherlands	USA (United States)	Milit Assistance	46UNTS291	100717
18 May	Ireland	UK Great Britain	Taxation	553UNTS209	108089
19 May	Austria	Italy	General Trade	50ITGU137	435031
20 May	Netherlands	Poland	General Trade	51NET67	447010
20 May	Iceland	Ireland	Visas	553UNTS99	108073
20 May	Ethiopia	USA (United States)	Milit Assistance	89UNTS99	101211
21 May	Sweden	Yugoslavia	General Trade	49SOFM157	461081
23 May	Norway	USSR (Soviet Union)	Territory Boundary	2NORT500	451206
23 May	Italy	Yugoslavia	Reparations	150UNTS179	101972
24 May	Philippines	UK Great Britain	Consul/Citizenship	2PTS145	465019
24 May	Pan Am Health Org	WHO (World Health)	Sanitation	32UNTS387	200178
25 May	Germany, West	Sweden	Finance	49SOFM457	461087
25 May	Norway	USA (United States)	Education	32UNTS345	100507
27 May	Pakistan	Turkey	Visas	141UNTS325	101922
30 May	France	Italy	Peace/Disarmament	50ITGU89	435115
31 May	Italy	Spain	Air Transport	231UNTS251	103224
31 May	United Arab Rep	UK Great Britain	Specific Resources	226UNTS273	103122

DATE	PARTY ONE	PARTY TWO	TOPIC	CITATION	NUMBER
1949 (Cont.)					
31 May	Belgium	Denmark	Visas	32UNTS337	100506
31 May	Costa Rica	USA (United States)	IGO Establishment	80UNTS3	101041
03 Jun	Australia	Pakistan	Air Transport	35UNTS23	100549
04 Jun	Canada	USA (United States)	Air Transport	200UNTS201	102704
04 Jun	Canada	USA (United States)	Air Transport	122UNTS237	101649
06 Jun	Mongolia	USSR (Soviet Union)	Specific Property	0SUST260	468268
06 Jun	Mongolia	USSR (Soviet Union)	Loans and Credits	0SUST439	468269
07 Jun	Philippines	USA (United States)	Direct Aid	45UNTS63	100692
07 Jun	Belgium	Luxembourg	Postal Service	34UNTS117	100531
07 Jun	Ethiopia	India	Air Transport	35UNTS13	100548
08 Jun	Norway	Pakistan	Visas	90UNTS131	101231
10 Jun	Greece	Lebanon	Culture	178UNTS29	102334
13 Jun	Philippines	Turkey	General Amity	2PTS155	465020
13 Jun	Sweden	Uruguay	Finance	49SOFM301	461083
13 Jun	Norway	USA (United States)	Taxation	127UNTS189	101705
13 Jun	Norway	USA (United States)	Taxation	127UNTS163	101704
13 Jun	UNICEF (Children)	UK Great Britain	Tech Assistance	65UNTS58	100825
13 Jun	Finland	Norway	Commodity Trade	34UNTS9	100523
14 Jun	Italy	UK Great Britain	Specific Property	135UNTS49	101813
14 Jun	Philippines	Thailand	General Amity	81UNTS53	101062
14 Jun	Panama	USA (United States)	Visas	89UNTS37	101207
15 Jun	Italy	Poland	General Trade	50ITGU130	435301
16 Jun	Multilateral		Land Transport	45UNTS149	100696
17 Jun	Denmark	Sweden	Commodity Trade	49SOFM307	461084
17 Jun	UNICEF (Children)	UK Great Britain	Tech Assistance	65UNTS56	100824
17 Jun	UNICEF (Children)	UK Great Britain	Tech Assistance	65UNTS54	100821
17 Jun	UNICEF (Children)	UK Great Britain	Tech Assistance	65UNTS54	100822
17 Jun	UNICEF (Children)	UK Great Britain	Tech Assistance	65UNTS50	100820
17 Jun	UNICEF (Children)	UK Great Britain	Tech Assistance	65UNTS56	100823
18 Jun	Italy	Switzerland	Specific Property	55SWRO611	462037
18 Jun	Multilateral		ILO Labor	605UNTS295	108768
18 Jun	Multilateral		ILO Labor	160UNTS223	102109
20 Jun	Multilateral		IGO Establishment	128UNTS141	101718
20 Jun	Peru	USA (United States)	Military Mission	92UNTS249	101276
20 Jun	Lebanon	UK Great Britain	Postal Service	90UNTS137	101232
20 Jun	Pakistan	UNICEF (Children)	Tech Assistance	65UNTS60	100826
21 Jun	Belgium	Greece	Air Transport	137UNTS215	101854
21 Jun	Mexico	USA (United States)	Scientific Project	89UNTS3	101204
22 Jun	Denmark	France	Milit Servic/Citiz	48UNTS3	100737
23 Jun	Norway	Pakistan	Air Transport	35UNTS49	100550
24 Jun	India	Switzerland	Air Transport	95UNTS109	101319
25 Jun	Poland	Switzerland	Claims and Debts	49SWRO839	462171
25 Jun	Poland	Switzerland	General Economic	49SWRO832	462151
25 Jun	Ireland	Sweden	General Trade	558UNTS299	108148
27 Jun	Sweden	USA (United States)	General Trade	49SOFM311	461085
27 Jun	France	Luxembourg	Education	49FRJO2510	416265
27 Jun	Taiwan	USA (United States)	Tech Assistance	0CTRC783	413035
27 Jun	Argentina	UK Great Britain	General Economic	83UNTS217	101110
29 Jun	Multilateral		ILO Labor	138UNTS207	101870
29 Jun	Greece	UK Great Britain	Finance	86UNTS203	101160
29 Jun	Korea, South	USA (United States)	Air Transport	55UNTS79	100809
30 Jun	France	Sweden	General Trade	49SOFM484	461088
30 Jun	Canada	Sweden	Visas	231UNTS37	103201
01 Jul	Multilateral		Non-ILO Labor	120UNTS71	101616
01 Jul	Multilateral		ILO Labor	138UNTS225	101871
01 Jul	Multilateral		ILO Labor	96UNTS257	101341
01 Jul	Multilateral		ILO Labor	96UNTS237	101340
02 Jul	Czechoslovakia	Poland	Land Transport	260UNTS179	103709
02 Jul	Czechoslovakia	Poland	Land Transport	260UNTS149	103708
04 Jul	Romania	USSR (Soviet Union)	Specific Property	16SUGG65	469890
04 Jul	France	Switzerland	Specific Property	50SWRO1334	462088
04 Jul	India	USA (United States)	Status of Forces	200UNTS181	102702
05 Jul	Mexico	USA (United States)	Military Mission	68UNTS55	100884
05 Jul	Greece	Syria	Air Transport	78UNTS71	101013
06 Jul	Netherlands	Sweden	Non-ILO Labor	197UNTS189	102639

DATE	PARTY ONE	PARTY TWO	TOPIC	CITATION	NUMBER
1949 (Cont.)					
07 Jul	Czechoslovakia	Netherlands	General Trade	51NET163	447011
09 Jul	France	Switzerland	Non-ILO Labor	50SWRO1164	462096
09 Jul	Multilateral		Telecommunications	168UNTS143	102218
11 Jul	Australia	India	Air Transport	35UNTS83	100552
12 Jul	France	San Marino	Non-ILO Labor	51FRJO203	416382
12 Jul	Austria	USA (United States)	Visas	84UNTS291	101138
12 Jul	Iraq	Norway	Air Transport	53UNTS137	100778
13 Jul	Czechoslovakia	Finland	Air Transport	53UNTS153	100779
15 Jul	Iceland	Sweden	General Trade	49SOFM497	461089
15 Jul	Multilateral		Health/Educ/Welfare	197UNTS3	102631
15 Jul	Belgium	Luxembourg	Visas	41UNTS13	100642
16 Jul	Pakistan	Philippines	Air Transport	35UNTS111	100553
18 Jul	Poland	Turkey	General Economic	49TURG1802	466082
19 Jul	Germany, East	Sweden	General Economic	49SOFM251	461082
19 Jul	Dominican Republic	USA (United States)	Air Transport	51UNTS145	100762
20 Jul	France	Netherlands	Mostfavored Nation	204UNTS287	102763
20 Jul	Israel	Syria	Peace/Disarmament	42UNTS327	100657
21 Jul	Greece	Turkey	General Trade	78UNTS55	101011
21 Jul	Greece	Turkey	Claims and Debts	78UNTS65	101012
22 Jul	Multilateral		General Trade	557UNTS211	108135
22 Jul	Liberia	USA (United States)	Visas	232UNTS283	103242
23 Jul	Syria	Turkey	Commodity Trade	50TURG403	466091
25 Jul	Argentina	Belgium	Taxation	46UNTS103	100703
26 Jul	Hungary	USSR (Soviet Union)	Scientific Project	0SUST261	468187
26 Jul	Netherlands	IBRD (World Bank)	IBRD Project	154UNTS178	102030
26 Jul	Colombia	USA (United States)	Admin Cooperation	73UNTS106	100949
27 Jul	El Salvador	USA (United States)	Sanitation	180UNTS219	102387
27 Jul	USA (United States)	Uruguay	Sanitation	151UNTS199	101995
27 Jul	India	Pakistan	Peace/Disarmament	81UNTS273	101076
27 Jul	Pakistan	UK Great Britain	Air Transport	44UNTS199	100685
30 Jul	Hungary	USSR (Soviet Union)	Territory Boundary	0SUST261	468188
01 Aug	Finland	IBRD (World Bank)	IBRD Project	156UNTS289	200480
01 Aug	Ireland	USA (United States)	Visas	82UNTS37	101083
01 Aug	Denmark	USA (United States)	Admin Cooperation	79UNTS147	101038
03 Aug	France	Netherlands	General Trade	51NET40	447012
03 Aug	Brazil	UK Great Britain	General Trade	86UNTS113	101154
04 Aug	Romania	USSR (Soviet Union)	Specific Property	16SUGG65	469891
04 Aug	Portugal	USA (United States)	Reparations	181UNTS15	102394
05 Aug	Multilateral		Finance	88UNTS229	101195
05 Aug	Ceylon (Sri Lanka)	UK Great Britain	Air Transport	35UNTS137	100554
06 Aug	Argentina	Canada	Taxation	231UNTS43	103202
06 Aug	France	Greece	General Trade	91UNTS95	101244
08 Aug	Austria	Turkey	Mostfavored Nation	49ABGB234	403199
08 Aug	Philippines	USA (United States)	Milit Installation	163UNTS103	102144
10 Aug	Multilateral		Finance	45UNTS3	100689
12 Aug	WHO (World Health)	Thailand	Sanitation	178UNTS347	102350
12 Aug	Multilateral		General Military	75UNTS135	100972
12 Aug	Australia	Netherlands	Reparations	34UNTS213	100539
12 Aug	Multilateral		Humanitarian	75UNTS31	100970
12 Aug	Multilateral		Humanitarian	75UNTS287	100973
12 Aug	Multilateral		IGO Establishment	87UNTS131	101169
12 Aug	Multilateral		Humanitarian	75UNTS85	100971
13 Aug	Denmark	UK Great Britain	General Trade	68UNTS105	100890
15 Aug	Mexico	USA (United States)	Scientific Project	66UNTS13	100846
16 Aug	Italy	Netherlands	Admin Cooperation	98UNTS21	101357
18 Aug	India	IBRD (World Bank)	IBRD Project	154UNTS269	102031
18 Aug	Czechoslovakia	UK Great Britain	Finance	86UNTS129	101155
19 Aug	Colombia	IBRD (World Bank)	IBRD Project	154UNTS329	102032
19 Aug	Canada	UK Great Britain	Air Transport	44UNTS223	100686
20 Aug	Belgium	Netherlands	Visas	46UNTS133	100706
21 Aug	Italy	Peru	General Amity	2ITMA387	437296
22 Aug	Poland	UK Great Britain	Admin Cooperation	404UNTS17	105801
23 Aug	Belgium	Chile	General Economic	46UNTS163	100708
24 Aug	Finland	Norway	Air Transport	53UNTS167	100780
24 Aug	Ecuador	Italy	General Amity	72UNTS35	100926

DATE	PARTY ONE	PARTY TWO	TOPIC	CITATION	NUMBER
1949 (Cont.)					
25 Aug	Taiwan	Italy	General Trade	0CTRC227	413010
26 Aug	Denmark	Finland	Air Transport	53UNTS191	100781
27 Aug	Colombia	Italy	General Amity	1ITMA551	437091
27 Aug	Multilateral		Non-ILO Labor	47UNTS127	100727
29 Aug	Belgium	France	Milit Servic/Citiz	93UNTS87	101293
30 Aug	Mexico	USA (United States)	IGO Establishment	98UNTS183	101364
30 Aug	Belgium	Canada	Air Transport	53UNTS221	100782
31 Aug	USSR (Soviet Union)	Yugoslavia	Admin Cooperation	116UNTS345	101580
31 Aug	Brazil	USA (United States)	Sanitation	102UNTS13	101407
31 Aug	Greece	Italy	Reparations	78UNTS89	101014
01 Sep	Iran	USA (United States)	Direct Aid	79UNTS155	101039
01 Sep	Australia	Philippines	Postal Service	46UNTS215	100711
02 Sep	Italy	Panama	General Amity	2ITMA442	437292
02 Sep	Multilateral		IGO Status/Immunit	250UNTS12	103515
02 Sep	Council of Europe	France	IGO Status/Immunit	249UNTS207	103510
06 Sep	Netherlands	Turkey	General Economic	50TURG1901	466079
07 Sep	Bulgaria	Turkey	General Economic	50TURG1001	466050
07 Sep	Belgium	UK Great Britain	Loans and Credits	106UNTS61	101457
07 Sep	Belgium	Netherlands	Loans and Credits	117UNTS3	101581
07 Sep	Belgium	France	Loans and Credits	123UNTS13	101651
09 Sep	Denmark	ICAO (Civil Aviat)	Air Transport	53UNTS341	100791
09 Sep	Argentina	Norway	Finance	42UNTS125	100646
10 Sep	Guatemala	Italy	General Amity	102UNTS53	101410
12 Sep	San Marino	UK Great Britain	Visas	87UNTS37	101164
13 Sep	Ireland	USA (United States)	Taxation	127UNTS119	101702
13 Sep	Ireland	USA (United States)	Taxation	127UNTS89	101701
14 Sep	United Nations	Switzerland	IGO Operations	43UNTS327	200183
15 Sep	Italy	Mexico	General Trade	52ITGU69	435273
15 Sep	Netherlands	Switzerland	Visas	252UNTS13	103555
15 Sep	Multilateral		Air Transport	53UNTS235	100783
16 Sep	Allied Milit Occup	Norway	General Trade	53UNTS3	100769
17 Sep	IBRD (World Bank)	Yugoslavia	IBRD Project	155UNTS3	102034
19 Sep	Cuba	Italy	General Amity	1ITMA616	437100
19 Sep	Multilateral		Land Transport	125UNTS3	101671
19 Sep	Belgium	United Arab Rep	Air Transport	137UNTS189	101853
19 Sep	UK Great Britain	USA (United States)	Milit Installation	68UNTS31	100882
20 Sep	Netherlands	UK Great Britain	Reparations	51NET137	447013
20 Sep	Lebanon	Netherlands	Air Transport	108UNTS205	101474
24 Sep	Multilateral		IGO Establishment	126UNTS237	101691
26 Sep	France	Italy	Patents/Copyrights	52ITGU124	435116
26 Sep	Bulgaria	Poland	Sanitation	260UNTS249	103712
26 Sep	Bulgaria	Poland	Sanitation	260UNTS227	103711
27 Sep	Dominican Republic	Italy	Peace/Disarmament	51ITGU15	435104
27 Sep	USA (United States)	USSR (Soviet Union)	Milit Assistance	149UNTS23	101948
28 Sep	Czechoslovakia	UK Great Britain	Claims and Debts	86UNTS175	101158
28 Sep	Czechoslovakia	UK Great Britain	General Economic	86UNTS141	101156
28 Sep	Burma	USA (United States)	Air Transport	55UNTS3	100806
28 Sep	Czechoslovakia	UK Great Britain	Reparations	86UNTS161	101157
29 Sep	India	IBRD (World Bank)	IBRD Project	154UNTS393	102033
02 Oct	China People's Rep	USSR (Soviet Union)	Consul/Citizenship	0SUST263	468068
08 Oct	Brazil	Italy	Peace/Disarmament	50ITGU195	435054
08 Oct	Greece	Philippines	Air Transport	187UNTS221	102515
11 Oct	Bulgaria	Sweden	General Trade	49SOFM519	461090
12 Oct	Paraguay	Spain	General Amity	51SPBO908	460215
12 Oct	Brazil	Italy	General Amity	1ITMA365	437055
12 Oct	Colombia	USA (United States)	General Trade	133UNTS15	101774
12 Oct	Ecuador	UNICEF (Children)	Tech Assistance	65UNTS62	100827
14 Oct	Canada	Denmark	Visas	46UNTS97	100702
15 Oct	Finland	Germany, East	General Trade	1EGDA498	419099
17 Oct	Finland	IBRD (World Bank)	IBRD Project	156UNTS355	200481
17 Oct	Greece	UK Great Britain	Postal Service	93UNTS185	101300
18 Oct	Poland	Sweden	Finance	49SOFM529	461091
18 Oct	Pakistan	USA (United States)	Visas	141UNTS333	101923
19 Oct	Germany, East	Hungary	General Economic	1EGDA426	419431
20 Oct	India	Philippines	Air Transport	72UNTS191	100934

DATE	PARTY ONE	PARTY TWO	TOPIC	CITATION	NUMBER
1949 (Cont.)					
21 Oct	Switzerland	USA (United States)	Reparations	132UNTS163	101757
22 Oct	Poland	USSR (Soviet Union)	Mass Media	0SUST263	468327
25 Oct	Ecuador	France	Finance	49FRMD2411	417154
27 Oct	Multilateral		Air Transport	53UNTS241	100784
29 Oct	Hungary	Poland	Sanitation	260UNTS113	103706
29 Oct	Hungary	Poland	Sanitation	260UNTS91	103705
31 Oct	Iran	Sweden	Air Transport	49SOFM767	461097
31 Oct	Iran	Netherlands	Air Transport	0IRTB35	433046
31 Oct	Iran	Netherlands	Air Transport	254UNTS257	103596
31 Oct	Norway	USA (United States)	Direct Aid	68UNTS3	100879
01 Nov	Finland	USA (United States)	Claims and Debts	68UNTS11	100880
02 Nov	Indonesia	Netherlands	Recognition	69UNTS3	100894
03 Nov	Czechoslovakia	USSR (Soviet Union)	Mass Media	16SUGG65	469892
03 Nov	Poland	Sweden	General Economic	49SOFM549	461092
03 Nov	United Arab Rep	USA (United States)	Education	71UNTS31	100908
04 Nov	France	Italy	Culture	52ITGU213	435117
05 Nov	Austria	Belgium	Extradition	48UNTS107	100739
07 Nov	Multilateral		Sanitation	132UNTS3	101748
07 Nov	Multilateral		Non-ILO Labor	132UNTS31	101749
08 Nov	Cambodia	France	Recognition	53FRJO1403	416094
08 Nov	USA (United States)	Uruguay	Visas	82UNTS45	101084
09 Nov	India	WHO (World Health)	IGO Status/Immunit	67UNTS43	100865
09 Nov	Denmark	Pakistan	Air Transport	44UNTS255	100687
12 Nov	France	Luxembourg	Non-ILO Labor	50FRJO110	416266
14 Nov	Germany, West	Turkey	Mostfavored Nation	50TURG1002	466029
14 Nov	Belgium	Czechoslovakia	Visas	46UNTS319	100718
15 Nov	Italy	Sweden	Finance	50SOFM840	461115
15 Nov	Italy	Sweden	General Trade	50SOFM817	461114
15 Nov	France	New Zealand	Air Transport	53UNTS247	100785
16 Nov	Poland	Sweden	Claims and Debts	50SOFM921	461119
16 Nov	Iran	Jordan	General Amity	0IRTB47	433070
16 Nov	South Africa	USA (United States)	Admin Cooperation	73UNTS97	100948
16 Nov	Belgium	Canada	Reparations	51UNTS3	100748
17 Nov	Finland	Sweden	Claims and Debts	50SOFM849	461116
19 Nov	Germany, East	USSR (Soviet Union)	Consul/Citizenship	1EGDA329	419376
19 Nov	Belgium	Canada	Visas	150UNTS231	101977
19 Nov	Italy	Norway	Finance	47UNTS89	100724
19 Nov	Italy	Norway	General Trade	47UNTS75	100723
21 Nov	France	Switzerland	Claims and Debts	49SWRO1953	462168
21 Nov	France	Ireland	Non-ILO Labor	553UNTS59	108069
22 Nov	Multilateral		Recognition	185UNTS307	102477
22 Nov	New Zealand	Norway	Visas	51UNTS123	100760
23 Nov	Sweden	Thailand	Air Transport	72UNTS217	100935
23 Nov	Denmark	Thailand	Air Transport	53UNTS255	100786
25 Nov	Romania	USSR (Soviet Union)	Dispute Settlement	0SUST264	468377
25 Nov	Romania	USSR (Soviet Union)	Admin Cooperation	0SUST264	468376
25 Nov	Ireland	Netherlands	General Trade	558UNTS256	108146
25 Nov	Italy	Turkey	Air Transport	192UNTS39	102594
26 Nov	Australia	New Zealand	Territory Boundary	198UNTS161	102662
26 Nov	Canada	Luxembourg	Visas	231UNTS51	103203
26 Nov	Australia	USA (United States)	Reparations	45UNTS133	100695
26 Nov	Norway	Thailand	Air Transport	53UNTS269	100787
28 Nov	Ireland	Italy	Visas	553UNTS105	108074
28 Nov	Brazil	Spain	Air Transport	215UNTS303	102923
28 Nov	Belgium	United Arab Rep	Culture	76UNTS91	100982
28 Nov	Norway	Portugal	Finance	47UNTS117	100726
30 Nov	Norway	USSR (Soviet Union)	Finance	16SUGG65	469893
30 Nov	Hungary	Sweden	General Trade	49SOFM561	461093
01 Dec	Chile	Italy	Health/Educ/Welfare	1ITMA526	437086
02 Dec	Belgium	USSR (Soviet Union)	Finance	16SUGG66	469894
02 Dec	Austria	Sweden	Air Transport	108UNTS3	101465
02 Dec	Austria	Denmark	Air Transport	53UNTS281	100788
02 Dec	Austria	Norway	Air Transport	72UNTS230	100936
03 Dec	Belgium	Luxembourg	Non-ILO Labor	91UNTS31	101241
04 Dec	Afghanistan	WHO (World Health)	Direct Aid	102UNTS117	101414

DATE	PARTY ONE	PARTY TWO	TOPIC	CITATION	NUMBER
1949 (Cont.)					
07 Dec	India	UK Great Britain	Postal Service	281UNTS245	104082
07 Dec	Denmark	Poland	Commodity Trade	81UNTS21	101059
08 Dec	Netherlands	United Arab Rep	Air Transport	95UNTS123	101320
09 Dec	Mongolia	USSR (Soviet Union)	General Trade	0SUST265	468270
12 Dec	Sweden	United Arab Rep	Air Transport	108UNTS15	101466
12 Dec	UK Great Britain	USA (United States)	Visas	92UNTS191	101271
13 Dec	Belgium	Denmark	Admin Cooperation	173UNTS193	102266
13 Dec	Colombia	UK Great Britain	Finance	88UNTS133	101189
13 Dec	Canada	Denmark	Air Transport	72UNTS247	100937
14 Dec	Canada	Netherlands	Visas	230UNTS337	103192
14 Dec	Norway	Sweden	Specific Resources	196UNTS19	102618
14 Dec	El Salvador	IBRD (World Bank)	IBRD Project	155UNTS43	102035
14 Dec	Belgium	San Marino	Visas	51UNTS107	100757
14 Dec	Afghanistan	India	Telecommunications	53UNTS95	100774
15 Dec	Germany, West	USA (United States)	Direct Aid	92UNTS269	101277
15 Dec	Denmark	Germany, West	Finance	51UNTS11	100749
16 Dec	Multilateral		Admin Cooperation	72UNTS3	100924
17 Dec	France	Sweden	General Trade	49SOFM584	461095
17 Dec	Norway	Sweden	Taxation	197UNTS197	102640
17 Dec	Norway	Sweden	Taxation	197UNTS215	102641
17 Dec	Czechoslovakia	Denmark	General Trade	74UNTS147	100961
17 Dec	Czechoslovakia	Denmark	Finance	74UNTS159	100962
19 Dec	Netherlands	Sweden	General Trade	49SOFM625	461096
19 Dec	Austria	Switzerland	Air Transport	254UNTS287	103597
19 Dec	UNICEF (Children)	UK Great Britain	Tech Assistance	65UNTS64	100828
20 Dec	Philippines	USA (United States)	Finance	2PTS517	465021
20 Dec	Guatemala	USA (United States)	Status of Forces	70UNTS71	100897
20 Dec	Haiti	UNICEF (Children)	Tech Assistance	65UNTS68	100829
21 Dec	France	UK Great Britain	Milit Servic/Citiz	264UNTS37	103786
21 Dec	Finland	Sweden	Taxation	197UNTS243	102642
21 Dec	Norway	Poland	Finance	47UNTS107	100725
21 Dec	Denmark	Finland	Visas	46UNTS125	100705
22 Dec	Czechoslovakia	Switzerland	General Economic	50SWRO15	462158
22 Dec	Austria	Belgium	Admin Cooperation	46UNTS233	100712
23 Dec	Belgium	UK Great Britain	Status of Forces	99UNTS61	101371
24 Dec	USA (United States)	Yugoslavia	Air Transport	89UNTS209	101219
25 Dec	Iran	Turkey	General Transport	51TURG1512	466136
25 Dec	Iran	Turkey	Customs	51TURG1512	466099
25 Dec	Iran	Turkey	Finance	51TURG1512	466071
25 Dec	China People's Rep	Korea, North	Postal Service	49CCJC1	410383
25 Dec	China People's Rep	Korea, North	Telecommunications	49CCJC3	410384
25 Dec	China People's Rep	Korea, North	Telecommunications	49CCJC4	410385
26 Dec	UK Great Britain	Yugoslavia	General Trade	87UNTS71	101167
27 Dec	Turkey	USA (United States)	Direct Aid	98UNTS141	101361
28 Dec	Finland	UK Great Britain	Peace/Disarmament	86UNTS191	101159
29 Dec	Haiti	USA (United States)	General Trade	133UNTS21	101775
29 Dec	Norway	USSR (Soviet Union)	Territory Boundary	83UNTS291	101112
29 Dec	Australia	USA (United States)	Patents/Copyrights	71UNTS45	100909
30 Dec	France	Netherlands	Taxation	203UNTS85	102742
30 Dec	France	Netherlands	Taxation	203UNTS133	102743
30 Dec	Finland	Norway	Visas	90UNTS175	101234
30 Dec	Belgium	France	Taxation	46UNTS111	100704
30 Dec	Sweden	UK Great Britain	Finance	87UNTS59	101166
30 Dec	Belgium	Italy	Visas	51UNTS83	100754
31 Dec	Greece	Portugal	General Trade	92UNTS71	101262
31 Dec	Greece	Portugal	Finance	92UNTS83	101263
1950					
02 Jan	Sweden	Yugoslavia	General Trade	50SOFM1	461098
04 Jan	Afghanistan	India	General Amity	81UNTS75	101064
05 Jan	Turkey	Yugoslavia	General Economic	50TURG1803	466030
05 Jan	Turkey	Yugoslavia	General Economic	50TURG2503	466097
05 Jan	France	Yugoslavia	Non-ILO Labor	51FRJO2404	416483
05 Jan	France	Yugoslavia	Non-ILO Labor	0UNTS0	109502
07 Jan	France	Netherlands	Non-ILO Labor	120UNTS25	101614

DATE	PARTY ONE	PARTY TWO	TOPIC	CITATION	NUMBER
1950 (Cont.)					
12 Jan	Australia	Ceylon (Sri Lanka)	Air Transport	53UNTS295	100789
13 Jan	Argentina	Switzerland	Taxation	50SWR0584	462042
13 Jan	France	New Zealand	Reparations	150UNTS151	101969
14 Jan	Costa Rica	UNICEF (Children)	Tech Assistance	65UNTS70	100830
17 Jan	Honduras	UNICEF (Children)	Tech Assistance	65UNTS74	100831
17 Jan	Nicaragua	UNICEF (Children)	Tech Assistance	65UNTS76	100832
18 Jan	El Salvador	UNICEF (Children)	Tech Assistance	65UNTS78	100833
18 Jan	Finland	USA (United States)	General Economic	92UNTS197	101272
21 Jan	Turkey	USA (United States)	Direct Aid	50TURG3003	466118
21 Jan	Ireland	USA (United States)	General Amity	206UNTS269	102792
23 Jan	Dominican Republic	USA (United States)	Consul/Citizenship	236UNTS3	103312
23 Jan	France	UK Great Britain	Reparations	97UNTS149	101348
24 Jan	Canada	USA (United States)	Specif Claim/Waive	151UNTS171	101992
26 Jan	Taiwan	USA (United States)	Direct Aid	0CTRC772	413034
26 Jan	Korea, South	USA (United States)	Military Mission	178UNTS97	102337
26 Jan	Panama	USA (United States)	Claims and Debts	132UNTS233	101763
26 Jan	Korea, South	USA (United States)	Milit Assistance	80UNTS205	101053
26 Jan	Austria	UK Great Britain	Finance	97UNTS183	101350
27 Jan	Mexico	Netherlands	General Trade	123UNTS197	101661
27 Jan	Norway	USA (United States)	Milit Assistance	80UNTS241	101055
27 Jan	Italy	USA (United States)	Milit Assistance	80UNTS145	101050
27 Jan	Denmark	USA (United States)	Milit Assistance	48UNTS115	100740
27 Jan	UK Great Britain	USA (United States)	Milit Assistance	80UNTS261	101056
27 Jan	France	USA (United States)	Milit Assistance	80UNTS171	101051
27 Jan	Luxembourg	USA (United States)	Milit Assistance	80UNTS187	101052
27 Jan	Belgium	USA (United States)	Milit Assistance	51UNTS213	100767
27 Jan	Netherlands	USA (United States)	Milit Assistance	80UNTS219	101054
28 Jan	Norway	Sweden	Land Transport	202UNTS151	102730
28 Jan	France	UK Great Britain	Non-ILO Labor	97UNTS155	101349
30 Jan	USSR (Soviet Union)	Vietnam, North	Consul/Citizenship	0SUST268	468446
31 Jan	Peru	UNICEF (Children)	Tech Assistance	65UNTS80	100834
01 Feb	Nicaragua	USA (United States)	Tech Assistance	99UNTS25	101368
02 Feb	India	USA (United States)	Education	89UNTS127	101214
03 Feb	Indonesia	USSR (Soviet Union)	Consul/Citizenship	0SUST268	468219
03 Feb	Bolivia	UNICEF (Children)	Tech Assistance	65UNTS82	100835
06 Feb	Belgium	Monaco	Visas	51UNTS93	100755
07 Feb	China People's Rep	USSR (Soviet Union)	Postal Service	0SUST268	468069
07 Feb	China People's Rep	USSR (Soviet Union)	Telecommunications	0SUST268	468070
07 Feb	China People's Rep	USSR (Soviet Union)	Gen Communications	50CCJC1	410386
07 Feb	China People's Rep	USSR (Soviet Union)	Gen Communications	50CCJC2	410002
09 Feb	Belgium	Finland	Visas	51UNTS77	100753
09 Feb	UK Great Britain	Yugoslavia	Finance	88UNTS287	101200
09 Feb	Guatemala	UNICEF (Children)	Tech Assistance	65UNTS84	100836
10 Feb	United Nations	WHO (World Health)	IGO Operations	46UNTS327	200188
10 Feb	Israel	UK Great Britain	Taxation	86UNTS211	101161
10 Feb	Australia	USA (United States)	Visas	51UNTS167	100763
10 Feb	UNICEF (Children)	UK Great Britain	Direct Aid	65UNTS86	100837
13 Feb	Netherlands	Syria	Air Transport	108UNTS53	101467
14 Feb	China People's Rep	USSR (Soviet Union)	Specific Property	0SUST270	468071
14 Feb	China People's Rep	USSR (Soviet Union)	Milit Installation	0SUST270	468072
14 Feb	China People's Rep	USSR (Soviet Union)	Loans and Credits	50CCJC6	410005
14 Feb	China People's Rep	USSR (Soviet Union)	General Amity	50CCJC4	410003
14 Feb	China People's Rep	USSR (Soviet Union)	Consul/Citizenship	50CCJC5	410004
14 Feb	China People's Rep	USSR (Soviet Union)	General Amity	226UNTS3	103103
14 Feb	China People's Rep	USSR (Soviet Union)	Loans and Credits	226UNTS21	103104
14 Feb	China People's Rep	USSR (Soviet Union)	Privil/Immunities	226UNTS31	103105
14 Feb	Canada	Norway	Air Transport	53UNTS329	100790
17 Feb	Romania	USSR (Soviet Union)	Scientific Project	0SUST270	468378
17 Feb	Romania	USSR (Soviet Union)	General Economic	0SUST270	468379
17 Feb	Ceylon (Sri Lanka)	WHO (World Health)	Direct Aid	102UNTS309	200309
17 Feb	Belgium	Netherlands	Water Transport	51UNTS101	100756
18 Feb	Bulgaria	USSR (Soviet Union)	Tech Assistance	0SUST271	468036
18 Feb	Spain	Sweden	Air Transport	166UNTS15	102184
18 Feb	Multilateral		Customs	123UNTS45	101654
18 Feb	Iran	Pakistan	General Amity	161UNTS23	102119

DATE	PARTY ONE	PARTY TWO	TOPIC	CITATION	NUMBER
1950 (Cont.)					
19 Feb	Israel	USA (United States)	Admin Cooperation	122UNTS117	101641
20 Feb	Bulgaria	Germany, West	Health/Educ/Welfare	0UNTS0	109871
20 Feb	Greece	USA (United States)	Taxation	196UNTS269	102629
20 Feb	Greece	USA (United States)	Taxation	196UNTS291	102630
22 Feb	Australia	Yugoslavia	Claims and Debts	51UNTS201	100766
23 Feb	Austria	Denmark	General Trade	74UNTS269	100969
24 Feb	India	Sweden	General Trade	50SOFM43	461099
24 Feb	Hungary	USSR (Soviet Union)	Admin Cooperation	0SUST271	468190
24 Feb	Hungary	USSR (Soviet Union)	Admin Cooperation	0SUST271	468189
24 Feb	Norway	Sweden	Claims and Debts	2NORT530	451160
24 Feb	Switzerland	USA (United States)	Admin Cooperation	93UNTS3	101282
24 Feb	Portugal	USA (United States)	Visas	92UNTS219	101274
24 Feb	Ceylon (Sri Lanka)	Thailand	Air Transport	72UNTS261	100938
26 Feb	Iraq	Pakistan	General Amity	214UNTS3	102896
27 Feb	Canada	USA (United States)	Specific Resources	132UNTS223	101762
28 Feb	Nicaragua	USA (United States)	General Trade	132UNTS169	101758
02 Mar	Austria	Sweden	General Trade	50SOFM59	461100
03 Mar	Chile	UNICEF (Children)	Direct Aid	126UNTS119	101685
04 Mar	Germany, West	Pakistan	General Trade	50WGBB717	425562
04 Mar	Italy	Netherlands	Air Transport	254UNTS305	103598
06 Mar	Honduras	USA (United States)	Military Mission	80UNTS51	101044
06 Mar	Honduras	USA (United States)	Military Mission	80UNTS71	101045
07 Mar	France	Italy	Gen Communications	53ITGU296	435118
07 Mar	Bulgaria	France	Admin Cooperation	50FRJO1607	416085
08 Mar	Denmark	Sweden	Finance	50SOFM93	461103
08 Mar	Denmark	Sweden	General Trade	50SOFM89	461102
10 Mar	ICJ Option Clause	Liechtenstein	ICJ Option Clause	51UNTS115	100758
10 Mar	ICJ Option Clause	Liechtenstein	ICJ Option Clause	51UNTS119	100759
11 Mar	Norway	United Arab Rep	Air Transport	95UNTS157	101321
13 Mar	Burma	UK Great Britain	Taxation	131UNTS53	101735
13 Mar	Canada	Norway	Visas	90UNTS181	101235
14 Mar	France	Italy	Patents/Copyrights	52ITGU127	435119
14 Mar	Belgium	France	Visas	65UNTS139	100842
14 Mar	Denmark	United Arab Rep	Air Transport	95UNTS197	101322
15 Mar	India	Iran	General Amity	161UNTS15	102118
15 Mar	Belgium	UK Great Britain	Patents/Copyrights	76UNTS85	100981
15 Mar	Colombia	UNICEF (Children)	Tech Assistance	65UNTS104	100838
16 Mar	Philippines	USA (United States)	Air Transport	89UNTS199	101218
17 Mar	Mexico	Yugoslavia	General Trade	54MEXD2202	444044
18 Mar	Canada	Norway	Reparations	230UNTS349	103194
20 Mar	United Arab Rep	UK Great Britain	Tech Assistance	226UNTS287	103123
20 Mar	Italy	UK Great Britain	Territory Boundary	128UNTS201	101721
21 Mar	Argentina	Greece	Taxation	187UNTS213	102514
21 Mar	Italy	UK Great Britain	Territory Boundary	128UNTS225	101722
21 Mar	Multilateral		Admin Cooperation	96UNTS271	101342
22 Mar	Denmark	Iceland	Air Transport	72UNTS273	100939
22 Mar	Iceland	Netherlands	Air Transport	95UNTS237	101323
24 Mar	Italy	Switzerland	Water Transport	52ITGU29	435367
24 Mar	Canada	USA (United States)	Customs	200UNTS211	102705
24 Mar	Honduras	USA (United States)	Admin Cooperation	93UNTS11	101283
24 Mar	Indonesia	USA (United States)	Direct Aid	92UNTS387	101281
24 Mar	Italy	Turkey	General Amity	96UNTS207	101338
25 Mar	Korea, South	UNICEF (Children)	IGO Operations	65UNTS171	200209
25 Mar	Canada	Denmark	Reparations	230UNTS343	103193
25 Mar	USA (United States)	Yugoslavia	Visas	98UNTS195	101365
27 Mar	China People's Rep	USSR (Soviet Union)	Specific Property	0SUST272	468074
27 Mar	China People's Rep	USSR (Soviet Union)	Specific Property	0SUST272	468075
27 Mar	China People's Rep	USSR (Soviet Union)	Privil/Immunities	0SUST272	468076
27 Mar	China People's Rep	USSR (Soviet Union)	Specific Property	0SUST272	468073
27 Mar	China People's Rep	USSR (Soviet Union)	Non-ILO Labor	50CCJC16	410012
27 Mar	China People's Rep	USSR (Soviet Union)	Specif Goods/Equip	50CCJC15	410011
27 Mar	China People's Rep	USSR (Soviet Union)	Specif Goods/Equip	50CCJC13	410009
27 Mar	China People's Rep	USSR (Soviet Union)	Specif Goods/Equip	50CCJC14	410010
27 Mar	Denmark	UK Great Britain	Taxation	68UNTS117	100891
28 Mar	Hungary	Italy	Customs	52ITGU68	435415

DATE	PARTY ONE	PARTY TWO	TOPIC	CITATION	NUMBER
1950 (Cont.)					
29 Mar	Canada	Yugoslavia	Reparations	230UNTS357	103195
29 Mar	Belgium	Netherlands	Visas	68UNTS45	100883
30 Mar	Czechoslovakia	Sweden	General Trade	50SOFM95	461104
30 Mar	Czechoslovakia	Sweden	Finance	50SOFM116	461105
30 Mar	Austria	Czechoslovakia	Sanitation	495UNTS85	107240
30 Mar	Bolivia	USA (United States)	Military Mission	241UNTS77	103425
30 Mar	Israel	UK Great Britain	Claims and Debts	86UNTS231	101162
31 Mar	Iceland	Sweden	General Trade	50SOFM118	461106
31 Mar	Finland	Sweden	Taxation	197UNTS285	102643
01 Apr	Japan	Sweden	General Trade	50SOFM153	461107
01 Apr	Finland	Sweden	General Economic	50SOFM169	461109
01 Apr	Japan	Sweden	Finance	50SOFM165	461108
01 Apr	France	Monaco	Taxation	53FRJO1006	416330
03 Apr	Paraguay	UK Great Britain	General Economic	99UNTS81	101372
04 Apr	Costa Rica	USA (United States)	General Trade	132UNTS177	101759
04 Apr	Afghanistan	India	General Trade	167UNTS105	102201
05 Apr	Switzerland	UK Great Britain	Air Transport	51SWRO573	462091
05 Apr	Italy	Portugal	Air Transport	254UNTS329	103599
05 Apr	Sweden	UK Great Britain	Air Transport	99UNTS107	101374
06 Apr	Switzerland	United Arab Rep	Finance	50SWRO329	462129
06 Apr	Indonesia	UNICEF (Children)	IGO Operations	68UNTS254	200238
06 Apr	Multilateral		Admin Cooperation	119UNTS99	101610
06 Apr	Belgium	Luxembourg	Visas	65UNTS147	100843
06 Apr	Denmark	Switzerland	General Trade	87UNTS197	101173
08 Apr	India	Pakistan	Visas	131UNTS3	101733
08 Apr	Multilateral		Specif Goods/Equip	68UNTS99	100889
08 Apr	Multilateral		IGO Establishment	66UNTS285	100860
12 Apr	Hungary	USSR (Soviet Union)	Mass Media	0SUST273	468191
12 Apr	Germany, East	USSR (Soviet Union)	General Economic	1EGDA245	419377
12 Apr	Turkey	United Arab Rep	Air Transport	128UNTS3	101711
14 Apr	Australia	Philippines	Air Transport	127UNTS281	101709
15 Apr	Finland	France	Education	50FRJO206	416188
17 Apr	Canada	France	Visas	230UNTS365	103196
17 Apr	Multilateral		Non-ILO Labor	126UNTS285	101694
17 Apr	Multilateral		Visas	131UNTS99	101738
18 Apr	Netherlands	Sweden	General Trade	50SOFM781	461113
18 Apr	Italy	Sweden	General Trade	50SOFM69	461101
18 Apr	India	IBRD (World Bank)	IBRD Project	155UNTS117	102036
19 Apr	China People's Rep	USSR (Soviet Union)	General Trade	0SUST273	468077
19 Apr	China People's Rep	USSR (Soviet Union)	General Trade	50CCJC17	410013
19 Apr	China People's Rep	USSR (Soviet Union)	General Trade	50CCJC18	410014
19 Apr	China People's Rep	USSR (Soviet Union)	General Aid	50CCJC20	410015
19 Apr	Italy	New Zealand	Claims and Debts	67UNTS81	100867
20 Apr	Philippines	USA (United States)	Specif Goods/Equip	2PTS553	465071
20 Apr	United Nations	WHO (World Health)	IGO Operations	139UNTS445	200470
21 Apr	El Salvador	WHO (World Health)	Sanitation	103UNTS13	101420
22 Apr	Burma	UNICEF (Children)	IGO Operations	68UNTS96	100888
24 Apr	Greece	United Arab Rep	Air Transport	163UNTS229	102149
26 Apr	Australia	Netherlands	Claims and Debts	54UNTS83	100796
28 Apr	Mexico	IBRD (World Bank)	IBRD Project	155UNTS185	102037
28 Apr	Australia	UK Great Britain	Air Transport	95UNTS249	101324
28 Apr	Korea, South	USA (United States)	Education	93UNTS21	101284
01 May	Ireland	USA (United States)	Consul/Citizenship	222UNTS107	103026
03 May	Mexico	USA (United States)	Visas	98UNTS201	101366
04 May	Israel	USA (United States)	Patents/Copyrights	132UNTS189	101760
06 May	Lebanon	Spain	General Amity	51SPBO607	460181
08 May	Spain	USA (United States)	Admin Cooperation	98UNTS175	101363
11 May	Ireland	Spain	Scientific Project	553UNTS147	108081
11 May	Austria	Greece	General Trade	184UNTS217	102450
12 May	Chile	USA (United States)	Consul/Citizenship	177UNTS103	102312
13 May	Multilateral		Land Transport	128UNTS171	101719
15 May	Germany, East	USSR (Soviet Union)	Reparations	0SUST274	468160
15 May	Switzerland	United Arab Rep	Air Transport	95UNTS255	101325
18 May	Portugal	Sweden	General Trade	50SOFM931	461120
18 May	Philippines	SCAP Japan	General Economic	2PTS555	465022

DATE	PARTY ONE	PARTY TWO	TOPIC	CITATION	NUMBER
1950 (Cont.)					
18 May	Portugal	Sweden	Finance	50SOFM933	461121
19 May	Germany, East	USSR (Soviet Union)	Claims and Debts	0SUST274	468161
20 May	ICJ Option Clause	Thailand	ICJ Option Clause	65UNTS157	100844
23 May	Brazil	USA (United States)	Admin Cooperation	151UNTS141	101989
23 May	Iran	USA (United States)	Milit Assistance	81UNTS3	101057
24 May	Bulgaria	USSR (Soviet Union)	Admin Cooperation	0SUST274	468037
24 May	Panama	USA (United States)	Territory Boundary	241UNTS139	103430
25 May	Italy	United Arab Rep	Air Transport	53ITGU67	435313
25 May	Sweden	USA (United States)	General Trade	88UNTS43	101184
26 May	Brazil	IBRD (World Bank)	IBRD Project	301UNTS165	104345
26 May	Iceland	UK Great Britain	Air Transport	95UNTS277	101326
27 May	Romania	USSR (Soviet Union)	Sanitation	221UNTS13	103000
30 May	France	Vietnam, South	Education	0VKNG9	496001
30 May	Austria	Switzerland	Land Transport	50SWRO781	462069
30 May	Canada	Italy	Culture	53ITDI80	436072
31 May	Iran	Norway	Air Transport	2NORT535	451084
31 May	Multilateral		General Trade	74UNTS95	100957
02 Jun	Czechoslovakia	France	Claims and Debts	63FRRT51	415440
02 Jun	Denmark	Portugal	General Trade	74UNTS229	100966
03 Jun	Sweden	Switzerland	General Trade	50SOFM853	461117
06 Jun	Germany, East	Poland	General Economic	4EGDA114	419229
06 Jun	Germany, East	Poland	Finance	4EGDA115	419228
06 Jun	Germany, East	Poland	Culture	4EGDA118	419230
06 Jun	Germany, East	Poland	Territory Boundary	4EGDA113	419227
06 Jun	Austria	USA (United States)	Education	92UNTS201	101273
07 Jun	ILO (Labor Org)	OAS (Am States)	IGO Operations	70UNTS223	200240
07 Jun	ILO (Labor Org)	United Nations	Visas	68UNTS213	200231
07 Jun	Ceylon (Sri Lanka)	UNICEF (Children)	IGO Operations	68UNTS256	200239
07 Jun	Indonesia	USA (United States)	Admin Cooperation	98UNTS167	101362
09 Jun	Hungary	USSR (Soviet Union)	Specific Resources	0SUST274	468192
09 Jun	Brazil	UNICEF (Children)	IGO Operations	66UNTS75	100848
12 Jun	France	Hungary	Claims and Debts	52FRJO2509	416221
12 Jun	Canada	USA (United States)	Taxation	127UNTS67	101700
12 Jun	Canada	USA (United States)	Taxation	127UNTS57	101699
12 Jun	South Africa	UK Great Britain	Customs	93UNTS67	101290
13 Jun	Finland	USSR (Soviet Union)	General Trade	0SUST275	468147
13 Jun	Israel	USA (United States)	Air Transport	212UNTS93	102863
14 Jun	China People's Rep	Czechoslovakia	General Trade	50CCJC22	410017
15 Jun	France	Vietnam, South	Education	0VKNG10	496002
15 Jun	Iraq	IBRD (World Bank)	IBRD Project	155UNTS267	102038
16 Jun	France	Vietnam, South	Water Transport	0VKNG11	496003
17 Jun	France	Vietnam, South	IGO Establishment	0VKNG13	496004
19 Jun	Bulgaria	Germany, East	Health/Educ/Welfare	4EGDA459	419031
20 Jun	France	Italy	Other Military	52ITGU203	435121
20 Jun	Netherlands	Spain	Air Transport	95UNTS303	101327
20 Jun	Iraq	Pakistan	Air Transport	77UNTS215	101001
20 Jun	Netherlands	IRO (Refugee Org)	Refugees	76UNTS55	100979
21 Jun	Haiti	WHO (World Health)	Sanitation	103UNTS61	101424
22 Jun	Canada	USA (United States)	Scientific Project	70UNTS115	100900
22 Jun	Denmark	Switzerland	Air Transport	96UNTS3	101328
23 Jun	Czechoslovakia	Germany, East	Scientific Project	4EGDA248	419325
23 Jun	Czechoslovakia	Germany, East	Culture	4EGDA252	419328
23 Jun	Czechoslovakia	Germany, East	Finance	4EGDA250	419327
23 Jun	Czechoslovakia	Germany, East	Finance	1EGDA376	419326
23 Jun	Czechoslovakia	Germany, East	General Amity	504UNTS163	107357
23 Jun	Germany, East	Poland	Sanitation	304UNTS91	104393
24 Jun	Germany, East	Hungary	Finance	4EGDA380	419433
24 Jun	Germany, East	Hungary	General Trade	1EGDA428	419434
24 Jun	Germany, East	Hungary	Culture	4EGDA382	419435
24 Jun	Germany, East	Hungary	Scientific Project	4EGDA378	419432
27 Jun	Albania	USSR (Soviet Union)	Mass Media	0SUST275	468009
27 Jun	Hungary	Switzerland	General Economic	50SWRO612	462139
27 Jun	Luxembourg	UK Great Britain	Culture	183UNTS217	102431
27 Jun	Haiti	WHO (World Health)	Tech Assistance	110UNTS99	101504
28 Jun	Multilateral		Loans and Credits	87UNTS153	101170

DATE	PARTY ONE	PARTY TWO	TOPIC	CITATION	NUMBER
1950 (Cont.)					
29 Jun	Poland	USSR (Soviet Union)	General Trade	0SUST275	468328
29 Jun	Poland	USSR (Soviet Union)	Loans and Credits	0SUST275	468329
29 Jun	Burma	Ceylon (Sri Lanka)	Air Transport	73UNTS3	100940
01 Jul	India	Sweden	General Trade	50SOFM178	461110
01 Jul	Germany, East	USSR (Soviet Union)	Postal Service	4EGDA11	419378
01 Jul	Germany, East	USSR (Soviet Union)	Postal Service	4EGDA16	419379
01 Jul	Germany, East	USSR (Soviet Union)	Telecommunications	4EGDA27	419380
01 Jul	Denmark	Italy	Patents/Copyrights	133UNTS181	101788
01 Jul	Thailand	USA (United States)	Education	81UNTS61	101063
04 Jul	Israel	Turkey	Mostfavored Nation	220UNTS3	102982
04 Jul	Afghanistan	UNICEF (Children)	IGO Operations	71UNTS3	100906
05 Jul	Brazil	Italy	General Economic	51ITGU38	435057
05 Jul	Brazil	Italy	General Economic	51ITGU36	435056
05 Jul	Belgium	Iraq	Claims and Debts	68UNTS165	100893
06 Jul	Germany, East	Poland	Telecommunications	4EGDA128	419232
06 Jul	Germany, East	Poland	Territory Boundary	319UNTS93	104631
07 Jul	IBRD (World Bank)	Turkey	IBRD Project	156UNTS75	102040
07 Jul	Finland	UK Great Britain	Finance	138UNTS171	101868
07 Jul	IBRD (World Bank)	Turkey	IBRD Project	156UNTS3	102039
08 Jul	Luxembourg	Netherlands	Non-ILO Labor	135UNTS229	101824
08 Jul	Denmark	Finland	General Trade	73UNTS191	100953
10 Jul	France	Germany, West	Non-ILO Labor	51WGBB177	425134
10 Jul	France	Germany, West	Visas	51WGBB87	425135
10 Jul	France	Germany, West	Non-ILO Labor	51WGBB69	425137
10 Jul	France	Germany, West	Non-ILO Labor	51WGBB98	425136
10 Jul	France	Germany, West	Education	51FRJO706	416033
12 Jul	Czechoslovakia	Germany, East	Sanitation	4EGDA255	419329
12 Jul	Germany, West	Ireland	General Trade	557UNTS221	108136
12 Jul	Korea, South	USA (United States)	Status of Forces	222UNTS229	103029
12 Jul	Denmark	Spain	General Trade	71UNTS135	100914
12 Jul	Denmark	Spain	Finance	71UNTS129	100913
13 Jul	Hungary	USSR (Soviet Union)	Sanitation	221UNTS35	103001
14 Jul	Indonesia	Netherlands	Status of Forces	51NET4	447014
15 Jul	Austria	Switzerland	Non-ILO Labor	51SWRO787	462093
15 Jul	Austria	Switzerland	Non-ILO Labor	51ABGB232	403179
17 Jul	Afghanistan	USSR (Soviet Union)	General Economic	0SUST276	468002
19 Jul	Hungary	Switzerland	Claims and Debts	50SWRO736	462169
19 Jul	Taiwan	UNICEF (Children)	IGO Operations	94UNTS21	101304
20 Jul	Spain	UK Great Britain	Air Transport	398UNTS101	105719
20 Jul	Argentina	USA (United States)	Taxation	89UNTS63	101209
21 Jul	UK Great Britain	USA (United States)	Milit Installation	97UNTS193	101351
24 Jul	Italy	Norway	Visas	90UNTS187	101236
26 Jul	Lebanon	Mexico	Culture	52MEXD1502	444030
26 Jul	France	Venezuela	General Economic	50FRMD2408	417479
26 Jul	Ceylon (Sri Lanka)	UK Great Britain	Taxation	337UNTS77	104818
27 Jul	Multilateral		Non-ILO Labor	166UNTS73	102186
28 Jul	Korea, South	USA (United States)	Finance	140UNTS57	101883
28 Jul	Belgium	Switzerland	Visas	71UNTS91	100911
28 Jul	Italy	UK Great Britain	Non-ILO Labor	101UNTS25	101399
31 Jul	India	Nepal	General Economic	104UNTS3	101430
31 Jul	France	Pakistan	Air Transport	96UNTS23	101329
31 Jul	India	Nepal	General Amity	94UNTS3	101302
01 Aug	Canada	France	Air Transport	73UNTS21	100941
01 Aug	UK Great Britain	USA (United States)	Milit Installation	88UNTS273	101199
02 Aug	FAO (Food Agri)	United Nations	IGO Operations	139UNTS407	200467
03 Aug	Spain	Switzerland	Air Transport	254UNTS365	103600
05 Aug	Spain	Vatican/Holy See	Admin Cooperation	50SPBO1811	460270
08 Aug	France	United Arab Rep	Air Transport	127UNTS293	101710
09 Aug	Iran	USSR (Soviet Union)	Admin Cooperation	16SUGG66	469895
09 Aug	Chile	Spain	General Economic	54SPBO1308	460073
11 Aug	Dominican Republic	USA (United States)	Status of Forces	92UNTS329	101278
14 Aug	USA (United States)	Yugoslavia	Postal Service	137UNTS131	101851
15 Aug	Indonesia	USA (United States)	Milit Assistance	134UNTS255	101804
16 Aug	Denmark	Sweden	Commodity Trade	50SOFM943	461122
16 Aug	Brazil	USA (United States)	Tech Assistance	140UNTS223	101890

DATE	PARTY ONE	PARTY TWO	TOPIC	CITATION	NUMBER
1950 (Cont.)					
16 Aug	Canada	New Zealand	Air Transport	77UNTS239	101002
17 Aug	Brazil	Germany, West	General Trade	51WGBB11	425050
18 Aug	China People's Rep	Korea, North	General Trade	50CCJC25	410020
19 Aug	Sweden	Yugoslavia	General Economic	50SOFM945	461123
23 Aug	USA (United States)	Venezuela	Military Mission	92UNTS341	101279
24 Aug	Germany, West	Portugal	General Economic	50WBGA164	424588
25 Aug	Paraguay	Spain	General Economic	52SPBO1211	460216
25 Aug	Czechoslovakia	Germany, East	Telecommunications	4EGDA267	419332
25 Aug	Czechoslovakia	Germany, East	Postal Service	4EGDA263	419331
25 Aug	Czechoslovakia	Germany, East	Postal Service	4EGDA259	419330
25 Aug	Bulgaria	USSR (Soviet Union)	Sanitation	221UNTS57	103002
25 Aug	IBRD (World Bank)	Uruguay	IBRD Project	156UNTS203	102042
25 Aug	WHO (World Health)	United Arab Rep	IGO Operations	92UNTS39	101259
25 Aug	Luxembourg	Netherlands	Non-ILO Labor	81UNTS13	101058
28 Aug	China People's Rep	USSR (Soviet Union)	Specific Property	50CCJC26	410021
28 Aug	Greece	Philippines	General Amity	225UNTS155	103097
29 Aug	Chile	USA (United States)	Visas	122UNTS43	101634
29 Aug	Belgium	Japan	General Trade	76UNTS113	100984
29 Aug	Belgium	Japan	General Trade	82UNTS147	101089
29 Aug	Pakistan	Syria	General Amity	109UNTS95	101494
29 Aug	India	Norway	General Trade	73UNTS179	100952
02 Sep	Mexico	Switzerland	General Trade	50SWRO915	462147
04 Sep	Germany, West	Sweden	General Trade	50SOFM181	461111
04 Sep	Germany, West	Sweden	Finance	50SOFM196	461112
04 Sep	ICJ Option Clause	Israel	ICJ Option Clause	108UNTS239	101477
11 Sep	WHO (World Health)	Venezuela	Tech Assistance	110UNTS237	101513
12 Sep	UN Relief Palestin	United Arab Rep	Refugees	121UNTS107	101630
12 Sep	Belgium	Luxembourg	Customs	110UNTS21	101497
13 Sep	France	Monaco	Claims and Debts	54FRJO2706	416331
13 Sep	Ethiopia	IBRD (World Bank)	IBRD Project	157UNTS213	102055
13 Sep	UK Great Britain	USA (United States)	Visas	122UNTS51	101635
13 Sep	Ethiopia	IBRD (World Bank)	IBRD Project	157UNTS233	102056
13 Sep	Burma	USA (United States)	Direct Aid	92UNTS361	101280
14 Sep	Austria	Switzerland	Admin Cooperation	51SWRO639	462010
14 Sep	Austria	Switzerland	Visas	51SWRO642	462013
14 Sep	Panama	USA (United States)	Land Transport	241UNTS159	103431
14 Sep	Panama	USA (United States)	Land Transport	124UNTS25	101664
14 Sep	Burma	Sweden	Air Transport	96UNTS45	101330
16 Sep	Belgium	Mexico	General Trade	188UNTS119	102523
16 Sep	Multilateral		General Transport	92UNTS91	101264
18 Sep	Brazil	UK Great Britain	General Trade	88UNTS115	101188
19 Sep	Thailand	USA (United States)	Tech Assistance	132UNTS199	101761
21 Sep	Brazil	Turkey	Air Transport	150UNTS299	101981
22 Sep	Australia	Sweden	General Trade	50SOFM1075	461131
22 Sep	Germany, East	Romania	Scientific Project	4EGDA419	419279
22 Sep	Germany, East	Romania	Finance	4EGDA420	419280
22 Sep	Germany, East	Romania	Culture	4EGDA422	419281
23 Sep	UN Relief Palestin	WHO (World Health)	Sanitation	103UNTS129	200310
23 Sep	Pakistan	USA (United States)	Education	82UNTS131	101088
24 Sep	Iran	Italy	General Amity	281UNTS157	104077
25 Sep	Bulgaria	Germany, East	Finance	4EGDA462	419032
25 Sep	Bulgaria	Germany, East	Culture	4EGDA465	419033
25 Sep	Accept UN Charter	Indonesia	UN Charter	71UNTS153	100916
26 Sep	France	Guatemala	Culture	60FRRT82	415207
26 Sep	Ceylon (Sri Lanka)	United Arab Rep	Air Transport	192UNTS53	102595
26 Sep	Belgium	France	Visas	79UNTS3	101026
26 Sep	Peru	WHO (World Health)	Sanitation	104UNTS233	101444
28 Sep	Haiti	USA (United States)	Sanitation	162UNTS85	102132
29 Sep	Bulgaria	Romania	Scientific Project	342UNTS141	104905
29 Sep	Czechoslovakia	USA (United States)	Postal Service	290UNTS3	104227
29 Sep	Canada	USSR (Soviet Union)	Claims and Debts	230UNTS371	103197
01 Oct	Denmark	Poland	General Economic	81UNTS43	101061
03 Oct	Lebanon	Pakistan	Visas	219UNTS41	102964
04 Oct	France	Italy	Non-ILO Labor	50ITGU240	435122
04 Oct	Austria	Italy	Finance	50ABGB220	403112

DATE	PARTY ONE	PARTY TWO	TOPIC	CITATION	NUMBER
1950 (Cont.)					
04 Oct	Denmark	Italy	Finance	78UNTS353	101025
04 Oct	Denmark	Italy	General Trade	78UNTS341	101024
06 Oct	Netherlands	USA (United States)	Finance	51NET1	447015
06 Oct	Austria	Ireland	General Trade	557UNTS173	108133
06 Oct	France	UK Great Britain	Air Transport	96UNTS63	101331
06 Oct	Iceland	WHO (World Health)	Tech Assistance	110UNTS127	101506
07 Oct	Jordan	Spain	General Amity	51SPBO1710	460179
07 Oct	Netherlands	USA (United States)	Loans and Credits	79UNTS33	101029
09 Oct	USA (United States)	Yugoslavia	Admin Cooperation	133UNTS25	101776
10 Oct	China People's Rep	Germany, East	General Economic	50CCJC27	410022
11 Oct	Canada	Venezuela	General Economic	231UNTS3	103198
12 Oct	ILO (Labor Org)	United Nations	IGO Operations	139UNTS395	200466
12 Oct	Spain	Sweden	Scientific Project	197UNTS305	102644
13 Oct	Switzerland	USA (United States)	General Trade	133UNTS33	101777
16 Oct	Indonesia	USA (United States)	Direct Aid	281UNTS105	104074
16 Oct	Netherlands	New Zealand	Non-ILO Labor	83UNTS269	101111
17 Oct	Thailand	USA (United States)	Milit Assistance	79UNTS41	101030
18 Oct	Multilateral		Specific Resources	638UNTS185	109134
18 Oct	Mexico	IBRD (World Bank)	IBRD Project	157UNTS259	102057
18 Oct	Sweden	Switzerland	Air Transport	166UNTS49	102185
19 Oct	IBRD (World Bank)	Turkey	IBRD Project	157UNTS333	102058
19 Oct	Denmark	UK Great Britain	Finance	79UNTS25	101028
19 Oct	WHO (World Health)	Turkey	Tech Assistance	110UNTS215	101512
19 Oct	Iran	USA (United States)	Tech Assistance	92UNTS135	101266
20 Oct	Belgium	Italy	Non-ILO Labor	50ITGU296	435041
21 Oct	Italy	Switzerland	General Trade	52ITGU57	435368
21 Oct	Luxembourg	Portugal	Air Transport	108UNTS67	101468
23 Oct	Israel	Netherlands	Air Transport	189UNTS89	102543
23 Oct	Taiwan	Philippines	Air Transport	215UNTS159	102918
23 Oct	Belgium	Netherlands	Territory Boundary	136UNTS31	101831
24 Oct	Germany, West	Switzerland	Non-ILO Labor	51SWRO937	462092
24 Oct	Greece	USA (United States)	Admin Cooperation	133UNTS41	101778
24 Oct	Belgium	Italy	Admin Cooperation	110UNTS39	101499
25 Oct	China People's Rep	USSR (Soviet Union)	Privil/Immunities	0SUST278	468078
26 Oct	Canada	USA (United States)	Direct Aid	132UNTS247	101764
27 Oct	IBRD (World Bank)	Thailand	IBRD Project	158UNTS25	102060
27 Oct	IBRD (World Bank)	Thailand	IBRD Project	158UNTS43	102061
27 Oct	IBRD (World Bank)	Thailand	IBRD Project	158UNTS3	102059
30 Oct	Nepal	UK Great Britain	General Amity	97UNTS121	101346
31 Oct	France	Sweden	General Trade	50SOFM981	461124
31 Oct	Austria	Sweden	Non-ILO Labor	197UNTS311	102645
01 Nov	Mongolia	USSR (Soviet Union)	Specific Property	0SUST439	468271
02 Nov	Germany, West	Switzerland	Patents/Copyrights	51WGBB63	425752
02 Nov	Colombia	IBRD (World Bank)	IBRD Project	158UNTS59	102062
02 Nov	Multilateral		Tech Assistance	81UNTS160	101071
03 Nov	Czechoslovakia	USSR (Soviet Union)	General Economic	0SUST278	468107
04 Nov	Iran	USSR (Soviet Union)	General Trade	0SUST278	468225
04 Nov	Multilateral		Humanitarian	213UNTS221	102889
06 Nov	Germany, East	Romania	General Trade	1EGDA453	419282
06 Nov	Philippines	USA (United States)	Finance	122UNTS63	101637
06 Nov	Burma	USA (United States)	Milit Assistance	122UNTS81	101638
06 Nov	Norway	UK Great Britain	Finance	88UNTS257	101197
07 Nov	Ceylon (Sri Lanka)	USA (United States)	Tech Assistance	92UNTS125	101265
10 Nov	Canada	Ecuador	General Economic	231UNTS15	103199
10 Nov	Thailand	UK Great Britain	Air Transport	96UNTS77	101332
10 Nov	Peru	WHO (World Health)	Tech Assistance	110UNTS187	101510
10 Nov	Nicaragua	WHO (World Health)	Tech Assistance	110UNTS155	101508
10 Nov	Sweden	UK Great Britain	Finance	88UNTS265	101198
14 Nov	Belgium	USSR (Soviet Union)	General Trade	0SUST278	468026
14 Nov	Australia	IBRD (World Bank)	IBRD Project	156UNTS147	102041
16 Nov	Greece	UK Great Britain	Taxation	166UNTS281	102193
17 Nov	Czechoslovakia	Poland	Sanitation	530UNTS195	107682
18 Nov	Canada	Costa Rica	General Economic	231UNTS25	103200
21 Nov	USA (United States)	Yugoslavia	Milit Assistance	93UNTS45	101286
21 Nov	USA (United States)	Yugoslavia	Direct Aid	93UNTS39	101285

DATE	PARTY ONE	PARTY TWO	TOPIC	CITATION	NUMBER
1950 (Cont.)					
22 Nov	Multilateral		Culture	131UNTS25	101734
22 Nov	Bolivia	USA (United States)	Education	152UNTS17	102008
24 Nov	Colombia	USA (United States)	Scientific Project	133UNTS49	101779
24 Nov	Multilateral		Tech Assistance	81UNTS188	101072
25 Nov	Belgium	Netherlands	Non-ILO Labor	51NET15	447016
25 Nov	Italy	Romania	Customs	52ITGU39	435323
27 Nov	Paraguay	USA (United States)	Direct Aid	122UNTS147	101644
28 Nov	Guatemala	WHO (World Health)	Sanitation	103UNTS51	101423
29 Nov	Multilateral		Patents/Copyrights	88UNTS221	101194
30 Nov	Denmark	South Africa	Taxation	84UNTS51	101118
02 Dec	France	Sweden	Non-ILO Labor	50SOFM1061	461129
02 Dec	Italy	Sweden	General Trade	50SOFM1017	461125
02 Dec	Multilateral		Trusteeship	118UNTS255	200381
02 Dec	Iceland	Ireland	General Trade	558UNTS231	108143
02 Dec	Albania	Poland	Culture	260UNTS131	103707
02 Dec	Costa Rica	USA (United States)	Admin Cooperation	133UNTS61	101780
06 Dec	Italy	Sweden	Finance	50SOFM1036	461126
06 Dec	Israel	UK Great Britain	Air Transport	151UNTS33	101983
07 Dec	Multilateral		Admin Cooperation	212UNTS17	102861
08 Dec	Greece	Sweden	Finance	50SOFM1056	461128
08 Dec	Greece	Sweden	General Trade	50SOFM1045	461127
08 Dec	Switzerland	UK Great Britain	Claims and Debts	175UNTS55	102295
09 Dec	France	Greece	Taxation	166UNTS315	102196
09 Dec	Germany, West	UK Great Britain	Finance	88UNTS247	101196
10 Dec	Israel	UK Great Britain	Patents/Copyrights	88UNTS211	101193
11 Dec	France	Mexico	Patents/Copyrights	51FRJO1111	416322
13 Dec	El Salvador	USA (United States)	Sanitation	166UNTS149	102188
14 Dec	El Salvador	Mexico	General Trade	52MEXD605	444016
14 Dec	France	UK Great Britain	Taxation	51FRJO2108	416198
14 Dec	Germany, West	Netherlands	Water Transport	87UNTS257	101177
15 Dec	Multilateral		Customs	347UNTS127	104994
15 Dec	Multilateral		Customs	171UNTS305	102234
15 Dec	Brazil	Netherlands	Non-ILO Labor	123UNTS101	101657
15 Dec	Multilateral		Customs	157UNTS129	102052
15 Dec	Multilateral		IGO Operations	160UNTS267	102111
15 Dec	Pakistan	USA (United States)	Milit Assistance	122UNTS89	101639
15 Dec	Multilateral		Tech Assistance	76UNTS120	100985
15 Dec	Norway	UK Great Britain	General Trade	106UNTS87	101459
19 Dec	Norway	Sweden	General Trade	50SOFM1065	461130
19 Dec	Germany, West	Iceland	Patents/Copyrights	56WGBB899	425278
19 Dec	Bulgaria	Italy	Customs	52ITGU224	435068
19 Dec	Germany, West	Iceland	General Amity	51WGBB153	425279
19 Dec	Taiwan	USA (United States)	Air Transport	0CTRC792	413037
19 Dec	Brazil	USA (United States)	Tech Assistance	141UNTS3	101900
19 Dec	Brazil	USA (United States)	Direct Aid	140UNTS365	101899
19 Dec	Australia	UK Great Britain	Territory Boundary	93UNTS81	101292
20 Dec	Germany, West	Norway	General Trade	2NORT545	451183
20 Dec	Panama	USA (United States)	Tech Assistance	92UNTS167	101269
20 Dec	Norway	Sweden	Specific Resources	92UNTS3	101256
21 Dec	Italy	UK Great Britain	Finance	175UNTS187	102301
21 Dec	Multilateral		Admin Cooperation	90UNTS3	101222
22 Dec	Ireland	Netherlands	General Trade	51NET11	447017
22 Dec	Liberia	USA (United States)	Direct Aid	133UNTS69	101781
22 Dec	Liberia	USA (United States)	Tech Assistance	92UNTS145	101267
22 Dec	France	Turkey	Non-ILO Labor	98UNTS11	101356
22 Dec	Cuba	USA (United States)	Military Mission	122UNTS97	101640
23 Dec	Italy	Yugoslavia	Air Transport	52ITGU142	435222
23 Dec	Italy	Yugoslavia	Consul/Citizenship	58ITGU136	435223
23 Dec	Italy	Yugoslavia	Peace/Disarmament	55ITGU73	435220
23 Dec	Italy	Yugoslavia	Patents/Copyrights	55ITGU73	435221
23 Dec	Italy	Yugoslavia	Admin Cooperation	171UNTS291	102233
23 Dec	Italy	Yugoslavia	Reparations	150UNTS213	101975
23 Dec	Italy	Yugoslavia	Finance	150UNTS191	101973
23 Dec	Italy	Yugoslavia	Admin Cooperation	150UNTS199	101974
23 Dec	Multilateral		Tech Assistance	185UNTS3	102456

DATE	PARTY ONE	PARTY TWO	TOPIC	CITATION	NUMBER
1950 (Cont.)					
23 Dec	Nicaragua	USA (United States)	Tech Assistance	92UNTS155	101268
27 Dec	Brazil	USA (United States)	Sanitation	147UNTS33	101926
28 Dec	Norway	USA (United States)	Milit Assistance	240UNTS391	103414
28 Dec	Colombia	IBRD (World Bank)	IBRD Project	158UNTS87	102063
28 Dec	India	USA (United States)	Tech Assistance	99UNTS39	101369
28 Dec	Philippines	WHO (World Health)	Tech Assistance	110UNTS203	101511
28 Dec	UK Great Britain	Yugoslavia	Loans and Credits	88UNTS329	101201
29 Dec	Belgium	Sweden	Finance	50SOFM900	461118
29 Dec	Finland	Sweden	Taxation	197UNTS333	102646
29 Dec	Netherlands	Norway	Taxation	134UNTS19	101795
29 Dec	France	UK Great Britain	Dispute Settlement	118UNTS149	101603
29 Dec	Paraguay	USA (United States)	Tech Assistance	122UNTS157	101645
30 Dec	Austria	Italy	Non-ILO Labor	54ITGU278	435032
30 Dec	Czechoslovakia	Germany, East	Visas	4EGDA272	419333
1951					
02 Jan	China People's Rep	USSR (Soviet Union)	Water Transport	0SUST279	468079
02 Jan	China People's Rep	USSR (Soviet Union)	Water Transport	51CCJC1	410024
02 Jan	Nicaragua	WHO (World Health)	Sanitation	103UNTS107	101428
02 Jan	El Salvador	WHO (World Health)	Sanitation	103UNTS29	101421
03 Jan	Pakistan	Philippines	General Amity	2PTS605	465023
04 Jan	Brazil	USA (United States)	Milit Assistance	165UNTS97	102171
04 Jan	Chile	USA (United States)	Milit Assistance	165UNTS105	102172
04 Jan	Australia	Finland	Claims and Debts	80UNTS27	101042
05 Jan	Portugal	USA (United States)	Milit Assistance	133UNTS75	101782
05 Jan	Colombia	WHO (World Health)	Sanitation	102UNTS139	101417
06 Jan	Finland	Ireland	General Trade	558UNTS120	108140
06 Jan	United Nations	Yugoslavia	Direct Aid	78UNTS165	101015
06 Jan	USA (United States)	Yugoslavia	Direct Aid	122UNTS137	101643
08 Jan	Argentina	USA (United States)	Milit Assistance	165UNTS89	102170
09 Jan	Multilateral		Humanitarian	197UNTS341	102647
10 Jan	Liberia	USA (United States)	Gen Communications	132UNTS255	101765
11 Jan	Sweden	Switzerland	General Economic	51SOFM1	461132
11 Jan	India	USA (United States)	Admin Cooperation	148UNTS49	101934
11 Jan	Costa Rica	USA (United States)	Tech Assistance	92UNTS179	101270
11 Jan	Liberia	USA (United States)	Military Mission	122UNTS125	101642
13 Jan	Norway	Switzerland	General Trade	2NORT547	451154
15 Jan	Ecuador	Norway	General Trade	2NORT548	451041
16 Jan	Chile	USA (United States)	Education	147UNTS11	101925
16 Jan	Chile	USA (United States)	Tech Assistance	151UNTS147	101990
16 Jan	Chile	USA (United States)	Direct Aid	157UNTS3	102043
17 Jan	Cuba	France	Claims and Debts	52FRJO2609	416143
17 Jan	Saudi Arabia	USA (United States)	Direct Aid	140UNTS335	101897
17 Jan	Costa Rica	USA (United States)	Land Transport	134UNTS215	101801
17 Jan	Sweden	UK Great Britain	Postal Service	93UNTS225	101301
18 Jan	Denmark	Norway	Non-ILO Labor	82UNTS153	101090
18 Jan	Multilateral		Tech Assistance	81UNTS233	101073
19 Jan	Belgium	Italy	Non-ILO Labor	51ITGU45	435042
19 Jan	Belgium	Italy	Non-ILO Labor	51ITGU46	435043
19 Jan	Germany, East	Poland	Territory Boundary	4EGDA130	419233
19 Jan	Netherlands	USA (United States)	Reparations	141UNTS221	101917
20 Jan	Denmark	Switzerland	Finance	87UNTS223	101174
20 Jan	UK Great Britain	Yemen	General Amity	101UNTS39	101400
22 Jan	China People's Rep	Hungary	General Economic	51CCJC3	410026
22 Jan	Italy	Norway	Finance	88UNTS339	101202
23 Jan	Philippines	UK Great Britain	Admin Cooperation	2PTS609	465024
23 Jan	Nepal	USA (United States)	Tech Assistance	184UNTS65	102439
23 Jan	IBRD (World Bank)	South Africa	IBRD Project	158UNTS115	102064
23 Jan	IBRD (World Bank)	South Africa	IBRD Project	158UNTS135	102065
24 Jan	Spain	Sweden	General Economic	51SOFM18	461133
24 Jan	Ceylon (Sri Lanka)	ILO (Labor Org)	Tech Assistance	117UNTS355	200380
24 Jan	France	UK Great Britain	Postal Service	90UNTS193	101237
25 Jan	Brazil	Italy	Air Transport	52ITGU169	435058
25 Jan	Albania	Poland	Scientific Project	260UNTS217	103710
25 Jan	Paraguay	UNICEF (Children)	IGO Operations	79UNTS9	101027

DATE	PARTY ONE	PARTY TWO	TOPIC	CITATION	NUMBER
1951 (Cont.)					
26 Jan	Germany, West	Sweden	General Trade	51WBGA23	424613
26 Jan	Canada	France	Claims and Debts	233UNTS65	103251
26 Jan	Canada	India	Visas	248UNTS89	103486
26 Jan	Panama	USA (United States)	Land Transport	137UNTS69	101849
26 Jan	Colombia	Denmark	Finance	87UNTS161	101171
26 Jan	Honduras	USA (United States)	Tech Assistance	99UNTS49	101370
29 Jan	France	Italy	Visas	52ITGU10	435124
29 Jan	France	Italy	Sanitation	52ITGU24	435125
29 Jan	France	Italy	Land Transport	52ITGU287	435123
29 Jan	China People's Rep	Poland	Water Transport	51CCJC7	410030
29 Jan	China People's Rep	Poland	Telecommunications	51CCJC5	410028
29 Jan	China People's Rep	Poland	Postal Service	51CCJC6	410029
29 Jan	China People's Rep	Poland	General Economic	51CCJC4	410027
30 Jan	Bulgaria	Germany, East	Telecommunications	4EGDA477	419036
30 Jan	Bulgaria	Germany, East	Postal Service	4EGDA472	419035
30 Jan	France	UK Great Britain	Specific Resources	51FRJO2010	416199
30 Jan	Bulgaria	Germany, East	Postal Service	4EGDA468	419034
30 Jan	Honduras	USA (United States)	Direct Aid	124UNTS63	101667
30 Jan	France	UK Great Britain	Privil/Immunities	121UNTS97	101629
31 Jan	Nicaragua	USA (United States)	Sanitation	160UNTS121	102105
31 Jan	Nicaragua	USA (United States)	Education	150UNTS3	101960
31 Jan	Austria	UK Great Britain	Finance	88UNTS107	101187
02 Feb	France	Italy	General Trade	52ITGU68	435126
02 Feb	Chile	Germany, West	General Trade	52WGBB325	425078
02 Feb	Germany, West	Sweden	Patents/Copyrights	51WGBB105	425614
02 Feb	France	India	Territory Boundary	203UNTS155	102744
02 Feb	Ethiopia	ICAO (Civil Aviat)	Tech Assistance	96UNTS123	101333
03 Feb	Germany, East	Poland	Postal Service	4EGDA137	419234
03 Feb	Germany, East	Poland	Telecommunications	4EGDA144	419235
05 Feb	Israel	Turkey	Air Transport	193UNTS3	102607
07 Feb	Afghanistan	USA (United States)	Tech Assistance	132UNTS265	101766
07 Feb	Bolivia	WHO (World Health)	Sanitation	104UNTS167	101438
08 Feb	Canada	USA (United States)	Telecommunications	207UNTS17	102797
09 Feb	Canada	Turkey	Visas	233UNTS95	103252
09 Feb	Taiwan	USA (United States)	Milit Assistance	132UNTS273	101767
09 Feb	Pakistan	USA (United States)	Tech Assistance	100UNTS67	101388
10 Feb	Denmark	Sweden	General Trade	51SOFM94	461134
10 Feb	Denmark	Sweden	Finance	51SOFM104	461135
10 Feb	Denmark	Hungary	General Trade	85UNTS49	101145
12 Feb	Germany, West	Greece	General Trade	198UNTS193	102665
13 Feb	Costa Rica	USA (United States)	Sanitation	141UNTS169	101914
13 Feb	Italy	USA (United States)	IGO Establishment	148UNTS57	101935
13 Feb	Netherlands	IRO (Refugee Org)	IGO Operations	87UNTS239	101175
14 Feb	Denmark	WHO (World Health)	Sanitation	104UNTS243	101445
15 Feb	Poland	USSR (Soviet Union)	Territory Boundary	432UNTS199	106222
15 Feb	Chile	USA (United States)	Military Mission	133UNTS95	101783
15 Feb	Chile	USA (United States)	Military Mission	133UNTS117	101784
15 Feb	Multilateral		Tech Assistance	81UNTS245	101074
15 Feb	Paraguay	WHO (World Health)	Tech Assistance	110UNTS171	101509
17 Feb	Albania	USSR (Soviet Union)	Loans and Credits	0SUST280	468010
17 Feb	France	UK Great Britain	Finance	88UNTS199	101191
19 Feb	Norway	Sweden	Finance	51SOFM567	461155
19 Feb	Ethiopia	IBRD (World Bank)	IBRD Project	186UNTS101	102486
19 Feb	Israel	ICAO (Civil Aviat)	Tech Assistance	96UNTS141	101334
19 Feb	Israel	ILO (Labor Org)	Tech Assistance	100UNTS105	101391
20 Feb	Australia	USA (United States)	Milit Assistance	132UNTS297	101769
20 Feb	Dominican Republic	USA (United States)	Tech Assistance	132UNTS305	101770
20 Feb	Australia	Netherlands	Visas	97UNTS283	101354
21 Feb	Greece	UK Great Britain	General Economic	88UNTS205	101192
22 Feb	Norway	UK Great Britain	Consul/Citizenship	326UNTS209	104713
22 Feb	Australia	Netherlands	Non-ILO Labor	128UNTS115	101717
24 Feb	Lebanon	USA (United States)	Tech Assistance	223UNTS121	103060
26 Feb	Israel	USA (United States)	Tech Assistance	137UNTS57	101848
26 Feb	Panama	USA (United States)	Sanitation	160UNTS153	102106
27 Feb	France	USA (United States)	Milit Installation	0UNTS0	109598

DATE	PARTY ONE	PARTY TWO	TOPIC	CITATION	NUMBER
1951 (Cont.)					
27 Feb	Jordan	USA (United States)	Tech Assistance	141UNTS55	101905
27 Feb	New Zealand	Yugoslavia	Reparations	150UNTS165	101971
28 Feb	India	Sweden	General Trade	51SOFM123	461137
28 Feb	ICAO (Civil Aviat)	United Nations	IGO Operations	139UNTS429	200469
28 Feb	Israel	USA (United States)	Taxation	220UNTS79	102991
02 Mar	Cuba	UK Great Britain	Visas	88UNTS191	101190
03 Mar	Philippines	SCAP Japan	General Trade	2PTS613	465025
03 Mar	Germany, East	Hungary	Mass Media	4EGDA384	419436
03 Mar	Indonesia	Pakistan	General Amity	188UNTS333	102537
03 Mar	India	Indonesia	General Amity	167UNTS3	102197
03 Mar	ILO (Labor Org)	Syria	Tech Assistance	110UNTS69	101502
05 Mar	Multilateral		Tech Assistance	81UNTS261	101075
06 Mar	Multilateral		Milit Assistance	138UNTS67	101860
06 Mar	UK Great Britain	USA (United States)	Status of Forces	97UNTS137	101347
06 Mar	Multilateral		Claims and Debts	106UNTS141	101461
07 Mar	Bulgaria	USSR (Soviet Union)	Education	0SUST285	468040
07 Mar	UNESCO (Educ/Cult)	United Nations	IGO Operations	139UNTS417	200468
07 Mar	USA (United States)	Uruguay	Sanitation	165UNTS113	102173
09 Mar	Colombia	USA (United States)	Tech Assistance	141UNTS15	101901
09 Mar	Colombia	Portugal	Air Transport	108UNTS87	101469
12 Mar	France	Vietnam, South	Specific Property	0VKNG25	496005
12 Mar	Philippines	SCAP Japan	General Trade	2PTS615	465026
14 Mar	China People's Rep	USSR (Soviet Union)	Land Transport	0SUST280	468080
14 Mar	Bolivia	USA (United States)	Tech Assistance	132UNTS319	101771
15 Mar	Romania	USSR (Soviet Union)	General Economic	0SUST280	468380
15 Mar	Greece	Yugoslavia	Air Transport	187UNTS237	102516
15 Mar	Belgium	Netherlands	Reparations	93UNTS97	101294
16 Mar	Czechoslovakia	Sweden	General Trade	51SOFM125	461138
16 Mar	Finland	Sweden	General Economic	51SOFM109	461136
16 Mar	Canada	France	Taxation	236UNTS297	103331
16 Mar	Canada	France	Taxation	236UNTS267	103330
16 Mar	India	USA (United States)	Milit Assistance	141UNTS47	101904
16 Mar	Dominican Republic	USA (United States)	Education	148UNTS15	101932
16 Mar	Austria	Belgium	Visas	88UNTS357	101203
16 Mar	Belgium	USA (United States)	Reparations	93UNTS109	101295
19 Mar	El Salvador	USA (United States)	Land Transport	134UNTS245	101803
20 Mar	Iran	Turkey	Air Transport	51TURG1512	466137
20 Mar	Luxembourg	USA (United States)	Other Military	180UNTS283	102392
20 Mar	Multilateral		IGO Operations	82UNTS172	101091
20 Mar	Belgium	Finland	Non-ILO Labor	110UNTS27	101498
21 Mar	France	Italy	Non-ILO Labor	53ITGU22	435129
21 Mar	France	Italy	Non-ILO Labor	53ITGU22	435128
21 Mar	France	Italy	Health/Educ/Welfare	53ITGU22	435127
22 Mar	Austria	Netherlands	Finance	51NET60	447019
22 Mar	Austria	Netherlands	General Transport	51NET59	447018
25 Mar	WHO (World Health)	United Arab Rep	IGO Status/Immunit	223UNTS87	103058
27 Mar	Albania	Germany, East	General Trade	1EGDA474	419006
27 Mar	Canada	USA (United States)	Milit Assistance	132UNTS333	101772
28 Mar	Multilateral		Tech Assistance	181UNTS61	102399
28 Mar	United Nations	USA (United States)	Postal Service	108UNTS231	101476
28 Mar	Indonesia	WHO (World Health)	Tech Assistance	103UNTS71	101425
29 Mar	Jordan	ILO (Labor Org)	Tech Assistance	100UNTS247	200287
29 Mar	Jordan	United Nations	Tech Assistance	137UNTS267	200448
29 Mar	Germany, West	Netherlands	Non-ILO Labor	149UNTS71	101952
29 Mar	Australia	Italy	Non-ILO Labor	131UNTS187	101741
31 Mar	Hungary	Sweden	Claims and Debts	51SOFM145	461139
02 Apr	Pakistan	UK Great Britain	General Trade	168UNTS281	102219
02 Apr	Liberia	ILO (Labor Org)	Tech Assistance	100UNTS117	101392
03 Apr	China People's Rep	Poland	Culture	51CCJC12	410033
03 Apr	Jordan	WHO (World Health)	Tech Assistance	110UNTS297	200367
03 Apr	China People's Rep	Poland	Culture	304UNTS187	104396
03 Apr	Multilateral		Milit Occupation	141UNTS303	101920
04 Apr	Japan	USA (United States)	Specific Resources	57JAIL85	440064
05 Apr	Italy	Switzerland	Territory Boundary	53SWRO409	462178
05 Apr	Italy	Switzerland	Territory Boundary	53SWRO403	462177

DATE	PARTY ONE	PARTY TWO	TOPIC	CITATION	NUMBER
1951 (Cont.)					
05 Apr	Indonesia	Sweden	General Trade	51SOFM193	461140
05 Apr	Italy	Switzerland	Territory Boundary	53ITGU91	435372
05 Apr	Italy	Tunisia	Telecommunications	52ITGU206	435398
05 Apr	Multilateral		Tech Assistance	84UNTS299	101139
06 Apr	Ceylon (Sri Lanka)	ILO (Labor Org)	Tech Assistance	100UNTS235	200286
06 Apr	Canada	Sweden	Taxation	197UNTS393	102648
06 Apr	Belgium	UK Great Britain	Specific Property	110UNTS3	101496
06 Apr	Mexico	ILO (Labor Org)	Tech Assistance	100UNTS131	101393
09 Apr	Luxembourg	Switzerland	Air Transport	254UNTS389	103601
10 Apr	Bulgaria	USSR (Soviet Union)	Scientific Project	0SUST281	468039
10 Apr	United Nations	WMO (Meteorology)	IGO Status/Immunit	103UNTS245	200415
10 Apr	Colombia	IBRD (World Bank)	IBRD Project	158UNTS155	102066
10 Apr	Iraq	USA (United States)	Tech Assistance	151UNTS179	101993
11 Apr	France	Sweden	General Trade	51SOFM203	461141
11 Apr	France	UK Great Britain	Claims and Debts	106UNTS3	101456
12 Apr	Iceland	Sweden	General Trade	51SOFM211	461142
13 Apr	Japan	Netherlands	Finance	51NET51	447021
13 Apr	Japan	Netherlands	General Trade	51NET50	447020
13 Apr	Peru	ILO (Labor Org)	Tech Assistance	100UNTS31	101385
13 Apr	Costa Rica	WHO (World Health)	Sanitation	103UNTS3	101419
13 Apr	Guatemala	ILO (Labor Org)	Tech Assistance	126UNTS249	101692
14 Apr	FAO (Food Agri)	Turkey	Tech Assistance	51TURG407	466134
14 Apr	France	Yugoslavia	Claims and Debts	53FRJO3107	416484
14 Apr	Canada	ICAO (Civil Aviat)	IGO Status/Immunit	96UNTS155	101335
17 Apr	USA (United States)	Yugoslavia	Milit Assistance	162UNTS173	102134
18 Apr	Multilateral		IGO Establishment	261UNTS140	103729
18 Apr	El Salvador	USA (United States)	Tech Assistance	141UNTS37	101903
18 Apr	Canada	USA (United States)	Milit Assistance	134UNTS205	101800
18 Apr	Greece	India	Reparations	166UNTS305	102195
19 Apr	Iraq	UK Great Britain	Air Transport	108UNTS121	101470
19 Apr	Ecuador	ILO (Labor Org)	Tech Assistance	100UNTS77	101389
19 Apr	ICAO (Civil Aviat)	Thailand	Tech Assistance	96UNTS181	101336
20 Apr	Greece	Turkey	Culture	178UNTS17	102333
20 Apr	Nicaragua	USA (United States)	Land Transport	138UNTS57	101859
20 Apr	Honduras	WHO (World Health)	Tech Assistance	110UNTS111	101505
20 Apr	France	UK Great Britain	Air Transport	106UNTS81	101458
21 Apr	Belgium	Netherlands	Non-ILO Labor	51NET64	447022
21 Apr	Germany, West	United Arab Rep	General Trade	52WGBB525	425710
21 Apr	Austria	Germany, West	Non-ILO Labor	52WGBB317	425523
21 Apr	Cuba	ILO (Labor Org)	Tech Assistance	99UNTS205	101382
24 Apr	Canada	Ceylon (Sri Lanka)	Visas	248UNTS101	103488
24 Apr	Honduras	USA (United States)	Education	140UNTS287	101894
25 Apr	Finland	Norway	Specific Resources	2NORT551	451048
25 Apr	Multilateral		Reparations	91UNTS21	101240
25 Apr	Greece	ILO (Labor Org)	Tech Assistance	100UNTS93	101390
25 Apr	UK Great Britain	USA (United States)	Specific Property	99UNTS97	101373
26 Apr	India	ILO (Labor Org)	Tech Assistance	100UNTS19	101384
27 Apr	Philippines	USA (United States)	Direct Aid	174UNTS251	102290
27 Apr	Denmark	USA (United States)	General Military	94UNTS35	101305
30 Apr	Indonesia	Norway	General Trade	2NORT552	451082
30 Apr	Ceylon (Sri Lanka)	India	General Trade	196UNTS199	102625
30 Apr	Mexico	WHO (World Health)	Tech Assistance	103UNTS95	101427
30 Apr	Netherlands	UK Great Britain	Consul/Citizenship	91UNTS177	101250
01 May	Jordan	UK Great Britain	Finance	117UNTS19	101582
02 May	Norway	Sierra Leone	Taxation	2NORT553	451139
02 May	Haiti	USA (United States)	Tech Assistance	151UNTS191	101994
02 May	Ethiopia	USA (United States)	Direct Aid	139UNTS85	101877
02 May	Belgium	Czechoslovakia	Taxation	109UNTS3	101483
02 May	WHO (World Health)	Yugoslavia	Tech Assistance	103UNTS117	101429
02 May	Norway	UK Great Britain	Taxation	106UNTS101	101460
03 May	Ecuador	USA (United States)	Tech Assistance	141UNTS27	101902
04 May	Colombia	WHO (World Health)	Tech Assistance	110UNTS83	101503
05 May	Iceland	USA (United States)	Milit Assistance	205UNTS173	102776
05 May	United Arab Rep	USA (United States)	Tech Assistance	198UNTS265	102670
07 May	Germany, West	Norway	Claims and Debts	92UNTS51	101260

DATE	PARTY ONE	PARTY TWO	TOPIC	CITATION	NUMBER
1951 (Cont.)					
08 May	Belgium	UK Great Britain	Air Transport	158UNTS451	102079
08 May	Belgium	Brazil	Consul/Citizenship	91UNTS75	101242
10 May	UK Great Britain	Yugoslavia	Loans and Credits	102UNTS29	101408
11 May	El Salvador	USA (United States)	Direct Aid	141UNTS191	101915
14 May	Italy	Switzerland	Admin Cooperation	51SWRO644	462031
14 May	Ceylon (Sri Lanka)	USA (United States)	Gen Communications	141UNTS159	101913
15 May	Austria	USA (United States)	Direct Aid	139UNTS79	101876
16 May	Italy	USA (United States)	Reparations	206UNTS325	102795
16 May	Pakistan	ILO (Labor Org)	Tech Assistance	100UNTS147	101394
17 May	Netherlands	UK Great Britain	Air Transport	118UNTS103	101599
19 May	Italy	Netherlands	Finance	51NET97	447023
19 May	Austria	Germany, West	Non-ILO Labor	52WGBB612	425524
20 May	Mexico	United Nations	IGO Operations	102UNTS103	101413
21 May	Norway	Pakistan	General Trade	318UNTS163	104613
22 May	Norway	Pakistan	General Trade	2NORT555	451125
23 May	Austria	Sweden	General Trade	51SOFM243	461143
23 May	Austria	Sweden	Finance	51SOFM251	461144
23 May	Pakistan	USA (United States)	Admin Cooperation	134UNTS265	101805
24 May	·Austria	Netherlands	Visas	51NET88	447024
24 May	Austria	Netherlands	Visas	52ABGB26	403142
24 May	Switzerland	USA (United States)	Taxation	127UNTS227	101706
24 May	India	Netherlands	Air Transport	108UNTS151	101471
25 May	South Africa	Sweden	Taxation	197UNTS425	102649
25 May	Multilateral		Status of Forces	175UNTS215	102303
25 May	Nicaragua	UK Great Britain	Sanitation	101UNTS77	101404
28 May	Greece	Norway	Air Transport	187UNTS141	102507
29 May	Netherlands	Sweden	General Trade	51SOFM253	461145
29 May	Italy	Luxembourg	Non-ILO Labor	54ITGU194	435262
29 May	Austria	Sweden	General Amity	197UNTS431	102650
29 May	Lebanon	USA (United States)	Tech Assistance	160UNTS49	102101
30 May	Finland	Netherlands	General Trade	51NET83	447025
31 May	Norway	Yugoslavia	Claims and Debts	2NORT558	451093
31 May	Cambodia	WHO (World Health)	Tech Assistance	102UNTS279	200307
31 May	Netherlands	South Africa	Culture	188UNTS289	102533
01 Jun	Israel	USA (United States)	Visas	212UNTS129	102864
01 Jun	Multilateral		Tech Assistance	118UNTS57	101596
03 Jun	France	Israel	Extradition	219UNTS215	102977
03 Jun	UK Great Britain	USA (United States)	Postal Service	137UNTS81	101850
05 Jun	India	UK Great Britain	Postal Service	135UNTS3	101811
05 Jun	Denmark	Portugal	General Trade	101UNTS61	101402
05 Jun	Lebanon	WHO (World Health)	Scientific Project	104UNTS225	101443
06 Jun	UK Great Britain	USA (United States)	Consul/Citizenship	165UNTS121	102174
07 Jun	Germany, West	USA (United States)	Direct Aid	238UNTS161	103360
07 Jun	Nicaragua	IBRD (World Bank)	IBRD Project	158UNTS215	102067
07 Jun	Nicaragua	IBRD (World Bank)	IBRD Project	158UNTS277	102068
07 Jun	USA (United States)	Venezuela	Tech Assistance	141UNTS273	101918
07 Jun	Lebanon	WHO (World Health)	Tech Assistance	126UNTS221	101690
07 Jun	Iceland	ICAO (Civil Aviat)	Tech Assistance	96UNTS193	101337
11 Jun	United Nations	Thailand	Tech Assistance	90UNTS45	101225
11 Jun	WHO (World Health)	Uruguay	Tech Assistance	128UNTS251	101724
11 Jun	Liberia	WHO (World Health)	Tech Assistance	103UNTS83	101426
13 Jun	Burma	WHO (World Health)	Sanitation	117UNTS115	101588
14 Jun	Panama	UNICEF (Children)	IGO Operations	97UNTS3	101343
14 Jun	Belgium	Netherlands	Reparations	101UNTS3	101397
14 Jun	Costa Rica	WHO (World Health)	Sanitation	102UNTS151	101418
15 Jun	Belgium	Netherlands	Claims and Debts	51NET106	447026
15 Jun	China People's Rep	USSR (Soviet Union)	General Trade	51CCJC17	410038
15 Jun	Finland	Sweden	Visas	198UNTS3	102651
15 Jun	UK Great Britain	USA (United States)	Tech Assistance	141UNTS79	101907
15 Jun	Multilateral		Tech Assistance	148UNTS67	101936
15 Jun	Italy	Netherlands	Reparations	150UNTS103	101964
16 Jun	Mongolia	USSR (Soviet Union)	Specific Property	16SUGG66	469896
16 Jun	Italy	UK Great Britain	Patents/Copyrights	172UNTS293	102253
16 Jun	Ethiopia	USA (United States)	Tech Assistance	148UNTS39	101933
18 Jun	Denmark	Iran	Air Transport	255UNTS3	103602

DATE	PARTY ONE	PARTY TWO	TOPIC	CITATION	NUMBER
1951 (Cont.)					
18 Jun	Saudi Arabia	USA (United States)	Milit Assistance	141UNTS67	101906
18 Jun	Saudi Arabia	USA (United States)	Specific Property	102UNTS73	101412
18 Jun	Dominican Republic	ILO (Labor Org)	Tech Assistance	100UNTS3	101383
19 Jun	Spain	Turkey	General Economic	52TURG2805	466086
19 Jun	Cuba	Spain	Air Transport	53SPBO2504	460068
19 Jun	Norway	South Africa	Taxation	2NORT560	451170
19 Jun	Multilateral		Status of Forces	199UNTS67	102678
19 Jun	Australia	Italy	Visas	184UNTS185	102447
20 Jun	Sweden	Switzerland	General Trade	51SOFM277	461146
20 Jun	Sweden	Switzerland	Finance	51SOFM296	461147
20 Jun	Sweden	Switzerland	General Trade	51SWRO619	462156
20 Jun	Iceland	IBRD (World Bank)	IBRD Project	158UNTS301	102069
20 Jun	Cuba	USA (United States)	Tech Assistance	148UNTS3	101931
21 Jun	Indonesia	Philippines	General Amity	2PTS689	465027
21 Jun	China People's Rep	Czechoslovakia	General Trade	51CCJC19	410040
25 Jun	Multilateral		Tech Assistance	92UNTS27	101258
25 Jun	Israel	United Nations	Tech Assistance	97UNTS21	101344
26 Jun	ILO (Labor Org)	Vietnam, South	Tech Assistance	100UNTS223	200285
26 Jun	Cuba	Portugal	Air Transport	192UNTS115	102598
27 Jun	Mexico	USA (United States)	Tech Assistance	141UNTS211	101916
27 Jun	Sweden	USA (United States)	Milit Assistance	148UNTS77	101937
28 Jun	Netherlands	Norway	Non-ILO Labor	51NET98	447027
28 Jun	Netherlands	Norway	Non-ILO Labor	2NORT562	451118
28 Jun	Multilateral		ILO Labor	172UNTS159	102244
28 Jun	Austria	UK Great Britain	Admin Cooperation	117UNTS99	101586
28 Jun	Italy	UK Great Britain	Claims and Debts	118UNTS115	101600
28 Jun	Multilateral		Tech Assistance	118UNTS154	101604
29 Jun	Germany, West	Netherlands	General Trade	51NET119	447028
29 Jun	IBRD (World Bank)	Switzerland	IGO Status/Immunit	216UNTS347	200529
29 Jun	India	Turkey	Culture	213UNTS183	102886
29 Jun	Multilateral		ILO Labor	165UNTS303	102181
29 Jun	Brazil	USA (United States)	Tech Assistance	184UNTS303	102455
29 Jun	Luxembourg	New Zealand	Visas	101UNTS71	101403
30 Jun	Denmark	France	Non-ILO Labor	151UNTS241	102000
01 Jul	United Arab Rep	UK Great Britain	Finance	249UNTS143	103504
01 Jul	United Arab Rep	UK Great Britain	Finance	249UNTS125	103503
01 Jul	Iraq	WHO (World Health)	Tech Assistance	110UNTS139	101507
02 Jul	Multilateral		Refugees	189UNTS137	102545
02 Jul	Ireland	Norway	General Trade	100UNTS53	101387
02 Jul	Ethiopia	WHO (World Health)	Tech Assistance	103UNTS39	101422
03 Jul	France	Netherlands	Finance	63FRRT76	415358
03 Jul	Denmark	Spain	General Trade	101UNTS51	101401
03 Jul	Belgium	Portugal	Visas	101UNTS17	101398
04 Jul	Canada	France	Reparations	233UNTS101	103253
07 Jul	Cuba	Germany, West	General Trade	52WGBB958	425399
07 Jul	Burma	India	General Amity	149UNTS35	101949
09 Jul	Switzerland	USA (United States)	Taxation	165UNTS51	102167
09 Jul	India	USA (United States)	Customs	147UNTS43	101927
09 Jul	Burma	WHO (World Health)	Sanitation	104UNTS175	101439
09 Jul	Burma	WHO (World Health)	Sanitation	102UNTS131	101416
09 Jul	Burma	WHO (World Health)	Sanitation	107UNTS9	101463
09 Jul	Burma	WHO (World Health)	Sanitation	104UNTS187	101440
10 Jul	Spain	Sweden	General Trade	51SOFM307	461148
10 Jul	Multilateral		Other Military	108UNTS287	101481
11 Jul	Finland	Netherlands	Non-ILO Labor	51NET113	447029
11 Jul	ILO (Labor Org)	Thailand	Tech Assistance	100UNTS159	101395
12 Jul	China People's Rep	Hungary	Culture	51CCJC21	410041
12 Jul	Paraguay	ILO (Labor Org)	Tech Assistance	117UNTS155	101591
13 Jul	UK Great Britain	USA (United States)	Tech Assistance	105UNTS71	101454
14 Jul	Iceland	Norway	Air Transport	163UNTS265	102150
17 Jul	Greece	Sweden	General Trade	51SOFM343	461149
17 Jul	Italy	Turkey	Culture	52ITGU203	435404
17 Jul	Burma	WHO (World Health)	Tech Assistance	102UNTS127	101415
18 Jul	Multilateral		Direct Aid	102UNTS291	200308
18 Jul	UK Great Britain	USA (United States)	Land Transport	117UNTS49	101583

DATE	PARTY ONE	PARTY TWO	TOPIC	CITATION	NUMBER
1951 (Cont.)					
19 Jul	Austria	Sweden	Taxation	198UNTS9	102652
19 Jul	El Salvador	USA (United States)	Tech Assistance	140UNTS259	101892
20 Jul	Germany, West	Peru	General Trade	52WGBB333	425576
20 Jul	Portugal	UK Great Britain	Finance	105UNTS61	101453
22 Jul	Philippines	WHO (World Health)	IGO Status/Immunit	149UNTS197	101953
23 Jul	Germany, West	Ireland	General Trade	558UNTS3	108137
23 Jul	El Salvador	USA (United States)	Direct Aid	138UNTS127	101865
24 Jul	Brazil	USA (United States)	Direct Aid	134UNTS195	101799
25 Jul	Australia	Belgium	Visas	108UNTS303	101482
26 Jul	Pakistan	Turkey	General Amity	188UNTS323	102536
26 Jul	Greece	Netherlands	Taxation	109UNTS103	101495
27 Jul	Multilateral		Tech Assistance	97UNTS291	200273
28 Jul	China People's Rep	USSR (Soviet Union)	Specific Property	0SUST282	468081
29 Jul	Israel	Yugoslavia	Mostfavored Nation	220UNTS7	102983
29 Jul	Multilateral		Other Military	117UNTS85	101585
30 Jul	Panama	USA (United States)	Direct Aid	140UNTS321	101896
30 Jul	Paraguay	USA (United States)	Military Mission	178UNTS163	102340
30 Jul	Burma	Denmark	Air Transport	108UNTS167	101472
30 Jul	UK Great Britain	USA (United States)	Admin Cooperation	105UNTS81	101455
01 Aug	Germany, East	Hungary	Finance	1EGDA438	419437
01 Aug	Canada	USA (United States)	Milit Installation	233UNTS109	103254
01 Aug	Austria	Sweden	Taxation	198UNTS13	102653
01 Aug	Multilateral		Sanitation	107UNTS19	101464
02 Aug	Austria	Italy	General Trade	53ITGU78	435033
02 Aug	Austria	Italy	Visas	51ABGB253	403113
02 Aug	Iran	UNICEF (Children)	Direct Aid	247UNTS11	103457
03 Aug	Romania	Switzerland	General Economic	51SWRO827	462153
03 Aug	Greece	USA (United States)	General Amity	224UNTS279	103080
04 Aug	Multilateral		Sanitation	104UNTS197	101441
07 Aug	Israel	Philippines	Air Transport	192UNTS81	102596
07 Aug	Israel	WHO (World Health)	Tech Assistance	104UNTS213	101442
08 Aug	Czechoslovakia	USSR (Soviet Union)	Postal Service	0SUST282	468108
08 Aug	Iraq	USA (United States)	Visas	229UNTS185	103166
10 Aug	USA (United States)	Venezuela	Military Mission	140UNTS345	101898
10 Aug	Mexico	USA (United States)	Telecommunications	152UNTS27	102009
10 Aug	Cuba	UK Great Britain	General Trade	108UNTS243	101478
11 Aug	Mexico	USA (United States)	Non-ILO Labor	162UNTS103	102133
11 Aug	Belgium	Brazil	Consul/Citizenship	104UNTS17	101431
14 Aug	Greece	Netherlands	Finance	51NET104	447030
14 Aug	India	United Nations	Tech Assistance	98UNTS115	101359
15 Aug	Lebanon	UK Great Britain	Air Transport	160UNTS327	102116
16 Aug	Iraq	USA (United States)	Education	147UNTS65	101929
17 Aug	France	United Nations	IGO Operations	122UNTS191	101647
20 Aug	Jordan	UN Relief Palestin	Refugees	120UNTS277	200394
20 Aug	France	UK Great Britain	Finance	108UNTS263	101479
23 Aug	France	Italy	Consul/Citizenship	291UNTS143	104249
23 Aug	Israel	USA (United States)	General Amity	219UNTS237	102979
23 Aug	Denmark	USA (United States)	Education	147UNTS49	101928
24 Aug	Romania	USSR (Soviet Union)	General Aid	0SUST282	468381
28 Aug	Iraq	Sweden	Air Transport	52SOFM483	461171
28 Aug	Germany, West	South Africa	General Economic	51WBGA216	424645
28 Aug	Pakistan	United Arab Rep	General Amity	214UNTS247	102902
28 Aug	Multilateral		Non-ILO Labor	198UNTS17	102654
28 Aug	Cuba	USA (United States)	Military Mission	140UNTS239	101891
28 Aug	Cuba	USA (United States)	Military Mission	134UNTS225	101802
28 Aug	Japan	USA (United States)	Education	147UNTS81	101930
29 Aug	WHO (World Health)	Saudi Arabia	Tech Assistance	110UNTS277	101516
30 Aug	Philippines	USA (United States)	Milit Assistance	177UNTS133	102315
31 Aug	Japan	UK Great Britain	Finance	149UNTS227	101955
31 Aug	Japan	UK Great Britain	Finance	108UNTS273	101480
01 Sep	Multilateral		General Military	131UNTS83	101736
03 Sep	Iraq	Spain	General Amity	55SPBO101	460163
03 Sep	France	USSR (Soviet Union)	General Trade	221UNTS79	103003
03 Sep	France	Greece	Mostfavored Nation	187UNTS113	102505
05 Sep	UNICEF (Children)	Turkey	Direct Aid	193UNTS55	102610

DATE	PARTY ONE	PARTY TWO	TOPIC	CITATION	NUMBER
1951 (Cont.)					
05 Sep	Multilateral		Tech Assistance	173UNTS15	102256
05 Sep	Australia	Luxembourg	Visas	109UNTS31	101487
06 Sep	Portugal	USA (United States)	Milit Assistance	237UNTS217	103348
06 Sep	Australia	Israel	Mostfavored Nation	188UNTS303	102534
06 Sep	Burma	Netherlands	Air Transport	108UNTS187	101473
07 Sep	France	Poland	Claims and Debts	57FRJO708	416361
07 Sep	Ethiopia	USA (United States)	General Amity	206UNTS41	102785
07 Sep	USA (United States)	Vietnam, South	Direct Aid	174UNTS165	102284
08 Sep	Multilateral		General Military	136UNTS165	101833
08 Sep	Japan	USA (United States)	General Military	136UNTS211	101835
08 Sep	Cambodia	USA (United States)	Direct Aid	174UNTS115	102282
08 Sep	Multilateral		Peace/Disarmament	136UNTS45	101832
08 Sep	Pakistan	United Arab Rep	Postal Service	133UNTS257	101793
08 Sep	Japan	USA (United States)	Milit Assistance	136UNTS203	101834
09 Sep	Laos	USA (United States)	Direct Aid	174UNTS141	102283
10 Sep	Canada	India	General Aid	391UNTS237	105629
10 Sep	Canada	Pakistan	Direct Aid	122UNTS21	101632
11 Sep	Costa Rica	USA (United States)	Air Transport	234UNTS255	103288
11 Sep	Canada	USA (United States)	Non-ILO Labor	206UNTS311	102793
13 Sep	Belgium	IBRD (World Bank)	IBRD Project	158UNTS323	102070
13 Sep	Belgium	IBRD (World Bank)	IBRD Project	158UNTS349	102071
15 Sep	Panama	UK Great Britain	Air Transport	560UNTS143	108172
15 Sep	Denmark	Switzerland	General Trade	110UNTS55	101501
17 Sep	Luxembourg	Norway	Finance	2NORT568	451107
17 Sep	Norway	USA (United States)	Milit Assistance	140UNTS313	101895
18 Sep	Colombia	WHO (World Health)	Tech Assistance	109UNTS45	101489
18 Sep	Belgium	Sweden	Non-ILO Labor	133UNTS187	101789
18 Sep	Iraq	ICAO (Civil Aviat)	Tech Assistance	108UNTS219	101475
19 Sep	Korea, South	WHO (World Health)	Sanitation	109UNTS297	200366
19 Sep	Germany, West	USA (United States)	General Trade	180UNTS161	102381
20 Sep	Multilateral		IGO Status/Immunit	200UNTS3	102691
20 Sep	Canada	Italy	Reparations	236UNTS251	103328
21 Sep	Korea, South	United Nations	IGO Status/Immunit	104UNTS323	200322
21 Sep	WHO (World Health)	Vietnam, South	Tech Assistance	107UNTS63	200352
25 Sep	Australia	Netherlands	Air Transport	128UNTS63	101713
26 Sep	Germany, West	Portugal	Customs	52WGBB505	425589
26 Sep	Netherlands	USA (United States)	Milit Installation	158UNTS469	102080
26 Sep	Australia	Sweden	Visas	109UNTS39	101488
26 Sep	Pakistan	UK Great Britain	Postal Service	118UNTS221	101608
27 Sep	Germany, East	USSR (Soviet Union)	Scientific Project	4EGDA33	419382
27 Sep	Germany, East	USSR (Soviet Union)	General Trade	1EGDA256	419381
27 Sep	Paraguay	United Nations	Tech Assistance	120UNTS105	101617
28 Sep	Australia	France	Reparations	161UNTS185	102128
28 Sep	Peru	USA (United States)	General Trade	160UNTS35	102099
28 Sep	UK Great Britain	Yugoslavia	Finance	117UNTS107	101587
29 Sep	Taiwan	Thailand	Air Transport	215UNTS166	102919
29 Sep	Greece	UK Great Britain	Culture	190UNTS260	102570
29 Sep	Burma	India	General Trade	132UNTS71	101752
29 Sep	Pakistan	UK Great Britain	Finance	134UNTS183	101798
01 Oct	Denmark	USA (United States)	General Amity	421UNTS105	106056
01 Oct	Multilateral		Tech Assistance	104UNTS249	101446
01 Oct	Bolivia	United Nations	Tech Assistance	104UNTS263	101447
02 Oct	UNICEF (Children)	UK Great Britain	Direct Aid	104UNTS301	101448
04 Oct	WHO (World Health)	Thailand	Sanitation	109UNTS77	101492
04 Oct	WHO (World Health)	Thailand	Scientific Project	109UNTS85	101493
06 Oct	Philippines	Spain	Postal Service	54SPBO2101	460098
06 Oct	Philippines	Spain	Air Transport	215UNTS193	102920
07 Oct	Germany, West	Iraq	General Trade	53WGBB543	425269
07 Oct	Pakistan	WHO (World Health)	Tech Assistance	126UNTS101	101684
08 Oct	Italy	Vatican/Holy See	Telecommunications	52ITGU150	435339
09 Oct	China People's Rep	Germany, East	Culture	4EGDA73	419080
09 Oct	China People's Rep	Germany, East	Culture	51CCJC23	410043
09 Oct	Multilateral		IGO Establishment	220UNTS121	102997
10 Oct	Italy	IBRD (World Bank)	IBRD Project	159UNTS383	200482
10 Oct	Chile	IBRD (World Bank)	IBRD Project	158UNTS369	102072

DATE	PARTY ONE	PARTY TWO	TOPIC	CITATION	NUMBER
1951 (Cont.)					
11 Oct	IBRD (World Bank)	Yugoslavia	IBRD Project	159UNTS3	102081
11 Oct	Austria	Belgium	Visas	110UNTS45	101500
11 Oct	India	WHO (World Health)	Non-IBRD Project	118UNTS27	101594
12 Oct	China People's Rep	Germany, East	Telecommunications	4EGDA81	419082
12 Oct	China People's Rep	Germany, East	Postal Service	4EGDA73	419081
12 Oct	China People's Rep	Germany, East	Postal Service	51CCJC24	410044
13 Oct	Colombia	IBRD (World Bank)	IBRD Project	159UNTS75	102084
14 Oct	Multilateral		IGO Establishment	122UNTS3	101631
16 Oct	India	WHO (World Health)	Tech Assistance	109UNTS49	101490
16 Oct	Ecuador	WHO (World Health)	Tech Assistance	110UNTS263	101515
17 Oct	Italy	Switzerland	Non-ILO Labor	54SWRO250	462097
17 Oct	United Nations	Uruguay	Tech Assistance	122UNTS29	101633
18 Oct	Sweden	Switzerland	Air Transport	51SOFM477	461154
19 Oct	Australia	Norway	Visas	128UNTS109	101716
21 Oct	China People's Rep	Germany, East	Telecommunications	51CCJC25	410045
22 Oct	Italy	Turkey	Visas	52ITDI481	436405
22 Oct	Pakistan	Turkey	Visas	219UNTS47	102965
22 Oct	Greece	Luxembourg	Air Transport	187UNTS119	102506
22 Oct	ILO (Labor Org)	Venezuela	Tech Assistance	117UNTS139	101590
23 Oct	Canada	Pakistan	Visas	248UNTS95	103487
23 Oct	El Salvador	USA (United States)	Direct Aid	137UNTS43	101847
23 Oct	Panama	USA (United States)	Direct Aid	140UNTS3	101880
23 Oct	India	WHO (World Health)	Sanitation	109UNTS59	101491
24 Oct	Denmark	Italy	General Trade	118UNTS91	101598
24 Oct	Italy	UK Great Britain	Air Transport	118UNTS143	101602
25 Oct	Taiwan	WHO (World Health)	Sanitation	126UNTS77	101683
26 Oct	Argentina	Germany, West	General Trade	51WBGA227	424006
26 Oct	Germany, West	Italy	Non-ILO Labor	53ITGU90	435162
26 Oct	Canada	USA (United States)	Extradition	206UNTS319	102794
29 Oct	Sweden	Yugoslavia	General Trade	51SOFM401	461150
29 Oct	Ireland	Netherlands	General Trade	52NET27	447031
29 Oct	Nicaragua	IBRD (World Bank)	IBRD Project	159UNTS35	102082
31 Oct	Multilateral		Other Military	172UNTS193	102247
01 Nov	Iceland	IBRD (World Bank)	IBRD Project	159UNTS55	102083
01 Nov	India	WHO (World Health)	Scientific Project	118UNTS13	101593
01 Nov	Belgium	New Zealand	Visas	118UNTS169	101605
05 Nov	Denmark	WHO (World Health)	Sanitation	110UNTS253	101514
06 Nov	France	Norway	Education	2NORT572	451057
07 Nov	Italy	UK Great Britain	Claims and Debts	118UNTS133	101601
08 Nov	Israel	Italy	Mostfavored Nation	219UNTS293	102980
09 Nov	South Africa	USA (United States)	Milit Assistance	160UNTS41	102100
09 Nov	Panama	WHO (World Health)	Sanitation	118UNTS43	101595
10 Nov	Saudi Arabia	USA (United States)	Scientific Project	180UNTS263	102390
10 Nov	Panama	ILO (Labor Org)	Tech Assistance	126UNTS269	101693
12 Nov	Netherlands	Switzerland	Taxation	126UNTS157	101688
12 Nov	Netherlands	Switzerland	Taxation	126UNTS173	101689
12 Nov	Italy	UK Great Britain	Specif Claim/Waive	135UNTS55	101814
13 Nov	Japan	Sweden	Consul/Citizenship	51SOFM623	461156
14 Nov	USA (United States)	Yugoslavia	Milit Assistance	174UNTS201	102286
14 Nov	Belgium	Netherlands	Admin Cooperation	123UNTS91	101656
15 Nov	Turkey	USA (United States)	Direct Aid	177UNTS315	102331
16 Nov	France	Sweden	General Trade	51SOFM411	461151
16 Nov	Germany, West	Lebanon	Mostfavored Nation	53WGBB540	425403
16 Nov	Australia	USA (United States)	Tech Assistance	168UNTS75	102214
16 Nov	Denmark	USA (United States)	Milit Assistance	180UNTS275	102391
16 Nov	Finland	USA (United States)	Patents/Copyrights	140UNTS273	101893
17 Nov	Australia	Austria	Admin Cooperation	133UNTS137	101785
18 Nov	Denmark	Iraq	Air Transport	232UNTS25	103227
19 Nov	France	Germany, West	Extradition	53WGBB151	425138
19 Nov	Liberia	USA (United States)	Milit Assistance	167UNTS141	102204
20 Nov	France	Switzerland	Land Transport	52SWRO623	462083
23 Nov	Austria	Germany, West	Non-ILO Labor	52WGBB609	425525
23 Nov	Austria	Germany, West	Non-ILO Labor	59WBGA13	424526
23 Nov	Austria	Germany, West	Non-ILO Labor	53ABGB10	403060
23 Nov	Council of Europe	ILO (Labor Org)	IGO Operations	126UNTS331	200435

DATE	PARTY ONE	PARTY TWO	TOPIC	CITATION	NUMBER
1951 (Cont.)					
24 Nov	ICJ Option Clause	Japan	ICJ Option Clause	137UNTS3	101842
25 Nov	Pakistan	Saudi Arabia	General Amity	177UNTS3	102304
26 Nov	Canada	South Africa	Taxation	248UNTS107	103489
26 Nov	Dominican Republic	USA (United States)	Milit Installation	150UNTS227	101976
26 Nov	Dominican Republic	UK Great Britain	Milit Installation	133UNTS205	101791
28 Nov	Dominican Republic	Turkey	General Amity	52TURG605	466001
28 Nov	Italy	UK Great Britain	Culture	172UNTS27	102238
28 Nov	Italy	UK Great Britain	Non-ILO Labor	172UNTS205	102248
28 Nov	New Zealand	UK Great Britain	General Trade	127UNTS263	101707
29 Nov	France	Mexico	General Trade	53FRJO2905	416323
30 Nov	Netherlands	UK Great Britain	Postal Service	123UNTS177	101659
30 Nov	Denmark	WHO (World Health)	Scientific Project	118UNTS3	101592
01 Dec	Czechoslovakia	Germany, East	General Economic	1EGDA393	419334
01 Dec	India	UK Great Britain	Air Transport	128UNTS39	101712
03 Dec	Poland	Sweden	Finance	51SOFM461	461153
04 Dec	Italy	Monaco	Reparations	52ITGU226	435280
04 Dec	USA (United States)	Uruguay	Military Mission	152UNTS41	102010
05 Dec	Italy	Netherlands	Culture	52ITGU207	435286
05 Dec	Italy	Netherlands	Culture	0UNTS0	109323
06 Dec	China People's Rep	USSR (Soviet Union)	Education	0SUST283	468082
06 Dec	China People's Rep	USSR (Soviet Union)	Tech Assistance	51CCJC26	410046
06 Dec	Multilateral		IGO Establishment	425UNTS61	106119
06 Dec	Multilateral		Admin Cooperation	150UNTS67	101963
07 Dec	Norway	Sweden	General Trade	51SOFM447	461152
07 Dec	Israel	USA (United States)	Tech Assistance	157UNTS53	102046
07 Dec	Paraguay	IBRD (World Bank)	IBRD Project	159UNTS103	102085
10 Dec	Iraq	UNICEF (Children)	Direct Aid	126UNTS57	101682
11 Dec	Colombia	Spain	Air Transport	216UNTS73	102933
12 Dec	China People's Rep	Romania	Culture	51CCJC27	410047
12 Dec	Italy	USA (United States)	Patents/Copyrights	137UNTS175	101852
12 Dec	Nicaragua	USA (United States)	Status of Forces	167UNTS151	102205
12 Dec	Finland	UK Great Britain	Taxation	172UNTS45	102239
12 Dec	El Salvador	USA (United States)	Education	132UNTS287	101768
13 Dec	Portugal	Sweden	General Trade	52SOFM193	461163
13 Dec	Libya	UK Great Britain	Direct Aid	123UNTS167	101658
14 Dec	India	Turkey	General Amity	137UNTS15	101845
14 Dec	El Salvador	Guatemala	General Economic	131UNTS131	101740
17 Dec	Cuba	USA (United States)	Visas	152UNTS87	102012
17 Dec	Mexico	WHO (World Health)	Tech Assistance	124UNTS121	101670
17 Dec	Guatemala	WHO (World Health)	Sanitation	120UNTS133	101619
18 Dec	Cuba	USA (United States)	General Military	165UNTS3	102164
19 Dec	Ireland	Spain	General Trade	0UNTS0	109228
20 Dec	Germany, West	Switzerland	Customs	52SWRO367	462114
20 Dec	Jordan	USA (United States)	Tech Assistance	157UNTS69	102048
20 Dec	Italy	New Zealand	Peace/Disarmament	150UNTS157	101970
20 Dec	Multilateral		Air Transport	163UNTS293	102151
20 Dec	Muscat and Oman	UK Great Britain	General Amity	149UNTS247	101956
20 Dec	Australia	Italy	Peace/Disarmament	190UNTS223	102566
20 Dec	Multilateral		Air Transport	163UNTS309	102152
20 Dec	India	WHO (World Health)	Tech Assistance	124UNTS109	101669
20 Dec	Spain	UK Great Britain	Finance	123UNTS187	101660
21 Dec	Mongolia	USSR (Soviet Union)	Non-ILO Labor	0SUST440	468272
21 Dec	Italy	USA (United States)	Peace/Disarmament	167UNTS163	102206
21 Dec	Italy	UK Great Britain	Peace/Disarmament	121UNTS89	101628
24 Dec	Multilateral		Tech Assistance	118UNTS290	200383
24 Dec	Accept UN Charter	Libya	UN Charter	223UNTS51	103050
26 Dec	Ireland	Switzerland	General Trade	558UNTS305	108149
28 Dec	Cambodia	USA (United States)	Milit Assistance	179UNTS97	102358
28 Dec	Germany, West	USA (United States)	Milit Assistance	181UNTS45	102397
28 Dec	Italy	USA (United States)	General Economic	157UNTS63	102047
29 Dec	Mongolia	USSR (Soviet Union)	General Trade	0SUST440	468273
29 Dec	Thailand	USA (United States)	Milit Assistance	179UNTS113	102360
29 Dec	Guatemala	WHO (World Health)	Sanitation	124UNTS89	101668
31 Dec	France	UK Great Britain	Consul/Citizenship	330UNTS145	104744
31 Dec	Laos	USA (United States)	Tech Assistance	198UNTS243	102668

DATE	PARTY ONE	PARTY TWO	TOPIC	CITATION	NUMBER
1952					
02 Jan	Jordan	United Arab Rep	Air Transport	192UNTS157	102599
02 Jan	Taiwan	USA (United States)	Milit Assistance	181UNTS161	102407
04 Jan	Belgium	Spain	Visas	121UNTS25	101622
05 Jan	Iran	USA (United States)	Direct Aid	0IRTB24	433038
05 Jan	Indonesia	USA (United States)	Tech Assistance	215UNTS121	102916
05 Jan	India	USA (United States)	Tech Assistance	157UNTS39	102045
05 Jan	France	USA (United States)	Milit Assistance	181UNTS177	102408
05 Jan	Lebanon	USA (United States)	Tech Assistance	180UNTS199	102385
05 Jan	Austria	USA (United States)	Milit Assistance	179UNTS73	102355
07 Jan	El Salvador	USA (United States)	Tech Assistance	198UNTS231	102667
07 Jan	Philippines	USA (United States)	Milit Assistance	179UNTS193	102368
07 Jan	Turkey	USA (United States)	Milit Assistance	179UNTS121	102361
07 Jan	Belgium	USA (United States)	Milit Assistance	179UNTS81	102356
07 Jan	Italy	USA (United States)	Milit Assistance	179UNTS165	102365
07 Jan	Dominican Republic	USA (United States)	Direct Aid	174UNTS243	102289
07 Jan	Greece	USA (United States)	Milit Assistance	180UNTS171	102382
07 Jan	Korea, South	USA (United States)	Milit Assistance	179UNTS105	102359
07 Jan	Greece	USA (United States)	Milit Assistance	177UNTS249	102323
08 Jan	Germany, East	Poland	Culture	304UNTS113	104394
08 Jan	Portugal	USA (United States)	General Military	207UNTS51	102799
08 Jan	Norway	USA (United States)	Milit Assistance	179UNTS185	102367
08 Jan	Iceland	USA (United States)	Milit Assistance	180UNTS183	102383
08 Jan	UK Great Britain	USA (United States)	Milit Assistance	179UNTS201	102369
08 Jan	Luxembourg	USA (United States)	Milit Assistance	180UNTS191	102384
08 Jan	Denmark	USA (United States)	Milit Assistance	179UNTS65	102354
08 Jan	Netherlands	USA (United States)	Milit Assistance	179UNTS175	102366
08 Jan	Guatemala	USA (United States)	Tech Assistance	181UNTS31	102395
08 Jan	USA (United States)	Yugoslavia	Direct Aid	152UNTS61	102011
08 Jan	UK Great Britain	USA (United States)	Direct Aid	126UNTS307	101696
10 Jan	Austria	WHO (World Health)	Tech Assistance	131UNTS295	200438
10 Jan	Multilateral		Visas	163UNTS3	102138
10 Jan	Multilateral		Visas	163UNTS27	102139
11 Jan	Mexico	IBRD (World Bank)	IBRD Project	159UNTS129	102086
12 Jan	Colombia	USA (United States)	Education	168UNTS109	102216
12 Jan	India	United Nations	Tech Assistance	118UNTS175	101606
14 Jan	Denmark	Norway	Claims and Debts	120UNTS119	101618
15 Jan	UK Great Britain	USA (United States)	Milit Installation	127UNTS3	101697
16 Jan	Finland	Norway	General Ad Hoc	2NORT578	451049
16 Jan	Australia	Pakistan	Postal Service	151UNTS281	102001
18 Jan	Italy	Sweden	General Trade	52SOFM103	461158
18 Jan	Germany, East	Poland	Finance	4EGDA153	419236
18 Jan	Belgium	Germany, West	Visas	243UNTS3	103443
18 Jan	Austria	Canada	Admin Cooperation	236UNTS245	103327
18 Jan	UK Great Britain	USA (United States)	Commodity Trade	184UNTS79	102440
18 Jan	Germany, West	Netherlands	Specific Property	179UNTS147	102364
18 Jan	Belgium	Germany, West	Education	124UNTS9	101663
19 Jan	USA (United States)	Vietnam, South	Milit Assistance	205UNTS127	102772
20 Jan	Hungary	USSR (Soviet Union)	General Aid	0SUST284	468194
20 Jan	Iran	USA (United States)	Tech Assistance	200UNTS191	102703
21 Jan	Ceylon (Sri Lanka)	United Nations	Tech Assistance	118UNTS281	200382
21 Jan	Libya	USA (United States)	Tech Assistance	183UNTS177	102427
21 Jan	Spain	USA (United States)	Visas	160UNTS63	102102
21 Jan	Belgium	Norway	Claims and Debts	123UNTS39	101653
23 Jan	Hungary	USSR (Soviet Union)	General Trade	0SUST284	468193
23 Jan	Germany, East	Romania	General Trade	1EGDA454	419283
23 Jan	Peru	IBRD (World Bank)	IBRD Project	159UNTS163	102087
23 Jan	Multilateral		Tech Assistance	127UNTS269	101708
23 Jan	Costa Rica	WHO (World Health)	Sanitation	135UNTS265	101826
24 Jan	Italy	Turkey	General Trade	53ITGU27	435406
24 Jan	Belgium	Italy	Peace/Disarmament	53ITGU51	435046
24 Jan	France	Israel	Taxation	220UNTS55	102988
25 Jan	Germany, West	Switzerland	Land Transport	53SWRO4	462067
25 Jan	Germany, West	Spain	Non-ILO Labor	53SPBO1616	460002
29 Jan	Canada	Spain	Claims and Debts	233UNTS117	103255

DATE	PARTY ONE	PARTY TWO	TOPIC	CITATION	NUMBER
1952 (Cont.)					
30 Jan	WHO (World Health)	Spain	Tech Assistance	124UNTS259	200425
31 Jan	Germany, West	Netherlands	Admin Cooperation	492UNTS295	107199
01 Feb	Belgium	Germany, West	Land Transport	52WGBB437	425019
01 Feb	Austria	Italy	Patents/Copyrights	54ITGU143	435034
01 Feb	Austria	Italy	Patents/Copyrights	53ABGB130	403114
01 Feb	Austria	Italy	Admin Cooperation	54ABGB235	403254
02 Feb	France	USA (United States)	Reparations	247UNTS223	103472
02 Feb	Greece	Yugoslavia	Sanitation	188UNTS311	102535
04 Feb	Peru	USA (United States)	Education	121UNTS255	200403
04 Feb	Denmark	USA (United States)	Patents/Copyrights	157UNTS25	102044
04 Feb	UNICEF (Children)	UK Great Britain	Direct Aid	120UNTS147	101620
04 Feb	Multilateral		General Economic	124UNTS3	101662
06 Feb	Ireland	Portugal	General Trade	558UNTS289	108147
06 Feb	Germany, East	Poland	Water Transport	304UNTS131	104395
06 Feb	ICAO (Civil Aviat)	Yugoslavia	Tech Assistance	128UNTS97	101715
06 Feb	Indonesia	United Nations	Tech Assistance	121UNTS3	101621
07 Feb	France	Netherlands	General Trade	54NET90	447032
07 Feb	Belgium	Luxembourg	Taxation	147UNTS3	101924
07 Feb	WHO (World Health)	UK Great Britain	Tech Assistance	121UNTS75	101627
08 Feb	France	Vietnam, South	Education	0VKNG41	496006
09 Feb	Burma	USA (United States)	Milit Assistance	179UNTS91	102357
11 Feb	Multilateral		Direct Aid	165UNTS77	102169
12 Feb	Jordan	USA (United States)	Tech Assistance	168UNTS25	102211
12 Feb	Italy	UK Great Britain	Claims and Debts	126UNTS297	101695
14 Feb	Lebanon	ICAO (Civil Aviat)	Tech Assistance	128UNTS83	101714
15 Feb	Denmark	Germany, West	Land Transport	61WBGA58	424097
15 Feb	Germany, West	Norway	Land Transport	61WBGA58	424516
15 Feb	Dominican Republic	UNICEF (Children)	Humanitarian	121UNTS43	101625
15 Feb	UNICEF (Children)	UK Great Britain	Direct Aid	121UNTS63	101626
15 Feb	Dominican Republic	WHO (World Health)	Sanitation	134UNTS291	101808
15 Feb	Multilateral		Scientific Project	132UNTS51	101751
16 Feb	Germany, West	Turkey	Admin Cooperation	52TURG1602	466033
16 Feb	Germany, West	Turkey	General Trade	53TURG202	466028
16 Feb	Germany, West	Turkey	Extradition	52TURG305	466006
16 Feb	Germany, West	Turkey	General Economic	52TURG305	466067
16 Feb	Germany, West	Turkey	Customs	52WGBB616	425768
16 Feb	Germany, West	Turkey	Finance	52WBGA50	424769
16 Feb	Austria	USA (United States)	Direct Aid	177UNTS299	102329
18 Feb	Multilateral		Tech Assistance	126UNTS319	200434
18 Feb	Burma	WHO (World Health)	Scientific Project	127UNTS43	101698
19 Feb	El Salvador	Spain	General Amity	52SPBO1611	460091
19 Feb	Philippines	USA (United States)	Direct Aid	177UNTS307	102330
20 Feb	Ecuador	USA (United States)	Milit Assistance	177UNTS43	102308
20 Feb	Belgium	Pakistan	Extradition	133UNTS199	101790
21 Feb	Canada	USA (United States)	Humanitarian	205UNTS293	102781
21 Feb	Iraq	USA (United States)	Tech Assistance	198UNTS225	102666
21 Feb	Pakistan	WHO (World Health)	IGO Operations	131UNTS221	101742
22 Feb	Peru	USA (United States)	Milit Assistance	165UNTS31	102166
25 Feb	India	Syria	General Amity	163UNTS55	102141
25 Feb	Costa Rica	USA (United States)	Status of Forces	174UNTS233	102288
26 Feb	Albania	Germany, East	Tech Assistance	4EGDA547	419007
27 Feb	Cuba	USA (United States)	Gen Communications	168UNTS3	102209
27 Feb	IBRD (World Bank)	UK Great Britain	IBRD Project	159UNTS181	102088
27 Feb	Israel	USA (United States)	Direct Aid	177UNTS123	102314
28 Feb	Japan	USA (United States)	Milit Assistance	208UNTS255	102817
29 Feb	Poland	USSR (Soviet Union)	General Trade	0SUST285	468332
29 Feb	Denmark	Japan	Consul/Citizenship	126UNTS139	101686
01 Mar	Philippines	UNTAB (Tech Assis)	Tech Assistance	2PTS775	465072
01 Mar	Taiwan	Korea, South	Air Transport	255UNTS35	103603
01 Mar	Multilateral		Specific Resources	168UNTS9	102210
03 Mar	ICJ Option Clause	Liberia	ICJ Option Clause	163UNTS117	102145
03 Mar	OAS (Am States)	USA (United States)	Tech Assistance	165UNTS67	102168
03 Mar	Finland	USA (United States)	Taxation	177UNTS163	102317
03 Mar	Finland	USA (United States)	Taxation	177UNTS141	102316
04 Mar	Ceylon (Sri Lanka)	WHO (World Health)	Direct Aid	128UNTS281	200437

DATE	PARTY ONE	PARTY TWO	TOPIC	CITATION	NUMBER
1952 (Cont.)					
05 Mar	Japan	Sweden	General Trade	52SOFM127	461159
05 Mar	Japan	Sweden	Finance	52SOFM142	461160
05 Mar	Netherlands	Paraguay	Air Transport	52NET67	447033
05 Mar	Italy	USA (United States)	Taxation	179UNTS3	102351
05 Mar	Greece	United Nations	Tech Assistance	123UNTS3	101650
06 Mar	ICAO (Civil Aviat)	United Arab Rep	Tech Assistance	151UNTS111	101986
07 Mar	Germany, East	Hungary	General Trade	1EGDA439	419438
07 Mar	Ecuador	Italy	Education	55ITGU80	435107
07 Mar	Finland	WHO (World Health)	Tech Assistance	128UNTS269	200436
07 Mar	Honduras	USA (United States)	Tech Assistance	233UNTS151	103260
07 Mar	Cuba	USA (United States)	Milit Assistance	165UNTS11	102165
07 Mar	Multilateral		Specific Resources	175UNTS205	102302
07 Mar	Taiwan	WHO (World Health)	Sanitation	128UNTS233	101723
07 Mar	Netherlands	USA (United States)	Taxation	135UNTS199	101821
08 Mar	Philippines	Switzerland	Air Transport	231UNTS301	103225
10 Mar	Belgium	Spain	Air Transport	178UNTS243	102342
13 Mar	Luxembourg	USA (United States)	Taxation	168UNTS57	102212
13 Mar	France	USA (United States)	Milit Assistance	177UNTS21	102306
14 Mar	Czechoslovakia	Sweden	General Trade	52SOFM83	461157
14 Mar	Austria	Italy	Culture	54ABGB270	403115
14 Mar	Austria	Italy	Admin Cooperation	56ABGB87	403116
14 Mar	Netherlands	Portugal	Visas	309UNTS117	104470
14 Mar	Sweden	UK Great Britain	Consul/Citizenship	202UNTS157	102731
15 Mar	Belgium	Pakistan	General Trade	316UNTS65	104578
15 Mar	Brazil	USA (United States)	Milit Assistance	199UNTS221	102687
17 Mar	Pakistan	Switzerland	Air Transport	192UNTS237	102603
17 Mar	Ecuador	USA (United States)	Telecommunications	177UNTS115	102313
18 Mar	Iraq	USA (United States)	Tech Assistance	223UNTS131	103061
18 Mar	Finland	Norway	Specific Resources	188UNTS187	102527
18 Mar	Iceland	USA (United States)	Taxation	177UNTS263	102325
18 Mar	UK Great Britain	USA (United States)	Milit Assistance	177UNTS33	102307
19 Mar	Philippines	SCAP Japan	Finance	2PTS783	465029
19 Mar	Germany, West	India	General Trade	52WBGA83	424251
19 Mar	Canada	USA (United States)	Status of Forces	174UNTS267	102291
20 Mar	Romania	USSR (Soviet Union)	Education	0SUST285	468382
20 Mar	Norway	Uruguay	Air Transport	310UNTS279	104496
20 Mar	Sweden	Uruguay	Air Transport	311UNTS3	104497
20 Mar	Canada	Monaco	Visas	233UNTS123	103256
20 Mar	Netherlands	IBRD (World Bank)	IBRD Project	159UNTS207	102089
21 Mar	ILO (Labor Org)	Turkey	Tech Assistance	52TURG1306	466135
21 Mar	Belgium	France	Land Transport	137UNTS249	101856
22 Mar	France	Italy	Consul/Citizenship	52ITDI336	436131
22 Mar	Austria	Greece	General Economic	187UNTS255	102517
25 Mar	Germany, East	Hungary	Postal Service	4EGDA387	419439
25 Mar	Germany, East	Hungary	Postal Service	4EGDA390	419440
26 Mar	Germany, East	Hungary	Telecommunications	4EGDA394	419441
26 Mar	Ceylon (Sri Lanka)	WHO (World Health)	Sanitation	134UNTS341	200442
26 Mar	South Africa	USA (United States)	Education	165UNTS187	102176
26 Mar	Denmark	WHO (World Health)	Scientific Project	134UNTS285	101807
27 Mar	Pakistan	IBRD (World Bank)	IBRD Project	159UNTS251	102090
31 Mar	Iceland	Sweden	General Trade	52SOFM191	461162
31 Mar	Netherlands	Sweden	General Trade	52SOFM167	461161
31 Mar	Iraq	Switzerland	Air Transport	311UNTS43	104498
31 Mar	Libya	UK Great Britain	Air Transport	151UNTS69	101984
31 Mar	Monaco	USA (United States)	Visas	177UNTS195	102318
01 Apr	Norway	USA (United States)	Direct Aid	177UNTS291	102328
01 Apr	Belgium	Germany, West	Visas	132UNTS45	101750
02 Apr	India	United Nations	Tech Assistance	126UNTS145	101687
02 Apr	India	WHO (World Health)	Sanitation	131UNTS227	101743
03 Apr	Philippines	FAO (Food Agri)	Tech Assistance	2PTS785	465073
04 Apr	El Salvador	USA (United States)	Tech Assistance	177UNTS219	102320
04 Apr	Greece	Switzerland	Finance	166UNTS271	102192
04 Apr	Denmark	USA (United States)	Telecommunications	177UNTS13	102305
04 Apr	Czechoslovakia	Denmark	General Trade	133UNTS245	101792
05 Apr	Poland	USSR (Soviet Union)	Culture	0SUST285	468333

DATE	PARTY ONE	PARTY TWO	TOPIC	CITATION	NUMBER
1952 (Cont.)					
05 Apr	France	Italy	Patents/Copyrights	52ITGU127	435132
05 Apr	Libya	UNICEF (Children)	Direct Aid	133UNTS287	200441
07 Apr	Belgium	USA (United States)	Taxation	205UNTS3	102765
07 Apr	Denmark	USA (United States)	Milit Assistance	177UNTS257	102324
08 Apr	France	Haiti	Education	52FRJO2404	416212
09 Apr	Finland	Sweden	General Trade	52SOFM203	461164
09 Apr	Peru	USA (United States)	Tech Assistance	184UNTS295	102454
09 Apr	Chile	USA (United States)	Milit Assistance	186UNTS53	102482
10 Apr	Finland	Italy	Consul/Citizenship	52ITDI295	436109
10 Apr	Canada	Netherlands	Reparations	233UNTS129	103257
10 Apr	United Nations	Yugoslavia	Tech Assistance	141UNTS89	101908
11 Apr	Czechoslovakia	USSR (Soviet Union)	Education	0SUST286	468109
11 Apr	Multilateral		Tech Assistance	173UNTS2	102255
12 Apr	China People's Rep	USSR (Soviet Union)	General Trade	52CCJC5	410050
14 Apr	India	WHO (World Health)	Tech Assistance	131UNTS265	101746
16 Apr	Finland	Germany, West	General Economic	52WBGA81	424131
16 Apr	Multilateral		General Economic	139UNTS35	101874
17 Apr	Colombia	USA (United States)	Milit Assistance	174UNTS215	102287
17 Apr	France	Mexico	Air Transport	163UNTS321	102153
17 Apr	India	WHO (World Health)	Tech Assistance	131UNTS241	101744
17 Apr	Liberia	UNICEF (Children)	Direct Aid	133UNTS3	101773
18 Apr	Spain	Syria	General Amity	53SPBO2401	460242
18 Apr	Spain	Syria	Culture	53SPBO2401	460243
19 Apr	Albania	USSR (Soviet Union)	Tech Assistance	0SUST286	468011
19 Apr	India	WHO (World Health)	Tech Assistance	131UNTS253	101745
21 Apr	Belgium	Sweden	Air Transport	166UNTS9	102183
23 Apr	Honduras	USA (United States)	Status of Forces	198UNTS251	102669
23 Apr	Greece	USA (United States)	Direct Aid	177UNTS283	102327
23 Apr	ICJ Option Clause	Ceylon (Sri Lanka)	UN Charter	137UNTS7	101843
24 Apr	Philippines	UNTAB (Tech Assis)	Tech Assistance	2PTS789	465074
24 Apr	Iran	USA (United States)	Milit Assistance	0IRTB23	433035
24 Apr	Taiwan	Japan	General Trade	0CTCY447	414048
24 Apr	Italy	Jordan	General Amity	281UNTS167	104078
24 Apr	Belgium	Greece	Finance	166UNTS261	102191
25 Apr	Netherlands	Sweden	Taxation	163UNTS131	102147
25 Apr	Netherlands	Sweden	Taxation	163UNTS195	102148
26 Apr	Spain	United Arab Rep	Culture	53SPBO2006	460095
28 Apr	Japan	Sweden	Air Transport	52SOFM231	461165
28 Apr	Denmark	Japan	Air Transport	166UNTS3	102182
28 Apr	Pakistan	United Nations	Tech Assistance	128UNTS191	101720
28 Apr	Taiwan	Japan	Peace/Disarmament	138UNTS3	101858
29 Apr	Austria	Sweden	General Trade	52SOFM235	461166
29 Apr	France	Luxembourg	Customs	55FRJO601	416267
29 Apr	United Arab Rep	USA (United States)	Milit Assistance	241UNTS3	103418
29 Apr	France	Israel	Air Transport	189UNTS55	102542
29 Apr	India	ICAO (Civil Aviat)	Tech Assistance	151UNTS123	101987
30 Apr	Mongolia	USSR (Soviet Union)	Education	0SUST286	468277
30 Apr	Germany, West	Italy	Patents/Copyrights	52WGBB975	425286
30 Apr	Germany, West	Luxembourg	General Transport	61WBGA173	424417
30 Apr	Finland	IBRD (World Bank)	IBRD Project	159UNTS408	200483
30 Apr	Canada	USA (United States)	Milit Installation	235UNTS269	103308
01 May	Australia	Denmark	Visas	152UNTS3	102006
01 May	Israel	USA (United States)	Direct Aid	177UNTS89	102311
06 May	Korea, North	USSR (Soviet Union)	Education	0SUST287	468249
06 May	China People's Rep	Czechoslovakia	Scientific Project	52CCJC19	410064
06 May	China People's Rep	Czechoslovakia	Telecommunications	52CCJC18	410063
06 May	China People's Rep	Czechoslovakia	Postal Service	52CCJC17	410062
08 May	Denmark	Netherlands	Reparations	131UNTS91	101737
09 May	Multilateral		Specific Resources	205UNTS65	102770
09 May	Israel	USA (United States)	Tech Assistance	177UNTS269	102326
09 May	Multilateral		Milit Occupation	168UNTS65	102213
09 May	Israel	USA (United States)	Tech Assistance	177UNTS63	102309
09 May	Norway	WHO (World Health)	Tech Assistance	131UNTS281	101747
10 May	Belgium	Italy	Non-ILO Labor	54ITGU244	435044
10 May	Multilateral		Admin Cooperation	439UNTS217	106331

1952 (Cont.)

DATE	PARTY ONE	PARTY TWO	TOPIC	CITATION	NUMBER
10 May	Multilateral		Taxation	439UNTS233	106332
10 May	Multilateral		Admin Cooperation	439UNTS193	106330
12 May	Germany, East	USSR (Soviet Union)	Education	4EGDA428	419383
12 May	Belgium	USA (United States)	Finance	179UNTS15	102352
13 May	Switzerland	UK Great Britain	Air Transport	164UNTS91	102160
15 May	Multilateral		Sanitation	0UNTS0	110476
15 May	Netherlands	USA (United States)	Milit Assistance	177UNTS233	102321
15 May	Ethiopia	USA (United States)	Education	180UNTS227	102388
17 May	Austria	Switzerland	Admin Cooperation	52SWRO529	462030
18 May	UNICEF (Children)	United Arab Rep	Direct Aid	324UNTS161	104684
19 May	Poland	USSR (Soviet Union)	Education	0SUST287	468334
19 May	Spain	Yemen	General Amity	55SPBO1505	460266
19 May	Hungary	USSR (Soviet Union)	Education	0SUST284	468195
19 May	Germany, West	Netherlands	Reparations	134UNTS3	101794
20 May	Netherlands	Switzerland	Land Transport	52SWRO603	462085
20 May	Multilateral		Sanitation	219UNTS55	102966
20 May	Libya	USA (United States)	Direct Aid	178UNTS307	102346
20 May	Libya	USA (United States)	Tech Assistance	178UNTS155	102339
20 May	Libya	USA (United States)	Tech Assistance	177UNTS81	102310
21 May	Iraq	USA (United States)	Tech Assistance	206UNTS3	102782
21 May	Iraq	USA (United States)	Tech Assistance	205UNTS33	102768
21 May	Iraq	USA (United States)	Tech Assistance	212UNTS183	102870
21 May	Iraq	USA (United States)	Tech Assistance	205UNTS25	102767
22 May	Iraq	UK Great Britain	Claims and Debts	175UNTS97	102298
22 May	Multilateral		Tech Assistance	131UNTS115	101739
23 May	Australia	Greece	Visas	223UNTS17	103042
24 May	China People's Rep	Czechoslovakia	Culture	52CCJC20	410065
24 May	Korea, South	USA (United States)	Direct Aid	179UNTS23	102353
24 May	Australia	Italy	Reparations	161UNTS65	102123
26 May	France	Vietnam, South	Land Transport	0VKNG45	496007
27 May	Brazil	Norway	Consul/Citizenship	2NORT583	451009
27 May	Australia	USA (United States)	Postal Service	178UNTS113	102338
28 May	China People's Rep	Germany, East	General Economic	52CCJC23	410068
28 May	Mexico	WHO (World Health)	Sanitation	134UNTS319	101810
29 May	Ecuador	USA (United States)	Tech Assistance	185UNTS203	102471
31 May	Chile	WHO (World Health)	Sanitation	136UNTS323	101841
02 Jun	Greece	Syria	General Trade	183UNTS251	102434
02 Jun	Brazil	USA (United States)	Scientific Project	181UNTS109	102403
03 Jun	Iceland	Sweden	Air Transport	215UNTS223	102921
04 Jun	India	WHO (World Health)	Sanitation	135UNTS279	101827
07 Jun	France	Vietnam, South	Education	0VKNG47	496008
08 Jun	Multilateral		Other Military	210UNTS317	102843
09 Jun	India	Japan	Peace/Disarmament	0JGJI1000	441070
09 Jun	Iraq	USA (United States)	Tech Assistance	212UNTS193	102871
09 Jun	Israel	USA (United States)	Mass Media	178UNTS297	102345
09 Jun	Denmark	Poland	General Trade	135UNTS209	101822
09 Jun	Burma	WHO (World Health)	Sanitation	134UNTS273	101806
09 Jun	Denmark	Poland	Finance	135UNTS221	101823
10 Jun	Austria	New Zealand	Admin Cooperation	171UNTS263	102229
11 Jun	France	Japan	Admin Cooperation	0JGJI1021	441144
11 Jun	Germany, West	Yugoslavia	General Trade	52WBGA169	424319
11 Jun	Germany, West	USA (United States)	Mass Media	273UNTS105	103947
12 Jun	Japan	Vietnam, South	Dispute Settlement	0VKNG48	496009
12 Jun	Mexico	UK Great Britain	Telecommunications	196UNTS149	102622
12 Jun	Brazil	WHO (World Health)	Scientific Project	151UNTS333	102003
12 Jun	Multilateral		Dispute Settlement	138UNTS183	101869
13 Jun	Mongolia	USSR (Soviet Union)	Tech Assistance	0SUST440	468274
13 Jun	Monaco	New Zealand	Visas	171UNTS269	102230
13 Jun	Ethiopia	USA (United States)	Milit Assistance	205UNTS17	102766
13 Jun	Pakistan	IBRD (World Bank)	IBRD Project	191UNTS85	102578
13 Jun	France	USA (United States)	Taxation	181UNTS3	102393
14 Jun	Australia	United Arab Rep	Air Transport	173UNTS241	102269
14 Jun	India	United Arab Rep	Air Transport	173UNTS209	102268
15 Jun	Accept UN Charter	Cambodia	UN Charter	223UNTS35	103046
16 Jun	Jordan	WHO (World Health)	Direct Aid	135UNTS323	200445

1952 (Cont.)

DATE	PARTY ONE	PARTY TWO	TOPIC	CITATION	NUMBER
16 Jun	Accept UN Charter	Japan	UN Charter	256UNTS167	103626
17 Jun	Italy	Sweden	Finance	54ITGU144	435362
17 Jun	France	Turkey	Culture	60FRRT2	415515
17 Jun	Belgium	Switzerland	Non-ILO Labor	180UNTS23	102373
17 Jun	Belgium	UNICEF (Children)	Direct Aid	171UNTS249	102228
18 Jun	Philippines	Vatican/Holy See	Status of Forces	543UNTS165	107900
18 Jun	Bolivia	USA (United States)	Tech Assistance	199UNTS211	102686
18 Jun	Ethiopia	USA (United States)	Tech Assistance	181UNTS207	102410
18 Jun	IBRD (World Bank)	Turkey	IBRD Project	159UNTS269	102091
19 Jun	Colombia	Italy	General Trade	53ITGU77	435092
19 Jun	New Zealand	USA (United States)	Milit Assistance	178UNTS315	102347
19 Jun	India	WHO (World Health)	Sanitation	134UNTS307	101809
19 Jun	Multilateral		Tech Assistance	133UNTS165	101787
20 Jun	WHO (World Health)	Syria	Tech Assistance	165UNTS219	102178
20 Jun	Germany, West	Netherlands	Reparations	136UNTS221	101836
21 Jun	Netherlands	South Africa	Visas	309UNTS123	104471
21 Jun	Norway	USA (United States)	Reparations	236UNTS9	103313
21 Jun	Iraq	UK Great Britain	Admin Cooperation	149UNTS221	101954
22 Jun	OAS (Am States)	USA (United States)	IGO Status/Immunit	181UNTS147	102405
23 Jun	Sweden	UK Great Britain	Air Transport	52SOFM468	461170
23 Jun	Canada	USA (United States)	Telecommunications	207UNTS25	102798
23 Jun	Norway	UK Great Britain	Air Transport	151UNTS81	101985
23 Jun	Denmark	UK Great Britain	Air Transport	151UNTS3	101982
24 Jun	South Africa	USA (United States)	Milit Assistance	177UNTS241	102322
24 Jun	Ethiopia	USA (United States)	Tech Assistance	181UNTS215	102411
25 Jun	Argentina	Italy	Health/Educ/Welfare	52ITDI223	436015
25 Jun	Burma	Pakistan	General Amity	173UNTS41	102259
25 Jun	Greece	USA (United States)	Air Transport	181UNTS53	102398
25 Jun	Taiwan	USA (United States)	Direct Aid	136UNTS229	101837
25 Jun	Belgium	Italy	Visas	137UNTS239	101855
26 Jun	Multilateral		ILO Labor	196UNTS183	102624
26 Jun	Lebanon	USA (United States)	Tech Assistance	181UNTS187	102409
27 Jun	Norway	USA (United States)	Tech Assistance	184UNTS271	102452
27 Jun	Brazil	IBRD (World Bank)	IBRD Project	190UNTS85	102560
27 Jun	Brazil	IBRD (World Bank)	IBRD Project	190UNTS115	102561
28 Jun	Multilateral		ILO Labor	210UNTS132	102838
28 Jun	Multilateral		ILO Labor	214UNTS321	102907
30 Jun	Canada	USA (United States)	Water Transport	234UNTS199	103283
30 Jun	Accept UN Charter	Laos	UN Charter	223UNTS47	103049
30 Jun	USA (United States)	Uruguay	Milit Assistance	207UNTS139	102804
30 Jun	Brazil	USA (United States)	Tech Assistance	185UNTS79	102460
30 Jun	Chile	USA (United States)	Tech Assistance	199UNTS241	102688
30 Jun	Belgium	Israel	Air Transport	183UNTS263	102435
30 Jun	Belgium	UK Great Britain	Milit Assistance	199UNTS113	102679
30 Jun	Panama	USA (United States)	Tech Assistance	181UNTS121	102404
30 Jun	Belgium	France	General Transport	137UNTS259	101857
30 Jun	Austria	UK Great Britain	Reparations	138UNTS153	101867
01 Jul	Indonesia	Sweden	General Trade	52SOFM265	461167
01 Jul	Sweden	USA (United States)	Milit Assistance	187UNTS3	102497
02 Jul	Sweden	Switzerland	General Trade	52SOFM289	461168
02 Jul	Finland	USA (United States)	Education	165UNTS203	102177
03 Jul	Ethiopia	UK Great Britain	Status of Forces	151UNTS207	101996
04 Jul	Italy	Switzerland	Territory Boundary	55SWRO557	462180
05 Jul	Albania	USSR (Soviet Union)	Education	0SUST288	468012
05 Jul	Greece	Italy	Visas	187UNTS157	102508
07 Jul	Australia	FAO (Food Agri)	Tech Assistance	184UNTS209	102449
08 Jul	Jordan	UNICEF (Children)	Direct Aid	173UNTS353	200503
08 Jul	Peru	IBRD (World Bank)	IBRD Project	159UNTS321	102093
08 Jul	Australia	IBRD (World Bank)	IBRD Project	159UNTS295	102092
09 Jul	Portugal	USA (United States)	Milit Assistance	180UNTS251	102389
10 Jul	Iraq	UK Great Britain	Finance	151UNTS227	101998
10 Jul	UNICEF (Children)	Syria	Direct Aid	136UNTS17	101830
11 Jul	Canada	Ceylon (Sri Lanka)	General Aid	391UNTS245	105630
11 Jul	Multilateral		Postal Service	171UNTS191	102227
11 Jul	India	Philippines	General Amity	203UNTS73	102741

DATE	PARTY ONE	PARTY TWO	TOPIC	CITATION	NUMBER
1952 (Cont.)					
11 Jul	Multilateral		Postal Service	170UNTS3	102221
11 Jul	Multilateral		Postal Service	171UNTS3	102224
11 Jul	Multilateral		Postal Service	170UNTS63	102222
11 Jul	Multilateral		Postal Service	171UNTS89	102225
11 Jul	Multilateral		Postal Service	171UNTS143	102226
11 Jul	Multilateral		Postal Service	170UNTS269	102223
11 Jul	Multilateral		IGO Establishment	169UNTS3	102220
11 Jul	Chile	WHO (World Health)	Tech Assistance	137UNTS27	101846
14 Jul	Germany, West	Switzerland	Non-ILO Labor	53SWRO423	462103
14 Jul	Spain	Sweden	General Economic	52SOFM303	461169
14 Jul	Bulgaria	China People's Rep	Culture	52CCJC35	410070
14 Jul	Multilateral		Visas	198UNTS37	102655
14 Jul	Multilateral		Consul/Citizenship	198UNTS47	102656
15 Jul	Mexico	USA (United States)	Air Transport	181UNTS263	102416
16 Jul	India	WHO (World Health)	Tech Assistance	135UNTS291	101828
17 Jul	Netherlands	Pakistan	Air Transport	150UNTS277	101980
17 Jul	Colombia	United Nations	Tech Assistance	135UNTS61	101815
17 Jul	ICJ Option Clause	Cambodia	UN Charter	137UNTS11	101844
18 Jul	Germany, West	USA (United States)	Education	165UNTS167	102175
19 Jul	Germany, West	Switzerland	Claims and Debts	53SWRO413	462026
21 Jul	Bulgaria	China People's Rep	General Economic	52CCJC40	410071
21 Jul	Panama	USA (United States)	Tech Assistance	181UNTS285	102417
22 Jul	Netherlands	Switzerland	Land Transport	52NET97	447034
22 Jul	Greece	Israel	Taxation	215UNTS365	102924
22 Jul	Greece	Israel	General Economic	219UNTS231	102978
22 Jul	France	USA (United States)	Direct Aid	181UNTS319	102420
22 Jul	Pakistan	UK Great Britain	Postal Service	157UNTS185	102054
23 Jul	France	WHO (World Health)	IGO Status/Immunit	209UNTS231	102829
23 Jul	Israel	USA (United States)	Milit Assistance	179UNTS139	102363
23 Jul	Chile	ILO (Labor Org)	Tech Assistance	178UNTS323	102348
24 Jul	Finland	Netherlands	Visas	52NET106	447035
25 Jul	Japan	United Nations	IGO Status/Immunit	135UNTS305	200443
25 Jul	Japan	USA (United States)	Milit Assistance	198UNTS281	102671
25 Jul	UNICEF (Children)	UK Great Britain	Direct Aid	135UNTS37	101812
28 Jul	Germany, West	Greece	General Trade	182UNTS85	102424
28 Jul	Denmark	Spain	Commodity Trade	135UNTS255	101825
29 Jul	UK Great Britain	USA (United States)	Status of Forces	179UNTS129	102362
30 Jul	China People's Rep	Romania	General Economic	52CCJC42	410072
31 Jul	Czechoslovakia	Romania	Sanitation	362UNTS123	105185
31 Jul	France	Greece	General Trade	187UNTS169	102510
01 Aug	Belgium	Italy	Non-ILO Labor	54ITGU185	435045
04 Aug	Brazil	United Nations	Tech Assistance	135UNTS185	101820
05 Aug	Greece	Turkey	Visas	187UNTS163	102509
06 Aug	Accept UN Charter	Austria	UN Charter	223UNTS27	103044
08 Aug	Germany, West	Japan	Admin Cooperation	0JGJI4507	441071
08 Aug	Panama	USA (United States)	Air Transport	181UNTS257	102415
08 Aug	Denmark	USA (United States)	Direct Aid	181UNTS249	102414
08 Aug	Israel	USA (United States)	Direct Aid	181UNTS37	102396
09 Aug	China People's Rep	USSR (Soviet Union)	Education	0SUST289	468083
09 Aug	China People's Rep	USSR (Soviet Union)	Education	52CCJC45	410073
11 Aug	Japan	USA (United States)	Air Transport	212UNTS27	102862
14 Aug	Belgium	Germany, West	Admin Cooperation	139UNTS29	101873
15 Aug	Romania	USSR (Soviet Union)	Specific Property	16SUGG66	469897
15 Aug	Laos	UNICEF (Children)	Direct Aid	161UNTS323	200491
15 Aug	Burma	Philippines	Air Transport	200UNTS97	102696
15 Aug	USA (United States)	Yugoslavia	Direct Aid	184UNTS97	102441
18 Aug	Iraq	USA (United States)	Direct Aid	184UNTS131	102444
19 Aug	Greece	Sweden	General Trade	189UNTS117	102544
20 Aug	Mongolia	USSR (Soviet Union)	Air Transport	16SUGG66	469898
20 Aug	UK Great Britain	Yugoslavia	Finance	158UNTS439	102077
20 Aug	Panama	United Nations	Tech Assistance	136UNTS3	101829
21 Aug	Jordan	WHO (World Health)	Direct Aid	141UNTS341	200472
21 Aug	India	Pakistan	Territory Boundary	207UNTS161	102805
21 Aug	Multilateral		Tech Assistance	141UNTS129	101912
23 Aug	Norway	Turkey	Visas	2NORT588	451175

DATE	PARTY ONE	PARTY TWO	TOPIC	CITATION	NUMBER
1952 (Cont.)					
26 Aug	Germany, West	Switzerland	Finance	53SWRO134	462116
26 Aug	Germany, West	Switzerland	Claims and Debts	53SWRO119	462115
26 Aug	Germany, West	Switzerland	Claims and Debts	53WGBB703	425753
26 Aug	Mexico	USA (United States)	IGO Establishment	264UNTS269	103797
26 Aug	Iceland	IBRD (World Bank)	IBRD Project	159UNTS363	102095
26 Aug	Colombia	IBRD (World Bank)	IBRD Project	159UNTS339	102094
28 Aug	USA (United States)	Venezuela	General Trade	178UNTS51	102336
28 Aug	Multilateral		Claims and Debts	175UNTS69	102296
29 Aug	UNICEF (Children)	Vietnam, South	Direct Aid	161UNTS335	200492
29 Aug	Haiti	USA (United States)	Direct Aid	186UNTS35	102480
29 Aug	Ethiopia	Pakistan	Air Transport	150UNTS257	101979
29 Aug	Denmark	Portugal	General Trade	149UNTS49	101950
29 Aug	Ethiopia	UK Great Britain	Trusteeship	190UNTS329	102573
29 Aug	Australia	Germany, West	Non-ILO Labor	184UNTS147	102446
03 Sep	Cuba	Philippines	General Amity	3PTS3	465030
04 Sep	Italy	ILO (Labor Org)	Tech Assistance	178UNTS371	200505
05 Sep	Multilateral		Taxation	256UNTS3	103619
05 Sep	Multilateral		Customs	247UNTS329	103479
06 Sep	Chile	Germany, West	Customs	53WGBB292	425079
06 Sep	Ceylon (Sri Lanka)	Japan	General Economic	314UNTS279	104552
06 Sep	Multilateral		Patents/Copyrights	216UNTS132	102937
06 Sep	Ethiopia	UK Great Britain	Finance	149UNTS57	101951
08 Sep	Greece	Sweden	General Trade	52SOFM491	461172
08 Sep	Greece	Sweden	Finance	52SOFM506	461173
09 Sep	Germany, West	UK Great Britain	Milit Installation	151UNTS215	101997
10 Sep	Germany, West	Israel	Consul/Citizenship	345UNTS91	104961
10 Sep	Germany, West	Israel	Reparations	162UNTS205	102137
12 Sep	Germany, East	Romania	General Economic	1EGDA455	419284
15 Sep	Mongolia	USSR (Soviet Union)	Specific Property	16SUGG67	469899
15 Sep	China People's Rep	USSR (Soviet Union)	Specific Property	0SUST290	468084
15 Sep	China People's Rep	USSR (Soviet Union)	Milit Installation	52CCJC49	410076
15 Sep	France	Israel	Customs	220UNTS65	102989
15 Sep	China People's Rep	USSR (Soviet Union)	Milit Installation	226UNTS45	103106
15 Sep	Denmark	Greece	General Trade	187UNTS207	102513
17 Sep	Pakistan	USA (United States)	Loans and Credits	227UNTS77	103132
18 Sep	Japan	USA (United States)	Visas	227UNTS85	103133
20 Sep	ILO (Labor Org)	Uruguay	Tech Assistance	187UNTS25	102499
20 Sep	Austria	Greece	General Trade	187UNTS191	102512
22 Sep	Netherlands	Peru	Air Transport	255UNTS49	103604
22 Sep	Italy	Netherlands	Reparations	150UNTS113	101965
22 Sep	Belgium	Italy	Customs	157UNTS121	102051
24 Sep	France	Spain	Territory Boundary	54SPBO1230	460102
24 Sep	Monaco	USA (United States)	Patents/Copyrights	186UNTS43	102481
26 Sep	Germany, West	Ireland	General Trade	558UNTS27	108138
26 Sep	Belgium	Luxembourg	Reparations	141UNTS111	101910
29 Sep	USA (United States)	Venezuela	Tech Assistance	186UNTS23	102479
29 Sep	Thailand	UK Great Britain	General Economic	173UNTS31	102257
30 Sep	Hungary	USSR (Soviet Union)	Specific Property	0SUST291	468196
30 Sep	United Nations	Trieste	Tech Assistance	140UNTS11	101881
04 Oct	Ceylon (Sri Lanka)	China People's Rep	General Trade	52CCJC55	410079
04 Oct	China People's Rep	Mongolia	Health/Educ/Welfare	52CCJC54	410078
04 Oct	France	USA (United States)	Milit Installation	0UNTS0	109599
07 Oct	Multilateral		Admin Cooperation	310UNTS181	104493
08 Oct	Germany, West	Switzerland	Admin Cooperation	53WGBB519	425754
09 Oct	Turkey	Yemen	General Amity	53TURG2107	466004
09 Oct	Turkey	UK Great Britain	Visas	151UNTS233	101999
09 Oct	New Zealand	Switzerland	General Trade	171UNTS275	102231
09 Oct	Nicaragua	USA (United States)	Consul/Citizenship	184UNTS105	102442
10 Oct	Canada	Italy	Visas	233UNTS137	103258
10 Oct	Dominican Republic	WHO (World Health)	Sanitation	150UNTS133	101967
11 Oct	USA (United States)	Yugoslavia	Direct Aid	235UNTS277	103309
13 Oct	Mexico	Netherlands	Air Transport	163UNTS341	102154
13 Oct	Austria	Luxembourg	Air Transport	192UNTS291	102606
15 Oct	Costa Rica	Norway	General Trade	2NORT590	451027
15 Oct	Multilateral		Tech Assistance	141UNTS96	101909

DATE	PARTY ONE	PARTY TWO	TOPIC	CITATION	NUMBER
1952 (Cont.)					
16 Oct	Belgium	Turkey	Visas	149UNTS289	101958
17 Oct	Italy	United Arab Rep	Other Military	52ITDI291	436314
17 Oct	Austria	Belgium	Culture	162UNTS183	102135
17 Oct	Multilateral		Direct Aid	141UNTS121	101911
18 Oct	Poland	Sweden	General Trade	52SOFM529	461174
19 Oct	United Arab Rep	UK Great Britain	General Trade	158UNTS423	102075
23 Oct	Iceland	Luxembourg	Air Transport	193UNTS39	102609
23 Oct	Iraq	USA (United States)	Tech Assistance	212UNTS201	102872
24 Oct	Brazil	Poland	General Economic	53PZUM59	458006
24 Oct	Burma	USA (United States)	Tech Assistance	222UNTS55	103022
24 Oct	Chile	WHO (World Health)	Sanitation	151UNTS339	102004
24 Oct	ICJ Option Clause	Laos	UN Charter	149UNTS285	101957
25 Oct	Multilateral		Land Transport	241UNTS336	103442
25 Oct	Burma	UK Great Britain	Air Transport	150UNTS237	101978
27 Oct	Chile	Norway	Air Transport	2NORT592	451020
27 Oct	Chile	Denmark	Air Transport	271UNTS93	103911
27 Oct	Chile	Sweden	Air Transport	311UNTS63	104499
28 Oct	Italy	Netherlands	Non-ILO Labor	289UNTS144	104218
28 Oct	Denmark	Italy	General Trade	167UNTS125	102202
29 Oct	Argentina	Poland	General Economic	53PZUM67	458007
30 Oct	Philippines	FAO (Food Agri)	Tech Assistance	3PTS36	465075
30 Oct	United Arab Rep	UK Great Britain	Finance	172UNTS3	102236
31 Oct	El Salvador	Germany, West	Mostfavored Nation	54WGBB49	425128
31 Oct	Germany, East	Romania	Telecommunications	4EGDA431	419286
31 Oct	Germany, East	Romania	Postal Service	4EGDA425	419285
01 Nov	Taiwan	USA (United States)	Admin Cooperation	0CTRC809	413039
02 Nov	Dominican Republic	Philippines	General Amity	543UNTS175	107901
04 Nov	Japan	UK Great Britain	Specific Property	164UNTS101	102161
04 Nov	Japan	UK Great Britain	Specific Property	164UNTS107	102162
04 Nov	Chile	WHO (World Health)	Sanitation	150UNTS119	101966
05 Nov	Philippines	UNTAB (Tech Assis)	Tech Assistance	3PTS45	465077
05 Nov	Philippines	UNTAB (Tech Assis)	Tech Assistance	3PTS41	465076
05 Nov	Ethiopia	USA (United States)	Sanitation	184UNTS139	102445
05 Nov	ICJ Option Clause	Vietnam, South	ICJ Option Clause	150UNTS147	101968
06 Nov	Italy	UK Great Britain	Specif Claim/Waive	158UNTS431	102076
07 Nov	Multilateral		General Trade	221UNTS255	103010
07 Nov	Ethiopia	USA (United States)	Tech Assistance	184UNTS285	102453
08 Nov	Canada	USA (United States)	Gen Communications	207UNTS3	102796
10 Nov	Norway	Sweden	Scientific Project	52SOFM893	461179
10 Nov	Dominican Republic	Spain	General Amity	53SPBO309	460080
10 Nov	France	UK Great Britain	Admin Cooperation	214UNTS255	102903
10 Nov	Multilateral		Admin Cooperation	214UNTS265	102904
10 Nov	Saudi Arabia	USA (United States)	Direct Aid	181UNTS307	102419
10 Nov	Saudi Arabia	USA (United States)	Direct Aid	181UNTS295	102418
10 Nov	Saudi Arabia	USA (United States)	Tech Assistance	181UNTS235	102413
10 Nov	Saudi Arabia	USA (United States)	Tech Assistance	181UNTS225	102412
10 Nov	India	Iraq	General Amity	172UNTS103	102242
12 Nov	Japan	IBRD (World Bank)	IBRD Project	354UNTS313	105068
12 Nov	USA (United States)	Uruguay	Visas	231UNTS145	103213
12 Nov	Japan	USA (United States)	Milit Assistance	184UNTS111	102443
12 Nov	Belgium	UK Great Britain	Status of Forces	180UNTS15	102372
13 Nov	France	Monaco	Claims and Debts	54FRJO508	416332
13 Nov	Australia	Iceland	General Trade	161UNTS59	102122
14 Nov	Philippines	FAO (Food Agri)	Tech Assistance	3PTS49	465078
14 Nov	Denmark	Israel	General Trade	160UNTS279	102113
14 Nov	Denmark	Israel	Finance	160UNTS289	102114
14 Nov	Belgium	Germany, West	Visas	160UNTS217	102108
14 Nov	Denmark	Israel	General Economic	160UNTS275	102112
17 Nov	Luxembourg	Norway	Air Transport	311UNTS95	104500
17 Nov	Luxembourg	Sweden	Air Transport	173UNTS277	102270
17 Nov	Ceylon (Sri Lanka)	USA (United States)	Education	180UNTS207	102386
19 Nov	Israel	Switzerland	Air Transport	232UNTS3	103226
19 Nov	Nicaragua	USA (United States)	Military Mission	186UNTS3	102478
20 Nov	Netherlands	Switzerland	Non-ILO Labor	163UNTS121	102146
20 Nov	Sweden	USA (United States)	Education	177UNTS203	102319

DATE	PARTY ONE	PARTY TWO	TOPIC	CITATION	NUMBER
1952 (Cont.)					
21 Nov	Ceylon (Sri Lanka)	WHO (World Health)	Sanitation	161UNTS315	200490
21 Nov	Portugal	UK Great Britain	Milit Assistance	404UNTS27	105802
21 Nov	Japan	UK Great Britain	Reparations	172UNTS303	102254
22 Nov	Norway	Sweden	General Trade	52SOFM535	461175
22 Nov	Japan	USA (United States)	Milit Installation	52JHZ12	439001
22 Nov	Ceylon (Sri Lanka)	Germany, West	General Trade	55WGBB189	425070
24 Nov	Philippines	USA (United States)	Visas	181UNTS155	102406
25 Nov	Italy	Switzerland	Territory Boundary	55SWRO626	462176
26 Nov	South Africa	Sweden	Air Transport	52SOFM541	461176
26 Nov	Japan	WHO (World Health)	Tech Assistance	204UNTS301	200521
28 Nov	Mexico	ICAO (Civil Aviat)	Tech Assistance	164UNTS15	102156
29 Nov	France	Sweden	General Trade	52SOFM545	461177
29 Nov	Belgium	France	Visas	160UNTS261	102110
02 Dec	El Salvador	Spain	General Trade	53SPBO511	460092
02 Dec	El Salvador	Spain	Finance	53SPBO511	460093
02 Dec	France	Italy	Claims and Debts	53ITGU51	435133
03 Dec	Bulgaria	China People's Rep	General Economic	52CCJC60	410084
03 Dec	Canada	United Arab Rep	Mostfavored Nation	233UNTS145	103259
03 Dec	USA (United States)	Yugoslavia	Direct Aid	185UNTS183	102469
04 Dec	Finland	USA (United States)	General Amity	205UNTS149	102774
05 Dec	Argentina	Italy	Mass Media	52ITDI225	436016
05 Dec	Canada	USA (United States)	Milit Installation	206UNTS11	102783
06 Dec	Belgium	Germany, West	Visas	152UNTS11	102007
10 Dec	Belgium	Iceland	Patents/Copyrights	158UNTS445	102078
11 Dec	India	WHO (World Health)	Sanitation	158UNTS391	102073
12 Dec	Taiwan	USA (United States)	Direct Aid	0CTRC807	413038
12 Dec	Austria	UK Great Britain	Culture	172UNTS9	102237
15 Dec	Liberia	USA (United States)	Tech Assistance	185UNTS45	102457
15 Dec	Saudi Arabia	USA (United States)	Direct Aid	185UNTS55	102458
15 Dec	Saudi Arabia	USA (United States)	Tech Assistance	185UNTS67	102459
16 Dec	Multilateral		Tech Assistance	158UNTS407	102074
16 Dec	UNICEF (Children)	UK Great Britain	Direct Aid	151UNTS359	102005
17 Dec	Australia	Germany, West	Visas	188UNTS267	102530
18 Dec	Ceylon (Sri Lanka)	China People's Rep	Commodity Trade	52CCJC62	410085
18 Dec	India	IBRD (World Bank)	IBRD Project	201UNTS241	102719
20 Dec	Sweden	Yugoslavia	General Trade	52SOFM569	461178
20 Dec	Czechoslovakia	Poland	General Economic	53PZUM77	458008
23 Dec	France	Greece	General Trade	187UNTS175	102511
23 Dec	Belgium	Germany, West	Claims and Debts	186UNTS69	102483
24 Dec	Greece	USA (United States)	Milit Assistance	185UNTS193	102470
24 Dec	Israel	South Africa	Taxation	207UNTS303	102813
25 Dec	Romania	USSR (Soviet Union)	Specific Resources	0SUST292	468383
29 Dec	Japan	UK Great Britain	Air Transport	175UNTS129	102299
29 Dec	Multilateral		Tech Assistance	151UNTS317	102002
31 Dec	ILO (Labor Org)	UN Relief Palestin	Tech Assistance	182UNTS201	200506
1953					
31 Dec	China People's Rep	USSR (Soviet Union)	Direct Aid	53CCJC29	410104
05 Jan	United Arab Rep	UK Great Britain	Specific Property	207UNTS277	102810
08 Jan	Netherlands	Portugal	General Trade	53NET37	447036
09 Jan	Costa Rica	Spain	General Amity	54SPBO303	460066
09 Jan	China People's Rep	Romania	Scientific Project	53CCJC1	410086
09 Jan	South Africa	Sweden	Air Transport	173UNTS299	102271
09 Jan	Germany, West	USA (United States)	Visas	212UNTS3	102859
13 Jan	Germany, East	USSR (Soviet Union)	Mass Media	4EGDA34	419384
16 Jan	China People's Rep	Mongolia	Telecommunications	53CCJC3	410088
16 Jan	China People's Rep	Mongolia	Postal Service	53CCJC2	410087
16 Jan	Lebanon	Pakistan	General Amity	284UNTS193	104137
16 Jan	Switzerland	UK Great Britain	Non-ILO Labor	196UNTS119	102621
16 Jan	USA (United States)	Venezuela	Military Mission	199UNTS287	102690
19 Jan	China People's Rep	Romania	General Trade	53CCJC4	410089
19 Jan	UK Great Britain	USA (United States)	General Military	161UNTS3	102117
21 Jan	Portugal	UK Great Britain	Non-IBRD Project	175UNTS13	102293
23 Jan	India	IBRD (World Bank)	IBRD Project	201UNTS145	102715
24 Jan	Japan	Philippines	Water Transport	3PTS63	465031

DATE	PARTY ONE	PARTY TWO	TOPIC	CITATION	NUMBER
1953 (Cont.)					
25 Jan	Saudi Arabia	USA (United States)	Education	201UNTS3	102706
27 Jan	Colombia	Sweden	General Trade	53SOFM1	461180
27 Jan	Dominican Republic	Spain	Culture	53SPBO112	460081
27 Jan	Greece	South Africa	Mostfavored Nation	533UNTS303	107748
28 Jan	FAO (Food Agri)	Vietnam, South	Tech Assistance	OVKNG52	496010
30 Jan	Germany, West	Liechtenstein	Claims and Debts	54WGBB522	425415
30 Jan	Belgium	France	Visas	188UNTS141	102525
31 Jan	Bolivia	Italy	Culture	281UNTS181	104079
03 Feb	Greece	Spain	Claims and Debts	225UNTS3	103081
04 Feb	Taiwan	USA (United States)	Patents/Copyrights	OCTRC815	413040
04 Feb	Greece	Italy	General Trade	189UNTS269	102551
04 Feb	Greece	Italy	Finance	189UNTS295	102552
04 Feb	Greece	USA (United States)	Milit Assistance	189UNTS3	102538
05 Feb	Greece	Netherlands	General Trade	263UNTS361	103783
05 Feb	Netherlands	Philippines	Air Transport	216UNTS99	102934
07 Feb	Multilateral		Territory Boundary	173UNTS143	102264
11 Feb	Denmark	Sweden	General Trade	53SOFM5	461181
11 Feb	United Nations	Sweden	Tech Assistance	160UNTS3	102096
11 Feb	IBRD (World Bank)	Yugoslavia	IBRD Project	165UNTS231	102179
11 Feb	India	WHO (World Health)	Tech Assistance	163UNTS43	102140
12 Feb	United Arab Rep	UK Great Britain	Recognition	161UNTS157	102127
13 Feb	Taiwan	ILO (Labor Org)	Tech Assistance	178UNTS337	102349
14 Feb	Albania	Romania	Culture	342UNTS107	104903
16 Feb	Chile	United Nations	IGO Operations	314UNTS49	104541
17 Feb	Japan	Netherlands	Air Transport	192UNTS215	102602
19 Feb	Czechoslovakia	Germany, East	Culture	4EGDA282	419335
19 Feb	Taiwan	Spain	General Amity	181UNTS81	102400
20 Feb	Costa Rica	Italy	General Trade	54ITGU198	435098
20 Feb	India	Pakistan	Air Transport	164UNTS3	102155
20 Feb	Japan	Sweden	Air Transport	173UNTS307	102272
21 Feb	Libya	UK Great Britain	Air Transport	311UNTS115	104501
23 Feb	Japan	Norway	Air Transport	192UNTS191	102601
25 Feb	France	Switzerland	Territory Boundary	57SWRO884	462002
25 Feb	France	Switzerland	Territory Boundary	60SWRO1546	462174
25 Feb	UK Great Britain	USA (United States)	Direct Aid	212UNTS157	102868
26 Feb	Turkey	Yugoslavia	General Trade	247UNTS54	103460
26 Feb	Denmark	Japan	Air Transport	173UNTS329	102273
26 Feb	Denmark	Poland	Claims and Debts	186UNTS301	102496
26 Feb	Multilateral		Tech Assistance	161UNTS31	102120
26 Feb	Denmark	Germany, West	Claims and Debts	178UNTS3	102332
27 Feb	Germany, West	Switzerland	Claims and Debts	54SWRO3	462118
27 Feb	France	Germany, West	Specif Claim/Waive	53WGBB508	425139
27 Feb	Germany, West	UK Great Britain	Claims and Debts	330UNTS217	104747
27 Feb	Multilateral		Claims and Debts	333UNTS3	104764
27 Feb	Germany, West	USA (United States)	Claims and Debts	224UNTS13	103067
27 Feb	Germany, West	USA (United States)	Claims and Debts	224UNTS31	103068
27 Feb	Germany, West	USA (United States)	Claims and Debts	223UNTS167	103065
27 Feb	Germany, West	USA (United States)	Claims and Debts	205UNTS103	102771
27 Feb	Belgium	France	Non-ILO Labor	164UNTS49	102158
27 Feb	Costa Rica	United Nations	Tech Assistance	161UNTS45	102121
28 Feb	Greece	Yugoslavia	General Economic	252UNTS27	103557
28 Feb	Multilateral		General Amity	167UNTS21	102199
02 Mar	Nepal	United Nations	Tech Assistance	161UNTS347	200493
02 Mar	Canada	USA (United States)	Specific Resources	222UNTS77	103024
02 Mar	UK Great Britain	USA (United States)	Milit Installation	172UNTS257	102249
04 Mar	Denmark	Uruguay	General Economic	250UNTS51	103517
06 Mar	Cuba	Norway	Visas	2NORT599	451030
06 Mar	Dominican Republic	USA (United States)	Milit Assistance	199UNTS267	102689
09 Mar	Philippines	USA (United States)	Milit Servic/Citiz	227UNTS101	103134
11 Mar	IBRD (World Bank)	UK Great Britain	IBRD Project	172UNTS115	102243
11 Mar	Belgium	France	Reparations	191UNTS329	102590
12 Mar	Japan	Philippines	Reparations	3PTS85	465032
12 Mar	Netherlands	USA (United States)	Claims and Debts	53NET135	447037
12 Mar	United Arab Rep	USA (United States)	Tech Assistance	204UNTS3	102747
13 Mar	Germany, West	Netherlands	Visas	293UNTS123	104289

DATE	PARTY ONE	PARTY TWO	TOPIC	CITATION	NUMBER
1953 (Cont.)					
13 Mar	Haiti	USA (United States)	Direct Aid	212UNTS143	102866
14 Mar	Austria	Italy	Culture	54ITGU215	435035
14 Mar	China People's Rep	Pakistan	Commodity Trade	53CCJC11	410094
14 Mar	France	Italy	Land Transport	284UNTS221	104140
15 Mar	India	Muscat and Oman	General Amity	190UNTS69	102559
16 Mar	Chile	Norway	Visas	167UNTS13	102198
17 Mar	Germany, West	Netherlands	Visas	293UNTS129	104290
17 Mar	Canada	USA (United States)	Telecommunications	236UNTS259	103329
18 Mar	Panama	Spain	General Amity	54SPBO607	460214
18 Mar	Japan	USA (United States)	Tech Assistance	212UNTS149	102867
19 Mar	UK Great Britain	USSR (Soviet Union)	Refugees	OSUST293	468430
19 Mar	Austria	Yugoslavia	Visas	467UNTS293	106767
19 Mar	Austria	Yugoslavia	Visas	467UNTS323	106768
19 Mar	United Arab Rep	USA (United States)	Tech Assistance	215UNTS17	102909
20 Mar	Belgium	Germany, West	Customs	53WGBB534	425020
20 Mar	Czechoslovakia	Germany, East	General Trade	1EGDA421	419336
21 Mar	China People's Rep	USSR (Soviet Union)	Direct Aid	OSUST294	468085
21 Mar	United Arab Rep	Netherlands	Finance	53NET44	447039
21 Mar	United Arab Rep	Netherlands	General Trade	53NET43	447038
21 Mar	China People's Rep	USSR (Soviet Union)	General Trade	53CCJC13	410095
21 Mar	Libya	UK Great Britain	General Military	172UNTS85	102240
23 Mar	El Salvador	France	General Trade	54FRJO1902	416386
23 Mar	Lebanon	Sweden	Air Transport	255UNTS83	103605
23 Mar	Lebanon	USA (United States)	Milit Assistance	239UNTS45	103370
23 Mar	Japan	USA (United States)	Direct Aid	185UNTS93	102461
23 Mar	Multilateral		Admin Cooperation	202UNTS241	102732
25 Mar	Libya	UK Great Britain	Finance	172UNTS281	102252
26 Mar	Belgium	Netherlands	Visas	165UNTS297	102180
27 Mar	United Nations	WMO (Meteorology)	IGO Operations	178UNTS361	200504
27 Mar	Japan	South Africa	Admin Cooperation	173UNTS37	102258
27 Mar	Belgium	UK Great Britain	Taxation	188UNTS153	102526
30 Mar	El Salvador	Italy	General Trade	53ITDI410	436106
30 Mar	China People's Rep	Hungary	General Economic	53CCJC17	410098
30 Mar	Jordan	UN Relief Palestin	Direct Aid	165UNTS317	200495
30 Mar	Germany, West	USA (United States)	Reparations	235UNTS285	103310
30 Mar	Belgium	Canada	Status of Forces	181UNTS95	102401
31 Mar	Norway	Switzerland	Milit Servic/Citiz	2NORT602	451155
31 Mar	Multilateral		Mass Media	435UNTS191	106280
31 Mar	Multilateral		Privil/Immunities	193UNTS136	102613
01 Apr	Colombia	Spain	Culture	65SPBO1201	460064
01 Apr	Czechoslovakia	Germany, East	Finance	4EGDA288	419337
01 Apr	Germany, West	USA (United States)	Claims and Debts	224UNTS3	103066
01 Apr	Multilateral		Non-ILO Labor	227UNTS169	103138
01 Apr	Belgium	Sweden	Taxation	185UNTS225	102473
01 Apr	Portugal	USA (United States)	Taxation	205UNTS41	102769
02 Apr	Liberia	Spain	General Amity	53SPBO912	460182
02 Apr	Japan	USA (United States)	General Amity	206UNTS143	102788
02 Apr	France	WHO (World Health)	Tech Assistance	174UNTS83	102279
07 Apr	United Nations	Yemen	Tech Assistance	163UNTS73	102142
08 Apr	Mongolia	USSR (Soviet Union)	Specific Property	OSUST441	468275
09 Apr	Netherlands	United Nations	Direct Aid	163UNTS89	102143
09 Apr	Germany, West	USA (United States)	Culture	204UNTS79	102750
09 Apr	Finland	Sweden	Dispute Settlement	198UNTS61	102657
10 Apr	Netherlands	Sweden	General Trade	53SOFM81	461182
13 Apr	Italy	UK Great Britain	Reparations	172UNTS271	102251
13 Apr	France	UK Great Britain	Admin Cooperation	172UNTS173	102245
15 Apr	Canada	Germany, West	Visas	236UNTS323	103333
16 Apr	France	Tunisia	Health/Educ/Welfare	53FRJO2407	416452
16 Apr	Turkey	Yugoslavia	Air Transport	255UNTS99	103606
17 Apr	Greece	UK Great Britain	Consul/Citizenship	191UNTS151	102582
18 Apr	Germany, West	Uruguay	General Trade	54WGBB51	425707
18 Apr	Germany, West	Uruguay	General Trade	53WBGA94	424708
20 Apr	Italy	Norway	General Trade	54ITGU107	435284
21 Apr	Germany, West	Yemen	General Amity	54WGBB573	425310
22 Apr	Germany, West	Indonesia	General Trade	53WBGA163	424261

DATE	PARTY ONE	PARTY TWO	TOPIC	CITATION	NUMBER
1953 (Cont.)					
22 Apr	Japan	USA (United States)	Admin Cooperation	178UNTS169	102341
23 Apr	Czechoslovakia	Denmark	General Trade	174UNTS95	102280
23 Apr	Czechoslovakia	Denmark	Finance	174UNTS107	102281
24 Apr	France	Sweden	General Trade	53SOFM577	461183
24 Apr	Japan	Pakistan	Admin Cooperation	221UNTS325	103013
25 Apr	France	Japan	Admin Cooperation	187UNTS41	102500
27 Apr	Japan	UK Great Britain	Admin Cooperation	228UNTS227	103154
27 Apr	Australia	Japan	Admin Cooperation	193UNTS78	102612
27 Apr	Ethiopia	UNICEF (Children)	Direct Aid	213UNTS169	102885
27 Apr	Philippines	Thailand	Air Transport	174UNTS3	102274
28 Apr	Colombia	France	Patents/Copyrights	62FRRT16	415119
28 Apr	Syria	Turkey	Telecommunications	204UNTS255	102760
29 Apr	Ethiopia	USA (United States)	Sanitation	224UNTS121	103073
29 Apr	Belgium	Netherlands	Admin Cooperation	173UNTS61	102261
29 Apr	Greece	Netherlands	Culture	191UNTS235	102583
30 Apr	Costa Rica	France	General Trade	54FRJO1902	416134
30 Apr	China People's Rep	Germany, East	General Economic	53CCJC20	410099
30 Apr	Israel	Uruguay	Culture	280UNTS269	104064
30 Apr	Brazil	IBRD (World Bank)	IBRD Project	190UNTS133	102562
30 Apr	France	WHO (World Health)	Tech Assistance	174UNTS71	102278
30 Apr	Denmark	South Africa	Air Transport	174UNTS19	102275
30 Apr	Multilateral		Admin Cooperation	175UNTS89	102297
01 May	Netherlands	Pakistan	Visas	293UNTS11	104281
04 May	Brazil	Ecuador	General Trade	369UNTS37	105249
05 May	Ecuador	Spain	Culture	54SPBO3001	460084
05 May	Germany, West	Italy	Non-ILO Labor	54WGBB485	425287
05 May	Germany, West	Italy	Non-ILO Labor	53WBGA134	424288
05 May	Germany, West	Italy	Non-ILO Labor	267UNTS9	103835
05 May	Israel	South Africa	Air Transport	192UNTS183	102600
06 May	Japan	Sweden	General Trade	53SOFM1155	461195
06 May	Indonesia	Poland	General Economic	53PZUM85	458009
07 May	China People's Rep	Czechoslovakia	Telecommunications	53CCJC24	410101
07 May	China People's Rep	Czechoslovakia	General Trade	53CCJC22	410100
08 May	Korea, North	Poland	Tech Assistance	53PZUM109	458010
08 May	Germany, West	Japan	Patents/Copyrights	0JGJI1172	441073
09 May	France	Vietnam, South	General Military	0VKNG53	496011
11 May	Cuba	Germany, West	General Economic	55WGBB1055	425400
11 May	Multilateral		Sanitation	456UNTS3	106555
12 May	France	Japan	Culture	53FRJO610	416254
13 May	Israel	UK Great Britain	Finance	175UNTS179	102300
14 May	El Salvador	USA (United States)	Direct Aid	234UNTS71	103273
14 May	Australia	USA (United States)	Taxation	205UNTS253	102779
14 May	Australia	USA (United States)	Taxation	205UNTS237	102778
14 May	Australia	USA (United States)	Taxation	205UNTS277	102780
15 May	France	Spain	Admin Cooperation	55SPBO1508	460103
15 May	Bulgaria	Germany, East	Mass Media	4EGDA482	419037
15 May	Germany, West	Sweden	Non-ILO Labor	227UNTS195	103139
20 May	Finland	Norway	Specific Resources	173UNTS163	102265
20 May	Belgium	Germany, West	Admin Cooperation	180UNTS3	102370
21 May	Greece	United Arab Rep	General Trade	256UNTS17	103620
21 May	Greece	United Arab Rep	Finance	256UNTS25	103621
21 May	United Arab Rep	USA (United States)	Tech Assistance	204UNTS29	102748
21 May	El Salvador	USA (United States)	Military Mission	213UNTS15	102878
22 May	Israel	Italy	Mostfavored Nation	219UNTS297	102981
22 May	Ethiopia	USA (United States)	Milit Assistance	207UNTS127	102803
22 May	Germany, West	UK Great Britain	Finance	172UNTS179	102246
22 May	Ethiopia	USA (United States)	Milit Installation	191UNTS59	102577
23 May	Peru	Spain	General Trade	54SPBO1810	460226
25 May	Australia	Sweden	General Trade	53SOFM1099	461194
25 May	China People's Rep	Poland	General Economic	53CCJC27	410103
26 May	Cuba	USA (United States)	Air Transport	224UNTS75	103070
28 May	Netherlands	Switzerland	General Trade	54NET25	447040
28 May	Switzerland	Yugoslavia	Air Transport	232UNTS45	103228
28 May	ICAO (Civil Aviat)	Syria	Tech Assistance	173UNTS199	102267
29 May	Belgium	Vietnam, South	General Trade	0VKNG56	496012

DATE	PARTY ONE	PARTY TWO	TOPIC	CITATION	NUMBER
1953 (Cont.)					
29 May	Belgium	Israel	Admin Cooperation	219UNTS197	102975
30 May	Brazil	USA (United States)	Tech Assistance	460UNTS89	106633
30 May	Netherlands	Thailand	Reparations	293UNTS17	104282
01 Jun	Austria	Sweden	General Trade	53SOFM699	461184
01 Jun	Greece	UK Great Britain	Visas	172UNTS265	102250
02 Jun	Germany, West	USA (United States)	General Amity	231UNTS151	103214
03 Jun	Germany, West	USA (United States)	General Amity	253UNTS89	103578
04 Jun	India	Turkey	General Trade	54TURG2203	466069
04 Jun	Jordan	Syria	Specific Resources	184UNTS15	102437
05 Jun	Sweden	Switzerland	General Trade	53SOFM708	461185
05 Jun	China People's Rep	Finland	Finance	53CCJC32	410106
05 Jun	China People's Rep	Finland	General Trade	53CCJC30	410105
05 Jun	China People's Rep	France	General Trade	53CCJC33	410107
08 Jun	Japan	Syria	General Trade	184UNTS3	102436
08 Jun	Australia	UK Great Britain	Non-ILO Labor	201UNTS187	102718
09 Jun	Colombia	USA (United States)	Tech Assistance	213UNTS3	102877
12 Jun	Canada	India	Admin Cooperation	248UNTS113	103490
13 Jun	Taiwan	Japan	Finance	0CTCY447	414049
13 Jun	Taiwan	Japan	General Economic	0CTRC263	413012
14 Jun	USSR (Soviet Union)	Yugoslavia	Consul/Citizenship	0SUST296	468464
16 Jun	Ecuador	United Nations	Tech Assistance	166UNTS289	102194
16 Jun	Israel	Netherlands	Visas	220UNTS93	102993
17 Jun	France	USA (United States)	Milit Installation	0UNTS0	109600
18 Jun	United Arab Rep	USA (United States)	Education	204UNTS55	102749
18 Jun	Belgium	USA (United States)	Milit Assistance	222UNTS3	103019
18 Jun	United Arab Rep	USA (United States)	Sanitation	215UNTS45	102910
18 Jun	Israel	Netherlands	Visas	220UNTS99	102994
19 Jun	Philippines	UNTAB (Tech Assis)	Tech Assistance	3PTS137	465079
19 Jun	Korea, North	USSR (Soviet Union)	Direct Aid	0SUST302	468250
19 Jun	Japan	Thailand	Air Transport	174UNTS29	102276
19 Jun	Netherlands	USA (United States)	Admin Cooperation	212UNTS249	102875
20 Jun	France	Netherlands	Land Transport	187UNTS97	102503
22 Jun	Burma	Norway	Air Transport	174UNTS49	102277
22 Jun	Ethiopia	United Nations	Tech Assistance	172UNTS93	102241
23 Jun	Liberia	USA (United States)	Education	213UNTS57	102880
23 Jun	Liberia	USA (United States)	Tech Assistance	213UNTS37	102879
24 Jun	Japan	United Nations	Tech Assistance	167UNTS249	200499
24 Jun	Cambodia	United Nations	Tech Assistance	168UNTS309	200500
24 Jun	UK Great Britain	USA (United States)	Tech Assistance	224UNTS141	103074
25 Jun	Philippines	FAO (Food Agri)	Tech Assistance	3PTS165	465081
25 Jun	Philippines	UNTAB (Tech Assis)	Tech Assistance	3PTS161	465080
25 Jun	Japan	Switzerland	Claims and Debts	54SWRO530	462027
25 Jun	Ethiopia	USA (United States)	Tech Assistance	212UNTS175	102869
25 Jun	Pakistan	USA (United States)	Direct Aid	205UNTS139	102773
25 Jun	Greece	UK Great Britain	Taxation	190UNTS281	102571
25 Jun	Multilateral		ILO Labor	191UNTS143	102581
26 Jun	Brazil	USA (United States)	Direct Aid	336UNTS241	104808
26 Jun	Panama	USA (United States)	Tech Assistance	215UNTS77	102912
26 Jun	UK Great Britain	USA (United States)	Loans and Credits	183UNTS225	102432
26 Jun	Philippines	USA (United States)	Milit Assistance	213UNTS77	102881
26 Jun	Italy	South Africa	Taxation	211UNTS255	102857
27 Jun	Chile	USA (United States)	Tech Assistance	229UNTS53	103160
27 Jun	Chile	USA (United States)	Tech Assistance	229UNTS193	103167
28 Jun	Fed Rhod/Nyasaland	South Africa	General Trade	267UNTS270	103848
29 Jun	Burma	Yugoslavia	General Trade	378UNTS83	105418
29 Jun	Saudi Arabia	USA (United States)	Sanitation	206UNTS23	102784
29 Jun	Pakistan	Turkey	Culture	211UNTS225	102854
30 Jun	India	Sweden	General Trade	53SOFM1067	461193
30 Jun	France	USA (United States)	Milit Installation	0UNTS0	109601
30 Jun	Canada	USA (United States)	Specific Property	206UNTS93	102786
30 Jun	UN Relief Palestin	United Arab Rep	Tech Assistance	190UNTS3	102554
30 Jun	Canada	USA (United States)	General Military	215UNTS103	102914
30 Jun	Afghanistan	USA (United States)	Tech Assistance	215UNTS3	102908
30 Jun	Ethiopia	USA (United States)	Direct Aid	212UNTS135	102865
30 Jun	Nicaragua	USA (United States)	Tech Assistance	215UNTS133	102917

DATE	PARTY ONE	PARTY TWO	TOPIC	CITATION	NUMBER
1953 (Cont.)					
01 Jul	Israel	Switzerland	Postal Service	220UNTS41	102986
01 Jul	Multilateral		IGO Establishment	200UNTS149	102701
02 Jul	Norway	USSR (Soviet Union)	Other Military	0SUST441	468294
02 Jul	Italy	Switzerland	Customs	257UNTS99	103653
03 Jul	Iceland	Sweden	General Trade	53SOFM733	461186
06 Jul	China People's Rep	UK Great Britain	General Trade	53CCJC39	410111
09 Jul	France	Vietnam, South	Education	0VKNG59	496013
10 Jul	France	Panama	Consul/Citizenship	58FRRT19	415352
10 Jul	France	Israel	General Economic	53FRMD2307	417244
11 Jul	Germany, West	Switzerland	Claims and Debts	53SWRO936	462117
11 Jul	Austria	Germany, West	Non-ILO Labor	54ABGB250	403059
15 Jul	Israel	USSR (Soviet Union)	Consul/Citizenship	0SUST297	468238
15 Jul	France	USSR (Soviet Union)	General Trade	0UNTS0	110492
16 Jul	Philippines	WHO (World Health)	Tech Assistance	3PTS175	465082
16 Jul	Philippines	WHO (World Health)	Tech Assistance	3PTS175	465033
16 Jul	China People's Rep	Hungary	Telecommunications	53CCJC41	410113
16 Jul	ECSC (Coal/Steel)	ILO (Labor Org)	IGO Operations	412UNTS273	200591
16 Jul	China People's Rep	Hungary	Postal Service	53CCJC40	410112
17 Jul	Austria	USSR (Soviet Union)	Specif Goods/Equip	0SUST297	468051
17 Jul	Denmark	USSR (Soviet Union)	General Trade	175UNTS3	102292
17 Jul	Brazil	IBRD (World Bank)	IBRD Project	190UNTS149	102563
18 Jul	Turkey	USSR (Soviet Union)	Dispute Settlement	0SUST298	468422
18 Jul	Belgium	USA (United States)	Taxation	180UNTS9	102371
20 Jul	Peru	Switzerland	General Trade	55SWRO287	462150
20 Jul	Germany, East	USSR (Soviet Union)	Direct Aid	1EGDA273	419385
20 Jul	Multilateral		Non-ILO Labor	228UNTS3	103141
20 Jul	Multilateral		Non-ILO Labor	227UNTS217	103140
20 Jul	Multilateral		Non-ILO Labor	228UNTS41	103142
20 Jul	India	UK Great Britain	Finance	196UNTS251	102628
23 Jul	USA (United States)	Yugoslavia	Taxation	221UNTS365	103018
24 Jul	India	Yugoslavia	General Trade	394UNTS13	105665
24 Jul	Multilateral		General Amity	250UNTS108	103520
24 Jul	Greece	Sweden	General Trade	189UNTS309	102553
27 Jul	Ireland	Italy	General Trade	558UNTS237	108144
27 Jul	Canada	Mexico	Air Transport	192UNTS255	102604
28 Jul	Greece	USSR (Soviet Union)	General Economic	0SUST298	468170
29 Jul	France	Italy	Peace/Disarmament	53ITDI289	436134
29 Jul	Libya	UK Great Britain	Status of Forces	186UNTS201	102492
29 Jul	Libya	UK Great Britain	Finance	186UNTS277	102493
29 Jul	Libya	UK Great Britain	General Amity	186UNTS185	102491
30 Jul	Austria	USSR (Soviet Union)	Milit Occupation	0SUST298	468052
30 Jul	Ceylon (Sri Lanka)	Yugoslavia	General Trade	337UNTS103	104819
30 Jul	Multilateral		Reparations	215UNTS97	102913
31 Jul	Albania	Germany, East	Culture	4EGDA548	419008
01 Aug	Iceland	USSR (Soviet Union)	General Economic	0SUST298	468205
01 Aug	Ecuador	Germany, West	General Trade	53WBGA192	424108
01 Aug	Ecuador	Germany, West	Patents/Copyrights	53WBGA192	424109
01 Aug	Ecuador	Germany, West	General Trade	54WGBB712	425107
05 Aug	Belgium	Greece	Visas	173UNTS53	102260
05 Aug	Argentina	USSR (Soviet Union)	General Economic	221UNTS99	103004
06 Aug	Philippines	UNTAB (Tech Assis)	Tech Assistance	3PTS191	465084
06 Aug	Germany, West	Turkey	Commodity Trade	54TURG2203	466043
06 Aug	Philippines	UNTAB (Tech Assis)	Tech Assistance	3PTS187	465083
06 Aug	Belgium	Italy	Non-ILO Labor	54ITGU123	435047
07 Aug	Italy	Netherlands	General Trade	53NET95	447041
12 Aug	Austria	Greece	Visas	53ABGB158	403084
12 Aug	Sweden	Switzerland	Customs	232UNTS59	103229
14 Aug	USA (United States)	Venezuela	Air Transport	213UNTS99	102883
14 Aug	Denmark	Germany, West	Non-ILO Labor	202UNTS3	102725
15 Aug	Turkey	United Arab Rep	General Economic	55TURG204	466094
17 Aug	Romania	USSR (Soviet Union)	Mass Media	0SUST299	468384
17 Aug	Luxembourg	USA (United States)	Mass Media	234UNTS219	103284
18 Aug	United Arab Rep	USSR (Soviet Union)	General Trade	16SUGG67	469900
18 Aug	United Arab Rep	USSR (Soviet Union)	Finance	0SUST299	468124
18 Aug	Cuba	Spain	General Economic	54SPBO408	460069

DATE	PARTY ONE	PARTY TWO	TOPIC	CITATION	NUMBER
1953 (Cont.)					
18 Aug	China People's Rep	Czechoslovakia	Sanitation	53CCJC48	410114
20 Aug	Germany, West	USA (United States)	Milit Assistance	224UNTS49	103069
21 Aug	Ethiopia	Yugoslavia	General Economic	378UNTS105	105421
22 Aug	Germany, East	USSR (Soviet Union)	Consul/Citizenship	1EGDA286	419386
22 Aug	Germany, East	USSR (Soviet Union)	Other Military	1EGDA286	419387
22 Aug	Germany, East	USSR (Soviet Union)	Reparations	221UNTS129	103005
25 Aug	China People's Rep	Vietnam, North	General Trade	53CCJC51	410116
26 Aug	Netherlands	Switzerland	Finance	53NET84	447042
27 Aug	Mongolia	USSR (Soviet Union)	Education	16SUGG67	469901
27 Aug	Spain	Vatican/Holy See	General Amity	53SPBO1910	460271
27 Aug	India	Italy	Other Military	275UNTS279	103987
27 Aug	Australia	Italy	Other Military	225UNTS47	103086
27 Aug	ICAO (Civil Aviat)	United Arab Rep	IGO Status/Immunit	215UNTS371	102925
27 Aug	Multilateral		Other Military	213UNTS137	102884
27 Aug	Italy	South Africa	Other Military	212UNTS211	102873
28 Aug	IBRD (World Bank)	South Africa	IBRD Project	180UNTS73	102376
28 Aug	IBRD (World Bank)	South Africa	IBRD Project	180UNTS91	102377
29 Aug	Cambodia	France	Recognition	59FRRT7	415095
01 Sep	Belgium	New Zealand	Air Transport	192UNTS283	102605
02 Sep	Belgium	USA (United States)	Milit Assistance	200UNTS127	102700
02 Sep	France	USA (United States)	Milit Assistance	224UNTS153	103075
02 Sep	Nicaragua	USA (United States)	Land Transport	215UNTS69	102911
04 Sep	Brazil	Germany, West	Patents/Copyrights	54WGBB533	425051
04 Sep	Brazil	Germany, West	Claims and Debts	50WBGA212	424052
04 Sep	Iceland	IBRD (World Bank)	IBRD Project	178UNTS275	102344
04 Sep	Nicaragua	IBRD (World Bank)	IBRD Project	186UNTS117	102487
04 Sep	Iceland	IBRD (World Bank)	IBRD Project	188UNTS3	102519
04 Sep	Nicaragua	IBRD (World Bank)	IBRD Project	186UNTS137	102488
05 Sep	Poland	USSR (Soviet Union)	Mass Media	0SUST301	468335
09 Sep	Cambodia	France	Admin Cooperation	59FRRT7	415096
09 Sep	Denmark	Uruguay	Finance	256UNTS149	103625
10 Sep	Belgium	UK Great Britain	Admin Cooperation	183UNTS203	102429
10 Sep	Chile	IBRD (World Bank)	IBRD Project	188UNTS25	102520
10 Sep	IBRD (World Bank)	Turkey	IBRD Project	187UNTS71	102502
10 Sep	Colombia	IBRD (World Bank)	IBRD Project	203UNTS3	102738
11 Sep	Mongolia	USSR (Soviet Union)	Mass Media	0SUST301	468278
14 Sep	Ceylon (Sri Lanka)	Netherlands	Air Transport	193UNTS21	102608
15 Sep	Turkey	USSR (Soviet Union)	Specific Resources	0SUST301	468423
20 Sep	China People's Rep	UK Great Britain	Reparations	53CCJC54	410118
21 Sep	Norway	South Africa	Air Transport	192UNTS105	102597
22 Sep	France	Norway	Taxation	2NORT607	451058
22 Sep	Finland	Norway	Milit Servic/Citiz	183UNTS245	102433
24 Sep	Denmark	Finland	Dispute Settlement	188UNTS283	102532
25 Sep	Panama	IBRD (World Bank)	IBRD Project	188UNTS71	102521
25 Sep	Panama	IBRD (World Bank)	IBRD Project	188UNTS95	102522
26 Sep	Greece	Netherlands	Visas	292UNTS23	104263
26 Sep	Spain	USA (United States)	Milit Assistance	207UNTS83	102801
26 Sep	Spain	USA (United States)	Direct Aid	207UNTS93	102802
26 Sep	Spain	USA (United States)	Milit Assistance	207UNTS61	102800
01 Oct	Korea, South	USA (United States)	General Military	238UNTS199	103363
01 Oct	Multilateral		Commodity Trade	258UNTS153	103677
01 Oct	Brazil	UK Great Britain	Claims and Debts	183UNTS207	102430
03 Oct	Czechoslovakia	Germany, East	Land Transport	4EGDA194	419338
03 Oct	China People's Rep	Hungary	Scientific Project	53CCJC56	410119
05 Oct	China People's Rep	Germany, East	Consul/Citizenship	1EGDA327	419083
05 Oct	Greece	UK Great Britain	Reparations	243UNTS73	103447
06 Oct	Germany, East	Poland	Consul/Citizenship	53PZUM113	458011
06 Oct	Germany, East	Poland	Consul/Citizenship	1EGDA370	419237
06 Oct	Italy	IBRD (World Bank)	IBRD Project	301UNTS135	104344
07 Oct	Iran	Lebanon	General Amity	0IRTB49	433076
07 Oct	UNICEF (Children)	UK Great Britain	Tech Assistance	180UNTS59	102375
09 Oct	Multilateral		Tech Assistance	190UNTS49	102557
10 Oct	Germany, West	Netherlands	Visas	293UNTS115	104288
12 Oct	Greece	USA (United States)	Milit Installation	191UNTS319	102589
13 Oct	Czechoslovakia	Germany, East	Consul/Citizenship	1EGDA422	419339

DATE	PARTY ONE	PARTY TWO	TOPIC	CITATION	NUMBER
1953 (Cont.)					
13 Oct	Iran	USA (United States)	Customs	222UNTS67	103023
13 Oct	Luxembourg	UK Great Britain	Non-ILO Labor	209UNTS87	102825
14 Oct	France	UK Great Britain	Admin Cooperation	186UNTS151	102489
14 Oct	UN Relief Palestin	United Arab Rep	Tech Assistance	190UNTS13	102555
15 Oct	China People's Rep	Poland	Mass Media	53PZUM115	458012
15 Oct	Bulgaria	China People's Rep	Mass Media	53CCJC60	410123
15 Oct	China People's Rep	Hungary	Mass Media	53CCJC57	410120
15 Oct	China People's Rep	Romania	Mass Media	53CCJC59	410122
15 Oct	China People's Rep	Poland	Mass Media	53CCJC58	410121
15 Oct	Japan	IBRD (World Bank)	IBRD Project	187UNTS271	200511
15 Oct	Japan	IBRD (World Bank)	IBRD Project	187UNTS321	200512
15 Oct	Japan	IBRD (World Bank)	IBRD Project	187UNTS367	200513
15 Oct	Denmark	USA (United States)	Patents/Copyrights	215UNTS111	102915
16 Oct	Sweden	Yugoslavia	General Trade	53SOFM1013	461197
16 Oct	Germany, East	Mongolia	Consul/Citizenship	1EGDA482	419211
17 Oct	Germany, East	Romania	Consul/Citizenship	1EGDA457	419287
17 Oct	Bulgaria	Germany, East	Commodity Trade	1EGDA467	419038
17 Oct	Germany, East	Hungary	Consul/Citizenship	1EGDA446	419442
17 Oct	Multilateral		General Transport	184UNTS42	102438
19 Oct	France	Vietnam, South	Admin Cooperation	0VKNG62	496014
19 Oct	Bulgaria	Poland	Gen Communications	53PZUM117	458013
19 Oct	Netherlands	UK Great Britain	Customs	306UNTS99	104435
19 Oct	Libya	UK Great Britain	Admin Cooperation	186UNTS285	102494
19 Oct	Denmark	Greece	General Trade	225UNTS9	103082
19 Oct	Multilateral		IGO Establishment	207UNTS189	102807
20 Oct	Italy	San Marino	Telecommunications	55ITGU45	435328
21 Oct	Denmark	Japan	Patents/Copyrights	0JGJI1171	441076
21 Oct	Jordan	USA (United States)	Direct Aid	222UNTS31	103020
22 Oct	France	Laos	Admin Cooperation	59FRRT7	415259
22 Oct	Chile	Denmark	Milit Servic/Citiz	348UNTS261	105004
22 Oct	Australia	Netherlands	Postal Service	184UNTS193	102448
23 Oct	Japan	USA (United States)	Visas	57JAIL86	440065
23 Oct	Bulgaria	Germany, East	Consul/Citizenship	1EGDA468	419039
26 Oct	Japan	United Nations	IGO Operations	57JAIL86	440066
26 Oct	Albania	Germany, East	Tech Assistance	1EGDA474	419009
26 Oct	Australia	Thailand	Air Transport	255UNTS117	103607
26 Oct	Multilateral		Status of Forces	207UNTS237	102809
26 Oct	Korea, South	Netherlands	Air Transport	200UNTS103	102697
27 Oct	Finland	Turkey	General Trade	55TURG702	466055
27 Oct	Denmark	Sweden	Taxation	198UNTS111	102659
27 Oct	Netherlands	USA (United States)	Tech Assistance	221UNTS357	103017
27 Oct	Denmark	Sweden	Taxation	198UNTS129	102660
27 Oct	Denmark	Sweden	Taxation	198UNTS71	102658
29 Oct	Japan	USA (United States)	Postal Service	57JAIL86	440067
30 Oct	China People's Rep	Germany, East	Health/Educ/Welfare	4EGDA85	419084
30 Oct	China People's Rep	Germany, East	Scientific Project	53CCJC63	410125
30 Oct	Canada	Germany, West	Admin Cooperation	236UNTS317	103332
31 Oct	Austria	Germany, West	Non-ILO Labor	55ABGB248	403058
31 Oct	Austria	Germany, West	Non-ILO Labor	55ABGB74	403061
03 Nov	Chile	Germany, West	Customs	54WGBB631	425080
03 Nov	Netherlands	Switzerland	Customs	293UNTS53	104285
04 Nov	Netherlands	Turkey	Visas	293UNTS3	104280
05 Nov	Albania	Germany, East	Consul/Citizenship	1EGDA478	419010
06 Nov	El Salvador	Spain	Consul/Citizenship	54SPBO508	460094
06 Nov	Bolivia	USA (United States)	Direct Aid	222UNTS41	103021
06 Nov	Luxembourg	Netherlands	Admin Cooperation	198UNTS187	102664
07 Nov	France	Sweden	General Trade	53SOFM1023	461188
07 Nov	Greece	Turkey	General Trade	225UNTS163	103098
07 Nov	Australia	Ceylon (Sri Lanka)	Admin Cooperation	191UNTS249	102585
10 Nov	Japan	USA (United States)	Patents/Copyrights	224UNTS161	103076
11 Nov	Germany, West	Greece	General Economic	53WBGA228	424228
11 Nov	Austria	Yugoslavia	Air Transport	363UNTS149	105206
12 Nov	Austria	Switzerland	Taxation	54SWRO1109	462043
12 Nov	Germany, West	Italy	Patents/Copyrights	56WGBB1883	425289
12 Nov	Canada	USA (United States)	IGO Establishment	234UNTS97	103274

DATE	PARTY ONE	PARTY TWO	TOPIC	CITATION	NUMBER
1953 (Cont.)					
12 Nov	Canada	USA (United States)	General Economic	223UNTS139	103062
12 Nov	Mexico	USA (United States)	Visas	224UNTS187	103077
14 Nov	Italy	Vietnam, South	General Trade	0VKNG63	496015
14 Nov	Netherlands	Vietnam, South	General Trade	0VKNG64	496016
14 Nov	Pakistan	United Arab Rep	Culture	485UNTS55	107046
16 Nov	Norway	Sweden	General Trade	53SOFM1047	461189
17 Nov	Hungary	Sweden	General Economic	53SOFM1049	461190
17 Nov	Belgium	USA (United States)	Milit Assistance	251UNTS105	103536
19 Nov	Nicaragua	USA (United States)	Military Mission	206UNTS117	102787
19 Nov	Australia	Yugoslavia	Admin Cooperation	191UNTS241	102584
19 Nov	Dominican Republic	United Nations	Tech Assistance	180UNTS45	102374
20 Nov	Belgium	Sweden	General Trade	53SOFM1057	461191
20 Nov	Ceylon (Sri Lanka)	Ireland	General Economic	345UNTS189	104967
21 Nov	Japan	UNICEF (Children)	Direct Aid	183UNTS297	200507
23 Nov	China People's Rep	Korea, North	Health/Educ/Welfare	53CCJC66	410126
23 Nov	Germany, West	USA (United States)	Milit Installation	224UNTS107	103071
24 Nov	Czechoslovakia	Switzerland	General Trade	54SWRO745	462157
25 Nov	Israel	USA (United States)	Direct Aid	219UNTS205	102976
26 Nov	Cuba	USA (United States)	Air Transport	205UNTS213	102777
27 Nov	Italy	Sweden	General Trade	53SOFM1063	461192
27 Nov	France	Netherlands	Reparations	302UNTS245	104363
28 Nov	Mongolia	USSR (Soviet Union)	Loans and Credits	16SUGG67	469902
28 Nov	China People's Rep	Germany, East	Culture	53CCJC67	410127
30 Nov	China People's Rep	Indonesia	General Trade	53CCJC68	410128
30 Nov	USA (United States)	Uruguay	General Trade	229UNTS25	103158
02 Dec	India	USSR (Soviet Union)	General Trade	0SUST304	468211
02 Dec	Germany, West	Ireland	General Trade	558UNTS38	108139
02 Dec	India	USSR (Soviet Union)	General Trade	240UNTS143	103402
03 Dec	Greece	Italy	General Economic	53ITDI374	436197
03 Dec	Thailand	USA (United States)	Tech Assistance	213UNTS91	102882
04 Dec	Poland	Turkey	Commodity Trade	55TURG204	466083
04 Dec	France	Norway	Culture	2NORT611	451059
05 Dec	Romania	USSR (Soviet Union)	Specific Property	0SUST304	468385
05 Dec	Romania	USSR (Soviet Union)	Admin Cooperation	0SUST304	468386
05 Dec	Italy	Japan	General Military	53ITDI336	436181
05 Dec	Bulgaria	Greece	General Trade	225UNTS135	103095
05 Dec	Bulgaria	Greece	Finance	225UNTS145	103096
07 Dec	Multilateral		Admin Cooperation	182UNTS51	102422
08 Dec	Netherlands	Spain	General Trade	53NET134	447043
09 Dec	Germany, West	Luxembourg	Extradition	63WBGA47	424418
09 Dec	Austria	Switzerland	Admin Cooperation	54ABGB164	403181
09 Dec	Multilateral		General Economic	249UNTS197	103509
10 Dec	Germany, West	Vietnam, South	General Trade	0VKNG66	496017
11 Dec	Multilateral		Non-ILO Labor	218UNTS255	102958
11 Dec	Multilateral		Education	218UNTS125	102954
11 Dec	Multilateral		Non-ILO Labor	218UNTS153	102956
11 Dec	Multilateral		Sanitation	191UNTS285	102588
11 Dec	Multilateral		Patents/Copyrights	218UNTS27	102952
11 Dec	Multilateral		Non-ILO Labor	218UNTS211	102957
14 Dec	Hungary	Romania	Sanitation	342UNTS151	104906
15 Dec	El Salvador	USA (United States)	Visas	236UNTS25	103314
15 Dec	Denmark	UK Great Britain	Non-ILO Labor	196UNTS105	102620
16 Dec	Indonesia	Japan	Reparations	57JAIL78	440154
16 Dec	Belgium	Cuba	Visas	185UNTS285	102475
17 Dec	Germany, West	Switzerland	Land Transport	54SWRO449	462079
17 Dec	Indonesia	USSR (Soviet Union)	Consul/Citizenship	0SUST304	468220
18 Dec	Germany, West	Yugoslavia	Admin Cooperation	55WBGA36	424320
18 Dec	Brazil	IBRD (World Bank)	IBRD Project	301UNTS229	104346
18 Dec	Cuba	UK Great Britain	General Trade	186UNTS157	102490
18 Dec	Brazil	IBRD (World Bank)	IBRD Project	190UNTS179	102564
19 Dec	Germany, East	Poland	Culture	4EGDA171	419238
19 Dec	Belgium	Germany, West	Visas	185UNTS277	102474
20 Dec	Italy	South Africa	Postal Service	277UNTS293	104014
21 Dec	Germany, East	Romania	Mass Media	4EGDA437	419288
21 Dec	Italy	Netherlands	Visas	189UNTS25	102540

DATE	PARTY ONE	PARTY TWO	TOPIC	CITATION	NUMBER
1953 (Cont.)					
23 Dec	Jordan	Syria	Admin Cooperation	204UNTS207	102759
24 Dec	Belgium	Lebanon	Extradition	539UNTS321	107842
24 Dec	Japan	USA (United States)	Territory Boundary	222UNTS193	103028
24 Dec	Belgium	Lebanon	Air Transport	219UNTS153	102972
26 Dec	USA (United States)	USSR (Soviet Union)	Specif Goods/Equip	0SUST305	468438
28 Dec	France	Italy	Milit Servic/Citiz	267UNTS89	103836
30 Dec	Germany, West	Norway	Customs	2NORT618	451184
30 Dec	Chile	USA (United States)	Tech Assistance	236UNTS41	103315
31 Dec	Mongolia	USSR (Soviet Union)	Specific Property	16SUGG68	469903
31 Dec	France	Switzerland	Taxation	55SWRO138	462050
31 Dec	France	Switzerland	Taxation	55SWRO115	462049
31 Dec	France	Switzerland	Taxation	55SWRO132	462051
31 Dec	Germany, East	USSR (Soviet Union)	Specif Goods/Equip	1EGDA299	419388
31 Dec	UK Great Britain	Yugoslavia	Education	190UNTS335	102574
1954					
04 Jan	Belgium	UK Great Britain	Sanitation	247UNTS47	103459
05 Jan	USA (United States)	Yugoslavia	Direct Aid	234UNTS267	103289
07 Jan	Libya	Netherlands	Air Transport	54NET157	447044
11 Jan	ICJ Option Clause	San Marino	ICJ Option Clause	186UNTS295	102495
11 Jan	Libya	USA (United States)	Direct Aid	229UNTS15	103157
13 Jan	Belgium	Taiwan	Milit Assistance	223UNTS111	103059
14 Jan	Dominican Republic	Spain	General Trade	54SPBO1808	460082
15 Jan	France	San Marino	Consul/Citizenship	56FRJO106	416383
15 Jan	Bolivia	USA (United States)	Tech Assistance	229UNTS213	103168
18 Jan	France	Turkey	Claims and Debts	54TURG1003	466104
18 Jan	Multilateral		IGO Establishment	330UNTS121	104743
19 Jan	France	Turkey	Commodity Trade	55TURG3105	466062
20 Jan	Ethiopia	Greece	Air Transport	222UNTS281	103035
20 Jan	UK Great Britain	USA (United States)	Tech Assistance	196UNTS95	102619
21 Jan	Japan	USA (United States)	Tech Assistance	223UNTS145	103063
22 Jan	Netherlands	USA (United States)	Tech Assistance	190UNTS207	102565
23 Jan	Sweden	USSR (Soviet Union)	Air Transport	0SUST306	468412
23 Jan	Spain	Turkey	Commodity Trade	55TURG204	466087
25 Jan	Pakistan	United Nations	Tech Assistance	185UNTS213	102472
27 Jan	Afghanistan	USSR (Soviet Union)	Loans and Credits	0SUST306	468003
27 Jan	Belgium	Netherlands	Non-ILO Labor	54NET46	447045
27 Jan	Denmark	Yugoslavia	Admin Cooperation	193UNTS181	102615
29 Jan	Japan	UK Great Britain	Finance	190UNTS319	102572
30 Jan	Syria	UK Great Britain	Air Transport	449UNTS47	106452
00 Feb	Czechoslovakia	Poland	Mass Media	54PZUM11	458014
01 Feb	Czechoslovakia	Greece	General Trade	225UNTS77	103091
01 Feb	Czechoslovakia	Greece	Finance	225UNTS95	103092
04 Feb	Brazil	WHO (World Health)	Tech Assistance	233UNTS49	103250
04 Feb	Pakistan	Turkey	General Amity	211UNTS263	102858
05 Feb	Iceland	USSR (Soviet Union)	General Economic	0SUST307	468206
05 Feb	Syria	UK Great Britain	Telecommunications	204UNTS267	102761
05 Feb	Taiwan	United Nations	Tech Assistance	186UNTS85	102485
06 Feb	Finland	USSR (Soviet Union)	Loans and Credits	221UNTS143	103006
06 Feb	ICJ Option Clause	Australia	ICJ Option Clause	186UNTS77	102484
08 Feb	France	Luxembourg	Culture	55FRJO1603	416268
08 Feb	France	Greece	Status of Forces	225UNTS107	103093
08 Feb	France	Greece	Status of Forces	225UNTS121	103094
08 Feb	Belgium	Israel	Extradition	188UNTS251	102528
10 Feb	Ecuador	IBRD (World Bank)	IBRD Project	209UNTS261	102830
11 Feb	El Salvador	Switzerland	General Trade	54SWRO687	462154
11 Feb	Belgium	Finland	Taxation	211UNTS63	102848
11 Feb	Turkey	UK Great Britain	Milit Assistance	190UNTS343	102575
12 Feb	Canada	Italy	Culture	55ITGU53	435074
12 Feb	Germany, West	USA (United States)	Milit Assistance	223UNTS153	103064
16 Feb	France	Sweden	General Transport	228UNTS137	103147
17 Feb	Czechoslovakia	Germany, East	Sanitation	4EGDA302	419340
18 Feb	Dominican Republic	Italy	General Trade	55ITGU124	435105
18 Feb	Canada	Peru	Air Transport	411UNTS64	105915
18 Feb	Multilateral		Other Military	226UNTS297	103124

DATE	PARTY ONE	PARTY TWO	TOPIC	CITATION	NUMBER
1954 (Cont.)					
19 Feb	Japan	United Nations	Status of Forces	0JGJI1162	441077
19 Feb	Japan	United Nations	Status of Forces	0JGJI7	441078
19 Feb	China People's Rep	Poland	General Economic	54CCJC5	410133
19 Feb	Multilateral		Status of Forces	214UNTS51	102899
20 Feb	Bulgaria	Yugoslavia	Territory Boundary	397UNTS13	105700
22 Feb	Multilateral		Other Military	188UNTS273	102531
24 Feb	Spain	Uruguay	Finance	57SPBO2502	460259
24 Feb	Spain	Uruguay	General Trade	57SPBO2502	460260
24 Feb	Spain	Uruguay	General Trade	57SPBO2502	460261
24 Feb	Brazil	IBRD (World Bank)	IBRD Project	301UNTS249	104347
24 Feb	United Arab Rep	USA (United States)	Tech Assistance	236UNTS61	103316
25 Feb	Multilateral		Air Transport	215UNTS249	102922
26 Feb	ICJ Option Clause	Finland	Dispute Settlement	189UNTS223	102546
01 Mar	Multilateral		Admin Cooperation	286UNTS265	104173
01 Mar	Multilateral		Commodity Trade	256UNTS31	103622
02 Mar	Australia	IBRD (World Bank)	IBRD Project	191UNTS103	102579
03 Mar	Lebanon	Switzerland	Air Transport	255UNTS127	103608
03 Mar	Belgium	Germany, West	Admin Cooperation	188UNTS259	102529
03 Mar	Indonesia	Thailand	General Amity	213UNTS297	102893
05 Mar	Israel	Italy	General Trade	55ITGU17	435218
05 Mar	United Nations	Venezuela	Tech Assistance	187UNTS9	102498
08 Mar	Japan	USA (United States)	Direct Aid	232UNTS243	103239
08 Mar	Japan	USA (United States)	Milit Assistance	232UNTS169	103236
08 Mar	Japan	USA (United States)	Milit Assistance	232UNTS215	103237
08 Mar	Japan	USA (United States)	General Economic	232UNTS267	103241
08 Mar	Japan	USA (United States)	Claims and Debts	232UNTS251	103240
08 Mar	Japan	USA (United States)	Direct Aid	232UNTS227	103238
09 Mar	Liberia	United Nations	Tech Assistance	187UNTS61	102501
10 Mar	Guatemala	United Nations	Tech Assistance	191UNTS271	102587
20 Mar	Mexico	UK Great Britain	Consul/Citizenship	331UNTS21	104750
20 Mar	Afghanistan	USA (United States)	Direct Aid	229UNTS7	103156
22 Mar	Cuba	Germany, West	Patents/Copyrights	54WGBB1112	425401
23 Mar	United Arab Rep	USSR (Soviet Union)	Consul/Citizenship	0SUST308	468125
24 Mar	United Nations	Vietnam, South	Tech Assistance	188UNTS345	200514
24 Mar	Finland	South Africa	Admin Cooperation	230UNTS121	103179
24 Mar	Belgium	Norway	Sanitation	219UNTS73	102967
25 Mar	Bulgaria	China People's Rep	General Economic	54CCJC8	410135
25 Mar	Panama	USA (United States)	Specific Property	232UNTS289	103243
25 Mar	ICJ Option Clause	Japan	ICJ Option Clause	188UNTS137	102524
26 Mar	USA (United States)	USSR (Soviet Union)	Milit Assistance	247UNTS263	103475
26 Mar	Australia	Belgium	General Trade	198UNTS305	102673
27 Mar	United Arab Rep	USSR (Soviet Union)	General Trade	0SUST309	468126
27 Mar	United Arab Rep	USSR (Soviet Union)	General Trade	0SUST309	468127
27 Mar	United Arab Rep	USSR (Soviet Union)	Non-ILO Labor	0SUST309	468128
27 Mar	Austria	Denmark	Visas	55ABGB192	403032
29 Mar	Finland	Norway	Taxation	2NORT625	451053
29 Mar	Finland	Norway	Taxation	2NORT623	451051
29 Mar	Finland	Norway	Taxation	2NORT624	451052
29 Mar	Finland	Netherlands	Taxation	252UNTS185	103567
29 Mar	Finland	Netherlands	Taxation	252UNTS239	103568
30 Mar	Cuba	Switzerland	General Trade	54SWRO537	462128
30 Mar	China People's Rep	Germany, East	General Economic	54CCJC12	410138
30 Mar	China People's Rep	Korea, North	Postal Service	54CCJC11	410137
30 Mar	Belgium	Germany, West	Admin Cooperation	190UNTS63	102558
31 Mar	Romania	USSR (Soviet Union)	Finance	0SUST309	468387
31 Mar	Romania	USSR (Soviet Union)	Loans and Credits	0SUST310	468388
31 Mar	Italy	USA (United States)	Milit Assistance	235UNTS293	103311
31 Mar	Peru	Spain	Air Transport	232UNTS65	103230
31 Mar	Japan	Sweden	Claims and Debts	262UNTS187	103744
31 Mar	Canada	Japan	General Trade	236UNTS329	103334
01 Apr	Belgium	Germany, West	Admin Cooperation	190UNTS43	102556
03 Apr	Belgium	Germany, West	Admin Cooperation	190UNTS247	102568
05 Apr	France	Vietnam, South	Admin Cooperation	0VKNG67	496018
05 Apr	Romania	Turkey	General Economic	55TURG1602	466084
06 Apr	Austria	Germany, West	Visas	55ABGB247	403062

DATE	PARTY ONE	PARTY TWO	TOPIC	CITATION	NUMBER
1954 (Cont.)					
06 Apr	Ireland	UK Great Britain	Sanitation	553UNTS197	108088
06 Apr	Mexico	USA (United States)	Tech Assistance	236UNTS69	103317
06 Apr	Mexico	USA (United States)	Non-IBRD Project	233UNTS163	103261
07 Apr	China People's Rep	Mongolia	General Economic	54CCJC14	410139
07 Apr	Austria	Turkey	Visas	55ABGB194	403200
08 Apr	Austria	Switzerland	Taxation	54SWRO1125	462044
08 Apr	Norway	IBRD (World Bank)	IBRD Project	201UNTS131	102714
09 Apr	Austria	Sweden	Visas	55ABGB193	403173
10 Apr	Turkey	Yugoslavia	General Trade	55TURG1602	466098
10 Apr	Austria	Switzerland	Specific Resources	55SWRO741	462035
10 Apr	Denmark	Italy	General Trade	196UNTS175	102623
12 Apr	Peru	IBRD (World Bank)	IBRD Project	190UNTS231	102567
13 Apr	Bulgaria	Czechoslovakia	Admin Cooperation	501UNTS3	107314
13 Apr	Peru	USA (United States)	Tech Assistance	236UNTS87	103318
13 Apr	Norway	USA (United States)	Status of Forces	229UNTS223	103169
15 Apr	Belgium	Germany, West	Admin Cooperation	190UNTS253	102569
16 Apr	Czechoslovakia	Hungary	Specific Resources	504UNTS231	107360
16 Apr	USA (United States)	Yugoslavia	Direct Aid	237UNTS77	103337
16 Apr	Japan	USA (United States)	Taxation	238UNTS39	103354
16 Apr	Japan	USA (United States)	Taxation	238UNTS3	103353
17 Apr	Lebanon	Yugoslavia	Air Transport	602UNTS199	108713
17 Apr	Luxembourg	USA (United States)	Milit Assistance	257UNTS255	103661
19 Apr	China People's Rep	Romania	General Economic	54CCJC16	410140
20 Apr	Germany, West	Italy	Admin Cooperation	55WGBB108	425290
20 Apr	Multilateral		Tech Assistance	189UNTS11	102539
21 Apr	Ethiopia	USA (United States)	Tech Assistance	232UNTS299	103244
21 Apr	Iraq	USA (United States)	Milit Assistance	222UNTS251	103032
22 Apr	Burma	China People's Rep	Finance	54CCJC19	410142
22 Apr	Burma	China People's Rep	General Trade	54CCJC18	410141
22 Apr	Bulgaria	Yugoslavia	Dispute Settlement	397UNTS43	105701
22 Apr	Netherlands	South Africa	Taxation	211UNTS215	102853
23 Apr	Austria	Norway	Visas	2NORT626	451222
23 Apr	Nicaragua	USA (United States)	Milit Assistance	229UNTS37	103159
23 Apr	ECSC (Coal/Steel)	USA (United States)	Loans and Credits	229UNTS229	103170
27 Apr	China People's Rep	Czechoslovakia	General Economic	54CCJC20	410143
27 Apr	Italy	USA (United States)	Milit Assistance	234UNTS103	103275
29 Apr	Finland	USSR (Soviet Union)	Specific Resources	0SUST311	468148
29 Apr	China People's Rep	India	General Economic	54CCJC22	410144
29 Apr	China People's Rep	India	Specif Claim/Waive	54CCJC23	410145
29 Apr	China People's Rep	India	General Trade	299UNTS57	104307
30 Apr	Germany, East	USSR (Soviet Union)	Specif Goods/Equip	4EGDA41	419389
30 Apr	France	Netherlands	Reparations	202UNTS115	102727
30 Apr	Lebanon	USSR (Soviet Union)	General Economic	226UNTS109	103111
01 May	Pakistan	USA (United States)	Mass Media	237UNTS231	103349
03 May	Intgov Eur Migrat	Switzerland	IGO Status/Immunit	56SWRO1213	462192
03 May	Canada	USA (United States)	Milit Assistance	221UNTS339	103015
04 May	Monaco	Netherlands	Admin Cooperation	291UNTS3	104240
05 May	France	South Africa	Air Transport	215UNTS401	102926
06 May	Argentina	Netherlands	General Economic	54NET175	447046
07 May	UNICEF (Children)	Spain	Direct Aid	190UNTS357	200515
07 May	Netherlands	USA (United States)	Milit Assistance	213UNTS325	102895
07 May	Norway	USA (United States)	Milit Assistance	231UNTS157	103215
08 May	India	Pakistan	Extradition	203UNTS167	102745
09 May	Japan	Philippines	Reparations	57JAIL78	440155
10 May	Chile	USA (United States)	Customs	247UNTS299	103477
11 May	France	Switzerland	Land Transport	54SWRO1148	462077
11 May	Panama	USA (United States)	Direct Aid	236UNTS107	103319
12 May	Norway	UK Great Britain	General Trade	2NORT627	451150
12 May	Taiwan	France	General Trade	0CTRC174	413003
12 May	Taiwan	France	Finance	0CTRC178	413004
12 May	Multilateral		Admin Cooperation	327UNTS3	104714
12 May	Norway	Sweden	Visas	198UNTS157	102661
13 May	Israel	USSR (Soviet Union)	Consul/Citizenship	0SUST312	468239
13 May	Ecuador	Germany, West	Visas	57WBGA193	424110
13 May	Austria	Germany, West	General Trade	54WBGA99	424527

DATE	PARTY ONE	PARTY TWO	TOPIC	CITATION	NUMBER
1954 (Cont.)					
13 May	Nepal	WHO (World Health)	Tech Assistance	204UNTS311	200522
13 May	Jordan	USA (United States)	Direct Aid	234UNTS225	103285
13 May	France	Greece	Non-ILO Labor	222UNTS299	103036
14 May	Japan	USA (United States)	Milit Assistance	247UNTS273	103476
14 May	Multilateral		Culture	249UNTS215	103511
14 May	Taiwan	USA (United States)	Milit Installation	231UNTS165	103216
15 May	Greece	Spain	General Trade	299UNTS261	104318
15 May	Greece	Spain	Finance	299UNTS277	104319
15 May	Pakistan	Yugoslavia	General Trade	286UNTS3	104158
19 May	Colombia	Germany, West	Patents/Copyrights	54WBGA184	424367
19 May	Spain	USA (United States)	Tech Assistance	235UNTS87	103296
19 May	Pakistan	USA (United States)	Milit Assistance	202UNTS301	102736
19 May	Greece	Romania	General Trade	225UNTS17	103083
19 May	Greece	Romania	Finance	225UNTS27	103084
20 May	Germany, West	Iceland	General Trade	54WBGA124	424280
20 May	Honduras	USA (United States)	Milit Assistance	222UNTS87	103025
20 May	Mexico	UNICEF (Children)	Direct Aid	192UNTS3	102591
21 May	Denmark	Switzerland	Non-ILO Labor	55SWRO290	462094
21 May	Multilateral		Non-ILO Labor	345UNTS285	104973
22 May	Colombia	USA (United States)	Visas	354UNTS21	105050
22 May	Multilateral		Non-ILO Labor	199UNTS3	102674
22 May	Multilateral		Visas	199UNTS29	102675
24 May	Germany, West	Japan	Admin Cooperation	0JGJI4508	441080
24 May	Honduras	USA (United States)	Milit Installation	433UNTS155	106238
24 May	Australia	Greece	Postal Service	191UNTS255	102586
24 May	Australia	Greece	Visas	193UNTS175	102614
24 May	Australia	Japan	Specif Claim/Waive	191UNTS125	102580
25 May	Germany, West	Norway	Visas	2NORT633	451185
25 May	Austria	Yugoslavia	Specific Resources	227UNTS111	103135
26 May	Mongolia	Poland	Mass Media	54PZUM14	458015
26 May	Liberia	Spain	General Trade	56SPBO2603	460183
26 May	Canada	Spain	General Trade	391UNTS273	105632
26 May	Switzerland	Syria	Air Transport	255UNTS145	103609
26 May	United Nations	Thailand	IGO Status/Immunit	260UNTS35	103703
27 May	Germany, East	Poland	Water Transport	54PZUM16	458016
27 May	Germany, East	Poland	Water Transport	54PZUM22	458017
27 May	Germany, East	Poland	Water Transport	4EGDA193	419240
27 May	Germany, East	Poland	Water Transport	4EGDA175	419239
27 May	Iran	Switzerland	Air Transport	496UNTS273	107257
27 May	Greece	Sweden	Taxation	219UNTS147	102971
28 May	Belgium	Germany, West	Other Military	54WBGA128	424021
28 May	Canada	Portugal	General Trade	391UNTS253	105631
28 May	Belgium	Germany, West	Non-ILO Labor	249UNTS387	103512
28 May	Haiti	USA (United States)	Non-IBRD Project	233UNTS281	103267
29 May	Czechoslovakia	Poland	Postal Service	54PZUM34	458018
29 May	Afghanistan	USA (United States)	Direct Aid	234UNTS3	103268
31 May	Denmark	Japan	Patents/Copyrights	0JGJI1173	441079
31 May	Austria	UK Great Britain	Claims and Debts	54ABGB259	403213
31 May	France	USA (United States)	Milit Assistance	236UNTS141	103321
31 May	Multilateral		Tech Assistance	192UNTS20	102592
31 May	Denmark	Germany, West	Extradition	200UNTS53	102694
31 May	Germany, West	Sweden	Extradition	200UNTS39	102693
01 Jun	Multilateral		Tech Assistance	200UNTS235	200520
01 Jun	Italy	UK Great Britain	Consul/Citizenship	403UNTS275	105798
01 Jun	Italy	UK Great Britain	Admin Cooperation	312UNTS353	104525
01 Jun	Ethiopia	USA (United States)	Direct Aid	232UNTS311	103245
01 Jun	Belgium	South Africa	Culture	201UNTS25	102708
02 Jun	Pakistan	IBRD (World Bank)	IBRD Project	324UNTS59	104678
03 Jun	Argentina	USSR (Soviet Union)	Culture	0SUST316	468019
04 Jun	France	Vietnam, South	General Amity	0VKNG68	496019
04 Jun	Austria	Monaco	Visas	55ABGB215	403140
04 Jun	Multilateral		Customs	282UNTS249	104101
04 Jun	Italy	Netherlands	Non-ILO Labor	289UNTS261	104222
04 Jun	Multilateral		Customs	276UNTS191	103992
05 Jun	Italy	Luxembourg	Reparations	55ITGU162	435263

DATE	PARTY ONE	PARTY TWO	TOPIC	CITATION	NUMBER
1954 (Cont.)					
05 Jun	Greece	Hungary	General Trade	299UNTS285	104320
05 Jun	Greece	Hungary	Finance	299UNTS295	104321
07 Jun	Belgium	France	Admin Cooperation	69FRJO2006	416061
07 Jun	Mexico	USA (United States)	Tech Assistance	234UNTS11	103269
08 Jun	Indonesia	Netherlands	Taxation	54NET92	447047
08 Jun	China People's Rep	Germany, East	Mass Media	4EGDA86	419085
08 Jun	Denmark	USA (United States)	Milit Assistance	307UNTS133	104448
09 Jun	Czechoslovakia	Norway	Claims and Debts	2NORT636	451033
09 Jun	Belgium	France	Visas	0UNTS0	110703
09 Jun	Netherlands	Norway	Finance	287UNTS179	104184
09 Jun	Belgium	Netherlands	Milit Servic/Citiz	216UNTS121	102936
10 Jun	China People's Rep	Germany, East	Mass Media	54CCJC35	410155
10 Jun	France	IBRD (World Bank)	IBRD Project	210UNTS89	102836
12 Jun	Ethiopia	USA (United States)	Tech Assistance	234UNTS25	103270
14 Jun	Multilateral		Air Transport	320UNTS209	104643
14 Jun	Multilateral		Air Transport	320UNTS217	104644
14 Jun	Haiti	Italy	General Economic	267UNTS97	103837
15 Jun	UK Great Britain	USA (United States)	Milit Assistance	236UNTS133	103320
16 Jun	Italy	USA (United States)	Loans and Credits	236UNTS149	103322
16 Jun	Bolivia	USA (United States)	Direct Aid	234UNTS35	103271
17 Jun	China People's Rep	Finland	General Trade	54CCJC36	410156
17 Jun	Jordan	USA (United States)	Direct Aid	266UNTS137	103828
17 Jun	Mexico	USA (United States)	Non-IBRD Project	237UNTS275	103352
17 Jun	Ireland	USA (United States)	Direct Aid	241UNTS173	103432
18 Jun	Chile	Netherlands	Visas	292UNTS37	104265
18 Jun	Lebanon	USA (United States)	Direct Aid	233UNTS177	103262
18 Jun	Luxembourg	UK Great Britain	Reparations	192UNTS33	102593
18 Jun	Australia	Israel	Postal Service	220UNTS29	102985
21 Jun	China People's Rep	Finland	General Trade	54CCJC37	410157
21 Jun	UK Great Britain	USA (United States)	Other Military	209UNTS61	102821
22 Jun	Indonesia	Norway	Finance	2NORT621	451083
22 Jun	Belgium	Israel	Visas	196UNTS245	102627
23 Jun	China People's Rep	Germany, East	Health/Educ/Welfare	2EGDA368	419086
23 Jun	China People's Rep	Germany, East	Scientific Project	54CCJC38	410158
23 Jun	Turkey	USA (United States)	Status of Forces	233UNTS189	103263
23 Jun	Turkey	USA (United States)	Taxation	222UNTS161	103027
23 Jun	Belgium	Greece	Taxation	199UNTS43	102676
24 Jun	Italy	USA (United States)	Tech Assistance	235UNTS3	103290
25 Jun	France	UNESCO (Educ/Cult)	Specific Property	55FRJO1208	416497
26 Jun	Germany, West	Yugoslavia	Water Transport	59WGBB735	425321
28 Jun	Israel	Italy	Dispute Settlement	56ITGU292	435219
28 Jun	Germany, West	Italy	Loans and Credits	288UNTS83	104199
28 Jun	Italy	USA (United States)	Tech Assistance	237UNTS121	103340
28 Jun	Belgium	Netherlands	Territory Boundary	272UNTS235	103942
28 Jun	Chile	USA (United States)	Tech Assistance	233UNTS3	103246
29 Jun	France	USSR (Soviet Union)	Air Transport	0SUST313	468155
29 Jun	Jordan	USA (United States)	Direct Aid	237UNTS111	103339
30 Jun	China People's Rep	Korea, North	General Trade	54CCJC41	410159
30 Jun	Costa Rica	USA (United States)	Tech Assistance	235UNTS35	103294
30 Jun	Colombia	USA (United States)	Non-IBRD Project	237UNTS263	103351
30 Jun	Brazil	USA (United States)	Non-IBRD Project	237UNTS137	103341
30 Jun	Ecuador	USA (United States)	Tech Assistance	236UNTS163	103323
30 Jun	France	Greece	Non-ILO Labor	257UNTS83	103651
30 Jun	Multilateral		Admin Cooperation	204UNTS99	102752
30 Jun	Multilateral		Tech Assistance	193UNTS67	102611
30 Jun	Belgium	Ireland	Air Transport	212UNTS255	102876
01 Jul	Turkey	USA (United States)	Milit Assistance	234UNTS147	103280
02 Jul	France	UNESCO (Educ/Cult)	IGO Status/Immunit	357UNTS3	105103
06 Jul	Cuba	Spain	General Economic	56SPBO1702	460070
06 Jul	Canada	Norway	Privil/Immunities	2NORT637	451017
06 Jul	Ireland	Monaco	Visas	553UNTS117	108076
07 Jul	China People's Rep	Vietnam, North	General Trade	54CCJC44	410161
07 Jul	Laos	Thailand	Air Transport	200UNTS115	102698
07 Jul	Luxembourg	USA (United States)	Milit Assistance	233UNTS23	103247
08 Jul	Multilateral		Finance	287UNTS27	104178

DATE	PARTY ONE	PARTY TWO	TOPIC	CITATION	NUMBER
1954 (Cont.)					
09 Jul	Norway	Sweden	Claims and Debts	2NORT638	451161
09 Jul	Netherlands	Norway	Claims and Debts	54NET187	447048
09 Jul	Ceylon (Sri Lanka)	IBRD (World Bank)	IBRD Project	198UNTS313	200517
09 Jul	France	Netherlands	Finance	287UNTS169	104183
09 Jul	Austria	UK Great Britain	Finance	201UNTS277	102720
09 Jul	Netherlands	UK Great Britain	Finance	199UNTS157	102682
09 Jul	Belgium	UK Great Britain	Finance	201UNTS299	102721
10 Jul	Austria	Italy	Admin Cooperation	55ITGU75	435036
10 Jul	Portugal	UK Great Britain	Finance	199UNTS169	102683
10 Jul	Germany, West	UK Great Britain	Finance	199UNTS135	102680
12 Jul	Ecuador	Spain	Finance	55SPBO1909	460086
12 Jul	Denmark	Mexico	Patents/Copyrights	55MEXD2608	444013
12 Jul	Ecuador	Spain	General Trade	55SPBO1909	460085
12 Jul	Belgium	Italy	Finance	288UNTS59	104198
12 Jul	UK Great Britain	USA (United States)	Tech Assistance	204UNTS123	102753
13 Jul	Austria	Switzerland	Finance	55ABGB42	403184
13 Jul	Greece	Portugal	General Trade	230UNTS19	103173
14 Jul	India	Iran	Sanitation	0IRTB38	433058
15 Jul	Denmark	Italy	Milit Servic/Citiz	250UNTS43	103516
16 Jul	Austria	Italy	Admin Cooperation	67ITGU3	435037
16 Jul	El Salvador	USA (United States)	Non-IBRD Project	237UNTS237	103350
16 Jul	Switzerland	UK Great Britain	Claims and Debts	199UNTS197	102685
17 Jul	Finland	USSR (Soviet Union)	General Trade	240UNTS173	103403
19 Jul	UK Great Britain	USA (United States)	Territory Boundary	250UNTS193	103523
20 Jul	France	Vietnam, South	Peace/Disarmament	0VKNG72	496020
20 Jul	China People's Rep	Poland	Scientific Project	54PZUM50	458019
20 Jul	China People's Rep	Poland	Scientific Project	54CCJC47	410164
21 Jul	Germany, West	Yugoslavia	Patents/Copyrights	55WGBB89	425322
21 Jul	Czechoslovakia	Germany, East	General Economic	2EGDA442	419341
21 Jul	UK Great Britain	USA (United States)	Status of Forces	222UNTS243	103031
22 Jul	Bulgaria	Romania	Sanitation	362UNTS101	105184
22 Jul	Germany, West	USA (United States)	Taxation	239UNTS3	103369
22 Jul	Germany, West	USA (United States)	Taxation	221UNTS351	103016
22 Jul	France	Greece	General Trade	225UNTS199	103099
23 Jul	Denmark	UK Great Britain	Specific Resources	213UNTS313	102894
27 Jul	Germany, West	Norway	Privil/Immunities	2NORT639	451186
27 Jul	Ireland	Luxembourg	Air Transport	232UNTS91	103231
28 Jul	Uruguay	USSR (Soviet Union)	Finance	0SUST315	468442
28 Jul	Sweden	UK Great Britain	Finance	199UNTS181	102684
29 Jul	Multilateral		Sanitation	249UNTS45	103500
29 Jul	India	USA (United States)	Postal Service	239UNTS69	103373
30 Jul	Guatemala	USA (United States)	Milit Assistance	234UNTS235	103286
30 Jul	Mexico	USA (United States)	Sanitation	269UNTS39	103871
30 Jul	Spain	USA (United States)	Milit Assistance	235UNTS45	103295
30 Jul	Greece	USA (United States)	Milit Assistance	234UNTS43	103272
30 Jul	Saudi Arabia	UK Great Britain	Dispute Settlement	201UNTS317	102722
31 Jul	Italy	Japan	Culture	55ITGU286	435182
31 Jul	Germany, West	United Arab Rep	Customs	55WGBB857	425711
31 Jul	Chile	UK Great Britain	Milit Servic/Citiz	618UNTS353	108934
31 Jul	Ethiopia	Greece	Culture	241UNTS319	103439
02 Aug	Germany, East	Poland	Specific Resources	54PZUM53	458020
02 Aug	Germany, East	Poland	Specific Resources	2EGDA426	419241
04 Aug	Canada	South Africa	Postal Service	261UNTS3	103722
06 Aug	Norway	USA (United States)	Air Transport	222UNTS269	103034
06 Aug	Denmark	USA (United States)	Air Transport	222UNTS235	103030
06 Aug	Sweden	USA (United States)	Air Transport	221UNTS331	103014
06 Aug	Norway	USA (United States)	Air Transport	222UNTS261	103033
09 Aug	Multilateral		General Amity	211UNTS237	102855
10 Aug	Indonesia	Netherlands	General Amity	54NET113	447049
11 Aug	Indonesia	Netherlands	Claims and Debts	241UNTS129	103429
11 Aug	Thailand	USA (United States)	Commodity Trade	234UNTS155	103281
11 Aug	Netherlands	UK Great Britain	Non-ILO Labor	248UNTS235	103497
13 Aug	Germany, West	Netherlands	Admin Cooperation	492UNTS305	107200
13 Aug	Netherlands	USA (United States)	Milit Installation	251UNTS91	103535
17 Aug	Germany, West	USA (United States)	Direct Aid	233UNTS31	103248

DATE	PARTY ONE	PARTY TWO	TOPIC	CITATION	NUMBER
1954 (Cont.)					
18 Aug	Greece	USA (United States)	Telecommunications	234UNTS161	103282
19 Aug	Hungary	UK Great Britain	Finance	199UNTS149	102681
19 Aug	Multilateral		Tech Assistance	201UNTS51	102710
20 Aug	USA (United States)	Vietnam, South	Humanitarian	0VKNG74	496021
20 Aug	Brazil	USA (United States)	Commodity Trade	410UNTS79	105898
20 Aug	Philippines	Sweden	Air Transport	200UNTS121	102699
21 Aug	China People's Rep	USSR (Soviet Union)	Mass Media	0SUST315	468086
21 Aug	China People's Rep	USSR (Soviet Union)	Mass Media	54CCJC51	410166
23 Aug	Ceylon (Sri Lanka)	USA (United States)	Mass Media	314UNTS297	104553
23 Aug	Pakistan	USA (United States)	Direct Aid	234UNTS243	103287
24 Aug	Mexico	IBRD (World Bank)	IBRD Project	286UNTS211	104168
24 Aug	Multilateral		Other Military	247UNTS213	103471
26 Aug	South Africa	Switzerland	Air Transport	216UNTS19	102929
26 Aug	New Zealand	UNICEF (Children)	Direct Aid	198UNTS173	102663
26 Aug	USA (United States)	Vietnam, South	Direct Aid	234UNTS111	103276
28 Aug	Germany, West	USA (United States)	Milit Installation	299UNTS377	104325
30 Aug	Denmark	Pakistan	Visas	203UNTS59	102740
31 Aug	France	Germany, West	Admin Cooperation	54FRJO1909	416034
31 Aug	El Salvador	USA (United States)	Non-IBRD Project	237UNTS49	103336
01 Sep	China People's Rep	Indonesia	General Trade	54CCJC54	410168
01 Sep	China People's Rep	Indonesia	Finance	54CCJC55	410169
01 Sep	Thailand	USA (United States)	Claims and Debts	237UNTS209	103347
01 Sep	Guatemala	USA (United States)	Tech Assistance	199UNTS51	102677
02 Sep	Greece	USSR (Soviet Union)	General Trade	230UNTS33	103175
07 Sep	Austria	Denmark	Non-ILO Labor	201UNTS39	102709
08 Sep	Multilateral		Milit Assistance	209UNTS23	102819
09 Sep	Libya	USA (United States)	Direct Aid	238UNTS217	103365
09 Sep	Libya	USA (United States)	Milit Installation	224UNTS217	103078
10 Sep	Belgium	Netherlands	Customs	54NET153	447050
10 Sep	Canada	USA (United States)	Specific Resources	238UNTS97	103355
11 Sep	Greece	Italy	Culture	284UNTS313	104145
13 Sep	Belgium	South Africa	Air Transport	201UNTS15	102707
14 Sep	Austria	Germany, West	Admin Cooperation	57ABGB245	403063
15 Sep	Austria	Switzerland	General Economic	54SWRO1005	462122
15 Sep	Austria	Germany, West	Visas	55WBGA148	424528
16 Sep	France	Vietnam, South	Recognition	59FRRT7	415480
17 Sep	France	South Africa	Air Transport	216UNTS29	102930
23 Sep	El Salvador	USA (United States)	Military Mission	237UNTS91	103338
24 Sep	UK Great Britain	USA (United States)	Milit Installation	300UNTS3	104326
25 Sep	Sweden	Switzerland	Patents/Copyrights	262UNTS205	103746
28 Sep	Multilateral		Refugees	360UNTS117	105158
28 Sep	Multilateral		Reparations	207UNTS293	102812
29 Sep	Finland	Turkey	Visas	59TURG1006	466012
29 Sep	UNESCO (Educ/Cult)	UN Special Fund	IGO Operations	363UNTS367	200572
29 Sep	Sweden	USSR (Soviet Union)	Humanitarian	202UNTS259	102733
30 Sep	France	Norway	Non-ILO Labor	2NORT641	451060
30 Sep	Germany, East	USSR (Soviet Union)	Consul/Citizenship	2EGDA275	419390
30 Sep	Germany, East	USSR (Soviet Union)	Finance	4EGDA42	419391
30 Sep	Denmark	Sweden	Patents/Copyrights	262UNTS199	103745
30 Sep	Switzerland	UK Great Britain	Taxation	209UNTS197	102828
01 Oct	USSR (Soviet Union)	Yugoslavia	General Trade	0SUST316	468465
02 Oct	Pakistan	USA (United States)	Direct Aid	236UNTS187	103324
02 Oct	Multilateral		IBRD Project	201UNTS171	102716
02 Oct	Multilateral		IBRD Project	201UNTS179	102717
04 Oct	Australia	Vietnam, South	Admin Cooperation	0VKNG81	496022
04 Oct	Austria	Germany, West	Admin Cooperation	55WGBB833	425531
04 Oct	Austria	Germany, West	Taxation	55WGBB749	425529
04 Oct	Austria	Germany, West	Taxation	55WGBB755	425530
04 Oct	Australia	Vietnam, South	Admin Cooperation	201UNTS349	102723
05 Oct	Multilateral		Territory Boundary	235UNTS99	103297
06 Oct	Multilateral		Tech Assistance	201UNTS75	102711
09 Oct	Bulgaria	USSR (Soviet Union)	Specific Property	0SUST317	468041
09 Oct	Austria	Turkey	General Aid	56TURG404	466100
11 Oct	Germany, West	Netherlands	Other Military	291UNTS9	104241
12 Oct	China People's Rep	USSR (Soviet Union)	Specific Property	0SUST317	468087

DATE	PARTY ONE	PARTY TWO	TOPIC	CITATION	NUMBER
1954 (Cont.)					
12 Oct	China People's Rep	USSR (Soviet Union)	Tech Assistance	0SUST318	468091
12 Oct	China People's Rep	USSR (Soviet Union)	Health/Educ/Welfare	0SUST318	468088
12 Oct	China People's Rep	USSR (Soviet Union)	General Ad Hoc	0SUST318	468089
12 Oct	China People's Rep	USSR (Soviet Union)	Loans and Credits	0SUST318	468090
12 Oct	China People's Rep	USSR (Soviet Union)	Scientific Project	54CCJC65	410174
12 Oct	China People's Rep	USSR (Soviet Union)	General Amity	226UNTS69	103109
12 Oct	El Salvador	IBRD (World Bank)	IBRD Project	203UNTS37	102739
12 Oct	China People's Rep	USSR (Soviet Union)	General Amity	226UNTS57	103108
12 Oct	China People's Rep	USSR (Soviet Union)	Milit Installation	226UNTS51	103107
12 Oct	Belgium	USA (United States)	Patents/Copyrights	202UNTS289	102735
13 Oct	Ethiopia	Sweden	Tech Assistance	202UNTS273	102734
14 Oct	Albania	China People's Rep	Scientific Project	54CCJC70	410177
14 Oct	Albania	China People's Rep	Culture	54CCJC71	410178
14 Oct	China People's Rep	India	Privil/Immunities	54CCJC73	410180
14 Oct	China People's Rep	India	General Trade	54CCJC74	410181
14 Oct	China People's Rep	India	General Trade	54CCJC72	410179
14 Oct	Austria	UK Great Britain	Claims and Debts	204UNTS87	102751
15 Oct	Czechoslovakia	Germany, East	Water Transport	4EGDA308	419342
15 Oct	Germany, West	USA (United States)	Milit Assistance	239UNTS135	103375
15 Oct	Belgium	France	Admin Cooperation	218UNTS19	102951
16 Oct	Iraq	Netherlands	Air Transport	55NET23	447051
16 Oct	Germany, East	India	General Economic	2EGDA521	419125
16 Oct	Germany, East	India	Tech Assistance	2EGDA521	419126
18 Oct	Ireland	Norway	Taxation	553UNTS123	108077
18 Oct	Ireland	Sweden	Taxation	262UNTS259	103753
18 Oct	USA (United States)	Yugoslavia	Milit Assistance	273UNTS163	103951
18 Oct	Germany, West	UK Great Britain	Taxation	218UNTS301	102960
18 Oct	Denmark	Ireland	Taxation	218UNTS295	102959
19 Oct	United Arab Rep	UK Great Britain	Milit Installation	221UNTS227	103008
19 Oct	United Arab Rep	UK Great Britain	General Amity	210UNTS3	102833
19 Oct	Canada	UK Great Britain	Milit Assistance	214UNTS309	102906
20 Oct	Denmark	Philippines	Air Transport	216UNTS3	102927
20 Oct	Norway	Philippines	Air Transport	216UNTS11	102928
21 Oct	France	India	Specific Property	62FRRT33	415229
21 Oct	India	USA (United States)	Patents/Copyrights	234UNTS119	103277
22 Oct	NATO (North Atlan)	USA (United States)	IGO Establishment	249UNTS175	103507
23 Oct	France	Germany, West	Territory Boundary	55WGBB295	425140
23 Oct	France	Germany, West	Extradition	57WBGA225	424141
23 Oct	France	Germany, West	Other Military	58WBGA64	424143
23 Oct	France	Germany, West	Culture	55WGBB885	425142
23 Oct	Germany, East	Hungary	General Economic	2EGDA448	419443
23 Oct	Multilateral		Milit Occupation	332UNTS157	104761
23 Oct	Multilateral		Reparations	332UNTS219	104762
23 Oct	Multilateral		Status of Forces	332UNTS387	104763
23 Oct	Multilateral		Milit Occupation	331UNTS253	104758
23 Oct	Multilateral		Status of Forces	334UNTS3	104765
23 Oct	Multilateral		Milit Occupation	331UNTS327	104759
23 Oct	Multilateral		Status of Forces	332UNTS3	104760
25 Oct	Germany, West	Switzerland	Extradition	55SWRO25	462007
25 Oct	Japan	Mexico	Culture	0JGJI1250	441082
25 Oct	Austria	Chile	Visas	55ABGB173	403019
25 Oct	Peru	USA (United States)	Direct Aid	238UNTS247	103368
25 Oct	Iran	UK Great Britain	Finance	204UNTS131	102754
26 Oct	Taiwan	USA (United States)	Direct Aid	0CTRC823	413041
26 Oct	Netherlands	Venezuela	Air Transport	232UNTS103	103232
27 Oct	Germany, West	USA (United States)	Admin Cooperation	234UNTS131	103278
27 Oct	Multilateral		Tech Assistance	201UNTS95	102712
27 Oct	Israel	Luxembourg	Visas	226UNTS241	103117
28 Oct	Canada	Ireland	Taxation	304UNTS317	104406
28 Oct	Canada	Ireland	Taxation	305UNTS3	104407
28 Oct	Denmark	Sweden	Sanitation	262UNTS211	103747
29 Oct	Germany, West	USA (United States)	General Amity	273UNTS3	103943
29 Oct	Germany, West	Netherlands	Non-ILO Labor	237UNTS3	103335
29 Oct	Multilateral		Tech Assistance	201UNTS115	102713
29 Oct	Sweden	UK Great Britain	Visas	209UNTS75	102823

DATE	PARTY ONE	PARTY TWO	TOPIC	CITATION	NUMBER
1954 (Cont.)					
30 Oct	United Arab Rep	USA (United States)	Direct Aid	234UNTS139	103279
01 Nov	Belgium	Yugoslavia	Non-ILO Labor	251UNTS123	103538
01 Nov	Greece	Netherlands	General Trade	223UNTS79	103057
02 Nov	Austria	Yugoslavia	Patents/Copyrights	55ABGB199	403229
02 Nov	Bulgaria	Yugoslavia	Patents/Copyrights	375UNTS333	105371
03 Nov	Burma	China People's Rep	Commodity Trade	54CCJC77	410184
03 Nov	Libya	USA (United States)	Direct Aid	238UNTS227	103366
03 Nov	Belgium	Germany, West	Admin Cooperation	201UNTS359	102724
04 Nov	Germany, West	Mexico	Patents/Copyrights	55WGBB903	425477
04 Nov	Germany, West	Iran	Direct Aid	56WGBB2091	425271
05 Nov	Germany, East	Poland	Land Transport	4EGDA204	419242
05 Nov	Austria	Finland	Visas	56ABGB47	403045
05 Nov	France	Sweden	Taxation	262UNTS229	103748
05 Nov	Burma	Japan	Reparations	251UNTS215	103543
05 Nov	Burma	Japan	Peace/Disarmament	251UNTS201	103542
05 Nov	Belgium	UK Great Britain	Visas	209UNTS69	102822
06 Nov	Hungary	USSR (Soviet Union)	Finance	0SUST319	468197
06 Nov	United Arab Rep	USA (United States)	Tech Assistance	237UNTS183	103344
08 Nov	Austria	IBRD (World Bank)	IBRD Project	216UNTS305	200528
10 Nov	Austria	Yugoslavia	Water Transport	56ABGB118	403230
10 Nov	Greece	Italy	General Trade	227UNTS9	103128
11 Nov	Poland	UK Great Britain	Finance	204UNTS137	102755
12 Nov	Belgium	France	Reparations	306UNTS85	104434
12 Nov	Peru	IBRD (World Bank)	IBRD Project	209UNTS287	102831
15 Nov	Turkey	USA (United States)	Commodity Trade	238UNTS135	103358
16 Nov	Finland	UK Great Britain	Visas	204UNTS177	102756
17 Nov	Austria	Netherlands	Non-ILO Labor	292UNTS45	104266
17 Nov	Ceylon (Sri Lanka)	United Arab Rep	General Trade	315UNTS3	104554
17 Nov	Korea, South	USA (United States)	Milit Assistance	256UNTS251	103635
18 Nov	Portugal	UK Great Britain	Territory Boundary	325UNTS307	104706
18 Nov	Portugal	UK Great Britain	Territory Boundary	210UNTS265	102841
19 Nov	Mongolia	USSR (Soviet Union)	General Trade	0SUST319	468279
19 Nov	France	Spain	General Trade	55SPBO1301	460104
19 Nov	India	IBRD (World Bank)	IBRD Project	309UNTS159	104473
19 Nov	Japan	USA (United States)	Milit Installation	238UNTS207	103364
19 Nov	Mexico	USA (United States)	Non-ILO Labor	238UNTS237	103367
19 Nov	Portugal	UK Great Britain	Culture	226UNTS305	103125
22 Nov	USA (United States)	Vietnam, South	Patents/Copyrights	235UNTS11	103291
22 Nov	France	South Africa	Taxation	219UNTS35	102963
23 Nov	Belgium	USA (United States)	Tech Assistance	235UNTS19	103292
23 Nov	Belgium	Germany, West	Admin Cooperation	202UNTS109	102726
23 Nov	Portugal	UK Great Britain	Visas	204UNTS183	102757
24 Nov	Portugal	UK Great Britain	Visas	313UNTS125	104533
24 Nov	Brazil	Italy	Dispute Settlement	284UNTS325	104146
25 Nov	Australia	Poland	Postal Service	521UNTS281	107526
26 Nov	Bulgaria	Switzerland	General Economic	54SWRO1171	462123
26 Nov	Lebanon	UN Relief Palestin	Direct Aid	202UNTS123	102728
27 Nov	Spain	Switzerland	General Economic	55SPBO1001	460251
27 Nov	France	Germany, West	Visas	55WBGA34	424144
27 Nov	Austria	Yugoslavia	Specific Resources	396UNTS75	105694
29 Nov	Multilateral		General Trade	287UNTS209	104187
29 Nov	Ethiopia	UK Great Britain	Status of Forces	207UNTS283	102811
01 Dec	Guatemala	USA (United States)	Visas	237UNTS161	103342
01 Dec	Multilateral		Admin Cooperation	210UNTS197	102839
02 Dec	Iran	USSR (Soviet Union)	Territory Boundary	0SUST320	468228
02 Dec	Germany, West	Switzerland	General Trade	54SWRO1291	462112
02 Dec	Iran	USSR (Soviet Union)	Finance	0SUST320	468227
02 Dec	Iran	USSR (Soviet Union)	Admin Cooperation	0IRTB74	433115
02 Dec	Iran	USSR (Soviet Union)	Territory Boundary	451UNTS227	106497
02 Dec	Multilateral		General Amity	226UNTS153	103112
03 Dec	Albania	China People's Rep	Loans and Credits	54CCJC80	410187
03 Dec	Albania	China People's Rep	General Economic	54CCJC79	410186
04 Dec	India	Netherlands	Reparations	289UNTS221	104219
06 Dec	Ecuador	Spain	Culture	56SPBO706	460088
06 Dec	France	Norway	Milit Servic/Citiz	202UNTS313	102737
09 Dec	Belgium	Greece	Culture	257UNTS243	103660
09 Dec	Taiwan	El Salvador	General Amity	214UNTS217	102900
10 Dec	Liechtenstein	Switzerland	Non-ILO Labor	55SWRO537	462186
10 Dec	Germany, West	Spain	Culture	56SPBO2503	460003
10 Dec	Iceland	USA (United States)	Milit Assistance	237UNTS191	103345
10 Dec	Taiwan	USA (United States)	General Military	248UNTS213	103496
13 Dec	Guatemala	USA (United States)	Direct Aid	237UNTS169	103343
13 Dec	Pakistan	United Arab Rep	Air Transport	255UNTS167	103610
14 Dec	Austria	Portugal	Visas	55ABGB175	403155
14 Dec	Netherlands	Portugal	Visas	289UNTS121	104216
14 Dec	Netherlands	USA (United States)	Milit Assistance	262UNTS35	103737
14 Dec	Belgium	IBRD (World Bank)	IBRD Project	210UNTS113	102837
14 Dec	Belgium	Israel	Admin Cooperation	220UNTS49	102987
14 Dec	Ecuador	Netherlands	Air Transport	232UNTS115	103233
15 Dec	France	Netherlands	Reparations	288UNTS37	104195
15 Dec	India	Iran	General Economic	327UNTS245	104724
15 Dec	Denmark	USA (United States)	Air Transport	213UNTS273	102890
16 Dec	France	Germany, West	Visas	55WBGA41	424145
16 Dec	Austria	Yugoslavia	Admin Cooperation	55ABGB224	403232
16 Dec	China People's Rep	Mongolia	General Trade	54CCJC85	410190
16 Dec	Austria	Yugoslavia	Territory Boundary	56ABGB119	403231
16 Dec	Multilateral		Tech Assistance	204UNTS323	200523
16 Dec	Belgium	Greece	Claims and Debts	223UNTS73	103056
17 Dec	France	Spain	Mass Media	55SPBO2101	460105
17 Dec	Sweden	Switzerland	Non-ILO Labor	369UNTS233	105260
18 Dec	Italy	Yugoslavia	Peace/Disarmament	284UNTS239	104141
19 Dec	Multilateral		Culture	218UNTS139	102955
19 Dec	Multilateral		Patents/Copyrights	218UNTS51	102953
20 Dec	Australia	Austria	Postal Service	205UNTS157	102775
21 Dec	Spain	UK Great Britain	General Trade	55SPBO301	460238
21 Dec	Iceland	Spain	General Trade	55SPBO401	460165
21 Dec	Multilateral		General Amity	258UNTS322	103678
22 Dec	USA (United States)	USSR (Soviet Union)	Milit Assistance	251UNTS41	103532
22 Dec	UK Great Britain	Yugoslavia	Claims and Debts	207UNTS227	102808
22 Dec	Sweden	USA (United States)	Air Transport	228UNTS85	103143
24 Dec	Italy	Netherlands	Non-ILO Labor	55NET26	447052
24 Dec	China People's Rep	Vietnam, North	Telecommunications	54CCJC88	410192
24 Dec	China People's Rep	Vietnam, North	Direct Aid	54CCJC90	410194
24 Dec	China People's Rep	Vietnam, North	Postal Service	54CCJC86	410191
27 Dec	China People's Rep	Germany, East	Education	2EGDA407	419087
27 Dec	China People's Rep	Germany, East	Education	54CCJC95	410199
28 Dec	Korea, North	USSR (Soviet Union)	Telecommunications	0SUST321	468252
28 Dec	Korea, North	USSR (Soviet Union)	Postal Service	0SUST321	468251
28 Dec	Germany, West	Switzerland	Extradition	55WBGA19	424755
28 Dec	China People's Rep	Hungary	Sanitation	54CCJC96	410200
28 Dec	Iceland	Netherlands	Finance	287UNTS159	104182
29 Dec	Cambodia	Vietnam, South	Water Transport	0VKNG85	496023
29 Dec	Laos	Vietnam, South	Water Transport	0VKNG85	496026
29 Dec	Colombia	IBRD (World Bank)	IBRD Project	211UNTS135	102851
30 Dec	France	Vietnam, South	General Economic	0VKNG85	496024
30 Dec	France	Vietnam, South	Status of Forces	0VKNG85	496025
30 Dec	Indonesia	Switzerland	General Trade	55SWRO64	462141
30 Dec	China People's Rep	USSR (Soviet Union)	Air Transport	0SUST321	468092
30 Dec	Brazil	Spain	General Economic	55SPBO2201	460056
30 Dec	Germany, East	Korea, North	Finance	4EGDA505	419171
30 Dec	China People's Rep	USSR (Soviet Union)	Air Transport	54CCJC99	410202
30 Dec	Norway	Switzerland	Air Transport	311UNTS147	104502
31 Dec	Norway	Spain	General Trade	55SPBO2101	460202
31 Dec	Peru	USA (United States)	Non-ILO Labor	251UNTS51	103533
31 Dec	Israel	South Africa	Postal Service	220UNTS11	102984
31 Dec	UK Great Britain	Yugoslavia	Education	209UNTS81	102824
31 Dec	Netherlands	UNICEF (Children)	Direct Aid	202UNTS135	102729
1955					
04 Jan	Japan	USA (United States)	Specif Claim/Waive	237UNTS197	103346

DATE	PARTY ONE	PARTY TWO	TOPIC	CITATION	NUMBER
1955 (Cont.)					
05 Jan	USSR (Soviet Union)	Yugoslavia	General Trade	0SUST322	468466
05 Jan	Austria	Switzerland	Extradition	55SWR061	462009
05 Jan	USSR (Soviet Union)	Yugoslavia	General Trade	240UNTS207	103404
05 Jan	USSR (Soviet Union)	Yugoslavia	Finance	240UNTS225	103405
05 Jan	USA (United States)	Yugoslavia	US Agri Commod Aid	251UNTS29	103531
05 Jan	Mexico	ILO (Labor Org)	IGO Status/Immunit	208UNTS225	102815
05 Jan	Switzerland	United Arab Rep	Taxation	216UNTS41	102931
07 Jan	Austria	Belgium	Air Transport	380UNTS219	105458
07 Jan	Peru	USA (United States)	Milit Assistance	261UNTS321	103730
08 Jan	France	Italy	Patents/Copyrights	57ITGU68	435138
08 Jan	France	Italy	Patents/Copyrights	57ITGU137	435137
10 Jan	USSR (Soviet Union)	Yugoslavia	Air Transport	0SUST322	468468
10 Jan	USSR (Soviet Union)	Yugoslavia	Air Transport	0SUST322	468467
10 Jan	Belgium	Brazil	Admin Cooperation	272UNTS181	103937
10 Jan	Norway	Sweden	Patents/Copyrights	204UNTS293	102764
11 Jan	Pakistan	USA (United States)	Milit Assistance	251UNTS111	103537
12 Jan	France	Italy	Specific Resources	56ITGU13	435141
12 Jan	France	Italy	Consul/Citizenship	58ITGU99	435139
12 Jan	France	Italy	Admin Cooperation	57ITGU87	435140
12 Jan	Algeria	Italy	Admin Cooperation	57ITGU87	435009
12 Jan	Canada	Japan	Air Transport	311UNTS167	104503
13 Jan	Belgium	Netherlands	Visas	210UNTS63	102834
14 Jan	Chile	USA (United States)	Mass Media	238UNTS191	103362
17 Jan	Turkey	UK Great Britain	Finance	204UNTS195	102758
18 Jan	United Arab Rep	Philippines	General Amity	3PTS399	465034
18 Jan	Austria	Yugoslavia	Mass Media	378UNTS31	105416
18 Jan	Pakistan	USA (United States)	US Agri Commod Aid	239UNTS61	103372
18 Jan	Pakistan	USA (United States)	Direct Aid	241UNTS53	103423
20 Jan	China People's Rep	Romania	General Economic	55CCJC3	410210
20 Jan	Denmark	UK Great Britain	Milit Servic/Citiz	210UNTS303	102842
21 Jan	Japan	Switzerland	Claims and Debts	55SWR0357	462170
24 Jan	Spain	Uruguay	Customs	55SPBO1902	460262
24 Jan	India	USSR (Soviet Union)	Non-IBRD Project	0SUST322	468212
24 Jan	Finland	USSR (Soviet Union)	Loans and Credits	240UNTS243	103406
25 Jan	Romania	USSR (Soviet Union)	Air Transport	0SUST323	468389
25 Jan	Panama	USA (United States)	General Ad Hoc	243UNTS211	103454
26 Jan	Iran	Italy	General Trade	57ITGU149	435208
26 Jan	Italy	USA (United States)	Air Transport	238UNTS179	103361
27 Jan	Belgium	Spain	General Economic	55SPBO2302	460044
27 Jan	Germany, East	Korea, North	Tech Assistance	4EGDA507	419172
27 Jan	Bulgaria	China People's Rep	General Economic	55CCJC6	410212
27 Jan	Chile	USA (United States)	US Agri Commod Aid	262UNTS3	103735
28 Jan	Czechoslovakia	Germany, East	Mass Media	4EGDA320	419343
28 Jan	Haiti	USA (United States)	Milit Assistance	270UNTS83	103894
29 Jan	Italy	Turkey	General Aid	56TURG202	466109
29 Jan	Korea, South	USA (United States)	Milit Assistance	239UNTS53	103371
31 Jan	Philippines	UK Great Britain	Air Transport	216UNTS51	102932
01 Feb	Finland	Ireland	Visas	553UNTS45	108067
02 Feb	Germany, West	Switzerland	Non-ILO Labor	55SWR0315	462008
02 Feb	Germany, West	Switzerland	Non-ILO Labor	55WBGA48	424756
04 Feb	Bulgaria	Germany, East	General Transport	58EGDZ172	420040
05 Feb	Bulgaria	Germany, East	Culture	58EGDZ172	420041
05 Feb	Austria	Italy	Specific Resources	56ABGB42	403117
07 Feb	Peru	USA (United States)	Direct Aid	241UNTS63	103424
08 Feb	Japan	Turkey	General Economic	56TURG301	466078
09 Feb	USA (United States)	Yugoslavia	Direct Aid	241UNTS13	103419
10 Feb	Greece	Turkey	Visas	55TURG1402	466015
10 Feb	Australia	Hungary	Postal Service	207UNTS173	102806
11 Feb	Italy	USA (United States)	Direct Aid	241UNTS91	103426
11 Feb	Italy	USA (United States)	Milit Assistance	240UNTS87	103396
12 Feb	China People's Rep	USSR (Soviet Union)	General Trade	16SUGG68	469904
12 Feb	China People's Rep	USSR (Soviet Union)	General Trade	55CCJC10	410215
14 Feb	Iraq	Spain	Culture	57SPBO1502	460164
15 Feb	Iran	USSR (Soviet Union)	Commodity Trade	0SUST323	468229
16 Feb	Belgium	Netherlands	Refugees	211UNTS49	102846

DATE	PARTY ONE	PARTY TWO	TOPIC	CITATION	NUMBER
1955 (Cont.)					
17 Feb	France	Spain	Specific Resources	55SPBO1503	460106
18 Feb	Poland	USSR (Soviet Union)	Air Transport	0SUST323	468336
18 Feb	Poland	USSR (Soviet Union)	Air Transport	55PZUM9	458021
18 Feb	Austria	Netherlands	Finance	55NET95	447053
18 Feb	Germany, West	USA (United States)	Milit Assistance	247UNTS257	103474
20 Feb	United Arab Rep	Yugoslavia	Air Transport	255UNTS199	103611
21 Feb	Portugal	Spain	General Economic	55SPBO2803	460229
21 Feb	Germany, East	Poland	General Economic	2EGDA431	419244
22 Feb	South Africa	USA (United States)	Air Transport	247UNTS247	103473
23 Feb	Bulgaria	Turkey	General Economic	56TURG202	466047
24 Feb	Greece	UK Great Britain	Specif Claim/Waive	209UNTS187	102827
24 Feb	Iraq	Turkey	General Military	233UNTS199	103264
26 Feb	Costa Rica	USA (United States)	Claims and Debts	252UNTS129	103562
02 Mar	Iraq	USA (United States)	Non-IBRD Project	250UNTS229	103526
02 Mar	Multilateral		IGO Establishment	225UNTS233	103101
02 Mar	Israel	Sweden	Visas	220UNTS105	102995
02 Mar	Israel	USA (United States)	Visas	220UNTS113	102996
05 Mar	France	Sweden	Consul/Citizenship	427UNTS133	106150
05 Mar	Netherlands	Vietnam, South	Patents/Copyrights	288UNTS53	104197
07 Mar	USA (United States)	Vietnam, South	Direct Aid	277UNTS285	104013
07 Mar	United Arab Rep	USA (United States)	Mass Media	252UNTS159	103565
07 Mar	Greece	UK Great Britain	General Military	211UNTS249	102856
08 Mar	Germany, West	Lebanon	Patents/Copyrights	55WGBB897	425404
09 Mar	Mexico	USA (United States)	Tech Assistance	263UNTS247	103776
10 Mar	Austria	Bulgaria	Water Transport	56ABGB140	403010
10 Mar	WMO (Meteorology)	Switzerland	IGO Status/Immunit	211UNTS277	200524
12 Mar	Multilateral		Land Transport	211UNTS3	102844
12 Mar	Greece	Japan	General Trade	227UNTS33	103130
14 Mar	India	IBRD (World Bank)	IBRD Project	309UNTS129	104472
15 Mar	France	Spain	General Trade	55SPBO304	460107
15 Mar	Taiwan	Japan	Air Transport	0CTRC281	413013
15 Mar	IBRD (World Bank)	UK Great Britain	IBRD Project	265UNTS85	103808
16 Mar	Bulgaria	Yugoslavia	General Economic	397UNTS83	105702
16 Mar	Peru	USA (United States)	Claims and Debts	252UNTS151	103564
18 Mar	Austria	Norway	Finance	2NORT650	451223
18 Mar	Germany, West	Norway	Extradition	209UNTS309	102832
18 Mar	Australia	IBRD (World Bank)	IBRD Project	220UNTS131	102998
19 Mar	Multilateral		Sanitation	228UNTS95	103144
21 Mar	China People's Rep	Poland	General Economic	55CCJC16	410221
21 Mar	Netherlands	USA (United States)	Telecommunications	289UNTS129	104217
21 Mar	Honduras	USA (United States)	Direct Aid	253UNTS3	103572
21 Mar	El Salvador	USA (United States)	Non-IBRD Project	250UNTS261	103528
21 Mar	Canada	South Africa	Commodity Trade	213UNTS291	102892
22 Mar	Australia	Taiwan	Postal Service	209UNTS3	102818
23 Mar	Bulgaria	China People's Rep	Scientific Project	55CCJC18	410222
23 Mar	Iraq	United Arab Rep	Air Transport	311UNTS199	104504
23 Mar	Guatemala	USA (United States)	Claims and Debts	252UNTS143	103563
24 Mar	Finland	IBRD (World Bank)	IBRD Project	211UNTS305	200525
24 Mar	Colombia	IBRD (World Bank)	IBRD Project	212UNTS217	102874
26 Mar	Italy	Yugoslavia	Sanitation	379UNTS3	105432
28 Mar	Albania	Germany, East	Consul/Citizenship	2EGDA477	419011
29 Mar	Ecuador	USA (United States)	Claims and Debts	261UNTS343	103732
30 Mar	Germany, West	New Zealand	Admin Cooperation	271UNTS207	103916
30 Mar	Italy	USA (United States)	Taxation	257UNTS169	103654
30 Mar	Italy	USA (United States)	Taxation	257UNTS199	103655
30 Mar	Israel	Luxembourg	Visas	226UNTS247	103118
31 Mar	France	Spain	General Trade	55SPBO105	460108
31 Mar	France	Spain	Mass Media	55SPBO105	460109
31 Mar	Italy	Yugoslavia	General Trade	57ITGU32	435230
31 Mar	Germany, West	India	General Trade	55WBGA174	424252
31 Mar	Italy	Yugoslavia	General Trade	57ITGU32	435229
31 Mar	Czechoslovakia	Germany, East	Postal Service	4EGDA267	419344
31 Mar	Italy	Yugoslavia	Visas	386UNTS307	105550
31 Mar	Italy	Yugoslavia	General Trade	386UNTS317	105551
31 Mar	Chile	USA (United States)	Education	262UNTS19	103736

DATE	PARTY ONE	PARTY TWO	TOPIC	CITATION	NUMBER
1955 (Cont.)					
31 Mar	Argentina	UK Great Britain	General Economic	210UNTS223	102840
01 Apr	Guatemala	Switzerland	General Trade	55SWRO407	462137
01 Apr	Hungary	Netherlands	General Trade	55NET62	447054
01 Apr	China People's Rep	India	Specific Property	55CCJC20	410223
01 Apr	Austria	Liechtenstein	Admin Cooperation	56ABGB212	403124
01 Apr	Austria	Liechtenstein	Admin Cooperation	56ABGB213	403123
01 Apr	Ceylon (Sri Lanka)	Germany, West	General Trade	369UNTS57	105251
01 Apr	Haiti	USA (United States)	Direct Aid	261UNTS361	103734
01 Apr	Australia	Czechoslovakia	Postal Service	213UNTS199	102888
04 Apr	Germany, West	USA (United States)	Milit Assistance	279UNTS73	104034
04 Apr	Denmark	Israel	Taxation	213UNTS283	102891
04 Apr	Multilateral		Tech Assistance	208UNTS239	102816
04 Apr	Iraq	UK Great Britain	General Military	233UNTS118	103265
04 Apr	Belgium	Luxembourg	Refugees	211UNTS57	102847
05 Apr	Brazil	UK Great Britain	Milit Servic/Citiz	403UNTS139	105793
05 Apr	Chile	USA (United States)	Direct Aid	250UNTS253	103527
05 Apr	Haiti	USA (United States)	Milit Assistance	270UNTS97	103895
05 Apr	Peru	IBRD (World Bank)	IBRD Project	211UNTS115	102850
06 Apr	China People's Rep	Czechoslovakia	General Economic	55CCJC21	410224
06 Apr	China People's Rep	Czechoslovakia	General Trade	55CCJC22	410225
06 Apr	Norway	USA (United States)	General Military	269UNTS65	103874
06 Apr	Multilateral		General Amity	261UNTS55	103725
06 Apr	Japan	Thailand	Culture	230UNTS219	103187
07 Apr	Japan	USA (United States)	Tech Assistance	263UNTS285	103778
10 Apr	Italy	Turkey	Commodity Trade	56TURG409	466076
14 Apr	Bulgaria	Germany, East	General Economic	2EGDA462	419043
14 Apr	Germany, West	USA (United States)	General Military	263UNTS351	103782
15 Apr	Belgium	Turkey	General Economic	58TURG2903	466046
15 Apr	Austria	USSR (Soviet Union)	General Ad Hoc	0SUST325	468053
15 Apr	Taiwan	France	General Economic	0CTRC183	413021
15 Apr	Taiwan	USA (United States)	Air Transport	0CTRC827	413042
15 Apr	China People's Rep	Japan	Territory Boundary	55CCJC25	410227
15 Apr	China People's Rep	Japan	Specif Claim/Waive	55CCJC26	410228
15 Apr	China People's Rep	Japan	Specific Resources	55CCJC24	410226
15 Apr	India	Pakistan	Land Transport	247UNTS25	103458
15 Apr	Belgium	Israel	Visas	211UNTS43	102845
19 Apr	Norway	IBRD (World Bank)	IBRD Project	211UNTS159	102852
19 Apr	Peru	IBRD (World Bank)	IBRD Project	221UNTS153	103007
20 Apr	Italy	Spain	Mass Media	55SPBO505	460169
20 Apr	Spain	USA (United States)	US Agri Commod Aid	239UNTS117	103374
21 Apr	Taiwan	WHO (World Health)	Tech Assistance	210UNTS71	102835
22 Apr	Romania	USSR (Soviet Union)	Atomic Energy	0SUST326	468390
22 Apr	China People's Rep	Indonesia	Consul/Citizenship	55CCJC28	410230
22 Apr	Belgium	San Marino	Non-ILO Labor	253UNTS41	103574
22 Apr	Dominican Republic	USA (United States)	Milit Assistance	239UNTS325	103389
23 Apr	Czechoslovakia	USSR (Soviet Union)	Atomic Energy	0SUST326	468110
23 Apr	Poland	USSR (Soviet Union)	Atomic Energy	0SUST326	468337
23 Apr	USA (United States)	Vietnam, South	Milit Assistance	277UNTS279	104012
24 Apr	China People's Rep	Germany, East	General Economic	55CCJC30	410231
25 Apr	Germany, West	Philippines	General Trade	3PTS417	465035
25 Apr	Turkey	USA (United States)	Milit Assistance	263UNTS299	103779
25 Apr	Argentina	USA (United States)	US Agri Commod Aid	251UNTS283	103546
26 Apr	China People's Rep	Hungary	General Economic	55CCJC32	410232
27 Apr	Germany, East	USSR (Soviet Union)	Specific Property	2EGDA337	419392
27 Apr	Philippines	USA (United States)	Direct Aid	261UNTS351	103733
27 Apr	Haiti	USA (United States)	IGO Establishment	240UNTS17	103391
28 Apr	Czechoslovakia	USSR (Soviet Union)	Specific Resources	16SUGG68	469905
28 Apr	Germany, East	USSR (Soviet Union)	Atomic Energy	0SUST327	468162
28 Apr	Czechoslovakia	Hungary	Sanitation	477UNTS197	106923
29 Apr	Bulgaria	Germany, East	Finance	4EGDA486	419044
29 Apr	Netherlands	USA (United States)	Milit Assistance	251UNTS357	103553
29 Apr	Israel	USA (United States)	US Agri Commod Aid	261UNTS331	103731
29 Apr	Brazil	Sweden	Patents/Copyrights	228UNTS115	103145
29 Apr	Denmark	Israel	Visas	220UNTS87	102992
29 Apr	Netherlands	USA (United States)	Milit Installation	219UNTS105	102969

DATE	PARTY ONE	PARTY TWO	TOPIC	CITATION	NUMBER
1955 (Cont.)					
30 Apr	Peru	USA (United States)	General Aid	263UNTS309	103780
30 Apr	Iraq	UK Great Britain	Claims and Debts	226UNTS319	103126
01 May	Multilateral		Admin Cooperation	0UNTS0	110416
02 May	Korea, South	USA (United States)	Direct Aid	258UNTS3	103666
04 May	China People's Rep	Japan	General Trade	55CCJC36	410234
04 May	Luxembourg	Netherlands	Refugees	292UNTS17	104262
05 May	Canada	USA (United States)	Milit Installation	241UNTS179	103433
06 May	Finland	USA (United States)	US Agri Commod Aid	251UNTS3	103529
07 May	Liechtenstein	Switzerland	Territory Boundary	56SWRO143	462181
10 May	Austria	Germany, West	Visas	55WBGA103	424532
10 May	Multilateral		Claims and Debts	273UNTS121	103948
10 May	USA (United States)	Vietnam, South	Milit Assistance	273UNTS157	103950
11 May	France	Vietnam, South	Education	0VKNG91	496027
11 May	Austria	Romania	Water Transport	342UNTS119	104904
12 May	USA (United States)	Yugoslavia	Direct Aid	251UNTS337	103550
12 May	USA (United States)	Yugoslavia	Direct Aid	251UNTS343	103551
12 May	Honduras	USA (United States)	Direct Aid	270UNTS3	103886
12 May	USA (United States)	Yugoslavia	Direct Aid	251UNTS331	103549
13 May	France	Spain	Customs	55FRJO2408	416161
14 May	Germany, West	Yugoslavia	Extradition	57WBGA146	424323
14 May	Multilateral		General Amity	219UNTS3	102962
15 May	France	Vietnam, South	Status of Forces	0VKNG92	496028
15 May	Austria	USSR (Soviet Union)	Recognition	0SUST328	468054
15 May	Austria	UK Great Britain	Claims and Debts	344UNTS9	104940
15 May	Multilateral		Recognition	217UNTS223	102949
16 May	Germany, West	Spain	Finance	55SPBO2106	460007
16 May	Germany, West	Spain	General Trade	55SPBO2106	460006
16 May	Cambodia	USA (United States)	Milit Assistance	263UNTS273	103777
18 May	Nigeria	Norway	Taxation	2NORT553	451123
18 May	Cyprus	Norway	Taxation	2NORT553	451031
18 May	Gambia	Norway	Taxation	2NORT553	451063
18 May	Austria	Hungary	Water Transport	55ABGB195	403088
18 May	Netherlands	Norway	Culture	252UNTS269	103569
19 May	Argentina	USSR (Soviet Union)	General Trade	0SUST328	468020
19 May	Italy	USA (United States)	Direct Aid	269UNTS83	103876
23 May	Ceylon (Sri Lanka)	Pakistan	General Trade	286UNTS15	104159
23 May	Italy	USA (United States)	US Agri Commod Aid	251UNTS303	103547
24 May	Israel	Norway	Taxation	220UNTS71	102990
25 May	China People's Rep	Vietnam, North	Land Transport	55CCJC38	410235
25 May	Greece	Norway	Taxation	423UNTS77	106085
25 May	Italy	Sweden	Non-ILO Labor	291UNTS235	104259
25 May	Netherlands	USA (United States)	Claims and Debts	289UNTS227	104220
25 May	Multilateral		IGO Establishment	264UNTS117	103791
26 May	Bulgaria	Germany, East	General Economic	3EGDA545	419045
26 May	Pakistan	USA (United States)	General Economic	257UNTS93	103652
26 May	USA (United States)	USSR (Soviet Union)	Milit Assistance	270UNTS61	103892
26 May	Turkey	USA (United States)	Milit Assistance	262UNTS97	103739
27 May	Japan	Yemen	General Amity	57JAIL80	440156
27 May	Hungary	USSR (Soviet Union)	Status of Forces	407UNTS156	105864
27 May	Greece	USA (United States)	Milit Assistance	251UNTS349	103552
28 May	Germany, East	Poland	Postal Service	3EGDA458	419245
28 May	Norway	Sweden	Scientific Project	262UNTS151	103743
29 May	Korea, South	USA (United States)	Milit Installation	256UNTS263	103636
30 May	Libya	USA (United States)	Direct Aid	270UNTS43	103890
31 May	Korea, North	USSR (Soviet Union)	Finance	0SUST329	468253
31 May	Japan	USA (United States)	Direct Aid	241UNTS243	103435
31 May	Japan	USA (United States)	Direct Aid	241UNTS197	103434
31 May	Korea, South	USA (United States)	US Agri Commod Aid	251UNTS321	103548
01 Jun	Greece	Spain	General Trade	56SPBO2701	460155
01 Jun	Italy	IBRD (World Bank)	IBRD Project	358UNTS203	105137
02 Jun	Costa Rica	France	General Amity	55FRRT9002	415135
02 Jun	ICJ Option Clause	UK Great Britain	ICJ Option Clause	211UNTS109	102849
03 Jun	France	Tunisia	General Amity	55FRJO609	416453
03 Jun	Germany, East	Romania	Scientific Project	3EGDA577	419290
03 Jun	Multilateral		Specific Resources	310UNTS145	104491

DATE	PARTY ONE	PARTY TWO	TOPIC	CITATION	NUMBER
1955 (Cont.)					
03 Jun	Canada	Ethiopia	General Economic	247UNTS157	103465
03 Jun	Japan	USA (United States)	Milit Assistance	270UNTS51	103891
04 Jun	Pakistan	Sweden	Tech Assistance	228UNTS121	103146
06 Jun	Germany, West	USA (United States)	Humanitarian	315UNTS155	104566
06 Jun	Multilateral		IGO Establishment	219UNTS79	102968
07 Jun	France	Ireland	General Trade	558UNTS217	108142
07 Jun	UK Great Britain	USA (United States)	General Military	265UNTS27	103804
08 Jun	Switzerland	USA (United States)	General Trade	55SWRO579	462133
08 Jun	Canada	USA (United States)	Customs	247UNTS163	103466
09 Jun	Iran	USSR (Soviet Union)	Specific Property	0SUST329	468230
09 Jun	Ecuador	Spain	General Economic	55SPBO3009	460087
10 Jun	Germany, East	Sudan	Finance	3EGDA660	419308
10 Jun	Germany, West	New Zealand	Visas	380UNTS307	105462
10 Jun	Honduras	USA (United States)	Claims and Debts	258UNTS51	103669
10 Jun	Israel	Italy	Taxation	280UNTS219	104061
10 Jun	Pakistan	UK Great Britain	Taxation	243UNTS15	103444
10 Jun	Turkey	USA (United States)	Atomic Energy	238UNTS149	103359
11 Jun	Spain	Sweden	General Economic	55SPBO1108	460245
11 Jun	CERN (Nuc Resrch)	Switzerland	IGO Status/Immunit	249UNTS405	200544
12 Jun	India	Pakistan	Finance	228UNTS211	103153
13 Jun	France	Vietnam, South	Milit Installation	0VKNG94	496029
13 Jun	Hungary	USSR (Soviet Union)	Atomic Energy	0SUST330	468198
13 Jun	Canada	Japan	Visas	247UNTS151	103464
13 Jun	Canada	USA (United States)	Specif Goods/Equip	268UNTS87	103851
14 Jun	Multilateral		Tech Assistance	212UNTS263	200526
14 Jun	Austria	IBRD (World Bank)	IBRD Project	221UNTS375	200531
14 Jun	Burma	Yugoslavia	Direct Aid	378UNTS93	105419
14 Jun	Italy	Norway	Culture	260UNTS307	103713
14 Jun	Colombia	USA (United States)	Non-IBRD Project	256UNTS211	103630
14 Jun	Austria	USA (United States)	US Agri Commod Aid	258UNTS37	103668
15 Jun	Luxembourg	USA (United States)	Reparations	264UNTS279	103798
15 Jun	Canada	USA (United States)	Specif Goods/Equip	268UNTS101	103852
15 Jun	Colombia	IBRD (World Bank)	IBRD Project	248UNTS161	103494
15 Jun	UK Great Britain	USA (United States)	Atomic Energy	214UNTS301	102905
15 Jun	UK Great Britain	USA (United States)	Atomic Energy	229UNTS73	103161
15 Jun	Canada	USA (United States)	Atomic Energy	235UNTS176	103301
15 Jun	Belgium	USA (United States)	Atomic Energy	235UNTS133	103299
15 Jun	Canada	USA (United States)	Milit Assistance	235UNTS201	103302
16 Jun	Italy	Spain	General Trade	55SPBO2908	460170
16 Jun	Greece	USA (United States)	Patents/Copyrights	262UNTS137	103742
17 Jun	Chile	Switzerland	General Trade	55SWRO705	462125
17 Jun	Bulgaria	Germany, East	Sanitation	4EGDA490	419046
17 Jun	Bulgaria	Yugoslavia	Sanitation	375UNTS287	105370
18 Jun	Germany, West	Japan	Visas	0JGJI1262	441085
18 Jun	Guatemala	USA (United States)	Milit Assistance	262UNTS105	103740
20 Jun	France	Vietnam, South	Air Transport	0VKNG95	496030
20 Jun	Germany, East	Poland	Air Transport	55PZUM13	458022
20 Jun	Czechoslovakia	Germany, East	General Economic	3EGDA511	419345
20 Jun	Germany, East	Poland	Air Transport	4EGDA224	419246
20 Jun	Pakistan	IBRD (World Bank)	IBRD Project	230UNTS41	103176
21 Jun	Multilateral		ILO Labor	305UNTS265	104423
21 Jun	Thailand	USA (United States)	US Agri Commod Aid	262UNTS87	103738
22 Jun	India	USSR (Soviet Union)	General Amity	0SUST330	468213
22 Jun	Belgium	Spain	Finance	55SPBO908	460045
22 Jun	Multilateral		Atomic Energy	249UNTS3	103498
23 Jun	Colombia	USA (United States)	US Agri Commod Aid	263UNTS337	103781
24 Jun	Canada	USSR (Soviet Union)	Postal Service	16SUGG68	469906
24 Jun	Norway	Yugoslavia	Culture	2NORT660	451094
24 Jun	France	Germany, West	Commodity Trade	55WBGA159	424146
24 Jun	China People's Rep	Sweden	Consul/Citizenship	55CCJC45	410239
24 Jun	Greece	USA (United States)	US Agri Commod Aid	270UNTS351	103905
24 Jun	Greece	USA (United States)	US Agri Commod Aid	270UNTS361	103906
24 Jun	Haiti	USA (United States)	Non-IBRD Project	264UNTS291	103800
24 Jun	China People's Rep	Sweden	Consul/Citizenship	228UNTS153	103148
25 Jun	Norway	Spain	General Trade	55SPBO2607	460203

DATE	PARTY ONE	PARTY TWO	TOPIC	CITATION	NUMBER
1955 (Cont.)					
25 Jun	Spain	Uruguay	General Trade	55SPBO1508	460263
25 Jun	USA (United States)	USSR (Soviet Union)	Territory Boundary	270UNTS15	103887
28 Jun	Afghanistan	USSR (Soviet Union)	General Transport	240UNTS253	103407
28 Jun	France	Greece	General Trade	225UNTS219	103100
29 Jun	Finland	Netherlands	Finance	55NET91	447055
29 Jun	Denmark	WHO (World Health)	IGO Status/Immunit	247UNTS168	103467
29 Jun	Turkey	USA (United States)	Milit Assistance	269UNTS97	103878
30 Jun	Germany, East	USSR (Soviet Union)	Specif Goods/Equip	3EGDA205	419393
30 Jun	Dominican Republic	USA (United States)	Non-IBRD Project	257UNTS313	103664
30 Jun	South Africa	UK Great Britain	General Military	248UNTS191	103495
30 Jun	Italy	USA (United States)	US Agri Commod Aid	258UNTS15	103667
30 Jun	Germany, West	USA (United States)	Milit Assistance	240UNTS69	103394
30 Jun	Australia	Fed Rhod/Nyasaland	General Trade	226UNTS215	103115
30 Jun	Germany, West	USA (United States)	Milit Assistance	240UNTS47	103393
01 Jul	Burma	USSR (Soviet Union)	General Trade	0SUST331	468062
01 Jul	Spain	UK Great Britain	General Economic	55SPBO608	460239
01 Jul	Brazil	Germany, West	General Trade	55WBGA141	424053
01 Jul	Germany, East	USSR (Soviet Union)	Culture	2EGDA206	419394
01 Jul	France	USA (United States)	Other Military	270UNTS19	103888
03 Jul	Syria	United Arab Rep	Air Transport	393UNTS67	105652
04 Jul	Indonesia	UNICEF (Children)	Admin Cooperation	212UNTS13	102860
04 Jul	Iran	WHO (World Health)	Tech Assistance	227UNTS65	103131
04 Jul	Multilateral		Tech Assistance	214UNTS10	102897
05 Jul	Libya	WHO (World Health)	Tech Assistance	219UNTS305	200530
06 Jul	Export-Import Bank	Japan	Loans and Credits	0JGJI1234	441145
07 Jul	China People's Rep	Vietnam, North	Culture	55CCJC47	410240
07 Jul	China People's Rep	Vietnam, North	General Trade	55CCJC49	410242
07 Jul	China People's Rep	Vietnam, North	General Trade	55CCJC48	410241
07 Jul	Germany, West	USA (United States)	Air Transport	275UNTS3	103973
08 Jul	USSR (Soviet Union)	Vietnam, North	General Trade	0SUST331	468448
08 Jul	USSR (Soviet Union)	Vietnam, North	General Trade	0SUST331	468447
08 Jul	Ecuador	USA (United States)	Milit Assistance	265UNTS49	103806
08 Jul	Laos	USA (United States)	Direct Aid	278UNTS59	104021
08 Jul	Italy	USA (United States)	Milit Installation	270UNTS29	103889
08 Jul	Nicaragua	IBRD (World Bank)	IBRD Project	229UNTS123	103163
08 Jul	Nicaragua	IBRD (World Bank)	IBRD Project	229UNTS97	103162
09 Jul	Germany, East	Poland	Sanitation	55PZUM19	458023
09 Jul	Germany, East	Poland	Sanitation	4EGDA230	419247
09 Jul	Japan	Thailand	Finance	230UNTS13	103172
11 Jul	Switzerland	Venezuela	General Trade	55SWRO729	462163
11 Jul	Bulgaria	China People's Rep	Sanitation	55CCJC50	410243
12 Jul	Netherlands	Spain	Finance	55SPBO2908	460211
12 Jul	Netherlands	Spain	General Trade	55SPBO2908	460210
12 Jul	Panama	IBRD (World Bank)	IBRD Project	219UNTS127	102970
12 Jul	Israel	USA (United States)	Atomic Energy	219UNTS185	102974
14 Jul	Greece	Netherlands	General Trade	227UNTS27	103129
15 Jul	Belgium	USA (United States)	Milit Assistance	223UNTS3	103040
15 Jul	Israel	USSR (Soviet Union)	Mostfavored Nation	226UNTS253	103119
16 Jul	Spain	USA (United States)	Postal Service	270UNTS211	103899
18 Jul	USSR (Soviet Union)	Vietnam, North	General Trade	0SUST333	468450
18 Jul	USSR (Soviet Union)	Vietnam, North	Direct Aid	0SUST333	468449
18 Jul	Germany, East	Mongolia	Mass Media	4EGDA559	419212
18 Jul	Libya	USA (United States)	Direct Aid	241UNTS305	103437
18 Jul	Denmark	Finland	Taxation	250UNTS149	103521
18 Jul	Denmark	Finland	Taxation	250UNTS167	103522
18 Jul	Ceylon (Sri Lanka)	USA (United States)	Postal Service	281UNTS295	104086
18 Jul	Taiwan	USA (United States)	Atomic Energy	235UNTS221	103304
18 Jul	Switzerland	USA (United States)	Atomic Energy	239UNTS311	103388
18 Jul	Netherlands	USA (United States)	Atomic Energy	240UNTS347	103412
18 Jul	Lebanon	USA (United States)	Atomic Energy	239UNTS247	103383
19 Jul	Colombia	USA (United States)	Atomic Energy	235UNTS233	103305
19 Jul	Spain	USA (United States)	Atomic Energy	239UNTS299	103387
20 Jul	Iceland	USA (United States)	General Military	256UNTS245	103634
20 Jul	Pakistan	USA (United States)	Postal Service	241UNTS255	103436
21 Jul	Poland	USSR (Soviet Union)	Direct Aid	16SUGG68	469907

1955 (Cont.)

DATE	PARTY ONE	PARTY TWO	TOPIC	CITATION	NUMBER
21 Jul	Cuba	Spain	General Economic	55SPBO1508	460071
21 Jul	Libya	USA (United States)	Tech Assistance	264UNTS247	103796
21 Jul	Canada	USA (United States)	Milit Assistance	269UNTS53	103873
21 Jul	USA (United States)	Venezuela	Atomic Energy	238UNTS121	103357
21 Jul	Portugal	USA (United States)	Atomic Energy	239UNTS283	103386
22 Jul	Ceylon (Sri Lanka)	Spain	General Trade	56SPBO2310	460063
22 Jul	Paraguay	USA (United States)	Military Mission	265UNTS15	103803
22 Jul	Germany, West	UK Great Britain	Air Transport	269UNTS189	103881
22 Jul	Paraguay	USA (United States)	Military Mission	265UNTS3	103802
22 Jul	Germany, West	UK Great Britain	Air Transport	269UNTS223	103882
23 Jul	Italy	Switzerland	Land Transport	284UNTS279	104142
25 Jul	Germany, West	Paraguay	Finance	55WBGA187	424572
25 Jul	Germany, West	Paraguay	General Trade	55WBGA187	424571
25 Jul	Denmark	USA (United States)	Atomic Energy	235UNTS245	103306
26 Jul	Netherlands	Turkey	General Economic	55NET140	447056
26 Jul	Israel	Norway	Visas	226UNTS257	103120
27 Jul	Philippines	USA (United States)	Atomic Energy	239UNTS271	103385
28 Jul	Bulgaria	France	Finance	59FRRT4	415086
28 Jul	Germany, East	Romania	Air Transport	342UNTS207	104909
28 Jul	Libya	USA (United States)	Non-IBRD Project	270UNTS317	103903
28 Jul	Libya	USA (United States)	Non-IBRD Project	270UNTS245	103900
28 Jul	Libya	USA (United States)	Non-IBRD Project	270UNTS269	103901
28 Jul	Libya	USA (United States)	Non-IBRD Project	270UNTS293	103902
28 Jul	Italy	USA (United States)	Atomic Energy	239UNTS235	103382
28 Jul	South Africa	Sweden	Taxation	230UNTS287	103191
29 Jul	Ireland	Portugal	Visas	553UNTS135	108079
29 Jul	Guatemala	IBRD (World Bank)	IBRD Project	229UNTS167	103165
29 Jul	Argentina	USA (United States)	Atomic Energy	235UNTS121	103298
29 Jul	Australia	Taiwan	Patents/Copyrights	213UNTS193	102887
30 Jul	USSR (Soviet Union)	Yugoslavia	General Trade	0SUST334	468469
30 Jul	Germany, West	Paraguay	Mostfavored Nation	57WGBB1273	425573
30 Jul	Bulgaria	Germany, East	Air Transport	4EGDA495	419047
30 Jul	China People's Rep	Romania	Gen Communications	55CCJC53	410246
30 Jul	Belgium	Portugal	Culture	250UNTS213	103525
30 Jul	Greece	Sweden	General Trade	225UNTS243	103102
02 Aug	Germany, West	USA (United States)	Specif Goods/Equip	268UNTS121	103854
02 Aug	Canada	Israel	Visas	226UNTS265	103121
03 Aug	Cuba	USA (United States)	Military Mission	265UNTS41	103805
03 Aug	Brazil	USA (United States)	Scientific Project	270UNTS71	103893
03 Aug	Bolivia	USA (United States)	Non-IBRD Project	264UNTS225	103795
03 Aug	Brazil	USA (United States)	Atomic Energy	235UNTS159	103300
04 Aug	Pakistan	IBRD (World Bank)	IBRD Project	230UNTS79	103177
04 Aug	Greece	USA (United States)	Atomic Energy	235UNTS257	103307
05 Aug	Germany, East	Romania	Sanitation	342UNTS229	104910
05 Aug	Germany, West	Sweden	Land Transport	262UNTS265	103754
05 Aug	Peru	IBRD (World Bank)	IBRD Project	218UNTS3	102950
06 Aug	Pakistan	IBRD (World Bank)	IBRD Project	236UNTS195	103325
08 Aug	Czechoslovakia	Germany, East	Air Transport	4EGDA325	419346
08 Aug	China People's Rep	Finland	General Trade	55CCJC54	410247
08 Aug	El Salvador	USA (United States)	Non-IBRD Project	264UNTS301	103801
08 Aug	Chile	USA (United States)	Atomic Energy	235UNTS209	103303
09 Aug	IBRD (World Bank)	Thailand	IBRD Project	221UNTS283	103011
10 Aug	France	Libya	General Amity	57FRJO704	416263
11 Aug	Italy	Spain	Culture	267UNTS125	103839
11 Aug	France	USA (United States)	US Agri Commod Aid	251UNTS15	103530
11 Aug	Pakistan	USA (United States)	Atomic Energy	239UNTS259	103384
12 Aug	Mongolia	USSR (Soviet Union)	General Aid	0SUST443	468280
12 Aug	Ethiopia	UK Great Britain	Territory Boundary	227UNTS3	103127
15 Aug	France	Honduras	Consul/Citizenship	60FRRT29	415219
15 Aug	Iran	USA (United States)	General Amity	284UNTS93	104132
16 Aug	China People's Rep	USSR (Soviet Union)	Sanitation	0SUST334	468093
16 Aug	France	Vietnam, South	Consul/Citizenship	59FRRT7	415481
16 Aug	China People's Rep	USSR (Soviet Union)	Sanitation	55CCJC56	410249
17 Aug	France	Vietnam, South	Finance	0VKNG98	496031
18 Aug	Denmark	USSR (Soviet Union)	Consul/Citizenship	16SUGG69	469908

1955 (Cont.)

DATE	PARTY ONE	PARTY TWO	TOPIC	CITATION	NUMBER
20 Aug	China People's Rep	Germany, East	Scientific Project	55CCJC57	410250
20 Aug	Australia	USA (United States)	Visas	268UNTS133	103855
21 Aug	Israel	Netherlands	Visas	299UNTS51	104306
22 Aug	Cambodia	Vietnam, South	Finance	0VKNG100	496032
22 Aug	Bulgaria	Germany, East	General Economic	3EGDA546	419048
22 Aug	China People's Rep	United Arab Rep	General Trade	55CCJC59	410252
22 Aug	China People's Rep	United Arab Rep	General Trade	55CCJC58	410251
23 Aug	Greece	USSR (Soviet Union)	General Trade	233UNTS39	103249
24 Aug	Japan	USA (United States)	Specif Claim/Waive	257UNTS297	103662
24 Aug	Ecuador	USA (United States)	Military Mission	256UNTS299	103640
25 Aug	Germany, East	USSR (Soviet Union)	Claims and Debts	0SUST334	468163
25 Aug	Lebanon	IBRD (World Bank)	IBRD Project	230UNTS233	103188
26 Aug	France	IBRD (World Bank)	IBRD Project	247UNTS305	103478
26 Aug	Nicaragua	IBRD (World Bank)	IBRD Project	229UNTS145	103164
27 Aug	USSR (Soviet Union)	Vietnam, North	Education	16SUGG69	469909
27 Aug	Albania	USSR (Soviet Union)	Sanitation	0SUST334	468013
29 Aug	Denmark	Greece	General Trade	230UNTS25	103174
29 Aug	Philippines	UK Great Britain	Non-ILO Labor	221UNTS241	103009
29 Aug	IBRD (World Bank)	Uruguay	IBRD Project	243UNTS123	103450
30 Aug	Czechoslovakia	Germany, East	Sanitation	504UNTS279	107361
31 Aug	Korea, North	USSR (Soviet Union)	Finance	0SUST335	468254
31 Aug	Austria	USSR (Soviet Union)	Specific Property	0SUST335	468055
31 Aug	Austria	France	Non-ILO Labor	55ABGB208	403050
31 Aug	Belgium	USA (United States)	Milit Assistance	223UNTS111	103041
03 Sep	Germany, East	USSR (Soviet Union)	Scientific Project	3EGDA242	419395
03 Sep	USSR (Soviet Union)	Yugoslavia	Air Transport	240UNTS267	103408
04 Sep	Libya	USSR (Soviet Union)	Consul/Citizenship	16SUGG69	469910
05 Sep	USA (United States)	USSR (Soviet Union)	Sanitation	256UNTS307	103641
06 Sep	Czechoslovakia	Poland	Visas	55PZUM23	458024
06 Sep	Japan	Thailand	Culture	55JHZ9	439002
06 Sep	Ecuador	USA (United States)	Direct Aid	256UNTS187	103628
06 Sep	Philippines	USA (United States)	Visas	238UNTS109	103356
07 Sep	Iran	WHO (World Health)	Tech Assistance	0IRTB87	433145
09 Sep	Thailand	USA (United States)	Commodity Trade	264UNTS285	103799
09 Sep	Bolivia	USA (United States)	Military Mission	256UNTS239	103633
10 Sep	China People's Rep	USA (United States)	Extradition	55CCJC63	410255
10 Sep	Germany, East	Hungary	Air Transport	407UNTS132	105863
10 Sep	Belgium	Ireland	Air Transport	255UNTS235	103612
12 Sep	ICJ Option Clause	South Africa	ICJ Option Clause	216UNTS115	102935
13 Sep	Germany, West	USSR (Soviet Union)	Consul/Citizenship	0SUST334	468159
14 Sep	Austria	Germany, West	Customs	57WGBB581	421533
14 Sep	Austria	Germany, West	Visas	57WGBB594	425537
14 Sep	Austria	Germany, West	Privil/Immunities	57WGBB596	425538
14 Sep	Austria	Germany, West	Visas	57WGBB585	425534
14 Sep	Austria	Germany, West	Privil/Immunities	57WGBB592	425536
14 Sep	Austria	Germany, West	Visas	57WGBB589	425535
14 Sep	Bulgaria	China People's Rep	Gen Communications	55CCJC64	410256
15 Sep	Multilateral		Non-ILO Labor	254UNTS55	103593
15 Sep	Indonesia	USA (United States)	Mass Media	256UNTS293	103639
16 Sep	China People's Rep	Germany, East	General Trade	55CCJC65	410257
16 Sep	Colombia	USA (United States)	Military Mission	256UNTS221	103631
17 Sep	Denmark	USSR (Soviet Union)	Consul/Citizenship	0SUST336	468119
17 Sep	Iceland	Norway	Taxation	2NORT664	451076
17 Sep	Italy	Switzerland	Specific Resources	291UNTS213	104257
17 Sep	Iceland	Sweden	Taxation	262UNTS273	103755
19 Sep	Finland	USSR (Soviet Union)	Milit Installation	226UNTS187	103113
20 Sep	Germany, East	USSR (Soviet Union)	Admin Cooperation	0SUST338	468164
20 Sep	Brazil	USA (United States)	Military Mission	257UNTS349	103665
20 Sep	Germany, East	USSR (Soviet Union)	General Amity	226UNTS201	103114
21 Sep	Japan	UK Great Britain	Other Military	0JGJI1287	441086
21 Sep	Germany, West	Greece	Admin Cooperation	55WBGA203	424229
21 Sep	Multilateral		Other Military	269UNTS241	103885
22 Sep	Bulgaria	Germany, East	General Economic	58EGDZ172	420049
22 Sep	Canada	USA (United States)	Specif Goods/Equip	256UNTS227	103632
22 Sep	Bulgaria	UK Great Britain	Finance	222UNTS349	103039

DATE	PARTY ONE	PARTY TWO	TOPIC	CITATION	NUMBER
1955 (Cont.)					
23 Sep	Iceland	USSR (Soviet Union)	General Economic	0SUST338	468207
23 Sep	Czechoslovakia	Poland	Territory Boundary	55PZUM27	458025
23 Sep	Germany, East	Hungary	Mass Media	4EGDA405	419444
23 Sep	Bolivia	USA (United States)	Claims and Debts	256UNTS275	103637
23 Sep	France	USA (United States)	Milit Assistance	270UNTS341	103904
23 Sep	Iceland	Sweden	Admin Cooperation	262UNTS241	103750
23 Sep	Accept UN Charter	Spain	UN Charter	223UNTS63	103053
26 Sep	Austria	USA (United States)	Specific Property	272UNTS31	103930
27 Sep	USSR (Soviet Union)	Yugoslavia	Gen Communications	0SUST338	468470
27 Sep	USSR (Soviet Union)	Yugoslavia	Postal Service	0SUST339	468471
27 Sep	Ireland	Turkey	Visas	553UNTS193	108087
28 Sep	Albania	China People's Rep	Mass Media	55CCJC66	410258
28 Sep	Multilateral		Air Transport	478UNTS371	106943
28 Sep	Guatemala	USA (United States)	General Trade	257UNTS307	103663
29 Sep	Multilateral		Air Transport	222UNTS313	103037
30 Sep	Czechoslovakia	Poland	Non-ILO Labor	55PZUM33	458026
30 Sep	USA (United States)	Yugoslavia	General Military	269UNTS89	103877
30 Sep	Canada	Denmark	Taxation	258UNTS115	103675
01 Oct	Bulgaria	Yugoslavia	Air Transport	396UNTS223	105698
04 Oct	France	Germany, West	Air Transport	353UNTS203	105044
04 Oct	India	USA (United States)	Direct Aid	268UNTS115	103853
05 Oct	Iceland	USA (United States)	Claims and Debts	256UNTS285	103638
06 Oct	Liberia	USA (United States)	Tech Assistance	275UNTS93	103978
06 Oct	Liberia	USA (United States)	Direct Aid	275UNTS87	103977
07 Oct	Germany, East	Poland	Sanitation	55PZUM41	458027
07 Oct	Germany, East	Poland	Sanitation	4EGDA234	419248
07 Oct	Norway	Sweden	Admin Cooperation	262UNTS253	103752
07 Oct	Ecuador	USA (United States)	US Agri Commod Aid	256UNTS197	103629
10 Oct	Denmark	Iceland	Taxation	230UNTS3	103171
11 Oct	Turkey	USA (United States)	Visas	272UNTS145	103935
11 Oct	Accept UN Charter	Jordan	UN Charter	223UNTS43	103048
12 Oct	Ceylon (Sri Lanka)	China People's Rep	Commodity Trade	55CCJC68	410260
12 Oct	Multilateral		IGO Establishment	560UNTS3	108165
14 Oct	Taiwan	USA (United States)	Milit Installation	268UNTS165	103857
14 Oct	UK Great Britain	Vietnam, South	Patents/Copyrights	231UNTS193	103220
15 Oct	Finland	Switzerland	General Trade	55SWRO1017	462135
15 Oct	Finland	Switzerland	Finance	55SWRO1014	462134
17 Oct	Mongolia	USSR (Soviet Union)	Land Transport	0SUST340	468281
17 Oct	Germany, East	Mongolia	Consul/Citizenship	3EGDA600	419213
17 Oct	Bulgaria	Germany, East	Commodity Trade	58EGDZ172	420050
17 Oct	Austria	USSR (Soviet Union)	Finance	56ABGB86	403221
17 Oct	Austria	USSR (Soviet Union)	Non-IBRD Project	0UNTS0	109254
17 Oct	Austria	USSR (Soviet Union)	Finance	0UNTS0	109255
17 Oct	Austria	Sweden	Taxation	262UNTS283	103756
17 Oct	Austria	USSR (Soviet Union)	General Economic	240UNTS289	103409
18 Oct	Burma	Japan	Admin Cooperation	0JGJI1254	441146
18 Oct	Germany, West	Italy	Commodity Trade	56WBGA17	424291
18 Oct	Germany, East	USSR (Soviet Union)	Air Transport	3EGDA327	419397
19 Oct	Finland	USSR (Soviet Union)	Air Transport	353UNTS185	105043
20 Oct	Norway	Uruguay	Consul/Citizenship	2NORT666	451197
20 Oct	Multilateral		IGO Establishment	378UNTS159	105425
20 Oct	Denmark	Syria	Air Transport	250UNTS61	103518
20 Oct	Syria	United Arab Rep	General Military	247UNTS117	103461
21 Oct	Taiwan	France	Telecommunications	0CTRC186	413005
21 Oct	Denmark	Lebanon	Air Transport	248UNTS17	103482
22 Oct	Nicaragua	USA (United States)	Visas	358UNTS51	105123
22 Oct	Austria	Italy	Specific Property	260UNTS327	103716
24 Oct	Czechoslovakia	Germany, East	Land Transport	504UNTS173	107358
25 Oct	Japan	IBRD (World Bank)	IBRD Project	230UNTS379	200534
28 Oct	Austria	Germany, West	Visas	57WGBB598	425539
28 Oct	Paraguay	USA (United States)	Claims and Debts	273UNTS97	103946
28 Oct	Philippines	USA (United States)	Milit Installation	239UNTS165	103376
28 Oct	Peru	USA (United States)	Military Mission	239UNTS181	103378
29 Oct	France	Switzerland	General Trade	55SWRO1092	462136
29 Oct	Netherlands	Poland	Finance	56NET19	447058

DATE	PARTY ONE	PARTY TWO	TOPIC	CITATION	NUMBER
1955 (Cont.)					
29 Oct	Netherlands	Poland	General Trade	56NET18	447057
31 Oct	ICJ Option Clause	UK Great Britain	ICJ Option Clause	219UNTS179	102973
31 Oct	USSR (Soviet Union)	Yemen	General Amity	240UNTS317	103410
02 Nov	Pakistan	Turkey	Air Transport	311UNTS217	104505
02 Nov	Fed Rhod/Nyasaland	Netherlands	Non-ILO Labor	263UNTS381	103784
03 Nov	Austria	Sweden	Non-ILO Labor	262UNTS289	103757
03 Nov	USA (United States)	Vietnam, South	Mass Media	239UNTS195	103379
04 Nov	Netherlands	USA (United States)	Air Transport	269UNTS3	103867
04 Nov	Italy	Lebanon	General Trade	267UNTS113	103838
04 Nov	Italy	Lebanon	Tech Assistance	267UNTS147	103840
04 Nov	Australia	South Africa	Air Transport	232UNTS143	103234
05 Nov	Multilateral		IGO Establishment	250UNTS201	103524
07 Nov	South Africa	Switzerland	Taxation	56SWRO655	462041
07 Nov	Germany, East	Syria	Consul/Citizenship	3EGDA668	419310
07 Nov	South Africa	Switzerland	Taxation	230UNTS279	103190
08 Nov	Iran	Turkey	Water Transport	0TURG217	466139
08 Nov	Burma	China People's Rep	Air Transport	55CCJC77	410265
08 Nov	Burma	China People's Rep	Consul/Citizenship	55CCJC79	410267
08 Nov	Burma	China People's Rep	Air Transport	55CCJC78	410266
08 Nov	Burma	China People's Rep	Air Transport	306UNTS11	104430
09 Nov	Austria	USSR (Soviet Union)	Air Transport	255UNTS247	103613
10 Nov	Colombia	Spain	Telecommunications	56SPBO1704	460065
10 Nov	United Arab Rep	Germany, East	General Trade	3EGDA621	419001
10 Nov	Germany, East	Hungary	Other Military	3EGDA527	419445
10 Nov	Belgium	UK Great Britain	Status of Forces	331UNTS209	104756
10 Nov	Italy	Syria	General Trade	267UNTS157	103841
10 Nov	Israel	USA (United States)	US Agri Commod Aid	240UNTS3	103390
11 Nov	China People's Rep	Czechoslovakia	General Economic	55CCJC81	410269
12 Nov	USSR (Soviet Union)	Yugoslavia	Culture	0SUST340	468472
12 Nov	United Arab Rep	Germany, East	Consul/Citizenship	3EGDA624	419002
14 Nov	Luxembourg	Switzerland	Non-ILO Labor	57SWRO282	462099
14 Nov	Poland	Yugoslavia	Scientific Project	55PZUM45	458028
14 Nov	Poland	Yugoslavia	Air Transport	55PZUM49	458029
14 Nov	Czechoslovakia	Germany, East	Specific Resources	4EGDA345	419347
14 Nov	Japan	USA (United States)	Atomic Energy	240UNTS361	103413
14 Nov	Thailand	USA (United States)	Commodity Trade	239UNTS201	103380
15 Nov	Norway	USSR (Soviet Union)	General Trade	0SUST341	468295
15 Nov	Bulgaria	Yugoslavia	Consul/Citizenship	396UNTS179	105696
15 Nov	Bulgaria	Yugoslavia	General Transport	396UNTS191	105697
15 Nov	UK Great Britain	USA (United States)	Scientific Project	231UNTS185	103219
16 Nov	Austria	Japan	Recognition	0JGJI1280	441087
16 Nov	Finland	Israel	Visas	257UNTS39	103647
16 Nov	Syria	USSR (Soviet Union)	General Economic	259UNTS71	103683
16 Nov	Brazil	USA (United States)	Commodity Trade	239UNTS207	103381
17 Nov	Austria	Israel	Air Transport	232UNTS153	103235
18 Nov	France	Japan	Visas	0JGJI1263	441088
18 Nov	Belgium	UK Great Britain	Atomic Energy	222UNTS327	103038
18 Nov	Colombia	USA (United States)	Claims and Debts	239UNTS173	103377
19 Nov	Syria	USSR (Soviet Union)	Consul/Citizenship	0SUST444	468416
20 Nov	China People's Rep	Germany, East	General Economic	55CCJC84	410271
21 Nov	Paraguay	UK Great Britain	General Economic	252UNTS107	103560
22 Nov	Greece	Netherlands	Visas	292UNTS31	104264
22 Nov	Guatemala	UNICEF (Children)	Direct Aid	221UNTS305	103012
23 Nov	Czechoslovakia	Germany, East	Scientific Project	3EGDA516	419348
23 Nov	Chile	France	Culture	60FRRT61	415115
23 Nov	Netherlands	Sweden	Admin Cooperation	262UNTS247	103751
25 Nov	France	Spain	General Trade	56SPBO202	460110
26 Nov	Bulgaria	USSR (Soviet Union)	Specific Property	0SUST342	468042
26 Nov	India	Japan	Air Transport	311UNTS243	104506
27 Nov	Germany, East	Syria	General Economic	3EGDA668	419311
27 Nov	Germany, East	USSR (Soviet Union)	Specif Goods/Equip	4EGDA51	419398
27 Nov	China People's Rep	Japan	Culture	55CCJC90	410275
28 Nov	IBRD (World Bank)	South Africa	IBRD Project	230UNTS101	103178
28 Nov	Colombia	USA (United States)	Non-IBRD Project	241UNTS39	103422
29 Nov	Brazil	Netherlands	General Economic	56NET96	447059

DATE	PARTY ONE	PARTY TWO	TOPIC	CITATION	NUMBER
1955 (Cont.)					
30 Nov	Korea, North	USSR (Soviet Union)	Sanitation	0SUST342	468255
30 Nov	China People's Rep	Syria	Finance	55CCJC93	410278
30 Nov	China People's Rep	Syria	General Trade	55CCJC92	410277
01 Dec	Germany, East	Hungary	Mass Media	4EGDA410	419446
01 Dec	Germany, East	Korea, North	Postal Service	4EGDA508	419173
01 Dec	Germany, East	Korea, North	Telecommunications	4EGDA516	419174
03 Dec	Iceland	USSR (Soviet Union)	Consul/Citizenship	0SUST343	468208
03 Dec	China People's Rep	Czechoslovakia	Scientific Project	55CCJC94	410279
03 Dec	Iraq	USA (United States)	Milit Assistance	241UNTS19	103420
05 Dec	Korea, North	Romania	Telecommunications	362UNTS141	105186
05 Dec	Korea, North	Romania	Postal Service	362UNTS163	105187
06 Dec	Austria	USSR (Soviet Union)	General Amity	0SUST444	468058
06 Dec	Germany, West	Switzerland	Admin Cooperation	57SWR0821	462025
07 Dec	Austria	Liechtenstein	Taxation	56ABGB214	403126
07 Dec	Denmark	Sweden	Admin Cooperation	262UNTS235	103749
08 Dec	Japan	Philippines	General Trade	3PTS529	465036
09 Dec	Korea, North	USSR (Soviet Union)	Air Transport	0SUST343	468256
09 Dec	Cambodia	Japan	General Amity	0JGJI1301	441089
10 Dec	Belgium	France	Taxation	231UNTS101	103211
11 Dec	Bulgaria	Yugoslavia	Sanitation	378UNTS49	105417
12 Dec	Pakistan	Turkey	Visas	55TURG1912	466024
12 Dec	Germany, East	Hungary	General Economic	3EGDA528	419447
13 Dec	Romania	USSR (Soviet Union)	Finance	0SUST344	468391
13 Dec	Multilateral		IGO Operations	529UNTS141	107660
13 Dec	Multilateral		Tech Assistance	407UNTS8	105857
13 Dec	Multilateral		Humanitarian	250UNTS3	103514
14 Dec	Finland	USA (United States)	Visas	335UNTS263	104794
14 Dec	United Arab Rep	USA (United States)	US Agri Commod Aid	240UNTS37	103392
14 Dec	Accept UN Charter	Romania	UN Charter	223UNTS59	103052
15 Dec	Accept UN Charter	Romania	UN Charter	223UNTS69	103055
15 Dec	Accept UN Charter	Nepal	UN Charter	223UNTS65	103054
16 Dec	USA (United States)	USSR (Soviet Union)	Culture	0SUST344	468439
16 Dec	Italy	Vatican/Holy See	Taxation	260UNTS319	103715
16 Dec	Dominican Republic	USA (United States)	Visas	241UNTS101	103427
18 Dec	Pakistan	Syria	General Trade	320UNTS269	104647
18 Dec	Afghanistan	USSR (Soviet Union)	Admin Cooperation	259UNTS101	103684
19 Dec	USSR (Soviet Union)	Yugoslavia	Scientific Project	378UNTS127	105423
19 Dec	ICJ Option Clause	Portugal	ICJ Option Clause	224UNTS275	103079
20 Dec	Canada	Norway	Milit Assistance	305UNTS17	104408
20 Dec	Colombia	Italy	Specif Goods/Equip	260UNTS315	103714
20 Dec	New Zealand	UK Great Britain	Non-ILO Labor	268UNTS243	103860
20 Dec	Costa Rica	Guatemala	General Economic	280UNTS121	104056
20 Dec	Colombia	USA (United States)	US Agri Commod Aid	241UNTS25	103421
21 Dec	Germany, East	Romania	Finance	4EGDA451	419291
21 Dec	China People's Rep	Poland	General Trade	55CCJC99	410283
21 Dec	China People's Rep	Mongolia	Mass Media	55CCJC98	410282
21 Dec	Multilateral		General Trade	292UNTS63	104267
21 Dec	Argentina	USA (United States)	Commodity Trade	240UNTS329	103411
22 Dec	Germany, West	Italy	Other Military	57WGBB1277	425292
22 Dec	Italy	Switzerland	Finance	260UNTS339	103717
22 Dec	Honduras	IBRD (World Bank)	IBRD Project	230UNTS262	103189
22 Dec	Libya	USA (United States)	Direct Aid	240UNTS111	103399
22 Dec	Sweden	UK Great Britain	Claims and Debts	231UNTS179	103218
23 Dec	India	USSR (Soviet Union)	Specif Goods/Equip	0SUST345	468214
23 Dec	Norway	Poland	Claims and Debts	2NORT671	451130
23 Dec	Germany, East	USSR (Soviet Union)	Commodity Trade	3EGDA353	419399
23 Dec	Germany, West	USA (United States)	US Agri Commod Aid	240UNTS79	103395
24 Dec	Japan	Spain	General Trade	56SPBO801	460178
25 Dec	China People's Rep	Germany, East	Sanitation	4EGDA100	419091
25 Dec	China People's Rep	Germany, East	General Amity	4EGDA95	419089
25 Dec	China People's Rep	Germany, East	Culture	4EGDA98	419090
25 Dec	China People's Rep	Germany, East	Culture	55CCJC103	410285
25 Dec	China People's Rep	Germany, East	Sanitation	55CCJC104	410286
25 Dec	China People's Rep	Germany, East	General Amity	55CCJC102	410284
27 Dec	China People's Rep	USSR (Soviet Union)	General Trade	16SUGG70	469911

DATE	PARTY ONE	PARTY TWO	TOPIC	CITATION	NUMBER
1955 (Cont.)					
27 Dec	China People's Rep	USSR (Soviet Union)	General Trade	55CCJC105	410287
27 Dec	Australia	France	Admin Cooperation	241UNTS325	103440
28 Dec	Austria	USSR (Soviet Union)	Postal Service	0SUST345	468059
28 Dec	Austria	Italy	Visas	260UNTS345	103718
28 Dec	Haiti	USA (United States)	Non-IBRD Project	240UNTS95	103397
29 Dec	Burma	China People's Rep	Commodity Trade	55CCJC107	410288
29 Dec	Iceland	Israel	Visas	227UNTS147	103136
30 Dec	Korea, North	Poland	Postal Service	55PZUM57	458031
30 Dec	Korea, North	Poland	Telecommunications	55PZUM67	458030
30 Dec	Italy	Thailand	Visas	260UNTS351	103719
31 Dec	Guatemala	Spain	General Trade	56SPBO2801	460158
31 Dec	Iceland	Spain	General Trade	56SPBO2701	460166
31 Dec	China People's Rep	Lebanon	General Trade	55CCJC110	410291
31 Dec	China People's Rep	Lebanon	General Trade	55CCJC112	410293
31 Dec	China People's Rep	Lebanon	General Trade	55CCJC111	410292
1956					
02 Jan	Belgium	Turkey	Visas	228UNTS203	103152
03 Jan	Romania	USSR (Soviet Union)	Air Transport	0SUST346	468392
03 Jan	China People's Rep	Romania	General Economic	56CCJC2	410295
04 Jan	Multilateral		Scientific Project	256UNTS171	103627
04 Jan	Germany, West	USA (United States)	General Military	268UNTS143	103856
05 Jan	Belgium	Switzerland	Reparations	228UNTS159	103149
07 Jan	Sudan	USSR (Soviet Union)	Consul/Citizenship	0SUST351	468415
07 Jan	ICJ Option Clause	India	ICJ Option Clause	226UNTS235	103116
09 Jan	Canada	UK Great Britain	Status of Forces	331UNTS192	104755
09 Jan	Canada	Finland	Visas	305UNTS33	104410
10 Jan	Cuba	USA (United States)	Milit Assistance	240UNTS101	103398
11 Jan	Italy	Japan	Visas	267UNTS175	103842
12 Jan	USSR (Soviet Union)	Yugoslavia	Direct Aid	0SUST347	468474
12 Jan	Germany, East	Poland	Water Transport	56PZUM11	458032
12 Jan	Germany, East	Poland	Water Transport	4EGDA237	419249
12 Jan	Accept UN Charter	Sudan	UN Charter	253UNTS81	103576
13 Jan	Czechoslovakia	Poland	Water Transport	56PZUM25	458033
13 Jan	Czechoslovakia	Poland	Land Transport	56PZUM30	458034
13 Jan	Romania	Yugoslavia	Postal Service	342UNTS265	104912
13 Jan	Czechoslovakia	Poland	Gen Communications	265UNTS157	103811
13 Jan	USA (United States)	Uruguay	Atomic Energy	240UNTS401	103415
14 Jan	China People's Rep	Korea, North	Specific Resources	56CCJC10	410299
17 Jan	Austria	Israel	Air Transport	59ABGB162	403106
17 Jan	France	Japan	Air Transport	255UNTS275	103614
17 Jan	Germany, West	Sweden	Reparations	262UNTS301	103758
18 Jan	Sweden	UK Great Britain	Admin Cooperation	428UNTS301	106181
18 Jan	Belgium	Sweden	Taxation	293UNTS23	104283
18 Jan	Sweden	USA (United States)	Atomic Energy	240UNTS413	103416
19 Jan	Australia	Japan	Air Transport	311UNTS291	104507
19 Jan	USA (United States)	Yugoslavia	Direct Aid	240UNTS121	103400
20 Jan	Austria	Belgium	Non-ILO Labor	248UNTS3	103481
21 Jan	Spain	Uruguay	General Trade	56SPBO1003	460264
21 Jan	Bulgaria	China People's Rep	General Economic	56CCJC13	410302
21 Jan	Nicaragua	USA (United States)	General Amity	367UNTS3	105224
22 Jan	Netherlands	USA (United States)	Atomic Energy	287UNTS121	104181
23 Jan	Austria	Italy	Air Transport	393UNTS97	105653
24 Jan	Poland	Vietnam, North	Gen Communications	56PZUM66	458037
24 Jan	Poland	Vietnam, North	Telecommunications	56PZUM50	458036
24 Jan	Poland	Vietnam, North	Postal Service	56PZUM32	458035
25 Jan	Finland	Germany, East	Finance	3EGDA646	419100
25 Jan	Argentina	Switzerland	Air Transport	559UNTS121	108157
25 Jan	Peru	USA (United States)	Atomic Energy	240UNTS425	103417
26 Jan	Norway	Sweden	General Ad Hoc	3NORT673	451162
26 Jan	Canada	USA (United States)	Status of Forces	241UNTS115	103428
27 Jan	Germany, East	Poland	Scientific Project	3EGDA504	419250
27 Jan	China People's Rep	Hungary	General Economic	56CCJC15	410303
28 Jan	Afghanistan	USSR (Soviet Union)	Loans and Credits	0SUST347	468005
28 Jan	USSR (Soviet Union)	Yugoslavia	Atomic Energy	0SUST348	468475

DATE	PARTY ONE	PARTY TWO	TOPIC	CITATION	NUMBER
1956 (Cont.)					
30 Jan	Belgium	Spain	General Economic	56SPBO803	460046
30 Jan	Germany, East	Hungary	General Economic	3EGDA530	419448
31 Jan	Germany, East	Poland	Water Transport	3EGDA504	419251
31 Jan	Denmark	Netherlands	Finance	286UNTS255	104172
01 Feb	Dominican Republic	Spain	Health/Educ/Welfare	57SPBO2901	460083
01 Feb	Poland	USSR (Soviet Union)	Specific Property	56PZUM70	458038
01 Feb	Romania	Yugoslavia	Air Transport	362UNTS203	105189
02 Feb	Lebanon	Norway	Air Transport	3NORT674	451104
02 Feb	Italy	Switzerland	Sanitation	291UNTS113	104247
02 Feb	USSR (Soviet Union)	Yugoslavia	Loans and Credits	259UNTS111	103685
02 Feb	Multilateral		Tech Assistance	227UNTS153	103137
03 Feb	Bulgaria	USSR (Soviet Union)	General Aid	0SUST348	468043
03 Feb	Hungary	Romania	Air Transport	362UNTS233	105190
03 Feb	India	USA (United States)	Air Transport	272UNTS75	103932
03 Feb	Korea, South	USA (United States)	Atomic Energy	240UNTS129	103401
04 Feb	Accept UN Charter	Portugal	UN Charter	229UNTS3	103155
06 Feb	Luxembourg	Netherlands	Reparations	261UNTS17	103723
07 Feb	Poland	USSR (Soviet Union)	Mass Media	0SUST349	468338
07 Feb	China People's Rep	Mongolia	General Trade	56CCJC20	410307
07 Feb	Austria	USA (United States)	US Agri Commod Aid	272UNTS117	103933
08 Feb	Germany, West	Italy	Culture	58WGBB77	425293
08 Feb	Austria	Poland	Air Transport	334UNTS221	104770
10 Feb	Bulgaria	Yugoslavia	Scientific Project	349UNTS21	105007
10 Feb	Japan	USA (United States)	Direct Aid	275UNTS181	103981
10 Feb	Japan	USA (United States)	Direct Aid	275UNTS105	103979
10 Feb	Japan	USA (United States)	Direct Aid	275UNTS157	103980
10 Feb	Multilateral		Tech Assistance	228UNTS189	103151
10 Feb	Multilateral		Tech Assistance	228UNTS167	103150
11 Feb	Czechoslovakia	Yugoslavia	Admin Cooperation	397UNTS135	105703
12 Feb	Netherlands	Sudan	Air Transport	311UNTS319	104508
13 Feb	Germany, West	USA (United States)	Atomic Energy	253UNTS119	103580
14 Feb	United Arab Rep	Poland	Air Transport	56PZUM82	458039
14 Feb	France	Italy	Culture	57ITGU139	435142
14 Feb	China People's Rep	Yugoslavia	Postal Service	56CCJC23	410309
14 Feb	China People's Rep	Yugoslavia	Telecommunications	56CCJC24	410310
15 Feb	Albania	Germany, East	Tech Assistance	3EGDA596	419012
17 Feb	China People's Rep	Yugoslavia	Dispute Settlement	56CCJC28	410314
17 Feb	China People's Rep	Yugoslavia	Dispute Settlement	56CCJC30	410316
17 Feb	China People's Rep	Yugoslavia	Dispute Settlement	56CCJC26	410312
17 Feb	China People's Rep	Yugoslavia	Scientific Project	56CCJC29	410315
17 Feb	China People's Rep	Yugoslavia	General Trade	56CCJC25	410311
17 Feb	China People's Rep	Yugoslavia	Finance	56CCJC27	410313
17 Feb	Ethiopia	WHO (World Health)	Tech Assistance	243UNTS91	103448
17 Feb	Norway	South Africa	Visas	230UNTS213	103186
18 Feb	Germany, West	United Arab Rep	General Trade	56WBGA110	424712
19 Feb	China People's Rep	France	Finance	56CCJC33	410317
19 Feb	China People's Rep	France	Finance	56CCJC34	410318
20 Feb	Iran	USA (United States)	US Agri Commod Aid	272UNTS135	103934
20 Feb	Taiwan	USA (United States)	Visas	275UNTS73	103976
21 Feb	Japan	IBRD (World Bank)	IBRD Project	248UNTS321	200543
22 Feb	Germany, West	United Arab Rep	Other Military	57WBGA48	424713
22 Feb	Luxembourg	Netherlands	Visas	286UNTS249	104171
22 Feb	Accept UN Charter	Italy	UN Charter	231UNTS175	103217
24 Feb	China People's Rep	Poland	Gen Communications	56CCJC35	410319
24 Feb	Israel	Italy	Extradition	316UNTS97	104580
24 Feb	Multilateral		Specific Resources	243UNTS147	103451
25 Feb	Norway	Syria	Air Transport	3NORT676	451169
25 Feb	China People's Rep	Poland	Postal Service	56PZUM109	458040
25 Feb	China People's Rep	Poland	Gen Communications	56CCJC36	410320
25 Feb	China People's Rep	Mongolia	Postal Service	56CCJC37	410321
25 Feb	Norway	Syria	Air Transport	463UNTS217	106706
27 Feb	Italy	USA (United States)	Direct Aid	291UNTS287	104260
27 Feb	Denmark	UK Great Britain	Commodity Trade	252UNTS83	103558
28 Feb	Portugal	Spain	Sanitation	57SPBO802	460230
28 Feb	Australia	Yugoslavia	Postal Service	243UNTS53	103446

DATE	PARTY ONE	PARTY TWO	TOPIC	CITATION	NUMBER
1956 (Cont.)					
29 Feb	San Marino	USSR (Soviet Union)	Consul/Citizenship	16SUGG70	469912
29 Feb	Canada	USSR (Soviet Union)	General Trade	252UNTS165	103566
01 Mar	Multilateral		Customs	343UNTS129	104923
01 Mar	Belgium	France	Admin Cooperation	337UNTS53	104815
02 Mar	Pakistan	USA (United States)	US Agri Commod Aid	271UNTS371	103927
02 Mar	Germany, West	USA (United States)	Claims and Debts	273UNTS209	103952
02 Mar	Indonesia	USA (United States)	US Agri Commod Aid	271UNTS345	103925
03 Mar	Syria	Turkey	General Trade	57TURG701	466092
03 Mar	USSR (Soviet Union)	Yugoslavia	Water Transport	0SUST350	468477
03 Mar	France	Italy	Non-ILO Labor	267UNTS181	103843
03 Mar	Multilateral		Milit Servic/Citiz	243UNTS169	103452
05 Mar	Germany, West	Pakistan	Other Military	68WBGA203	424563
05 Mar	Cameroon	Germany, West	Other Military	68WBGA203	424348
05 Mar	Germany, West	India	Other Military	68WBGA202	424253
05 Mar	Germany, West	South Africa	Other Military	68WBGA205	424646
05 Mar	Germany, West	New Zealand	Other Military	402UNTS103	105779
05 Mar	Multilateral		Other Military	326UNTS169	104711
05 Mar	Australia	Germany, West	Other Military	328UNTS241	104737
05 Mar	Multilateral		Other Military	326UNTS181	104712
05 Mar	Burma	Israel	Direct Aid	280UNTS209	104060
05 Mar	Spain	USA (United States)	US Agri Commod Aid	271UNTS329	103924
05 Mar	Ethiopia	Italy	Reparations	267UNTS189	103844
06 Mar	Denmark	USSR (Soviet Union)	Health/Educ/Welfare	0SUST350	468120
06 Mar	Burma	Sweden	General Trade	369UNTS275	105261
06 Mar	Iceland	USA (United States)	General Trade	270UNTS205	103898
07 Mar	Poland	Yugoslavia	Telecommunications	56PZUM115	458041
07 Mar	Poland	Yugoslavia	Postal Service	56PZUM121	458042
07 Mar	Burma	Yugoslavia	Commodity Trade	386UNTS207	105542
07 Mar	France	Sweden	Admin Cooperation	369UNTS155	105256
07 Mar	France	Sweden	Admin Cooperation	369UNTS171	105257
07 Mar	Burma	Yugoslavia	Tech Assistance	386UNTS235	105543
07 Mar	Burma	Yugoslavia	Direct Aid	378UNTS99	105420
07 Mar	Germany, West	USA (United States)	Sanitation	271UNTS361	103926
08 Mar	USSR (Soviet Union)	Yemen	General Trade	0SUST350	468457
08 Mar	Canada	Hungary	Commodity Trade	305UNTS27	104409
09 Mar	USSR (Soviet Union)	Yugoslavia	Claims and Debts	0SUST351	468478
09 Mar	Iran	Pakistan	Culture	449UNTS183	106460
09 Mar	Norway	Sweden	Land Transport	369UNTS285	105262
10 Mar	Germany, West	Yugoslavia	General Economic	56WGBB967	425325
10 Mar	Germany, West	Yugoslavia	General Economic	57WBGA9	424326
10 Mar	Germany, West	Yugoslavia	Claims and Debts	57WBGA9	424327
10 Mar	Germany, West	Yugoslavia	Specif Claim/Waive	57WBGA9	424328
10 Mar	Germany, West	Yugoslavia	Non-ILO Labor	58WGBB168	425324
10 Mar	Bolivia	USA (United States)	Mass Media	270UNTS199	103897
12 Mar	Iran	Spain	General Amity	57SPBO1912	460162
12 Mar	Iran	Spain	Culture	0IRTB21	433033
12 Mar	Turkey	UK Great Britain	Culture	313UNTS73	104530
12 Mar	Turkey	USA (United States)	US Agri Commod Aid	272UNTS21	103929
13 Mar	Albania	China People's Rep	General Economic	56CCJC40	410324
13 Mar	Multilateral		Humanitarian	427UNTS245	106158
13 Mar	Japan	Netherlands	Claims and Debts	252UNTS3	103554
13 Mar	Korea, South	USA (United States)	US Agri Commod Aid	272UNTS3	103928
13 Mar	Chile	USA (United States)	US Agri Commod Aid	275UNTS49	103975
13 Mar	Thailand	USA (United States)	Atomic Energy	253UNTS105	103579
14 Mar	Germany, East	Vietnam, North	Tech Assistance	4EGDA567	419486
14 Mar	Colombia	USA (United States)	Scientific Project	271UNTS303	103922
15 Mar	Australia	Austria	Visas	241UNTS331	103441
15 Mar	Australia	Greece	Consul/Citizenship	241UNTS313	103438
16 Mar	Ceylon (Sri Lanka)	Romania	General Trade	315UNTS41	104558
16 Mar	Ireland	USA (United States)	Atomic Energy	317UNTS195	104604
16 Mar	Ceylon (Sri Lanka)	Romania	Finance	315UNTS51	104559
19 Mar	Austria	Switzerland	Non-ILO Labor	56SWRO663	462012
19 Mar	China People's Rep	Pakistan	Direct Aid	56CCJC41	410325
19 Mar	Nicaragua	USA (United States)	Postal Service	275UNTS231	103984
19 Mar	France	USA (United States)	Other Military	275UNTS37	103974

DATE	PARTY ONE	PARTY TWO	TOPIC	CITATION	NUMBER
1956 (Cont.)					
20 Mar	Iran	Pakistan	Sanitation	0IRTB55	433084
20 Mar	Canada	Japan	Postal Service	517UNTS33	107482
21 Mar	Austria	Spain	Finance	56SPBO2404	460040
21 Mar	Austria	Spain	General Trade	56SPBO2404	460039
22 Mar	Germany, West	Sweden	Reparations	262UNTS401	103762
22 Mar	Japan	USA (United States)	Patents/Copyrights	275UNTS195	103983
22 Mar	Germany, West	Sweden	Patents/Copyrights	262UNTS423	103763
22 Mar	Germany, West	Sweden	Claims and Debts	262UNTS361	103761
23 Mar	USA (United States)	Uruguay	Tech Assistance	376UNTS311	105386
23 Mar	Bulgaria	Yugoslavia	Admin Cooperation	367UNTS213	105230
23 Mar	France	USA (United States)	Specific Property	278UNTS131	104029
24 Mar	Afghanistan	USSR (Soviet Union)	Air Transport	0SUST351	468006
26 Mar	Multilateral		IGO Establishment	259UNTS125	103686
26 Mar	Ecuador	IBRD (World Bank)	IBRD Project	292UNTS391	104277
26 Mar	Belgium	Israel	Extradition	260UNTS3	103702
27 Mar	Colombia	USA (United States)	Air Transport	273UNTS235	103954
27 Mar	Netherlands	USA (United States)	General Amity	285UNTS231	104154
28 Mar	Spain	Turkey	Culture	58SPBO908	460257
28 Mar	France	Spain	General Trade	56SPBO2704	460111
30 Mar	Multilateral		IGO Operations	604UNTS114	108748
31 Mar	France	USSR (Soviet Union)	Culture	0SUST355	468157
31 Mar	France	USSR (Soviet Union)	General Trade	0SUST351	468156
31 Mar	China People's Rep	Finland	Mostfavored Nation	56CCJC44	410326
31 Mar	Norway	USSR (Soviet Union)	Air Transport	259UNTS205	103690
31 Mar	Sweden	USSR (Soviet Union)	Air Transport	259UNTS239	103691
31 Mar	Denmark	USSR (Soviet Union)	Air Transport	259UNTS169	103689
01 Apr	Burma	USSR (Soviet Union)	Commodity Trade	0SUST352	468063
03 Apr	Taiwan	USA (United States)	Milit Assistance	268UNTS315	103864
03 Apr	South Africa	USA (United States)	Visas	249UNTS395	103513
04 Apr	Japan	Pakistan	General Trade	57JAIL82	440161
04 Apr	Bulgaria	Yugoslavia	Air Transport	391UNTS47	105616
05 Apr	France	Vietnam, South	Mass Media	0VKNG104	496033
05 Apr	China People's Rep	Vietnam, North	Air Transport	56CCJC45	410327
06 Apr	India	USSR (Soviet Union)	Water Transport	0SUST352	468215
06 Apr	France	Italy	Admin Cooperation	60FRRT15	415246
07 Apr	China People's Rep	USSR (Soviet Union)	Direct Aid	0SUST353	468095
07 Apr	China People's Rep	USSR (Soviet Union)	Direct Aid	0SUST353	468094
07 Apr	Morocco	Spain	Recognition	57SPBO403	460188
07 Apr	Morocco	Spain	Recognition	57SPBO403	460189
07 Apr	Morocco	Spain	Recognition	57SPBO403	460187
07 Apr	Romania	USSR (Soviet Union)	Culture	259UNTS377	103698
09 Apr	Japan	Thailand	General Trade	57JAIL82	440162
09 Apr	Austria	Hungary	Specific Resources	438UNTS123	106315
10 Apr	Australia	Turkey	Visas	247UNTS139	103462
11 Apr	Spain	Sweden	General Economic	56SPBO705	460246
12 Apr	China People's Rep	Sudan	General Trade	56CCJC50	410330
13 Apr	Italy	Spain	General Trade	56SPBO3004	460171
13 Apr	Japan	USA (United States)	Milit Assistance	273UNTS223	103953
14 Apr	Romania	USSR (Soviet Union)	Gen Communications	0SUST353	468393
14 Apr	Belgium	Germany, West	Air Transport	344UNTS103	104945
15 Apr	China People's Rep	United Arab Rep	Culture	56CCJC51	410331
16 Apr	Italy	Spain	Mass Media	57SPBO102	460172
16 Apr	New Zealand	Sweden	Taxation	274UNTS259	103971
17 Apr	Indonesia	United Nations	Non-IBRD Project	233UNTS267	103266
18 Apr	Germany, West	USA (United States)	Admin Cooperation	271UNTS319	103923
19 Apr	Bulgaria	Greece	Sanitation	594UNTS131	108600
19 Apr	Canada	USA (United States)	Milit Installation	274UNTS3	103955
19 Apr	Germany, West	Italy	General Trade	281UNTS195	104080
20 Apr	Chile	USA (United States)	Atomic Energy	293UNTS277	104295
23 Apr	Mongolia	USSR (Soviet Union)	Tech Assistance	16SUGG70	469914
23 Apr	Mongolia	USSR (Soviet Union)	Specific Property	16SUGG70	469913
23 Apr	China People's Rep	Poland	Scientific Project	56CCJC53	410332
23 Apr	Canada	USA (United States)	Non-ILO Labor	300UNTS29	104329
24 Apr	Cambodia	China People's Rep	General Trade	56CCJC54	410333
24 Apr	Cambodia	China People's Rep	General Trade	56CCJC55	410334

DATE	PARTY ONE	PARTY TWO	TOPIC	CITATION	NUMBER
1956 (Cont.)					
24 Apr	Mongolia	USSR (Soviet Union)	Culture	259UNTS297	103693
25 Apr	France	Switzerland	Specific Property	58SWRO135	462004
25 Apr	France	Switzerland	Specific Property	58SWRO135	462087
25 Apr	Hungary	Poland	Telecommunications	56PZUM140	458044
25 Apr	Hungary	Poland	Gen Communications	56PZUM156	458045
25 Apr	Belgium	Spain	Finance	56SPBO2405	460047
25 Apr	Hungary	Poland	Postal Service	56PZUM128	458043
25 Apr	Czechoslovakia	Germany, East	Land Transport	4EGDA359	419349
25 Apr	Honduras	USA (United States)	Military Mission	269UNTS25	103869
25 Apr	Multilateral		Commodity Trade	270UNTS103	103896
26 Apr	Germany, East	USSR (Soviet Union)	Health/Educ/Welfare	259UNTS279	103692
26 Apr	Germany, West	USA (United States)	Culture	283UNTS267	104122
27 Apr	Italy	USA (United States)	Direct Aid	273UNTS149	103949
28 Apr	Cambodia	UNICEF (Children)	Direct Aid	136UNTS341	200446
28 Apr	Ceylon (Sri Lanka)	USA (United States)	Direct Aid	274UNTS35	103956
28 Apr	Bulgaria	USSR (Soviet Union)	Culture	259UNTS363	103697
30 Apr	Multilateral		Air Transport	310UNTS229	104494
02 May	Germany, West	Switzerland	Air Transport	559UNTS157	108158
02 May	Paraguay	USA (United States)	US Agri Commod Aid	268UNTS299	103863
03 May	Germany, West	Spain	Mass Media	56SPBO706	460005
03 May	Germany, West	Spain	Mass Media	56SPBO706	460004
03 May	Italy	Luxembourg	Culture	58ITGU121	435265
03 May	Peru	USA (United States)	Direct Aid	272UNTS59	103931
03 May	Albania	USSR (Soviet Union)	Culture	259UNTS391	103699
03 May	Norway	IBRD (World Bank)	IBRD Project	243UNTS281	103455
04 May	Czechoslovakia	Germany, East	Consul/Citizenship	4EGDA366	419350
04 May	Brazil	France	Finance	323UNTS339	104675
04 May	Burma	IBRD (World Bank)	IBRD Project	253UNTS209	103585
04 May	Burma	IBRD (World Bank)	IBRD Project	253UNTS179	103584
07 May	Haiti	IBRD (World Bank)	IBRD Project	252UNTS279	103570
07 May	Austria	Italy	Finance	284UNTS351	104147
07 May	Peru	USA (United States)	US Agri Commod Aid	268UNTS285	103862
08 May	Mongolia	Romania	Culture	342UNTS291	104913
08 May	Peru	USA (United States)	Direct Aid	278UNTS117	104028
09 May	Japan	Philippines	Direct Aid	0JGJI1291	441090
09 May	Austria	Italy	Education	267UNTS227	103845
09 May	Japan	Philippines	Reparations	285UNTS3	104148
10 May	Greece	Japan	Visas	0JGJI1302	441091
10 May	Multilateral		Tech Assistance	243UNTS103	103449
11 May	Korea, North	Poland	Culture	432UNTS161	106219
11 May	Paraguay	USA (United States)	Visas	269UNTS33	103870
12 May	Korea, North	Romania	Culture	342UNTS189	104908
12 May	Denmark	Italy	General Trade	260UNTS357	103720
13 May	Cambodia	USSR (Soviet Union)	Consul/Citizenship	16SUGG70	469915
14 May	Japan	USSR (Soviet Union)	Specific Resources	0JGJI1314	441092
14 May	Greece	Spain	General Trade	56SPBO1406	460156
14 May	Japan	USSR (Soviet Union)	Humanitarian	0JGJI1315	441093
14 May	Denmark	USSR (Soviet Union)	General Trade	271UNTS125	103912
15 May	Belgium	Germany, West	Visas	58WGBB190	425022
16 May	Portugal	Venezuela	Air Transport	463UNTS239	106707
16 May	Japan	Netherlands	Visas	305UNTS97	104417
17 May	Thailand	USSR (Soviet Union)	Consul/Citizenship	16SUGG71	469916
17 May	Germany, West	Greece	Culture	57WGBB501	425230
17 May	USSR (Soviet Union)	Yugoslavia	Culture	259UNTS145	103687
18 May	Ethiopia	USSR (Soviet Union)	Consul/Citizenship	16SUGG71	469917
18 May	Germany, West	Spain	General Trade	56SPBO307	460008
18 May	Germany, West	Spain	Finance	56SPBO307	460009
18 May	Multilateral		Customs	327UNTS123	104721
18 May	Costa Rica	USA (United States)	Atomic Energy	404UNTS237	105814
18 May	Multilateral		Land Transport	339UNTS3	104844
18 May	Multilateral		Customs	338UNTS103	104834
18 May	Multilateral		Customs	319UNTS21	104630
18 May	Turkey	USA (United States)	Patents/Copyrights	283UNTS167	104115
19 May	Multilateral		Land Transport	399UNTS189	105742
20 May	Thailand	USSR (Soviet Union)	Consul/Citizenship	0SUST355	468421

DATE	PARTY ONE	PARTY TWO	TOPIC	CITATION	NUMBER
1956 (Cont.)					
20 May	China People's Rep	United Arab Rep	Culture	56CCJC66	410337
21 May	India	USSR (Soviet Union)	Specif Goods/Equip	OSUST356	468216
21 May	Finland	Spain	Finance	56SPBO906	460100
21 May	Finland	Spain	General Trade	56SPBO906	460099
21 May	USA (United States)	Yugoslavia	Visas	281UNTS93	104072
21 May	Italy	South Africa	Air Transport	255UNTS323	103616
22 May	China People's Rep	Germany, East	General Trade	56CCJC67	410338
22 May	Bulgaria	Yugoslavia	Visas	367UNTS119	105229
22 May	USSR (Soviet Union)	Yugoslavia	Consul/Citizenship	259UNTS155	103688
22 May	Fed Rhod/Nyasaland	South Africa	Taxation	254UNTS227	103595
22 May	Nicaragua	IBRD (World Bank)	IBRD Project	253UNTS233	103586
22 May	Finland	IBRD (World Bank)	IBRD Project	248UNTS57	103485
23 May	Argentina	Italy	Claims and Debts	267UNTS255	103846
23 May	Denmark	Norway	Taxation	271UNTS75	103910
23 May	Denmark	Norway	Taxation	271UNTS49	103909
24 May	Japan	Switzerland	Air Transport	312UNTS3	104509
24 May	Portugal	USA (United States)	US Agri Commod Aid	268UNTS323	103865
25 May	Panama	USA (United States)	Visas	268UNTS333	103866
25 May	UK Great Britain	USSR (Soviet Union)	Specific Resources	266UNTS209	103831
26 May	Greece	Italy	Air Transport	496UNTS301	107258
28 May	France	India	Specific Property	62FRRT33	415230
28 May	Pakistan	USA (United States)	Milit Assistance	269UNTS15	103868
28 May	Italy	UNICEF (Children)	Direct Aid	243UNTS43	103445
29 May	Germany, West	Norway	Culture	3NORT688	451187
30 May	Norway	Yugoslavia	General Trade	3NORT689	451095
30 May	China People's Rep	Korea, North	Culture	56CCJC68	410339
30 May	Guatemala	USA (United States)	Visas	275UNTS271	103986
30 May	Germany, East	USSR (Soviet Union)	Sanitation	263UNTS143	103771
30 May	Fed Rhod/Nyasaland	South Africa	Air Transport	255UNTS317	103615
31 May	Japan	Tunisia	Visas	OJGJI1294	441094
31 May	Multilateral		Tech Assistance	251UNTS181	103541
01 Jun	Italy	Switzerland	Telecommunications	57ITGU159	435376
01 Jun	China People's Rep	UK Great Britain	Patents/Copyrights	56CCJC69	410340
01 Jun	Netherlands	Yugoslavia	Non-ILO Labor	276UNTS319	103994
01 Jun	Czechoslovakia	USSR (Soviet Union)	Culture	259UNTS341	103696
02 Jun	Ethiopia	USSR (Soviet Union)	Consul/Citizenship	OSUST357	468131
02 Jun	France	Spain	Mass Media	56SPBO2406	460112
04 Jun	Chile	Italy	Milit Servic/Citiz	362UNTS309	105195
04 Jun	Ceylon (Sri Lanka)	Hungary	General Trade	315UNTS13	104555
04 Jun	Italy	Switzerland	Air Transport	378UNTS311	105429
04 Jun	Canada	Germany, West	Taxation	316UNTS231	104589
04 Jun	Iceland	USA (United States)	Visas	275UNTS189	103982
05 Jun	Greece	Ireland	Visas	553UNTS93	108072
05 Jun	UK Great Britain	USA (United States)	Milit Installation	247UNTS205	103470
06 Jun	Germany, West	Switzerland	Admin Cooperation	60SWRO617	462023
06 Jun	Iraq	USA (United States)	Visas	275UNTS265	103985
06 Jun	Colombia	IBRD (World Bank)	IBRD Project	248UNTS139	103493
07 Jun	Multilateral		Non-ILO Labor	381UNTS145	105470
08 Jun	Multilateral		Tech Assistance	247UNTS366	200541
08 Jun	Poland	Sweden	Air Transport	334UNTS257	104771
08 Jun	Austria	USA (United States)	Atomic Energy	253UNTS139	103581
09 Jun	Sweden	UK Great Britain	Non-ILO Labor	309UNTS301	104479
11 Jun	Netherlands	UK Great Britain	Status of Forces	306UNTS107	104436
12 Jun	Indonesia	USSR (Soviet Union)	Mostfavored Nation	OSUST367	468222
12 Jun	Germany, West	Lebanon	Admin Cooperation	57WBGA173	424405
12 Jun	Germany, East	Korea, North	Health/Educ/Welfare	4EGDA532	419175
12 Jun	Germany, East	Korea, North	Mass Media	1EGDA534	419176
12 Jun	China People's Rep	Syria	Culture	56CCJC71	410341
12 Jun	China People's Rep	Syria	Culture	56CCJC72	410342
12 Jun	Germany, West	Ireland	Air Transport	353UNTS121	105040
12 Jun	India	Thailand	Air Transport	255UNTS341	103617
12 Jun	Switzerland	UK Great Britain	Taxation	269UNTS133	103879
12 Jun	Netherlands	UK Great Britain	Non-ILO Labor	250UNTS81	103519
12 Jun	Multilateral		Tech Assistance	243UNTS187	103453
13 Jun	New Zealand	USA (United States)	Atomic Energy	253UNTS155	103582

DATE	PARTY ONE	PARTY TWO	TOPIC	CITATION	NUMBER
1956 (Cont.)					
14 Jun	China People's Rep	USSR (Soviet Union)	Commodity Trade	16SUGG71	469918
14 Jun	Hungary	USSR (Soviet Union)	Mass Media	OSUST385	468199
14 Jun	China People's Rep	USSR (Soviet Union)	General Trade	56CCJC73	410343
14 Jun	Multilateral		Tech Assistance	265UNTS125	103809
15 Jun	Germany, East	Vietnam, North	Finance	3EGDA612	419487
15 Jun	Austria	Yugoslavia	Sanitation	396UNTS117	105695
15 Jun	Dominican Republic	USA (United States)	Atomic Energy	265UNTS227	103815
16 Jun	Czechoslovakia	Yugoslavia	Health/Educ/Welfare	552UNTS325	108064
16 Jun	Bulgaria	Yugoslavia	Territory Boundary	391UNTS3	105613
16 Jun	Bulgaria	Yugoslavia	Territory Boundary	375UNTS235	105368
17 Jun	Israel	Sweden	Taxation	257UNTS47	103648
18 Jun	Hungary	Poland	Telecommunications	56PZUM185	458046
18 Jun	Germany, East	USSR (Soviet Union)	Air Transport	4EGDA61	419400
18 Jun	China People's Rep	Vietnam, North	General Trade	56CCJC74	410344
18 Jun	Burma	UK Great Britain	Commodity Trade	256UNTS125	103623
19 Jun	Bulgaria	Ceylon (Sri Lanka)	Finance	315UNTS33	104557
19 Jun	Austria	Canada	Visas	305UNTS51	104412
19 Jun	Bulgaria	Ceylon (Sri Lanka)	General Trade	315UNTS23	104556
19 Jun	France	USA (United States)	Atomic Energy	281UNTS341	104087
20 Jun	USSR (Soviet Union)	Yugoslavia	Admin Cooperation	OSUST358	468479
20 Jun	Burma	Japan	Admin Cooperation	306UNTS61	104431
20 Jun	Multilateral		Admin Cooperation	268UNTS3	103850
21 Jun	Cambodia	China People's Rep	Direct Aid	56CCJC76	410345
21 Jun	Canada	UK Great Britain	Postal Service	381UNTS111	105467
21 Jun	Fed Rhod/Nyasaland	IBRD (World Bank)	IBRD Project	285UNTS317	104156
21 Jun	IBRD (World Bank)	UK Great Britain	IBRD Project	285UNTS355	104157
21 Jun	Switzerland	USA (United States)	Atomic Energy	279UNTS41	104033
22 Jun	Brazil	Switzerland	Taxation	56SWRO1087	462045
22 Jun	Australia	USA (United States)	Atomic Energy	283UNTS275	104123
22 Jun	France	USA (United States)	Taxation	291UNTS101	104246
23 Jun	Afghanistan	USA (United States)	Direct Aid	271UNTS295	103921
25 Jun	Honduras	USA (United States)	Taxation	279UNTS113	104036
25 Jun	Cambodia	UNICEF (Children)	Direct Aid	249UNTS153	103505
25 Jun	UK Great Britain	USA (United States)	Milit Installation	249UNTS91	103502
25 Jun	UK Great Britain	USA (United States)	Milit Installation	249UNTS59	103501
25 Jun	France	Greece	General Trade	251UNTS167	103540
26 Jun	Afghanistan	Iran	Admin Cooperation	OIRTB2	433002
26 Jun	Multilateral		Tech Assistance	321UNTS2	104650
26 Jun	Israel	USA (United States)	Education	257UNTS55	103649
26 Jun	India	IBRD (World Bank)	IBRD Project	301UNTS3	104341
26 Jun	Cuba	USA (United States)	Atomic Energy	293UNTS257	104294
26 Jun	Multilateral		Tech Assistance	253UNTS12	103573
27 Jun	Pakistan	USSR (Soviet Union)	General Trade	16SUGG71	469919
27 Jun	Pakistan	USSR (Soviet Union)	Finance	16SUGG71	469920
27 Jun	Pakistan	USSR (Soviet Union)	General Trade	OSUST359	468304
27 Jun	Netherlands	USSR (Soviet Union)	General Trade	OSUST359	468291
27 Jun	Libya	USA (United States)	Direct Aid	273UNTS89	103945
27 Jun	Hungary	UK Great Britain	Claims and Debts	249UNTS19	103499
28 Jun	Poland	USA (United States)	Claims and Debts	273UNTS79	103944
28 Jun	Hungary	USSR (Soviet Union)	Health/Educ/Welfare	259UNTS405	103700
29 Jun	Chile	Germany, West	Customs	58WGBB108	425081
29 Jun	Italy	Netherlands	Finance	287UNTS193	104185
29 Jun	Italy	Switzerland	Finance	284UNTS299	104144
29 Jun	Norway	Sweden	Specific Resources	262UNTS335	103759
30 Jun	Poland	USSR (Soviet Union)	Culture	259UNTS311	103694
30 Jun	Bolivia	USA (United States)	Military Mission	271UNTS269	103920
30 Jun	Burma	USA (United States)	Tech Assistance	281UNTS65	104070
30 Jun	Argentina	UK Great Britain	General Economic	269UNTS235	103884
30 Jun	Denmark	Germany, West	Visas	258UNTS65	103671
30 Jun	Bolivia	USA (United States)	Military Mission	271UNTS243	103919
02 Jul	Multilateral		Tech Assistance	540UNTS110	107846
02 Jul	Indonesia	UK Great Britain	Commodity Trade	265UNTS285	103820
02 Jul	Korea, South	USA (United States)	Milit Assistance	281UNTS41	104067
02 Jul	Indonesia	UK Great Britain	Commodity Trade	265UNTS271	103819
02 Jul	Multilateral		Tech Assistance	248UNTS37	103484

DATE	PARTY ONE	PARTY TWO	TOPIC	CITATION	NUMBER
1956 (Cont.)					
03 Jul	Czechoslovakia	Yugoslavia	General Economic	397UNTS165	105704
03 Jul	Lebanon	UNICEF (Children)	Direct Aid	324UNTS145	104683
04 Jul	Austria	Brazil	General Economic	57ABGB46	403007
04 Jul	Austria	Brazil	Finance	57ABGB47	403008
04 Jul	Indonesia	Philippines	Admin Cooperation	401UNTS59	105763
05 Jul	Bulgaria	Germany, East	Sanitation	5EGDA311	419051
05 Jul	China People's Rep	USSR (Soviet Union)	Culture	56CCJC84	410349
05 Jul	China People's Rep	USSR (Soviet Union)	Culture	263UNTS129	103770
05 Jul	Multilateral		Patents/Copyrights	258UNTS371	103679
06 Jul	Germany, East	Hungary	Health/Educ/Welfare	5EGDA582	419449
06 Jul	Multilateral		Admin Cooperation	312UNTS109	104514
06 Jul	Poland	Yugoslavia	Culture	281UNTS143	104076
07 Jul	Cambodia	USSR (Soviet Union)	Direct Aid	OSUST363	468064
07 Jul	Finland	Sweden	General Transport	258UNTS83	103672
08 Jul	Germany, East	Syria	Culture	5EGDA485	419312
09 Jul	Nepal	USSR (Soviet Union)	Consul/Citizenship	16SUGG72	469921
09 Jul	USA (United States)	USSR (Soviet Union)	Specif Goods/Equip	OSUST363	468440
09 Jul	United Nations	Switzerland	Telecommunications	56SWRO1273	462191
09 Jul	Austria	UK Great Britain	Non-ILO Labor	310UNTS61	104487
09 Jul	Multilateral		Non-ILO Labor	314UNTS3	104539
09 Jul	Denmark	UK Great Britain	Non-ILO Labor	264UNTS45	103787
10 Jul	France	UK Great Britain	Non-ILO Labor	326UNTS23	104708
11 Jul	Tunisia	USSR (Soviet Union)	Recognition	16SUGG72	469922
11 Jul	USSR (Soviet Union)	Yemen	General Economic	OSUST363	468458
11 Jul	Canada	Honduras	Mostfavored Nation	305UNTS39	104411
11 Jul	Belgium	Japan	Visas	248UNTS129	103492
12 Jul	Korea, North	USSR (Soviet Union)	Direct Aid	OSUST363	468257
12 Jul	United Arab Rep	USSR (Soviet Union)	Atomic Energy	OSUST363	468129
12 Jul	Austria	Italy	Non-ILO Labor	378UNTS249	105426
13 Jul	Turkey	Yugoslavia	Claims and Debts	57TURG1309	466031
13 Jul	Multilateral		Dispute Settlement	281UNTS3	104066
14 Jul	France	Vietnam, South	Consul/Citizenship	OVKNG109	496034
14 Jul	China People's Rep	Poland	Education	56CCJC86	410351
14 Jul	Accept UN Charter	Tunisia	UN Charter	253UNTS85	103577
15 Jul	United Arab Rep	USSR (Soviet Union)	General Trade	OUNTSO	109824
16 Jul	Germany, West	Switzerland	Finance	57SWRO399	462113
17 Jul	Norway	Spain	General Trade	56SPBO808	460204
17 Jul	Germany, West	Yugoslavia	Customs	59WGBB735	425329
17 Jul	Germany, West	Yugoslavia	Finance	56WBGA160	424330
17 Jul	Germany, East	USSR (Soviet Union)	Milit Occupation	5EGDA645	419401
17 Jul	Accept UN Charter	Morocco	UN Charter	253UNTS77	103575
18 Jul	Belgium	France	Non-ILO Labor	248UNTS121	103491
19 Jul	Ecuador	USA (United States)	Milit Assistance	372UNTS149	105295
20 Jul	Denmark	Japan	Visas	OJGJI1296	441095
20 Jul	UK Great Britain	Venezuela	Admin Cooperation	351UNTS289	105029
20 Jul	Austria	UK Great Britain	Taxation	269UNTS147	103880
21 Jul	Romania	USSR (Soviet Union)	Commodity Trade	OSUST364	468394
21 Jul	Italy	Spain	Non-ILO Labor	58SPBO1503	460173
21 Jul	Germany, West	Switzerland	Visas	57WBGA107	424757
23 Jul	France	Luxembourg	Admin Cooperation	60FRRT45	415269
23 Jul	France	USSR (Soviet Union)	Culture	65FRRT52	415469
25 Jul	Germany, West	Luxembourg	Visas	51WBGA114	424419
26 Jul	Israel	Luxembourg	Extradition	550UNTS239	108020
26 Jul	Belgium	Germany, West	Visas	249UNTS187	103508
27 Jul	Iran	Netherlands	Taxation	OIRTB35	433047
27 Jul	Germany, West	USA (United States)	Admin Cooperation	278UNTS3	104017
28 Jul	France	Vietnam, South	Air Transport	OVKNG110	496035
30 Jul	Belgium	Spain	Finance	56SPBO610	460048
30 Jul	Germany, West	Malawi	Consul/Citizenship	57WGBB284	425444
30 Jul	Germany, West	UK Great Britain	Consul/Citizenship	330UNTS233	104748
31 Jul	China People's Rep	Finland	General Trade	56CCJC91	410355
31 Jul	Germany, West	UK Great Britain	Atomic Energy	252UNTS93	103559
01 Aug	Panama	USA (United States)	Telecommunications	281UNTS49	104068
01 Aug	Australia	Netherlands	Non-ILO Labor	280UNTS3	104047
01 Aug	ICJ Option Clause	Netherlands	ICJ Option Clause	248UNTS33	103483

DATE	PARTY ONE	PARTY TWO	TOPIC	CITATION	NUMBER
1956 (Cont.)					
02 Aug	Bolivia	Japan	Health/Educ/Welfare	OJGJI1299	441096
02 Aug	Nicaragua	USA (United States)	Land Transport	281UNTS99	104073
04 Aug	Korea, North	USSR (Soviet Union)	Direct Aid	16SUGG72	469923
04 Aug	Romania	Yugoslavia	Sanitation	395UNTS99	105682
06 Aug	United Arab Rep	Germany, East	Mass Media	5EGDA278	419003
07 Aug	Belgium	Spain	General Trade	56SPBO3108	460049
07 Aug	UNICEF (Children)	Sudan	Direct Aid	248UNTS307	200542
07 Aug	Netherlands	USA (United States)	US Agri Commod Aid	281UNTS57	104069
07 Aug	Pakistan	USA (United States)	US Agri Commod Aid	281UNTS75	104071
08 Aug	Japan	Sweden	Visas	OJGJI1303	441097
08 Aug	Greece	USA (United States)	US Agri Commod Aid	277UNTS203	104007
08 Aug	Belgium	Czechoslovakia	Visas	257UNTS215	103656
09 Aug	Spain	Uruguay	General Trade	56SPBO2310	460265
09 Aug	Dominican Republic	UK Great Britain	Consul/Citizenship	252UNTS127	103561
09 Aug	UNESCO (Educ/Cult)	UK Great Britain	Direct Aid	256UNTS139	103624
10 Aug	Export-Import Bank	Japan	Loans and Credits	OJGJI1300	441147
11 Aug	Uruguay	USSR (Soviet Union)	General Trade	OSUST366	468443
11 Aug	Uruguay	USSR (Soviet Union)	General Economic	OSUST366	468444
11 Aug	Dominican Republic	USA (United States)	Scientific Project	263UNTS181	103773
12 Aug	Indonesia	USSR (Soviet Union)	General Trade	16SUGG72	469924
13 Aug	China People's Rep	Korea, North	Mass Media	56CCJC92	410356
14 Aug	Cuba	Spain	General Economic	56SPBO609	460072
14 Aug	Austria	Sweden	Taxation	262UNTS355	103760
14 Aug	Taiwan	USA (United States)	US Agri Commod Aid	281UNTS257	104083
15 Aug	Guatemala	USA (United States)	Atomic Energy	288UNTS181	104205
16 Aug	Netherlands	USA (United States)	Specific Property	279UNTS3	104031
16 Aug	Multilateral		General Trade	287UNTS223	104188
18 Aug	Indonesia	USSR (Soviet Union)	General Economic	OSUST366	468221
18 Aug	China People's Rep	USSR (Soviet Union)	Scientific Project	OSUST366	468096
20 Aug	Syria	USSR (Soviet Union)	Culture	274UNTS105	103961
21 Aug	Canada	Turkey	Visas	305UNTS89	104416
22 Aug	Japan	Norway	Visas	3NORT692	451091
22 Aug	Guatemala	Honduras	General Economic	263UNTS49	103767
23 Aug	Brazil	France	General Economic	56FRMD1009	417077
24 Aug	Czechoslovakia	Germany, East	Customs	5EGDA486	419351
25 Aug	Greece	Romania	Reparations	299UNTS231	104315
27 Aug	USSR (Soviet Union)	Yugoslavia	Specif Goods/Equip	16SUGG73	469925
29 Aug	China People's Rep	Mongolia	Direct Aid	56CCJC96	410359
29 Aug	India	USA (United States)	US Agri Commod Aid	278UNTS25	104019
30 Aug	France	Iran	Taxation	OIRTB30	433041
30 Aug	Philippines	Switzerland	General Amity	293UNTS43	104284
30 Aug	Canada	India	Patents/Copyrights	305UNTS59	104413
31 Aug	Czechoslovakia	Germany, East	Finance	5EGDA491	419352
31 Aug	Multilateral		Tech Assistance	249UNTS158	103506
01 Sep	Israel	South Africa	Visas	251UNTS161	103539
02 Sep	China People's Rep	Korea, North	Specific Resources	56CCJC97	410360
03 Sep	Denmark	WHO (World Health)	Sanitation	258UNTS103	103674
04 Sep	Greece	United Arab Rep	Culture	299UNTS253	104317
04 Sep	Denmark	Greece	General Trade	256UNTS319	103643
04 Sep	Canada	France	Other Military	305UNTS79	104415
05 Sep	Japan	USA (United States)	Admin Cooperation	277UNTS267	104011
05 Sep	Italy	Spain	Mass Media	302UNTS195	104359
05 Sep	Korea, North	USSR (Soviet Union)	Culture	259UNTS329	103695
06 Sep	Greece	USSR (Soviet Union)	Humanitarian	16SUGG73	469926
06 Sep	France	USA (United States)	Milit Installation	335UNTS173	104784
06 Sep	Peru	USA (United States)	Military Mission	277UNTS231	104009
07 Sep	Multilateral		Humanitarian	266UNTS3	103822
07 Sep	Ceylon (Sri Lanka)	USA (United States)	Visas	280UNTS35	104048
07 Sep	Greece	USA (United States)	Status of Forces	278UNTS141	104030
10 Sep	Ceylon (Sri Lanka)	India	Taxation	315UNTS59	104560
10 Sep	Pakistan	USA (United States)	Milit Assistance	277UNTS259	104010
11 Sep	Czechoslovakia	Germany, East	Consul/Citizenship	5EGDA506	419353
11 Sep	Czechoslovakia	Germany, East	Health/Educ/Welfare	5EGDA539	419356
11 Sep	Czechoslovakia	Germany, East	General Economic	5EGDA507	419354
11 Sep	France	Paraguay	General Trade	58FRRT18	415353

DATE	PARTY ONE	PARTY TWO	TOPIC	CITATION	NUMBER
1956 (Cont.)					
11 Sep	Czechoslovakia	Germany, East	Admin Cooperation	5EGDA511	419355
11 Sep	Greece	Yugoslavia	Health/Educ/Welfare	552UNTS311	108063
11 Sep	Greece	Yugoslavia	Admin Cooperation	391UNTS117	105620
11 Sep	Israel	USA (United States)	US Agri Commod Aid	277UNTS215	104008
11 Sep	Multilateral		Humanitarian	266UNTS221	103832
13 Sep	Austria	China People's Rep	General Trade	56CCJC99	410362
14 Sep	Israel	Switzerland	General Trade	56SWRO1281	462143
14 Sep	Germany, West	Iceland	Visas	57WBGA192	424281
14 Sep	Taiwan	USA (United States)	Loans and Credits	0CTRC868	413043
14 Sep	Finland	USSR (Soviet Union)	Land Transport	255UNTS365	103618
15 Sep	Indonesia	USSR (Soviet Union)	General Aid	0SUST368	468223
15 Sep	Denmark	Finland	General Transport	254UNTS3	103589
15 Sep	Multilateral		Admin Cooperation	254UNTS45	103592
15 Sep	Denmark	Norway	General Transport	259UNTS3	103680
15 Sep	Finland	Norway	Admin Cooperation	254UNTS17	103590
15 Sep	Norway	Sweden	Admin Cooperation	263UNTS17	103765
15 Sep	Denmark	Sweden	General Transport	263UNTS3	103764
15 Sep	Finland	Sweden	Admin Cooperation	254UNTS31	103591
16 Sep	Denmark	Iran	Taxation	0IRTB19	433030
16 Sep	Iran	Sweden	Taxation	0IRTB63	433101
17 Sep	IBRD (World Bank)	Switzerland	Loans and Credits	340UNTS311	200560
18 Sep	China People's Rep	USSR (Soviet Union)	Specif Goods/Equip	16SUGG73	469927
18 Sep	Poland	USSR (Soviet Union)	Loans and Credits	0SUST368	468339
18 Sep	Costa Rica	IBRD (World Bank)	IBRD Project	260UNTS369	103721
20 Sep	China People's Rep	Nepal	Consul/Citizenship	56CCJC105	410366
20 Sep	China People's Rep	Nepal	Consul/Citizenship	56CCJC106	410367
20 Sep	China People's Rep	Nepal	General Amity	56CCJC104	410365
20 Sep	Germany, West	Netherlands	Specific Property	509UNTS269	107405
21 Sep	Austria	IBRD (World Bank)	IBRD Project	259UNTS43	103682
21 Sep	Austria	IBRD (World Bank)	IBRD Project	259UNTS17	103681
22 Sep	Liberia	USA (United States)	Specific Property	278UNTS109	104027
24 Sep	Romania	USSR (Soviet Union)	Specific Resources	16SUGG73	469928
24 Sep	Belgium	Germany, West	Territory Boundary	314UNTS195	104549
24 Sep	Belgium	Germany, West	Culture	263UNTS31	103766
24 Sep	Jordan	USA (United States)	Milit Assistance	278UNTS51	104020
24 Sep	Multilateral		Patents/Copyrights	253UNTS171	103583
25 Sep	Multilateral		Air Transport	334UNTS89	104767
25 Sep	Romania	Yugoslavia	Sanitation	395UNTS147	105683
25 Sep	Multilateral		Air Transport	334UNTS13	104766
26 Sep	Costa Rica	Denmark	General Economic	341UNTS305	104893
27 Sep	India	USA (United States)	Direct Aid	281UNTS289	104085
27 Sep	Norway	Sweden	Taxation	261UNTS71	103726
28 Sep	Int Rail Transport	Switzerland	IGO Status/Immunit	56SWRO1367	462188
28 Sep	Germany, West	South Africa	Taxation	327UNTS83	104718
28 Sep	Germany, West	Netherlands	Air Transport	327UNTS185	104722
28 Sep	Canada	South Africa	Taxation	299UNTS17	104304
28 Sep	Canada	South Africa	Taxation	299UNTS3	104303
29 Sep	India	Poland	Telecommunications	276UNTS305	103993
02 Oct	Poland	USSR (Soviet Union)	Specific Property	56PZUM205	458047
02 Oct	Italy	Libya	Tech Assistance	57ITGU237	435259
03 Oct	ICJ Option Clause	Israel	ICJ Option Clause	252UNTS301	103571
03 Oct	Argentina	USA (United States)	Military Mission	279UNTS13	104032
04 Oct	Canada	France	Non-ILO Labor	305UNTS65	104414
05 Oct	Hungary	USSR (Soviet Union)	Loans and Credits	0SUST368	468200
05 Oct	Germany, East	Hungary	Finance	5EGDA583	419450
05 Oct	Multilateral		Tech Assistance	251UNTS267	103545
05 Oct	Multilateral		Tech Assistance	251UNTS245	103544
06 Oct	Czechoslovakia	Germany, East	Humanitarian	501UNTS109	107315
07 Oct	China People's Rep	Nepal	Finance	56CCJC113	410370
07 Oct	China People's Rep	Nepal	Direct Aid	56CCJC111	410368
07 Oct	China People's Rep	Nepal	Finance	56CCJC112	410369
08 Oct	Germany, East	India	General Trade	5EGDA342	419127
08 Oct	UN Hi Com Refugees	Sweden	Refugees	428UNTS307	106182
08 Oct	Denmark	UK Great Britain	Consul/Citizenship	331UNTS181	104754
08 Oct	Germany, West	USA (United States)	Milit Assistance	278UNTS9	104018

DATE	PARTY ONE	PARTY TWO	TOPIC	CITATION	NUMBER
1956 (Cont.)					
09 Oct	Peru	USA (United States)	Visas	288UNTS165	104204
09 Oct	Germany, West	Thailand	Direct Aid	258UNTS143	103676
09 Oct	Belgium	Chile	Visas	257UNTS227	103658
11 Oct	Italy	IBRD (World Bank)	IBRD Project	359UNTS3	105138
12 Oct	Germany, East	USSR (Soviet Union)	Mass Media	0SUST369	468165
12 Oct	Germany, East	USSR (Soviet Union)	Mass Media	0SUST369	468166
12 Oct	Romania	Vietnam, North	Culture	342UNTS173	104907
12 Oct	IBRD (World Bank)	Thailand	IBRD Project	261UNTS117	103728
12 Oct	Norway	USSR (Soviet Union)	Culture	308UNTS95	104457
13 Oct	Iran	Turkey	General Economic	57TURG2506	466072
13 Oct	Switzerland	Thailand	Air Transport	312UNTS43	104510
13 Oct	Czechoslovakia	Hungary	Territory Boundary	300UNTS177	104337
13 Oct	Czechoslovakia	Hungary	Territory Boundary	300UNTS125	104336
15 Oct	Iran	USSR (Soviet Union)	Territory Boundary	0IRTB75	433117
15 Oct	Burma	Thailand	General Amity	277UNTS87	104000
16 Oct	Nicaragua	USA (United States)	Gen Communications	282UNTS29	104090
17 Oct	Iran	Lebanon	Culture	0IRTB49	433077
17 Oct	Belgium	Poland	Air Transport	356UNTS279	105100
18 Oct	Taiwan	Philippines	General Trade	541UNTS57	107860
18 Oct	Philippines	USA (United States)	Taxation	280UNTS55	104050
19 Oct	Mongolia	USSR (Soviet Union)	Scientific Project	16SUGG74	469929
19 Oct	Austria	Turkey	Visas	56TURG2710	466010
19 Oct	Japan	USSR (Soviet Union)	General Economic	263UNTS119	103769
19 Oct	Japan	USSR (Soviet Union)	General Amity	263UNTS99	103768
19 Oct	Costa Rica	USA (United States)	Gen Communications	278UNTS65	104022
19 Oct	Belgium	Pakistan	Visas	257UNTS221	103657
19 Oct	Norway	USSR (Soviet Union)	Humanitarian	257UNTS3	103644
20 Oct	Canada	UK Great Britain	Postal Service	381UNTS99	105466
22 Oct	Romania	USSR (Soviet Union)	Finance	0SUST370	468395
22 Oct	China People's Rep	United Arab Rep	Finance	56CCJC118	410372
22 Oct	China People's Rep	United Arab Rep	General Trade	56CCJC117	410371
23 Oct	Spain	USA (United States)	US Agri Commod Aid	277UNTS105	104001
23 Oct	Netherlands	Switzerland	Admin Cooperation	287UNTS203	104186
23 Oct	Burma	USA (United States)	Mass Media	282UNTS37	104091
24 Oct	Colombia	USA (United States)	Air Transport	476UNTS77	106905
24 Oct	Multilateral		Admin Cooperation	510UNTS161	107412
24 Oct	Canada	USA (United States)	Specif Goods/Equip	281UNTS281	104084
25 Oct	Belgium	Turkey	Air Transport	380UNTS3	105447
25 Oct	Austria	USA (United States)	Taxation	299UNTS123	104310
25 Oct	IBRD (World Bank)	Uruguay	IBRD Project	265UNTS59	103807
26 Oct	Denmark	Italy	Culture	267UNTS261	103847
26 Oct	Multilateral		IGO Establishment	276UNTS3	103988
27 Oct	France	Germany, West	Territory Boundary	56WGBB1587	425147
27 Oct	France	Germany, West	General Amity	57WGBB1661	425149
27 Oct	France	Germany, West	Specific Resources	56WGBB1863	425148
27 Oct	Romania	Yugoslavia	Culture	389UNTS33	105590
27 Oct	Romania	Yugoslavia	Scientific Project	389UNTS55	105592
27 Oct	Austria	UK Great Britain	Air Transport	264UNTS67	103789
29 Oct	India	Japan	Culture	318UNTS289	104622
29 Oct	Multilateral		Territory Boundary	263UNTS165	103772
30 Oct	Italy	USA (United States)	US Agri Commod Aid	263UNTS221	103775
31 Oct	Italy	Switzerland	Taxation	58ITGU50	435377
31 Oct	Argentina	UK Great Britain	Finance	269UNTS229	103883
31 Oct	Germany, West	Netherlands	Admin Cooperation	287UNTS21	104177
31 Oct	Ecuador	USA (United States)	Education	283UNTS151	104114
31 Oct	Belgium	United Arab Rep	Taxation	257UNTS235	103659
01 Nov	UK Great Britain	USA (United States)	Scientific Project	264UNTS3	103785
01 Nov	Chile	IBRD (World Bank)	IBRD Project	261UNTS27	103724
02 Nov	Belgium	USSR (Soviet Union)	General Amity	0SUST371	468023
02 Nov	Germany, West	Japan	Non-ILO Labor	0JGJI1325	441099
02 Nov	Chile	Germany, West	General Economic	56WBGA230	424082
02 Nov	Ceylon (Sri Lanka)	USA (United States)	Milit Assistance	282UNTS93	104094
03 Nov	China People's Rep	Indonesia	Direct Aid	56CCJC129	410379
03 Nov	China People's Rep	Indonesia	Finance	56CCJC128	410378
03 Nov	China People's Rep	Indonesia	General Trade	56CCJC126	410377

DATE	PARTY ONE	PARTY TWO	TOPIC	CITATION	NUMBER
1956 (Cont.)					
03 Nov	USA (United States)	Yugoslavia	US Agri Commod Aid	277UNTS119	104002
04 Nov	Iran	Norway	Taxation	3NORT699	451085
05 Nov	Argentina	USA (United States)	Education	277UNTS143	104004
06 Nov	Accept UN Charter	Ireland	UN Charter	254UNTS223	103594
07 Nov	Portugal	USA (United States)	Milit Assistance	277UNTS133	104003
08 Nov	Multilateral		Commodity Trade	470UNTS171	106809
08 Nov	France	USA (United States)	Direct Aid	280UNTS189	104058
09 Nov	Austria	Spain	Visas	56ABGB241	403165
09 Nov	Israel	UN Relief Palestin	Direct Aid	280UNTS261	104063
12 Nov	Poland	Yugoslavia	General Economic	57PZUM114	458056
12 Nov	Turkey	USA (United States)	US Agri Commod Aid	282UNTS77	104093
15 Nov	Chile	USA (United States)	Military Mission	282UNTS3	104089
15 Nov	Australia	IBRD (World Bank)	IBRD Project	288UNTS117	104201
16 Nov	Germany, West	Poland	General Economic	57WBGA1	424584
16 Nov	France	Laos	Admin Cooperation	60FRRT22	415260
16 Nov	Canada	UK Great Britain	Postal Service	412UNTS166	105930
18 Nov	United Nations	Venezuela	IGO Operations	588UNTS243	108529
19 Nov	Austria	Italy	Admin Cooperation	284UNTS293	104143
20 Nov	France	Norway	Patents/Copyrights	3NORT699	451061
20 Nov	Chile	Germany, West	Culture	59WGBB549	425083
20 Nov	Greece	Iran	Culture	0IRTB34	433043
20 Nov	Belgium	Sweden	Taxation	281UNTS239	104081
21 Nov	Austria	USA (United States)	Claims and Debts	290UNTS181	104237
21 Nov	Taiwan	USA (United States)	Milit Installation	265UNTS241	103816
21 Nov	Multilateral		Tech Assistance	253UNTS266	103588
22 Nov	Bulgaria	USSR (Soviet Union)	Mass Media	16SUGG74	469930
23 Nov	Peru	Switzerland	Air Transport	411UNTS97	105916
23 Nov	Japan	USA (United States)	Atomic Energy	324UNTS177	104685
23 Nov	Albania	Yugoslavia	Air Transport	386UNTS73	105539
23 Nov	Albania	Yugoslavia	Air Transport	363UNTS123	105204
23 Nov	Turkey	USA (United States)	Direct Aid	290UNTS273	104239
23 Nov	Iceland	USA (United States)	Specif Claim/Waive	281UNTS361	104088
27 Nov	UK Great Britain	USA (United States)	Scientific Project	282UNTS43	104092
28 Nov	Belgium	Spain	Non-ILO Labor	58SPBO2605	460050
28 Nov	Belgium	Spain	Non-ILO Labor	58SPBO2705	460052
28 Nov	Belgium	Spain	Non-ILO Labor	58SPBO2705	460051
28 Nov	Korea, South	USA (United States)	General Amity	302UNTS281	104367
28 Nov	Belgium	Spain	Non-ILO Labor	308UNTS239	104464
28 Nov	Belgium	Spain	Non-ILO Labor	308UNTS285	104465
29 Nov	Australia	Netherlands	Air Transport	302UNTS141	104356
30 Nov	Japan	Philippines	Reparations	0JGJI1313	441148
30 Nov	Czechoslovakia	USSR (Soviet Union)	Territory Boundary	266UNTS243	103833
01 Dec	Mongolia	USSR (Soviet Union)	Air Transport	0SUST373	468282
01 Dec	USSR (Soviet Union)	Vietnam, North	Loans and Credits	0SUST445	468451
01 Dec	France	Spain	General Trade	57SPBO301	460113
01 Dec	India	Iran	Culture	0IRTB38	433056
01 Dec	Germany, West	Netherlands	Extradition	276UNTS127	103989
03 Dec	Romania	USSR (Soviet Union)	Loans and Credits	0SUST373	468396
03 Dec	Taiwan	Spain	General Trade	56SPBO1512	460077
03 Dec	Australia	IBRD (World Bank)	IBRD Project	288UNTS99	104200
04 Dec	Belgium	Romania	Air Transport	317UNTS161	104602
04 Dec	Burma	USA (United States)	US Agri Commod Aid	268UNTS189	103858
05 Dec	Finland	South Africa	Visas	258UNTS59	103670
06 Dec	Ceylon (Sri Lanka)	USSR (Soviet Union)	Consul/Citizenship	16SUGG74	469931
06 Dec	Iceland	USA (United States)	General Military	265UNTS261	103818
07 Dec	Norway	Switzerland	Taxation	57SWRO728	462059
07 Dec	Norway	Switzerland	Taxation	57SWRO715	462058
07 Dec	Norway	Switzerland	Taxation	3NORT700	451156
07 Dec	Norway	Switzerland	Taxation	3NORT701	451157
07 Dec	Finland	USSR (Soviet Union)	Humanitarian	258UNTS89	103673
07 Dec	Luxembourg	USA (United States)	General Military	265UNTS255	103817
07 Dec	Dominican Republic	USA (United States)	Military Mission	263UNTS193	103774
08 Dec	France	Germany, West	Land Transport	58WBGA4	424150
08 Dec	Germany, East	Romania	Sanitation	362UNTS189	105188
08 Dec	Sweden	UK Great Britain	Claims and Debts	264UNTS61	103788

DATE	PARTY ONE	PARTY TWO	TOPIC	CITATION	NUMBER
1956 (Cont.)					
10 Dec	Japan	USA (United States)	Postal Service	0JGJI1146	441100
10 Dec	Canada	Germany, West	Milit Assistance	392UNTS3	105633
10 Dec	ICJ Option Clause	Denmark	ICJ Option Clause	257UNTS35	103646
11 Dec	Greece	Sweden	Dispute Settlement	299UNTS247	104316
12 Dec	Austria	Norway	Patents/Copyrights	3NORT701	451224
12 Dec	Germany, East	Indonesia	General Trade	5EGDA344	419132
12 Dec	Japan	Sweden	Taxation	318UNTS309	104623
12 Dec	Denmark	USA (United States)	Status of Forces	304UNTS311	104405
12 Dec	Germany, West	USA (United States)	Milit Assistance	280UNTS71	104052
12 Dec	Germany, West	USA (United States)	Milit Assistance	280UNTS63	104051
14 Dec	Brazil	Japan	Air Transport	0JGJI1485	441101
14 Dec	Multilateral		Taxation	436UNTS115	106292
14 Dec	Multilateral		Taxation	436UNTS131	106293
14 Dec	Indonesia	Yugoslavia	General Trade	378UNTS117	105422
14 Dec	France	USA (United States)	Air Transport	266UNTS117	103826
15 Dec	Multilateral		Education	278UNTS73	104023
16 Dec	Italy	Norway	Patents/Copyrights	291UNTS207	104256
17 Dec	ICJ Option Clause	Norway	ICJ Option Clause	256UNTS315	103642
17 Dec	Poland	USSR (Soviet Union)	Status of Forces	266UNTS179	103830
18 Dec	Germany, West	Mexico	Admin Cooperation	57WGBB500	425478
18 Dec	UNICEF (Children)	Uruguay	IGO Operations	0UNTSO	109398
18 Dec	Japan	Luxembourg	Visas	318UNTS227	104616
18 Dec	Israel	Netherlands	Extradition	276UNTS153	103991
19 Dec	Brazil	Norway	Patents/Copyrights	3NORT705	451010
19 Dec	Multilateral		Non-ILO Labor	427UNTS93	106148
19 Dec	Japan	IBRD (World Bank)	IBRD Project	264UNTS179	103793
19 Dec	India	IBRD (World Bank)	IBRD Project	310UNTS75	104489
19 Dec	Japan	IBRD (World Bank)	IBRD Project	268UNTS203	103859
20 Dec	Germany, West	Peru	Admin Cooperation	61WBGA200	424577
20 Dec	China People's Rep	Vietnam, North	Water Transport	56CCJC139	410388
20 Dec	Mexico	ICAO (Civil Aviat)	IGO Operations	497UNTS3	107259
20 Dec	Italy	Sweden	Taxation	369UNTS357	105265
20 Dec	Italy	Sweden	Taxation	369UNTS305	105263
20 Dec	Australia	Thailand	Admin Cooperation	265UNTS149	103810
21 Dec	Norway	Spain	Patents/Copyrights	56SPBO803	460205
21 Dec	Norway	Spain	Patents/Copyrights	3NORT705	451143
21 Dec	Spain	UK Great Britain	General Trade	57SPBO1601	460240
21 Dec	Japan	Spain	General Military	57JAIL88	440068
21 Dec	Czechoslovakia	Germany, East	Scientific Project	5EGDA554	419357
21 Dec	Multilateral		Humanitarian	427UNTS81	106147
22 Dec	Italy	Switzerland	Taxation	57SWRO44	462020
22 Dec	China People's Rep	Mongolia	General Trade	56CCJC141	410390
24 Dec	China People's Rep	USSR (Soviet Union)	Scientific Project	56CCJC143	410391
24 Dec	Bulgaria	Yugoslavia	Culture	397UNTS3	105699
24 Dec	Austria	Pakistan	General Trade	316UNTS83	104579
26 Dec	France	Libya	Territory Boundary	300UNTS263	104340
27 Dec	Taiwan	USA (United States)	Admin Cooperation	0CTRC874	413044
27 Dec	Finland	Switzerland	Taxation	277UNTS59	103997
27 Dec	Finland	Switzerland	Taxation	277UNTS7	103996
28 Dec	France	Italy	Non-ILO Labor	291UNTS203	104255
28 Dec	Haiti	USA (United States)	Direct Aid	279UNTS107	104035
28 Dec	Canada	USA (United States)	Specific Resources	290UNTS103	104229
29 Dec	USA (United States)	USSR (Soviet Union)	Privil/Immunities	0SUST371	468441
29 Dec	Ceylon (Sri Lanka)	China People's Rep	Commodity Trade	56CCJC146	410392
31 Dec	Brazil	USA (United States)	US Agri Commod Aid	266UNTS151	103829
31 Dec	Australia	USA (United States)	Milit Assistance	266UNTS89	103823
1957					
03 Jan	UNESCO (Educ/Cult)	Tunisia	Direct Aid	257UNTS21	103645
04 Jan	Italy	Portugal	Visas	59ITDI369	436311
04 Jan	China People's Rep	Yugoslavia	General Trade	57CCJC1	410393
04 Jan	China People's Rep	Yugoslavia	General Transport	57CCJC2	410394
08 Jan	Japan	Spain	Claims and Debts	318UNTS221	104615
08 Jan	United Nations	United Arab Rep	Specific Property	257UNTS75	103650
09 Jan	Colombia	USA (United States)	Education	462UNTS151	106676

DATE	PARTY ONE	PARTY TWO	TOPIC	CITATION	NUMBER
1957 (Cont.)					
10 Jan	Bulgaria	Germany, East	Patents/Copyrights	5EGDA790	419052
11 Jan	France	Italy	Non-ILO Labor	59ITDI264	436144
14 Jan	Czechoslovakia	USSR (Soviet Union)	General Trade	0SUST376	468111
14 Jan	France	Germany, West	Visas	57WBGA137	424151
14 Jan	Denmark	Switzerland	Taxation	286UNTS27	104160
14 Jan	Denmark	Switzerland	Taxation	286UNTS85	104161
15 Jan	Multilateral		Tech Assistance	376UNTS122	105378
15 Jan	Turkey	USA (United States)	Claims and Debts	280UNTS79	104053
16 Jan	Italy	Luxembourg	Non-ILO Labor	59ITDI347	436266
16 Jan	Brazil	USA (United States)	Milit Assistance	266UNTS99	103824
16 Jan	Iran	USA (United States)	Air Transport	308UNTS147	104460
17 Jan	Canada	USA (United States)	Specif Goods/Equip	266UNTS109	103825
19 Jan	Greece	USA (United States)	Milit Installation	280UNTS45	104049
21 Jan	Portugal	Spain	Customs	57SPBO209	460231
21 Jan	Brazil	USA (United States)	Milit Installation	278UNTS97	104025
22 Jan	Iran	IBRD (World Bank)	IBRD Project	317UNTS129	104600
22 Jan	Iceland	Thailand	Air Transport	312UNTS63	104511
23 Jan	Multilateral		Tech Assistance	259UNTS426	103701
24 Jan	Italy	Netherlands	Taxation	485UNTS67	107047
25 Jan	Czechoslovakia	USSR (Soviet Union)	Mass Media	16SUGG118	469932
25 Jan	Bulgaria	Czechoslovakia	Non-ILO Labor	501UNTS149	107316
28 Jan	Lebanon	Turkey	Consul/Citizenship	57TURG1309	466008
28 Jan	Bulgaria	China People's Rep	General Economic	57CCJC13	410398
28 Jan	Sweden	USSR (Soviet Union)	Finance	428UNTS315	106183
28 Jan	Ethiopia	IBRD (World Bank)	IBRD Project	286UNTS307	104175
29 Jan	Czechoslovakia	Germany, East	Culture	5EGDA557	419358
29 Jan	Mexico	USA (United States)	Telecommunications	418UNTS253	106025
29 Jan	Germany, West	Norway	Air Transport	353UNTS39	105037
29 Jan	Italy	UK Great Britain	Non-ILO Labor	326UNTS119	104710
29 Jan	Germany, West	Sweden	Air Transport	393UNTS113	105654
29 Jan	Czechoslovakia	Yugoslavia	Culture	300UNTS249	104339
29 Jan	Germany, West	Netherlands	Status of Forces	314UNTS173	104548
29 Jan	Denmark	Germany, West	Air Transport	302UNTS75	104354
30 Jan	Korea, South	USA (United States)	US Agri Commod Aid	278UNTS85	104024
31 Jan	Multilateral		Claims and Debts	278UNTS105	104026
01 Feb	Germany, East	Poland	Admin Cooperation	319UNTS115	104632
02 Feb	Taiwan	Italy	General Trade	0CTRC229	413011
02 Feb	Poland	United Arab Rep	Culture	319UNTS221	104633
04 Feb	Cuba	USA (United States)	Admin Cooperation	302UNTS273	104366
05 Feb	Norway	USA (United States)	Air Transport	279UNTS169	104038
05 Feb	Belgium	Yugoslavia	Culture	276UNTS143	103990
05 Feb	Belgium	Philippines	Patents/Copyrights	269UNTS49	103872
06 Feb	France	Morocco	Admin Cooperation	60FRRT11	415295
06 Feb	France	Morocco	Admin Cooperation	0UNTS0	109933
06 Feb	Philippines	USA (United States)	Status of Forces	303UNTS237	104383
07 Feb	Iran	Switzerland	Taxation	57SWRO213	462055
07 Feb	Taiwan	Spain	Culture	0CTRC439	413025
07 Feb	Taiwan	Spain	Culture	314UNTS161	104547
08 Feb	Denmark	France	Taxation	58FRRT27	415151
08 Feb	Japan	Poland	General Amity	318UNTS251	104620
08 Feb	United Nations	United Arab Rep	Status of Forces	260UNTS61	103704
09 Feb	USSR (Soviet Union)	Yugoslavia	Scientific Project	0SUST377	468480
09 Feb	Multilateral		Specific Resources	314UNTS105	104546
09 Feb	Nicaragua	USA (United States)	Milit Assistance	279UNTS191	104040
11 Feb	France	USSR (Soviet Union)	General Trade	0SUST377	468158
11 Feb	Morocco	Spain	General Amity	57SPBO403	460190
11 Feb	Morocco	Spain	Admin Cooperation	57SPBO403	460191
12 Feb	Taiwan	Turkey	Culture	282UNTS125	104097
13 Feb	Iceland	Spain	General Trade	57SPBO103	460167
13 Feb	Germany, West	Sweden	Admin Cooperation	428UNTS149	106174
13 Feb	Czechoslovakia	Japan	General Amity	300UNTS119	104335
14 Feb	Germany, West	Japan	Culture	318UNTS361	104626
15 Feb	China People's Rep	USSR (Soviet Union)	Gen Communications	57CCJC17	410399
15 Feb	France	Netherlands	Refugees	286UNTS243	104170
15 Feb	Norway	USSR (Soviet Union)	Territory Boundary	312UNTS289	104523

DATE	PARTY ONE	PARTY TWO	TOPIC	CITATION	NUMBER
1957 (Cont.)					
15 Feb	Netherlands	USA (United States)	Atomic Energy	287UNTS239	104190
15 Feb	USSR (Soviet Union)	Vietnam, North	Culture	274UNTS115	103962
15 Feb	Ecuador	USA (United States)	US Agri Commod Aid	279UNTS155	104037
15 Feb	Belgium	France	Refugees	267UNTS3	103834
17 Feb	Multilateral		Tech Assistance	271UNTS2	103907
20 Feb	Bulgaria	USSR (Soviet Union)	General Economic	0SUST378	468045
20 Feb	IBRD (World Bank)	United Nations	IGO Operations	265UNTS312	200546
20 Feb	Denmark	Netherlands	Taxation	287UNTS41	104179
20 Feb	Multilateral		Consul/Citizenship	309UNTS65	104468
21 Feb	USA (United States)	Venezuela	Water Transport	279UNTS199	104041
22 Feb	Hungary	Norway	Claims and Debts	3NORT712	451072
22 Feb	Albania	Germany, East	Tech Assistance	5EGDA284	419013
22 Feb	Germany, East	Korea, North	General Trade	5EGDA355	419177
22 Feb	Multilateral		Tech Assistance	274UNTS93	103960
22 Feb	Denmark	Norway	Taxation	286UNTS127	104164
23 Feb	Iceland	USA (United States)	Education	283UNTS73	104107
25 Feb	Norway	USA (United States)	Atomic Energy	284UNTS19	104126
26 Feb	Germany, East	USSR (Soviet Union)	Specific Property	5EGDA686	419402
26 Feb	Canada	USA (United States)	Water Transport	279UNTS179	104039
26 Feb	Australia	UK Great Britain	General Trade	265UNTS197	103813
27 Feb	France	Italy	Non-ILO Labor	59ITDI264	436145
27 Feb	Belgium	Brazil	Visas	265UNTS189	103812
28 Feb	France	Italy	Visas	291UNTS191	104253
28 Feb	Japan	Norway	General Economic	280UNTS87	104054
28 Feb	Turkey	UK Great Britain	Customs	310UNTS29	104483
28 Feb	Turkey	UK Great Britain	General Economic	310UNTS69	104488
01 Mar	Czechoslovakia	USSR (Soviet Union)	Specif Goods/Equip	16SUGG119	469933
01 Mar	Chile	USA (United States)	Non-ILO Labor	283UNTS127	104112
01 Mar	Accept UN Charter	Ghana	IGO Establishment	261UNTS113	103727
01 Mar	Multilateral		Tech Assistance	264UNTS94	103790
01 Mar	Morocco	UK Great Britain	General Economic	310UNTS3	104480
04 Mar	Romania	USSR (Soviet Union)	General Trade	0SUST379	468397
04 Mar	Thailand	USA (United States)	US Agri Commod Aid	279UNTS235	104043
05 Mar	Iran	USA (United States)	Atomic Energy	342UNTS29	104898
05 Mar	India	IBRD (World Bank)	IBRD Project	272UNTS201	103939
05 Mar	Poland	USSR (Soviet Union)	Territory Boundary	274UNTS133	103963
06 Mar	China People's Rep	Czechoslovakia	General Economic	57CCJC22	410404
07 Mar	Mexico	USA (United States)	Air Transport	279UNTS205	104042
07 Mar	Belgium	Netherlands	Dispute Settlement	282UNTS241	104100
08 Mar	Albania	China People's Rep	General Economic	57CCJC25	410407
09 Mar	Germany, West	Pakistan	General Trade	52WBGA132	424564
09 Mar	France	Tunisia	General Amity	58FRRT8	415454
09 Mar	Dominican Republic	USA (United States)	Gen Communications	279UNTS249	104044
09 Mar	Spain	USA (United States)	Milit Assistance	283UNTS89	104108
10 Mar	Finland	Germany, East	General Economic	5EGDA790	419101
11 Mar	USSR (Soviet Union)	Vietnam, North	Finance	0SUST379	468452
12 Mar	Germany, East	Korea, North	Tech Assistance	5EGDA355	419178
12 Mar	France	USA (United States)	Patents/Copyrights	279UNTS275	104045
12 Mar	Germany, East	USSR (Soviet Union)	Status of Forces	285UNTS105	104150
12 Mar	Belgium	Czechoslovakia	Air Transport	312UNTS75	104512
12 Mar	Burma	India	Finance	312UNTS131	104515
13 Mar	Sweden	Venezuela	Admin Cooperation	428UNTS351	106185
13 Mar	Netherlands	Yugoslavia	Air Transport	327UNTS227	104723
13 Mar	Peru	IBRD (World Bank)	IBRD Project	274UNTS59	103958
14 Mar	Romania	USSR (Soviet Union)	Mass Media	16SUGG119	469934
16 Mar	Liberia	USA (United States)	Postal Service	290UNTS59	104228
16 Mar	Ethiopia	Sweden	Tech Assistance	304UNTS214	104398
20 Mar	Dominican Republic	Japan	Visas	318UNTS245	104619
20 Mar	Japan	United Arab Rep	Culture	318UNTS345	104625
21 Mar	Burma	USA (United States)	Direct Aid	300UNTS11	104327
22 Mar	Japan	USA (United States)	Visas	288UNTS201	104206
25 Mar	Austria	Germany, West	Specific Resources	58ABGB197	403003
25 Mar	Multilateral		IGO Status/Immunit	294UNTS411	104302
25 Mar	Multilateral		IGO Establishment	294UNTS259	104301
25 Mar	Multilateral		IGO Establishment	294UNTS2	104300

DATE	PARTY ONE	PARTY TWO	TOPIC	CITATION	NUMBER
1957 (Cont.)					
25 Mar	Japan	Switzerland	Visas	318UNTS239	104618
25 Mar	Poland	USSR (Soviet Union)	Extradition	281UNTS121	104075
26 Mar	Paraguay	Spain	Culture	58SPBO2904	460217
26 Mar	Tunisia	USA (United States)	General Aid	283UNTS117	104111
26 Mar	Netherlands	Portugal	Visas	288UNTS47	104196
27 Mar	China People's Rep	USSR (Soviet Union)	Specific Property	16SUGG119	469935
27 Mar	Poland	USSR (Soviet Union)	Education	0SUST379	468340
27 Mar	China People's Rep	Czechoslovakia	Sanitation	57CCJC31	410411
27 Mar	China People's Rep	Czechoslovakia	Culture	57CCJC30	410410
27 Mar	China People's Rep	Czechoslovakia	General Amity	57CCJC29	410409
27 Mar	India	Poland	Culture	319UNTS263	104635
27 Mar	France	Japan	Specif Claim/Waive	318UNTS233	104617
28 Mar	Austria	Spain	General Trade	57SPBO2004	460041
28 Mar	Multilateral		Tech Assistance	271UNTS30	103908
29 Mar	Multilateral		Claims and Debts	283UNTS137	104113
29 Mar	Italy	UK Great Britain	Reparations	310UNTS11	104481
29 Mar	Italy	USA (United States)	Reparations	299UNTS157	104311
01 Apr	Italy	Switzerland	Loans and Credits	59ITDI411	436378
01 Apr	China People's Rep	Poland	General Trade	57CCJC34	410414
01 Apr	Australia	UK Great Britain	Non-ILO Labor	271UNTS235	103918
02 Apr	Canada	Netherlands	Taxation	285UNTS193	104153
02 Apr	Saudi Arabia	USA (United States)	Milit Installation	283UNTS97	104109
02 Apr	Brazil	USA (United States)	Patents/Copyrights	290UNTS119	104231
02 Apr	Morocco	USA (United States)	General Aid	288UNTS157	104203
03 Apr	Netherlands	USA (United States)	Air Transport	410UNTS193	105904
04 Apr	Germany, East	USSR (Soviet Union)	Specif Goods/Equip	16SUGG119	469936
04 Apr	Poland	Yugoslavia	Atomic Energy	57PZUM62	458048
04 Apr	Libya	USA (United States)	Tech Assistance	283UNTS181	104116
04 Apr	Paraguay	USA (United States)	Taxation	283UNTS193	104117
04 Apr	Paraguay	USA (United States)	Education	284UNTS161	104135
05 Apr	China People's Rep	Germany, East	General Economic	57CCJC36	410415
06 Apr	Japan	USSR (Soviet Union)	Specific Resources	0SUST380	468243
06 Apr	France	Turkey	General Economic	58TURG407	466063
06 Apr	Austria	Turkey	Admin Cooperation	58TURG2602	466032
06 Apr	Taiwan	Lebanon	General Trade	0CTRC305	413015
06 Apr	Luxembourg	Sweden	Admin Cooperation	427UNTS173	106152
06 Apr	Poland	Vietnam, North	Culture	432UNTS255	106224
06 Apr	ICJ Option Clause	Sweden	ICJ Option Clause	264UNTS221	103794
07 Apr	Germany, West	Iran	Taxation	0IRTB7	433011
08 Apr	USSR (Soviet Union)	Vietnam, North	General Trade	0SUST380	468453
08 Apr	China People's Rep	Sweden	Patents/Copyrights	57CCJC38	410416
08 Apr	China People's Rep	Sweden	Patents/Copyrights	428UNTS267	106179
08 Apr	Czechoslovakia	Mongolia	General Amity	501UNTS171	107317
08 Apr	Philippines	USA (United States)	Specific Resources	303UNTS227	104382
09 Apr	Multilateral		Tech Assistance	274UNTS172	103965
09 Apr	Canada	USA (United States)	Water Transport	283UNTS217	104119
10 Apr	USSR (Soviet Union)	Yugoslavia	General Trade	0SUST381	468481
10 Apr	China People's Rep	USSR (Soviet Union)	General Trade	57CCJC39	410417
10 Apr	China People's Rep	Korea, North	Sanitation	57CCJC40	410418
10 Apr	Austria	Sweden	Admin Cooperation	427UNTS343	106165
10 Apr	Germany, West	Yugoslavia	Air Transport	463UNTS269	106708
10 Apr	Denmark	Pakistan	Air Transport	302UNTS53	104353
11 Apr	Iran	USSR (Soviet Union)	Territory Boundary	0SUST381	468231
11 Apr	Germany, West	UK Great Britain	Status of Forces	331UNTS173	104753
11 Apr	Netherlands	Venezuela	Admin Cooperation	288UNTS23	104193
11 Apr	Germany, West	USA (United States)	Admin Cooperation	283UNTS233	104120
11 Apr	Iceland	USA (United States)	US Agri Commod Aid	283UNTS107	104110
12 Apr	Multilateral		Education	443UNTS128	106362
13 Apr	Netherlands	Paraguay	Finance	593UNTS85	108577
13 Apr	Canada	Netherlands	Milit Assistance	316UNTS223	104588
14 Apr	China People's Rep	Switzerland	Patents/Copyrights	57CCJC23	410405
15 Apr	Italy	Turkey	General Trade	58TURG407	466077
15 Apr	Romania	United Arab Rep	Culture	389UNTS21	105589
15 Apr	Romania	Sweden	Air Transport	342UNTS325	104915
15 Apr	Romania	USSR (Soviet Union)	Status of Forces	274UNTS143	103964

DATE	PARTY ONE	PARTY TWO	TOPIC	CITATION	NUMBER
1957 (Cont.)					
16 Apr	Iran	USSR (Soviet Union)	General Trade	0SUST381	468232
16 Apr	Mongolia	USSR (Soviet Union)	Specific Property	0SUST381	468283
16 Apr	Iran	Japan	Culture	325UNTS113	104697
16 Apr	Colombia	USA (United States)	US Agri Commod Aid	283UNTS245	104121
17 Apr	Albania	USSR (Soviet Union)	General Amity	0SUST381	468014
17 Apr	Korea, North	Poland	Scientific Project	57PZUM67	458049
17 Apr	Germany, East	Poland	Specific Resources	5EGDA407	419252
17 Apr	Bulgaria	Sweden	Air Transport	464UNTS3	106709
17 Apr	Peru	USA (United States)	Scientific Project	283UNTS3	104102
17 Apr	Canada	Denmark	Milit Assistance	316UNTS207	104586
17 Apr	Canada	Norway	Milit Assistance	316UNTS215	104587
18 Apr	Morocco	USSR (Soviet Union)	General Trade	0SUST381	468289
18 Apr	ICJ Option Clause	UK Great Britain	ICJ Option Clause	265UNTS221	103814
19 Apr	China People's Rep	Romania	General Economic	57CCJC46	410422
19 Apr	Bulgaria	Yugoslavia	Water Transport	349UNTS3	105006
20 Apr	Korea, North	USSR (Soviet Union)	Mass Media	16SUGG120	469937
20 Apr	Mongolia	USSR (Soviet Union)	Air Transport	0SUST382	468285
22 Apr	Mongolia	USSR (Soviet Union)	Air Transport	0SUST381	468284
22 Apr	Greece	Yugoslavia	Postal Service	391UNTS109	105619
23 Apr	Ceylon (Sri Lanka)	Italy	General Trade	337UNTS115	104820
24 Apr	Norway	Turkey	General Trade	2NORT715	451176
24 Apr	Ecuador	USA (United States)	Scientific Project	284UNTS3	104124
24 Apr	Other Unilat Decla	United Arab Rep	General Ad Hoc	265UNTS299	103821
24 Apr	Korea, South	USA (United States)	Air Transport	288UNTS219	104207
25 Apr	Korea, North	USSR (Soviet Union)	Specific Property	0SUST382	468258
25 Apr	Iran	USSR (Soviet Union)	Land Transport	0UNTS0	109578
25 Apr	Ethiopia	USA (United States)	Direct Aid	283UNTS205	104118
27 Apr	Austria	USSR (Soviet Union)	General Amity	0SUST382	468060
27 Apr	Iran	USSR (Soviet Union)	General Trade	0SUST382	468233
27 Apr	Bulgaria	Germany, East	General Economic	58EGDZ172	420053
27 Apr	Argentina	Uruguay	Non-ILO Labor	635UNTS69	109072
28 Apr	Germany, East	Romania	Health/Educ/Welfare	5EGDA468	419292
28 Apr	Germany, East	Romania	Sanitation	5EGDA479	419293
29 Apr	Multilateral		Dispute Settlement	320UNTS243	104646
29 Apr	Jordan	USA (United States)	Direct Aid	290UNTS111	104230
29 Apr	Israel	UK Great Britain	Non-ILO Labor	280UNTS227	104062
30 Apr	India	Romania	Culture	342UNTS251	104911
01 May	Lebanon	United Nations	IGO Establishment	266UNTS125	103827
01 May	Germany, West	USA (United States)	Milit Assistance	284UNTS85	104131
01 May	Multilateral		Admin Cooperation	284UNTS201	104138
02 May	Czechoslovakia	Romania	Health/Educ/Welfare	387UNTS167	105562
02 May	Peru	USA (United States)	US Agri Commod Aid	283UNTS55	104106
03 May	Taiwan	USA (United States)	Claims and Debts	0CTRC877	413045
03 May	Belgium	Peru	Visas	274UNTS251	103970
04 May	Philippines	UNTAB (Tech Assis)	Tech Assistance	3PTS661	465085
06 May	Romania	USSR (Soviet Union)	Commodity Trade	16SUGG120	469938
06 May	Czechoslovakia	United Arab Rep	Tech Assistance	292UNTS317	104278
07 May	Czechoslovakia	Poland	General Economic	57PZUM69	458050
08 May	Greece	Spain	General Trade	57SPBO3005	460157
08 May	Germany, West	Turkey	Culture	58WBGA336	424770
08 May	Japan	USA (United States)	Atomic Energy	318UNTS257	104621
10 May	France	Sweden	Admin Cooperation	427UNTS127	106149
10 May	Finland	USA (United States)	US Agri Commod Aid	283UNTS43	104105
10 May	Austria	USA (United States)	US Agri Commod Aid	283UNTS15	104103
10 May	Austria	USA (United States)	Direct Aid	283UNTS33	104104
10 May	Germany, East	USSR (Soviet Union)	Consul/Citizenship	285UNTS135	104151
13 May	Germany, West	Luxembourg	Sanitation	60WBGA180	424420
14 May	Iran	USSR (Soviet Union)	Admin Cooperation	16SUGG120	469939
14 May	Iran	USSR (Soviet Union)	Dispute Settlement	457UNTS161	106586
14 May	Belgium	Bulgaria	Air Transport	317UNTS81	104596
15 May	Mongolia	USSR (Soviet Union)	Specific Property	16SUGG120	469940
15 May	Mongolia	USSR (Soviet Union)	Direct Aid	16SUGG120	469941
15 May	Brazil	Germany, West	Admin Cooperation	58WBGA91	424054
15 May	Netherlands	United Arab Rep	Taxation	288UNTS29	104194
15 May	Netherlands	IBRD (World Bank)	IBRD Project	274UNTS211	103967

DATE	PARTY ONE	PARTY TWO	TOPIC	CITATION	NUMBER
1957 (Cont.)					
17 May	France	Spain	General Trade	57SPBO606	460114
18 May	Iran	Pakistan	Air Transport	0IRTB54	433081
18 May	Denmark	Paraguay	Finance	286UNTS117	104163
18 May	Ceylon (Sri Lanka)	Sweden	Taxation	315UNTS85	104561
20 May	Albania	Yugoslavia	Sanitation	363UNTS99	105203
20 May	Belgium	UK Great Britain	Non-ILO Labor	303UNTS53	104371
21 May	France	Netherlands	Visas	299UNTS43	104305
21 May	Netherlands	Sweden	Land Transport	286UNTS237	104169
22 May	Czechoslovakia	Yugoslavia	Non-ILO Labor	391UNTS57	105617
22 May	Australia	Germany, West	Air Transport	357UNTS45	105105
22 May	Czechoslovakia	Yugoslavia	Non-ILO Labor	391UNTS33	105615
22 May	Iraq	USA (United States)	Direct Aid	284UNTS13	104125
23 May	Poland	USSR (Soviet Union)	Education	0SUST388	468341
23 May	Cuba	Germany, West	Postal Service	61WGBB441	425402
23 May	Argentina	Israel	Culture	280UNTS199	104059
23 May	ICJ Option Clause	Pakistan	ICJ Option Clause	269UNTS77	103875
24 May	Czechoslovakia	Germany, East	Consul/Citizenship	292UNTS327	104279
24 May	Multilateral		Tech Assistance	268UNTS270	103861
24 May	Belgium	Colombia	Visas	274UNTS245	103969
25 May	Finland	Spain	General Trade	57SPBO2007	460279
25 May	Germany, East	USSR (Soviet Union)	General Economic	5EGDA697	419403
25 May	Hungary	Yugoslavia	Sanitation	477UNTS219	106924
27 May	Italy	Switzerland	Specific Resources	59SWRO432	462036
27 May	Hungary	USSR (Soviet Union)	Status of Forces	0SUST383	468201
27 May	Germany, West	Spain	General Trade	57SPBO1007	460010
27 May	Taiwan	Morocco	General Trade	0CTRC317	413016
27 May	Japan	Pakistan	Culture	325UNTS21	104692
28 May	Luxembourg	Norway	General Trade	3NORT717	451108
28 May	Belgium	Norway	General Trade	3NORTO	451006
28 May	Netherlands	Norway	General Trade	3NORT717	451119
28 May	Hungary	Netherlands	Air Transport	334UNTS291	104773
29 May	India	IBRD (World Bank)	IBRD Project	309UNTS201	104474
31 May	Cambodia	USSR (Soviet Union)	Health/Educ/Welfare	0SUST384	468066
31 May	Cambodia	USSR (Soviet Union)	Finance	0SUST384	468067
31 May	Cambodia	USSR (Soviet Union)	General Trade	0SUST384	468065
31 May	Albania	China People's Rep	Gen Communications	57CCJC54	410425
31 May	Austria	Germany, West	Visas	57ABGB192	403064
31 May	Ecuador	USA (United States)	Atomic Energy	304UNTS61	104391
01 Jun	Austria	Switzerland	Visas	57ABGB159	403185
01 Jun	Italy	Monaco	Visas	291UNTS197	104254
01 Jun	Belgium	Hungary	Air Transport	291UNTS17	104242
03 Jun	Ghana	USA (United States)	Tech Assistance	284UNTS63	104129
03 Jun	Bulgaria	Czechoslovakia	Sanitation	292UNTS3	104261
03 Jun	Argentina	USA (United States)	Tech Assistance	291UNTS61	104244
04 Jun	Morocco	Spain	General Trade	57SPBO1706	460192
04 Jun	Bulgaria	Yugoslavia	Sanitation	349UNTS35	105008
04 Jun	Denmark	Uruguay	Finance	286UNTS107	104162
05 Jun	Albania	Germany, East	Postal Service	5EGDA285	419014
05 Jun	Albania	Germany, East	Telecommunications	5EGDA292	419015
06 Jun	Lebanon	USA (United States)	Tech Assistance	284UNTS155	104134
07 Jun	Norway	USSR (Soviet Union)	Specific Resources	0SUST384	468298
07 Jun	Denmark	Germany, West	General Military	59WGBB409	425098
07 Jun	France	Germany, West	General Military	59WGBB409	425152
07 Jun	China People's Rep	Yugoslavia	Culture	57CCJC62	410429
07 Jun	China People's Rep	Korea, North	Postal Service	57CCJC59	410427
07 Jun	China People's Rep	Korea, North	Telecommunications	57CCJC60	410428
07 Jun	Germany, West	USA (United States)	Milit Assistance	346UNTS241	104984
07 Jun	Germany, West	UK Great Britain	Milit Assistance	398UNTS275	105730
07 Jun	Poland	USA (United States)	Direct Aid	291UNTS41	104243
07 Jun	Ceylon (Sri Lanka)	UK Great Britain	Milit Installation	280UNTS107	104055
07 Jun	Bolivia	USA (United States)	US Agri Commod Aid	291UNTS77	104245
08 Jun	China People's Rep	Hungary	General Economic	57CCJC65	410432
09 Jun	Afghanistan	USA (United States)	Admin Cooperation	307UNTS97	104445
10 Jun	Denmark	Peru	General Economic	406UNTS63	105839
11 Jun	Czechoslovakia	Yugoslavia	Sanitation	504UNTS107	107355

DATE	PARTY ONE	PARTY TWO	TOPIC	CITATION	NUMBER
1957 (Cont.)					
11 Jun	Nicaragua	USA (United States)	Atomic Energy	304UNTS267	104402
11 Jun	Austria	South Africa	Visas	272UNTS229	103941
11 Jun	Belgium	South Africa	Taxation	292UNTS165	104272
12 Jun	Honduras	Spain	Culture	63SPBO1105	460161
12 Jun	Italy	UK Great Britain	Non-ILO Labor	310UNTS35	104484
13 Jun	Afghanistan	Pakistan	Air Transport	327UNTS51	104717
14 Jun	Finland	India	Tech Assistance	277UNTS327	104016
14 Jun	Austria	USSR (Soviet Union)	Water Transport	285UNTS169	104152
15 Jun	Hungary	USSR (Soviet Union)	Mass Media	16SUGG121	469942
15 Jun	Austria	Germany, West	Finance	58WGBB129	425540
15 Jun	Multilateral		General Trade	550UNTS45	108008
15 Jun	Multilateral		Patents/Copyrights	583UNTS3	108470
16 Jun	Iraq	USA (United States)	Tech Assistance	284UNTS39	104127
17 Jun	Finland	Switzerland	Taxation	57SWRO756	462048
17 Jun	Bulgaria	Yugoslavia	Territory Boundary	375UNTS249	105369
18 Jun	Romania	USSR (Soviet Union)	Specific Property	0SUST385	468398
18 Jun	Philippines	USA (United States)	Milit Installation	289UNTS289	104225
18 Jun	Czechoslovakia	Syria	Culture	303UNTS119	104374
18 Jun	Special Decla ICJ	United Arab Rep	ICJ Option Clause	272UNTS225	103940
21 Jun	Belgium	Switzerland	General Trade	57SWRO521	462162
21 Jun	Netherlands	Switzerland	General Trade	57SWRO521	462149
21 Jun	France	Spain	Patents/Copyrights	51FRJO1108	416162
22 Jun	Poland	USSR (Soviet Union)	Mass Media	16SUGG121	469943
22 Jun	Albania	Italy	Peace/Disarmament	57ITGU263	435003
22 Jun	Albania	Italy	Admin Cooperation	59ITDI216	436004
22 Jun	Albania	Italy	Other Military	59ITDI216	436005
22 Jun	Honduras	Nicaragua	Specif Claim/Waive	277UNTS159	104005
22 Jun	Italy	USA (United States)	Milit Assistance	284UNTS51	104128
25 Jun	France	Spain	Patents/Copyrights	58SPBO2203	460115
25 Jun	Multilateral		ILO Labor	320UNTS291	104648
25 Jun	Philippines	USA (United States)	US Agri Commod Aid	289UNTS279	104224
26 Jun	Multilateral		ILO Labor	328UNTS247	104738
26 Jun	Multilateral		ILO Labor	325UNTS279	104704
26 Jun	Belgium	IBRD (World Bank)	IBRD Project	322UNTS301	104661
27 Jun	France	Spain	Non-ILO Labor	57SPBO1409	460117
27 Jun	France	Spain	Non-ILO Labor	57SPBO1409	460118
27 Jun	France	Spain	Non-ILO Labor	59SPBO3003	460276
27 Jun	France	Spain	Non-ILO Labor	59SPBO3003	460116
27 Jun	France	Spain	Non-ILO Labor	59SPBO1104	460277
27 Jun	France	Spain	Non-ILO Labor	0UNTSO	110704
27 Jun	Pakistan	USSR (Soviet Union)	General Trade	0UNTSO	109823
27 Jun	Jordan	USA (United States)	General Aid	288UNTS269	104209
27 Jun	Finland	United Nations	Status of Forces	271UNTS135	103913
27 Jun	Multilateral		General Economic	284UNTS139	104133
27 Jun	Germany, West	Japan	Admin Cooperation	318UNTS335	104624
27 Jun	UK Great Britain	USA (United States)	Direct Aid	290UNTS133	104232
27 Jun	UK Great Britain	USA (United States)	General Economic	284UNTS75	104130
28 Jun	Taiwan	USA (United States)	Loans and Credits	0CTRC880	413046
28 Jun	Germany, West	USA (United States)	Atomic Energy	288UNTS339	104213
28 Jun	Tunisia	USA (United States)	Direct Aid	289UNTS301	104226
28 Jun	Finland	Norway	Non-IBRD Project	272UNTS191	103938
29 Jun	Syria	USSR (Soviet Union)	Telecommunications	0SUST385	468417
29 Jun	Germany, East	Hungary	Patents/Copyrights	5EGDA792	419451
29 Jun	Jordan	USA (United States)	Direct Aid	288UNTS263	104208
30 Jun	Czechoslovakia	United Arab Rep	Air Transport	411UNTS126	105917
30 Jun	Multilateral		Tech Assistance	286UNTS171	104165
30 Jun	Libya	USA (United States)	Milit Assistance	284UNTS177	104136
01 Jul	Denmark	Spain	General Trade	57SPBO1009	460078
01 Jul	Multilateral		Culture	0UNTSO	110418
01 Jul	Pakistan	USA (United States)	Taxation	344UNTS203	104951
01 Jul	United Nations	Sweden	Status of Forces	271UNTS187	103914
01 Jul	Canada	Greece	Visas	316UNTS201	104585
03 Jul	Norway	Switzerland	Taxation	57SWRO733	462060
03 Jul	China People's Rep	Syria	General Trade	57CCJC69	410434
03 Jul	Germany, East	Hungary	Consul/Citizenship	407UNTS186	105865

DATE	PARTY ONE	PARTY TWO	TOPIC	CITATION	NUMBER
1957 (Cont.)					
03 Jul	Italy	USA (United States)	Atomic Energy	308UNTS195	104462
03 Jul	Germany, West	USA (United States)	Atomic Energy	288UNTS305	104212
04 Jul	Germany, West	Italy	General Transport	64WBGA97	424294
04 Jul	New Zealand	UK Great Britain	Milit Assistance	402UNTS109	105780
05 Jul	Germany, West	Turkey	Air Transport	62WGBB2376	425771
05 Jul	Germany, West	Turkey	Air Transport	0UNTS0	110464
06 Jul	Czechoslovakia	USSR (Soviet Union)	Claims and Debts	0SUST385	468112
06 Jul	Spain	Vatican/Holy See	Admin Cooperation	57SPBO1207	460272
06 Jul	Australia	Japan	General Trade	318UNTS381	104627
06 Jul	Italy	United Arab Rep	Finance	302UNTS147	104357
07 Jul	Morocco	Spain	Commodity Trade	57SPBO709	460197
07 Jul	Morocco	Spain	Specific Resources	57SPBO709	460198
07 Jul	Morocco	Spain	General Trade	57SPBO709	460196
07 Jul	Morocco	Spain	Culture	58SPBO402	460199
07 Jul	Morocco	Spain	Finance	57SPBO709	460193
07 Jul	Morocco	Spain	Finance	57SPBO709	460194
07 Jul	Morocco	Spain	Tech Assistance	58SPBO502	460200
07 Jul	Morocco	Spain	General Trade	57SPBO709	460195
08 Jul	Pakistan	Spain	General Amity	59SPBO1706	460213
08 Jul	Albania	Poland	Air Transport	57PZUM74	458051
08 Jul	Australia	FAO (Food Agri)	Tech Assistance	277UNTS315	104015
08 Jul	South Africa	USA (United States)	Atomic Energy	290UNTS147	104234
09 Jul	Belgium	Germany, West	General Military	59WGBB409	425023
09 Jul	Austria	Germany, West	Admin Cooperation	57ABGB198	403065
09 Jul	Norway	United Nations	Status of Forces	271UNTS223	103917
09 Jul	Multilateral		Tech Assistance	274UNTS300	103972
10 Jul	USSR (Soviet Union)	Yugoslavia	Mass Media	0SUST386	468482
10 Jul	Germany, West	Netherlands	Status of Forces	339UNTS97	104848
12 Jul	Denmark	Italy	General Trade	291UNTS169	104251
12 Jul	Australia	USA (United States)	Milit Assistance	290UNTS139	104233
12 Jul	India	IBRD (World Bank)	IBRD Project	288UNTS135	104202
12 Jul	Multilateral		Visas	322UNTS245	104660
12 Jul	Germany, West	Italy	Finance	291UNTS181	104252
12 Jul	Norway	UK Great Britain	Atomic Energy	310UNTS41	104485
13 Jul	Germany, East	Poland	Health/Educ/Welfare	319UNTS229	104634
15 Jul	Denmark	Spain	General Trade	57SPBO1009	460079
16 Jul	Denmark	United Nations	Milit Assistance	274UNTS81	103959
18 Jul	Romania	USSR (Soviet Union)	Admin Cooperation	0SUST386	468399
18 Jul	Italy	Yugoslavia	Specific Resources	58ITGU64	435231
19 Jul	Germany, West	Yugoslavia	Commodity Trade	57WBGA183	424331
19 Jul	Peru	USA (United States)	Direct Aid	289UNTS271	104223
22 Jul	Austria	Switzerland	Land Transport	57SWRO906	462076
22 Jul	Norway	Spain	General Trade	57SPBO808	460206
22 Jul	Austria	Switzerland	Land Transport	57ABGB268	403186
24 Jul	Chile	IBRD (World Bank)	IBRD Project	282UNTS139	104098
24 Jul	Chile	IBRD (World Bank)	IBRD Project	282UNTS189	104099
25 Jul	Norway	UK Great Britain	Non-ILO Labor	313UNTS3	104528
25 Jul	Thailand	UK Great Britain	Customs	277UNTS81	103999
26 Jul	Germany, West	Japan	Visas	0JGJI1262	441102
26 Jul	Belgium	Spain	Finance	57SPBO2208	460053
26 Jul	Austria	ECSC (Coal/Steel)	Land Transport	58ABGB63	403141
26 Jul	Multilateral		Land Transport	386UNTS3	105535
27 Jul	Germany, West	Hungary	Commodity Trade	57WBGA164	424704
28 Jul	Afghanistan	China People's Rep	General Economic	57CCJC72	410437
29 Jul	USSR (Soviet Union)	Yugoslavia	Direct Aid	0SUST386	468483
29 Jul	Canada	United Nations	Milit Assistance	274UNTS47	103957
29 Jul	France	Italy	Patents/Copyrights	291UNTS163	104250
30 Jul	Norway	Venezuela	General Trade	3NORT725	451217
30 Jul	Taiwan	USA (United States)	Postal Service	300UNTS61	104331
31 Jul	Romania	USSR (Soviet Union)	Specific Resources	16SUGG121	469944
31 Jul	Germany, East	Vietnam, North	Culture	5EGDA780	419488
31 Jul	China People's Rep	Vietnam, North	General Trade	57CCJC75	410440
31 Jul	China People's Rep	Vietnam, North	General Economic	57CCJC73	410438
31 Jul	Morocco	UNICEF (Children)	Direct Aid	282UNTS99	104095
01 Aug	Romania	USSR (Soviet Union)	Admin Cooperation	0SUST386	468400

DATE	PARTY ONE	PARTY TWO	TOPIC	CITATION	NUMBER
1957 (Cont.)					
01 Aug	Norway	USSR (Soviet Union)	Territory Boundary	0SUST386	468299
01 Aug	France	Italy	Non-ILO Labor	302UNTS221	104360
02 Aug	Germany, East	USSR (Soviet Union)	Status of Forces	5EGDA699	419404
02 Aug	Greece	Italy	Air Transport	533UNTS217	107744
02 Aug	Hungary	Sweden	Air Transport	334UNTS307	104774
03 Aug	Italy	Yugoslavia	Finance	59ITDI327	436234
05 Aug	Germany, West	USSR (Soviet Union)	Admin Cooperation	16SUGG121	469945
05 Aug	Greece	USA (United States)	Milit Assistance	290UNTS167	104235
05 Aug	Panama	USA (United States)	Visas	299UNTS113	104309
09 Aug	Austria	USA (United States)	Milit Assistance	288UNTS299	104211
09 Aug	Japan	IBRD (World Bank)	IBRD Project	293UNTS59	104286
11 Aug	Iran	USSR (Soviet Union)	Specific Resources	0SUST387	468235
13 Aug	Brazil	United Nations	Milit Assistance	274UNTS199	103966
14 Aug	Korea, North	USSR (Soviet Union)	Tech Assistance	0SUST387	468259
14 Aug	Korea, North	USSR (Soviet Union)	Non-IBRD Project	0SUST387	468260
14 Aug	Taiwan	Iraq	Culture	0CTRC210	413008
14 Aug	India	United Nations	Milit Assistance	274UNTS233	103968
15 Aug	USA (United States)	Vietnam, South	Admin Cooperation	0VKNG122	496036
16 Aug	Turkey	UK Great Britain	Milit Assistance	310UNTS21	104482
16 Aug	Spain	USA (United States)	Atomic Energy	307UNTS169	104449
16 Aug	Austria	Pakistan	Visas	306UNTS3	104429
17 Aug	Albania	Germany, East	Sanitation	5EGDA302	419016
21 Aug	Poland	Sweden	Admin Cooperation	427UNTS277	106159
22 Aug	Germany, East	Mongolia	Health/Educ/Welfare	5EGDA363	419214
22 Aug	Germany, East	Mongolia	General Amity	521UNTS351	107530
23 Aug	Poland	USSR (Soviet Union)	Education	56PZUM90	458052
24 Aug	Hungary	USSR (Soviet Union)	Consul/Citizenship	318UNTS35	104608
24 Aug	Hungary	USSR (Soviet Union)	Consul/Citizenship	318UNTS3	104607
27 Aug	Netherlands	Romania	Air Transport	342UNTS309	104914
29 Aug	Morocco	Switzerland	Mostfavored Nation	58SWRO271	462146
29 Aug	Brazil	Germany, West	Air Transport	59WGBB73	425055
29 Aug	Germany, West	Indonesia	Direct Aid	57WBGA228	424262
29 Aug	Albania	Yugoslavia	Postal Service	391UNTS127	105621
29 Aug	Albania	Yugoslavia	Postal Service	391UNTS167	105622
30 Aug	Japan	UK Great Britain	Visas	313UNTS63	104529
31 Aug	Germany, West	Uruguay	Air Transport	59WGBB80	425709
31 Aug	Czechoslovakia	USSR (Soviet Union)	Admin Cooperation	308UNTS3	104456
31 Aug	Accept UN Charter	Fed of Malaya	UN Charter	277UNTS3	103995
03 Sep	Germany, East	Syria	General Trade	5EGDA485	419313
04 Sep	Romania	USSR (Soviet Union)	Consul/Citizenship	318UNTS55	104609
04 Sep	Romania	USSR (Soviet Union)	Consul/Citizenship	318UNTS89	104610
05 Sep	Germany, East	Poland	Customs	57PZUM94	458053
05 Sep	Germany, East	Poland	Customs	5EGDA433	419253
06 Sep	Belgium	France	Specific Resources	59FRRT39	415062
07 Sep	United Arab Rep	Germany, East	General Economic	5EGDA280	419005
07 Sep	United Arab Rep	Germany, East	Consul/Citizenship	5EGDA281	419004
09 Sep	ICJ Option Clause	Cambodia	ICJ Option Clause	277UNTS77	103998
10 Sep	Belgium	Spain	Non-ILO Labor	58SPBO3005	460054
10 Sep	Belgium	IBRD (World Bank)	IBRD Project	286UNTS291	104174
11 Sep	Lebanon	Switzerland	Taxation	57SWRO846	462057
12 Sep	Turkey	USA (United States)	Direct Aid	58TURG1004	466119
12 Sep	Fed of Malaya	UK Great Britain	Recognition	279UNTS287	104046
12 Sep	IBRD (World Bank)	Thailand	IBRD Project	299UNTS349	104324
14 Sep	Japan	USA (United States)	Admin Cooperation	293UNTS247	104293
16 Sep	Norway	Sweden	Territory Boundary	428UNTS263	106178
17 Sep	Germany, East	Poland	Atomic Energy	57PZUM99	458054
17 Sep	Germany, East	Poland	Atomic Energy	5EGDA438	419254
18 Sep	Albania	USSR (Soviet Union)	Consul/Citizenship	307UNTS265	104455
18 Sep	Albania	USSR (Soviet Union)	Consul/Citizenship	307UNTS251	104454
19 Sep	Ceylon (Sri Lanka)	China People's Rep	Direct Aid	57CCJC87	410448
19 Sep	Ceylon (Sri Lanka)	China People's Rep	General Trade	57CCJC85	410446
19 Sep	Ceylon (Sri Lanka)	China People's Rep	General Trade	57CCJC86	410447
19 Sep	Ceylon (Sri Lanka)	China People's Rep	Customs	57CCJC84	410445
19 Sep	Ceylon (Sri Lanka)	China People's Rep	General Economic	337UNTS137	104821
19 Sep	Ceylon (Sri Lanka)	China People's Rep	Direct Aid	337UNTS169	104822

DATE	PARTY ONE	PARTY TWO	TOPIC	CITATION	NUMBER
1957 (Cont.)					
19 Sep	Italy	Switzerland	Land Transport	363UNTS69	105200
19 Sep	India	USA (United States)	Claims and Debts	290UNTS175	104236
19 Sep	France	Italy	Non-ILO Labor	302UNTS225	104361
20 Sep	Belgium	France	Postal Service	57FRJO1910	416063
20 Sep	Sweden	UK Great Britain	Atomic Energy	310UNTS49	104486
20 Sep	New Zealand	UK Great Britain	Sanitation	287UNTS105	104180
20 Sep	Ecuador	IBRD (World Bank)	IBRD Project	289UNTS237	104221
20 Sep	Japan	Netherlands	Visas	305UNTS105	104418
20 Sep	Ecuador	IBRD (World Bank)	IBRD Project	293UNTS135	104291
20 Sep	Japan	Sweden	Reparations	325UNTS29	104693
20 Sep	Burma	WHO (World Health)	Tech Assistance	282UNTS113	104096
21 Sep	Iran	USA (United States)	Claims and Debts	293UNTS287	104296
23 Sep	Spain	USA (United States)	Air Transport	290UNTS261	104238
23 Sep	France	USA (United States)	Tech Assistance	293UNTS297	104297
24 Sep	USA (United States)	Venezuela	Tech Assistance	293UNTS307	104298
26 Sep	China People's Rep	Germany, East	Commodity Trade	5EGDA332	419092
26 Sep	Austria	South Africa	Postal Service	287UNTS3	104176
27 Sep	Germany, East	USSR (Soviet Union)	General Economic	5EGDA730	419405
27 Sep	China People's Rep	Germany, West	Dispute Settlement	57CCJC92	410452
27 Sep	China People's Rep	Germany, West	General Trade	57CCJC91	410451
27 Sep	China People's Rep	Germany, West	General Trade	57CCJC90	410450
27 Sep	Germany, East	USSR (Soviet Union)	General Economic	292UNTS75	104268
27 Sep	Multilateral		Admin Cooperation	299UNTS211	104314
30 Sep	Burma	USSR (Soviet Union)	Specif Goods/Equip	16SUGG121	469946
30 Sep	Brazil	Spain	General Economic	57SPBO1810	460057
30 Sep	Multilateral		General Transport	619UNTS77	108940
01 Oct	Australia	Canada	Taxation	392UNTS41	105638
01 Oct	United Nations	Yugoslavia	Milit Assistance	277UNTS191	104006
01 Oct	IBRD (World Bank)	South Africa	IBRD Project	280UNTS285	104065
03 Oct	Multilateral		Postal Service	366UNTS193	105218
03 Oct	Multilateral		Postal Service	366UNTS255	105219
03 Oct	Multilateral		Postal Service	365UNTS207	105214
03 Oct	Multilateral		Postal Service	365UNTS3	105213
03 Oct	Multilateral		Postal Service	366UNTS87	105216
03 Oct	Multilateral		Postal Service	366UNTS3	105215
03 Oct	Belgium	UK Great Britain	Reparations	394UNTS69	105669
03 Oct	Multilateral		Postal Service	364UNTS3	105211
03 Oct	Multilateral		Postal Service	366UNTS141	105217
03 Oct	Multilateral		Postal Service	364UNTS331	105212
04 Oct	Brazil	Italy	Taxation	62ITGU240	435059
05 Oct	France	Morocco	Admin Cooperation	60FRRT4	415296
05 Oct	France	Morocco	Admin Cooperation	0UNTSO	110712
05 Oct	France	Morocco	Admin Cooperation	0UNTSO	110713
05 Oct	Italy	Pakistan	Air Transport	353UNTS91	105039
05 Oct	Czechoslovakia	USSR (Soviet Union)	Consul/Citizenship	320UNTS129	104641
05 Oct	Czechoslovakia	USSR (Soviet Union)	Consul/Citizenship	320UNTS111	104640
07 Oct	Hungary	Yugoslavia	Non-ILO Labor	439UNTS61	106325
08 Oct	Ecuador	Switzerland	General Trade	59SWRO194	462130
08 Oct	Taiwan	USA (United States)	Postal Service	304UNTS241	104400
09 Oct	Australia	Netherlands	Dispute Settlement	312UNTS225	104520
10 Oct	Germany, East	Yugoslavia	Consul/Citizenship	5EGDA348	419144
10 Oct	Austria	IBRD (World Bank)	IBRD Project	301UNTS95	104343
11 Oct	Korea, North	USSR (Soviet Union)	Education	0SUST390	468261
12 Oct	Italy	Spain	Patents/Copyrights	291UNTS229	104258
12 Oct	Fed of Malaya	UK Great Britain	Milit Assistance	285UNTS59	104149
14 Oct	Korea, North	USSR (Soviet Union)	Admin Cooperation	0SUST390	468262
14 Oct	France	Switzerland	Visas	58FRRT4	415406
15 Oct	China People's Rep	USSR (Soviet Union)	Atomic Energy	16SUGG122	469947
17 Oct	Cambodia	USA (United States)	Scientific Project	299UNTS203	104313
18 Oct	Fed of Malaya	UK Great Britain	Air Transport	335UNTS3	104775
18 Oct	Pakistan	IBRD (World Bank)	IBRD Project	299UNTS303	104322
19 Oct	United Arab Rep	USSR (Soviet Union)	Culture	0SUST391	468130
19 Oct	Germany, East	Yugoslavia	Finance	5EGDA352	419146
19 Oct	Germany, East	Yugoslavia	General Trade	5EGDA352	419145
19 Oct	Czechoslovakia	United Arab Rep	Culture	530UNTS181	107681

DATE	PARTY ONE	PARTY TWO	TOPIC	CITATION	NUMBER
1957 (Cont.)					
19 Oct	United Arab Rep	USSR (Soviet Union)	Culture	292UNTS151	104271
20 Oct	Poland	Yugoslavia	Sanitation	57PZUM102	458055
22 Oct	Netherlands	UK Great Britain	Air Transport	313UNTS309	104538
23 Oct	Belgium	Netherlands	Water Transport	0UNTSO	109725
23 Oct	IAEA (Atom Energy)	United Nations	IGO Operations	281UNTS369	200548
23 Oct	Netherlands	Sweden	Land Transport	306UNTS75	104433
23 Oct	Mexico	USA (United States)	US Agri Commod Aid	300UNTS35	104330
24 Oct	Belgium	Netherlands	Water Transport	489UNTS11	107132
24 Oct	Belgium	Netherlands	Water Transport	489UNTS3	107131
24 Oct	Belgium	Netherlands	Water Transport	292UNTS199	104274
25 Oct	France	Morocco	Air Transport	559UNTS95	108156
25 Oct	Austria	Belgium	Admin Cooperation	372UNTS177	105297
25 Oct	Germany, East	Hungary	Sanitation	408UNTS156	105869
26 Oct	Albania	USSR (Soviet Union)	Mass Media	16SUGG122	469948
26 Oct	Switzerland	Tunisia	Mostfavored Nation	58SWRO260	462159
26 Oct	Poland	USSR (Soviet Union)	Status of Forces	432UNTS221	106223
28 Oct	Syria	USSR (Soviet Union)	General Aid	0SUST391	468418
28 Oct	Afghanistan	Spain	General Amity	58SPBO2507	460001
29 Oct	China People's Rep	Poland	Sanitation	57CCJC102	410457
30 Oct	Germany, West	Norway	Milit Installation	3NORT728	451188
30 Oct	Germany, East	Mongolia	Finance	5EGDA366	419215
30 Oct	Germany, East	Hungary	Admin Cooperation	408UNTS4	105867
31 Oct	Iran	USA (United States)	Milit Installation	0IRTB23	433036
01 Nov	Germany, West	Switzerland	Specific Resources	59SWRO369	462105
01 Nov	China People's Rep	Yugoslavia	Scientific Project	57CCJC103	410458
01 Nov	Burma	China People's Rep	Postal Service	57CCJC105	410460
01 Nov	Burma	China People's Rep	Postal Service	57CCJC104	410459
01 Nov	UK Great Britain	USA (United States)	Scientific Project	299UNTS167	104312
01 Nov	Philippines	USA (United States)	Status of Forces	307UNTS39	104440
05 Nov	Japan	Turkey	Visas	318UNTS411	104628
05 Nov	Multilateral		Tech Assistance	285UNTS301	104155
05 Nov	Brazil	USA (United States)	Education	303UNTS3	104368
05 Nov	USA (United States)	Vietnam, South	Finance	300UNTS23	104328
06 Nov	Germany, East	Mongolia	General Trade	5EGDA370	419216
06 Nov	Ecuador	USA (United States)	Consul/Citizenship	307UNTS49	104441
07 Nov	Israel	USA (United States)	US Agri Commod Aid	302UNTS255	104365
08 Nov	China People's Rep	Sweden	General Trade	57CCJC108	410462
08 Nov	France	Italy	Mass Media	305UNTS393	104427
09 Nov	India	USSR (Soviet Union)	General Economic	0SUST391	468217
09 Nov	Colombia	Germany, West	General Trade	58WBGA49	424368
11 Nov	Taiwan	Iran	Culture	563UNTS31	108202
11 Nov	Ireland	Portugal	Mostfavored Nation	553UNTS141	108080
12 Nov	Belgium	France	Non-ILO Labor	328UNTS167	104734
13 Nov	Germany, East	Hungary	Sanitation	407UNTS216	105866
13 Nov	Denmark	Netherlands	Land Transport	306UNTS67	104432
14 Nov	Italy	Yugoslavia	Non-ILO Labor	60ITGU210	435232
15 Nov	Ireland	Italy	Air Transport	59ITDI320	436216
15 Nov	Pakistan	USA (United States)	US Agri Commod Aid	303UNTS173	104380
16 Nov	Germany, East	Poland	General Economic	5EGDA440	419255
16 Nov	France	Portugal	Non-ILO Labor	59FRRT16	415368
18 Nov	Denmark	UK Great Britain	General Trade	403UNTS153	105794
19 Nov	Bulgaria	USSR (Soviet Union)	General Trade	0SUST391	468046
19 Nov	France	Spain	General Economic	58SPBO301	460119
19 Nov	Taiwan	Jordan	General Amity	308UNTS227	104463
19 Nov	Argentina	UNICEF (Children)	Direct Aid	300UNTS229	104338
20 Nov	Hungary	Yugoslavia	Sanitation	477UNTS267	106925
20 Nov	India	IBRD (World Bank)	IBRD Project	301UNTS47	104342
21 Nov	Germany, West	Italy	General Amity	59WGBB949	425295
21 Nov	El Salvador	USA (United States)	Military Mission	303UNTS19	104369
22 Nov	Albania	USSR (Soviet Union)	General Aid	0SUST392	468017
22 Nov	Brazil	Iran	Culture	0IRTB15	433024
22 Nov	Philippines	IBRD (World Bank)	IBRD Project	293UNTS83	104287
22 Nov	Norway	USSR (Soviet Union)	Specific Resources	309UNTS269	104476
23 Nov	Multilateral		Refugees	506UNTS125	107384
25 Nov	Argentina	Switzerland	General Economic	58SWRO38	462120

DATE	PARTY ONE	PARTY TWO	TOPIC	CITATION	NUMBER
1957 (Cont.)					
25 Nov	Italy	Spain	Non-ILO Labor	59SPBO1601	460174
25 Nov	Argentina	Italy	Health/Educ/Welfare	58ITGU120	435017
25 Nov	Argentina	Germany, West	General Trade	58WBGA6	424007
25 Nov	Argentina	France	General Trade	57FRMD1112	417053
25 Nov	Argentina	France	Finance	57FRMD1112	417052
25 Nov	Multilateral		General Trade	403UNTS169	105795
25 Nov	Italy	Spain	Non-ILO Labor	378UNTS289	105428
25 Nov	Germany, East	Poland	Consul/Citizenship	340UNTS99	104862
25 Nov	Ghana	UK Great Britain	Recognition	287UNTS233	104189
25 Nov	Argentina	Italy	General Economic	305UNTS275	104424
25 Nov	Argentina	UK Great Britain	Claims and Debts	313UNTS95	104531
25 Nov	Austria	Israel	Visas	314UNTS81	104542
25 Nov	Argentina	Denmark	General Economic	299UNTS83	104308
26 Nov	Israel	Norway	Culture	345UNTS99	104962
27 Nov	Belgium	IBRD (World Bank)	IBRD Project	292UNTS175	104273
28 Nov	Germany, East	USSR (Soviet Union)	Admin Cooperation	305UNTS113	104419
29 Nov	Norway	USSR (Soviet Union)	Territory Boundary	0SUST392	468301
29 Nov	France	Spain	Non-ILO Labor	57SPBO3112	460120
30 Nov	Taiwan	Greece	General Trade	0CTRC202	413007
30 Nov	Taiwan	USA (United States)	Culture	0CTRC885	413047
01 Dec	Germany, West	Luxembourg	Non-ILO Labor	60WGBB2305	425421
01 Dec	China People's Rep	Denmark	General Economic	57CCJC111	410465
01 Dec	China People's Rep	Denmark	Mostfavored Nation	57CCJC112	410466
01 Dec	China People's Rep	Denmark	General Economic	309UNTS241	104475
03 Dec	Germany, East	Poland	General Economic	5EGDA794	419256
03 Dec	Belgium	USA (United States)	Air Transport	303UNTS45	104370
04 Dec	France	Switzerland	Specific Resources	58SWRO49	462106
04 Dec	France	Spain	General Trade	58SPBO301	460121
04 Dec	Czechoslovakia	USSR (Soviet Union)	Sanitation	313UNTS291	104537
05 Dec	Ireland	Sweden	Non-ILO Labor	428UNTS221	106176
05 Dec	Belgium	Switzerland	Taxation	293UNTS317	104299
06 Dec	Japan	USSR (Soviet Union)	Water Transport	16SUGG122	469949
06 Dec	Japan	USSR (Soviet Union)	General Economic	0SUST392	468245
06 Dec	Hungary	Yugoslavia	Sanitation	519UNTS215	107509
06 Dec	Italy	Monaco	Non-ILO Labor	363UNTS45	105198
06 Dec	Italy	Monaco	Non-ILO Labor	363UNTS59	105199
06 Dec	Japan	USSR (Soviet Union)	General Economic	325UNTS35	104694
07 Dec	Belgium	Germany, West	Non-ILO Labor	64WGBB170	425025
07 Dec	Belgium	Germany, West	Non-ILO Labor	63WGBB404	425024
09 Dec	Belgium	Italy	Non-ILO Labor	58ITGU9	435048
09 Dec	Netherlands	Thailand	Visas	309UNTS291	104477
10 Dec	Belgium	Italy	Non-ILO Labor	58ITGU19	435049
10 Dec	Germany, West	USA (United States)	Milit Assistance	307UNTS59	104442
11 Dec	Cameroon	Germany, West	Atomic Energy	58WBGA46	424349
11 Dec	Belgium	Italy	Health/Educ/Welfare	59ITDI245	436050
11 Dec	China People's Rep	USSR (Soviet Union)	Scientific Project	57CCJC114	410468
11 Dec	Austria	IAEA (Atom Energy)	Atomic Energy	339UNTS110	104849
12 Dec	Poland	Org Rail Collabor	IGO Operations	57PZUM125	458057
12 Dec	Italy	Yugoslavia	Mass Media	386UNTS293	105549
12 Dec	Bulgaria	USSR (Soviet Union)	Consul/Citizenship	302UNTS3	104351
12 Dec	Bulgaria	USSR (Soviet Union)	Consul/Citizenship	302UNTS21	104352
12 Dec	Bulgaria	USSR (Soviet Union)	Admin Cooperation	317UNTS217	104606
13 Dec	Multilateral		Land Transport	372UNTS159	105296
13 Dec	Multilateral		Extradition	359UNTS273	105146
13 Dec	Multilateral		Visas	315UNTS139	104565
16 Dec	Austria	Switzerland	Claims and Debts	58SWRO239	462121
16 Dec	Mongolia	USSR (Soviet Union)	Health/Educ/Welfare	0SUST393	468286
16 Dec	China People's Rep	Germany, East	Sanitation	5EGDA333	419093
16 Dec	China People's Rep	Germany, East	Sanitation	57CCJC118	410471
16 Dec	Korea, North	USSR (Soviet Union)	Consul/Citizenship	292UNTS107	104269
16 Dec	Korea, North	USSR (Soviet Union)	Consul/Citizenship	292UNTS121	104270
16 Dec	Korea, North	USSR (Soviet Union)	Admin Cooperation	301UNTS301	104349
17 Dec	Mongolia	USSR (Soviet Union)	General Trade	0SUST394	468287
17 Dec	Mongolia	USSR (Soviet Union)	General Trade	0SUST394	468288
17 Dec	Cambodia	Poland	Tech Assistance	57PZUM130	458058

DATE	PARTY ONE	PARTY TWO	TOPIC	CITATION	NUMBER
1957 (Cont.)					
17 Dec	Hungary	Italy	Finance	58ITGU19	435416
17 Dec	Hungary	Romania	Sanitation	477UNTS303	106926
17 Dec	Finland	Italy	Finance	291UNTS133	104248
17 Dec	Pakistan	IBRD (World Bank)	IBRD Project	299UNTS321	104323
18 Dec	Hungary	USSR (Soviet Union)	General Aid	0SUST394	468204
18 Dec	China People's Rep	Finland	General Trade	57CCJC119	410472
18 Dec	Bulgaria	Yugoslavia	Non-ILO Labor	376UNTS3	105372
18 Dec	Norway	USSR (Soviet Union)	Specific Resources	312UNTS257	104522
18 Dec	Greece	USA (United States)	US Agri Commod Aid	303UNTS159	104379
19 Dec	Romania	USSR (Soviet Union)	Tech Assistance	16SUGG123	469950
19 Dec	Romania	USSR (Soviet Union)	Education	16SUGG123	469951
19 Dec	Syria	USSR (Soviet Union)	General Trade	0SUST394	468419
19 Dec	UK Great Britain	USSR (Soviet Union)	Air Transport	351UNTS235	105026
19 Dec	Ethiopia	Japan	General Amity	325UNTS91	104695
20 Dec	Czechoslovakia	Germany, East	IGO Establishment	5EGDA580	419359
21 Dec	China People's Rep	USSR (Soviet Union)	Water Transport	57CCJC120	410473
21 Dec	China People's Rep	United Arab Rep	General Trade	57CCJC122	410474
21 Dec	China People's Rep	USSR (Soviet Union)	Visas	305UNTS213	104420
23 Dec	Dominican Republic	Germany, West	General Amity	59WGBB1468	425106
25 Dec	USSR (Soviet Union)	Vietnam, North	Culture	0SUST395	468454
26 Dec	USSR (Soviet Union)	Vietnam, North	Postal Service	0SUST395	468456
26 Dec	USSR (Soviet Union)	Vietnam, North	Telecommunications	0SUST395	468455
26 Dec	Ethiopia	USA (United States)	Milit Assistance	307UNTS71	104443
27 Dec	Germany, East	USSR (Soviet Union)	Admin Cooperation	0SUST395	468169
27 Dec	China People's Rep	Yugoslavia	Scientific Project	57CCJC125	410475
27 Dec	France	USA (United States)	US Agri Commod Aid	307UNTS79	104444
28 Dec	China People's Rep	USSR (Soviet Union)	Education	16SUGG124	469954
28 Dec	China People's Rep	USSR (Soviet Union)	Tech Assistance	16SUGG124	469953
28 Dec	Italy	USSR (Soviet Union)	Finance	58ITGU10	435421
28 Dec	Italy	USSR (Soviet Union)	Finance	0UNTS0	109579
28 Dec	Poland	USSR (Soviet Union)	Admin Cooperation	320UNTS3	104638
28 Dec	Italy	UK Great Britain	Atomic Energy	305UNTS357	104425
30 Dec	Australia	Ireland	Air Transport	497UNTS29	107260
30 Dec	ICJ Option Clause	Sudan	ICJ Option Clause	284UNTS215	104139
31 Dec	Japan	Korea, South	Admin Cooperation	0JGJI1369	441103
31 Dec	China People's Rep	Korea, North	Scientific Project	57CCJC129	410479
31 Dec	China People's Rep	Korea, North	Scientific Project	57CCJC130	410480
31 Dec	Belgium	Denmark	Culture	305UNTS247	104422
31 Dec	Ceylon (Sri Lanka)	China People's Rep	General Economic	57CCJC83	410444
1958					
06 Jan	Multilateral		General Transport	304UNTS227	104399
07 Jan	Japan	Philippines	General Trade	3PTS699	465037
08 Jan	Brazil	Italy	Reparations	362UNTS273	105192
10 Jan	OECD (Econ Coop)	Spain	IGO Operations	58SPBO1207	460274
10 Jan	Bulgaria	Germany, East	Finance	6EGDA216	419054
10 Jan	Canada	Switzerland	Air Transport	464UNTS21	106710
10 Jan	Norway	Turkey	Culture	351UNTS229	105025
11 Jan	Laos	UNICEF (Children)	Claims and Debts	287UNTS255	104191
11 Jan	Japan	USA (United States)	Education	304UNTS35	104390
12 Jan	China People's Rep	Yemen	General Amity	58CCJC3	410481
12 Jan	China People's Rep	Yemen	Health/Educ/Welfare	58CCJC5	410483
12 Jan	China People's Rep	Yemen	General Trade	58CCJC4	410482
13 Jan	Hungary	USSR (Soviet Union)	General Trade	7SUGG101	469484
13 Jan	Ceylon (Sri Lanka)	India	Commodity Trade	315UNTS107	104562
14 Jan	Ghana	USSR (Soviet Union)	Consul/Citizenship	7SUGG102	469485
14 Jan	Mexico	IBRD (World Bank)	IBRD Project	293UNTS167	104292
15 Jan	Multilateral		Customs	383UNTS229	105503
15 Jan	Canada	Pakistan	Patents/Copyrights	392UNTS35	105637
15 Jan	Ceylon (Sri Lanka)	USSR (Soviet Union)	Culture	305UNTS235	104421
16 Jan	Poland	Yugoslavia	Non-ILO Labor	340UNTS137	104863
16 Jan	Poland	Yugoslavia	Non-ILO Labor	340UNTS181	104864
17 Jan	China People's Rep	Mongolia	Air Transport	58CCJC6	410484
17 Jan	Belgium	Germany, West	Extradition	328UNTS173	104735
18 Jan	China People's Rep	USSR (Soviet Union)	Scientific Project	7SUGG102	469488

DATE	PARTY ONE	PARTY TWO	TOPIC	CITATION	NUMBER
1958 (Cont.)					
18 Jan	Bulgaria	USSR (Soviet Union)	Claims and Debts	7SUGG102	469487
18 Jan	Afghanistan	USSR (Soviet Union)	Admin Cooperation	7SUGG102	469486
18 Jan	Afghanistan	USSR (Soviet Union)	Visas	321UNTS77	104655
20 Jan	Iran	USSR (Soviet Union)	Land Transport	7SUGG103	469489
20 Jan	Indonesia	Japan	Loans and Credits	0JGJI1365	441104
20 Jan	Indonesia	Japan	Peace/Disarmament	324UNTS227	104688
20 Jan	Indonesia	Japan	Reparations	324UNTS247	104689
20 Jan	Indonesia	Japan	Loans and Credits	325UNTS13	104691
20 Jan	Lebanon	United Nations	Postal Service	286UNTS199	104167
20 Jan	Belgium	Morocco	Air Transport	288UNTS3	104192
20 Jan	Indonesia	Japan	Claims and Debts	325UNTS3	104690
20 Jan	Turkey	USA (United States)	US Agri Commod Aid	304UNTS15	104389
20 Jan	UK Great Britain	USA (United States)	Specific Property	304UNTS3	104387
20 Jan	Lebanon	United Nations	Milit Installation	286UNTS189	104166
21 Jan	China People's Rep	Korea, North	General Trade	58CCJC10	410488
21 Jan	Ghana	WHO (World Health)	Tech Assistance	307UNTS3	104437
21 Jan	Poland	USSR (Soviet Union)	Consul/Citizenship	319UNTS277	104636
21 Jan	Poland	USSR (Soviet Union)	Consul/Citizenship	319UNTS291	104637
22 Jan	Poland	USSR (Soviet Union)	Atomic Energy	7SUGG103	469492
22 Jan	Brazil	IBRD (World Bank)	IBRD Project	323UNTS99	104666
23 Jan	Argentina	Paraguay	Scientific Project	0UNTS0	109294
24 Jan	China People's Rep	Mongolia	Air Transport	58CCJC13	410490
24 Jan	Canada	Portugal	Visas	392UNTS15	105634
24 Jan	Australia	USA (United States)	Patents/Copyrights	307UNTS105	104446
25 Jan	France	Italy	Non-ILO Labor	58ITGU123	435146
25 Jan	Japan	USA (United States)	Milit Assistance	304UNTS81	104392
27 Jan	Bulgaria	Germany, East	Admin Cooperation	6EGDA221	419055
27 Jan	Germany, East	Syria	Mass Media	6EGDA515	419314
27 Jan	USA (United States)	USSR (Soviet Union)	Health/Educ/Welfare	301UNTS405	104350
27 Jan	Spain	USA (United States)	US Agri Commod Aid	303UNTS247	104384
28 Jan	China People's Rep	Mongolia	General Trade	58CCJC14	410491
28 Jan	Germany, West	Netherlands	Specif Goods/Equip	453UNTS183	106525
28 Jan	Italy	Romania	Finance	302UNTS231	104362
29 Jan	United Arab Rep	USSR (Soviet Union)	General Aid	7SUGG103	469493
29 Jan	Iran	Italy	General Economic	58ITGU39	435210
29 Jan	Australia	UK Great Britain	Non-ILO Labor	292UNTS233	104275
29 Jan	Multilateral		Specific Resources	339UNTS23	104845
29 Jan	Iran	Italy	Finance	302UNTS181	104358
29 Jan	Japan	IBRD (World Bank)	IBRD Project	310UNTS111	104490
30 Jan	France	USA (United States)	Specif Claim/Waive	304UNTS9	104388
30 Jan	Germany, West	Netherlands	Humanitarian	315UNTS117	104563
31 Jan	Afghanistan	Germany, West	Direct Aid	58WGBB83	425002
31 Jan	Afghanistan	Germany, West	General Economic	58WBGA83	424001
31 Jan	Burma	China People's Rep	Telecommunications	58CCJC15	410492
31 Jan	Czechoslovakia	Poland	Land Transport	431UNTS99	106214
03 Feb	Multilateral		IGO Establishment	381UNTS165	105471
03 Feb	Belgium	Netherlands	Territory Boundary	381UNTS305	105472
03 Feb	UK Great Britain	USA (United States)	US Agri Commod Aid	307UNTS199	104450
03 Feb	USA (United States)	Yugoslavia	US Agri Commod Aid	304UNTS293	104404
04 Feb	Poland	USSR (Soviet Union)	General Trade	7SUGG104	469494
04 Feb	Belgium	Netherlands	Extradition	330UNTS83	104740
04 Feb	India	Japan	General Trade	324UNTS215	104687
05 Feb	Germany, West	Switzerland	Land Transport	60SWRO1639	462065
05 Feb	Poland	USSR (Soviet Union)	Scientific Project	7SUGG105	469495
05 Feb	Germany, West	Switzerland	Land Transport	60SWRO1671	462066
05 Feb	Indonesia	WHO (World Health)	Tech Assistance	307UNTS15	104438
05 Feb	Korea, South	USA (United States)	US Agri Commod Aid	307UNTS121	104447
06 Feb	Iran	Pakistan	Territory Boundary	0IRTB54	433079
06 Feb	Iran	Netherlands	Consul/Citizenship	0IRTB36	433050
06 Feb	Canada	Fed Rhod/Nyasaland	General Trade	392UNTS27	105636
07 Feb	Australia	UK Great Britain	Air Transport	335UNTS23	104776
07 Feb	Bulgaria	Netherlands	Air Transport	335UNTS45	104777
08 Feb	Ceylon (Sri Lanka)	USSR (Soviet Union)	General Trade	16SUGG124	469955
08 Feb	Ceylon (Sri Lanka)	USSR (Soviet Union)	General Trade	7SUGG105	469496
08 Feb	Ceylon (Sri Lanka)	USSR (Soviet Union)	Finance	0UNTS0	110491

DATE	PARTY ONE	PARTY TWO	TOPIC	CITATION	NUMBER
1958 (Cont.)					
08 Feb	Afghanistan	Turkey	Air Transport	464UNTS39	106711
08 Feb	Ceylon (Sri Lanka)	USSR (Soviet Union)	General Trade	348UNTS159	104999
09 Feb	Libya	Turkey	Culture	59TURG206	466039
12 Feb	Ghana	USA (United States)	Admin Cooperation	442UNTS175	106348
12 Feb	Poland	USA (United States)	Mass Media	304UNTS287	104403
14 Feb	Greece	India	General Trade	609UNTS94	108827
15 Feb	Albania	USSR (Soviet Union)	General Trade	7SUGG105	469497
15 Feb	Albania	USSR (Soviet Union)	General Economic	313UNTS261	104536
15 Feb	Poland	USA (United States)	US Agri Commod Aid	307UNTS217	104452
17 Feb	France	Pakistan	General Trade	58FRMD2202	417349
17 Feb	Sudan	Sweden	Air Transport	393UNTS161	105655
18 Feb	Austria	Sweden	Land Transport	427UNTS349	106166
19 Feb	Spain	UK Great Britain	General Trade	58SPBO803	460241
19 Feb	Austria	Sweden	Land Transport	427UNTS211	106155
20 Feb	Poland	Yugoslavia	General Economic	58PZUM48	458059
20 Feb	Bulgaria	Germany, East	Health/Educ/Welfare	6EGDA250	419056
20 Feb	Canada	India	Loans and Credits	391UNTS231	105628
20 Feb	Philippines	USA (United States)	Status of Forces	303UNTS261	104385
21 Feb	Germany, East	USSR (Soviet Union)	Specific Property	6EGDA429	419406
21 Feb	Germany, East	USSR (Soviet Union)	Education	6EGDA425	419407
21 Feb	Burma	China People's Rep	General Trade	58CCJC21	410496
21 Feb	China People's Rep	Mongolia	Culture	58CCJC19	410494
21 Feb	Finland	USA (United States)	US Agri Commod Aid	304UNTS253	104401
22 Feb	UK Great Britain	USA (United States)	Milit Assistance	307UNTS207	104451
25 Feb	Italy	Poland	Admin Cooperation	58ITGU105	435303
25 Feb	Italy	Poland	Finance	58ITGU105	435302
25 Feb	Germany, East	USSR (Soviet Union)	General Economic	6EGDA431	419408
25 Feb	Bulgaria	Italy	Finance	362UNTS279	105193
25 Feb	Bulgaria	Italy	General Trade	362UNTS291	105194
25 Feb	Australia	USA (United States)	Tech Assistance	317UNTS153	104601
26 Feb	Israel	Philippines	General Amity	507UNTS135	107398
28 Feb	Italy	IBRD (World Bank)	IBRD Project	359UNTS47	105139
28 Feb	France	USA (United States)	US Agri Commod Aid	366UNTS343	105222
01 Mar	France	Israel	Visas	314UNTS87	104543
04 Mar	Fed of Malaya	UK Great Britain	Admin Cooperation	314UNTS253	104550
05 Mar	Iran	USSR (Soviet Union)	Specific Resources	7SUGG107	469499
05 Mar	China People's Rep	Japan	General Trade	58CCJC24	410499
05 Mar	Brazil	Ecuador	General Economic	369UNTS43	105250
05 Mar	Norway	Pakistan	Air Transport	334UNTS199	104769
06 Mar	Canada	Switzerland	Atomic Energy	58SWRO724	462040
06 Mar	Pakistan	Sweden	Air Transport	393UNTS181	105656
07 Mar	Romania	USSR (Soviet Union)	Claims and Debts	7SUGG107	469500
07 Mar	Italy	USA (United States)	US Agri Commod Aid	303UNTS205	104381
12 Mar	Albania	China People's Rep	General Economic	58CCJC25	410500
12 Mar	Luxembourg	Sweden	Admin Cooperation	427UNTS179	106153
12 Mar	Czechoslovakia	Hungary	Sanitation	408UNTS178	105870
12 Mar	USSR (Soviet Union)	Vietnam, North	General Economic	356UNTS149	105094
13 Mar	Iceland	USSR (Soviet Union)	Consul/Citizenship	16SUGG124	469956
13 Mar	Bulgaria	China People's Rep	General Economic	58CCJC27	410501
13 Mar	Bulgaria	Hungary	Sanitation	438UNTS191	106317
13 Mar	Bulgaria	Hungary	Sanitation	438UNTS173	106316
14 Mar	Germany, East	Poland	Health/Educ/Welfare	6EGDA332	419257
14 Mar	Colombia	USA (United States)	US Agri Commod Aid	308UNTS115	104459
15 Mar	China People's Rep	Vietnam, North	Mass Media	58CCJC28	410502
15 Mar	Multilateral		Tech Assistance	292UNTS273	104276
18 Mar	Belgium	Japan	Admin Cooperation	303UNTS149	104378
18 Mar	Poland	USSR (Soviet Union)	Territory Boundary	340UNTS89	104861
18 Mar	Belgium	Mexico	Visas	301UNTS291	104348
19 Mar	Austria	Yugoslavia	Territory Boundary	58ABGB144	403233
20 Mar	Belgium	Ecuador	Visas	304UNTS207	104397
20 Mar	Israel	Sweden	Admin Cooperation	314UNTS99	104545
20 Mar	Austria	Japan	Visas	324UNTS205	104686
20 Mar	Multilateral		Admin Cooperation	335UNTS211	104789
21 Mar	China People's Rep	Hungary	General Economic	58CCJC30	410504
21 Mar	Czechoslovakia	Poland	Specific Resources	538UNTS89	107811

DATE	PARTY ONE	PARTY TWO	TOPIC	CITATION	NUMBER
1958 (Cont.)					
21 Mar	Germany, West	Portugal	Air Transport	464UNTS71	106712
21 Mar	Bulgaria	Yugoslavia	Land Transport	349UNTS61	105009
21 Mar	Bulgaria	Yugoslavia	Land Transport	386UNTS119	105541
21 Mar	Bulgaria	Yugoslavia	Customs	376UNTS53	105373
25 Mar	Czechoslovakia	Romania	Sanitation	339UNTS77	104846
26 Mar	Jordan	UK Great Britain	Loans and Credits	312UNTS373	104526
27 Mar	Sweden	USSR (Soviet Union)	Specific Property	7SUGG108	469501
27 Mar	Czechoslovakia	Poland	Culture	58PZUM61	458060
27 Mar	Germany, East	United Arab Rep	Water Transport	6EGDA474	419471
27 Mar	China People's Rep	Germany, East	Finance	58CCJC34	410506
27 Mar	France	Italy	Visas	305UNTS387	104426
27 Mar	France	Italy	Non-ILO Labor	305UNTS409	104428
28 Mar	France	Spain	Non-ILO Labor	58SPBO1504	460122
28 Mar	France	Spain	Non-ILO Labor	58SPBO2204	460123
28 Mar	Italy	Spain	Non-ILO Labor	58SPBO2605	460175
28 Mar	Sweden	USSR (Soviet Union)	Privil/Immunities	428UNTS321	106184
28 Mar	South Africa	Sweden	Air Transport	300UNTS95	104333
28 Mar	Denmark	South Africa	Air Transport	300UNTS107	104334
28 Mar	Norway	South Africa	Air Transport	300UNTS83	104332
28 Mar	Belgium	Luxembourg	General Trade	303UNTS101	104372
28 Mar	Netherlands	Switzerland	Non-ILO Labor	318UNTS175	104614
29 Mar	China People's Rep	Yugoslavia	Culture	58CCJC35	410507
29 Mar	Czechoslovakia	Poland	Reparations	340UNTS199	104865
29 Mar	Netherlands	Switzerland	Visas	330UNTS101	104741
30 Mar	China People's Rep	Romania	General Economic	58CCJC36	410508
31 Mar	France	Germany, West	Specific Property	59WGBB189	425153
31 Mar	China People's Rep	Vietnam, North	General Economic	58CCJC38	410509
31 Mar	Multilateral		Specific Property	320UNTS103	104639
31 Mar	Sudan	USA (United States)	General Aid	308UNTS105	104458
01 Apr	Czechoslovakia	USSR (Soviet Union)	Customs	7SUGG108	469502
01 Apr	France	Luxembourg	Taxation	60FRRT18	415270
01 Apr	Belgium	Greece	Non-ILO Labor	388UNTS93	105574
03 Apr	Germany, West	Portugal	Finance	59WGBB264	425592
03 Apr	Germany, West	Portugal	Patents/Copyrights	59WGBB264	425591
03 Apr	Morocco	Portugal	Air Transport	393UNTS203	105657
03 Apr	ICJ Option Clause	Belgium	ICJ Option Clause	302UNTS251	104364
03 Apr	Multilateral		Commodity Trade	336UNTS177	104806
03 Apr	Romania	USSR (Soviet Union)	Admin Cooperation	313UNTS167	104535
03 Apr	Multilateral		Commodity Trade	302UNTS121	104355
04 Apr	Bulgaria	Yugoslavia	Water Transport	367UNTS89	105228
05 Apr	USA (United States)	Yugoslavia	Tech Assistance	338UNTS233	104838
07 Apr	China People's Rep	Poland	General Trade	58CCJC47	410514
08 Apr	Germany, West	Spain	Finance	59SPBO2606	460013
08 Apr	Germany, West	Spain	Finance	59SPBO2606	460017
08 Apr	Germany, West	Spain	Patents/Copyrights	59SPBO2606	460020
08 Apr	Germany, West	Spain	Specif Goods/Equip	59SPBO2606	460014
08 Apr	Germany, West	Spain	Claims and Debts	59SPBO2606	460011
08 Apr	Germany, West	Spain	Patents/Copyrights	59SPBO2606	460016
08 Apr	Germany, West	Spain	Finance	59SPBO2606	460012
08 Apr	Germany, West	Spain	Finance	59SPBO2606	460018
08 Apr	Germany, West	Spain	Finance	59SPBO2606	460015
08 Apr	Germany, West	Spain	Finance	59SPBO2606	460019
08 Apr	Italy	Monaco	Visas	60ITDI263	436281
08 Apr	Italy	Tunisia	General Trade	378UNTS327	105430
09 Apr	Germany, West	Netherlands	Visas	335UNTS237	104791
09 Apr	Peru	USA (United States)	US Agri Commod Aid	316UNTS37	104576
10 Apr	United Arab Rep	USSR (Soviet Union)	Culture	7SUGG109	469503
10 Apr	Taiwan	Costa Rica	Culture	315UNTS165	104567
11 Apr	Mongolia	USSR (Soviet Union)	Tech Assistance	16SUGG124	469957
11 Apr	Mongolia	USSR (Soviet Union)	Education	16SUGG125	469958
11 Apr	Israel	WHO (World Health)	Tech Assistance	307UNTS27	104439
12 Apr	China People's Rep	Denmark	Patents/Copyrights	58CCJC49	410515
12 Apr	Belgium	Morocco	Visas	303UNTS141	104377
14 Apr	Philippines	UK Great Britain	Air Transport	3PTS715	465038
14 Apr	Italy	Sweden	Admin Cooperation	427UNTS167	106151

DATE	PARTY ONE	PARTY TWO	TOPIC	CITATION	NUMBER
1958 (Cont.)					
14 Apr	Belgium	Iran	Air Transport	381UNTS309	105473
15 Apr	Iran	USSR (Soviet Union)	General Trade	7SUGG110	469504
15 Apr	Multilateral		Health/Educ/Welfare	539UNTS27	107822
16 Apr	Ethiopia	Germany, West	Air Transport	59WGBB1065	425014
16 Apr	China People's Rep	Czechoslovakia	General Economic	58CCJC51	410517
16 Apr	Germany, West	Netherlands	Sanitation	486UNTS331	107084
17 Apr	Tunisia	Turkey	Mostfavored Nation	59TURG606	466093
18 Apr	France	Germany, West	Visas	60WGBB1533	425154
18 Apr	Germany, East	Korea, North	Health/Educ/Welfare	6EGDA323	419179
18 Apr	Bulgaria	Germany, East	Health/Educ/Welfare	6EGDA278	419058
18 Apr	Bulgaria	Germany, East	Consul/Citizenship	6EGDA270	419057
18 Apr	Bulgaria	Germany, East	Sanitation	6EGDA282	419059
18 Apr	Bulgaria	Germany, West	Consul/Citizenship	0UNTS0	109872
18 Apr	France	Germany, West	General Transport	0UNTS0	110714
18 Apr	Sweden	Yugoslavia	Air Transport	393UNTS225	105658
18 Apr	Taiwan	USA (United States)	US Agri Commod Aid	308UNTS179	104461
18 Apr	Germany, West	UK Great Britain	Culture	343UNTS241	104928
19 Apr	Morocco	USSR (Soviet Union)	Finance	7SUGG110	469506
19 Apr	Morocco	USSR (Soviet Union)	General Trade	7SUGG110	469505
19 Apr	France	Spain	General Trade	58SPBO805	460124
19 Apr	France	Greece	Non-ILO Labor	59FRRT14	415204
22 Apr	Bolivia	USA (United States)	Milit Assistance	317UNTS209	104605
23 Apr	China People's Rep	Germany, East	General Economic	58CCJC58	410522
23 Apr	China People's Rep	USSR (Soviet Union)	General Trade	58CCJC57	410521
23 Apr	China People's Rep	USSR (Soviet Union)	General Trade	58CCJC56	410520
23 Apr	Pakistan	IBRD (World Bank)	IBRD Project	323UNTS253	104672
23 Apr	China People's Rep	USSR (Soviet Union)	General Economic	313UNTS135	104534
24 Apr	FAO (Food Agri)	UK Great Britain	IGO Operations	642UNTS245	109177
24 Apr	Hungary	USSR (Soviet Union)	Status of Forces	408UNTS118	105868
25 Apr	Germany, West	USSR (Soviet Union)	General Economic	346UNTS71	104978
25 Apr	Germany, West	USSR (Soviet Union)	Consul/Citizenship	338UNTS49	104832
26 Apr	Bulgaria	USSR (Soviet Union)	Commodity Trade	7SUGG111	469507
26 Apr	Bulgaria	USSR (Soviet Union)	General Trade	7SUGG111	469508
26 Apr	Japan	Poland	General Economic	340UNTS221	104866
28 Apr	Austria	IBRD (World Bank)	IBRD Project	359UNTS145	105142
28 Apr	Albania	Yugoslavia	Consul/Citizenship	386UNTS103	105540
28 Apr	Chile	IBRD (World Bank)	IBRD Project	359UNTS89	105140
28 Apr	Argentina	USA (United States)	Status of Forces	315UNTS211	104570
28 Apr	Belgium	South Africa	Visas	303UNTS131	104375
29 Apr	Multilateral		Specific Resources	559UNTS285	108164
29 Apr	Multilateral		Water Transport	450UNTS11	106465
29 Apr	Multilateral		Dispute Settlement	450UNTS169	106466
29 Apr	Multilateral		Territory Boundary	499UNTS311	107302
29 Apr	Multilateral		Territory Boundary	516UNTS205	107477
29 Apr	Israel	New Zealand	Visas	314UNTS93	104544
30 Apr	Sweden	Switzerland	Land Transport	427UNTS295	106161
30 Apr	Belgium	Japan	Finance	303UNTS109	104373
01 May	Ireland	South Africa	Taxation	398UNTS3	105714
01 May	Saudi Arabia	USA (United States)	Direct Aid	315UNTS221	104571
02 May	IBRD (World Bank)	UK Great Britain	IBRD Project	324UNTS25	104677
03 May	Iceland	USA (United States)	US Agri Commod Aid	316UNTS137	104581
03 May	Austria	Netherlands	Admin Cooperation	342UNTS3	104895
05 May	Czechoslovakia	Italy	Finance	58ITGU129	435078
05 May	Mexico	IBRD (World Bank)	IBRD Project	309UNTS3	104466
05 May	New Zealand	USA (United States)	Visas	317UNTS59	104594
07 May	Germany, West	Turkey	Culture	58TURG1505	466036
07 May	Iran	Italy	General Trade	60ITDI329	436211
07 May	Jordan	UK Great Britain	Loans and Credits	312UNTS379	104527
08 May	Italy	Spain	General Trade	56SPBO406	460176
08 May	Norway	USA (United States)	Milit Installation	2NORT528	451199
08 May	Italy	Spain	Finance	58ITGU237	435352
08 May	Hungary	Poland	Sanitation	408UNTS212	105872
08 May	Czechoslovakia	Hungary	Customs	407UNTS92	105862
08 May	Italy	USA (United States)	Direct Aid	316UNTS177	104584
08 May	Belgium	Sweden	Land Transport	312UNTS145	104516

DATE	PARTY ONE	PARTY TWO	TOPIC	CITATION	NUMBER
1958 (Cont.)					
09 May	El Salvador	USA (United States)	Visas	316UNTS29	104575
09 May	Honduras	IBRD (World Bank)	IBRD Project	323UNTS4	104662
10 May	Portugal	Switzerland	Water Transport	58SWRO781	462078
10 May	Finland	Spain	General Trade	58SPBO2405	460278
11 May	Korea, North	USSR (Soviet Union)	General Economic	7SUGG112	469510
11 May	Hungary	USSR (Soviet Union)	Atomic Energy	7SUGG112	469509
12 May	Canada	USA (United States)	General Military	316UNTS151	104582
13 May	Multilateral		ILO Labor	389UNTS277	105598
14 May	Germany, East	Vietnam, North	Telecommunications	6EGDA505	419490
14 May	Germany, East	Vietnam, North	Postal Service	6EGDA494	419489
14 May	Austria	New Zealand	Visas	317UNTS117	104598
15 May	Philippines	USA (United States)	Milit Assistance	316UNTS163	104583
17 May	China People's Rep	Hungary	Scientific Project	58CCJC62	410526
19 May	Lebanon	UK Great Britain	Milit Assistance	327UNTS43	104716
22 May	Poland	USSR (Soviet Union)	Culture	7SUGG112	469511
22 May	Ceylon (Sri Lanka)	Sweden	Tech Assistance	428UNTS65	106168
23 May	Italy	Switzerland	Land Transport	363UNTS81	105201
24 May	Chile	Spain	Health/Educ/Welfare	58SPBO1411	460074
24 May	Taiwan	France	Patents/Copyrights	0CTRC10	413006
24 May	UK Great Britain	Yugoslavia	Non-ILO Labor	326UNTS69	104709
26 May	Arab League	ILO (Labor Org)	IGO Operations	302UNTS343	200549
26 May	Albania	Italy	Finance	362UNTS259	105191
27 May	Burma	USA (United States)	US Agri Commod Aid	315UNTS197	104569
28 May	Italy	Syria	Sanitation	60ITDI265	436342
28 May	Brazil	Colombia	Tech Assistance	369UNTS141	105255
28 May	Bulgaria	Denmark	Air Transport	312UNTS235	104521
29 May	Denmark	Germany, West	Specific Resources	59WGBB1072	425099
29 May	Germany, West	Liechtenstein	Admin Cooperation	59WBGA73	424416
29 May	Denmark	Germany, West	Specific Resources	0UNTSO	109731
29 May	Fed of Malaya	United Nations	Tech Assistance	330UNTS109	104742
29 May	Euratom	USA (United States)	Atomic Energy	335UNTS161	104783
30 May	Germany, West	Netherlands	Visas	570UNTS127	108291
30 May	Austria	Netherlands	Visas	458UNTS147	106598
30 May	Poland	USA (United States)	Mass Media	315UNTS231	104572
31 May	Belgium	France	Patents/Copyrights	60FRRT20	415064
31 May	Sweden	Yugoslavia	Admin Cooperation	428UNTS357	106186
02 Jun	India	USSR (Soviet Union)	Air Transport	393UNTS3	105650
03 Jun	Japan	USSR (Soviet Union)	Water Transport	7SUGG113	469512
03 Jun	Germany, West	Portugal	Claims and Debts	59WGBB264	425590
03 Jun	China People's Rep	Pakistan	Commodity Trade	58CCJC64	410431
03 Jun	Philippines	USA (United States)	US Agri Commod Aid	316UNTS3	104573
04 Jun	China People's Rep	Norway	General Economic	3NORT742	451022
04 Jun	China People's Rep	Norway	General Economic	58CCJC65	410527
05 Jun	Belgium	USSR (Soviet Union)	Air Transport	345UNTS145	104965
05 Jun	New Zealand	Turkey	Visas	317UNTS123	104599
06 Jun	Austria	Mexico	Visas	59ABGB44	403139
07 Jun	Pakistan	Portugal	Air Transport	320UNTS225	104645
09 Jun	France	WEU (West Europe)	Non-ILO Labor	58FRRT32	415498
09 Jun	Norway	Sweden	Water Transport	427UNTS221	106156
10 Jun	Multilateral		Land Transport	454UNTS211	106541
10 Jun	Multilateral		General Economic	454UNTS47	106539
10 Jun	Multilateral		Land Transport	454UNTS115	106540
10 Jun	Denmark	Luxembourg	Air Transport	356UNTS193	105096
10 Jun	Multilateral		Admin Cooperation	330UNTS3	104739
11 Jun	Albania	Italy	Water Transport	58ITGU244	435006
11 Jun	Belgium	South Africa	Air Transport	335UNTS63	104778
13 Jun	Czechoslovakia	Poland	Territory Boundary	354UNTS221	105064
13 Jun	Lebanon	United Nations	IGO Status/Immunit	303UNTS271	104386
13 Jun	Japan	IBRD (World Bank)	IBRD Project	312UNTS159	104518
14 Jun	Poland	USSR (Soviet Union)	Water Transport	7SUGG114	469513
14 Jun	Germany, East	Hungary	Sanitation	407UNTS78	105861
16 Jun	Norway	Romania	Air Transport	405UNTS223	105835
16 Jun	Japan	UK Great Britain	Atomic Energy	325UNTS185	104700
16 Jun	IBRD (World Bank)	UK Great Britain	IBRD Project	309UNTS35	104467
16 Jun	USA (United States)	Yugoslavia	Admin Cooperation	317UNTS31	104591

DATE	PARTY ONE	PARTY TWO	TOPIC	CITATION	NUMBER
1958 (Cont.)					
17 Jun	USA (United States)	Vietnam, South	Atomic Energy	321UNTS35	104652
17 Jun	Netherlands	USSR (Soviet Union)	Air Transport	335UNTS77	104779
18 Jun	Poland	USSR (Soviet Union)	Status of Forces	7SUGG114	469514
18 Jun	Austria	Sweden	Visas	59ABGB30	403174
18 Jun	Ireland	Switzerland	Taxation	553UNTS183	108086
18 Jun	Multilateral		General Trade	386UNTS345	105552
18 Jun	Multilateral		Finance	386UNTS355	105553
18 Jun	Ethiopia	United Nations	IGO Operations	317UNTS101	104597
18 Jun	Ceylon (Sri Lanka)	USA (United States)	US Agri Commod Aid	316UNTS15	104574
19 Jun	Bulgaria	Norway	Air Transport	3NORT746	451014
19 Jun	Multilateral		Tech Assistance	306UNTS236	200550
19 Jun	Japan	USA (United States)	Atomic Energy	325UNTS143	104699
20 Jun	Greece	Norway	Visas	3NORT747	451066
20 Jun	Canada	USA (United States)	Milit Assistance	317UNTS37	104592
20 Jun	Austria	Belgium	Land Transport	312UNTS95	104513
20 Jun	Australia	USA (United States)	Postal Service	336UNTS97	104802
21 Jun	WHO (World Health)	Sudan	Tech Assistance	307UNTS235	104453
23 Jun	Japan	USSR (Soviet Union)	General Trade	16SUGG125	469959
23 Jun	Chile	Spain	Health/Educ/Welfare	58SPBO1411	460075
23 Jun	Canada	Switzerland	Admin Cooperation	391UNTS213	105625
23 Jun	India	USA (United States)	US Agri Commod Aid	317UNTS181	104603
24 Jun	Germany, East	USSR (Soviet Union)	Milit Occupation	6EGDA447	419409
24 Jun	Italy	Morocco	General Trade	363UNTS23	105197
24 Jun	Multilateral		ILO Labor	348UNTS275	105005
24 Jun	Burma	USA (United States)	Milit Assistance	335UNTS193	104786
25 Jun	Afghanistan	USSR (Soviet Union)	Specific Resources	7SUGG114	469515
25 Jun	Multilateral		ILO Labor	362UNTS31	105181
25 Jun	ICJ Option Clause	Finland	ICJ Option Clause	303UNTS137	104376
25 Jun	Denmark	Romania	Air Transport	345UNTS231	104970
25 Jun	India	IBRD (World Bank)	IBRD Project	323UNTS131	104667
25 Jun	India	IBRD (World Bank)	IBRD Project	323UNTS157	104668
26 Jun	Finland	USSR (Soviet Union)	Commodity Trade	7SUGG114	469516
26 Jun	Austria	France	Admin Cooperation	60FRRT19	415056
26 Jun	Czechoslovakia	Germany, East	Patents/Copyrights	504UNTS221	107359
26 Jun	Afghanistan	USA (United States)	Culture	321UNTS67	104654
26 Jun	Multilateral		Admin Cooperation	324UNTS97	104679
27 Jun	Czechoslovakia	Hungary	Consul/Citizenship	477UNTS321	106927
27 Jun	Bulgaria	Hungary	Culture	438UNTS235	106318
27 Jun	Ecuador	USA (United States)	Direct Aid	317UNTS51	104593
27 Jun	Japan	IBRD (World Bank)	IBRD Project	312UNTS193	104519
30 Jun	Czechoslovakia	USSR (Soviet Union)	Claims and Debts	7SUGG115	469517
30 Jun	Belgium	Germany, West	Admin Cooperation	387UNTS245	105566
30 Jun	Romania	Vietnam, North	Scientific Project	389UNTS43	105591
30 Jun	Germany, West	Netherlands	Non-ILO Labor	315UNTS179	104568
30 Jun	Netherlands	Norway	Reparations	346UNTS217	104982
30 Jun	Netherlands	Norway	Reparations	348UNTS3	104995
30 Jun	Albania	USSR (Soviet Union)	Admin Cooperation	328UNTS3	104729
30 Jun	Philippines	USA (United States)	Direct Aid	321UNTS51	104653
30 Jun	Ecuador	USA (United States)	US Agri Commod Aid	336UNTS11	104796
01 Jul	Germany, East	Mongolia	Health/Educ/Welfare	6EGDA518	419217
03 Jul	Iran	USSR (Soviet Union)	Territory Boundary	7SUGG115	469518
03 Jul	UK Great Britain	USA (United States)	Atomic Energy	326UNTS3	104707
04 Jul	Belgium	Pakistan	Air Transport	387UNTS305	105569
07 Jul	Austria	Norway	Admin Cooperation	3NORT750	451225
07 Jul	EEC (Econ Commnty)	ILO (Labor Org)	IGO Operations	312UNTS387	200551
07 Jul	Ethiopia	UK Great Britain	Air Transport	331UNTS3	104749
08 Jul	Iraq	USSR (Soviet Union)	Consul/Citizenship	7SUGG116	469520
09 Jul	Denmark	El Salvador	General Economic	341UNTS289	104892
09 Jul	Fed of Malaya	USA (United States)	Milit Assistance	336UNTS79	104799
10 Jul	Austria	Romania	Air Transport	353UNTS155	105041
11 Jul	Japan	IBRD (World Bank)	IBRD Project	318UNTS103	104611
15 Jul	Germany, East	Romania	Health/Educ/Welfare	387UNTS115	105560
15 Jul	Germany, East	Romania	Admin Cooperation	395UNTS3	105681
15 Jul	Germany, East	Romania	Consul/Citizenship	387UNTS133	105561
15 Jul	Hungary	USSR (Soviet Union)	Admin Cooperation	322UNTS3	104656

1958 (Cont.)

DATE	PARTY ONE	PARTY TWO	TOPIC	CITATION	NUMBER
16 Jul	Iceland	USSR (Soviet Union)	Specific Resources	7SUGG116	469519
16 Jul	Mexico	USA (United States)	Telecommunications	335UNTS139	104782
17 Jul	Germany, West	Morocco	Admin Cooperation	59WGBB118	425463
17 Jul	Denmark	Hungary	Air Transport	344UNTS281	104954
17 Jul	Philippines	USA (United States)	Specific Property	335UNTS199	104787
18 Jul	Portugal	UK Great Britain	Atomic Energy	313UNTS109	104532
19 Jul	Bulgaria	USSR (Soviet Union)	Tech Assistance	7SUGG116	469521
21 Jul	Hungary	USSR (Soviet Union)	Customs	16SUGG125	469960
21 Jul	Ecuador	Germany, West	Admin Cooperation	58WBGA218	424111
21 Jul	Afghanistan	Austria	Air Transport	0UNTS0	109236
21 Jul	Sweden	United Arab Rep	Mostfavored Nation	427UNTS285	106160
21 Jul	Hungary	USSR (Soviet Union)	Customs	408UNTS194	105871
21 Jul	IBRD (World Bank)	Sudan	IBRD Project	323UNTS183	104669
21 Jul	Denmark	Sweden	Taxation	320UNTS163	104642
22 Jul	Netherlands	Yugoslavia	Claims and Debts	386UNTS263	105546
23 Jul	Philippines	UNTAB (Tech Assis)	Tech Assistance	3PTS749	465086
23 Jul	Australia	Netherlands	Postal Service	328UNTS227	104736
23 Jul	India	IBRD (World Bank)	IBRD Project	317UNTS3	104590
24 Jul	Japan	Philippines	Visas	325UNTS103	104696
25 Jul	France	Luxembourg	Postal Service	58FRJO2507	416271
25 Jul	Multilateral		Customs	352UNTS3	105035
25 Jul	Muscat and Oman	UK Great Britain	General Military	312UNTS347	104524
28 Jul	Multilateral		General Military	335UNTS205	104788
29 Jul	Sweden	United Arab Rep	Taxation	369UNTS323	105264
30 Jul	India	Sweden	Taxation	369UNTS211	105259
31 Jul	Italy	Switzerland	Taxation	61SWRO413	462056
01 Aug	France	Switzerland	Milit Servic/Citiz	59SWRO223	462006
02 Aug	France	Yugoslavia	Claims and Debts	59FRRT11	415485
05 Aug	Taiwan	Philippines	Postal Service	3PTS761	465039
06 Aug	Taiwan	USA (United States)	Milit Installation	462UNTS3	106666
06 Aug	Lebanon	USA (United States)	Status of Forces	366UNTS361	105223
07 Aug	Germany, West	India	Education	58WBGA178	424254
07 Aug	Germany, West	Pakistan	Taxation	60WGBB1799	425565
08 Aug	China People's Rep	USSR (Soviet Union)	Tech Assistance	7SUGG118	469522
09 Aug	Jordan	UNICEF (Children)	Direct Aid	309UNTS297	104478
10 Aug	United Arab Rep	USSR (Soviet Union)	General Trade	7SUGG118	469524
11 Aug	Paraguay	Spain	Commodity Trade	59SPBO1007	460218
12 Aug	Ghana	UNICEF (Children)	Direct Aid	309UNTS103	104469
13 Aug	Mexico	Paraguay	Culture	60MEXD907	444036
13 Aug	Indonesia	USA (United States)	Milit Assistance	335UNTS187	104785
14 Aug	Romania	United Arab Rep	Air Transport	405UNTS189	105834
15 Aug	Cuba	USA (United States)	Specific Resources	358UNTS63	105124
15 Aug	Finland	USA (United States)	Visas	314UNTS43	104540
18 Aug	Iceland	USSR (Soviet Union)	Loans and Credits	7SUGG118	469523
18 Aug	Nepal	United Nations	Admin Cooperation	508UNTS3	107403
18 Aug	Japan	IBRD (World Bank)	IBRD Project	323UNTS205	104670
20 Aug	USA (United States)	USSR (Soviet Union)	Visas	336UNTS269	104809
22 Aug	France	Germany, West	Finance	58FRRT28	415047
22 Aug	France	United Arab Rep	General Amity	0UNTS0	110511
25 Aug	Finland	France	Taxation	59FRRT28	415190
25 Aug	Finland	France	Taxation	59FRRT28	415189
25 Aug	China People's Rep	United Arab Rep	Postal Service	58CCJC81	410538
25 Aug	Pakistan	Sweden	Taxation	369UNTS183	105258
25 Aug	Mongolia	USSR (Soviet Union)	Consul/Citizenship	322UNTS215	104659
25 Aug	Mongolia	USSR (Soviet Union)	Consul/Citizenship	322UNTS201	104658
25 Aug	Mongolia	USSR (Soviet Union)	Admin Cooperation	322UNTS105	104657
25 Aug	Burma	USA (United States)	Commodity Trade	336UNTS3	104795
26 Aug	Australia	Fed of Malaya	General Trade	325UNTS253	104703
27 Aug	Australia	Germany, West	Non-ILO Labor	320UNTS303	104649
28 Aug	India	Switzerland	Taxation	58SWRO795	462054
28 Aug	Italy	Spain	Customs	60ITDI282	436353
28 Aug	Germany, West	Luxembourg	Taxation	59WGBB1269	425422
28 Aug	Pakistan	Thailand	General Amity	394UNTS53	105668
28 Aug	Denmark	USA (United States)	Reparations	335UNTS133	104781
29 Aug	Germany, West	Sweden	Admin Cooperation	59WGBB401	425615

1958 (Cont.)

DATE	PARTY ONE	PARTY TWO	TOPIC	CITATION	NUMBER
29 Aug	Germany, East	United Arab Rep	Tech Assistance	6EGDA484	419473
29 Aug	Germany, East	United Arab Rep	General Aid	6EGDA484	419472
02 Sep	Canada	USA (United States)	General Military	335UNTS249	104792
03 Sep	Belgium	France	Health/Educ/Welfare	58FRJO1910	416065
03 Sep	Lebanon	USA (United States)	Direct Aid	336UNTS91	104801
04 Sep	Morocco	USSR (Soviet Union)	Consul/Citizenship	7SUGG120	469525
05 Sep	Czechoslovakia	USSR (Soviet Union)	Scientific Project	7SUGG120	469526
05 Sep	Czechoslovakia	USSR (Soviet Union)	Scientific Project	7SUGG120	469527
05 Sep	Nicaragua	USA (United States)	Milit Installation	336UNTS33	104797
06 Sep	Brazil	Italy	Atomic Energy	60ITGU96	435061
06 Sep	Brazil	Italy	Milit Servic/Citiz	60ITGU215	435060
06 Sep	Brazil	Italy	Culture	62ITGU153	435062
06 Sep	Turkey	USA (United States)	Loans and Credits	336UNTS85	104800
08 Sep	Germany, East	USSR (Soviet Union)	Specif Goods/Equip	6EGDA452	419410
09 Sep	United Arab Rep	Iran	Culture	0IRTB20	433032
09 Sep	Italy	UK Great Britain	Non-ILO Labor	60ITDI243	436190
09 Sep	Haiti	USA (United States)	Direct Aid	335UNTS257	104793
09 Sep	Japan	New Zealand	General Trade	325UNTS119	104698
10 Sep	France	Vietnam, South	Finance	0VKNG130	496037
10 Sep	USA (United States)	USSR (Soviet Union)	Culture	7SUGG121	469529
10 Sep	Poland	USSR (Soviet Union)	Territory Boundary	7SUGG120	469528
10 Sep	India	Pakistan	Territory Boundary	369UNTS81	105252
10 Sep	Japan	IBRD (World Bank)	IBRD Project	318UNTS133	104612
10 Sep	Japan	IBRD (World Bank)	IBRD Project	323UNTS297	104673
11 Sep	United Arab Rep	USSR (Soviet Union)	Air Transport	7SUGG121	469530
12 Sep	Laos	Vietnam, South	Admin Cooperation	0VKNG131	496038
12 Sep	Cambodia	USSR (Soviet Union)	Non-IBRD Project	7SUGG121	469531
12 Sep	Austria	Luxembourg	Non-ILO Labor	59ABGB27	403136
12 Sep	Austria	Bulgaria	Air Transport	353UNTS3	105036
15 Sep	ICJ Option Clause	Japan	ICJ Option Clause	312UNTS155	104517
16 Sep	India	IBRD (World Bank)	IBRD Project	323UNTS235	104671
17 Sep	Ceylon (Sri Lanka)	China People's Rep	Loans and Credits	58CCJC83	410540
17 Sep	Peru	IBRD (World Bank)	IBRD Project	323UNTS27	104663
17 Sep	Ceylon (Sri Lanka)	IBRD (World Bank)	IBRD Project	323UNTS51	104664
18 Sep	United Arab Rep	USSR (Soviet Union)	Water Transport	338UNTS29	104831
19 Sep	Argentina	Brazil	Tech Assistance	374UNTS57	105329
20 Sep	Belgium	France	Reparations	376UNTS331	105387
22 Sep	Austria	Germany, West	Admin Cooperation	60WGBB1341	425542
22 Sep	Austria	Germany, West	Extradition	60WGBB1341	425541
22 Sep	IAEA (Atom Energy)	United Nations	IGO Operations	313UNTS323	200552
22 Sep	Finland	Sweden	Water Transport	428UNTS119	106170
22 Sep	Fed of Malaya	IBRD (World Bank)	IBRD Project	323UNTS71	104665
24 Sep	France	Switzerland	Non-ILO Labor	62SWRO1016	462102
24 Sep	Norway	Portugal	Visas	3NORT751	451134
24 Sep	Ghana	UK Great Britain	Air Transport	411UNTS146	105918
25 Sep	Bulgaria	Germany, East	Commodity Trade	6EGDA519	419060
25 Sep	China People's Rep	Tunisia	General Trade	58CCJC84	410541
26 Sep	Australia	South Africa	Air Transport	335UNTS121	104780
26 Sep	India	USA (United States)	US Agri Commod Aid	336UNTS59	104798
27 Sep	China People's Rep	Korea, North	Specif Goods/Equip	58CCJC88	410545
30 Sep	Ghana	USA (United States)	Admin Cooperation	336UNTS169	104805
30 Sep	Australia	New Zealand	Territory Boundary	340UNTS61	104859
01 Oct	IAEA (Atom Energy)	UNESCO (Educ/Cult)	IGO Operations	339UNTS373	200558
01 Oct	FAO (Food Agri)	IAEA (Atom Energy)	IGO Operations	361UNTS211	200571
01 Oct	Morocco	UK Great Britain	Visas	331UNTS119	104751
02 Oct	Poland	USSR (Soviet Union)	General Trade	7SUGG121	469532
03 Oct	Germany, West	UK Great Britain	Milit Assistance	398UNTS293	105731
03 Oct	Brazil	IBRD (World Bank)	IBRD Project	337UNTS177	104823
04 Oct	Guinea	USSR (Soviet Union)	Consul/Citizenship	7SUGG121	469533
04 Oct	China People's Rep	Pakistan	Mostfavored Nation	58CCJC89	410546
07 Oct	Hungary	Romania	Admin Cooperation	416UNTS199	106004
08 Oct	USA (United States)	Venezuela	Atomic Energy	371UNTS69	105271
09 Oct	USA (United States)	USSR (Soviet Union)	Mass Media	7SUGG122	469534
09 Oct	China People's Rep	Germany, East	Commodity Trade	18EGDZ198	420094
09 Oct	Ecuador	IBRD (World Bank)	IBRD Project	337UNTS299	104827

DATE	PARTY ONE	PARTY TWO	TOPIC	CITATION	NUMBER
1958 (Cont.)					
10 Oct	Austria	Germany, West	Admin Cooperation	58WBGA228	424543
10 Oct	Germany, West	Netherlands	Visas	486UNTS345	107085
11 Oct	Fed Rhod/Nyasaland	South Africa	Non-ILO Labor	373UNTS75	105315
11 Oct	Iraq	USSR (Soviet Union)	General Trade	328UNTS117	104731
11 Oct	Iraq	USSR (Soviet Union)	General Trade	328UNTS95	104730
14 Oct	Czechoslovakia	USSR (Soviet Union)	Commodity Trade	7SUGG122	469535
14 Oct	Italy	UK Great Britain	Patents/Copyrights	60ITDI245	436191
14 Oct	Germany, East	Hungary	General Economic	6EGDA422	419453
14 Oct	Germany, East	Hungary	General Trade	6EGDA422	419452
14 Oct	Turkey	USA (United States)	Milit Assistance	336UNTS145	104803
15 Oct	Japan	Laos	General Aid	341UNTS25	104875
16 Oct	France	Switzerland	Land Transport	58SWRO1087	462084
16 Oct	Finland	Sweden	Culture	428UNTS125	106171
16 Oct	Spain	USA (United States)	Education	336UNTS153	104804
18 Oct	Canada	UK Great Britain	General Aid	392UNTS61	105639
20 Oct	Norway	USSR (Soviet Union)	Culture	7SUGG122	469536
21 Oct	Germany, East	USSR (Soviet Union)	Sanitation	16SUGG125	469961
21 Oct	Germany, East	USSR (Soviet Union)	Sanitation	6EGDA457	419411
22 Oct	Austria	Switzerland	Land Transport	59SWRO329	462080
22 Oct	Germany, East	USSR (Soviet Union)	Tech Assistance	6EGDA521	419412
22 Oct	Canada	India	Finance	392UNTS21	105635
24 Oct	Germany, East	Poland	Commodity Trade	6EGDA332	419258
24 Oct	Germany, East	Poland	General Economic	6EGDA332	419259
25 Oct	Hungary	Poland	General Economic	58PZUM87	458061
25 Oct	Czechoslovakia	Romania	Admin Cooperation	417UNTS37	106006
25 Oct	Czechoslovakia	Romania	Culture	338UNTS301	104843
26 Oct	Germany, East	Iraq	Consul/Citizenship	6EGDA314	419137
26 Oct	Germany, East	Iraq	General Trade	6EGDA314	419138
27 Oct	Argentina	USSR (Soviet Union)	Loans and Credits	7SUGG122	469537
27 Oct	France	Tunisia	Water Transport	60FRRT17	415455
27 Oct	Haiti	USA (United States)	Military Mission	336UNTS235	104807
27 Oct	Multilateral		Reparations	351UNTS303	105031
27 Oct	Belgium	Spain	Culture	327UNTS107	104720
29 Oct	France	Italy	Taxation	68FRJO1403	416247
30 Oct	France	Portugal	Non-ILO Labor	59FRRT16	415369
30 Oct	France	Italy	Visas	363UNTS3	105196
31 Oct	Denmark	Norway	Privil/Immunities	3NORT752	451036
31 Oct	Canada	USA (United States)	Non-ILO Labor	391UNTS219	105626
31 Oct	United Arab Rep	USA (United States)	Postal Service	355UNTS355	105086
03 Nov	Japan	USA (United States)	Postal Service	341UNTS83	104879
05 Nov	Hungary	USSR (Soviet Union)	General Aid	7SUGG124	469538
05 Nov	Hungary	USSR (Soviet Union)	Tech Assistance	7SUGG125	469539
05 Nov	Spain	Sweden	General Economic	58SPBO1612	460247
05 Nov	Multilateral		Admin Cooperation	613UNTS385	200630
05 Nov	Multilateral		Land Transport	428UNTS73	106169
05 Nov	Canada	Ceylon (Sri Lanka)	Loans and Credits	391UNTS225	105627
06 Nov	Israel	USA (United States)	US Agri Commod Aid	336UNTS275	104810
07 Nov	Germany, West	Iraq	Admin Cooperation	59WBGA93	424270
08 Nov	Fed of Malaya	UK Great Britain	Recognition	327UNTS301	104728
08 Nov	Euratom	USA (United States)	Atomic Energy	338UNTS135	104835
12 Nov	France	Israel	Admin Cooperation	345UNTS79	104960
14 Nov	France	USSR (Soviet Union)	General Trade	7SUGG125	469541
14 Nov	France	USSR (Soviet Union)	General Trade	7SUGG125	469540
14 Nov	El Salvador	Israel	Culture	345UNTS67	104959
16 Nov	India	USSR (Soviet Union)	General Trade	16SUGG125	469962
16 Nov	India	USSR (Soviet Union)	General Trade	7SUGG126	469542
17 Nov	Germany, East	Guinea	Culture	6EGDA309	419116
17 Nov	Germany, East	Guinea	General Economic	6EGDA309	419115
17 Nov	Germany, East	Guinea	Consul/Citizenship	6EGDA309	419114
17 Nov	Poland	Yugoslavia	Consul/Citizenship	432UNTS267	106225
18 Nov	Germany, West	Norway	Taxation	357UNTS205	105119
18 Nov	Jordan	United Nations	IGO Operations	315UNTS125	104564
19 Nov	Mongolia	USSR (Soviet Union)	Loans and Credits	7SUGG126	469543
19 Nov	China People's Rep	Korea, North	General Trade	58CCJC99	410554
20 Nov	Italy	San Marino	Land Transport	62ITGU6	435329
1958 (Cont.)					
20 Nov	Italy	Yugoslavia	Territory Boundary	379UNTS23	105433
21 Nov	Germany, West	Switzerland	Customs	60WGBB941	425758
22 Nov	Italy	Switzerland	Commodity Trade	62ITGU312	435382
25 Nov	Czechoslovakia	Poland	Customs	372UNTS205	105299
25 Nov	Turkey	UK Great Britain	Loans and Credits	327UNTS35	104715
26 Nov	Pakistan	USA (United States)	US Agri Commod Aid	337UNTS3	104812
26 Nov	ICJ Option Clause	UK Great Britain	ICJ Option Clause	316UNTS59	104577
27 Nov	Germany, West	Turkey	Direct Aid	64TURG909	466106
27 Nov	Germany, West	Greece	General Economic	59WBGA3	424231
27 Nov	Germany, East	United Arab Rep	Specific Property	6EGDA521	419474
28 Nov	Belgium	Turkey	Loans and Credits	64TURG909	466102
28 Nov	Liberia	Netherlands	Air Transport	393UNTS55	105651
28 Nov	France	UK Great Britain	Taxation	351UNTS263	105027
29 Nov	Italy	Turkey	Direct Aid	60ITDI306	436408
29 Nov	Iran	Italy	Culture	0IRTB43	433062
29 Nov	Netherlands	Turkey	Direct Aid	335UNTS229	104790
29 Nov	Fed Rhod/Nyasaland	Portugal	General Trade	354UNTS137	105060
01 Dec	Germany, East	Vietnam, North	General Economic	7EGDA559	419491
01 Dec	Multilateral		Commodity Trade	385UNTS137	105534
01 Dec	Denmark	United Arab Rep	Taxation	337UNTS69	104817
02 Dec	Austria	IBRD (World Bank)	IBRD Project	340UNTS3	104856
02 Dec	IBRD (World Bank)	South Africa	IBRD Project	324UNTS3	104676
03 Dec	Bulgaria	Romania	Admin Cooperation	417UNTS133	106007
03 Dec	Multilateral		Admin Cooperation	398UNTS9	105715
03 Dec	Multilateral		Admin Cooperation	416UNTS51	105995
03 Dec	Accept UN Charter	Guinea	UN Charter	317UNTS77	104595
08 Dec	China People's Rep	Vietnam, North	Land Transport	58CCJC102	410556
08 Dec	France	USA (United States)	Milit Installation	0UNTS0	109602
09 Dec	Poland	Romania	General Economic	58PZUM111	458062
09 Dec	Iran	Japan	General Aid	325UNTS221	104701
09 Dec	Canada	Finland	Visas	323UNTS331	104674
10 Dec	Italy	Switzerland	Admin Cooperation	60ITDI306	436383
11 Dec	Israel	Yugoslavia	Finance	386UNTS283	105548
11 Dec	Israel	Yugoslavia	General Trade	386UNTS271	105547
11 Dec	Germany, West	USA (United States)	Air Transport	337UNTS31	104813
12 Dec	India	USSR (Soviet Union)	General Aid	7SUGG128	469544
13 Dec	Italy	Yugoslavia	Specific Resources	60ITDI345	436235
13 Dec	Germany, East	United Arab Rep	Finance	6EGDA485	419475
13 Dec	Germany, East	United Arab Rep	General Trade	8EGDA559	419476
15 Dec	China People's Rep	United Arab Rep	General Trade	58CCJC106	410559
15 Dec	China People's Rep	United Arab Rep	Finance	58CCJC105	410558
15 Dec	China People's Rep	United Arab Rep	General Trade	58CCJC104	410557
15 Dec	Multilateral		Mass Media	546UNTS235	107950
15 Dec	Colombia	IBRD (World Bank)	IBRD Project	354UNTS233	105065
15 Dec	Multilateral		Sanitation	351UNTS159	105022
15 Dec	Burma	United Nations	Tech Assistance	319UNTS3	104629
17 Dec	Sweden	Turkey	Direct Aid	64TURG909	466114
17 Dec	Denmark	Turkey	Direct Aid	64TURG909	466103
17 Dec	Haiti	Japan	General Economic	518UNTS91	107492
17 Dec	Norway	Poland	Culture	432UNTS193	106221
17 Dec	India	USA (United States)	Milit Assistance	358UNTS77	105125
18 Dec	Portugal	Turkey	Direct Aid	64TURG909	466113
18 Dec	Bulgaria	China People's Rep	General Economic	58CCJC108	410561
18 Dec	Afghanistan	WHO (World Health)	Tech Assistance	324UNTS121	104681
18 Dec	Korea, South	USA (United States)	Reparations	325UNTS233	104702
19 Dec	Norway	Turkey	Loans and Credits	2NORT758	451177
20 Dec	Muscat and Oman	USA (United States)	General Amity	380UNTS181	105457
22 Dec	Switzerland	Turkey	Direct Aid	64TURG909	466115
22 Dec	Germany, East	USSR (Soviet Union)	Scientific Project	7SUGG129	469545
22 Dec	Denmark	Germany, West	General Trade	59WBGA37	424100
22 Dec	Austria	Switzerland	Land Transport	59ABGB123	403187
22 Dec	Argentina	Brazil	Water Transport	0UNTS0	109545
22 Dec	USA (United States)	Yugoslavia	US Agri Commod Aid	338UNTS243	104839
22 Dec	Finland	Japan	Visas	341UNTS41	104876
23 Dec	Mongolia	Poland	Culture	432UNTS177	106220

DATE	PARTY ONE	PARTY TWO	TOPIC	CITATION	NUMBER
1958 (Cont.)					
23 Dec	United Nations	Tunisia	Tech Assistance	321UNTS23	104651
24 Dec	Iraq	Romania	General Trade	405UNTS243	105836
24 Dec	New Zealand	USA (United States)	Scientific Project	324UNTS111	104680
24 Dec	Taiwan	USA (United States)	Loans and Credits	340UNTS251	104868
24 Dec	United Arab Rep	USA (United States)	US Agri Commod Aid	338UNTS221	104837
24 Dec	Haiti	USA (United States)	Military Mission	338UNTS265	104840
26 Dec	Bulgaria	USSR (Soviet Union)	Non-IBRD Project	7SUGG130	469547
26 Dec	Bulgaria	USSR (Soviet Union)	Non-IBRD Project	7SUGG130	469546
29 Dec	USA (United States)	USSR (Soviet Union)	Culture	7SUGG131	469548
29 Dec	Indonesia	Iran	General Amity	OIRTB39	433059
29 Dec	Belgium	Turkey	Culture	357UNTS195	105118
30 Dec	Bulgaria	Poland	General Economic	58PZUM124	458064
30 Dec	Australia	Poland	Privil/Immunities	58PZUM122	458063
30 Dec	New Zealand	Switzerland	Taxation	380UNTS313	105463
30 Dec	Finland	USA (United States)	US Agri Commod Aid	340UNTS259	104869
30 Dec	UK Great Britain	USA (United States)	Specific Property	338UNTS281	104841
31 Dec	Israel	Switzerland	Extradition	377UNTS305	105408
1959					
02 Jan	Iran	Turkey	Culture	64TURG601	466037
03 Jan	Indonesia	USSR (Soviet Union)	General Aid	8SUGG132	469549
03 Jan	Iraq	Poland	General Economic	59PZUM9	458065
03 Jan	China People's Rep	Iraq	General Economic	59CCJC2	410566
03 Jan	China People's Rep	Iraq	General Trade	59CCJC3	410567
06 Jan	Afghanistan	France	General Aid	61FRRT40	415001
07 Jan	Czechoslovakia	USSR (Soviet Union)	Non-IBRD Project	8SUGG133	469550
07 Jan	Canada	USA (United States)	Specific Property	391UNTS207	105624
07 Jan	El Salvador	IBRD (World Bank)	IBRD Project	346UNTS51	104977
07 Jan	Finland	Switzerland	Air Transport	353UNTS173	105042
08 Jan	Italy	United Arab Rep	Admin Cooperation	61ITDI289	436316
08 Jan	Italy	United Arab Rep	Claims and Debts	61ITDI289	436317
08 Jan	Italy	United Arab Rep	Culture	61ITDI342	436315
11 Jan	Albania	Germany, East	Consul/Citizenship	7EGDA275	419017
11 Jan	Albania	Germany, East	Admin Cooperation	7EGDA283	419018
12 Jan	Portugal	USA (United States)	Postal Service	343UNTS49	104921
13 Jan	IMCO (Maritime Org)	United Nations	IGO Operations	324UNTS273	200553
13 Jan	United Arab Rep	USA (United States)	Postal Service	358UNTS3	105122
13 Jan	Spain	USA (United States)	US Agri Commod Aid	341UNTS241	104887
14 Jan	ILO (Labor Org)	UK Great Britain	IGO Operations	355UNTS283	105081
15 Jan	Canada	USSR (Soviet Union)	Consul/Citizenship	8SUGG133	469551
15 Jan	Colombia	Switzerland	Milit Servic/Citiz	63SWRO143	462005
15 Jan	Greece	USA (United States)	Milit Assistance	357UNTS281	105120
15 Jan	Multilateral		Customs	348UNTS13	104996
16 Jan	Austria	Germany, West	Specific Property	59WBGA51	424544
16 Jan	China People's Rep	Vietnam, North	Culture	59CCJC11	410573
16 Jan	Albania	China People's Rep	Loans and Credits	59CCJC7	410571
16 Jan	Albania	China People's Rep	General Economic	59CCJC8	410572
16 Jan	Albania	China People's Rep	General Trade	59CCJC6	410570
16 Jan	ILO (Labor Org)	IMCO (Maritime Org)	IGO Operations	327UNTS309	200554
16 Jan	India	Netherlands	Tech Assistance	506UNTS153	107386
16 Jan	Argentina	Sweden	Milit Servic/Citiz	427UNTS327	106163
16 Jan	Albania	Czechoslovakia	Admin Cooperation	363UNTS195	105208
16 Jan	Albania	Czechoslovakia	Consul/Citizenship	363UNTS165	105207
17 Jan	China People's Rep	USSR (Soviet Union)	General Trade	16SUGG126	469963
17 Jan	Czechoslovakia	USSR (Soviet Union)	General Trade	8SUGG134	469552
18 Jan	United Arab Rep	USSR (Soviet Union)	Non-IBRD Project	8SUGG134	469553
20 Jan	Malaysia	Netherlands	Visas	493UNTS147	107212
20 Jan	Belgium	France	Taxation	361UNTS155	105178
20 Jan	Burma	UK Great Britain	Commodity Trade	343UNTS201	104926
21 Jan	Finland	Norway	Non-ILO Labor	325UNTS295	104705
21 Jan	Philippines	USA (United States)	Specif Claim/Waive	341UNTS255	104888
24 Jan	Multilateral		IGO Establishment	486UNTS157	107078
26 Jan	France	UK Great Britain	Admin Cooperation	330UNTS207	104745
26 Jan	France	UK Great Britain	Admin Cooperation	330UNTS213	104746
27 Jan	China People's Rep	Germany, East	Consul/Citizenship	7EGDA335	419095

DATE	PARTY ONE	PARTY TWO	TOPIC	CITATION	NUMBER
1959 (Cont.)					
27 Jan	China People's Rep	Germany, East	Consul/Citizenship	59CCJC19	410579
28 Jan	Hungary	USSR (Soviet Union)	Scientific Project	8SUGG135	469554
29 Jan	Norway	Switzerland	Visas	3NORT761	451158
29 Jan	Czechoslovakia	Germany, East	General Economic	7EGDA447	419360
30 Jan	Afghanistan	Italy	Air Transport	61ITDI347	436001
30 Jan	China People's Rep	Mongolia	General Trade	59CCJC21	410581
30 Jan	Multilateral		General Trade	OUNTSO	109234
30 Jan	Austria	USA (United States)	Claims and Debts	511UNTS145	107432
30 Jan	Czechoslovakia	Hungary	Non-ILO Labor	351UNTS3	105016
30 Jan	Colombia	IBRD (World Bank)	IBRD Project	337UNTS327	104828
02 Feb	Romania	USSR (Soviet Union)	General Trade	8SUGG136	469555
03 Feb	Italy	Poland	Finance	61ITDI382	436304
03 Feb	UK Great Britain	Yugoslavia	Loans and Credits	343UNTS153	104924
03 Feb	UK Great Britain	Yugoslavia	Air Transport	359UNTS339	105151
04 Feb	Afghanistan	USSR (Soviet Union)	Telecommunications	8SUGG136	469556
04 Feb	Euratom	UK Great Britain	Atomic Energy	331UNTS125	104752
04 Feb	Denmark	IBRD (World Bank)	IBRD Project	328UNTS143	104733
05 Feb	China People's Rep	Germany, East	General Economic	59CCJC22	410582
06 Feb	Albania	USSR (Soviet Union)	General Trade	8SUGG136	469557
06 Feb	Burma	UK Great Britain	Commodity Trade	343UNTS223	104927
07 Feb	China People's Rep	USSR (Soviet Union)	Tech Assistance	8SUGG136	469558
07 Feb	China People's Rep	USSR (Soviet Union)	Direct Aid	59CCJC24	410583
07 Feb	Czechoslovakia	United Arab Rep	General Economic	372UNTS243	105301
07 Feb	Taiwan	USA (United States)	Milit Assistance	341UNTS225	104885
09 Feb	France	Romania	Finance	59FRJO1903	416374
09 Feb	Finland	Germany, East	Finance	7EGDA356	419102
10 Feb	Mongolia	USSR (Soviet Union)	General Aid	8SUGG136	469559
11 Feb	Costa Rica	IBRD (World Bank)	IBRD Project	337UNTS245	104825
12 Feb	Australia	Italy	Commodity Trade	328UNTS133	104732
13 Feb	Guinea	USSR (Soviet Union)	General Economic	8SUGG137	469560
13 Feb	Turkey	USA (United States)	US Agri Commod Aid	340UNTS235	104867
14 Feb	China People's Rep	Poland	General Trade	59CCJC26	410585
14 Feb	Hungary	Poland	Non-ILO Labor	431UNTS157	106215
16 Feb	Iran	Pakistan	Specific Property	OIRTB55	433087
17 Feb	Japan	Pakistan	Taxation	341UNTS127	104880
17 Feb	Japan	IBRD (World Bank)	IBRD Project	337UNTS205	104824
18 Feb	China People's Rep	Vietnam, North	General Economic	59CCJC28	410587
18 Feb	China People's Rep	Korea, North	Air Transport	59CCJC34	410589
18 Feb	Norway	Philippines	Visas	359UNTS305	105147
19 Feb	Chile	USA (United States)	Specific Property	343UNTS17	104918
20 Feb	El Salvador	IBRD (World Bank)	IBRD Project	362UNTS75	105183
20 Feb	USA (United States)	Uruguay	US Agri Commod Aid	341UNTS201	104884
21 Feb	China People's Rep	Korea, North	Culture	59CCJC38	410592
21 Feb	Finland	USSR (Soviet Union)	Specific Resources	338UNTS3	104830
21 Feb	Japan	Norway	Taxation	356UNTS231	105098
25 Feb	Germany, East	Ghana	Consul/Citizenship	7EGDA363	419105
25 Feb	Finland	Germany, East	Finance	7EGDA357	419103
27 Feb	Belgium	Morocco	Extradition	390UNTS275	105611
27 Feb	Ghana	United Nations	Tech Assistance	324UNTS133	104682
27 Feb	Canada	USA (United States)	Specific Resources	341UNTS3	104873
28 Feb	Austria	USSR (Soviet Union)	Consul/Citizenship	356UNTS39	105091
28 Feb	United Arab Rep	UK Great Britain	Finance	343UNTS159	104925
28 Feb	Japan	Yugoslavia	General Economic	341UNTS179	104883
02 Mar	Cambodia	Japan	General Economic	341UNTS163	104882
02 Mar	Indonesia	USA (United States)	Air Transport	357UNTS145	105113
02 Mar	Japan	Philippines	Air Transport	341UNTS49	104877
03 Mar	Poland	USSR (Soviet Union)	Tech Assistance	8SUGG138	469561
03 Mar	UK Great Britain	USSR (Soviet Union)	Culture	8SUGG138	469562
03 Mar	Germany, East	Guinea	General Trade	7EGDA365	419117
03 Mar	China People's Rep	Czechoslovakia	Scientific Project	59CCJC41	410595
03 Mar	India	USA (United States)	US Agri Commod Aid	341UNTS235	104886
03 Mar	Iceland	USA (United States)	US Agri Commod Aid	341UNTS261	104889
05 Mar	France	OECD (Econ Coop)	Non-ILO Labor	59FRRT40	415499
05 Mar	Turkey	USA (United States)	General Military	327UNTS293	104727
05 Mar	France	UK Great Britain	Finance	343UNTS277	104932

DATE	PARTY ONE	PARTY TWO	TOPIC	CITATION	NUMBER
1959 (Cont.)					
05 Mar	Iran	USA (United States)	General Military	327UNTS277	104725
05 Mar	Pakistan	USA (United States)	General Military	327UNTS285	104726
05 Mar	Greece	Pakistan	Visas	338UNTS97	104833
06 Mar	China People's Rep	Poland	General Trade	59CCJC43	410597
06 Mar	Hungary	Poland	Admin Cooperation	432UNTS3	106216
07 Mar	USSR (Soviet Union)	Vietnam, North	Tech Assistance	8SUGG139	469563
07 Mar	Germany, East	Vietnam, North	General Economic	7EGDA541	419492
09 Mar	WHO (World Health)	Vietnam, South	Sanitation	0VKNG135	496039
09 Mar	Canada	USA (United States)	Territory Boundary	340UNTS295	104872
10 Mar	Denmark	Japan	Taxation	341UNTS55	104878
12 Mar	China People's Rep	Czechoslovakia	General Economic	59CCJC48	410601
13 Mar	Australia	USSR (Soviet Union)	Consul/Citizenship	8SUGG139	469564
13 Mar	Ceylon (Sri Lanka)	USA (United States)	US Agri Commod Aid	342UNTS51	104900
14 Mar	Italy	Spain	Non-ILO Labor	59SPBO904	460177
14 Mar	Austria	Yugoslavia	Admin Cooperation	59ABGB163	403234
14 Mar	Austria	UK Great Britain	Claims and Debts	343UNTS263	104930
16 Mar	Sudan	USSR (Soviet Union)	General Trade	8SUGG140	469565
16 Mar	Germany, East	Romania	General Economic	7EGDA432	419294
16 Mar	Brazil	Netherlands	Admin Cooperation	499UNTS219	107300
16 Mar	Iraq	USSR (Soviet Union)	General Aid	346UNTS107	104979
16 Mar	Finland	IBRD (World Bank)	IBRD Project	337UNTS269	104826
17 Mar	Korea, North	USSR (Soviet Union)	Tech Assistance	8SUGG140	469566
17 Mar	China People's Rep	Germany, East	Scientific Project	59CCJC51	410603
17 Mar	China People's Rep	Hungary	General Economic	59CCJC49	410602
17 Mar	Sudan	USA (United States)	Admin Cooperation	342UNTS13	104896
18 Mar	Germany, West	India	Taxation	60WGBB1828	425255
18 Mar	Germany, East	Romania	Mass Media	7EGDA438	419295
18 Mar	Germany West	Guinea	Direct Aid	59WBGA77	424242
18 Mar	China People's Rep	Yugoslavia	General Trade	59CCJC53	410605
18 Mar	Hungary	Romania	Consul/Citizenship	417UNTS3	106005
18 Mar	IAEA (Atom Energy)	Thailand	Tech Assistance	339UNTS307	104850
18 Mar	Tunisia	USA (United States)	Admin Cooperation	344UNTS179	104948
19 Mar	Austria	Netherlands	Admin Cooperation	485UNTS117	107048
19 Mar	Netherlands	Tunisia	Air Transport	497UNTS61	107262
19 Mar	Sweden	Tunisia	Air Transport	497UNTS43	107261
20 Mar	Romania	USSR (Soviet Union)	Tech Assistance	8SUGG141	469567
20 Mar	Bulgaria	Germany, East	General Economic	7EGDA319	419061
20 Mar	Ecuador	France	General Trade	59FRRT42	415155
20 Mar	Germany, West	USA (United States)	Claims and Debts	341UNTS15	104874
21 Mar	France	USA (United States)	US Agri Commod Aid	342UNTS71	104901
22 Mar	China People's Rep	Romania	General Economic	59CCJC55	410607
24 Mar	Japan	IAEA (Atom Energy)	Atomic Energy	339UNTS327	104852
24 Mar	Canada	IAEA (Atom Energy)	Atomic Energy	339UNTS315	104851
25 Mar	Germany, West	USSR (Soviet Union)	Scientific Project	8SUGG141	469568
26 Mar	Ceylon (Sri Lanka)	China People's Rep	Air Transport	59CCJC57	410608
27 Mar	Czechoslovakia	Hungary	Consul/Citizenship	351UNTS57	105017
28 Mar	UK Great Britain	USSR (Soviet Union)	Health/Educ/Welfare	8SUGG141	469569
28 Mar	Norway	Tunisia	Air Transport	497UNTS77	107263
28 Mar	Canada	Finland	Taxation	355UNTS3	105072
28 Mar	United Nations	Sudan	Tech Assistance	327UNTS95	104719
01 Apr	Germany, East	Iraq	Health/Educ/Welfare	7EGDA370	419139
02 Apr	Iraq	Poland	Culture	432UNTS147	106218
03 Apr	Poland	USSR (Soviet Union)	Non-IBRD Project	8SUGG141	469571
03 Apr	Albania	USSR (Soviet Union)	General Economic	8SUGG141	469570
03 Apr	Bulgaria	Hungary	Sanitation	438UNTS269	106319
03 Apr	Poland	UK Great Britain	Air Transport	351UNTS295	105030
04 Apr	China People's Rep	Iraq	Culture	59CCJC61	410610
04 Apr	Morocco	UN Special Fund	Direct Aid	354UNTS347	105069
05 Apr	Norway	Sudan	Air Transport	3NORT765	451153
06 Apr	Austria	Switzerland	Taxation	59ABGB196	403182
06 Apr	China People's Rep	Hungary	Mass Media	59CCJC62	410611
06 Apr	Multilateral		Commodity Trade	349UNTS167	105013
07 Apr	Mexico	United Nations	IGO Operations	381UNTS123	105468
08 Apr	Czechoslovakia	Poland	Sanitation	59PZUM60	458066
08 Apr	Multilateral		IGO Establishment	389UNTS69	105593

DATE	PARTY ONE	PARTY TWO	TOPIC	CITATION	NUMBER
1959 (Cont.)					
08 Apr	India	IBRD (World Bank)	IBRD Project	348UNTS131	104998
09 Apr	Israel	Liberia	General Amity	448UNTS95	106427
09 Apr	Ghana	USA (United States)	Customs	342UNTS21	104897
10 Apr	Germany, West	UK Great Britain	Claims and Debts	343UNTS295	104935
11 Apr	Germany, East	Mongolia	Tech Assistance	7EGDA399	419218
11 Apr	Hungary	Iraq	Culture	439UNTS25	106323
13 Apr	Ecuador	France	Tech Assistance	65FRRT16	415156
13 Apr	China People's Rep	Romania	Scientific Project	59CCJC64	410613
13 Apr	Canada	USA (United States)	Specific Property	342UNTS43	104899
14 Apr	Netherlands	Switzerland	Finance	486UNTS367	107086
14 Apr	Denmark	Tunisia	Air Transport	340UNTS273	104870
14 Apr	Italy	UK Great Britain	Claims and Debts	343UNTS289	104934
14 Apr	Nicaragua	USA (United States)	Admin Cooperation	343UNTS119	104922
15 Apr	France	Tunisia	Health/Educ/Welfare	59FRRT47	415456
15 Apr	China People's Rep	Poland	Mass Media	59CCJC66	410615
16 Apr	USA (United States)	USSR (Soviet Union)	Culture	8SUGG142	469572
16 Apr	France	Switzerland	Non-ILO Labor	61SWRO24	462101
16 Apr	Spain	Turkey	General Amity	61SPBO803	460258
16 Apr	UK Great Britain	USA (United States)	IGO Status/Immunit	343UNTS11	104917
17 Apr	Hungary	USSR (Soviet Union)	Sanitation	16SUGG126	469964
17 Apr	Germany, West	Italy	Status of Forces	60WGBB1961	425296
17 Apr	Ireland	Spain	Visas	553UNTS157	108082
17 Apr	Hungary	USSR (Soviet Union)	Sanitation	439UNTS41	106324
17 Apr	Italy	Netherlands	Admin Cooperation	474UNTS207	106883
17 Apr	Indonesia	Malaysia	General Amity	470UNTS273	106813
17 Apr	Germany, West	Sweden	Taxation	428UNTS155	106175
17 Apr	Ghana	UK Great Britain	Status of Forces	337UNTS353	104829
17 Apr	USA (United States)	Venezuela	Visas	358UNTS83	105126
18 Apr	Sweden	UK Great Britain	Claims and Debts	360UNTS89	105156
20 Apr	Iran	Pakistan	Extradition	0IRTB54	433080
20 Apr	Multilateral		Land Transport	0UNTS0	110345
20 Apr	Multilateral		Admin Cooperation	472UNTS185	106841
20 Apr	Multilateral		Visas	376UNTS85	105375
20 Apr	Germany, West	New Zealand	General Trade	402UNTS125	105782
21 Apr	Denmark	Philippines	Visas	3PTS827	465040
21 Apr	Italy	Yugoslavia	Visas	61ITDI284	436237
21 Apr	Italy	IBRD (World Bank)	IBRD Project	359UNTS191	105143
21 Apr	Fed of Malaya	USA (United States)	Admin Cooperation	343UNTS3	104916
22 Apr	Multilateral		Admin Cooperation	613UNTS391	200631
22 Apr	USA (United States)	Vietnam, South	Atomic Energy	347UNTS113	104993
22 Apr	Austria	Belgium	Extradition	356UNTS309	105102
23 Apr	France	Peru	Air Transport	61FRRT19	415359
23 Apr	Bulgaria	China People's Rep	Scientific Project	59CCJC69	410617
23 Apr	Bulgaria	Romania	Consul/Citizenship	387UNTS81	105559
23 Apr	Norway	UK Great Britain	Finance	343UNTS283	104933
23 Apr	Belgium	UK Great Britain	Finance	343UNTS271	104931
24 Apr	Norway	Turkey	Visas	59TURG1006	466023
24 Apr	Nepal	USSR (Soviet Union)	Non-IBRD Project	8SUGG143	469574
24 Apr	Nepal	USSR (Soviet Union)	General Aid	8SUGG143	469573
25 Apr	Belgium	Germany, West	Admin Cooperation	59WGBB1524	425026
25 Apr	China People's Rep	Germany, East	Mass Media	59CCJC70	410618
25 Apr	China People's Rep	Germany, East	Mass Media	59CCJC71	410619
26 Apr	Philippines	Vietnam, South	General Amity	3PTS829	465041
27 Apr	India	Netherlands	Tech Assistance	506UNTS141	107385
28 Apr	Belgium	Netherlands	Finance	485UNTS123	107049
28 Apr	Denmark	UK Great Britain	Finance	343UNTS257	104929
29 Apr	Italy	United Arab Rep	General Trade	61ITDI291	436318
29 Apr	Belgium	Switzerland	Admin Cooperation	443UNTS35	106356
29 Apr	France	Netherlands	Finance	486UNTS379	107088
29 Apr	Italy	Netherlands	Finance	486UNTS387	107089
29 Apr	Austria	Netherlands	Finance	486UNTS373	107087
29 Apr	Italy	United Arab Rep	Tech Assistance	363UNTS91	105202
29 Apr	Multilateral		Specific Property	346UNTS167	104980
29 Apr	Finland	USSR (Soviet Union)	Specif Claim/Waive	346UNTS209	104981
30 Apr	Hungary	Norway	Air Transport	3NORT769	451073

DATE	PARTY ONE	PARTY TWO	TOPIC	CITATION	NUMBER
1959 (Cont.)					
30 Apr	China People's Rep	Czechoslovakia	Mass Media	59CCJC73	410620
30 Apr	Iceland	Netherlands	Finance	487UNTS13	107091
30 Apr	Germany, West	Netherlands	Finance	485UNTS141	107052
30 Apr	Greece	Netherlands	Finance	485UNTS135	107051
30 Apr	Denmark	Netherlands	Finance	487UNTS23	107092
30 Apr	Netherlands	Sweden	Finance	485UNTS147	107053
30 Apr	Netherlands	Norway	Finance	487UNTS3	107090
30 Apr	Netherlands	Portugal	Finance	485UNTS129	107050
30 Apr	Netherlands	UK Great Britain	Claims and Debts	343UNTS307	104937
30 Apr	Austria	USA (United States)	Air Transport	343UNTS41	104920
01 May	Canada	USA (United States)	Specific Property	343UNTS27	104919
01 May	Fed of Malaya	UK Great Britain	Loans and Credits	345UNTS57	104958
05 May	Libya	Spain	Culture	62SPBO2307	460184
05 May	Ceylon (Sri Lanka)	Yugoslavia	Scientific Project	391UNTS101	105618
05 May	Germany, West	USA (United States)	Atomic Energy	355UNTS307	105083
05 May	Turkey	USA (United States)	Milit Assistance	355UNTS341	105085
05 May	Iraq	USSR (Soviet Union)	Culture	356UNTS179	105095
06 May	Germany, East	Poland	Culture	7EGDA409	419260
06 May	China People's Rep	Hungary	General Amity	59CCJC75	410621
06 May	Austria	Netherlands	Land Transport	485UNTS175	107055
06 May	Austria	Netherlands	Land Transport	485UNTS153	107054
06 May	Iran	UK Great Britain	Culture	398UNTS51	105717
06 May	Greece	USA (United States)	Milit Assistance	357UNTS163	105115
06 May	Switzerland	UK Great Britain	Claims and Debts	343UNTS315	104938
06 May	Netherlands	USA (United States)	Milit Installation	355UNTS327	105084
07 May	France	USA (United States)	Milit Assistance	354UNTS83	105055
08 May	Germany, East	Poland	Culture	59PZUM64	458067
08 May	IAEA (Atom Energy)	ILO (Labor Org)	IGO Operations	328UNTS273	200555
08 May	Denmark	USA (United States)	Milit Assistance	344UNTS185	104949
08 May	Colombia	USA (United States)	Direct Aid	344UNTS193	104950
09 May	Argentina	Belgium	Visas	340UNTS53	104858
11 May	Colombia	Germany, West	Patents/Copyrights	61WGBB13	425369
11 May	Denmark	Sudan	Air Transport	445UNTS105	106380
11 May	Multilateral		Claims and Debts	527UNTS145	107623
11 May	IAEA (Atom Energy)	UK Great Britain	Atomic Energy	339UNTS351	104854
11 May	IAEA (Atom Energy)	USA (United States)	Atomic Energy	339UNTS359	104855
11 May	IAEA (Atom Energy)	USSR (Soviet Union)	Atomic Energy	339UNTS341	104853
12 May	France	Iran	General Trade	0IRTB31	433042
13 May	Japan	USSR (Soviet Union)	Specific Resources	8SUGG145	469575
13 May	Japan	Vietnam, South	Reparations	373UNTS101	105317
13 May	Japan	Vietnam, South	Loans and Credits	373UNTS149	105318
13 May	Japan	Vietnam, South	Loans and Credits	373UNTS173	105319
14 May	Germany, West	Monaco	Visas	60WBGA85	424481
14 May	Austria	Sweden	Taxation	428UNTS3	106167
14 May	Canada	Pakistan	Atomic Energy	426UNTS129	106133
14 May	Greece	UK Great Britain	Specif Claim/Waive	360UNTS69	105154
14 May	Iceland	UK Great Britain	Finance	343UNTS301	104936
15 May	China People's Rep	Finland	General Trade	59CCJC76	410622
16 May	Peru	Spain	Consul/Citizenship	60SPBO1904	460227
16 May	Cambodia	Japan	General Economic	0JGJI1401	441149
18 May	Belgium	Sweden	Admin Cooperation	341UNTS277	104890
19 May	France	Israel	Admin Cooperation	377UNTS231	105403
19 May	Thailand	USA (United States)	Milit Assistance	346UNTS271	104986
20 May	Hungary	Poland	Consul/Citizenship	432UNTS115	106217
20 May	Colombia	IBRD (World Bank)	IBRD Project	344UNTS251	104953
20 May	Panama	USA (United States)	Milit Assistance	346UNTS235	104983
20 May	Honduras	IBRD (World Bank)	IBRD Project	359UNTS119	105141
21 May	Australia	Switzerland	Taxation	341UNTS283	104891
21 May	Greece	UK Great Britain	Claims and Debts	344UNTS3	104939
21 May	Libya	USA (United States)	Tech Assistance	361UNTS123	105176
22 May	Norway	Spain	Visas	3NORT771	451144
22 May	Iran	Netherlands	Culture	0IRTB35	433045
22 May	Iran	Netherlands	Culture	474UNTS195	106882
22 May	Fed of Malaya	USA (United States)	Tech Assistance	346UNTS263	104985
22 May	Austria	USA (United States)	Reparations	347UNTS3	104988
1959 (Cont.)					
22 May	Canada	USA (United States)	Milit Assistance	354UNTS63	105054
24 May	UK Great Britain	USSR (Soviet Union)	General Trade	374UNTS305	105344
25 May	Denmark	Japan	Reparations	341UNTS157	104881
26 May	Turkey	USA (United States)	Direct Aid	354UNTS57	105053
27 May	Germany, West	Vietnam, South	Education	0VKNG141	496040
27 May	Germany, East	Poland	Commodity Trade	7EGDA568	419261
27 May	Netherlands	Spain	Visas	458UNTS165	106599
27 May	Belgium	Spain	Visas	340UNTS81	104860
27 May	Bulgaria	Czechoslovakia	Consul/Citizenship	360UNTS335	105167
28 May	Afghanistan	USSR (Soviet Union)	General Aid	8SUGG145	469576
28 May	IAEA (Atom Energy)	WHO (World Health)	IGO Operations	339UNTS387	200559
28 May	Ireland	Netherlands	Non-ILO Labor	344UNTS95	104944
29 May	India	USSR (Soviet Union)	General Aid	8SUGG146	469577
29 May	Brazil	Norway	Visas	3NORT772	451011
29 May	Denmark	France	General Trade	59FRMD1706	417152
29 May	Ceylon (Sri Lanka)	Sweden	Air Transport	464UNTS109	106713
29 May	Ceylon (Sri Lanka)	Norway	Air Transport	411UNTS165	105919
29 May	SEATO (SE Asia)	USA (United States)	Sanitation	347UNTS77	104991
29 May	Indonesia	USA (United States)	US Agri Commod Aid	347UNTS85	104992
29 May	Iran	IBRD (World Bank)	IBRD Project	348UNTS103	104997
29 May	Ceylon (Sri Lanka)	Denmark	Air Transport	348UNTS225	105002
30 May	Germany, West	USSR (Soviet Union)	Health/Educ/Welfare	8SUGG146	469579
30 May	Denmark	USSR (Soviet Union)	Finance	8SUGG146	469578
30 May	Germany, West	Portugal	General Economic	59WBGA131	424593
01 Jun	Ceylon (Sri Lanka)	Italy	Air Transport	63ITDI14	436083
01 Jun	China People's Rep	USSR (Soviet Union)	Scientific Project	59CCJC81	410625
03 Jun	United Nations	Vietnam, South	IGO Status/Immunit	337UNTS361	200557
04 Jun	Czechoslovakia	Korea, North	Sanitation	338UNTS291	104842
04 Jun	Czechoslovakia	Switzerland	Non-ILO Labor	349UNTS121	105012
05 Jun	Poland	USSR (Soviet Union)	Non-IBRD Project	8SUGG147	469580
05 Jun	USSR (Soviet Union)	Vietnam, North	Consul/Citizenship	356UNTS111	105093
06 Jun	Austria	USSR (Soviet Union)	Air Transport	8SUGG147	469581
06 Jun	Austria	Germany, West	Admin Cooperation	60WGBB1245	425546
06 Jun	Austria	Germany, West	Admin Cooperation	59WGBB1523	425545
06 Jun	Ethiopia	Yugoslavia	Loans and Credits	386UNTS243	105544
08 Jun	Guinea	UNICEF (Children)	Direct Aid	334UNTS277	104772
09 Jun	Taiwan	USA (United States)	US Agri Commod Aid	353UNTS257	105046
10 Jun	Ghana	USSR (Soviet Union)	General Trade	8SUGG147	469582
10 Jun	Italy	Turkey	Tech Assistance	61ITDI302	436409
10 Jun	Austria	Spain	Visas	59ABGB223	403166
10 Jun	Finland	Hungary	Culture	439UNTS3	106321
10 Jun	Poland	USA (United States)	US Agri Commod Aid	347UNTS41	104989
10 Jun	IBRD (World Bank)	South Africa	IBRD Project	340UNTS33	104857
11 Jun	Laos	Vietnam, South	General Amity	0VKNG143	496041
11 Jun	Jordan	UK Great Britain	Loans and Credits	351UNTS283	105028
12 Jun	Germany, East	Mongolia	Postal Service	7EGDA392	419219
12 Jun	Germany, East	Mongolia	Telecommunications	7EGDA399	419220
12 Jun	Italy	Norway	Non-ILO Labor	428UNTS363	106187
12 Jun	Argentina	Sweden	Culture	427UNTS337	106164
12 Jun	Taiwan	Ecuador	Culture	387UNTS3	105554
12 Jun	Argentina	USA (United States)	US Agri Commod Aid	347UNTS59	104990
13 Jun	Ceylon (Sri Lanka)	China People's Rep	General Trade	59CCJC83	410626
13 Jun	Ceylon (Sri Lanka)	China People's Rep	Commodity Trade	59CCJC84	410627
13 Jun	Turkey	UK Great Britain	Claims and Debts	551UNTS59	108033
15 Jun	Israel	Mexico	Culture	377UNTS267	105406
15 Jun	Peru	USA (United States)	Milit Assistance	346UNTS279	104987
16 Jun	Norway	Panama	Visas	3NORT775	451126
16 Jun	Germany, West	Netherlands	Taxation	593UNTS3	108576
16 Jun	Austria	Belgium	Admin Cooperation	419UNTS45	106029
17 Jun	Brazil	IBRD (World Bank)	IBRD Project	377UNTS111	105398
18 Jun	South Africa	UK Great Britain	Taxation	380UNTS81	105451
18 Jun	South Africa	UK Great Britain	Taxation	380UNTS103	105452
18 Jun	Greece	Yugoslavia	Visas	388UNTS3	105570
18 Jun	South Africa	UK Great Britain	Taxation	380UNTS59	105450
18 Jun	Greece	Yugoslavia	Admin Cooperation	368UNTS125	105237

DATE	PARTY ONE	PARTY TWO	TOPIC	CITATION	NUMBER
1959 (Cont.)					
18 Jun	Greece	Yugoslavia	Admin Cooperation	368UNTS69	105235
18 Jun	Greece	Yugoslavia	Culture	368UNTS137	105238
18 Jun	Greece	Yugoslavia	Claims and Debts	368UNTS9	105232
18 Jun	Greece	Yugoslavia	Admin Cooperation	368UNTS81	105236
18 Jun	Greece	Yugoslavia	IGO Establishment	368UNTS17	105233
18 Jun	Greece	Yugoslavia	Land Transport	368UNTS27	105234
18 Jun	Greece	Yugoslavia	Specific Resources	363UNTS133	105205
18 Jun	Greece	Yugoslavia	Claims and Debts	368UNTS3	105231
19 Jun	Multilateral		ILO Labor	413UNTS148	105949
19 Jun	Multilateral		ILO Labor	413UNTS158	105950
19 Jun	Multilateral		ILO Labor	413UNTS168	105951
20 Jun	Bulgaria	Poland	Customs	59PZUM78	458068
20 Jun	China People's Rep	Vietnam, North	Finance	59CCJC85	410628
20 Jun	Belgium	Japan	Air Transport	411UNTS3	105911
22 Jun	Ethiopia	Greece	General Economic	534UNTS147	107759
23 Jun	India	USSR (Soviet Union)	Non-IBRD Project	8SUGG147	469583
23 Jun	China People's Rep	USSR (Soviet Union)	Consul/Citizenship	59CCJC86	410629
23 Jun	IMCO (Maritime Org)	United Nations	IGO Operations	336UNTS317	200556
23 Jun	China People's Rep	USSR (Soviet Union)	Consul/Citizenship	356UNTS83	105092
23 Jun	Spain	USA (United States)	Milit Assistance	354UNTS11	105049
23 Jun	Iceland	USA (United States)	Direct Aid	354UNTS3	105048
24 Jun	Panama	USA (United States)	Scientific Project	479UNTS145	106950
24 Jun	Panama	United Nations	IGO Operations	507UNTS245	107402
24 Jun	Brazil	Israel	Culture	515UNTS151	107458
24 Jun	Burma	USA (United States)	Direct Aid	358UNTS91	105127
25 Jun	Paraguay	Spain	General Trade	60SPBO1804	460220
25 Jun	Paraguay	Spain	Non-ILO Labor	60SPBO1804	460219
25 Jun	Paraguay	Spain	Water Transport	60SPBO1904	460223
25 Jun	Paraguay	Spain	General Trade	60SPBO1804	460221
25 Jun	Paraguay	Spain	Consul/Citizenship	60SPBO1904	460222
26 Jun	Germany, West	Turkey	Claims and Debts	60WGBB2365	425772
27 Jun	China People's Rep	Vietnam, North	Scientific Project	59CCJC87	410630
27 Jun	Libya	United Nations	Tech Assistance	336UNTS291	104811
29 Jun	Congo (Zaire)	Switzerland	Taxation	59SWRO639	462046
30 Jun	France	Germany, West	Visas	59WGBB389	425155
30 Jun	France	Israel	Milit Servic/Citiz	448UNTS107	106428
30 Jun	France	IBRD (World Bank)	IBRD Project	452UNTS67	106505
30 Jun	Congo (Brazzaville)	IBRD (World Bank)	IBRD Project	452UNTS123	106506
30 Jun	Gabon	IBRD (World Bank)	IBRD Project	452UNTS135	106507
30 Jun	Korea, South	USA (United States)	US Agri Commod Aid	353UNTS297	105047
30 Jun	USA (United States)	Yemen	Direct Aid	357UNTS137	105112
01 Jul	Multilateral		IGO Status/Immunit	374UNTS147	105334
02 Jul	Canada	Japan	Atomic Energy	383UNTS243	105504
03 Jul	Albania	USSR (Soviet Union)	Culture	8SUGG148	469584
03 Jul	Albania	USSR (Soviet Union)	Non-IBRD Project	8SUGG148	469587
03 Jul	Albania	USSR (Soviet Union)	Tech Assistance	8SUGG148	469585
03 Jul	Albania	USSR (Soviet Union)	Non-IBRD Project	8SUGG148	469586
04 Jul	Czechoslovakia	Poland	Visas	363UNTS333	105210
06 Jul	Laos	United Nations	Tech Assistance	337UNTS41	104814
07 Jul	Multilateral		Specific Resources	377UNTS203	105402
07 Jul	Czechoslovakia	India	Culture	359UNTS259	105145
07 Jul	Australia	Monaco	Visas	354UNTS105	105057
07 Jul	Iraq	USA (United States)	Milit Assistance	357UNTS153	105114
08 Jul	Italy	Paraguay	General Trade	61ITGU76	435294
08 Jul	Italy	Paraguay	Finance	63ITDI293	436295
08 Jul	Norway	IBRD (World Bank)	IBRD Project	344UNTS229	104952
08 Jul	Taiwan	USA (United States)	Milit Assistance	354UNTS47	105052
08 Jul	Liberia	USA (United States)	Milit Assistance	357UNTS93	105108
09 Jul	Bulgaria	United Arab Rep	Air Transport	411UNTS187	105920
10 Jul	France	USA (United States)	Patents/Copyrights	62FRRT12	415179
10 Jul	ICJ Option Clause	France	ICJ Option Clause	337UNTS65	104816
11 Jul	Ethiopia	USSR (Soviet Union)	General Trade	8SUGG149	469588
11 Jul	Germany, West	Luxembourg	Admin Cooperation	60WGBB2077	425423
11 Jul	Albania	China People's Rep	Mass Media	59CCJC89	410632
11 Jul	Ethiopia	USSR (Soviet Union)	General Trade	0UNTS0	110494

DATE	PARTY ONE	PARTY TWO	TOPIC	CITATION	NUMBER
1959 (Cont.)					
12 Jul	Ethiopia	USSR (Soviet Union)	Culture	8SUGG149	469590
12 Jul	Ethiopia	USSR (Soviet Union)	General Aid	8SUGG149	469589
13 Jul	Denmark	Yugoslavia	Specif Claim/Waive	386UNTS251	105545
13 Jul	Canada	USA (United States)	Milit Assistance	353UNTS237	105045
14 Jul	Norway	Turkey	Claims and Debts	2NORT770	451178
14 Jul	France	Spain	Visas	60SPBO404	460128
14 Jul	France	Spain	Sanitation	60SPBO305	460126
14 Jul	France	Spain	Specific Resources	65SPBO202	460125
14 Jul	France	Spain	Health/Educ/Welfare	60SPBO404	460127
14 Jul	Italy	Philippines	Visas	490UNTS237	107157
15 Jul	India	IBRD (World Bank)	IBRD Project	355UNTS95	105075
15 Jul	India	IBRD (World Bank)	IBRD Project	346UNTS33	104976
16 Jul	Bulgaria	Germany, East	General Economic	7EGDA320	419062
16 Jul	India	Italy	Air Transport	464UNTS129	106714
17 Jul	Austria	Hungary	Air Transport	60ABGB76	403089
17 Jul	Austria	Hungary	Air Transport	0UNTS0	109237
18 Jul	Afghanistan	USSR (Soviet Union)	Non-IBRD Project	8SUGG149	469591
18 Jul	Pakistan	USA (United States)	Gen Communications	355UNTS367	105087
20 Jul	India	Norway	Taxation	356UNTS257	105099
21 Jul	France	Germany, West	Taxation	61WGBB397	425156
22 Jul	Japan	Paraguay	Loans and Credits	0JGJI9	441105
22 Jul	Afghanistan	Germany, West	Air Transport	464UNTS177	106715
22 Jul	Japan	Paraguay	Visas	373UNTS85	105316
22 Jul	UK Great Britain	Yugoslavia	Admin Cooperation	374UNTS319	105345
22 Jul	Taiwan	USA (United States)	Milit Assistance	357UNTS293	105121
22 Jul	Austria	USA (United States)	Atomic Energy	368UNTS199	105242
22 Jul	Finland	USA (United States)	Admin Cooperation	354UNTS39	105051
23 Jul	India	USSR (Soviet Union)	Tech Assistance	8SUGG150	469592
25 Jul	Iran	Italy	Visas	61ITDI281	436213
25 Jul	Austria	Peru	Visas	59ABGB242	403150
25 Jul	Subsahara Tech Com	ILO (Labor Org)	IGO Operations	409UNTS290	200590
27 Jul	Norway	Peru	Visas	3NORT778	451129
27 Jul	Fed of Malaya	UK Great Britain	Non-ILO Labor	374UNTS21	105324
28 Jul	Mongolia	USSR (Soviet Union)	Tech Assistance	16SUGG126	469965
28 Jul	Indonesia	USSR (Soviet Union)	Loans and Credits	8SUGG150	469594
28 Jul	Indonesia	USSR (Soviet Union)	Loans and Credits	8SUGG150	469593
28 Jul	Pakistan	USA (United States)	Visas	360UNTS327	105166
28 Jul	Finland	UK Great Britain	Non-ILO Labor	355UNTS31	105073
28 Jul	Australia	Thailand	Customs	339UNTS91	104847
29 Jul	United Arab Rep	USA (United States)	US Agri Commod Aid	357UNTS121	105111
30 Jul	Italy	USA (United States)	Direct Aid	355UNTS393	105088
31 Jul	Morocco	USSR (Soviet Union)	General Trade	8SUGG150	469595
31 Jul	Mexico	USA (United States)	Gen Communications	357UNTS187	105117
31 Jul	Japan	USA (United States)	Milit Assistance	357UNTS107	105110
01 Aug	Denmark	Germany, West	Non-ILO Labor	60WGBB2109	425101
01 Aug	Paraguay	United Nations	Tech Assistance	341UNTS319	104894
03 Aug	France	Germany, West	Dispute Settlement	61WGBB1183	425157
03 Aug	Cameroon	Germany, West	General Military	61WGBB1183	425350
03 Aug	Belgium	Germany, West	Admin Cooperation	61WGBB1183	425027
03 Aug	Multilateral		Status of Forces	481UNTS262	106986
03 Aug	Germany, West	USA (United States)	Status of Forces	490UNTS28	107153
03 Aug	Germany, West	UK Great Britain	Dispute Settlement	502UNTS197	107331
04 Aug	Austria	Spain	Culture	61ABGB256	403167
04 Aug	Iraq	Romania	Culture	502UNTS17	107324
04 Aug	Australia	Canada	Atomic Energy	391UNTS191	105623
05 Aug	Mexico	USA (United States)	Customs	356UNTS3	105089
06 Aug	Bulgaria	China People's Rep	Mass Media	59CCJC90	410633
07 Aug	Hungary	USSR (Soviet Union)	General Trade	8SUGG151	469596
07 Aug	Hungary	USSR (Soviet Union)	Tech Assistance	8SUGG151	469597
07 Aug	Germany, West	Norway	Reparations	358UNTS185	105136
12 Aug	IAEA (Atom Energy)	WMO (Meteorology)	IGO Operations	341UNTS341	200561
12 Aug	Netherlands	Turkey	Admin Cooperation	527UNTS181	107624
12 Aug	Germany, West	Iceland	Air Transport	411UNTS224	105921
12 Aug	Ghana	UN Special Fund	Direct Aid	338UNTS203	104836
12 Aug	New Zealand	UK Great Britain	General Trade	354UNTS161	105062

DATE	PARTY ONE	PARTY TWO	TOPIC	CITATION	NUMBER
1959 (Cont.)					
13 Aug	Liberia	USA (United States)	Telecommunications	357UNTS181	105116
13 Aug	Pakistan	IBRD (World Bank)	IBRD Project	355UNTS129	105076
14 Aug	Indonesia	USSR (Soviet Union)	Tech Assistance	8SUGG152	469598
17 Aug	Iraq	USSR (Soviet Union)	Atomic Energy	8SUGG152	469599
17 Aug	Iraq	USSR (Soviet Union)	Atomic Energy	0UNTS0	110362
18 Aug	Italy	USA (United States)	Milit Assistance	361UNTS11	105169
19 Aug	Australia	USA (United States)	Visas	388UNTS183	105578
19 Aug	Norway	Spain	Culture	376UNTS145	105379
20 Aug	Turkey	USA (United States)	Claims and Debts	61TURG2207	466120
20 Aug	Multilateral		Air Transport	376UNTS99	105376
22 Aug	Peru	USA (United States)	Atomic Energy	357UNTS99	105109
24 Aug	Guinea	USSR (Soviet Union)	General Aid	8SUGG152	469600
24 Aug	Guinea	USSR (Soviet Union)	Loans and Credits	8SUGG152	469601
24 Aug	Denmark	Germany, West	Specif Claim/Waive	60WGBB1333	425102
25 Aug	USA (United States)	Yugoslavia	Milit Assistance	357UNTS87	105107
25 Aug	USA (United States)	Yugoslavia	Milit Assistance	357UNTS77	105106
27 Aug	Denmark	UK Great Britain	Non-ILO Labor	360UNTS11	105153
29 Aug	Turkey	USA (United States)	Claims and Debts	61TURG2207	466121
01 Sep	Multilateral		Customs	454UNTS289	106542
04 Sep	Canada	Germany, West	Air Transport	411UNTS260	105922
05 Sep	Denmark	Pakistan	Admin Cooperation	354UNTS377	105071
07 Sep	Korea, North	USSR (Soviet Union)	Atomic Energy	8SUGG153	469602
07 Sep	Japan	Philippines	Loans and Credits	0JGJI9	441106
08 Sep	Multilateral		Non-ILO Labor	383UNTS203	105502
09 Sep	Austria	Iran	General Amity	66ABGB45	403103
09 Sep	Turkey	UK Great Britain	Non-ILO Labor	424UNTS267	106113
11 Sep	Belgium	Spain	Visas	345UNTS29	104956
12 Sep	India	USSR (Soviet Union)	Loans and Credits	8SUGG153	469603
12 Sep	Czechoslovakia	Germany, East	General Aid	7EGDA449	419361
14 Sep	Indonesia	Turkey	General Trade	64TURG2909	466070
14 Sep	ICJ Option Clause	India	ICJ Option Clause	340UNTS289	104871
16 Sep	Italy	IBRD (World Bank)	IBRD Project	375UNTS159	105366
16 Sep	Denmark	India	Taxation	405UNTS13	105820
16 Sep	Lebanon	USA (United States)	Scientific Project	358UNTS175	105135
17 Sep	Denmark	France	Taxation	410UNTS141	105901
18 Sep	Canada	Vietnam, South	Direct Aid	0VKNG146	496042
18 Sep	Israel	South Africa	Extradition	373UNTS47	105314
18 Sep	Czechoslovakia	Germany, East	Customs	363UNTS287	105209
19 Sep	Bulgaria	Czechoslovakia	Sanitation	355UNTS77	105074
21 Sep	Spain	Switzerland	Non-ILO Labor	60SPBO1406	460252
21 Sep	New Zealand	UK Great Britain	Milit Assistance	401UNTS51	105762
21 Sep	Bulgaria	Romania	Consul/Citizenship	387UNTS61	105558
22 Sep	Canada	Switzerland	Taxation	470UNTS101	106800
23 Sep	Germany, East	Poland	Land Transport	59PZUM90	458069
23 Sep	Germany, East	Poland	Visas	7EGDA416	419262
25 Sep	Korea, South	USA (United States)	Mass Media	358UNTS163	105133
25 Sep	Pakistan	IBRD (World Bank)	IBRD Project	355UNTS169	105077
25 Sep	Austria	IBRD (World Bank)	IBRD Project	355UNTS223	105079
28 Sep	India	USSR (Soviet Union)	Non-IBRD Project	8SUGG154	469604
28 Sep	FAO (Food Agri)	UN Special Fund	IGO Operations	341UNTS353	200562
28 Sep	United Arab Rep	USA (United States)	Education	358UNTS97	105128
29 Sep	France	Vietnam, South	Scientific Project	0VKNG151	496043
29 Sep	Australia	Fed of Malaya	Air Transport	357UNTS29	105104
30 Sep	Norway	USSR (Soviet Union)	Claims and Debts	3NORT784	451209
30 Sep	Austria	Netherlands	Specific Property	507UNTS111	107397
30 Sep	Canada	Greece	Visas	470UNTS87	106798
01 Oct	Colombia	Norway	Visas	3NORT785	451026
01 Oct	Austria	France	Patents/Copyrights	60FRRT21	415057
01 Oct	IAEA (Atom Energy)	ICAO (Civil Aviat)	IGO Operations	361UNTS193	200570
01 Oct	Korea, South	USA (United States)	Direct Aid	358UNTS115	105129
01 Oct	Germany, West	USA (United States)	Air Transport	358UNTS129	105130
05 Oct	Italy	Yemen	General Economic	61ITDI306	436429
05 Oct	Italy	Yugoslavia	Land Transport	62ITGU255	435238
06 Oct	Iran	UN Special Fund	Direct Aid	0IRTB86	433139
06 Oct	Canada	Euratom	Scientific Project	475UNTS187	106894

DATE	PARTY ONE	PARTY TWO	TOPIC	CITATION	NUMBER
1959 (Cont.)					
06 Oct	India	Italy	General Trade	378UNTS267	105427
06 Oct	Colombia	USA (United States)	US Agri Commod Aid	358UNTS145	105132
06 Oct	Iran	UN Special Fund	Direct Aid	342UNTS89	104902
07 Oct	China People's Rep	Guinea	Culture	29CCJC595	410637
08 Oct	Albania	Germany, East	General Economic	7EGDA311	419019
08 Oct	Austria	France	Taxation	453UNTS95	106521
08 Oct	Canada	Venezuela	Visas	470UNTS93	106799
09 Oct	Germany, East	Vietnam, North	Consul/Citizenship	7EGDA547	419493
09 Oct	Multilateral		Tech Assistance	376UNTS382	105391
12 Oct	Philippines	USA (United States)	General Military	4PTS11	465042
12 Oct	ILO (Labor Org)	UN Special Fund	IGO Operations	343UNTS325	200563
14 Oct	Nicaragua	Peru	Air Transport	392UNTS303	105649
14 Oct	Australia	Germany, West	General Trade	345UNTS35	104957
15 Oct	Romania	USSR (Soviet Union)	Specific Resources	16SUGG126	469966
15 Oct	Guinea	United Nations	Tech Assistance	344UNTS47	104942
15 Oct	Poland	UN Special Fund	Direct Aid	344UNTS29	104941
16 Oct	Austria	Netherlands	Admin Cooperation	458UNTS173	106600
16 Oct	Germany, West	UK Great Britain	Other Military	385UNTS21	105526
16 Oct	USA (United States)	Vietnam, South	US Agri Commod Aid	360UNTS271	105163
18 Oct	Italy	USSR (Soviet Union)	Refugees	8SUGG155	469605
19 Oct	South Africa	Switzerland	Air Transport	61SWRO907	462090
19 Oct	South Africa	Switzerland	Air Transport	559UNTS257	108162
19 Oct	Brazil	USA (United States)	Milit Assistance	372UNTS131	105293
20 Oct	Portugal	Spain	Sanitation	61SPBO1107	460232
20 Oct	France	Spain	Non-ILO Labor	60SPBO2603	460129
20 Oct	Monaco	Netherlands	Visas	487UNTS29	107093
20 Oct	India	UN Special Fund	Direct Aid	344UNTS143	104946
21 Oct	El Salvador	Norway	Visas	3NORT786	451138
21 Oct	Costa Rica	Norway	Visas	3NORT785	451028
21 Oct	France	Italy	General Economic	61ITDI264	436147
22 Oct	Finland	USSR (Soviet Union)	General Trade	8SUGG155	469606
22 Oct	Italy	Netherlands	Visas	61ITDI288	436288
22 Oct	Guinea	UK Great Britain	General Trade	351UNTS341	105033
22 Oct	USA (United States)	Yugoslavia	Tech Assistance	360UNTS259	105161
23 Oct	Switzerland	Yugoslavia	Claims and Debts	60SWRO475	462166
23 Oct	India	Pakistan	Territory Boundary	362UNTS3	105180
27 Oct	Dominican Republic	Norway	Visas	3NORT786	451039
27 Oct	France	Germany, West	Visas	61WBGA11	424158
27 Oct	UN Special Fund	Yugoslavia	Direct Aid	344UNTS159	104947
28 Oct	Norway	Sweden	Visas	427UNTS225	106157
28 Oct	Turkey	USA (United States)	Milit Assistance	360UNTS265	105162
28 Oct	Guinea	USA (United States)	Culture	358UNTS169	105134
29 Oct	Germany, West	Spain	Non-ILO Labor	61SPBO2312	460024
29 Oct	Germany, West	Spain	Non-ILO Labor	61SPBO1110	460023
29 Oct	Germany, West	Spain	Non-ILO Labor	61SPBO1110	460021
29 Oct	Germany, West	Spain	Non-ILO Labor	61SPBO1110	460022
30 Oct	New Zealand	USA (United States)	Tech Assistance	361UNTS21	105170
30 Oct	Norway	South Africa	Specific Property	346UNTS21	104975
31 Oct	Italy	Tunisia	General Trade	378UNTS349	105431
04 Nov	Bulgaria	USSR (Soviet Union)	Tech Assistance	8SUGG156	469608
04 Nov	Bulgaria	USSR (Soviet Union)	General Trade	8SUGG156	469607
06 Nov	Netherlands	USSR (Soviet Union)	General Trade	8SUGG157	469609
06 Nov	Korea, South	United Nations	Other Military	346UNTS289	200565
06 Nov	Ireland	Sweden	Taxation	428UNTS231	106177
07 Nov	Afghanistan	Turkey	Culture	64TURG601	466034
08 Nov	Sudan	United Arab Rep	Specific Resources	453UNTS51	106519
10 Nov	Germany, East	Poland	Specific Resources	59PZUM100	458070
10 Nov	Germany, East	Poland	Specific Resources	7EGDA426	419263
10 Nov	Ecuador	UN Special Fund	Direct Aid	345UNTS3	104955
11 Nov	Germany, West	United Arab Rep	Culture	60WGBB2351	425714
12 Nov	France	Poland	Taxation	59PZUM106	458071
12 Nov	Ethiopia	France	Land Transport	60FRRT30	415183
12 Nov	Germany, East	Romania	Atomic Energy	7EGDA443	419296
12 Nov	Ethiopia	France	Specific Property	381UNTS3	105465
12 Nov	Pakistan	USA (United States)	General Amity	404UNTS259	105816

DATE	PARTY ONE	PARTY TWO	TOPIC	CITATION	NUMBER
1959 (Cont.)					
12 Nov	Japan	USA (United States)	Direct Aid	361UNTS27	105171
12 Nov	Japan	IBRD (World Bank)	IBRD Project	354UNTS279	105067
12 Nov	USA (United States)	Venezuela	Gen Communications	367UNTS81	105227
13 Nov	Mexico	UK Great Britain	Visas	360UNTS3	105152
13 Nov	India	USA (United States)	US Agri Commod Aid	360UNTS287	105164
13 Nov	Greece	UN Special Fund	Direct Aid	345UNTS171	104966
13 Nov	Turkey	USA (United States)	Milit Assistance	361UNTS3	105168
14 Nov	France	Vietnam, South	General Economic	0VKNG153	496044
14 Nov	Austria	Denmark	Commodity Trade	630UNTS29	108962
14 Nov	United Arab Rep	USA (United States)	US Agri Commod Aid	360UNTS311	105165
16 Nov	Tunisia	UK Great Britain	General Trade	354UNTS367	105070
17 Nov	Germany, West	Liberia	Direct Aid	60WBGA69	424408
17 Nov	Germany, West	United Arab Rep	Taxation	61WGBB420	425715
17 Nov	UN Special Fund	WMO (Meteorology)	IGO Operations	345UNTS311	200564
18 Nov	Multilateral		IGO Establishment	390UNTS227	105610
18 Nov	Norway	Yugoslavia	Finance	383UNTS131	105499
19 Nov	Germany, West	Mexico	Visas	60WBGA101	424479
19 Nov	Argentina	Italy	Visas	61ITDI245	436018
19 Nov	Multilateral		IGO Operations	410UNTS156	105902
20 Nov	Japan	USSR (Soviet Union)	General Trade	8SUGG158	469610
20 Nov	Australia	USA (United States)	Air Transport	349UNTS293	105015
20 Nov	UN Special Fund	Turkey	Direct Aid	345UNTS105	104963
21 Nov	Spain	Switzerland	General Trade	59SWRO2095	462131
21 Nov	Germany, East	USSR (Soviet Union)	General Trade	7EGDA531	419414
21 Nov	Cambodia	China People's Rep	Customs	59CCJC104	410645
21 Nov	USA (United States)	USSR (Soviet Union)	Culture	361UNTS35	105172
23 Nov	Iran	IBRD (World Bank)	IBRD Project	380UNTS245	105459
24 Nov	Afghanistan	United Nations	Tech Assistance	397UNTS187	105705
25 Nov	Germany, West	Pakistan	General Economic	457UNTS22	106575
25 Nov	France	USA (United States)	Admin Cooperation	401UNTS75	105764
25 Nov	Czechoslovakia	Germany, East	General Economic	374UNTS101	105331
25 Nov	UN Special Fund	United Arab Rep	Direct Aid	345UNTS125	104964
26 Nov	Guinea	USSR (Soviet Union)	Culture	8SUGG159	469611
26 Nov	Argentina	Brazil	General Trade	374UNTS31	105325
26 Nov	Argentina	Brazil	General Trade	374UNTS45	105327
26 Nov	Argentina	Brazil	Visas	374UNTS51	105328
26 Nov	Argentina	Brazil	General Trade	374UNTS39	105326
27 Nov	Belgium	USA (United States)	Other Military	366UNTS331	105221
30 Nov	Czechoslovakia	Guinea	Culture	386UNTS63	105538
30 Nov	France	Israel	Culture	377UNTS237	105404
30 Nov	Pakistan	IBRD (World Bank)	IBRD Project	355UNTS203	105078
30 Nov	Turkey	USA (United States)	Tech Assistance	361UNTS107	105174
01 Dec	Romania	USSR (Soviet Union)	Tech Assistance	8SUGG159	469612
01 Dec	USSR (Soviet Union)	Yemen	Tech Assistance	8SUGG160	469613
01 Dec	Norway	Venezuela	Visas	3NORT790	451218
01 Dec	Italy	Netherlands	Sanitation	455UNTS241	106545
01 Dec	Hague Private IL	Netherlands	IGO Status/Immunit	510UNTS191	107414
01 Dec	Multilateral		Territory Boundary	402UNTS71	105778
01 Dec	UK Great Britain	USSR (Soviet Union)	Health/Educ/Welfare	351UNTS313	105032
01 Dec	Israel	UN Special Fund	Direct Aid	345UNTS197	104968
02 Dec	Romania	USSR (Soviet Union)	Tech Assistance	8SUGG160	469614
02 Dec	Guinea	UN Special Fund	Direct Aid	345UNTS215	104969
02 Dec	Belgium	Thailand	Visas	351UNTS89	105018
02 Dec	Taiwan	USA (United States)	Atomic Energy	361UNTS115	105175
02 Dec	Czechoslovakia	USSR (Soviet Union)	Non-ILO Labor	374UNTS63	105330
03 Dec	France	Switzerland	Territory Boundary	60SWRO1555	462175
03 Dec	France	Switzerland	Territory Boundary	60SWRO1554	462173
03 Dec	France	Switzerland	Specific Resources	60SWRO1552	462034
03 Dec	France	Switzerland	Territory Boundary	60SWRO1550	462003
03 Dec	France	Switzerland	Specific Resources	60SWRO1548	462033
03 Dec	Multilateral		Tech Assistance	348UNTS246	105003
03 Dec	Multilateral		Tech Assistance	345UNTS251	104971
04 Dec	Argentina	UN Special Fund	Direct Aid	345UNTS263	104972
07 Dec	Germany, East	Korea, North	Education	7EGDA384	419180
07 Dec	Austria	Brazil	Visas	67ABGB332	403009
07 Dec	Philippines	USA (United States)	Milit Installation	359UNTS227	105144
08 Dec	Italy	Netherlands	Land Transport	484UNTS309	107039
09 Dec	Mongolia	USSR (Soviet Union)	General Aid	16SUGG126	469967
09 Dec	Brazil	USSR (Soviet Union)	General Economic	8SUGG160	469615
09 Dec	Liberia	Sweden	Air Transport	464UNTS219	106716
09 Dec	Norway	USSR (Soviet Union)	Specif Claim/Waive	361UNTS93	105173
10 Dec	Mexico	Norway	Visas	3NORT792	451116
10 Dec	Italy	Switzerland	Water Transport	61ITDI298	436384
10 Dec	France	IBRD (World Bank)	IBRD Project	380UNTS319	105464
10 Dec	Canada	UK Great Britain	Non-ILO Labor	379UNTS201	105440
11 Dec	Czechoslovakia	Ethiopia	Scientific Project	386UNTS45	105536
11 Dec	Czechoslovakia	Ethiopia	General Amity	386UNTS51	105537
11 Dec	Czechoslovakia	Ethiopia	Culture	399UNTS93	105736
11 Dec	Bulgaria	USSR (Soviet Union)	Non-ILO Labor	368UNTS287	105246
14 Dec	Multilateral		Admin Cooperation	444UNTS193	106369
14 Dec	Multilateral		Sanitation	422UNTS33	106067
14 Dec	Multilateral		Sanitation	422UNTS57	106068
14 Dec	Multilateral		Land Transport	422UNTS75	106069
14 Dec	Multilateral		IGO Establishment	368UNTS253	105245
14 Dec	Multilateral		IGO Status/Immunit	368UNTS237	105244
14 Dec	Iraq	UK Great Britain	Culture	374UNTS253	105339
15 Dec	Czechoslovakia	Japan	General Trade	383UNTS277	105505
15 Dec	Jordan	UN Special Fund	Direct Aid	346UNTS3	104974
16 Dec	Iraq	USSR (Soviet Union)	Tech Assistance	8SUGG162	469616
16 Dec	China People's Rep	Finland	General Trade	59CCJC111	410650
16 Dec	Czechoslovakia	Poland	Admin Cooperation	372UNTS223	105300
17 Dec	Australia	Indonesia	General Trade	354UNTS109	105058
18 Dec	Taiwan	Philippines	Consul/Citizenship	4PTS25	465043
18 Dec	Germany, East	India	General Economic	7EGDA367	419128
18 Dec	Canada	Spain	Visas	470UNTS117	106802
18 Dec	Australia	Austria	Reparations	348UNTS201	105001
19 Dec	Germany, East	Hungary	Health/Educ/Welfare	7EGDA490	419454
19 Dec	Germany, East	Hungary	Health/Educ/Welfare	409UNTS4	105874
21 Dec	Norway	Yugoslavia	General Trade	3NORT794	451096
21 Dec	Council of Europe	France	Non-ILO Labor	60FRRT34	415500
21 Dec	Germany, West	Ghana	Direct Aid	60WBGA196	424214
21 Dec	Germany, West	Ghana	General Trade	60WBGA241	424215
21 Dec	Denmark	Switzerland	Commodity Trade	633UNTS351	109045
21 Dec	Ceylon (Sri Lanka)	WHO (World Health)	Tech Assistance	349UNTS109	105011
22 Dec	USA (United States)	USSR (Soviet Union)	Claims and Debts	8SUGG163	469619
22 Dec	UK Great Britain	USSR (Soviet Union)	General Trade	8SUGG163	469618
22 Dec	Finland	USSR (Soviet Union)	Loans and Credits	8SUGG163	469617
22 Dec	Germany, West	Iran	Admin Cooperation	61WGBB105	425272
22 Dec	Argentina	USA (United States)	Admin Cooperation	411UNTS42	105912
22 Dec	Turkey	USA (United States)	US Agri Commod Aid	367UNTS57	105225
22 Dec	Israel	Sweden	Taxation	377UNTS277	105407
22 Dec	IBRD (World Bank)	United Arab Rep	IBRD Project	354UNTS197	105063
23 Dec	Canada	USSR (Soviet Union)	Visas	16SUGG127	469968
24 Dec	New Zealand	Thailand	Customs	351UNTS197	105023
27 Dec	Iraq	USSR (Soviet Union)	Tech Assistance	8SUGG164	469620
29 Dec	Albania	Yugoslavia	General Trade	396UNTS63	105693
30 Dec	Pakistan	Switzerland	Taxation	60SWRO1058	462061
30 Dec	IBRD (World Bank)	Uruguay	IBRD Project	384UNTS275	105523
1960					
04 Jan	Denmark	Sweden	General Trade	376UNTS375	105390
04 Jan	Multilateral		IGO Establishment	370UNTS3	105266
05 Jan	India	Japan	Taxation	384UNTS3	105507
06 Jan	Costa Rica	Norway	Visas	3NORT785	451029
06 Jan	Belgium	Brazil	Culture	531UNTS149	107701
06 Jan	Haiti	USA (United States)	Gen Communications	367UNTS75	105226
07 Jan	UN Special Fund	UK Great Britain	Direct Aid	348UNTS177	105000
07 Jan	Greece	USA (United States)	US Agri Commod Aid	368UNTS221	105243
07 Jan	Israel	USA (United States)	US Agri Commod Aid	368UNTS181	105241
09 Jan	Germany, East	Poland	Water Transport	8EGDA419	419265

DATE	PARTY ONE	PARTY TWO	TOPIC	CITATION	NUMBER
1960 (Cont.)					
09 Jan	Germany, East	Poland	Water Transport	8EGDA414	419264
10 Jan	Germany, East	Guinea	General Economic	8EGDA345	419118
11 Jan	India	Pakistan	Territory Boundary	375UNTS119	105364
11 Jan	Colombia	USA (United States)	Tech Assistance	371UNTS37	105268
12 Jan	Albania	Hungary	Admin Cooperation	520UNTS3	107511
12 Jan	Guinea	Hungary	Culture	519UNTS131	107505
12 Jan	Germany, East	Hungary	Patents/Copyrights	409UNTS22	105875
13 Jan	Accept UN Charter	Cameroon	UN Charter	375UNTS79	105354
14 Jan	ITU (Telecommun)	United Nations	IGO Operations	348UNTS331	200566
15 Jan	Czechoslovakia	UK Great Britain	Air Transport	374UNTS207	105336
16 Jan	Tunisia	USSR (Soviet Union)	General Trade	9SUGG121	469622
17 Jan	United Arab Rep	USSR (Soviet Union)	Non-IBRD Project	9SUGG121	469621
18 Jan	China People's Rep	Germany, East	General Economic	8EGDA333	419096
18 Jan	China People's Rep	Germany, East	General Amity	60CCJC2	410656
19 Jan	Afghanistan	USSR (Soviet Union)	General Aid	9SUGG121	469623
19 Jan	Spain	UK Great Britain	Atomic Energy	404UNTS41	105804
19 Jan	Peru	UN Special Fund	Direct Aid	349UNTS83	105010
19 Jan	Japan	USA (United States)	General Military	373UNTS179	105320
19 Jan	Japan	USA (United States)	Status of Forces	373UNTS207	105321
20 Jan	Italy	USSR (Soviet Union)	Visas	16SUGG127	469969
20 Jan	Bulgaria	USSR (Soviet Union)	Tech Assistance	9SUGG22	469624
20 Jan	Czechoslovakia	USSR (Soviet Union)	General Trade	9SUGG122	469625
20 Jan	Brazil	Mexico	Culture	65MEXD2306	444002
20 Jan	Italy	USSR (Soviet Union)	Visas	62ITDI382	436422
20 Jan	Colombia	IBRD (World Bank)	IBRD Project	375UNTS49	105353
20 Jan	Belgium	Netherlands	Admin Cooperation	373UNTS3	105310
20 Jan	Pakistan	WHO (World Health)	Tech Assistance	351UNTS355	105034
21 Jan	Argentina	Italy	General Economic	62ITDI313	436019
21 Jan	Albania	Germany, East	Air Transport	8EGDA310	419020
22 Jan	France	Germany, West	Extradition	60WBGA63	424159
22 Jan	Chile	UN Special Fund	Direct Aid	351UNTS115	105020
23 Jan	Austria	Czechoslovakia	Specific Resources	495UNTS125	107242
23 Jan	Austria	Czechoslovakia	Scientific Project	495UNTS99	107241
25 Jan	Albania	USSR (Soviet Union)	General Trade	9SUGG122	469626
25 Jan	Spain	Switzerland	Non-ILO Labor	60SPBO2707	460253
25 Jan	India	Japan	Tech Assistance	384UNTS31	105508
26 Jan	Argentina	Mexico	Culture	635UNTS79	109073
26 Jan	Multilateral		IGO Establishment	439UNTS249	106333
28 Jan	Chile	Mexico	Culture	63MEXD3010	444012
28 Jan	Burma	China People's Rep	Territory Boundary	60CCJC8	410659
28 Jan	Burma	China People's Rep	General Amity	60CCJC7	410658
28 Jan	Germany, West	UK Great Britain	Reparations	420UNTS29	106038
29 Jan	China People's Rep	USSR (Soviet Union)	Specific Resources	16SUGG127	469970
29 Jan	Germany, West	Tunisia	General Trade	60WBGA107	424678
29 Jan	China People's Rep	USSR (Soviet Union)	Specific Resources	60CCJC9	410660
29 Jan	El Salvador	USA (United States)	Claims and Debts	372UNTS3	105283
30 Jan	Germany, East	Hungary	Health/Educ/Welfare	408UNTS230	105873
02 Feb	Canada	Italy	Air Transport	62ITGU22	435075
02 Feb	China People's Rep	Czechoslovakia	General Economic	60CCJC10	410661
03 Feb	Mexico	Peru	Culture	62MEXD3010	444037
04 Feb	Germany, West	Iran	Non-IBRD Project	0IRTB8	433013
04 Feb	Mexico	USA (United States)	Scientific Project	586UNTS57	108496
04 Feb	Colombia	UN Special Fund	Direct Aid	355UNTS257	105080
06 Feb	France	Italy	Non-ILO Labor	62ITDI325	436151
06 Feb	Germany, East	Yugoslavia	Air Transport	8EGDA354	419147
06 Feb	Poland	Yugoslavia	Admin Cooperation	521UNTS37	107517
06 Feb	Multilateral		General Economic	383UNTS3	105494
09 Feb	Italy	USSR (Soviet Union)	Visas	9SUGG124	469627
09 Feb	Germany, West	Panama	Admin Cooperation	60WBGA169	424567
09 Feb	Italy	USSR (Soviet Union)	Culture	399UNTS75	105735
09 Feb	Bolivia	UN Special Fund	Direct Aid	351UNTS203	105024
11 Feb	Mongolia	USSR (Soviet Union)	General Aid	9SUGG124	469628
11 Feb	Mongolia	USSR (Soviet Union)	General Aid	9SUGG124	469629
11 Feb	Morocco	Norway	Visas	3NORT798	451115
11 Feb	Cuba	UNICEF (Children)	Direct Aid	349UNTS277	105014

DATE	PARTY ONE	PARTY TWO	TOPIC	CITATION	NUMBER
1960 (Cont.)					
11 Feb	Ecuador	USA (United States)	Milit Assistance	372UNTS141	105294
12 Feb	India	USSR (Soviet Union)	General Aid	9SUGG125	469630
12 Feb	Argentina	Philippines	General Amity	535UNTS293	107785
12 Feb	India	USSR (Soviet Union)	Culture	392UNTS153	105642
12 Feb	Italy	Yugoslavia	Other Military	379UNTS77	105434
12 Feb	Australia	Canada	General Trade	369UNTS89	105253
12 Feb	Peru	USA (United States)	US Agri Commod Aid	372UNTS83	105290
13 Feb	Italy	Lebanon	Air Transport	62ITDI353	436258
13 Feb	Norway	USA (United States)	Milit Assistance	388UNTS255	105583
13 Feb	Cuba	USSR (Soviet Union)	Claims and Debts	369UNTS3	105247
13 Feb	Cuba	USSR (Soviet Union)	General Economic	369UNTS17	105248
13 Feb	Spain	USA (United States)	Milit Installation	371UNTS185	105279
14 Feb	Germany, West	Luxembourg	Non-ILO Labor	63WGBB385	425424
15 Feb	UK Great Britain	USA (United States)	Milit Assistance	371UNTS45	105269
15 Feb	Greece	USA (United States)	Milit Assistance	377UNTS95	105397
16 Feb	Germany, West	United Arab Rep	Air Transport	464UNTS233	106717
17 Feb	Portugal	Spain	Customs	60SPBO312	460233
17 Feb	Belgium	Philippines	Visas	356UNTS303	105101
17 Feb	Netherlands	Philippines	Visas	359UNTS317	105149
17 Feb	Luxembourg	Philippines	Visas	359UNTS311	105148
18 Feb	Afghanistan	USSR (Soviet Union)	Education	9SUGG126	469631
18 Feb	Italy	Peru	Admin Cooperation	62ITDI362	436298
18 Feb	Italy	Peru	Visas	62ITDI361	436297
18 Feb	Germany, West	Greece	Non-ILO Labor	60WBGA173	424232
18 Feb	Japan	USA (United States)	Direct Aid	372UNTS117	105292
19 Feb	Poland	USSR (Soviet Union)	Customs	16SUGG127	469971
19 Feb	Poland	USSR (Soviet Union)	Customs	60PZUM11	458072
19 Feb	Denmark	USA (United States)	Patents/Copyrights	354UNTS151	105061
19 Feb	Korea, South	USA (United States)	Claims and Debts	372UNTS109	105291
19 Feb	Honduras	USA (United States)	Gen Communications	371UNTS109	105273
19 Feb	Chile	USA (United States)	Atomic Energy	371UNTS255	105282
20 Feb	Cuba	USSR (Soviet Union)	General Trade	9SUGG126	469632
20 Feb	Iran	IBRD (World Bank)	IBRD Project	384UNTS213	105521
21 Feb	Afghanistan	UN Special Fund	Direct Aid	351UNTS93	105019
22 Feb	Austria	Sweden	Taxation	60ABGB143	403175
23 Feb	China People's Rep	Mongolia	General Trade	60CCJC23	410673
23 Feb	Germany, West	UK Great Britain	Extradition	385UNTS39	105527
23 Feb	Australia	Philippines	Visas	358UNTS139	105131
24 Feb	Ecuador	USA (United States)	Tech Assistance	371UNTS55	105270
25 Feb	Italy	USSR (Soviet Union)	Visas	16SUGG127	469972
25 Feb	Austria	Norway	Taxation	60ABGB205	403145
25 Feb	Pakistan	UN Special Fund	Direct Aid	351UNTS141	105021
25 Feb	Austria	Norway	Taxation	376UNTS155	105380
26 Feb	Taiwan	Panama	Culture	435UNTS281	106285
26 Feb	Peru	USA (United States)	Milit Assistance	394UNTS141	105674
26 Feb	France	Thailand	Air Transport	392UNTS279	105648
26 Feb	Multilateral		Air Transport	418UNTS171	106022
26 Feb	Australia	Thailand	Air Transport	392UNTS255	105647
26 Feb	Australia	USA (United States)	Specific Property	354UNTS95	105056
27 Feb	Brazil	USA (United States)	Direct Aid	384UNTS131	105515
28 Feb	China People's Rep	Hungary	General Economic	60CCJC29	410677
28 Feb	Indonesia	USSR (Soviet Union)	Culture	392UNTS191	105644
28 Feb	Indonesia	USSR (Soviet Union)	General Aid	392UNTS173	105643
29 Feb	Cuba	Germany, East	Consul/Citizenship	8EGDA394	419184
29 Feb	China People's Rep	Korea, North	General Trade	60CCJC31	410678
01 Mar	Guinea	USSR (Soviet Union)	Tech Assistance	9SUGG127	469633
01 Mar	Guinea	USSR (Soviet Union)	Tech Assistance	9SUGG128	469635
01 Mar	Guinea	USSR (Soviet Union)	Direct Aid	9SUGG128	469634
01 Mar	Germany, East	USSR (Soviet Union)	Tech Assistance	8EGDA538	419415
01 Mar	Turkey	UK Great Britain	Visas	374UNTS295	105343
02 Mar	Japan	USSR (Soviet Union)	General Trade	9SUGG128	469637
02 Mar	Japan	USSR (Soviet Union)	General Trade	9SUGG128	469636
02 Mar	Greece	Tunisia	General Trade	483UNTS89	107008
02 Mar	Turkey	USA (United States)	Milit Assistance	372UNTS37	105286
03 Mar	Germany, East	Sudan	Scientific Project	46EGDZ364	420309

DATE	PARTY ONE	PARTY TWO	TOPIC	CITATION	NUMBER
1960 (Cont.)					
04 Mar	Afghanistan	USSR (Soviet Union)	Culture	9SUGG129	469638
04 Mar	Italy	Switzerland	Land Transport	62ITGU212	435385
07 Mar	Czechoslovakia	USSR (Soviet Union)	Tech Assistance	9SUGG129	469639
07 Mar	China People's Rep	Vietnam, North	General Economic	60CCJC36	410682
08 Mar	Ethiopia	USSR (Soviet Union)	Non-IBRD Project	9SUGG129	469640
08 Mar	France	Germany, West	Patents/Copyrights	61WGBB22	425160
08 Mar	France	Germany, West	Patents/Copyrights	0UNTS0	110715
09 Mar	Taiwan	Thailand	Air Transport	0CTRC46	413027
09 Mar	Guinea	Netherlands	Air Transport	392UNTS243	105646
09 Mar	Germany, West	UK Great Britain	Admin Cooperation	403UNTS253	105796
10 Mar	Poland	USSR (Soviet Union)	General Trade	9SUGG129	469641
10 Mar	Poland	USSR (Soviet Union)	Tech Assistance	9SUGG130	469642
10 Mar	Finland	Iceland	Air Transport	497UNTS95	107264
11 Mar	Czechoslovakia	Iraq	Air Transport	464UNTS267	106718
14 Mar	Iceland	USSR (Soviet Union)	Consul/Citizenship	16SUGG127	469973
14 Mar	India	USSR (Soviet Union)	General Trade	9SUGG130	469643
14 Mar	Bulgaria	Romania	Admin Cooperation	472UNTS279	106844
15 Mar	Bulgaria	China People's Rep	General Trade	60CCJC45	410689
15 Mar	Albania	China People's Rep	General Economic	60CCJC41	410686
15 Mar	China People's Rep	Romania	General Economic	60CCJC39	410685
15 Mar	Multilateral		Water Transport	572UNTS133	108310
16 Mar	Norway	Spain	Claims and Debts	3NORT801	451145
16 Mar	Germany, West	USA (United States)	Specific Property	371UNTS101	105272
17 Mar	Austria	Liechtenstein	Territory Boundary	60ABGB228	403128
17 Mar	France	IBRD (World Bank)	IBRD Project	452UNTS147	106508
17 Mar	Mauritania	IBRD (World Bank)	IBRD Project	452UNTS211	106509
17 Mar	Japan	IBRD (World Bank)	IBRD Project	362UNTS43	105182
17 Mar	France	UN Special Fund	Direct Aid	354UNTS119	105059
18 Mar	Germany, West	Greece	Specif Claim/Waive	61WGBB1596	425233
18 Mar	Germany, West	Greece	General Economic	62WGBB1505	425234
18 Mar	Austria	Yugoslavia	Consul/Citizenship	68ABGB378	403251
18 Mar	Austria	Yugoslavia	Admin Cooperation	61ABGB115	403235
18 Mar	Austria	Yugoslavia	Visas	60ABGB232	403226
18 Mar	Austria	Yugoslavia	Admin Cooperation	60ABGB265	403255
18 Mar	Spain	USA (United States)	Scientific Project	372UNTS13	105284
18 Mar	Bolivia	UK Great Britain	Visas	374UNTS199	105335
18 Mar	Austria	Guatemala	General Trade	379UNTS89	105435
19 Mar	Portugal	USA (United States)	Education	371UNTS131	105275
20 Mar	Iraq	USSR (Soviet Union)	Non-IBRD Project	9SUGG131	469644
21 Mar	United Arab Rep	USSR (Soviet Union)	Visas	16SUGG127	469974
21 Mar	China People's Rep	Nepal	Direct Aid	60CCJC48	410691
21 Mar	China People's Rep	Nepal	Territory Boundary	60CCJC47	410690
23 Mar	China People's Rep	Germany, East	General Trade	60CCJC49	410692
23 Mar	Austria	El Salvador	General Trade	390UNTS3	105599
23 Mar	Finland	USA (United States)	US Agri Commod Aid	371UNTS117	105274
23 Mar	Japan	USA (United States)	Tech Assistance	372UNTS289	105305
23 Mar	New Zealand	USA (United States)	Atomic Energy	371UNTS147	105276
24 Mar	France	Vietnam, South	General Economic	0VKNG153	496045
24 Mar	France	Vietnam, South	Specific Property	70FRJO2203	416482
24 Mar	France	Vietnam, South	Claims and Debts	0UNTS0	110473
24 Mar	Belgium	Switzerland	Air Transport	416UNTS81	105996
24 Mar	Netherlands	USA (United States)	Milit Assistance	406UNTS165	105847
24 Mar	Ireland	USA (United States)	Atomic Energy	371UNTS237	105280
25 Mar	Ethiopia	USSR (Soviet Union)	Tech Assistance	9SUGG131	469645
25 Mar	China People's Rep	Yugoslavia	General Trade	60CCJC52	410694
26 Mar	Mexico	Yugoslavia	Culture	66MEXD1607	444045
28 Mar	Mongolia	USSR (Soviet Union)	Direct Aid	9SUGG131	469646
28 Mar	Chile	USA (United States)	Scientific Project	401UNTS105	105765
29 Mar	Germany, West	Spain	Non-ILO Labor	60SPBO505	460025
29 Mar	Ireland	UK Great Britain	Non-ILO Labor	371UNTS3	105267
29 Mar	Switzerland	USA (United States)	General Trade	371UNTS155	105277
30 Mar	Germany, West	Greece	Non-ILO Labor	61WBGA25	424235
30 Mar	Belgium	IBRD (World Bank)	IBRD Project	379UNTS161	105439
30 Mar	Romania	USA (United States)	Claims and Debts	371UNTS163	105278
30 Mar	Belgium	IBRD (World Bank)	IBRD Project	379UNTS103	105437
30 Mar	Belgium	IBRD (World Bank)	IBRD Project	379UNTS129	105438
31 Mar	Czechoslovakia	USSR (Soviet Union)	Non-IBRD Project	9SUGG132	469647
31 Mar	Canada	USA (United States)	Specif Goods/Equip	400UNTS315	105755
01 Apr	Poland	USSR (Soviet Union)	Finance	9SUGG132	469648
01 Apr	Ecuador	Spain	Non-ILO Labor	62SPBO2310	460089
01 Apr	Argentina	USA (United States)	Milit Assistance	371UNTS245	105281
01 Apr	Belgium	UK Great Britain	Visas	361UNTS135	105177
01 Apr	Luxembourg	UK Great Britain	Visas	374UNTS267	105340
01 Apr	Italy	UN Special Fund	Direct Aid	354UNTS261	105066
01 Apr	Netherlands	UK Great Britain	Visas	374UNTS277	105341
01 Apr	IBRD (World Bank)	UK Great Britain	IBRD Project	379UNTS397	105446
02 Apr	France	USSR (Soviet Union)	Finance	9SUGG132	469649
02 Apr	Spain	Switzerland	General Trade	60SWRO457	462132
02 Apr	Czechoslovakia	Poland	General Economic	60PZUM16	458073
02 Apr	France	Malagasy	Recognition	60FRRT38	415278
02 Apr	France	Norway	General Trade	60FRMD904	417346
02 Apr	France	USSR (Soviet Union)	Finance	0UNTS0	110493
04 Apr	USSR (Soviet Union)	Yemen	Non-IBRD Project	9SUGG133	469650
04 Apr	Israel	UK Great Britain	Extradition	377UNTS331	105410
06 Apr	Iceland	USA (United States)	US Agri Commod Aid	372UNTS71	105289
07 Apr	Colombia	USA (United States)	Milit Assistance	372UNTS27	105285
08 Apr	Mexico	United Arab Rep	Culture	64MEXD1408	444038
08 Apr	Germany, East	Hungary	General Trade	8EGDA478	419455
08 Apr	Germany, West	Netherlands	Territory Boundary	508UNTS14	107404
08 Apr	Denmark	UK Great Britain	Customs	374UNTS233	105337
09 Apr	Luxembourg	Yugoslavia	Air Transport	464UNTS293	106719
09 Apr	Iran	UK Great Britain	Taxation	385UNTS63	105529
11 Apr	France	Spain	Non-ILO Labor	60SPBO2007	460130
11 Apr	Bulgaria	Germany, East	General Trade	8EGDA325	419063
11 Apr	Pakistan	USA (United States)	US Agri Commod Aid	372UNTS251	105302
11 Apr	Multilateral		Visas	374UNTS3	105323
12 Apr	Greece	Mexico	General Trade	64MEXD3012	444025
12 Apr	France	Switzerland	Refugees	60FRRT41	415407
12 Apr	UK Great Britain	Yugoslavia	Culture	360UNTS79	105155
12 Apr	Mexico	USA (United States)	Scientific Project	372UNTS47	105287
12 Apr	Iran	USA (United States)	General Trade	372UNTS63	105288
12 Apr	Denmark	USA (United States)	Milit Assistance	373UNTS9	105311
12 Apr	Multilateral		Tech Assistance	359UNTS323	105150
12 Apr	UN Special Fund	Tunisia	Direct Aid	355UNTS289	105082
13 Apr	Finland	Sweden	Culture	428UNTS131	106172
13 Apr	Ireland	South Africa	Postal Service	390UNTS307	105612
15 Apr	Multilateral		Finance	470UNTS239	106811
15 Apr	Taiwan	USA (United States)	Milit Installation	462UNTS19	106667
15 Apr	Japan	USA (United States)	Milit Assistance	372UNTS267	105303
16 Apr	Germany, West	Iran	Non-IBRD Project	0IRTB9	433014
19 Apr	Germany, West	Turkey	Direct Aid	60TURG2208	466107
19 Apr	Libya	UN Special Fund	Direct Aid	356UNTS11	105090
20 Apr	Germany, West	UK Great Britain	Non-ILO Labor	449UNTS77	106453
20 Apr	Germany, West	UK Great Britain	Non-ILO Labor	413UNTS236	105958
21 Apr	Brazil	Italy	Visas	62ITDI319	436063
21 Apr	France	Iran	Air Transport	86FRRT5009	415238
21 Apr	ICAO (Civil Aviat)	UN Special Fund	IGO Operations	360UNTS367	200569
21 Apr	UN Special Fund	Sudan	Direct Aid	356UNTS213	105097
22 Apr	Argentina	Spain	Mass Media	61SPBO2109	460037
22 Apr	Germany, East	Poland	General Economic	60PZUM20	458074
22 Apr	France	Germany, West	Admin Cooperation	60WGBB2325	425181
22 Apr	Germany, East	Poland	General Economic	8EGDA423	419266
22 Apr	Cuba	Japan	General Trade	442UNTS261	106354
22 Apr	Multilateral		Air Transport	418UNTS211	106023
22 Apr	Belgium	USA (United States)	Milit Assistance	372UNTS277	105304
23 Apr	Guatemala	USA (United States)	Atomic Energy	373UNTS23	105312
25 Apr	Albania	Germany, East	Finance	8EGDA316	419021
25 Apr	Canada	Norway	Milit Installation	470UNTS109	106801
26 Apr	Czechoslovakia	Switzerland	Taxation	60SWRO538	462063
26 Apr	Iran	Jordan	Culture	0IRTB47	433071

DATE	PARTY ONE	PARTY TWO	TOPIC	CITATION	NUMBER
1960 (Cont.)					
26 Apr	Greece	USA (United States)	Patents/Copyrights	372UNTS299	105306
27 Apr	Germany, East	Hungary	Specif Goods/Equip	8EGDA479	419456
28 Apr	Czechoslovakia	USSR (Soviet Union)	General Trade	9SUGG134	469651
28 Apr	Dominican Republic	Norway	Visas	3NORT786	451040
28 Apr	China People's Rep	Nepal	General Amity	60CCJC58	410698
28 Apr	Germany, West	Spain	Air Transport	465UNTS3	106720
28 Apr	Multilateral		Health/Educ/Welfare	376UNTS111	105377
29 Apr	UN Special Fund	Vietnam, South	Direct Aid	0VKNG154	496046
29 Apr	UN Special Fund	Vietnam, South	Direct Aid	357UNTS311	200567
30 Apr	Laos	UN Special Fund	Tech Assistance	361UNTS171	105179
01 May	Togo	USSR (Soviet Union)	Consul/Citizenship	9SUGG134	469652
02 May	France	Hungary	Air Transport	60FRRT63	415222
02 May	Iran	UK Great Britain	Air Transport	566UNTS129	108241
02 May	Greece	Romania	Air Transport	485UNTS17	107043
03 May	Japan	United Nations	IGO Operations	0JGJI1413	441107
04 May	Tunisia	USSR (Soviet Union)	Consul/Citizenship	9SUGG134	469654
04 May	Burma	USSR (Soviet Union)	Direct Aid	9SUGG134	469653
04 May	Jordan	UK Great Britain	Loans and Credits	385UNTS81	105531
04 May	Costa Rica	IBRD (World Bank)	IBRD Project	390UNTS201	105609
04 May	India	USA (United States)	US Agri Commod Aid	376UNTS279	105384
05 May	Poland	Yugoslavia	Sanitation	423UNTS229	106095
06 May	Hungary	USSR (Soviet Union)	General Trade	9SUGG135	469655
06 May	China People's Rep	Mongolia	Mass Media	60CCJC60	410699
06 May	United Nations	Togo	Tech Assistance	388UNTS53	105571
07 May	China People's Rep	Czechoslovakia	Consul/Citizenship	60CCJC61	410700
07 May	Hungary	Yugoslavia	Admin Cooperation	519UNTS237	107510
07 May	China People's Rep	Czechoslovakia	Consul/Citizenship	402UNTS209	105787
07 May	Lebanon	UN Special Fund	Tech Assistance	360UNTS225	105160
08 May	Cuba	USSR (Soviet Union)	Consul/Citizenship	9SUGG135	469656
09 May	France	Uruguay	Finance	60FRRT43	415478
09 May	New Zealand	Philippines	Postal Service	486UNTS65	107073
10 May	Denmark	USSR (Soviet Union)	Taxation	16SUGG127	469975
10 May	Cambodia	USSR (Soviet Union)	Direct Aid	9SUGG165	469658
10 May	Cambodia	USSR (Soviet Union)	Direct Aid	9SUGG135	469657
10 May	Fed of Malaya	Japan	General Trade	383UNTS293	105506
10 May	Colombia	IBRD (World Bank)	IBRD Project	379UNTS218	105441
11 May	Germany, West	Ireland	Non-ILO Labor	553UNTS69	108070
12 May	Czechoslovakia	USSR (Soviet Union)	Tech Assistance	9SUGG135	469659
12 May	Netherlands	Turkey	Culture	463UNTS207	106704
12 May	Australia	New Zealand	Taxation	369UNTS119	105254
13 May	Finland	Turkey	General Trade	60TURG1908	466056
13 May	Finland	Turkey	Finance	60TURG1908	466057
13 May	Spain	UK Great Britain	Visas	374UNTS287	105342
14 May	France	Morocco	Non-IBRD Project	60FRRT40	415297
14 May	Belgium	Iran	Culture	522UNTS249	107551
16 May	Fed Rhod/Nyasaland	South Africa	General Trade	376UNTS217	105381
17 May	Iceland	USSR (Soviet Union)	Finance	9SUGG136	469660
17 May	Norway	Spain	General Trade	3NORT805	451146
17 May	Czechoslovakia	Poland	Consul/Citizenship	424UNTS3	106096
17 May	Nepal	USA (United States)	Claims and Debts	372UNTS313	105307
18 May	Japan	USSR (Soviet Union)	Specific Resources	9SUGG136	469661
18 May	Ireland	Italy	Visas	62ITDI327	436217
18 May	Taiwan	Japan	Air Transport	0CTRC26	413022
18 May	Belgium	USA (United States)	Patents/Copyrights	373UNTS31	105313
19 May	Morocco	United Arab Rep	Air Transport	563UNTS121	108208
19 May	Cambodia	WHO (World Health)	Tech Assistance	372UNTS193	105298
20 May	Denmark	UK Great Britain	Atomic Energy	374UNTS245	105338
21 May	Switzerland	Tunisia	Air Transport	497UNTS109	107265
21 May	Czechoslovakia	Romania	Consul/Citizenship	397UNTS245	105709
21 May	Accept UN Charter	Togo	UN Charter	375UNTS83	105355
23 May	China People's Rep	Korea, North	Water Transport	60CCJC66	410702
23 May	Argentina	USA (United States)	Atomic Energy	377UNTS3	105392
24 May	Canada	Norway	Milit Installation	470UNTS125	106803
24 May	Kuwait	UK Great Britain	Air Transport	412UNTS4	105923
24 May	Germany, East	USSR (Soviet Union)	Non-ILO Labor	392UNTS205	105645

DATE	PARTY ONE	PARTY TWO	TOPIC	CITATION	NUMBER
1960 (Cont.)					
25 May	Afghanistan	USSR (Soviet Union)	Non-IBRD Project	9SUGG136	469662
25 May	UN Special Fund	WHO (World Health)	IGO Operations	359UNTS375	200568
27 May	Argentina	USSR (Soviet Union)	Loans and Credits	9SUGG137	469663
27 May	Norway	Tunisia	Visas	3NORT807	451173
27 May	IBRD (World Bank)	UK Great Britain	IBRD Project	375UNTS201	105367
27 May	Germany, West	USA (United States)	Milit Assistance	377UNTS45	105395
27 May	Finland	USSR (Soviet Union)	Culture	379UNTS381	105444
28 May	China People's Rep	USSR (Soviet Union)	Visas	16SUGG128	469976
28 May	Afghanistan	Czechoslovakia	Air Transport	497UNTS129	107266
31 May	China People's Rep	Mongolia	General Amity	60CCJC72	410705
31 May	China People's Rep	Mongolia	Tech Assistance	60CCJC74	410707
31 May	Japan	USA (United States)	Direct Aid	376UNTS301	105385
01 Jun	Sweden	Turkey	Visas	60TURG2106	466027
01 Jun	France	Italy	General Military	62ITDI325	436152
01 Jun	Belgium	Germany, West	Admin Cooperation	60WBGA150	424028
01 Jun	Czechoslovakia	Germany, East	General Trade	8EGDA438	419362
01 Jun	Peru	IBRD (World Bank)	IBRD Project	380UNTS15	105448
02 Jun	Chile	USA (United States)	US Agri Commod Aid	377UNTS11	105393
03 Jun	Germany, East	Korea, North	Consul/Citizenship	8EGDA381	419181
03 Jun	Germany, West	Netherlands	Visas	487UNTS37	107094
03 Jun	USA (United States)	Yugoslavia	US Agri Commod Aid	376UNTS243	105382
04 Jun	Multilateral		Tech Assistance	360UNTS208	105159
04 Jun	UN Special Fund	Thailand	Tech Assistance	360UNTS97	105157
04 Jun	Ghana	UK Great Britain	Admin Cooperation	377UNTS197	105401
07 Jun	Germany, West	Sweden	Admin Cooperation	60WGBB2299	425616
07 Jun	Fed of Malaya	UK Great Britain	Scientific Project	375UNTS141	105365
08 Jun	UN Special Fund	Togo	Tech Assistance	369UNTS401	200574
08 Jun	Denmark	Poland	Culture	424UNTS37	106097
08 Jun	Indonesia	USA (United States)	Atomic Energy	388UNTS287	105585
08 Jun	Burma	Thailand	Visas	372UNTS321	105308
09 Jun	Norway	Tunisia	General Trade	3NORT808	451174
10 Jun	Cuba	Czechoslovakia	General Trade	447UNTS75	106412
13 Jun	Luxembourg	Tunisia	Air Transport	497UNTS143	107267
13 Jun	India	USA (United States)	Atomic Energy	377UNTS37	105394
14 Jun	USSR (Soviet Union)	Vietnam, North	Loans and Credits	9SUGG138	469664
14 Jun	Argentina	Italy	Atomic Energy	62ITDI314	436020
14 Jun	Canada	USA (United States)	Scientific Project	377UNTS365	105413
15 Jun	Austria	USA (United States)	Patents/Copyrights	376UNTS267	105383
15 Jun	Iceland	Israel	Patents/Copyrights	377UNTS261	105405
16 Jun	Hungary	USSR (Soviet Union)	Mass Media	16SUGG128	469977
16 Jun	India	USSR (Soviet Union)	Tech Assistance	9SUGG138	469665
16 Jun	Czechoslovakia	Germany, East	General Economic	415UNTS248	105988
17 Jun	Argentina	Austria	Visas	60ABGB215	403001
17 Jun	Multilateral		Humanitarian	536UNTS27	107794
17 Jun	Austria	Spain	General Trade	390UNTS17	105600
17 Jun	IBRD (World Bank)	Sudan	IBRD Project	379UNTS253	105442
18 Jun	Cuba	USSR (Soviet Union)	General Trade	9SUGG139	469666
18 Jun	Cuba	USSR (Soviet Union)	Finance	9SUGG139	469667
19 Jun	Multilateral		IGO Operations	537UNTS214	107803
19 Jun	Iraq	UN Special Fund	Direct Aid	376UNTS357	105389
20 Jun	Belgium	Netherlands	Specific Property	423UNTS19	106084
20 Jun	Germany, West	UK Great Britain	Visas	385UNTS55	105528
21 Jun	Austria	El Salvador	Visas	60ABGB189	403161
21 Jun	Multilateral		IGO Establishment	418UNTS109	106019
22 Jun	France	Senegal	General Amity	60FRRT47	415388
22 Jun	Multilateral		Mass Media	546UNTS247	107951
22 Jun	Denmark	Peru	Air Transport	439UNTS113	106326
22 Jun	Multilateral		Sanitation	431UNTS41	106208
22 Jun	Peru	ILO (Labor Org)	IGO Status/Immunit	423UNTS165	106092
22 Jun	Korea, North	USSR (Soviet Union)	General Economic	399UNTS3	105732
22 Jun	Spain	USA (United States)	US Agri Commod Aid	378UNTS3	105414
22 Jun	Nicaragua	IBRD (World Bank)	IBRD Project	384UNTS243	105522
23 Jun	Austria	Vatican/Holy See	Admin Cooperation	60ABGB196	403209
23 Jun	Austria	Vatican/Holy See	Claims and Debts	60ABGB195	403207
23 Jun	Finland	USSR (Soviet Union)	Territory Boundary	379UNTS277	105443

DATE	PARTY ONE	PARTY TWO	TOPIC	CITATION	NUMBER
1960 (Cont.)					
24 Jun	Austria	UK Great Britain	Consul/Citizenship	502UNTS79	107327
24 Jun	Ireland	Portugal	Air Transport	412UNTS30	105924
24 Jun	UK Great Britain	USA (United States)	Gen Communications	377UNTS63	105396
25 Jun	USSR (Soviet Union)	Yemen	Tech Assistance	9SUGG140	469668
25 Jun	Brazil	Spain	Culture	65SPBO907	460058
25 Jun	France	Poland	Air Transport	60PZUM53	458075
25 Jun	France	Poland	Air Transport	61FRRT20	415362
25 Jun	Brazil	Spain	Culture	0UNTS0	109427
26 Jun	Somalia	UK Great Britain	Finance	374UNTS363	105350
26 Jun	Somalia	UK Great Britain	Non-ILO Labor	374UNTS347	105348
26 Jun	Somalia	UK Great Britain	Recognition	374UNTS357	105349
26 Jun	Accept UN Charter	Malagasy	UN Charter	375UNTS87	105356
26 Jun	Somalia	UK Great Britain	Direct Aid	374UNTS331	105346
26 Jun	Somalia	UK Great Britain	Non-ILO Labor	374UNTS339	105347
27 Jun	India	Poland	Water Transport	60PZUM63	458076
27 Jun	France	Malagasy	General Amity	60FRRT46	415279
28 Jun	Bulgaria	USSR (Soviet Union)	Tech Assistance	9SUGG140	469669
28 Jun	Italy	Spain	General Trade	62ITDI370	436354
28 Jun	IAEA (Atom Energy)	USA (United States)	Direct Aid	374UNTS133	105333
29 Jun	Kuwait	UN Special Fund	Tech Assistance	369UNTS419	200575
29 Jun	Australia	USSR (Soviet Union)	Postal Service	392UNTS131	105641
29 Jun	Peru	IBRD (World Bank)	IBRD Project	400UNTS99	105750
29 Jun	Honduras	IBRD (World Bank)	IBRD Project	400UNTS137	105751
29 Jun	Chile	USA (United States)	Direct Aid	377UNTS355	105411
30 Jun	Italy	USSR (Soviet Union)	Patents/Copyrights	62ITDI385	436423
01 Jul	Indonesia	USSR (Soviet Union)	Atomic Energy	9SUGG141	469670
01 Jul	Cuba	Poland	Tech Assistance	60PZUM71	458077
01 Jul	Italy	Somalia	General Amity	62ITGU148	435343
01 Jul	Italy	Somalia	General Economic	62ITGU148	435345
01 Jul	Italy	Somalia	Air Transport	62ITGU148	435347
01 Jul	Italy	Somalia	Consul/Citizenship	62ITGU148	435344
01 Jul	Germany, West	Japan	General Trade	60WBGA156	424750
01 Jul	Italy	Somalia	Admin Cooperation	62ITDI366	436346
02 Jul	Poland	UK Great Britain	Air Transport	385UNTS87	105532
04 Jul	Italy	UK Great Britain	Taxation	466UNTS195	106745
05 Jul	Ghana	UK Great Britain	Admin Cooperation	402UNTS17	105774
06 Jul	Norway	USA (United States)	Milit Assistance	378UNTS25	105415
07 Jul	Congo (Zaire)	USSR (Soviet Union)	Consul/Citizenship	9SUGG141	469671
07 Jul	Congo (Zaire)	USSR (Soviet Union)	Recognition	16SUGG128	469978
07 Jul	France	Israel	Visas	413UNTS79	105942
07 Jul	Italy	USA (United States)	Milit Assistance	380UNTS143	105455
07 Jul	Israel	Thailand	Visas	377UNTS325	105409
07 Jul	Denmark	USA (United States)	Air Transport	380UNTS39	105449
08 Jul	United Arab Rep	USSR (Soviet Union)	Loans and Credits	9SUGG154	469720
08 Jul	Argentina	Spain	Health/Educ/Welfare	60SPBO508	460036
08 Jul	Germany, West	Libya	Direct Aid	61WBGA21	424414
08 Jul	Multilateral		Tech Assistance	366UNTS310	105220
08 Jul	Haiti	USA (United States)	Milit Assistance	380UNTS135	105454
09 Jul	Indonesia	USSR (Soviet Union)	General Trade	9SUGG141	469672
09 Jul	Indonesia	USSR (Soviet Union)	Tech Assistance	9SUGG142	469673
09 Jul	Germany, East	Hungary	Mass Media	8EGDA480	419457
11 Jul	Korea, North	USSR (Soviet Union)	Tech Assistance	9SUGG142	469674
11 Jul	France	Upper Volta	Recognition	60FRRT52	415214
11 Jul	France	Niger	Recognition	60FRRT52	415339
11 Jul	France	Ivory Coast	Recognition	60FRRT52	415138
11 Jul	Dahomey	France	Recognition	60FRRT52	415145
12 Jul	France	USSR (Soviet Union)	Culture	9SUGG142	469675
12 Jul	Congo (Brazzaville)	France	Recognition	60FRRT50	415121
12 Jul	Central Afri Rep	France	Recognition	60FRRT50	415110
12 Jul	Chad	France	Recognition	60FRRT50	415426
12 Jul	Spain	UK Great Britain	Culture	414UNTS123	105971
13 Jul	ITU (Telecommun)	UN Special Fund	IGO Operations	368UNTS329	200573
13 Jul	Ethiopia	United Nations	Tech Assistance	368UNTS143	105239
13 Jul	Ethiopia	UN Special Fund	Tech Assistance	368UNTS159	105240
14 Jul	Germany, West	Luxembourg	Non-ILO Labor	63WGBB397	425425

DATE	PARTY ONE	PARTY TWO	TOPIC	CITATION	NUMBER
1960 (Cont.)					
14 Jul	Switzerland	United Arab Rep	Air Transport	497UNTS161	107268
14 Jul	Germany, West	UK Great Britain	Admin Cooperation	414UNTS144	105972
15 Jul	France	Germany, West	Specif Claim/Waive	61WGBB1029	425182
15 Jul	France	Gabon	Recognition	60FRRT51	415191
15 Jul	Peru	USA (United States)	Military Mission	384UNTS159	105517
15 Jul	Cambodia	USA (United States)	Admin Cooperation	380UNTS129	105453
16 Jul	Chile	USA (United States)	Milit Assistance	393UNTS271	105661
16 Jul	Poland	USA (United States)	Specif Claim/Waive	384UNTS169	105518
19 Jul	Albania	USSR (Soviet Union)	Tech Assistance	9SUGG142	469676
19 Jul	Italy	USA (United States)	Direct Aid	389UNTS237	105595
19 Jul	Belgium	Fed of Malaya	Visas	379UNTS391	105445
20 Jul	Denmark	USSR (Soviet Union)	Consul/Citizenship	16SUGG128	469979
20 Jul	Germany, West	Togo	Water Transport	60WBGA237	424659
20 Jul	Germany, West	Togo	Direct Aid	60WBGA243	424660
20 Jul	Germany, West	Pakistan	Air Transport	465UNTS41	106721
21 Jul	USSR (Soviet Union)	Yugoslavia	Consul/Citizenship	9SUGG142	469677
21 Jul	Netherlands	Poland	Air Transport	497UNTS189	107269
21 Jul	Spain	USA (United States)	Milit Assistance	393UNTS289	105663
21 Jul	Poland	USA (United States)	US Agri Commod Aid	380UNTS157	105456
21 Jul	Japan	Luxembourg	Visas	384UNTS55	105510
22 Jul	Bulgaria	USSR (Soviet Union)	Tech Assistance	9SUGG143	469678
22 Jul	USA (United States)	Uruguay	Education	388UNTS315	105587
23 Jul	China People's Rep	Cuba	Culture	60CCJC83	410714
23 Jul	China People's Rep	Cuba	General Economic	60CCJC81	410712
23 Jul	China People's Rep	Cuba	Tech Assistance	60CCJC82	410713
25 Jul	France	Greece	General Aid	533UNTS227	107745
26 Jul	Iran	USA (United States)	US Agri Commod Aid	384UNTS141	105516
27 Jul	Indonesia	Philippines	Admin Cooperation	4PTS349	465044
27 Jul	Italy	Yugoslavia	Land Transport	6ITGU6	435024
28 Jul	Multilateral		IGO Establishment	485UNTS3	107042
28 Jul	Multilateral		IGO Status/Immunit	394UNTS37	105667
28 Jul	Sweden	UK Great Britain	Taxation	404UNTS113	105808
28 Jul	Sweden	UK Great Britain	Taxation	404UNTS85	105806
29 Jul	Germany, East	USSR (Soviet Union)	Specif Goods/Equip	8EGDA577	419416
29 Jul	El Salvador	IBRD (World Bank)	IBRD Project	390UNTS101	105605
29 Jul	Chile	USA (United States)	Admin Cooperation	405UNTS127	105829
29 Jul	Multilateral		Water Transport	392UNTS69	105640
29 Jul	India	IBRD (World Bank)	IBRD Project	377UNTS153	105399
30 Jul	India	Switzerland	Finance	60SWRO1678	462140
30 Jul	Brazil	Greece	General Trade	607UNTS245	108808
30 Jul	Ghana	Netherlands	Air Transport	412UNTS51	105925
30 Jul	Japan	Pakistan	Education	384UNTS63	105511
01 Aug	Argentina	Italy	Taxation	63ITGU9	435021
01 Aug	United Arab Rep	USA (United States)	US Agri Commod Aid	384UNTS189	105519
02 Aug	USSR (Soviet Union)	Vietnam, North	Tech Assistance	9SUGG143	469680
02 Aug	Chile	Italy	General Aid	62ITDI320	436087
02 Aug	Accept UN Charter	Dahomey	UN Charter	375UNTS91	105357
02 Aug	Argentina	USA (United States)	Military Mission	384UNTS105	105514
03 Aug	Austria	Bolivia	Visas	60ABGB216	403006
03 Aug	WHO (World Health)	United Arab Rep	Tech Assistance	385UNTS3	105524
03 Aug	Jordan	WHO (World Health)	Tech Assistance	381UNTS133	105469
04 Aug	Italy	USA (United States)	Admin Cooperation	62ITDI376	436357
04 Aug	Ghana	USSR (Soviet Union)	General Aid	399UNTS61	105734
04 Aug	Ghana	USSR (Soviet Union)	General Trade	421UNTS27	106050
04 Aug	WHO (World Health)	Tunisia	Tech Assistance	381UNTS335	105474
04 Aug	Laos	WHO (World Health)	Tech Assistance	373UNTS313	105322
05 Aug	Canada	UK Great Britain	Milit Installation	470UNTS133	106804
06 Aug	Italy	Netherlands	Non-ILO Labor	455UNTS259	106546
07 Aug	Accept UN Charter	Niger	UN Charter	375UNTS95	105358
07 Aug	Accept UN Charter	Ivory Coast	UN Charter	375UNTS103	105360
07 Aug	Accept UN Charter	Upper Volta	UN Charter	375UNTS99	105359
08 Aug	Germany, East	Morocco	Finance	8EGDA401	419207
09 Aug	Guatemala	USA (United States)	Finance	461UNTS15	106648
09 Aug	United Arab Rep	USA (United States)	US Agri Commod Aid	388UNTS271	105584
11 Aug	United Arab Rep	USSR (Soviet Union)	Tech Assistance	9SUGG144	469681

DATE	PARTY ONE	PARTY TWO	TOPIC	CITATION	NUMBER
1960 (Cont.)					
11 Aug	Chad	France	General Amity	60FRRT76	415427
12 Aug	Afghanistan	USSR (Soviet Union)	General Trade	9SUGG144	469682
12 Aug	Nepal	USSR (Soviet Union)	Tech Assistance	9SUGG144	469683
12 Aug	Accept UN Charter	Chad	UN Charter	375UNTS107	105361
12 Aug	Netherlands	UN Special Fund	Tech Assistance	372UNTS331	105309
12 Aug	Accept UN Charter	Congo (Brazzaville)	UN Charter	375UNTS111	105362
13 Aug	Central Afri Rep	France	General Amity	60FRRT76	415111
13 Aug	Accept UN Charter	Central Afri Rep	UN Charter	375UNTS115	105363
15 Aug	Congo (Brazzaville)	France	General Military	60FRRT76	415122
15 Aug	Mexico	USA (United States)	Air Transport	402UNTS177	105786
16 Aug	Multilateral		General Amity	397UNTS287	105712
16 Aug	Germany, West	USA (United States)	Claims and Debts	418UNTS235	106024
16 Aug	Multilateral		Recognition	382UNTS3	105475
16 Aug	Multilateral		Recognition	382UNTS8	105476
16 Aug	Cyprus	UK Great Britain	Customs	382UNTS215	105482
16 Aug	Cyprus	UK Great Britain	Consul/Citizenship	382UNTS247	105486
16 Aug	Cyprus	UK Great Britain	Specific Property	382UNTS177	105477
16 Aug	Cyprus	UK Great Britain	Privil/Immunities	382UNTS225	105483
16 Aug	Cyprus	UK Great Britain	Dispute Settlement	382UNTS183	105478
16 Aug	Cyprus	UK Great Britain	Direct Aid	382UNTS231	105484
16 Aug	Cyprus	UK Great Britain	Specific Property	382UNTS207	105481
16 Aug	Cyprus	UK Great Britain	Claims and Debts	382UNTS239	105485
16 Aug	Cyprus	UK Great Britain	Specific Property	382UNTS201	105480
16 Aug	Cyprus	UK Great Britain	Specific Property	382UNTS189	105479
17 Aug	Guinea	USSR (Soviet Union)	Consul/Citizenship	16SUGG128	469980
17 Aug	France	Gabon	General Amity	60FRRT77	415192
17 Aug	Belgium	Burma	Air Transport	540UNTS185	107850
17 Aug	Korea, South	USA (United States)	Postal Service	400UNTS339	105757
18 Aug	Iraq	USSR (Soviet Union)	Loans and Credits	9SUGG144	469684
18 Aug	Cyprus	USSR (Soviet Union)	Recognition	16SUGG128	469981
19 Aug	Panama	IBRD (World Bank)	IBRD Project	390UNTS153	105607
22 Aug	India	USSR (Soviet Union)	Education	9SUGG145	469685
23 Aug	Congo (Zaire)	United Nations	Direct Aid	373UNTS327	200576
23 Aug	Australia	USA (United States)	General Military	388UNTS237	105581
24 Aug	Japan	Thailand	Education	384UNTS73	105512
24 Aug	Canada	USA (United States)	Scientific Project	388UNTS225	105580
25 Aug	Ghana	USSR (Soviet Union)	Culture	9SUGG145	469686
26 Aug	USSR (Soviet Union)	Vietnam, North	General Aid	9SUGG145	469687
26 Aug	Burma	Germany, East	Consul/Citizenship	45EGDZ255	420074
26 Aug	Afghanistan	China People's Rep	General Amity	60CCJC88	410716
27 Aug	United Arab Rep	USSR (Soviet Union)	Tech Assistance	399UNTS37	105733
29 Aug	Cambodia	Germany, East	Tech Assistance	8EGDA371	419167
29 Aug	Cambodia	Germany, East	General Trade	8EGDA371	419165
29 Aug	Cambodia	Germany, East	Finance	8EGDA372	419166
29 Aug	Cuba	Korea, North	Culture	473UNTS117	106860
29 Aug	Cuba	Korea, North	Consul/Citizenship	469UNTS163	106790
29 Aug	Ghana	United Arab Rep	Air Transport	412UNTS71	105926
30 Aug	Germany, East	USSR (Soviet Union)	Education	9SUGG146	469688
30 Aug	Taiwan	USA (United States)	US Agri Commod Aid	388UNTS191	105579
31 Aug	Korea, North	USSR (Soviet Union)	Tech Assistance	9SUGG146	469690
31 Aug	Albania	USSR (Soviet Union)	Tech Assistance	9SUGG146	469689
31 Aug	Canada	USA (United States)	Milit Assistance	393UNTS247	105659
31 Aug	Israel	UK Great Britain	Culture	385UNTS71	105530
01 Sep	Multilateral		Commodity Trade	403UNTS3	105792
01 Sep	Haiti	USA (United States)	Milit Assistance	388UNTS249	105582
02 Sep	Italy	Peru	Visas	62ITDI363	436299
05 Sep	El Salvador	Israel	Visas	413UNTS73	105941
06 Sep	WHO (World Health)	Saudi Arabia	Tech Assistance	395UNTS169	105684
06 Sep	Liberia	USA (United States)	Admin Cooperation	389UNTS245	105596
06 Sep	Sweden	Tunisia	Taxation	427UNTS301	106162
07 Sep	Argentina	Bolivia	Land Transport	0UNTS0	109516
08 Sep	Guinea	USSR (Soviet Union)	General Trade	9SUGG147	469691
08 Sep	Lebanon	WHO (World Health)	Tech Assistance	387UNTS49	105557
09 Sep	Mongolia	USSR (Soviet Union)	General Aid	9SUGG147	469692
09 Sep	Israel	IBRD (World Bank)	IBRD Project	406UNTS3	105837

DATE	PARTY ONE	PARTY TWO	TOPIC	CITATION	NUMBER
1960 (Cont.)					
09 Sep	New Zealand	Yugoslavia	General Trade	402UNTS119	105781
10 Sep	Czechoslovakia	Poland	General Economic	60PZUM110	458078
11 Sep	Somalia	USSR (Soviet Union)	Consul/Citizenship	9SUGG149	469701
12 Sep	ICJ Option Clause	Pakistan	ICJ Option Clause	374UNTS127	105332
12 Sep	Iran	Japan	Education	384UNTS43	105509
13 Sep	Poland	USSR (Soviet Union)	Tech Assistance	9SUGG148	469693
13 Sep	Poland	USSR (Soviet Union)	Tech Assistance	9SUGG148	469694
13 Sep	China People's Rep	Guinea	Direct Aid	60CCJC94	410718
13 Sep	China People's Rep	Guinea	General Amity	60CCJC93	410717
13 Sep	China People's Rep	Guinea	General Trade	60CCJC95	410719
13 Sep	South Africa	USA (United States)	Specific Property	388UNTS65	105572
14 Sep	France	Italy	General Ad Hoc	61ITDI213	436153
14 Sep	Multilateral		IGO Establishment	443UNTS247	106363
14 Sep	Austria	Czechoslovakia	Commodity Trade	495UNTS143	107243
16 Sep	Brazil	UN Special Fund	Tech Assistance	375UNTS3	105351
19 Sep	Afghanistan	Poland	Tech Assistance	60PZUM116	458079
19 Sep	Malaysia	Norway	Visas	3NORT812	451113
19 Sep	France	Senegal	Admin Cooperation	61FRRT22	415389
19 Sep	Pakistan	IBRD (World Bank)	IBRD Project	444UNTS207	106370
19 Sep	Czechoslovakia	India	Air Transport	465UNTS67	106722
19 Sep	Multilateral		IBRD Project	444UNTS259	106371
19 Sep	Multilateral		IBRD Project	419UNTS125	106032
19 Sep	France	USA (United States)	Milit Assistance	400UNTS21	105745
20 Sep	Argentina	Germany, West	Air Transport	61WGBB1045	425008
20 Sep	France	Morocco	Health/Educ/Welfare	60FRRT80	415298
20 Sep	Colombia	IBRD (World Bank)	IBRD Project	390UNTS173	105608
20 Sep	Taiwan	UN Special Fund	Tech Assistance	375UNTS29	105352
20 Sep	Accept UN Charter	Senegal	UN Charter	376UNTS79	105374
21 Sep	Multilateral		Patents/Copyrights	394UNTS3	105664
22 Sep	Bulgaria	USSR (Soviet Union)	Education	16SUGG129	469982
22 Sep	Turkey	Yugoslavia	Sanitation	61TURG504	466041
22 Sep	Czechoslovakia	Italy	Finance	62ITDI470	436079
23 Sep	Belgium	Ireland	Commodity Trade	557UNTS180	108134
26 Sep	Portugal	USA (United States)	Milit Assistance	393UNTS257	105660
27 Sep	Mongolia	USSR (Soviet Union)	Tech Assistance	9SUGG148	469697
27 Sep	Germany, East	USSR (Soviet Union)	Tech Assistance	9SUGG148	469695
27 Sep	Mongolia	USSR (Soviet Union)	Tech Assistance	9SUGG148	469696
27 Sep	Ecuador	USA (United States)	US Agri Commod Aid	401UNTS115	105766
28 Sep	France	Switzerland	Customs	61SWRO574	462074
28 Sep	Belgium	Germany, West	Specif Claim/Waive	61WGBB2640	425029
28 Sep	France	Switzerland	General Transport	0UNTS0	110716
29 Sep	Poland	USSR (Soviet Union)	Commodity Trade	9SUGG148	469698
30 Sep	Korea, North	USSR (Soviet Union)	Tech Assistance	9SUGG148	469700
30 Sep	USSR (Soviet Union)	Vietnam, North	Tech Assistance	9SUGG148	469699
30 Sep	Netherlands	Romania	General Economic	479UNTS91	106948
30 Sep	Guinea	USA (United States)	General Aid	394UNTS103	105671
30 Sep	Ceylon (Sri Lanka)	USA (United States)	US Agri Commod Aid	389UNTS[illegible]21	105594
01 Oct	Burma	China People's Rep	Territory Boundary	60CCJC9[illegible]	410722
01 Oct	Burma	China People's Rep	Territory Boundary	60CCJC98	410721
01 Oct	Nigeria	UK Great Britain	Recognition	384UNTS207	105520
03 Oct	Mongolia	USSR (Soviet Union)	Education	16SUGG129	469983
06 Oct	Multilateral		Customs	473UNTS131	106861
06 Oct	Paraguay	USA (United States)	Gen Communications	393UNTS281	105662
07 Oct	Laos	USSR (Soviet Union)	Consul/Citizenship	9SUGG149	469702
07 Oct	Indonesia	UN Special Fund	Direct Aid	378UNTS141	105424
07 Oct	Japan	UK Great Britain	Reparations	384UNTS89	105513
08 Oct	Mongolia	USSR (Soviet Union)	Education	9SUGG149	469704
08 Oct	Bulgaria	USSR (Soviet Union)	Tech Assistance	9SUGG149	469703
08 Oct	Multilateral		General Trade	450UNTS309	106476
11 Oct	Colombia	Germany, West	Culture	65WGBB1948	425370
11 Oct	Iran	Japan	General Economic	0IRTB45	433066
11 Oct	Liberia	UN Special Fund	Direct Aid	376UNTS341	105388
13 Oct	Korea, North	USSR (Soviet Union)	Finance	9SUGG149	469705
13 Oct	Brazil	Spain	Visas	0UNTS0	109416
13 Oct	Belgium	Tunisia	Visas	421UNTS71	106052

DATE	PARTY ONE	PARTY TWO	TOPIC	CITATION	NUMBER
1960 (Cont.)					
14 Oct	Indonesia	USSR (Soviet Union)	Non-IBRD Project	9SUGG150	469706
14 Oct	Mali	USSR (Soviet Union)	Recognition	16SUGG129	469984
14 Oct	UK Great Britain	USA (United States)	Scientific Project	398UNTS165	105721
17 Oct	Nicaragua	Norway	Visas	3NORT815	451120
17 Oct	United Nations	United Arab Rep	Specif Claim/Waive	388UNTS143	105575
18 Oct	Mexico	IBRD (World Bank)	IBRD Project	422UNTS177	106075
19 Oct	France	Mauritania	Recognition	60FRRT75	415311
19 Oct	Belgium	Jordan	Air Transport	479UNTS277	106959
19 Oct	Nigeria	USA (United States)	Scientific Project	394UNTS113	105672
21 Oct	Chile	UK Great Britain	Loans and Credits	385UNTS15	105525
22 Oct	Accept UN Charter	Mali	UN Charter	377UNTS361	105412
24 Oct	Germany, West	Spain	Non-ILO Labor	61SPBO710	460026
24 Oct	Mexico	USA (United States)	Specific Property	401UNTS137	105767
24 Oct	El Salvador	UN Special Fund	Direct Aid	377UNTS171	105400
25 Oct	Hungary	UK Great Britain	Air Transport	419UNTS309	106034
28 Oct	Cuba	Romania	Culture	457UNTS9	106574
28 Oct	USA (United States)	Vietnam, South	US Agri Commod Aid	401UNTS3	105758
28 Oct	India	IBRD (World Bank)	IBRD Project	406UNTS27	105838
28 Oct	Chile	USA (United States)	Direct Aid	401UNTS177	105770
31 Oct	Kuwait	United Nations	Tech Assistance	391UNTS295	200581
31 Oct	Burma	Switzerland	Air Transport	465UNTS97	106723
31 Oct	Portugal	USA (United States)	Patents/Copyrights	394UNTS127	105673
31 Oct	Panama	USA (United States)	Admin Cooperation	405UNTS63	105823
02 Nov	Norway	Peru	Air Transport	497UNTS207	107270
02 Nov	Accept UN Charter	Gabon	UN Charter	379UNTS99	105436
04 Nov	Hungary	USSR (Soviet Union)	Education	16SUGG129	469985
04 Nov	France	USA (United States)	US Agri Commod Aid	400UNTS323	105756
04 Nov	Czechoslovakia	Hungary	Consul/Citizenship	397UNTS227	105708
05 Nov	Indonesia	USA (United States)	US Agri Commod Aid	400UNTS35	105746
07 Nov	Greece	USA (United States)	US Agri Commod Aid	400UNTS57	105748
08 Nov	Greece	Poland	General Trade	483UNTS127	107010
08 Nov	Greece	Poland	Finance	483UNTS141	107011
08 Nov	Chile	USA (United States)	US Agri Commod Aid	405UNTS85	105825
08 Nov	Czechoslovakia	Germany, East	Admin Cooperation	424UNTS71	106100
10 Nov	Australia	Italy	Air Transport	497UNTS247	107271
10 Nov	Denmark	Germany, West	Consul/Citizenship	431UNTS21	106205
10 Nov	Romania	UK Great Britain	Finance	385UNTS113	105533
11 Nov	Romania	USSR (Soviet Union)	Tech Assistance	9SUGG151	469710
11 Nov	Romania	USSR (Soviet Union)	General Trade	9SUGG151	469707
11 Nov	Korea, South	Philippines	Visas	490UNTS249	107159
13 Nov	Afghanistan	USSR (Soviet Union)	Tech Assistance	9SUGG151	469708
13 Nov	Cyprus	USSR (Soviet Union)	Consul/Citizenship	9SUGG151	469709
13 Nov	Cameroon	France	General Amity	61FRRT29	415099
13 Nov	Cameroon	France	Military Mission	0UNTS0	110640
13 Nov	Cameroon	France	Military Mission	0UNTS0	110641
13 Nov	Cameroon	France	General Amity	0UNTS0	110634
13 Nov	Cameroon	France	Air Transport	0UNTS0	110642
13 Nov	Cameroon	France	General Economic	0UNTS0	110638
13 Nov	Cameroon	France	Admin Cooperation	0UNTS0	110637
13 Nov	Cameroon	France	Admin Cooperation	0UNTS0	110643
13 Nov	Cameroon	France	General Economic	0UNTS0	110639
13 Nov	Cameroon	France	Consul/Citizenship	0UNTS0	110635
13 Nov	Cameroon	France	Culture	0UNTS0	110636
14 Nov	Mongolia	USSR (Soviet Union)	Tech Assistance	9SUGG151	469711
14 Nov	Brazil	Japan	Consul/Citizenship	518UNTS29	107491
14 Nov	Czechoslovakia	Poland	Sanitation	413UNTS4	105938
15 Nov	Morocco	USSR (Soviet Union)	Milit Assistance	9SUGG151	469712
15 Nov	UNICEF (Children)	Upper Volta	Direct Aid	402UNTS33	105776
15 Nov	Belgium	Congo (Zaire)	Finance	394UNTS79	105670
15 Nov	Finland	Norway	Specific Resources	383UNTS159	105501
15 Nov	WHO (World Health)	Upper Volta	Tech Assistance	383UNTS91	105496
16 Nov	Cuba	USSR (Soviet Union)	Education	9SUGG152	469714
16 Nov	Cuba	USSR (Soviet Union)	Tech Assistance	9SUGG152	469713
17 Nov	Mali	UNICEF (Children)	Direct Aid	402UNTS23	105775
17 Nov	Norway	UK Great Britain	Specific Resources	398UNTS189	105723

DATE	PARTY ONE	PARTY TWO	TOPIC	CITATION	NUMBER
1960 (Cont.)					
17 Nov	Pakistan	United Nations	Tech Assistance	380UNTS277	105460
17 Nov	Nepal	UN Special Fund	Direct Aid	380UNTS289	105461
17 Nov	Guatemala	UN Special Fund	Direct Aid	383UNTS67	105495
18 Nov	Korea, South	USA (United States)	Atomic Energy	400UNTS49	105747
21 Nov	Netherlands	Paraguay	Visas	450UNTS201	106467
21 Nov	Finland	Sweden	Territory Boundary	383UNTS125	105498
21 Nov	Belgium	Paraguay	Visas	387UNTS237	105565
23 Nov	Argentina	Uruguay	Non-IBRD Project	0UNTS0	109519
23 Nov	Indonesia	UK Great Britain	Air Transport	398UNTS71	105718
23 Nov	Czechoslovakia	Ghana	Culture	431UNTS91	106213
23 Nov	Czechoslovakia	Ghana	Tech Assistance	431UNTS85	106212
24 Nov	Finland	USSR (Soviet Union)	Customs	9SUGG152	469715
24 Nov	IAEA (Atom Energy)	OECD (Econ Coop)	IGO Operations	396UNTS273	200585
24 Nov	Israel	Mali	Tech Assistance	413UNTS95	105944
24 Nov	Israel	Mali	Culture	413UNTS104	105945
24 Nov	Cambodia	UN Special Fund	Direct Aid	382UNTS255	105487
25 Nov	Italy	Morocco	Visas	62ITDI356	436270
25 Nov	Fed of Malaya	WHO (World Health)	Tech Assistance	387UNTS37	105556
26 Nov	Czechoslovakia	Germany, East	Specific Property	8EGDA452	419363
26 Nov	Multilateral		Taxation	500UNTS25	107304
27 Nov	Italy	Poland	Scientific Project	58PZUM132	458080
27 Nov	Italy	Poland	Tech Assistance	62ITDI437	436305
27 Nov	Cambodia	Czechoslovakia	Culture	410UNTS263	105910
27 Nov	Cambodia	Czechoslovakia	General Amity	412UNTS179	105931
28 Nov	Brazil	Italy	Consul/Citizenship	62ITDI468	436064
28 Nov	China People's Rep	Vietnam, North	Scientific Project	60CCJC118	410735
29 Nov	Bulgaria	USSR (Soviet Union)	Tech Assistance	9SUGG152	469716
29 Nov	Norway	USA (United States)	Milit Assistance	404UNTS251	105815
30 Nov	Bulgaria	USSR (Soviet Union)	General Aid	9SUGG153	469717
30 Nov	Bulgaria	USSR (Soviet Union)	Tech Assistance	9SUGG153	469718
30 Nov	China People's Rep	Cuba	Direct Aid	60CCJC122	410737
30 Nov	Cambodia	United Nations	Tech Assistance	383UNTS147	105500
01 Dec	Luxembourg	USSR (Soviet Union)	Consul/Citizenship	10SUGG118	469736
01 Dec	Japan	Pakistan	Visas	450UNTS337	106477
01 Dec	Multilateral		Scientific Project	414UNTS110	105970
02 Dec	Germany, East	Yugoslavia	General Economic	8EGDA364	419148
02 Dec	Denmark	USA (United States)	Milit Installation	402UNTS245	105789
02 Dec	Norway	IBRD (World Bank)	IBRD Project	390UNTS131	105606
03 Dec	Italy	Yugoslavia	Consul/Citizenship	63ITGU15	435242
03 Dec	Italy	Yugoslavia	Admin Cooperation	62ITGU237	435243
03 Dec	Italy	Yugoslavia	Culture	63ITGU30	435241
03 Dec	WHO (World Health)	Yemen	Tech Assistance	395UNTS187	105685
03 Dec	Italy	USA (United States)	Atomic Energy	410UNTS3	105893
03 Dec	Japan	UK Great Britain	Culture	414UNTS61	105966
06 Dec	Philippines	USA (United States)	Other Economic	4PTS371	465045
06 Dec	Bolivia	Italy	Visas	62ITDI317	436053
07 Dec	Central Afri Rep	USSR (Soviet Union)	Consul/Citizenship	9SUGG154	469721
07 Dec	Dahomey	WHO (World Health)	Tech Assistance	387UNTS277	105567
08 Dec	Romania	USSR (Soviet Union)	Education	16SUGG129	469986
08 Dec	Council of Europe	ILO (Labor Org)	IGO Operations	389UNTS291	200579
08 Dec	Netherlands	United Arab Rep	Culture	455UNTS276	106547
08 Dec	Cyprus	USA (United States)	Direct Aid	405UNTS145	105831
09 Dec	Japan	Philippines	General Amity	4PTS383	465046
09 Dec	Brazil	Italy	Health/Educ/Welfare	63ITGU109	435065
09 Dec	Argentina	Bolivia	General Trade	0UNTS0	109549
09 Dec	Romania	USA (United States)	Culture	401UNTS19	105759
09 Dec	Multilateral		Customs	429UNTS211	106200
10 Dec	Afghanistan	Italy	Tech Assistance	63ITGU9	435002
11 Dec	Libya	USA (United States)	Health/Educ/Welfare	445UNTS125	106381
12 Dec	Cuba	USSR (Soviet Union)	Culture	421UNTS3	106048
12 Dec	Congo (Brazzaville)	WHO (World Health)	Tech Assistance	399UNTS105	105737
12 Dec	Nepal	UNICEF (Children)	Direct Aid	382UNTS273	105488
13 Dec	Austria	USSR (Soviet Union)	General Trade	9SUGG154	469722
13 Dec	Multilateral		General Economic	455UNTS3	106543
13 Dec	Multilateral		IGO Establishment	455UNTS204	106544

DATE	PARTY ONE	PARTY TWO	TOPIC	CITATION	NUMBER
1960 (Cont.)					
13 Dec	Multilateral		Air Transport	523UNTS117	107557
14 Dec	Iran	Pakistan	Sanitation	OIRTB55	433085
14 Dec	Israel	Philippines	Visas	449UNTS23	106448
14 Dec	Multilateral		Education	429UNTS93	106193
14 Dec	Bolivia	United Nations	Tech Assistance	382UNTS283	105489
15 Dec	Czechoslovakia	Germany, East	Finance	8EGDA457	419364
15 Dec	Cambodia	Thailand	Extradition	382UNTS321	105493
15 Dec	Cambodia	Thailand	Mass Media	382UNTS301	105490
15 Dec	Cambodia	Thailand	Extradition	382UNTS315	105492
15 Dec	Cambodia	Thailand	Admin Cooperation	382UNTS307	105491
16 Dec	Austria	Switzerland	Admin Cooperation	62SWRO270	462029
17 Dec	Germany, West	Norway	Milit Installation	3NORT822	451189
17 Dec	Cuba	Germany, East	Tech Assistance	8EGDA397	419185
18 Dec	Japan	Pakistan	General Amity	423UNTS197	106093
19 Dec	Cuba	USSR (Soviet Union)	Education	9SUGG155	469724
19 Dec	Cuba	USSR (Soviet Union)	General Aid	9SUGG155	469723
19 Dec	Cambodia	China People's Rep	General Amity	60CCJC129	410741
19 Dec	Peru	IBRD (World Bank)	IBRD Project	417UNTS275	106010
19 Dec	Israel	USA (United States)	Direct Aid	401UNTS195	105772
20 Dec	Mongolia	USSR (Soviet Union)	General Trade	9SUGG156	469725
20 Dec	Italy	San Marino	Finance	62ITGU6	435311
20 Dec	Italy	San Marino	Reparations	62ITGU6	435332
20 Dec	Japan	IBRD (World Bank)	IBRD Project	400UNTS167	105752
20 Dec	Japan	IBRD (World Bank)	IBRD Project	400UNTS279	105754
20 Dec	Honduras	UN Special Fund	Direct Aid	383UNTS103	105497
21 Dec	Canada	Pakistan	Air Transport	465UNTS115	106724
22 Dec	Romania	USSR (Soviet Union)	Customs	16SUGG130	469987
22 Dec	Germany, West	Malaysia	Claims and Debts	62WGBB1064	425450
22 Dec	IMF (Fund)	United Nations	IGO Operations	384UNTS315	200578
22 Dec	Inter-Am Nuc Energ	IAEA (Atom Energy)	IGO Operations	396UNTS285	200586
22 Dec	Cuba	Czechoslovakia	Culture	426UNTS145	106134
22 Dec	Togo	USA (United States)	Direct Aid	401UNTS33	105760
23 Dec	USSR (Soviet Union)	Vietnam, North	General Aid	9SUGG157	469726
23 Dec	USSR (Soviet Union)	Vietnam, North	General Trade	9SUGG157	469727
23 Dec	Thailand	USA (United States)	IGO Establishment	405UNTS135	105830
24 Dec	Korea, North	USSR (Soviet Union)	Tech Assistance	9SUGG158	469728
24 Dec	Korea, North	USSR (Soviet Union)	General Trade	9SUGG158	469729
24 Dec	Romania	USSR (Soviet Union)	Admin Cooperation	472UNTS245	106843
27 Dec	Brazil	Spain	Health/Educ/Welfare	64SPBO508	460060
27 Dec	Brazil	Spain	Health/Educ/Welfare	64SPBO508	460061
27 Dec	Brazil	Spain	Health/Educ/Welfare	64SPBO508	460059
27 Dec	Brazil	Spain	Visas	0UNTS0	109428
27 Dec	Kuwait	USA (United States)	Visas	401UNTS185	105771
28 Dec	Niger	WHO (World Health)	Tech Assistance	394UNTS195	105679
28 Dec	Korea, South	USA (United States)	US Agri Commod Aid	402UNTS3	105773
29 Dec	Luxembourg	Thailand	Air Transport	465UNTS131	106725
30 Dec	Multilateral		Atomic Energy	395UNTS241	105689
30 Dec	Finland	IAEA (Atom Energy)	Atomic Energy	395UNTS257	105690
30 Dec	Iceland	USA (United States)	Direct Aid	401UNTS43	105761
31 Dec	Turkey	USA (United States)	Loans and Credits	61TURG2407	466122
31 Dec	Bulgaria	USSR (Soviet Union)	Loans and Credits	9SUGG158	469730
31 Dec	Germany, East	USSR (Soviet Union)	General Economic	9SUGG159	469731
31 Dec	Germany, West	USSR (Soviet Union)	General Economic	61WBGA12	424644
1961					
03 Jan	Germany, West	USA (United States)	Admin Cooperation	416UNTS93	105997
03 Jan	Burma	UN Special Fund	Direct Aid	387UNTS219	105564
04 Jan	Albania	USSR (Soviet Union)	General Economic	10SUGG117	469732
04 Jan	Poland	USSR (Soviet Union)	Health/Educ/Welfare	10SUGG117	469733
04 Jan	Mali	USA (United States)	General Aid	405UNTS165	105832
05 Jan	IBRD (World Bank)	United Nations	IGO Operations	384UNTS303	200577
06 Jan	Indonesia	USSR (Soviet Union)	Milit Assistance	10SUGG117	469734
07 Jan	Poland	USSR (Soviet Union)	Direct Aid	10SUGG117	469735
09 Jan	Turkey	USA (United States)	General Economic	61TURG1707	466123
09 Jan	Saudi Arabia	Spain	General Amity	62SPBO606	460038

DATE	PARTY ONE	PARTY TWO	TOPIC	CITATION	NUMBER
1961 (Cont.)					
09 Jan	Burma	China People's Rep	Direct Aid	61CCJC2	410745
09 Jan	Burma	China People's Rep	Finance	61CCJC3	410746
09 Jan	Jordan	Sweden	Air Transport	465UNTS155	106726
09 Jan	UK Great Britain	USSR (Soviet Union)	Health/Educ/Welfare	404UNTS175	105810
10 Jan	Tunisia	USSR (Soviet Union)	Consul/Citizenship	16SUGG130	469988
10 Jan	Italy	Pakistan	General Trade	62ITDI516	436290
10 Jan	Costa Rica	UN Special Fund	Direct Aid	389UNTS253	105597
11 Jan	Albania	Germany, East	General Trade	9EGDA309	419022
11 Jan	Turkey	USA (United States)	US Agri Commod Aid	405UNTS173	105833
12 Jan	Nigeria	USSR (Soviet Union)	Recognition	16SUGG130	469989
12 Jan	UK Great Britain	USSR (Soviet Union)	Culture	398UNTS157	105720
13 Jan	Albania	Germany, East	Sanitation	9EGDA310	419023
13 Jan	Brazil	USA (United States)	Extradition	532UNTS177	107718
13 Jan	Ethiopia	USSR (Soviet Union)	Culture	421UNTS13	106049
13 Jan	Canada	USA (United States)	Postal Service	410UNTS62	105897
16 Jan	Albania	Cuba	General Trade	448UNTS67	106425
16 Jan	Sudan	UK Great Britain	Air Transport	424UNTS233	106112
16 Jan	Mexico	IBRD (World Bank)	IBRD Project	422UNTS203	106076
16 Jan	Burma	IBRD (World Bank)	IBRD Project	400UNTS73	105749
17 Jan	Austria	Czechoslovakia	Customs	61ABGB222	403023
17 Jan	Austria	Hungary	Customs	61ABGB42	403091
17 Jan	Ghana	Poland	Culture	572UNTS209	108314
17 Jan	Canada	USA (United States)	Specific Resources	542UNTS224	107894
17 Jan	Tunisia	UK Great Britain	General Trade	566UNTS2	108236
17 Jan	Denmark	Poland	Air Transport	412UNTS111	105927
17 Jan	Norway	Poland	Air Transport	412UNTS130	105928
18 Jan	Bulgaria	USSR (Soviet Union)	General Trade	10SUGG118	469737
18 Jan	Germany, East	Poland	Specific Property	9EGDA379	419267
18 Jan	Germany, West	Japan	Air Transport	465UNTS173	106727
18 Jan	Honduras	USA (United States)	General Trade	402UNTS169	105785
19 Jan	USA (United States)	Yugoslavia	General Aid	402UNTS163	105784
19 Jan	UN Special Fund	Saudi Arabia	Direct Aid	396UNTS27	105692
20 Jan	Korea, South	WHO (World Health)	Tech Assistance	406UNTS269	200589
20 Jan	UK Great Britain	USA (United States)	Scientific Project	402UNTS153	105783
20 Jan	Nicaragua	UN Special Fund	Direct Aid	387UNTS15	105555
21 Jan	Turkey	USA (United States)	Loans and Credits	61TURG2407	466124
23 Jan	Greece	USSR (Soviet Union)	Postal Service	16SUGG130	469990
23 Jan	Brazil	Japan	Culture	569UNTS81	108281
23 Jan	Multilateral		Postal Service	530UNTS141	107679
23 Jan	Panama	USA (United States)	Admin Cooperation	445UNTS135	106382
23 Jan	Chad	UN Special Fund	Direct Aid	390UNTS69	105603
24 Jan	Norway	Uruguay	Visas	3NORT824	451198
24 Jan	Italy	Netherlands	Milit Servic/Citiz	450UNTS207	106468
25 Jan	France	Spain	Non-ILO Labor	62SPBO2103	460132
25 Jan	France	Spain	Non-ILO Labor	61SPBO2802	460131
25 Jan	Italy	New Zealand	Visas	435UNTS255	106282
26 Jan	Euratom	ILO (Labor Org)	IGO Operations	390UNTS323	200580
27 Jan	USSR (Soviet Union)	Vietnam, North	Direct Aid	10SUGG119	469738
27 Jan	Burma	China People's Rep	General Trade	61CCJC6	410749
28 Jan	France	Vietnam, South	Atomic Energy	0VKNG159	496047
28 Jan	Italy	Morocco	General Trade	62ITDI511	436271
28 Jan	UN Special Fund	Somalia	Direct Aid	388UNTS75	105573
28 Jan	Multilateral		Tech Assistance	387UNTS202	105563
30 Jan	Indonesia	Philippines	General Military	4PTS425	465047
30 Jan	Ivory Coast	WHO (World Health)	Tech Assistance	395UNTS205	105686
31 Jan	China People's Rep	Vietnam, North	Land Transport	61CCJC12	410753
01 Feb	Ghana	USSR (Soviet Union)	Specif Goods/Equip	10SUGG120	469739
01 Feb	France	Korea, South	Patents/Copyrights	61FRRT11	415130
02 Feb	Albania	China People's Rep	Loans and Credits	61CCJC18	410756
02 Feb	Albania	China People's Rep	General Trade	61CCJC17	410755
02 Feb	Albania	China People's Rep	General Amity	61CCJC16	410754
02 Feb	Gabon	UN Special Fund	Direct Aid	387UNTS289	105568
02 Feb	New Zealand	United Nations	Humanitarian	391UNTS23	105614
03 Feb	Finland	USSR (Soviet Union)	Specific Property	10SUGG120	469740
03 Feb	Malaysia	New Zealand	General Trade	447UNTS251	106418

DATE	PARTY ONE	PARTY TWO	TOPIC	CITATION	NUMBER
1961 (Cont.)					
03 Feb	Chad	WHO (World Health)	Tech Assistance	394UNTS161	105676
03 Feb	Costa Rica	IBRD (World Bank)	IBRD Project	414UNTS314	105977
03 Feb	WHO (World Health)	Togo	Tech Assistance	394UNTS207	105680
04 Feb	Somalia	USA (United States)	Tech Assistance	433UNTS179	106241
05 Feb	China People's Rep	United Arab Rep	General Trade	61CCJC23	410758
05 Feb	Poland	USSR (Soviet Union)	Territory Boundary	420UNTS161	106046
07 Feb	Turkey	USA (United States)	Atomic Energy	61TURG509	466040
07 Feb	Australia	Japan	Postal Service	450UNTS343	106478
07 Feb	India	USA (United States)	Scientific Project	462UNTS57	106671
08 Feb	Korea, South	USA (United States)	General Aid	405UNTS37	105821
09 Feb	Germany, East	Vietnam, North	General Economic	9EGDA448	419494
09 Feb	Netherlands	Yugoslavia	Claims and Debts	453UNTS221	106526
09 Feb	Iceland	UK Great Britain	Visas	398UNTS259	105728
09 Feb	Bolivia	USA (United States)	Milit Assistance	405UNTS113	105827
10 Feb	Italy	Morocco	Tech Assistance	62ITDI513	436272
10 Feb	UK Great Britain	USA (United States)	Milit Installation	409UNTS68	105879
10 Feb	UK Great Britain	USA (United States)	Milit Installation	409UNTS129	105880
10 Feb	Nigeria	UN Special Fund	Direct Aid	390UNTS85	105604
11 Feb	France	Vietnam, South	Culture	0VKNG160	496048
11 Feb	Guinea	WHO (World Health)	Tech Assistance	394UNTS173	105677
11 Feb	Accept UN Charter	Somalia	UN Charter	388UNTS179	105577
13 Feb	Multilateral		ILO Labor	0UNTSO	110306
13 Feb	Peru	USA (United States)	Visas	406UNTS177	105848
13 Feb	Central Afri Rep	WHO (World Health)	Tech Assistance	394UNTS149	105675
14 Feb	France	UK Great Britain	Visas	398UNTS267	105729
15 Feb	Korea, North	USSR (Soviet Union)	Education	16SUGG130	469991
15 Feb	Poland	USSR (Soviet Union)	Admin Cooperation	10SUGG121	469741
15 Feb	Spain	UK Great Britain	Visas	404UNTS75	105805
15 Feb	Afghanistan	USA (United States)	Mass Media	406UNTS235	105852
16 Feb	Germany, East	Indonesia	Commodity Trade	9EGDA351	419135
16 Feb	Germany, East	Indonesia	Health/Educ/Welfare	9EGDA350	419134
16 Feb	Germany, East	Indonesia	General Trade	9EGDA350	419133
16 Feb	Germany, East	Indonesia	Water Transport	9EGDA351	419136
17 Feb	Germany, East	Romania	General Trade	9EGDA388	419297
17 Feb	Canada	USA (United States)	Taxation	445UNTS143	106383
18 Feb	Bulgaria	USSR (Soviet Union)	Tech Assistance	10SUGG122	469742
18 Feb	Finland	Sweden	Visas	428UNTS145	106173
18 Feb	Finland	Italy	Non-ILO Labor	434UNTS199	106263
20 Feb	FAO (Food Agri)	UK Great Britain	IGO Operations	642UNTS253	109178
20 Feb	Germany, West	UK Great Britain	Visas	398UNTS249	105727
21 Feb	Czechoslovakia	USSR (Soviet Union)	Scientific Project	10SUGG122	469743
21 Feb	India	USSR (Soviet Union)	General Aid	10SUGG122	469744
21 Feb	Belgium	USA (United States)	General Amity	480UNTS149	106967
21 Feb	Netherlands	UK Great Britain	Visas	398UNTS235	105725
21 Feb	Belgium	UK Great Britain	Visas	398UNTS229	105724
21 Feb	Luxembourg	UK Great Britain	Visas	398UNTS243	105726
21 Feb	Australia	Finland	Visas	390UNTS61	105602
23 Feb	IBRD (World Bank)	Yugoslavia	IBRD Project	415UNTS92	105982
23 Feb	Mexico	UN Special Fund	Direct Aid	388UNTS151	105576
24 Feb	Indonesia	USSR (Soviet Union)	General Aid	10SUGG123	469745
24 Feb	Belgium	Netherlands	Admin Cooperation	474UNTS161	106880
24 Feb	Belgium	Netherlands	Water Transport	474UNTS167	106881
24 Feb	Korea, South	Philippines	General Trade	423UNTS217	106094
24 Feb	Czechoslovakia	Hungary	Culture	422UNTS15	106066
24 Feb	Cyprus	UN Special Fund	Direct Aid	389UNTS3	105588
25 Feb	Mongolia	USSR (Soviet Union)	Non-IBRD Project	10SUGG123	469746
27 Feb	Romania	USSR (Soviet Union)	Admin Cooperation	10SUGG123	469747
27 Feb	Switzerland	UK Great Britain	Visas	404UNTS167	105809
27 Feb	Austria	United Nations	IGO Status/Immunit	394UNTS27	105666
27 Feb	Portugal	UK Great Britain	Visas	404UNTS33	105803
28 Feb	Ghana	USSR (Soviet Union)	Atomic Energy	10SUGG124	469748
28 Feb	Mongolia	Poland	Tech Assistance	61PZUM88	458081
28 Feb	China People's Rep	Mali	General Trade	61CCJC27	410761
02 Mar	Spain	Switzerland	Non-ILO Labor	61SPBO912	460254
02 Mar	Germany, East	Romania	Scientific Project	9EGDA389	419298

DATE	PARTY ONE	PARTY TWO	TOPIC	CITATION	NUMBER
1961 (Cont.)					
03 Mar	Taiwan	Korea, South	General Trade	0CTRC33	413014
04 Mar	Pakistan	USSR (Soviet Union)	General Aid	10SUGG124	469749
04 Mar	Cuba	Czechoslovakia	Air Transport	465UNTS209	106728
04 Mar	Denmark	Greece	Taxation	534UNTS157	107760
05 Mar	Iraq	United Nations	Tech Assistance	409UNTS56	105878
06 Mar	USSR (Soviet Union)	Vietnam, North	Tech Assistance	10SUGG124	469750
06 Mar	Cuba	Poland	Culture	484UNTS123	107020
06 Mar	Italy	UK Great Britain	Visas	404UNTS3	105799
07 Mar	Italy	Korea, South	Patents/Copyrights	62ITDI497	436095
07 Mar	Japan	Pakistan	Postal Service	450UNTS359	106479
08 Mar	China People's Rep	Cuba	Finance	61CCJC32	410764
08 Mar	Bulgaria	China People's Rep	General Trade	61CCJC34	410766
08 Mar	Multilateral		Scientific Project	396UNTS255	200584
08 Mar	Belgium	UK Great Britain	Consul/Citizenship	523UNTS17	107554
08 Mar	San Marino	UK Great Britain	Visas	414UNTS46	105964
09 Mar	USSR (Soviet Union)	Vietnam, North	Tech Assistance	10SUGG124	469751
09 Mar	Germany, West	Guinea	Water Transport	61WBGA160	424243
09 Mar	Germany, West	Netherlands	Admin Cooperation	485UNTS185	107056
09 Mar	Panama	UN Special Fund	Direct Aid	396UNTS3	105691
10 Mar	Argentina	Norway	Milit Servic/Citiz	3NORT826	451003
10 Mar	France	Morocco	Air Transport	61FRRT52	415299
10 Mar	Canada	Iran	Visas	470UNTS139	106805
10 Mar	Cuba	UN Special Fund	Direct Aid	390UNTS35	105601
11 Mar	Italy	Switzerland	Customs	63SWRO711	462075
11 Mar	Iceland	UK Great Britain	Dispute Settlement	397UNTS275	105710
12 Mar	Philippines	USA (United States)	Postal Service	288UNTS285	104210
14 Mar	Burma	Germany, East	Water Transport	9EGDA459	419075
15 Mar	Germany, West	Lebanon	Air Transport	62WGBB184	425406
15 Mar	Afghanistan	Japan	Education	450UNTS373	106480
15 Mar	Japan	United Nations	IGO Operations	397UNTS199	105706
15 Mar	UK Great Britain	USA (United States)	Scientific Project	404UNTS207	105811
16 Mar	Norway	Sweden	Customs	3NORT827	451163
16 Mar	Kuwait	WHO (World Health)	Tech Assistance	397UNTS315	200588
16 Mar	Multilateral		General Trade	638UNTS235	109139
16 Mar	Japan	IBRD (World Bank)	IBRD Project	400UNTS201	105753
17 Mar	Brazil	USA (United States)	Atomic Energy	406UNTS241	105853
18 Mar	Mali	USSR (Soviet Union)	General Aid	10SUGG125	469752
18 Mar	Mali	USSR (Soviet Union)	Culture	10SUGG125	469754
18 Mar	Mali	USSR (Soviet Union)	General Trade	10SUGG125	469753
18 Mar	Mali	USSR (Soviet Union)	General Trade	0UNTSO	109826
20 Mar	China People's Rep	USSR (Soviet Union)	Finance	61CCJC38	410770
20 Mar	Ceylon (Sri Lanka)	Japan	Education	450UNTS385	106481
21 Mar	Accept UN Charter	Nigeria	UN Charter	395UNTS237	105688
22 Mar	Iraq	USSR (Soviet Union)	Consul/Citizenship	16SUGG131	469992
23 Mar	Austria	Yugoslavia	Land Transport	61ABGB223	403236
25 Mar	USA (United States)	Vietnam, South	US Agri Commod Aid	406UNTS187	105849
27 Mar	Germany, West	Greece	Claims and Debts	63WGBB216	425236
27 Mar	Denmark	Finland	Commodity Trade	630UNTS3	108961
27 Mar	Multilateral		IGO Establishment	420UNTS109	106043
28 Mar	Romania	USSR (Soviet Union)	Tech Assistance	10SUGG126	469755
29 Mar	Austria	USA (United States)	Direct Aid	459UNTS45	106612
29 Mar	UK Great Britain	USA (United States)	Scientific Project	405UNTS107	105826
29 Mar	IBRD (World Bank)	UK Great Britain	IBRD Project	415UNTS300	105990
29 Mar	Cuba	Germany, East	Culture	448UNTS81	106426
30 Mar	USSR (Soviet Union)	Yugoslavia	General Trade	10SUGG126	469756
30 Mar	Multilateral		Sanitation	520UNTS151	107515
30 Mar	Morocco	Sweden	Taxation	427UNTS185	106154
31 Mar	Indonesia	USA (United States)	Visas	405UNTS119	105828
31 Mar	Morocco	USA (United States)	Admin Cooperation	406UNTS249	105854
31 Mar	France	USA (United States)	Scientific Project	409UNTS136	105881
01 Apr	Finland	USSR (Soviet Union)	Customs	10SUGG127	469757
01 Apr	Germany, East	Mali	Consul/Citizenship	9EGDA462	419197
01 Apr	China People's Rep	Indonesia	General Amity	61CCJC43	410774
01 Apr	China People's Rep	Indonesia	Culture	61CCJC44	410775
03 Apr	Nigeria	USSR (Soviet Union)	Consul/Citizenship	10SUGG127	469759

1961 (Cont.)

DATE	PARTY ONE	PARTY TWO	TOPIC	CITATION	NUMBER
03 Apr	USA (United States)	Vietnam, South	General Amity	424UNTS137	106106
03 Apr	Colombia	USA (United States)	Milit Assistance	407UNTS3	105856
03 Apr	Ecuador	USA (United States)	US Agri Commod Aid	409UNTS140	105882
04 Apr	China People's Rep	Norway	Visas	3NORT829	451023
04 Apr	China People's Rep	Norway	Visas	61CCJC45	410776
04 Apr	Ceylon (Sri Lanka)	China People's Rep	General Trade	61CCJC47	410777
04 Apr	Colombia	USA (United States)	Direct Aid	405UNTS55	105822
04 Apr	USA (United States)	Vietnam, South	Admin Cooperation	405UNTS77	105824
05 Apr	Cuba	Czechoslovakia	Sanitation	442UNTS201	106350
06 Apr	Finland	USSR (Soviet Union)	Tech Assistance	10SUGG127	469758
06 Apr	Greece	UK Great Britain	Visas	403UNTS267	105797
06 Apr	UK Great Britain	USA (United States)	Scientific Project	404UNTS215	105812
07 Apr	China People's Rep	USSR (Soviet Union)	Finance	10SUGG127	469760
07 Apr	China People's Rep	USSR (Soviet Union)	Direct Aid	10SUGG127	469761
07 Apr	Argentina	Uruguay	Territory Boundary	635UNTS91	109074
07 Apr	Chile	Netherlands	Visas	453UNTS239	106527
07 Apr	Belgium	Chile	Visas	410UNTS255	105909
07 Apr	Bolivia	USA (United States)	US Agri Commod Aid	433UNTS3	106227
07 Apr	Iceland	USA (United States)	US Agri Commod Aid	406UNTS203	105850
08 Apr	France	Turkey	Commodity Trade	61TURG1109	466064
08 Apr	Italy	Peru	Culture	63ITGU36	435300
08 Apr	Netherlands	Spain	Non-ILO Labor	482UNTS193	106996
10 Apr	IDA (Devel Assoc)	United Nations	IGO Operations	394UNTS221	200582
10 Apr	Multilateral		Atomic Energy	402UNTS281	105791
10 Apr	Norway	IAEA (Atom Energy)	Scientific Project	402UNTS255	105790
11 Apr	China People's Rep	Finland	General Trade	61CCJC55	410784
11 Apr	Monaco	UK Great Britain	Visas	404UNTS11	105800
11 Apr	Japan	UK Great Britain	Taxation	420UNTS75	106042
12 Apr	Argentina	Italy	Culture	63ITGU86	435022
12 Apr	Argentina	Italy	Non-ILO Labor	63ITGU8	435023
12 Apr	Argentina	Italy	Loans and Credits	62ITDI490	436024
12 Apr	Argentina	Italy	Non-ILO Labor	0UNTS0	109522
12 Apr	Honduras	USA (United States)	Direct Aid	413UNTS182	105952
13 Apr	Mongolia	USSR (Soviet Union)	Direct Aid	10SUGG128	469762
13 Apr	IAEA (Atom Energy)	IMCO (Maritime Org)	IGO Operations	425UNTS281	200595
14 Apr	Multilateral		IGO Establishment	422UNTS101	106071
15 Apr	Germany, West	Morocco	General Trade	61WBGA150	424464
17 Apr	France	Spain	Admin Cooperation	61SPBO2505	460133
17 Apr	Germany, East	Mali	Finance	9EGDA372	419198
17 Apr	Mauritania	WHO (World Health)	Tech Assistance	396UNTS301	200587
18 Apr	Afghanistan	Germany, West	Culture	63WGBB1069	425003
18 Apr	Multilateral		Consul/Citizenship	500UNTS95	107310
18 Apr	Multilateral		Consul/Citizenship	500UNTS223	107311
18 Apr	Multilateral		Dispute Settlement	500UNTS243	107312
19 Apr	Ghana	Poland	Tech Assistance	61PZUM94	458082
19 Apr	Italy	United Arab Rep	Specific Resources	62ITDI518	436319
19 Apr	India	Norway	Culture	404UNTS307	105818
19 Apr	USA (United States)	Yugoslavia	Direct Aid	409UNTS163	105883
19 Apr	Cyprus	UNICEF (Children)	Direct Aid	394UNTS185	105678
20 Apr	Italy	UK Great Britain	Other Military	63ITGU99	435192
21 Apr	Poland	USSR (Soviet Union)	Non-IBRD Project	10SUGG128	469763
21 Apr	Korea, South	UN Special Fund	Direct Aid	394UNTS231	200583
21 Apr	Multilateral		IGO Establishment	484UNTS349	107041
23 Apr	Afghanistan	Czechoslovakia	Culture	437UNTS25	106297
24 Apr	Switzerland	Yugoslavia	Loans and Credits	62SWRO99	462110
24 Apr	France	Upper Volta	General Amity	62FRRT8	415215
24 Apr	Dahomey	France	General Amity	62FRRT8	415146
24 Apr	France	Niger	General Amity	62FRRT8	415340
24 Apr	France	Ivory Coast	General Amity	62FRRT8	415139
24 Apr	France	Ivory Coast	Admin Cooperation	0UNTS0	110717
24 Apr	France	Ivory Coast	Culture	0UNTS0	110718
25 Apr	Iceland	USSR (Soviet Union)	Health/Educ/Welfare	10SUGG129	469764
25 Apr	Italy	Switzerland	Commodity Trade	62SWRO189	462144
25 Apr	Germany, West	Greece	Non-ILO Labor	63WGBB678	425237
25 Apr	Taiwan	Nicaragua	Culture	423UNTS139	106090

1961 (Cont.)

DATE	PARTY ONE	PARTY TWO	TOPIC	CITATION	NUMBER
26 Apr	Italy	Somalia	Culture	63ITGU36	435348
26 Apr	Germany, East	Hungary	General Economic	9EGDA402	419458
26 Apr	China People's Rep	Mongolia	General Amity	61CCJC69	410792
26 Apr	China People's Rep	Mongolia	General Trade	61CCJC70	410793
27 Apr	Germany, West	Netherlands	Culture	487UNTS77	107095
27 Apr	Gabon	WHO (World Health)	Tech Assistance	397UNTS215	105707
27 Apr	Turkey	USSR (Soviet Union)	Land Transport	420UNTS307	106047
27 Apr	Accept UN Charter	Sierra Leone	UN Charter	409UNTS44	105876
27 Apr	Mali	WHO (World Health)	Tech Assistance	407UNTS66	105860
27 Apr	Ghana	Hungary	Culture	439UNTS17	106322
28 Apr	USA (United States)	Yugoslavia	US Agri Commod Aid	409UNTS172	105884
28 Apr	IBRD (World Bank)	Thailand	IBRD Project	415UNTS121	105983
29 Apr	Guinea	USSR (Soviet Union)	Non-IBRD Project	10SUGG130	469765
02 May	Japan	IBRD (World Bank)	IBRD Project	415UNTS144	105984
02 May	Germany, West	UK Great Britain	Admin Cooperation	414UNTS3	105959
03 May	Albania	Romania	Non-ILO Labor	592UNTS21	108567
03 May	Taiwan	Uruguay	Culture	596UNTS121	108630
03 May	Ceylon (Sri Lanka)	UN Special Fund	Direct Aid	395UNTS217	105687
04 May	Brazil	USA (United States)	US Agri Commod Aid	433UNTS91	106233
05 May	Finland	UK Great Britain	Visas	414UNTS101	105969
05 May	Sweden	UK Great Britain	Visas	404UNTS105	105807
05 May	Sierra Leone	USA (United States)	General Aid	409UNTS194	105885
05 May	Sierra Leone	UK Great Britain	Recognition	420UNTS11	106036
05 May	Canada	USA (United States)	Admin Cooperation	419UNTS9	106027
05 May	Sierra Leone	UK Great Britain	Consul/Citizenship	420UNTS17	106037
06 May	France	Germany, West	Admin Cooperation	61WGBB1040	425183
09 May	Germany, West	Spain	General Economic	61SPBO2905	460027
09 May	Australia	USA (United States)	Scientific Project	409UNTS203	105886
09 May	Chile	UK Great Britain	Visas	414UNTS37	105963
10 May	Denmark	UK Great Britain	Visas	414UNTS17	105961
10 May	Norway	UK Great Britain	Visas	414UNTS9	105960
10 May	Israel	USA (United States)	US Agri Commod Aid	409UNTS213	105887
12 May	Norway	USSR (Soviet Union)	Consul/Citizenship	3NORT833	451210
12 May	Honduras	IDA (Devel Assoc)	Loans and Credits	414UNTS180	105973
12 May	Colombia	IBRD (World Bank)	IBRD Project	415UNTS172	105985
13 May	Germany, West	Portugal	Admin Cooperation	61WBGA125	424594
13 May	Germany, East	Poland	Admin Cooperation	9EGDA469	419268
13 May	Senegal	USA (United States)	General Aid	409UNTS232	105888
15 May	Afghanistan	France	Air Transport	62FRRT4	415002
15 May	China People's Rep	Poland	Finance	61CCJC75	410796
15 May	China People's Rep	Germany, East	General Economic	61CCJC76	410797
15 May	Japan	Peru	General Trade	451UNTS3	106482
16 May	Italy	Switzerland	Territory Boundary	63SWRO520	462179
16 May	Germany, West	Togo	Claims and Debts	64WGBB154	425661
16 May	Germany, West	Netherlands	General Military	64WBGA168	424487
17 May	Mali	USSR (Soviet Union)	Consul/Citizenship	16SUGG131	469993
17 May	Ghana	Switzerland	Air Transport	559UNTS193	108159
17 May	Ivory Coast	USA (United States)	General Aid	409UNTS241	105889
18 May	Poland	Switzerland	Air Transport	559UNTS233	108161
19 May	UK Great Britain	USSR (Soviet Union)	Atomic Energy	10SUGG131	469768
19 May	Poland	USSR (Soviet Union)	Tech Assistance	10SUGG130	469767
19 May	Poland	USSR (Soviet Union)	Direct Aid	10SUGG130	469766
19 May	Japan	USA (United States)	Atomic Energy	0JGJI1445	441108
19 May	Sierra Leone	USA (United States)	Admin Cooperation	409UNTS251	105890
20 May	France	Tunisia	Air Transport	65FRRT53	415457
20 May	Mali	USA (United States)	Milit Assistance	413UNTS205	105954
22 May	Australia	USA (United States)	Scientific Project	419UNTS3	106026
22 May	Spain	USA (United States)	US Agri Commod Aid	409UNTS260	105891
25 May	France	Poland	Non-ILO Labor	61PZUM118	458083
25 May	China People's Rep	USSR (Soviet Union)	Mass Media	61CCJC79	410799
25 May	France	Poland	Non-ILO Labor	0UNTS0	110701
26 May	Germany, East	Tunisia	Mass Media	9EGDA400	419372
26 May	Niger	USA (United States)	General Aid	410UNTS213	105905
26 May	Cameroon	USA (United States)	General Aid	413UNTS195	105953
26 May	Colombia	UK Great Britain	Visas	414UNTS85	105967

DATE	PARTY ONE	PARTY TWO	TOPIC	CITATION	NUMBER
1961 (Cont.)					
27 May	Brazil	USSR (Soviet Union)	General Trade	10SUGG131	469770
27 May	Brazil	USSR (Soviet Union)	General Trade	10SUGG131	469771
27 May	Brazil	USSR (Soviet Union)	Loans and Credits	10SUGG131	469769
27 May	Dahomey	USA (United States)	General Aid	445UNTS23	106373
29 May	Guinea	USSR (Soviet Union)	General Aid	10SUGG132	469772
29 May	Czechoslovakia	Indonesia	General Amity	479UNTS337	106962
29 May	Nigeria	UK Great Britain	Recognition	478UNTS3	106931
29 May	Romania	United Nations	IGO Operations	406UNTS147	105845
29 May	South Africa	Sweden	Taxation	442UNTS15	106335
29 May	Accept UN Charter	Cyprus	UN Charter	397UNTS283	105711
30 May	France	Spain	Customs	63SPBO1009	460134
30 May	Germany, East	USSR (Soviet Union)	General Economic	9EGDA418	419417
30 May	Spain	UK Great Britain	Consul/Citizenship	562UNTS169	108198
30 May	Luxembourg	South Africa	Visas	412UNTS203	105933
31 May	Germany, West	Greece	Non-ILO Labor	62WGBB1109	425238
31 May	Germany, West	Luxembourg	Consul/Citizenship	61WBGA141	424426
31 May	Germany, West	Luxembourg	Admin Cooperation	62WBGA23	424427
01 Jun	Cuba	USSR (Soviet Union)	Tech Assistance	10SUGG132	469773
01 Jun	Germany, West	Switzerland	Customs	64SWRO387	462072
01 Jun	Jamaica	UK Great Britain	Recognition	478UNTS9	106932
01 Jun	USA (United States)	Upper Volta	General Aid	410UNTS223	105906
02 Jun	Germany, West	Italy	Claims and Debts	63WGBB668	425298
02 Jun	Germany, West	Italy	Specif Claim/Waive	63WGBB791	425297
02 Jun	Somalia	USSR (Soviet Union)	General Trade	493UNTS173	107214
02 Jun	Somalia	USSR (Soviet Union)	Culture	528UNTS147	107638
02 Jun	Somalia	USSR (Soviet Union)	Tech Assistance	457UNTS263	106587
04 Jun	USSR (Soviet Union)	Yemen	Non-IBRD Project	10SUGG134	469774
04 Jun	Czechoslovakia	Somalia	Tech Assistance	480UNTS261	106973
04 Jun	Czechoslovakia	Somalia	Culture	479UNTS291	106960
05 Jun	Australia	USA (United States)	Scientific Project	409UNTS279	105892
06 Jun	Germany, West	Turkey	Loans and Credits	61TURG1907	466108
06 Jun	France	Gabon	Specific Property	63FRRT20	415193
06 Jun	Ceylon (Sri Lanka)	IBRD (World Bank)	IBRD Project	414UNTS349	105978
07 Jun	Italy	USSR (Soviet Union)	General Trade	10SUGG134	469775
07 Jun	Chile	Spain	Health/Educ/Welfare	65SPBO1911	460076
08 Jun	Mongolia	USSR (Soviet Union)	Tech Assistance	10SUGG134	469776
08 Jun	Germany, West	Upper Volta	Direct Aid	61WBGA193	424522
08 Jun	Germany, West	Upper Volta	General Economic	61WBGA193	424521
08 Jun	Multilateral		Customs	473UNTS153	106862
08 Jun	Multilateral		Customs	473UNTS187	106863
08 Jun	Czechoslovakia	Morocco	Air Transport	497UNTS275	107272
08 Jun	UK Great Britain	Yugoslavia	Mass Media	437UNTS111	106300
08 Jun	Japan	USA (United States)	Reparations	410UNTS183	105903
09 Jun	Nepal	USA (United States)	Education	421UNTS223	106061
09 Jun	Finland	UK Great Britain	Visas	414UNTS53	105965
11 Jun	Israel	Upper Volta	Tech Assistance	413UNTS113	105946
12 Jun	Togo	USSR (Soviet Union)	General Trade	0SUST135	471030
12 Jun	Ghana	USSR (Soviet Union)	Tech Assistance	10SUGG135	469777
12 Jun	Togo	USSR (Soviet Union)	General Trade	0UNTS0	110495
12 Jun	Congo (Zaire)	United Nations	General Aid	494UNTS205	107234
12 Jun	Canada	USA (United States)	Milit Assistance	410UNTS21	105894
12 Jun	Norway	UK Great Britain	Admin Cooperation	424UNTS173	106107
13 Jun	Poland	Switzerland	Taxation	61PZUM121	458084
13 Jun	Poland	Switzerland	Taxation	61SWRO570	462062
13 Jun	France	Germany, West	Visas	66WBGA245	424184
13 Jun	New Zealand	UK Great Britain	Air Transport	497UNTS293	107273
13 Jun	Cameroon	UN Special Fund	Direct Aid	397UNTS297	105713
14 Jun	Germany, West	Niger	General Economic	61WBGA195	424502
14 Jun	Germany, West	Niger	Direct Aid	61WBGA195	424503
14 Jun	Togo	USSR (Soviet Union)	General Trade	0UNTS0	110496
14 Jun	USA (United States)	Yugoslavia	Admin Cooperation	0UNTS0	110400
14 Jun	IDA (Devel Assoc)	Sudan	Loans and Credits	415UNTS50	105981
14 Jun	Ethiopia	United Nations	Direct Aid	406UNTS81	105840
14 Jun	IBRD (World Bank)	Sudan	IBRD Project	415UNTS26	105980
14 Jun	Multilateral		IBRD Project	415UNTS4	105979

DATE	PARTY ONE	PARTY TWO	TOPIC	CITATION	NUMBER
1961 (Cont.)					
15 Jun	Israel	Norway	General Economic	3NORT836	451088
15 Jun	France	Poland	Consul/Citizenship	61PZUM127	458085
15 Jun	France	Spain	Admin Cooperation	61FRRT42	415163
15 Jun	China People's Rep	Germany, East	Finance	61CCJC84	410801
15 Jun	Cyprus	United Nations	Tech Assistance	398UNTS39	105716
16 Jun	Finland	USA (United States)	Claims and Debts	413UNTS211	105955
16 Jun	Cameroon	France	Air Transport	412UNTS148	105929
17 Jun	Guinea	Sweden	Air Transport	465UNTS236	106729
17 Jun	Liberia	USA (United States)	Milit Assistance	410UNTS233	105907
17 Jun	Ecuador	USA (United States)	Direct Aid	411UNTS49	105913
19 Jun	China People's Rep	USSR (Soviet Union)	General Aid	16SUGG131	469995
19 Jun	China People's Rep	USSR (Soviet Union)	General Economic	10SUGG136	469778
19 Jun	China People's Rep	USSR (Soviet Union)	Tech Assistance	16SUGG131	469994
19 Jun	China People's Rep	USSR (Soviet Union)	Scientific Project	10SUGG136	469779
19 Jun	Dahomey	Germany, West	Water Transport	61WBGA196	424094
19 Jun	France	Mauritania	General Amity	62FRRT9	415312
19 Jun	Dahomey	Germany, West	General Economic	61WBGA196	424093
19 Jun	Dahomey	Germany, West	General Economic	64WBGA196	424092
19 Jun	China People's Rep	USSR (Soviet Union)	Scientific Project	61CCJC87	410803
19 Jun	Argentina	UK Great Britain	Culture	470UNTS71	106797
19 Jun	Kuwait	UK Great Britain	General Amity	399UNTS239	105743
19 Jun	Inter-Am Devel Bnk	USA (United States)	Direct Aid	410UNTS34	105895
20 Jun	Hungary	USSR (Soviet Union)	General Aid	10SUGG136	469785
21 Jun	France	Morocco	Customs	61FRRT38	415300
21 Jun	China People's Rep	USSR (Soviet Union)	Scientific Project	61CCJC88	410804
21 Jun	Multilateral		IGO Establishment	514UNTS209	107449
21 Jun	India	IDA (Devel Assoc)	Loans and Credits	418UNTS61	106017
22 Jun	Poland	USSR (Soviet Union)	Non-IBRD Project	10SUGG136	469780
22 Jun	Madagascar	USA (United States)	General Aid	413UNTS219	105956
22 Jun	Japan	USA (United States)	General Economic	410UNTS53	105896
22 Jun	Paraguay	UN Special Fund	Direct Aid	399UNTS117	105738
23 Jun	Finland	India	Taxation	421UNTS49	106051
23 Jun	IBRD (World Bank)	UK Great Britain	IBRD Project	415UNTS358	105991
24 Jun	Cambodia	USSR (Soviet Union)	Non-IBRD Project	10SUGG136	469781
26 Jun	Multilateral		ILO Labor	423UNTS11	106083
26 Jun	Mexico	USA (United States)	Direct Aid	413UNTS229	105957
26 Jun	UN Special Fund	Upper Volta	Direct Aid	400UNTS3	105744
27 Jun	Germany, West	Senegal	Direct Aid	61WBGA194	424619
27 Jun	Germany, West	Senegal	Water Transport	61WBGA171	424620
27 Jun	Pakistan	IBRD (World Bank)	IBRD Project	425UNTS241	106127
28 Jun	Czechoslovakia	USSR (Soviet Union)	Non-IBRD Project	10SUGG136	469782
28 Jun	Italy	Spain	Taxation	66ITGU159	435355
28 Jun	Philippines	UN Special Fund	Direct Aid	399UNTS141	105739
28 Jun	Haiti	United Nations	Tech Assistance	399UNTS159	105740
28 Jun	Turkey	UK Great Britain	Visas	414UNTS93	105968
28 Jun	Chile	IDA (Devel Assoc)	Loans and Credits	426UNTS89	106131
28 Jun	Haiti	UN Special Fund	Direct Aid	399UNTS171	105741
28 Jun	Chile	IBRD (World Bank)	IBRD Project	426UNTS33	106129
29 Jun	Germany, West	Switzerland	Claims and Debts	62SWRO1311	462167
29 Jun	Finland	Norway	Extradition	2NORT241	451055
29 Jun	Cyprus	USA (United States)	General Aid	411UNTS56	105914
29 Jun	Indonesia	UK Great Britain	General Economic	443UNTS255	106364
30 Jun	Poland	USSR (Soviet Union)	Specif Goods/Equip	10SUGG137	469783
30 Jun	Argentina	IBRD (World Bank)	IBRD Project	445UNTS85	106379
30 Jun	Tunisia	USA (United States)	US Agri Commod Aid	434UNTS85	106257
30 Jun	Austria	Yugoslavia	Admin Cooperation	443UNTS51	106358
30 Jun	Bulgaria	Hungary	Admin Cooperation	438UNTS287	106320
01 Jul	Germany, West	Iran	Air Transport	63WGBB1086	425273
01 Jul	Germany, West	Iran	Air Transport	0UNTS0	110465
01 Jul	Indonesia	Japan	General Amity	517UNTS107	107484
02 Jul	Ghana	USSR (Soviet Union)	General Trade	16SUGG131	469996
02 Jul	Ghana	USSR (Soviet Union)	General Trade	0UNTS0	109380
04 Jul	Czechoslovakia	Poland	Admin Cooperation	436UNTS189	106295
04 Jul	UNICEF (Children)	Saudi Arabia	Direct Aid	413UNTS122	105947
05 Jul	Germany, West	Luxembourg	Air Transport	62WGBB195	425428

DATE	PARTY ONE	PARTY TWO	TOPIC	CITATION	NUMBER
1961 (Cont.)					
05 Jul	Hungary	Poland	Consul/Citizenship	437UNTS3	106296
06 Jul	Korea, North	USSR (Soviet Union)	General Aid	10SUGG137	469784
06 Jul	Korea, North	USSR (Soviet Union)	General Aid	10SUGG137	469786
06 Jul	Austria	Uruguay	Visas	63ABGB223	403206
06 Jul	Argentina	Brazil	Postal Service	0UNTS0	109410
06 Jul	Korea, North	USSR (Soviet Union)	General Amity	420UNTS145	106045
07 Jul	Poland	USSR (Soviet Union)	Atomic Energy	10SUGG137	469787
07 Jul	China People's Rep	Romania	General Economic	61CCJC93	410807
07 Jul	Bulgaria	Netherlands	Finance	489UNTS21	107133
07 Jul	Belgium	France	Taxation	406UNTS157	105846
07 Jul	Paraguay	USA (United States)	US Agri Commod Aid	433UNTS53	106231
08 Jul	Germany, East	Ghana	General Trade	9EGDA338	419106
10 Jul	China People's Rep	Poland	General Trade	61CCJC95	410808
11 Jul	China People's Rep	Korea, North	General Amity	61CCJC96	410809
11 Jul	Israel	IBRD (World Bank)	IBRD Project	429UNTS3	106188
12 Jul	Germany, West	Italy	Privil/Immunities	65WGBB843	425299
12 Jul	Germany, West	UK Great Britain	Status of Forces	424UNTS211	106109
12 Jul	Bulgaria	Poland	Admin Cooperation	436UNTS147	106294
14 Jul	USA (United States)	Vietnam, South	US Agri Commod Aid	416UNTS133	105999
14 Jul	Austria	UK Great Britain	Admin Cooperation	453UNTS267	106530
15 Jul	China People's Rep	Hungary	General Economic	61CCJC102	410813
15 Jul	China People's Rep	Yugoslavia	General Trade	61CCJC103	410814
15 Jul	China People's Rep	Hungary	Finance	61CCJC100	410812
17 Jul	Mongolia	USSR (Soviet Union)	Tech Assistance	10SUGG138	469788
17 Jul	Jordan	UK Great Britain	Loans and Credits	420UNTS53	106039
18 Jul	Germany, West	Netherlands	Sanitation	487UNTS95	107096
18 Jul	UK Great Britain	USA (United States)	Milit Assistance	404UNTS227	105813
19 Jul	Bolivia	Norway	Visas	3NORT838	451008
19 Jul	Austria	Germany, West	Extradition	61WBGA169	424548
19 Jul	Ghana	USA (United States)	Direct Aid	416UNTS167	106002
19 Jul	Mexico	USA (United States)	Air Transport	433UNTS43	106230
19 Jul	Germany, West	Iceland	Specific Resources	409UNTS47	105877
19 Jul	Austria	Germany, West	Visas	414UNTS211	105974
20 Jul	Poland	USSR (Soviet Union)	Non-IBRD Project	10SUGG138	469789
21 Jul	Taiwan	USA (United States)	US Agri Commod Aid	416UNTS101	105998
21 Jul	Austria	Romania	General Trade	421UNTS161	106057
21 Jul	Mali	UN Special Fund	Direct Aid	401UNTS141	105768
21 Jul	UK Great Britain	Yugoslavia	Loans and Credits	420UNTS61	106040
21 Jul	Tanganyika	USA (United States)	Direct Aid	445UNTS33	106374
21 Jul	Brazil	UK Great Britain	Loans and Credits	414UNTS26	105962
22 Jul	Mongolia	USSR (Soviet Union)	Tech Assistance	10SUGG139	469790
22 Jul	San Marino	UK Great Britain	Reparations	420UNTS3	106035
24 Jul	Ghana	USSR (Soviet Union)	Finance	10SUGG139	469791
25 Jul	Nicaragua	Spain	Consul/Citizenship	62SPBO205	460201
25 Jul	Australia	New Zealand	Air Transport	523UNTS271	107561
25 Jul	Netherlands	Euratom	Scientific Project	462UNTS263	106686
25 Jul	Netherlands	Euratom	IGO Status/Immunit	462UNTS313	106687
25 Jul	Fed of Malaya	UN Special Fund	Direct Aid	401UNTS159	105769
26 Jul	Philippines	IBRD (World Bank)	IBRD Project	414UNTS253	105976
27 Jul	Iraq	Poland	Air Transport	61PZUM183	458086
27 Jul	France	Germany, West	Claims and Debts	63FRJO33	416039
27 Jul	Germany, East	Yugoslavia	General Economic	9EGDA484	419149
27 Jul	France	USA (United States)	Milit Assistance	433UNTS29	106229
27 Jul	Albania	Austria	General Economic	407UNTS37	105858
28 Jul	Guatemala	Spain	Consul/Citizenship	62SPBO1003	460159
29 Jul	France	Guinea	Culture	62FRRT17	415208
29 Jul	Turkey	USA (United States)	US Agri Commod Aid	416UNTS151	106001
31 Jul	Portugal	UK Great Britain	Taxation	449UNTS119	106454
01 Aug	Hungary	USSR (Soviet Union)	General Trade	10SUGG140	469792
01 Aug	Colombia	USA (United States)	Taxation	433UNTS123	106235
01 Aug	Denmark	Iceland	Specific Resources	425UNTS191	106124
02 Aug	Czechoslovakia	Ghana	Air Transport	465UNTS249	106730
02 Aug	UN Special Fund	Yemen	Direct Aid	402UNTS43	105777
03 Aug	Germany, West	Netherlands	Admin Cooperation	492UNTS321	107201
03 Aug	Israel	Liberia	Visas	484UNTS203	107030

DATE	PARTY ONE	PARTY TWO	TOPIC	CITATION	NUMBER
1961 (Cont.)					
03 Aug	Chile	USA (United States)	Direct Aid	433UNTS21	106228
04 Aug	Finland	USA (United States)	US Agri Commod Aid	418UNTS19	106014
05 Aug	Japan	Morocco	Milit Installation	61JGJI38	441301
05 Aug	Congo (Brazzaville)	USA (United States)	Admin Cooperation	603UNTS19	108720
09 Aug	India	IBRD (World Bank)	IBRD Project	417UNTS297	106011
09 Aug	Morocco	WHO (World Health)	Tech Assistance	412UNTS192	105932
09 Aug	Finland	IBRD (World Bank)	IBRD Project	415UNTS204	105986
10 Aug	Germany, West	Vietnam, South	Tech Assistance	OVKNG171	496051
10 Aug	EFTA (Free Trade)	Switzerland	IGO Status/Immunit	61SWRO763	462193
10 Aug	France	Vietnam, South	Tech Assistance	OVKNG170	496050
11 Aug	Brazil	Norway	Finance	3NORT839	451012
12 Aug	Chile	USA (United States)	Scientific Project	421UNTS209	106059
12 Aug	Cameroon	UNICEF (Children)	Direct Aid	402UNTS235	105788
15 Aug	Finland	Luxembourg	Air Transport	541UNTS45	107859
15 Aug	Pakistan	Philippines	Culture	522UNTS35	107534
16 Aug	IBRD (World Bank)	UK Great Britain	IBRD Project	426UNTS287	106143
17 Aug	Cyprus	Israel	Visas	484UNTS169	107025
17 Aug	India	IBRD (World Bank)	IBRD Project	417UNTS319	106012
17 Aug	WHO (World Health)	Somalia	Tech Assistance	423UNTS111	106088
18 Aug	China People's Rep	Ghana	General Aid	61CCJC109	410818
18 Aug	China People's Rep	Ghana	Milit Assistance	61CCJC110	410819
18 Aug	China People's Rep	Ghana	General Amity	61CCJC108	410817
18 Aug	China People's Rep	Ghana	Culture	61CCJC111	410820
18 Aug	Mexico	United Nations	Humanitarian	404UNTS297	105817
18 Aug	Taiwan	Paraguay	Culture	438UNTS109	106314
21 Aug	Czechoslovakia	USSR (Soviet Union)	Non-IBRD Project	10SUGG140	469793
21 Aug	Jordan	Norway	Air Transport	465UNTS275	106731
21 Aug	El Salvador	USA (United States)	US Agri Commod Aid	418UNTS35	106015
21 Aug	Central Afri Rep	UNICEF (Children)	Direct Aid	413UNTS48	105939
22 Aug	France	Mali	Claims and Debts	63FRRT27	415288
23 Aug	Hungary	Indonesia	General Amity	519UNTS163	107507
23 Aug	Italy	United Nations	IGO Operations	405UNTS3	105819
24 Aug	Jordan	Netherlands	Air Transport	466UNTS3	106733
24 Aug	Mexico	Netherlands	Air Transport	465UNTS291	106732
24 Aug	Poland	UNICEF (Children)	Direct Aid	406UNTS95	105841
25 Aug	Italy	Norway	Taxation	475UNTS269	106896
25 Aug	UNESCO (Educ/Cult)	Thailand	IGO Operations	410UNTS125	105899
26 Aug	Central Afri Rep	France	Specific Property	63FRRT19	415112
26 Aug	Chad	UNICEF (Children)	Direct Aid	422UNTS231	106077
26 Aug	Lebanon	United Nations	Tech Assistance	406UNTS105	105842
27 Aug	Israel	Malagasy	General Amity	484UNTS217	107032
27 Aug	Israel	Malagasy	Direct Aid	413UNTS86	105943
28 Aug	Colombia	IDA (Devel Assoc)	Loans and Credits	416UNTS3	105992
28 Aug	Colombia	IBRD (World Bank)	IBRD Project	416UNTS23	105993
28 Aug	Multilateral		IBRD Project	416UNTS45	105994
28 Aug	UK Great Britain	USA (United States)	Finance	434UNTS103	106258
29 Aug	Ivory Coast	UN Special Fund	Direct Aid	406UNTS129	105844
29 Aug	Ghana	United Nations	Tech Assistance	406UNTS117	105843
30 Aug	Israel	Italy	Visas	484UNTS197	107029
30 Aug	Tunisia	USSR (Soviet Union)	General Aid	437UNTS243	106310
30 Aug	Taiwan	IDA (Devel Assoc)	Loans and Credits	417UNTS227	106008
30 Aug	Taiwan	IDA (Devel Assoc)	Loans and Credits	416UNTS175	106003
30 Aug	ILO (Labor Org)	Thailand	IGO Operations	422UNTS125	106072
31 Aug	Germany, West	Morocco	Claims and Debts	67WGBB1641	425465
31 Aug	Liberia	Switzerland	Air Transport	559UNTS215	108160
01 Sep	Canada	USA (United States)	Claims and Debts	421UNTS199	106058
01 Sep	Costa Rica	Israel	Visas	448UNTS247	106436
02 Sep	United Arab Rep	USA (United States)	US Agri Commod Aid	421UNTS251	106063
04 Sep	Denmark	Pakistan	Taxation	455UNTS305	106549
04 Sep	Fed of Malaya	USA (United States)	Direct Aid	421UNTS215	106060
05 Sep	Canada	Japan	Reparations	451UNTS47	106483
05 Sep	Sweden	USA (United States)	General Economic	421UNTS241	106062
06 Sep	Argentina	Norway	Visas	3NORT842	451004
06 Sep	Taiwan	IDA (Devel Assoc)	Loans and Credits	417UNTS253	106009
06 Sep	India	IDA (Devel Assoc)	Loans and Credits	418UNTS81	106018

DATE	PARTY ONE	PARTY TWO	TOPIC	CITATION	NUMBER
1961 (Cont.)					
06 Sep	Costa Rica	IBRD (World Bank)	IBRD Project	446UNTS345	106408
07 Sep	Hungary	Romania	Non-ILO Labor	519UNTS141	107506
08 Sep	UK Great Britain	USA (United States)	Scientific Project	418UNTS53	106016
11 Sep	Jordan	United Nations	Tech Assistance	406UNTS255	105855
12 Sep	USA (United States)	Uruguay	Gen Communications	607UNTS175	108805
12 Sep	Denmark	Germany, West	Non-ILO Labor	516UNTS283	107478
13 Sep	Iraq	WHO (World Health)	Tech Assistance	419UNTS69	106030
15 Sep	Italy	Yugoslavia	Culture	62ITGU80	435244
15 Sep	Korea, South	Thailand	General Trade	413UNTS137	105948
16 Sep	Poland	Tunisia	Tech Assistance	61PZUM192	458087
18 Sep	Multilateral		Air Transport	500UNTS31	107305
19 Sep	Bulgaria	Poland	Consul/Citizenship	483UNTS249	107018
20 Sep	Multilateral		Tech Assistance	407UNTS52	105859
21 Sep	Italy	USSR (Soviet Union)	Specif Goods/Equip	10SUGG142	469794
21 Sep	Hungary	Italy	General Economic	66ITDI247	436417
21 Sep	France	USA (United States)	Visas	433UNTS243	106247
22 Sep	Germany, West	Korea, South	Visas	62WBGA8	424389
22 Sep	China People's Rep	Mali	General Aid	61CCJC125	410830
23 Sep	China People's Rep	Denmark	Taxation	61CCJC126	410831
23 Sep	China People's Rep	Denmark	Taxation	446UNTS3	106397
23 Sep	Canada	USA (United States)	Milit Installation	421UNTS79	106053
25 Sep	Canada	Vietnam, South	Direct Aid	0VKNG172	496052
26 Sep	Paraguay	USA (United States)	General Aid	461UNTS91	106653
26 Sep	UK Great Britain	USA (United States)	Scientific Project	421UNTS99	106055
26 Sep	Germany, West	UK Great Britain	Milit Assistance	424UNTS201	106108
27 Sep	Afghanistan	Switzerland	Air Transport	63SWR0874	462089
27 Sep	Australia	Spain	Visas	426UNTS159	106135
27 Sep	Canada	USA (United States)	Milit Assistance	421UNTS85	106054
28 Sep	France	Germany, West	General Military	63WBGA171	424185
28 Sep	Dahomey	Israel	Tech Assistance	448UNTS151	106429
29 Sep	Bulgaria	USSR (Soviet Union)	Tech Assistance	10SUGG142	469795
29 Sep	Germany, West	USA (United States)	Scientific Project	424UNTS113	106103
29 Sep	Pakistan	Philippines	General Trade	422UNTS3	106065
30 Sep	Ghana	Romania	Air Transport	467UNTS443	106769
30 Sep	Bolivia	Netherlands	Visas	487UNTS105	107097
30 Sep	Ghana	Romania	Culture	457UNTS3	106573
30 Sep	Belgium	Bolivia	Visas	425UNTS53	106118
02 Oct	New Zealand	Spain	Visas	453UNTS11	106516
02 Oct	UN Special Fund	Sierra Leone	Direct Aid	422UNTS131	106073
03 Oct	Hungary	USSR (Soviet Union)	Admin Cooperation	10SUGG142	469796
03 Oct	Austria	USA (United States)	Direct Aid	426UNTS187	106137
04 Oct	Poland	USSR (Soviet Union)	Specific Property	61PZUM209	458088
04 Oct	France	Spain	Non-ILO Labor	62SPBO401	460135
04 Oct	Japan	United Nations	Education	410UNTS133	105900
04 Oct	IAEA (Atom Energy)	Yugoslavia	Scientific Project	412UNTS226	105935
04 Oct	Philippines	USA (United States)	Specif Goods/Equip	433UNTS83	106232
04 Oct	Multilateral		Scientific Project	412UNTS210	105934
04 Oct	El Salvador	Israel	Visas	448UNTS253	106437
05 Oct	China People's Rep	Nepal	Territory Boundary	61CCJC128	410832
05 Oct	Multilateral		Admin Cooperation	0UNTS0	109431
05 Oct	Multilateral		Patents/Copyrights	527UNTS181	107625
05 Oct	Multilateral		Dispute Settlement	510UNTS175	107413
06 Oct	India	USSR (Soviet Union)	Atomic Energy	10SUGG143	469797
06 Oct	Greece	Sweden	Taxation	481UNTS137	106981
07 Oct	Syria	USSR (Soviet Union)	Consul/Citizenship	10SUGG143	469798
07 Oct	Ceylon (Sri Lanka)	China People's Rep	General Trade	61CCJC132	410836
10 Oct	Indonesia	Poland	Tech Assistance	61PZUM211	458089
10 Oct	Bulgaria	Germany, East	Education	9EGDA319	419064
10 Oct	Austria	Yugoslavia	Admin Cooperation	62ABGB310	403237
10 Oct	Austria	Israel	Extradition	448UNTS161	106430
11 Oct	Cuba	USSR (Soviet Union)	Tech Assistance	10SUGG143	469799
11 Oct	Italy	Monaco	Non-ILO Labor	63ITGU122	435282
11 Oct	China People's Rep	Indonesia	General Aid	61CCJC134	410837
11 Oct	IBRD (World Bank)	Switzerland	IBRD Project	415UNTS396	200592
11 Oct	Hungary	Iraq	Gen Communications	577UNTS231	108380

DATE	PARTY ONE	PARTY TWO	TOPIC	CITATION	NUMBER
1961 (Cont.)					
12 Oct	Bolivia	Spain	Consul/Citizenship	64SPBO1406	460055
12 Oct	Germany, West	Morocco	Air Transport	523UNTS289	107562
13 Oct	Burma	China People's Rep	Territory Boundary	61CCJC135	410838
13 Oct	Switzerland	USA (United States)	Air Transport	459UNTS219	106625
13 Oct	Costa Rica	IDA (Devel Assoc)	Non-IBRD Project	431UNTS3	106204
13 Oct	Philippines	IBRD (World Bank)	IBRD Project	415UNTS269	105989
13 Oct	Costa Rica	IBRD (World Bank)	IBRD Project	430UNTS27	106202
13 Oct	Malagasy	WHO (World Health)	Tech Assistance	421UNTS273	106064
13 Oct	India	IBRD (World Bank)	IBRD Project	418UNTS3	106013
14 Oct	Pakistan	USA (United States)	US Agri Commod Aid	426UNTS237	106141
15 Oct	China People's Rep	Nepal	Non-IBRD Project	61CCJC138	410839
16 Oct	Afghanistan	USSR (Soviet Union)	General Aid	10SUGG143	469800
16 Oct	Japan	USA (United States)	General Trade	433UNTS287	106250
16 Oct	Multilateral		Tech Assistance	410UNTS242	105908
17 Oct	Japan	Pakistan	Air Transport	466UNTS17	106734
17 Oct	Taiwan	Jordan	Culture	435UNTS267	106284
17 Oct	Canada	USA (United States)	Specific Property	426UNTS201	106138
17 Oct	Canada	USA (United States)	Water Transport	424UNTS101	106102
18 Oct	France	Malagasy	Specific Property	63FRRT21	415280
18 Oct	China People's Rep	Iraq	General Trade	61CCJC140	410840
18 Oct	Multilateral		IGO Establishment	529UNTS89	107659
18 Oct	Greece	USA (United States)	US Agri Commod Aid	426UNTS209	106139
19 Oct	Germany, East	Ghana	Culture	9EGDA344	419110
19 Oct	Germany, East	Ghana	Finance	9EGDA338	419108
19 Oct	Germany, East	Ghana	Tech Assistance	9EGDA342	419109
19 Oct	Germany, East	Ghana	General Trade	9EGDA333	419107
19 Oct	Brazil	Poland	Culture	552UNTS75	108050
19 Oct	Pakistan	IDA (Devel Assoc)	Non-IBRD Project	447UNTS161	106415
20 Oct	China People's Rep	Czechoslovakia	General Trade	61CCJC141	410841
20 Oct	Sweden	Thailand	Taxation	428UNTS275	106180
20 Oct	Switzerland	UK Great Britain	Loans and Credits	431UNTS29	106206
21 Oct	China People's Rep	Cuba	Telecommunications	61CCJC143	410842
21 Oct	China People's Rep	Cuba	Postal Service	61CCJC144	410843
23 Oct	Italy	UK Great Britain	Admin Cooperation	424UNTS225	106111
23 Oct	Belgium	Denmark	Taxation	425UNTS181	106123
23 Oct	Austria	Denmark	Taxation	425UNTS115	106122
23 Oct	Bolivia	USA (United States)	Telecommunications	424UNTS93	106101
24 Oct	Sweden	USA (United States)	Extradition	494UNTS141	107231
25 Oct	Chad	France	Specific Property	63FRRT23	415428
26 Oct	France	Ivory Coast	Customs	62FRRT37	415140
26 Oct	Israel	Ivory Coast	Visas	515UNTS251	107462
26 Oct	Multilateral		Patents/Copyrights	496UNTS43	107247
26 Oct	Paraguay	IDA (Devel Assoc)	Non-IBRD Project	447UNTS277	106419
26 Oct	Indonesia	USA (United States)	US Agri Commod Aid	433UNTS249	106248
27 Oct	China People's Rep	Morocco	Finance	61CCJC145	410844
27 Oct	Brazil	USA (United States)	Telecommunications	433UNTS113	106234
28 Oct	Belgium	Italy	Culture	429UNTS199	106199
30 Oct	Cyprus	Germany, West	Tech Assistance	62WBGA3	424738
30 Oct	Cyprus	Germany, West	General Economic	62WBGA3	424737
30 Oct	Cyprus	Germany, West	General Trade	62WBGA3	424736
31 Oct	IBRD (World Bank)	Turkey	IBRD Project	0UNTS0	109630
31 Oct	Accept UN Charter	Congo (Zaire)	UN Charter	418UNTS157	106020
31 Oct	Philippines	USA (United States)	Direct Aid	424UNTS129	106105
31 Oct	Belgium	Yugoslavia	Sanitation	426UNTS165	106136
01 Nov	Sudan	USSR (Soviet Union)	General Trade	10SUGG143	469801
01 Nov	Sudan	USSR (Soviet Union)	General Trade	0UNTS0	109827
01 Nov	Greece	Morocco	General Trade	483UNTS113	107009
02 Nov	Mali	Poland	Tech Assistance	61PZUM217	458091
02 Nov	Mali	Poland	Culture	64PDZU361	457090
02 Nov	Czechoslovakia	Hungary	Admin Cooperation	438UNTS3	106313
02 Nov	Gabon	UNICEF (Children)	Direct Aid	422UNTS241	106078
03 Nov	Iraq	Syria	General Trade	489UNTS45	107134
03 Nov	Peru	IBRD (World Bank)	IBRD Project	430UNTS47	106203
04 Nov	Ghana	USSR (Soviet Union)	Finance	10SUGG144	469802
04 Nov	Ghana	USSR (Soviet Union)	Commodity Trade	10SUGG144	469803

DATE	PARTY ONE	PARTY TWO	TOPIC	CITATION	NUMBER
1961 (Cont.)					
04 Nov	Germany, West	Greece	Admin Cooperation	63WGBB109	425239
04 Nov	Ghana	USSR (Soviet Union)	Finance	0UNTS0	109381
04 Nov	Ghana	USSR (Soviet Union)	General Trade	437UNTS213	106308
06 Nov	Iceland	USA (United States)	US Agri Commod Aid	426UNTS225	106140
07 Nov	Mauritania	UN Special Fund	Direct Aid	412UNTS240	105936
07 Nov	Multilateral		Tech Assistance	412UNTS258	105937
09 Nov	Niger	Poland	Health/Educ/Welfare	61PZUM229	458092
09 Nov	Germany, West	Pakistan	Culture	63WGBB43	425566
09 Nov	Syria	USA (United States)	US Agri Commod Aid	435UNTS75	106271
09 Nov	Congo (Brazzaville)	UN Special Fund	Direct Aid	413UNTS58	105940
10 Nov	Germany, East	USSR (Soviet Union)	Tech Assistance	10SUGG145	469804
10 Nov	Indonesia	Mexico	General Trade	62MEXD1602	444028
10 Nov	Chile	Germany, West	Admin Cooperation	62WBGA35	424084
10 Nov	Austria	Czechoslovakia	Admin Cooperation	455UNTS337	106550
11 Nov	Brazil	USA (United States)	Direct Aid	433UNTS199	106243
14 Nov	Australia	UK Great Britain	Air Transport	466UNTS35	106735
14 Nov	Sudan	USA (United States)	US Agri Commod Aid	434UNTS51	106255
14 Nov	United Arab Rep	UK Great Britain	Education	449UNTS129	106455
15 Nov	Argentina	Brazil	Extradition	0UNTS0	109424
15 Nov	Argentina	Brazil	Admin Cooperation	0UNTS0	109546
15 Nov	Denmark	UK Great Britain	Dispute Settlement	420UNTS67	106041
15 Nov	Bolivia	USA (United States)	US Agri Commod Aid	456UNTS192	106557
15 Nov	Mexico	USA (United States)	Non-IBRD Project	460UNTS113	106634
16 Nov	Saudi Arabia	Syria	General Economic	491UNTS163	107177
16 Nov	Malagasy	UNICEF (Children)	Direct Aid	422UNTS251	106079
18 Nov	United Nations	USA (United States)	US Agri Commod Aid	494UNTS213	107235
18 Nov	Congo (Zaire)	USA (United States)	US Agri Commod Aid	433UNTS207	106244
20 Nov	El Salvadcr	USA (United States)	Direct Aid	433UNTS221	106245
21 Nov	Sudan	USSR (Soviet Union)	Direct Aid	10SUGG145	469805
21 Nov	Italy	Korea, South	General Economic	62ITDI577	436096
22 Nov	Canada	Venezuela	Telecommunications	470UNTS148	106806
22 Nov	India	IDA (Devel Assoc)	Loans and Credits	427UNTS55	106146
22 Nov	Ethiopia	IBRD (World Bank)	IBRD Project	426UNTS255	106142
22 Nov	Pakistan	IDA (Devel Assoc)	Non-IBRD Project	447UNTS295	106420
22 Nov	India	IDA (Devel Assoc)	Loans and Credits	427UNTS3	106144
22 Nov	India	IDA (Devel Assoc)	Loans and Credits	427UNTS29	106145
23 Nov	Brazil	USSR (Soviet Union)	Consul/Citizenship	10SUGG145	469806
23 Nov	Italy	Tunisia	Tech Assistance	62ITDI530	436400
23 Nov	Cyprus	Greece	Air Transport	497UNTS311	107274
24 Nov	Chile	Switzerland	Loans and Credits	62SWRO77	462107
24 Nov	Philippines	USA (United States)	US Agri Commod Aid	433UNTS315	106251
25 Nov	Japan	Thailand	Sanitation	451UNTS55	106484
27 Nov	France	Germany, West	Admin Cooperation	62WGBB705	425186
27 Nov	Austria	Germany, West	Refugees	62WGBB1041	425549
27 Nov	Czechoslovakia	Mali	Air Transport	466UNTS41	106736
27 Nov	Taiwan	El Salvador	Culture	437UNTS161	106306
27 Nov	Guatemala	Israel	Culture	448UNTS191	106431
27 Nov	Congo (Zaire)	United Nations	IGO Status/Immunit	414UNTS229	105975
28 Nov	Thailand	USA (United States)	Direct Aid	434UNTS77	106256
28 Nov	Portugal	USA (United States)	US Agri Commod Aid	434UNTS31	106253
29 Nov	IAEA (Atom Energy)	UN Special Fund	IGO Operations	415UNTS408	200593
29 Nov	Belgium	Luxembourg	Visas	486UNTS37	107071
29 Nov	Japan	IBRD (World Bank)	IBRD Project	426UNTS3	106128
29 Nov	IBRD (World Bank)	UK Great Britain	IBRD Project	426UNTS49	106130
29 Nov	OAS (Am States)	USA (United States)	Direct Aid	424UNTS119	106104
30 Nov	Morocco	USA (United States)	Postal Service	451UNTS167	106492
01 Dec	Romania	USSR (Soviet Union)	Tech Assistance	10SUGG145	469807
01 Dec	IBRD (World Bank)	South Africa	IBRD Project	425UNTS197	106125
01 Dec	IBRD (World Bank)	South Africa	IBRD Project	425UNTS215	106126
01 Dec	Ivory Coast	USA (United States)	Claims and Debts	462UNTS221	106681
01 Dec	Taiwan	IDA (Devel Assoc)	Loans and Credits	426UNTS105	106132
02 Dec	Switzerland	Tunisia	Tech Assistance	64SWRO70	462109
02 Dec	Switzerland	Tunisia	Finance	64SWRO67	462108
02 Dec	Switzerland	Tunisia	General Trade	62SWRO1517	462160
03 Dec	Poland	USSR (Soviet Union)	Atomic Energy	10SUGG145	469808

DATE	PARTY ONE	PARTY TWO	TOPIC	CITATION	NUMBER
1961 (Cont.)					
04 Dec	Bulgaria	Poland	Admin Cooperation	484UNTS3	107019
04 Dec	Accept UN Charter	Mongolia	UN Charter	434UNTS141	106261
04 Dec	Ceylon (Sri Lanka)	United Nations	Tech Assistance	415UNTS236	105987
05 Dec	Finland	UK Great Britain	Admin Cooperation	424UNTS217	106110
06 Dec	Multilateral		Customs	473UNTS219	106864
06 Dec	Greece	New Zealand	Visas	486UNTS3	107067
06 Dec	Ethiopia	USA (United States)	Education	433UNTS231	106246
06 Dec	Japan	Philippines	Visas	449UNTS29	106449
07 Dec	Denmark	Jordan	Air Transport	631UNTS333	109003
07 Dec	COMECON (Econ Aid)	USSR (Soviet Union)	IGO Operations	506UNTS325	107392
09 Dec	Italy	Poland	Culture	61PZUM266	458093
09 Dec	Italy	Poland	Culture	62ITDI517	436306
09 Dec	Czechoslovakia	Germany, East	Specific Property	9EGDA395	419365
09 Dec	Tanganyika	UK Great Britain	IGO Establishment	437UNTS47	106299
09 Dec	Accept UN Charter	Tanganyika	UN Charter	416UNTS147	106000
10 Dec	Tanganyika	USSR (Soviet Union)	Recognition	16SUGG132	469997
10 Dec	Argentina	Thailand	General Trade	422UNTS87	106070
11 Dec	UN Special Fund	Venezuela	Direct Aid	422UNTS149	106074
11 Dec	Panama	USA (United States)	General Aid	445UNTS161	106384
12 Dec	Germany, West	Liberia	Claims and Debts	67WGBB1537	425409
12 Dec	Germany, West	Liberia	General Transport	62WBGA46	424410
12 Dec	Germany, West	Liberia	Direct Aid	62WBGA46	424411
13 Dec	Poland	USSR (Soviet Union)	General Aid	10SUGG146	469809
13 Dec	Germany, West	Thailand	Claims and Debts	541UNTS181	107870
13 Dec	IBRD (World Bank)	Venezuela	IBRD Project	446UNTS371	106409
14 Dec	France	Spain	Non-ILO Labor	62SPBO2002	460137
14 Dec	France	Spain	Non-ILO Labor	62SPBO1902	460136
14 Dec	Bulgaria	Germany, East	General Economic	9EGDA325	419065
15 Dec	Italy	Switzerland	Customs	63SWRO724	462064
15 Dec	Multilateral		Admin Cooperation	424UNTS43	106098
15 Dec	Poland	USA (United States)	US Agri Commod Aid	434UNTS3	106252
16 Dec	Czechoslovakia	Guinea	Air Transport	559UNTS49	108154
16 Dec	Multilateral		Visas	544UNTS19	107909
16 Dec	UN Special Fund	Senegal	Direct Aid	425UNTS97	106121
18 Dec	France	Italy	Culture	62ITDI506	436154
18 Dec	Germany, West	Ivory Coast	General Economic	62WBGA58	424120
18 Dec	Germany, West	Ivory Coast	Water Transport	62WBGA58	424122
18 Dec	Germany, West	Ivory Coast	Direct Aid	62WBGA58	424121
18 Dec	Canada	Italy	Specific Resources	470UNTS153	106807
18 Dec	Dahomey	Israel	Visas	448UNTS259	106438
19 Dec	El Salvador	USA (United States)	General Aid	445UNTS175	106385
20 Dec	France	Germany, West	IGO Establishment	62WGBB1106	425187
20 Dec	Argentina	Japan	Health/Educ/Welfare	0JGJI1504	441112
20 Dec	Argentina	Japan	Sanitation	0JGJI1462	441111
20 Dec	Argentina	Japan	General Amity	67JHZ9	439038
20 Dec	Argentina	Japan	Sanitation	0JGJI1460	441109
20 Dec	Argentina	Japan	Commodity Trade	0JGJI1461	441110
20 Dec	Argentina	Japan	General Amity	613UNTS323	108859
20 Dec	Austria	Japan	Taxation	517UNTS155	107485
20 Dec	Multilateral		Water Transport	419UNTS79	106031
20 Dec	Argentina	Japan	Sanitation	451UNTS77	106486
20 Dec	Argentina	Japan	Visas	451UNTS71	106485
20 Dec	Argentina	Japan	Taxation	451UNTS91	106487
21 Dec	Czechoslovakia	USSR (Soviet Union)	Non-IBRD Project	10SUGG147	469811
21 Dec	Indonesia	USSR (Soviet Union)	Gen Communications	10SUGG147	469812
21 Dec	Canada	Mexico	Air Transport	64MEXD607	444004
21 Dec	Iran	USA (United States)	Direct Aid	433UNTS269	106249
22 Dec	Cyprus	USSR (Soviet Union)	General Economic	10SUGG147	469813
22 Dec	Cyprus	USSR (Soviet Union)	General Trade	0UNTS0	109828
22 Dec	India	IBRD (World Bank)	IBRD Project	481UNTS85	106979
22 Dec	Costa Rica	USA (United States)	General Aid	460UNTS277	106646
22 Dec	Jordan	IDA (Devel Assoc)	Non-IBRD Project	448UNTS21	106423
23 Dec	Romania	USSR (Soviet Union)	Non-IBRD Project	10SUGG148	469814
27 Dec	Multilateral		Tech Assistance	425UNTS83	106120
27 Dec	USA (United States)	Vietnam, South	US Agri Commod Aid	433UNTS185	106242

DATE	PARTY ONE	PARTY TWO	TOPIC	CITATION	NUMBER
1961 (Cont.)					
28 Dec	Germany, East	USSR (Soviet Union)	Atomic Energy	9EGDA442	419418
28 Dec	USA (United States)	Yugoslavia	US Agri Commod Aid	434UNTS111	106259
29 Dec	Germany, East	Korea, North	General Economic	10EGDA399	419182
29 Dec	Argentina	Chile	Territory Boundary	635UNTS111	109075
29 Dec	Sierra Leone	USA (United States)	Direct Aid	434UNTS43	106254
1962					
01 Jan	USSR (Soviet Union)	Western Samoa	Recognition	11SUGG130	469815
03 Jan	Ghana	USA (United States)	Scientific Project	433UNTS147	106237
05 Jan	Malagasy	UN Special Fund	Direct Aid	419UNTS29	106028
08 Jan	China People's Rep	Korea, North	General Trade	62CCJC1	410854
08 Jan	Canada	Ghana	Military Mission	528UNTS221	107645
08 Jan	Mexico	USA (United States)	Humanitarian	433UNTS163	106239
08 Jan	Netherlands	Sweden	Air Transport	466UNTS65	106737
09 Jan	Japan	USA (United States)	Direct Aid	451UNTS97	106488
10 Jan	Ivory Coast	UNICEF (Children)	Direct Aid	422UNTS261	106080
11 Jan	Dominican Republic	USA (United States)	General Aid	433UNTS133	106236
11 Jan	Ethiopia	WHO (World Health)	Tech Assistance	423UNTS99	106087
12 Jan	Thailand	USA (United States)	Postal Service	459UNTS95	106615
13 Jan	Afghanistan	USSR (Soviet Union)	General Trade	11SUGG130	469816
15 Jan	Austria	Greece	Air Transport	498UNTS3	107275
15 Jan	Cyprus	USA (United States)	Commodity Trade	435UNTS15	106267
16 Jan	Guinea	USSR (Soviet Union)	Air Transport	11SUGG130	469817
16 Jan	Paraguay	USA (United States)	Scientific Project	433UNTS169	106240
17 Jan	Indonesia	USSR (Soviet Union)	Education	16SUGG132	469998
17 Jan	Multilateral		Tech Assistance	419UNTS294	106033
18 Jan	Sierra Leone	USSR (Soviet Union)	Recognition	16SUGG132	469999
18 Jan	Cyprus	USA (United States)	Education	435UNTS3	106266
19 Jan	Germany, West	Somalia	Direct Aid	62WBGA113	424636
19 Jan	Germany, West	Somalia	General Trade	62WBGA113	424635
19 Jan	Germany, West	Somalia	General Transport	62WBGA113	424637
19 Jan	Germany, West	Somalia	Loans and Credits	62WBGA113	424638
19 Jan	France	Germany, West	Admin Cooperation	62FRJO13	416040
19 Jan	United Arab Rep	USA (United States)	US Agri Commod Aid	435UNTS107	106273
19 Jan	Argentina	IBRD (World Bank)	IBRD Project	446UNTS305	106407
19 Jan	UNESCO (Educ/Cult)	USA (United States)	Culture	435UNTS99	106272
20 Jan	Portugal	Spain	Non-ILO Labor	62SPBO1809	460234
20 Jan	Multilateral		Tech Assistance	429UNTS230	200596
20 Jan	United Nations	Somalia	Tech Assistance	420UNTS133	106044
23 Jan	Indonesia	Japan	Air Transport	559UNTS77	108155
23 Jan	Australia	IBRD (World Bank)	IBRD Project	430UNTS3	106201
24 Jan	Ghana	USA (United States)	Education	435UNTS23	106268
25 Jan	Peru	USA (United States)	Tech Assistance	473UNTS57	106855
25 Jan	Poland	Romania	Admin Cooperation	468UNTS3	106770
27 Jan	China People's Rep	Cuba	Mass Media	62CCJC15	410864
29 Jan	Iran	USA (United States)	US Agri Commod Aid	435UNTS53	106270
30 Jan	Norway	Panama	Visas	3NORT848	451127
30 Jan	Denmark	Germany, West	Taxation	63WGBB1311	425103
30 Jan	UK Great Britain	Zambia	Non-ILO Labor	590UNTS173	108553
31 Jan	Luxembourg	South Africa	Air Transport	563UNTS153	108209
31 Jan	Italy	Japan	Air Transport	498UNTS23	107276
31 Jan	UNICEF (Children)	Yemen	Direct Aid	422UNTS271	106081
01 Feb	United Arab Rep	USSR (Soviet Union)	Consul/Citizenship	16SUGG132	470001
01 Feb	Afghanistan	Iran	General Transport	OIRTB2	433005
01 Feb	Israel	IBRD (World Bank)	IBRD Project	435UNTS155	106277
01 Feb	Austria	Finland	Non-ILO Labor	425UNTS33	106116
02 Feb	Sweden	USSR (Soviet Union)	General Trade	11SUGG131	469818
02 Feb	Guinea	USA (United States)	US Agri Commod Aid	435UNTS35	106269
05 Feb	Chile	Norway	Claims and Debts	3NORT849	451021
06 Feb	Nepal	USSR (Soviet Union)	Direct Aid	11SUGG131	469819
07 Feb	Ceylon (Sri Lanka)	China People's Rep	Admin Cooperation	62CCJC18	410867
08 Feb	Turkey	USA (United States)	Loans and Credits	63TURG106	466125
08 Feb	Ghana	IBRD (World Bank)	IBRD Project	449UNTS207	106462
09 Feb	Japan	USA (United States)	General Trade	13UST948	486001
09 Feb	Hungary	Yugoslavia	Land Transport	577UNTS3	108370

DATE	PARTY ONE	PARTY TWO	TOPIC	CITATION	NUMBER
1962 (Cont.)					
09 Feb	Morocco	USA (United States)	Direct Aid	442UNTS135	106345
12 Feb	India	USSR (Soviet Union)	General Aid	11SUGG132	469820
12 Feb	Ivory Coast	Netherlands	Visas	485UNTS219	107057
12 Feb	Bolivia	USA (United States)	US Agri Commod Aid	451UNTS281	106499
12 Feb	Belgium	Ivory Coast	Visas	429UNTS193	106198
13 Feb	Japan	Morocco	Tech Assistance	62JGJI18	441302
13 Feb	Multilateral		Tech Assistance	422UNTS288	200594
13 Feb	Austria	Czechoslovakia	Education	455UNTS381	106551
13 Feb	Finland	Hungary	Air Transport	463UNTS61	106693
13 Feb	UK Great Britain	Yugoslavia	Culture	431UNTS35	106207
13 Feb	Tunisia	USA (United States)	Direct Aid	442UNTS155	106346
14 Feb	Germany, West	Mali	Loans and Credits	62WBGA75	424456
14 Feb	India	IDA (Devel Assoc)	Non-IBRD Project	468UNTS177	106773
14 Feb	Central Afri Rep	Israel	Visas	484UNTS143	107022
14 Feb	Iceland	IBRD (World Bank)	IBRD Project	447UNTS95	106413
16 Feb	Germany, West	Luxembourg	Visas	63WGBB141	425429
16 Feb	Tunisia	USA (United States)	US Agri Commod Aid	442UNTS161	106347
17 Feb	Japan	Morocco	Non-IBRD Project	62JGJI19	441303
19 Feb	Burma	USSR (Soviet Union)	Direct Aid	11SUGG133	469821
19 Feb	Austria	Spain	Air Transport	62SPBO2910	460042
19 Feb	Austria	Spain	Air Transport	OUNTSO	109238
19 Feb	India	United Nations	Direct Aid	423UNTS3	106082
19 Feb	Indonesia	USA (United States)	US Agri Commod Aid	435UNTS137	106276
20 Feb	Multilateral		Water Transport	597UNTS159	108644
21 Feb	Multilateral		Tech Assistance	423UNTS151	106091
22 Feb	Ceylon (Sri Lanka)	USSR (Soviet Union)	General Trade	11SUGG133	469822
22 Feb	Norway	USSR (Soviet Union)	Specific Resources	11SUGG133	469823
22 Feb	Portugal	Switzerland	Commodity Trade	62SWRO257	462152
22 Feb	UK Great Britain	USA (United States)	Direct Aid	435UNTS127	106275
23 Feb	Luxembourg	USA (United States)	General Amity	474UNTS3	106868
24 Feb	USSR (Soviet Union)	Yugoslavia	Admin Cooperation	471UNTS195	106833
25 Feb	China People's Rep	Mongolia	General Trade	62CCJC20	410869
26 Feb	Guinea	USSR (Soviet Union)	General Aid	11SUGG134	469824
26 Feb	Niger	UN Special Fund	Direct Aid	423UNTS83	106086
28 Feb	Syria	USSR (Soviet Union)	Consul/Citizenship	16SUGG132	470002
28 Feb	Germany, East	Tunisia	Finance	10EGDA566	419373
28 Feb	Taiwan	USA (United States)	Milit Installation	462UNTS25	106668
28 Feb	Jordan	UK Great Britain	Postal Service	466UNTS249	106748
28 Feb	India	IBRD (World Bank)	IBRD Project	447UNTS3	106410
01 Mar	Austria	Czechoslovakia	Air Transport	62ABGB319	403024
01 Mar	Australia	Japan	Postal Service	517UNTS81	107483
01 Mar	Multilateral		Tech Assistance	423UNTS122	106089
02 Mar	Korea, South	USA (United States)	US Agri Commod Aid	442UNTS185	106349
02 Mar	Cyprus	USA (United States)	Direct Aid	445UNTS189	106386
05 Mar	Germany, East	USSR (Soviet Union)	Loans and Credits	10EGDA504	419419
05 Mar	Germany, West	Thailand	Air Transport	563UNTS165	108210
05 Mar	Multilateral		Scientific Project	425UNTS3	106114
05 Mar	Finland	USA (United States)	General Economic	446UNTS19	106399
05 Mar	Peru	USA (United States)	General Economic	446UNTS65	106404
05 Mar	Denmark	USA (United States)	General Economic	446UNTS9	106398
05 Mar	Sweden	USA (United States)	Commodity Trade	459UNTS17	106610
05 Mar	Israel	USA (United States)	General Economic	446UNTS29	106400
05 Mar	Norway	USA (United States)	General Economic	446UNTS47	106402
05 Mar	New Zealand	USA (United States)	General Economic	446UNTS39	106401
05 Mar	Pakistan	USA (United States)	General Trade	446UNTS57	106403
05 Mar	Portugal	USA (United States)	General Trade	436UNTS101	106290
05 Mar	Pakistan	IAEA (Atom Energy)	Scientific Project	425UNTS17	106115
07 Mar	China People's Rep	Czechoslovakia	Finance	62CCJC22	410871
07 Mar	EEC (Econ Commnty)	USA (United States)	General Trade	436UNTS49	106288
07 Mar	EEC (Econ Commnty)	USA (United States)	General Trade	445UNTS195	106387
07 Mar	EEC (Econ Commnty)	USA (United States)	General Economic	446UNTS81	106405
07 Mar	UK Great Britain	USA (United States)	General Economic	446UNTS231	106406
07 Mar	Canada	USA (United States)	General Trade	436UNTS3	106286
07 Mar	Multilateral		Commodity Trade	445UNTS199	106388
07 Mar	Multilateral		Commodity Trade	445UNTS205	106389

DATE	PARTY ONE	PARTY TWO	TOPIC	CITATION	NUMBER
1962 (Cont.)					
08 Mar	Cameroon	Germany, West	Water Transport	62WBGA126	424343
08 Mar	Cameroon	Germany, West	General Trade	62WBGA126	424342
08 Mar	Dominican Republic	USA (United States)	Milit Assistance	527UNTS29	107615
08 Mar	Germany, West	Greece	Land Transport	533UNTS269	107747
08 Mar	USA (United States)	USSR (Soviet Union)	Health/Educ/Welfare	460UNTS3	106630
08 Mar	Liberia	USA (United States)	Direct Aid	445UNTS41	106375
09 Mar	France	Mali	General Amity	64FRRT49	415289
09 Mar	Japan	New Zealand	General Trade	485UNTS339	107065
09 Mar	Japan	New Zealand	General Trade	485UNTS351	107066
09 Mar	Germany, West	Philippines	Visas	449UNTS35	106450
10 Mar	India	USSR (Soviet Union)	Consul/Citizenship	16SUGG132	470003
11 Mar	WHO (World Health)	Sudan	Tech Assistance	432UNTS325	106226
13 Mar	IDA (Devel Assoc)	UK Great Britain	Direct Aid	466UNTS331	106753
14 Mar	Tunisia	USSR (Soviet Union)	Finance	11SUGG135	469827
14 Mar	Tunisia	USSR (Soviet Union)	Mostfavored Nation	11SUGG135	469826
14 Mar	Tunisia	USSR (Soviet Union)	General Trade	11SUGG135	469825
14 Mar	Tanganyika	UK Great Britain	Admin Cooperation	449UNTS147	106456
15 Mar	Brazil	USA (United States)	US Agri Commod Aid	456UNTS209	106558
16 Mar	Argentina	USA (United States)	Scientific Project	454UNTS3	106535
16 Mar	United Nations	Saudi Arabia	Tech Assistance	456UNTS379	106566
16 Mar	Iceland	USA (United States)	US Agri Commod Aid	445UNTS49	106376
17 Mar	China People's Rep	United Arab Rep	General Trade	62CCJC26	410875
17 Mar	China People's Rep	United Arab Rep	Finance	62CCJC25	410874
17 Mar	China People's Rep	United Arab Rep	General Trade	62CCJC24	410873
19 Mar	Algeria	France	Recognition	62FRJO2003	416006
19 Mar	Multilateral		Patents/Copyrights	0UNTS0	110108
19 Mar	Australia	Germany, West	Postal Service	488UNTS203	107130
20 Mar	Mali	USSR (Soviet Union)	Air Transport	16SUGG132	470004
20 Mar	Peru	USA (United States)	US Agri Commod Aid	445UNTS61	106377
20 Mar	Togo	USA (United States)	Admin Cooperation	445UNTS79	106378
21 Mar	France	Guinea	Air Transport	63FRRT59	415209
23 Mar	Algeria	USSR (Soviet Union)	Recognition	11SUGG136	469828
23 Mar	Multilateral		Admin Cooperation	470UNTS25	106793
23 Mar	Multilateral		General Amity	434UNTS145	106262
26 Mar	Luxembourg	Spain	Air Transport	563UNTS205	108211
26 Mar	Multilateral		IGO Establishment	539UNTS67	107825
27 Mar	Somalia	USSR (Soviet Union)	Direct Aid	11SUGG136	469830
27 Mar	Somalia	USSR (Soviet Union)	General Aid	11SUGG136	469829
27 Mar	New Zealand	USSR (Soviet Union)	Visas	16SUGG132	470005
27 Mar	Nigeria	WHO (World Health)	Tech Assistance	429UNTS123	106194
28 Mar	Morocco	USSR (Soviet Union)	Air Transport	11SUGG136	469831
28 Mar	Niger	Switzerland	General Economic	63SWRO46	462148
28 Mar	Dahomey	France	Customs	63FRRT30	415147
28 Mar	Brazil	Japan	Education	451UNTS125	106489
28 Mar	Dahomey	UN Special Fund	Tech Assistance	424UNTS55	106099
29 Mar	Turkey	USA (United States)	Loans and Credits	63TURG106	466126
29 Mar	Switzerland	Yugoslavia	Land Transport	62SWRO1359	462086
29 Mar	China People's Rep	Finland	General Trade	62CCJC30	410878
29 Mar	France	Luxembourg	Air Transport	563UNTS227	108212
29 Mar	Multilateral		IGO Establishment	507UNTS177	107401
29 Mar	FAO (Food Agri)	USA (United States)	IGO Operations	454UNTS13	106536
30 Mar	France	Spain	General Transport	62SPBO1911	460138
30 Mar	France	Spain	Admin Cooperation	62SPBO1711	460140
30 Mar	France	Spain	General Transport	62SPBO2311	460139
30 Mar	Japan	Morocco	Education	62JGJI20	441304
30 Mar	China People's Rep	Hungary	General Economic	62CCJC33	410880
30 Mar	Bulgaria	China People's Rep	General Economic	62CCJC31	410879
30 Mar	Belgium	France	Visas	502UNTS297	107335
30 Mar	Hungary	India	Culture	519UNTS119	107504
30 Mar	IAEA (Atom Energy)	USA (United States)	Specific Property	442UNTS49	106338
30 Mar	Nicaragua	USA (United States)	Tech Assistance	456UNTS241	106559
31 Mar	Japan	USSR (Soviet Union)	Admin Cooperation	16SUGG133	470006
31 Mar	France	Upper Volta	Customs	62FRRT42	415216
31 Mar	India	Japan	Education	451UNTS143	106490
01 Apr	UNICEF (Children)	Somalia	Direct Aid	431UNTS75	106211

DATE	PARTY ONE	PARTY TWO	TOPIC	CITATION	NUMBER
1962 (Cont.)					
04 Apr	Taiwan	Malagasy	General Amity	463UNTS195	106703
05 Apr	Spain	Vatican/Holy See	Education	62SPBO2007	460273
05 Apr	El Salvador	USA (United States)	Telecommunications	442UNTS41	106337
05 Apr	Sierra Leone	UK Great Britain	Air Transport	434UNTS227	106265
06 Apr	Austria	Switzerland	Admin Cooperation	62SWRO1659	462024
06 Apr	Belgium	Italy	Admin Cooperation	490UNTS317	107161
06 Apr	Ghana	USSR (Soviet Union)	Air Transport	498UNTS41	107277
09 Apr	France	Togo	Direct Aid	62FRRT41	415449
09 Apr	Colombia	USA (United States)	Scientific Project	476UNTS9	106899
09 Apr	Congo (Brazzaville)	UNICEF (Children)	Direct Aid	431UNTS65	106210
10 Apr	Dahomey	France	Claims and Debts	62FRRT38	415148
10 Apr	Multilateral		Tech Assistance	429UNTS78	106192
11 Apr	Afghanistan	USSR (Soviet Union)	Tech Assistance	11SUGG137	469832
11 Apr	Denmark	Senegal	General Trade	0UNTS0	110769
11 Apr	Japan	United Nations	IGO Operations	425UNTS45	106117
11 Apr	Israel	Vietnam, South	Mostfavored Nation	448UNTS205	106432
11 Apr	UNICEF (Children)	Sierra Leone	Direct Aid	431UNTS55	106209
12 Apr	France	Spain	Non-ILO Labor	62SPBO3107	460141
12 Apr	Bolivia	Mexico	Culture	66MEXD1708	444001
12 Apr	Liberia	USA (United States)	US Agri Commod Aid	445UNTS213	106390
13 Apr	Italy	United Arab Rep	Claims and Debts	63ITDI380	436320
13 Apr	Brazil	USA (United States)	Non-IBRD Project	445UNTS227	106391
13 Apr	El Salvador	USA (United States)	Milit Assistance	451UNTS307	106500
16 Apr	Italy	Switzerland	Land Transport	63ITDI301	436390
16 Apr	Norway	USSR (Scviet Union)	Specific Resources	437UNTS175	106307
16 Apr	Taiwan	USA (United States)	General Trade	445UNTS249	106392
16 Apr	India	USA (United States)	General Trade	445UNTS257	106393
17 Apr	Czechoslovakia	USSR (Soviet Union)	Atomic Energy	11SUGG138	469833
17 Apr	Ecuador	USA (United States)	General Aid	442UNTS69	106339
17 Apr	Somalia	USA (United States)	Direct Aid	436UNTS107	106291
18 Apr	Multilateral		Tech Assistance	463UNTS44	106692
18 Apr	Mexico	USA (United States)	Telecommunications	452UNTS3	106501
19 Apr	Romania	USSR (Soviet Union)	Atomic Energy	11SUGG138	469834
19 Apr	Germany, West	Guinea	Claims and Debts	64WGBB145	425244
19 Apr	Germany, West	Guinea	General Economic	62WBGA134	424245
19 Apr	Germany, West	Guinea	Air Transport	62WBGA134	424247
19 Apr	Germany, West	Guinea	Loans and Credits	62WBGA134	424246
19 Apr	Brazil	USA (United States)	General Trade	456UNTS255	106560
19 Apr	Canada	USA (United States)	Specific Property	445UNTS265	106394
21 Apr	Albania	Italy	Air Transport	63ITDI273	436007
21 Apr	Ivory Coast	USA (United States)	General Aid	526UNTS39	107598
21 Apr	USA (United States)	Yugoslavia	US Agri Commod Aid	442UNTS123	106344
23 Apr	India	Japan	Education	451UNTS155	106491
24 Apr	Netherlands	USA (United States)	Specific Property	436UNTS93	106289
24 Apr	Greece	USA (United States)	Water Transport	459UNTS3	106609
25 Apr	Greece	USSR (Soviet Union)	General Trade	11SUGG139	469835
26 Apr	Guinea	Switzerland	General Economic	63SWRO732	462138
26 Apr	Austria	Switzerland	Admin Cooperation	62ABGB320	403189
26 Apr	Niger	USA (United States)	Claims and Debts	459UNTS129	106618
26 Apr	Bolivia	USA (United States)	Milit Assistance	461UNTS105	106654
26 Apr	UK Great Britain	USA (United States)	General Trade	445UNTS273	106395
27 Apr	USA (United States)	Uruguay	US Agri Commod Aid	452UNTS25	106502
27 Apr	Taiwan	USA (United States)	US Agri Commod Aid	436UNTS25	106287
27 Apr	France	Germany, West	Admin Cooperation	62FRRT23	415041
30 Apr	Germany, West	Peru	Air Transport	63WGBB373	425578
30 Apr	Germany, West	Peru	Air Transport	0UNTS0	110466
30 Apr	Honduras	UK Great Britain	Visas	449UNTS159	106457
01 May	India	USA (United States)	US Agri Commod Aid	451UNTS179	106493
02 May	Austria	Spain	Non-ILO Labor	62SPBO606	460043
02 May	Congo (Brazzaville)	France	Air Transport	63FRRT25	415123
02 May	Dominican Republic	USA (United States)	Direct Aid	442UNTS107	106342
02 May	Dominican Republic	USA (United States)	Claims and Debts	442UNTS99	106341
03 May	Philippines	United Arab Rep	Culture	4PTS551	465048
03 May	Germany, East	USSR (Soviet Union)	Tech Assistance	10EGDA574	419420
03 May	ILO (Labor Org)	Tanganyika	IGO Operations	429UNTS73	106191

DATE	PARTY ONE	PARTY TWO	TOPIC	CITATION	NUMBER
1962 (Cont.)					
03 May	Ireland	USA (United States)	General Trade	442UNTS117	106343
03 May	Israel	USA (United States)	US Agri Commod Aid	442UNTS83	106340
04 May	UN Special Fund	Uruguay	Direct Aid	429UNTS143	106196
08 May	Cuba	USSR (Soviet Union)	Direct Aid	11SUGG139	469836
08 May	Indonesia	USSR (Soviet Union)	Direct Aid	11SUGG139	469837
09 May	Germany, East	Poland	Visas	10EGDA575	419269
09 May	Guinea	USA (United States)	Claims and Debts	451UNTS197	106494
09 May	Multilateral		IGO Establishment	453UNTS299	106531
10 May	Japan	United Arab Rep	Air Transport	498UNTS69	107278
11 May	Germany, East	Hungary	Education	10EGDA497	419459
14 May	Cuba	USSR (Soviet Union)	General Trade	11SUGG140	469838
14 May	Multilateral		Scientific Project	544UNTS39	107910
14 May	Multilateral		Sanitation	544UNTS81	107911
15 May	Gabon	Israel	General Amity	484UNTS181	107027
15 May	Israel	Sweden	Taxation	484UNTS261	107036
15 May	El Salvador	USA (United States)	General Trade	452UNTS49	106503
15 May	Multilateral		Commodity Trade	444UNTS3	106367
15 May	Gabon	Israel	Tech Assistance	448UNTS211	106433
15 May	Colombia	USA (United States)	General Trade	445UNTS279	106396
17 May	Afghanistan	USSR (Soviet Union)	General Aid	11SUGG140	469839
17 May	USA (United States)	Venezuela	US Agri Commod Aid	456UNTS275	106562
17 May	Belgium	USA (United States)	Milit Assistance	461UNTS3	106647
17 May	Multilateral		Tech Assistance	429UNTS46	106189
18 May	Congo (Brazzaville)	France	Admin Cooperation	65FRRT9	415124
18 May	France	Romania	Air Transport	498UNTS115	107279
18 May	Greece	United Nations	Tech Assistance	429UNTS61	106190
19 May	Indonesia	USSR (Soviet Union)	Consul/Citizenship	16SUGG133	470007
20 May	Iran	Pakistan	General Trade	0IRTB55	433083
21 May	Germany, West	Monaco	Extradition	64WGBB1297	425482
21 May	Germany, West	Monaco	Admin Cooperation	64WGBB1297	425483
21 May	Guatemala	USA (United States)	General Trade	451UNTS205	106495
21 May	United Arab Rep	USA (United States)	Culture	458UNTS197	106601
23 May	France	Malagasy	Customs	62FRRT40	415281
23 May	China People's Rep	Sudan	General Trade	62CCJC49	410891
23 May	Cambodia	China People's Rep	Admin Cooperation	62CCJC50	410892
23 May	Panama	USA (United States)	Milit Assistance	458UNTS225	106604
23 May	Colombia	IBRD (World Bank)	IBRD Project	447UNTS39	106411
23 May	Belgium	USA (United States)	Visas	434UNTS133	106260
23 May	Ethiopia	USA (United States)	General Aid	456UNTS293	106563
24 May	Germany, East	Iraq	Consul/Citizenship	10EGDA384	419140
25 May	Cyprus	Norway	Visas	3NORT857	451032
25 May	Colombia	Italy	Visas	63ITDI279	436093
25 May	Multilateral		IGO Establishment	486UNTS103	107075
25 May	Ghana	Israel	Tech Assistance	515UNTS237	107461
25 May	Korea, South	USA (United States)	Visas	454UNTS25	106537
25 May	Germany, West	USA (United States)	Milit Assistance	458UNTS259	106608
25 May	Canada	France	Other Military	470UNTS163	106808
26 May	Greece	Tunisia	General Aid	534UNTS163	107761
26 May	Romania	USA (United States)	Visas	456UNTS265	106561
28 May	USA (United States)	Vietnam, South	US Agri Commod Aid	0VKNG168	496049
28 May	France	Niger	Air Transport	63FRRT1	415341
28 May	Chile	Netherlands	Admin Cooperation	0UNTS0	110029
28 May	USA (United States)	Venezuela	Tech Assistance	458UNTS249	106607
28 May	Denmark	USA (United States)	Education	450UNTS215	106469
28 May	South Africa	UK Great Britain	Taxation	443UNTS79	106361
28 May	Israel	Netherlands	Postal Service	448UNTS219	106434
28 May	Australia	UK Great Britain	Admin Cooperation	434UNTS219	106264
29 May	Germany, West	Spain	Humanitarian	65SPBO706	460028
29 May	France	Upper Volta	Air Transport	63FRRT2	415217
29 May	China People's Rep	Romania	General Economic	62CCJC52	410893
30 May	France	Spain	Customs	63FRRT68	415164
30 May	Jordan	UK Great Britain	Loans and Credits	449UNTS167	106458
31 May	Ethiopia	IBRD (World Bank)	IBRD Project	467UNTS237	106765
31 May	Thailand	USA (United States)	Postal Service	459UNTS135	106619
31 May	Pakistan	USA (United States)	General Aid	460UNTS75	106631

DATE	PARTY ONE	PARTY TWO	TOPIC	CITATION	NUMBER
1962 (Cont.)					
01 Jun	United Nations	Tanganyika	Tech Assistance	479UNTS3	106944
01 Jun	Germany, West	Israel	Specific Property	448UNTS227	106435
01 Jun	United Nations	Sweden	Admin Cooperation	429UNTS135	106195
04 Jun	Dahomey	USSR (Soviet Union)	Consul/Citizenship	11SUGG141	469840
06 Jun	Germany, West	Malagasy	General Economic	62WBGA153	424438
06 Jun	Germany, West	Malagasy	Direct Aid	62WBGA153	424439
06 Jun	Germany, West	Malagasy	Water Transport	62WBGA153	424440
06 Jun	Multilateral		Privil/Immunities	486UNTS263	107080
06 Jun	Multilateral		Privil/Immunities	486UNTS271	107081
06 Jun	Germany, West	UK Great Britain	Status of Forces	437UNTS39	106298
06 Jun	Dominican Republic	UN Special Fund	Direct Aid	429UNTS169	106197
06 Jun	Haiti	USA (United States)	General Trade	452UNTS59	106504
08 Jun	Switzerland	Yugoslavia	Non-ILO Labor	64SWRO157	462100
08 Jun	Italy	Poland	General Trade	63ITDI294	436307
08 Jun	New Zealand	USA (United States)	Loans and Credits	458UNTS209	106602
09 Jun	Turkey	USSR (Soviet Union)	Telecommunications	493UNTS155	107213
11 Jun	Germany, West	South Africa	Culture	64WGBB13	425647
12 Jun	Ceylon (Sri Lanka)	USSR (Soviet Union)	General Aid	11SUGG143	469841
12 Jun	Greece	Switzerland	Taxation	492UNTS47	107186
13 Jun	Central Afri Rep	Israel	Tech Assistance	448UNTS265	106439
13 Jun	Dahomey	USA (United States)	Milit Assistance	458UNTS219	106603
14 Jun	Senegal	USSR (Soviet Union)	General Aid	11SUGG143	469843
14 Jun	Senegal	USSR (Soviet Union)	Consul/Citizenship	16SUGG133	470008
14 Jun	Senegal	USSR (Soviet Union)	General Trade	11SUGG143	469842
14 Jun	France	Senegal	Admin Cooperation	65FRRT28	415390
14 Jun	Multilateral		IGO Establishment	528UNTS33	107634
14 Jun	Senegal	USSR (Soviet Union)	Culture	437UNTS233	106309
14 Jun	Niger	USA (United States)	Milit Assistance	458UNTS233	106605
15 Jun	France	Senegal	Air Transport	524UNTS3	107563
15 Jun	Austria	IBRD (World Bank)	IBRD Project	447UNTS127	106414
16 Jun	Libya	WHO (World Health)	Tech Assistance	437UNTS127	106301
18 Jun	Poland	Senegal	General Economic	62PZUM51	458095
18 Jun	Poland	Senegal	Culture	62PZUM48	458094
18 Jun	Costa Rica	USA (United States)	Milit Assistance	461UNTS155	106659
19 Jun	WHO (World Health)	Sierra Leone	Tech Assistance	439UNTS151	106327
19 Jun	Bolivia	USA (United States)	General Aid	458UNTS239	106606
20 Jun	Bulgaria	USSR (Soviet Union)	Commodity Trade	11SUGG144	469845
20 Jun	Bulgaria	USSR (Soviet Union)	General Trade	11SUGG144	469844
20 Jun	Germany, West	Turkey	Loans and Credits	65WGBB1193	425774
20 Jun	Greece	Italy	General Trade	62ITDI289	436198
20 Jun	Czechoslovakia	Senegal	Air Transport	498UNTS145	107280
20 Jun	Mexico	IBRD (World Bank)	IBRD Project	468UNTS109	106771
20 Jun	Mexico	IBRD (World Bank)	IBRD Project	467UNTS205	106764
21 Jun	Guinea	Norway	Air Transport	466UNTS81	106738
22 Jun	Multilateral		ILO Labor	494UNTS249	107237
22 Jun	Multilateral		IGO Establishment	466UNTS323	106752
22 Jun	Argentina	USA (United States)	Atomic Energy	458UNTS97	106594
22 Jun	Israel	USA (United States)	Education	448UNTS273	106440
23 Jun	United Arab Rep	USSR (Soviet Union)	Finance	11SUGG144	469846
23 Jun	United Arab Rep	USSR (Soviet Union)	General Trade	11SUGG145	469847
23 Jun	United Arab Rep	USSR (Soviet Union)	Finance	472UNTS19	106835
23 Jun	United Arab Rep	USSR (Soviet Union)	General Trade	472UNTS43	106836
25 Jun	Germany, West	Syria	Tech Assistance	489UNTS71	107135
25 Jun	Israel	Peru	Culture	515UNTS263	107464
25 Jun	Israel	Liberia	Culture	448UNTS295	106442
25 Jun	Israel	Liberia	Tech Assistance	448UNTS287	106441
26 Jun	Ivory Coast	Switzerland	General Economic	63SWRO53	462127
27 Jun	Afghanistan	Poland	Air Transport	62PZUM57	458096
27 Jun	Denmark	UK Great Britain	Consul/Citizenship	562UNTS75	108197
27 Jun	Multilateral		Extradition	616UNTS79	108893
27 Jun	Multilateral		Atomic Energy	463UNTS17	106690
27 Jun	Multilateral		Atomic Energy	463UNTS11	106689
27 Jun	Congo (Zaire)	IAEA (Atom Energy)	Direct Aid	463UNTS31	106691
27 Jun	Multilateral		Atomic Energy	463UNTS3	106688
28 Jun	China People's Rep	Yugoslavia	General Trade	62CCJC60	410898

DATE	PARTY ONE	PARTY TWO	TOPIC	CITATION	NUMBER
1962 (Cont.)					
28 Jun	Bulgaria	Syria	Culture	0UNTS0	109954
28 Jun	Germany, West	United Nations	IGO Operations	434UNTS249	200597
28 Jun	Multilateral		ILO Labor	494UNTS271	107238
29 Jun	Cameroon	Germany, West	Claims and Debts	63WGBB911	425344
29 Jun	Cameroon	Germany, West	Direct Aid	62WBGA172	424345
29 Jun	Israel	Switzerland	Visas	448UNTS303	106443
29 Jun	Pakistan	IDA (Devel Assoc)	Non-IBRD Project	447UNTS325	106421
29 Jun	India	IDA (Devel Assoc)	Non-IBRD Project	447UNTS221	106417
29 Jun	Liberia	Norway	Air Transport	466UNTS95	106739
30 Jun	Burundi	USSR (Soviet Union)	Recognition	11SUGG145	469848
30 Jun	Rwanda	USSR (Soviet Union)	Recognition	11SUGG145	469849
01 Jul	Accept UN Charter	Rwanda	UN Charter	437UNTS145	106302
03 Jul	Algeria	France	Recognition	507UNTS25	107395
04 Jul	Italy	Venezuela	Air Transport	65ITGU194	435427
04 Jul	Ceylon (Sri Lanka)	Germany, West	Taxation	64WGBB789	425071
04 Jul	Philippines	Spain	Visas	490UNTS243	107158
04 Jul	Accept UN Charter	Burundi	UN Charter	437UNTS149	106303
05 Jul	Morocco	Switzerland	Air Transport	498UNTS189	107282
05 Jul	Morocco	Switzerland	Air Transport	498UNTS171	107281
06 Jul	Italy	USA (United States)	Commodity Trade	459UNTS123	106617
07 Jul	UN Special Fund	Syria	Direct Aid	443UNTS3	106355
09 Jul	Austria	Vatican/Holy See	Education	62ABGB273	403210
09 Jul	Germany, West	Israel	Taxation	630UNTS87	108968
11 Jul	Gabon	Germany, West	Direct Aid	63WBGA58	424206
11 Jul	Gabon	Germany, West	General Transport	63WBGA58	424207
11 Jul	Gabon	Germany, West	General Economic	63WBGA58	424205
11 Jul	Taiwan	Paraguay	General Trade	458UNTS41	106591
11 Jul	IBRD (World Bank)	Yugoslavia	IBRD Project	468UNTS143	106772
12 Jul	Germany, West	Netherlands	Non-ILO Labor	63WBGA75	424488
12 Jul	Germany, West	Italy	Non-ILO Labor	63WBGA75	424300
12 Jul	France	Germany, West	Non-ILO Labor	63WBGA75	424188
12 Jul	Burma	Germany, West	Direct Aid	62WBGA161	424043
12 Jul	Germany, West	Luxembourg	Non-ILO Labor	63WBGA75	424430
12 Jul	Belgium	Germany, West	Non-ILO Labor	63WBGA48	424030
13 Jul	Canada	USA (United States)	Water Transport	460UNTS83	106632
13 Jul	Chile	Netherlands	Air Transport	466UNTS109	106740
14 Jul	Tunisia	UK Great Britain	Visas	466UNTS235	106746
16 Jul	Belgium	India	Admin Cooperation	453UNTS259	106529
17 Jul	Cuba	USSR (Soviet Union)	Air Transport	11SUGG147	469850
17 Jul	France	Spain	Culture	66FRRT17	415165
17 Jul	China People's Rep	Czechoslovakia	General Economic	62CCJC64	410901
17 Jul	Cuba	USSR (Soviet Union)	Air Transport	0UNTS0	110123
17 Jul	UN Special Fund	Tanganyika	Direct Aid	435UNTS237	106281
18 Jul	Canada	Greece	General Military	528UNTS265	107647
18 Jul	India	IDA (Devel Assoc)	Non-IBRD Project	447UNTS191	106416
19 Jul	Ceylon (Sri Lanka)	USA (United States)	US Agri Commod Aid	454UNTS31	106538
20 Jul	Czechoslovakia	COMECON (Econ Aid)	IGO Operations	506UNTS345	107393
20 Jul	Senegal	USA (United States)	Milit Assistance	458UNTS137	106596
20 Jul	Honduras	USA (United States)	General Aid	460UNTS125	106635
23 Jul	Turkey	USA (United States)	Loans and Credits	63TURG106	466127
23 Jul	Niger	USA (United States)	Tech Assistance	487UNTS325	107114
23 Jul	Colombia	USA (United States)	General Aid	458UNTS123	106595
23 Jul	Multilateral		Recognition	456UNTS302	106564
24 Jul	France	Lebanon	Taxation	64FRRT6	415261
25 Jul	Multilateral		Specific Property	506UNTS177	107387
25 Jul	Pakistan	USA (United States)	Direct Aid	459UNTS87	106614
26 Jul	Italy	Tunisia	Loans and Credits	63ITDI398	436401
26 Jul	Italy	Tunisia	Non-ILO Labor	63ITDI397	436403
26 Jul	Italy	Tunisia	Non-ILO Labor	63ITDI399	436402
27 Jul	Ghana	USSR (Soviet Union)	Consul/Citizenship	16SUGG133	470009
28 Jul	Multilateral		Specific Resources	460UNTS219	106642
30 Jul	Canada	Mexico	Gen Communications	528UNTS257	107646
31 Jul	Italy	Vatican/Holy See	Finance	64ITGU281	435340
31 Jul	Costa Rica	Israel	Education	484UNTS155	107024
31 Jul	Philippines	Thailand	Visas	452UNTS235	106511

DATE	PARTY ONE	PARTY TWO	TOPIC	CITATION	NUMBER
1962 (Cont.)					
31 Jul	Malaysia	Philippines	Visas	452UNTS223	106510
01 Aug	Japan	Pakistan	Visas	0JGJI1477	441113
01 Aug	New Zealand	Western Samoa	General Amity	453UNTS3	106515
02 Aug	Germany, East	United Arab Rep	Mass Media	10EGDA547	419477
02 Aug	Brazil	Colombia	Visas	0UNTS0	109422
02 Aug	Guatemala	USA (United States)	Milit Assistance	461UNTS199	106664
03 Aug	Cuba	USSR (Soviet Union)	Tech Assistance	16SUGG134	470010
03 Aug	Colombia	Netherlands	Visas	485UNTS225	107058
03 Aug	Ethiopia	USA (United States)	Claims and Debts	459UNTS79	106613
03 Aug	Ecuador	USA (United States)	General Aid	460UNTS133	106636
04 Aug	Cuba	USSR (Soviet Union)	Education	11SUGG149	469852
04 Aug	Colombia	Germany, West	Claims and Debts	64WGBB257	425371
04 Aug	China People's Rep	Germany, East	General Economic	62CCJC77	410910
05 Aug	Jamaica	USSR (Soviet Union)	Recognition	11SUGG149	469853
06 Aug	WHO (World Health)	Senegal	Tech Assistance	435UNTS179	106279
06 Aug	Accept UN Charter	Jamaica	UN Charter	437UNTS153	106304
07 Aug	Australia	Japan	Atomic Energy	435UNTS261	106283
07 Aug	Multilateral		Recognition	457UNTS117	106580
07 Aug	Chile	USA (United States)	US Agri Commod Aid	461UNTS61	106652
07 Aug	Nigeria	United Nations	Tech Assistance	435UNTS167	106278
08 Aug	Germany, East	USSR (Soviet Union)	Scientific Project	10EGDA521	419421
08 Aug	India	IDA (Devel Assoc)	Non-IBRD Project	478UNTS335	106941
09 Aug	Iran	USSR (Soviet Union)	General Trade	11SUGG149	469855
09 Aug	Ceylon (Sri Lanka)	USSR (Soviet Union)	General Aid	11SUGG149	469854
12 Aug	Multilateral		Tech Assistance	443UNTS266	106365
13 Aug	Ethiopia	USA (United States)	US Agri Commod Aid	459UNTS31	106611
14 Aug	Italy	Switzerland	Land Transport	63ITDI302	436391
14 Aug	China People's Rep	Nepal	Consul/Citizenship	62CCJC79	410911
14 Aug	WHO (World Health)	Western Samoa	Tech Assistance	437UNTS317	200598
15 Aug	UK Great Britain	USA (United States)	General Aid	580UNTS189	108421
15 Aug	Multilateral		Territory Boundary	437UNTS292	106312
15 Aug	Taiwan	USA (United States)	Loans and Credits	460UNTS237	106643
15 Aug	Indonesia	Netherlands	Territory Boundary	437UNTS273	106311
15 Aug	Finland	IBRD (World Bank)	IBRD Project	467UNTS177	106763
16 Aug	Senegal	Switzerland	General Economic	64SWRO718	462155
16 Aug	Australia	UK Great Britain	Non-ILO Labor	439UNTS163	106328
17 Aug	Korea, South	IDA (Devel Assoc)	Non-IBRD Project	468UNTS387	200603
19 Aug	Syria	USSR (Soviet Union)	Culture	457UNTS285	106588
20 Aug	El Salvador	UK Great Britain	Visas	453UNTS309	106532
20 Aug	IAEA (Atom Energy)	USA (United States)	Commodity Trade	456UNTS447	106570
21 Aug	Philippines	USA (United States)	Milit Assistance	461UNTS163	106660
23 Aug	Cyprus	Greece	General Trade	609UNTS15	108825
23 Aug	Cyprus	USA (United States)	General Aid	461UNTS147	106658
24 Aug	Nepal	USA (United States)	General Aid	460UNTS143	106637
25 Aug	Paraguay	USA (United States)	Milit Assistance	461UNTS207	106665
27 Aug	Belgium	Colombia	Visas	449UNTS199	106461
27 Aug	Turkey	USA (United States)	General Aid	461UNTS55	106651
28 Aug	Algeria	France	Specific Resources	62FRRT27	415007
28 Aug	Israel	USA (United States)	US Agri Commod Aid	448UNTS317	106445
28 Aug	Japan	USA (United States)	Loans and Credits	460UNTS267	106645
28 Aug	Italy	USA (United States)	Sanitation	461UNTS137	106657
29 Aug	Ethiopia	USSR (Soviet Union)	Non-IBRD Project	11SUGG150	469856
29 Aug	UK Great Britain	USA (United States)	Milit Installation	449UNTS177	106459
29 Aug	Cameroon	United Nations	Tech Assistance	442UNTS3	106334
29 Aug	Multilateral		Tech Assistance	443UNTS280	106366
30 Aug	Cuba	USSR (Soviet Union)	Non-IBRD Project	11SUGG150	469858
30 Aug	Burma	USSR (Soviet Union)	Non-IBRD Project	11SUGG150	469857
30 Aug	Trinidad/Tobago	USSR (Soviet Union)	Recognition	11SUGG150	469859
30 Aug	Germany, West	Netherlands	Admin Cooperation	547UNTS173	107957
30 Aug	Belgium	Luxembourg	Taxation	485UNTS313	107062
30 Aug	Germany, West	Netherlands	Admin Cooperation	500UNTS3	107303
30 Aug	Israel	Sierra Leone	Visas	448UNTS309	106444
31 Aug	Multilateral		Recognition	457UNTS123	106581
31 Aug	Austria	South Africa	Visas	443UNTS65	106359
31 Aug	Taiwan	USA (United States)	US Agri Commod Aid	460UNTS247	106644

DATE	PARTY ONE	PARTY TWO	TOPIC	CITATION	NUMBER
1962 (Cont.)					
01 Sep	Congo (Brazzaville)	USA (United States)	Claims and Debts	459UNTS117	106616
04 Sep	Japan	UK Great Britain	Taxation	475UNTS31	106888
05 Sep	Denmark	Norway	Water Transport	3NORT863	451037
05 Sep	Italy	USA (United States)	Scientific Project	461UNTS185	106663
05 Sep	Iran	United Nations	Specific Resources	442UNTS249	106353
05 Sep	Togo	USA (United States)	General Aid	461UNTS47	106650
06 Sep	Germany, West	Tanzania	Tech Assistance	62WBGA225	424652
06 Sep	Austria	Germany, West	Visas	63WGBB1279	425550
06 Sep	Germany, West	Tanzania	General Economic	62WBGA225	424651
06 Sep	Accept UN Charter	Trinidad/Tobago	UN Charter	437UNTS157	106305
07 Sep	Algeria	France	Education	0UNTS0	110819
07 Sep	Nicaragua	IDA (Devel Assoc)	Non-IBRD Project	478UNTS313	106940
10 Sep	Multilateral		Other Military	502UNTS3	107323
10 Sep	Cameroon	USA (United States)	Tech Assistance	461UNTS177	106662
11 Sep	Germany, West	Tanzania	Water Transport	62WBGA225	424654
11 Sep	Germany, West	Turkey	Visas	62WBGA217	424775
11 Sep	Germany, West	Tanzania	Loans and Credits	62WBGA225	424653
11 Sep	Bulgaria	Germany, East	Air Transport	10EGDA368	419066
11 Sep	Canada	Sweden	Atomic Energy	529UNTS9	107651
11 Sep	Morocco	USA (United States)	US Agri Commod Aid	462UNTS207	106680
11 Sep	Denmark	USSR (Soviet Union)	Culture	458UNTS3	106589
11 Sep	Multilateral		Tech Assistance	455UNTS402	106553
11 Sep	Afghanistan	USA (United States)	General Aid	461UNTS169	106661
13 Sep	Chile	Germany, West	Admin Cooperation	63WBGA13	424085
14 Sep	Chile	France	Tech Assistance	65FRRT17	415116
14 Sep	Multilateral		IGO Status/Immunit	494UNTS219	107236
14 Sep	Panama	IBRD (World Bank)	IBRD Project	476UNTS153	106908
14 Sep	Pakistan	IBRD (World Bank)	IBRD Project	467UNTS152	106762
14 Sep	Multilateral		Visas	443UNTS73	106360
14 Sep	India	IDA (Devel Assoc)	Non-IBRD Project	448UNTS3	106422
14 Sep	India	IDA (Devel Assoc)	IBRD Project	467UNTS265	106766
14 Sep	Tunisia	USA (United States)	US Agri Commod Aid	461UNTS31	106649
14 Sep	Pakistan	IBRD (World Bank)	IBRD Project	467UNTS125	106761
15 Sep	USSR (Soviet Union)	Vietnam, North	General Aid	11SUGG152	469860
16 Sep	Iran	USA (United States)	Tech Assistance	0IRTB23	433037
17 Sep	France	Switzerland	Customs	62SWRO1657	462070
17 Sep	IDA (Devel Assoc)	Tunisia	Non-IBRD Project	469UNTS33	106783
18 Sep	France	Senegal	Specific Property	63FRRT22	415391
18 Sep	Israel	Liberia	Postal Service	484UNTS209	107031
18 Sep	Multilateral		Water Transport	442UNTS215	106351
20 Sep	Belgium	France	Culture	65FRRT34	415066
20 Sep	Ecuador	Germany, West	Air Transport	498UNTS199	107283
20 Sep	Germany, West	UK Great Britain	Admin Cooperation	453UNTS317	106533
21 Sep	Germany, West	Malagasy	Claims and Debts	65WGBB369	425441
21 Sep	Belgium	Germany, West	Reparations	502UNTS63	107326
22 Sep	Ceylon (Sri Lanka)	USSR (Soviet Union)	Non-IBRD Project	11SUGG153	469861
22 Sep	Austria	Czechoslovakia	Land Transport	495UNTS157	107244
24 Sep	Cameroon	USSR (Soviet Union)	General Trade	11SUGG153	469862
24 Sep	Cameroon	USSR (Soviet Union)	General Trade	11SUGG153	469863
24 Sep	Ghana	Japan	Direct Aid	0JGJI1501	441114
24 Sep	Algeria	France	Tech Assistance	62FRRT30	415008
24 Sep	Algeria	France	Tech Assistance	0UNTS0	109507
24 Sep	Cameroon	USSR (Soviet Union)	General Trade	0UNTS0	109580
25 Sep	Cuba	USSR (Soviet Union)	Specific Resources	11SUGG153	469864
25 Sep	Cuba	USSR (Soviet Union)	Non-IBRD Project	11SUGG153	469865
25 Sep	Finland	Germany, West	Land Transport	62WBGA217	424132
26 Sep	Cuba	USSR (Soviet Union)	Specific Resources	16SUGG134	470011
26 Sep	Israel	UK Great Britain	Taxation	474UNTS233	106885
27 Sep	Finland	USSR (Soviet Union)	Territory Boundary	479UNTS99	106949
28 Sep	France	Gabon	Customs	62FRRT39	415194
28 Sep	Multilateral		IGO Establishment	469UNTS169	106791
29 Sep	Czechoslovakia	Poland	Specific Property	62PZUM81	458097
29 Sep	France	Malagasy	General Economic	65FRRT69	415282
30 Sep	China People's Rep	Czechoslovakia	Scientific Project	62CCJC90	410918
30 Sep	Accept UN Charter	Algeria	UN Charter	442UNTS37	106336

DATE	PARTY ONE	PARTY TWO	TOPIC	CITATION	NUMBER
1962 (Cont.)					
01 Oct	Burundi	USSR (Soviet Union)	Consul/Citizenship	11SUGG154	469866
01 Oct	Niger	United Nations	Tech Assistance	439UNTS181	106329
02 Oct	Czechoslovakia	Italy	Admin Cooperation	63ITDI277	436080
02 Oct	Italy	Senegal	Tech Assistance	63ITDI347	436341
03 Oct	Ceylon (Sri Lanka)	China People's Rep	General Economic	62CCJC93	410919
03 Oct	Ceylon (Sri Lanka)	China People's Rep	General Trade	62CCJC95	410921
03 Oct	Ceylon (Sri Lanka)	China People's Rep	Direct Aid	62CCJC94	410920
03 Oct	Denmark	Germany, West	Other Military	450UNTS291	106475
04 Oct	USSR (Soviet Union)	Yemen	Recognition	11SUGG155	469867
04 Oct	Cuba	Germany, East	Mass Media	10EGDA407	419186
04 Oct	Gabon	USA (United States)	General Aid	459UNTS185	106620
04 Oct	Chile	USA (United States)	Tech Assistance	461UNTS129	106656
04 Oct	Sweden	USA (United States)	Milit Assistance	462UNTS31	106669
05 Oct	Poland	Romania	Consul/Citizenship	521UNTS3	107516
05 Oct	Multilateral		IGO Establishment	502UNTS225	107333
05 Oct	Colombia	USA (United States)	Finance	459UNTS191	106621
06 Oct	Japan	Kuwait	Air Transport	498UNTS235	107284
08 Oct	Uganda	USSR (Soviet Union)	Recognition	11SUGG155	469868
08 Oct	Cameroon	Denmark	General Trade	0UNTS0	110770
08 Oct	United Arab Rep	USA (United States)	US Agri Commod Aid	462UNTS39	106670
08 Oct	Trinidad/Tobago	USA (United States)	Air Transport	462UNTS145	106675
09 Oct	India	USA (United States)	Scientific Project	471UNTS39	106820
09 Oct	Accept UN Charter	Uganda	UN Charter	443UNTS47	106357
10 Oct	Honduras	Israel	Visas	484UNTS189	107028
10 Oct	Mali	USSR (Soviet Union)	Tech Assistance	493UNTS219	107216
10 Oct	Gabon	Israel	Visas	484UNTS175	107026
10 Oct	Uganda	UK Great Britain	Admin Cooperation	475UNTS177	106893
11 Oct	Israel	OAS (Am States)	Tech Assistance	484UNTS241	107035
12 Oct	Cuba	Poland	Mass Media	62PZUM93	458098
12 Oct	Belgium	France	Milit Servic/Citiz	64FRRT61	415067
12 Oct	Finland	France	Air Transport	498UNTS299	107285
12 Oct	Belgium	Romania	Sanitation	502UNTS31	107325
13 Oct	Uganda	USSR (Soviet Union)	Consul/Citizenship	11SUGG156	469869
13 Oct	France	Senegal	Customs	63FRRT55	415392
13 Oct	Belgium	Rwanda	Tech Assistance	456UNTS425	106568
13 Oct	Belgium	Rwanda	Tech Assistance	456UNTS431	106569
14 Oct	Canada	Chile	Gen Communications	528UNTS273	107648
15 Oct	Morocco	Poland	Tech Assistance	62PZUM100	458099
15 Oct	Iran	USA (United States)	US Agri Commod Aid	473UNTS291	106866
16 Oct	Canada	San Marino	Visas	529UNTS3	107650
16 Oct	Austria	United Arab Rep	Taxation	491UNTS63	107174
16 Oct	Czechoslovakia	Hungary	Visas	479UNTS301	106961
16 Oct	Multilateral		Postal Service	470UNTS336	106816
16 Oct	Multilateral		Postal Service	470UNTS291	106814
16 Oct	Multilateral		Postal Service	470UNTS321	106815
17 Oct	Germany, West	Ireland	Taxation	604UNTS135	108749
17 Oct	Canada	Iceland	Visas	528UNTS281	107649
17 Oct	Israel	IBRD (World Bank)	IBRD Project	467UNTS107	106760
18 Oct	Congo (Brazzaville)	Switzerland	General Economic	64SWRO635	462126
18 Oct	Austria	Luxembourg	Taxation	496UNTS97	107248
18 Oct	Hungary	Syria	Air Transport	491UNTS209	107178
18 Oct	Netherlands	Norway	Air Transport	466UNTS145	106741
19 Oct	France	Ivory Coast	Air Transport	498UNTS317	107286
20 Oct	Sudan	USSR (Soviet Union)	Air Transport	11SUGG156	469870
22 Oct	Greece	USA (United States)	US Agri Commod Aid	462UNTS187	106678
22 Oct	Czechoslovakia	Yugoslavia	Land Transport	480UNTS267	106974
23 Oct	Israel	Rwanda	Tech Assistance	515UNTS291	107466
24 Oct	Haiti	Norway	Visas	3NORT868	451070
24 Oct	Cameroon	Israel	General Aid	449UNTS3	106446
24 Oct	Honduras	USA (United States)	Milit Assistance	459UNTS211	106624
24 Oct	Cameroon	Israel	Culture	449UNTS15	106447
24 Oct	Canada	USA (United States)	Telecommunications	462UNTS67	106672
24 Oct	Japan	USA (United States)	Sanitation	462UNTS119	106673
25 Oct	Guatemala	Norway	Visas	3NORT869	451067
25 Oct	Czechoslovakia	Sweden	Air Transport	498UNTS343	107288

DATE	PARTY ONE	PARTY TWO	TOPIC	CITATION	NUMBER
1962 (Cont.)					
25 Oct	Czechoslovakia	Norway	Taxation	498UNTS335	107287
25 Oct	Multilateral		Tech Assistance	457UNTS129	106582
25 Oct	Czechoslovakia	Denmark	Taxation	456UNTS457	106571
25 Oct	Multilateral		General Aid	457UNTS137	106583
25 Oct	Dominican Republic	USA (United States)	Scientific Project	459UNTS247	106627
26 Oct	IBRD (World Bank)	Uruguay	IBRD Project	481UNTS39	106977
29 Oct	Cameroon	Greece	General Trade	538UNTS185	107815
29 Oct	Tunisia	USA (United States)	Direct Aid	462UNTS201	106679
30 Oct	USA (United States)	USSR (Soviet Union)	Scientific Project	11SUGG156	469871
30 Oct	Guinea	Italy	Air Transport	65ITGU280	435200
30 Oct	Congo (Brazzaville)	Germany, West	General Transport	63WBGA59	424380
30 Oct	Congo (Brazzaville)	Germany, West	Tech Assistance	63WBGA59	424381
30 Oct	Congo (Brazzaville)	Germany, West	General Economic	63WBGA59	424379
31 Oct	Italy	Yugoslavia	Visas	65ITGU192	435245
31 Oct	Norway	Sweden	Claims and Debts	466UNTS361	106755
31 Oct	Japan	UN Special Fund	Tech Assistance	444UNTS171	106368
01 Nov	China People's Rep	Indonesia	Scientific Project	62CCJC98	410924
02 Nov	France	Spain	Non-ILO Labor	63SPBO403	460142
02 Nov	Mali	Poland	Culture	572UNTS219	108315
02 Nov	Pakistan	IDA (Devel Assoc)	Non-IBRD Project	468UNTS351	106781
02 Nov	Japan	UK Great Britain	Visas	466UNTS277	106749
02 Nov	El Salvador	IDA (Devel Assoc)	Non-IBRD Project	468UNTS331	106780
02 Nov	Haiti	IDA (Devel Assoc)	Non-IBRD Project	468UNTS205	106774
03 Nov	Guinea	USA (United States)	Mass Media	459UNTS259	106628
05 Nov	China People's Rep	Korea, North	General Amity	62CCJC100	410925
05 Nov	United Nations	Western Samoa	Tech Assistance	443UNTS297	200599
05 Nov	Finland	Sweden	Customs	455UNTS289	106548
06 Nov	Japan	USA (United States)	Telecommunications	459UNTS203	106623
07 Nov	Ethiopia	Greece	Taxation	550UNTS179	108014
07 Nov	Ethiopia	Greece	Taxation	550UNTS189	108015
07 Nov	Philippines	IBRD (World Bank)	Loans and Credits	468UNTS281	106777
07 Nov	Korea, South	USA (United States)	US Agri Commod Aid	462UNTS129	106674
08 Nov	Romania	Yugoslavia	Consul/Citizenship	472UNTS305	106845
09 Nov	China People's Rep	Japan	General Trade	62CCJC103	410928
09 Nov	Burma	USA (United States)	US Agri Commod Aid	461UNTS113	106655
10 Nov	Indonesia	USSR (Soviet Union)	Mass Media	16SUGG134	470012
10 Nov	Poland	Syria	Air Transport	491UNTS228	107179
12 Nov	Finland	New Zealand	Water Transport	485UNTS331	107064
13 Nov	Saudi Arabia	USA (United States)	Loans and Credits	488UNTS175	107127
14 Nov	Ceylon (Sri Lanka)	USSR (Soviet Union)	Water Transport	11SUGG156	469872
14 Nov	Italy	USA (United States)	Telecommunications	459UNTS197	106622
14 Nov	Japan	UK Great Britain	General Trade	478UNTS29	106934
15 Nov	Hungary	USSR (Soviet Union)	General Trade	11SUGG157	469873
15 Nov	Algeria	UN Special Fund	Tech Assistance	452UNTS243	106512
15 Nov	Multilateral		Tech Assistance	448UNTS50	106424
16 Nov	France	Switzerland	Specific Resources	63SWRO961	462039
16 Nov	Czechoslovakia	Poland	Land Transport	526UNTS3	107597
17 Nov	Hungary	USSR (Soviet Union)	General Trade	11SUGG157	469874
17 Nov	Ivory Coast	Switzerland	Air Transport	499UNTS3	107289
17 Nov	United Nations	Syria	IGO Status/Immunit	456UNTS359	106565
17 Nov	Congo (Zaire)	USA (United States)	Finance	474UNTS41	106870
18 Nov	WHO (World Health)	Syria	Tech Assistance	480UNTS249	106972
19 Nov	Fed Rhod/Nyasaland	South Africa	Extradition	458UNTS59	106592
19 Nov	Taiwan	USA (United States)	US Agri Commod Aid	459UNTS263	106629
20 Nov	India	USSR (Soviet Union)	Water Transport	11SUGG157	469875
20 Nov	Germany, West	USA (United States)	Education	505UNTS263	107377
20 Nov	Thailand	UK Great Britain	Tech Assistance	466UNTS243	106747
20 Nov	Algeria	UNICEF (Children)	Direct Aid	453UNTS151	106522
21 Nov	Austria	Sweden	Taxation	63ABGB212	403176
21 Nov	USA (United States)	Vietnam, South	US Agri Commod Aid	469UNTS101	106786
21 Nov	India	USA (United States)	General Aid	462UNTS255	106685
21 Nov	Ceylon (Sri Lanka)	USA (United States)	General Aid	462UNTS237	106683
21 Nov	Ceylon (Sri Lanka)	ILO (Labor Org)	IGO Operations	449UNTS263	106463
22 Nov	France	Vietnam, South	Education	0VKNG184	496054
23 Nov	Turkey	USA (United States)	Loans and Credits	63TURG404	466128

DATE	PARTY ONE	PARTY TWO	TOPIC	CITATION	NUMBER
1962 (Cont.)					
23 Nov	France	Spain	Non-ILO Labor	63SPBO202	460143
23 Nov	Costa Rica	USA (United States)	General Aid	541UNTS67	107861
23 Nov	IDA (Devel Assoc)	Turkey	Non-IBRD Project	469UNTS3	106782
24 Nov	Paraguay	USA (United States)	US Agri Commod Aid	471UNTS49	106821
26 Nov	Ecuador	United Nations	Tech Assistance	445UNTS3	106372
26 Nov	India	USA (United States)	US Agri Commod Aid	460UNTS203	106641
26 Nov	Australia	Fed of Malaya	Specif Goods/Equip	453UNTS161	106523
27 Nov	India	UK Great Britain	Milit Installation	466UNTS189	106744
28 Nov	Czechoslovakia	Germany, East	Specific Resources	52EGDZ276	420366
28 Nov	UK Great Britain	Yugoslavia	Commodity Trade	470UNTS65	106796
28 Nov	Rwanda	United Nations	Tech Assistance	450UNTS267	106473
28 Nov	USA (United States)	Yugoslavia	US Agri Commod Aid	460UNTS185	106640
28 Nov	Argentina	Denmark	Milit Servic/Citiz	455UNTS429	106554
29 Nov	Honduras	Norway	Visas	3NORT873	451071
29 Nov	France	Niger	Customs	63FRRT28	415342
29 Nov	USA (United States)	Venezuela	Finance	474UNTS107	106875
29 Nov	Multilateral		Visas	457UNTS63	106577
29 Nov	Jamaica	USA (United States)	Air Transport	462UNTS229	106682
29 Nov	France	UK Great Britain	Scientific Project	453UNTS325	106534
29 Nov	Germany, West	USA (United States)	Water Transport	460UNTS169	106639
30 Nov	Dominican Republic	USA (United States)	US Agri Commod Aid	471UNTS25	106819
30 Nov	India	USA (United States)	US Agri Commod Aid	459UNTS231	106626
30 Nov	New Zealand	Western Samoa	Recognition	476UNTS3	106898
30 Nov	Austria	France	Visas	463UNTS173	106701
30 Nov	UK Great Britain	Vietnam, South	Admin Cooperation	470UNTS51	106794
01 Dec	Laos	USSR (Soviet Union)	Direct Aid	11SUGG158	469876
01 Dec	Laos	USSR (Soviet Union)	General Trade	458UNTS21	106590
01 Dec	Laos	USSR (Soviet Union)	Direct Aid	472UNTS3	106834
01 Dec	Laos	USSR (Soviet Union)	Finance	471UNTS181	106832
04 Dec	France	Rwanda	General Amity	65FRRT20	415381
05 Dec	Indonesia	USSR (Soviet Union)	Education	16SUGG134	470013
05 Dec	China People's Rep	Vietnam, North	General Amity	62CCJC108	410931
05 Dec	China People's Rep	Vietnam, North	General Economic	62CCJC109	410932
05 Dec	Niger	UNICEF (Children)	IGO Operations	503UNTS195	107344
06 Dec	Multilateral		Tech Assistance	450UNTS240	106471
06 Dec	Australia	UK Great Britain	Postal Service	457UNTS145	106584
06 Dec	Israel	USA (United States)	US Agri Commod Aid	460UNTS151	106638
07 Dec	Turkey	USA (United States)	Loans and Credits	63TURG504	466129
07 Dec	Germany, West	Luxembourg	Admin Cooperation	64WGBB193	425431
07 Dec	Congo (Zaire)	Italy	Air Transport	66ITGU211	435094
08 Dec	Multilateral		Finance	510UNTS235	107418
08 Dec	Cameroon	WHO (World Health)	Tech Assistance	451UNTS215	106496
10 Dec	France	Luxembourg	Humanitarian	63FRRT9	415272
10 Dec	Multilateral		Culture	521UNTS231	107525
10 Dec	UK Great Britain	USA (United States)	Mostfavored Nation	471UNTS91	106824
10 Dec	Nigeria	IBRD (World Bank)	IBRD Project	468UNTS255	106776
10 Dec	Ivory Coast	United Nations	Tech Assistance	451UNTS269	106498
10 Dec	Israel	USA (United States)	Extradition	484UNTS283	107038
11 Dec	Norway	Thailand	Visas	3NORT875	451171
11 Dec	Ghana	Tunisia	Air Transport	563UNTS243	108213
11 Dec	Austria	Yugoslavia	Land Transport	546UNTS3	107938
12 Dec	Multilateral		IGO Establishment	552UNTS15	108048
12 Dec	Multilateral		Tech Assistance	457UNTS72	106578
13 Dec	China People's Rep	Tanganyika	Culture	62CCJC114	410935
14 Dec	Italy	Switzerland	Non-ILO Labor	64SWRO730	462098
14 Dec	Guinea	USA (United States)	General Aid	462UNTS247	106684
16 Dec	Italy	Switzerland	General Ad Hoc	63ITDI303	436392
16 Dec	Germany, East	United Arab Rep	General Trade	10EGDA620	419478
17 Dec	Algeria	France	Tech Assistance	63FRRT8	415009
17 Dec	Multilateral		Admin Cooperation	590UNTS81	108548
17 Dec	Multilateral		General Economic	523UNTS93	107555
17 Dec	Netherlands	Spain	Health/Educ/Welfare	499UNTS227	107301
17 Dec	Multilateral		Sanitation	486UNTS119	107076
17 Dec	Bolivia	USA (United States)	US Agri Commod Aid	469UNTS121	106788
18 Dec	Germany, East	Romania	IGO Establishment	51EGDZ278	420299

DATE	PARTY ONE	PARTY TWO	TOPIC	CITATION	NUMBER
1962 (Cont.)					
18 Dec	Luxembourg	USA (United States)	Taxation	532UNTS277	107723
19 Dec	Korea, South	Vietnam, South	General Trade	0VKNG187	496055
19 Dec	Iceland	USSR (Soviet Union)	General Trade	11SUGG159	469877
19 Dec	France	Germany, West	Postal Service	62FRJO2812	416042
19 Dec	UN Special Fund	Uganda	Admin Cooperation	449UNTS41	106451
20 Dec	Hungary	USSR (Soviet Union)	Non-ILO Labor	11SUGG160	469878
20 Dec	Hungary	USSR (Soviet Union)	Non-ILO Labor	577UNTS245	108381
20 Dec	Algeria	WHO (World Health)	Tech Assistance	463UNTS135	106698
20 Dec	Peru	USA (United States)	Milit Installation	471UNTS75	106822
21 Dec	France	Japan	Taxation	0JGJI1502	441115
21 Dec	Morocco	IBRD (World Bank)	IBRD Project	478UNTS205	106937
21 Dec	IBRD (World Bank)	Thailand	IBRD Project	467UNTS63	106758
21 Dec	IBRD (World Bank)	Thailand	IBRD Project	467UNTS43	106757
21 Dec	Czechoslovakia	USA (United States)	Visas	469UNTS115	106787
21 Dec	Belgium	Tunisia	Culture	482UNTS3	106987
21 Dec	Colombia	Israel	Visas	484UNTS149	107023
24 Dec	Nigeria	USA (United States)	Claims and Debts	462UNTS180	106677
25 Dec	Bulgaria	USSR (Soviet Union)	Mass Media	11SUGG160	469879
26 Dec	China People's Rep	Mongolia	Territory Boundary	62CCJC117	410938
27 Dec	China People's Rep	Japan	General Trade	62CCJC118	410939
27 Dec	Syria	United Arab Rep	Air Transport	491UNTS245	107180
27 Dec	Iceland	USA (United States)	Taxation	469UNTS91	106785
27 Dec	India	United Nations	Scientific Project	450UNTS3	106464
28 Dec	Brazil	Taiwan	General Trade	500UNTS61	107307
28 Dec	Canada	USA (United States)	Scientific Project	471UNTS13	106818
29 Dec	Central Afri Rep	Germany, West	Direct Aid	63WBGA210	424731
29 Dec	Italy	Poland	Customs	63ITDI295	436308
29 Dec	Central Afri Rep	Germany, West	General Economic	63WBGA210	424730
29 Dec	Burundi	United Nations	Tech Assistance	450UNTS279	106474
29 Dec	Guatemala	USA (United States)	Tech Assistance	474UNTS31	106869
31 Dec	Algeria	France	Tech Assistance	63FRRT13	415010
31 Dec	Spain	USA (United States)	Commodity Trade	471UNTS99	106825
31 Dec	Japan	USA (United States)	Mostfavored Nation	471UNTS83	106823
1963					
04 Jan	Jamaica	USA (United States)	Finance	471UNTS119	106826
05 Jan	China People's Rep	United Arab Rep	Telecommunications	63CCJC2	410942
07 Jan	Germany, East	Mongolia	Consul/Citizenship	11EGDA430	419221
07 Jan	Ecuador	USA (United States)	Visas	477UNTS101	106917
07 Jan	Israel	United Nations	Tech Assistance	450UNTS229	106470
08 Jan	France	Spain	Taxation	64SPBO701	460144
08 Jan	Chad	France	Air Transport	63FRRT31	415430
08 Jan	France	Tunisia	Health/Educ/Welfare	63FRRT10	415458
08 Jan	Korea, South	USA (United States)	Consul/Citizenship	493UNTS105	107211
09 Jan	Austria	UK Great Britain	Extradition	0UNTSO	110806
09 Jan	Thailand	UK Great Britain	Admin Cooperation	470UNTS59	106795
09 Jan	Ghana	Mali	Air Transport	466UNTS165	106742
10 Jan	China People's Rep	Somalia	Culture	63CCJC6	410943
10 Jan	Israel	Philippines	Atomic Energy	588UNTS205	108526
10 Jan	Belgium	Ecuador	Visas	457UNTS153	106585
11 Jan	Philippines	USA (United States)	Specific Resources	473UNTS43	106853
11 Jan	Cyprus	USA (United States)	Visas	471UNTS127	106827
11 Jan	Gabon	United Nations	IGO Operations	450UNTS257	106472
14 Jan	Czechoslovakia	Vietnam, North	Consul/Citizenship	501UNTS181	107318
15 Jan	Trinidad/Tobago	USA (United States)	Finance	471UNTS141	106829
15 Jan	UK Great Britain	USA (United States)	Scientific Project	466UNTS181	106743
15 Jan	Multilateral		Tech Assistance	456UNTS409	106567
16 Jan	Algeria	France	Direct Aid	63FRRT11	415011
16 Jan	Cameroon	France	Education	63FRRT53	415100
16 Jan	Cameroon	France	Customs	63FRRT15	415101
16 Jan	Pakistan	USA (United States)	Milit Assistance	471UNTS133	106828
17 Jan	Argentina	France	Culture	65FRRT44	415054
17 Jan	Greece	Pakistan	General Trade	538UNTS175	107814
17 Jan	Senegal	USA (United States)	General Aid	493UNTS97	107210
19 Jan	Algeria	France	Finance	63FRRT17	415012

DATE	PARTY ONE	PARTY TWO	TOPIC	CITATION	NUMBER
1963 (Cont.)					
19 Jan	Japan	Philippines	Postal Service	517UNTS281	107489
19 Jan	Mauritania	UNICEF (Children)	Direct Aid	452UNTS271	106514
20 Jan	China People's Rep	Nepal	Territory Boundary	63CCJC10	410947
21 Jan	Hungary	USSR (Soviet Union)	Consul/Citizenship	577UNTS201	108378
21 Jan	Ecuador	Netherlands	Visas	514UNTS87	107443
21 Jan	Poland	USA (United States)	Visas	471UNTS151	106830
21 Jan	UK Great Britain	USSR (Soviet Union)	Health/Educ/Welfare	475UNTS3	106887
21 Jan	Multilateral		Tech Assistance	453UNTS20	106517
22 Jan	France	Germany, West	General Amity	63WGBB405	425189
22 Jan	Brazil	France	Tech Assistance	69FRJO2005	416078
22 Jan	Brazil	France	Privil/Immunities	0UNTSO	110229
22 Jan	France	USA (United States)	Dispute Settlement	473UNTS3	106849
23 Jan	Spain	Switzerland	Land Transport	63SPBO1109	460255
23 Jan	Algeria	France	Mass Media	63FRRT12	415013
23 Jan	Senegal	Switzerland	Air Transport	524UNTS23	107564
23 Jan	Iraq	USA (United States)	Culture	488UNTS163	107126
23 Jan	Australia	India	Patents/Copyrights	456UNTS185	106556
24 Jan	France	USSR (Soviet Union)	Finance	63FRMD1302	417470
24 Jan	United Nations	South Pacific Com	Tech Assistance	470UNTS361	200604
24 Jan	New Zealand	Western Samoa	Air Transport	499UNTS21	107290
25 Jan	Italy	Libya	General Trade	61ITDI272	436260
25 Jan	UNICEF (Children)	Tanganyika	Direct Aid	453UNTS249	106528
25 Jan	Ethiopia	USA (United States)	Scientific Project	473UNTS27	106851
26 Jan	Algeria	Poland	Tech Assistance	63PZUM11	458100
28 Jan	Cameroon	Switzerland	General Economic	64SWRO400	462124
28 Jan	Israel	Tanganyika	Tech Assistance	516UNTS39	107468
28 Jan	Malaysia	USA (United States)	Education	473UNTS15	106850
29 Jan	Belgium	Luxembourg	Direct Aid	0UNTSO	110432
29 Jan	Belgium	Luxembourg	IGO Establishment	547UNTS39	107955
29 Jan	Austria	United Nations	Consul/Citizenship	452UNTS261	106513
30 Jan	Japan	New Zealand	Taxation	517UNTS183	107486
31 Jan	France	Tunisia	Customs	63FRRT32	415459
31 Jan	Sudan	USA (United States)	US Agri Commod Aid	494UNTS119	107230
01 Feb	Belgium	Germany, West	General Military	63WBGA171	424031
01 Feb	Guinea	Switzerland	Air Transport	499UNTS35	107291
01 Feb	IDA (Devel Assoc)	Turkey	Non-IBRD Project	468UNTS223	106775
01 Feb	Japan	USA (United States)	Air Transport	473UNTS49	106854
01 Feb	Poland	USA (United States)	US Agri Commod Aid	487UNTS143	107100
01 Feb	India	USA (United States)	Scientific Project	473UNTS37	106852
04 Feb	Bolivia	USA (United States)	US Agri Commod Aid	473UNTS65	106856
04 Feb	Israel	Uganda	Tech Assistance	484UNTS273	107037
05 Feb	Germany, West	Philippines	Tech Assistance	4PTS639	465049
05 Feb	Multilateral		Tech Assistance	453UNTS36	106518
06 Feb	Austria	Netherlands	Admin Cooperation	570UNTS101	108290
06 Feb	Iceland	USA (United States)	US Agri Commod Aid	473UNTS93	106858
06 Feb	Netherlands	USA (United States)	Status of Forces	487UNTS113	107098
07 Feb	Germany, West	Sudan	Claims and Debts	66WGBB889	425648
07 Feb	Germany, West	Sudan	Tech Assistance	64WBGA6	424649
07 Feb	Mali	Senegal	Air Transport	524UNTS41	107565
08 Feb	South Africa	Spain	Mostfavored Nation	458UNTS79	106593
08 Feb	United Nations	United Arab Rep	Direct Aid	453UNTS79	106520
10 Feb	Central Afri Rep	USA (United States)	Direct Aid	473UNTS83	106857
11 Feb	Germany, East	Guinea	General Economic	11EGDA584	419119
11 Feb	Burundi	France	Health/Educ/Welfare	65FRRT18	415093
13 Feb	Cuba	Germany, East	General Trade	11EGDA585	419187
13 Feb	Pakistan	IBRD (World Bank)	IBRD Project	467UNTS3	106756
14 Feb	Multilateral		Tech Assistance	453UNTS168	106524
15 Feb	Philippines	IBRD (World Bank)	IBRD Project	478UNTS161	106936
16 Feb	France	Senegal	Consul/Citizenship	65FRRT51	415393
16 Feb	UK Great Britain	Yugoslavia	Air Transport	507UNTS171	107400
16 Feb	Ceylon (Sri Lanka)	Denmark	Taxation	486UNTS285	107083
18 Feb	Albania	China People's Rep	Sanitation	63CCJC14	410948
18 Feb	Sudan	Switzerland	Air Transport	563UNTS281	108215
18 Feb	Algeria	France	Air Transport	563UNTS263	108214
19 Feb	Japan	USA (United States)	Direct Aid	473UNTS107	106859

DATE	PARTY ONE	PARTY TWO	TOPIC	CITATION	NUMBER
1963 (Cont.)					
20 Feb	United Nations	South Pacific Com	Tech Assistance	453UNTS333	200600
20 Feb	Bulgaria	India	Culture	0UNTS0	109955
21 Feb	China People's Rep	Syria	General Trade	63CCJC15	410949
21 Feb	China People's Rep	Syria	Direct Aid	63CCJC17	410951
21 Feb	China People's Rep	Syria	Finance	63CCJC16	410950
21 Feb	Turkey	USA (United States)	US Agri Commod Aid	473UNTS311	106867
22 Feb	Poland	COMECON (Econ Aid)	IGO Operations	506UNTS303	107391
22 Feb	India	New Zealand	Loans and Credits	486UNTS19	107069
22 Feb	Bolivia	Philippines	Visas	490UNTS231	107156
22 Feb	ILO (Labor Org)	USA (United States)	IGO Operations	489UNTS347	107149
23 Feb	Congo (Zaire)	USA (United States)	US Agri Commod Aid	493UNTS17	107204
23 Feb	Congo (Zaire)	USA (United States)	US Agri Commod Aid	493UNTS3	107203
27 Feb	Portugal	Spain	Non-ILO Labor	63SPBO3010	460235
27 Feb	Ethiopia	IDA (Devel Assoc)	Non-IBRD Project	478UNTS289	106939
28 Feb	France	Switzerland	Visas	63FRRT34	415408
28 Feb	France	Switzerland	Visas	63FRRT37	415409
28 Feb	Hungary	COMECON (Econ Aid)	IGO Operations	506UNTS281	107390
01 Mar	Norway	USA (United States)	Water Transport	524UNTS185	107573
01 Mar	Nicaragua	IBRD (World Bank)	IBRD Project	481UNTS15	106976
01 Mar	Japan	Thailand	Taxation	475UNTS233	106895
02 Mar	China People's Rep	Pakistan	Territory Boundary	63CCJC28	410957
04 Mar	IAEA (Atom Energy)	Yugoslavia	Atomic Energy	490UNTS333	107162
05 Mar	Bulgaria	China People's Rep	General Economic	63CCJC31	410959
05 Mar	Cyprus	Norway	Air Transport	563UNTS305	108216
06 Mar	Multilateral		Tech Assistance	455UNTS386	106552
07 Mar	Germany, West	Poland	General Economic	63WBGA64	424585
07 Mar	IBRD (World Bank)	Thailand	IBRD Project	467UNTS83	106759
08 Mar	France	Mali	Visas	63FRRT42	415290
08 Mar	France	Philippines	Visas	569UNTS77	108280
08 Mar	Austria	Czechoslovakia	General Economic	495UNTS219	107245
11 Mar	Germany, East	USSR (Soviet Union)	Commodity Trade	11EGDA588	419422
11 Mar	Canada	El Salvador	Gen Communications	529UNTS25	107652
13 Mar	Peru	IBRD (World Bank)	IBRD Project	478UNTS245	106938
13 Mar	Pakistan	UK Great Britain	Atomic Energy	482UNTS347	107003
14 Mar	Indonesia	USA (United States)	General Aid	505UNTS79	107365
14 Mar	Germany, West	USA (United States)	Status of Forces	474UNTS71	106872
15 Mar	Italy	Japan	Visas	64ITDI258	436183
15 Mar	Japan	New Zealand	Postal Service	517UNTS229	107487
17 Mar	Germany, East	Poland	Non-ILO Labor	11EGDA589	419270
18 Mar	China People's Rep	Mongolia	General Trade	63CCJC34	410961
19 Mar	USSR (Soviet Union)	Yemen	General Trade	0UNTS0	109581
20 Mar	Dahomey	USSR (Soviet Union)	Culture	528UNTS181	107641
20 Mar	Accept UN Charter	Mauritania	UN Charter	457UNTS59	106576
21 Mar	Norway	Paraguay	Visas	3NORT880	451128
21 Mar	Israel	USA (United States)	Education	476UNTS131	106907
22 Mar	Japan	USA (United States)	Consul/Citizenship	518UNTS179	107495
22 Mar	India	IDA (Devel Assoc)	Non-IBRD Project	477UNTS3	106911
22 Mar	UN Special Fund	Uganda	Direct Aid	456UNTS466	106572
23 Mar	Philippines	USA (United States)	Education	474UNTS80	106873
25 Mar	Italy	Jordan	Air Transport	64ITDI258	436184
25 Mar	Germany, West	Nigeria	General Trade	64WBGA5	424508
25 Mar	Germany, West	Nigeria	Tech Assistance	64WBGA5	424510
25 Mar	Germany, West	Nigeria	Loans and Credits	64WBGA5	424509
25 Mar	Germany, West	Nigeria	General Transport	64WBGA5	424511
25 Mar	ICJ Option Clause	Somalia	ICJ Option Clause	458UNTS143	106597
26 Mar	China People's Rep	Ghana	Water Transport	63CCJC36	410963
27 Mar	Congo (Brazzaville)	France	Customs	63FRRT43	415125
27 Mar	Central Afri Rep	France	Customs	63FRRT43	415113
27 Mar	Colombia	USA (United States)	US Agri Commod Aid	489UNTS289	107145
29 Mar	Chad	France	Customs	63FRRT43	415429
29 Mar	Hungary	Korea, North	Sanitation	577UNTS219	108379
29 Mar	Burma	Japan	General Aid	518UNTS3	107490
29 Mar	Australia	Portugal	Visas	468UNTS313	106778
29 Mar	Brazil	USA (United States)	Scientific Project	476UNTS67	106904
30 Mar	China People's Rep	Morocco	General Trade	63CCJC39	410966
1963 (Cont.)					
30 Mar	Bulgaria	COMECON (Econ Aid)	IGO Operations	506UNTS257	107389
01 Apr	Ethiopia	UNICEF (Children)	IGO Operations	457UNTS103	106579
02 Apr	Israel	Peru	Tech Assistance	515UNTS279	107465
02 Apr	Romania	USA (United States)	Culture	474UNTS95	106874
02 Apr	Burma	UK Great Britain	Commodity Trade	475UNTS139	106890
02 Apr	Multilateral		Commodity Trade	475UNTS121	106889
03 Apr	Tanganyika	UK Great Britain	Admin Cooperation	478UNTS23	106933
04 Apr	France	Switzerland	Claims and Debts	63FRRT45	415410
05 Apr	France	Paraguay	Visas	63FRRT50	415354
05 Apr	Ecuador	USA (United States)	US Agri Commod Aid	477UNTS135	106919
05 Apr	Austria	Bulgaria	General Trade	480UNTS3	106963
06 Apr	Czechoslovakia	Tunisia	Culture	555UNTS111	108106
06 Apr	Japan	South Africa	Postal Service	484UNTS319	107040
06 Apr	UK Great Britain	USA (United States)	Milit Installation	474UNTS49	106871
08 Apr	China People's Rep	Romania	General Economic	63CCJC40	410967
10 Apr	China People's Rep	Hungary	General Economic	63CCJC42	410968
10 Apr	Gabon	USA (United States)	Finance	474UNTS113	106876
17 Apr	France	UK Great Britain	Admin Cooperation	474UNTS295	106886
17 Apr	Cyprus	IBRD (World Bank)	IBRD Project	476UNTS185	106909
18 Apr	Pakistan	United Nations	IGO Operations	503UNTS25	107339
18 Apr	Multilateral		Tech Assistance	463UNTS121	106697
19 Apr	Indonesia	Italy	Admin Cooperation	64ITDI260	436207
19 Apr	China People's Rep	Czechoslovakia	General Economic	63CCJC44	410969
19 Apr	Algeria	France	Tech Assistance	64FRRT20	415014
19 Apr	Belgium	USA (United States)	Water Transport	493UNTS83	107209
19 Apr	Belgium	USA (United States)	Gen Communications	476UNTS29	106900
20 Apr	Brazil	USSR (Soviet Union)	General Trade	0UNTS0	109256
20 Apr	Brazil	USSR (Soviet Union)	General Trade	0UNTS0	109257
20 Apr	Multilateral		IGO Establishment	495UNTS3	107239
20 Apr	Accept UN Charter	Kuwait	UN Charter	463UNTS213	106705
22 Apr	Algeria	France	Education	0UNTS0	110349
22 Apr	Poland	USSR (Soviet Union)	Land Transport	493UNTS229	107217
22 Apr	Dominican Republic	USA (United States)	Telecommunications	487UNTS169	107101
22 Apr	Austria	Italy	Visas	491UNTS53	107173
23 Apr	Cyprus	USA (United States)	Telecommunications	487UNTS291	107111
24 Apr	France	Senegal	Claims and Debts	65FRRT7	415394
24 Apr	Multilateral		Consul/Citizenship	596UNTS487	108640
24 Apr	Multilateral		Consul/Citizenship	596UNTS469	108639
24 Apr	Multilateral		Consul/Citizenship	596UNTS261	108638
25 Apr	Spain	Sweden	Taxation	64SPBO1801	460249
25 Apr	Spain	Sweden	Taxation	64SPBO1601	460248
25 Apr	France	Malagasy	Consul/Citizenship	65FRRT83	415283
25 Apr	Norway	Spain	Taxation	503UNTS41	107340
25 Apr	Israel	Netherlands	Admin Cooperation	484UNTS231	107034
25 Apr	Thailand	USA (United States)	Sanitation	476UNTS115	106906
26 Apr	Cameroon	Poland	Tech Assistance	63PZUM27	458101
26 Apr	Cameroon	Poland	Culture	63PZUM31	458102
26 Apr	France	Korea, South	Patents/Copyrights	64FRRT2	415131
26 Apr	Sweden	UK Great Britain	Extradition	590UNTS117	108551
26 Apr	Japan	USA (United States)	Milit Installation	477UNTS37	106914
27 Apr	Czechoslovakia	Poland	Mass Media	63PZUM34	458103
27 Apr	Czechoslovakia	Poland	Mass Media	63PZUM39	458104
27 Apr	Germany, West	Spain	Scientific Project	63SPBO2205	460029
27 Apr	Greece	Hungary	Air Transport	534UNTS3	107750
27 Apr	Greece	Hungary	Finance	550UNTS197	108016
27 Apr	Cyprus	Denmark	Air Transport	529UNTS255	107664
27 Apr	Jordan	UK Great Britain	Loans and Credits	475UNTS169	106892
29 Apr	Mexico	IBRD (World Bank)	IBRD Project	489UNTS151	107138
29 Apr	Australia	New Zealand	Customs	483UNTS241	107017
30 Apr	Multilateral		General Trade	570UNTS23	108285
30 Apr	Algeria	Morocco	Air Transport	564UNTS3	108217
01 May	Turkey	UK Great Britain	Loans and Credits	63TURG2109	466116
02 May	Austria	Bulgaria	Finance	535UNTS143	107778
03 May	Cameroon	Germany, West	Loans and Credits	63WBGA115	424346
04 May	Israel	Malagasy	Visas	484UNTS225	107033

DATE	PARTY ONE	PARTY TWO	TOPIC	CITATION	NUMBER
1963 (Cont.)					
05 May	Cameroon	France	Mass Media	65FRRT48	415102
06 May	Multilateral		Consul/Citizenship	634UNTS221	109065
06 May	Multilateral		Tech Assistance	463UNTS78	106694
06 May	UN Special Fund	Trinidad/Tobago	Direct Aid	463UNTS93	106695
06 May	Philippines	USA (United States)	Telecommunications	477UNTS67	106916
06 May	United Nations	Trinidad/Tobago	IGO Status/Immunit	463UNTS109	106696
07 May	Austria	Germany, West	Health/Educ/Welfare	64WGBB220	425551
07 May	Portugal	South Africa	Air Transport	499UNTS49	107292
07 May	El Salvador	USA (United States)	US Agri Commod Aid	476UNTS35	106901
08 May	Argentina	Finland	Milit Servic/Citiz	482UNTS309	107000
09 May	Hungary	Norway	Finance	3NORT883	451074
09 May	Australia	USA (United States)	Status of Forces	469UNTS55	106784
09 May	Mali	United Nations	Tech Assistance	463UNTS147	106699
09 May	Greece	UK Great Britain	Specific Property	398UNTS179	105722
09 May	India	USA (United States)	US Agri Commod Aid	476UNTS43	106902
09 May	Multilateral		Tech Assistance	463UNTS159	106700
09 May	Australia	USA (United States)	Milit Installation	475UNTS331	106897
10 May	Japan	Morocco	Claims and Debts	63JGJI46	441305
10 May	France	Mauritania	Specific Property	63FRRT72	415313
11 May	Cuba	Germany, East	Mass Media	11EGDA414	419188
11 May	Denmark	Norway	General Trade	613UNTS271	108856
13 May	Turkey	USA (United States)	Loans and Credits	65TURG1506	466130
13 May	Belgium	Netherlands	Territory Boundary	540UNTS3	107843
13 May	Australia	United Nations	Education	463UNTS187	106702
14 May	Canada	India	Loans and Credits	529UNTS31	107653
14 May	France	Japan	General Economic	518UNTS111	107493
15 May	France	Vietnam, South	Admin Cooperation	0VKNG190	496056
15 May	Germany, West	Ghana	Water Transport	63WBGA131	424217
15 May	Germany, West	Ghana	Air Transport	63WBGA131	424218
15 May	Germany, West	Ghana	Loans and Credits	63WBGA131	424216
15 May	China People's Rep	Somalia	General Economic	63CCJC61	410979
15 May	China People's Rep	Mali	Culture	63CCJC58	410976
15 May	Denmark	India	Tech Assistance	616UNTS49	108891
15 May	Denmark	India	Direct Aid	616UNTS39	108890
15 May	Denmark	India	Direct Aid	616UNTS23	108889
15 May	New Zealand	USA (United States)	Military Mission	477UNTS55	106915
15 May	New Zealand	UK Great Britain	Commodity Trade	486UNTS11	107068
15 May	Belgium	Venezuela	Culture	470UNTS259	106812
16 May	IBRD (World Bank)	UK Great Britain	IBRD Project	476UNTS211	106910
16 May	IBRD (World Bank)	UK Great Britain	IBRD Project	477UNTS361	106929
17 May	Burma	Thailand	Visas	468UNTS319	106779
17 May	Laos	UK Great Britain	Direct Aid	475UNTS155	106891
18 May	France	Monaco	Finance	63FRRT66	415333
18 May	France	Monaco	Non-ILO Labor	0UNTS0	110719
18 May	France	Monaco	Taxation	0UNTS0	109438
20 May	Germany, East	Lebanon	General Economic	11EGDA603	419196
20 May	Netherlands	USA (United States)	Specif Goods/Equip	487UNTS123	107099
21 May	Paraguay	Spain	Specif Goods/Equip	65SPBO2207	460224
21 May	Germany, West	Morocco	Non-ILO Labor	71WGBB1365	425466
21 May	Israel	USA (United States)	Telecommunications	487UNTS319	107113
22 May	France	Vietnam, South	Specific Property	0VKNG191	496057
22 May	Germany, East	Yugoslavia	General Ad Hoc	11EGDA603	419150
22 May	France	Guinea	General Trade	63FRRT62	415211
22 May	France	Guinea	Tech Assistance	63FRRT61	415210
22 May	Multilateral		Tech Assistance	483UNTS72	107007
22 May	Guinea	USA (United States)	US Agri Commod Aid	487UNTS251	107108
22 May	Jamaica	UN Special Fund	Direct Aid	489UNTS191	107140
22 May	Jamaica	United Nations	IGO Status/Immunit	479UNTS19	106945
23 May	Ghana	Japan	Education	0JGJI1506	441116
23 May	Netherlands	Tunisia	Finance	523UNTS237	107558
24 May	Austria	Norway	Visas	3NORT888	451226
24 May	Germany, West	Norway	Visas	3NORT887	451190
24 May	France	Norway	Visas	3NORT886	451062
24 May	Netherlands	UN Special Fund	Direct Aid	466UNTS289	106750
24 May	India	IDA (Devel Assoc)	Non-IBRD Project	483UNTS205	107014

DATE	PARTY ONE	PARTY TWO	TOPIC	CITATION	NUMBER
1963 (Cont.)					
24 May	Multilateral		Tech Assistance	470UNTS208	106810
24 May	Multilateral		Tech Assistance	466UNTS346	106754
24 May	Thailand	USA (United States)	Education	477UNTS123	106918
25 May	Norway	Switzerland	Visas	3NORT889	451159
25 May	Multilateral		IGO Establishment	479UNTS39	106947
27 May	Indonesia	Philippines	General Trade	4PTS739	465050
27 May	Indonesia	Philippines	Tech Assistance	4PTS749	465052
27 May	Indonesia	Philippines	General Economic	4PTS753	465053
27 May	Indonesia	Philippines	Admin Cooperation	4PTS747	465051
29 May	China People's Rep	Finland	General Trade	63CCJC68	410983
29 May	France	Mauritania	Direct Aid	65FRRT99	415314
29 May	United Nations	Uganda	IGO Status/Immunit	466UNTS311	106751
29 May	Cyprus	USA (United States)	Finance	487UNTS283	107110
30 May	Bulgaria	Italy	Tech Assistance	64ITDI344	436069
30 May	Afromalagasy Org	ILO (Labor Org)	IGO Operations	467UNTS482	200602
31 May	Italy	Switzerland	Customs	64ITDI283	436394
31 May	Germany, West	India	Air Transport	64WGBB677	425256
31 May	Japan	Morocco	Mass Media	65JGJI49	441306
31 May	Chad	Germany, West	General Economic	63WBGA224	424670
31 May	Chad	Germany, West	Tech Assistance	63WBGA224	424671
31 May	Bolivia	Canada	Gen Communications	529UNTS37	107654
31 May	IDA (Devel Assoc)	Turkey	Non-IBRD Project	480UNTS127	106966
01 Jun	Japan	Morocco	Non-ILO Labor	63JGJI52	441308
01 Jun	Japan	Morocco	Non-ILO Labor	63JGJI52	441307
03 Jun	Colombia	IBRD (World Bank)	IBRD Project	490UNTS199	107155
04 Jun	Japan	Malaysia	Taxation	517UNTS245	107488
04 Jun	IAEA (Atom Energy)	Yugoslavia	Atomic Energy	490UNTS343	107163
05 Jun	UN Special Fund	Western Samoa	Direct Aid	467UNTS463	200601
05 Jun	Canada	Finland	Water Transport	472UNTS345	106846
05 Jun	India	IBRD (World Bank)	IBRD Project	481UNTS191	106983
05 Jun	Argentina	UK Great Britain	Loans and Credits	482UNTS353	107004
06 Jun	Denmark	France	Milit Servic/Citiz	600UNTS213	108682
06 Jun	Jamaica	USA (United States)	Milit Assistance	477UNTS29	106913
06 Jun	Denmark	Netherlands	Patents/Copyrights	484UNTS137	107021
06 Jun	Australia	UK Great Britain	Sanitation	472UNTS157	106838
07 Jun	China People's Rep	Germany, East	Culture	63CCJC70	410984
07 Jun	Germany, West	Greece	Air Transport	544UNTS193	107919
07 Jun	Multilateral		Water Transport	472UNTS95	106837
08 Jun	China People's Rep	Romania	Scientific Project	63CCJC71	410985
08 Jun	Belgium	Cyprus	Air Transport	601UNTS311	108703
09 Jun	Multilateral		General Economic	538UNTS309	107818
10 Jun	India	USSR (Soviet Union)	General Trade	0UNTS0	109382
10 Jun	Finland	Poland	Air Transport	503UNTS179	107343
10 Jun	Denmark	Germany, West	Admin Cooperation	477UNTS405	106930
11 Jun	Algeria	France	Tech Assistance	64FRRT21	415015
11 Jun	Algeria	France	Education	0UNTS0	110820
11 Jun	Argentina	Belgium	Milit Servic/Citiz	635UNTS135	109077
11 Jun	Ethiopia	USA (United States)	US Agri Commod Aid	487UNTS269	107109
11 Jun	IBRD (World Bank)	Thailand	IBRD Project	481UNTS227	106984
12 Jun	Guatemala	Mexico	Telecommunications	65MEXD2901	444023
12 Jun	Germany, East	Romania	Non-ILO Labor	11EGDA605	419300
12 Jun	Senegal	USA (United States)	Finance	0UNTS0	109979
13 Jun	Hungary	Romania	Territory Boundary	576UNTS275	108369
14 Jun	Japan	USA (United States)	Finance	479UNTS165	106951
15 Jun	Taiwan	Liberia	Culture	521UNTS361	107531
17 Jun	Guinea	Poland	Tech Assistance	63PZUM61	458105
18 Jun	China People's Rep	Norway	Culture	3NORT890	451024
18 Jun	China People's Rep	Norway	Culture	63CCJC76	410987
18 Jun	Korea, South	USA (United States)	Education	487UNTS297	107112
18 Jun	Cyprus	USA (United States)	US Agri Commod Aid	479UNTS191	106953
19 Jun	Multilateral		Visas	482UNTS19	106988
19 Jun	El Salvador	IBRD (World Bank)	IBRD Project	481UNTS59	106978
19 Jun	India	USA (United States)	Education	479UNTS175	106952
20 Jun	Ghana	Italy	Air Transport	65ITGU193	435180
20 Jun	USA (United States)	USSR (Soviet Union)	Specif Goods/Equip	472UNTS163	106839

DATE	PARTY ONE	PARTY TWO	TOPIC	CITATION	NUMBER
1963 (Cont.)					
21 Jun	Italy	Turkey	General Economic	63TURG609	466111
21 Jun	Austria	Poland	Air Transport	63ABGB294	403151
21 Jun	France	UK Great Britain	Taxation	540UNTS311	107855
21 Jun	Colombia	IBRD (World Bank)	IBRD Project	482UNTS159	106994
21 Jun	Mongolia	WHO (World Health)	Tech Assistance	472UNTS373	106848
21 Jun	IBRD (World Bank)	Yugoslavia	IBRD Project	482UNTS43	106990
21 Jun	Austria	IAEA (Atom Energy)	Atomic Energy	490UNTS351	107164
22 Jun	Luxembourg	Spain	Non-ILO Labor	65SPBO2408	460185
22 Jun	Luxembourg	Spain	Non-ILO Labor	65SPBO1509	460186
22 Jun	China People's Rep	Germany, East	General Economic	63CCJC80	410991
24 Jun	Czechoslovakia	Yugoslavia	Consul/Citizenship	496UNTS3	107246
25 Jun	China People's Rep	Cuba	Scientific Project	63CCJC83	410992
25 Jun	Multilateral		ILO Labor	532UNTS159	107717
25 Jun	Austria	USA (United States)	Education	479UNTS223	106956
26 Jun	Guinea	Ivory Coast	Air Transport	499UNTS71	107293
26 Jun	Pakistan	IDA (Devel Assoc)	Non-IBRD Project	492UNTS115	107189
27 Jun	Czechoslovakia	Germany, East	Health/Educ/Welfare	11EGDA647	419367
27 Jun	Germany, West	Italy	Non-ILO Labor	63WBGA231	424301
27 Jun	Germany, West	Netherlands	Non-ILO Labor	63WBGA231	424489
27 Jun	France	Germany, West	Non-ILO Labor	63WBGA231	424190
27 Jun	Germany, West	Luxembourg	Non-ILO Labor	63WBGA231	424432
27 Jun	UNICEF (Children)	Togo	IGO Operations	540UNTS135	107847
27 Jun	United Nations	UK Great Britain	Trusteeship	469UNTS145	106789
27 Jun	India	USA (United States)	US Agri Commod Aid	479UNTS215	106955
28 Jun	Norway	Sweden	Specific Resources	3NORT891	451164
28 Jun	New Zealand	UN Special Fund	Non-IBRD Project	470UNTS3	106792
28 Jun	Colombia	IBRD (World Bank)	IBRD Project	489UNTS113	107137
29 Jun	Afghanistan	Bulgaria	Culture	0UNTS0	109873
29 Jun	Pakistan	USA (United States)	Milit Assistance	487UNTS243	107107
29 Jun	Finland	Sweden	Land Transport	477UNTS21	106912
29 Jun	United Arab Rep	USA (United States)	Finance	479UNTS207	106954
02 Jul	Bulgaria	USA (United States)	Claims and Debts	479UNTS245	106957
02 Jul	Finland	IAEA (Atom Energy)	Atomic Energy	490UNTS403	107167
03 Jul	Mexico	Yugoslavia	General Trade	67MEXD1711	444046
03 Jul	Austria	Romania	Claims and Debts	588UNTS3	108516
03 Jul	Senegal	USA (United States)	US Agri Commod Aid	527UNTS95	107620
03 Jul	Canada	Nigeria	Milit Assistance	529UNTS57	107656
03 Jul	IBRD (World Bank)	Tunisia	IBRD Project	480UNTS209	106970
05 Jul	France	Germany, West	Health/Educ/Welfare	63WGBB1612	425191
06 Jul	China People's Rep	Romania	Scientific Project	63CCJC86	410994
06 Jul	France	Malagasy	Claims and Debts	63FRRT81	415284
07 Jul	Iran	Jordan	General Trade	0IRTB47	433072
07 Jul	France	Saudi Arabia	Health/Educ/Welfare	65FRRT21	415051
08 Jul	France	Spain	Non-ILO Labor	63SPBO1312	460145
08 Jul	France	Spain	Non-ILO Labor	0UNTS0	110705
09 Jul	Germany, West	Togo	Loans and Credits	63WBGA199	424662
09 Jul	Multilateral		Admin Cooperation	0UNTS0	110760
09 Jul	Austria	Hungary	Sanitation	482UNTS29	106989
10 Jul	France	Togo	General Amity	64FRRT39	415450
10 Jul	France	Togo	Admin Cooperation	0UNTS0	110367
10 Jul	France	Togo	General Military	0UNTS0	110365
10 Jul	France	Togo	General Economic	0UNTS0	110371
10 Jul	France	Togo	Admin Cooperation	0UNTS0	110370
10 Jul	France	Togo	Culture	0UNTS0	110368
10 Jul	France	Togo	Finance	0UNTS0	110372
10 Jul	France	Togo	Consul/Citizenship	0UNTS0	110366
10 Jul	France	Togo	Tech Assistance	0UNTS0	110369
10 Jul	Hungary	Mongolia	Consul/Citizenship	519UNTS173	107508
10 Jul	Dahomey	USSR (Soviet Union)	General Trade	528UNTS167	107640
10 Jul	Costa Rica	IBRD (World Bank)	IBRD Project	482UNTS69	106991
11 Jul	Switzerland	USA (United States)	General Trade	487UNTS177	107102
12 Jul	France	Yugoslavia	Claims and Debts	64FRRT31	415486
12 Jul	Denmark	India	Loans and Credits	616UNTS3	108888
12 Jul	Austria	France	Air Transport	499UNTS91	107294
14 Jul	China People's Rep	United Arab Rep	General Trade	63CCJC88	410995

DATE	PARTY ONE	PARTY TWO	TOPIC	CITATION	NUMBER
1963 (Cont.)					
15 Jul	Turkey	USA (United States)	Loans and Credits	63TURG2809	466131
15 Jul	Bulgaria	Germany, East	Tech Assistance	11EGDA610	419067
15 Jul	Dahomey	Germany, West	Loans and Credits	63WBGA192	424095
15 Jul	France	Mauritania	Visas	64FRRT8	415315
15 Jul	Iceland	USA (United States)	General Trade	527UNTS45	107616
15 Jul	Malaysia	IBRD (World Bank)	IBRD Project	482UNTS123	106993
15 Jul	Austria	Mongolia	General Trade	496UNTS171	107251
16 Jul	France	Luxembourg	Territory Boundary	68FRJO1101	416273
16 Jul	Spain	USA (United States)	Commodity Trade	488UNTS77	107120
16 Jul	Poland	United Nations	IGO Operations	471UNTS3	106817
16 Jul	Colombia	IBRD (World Bank)	IBRD Project	482UNTS256	106998
17 Jul	France	Italy	Non-ILO Labor	64ITDI254	436156
17 Jul	France	Italy	Non-ILO Labor	64ITDI253	436155
17 Jul	Congo (Zaire)	France	Non-ILO Labor	67FRJO1511	416128
17 Jul	Austria	Denmark	Consul/Citizenship	479UNTS263	106958
18 Jul	Denmark	Italy	Privil/Immunities	64ITDI252	436103
18 Jul	Germany, East	USSR (Soviet Union)	Tech Assistance	11EGDA611	419423
18 Jul	Austria	Yugoslavia	Visas	63ABGB244	403227
19 Jul	Germany, West	Vietnam, South	Direct Aid	0VKNG192	496058
19 Jul	Austria	France	Culture	65FRRT43	415058
19 Jul	Taiwan	Luxembourg	Air Transport	564UNTS23	108218
19 Jul	El Salvador	Japan	General Economic	518UNTS135	107494
19 Jul	Congo (Zaire)	USA (United States)	Milit Installation	511UNTS47	107425
20 Jul	Germany, East	Yugoslavia	General Trade	51EGDZ292	420151
20 Jul	Greece	Romania	Taxation	609UNTS109	108829
22 Jul	Algeria	Mali	Air Transport	564UNTS29	108219
23 Jul	Iran	Japan	Admin Cooperation	0IRTB46	433067
23 Jul	Germany, West	Italy	Patents/Copyrights	65WGBB156	425302
23 Jul	France	Gabon	Admin Cooperation	65FRRT26	415195
23 Jul	France	Morocco	Non-ILO Labor	0UNTS0	109934
23 Jul	Israel	Niger	Visas	515UNTS257	107463
23 Jul	Multilateral		Tech Assistance	471UNTS158	106831
24 Jul	Mali	Tunisia	Air Transport	602UNTS91	108708
24 Jul	Denmark	IBRD (World Bank)	IBRD Project	481UNTS171	106982
24 Jul	Argentina	USA (United States)	General Trade	487UNTS183	107103
25 Jul	Indonesia	Philippines	General Military	4PTS761	465054
25 Jul	Ceylon (Sri Lanka)	China People's Rep	Water Transport	63CCJC92	410999
26 Jul	Italy	United Nations	IGO Operations	472UNTS173	106840
26 Jul	Pakistan	IDA (Devel Assoc)	Non-IBRD Project	492UNTS143	107190
26 Jul	Malagasy	USA (United States)	Finance	487UNTS189	107104
26 Jul	Congo (Zaire)	UN Special Fund	Direct Aid	474UNTS137	106878
27 Jul	Iran	USSR (Soviet Union)	Non-IBRD Project	0IRTB80	433128
29 Jul	France	Spain	Specific Resources	64SPBO108	460146
29 Jul	Cameroon	UK Great Britain	General Economic	478UNTS148	106935
30 Jul	Finland	IAEA (Atom Energy)	Atomic Energy	490UNTS413	107168
31 Jul	Multilateral		General Amity	550UNTS343	108029
31 Jul	Multilateral		Tech Assistance	472UNTS220	106842
31 Jul	Australia	Finland	Admin Cooperation	478UNTS363	106942
31 Jul	USA (United States)	Uruguay	Tech Assistance	488UNTS3	107115
01 Aug	France	USA (United States)	Taxation	527UNTS89	107619
01 Aug	New Zealand	USSR (Soviet Union)	General Trade	486UNTS27	107070
01 Aug	United Arab Rep	USA (United States)	Visas	488UNTS189	107128
02 Aug	Argentina	Bolivia	Claims and Debts	0UNTS0	109517
04 Aug	Multilateral		IGO Establishment	510UNTS3	107408
05 Aug	Multilateral		Sanitation	480UNTS43	106964
05 Aug	Dominican Republic	United Nations	IGO Status/Immunit	472UNTS353	106847
07 Aug	Malaysia	IBRD (World Bank)	IBRD Project	485UNTS253	107060
08 Aug	Burundi	WHO (World Health)	Tech Assistance	477UNTS346	106928
08 Aug	India	USA (United States)	Scientific Project	488UNTS21	107117
08 Aug	UNICEF (Children)	Trinidad/Tobago	IGO Operations	473UNTS281	106865
09 Aug	France	Tunisia	Education	63FRRT70	415460
09 Aug	France	Tunisia	Claims and Debts	65FRRT77	415461
09 Aug	Cameroon	Israel	Air Transport	499UNTS121	107295
10 Aug	Cameroon	France	Specific Property	64FRRT71	415103
13 Aug	France	Germany, West	Admin Cooperation	63FRRT69	415043

DATE	PARTY ONE	PARTY TWO	TOPIC	CITATION	NUMBER
1963 (Cont.)					
13 Aug	Multilateral		General Trade	592UNTS139	108572
13 Aug	Dominican Republic	USA (United States)	US Agri Commod Aid	492UNTS327	107202
14 Aug	Denmark	Switzerland	Land Transport	63SWRO797	462081
14 Aug	Tanganyika	USSR (Soviet Union)	General Trade	493UNTS195	107215
15 Aug	Philippines	USA (United States)	Tech Assistance	4PTS791	465055
16 Aug	Pakistan	IDA (Devel Assoc)	Non-IBRD Project	492UNTS205	107192
16 Aug	Pakistan	IDA (Devel Assoc)	Non-IBRD Project	492UNTS171	107191
17 Aug	Chad	France	Direct Aid	64FRRT16	415431
19 Aug	USA (United States)	Vietnam, South	Atomic Energy	0VKNG178	496053
20 Aug	Paraguay	USA (United States)	Education	531UNTS197	107704
20 Aug	Cameroon	UK Great Britain	Culture	539UNTS233	107834
20 Aug	France	Israel	Taxation	515UNTS173	107460
20 Aug	Afghanistan	USA (United States)	Education	488UNTS41	107118
21 Aug	France	Greece	Taxation	533UNTS235	107746
21 Aug	Argentina	USA (United States)	Education	488UNTS61	107119
22 Aug	Germany, West	Syria	Direct Aid	64WBGA79	424650
22 Aug	Austria	Israel	Air Transport	63ABGB260	403107
22 Aug	Burundi	UN Special Fund	Direct Aid	476UNTS49	106903
23 Aug	France	Switzerland	Specific Property	64SWRO1255	462032
23 Aug	France	Switzerland	Territory Boundary	64SWRO1272	462001
23 Aug	Canada	USA (United States)	Telecommunications	494UNTS13	107222
23 Aug	United Nations	Saudi Arabia	IGO Status/Immunit	474UNTS155	106879
27 Aug	Portugal	Spain	Non-ILO Labor	63SPBO3010	460236
27 Aug	Multilateral		Tech Assistance	511UNTS210	107435
27 Aug	Iraq	USA (United States)	US Agri Commod Aid	489UNTS271	107144
27 Aug	Colombia	United Nations	Education	481UNTS3	106975
27 Aug	Netherlands	UK Great Britain	Other Military	490UNTS3	107150
27 Aug	United Nations	United Arab Rep	Tech Assistance	474UNTS221	106884
27 Aug	Switzerland	UK Great Britain	General Transport	486UNTS183	107079
27 Aug	Japan	USA (United States)	Commodity Trade	487UNTS197	107105
28 Aug	Burma	China People's Rep	Admin Cooperation	63CCJC100	411004
28 Aug	Dahomey	UNICEF (Children)	IGO Operations	507UNTS101	107396
28 Aug	Japan	USA (United States)	Commodity Trade	487UNTS237	107106
29 Aug	China People's Rep	Pakistan	Air Transport	63CCJC101	411005
29 Aug	Mexico	USA (United States)	Territory Boundary	505UNTS185	107374
30 Aug	Burundi	WHO (World Health)	IGO Operations	490UNTS423	107169
30 Aug	Panama	USA (United States)	Taxation	488UNTS11	107116
30 Aug	Philippines	USA (United States)	Non-ILO Labor	489UNTS323	107147
31 Aug	China People's Rep	Mali	Mass Media	63CCJC103	411007
01 Sep	Algeria	Tunisia	Air Transport	601UNTS275	108701
02 Sep	Austria	Liechtenstein	Visas	65ABGB11	403129
02 Sep	Multilateral		General Transport	548UNTS129	107974
02 Sep	Austria	Switzerland	Visas	548UNTS91	107973
03 Sep	Cuba	Germany, East	Loans and Credits	11EGDA615	419189
03 Sep	Germany, West	Ivory Coast	Loans and Credits	63WBGA210	424123
04 Sep	Argentina	Uruguay	General Economic	0UNTS0	109541
05 Sep	Germany, East	Hungary	Non-ILO Labor	11EGDA648	419460
06 Sep	Brazil	Italy	Patents/Copyrights	64ITDI240	436066
06 Sep	IBRD (World Bank)	UK Great Britain	IBRD Project	483UNTS173	107013
10 Sep	Israel	Sweden	Extradition	516UNTS3	107467
10 Sep	Multilateral		Tech Assistance	480UNTS100	106965
11 Sep	Turkey	USA (United States)	Loans and Credits	63TURG2509	466132
11 Sep	Algeria	China People's Rep	Culture	63CCJC106	411009
11 Sep	Fed of Malaya	UK Great Britain	Admin Cooperation	0UNTS0	110761
11 Sep	Brazil	USA (United States)	US Agri Commod Aid	493UNTS267	107220
12 Sep	EEC (Econ Commnty)	Turkey	Other Economic	64TURG1202	466005
12 Sep	Austria	Germany, West	Visas	63ABGB296	403004
12 Sep	Argentina	UK Great Britain	Milit Servic/Citiz	601UNTS213	108698
12 Sep	Denmark	Norway	General Trade	613UNTS289	108857
13 Sep	Germany, West	Sierra Leone	Water Transport	63WBGA222	424631
13 Sep	Germany, West	Sierra Leone	General Economic	63WBGA222	424628
13 Sep	Germany, West	Sierra Leone	Tech Assistance	63WBGA222	424629
13 Sep	Germany, West	Sierra Leone	Loans and Credits	63WBGA222	424630
13 Sep	Ecuador	UK Great Britain	Visas	490UNTS19	107152
14 Sep	Multilateral		Air Transport	0UNTS0	110106

DATE	PARTY ONE	PARTY TWO	TOPIC	CITATION	NUMBER
1963 (Cont.)					
14 Sep	Multilateral		Telecommunications	488UNTS121	107123
16 Sep	Paraguay	USA (United States)	US Agri Commod Aid	494UNTS101	107229
17 Sep	Israel	Tanganyika	Visas	516UNTS47	107469
18 Sep	Canada	Italy	Specific Resources	64ITDI245	436076
18 Sep	Germany, East	Hungary	Visas	11EGDA619	419461
18 Sep	Colombia	France	Tech Assistance	65FRRT19	415120
18 Sep	Finland	IBRD (World Bank)	IBRD Project	491UNTS345	107183
19 Sep	France	Switzerland	Finance	63FRRT83	415411
20 Sep	Mexico	IBRD (World Bank)	IBRD Project	491UNTS317	107182
20 Sep	Ecuador	USA (United States)	Education	488UNTS147	107125
20 Sep	IBRD (World Bank)	Venezuela	IBRD Project	482UNTS227	106997
23 Sep	Belgium	Turkey	Direct Aid	566UNTS195	108244
23 Sep	IBRD (World Bank)	UK Great Britain	IBRD Project	503UNTS247	107348
23 Sep	Australia	UK Great Britain	Postal Service	483UNTS39	107006
23 Sep	Peru	USA (United States)	US Agri Commod Aid	488UNTS91	107121
23 Sep	Multilateral		Atomic Energy	488UNTS99	107122
24 Sep	El Salvador	Germany, West	Tech Assistance	64WBGA198	424129
24 Sep	Austria	India	Taxation	545UNTS199	107935
25 Sep	Jamaica	WHO (World Health)	Tech Assistance	481UNTS125	106980
26 Sep	Denmark	Greece	General Trade	534UNTS43	107752
26 Sep	Mali	Romania	Culture	528UNTS193	107642
26 Sep	Germany, West	Greece	Other Military	550UNTS203	108017
27 Sep	Japan	IBRD (World Bank)	IBRD Project	485UNTS283	107061
27 Sep	Taiwan	IBRD (World Bank)	IBRD Project	483UNTS151	107012
28 Sep	Germany, East	Yugoslavia	General Economic	11EGDA620	419152
28 Sep	Germany, East	Yugoslavia	Humanitarian	11EGDA620	419153
30 Sep	Iraq	Italy	General Trade	64ITDI261	436214
30 Sep	Iraq	Italy	Tech Assistance	64ITDI264	436215
30 Sep	Germany, East	Mali	Tech Assistance	11EGDA424	419199
30 Sep	Greece	Poland	General Trade	534UNTS23	107751
01 Oct	El Salvador	IBRD (World Bank)	IBRD Project	517UNTS3	107481
01 Oct	Jamaica	USA (United States)	Commodity Trade	488UNTS133	107124
03 Oct	Italy	Yemen	Admin Cooperation	64ITDI288	436430
03 Oct	Austria	El Salvador	Visas	64ABGB34	403162
03 Oct	ICJ Option Clause	Uganda	ICJ Option Clause	479UNTS35	106946
03 Oct	Guatemala	USA (United States)	Direct Aid	493UNTS45	107206
04 Oct	Iraq	Kuwait	Visas	485UNTS321	107063
05 Oct	Czechoslovakia	Yugoslavia	Sanitation	504UNTS151	107356
07 Oct	Malagasy	USA (United States)	Scientific Project	494UNTS3	107221
07 Oct	Pakistan	USSR (Soviet Union)	Air Transport	499UNTS161	107297
08 Oct	Philippines	USA (United States)	Non-ILO Labor	4PTS811	465056
08 Oct	Austria	Finland	Taxation	490UNTS255	107160
09 Oct	Ivory Coast	Netherlands	Air Transport	499UNTS141	107296
10 Oct	Ceylon (Sri Lanka)	China People's Rep	General Trade	63CCJC114	411015
11 Oct	France	Spain	Non-ILO Labor	63SPBO1612	460147
11 Oct	France	Italy	Land Transport	65ITGU181	435157
11 Oct	Algeria	China People's Rep	Loans and Credits	63CCJC116	411017
11 Oct	Italy	IAEA (Atom Energy)	IGO Establishment	639UNTS25	109142
11 Oct	Canada	France	Mass Media	529UNTS71	107657
11 Oct	UK Great Britain	USA (United States)	Scientific Project	483UNTS3	107005
14 Oct	Iran	EEC (Econ Commnty)	General Trade	0IRTB85	433138
14 Oct	China People's Rep	Korea, North	General Trade	63CCJC118	411019
15 Oct	Turkey	USA (United States)	Loans and Credits	64TURG904	466133
15 Oct	France	Monaco	Admin Cooperation	63FRRT77	415334
15 Oct	Hungary	Yugoslavia	Health/Educ/Welfare	577UNTS49	108372
15 Oct	Norway	IBRD (World Bank)	IBRD Project	482UNTS103	106992
17 Oct	Multilateral		Atomic Energy	525UNTS75	107585
19 Oct	Multilateral		Direct Aid	523UNTS249	107559
19 Oct	Taiwan	USA (United States)	Commodity Trade	494UNTS27	107224
21 Oct	Kuwait	USA (United States)	Postal Service	530UNTS281	107688
21 Oct	Multilateral		Tech Assistance	480UNTS197	106969
22 Oct	Czechoslovakia	Hungary	Land Transport	514UNTS95	107444
22 Oct	Sweden	USA (United States)	Taxation	530UNTS247	107686
23 Oct	Algeria	France	Health/Educ/Welfare	64FRRT24	415016
23 Oct	Multilateral		IGO Establishment	506UNTS197	107388

DATE	PARTY ONE	PARTY TWO	TOPIC	CITATION	NUMBER
1963 (Cont.)					
24 Oct	Austria	Italy	Mass Media	65ITGU152	435039
24 Oct	France	Mauritania	Air Transport	64FRRT10	415316
24 Oct	Lebanon	UK Great Britain	Taxation	535UNTS3	107772
24 Oct	Jamaica	USA (United States)	General Aid	489UNTS337	107148
24 Oct	Iran	USA (United States)	Culture	489UNTS303	107146
25 Oct	Austria	Poland	Land Transport	63PZUM67	458106
25 Oct	Mexico	United Arab Rep	General Trade	66MEXD1708	444039
25 Oct	IBRD (World Bank)	Spain	IBRD Project	491UNTS297	107181
26 Oct	Italy	San Marino	Commodity Trade	66ITGU21	435333
26 Oct	Multilateral		Water Transport	587UNTS9	108506
28 Oct	Germany, East	Yemen	Consul/Citizenship	11EGDA627	419143
28 Oct	China People's Rep	Finland	General Trade	63CCJC126	411025
28 Oct	IBRD (World Bank)	Yugoslavia	IBRD Project	503UNTS289	107349
30 Oct	Panama	USA (United States)	General Aid	530UNTS3	107668
30 Oct	Netherlands	UK Great Britain	Other Military	490UNTS11	107151
30 Oct	Greece	USA (United States)	US Agri Commod Aid	493UNTS29	107205
30 Oct	Multilateral		Tech Assistance	480UNTS180	106968
30 Oct	Central Afri Rep	UN Special Fund	Direct Aid	481UNTS247	106985
31 Oct	Afghanistan	Iran	Finance	0IRTB2	433004
31 Oct	Afghanistan	Iran	General Trade	0IRTB2	433003
31 Oct	Gabon	Germany, West	Loans and Credits	64WBGA155	424208
02 Nov	Afghanistan	Iran	Telecommunications	0IRTB2	433006
04 Nov	Austria	UNESCO (Educ/Cult)	IGO Establishment	63ABGB337	403204
05 Nov	China People's Rep	Yugoslavia	General Trade	63CCJC128	411027
05 Nov	Canada	Poland	Commodity Trade	529UNTS81	107658
05 Nov	France	UK Great Britain	Taxation	539UNTS277	107838
05 Nov	WHO (World Health)	Tanganyika	Tech Assistance	496UNTS193	107252
06 Nov	Liechtenstein	Switzerland	Consul/Citizenship	64SWRO5	462184
06 Nov	Liechtenstein	Switzerland	Consul/Citizenship	64SWRO1	462183
06 Nov	Tanganyika	USSR (Soviet Union)	Culture	528UNTS157	107639
06 Nov	Portugal	IBRD (World Bank)	IBRD Project	492UNTS89	107188
06 Nov	Portugal	IBRD (World Bank)	IBRD Project	491UNTS137	107176
07 Nov	Multilateral		Tech Assistance	480UNTS232	106971
08 Nov	Ceylon (Sri Lanka)	Germany, West	Loans and Credits	66WGBB909	425072
08 Nov	Ecuador	Germany, West	Finance	64WBGA41	424112
08 Nov	WHO (World Health)	Somalia	IGO Operations	493UNTS243	107218
08 Nov	Czechoslovakia	Mongolia	Consul/Citizenship	503UNTS125	107341
08 Nov	Multilateral		Tech Assistance	482UNTS286	106999
09 Nov	China People's Rep	Japan	Specific Resources	63CCJC129	411028
09 Nov	China People's Rep	Japan	General Ad Hoc	63CCJC130	411029
09 Nov	China People's Rep	Japan	Dispute Settlement	63CCJC131	411030
09 Nov	Multilateral		Direct Aid	489UNTS209	107141
09 Nov	UNESCO (Educ/Cult)	United Arab Rep	Culture	489UNTS233	107142
10 Nov	Germany, West	Hungary	General Economic	64WBGA14	424705
12 Nov	New Zealand	IBRD (World Bank)	IBRD Project	485UNTS233	107059
13 Nov	Belgium	Romania	Culture	520UNTS119	107513
14 Nov	Belgium	Poland	Claims and Debts	66PZUM85	458107
14 Nov	Multilateral		Finance	619UNTS299	108948
14 Nov	Belgium	Pakistan	Culture	535UNTS393	107792
14 Nov	Austria	Belgium	Specific Property	544UNTS97	107912
14 Nov	Belgium	USA (United States)	Extradition	522UNTS237	107549
14 Nov	Tanganyika	USA (United States)	Claims and Debts	493UNTS75	107208
14 Nov	Paraguay	USA (United States)	US Agri Commod Aid	505UNTS87	107366
15 Nov	France	Spain	Loans and Credits	64SPBO1403	460148
15 Nov	Switzerland	Tunisia	Claims and Debts	63SWRO1073	462161
15 Nov	Canada	USA (United States)	Other Military	493UNTS67	107207
16 Nov	Japan	Pakistan	Education	0JGJI1527	441117
17 Nov	Iran	USA (United States)	US Agri Commod Aid	530UNTS41	107671
18 Nov	Syria	USA (United States)	US Agri Commod Aid	494UNTS169	107232
18 Nov	Tunisia	USA (United States)	Education	494UNTS193	107233
20 Nov	Germany, East	Romania	Air Transport	11EGDA478	419301
20 Nov	China People's Rep	Czechoslovakia	Finance	63CCJC135	411032
20 Nov	Niger	United Nations	IGO Establishment	536UNTS3	107793
21 Nov	Iran	UNICEF (Children)	Direct Aid	0IRTB86	433140
21 Nov	Iran	UNICEF (Children)	IGO Operations	485UNTS35	107044

DATE	PARTY ONE	PARTY TWO	TOPIC	CITATION	NUMBER
1963 (Cont.)					
22 Nov	Afghanistan	China People's Rep	Territory Boundary	63CCJC136	411033
22 Nov	Netherlands	Portugal	Non-ILO Labor	492UNTS31	107185
22 Nov	Peru	IBRD (World Bank)	IBRD Project	491UNTS101	107175
22 Nov	WHO (World Health)	Sierra Leone	IGO Operations	493UNTS255	107219
22 Nov	Israel	USA (United States)	Commodity Trade	494UNTS89	107228
23 Nov	Germany, East	India	Water Transport	11EGDA388	419129
25 Nov	Cambodia	China People's Rep	Air Transport	63CCJC138	411034
26 Nov	Cambodia	China People's Rep	Air Transport	63CCJC141	411037
26 Nov	Netherlands	USA (United States)	Milit Assistance	388UNTS303	105586
27 Nov	Spain	Switzerland	Taxation	64SWRO953	462047
27 Nov	Spain	Switzerland	Taxation	65SPBO1201	460256
27 Nov	ICJ Option Clause	UK Great Britain	ICJ Option Clause	482UNTS187	106995
27 Nov	Czechoslovakia	USSR (Soviet Union)	General Amity	496UNTS161	107250
28 Nov	Canada	Denmark	Air Transport	496UNTS223	107254
29 Nov	Colombia	USA (United States)	Gen Communications	494UNTS49	107225
30 Nov	Germany, West	Norway	Milit Installation	3NORT896	451191
30 Nov	Brazil	Germany, West	Consul/Citizenship	65WGBB1565	425057
30 Nov	Brazil	Germany, West	Tech Assistance	64WBGA49	424056
30 Nov	Brazil	Germany, West	Finance	0UNTS0	109425
30 Nov	Brazil	Germany, West	Consul/Citizenship	0UNTS0	109423
30 Nov	Brazil	Germany, West	Tech Assistance	0UNTS0	109421
30 Nov	Brazil	Germany, West	Water Transport	0UNTS0	109426
30 Nov	Romania	Yugoslavia	Specific Property	512UNTS2	107438
30 Nov	Argentina	USA (United States)	Scientific Project	505UNTS131	107369
02 Dec	France	Gabon	Air Transport	64FRRT9	415196
03 Dec	Multilateral		IGO Establishment	529UNTS217	107663
03 Dec	Iraq	UNICEF (Children)	IGO Operations	482UNTS319	107001
03 Dec	Nicaragua	United Nations	IGO Status/Immunit	482UNTS329	107002
03 Dec	Australia	India	Milit Assistance	486UNTS279	107082
04 Dec	Germany, West	Vietnam, South	Loans and Credits	0VKNG194	496059
04 Dec	United Arab Rep	USA (United States)	Commodity Trade	505UNTS117	107368
05 Dec	Iran	Yugoslavia	Health/Educ/Welfare	0IRTB83	433135
06 Dec	Ghana	Switzerland	Taxation	64SWRO426	462052
06 Dec	Albania	China People's Rep	General Economic	63CCJC144	411039
07 Dec	IAEA (Atom Energy)	Yugoslavia	Scientific Project	501UNTS273	107322
09 Dec	Germany, West	Malaysia	Loans and Credits	64WBGA13	424451
09 Dec	Czechoslovakia	Germany, East	Air Transport	11EGDA501	419368
09 Dec	Dahomey	France	Air Transport	64FRRT13	415149
09 Dec	Belgium	Poland	Culture	514UNTS195	107448
09 Dec	Tanganyika	USA (United States)	Tech Assistance	526UNTS301	107612
09 Dec	Austria	Denmark	Admin Cooperation	520UNTS133	107514
10 Dec	France	Paraguay	Health/Educ/Welfare	65FRRT15	415355
10 Dec	Accept UN Charter	Zanzibar	UN Charter	483UNTS237	107016
11 Dec	Austria	Poland	Admin Cooperation	63PZUM76	458108
12 Dec	Jordan	IDA (Devel Assoc)	Non-IBRD Project	492UNTS3	107184
12 Dec	Accept UN Charter	Kenya	UN Charter	483UNTS233	107015
12 Dec	Jordan	IDA (Devel Assoc)	Non-IBRD Project	506UNTS51	107381
13 Dec	Greece	USA (United States)	Education	494UNTS55	107226
14 Dec	India	Japan	Claims and Debts	0JGJI1529	441118
14 Dec	Albania	France	General Amity	65FRRT41	415004
14 Dec	Multilateral		IGO Establishment	507UNTS149	107399
16 Dec	Germany, West	Korea, South	Non-ILO Labor	64WGBB143	425390
16 Dec	Canada	India	Atomic Energy	529UNTS45	107655
16 Dec	Czechoslovakia	Romania	General Trade	527UNTS285	107630
17 Dec	Congo (Zaire)	France	Health/Educ/Welfare	67FRJO1511	416129
18 Dec	Cameroon	Netherlands	General Aid	521UNTS303	107527
18 Dec	Mexico	IAEA (Atom Energy)	Atomic Energy	490UNTS361	107165
18 Dec	UK Great Britain	Yugoslavia	Commodity Trade	502UNTS177	107328
18 Dec	Finland	Poland	Non-ILO Labor	486UNTS57	107072
18 Dec	Multilateral		Atomic Energy	490UNTS383	107166
18 Dec	Chile	IBRD (World Bank)	IBRD Project	504UNTS3	107351
18 Dec	Chile	IBRD (World Bank)	IBRD Project	504UNTS29	107352
19 Dec	Germany, East	Yugoslavia	Sanitation	11EGDA395	419154
19 Dec	Germany, East	Romania	Education	11EGDA638	419302
19 Dec	Taiwan	USA (United States)	Status of Forces	527UNTS69	107617

DATE	PARTY ONE	PARTY TWO	TOPIC	CITATION	NUMBER
1963 (Cont.)					
19 Dec	IDA (Devel Assoc)	Tanganyika	Non-IBRD Project	492UNTS241	107193
20 Dec	France	Germany, West	Non-ILO Labor	65WGBB1287	425192
20 Dec	Germany, West	Tunisia	Claims and Debts	65WGBB1377	425679
20 Dec	France	Germany, West	Non-ILO Labor	64WGBB702	425193
20 Dec	Germany, West	Tunisia	Loans and Credits	64WBGA73	424680
20 Dec	Netherlands	Poland	Claims and Debts	514UNTS169	107446
20 Dec	Czechoslovakia	Hungary	General Economic	538UNTS127	107812
20 Dec	Romania	Yugoslavia	Visas	527UNTS245	107629
20 Dec	France	Israel	Customs	515UNTS165	107459
21 Dec	Norway	Zambia	Taxation	2NORT553	451219
21 Dec	Greece	Poland	Air Transport	538UNTS155	107813
23 Dec	Liechtenstein	Norway	Visas	3NORT889	451106
23 Dec	Italy	Yugoslavia	Visas	64ITDI321	436247
24 Dec	Norway	USSR (Soviet Union)	Territory Boundary	3NORT897	451211
24 Dec	Germany, West	Romania	General Trade	64WBGA57	424604
24 Dec	IDA (Devel Assoc)	Syria	Non-IBRD Project	534UNTS253	107764
24 Dec	Laos	UK Great Britain	Finance	502UNTS189	107330
24 Dec	Australia	Laos	Finance	503UNTS315	107350
25 Dec	Romania	Yugoslavia	Land Transport	576UNTS95	108366
25 Dec	Dominican Republic	Israel	Tech Assistance	550UNTS221	108018
26 Dec	Paraguay	IDA (Devel Assoc)	Non-IBRD Project	507UNTS3	107394
27 Dec	China People's Rep	Romania	General Economic	63CCJC151	411041
27 Dec	Canada	USA (United States)	Air Transport	494UNTS21	107223
30 Dec	Austria	Turkey	Direct Aid	64TURG903	466101
30 Dec	Belgium	Germany, West	Admin Cooperation	64WBGA78	424032
30 Dec	Germany, East	Poland	Air Transport	11EGDA416	419271
30 Dec	Multilateral		IBRD Project	568UNTS243	108272
30 Dec	Multilateral		IBRD Project	568UNTS215	108270
30 Dec	Multilateral		IBRD Project	568UNTS233	108271
30 Dec	Multilateral		IBRD Project	551UNTS75	108035
30 Dec	Multilateral		IBRD Project	551UNTS119	108037
30 Dec	Multilateral		IBRD Project	551UNTS105	108036
31 Dec	Afghanistan	Iran	Taxation	0IRTB3	433008
31 Dec	France	Portugal	Non-ILO Labor	64FRRT12	415370
31 Dec	New Zealand	Western Samoa	Scientific Project	521UNTS163	107519
1964					
02 Jan	Albania	China People's Rep	Sanitation	64CCJC3	411050
03 Jan	Congo (Zaire)	UK Great Britain	Loans and Credits	534UNTS417	107770
03 Jan	Australia	USA (United States)	Gen Communications	505UNTS159	107371
06 Jan	Italy	Panama	Visas	65ITDI155	436293
06 Jan	France	South Africa	Scientific Project	601UNTS229	108699
06 Jan	Belgium	Netherlands	Reparations	531UNTS119	107698
06 Jan	Saudi Arabia	USA (United States)	Telecommunications	531UNTS3	107689
06 Jan	Japan	UK Great Britain	Specific Resources	502UNTS183	107329
07 Jan	China People's Rep	Guinea	General Trade	64CCJC4	411157
08 Jan	Ceylon (Sri Lanka)	Finland	Water Transport	492UNTS285	107198
08 Jan	Liberia	IBRD (World Bank)	IBRD Project	504UNTS53	107353
08 Jan	Burundi	UNICEF (Children)	IGO Operations	485UNTS45	107045
08 Jan	Somalia	USA (United States)	Claims and Debts	505UNTS165	107372
09 Jan	Norway	Thailand	Taxation	522UNTS65	107537
09 Jan	USA (United States)	Vietnam, South	US Agri Commod Aid	505UNTS173	107373
11 Jan	Hungary	Netherlands	Taxation	522UNTS243	107550
15 Jan	France	Germany, West	Admin Cooperation	70WGBB1	425194
15 Jan	China People's Rep	Cuba	General Economic	64CCJC9	411106
15 Jan	Cambodia	France	Air Transport	64FRRT14	415097
15 Jan	Canada	France	Education	65FRRT37	415105
15 Jan	Mali	Niger	Air Transport	499UNTS197	107299
16 Jan	China People's Rep	Germany, East	Health/Educ/Welfare	12EGDA726	419097
16 Jan	Czechoslovakia	France	Dispute Settlement	64FRRT15	415441
16 Jan	Kenya	UK Great Britain	Admin Cooperation	502UNTS213	107332
17 Jan	Ghana	Poland	Culture	65PDZU393	457109
20 Jan	China People's Rep	Mongolia	General Trade	64CCJC13	411252
20 Jan	Czechoslovakia	Yugoslavia	Admin Cooperation	538UNTS197	107816
20 Jan	Austria	Belgium	Land Transport	509UNTS275	107406

DATE	PARTY ONE	PARTY TWO	TOPIC	CITATION	NUMBER
1964 (Cont.)					
21 Jan	France	Senegal	Education	64FRRT25	415396
21 Jan	France	Senegal	Visas	64FRRT32	415395
21 Jan	Greece	Poland	Taxation	533UNTS309	107749
22 Jan	Canada	USA (United States)	Specific Property	530UNTS89	107674
22 Jan	UNICEF (Children)	Senegal	IGO Operations	486UNTS91	107074
24 Jan	Germany, West	Senegal	Claims and Debts	65WGBB1391	425621
25 Jan	France	Yugoslavia	General Trade	64FRMD102	417487
27 Jan	Finland	IAEA (Atom Energy)	Scientific Project	501UNTS213	107319
28 Jan	Multilateral		Tech Assistance	502UNTS321	107336
29 Jan	Ecuador	Norway	Visas	3NORT899	451042
29 Jan	France	Tunisia	Visas	64FRRT26	415463
29 Jan	France	Tunisia	Visas	64FRRT30	415462
29 Jan	Spain	USA (United States)	Specific Property	511UNTS61	107427
30 Jan	Switzerland	Tanganyika	Admin Cooperation	64SWRO276	462028
30 Jan	Brazil	USA (United States)	Milit Assistance	511UNTS77	107428
31 Jan	China People's Rep	Hungary	Mass Media	64CCJC20	411195
31 Jan	Australia	Italy	Non-ILO Labor	488UNTS197	107129
01 Feb	Iran	Switzerland	General Economic	64SWRO87	462142
02 Feb	Cambodia	Germany, East	Health/Educ/Welfare	12EGDA826	419168
03 Feb	Ecuador	France	Air Transport	64FRRT38	415157
03 Feb	Poland	USA (United States)	US Agri Commod Aid	505UNTS215	107375
03 Feb	Poland	USA (United States)	US Agri Commod Aid	505UNTS245	107376
04 Feb	Germany, West	Korea, South	Claims and Debts	66WGBB841	425391
04 Feb	Lebanon	Pakistan	Air Transport	614UNTS55	108863
04 Feb	Denmark	Ireland	Taxation	525UNTS233	107596
05 Feb	Italy	USSR (Soviet Union)	General Trade	65ITDI165	436424
05 Feb	China People's Rep	Ghana	General Trade	64CCJC24	411158
05 Feb	Australia	USA (United States)	Status of Forces	511UNTS103	107430
05 Feb	IDA (Devel Assoc)	Tanganyika	Non-IBRD Project	506UNTS91	107382
06 Feb	Subsahara Tech Com	IAEA (Atom Energy)	IGO Operations	501UNTS285	200606
07 Feb	France	Mauritania	Consul/Citizenship	66FRJO1901	416317
07 Feb	Argentina	Paraguay	Air Transport	634UNTS127	109057
07 Feb	Colombia	IBRD (World Bank)	IBRD Project	516UNTS99	107473
10 Feb	Multilateral		Visas	496UNTS151	107249
10 Feb	Paraguay	USA (United States)	Milit Assistance	511UNTS53	107426
11 Feb	IMCO (Maritime Org)	United Nations	IGO Operations	489UNTS357	200605
11 Feb	Netherlands	Tunisia	Culture	570UNTS173	108293
11 Feb	Denmark	Yugoslavia	Air Transport	511UNTS241	107437
11 Feb	Jordan	USA (United States)	US Agri Commod Aid	511UNTS85	107429
12 Feb	Germany, East	Yugoslavia	Consul/Citizenship	12EGDA792	419155
13 Feb	Iran	Poland	General Economic	0IRTB57	433092
13 Feb	Iceland	USA (United States)	Education	524UNTS235	107576
13 Feb	Peru	USA (United States)	US Agri Commod Aid	511UNTS119	107431
13 Feb	Iceland	USA (United States)	US Agri Commod Aid	510UNTS295	107420
13 Feb	Iceland	USA (United States)	US Agri Commod Aid	511UNTS3	107421
14 Feb	Mexico	USA (United States)	Scientific Project	524UNTS197	107574
15 Feb	Multilateral		Milit Installation	533UNTS98	107736
17 Feb	Australia	USA (United States)	Commodity Trade	511UNTS17	107422
17 Feb	New Zealand	USA (United States)	Commodity Trade	511UNTS37	107424
19 Feb	El Salvador	France	Telecommunications	65FRRT38	415387
19 Feb	United Nations	Sierra Leone	IGO Status/Immunit	489UNTS91	107136
20 Feb	Guinea	Italy	Tech Assistance	65ITDI191	436201
20 Feb	Guinea	Italy	Claims and Debts	65ITDI130	436202
20 Feb	Germany, East	India	Culture	12EGDA1128	419130
20 Feb	Jamaica	UK Great Britain	Military Mission	496UNTS239	107256
20 Feb	Multilateral		Tech Assistance	491UNTS30	107172
21 Feb	Belgium	Italy	Health/Educ/Welfare	65ITDI119	436051
22 Feb	USA (United States)	USSR (Soviet Union)	Health/Educ/Welfare	526UNTS131	107605
24 Feb	Philippines	USA (United States)	Commodity Trade	505UNTS283	107378
25 Feb	Germany, West	Switzerland	Non-ILO Labor	65WGBB1293	425759
25 Feb	Ireland	USA (United States)	Commodity Trade	511UNTS27	107423
26 Feb	United Nations	Upper Volta	IGO Status/Immunit	489UNTS179	107139
27 Feb	Germany, West	Italy	Non-ILO Labor	65ITDI129	436177
27 Feb	France	Germany, West	Visas	64WBGA238	424195
27 Feb	UNESCO (Educ/Cult)	Yugoslavia	IGO Operations	489UNTS257	107143

DATE	PARTY ONE	PARTY TWO	TOPIC	CITATION	NUMBER
1964 (Cont.)					
27 Feb	France	New Zealand	Air Transport	499UNTS191	107298
27 Feb	Denmark	USSR (Soviet Union)	Specif Claim/Waive	509UNTS285	107407
28 Feb	Germany, West	Philippines	General Trade	4PTS831	465057
28 Feb	Multilateral		Atomic Energy	501UNTS245	107321
29 Feb	Germany, West	Philippines	Direct Aid	4PTS835	465058
29 Feb	Germany, West	Malta	General Trade	64WBGA87	424461
29 Feb	Cyprus	USSR (Soviet Union)	Air Transport	602UNTS45	108706
02 Mar	Sudan	USA (United States)	US Agri Commod Aid	524UNTS217	107575
02 Mar	Congo (Zaire)	United Nations	Milit Installation	533UNTS93	107735
03 Mar	Germany, West	Philippines	Water Transport	4PTS841	465060
03 Mar	Germany, West	Philippines	Visas	4PTS839	465059
03 Mar	Germany, West	Philippines	General Economic	4PTS843	465061
03 Mar	Germany, West	Philippines	Admin Cooperation	64WBGA89	424581
03 Mar	Germany, West	Philippines	General Amity	64WBGA89	424781
03 Mar	Multilateral		Consul/Citizenship	516UNTS53	107470
03 Mar	Netherlands	Tunisia	Tech Assistance	533UNTS133	107739
03 Mar	Morocco	United Nations	IGO Status/Immunit	490UNTS187	107154
04 Mar	Ecuador	Spain	Consul/Citizenship	65SPBO1301	460090
05 Mar	Albania	China People's Rep	Health/Educ/Welfare	64CCJC34	411051
06 Mar	Bulgaria	Germany, West	General Trade	64WBGA148	424064
06 Mar	Canada	USA (United States)	Specific Property	524UNTS255	107577
09 Mar	China People's Rep	Vietnam, North	Land Transport	64CCJC36	411363
09 Mar	Multilateral		Specific Resources	581UNTS57	108432
09 Mar	Algeria	Czechoslovakia	Air Transport	601UNTS247	108700
09 Mar	Multilateral		Specific Resources	581UNTS83	108433
09 Mar	Multilateral		Specific Resources	581UNTS89	108434
10 Mar	Belgium	France	Taxation	557UNTS13	108127
10 Mar	Ivory Coast	USA (United States)	US Agri Commod Aid	526UNTS285	107611
11 Mar	India	Iran	General Trade	0IRTB38	433057
11 Mar	IBRD (World Bank)	Thailand	IBRD Project	504UNTS73	107354
12 Mar	Portugal	USA (United States)	Commodity Trade	542UNTS3	107875
12 Mar	Nigeria	IBRD (World Bank)	IBRD Project	516UNTS325	107480
12 Mar	New Zealand	IBRD (World Bank)	IBRD Project	505UNTS3	107362
14 Mar	Germany, East	Poland	Visas	64PZUM16	458110
14 Mar	Czechoslovakia	Yugoslavia	Visas	544UNTS147	107917
16 Mar	Israel	Philippines	Tech Assistance	550UNTS269	108021
17 Mar	Jamaica	Japan	Consul/Citizenship	65JAIL233	440163
17 Mar	Germany, West	USA (United States)	Education	64WBGA113	424720
17 Mar	Germany, West	Portugal	Non-ILO Labor	64WBGA104	424595
17 Mar	Germany, West	Uganda	Water Transport	66WBGA167	424697
17 Mar	Germany, West	Uganda	General Trade	67WBGA89	424698
17 Mar	Cameroon	Mali	Air Transport	524UNTS61	107566
18 Mar	Korea, South	USA (United States)	US Agri Commod Aid	524UNTS263	107578
18 Mar	Spain	USA (United States)	Culture	535UNTS343	107789
18 Mar	Italy	United Nations	Education	491UNTS21	107171
18 Mar	Rwanda	UN Special Fund	Direct Aid	491UNTS3	107170
19 Mar	Indonesia	Philippines	IGO Establishment	4PTS855	465062
19 Mar	Indonesia	Philippines	Gen Communications	4PTS859	465063
20 Mar	Germany, West	Uganda	Loans and Credits	66WBGA167	424699
20 Mar	Germany, West	Uganda	Tech Assistance	66WBGA167	424700
20 Mar	Belgium	United Nations	Milit Installation	533UNTS83	107734
21 Mar	Argentina	Yugoslavia	Claims and Debts	635UNTS153	109078
21 Mar	USSR (Soviet Union)	Yemen	General Amity	553UNTS267	108094
23 Mar	Norway	Uganda	Tech Assistance	3NORT900	451196
24 Mar	Belgium	France	Non-ILO Labor	64FRJO51	416068
24 Mar	Luxembourg	Netherlands	Consul/Citizenship	548UNTS137	107975
25 Mar	Bolivia	USA (United States)	US Agri Commod Aid	532UNTS3	107710
25 Mar	Pakistan	IDA (Devel Assoc)	Non-IBRD Project	535UNTS43	107775
25 Mar	Pakistan	IDA (Devel Assoc)	Non-IBRD Project	534UNTS275	107765
28 Mar	China People's Rep	Hungary	General Economic	64CCJC42	411197
30 Mar	Chile	Germany, West	Air Transport	65WGBB79	425086
30 Mar	Cyprus	United Nations	IGO Status/Immunit	492UNTS261	107194
31 Mar	Cyprus	United Nations	IGO Status/Immunit	492UNTS57	107187
31 Mar	Greece	United Nations	IGO Status/Immunit	492UNTS267	107195
31 Mar	United Nations	Turkey	IGO Status/Immunit	492UNTS273	107196

DATE	PARTY ONE	PARTY TWO	TOPIC	CITATION	NUMBER
1964 (Cont.)					
02 Apr	Italy	Monaco	Non-ILO Labor	65ITDI131	436283
02 Apr	Ireland	Norway	Culture	553UNTS129	108078
02 Apr	Germany, West	Thailand	Tech Assistance	503UNTS3	107338
02 Apr	United Nations	UK Great Britain	IGO Status/Immunit	492UNTS279	107197
03 Apr	Indonesia	Netherlands	Tech Assistance	566UNTS45	108239
04 Apr	USA (United States)	Yugoslavia	Visas	526UNTS47	107599
07 Apr	Malaysia	Netherlands	Air Transport	524UNTS81	107567
07 Apr	Denmark	Finland	Taxation	525UNTS89	107586
07 Apr	Tunisia	USA (United States)	US Agri Commod Aid	527UNTS3	107613
07 Apr	Portugal	UK Great Britain	Land Transport	539UNTS167	107830
08 Apr	Germany, West	Japan	General Trade	65JAIL234	440164
08 Apr	Austria	Yugoslavia	Territory Boundary	66ABGB229	403238
08 Apr	Bulgaria	Yemen	General Amity	0UNTS0	110292
08 Apr	Bulgaria	Yemen	Culture	0UNTS0	110293
08 Apr	Mexico	Netherlands	Culture	575UNTS35	108353
08 Apr	Multilateral		Loans and Credits	501UNTS221	107320
08 Apr	Taiwan	UNICEF (Children)	IGO Operations	500UNTS49	107306
10 Apr	Austria	Luxembourg	Taxation	64ABGB143	403137
10 Apr	France	UK Great Britain	Specific Resources	0UNTS0	109272
13 Apr	UK Great Britain	USSR (Soviet Union)	Visas	539UNTS197	107832
14 Apr	Bulgaria	China People's Rep	General Economic	64CCJC46	411084
14 Apr	Algeria	China People's Rep	Mass Media	64CCJC48	411060
14 Apr	Liberia	USA (United States)	Specific Property	526UNTS221	107606
14 Apr	Congo (Zaire)	Israel	Visas	552UNTS305	108062
14 Apr	Australia	Israel	Visas	496UNTS233	107255
15 Apr	Norway	Yugoslavia	Air Transport	602UNTS177	108712
15 Apr	India	USA (United States)	Commodity Trade	527UNTS19	107614
15 Apr	Argentina	UK Great Britain	Commodity Trade	515UNTS3	107450
15 Apr	Canada	UK Great Britain	Commodity Trade	515UNTS39	107452
15 Apr	Australia	UK Great Britain	Commodity Trade	515UNTS23	107451
15 Apr	UK Great Britain	USA (United States)	Commodity Trade	515UNTS55	107453
16 Apr	Netherlands	Spain	Non-ILO Labor	64SPBO1306	460212
16 Apr	Ecuador	Italy	Visas	65ITDI127	436108
16 Apr	Germany, West	Greece	Other Economic	609UNTS27	108826
16 Apr	Multilateral		Visas	548UNTS27	107967
18 Apr	Hungary	Poland	Visas	64PZUM20	458111
18 Apr	Brazil	Italy	Mass Media	65ITDI120	436067
18 Apr	Germany, West	Honduras	Tech Assistance	66WBGA33	424250
20 Apr	Kenya	Poland	Tech Assistance	64PZUM23	458112
20 Apr	Kenya	USA (United States)	Claims and Debts	524UNTS165	107571
21 Apr	Ethiopia	Germany, West	Water Transport	68WBGA38	424017
21 Apr	Ethiopia	Germany, West	General Economic	68WBGA38	424016
21 Apr	Ethiopia	Germany, West	Air Transport	68WBGA38	424018
21 Apr	Ethiopia	Germany, West	Claims and Debts	65WGBB1521	425015
22 Apr	Peru	IBRD (World Bank)	IBRD Project	519UNTS95	107503
22 Apr	Japan	IBRD (World Bank)	IBRD Project	505UNTS21	107363
23 Apr	Taiwan	USA (United States)	Health/Educ/Welfare	524UNTS141	107570
24 Apr	Multilateral		Loans and Credits	617UNTS347	200633
24 Apr	Finland	USSR (Soviet Union)	Territory Boundary	537UNTS231	107804
25 Apr	Germany, West	Rwanda	Loans and Credits	64WBGA243	424600
25 Apr	Japan	USA (United States)	General Economic	530UNTS61	107672
26 Apr	Cuba	Germany, East	General Aid	12EGDA837	419190
27 Apr	Guatemala	Spain	Culture	65SPBO2506	460160
27 Apr	Japan	United Arab Rep	Taxation	0JGJI1536	441119
27 Apr	USA (United States)	Yugoslavia	US Agri Commod Aid	526UNTS89	107602
27 Apr	USA (United States)	Yugoslavia	US Agri Commod Aid	526UNTS73	107601
28 Apr	France	Italy	Territory Boundary	65ITDI128	436158
28 Apr	France	Italy	Patents/Copyrights	69FRJO2704	416248
28 Apr	France	Uganda	Air Transport	65FRRT95	415348
28 Apr	France	Tanzania	Air Transport	65FRRT97	415425
28 Apr	USA (United States)	Yugoslavia	US Agri Commod Aid	526UNTS103	107603
28 Apr	Congo (Zaire)	USA (United States)	US Agri Commod Aid	526UNTS55	107600
28 Apr	Afghanistan	United Nations	Education	494UNTS77	107227
30 Apr	Germany, West	Turkey	Health/Educ/Welfare	65WGBB1169	425776
30 Apr	Chile	Germany, West	Air Transport	0UNTS0	109476

DATE	PARTY ONE	PARTY TWO	TOPIC	CITATION	NUMBER
1964 (Cont.)					
04 May	Japan	UK Great Britain	Consul/Citizenship	561UNTS25	108179
05 May	Germany, East	USSR (Soviet Union)	Tech Assistance	12EGDA1137	419424
05 May	Austria	France	Patents/Copyrights	64FRRT46	415059
05 May	United Arab Rep	USA (United States)	Air Transport	531UNTS229	107706
06 May	Norway	Yugoslavia	Visas	3NORT909	451097
06 May	Canada	USA (United States)	Scientific Project	524UNTS173	107572
06 May	Multilateral		IGO Operations	514UNTS71	107442
08 May	Liberia	USA (United States)	Education	526UNTS239	107608
08 May	Ethiopia	IBRD (World Bank)	IBRD Project	505UNTS51	107364
09 May	Trinidad/Tobago	UK Great Britain	Admin Cooperation	633UNTS327	109043
10 May	China People's Rep	Kenya	Direct Aid	64CCJC64	411229
10 May	Argentina	USA (United States)	Milit Assistance	527UNTS77	107618
12 May	Korea, South	USA (United States)	Commodity Trade	529UNTS299	107667
13 May	Morocco	UNESCO (Educ/Cult)	Tech Assistance	0UNTS0	109220
13 May	Germany, West	Ireland	Other Military	553UNTS87	108071
13 May	Colombia	USA (United States)	Scientific Project	530UNTS77	107673
14 May	Germany, East	Ghana	Education	12EGDA746	419112
14 May	Germany, East	Ghana	Non-ILO Labor	12EGDA740	419111
14 May	Multilateral		Refugees	528UNTS13	107632
14 May	Pakistan	IBRD (World Bank)	IBRD Project	516UNTS145	107475
14 May	Multilateral		Refugees	528UNTS23	107633
14 May	Philippines	USA (United States)	US Agri Commod Aid	526UNTS113	107604
14 May	Multilateral		Visas	528UNTS3	107631
14 May	Algeria	IBRD (World Bank)	IBRD Project	522UNTS265	107552
14 May	Mexico	USA (United States)	Commodity Trade	526UNTS228	107607
14 May	Algeria	Czechoslovakia	Culture	538UNTS301	107817
15 May	Germany, West	Spain	Non-ILO Labor	65SPBO1907	460030
15 May	France	Senegal	Education	66FRJO1601	416397
15 May	Germany, East	Yugoslavia	IGO Establishment	12EGDA806	419156
15 May	Austria	Turkey	Non-ILO Labor	515UNTS109	107457
17 May	Germany, East	Tanzania	General Amity	12EGDA1139	419485
17 May	Germany, East	Zanzibar	General Aid	12EGDA1139	419306
18 May	Cuba	Italy	Loans and Credits	65ITDI219	436101
19 May	Chad	France	Non-ILO Labor	68FRJO1112	416432
19 May	Chad	France	Milit Assistance	68FRJO1112	416435
19 May	Chad	France	Culture	68FRJO1112	416434
19 May	Chad	France	IGO Establishment	0UNTS0	109440
19 May	Chad	France	General Aid	0UNTS0	109441
19 May	Chad	France	Culture	0UNTS0	109442
19 May	Chad	France	Milit Assistance	0UNTS0	109443
19 May	Jamaica	UNICEF (Children)	IGO Operations	500UNTS75	107308
20 May	Austria	Yugoslavia	Extradition	514UNTS3	107439
21 May	France	Luxembourg	Territory Boundary	0UNTS0	110527
21 May	Norway	Romania	Claims and Debts	563UNTS45	108203
23 May	France	Spain	General Trade	64FRRT48	415166
23 May	Italy	Eur Space Research	IGO Operations	528UNTS75	107635
25 May	Multilateral		Taxation	620UNTS149	108953
25 May	Netherlands	NATO (North Atlan)	Status of Forces	544UNTS237	107920
25 May	Canada	USA (United States)	Milit Installation	526UNTS251	107609
26 May	Multilateral		IBRD Project	541UNTS271	200613
26 May	Congo (Zaire)	USSR (Soviet Union)	General Trade	0UNTS0	109582
26 May	Ecuador	IDA (Devel Assoc)	Non-IBRD Project	534UNTS93	107757
26 May	Ecuador	IBRD (World Bank)	IBRD Project	534UNTS113	107758
27 May	Germany, West	Netherlands	Non-ILO Labor	64WBGA237	424490
27 May	France	Switzerland	Non-ILO Labor	64FRRT42	415412
27 May	Austria	Romania	Land Transport	588UNTS29	108517
27 May	Netherlands	United Nations	IGO Status/Immunit	548UNTS79	107971
28 May	Greece	USA (United States)	Claims and Debts	0UNTS0	109676
28 May	Netherlands	Yugoslavia	Visas	521UNTS191	107522
29 May	Germany, East	Guinea	Education	12EGDA765	419121
29 May	Germany, East	Guinea	Non-ILO Labor	12EGDA759	419120
29 May	Italy	Netherlands	Other Military	541UNTS147	107867
30 May	Hungary	Yemen	General Amity	577UNTS39	108371
01 Jun	USA (United States)	USSR (Soviet Union)	Consul/Citizenship	0UNTS0	109383
02 Jun	Cyprus	Hungary	Air Transport	602UNTS3	108704

DATE	PARTY ONE	PARTY TWO	TOPIC	CITATION	NUMBER
1964 (Cont.)					
02 Jun	France	Italy	Finance	634UNTS117	109056
03 Jun	Italy	Mali	Tech Assistance	65ITDI142	436269
03 Jun	Germany, East	Mali	Health/Educ/Welfare	12EGDA844	419200
03 Jun	Germany, East	Mali	Education	12EGDA849	419201
03 Jun	France	Luxembourg	Non-ILO Labor	67FRJO2412	416274
03 Jun	France	UK Great Britain	General Ad Hoc	65FRRT92	415200
03 Jun	France	UK Great Britain	Scientific Project	539UNTS253	107836
03 Jun	Taiwan	USA (United States)	US Agri Commod Aid	526UNTS257	107610
03 Jun	Cuba	Czechoslovakia	Sanitation	527UNTS205	107626
03 Jun	Ireland	UN Special Fund	Direct Aid	496UNTS205	107253
04 Jun	France	Spain	Scientific Project	65SPBO1805	460149
04 Jun	Chad	Italy	General Aid	65ITDI216	436084
05 Jun	IBRD (World Bank)	Tunisia	IBRD Project	539UNTS129	107827
07 Jun	Germany, East	Poland	Visas	12EGDA1144	419272
08 Jun	Costa Rica	Spain	Consul/Citizenship	65SPBO2506	460067
08 Jun	Taiwan	Peru	General Trade	548UNTS151	107976
09 Jun	China People's Rep	Yemen	General Amity	64CCJC78	411388
09 Jun	China People's Rep	Yemen	Culture	64CCJC80	411390
09 Jun	Germany, West	UK Great Britain	Reparations	539UNTS187	107831
09 Jun	Mali	USA (United States)	Claims and Debts	530UNTS133	107678
09 Jun	Finland	Norway	Specific Resources	503UNTS205	107345
09 Jun	India	IDA (Devel Assoc)	Non-IBRD Project	506UNTS31	107380
10 Jun	Iran	IBRD (World Bank)	IBRD Project	537UNTS111	107799
11 Jun	China People's Rep	Yugoslavia	General Trade	64CCJC82	411392
11 Jun	Multilateral		Atomic Energy	525UNTS61	107584
11 Jun	Ceylon (Sri Lanka)	Norway	Taxation	559UNTS23	108153
11 Jun	Czechoslovakia	Netherlands	Claims and Debts	556UNTS89	108120
11 Jun	Pakistan	IDA (Devel Assoc)	Non-IBRD Project	534UNTS309	107766
11 Jun	Austria	Belgium	Taxation	521UNTS157	107518
11 Jun	Austria	United Nations	IGO Status/Immunit	500UNTS85	107309
11 Jun	Pakistan	IDA (Devel Assoc)	Non-IBRD Project	506UNTS3	107379
12 Jun	Germany, East	USSR (Soviet Union)	General Amity	553UNTS249	108093
12 Jun	Finland	South Africa	Water Transport	505UNTS107	107367
13 Jun	Guinea	USA (United States)	US Agri Commod Aid	531UNTS263	107708
13 Jun	Israel	Yugoslavia	Visas	516UNTS91	107472
15 Jun	Germany, West	Portugal	Extradition	67WGBB2345	425596
15 Jun	Multilateral		Atomic Energy	573UNTS85	108324
15 Jun	IAEA (Atom Energy)	USA (United States)	Atomic Energy	525UNTS3	107580
16 Jun	China People's Rep	Tanzania	Direct Aid	64CCJC85	411335
16 Jun	Italy	Romania	Scientific Project	558UNTS313	108150
17 Jun	Iraq	Japan	General Trade	65JAIL235	440165
17 Jun	Taiwan	Ecuador	General Trade	533UNTS141	107740
18 Jun	Costa Rica	France	Telecommunications	65FRRT32	415136
18 Jun	Multilateral		Atomic Energy	542UNTS145	107886
18 Jun	Ireland	USA (United States)	Water Transport	530UNTS217	107684
19 Jun	France	Yugoslavia	Culture	65FRRT31	415488
19 Jun	France	Malagasy	Visas	64FRRT69	415285
19 Jun	UK Great Britain	USA (United States)	Water Transport	530UNTS99	107675
20 Jun	Iran	USSR (Soviet Union)	Finance	0IRTB80	433127
20 Jun	Multilateral		General Economic	539UNTS3	107819
22 Jun	Rwanda	WHO (World Health)	Tech Assistance	514UNTS11	107440
22 Jun	South Africa	UK Great Britain	Commodity Trade	515UNTS71	107454
23 Jun	WHO (World Health)	Trinidad/Tobago	Tech Assistance	503UNTS167	107342
23 Jun	Rwanda	WHO (World Health)	Tech Assistance	514UNTS157	107445
23 Jun	Multilateral		Tech Assistance	506UNTS108	107383
24 Jun	France	Iran	Extradition	67FRJO3003	416239
24 Jun	France	Iran	Water Transport	69FRJO511	416240
24 Jun	France	Iran	Consul/Citizenship	0UNTS0	110722
24 Jun	New Zealand	USA (United States)	Air Transport	524UNTS101	107568
24 Jun	Niger	IDA (Devel Assoc)	Non-IBRD Project	554UNTS93	108098
24 Jun	Pakistan	IDA (Devel Assoc)	Non-IBRD Project	533UNTS165	107742
24 Jun	Pakistan	IDA (Devel Assoc)	Non-IBRD Project	533UNTS191	107743
25 Jun	Japan	Yugoslavia	Visas	0JGJI1548	441120
25 Jun	Ireland	UK Great Britain	Commodity Trade	553UNTS221	108090
26 Jun	Denmark	Kenya	Education	573UNTS107	108325

DATE	PARTY ONE	PARTY TWO	TOPIC	CITATION	NUMBER
1964 (Cont.)					
27 Jun	Germany, East	Zanzibar	Tech Assistance	12EGDA1146	419307
28 Jun	Multilateral		Tech Assistance	519UNTS14	107499
30 Jun	Poland	Yugoslavia	General Economic	64PZUM29	458113
30 Jun	Germany, West	Niger	Loans and Credits	65WBGA14	424504
30 Jun	China People's Rep	Mongolia	Territory Boundary	64CCJC90	411255
30 Jun	France	Eur Plant Protect	IGO Status/Immunit	65FRRT74	415501
30 Jun	Ireland	UK Great Britain	Commodity Trade	522UNTS141	107541
30 Jun	Denmark	UK Great Britain	Water Transport	539UNTS203	107833
30 Jun	Pakistan	IBRD (World Bank)	IBRD Project	519UNTS57	107502
30 Jun	Sweden	UK Great Britain	Commodity Trade	515UNTS83	107455
01 Jul	Italy	Malagasy	Tech Assistance	65ITDI197	436268
01 Jul	Italy	Malagasy	General Economic	65ITDI195	436267
01 Jul	Malaysia	UNICEF (Children)	IGO Operations	503UNTS229	107346
02 Jul	Denmark	USA (United States)	Water Transport	529UNTS277	107665
02 Jul	Cyprus	UK Great Britain	Commodity Trade	522UNTS129	107540
03 Jul	France	Spain	Non-ILO Labor	64SPBO1509	460151
03 Jul	Mauritania	USA (United States)	Finance	532UNTS307	107724
03 Jul	United Nations	Togo	Education	502UNTS287	107334
04 Jul	Cambodia	France	General Aid	67FRJO2107	416098
06 Jul	Colombia	Netherlands	General Aid	543UNTS289	107906
06 Jul	India	IDA (Devel Assoc)	Non-IBRD Project	534UNTS49	107753
06 Jul	Sweden	USA (United States)	Water Transport	529UNTS287	107666
07 Jul	Bulgaria	Germany, West	General Trade	64WGBB781	425065
07 Jul	Aus.ria	Vatican/Holy See	Admin Cooperation	64ABGB227	403211
07 Jul	Nigeria	IBRD (World Bank)	IBRD Project	537UNTS3	107795
07 Jul	Peru	USA (United States)	Scientific Project	530UNTS113	107676
08 Jul	Multilateral		ILO Labor	602UNTS259	108718
08 Jul	Multilateral		ILO Labor	560UNTS201	108175
09 Jul	Bulgaria	Greece	Postal Service	0UNTS0	110294
09 Jul	Bulgaria	Greece	Visas	0UNTS0	110296
09 Jul	Bulgaria	Greece	Air Transport	0UNTS0	110297
09 Jul	Bulgaria	Greece	Land Transport	0UNTS0	110295
09 Jul	Malaysia	UK Great Britain	Consul/Citizenship	522UNTS213	107547
09 Jul	Ivory Coast	Mali	Air Transport	524UNTS121	107569
09 Jul	Malaysia	UK Great Britain	Consul/Citizenship	522UNTS189	107545
09 Jul	Malaysia	UK Great Britain	Consul/Citizenship	522UNTS201	107546
10 Jul	Germany, West	Guinea	Commodity Trade	64WBGA195	424248
10 Jul	Germany, East	Yugoslavia	Health/Educ/Welfare	12EGDA815	419157
10 Jul	Multilateral		Postal Service	612UNTS233	108848
10 Jul	Multilateral		Postal Service	612UNTS361	108849
10 Jul	Multilateral		Postal Service	613UNTS127	108853
10 Jul	Multilateral		Postal Service	613UNTS3	108850
10 Jul	Multilateral		Postal Service	611UNTS387	108846
10 Jul	Multilateral		Postal Service	613UNTS3	108851
10 Jul	Multilateral		Postal Service	613UNTS193	108852
10 Jul	Multilateral		Postal Service	611UNTS7	108844
10 Jul	Multilateral		Postal Service	611UNTS105	108845
10 Jul	Multilateral		Postal Service	612UNTS3	108847
10 Jul	Gabon	IBRD (World Bank)	IBRD Project	537UNTS63	107797
10 Jul	Finland	IBRD (World Bank)	IBRD Project	516UNTS125	107474
10 Jul	Iceland	UN Special Fund	IGO Operations	502UNTS343	107337
11 Jul	France	Spain	General Ad Hoc	67FRJO2502	416167
11 Jul	France	Spain	Specific Property	0UNTS0	110374
13 Jul	Multilateral		ILO Labor	569UNTS65	108279
14 Jul	IDA (Devel Assoc)	Turkey	Non-IBRD Project	534UNTS339	107767
15 Jul	Multilateral		IGO Establishment	610UNTS143	108840
15 Jul	Austria	Spain	Non-ILO Labor	589UNTS169	108541
15 Jul	Belgium	Tunisia	Tech Assistance	560UNTS65	108169
15 Jul	Belgium	Tunisia	Tech Assistance	560UNTS57	108168
15 Jul	Belgium	Tunisia	General Economic	561UNTS297	108190
16 Jul	Germany, West	Yugoslavia	Direct Aid	65WBGA17	424333
16 Jul	Germany, West	Yugoslavia	Visas	64WBGA192	424332
16 Jul	France	Luxembourg	Territory Boundary	0UNTS0	109225
16 Jul	Spain	USA (United States)	Water Transport	529UNTS187	107661
16 Jul	France	Norway	Patents/Copyrights	510UNTS229	107417

DATE	PARTY ONE	PARTY TWO	TOPIC	CITATION	NUMBER
1964 (Cont.)					
17 Jul	Mexico	United Nations	IGO Operations	533UNTS117	107738
17 Jul	Turkey	USA (United States)	Commodity Trade	530UNTS25	107670
17 Jul	Greece	USA (United States)	Commodity Trade	530UNTS13	107669
17 Jul	Poland	USSR (Soviet Union)	Specific Resources	552UNTS175	108054
20 Jul	Cuba	Germany, East	Loans and Credits	12EGDA1149	419191
21 Jul	Pakistan	IDA (Devel Assoc)	Non-IBRD Project	534UNTS373	107768
22 Jul	Algeria	Poland	Culture	64PDZU71	457114
22 Jul	Philippines	IBRD (World Bank)	IBRD Project	516UNTS171	107476
23 Jul	China People's Rep	Congo (Brazzaville)	General Economic	64CCJC100	411113
23 Jul	Austria	Finland	Taxation	65ABGB117	403046
23 Jul	New Zealand	Western Samoa	Non-IBRD Project	521UNTS173	107520
23 Jul	Austria	Netherlands	Admin Cooperation	544UNTS265	107921
24 Jul	Bolivia	IDA (Devel Assoc)	Non-IBRD Project	534UNTS171	107762
24 Jul	Bolivia	IDA (Devel Assoc)	Non-IBRD Project	534UNTS203	107763
27 Jul	Belgium	Germany, West	Commodity Trade	67WBGA236	424033
27 Jul	Germany, West	UK Great Britain	Status of Forces	539UNTS243	107835
28 Jul	France	Kenya	Air Transport	65FRJO2511	416258
28 Jul	Multilateral		IGO Operations	555UNTS183	108113
29 Jul	China People's Rep	Vietnam, North	Postal Service	64CCJC102	411370
29 Jul	China People's Rep	Vietnam, North	Telecommunications	64CCJC103	411371
29 Jul	Eur Space Research	Sweden	IGO Operations	528UNTS81	107636
30 Jul	Japan	Kenya	Education	0JGJI1550	441121
31 Jul	Germany, East	Morocco	Finance	12EGDA859	419209
31 Jul	Germany, East	Morocco	General Trade	12EGDA856	419208
31 Jul	China People's Rep	Vietnam, North	Sanitation	64CCJC105	411372
31 Jul	France	Romania	Tech Assistance	64FRRT64	415375
31 Jul	France	Romania	Education	0UNTS0	110723
31 Jul	India	UK Great Britain	Commodity Trade	522UNTS153	107542
31 Jul	IBRD (World Bank)	Spain	IBRD Project	537UNTS81	107798
31 Jul	IDA (Devel Assoc)	UK Great Britain	Non-IBRD Project	535UNTS205	107781
01 Aug	China People's Rep	Germany, East	General Economic	64CCJC106	411160
03 Aug	Germany, West	Sweden	Specif Claim/Waive	64WGBB1402	425617
03 Aug	Multilateral		Tech Assistance	503UNTS239	107347
04 Aug	Accept UN Charter	Malawi	UN Charter	519UNTS3	107496
04 Aug	Denmark	Tanganyika	Dispute Settlement	544UNTS123	107915
04 Aug	Denmark	Tanganyika	Taxation	544UNTS117	107914
04 Aug	Italy	USA (United States)	General Military	529UNTS205	107662
05 Aug	China People's Rep	Guinea	Mass Media	64CCJC107	411161
07 Aug	Mexico	USA (United States)	Taxation	530UNTS123	107677
08 Aug	Norway	USSR (Soviet Union)	Territory Boundary	3NORT921	451212
10 Aug	Italy	Switzerland	Non-ILO Labor	65ITGU54	435396
10 Aug	France	Eur Space Research	IGO Operations	528UNTS135	107637
11 Aug	China People's Rep	Cuba	General Economic	64CCJC108	411114
11 Aug	Brazil	Spain	Health/Educ/Welfare	0UNTS0	109417
11 Aug	Switzerland	UK Great Britain	Atomic Energy	552UNTS271	108059
17 Aug	Iran	USSR (Soviet Union)	Air Transport	0IRTB79	433123
17 Aug	Australia	USA (United States)	Scientific Project	530UNTS209	107683
17 Aug	Kenya	IDA (Devel Assoc)	Non-IBRD Project	535UNTS79	107776
18 Aug	Italy	USA (United States)	Admin Cooperation	65ITGU279	435358
18 Aug	Italy	USA (United States)	Admin Cooperation	0UNTS0	109836
18 Aug	IBRD (World Bank)	Sierra Leone	IBRD Project	516UNTS295	107479
19 Aug	Netherlands	Turkey	Non-ILO Labor	521UNTS197	107523
20 Aug	India	Italy	General Amity	66ITGU218	435206
20 Aug	UK Great Britain	USA (United States)	Specific Property	531UNTS85	107694
20 Aug	Multilateral		Telecommunications	514UNTS25	107441
24 Aug	Costa Rica	USA (United States)	Gen Communications	531UNTS107	107696
25 Aug	Kenya	UK Great Britain	Commodity Trade	522UNTS165	107543
25 Aug	Taiwan	Philippines	Tech Assistance	511UNTS233	107436
26 Aug	Germany, East	Mongolia	Tech Assistance	12EGDA1153	419222
26 Aug	Pakistan	IBRD (World Bank)	IBRD Project	632UNTS201	109023
26 Aug	Morocco	IBRD (World Bank)	IBRD Project	537UNTS193	107802
26 Aug	Pakistan	IDA (Devel Assoc)	Non-IBRD Project	535UNTS263	107784
26 Aug	Kenya	USA (United States)	General Aid	531UNTS51	107692
27 Aug	France	Pakistan	Visas	64FRMD67	417350
27 Aug	Algeria	France	Extradition	65FRRT72	415017

DATE	PARTY ONE	PARTY TWO	TOPIC	CITATION	NUMBER
1964 (Cont.)					
28 Aug	Cameroon	Germany, West	General Military	64WBGA195	424351
28 Aug	Malawi	UK Great Britain	Consul/Citizenship	522UNTS223	107548
28 Aug	Dominican Republic	USA (United States)	Scientific Project	531UNTS35	107691
28 Aug	IBRD (World Bank)	Venezuela	IBRD Project	520UNTS97	107512
28 Aug	IBRD (World Bank)	Venezuela	IBRD Project	537UNTS135	107800
28 Aug	Australia	USA (United States)	Education	510UNTS201	107415
29 Aug	France	Spain	Non-ILO Labor	65SPBO1602	460152
29 Aug	France	Spain	Non-ILO Labor	64SPBO112	460153
29 Aug	France	Spain	Non-ILO Labor	65SPBO302	460150
29 Aug	France	Spain	Non-ILO Labor	0UNTS0	110706
29 Aug	Ceylon (Sri Lanka)	USA (United States)	Education	531UNTS93	107695
31 Aug	France	Monaco	Visas	64FRRT66	415335
31 Aug	IDA (Devel Assoc)	Turkey	Non-IBRD Project	535UNTS111	107777
31 Aug	Jordan	UK Great Britain	Loans and Credits	541UNTS3	107856
31 Aug	Syria	UK Great Britain	Commodity Trade	539UNTS259	107837
01 Sep	France	Int Org Metrology	IGO Status/Immunit	65FRRT76	415502
01 Sep	Malawi	UK Great Britain	Commodity Trade	522UNTS117	107539
02 Sep	Tanganyika	UK Great Britain	Commodity Trade	522UNTS177	107544
04 Sep	Germany, West	Norway	Customs	3NORT923	451192
05 Sep	Canada	Japan	Visas	0JGJI1558	441122
05 Sep	Canada	Japan	Taxation	569UNTS99	108282
05 Sep	Paraguay	USA (United States)	US Agri Commod Aid	530UNTS225	107685
08 Sep	Canada	Spain	Atomic Energy	65SPBO2505	460062
11 Sep	Canada	UK Great Britain	Status of Forces	522UNTS99	107538
11 Sep	Rwanda	UNICEF (Children)	IGO Operations	510UNTS127	107409
12 Sep	Germany, East	India	General Economic	12EGDA771	419131
12 Sep	China People's Rep	Vietnam, North	Air Transport	64CCJC116	411374
12 Sep	Argentina	Colombia	Visas	635UNTS149	109079
12 Sep	Multilateral		Specific Resources	0UNTS0	109344
12 Sep	Finland	UK Great Britain	Commodity Trade	535UNTS13	107773
15 Sep	Israel	UK Great Britain	Taxation	539UNTS283	107839
15 Sep	Multilateral		General Trade	510UNTS147	107411
15 Sep	Philippines	United Nations	IGO Operations	510UNTS137	107410
16 Sep	Canada	USA (United States)	Gen Communications	530UNTS267	107687
16 Sep	Denmark	UK Great Britain	Commodity Trade	534UNTS427	107771
17 Sep	IAEA (Atom Energy)	United Arab Rep	Atomic Energy	525UNTS19	107581
18 Sep	Multilateral		IGO Operations	555UNTS205	108114
18 Sep	Multilateral		IGO Operations	556UNTS25	108117
19 Sep	Algeria	China People's Rep	General Trade	64CCJC118	411063
19 Sep	Algeria	China People's Rep	Finance	64CCJC119	411064
21 Sep	Malta	UK Great Britain	Military Mission	588UNTS55	108518
21 Sep	Malta	UK Great Britain	Direct Aid	588UNTS125	108519
21 Sep	Multilateral		IGO Operations	555UNTS227	108115
22 Sep	Pakistan	IDA (Devel Assoc)	Non-IBRD Project	594UNTS225	108605
23 Sep	China People's Rep	Iraq	General Trade	64CCJC123	411207
23 Sep	Algeria	United Nations	IGO Operations	510UNTS217	107416
24 Sep	Liechtenstein	Switzerland	Customs	64SWRO851	462182
24 Sep	Liechtenstein	Switzerland	Customs	64SWRO849	462185
24 Sep	China People's Rep	Korea, North	General Trade	64CCJC126	411232
25 Sep	Germany, West	Malawi	Loans and Credits	65WBGA67	424445
25 Sep	Greece	Norway	General Economic	610UNTS0	108835
25 Sep	Taiwan	Mexico	General Trade	547UNTS233	107960
26 Sep	Czechoslovakia	France	Culture	0UNTS0	110726
26 Sep	Poland	UK Great Britain	Specific Property	539UNTS153	107828
28 Sep	France	Switzerland	Admin Cooperation	64FRRT63	415413
28 Sep	Norway	UK Great Britain	Specific Property	548UNTS63	107970
29 Sep	China People's Rep	Central Afri Rep	General Economic	64CCJC130	411118
29 Sep	China People's Rep	Central Afri Rep	Direct Aid	64CCJC128	411116
29 Sep	China People's Rep	Central Afri Rep	Culture	64CCJC129	411117
29 Sep	Mali	IDA (Devel Assoc)	Non-IBRD Project	594UNTS187	108604
29 Sep	USA (United States)	Vietnam, South	US Agri Commod Aid	531UNTS183	107703
29 Sep	Accept UN Charter	Malta	UN Charter	519UNTS7	107497
29 Sep	Iran	USA (United States)	US Agri Commod Aid	531UNTS163	107702
30 Sep	Germany, West	Panama	Tech Assistance	65WBGA7	424568
30 Sep	Germany, West	Turkey	Non-ILO Labor	68WBGA22	424773

DATE	PARTY ONE	PARTY TWO	TOPIC	CITATION	NUMBER
1964 (Cont.)					
30 Sep	India	USA (United States)	US Agri Commod Aid	532UNTS321	107726
30 Sep	Multilateral		IGO Operations	556UNTS3	108116
30 Sep	Austria	Thailand	General Trade	527UNTS239	107628
30 Sep	UK Great Britain	USSR (Soviet Union)	Specific Property	539UNTS159	107829
30 Sep	Australia	UN Special Fund	Scientific Project	510UNTS277	107419
01 Oct	Germany, East	USSR (Soviet Union)	Health/Educ/Welfare	12EGDA1077	419425
01 Oct	Kenya	United Nations	IGO Operations	511UNTS199	107434
01 Oct	Kenya	UN Special Fund	IGO Operations	511UNTS181	107433
02 Oct	Central Afri Rep	Germany, West	Loans and Credits	64WBGA234	424732
02 Oct	China People's Rep	Congo (Brazzaville)	General Amity	64CCJC135	411095
02 Oct	China People's Rep	Congo (Brazzaville)	Water Transport	64CCJC136	411096
03 Oct	Bulgaria	Poland	Land Transport	64PZUM48	458115
03 Oct	Algeria	Germany, West	Finance	65WBGA116	424004
03 Oct	China People's Rep	Romania	Mass Media	64CCJC140	411310
03 Oct	Argentina	France	Culture	0UNTS0	109555
03 Oct	Argentina	France	Culture	635UNTS155	109080
05 Oct	Philippines	USA (United States)	Taxation	4PTS879	465064
05 Oct	Germany, West	Japan	Taxation	0JGJI1559	441123
05 Oct	Cuba	Germany, East	Sanitation	12EGDA841	419192
05 Oct	USA (United States)	Yugoslavia	Commodity Trade	531UNTS63	107693
06 Oct	Germany, West	Luxembourg	Non-ILO Labor	65WBGA157	424433
06 Oct	Belgium	Germany, West	Non-ILO Labor	65WBGA157	424034
06 Oct	Germany, West	Netherlands	Non-ILO Labor	65WBGA157	424491
06 Oct	Germany, East	Poland	Culture	552UNTS89	108051
06 Oct	Czechoslovakia	Germany, East	Culture	545UNTS113	107927
07 Oct	Chad	Israel	Tech Assistance	630UNTS175	108969
07 Oct	Germany, West	Jamaica	Air Transport	514UNTS187	107447
07 Oct	Israel	USSR (Soviet Union)	Specific Property	516UNTS59	107471
08 Oct	Iran	Turkey	Visas	64TURG2912	466017
08 Oct	Colombia	USA (United States)	US Agri Commod Aid	579UNTS3	108395
08 Oct	Czechoslovakia	Yugoslavia	Visas	544UNTS129	107916
11 Oct	China People's Rep	Nepal	Culture	64CCJC147	411276
12 Oct	France	Trinidad/Tobago	Air Transport	535UNTS25	107774
13 Oct	Pakistan	UK Great Britain	Atomic Energy	534UNTS71	107754
14 Oct	Austria	Spain	Non-ILO Labor	66ABGB9	403168
14 Oct	Austria	France	Land Transport	64ABGB324	403054
14 Oct	Brazil	UK Great Britain	Loans and Credits	539UNTS289	107840
14 Oct	Sweden	UK Great Britain	Taxation	543UNTS135	107898
15 Oct	Germany, West	India	Claims and Debts	64WBGA235	424257
15 Oct	Canada	Denmark	Water Transport	525UNTS227	107595
16 Oct	France	Portugal	Education	64FRRT68	415371
16 Oct	UNESCO (Educ/Cult)	USA (United States)	Specific Property	550UNTS23	108006
17 Oct	France	Yugoslavia	General Transport	65FRRT88	415489
17 Oct	France	Morocco	Non-ILO Labor	0UNTS0	109935
17 Oct	Czechoslovakia	Hungary	Land Transport	545UNTS21	107924
18 Oct	Iran	Pakistan	Visas	0IRTB55	433086
19 Oct	France	Sierra Leone	Health/Educ/Welfare	65FRRT30	415399
20 Oct	India	UK Great Britain	Customs	534UNTS77	107755
20 Oct	Norway	United Arab Rep	Taxation	543UNTS3	107895
21 Oct	Argentina	Paraguay	Specific Property	635UNTS189	109082
21 Oct	Argentina	Paraguay	Specific Property	635UNTS177	109081
21 Oct	Czechoslovakia	Mongolia	Sanitation	545UNTS91	107926
22 Oct	Cameroon	Germany, West	Air Transport	66WGBB109	425347
22 Oct	Burundi	China People's Rep	General Economic	64CCJC148	411086
23 Oct	Madagascar	USSR (Soviet Union)	General Trade	0UNTS0	109829
23 Oct	Taiwan	Ecuador	General Trade	543UNTS241	107904
24 Oct	Ceylon (Sri Lanka)	China People's Rep	General Trade	64CCJC150	411119
24 Oct	Multilateral		Tech Assistance	514UNTS220	200608
24 Oct	Malawi	UN Special Fund	Direct Aid	514UNTS235	200609
24 Oct	Italy	ILO (Labor Org)	IGO Establishment	541UNTS217	107871
24 Oct	Romania	UN Special Fund	IGO Operations	519UNTS29	107500
26 Oct	United Arab Rep	Poland	Tech Assistance	64PZUM63	458116
26 Oct	India	IDA (Devel Assoc)	Non-IBRD Project	535UNTS245	107783
26 Oct	Accept UN Charter	Zambia	UN Charter	519UNTS11	107498
27 Oct	Asian Productivity	ILO (Labor Org)	IGO Operations	516UNTS367	200610

DATE	PARTY ONE	PARTY TWO	TOPIC	CITATION	NUMBER
1964 (Cont.)					
27 Oct	Chile	USA (United States)	Military Mission	532UNTS347	107727
28 Oct	Germany, West	Thailand	Non-IBRD Project	521UNTS311	107528
28 Oct	Mongolia	Poland	Consul/Citizenship	552UNTS115	108052
28 Oct	Ethiopia	Netherlands	Tech Assistance	541UNTS235	107872
28 Oct	USA (United States)	Yugoslavia	US Agri Commod Aid	533UNTS3	107728
28 Oct	Philippines	IBRD (World Bank)	IBRD Project	537UNTS165	107801
28 Oct	Germany, West	Thailand	Loans and Credits	521UNTS333	107529
29 Oct	Germany, West	Niger	Claims and Debts	65WGBB1402	425505
29 Oct	Germany, West	Senegal	Air Transport	66WGBB118	425622
29 Oct	Guinea	Italy	Water Transport	65ITDI131	436203
29 Oct	Italy	Sweden	Non-ILO Labor	65ITDI161	436363
29 Oct	Cuba	Germany, East	Commodity Trade	12EGDA1166	419193
29 Oct	Germany, West	Senegal	Air Transport	0UNTS0	110467
29 Oct	USA (United States)	Yugoslavia	US Agri Commod Aid	533UNTS17	107729
30 Oct	Norway	Poland	Finance	3NORT928	451131
30 Oct	Japan	USA (United States)	Atomic Energy	0JGJI1563	441124
30 Oct	France	USSR (Soviet Union)	General Trade	64FRMD411	417471
30 Oct	Argentina	Guatemala	Culture	601UNTS175	108695
30 Oct	Netherlands	Pakistan	Tech Assistance	541UNTS243	107873
31 Oct	Korea, South	Vietnam, South	Milit Assistance	0VKNG323	496081
31 Oct	Austria	Hungary	Claims and Debts	605UNTS63	108759
31 Oct	Austria	Hungary	Claims and Debts	605UNTS77	108760
31 Oct	Austria	Hungary	Finance	605UNTS3	108758
31 Oct	Austria	Hungary	Visas	545UNTS241	107937
31 Oct	Austria	Hungary	Visas	545UNTS223	107936
03 Nov	China People's Rep	Mali	General Amity	64CCJC157	411246
03 Nov	USA (United States)	Western Samoa	Scientific Project	521UNTS181	107521
05 Nov	France	United Arab Rep	Claims and Debts	64FRRT73	415048
05 Nov	USA (United States)	Yugoslavia	Claims and Debts	550UNTS31	108007
05 Nov	Greece	Yugoslavia	Territory Boundary	539UNTS13	107820
05 Nov	Greece	Yugoslavia	Land Transport	539UNTS19	107821
06 Nov	Germany, West	Portugal	Non-ILO Labor	68WGBB473	425597
06 Nov	China People's Rep	Indonesia	Air Transport	64CCJC161	411203
07 Nov	Cyprus	Germany, East	General Economic	12EGDA1107	419498
07 Nov	Multilateral		Sanitation	548UNTS3	107965
08 Nov	Taiwan	Guatemala	General Trade	543UNTS227	107903
09 Nov	USA (United States)	Yugoslavia	Education	533UNTS39	107731
10 Nov	Argentina	Morocco	Culture	0UNTS0	110179
11 Nov	Austria	Hungary	Sanitation	576UNTS163	108368
11 Nov	Greece	South Africa	Taxation	631UNTS319	109001
11 Nov	Multilateral		Tech Assistance	515UNTS94	107456
12 Nov	Philippines	USA (United States)	Postal Service	574UNTS159	108349
12 Nov	Portugal	USA (United States)	Specific Property	541UNTS251	107874
13 Nov	Paraguay	Spain	Specif Goods/Equip	65SPBO1108	460225
13 Nov	Israel	Turkey	Tech Assistance	550UNTS303	108025
16 Nov	Japan	Thailand	Education	0JGJI1564	441125
16 Nov	France	Mauritania	Education	65FRRT91	415318
16 Nov	UK Great Britain	USA (United States)	General Trade	0UNTS0	109749
16 Nov	Uganda	USA (United States)	General Aid	586UNTS143	108501
16 Nov	Iran	USA (United States)	US Agri Commod Aid	532UNTS213	107719
17 Nov	Netherlands	Norway	Sanitation	579UNTS243	108412
17 Nov	Greece	USA (United States)	US Agri Commod Aid	532UNTS107	107714
18 Nov	USA (United States)	USSR (Soviet Union)	Atomic Energy	535UNTS307	107786
19 Nov	Belgium	Iran	Visas	0IRTB14	433022
19 Nov	Iran	Netherlands	Visas	0IRTB36	433049
19 Nov	Iran	Luxembourg	Visas	0IRTB50	433078
19 Nov	Brazil	Costa Rica	Culture	0UNTS0	109429
19 Nov	Multilateral		Visas	523UNTS3	107553
19 Nov	Belgium	Mexico	Culture	546UNTS217	107949
20 Nov	Germany, West	Peru	Culture	66WGBB76	425579
20 Nov	India	UK Great Britain	Milit Assistance	534UNTS85	107756
21 Nov	Argentina	Panama	Culture	635UNTS205	109083
23 Nov	Germany, West	Switzerland	Territory Boundary	67WGBB2029	425761
23 Nov	Germany, West	Switzerland	Territory Boundary	67WGBB2040	425760
23 Nov	Congo (Zaire)	Germany, West	Loans and Credits	65WBGA38	424384

DATE	PARTY ONE	PARTY TWO	TOPIC	CITATION	NUMBER
1964 (Cont.)					
23 Nov	Argentina	Costa Rica	Culture	635UNTS213	109084
23 Nov	Italy	USA (United States)	Milit Assistance	532UNTS133	107716
23 Nov	Afghanistan	IDA (Devel Assoc)	Non-IBRD Project	567UNTS155	108255
24 Nov	Chad	Japan	General Trade	0JGJI1591	441126
25 Nov	Multilateral		Water Transport	587UNTS19	108507
25 Nov	Argentina	Nicaragua	Culture	0UNTS0	109556
25 Nov	Japan	USA (United States)	Specific Property	533UNTS31	107730
25 Nov	Ethiopia	USA (United States)	Mass Media	532UNTS125	107715
25 Nov	IBRD (World Bank)	Thailand	IBRD Project	537UNTS273	107805
25 Nov	India	United Nations	Scientific Project	519UNTS47	107501
26 Nov	Argentina	Honduras	Culture	0UNTS0	109557
26 Nov	Germany, West	UK Great Britain	Taxation	603UNTS183	108734
26 Nov	Poland	Romania	Health/Educ/Welfare	552UNTS157	108053
26 Nov	Czechoslovakia	United Arab Rep	Sanitation	545UNTS11	107923
27 Nov	Germany, East	Tunisia	Finance	12EGDA903	419375
27 Nov	Germany, East	Tunisia	General Trade	12EGDA1171	419374
27 Nov	Austria	Yugoslavia	Visas	64ABGB325	403228
27 Nov	France	Japan	Taxation	65FRRT75	415255
27 Nov	Kenya	UK Great Britain	Milit Assistance	0UNTS0	110039
27 Nov	France	Japan	Taxation	569UNTS157	108283
27 Nov	Multilateral		Visas	548UNTS47	107968
27 Nov	Taiwan	Korea, South	General Amity	555UNTS3	108102
28 Nov	Italy	Yugoslavia	General Economic	65ITDI194	436249
28 Nov	Italy	Yugoslavia	General Economic	65ITDI140	436250
30 Nov	Ghana	Israel	Tech Assistance	550UNTS231	108019
01 Dec	Germany, West	Netherlands	Territory Boundary	550UNTS123	108011
01 Dec	Ireland	Vietnam, South	General Trade	553UNTS233	108091
01 Dec	Multilateral		Water Transport	550UNTS133	108012
02 Dec	Argentina	IAEA (Atom Energy)	Atomic Energy	525UNTS29	107582
02 Dec	Multilateral		Scientific Project	572UNTS229	108317
02 Dec	Multilateral		Atomic Energy	525UNTS51	107583
03 Dec	China People's Rep	Ghana	General Trade	64CCJC174	411163
04 Dec	Germany, West	Kenya	Claims and Debts	66WGBB899	425355
04 Dec	Germany, West	Kenya	Tech Assistance	66WBGA165	424357
04 Dec	Germany, West	Kenya	General Economic	66WBGA165	424356
04 Dec	Germany, West	Kenya	Loans and Credits	66WBGA165	424358
04 Dec	State/IGO Group	IAEA (Atom Energy)	Atomic Energy	637UNTS0	109111
04 Dec	Netherlands	Nigeria	Education	545UNTS155	107931
04 Dec	Japan	USA (United States)	Milit Installation	532UNTS249	107721
05 Dec	Trinidad/Tobago	USA (United States)	Milit Installation	535UNTS331	107788
07 Dec	Germany, West	Korea, South	Loans and Credits	65WBGA29	424393
07 Dec	Austria	China People's Rep	General Economic	64CCJC175	411080
07 Dec	Kenya	USA (United States)	US Agri Commod Aid	532UNTS263	107722
09 Dec	Congo (Zaire)	USA (United States)	US Agri Commod Aid	531UNTS249	107707
10 Dec	Ethiopia	ILO (Labor Org)	IGO Establishment	521UNTS217	107524
11 Dec	Multilateral		IGO Operations	547UNTS297	107964
11 Dec	IBRD (World Bank)	Yugoslavia	IBRD Project	537UNTS321	107807
11 Dec	India	Netherlands	Scientific Project	570UNTS165	108292
12 Dec	Bulgaria	China People's Rep	General Economic	64CCJC180	411088
12 Dec	Denmark	Pakistan	Tech Assistance	636UNTS313	109107
13 Dec	Bulgaria	Syria	Air Transport	0UNTS0	109956
14 Dec	USA (United States)	USSR (Soviet Union)	Specific Property	531UNTS213	107705
15 Dec	UN Special Fund	Zambia	Direct Aid	522UNTS3	107532
15 Dec	Multilateral		Tech Assistance	522UNTS20	107533
16 Dec	Algeria	France	Extradition	65FRRT4	415018
16 Dec	WMO (Meteorology)	UK Great Britain	Tech Assistance	548UNTS57	107969
16 Dec	Germany, West	Jamaica	Tech Assistance	531UNTS129	107699
16 Dec	Paraguay	IBRD (World Bank)	IBRD Project	549UNTS173	107999
17 Dec	India	Japan	Education	0JGJI1567	441127
17 Dec	Belgium	Germany, West	Taxation	66WGBB1508	425035
17 Dec	Algeria	Germany, West	Tech Assistance	65WBGA100	424005
17 Dec	Belgium	Germany, West	Land Transport	631UNTS229	108996
17 Dec	Taiwan	IBRD (World Bank)	IBRD Project	538UNTS3	107808
18 Dec	Austria	Romania	Sanitation	65ABGB34	403157
19 Dec	Albania	Italy	General Trade	65ITDI115	436008

DATE	PARTY ONE	PARTY TWO	TOPIC	CITATION	NUMBER
1964 (Cont.)					
19 Dec	Taiwan	USA (United States)	Status of Forces	532UNTS313	107725
20 Dec	Germany, West	Italy	Dispute Settlement	66ITGU214	435178
22 Dec	China People's Rep	United Arab Rep	General Trade	64CCJC186	411351
22 Dec	China People's Rep	United Arab Rep	Direct Aid	64CCJC184	411350
22 Dec	Cyprus	Syria	Air Transport	602UNTS25	108705
22 Dec	Israel	USA (United States)	US Agri Commod Aid	532UNTS231	107720
23 Dec	Norway	Turkey	Loans and Credits	2NORT931	451179
23 Dec	Romania	USA (United States)	Health/Educ/Welfare	535UNTS359	107790
23 Dec	Germany, West	Thailand	Non-IBRD Project	525UNTS193	107591
23 Dec	Germany, West	Thailand	Sanitation	525UNTS201	107592
23 Dec	Japan	IBRD (World Bank)	IBRD Project	538UNTS37	107809
23 Dec	Germany, West	Thailand	Tech Assistance	525UNTS185	107590
23 Dec	Germany, West	Thailand	Scientific Project	525UNTS177	107589
24 Dec	Norway	Turkey	Loans and Credits	2NORT953	451180
25 Dec	Algeria	China People's Rep	Scientific Project	64CCJC187	411068
27 Dec	China People's Rep	Korea, North	Mass Media	64CCJC188	411237
28 Dec	Mauritania	IDA (Devel Assoc)	Non-IBRD Project	540UNTS163	107849
29 Dec	Multilateral		IGO Operations	OUNTSO	109738
29 Dec	Morocco	USA (United States)	Commodity Trade	593UNTS185	108584
29 Dec	Laos	USA (United States)	Claims and Debts	542UNTS23	107876
29 Dec	Kenya	IDA (Devel Assoc)	Non-IBRD Project	535UNTS225	107782
30 Dec	Denmark	Peru	Tech Assistance	595UNTS47	108611
30 Dec	Iceland	USA (United States)	US Agri Commod Aid	542UNTS37	107878
30 Dec	Iceland	USA (United States)	US Agri Commod Aid	531UNTS287	107709
31 Dec	China People's Rep	Cuba	General Trade	64CCJC189	411124
31 Dec	Korea, South	USA (United States)	US Agri Commod Aid	535UNTS315	107787
31 Dec	Dahomey	USA (United States)	US Agri Commod Aid	541UNTS117	107865
31 Dec	Central Afri Rep	USA (United States)	Claims and Debts	542UNTS29	107877
31 Dec	Taiwan	USA (United States)	US Agri Commod Aid	532UNTS59	107712
31 Dec	Taiwan	USA (United States)	US Agri Commod Aid	532UNTS29	107711
31 Dec	Malta	UK Great Britain	Admin Cooperation	525UNTS221	107594
1965					
05 Jan	China People's Rep	Tanzania	Tech Assistance	65CCJC3	411332
05 Jan	China People's Rep	Tanzania	Direct Aid	65CCJC2	411331
06 Jan	Denmark	Germany, West	Admin Cooperation	528UNTS201	107643
06 Jan	Malawi	WHO (World Health)	Tech Assistance	525UNTS165	107588
06 Jan	Mongolia	United Nations	IGO Operations	522UNTS45	107535
06 Jan	UK Great Britain	USSR (Soviet Union)	Scientific Project	543UNTS77	107897
07 Jan	United Nations	Yugoslavia	IGO Operations	522UNTS55	107536
08 Jan	France	Turkey	Non-ILO Labor	65FRRT57	415468
08 Jan	Malawi	WHO (World Health)	Tech Assistance	524UNTS281	107579
11 Jan	Japan	Vietnam, South	Specific Resources	OVKNG208	496060
11 Jan	France	Romania	Culture	65FRRT46	415376
11 Jan	Int Exhibit Bureau	France	IGO Status/Immunit	66FRRT36	415513
11 Jan	France	Romania	Culture	OUNTSO	110528
11 Jan	Belgium	Sweden	Education	533UNTS157	107741
12 Jan	China People's Rep	Indonesia	Visas	65CCJC4	411209
12 Jan	Denmark	United Arab Rep	Sanitation	OUNTSO	109732
12 Jan	Argentina	UK Great Britain	Air Transport	597UNTS177	108645
13 Jan	China People's Rep	United Arab Rep	Tech Assistance	65CCJC5	411352
13 Jan	Japan	IBRD (World Bank)	IBRD Project	537UNTS293	107806
13 Jan	India	USA (United States)	Milit Assistance	541UNTS107	107864
14 Jan	Algeria	China People's Rep	Commodity Trade	65CCJC6	411069
14 Jan	China People's Rep	Central Afri Rep	Direct Aid	65CCJC7	411125
14 Jan	IAEA (Atom Energy)	United Arab Rep	Atomic Energy	603UNTS45	108723
14 Jan	Belgium	Luxembourg	Claims and Debts	620UNTS3	108949
14 Jan	Ecuador	Netherlands	Health/Educ/Welfare	551UNTS129	108038
15 Jan	Colombia	Israel	Tech Assistance	581UNTS173	108441
16 Jan	Canada	USA (United States)	Commodity Trade	606UNTS31	108772
18 Jan	Germany, East	Hungary	General Economic	51EGDZ328	420462
18 Jan	France	Germany, West	Admin Cooperation	67WBGA10	424196
18 Jan	Central Afri Rep	France	Admin Cooperation	67FRJO1905	416114
19 Jan	Algeria	France	Non-ILO Labor	65FRJO1905	416020
19 Jan	Algeria	France	Non-ILO Labor	65FRRT50	415019

DATE	PARTY ONE	PARTY TWO	TOPIC	CITATION	NUMBER
1965 (Cont.)					
20 Jan	France	Int Wine Office	IGO Status/Immunit	66FRRT35	415503
20 Jan	Malta	Switzerland	General Trade	548UNTS193	107978
21 Jan	China People's Rep	Nepal	Postal Service	65CCJC8	411277
21 Jan	Finland	Israel	Taxation	581UNTS275	108450
22 Jan	Belgium	Peru	Tech Assistance	OUNTSO	110565
22 Jan	Multilateral		Gen Communications	634UNTS239	109066
23 Jan	Italy	Turkey	Finance	66ITDI159	436411
25 Jan	France	Yugoslavia	Non-ILO Labor	65FRRT82	415490
25 Jan	Denmark	Thailand	Tech Assistance	530UNTS173	107680
26 Jan	India	Japan	Postal Service	OJGJI1606	441128
26 Jan	Burma	China People's Rep	Commodity Trade	65CCJC9	411089
26 Jan	France	Portugal	Admin Cooperation	65FRRT25	415372
26 Jan	Korea, South	USA (United States)	Commodity Trade	541UNTS77	107862
26 Jan	Spain	USA (United States)	Scientific Project	542UNTS81	107881
27 Jan	Ethiopia	WHO (World Health)	IGO Operations	541UNTS135	107866
27 Jan	Multilateral		Tech Assistance	523UNTS102	107556
27 Jan	WHO (World Health)	Tunisia	IGO Operations	528UNTS209	107644
28 Jan	China People's Rep	Indonesia	Loans and Credits	65CCJC12	411211
28 Jan	China People's Rep	Indonesia	Direct Aid	65CCJC11	411210
28 Jan	Peru	USA (United States)	Education	587UNTS273	108513
29 Jan	Norway	USSR (Soviet Union)	Finance	3NORT932	451213
29 Jan	Sierra Leone	USA (United States)	US Agri Commod Aid	542UNTS87	107882
30 Jan	Germany, West	Tanzania	Claims and Debts	66WGBB873	425655
30 Jan	Switzerland	USA (United States)	Atomic Energy	594UNTS55	108594
02 Feb	Dominican Republic	USA (United States)	Gen Communications	542UNTS117	107884
02 Feb	Honduras	IDA (Devel Assoc)	Non-IBRD Project	561UNTS279	108189
02 Feb	Multilateral		Tech Assistance	523UNTS256	107560
02 Feb	Honduras	IBRD (World Bank)	IBRD Project	561UNTS255	108188
03 Feb	Germany, West	Jamaica	Scientific Project	531UNTS143	107700
04 Feb	UN Special Fund	Zambia	Admin Cooperation	527UNTS115	107621
04 Feb	Mexico	IBRD (World Bank)	IBRD Project	549UNTS189	108000
05 Feb	USA (United States)	USSR (Soviet Union)	Specific Resources	541UNTS97	107863
06 Feb	Algeria	Poland	Air Transport	64PZUM9	458117
06 Feb	China People's Rep	Congo (Brazzaville)	Direct Aid	65CCJC14	411100
06 Feb	Brazil	USA (United States)	Direct Aid	OUNTSO	110324
06 Feb	Belgium	Congo (Zaire)	Claims and Debts	540UNTS227	107852
06 Feb	Belgium	Congo (Zaire)	Finance	540UNTS275	107853
06 Feb	Denmark	India	Water Transport	531UNTS23	107690
08 Feb	France	Romania	General Economic	65FRMD1302	417377
09 Feb	USA (United States)	Vietnam, South	Claims and Debts	542UNTS175	107888
09 Feb	Israel	Togo	Visas	550UNTS297	108024
10 Feb	China People's Rep	Tanzania	General Trade	65CCJC15	411336
10 Feb	China People's Rep	Tanzania	General Trade	65CCJC16	411337
10 Feb	Netherlands	Spain	Visas	545UNTS3	107922
11 Feb	Japan	Malaysia	Air Transport	OJGJI1614	441129
11 Feb	Japan	Malaysia	Air Transport	OUNTSO	109477
11 Feb	Greece	India	Taxation	606UNTS9	108771
11 Feb	Belgium	Hungary	Culture	544UNTS3	107908
12 Feb	Multilateral		Tech Assistance	525UNTS148	107587
12 Feb	Chile	IBRD (World Bank)	IBRD Project	537UNTS35	107796
12 Feb	Luxembourg	Portugal	Non-ILO Labor	571UNTS239	108305
13 Feb	UK Great Britain	USSR (Soviet Union)	Health/Educ/Welfare	543UNTS43	107896
15 Feb	Multilateral		Refugees	546UNTS277	107952
15 Feb	Multilateral		Visas	547UNTS3	107953
16 Feb	Germany, West	Rwanda	Tech Assistance	65WBGA90	424601
16 Feb	Iran	United Nations	Admin Cooperation	525UNTS211	107593
17 Feb	Cuba	USSR (Soviet Union)	Finance	OUNTSO	109830
17 Feb	Cuba	USSR (Soviet Union)	General Trade	OUNTSO	109583
17 Feb	Tunisia	USA (United States)	US Agri Commod Aid	542UNTS125	107885
17 Feb	Benelux Econ Union	Poland	General Economic	547UNTS165	107956
18 Feb	China People's Rep	Pakistan	Direct Aid	65CCJC19	411295
18 Feb	Accept UN Charter	Gambia	UN Charter	545UNTS143	107928
19 Feb	Brazil	Japan	Finance	OJGJI1585	441130
19 Feb	China People's Rep	Germany, East	General Economic	65CCJC20	411179
20 Feb	Austria	Switzerland	Non-ILO Labor	66ABGB41	403180

DATE	PARTY ONE	PARTY TWO	TOPIC	CITATION	NUMBER
1965 (Cont.)					
20 Feb	Austria	Switzerland	Non-ILO Labor	66ABGB41	403190
20 Feb	China People's Rep	Tanzania	General Amity	65CCJC21	411338
20 Feb	Denmark	Portugal	Commodity Trade	639UNTS43	109143
20 Feb	Belgium	United Nations	Finance	535UNTS191	107779
20 Feb	Belgium	United Nations	Claims and Debts	535UNTS197	107780
22 Feb	Italy	USSR (Soviet Union)	Air Transport	67ITGU231	435425
22 Feb	Ceylon (Sri Lanka)	Germany, East	General Economic	51EGDZ330	420077
22 Feb	Cyprus	USSR (Soviet Union)	General Trade	0UNTSO	109584
22 Feb	Japan	UK Great Britain	Finance	560UNTS123	108171
23 Feb	Germany, West	Italy	Non-ILO Labor	65WBGA63	424303
23 Feb	Multilateral		IGO Operations	527UNTS120	107622
24 Feb	Multilateral		IGO Operations	556UNTS47	108118
24 Feb	India	Japan	Postal Service	570UNTS3	108284
25 Feb	Italy	Poland	General Trade	66ITDI150	436309
25 Feb	France	UK Great Britain	Non-ILO Labor	543UNTS157	107899
26 Feb	Japan	USSR (Soviet Union)	Visas	0JGJI1622	441131
26 Feb	Malaysia	IBRD (World Bank)	IBRD Project	549UNTS239	108002
26 Feb	Pakistan	USA (United States)	Commodity Trade	542UNTS103	107883
26 Feb	Multilateral		IGO Operations	556UNTS69	108119
26 Feb	Brazil	IBRD (World Bank)	IBRD Project	567UNTS91	108253
26 Feb	Brazil	IBRD (World Bank)	IBRD Project	553UNTS3	108065
27 Feb	Canada	France	Education	65FRRT40	415106
27 Feb	Mexico	USA (United States)	Scientific Project	542UNTS181	107889
27 Feb	Mexico	USA (United States)	Scientific Project	546UNTS135	107940
01 Mar	Nigeria	IDA (Devel Assoc)	Non-IBRD Project	571UNTS3	108297
01 Mar	UK Great Britain	Yugoslavia	General Trade	548UNTS85	107972
01 Mar	Nigeria	IDA (Devel Assoc)	Non-IBRD Project	563UNTS3	108201
02 Mar	Colombia	Germany, West	Tech Assistance	65WBGA140	424372
05 Mar	Dahomey	Poland	Culture	66PDZU395	457118
05 Mar	France	Senegal	Non-ILO Labor	67FRJO3110	416398
05 Mar	Multilateral		IGO Operations	527UNTS221	107627
06 Mar	Norway	USSR (Soviet Union)	Consul/Citizenship	3NORT934	451214
09 Mar	Multilateral		Water Transport	591UNTS265	108564
10 Mar	Philippines	USA (United States)	Non-ILO Labor	4PTS925	465066
10 Mar	Dahomey	Italy	Tech Assistance	66ITDI175	436102
10 Mar	France	Switzerland	Admin Cooperation	67FRJO604	416414
10 Mar	Philippines	USA (United States)	Non-IBRD Project	0UNTSO	110124
10 Mar	Norway	UK Great Britain	Territory Boundary	551UNTS213	108043
11 Mar	Germany, East	Poland	Specific Resources	52EGDZ331	420273
11 Mar	France	Mali	Non-ILO Labor	67FRJO3008	416291
11 Mar	France	Eur Space Vehicle	Scientific Project	66FRRT21	415504
11 Mar	Belgium	Luxembourg	Taxation	540UNTS297	107854
12 Mar	Albania	China People's Rep	Culture	65CCJC26	411070
12 Mar	SEATO (SE Asia)	UK Great Britain	IGO Status/Immunit	561UNTS313	108191
13 Mar	Dahomey	USA (United States)	Claims and Debts	549UNTS43	107987
15 Mar	Austria	Germany, West	Air Transport	66WGBB126	425552
15 Mar	Cuba	Germany, East	Education	49EGDZ332	420194
15 Mar	Ceylon (Sri Lanka)	China People's Rep	Direct Aid	65CCJC27	411126
15 Mar	Peru	IBRD (World Bank)	IBRD Project	632UNTS209	109024
15 Mar	Austria	Germany, West	Air Transport	0UNTSO	109478
16 Mar	Japan	Spain	Visas	0JGJI1572	441132
16 Mar	France	Germany, West	Non-ILO Labor	65WBGA157	424197
16 Mar	China People's Rep	Poland	General Economic	65CCJC29	411296
16 Mar	China People's Rep	Indonesia	Tech Assistance	65CCJC28	411212
16 Mar	USA (United States)	Yugoslavia	US Agri Commod Aid	542UNTS161	107887
16 Mar	Philippines	USA (United States)	Status of Forces	542UNTS199	107890
16 Mar	Bolivia	USA (United States)	Gen Communications	542UNTS209	107891
17 Mar	China People's Rep	Mali	Direct Aid	65CCJC30	411257
18 Mar	China People's Rep	Syria	Culture	65CCJC31	411323
18 Mar	Dominican Republic	USA (United States)	US Agri Commod Aid	542UNTS215	107892
18 Mar	Multilateral		Dispute Settlement	575UNTS159	108359
19 Mar	Bulgaria	Germany, East	Health/Educ/Welfare	50EGDZ332	420068
22 Mar	Germany, East	Yugoslavia	Sanitation	50EGDZ332	420158
22 Mar	France	Germany, West	Culture	65FRRT79	415045
22 Mar	Albania	China People's Rep	General Transport	65CCJC34	411071

DATE	PARTY ONE	PARTY TWO	TOPIC	CITATION	NUMBER
1965 (Cont.)					
22 Mar	France	USSR (Soviet Union)	Mass Media	65FRRT60	415472
22 Mar	Cambodia	China People's Rep	Health/Educ/Welfare	65CCJC35	411127
22 Mar	IBRD (World Bank)	Thailand	IBRD Project	538UNTS63	107810
23 Mar	Italy	United Arab Rep	Claims and Debts	66ITDI231	436322
23 Mar	Italy	United Arab Rep	Claims and Debts	66ITGU215	435321
23 Mar	China People's Rep	Yemen	Direct Aid	65CCJC37	411393
24 Mar	Afghanistan	China People's Rep	Culture	65CCJC41	411046
24 Mar	China People's Rep	Finland	General Trade	65CCJC43	411152
24 Mar	Afghanistan	China People's Rep	Territory Boundary	65CCJC39	411044
24 Mar	Afghanistan	China People's Rep	Direct Aid	65CCJC40	411045
24 Mar	China People's Rep	Czechoslovakia	Scientific Project	65CCJC42	411128
24 Mar	China People's Rep	Mongolia	General Trade	65CCJC38	411258
25 Mar	Italy	Poland	Culture	69PZUM213	458119
25 Mar	France	Italy	Land Transport	65ITGU193	435159
25 Mar	France	Germany, West	Status of Forces	69FRJO1810	416044
25 Mar	Canada	USA (United States)	Dispute Settlement	607UNTS141	108802
25 Mar	Finland	UK Great Britain	Air Transport	539UNTS103	107826
26 Mar	Brazil	Japan	Finance	0JGJI1587	441133
26 Mar	China People's Rep	Hungary	General Economic	65CCJC46	411198
26 Mar	China People's Rep	Pakistan	Territory Boundary	65CCJC44	411297
26 Mar	China People's Rep	Pakistan	Culture	65CCJC45	411298
26 Mar	Denmark	Malaysia	Air Transport	540UNTS205	107851
26 Mar	Ecuador	USA (United States)	Gen Communications	542UNTS237	107893
27 Mar	Czechoslovakia	Italy	Tech Assistance	66ITDI123	436081
29 Mar	IDA (Devel Assoc)	Somalia	Non-IBRD Project	586UNTS101	108499
29 Mar	Ivory Coast	UK Great Britain	Visas	551UNTS53	108032
29 Mar	Multilateral		Non-IBRD Project	540UNTS145	107848
30 Mar	Italy	Mexico	Commodity Trade	66ITDI142	436274
30 Mar	IBRD (World Bank)	Uruguay	IBRD Project	567UNTS45	108251
31 Mar	Burundi	Germany, West	Tech Assistance	65WBGA142	424067
31 Mar	Jamaica	UK Great Britain	Military Mission	539UNTS59	107824
31 Mar	Poland	USSR (Soviet Union)	Consul/Citizenship	571UNTS217	108304
01 Apr	IDA (Devel Assoc)	Turkey	Non-IBRD Project	554UNTS137	108100
01 Apr	Finland	United Arab Rep	Taxation	562UNTS3	108193
02 Apr	Japan	USA (United States)	IGO Operations	16UST657	486002
02 Apr	Japan	USA (United States)	Admin Cooperation	0JGJI1588	441134
02 Apr	Jamaica	UK Great Britain	Taxation	552UNTS219	108056
03 Apr	Kenya	Norway	Tech Assistance	3NORT937	451100
05 Apr	Ivory Coast	USA (United States)	US Agri Commod Aid	546UNTS143	107941
07 Apr	Japan	Laos	Postal Service	0JGJI1589	441135
08 Apr	Germany, West	Sierra Leone	Claims and Debts	66WGBB861	425632
08 Apr	Germany, West	Korea, South	General Trade	65WBGA29	424394
08 Apr	Germany, West	Nicaragua	Tech Assistance	65WBGA169	424485
08 Apr	China People's Rep	Czechoslovakia	General Economic	65CCJC53	411101
08 Apr	Hungary	Yugoslavia	Territory Boundary	587UNTS169	108511
08 Apr	Poland	USSR (Soviet Union)	General Amity	540UNTS97	107845
08 Apr	Jamaica	IBRD (World Bank)	IBRD Project	539UNTS303	107841
08 Apr	Multilateral		IGO Operations	533UNTS66	107733
09 Apr	Greece	Japan	General Trade	0JGJI1584	441136
09 Apr	Germany, West	Korea, South	Water Transport	71WGBB1259	425395
09 Apr	Austria	Hungary	Recognition	638UNTS105	109132
09 Apr	Greece	Japan	General Trade	632UNTS61	109008
09 Apr	Austria	Hungary	Admin Cooperation	638UNTS135	109133
09 Apr	Austria	Hungary	Visas	638UNTS53	109131
09 Apr	Austria	Hungary	Visas	564UNTS179	108228
09 Apr	Taiwan	USA (United States)	General Economic	546UNTS81	107939
12 Apr	ICJ Option Clause	Kenya	ICJ Option Clause	531UNTS113	107697
13 Apr	Australia	France	Air Transport	601UNTS293	108702
14 Apr	Italy	Romania	Sanitation	66ITGU290	435324
15 Apr	Israel	UK Great Britain	Finance	551UNTS19	108031
17 Apr	China People's Rep	Mali	Culture	65CCJC54	411259
19 Apr	Afghanistan	UK Great Britain	Culture	633UNTS45	109033
20 Apr	Germany, West	Tunisia	Tech Assistance	65WBGA123	424681
20 Apr	UK Great Britain	Yugoslavia	Visas	551UNTS69	108034
20 Apr	Malawi	USA (United States)	General Aid	546UNTS175	107943

DATE	PARTY ONE	PARTY TWO	TOPIC	CITATION	NUMBER
1965 (Cont.)					
21 Apr	China People's Rep	Uganda	Direct Aid	65CCJC55	411353
21 Apr	Australia	Germany, West	Claims and Debts	598UNTS25	108654
21 Apr	UK Great Britain	Yugoslavia	Consul/Citizenship	595UNTS189	108620
22 Apr	France	Mexico	Tech Assistance	63FRRT13	415324
22 Apr	UK Great Britain	USA (United States)	Postal Service	0UNTS0	109750
22 Apr	Malta	UNICEF (Children)	IGO Operations	533UNTS107	107737
23 Apr	Belgium	Italy	Privil/Immunities	66ITGU165	435052
23 Apr	Morocco	USA (United States)	US Agri Commod Aid	594UNTS3	108591
23 Apr	Argentina	Brazil	IGO Establishment	0UNTS0	109411
23 Apr	Philippines	USA (United States)	US Agri Commod Aid	546UNTS157	107942
24 Apr	USA (United States)	Vietnam, South	Specific Resources	0VKNG216	496061
25 Apr	Multilateral		Finance	0UNTS0	110810
26 Apr	China People's Rep	Poland	Scientific Project	65CCJC56	411299
26 Apr	Sierra Leone	USSR (Soviet Union)	General Trade	0UNTS0	109831
26 Apr	Ivory Coast	Netherlands	General Economic	634UNTS81	109053
26 Apr	Multilateral		IGO Operations	533UNTS50	107732
27 Apr	Guatemala	Norway	Visas	3NORT869	451068
27 Apr	Belgium	Netherlands	Specific Resources	596UNTS235	108636
27 Apr	Netherlands	Tanzania	Tech Assistance	594UNTS123	108599
28 Apr	Bel-Lux Econ Union	Morocco	General Economic	620UNTS171	108954
28 Apr	Iran	IBRD (World Bank)	IBRD Project	555UNTS21	108103
28 Apr	Taiwan	IBRD (World Bank)	IBRD Project	549UNTS145	107998
28 Apr	Iran	IBRD (World Bank)	IBRD Project	555UNTS45	108104
28 Apr	Australia	Malta	Non-ILO Labor	548UNTS203	107979
29 Apr	Germany, West	Switzerland	Humanitarian	67WGBB773	425762
29 Apr	China People's Rep	USSR (Soviet Union)	General Trade	65CCJC57	411354
29 Apr	Portugal	IBRD (World Bank)	IBRD Project	549UNTS69	107991
29 Apr	Multilateral		Non-IBRD Project	586UNTS123	108500
30 Apr	Austria	Japan	General Trade	0JGJI1598	441137
02 May	China People's Rep	United Arab Rep	Air Transport	65CCJC58	411341
03 May	China People's Rep	Germany, East	Culture	65CCJC59	411164
03 May	China People's Rep	Yemen	Culture	65CCJC60	411391
03 May	France	Senegal	General Economic	0UNTS0	109489
04 May	Norway	Uganda	Visas	3NORT940	451195
04 May	Guatemala	USA (United States)	Status of Forces	545UNTS163	107932
04 May	Ghana	Malawi	Air Transport	541UNTS163	107869
05 May	Norway	Spain	Air Transport	3NORT941	451147
05 May	China People's Rep	Poland	Culture	65CCJC62	411287
05 May	Spain	Sweden	Air Transport	0UNTS0	109239
05 May	Denmark	Spain	Air Transport	543UNTS255	107905
06 May	Germany, East	United Arab Rep	Tech Assistance	43EGDZ335	420479
06 May	Congo (Brazzaville)	Germany, East	General Aid	43EGDZ335	420169
07 May	Chad	Germany, West	Loans and Credits	65WBGA135	424672
07 May	France	USA (United States)	Education	573UNTS183	108331
07 May	Malaysia	UK Great Britain	Admin Cooperation	552UNTS259	108058
08 May	Bulgaria	Cyprus	Air Transport	0UNTS0	109957
10 May	Hungary	Iran	General Economic	0IRTB37	433054
10 May	UK Great Britain	USA (United States)	Education	545UNTS181	107934
11 May	China People's Rep	Yugoslavia	General Trade	65CCJC63	411394
11 May	Mauritania	Spain	Air Transport	602UNTS111	108709
12 May	Argentina	Iran	Culture	0IRTB11	433019
12 May	Germany, East	Poland	Specific Property	44EGDZ335	420274
12 May	China People's Rep	Congo (Brazzaville)	Mass Media	65CCJC64	411129
12 May	Chad	USA (United States)	Finance	546UNTS183	107944
12 May	Canada	USA (United States)	Milit Installation	545UNTS169	107933
12 May	Bolivia	USA (United States)	US Agri Commod Aid	564UNTS143	108226
12 May	Multilateral		IGO Operations	534UNTS390	107769
13 May	Bulgaria	China People's Rep	Culture	65CCJC65	411090
14 May	France	Hungary	Claims and Debts	65FRRT68	415223
14 May	Multilateral		IGO Operations	550UNTS310	108026
15 May	Poland	Tanzania	Tech Assistance	65PZUM38	458120
15 May	China People's Rep	Romania	Scientific Project	65CCJC66	411314
17 May	Czechoslovakia	Poland	Consul/Citizenship	66PDZU135	457121
17 May	Germany, East	Mali	Mass Media	50EGDZ336	420202
17 May	Czechoslovakia	Poland	Consul/Citizenship	572UNTS181	108312
17 May	USA (United States)	Uruguay	Education	564UNTS69	108221
19 May	China People's Rep	Ghana	Scientific Project	65CCJC67	411180
19 May	Brazil	Ecuador	Visas	0UNTS0	109419
20 May	Germany, East	United Arab Rep	Air Transport	52EGDZ329	420480
20 May	Finland	USSR (Soviet Union)	Territory Boundary	566UNTS31	108238
21 May	Germany, West	Lebanon	General Economic	67WGBB1673	425407
21 May	Japan	Zambia	General Trade	0JGJI1607	441138
21 May	France	San Marino	Non-ILO Labor	65FRRT58	415384
21 May	China People's Rep	Cuba	Tech Assistance	65CCJC68	411130
22 May	Bulgaria	Czechoslovakia	Culture	545UNTS65	107925
22 May	Afghanistan	USA (United States)	US Agri Commod Aid	579UNTS29	108396
24 May	Korea, South	Norway	Patents/Copyrights	3NORT942	451103
25 May	China People's Rep	USSR (Soviet Union)	Culture	65CCJC69	411355
25 May	Belgium	South Africa	Non-ILO Labor	0UNTS0	110762
25 May	Ethiopia	Hungary	Health/Educ/Welfare	577UNTS193	108377
25 May	Multilateral		IGO Operations	535UNTS374	107791
25 May	Hungary	Yugoslavia	Customs	576UNTS145	108367
26 May	Italy	Jordan	Air Transport	66ITDI265	436185
26 May	Malaysia	Norway	Air Transport	602UNTS157	108711
26 May	Portugal	USA (United States)	Gen Communications	546UNTS189	107945
26 May	Japan	IBRD (World Bank)	IBRD Project	550UNTS95	108010
26 May	Brazil	USA (United States)	Visas	549UNTS125	107995
26 May	USA (United States)	Vietnam, South	US Agri Commod Aid	550UNTS3	108005
27 May	China People's Rep	Romania	Culture	65CCJC70	411315
27 May	China People's Rep	Romania	Culture	592UNTS3	108566
28 May	Germany, East	Mongolia	Education	51EGDZ336	420223
28 May	China People's Rep	Hungary	Scientific Project	65CCJC71	411199
28 May	Philippines	USA (United States)	Visas	0UNTS0	110248
28 May	India	IBRD (World Bank)	Loans and Credits	552UNTS39	108049
28 May	Multilateral		IGO Establishment	559UNTS273	108163
29 May	British Guiana	USA (United States)	Loans and Credits	605UNTS87	108761
29 May	Uganda	USA (United States)	Claims and Debts	546UNTS209	107948
29 May	Gambia	UNICEF (Children)	IGO Operations	547UNTS29	107954
30 May	Germany, East	Mali	Tech Assistance	51EGDZ336	420203
31 May	Bulgaria	Cuba	Visas	0UNTS0	110299
31 May	Bulgaria	Cuba	Air Transport	0UNTS0	110298
01 Jun	France	Spain	Non-ILO Labor	65SPBO2906	460154
01 Jun	Iran	Iraq	Visas	0IRTB40	433061
01 Jun	France	Niger	Finance	66FRRT48	415343
01 Jun	Denmark	Thailand	Taxation	551UNTS157	108040
01 Jun	Brazil	USA (United States)	Gen Communications	546UNTS195	107946
01 Jun	Australia	Netherlands	Consul/Citizenship	560UNTS85	108170
02 Jun	Multilateral		Tech Assistance	537UNTS348	200611
02 Jun	Multilateral		Tech Assistance	551UNTS2	108030
03 Jun	Norway	Spain	Patents/Copyrights	3NORT943	451148
03 Jun	Algeria	Italy	Air Transport	67ITGU137	435010
03 Jun	Germany, West	Guinea	Loans and Credits	65WBGA136	424249
03 Jun	Algeria	China People's Rep	Culture	65CCJC72	411052
03 Jun	Ivory Coast	Netherlands	Non-ILO Labor	634UNTS95	109054
03 Jun	Peru	IBRD (World Bank)	IBRD Project	551UNTS227	108045
04 Jun	Bulgaria	Czechoslovakia	Visas	0UNTS0	110515
04 Jun	Finland	USSR (Soviet Union)	Specific Resources	560UNTS169	108173
05 Jun	China People's Rep	Guinea	Culture	65CCJC74	411165
05 Jun	China People's Rep	Hungary	Culture	65CCJC73	411193
05 Jun	Pakistan	USSR (Soviet Union)	Culture	593UNTS115	108579
05 Jun	Saudi Arabia	USA (United States)	Milit Installation	548UNTS285	107984
05 Jun	Gambia	UK Great Britain	Admin Cooperation	551UNTS193	108041
06 Jun	Germany, East	Syria	Air Transport	43EGDZ337	420315
07 Jun	Italy	Mexico	Visas	66ITDI143	436275
07 Jun	Ivory Coast	Sweden	Air Transport	0UNTS0	109240
08 Jun	Bulgaria	Poland	Visas	65PZUM44	458122
08 Jun	Albania	China People's Rep	Loans and Credits	65CCJC75	411053
08 Jun	Albania	China People's Rep	General Economic	65CCJC77	411055
08 Jun	Albania	China People's Rep	General Economic	65CCJC76	411054
08 Jun	Bulgaria	Poland	Visas	0UNTS0	110300

DATE	PARTY ONE	PARTY TWO	TOPIC	CITATION	NUMBER
1965 (Cont.)					
08 Jun	Jordan	UK Great Britain	Loans and Credits	552UNTS251	108057
08 Jun	Canada	USA (United States)	Gen Communications	546UNTS201	107947
08 Jun	Greece	UK Great Britain	Visas	551UNTS205	108042
09 Jun	China People's Rep	Mongolia	Culture	65CCJC80	411249
09 Jun	Gambia	UN Special Fund	IGO Operations	538UNTS321	200612
09 Jun	Denmark	Germany, West	Territory Boundary	605UNTS95	108762
09 Jun	Argentina	Yugoslavia	General Trade	601UNTS3	108684
09 Jun	Colombia	USA (United States)	Commodity Trade	549UNTS3	107985
09 Jun	Denmark	Germany, West	Territory Boundary	570UNTS91	108289
09 Jun	Denmark	Germany, West	Water Transport	581UNTS141	108439
11 Jun	Colombia	Germany, West	Claims and Debts	67WGBB1552	425373
11 Jun	Colombia	Germany, West	Loans and Credits	66WBGA238	424374
11 Jun	Canada	USA (United States)	Scientific Project	564UNTS83	108222
11 Jun	India	IBRD (World Bank)	IBRD Project	557UNTS101	108130
11 Jun	India	IBRD (World Bank)	IBRD Project	557UNTS59	108128
12 Jun	China People's Rep	USSR (Soviet Union)	Scientific Project	65CCJC82	411356
12 Jun	Netherlands	Senegal	General Economic	602UNTS231	108715
13 Jun	China People's Rep	Congo (Brazzaville)	Direct Aid	65CCJC83	411131
15 Jun	Germany, East	Romania	Visas	44EGDZ337	420303
15 Jun	France	Haiti	Air Transport	67FRJO1205	416213
16 Jun	France	Jordan	Health/Educ/Welfare	65FRRT86	415256
16 Jun	Australia	Philippines	General Trade	541UNTS31	107858
16 Jun	United Nations	Sweden	Admin Cooperation	539UNTS45	107823
18 Jun	Poland	Syria	Tech Assistance	66PZUM33	458123
18 Jun	China People's Rep	Korea, North	Commodity Trade	65CCJC85	411238
18 Jun	China People's Rep	Czechoslovakia	Culture	65CCJC84	411132
18 Jun	Belgium	USA (United States)	Gen Communications	549UNTS95	107992
18 Jun	Multilateral		Atomic Energy	573UNTS3	108320
18 Jun	Peru	IBRD (World Bank)	IBRD Project	568UNTS191	108269
18 Jun	USA (United States)	Upper Volta	Finance	549UNTS133	107996
19 Jun	China People's Rep	Vietnam, North	Culture	65CCJC86	411376
21 Jun	Argentina	United Arab Rep	Commodity Trade	634UNTS177	109059
21 Jun	Argentina	United Arab Rep	General Economic	634UNTS161	109058
21 Jun	Australia	Germany, West	Visas	542UNTS53	107879
21 Jun	Australia	Malaysia	Humanitarian	542UNTS75	107880
22 Jun	Multilateral		ILO Labor	610UNTSO	108836
22 Jun	Japan	Korea, South	Dispute Settlement	584UNTS147	108476
22 Jun	Japan	Korea, South	Specific Resources	583UNTS51	108472
22 Jun	Japan	Korea, South	Claims and Debts	583UNTS173	108473
22 Jun	Japan	Korea, South	General Amity	583UNTS33	108471
22 Jun	Japan	Korea, South	Culture	584UNTS49	108475
22 Jun	Japan	Korea, South	Consul/Citizenship	584UNTS3	108474
23 Jun	Congo (Zaire)	Germany, West	Loans and Credits	65WBGA170	424385
23 Jun	Multilateral		General IGO	614UNTS239	108873
23 Jun	Mongolia	UNICEF (Children)	IGO Operations	540UNTS83	107844
23 Jun	Multilateral		Atomic Energy	548UNTS241	107981
24 Jun	Poland	USA (United States)	Commodity Trade	593UNTS147	108581
24 Jun	Austria	Petrol Export Org	IGO Operations	589UNTS135	108540
25 Jun	Argentina	Ireland	Visas	OUNTSO	109523
25 Jun	Ecuador	USA (United States)	US Agri Commod Aid	549UNTS23	107986
25 Jun	Australia	USA (United States)	Gen Communications	541UNTS155	107868
26 Jun	Greece	Italy	Finance	66ITDI138	436199
28 Jun	Ecuador	Germany, West	Claims and Debts	66WGBB825	425114
28 Jun	Ecuador	Germany, West	Loans and Credits	65WBGA185	424113
28 Jun	Austria	Tunisia	Admin Cooperation	65ABGB255	403196
28 Jun	Austria	Yugoslavia	Visas	66ABGB23	403240
28 Jun	Austria	Tunisia	Visas	65ABGB254	403197
28 Jun	Italy	IBRD (World Bank)	IBRD Project	567UNTS127	108254
29 Jun	Czechoslovakia	France	General Trade	65FRMD2807	417442
29 Jun	Czechoslovakia	France	Tech Assistance	66FRJO2502	416443
29 Jun	Czechoslovakia	France	Scientific Project	OUNTSO	110727
29 Jun	Guinea	USA (United States)	Milit Installation	549UNTS139	107997
29 Jun	Canada	USA (United States)	Scientific Project	549UNTS273	108003
30 Jun	Chile	Italy	Water Transport	66ITDI229	436089
30 Jun	Chile	Italy	Claims and Debts	66ITDI127	436088

DATE	PARTY ONE	PARTY TWO	TOPIC	CITATION	NUMBER
1965 (Cont.)					
30 Jun	France	Switzerland	Admin Cooperation	65FRRT78	415415
30 Jun	Finland	IBRD (World Bank)	IBRD Project	550UNTS63	108009
30 Jun	Kenya	IDA (Devel Assoc)	Non-IBRD Project	554UNTS75	108097
30 Jun	UN Special Fund	Spain	Direct Aid	544UNTS159	107918
30 Jun	India	Pakistan	Territory Boundary	548UNTS277	107983
30 Jun	Pakistan	IDA (Devel Assoc)	Non-IBRD Project	554UNTS111	108099
02 Jul	ILO (Labor Org)	LAFTA (Free Trade)	IGO Operations	563UNTS327	200619
02 Jul	Belgium	Sweden	Taxation	OUNTSO	109367
02 Jul	Hungary	Netherlands	Finance	564UNTS49	108220
02 Jul	Multilateral		Sanitation	592UNTS215	108575
05 Jul	Multilateral		General Aid	563UNTS104	108207
06 Jul	Cameroon	Netherlands	Tech Assistance	571UNTS75	108300
06 Jul	Cameroon	Netherlands	Tech Assistance	571UNTS63	108299
07 Jul	France	Spain	Admin Cooperation	66FRRT16	415168
07 Jul	Switzerland	UK Great Britain	Dispute Settlement	605UNTS205	108765
07 Jul	New Zealand	Poland	General Trade	548UNTS19	107966
07 Jul	Israel	USA (United States)	Gen Communications	549UNTS281	108004
07 Jul	UK Great Britain	USA (United States)	Specific Property	551UNTS221	108044
08 Jul	Brazil	USA (United States)	Atomic Energy	OUNTSO	109603
08 Jul	Multilateral		General Trade	597UNTS3	108641
08 Jul	Australia	Germany, West	Postal Service	543UNTS305	107907
09 Jul	Kenya	Norway	Taxation	2NORT553	451101
09 Jul	France	Morocco	Non-ILO Labor	67FRJO605	416309
09 Jul	France	Morocco	Non-ILO Labor	OUNTSO	109936
09 Jul	Pakistan	IBRD (World Bank)	IBRD Project	554UNTS39	108096
10 Jul	Cameroon	France	Finance	68FRJO2703	416104
10 Jul	Cameroon	France	Taxation	OUNTSO	109433
12 Jul	Malawi	Norway	Taxation	2NORT553	451111
12 Jul	Austria	Bulgaria	Sanitation	587UNTS51	108510
12 Jul	Austria	Bulgaria	Visas	587UNTS45	108509
12 Jul	Iran	IBRD (World Bank)	IBRD Project	554UNTS3	108095
13 Jul	Ceylon (Sri Lanka)	China People's Rep	Direct Aid	65CCJC91	411133
13 Jul	China People's Rep	Vietnam, North	Direct Aid	65CCJC90	411377
13 Jul	Australia	Eur Space Vehicle	IGO Operations	543UNTS183	107902
14 Jul	Italy	Poland	General Economic	65PZUM50	458124
14 Jul	Italy	Poland	General Economic	66ITDI154	436310
14 Jul	Germany, East	USSR (Soviet Union)	Atomic Energy	48EGDZ339	420426
14 Jul	Germany, West	Tunisia	Loans and Credits	65WBGA182	424682
14 Jul	Mali	USA (United States)	US Agri Commod Aid	564UNTS101	108223
15 Jul	Czechoslovakia	Italy	General Trade	66ITDI124	436082
15 Jul	China People's Rep	Germany, East	Education	48EGDZ339	420098
15 Jul	China People's Rep	Mali	Specific Property	65CCJC95	411260
15 Jul	China People's Rep	Germany, East	Education	65CCJC94	411181
15 Jul	Philippines	USA (United States)	Non-IBRD Project	OUNTSO	110125
15 Jul	Malta	Yugoslavia	General Trade	561UNTS223	108186
16 Jul	France	Italy	Visas	65FRRT71	415249
16 Jul	Multilateral		General Trade	600UNTS49	108675
16 Jul	USA (United States)	Yugoslavia	US Agri Commod Aid	549UNTS111	107994
16 Jul	Canada	Jamaica	Milit Assistance	548UNTS265	107982
18 Jul	Hungary	Poland	Land Transport	577UNTS161	108376
19 Jul	Congo (Zaire)	USA (United States)	Direct Aid	593UNTS215	108586
20 Jul	Italy	Mexico	IGO Establishment	66ITDI144	436276
20 Jul	Belgium	Germany, West	Non-ILO Labor	67WGBB813	425036
20 Jul	Multilateral		IGO Operations	541UNTS12	107857
20 Jul	Israel	USA (United States)	Milit Assistance	549UNTS55	107989
21 Jul	Germany, West	Peru	Tech Assistance	69WBGA126	424580
22 Jul	Italy	Sudan	Tech Assistance	66ITDI243	436360
22 Jul	France	Mauritania	Non-ILO Labor	67FRJO1202	416319
22 Jul	Multilateral		IBRD Project	561UNTS333	200618
22 Jul	France	Mauritania	Non-ILO Labor	OUNTSO	109329
23 Jul	France	Japan	Atomic Energy	OJGJI1604	441139
23 Jul	Albania	Germany, East	Water Transport	51EGDZ340	420024
23 Jul	Costa Rica	Germany, West	Tech Assistance	66WBGA66	424090
24 Jul	Germany, East	Ghana	Tech Assistance	51EGDZ340	420113
24 Jul	France	Switzerland	General Transport	65FRRT80	415416

DATE	PARTY ONE	PARTY TWO	TOPIC	CITATION	NUMBER
1965 (Cont.)					
24 Jul	France	Switzerland	Land Transport	65FRRT80	415417
24 Jul	China People's Rep	Indonesia	Water Transport	65CCJC100	411213
24 Jul	Uganda	USSR (Soviet Union)	Culture	596UNTS199	108633
26 Jul	ILO (Labor Org)	Org Ctrl Am States	IGO Operations	563UNTS341	200620
26 Jul	Israel	USA (United States)	Status of Forces	549UNTS49	107988
26 Jul	Maldive Islands	UK Great Britain	General Amity	548UNTS223	107980
27 Jul	Germany, East	Korea, North	Sanitation	52EGDZ340	420183
27 Jul	India	Netherlands	Direct Aid	0UNTS0	110196
27 Jul	Chile	USA (United States)	US Agri Commod Aid	574UNTS83	108342
28 Jul	Algeria	France	Non-IBRD Project	65FRRT107	415021
28 Jul	Algeria	France	Tech Assistance	0UNTS0	110609
29 Jul	Algeria	France	Specific Resources	65FRRT106	415022
29 Jul	Algeria	France	Non-IBRD Project	0UNTS0	110610
29 Jul	Luxembourg	USA (United States)	Gen Communications	573UNTS197	108332
29 Jul	Czechoslovakia	Poland	Dispute Settlement	572UNTS203	108313
30 Jul	China People's Rep	Korea, North	Culture	65CCJC102	411239
02 Aug	Austria	Italy	Air Transport	66ITDI118	436040
02 Aug	Germany, East	Syria	General Trade	51EGDZ341	420316
02 Aug	Germany, East	Syria	Tech Assistance	51EGDZ341	420317
02 Aug	Germany, East	Syria	Water Transport	51EGDZ341	420319
02 Aug	Germany, East	Syria	Finance	51EGDZ341	420318
04 Aug	Italy	Tanzania	Tech Assistance	66ITDI246	436397
04 Aug	Bulgaria	France	Air Transport	65FRRT81	415087
04 Aug	Bulgaria	France	Air Transport	0UNTS0	109958
05 Aug	China People's Rep	Japan	Specific Resources	65CCJC104	411218
05 Aug	China People's Rep	Ghana	Milit Assistance	65CCJC154	411166
05 Aug	Netherlands	United Arab Rep	Air Transport	0UNTS0	110161
07 Aug	Malaysia	Singapore	Recognition	563UNTS89	108206
09 Aug	Germany, East	Guinea	General Economic	52EGDZ341	420122
09 Aug	Rwanda	USA (United States)	Finance	0UNTS0	109895
09 Aug	Hungary	Yugoslavia	Visas	577UNTS103	108375
09 Aug	UK Great Britain	USA (United States)	General Aid	580UNTS181	108420
11 Aug	Germany, East	Mongolia	Sanitation	52EGDZ341	420224
11 Aug	France	Upper Volta	Finance	67FRJO106	416218
11 Aug	India	IDA (Devel Assoc)	Non-IBRD Project	562UNTS277	108199
11 Aug	Peru	USA (United States)	Gen Communications	564UNTS135	108225
12 Aug	Brazil	Spain	Visas	0UNTS0	109486
12 Aug	Philippines	USA (United States)	Milit Installation	579UNTS47	108397
12 Aug	Laos	Thailand	Specific Property	547UNTS209	107958
13 Aug	China People's Rep	Congo (Brazzaville)	Culture	65CCJC106	411134
14 Aug	ICJ Option Clause	Nigeria	ICJ Option Clause	544UNTS113	107913
16 Aug	Iraq	UK Great Britain	Commodity Trade	0UNTS0	109878
16 Aug	Sierra Leone	USA (United States)	Telecommunications	579UNTS55	108398
17 Aug	China People's Rep	Somalia	Culture	65CCJC107	411324
17 Aug	Bolivia	USA (United States)	US Agri Commod Aid	587UNTS289	108514
17 Aug	Ethiopia	USA (United States)	US Agri Commod Aid	564UNTS119	108224
19 Aug	Argentina	Turkey	Culture	0UNTS0	109558
19 Aug	Bulgaria	Hungary	Culture	577UNTS67	108373
19 Aug	Kenya	USA (United States)	Extradition	574UNTS153	108348
21 Aug	Bulgaria	Germany, East	Consul/Citizenship	43EGDZ342	420069
22 Aug	Israel	Sierra Leone	Culture	550UNTS275	108022
22 Aug	Israel	Sierra Leone	Tech Assistance	550UNTS285	108023
23 Aug	Central Afri Rep	Germany, West	Claims and Debts	67WGBB1657	425733
26 Aug	Accept UN Charter	Maldive Islands	UN Charter	545UNTS147	107929
26 Aug	Poland	WHO (World Health)	Tech Assistance	552UNTS3	108047
29 Aug	China People's Rep	Nepal	Non-IBRD Project	65CCJC109	411278
30 Aug	Japan	USA (United States)	Atomic Energy	0JGJI1609	441140
31 Aug	Chile	Japan	Finance	0JGJI1610	441141
31 Aug	Germany, East	Yugoslavia	Sanitation	44EGDZ342	420159
31 Aug	France	Luxembourg	Health/Educ/Welfare	68FRJO1910	416275
31 Aug	Australia	New Zealand	General Trade	554UNTS169	108101
31 Aug	China	USA (United States)	Status of Forces	572UNTS3	108308
31 Aug	Other Unilat Decla	United Nations	IGO Establishment	557UNTS143	108132
01 Sep	Belgium	Iran	Taxation	0IRTB14	433021
01 Sep	Italy	UK Great Britain	Customs	0UNTS0	109283

DATE	PARTY ONE	PARTY TWO	TOPIC	CITATION	NUMBER
1965 (Cont.)					
01 Sep	Italy	UK Great Britain	Taxation	0UNTS0	109284
02 Sep	Ecuador	France	Visas	65FRRT89	415158
03 Sep	China People's Rep	Nepal	Culture	65CCJC111	411272
04 Sep	Accept UN Charter	Singapore	UN Charter	545UNTS151	107930
06 Sep	Germany, West	Norway	General Aid	3NORT946	451193
06 Sep	Italy	Romania	General Economic	604UNTS49	108742
08 Sep	Multilateral		Visas	578UNTS3	108382
10 Sep	Philippines	USA (United States)	Gen Communications	4PTS919	465065
10 Sep	Colombia	Germany, West	Taxation	67WGBB762	425375
10 Sep	Japan	IBRD (World Bank)	Claims and Debts	566UNTS249	108246
13 Sep	Congo (Brazzaville)	Germany, West	Claims and Debts	67WGBB1733	425382
13 Sep	France	CERN (Nuc Resrch)	IGO Status/Immunit	69FRJO1004	416514
13 Sep	France	Switzerland	IGO Status/Immunit	69FRJO1004	416418
13 Sep	France	Switzerland	Atomic Energy	0UNTS0	109863
13 Sep	France	CERN (Nuc Resrch)	Atomic Energy	0UNTS0	109862
13 Sep	Multilateral		Tech Assistance	547UNTS264	107962
13 Sep	Multilateral		IGO Operations	547UNTS248	107961
14 Sep	Germany, West	Netherlands	Status of Forces	65WBGA203	424492
14 Sep	China People's Rep	Indonesia	Non-IBRD Project	65CCJC117	411214
14 Sep	China People's Rep	Guinea	Postal Service	65CCJC114	411182
14 Sep	China People's Rep	Guinea	Telecommunications	65CCJC115	411183
15 Sep	Finland	Ireland	Water Transport	604UNTS199	108750
15 Sep	Finland	Ireland	Taxation	0UNTS0	109372
16 Sep	China People's Rep	Vietnam, North	Sanitation	65CCJC118	411378
16 Sep	Cambodia	China People's Rep	Mass Media	65CCJC119	411135
16 Sep	Israel	IBRD (World Bank)	Claims and Debts	566UNTS212	108245
17 Sep	Czechoslovakia	USSR (Soviet Union)	Visas	549UNTS221	108001
17 Sep	Peru	IBRD (World Bank)	Loans and Credits	566UNTS311	108248
18 Sep	Italy	Turkey	Loans and Credits	66ITDI162	436413
18 Sep	Italy	Turkey	Finance	66ITDI161	436412
20 Sep	Belgium	Denmark	Taxation	549UNTS63	107990
21 Sep	Australia	Korea, South	General Trade	548UNTS163	107977
21 Sep	France	UK Great Britain	Culture	561UNTS3	108177
21 Sep	Norway	Eur Space Research	IGO Operations	579UNTS251	108413
21 Sep	Multilateral		IGO Operations	547UNTS280	107963
23 Sep	Czechoslovakia	Poland	Admin Cooperation	72PDZU237	457138
23 Sep	France	Niger	Extradition	65FRRT90	415344
24 Sep	Afghanistan	IAEA (Atom Energy)	Atomic Energy	556UNTS101	108121
24 Sep	IAEA (Atom Energy)	Uruguay	Atomic Energy	556UNTS117	108123
24 Sep	Multilateral		Atomic Energy	556UNTS141	108124
24 Sep	Morocco	IAEA (Atom Energy)	Atomic Energy	556UNTS109	108122
26 Sep	Nigeria	IBRD (World Bank)	IBRD Project	570UNTS233	108296
26 Sep	Nigeria	IBRD (World Bank)	IBRD Project	571UNTS39	108298
27 Sep	Poland	USA (United States)	Air Transport	564UNTS169	108227
28 Sep	Austria	Yugoslavia	Customs	66ABGB239	403239
29 Sep	East Afri Service	IBRD (World Bank)	IBRD Project	568UNTS327	200623
29 Sep	United Arab Rep	UK Great Britain	Culture	0UNTS0	109444
29 Sep	Kenya	IBRD (World Bank)	IBRD Project	568UNTS289	108274
29 Sep	IBRD (World Bank)	Spain	IBRD Project	568UNTS49	108264
29 Sep	IBRD (World Bank)	Uganda	IBRD Project	568UNTS317	108276
29 Sep	IBRD (World Bank)	Tanzania	IBRD Project	568UNTS309	108275
30 Sep	China People's Rep	Indonesia	General Trade	65CCJC123	411216
30 Sep	China People's Rep	Indonesia	Direct Aid	65CCJC122	411215
30 Sep	China People's Rep	Indonesia	Finance	65CCJC124	411217
30 Sep	Belgium	Luxembourg	Consul/Citizenship	590UNTS35	108545
01 Oct	Spain	USA (United States)	Scientific Project	65SPBO611	460280
01 Oct	China People's Rep	France	Culture	65CCJC126	411150
01 Oct	Mexico	IBRD (World Bank)	IBRD Project	589UNTS339	108542
01 Oct	Greece	Malta	Visas	550UNTS329	108027
02 Oct	China People's Rep	Guinea	Culture	65CCJC127	411167
02 Oct	Hungary	Mongolia	General Amity	587UNTS35	108508
05 Oct	Philippines	USA (United States)	General Trade	4PTS973	465067
06 Oct	China People's Rep	Syria	Mass Media	65CCJC130	411322
06 Oct	Albania	China People's Rep	Tech Assistance	65CCJC131	411056
06 Oct	Netherlands	UK Great Britain	Territory Boundary	595UNTS105	108615

DATE	PARTY ONE	PARTY TWO	TOPIC	CITATION	NUMBER
1965 (Cont.)					
06 Oct	Chile	IBRD (World Bank)	IBRD Project	567UNTS293	108261
06 Oct	Netherlands	UK Great Britain	Territory Boundary	595UNTS113	108616
07 Oct	Multilateral		Atomic Energy	556UNTS175	108125
08 Oct	France	Eur Space Research	Non-ILO Labor	66FRRT19	415505
11 Oct	Nigeria	Switzerland	Air Transport	602UNTS137	108710
11 Oct	Morocco	IDA (Devel Assoc)	Non-IBRD Project	562UNTS299	108200
12 Oct	Ceylon (Sri Lanka)	China People's Rep	General Trade	65CCJC132	411136
12 Oct	Argentina	Spain	Visas	635UNTS221	109085
13 Oct	France	Sweden	Culture	65FRRT103	415402
15 Oct	Argentina	Japan	Finance	0JGJI1613	441142
15 Oct	Australia	USSR (Soviet Union)	General Trade	553UNTS239	108092
17 Oct	Germany, East	Syria	General Economic	52EGDZ356	420320
18 Oct	Germany, West	Tunisia	Non-ILO Labor	66WBGA57	424683
18 Oct	ICAO (Civil Aviat)	Thailand	Air Transport	0UNTS0	110162
21 Oct	Dahomey	France	Finance	67FRRT905	415150
21 Oct	Turkey	UK Great Britain	Loans and Credits	561UNTS185	108180
21 Oct	Multilateral		Tech Assistance	547UNTS216	107959
22 Oct	Germany, West	Portugal	Culture	67WGBB721	425598
22 Oct	France	Poland	General Trade	65FRMD611	417363
23 Oct	Italy	Malta	Visas	550UNTS337	108028
23 Oct	United Nations	Zambia	IGO Operations	549UNTS101	107993
25 Oct	Iran	Romania	General Economic	0IRTB60	433099
26 Oct	China People's Rep	Czechoslovakia	Scientific Project	65CCJC133	411137
26 Oct	Brazil	France	Finance	66FRRT10	415079
27 Oct	Congo (Brazzaville)	Germany, West	Loans and Credits	66WBGA4	424383
28 Oct	Gambia	Norway	Visas	3NORT948	451064
28 Oct	Colombia	USA (United States)	Telecommunications	574UNTS109	108343
28 Oct	Netherlands	Nigeria	Scientific Project	578UNTS15	108383
29 Oct	Brazil	France	Air Transport	67FRJO1105	416080
29 Oct	France	Italy	Taxation	0UNTS0	109445
01 Nov	China People's Rep	Korea, North	Scientific Project	65CCJC135	411221
01 Nov	China People's Rep	Pakistan	Direct Aid	65CCJC134	411288
02 Nov	Philippines	IBRD (World Bank)	IBRD Project	567UNTS3	108249
03 Nov	Finland	USA (United States)	Air Transport	573UNTS175	108330
04 Nov	Germany, East	Poland	Education	65PZUM65	458125
04 Nov	Germany, East	Vietnam, North	Education	43EGDZ347	420495
05 Nov	Italy	Yugoslavia	Specific Resources	67ITGU210	435252
05 Nov	Argentina	Belgium	Culture	635UNTS229	109086
06 Nov	Afghanistan	China People's Rep	General Trade	65CCJC136	411042
06 Nov	Cuba	USA (United States)	Refugees	601UNTS81	108688
08 Nov	Germany, West	Malaysia	Loans and Credits	65WBGA242	424452
08 Nov	Bulgaria	Syria	Scientific Project	0UNTS0	109959
08 Nov	Morocco	IBRD (World Bank)	Claims and Debts	566UNTS279	108247
09 Nov	Bulgaria	China People's Rep	Scientific Project	65CCJC137	411081
09 Nov	China People's Rep	Korea, North	Sanitation	65CCJC138	411222
10 Nov	Italy	Yugoslavia	Admin Cooperation	66ITGU244	435253
10 Nov	Italy	Yugoslavia	Admin Cooperation	67ITGU169	435254
10 Nov	Argentina	Spain	Culture	0UNTS0	109559
10 Nov	UK Great Britain	USA (United States)	General Aid	580UNTS197	108422
11 Nov	Germany, West	Iran	Loans and Credits	67WGBB2549	425274
11 Nov	Saudi Arabia	USA (United States)	Milit Installation	606UNTS65	108775
12 Nov	Germany, East	Mali	Tech Assistance	44EGDZ347	420204
12 Nov	Albania	China People's Rep	General Trade	65CCJC140	411072
12 Nov	Multilateral		IGO Operations	550UNTS160	108013
13 Nov	China People's Rep	Vietnam, North	Scientific Project	65CCJC142	411379
15 Nov	OAU (Afri Unity)	United Nations	IGO Operations	548UNTS315	200614
15 Nov	Multilateral		Admin Cooperation	0UNTS0	109432
15 Nov	Philippines	USA (United States)	Milit Assistance	574UNTS205	108350
17 Nov	Canada	France	Culture	66FRJO1401	416107
17 Nov	Bulgaria	United Arab Rep	Visas	0UNTS0	109960
17 Nov	Austria	Romania	Admin Cooperation	0UNTS0	109625
17 Nov	Austria	Romania	Visas	564UNTS185	108229
17 Nov	Malaysia	IBRD (World Bank)	IBRD Project	568UNTS23	108263
18 Nov	China People's Rep	Korea, North	Land Transport	65CCJC144	411240
18 Nov	China People's Rep	USSR (Soviet Union)	Scientific Project	65CCJC143	411357

DATE	PARTY ONE	PARTY TWO	TOPIC	CITATION	NUMBER
1965 (Cont.)					
18 Nov	Multilateral		Customs	609UNTS115	108830
19 Nov	France	UK Great Britain	Non-ILO Labor	65FRRT105	415201
19 Nov	Austria	Yugoslavia	Non-ILO Labor	587UNTS239	108512
19 Nov	Saudi Arabia	USA (United States)	Non-IBRD Project	580UNTS35	108419
19 Nov	France	UK Great Britain	Non-ILO Labor	561UNTS19	108178
19 Nov	Austria	Yugoslavia	Non-ILO Labor	591UNTS3	108556
21 Nov	Israel	Paraguay	Visas	582UNTS65	108458
22 Nov	China People's Rep	Germany, East	Scientific Project	65CCJC146	411184
22 Nov	USA (United States)	Yugoslavia	US Agri Commod Aid	574UNTS211	108351
23 Nov	China People's Rep	Finland	General Trade	65CCJC145	411153
23 Nov	Hungary	Yugoslavia	Visas	577UNTS89	108374
23 Nov	Chile	UK Great Britain	Loans and Credits	560UNTS215	108176
24 Nov	Canada	France	Culture	66FRJO1401	416108
25 Nov	ILO (Labor Org)	OAU (Afri Unity)	General Amity	550UNTS389	200617
26 Nov	Belgium	Poland	Non-ILO Labor	620UNTS13	108950
26 Nov	UK Great Britain	USA (United States)	Gen Communications	561UNTS193	108181
26 Nov	Multilateral		Recognition	598UNTS81	108655
26 Nov	United Nations	United Arab Rep	IGO Operations	551UNTS253	108046
27 Nov	East Afri Service	United Nations	Health/Educ/Welfare	550UNTS375	200616
29 Nov	Germany, West	Bank Int Settlement	Claims and Debts	66WGBB209	425742
30 Nov	Brazil	El Salvador	Culture	0UNTS0	109430
30 Nov	Chile	UNICEF (Children)	IGO Operations	596UNTS215	108635
01 Dec	Ethiopia	Poland	Tech Assistance	65PZUM71	458126
01 Dec	Italy	Turkey	General Economic	66ITDI248	436418
01 Dec	Italy	Turkey	General Trade	66ITDI163	436419
01 Dec	China People's Rep	Romania	Scientific Project	65CCJC149	411312
01 Dec	Ceylon (Sri Lanka)	China People's Rep	Commodity Trade	65CCJC147	411102
01 Dec	Canada	USA (United States)	Milit Installation	574UNTS37	108340
02 Dec	China People's Rep	Korea, North	Water Transport	65CCJC150	411223
02 Dec	UK Great Britain	USSR (Soviet Union)	Consul/Citizenship	0UNTS0	109384
03 Dec	Germany, East	USSR (Soviet Union)	General Trade	61EGDZ349	420427
03 Dec	China People's Rep	Vietnam, North	Tech Assistance	65CCJC151	411364
03 Dec	Multilateral		Admin Cooperation	572UNTS105	108309
04 Dec	Multilateral		IGO Establishment	571UNTS123	108303
05 Dec	China People's Rep	Vietnam, North	Loans and Credits	65CCJC152	411365
05 Dec	China People's Rep	Vietnam, North	General Trade	65CCJC153	411366
06 Dec	Austria	Greece	Admin Cooperation	71ABGB2	403085
06 Dec	Tanzania	USA (United States)	Consul/Citizenship	592UNTS51	108568
06 Dec	Canada	UK Great Britain	Taxation	572UNTS161	108311
07 Dec	Belgium	Poland	Atomic Energy	65PZUM77	458127
08 Dec	Italy	Mexico	Tech Assistance	66ITDI146	436277
08 Dec	Italy	Mexico	Loans and Credits	66ITDI147	436278
08 Dec	Germany, West	Turkey	Admin Cooperation	67WGBB1692	425777
08 Dec	Denmark	Norway	Territory Boundary	634UNTS71	109052
08 Dec	Multilateral		IGO Establishment	600UNTS161	108680
08 Dec	Korea, South	Netherlands	Patents/Copyrights	571UNTS83	108301
08 Dec	Finland	Malta	Visas	561UNTS205	108183
09 Dec	Gambia	Italy	Visas	66ITDI131	436161
09 Dec	Germany, West	Luxembourg	Visas	67WGBB909	425434
09 Dec	Austria	Finland	Admin Cooperation	69ABGB3	403047
09 Dec	Austria	Finland	Education	0UNTS0	109462
10 Dec	Poland	Yugoslavia	Sanitation	66PDZU279	457128
10 Dec	Bulgaria	Italy	Water Transport	66ITDI121	436071
10 Dec	Bulgaria	Italy	General Trade	66ITDI120	436070
10 Dec	Germany, East	Guinea	General Economic	51EGDZ349	420123
10 Dec	Denmark	Madagascar	General Trade	0UNTS0	110553
12 Dec	Denmark	Zambia	Tech Assistance	574UNTS21	108339
13 Dec	IBRD (World Bank)	Venezuela	IBRD Project	568UNTS77	108265
14 Dec	Japan	UK Great Britain	Admin Cooperation	0JGJI1615	441143
14 Dec	France	Greece	Loans and Credits	67FRJO1005	416205
14 Dec	China People's Rep	Korea, North	General Trade	65CCJC154	411241
14 Dec	Ireland	UK Great Britain	General Trade	565UNTS58	108235
14 Dec	Ethiopia	USA (United States)	US Agri Commod Aid	574UNTS115	108344
15 Dec	Germany, East	Hungary	General Trade	52EGDZ349	420463
15 Dec	China People's Rep	Poland	Scientific Project	65CCJC155	411300

DATE	PARTY ONE	PARTY TWO	TOPIC	CITATION	NUMBER
1965 (Cont.)					
15 Dec	Burma	Czechoslovakia	Air Transport	602UNTS71	108707
15 Dec	Mexico	IBRD (World Bank)	IBRD Project	568UNTS125	108267
16 Dec	Philippines	USA (United States)	General Military	4PTS1037	465068
16 Dec	Paraguay	IBRD (World Bank)	IBRD Project	568UNTS165	108268
16 Dec	Multilateral		Postal Service	570UNTS201	108295
16 Dec	Italy	USA (United States)	Specif Claim/Waive	574UNTS139	108346
17 Dec	China People's Rep	Japan	Specific Resources	65CCJC156	411219
17 Dec	France	Tunisia	Non-ILO Labor	66FRRT37	415464
17 Dec	Austria	Yugoslavia	Non-ILO Labor	66ABGB290	403241
17 Dec	Monaco	United Nations	IGO Operations	550UNTS365	200615
17 Dec	France	Tunisia	Non-ILO Labor	0UNTS0	110665
17 Dec	Netherlands	Zambia	Non-ILO Labor	631UNTS311	109000
17 Dec	France	Israel	Non-ILO Labor	582UNTS3	108452
17 Dec	New Zealand	IBRD (World Bank)	IBRD Project	567UNTS255	108259
17 Dec	France	Israel	Non-ILO Labor	581UNTS311	108451
17 Dec	Canada	USA (United States)	General Trade	574UNTS49	108341
17 Dec	New Zealand	IBRD (World Bank)	IBRD Project	567UNTS275	108260
18 Dec	Germany, West	USA (United States)	Status of Forces	579UNTS193	108407
20 Dec	Philippines	USA (United States)	Admin Cooperation	4PTS1041	465069
20 Dec	Bulgaria	Germany, East	General Trade	59EGDZ350	420070
20 Dec	Austria	Yugoslavia	Visas	573UNTS165	108329
21 Dec	Czechoslovakia	Germany, East	General Trade	59EGDZ350	420369
21 Dec	China People's Rep	Romania	General Trade	65CCJC159	411316
21 Dec	Austria	Brazil	Admin Cooperation	595UNTS299	108624
23 Dec	Italy	Mexico	Air Transport	66ITDI210	436279
23 Dec	Burundi	Germany, West	Loans and Credits	66WBGA88	424068
23 Dec	China People's Rep	Czechoslovakia	Scientific Project	65CCJC160	411138
27 Dec	Italy	USA (United States)	Specific Property	574UNTS145	108347
27 Dec	IBRD (World Bank)	Sudan	IBRD Project	567UNTS27	108250
28 Dec	France	Korea, South	Health/Educ/Welfare	68FRJO1909	416132
28 Dec	Ethiopia	IBRD (World Bank)	IBRD Project	567UNTS229	108258
28 Dec	Denmark	Syria	Tech Assistance	588UNTS163	108523
29 Dec	Philippines	USA (United States)	Taxation	4PTS1051	465070
29 Dec	China People's Rep	Cuba	Culture	65CCJC161	411139
29 Dec	Chile	Israel	Scientific Project	0UNTS0	110375
29 Dec	Malta	Norway	Visas	561UNTS211	108184
29 Dec	Malta	Sweden	Visas	561UNTS217	108185
30 Dec	Germany, East	Poland	General Economic	60EGDZ350	420275
30 Dec	Austria	Tunisia	Tech Assistance	589UNTS119	108539
30 Dec	Multilateral		Atomic Energy	557UNTS3	108126
30 Dec	Denmark	Malta	Visas	561UNTS199	108182
30 Dec	Ethiopia	USA (United States)	Milit Installation	574UNTS129	108345
31 Dec	Multilateral		Specific Resources	616UNTS317	108904
31 Dec	UN Special Fund	Singapore	Admin Cooperation	552UNTS299	108061
31 Dec	Multilateral		Recognition	552UNTS292	108060
1966					
03 Jan	United Arab Rep	USA (United States)	US Agri Commod Aid	579UNTS63	108399
03 Jan	United Arab Rep	USA (United States)	US Agri Commod Aid	579UNTS83	108400
03 Jan	USA (United States)	Vietnam, South	Mass Media	579UNTS99	108401
06 Jan	Liberia	USA (United States)	US Agri Commod Aid	592UNTS101	108570
07 Jan	Japan	Sierra Leone	Commodity Trade	66JJS229	442166
07 Jan	France	Syria	Air Transport	67FRJO404	416424
07 Jan	Panama	UK Great Britain	Visas	565UNTS25	108233
08 Jan	Burma	Germany, East	General Economic	51EGDZ351	420076
10 Jan	India	Pakistan	General Amity	560UNTS39	108166
12 Jan	United Nations	Senegal	Health/Educ/Welfare	551UNTS147	108039
12 Jan	Italy	USA (United States)	Reparations	587UNTS309	108515
13 Jan	Iran	USSR (Soviet Union)	Non-IBRD Project	0IRTB81	433129
13 Jan	Iran	USSR (Soviet Union)	Commodity Trade	0IRTB81	433130
13 Jan	El Salvador	Mexico	Culture	67MEXD1711	444017
13 Jan	France	Liberia	Air Transport	68FRJO1904	416262
13 Jan	Iran	USSR (Soviet Union)	Non-IBRD Project	633UNTS123	109037
13 Jan	Pakistan	IDA (Devel Assoc)	Non-IBRD Project	567UNTS67	108252
13 Jan	IDA (Devel Assoc)	Tanzania	Non-IBRD Project	567UNTS177	108256

DATE	PARTY ONE	PARTY TWO	TOPIC	CITATION	NUMBER
1966 (Cont.)					
14 Jan	Iran	USSR (Soviet Union)	Visas	0IRTB80	433125
15 Jan	Honduras	Mexico	Culture	70MEXD703	444027
15 Jan	Mongolia	USSR (Soviet Union)	General Amity	562UNTS43	108194
15 Jan	Malta	USA (United States)	Specif Goods/Equip	579UNTS109	108402
17 Jan	Austria	Germany, West	Health/Educ/Welfare	69WGBB1	425553
17 Jan	Mexico	Nicaragua	Culture	68MEXD1005	444033
17 Jan	Iran	USSR (Soviet Union)	Admin Cooperation	0IRTB79	433121
17 Jan	Mexico	Nicaragua	Tech Assistance	68MEXD510	444032
17 Jan	Austria	Germany, West	Health/Educ/Welfare	0UNTS0	110163
17 Jan	Canada	USA (United States)	Air Transport	586UNTS151	108502
17 Jan	Multilateral		IGO Establishment	592UNTS101	108573
19 Jan	Poland	Sweden	Finance	66PZUM25	458129
19 Jan	Costa Rica	Mexico	Culture	67MEXD2511	444009
19 Jan	Costa Rica	Mexico	Tech Assistance	67MEXD2511	444008
20 Jan	Mexico	Panama	Culture	67MEXD807	444035
21 Jan	Japan	USSR (Soviet Union)	Air Transport	67JHZ3	439003
21 Jan	Japan	USSR (Soviet Union)	General Trade	633UNTS165	109038
22 Jan	Germany, East	Romania	General Trade	40EGDZ352	420304
22 Jan	Czechoslovakia	Poland	Culture	588UNTS175	108524
24 Jan	Finland	USSR (Soviet Union)	Consul/Citizenship	576UNTS35	108364
26 Jan	France	OECD (Econ Coop)	Non-ILO Labor	66FRRT12	415506
26 Jan	Mongolia	UN Special Fund	Direct Aid	552UNTS201	108055
27 Jan	UK Great Britain	Yugoslavia	Culture	573UNTS243	108337
29 Jan	Japan	Laos	Postal Service	66JJS201	442167
29 Jan	Czechoslovakia	Iran	General Economic	0IRTB66	433106
31 Jan	Norway	Eur Space Research	Specific Property	580UNTS3	108414
01 Feb	China People's Rep	Guinea	General Trade	66CCJC2	411168
02 Feb	UK Great Britain	Yugoslavia	Commodity Trade	571UNTS275	108306
03 Feb	France	Iran	Visas	66FRRT14	415241
04 Feb	China People's Rep	Czechoslovakia	General Economic	66CCJC3	411103
04 Feb	Guinea	USA (United States)	US Agri Commod Aid	579UNTS213	108409
04 Feb	Belgium	Denmark	Land Transport	561UNTS233	108187
07 Feb	Malaysia	Philippines	Admin Cooperation	608UNTS3	108809
07 Feb	Brazil	Korea, South	Culture	0UNTS0	109524
08 Feb	France	Yugoslavia	Sanitation	67FRJO102	416491
08 Feb	France	Yugoslavia	Health/Educ/Welfare	67FRJO1802	416492
08 Feb	Togo	USA (United States)	General Amity	0UNTS0	109677
08 Feb	France	Yugoslavia	Sanitation	0UNTS0	109503
08 Feb	UK Great Britain	USA (United States)	Finance	0UNTS0	109751
08 Feb	IDA (Devel Assoc)	UK Great Britain	Non-IBRD Project	567UNTS207	108257
08 Feb	IAEA (Atom Energy)	Turkey	Atomic Energy	573UNTS75	108323
10 Feb	Multilateral		Loans and Credits	575UNTS129	108356
10 Feb	Pakistan	IDA (Devel Assoc)	Non-IBRD Project	575UNTS89	108355
11 Feb	Germany, East	United Arab Rep	Water Transport	52EGDZ353	420481
11 Feb	China People's Rep	Romania	Culture	66CCJC4	411317
12 Feb	Cyprus	Germany, East	General Economic	52EGDZ353	420499
12 Feb	Argentina	Uruguay	Non-IBRD Project	0UNTS0	109520
15 Feb	Niger	Norway	Visas	3NORT956	451122
15 Feb	Japan	Philippines	Direct Aid	66JJS217	442168
15 Feb	Italy	UK Great Britain	Taxation	67ITGU230	435194
15 Feb	France	Hungary	General Trade	66FRMD2602	417224
15 Feb	Panama	USA (United States)	Scientific Project	586UNTS27	108494
16 Feb	Czechoslovakia	Germany, East	Finance	51EGDZ354	420370
16 Feb	United Arab Rep	Zambia	General Trade	0UNTS0	109535
16 Feb	Ethiopia	IDA (Devel Assoc)	Loans and Credits	569UNTS43	108278
17 Feb	Ecuador	France	Tech Assistance	66FRJO2206	416159
17 Feb	Austria	Germany, West	Land Transport	614UNTS263	108875
17 Feb	Austria	Germany, West	Land Transport	615UNTS3	108876
17 Feb	UK Great Britain	Venezuela	Territory Boundary	561UNTS321	108192
19 Feb	Germany, East	Hungary	Scientific Project	51EGDZ354	420464
20 Feb	China People's Rep	Hungary	General Economic	66CCJC5	411200
21 Feb	New Zealand	United Nations	IGO Operations	555UNTS163	108110
21 Feb	Denmark	United Nations	IGO Operations	555UNTS151	108108
21 Feb	United Nations	Sweden	IGO Operations	555UNTS169	108111
21 Feb	United Nations	UK Great Britain	General Economic	555UNTS177	108112

DATE	PARTY ONE	PARTY TWO	TOPIC	CITATION	NUMBER
1966 (Cont.)					
21 Feb	Canada	United Nations	IGO Operations	555UNTS119	108107
21 Feb	Austria	Finland	Claims and Debts	597UNTS273	108651
21 Feb	Finland	United Nations	IGO Operations	555UNTS157	108109
22 Feb	Japan	Spain	General Trade	66JJS257	442169
23 Feb	Finland	Israel	Visas	581UNTS219	108447
23 Feb	Ceylon (Sri Lanka)	USA (United States)	Finance	586UNTS91	108498
23 Feb	Israel	Sweden	Visas	581UNTS195	108444
23 Feb	Iceland	Israel	Visas	581UNTS211	108446
23 Feb	Israel	Norway	Visas	581UNTS203	108445
23 Feb	Algeria	USA (United States)	Direct Aid	592UNTS117	108571
23 Feb	Denmark	Israel	Visas	581UNTS187	108443
24 Feb	Austria	United Nations	IGO Operations	557UNTS129	108131
25 Feb	China People's Rep	Korea, North	Culture	66CCJC6	411242
25 Feb	Taiwan	Haiti	Admin Cooperation	0UNTS0	110433
25 Feb	Brazil	Denmark	Tech Assistance	590UNTS95	108549
25 Feb	Israel	Kenya	Tech Assistance	582UNTS23	108455
25 Feb	Australia	United Nations	IGO Operations	557UNTS85	108129
28 Feb	Ireland	UK Great Britain	Health/Educ/Welfare	565UNTS33	108234
01 Mar	Albania	Germany, East	General Trade	51EGDZ355	420025
01 Mar	France	Italy	Admin Cooperation	67FRJO1108	416250
01 Mar	Argentina	Germany, West	Tech Assistance	635UNTS247	109087
02 Mar	Netherlands	Philippines	Tech Assistance	631UNTS325	109002
03 Mar	Denmark	UK Great Britain	Territory Boundary	592UNTS207	108574
04 Mar	Multilateral		US Agri Commod Aid	578UNTS57	108387
04 Mar	Romania	USSR (Soviet Union)	Visas	591UNTS327	108565
04 Mar	Hungary	United Nations	IGO Operations	559UNTS3	108151
05 Mar	Germany, East	Poland	Commodity Trade	51EGDZ355	420276
07 Mar	Multilateral		Humanitarian	0UNTS0	109464
07 Mar	Argentina	Uruguay	General Trade	635UNTS275	109088
07 Mar	Korea, South	USA (United States)	US Agri Commod Aid	579UNTS137	108404
10 Mar	Guinea	Poland	Culture	67PDZU201	457130
10 Mar	Iran	Norway	Tech Assistance	3NORT958	451086
10 Mar	Germany, West	Malagasy	Loans and Credits	66WBGA151	424442
10 Mar	Colombia	USA (United States)	US Agri Commod Aid	0UNTS0	109604
10 Mar	Denmark	Italy	Taxation	0UNTS0	109217
10 Mar	Denmark	Italy	Taxation	643UNTS349	109201
10 Mar	Bulgaria	UNICEF (Children)	IGO Operations	559UNTS13	108152
11 Mar	Germany, East	Hungary	Specific Property	51EGDZ355	420465
12 Mar	Ceylon (Sri Lanka)	USA (United States)	US Agri Commod Aid	579UNTS117	108403
14 Mar	France	Romania	Land Transport	604UNTS33	108741
15 Mar	Brazil	IBRD (World Bank)	IBRD Project	599UNTS52	108664
15 Mar	Pakistan	IAEA (Atom Energy)	Claims and Debts	588UNTS261	108530
16 Mar	Germany, East	USSR (Soviet Union)	IGO Establishment	51EGDZ356	420428
16 Mar	Bulgaria	China People's Rep	General Economic	66CCJC7	411091
18 Mar	Brazil	Chile	Mass Media	0UNTS0	109418
19 Mar	Germany, East	Mongolia	Tech Assistance	51EGDZ356	420225
19 Mar	Argentina	Taiwan	Culture	635UNTS281	109089
19 Mar	USA (United States)	USSR (Soviet Union)	Scientific Project	0UNTS0	109617
20 Mar	Iran	Switzerland	Claims and Debts	0IRTB65	433103
21 Mar	China People's Rep	Vietnam, North	Land Transport	66CCJC8	411380
21 Mar	USA (United States)	Vietnam, South	US Agri Commod Aid	578UNTS165	108394
22 Mar	China People's Rep	Poland	General Economic	66CCJC9	411301
22 Mar	Romania	UK Great Britain	Commodity Trade	571UNTS281	108307
24 Mar	Japan	Korea, South	General Trade	66JJS183	442170
24 Mar	Austria	Spain	Land Transport	590UNTS203	108555
24 Mar	Brazil	United Nations	IGO Establishment	560UNTS47	108167
25 Mar	Germany, West	Togo	Non-IBRD Project	66WBGA111	424663
25 Mar	Germany, West	USA (United States)	Commodity Trade	66WBGA144	424721
25 Mar	China People's Rep	Germany, East	General Economic	66CCJC10	411185
25 Mar	Singapore	USA (United States)	Finance	580UNTS221	108425
26 Mar	Argentina	India	General Trade	601UNTS201	108697
28 Mar	Germany, West	Vietnam, South	Specif Goods/Equip	66WGBB322	425728
28 Mar	Germany, West	Tunisia	Other Military	66WBGA90	424684
28 Mar	China People's Rep	Mongolia	General Trade	66CCJC11	411261
28 Mar	Brazil	UNICEF (Children)	IGO Operations	607UNTS235	108807

DATE	PARTY ONE	PARTY TWO	TOPIC	CITATION	NUMBER
1966 (Cont.)					
28 Mar	WHO (World Health)	Singapore	Tech Assistance	562UNTS59	108195
30 Mar	Iceland	Norway	Taxation	3NORT959	451077
30 Mar	Belgium	United Arab Rep	Claims and Debts	632UNTS237	109026
30 Mar	Iceland	Norway	Taxation	566UNTS51	108240
30 Mar	Guinea	IBRD (World Bank)	IBRD Project	568UNTS3	108262
30 Mar	Multilateral		Scientific Project	593UNTS261	108588
31 Mar	Japan	Kenya	Direct Aid	66JJS177	442171
31 Mar	Cambodia	China People's Rep	Health/Educ/Welfare	66CCJC12	411140
31 Mar	Denmark	Netherlands	Territory Boundary	604UNTS209	108751
31 Mar	Burundi	IDA (Devel Assoc)	Loans and Credits	569UNTS3	108277
01 Apr	Ghana	USA (United States)	US Agri Commod Aid	579UNTS157	108405
02 Apr	Turkey	USA (United States)	US Agri Commod Aid	0UNTS0	109678
02 Apr	Singapore	USSR (Soviet Union)	General Trade	631UNTS125	108992
03 Apr	Israel	Uruguay	Visas	582UNTS73	108459
04 Apr	China People's Rep	USSR (Soviet Union)	Air Transport	66CCJC14	411342
04 Apr	Paraguay	IDA (Devel Assoc)	Non-IBRD Project	582UNTS331	108469
04 Apr	Paraguay	IBRD (World Bank)	IBRD Project	570UNTS41	108287
05 Apr	Multilateral		Water Transport	640UNTS133	109159
05 Apr	Netherlands	Turkey	Non-ILO Labor	0UNTS0	109204
05 Apr	Jordan	USA (United States)	Direct Aid	593UNTS239	108587
05 Apr	Philippines	United Nations	Health/Educ/Welfare	560UNTS191	108174
05 Apr	UK Great Britain	USA (United States)	General Trade	592UNTS61	108569
06 Apr	Germany, West	Ghana	Loans and Credits	66WBGA131	424219
06 Apr	France	Ivory Coast	Finance	69FRJO2201	416141
07 Apr	Bulgaria	Poland	Culture	66PZUM14	458131
08 Apr	Algeria	France	Health/Educ/Welfare	66FRRT34	415023
08 Apr	Algeria	France	Tech Assistance	0UNTS0	109508
11 Apr	USA (United States)	Yugoslavia	US Agri Commod Aid	580UNTS239	108427
11 Apr	Paraguay	USA (United States)	Milit Assistance	578UNTS99	108389
12 Apr	Philippines	Sweden	Taxation	0UNTS0	110197
13 Apr	Sudan	USA (United States)	US Agri Commod Aid	586UNTS39	108495
14 Apr	China People's Rep	Congo (Brazzaville)	Culture	66CCJC16	411141
14 Apr	Spain	USA (United States)	Scientific Project	586UNTS79	108497
14 Apr	Spain	USA (United States)	Specific Property	579UNTS173	108406
17 Apr	Portugal	UK Great Britain	Air Transport	573UNTS223	108335
18 Apr	Germany, West	Greece	Taxation	67WGBB852	425240
18 Apr	Germany, West	Greece	Taxation	0UNTS0	109395
18 Apr	Bulgaria	Turkey	Air Transport	631UNTS263	108999
18 Apr	Indonesia	USA (United States)	US Agri Commod Aid	578UNTS106	108390
18 Apr	IBRD (World Bank)	UK Great Britain	IGO Operations	573UNTS209	108334
18 Apr	Paraguay	USA (United States)	Gen Communications	586UNTS189	108503
19 Apr	France	Germany, West	Other Military	66WBGA161	424199
19 Apr	China People's Rep	USSR (Soviet Union)	General Trade	66CCJC18	411358
19 Apr	African Coffee Org	France	IGO Status/Immunit	67FRJO1903	416507
20 Apr	China People's Rep	Syria	Culture	66CCJC19	411325
21 Apr	France	Gabon	Finance	69FRJO2404	416197
21 Apr	Morocco	USA (United States)	US Agri Commod Aid	0UNTS0	109679
21 Apr	IBRD (World Bank)	Venezuela	IBRD Project	568UNTS257	108273
21 Apr	Romania	Tunisia	Scientific Project	604UNTS65	108744
21 Apr	Spain	USA (United States)	Milit Assistance	580UNTS231	108426
21 Apr	Romania	Tunisia	Culture	604UNTS57	108743
22 Apr	Germany, West	Japan	Taxation	68JAIL201	440069
22 Apr	Germany, East	Yugoslavia	Gen Communications	47EGDZ358	420160
22 Apr	France	Romania	Culture	66FRRT38	415378
22 Apr	China People's Rep	Tanzania	Water Transport	66CCJC21	411339
22 Apr	China People's Rep	Vietnam, North	Tech Assistance	66CCJC20	411381
22 Apr	Germany, West	Japan	Taxation	0UNTS0	109715
22 Apr	France	Gabon	Taxation	0UNTS0	109647
22 Apr	Romania	IAEA (Atom Energy)	Atomic Energy	603UNTS23	108721
22 Apr	Bolivia	USA (United States)	US Agri Commod Aid	578UNTS73	108388
23 Apr	Germany, East	Syria	Mass Media	47EGDZ358	420321
23 Apr	Brazil	USA (United States)	US Agri Commod Aid	607UNTS117	108801
23 Apr	Czechoslovakia	USSR (Soviet Union)	Culture	566UNTS159	108242
24 Apr	Iran	Yugoslavia	General Economic	0IRTB83	433136
24 Apr	Germany, West	Guatemala	Tech Assistance	67WBGA39	424241

DATE	PARTY ONE	PARTY TWO	TOPIC	CITATION	NUMBER
1966 (Cont.)					
25 Apr	Austria	Thailand	Admin Cooperation	66ABGB135	403195
26 Apr	Belgium	Israel	Admin Cooperation	566UNTS187	108243
27 Apr	Poland	Tunisia	Culture	67PDZU249	457132
27 Apr	Finland	IBRD (World Bank)	IBRD Project	568UNTS107	108266
27 Apr	Paraguay	USA (United States)	US Agri Commod Aid	578UNTS121	108391
28 Apr	France	Poland	Non-ILO Labor	66PZUM76	458133
28 Apr	France	Poland	Non-ILO Labor	0UNTS0	110702
28 Apr	Multilateral		Non-ILO Labor	604UNTS219	108752
29 Apr	Korea, South	Mexico	Culture	70MEXD2904	444005
29 Apr	Italy	Norway	Taxation	3NORT961	451090
29 Apr	Cambodia	China People's Rep	General Economic	66CCJC22	411142
30 Apr	Malawi	Norway	Visas	3NORT962	451112
30 Apr	Ivory Coast	Norway	General Trade	3NORT963	451043
30 Apr	China People's Rep	Norway	Culture	66CCJC23	411279
30 Apr	France	Jordan	Air Transport	66FRJO2606	416257
30 Apr	China People's Rep	Guinea	Culture	66CCJC24	411186
30 Apr	Multilateral		Specific Resources	620UNTS191	108956
02 May	China People's Rep	Nepal	General Trade	66CCJC26	411273
03 May	Germany, East	United Arab Rep	General Economic	33EGDZ359	420483
03 May	Germany, East	United Arab Rep	General Economic	33EGDZ359	420482
04 May	Albania	China People's Rep	Water Transport	66CCJC27	411057
04 May	China People's Rep	United Arab Rep	General Trade	66CCJC28	411343
04 May	Multilateral		IBRD Project	575UNTS49	108354
05 May	Bulgaria	Singapore	General Trade	631UNTS165	108993
05 May	France	USA (United States)	Admin Cooperation	593UNTS279	108589
06 May	Germany, West	Mali	Loans and Credits	66WBGA124	424457
06 May	Rwanda	USSR (Soviet Union)	Culture	633UNTS217	109039
06 May	Sierra Leone	USA (United States)	Admin Cooperation	594UNTS47	108593
07 May	Poland	USSR (Soviet Union)	Land Transport	66PZUM60	458134
07 May	China People's Rep	Tanzania	Culture	66CCJC29	411333
07 May	China People's Rep	United Arab Rep	Culture	66CCJC30	411344
07 May	France	Ivory Coast	Claims and Debts	66FRJO2011	416142
09 May	Nicaragua	USA (United States)	Finance	0UNTS0	110043
10 May	Tunisia	Vietnam, South	General Trade	0VKNG235	496062
11 May	China People's Rep	Czechoslovakia	Culture	66CCJC32	411143
12 May	Germany, West	Israel	Direct Aid	66WBGA111	424282
12 May	France	Switzerland	Visas	66FRJO2406	416419
12 May	Multilateral		General Aid	563UNTS54	108204
13 May	Malagasy	Norway	General Amity	3NORT964	451109
13 May	Malagasy	Norway	General Economic	3NORT965	451110
13 May	China People's Rep	Mali	Culture	66CCJC33	411262
13 May	Peru	IBRD (World Bank)	IBRD Project	570UNTS61	108288
14 May	Multilateral		Specific Resources	0UNTS0	109587
14 May	Lebanon	ILO (Labor Org)	IGO Establishment	600UNTS69	108676
16 May	Bulgaria	Hungary	Admin Cooperation	0UNTS0	110417
16 May	IBRD (World Bank)	Tunisia	IBRD Project	584UNTS155	108477
16 May	ICJ Option Clause	France	ICJ Option Clause	562UNTS299	108196
16 May	Colombia	IBRD (World Bank)	Loans and Credits	608UNTS249	108819
17 May	Germany, West	Luxembourg	Extradition	66WBGA131	424435
17 May	Multilateral		Visas	571UNTS89	108302
18 May	Norway	Yugoslavia	Taxation	3NORT970	451098
19 May	France	Iraq	Air Transport	67FRJO1901	416236
20 May	France	Poland	Scientific Project	66PZUM79	458135
20 May	Germany, East	Yugoslavia	Admin Cooperation	45EGDZ360	420161
20 May	France	Poland	Culture	67FRJO204	416365
20 May	France	Poland	Tech Assistance	67FRJO404	416364
20 May	Argentina	Portugal	Non-ILO Labor	635UNTS301	109090
22 May	France	Poland	Culture	66PZUM70	458136
23 May	China People's Rep	Yemen	Culture	66CCJC36	411395
23 May	Italy	United Nations	IGO Operations	565UNTS11	108231
23 May	Maldive Islands	WHO (World Health)	Tech Assistance	566UNTS19	108237
24 May	Albania	China People's Rep	Scientific Project	66CCJC38	411073
24 May	Afghanistan	China People's Rep	Culture	66CCJC37	411047
24 May	Austria	Ireland	Taxation	636UNTS149	109102
25 May	Germany, West	Switzerland	Territory Boundary	67WBGA165	424763

DATE	PARTY ONE	PARTY TWO	TOPIC	CITATION	NUMBER
1966 (Cont.)					
25 May	India	USA (United States)	Gen Communications	593UNTS157	108582
25 May	Mexico	IBRD (World Bank)	IBRD Project	596UNTS3	108627
26 May	China People's Rep	Cuba	General Trade	66CCJC39	411144
26 May	Bolivia	France	Health/Educ/Welfare	68FRJO1606	416075
26 May	Pakistan	USA (United States)	US Agri Commod Aid	594UNTS27	108592
26 May	Bulgaria	UN Special Fund	General Aid	563UNTS71	108205
26 May	Guyana	UK Great Britain	Admin Cooperation	588UNTS143	108521
26 May	Guyana	UK Great Britain	Status of Forces	595UNTS255	108621
27 May	China People's Rep	Cuba	Scientific Project	66CCJC40	411145
27 May	Multilateral		IGO Establishment	637UNTS0	109121
28 May	China People's Rep	Vietnam, North	Culture	66CCJC41	411382
28 May	Argentina	Spain	Non-ILO Labor	0UNTS0	109525
29 May	Thailand	USA (United States)	General Amity	0UNTS0	109345
30 May	China People's Rep	Mongolia	Tech Assistance	66CCJC42	411263
31 May	Colombia	IBRD (World Bank)	Loans and Credits	608UNTS279	108820
01 Jun	Germany, East	USSR (Soviet Union)	Land Transport	41EGDZ361	420429
01 Jun	Cuba	Germany, East	Gen Communications	41EGDZ361	420195
01 Jun	China People's Rep	Korea, North	Sanitation	66CCJC44	411224
01 Jun	China People's Rep	France	Air Transport	66CCJC43	411151
01 Jun	China People's Rep	Pakistan	Culture	66CCJC45	411289
01 Jun	China People's Rep	France	Air Transport	66FRRT23	415117
01 Jun	Austria	Liechtenstein	Admin Cooperation	68ABGB99	403125
01 Jun	Burma	USA (United States)	Loans and Credits	580UNTS253	108428
02 Jun	Mexico	Switzerland	Air Transport	68MEXD2702	444041
02 Jun	China People's Rep	Guinea	Scientific Project	66CCJC46	411169
02 Jun	UK Great Britain	USA (United States)	Atomic Energy	573UNTS229	108336
03 Jun	Germany, West	Tunisia	Loans and Credits	66WBGA148	424685
03 Jun	France	Italy	Visas	66FRRT30	415251
03 Jun	United Nations	Switzerland	Claims and Debts	564UNTS193	200621
04 Jun	China People's Rep	Iraq	Culture	66CCJC48	411204
04 Jun	China People's Rep	Iraq	Mass Media	66CCJC49	411205
04 Jun	Accept UN Charter	Guyana	UN Charter	572UNTS225	108316
06 Jun	Austria	Israel	Admin Cooperation	68ABGB349	403108
06 Jun	Austria	Israel	Admin Cooperation	68ABGB348	403109
06 Jun	Austria	Israel	Admin Cooperation	0UNTS0	109347
06 Jun	Austria	Israel	Admin Cooperation	0UNTS0	109346
06 Jun	Israel	USA (United States)	US Agri Commod Aid	593UNTS165	108583
06 Jun	Israel	USA (United States)	US Agri Commod Aid	578UNTS143	108392
06 Jun	Malta	Turkey	Visas	579UNTS237	108411
07 Jun	Ivory Coast	Norway	Air Transport	3NORT967	451044
07 Jun	Ivory Coast	Norway	Visas	3NORT968	451045
07 Jun	France	India	Health/Educ/Welfare	66FRRT32	415231
07 Jun	Ivory Coast	Norway	Air Transport	0UNTS0	109249
07 Jun	Poland	Singapore	General Trade	631UNTS189	108994
07 Jun	Denmark	Ivory Coast	Air Transport	595UNTS313	108626
08 Jun	Germany, East	Mali	Air Transport	42EGDZ361	420205
08 Jun	China People's Rep	Tanzania	General Economic	66CCJC50	411334
08 Jun	Liberia	UNICEF (Children)	General Amity	570UNTS31	108286
09 Jun	China People's Rep	Mali	Loans and Credits	66CCJC51	411250
09 Jun	Congo (Brazzaville)	France	Direct Aid	66FRJO6051	416126
09 Jun	Canada	USA (United States)	Non-IBRD Project	580UNTS263	108429
10 Jun	Germany, West	Ghana	Extradition	67WGBB1743	425220
10 Jun	China People's Rep	Yugoslavia	General Trade	66CCJC52	411396
10 Jun	Canada	USA (United States)	Water Transport	639UNTS13	109141
11 Jun	France	Germany, West	Admin Cooperation	66WBGA192	424198
11 Jun	China People's Rep	Somalia	Culture	66CCJC53	411326
11 Jun	Guyana	UN Special Fund	Non-IBRD Project	564UNTS201	200622
12 Jun	Bulgaria	Syria	Visas	0UNTS0	109961
13 Jun	Morocco	IBRD (World Bank)	IGO Operations	615UNTS205	108881
14 Jun	Denmark	France	General Trade	66FRMD2076	417153
14 Jun	Belgium	Bulgaria	Other HEW	607UNTS183	108806
14 Jun	Denmark	Iran	Tech Assistance	597UNTS283	108652
14 Jun	Bel-Lux Econ Union	Bulgaria	General Economic	601UNTS167	108694
14 Jun	Portugal	IBRD (World Bank)	IBRD Project	581UNTS3	108430
14 Jun	ICJ Option Clause	Gambia	ICJ Option Clause	565UNTS21	108232

DATE	PARTY ONE	PARTY TWO	TOPIC	CITATION	NUMBER
1966 (Cont.)					
14 Jun	Portugal	IBRD (World Bank)	IBRD Project	581UNTS29	108431
15 Jun	Germany, West	India	Water Transport	66WBGA190	424258
15 Jun	Argentina	Bolivia	Finance	0UNTS0	109518
15 Jun	Canada	USA (United States)	Milit Installation	594UNTS83	108595
15 Jun	Israel	USA (United States)	Telecommunications	578UNTS159	108393
17 Jun	Pakistan	IDA (Devel Assoc)	Non-IBRD Project	582UNTS297	108468
17 Jun	France	USA (United States)	Scientific Project	601UNTS113	108690
18 Jun	Fed Rhod/Nyasaland	Norway	Taxation	580UNTS9	108415
19 Jun	Israel	Venezuela	Culture	0UNTS0	110376
20 Jun	China People's Rep	Poland	Scientific Project	66CCJC54	411302
20 Jun	Australia	Poland	General Trade	638UNTS201	109136
20 Jun	Multilateral		Scientific Project	572UNTS263	108318
20 Jun	Mexico	IAEA (Atom Energy)	Atomic Energy	573UNTS25	108321
20 Jun	Multilateral		Atomic Energy	573UNTS41	108322
20 Jun	Ecuador	Israel	Visas	581UNTS265	108449
20 Jun	Gambia	UK Great Britain	Recognition	573UNTS203	108333
20 Jun	Greece	United Nations	Claims and Debts	565UNTS3	108230
20 Jun	Jamaica	IBRD (World Bank)	IBRD Project	582UNTS145	108462
20 Jun	IAEA (Atom Energy)	UK Great Britain	IGO Operations	588UNTS269	108531
21 Jun	Multilateral		ILO Labor	0UNTS0	109728
21 Jun	Multilateral		Non-ILO Labor	0UNTS0	109298
21 Jun	Romania	USSR (Soviet Union)	Land Transport	604UNTS81	108746
22 Jun	Netherlands	USA (United States)	Gen Communications	590UNTS109	108550
22 Jun	Australia	Bulgaria	General Trade	607UNTS69	108796
23 Jun	El Salvador	Mexico	Tech Assistance	68MEXD1403	444018
23 Jun	China People's Rep	Pakistan	Direct Aid	66CCJC56	411303
23 Jun	Austria	USA (United States)	Air Transport	601UNTS51	108687
24 Jun	Algeria	Germany, East	Education	44EGDZ362	420026
24 Jun	China People's Rep	Poland	Culture	66CCJC57	411304
24 Jun	IBRD (World Bank)	Thailand	IBRD Project	582UNTS259	108466
25 Jun	Afghanistan	Poland	Culture	72PDZU373	457137
27 Jun	China People's Rep	USSR (Soviet Union)	Culture	66CCJC59	411359
27 Jun	France	Yugoslavia	Tech Assistance	67FRJO504	416493
27 Jun	France	Germany, West	Culture	66FRRT24	415046
27 Jun	Denmark	Israel	Taxation	581UNTS227	108448
28 Jun	Germany, West	Vietnam, South	Direct Aid	0VKNG237	496063
28 Jun	Denmark	Jordan	Loans and Credits	574UNTS3	108338
28 Jun	Indonesia	USA (United States)	US Agri Commod Aid	593UNTS201	108585
29 Jun	India	IDA (Devel Assoc)	Non-IBRD Project	582UNTS277	108467
29 Jun	India	IDA (Devel Assoc)	Non-IBRD Project	585UNTS101	108484
30 Jun	Ceylon (Sri Lanka)	Germany, West	Loans and Credits	66WBGA160	424073
30 Jun	Germany, West	USA (United States)	Gen Communications	601UNTS107	108689
30 Jun	France	USSR (Soviet Union)	Scientific Project	589UNTS99	108537
30 Jun	France	USSR (Soviet Union)	Culture	589UNTS109	108538
01 Jul	Bulgaria	China People's Rep	Culture	66CCJC62	411082
02 Jul	China People's Rep	Vietnam, North	Direct Aid	66CCJC63	411367
04 Jul	China People's Rep	Pakistan	General Trade	66CCJC64	411290
04 Jul	China People's Rep	Germany, East	Scientific Project	66CCJC65	411170
04 Jul	Belgium	Turkey	Non-ILO Labor	0UNTS0	109397
05 Jul	China People's Rep	Korea, North	Tech Assistance	66CCJC66	411225
05 Jul	France	Refrigeration Inst	IGO Status/Immunit	67FRJO1203	416508
05 Jul	Ecuador	France	Culture	66FRJO2011	416160
05 Jul	Israel	UK Great Britain	Admin Cooperation	630UNTS189	108971
06 Jul	China People's Rep	Cuba	Tech Assistance	66CCJC67	411104
06 Jul	UK Great Britain	USA (United States)	Extradition	588UNTS137	108520
06 Jul	Bulgaria	USSR (Soviet Union)	Consul/Citizenship	596UNTS177	108632
07 Jul	Germany, East	Romania	Mass Media	48EGDZ363	420305
07 Jul	India	IBRD (World Bank)	IBRD Project	595UNTS3	108610
08 Jul	Multilateral		Atomic Energy	572UNTS283	108319
08 Jul	Brazil	Denmark	Loans and Credits	581UNTS95	108435
08 Jul	Netherlands	Tunisia	Tech Assistance	591UNTS235	108560
11 Jul	Israel	Mexico	Tech Assistance	68MEXD2510	444029
11 Jul	FAO (Food Agri)	IMCO (Maritime Org)	IGO Operations	575UNTS238	200627
11 Jul	Euratom	UK Great Britain	Taxation	639UNTS99	109147
11 Jul	Israel	Mexico	Tech Assistance	0UNTS0	109348

DATE	PARTY ONE	PARTY TWO	TOPIC	CITATION	NUMBER
1966 (Cont.)					
11 Jul	Gambia	Israel	Visas	582UNTS11	108453
12 Jul	Indonesia	Netherlands	Air Transport	0UNTS0	110164
12 Jul	Multilateral		Visas	578UNTS23	108384
12 Jul	Colombia	Israel	Visas	581UNTS181	108442
13 Jul	Norway	USA (United States)	Claims and Debts	3NORT972	451200
13 Jul	Argentina	Germany, West	Taxation	636UNTS3	109091
13 Jul	New Zealand	UK Great Britain	Taxation	598UNTS121	108658
15 Jul	Bulgaria	Tanzania	Scientific Project	0UNTS0	109962
15 Jul	Austria	France	Admin Cooperation	634UNTS3	109047
15 Jul	Austria	France	Admin Cooperation	604UNTS265	108755
17 Jul	Syria	Yugoslavia	Air Transport	0UNTS0	110165
18 Jul	France	USA (United States)	Consul/Citizenship	68FRRT7	415180
18 Jul	France	USA (United States)	Consul/Citizenship	0UNTS0	110044
19 Jul	Germany, West	Tunisia	Extradition	69WGBB1157	425689
19 Jul	Germany, West	Tunisia	Culture	67WGBB1210	425687
19 Jul	Germany, West	Tunisia	Admin Cooperation	69WGBB889	425688
19 Jul	Germany, West	Tunisia	Water Transport	67WBGA66	424686
19 Jul	Malawi	UK Great Britain	Admin Cooperation	637UNTS0	109125
19 Jul	Belgium	Spain	Land Transport	575UNTS3	108352
19 Jul	Colombia	Netherlands	Tech Assistance	591UNTS201	108558
20 Jul	Czechoslovakia	Germany, East	Admin Cooperation	45EGDZ364	420371
20 Jul	China People's Rep	Hungary	Culture	66CCJC69	411201
21 Jul	Dominican Republic	USA (United States)	Scientific Project	0UNTS0	109680
22 Jul	Benelux Econ Union	Japan	General Trade	66JJS31	442172
22 Jul	France	Spain	Admin Cooperation	67FRJO408	416169
22 Jul	France	Pakistan	Taxation	69FRMD25	417351
22 Jul	China People's Rep	Germany, East	Culture	66CCJC70	411187
22 Jul	France	Pakistan	Taxation	0UNTS0	109648
22 Jul	Iraq	IBRD (World Bank)	IBRD Project	584UNTS233	108480
24 Jul	Kuwait	USA (United States)	Gen Communications	593UNTS289	108590
25 Jul	China People's Rep	France	Air Transport	66CCJC71	411154
26 Jul	Jordan	UK Great Britain	Loans and Credits	597UNTS219	108647
26 Jul	Iran	IBRD (World Bank)	IBRD Project	582UNTS107	108461
26 Jul	Malaysia	IBRD (World Bank)	IBRD Project	586UNTS195	108504
27 Jul	Germany, West	Italy	Commodity Trade	67WBGA81	424304
27 Jul	China People's Rep	Sudan	General Trade	66CCJC72	411327
28 Jul	France	Hungary	Consul/Citizenship	67FRJO2210	416225
28 Jul	France	Hungary	Culture	67FRJO204	416227
28 Jul	France	United Arab Rep	Admin Cooperation	67FRJO810	416049
28 Jul	France	Hungary	Scientific Project	67FRJO201	416226
28 Jul	France	United Arab Rep	Visas	0UNTS0	110512
28 Jul	UK Great Britain	Zambia	Non-ILO Labor	590UNTS191	108554
28 Jul	Sweden	USA (United States)	Atomic Energy	603UNTS61	108725
29 Jul	Japan	USSR (Soviet Union)	Consul/Citizenship	67JHZ8	439004
29 Jul	Afghanistan	China People's Rep	General Economic	66CCJC73	411048
29 Jul	Bolivia	Taiwan	Admin Cooperation	0UNTS0	110434
29 Jul	Japan	USSR (Soviet Union)	Consul/Citizenship	608UNTS93	108815
29 Jul	Turkey	UK Great Britain	Loans and Credits	597UNTS241	108649
29 Jul	Japan	IBRD (World Bank)	IBRD Project	582UNTS209	108464
29 Jul	New Zealand	Western Samoa	Direct Aid	598UNTS115	108657
30 Jul	China People's Rep	Korea, North	Direct Aid	66CCJC74	411243
30 Jul	Tunisia	USA (United States)	US Agri Commod Aid	601UNTS133	108692
31 Jul	China People's Rep	Romania	Scientific Project	66CCJC75	411318
01 Aug	Germany, East	Hungary	Land Transport	49EGDZ365	420466
01 Aug	France	Italy	Culture	66FRRT40	415252
01 Aug	France	Italy	Mass Media	0UNTS0	110728
01 Aug	Ivory Coast	Netherlands	Education	591UNTS245	108561
02 Aug	Germany, East	United Arab Rep	Sanitation	49EGDZ365	420484
02 Aug	IDA (Devel Assoc)	Siam	Non-IBRD Project	585UNTS271	108492
02 Aug	Multilateral		Tech Assistance	582UNTS59	108457
03 Aug	Malta	USA (United States)	Milit Assistance	601UNTS125	108691
03 Aug	Israel	Malawi	Visas	582UNTS53	108456
04 Aug	Cyprus	Germany, East	Sanitation	50EGDZ365	420500
04 Aug	Bolivia	Germany, West	Culture	70WGBB977	425047
04 Aug	United Nations	Tunisia	IGO Operations	576UNTS23	108363

DATE	PARTY ONE	PARTY TWO	TOPIC	CITATION	NUMBER
1966 (Cont.)					
06 Aug	Multilateral		Tech Assistance	570UNTS178	108294
08 Aug	Iran	Romania	Specific Property	0IRTB60	433100
08 Aug	Germany, West	Malawi	Loans and Credits	66WBGA188	424446
08 Aug	Argentina	USA (United States)	Admin Cooperation	606UNTS209	108786
09 Aug	China People's Rep	Hungary	Scientific Project	66CCJC76	411194
10 Aug	IDA (Devel Assoc)	Turkey	Non-IBRD Project	585UNTS237	108491
10 Aug	IBRD (World Bank)	Turkey	IBRD Project	585UNTS199	108490
11 Aug	USA (United States)	Zambia	Finance	616UNTS267	108901
11 Aug	Netherlands	Yugoslavia	Culture	602UNTS243	108716
11 Aug	IBRD (World Bank)	Singapore	IBRD Project	585UNTS39	108482
12 Aug	India	Japan	Direct Aid	66JJS57	442173
12 Aug	Morocco	USA (United States)	US Agri Commod Aid	0UNTS0	109616
13 Aug	China People's Rep	Malagasy	Tech Assistance	66CCJC77	411264
19 Aug	Taiwan	Vietnam, South	Air Transport	0VKNG238	496064
19 Aug	Taiwan	Vietnam, South	Air Transport	0UNTS0	109241
19 Aug	India	IDA (Devel Assoc)	Non-IBRD Project	584UNTS193	108478
19 Aug	Kenya	IDA (Devel Assoc)	Non-IBRD Project	585UNTS119	108485
20 Aug	Ceylon (Sri Lanka)	Germany, West	Loans and Credits	66WBGA212	424074
21 Aug	Afghanistan	France	Health/Educ/Welfare	67FRJO801	416003
21 Aug	China People's Rep	Vietnam, North	Scientific Project	66CCJC78	411383
22 Aug	Iran	USSR (Soviet Union)	Culture	0IRTB79	433122
22 Aug	China People's Rep	Zambia	Culture	66CCJC80	411397
22 Aug	Multilateral		Tech Assistance	571UNTS298	200624
22 Aug	Guyana	United Nations	IGO Operations	571UNTS305	200625
22 Aug	Iran	USSR (Soviet Union)	Culture	643UNTS203	109192
23 Aug	Finland	Germany, East	Sanitation	40EGDZ366	420104
23 Aug	Japan	USA (United States)	Visas	606UNTS219	108787
24 Aug	Mexico	USA (United States)	Non-IBRD Project	606UNTS251	108789
25 Aug	Honduras	IBRD (World Bank)	IBRD Project	582UNTS79	108460
25 Aug	Jordan	USA (United States)	US Agri Commod Aid	606UNTS237	108788
26 Aug	UK Great Britain	USA (United States)	General Trade	0UNTS0	109769
26 Aug	Philippines	USA (United States)	Milit Installation	606UNTS259	108790
27 Aug	Ethiopia	France	Health/Educ/Welfare	67FRJO3103	416184
27 Aug	Ethiopia	France	Education	67FRJO3103	416185
27 Aug	Ethiopia	France	Culture	67FRJO3103	416186
27 Aug	Ethiopia	France	Culture	0UNTS0	110645
27 Aug	Ethiopia	France	Culture	0UNTS0	110644
27 Aug	Ethiopia	France	Culture	0UNTS0	110646
28 Aug	Kenya	Norway	Tech Assistance	3NORT973	451102
29 Aug	China People's Rep	Vietnam, North	Direct Aid	66CCJC81	411384
29 Aug	Bulgaria	United Arab Rep	Sanitation	0UNTS0	109963
29 Aug	Bulgaria	United Arab Rep	Sanitation	630UNTS325	108980
30 Aug	Germany, East	Syria	General Economic	42EGDZ366	420322
30 Aug	Singapore	USA (United States)	General Trade	616UNTS242	108899
31 Aug	Chad	USA (United States)	Direct Aid	606UNTS47	108773
01 Sep	Ireland	Japan	Visas	66JJS171	442174
01 Sep	Germany, East	USSR (Soviet Union)	Air Transport	34EGDZ367	420430
01 Sep	Malta	Portugal	Visas	579UNTS231	108410
01 Sep	Denmark	Malawi	Loans and Credits	586UNTS3	108493
01 Sep	Ireland	Japan	Visas	608UNTS339	108822
03 Sep	Romania	United Arab Rep	Direct Aid	604UNTS73	108745
06 Sep	Japan	USA (United States)	General Trade	616UNTS215	108898
07 Sep	Indonesia	Netherlands	Finance	0UNTS0	109779
07 Sep	Peru	IBRD (World Bank)	IBRD Project	585UNTS3	108481
08 Sep	Costa Rica	Mexico	Air Transport	70MEXD304	444010
08 Sep	Nigeria	Norway	Air Transport	3NORT974	451124
08 Sep	Netherlands	Yugoslavia	Land Transport	597UNTS147	108643
08 Sep	Denmark	Nigeria	Air Transport	591UNTS177	108557
08 Sep	IBRD (World Bank)	South Africa	IBRD Project	585UNTS71	108483
09 Sep	Norway	Singapore	Taxation	3NORT975	451140
09 Sep	Ceylon (Sri Lanka)	Japan	Loans and Credits	66JJS89	442175
09 Sep	France	Switzerland	Taxation	67FRJO1010	416420
09 Sep	Multilateral		IGO Status/Immunit	0UNTS0	109343
12 Sep	Canada	Israel	Telecommunications	581UNTS167	108440
12 Sep	Germany, West	Israel	Education	582UNTS17	108454

DATE	PARTY ONE	PARTY TWO	TOPIC	CITATION	NUMBER
1966 (Cont.)					
13 Sep	Germany, West	Morocco	Loans and Credits	66WBGA207	424467
13 Sep	Greece	Netherlands	Non-ILO Labor	0UNTS0	110746
13 Sep	Greece	Netherlands	Non-ILO Labor	0UNTS0	109833
13 Sep	Greece	Netherlands	Non-ILO Labor	596UNTS245	108637
14 Sep	Germany, East	Syria	Culture	37EGDZ367	420323
14 Sep	Korea, South	USA (United States)	Direct Aid	606UNTS55	108774
14 Sep	Iceland	IBRD (World Bank)	IBRD Project	598UNTS223	108660
15 Sep	Morocco	Senegal	General Amity	634UNTS105	109055
15 Sep	Argentina	UK Great Britain	Loans and Credits	603UNTS151	108732
16 Sep	IDA (Devel Assoc)	Tunisia	Loans and Credits	616UNTS285	108903
17 Sep	Germany, East	Mali	Mass Media	34EGDZ368	420206
18 Sep	Germany, East	Yugoslavia	Land Transport	34EGDZ368	420162
19 Sep	Japan	USA (United States)	Scientific Project	0TIAS6170	487003
19 Sep	El Salvador	Germany, West	Loans and Credits	67WBGA42	424130
19 Sep	Germany, West	Israel	Admin Cooperation	67WGBB719	425283
19 Sep	Japan	USA (United States)	Scientific Project	0UNTS0	109681
20 Sep	Bulgaria	Italy	General Economic	0UNTS0	109964
20 Sep	Nicaragua	USA (United States)	Gen Communications	607UNTS167	108804
20 Sep	Greece	Japan	Claims and Debts	609UNTS103	108828
21 Sep	Germany, West	Sweden	Other Military	66WBGA213	424618
21 Sep	UN Special Fund	UPU (Postal Union)	Non-IBRD Project	573UNTS259	200626
22 Sep	China People's Rep	France	Air Transport	68FRJO2801	416118
22 Sep	Germany, West	Netherlands	Land Transport	0UNTS0	109226
22 Sep	Netherlands	Norway	Taxation	600UNTS227	108683
23 Sep	Philippines	IBRD (World Bank)	IBRD Project	596UNTS71	108629
23 Sep	Multilateral		IGO Operations	573UNTS132	108327
23 Sep	Multilateral		General Aid	573UNTS148	108328
23 Sep	UN Special Fund	Singapore	General Aid	573UNTS115	108326
23 Sep	Belgium	France	Atomic Energy	588UNTS227	108528
24 Sep	Korea, South	USA (United States)	Admin Cooperation	607UNTS157	108803
26 Sep	IAEA (Atom Energy)	USA (United States)	Atomic Energy	589UNTS3	108532
26 Sep	Tunisia	USA (United States)	Scientific Project	616UNTS259	108900
26 Sep	Hungary	Yugoslavia	Sanitation	601UNTS21	108685
27 Sep	Austria	Germany, West	Commodity Trade	66WBGA235	424554
28 Sep	Philippines	IAEA (Atom Energy)	Atomic Energy	589UNTS25	108533
28 Sep	Multilateral		Specif Goods/Equip	589UNTS41	108534
29 Sep	Japan	Philippines	Education	66JJS221	442176
29 Sep	China People's Rep	Mongolia	Culture	66CCJC82	411265
29 Sep	IDA (Devel Assoc)	Senegal	Non-IBRD Project	594UNTS277	108607
29 Sep	USSR (Soviet Union)	Yugoslavia	General Aid	608UNTS219	108818
30 Sep	Cambodia	Japan	Tech Assistance	66JJS53	442177
30 Sep	Botswana	UK Great Britain	Consul/Citizenship	633UNTS339	109044
30 Sep	Botswana	USA (United States)	Admin Cooperation	0UNTS0	109682
30 Sep	Indonesia	USA (United States)	US Agri Commod Aid	616UNTS199	108897
30 Sep	Botswana	UN Special Fund	IGO Operations	576UNTS3	108360
30 Sep	Accept UN Charter	Botswana	UN Charter	575UNTS151	108357
30 Sep	Multilateral		IGO Operations	576UNTS8	108361
30 Sep	Botswana	United Nations	Tech Assistance	576UNTS17	108362
30 Sep	Jamaica	IBRD (World Bank)	IBRD Project	582UNTS179	108463
30 Sep	Canada	USA (United States)	Milit Installation	616UNTS193	108896
30 Sep	Botswana	UK Great Britain	Status of Forces	597UNTS211	108646
01 Oct	Germany, East	Yugoslavia	Consul/Citizenship	46EGDZ369	420163
03 Oct	Germany, East	Hungary	Mass Media	45EGDZ369	420467
03 Oct	Congo (Zaire)	USA (United States)	US Agri Commod Aid	0UNTS0	109683
03 Oct	Multilateral		Culture	610UNTS169	108841
03 Oct	Bulgaria	Poland	Culture	618UNTS3	108921
04 Oct	Lesotho	USA (United States)	Admin Cooperation	0UNTS0	109684
04 Oct	Accept UN Charter	Lesotho	UN Charter	575UNTS155	108358
04 Oct	Malawi	IDA (Devel Assoc)	Non-IBRD Project	584UNTS215	108479
04 Oct	IBRD (World Bank)	Zambia	IBRD Project	585UNTS181	108489
05 Oct	Nicaragua	IBRD (World Bank)	IBRD Project	582UNTS231	108465
06 Oct	Canada	USA (United States)	Scientific Project	0UNTS0	109607
07 Oct	Brazil	Japan	Loans and Credits	68JJS39	442178
07 Oct	Chile	UK Great Britain	Tech Assistance	603UNTS167	108733
08 Oct	France	Hungary	Land Transport	67FRJO3003	416228

DATE	PARTY ONE	PARTY TWO	TOPIC	CITATION	NUMBER
1966 (Cont.)					
10 Oct	Germany, East	Vietnam, North	Education	46EGDZ369	420497
10 Oct	Germany, East	Vietnam, North	Loans and Credits	46EGDZ369	420496
10 Oct	China People's Rep	Tanzania	Direct Aid	66CCJC83	411340
10 Oct	Austria	Yugoslavia	Visas	595UNTS273	108622
10 Oct	Argentina	Vatican/Holy See	Consul/Citizenship	601UNTS187	108696
12 Oct	Austria	Turkey	Non-ILO Labor	69ABGB338	403201
12 Oct	China People's Rep	Vietnam, North	Sanitation	66CCJC84	411385
12 Oct	Netherlands	Portugal	Non-ILO Labor	0UNTS0	109273
12 Oct	Brazil	Netherlands	Culture	643UNTS271	109197
12 Oct	Greece	UK Great Britain	Other Military	578UNTS33	108385
15 Oct	Japan	Singapore	Education	66JJS247	442179
15 Oct	Bulgaria	Germany, East	Finance	34EGDZ370	420071
15 Oct	Bulgaria	France	Culture	67FRJO204	416089
15 Oct	Bulgaria	France	Tech Assistance	67FRJO204	416088
17 Oct	Brazil	Mexico	Air Transport	71MEXD903	444003
17 Oct	Austria	Germany, West	Admin Cooperation	67WGBB2318	425555
17 Oct	Austria	Tunisia	Air Transport	67ABGB251	403198
17 Oct	Mauritania	USA (United States)	Direct Aid	0UNTS0	109618
17 Oct	Mauritania	USSR (Soviet Union)	General Trade	633UNTS231	109040
18 Oct	Japan	Korea, South	Specific Resources	66JJS187	442180
18 Oct	China People's Rep	Nepal	Direct Aid	66CCJC85	411280
18 Oct	Niger	Tunisia	Air Transport	0UNTS0	110468
18 Oct	Bulgaria	Mongolia	Visas	0UNTS0	110301
18 Oct	Netherlands	Nigeria	Education	603UNTS53	108724
19 Oct	Brazil	USA (United States)	Education	0UNTS0	109685
19 Oct	Italy	USA (United States)	Commodity Trade	0UNTS0	109686
19 Oct	IBRD (World Bank)	Thailand	IBRD Project	594UNTS347	108609
20 Oct	Japan	Tanzania	Direct Aid	66JJS317	442181
20 Oct	Albania	China People's Rep	Loans and Credits	66CCJC86	411074
21 Oct	China People's Rep	Pakistan	Water Transport	66CCJC87	411305
22 Oct	Germany, East	Iraq	Air Transport	36EGDZ370	420141
23 Oct	China People's Rep	Somalia	Non-ILO Labor	66CCJC88	411328
25 Oct	Bulgaria	Germany, East	Land Transport	36EGDZ370	420072
25 Oct	Colombia	USA (United States)	Tech Assistance	0UNTS0	109687
26 Oct	Mexico	USA (United States)	Education	0UNTS0	109619
27 Oct	Honduras	Mexico	Tech Assistance	68MEXD1902	444026
27 Oct	Germany, West	Ivory Coast	Claims and Debts	68WBGA61	424124
27 Oct	Morocco	USSR (Soviet Union)	Scientific Project	608UNTS197	108816
27 Oct	Paraguay	UK Great Britain	Visas	597UNTS229	108648
27 Oct	Morocco	USSR (Soviet Union)	Mass Media	608UNTS207	108817
27 Oct	UK Great Britain	USA (United States)	Claims and Debts	597UNTS265	108650
28 Oct	China People's Rep	Czechoslovakia	Scientific Project	66CCJC90	411146
28 Oct	IBRD (World Bank)	IFC (Finance Corp)	Loans and Credits	586UNTS225	200628
30 Oct	Germany, East	Syria	Tech Assistance	37EGDZ370	420324
02 Nov	Israel	Norway	Taxation	630UNTS225	108972
04 Nov	Austria	Japan	General Trade	66JJS1	442182
04 Nov	USA (United States)	USSR (Soviet Union)	Air Transport	0UNTS0	109606
04 Nov	Paraguay	USA (United States)	Direct Aid	0UNTS0	109620
04 Nov	IBRD (World Bank)	Singapore	IBRD Project	585UNTS155	108488
06 Nov	China People's Rep	USSR (Soviet Union)	Scientific Project	66CCJC91	411345
08 Nov	Ireland	Switzerland	Taxation	0UNTS0	109499
08 Nov	United Nations	Sudan	Scientific Project	576UNTS85	108365
11 Nov	Philippines	Sweden	Visas	587UNTS3	108505
14 Nov	Romania	United Arab Rep	General Trade	642UNTS129	109169
14 Nov	Romania	United Arab Rep	Finance	642UNTS141	109170
15 Nov	Iceland	Japan	Visas	66JJS153	442183
15 Nov	Bulgaria	Iraq	Air Transport	0UNTS0	109965
16 Nov	China People's Rep	Guinea	General Trade	66CCJC95	411191
16 Nov	China People's Rep	Guinea	General Economic	66CCJC92	411188
16 Nov	China People's Rep	Guinea	Direct Aid	66CCJC93	411189
16 Nov	China People's Rep	Guinea	Loans and Credits	66CCJC94	411190
16 Nov	Panama	USA (United States)	Gen Communications	0UNTS0	109688
16 Nov	Malta	USA (United States)	Finance	0UNTS0	109837
17 Nov	Indonesia	UNICEF (Children)	IGO Operations	578UNTS47	108386
17 Nov	Lesotho	UN Special Fund	Recognition	580UNTS17	108416

DATE	PARTY ONE	PARTY TWO	TOPIC	CITATION	NUMBER
1966 (Cont.)					
17 Nov	Multilateral		IGO Operations	580UNTS22	108417
17 Nov	Lesotho	United Nations	IGO Operations	580UNTS29	108418
19 Nov	Kenya	Netherlands	Admin Cooperation	643UNTS285	109198
21 Nov	Albania	China People's Rep	General Economic	66CCJC96	411075
21 Nov	Malawi	UK Great Britain	Admin Cooperation	637UNTS0	109126
21 Nov	Pakistan	USA (United States)	Commodity Trade	0UNTS0	109689
22 Nov	Afghanistan	IBRD (World Bank)	IBRD Project	632UNTS171	109019
22 Nov	ICJ Option Clause	Malawi	ICJ Option Clause	581UNTS135	108438
23 Nov	China People's Rep	Vietnam, North	General Economic	66CCJC99	411386
23 Nov	Denmark	Ivory Coast	General Trade	0UNTS0	110554
23 Nov	Ghana	Romania	Loans and Credits	642UNTS79	109166
23 Nov	Ghana	Romania	General Trade	642UNTS63	109165
23 Nov	Canada	Norway	Taxation	604UNTS295	108757
23 Nov	Taiwan	Thailand	General Trade	581UNTS125	108436
24 Nov	Germany, West	Morocco	General Economic	67WBGA49	424470
24 Nov	Germany, West	Morocco	Loans and Credits	67WBGA49	424468
24 Nov	Germany, West	Morocco	Water Transport	67WBGA49	424469
24 Nov	Central Afri Rep	USA (United States)	Direct Aid	0UNTS0	109690
26 Nov	Kuwait	UK Great Britain	Culture	633UNTS58	109034
28 Nov	Eur Space Research	USA (United States)	Scientific Project	0UNTS0	109691
29 Nov	Germany, West	Uganda	Claims and Debts	68WGBB449	425701
29 Nov	Ceylon (Sri Lanka)	China People's Rep	General Trade	66CCJC100	411147
29 Nov	Ceylon (Sri Lanka)	China People's Rep	Commodity Trade	66CCJC101	411148
29 Nov	Congo (Brazzaville)	Czechoslovakia	Culture	635UNTS3	109069
29 Nov	ICJ Option Clause	Malta	ICJ Option Clause	580UNTS205	108423
30 Nov	Albania	China People's Rep	Tech Assistance	66CCJC102	411076
30 Nov	Brazil	Bulgaria	Finance	0UNTS0.	109874
30 Nov	Accept UN Charter	United Arab Rep	UN Charter	581UNTS131	108437
30 Nov	Canada	Israel	Taxation	630UNTS267	108973
01 Dec	Guinea	Romania	General Trade	642UNTS89	109167
01 Dec	Singapore	UK Great Britain	Taxation	605UNTS153	108763
01 Dec	Indonesia	UK Great Britain	Claims and Debts	606UNTS125	108782
03 Dec	China People's Rep	Korea, North	General Trade	66CCJC103	411226
03 Dec	Mexico	USA (United States)	Admin Cooperation	0UNTS0	109692
03 Dec	Peru	UK Great Britain	Loans and Credits	617UNTS231	108915
05 Dec	Chile	Germany, East	Culture	34EGDZ373	420078
05 Dec	Germany, West	Liberia	Loans and Credits	67WBGA40	424412
05 Dec	Gambia	USA (United States)	Direct Aid	0UNTS0	109693
06 Dec	Jamaica	United Nations	IGO Operations	580UNTS211	108424
08 Dec	Germany, West	Kenya	Loans and Credits	67WBGA52	424359
08 Dec	France	USSR (Soviet Union)	Consul/Citizenship	69FRJO1610	416473
08 Dec	France	USSR (Soviet Union)	Consul/Citizenship	0UNTS0	110363
08 Dec	France	USSR (Soviet Union)	Consul/Citizenship	0UNTS0	110031
08 Dec	IAEA (Atom Energy)	Turkey	Atomic Energy	608UNTS69	108813
09 Dec	Hungary	Norway	General Trade	3NORT981	451075
09 Dec	France	Monaco	Finance	0UNTS0	109439
09 Dec	Czechoslovakia	Mongolia	Sanitation	637UNTS0	109124
09 Dec	IAEA (Atom Energy)	USA (United States)	Atomic Energy	589UNTS55	108535
09 Dec	India	IAEA (Atom Energy)	Atomic Energy	603UNTS35	108722
09 Dec	Australia	USA (United States)	Scientific Project	607UNTS83	108798
10 Dec	Germany, West	Zambia	Claims and Debts	68WGBB33	425610
10 Dec	Germany, West	Zambia	General Economic	67WBGA51	424607
10 Dec	Germany, West	Zambia	Loans and Credits	67WBGA51	424608
10 Dec	Germany, West	Zambia	Tech Assistance	67WBGA51	424609
12 Dec	Korea, South	Mexico	General Trade	70MEXD2904	444006
12 Dec	Algeria	Germany, East	General Trade	41EGDZ374	420027
12 Dec	UK Great Britain	USA (United States)	Scientific Project	603UNTS235	108735
13 Dec	Canada	UK Great Britain	Non-ILO Labor	0UNTS0	109274
14 Dec	Norway	Philippines	Visas	591UNTS253	108562
15 Dec	USA (United States)	Vietnam, South	US Agri Commod Aid	0VKNG319	496080
15 Dec	USA (United States)	Vietnam, South	US Agri Commod Aid	0UNTS0	109695
16 Dec	India	Japan	Loans and Credits	66JJS161	442184
16 Dec	Guatemala	Mexico	Culture	67MEXD402	444024
16 Dec	Germany, West	USA (United States)	Culture	0UNTS0	109694
18 Dec	Syria	USSR (Soviet Union)	Non-IBRD Project	633UNTS247	109041

DATE	PARTY ONE	PARTY TWO	TOPIC	CITATION	NUMBER
1966 (Cont.)					
19 Dec	Argentina	Bolivia	Air Transport	0UNTSO	110180
19 Dec	Iran	USA (United States)	US Agri Commod Aid	0UNTSO	109696
19 Dec	Argentina	Bolivia	Telecommunications	636UNTS89	109094
19 Dec	Argentina	Bolivia	Education	636UNTS83	109093
19 Dec	Argentina	Bolivia	Tech Assistance	636UNTS75	109092
19 Dec	Multilateral		Specific Resources	605UNTS313	108769
19 Dec	Denmark	Norway	Specific Resources	606UNTS3	108770
19 Dec	Brazil	IBRD (World Bank)	IBRD Project	599UNTS205	108668
19 Dec	Brazil	IBRD (World Bank)	IBRD Project	599UNTS149	108666
19 Dec	Brazil	IBRD (World Bank)	IBRD Project	599UNTS177	108667
19 Dec	Brazil	IBRD (World Bank)	IBRD Project	599UNTS107	108665
20 Dec	Norway	Singapore	Air Transport	3NORT985	451141
20 Dec	Norway	Singapore	Air Transport	0UNTSO	109242
20 Dec	Jamaica	USA (United States)	Admin Cooperation	0UNTSO	109698
20 Dec	Afghanistan	USA (United States)	US Agri Commod Aid	0UNTSO	109699
20 Dec	Singapore	Sweden	Air Transport	0UNTSO	109243
20 Dec	Iran	USA (United States)	US Agri Commod Aid	0UNTSO	109697
20 Dec	Austria	Spain	Taxation	636UNTS197	109103
20 Dec	Denmark	Singapore	Air Transport	593UNTS125	108580
20 Dec	Denmark	Philippines	Visas	591UNTS259	108563
21 Dec	Algeria	Germany, East	Air Transport	41EGDZ374	420029
21 Dec	Algeria	Germany, East	Culture	41EGDZ374	420028
21 Dec	China People's Rep	Nepal	Direct Aid	66CCJC104	411281
21 Dec	Austria	Malta	Visas	595UNTS307	108625
22 Dec	Austria	Germany, West	Non-ILO Labor	69WGBB1233	425556
22 Dec	France	Nicaragua	Health/Educ/Welfare	68FRJO1105	416338
22 Dec	Multilateral		Taxation	0UNTSO	109980
22 Dec	Austria	Germany, West	Non-ILO Labor	0UNTSO	110090
22 Dec	Guinea	UNICEF (Children)	IGO Operations	585UNTS137	108486
22 Dec	Asian Devel Bank	Philippines	IGO Establishment	615UNTS375	108887
22 Dec	Philippines	USA (United States)	Other Military	579UNTS203	108408
22 Dec	Philippines	USA (United States)	US Agri Commod Aid	591UNTS219	108559
23 Dec	Germany, West	USA (United States)	Education	68WBGA21	424722
23 Dec	Algeria	France	Health/Educ/Welfare	67FRJO3003	416024
23 Dec	India	IDA (Devel Assoc)	Non-IBRD Project	594UNTS165	108603
23 Dec	Denmark	Norway	General Trade	613UNTS265	108855
23 Dec	Chile	IBRD (World Bank)	IBRD Project	595UNTS141	108618
23 Dec	Pakistan	IDA (Devel Assoc)	Non-IBRD Project	594UNTS255	108606
24 Dec	Iran	USSR (Soviet Union)	Sanitation	0IRTB78	433120
27 Dec	Norway	Turkey	Loans and Credits	3NORT987	451181
28 Dec	Afghanistan	China People's Rep	General Trade	66CCJC105	411049
28 Dec	UK Great Britain	USA (United States)	Direct Aid	0UNTSO	109700
28 Dec	Malta	USA (United States)	General Military	0UNTSO	109838
28 Dec	Luxembourg	United Nations	Claims and Debts	585UNTS147	108487
29 Dec	Austria	Switzerland	Taxation	67ABGB355	403183
29 Dec	Germany, West	USA (United States)	General Aid	0UNTSO	109839
29 Dec	Trinidad/Tobago	UK Great Britain	Taxation	605UNTS237	108766
29 Dec	Kuwait	UK Great Britain	Postal Service	617UNTS203	108914
30 Dec	China People's Rep	Korea, North	Mass Media	66CCJC106	411244
30 Dec	UK Great Britain	USA (United States)	Scientific Project	603UNTS245	108736
30 Dec	UK Great Britain	USA (United States)	General Military	603UNTS273	108737
1967					
01 Jan	UK Great Britain	USA (United States)	Scientific Project	604UNTS3	108738
03 Jan	Austria	Czechoslovakia	Visas	67ABGB348	403025
03 Jan	AID (Int Devel)	IBRD (World Bank)	Direct Aid	619UNTS321	200635
04 Jan	Philippines	USA (United States)	Customs	590UNTS51	108546
05 Jan	Romania	Spain	Consul/Citizenship	642UNTS103	109168
05 Jan	UK Great Britain	Yugoslavia	Mass Media	604UNTS13	108739
07 Jan	Indonesia	USA (United States)	Finance	0UNTSO	109896
09 Jan	Congo (Brazzaville)	IBRD (World Bank)	IBRD Project	598UNTS161	108659
10 Jan	Gabon	Germany, West	Loans and Credits	67WBGA63	424209
10 Jan	UK Great Britain	USA (United States)	General Aid	0UNTSO	109840
11 Jan	Germany, West	UK Great Britain	Commodity Trade	67WBGA22	424716
11 Jan	UK Great Britain	USA (United States)	General Aid	0UNTSO	109841

DATE	PARTY ONE	PARTY TWO	TOPIC	CITATION	NUMBER
1967 (Cont.)					
12 Jan	Greece	USA (United States)	General Military	0UNTSO	109842
13 Jan	Australia	Mexico	Visas	607UNTS77	108797
16 Jan	Korea, South	Vietnam, South	Air Transport	0VKNG241	496066
16 Jan	Korea, South	Vietnam, South	Claims and Debts	0VKNG240	496065
16 Jan	Brazil	France	Tech Assistance	69FRJO2704	416081
16 Jan	Brazil	France	Tech Assistance	0UNTSO	110230
16 Jan	Finland	United Nations	Education	588UNTS153	108522
17 Jan	China People's Rep	Pakistan	Direct Aid	67CCJC1	411306
18 Jan	UK Great Britain	USA (United States)	General Aid	0UNTSO	109843
18 Jan	Italy	United Nations	Specif Claim/Waive	588UNTS197	108525
19 Jan	France	Germany, West	Atomic Energy	67WGBB2430	425200
23 Jan	Argentina	Paraguay	Water Transport	634UNTS181	109060
23 Jan	Argentina	Paraguay	General Trade	634UNTS193	109061
23 Jan	Trinidad/Tobago	UK Great Britain	Telecommunications	605UNTS277	108767
23 Jan	Jamaica	IBRD (World Bank)	IBRD Project	594UNTS311	108608
24 Jan	Brazil	Japan	Taxation	67JHZ12	439005
24 Jan	Brazil	Japan	Taxation	0UNTSO	109716
25 Jan	Multilateral		IGO Operations	588UNTS212	108527
26 Jan	China People's Rep	Finland	Patents/Copyrights	67CCJC2	411155
26 Jan	Morocco	IBRD (World Bank)	IBRD Project	642UNTS3	109160
26 Jan	IBRD (World Bank)	Venezuela	IBRD Project	596UNTS35	108628
27 Jan	Brazil	USA (United States)	Milit Installation	0UNTSO	109844
27 Jan	Brazil	Israel	Commodity Trade	0UNTSO	109845
27 Jan	Multilateral		Scientific Project	610UNTS205	108843
27 Jan	Netherlands	Uganda	Extradition	608UNTS345	108823
28 Jan	Israel	Mexico	Scientific Project	0UNTSO	109846
31 Jan	Central Afri Rep	Germany, West	Loans and Credits	67WBGA73	424734
31 Jan	Bulgaria	China People's Rep	General Economic	67CCJC3	411092
31 Jan	Korea, South	New Zealand	General Trade	598UNTS91	108656
31 Jan	Multilateral		Refugees	606UNTS267	108791
02 Feb	Denmark	Germany, West	Dispute Settlement	606UNTS97	108778
02 Feb	Germany, West	Netherlands	Dispute Settlement	606UNTS105	108779
02 Feb	UNICEF (Children)	Zambia	IGO Operations	589UNTS89	108536
02 Feb	Multilateral		Dispute Settlement	606UNTS89	108777
02 Feb	Iran	Thailand	General Amity	614UNTS251	108874
03 Feb	Germany, West	Togo	Loans and Credits	67WBGA136	424664
03 Feb	Czechoslovakia	USSR (Soviet Union)	Land Transport	617UNTS267	108917
06 Feb	Australia	UN Special Fund	IGO Operations	590UNTS3	108543
07 Feb	Nigeria	United Nations	IGO Operations	590UNTS25	108544
08 Feb	African Insur Org	France	IGO Status/Immunit	67FRJO212	416509
09 Feb	Bulgaria	Iran	General Trade	0IRTB16	433026
09 Feb	Bulgaria	Iran	General Economic	0IRTB16	433028
09 Feb	Bulgaria	Iran	Finance	0IRTB16	433027
09 Feb	Israel	UK Great Britain	Visas	0UNTSO	109349
09 Feb	Korea, South	USA (United States)	Milit Installation	0UNTSO	109605
09 Feb	Kenya	Netherlands	General Aid	0UNTSO	109780
09 Feb	Kenya	Netherlands	Non-ILO Labor	610UNTSO	108833
09 Feb	ILO (Labor Org)	Senegal	IGO Establishment	600UNTS75	108677
10 Feb	Morocco	USA (United States)	Culture	0UNTSO	109847
11 Feb	France	Korea, South	Visas	67FRJO1204	416133
12 Feb	Argentina	Uruguay	Water Transport	635UNTS125	109076
12 Feb	Bulgaria	United Arab Rep	Gen Communications	630UNTS353	108981
12 Feb	Bulgaria	United Arab Rep	Telecommunications	630UNTS363	108982
13 Feb	Greece	Japan	General Trade	67JJS201	442185
13 Feb	France	Romania	Sanitation	67FRJO508	416379
13 Feb	USA (United States)	USSR (Soviet Union)	Specific Resources	0UNTSO	109848
13 Feb	Netherlands	Romania	Culture	604UNTS287	108756
14 Feb	Japan	Singapore	Air Transport	67JHZ8	439006
14 Feb	China People's Rep	Romania	General Economic	67CCJC4	411319
14 Feb	India	USA (United States)	Scientific Project	0UNTSO	109752
14 Feb	France	UK Great Britain	Non-ILO Labor	0UNTSO	109493
14 Feb	Japan	Singapore	Air Transport	0UNTSO	109244
14 Feb	Multilateral		General Military	634UNTS281	109068
14 Feb	Denmark	Israel	Admin Cooperation	620UNTS211	108957
15 Feb	France	Mali	Finance	67FRJO2706	416292

DATE	PARTY ONE	PARTY TWO	TOPIC	CITATION	NUMBER
1967 (Cont.)					
15 Feb	Denmark	France	Culture	604UNTS247	108754
15 Feb	France	UK Great Britain	Admin Cooperation	606UNTS119	108781
16 Feb	China People's Rep	Mauritania	Direct Aid	67CCJC6	411267
16 Feb	China People's Rep	Mauritania	Culture	67CCJC7	411268
16 Feb	China People's Rep	Mauritania	General Trade	67CCJC5	411266
16 Feb	Algeria	Ivory Coast	Air Transport	0UNTS0	109245
17 Feb	East Afri Service	IBRD (World Bank)	IBRD Project	599UNTS335	200629
17 Feb	Bulgaria	Lebanon	Air Transport	0UNTS0	110538
17 Feb	India	Netherlands	Direct Aid	0UNTS0	109389
17 Feb	Lesotho	UK Great Britain	Admin Cooperation	632UNTS3	109004
17 Feb	Kenya	IBRD (World Bank)	IBRD Project	599UNTS233	108669
17 Feb	IBRD (World Bank)	Tanzania	IBRD Project	599UNTS287	108671
17 Feb	IBRD (World Bank)	Uganda	IBRD Project	599UNTS321	108673
17 Feb	Argentina	UK Great Britain	Visas	617UNTS193	108913
18 Feb	Romania	USA (United States)	Tech Assistance	0UNTS0	109849
20 Feb	India	USA (United States)	US Agri Commod Aid	0UNTS0	109850
20 Feb	Israel	Philippines	Atomic Energy	597UNTS139	108642
20 Feb	Poland	United Nations	IGO Operations	590UNTS71	108547
21 Feb	United Arab Rep	USA (United States)	Culture	0UNTS0	109851
21 Feb	IBRD (World Bank)	Tunisia	IBRD Project	618UNTS39	108923
21 Feb	Indonesia	Philippines	Gen Communications	593UNTS109	108578
21 Feb	IDA (Devel Assoc)	Tunisia	Non-IBRD Project	618UNTS69	108924
22 Feb	Belgium	Luxembourg	Culture	639UNTS3	109140
23 Feb	Poland	UK Great Britain	Consul/Citizenship	71PDZU186	457139
23 Feb	Korea, South	USA (United States)	General Aid	0UNTS0	109852
24 Feb	Turkey	USSR (Soviet Union)	Scientific Project	643UNTS153	109190
24 Feb	Lesotho	USA (United States)	Finance	0UNTS0	109853
24 Feb	Multilateral		Health/Educ/Welfare	596UNTS133	108631
24 Feb	IBRD (World Bank)	Yugoslavia	IBRD Project	599UNTS27	108663
24 Feb	UK Great Britain	USSR (Soviet Union)	Scientific Project	606UNTS171	108785
25 Feb	France	Niger	Mass Media	68FRJO204	416345
25 Feb	France	Niger	Mass Media	0UNTS0	109261
27 Feb	Bulgaria	China People's Rep	Scientific Project	67CCJC9	411093
27 Feb	Ghana	UK Great Britain	Claims and Debts	606UNTS133	108783
27 Feb	Multilateral		IGO Operations	590UNTS156	108552
27 Feb	Congo (Brazzaville)	Denmark	Air Transport	600UNTS189	108681
28 Feb	Germany, West	Luxembourg	Specif Claim/Waive	67WGBB1694	425436
01 Mar	Austria	UK Great Britain	Air Transport	67ABGB119	403214
01 Mar	Romania	Sweden	General Transport	642UNTS163	109172
01 Mar	Trinidad/Tobago	UK Great Britain	Air Transport	606UNTS149	108784
01 Mar	Czechoslovakia	Poland	General Amity	632UNTS255	109027
03 Mar	Ghana	USA (United States)	US Agri Commod Aid	0UNTS0	109854
03 Mar	Multilateral		Tech Assistance	594UNTS96	108597
03 Mar	Barbados	UN Special Fund	Tech Assistance	594UNTS91	108596
06 Mar	Norway	UK Great Britain	Non-ILO Labor	3NORT991	451151
06 Mar	Bulgaria	Sudan	Scientific Project	0UNTS0	109966
06 Mar	Taiwan	USA (United States)	Water Transport	0UNTS0	109753
07 Mar	Germany, West	Switzerland	Patents/Copyrights	69WGBB138	425764
07 Mar	Congo (Zaire)	Germany, West	Loans and Credits	67WBGA98	424386
07 Mar	Cameroon	USA (United States)	Finance	0UNTS0	109855
08 Mar	Germany, West	Mexico	Air Transport	69WGBB193	425480
09 Mar	Austria	UK Great Britain	Other Military	67ABGB192	403216
09 Mar	Romania	UK Great Britain	Scientific Project	605UNTS195	108764
09 Mar	Multilateral		Other Military	603UNTS135	108730
10 Mar	Canada	Israel	Extradition	0UNTS0	110380
10 Mar	State/IGO Group	IAEA (Atom Energy)	Atomic Energy	0UNTS0	109526
10 Mar	IBRD (World Bank)	Trinidad/Tobago	IBRD Project	599UNTS3	108662
10 Mar	Guatemala	IBRD (World Bank)	Loans and Credits	616UNTS139	108894
13 Mar	USA (United States)	Vietnam, South	US Agri Commod Aid	0VKNG244	496067
13 Mar	Germany, West	NATO (North Atlan)	Military Mission	69WGBB1997	425744
13 Mar	Iran	USSR (Soviet Union)	Sanitation	0IRTB78	433119
13 Mar	USA (United States)	Vietnam, South	US Agri Commod Aid	0UNTS0	109754
13 Mar	Nicaragua	IBRD (World Bank)	IBRD Project	632UNTS177	109020
14 Mar	Japan	OECD (Econ Coop)	IGO Status/Immunit	67JHZ7	439007
14 Mar	Germany, West	Jordan	Loans and Credits	67WBGA90	424314

DATE	PARTY ONE	PARTY TWO	TOPIC	CITATION	NUMBER
1967 (Cont.)					
14 Mar	China People's Rep	Nepal	Direct Aid	67CCJC10	411282
14 Mar	France	USSR (Soviet Union)	Patents/Copyrights	68FRJO2103	416474
14 Mar	France	WHO (World Health)	IGO Operations	0UNTS0	110667
14 Mar	France	USSR (Soviet Union)	Taxation	0UNTS0	109330
15 Mar	Congo (Zaire)	USA (United States)	US Agri Commod Aid	0UNTS0	109897
15 Mar	Poland	USA (United States)	Commodity Trade	0UNTS0	109856
15 Mar	Pakistan	IBRD (World Bank)	IBRD Project	599UNTS245	108670
15 Mar	Germany, East	Poland	General Amity	618UNTS21	108922
16 Mar	Germany, West	USA (United States)	Commodity Trade	67WBGA150	424723
16 Mar	Cuba	France	Claims and Debts	46FRJO7041	416144
16 Mar	Multilateral		Gen Communications	0UNTS0	109755
17 Mar	India	Norway	Specific Resources	3NORT992	451079
17 Mar	Tunisia	USA (United States)	US Agri Commod Aid	0UNTS0	109898
17 Mar	Romania	UK Great Britain	Air Transport	0UNTS0	109706
17 Mar	Multilateral		Non-IBRD Project	594UNTS105	108598
17 Mar	Czechoslovakia	Germany, East	General Amity	609UNTS187	108831
20 Mar	France	Spain	Specific Resources	67FRJO408	416170
20 Mar	France	Spain	Specific Resources	0UNTS0	110234
20 Mar	Belgium	Sweden	Land Transport	0UNTS0	109795
20 Mar	Belgium	Hungary	Land Transport	601UNTS37	108686
21 Mar	Pakistan	Poland	Admin Cooperation	67PZUM69	458140
21 Mar	China People's Rep	Cuba	General Trade	67CCJC11	411149
22 Mar	Australia	Austria	Air Transport	67ABGB152	403002
22 Mar	Australia	Austria	Air Transport	0UNTS0	109246
23 Mar	France	Yugoslavia	Air Transport	67FRJO410	416494
23 Mar	Portugal	USA (United States)	Commodity Trade	0UNTS0	109857
23 Mar	Belgium	Israel	Culture	630UNTS275	108974
24 Mar	France	USA (United States)	Specific Property	0UNTS0	109858
24 Mar	Netherlands	Vietnam, South	Sanitation	610UNTS0	108834
24 Mar	IBRD (World Bank)	Thailand	IBRD Project	599UNTS299	108672
25 Mar	Korea, South	USA (United States)	US Agri Commod Aid	0UNTS0	109756
27 Mar	Kuwait	USSR (Soviet Union)	Culture	643UNTS135	109189
28 Mar	Bulgaria	Japan	General Trade	67JJS103	442190
28 Mar	Philippines	USA (United States)	Water Transport	0UNTS0	109757
28 Mar	Cameroon	IDA (Devel Assoc)	Non-IBRD Project	618UNTS133	108926
28 Mar	Haiti	Israel	General Amity	630UNTS293	108975
28 Mar	Cameroon	IBRD (World Bank)	IBRD Project	618UNTS89	108925
29 Mar	Denmark	Lebanon	Taxation	602UNTS251	108717
30 Mar	Germany, West	Vietnam, South	Humanitarian	67WGBB2105	425729
30 Mar	Denmark	Germany, West	Customs	69WGBB937	425104
30 Mar	Denmark	Germany, West	Customs	0UNTS0	109975
31 Mar	Norway	Zambia	Tech Assistance	3NORT993	451220
31 Mar	Germany, West	UK Great Britain	Commodity Trade	67WBGA83	424717
31 Mar	Argentina	USA (United States)	Gen Communications	636UNTS103	109096
31 Mar	Argentina	USA (United States)	Gen Communications	636UNTS95	109095
01 Apr	Taiwan	USA (United States)	Water Transport	0UNTS0	109758
03 Apr	Malaysia	USSR (Soviet Union)	General Trade	0UNTS0	109832
03 Apr	Austria	Israel	Gen Communications	630UNTS301	108976
04 Apr	Malawi	USA (United States)	Recognition	0UNTS0	109899
05 Apr	France	Poland	Admin Cooperation	69PDZU29	457142
05 Apr	Norway	Sweden	Specific Resources	3NORT994	451165
05 Apr	Asian Productivity	Japan	IGO Status/Immunit	67JHZ7	439008
05 Apr	Norway	Sweden	Specific Resources	3NORT994	451166
05 Apr	France	Poland	Consul/Citizenship	69FRJO2202	416366
05 Apr	France	Poland	Admin Cooperation	0UNTS0	109510
05 Apr	France	Poland	Admin Cooperation	0UNTS0	109636
05 Apr	Canada	Israel	Gen Communications	0UNTS0	109350
05 Apr	Denmark	Tanzania	Tech Assistance	603UNTS111	108728
05 Apr	Denmark	Tanzania	Scientific Project	604UNTS19	108740
05 Apr	Philippines	IBRD (World Bank)	IBRD Project	598UNTS261	108661
06 Apr	Bulgaria	Poland	General Amity	617UNTS327	108920
06 Apr	Algeria	ILO (Labor Org)	IGO Establishment	595UNTS99	108614
08 Apr	Czechoslovakia	Poland	Land Transport	72PDZU240	457143
08 Apr	Austria	Yugoslavia	Visas	0UNTS0	109216
08 Apr	Ghana	United Nations	IGO Operations	594UNTS149	108601

DATE	PARTY ONE	PARTY TWO	TOPIC	CITATION	NUMBER
1967 (Cont.)					
08 Apr	Romania	United Nations	Privil/Immunities	594UNTS159	108602
11 Apr	Chad	Germany, West	Claims and Debts	68WGBB221	425673
11 Apr	Belgium	Germany, West	Taxation	69WGBB17	425037
11 Apr	Belgium	Germany, West	Taxation	0UNTS0	110109
13 Apr	China People's Rep	Syria	Tech Assistance	67CCJC12	411329
13 Apr	Canada	USA (United States)	Water Transport	0UNTS0	109759
13 Apr	Multilateral		IGO Operations	595UNTS60	108612
13 Apr	Austria	United Nations	IGO Establishment	600UNTS93	108679
14 Apr	Belgium	Germany, West	Admin Cooperation	67WGBB2545	425038
14 Apr	China People's Rep	Germany, East	General Economic	67CCJC13	411192
14 Apr	Afromalagasy Coffee	France	IGO Status/Immunit	69FRJO2204	416510
14 Apr	African Coffee Org	France	IGO Establishment	0UNTS0	110312
14 Apr	Indonesia	USA (United States)	Milit Assistance	0UNTS0	109859
14 Apr	Greece	United Nations	IGO Operations	595UNTS83	108613
15 Apr	Greece	Yugoslavia	Taxation	633UNTS373	109046
17 Apr	Multilateral		Consul/Citizenship	0UNTS0	110377
17 Apr	Honduras	USA (United States)	Gen Communications	0UNTS0	109760
18 Apr	Israel	Norway	Admin Cooperation	630UNTS307	108977
19 Apr	Gambia	Senegal	General Amity	640UNTS101	109156
19 Apr	Multilateral		Tech Assistance	595UNTS120	108617
20 Apr	France	USSR (Soviet Union)	Water Transport	67FRJO2709	416475
20 Apr	Romania	Somalia	Scientific Project	642UNTS155	109171
20 Apr	Morocco	USA (United States)	US Agri Commod Aid	0UNTS0	109761
20 Apr	Denmark	Norway	Specific Resources	604UNTS103	108747
21 Apr	Austria	Italy	Admin Cooperation	72ABGB15	403118
21 Apr	Turkey	UK Great Britain	Loans and Credits	610UNTS0	108838
21 Apr	IDA (Devel Assoc)	Uganda	General Aid	617UNTS161	108911
21 Apr	Austria	Bulgaria	Visas	603UNTS121	108729
24 Apr	Albania	China People's Rep	Culture	67CCJC14	411077
24 Apr	USA (United States)	Yugoslavia	Finance	0UNTS0	109900
24 Apr	Multilateral		Humanitarian	634UNTS255	109067
24 Apr	IBRD (World Bank)	UK Great Britain	IBRD Project	600UNTS3	108674
25 Apr	China People's Rep	Vietnam, North	Culture	67CCJC15	411387
25 Apr	China People's Rep	Finland	General Trade	67CCJC16	411156
25 Apr	Philippines	USA (United States)	Tech Assistance	0UNTS0	109860
26 Apr	Austria	Yugoslavia	Visas	67ABGB177	403243
26 Apr	Multilateral		General Trade	0UNTS0	109890
26 Apr	Czechoslovakia	Poland	Education	610UNTS0	108832
26 Apr	Austria	Yugoslavia	Admin Cooperation	603UNTS143	108731
27 Apr	Bulgaria	USSR (Soviet Union)	Atomic Energy	631UNTS3	108983
28 Apr	Japan	Korea, South	Scientific Project	67JJS249	442186
28 Apr	Japan	Korea, South	Scientific Project	67JJS251	442187
28 Apr	Austria	Yugoslavia	Visas	68ABGB173	403244
28 Apr	China People's Rep	Zambia	General Trade	67CCJC18	411398
28 Apr	Hungary	UN Special Fund	General Aid	595UNTS171	108619
29 Apr	Mongolia	Romania	Consul/Citizenship	0UNTS0	110204
01 May	Dominican Republic	Spain	Admin Cooperation	0UNTS0	110410
01 May	IBRD (World Bank)	Senegal	IGO Operations	615UNTS267	108883
01 May	Israel	Switzerland	Visas	630UNTS313	108978
02 May	Jordan	UK Great Britain	Finance	610UNTS0	108837
03 May	USA (United States)	Vietnam, South	Taxation	0VKNG246	496068
03 May	France	Spain	Admin Cooperation	67FRJO1108	416171
03 May	Multilateral		IGO Operations	0UNTS0	110764
03 May	USA (United States)	Vietnam, South	Taxation	0UNTS0	109762
03 May	Denmark	Paraguay	General Trade	608UNTS55	108812
04 May	Norway	USA (United States)	Atomic Energy	3NORT997	451201
04 May	Norway	USA (United States)	Atomic Energy	0UNTS0	109763
04 May	Multilateral		IGO Establishment	595UNTS287	108623
04 May	Malawi	IDA (Devel Assoc)	Loans and Credits	617UNTS141	108910
05 May	Germany, East	Poland	Scientific Project	48EGDZ383	420277
05 May	Finland	USSR (Soviet Union)	Specific Resources	640UNTS111	109157
05 May	Canada	USA (United States)	Non-ILO Labor	0UNTS0	109764
05 May	Germany, West	UK Great Britain	Finance	613UNTS313	108858
07 May	Cameroon	ILO (Labor Org)	IGO Operations	596UNTS209	108634
08 May	France	Malagasy	Non-ILO Labor	68FRJO708	416286

DATE	PARTY ONE	PARTY TWO	TOPIC	CITATION	NUMBER
1967 (Cont.)					
08 May	Netherlands	Romania	Finance	607UNTS105	108800
08 May	Belgium	Canada	Culture	637UNTS0	109119
09 May	Japan	USA (United States)	Specific Resources	18UST1309	486004
09 May	Poland	Yugoslavia	Customs	67PZUM88	458144
09 May	Japan	USA (United States)	Specific Resources	0UNTS0	109765
09 May	Japan	USA (United States)	Specific Resources	0UNTS0	109766
09 May	Jordan	IDA (Devel Assoc)	Loans and Credits	617UNTS47	108907
10 May	Iran	IAEA (Atom Energy)	Atomic Energy	0IRTB86	433141
10 May	Iran	IAEA (Atom Energy)	IGO Operations	614UNTS93	108865
10 May	Malta	WHO (World Health)	Tech Assistance	603UNTS99	108727
10 May	Congo (Brazzaville)	IBRD (World Bank)	IBRD Project	632UNTS185	109021
11 May	Japan	Norway	Taxation	68JHZ10	439009
11 May	Japan	Norway	Taxation	3NORT997	451092
11 May	Austria	Canada	Extradition	69ABGB324	403018
11 May	Pakistan	USA (United States)	US Agri Commod Aid	0UNTS0	109767
11 May	Japan	Norway	Taxation	0UNTS0	109717
11 May	Kenya	IDA (Devel Assoc)	General Aid	617UNTS91	108908
11 May	IBRD (World Bank)	Turkey	IBRD Project	632UNTS193	109022
11 May	Kenya	IDA (Devel Assoc)	General Aid	617UNTS111	108909
12 May	Bulgaria	USSR (Soviet Union)	General Amity	631UNTS239	108997
16 May	Japan	Korea, South	Air Transport	67JHZ8	439010
16 May	Switzerland	USA (United States)	Gen Communications	0UNTS0	109768
16 May	Japan	Korea, South	Air Transport	0UNTS0	109479
16 May	Italy	USSR (Soviet Union)	Admin Cooperation	608UNTS79	108814
16 May	Cyprus	IBRD (World Bank)	Loans and Credits	617UNTS21	108906
17 May	Belgium	United Arab Rep	Culture	0UNTS0	109501
17 May	Belgium	Bulgaria	Culture	631UNTS215	108995
17 May	Czechoslovakia	Yugoslavia	Customs	617UNTS305	108918
18 May	Germany, West	Rwanda	Claims and Debts	68WGBB1260	425602
18 May	Philippines	USA (United States)	Non-IBRD Project	0UNTS0	110126
18 May	France	Monaco	Culture	0UNTS0	110662
18 May	Australia	Romania	General Trade	642UNTS25	109162
18 May	Germany, East	Hungary	General Amity	617UNTS3	108905
19 May	Japan	USSR (Soviet Union)	Consul/Citizenship	68JAIL163	440188
19 May	Germany, West	Ghana	Loans and Credits	68WGBB1251	425221
19 May	Romania	Turkey	Sanitation	0UNTS0	109536
22 May	Ghana	Japan	Education	67JJS193	442189
22 May	France	Malaysia	Air Transport	67FRJO508	416277
23 May	Multilateral		Loans and Credits	617UNTS352	200634
24 May	Afghanistan	Denmark	Air Transport	0UNTS0	109951
24 May	Luxembourg	UK Great Britain	Taxation	0UNTS0	109341
24 May	Benelux Econ Union	Portugal	Visas	601UNTS153	108693
25 May	China People's Rep	United Arab Rep	General Trade	67CCJC19	411360
25 May	China People's Rep	Nepal	Non-IBRD Project	67CCJC20	411283
25 May	France	San Marino	Admin Cooperation	69FRJO1503	416385
25 May	France	San Marino	Admin Cooperation	0UNTS0	109527
26 May	Czechoslovakia	Iran	Culture	0IRTB66	433105
26 May	FAO (Food Agri)	USA (United States)	Direct Aid	0UNTS0	109901
26 May	USSR (Soviet Union)	Zambia	General Economic	643UNTS179	109191
26 May	Honduras	IBRD (World Bank)	IGO Operations	615UNTS145	108879
26 May	Pakistan	IBRD (World Bank)	Loans and Credits	616UNTS167	108895
26 May	Bolivia	IDA (Devel Assoc)	Non-IBRD Project	618UNTS159	108927
28 May	China People's Rep	Nepal	Non-IBRD Project	67CCJC21	411284
28 May	Albania	China People's Rep	Water Transport	67CCJC22	411078
30 May	Germany, East	Hungary	Admin Cooperation	38EGDZ384	420468
30 May	Cyprus	Germany, West	Commodity Trade	69WBGA2	424739
30 May	Czechoslovakia	France	Sanitation	68FRJO1101	416444
30 May	Bulgaria	Turkey	Sanitation	0UNTS0	109967
30 May	Argentina	Uruguay	Non-IBRD Project	0UNTS0	109521
30 May	Bulgaria	Turkey	Sanitation	631UNTS19	108984
31 May	Austria	Germany, West	Visas	70WGBB697	425557
31 May	Belgium	France	Admin Cooperation	67FRJO408	416069
01 Jun	Denmark	Pakistan	Water Transport	620UNTS217	108958
01 Jun	Norway	USA (United States)	Gen Communications	631UNTS119	108991
02 Jun	Japan	Lebanon	Air Transport	71JHZ3	439191

DATE	PARTY ONE	PARTY TWO	TOPIC	CITATION	NUMBER
1967 (Cont.)					
02 Jun	Germany, West	Tunisia	Loans and Credits	67WBGA128	424690
02 Jun	Germany, West	UK Great Britain	Land Transport	67WBGA135	424718
02 Jun	Mexico	USA (United States)	General Trade	0UNTS0	109770
03 Jun	Germany, East	Yugoslavia	Scientific Project	42EGDZ385	420164
05 Jun	Japan	Laos	Postal Service	67JJS299	442192
05 Jun	El Salvador	USA (United States)	Gen Communications	0UNTS0	109902
05 Jun	Iceland	USA (United States)	US Agri Commod Aid	0UNTS0	109903
05 Jun	Liberia	IBRD (World Bank)	Tech Assistance	633UNTS13	109031
06 Jun	France	Germany, West	Telecommunications	69WGBB84	425201
07 Jun	Iran	IAEA (Atom Energy)	Atomic Energy	0IRTB87	433143
07 Jun	Guyana	USA (United States)	Admin Cooperation	0UNTS0	109771
07 Jun	IAEA (Atom Energy)	USA (United States)	IGO Operations	614UNTS109	108866
08 Jun	Taiwan	USA (United States)	Water Transport	0UNTS0	109904
09 Jun	Indonesia	Japan	Loans and Credits	67JJS229	442193
10 Jun	Japan	Vietnam, South	Sanitation	67JJS537	442194
10 Jun	Multilateral		Direct Aid	602UNTS212	108714
12 Jun	UK Great Britain	USA (United States)	Land Transport	0UNTS0	110785
12 Jun	Canada	USA (United States)	Gen Communications	0UNTS0	109772
12 Jun	Multilateral		IGO Operations	615UNTS321	108885
13 Jun	Netherlands	Sierra Leone	Air Transport	0UNTS0	109247
14 Jun	Israel	UN Relief Palestin	Direct Aid	620UNTS183	108955
14 Jun	Malta	USA (United States)	Commodity Trade	604UNTS231	108753
14 Jun	Multilateral		Direct Aid	603UNTS2	108719
14 Jun	China	IBRD (World Bank)	IGO Operations	615UNTS243	108882
15 Jun	France	Spain	Visas	67FRJO608	416172
15 Jun	Ethiopia	USA (United States)	Postal Service	0UNTS0	109905
15 Jun	Colombia	IBRD (World Bank)	Gen Communications	615UNTS47	108877
15 Jun	Bulgaria	Romania	Visas	634UNTS57	109051
15 Jun	Malaysia	IBRD (World Bank)	IBRD Project	618UNTS235	108930
15 Jun	Guyana	UK Great Britain	Military Mission	632UNTS15	109005
16 Jun	France	Switzerland	Admin Cooperation	67FRJO1108	416421
16 Jun	Cameroon	UK Great Britain	Loans and Credits	618UNTS329	108933
19 Jun	Italy	USA (United States)	Scientific Project	0UNTS0	109773
19 Jun	Other Party Combin	Ecuador	IGO Operations	615UNTS75	108878
19 Jun	State/IGO Group	IAEA (Atom Energy)	Atomic Energy	637UNTS0	109112
20 Jun	France	Spain	Visas	67FRJO608	416173
20 Jun	Algeria	France	General Ad Hoc	68FRJO1008	416030
20 Jun	El Salvador	UK Great Britain	Tech Assistance	0UNTS0	109471
20 Jun	Multilateral		Tech Assistance	0UNTS0	109290
20 Jun	Denmark	Peru	Loans and Credits	0UNTS0	109446
20 Jun	Dominican Republic	UK Great Britain	Visas	619UNTS3	108935
20 Jun	Multilateral		Visas	607UNTS97	108799
20 Jun	Denmark	Netherlands	Non-ILO Labor	619UNTS67	108939
21 Jun	New Zealand	USA (United States)	Gen Communications	0UNTS0	109205
21 Jun	Multilateral		Tech Assistance	598UNTS2	108653
22 Jun	China People's Rep	Hungary	General Economic	67CCJC25	411202
22 Jun	Ascension Island	USA (United States)	Air Transport	0UNTS0	110021
22 Jun	Chad	USSR (Soviet Union)	Mostfavored Nation	643UNTS121	109188
22 Jun	Norway	South Africa	Scientific Project	643UNTS121	109888
23 Jun	Brazil	Japan	Customs	67JJS93	442195
23 Jun	Denmark	Iran	Visas	0IRTB19	433031
23 Jun	Albania	China People's Rep	Direct Aid	67CCJC23	411079
23 Jun	IAEA (Atom Energy)	Spain	IGO Operations	614UNTS169	108870
23 Jun	Multilateral		IGO Operations	614UNTS185	108871
24 Jun	Germany, East	Hungary	Admin Cooperation	42EGDZ386	420469
24 Jun	India	USA (United States)	US Agri Commod Aid	0UNTS0	109906
26 Jun	Algeria	France	Health/Educ/Welfare	67FRJO2809	416025
26 Jun	Philippines	USA (United States)	Non-IBRD Project	0UNTS0	110127
26 Jun	IDA (Devel Assoc)	Switzerland	Loans and Credits	0UNTS0	200648
26 Jun	France	Romania	Culture	642UNTS181	109173
28 Jun	Multilateral		ILO Labor	0UNTS0	110355
28 Jun	Brazil	USA (United States)	Water Transport	0UNTS0	109775
28 Jun	Brazil	USA (United States)	Water Transport	0UNTS0	109774
29 Jun	USA (United States)	Vietnam, South	Direct Aid	0VKNG251	496069
29 Jun	France	Singapore	Air Transport	67FRJO1110	416401

DATE	PARTY ONE	PARTY TWO	TOPIC	CITATION	NUMBER
1967 (Cont.)					
29 Jun	Multilateral		Non-ILO Labor	0UNTS0	110030
29 Jun	Philippines	USA (United States)	Claims and Debts	0UNTS0	109776
29 Jun	Colombia	IBRD (World Bank)	IBRD Project	619UNTS99	108941
29 Jun	Switzerland	UK Great Britain	Gen Communications	617UNTS261	108916
29 Jun	Belgium	Denmark	Specific Resources	606UNTS113	108780
30 Jun	Belgium	Norway	Taxation	3NORT999	451007
30 Jun	Japan	EEC (Econ Commnty)	General Trade	68JHZ5	439011
30 Jun	China People's Rep	Poland	General Economic	67CCJC26	411307
30 Jun	Austria	Czechoslovakia	Customs	67ABGB299	403026
30 Jun	Denmark	EEC (Econ Commnty)	General Trade	0UNTS0	109745
30 Jun	Denmark	EEC (Econ Commnty)	General Trade	0UNTS0	109746
30 Jun	Denmark	EEC (Econ Commnty)	General Trade	0UNTS0	109747
30 Jun	Multilateral		Commodity Trade	0UNTS0	109864
30 Jun	Belgium	Norway	Taxation	0UNTS0	110020
30 Jun	Denmark	EEC (Econ Commnty)	General Trade	0UNTS0	109748
30 Jun	UK Great Britain	Yugoslavia	Postal Service	642UNTS325	109182
03 Jul	Pakistan	USA (United States)	General Trade	0UNTS0	109777
03 Jul	Dahomey	USA (United States)	Direct Aid	0UNTS0	109907
03 Jul	Multilateral		Air Transport	0UNTS0	109248
03 Jul	South Africa	Switzerland	Taxation	643UNTS3	109184
04 Jul	Austria	USA (United States)	Taxation	0UNTS0	109981
05 Jul	Australia	Austria	Other Military	636UNTS117	109098
05 Jul	IBRD (World Bank)	Singapore	IBRD Project	618UNTS189	108928
06 Jul	United Nations	Zambia	IGO Operations	600UNTS81	108678
07 Jul	Germany, East	Hungary	Health/Educ/Welfare	48EGDZ387	420470
08 Jul	Algeria	France	Non-IBRD Project	69FRJO2006	416026
08 Jul	France	USSR (Soviet Union)	Culture	68FRJO1603	416476
08 Jul	Algeria	France	Education	0UNTS0	110351
08 Jul	France	USSR (Soviet Union)	Mass Media	0UNTS0	109378
10 Jul	Germany, West	Thailand	Taxation	68WGBB589	425657
10 Jul	Multilateral		Air Transport	0UNTS0	109971
10 Jul	Malta	UK Great Britain	Air Transport	619UNTS11	108936
12 Jul	Japan	New Zealand	Specific Resources	68JHZ7	439012
12 Jul	Ecuador	Germany, West	Visas	67WBGA166	424115
12 Jul	Germany, West	USA (United States)	Patents/Copyrights	0UNTS0	109908
12 Jul	Japan	New Zealand	Specific Resources	0UNTS0	109718
13 Jul	Israel	USA (United States)	General Trade	0UNTS0	109778
13 Jul	Czechoslovakia	UN Special Fund	Non-IBRD Project	606UNTS71	108776
13 Jul	FAO (Food Agri)	UK Great Britain	IGO Operations	642UNTS263	109179
14 Jul	India	Japan	Loans and Credits	67JJS207	442196
14 Jul	Netherlands	USSR (Soviet Union)	Culture	0UNTS0	110497
14 Jul	Argentina	Paraguay	Culture	0UNTS0	110181
14 Jul	Kenya	UK Great Britain	Military Mission	643UNTS254	109196
14 Jul	Kenya	UK Great Britain	Status of Forces	643UNTS231	109195
17 Jul	Malaysia	UK Great Britain	Taxation	637UNTS0	109127
18 Jul	France	Sierra Leone	Air Transport	67FRJO1410	416400
18 Jul	IBRD (World Bank)	Yugoslavia	IGO Operations	615UNTS343	108886
18 Jul	Barbados	WHO (World Health)	Tech Assistance	603UNTS87	108726
19 Jul	France	Switzerland	Admin Cooperation	67FRJO1108	416422
19 Jul	Afghanistan	USA (United States)	US Agri Commod Aid	0UNTS0	109909
20 Jul	Japan	USSR (Soviet Union)	Scientific Project	67JJS455	442197
20 Jul	Germany, West	UK Great Britain	General Trade	67WBGA176	424719
20 Jul	Algeria	France	Water Transport	67FRJO2510	416027
20 Jul	Argentina	Paraguay	Atomic Energy	0UNTS0	110182
20 Jul	Argentina	Paraguay	Tech Assistance	0UNTS0	110183
20 Jul	Multilateral		General Economic	0UNTS0	109259
20 Jul	Netherlands	Romania	Sanitation	633UNTS21	109032
21 Jul	Poland	UK Great Britain	Sanitation	70PDZU1	457145
21 Jul	Poland	UK Great Britain	Sanitation	0UNTS0	110421
21 Jul	Malawi	USA (United States)	Finance	0UNTS0	109910
21 Jul	Bulgaria	Mongolia	General Amity	610UNTS0	108839
24 Jul	Japan	Mexico	Tech Assistance	67JJS311	442198
25 Jul	Malta	USA (United States)	General Military	0UNTS0	109911
26 Jul	Multilateral		IGO Operations	614UNTS217	108872
27 Jul	China People's Rep	USSR (Soviet Union)	General Trade	67CCJC27	411361

DATE	PARTY ONE	PARTY TWO	TOPIC	CITATION	NUMBER
1967 (Cont.)					
28 Jul	Austria	Yugoslavia	Visas	68ABGB379	403245
28 Jul	France	USA (United States)	Taxation	68FRJO1210	416181
28 Jul	France	USA (United States)	Taxation	OUNTSO	110325
28 Jul	IDA (Devel Assoc)	Uganda	General Aid	617UNTS177	108912
29 Jul	Bulgaria	Italy	Mass Media	631UNTS33	108985
31 Jul	Germany, West	Togo	Loans and Credits	67WBGA218	424665
31 Jul	Germany, West	Panama	Visas	67WBGA171	424569
31 Jul	France	India	Air Transport	69FRJO709	416232
31 Jul	Argentina	IBRD (World Bank)	IBRD Project	633UNTS289	109042
01 Aug	Mexico	USA (United States)	Claims and Debts	OUNTSO	109982
01 Aug	Indonesia	UK Great Britain	Claims and Debts	638UNTS3	109128
01 Aug	Malaysia	UK Great Britain	Air Transport	633UNTS93	109036
01 Aug	Singapore	UK Great Britain	Air Transport	619UNTS29	108937
02 Aug	Taiwan	IBRD (World Bank)	IBRD Project	618UNTS301	108932
03 Aug	Czechoslovakia	Germany, West	General Economic	68WBGA61	424676
03 Aug	China People's Rep	Vietnam, North	Direct Aid	67CCJC28	411368
03 Aug	Pakistan	USA (United States)	US Agri Commod Aid	OUNTSO	109912
03 Aug	Germany, West	Romania	General Economic	642UNTS47	109164
04 Aug	Israel	USA (United States)	US Agri Commod Aid	OUNTSO	109351
04 Aug	IBRD (World Bank)	Spain	IBRD Project	619UNTS209	108944
05 Aug	China People's Rep	Vietnam, North	Direct Aid	67CCJC29	411369
07 Aug	Austria	Germany, West	Patents/Copyrights	68WGBB5	425558
07 Aug	Taiwan	IBRD (World Bank)	IBRD Project	620UNTS113	108952
08 Aug	Japan	USA (United States)	Milit Assistance	18UST1678	486005
08 Aug	Canada	USA (United States)	Scientific Project	OUNTSO	109913
08 Aug	Italy	Romania	Culture	642UNTS213	109175
08 Aug	Italy	Romania	Culture	642UNTS191	109174
09 Aug	Denmark	Ghana	Loans and Credits	610UNTSO	108842
09 Aug	Hungary	UK Great Britain	Scientific Project	632UNTS39	109006
09 Aug	Ecuador	Israel	Visas	630UNTS319	108979
10 Aug	Pakistan	IBRD (World Bank)	IBRD Project	618UNTS261	108931
11 Aug	Philippines	USA (United States)	Non-IBRD Project	OUNTSO	110128
11 Aug	Canada	USA (United States)	Scientific Project	OUNTSO	109914
14 Aug	China People's Rep	Mali	Direct Aid	67CCJC30	411269
15 Aug	Iran	Romania	Culture	OIRTB60	433096
15 Aug	Jordan	UK Great Britain	Loans and Credits	632UNTS269	109028
18 Aug	Ethiopia	Japan	General Trade	68JJS175	442199
18 Aug	Mexico	IAEA (Atom Energy)	IGO Operations	614UNTS123	108867
19 Aug	China People's Rep	Somalia	Culture	67CCJC32	411330
21 Aug	USA (United States)	Upper Volta	Scientific Project	OUNTSO	110045
22 Aug	Netherlands	Poland	General Economic	68PZUM26	458146
22 Aug	Netherlands	Poland	Culture	68PDZU209	457147
22 Aug	Multilateral		General Trade	OUNTSO	110687
22 Aug	Netherlands	Poland	General Economic	OUNTSO	109276
22 Aug	Austria	Brazil	Visas	OUNTSO	109528
22 Aug	Netherlands	Poland	Culture	OUNTSO	109275
22 Aug	Bulgaria	Romania	Visas	631UNTS49	108986
23 Aug	Austria	Switzerland	Tech Assistance	67ABGB333	403191
23 Aug	Mexico	IAEA (Atom Energy)	IGO Operations	614UNTS133	108868
23 Aug	Multilateral		IGO Operations	614UNTS145	108869
23 Aug	Madagascar	IBRD (World Bank)	IBRD Project	618UNTS215	108929
24 Aug	Philippines	USA (United States)	General Military	OUNTSO	109915
24 Aug	Ceylon (Sri Lanka)	IBRD (World Bank)	IBRD Project	632UNTS217	109025
25 Aug	UK Great Britain	USSR (Soviet Union)	Gen Communications	632UNTS49	109007
28 Aug	Czechoslovakia	USA (United States)	Consul/Citizenship	OUNTSO	110443
29 Aug	India	Japan	Claims and Debts	67JJS205	442200
29 Aug	Guatemala	Norway	Visas	3NORT869	451069
29 Aug	Belgium	UK Great Britain	Taxation	OUNTSO	110540
29 Aug	Denmark	Romania	General Economic	OUNTSO	109404
29 Aug	Denmark	Romania	Land Transport	OUNTSO	109231
29 Aug	New Zealand	WHO (World Health)	Direct Aid	607UNTS57	108795
29 Aug	Denmark	Romania	Culture	642UNTS357	109183
31 Aug	India	USA (United States)	Commodity Trade	OUNTSO	109916
31 Aug	Israel	IAEA (Atom Energy)	Atomic Energy	OUNTSO	109310
01 Sep	Germany, West	Ghana	Loans and Credits	67WBGA193	424222

DATE	PARTY ONE	PARTY TWO	TOPIC	CITATION	NUMBER
1967 (Cont.)					
01 Sep	Malaysia	Philippines	Commodity Trade	608UNTS13	108810
01 Sep	Denmark	India	Direct Aid	616UNTS69	108892
02 Sep	Bulgaria	Denmark	General Economic	OUNTSO	109726
02 Sep	Bulgaria	Denmark	Visas	631UNTS71	108987
05 Sep	India	Japan	Loans and Credits	67JJS221	442201
05 Sep	Germany, West	Sierra Leone	Loans and Credits	67WBGA214	424633
07 Sep	Hungary	USSR (Soviet Union)	General Amity	632UNTS89	109011
07 Sep	Bulgaria	Germany, East	General Amity	631UNTS81	108988
08 Sep	Germany, West	Eur Space Research	IGO Establishment	69WGBB92	425747
09 Sep	Argentina	Dominican Republic	Culture	OUNTSO	110412
11 Sep	Japan	Morocco	Direct Aid	67JJS325	442203
11 Sep	France	Portugal	Non-ILO Labor	67FRJO2910	416373
11 Sep	Peru	IBRD (World Bank)	IBRD Project	619UNTS171	108943
12 Sep	India	USA (United States)	US Agri Commod Aid	OUNTSO	109917
12 Sep	Argentina	Dominican Republic	Culture	OUNTSO	109560
14 Sep	China People's Rep	Pakistan	Culture	67CCJC34	411308
14 Sep	IBRD (World Bank)	Tunisia	IBRD Project	639UNTS147	109149
15 Sep	Indonesia	USA (United States)	US Agri Commod Aid	OUNTSO	109918
15 Sep	Argentina	Colombia	Taxation	OUNTSO	109529
15 Sep	IDA (Devel Assoc)	Uganda	Non-IBRD Project	639UNTS115	109148
15 Sep	IBRD (World Bank)	Singapore	IGO Operations	615UNTS295	108884
16 Sep	Hungary	Poland	Admin Cooperation	68PZUM32	458148
18 Sep	Thailand	Vietnam, South	Refugees	OVKNG252	496070
18 Sep	USA (United States)	Venezuela	Gen Communications	OUNTSO	109919
19 Sep	India	IBRD (World Bank)	IGO Operations	615UNTS165	108880
19 Sep	IBRD (World Bank)	Thailand	IBRD Project	619UNTS275	108946
20 Sep	Iran	Spain	Visas	OIRTB21	433034
21 Sep	Japan	Singapore	Reparations	68JHZ5	439013
21 Sep	Japan	Malaysia	General Economic	68JHZ5	439014
21 Sep	Norway	Poland	General Trade	3NORT1004	451132
21 Sep	Japan	Malaysia	General Economic	OUNTSO	109719
21 Sep	Japan	Singapore	Reparations	OUNTSO	109720
21 Sep	Philippines	USA (United States)	Commodity Trade	OUNTSO	109921
21 Sep	USA (United States)	Vietnam, South	US Agri Commod Aid	OUNTSO	109920
21 Sep	Iraq	IAEA (Atom Energy)	Atomic Energy	630UNTS41	108963
22 Sep	Ceylon (Sri Lanka)	Japan	Loans and Credits	67JJS119	442202
22 Sep	Lesotho	USA (United States)	Direct Aid	OUNTSO	109922
22 Sep	Multilateral		Non-IBRD Project	OUNTSO	109258
22 Sep	Belgium	Romania	Land Transport	637UNTSO	109109
23 Sep	Brazil	IBRD (World Bank)	IBRD Project	620UNTS77	108951
25 Sep	France	Iraq	General Trade	69FRJO1408	416237
25 Sep	France	Iraq	General Trade	OUNTSO	110822
25 Sep	Canada	USA (United States)	Commodity Trade	OUNTSO	110503
26 Sep	USA (United States)	Yugoslavia	Commodity Trade	OUNTSO	110046
26 Sep	Multilateral		Atomic Energy	633UNTS73	109035
26 Sep	Japan	IAEA (Atom Energy)	Atomic Energy	637UNTSO	109113
28 Sep	Lesotho	South Africa	Air Transport	OUNTSO	110166
29 Sep	Jamaica	USA (United States)	Commodity Trade	OUNTSO	109923
29 Sep	Swaziland	USA (United States)	Finance	OUNTSO	109924
30 Sep	Ceylon (Sri Lanka)	Germany, West	Loans and Credits	68WBGA15	424075
30 Sep	Italy	UK Great Britain	Culture	642UNTS271	109180
01 Oct	Algeria	France	Non-IBRD Project	70FRJO1004	416031
02 Oct	Germany, West	Mauritania	Loans and Credits	56WBGA91	424475
04 Oct	Korea, South	Vietnam, South	Finance	OVKNG255	496071
04 Oct	Jordan	USSR (Soviet Union)	Culture	OUNTSO	110278
05 Oct	Australia	Turkey	Visas	OUNTSO	109457
06 Oct	Germany, West	Nepal	Scientific Project	68WGBB81	425484
07 Oct	Cyprus	WHO (World Health)	Direct Aid	608UNTS327	108821
09 Oct	Costa Rica	Dominican Republic	Culture	OUNTSO	110413
10 Oct	Poland	UK Great Britain	Scientific Project	68PZUM35	458149
10 Oct	Poland	UK Great Britain	Scientific Project	OUNTSO	109496
10 Oct	Bel-Lux Econ Union	Czechoslovakia	Tech Assistance	OUNTSO	109362
10 Oct	Ecuador	Romania	General Trade	642UNTS33	109163
11 Oct	Burma	IAEA (Atom Energy)	Atomic Energy	630UNTS49	108964
12 Oct	Taiwan	USA (United States)	Commodity Trade	OUNTSO	110047

DATE	PARTY ONE	PARTY TWO	TOPIC	CITATION	NUMBER
1967 (Cont.)					
12 Oct	Multilateral		Direct Aid	607UNTS2	108792
12 Oct	Multilateral		Direct Aid	607UNTS20	108793
12 Oct	Botswana	UN Special Fund	Direct Aid	607UNTS37	108794
13 Oct	Spain	USA (United States)	Commodity Trade	0UNTS0	110049
13 Oct	Japan	USA (United States)	General Military	0UNTS0	110048
16 Oct	IAEA (Atom Energy)	Vietnam, South	Atomic Energy	630UNTS379	200636
16 Oct	IAEA (Atom Energy)	USA (United States)	Atomic Energy	630UNTS57	108965
16 Oct	Philippines	USA (United States)	General Military	632UNTS113	109013
17 Oct	Belgium	France	Culture	68FRJO1008	416070
17 Oct	Iran	IBRD (World Bank)	IBRD Project	0UNTS0	109331
17 Oct	Denmark	Zambia	Tech Assistance	620UNTS239	108960
18 Oct	Cyprus	Germany, West	Air Transport	69WGBB981	425740
18 Oct	Guinea	USA (United States)	US Agri Commod Aid	0UNTS0	110050
18 Oct	Denmark	Zambia	Loans and Credits	637UNTS0	109116
19 Oct	Malaysia	Norway	Air Transport	3NORT1005	451114
19 Oct	Germany, West	Italy	Specif Claim/Waive	67WGBB1997	425305
19 Oct	Germany, West	Uganda	Loans and Credits	68WBGA224	424702
19 Oct	Bulgaria	Sweden	Education	0UNTS0	109968
19 Oct	Austria	Czechoslovakia	Land Transport	634UNTS19	109048
19 Oct	Multilateral		Atomic Energy	630UNTS69	108966
20 Oct	Brazil	Norway	Taxation	3NORT1005	451013
20 Oct	Austria	Bulgaria	Admin Cooperation	0UNTS0	110601
20 Oct	Netherlands	USSR (Soviet Union)	Claims and Debts	0UNTS0	109391
21 Oct	Norway	Romania	General Trade	3NORT1006	451135
21 Oct	Denmark	Pakistan	Tech Assistance	632UNTS105	109012
23 Oct	Liberia	USA (United States)	US Agri Commod Aid	0UNTS0	110051
24 Oct	Germany, West	USA (United States)	Status of Forces	67WBGA213	424724
24 Oct	Germany, West	Jordan	Loans and Credits	68WBGA42	424315
24 Oct	Austria	Switzerland	Visas	68ABGB21	403192
24 Oct	Austria	Liechtenstein	Visas	68ABGB21	403130
24 Oct	Ceylon (Sri Lanka)	USA (United States)	US Agri Commod Aid	0UNTS0	109984
24 Oct	Ghana	USA (United States)	US Agri Commod Aid	0UNTS0	109985
24 Oct	USA (United States)	Vietnam, South	US Agri Commod Aid	0UNTS0	109983
25 Oct	Japan	Korea, South	Education	67JJS291	442204
25 Oct	Multilateral		Scientific Project	0UNTS0	110322
25 Oct	Canada	USA (United States)	Scientific Project	0UNTS0	110052
25 Oct	UNICEF (Children)	Venezuela	IGO Operations	0UNTS0	109337
26 Oct	Czechoslovakia	France	Culture	68FRJO2109	416445
26 Oct	Argentina	Bolivia	Land Transport	0UNTS0	109550
26 Oct	Sweden	UK Great Britain	Milit Assistance	632UNTS277	109029
27 Oct	Austria	Bulgaria	Customs	68ABGB23	403011
27 Oct	Mexico	USA (United States)	Specific Resources	0UNTS0	109925
27 Oct	Multilateral		Telecommunications	0UNTS0	109861
27 Oct	Morocco	USA (United States)	US Agri Commod Aid	0UNTS0	110053
27 Oct	Finland	France	General Transport	643UNTS75	109185
27 Oct	Multilateral		General Aid	608UNTS37	108811
28 Oct	Bulgaria	Norway	Visas	3NORT1007	451015
28 Oct	Bulgaria	Norway	Visas	0UNTS0	110302
29 Oct	Germany, East	Poland	Territory Boundary	69PDZU217	457160
30 Oct	Brazil	Norway	Taxation	0UNTS0	110602
31 Oct	Austria	Hungary	Claims and Debts	67ABGB293	403092
31 Oct	Indonesia	UK Great Britain	Claims and Debts	0UNTS0	109497
31 Oct	Netherlands	UK Great Britain	Taxation	0UNTS0	109222
01 Nov	Indonesia	USA (United States)	US Agri Commod Aid	0UNTS0	110054
01 Nov	Denmark	Tanzania	Loans and Credits	619UNTS47	108938
02 Nov	Gambia	Germany, West	Visas	68WBGA80	424213
02 Nov	Denmark	Iran	Loans and Credits	638UNTS217	109138
03 Nov	Australia	Singapore	Air Transport	0UNTS0	110167
03 Nov	Bulgaria	New Zealand	General Trade	0UNTS0	109207
04 Nov	France	Ireland	Culture	68FRJO2402	416243
04 Nov	France	Ireland	Culture	0UNTS0	109291
04 Nov	Gambia	USA (United States)	Finance	0UNTS0	110055
04 Nov	India	United Nations	IGO Operations	609UNTS3	108824
05 Nov	Multilateral		Atomic Energy	630UNTS77	108967
06 Nov	Tunisia	USA (United States)	US Agri Commod Aid	0UNTS0	110056

DATE	PARTY ONE	PARTY TWO	TOPIC	CITATION	NUMBER
1967 (Cont.)					
06 Nov	Argentina	Hungary	General Trade	0UNTS0	109561
06 Nov	Argentina	Chile	Taxation	636UNTS111	109097
06 Nov	Multilateral		Other Military	640UNTS87	109155
07 Nov	Lesotho	WHO (World Health)	Tech Assistance	632UNTS143	109016
08 Nov	Netherlands	Pakistan	Scientific Project	0UNTS0	110753
08 Nov	Australia	France	Scientific Project	0UNTS0	109668
08 Nov	United Nations	Senegal	Admin Cooperation	613UNTS255	108854
08 Nov	Austria	South Africa	Other Military	636UNTS125	109099
09 Nov	France	New Zealand	Air Transport	68FRJO103	416347
10 Nov	Indonesia	Japan	General Aid	67JJS243	442205
10 Nov	Kenya	Netherlands	Extradition	0UNTS0	109232
10 Nov	Finland	Hungary	Land Transport	643UNTS95	109186
11 Nov	Burma	Germany, West	Loans and Credits	68WBGA15	424044
13 Nov	Congo (Brazzaville)	France	Finance	70FRJO307	416127
13 Nov	Morocco	IBRD (World Bank)	IBRD Project	0UNTS0	110544
13 Nov	Congo (Brazzaville)	France	Taxation	0UNTS0	110315
13 Nov	Belgium	South Africa	Air Transport	0UNTS0	110168
14 Nov	Iran	Saudi Arabia	Culture	0IRTB10	433018
14 Nov	Multilateral		Admin Cooperation	614UNTS2	108860
15 Nov	France	Mauritania	Finance	69FRJO2704	416320
15 Nov	France	Mauritania	Taxation	0UNTS0	110244
15 Nov	Austria	Switzerland	Non-ILO Labor	69ABGB4	403193
15 Nov	Multilateral		General Trade	0UNTS0	109703
15 Nov	Finland	Spain	Taxation	0UNTS0	109375
15 Nov	Austria	Switzerland	Non-ILO Labor	0UNTS0	109434
15 Nov	Israel	IBRD (World Bank)	IBRD Project	619UNTS129	108942
15 Nov	Czechoslovakia	Netherlands	Land Transport	0UNTS0	109223
15 Nov	Muscat and Oman	UK Great Britain	Territory Boundary	617UNTS319	108919
15 Nov	South Africa	UK Great Britain	Consul/Citizenship	616UNTS277	108902
15 Nov	Denmark	Poland	General Economic	643UNTS383	109203
17 Nov	Netherlands	UK Great Britain	Admin Cooperation	0UNTS0	110356
17 Nov	Netherlands	UK Great Britain	Dispute Settlement	0UNTS0	110022
17 Nov	Czechoslovakia	Romania	Sanitation	0UNTS0	109280
21 Nov	Sweden	UK Great Britain	Land Transport	0UNTS0	109338
21 Nov	Austria	USA (United States)	Gen Communications	634UNTS43	109049
22 Nov	Indonesia	USA (United States)	US Agri Commod Aid	0UNTS0	109987
22 Nov	Ceylon (Sri Lanka)	IBRD (World Bank)	IBRD Project	639UNTS221	109151
22 Nov	France	UK Great Britain	Gen Communications	643UNTS225	109194
23 Nov	Czechoslovakia	USSR (Soviet Union)	Gen Communications	0UNTS0	109224
24 Nov	France	Indonesia	Air Transport	68FRJO3103	416234
24 Nov	Eur Space Research	UK Great Britain	Gen Communications	638UNTS17	109129
25 Nov	USA (United States)	USSR (Soviet Union)	Specific Resources	0UNTS0	110057
26 Nov	Bulgaria	Iran	Culture	0IRTB16	433025
30 Nov	Germany, West	Kenya	Loans and Credits	68WBGA47	424360
30 Nov	Germany, West	Somalia	Loans and Credits	68WBGA77	424639
30 Nov	Costa Rica	France	Education	68FRJO206	416137
30 Nov	France	WEU (West Europe)	Non-ILO Labor	68FRJO506	416511
30 Nov	Multilateral		Commodity Trade	0UNTS0	110455
30 Nov	Costa Rica	France	Education	0UNTS0	110668
30 Nov	Sweden	USSR (Soviet Union)	Consul/Citizenship	0UNTS0	109385
30 Nov	Chile	USA (United States)	Gen Communications	0UNTS0	110058
30 Nov	Denmark	Germany, West	Specific Resources	632UNTS153	109017
30 Nov	Accept UN Charter	Southern Yemen	UN Charter	614UNTS21	108861
02 Dec	Czechoslovakia	Poland	Admin Cooperation	71PDZU117	457150
02 Dec	China People's Rep	Norway	Consul/Citizenship	3NORT1008	451025
02 Dec	Indonesia	UK Great Britain	Loans and Credits	0UNTS0	109339
04 Dec	Ivory Coast	Norway	Privil/Immunities	3NORT1009	451046
04 Dec	Belgium	Ireland	Taxation	0UNTS0	110594
05 Dec	Israel	Jamaica	Visas	632UNTS83	109010
05 Dec	Denmark	Sweden	Specific Resources	631UNTS257	108998
05 Dec	Australia	Hungary	General Trade	638UNTS209	109137
05 Dec	Malaysia	UK Great Britain	Military Mission	642UNTS293	109181
06 Dec	Czechoslovakia	Romania	Land Transport	0UNTS0	109537
07 Dec	Austria	Czechoslovakia	Water Transport	0UNTS0	110475
07 Dec	Austria	Czechoslovakia	Specific Resources	70ABGB106	403027

DATE	PARTY ONE	PARTY TWO	TOPIC	CITATION	NUMBER
1967 (Cont.)					
07 Dec	Australia	UK Great Britain	Taxation	0UNTS0	109458
07 Dec	El Salvador	IBRD (World Bank)	Loans and Credits	0UNTS0	109299
08 Dec	Multilateral		Specific Resources	620UNTS225	108959
11 Dec	Guatemala	USA (United States)	Gen Communications	0UNTS0	110444
11 Dec	Korea, South	USA (United States)	Commodity Trade	0UNTS0	110060
11 Dec	Congo (Zaire)	USA (United States)	US Agri Commod Aid	0UNTS0	110059
11 Dec	Finland	Pakistan	Water Transport	631UNTS99	108989
12 Dec	Ceylon (Sri Lanka)	Japan	Taxation	68JHZ9	439015
12 Dec	Taiwan	USA (United States)	US Agri Commod Aid	0UNTS0	110062
12 Dec	Ceylon (Sri Lanka)	Japan	Taxation	0UNTS0	109721
12 Dec	Taiwan	USA (United States)	US Agri Commod Aid	0UNTS0	110061
13 Dec	Japan	USA (United States)	Milit Assistance	18UST2804	486006
13 Dec	IBRD (World Bank)	Tanzania	IBRD Project	619UNTS239	108945
14 Dec	Norway	Sweden	Admin Cooperation	3NORT1012	451167
14 Dec	Bulgaria	Finland	Visas	0UNTS0	109969
14 Dec	Denmark	Malaysia	Air Transport	614UNTS26	108862
14 Dec	Austria	Czechoslovakia	Visas	634UNTS51	109050
14 Dec	Austria	Cyprus	Visas	636UNTS267	109104
15 Dec	Bulgaria	Turkey	Land Transport	0UNTS0	110836
15 Dec	Taiwan	USA (United States)	Loans and Credits	0UNTS0	109989
15 Dec	Chile	Denmark	Scientific Project	643UNTS293	109199
16 Dec	UK Great Britain	USA (United States)	Direct Aid	0UNTS0	110063
17 Dec	Mongolia	USSR (Soviet Union)	General Trade	0UNTS0	109825
18 Dec	Norway	USSR (Soviet Union)	Territory Boundary	3NORT1013	451215
18 Dec	Korea, South	IDA (Devel Assoc)	Non-IBRD Project	639UNTS303	200639
18 Dec	Morocco	UNESCO (Educ/Cult)	IGO Operations	0UNTS0	109221
19 Dec	Belgium	France	Admin Cooperation	68FRJO2801	416071
19 Dec	Peru	UK Great Britain	Loans and Credits	0UNTS0	109447
20 Dec	ILO (Labor Org)	Zambia	IGO Operations	619UNTS293	108947
21 Dec	India	Netherlands	Direct Aid	0UNTS0	109390
21 Dec	Canada	Ireland	General Trade	0UNTS0	109448
21 Dec	Australia	UNICEF (Children)	IGO Operations	614UNTS83	108864
22 Dec	Philippines	USA (United States)	US Agri Commod Aid	0UNTS0	110133
23 Dec	Mongolia	Romania	Land Transport	0UNTS0	110205
26 Dec	Algeria	France	Air Transport	69FRJO1101	416028
26 Dec	Algeria	France	Admin Cooperation	0UNTS0	109509
26 Dec	Pakistan	USA (United States)	US Agri Commod Aid	0UNTS0	109990
27 Dec	Germany, West	Japan	General Trade	68JAIL169	440206
27 Dec	Germany, West	Japan	Water Transport	68WBGA43	424751
27 Dec	France	Iran	Tech Assistance	69FRJO1304	416242
27 Dec	Finland	USA (United States)	Gen Communications	0UNTS0	109991
28 Dec	Ghana	Netherlands	Education	0UNTS0	110747
28 Dec	Multilateral		Scientific Project	0UNTS0	109322
29 Dec	Austria	Switzerland	Admin Cooperation	68ABGB84	403188
29 Dec	Chile	USA (United States)	US Agri Commod Aid	0UNTS0	109992
29 Dec	Brazil	UK Great Britain	Taxation	643UNTS217	109193
30 Dec	India	USA (United States)	US Agri Commod Aid	0UNTS0	109993
30 Dec	Indonesia	USA (United States)	Finance	0UNTS0	109994
1968					
03 Jan	Ghana	USA (United States)	US Agri Commod Aid	0UNTS0	109986
04 Jan	Australia	Norway	Water Transport	3NORT999	451005
05 Jan	UK Great Britain	USSR (Soviet Union)	Claims and Debts	638UNTS41	109130
05 Jan	State/IGO Group	IAEA (Atom Energy)	Atomic Energy	637UNTS0	109114
06 Jan	USA (United States)	Vietnam, South	US Agri Commod Aid	0UNTS0	109995
09 Jan	Multilateral		IGO Establishment	0UNTS0	109707
10 Jan	Austria	Pakistan	Other Military	636UNTS133	109100
11 Jan	Bulgaria	Italy	Land Transport	0UNTS0	110303
12 Jan	Japan	USA (United States)	Commodity Trade	19UST4419	486007
12 Jan	Japan	Thailand	Loans and Credits	69JAIL169	440207
12 Jan	Japan	USA (United States)	General Trade	0UNTS0	109998
12 Jan	Botswana	USA (United States)	Finance	0UNTS0	109997
12 Jan	Austria	France	Scientific Project	0UNTS0	109531
13 Jan	France	Honduras	Health/Educ/Welfare	69FRJO1101	416220
13 Jan	France	Honduras	Culture	0UNTS0	109530

DATE	PARTY ONE	PARTY TWO	TOPIC	CITATION	NUMBER
1968 (Cont.)					
15 Jan	Japan	San Marino	Visas	68JJS421	442208
15 Jan	Italy	United Nations	Scientific Project	635UNTS11	109070
16 Jan	Bolivia	USA (United States)	US Agri Commod Aid	0UNTS0	110065
16 Jan	Bolivia	USA (United States)	US Agri Commod Aid	0UNTS0	110064
17 Jan	Mali	USA (United States)	Scientific Project	0UNTS0	110000
18 Jan	Brazil	UK Great Britain	Tech Assistance	0UNTS0	109472
19 Jan	Japan	USA (United States)	Military Mission	0TIAS6442	487008
19 Jan	Japan	USA (United States)	Admin Cooperation	0UNTS0	110001
19 Jan	USA (United States)	Uruguay	US Agri Commod Aid	0UNTS0	110002
19 Jan	UK Great Britain	USSR (Soviet Union)	Scientific Project	0UNTS0	109277
23 Jan	Sierra Leone	USA (United States)	US Agri Commod Aid	0UNTS0	110004
23 Jan	Philippines	USA (United States)	Finance	0UNTS0	110003
24 Jan	Iran	Romania	General Trade	0IRTB60	433097
24 Jan	Iran	Romania	Finance	0IRTB60	433098
25 Jan	Iran	Norway	Visas	3NORT0	451087
25 Jan	Argentina	Brazil	Culture	0UNTS0	109547
25 Jan	Argentina	IBRD (World Bank)	IBRD Project	639UNTS187	109150
26 Jan	Mexico	IBRD (World Bank)	IBRD Project	0UNTS0	109511
26 Jan	Brazil	IBRD (World Bank)	IBRD Project	0UNTS0	109613
26 Jan	Mexico	IBRD (World Bank)	IBRD Project	640UNTS3	109152
27 Jan	Iran	Pakistan	Admin Cooperation	0IRTB56	433088
29 Jan	Poland	Romania	Land Transport	68PZUM52	458152
29 Jan	Poland	Romania	Land Transport	68PZUM42	458151
29 Jan	Cameroon	IDA (Devel Assoc)	Non-IBRD Project	0UNTS0	109325
29 Jan	Poland	Romania	Land Transport	0UNTS0	109538
30 Jan	Bulgaria	France	Sanitation	68FRJO1808	416090
30 Jan	Denmark	Indonesia	General Economic	0UNTS0	110352
31 Jan	France	Mongolia	Culture	68FRJO1010	416337
31 Jan	Korea, South	IBRD (World Bank)	IBRD Project	639UNTS263	200638
01 Feb	Hungary	Romania	Customs	0UNTS0	109704
03 Feb	Denmark	Japan	Taxation	68JHZ7	439016
03 Feb	Denmark	Japan	Taxation	0UNTS0	109405
05 Feb	Austria	Poland	Taxation	68ABGB123	403152
05 Feb	Malawi	IDA (Devel Assoc)	Non-IBRD Project	0UNTS0	109309
05 Feb	Austria	Poland	Taxation	0UNTS0	109213
05 Feb	Malawi	IDA (Devel Assoc)	Non-IBRD Project	0UNTS0	109308
05 Feb	Malawi	IDA (Devel Assoc)	Non-IBRD Project	0UNTS0	109307
06 Feb	India	Netherlands	Scientific Project	0UNTS0	110754
06 Feb	Afghanistan	USSR (Soviet Union)	Tech Assistance	0UNTS0	110279
07 Feb	Belgium	Luxembourg	Finance	0UNTS0	110811
07 Feb	Austria	Ecuador	Visas	68ABGB108	403034
07 Feb	Multilateral		IGO Establishment	0UNTS0	109513
07 Feb	Austria	Ecuador	Visas	0UNTS0	109212
08 Feb	Austria	Turkey	Customs	68ABGB280	403202
08 Feb	Tanzania	USA (United States)	General Economic	0UNTS0	110005
12 Feb	Sweden	UK Great Britain	Taxation	0UNTS0	109449
12 Feb	State/IGO Group	IAEA (Atom Energy)	Atomic Energy	0UNTS0	109311
13 Feb	Germany, West	Senegal	Loans and Credits	68WBGA78	424623
13 Feb	Netherlands	Philippines	Non-ILO Labor	0UNTS0	110748
14 Feb	France	Malta	Culture	68FRRT60	415293
14 Feb	Hungary	Netherlands	Culture	0UNTS0	110419
15 Feb	Indonesia	USA (United States)	US Agri Commod Aid	0UNTS0	109988
15 Feb	Iran	United Nations	Consul/Citizenship	631UNTS103	108990
15 Feb	Italy	UK Great Britain	Taxation	0UNTS0	109263
17 Feb	France	Mauritania	Scientific Project	68FRJO706	416321
17 Feb	State/IGO Group	Chad	Direct Aid	0UNTS0	109658
21 Feb	Austria	Dominican Republic	Visas	68ABGB109	403033
21 Feb	Argentina	Italy	Visas	0UNTS0	109562
21 Feb	Switzerland	UK Great Britain	Non-ILO Labor	0UNTS0	110034
21 Feb	Austria	Dominican Republic	Visas	0UNTS0	109215
21 Feb	UK Great Britain	Zambia	Military Mission	0UNTS0	109264
22 Feb	Panama	USA (United States)	Air Transport	0UNTS0	110006
25 Feb	Germany, West	Israel	Admin Cooperation	69WBGA94	424284
26 Feb	Japan	USA (United States)	Atomic Energy	68JHZ7	439017
26 Feb	Japan	USA (United States)	Atomic Energy	0UNTS0	109722

DATE	PARTY ONE	PARTY TWO	TOPIC	CITATION	NUMBER
1968 (Cont.)					
26 Feb	Denmark	Poland	Water Transport	643UNTS371	109202
27 Feb	Algeria	Belgium	Non-ILO Labor	0UNTS0	110110
27 Feb	Germany, West	USA (United States)	Admin Cooperation	0UNTS0	110134
27 Feb	Czechoslovakia	Hungary	IGO Establishment	640UNTS49	109154
28 Feb	Japan	Laos	Loans and Credits	68JJS299	442209
28 Feb	Austria	Canada	Other Military	636UNTS141	109101
28 Feb	State/IGO Group	IAEA (Atom Energy)	Atomic Energy	637UNTS0	109115
29 Feb	Denmark	Malaysia	Loans and Credits	640UNTS29	109153
03 Mar	France	Poland	Land Transport	68PZUM65	458153
03 Mar	France	Poland	General Transport	68FRJO308	416367
03 Mar	Czechoslovakia	France	Culture	68FRJO1709	416446
04 Mar	Turkey	UK Great Britain	Loans and Credits	0UNTS0	109265
04 Mar	Turkey	UK Great Britain	Loans and Credits	0UNTS0	109266
05 Mar	India	Japan	Education	69JAIL171	440210
06 Mar	Japan	UK Great Britain	Atomic Energy	68JHZ10	439018
06 Mar	Japan	UK Great Britain	Atomic Energy	0UNTS0	109494
06 Mar	Czechoslovakia	France	Mass Media	0UNTS0	109379
07 Mar	Japan	Mexico	Specific Resources	68JHZ6	439019
07 Mar	Cyprus	UK Great Britain	Taxation	0UNTS0	109342
07 Mar	Japan	Mexico	Water Transport	0UNTS0	109723
07 Mar	Finland	USSR (Soviet Union)	General Transport	643UNTS107	109187
08 Mar	Upper Volta	USSR (Soviet Union)	General Trade	0UNTS0	110280
08 Mar	Multilateral		Visas	634UNTS199	109062
11 Mar	USA (United States)	Vietnam, South	US Agri Commod Aid	0UNTS0	110135
11 Mar	Barbados	USA (United States)	Finance	0UNTS0	110007
11 Mar	Cyprus	UK Great Britain	Military Mission	0UNTS0	109285
12 Mar	Austria	France	Scientific Project	69FRJO1001	416060
12 Mar	Brazil	USA (United States)	Scientific Project	0UNTS0	110138
12 Mar	Austria	United Nations	IGO Operations	632UNTS131	109015
12 Mar	United Nations	UK Great Britain	IGO Operations	632UNTS121	109014
12 Mar	Mauritius	UK Great Britain	Milit Assistance	0UNTS0	109267
12 Mar	Mauritius	UK Great Britain	Tech Assistance	0UNTS0	109268
12 Mar	Mauritius	UK Great Britain	Scientific Project	0UNTS0	109270
12 Mar	Mauritius	UK Great Britain	Admin Cooperation	0UNTS0	109269
12 Mar	Accept UN Charter	Mauritius	UN Charter	634UNTS217	109064
13 Mar	Bulgaria	UK Great Britain	Consul/Citizenship	0UNTS0	109708
13 Mar	Bulgaria	UK Great Britain	Sanitation	0UNTS0	109585
13 Mar	Congo (Brazzaville)	United Nations	IGO Operations	632UNTS161	109018
13 Mar	Netherlands	Yugoslavia	General Economic	0UNTS0	109297
14 Mar	Germany, West	Netherlands	Status of Forces	68WBGA81	424493
15 Mar	Bulgaria	Japan	Visas	68JJS3	442211
15 Mar	Japan	Yugoslavia	Culture	69JHZ5	439020
15 Mar	Germany, West	Netherlands	Admin Cooperation	68WBGA106	424494
15 Mar	France	Spain	Admin Cooperation	70FRJO2503	416174
15 Mar	Japan	Yugoslavia	Culture	0UNTS0	110575
15 Mar	Dominican Republic	Spain	Consul/Citizenship	0UNTS0	110411
15 Mar	Somalia	USA (United States)	US Agri Commod Aid	0UNTS0	110008
15 Mar	Jamaica	Mexico	Visas	0UNTS0	109235
16 Mar	Algeria	France	Tech Assistance	69FRJO2006	416029
16 Mar	Algeria	France	Scientific Project	0UNTS0	110821
18 Mar	Germany, West	Niger	Loans and Credits	68WBGA108	424506
18 Mar	Multilateral		Postal Service	0UNTS0	110009
18 Mar	Sierra Leone	UK Great Britain	Taxation	0UNTS0	109655
18 Mar	Greece	IBRD (World Bank)	IBRD Project	0UNTS0	109326
18 Mar	United Nations	Tunisia	IGO Operations	633UNTS3	109030
18 Mar	Multilateral		Commodity Trade	0UNTS0	109262
19 Mar	France	United Arab Rep	Health/Educ/Welfare	69FRJO3005	416050
19 Mar	France	Hungary	Admin Cooperation	0UNTS0	109532
19 Mar	France	United Arab Rep	Culture	0UNTS0	110101
19 Mar	France	United Arab Rep	Education	0UNTS0	110102
19 Mar	Iran	USA (United States)	Specific Resources	0UNTS0	110010
19 Mar	Bulgaria	Finland	Sanitation	0UNTS0	109970
20 Mar	France	Tunisia	Non-ILO Labor	0UNTS0	110730
21 Mar	Belgium	Netherlands	Non-ILO Labor	0UNTS0	109363
21 Mar	Argentina	Germany, West	Admin Cooperation	0UNTS0	109563

DATE	PARTY ONE	PARTY TWO	TOPIC	CITATION	NUMBER
1968 (Cont.)					
21 Mar	IDA (Devel Assoc)	Tanzania	Non-IBRD Project	0UNTS0	109327
22 Mar	Austria	USSR (Soviet Union)	Culture	0UNTS0	110281
22 Mar	IBRD (World Bank)	Yugoslavia	Loans and Credits	0UNTS0	109301
24 Mar	Multilateral		IGO Establishment	0UNTS0	109577
25 Mar	Denmark	India	Direct Aid	0UNTS0	109229
26 Mar	Czechoslovakia	UK Great Britain	Scientific Project	0UNTS0	109278
27 Mar	Nicaragua	Norway	Visas	3NORT815	451121
27 Mar	Portugal	UK Great Britain	Taxation	0UNTS0	109656
27 Mar	State/IGO Group	IAEA (Atom Energy)	Atomic Energy	0UNTS0	109312
27 Mar	Multilateral		Visas	0UNTS0	109293
27 Mar	France	South Africa	Scientific Project	643UNTS343	109200
28 Mar	Belgium	Japan	Taxation	70JHZ4	439021
28 Mar	Belgium	Japan	Taxation	0UNTS0	110513
28 Mar	Korea, South	USA (United States)	Visas	0UNTS0	109926
29 Mar	Israel	USA (United States)	US Agri Commod Aid	0UNTS0	109352
29 Mar	Germany, West	Thailand	Direct Aid	637UNTS0	109122
29 Mar	Turkey	UK Great Britain	Loans and Credits	0UNTS0	109286
30 Mar	France	Japan	General Trade	68JJS187	442212
30 Mar	Germany, West	Ghana	Tech Assistance	68WBGA147	424223
30 Mar	Cyprus	Greece	Taxation	0UNTS0	109465
30 Mar	Barbados	UNICEF (Children)	IGO Operations	637UNTS0	109123
31 Mar	Czechoslovakia	Mongolia	Sanitation	0UNTS0	109279
01 Apr	Jordan	Turkey	Land Transport	0UNTS0	110584
01 Apr	Gambia	UK Great Britain	Taxation	0UNTS0	109709
01 Apr	Dominican Republic	USA (United States)	General Aid	0UNTS0	110249
01 Apr	Finland	Romania	Land Transport	0UNTS0	109392
01 Apr	Israel	Peru	Visas	0UNTS0	109354
01 Apr	Denmark	Uganda	Loans and Credits	0UNTS0	109209
02 Apr	Malawi	UK Great Britain	Taxation	0UNTS0	109450
02 Apr	Czechoslovakia	Yemen	General Amity	0UNTS0	110172
02 Apr	Turkey	UK Great Britain	Taxation	0UNTS0	109452
02 Apr	New Zealand	UK Great Britain	General Military	0UNTS0	109206
03 Apr	France	Gabon	General Economic	0UNTS0	110529
03 Apr	State/IGO Group	Jordan	Direct Aid	632UNTS66	109009
03 Apr	Austria	UK Great Britain	Visas	0UNTS0	109214
04 Apr	Poland	Sweden	Land Transport	68PZUM71	458154
04 Apr	Jordan	USA (United States)	US Agri Commod Aid	0UNTS0	110011
04 Apr	New Zealand	Singapore	Air Transport	0UNTS0	109480
05 Apr	Japan	USA (United States)	Territory Boundary	68JHZ6	439022
05 Apr	Japan	USA (United States)	Territory Boundary	0UNTS0	109724
06 Apr	UK Great Britain	Zambia	Taxation	0UNTS0	110698
06 Apr	Costa Rica	Israel	Visas	0UNTS0	109355
09 Apr	Argentina	Colombia	General Military	0UNTS0	109566
10 Apr	Hungary	Iran	General Economic	0IRTB37	433055
10 Apr	Ecuador	Germany, West	Education	68WBGA148	424116
10 Apr	Chad	Germany, West	Loans and Credits	68WBGA152	424674
10 Apr	Bulgaria	Iceland	Visas	0UNTS0	110304
10 Apr	Nicaragua	IBRD (World Bank)	Loans and Credits	0UNTS0	109300
11 Apr	Germany, West	Zambia	Tech Assistance	68WBGA147	424611
11 Apr	Denmark	Yugoslavia	Taxation	0UNTS0	109406
11 Apr	Germany, West	UK Great Britain	Finance	0UNTS0	109288
15 Apr	Greece	UK Great Britain	Atomic Energy	0UNTS0	109782
16 Apr	Malta	USA (United States)	Military Mission	0UNTS0	110012
17 Apr	Belgium	Czechoslovakia	Land Transport	0UNTS0	109539
17 Apr	Malaysia	IBRD (World Bank)	IBRD Project	0UNTS0	109360
18 Apr	Argentina	Bolivia	Commodity Trade	0UNTS0	109551
19 Apr	UK Great Britain	Yugoslavia	Scientific Project	0UNTS0	109657
20 Apr	State/IGO Group	Nigeria	IGO Operations	636UNTS294	109106
22 Apr	Germany, West	Iran	Loans and Credits	68WBGA112	424275
22 Apr	Germany, West	Malawi	Loans and Credits	68WBGA129	424447
22 Apr	Austria	Yugoslavia	Customs	68ABGB400	403246
22 Apr	Australia	Taiwan	General Trade	0UNTS0	109734
22 Apr	Multilateral		Scientific Project	0UNTS0	109574
22 Apr	UN Special Fund	Syria	IGO Operations	634UNTS207	109063
22 Apr	Denmark	Morocco	Tech Assistance	0UNTS0	109218

DATE	PARTY ONE	PARTY TWO	TOPIC	CITATION	NUMBER
1968 (Cont.)					
23 Apr	Netherlands	Romania	Land Transport	0UNTS0	109481
24 Apr	Poland	USSR (Soviet Union)	Air Transport	68PZUM77	458155
24 Apr	Austria	Italy	Culture	68ABGB197	403119
24 Apr	Israel	Singapore	General Trade	642UNTS235	109176
26 Apr	Canada	Norway	Specific Resources	3NORT0	451018
26 Apr	Denmark	Norway	Specific Resources	3NORT0	451038
26 Apr	Bulgaria	Czechoslovakia	General Amity	0UNTS0	110344
26 Apr	Denmark	Norway	Specific Resources	0UNTS0	109211
28 Apr	Austria	Romania	Customs	0UNTS0	109377
29 Apr	Denmark	India	Direct Aid	0UNTS0	109230
30 Apr	Germany, West	Philippines	Visas	68WBGA135	424782
30 Apr	Germany, West	Philippines	Visas	68WBGA135	424582
30 Apr	France	Togo	Claims and Debts	69FRJO2006	416451
30 Apr	France	Togo	Territory Boundary	0UNTS0	110373
30 Apr	Philippines	USA (United States)	Milit Installation	0UNTS0	110129
30 Apr	Austria	Costa Rica	Visas	0UNTS0	109324
02 May	Morocco	USA (United States)	US Agri Commod Aid	0UNTS0	110013
02 May	State/IGO Group	IBRD (World Bank)	Direct Aid	637UNTS0	109110
02 May	Dominican Republic	Israel	Visas	0UNTS0	109357
03 May	Mexico	USA (United States)	Admin Cooperation	0UNTS0	110014
04 May	Germany, West	Iran	Taxation	0IRTB7	433012
06 May	Austria	Bulgaria	Tech Assistance	0UNTS0	109875
06 May	Indonesia	UK Great Britain	Loans and Credits	0UNTS0	109340
07 May	Germany, West	Ghana	Loans and Credits	68WBGA130	424224
07 May	USA (United States)	Uruguay	US Agri Commod Aid	0UNTS0	110015
07 May	Niger	United Nations	IGO Operations	639UNTS71	109145
08 May	Iran	Kuwait	Taxation	0IRTB48	433075
08 May	Luxembourg	Netherlands	Taxation	0UNTS0	110089
09 May	Germany, West	Malta	Water Transport	68WBGA119	424462
09 May	Austria	Bulgaria	Customs	68ABGB404	403012
09 May	Netherlands	Tanzania	Extradition	0UNTS0	109621
10 May	Dominican Republic	USA (United States)	US Agri Commod Aid	0UNTS0	110326
10 May	Colombia	Denmark	Loans and Credits	0UNTS0	110482
10 May	Korea, South	USA (United States)	US Agri Commod Aid	0UNTS0	110139
10 May	Colombia	USA (United States)	Customs	0UNTS0	110016
10 May	State/IGO Group	Malaysia	IGO Operations	636UNTS276	109105
13 May	Iran	Poland	Culture	69PDZU73	457156
13 May	United Nations	Switzerland	IGO Operations	636UNTS353	200637
13 May	Guyana	USA (United States)	Gen Communications	0UNTS0	110017
13 May	Denmark	Yugoslavia	Land Transport	0UNTS0	109727
16 May	Hungary	Poland	General Amity	68PDZU257	457157
16 May	UK Great Britain	USA (United States)	Admin Cooperation	0UNTS0	110018
16 May	Pakistan	USA (United States)	US Agri Commod Aid	0UNTS0	109996
16 May	Korea, South	Netherlands	Non-IBRD Project	0UNTS0	109260
16 May	Hungary	Poland	General Amity	0UNTS0	109292
17 May	Germany, West	Indonesia	Loans and Credits	68WBGA139	424263
17 May	Tunisia	USA (United States)	US Agri Commod Aid	0UNTS0	110019
18 May	France	Romania	Consul/Citizenship	0UNTS0	110724
21 May	State/IGO Group	Australia	Tech Assistance	636UNTS326	109108
22 May	France	Malagasy	Tech Assistance	68FRJO2211	416287
22 May	France	UK Great Britain	Finance	69FRJO2511	416202
22 May	France	UK Great Britain	Taxation	0UNTS0	110422
22 May	Colombia	IBRD (World Bank)	IBRD Project	0UNTS0	109614
22 May	Turkey	UK Great Britain	Loans and Credits	0UNTS0	109287
22 May	Israel	USA (United States)	Scientific Project	0UNTS0	109356
23 May	IBRD (World Bank)	Thailand	IBRD Project	0UNTS0	109332
24 May	Hungary	Iran	Culture	0IRTB37	433051
24 May	France	USA (United States)	Non-ILO Labor	69FRJO607	416182
24 May	Belgium	Greece	Taxation	0UNTS0	110552
24 May	Finland	UK Great Britain	Atomic Energy	0UNTS0	109575
25 May	Brazil	Poland	Water Transport	68PZUM88	458158
25 May	Nicaragua	USA (United States)	General Aid	0UNTS0	110143
25 May	Argentina	Peru	Atomic Energy	0UNTS0	110184
25 May	Austria	United Nations	IGO Operations	637UNTS0	109118
25 May	Congo (Zaire)	Denmark	Tech Assistance	0UNTS0	109289

DATE	PARTY ONE	PARTY TWO	TOPIC	CITATION	NUMBER
1968 (Cont.)					
25 May	Austria	United Nations	IGO Operations	637UNTS0	109117
27 May	Austria	Bulgaria	Scientific Project	72ABGB86	403013
27 May	Philippines	USA (United States)	Non-ILO Labor	0UNTS0	109435
27 May	UK Great Britain	USA (United States)	General Aid	0UNTS0	110144
27 May	Iran	USA (United States)	Scientific Project	0UNTS0	109883
28 May	Mexico	USSR (Soviet Union)	Health/Educ/Welfare	70MEXD808	444042
28 May	Germany, West	Tunisia	Loans and Credits	68WBGA156	424691
28 May	Mexico	USSR (Soviet Union)	Culture	0UNTS0	110282
29 May	Indonesia	Japan	Tech Assistance	68JJS247	442213
29 May	Iceland	USA (United States)	US Agri Commod Aid	0UNTS0	110066
29 May	State/IGO Group	Sierra Leone	Direct Aid	637UNTS0	109120
30 May	Singapore	United Arab Rep	General Trade	0UNTS0	110420
30 May	Denmark	Netherlands	Specific Resources	0UNTS0	109233
31 May	Colombia	USA (United States)	US Agri Commod Aid	0UNTS0	110067
01 Jun	Multilateral		General Trade	0UNTS0	110835
01 Jun	Finland	Tanzania	Non-ILO Labor	0UNTS0	109791
03 Jun	Colombia	IBRD (World Bank)	IBRD Project	0UNTS0	109333
03 Jun	Colombia	IBRD (World Bank)	IBRD Project	0UNTS0	109334
05 Jun	Costa Rica	IBRD (World Bank)	IBRD Project	0UNTS0	109365
05 Jun	Iran	IBRD (World Bank)	IBRD Project	0UNTS0	109373
06 Jun	Ethiopia	Iran	General Amity	0IRTB28	433039
06 Jun	Germany, West	Somalia	Loans and Credits	68WBGA149	424640
07 Jun	Multilateral		Admin Cooperation	0UNTS0	110346
07 Jun	Taiwan	Paraguay	General Amity	0UNTS0	110435
07 Jun	Denmark	Tunisia	Loans and Credits	0UNTS0	109407
08 Jun	Austria	Hungary	Customs	68ABGB293	403093
10 Jun	Denmark	India	Sanitation	0UNTS0	109219
11 Jun	Germany, West	Ivory Coast	Loans and Credits	68WGBB167	425125
11 Jun	France	Eur Space Vehicle	Specific Property	69FRJO1903	416512
11 Jun	Eur Space Vehicle	France	Gen Communications	0UNTS0	110028
11 Jun	Philippines	USA (United States)	Non-IBRD Project	0UNTS0	110130
11 Jun	Dominican Republic	USA (United States)	General Aid	0UNTS0	110250
11 Jun	Multilateral		Scientific Project	0UNTS0	109884
12 Jun	Other Party Combin	IBRD (World Bank)	IBRD Project	0UNTS0	200644
12 Jun	Honduras	IDA (Devel Assoc)	Non-IBRD Project	0UNTS0	109409
13 Jun	Norway	Turkey	Loans and Credits	3NORT0	451182
13 Jun	Philippines	USA (United States)	Atomic Energy	0UNTS0	110131
14 Jun	Australia	Indonesia	Culture	0UNTS0	110173
14 Jun	Czechoslovakia	Hungary	General Amity	0UNTS0	109645
14 Jun	Ghana	IDA (Devel Assoc)	Non-IBRD Project	0UNTS0	109303
15 Jun	Norway	USA (United States)	Scientific Project	3NORT0	451202
15 Jun	Norway	USA (United States)	Scientific Project	0UNTS0	110145
17 Jun	Germany, West	Ivory Coast	Loans and Credits	68WBGA153	424126
17 Jun	Romania	Southern Yemen	General Trade	0UNTS0	110206
17 Jun	Kenya	IDA (Devel Assoc)	Non-IBRD Project	0UNTS0	109304
17 Jun	State/IGO Group	IAEA (Atom Energy)	Atomic Energy	0UNTS0	109313
17 Jun	Pakistan	IAEA (Atom Energy)	Atomic Energy	0UNTS0	109314
17 Jun	Kenya	IDA (Devel Assoc)	Non-IBRD Project	0UNTS0	109320
18 Jun	Taiwan	USA (United States)	Milit Assistance	0UNTS0	110146
19 Jun	Ceylon (Sri Lanka)	IDA (Devel Assoc)	Non-IBRD Project	0UNTS0	109622
20 Jun	Ceylon (Sri Lanka)	Germany, West	Loans and Credits	68WBGA170	424076
20 Jun	Brazil	France	Specific Property	69FRJO1903	416082
20 Jun	Brazil	France	Scientific Project	0UNTS0	110231
21 Jun	Ceylon (Sri Lanka)	USA (United States)	US Agri Commod Aid	0UNTS0	110327
21 Jun	Ivory Coast	IBRD (World Bank)	IBRD Project	0UNTS0	109412
21 Jun	Nicaragua	IBRD (World Bank)	IBRD Project	0UNTS0	109366
22 Jun	Iran	USSR (Soviet Union)	General Economic	0IRTB81	433131
22 Jun	Germany, West	Morocco	Loans and Credits	68WBGA154	424471
23 Jun	Iran	Japan	General Trade	68JJS283	442214
24 Jun	Italy	USA (United States)	Scientific Project	0UNTS0	110328
24 Jun	IDA (Devel Assoc)	Sudan	Non-IBRD Project	0UNTS0	109649
25 Jun	Spain	USA (United States)	Non-IBRD Project	0UNTS0	110147
25 Jun	Botswana	UNICEF (Children)	IGO Operations	639UNTS61	109144
25 Jun	UK Great Britain	USA (United States)	Direct Aid	0UNTS0	109271
26 Jun	Norway	USA (United States)	Non-ILO Labor	3NORT0	451203

DATE	PARTY ONE	PARTY TWO	TOPIC	CITATION	NUMBER
1968 (Cont.)					
26 Jun	Japan	Philippines	Postal Service	69JHZ8	439023
26 Jun	IDA (Devel Assoc)	Somalia	Non-IBRD Project	0UNTS0	109634
26 Jun	Denmark	Kenya	Loans and Credits	0UNTS0	109210
27 Jun	UK Great Britain	USA (United States)	Finance	0UNTS0	110498
27 Jun	Australia	Singapore	Health/Educ/Welfare	0UNTS0	109669
27 Jun	Romania	IAEA (Atom Energy)	Atomic Energy	0UNTS0	109315
27 Jun	Ecuador	IDA (Devel Assoc)	Non-IBRD Project	0UNTS0	109321
28 Jun	Japan	Uganda	Education	68JJS445	442215
28 Jun	Australia	IBRD (World Bank)	IBRD Project	0UNTS0	109483
28 Jun	Malawi	Netherlands	Extradition	0UNTS0	109504
28 Jun	Guatemala	IBRD (World Bank)	IBRD Project	0UNTS0	109482
28 Jun	Mexico	IBRD (World Bank)	IBRD Project	0UNTS0	109335
28 Jun	Denmark	Kenya	Direct Aid	0UNTS0	109393
29 Jun	Ghana	Norway	Tech Assistance	3NORT0	451065
01 Jul	Multilateral		Peace/Disarmament	0UNTS0	110485
02 Jul	Indonesia	Japan	Loans and Credits	68JJS263	442216
02 Jul	Austria	USSR (Soviet Union)	Air Transport	68ABGB295	403222
02 Jul	Afghanistan	USA (United States)	US Agri Commod Aid	0UNTS0	110148
02 Jul	Nigeria	United Nations	General Economic	639UNTS81	109146
03 Jul	Denmark	Uganda	Tech Assistance	0UNTS0	109466
03 Jul	Lesotho	UK Great Britain	Taxation	0UNTS0	109783
03 Jul	Denmark	Uganda	Non-IBRD Project	0UNTS0	109467
03 Jul	Denmark	Uganda	Direct Aid	0UNTS0	109305
03 Jul	Guyana	WHO (World Health)	Direct Aid	642UNTS13	109161
03 Jul	IBRD (World Bank)	Singapore	IBRD Project	0UNTS0	109364
05 Jul	Germany, West	Panama	Air Transport	69WGBB1560	425570
07 Jul	Indonesia	Netherlands	Culture	0UNTS0	110604
07 Jul	Gabon	IBRD (World Bank)	IBRD Project	0UNTS0	109361
08 Jul	Argentina	Uruguay	Visas	0UNTS0	109544
08 Jul	Argentina	Korea, South	Culture	0UNTS0	110186
08 Jul	Argentina	Uruguay	Non-IBRD Project	0UNTS0	109542
08 Jul	Argentina	Uruguay	Territory Boundary	0UNTS0	110185
09 Jul	Norway	USSR (Soviet Union)	Admin Cooperation	3NORT0	451216
09 Jul	Barbados	USA (United States)	Scientific Project	0UNTS0	110068
09 Jul	Argentina	Bolivia	Telecommunications	0UNTS0	109552
09 Jul	New Zealand	USA (United States)	Scientific Project	0UNTS0	109208
10 Jul	Bulgaria	France	General Economic	69FRJ03007	416091
10 Jul	Austria	India	Other Military	68ABGB326	403100
10 Jul	Bulgaria	France	General Economic	0UNTS0	110731
10 Jul	Pakistan	IBRD (World Bank)	IBRD Project	0UNTS0	109588
10 Jul	Austria	India	Other Military	0UNTS0	109227
10 Jul	Pakistan	IBRD (World Bank)	IBRD Project	0UNTS0	109302
10 Jul	State/IGO Group	IAEA (Atom Energy)	Atomic Energy	0UNTS0	109316
11 Jul	Denmark	Zambia	Tech Assistance	0UNTS0	110794
11 Jul	Denmark	Zambia	Direct Aid	0UNTS0	109306
12 Jul	Austria	Yugoslavia	Visas	68ABGB345	403247
12 Jul	Honduras	IBRD (World Bank)	IBRD Project	0UNTS0	109408
13 Jul	Italy	Poland	Land Transport	68PZUM94	458159
13 Jul	Iran	Netherlands	Taxation	0IRTB36	433048
15 Jul	Austria	Costa Rica	Visas	68ABGB344	403020
15 Jul	Spain	USA (United States)	General Economic	0UNTS0	110252
15 Jul	USA (United States)	USSR (Soviet Union)	Scientific Project	0UNTS0	110069
15 Jul	IBRD (World Bank)	Sudan	IBRD Project	0UNTS0	109319
15 Jul	State/IGO Group	IAEA (Atom Energy)	Atomic Energy	0UNTS0	109317
16 Jul	Inter-Am Devel Bnk	UN Special Fund	Non-IBRD Project	640UNTS305	200640
16 Jul	Germany, West	Romania	Land Transport	0UNTS0	110207
16 Jul	Romania	UK Great Britain	Atomic Energy	0UNTS0	109710
17 Jul	Tunisia	USA (United States)	Scientific Project	0UNTS0	110149
18 Jul	Germany, West	Malagasy	Loans and Credits	68WBGA175	424443
18 Jul	Germany, West	Israel	Direct Aid	68WBGA165	424285
19 Jul	Costa Rica	Germany, West	Loans and Credits	68WBGA185	424091
20 Jul	Iran	Tunisia	General Trade	0IRTB69	433113
22 Jul	Bulgaria	France	Consul/Citizenship	0UNTS0	110732
22 Jul	India	United Nations	IGO Operations	640UNTS121	109158
23 Jul	Germany, West	Malaysia	Air Transport	70WGBB681	425453

DATE	PARTY ONE	PARTY TWO	TOPIC	CITATION	NUMBER
1968 (Cont.)					
23 Jul	Israel	USA (United States)	Air Transport	0UNTS0	109358
24 Jul	Norway	Sweden	Territory Boundary	3NORT0	451168
24 Jul	Germany, West	India	Customs	69WGBB1012	425259
24 Jul	Korea, South	IDA (Devel Assoc)	Non-IBRD Project	0UNTS0	200647
24 Jul	Denmark	Int Coun Expl Sea	IGO Status/Immunit	0UNTS0	109413
25 Jul	Germany, West	Jordan	Loans and Credits	68WBGA199	424316
25 Jul	Saudi Arabia	USA (United States)	Culture	0UNTS0	110401
25 Jul	Colombia	IBRD (World Bank)	IBRD Project	0UNTS0	109484
25 Jul	Canada	Denmark	Admin Cooperation	0UNTS0	109701
26 Jul	El Salvador	Japan	Direct Aid	68JJS165	442217
27 Jul	Colombia	IBRD (World Bank)	IBRD Project	0UNTS0	109485
30 Jul	Jordan	UK Great Britain	Loans and Credits	0UNTS0	109784
31 Jul	Colombia	IBRD (World Bank)	IBRD Project	0UNTS0	109512
31 Jul	Argentina	Chile	Land Transport	0UNTS0	109570
01 Aug	Multilateral		Culture	0UNTS0	109368
02 Aug	France	Spain	Non-ILO Labor	69FRJ01809	416175
02 Aug	Algeria	France	Scientific Project	0UNTS0	110474
03 Aug	Denmark	Senegal	Loans and Credits	0UNTS0	109282
05 Aug	Argentina	Bolivia	Specific Resources	0UNTS0	109553
05 Aug	IBRD (World Bank)	Sierra Leone	IBRD Project	0UNTS0	109487
05 Aug	Indonesia	USA (United States)	US Agri Commod Aid	0UNTS0	110070
06 Aug	Germany, West	Ghana	Air Transport	69WGBB1553	425225
06 Aug	Turkey	UK Great Britain	Loans and Credits	0UNTS0	109451
08 Aug	Japan	Philippines	Postal Service	69JJS349	442247
08 Aug	Algeria	Iran	Culture	0IRTB5	433010
08 Aug	Germany, West	Kenya	Visas	68WBGA184	424361
08 Aug	Japan	Philippines	Postal Service	0UNTS0	109834
09 Aug	Czechoslovakia	Mexico	Culture	71MEXD903	444011
09 Aug	UK Great Britain	USA (United States)	Finance	0UNTS0	110499
12 Aug	Congo (Zaire)	USA (United States)	US Agri Commod Aid	0UNTS0	110150
12 Aug	Turkey	UK Great Britain	Loans and Credits	0UNTS0	109495
13 Aug	Iran	Poland	Taxation	0IRTB58	433094
14 Aug	Chad	IDA (Devel Assoc)	Non-IBRD Project	0UNTS0	109641
15 Aug	Ireland	Mexico	Visas	0UNTS0	109937
15 Aug	UK Great Britain	USSR (Soviet Union)	Visas	0UNTS0	109473
15 Aug	IBRD (World Bank)	Yugoslavia	IBRD Project	0UNTS0	109595
16 Aug	Czechoslovakia	Romania	General Amity	0UNTS0	110392
16 Aug	Indonesia	USA (United States)	US Agri Commod Aid	0UNTS0	110071
16 Aug	Multilateral		Non-ILO Labor	0UNTS0	109281
20 Aug	Ecuador	USA (United States)	Scientific Project	0UNTS0	110504
21 Aug	Norway	Yugoslavia	General Economic	3NORT0	451099
23 Aug	IAEA (Atom Energy)	USA (United States)	Atomic Energy	0UNTS0	110516
25 Aug	Muscat and Oman	Netherlands	Consul/Citizenship	0UNTS0	109835
26 Aug	Austria	Switzerland	Admin Cooperation	0UNTS0	110354
28 Aug	Germany, West	Togo	Tech Assistance	68WBGA219	424666
29 Aug	Argentina	Germany, West	Tech Assistance	0UNTS0	109564
29 Aug	Chad	IDA (Devel Assoc)	Non-IBRD Project	0UNTS0	109642
30 Aug	India	Netherlands	Non-IBRD Project	0UNTS0	109475
02 Sep	Japan	USA (United States)	Scientific Project	19UST6011	486009
02 Sep	Japan	USA (United States)	Scientific Project	0UNTS0	110073
03 Sep	Japan	United Arab Rep	Taxation	69JHZ8	439024
03 Sep	Ceylon (Sri Lanka)	Japan	Loans and Credits	68JJS113	442218
03 Sep	Japan	United Arab Rep	Taxation	0UNTS0	110576
03 Sep	Mauritius	USA (United States)	Milit Installation	0UNTS0	109737
03 Sep	Denmark	Malawi	Education	0UNTS0	109414
04 Sep	Germany, West	Malawi	Loans and Credits	68WBGA215	424448
04 Sep	Argentina	India	Visas	0UNTS0	109571
05 Sep	France	United Arab Rep	Taxation	0UNTS0	110801
05 Sep	Argentina	Switzerland	Loans and Credits	0UNTS0	109572
05 Sep	Indonesia	USA (United States)	US Agri Commod Aid	0UNTS0	110072
05 Sep	Ecuador	IBRD (World Bank)	IBRD Project	0UNTS0	110112
05 Sep	Denmark	Pakistan	Tech Assistance	0UNTS0	109396
06 Sep	IBRD (World Bank)	Sudan	IBRD Project	0UNTS0	110595
06 Sep	Indonesia	IDA (Devel Assoc)	Non-IBRD Project	0UNTS0	109626
06 Sep	ICJ Option Clause	Swaziland	UN Charter	0UNTS0	109252

DATE	PARTY ONE	PARTY TWO	TOPIC	CITATION	NUMBER
1968 (Cont.)					
06 Sep	Mexico	IAEA (Atom Energy)	Atomic Energy	0UNTS0	109318
08 Sep	Germany, West	Iran	Loans and Credits	69WBGA216	424276
08 Sep	Swaziland	UK Great Britain	Admin Cooperation	0UNTS0	109474
09 Sep	Iceland	Norway	Gen Communications	3NORT0	451078
10 Sep	Brazil	USA (United States)	Scientific Project	0UNTS0	110074
12 Sep	Germany, East	Mongolia	General Amity	0UNTS0	109453
12 Sep	Barbados	USA (United States)	Gen Communications	0UNTS0	110075
13 Sep	France	UK Great Britain	Culture	69FRJ01001	416203
13 Sep	Central Afri Rep	Romania	General Trade	0UNTS0	110208
13 Sep	Central Afri Rep	Romania	Tech Assistance	0UNTS0	110209
16 Sep	India	Norway	Loans and Credits	3NORT0	451080
16 Sep	Mauritius	UK Great Britain	Finance	0UNTS0	109797
16 Sep	Bel-Lux Econ Union	Romania	General Economic	0UNTS0	110042
16 Sep	Bel-Lux Econ Union	Romania	Tech Assistance	0UNTS0	110212
17 Sep	Germany, West	Italy	Taxation	70WGBB723	425307
17 Sep	Guyana	USA (United States)	US Agri Commod Aid	0UNTS0	110076
18 Sep	Guinea	IBRD (World Bank)	IBRD Project	0UNTS0	110596
18 Sep	Ceylon (Sri Lanka)	UK Great Britain	Finance	0UNTS0	109798
18 Sep	Colombia	USA (United States)	Commodity Trade	0UNTS0	110077
19 Sep	Iceland	UK Great Britain	Finance	0UNTS0	109800
19 Sep	Chile	IBRD (World Bank)	IBRD Project	0UNTS0	109590
19 Sep	Singapore	UK Great Britain	Finance	0UNTS0	109801
19 Sep	Gambia	UK Great Britain	Finance	0UNTS0	109799
19 Sep	Ghana	United Nations	IGO Operations	0UNTS0	109250
20 Sep	Belgium	France	Admin Cooperation	68FRJ02211	416072
20 Sep	Jamaica	UK Great Britain	Finance	0UNTS0	109804
20 Sep	Sierra Leone	UK Great Britain	Finance	0UNTS0	109806
20 Sep	Kenya	UK Great Britain	Finance	0UNTS0	109805
20 Sep	Brazil	USA (United States)	Gen Communications	0UNTS0	110078
20 Sep	Guyana	UK Great Britain	Finance	0UNTS0	109803
21 Sep	Czechoslovakia	France	General Transport	69FRJ02006	416447
21 Sep	Ghana	UK Great Britain	Finance	0UNTS0	109807
21 Sep	Cyprus	UK Great Britain	Finance	0UNTS0	109808
21 Sep	Czechoslovakia	France	Land Transport	0UNTS0	110347
21 Sep	Uganda	UK Great Britain	Finance	0UNTS0	109810
21 Sep	India	UK Great Britain	Finance	0UNTS0	109809
22 Sep	Jordan	UK Great Britain	Finance	0UNTS0	109811
22 Sep	Malta	UK Great Britain	Finance	0UNTS0	109812
23 Sep	Germany, West	Senegal	Culture	70WGBB1224	425624
23 Sep	UK Great Britain	Zambia	Finance	0UNTS0	109814
23 Sep	Tanzania	UK Great Britain	Finance	0UNTS0	109813
23 Sep	Niger	IDA (Devel Assoc)	Non-IBRD Project	0UNTS0	109627
23 Sep	Ireland	UK Great Britain	Finance	0UNTS0	109374
23 Sep	ICJ Option Clause	Mauritius	ICJ Option Clause	0UNTS0	109251
24 Sep	France	Jamaica	Visas	69FRJ02810	416253
24 Sep	Austria	United Nations	IGO Operations	68ABGB377	403249
24 Sep	Multilateral		Air Transport	0UNTS0	110612
24 Sep	Turkey	USA (United States)	Status of Forces	0UNTS0	110079
24 Sep	Nigeria	UK Great Britain	Finance	0UNTS0	109819
24 Sep	New Zealand	UK Great Britain	Finance	0UNTS0	109818
24 Sep	Libya	UK Great Britain	Finance	0UNTS0	109815
24 Sep	Malaysia	UK Great Britain	Finance	0UNTS0	109817
24 Sep	Malawi	UK Great Britain	Finance	0UNTS0	109816
24 Sep	Austria	United Nations	IGO Operations	0UNTS0	109253
24 Sep	France	Jamaica	Visas	0UNTS0	109336
25 Sep	Iraq	Turkey	Land Transport	0UNTS0	110585
25 Sep	Pakistan	UK Great Britain	Finance	0UNTS0	109820
25 Sep	India	Romania	Taxation	0UNTS0	109882
25 Sep	Barbados	UK Great Britain	Finance	0UNTS0	109802
25 Sep	Belgium	Israel	Consul/Citizenship	0UNTS0	109359
26 Sep	France	Monaco	General Economic	70FRJ01601	416336
26 Sep	Austria	Liechtenstein	Non-ILO Labor	69ABGB72	403131
26 Sep	France	Monaco	Non-ILO Labor	0UNTS0	110720
26 Sep	Austria	Liechtenstein	Non-ILO Labor	0UNTS0	109492
27 Sep	Norway	Trinidad/Tobago	Visas	3NORT0	451172

DATE	PARTY ONE	PARTY TWO	TOPIC	CITATION	NUMBER
1968 (Cont.)					
27 Sep	Malaysia	IBRD (World Bank)	IBRD Project	0UNTS0	109505
27 Sep	Malaysia	IBRD (World Bank)	IBRD Project	0UNTS0	109506
27 Sep	Guyana	IBRD (World Bank)	IBRD Project	0UNTS0	109612
27 Sep	Malawi	UK Great Britain	Air Transport	0UNTS0	109713
27 Sep	Argentina	Brazil	Water Transport	0UNTS0	109420
28 Sep	Multilateral		Tech Assistance	0UNTS0	109296
30 Sep	Malta	USA (United States)	Military Mission	0UNTS0	110080
30 Sep	IAEA (Atom Energy)	USA (United States)	Atomic Energy	0UNTS0	109944
01 Oct	Austria	Switzerland	Non-ILO Labor	69ABGB5	403194
01 Oct	Algeria	France	Education	0UNTS0	110477
03 Oct	Australia	UK Great Britain	Finance	0UNTS0	109821
05 Oct	IBRD (World Bank)	Zambia	IBRD Project	0UNTS0	109650
05 Oct	IBRD (World Bank)	Zambia	IBRD Project	0UNTS0	109608
05 Oct	IDA (Devel Assoc)	Uganda	Non-IBRD Project	0UNTS0	109635
07 Oct	Austria	Vatican/Holy See	Admin Cooperation	68ABGB417	403212
07 Oct	Finland	Sweden	General Ad Hoc	0UNTS0	109376
08 Oct	Canada	Norway	Gen Communications	3NORT0	451019
08 Oct	Germany, West	San Marino	Visas	69WGBB203	425612
08 Oct	Germany, West	Thailand	Loans and Credits	68WBGA234	424658
08 Oct	Germany, West	Thailand	Loans and Credits	0UNTS0	109637
09 Oct	Germany, West	Nicaragua	Loans and Credits	69WBGA11	424486
09 Oct	African Devel Bank	UN Special Fund	Non-IBRD Project	0UNTS0	200641
09 Oct	Multilateral		Finance	0UNTS0	109822
09 Oct	Botswana	UK Great Britain	Military Mission	0UNTS0	109711
09 Oct	UK Great Britain	USA (United States)	Finance	0UNTS0	110081
10 Oct	Ireland	USA (United States)	Gen Communications	0UNTS0	109938
10 Oct	IDA (Devel Assoc)	Togo	Non-IBRD Project	0UNTS0	109643
10 Oct	Ireland	USA (United States)	Gen Communications	0UNTS0	110082
11 Oct	UK Great Britain	USA (United States)	Finance	0UNTS0	110083
11 Oct	Israel	Uganda	Culture	0UNTS0	110378
12 Oct	Germany, West	Yugoslavia	Non-ILO Labor	69WGBB1107	425337
15 Oct	Central Afri Rep	Japan	General Economic	68JJS57	442219
15 Oct	Finland	Sweden	Atomic Energy	0UNTS0	110798
15 Oct	State/IGO Group	IAEA (Atom Energy)	Atomic Energy	0UNTS0	109533
16 Oct	Monaco	USA (United States)	Gen Communications	0UNTS0	110329
16 Oct	Denmark	Thailand	Scientific Project	0UNTS0	109463
16 Oct	IBRD (World Bank)	Trinidad/Tobago	IBRD Project	0UNTS0	109651
16 Oct	Australia	UK Great Britain	Scientific Project	0UNTS0	109459
16 Oct	Argentina	Uruguay	Territory Boundary	0UNTS0	109543
17 Oct	Greece	Syria	Taxation	0UNTS0	110032
18 Oct	Norway	Poland	General Trade	3NORT0	451133
18 Oct	Chile	Germany, West	General Aid	70WBGA64	424087
18 Oct	Chile	Germany, West	Loans and Credits	69WBGA146	424088
18 Oct	Romania	UK Great Britain	General Trade	0UNTS0	110210
18 Oct	Finland	USSR (Soviet Union)	Land Transport	0UNTS0	109609
21 Oct	Japan	South Africa	Taxation	68JJS439	442220
23 Oct	Germany, West	Yugoslavia	Visas	69WBGA59	424338
23 Oct	Austria	Germany, West	Customs	68ABGB410	403067
23 Oct	Austria	Germany, West	Customs	68ABGB409	403066
23 Oct	Brazil	IBRD (World Bank)	IBRD Project	0UNTS0	109629
23 Oct	Korea, South	USA (United States)	US Agri Commod Aid	0UNTS0	110140
23 Oct	Brazil	IBRD (World Bank)	IBRD Project	0UNTS0	109628
23 Oct	Brazil	IBRD (World Bank)	IBRD Project	0UNTS0	110119
24 Oct	Iran	Saudi Arabia	Territory Boundary	0IRTB10	433017
24 Oct	Iran	Saudi Arabia	Territory Boundary	0UNTS0	109976
25 Oct	Austria	Germany, West	Health/Educ/Welfare	69ABGB259	403068
25 Oct	Bulgaria	Denmark	Land Transport	0UNTS0	109876
25 Oct	Accept UN Charter	Guinea	UN Charter	0UNTS0	109295
28 Oct	Germany, West	Netherlands	Specific Property	69WGBB1121	425495
28 Oct	Switzerland	USA (United States)	General Economic	0UNTS0	110084
29 Oct	Germany, West	Norway	Gen Communications	3NORT0	451194
29 Oct	France	Philippines	Air Transport	0UNTS0	109972
30 Oct	Iran	Sweden	Visas	0IRTB63	433102
30 Oct	Austria	Liechtenstein	Non-ILO Labor	69ABGB73	403132
30 Oct	Belgium	Poland	Land Transport	0UNTS0	109597

DATE	PARTY ONE	PARTY TWO	TOPIC	CITATION	NUMBER
1968 (Cont.)					
31 Oct	Hungary	Poland	Health/Educ/Welfare	70PDZU91	457161
31 Oct	IDA (Devel Assoc)	Tanzania	Non-IBRD Project	0UNTS0	109652
02 Nov	Cambodia	Japan	Tech Assistance	68JJS49	442221
05 Nov	Germany, West	Italy	Non-ILO Labor	70WGBB797	425308
05 Nov	Argentina	Romania	Culture	0UNTS0	109573
05 Nov	Denmark	Morocco	Loans and Credits	0UNTS0	109415
06 Nov	Norway	UK Great Britain	Commodity Trade	3NORT0	451152
06 Nov	Iran	Kuwait	General Trade	0IRTB48	433074
07 Nov	Germany, West	Iran	Tech Assistance	0IRTB9	433015
08 Nov	Germany, West	Indonesia	Loans and Credits	70WGBB492	425264
08 Nov	Japan	USA (United States)	Culture	0UNTS0	110085
09 Nov	USA (United States)	Vietnam, South	Status of Forces	0VKNG281	496073
09 Nov	USA (United States)	Vietnam, South	Milit Servic/Citiz	0UNTS0	110086
11 Nov	Indonesia	UK Great Britain	Loans and Credits	0UNTS0	109659
12 Nov	Turkey	USA (United States)	Milit Installation	0UNTS0	110087
12 Nov	Ceylon (Sri Lanka)	IBRD (World Bank)	IBRD Project	0UNTS0	109623
12 Nov	Ceylon (Sri Lanka)	IDA (Devel Assoc)	Non-IBRD Project	0UNTS0	109624
12 Nov	Madagascar	IDA (Devel Assoc)	Non-IBRD Project	0UNTS0	109671
12 Nov	Madagascar	IBRD (World Bank)	IBRD Project	0UNTS0	109670
13 Nov	Japan	Malta	General Trade	68JJS327	442222
13 Nov	Austria	Germany, West	General Transport	69WGBB1457	425559
14 Nov	India	Norway	Visas	3NORT0	451081
14 Nov	Morocco	IBRD (World Bank)	IBRD Project	0UNTS0	110597
14 Nov	United Nations	United Arab Rep	IGO Operations	0UNTS0	109371
15 Nov	Bulgaria	Norway	General Trade	3NORT0	451016
15 Nov	Bolivia	Germany, West	Air Transport	70WGBB1197	425048
15 Nov	Belgium	Finland	Land Transport	0UNTS0	109673
16 Nov	Hungary	USSR (Soviet Union)	Culture	0UNTS0	110283
18 Nov	Chile	UK Great Britain	Atomic Energy	0UNTS0	110236
19 Nov	Costa Rica	UK Great Britain	Visas	0UNTS0	109661
20 Nov	Germany, West	Senegal	Loans and Credits	69WBGA28	424625
21 Nov	Burundi	Germany, West	Loans and Credits	69WBGA14	424069
21 Nov	South Africa	UK Great Britain	Taxation	0UNTS0	110023
21 Nov	UK Great Britain	USA (United States)	Finance	0UNTS0	110088
22 Nov	Austria	Israel	Visas	68ABGB438	403110
22 Nov	Hungary	Mongolia	Admin Cooperation	0UNTS0	109646
22 Nov	Costa Rica	USA (United States)	Finance	0UNTS0	110445
22 Nov	Austria	Israel	Visas	0UNTS0	109388
23 Nov	Czechoslovakia	Romania	Culture	0UNTS0	110211
25 Nov	Colombia	Germany, West	Air Transport	70WGBB673	425376
25 Nov	Ethiopia	Finland	Tech Assistance	0UNTS0	109674
26 Nov	Norway	Romania	Visas	3NORT0	451136
26 Nov	Multilateral		Humanitarian	0UNTS0	110823
26 Nov	Romania	USA (United States)	Education	0UNTS0	110402
26 Nov	Switzerland	UK Great Britain	Taxation	0UNTS0	109662
27 Nov	UK Great Britain	Vietnam, South	Air Transport	0VKNG278	496072
27 Nov	Afghanistan	Japan	Loans and Credits	69JJS3	442257
27 Nov	Australia	Japan	Specific Resources	69JHZ8	439025
27 Nov	Gabon	Germany, West	Loans and Credits	69WBGA27	424210
27 Nov	Austria	Hungary	Customs	69ABGB261	403094
27 Nov	Australia	Japan	Specific Resources	0UNTS0	110174
27 Nov	Bulgaria	Mongolia	Admin Cooperation	0UNTS0	109885
27 Nov	Bulgaria	Mongolia	Admin Cooperation	0UNTS0	109633
27 Nov	Nigeria	IBRD (World Bank)	IBRD Project	0UNTS0	109591
28 Nov	Norway	Singapore	Visas	3NORT0	451142
28 Nov	Germany, West	Somalia	Loans and Credits	69WBGA157	424641
28 Nov	Int Wheat Coun	UK Great Britain	General IGO	0UNTS0	109498
28 Nov	IMCO (Maritime Org)	UK Great Britain	IGO Operations	0UNTS0	109632
29 Nov	Japan	Philippines	Tech Assistance	68JJS417	442223
29 Nov	Norway	Romania	General Economic	3NORT0	451137
29 Nov	Int Bureau Educ	UNESCO (Educ/Cult)	IGO Operations	0UNTS0	200642
29 Nov	IBRD (World Bank)	Tunisia	IBRD Project	0UNTS0	110598
29 Nov	Norway	Romania	General Economic	0UNTS0	109705
02 Dec	Belgium	France	Admin Cooperation	69FRJO2006	416073
02 Dec	Taiwan	IBRD (World Bank)	IBRD Project	0UNTS0	109639

DATE	PARTY ONE	PARTY TWO	TOPIC	CITATION	NUMBER
1968 (Cont.)					
02 Dec	Colombia	IBRD (World Bank)	IBRD Project	0UNTS0	109592
03 Dec	Czechoslovakia	Norway	Air Transport	3NORT0	451034
03 Dec	Czechoslovakia	Norway	General Trade	3NORT0	451035
03 Dec	Japan	Korea, South	Patents/Copyrights	68JJS293	442224
04 Dec	Argentina	Germany, West	Loans and Credits	69WBGA39	424009
04 Dec	Germany, West	Thailand	Loans and Credits	0UNTS0	109638
04 Dec	Argentina	Germany, West	Direct Aid	0UNTS0	109569
05 Dec	Multilateral		Scientific Project	0UNTS0	109952
05 Dec	India	USA (United States)	Customs	0UNTS0	110253
06 Dec	Bulgaria	Poland	Sanitation	70PDZU13	457162
10 Dec	Finland	Norway	Customs	3NORT0	451056
10 Dec	Lebanon	Norway	Taxation	3NORT0	451105
10 Dec	Finland	Norway	Territory Boundary	0UNTS0	109977
10 Dec	Indonesia	USA (United States)	Gen Communications	0UNTS0	110151
10 Dec	Ghana	USA (United States)	General Aid	0UNTS0	110254
10 Dec	Norway	Sweden	Taxation	0UNTS0	109615
10 Dec	Multilateral		Visas	0UNTS0	109387
11 Dec	Mexico	USA (United States)	Telecommunications	71MEXD2001	444020
11 Dec	United Nations	Switzerland	Postal Service	0UNTS0	200649
11 Dec	Sudan	UK Great Britain	Loans and Credits	0UNTS0	109786
11 Dec	Argentina	Bolivia	General Trade	0UNTS0	109554
11 Dec	Belgium	UK Great Britain	Land Transport	0UNTS0	109586
12 Dec	Switzerland	UK Great Britain	Atomic Energy	0UNTS0	109787
12 Dec	Multilateral		IGO Establishment	0UNTS0	109733
12 Dec	Belgium	Netherlands	Water Transport	0UNTS0	109793
13 Dec	Netherlands	Pakistan	Water Transport	0UNTS0	109739
13 Dec	India	Thailand	General Trade	0UNTS0	109386
15 Dec	Indonesia	USA (United States)	Air Transport	0UNTS0	109999
16 Dec	Iran	UNESCO (Educ/Cult)	Non-IBRD Project	0IRTB87	433144
16 Dec	France	Sweden	General Transport	69FRJO2702	416403
16 Dec	France	Sweden	Land Transport	0UNTS0	109865
16 Dec	Denmark	Malawi	Loans and Credits	0UNTS0	109461
16 Dec	Taiwan	USA (United States)	Milit Assistance	0UNTS0	110256
16 Dec	Guatemala	IBRD (World Bank)	IBRD Project	0UNTS0	110214
17 Dec	Austria	Romania	Visas	69ABGB39	403158
17 Dec	Ghana	UK Great Britain	Claims and Debts	0UNTS0	109712
17 Dec	Austria	Romania	Visas	0UNTS0	109468
19 Dec	Argentina	IBRD (World Bank)	IBRD Project	0UNTS0	109631
19 Dec	Colombia	USA (United States)	Scientific Project	0UNTS0	110257
20 Dec	Germany, West	Netherlands	Admin Cooperation	69WGBB609	425496
20 Dec	Germany, West	Iran	Taxation	69WGBB2133	425277
20 Dec	Mexico	USA (United States)	Scientific Project	0UNTS0	110258
20 Dec	Pakistan	IBRD (World Bank)	IBRD Project	0UNTS0	109593
21 Dec	Spain	UK Great Britain	Taxation	0UNTS0	109663
23 Dec	Japan	USA (United States)	Specific Resources	0TIAS6600	487010
23 Dec	Denmark	Ivory Coast	Loans and Credits	0UNTS0	110178
23 Dec	India	USA (United States)	General Aid	0UNTS0	110259
23 Dec	India	USA (United States)	Commodity Trade	0UNTS0	110260
23 Dec	Argentina	Germany, West	Tech Assistance	0UNTS0	109565
24 Dec	Austria	Japan	General Trade	68JJS1	442225
24 Dec	Japan	Laos	General Aid	68JJS305	442226
24 Dec	Int Relief Union	UNESCO (Educ/Cult)	IGO Operations	0UNTS0	200643
24 Dec	Tunisia	USA (United States)	Commodity Trade	0UNTS0	110261
24 Dec	Multilateral		Commodity Trade	0UNTS0	109369
27 Dec	Ceylon (Sri Lanka)	Japan	Loans and Credits	68JJS121	442227
27 Dec	Algeria	France	Non-ILO Labor	69FRJO2203	416032
27 Dec	Indonesia	IDA (Devel Assoc)	Non-IBRD Project	0UNTS0	109653
27 Dec	Algeria	France	Privil/Immunities	0UNTS0	109640
28 Dec	Ceylon (Sri Lanka)	Denmark	Loans and Credits	0UNTS0	109490
28 Dec	Philippines	USA (United States)	Milit Installation	0UNTS0	109436
31 Dec	Iran	Switzerland	Visas	0IRTB65	433104
31 Dec	Israel	Trinidad/Tobago	Visas	0UNTS0	110379
1969					
01 Jan	ICJ Option Clause	UK Great Britain	ICJ Option Clause	0UNTS0	109370

DATE	PARTY ONE	PARTY TWO	TOPIC	CITATION	NUMBER
1969 (Cont.)					
09 Jan	France	USSR (Soviet Union)	Health/Educ/Welfare	69FRJO3007	416477
09 Jan	Paraguay	IBRD (World Bank)	IBRD Project	0UNTS0	110825
09 Jan	France	USSR (Soviet Union)	Health/Educ/Welfare	0UNTS0	110733
09 Jan	Malaysia	IBRD (World Bank)	IBRD Project	0UNTS0	109594
10 Jan	Japan	Norway	General Trade	70JAIL190	440228
10 Jan	Australia	Japan	Visas	69JJS35	442229
10 Jan	Gabon	IBRD (World Bank)	IBRD Project	0UNTS0	109654
11 Jan	Afghanistan	Iran	Telecommunications	0IRTB3	433007
13 Jan	Austria	Singapore	Admin Cooperation	69ABGB435	403164
13 Jan	Austria	Singapore	Admin Cooperation	0UNTS0	110409
13 Jan	Australia	USA (United States)	Scientific Project	0UNTS0	110262
13 Jan	Australia	USA (United States)	Scientific Project	0UNTS0	109460
13 Jan	Pakistan	IDA (Devel Assoc)	Non-IBRD Project	0UNTS0	109610
14 Jan	Jordan	UK Great Britain	Loans and Credits	0UNTS0	109785
14 Jan	USA (United States)	Vietnam, South	US Agri Commod Aid	0UNTS0	110136
14 Jan	Israel	Philippines	Atomic Energy	0UNTS0	109437
15 Jan	Germany, West	Uganda	Loans and Credits	69WBGA123	424703
15 Jan	France	Yugoslavia	Visas	69FRJO2205	416496
15 Jan	France	Yugoslavia	General Economic	69FRJO2811	416495
15 Jan	Austria	UK Great Britain	Extradition	70ABGB169	403215
15 Jan	France	Yugoslavia	Scientific Project	0UNTS0	110530
15 Jan	Multilateral		Consul/Citizenship	0UNTS0	109491
15 Jan	Algeria	Morocco	General Amity	0UNTS0	110095
16 Jan	Indonesia	UK Great Britain	Loans and Credits	0UNTS0	109660
17 Jan	France	Romania	Admin Cooperation	0UNTS0	110725
17 Jan	Austria	Paraguay	Visas	69ABGB92	403149
17 Jan	Israel	USA (United States)	Commodity Trade	0UNTS0	110263
20 Jan	Greece	Israel	Visas	0UNTS0	110382
21 Jan	Japan	Kenya	Direct Aid	69JJS275	442230
21 Jan	Germany, West	Netherlands	Non-ILO Labor	70WGBB277	425497
21 Jan	Germany, West	Netherlands	Non-ILO Labor	0UNTS0	110751
21 Jan	Czechoslovakia	Denmark	Land Transport	0UNTS0	109469
21 Jan	Australia	IDA (Devel Assoc)	Non-IBRD Project	0UNTS0	110486
21 Jan	Jordan	USSR (Soviet Union)	General Trade	0UNTS0	110364
22 Jan	Japan	FAO (Food Agri)	Direct Aid	69JJS561	442231
22 Jan	Bulgaria	Hungary	Visas	0UNTS0	110837
22 Jan	India	IDA (Devel Assoc)	Non-IBRD Project	0UNTS0	109611
22 Jan	Norway	UK Great Britain	Taxation	0UNTS0	110436
23 Jan	Taiwan	USA (United States)	Scientific Project	0UNTS0	110264
24 Jan	Finland	IBRD (World Bank)	IBRD Project	0UNTS0	109596
24 Jan	Argentina	Brazil	Telecommunications	0UNTS0	109548
26 Jan	Kuwait	UNICEF (Children)	IGO Operations	0UNTS0	109792
27 Jan	Multilateral		Telecommunications	0UNTS0	109664
27 Jan	Ceylon (Sri Lanka)	UNICEF (Children)	IGO Operations	0UNTS0	109394
29 Jan	Belgium	Germany, West	Non-ILO Labor	71WGBB857	425039
30 Jan	Japan	Mexico	General Trade	69JHZ12	439026
30 Jan	Eur Space Research	UK Great Britain	Scientific Project	0UNTS0	109665
30 Jan	Canada	USA (United States)	Sanitation	0UNTS0	110265
31 Jan	Guyana	IDA (Devel Assoc)	Non-IBRD Project	0UNTS0	110097
31 Jan	Guyana	IBRD (World Bank)	IBRD Project	0UNTS0	110096
03 Feb	France	Togo	Scientific Project	0UNTS0	110670
03 Feb	Guinea	USA (United States)	Commodity Trade	0UNTS0	110266
03 Feb	Congo (Zaire)	Netherlands	Air Transport	0UNTS0	110469
03 Feb	UK Great Britain	Yugoslavia	Land Transport	0UNTS0	110437
04 Feb	Belgium	Netherlands	Non-ILO Labor	0UNTS0	109714
05 Feb	Nicaragua	UK Great Britain	Visas	0UNTS0	109666
05 Feb	USA (United States)	Vietnam, South	US Agri Commod Aid	0UNTS0	110137
05 Feb	Asian Devel Bank	Denmark	Loans and Credits	0UNTS0	109702
06 Feb	Brazil	France	Culture	69FRJO506	416083
06 Feb	Brazil	France	Culture	0UNTS0	110555
06 Feb	Turkey	USA (United States)	Commodity Trade	0UNTS0	110267
07 Feb	Austria	Germany, West	Health/Educ/Welfare	70ABGB210	403069
07 Feb	Multilateral		Status of Forces	0UNTS0	110587
07 Feb	France	Spain	Culture	0UNTS0	110707
07 Feb	Multilateral		Status of Forces	0UNTS0	110586

DATE	PARTY ONE	PARTY TWO	TOPIC	CITATION	NUMBER
1969 (Cont.)					
10 Feb	Japan	UK Great Britain	Taxation	70JHZ12	439027
10 Feb	Germany, West	Yugoslavia	General Economic	69WBGA145	424339
10 Feb	Albania	France	General Trade	69FRMD2402	417005
10 Feb	IDA (Devel Assoc)	Senegal	Non-IBRD Project	0UNTS0	110121
10 Feb	Poland	Romania	Specific Resources	0UNTS0	110213
10 Feb	IBRD (World Bank)	Senegal	IBRD Project	0UNTS0	110120
11 Feb	Ireland	Netherlands	Taxation	0UNTS0	110605
11 Feb	Australia	Singapore	Taxation	0UNTS0	110175
13 Feb	Multilateral		Education	0UNTS0	110462
13 Feb	Ethiopia	UK Great Britain	Admin Cooperation	0UNTS0	109788
14 Feb	India	Japan	Loans and Credits	69JJS211	442232
14 Feb	Madagascar	IBRD (World Bank)	IBRD Project	0UNTS0	110103
14 Feb	France	Tunisia	Culture	0UNTS0	110316
15 Feb	Burma	Japan	Loans and Credits	69JJS69	442233
15 Feb	Germany, West	Singapore	Air Transport	71WGBB184	425643
17 Feb	France	Tunisia	Culture	69FRJO110	416465
18 Feb	IDA (Devel Assoc)	Upper Volta	Non-IBRD Project	0UNTS0	110215
19 Feb	Ceylon (Sri Lanka)	USA (United States)	US Agri Commod Aid	0UNTS0	110152
20 Feb	India	United Arab Rep	Taxation	0UNTS0	110590
21 Feb	Japan	Philippines	Loans and Credits	69JJS357	442234
25 Feb	Morocco	USA (United States)	Commodity Trade	0UNTS0	110268
26 Feb	Greece	Israel	Visas	0UNTS0	110383
26 Feb	Korea, South	USA (United States)	US Agri Commod Aid	0UNTS0	110141
28 Feb	IBRD (World Bank)	Turkey	IBRD Project	0UNTS0	110091
28 Feb	IDA (Devel Assoc)	Turkey	Non-IBRD Project	0UNTS0	110092
28 Feb	Czechoslovakia	USA (United States)	Air Transport	0UNTS0	110269
28 Feb	Bulgaria	UK Great Britain	Scientific Project	0UNTS0	109789
03 Mar	Israel	Uruguay	Taxation	0UNTS0	110381
03 Mar	Multilateral		Commodity Trade	0UNTS0	110233
04 Mar	Iran	IAEA (Atom Energy)	Atomic Energy	0IRTB87	433142
04 Mar	IAEA (Atom Energy)	USA (United States)	Atomic Energy	0UNTS0	109945
05 Mar	Austria	Yugoslavia	Visas	70ABGB82	403242
05 Mar	Nigeria	IBRD (World Bank)	IBRD Project	0UNTS0	109644
05 Mar	Dahomey	IDA (Devel Assoc)	Non-IBRD Project	0UNTS0	110216
05 Mar	France	IDA (Devel Assoc)	Non-IBRD Project	0UNTS0	110217
06 Mar	Pakistan	IDA (Devel Assoc)	Non-IBRD Project	0UNTS0	109667
07 Mar	Japan	USSR (Soviet Union)	Air Transport	69JJS397	442235
07 Mar	Belgium	Germany, West	Admin Cooperation	69WGBB1147	425040
07 Mar	Denmark	Singapore	Taxation	0UNTS0	110771
07 Mar	Bolivia	USA (United States)	US Agri Commod Aid	0UNTS0	110154
07 Mar	Australia	Indonesia	Air Transport	0UNTS0	109735
07 Mar	Bolivia	USA (United States)	US Agri Commod Aid	0UNTS0	110153
11 Mar	France	Spain	Specific Resources	69FRJO909	416176
12 Mar	Czechoslovakia	Iran	General Economic	0IRTB66	433107
12 Mar	Czechoslovakia	Iran	Finance	0IRTB67	433109
12 Mar	Czechoslovakia	Iran	General Trade	0IRTB66	433108
12 Mar	France	Romania	Sanitation	69FRJO609	416380
12 Mar	France	Romania	Sanitation	0UNTS0	110531
12 Mar	IBRD (World Bank)	Turkey	IBRD Project	0UNTS0	110113
13 Mar	Ecuador	Germany, West	Culture	70WGBB1025	425117
13 Mar	Indonesia	UK Great Britain	Loans and Credits	0UNTS0	109879
13 Mar	Indonesia	UK Great Britain	Claims and Debts	0UNTS0	109790
14 Mar	Japan	USSR (Soviet Union)	General Trade	70JAIL191	440236
14 Mar	ILO (Labor Org)	Trinidad/Tobago	IGO Operations	0UNTS0	109500
14 Mar	India	Philippines	Atomic Energy	0UNTS0	109796
18 Mar	Congo (Zaire)	Germany, West	Claims and Debts	70WGBB509	425388
18 Mar	Germany, West	Malaysia	Loans and Credits	69WBGA99	424454
18 Mar	Congo (Zaire)	Germany, West	Loans and Credits	69WBGA84	424387
20 Mar	Australia	Japan	Taxation	70JHZ7	439028
20 Mar	Germany, West	India	Culture	69WGBB1713	425260
20 Mar	Panama	USA (United States)	Scientific Project	0UNTS0	110155
20 Mar	Canada	Czechoslovakia	Air Transport	0UNTS0	110470
21 Mar	Cambodia	Japan	Direct Aid	69JJS75	442237
21 Mar	Argentina	France	Scientific Project	69FRJO1609	416055
21 Mar	Brazil	France	Specific Property	69FRJO1609	416084

DATE	PARTY ONE	PARTY TWO	TOPIC	CITATION	NUMBER
1969 (Cont.)					
21 Mar	Pakistan	IBRD (World Bank)	IBRD Project	0UNTS0	109672
21 Mar	Argentina	France	Culture	0UNTS0	110187
21 Mar	Canada	USA (United States)	Other Ad Hoc	0UNTS0	110271
21 Mar	Canada	USA (United States)	Other Ad Hoc	0UNTS0	110270
21 Mar	Cambodia	Japan	Non-IBRD Project	0UNTS0	110577
24 Mar	France	Malta	Visas	0UNTS0	110734
24 Mar	Ireland	IBRD (World Bank)	IBRD Project	0UNTS0	110222
24 Mar	Jordan	UNICEF (Children)	IGO Operations	0UNTS0	109488
25 Mar	Denmark	Jamaica	Visas	0UNTS0	109940
26 Mar	Germany, West	Switzerland	Admin Cooperation	69WBGA142	424765
26 Mar	France	India	Taxation	70FRJO2803	416233
26 Mar	France	India	Taxation	0UNTS0	110735
26 Mar	IAEA (Atom Energy)	OAU (Afri Unity)	Atomic Energy	0UNTS0	200646
26 Mar	Austria	South Africa	Air Transport	0UNTS0	110471
27 Mar	Japan	UN Special Fund	IGO Operations	70JAIL191	440238
27 Mar	Bulgaria	France	Water Transport	69FRJO1906	416092
27 Mar	France	Malta	Visas	69FRRT50	415294
27 Mar	Jordan	UK Great Britain	Loans and Credits	0UNTS0	110114
27 Mar	Argentina	Colombia	Visas	0UNTS0	109567
27 Mar	Bulgaria	France	Land Transport	0UNTS0	110556
27 Mar	Argentina	Colombia	Culture	0UNTS0	109568
28 Mar	Ethiopia	France	Health/Educ/Welfare	69FRJO2412	416187
28 Mar	Ethiopia	France	Education	0UNTS0	110647
28 Mar	Austria	Ecuador	General Trade	71ABGB121	403035
28 Mar	Dominican Republic	USA (United States)	General Aid	0UNTS0	110251
28 Mar	UK Great Britain	USSR (Soviet Union)	Scientific Project	0UNTS0	109880
28 Mar	France	UK Great Britain	Land Transport	0UNTS0	110599
31 Mar	Argentina	Germany, West	Scientific Project	70WGBB5	425010
31 Mar	Bolivia	Netherlands	Non-ILO Labor	0UNTS0	110749
31 Mar	Austria	Germany, West	Admin Cooperation	70ABGB340	403070
31 Mar	Argentina	Germany, West	Scientific Project	0UNTS0	110188
31 Mar	Jamaica	Norway	Visas	0UNTS0	109941
31 Mar	Germany, West	Israel	Admin Cooperation	0UNTS0	110384
31 Mar	Nepal	UK Great Britain	Loans and Credits	0UNTS0	109881
31 Mar	Finland	France	Taxation	0UNTS0	110035
01 Apr	Japan	Korea, South	Taxation	69JJS287	442239
01 Apr	Jamaica	Sweden	Visas	0UNTS0	109942
01 Apr	Asian Devel Bank	Denmark	Loans and Credits	0UNTS0	109877
03 Apr	Canada	France	Sanitation	69FRJO2512	416109
03 Apr	France	Indonesia	Atomic Energy	69FRJO2707	416235
03 Apr	France	Indonesia	Atomic Energy	0UNTS0	110736
03 Apr	Argentina	Romania	General Trade	0UNTS0	110189
03 Apr	Canada	France	Sanitation	0UNTS0	110532
03 Apr	IDA (Devel Assoc)	Somalia	Loans and Credits	0UNTS0	110284
04 Apr	Japan	USA (United States)	Milit Installation	20UST545	486011
04 Apr	UN Special Fund	Southern Yemen	Direct Aid	0UNTS0	109456
04 Apr	State/IGO Group	Southern Yemen	Direct Aid	0UNTS0	109455
04 Apr	Japan	USA (United States)	Milit Assistance	0UNTS0	110156
04 Apr	State/IGO Group	Southern Yemen	Direct Aid	0UNTS0	109454
08 Apr	Greece	USA (United States)	Commodity Trade	0UNTS0	110157
08 Apr	Korea, South	USA (United States)	US Agri Commod Aid	0UNTS0	110142
08 Apr	Sierra Leone	USA (United States)	US Agri Commod Aid	0UNTS0	110158
09 Apr	Brazil	Germany, West	Loans and Credits	69WBGA106	424058
09 Apr	France	Greece	Land Transport	69FRJO3007	416206
09 Apr	France	Spain	Admin Cooperation	0UNTS0	110708
09 Apr	France	Spain	Milit Servic/Citiz	0UNTS0	110709
09 Apr	France	Greece	Land Transport	0UNTS0	110738
11 Apr	Germany, West	Kenya	Loans and Credits	69WBGA115	424362
11 Apr	Burundi	IDA (Devel Assoc)	Non-IBRD Project	0UNTS0	110218
11 Apr	IBRD (World Bank)	Zambia	IBRD Project	0UNTS0	109891
11 Apr	Dominican Republic	USA (United States)	Scientific Project	0UNTS0	110159
12 Apr	Denmark	United Arab Rep	Loans and Credits	0UNTS0	109953
15 Apr	Bulgaria	Germany, East	Gen Communications	0UNTS0	110838
15 Apr	Dahomey	Denmark	Loans and Credits	0UNTS0	110200
15 Apr	Dahomey	United Nations	IGO Operations	0UNTS0	110170

DATE	PARTY ONE	PARTY TWO	TOPIC	CITATION	NUMBER
1969 (Cont.)					
15 Apr	Cameroon	IBRD (World Bank)	IBRD Project	0UNTS0	110171
17 Apr	Iran	Tunisia	Culture	0IRTB69	433112
17 Apr	Iran	Tunisia	General Amity	0IRTB69	433111
17 Apr	Iran	Tunisia	Visas	0IRTB69	433114
17 Apr	Germany, West	Senegal	Admin Cooperation	71WGBB1309	425626
17 Apr	Indonesia	USA (United States)	General Military	0UNTS0	110330
18 Apr	Japan	USSR (Soviet Union)	Specific Resources	69JJS423	442240
18 Apr	Japan	USA (United States)	Territory Boundary	69JHZ7	439029
18 Apr	Chad	Germany, West	Loans and Credits	69WBGA143	424675
18 Apr	Cyprus	Netherlands	Air Transport	0UNTS0	110472
18 Apr	Iran	IBRD (World Bank)	IBRD Project	0UNTS0	110198
18 Apr	Japan	USA (United States)	Territory Boundary	0UNTS0	110331
21 Apr	Finland	Ireland	Taxation	0UNTS0	110818
21 Apr	Jordan	USA (United States)	US Agri Commod Aid	0UNTS0	110160
23 Apr	State/IGO Group	Yemen	Direct Aid	0UNTS0	109514
24 Apr	Germany, West	Tunisia	Loans and Credits	69WBGA144	424692
24 Apr	France	Iraq	Culture	0UNTS0	110739
24 Apr	Philippines	USA (United States)	Customs	0UNTS0	110403
24 Apr	Philippines	USA (United States)	Non-IBRD Project	0UNTS0	110132
25 Apr	Finland	Iran	Visas	0IRTB29	433040
25 Apr	IBRD (World Bank)	Singapore	IBRD Project	0UNTS0	109946
25 Apr	Romania	USA (United States)	Visas	0UNTS0	110272
27 Apr	Canada	Thailand	General Economic	0UNTS0	109675
28 Apr	Bolivia	IDA (Devel Assoc)	Non-IBRD Project	0UNTS0	110235
28 Apr	Denmark	Norway	Admin Cooperation	0UNTS0	110578
29 Apr	Bulgaria	Tunisia	Water Transport	0UNTS0	110839
29 Apr	Austria	Hungary	Visas	69ABGB167	403095
29 Apr	UK Great Britain	Yugoslavia	Visas	0UNTS0	110024
29 Apr	Indonesia	UK Great Britain	Loans and Credits	0UNTS0	110036
29 Apr	Chile	USA (United States)	Commodity Trade	0UNTS0	110273
29 Apr	Australia	Iceland	Visas	0UNTS0	110176
30 Apr	Austria	UK Great Britain	Taxation	70ABGB390	403250
30 Apr	Germany, East	Mongolia	Admin Cooperation	0UNTS0	110320
01 May	Netherlands	UK Great Britain	Taxation	0UNTS0	110438
03 May	State/IGO Group	Spain	Tech Assistance	0UNTS0	109534
05 May	Iran	Korea, South	General Amity	0IRTB17	433029
06 May	Germany, West	UNESCO (Educ/Cult)	IGO Operations	69WBGA207	424745
06 May	Burundi	USA (United States)	Finance	0UNTS0	110799
06 May	Denmark	Malta	Air Transport	0UNTS0	109931
08 May	Germany, West	Indonesia	Loans and Credits	69WBGA189	424265
08 May	Norway	Philippines	Air Transport	0UNTS0	109867
08 May	Denmark	India	General Aid	0UNTS0	109887
08 May	Philippines	Sweden	Air Transport	0UNTS0	109868
08 May	Denmark	Philippines	Air Transport	0UNTS0	109866
09 May	Ethiopia	IBRD (World Bank)	IBRD Project	0UNTS0	110219
09 May	ICJ Option Clause	Swaziland	ICJ Option Clause	0UNTS0	109589
09 May	Costa Rica	ILO (Labor Org)	IGO Establishment	0UNTS0	110307
13 May	Pakistan	IBRD (World Bank)	IBRD Project	0UNTS0	110098
14 May	Congo (Brazzaville)	USA (United States)	Commodity Trade	0UNTS0	110274
14 May	Morocco	Netherlands	Non-ILO Labor	0UNTS0	109781
14 May	Finland	USSR (Soviet Union)	Atomic Energy	0UNTS0	110040
14 May	Jamaica	IBRD (World Bank)	IBRD Project	0UNTS0	109889
15 May	Germany, East	Poland	Water Transport	70PDZU96	457163
15 May	Israel	Mauritius	Visas	0UNTS0	110385
16 May	Gabon	Germany, West	Claims and Debts	70WGBB657	425211
16 May	USA (United States)	USSR (Soviet Union)	Consul/Citizenship	0UNTS0	110275
19 May	France	Mauritius	General Trade	69FRMD3107	417310
19 May	Argentina	Germany, West	Non-IBRD Project	0UNTS0	110190
19 May	Germany, West	UK Great Britain	Finance	0UNTS0	110025
21 May	Hungary	Iran	General Trade	0IRTB7	433052
21 May	Hungary	Iran	Finance	0IRTB7	433053
21 May	Other Party Combin	IAEA (Atom Energy)	Scientific Project	0UNTS0	200650
22 May	Central Afri Rep	Germany, West	Loans and Credits	69WBGA148	424735
23 May	Korea, South	IBRD (World Bank)	Loans and Credits	0UNTS0	200655
23 May	Iceland	USA (United States)	Commodity Trade	0UNTS0	110276

DATE	PARTY ONE	PARTY TWO	TOPIC	CITATION	NUMBER
1969 (Cont.)					
23 May	Malaysia	IBRD (World Bank)	IBRD Project	0UNTS0	110169
24 May	Bulgaria	United Arab Rep	Water Transport	0UNTS0	110566
24 May	Jordan	UK Great Britain	Loans and Credits	0UNTS0	110115
26 May	Germany, West	Switzerland	Admin Cooperation	71WGBB90	425766
26 May	Germany, West	Tunisia	Air Transport	71WGBB177	425693
26 May	Congo (Zaire)	IDA (Devel Assoc)	Loans and Credits	0UNTS0	110285
27 May	Denmark	Tanzania	Education	0UNTS0	110763
28 May	Austria	Hungary	Health/Educ/Welfare	72ABGB111	403096
28 May	France	Spain	Admin Cooperation	0UNTS0	110710
28 May	France	UK Great Britain	Taxation	0UNTS0	110423
28 May	Iran	IBRD (World Bank)	IBRD Project	0UNTS0	110308
28 May	IBRD (World Bank)	Trinidad/Tobago	IBRD Project	0UNTS0	110220
29 May	Austria	UK Great Britain	Land Transport	70ABGB39	403218
29 May	Taiwan	IBRD (World Bank)	IBRD Project	0UNTS0	109892
29 May	IDA (Devel Assoc)	Tanzania	Non-IBRD Project	0UNTS0	110224
29 May	Int Coffee Org	UK Great Britain	IGO Operations	0UNTS0	110037
29 May	Int Sugar Council	UK Great Britain	IGO Operations	0UNTS0	110038
30 May	Brazil	Germany, West	Loans and Credits	69WBGA138	424059
30 May	France	Spain	Specific Resources	76FRJ09070	416177
30 May	Costa Rica	France	Culture	0UNTS0	110741
30 May	Finland	USSR (Soviet Union)	Education	0UNTS0	110041
02 Jun	Cameroon	IBRD (World Bank)	IBRD Project	0UNTS0	110122
02 Jun	Sweden	USA (United States)	Telecommunications	0UNTS0	110277
03 Jun	Germany, West	Turkey	Loans and Credits	69WBGA133	424778
03 Jun	Argentina	IAEA (Atom Energy)	Atomic Energy	0UNTS0	109947
03 Jun	UK Great Britain	USSR (Soviet Union)	General Trade	0UNTS0	110026
04 Jun	Austria	Finland	Air Transport	69ABGB257	403048
04 Jun	Korea, South	IDA (Devel Assoc)	Non-IBRD Project	0UNTS0	200657
04 Jun	IDA (Devel Assoc)	Tunisia	IBRD Project	0UNTS0	110287
04 Jun	Philippines	IBRD (World Bank)	IBRD Project	0UNTS0	109893
04 Jun	IBRD (World Bank)	Tunisia	IBRD Project	0UNTS0	110648
04 Jun	Austria	Finland	Air Transport	0UNTS0	109886
04 Jun	IBRD (World Bank)	Tunisia	IBRD Project	0UNTS0	110286
05 Jun	France	Tunisia	Tech Assistance	69FRJ02109	416466
05 Jun	IBRD (World Bank)	Yugoslavia	IBRD Project	0UNTS0	110480
05 Jun	France	Tunisia	Tech Assistance	0UNTS0	110317
06 Jun	Belgium	France	Admin Cooperation	69FRJ02009	416074
07 Jun	Paraguay	USA (United States)	US Agri Commod Aid	0UNTS0	110333
09 Jun	Brazil	Germany, West	Culture	71WGBB117	425061
09 Jun	Brazil	Germany, West	Scientific Project	69WBGA2118	424060
09 Jun	Austria	UK Great Britain	Visas	69ABGB260	403217
09 Jun	Congo (Zaire)	IDA (Devel Assoc)	Non-IBRD Project	0UNTS0	110588
09 Jun	Ghana	USA (United States)	General Aid	0UNTS0	110255
09 Jun	Multilateral		Specific Resources	0UNTS0	110099
10 Jun	Germany, West	Romania	Tech Assistance	69WBGA72	424605
10 Jun	Denmark	Tunisia	Loans and Credits	0UNTS0	110772
10 Jun	Singapore	USA (United States)	Extradition	0UNTS0	110404
10 Jun	Israel	UK Great Britain	Culture	0UNTS0	110386
11 Jun	Multilateral		Scientific Project	0UNTS0	110100
11 Jun	El Salvador	IBRD (World Bank)	IBRD Project	0UNTS0	110288
12 Jun	Poland	USA (United States)	Specific Resources	0UNTS0	110335
12 Jun	Mexico	IBRD (World Bank)	IBRD Project	0UNTS0	110289
12 Jun	Multilateral		Visas	0UNTS0	110305
13 Jun	Ivory Coast	IBRD (World Bank)	IBRD Project	0UNTS0	110567
13 Jun	Ivory Coast	IBRD (World Bank)	IBRD Project	0UNTS0	110569
13 Jun	State/IGO Group	IAEA (Atom Energy)	Atomic Energy	0UNTS0	109948
13 Jun	Finland	USSR (Soviet Union)	Specific Resources	0UNTS0	110606
13 Jun	Ivory Coast	IBRD (World Bank)	IBRD Project	0UNTS0	110568
16 Jun	Denmark	Thailand	Scientific Project	0UNTS0	109794
17 Jun	Japan	Philippines	Tech Assistance	69JJS367	442241
17 Jun	France	Spain	General Ad Hoc	64FRJ01010	416178
18 Jun	Barbados	Israel	Visas	0UNTS0	110387
18 Jun	IBRD (World Bank)	Venezuela	IBRD Project	0UNTS0	110221
18 Jun	Multilateral		IGO Operations	0UNTS0	109741
18 Jun	Malawi	Netherlands	Taxation	0UNTS0	110429

DATE	PARTY ONE	PARTY TWO	TOPIC	CITATION	NUMBER
1969 (Cont.)					
18 Jun	India	IBRD (World Bank)	IBRD Project	0UNTS0	109894
18 Jun	India	IBRD (World Bank)	IBRD Project	0UNTS0	110093
18 Jun	India	IDA (Devel Assoc)	Non-IBRD Project	0UNTS0	110094
18 Jun	Multilateral		IGO Operations	0UNTS0	109740
18 Jun	Taiwan	USA (United States)	Milit Installation	0UNTS0	110334
18 Jun	Malta	USA (United States)	Specific Property	0UNTS0	110332
18 Jun	Guinea	UN Special Fund	General Aid	0UNTS0	109742
19 Jun	Japan	Lebanon	Taxation	69JJS317	442242
19 Jun	Germany, West	Morocco	Loans and Credits	69WBGA165	424472
19 Jun	France	Iraq	Tech Assistance	0UNTS0	110740
19 Jun	New Zealand	UK Great Britain	Non-ILO Labor	0UNTS0	110439
20 Jun	Indonesia	IDA (Devel Assoc)	Non-IBRD Project	0UNTS0	110571
20 Jun	Liberia	IBRD (World Bank)	IBRD Project	0UNTS0	109949
20 Jun	Indonesia	IDA (Devel Assoc)	Non-IBRD Project	0UNTS0	110570
20 Jun	Denmark	Uganda	Education	0UNTS0	109932
23 Jun	Turkey	UK Great Britain	Loans and Credits	0UNTS0	110027
23 Jun	Ghana	IBRD (World Bank)	IBRD Project	0UNTS0	110107
24 Jun	Greece	Japan	General Economic	69JJS183	442243
24 Jun	Germany, West	USA (United States)	Specific Property	69WBGA156	424725
24 Jun	Multilateral		IGO Operations	0UNTS0	109743
24 Jun	Argentina	IBRD (World Bank)	IBRD Project	0UNTS0	110290
25 Jun	Argentina	USA (United States)	Atomic Energy	0UNTS0	110336
25 Jun	France	Romania	Culture	0UNTS0	110533
25 Jun	Paraguay	IDA (Devel Assoc)	Non-IBRD Project	0UNTS0	110226
25 Jun	Indonesia	UK Great Britain	Loans and Credits	0UNTS0	110116
25 Jun	Paraguay	IBRD (World Bank)	IBRD Project	0UNTS0	110225
26 Jun	Austria	EEC (Econ Commnty)	General Trade	70ABGB128	403041
26 Jun	Pakistan	IDA (Devel Assoc)	Non-IBRD Project	0UNTS0	110227
26 Jun	Mauritius	IDA (Devel Assoc)	Non-IBRD Project	0UNTS0	110572
26 Jun	Afghanistan	IBRD (World Bank)	IBRD Project	0UNTS0	110649
26 Jun	Pakistan	IBRD (World Bank)	IBRD Project	0UNTS0	110357
27 Jun	Colombia	IBRD (World Bank)	IBRD Project	0UNTS0	110500
27 Jun	Colombia	IBRD (World Bank)	IBRD Project	0UNTS0	110104
27 Jun	IBRD (World Bank)	Thailand	IBRD Project	0UNTS0	110311
27 Jun	Argentina	Uruguay	Commodity Trade	0UNTS0	110191
27 Jun	IBRD (World Bank)	Turkey	IBRD Project	0UNTS0	110559
28 Jun	Iran	Italy	Visas	0IRTB43	433063
30 Jun	IBRD (World Bank)	Zambia	IBRD Project	0UNTS0	110310
30 Jun	Cyprus	IBRD (World Bank)	IBRD Project	0UNTS0	110309
30 Jun	Ecuador	USA (United States)	US Agri Commod Aid	0UNTS0	110690
30 Jun	IBRD (World Bank)	Venezuela	IGO Operations	0UNTS0	110514
02 Jul	Austria	Czechoslovakia	General Trade	70ABGB129	403028
02 Jul	Guyana	UNICEF (Children)	IGO Operations	0UNTS0	109744
02 Jul	Iceland	Jamaica	Visas	0UNTS0	109943
03 Jul	Portugal	USA (United States)	Atomic Energy	0UNTS0	110337
03 Jul	Pakistan	USA (United States)	US Agri Commod Aid	0UNTS0	110446
04 Jul	Indonesia	Japan	Direct Aid	69JJS211	442244
04 Jul	France	Germany, West	Specific Resources	70WGBB726	425202
04 Jul	Austria	France	Land Transport	69ABGB335	403055
04 Jul	Cambodia	Netherlands	Non-IBRD Project	0UNTS0	110391
08 Jul	Cameroon	Germany, West	Scientific Project	70WGBB97	425352
09 Jul	Cambodia	UK Great Britain	Loans and Credits	0UNTS0	110117
10 Jul	Bulgaria	Hungary	General Amity	0UNTS0	110111
10 Jul	Costa Rica	IBRD (World Bank)	IBRD Project	0UNTS0	110488
10 Jul	Philippines	IBRD (World Bank)	IBRD Project	0UNTS0	110105
10 Jul	Ethiopia	France	Tech Assistance	0UNTS0	110318
10 Jul	Costa Rica	IBRD (World Bank)	IBRD Project	0UNTS0	110487
11 Jul	Germany, West	Ghana	Loans and Credits	69WBGA176	424226
11 Jul	Tunisia	USA (United States)	US Agri Commod Aid	0UNTS0	110338
11 Jul	State/IGO Group	IAEA (Atom Energy)	Atomic Energy	0UNTS0	109950
11 Jul	Austria	USA (United States)	Atomic Energy	0UNTS0	110431
15 Jul	IAEA (Atom Energy)	UNESCO (Educ/Cult)	IGO Operations	0UNTS0	200654
15 Jul	Argentina	Paraguay	Territory Boundary	0UNTS0	110193
16 Jul	Belgium	Greece	General Transport	0UNTS0	109869
17 Jul	Germany, West	Italy	Admin Cooperation	69WBGA197	424309

DATE	PARTY ONE	PARTY TWO	TOPIC	CITATION	NUMBER
1969 (Cont.)					
17 Jul	Multilateral		Visas	0UNTS0	109729
17 Jul	IBRD (World Bank)	Spain	IBRD Project	0UNTS0	110489
17 Jul	Finland	UK Great Britain	Taxation	0UNTS0	110321
18 Jul	Indonesia	Japan	Tech Assistance	69JJS235	442245
18 Jul	Ceylon (Sri Lanka)	IBRD (World Bank)	IBRD Project	0UNTS0	110484
19 Jul	Germany, West	Niger	Loans and Credits	69WBGA193	424507
21 Jul	Trinidad/Tobago	USA (United States)	Non-ILO Labor	0UNTS0	110339
22 Jul	USA (United States)	Western Samoa	Loans and Credits	0UNTS0	110340
22 Jul	Korea, South	Philippines	Air Transport	0UNTS0	110199
23 Jul	Kenya	Netherlands	Sanitation	0UNTS0	110750
23 Jul	UK Great Britain	Western Samoa	Finance	0UNTS0	110118
25 Jul	Japan	Pakistan	Finance	69JJS341	442246
25 Jul	Denmark	France	Land Transport	0UNTS0	110033
26 Jul	UNICEF (Children)	Southern Yemen	IGO Operations	0UNTS0	109730
28 Jul	Germany, West	Yugoslavia	Consul/Citizenship	70WGBB1191	425340
28 Jul	Germany, West	Yugoslavia	Health/Educ/Welfare	70WGBB1375	425341
28 Jul	France	Spain	Non-ILO Labor	0UNTS0	110711
28 Jul	Ceylon (Sri Lanka)	IBRD (World Bank)	IBRD Project	0UNTS0	110483
29 Jul	Ghana	IDA (Devel Assoc)	Loans and Credits	0UNTS0	110291
31 Jul	Japan	USA (United States)	Scientific Project	20UST2720	486012
31 Jul	Germany, West	Nigeria	Loans and Credits	69WBGA193	424512
31 Jul	Canada	USA (United States)	Water Transport	0UNTS0	110341
31 Jul	Chad	Denmark	Loans and Credits	0UNTS0	110201
31 Jul	Belgium	Bulgaria	Land Transport	0UNTS0	109870
31 Jul	UNICEF (Children)	Singapore	IGO Operations	0UNTS0	109736
31 Jul	Japan	USA (United States)	Scientific Project	0UNTS0	110342
01 Aug	Cambodia	Japan	Non-IBRD Project	69JHZ8	439030
03 Aug	Ceylon (Sri Lanka)	Germany, West	Loans and Credits	69WBGA199	424077
03 Aug	Romania	USA (United States)	Education	0UNTS0	110343
05 Aug	Bolivia	Germany, West	Loans and Credits	69WBGA204	424049
06 Aug	Greece	Iran	Visas	0IRTB34	433044
07 Aug	Belgium	Tunisia	Non-ILO Labor	0UNTS0	109973
07 Aug	Belgium	Tunisia	Education	0UNTS0	109974
08 Aug	Nepal	UK Great Britain	Direct Aid	0UNTS0	110237
09 Aug	Laos	UK Great Britain	Finance	0UNTS0	110238
09 Aug	Jordan	UK Great Britain	Air Transport	0UNTS0	110424
12 Aug	Hungary	UK Great Britain	Commodity Trade	0UNTS0	110239
14 Aug	Ecuador	Germany, West	Loans and Credits	69WBGA232	424118
15 Aug	Australia	Brazil	Visas	0UNTS0	110177
15 Aug	Burma	Thailand	Air Transport	0UNTS0	109978
18 Aug	UN Special Fund	Swaziland	Direct Aid	0UNTS0	109929
18 Aug	State/IGO Group	Swaziland	IGO Operations	0UNTS0	109928
18 Aug	Philippines	IBRD (World Bank)	IBRD Project	0UNTS0	110490
18 Aug	State/IGO Group	Swaziland	Tech Assistance	0UNTS0	109927
22 Aug	Taiwan	USA (United States)	Education	0UNTS0	110405
23 Aug	Sudan	UK Great Britain	Loans and Credits	0UNTS0	110425
28 Aug	Ghana	IDA (Devel Assoc)	Non-IBRD Project	0UNTS0	110573
28 Aug	Argentina	Spain	Culture	0UNTS0	110194
29 Aug	Poland	USSR (Soviet Union)	Territory Boundary	70PDZU165	457164
29 Aug	Mauritius	United Nations	Tech Assistance	0UNTS0	110246
29 Aug	Mauritius	United Nations	General Aid	0UNTS0	110247
29 Aug	Mauritius	United Nations	Tech Assistance	0UNTS0	110245
29 Aug	Czechoslovakia	USA (United States)	General Trade	0UNTS0	110406
01 Sep	Japan	Romania	General Economic	70JHZ7	439031
01 Sep	Germany, West	UK Great Britain	Finance	0UNTS0	110241
01 Sep	Botswana	UK Great Britain	Finance	0UNTS0	110240
03 Sep	Germany, West	Netherlands	Non-ILO Labor	71WGBB37	425498
03 Sep	New Zealand	USA (United States)	Milit Assistance	0UNTS0	110407
05 Sep	Philippines	USA (United States)	Education	0UNTS0	110408
09 Sep	Japan	IBRD (World Bank)	IGO Establishment	70JHZ5	439032
09 Sep	Japan	UN Special Fund	Education	0UNTS0	109930
11 Sep	Germany, West	Poland	Land Transport	69WBGA191	424586
11 Sep	Italy	USA (United States)	Scientific Project	0UNTS0	110506
15 Sep	Turkey	UK Great Britain	Loans and Credits	0UNTS0	110242
17 Sep	Austria	Costa Rica	Telecommunications	69ABGB357	403021

DATE	PARTY ONE	PARTY TWO	TOPIC	CITATION	NUMBER
1969 (Cont.)					
18 Sep	Argentina	Uruguay	Commodity Trade	0UNTS0	110192
18 Sep	France	Kuwait	Culture	0UNTS0	110742
19 Sep	Hungary	USA (United States)	Consul/Citizenship	0UNTS0	110447
19 Sep	Netherlands	UK Great Britain	Land Transport	0UNTS0	110807
20 Sep	Iran	Qatar	Territory Boundary	0IRTB59	433095
20 Sep	France	Indonesia	Culture	0UNTS0	110737
23 Sep	Costa Rica	France	Education	0UNTS0	110669
23 Sep	Cameroon	IDA (Devel Assoc)	Non-IBRD Project	0UNTS0	110580
24 Sep	OAU (Afri Unity)	WHO (World Health)	IGO Operations	0UNTS0	200651
24 Sep	India	IDA (Devel Assoc)	Non-IBRD Project	0UNTS0	110574
25 Sep	Finland	Romania	General Economic	0UNTS0	110398
25 Sep	Ghana	IDA (Devel Assoc)	Non-IBRD Project	0UNTS0	110591
25 Sep	UK Great Britain	USA (United States)	Finance	0UNTS0	110243
29 Sep	Austria	Vatican/Holy See	Claims and Debts	70ABGB107	403208
29 Sep	Belgium	Eur Space Vehicle	IGO Operations	0UNTS0	110203
29 Sep	IDA (Devel Assoc)	Uganda	Non-IBRD Project	0UNTS0	110589
30 Sep	France	Japan	Commodity Trade	69JJS155	442248
30 Sep	Denmark	India	Non-IBRD Project	0UNTS0	110541
01 Oct	Finland	Hungary	Visas	0UNTS0	110358
01 Oct	Finland	Hungary	General Economic	0UNTS0	110481
01 Oct	Costa Rica	USA (United States)	Commodity Trade	0UNTS0	110507
02 Oct	Jamaica	USA (United States)	Air Transport	0UNTS0	110448
03 Oct	Pakistan	USA (United States)	US Agri Commod Aid	0UNTS0	110508
04 Oct	Afghanistan	Japan	Direct Aid	69JJS11	442249
04 Oct	Iran	Poland	Taxation	0IRTB57	433093
06 Oct	Cyprus	UK Great Britain	Non-ILO Labor	0UNTS0	110426
07 Oct	Iran	Italy	Taxation	0IRTB43	433064
07 Oct	Burundi	France	Milit Assistance	0UNTS0	110534
10 Oct	Kenya	IBRD (World Bank)	IBRD Project	0UNTS0	110671
13 Oct	Jordan	UK Great Britain	Loans and Credits	0UNTS0	110427
13 Oct	France	USSR (Soviet Union)	Other Military	0UNTS0	110319
13 Oct	India	USA (United States)	US Agri Commod Aid	0UNTS0	110449
13 Oct	Taiwan	IAEA (Atom Energy)	Atomic Energy	0UNTS0	110517
17 Oct	USA (United States)	Vietnam, South	US Agri Commod Aid	0SUGG304	469074
17 Oct	Multilateral		Atomic Energy	0UNTS0	110518
18 Oct	Multilateral		IGO Establishment	0UNTS0	110232
18 Oct	Finland	Poland	Land Transport	0UNTS0	110463
20 Oct	Denmark	Hungary	Scientific Project	0UNTS0	110525
21 Oct	Congo (Zaire)	USA (United States)	US Agri Commod Aid	0UNTS0	110450
22 Oct	Chile	Japan	Visas	69JJS133	442252
22 Oct	Italy	Japan	Commodity Trade	69JJS259	442253
22 Oct	Benelux Econ Union	Japan	Commodity Trade	69JJS45	442250
22 Oct	Germany, West	Japan	Commodity Trade	69JJS169	442251
22 Oct	Indonesia	UK Great Britain	Loans and Credits	0UNTS0	110440
22 Oct	Denmark	Indonesia	Loans and Credits	0UNTS0	110393
22 Oct	France	Pakistan	Water Transport	0UNTS0	110633
23 Oct	Argentina	Germany, West	Non-IBRD Project	70WBGA6	424011
23 Oct	Germany, West	Indonesia	Loans and Credits	70WBGA28	424266
23 Oct	Cameroon	Germany, West	Admin Cooperation	70WGBB846	425353
23 Oct	Austria	Spain	Non-ILO Labor	70ABGB358	403169
23 Oct	Argentina	Germany, West	Non-IBRD Project	0UNTS0	110195
24 Oct	Ceylon (Sri Lanka)	Japan	Loans and Credits	69JJS117	442254
24 Oct	France	USSR (Soviet Union)	Scientific Project	0UNTS0	110460
25 Oct	Belgium	Romania	Visas	0UNTS0	110557
27 Oct	Barbados	Denmark	Air Transport	0UNTS0	110394
28 Oct	Germany, East	Poland	Admin Cooperation	70PDZU221	457165
29 Oct	Cyprus	France	Culture	0UNTS0	110461
29 Oct	USA (United States)	Vietnam, South	US Agri Commod Aid	0UNTS0	110451
29 Oct	Indonesia	IDA (Devel Assoc)	Non-IBRD Project	0UNTS0	110650
30 Oct	Japan	Syria	Direct Aid	69JJS391	442255
02 Nov	Ceylon (Sri Lanka)	Japan	Direct Aid	69JJS125	442256
02 Nov	Denmark	Trinidad/Tobago	Air Transport	0UNTS0	110395
03 Nov	France	Germany, West	Taxation	70WGBB1317	425203
03 Nov	Turkey	USA (United States)	US Agri Commod Aid	0UNTS0	110452
05 Nov	Austria	Liechtenstein	Taxation	71ABGB24	403133

DATE	PARTY ONE	PARTY TWO	TOPIC	CITATION	NUMBER
1969 (Cont.)					
06 Nov	Barbados	Germany, West	Visas	70WBGA8	424460
06 Nov	Austria	Liechtenstein	Taxation	69ABGB479	403134
06 Nov	Nigeria	IBRD (World Bank)	IBRD Project	0UNTS0	110672
06 Nov	Austria	Liechtenstein	Taxation	0UNTS0	110323
07 Nov	Austria	Turkey	Land Transport	70ABGB274	403203
07 Nov	Kenya	IBRD (World Bank)	IBRD Project	0UNTS0	110673
10 Nov	Nepal	IDA (Devel Assoc)	Non-IBRD Project	0UNTS0	110581
10 Nov	Australia	USA (United States)	General Military	0UNTS0	110479
11 Nov	Germany, West	Paraguay	Loans and Credits	70WBGA41	424574
12 Nov	Iran	Thailand	General Trade	0IRTB68	433110
12 Nov	Iran	Thailand	General Trade	0UNTS0	110563
13 Nov	Morocco	IDA (Devel Assoc)	Non-IBRD Project	0UNTS0	110545
13 Nov	Ceylon (Sri Lanka)	IDA (Devel Assoc)	Non-IBRD Project	0UNTS0	110582
13 Nov	Morocco	IBRD (World Bank)	IBRD Project	0UNTS0	110674
14 Nov	Turkey	UK Great Britain	Loans and Credits	0UNTS0	110441
14 Nov	Argentina	IBRD (World Bank)	IBRD Project	0UNTS0	110675
14 Nov	Bulgaria	Finland	Scientific Project	0UNTS0	110550
15 Nov	Ecuador	UK Great Britain	Loans and Credits	0UNTS0	110600
17 Nov	Indonesia	USA (United States)	US Agri Commod Aid	0UNTS0	110453
18 Nov	Austria	Germany, West	Taxation	70WGBB1370	425560
18 Nov	Denmark	Thailand	Culture	0UNTS0	110766
18 Nov	Denmark	Thailand	Admin Cooperation	0UNTS0	110765
18 Nov	Korea, South	UK Great Britain	Visas	0UNTS0	110428
20 Nov	Germany, West	Mauritius	Visas	70WBGA84	424476
20 Nov	Cambodia	Denmark	Loans and Credits	0UNTS0	110353
20 Nov	IBRD (World Bank)	Zambia	Loans and Credits	0UNTS0	110546
21 Nov	Germany, West	Mali	Loans and Credits	70WBGA15	424458
24 Nov	Denmark	United Arab Rep	Direct Aid	0UNTS0	110456
25 Nov	Cambodia	Singapore	General Economic	0UNTS0	110561
26 Nov	Ethiopia	IDA (Devel Assoc)	Non-IBRD Project	0UNTS0	110583
27 Nov	Germany, West	Iran	Non-IBRD Project	0IRTB9	433016
27 Nov	Honduras	USA (United States)	Commodity Trade	0UNTS0	110454
27 Nov	Multilateral		Atomic Energy	0UNTS0	110519
27 Nov	Algeria	France	Tech Assistance	0UNTS0	110478
28 Nov	Germany, West	Yemen	Loans and Credits	70WBGA37	424311
28 Nov	France	Israel	Visas	0UNTS0	110388
03 Dec	Finland	Germany, West	General Economic	70WBGA31	424133
03 Dec	Multilateral		Visas	0UNTS0	110526
04 Dec	Germany, West	Indonesia	Air Transport	71WGBB192	425267
04 Dec	Denmark	Korea, South	Loans and Credits	0UNTS0	110396
05 Dec	Japan	Laos	Loans and Credits	69JJS303	442259
05 Dec	Taiwan	Japan	Education	69JJS145	442258
09 Dec	Germany, West	Luxembourg	Non-ILO Labor	71WGBB40	425437
10 Dec	Dominican Republic	IBRD (World Bank)	IBRD Project	0UNTS0	110689
10 Dec	Israel	Philippines	Visas	0UNTS0	110389
12 Dec	Multilateral		General Economic	0UNTS0	110755
15 Dec	Indonesia	IDA (Devel Assoc)	Non-IBRD Project	0UNTS0	110651
16 Dec	Iran	Poland	General Trade	0IRTB57	433090
16 Dec	Iran	Poland	Finance	0IRTB57	433091
18 Dec	Tunisia	USA (United States)	US Agri Commod Aid	0UNTS0	110510
19 Dec	Cameroon	Germany, West	Non-ILO Labor	70WGBB253	425354
19 Dec	Indonesia	IAEA (Atom Energy)	Atomic Energy	0UNTS0	110523
19 Dec	IAEA (Atom Energy)	Sweden	Atomic Energy	0UNTS0	110524
19 Dec	Multilateral		Atomic Energy	0UNTS0	110520
19 Dec	IBRD (World Bank)	Singapore	Loans and Credits	0UNTS0	110547
19 Dec	Chile	IAEA (Atom Energy)	Atomic Energy	0UNTS0	110521
19 Dec	Eur Space Research	UK Great Britain	Scientific Project	0UNTS0	110442
19 Dec	Multilateral		Atomic Energy	0UNTS0	110522
22 Dec	France	Sudan	Culture	0UNTS0	110743
23 Dec	Japan	Laos	Direct Aid	69JJS309	442260
23 Dec	IBRD (World Bank)	IFC (Finance Corp)	IBRD Project	0UNTS0	200653
23 Dec	USA (United States)	Vietnam, South	Commodity Trade	0UNTS0	110613
24 Dec	Belgium	Germany, West	Specific Resources	70WGBB1205	425041
24 Dec	IBRD (World Bank)	Tunisia	Non-IBRD Project	0UNTS0	110548
24 Dec	Cyprus	IBRD (World Bank)	IBRD Project	0UNTS0	110676

DATE	PARTY ONE	PARTY TWO	TOPIC	CITATION	NUMBER
1969 (Cont.)					
29 Dec	Mauritius	USA (United States)	Scientific Project	0UNTS0	110615
1970					
06 Jan	Lesotho	UK Great Britain	Finance	0UNTS0	110699
08 Jan	Kenya	Netherlands	Sanitation	0UNTS0	110752
08 Jan	Algeria	Belgium	Non-ILO Labor	0UNTS0	110314
08 Jan	Algeria	Belgium	Tech Assistance	0UNTS0	110313
10 Jan	Pakistan	USA (United States)	US Agri Commod Aid	0UNTS0	110509
12 Jan	Multilateral		Commodity Trade	0UNTS0	110603
12 Jan	Lat Am Nuclear Arm	Mexico	IGO Establishment	0UNTS0	110564
13 Jan	Thailand	Vietnam, South	Air Transport	0VKNG312	496076
13 Jan	Bolivia	IDA (Devel Assoc)	Non-IBRD Project	0UNTS0	110652
14 Jan	ICJ Option Clause	Botswana	ICJ Option Clause	0UNTS0	110359
15 Jan	Austria	USSR (Soviet Union)	Air Transport	70ABGB109	403223
15 Jan	State/IGO Group	Mongolia	Tech Assistance	0UNTS0	110202
16 Jan	Indonesia	USA (United States)	Scientific Project	0UNTS0	110616
20 Jan	USA (United States)	Vietnam, South	Commodity Trade	0VKNG311	496075
20 Jan	Japan	Philippines	Air Transport	70JHZ5	439033
20 Jan	Germany, West	Somalia	Loans and Credits	70WBGA48	424642
20 Jan	Ecuador	IDA (Devel Assoc)	Non-IBRD Project	0UNTS0	110653
21 Jan	Israel	Lesotho	Visas	0UNTS0	110390
23 Jan	France	Monaco	Education	0UNTS0	110664
23 Jan	France	Monaco	Culture	0UNTS0	110663
23 Jan	Philippines	ILO (Labor Org)	IGO Establishment	0UNTS0	110348
26 Jan	Germany, West	Eur Space Vehicle	IGO Operations	70WGBB185	425743
27 Jan	Colombia	Germany, West	Loans and Credits	70WBGA74	424377
27 Jan	Chile	Denmark	Non-IBRD Project	0UNTS0	110558
29 Jan	Germany, West	Jordan	Air Transport	71WGBB1080	425318
29 Jan	Germany, West	Jordan	Loans and Credits	70WBGA54	424317
29 Jan	Austria	Israel	Taxation	71ABGB85	403111
29 Jan	Canada	USA (United States)	Specific Resources	0UNTS0	110800
29 Jan	New Zealand	USA (United States)	General Trade	0UNTS0	110617
30 Jan	Japan	Malaysia	Taxation	70JHZ12	439034
30 Jan	Ireland	USA (United States)	General Trade	0UNTS0	110619
30 Jan	IBRD (World Bank)	Yugoslavia	Non-IBRD Project	0UNTS0	110549
30 Jan	Australia	USA (United States)	General Trade	0UNTS0	110618
30 Jan	Australia	IDA (Devel Assoc)	Non-IBRD Project	0UNTS0	110654
02 Feb	Austria	Netherlands	Land Transport	70ABGB86	403143
02 Feb	Malaysia	USA (United States)	Air Transport	0UNTS0	110620
03 Feb	Argentina	Germany, West	Loans and Credits	70WBGA82	424012
03 Feb	New Zealand	USA (United States)	Education	0UNTS0	110621
04 Feb	Mexico	Norway	Air Transport	71MEXD603	444034
04 Feb	Denmark	Mexico	Air Transport	71MEXD503	444014
04 Feb	Mexico	Sweden	Air Transport	71MEXD803	444040
09 Feb	Austria	Spain	Culture	70ABGB87	403170
10 Feb	Austria	Belgium	Land Transport	70ABGB70	403005
10 Feb	IBRD (World Bank)	Thailand	IBRD Project	0UNTS0	110677
10 Feb	USA (United States)	USSR (Soviet Union)	Scientific Project	0UNTS0	110774
10 Feb	Austria	Belgium	Land Transport	0UNTS0	110539
11 Feb	Pakistan	IDA (Devel Assoc)	Non-IBRD Project	0UNTS0	110656
11 Feb	Malawi	IDA (Devel Assoc)	Non-IBRD Project	0UNTS0	110655
12 Feb	USA (United States)	Vietnam, South	Claims and Debts	0VKNG314	496077
12 Feb	Australia	Yugoslavia	Non-ILO Labor	0UNTS0	110660
16 Feb	Brazil	IBRD (World Bank)	IBRD Project	0UNTS0	110826
16 Feb	Denmark	India	Tech Assistance	0UNTS0	110697
16 Feb	France	Niger	Visas	0UNTS0	110535
16 Feb	France	Italy	Mass Media	0UNTS0	110729
17 Feb	USA (United States)	Vietnam, South	US Agri Commod Aid	0VKNG315	496078
18 Feb	Germany, West	Korea, South	Non-ILO Labor	70WBGA99	424396
19 Feb	Japan	Zambia	Taxation	71JHZ1	439261
21 Feb	France	Ivory Coast	Visas	0UNTS0	110536
24 Feb	Multilateral		Non-IBRD Project	0UNTS0	110623
25 Feb	Nicaragua	USA (United States)	General Trade	0UNTS0	110812
25 Feb	Ceylon (Sri Lanka)	USSR (Soviet Union)	General Economic	0UNTS0	110361
25 Feb	IBRD (World Bank)	Singapore	IBRD Project	0UNTS0	110678

DATE	PARTY ONE	PARTY TWO	TOPIC	CITATION	NUMBER
1970 (Cont.)					
25 Feb	France	Togo	Visas	0UNTS0	110537
26 Feb	Norway	USA (United States)	Admin Cooperation	0UNTS0	110624
28 Feb	Bulgaria	Japan	General Economic	70JHZ8	439035
02 Mar	Greece	UK Great Britain	Land Transport	0UNTS0	110756
03 Mar	Japan	USA (United States)	IGO Operations	21UST473	486013
03 Mar	Japan	Korea, South	Taxation	70JHZ10	439036
03 Mar	Japan	Netherlands	Taxation	70JHZ10	439037
03 Mar	Japan	USA (United States)	Recognition	0UNTS0	110625
04 Mar	Austria	Greece	Land Transport	71ABGB83	403086
04 Mar	Panama	USA (United States)	Commodity Trade	0UNTS0	110626
05 Mar	Austria	Iran	General Amity	70ABGB111	403104
05 Mar	France	Yugoslavia	Non-ILO Labor	0UNTS0	110803
06 Mar	Denmark	Turkey	Finance	0UNTS0	110542
06 Mar	Costa Rica	USA (United States)	Commodity Trade	0UNTS0	110627
06 Mar	Morocco	IBRD (World Bank)	IBRD Project	0UNTS0	110679
07 Mar	Japan	Vietnam, South	Tech Assistance	0VKNG316	496079
09 Mar	Netherlands	Yugoslavia	Non-ILO Labor	0UNTS0	110804
09 Mar	Dominican Republic	USA (United States)	Commodity Trade	0UNTS0	110691
11 Mar	Austria	USSR (Soviet Union)	Admin Cooperation	72ABGB112	403224
11 Mar	Austria	Germany, West	Visas	70ABGB130	403071
12 Mar	Belgium	Iran	Health/Educ/Welfare	0IRTB14	433023
13 Mar	Germany, West	Kenya	Loans and Credits	70WBGA98	424363
13 Mar	Indonesia	UK Great Britain	Finance	0UNTS0	110757
14 Mar	State/IGO Group	Dahomey	IGO Operations	0UNTS0	110457
16 Mar	Turkey	USA (United States)	US Agri Commod Aid	0UNTS0	110628
16 Mar	United Nations	Yugoslavia	Humanitarian	0UNTS0	110360
16 Mar	Panama	IBRD (World Bank)	IBRD Project	0UNTS0	110680
17 Mar	Iran	Japan	Taxation	0IRTB46	433068
18 Mar	Algeria	Benelux Econ Union	General Economic	0UNTS0	110773
19 Mar	Bulgaria	Finland	Air Transport	0UNTS0	110611
20 Mar	France	Tunisia	Finance	0UNTS0	110666
20 Mar	Mexico	USA (United States)	Commodity Trade	0UNTS0	110629
20 Mar	New Zealand	USA (United States)	Air Transport	0UNTS0	110630
20 Mar	Korea, South	USA (United States)	US Agri Commod Aid	0UNTS0	110631
20 Mar	Romania	Thailand	General Trade	0UNTS0	110458
24 Mar	Laos	UK Great Britain	Loans and Credits	0UNTS0	110758
24 Mar	Philippines	USA (United States)	US Agri Commod Aid	0UNTS0	110692
25 Mar	Gambia	UN Special Fund	Tech Assistance	0UNTS0	110397
25 Mar	Jamaica	UK Great Britain	Air Transport	0UNTS0	110759
25 Mar	USA (United States)	Vietnam, South	Commodity Trade	0UNTS0	110614
25 Mar	Australia	USA (United States)	Gen Communications	0UNTS0	110693
26 Mar	Belgium	India	Scientific Project	0UNTS0	110551
27 Mar	Cameroon	IBRD (World Bank)	IBRD Project	0UNTS0	110681
27 Mar	Cameroon	IDA (Devel Assoc)	Non-IBRD Project	0UNTS0	110682
27 Mar	Australia	France	Taxation	0UNTS0	110802
30 Mar	United Nations	Zambia	Humanitarian	0UNTS0	110399
31 Mar	Dominican Republic	USA (United States)	US Agri Commod Aid	0UNTS0	110632
02 Apr	Costa Rica	IBRD (World Bank)	IBRD Project	0UNTS0	110683
03 Apr	Austria	Yugoslavia	Visas	70ABGB141	403248
06 Apr	Austria	Sweden	Taxation	70ABGB341	403177
06 Apr	Argentina	ILO (Labor Org)	IGO Operations	0UNTS0	110430
06 Apr	Maldive Islands	UNICEF (Children)	IGO Operations	0UNTS0	110414
06 Apr	Botswana	UK Great Britain	Taxation	0UNTS0	110808
07 Apr	ICJ Option Clause	Canada	ICJ Option Clause	0UNTS0	110415
08 Apr	Finland	USA (United States)	Atomic Energy	0UNTS0	110767
10 Apr	Indonesia	USA (United States)	Commodity Trade	0UNTS0	110813
13 Apr	Multilateral		Education	0UNTS0	110793
13 Apr	Indonesia	UK Great Britain	Finance	0UNTS0	110786
16 Apr	Iran	Yugoslavia	Visas	0IRTB83	433137
16 Apr	France	Monaco	Admin Cooperation	0UNTS0	110721
17 Apr	Austria	Bulgaria	Culture	70ABGB204	403014
17 Apr	USA (United States)	Uruguay	General Trade	0UNTS0	110775
23 Apr	Germany, West	Tunisia	Tech Assistance	70WBGA196	424695
23 Apr	Germany, West	Tunisia	Finance	70WBGA126	424694
23 Apr	Malta	USA (United States)	Military Mission	0UNTS0	110694

DATE	PARTY ONE	PARTY TWO	TOPIC	CITATION	NUMBER
1970 (Cont.)					
23 Apr	Peru	USA (United States)	Visas	0UNTS0	110776
23 Apr	Chile	IBRD (World Bank)	IBRD Project	0UNTS0	110827
24 Apr	Ecuador	Germany, West	Loans and Credits	70WBGA135	424119
24 Apr	India	IDA (Devel Assoc)	Non-IBRD Project	0UNTS0	110657
27 Apr	Bulgaria	UK Great Britain	General Trade	0UNTS0	110787
28 Apr	Multilateral		Visas	0UNTS0	110805
30 Apr	Honduras	USA (United States)	General Trade	0UNTS0	110778
01 May	Japan	USA (United States)	IGO Operations	21UST1167	486014
01 May	Japan	USA (United States)	Admin Cooperation	0UNTS0	110695
04 May	Belgium	Germany, West	General Military	70WBGA85	424042
04 May	United Nations	USSR (Soviet Union)	Education	0UNTS0	110459
04 May	Multilateral		Visas	0UNTS0	110579
05 May	Germany, West	Ivory Coast	Loans and Credits	70WBGA145	424127
05 May	Argentina	USA (United States)	General Military	0UNTS0	110779
06 May	Pakistan	USA (United States)	Commodity Trade	0UNTS0	110780
06 May	Czechoslovakia	USSR (Soviet Union)	General Amity	0UNTS0	110560
07 May	Iran	USSR (Soviet Union)	Territory Boundary	0IRTB74	433116
07 May	Israel	USA (United States)	US Agri Commod Aid	0UNTS0	110696
09 May	Burma	Germany, West	Loans and Credits	70WBGA145	424045
11 May	Mauritius	USA (United States)	Finance	0UNTS0	110781
14 May	Austria	Spain	Non-ILO Labor	70ABGB358	403171
15 May	USA (United States)	Vietnam, South	US Agri Commod Aid	0VKNG327	496083
16 May	Taiwan	IBRD (World Bank)	IBRD Project	0UNTS0	110688
19 May	France	UK Great Britain	Consul/Citizenship	0UNTS0	110809
20 May	Japan	Vietnam, South	Refugees	0VKNG326	496082
20 May	Kenya	IDA (Devel Assoc)	Non-IBRD Project	0UNTS0	110684
20 May	Malaysia	IBRD (World Bank)	IBRD Project	0UNTS0	110829
20 May	Malaysia	IBRD (World Bank)	IBRD Project	0UNTS0	110828
21 May	Germany, West	Switzerland	Visas	70WGBB745	425767
21 May	France	Philippines	Visas	0UNTS0	110744
21 May	Indonesia	ILO (Labor Org)	IGO Establishment	0UNTS0	110543
22 May	Pakistan	IDA (Devel Assoc)	Non-IBRD Project	0UNTS0	110658
22 May	Australia	USA (United States)	General Military	0UNTS0	110661
27 May	Cambodia	Vietnam, South	Consul/Citizenship	0VKNG334	496086
27 May	Cambodia	Vietnam, South	Consul/Citizenship	0VKNG332	496084
27 May	Cambodia	Vietnam, South	General Economic	0VKNG333	496085
27 May	Germany, West	Liberia	Specific Property	71WGBB953	425413
27 May	Austria	UK Great Britain	Visas	70ABGB167	403219
28 May	Bulgaria	UK Great Britain	Air Transport	0UNTS0	110788
28 May	Congo (Zaire)	IDA (Devel Assoc)	Non-IBRD Project	0UNTS0	110659
29 May	State/IGO Group	Zambia	Tech Assistance	0UNTS0	110502
29 May	State/IGO Group	Zambia	Tech Assistance	0UNTS0	110501
30 May	France	Upper Volta	Visas	0UNTS0	110745
03 Jun	India	IBRD (World Bank)	IBRD Project	0UNTS0	110830
04 Jun	Korea, South	Vietnam, South	General Economic	0VKNG384	496098
04 Jun	Korea, South	Vietnam, South	General Economic	0VKNG337	496087
04 Jun	Liberia	IBRD (World Bank)	IBRD Project	0UNTS0	110685
09 Jun	Japan	Vietnam, South	Direct Aid	0VKNG339	496088
09 Jun	Austria	Poland	General Amity	70ABGB278	403153
10 Jun	Pakistan	IDA (Devel Assoc)	Non-IBRD Project	0UNTS0	110686
15 Jun	Israel	IBRD (World Bank)	IBRD Project	0UNTS0	110831
16 Jun	Germany, West	Turkey	Loans and Credits	70WBGA135	424779
18 Jun	Germany, West	Togo	Loans and Credits	70WBGA196	424667
19 Jun	Bolivia	Denmark	Finance	0UNTS0	110795
20 Jun	Germany, West	Kenya	Admin Cooperation	71WGBB924	425364
20 Jun	Italy	USA (United States)	Scientific Project	0UNTS0	110814
22 Jun	Ghana	USA (United States)	Commodity Trade	0UNTS0	110782
23 Jun	Mexico	USA (United States)	Direct Aid	0UNTS0	110815
24 Jun	Cyprus	Germany, West	Loans and Credits	70WBGA163	424741
24 Jun	Iceland	USA (United States)	Air Transport	0UNTS0	110783
24 Jun	Kenya	UNICEF (Children)	IGO Operations	0UNTS0	110562
24 Jun	Malta	USA (United States)	Non-ILO Labor	0UNTS0	110816
25 Jun	Canada	USA (United States)	Scientific Project	0UNTS0	110817
26 Jun	Nigeria	IBRD (World Bank)	IBRD Project	0UNTS0	110832
29 Jun	Austria	Korea, South	Visas	70ABGB242	403121

DATE	PARTY ONE	PARTY TWO	TOPIC	CITATION	NUMBER
1970 (Cont.)					
29 Jun	Pakistan	IBRD (World Bank)	IBRD Project	0UNTSO	110833
01 Jul	Germany, West	Kenya	Loans and Credits	70WBGA151	424365
02 Jul	Germany, West	Morocco	Loans and Credits	70WBGA165	424473
06 Jul	Austria	Pakistan	Taxation	71ABGB297	403147
06 Jul	Austria	Germany, West	Visas	70ABGB285	403072
08 Jul	Austria	Bulgaria	Land Transport	70ABGB279	403015
09 Jul	Belgium	Iceland	Taxation	0UNTSO	110607
17 Jul	Mexico	USA (United States)	Admin Cooperation	71MEXD906	444021
17 Jul	Denmark	USSR (Soviet Union)	Scientific Project	0UNTSO	110784
17 Jul	State/IGO Group	New Zealand	IGO Operations	0UNTSO	110592
17 Jul	State/IGO Group	New Zealand	Tech Assistance	0UNTSO	110593
20 Jul	UK Great Britain	Vietnam, South	Air Transport	0VKNG351	496089
22 Jul	Central Am Bank	Germany, West	Loans and Credits	70WBGA149	424749
23 Jul	Dahomey	Germany, West	Loans and Credits	70WBGA215	424096
24 Jul	Mexico	Poland	Health/Educ/Welfare	71PDZU321	457166
29 Jul	Multilateral		Tech Assistance	0UNTSO	110608
30 Jul	Iran	USSR (Soviet Union)	General Trade	0IRTB80	433126
30 Jul	Iran	USSR (Soviet Union)	General Trade	0IRTB81	433132
30 Jul	Iran	USSR (Soviet Union)	Specific Property	0IRTB82	433134
30 Jul	State/IGO Group	Western Samoa	IGO Operations	0UNTSO	200656
05 Aug	Austria	USSR (Soviet Union)	General Economic	70ABGB317	403225
07 Aug	Belgium	Rwanda	Admin Cooperation	0UNTSO	110834
16 Aug	Iran	Japan	Telecommunications	0IRTB46	433069
25 Aug	Austria	Jamaica	Visas	70ABGB306	403120
27 Aug	Germany, West	Indonesia	Loans and Credits	70WBGA226	424268
28 Aug	Chile	Germany, West	Scientific Project	71WGBB106	425089
29 Aug	Finland	Zambia	Tech Assistance	0UNTSO	110841
01 Sep	Austria	Netherlands	Taxation	71ABGB191	403144
08 Sep	Eurocontrol	Germany, West	Admin Cooperation	71WGBB1153	425748
11 Sep	Germany, West	USA (United States)	Non-ILO Labor	70WGBB2778	425726
11 Sep	Austria	Germany, West	Admin Cooperation	71WGBB1001	425561
11 Sep	Denmark	Sweden	General Military	0UNTSO	110840
18 Sep	Burma	Germany, West	Loans and Credits	70WBGA220	424046
21 Sep	Austria	Finland	Taxation	72ABGB110	403049
22 Sep	Germany, West	Netherlands	Land Transport	70WGBB1056	425499
22 Sep	Germany, West	Netherlands	Land Transport	70WGBB1056	425500
22 Sep	Austria	Greece	Taxation	72ABGB39	403087
22 Sep	Austria	United Nations	IGO Operations	70ABGB318	403252
24 Sep	Austria	Romania	General Trade	70ABGB328	403159
26 Sep	Multilateral		IGO Operations	0UNTSO	110768
27 Sep	Iran	Italy	Scientific Project	0IRTB44	433065
28 Sep	Germany, West	Yemen	Loans and Credits	70WBGA226	424312
28 Sep	Germany, West	Senegal	Loans and Credits	70WBGA214	424627
02 Oct	Brazil	Germany, West	Loans and Credits	70WBGA232	424062
02 Oct	Austria	Romania	Customs	70ABGB338	403160
05 Oct	Poland	Sweden	Specific Property	71PDZU37	457167
07 Oct	Germany, West	Malawi	Loans and Credits	70WBGA221	424449
07 Oct	Switzerland	Thailand	General Economic	0UNTSO	110824
10 Oct	Accept UN Charter	Fiji Islands	UN Charter	0UNTSO	110789
12 Oct	Germany, West	Romania	Land Transport	70WGBB1217	425606
13 Oct	Fiji Islands	UN Special Fund	IGO Operations	0UNTSO	110792
13 Oct	State/IGO Group	Fiji Islands	General Aid	0UNTSO	110791
14 Oct	Poland	USSR (Soviet Union)	Health/Educ/Welfare	71PDZU213	457170
15 Oct	Germany, West	Poland	General Economic	70WBGA211	424587
17 Oct	Japan	Vietnam, South	Direct Aid	0VKNG391	496090
22 Oct	State/IGO Group	El Salvador	Tech Assistance	0UNTSO	110796
22 Oct	Afghanistan	UNICEF (Children)	IGO Operations	0UNTSO	110797
27 Oct	Germany, West	Hungary	General Economic	70WBGA218	424706
30 Oct	Austria	France	Taxation	72ABGB147	403056
30 Oct	State/IGO Group	Fiji Islands	Tech Assistance	0UNTSO	110790
04 Nov	Austria	EEC (Econ Commnty)	Commodity Trade	71ABGB157	403043
04 Nov	Austria	EEC (Econ Commnty)	Commodity Trade	71ABGB156	403042
05 Nov	Gabon	Germany, West	Loans and Credits	70WBGA235	424212
12 Nov	Poland	Romania	General Amity	71PDZU53	457168
21 Nov	Austria	Iraq	Air Transport	71ABGB270	403102

DATE	PARTY ONE	PARTY TWO	TOPIC	CITATION	NUMBER
1970 (Cont.)					
23 Nov	Mexico	USA (United States)	Territory Boundary	72MEXD1501	444022
03 Dec	Germany, West	USA (United States)	Milit Installation	71WGBB407	425727
07 Dec	Germany, West	Poland	Territory Boundary	72PDZU229	457169
08 Dec	Germany, West	Ghana	Loans and Credits	71WBGA64	424227
10 Dec	Malaysia	Vietnam, South	Air Transport	0VKNG368	496092
10 Dec	Colombia	Germany, West	Loans and Credits	71WBGA58	424378
10 Dec	Austria	Ireland	Visas	70ABGB428	403105
11 Dec	Japan	USA (United States)	Specific Resources	0TIAS7019	487015
11 Dec	Japan	USA (United States)	Specific Resources	0TIAS7021	487017
11 Dec	Japan	USA (United States)	Specific Resources	0TIAS7020	487016
15 Dec	Germany, West	Sierra Leone	Loans and Credits	71WBGA64	424634
15 Dec	Austria	United Nations	Non-ILO Labor	71ABGB424	403253
16 Dec	Asian Devel Bank	Vietnam, South	Loans and Credits	0VKNG381	496095
16 Dec	Japan	Vietnam, South	Direct Aid	0VKNG366	496091
16 Dec	Austria	Czechoslovakia	Customs	71ABGB84	403029
16 Dec	Austria	Norway	Taxation	71ABGB414	403146
17 Dec	Czechoslovakia	Germany, West	General Economic	71WBGA1	424677
18 Dec	Germany, West	Netherlands	Specific Property	71WGBB122	425501
29 Dec	Austria	Portugal	Taxation	72ABGB85	403156
1971					
22 Jan	Cambodia	Vietnam, South	General Amity	0VKNG370	496093
25 Jan	Austria	Germany, West	Visas	71ABGB100	403076
25 Jan	Austria	Germany, West	Visas	71ABGB99	403075
25 Jan	Austria	Germany, West	Visas	71ABGB97	403073
25 Jan	Austria	Germany, West	Visas	71ABGB102	403078
25 Jan	Austria	Germany, West	Visas	71ABGB98	403074
25 Jan	Austria	Germany, West	Visas	71ABGB101	403077
02 Feb	France	Germany, West	Admin Cooperation	71WGBB2434	425204
06 Feb	Germany, West	Tanzania	Loans and Credits	71WBGA114	424656
11 Feb	Germany, West	Malaysia	Loans and Credits	71WBGA82	424455
12 Feb	Germany, West	Nigeria	Loans and Credits	71WBGA102	424513
12 Feb	Bulgaria	Germany, West	General Trade	71WBGA69	424066
25 Feb	Iran	USSR (Soviet Union)	Scientific Project	0IRTB81	433133
13 Mar	Germany, West	Mali	Loans and Credits	71WBGA86	424459
20 Mar	Germany, West	Togo	Loans and Credits	71WBGA115	424668
30 Mar	Japan	Vietnam, South	Privil/Immunities	0VKNG377	496094
31 Mar	Austria	Eurocontrol	Air Transport	72ABGB56	403044
01 Apr	Austria	ICAO (Civil Aviat)	IGO Operations	71ABGB152	403101
08 Apr	Germany, West	Rwanda	Loans and Credits	71WBGA112	424603
23 Apr	Brazil	Germany, West	Loans and Credits	71WBGA109	424063
27 Apr	Indonesia	Iran	Culture	0IRTB39	433060
28 Apr	Austria	Hungary	Visas	71ABGB203	403097
29 Apr	Germany, West	Paraguay	Loans and Credits	71WBGA114	424575
05 May	Austria	Hungary	Air Transport	71ABGB403	403090
07 May	Germany, West	Tunisia	Finance	71WBGA116	424696
13 May	Germany, West	Nigeria	Loans and Credits	71WBGA115	424514
13 May	Germany, West	Kenya	Loans and Credits	71WBGA114	424366
17 May	Austria	Hungary	Visas	71ABGB252	403098
21 May	Argentina	Germany, West	Water Transport	71WGBB2655	425013
21 May	Germany, West	Korea, South	Loans and Credits	71WBGA142	424397
27 May	Poland	USSR (Soviet Union)	Consul/Citizenship	72PDZU125	457171
27 May	Germany, West	Togo	Loans and Credits	71WBGA114	424669
27 May	Germany, West	Philippines	Loans and Credits	71WBGA158	424583
27 May	Germany, West	Philippines	Loans and Credits	71WBGA158	424783
28 May	Austria	Pakistan	Air Transport	71ABGB296	403148
01 Jun	Denmark	Poland	Specific Property	72PDZU33	457172
02 Jun	Germany, West	Korea, South	Non-ILO Labor	71WGBB927	425398
03 Jun	Germany, West	Yemen	Loans and Credits	71WBGA146	424313
04 Jun	Cambodia	Vietnam, South	Visas	0VKNG383	496097
04 Jun	Cambodia	Vietnam, South	Customs	0VKNG382	496096
10 Jun	Germany, West	Morocco	Loans and Credits	71WBGA151	424474
11 Jun	Denmark	Germany, West	Status of Forces	71WGBB1092	425105
28 Jun	Poland	Romania	Visas	72PDZU1	457173
02 Jul	Chad	Vietnam, South	Consul/Citizenship	0VKNG387	496099

DATE	PARTY ONE	PARTY TWO	TOPIC	CITATION	NUMBER
1971 (Cont.)					
05 Jul	Austria	France	Telecommunications	71ABGB325	403057
10 Jul	Iran	Jordan	Taxation	0IRTB47	433073
12 Jul	Austria	UK Great Britain	Visas	71ABGB278	403220
16 Jul	Germany, East	Poland	Gen Communications	72PDZU41	457174
16 Jul	Austria	Luxembourg	Land Transport	71ABGB404	403138
18 Jul	Iran	USSR (Soviet Union)	Taxation	0IRTB79	433124
01 Sep	Austria	Korea, South	General Trade	71ABGB398	403122
09 Sep	Germany, West	Norway	Admin Cooperation	71WGBB1266	425520
09 Sep	Austria	Poland	General Economic	71ABGB495	403154
12 Sep	Austria	Czechoslovakia	General Economic	72ABGB24	403030
14 Sep	Mongolia	Poland	Admin Cooperation	72PDZU321	457175
18 Sep	Japan	Vietnam, South	Direct Aid	0VKNG389	496100
02 Oct	Japan	Vietnam, South	Direct Aid	0VKNG391	496101
11 Oct	Iran	South Africa	Visas	0IRTB4	433009
12 Oct	Austria	Liechtenstein	Taxation	71ABGB493	403135
13 Oct	Austria	Bulgaria	Finance	71ABGB442	403016
22 Oct	Austria	Czechoslovakia	Finance	71ABGB496	403031
28 Oct	Austria	Hungary	Finance	71ABGB421	403099

DATE	PARTY ONE	PARTY TWO	TOPIC	CITATION	NUMBER
1971 (Cont.)					
01 Nov	Iran	Pakistan	Taxation	0IRTB54	433082
25 Nov	Germany, East	Poland	Visas	71PDZU357	457177
25 Nov	Germany, East	Poland	Admin Cooperation	72PDZU48	457176
27 Nov	Japan	Vietnam, South	Direct Aid	0VKNG394	496102
03 Dec	Germany, West	Turkey	Loans and Credits	71WBGA242	424780
24 Dec	Japan	Vietnam, South	Direct Aid	0VKNG397	496103
1972					
07 Feb	Bulgaria	Poland	Consul/Citizenship	72PDZU401	457178
22 Feb	Austria	Bulgaria	Admin Cooperation	72ABGB113	403017
14 Mar	Austria	Spain	Admin Cooperation	72ABGB249	403172
14 Mar	Austria	Sweden	Taxation	72ABGB298	403178
30 May	Austria	San Marino	Visas	72ABGB259	403163
05 Jul	Austria	Germany, West	Visas	72ABGB309	403080
05 Jul	Austria	Germany, West	Visas	72ABGB311	403082
05 Jul	Austria	Germany, West	Visas	72ABGB312	403083
05 Jul	Austria	Germany, West	Visas	72ABGB308	403079
05 Jul	Austria	Germany, West	Visas	72ABGB310	403081

PARTY SECTION

User's Guide

This is one of the five specialized sections of the INDEX. Each specialized section lists treaties in a different order: (1) by date of signature, (2) by party, (3) by international organizations mentioned in the treaty text, (4) by the topical categories of the UNTS Index and (5) by the topical categories of this INDEX.

Within each section there is a standard set of information per treaty: (1) parties, (2) date of signature, (3) topic, (4) citation and (5) treaty number.

In many cases a user will satisfy a query within one of the five specialized sections and will not need to go to the Main Entry Section (Volumes 1–3). It is for limited use of this kind that the present USER'S GUIDE has been designed. However, if the user is unfamiliar with the general format and search techniques of this INDEX, or if the search involves more than one specialized section, it is advisable to consult the Introduction in Volume 1.

Sample of Party Section

PARTY ONE	PARTY TWO	DATE	TOPIC	CITATION	NUMBER
Afghanistan		19 Nov 46	UN Charter	1UNTS39	100007
	Austria	21 Jul 58	Air Transport	0UNTS0	109236
	Bulgaria	29 Jun 63	Culture	0UNTS0	109873
	China People's Rep	28 Jul 57	General Economic	57CCJC72	410437
	China People's Rep	26 Aug 60	General Amity	60CCJC88	410716
	Czechoslovakia	28 May 60	Air Transport	497UNTS129	107266
	Czechoslovakia	23 Apr 61	Culture	437UNTS25	106297
	Denmark	24 May 67	Air Transport	0UNTS0	109951
	France	06 Jan 59	General Aid	61FRRT40	415001
	Multilateral	07 Dec 44	Air Transport	84UNTS389	200252
Asian Devel Bank	Philippines	22 Dec 66	IGO Establishment	615UNTS375	108887

Party One. This section is arranged in a three-fold order: (1) in alphabetical order of the first party; (2) within any one block of the first party, in alphabetical order of the second party; and (3) within any block of identical pairs of both parties, in order of date of signature. The format varies depending on the number of parties (laterality) of a given treaty. Unilateral instruments appear only once under the single party (PARTY ONE), and PARTY TWO remains blank. For instance, the first treaty in the above sample is a unilateral declaration by Afghanistan to accept the obligations of the UN Charter. Bilateral treaties appear *twice.* For instance, the second treaty in the above sample appears once under Afghanistan (as shown) and again later under Austria (not shown). Multilateral treaties appear as many times as there are *original* signatories. For instance, the last treaty under Afghanistan in the above sample appears also under Argentina, Australia, Belgium, Bolivia, and so forth to Venezuela (all parties to this treaty at the time of its original registration with the UNTS) but *not* under Austria or any of those other countries which acceded *later* to the same treaty. Subsequent accessions can be found only in the Main Entry Section under "Annex."

Party Two. In case of a bilateral treaty this column identifies the other of the two parties. In a multilateral treaty it remains blank.

Date. This column identifies the date of signature. Other dates (ratification, force, registration, accession, etc.) can be found in the Main Entry Section. Multiple dates of signature are represented only by the most recent date.

Topic. This column identifies the single dominant theme of each treaty. For a full list of INDEX topics see Volume 1, Introduction, Thesaurus, Topic List. The same information is reproduced also in the beginning of Volume 5.

Citation. This column identifies the printed source where the full text of the treaty can be found. For details on abbreviations see Volume 1, Introduction, Thesaurus, Sources and Citations.

Treaty Number. This column identifies the serial number of each treaty under which it is listed in the Main Entry Section. See that location for all further information on any treaty.

League of Nations Treaty Series

PARTY ONE	PARTY TWO	DATE	TOPIC	CITATION	NUMBER
Abyssinia	Italy	02 Aug 28	Land Transport	94LTS423	302159
Abyssinia	Italy	02 Aug 28	General Amity	94LTS413	302158
Abyssinia	Japan	15 Nov 30	General Trade	133LTS135	303063
Abyssinia	Multilateral	16 Dec 20	General IGO	6LTS379	300170
Abyssinia	Multilateral	20 Apr 21	Land Transport	7LTS11	300171
Abyssinia	Multilateral	09 Dec 23	Land Transport	47LTS55	301129
Abyssinia	Multilateral	28 Aug 24	Postal Service	40LTS307	301004
Abyssinia	Multilateral	28 Aug 24	Postal Service	40LTS437	301005
Abyssinia	Multilateral	28 Aug 24	Postal Service	40LTS19	301002
Abyssinia	Multilateral	28 Aug 24	Postal Service	40LTS249	301003
Abyssinia	Multilateral	17 Jun 25	Peace/Disarmament	94LTS65	302138
Abyssinia	Multilateral	21 Jun 26	Sanitation	78LTS229	301793
Abyssinia	Multilateral	25 Sep 26	ILO Labor	60LTS253	301414
Abyssinia	Multilateral	27 Aug 28	General Military	94LTS57	302137
Abyssinia	Multilateral	28 Jun 29	Postal Service	103LTS429	302374
Abyssinia	Multilateral	28 Jun 29	Postal Service	103LTS71	302370
Abyssinia	Multilateral	28 Jun 29	Postal Service	103LTS5	302369
Abyssinia	Multilateral	28 Jun 29	Postal Service	102LTS245	302368
Abyssinia	Multilateral	28 Jun 29	Postal Service	103LTS321	302372
Abyssinia	Multilateral	28 Jun 29	Postal Service	103LTS377	302373
Abyssinia	Multilateral	28 Jun 29	Postal Service	103LTS249	302371
Abyssinia	Multilateral	27 Jul 29	Other Military	118LTS303	302733
Abyssinia	Multilateral	13 Jul 31	Other HEW	139LTS301	303219
Abyssinia	Netherlands	30 Sep 26	General Trade	78LTS89	301780
Aden	Multilateral	12 Oct 29	General Transport	137LTS11	303145
Aden	Multilateral	28 Oct 33	Refugees	159LTS199	303663
Aden	Multilateral	23 Sep 36	Gen Communications	186LTS301	304319
Aden	Multilateral	10 Feb 38	Refugees	192LTS59	304461
Aden	United Arab Rep	03 Nov 38	Postal Service	197LTS241	304617
Aden	United Arab Rep	25 Aug 40	Postal Service	204LTS297	304810
Aden Colony	Multilateral	20 Mar 34	Postal Service	175LTS5	304049
Aden Colony	Multilateral	20 Mar 34	Postal Service	174LTS171	304048
Aegean	Multilateral	06 Nov 25	Patents/Copyrights	74LTS327	301745
Aegean	Multilateral	06 Nov 25	Patents/Copyrights	74LTS289	301743
Afghanistan	Belgium	16 Jun 28	Education	97LTS97	302221
Afghanistan	Brazil	20 Feb 33	General Amity	186LTS385	304322
Afghanistan	Czechoslovakia	13 Oct 37	General Amity	191LTS9	304431
Afghanistan	Estonia	06 Dec 30	General Amity	137LTS445	303174
Afghanistan	Finland	17 Jul 28	General Amity	112LTS9	302601
Afghanistan	France	28 Apr 22	Consul/Citizenship	105LTS147	302408
Afghanistan	France	09 Sep 22	Education	105LTS153	302409
Afghanistan	Germany	03 Mar 26	General Amity	62LTS115	301460
Afghanistan	Iraq	20 Dec 32	General Amity	155LTS375	303588
Afghanistan	Japan	19 Nov 30	General Amity	121LTS237	302789
Afghanistan	Latvia	16 Feb 28	General Amity	78LTS99	301781
Afghanistan	Lithuania	09 Dec 30	General Amity	138LTS29	303178
Afghanistan	Multilateral	23 Jan 12	Sanitation	8LTS187	300222
Afghanistan	Multilateral	31 Mar 24	Sanitation	27LTS211	300685
Afghanistan	Multilateral	21 Jun 26	Sanitation	78LTS229	301793
Afghanistan	Multilateral	25 Sep 26	ILO Labor	60LTS253	301414
Afghanistan	Multilateral	27 Aug 28	General Military	94LTS57	302137
Afghanistan	Multilateral	03 Jul 33	Peace/Disarmament	147LTS67	303391
Afghanistan	Multilateral	11 Oct 33	Consul/Citizenship	150LTS431	303476
Afghanistan	Multilateral	03 Feb 34	Territory Boundary	154LTS349	303560
Afghanistan	Multilateral	06 Nov 36	General Military	173LTS353	304025
Afghanistan	Multilateral	08 Jul 37	General Amity	190LTS21	304402
Afghanistan	Multilateral	02 Oct 37	Education	182LTS263	304216
Afghanistan	Persia	22 Jun 21	General Amity	33LTS285	300853
Afghanistan	Persia	27 Nov 27	General Military	107LTS433	302500
Afghanistan	Persia	26 Jun 28	Admin Cooperation	106LTS321	302453
Afghanistan	Poland	03 Nov 27	General Amity	74LTS83	301734
Afghanistan	Switzerland	17 Feb 28	General Amity	73LTS323	301722
Afghanistan	UK Great Britain	22 Nov 21	General Amity	14LTS47	300367
Afghanistan	UK Great Britain	05 Jun 23	General Trade	21LTS89	300533
Afghanistan	UK Great Britain	06 May 30	Admin Cooperation	105LTS265	302418
Afghanistan	USA (United States)	26 Mar 36	General Amity	168LTS143	303895
Afghanistan	USSR (Soviet Union)	24 Jun 31	General Amity	157LTS371	303611
Afghanistan	USSR (Soviet Union)	06 May 35	Sanitation	164LTS335	303800
Albania	Austria	30 Jan 31	Visas	114LTS65	302655
Albania	Bel-Lux Econ Union	19 Feb 29	General Trade	90LTS429	302053
Albania	Czechoslovakia	19 Jan 26	General Trade	64LTS349	301507
Albania	Czechoslovakia	09 Apr 34	General Trade	158LTS59	303626
Albania	Czechoslovakia	14 Apr 34	Extradition	188LTS255	304362
Albania	France	15 Feb 28	Consul/Citizenship	107LTS307	302487
Albania	Greece	25 Jun 26	Extradition	83LTS305	301898
Albania	Greece	13 Oct 26	General Trade	83LTS325	301899
Albania	Greece	13 Oct 26	Consul/Citizenship	83LTS361	301900
Albania	Hungary	02 Jun 28	Water Transport	82LTS201	301870
Albania	Italy	04 Dec 22	Telecommunications	15LTS213	300395
Albania	Italy	05 Dec 22	Postal Service	15LTS203	300394
Albania	Italy	29 Feb 24	General Trade	44LTS331	301092
Albania	Italy	29 Feb 24	Consul/Citizenship	44LTS343	301093
Albania	Italy	06 Mar 25	General Economic	44LTS359	301094
Albania	Italy	27 Nov 26	General Amity	60LTS15	301402
Albania	Italy	19 Mar 36	Loans and Credits	173LTS83	304005
Albania	Italy	19 Mar 36	General Trade	173LTS131	304008
Albania	Italy	19 Mar 36	Water Transport	173LTS93	304006
Albania	Italy	19 Mar 36	Loans and Credits	173LTS73	304004
Albania	Italy	19 Mar 36	Finance	173LTS63	304003
Albania	Italy	19 Mar 36	Sanitation	173LTS107	304007
Albania	Italy	19 Mar 36	Finance	173LTS51	304002
Albania	Japan	20 Jun 30	General Trade	123LTS295	302820
Albania	Multilateral	23 Jan 12	Sanitation	8LTS187	300222
Albania	Multilateral	05 Jun 12	Telecommunications	1LTS135	300013
Albania	Multilateral	16 Dec 20	General IGO	6LTS379	300170
Albania	Multilateral	20 Apr 21	Water Transport	7LTS65	300173

PARTY ONE	PARTY TWO	DATE	TOPIC	CITATION	NUMBER
Albania	Multilateral	20 Apr 21	Water Transport	7LTS73	300174
Albania	Multilateral	20 Apr 21	Land Transport	7LTS11	300171
Albania	Multilateral	20 Apr 21	Water Transport	7LTS35	300172
Albania	Multilateral	05 Aug 21	Admin Cooperation	27LTS349	300695
Albania	Multilateral	05 Oct 21	IGO Establishment	51LTS361	301241
Albania	Multilateral	05 Oct 21	Admin Cooperation	29LTS73	300734
Albania	Multilateral	31 Mar 22	Humanitarian	9LTS415	300269
Albania	Multilateral	31 Mar 24	Sanitation	27LTS211	300685
Albania	Multilateral	28 Aug 24	Postal Service	40LTS437	301005
Albania	Multilateral	28 Aug 24	Postal Service	40LTS307	301004
Albania	Multilateral	28 Aug 24	Postal Service	41LTS9	301006
Albania	Multilateral	28 Aug 24	Postal Service	40LTS249	301003
Albania	Multilateral	28 Aug 24	Postal Service	40LTS19	301002
Albania	Multilateral	28 Aug 24	Postal Service	41LTS97	301008
Albania	Multilateral	19 Feb 25	Admin Cooperation	81LTS317	301845
Albania	Multilateral	29 Oct 25	Telecommunications	57LTS201	301365
Albania	Multilateral	21 Jun 26	Sanitation	78LTS229	301793
Albania	Multilateral	25 Sep 26	ILO Labor	60LTS253	301414
Albania	Multilateral	12 Jul 27	Direct Aid	135LTS247	303115
Albania	Multilateral	29 Oct 27	Scientific Project	127LTS27	302903
Albania	Multilateral	27 Aug 28	General Military	94LTS57	302137
Albania	Multilateral	22 Nov 28	Culture	111LTS343	302598
Albania	Multilateral	20 Apr 29	Admin Cooperation	112LTS371	302623
Albania	Multilateral	28 Jun 29	Postal Service	103LTS321	302372
Albania	Multilateral	28 Jun 29	Postal Service	103LTS71	302370
Albania	Multilateral	28 Jun 29	Postal Service	103LTS249	302371
Albania	Multilateral	28 Jun 29	Postal Service	103LTS429	302374
Albania	Multilateral	28 Jun 29	Postal Service	103LTS5	302369
Albania	Multilateral	28 Jun 29	Postal Service	103LTS377	302373
Albania	Multilateral	28 Jun 29	Postal Service	102LTS245	302368
Albania	Multilateral	14 Sep 29	UN Charter	165LTS353	303822
Albania	Multilateral	13 Jul 31	Other HEW	139LTS301	303219
Albania	Multilateral	24 Sep 31	Specific Resources	155LTS349	303586
Albania	Multilateral	09 Dec 32	Telecommunications	151LTS5	303479
Albania	Multilateral	11 Oct 33	Education	155LTS331	303585
Albania	Multilateral	11 Oct 33	Consul/Citizenship	150LTS431	303476
Albania	Multilateral	20 Mar 34	Postal Service	175LTS269	304051
Albania	Multilateral	20 Mar 34	Postal Service	175LTS5	304049
Albania	Multilateral	20 Mar 34	Postal Service	174LTS171	304048
Albania	Multilateral	20 Mar 34	Finance	176LTS9	304053
Albania	Multilateral	20 Mar 34	Postal Service	176LTS55	304054
Albania	Multilateral	20 Mar 34	Postal Service	175LTS363	304052
Albania	Multilateral	20 Mar 34	Postal Service	175LTS73	304050
Albania	Multilateral	25 Jul 34	Other HEW	177LTS59	304080
Albania	Multilateral	23 Sep 36	Gen Communications	186LTS301	304319
Albania	Multilateral	06 Nov 36	General Military	173LTS353	304025
Albania	Multilateral	31 Oct 38	Sanitation	198LTS205	304642
Albania	Multilateral	03 Dec 38	Education	200LTS249	304694
Albania	Other Unilat Decla	02 Oct 22	Consul/Citizenship	9LTS173	300249
Albania	Romania	03 Nov 30	Mostfavored Nation	118LTS39	302712
Albania	Serb/Croat/Slovene	22 Jun 26	Extradition	91LTS81	302056
Albania	Serb/Croat/Slovene	22 Jun 26	Consul/Citizenship	91LTS55	302055
Albania	Serb/Croat/Slovene	22 Jun 26	General Economic	91LTS9	302054
Albania	Serb/Croat/Slovene	11 Aug 29	Territory Boundary	101LTS439	302342
Albania	Switzerland	10 Jun 29	General Trade	104LTS145	302384
Albania	UK Great Britain	10 Jun 25	General Economic	43LTS81	301049
Albania	UK Great Britain	22 Jul 26	Admin Cooperation	67LTS165	301545
Albania	USA (United States)	22 Oct 28	Dispute Settlement	92LTS223	302090
Albania	USA (United States)	22 Oct 28	Dispute Settlement	92LTS217	302089
Albania	USA (United States)	05 Apr 32	Consul/Citizenship	162LTS31	303732
Albania	USA (United States)	01 Mar 33	Extradition	166LTS195	303839
Albania	Yugoslavia	05 May 34	General Economic	187LTS179	304337
Albania	Yugoslavia	08 May 34	General Economic	159LTS9	303649
Algeria	Multilateral	21 Jun 20	Health/Educ/Welfare	8LTS65	300207
Algeria	Multilateral	31 Oct 20	Sanitation	164LTS85	303790

PARTY ONE	PARTY TWO	DATE	TOPIC	CITATION	NUMBER
Algeria	Multilateral	28 Aug 24	Postal Service	41LTS97	301008
Algeria	Multilateral	28 Aug 24	Postal Service	40LTS249	301003
Algeria	Multilateral	28 Aug 24	Postal Service	40LTS307	301004
Algeria	Multilateral	28 Aug 24	Postal Service	40LTS437	301005
Algeria	Multilateral	28 Aug 24	Postal Service	41LTS55	301007
Algeria	Multilateral	28 Aug 24	Postal Service	40LTS19	301002
Algeria	Multilateral	21 Jun 26	Sanitation	78LTS229	301793
Algeria	Multilateral	20 Apr 29	Admin Cooperation	112LTS371	302623
Algeria	Multilateral	20 Apr 29	Admin Cooperation	112LTS395	302624
Algeria	Multilateral	28 Jun 29	Postal Service	102LTS245	302368
Algeria	Multilateral	28 Jun 29	Postal Service	103LTS71	302370
Algeria	Multilateral	28 Jun 29	Postal Service	103LTS377	302373
Algeria	Multilateral	28 Jun 29	Postal Service	103LTS321	302372
Algeria	Multilateral	28 Jun 29	Postal Service	103LTS5	302369
Algeria	Multilateral	28 Jun 29	Postal Service	103LTS429	302374
Algeria	Multilateral	28 Jun 29	Postal Service	103LTS249	302371
Algeria	Multilateral	30 Mar 31	Land Transport	150LTS247	303459
Algeria	Multilateral	11 Dec 31	Commodity Trade	170LTS251	303941
Algeria	Multilateral	19 Jun 33	Gen Communications	154LTS133	303544
Algeria	Multilateral	20 Mar 34	Postal Service	175LTS363	304052
Algeria	Multilateral	20 Mar 34	Finance	176LTS9	304053
Algeria	Multilateral	20 Mar 34	Postal Service	175LTS5	304049
Algeria	Multilateral	20 Mar 34	Postal Service	176LTS55	304054
Algeria	Multilateral	20 Mar 34	Postal Service	174LTS171	304048
Algeria	Multilateral	20 Mar 34	Postal Service	175LTS73	304050
Algeria	Multilateral	20 Mar 34	Postal Service	175LTS269	304051
Algeria	Multilateral	31 Mar 37	Commodity Trade	189LTS359	304394
Algeria	Multilateral	23 May 39	Postal Service	202LTS159	304742
Allied Powers	Germany	17 Dec 20	Territory Boundary	12LTS39	300306
Allied Powers	Germany	28 Oct 24	General Military	41LTS461	301025
Allied Powers	Poland	01 Apr 22	Reparations	9LTS325	300265
Angola	Multilateral	29 Oct 25	Telecommunications	57LTS201	301365
Angola	Multilateral	30 Oct 35	Postal Service	189LTS85	304376
Angola	Multilateral	30 Oct 35	Telecommunications	189LTS51	304375
Anguilla	Multilateral	30 Oct 35	Telecommunications	189LTS51	304375
Antigua	Multilateral	26 Sep 27	Dispute Settlement	92LTS301	302096
Argentina	Austria	22 Mar 26	Non-ILO Labor	143LTS157	303306
Argentina	Bel-Lux Econ Union	16 Jan 34	Mostfavored Nation	147LTS79	303392
Argentina	Bel-Lux Econ Union	16 Jan 34	Finance	145LTS145	303352
Argentina	Belgium	20 Oct 24	Health/Educ/Welfare	137LTS381	303166
Argentina	Brazil	10 Oct 33	Customs	179LTS185	304146
Argentina	Brazil	10 Oct 33	Education	179LTS165	304144
Argentina	Brazil	10 Oct 33	Education	179LTS175	304145
Argentina	Chile	02 Jul 35	Sanitation	167LTS173	303864
Argentina	Czechoslovakia	31 Mar 32	Non-ILO Labor	155LTS379	303589
Argentina	Denmark	16 Nov 27	Non-ILO Labor	165LTS177	303809
Argentina	Denmark	03 May 28	Sanitation	168LTS309	303907
Argentina	Finland	03 Nov 31	Customs	126LTS101	302874
Argentina	France	26 Jun 27	Milit Servic/Citiz	62LTS85	301457
Argentina	Italy	26 Mar 20	Non-ILO Labor	15LTS271	300400
Argentina	Lithuania	20 Oct 32	Non-ILO Labor	154LTS113	303542
Argentina	Multilateral	20 Aug 10	Patents/Copyrights	155LTS179	303576
Argentina	Multilateral	12 Jan 12	Sanitation	4LTS281	300112
Argentina	Multilateral	23 Jan 12	Sanitation	8LTS187	300222
Argentina	Multilateral	05 Jun 12	Telecommunications	1LTS135	300013
Argentina	Multilateral	21 Apr 14	Sanitation	5LTS394	300144
Argentina	Multilateral	[illegible]9 Feb 20	Admin Cooperation	127LTS433	302930
Argentina	Multilateral	21 Jun 20	Health/Educ/Welfare	8LTS65	300207
Argentina	Multilateral	31 Oct 20	Sanitation	164LTS85	303790
Argentina	Multilateral	16 Dec 20	General IGO	6LTS379	300170
Argentina	Multilateral	15 Sep 21	Postal Service	30LTS141	300767
Argentina	Multilateral	06 Oct 21	General Economic	17LTS45	300427
Argentina	Multilateral	31 Mar 22	Humanitarian	9LTS415	300269
Argentina	Multilateral	28 Apr 23	Patents/Copyrights	33LTS47	300832
Argentina	Multilateral	03 May 23	General Trade	33LTS81	300833

PARTY ONE	PARTY TWO	DATE	TOPIC	CITATION	NUMBER
Argentina	Multilateral	03 May 23	General Amity	33LTS25	300831
Argentina	Multilateral	03 May 23	Customs	33LTS11	300830
Argentina	Multilateral	25 Jan 24	Sanitation	57LTS135	301360
Argentina	Multilateral	31 Mar 24	Sanitation	27LTS211	300685
Argentina	Multilateral	25 Aug 24	Water Transport	120LTS123	302763
Argentina	Multilateral	25 Aug 24	Water Transport	120LTS155	302764
Argentina	Multilateral	28 Aug 24	Postal Service	40LTS19	301002
Argentina	Multilateral	28 Aug 24	Postal Service	40LTS249	301003
Argentina	Multilateral	28 Aug 24	Postal Service	40LTS437	301005
Argentina	Multilateral	28 Aug 24	Postal Service	40LTS307	301004
Argentina	Multilateral	28 Aug 24	Postal Service	41LTS97	301008
Argentina	Multilateral	14 Nov 24	Sanitation	86LTS43	301949
Argentina	Multilateral	01 Dec 24	Sanitation	78LTS351	301794
Argentina	Multilateral	19 Feb 25	Admin Cooperation	81LTS317	301845
Argentina	Multilateral	29 Oct 25	Telecommunications	57LTS201	301365
Argentina	Multilateral	24 Apr 26	Land Transport	108LTS123	302505
Argentina	Multilateral	21 Jun 26	Sanitation	78LTS229	301793
Argentina	Multilateral	29 Oct 27	Scientific Project	127LTS27	302903
Argentina	Multilateral	25 Nov 27	Telecommunications	84LTS97	301905
Argentina	Multilateral	18 Feb 28	Patents/Copyrights	132LTS275	303044
Argentina	Multilateral	20 Feb 28	Consul/Citizenship	132LTS323	303046
Argentina	Multilateral	20 Feb 28	Privil/Immunities	132LTS301	303045
Argentina	Multilateral	20 Feb 28	Consul/Citizenship	155LTS259	303581
Argentina	Multilateral	20 Feb 28	Consul/Citizenship	155LTS289	303582
Argentina	Multilateral	20 Feb 28	Air Transport	129LTS223	302963
Argentina	Multilateral	20 Feb 28	Other Ad Hoc	86LTS111	301950
Argentina	Multilateral	20 Feb 28	Admin Cooperation	134LTS45	303082
Argentina	Multilateral	20 Feb 28	General Amity	135LTS187	303111
Argentina	Multilateral	31 May 29	Water Transport	136LTS81	303127
Argentina	Multilateral	28 Jun 29	Postal Service	102LTS245	302368
Argentina	Multilateral	28 Jun 29	Postal Service	103LTS5	302369
Argentina	Multilateral	27 Jul 29	Other Military	118LTS303	302733
Argentina	Multilateral	27 Jul 29	Other Military	118LTS343	302734
Argentina	Multilateral	14 Sep 29	UN Charter	165LTS353	303822
Argentina	Multilateral	13 Jul 31	Other HEW	139LTS301	303219
Argentina	Multilateral	10 Nov 31	Postal Service	131LTS447	303025
Argentina	Multilateral	10 Nov 31	Postal Service	131LTS389	303024
Argentina	Multilateral	10 Nov 31	Postal Service	131LTS327	303023
Argentina	Multilateral	09 Dec 32	Telecommunications	151LTS5	303479
Argentina	Multilateral	25 Aug 33	Commodity Trade	141LTS71	303262
Argentina	Multilateral	10 Oct 33	General Amity	163LTS393	303781
Argentina	Multilateral	26 Dec 33	Recognition	165LTS19	303802
Argentina	Multilateral	26 Dec 33	Extradition	165LTS45	303803
Argentina	Multilateral	20 Mar 34	Postal Service	175LTS363	304052
Argentina	Multilateral	20 Mar 34	Postal Service	176LTS55	304054
Argentina	Multilateral	20 Mar 34	Postal Service	175LTS5	304049
Argentina	Multilateral	20 Mar 34	Postal Service	174LTS171	304048
Argentina	Multilateral	20 Mar 34	Postal Service	175LTS269	304051
Argentina	Multilateral	20 Mar 34	Postal Service	175LTS73	304050
Argentina	Multilateral	20 Mar 34	Finance	176LTS9	304053
Argentina	Multilateral	15 Apr 35	Culture	167LTS289	303874
Argentina	Multilateral	23 Sep 36	Gen Communications	186LTS301	304319
Argentina	Multilateral	23 Dec 36	General Amity	188LTS31	304351
Argentina	Multilateral	23 Dec 36	Culture	188LTS125	304355
Argentina	Multilateral	23 Dec 36	Dispute Settlement	195LTS229	304548
Argentina	Multilateral	23 Dec 36	Admin Cooperation	201LTS295	304721
Argentina	Multilateral	23 Dec 36	Culture	188LTS151	304356
Argentina	Multilateral	23 Dec 36	Land Transport	188LTS99	304354
Argentina	Multilateral	23 Dec 36	Dispute Settlement	188LTS53	304352
Argentina	Multilateral	23 Dec 36	Dispute Settlement	188LTS75	304353
Argentina	Multilateral	23 Dec 36	Peace/Disarmament	188LTS9	304350
Argentina	Multilateral	31 Mar 37	Commodity Trade	189LTS359	304394
Argentina	Multilateral	08 Jun 37	Specific Resources	190LTS79	304406
Argentina	Multilateral	02 Oct 37	Education	182LTS263	304216
Argentina	Multilateral	24 Jun 38	Specific Resources	196LTS131	304575

PARTY ONE	PARTY TWO	DATE	TOPIC	CITATION	NUMBER
Argentina	Multilateral	03 Dec 38	Education	200LTS249	304694
Argentina	Multilateral	23 May 39	Postal Service	202LTS159	304742
Argentina	Netherlands	31 Jan 34	Mostfavored Nation	148LTS355	303421
Argentina	Netherlands	31 Jan 34	Finance	148LTS361	303422
Argentina	Netherlands	05 Feb 37	Finance	179LTS383	304165
Argentina	Netherlands	06 Sep 38	Visas	194LTS409	304531
Argentina	Norway	07 Oct 24	Admin Cooperation	33LTS191	300843
Argentina	Serb/Croat/Slovene	13 Mar 35	Non-ILO Labor	158LTS189	303631
Argentina	Spain	17 Feb 35	Extradition	166LTS375	303853
Argentina	Sweden	14 May 28	Non-ILO Labor	155LTS109	303573
Argentina	UK Great Britain	07 Apr 12	Postal Service	6LTS337	300165
Argentina	UK Great Britain	29 Jul 21	Admin Cooperation	8LTS315	300229
Argentina	UK Great Britain	15 Nov 29	Non-ILO Labor	160LTS257	303694
Argentina	UK Great Britain	01 May 33	General Trade	143LTS67	303305
Argentina	UK Great Britain	28 Jun 37	Commodity Trade	196LTS263	304588
Argentina	Uruguay	11 Apr 18	Territory Boundary	14LTS367	300385
Argentina	USA (United States)	03 Sep 34	Patents/Copyrights	160LTS57	303682
Argentina	USA (United States)	08 Apr 39	Postal Service	198LTS55	304623
Argentina	USA (United States)	12 Sep 39	Military Mission	201LTS213	304715
Argentina	USA (United States)	17 Oct 39	Admin Cooperation	201LTS273	304720
Argentina	USA (United States)	29 Jun 40	Milit Assistance	203LTS57	304750
Argentina	Venezuela	22 Jul 11	Dispute Settlement	28LTS287	300715
Ascension Island	Multilateral	25 Nov 27	Telecommunications	84LTS97	301905
Australia	Bel-Lux Econ Union	03 Oct 36	General Trade	177LTS271	304094
Australia	Belgium	14 Dec 33	General Trade	147LTS21	303386
Australia	Belgium	19 Nov 34	Customs	155LTS385	303590
Australia	Brazil	19 Jul 39	General Trade	200LTS191	304690
Australia	Czechoslovakia	19 Aug 36	General Trade	177LTS245	304093
Australia	Dutch Indies	19 Sep 33	Postal Service	144LTS335	303337
Australia	France	30 May 34	Postal Service	165LTS81	303804
Australia	France	27 Nov 36	General Trade	177LTS301	304095
Australia	Germany	31 May 26	Postal Service	60LTS121	301409
Australia	Indochina	20 May 36	Visas	170LTS221	303937
Australia	Italy	22 Jun 34	Postal Service	165LTS107	303806
Australia	Malay States	24 Jan 21	Postal Service	23LTS209	300590
Australia	Multilateral	09 Sep 86*	Patents/Copyrights	123LTS233	302816
Australia	Multilateral	18 Mar 04	Humanitarian	1LTS83	300011
Australia	Multilateral	12 Jan 12	Sanitation	4LTS281	300112
Australia	Multilateral	05 Jun 12	Telecommunications	1LTS135	300013
Australia	Multilateral	10 Sep 19	Health/Educ/Welfare	8LTS11	300201
Australia	Multilateral	10 Sep 19	General Trade	7LTS331	300200
Australia	Multilateral	09 Feb 20	Territory Boundary	2LTS7	300041
Australia	Multilateral	01 May 20	Air Transport	11LTS173	300297
Australia	Multilateral	21 Jun 20	Health/Educ/Welfare	8LTS65	300207
Australia	Multilateral	30 Jun 20	Patents/Copyrights	1LTS59	300008
Australia	Multilateral	10 Aug 20	Territory Boundary	28LTS225	300710
Australia	Multilateral	10 Aug 20	Consul/Citizenship	28LTS223	300711
Australia	Multilateral	31 Oct 20	Sanitation	164LTS85	303790
Australia	Multilateral	16 Dec 20	General IGO	6LTS379	300170
Australia	Multilateral	20 Apr 21	Water Transport	7LTS73	300174
Australia	Multilateral	05 Aug 21	Admin Cooperation	27LTS349	300695
Australia	Multilateral	05 Oct 21	IGO Establishment	51LTS361	301241
Australia	Multilateral	05 Oct 21	Admin Cooperation	29LTS67	300733
Australia	Multilateral	05 Oct 21	Admin Cooperation	29LTS73	300734
Australia	Multilateral	05 Oct 21	Admin Cooperation	29LTS79	300735
Australia	Multilateral	06 Feb 22	General Trade	38LTS277	300982
Australia	Multilateral	06 Feb 22	Customs	38LTS267	300981
Australia	Multilateral	31 Mar 22	Humanitarian	9LTS415	300269
Australia	Multilateral	02 Nov 22	Peace/Disarmament	149LTS35	303431
Australia	Multilateral	03 Nov 23	Customs	30LTS371	300775
Australia	Multilateral	16 Aug 24	Taxation	41LTS429	301024
Australia	Multilateral	28 Aug 24	Postal Service	40LTS19	301002
Australia	Multilateral	30 Aug 24	Admin Cooperation	30LTS75	300760
Australia	Multilateral	30 Aug 24	Admin Cooperation	30LTS79	300761
Australia	Multilateral	01 Dec 24	Sanitation	78LTS351	301794

PARTY ONE	PARTY TWO	DATE	TOPIC	CITATION	NUMBER
Australia	Multilateral	19 Feb 25	Admin Cooperation	81LTS317	301845
Australia	Multilateral	17 Jun 25	Peace/Disarmament	94LTS65	302138
Australia	Multilateral	29 Oct 25	Telecommunications	57LTS201	301365
Australia	Multilateral	06 Nov 25	Patents/Copyrights	74LTS289	301743
Australia	Multilateral	21 Jun 26	Sanitation	78LTS229	301793
Australia	Multilateral	25 Sep 26	ILO Labor	60LTS253	301414
Australia	Multilateral	25 Nov 27	Telecommunications	84LTS97	301905
Australia	Multilateral	27 Aug 28	General Military	94LTS57	302137
Australia	Multilateral	26 Sep 28	Dispute Settlement	93LTS343	302123
Australia	Multilateral	22 Nov 28	Culture	111LTS343	302598
Australia	Multilateral	14 Dec 28	General Economic	110LTS171	302560
Australia	Multilateral	31 May 29	Water Transport	136LTS81	303127
Australia	Multilateral	28 Jun 29	Postal Service	102LTS245	302368
Australia	Multilateral	27 Jul 29	Other Military	118LTS303	302733
Australia	Multilateral	27 Jul 29	Other Military	118LTS343	302734
Australia	Multilateral	14 Sep 29	UN Charter	165LTS353	303822
Australia	Multilateral	12 Oct 29	General Transport	137LTS11	303145
Australia	Multilateral	20 Jan 30	Reparations	112LTS361	302622
Australia	Multilateral	20 Jan 30	Reparations	113LTS389	302650
Australia	Multilateral	20 Jan 30	Finance	104LTS433	302397
Australia	Multilateral	20 Jan 30	Reparations	104LTS243	302394
Australia	Multilateral	12 Apr 30	Admin Cooperation	179LTS115	304138
Australia	Multilateral	12 Apr 30	Admin Cooperation	179LTS89	304137
Australia	Multilateral	17 Apr 30	Extradition	126LTS201	302883
Australia	Multilateral	22 Apr 30	Peace/Disarmament	112LTS65	302608
Australia	Multilateral	28 Apr 30	Claims and Debts	121LTS69	302785
Australia	Multilateral	07 Jun 30	Finance	143LTS337	303315
Australia	Multilateral	10 Jun 30	Loans and Credits	112LTS237	302618
Australia	Multilateral	27 Nov 30	Extradition	121LTS39	302781
Australia	Multilateral	19 Mar 31	Admin Cooperation	143LTS7	303301
Australia	Multilateral	30 Mar 31	Land Transport	150LTS247	303459
Australia	Multilateral	13 Apr 31	Air Transport	119LTS275	302751
Australia	Multilateral	13 Jul 31	Other HEW	139LTS301	303219
Australia	Multilateral	24 Sep 31	Specific Resources	155LTS349	303586
Australia	Multilateral	10 Dec 31	Water Transport	129LTS177	302961
Australia	Multilateral	20 Jan 32	Extradition	141LTS267	303269
Australia	Multilateral	09 Dec 32	Telecommunications	151LTS5	303479
Australia	Multilateral	11 Mar 33	Water Transport	135LTS301	303119
Australia	Multilateral	12 Apr 33	Sanitation	161LTS65	303706
Australia	Multilateral	22 Jul 33	Specific Resources	153LTS107	303511
Australia	Multilateral	25 Aug 33	Commodity Trade	141LTS71	303262
Australia	Multilateral	30 Sep 33	Extradition	205LTS155	304832
Australia	Multilateral	11 Oct 33	Consul/Citizenship	150LTS431	303476
Australia	Multilateral	20 Mar 34	Postal Service	174LTS171	304048
Australia	Multilateral	16 Apr 34	Water Transport	163LTS185	303767
Australia	Multilateral	02 Jun 34	Patents/Copyrights	205LTS179	304834
Australia	Multilateral	02 Jun 34	Patents/Copyrights	192LTS17	304459
Australia	Multilateral	04 Jun 34	Extradition	184LTS437	304264
Australia	Multilateral	19 Jun 34	Admin Cooperation	154LTS381	303564
Australia	Multilateral	22 Dec 34	Visas	183LTS145	304230
Australia	Multilateral	22 Dec 34	Admin Cooperation	183LTS153	304231
Australia	Multilateral	15 Mar 35	Other Military	170LTS9	303926
Australia	Multilateral	20 Dec 35	Other Military	167LTS141	303862
Australia	Multilateral	25 Mar 36	Peace/Disarmament	184LTS115	304246
Australia	Multilateral	27 May 36	Admin Cooperation	203LTS367	304779
Australia	Multilateral	20 Jul 36	Territory Boundary	173LTS213	304015
Australia	Multilateral	30 Jul 36	IGO Status/Immunit	197LTS31	304602
Australia	Multilateral	23 Sep 36	Gen Communications	186LTS301	304319
Australia	Multilateral	06 Nov 36	General Military	173LTS353	304025
Australia	Multilateral	23 Jan 37	Extradition	191LTS219	304446
Australia	Multilateral	31 Mar 37	Commodity Trade	189LTS359	304394
Australia	Multilateral	08 May 37	Privil/Immunities	182LTS37	304202
Australia	Multilateral	02 Jun 37	Specific Property	184LTS445	304265
Australia	Multilateral	08 Jun 37	Specific Resources	190LTS79	304406
Australia	Multilateral	21 Jul 37	Admin Cooperation	184LTS271	304250

PARTY ONE	PARTY TWO	DATE	TOPIC	CITATION	NUMBER
Australia	Multilateral	02 Oct 37	Education	182LTS263	304216
Australia	Multilateral	11 Oct 37	Air Transport	182LTS173	304210
Australia	Multilateral	29 Apr 38	Visas	190LTS115	304410
Australia	Multilateral	17 May 38	Visas	192LTS319	304481
Australia	Multilateral	30 May 38	Visas	191LTS299	304451
Australia	Multilateral	24 Jun 38	Specific Resources	196LTS131	304575
Australia	Multilateral	12 Sep 38	Culture	198LTS111	304630
Australia	Multilateral	25 Oct 38	Air Transport	192LTS323	304482
Australia	Multilateral	31 Oct 38	Sanitation	198LTS205	304642
Australia	Multilateral	28 Dec 38	Other Military	196LTS221	304585
Australia	Multilateral	23 May 39	Postal Service	202LTS159	304742
Australia	Multilateral	21 Aug 39	Visas	198LTS343	304652
Australia	Multilateral	08 Jan 40	Visas	203LTS133	304756
Australia	Multilateral	01 Jan 42	General Military	204LTS381	304817
Australia	Multilateral	02 Jun 42	Patents/Copyrights	205LTS163	304833
Australia	Nauru	27 Oct 21	Postal Service	23LTS229	300591
Australia	Netherlands	30 May 23	Postal Service	22LTS129	300556
Australia	Netherlands	14 Sep 36	Territory Boundary	173LTS325	304022
Australia	Norway	13 Dec 27	Non-ILO Labor	69LTS307	301612
Australia	Switzerland	22 Nov 38	General Trade	194LTS35	304505
Australia	United Arab Rep	08 Jun 34	Postal Service	165LTS95	303805
Australia	USA (United States)	06 Sep 40	General Amity	204LTS245	304803
Austria	Albania	30 Jan 31	Visas	114LTS65	302655
Austria	Argentina	22 Mar 26	Non-ILO Labor	143LTS157	303306
Austria	Belgium	04 Oct 20	Claims and Debts	5LTS371	300142
Austria	Belgium	29 Mar 24	Peace/Disarmament	91LTS245	302066
Austria	Belgium	10 Oct 27	Claims and Debts	91LTS271	302067
Austria	Belgium	18 Jan 30	Admin Cooperation	104LTS231	302393
Austria	Belgium	01 Dec 30	Admin Cooperation	112LTS43	302606
Austria	Belgium	01 Dec 30	Extradition	112LTS37	302605
Austria	Belgium	26 Jan 32	Extradition	129LTS141	302959
Austria	Brazil	06 Jul 31	Visas	123LTS9	302801
Austria	Brazil	02 Jan 32	Mostfavored Nation	140LTS15	303224
Austria	China	19 Oct 25	General Economic	55LTS9	301301
Austria	Czechoslovakia	07 Jun 20	Consul/Citizenship	3LTS189	300098
Austria	Czechoslovakia	02 Aug 20	Finance	32LTS365	300826
Austria	Czechoslovakia	23 Aug 20	Health/Educ/Welfare	3LTS229	300099
Austria	Czechoslovakia	10 Mar 21	Territory Boundary	9LTS333	300267
Austria	Czechoslovakia	04 May 21	General Economic	15LTS13	300388
Austria	Czechoslovakia	16 Dec 21	General Amity	9LTS247	300257
Austria	Czechoslovakia	17 Dec 21	Finance	22LTS401	300570
Austria	Czechoslovakia	11 Feb 22	Taxation	152LTS175	303492
Austria	Czechoslovakia	18 Feb 22	Taxation	14LTS129	300371
Austria	Czechoslovakia	18 Jan 23	Visas	88LTS237	302000
Austria	Czechoslovakia	30 Nov 23	Non-ILO Labor	126LTS171	302880
Austria	Czechoslovakia	29 Mar 24	Non-ILO Labor	94LTS103	302140
Austria	Czechoslovakia	29 Mar 24	Non-ILO Labor	94LTS75	302139
Austria	Czechoslovakia	15 Jun 24	Non-ILO Labor	94LTS131	302141
Austria	Czechoslovakia	15 Jun 24	Non-ILO Labor	94LTS143	302142
Austria	Czechoslovakia	15 Jun 24	Non-ILO Labor	94LTS165	302143
Austria	Czechoslovakia	12 Jul 24	Finance	50LTS111	301199
Austria	Czechoslovakia	27 Nov 24	General Economic	42LTS201	301041
Austria	Czechoslovakia	22 Dec 24	Non-ILO Labor	94LTS179	302144
Austria	Czechoslovakia	17 Jan 25	Non-ILO Labor	94LTS245	302146
Austria	Czechoslovakia	17 Jan 25	Non-ILO Labor	94LTS185	302145
Austria	Czechoslovakia	14 May 25	Finance	50LTS39	301198
Austria	Czechoslovakia	29 May 25	Non-ILO Labor	98LTS91	302242
Austria	Czechoslovakia	07 Dec 25	Admin Cooperation	86LTS7	301947
Austria	Czechoslovakia	05 Mar 26	General Amity	51LTS349	301240
Austria	Czechoslovakia	12 Jul 26	Taxation	86LTS383	301951
Austria	Czechoslovakia	12 Jul 26	Admin Cooperation	86LTS395	301952
Austria	Czechoslovakia	15 Feb 27	Air Transport	73LTS349	301724
Austria	Czechoslovakia	15 Feb 27	Air Transport	73LTS381	301725
Austria	Czechoslovakia	21 Jul 27	General Trade	81LTS7	301842
Austria	Czechoslovakia	30 Mar 28	Visas	73LTS87	301709

PARTY ONE	PARTY TWO	DATE	TOPIC	CITATION	NUMBER
Austria	Czechoslovakia	12 Dec 28	Territory Boundary	107LTS137	302474
Austria	Czechoslovakia	12 Dec 28	Territory Boundary	108LTS9	302501
Austria	Czechoslovakia	03 Feb 29	Non-ILO Labor	101LTS285	302329
Austria	Czechoslovakia	03 Feb 29	Non-ILO Labor	102LTS191	302362
Austria	Czechoslovakia	12 Sep 30	Admin Cooperation	107LTS341	302489
Austria	Czechoslovakia	22 Jul 31	General Trade	128LTS59	302938
Austria	Czechoslovakia	18 Jan 33	Non-ILO Labor	142LTS41	303278
Austria	Czechoslovakia	02 Apr 36	General Economic	180LTS51	304173
Austria	Denmark	30 Jun 23	General Trade	18LTS195	300464
Austria	Denmark	30 Jun 23	General Trade	18LTS189	300463
Austria	Denmark	19 Dec 25	Education	57LTS121	301358
Austria	Denmark	11 Jun 27	Visas	68LTS87	301572
Austria	Denmark	06 Apr 28	General Trade	85LTS423	301943
Austria	Denmark	05 Aug 32	Air Transport	132LTS165	303036
Austria	Estonia	15 Oct 26	Consul/Citizenship	93LTS137	302106
Austria	Estonia	15 Oct 26	Extradition	74LTS213	301739
Austria	Estonia	11 Dec 28	General Trade	92LTS229	302091
Austria	Estonia	22 Mar 29	Visas	89LTS301	302025
Austria	Finland	21 Jul 27	Visas	66LTS419	301535
Austria	Finland	08 Aug 27	General Trade	70LTS349	301645
Austria	Finland	22 Oct 28	Extradition	89LTS69	302007
Austria	France	03 Aug 20	Claims and Debts	5LTS355	300141
Austria	France	07 Feb 21	General Military	4LTS251	300108
Austria	France	11 Aug 24	General Trade	44LTS7	301079
Austria	France	04 Mar 25	Admin Cooperation	75LTS97	301755
Austria	France	04 Mar 25	Admin Cooperation	44LTS205	301084
Austria	France	16 May 28	General Trade	88LTS21	301986
Austria	France	29 Dec 32	Commodity Trade	147LTS101	303394
Austria	Germany	01 Sep 20	General Economic	4LTS201	300107
Austria	Germany	01 Sep 20	Finance	2LTS132	300057
Austria	Germany	11 Aug 21	Non-ILO Labor	29LTS429	300753
Austria	Germany	17 Aug 21	Claims and Debts	19LTS237	300497
Austria	Germany	23 May 22	Taxation	26LTS405	300660
Austria	Germany	28 May 22	Taxation	26LTS445	300661
Austria	Germany	21 Jun 23	Admin Cooperation	27LTS88	300669
Austria	Germany	21 Jun 23	Admin Cooperation	27LTS57	300668
Austria	Germany	18 Feb 24	Non-ILO Labor	29LTS435	300754
Austria	Germany	30 Apr 24	Admin Cooperation	46LTS175	301119
Austria	Germany	12 Jul 24	General Trade	41LTS287	301022
Austria	Germany	19 May 25	Air Transport	52LTS121	301253
Austria	Germany	03 Oct 25	Customs	52LTS171	301255
Austria	Germany	08 Jan 26	Admin Cooperation	62LTS95	301459
Austria	Germany	21 May 26	General Economic	53LTS397	301269
Austria	Germany	05 Feb 27	Territory Boundary	73LTS205	301714
Austria	Germany	05 Feb 27	Admin Cooperation	73LTS227	301715
Austria	Germany	29 Feb 28	Non-ILO Labor	79LTS405	301816
Austria	Germany	17 Jan 30	Reparations	107LTS325	302488
Austria	Germany	05 Feb 30	Non-ILO Labor	119LTS201	302746
Austria	Germany	15 Feb 30	Patents/Copyrights	109LTS501	302552
Austria	Germany	12 Apr 30	General Transport	115LTS277	302692
Austria	Germany	12 Apr 30	Privil/Immunities	115LTS297	302693
Austria	Germany	12 Apr 30	Customs	115LTS333	302694
Austria	Germany	01 Aug 30	Admin Cooperation	115LTS465	302695
Austria	Germany	07 Dec 32	Extradition	137LTS69	303147
Austria	Germany	26 Aug 36	Visas	171LTS357	303972
Austria	Great Britain	18 Jul 27	Visas	68LTS97	301573
Austria	Great Britain	13 Apr 28	Patents/Copyrights	80LTS247	301830
Austria	Greece	12 Jun 56*	Specif Goods/Equip	2LTS157	300061
Austria	Greece	28 Mar 74*	Extradition	2LTS169	300063
Austria	Greece	16 Sep 04	Claims and Debts	2LTS161	300062
Austria	Greece	27 May 24	Patents/Copyrights	27LTS99	300671
Austria	Greece	18 Apr 25	General Trade	38LTS311	300986
Austria	Greece	27 Dec 29	Claims and Debts	100LTS423	302311
Austria	Greece	26 Jun 30	Dispute Settlement	119LTS353	302755
Austria	Greece	15 Sep 33	General Trade	161LTS251	303717

PARTY ONE	PARTY TWO	DATE	TOPIC	CITATION	NUMBER
Austria	Hungary	08 Oct 21	General Economic	16LTS19	300402
Austria	Hungary	13 Oct 21	Territory Boundary	9LTS203	300254
Austria	Hungary	08 Feb 22	General Economic	55LTS367	301320
Austria	Hungary	10 Apr 23	Dispute Settlement	18LTS93	300457
Austria	Hungary	30 Sep 24	Consul/Citizenship	42LTS177	301040
Austria	Hungary	08 Nov 24	Taxation	45LTS21	301097
Austria	Hungary	08 Nov 24	Taxation	44LTS407	301096
Austria	Hungary	10 May 26	General Trade	56LTS39	301321
Austria	Hungary	14 Jul 26	Visas	61LTS159	301431
Austria	Hungary	14 Jul 26	Visas	61LTS123	301430
Austria	Hungary	11 Mar 27	Admin Cooperation	80LTS67	301823
Austria	Hungary	14 Jun 28	General Trade	79LTS17	301802
Austria	Hungary	25 Jun 28	Admin Cooperation	100LTS85	302296
Austria	Hungary	11 Apr 30	Visas	101LTS309	302332
Austria	Hungary	03 Jun 30	Land Transport	122LTS69	302799
Austria	Hungary	26 Jan 31	General Amity	123LTS171	302814
Austria	Hungary	30 Jun 31	General Trade	122LTS123	302800
Austria	Hungary	27 Nov 32	Culture	162LTS387	303752
Austria	Hungary	27 Nov 32	Culture	162LTS395	303753
Austria	Hungary	21 Dec 32	General Economic	169LTS161	303919
Austria	Hungary	12 Jan 34	Admin Cooperation	162LTS419	303754
Austria	Hungary	04 Mar 35	Education	163LTS33	303759
Austria	Iceland	06 Apr 28	General Trade	87LTS343	301980
Austria	Italy	16 Jul 23	General Trade	27LTS383	300699
Austria	Italy	29 Mar 24	Other HEW	84LTS321	301911
Austria	Italy	29 Mar 24	Non-ILO Labor	84LTS293	301910
Austria	Italy	18 Jun 24	Non-ILO Labor	84LTS349	301912
Austria	Italy	18 Jun 24	Finance	84LTS381	301914
Austria	Italy	18 Jun 24	Non-ILO Labor	84LTS367	301913
Austria	Italy	27 Sep 24	Non-ILO Labor	84LTS397	301915
Austria	Italy	27 Sep 24	Non-ILO Labor	84LTS409	301916
Austria	Italy	17 Jan 25	Non-ILO Labor	84LTS419	301917
Austria	Italy	17 Jan 25	Non-ILO Labor	85LTS19	301919
Austria	Italy	17 Jan 25	Non-ILO Labor	85LTS9	301918
Austria	Italy	22 Dec 27	General Economic	91LTS283	302068
Austria	Italy	30 Dec 27	General Economic	87LTS109	301964
Austria	Italy	11 May 28	Air Transport	100LTS41	302293
Austria	Italy	11 May 28	Air Transport	100LTS375	302307
Austria	Italy	22 Feb 29	Territory Boundary	89LTS271	302021
Austria	Italy	06 Feb 30	Dispute Settlement	105LTS97	302405
Austria	Italy	06 Jun 30	Visas	105LTS329	302425
Austria	Italy	07 May 31	General Trade	132LTS9	303026
Austria	Italy	19 Nov 31	Extradition	126LTS163	302879
Austria	Italy	17 Mar 34	General Economic	154LTS297	303556
Austria	Japan	02 Oct 23	General Trade	22LTS349	300563
Austria	Japan	06 Jul 28	Visas	81LTS425	301851
Austria	Japan	16 Aug 30	General Economic	126LTS351	302894
Austria	Latvia	09 Aug 24	General Economic	65LTS7	301516
Austria	Latvia	30 Jun 27	Visas	66LTS97	301526
Austria	Latvia	05 Jan 32	Extradition	133LTS59	303056
Austria	Luxembourg	30 Jan 30	Admin Cooperation	99LTS357	302279
Austria	Luxembourg	07 Mar 30	Visas	101LTS237	302325
Austria	Monaco	07 Feb 36	Visas	167LTS389	303880
Austria	Multilateral	09 Sep 86*	Patents/Copyrights	123LTS233	302816
Austria	Multilateral	13 Nov 08	General Ad Hoc	1LTS217	300015
Austria	Multilateral	12 Jan 12	Sanitation	4LTS281	300112
Austria	Multilateral	05 Jun 12	Telecommunications	1LTS135	300013
Austria	Multilateral	20 Mar 14	Patents/Copyrights	1LTS243	300016
Austria	Multilateral	30 Jun 20	Patents/Copyrights	1LTS59	300008
Austria	Multilateral	16 Dec 20	General IGO	6LTS379	300170
Austria	Multilateral	20 Apr 21	Land Transport	7LTS11	300171
Austria	Multilateral	20 Apr 21	Water Transport	7LTS73	300174
Austria	Multilateral	20 Apr 21	Water Transport	7LTS35	300172
Austria	Multilateral	23 Jul 21	Water Transport	26LTS173	300647
Austria	Multilateral	06 Oct 21	General Economic	17LTS45	300427

PARTY ONE	PARTY TWO	DATE	TOPIC	CITATION	NUMBER
Austria	Multilateral	27 Jan 22	Visas	9LTS291	300262
Austria	Multilateral	31 Mar 22	Humanitarian	9LTS415	300269
Austria	Multilateral	06 Apr 22	Admin Cooperation	123LTS277	302818
Austria	Multilateral	05 Jul 22	Reparations	13LTS237	300355
Austria	Multilateral	04 Oct 22	Territory Boundary	12LTS385	300334
Austria	Multilateral	04 Oct 22	Territory Boundary	12LTS391	300335
Austria	Multilateral	29 Mar 23	Land Transport	23LTS378	300594
Austria	Multilateral	29 Mar 23	Land Transport	23LTS256	300593
Austria	Multilateral	24 Sep 23	Dispute Settlement	27LTS157	300678
Austria	Multilateral	03 Nov 23	Customs	30LTS371	300775
Austria	Multilateral	30 Nov 23	Non-ILO Labor	102LTS183	302361
Austria	Multilateral	30 Nov 23	Non-ILO Labor	102LTS153	302360
Austria	Multilateral	09 Dec 23	Non-IBRD Project	36LTS76	300905
Austria	Multilateral	09 Dec 23	General Economic	58LTS315	301380
Austria	Multilateral	09 Dec 23	Land Transport	47LTS55	301129
Austria	Multilateral	14 Dec 23	General Trade	29LTS37	300732
Austria	Multilateral	31 Mar 24	Sanitation	27LTS211	300685
Austria	Multilateral	22 May 24	General Trade	35LTS175	300895
Austria	Multilateral	25 Aug 24	Water Transport	120LTS155	302764
Austria	Multilateral	28 Aug 24	Postal Service	40LTS249	301003
Austria	Multilateral	28 Aug 24	Postal Service	40LTS307	301004
Austria	Multilateral	28 Aug 24	Postal Service	41LTS97	301008
Austria	Multilateral	28 Aug 24	Postal Service	40LTS19	301002
Austria	Multilateral	28 Aug 24	Postal Service	41LTS9	301006
Austria	Multilateral	28 Aug 24	Postal Service	41LTS55	301007
Austria	Multilateral	28 Aug 24	Postal Service	40LTS437	301005
Austria	Multilateral	23 Oct 24	General Transport	77LTS367	301778
Austria	Multilateral	23 Oct 24	Land Transport	78LTS17	301779
Austria	Multilateral	26 Nov 24	Finance	48LTS69	301151
Austria	Multilateral	19 Feb 25	Admin Cooperation	81LTS317	301845
Austria	Multilateral	17 Jun 25	Peace/Disarmament	94LTS65	302138
Austria	Multilateral	29 Oct 25	Telecommunications	57LTS201	301365
Austria	Multilateral	06 Nov 25	Patents/Copyrights	74LTS327	301745
Austria	Multilateral	06 Nov 25	Patents/Copyrights	74LTS289	301743
Austria	Multilateral	27 Nov 25	Water Transport	67LTS63	301539
Austria	Multilateral	24 Apr 26	Land Transport	108LTS123	302505
Austria	Multilateral	24 Apr 26	Land Transport	97LTS83	302220
Austria	Multilateral	12 May 26	Refugees	89LTS47	302004
Austria	Multilateral	21 Jun 26	Sanitation	78LTS229	301793
Austria	Multilateral	25 Sep 26	ILO Labor	60LTS253	301414
Austria	Multilateral	22 Jan 27	Telecommunications	68LTS129	301576
Austria	Multilateral	25 Feb 27	Telecommunications	78LTS123	301783
Austria	Multilateral	10 Sep 27	Postal Service	75LTS7	301749
Austria	Multilateral	10 Sep 27	Postal Service	75LTS39	301750
Austria	Multilateral	26 Sep 27	Dispute Settlement	92LTS301	302096
Austria	Multilateral	27 Oct 27	Air Transport	148LTS265	303417
Austria	Multilateral	08 Nov 27	General Trade	97LTS391	302238
Austria	Multilateral	21 Nov 27	Telecommunications	78LTS163	301787
Austria	Multilateral	25 Nov 27	Telecommunications	84LTS97	301905
Austria	Multilateral	10 Mar 28	Telecommunications	132LTS405	303049
Austria	Multilateral	30 Jun 28	Refugees	89LTS53	302005
Austria	Multilateral	11 Jul 28	Commodity Trade	95LTS373	302185
Austria	Multilateral	11 Jul 28	Commodity Trade	95LTS357	302184
Austria	Multilateral	15 Jul 28	Patents/Copyrights	79LTS133	301806
Austria	Multilateral	27 Aug 28	General Military	94LTS57	302137
Austria	Multilateral	30 Oct 28	Non-ILO Labor	130LTS405	302999
Austria	Multilateral	14 Dec 28	General Economic	110LTS171	302560
Austria	Multilateral	16 Apr 29	Specific Resources	126LTS305	302891
Austria	Multilateral	20 Apr 29	Admin Cooperation	112LTS371	302623
Austria	Multilateral	20 Apr 29	Admin Cooperation	112LTS395	302624
Austria	Multilateral	14 Jun 29	Visas	94LTS275	302148
Austria	Multilateral	28 Jun 29	Postal Service	103LTS377	302373
Austria	Multilateral	28 Jun 29	Postal Service	102LTS245	302368
Austria	Multilateral	28 Jun 29	Postal Service	103LTS5	302369
Austria	Multilateral	28 Jun 29	Postal Service	103LTS321	302372

PARTY ONE	PARTY TWO	DATE	TOPIC	CITATION	NUMBER
Austria	Multilateral	28 Jun 29	Postal Service	103LTS71	302370
Austria	Multilateral	28 Jun 29	Postal Service	103LTS429	302374
Austria	Multilateral	28 Jun 29	Postal Service	103LTS249	302371
Austria	Multilateral	27 Jul 29	Other Military	118LTS343	302734
Austria	Multilateral	27 Jul 29	Other Military	118LTS303	302733
Austria	Multilateral	14 Sep 29	UN Charter	165LTS353	303822
Austria	Multilateral	26 Sep 29	Telecommunications	98LTS395	302259
Austria	Multilateral	12 Oct 29	General Transport	137LTS11	303145
Austria	Multilateral	20 Jan 30	Finance	104LTS413	302395
Austria	Multilateral	15 Mar 30	Finance	113LTS395	302651
Austria	Multilateral	12 Apr 30	Milit Servic/Citiz	178LTS227	304117
Austria	Multilateral	12 Apr 30	Admin Cooperation	179LTS89	304137
Austria	Multilateral	07 Jun 30	Finance	143LTS337	303315
Austria	Multilateral	07 Jun 30	Finance	143LTS317	303314
Austria	Multilateral	07 Jun 30	Finance	143LTS257	303313
Austria	Multilateral	31 Oct 30	Dispute Settlement	120LTS9	302760
Austria	Multilateral	19 Mar 31	Finance	143LTS355	303316
Austria	Multilateral	19 Mar 31	Finance	143LTS407	303317
Austria	Multilateral	19 Mar 31	Admin Cooperation	143LTS7	303301
Austria	Multilateral	27 Mar 31	ICJ Option Clause	167LTS341	303877
Austria	Multilateral	28 Mar 31	Customs	119LTS47	302739
Austria	Multilateral	30 Mar 31	Land Transport	150LTS247	303459
Austria	Multilateral	13 Jul 31	Other HEW	139LTS301	303219
Austria	Multilateral	15 Jul 32	Direct Aid	135LTS285	303118
Austria	Multilateral	02 Sep 32	Land Transport	154LTS123	303543
Austria	Multilateral	09 Dec 32	Telecommunications	151LTS5	303479
Austria	Multilateral	12 Apr 33	Sanitation	161LTS65	303706
Austria	Multilateral	29 May 33	Admin Cooperation	192LTS289	304479
Austria	Multilateral	19 Jun 33	Gen Communications	154LTS133	303544
Austria	Multilateral	25 Aug 33	Commodity Trade	141LTS71	303262
Austria	Multilateral	11 Oct 33	Consul/Citizenship	150LTS431	303476
Austria	Multilateral	11 Oct 33	Education	155LTS331	303585
Austria	Multilateral	23 Nov 33	Land Transport	192LTS389	304484
Austria	Multilateral	23 Nov 33	Land Transport	192LTS327	304483
Austria	Multilateral	17 Mar 34	General Economic	154LTS287	303555
Austria	Multilateral	17 Mar 34	General Amity	154LTS281	303554
Austria	Multilateral	20 Mar 34	Postal Service	175LTS5	304049
Austria	Multilateral	20 Mar 34	Finance	176LTS9	304053
Austria	Multilateral	20 Mar 34	Postal Service	174LTS171	304048
Austria	Multilateral	20 Mar 34	Postal Service	175LTS363	304052
Austria	Multilateral	20 Mar 34	Postal Service	175LTS73	304050
Austria	Multilateral	20 Mar 34	Postal Service	176LTS55	304054
Austria	Multilateral	20 Mar 34	Postal Service	175LTS269	304051
Austria	Multilateral	02 Jun 34	Patents/Copyrights	192LTS17	304459
Austria	Multilateral	20 Feb 35	Sanitation	193LTS37	304486
Austria	Multilateral	20 Feb 35	Sanitation	193LTS59	304487
Austria	Multilateral	20 Feb 35	Sanitation	186LTS173	304310
Austria	Multilateral	26 Jun 36	Other HEW	198LTS299	304648
Austria	Multilateral	23 Sep 36	Gen Communications	186LTS301	304319
Austria	Multilateral	06 Nov 36	General Military	173LTS353	304025
Austria	Netherlands	01 Dec 21	Extradition	9LTS167	300248
Austria	Netherlands	06 Nov 22	Consul/Citizenship	17LTS375	300444
Austria	Netherlands	05 Sep 23	General Trade	20LTS147	300514
Austria	Netherlands	04 Aug 26	Customs	59LTS243	301394
Austria	Netherlands	01 Mar 27	Visas	68LTS75	301570
Austria	Netherlands	28 Mar 29	General Economic	109LTS39	302527
Austria	Netherlands	31 Dec 29	Air Transport	111LTS177	302586
Austria	Netherlands	26 Jun 31	Land Transport	127LTS225	302922
Austria	Netherlands	28 Jun 33	Land Transport	152LTS193	303493
Austria	Netherlands	02 Apr 37	Customs	179LTS81	304136
Austria	Norway	20 Jun 24	Admin Cooperation	27LTS123	300675
Austria	Norway	03 Dec 24	General Trade	31LTS151	300792
Austria	Norway	06 Dec 24	Consul/Citizenship	31LTS179	300794
Austria	Norway	17 Dec 25	Extradition	48LTS77	301152
Austria	Norway	08 Feb 28	Visas	71LTS211	301664

PARTY ONE	PARTY TWO	DATE	TOPIC	CITATION	NUMBER
Austria	Norway	01 Oct 30	Extradition	119LTS15	302737
Austria	Norway	03 Sep 32	Finance	137LTS403	303170
Austria	Other Unilat Decla	04 Oct 22	Territory Boundary	12LTS405	300336
Austria	Panama	05 Mar 30	Visas	101LTS293	302330
Austria	Persia	17 Jun 28	Dispute Settlement	112LTS101	302610
Austria	Poland	09 Jan 20	General Economic	7LTS163	300185
Austria	Poland	23 Sep 21	General Economic	7LTS181	300186
Austria	Poland	25 Sep 22	General Trade	59LTS307	301400
Austria	Poland	13 Nov 23	Dispute Settlement	34LTS399	300888
Austria	Poland	19 Mar 24	Admin Cooperation	56LTS95	301326
Austria	Poland	29 Mar 24	Non-ILO Labor	130LTS223	302992
Austria	Poland	29 Mar 24	Non-ILO Labor	130LTS251	302993
Austria	Poland	18 Jun 24	Non-ILO Labor	130LTS279	302994
Austria	Poland	18 Jun 24	Non-ILO Labor	130LTS293	302995
Austria	Poland	18 Jun 24	Non-ILO Labor	130LTS309	302996
Austria	Poland	17 Jan 25	Non-ILO Labor	130LTS387	302998
Austria	Poland	17 Jan 25	Non-ILO Labor	130LTS327	302997
Austria	Poland	05 May 25	Air Transport	46LTS269	301121
Austria	Poland	16 Apr 26	Dispute Settlement	62LTS329	301471
Austria	Poland	24 Nov 26	Customs	77LTS359	301777
Austria	Poland	24 Feb 28	Claims and Debts	81LTS417	301850
Austria	Poland	20 Jan 30	Claims and Debts	133LTS223	303067
Austria	Poland	10 Apr 30	Air Transport	108LTS289	302514
Austria	Poland	22 Apr 32	Taxation	143LTS45	303304
Austria	Poland	26 Oct 32	Admin Cooperation	138LTS193	303188
Austria	Portugal	18 Dec 25	General Economic	54LTS91	301277
Austria	Portugal	28 Mar 27	Visas	68LTS81	301571
Austria	Romania	26 Jul 24	Finance	85LTS243	301934
Austria	Romania	26 Jul 24	Claims and Debts	85LTS223	301933
Austria	Romania	30 Aug 30	Mostfavored Nation	118LTS17	302709
Austria	Romania	10 Oct 34	Admin Cooperation	158LTS281	303638
Austria	Serb/Croat/Slovene	29 Mar 24	Non-ILO Labor	114LTS451	302671
Austria	Serb/Croat/Slovene	29 Mar 24	Land Transport	114LTS421	302670
Austria	Serb/Croat/Slovene	18 Jun 24	Non-ILO Labor	114LTS481	302672
Austria	Serb/Croat/Slovene	18 Jun 24	Non-ILO Labor	115LTS25	302674
Austria	Serb/Croat/Slovene	18 Jun 24	Non-ILO Labor	115LTS9	302673
Austria	Serb/Croat/Slovene	27 Jun 24	Non-ILO Labor	115LTS49	302676
Austria	Serb/Croat/Slovene	27 Jun 24	Non-ILO Labor	115LTS39	302675
Austria	Serb/Croat/Slovene	17 Jan 25	Health/Educ/Welfare	128LTS453	302949
Austria	Serb/Croat/Slovene	17 Jan 25	Health/Educ/Welfare	128LTS445	302948
Austria	Serb/Croat/Slovene	01 May 28	Admin Cooperation	96LTS373	302214
Austria	Serb/Croat/Slovene	06 Jun 28	Non-ILO Labor	129LTS11	302950
Austria	Serb/Croat/Slovene	09 Jul 28	General Trade	85LTS265	301936
Austria	Spain	03 Feb 25	General Economic	43LTS313	301067
Austria	Spain	11 Jun 28	Dispute Settlement	87LTS393	301984
Austria	Spain	23 Aug 29	Visas	97LTS353	302232
Austria	Sweden	04 Oct 22	Humanitarian	9LTS317	300264
Austria	Sweden	10 Nov 24	General Economic	31LTS57	300782
Austria	Sweden	06 Mar 26	Admin Cooperation	47LTS39	301128
Austria	Sweden	28 May 26	Dispute Settlement	61LTS193	301434
Austria	Sweden	20 Dec 27	Visas	71LTS293	301670
Austria	Sweden	24 Mar 30	Extradition	105LTS313	302424
Austria	Sweden	15 Jan 37	Non-ILO Labor	174LTS125	304043
Austria	Switzerland	11 Oct 24	Dispute Settlement	33LTS423	300862
Austria	Switzerland	19 Nov 24	Water Transport	39LTS26	300994
Austria	Switzerland	06 Jan 26	General Economic	46LTS299	301124
Austria	Switzerland	15 Mar 27	Admin Cooperation	87LTS351	301981
Austria	Switzerland	24 Oct 27	Taxation	85LTS253	301935
Austria	Switzerland	21 Nov 36	Land Transport	179LTS341	304162
Austria	Turkey	28 Jan 24	Consul/Citizenship	32LTS303	300822
Austria	Turkey	28 Jan 24	General Amity	32LTS297	300821
Austria	Turkey	28 Jan 24	General Trade	32LTS313	300823
Austria	Turkey	14 Sep 32	Admin Cooperation	135LTS275	303116
Austria	UK Great Britain	22 Sep 20	Admin Cooperation	5LTS309	300136
Austria	UK Great Britain	14 Jul 21	Sanitation	16LTS151	300405

PARTY ONE	PARTY TWO	DATE	TOPIC	CITATION	NUMBER
Austria	UK Great Britain	02 Oct 22	Reparations	12LTS413	300337
Austria	UK Great Britain	28 Mar 23	Customs	17LTS385	300445
Austria	UK Great Britain	31 Mar 31	Admin Cooperation	127LTS167	302918
Austria	UK Great Britain	14 Jul 31	Dispute Settlement	123LTS383	302824
Austria	UK Great Britain	16 Jul 32	Air Transport	144LTS9	303318
Austria	UK Great Britain	27 Jul 33	Patents/Copyrights	142LTS157	303287
Austria	UK Great Britain	15 Dec 33	Postal Service	146LTS9	303360
Austria	UK Great Britain	29 Oct 34	Extradition	165LTS373	303823
Austria	United Arab Rep	07 Mar 30	General Economic	100LTS417	302310
Austria	United Arab Rep	13 Oct 34	Admin Cooperation	153LTS279	303522
Austria	Uruguay	25 May 29	Visas	93LTS229	302112
Austria	USA (United States)	24 Aug 21	General Amity	7LTS155	300184
Austria	USA (United States)	19 Jun 28	Consul/Citizenship	118LTS241	302728
Austria	USA (United States)	16 Aug 28	Dispute Settlement	88LTS101	301989
Austria	USA (United States)	16 Aug 28	Dispute Settlement	88LTS95	301988
Austria	USA (United States)	30 Jan 30	Extradition	106LTS379	302457
Austria	USA (United States)	19 May 34	Extradition	153LTS247	303517
Austria	USSR (Soviet Union)	08 Sep 23	Consul/Citizenship	20LTS153	300515
Austria	Vatican/Holy See	23 Mar 35	Visas	167LTS385	303879
Austria	Yugoslavia	21 Jul 31	Non-ILO Labor	147LTS123	303397
Austria	Yugoslavia	09 Mar 32	General Trade	157LTS145	303609
Austria	Yugoslavia	20 Apr 32	Claims and Debts	132LTS217	303040
Austria	Yugoslavia	14 Oct 32	Air Transport	147LTS173	303398
Austria	Yugoslavia	09 Aug 33	General Trade	158LTS195	303632
Austria-Hungary	Greece	21 Dec 04	Extradition	2LTS173	300064
Austria-Hungary	Multilateral	18 Mar 04	Humanitarian	1LTS83	300011
Austria-Hungary	Multilateral	12 Jan 12	Sanitation	4LTS281	300112
Bahamas	Multilateral	30 Jun 20	Patents/Copyrights	1LTS59	300008
Bahamas	Multilateral	31 Mar 22	Humanitarian	9LTS415	300269
Bahamas	Multilateral	24 Sep 23	Dispute Settlement	27LTS157	300678
Bahamas	Multilateral	25 Aug 24	Water Transport	120LTS155	302764
Bahamas	Multilateral	01 Dec 24	Sanitation	78LTS351	301794
Bahamas	Multilateral	19 Feb 25	Admin Cooperation	81LTS317	301845
Bahamas	Multilateral	26 Sep 27	Dispute Settlement	92LTS301	302096
Bahamas	Multilateral	25 Nov 27	Telecommunications	84LTS97	301905
Bahamas	Multilateral	28 Oct 33	Refugees	159LTS199	303663
Bahamas	Multilateral	23 Sep 36	Gen Communications	186LTS301	304319
Bahamas	Multilateral	10 Feb 38	Refugees	192LTS59	304461
Bahamas	USA (United States)	21 Dec 36	Postal Service	176LTS411	304077
Balkan States	Bulgaria	31 Jul 38	General Amity	196LTS371	304596
Barbados	Curacao	10 Oct 33	Postal Service	145LTS245	303357
Barbados	Martinique	21 Oct 39	Postal Service	201LTS65	304704
Barbados	Multilateral	30 Jun 20	Patents/Copyrights	1LTS59	300008
Barbados	Multilateral	31 Mar 22	Humanitarian	9LTS415	300269
Barbados	Multilateral	25 Aug 24	Water Transport	120LTS155	302764
Barbados	Multilateral	25 Nov 27	Telecommunications	84LTS97	301905
Barbados	Multilateral	30 Mar 31	Taxation	138LTS149	303185
Barbados	Multilateral	23 Sep 36	Gen Communications	186LTS301	304319
Barbados	USA (United States)	13 Sep 39	Postal Service	199LTS375	304685
Basutoland	Multilateral	25 Nov 27	Telecommunications	84LTS97	301905
Basutoland	Multilateral	28 Oct 33	Refugees	159LTS199	303663
Basutoland	Multilateral	30 Oct 35	Telecommunications	189LTS51	304375
Basutoland	Multilateral	30 Oct 35	Postal Service	189LTS85	304376
Basutoland	Multilateral	23 Sep 36	Gen Communications	186LTS301	304319
Basutoland	Multilateral	10 Feb 38	Refugees	192LTS59	304461
Bechuanaland	Multilateral	25 Nov 27	Telecommunications	84LTS97	301905
Bechuanaland	Multilateral	28 Oct 33	Refugees	159LTS199	303663
Bechuanaland	Multilateral	30 Oct 35	Telecommunications	189LTS51	304375
Bechuanaland	Multilateral	30 Oct 35	Postal Service	189LTS85	304376
Bechuanaland	Multilateral	23 Sep 36	Gen Communications	186LTS301	304319
Bechuanaland	Multilateral	10 Feb 38	Refugees	192LTS59	304461
Bel-Lux Econ Union		07 Jul 25	General Economic	54LTS267	301290
Bel-Lux Econ Union	Albania	19 Feb 29	General Trade	90LTS429	302053
Bel-Lux Econ Union	Argentina	16 Jan 34	Mostfavored Nation	147LTS79	303392
Bel-Lux Econ Union	Argentina	16 Jan 34	Finance	145LTS145	303352

PARTY ONE	PARTY TWO	DATE	TOPIC	CITATION	NUMBER
Bel-Lux Econ Union	Australia	03 Oct 36	General Trade	177LTS271	304094
Bel-Lux Econ Union	Brazil	14 Jan 32	Mostfavored Nation	128LTS21	302933
Bel-Lux Econ Union	Bulgaria	21 Jun 33	Claims and Debts	140LTS375	303247
Bel-Lux Econ Union	Bulgaria	01 Apr 36	Finance	169LTS23	303912
Bel-Lux Econ Union	Canada	03 Jul 24	General Trade	32LTS35	300803
Bel-Lux Econ Union	Chile	14 Dec 31	Mostfavored Nation	126LTS247	302887
Bel-Lux Econ Union	China	22 Nov 28	General Amity	87LTS287	301975
Bel-Lux Econ Union	Czechoslovakia	28 Dec 25	General Economic	58LTS189	301372
Bel-Lux Econ Union	Estonia	28 Sep 26	General Economic	62LTS433	301475
Bel-Lux Econ Union	Estonia	19 Jun 35	Finance	170LTS243	303940
Bel-Lux Econ Union	Estonia	13 Jan 38	General Trade	185LTS63	304275
Bel-Lux Econ Union	France	04 Apr 25	General Trade	44LTS213	301085
Bel-Lux Econ Union	France	23 Feb 28	General Trade	72LTS61	301689
Bel-Lux Econ Union	France	28 Mar 29	General Trade	96LTS41	302190
Bel-Lux Econ Union	France	16 Jul 35	Territory Boundary	162LTS19	303731
Bel-Lux Econ Union	Germany	05 Sep 34	General Trade	154LTS187	303547
Bel-Lux Econ Union	Greece	22 Nov 27	Milit Assistance	69LTS341	301616
Bel-Lux Econ Union	Guatemala	07 Nov 24	General Economic	69LTS17	301596
Bel-Lux Econ Union	Hungary	26 Mar 32	Finance	136LTS405	303139
Bel-Lux Econ Union	Hungary	24 May 33	Claims and Debts	140LTS169	303234
Bel-Lux Econ Union	Italy	30 Jun 37	General Trade	197LTS23	304601
Bel-Lux Econ Union	Italy	30 Jun 37	Finance	182LTS106	304203
Bel-Lux Econ Union	Japan	27 Jun 25	Water Transport	36LTS95	300907
Bel-Lux Econ Union	Latvia	16 Aug 28	General Trade	81LTS411	301849
Bel-Lux Econ Union	Latvia	22 Feb 36	General Trade	171LTS147	303956
Bel-Lux Econ Union	Latvia	31 Jan 39	General Economic	195LTS401	304559
Bel-Lux Econ Union	Multilateral	15 Jul 34	Mostfavored Nation	165LTS9	303801
Bel-Lux Econ Union	New Zealand	05 Dec 33	Mostfavored Nation	149LTS435	303445
Bel-Lux Econ Union	Persia	09 May 29	General Economic	110LTS377	302569
Bel-Lux Econ Union	Poland	10 Jun 33	General Trade	144LTS137	303324
Bel-Lux Econ Union	Poland	02 Mar 36	General Economic	168LTS67	303887
Bel-Lux Econ Union	Portugal	06 Jan 27	General Trade	91LTS239	302065
Bel-Lux Econ Union	Romania	28 Aug 30	Mostfavored Nation	107LTS221	302479
Bel-Lux Econ Union	Romania	24 Aug 37	Finance	193LTS189	304496
Bel-Lux Econ Union	Serb/Croat/Slovene	16 Dec 26	General Trade	70LTS371	301647
Bel-Lux Econ Union	Siam	13 Jul 26	General Economic	62LTS287	301468
Bel-Lux Econ Union	Siam	05 Nov 37	General Amity	190LTS151	304413
Bel-Lux Econ Union	South Africa	13 Jul 37	General Trade	182LTS247	304214
Bel-Lux Econ Union	Spain	15 Dec 28	General Trade	84LTS287	301909
Bel-Lux Econ Union	Spain	04 Apr 36	Finance	168LTS339	303909
Bel-Lux Econ Union	Switzerland	26 Aug 29	General Economic	105LTS9	302401
Bel-Lux Econ Union	Turkey	28 Aug 27	General Trade	82LTS77	301862
Bel-Lux Econ Union	Turkey	24 May 34	Mostfavored Nation	150LTS269	303460
Bel-Lux Econ Union	Turkey	31 May 34	Claims and Debts	150LTS277	303461
Bel-Lux Econ Union	Turkey	31 May 34	General Trade	150LTS289	303462
Bel-Lux Econ Union	Uruguay	22 Feb 37	General Trade	196LTS391	304600
Bel-Lux Econ Union	USA (United States)	27 Feb 35	General Trade	160LTS27	303681
Bel-Lux Econ Union	USSR (Soviet Union)	05 Sep 35	General Trade	173LTS169	304010
Bel-Lux Econ Union	Yugoslavia	07 Aug 32	Finance	139LTS223	303212
Bel-Lux Econ Union	Yugoslavia	21 Feb 33	Claims and Debts	147LTS203	303399
Bel-Lux Econ Union	Yugoslavia	26 Nov 37	Finance	196LTS19	304567
Belgian Colonies	Fr Equatorial Afri	04 May 22	Telecommunications	148LTS61	303403
Belgian Colonies	Multilateral	23 Jan 12	Sanitation	8LTS187	300222
Belgian Colonies	Multilateral	01 Dec 24	Sanitation	78LTS351	301794
Belgian Colonies	Multilateral	19 Feb 25	Admin Cooperation	81LTS317	301845
Belgian Colonies	Multilateral	29 Oct 25	Telecommunications	57LTS201	301365
Belgian Colonies	Multilateral	25 Nov 27	Telecommunications	84LTS97	301905
Belgian Colonies	Multilateral	28 Jun 29	Postal Service	103LTS71	302370
Belgian Colonies	Multilateral	28 Jun 29	Postal Service	103LTS5	302369
Belgian Colonies	Multilateral	28 Jun 29	Postal Service	102LTS245	302368
Belgian Colonies	Multilateral	13 Jul 31	Other HEW	139LTS301	303219
Belgian Colonies	Multilateral	09 Dec 32	Telecommunications	151LTS5	303479
Belgian Colonies	Multilateral	20 Mar 34	Postal Service	174LTS171	304048
Belgian Colonies	Multilateral	20 Mar 34	Postal Service	175LTS5	304049
Belgian Colonies	Multilateral	20 Mar 34	Postal Service	175LTS73	304050

PARTY ONE	PARTY TWO	DATE	TOPIC	CITATION	NUMBER
Belgian Colonies	Multilateral	30 Oct 35	Telecommunications	189LTS51	304375
Belgian Colonies	Multilateral	30 Oct 35	Postal Service	189LTS85	304376
Belgian Colonies	Multilateral	02 Jan 39	Postal Service	196LTS235	304587
Belgian Colonies	Multilateral	23 May 39	Postal Service	202LTS159	304742
Belgian Colonies	Ruanda-Urundi	06 Aug 35	Admin Cooperation	164LTS49	303787
Belgian Colonies	Tanganyika	10 Jul 22	Telecommunications	148LTS71	303404
Belgium	Afghanistan	16 Jun 28	Education	97LTS97	302221
Belgium	Argentina	20 Oct 24	Health/Educ/Welfare	137LTS381	303166
Belgium	Australia	14 Dec 33	General Trade	147LTS21	303386
Belgium	Australia	19 Nov 34	Customs	155LTS385	303590
Belgium	Austria	04 Oct 20	Claims and Debts	5LTS371	300142
Belgium	Austria	29 Mar 24	Peace/Disarmament	91LTS245	302066
Belgium	Austria	10 Oct 27	Claims and Debts	91LTS271	302067
Belgium	Austria	18 Jan 30	Admin Cooperation	104LTS231	302393
Belgium	Austria	01 Dec 30	Extradition	112LTS37	302605
Belgium	Austria	01 Dec 30	Admin Cooperation	112LTS43	302606
Belgium	Austria	26 Jan 32	Extradition	129LTS141	302959
Belgium	Bolivia	06 Jan 33	Territory Boundary	147LTS59	303390
Belgium	Bulgaria	02 Jul 30	Admin Cooperation	130LTS191	302990
Belgium	Bulgaria	23 Jun 31	Dispute Settlement	137LTS191	303156
Belgium	Bulgaria	04 Jun 32	Extradition	134LTS241	303094
Belgium	Bulgaria	26 Oct 34	Admin Cooperation	155LTS99	303571
Belgium	Bulgaria	26 Oct 34	Admin Cooperation	155LTS105	303572
Belgium	Chile	21 Feb 33	Extradition	162LTS339	303747
Belgium	China	31 Aug 29	Privil/Immunities	123LTS105	302810
Belgium	China	18 Dec 37	Air Transport	190LTS109	304409
Belgium	Colombia	21 Nov 31	Extradition	182LTS165	304209
Belgium	Costa Rica	03 Feb 33	Extradition	166LTS325	303848
Belgium	Cuba	23 Feb 33	Admin Cooperation	185LTS279	304294
Belgium	Czechoslovakia	19 Jul 27	Extradition	73LTS283	301720
Belgium	Czechoslovakia	19 Jul 27	Admin Cooperation	73LTS307	301721
Belgium	Czechoslovakia	26 Jun 28	Visas	80LTS9	301819
Belgium	Czechoslovakia	29 Apr 29	Dispute Settlement	110LTS113	302556
Belgium	Czechoslovakia	16 Oct 37	Visas	184LTS73	304243
Belgium	Denmark	28 Jun 23	Air Transport	20LTS59	300507
Belgium	Denmark	25 Oct 26	Extradition	58LTS259	301376
Belgium	Denmark	13 Mar 27	Dispute Settlement	67LTS117	301542
Belgium	Denmark	12 Dec 28	Taxation	107LTS363	302492
Belgium	Denmark	14 Mar 32	Extradition	139LTS39	303202
Belgium	Denmark	27 Jul 34	Health/Educ/Welfare	150LTS351	303467
Belgium	Denmark	22 May 35	Admin Cooperation	159LTS255	303669
Belgium	Denmark	16 Sep 37	Visas	197LTS67	304606
Belgium	Ecuador	05 Dec 29	Visas	97LTS385	302237
Belgium	Ecuador	06 Jun 33	Extradition	159LTS249	303668
Belgium	El Salvador	31 Aug 33	Extradition	145LTS129	303350
Belgium	Estonia	28 Sep 26	Water Transport	60LTS9	301401
Belgium	Estonia	11 Nov 26	Extradition	65LTS405	301523
Belgium	Estonia	08 Feb 27	Consul/Citizenship	74LTS227	301740
Belgium	Estonia	24 Apr 31	Customs	119LTS371	302756
Belgium	Finland	04 Mar 27	Dispute Settlement	69LTS361	301618
Belgium	Finland	23 Jan 28	Extradition	74LTS353	301747
Belgium	Finland	01 Jun 28	Visas	77LTS327	301774
Belgium	Finland	19 Feb 29	Taxation	111LTS31	302577
Belgium	Finland	03 Jun 32	Extradition	132LTS269	303043
Belgium	France	24 Jul 20	Reparations	1LTS311	300026
Belgium	France	07 Sep 20	General Military	2LTS127	300056
Belgium	France	14 Feb 21	Admin Cooperation	12LTS245	300317
Belgium	France	04 Oct 21	Milit Servic/Citiz	8LTS157	300219
Belgium	France	30 Nov 21	Humanitarian	27LTS173	300680
Belgium	France	24 Dec 24	Non-ILO Labor	78LTS367	301795
Belgium	France	24 Jun 26	Extradition	94LTS349	302153
Belgium	France	11 Apr 27	Land Transport	143LTS215	303309
Belgium	France	21 May 27	Non-ILO Labor	105LTS125	302407
Belgium	France	21 May 27	Non-ILO Labor	95LTS283	302180

PARTY ONE	PARTY TWO	DATE	TOPIC	CITATION	NUMBER
Belgium	France	06 Oct 27	Admin Cooperation	69LTS49	301599
Belgium	France	23 May 28	Sanitation	88LTS145	301993
Belgium	France	30 May 28	Education	95LTS195	302173
Belgium	France	30 Jun 28	IGO Operations	93LTS377	302126
Belgium	France	04 Jul 28	Visas	85LTS205	301931
Belgium	France	12 Sep 28	Consul/Citizenship	123LTS91	302808
Belgium	France	12 Sep 28	Milit Servic/Citiz	123LTS97	302809
Belgium	France	01 Jul 29	Non-ILO Labor	93LTS371	302125
Belgium	France	07 Oct 29	Taxation	111LTS43	302579
Belgium	France	07 Nov 29	Reparations	134LTS257	303096
Belgium	France	23 May 30	Telecommunications	119LTS33	302738
Belgium	France	23 Aug 30	Non-ILO Labor	166LTS11	303825
Belgium	France	30 Mar 31	Non-ILO Labor	126LTS195	302882
Belgium	France	15 Apr 31	Territory Boundary	119LTS161	302743
Belgium	France	16 May 31	Taxation	141LTS333	303274
Belgium	France	29 Jul 31	Sanitation	127LTS85	302909
Belgium	France	07 Sep 31	Non-ILO Labor	134LTS65	303083
Belgium	France	17 Nov 31	Reparations	152LTS121	303490
Belgium	France	23 Dec 31	Taxation	137LTS277	303162
Belgium	France	18 Jun 32	Taxation	137LTS289	303163
Belgium	France	28 Jul 34	Visas	152LTS27	303481
Belgium	France	09 May 35	Territory Boundary	162LTS437	303755
Belgium	France	25 Aug 35	Extradition	161LTS369	303725
Belgium	France	30 Dec 35	General Trade	166LTS25	303826
Belgium	France	16 Jul 36	Admin Cooperation	171LTS287	303965
Belgium	France	07 Jul 37	Admin Cooperation	181LTS111	304182
Belgium	France	02 Oct 37	Water Transport	184LTS65	304242
Belgium	France	06 Mar 39	Non-ILO Labor	195LTS353	304555
Belgium	Germany	23 Apr 20	Admin Cooperation	12LTS29	300305
Belgium	Germany	09 Jul 20	Peace/Disarmament	12LTS45	300307
Belgium	Germany	11 Sep 22	General Amity	41LTS141	301009
Belgium	Germany	18 Apr 25	Admin Cooperation	42LTS49	301031
Belgium	Germany	03 Oct 25	Visas	38LTS285	300983
Belgium	Germany	16 Oct 25	General Military	54LTS303	301293
Belgium	Germany	29 May 26	Air Transport	127LTS149	302916
Belgium	Germany	01 Jul 26	General Transport	62LTS127	301461
Belgium	Germany	09 Jul 27	Admin Cooperation	75LTS367	301759
Belgium	Germany	13 Jul 29	Finance	104LTS201	302390
Belgium	Germany	13 Jul 29	Consul/Citizenship	104LTS211	302391
Belgium	Germany	07 Nov 29	Territory Boundary	121LTS327	302795
Belgium	Germany	16 Jan 30	Admin Cooperation	104LTS223	302392
Belgium	Germany	20 Jun 30	Land Transport	110LTS107	302555
Belgium	Germany	16 Jul 31	Non-ILO Labor	145LTS137	303351
Belgium	Germany	21 Dec 34	Taxation	162LTS9	303730
Belgium	Germany	10 May 35	Territory Boundary	182LTS323	304220
Belgium	Germany	10 May 35	Territory Boundary	165LTS169	303808
Belgium	Germany	10 May 35	Territory Boundary	182LTS335	304221
Belgium	Germany	10 May 35	Territory Boundary	165LTS143	303807
Belgium	Great Britain	21 Dec 28	Admin Cooperation	85LTS415	301942
Belgium	Greece	25 Jun 29	Dispute Settlement	113LTS117	302640
Belgium	Greece	04 Aug 33	Extradition	153LTS325	303528
Belgium	Greece	01 Aug 34	Water Transport	153LTS273	303521
Belgium	Greece	09 Sep 37	Visas	197LTS63	304605
Belgium	Guatemala	26 Apr 34	Extradition	161LTS415	303729
Belgium	Honduras	17 Jun 33	Extradition	167LTS69	303857
Belgium	Hungary	05 Dec 25	Admin Cooperation	43LTS173	301053
Belgium	Hungary	30 Sep 26	Claims and Debts	97LTS215	302225
Belgium	Iceland	21 Dec 28	Taxation	107LTS369	302493
Belgium	Irish Free State	24 Sep 29	Postal Service	102LTS213	302364
Belgium	Italy	28 Jan 29	Extradition	92LTS263	302094
Belgium	Italy	11 Jul 31	Taxation	136LTS9	303120
Belgium	Italy	07 Feb 34	Consul/Citizenship	147LTS107	303395
Belgium	Italy	04 May 35	Air Transport	159LTS165	303660
Belgium	Italy	02 Dec 35	Extradition	172LTS209	303992
Belgium	Italy	01 May 37	Visas	198LTS73	304624

PARTY ONE	PARTY TWO	DATE	TOPIC	CITATION	NUMBER
Belgium	Japan	28 Aug 34	Health/Educ/Welfare	155LTS395	303591
Belgium	Latvia	11 Dec 26	Extradition	63LTS299	301497
Belgium	Liechtenstein	05 Aug 36	Extradition	185LTS33	304302
Belgium	Lithuania	17 May 27	Extradition	77LTS123	301767
Belgium	Lithuania	24 Sep 30	Dispute Settlement	129LTS399	302974
Belgium	Lithuania	12 Dec 30	Admin Cooperation	135LTS231	303114
Belgium	Lithuania	21 Jul 31	Patents/Copyrights	137LTS225	303158
Belgium	Lithuania	16 Jun 32	Extradition	137LTS439	303173
Belgium	Lithuania	20 Sep 34	Water Transport	153LTS289	303524
Belgium	Luxembourg	25 Jul 21	General Economic	9LTS223	300256
Belgium	Luxembourg	27 Dec 21	Telecommunications	12LTS253	300318
Belgium	Luxembourg	17 Jul 23	Humanitarian	27LTS235	300686
Belgium	Luxembourg	24 Aug 26	Extradition	61LTS311	301442
Belgium	Luxembourg	20 Oct 26	Non-ILO Labor	78LTS375	301796
Belgium	Luxembourg	17 Oct 27	Dispute Settlement	124LTS203	302834
Belgium	Luxembourg	13 Apr 28	Admin Cooperation	72LTS237	301695
Belgium	Luxembourg	26 Apr 28	Admin Cooperation	93LTS159	302107
Belgium	Luxembourg	18 May 28	Postal Service	89LTS213	302016
Belgium	Luxembourg	18 May 28	Postal Service	89LTS207	302015
Belgium	Luxembourg	18 May 29	Customs	119LTS377	302757
Belgium	Luxembourg	09 Mar 31	Taxation	137LTS267	303161
Belgium	Luxembourg	31 May 33	Consul/Citizenship	141LTS9	303256
Belgium	Luxembourg	23 May 35	Direct Aid	161LTS327	303721
Belgium	Luxembourg	23 May 35	Taxation	161LTS347	303723
Belgium	Luxembourg	23 May 35	General Trade	161LTS335	303722
Belgium	Luxembourg	22 Jul 38	Territory Boundary	191LTS113	304440
Belgium	Luxembourg	04 Mar 39	Admin Cooperation	197LTS141	304610
Belgium	Mexico	22 Sep 38	Extradition	198LTS399	304658
Belgium	Monaco	28 May 32	Claims and Debts	136LTS415	303140
Belgium	Monaco	16 Dec 37	Extradition	187LTS195	304339
Belgium	Multilateral	09 Sep 86*	Patents/Copyrights	123LTS233	302816
Belgium	Multilateral	18 Mar 04	Humanitarian	1LTS83	300011
Belgium	Multilateral	13 Nov 08	General Ad Hoc	1LTS217	300015
Belgium	Multilateral	12 Jan 12	Sanitation	4LTS281	300112
Belgium	Multilateral	05 Jun 12	Telecommunications	1LTS135	300013
Belgium	Multilateral	20 Mar 14	Patents/Copyrights	1LTS243	300016
Belgium	Multilateral	10 Sep 19	General Trade	7LTS331	300200
Belgium	Multilateral	10 Sep 19	Reparations	2LTS29	300043
Belgium	Multilateral	10 Sep 19	Reparations	2LTS21	300042
Belgium	Multilateral	10 Sep 19	Reparations	2LTS44	300045
Belgium	Multilateral	10 Sep 19	General Economic	2LTS35	300044
Belgium	Multilateral	10 Sep 19	Admin Cooperation	8LTS25	300202
Belgium	Multilateral	10 Sep 19	Health/Educ/Welfare	8LTS11	300201
Belgium	Multilateral	01 May 20	Air Transport	11LTS173	300297
Belgium	Multilateral	04 Jun 20	Peace/Disarmament	6LTS187	300152
Belgium	Multilateral	21 Jun 20	Health/Educ/Welfare	8LTS65	300207
Belgium	Multilateral	30 Jun 20	Patents/Copyrights	1LTS59	300008
Belgium	Multilateral	16 Dec 20	General IGO	6LTS379	300170
Belgium	Multilateral	20 Apr 21	Water Transport	7LTS73	300174
Belgium	Multilateral	20 Apr 21	Water Transport	7LTS35	300172
Belgium	Multilateral	20 Apr 21	Land Transport	7LTS11	300171
Belgium	Multilateral	20 Apr 21	Water Transport	7LTS65	300173
Belgium	Multilateral	05 May 21	Peace/Disarmament	12LTS419	300338
Belgium	Multilateral	10 Jun 21	Customs	8LTS297	300227
Belgium	Multilateral	23 Jul 21	Water Transport	26LTS173	300647
Belgium	Multilateral	05 Oct 21	Admin Cooperation	29LTS79	300735
Belgium	Multilateral	05 Oct 21	Admin Cooperation	29LTS67	300733
Belgium	Multilateral	05 Oct 21	Admin Cooperation	29LTS73	300734
Belgium	Multilateral	06 Oct 21	General Economic	17LTS45	300427
Belgium	Multilateral	06 Feb 22	General Trade	38LTS277	300982
Belgium	Multilateral	06 Feb 22	Customs	38LTS267	300981
Belgium	Multilateral	22 Feb 22	Water Transport	26LTS219	300649
Belgium	Multilateral	31 Mar 22	Humanitarian	9LTS415	300269
Belgium	Multilateral	04 Oct 22	Territory Boundary	12LTS391	300335
Belgium	Multilateral	04 Oct 22	Territory Boundary	12LTS385	300334

PARTY ONE	PARTY TWO	DATE	TOPIC	CITATION	NUMBER
Belgium	Multilateral	14 Dec 22	Water Transport	36LTS457	300943
Belgium	Multilateral	30 Dec 22	General Trade	21LTS183	300542
Belgium	Multilateral	27 Jan 23	Water Transport	26LTS253	300651
Belgium	Multilateral	29 Mar 23	Admin Cooperation	20LTS111	300510
Belgium	Multilateral	24 Jul 23	Admin Cooperation	28LTS197	300706
Belgium	Multilateral	24 Sep 23	Dispute Settlement	27LTS157	300678
Belgium	Multilateral	03 Nov 23	Customs	30LTS371	300775
Belgium	Multilateral	28 Nov 23	Admin Cooperation	51LTS221	301230
Belgium	Multilateral	09 Dec 23	Land Transport	47LTS55	301129
Belgium	Multilateral	09 Dec 23	Non-IBRD Project	36LTS76	300905
Belgium	Multilateral	09 Dec 23	General Economic	58LTS315	301380
Belgium	Multilateral	09 Dec 23	Water Transport	58LTS284	301379
Belgium	Multilateral	14 Dec 23	General Trade	29LTS37	300732
Belgium	Multilateral	25 Jan 24	Sanitation	57LTS135	301360
Belgium	Multilateral	07 Feb 24	Water Transport	25LTS265	300614
Belgium	Multilateral	12 Mar 24	General Trade	24LTS17	300595
Belgium	Multilateral	31 Mar 24	Sanitation	27LTS211	300685
Belgium	Multilateral	04 Jul 24	Admin Cooperation	51LTS227	301231
Belgium	Multilateral	16 Aug 24	Taxation	41LTS429	301024
Belgium	Multilateral	25 Aug 24	Water Transport	120LTS123	302763
Belgium	Multilateral	25 Aug 24	Water Transport	120LTS155	302764
Belgium	Multilateral	28 Aug 24	Postal Service	41LTS97	301008
Belgium	Multilateral	28 Aug 24	Postal Service	41LTS9	301006
Belgium	Multilateral	28 Aug 24	Postal Service	40LTS437	301005
Belgium	Multilateral	28 Aug 24	Postal Service	40LTS249	301003
Belgium	Multilateral	28 Aug 24	Postal Service	41LTS55	301007
Belgium	Multilateral	28 Aug 24	Postal Service	40LTS19	301002
Belgium	Multilateral	28 Aug 24	Postal Service	40LTS307	301004
Belgium	Multilateral	30 Aug 24	Admin Cooperation	30LTS79	300761
Belgium	Multilateral	30 Aug 24	Reparations	30LTS97	300762
Belgium	Multilateral	30 Aug 24	General Economic	30LTS63	300759
Belgium	Multilateral	30 Aug 24	Admin Cooperation	30LTS75	300760
Belgium	Multilateral	30 Sep 24	Mostfavored Nation	30LTS135	300766
Belgium	Multilateral	23 Oct 24	Land Transport	78LTS17	301779
Belgium	Multilateral	23 Oct 24	General Transport	77LTS367	301778
Belgium	Multilateral	01 Dec 24	Sanitation	78LTS351	301794
Belgium	Multilateral	12 Dec 24	Gen Communications	37LTS113	300950
Belgium	Multilateral	19 Feb 25	Admin Cooperation	81LTS317	301845
Belgium	Multilateral	00 Apr 25	Water Transport	37LTS21	300945
Belgium	Multilateral	23 Apr 25	Water Transport	37LTS9	300944
Belgium	Multilateral	05 May 25	Finance	55LTS225	301318
Belgium	Multilateral	17 Jun 25	Peace/Disarmament	94LTS65	302138
Belgium	Multilateral	16 Oct 25	Peace/Disarmament	54LTS289	301292
Belgium	Multilateral	29 Oct 25	Telecommunications	57LTS201	301365
Belgium	Multilateral	06 Nov 25	Patents/Copyrights	74LTS289	301743
Belgium	Multilateral	06 Nov 25	Other Economic	74LTS341	301746
Belgium	Multilateral	06 Nov 25	Patents/Copyrights	74LTS327	301745
Belgium	Multilateral	27 Nov 25	Water Transport	67LTS63	301539
Belgium	Multilateral	00 Apr 26	Water Transport	57LTS437	301366
Belgium	Multilateral	10 Apr 26	Water Transport	176LTS199	304062
Belgium	Multilateral	10 Apr 26	Water Transport	120LTS187	302765
Belgium	Multilateral	24 Apr 26	Land Transport	108LTS123	302505
Belgium	Multilateral	12 May 26	Refugees	89LTS47	302004
Belgium	Multilateral	22 May 26	Air Transport	58LTS331	301381
Belgium	Multilateral	21 Jun 26	Sanitation	78LTS229	301793
Belgium	Multilateral	25 Sep 26	ILO Labor	60LTS253	301414
Belgium	Multilateral	18 Mar 27	Telecommunications	68LTS179	301581
Belgium	Multilateral	02 May 27	Telecommunications	68LTS189	301582
Belgium	Multilateral	12 Jul 27	Direct Aid	135LTS247	303115
Belgium	Multilateral	10 Sep 27	Postal Service	75LTS7	301749
Belgium	Multilateral	10 Sep 27	Postal Service	75LTS39	301750
Belgium	Multilateral	26 Sep 27	Dispute Settlement	92LTS301	302096
Belgium	Multilateral	29 Oct 27	Scientific Project	127LTS27	302903
Belgium	Multilateral	08 Nov 27	General Trade	97LTS391	302238
Belgium	Multilateral	25 Nov 27	Telecommunications	84LTS97	301905

PARTY ONE	PARTY TWO	DATE	TOPIC	CITATION	NUMBER
Belgium	Multilateral	19 Mar 28	Telecommunications	78LTS177	301788
Belgium	Multilateral	25 Apr 28	Telecommunications	78LTS207	301791
Belgium	Multilateral	30 Jun 28	Refugees	89LTS63	302006
Belgium	Multilateral	30 Jun 28	Refugees	89LTS53	302005
Belgium	Multilateral	11 Jul 28	Commodity Trade	95LTS373	302185
Belgium	Multilateral	11 Jul 28	Commodity Trade	95LTS357	302184
Belgium	Multilateral	15 Jul 28	Patents/Copyrights	79LTS133	301806
Belgium	Multilateral	27 Aug 28	General Military	94LTS57	302137
Belgium	Multilateral	26 Sep 28	Dispute Settlement	93LTS343	302123
Belgium	Multilateral	22 Nov 28	Culture	111LTS343	302598
Belgium	Multilateral	27 Nov 28	Telecommunications	92LTS321	302098
Belgium	Multilateral	14 Dec 28	General Economic	110LTS171	302560
Belgium	Multilateral	16 Apr 29	Specific Resources	126LTS305	302891
Belgium	Multilateral	20 Apr 29	Admin Cooperation	112LTS371	302623
Belgium	Multilateral	31 May 29	Water Transport	136LTS81	303127
Belgium	Multilateral	14 Jun 29	Visas	94LTS275	302148
Belgium	Multilateral	28 Jun 29	Postal Service	102LTS245	302368
Belgium	Multilateral	28 Jun 29	Postal Service	103LTS429	302374
Belgium	Multilateral	28 Jun 29	Postal Service	103LTS249	302371
Belgium	Multilateral	28 Jun 29	Postal Service	103LTS71	302370
Belgium	Multilateral	28 Jun 29	Postal Service	103LTS321	302372
Belgium	Multilateral	28 Jun 29	Postal Service	103LTS377	302373
Belgium	Multilateral	28 Jun 29	Postal Service	103LTS5	302369
Belgium	Multilateral	27 Jul 29	Other Military	118LTS303	302733
Belgium	Multilateral	27 Jul 29	Other Military	118LTS343	302734
Belgium	Multilateral	20 Aug 29	Sanitation	98LTS125	302243
Belgium	Multilateral	30 Aug 29	General Amity	104LTS487	302400
Belgium	Multilateral	30 Aug 29	Consul/Citizenship	104LTS473	302399
Belgium	Multilateral	14 Sep 29	UN Charter	165LTS353	303822
Belgium	Multilateral	30 Sep 29	Postal Service	99LTS71	302269
Belgium	Multilateral	12 Oct 29	General Transport	137LTS11	303145
Belgium	Multilateral	20 Jan 30	Finance	104LTS433	302397
Belgium	Multilateral	20 Jan 30	Finance	104LTS413	302395
Belgium	Multilateral	20 Jan 30	Reparations	104LTS243	302394
Belgium	Multilateral	20 Jan 30	Other Economic	104LTS441	302398
Belgium	Multilateral	20 Jan 30	Reparations	104LTS421	302396
Belgium	Multilateral	20 Jan 30	Reparations	112LTS361	302622
Belgium	Multilateral	20 Jan 30	Reparations	113LTS389	302650
Belgium	Multilateral	24 Jan 30	Peace/Disarmament	106LTS85	302437
Belgium	Multilateral	12 Apr 30	Admin Cooperation	179LTS89	304137
Belgium	Multilateral	12 Apr 30	Admin Cooperation	179LTS115	304138
Belgium	Multilateral	12 Apr 30	Milit Servic/Citiz	178LTS227	304117
Belgium	Multilateral	28 Apr 30	Claims and Debts	121LTS69	302785
Belgium	Multilateral	07 Jun 30	Finance	143LTS257	303313
Belgium	Multilateral	07 Jun 30	Finance	143LTS317	303314
Belgium	Multilateral	07 Jun 30	Finance	143LTS337	303315
Belgium	Multilateral	01 Aug 30	Health/Educ/Welfare	128LTS9	302932
Belgium	Multilateral	23 Oct 30	Water Transport	125LTS95	302849
Belgium	Multilateral	23 Oct 30	Water Transport	112LTS21	302603
Belgium	Multilateral	22 Dec 30	General Trade	126LTS341	302893
Belgium	Multilateral	19 Mar 31	Finance	143LTS407	303317
Belgium	Multilateral	19 Mar 31	Finance	143LTS355	303316
Belgium	Multilateral	19 Mar 31	Admin Cooperation	143LTS7	303301
Belgium	Multilateral	27 Mar 31	ICJ Option Clause	167LTS341	303877
Belgium	Multilateral	28 Mar 31	Customs	119LTS47	302739
Belgium	Multilateral	30 Mar 31	Land Transport	150LTS247	303459
Belgium	Multilateral	30 Mar 31	Taxation	138LTS149	303185
Belgium	Multilateral	13 Jul 31	Other HEW	139LTS301	303219
Belgium	Multilateral	24 Sep 31	Specific Resources	155LTS349	303586
Belgium	Multilateral	11 Dec 31	Commodity Trade	170LTS251	303941
Belgium	Multilateral	15 Jul 32	Direct Aid	135LTS285	303118
Belgium	Multilateral	02 Sep 32	Land Transport	154LTS123	303543
Belgium	Multilateral	09 Dec 32	Telecommunications	151LTS5	303479
Belgium	Multilateral	11 Mar 33	Water Transport	135LTS301	303119
Belgium	Multilateral	12 Apr 33	Sanitation	161LTS65	303706

PARTY ONE	PARTY TWO	DATE	TOPIC	CITATION	NUMBER
Belgium	Multilateral	29 May 33	Admin Cooperation	192LTS289	304479
Belgium	Multilateral	19 Jun 33	Gen Communications	154LTS133	303544
Belgium	Multilateral	25 Aug 33	Commodity Trade	141LTS71	303262
Belgium	Multilateral	11 Oct 33	Education	155LTS331	303585
Belgium	Multilateral	11 Oct 33	Consul/Citizenship	150LTS431	303476
Belgium	Multilateral	28 Oct 33	Refugees	159LTS199	303663
Belgium	Multilateral	08 Nov 33	Specific Resources	172LTS241	303995
Belgium	Multilateral	23 Nov 33	Land Transport	192LTS389	304484
Belgium	Multilateral	23 Nov 33	Land Transport	192LTS327	304483
Belgium	Multilateral	20 Mar 34	Postal Service	174LTS171	304048
Belgium	Multilateral	20 Mar 34	Postal Service	175LTS363	304052
Belgium	Multilateral	20 Mar 34	Finance	176LTS9	304053
Belgium	Multilateral	20 Mar 34	Postal Service	175LTS269	304051
Belgium	Multilateral	20 Mar 34	Postal Service	175LTS5	304049
Belgium	Multilateral	20 Mar 34	Postal Service	176LTS55	304054
Belgium	Multilateral	20 Mar 34	Postal Service	175LTS73	304050
Belgium	Multilateral	26 Apr 34	Admin Cooperation	164LTS63	303789
Belgium	Multilateral	02 Jun 34	Patents/Copyrights	205LTS179	304834
Belgium	Multilateral	02 Jun 34	Patents/Copyrights	192LTS17	304459
Belgium	Multilateral	12 Jun 34	Milit Installation	155LTS367	303587
Belgium	Multilateral	20 Feb 35	Sanitation	193LTS59	304487
Belgium	Multilateral	20 Feb 35	Sanitation	193LTS37	304486
Belgium	Multilateral	20 Feb 35	Sanitation	186LTS173	304310
Belgium	Multilateral	26 Jun 36	Other HEW	198LTS299	304648
Belgium	Multilateral	04 Jul 36	Refugees	171LTS75	303952
Belgium	Multilateral	30 Jul 36	IGO Status/Immunit	197LTS31	304602
Belgium	Multilateral	23 Sep 36	Gen Communications	186LTS301	304319
Belgium	Multilateral	06 Nov 36	General Military	173LTS353	304025
Belgium	Multilateral	10 Feb 37	General Transport	189LTS313	304391
Belgium	Multilateral	31 Mar 37	Commodity Trade	189LTS359	304394
Belgium	Multilateral	08 May 37	Privil/Immunities	182LTS37	304202
Belgium	Multilateral	28 May 37	General Trade	180LTS5	304170
Belgium	Multilateral	02 Oct 37	Education	182LTS263	304216
Belgium	Multilateral	10 Feb 38	Refugees	192LTS59	304461
Belgium	Multilateral	29 Apr 38	Visas	190LTS115	304410
Belgium	Multilateral	11 May 38	General Trade	189LTS237	304386
Belgium	Multilateral	27 Jun 38	Visas	191LTS199	304443
Belgium	Multilateral	31 Oct 38	Sanitation	198LTS205	304642
Belgium	Multilateral	03 Dec 38	Education	200LTS249	304694
Belgium	Multilateral	03 Apr 39	Water Transport	195LTS471	304566
Belgium	Multilateral	06 May 39	Finance	198LTS81	304626
Belgium	Multilateral	23 May 39	Postal Service	202LTS159	304742
Belgium	Multilateral	01 Jan 42	General Military	204LTS381	304817
Belgium	Multilateral	02 Jun 42	Patents/Copyrights	205LTS163	304833
Belgium	Multilateral	09 Sep 42	Commodity Trade	205LTS137	304831
Belgium	Netherlands	31 May 89*	Extradition	137LTS261	303160
Belgium	Netherlands	08 Mar 20	Telecommunications	1LTS25	300003
Belgium	Netherlands	06 Oct 20	Land Transport	18LTS247	300467
Belgium	Netherlands	09 Feb 21	Non-ILO Labor	11LTS333	300299
Belgium	Netherlands	15 Oct 21	Postal Service	12LTS233	300315
Belgium	Netherlands	08 Jul 22	Air Transport	13LTS273	300358
Belgium	Netherlands	14 Jul 23	Water Transport	20LTS119	300511
Belgium	Netherlands	02 May 24	Admin Cooperation	27LTS113	300673
Belgium	Netherlands	28 Aug 25	Dispute Settlement	93LTS431	302131
Belgium	Netherlands	05 Mar 26	Postal Service	50LTS213	301203
Belgium	Netherlands	28 Feb 27	Telecommunications	68LTS169	301580
Belgium	Netherlands	24 Mar 27	Sanitation	84LTS34	301902
Belgium	Netherlands	25 Oct 27	Extradition	69LTS29	301597
Belgium	Netherlands	26 Oct 27	Education	89LTS37	302003
Belgium	Netherlands	16 Apr 28	Admin Cooperation	75LTS61	301751
Belgium	Netherlands	27 Mar 29	Finance	89LTS201	302014
Belgium	Netherlands	28 May 29	Sanitation	89LTS191	302013
Belgium	Netherlands	16 Oct 31	Admin Cooperation	137LTS411	303171
Belgium	Netherlands	22 Oct 31	Customs	125LTS367	302865
Belgium	Netherlands	29 Dec 31	General Trade	127LTS163	302917

PARTY ONE	PARTY TWO	DATE	TOPIC	CITATION	NUMBER
Belgium	Netherlands	04 Aug 32	Postal Service	134LTS117	303086
Belgium	Netherlands	20 Feb 33	Non-ILO Labor	165LTS383	303824
Belgium	Netherlands	20 Feb 33	Taxation	164LTS223	303796
Belgium	Netherlands	01 Aug 34	Telecommunications	153LTS267	303520
Belgium	Netherlands	06 Apr 35	Water Transport	160LTS137	303687
Belgium	Netherlands	15 May 36	Humanitarian	179LTS41	304131
Belgium	Netherlands	13 Jul 36	Postal Service	177LTS93	304083
Belgium	Netherlands	26 Mar 37	Customs	179LTS52	304132
Belgium	Netherlands	09 Jun 37	Consul/Citizenship	181LTS153	304186
Belgium	Netherlands	31 Dec 37	Land Transport	189LTS387	304396
Belgium	Netherlands	07 Feb 38	Admin Cooperation	187LTS9	304328
Belgium	Netherlands	30 Apr 38	Taxation	190LTS199	304418
Belgium	Netherlands	17 Dec 38	Water Transport	198LTS177	304638
Belgium	Nicaragua	13 Jul 33	Extradition	161LTS361	303724
Belgium	Norway	29 Oct 28	Taxation	107LTS75	302469
Belgium	Norway	20 Jul 34	Consul/Citizenship	150LTS369	303469
Belgium	Norway	17 Dec 36	Taxation	178LTS153	304110
Belgium	Norway	10 Mar 37	Customs	178LTS12	304101
Belgium	Paraguay	20 Jan 26	Extradition	97LTS197	302224
Belgium	Persia	15 May 28	General Amity	94LTS447	302160
Belgium	Persia	09 May 29	Privil/Immunities	110LTS391	302570
Belgium	Persia	23 May 29	General Amity	110LTS369	302568
Belgium	Poland	30 Dec 22	Finance	21LTS201	300543
Belgium	Poland	01 Sep 25	Admin Cooperation	54LTS69	301274
Belgium	Poland	12 Jun 28	Consul/Citizenship	123LTS25	302803
Belgium	Poland	18 Dec 30	Health/Educ/Welfare	134LTS177	303090
Belgium	Poland	13 May 31	Extradition	131LTS109	303005
Belgium	Portugal	22 Jan 20	Customs	3LTS149	300096
Belgium	Portugal	27 Feb 25	Water Transport	91LTS201	302061
Belgium	Portugal	09 Jul 27	Dispute Settlement	74LTS39	301730
Belgium	Portugal	19 Jul 27	Sanitation	71LTS419	301680
Belgium	Portugal	20 Jul 27	General Economic	71LTS431	301681
Belgium	Portugal	21 Jul 27	Water Transport	71LTS439	301682
Belgium	Portugal	22 Jul 27	Territory Boundary	71LTS449	301683
Belgium	Portugal	28 Mar 28	Admin Cooperation	92LTS185	302085
Belgium	Romania	08 Jul 30	Dispute Settlement	128LTS403	302944
Belgium	Shereefian	24 Jul 30	Non-ILO Labor	138LTS35	303179
Belgium	Siam	14 Jan 37	Extradition	179LTS419	304168
Belgium	Siam	05 Nov 37	Privil/Immunities	190LTS163	304414
Belgium	South Africa	04 Feb 32	Admin Cooperation	127LTS121	302912
Belgium	Spain	19 Jul 27	Dispute Settlement	80LTS17	301820
Belgium	Spain	31 Jan 30	Taxation	99LTS369	302281
Belgium	Spain	27 Feb 32	Air Transport	137LTS111	303149
Belgium	Spain	27 Feb 32	Air Transport	137LTS129	303150
Belgium	Sweden	03 Jan 21	Land Transport	2LTS301	300083
Belgium	Sweden	25 Oct 22	Admin Cooperation	18LTS121	300459
Belgium	Sweden	30 Apr 26	Dispute Settlement	67LTS91	301540
Belgium	Sweden	13 May 29	Taxation	111LTS37	302578
Belgium	Sweden	22 Sep 34	Water Transport	153LTS261	303519
Belgium	Sweden	15 Jun 37	Visas	198LTS77	304625
Belgium	Switzerland	13 Jun 22	Air Transport	12LTS295	300321
Belgium	Switzerland	05 Feb 27	Dispute Settlement	68LTS45	301567
Belgium	Switzerland	30 Aug 35	Taxation	162LTS293	303741
Belgium	Switzerland	14 May 38	Extradition	190LTS217	304420
Belgium	Turkey	27 May 30	General Economic	111LTS49	302580
Belgium	Turkey	09 Feb 38	Extradition	198LTS181	304639
Belgium	UK Great Britain	05 Oct 20	Postal Service	5LTS147	300123
Belgium	UK Great Britain	15 Mar 21	Land Transport	5LTS319	300138
Belgium	UK Great Britain	20 Jul 21	Reparations	8LTS301	300228
Belgium	UK Great Britain	21 Jun 22	Admin Cooperation	24LTS91	300597
Belgium	UK Great Britain	28 Mar 23	Reparations	16LTS439	300421
Belgium	UK Great Britain	08 Aug 23	Extradition	22LTS375	300566
Belgium	UK Great Britain	29 Jul 24	Telecommunications	29LTS389	300749
Belgium	UK Great Britain	18 Feb 25	Postal Service	33LTS341	300857
Belgium	UK Great Britain	18 Feb 25	Postal Service	33LTS361	300858

PARTY ONE	PARTY TWO	DATE	TOPIC	CITATION	NUMBER
Belgium	UK Great Britain	26 Feb 25	Telecommunications	71LTS83	301656
Belgium	UK Great Britain	11 May 26	Postal Service	71LTS97	301657
Belgium	UK Great Britain	17 May 26	Territory Boundary	54LTS239	301287
Belgium	UK Great Britain	09 Apr 27	Telecommunications	67LTS209	301548
Belgium	UK Great Britain	03 May 27	Territory Boundary	140LTS71	303229
Belgium	UK Great Britain	06 May 27	Admin Cooperation	63LTS153	301486
Belgium	UK Great Britain	04 Nov 32	Admin Cooperation	153LTS251	303518
Belgium	UK Great Britain	13 Apr 34	Dispute Settlement	154LTS361	303561
Belgium	UK Great Britain	02 May 34	Admin Cooperation	173LTS291	304020
Belgium	UK Great Britain	22 Nov 34	Territory Boundary	190LTS95	304407
Belgium	UK Great Britain	22 Nov 34	Specific Resources	190LTS99	304408
Belgium	UK Great Britain	01 Jun 37	Taxation	196LTS209	304583
Belgium	UK Great Britain	29 Jul 38	Postal Service	201LTS317	304722
Belgium	UK Great Britain	19 Jun 39	Admin Cooperation	198LTS171	304637
Belgium	UK Great Britain	04 Jun 42	Commodity Trade	204LTS363	304814
Belgium	United Arab Rep	20 May 37	Taxation	182LTS153	304207
Belgium	USA (United States)	30 Mar 22	General Transport	12LTS259	300319
Belgium	USA (United States)	21 Jan 24	Territory Boundary	31LTS137	300791
Belgium	USA (United States)	18 Nov 25	Extradition	50LTS225	301205
Belgium	USA (United States)	09 Dec 25	Other Ad Hoc	72LTS171	301690
Belgium	USA (United States)	20 Mar 29	Dispute Settlement	109LTS261	302542
Belgium	USA (United States)	20 Mar 29	Dispute Settlement	109LTS267	302543
Belgium	USA (United States)	04 Oct 29	Other Military	105LTS189	302412
Belgium	USA (United States)	19 Apr 32	Water Transport	134LTS19	303080
Belgium	USA (United States)	22 Oct 32	Air Transport	137LTS389	303167
Belgium	USA (United States)	20 Jun 35	Extradition	164LTS205	303794
Belgium	USA (United States)	28 Jan 36	Taxation	166LTS333	303849
Belgium	USA (United States)	15 Jan 39	Postal Service	199LTS321	304682
Belgium	Yugoslavia	25 Mar 30	Dispute Settlement	106LTS343	302455
Belgium	Yugoslavia	29 Feb 36	Admin Cooperation	184LTS379	304258
Benelux Econ Union	Germany	04 Apr 25	General Trade	37LTS203	300957
Benelux Econ Union	Germany	15 Jul 26	Visas	63LTS137	301485
Bermuda	Multilateral	25 Aug 24	Water Transport	120LTS155	302764
Bermuda	Multilateral	25 Nov 27	Telecommunications	84LTS97	301905
Bermuda	Multilateral	30 Mar 31	Taxation	138LTS149	303185
Bermuda	Multilateral	23 Sep 36	Gen Communications	186LTS301	304319
Bolivia	Belgium	06 Jan 33	Territory Boundary	147LTS59	303390
Bolivia	Denmark	09 Nov 31	General Economic	147LTS27	303387
Bolivia	Germany	20 Jul 21	General Amity	10LTS301	300275
Bolivia	Germany	12 Mar 24	General Amity	73LTS95	301710
Bolivia	Germany	20 Feb 25	General Trade	42LTS43	301030
Bolivia	Iceland	09 Nov 31	Mostfavored Nation	147LTS43	303388
Bolivia	Multilateral	20 Aug 10	Patents/Copyrights	155LTS179	303576
Bolivia	Multilateral	12 Jan 12	Sanitation	4LTS281	300112
Bolivia	Multilateral	05 Jun 12	Telecommunications	1LTS135	300013
Bolivia	Multilateral	10 Sep 19	General Trade	7LTS331	300200
Bolivia	Multilateral	29 Feb 20	Admin Cooperation	127LTS433	302930
Bolivia	Multilateral	01 May 20	Air Transport	11LTS173	300297
Bolivia	Multilateral	16 Dec 20	General IGO	6LTS379	300170
Bolivia	Multilateral	20 Apr 21	Water Transport	7LTS35	300172
Bolivia	Multilateral	20 Apr 21	Land Transport	7LTS11	300171
Bolivia	Multilateral	20 Apr 21	Water Transport	7LTS73	300174
Bolivia	Multilateral	05 Aug 21	Admin Cooperation	27LTS349	300695
Bolivia	Multilateral	15 Sep 21	Postal Service	30LTS141	300767
Bolivia	Multilateral	05 Oct 21	IGO Establishment	51LTS361	301241
Bolivia	Multilateral	05 Oct 21	Admin Cooperation	29LTS67	300733
Bolivia	Multilateral	05 Oct 21	Admin Cooperation	29LTS79	300735
Bolivia	Multilateral	05 Oct 21	Admin Cooperation	29LTS73	300734
Bolivia	Multilateral	03 May 23	General Amity	33LTS25	300831
Bolivia	Multilateral	28 Aug 24	Postal Service	41LTS97	301008
Bolivia	Multilateral	28 Aug 24	Postal Service	40LTS307	301004
Bolivia	Multilateral	28 Aug 24	Postal Service	41LTS55	301007
Bolivia	Multilateral	28 Aug 24	Postal Service	40LTS19	301002
Bolivia	Multilateral	28 Aug 24	Postal Service	40LTS249	301003
Bolivia	Multilateral	28 Aug 24	Postal Service	41LTS9	301006

PARTY ONE	PARTY TWO	DATE	TOPIC	CITATION	NUMBER
Bolivia	Multilateral	28 Aug 24	Postal Service	40LTS437	301005
Bolivia	Multilateral	14 Nov 24	Sanitation	86LTS43	301949
Bolivia	Multilateral	19 Feb 25	Admin Cooperation	81LTS317	301845
Bolivia	Multilateral	29 Oct 25	Telecommunications	57LTS201	301365
Bolivia	Multilateral	25 Nov 27	Telecommunications	84LTS97	301905
Bolivia	Multilateral	18 Feb 28	Patents/Copyrights	132LTS275	303044
Bolivia	Multilateral	20 Feb 28	Consul/Citizenship	155LTS289	303582
Bolivia	Multilateral	20 Feb 28	Consul/Citizenship	155LTS259	303581
Bolivia	Multilateral	20 Feb 28	Privil/Immunities	132LTS301	303045
Bolivia	Multilateral	20 Feb 28	Admin Cooperation	134LTS45	303082
Bolivia	Multilateral	20 Feb 28	General Amity	135LTS187	303111
Bolivia	Multilateral	20 Feb 28	Consul/Citizenship	132LTS323	303046
Bolivia	Multilateral	20 Feb 28	Air Transport	129LTS223	302963
Bolivia	Multilateral	20 Feb 28	Other Ad Hoc	86LTS111	301950
Bolivia	Multilateral	05 Jan 29	Dispute Settlement	130LTS135	302988
Bolivia	Multilateral	05 Jan 29	Dispute Settlement	100LTS399	302309
Bolivia	Multilateral	20 Feb 29	Patents/Copyrights	124LTS357	302840
Bolivia	Multilateral	28 Jun 29	Postal Service	103LTS377	302373
Bolivia	Multilateral	28 Jun 29	Postal Service	102LTS245	302368
Bolivia	Multilateral	28 Jun 29	Postal Service	103LTS429	302374
Bolivia	Multilateral	28 Jun 29	Postal Service	103LTS321	302372
Bolivia	Multilateral	28 Jun 29	Postal Service	103LTS249	302371
Bolivia	Multilateral	28 Jun 29	Postal Service	103LTS5	302369
Bolivia	Multilateral	28 Jun 29	Postal Service	103LTS71	302370
Bolivia	Multilateral	27 Jul 29	Other Military	118LTS343	302734
Bolivia	Multilateral	27 Jul 29	Other Military	118LTS303	302733
Bolivia	Multilateral	14 Sep 29	UN Charter	165LTS353	303822
Bolivia	Multilateral	13 Jul 31	Other HEW	139LTS301	303219
Bolivia	Multilateral	10 Nov 31	Postal Service	131LTS447	303025
Bolivia	Multilateral	10 Nov 31	Postal Service	131LTS389	303024
Bolivia	Multilateral	10 Nov 31	Postal Service	131LTS327	303023
Bolivia	Multilateral	09 Dec 32	Telecommunications	151LTS5	303479
Bolivia	Multilateral	12 Apr 33	Sanitation	161LTS65	303706
Bolivia	Multilateral	10 Oct 33	General Amity	163LTS393	303781
Bolivia	Multilateral	20 Mar 34	Postal Service	175LTS363	304052
Bolivia	Multilateral	20 Mar 34	Postal Service	174LTS171	304048
Bolivia	Multilateral	20 Mar 34	Postal Service	175LTS5	304049
Bolivia	Multilateral	20 Mar 34	Finance	176LTS9	304053
Bolivia	Multilateral	20 Mar 34	Postal Service	175LTS269	304051
Bolivia	Multilateral	20 Mar 34	Postal Service	175LTS73	304050
Bolivia	Multilateral	20 Mar 34	Postal Service	176LTS55	304054
Bolivia	Multilateral	15 Apr 35	Culture	167LTS289	303874
Bolivia	Multilateral	23 Dec 36	Admin Cooperation	201LTS295	304721
Bolivia	Multilateral	23 Dec 36	Dispute Settlement	195LTS229	304548
Bolivia	Multilateral	23 Dec 36	Culture	188LTS151	304356
Bolivia	Multilateral	23 Dec 36	General Amity	188LTS31	304351
Bolivia	Multilateral	23 Dec 36	Dispute Settlement	188LTS53	304352
Bolivia	Multilateral	23 Dec 36	Land Transport	188LTS99	304354
Bolivia	Multilateral	23 Dec 36	Culture	188LTS125	304355
Bolivia	Multilateral	23 Dec 36	Dispute Settlement	188LTS75	304353
Bolivia	Multilateral	23 Dec 36	Peace/Disarmament	188LTS9	304350
Bolivia	Multilateral	23 May 39	Postal Service	202LTS159	304742
Bolivia	Multilateral	09 Sep 42	Commodity Trade	205LTS137	304831
Bolivia	Netherlands	30 May 29	General Trade	133LTS113	303062
Bolivia	Spain	13 Mar 36	Patents/Copyrights	170LTS179	303933
Bolivia	UK Great Britain	05 Apr 20	General Trade	1LTS271	300020
Bolivia	UK Great Britain	11 Aug 21	Admin Cooperation	8LTS323	300231
Bolivia	UK Great Britain	14 Mar 21	Patents/Copyrights	5LTS315	300137
Bolivia	UK Great Britain	18 Jan 29	Postal Service	95LTS9	302161
Bosnia-Herzegovina	Multilateral	05 Jun 12	Telecommunications	1LTS135	300013
Brazil	Afghanistan	20 Feb 33	General Amity	186LTS385	304322
Brazil	Argentina	10 Oct 33	Customs	179LTS185	304146
Brazil	Argentina	10 Oct 33	Education	179LTS175	304145
Brazil	Argentina	10 Oct 33	Education	179LTS165	304144
Brazil	Australia	19 Jul 39	General Trade	200LTS191	304690

PARTY ONE	PARTY TWO	DATE	TOPIC	CITATION	NUMBER
Brazil	Austria	06 Jul 31	Visas	123LTS9	302801
Brazil	Austria	02 Jan 32	Mostfavored Nation	140LTS15	303224
Brazil	Bel-Lux Econ Union	14 Jan 32	Mostfavored Nation	128LTS21	302933
Brazil	Canada	04 Dec 31	General Trade	139LTS241	303214
Brazil	Chile	08 Nov 35	Extradition	181LTS297	304197
Brazil	Colombia	15 Nov 28	Water Transport	100LTS123	302299
Brazil	Czechoslovakia	27 Nov 31	General Trade	136LTS453	303144
Brazil	Czechoslovakia	22 Jul 36	General Trade	188LTS275	304363
Brazil	Denmark	29 Apr 29	Admin Cooperation	89LTS295	302024
Brazil	Denmark	30 Nov 31	Customs	128LTS29	302934
Brazil	Denmark	05 Aug 32	Health/Educ/Welfare	132LTS211	303039
Brazil	Denmark	30 Jul 36	General Trade	194LTS81	304510
Brazil	Estonia	30 Sep 32	General Trade	134LTS247	303095
Brazil	Finland	26 Nov 31	General Trade	126LTS239	302886
Brazil	France	27 Aug 27	Dispute Settlement	75LTS91	301754
Brazil	Germany	22 Oct 31	General Trade	136LTS443	303143
Brazil	Germany	14 Jun 33	Admin Cooperation	178LTS19	304102
Brazil	Hungary	24 Dec 31	Mostfavored Nation	147LTS51	303389
Brazil	Hungary	30 Jul 36	General Trade	177LTS53	304079
Brazil	Iceland	30 Nov 31	Customs	128LTS369	302942
Brazil	India	21 Jul 32	General Trade	133LTS93	303059
Brazil	Irish Free State	16 Oct 31	Mostfavored Nation	134LTS75	303084
Brazil	Italy	08 Oct 21	Non-ILO Labor	16LTS9	300401
Brazil	Italy	08 Feb 30	Visas	101LTS57	302319
Brazil	Italy	28 Nov 31	Extradition	132LTS345	303047
Brazil	Italy	28 Nov 31	Mostfavored Nation	131LTS273	303017
Brazil	Latvia	21 Sep 32	General Trade	137LTS61	303146
Brazil	Lithuania	28 Sep 37	General Trade	186LTS403	304324
Brazil	Mexico	07 Dec 31	General Trade	139LTS247	303215
Brazil	Mexico	18 Dec 33	Education	186LTS395	304323
Brazil	Multilateral	09 Sep 86*	Patents/Copyrights	123LTS233	302816
Brazil	Multilateral	18 Mar 04	Humanitarian	1LTS83	300011
Brazil	Multilateral	13 Nov 08	General Ad Hoc	1LTS217	300015
Brazil	Multilateral	20 Aug 10	Patents/Copyrights	155LTS179	303576
Brazil	Multilateral	12 Jan 12	Sanitation	4LTS281	300112
Brazil	Multilateral	05 Jun 12	Telecommunications	1LTS135	300013
Brazil	Multilateral	20 Mar 14	Patents/Copyrights	1LTS243	300016
Brazil	Multilateral	21 Apr 14	Sanitation	5LTS394	300144
Brazil	Multilateral	10 Sep 19	General Trade	7LTS331	300200
Brazil	Multilateral	29 Feb 20	Admin Cooperation	127LTS433	302930
Brazil	Multilateral	01 May 20	Air Transport	11LTS173	300297
Brazil	Multilateral	30 Jun 20	Patents/Copyrights	1LTS59	300008
Brazil	Multilateral	16 Dec 20	General IGO	6LTS379	300170
Brazil	Multilateral	15 Sep 21	Postal Service	30LTS141	300767
Brazil	Multilateral	05 Oct 21	Admin Cooperation	29LTS79	300735
Brazil	Multilateral	05 Oct 21	Admin Cooperation	29LTS73	300734
Brazil	Multilateral	05 Oct 21	Admin Cooperation	29LTS67	300733
Brazil	Multilateral	06 Oct 21	General Economic	17LTS45	300427
Brazil	Multilateral	31 Mar 22	Humanitarian	9LTS415	300269
Brazil	Multilateral	28 Apr 23	Patents/Copyrights	33LTS47	300832
Brazil	Multilateral	03 May 23	General Trade	33LTS81	300833
Brazil	Multilateral	03 May 23	General Amity	33LTS25	300831
Brazil	Multilateral	03 May 23	Customs	33LTS11	300830
Brazil	Multilateral	24 Sep 23	Dispute Settlement	27LTS157	300678
Brazil	Multilateral	03 Nov 23	Customs	30LTS371	300775
Brazil	Multilateral	09 Dec 23	Water Transport	58LTS284	301379
Brazil	Multilateral	09 Dec 23	Land Transport	47LTS55	301129
Brazil	Multilateral	25 Jan 24	Sanitation	57LTS135	301360
Brazil	Multilateral	31 Mar 24	Sanitation	27LTS211	300685
Brazil	Multilateral	25 Aug 24	Water Transport	120LTS123	302763
Brazil	Multilateral	28 Aug 24	Postal Service	40LTS19	301002
Brazil	Multilateral	28 Aug 24	Postal Service	40LTS249	301003
Brazil	Multilateral	28 Aug 24	Postal Service	40LTS307	301004
Brazil	Multilateral	14 Nov 24	Sanitation	86LTS43	301949
Brazil	Multilateral	19 Feb 25	Admin Cooperation	81LTS317	301845

PARTY ONE	PARTY TWO	DATE	TOPIC	CITATION	NUMBER
Brazil	Multilateral	17 Jun 25	Peace/Disarmament	94LTS65	302138
Brazil	Multilateral	29 Oct 25	Telecommunications	57LTS201	301365
Brazil	Multilateral	06 Nov 25	Patents/Copyrights	74LTS289	301743
Brazil	Multilateral	06 Nov 25	Other Economic	74LTS319	301744
Brazil	Multilateral	06 Nov 25	Patents/Copyrights	74LTS327	301745
Brazil	Multilateral	10 Apr 26	Water Transport	176LTS199	304062
Brazil	Multilateral	10 Apr 26	Water Transport	120LTS187	302765
Brazil	Multilateral	24 Apr 26	Land Transport	108LTS123	302505
Brazil	Multilateral	21 Jun 26	Sanitation	78LTS229	301793
Brazil	Multilateral	12 Jul 27	Direct Aid	135LTS247	303115
Brazil	Multilateral	25 Nov 27	Telecommunications	84LTS97	301905
Brazil	Multilateral	18 Feb 28	Patents/Copyrights	132LTS275	303044
Brazil	Multilateral	20 Feb 28	Consul/Citizenship	155LTS289	303582
Brazil	Multilateral	20 Feb 28	Consul/Citizenship	155LTS259	303581
Brazil	Multilateral	20 Feb 28	General Amity	135LTS187	303111
Brazil	Multilateral	20 Feb 28	Consul/Citizenship	132LTS323	303046
Brazil	Multilateral	20 Feb 28	Air Transport	129LTS223	302963
Brazil	Multilateral	20 Feb 28	Admin Cooperation	134LTS45	303082
Brazil	Multilateral	20 Feb 28	Privil/Immunities	132LTS301	303045
Brazil	Multilateral	20 Feb 28	Other Ad Hoc	86LTS111	301950
Brazil	Multilateral	22 Nov 28	Culture	111LTS343	302598
Brazil	Multilateral	05 Jan 29	Dispute Settlement	130LTS135	302988
Brazil	Multilateral	05 Jan 29	Dispute Settlement	100LTS399	302309
Brazil	Multilateral	20 Feb 29	Patents/Copyrights	124LTS357	302840
Brazil	Multilateral	16 Apr 29	Specific Resources	126LTS305	302891
Brazil	Multilateral	20 Apr 29	Admin Cooperation	112LTS395	302624
Brazil	Multilateral	20 Apr 29	Admin Cooperation	112LTS371	302623
Brazil	Multilateral	31 May 29	Water Transport	136LTS81	303127
Brazil	Multilateral	28 Jun 29	Postal Service	102LTS245	302368
Brazil	Multilateral	28 Jun 29	Postal Service	103LTS71	302370
Brazil	Multilateral	28 Jun 29	Postal Service	103LTS5	302369
Brazil	Multilateral	27 Jul 29	Other Military	118LTS303	302733
Brazil	Multilateral	27 Jul 29	Other Military	118LTS343	302734
Brazil	Multilateral	14 Sep 29	UN Charter	165LTS353	303822
Brazil	Multilateral	12 Oct 29	General Transport	137LTS11	303145
Brazil	Multilateral	17 Feb 30	Dispute Settlement	102LTS87	302354
Brazil	Multilateral	12 Apr 30	Admin Cooperation	179LTS115	304138
Brazil	Multilateral	12 Apr 30	Admin Cooperation	179LTS89	304137
Brazil	Multilateral	07 Jun 30	Finance	143LTS317	303314
Brazil	Multilateral	07 Jun 30	Finance	143LTS257	303313
Brazil	Multilateral	07 Jun 30	Finance	143LTS337	303315
Brazil	Multilateral	23 Oct 30	Water Transport	125LTS95	302849
Brazil	Multilateral	23 Oct 30	Water Transport	112LTS21	302603
Brazil	Multilateral	19 Mar 31	Finance	143LTS407	303317
Brazil	Multilateral	19 Mar 31	Finance	143LTS355	303316
Brazil	Multilateral	13 Jul 31	Other HEW	139LTS301	303219
Brazil	Multilateral	24 Sep 31	Specific Resources	155LTS349	303586
Brazil	Multilateral	10 Nov 31	Postal Service	131LTS327	303023
Brazil	Multilateral	10 Nov 31	Postal Service	131LTS447	303025
Brazil	Multilateral	09 Dec 32	Telecommunications	151LTS5	303479
Brazil	Multilateral	11 Mar 33	Water Transport	135LTS301	303119
Brazil	Multilateral	12 Apr 33	Sanitation	161LTS65	303706
Brazil	Multilateral	29 May 33	Admin Cooperation	192LTS289	304479
Brazil	Multilateral	10 Oct 33	General Amity	163LTS393	303781
Brazil	Multilateral	11 Oct 33	Consul/Citizenship	150LTS431	303476
Brazil	Multilateral	26 Dec 33	Recognition	165LTS19	303802
Brazil	Multilateral	26 Dec 33	Extradition	165LTS45	303803
Brazil	Multilateral	20 Mar 34	Postal Service	174LTS171	304048
Brazil	Multilateral	20 Mar 34	Postal Service	175LTS73	304050
Brazil	Multilateral	20 Mar 34	Postal Service	175LTS5	304049
Brazil	Multilateral	02 Jun 34	Patents/Copyrights	205LTS179	304834
Brazil	Multilateral	02 Jun 34	General Trade	192LTS9	304458
Brazil	Multilateral	02 Jun 34	Patents/Copyrights	192LTS17	304459
Brazil	Multilateral	15 Apr 35	Culture	167LTS289	303874
Brazil	Multilateral	26 Jun 36	Other HEW	198LTS299	304648

PARTY ONE	PARTY TWO	DATE	TOPIC	CITATION	NUMBER
Brazil	Multilateral	23 Sep 36	Gen Communications	186LTS301	304319
Brazil	Multilateral	06 Nov 36	General Military	173LTS353	304025
Brazil	Multilateral	23 Dec 36	Dispute Settlement	188LTS75	304353
Brazil	Multilateral	23 Dec 36	Land Transport	188LTS99	304354
Brazil	Multilateral	23 Dec 36	Culture	188LTS151	304356
Brazil	Multilateral	23 Dec 36	Dispute Settlement	188LTS53	304352
Brazil	Multilateral	23 Dec 36	General Amity	188LTS31	304351
Brazil	Multilateral	23 Dec 36	Culture	188LTS125	304355
Brazil	Multilateral	23 Dec 36	Dispute Settlement	195LTS229	304548
Brazil	Multilateral	23 Dec 36	Admin Cooperation	201LTS295	304721
Brazil	Multilateral	23 Dec 36	Peace/Disarmament	188LTS9	304350
Brazil	Multilateral	31 Mar 37	Commodity Trade	189LTS359	304394
Brazil	Multilateral	12 Sep 38	Culture	198LTS111	304630
Brazil	Multilateral	31 Oct 38	Sanitation	198LTS205	304642
Brazil	Multilateral	03 Dec 38	Education	200LTS249	304694
Brazil	Multilateral	23 May 39	Postal Service	202LTS159	304742
Brazil	Netherlands	16 Sep 30	Mostfavored Nation	125LTS197	302854
Brazil	Netherlands	22 Sep 31	Territory Boundary	130LTS113	302986
Brazil	Netherlands	15 Mar 37	Finance	179LTS405	304167
Brazil	Netherlands	15 Mar 37	General Trade	179LTS395	304166
Brazil	Norway	31 Dec 31	General Trade	126LTS385	302896
Brazil	Norway	27 Jul 36	General Trade	176LTS125	304056
Brazil	Paraguay	24 Feb 22	Extradition	138LTS211	303189
Brazil	Paraguay	09 Dec 31	Territory Boundary	136LTS427	303142
Brazil	Peru	31 Dec 28	Gen Communications	127LTS455	302931
Brazil	Poland	03 Feb 32	Mostfavored Nation	147LTS113	303396
Brazil	Poland	15 Oct 32	Admin Cooperation	176LTS373	304074
Brazil	Poland	27 Jan 33	Dispute Settlement	142LTS255	303299
Brazil	Portugal	26 Sep 22	Patents/Copyrights	25LTS229	300610
Brazil	Portugal	26 Aug 33	General Trade	179LTS63	304134
Brazil	Romania	16 Dec 31	General Trade	139LTS255	303216
Brazil	South Africa	11 Apr 32	Mostfavored Nation	135LTS219	303112
Brazil	South Africa	18 Apr 39	General Trade	198LTS289	304646
Brazil	Spain	08 Apr 09	Dispute Settlement	88LTS86	301987
Brazil	Sweden	16 Oct 31	Mostfavored Nation	125LTS51	302845
Brazil	Sweden	27 Jan 32	Admin Cooperation	177LTS119	304086
Brazil	Switzerland	23 Jun 24	Dispute Settlement	33LTS415	300861
Brazil	Switzerland	29 Oct 30	General Trade	140LTS265	303241
Brazil	Switzerland	23 Jul 32	Extradition	145LTS167	303354
Brazil	UK Great Britain	04 Apr 19	General Amity	5LTS45	300116
Brazil	UK Great Britain	01 Mar 21	Postal Service	8LTS265	300225
Brazil	UK Great Britain	16 Jul 21	Admin Cooperation	10LTS407	300279
Brazil	UK Great Britain	22 Apr 27	Territory Boundary	92LTS311	302097
Brazil	UK Great Britain	21 Feb 30	Consul/Citizenship	101LTS11	302315
Brazil	UK Great Britain	18 Mar 30	Territory Boundary	101LTS401	302339
Brazil	UK Great Britain	11 Sep 31	Mostfavored Nation	130LTS103	302985
Brazil	UK Great Britain	01 Nov 32	Territory Boundary	177LTS127	304087
Brazil	UK Great Britain	27 Mar 35	Finance	160LTS311	303700
Brazil	UK Great Britain	10 Aug 36	General Economic	172LTS283	303997
Brazil	UK Great Britain	10 Aug 36	Mostfavored Nation	172LTS273	303996
Brazil	Uruguay	01 Aug 21	Education	177LTS109	304085
Brazil	Uruguay	07 Dec 21	Extradition	63LTS223	301492
Brazil	Uruguay	25 Aug 33	General Trade	176LTS381	304075
Brazil	Uruguay	20 Dec 33	Customs	181LTS45	304176
Brazil	Uruguay	20 Dec 33	Admin Cooperation	181LTS91	304179
Brazil	Uruguay	20 Dec 33	Culture	181LTS35	304175
Brazil	Uruguay	20 Dec 33	Territory Boundary	181LTS69	304178
Brazil	Uruguay	20 Dec 33	Visas	181LTS55	304177
Brazil	USA (United States)	10 May 34	Military Mission	150LTS445	303477
Brazil	USA (United States)	02 Feb 35	General Trade	166LTS211	303840
Brazil	USA (United States)	27 May 36	Military Mission	171LTS343	303971
Brazil	USA (United States)	12 Nov 36	Military Mission	176LTS133	304057
Brazil	USA (United States)	17 Dec 37	Visas	186LTS413	304325
Brazil	USA (United States)	12 Nov 38	Military Mission	195LTS375	304557
Brazil	USA (United States)	24 Jun 40	Admin Cooperation	203LTS227	304766

PARTY ONE	PARTY TWO	DATE	TOPIC	CITATION	NUMBER
Brazil	USA (United States)	11 Oct 40	Privil/Immunities	203LTS261	304768
Brazil	USA (United States)	17 Jan 41	Military Mission	204LTS97	304788
Brazil	Venezuela	13 Apr 26	General Amity	80LTS283	301834
Brazil	Venezuela	07 Nov 29	Territory Boundary	99LTS427	302288
Brazil	Yugoslavia	16 May 32	Mostfavored Nation	144LTS303	303333
Brit Solomon Is	Multilateral	25 Aug 24	Water Transport	120LTS155	302764
Brit Solomon Is	Multilateral	01 Dec 24	Sanitation	78LTS351	301794
Brit Solomon Is	Multilateral	12 Apr 33	Sanitation	161LTS65	303706
Brit Solomon Is	Multilateral	28 Oct 33	Refugees	159LTS199	303663
Brit Solomon Is	Multilateral	23 Sep 36	Gen Communications	186LTS301	304319
Brit Solomon Is	Multilateral	10 Feb 38	Refugees	192LTS59	304461
British Empire	Greece	26 Nov 25	General Trade	63LTS167	301488
British Empire	Hedjaz	20 May 27	General Amity	71LTS131	301658
British Empire	Japan	30 Nov 22	Water Transport	16LTS207	300412
British Empire	Multilateral	21 Apr 14	Sanitation	5LTS394	300144
British Empire	Multilateral	10 Sep 19	Admin Cooperation	8LTS25	300202
British Empire	Multilateral	10 Sep 19	Reparations	2LTS44	300045
British Empire	Multilateral	10 Sep 19	General Economic	2LTS35	300044
British Empire	Multilateral	10 Sep 19	Reparations	2LTS29	300043
British Empire	Multilateral	10 Sep 19	Reparations	2LTS21	300042
British Empire	Multilateral	09 Dec 19	Territory Boundary	5LTS335	300140
British Empire	Multilateral	01 May 20	Air Transport	11LTS173	300297
British Empire	Multilateral	04 Jun 20	Peace/Disarmament	6LTS187	300152
British Empire	Multilateral	05 Jul 20	Dispute Settlement	2LTS241	300070
British Empire	Multilateral	05 Aug 20	Territory Boundary	2LTS49	300046
British Empire	Multilateral	10 Aug 20	Territory Boundary	28LTS225	300710
British Empire	Multilateral	10 Aug 20	Consul/Citizenship	28LTS223	300711
British Empire	Multilateral	16 Dec 20	General IGO	6LTS379	300170
British Empire	Multilateral	20 Apr 21	Land Transport	7LTS11	300171
British Empire	Multilateral	05 Aug 21	Admin Cooperation	27LTS349	300695
British Empire	Multilateral	05 Oct 21	Admin Cooperation	29LTS73	300734
British Empire	Multilateral	05 Oct 21	Admin Cooperation	29LTS79	300735
British Empire	Multilateral	05 Oct 21	IGO Establishment	51LTS361	301241
British Empire	Multilateral	05 Oct 21	Admin Cooperation	29LTS67	300733
British Empire	Multilateral	20 Oct 21	Peace/Disarmament	9LTS211	300255
British Empire	Multilateral	09 Nov 21	Territory Boundary	12LTS381	300333
British Empire	Multilateral	13 Dec 21	Territory Boundary	25LTS184	300607
British Empire	Multilateral	06 Feb 22	General Trade	38LTS277	300982
British Empire	Multilateral	06 Feb 22	Peace/Disarmament	25LTS201	300609
British Empire	Multilateral	06 Feb 22	Customs	38LTS267	300981
British Empire	Multilateral	06 Feb 22	Admin Cooperation	25LTS195	300608
British Empire	Multilateral	31 Mar 22	Humanitarian	9LTS415	300269
British Empire	Multilateral	02 Nov 22	Peace/Disarmament	149LTS35	303431
British Empire	Multilateral	15 Mar 23	Territory Boundary	15LTS259	300398
British Empire	Multilateral	24 Jul 23	Peace/Disarmament	28LTS11	300701
British Empire	Multilateral	24 Jul 23	General Amity	36LTS145	300913
British Empire	Multilateral	24 Jul 23	Territory Boundary	28LTS139	300703
British Empire	Multilateral	24 Jul 23	Admin Cooperation	28LTS197	300706
British Empire	Multilateral	24 Jul 23	General Trade	28LTS203	300707
British Empire	Multilateral	24 Jul 23	Territory Boundary	28LTS215	300708
British Empire	Multilateral	24 Jul 23	General Trade	28LTS171	300705
British Empire	Multilateral	24 Jul 23	Admin Cooperation	28LTS283	300714
British Empire	Multilateral	24 Jul 23	General Trade	28LTS151	300704
British Empire	Multilateral	24 Jul 23	Water Transport	28LTS115	300702
British Empire	Multilateral	24 Jul 23	Consul/Citizenship	28LTS221	300709
British Empire	Multilateral	24 Sep 23	Dispute Settlement	27LTS157	300678
British Empire	Multilateral	23 Nov 23	Reparations	28LTS273	300713
British Empire	Multilateral	23 Nov 23	Claims and Debts	28LTS267	300712
British Empire	Multilateral	09 Dec 23	Land Transport	47LTS55	301129
British Empire	Multilateral	09 Dec 23	Non-IBRD Project	36LTS76	300905
British Empire	Multilateral	09 Dec 23	Water Transport	58LTS284	301379
British Empire	Multilateral	09 Dec 23	General Economic	58LTS315	301380
British Empire	Multilateral	08 May 24	Territory Boundary	29LTS85	300736
British Empire	Multilateral	16 Aug 24	Taxation	41LTS429	301024
British Empire	Multilateral	25 Aug 24	Water Transport	120LTS155	302764

PARTY ONE	PARTY TWO	DATE	TOPIC	CITATION	NUMBER
British Empire	Multilateral	28 Aug 24	Postal Service	40LTS19	301002
British Empire	Multilateral	30 Aug 24	General Economic	30LTS63	300759
British Empire	Multilateral	11 Feb 25	Sanitation	51LTS337	301239
British Empire	Multilateral	19 Feb 25	Admin Cooperation	81LTS317	301845
British Empire	Multilateral	05 May 25	Finance	55LTS225	301318
British Empire	Multilateral	17 Jun 25	Peace/Disarmament	94LTS65	302138
British Empire	Multilateral	22 May 26	Air Transport	58LTS331	301381
British Empire	Multilateral	21 Jun 26	Sanitation	78LTS229	301793
British Empire	Multilateral	25 Sep 26	ILO Labor	60LTS253	301414
British Empire	Multilateral	18 Dec 26	Telecommunications	63LTS185	301489
British Empire	Multilateral	31 Mar 27	Air Transport	66LTS59	301525
British Empire	Multilateral	19 May 27	Air Transport	68LTS407	301595
British Empire	Multilateral	14 Dec 28	General Economic	110LTS171	302560
British Empire	Multilateral	14 Sep 29	UN Charter	165LTS353	303822
British Empire	Multilateral	12 Apr 33	Sanitation	161LTS65	303706
British Empire	USA (United States)	15 Nov 23	Postal Service	33LTS304	300854
British Guiana	Curacao	16 Jul 42	Postal Service	205LTS13	304823
British Guiana	Multilateral	30 Jun 20	Patents/Copyrights	1LTS59	300008
British Guiana	Multilateral	31 Mar 22	Humanitarian	9LTS415	300269
British Guiana	Multilateral	25 Aug 24	Water Transport	120LTS155	302764
British Guiana	Multilateral	01 Dec 24	Sanitation	78LTS351	301794
British Guiana	Multilateral	26 Sep 27	Dispute Settlement	92LTS301	302096
British Guiana	Multilateral	25 Nov 27	Telecommunications	84LTS97	301905
British Guiana	Multilateral	30 Mar 31	Taxation	138LTS149	303185
British Guiana	Multilateral	28 Oct 33	Refugees	159LTS199	303663
British Guiana	Multilateral	23 Sep 36	Gen Communications	186LTS301	304319
British Guiana	Multilateral	10 Feb 38	Refugees	192LTS59	304461
British Guiana	USA (United States)	06 Sep 38	Postal Service	193LTS117	304490
British Honduras	Mexico	25 Mar 25	Postal Service	43LTS61	301047
British Honduras	Multilateral	30 Jun 20	Patents/Copyrights	1LTS59	300008
British Honduras	Multilateral	31 Mar 22	Humanitarian	9LTS415	300269
British Honduras	Multilateral	25 Aug 24	Water Transport	120LTS155	302764
British Honduras	Multilateral	01 Dec 24	Sanitation	78LTS351	301794
British Honduras	Multilateral	26 Sep 27	Dispute Settlement	92LTS301	302096
British Honduras	Multilateral	25 Nov 27	Telecommunications	84LTS97	301905
British Honduras	Multilateral	28 Oct 33	Refugees	159LTS199	303663
British Honduras	Multilateral	23 Sep 36	Gen Communications	186LTS301	304319
British Honduras	Multilateral	10 Feb 38	Refugees	192LTS59	304461
British India	Multilateral	09 Dec 32	Telecommunications	151LTS5	303479
British India	Multilateral	20 Mar 34	Postal Service	174LTS171	304048
British Indies	Multilateral	28 Aug 24	Postal Service	40LTS19	301002
British Indies	Multilateral	29 Oct 25	Telecommunications	57LTS201	301365
British Indies	Multilateral	09 Dec 32	Telecommunications	151LTS5	303479
British Indies	Multilateral	20 Mar 34	Postal Service	174LTS171	304048
Brunei	Multilateral	05 Jun 12	Telecommunications	1LTS135	300013
Bulgaria		09 Sep 26	Refugees	58LTS245	301375
Bulgaria		08 Sep 28	Loans and Credits	74LTS167	301738
Bulgaria	Balkan States	31 Jul 38	General Amity	196LTS371	304596
Bulgaria	Bel-Lux Econ Union	21 Jun 33	Claims and Debts	140LTS375	303247
Bulgaria	Bel-Lux Econ Union	01 Apr 36	Finance	169LTS23	303912
Bulgaria	Belgium	02 Jul 30	Admin Cooperation	130LTS191	302990
Bulgaria	Belgium	23 Jun 31	Dispute Settlement	137LTS191	303156
Bulgaria	Belgium	04 Jun 32	Extradition	134LTS241	303094
Bulgaria	Belgium	26 Oct 34	Admin Cooperation	155LTS99	303571
Bulgaria	Belgium	26 Oct 34	Admin Cooperation	155LTS105	303572
Bulgaria	Czechoslovakia	06 Sep 25	Health/Educ/Welfare	50LTS253	301208
Bulgaria	Czechoslovakia	16 Oct 25	General Economic	56LTS265	301334
Bulgaria	Czechoslovakia	15 May 26	Extradition	60LTS169	301412
Bulgaria	Czechoslovakia	15 May 26	Admin Cooperation	60LTS203	301413
Bulgaria	Czechoslovakia	29 Aug 33	General Economic	148LTS15	303402
Bulgaria	Denmark	11 Jul 22	Mostfavored Nation	12LTS225	300314
Bulgaria	Denmark	07 Dec 35	Dispute Settlement	182LTS183	304211
Bulgaria	Estonia	11 Feb 28	General Trade	79LTS43	301803
Bulgaria	Finland	22 Mar 35	Mostfavored Nation	159LTS123	303654
Bulgaria	Finland	27 Oct 36	Finance	173LTS201	304013

PARTY ONE	PARTY TWO	DATE	TOPIC	CITATION	NUMBER
Bulgaria	Finland	27 Oct 36	General Trade	179LTS309	304158
Bulgaria	France	22 Oct 25	General Trade	44LTS257	301087
Bulgaria	France	06 Jul 36	Finance	171LTS269	303963
Bulgaria	Germany	19 Feb 21	Other Economic	6LTS227	300157
Bulgaria	Germany	22 Dec 26	Admin Cooperation	64LTS77	301502
Bulgaria	Germany	04 Jun 29	Consul/Citizenship	106LTS49	302436
Bulgaria	Germany	24 Jun 32	General Economic	147LTS211	303400
Bulgaria	Great Britain	07 May 25	Postal Service	38LTS153	300973
Bulgaria	Greece	27 Nov 19	Consul/Citizenship	1LTS67	300009
Bulgaria	Greece	28 Feb 27	Mostfavored Nation	68LTS59	301568
Bulgaria	Greece	09 Dec 27	Finance	87LTS199	301970
Bulgaria	Greece	21 Feb 29	Extradition	106LTS443	302461
Bulgaria	Greece	16 Sep 38	General Trade	195LTS27	304534
Bulgaria	Hungary	03 Sep 21	Mostfavored Nation	7LTS229	300188
Bulgaria	Hungary	10 Sep 26	General Economic	69LTS333	301615
Bulgaria	Hungary	05 Jan 29	Health/Educ/Welfare	118LTS279	302730
Bulgaria	Hungary	17 May 29	Extradition	92LTS197	302087
Bulgaria	Hungary	22 Jul 29	Dispute Settlement	101LTS41	302317
Bulgaria	Hungary	12 Jun 34	Finance	160LTS73	303684
Bulgaria	Italy	20 May 31	Mostfavored Nation	129LTS371	302971
Bulgaria	Italy	20 May 31	Patents/Copyrights	129LTS361	302970
Bulgaria	Latvia	22 Jun 28	General Trade	97LTS379	302236
Bulgaria	Latvia	17 May 38	General Trade	189LTS249	304388
Bulgaria	Mexico	05 Nov 36	General Amity	187LTS37	304331
Bulgaria	Multilateral	09 Sep 86*	Patents/Copyrights	123LTS233	302816
Bulgaria	Multilateral	18 Mar 04	Humanitarian	1LTS83	300011
Bulgaria	Multilateral	12 Jan 12	Sanitation	4LTS281	300112
Bulgaria	Multilateral	05 Jun 12	Telecommunications	1LTS135	300013
Bulgaria	Multilateral	10 Sep 19	General Trade	7LTS331	300200
Bulgaria	Multilateral	01 May 20	Air Transport	11LTS173	300297
Bulgaria	Multilateral	30 Jun 20	Patents/Copyrights	1LTS59	300008
Bulgaria	Multilateral	31 Oct 20	Sanitation	164LTS85	303790
Bulgaria	Multilateral	16 Dec 20	General IGO	6LTS379	300170
Bulgaria	Multilateral	20 Apr 21	Land Transport	7LTS11	300171
Bulgaria	Multilateral	20 Apr 21	Water Transport	7LTS73	300174
Bulgaria	Multilateral	20 Apr 21	Water Transport	7LTS35	300172
Bulgaria	Multilateral	23 Jul 21	Water Transport	26LTS173	300647
Bulgaria	Multilateral	05 Aug 21	Admin Cooperation	27LTS349	300695
Bulgaria	Multilateral	05 Oct 21	IGO Establishment	51LTS361	301241
Bulgaria	Multilateral	05 Oct 21	Admin Cooperation	29LTS79	300735
Bulgaria	Multilateral	05 Oct 21	Admin Cooperation	29LTS67	300733
Bulgaria	Multilateral	05 Oct 21	Admin Cooperation	29LTS73	300734
Bulgaria	Multilateral	06 Oct 21	General Economic	17LTS45	300427
Bulgaria	Multilateral	05 Jul 22	Reparations	13LTS237	300355
Bulgaria	Multilateral	24 Jul 23	Admin Cooperation	28LTS283	300714
Bulgaria	Multilateral	24 Jul 23	Territory Boundary	28LTS139	300703
Bulgaria	Multilateral	24 Jul 23	Water Transport	28LTS115	300702
Bulgaria	Multilateral	03 Nov 23	Customs	30LTS371	300775
Bulgaria	Multilateral	09 Dec 23	Water Transport	58LTS284	301379
Bulgaria	Multilateral	09 Dec 23	General Economic	58LTS315	301380
Bulgaria	Multilateral	09 Dec 23	Land Transport	47LTS55	301129
Bulgaria	Multilateral	09 Dec 23	Non-IBRD Project	36LTS76	300905
Bulgaria	Multilateral	25 Jan 24	Sanitation	57LTS135	301360
Bulgaria	Multilateral	28 Mar 24	Finance	31LTS46	300780
Bulgaria	Multilateral	31 Mar 24	Sanitation	27LTS211	300685
Bulgaria	Multilateral	28 Aug 24	Postal Service	40LTS249	301003
Bulgaria	Multilateral	28 Aug 24	Postal Service	40LTS307	301004
Bulgaria	Multilateral	28 Aug 24	Postal Service	41LTS97	301008
Bulgaria	Multilateral	28 Aug 24	Postal Service	40LTS437	301005
Bulgaria	Multilateral	28 Aug 24	Postal Service	40LTS19	301002
Bulgaria	Multilateral	23 Oct 24	Land Transport	78LTS17	301779
Bulgaria	Multilateral	23 Oct 24	General Transport	77LTS367	301778
Bulgaria	Multilateral	19 Feb 25	Admin Cooperation	81LTS317	301845
Bulgaria	Multilateral	17 Jun 25	Peace/Disarmament	94LTS65	302138
Bulgaria	Multilateral	29 Oct 25	Telecommunications	57LTS201	301365

PARTY ONE	PARTY TWO	DATE	TOPIC	CITATION	NUMBER
Bulgaria	Multilateral	27 Nov 25	Water Transport	67LTS63	301539
Bulgaria	Multilateral	24 Apr 26	Land Transport	108LTS123	302505
Bulgaria	Multilateral	24 Apr 26	Land Transport	97LTS83	302220
Bulgaria	Multilateral	12 May 26	Refugees	89LTS47	302004
Bulgaria	Multilateral	21 Jun 26	Sanitation	78LTS229	301793
Bulgaria	Multilateral	25 Sep 26	ILO Labor	60LTS253	301414
Bulgaria	Multilateral	31 Mar 27	Air Transport	66LTS59	301525
Bulgaria	Multilateral	12 Jul 27	Direct Aid	135LTS247	303115
Bulgaria	Multilateral	10 Sep 27	Postal Service	75LTS39	301750
Bulgaria	Multilateral	10 Sep 27	Postal Service	75LTS7	301749
Bulgaria	Multilateral	08 Nov 27	General Trade	97LTS391	302238
Bulgaria	Multilateral	25 Nov 27	Telecommunications	84LTS97	301905
Bulgaria	Multilateral	30 Jun 28	Refugees	89LTS63	302006
Bulgaria	Multilateral	30 Jun 28	Refugees	89LTS53	302005
Bulgaria	Multilateral	11 Jul 28	Commodity Trade	95LTS357	302184
Bulgaria	Multilateral	11 Jul 28	Commodity Trade	95LTS373	302185
Bulgaria	Multilateral	27 Aug 28	General Military	94LTS57	302137
Bulgaria	Multilateral	14 Dec 28	General Economic	110LTS171	302560
Bulgaria	Multilateral	20 Apr 29	Admin Cooperation	112LTS395	302624
Bulgaria	Multilateral	20 Apr 29	Admin Cooperation	112LTS371	302623
Bulgaria	Multilateral	31 May 29	Water Transport	136LTS81	303127
Bulgaria	Multilateral	28 Jun 29	Postal Service	103LTS5	302369
Bulgaria	Multilateral	28 Jun 29	Postal Service	103LTS71	302370
Bulgaria	Multilateral	28 Jun 29	Postal Service	102LTS245	302368
Bulgaria	Multilateral	28 Jun 29	Postal Service	103LTS429	302374
Bulgaria	Multilateral	28 Jun 29	Postal Service	103LTS249	302371
Bulgaria	Multilateral	27 Jul 29	Other Military	118LTS303	302733
Bulgaria	Multilateral	27 Jul 29	Other Military	118LTS343	302734
Bulgaria	Multilateral	20 Aug 29	Sanitation	98LTS125	302243
Bulgaria	Multilateral	14 Sep 29	UN Charter	165LTS353	303822
Bulgaria	Multilateral	12 Oct 29	General Transport	137LTS11	303145
Bulgaria	Multilateral	20 Jan 30	Reparations	112LTS361	302622
Bulgaria	Multilateral	01 Aug 30	Health/Educ/Welfare	128LTS9	302932
Bulgaria	Multilateral	28 Mar 31	Customs	119LTS47	302739
Bulgaria	Multilateral	30 Mar 31	Taxation	138LTS149	303185
Bulgaria	Multilateral	13 Jul 31	Other HEW	139LTS301	303219
Bulgaria	Multilateral	11 Dec 31	Commodity Trade	170LTS251	303941
Bulgaria	Multilateral	02 Sep 32	Land Transport	154LTS123	303543
Bulgaria	Multilateral	09 Dec 32	Telecommunications	151LTS5	303479
Bulgaria	Multilateral	11 Mar 33	Water Transport	135LTS301	303119
Bulgaria	Multilateral	25 Aug 33	Commodity Trade	141LTS71	303262
Bulgaria	Multilateral	10 Oct 33	General Amity	163LTS393	303781
Bulgaria	Multilateral	11 Oct 33	Consul/Citizenship	150LTS431	303476
Bulgaria	Multilateral	11 Oct 33	Education	155LTS331	303585
Bulgaria	Multilateral	28 Oct 33	Refugees	159LTS199	303663
Bulgaria	Multilateral	23 Nov 33	Land Transport	192LTS327	304483
Bulgaria	Multilateral	23 Nov 33	Land Transport	192LTS389	304484
Bulgaria	Multilateral	20 Mar 34	Postal Service	175LTS269	304051
Bulgaria	Multilateral	20 Mar 34	Postal Service	174LTS171	304048
Bulgaria	Multilateral	20 Mar 34	Postal Service	175LTS5	304049
Bulgaria	Multilateral	20 Mar 34	Postal Service	176LTS55	304054
Bulgaria	Multilateral	20 Mar 34	Postal Service	175LTS73	304050
Bulgaria	Multilateral	25 Jul 34	Other HEW	177LTS59	304080
Bulgaria	Multilateral	20 Feb 35	Sanitation	193LTS37	304486
Bulgaria	Multilateral	20 Feb 35	Sanitation	193LTS59	304487
Bulgaria	Multilateral	20 Feb 35	Sanitation	186LTS173	304310
Bulgaria	Multilateral	26 Jun 36	Other HEW	198LTS299	304648
Bulgaria	Multilateral	20 Jul 36	Territory Boundary	173LTS213	304015
Bulgaria	Multilateral	06 Nov 36	General Military	173LTS353	304025
Bulgaria	Multilateral	31 Mar 37	Commodity Trade	189LTS359	304394
Bulgaria	Multilateral	14 Sep 37	General Military	181LTS137	304184
Bulgaria	Multilateral	17 Sep 37	Milit Installation	181LTS150	304185
Bulgaria	Multilateral	23 May 39	Postal Service	202LTS159	304742
Bulgaria	Netherlands	13 Nov 20	Customs	7LTS107	300178
Bulgaria	Netherlands	09 Mar 22	Customs	9LTS265	300260

PARTY ONE	PARTY TWO	DATE	TOPIC	CITATION	NUMBER
Bulgaria	Netherlands	23 Sep 35	Finance	166LTS51	303829
Bulgaria	Norway	02 Oct 24	General Trade	30LTS103	300763
Bulgaria	Norway	26 Nov 31	Dispute Settlement	134LTS27	303081
Bulgaria	Norway	05 Dec 32	Patents/Copyrights	136LTS281	303130
Bulgaria	Other Unilat Decla	29 Sep 24	Consul/Citizenship	29LTS117	300737
Bulgaria	Poland	29 Apr 25	General Economic	60LTS103	301408
Bulgaria	Poland	31 Dec 29	Dispute Settlement	113LTS89	302638
Bulgaria	Poland	07 Apr 31	Air Transport	127LTS45	302905
Bulgaria	Poland	22 Dec 34	Consul/Citizenship	159LTS265	303671
Bulgaria	Poland	08 Apr 35	Education	161LTS319	303720
Bulgaria	Romania	19 Apr 24	Admin Cooperation	33LTS209	300845
Bulgaria	Romania	19 Apr 24	Extradition	33LTS221	300846
Bulgaria	Romania	27 Sep 30	Mostfavored Nation	118LTS27	302710
Bulgaria	Romania	26 Jul 35	Land Transport	198LTS9	304621
Bulgaria	Romania	22 May 37	Air Transport	188LTS173	304357
Bulgaria	Romania	20 Jul 37	Water Transport	202LTS33	304733
Bulgaria	Serb/Croat/Slovene	26 Nov 23	Reparations	21LTS163	300540
Bulgaria	Serb/Croat/Slovene	26 Nov 23	Humanitarian	26LTS141	300644
Bulgaria	Serb/Croat/Slovene	26 Nov 23	Extradition	26LTS119	300643
Bulgaria	Serb/Croat/Slovene	26 Nov 23	Reparations	21LTS153	300539
Bulgaria	Serb/Croat/Slovene	26 Nov 23	Admin Cooperation	26LTS85	300642
Bulgaria	Spain	17 Jul 30	Extradition	114LTS41	302653
Bulgaria	Spain	26 Jun 31	Dispute Settlement	166LTS341	303850
Bulgaria	Spain	19 Nov 34	Finance	166LTS277	303843
Bulgaria	Sweden	14 Apr 21	Mostfavored Nation	5LTS240	300131
Bulgaria	Sweden	30 Sep 21	General Economic	7LTS137	300182
Bulgaria	Sweden	31 Dec 23	General Trade	22LTS323	300561
Bulgaria	Sweden	07 Dec 36	General Trade	173LTS393	304030
Bulgaria	Turkey	27 Dec 24	Admin Cooperation	54LTS135	301281
Bulgaria	Turkey	18 Oct 25	General Amity	54LTS125	301280
Bulgaria	Turkey	12 Feb 28	General Trade	81LTS383	301848
Bulgaria	Turkey	06 Mar 29	Dispute Settlement	114LTS399	302668
Bulgaria	Turkey	23 Dec 29	Extradition	122LTS17	302796
Bulgaria	Turkey	21 Dec 33	General Trade	148LTS9	303401
Bulgaria	UK Great Britain	05 Apr 22	Sanitation	16LTS191	300410
Bulgaria	UK Great Britain	12 Nov 25	General Trade	43LTS165	301052
Bulgaria	UK Great Britain	17 Jun 27	Dispute Settlement	67LTS239	301551
Bulgaria	UK Great Britain	24 Nov 38	General Military	195LTS117	304539
Bulgaria	USA (United States)	23 Nov 23	Consul/Citizenship	25LTS238	300611
Bulgaria	USA (United States)	19 Mar 24	Extradition	26LTS27	300638
Bulgaria	USA (United States)	21 Jan 29	Dispute Settlement	93LTS337	302122
Bulgaria	USA (United States)	21 Jan 29	Dispute Settlement	93LTS331	302121
Bulgaria	USA (United States)	18 Aug 32	Mostfavored Nation	136LTS73	303126
Bulgaria	USA (United States)	08 Jun 34	Extradition	161LTS409	303728
Bulgaria	USA (United States)	05 Jan 38	Admin Cooperation	191LTS207	304444
Bulgaria	USSR (Soviet Union)	10 Jul 35	Postal Service	168LTS275	303905
Bulgaria	Yugoslavia	26 Sep 29	Territory Boundary	101LTS217	302324
Bulgaria	Yugoslavia	14 Feb 30	Claims and Debts	101LTS135	302323
Bulgaria	Yugoslavia	09 Nov 35	Territory Boundary	194LTS89	304511
Bulgaria	Yugoslavia	24 Jan 37	General Amity	176LTS221	304063
Burma	France	26 Jan 39	Postal Service	201LTS9	304701
Burma	Multilateral	24 Sep 23	Dispute Settlement	27LTS157	300678
Burma	Multilateral	12 Jul 27	Direct Aid	135LTS247	303115
Burma	Multilateral	26 Sep 27	Dispute Settlement	92LTS301	302096
Burma	Multilateral	31 May 29	Water Transport	136LTS81	303127
Burma	Multilateral	12 Oct 29	General Transport	137LTS11	303145
Burma	Multilateral	11 Mar 33	Water Transport	135LTS301	303119
Burma	Multilateral	12 Apr 33	Sanitation	161LTS65	303706
Burma	Multilateral	20 Mar 34	Postal Service	175LTS5	304049
Burma	Multilateral	20 Mar 34	Postal Service	174LTS171	304048
Burma	Multilateral	23 Sep 36	Gen Communications	186LTS301	304319
Burma	Multilateral	03 Dec 37	Air Transport	186LTS293	304318
Burma	Multilateral	12 Sep 38	Culture	198LTS111	304630
Burma	Siam	14 Feb 39	Postal Service	197LTS255	304618
Burma	United Arab Rep	30 Sep 38	Postal Service	203LTS373	304780

PARTY ONE	PARTY TWO	DATE	TOPIC	CITATION	NUMBER
Byelorussia	Multilateral	24 May 23	Postal Service	50LTS341	301218
Cameroon	Multilateral	24 Apr 26	Land Transport	108LTS123	302505
Cameroon	Multilateral	24 Apr 26	Land Transport	97LTS83	302220
Cameroon	Multilateral	25 Sep 26	ILO Labor	60LTS253	301414
Cameroon	Multilateral	28 Jun 29	Postal Service	103LTS71	302370
Cameroon	Multilateral	28 Jun 29	Postal Service	102LTS245	302368
Cameroon	Multilateral	28 Jun 29	Postal Service	103LTS5	302369
Cameroon	Multilateral	28 Jun 29	Postal Service	103LTS249	302371
Cameroon	Multilateral	23 Oct 30	Water Transport	125LTS95	302849
Cameroon	Multilateral	11 Oct 33	Consul/Citizenship	150LTS431	303476
Canada	Bel-Lux Econ Union	03 Jul 24	General Trade	32LTS35	300803
Canada	Brazil	04 Dec 31	General Trade	139LTS241	303214
Canada	Czechoslovakia	15 Mar 28	General Trade	82LTS147	301865
Canada	Denmark	18 Jun 29	Taxation	95LTS81	302167
Canada	Finland	18 Dec 25	Postal Service	47LTS319	301137
Canada	France	19 Sep 07	Customs	1LTS95	300012
Canada	France	29 Jan 21	General Trade	8LTS105	300212
Canada	France	15 Dec 22	General Trade	21LTS38	300532
Canada	Germany	17 Jan 30	Reparations	109LTS473	302550
Canada	Germany	17 Apr 30	Taxation	101LTS245	302326
Canada	Germany	22 Oct 36	Finance	173LTS311	304021
Canada	Greece	30 Sep 29	Taxation	96LTS159	302198
Canada	Guatemala	28 Sep 37	General Trade	194LTS65	304508
Canada	Haiti	23 Apr 37	General Trade	194LTS59	304507
Canada	Irish Free State	12 Oct 23	Postal Service	56LTS291	301338
Canada	Irish Free State	12 Nov 24	Postal Service	56LTS333	301340
Canada	Italy	04 Jan 23	General Economic	25LTS375	300626
Canada	Japan	21 Sep 29	Taxation	96LTS143	302196
Canada	Multilateral	09 Sep 86*	Patents/Copyrights	123LTS233	302816
Canada	Multilateral	18 Mar 04	Humanitarian	1LTS83	300011
Canada	Multilateral	13 Nov 08	General Ad Hoc	1LTS217	300015
Canada	Multilateral	05 Jun 12	Telecommunications	1LTS135	300013
Canada	Multilateral	20 Mar 14	Patents/Copyrights	1LTS243	300016
Canada	Multilateral	10 Sep 19	Health/Educ/Welfare	8LTS11	300201
Canada	Multilateral	10 Sep 19	General Trade	7LTS331	300200
Canada	Multilateral	09 Feb 20	Territory Boundary	2LTS7	300041
Canada	Multilateral	01 May 20	Air Transport	11LTS173	300297
Canada	Multilateral	21 Jun 20	Health/Educ/Welfare	8LTS65	300207
Canada	Multilateral	30 Jun 20	Patents/Copyrights	1LTS59	300008
Canada	Multilateral	10 Aug 20	Territory Boundary	28LTS225	300710
Canada	Multilateral	10 Aug 20	Consul/Citizenship	28LTS223	300711
Canada	Multilateral	16 Dec 20	General IGO	6LTS379	300170
Canada	Multilateral	20 Apr 21	Water Transport	7LTS73	300174
Canada	Multilateral	05 Aug 21	Admin Cooperation	27LTS349	300695
Canada	Multilateral	05 Oct 21	IGO Establishment	51LTS361	301241
Canada	Multilateral	05 Oct 21	Admin Cooperation	29LTS79	300735
Canada	Multilateral	05 Oct 21	Admin Cooperation	29LTS73	300734
Canada	Multilateral	05 Oct 21	Admin Cooperation	29LTS67	300733
Canada	Multilateral	06 Oct 21	General Economic	17LTS45	300427
Canada	Multilateral	06 Feb 22	General Trade	38LTS277	300982
Canada	Multilateral	06 Feb 22	Customs	38LTS267	300981
Canada	Multilateral	31 Mar 22	Humanitarian	9LTS415	300269
Canada	Multilateral	02 Nov 22	Peace/Disarmament	149LTS35	303431
Canada	Multilateral	16 Aug 24	Taxation	41LTS429	301024
Canada	Multilateral	28 Aug 24	Postal Service	40LTS19	301002
Canada	Multilateral	30 Aug 24	Admin Cooperation	30LTS75	300760
Canada	Multilateral	30 Aug 24	Admin Cooperation	30LTS79	300761
Canada	Multilateral	01 Dec 24	Sanitation	78LTS351	301794
Canada	Multilateral	19 Feb 25	Admin Cooperation	81LTS317	301845
Canada	Multilateral	17 Jun 25	Peace/Disarmament	94LTS65	302138
Canada	Multilateral	06 Nov 25	Patents/Copyrights	74LTS289	301743
Canada	Multilateral	12 May 26	Refugees	89LTS47	302004
Canada	Multilateral	21 Jun 26	Sanitation	78LTS229	301793
Canada	Multilateral	25 Sep 26	ILO Labor	60LTS253	301414
Canada	Multilateral	25 Nov 27	Telecommunications	84LTS97	301905

PARTY ONE	PARTY TWO	DATE	TOPIC	CITATION	NUMBER
Canada	Multilateral	27 Aug 28	General Military	94LTS57	302137
Canada	Multilateral	26 Sep 28	Dispute Settlement	93LTS343	302123
Canada	Multilateral	22 Nov 28	Culture	111LTS343	302598
Canada	Multilateral	14 Dec 28	General Economic	110LTS171	302560
Canada	Multilateral	28 Feb 29	Telecommunications	97LTS301	302228
Canada	Multilateral	31 May 29	Water Transport	136LTS81	303127
Canada	Multilateral	28 Jun 29	Postal Service	102LTS245	302368
Canada	Multilateral	27 Jul 29	Other Military	118LTS343	302734
Canada	Multilateral	27 Jul 29	Other Military	118LTS303	302733
Canada	Multilateral	14 Sep 29	UN Charter	165LTS353	303822
Canada	Multilateral	20 Jan 30	Reparations	104LTS243	302394
Canada	Multilateral	20 Jan 30	Finance	104LTS413	302395
Canada	Multilateral	20 Jan 30	Finance	104LTS433	302397
Canada	Multilateral	20 Jan 30	Reparations	113LTS389	302650
Canada	Multilateral	20 Jan 30	Reparations	112LTS361	302622
Canada	Multilateral	12 Apr 30	Milit Servic/Citiz	178LTS227	304117
Canada	Multilateral	12 Apr 30	Admin Cooperation	179LTS89	304137
Canada	Multilateral	12 Apr 30	Admin Cooperation	179LTS115	304138
Canada	Multilateral	22 Apr 30	Peace/Disarmament	112LTS65	302608
Canada	Multilateral	28 Apr 30	Claims and Debts	121LTS69	302785
Canada	Multilateral	10 Jun 30	Loans and Credits	112LTS237	302618
Canada	Multilateral	13 Apr 31	Air Transport	119LTS275	302751
Canada	Multilateral	13 Jul 31	Other HEW	139LTS301	303219
Canada	Multilateral	24 Sep 31	Specific Resources	155LTS349	303586
Canada	Multilateral	10 Nov 31	Postal Service	131LTS327	303023
Canada	Multilateral	10 Nov 31	Postal Service	131LTS447	303025
Canada	Multilateral	10 Dec 31	Water Transport	129LTS177	302961
Canada	Multilateral	09 Dec 32	Telecommunications	151LTS5	303479
Canada	Multilateral	11 Mar 33	Water Transport	135LTS301	303119
Canada	Multilateral	22 Jul 33	Specific Resources	153LTS107	303511
Canada	Multilateral	25 Aug 33	Commodity Trade	141LTS71	303262
Canada	Multilateral	20 Mar 34	Postal Service	174LTS171	304048
Canada	Multilateral	16 Apr 34	Water Transport	163LTS185	303767
Canada	Multilateral	19 Jun 34	Admin Cooperation	154LTS381	303564
Canada	Multilateral	15 Mar 35	Other Military	170LTS9	303926
Canada	Multilateral	20 Dec 35	Other Military	167LTS141	303862
Canada	Multilateral	25 Mar 36	Peace/Disarmament	184LTS115	304246
Canada	Multilateral	26 Jun 36	Other HEW	198LTS299	304648
Canada	Multilateral	30 Jul 36	IGO Status/Immunit	197LTS31	304602
Canada	Multilateral	06 Nov 36	General Military	173LTS353	304025
Canada	Multilateral	08 May 37	Privil/Immunities	182LTS37	304202
Canada	Multilateral	02 Jun 37	Specific Property	184LTS445	304265
Canada	Multilateral	08 Jun 37	Specific Resources	190LTS79	304406
Canada	Multilateral	24 Jun 38	Specific Resources	196LTS131	304575
Canada	Multilateral	28 Dec 38	Other Military	196LTS221	304585
Canada	Multilateral	23 May 39	Postal Service	202LTS159	304742
Canada	Multilateral	01 Jan 42	General Military	204LTS381	304817
Canada	Netherlands	11 Jul 24	General Trade	39LTS45	300995
Canada	Netherlands	23 Sep 29	Taxation	96LTS151	302197
Canada	Norway	30 Apr 26	Postal Service	51LTS203	301227
Canada	Norway	02 May 29	Taxation	91LTS329	302073
Canada	Norway	13 Mar 33	Postal Service	141LTS211	303266
Canada	Poland	03 Jul 35	General Trade	172LTS69	303980
Canada	Spain	11 Apr 25	General Economic	43LTS333	301068
Canada	Sweden	21 Nov 29	Taxation	97LTS331	302230
Canada	USA (United States)	02 Mar 23	Specific Resources	32LTS93	300809
Canada	USA (United States)	06 Jun 24	Customs	43LTS225	301057
Canada	USA (United States)	08 Jan 25	Extradition	43LTS233	301058
Canada	USA (United States)	24 Feb 25	Territory Boundary	43LTS239	301059
Canada	USA (United States)	24 Feb 25	Territory Boundary	43LTS251	301060
Canada	USA (United States)	17 Sep 28	Taxation	95LTS209	302175
Canada	USA (United States)	12 Jan 29	Telecommunications	102LTS143	302359
Canada	USA (United States)	22 Oct 29	Air Transport	97LTS321	302229
Canada	USA (United States)	23 Oct 29	Sanitation	96LTS167	302199
Canada	USA (United States)	09 May 30	Specific Resources	121LTS45	302782

PARTY ONE	PARTY TWO	DATE	TOPIC	CITATION	NUMBER
Canada	USA (United States)	09 Dec 33	Water Transport	152LTS39	303483
Canada	USA (United States)	15 Apr 35	Dispute Settlement	162LTS73	303735
Canada	USA (United States)	15 Nov 35	General Trade	168LTS355	303910
Canada	USA (United States)	30 Dec 36	Taxation	184LTS473	304268
Canada	USA (United States)	29 Jan 37	Specific Resources	181LTS209	304190
Canada	USA (United States)	09 Oct 37	Admin Cooperation	185LTS33	304271
Canada	USA (United States)	07 Jan 38	Specific Resources	184LTS305	304255
Canada	USA (United States)	24 Jan 38	Admin Cooperation	187LTS27	304330
Canada	USA (United States)	28 Jul 38	Admin Cooperation	192LTS125	304466
Canada	USA (United States)	28 Jul 38	Admin Cooperation	192LTS115	304465
Canada	USA (United States)	28 Jul 38	Air Transport	192LTS94	304464
Canada	USA (United States)	15 Sep 38	Specific Resources	203LTS207	304763
Canada	USA (United States)	17 Nov 38	General Trade	199LTS91	304670
Canada	USA (United States)	20 Dec 38	Telecommunications	196LTS171	304580
Canada	USA (United States)	20 Feb 39	Gen Communications	197LTS181	304613
Canada	USA (United States)	22 Jun 39	Other Military	199LTS197	304673
Canada	USA (United States)	18 Aug 39	Air Transport	199LTS367	304684
Canada	USA (United States)	30 Dec 39	General Trade	203LTS211	304764
Canada	USA (United States)	29 Feb 40	Admin Cooperation	203LTS119	304754
Canada	USA (United States)	04 Mar 40	Admin Cooperation	202LTS429	304745
Canada	USA (United States)	18 Jun 40	Finance	203LTS41	304748
Canada	USA (United States)	06 Sep 40	General Amity	204LTS249	304804
Canada	USA (United States)	07 Nov 40	Specific Resources	203LTS267	304769
Canada	USA (United States)	02 Dec 40	Air Transport	203LTS219	304765
Canada	USA (United States)	20 May 41	Specific Resources	204LTS199	304800
Central Afri Rep	Multilateral	25 Sep 26	ILO Labor	60LTS253	301414
Central Afri Rep	Multilateral	11 Oct 33	Consul/Citizenship	150LTS431	303476
Ceylon (Sri Lanka)	Germany	02 May 27	Postal Service	69LTS203	301606
Ceylon (Sri Lanka)	Multilateral	30 Jun 20	Patents/Copyrights	1LTS59	300008
Ceylon (Sri Lanka)	Multilateral	31 Mar 22	Humanitarian	9LTS415	300269
Ceylon (Sri Lanka)	Multilateral	25 Aug 24	Water Transport	120LTS155	302764
Ceylon (Sri Lanka)	Multilateral	01 Dec 24	Sanitation	78LTS351	301794
Ceylon (Sri Lanka)	Multilateral	29 Oct 25	Telecommunications	57LTS201	301365
Ceylon (Sri Lanka)	Multilateral	25 Nov 27	Telecommunications	84LTS97	301905
Ceylon (Sri Lanka)	Multilateral	12 Apr 33	Sanitation	161LTS65	303706
Ceylon (Sri Lanka)	Multilateral	28 Oct 33	Refugees	159LTS199	303663
Ceylon (Sri Lanka)	Multilateral	02 Jun 34	General Trade	192LTS9	304458
Ceylon (Sri Lanka)	Multilateral	23 Sep 36	Gen Communications	186LTS301	304319
Ceylon (Sri Lanka)	Multilateral	10 Feb 38	Refugees	192LTS59	304461
Chile	Argentina	02 Jul 35	Sanitation	167LTS173	303864
Chile	Bel-Lux Econ Union	14 Dec 31	Mostfavored Nation	126LTS247	302887
Chile	Belgium	21 Feb 33	Extradition	162LTS339	303747
Chile	Brazil	08 Nov 35	Extradition	181LTS297	304197
Chile	Colombia	16 Nov 14	Dispute Settlement	114LTS111	302659
Chile	Colombia	16 Nov 14	Extradition	82LTS243	301875
Chile	Cuba	13 Mar 37	General Trade	195LTS389	304558
Chile	Czechoslovakia	18 Sep 30	General Trade	140LTS161	303233
Chile	Denmark	23 Dec 31	Dispute Settlement	145LTS77	303346
Chile	Denmark	22 Aug 34	Patents/Copyrights	154LTS181	303546
Chile	Finland	01 Mar 35	Mostfavored Nation	159LTS113	303653
Chile	France	24 Feb 27	Dispute Settlement	69LTS277	301610
Chile	France	22 May 31	Customs	124LTS31	302831
Chile	France	19 Nov 37	Admin Cooperation	185LTS261	304291
Chile	Germany	18 Apr 28	Sanitation	79LTS411	301817
Chile	Italy	10 Nov 27	Postal Service	69LTS289	301611
Chile	Multilateral	20 Aug 10	Patents/Copyrights	155LTS179	303576
Chile	Multilateral	12 Jan 12	Sanitation	4LTS281	300112
Chile	Multilateral	23 Jan 12	Sanitation	8LTS187	300222
Chile	Multilateral	05 Jun 12	Telecommunications	1LTS135	300013
Chile	Multilateral	10 Sep 19	General Trade	7LTS331	300200
Chile	Multilateral	29 Feb 20	Admin Cooperation	127LTS433	302930
Chile	Multilateral	01 May 20	Air Transport	11LTS173	300297
Chile	Multilateral	21 Jun 20	Health/Educ/Welfare	8LTS65	300207
Chile	Multilateral	16 Dec 20	General IGO	6LTS379	300170
Chile	Multilateral	20 Apr 21	Land Transport	7LTS11	300171

PARTY ONE	PARTY TWO	DATE	TOPIC	CITATION	NUMBER
Chile	Multilateral	20 Apr 21	Water Transport	7LTS35	300172
Chile	Multilateral	20 Apr 21	Water Transport	7LTS73	300174
Chile	Multilateral	20 Apr 21	Water Transport	7LTS65	300173
Chile	Multilateral	15 Sep 21	Postal Service	30LTS141	300767
Chile	Multilateral	06 Oct 21	General Economic	17LTS45	300427
Chile	Multilateral	31 Mar 22	Humanitarian	9LTS415	300269
Chile	Multilateral	28 Apr 23	Patents/Copyrights	33LTS47	300832
Chile	Multilateral	03 May 23	Customs	33LTS11	300830
Chile	Multilateral	03 May 23	General Amity	33LTS25	300831
Chile	Multilateral	03 May 23	General Trade	33LTS81	300833
Chile	Multilateral	24 Sep 23	Dispute Settlement	27LTS157	300678
Chile	Multilateral	03 Nov 23	Customs	30LTS371	300775
Chile	Multilateral	09 Dec 23	Land Transport	47LTS55	301129
Chile	Multilateral	09 Dec 23	Non-IBRD Project	36LTS76	300905
Chile	Multilateral	09 Dec 23	General Economic	58LTS315	301380
Chile	Multilateral	09 Dec 23	Water Transport	58LTS284	301379
Chile	Multilateral	25 Aug 24	Water Transport	120LTS123	302763
Chile	Multilateral	25 Aug 24	Water Transport	120LTS155	302764
Chile	Multilateral	28 Aug 24	Postal Service	40LTS307	301004
Chile	Multilateral	28 Aug 24	Postal Service	41LTS9	301006
Chile	Multilateral	28 Aug 24	Postal Service	40LTS249	301003
Chile	Multilateral	28 Aug 24	Postal Service	41LTS97	301008
Chile	Multilateral	28 Aug 24	Postal Service	40LTS437	301005
Chile	Multilateral	28 Aug 24	Postal Service	40LTS19	301002
Chile	Multilateral	28 Aug 24	Postal Service	41LTS55	301007
Chile	Multilateral	14 Nov 24	Sanitation	86LTS43	301949
Chile	Multilateral	19 Feb 25	Admin Cooperation	81LTS317	301845
Chile	Multilateral	17 Jun 25	Peace/Disarmament	94LTS65	302138
Chile	Multilateral	29 Oct 25	Telecommunications	57LTS201	301365
Chile	Multilateral	10 Apr 26	Water Transport	176LTS199	304062
Chile	Multilateral	10 Apr 26	Water Transport	120LTS187	302765
Chile	Multilateral	24 Apr 26	Land Transport	108LTS123	302505
Chile	Multilateral	24 Apr 26	Land Transport	97LTS83	302220
Chile	Multilateral	21 Jun 26	Sanitation	78LTS229	301793
Chile	Multilateral	08 Nov 27	General Trade	97LTS391	302238
Chile	Multilateral	25 Nov 27	Telecommunications	84LTS97	301905
Chile	Multilateral	18 Feb 28	Patents/Copyrights	132LTS275	303044
Chile	Multilateral	20 Feb 28	Consul/Citizenship	155LTS289	303582
Chile	Multilateral	20 Feb 28	Consul/Citizenship	155LTS259	303581
Chile	Multilateral	20 Feb 28	Admin Cooperation	134LTS45	303082
Chile	Multilateral	20 Feb 28	Air Transport	129LTS223	302963
Chile	Multilateral	20 Feb 28	Consul/Citizenship	132LTS323	303046
Chile	Multilateral	20 Feb 28	General Amity	135LTS187	303111
Chile	Multilateral	20 Feb 28	Privil/Immunities	132LTS301	303045
Chile	Multilateral	20 Feb 28	Other Ad Hoc	86LTS111	301950
Chile	Multilateral	27 Aug 28	General Military	94LTS57	302137
Chile	Multilateral	05 Jan 29	Dispute Settlement	130LTS135	302988
Chile	Multilateral	05 Jan 29	Dispute Settlement	100LTS399	302309
Chile	Multilateral	20 Feb 29	Patents/Copyrights	124LTS357	302840
Chile	Multilateral	16 Apr 29	Specific Resources	126LTS305	302891
Chile	Multilateral	31 May 29	Water Transport	136LTS81	303127
Chile	Multilateral	28 Jun 29	Postal Service	103LTS429	302374
Chile	Multilateral	28 Jun 29	Postal Service	103LTS71	302370
Chile	Multilateral	28 Jun 29	Postal Service	102LTS245	302368
Chile	Multilateral	28 Jun 29	Postal Service	103LTS249	302371
Chile	Multilateral	28 Jun 29	Postal Service	103LTS377	302373
Chile	Multilateral	28 Jun 29	Postal Service	103LTS5	302369
Chile	Multilateral	27 Jul 29	Other Military	118LTS343	302734
Chile	Multilateral	27 Jul 29	Other Military	118LTS303	302733
Chile	Multilateral	14 Sep 29	UN Charter	165LTS353	303822
Chile	Multilateral	12 Apr 30	Admin Cooperation	179LTS89	304137
Chile	Multilateral	12 Apr 30	Milit Servic/Citiz	178LTS227	304117
Chile	Multilateral	12 Apr 30	Admin Cooperation	179LTS115	304138
Chile	Multilateral	13 Jul 31	Other HEW	139LTS301	303219
Chile	Multilateral	10 Nov 31	Postal Service	131LTS327	303023

PARTY ONE	PARTY TWO	DATE	TOPIC	CITATION	NUMBER
Chile	Multilateral	10 Nov 31	Postal Service	131LTS447	303025
Chile	Multilateral	10 Nov 31	Postal Service	131LTS389	303024
Chile	Multilateral	09 Dec 32	Telecommunications	151LTS5	303479
Chile	Multilateral	11 Mar 33	Water Transport	135LTS301	303119
Chile	Multilateral	12 Apr 33	Sanitation	161LTS65	303706
Chile	Multilateral	10 Oct 33	General Amity	163LTS393	303781
Chile	Multilateral	11 Oct 33	Consul/Citizenship	150LTS431	303476
Chile	Multilateral	11 Oct 33	Education	155LTS331	303585
Chile	Multilateral	26 Dec 33	Extradition	165LTS45	303803
Chile	Multilateral	26 Dec 33	Recognition	165LTS19	303802
Chile	Multilateral	20 Mar 34	Postal Service	175LTS269	304051
Chile	Multilateral	20 Mar 34	Postal Service	175LTS73	304050
Chile	Multilateral	20 Mar 34	Postal Service	174LTS171	304048
Chile	Multilateral	20 Mar 34	Postal Service	175LTS5	304049
Chile	Multilateral	20 Mar 34	Postal Service	176LTS55	304054
Chile	Multilateral	20 Mar 34	Finance	176LTS9	304053
Chile	Multilateral	19 Jun 34	Admin Cooperation	154LTS381	303564
Chile	Multilateral	20 Feb 35	Sanitation	193LTS59	304487
Chile	Multilateral	20 Feb 35	Sanitation	193LTS37	304486
Chile	Multilateral	20 Feb 35	Sanitation	186LTS173	304310
Chile	Multilateral	15 Apr 35	Culture	167LTS289	303874
Chile	Multilateral	23 Sep 36	Gen Communications	186LTS301	304319
Chile	Multilateral	23 Dec 36	Admin Cooperation	201LTS295	304721
Chile	Multilateral	23 Dec 36	General Amity	188LTS31	304351
Chile	Multilateral	23 Dec 36	Culture	188LTS151	304356
Chile	Multilateral	23 Dec 36	Dispute Settlement	195LTS229	304548
Chile	Multilateral	23 Dec 36	Culture	188LTS125	304355
Chile	Multilateral	23 Dec 36	Dispute Settlement	188LTS75	304353
Chile	Multilateral	23 Dec 36	Land Transport	188LTS99	304354
Chile	Multilateral	23 Dec 36	Peace/Disarmament	188LTS9	304350
Chile	Multilateral	23 Dec 36	Dispute Settlement	188LTS53	304352
Chile	Multilateral	10 Feb 37	General Transport	189LTS313	304391
Chile	Multilateral	08 Jun 37	Specific Resources	190LTS79	304406
Chile	Multilateral	02 Oct 37	Education	182LTS263	304216
Chile	Multilateral	24 Jun 38	Specific Resources	196LTS131	304575
Chile	Multilateral	12 Sep 38	Culture	198LTS111	304630
Chile	Multilateral	03 Dec 38	Education	200LTS249	304694
Chile	Multilateral	23 May 39	Postal Service	202LTS159	304742
Chile	Netherlands	04 Nov 13	Consul/Citizenship	84LTS79	301904
Chile	Netherlands	17 Dec 31	Mostfavored Nation	127LTS79	302908
Chile	Netherlands	01 Jun 34	Claims and Debts	154LTS325	303559
Chile	Netherlands	30 Dec 36	General Trade	177LTS87	304082
Chile	Netherlands	05 May 37	General Trade	182LTS385	304223
Chile	Norway	27 Jul 23	Admin Cooperation	33LTS249	300848
Chile	Norway	09 Feb 27	General Trade	80LTS325	301837
Chile	Norway	27 Jan 36	Dispute Settlement	179LTS433	304169
Chile	Peru	20 Jul 22	Dispute Settlement	21LTS141	300537
Chile	Peru	03 Jun 29	Dispute Settlement	94LTS401	302157
Chile	Peru	29 Apr 30	Admin Cooperation	112LTS133	302612
Chile	Poland	19 Oct 29	Dispute Settlement	113LTS79	302637
Chile	Spain	28 May 27	Dispute Settlement	71LTS329	301673
Chile	Spain	18 Feb 36	Mass Media	169LTS321	303920
Chile	Sweden	26 Mar 20	Dispute Settlement	4LTS271	300111
Chile	Sweden	08 Mar 33	Claims and Debts	142LTS147	303286
Chile	Sweden	21 Oct 36	Patents/Copyrights	174LTS109	304041
Chile	Sweden	30 Oct 36	General Trade	188LTS283	304364
Chile	Turkey	30 Jan 26	General Amity	59LTS249	301395
Chile	UK Great Britain	12 Apr 22	Admin Cooperation	11LTS17	300287
Chile	UK Great Britain	15 Oct 31	Mostfavored Nation	128LTS439	302947
Chile	UK Great Britain	26 Nov 37	General Trade	186LTS285	304317
Chile	UK Great Britain	09 Jan 39	General Trade	196LTS277	304589
Chile	UK Great Britain	17 Jun 42	General Trade	204LTS371	304815
Chile	UK Great Britain	28 Jun 43	General Trade	205LTS109	304827
Chile	United Arab Rep	05 Mar 30	Mostfavored Nation	124LTS25	302830
Chile	USA (United States)	27 May 30	Other Economic	133LTS141	303064

PARTY ONE	PARTY TWO	DATE	TOPIC	CITATION	NUMBER
Chile	USA (United States)	28 Sep 31	General Trade	144LTS147	303325
Chile	USA (United States)	17 Aug 34	Gen Communications	157LTS15	303602
Chile	USA (United States)	27 Oct 37	Admin Cooperation	186LTS219	304314
Chile	USA (United States)	01 Feb 38	General Trade	190LTS9	304401
Chile	USA (United States)	24 Feb 39	General Trade	197LTS217	304614
Chile	USA (United States)	23 Apr 40	Military Mission	203LTS29	304747
China	Austria	19 Oct 25	General Economic	55LTS9	301301
China	Bel-Lux Econ Union	22 Nov 28	General Amity	87LTS287	301975
China	Belgium	31 Aug 29	Privil/Immunities	123LTS105	302810
China	Belgium	18 Dec 37	Air Transport	190LTS109	304409
China	Czechoslovakia	12 Feb 30	General Economic	110LTS285	302561
China	Denmark	12 Dec 28	General Amity	91LTS207	302062
China	Estonia	21 Dec 37	General Amity	194LTS123	304516
China	Finland	29 Oct 26	General Amity	67LTS345	301556
China	France	23 Dec 28	Customs	92LTS267	302095
China	France	16 May 30	General Amity	162LTS99	303738
China	Germany	20 May 21	Peace/Disarmament	9LTS271	300261
China	Germany	31 Dec 24	Customs	42LTS7	301027
China	Germany	17 Aug 28	General Trade	91LTS93	302057
China	Germany	20 Dec 28	Customs	90LTS337	302047
China	Greece	30 Sep 29	General Amity	123LTS127	302811
China	India	13 Jun 34	Postal Service	157LTS77	303606
China	Italy	27 Nov 28	General Amity	93LTS173	302109
China	Japan	04 Feb 22	Dispute Settlement	10LTS309	300277
China	Japan	28 Mar 22	Reparations	13LTS213	300353
China	Japan	01 Dec 22	Territory Boundary	22LTS179	300559
China	Japan	05 Dec 22	Land Transport	22LTS293	300560
China	Japan	08 Dec 22	Postal Service	20LTS289	300522
China	Japan	08 Dec 22	Postal Service	20LTS233	300520
China	Japan	08 Dec 22	Postal Service	20LTS205	300519
China	Japan	08 Dec 22	Postal Service	20LTS253	300521
China	Japan	06 May 30	Customs	106LTS295	302452
China	Latvia	25 Jun 36	General Amity	176LTS275	304066
China	Malaya	30 Mar 35	Postal Service	163LTS159	303765
China	Malaya	12 Feb 36	Postal Service	170LTS19	303927
China	Mexico	26 Sep 21	General Amity	13LTS201	300352
China	Multilateral	18 Mar 04	Humanitarian	1LTS83	300011
China	Multilateral	23 Jan 12	Sanitation	8LTS187	300222
China	Multilateral	05 Jun 12	Telecommunications	1LTS135	300013
China	Multilateral	10 Sep 19	General Trade	7LTS331	300200
China	Multilateral	10 Sep 19	Reparations	2LTS21	300042
China	Multilateral	10 Sep 19	Reparations	2LTS44	300045
China	Multilateral	10 Sep 19	Reparations	2LTS29	300043
China	Multilateral	01 May 20	Air Transport	11LTS173	300297
China	Multilateral	21 Jun 20	Health/Educ/Welfare	8LTS65	300207
China	Multilateral	30 Jun 20	Patents/Copyrights	1LTS59	300008
China	Multilateral	16 Dec 20	General IGO	6LTS379	300170
China	Multilateral	20 Apr 21	Land Transport	7LTS11	300171
China	Multilateral	20 Apr 21	Water Transport	7LTS35	300172
China	Multilateral	20 Apr 21	Water Transport	7LTS73	300174
China	Multilateral	05 Aug 21	Admin Cooperation	27LTS349	300695
China	Multilateral	05 Oct 21	IGO Establishment	51LTS361	301241
China	Multilateral	05 Oct 21	Admin Cooperation	29LTS67	300733
China	Multilateral	05 Oct 21	Admin Cooperation	29LTS79	300735
China	Multilateral	05 Oct 21	Admin Cooperation	29LTS73	300734
China	Multilateral	06 Feb 22	Customs	38LTS267	300981
China	Multilateral	06 Feb 22	General Trade	38LTS277	300982
China	Multilateral	31 Mar 22	Humanitarian	9LTS415	300269
China	Multilateral	05 Jul 22	Reparations	13LTS237	300355
China	Multilateral	02 Nov 22	Peace/Disarmament	149LTS35	303431
China	Multilateral	03 Nov 23	Customs	30LTS371	300775
China	Multilateral	31 Mar 24	Sanitation	27LTS211	300685
China	Multilateral	28 Aug 24	Postal Service	40LTS249	301003
China	Multilateral	28 Aug 24	Postal Service	40LTS307	301004
China	Multilateral	28 Aug 24	Postal Service	40LTS19	301002

PARTY ONE	PARTY TWO	DATE	TOPIC	CITATION	NUMBER
China	Multilateral	28 Aug 24	Postal Service	40LTS437	301005
China	Multilateral	11 Feb 25	Sanitation	51LTS337	301239
China	Multilateral	17 Jun 25	Peace/Disarmament	94LTS65	302138
China	Multilateral	29 Oct 25	Telecommunications	57LTS201	301365
China	Multilateral	21 Jun 26	Sanitation	78LTS229	301793
China	Multilateral	25 Sep 26	ILO Labor	60LTS253	301414
China	Multilateral	25 Nov 27	Telecommunications	84LTS97	301905
China	Multilateral	27 Aug 28	General Military	94LTS57	302137
China	Multilateral	20 Apr 29	Admin Cooperation	112LTS371	302623
China	Multilateral	31 May 29	Water Transport	136LTS81	303127
China	Multilateral	28 Jun 29	Postal Service	103LTS249	302371
China	Multilateral	28 Jun 29	Postal Service	103LTS71	302370
China	Multilateral	28 Jun 29	Postal Service	103LTS5	302369
China	Multilateral	28 Jun 29	Postal Service	102LTS245	302368
China	Multilateral	27 Jul 29	Other Military	118LTS343	302734
China	Multilateral	27 Jul 29	Other Military	118LTS303	302733
China	Multilateral	14 Sep 29	UN Charter	165LTS353	303822
China	Multilateral	12 Oct 29	General Transport	137LTS11	303145
China	Multilateral	17 Feb 30	Dispute Settlement	102LTS87	302354
China	Multilateral	12 Apr 30	Admin Cooperation	179LTS89	304137
China	Multilateral	12 Apr 30	Admin Cooperation	179LTS115	304138
China	Multilateral	23 Oct 30	Water Transport	125LTS95	302849
China	Multilateral	23 Oct 30	Water Transport	112LTS21	302603
China	Multilateral	13 Jul 31	Other HEW	139LTS301	303219
China	Multilateral	09 Dec 32	Telecommunications	151LTS5	303479
China	Multilateral	22 Jul 33	Specific Resources	153LTS107	303511
China	Multilateral	11 Oct 33	Consul/Citizenship	150LTS431	303476
China	Multilateral	20 Mar 34	Postal Service	174LTS171	304048
China	Multilateral	20 Mar 34	Postal Service	175LTS5	304049
China	Multilateral	20 Mar 34	Postal Service	175LTS269	304051
China	Multilateral	20 Mar 34	Postal Service	175LTS73	304050
China	Multilateral	09 Apr 35	Territory Boundary	163LTS177	303766
China	Multilateral	26 Jun 36	Other HEW	198LTS299	304648
China	Multilateral	31 Mar 37	Commodity Trade	189LTS359	304394
China	Multilateral	03 Dec 38	Education	200LTS249	304694
China	Multilateral	23 May 39	Postal Service	202LTS159	304742
China	Multilateral	01 Jan 42	General Military	204LTS381	304817
China	Netherlands	19 Dec 28	Customs	111LTS161	302585
China	Norway	12 Nov 28	Customs	87LTS381	301983
China	Norway	23 Apr 31	Privil/Immunities	119LTS9	302736
China	Persia	01 Jun 20	General Amity	9LTS17	300240
China	Poland	18 Sep 29	General Economic	120LTS331	302774
China	Portugal	19 Dec 28	General Economic	107LTS93	302471
China	Strait Settlements	16 Jan 25	Postal Service	36LTS395	300937
China	Sweden	20 Dec 28	Customs	107LTS81	302470
China	Switzerland	12 Apr 27	Sanitation	66LTS427	301536
China	Turkey	04 Apr 34	Consul/Citizenship	153LTS161	303515
China	UK Great Britain	26 Apr 20	Postal Service	5LTS83	300120
China	UK Great Britain	07 Jan 24	Postal Service	24LTS115	300599
China	UK Great Britain	23 May 24	Postal Service	28LTS481	300724
China	UK Great Britain	26 Nov 24	Admin Cooperation	32LTS281	300818
China	UK Great Britain	31 Oct 29	Admin Cooperation	99LTS441	302289
China	UK Great Britain	09 Nov 29	Claims and Debts	99LTS453	302290
China	UK Great Britain	18 Apr 30	Recognition	112LTS49	302607
China	UK Great Britain	17 Sep 30	Admin Cooperation	111LTS153	302584
China	UK Great Britain	22 Sep 30	Reparations	115LTS493	302697
China	UK Great Britain	28 Apr 32	Postal Service	137LTS319	303165
China	UK Great Britain	27 Oct 34	Taxation	160LTS265	303695
China	UK Great Britain	17 Jul 36	Postal Service	173LTS343	304024
China	UK Great Britain	24 Jan 39	Air Transport	199LTS53	304664
China	UK Great Britain	11 Jan 43	Privil/Immunities	205LTS67	304826
China	USA (United States)	25 Jul 28	Customs	107LTS121	302472
China	USA (United States)	27 Jun 30	Dispute Settlement	140LTS184	303236
China	USSR (Soviet Union)	31 May 24	General Amity	37LTS175	300955
China	USSR (Soviet Union)	31 May 24	Land Transport	37LTS193	300956

PARTY ONE	PARTY TWO	DATE	TOPIC	CITATION	NUMBER
China	USSR (Soviet Union)	21 Aug 37	General Amity	181LTS101	304180
Chosen	Multilateral	28 Aug 24	Postal Service	40LTS437	301005
Chosen	Multilateral	28 Aug 24	Postal Service	40LTS307	301004
Chosen	Multilateral	28 Jun 29	Postal Service	103LTS249	302371
Chosen	Multilateral	28 Jun 29	Postal Service	103LTS71	302370
Chosen	Multilateral	28 Jun 29	Postal Service	102LTS245	302368
Chosen	Multilateral	28 Jun 29	Postal Service	103LTS321	302372
Chosen	Multilateral	28 Jun 29	Postal Service	103LTS5	302369
Chosen	Multilateral	20 Mar 34	Postal Service	175LTS5	304049
Chosen	Multilateral	20 Mar 34	Postal Service	175LTS269	304051
Chosen	Multilateral	20 Mar 34	Postal Service	174LTS171	304048
Chosen	Multilateral	20 Mar 34	Postal Service	175LTS73	304050
Chosen	Multilateral	23 May 39	Postal Service	202LTS159	304742
Colombia	Belgium	21 Nov 31	Extradition	182LTS165	304209
Colombia	Brazil	15 Nov 28	Water Transport	100LTS123	302299
Colombia	Chile	16 Nov 14	Dispute Settlement	114LTS111	302659
Colombia	Chile	16 Nov 14	Extradition	82LTS243	301875
Colombia	Costa Rica	13 Oct 26	Education	95LTS325	302182
Colombia	Cuba	02 Jul 32	Extradition	174LTS69	304038
Colombia	Denmark	21 Jun 29	General Economic	125LTS113	302850
Colombia	Multilateral	20 Aug 10	Patents/Copyrights	155LTS179	303576
Colombia	Multilateral	12 Jan 12	Sanitation	4LTS281	300112
Colombia	Multilateral	23 Jan 12	Sanitation	8LTS187	300222
Colombia	Multilateral	05 Jun 12	Telecommunications	1LTS135	300013
Colombia	Multilateral	21 Jun 20	Health/Educ/Welfare	8LTS65	300207
Colombia	Multilateral	16 Dec 20	General IGO	6LTS379	300170
Colombia	Multilateral	05 Aug 21	Admin Cooperation	27LTS349	300695
Colombia	Multilateral	15 Sep 21	Postal Service	30LTS141	300767
Colombia	Multilateral	05 Oct 21	IGO Establishment	51LTS361	301241
Colombia	Multilateral	05 Oct 21	Admin Cooperation	29LTS79	300735
Colombia	Multilateral	05 Oct 21	Admin Cooperation	29LTS73	300734
Colombia	Multilateral	05 Oct 21	Admin Cooperation	29LTS67	300733
Colombia	Multilateral	31 Mar 22	Humanitarian	9LTS415	300269
Colombia	Multilateral	28 Apr 23	Patents/Copyrights	33LTS47	300832
Colombia	Multilateral	03 May 23	General Amity	33LTS25	300831
Colombia	Multilateral	03 May 23	Customs	33LTS11	300830
Colombia	Multilateral	03 May 23	General Trade	33LTS81	300833
Colombia	Multilateral	31 Mar 24	Sanitation	27LTS211	300685
Colombia	Multilateral	28 Aug 24	Postal Service	40LTS249	301003
Colombia	Multilateral	28 Aug 24	Postal Service	41LTS97	301008
Colombia	Multilateral	28 Aug 24	Postal Service	40LTS19	301002
Colombia	Multilateral	28 Aug 24	Postal Service	40LTS437	301005
Colombia	Multilateral	28 Aug 24	Postal Service	40LTS307	301004
Colombia	Multilateral	14 Nov 24	Sanitation	86LTS43	301949
Colombia	Multilateral	19 Feb 25	Admin Cooperation	81LTS317	301845
Colombia	Multilateral	17 Jun 25	Peace/Disarmament	94LTS65	302138
Colombia	Multilateral	29 Oct 25	Telecommunications	57LTS201	301365
Colombia	Multilateral	21 Jun 26	Sanitation	78LTS229	301793
Colombia	Multilateral	25 Sep 26	ILO Labor	60LTS253	301414
Colombia	Multilateral	12 Jul 27	Direct Aid	135LTS247	303115
Colombia	Multilateral	29 Oct 27	Scientific Project	127LTS27	302903
Colombia	Multilateral	25 Nov 27	Telecommunications	84LTS97	301905
Colombia	Multilateral	18 Feb 28	Patents/Copyrights	132LTS275	303044
Colombia	Multilateral	20 Feb 28	Consul/Citizenship	155LTS289	303582
Colombia	Multilateral	20 Feb 28	Consul/Citizenship	155LTS259	303581
Colombia	Multilateral	20 Feb 28	Privil/Immunities	132LTS301	303045
Colombia	Multilateral	20 Feb 28	Other Ad Hoc	86LTS111	301950
Colombia	Multilateral	20 Feb 28	Consul/Citizenship	132LTS323	303046
Colombia	Multilateral	20 Feb 28	Air Transport	129LTS223	302963
Colombia	Multilateral	20 Feb 28	Admin Cooperation	134LTS45	303082
Colombia	Multilateral	20 Feb 28	General Amity	135LTS187	303111
Colombia	Multilateral	27 Aug 28	General Military	94LTS57	302137
Colombia	Multilateral	22 Nov 28	Culture	111LTS343	302598
Colombia	Multilateral	05 Jan 29	Dispute Settlement	130LTS135	302988
Colombia	Multilateral	05 Jan 29	Dispute Settlement	100LTS399	302309

PARTY ONE	PARTY TWO	DATE	TOPIC	CITATION	NUMBER
Colombia	Multilateral	20 Feb 29	Patents/Copyrights	124LTS357	302840
Colombia	Multilateral	20 Apr 29	Admin Cooperation	112LTS395	302624
Colombia	Multilateral	20 Apr 29	Admin Cooperation	112LTS371	302623
Colombia	Multilateral	28 Jun 29	Postal Service	103LTS249	302371
Colombia	Multilateral	28 Jun 29	Postal Service	103LTS5	302369
Colombia	Multilateral	28 Jun 29	Postal Service	102LTS245	302368
Colombia	Multilateral	28 Jun 29	Postal Service	103LTS71	302370
Colombia	Multilateral	28 Jun 29	Postal Service	103LTS429	302374
Colombia	Multilateral	27 Jul 29	Other Military	118LTS303	302733
Colombia	Multilateral	27 Jul 29	Other Military	118LTS343	302734
Colombia	Multilateral	14 Sep 29	UN Charter	165LTS353	303822
Colombia	Multilateral	12 Apr 30	Admin Cooperation	179LTS115	304138
Colombia	Multilateral	12 Apr 30	Milit Servic/Citiz	178LTS227	304117
Colombia	Multilateral	12 Apr 30	Admin Cooperation	179LTS89	304137
Colombia	Multilateral	07 Jun 30	Finance	143LTS317	303314
Colombia	Multilateral	07 Jun 30	Finance	143LTS257	303313
Colombia	Multilateral	07 Jun 30	Finance	143LTS337	303315
Colombia	Multilateral	13 Jul 31	Other HEW	139LTS301	303219
Colombia	Multilateral	24 Sep 31	Specific Resources	155LTS349	303586
Colombia	Multilateral	10 Nov 31	Postal Service	131LTS389	303024
Colombia	Multilateral	10 Nov 31	Postal Service	131LTS327	303023
Colombia	Multilateral	10 Nov 31	Postal Service	131LTS447	303025
Colombia	Multilateral	09 Dec 32	Telecommunications	151LTS5	303479
Colombia	Multilateral	10 Oct 33	General Amity	163LTS393	303781
Colombia	Multilateral	26 Dec 33	Recognition	165LTS19	303802
Colombia	Multilateral	26 Dec 33	Extradition	165LTS45	303803
Colombia	Multilateral	20 Mar 34	Postal Service	175LTS73	304050
Colombia	Multilateral	20 Mar 34	Postal Service	176LTS55	304054
Colombia	Multilateral	20 Mar 34	Postal Service	174LTS171	304048
Colombia	Multilateral	20 Mar 34	Postal Service	175LTS269	304051
Colombia	Multilateral	20 Mar 34	Postal Service	175LTS5	304049
Colombia	Multilateral	15 Jul 34	Mostfavored Nation	165LTS9	303801
Colombia	Multilateral	15 Apr 35	Culture	167LTS289	303874
Colombia	Multilateral	26 Jun 36	Other HEW	198LTS299	304648
Colombia	Multilateral	23 Sep 36	Gen Communications	186LTS301	304319
Colombia	Multilateral	23 Dec 36	Dispute Settlement	195LTS229	304548
Colombia	Multilateral	23 Dec 36	Admin Cooperation	201LTS295	304721
Colombia	Multilateral	23 Dec 36	Dispute Settlement	188LTS53	304352
Colombia	Multilateral	23 Dec 36	Culture	188LTS151	304356
Colombia	Multilateral	23 Dec 36	Dispute Settlement	188LTS75	304353
Colombia	Multilateral	23 Dec 36	General Amity	188LTS31	304351
Colombia	Multilateral	23 Dec 36	Culture	188LTS125	304355
Colombia	Multilateral	23 Dec 36	Peace/Disarmament	188LTS9	304350
Colombia	Multilateral	23 Dec 36	Land Transport	188LTS99	304354
Colombia	Multilateral	02 Oct 37	Education	182LTS263	304216
Colombia	Multilateral	03 Dec 38	Education	200LTS249	304694
Colombia	Multilateral	23 May 39	Postal Service	202LTS159	304742
Colombia	Nicaragua	25 Mar 29	Extradition	132LTS255	303042
Colombia	Nicaragua	05 May 30	Territory Boundary	105LTS337	302426
Colombia	Panama	20 Aug 24	Territory Boundary	33LTS167	300841
Colombia	Panama	24 Dec 27	Extradition	87LTS409	301985
Colombia	Panama	17 Jun 38	Territory Boundary	193LTS231	304500
Colombia	Peru	24 Mar 22	Territory Boundary	74LTS9	301726
Colombia	Peru	25 May 33	Admin Cooperation	138LTS251	303192
Colombia	Peru	24 May 34	General Amity	164LTS21	303786
Colombia	Spain	19 Jul 29	Dispute Settlement	114LTS105	302658
Colombia	Spain	30 Sep 35	Education	163LTS337	303776
Colombia	Sweden	13 Sep 27	Dispute Settlement	132LTS123	303032
Colombia	Sweden	09 Mar 28	General Trade	85LTS443	301944
Colombia	Switzerland	20 Aug 27	Dispute Settlement	111LTS229	302589
Colombia	UK Great Britain	27 Sep 21	Admin Cooperation	10LTS417	300281
Colombia	UK Great Britain	08 Mar 23	Sanitation	17LTS167	300434
Colombia	UK Great Britain	02 Dec 29	Extradition	110LTS401	302571
Colombia	UK Great Britain	30 Dec 38	General Economic	196LTS231	304586
Colombia	USA (United States)	06 Apr 14	Dispute Settlement	9LTS302	300263
Colombia	USA (United States)	13 Sep 35	General Trade	170LTS293	303944
Colombia	USA (United States)	11 Jan 36	Postal Service	169LTS79	303914
Colombia	USA (United States)	23 Nov 38	Military Mission	196LTS157	304579
Colombia	USA (United States)	23 Nov 38	Military Mission	196LTS147	304578
Colombia	USA (United States)	07 Feb 39	Postal Service	196LTS53	304569
Colombia	Vatican/Holy See	05 May 28	Consul/Citizenship	79LTS157	301808
Colombia	Venezuela	20 Jul 25	General Transport	39LTS15	300993
Congo (Brazzaville)	Multilateral	25 Sep 26	ILO Labor	60LTS253	301414
Congo (Brazzaville)	Multilateral	11 Oct 33	Consul/Citizenship	150LTS431	303476
Costa Rica	Belgium	03 Feb 33	Extradition	166LTS325	303848
Costa Rica	Colombia	13 Oct 26	Education	95LTS325	302182
Costa Rica	Multilateral	20 Aug 10	Patents/Copyrights	155LTS179	303576
Costa Rica	Multilateral	12 Jan 12	Sanitation	4LTS281	300112
Costa Rica	Multilateral	23 Jan 12	Sanitation	8LTS187	300222
Costa Rica	Multilateral	21 Jun 20	Health/Educ/Welfare	8LTS65	300207
Costa Rica	Multilateral	16 Dec 20	General IGO	6LTS379	300170
Costa Rica	Multilateral	19 Jan 21	Recognition	5LTS9	300113
Costa Rica	Multilateral	05 Aug 21	Admin Cooperation	27LTS349	300695
Costa Rica	Multilateral	15 Sep 21	Postal Service	30LTS141	300767
Costa Rica	Multilateral	05 Oct 21	IGO Establishment	51LTS361	301241
Costa Rica	Multilateral	05 Oct 21	Admin Cooperation	29LTS67	300733
Costa Rica	Multilateral	05 Oct 21	Admin Cooperation	29LTS79	300735
Costa Rica	Multilateral	31 Mar 22	Humanitarian	9LTS415	300269
Costa Rica	Multilateral	28 Apr 23	Patents/Copyrights	33LTS47	300832
Costa Rica	Multilateral	03 May 23	General Amity	33LTS25	300831
Costa Rica	Multilateral	03 May 23	Customs	33LTS11	300830
Costa Rica	Multilateral	03 May 23	General Trade	33LTS81	300833
Costa Rica	Multilateral	31 Mar 24	Sanitation	27LTS211	300685
Costa Rica	Multilateral	28 Aug 24	Postal Service	40LTS307	301004
Costa Rica	Multilateral	28 Aug 24	Postal Service	40LTS19	301002
Costa Rica	Multilateral	14 Nov 24	Sanitation	86LTS43	301949
Costa Rica	Multilateral	25 Nov 27	Telecommunications	84LTS97	301905
Costa Rica	Multilateral	18 Feb 28	Patents/Copyrights	132LTS275	303044
Costa Rica	Multilateral	20 Feb 28	Consul/Citizenship	155LTS289	303582
Costa Rica	Multilateral	20 Feb 28	Admin Cooperation	134LTS45	303082
Costa Rica	Multilateral	20 Feb 28	Consul/Citizenship	132LTS323	303046
Costa Rica	Multilateral	20 Feb 28	Consul/Citizenship	155LTS259	303581
Costa Rica	Multilateral	20 Feb 28	General Amity	135LTS187	303111
Costa Rica	Multilateral	20 Feb 28	Other Ad Hoc	86LTS111	301950
Costa Rica	Multilateral	20 Feb 28	Privil/Immunities	132LTS301	303045
Costa Rica	Multilateral	20 Feb 28	Air Transport	129LTS223	302963
Costa Rica	Multilateral	27 Aug 28	General Military	94LTS57	302137
Costa Rica	Multilateral	05 Jan 29	Dispute Settlement	130LTS135	302988
Costa Rica	Multilateral	05 Jan 29	Dispute Settlement	100LTS399	302309
Costa Rica	Multilateral	20 Feb 29	Patents/Copyrights	124LTS357	302840
Costa Rica	Multilateral	28 Jun 29	Postal Service	103LTS71	302370
Costa Rica	Multilateral	28 Jun 29	Postal Service	102LTS245	302368
Costa Rica	Multilateral	13 Jul 31	Other HEW	139LTS301	303219
Costa Rica	Multilateral	10 Nov 31	Postal Service	131LTS389	303024
Costa Rica	Multilateral	10 Nov 31	Postal Service	131LTS327	303023
Costa Rica	Multilateral	10 Nov 31	Postal Service	131LTS447	303025
Costa Rica	Multilateral	09 Dec 32	Telecommunications	151LTS5	303479
Costa Rica	Multilateral	10 Oct 33	General Amity	163LTS393	303781
Costa Rica	Multilateral	20 Mar 34	Postal Service	174LTS171	304048
Costa Rica	Multilateral	20 Mar 34	Postal Service	175LTS73	304050
Costa Rica	Multilateral	15 Apr 35	Culture	167LTS289	303874
Costa Rica	Multilateral	06 Nov 36	General Military	173LTS353	304025
Costa Rica	Multilateral	23 Dec 36	Admin Cooperation	201LTS295	304721
Costa Rica	Multilateral	23 Dec 36	Dispute Settlement	188LTS53	304352
Costa Rica	Multilateral	23 Dec 36	Land Transport	188LTS99	304354
Costa Rica	Multilateral	23 Dec 36	Dispute Settlement	195LTS229	304548
Costa Rica	Multilateral	23 Dec 36	Culture	188LTS125	304355
Costa Rica	Multilateral	23 Dec 36	General Amity	188LTS31	304351
Costa Rica	Multilateral	23 Dec 36	Peace/Disarmament	188LTS9	304350
Costa Rica	Multilateral	23 Dec 36	Culture	188LTS151	304356

PARTY ONE	PARTY TWO	DATE	TOPIC	CITATION	NUMBER
Costa Rica	Multilateral	23 Dec 36	Dispute Settlement	188LTS75	304353
Costa Rica	Multilateral	31 Mar 37	Commodity Trade	189LTS359	304394
Costa Rica	Multilateral	08 Dec 38	Gen Communications	202LTS49	304734
Costa Rica	Multilateral	23 May 39	Postal Service	202LTS159	304742
Costa Rica	Multilateral	01 Jan 42	General Military	204LTS381	304817
Costa Rica	Spain	21 Mar 30	Milit Servic/Citiz	168LTS61	303886
Costa Rica	UK Great Britain	12 Jan 22	Claims and Debts	17LTS151	300432
Costa Rica	UK Great Britain	25 Apr 23	General Trade	20LTS19	300502
Costa Rica	UK Great Britain	29 Sep 24	Postal Service	31LTS121	300789
Costa Rica	UK Great Britain	27 Dec 28	General Economic	108LTS375	302520
Costa Rica	USA (United States)	28 Nov 36	General Trade	181LTS183	304189
Costa Rica	USA (United States)	14 Jul 41	Military Mission	204LTS231	304802
Cuba	Belgium	23 Feb 33	Admin Cooperation	185LTS279	304294
Cuba	Chile	13 Mar 37	General Trade	195LTS389	304558
Cuba	Colombia	02 Jul 32	Extradition	174LTS69	304038
Cuba	France	06 Nov 29	General Economic	114LTS345	302665
Cuba	Germany	14 Jun 28	Postal Service	124LTS47	302832
Cuba	Japan	21 Dec 29	Mostfavored Nation	111LTS13	302575
Cuba	Mexico	29 Jun 28	Telecommunications	124LTS189	302833
Cuba	Multilateral	20 Aug 10	Patents/Copyrights	155LTS179	303576
Cuba	Multilateral	12 Jan 12	Sanitation	4LTS281	300112
Cuba	Multilateral	05 Jun 12	Telecommunications	1LTS135	300013
Cuba	Multilateral	10 Sep 19	General Trade	7LTS331	300200
Cuba	Multilateral	10 Sep 19	Reparations	2LTS44	300045
Cuba	Multilateral	10 Sep 19	General Economic	2LTS35	300044
Cuba	Multilateral	10 Sep 19	Reparations	2LTS29	300043
Cuba	Multilateral	10 Sep 19	Reparations	2LTS21	300042
Cuba	Multilateral	01 May 20	Air Transport	11LTS173	300297
Cuba	Multilateral	21 Jun 20	Health/Educ/Welfare	8LTS65	300207
Cuba	Multilateral	30 Jun 20	Patents/Copyrights	1LTS59	300008
Cuba	Multilateral	31 Oct 20	Sanitation	164LTS85	303790
Cuba	Multilateral	16 Dec 20	General IGO	6LTS379	300170
Cuba	Multilateral	15 Sep 21	Postal Service	30LTS141	300767
Cuba	Multilateral	05 Oct 21	Admin Cooperation	29LTS67	300733
Cuba	Multilateral	05 Oct 21	Admin Cooperation	29LTS73	300734
Cuba	Multilateral	05 Oct 21	IGO Establishment	51LTS361	301241
Cuba	Multilateral	05 Oct 21	Admin Cooperation	29LTS79	300735
Cuba	Multilateral	31 Mar 22	Humanitarian	9LTS415	300269
Cuba	Multilateral	02 Nov 22	Peace/Disarmament	149LTS35	303431
Cuba	Multilateral	28 Apr 23	Patents/Copyrights	33LTS47	300832
Cuba	Multilateral	03 May 23	Customs	33LTS11	300830
Cuba	Multilateral	03 May 23	General Amity	33LTS25	300831
Cuba	Multilateral	03 May 23	General Trade	33LTS81	300833
Cuba	Multilateral	31 Mar 24	Sanitation	27LTS211	300685
Cuba	Multilateral	25 Aug 24	Water Transport	120LTS123	302763
Cuba	Multilateral	28 Aug 24	Postal Service	40LTS307	301004
Cuba	Multilateral	28 Aug 24	Postal Service	40LTS249	301003
Cuba	Multilateral	28 Aug 24	Postal Service	41LTS55	301007
Cuba	Multilateral	28 Aug 24	Postal Service	41LTS9	301006
Cuba	Multilateral	28 Aug 24	Postal Service	40LTS19	301002
Cuba	Multilateral	28 Aug 24	Postal Service	40LTS437	301005
Cuba	Multilateral	28 Aug 24	Postal Service	41LTS97	301008
Cuba	Multilateral	14 Nov 24	Sanitation	86LTS43	301949
Cuba	Multilateral	01 Dec 24	Sanitation	78LTS351	301794
Cuba	Multilateral	19 Feb 25	Admin Cooperation	81LTS317	301845
Cuba	Multilateral	06 Nov 25	Other Economic	74LTS319	301744
Cuba	Multilateral	06 Nov 25	Patents/Copyrights	74LTS289	301743
Cuba	Multilateral	06 Nov 25	Patents/Copyrights	74LTS327	301745
Cuba	Multilateral	24 Apr 26	Land Transport	108LTS123	302505
Cuba	Multilateral	24 Apr 26	Land Transport	97LTS83	302220
Cuba	Multilateral	12 May 26	Refugees	89LTS47	302004
Cuba	Multilateral	21 Jun 26	Sanitation	78LTS229	301793
Cuba	Multilateral	25 Sep 26	ILO Labor	60LTS253	301414
Cuba	Multilateral	12 Jul 27	Direct Aid	135LTS247	303115
Cuba	Multilateral	25 Nov 27	Telecommunications	84LTS97	301905

PARTY ONE	PARTY TWO	DATE	TOPIC	CITATION	NUMBER
Cuba	Multilateral	18 Feb 28	Patents/Copyrights	132LTS275	303044
Cuba	Multilateral	20 Feb 28	Consul/Citizenship	155LTS289	303582
Cuba	Multilateral	20 Feb 28	Consul/Citizenship	155LTS259	303581
Cuba	Multilateral	20 Feb 28	General Amity	135LTS187	303111
Cuba	Multilateral	20 Feb 28	Consul/Citizenship	132LTS323	303046
Cuba	Multilateral	20 Feb 28	Privil/Immunities	132LTS301	303045
Cuba	Multilateral	20 Feb 28	Admin Cooperation	134LTS45	303082
Cuba	Multilateral	20 Feb 28	Air Transport	129LTS223	302963
Cuba	Multilateral	20 Feb 28	Other Ad Hoc	86LTS111	301950
Cuba	Multilateral	27 Aug 28	General Military	94LTS57	302137
Cuba	Multilateral	22 Nov 28	Culture	111LTS343	302598
Cuba	Multilateral	14 Dec 28	General Economic	110LTS171	302560
Cuba	Multilateral	05 Jan 29	Dispute Settlement	130LTS135	302988
Cuba	Multilateral	05 Jan 29	Dispute Settlement	100LTS399	302309
Cuba	Multilateral	20 Feb 29	Patents/Copyrights	124LTS357	302840
Cuba	Multilateral	28 Feb 29	Telecommunications	97LTS301	302228
Cuba	Multilateral	20 Apr 29	Admin Cooperation	112LTS371	302623
Cuba	Multilateral	20 Apr 29	Admin Cooperation	112LTS395	302624
Cuba	Multilateral	28 Jun 29	Postal Service	103LTS71	302370
Cuba	Multilateral	28 Jun 29	Postal Service	103LTS377	302373
Cuba	Multilateral	28 Jun 29	Postal Service	103LTS321	302372
Cuba	Multilateral	28 Jun 29	Postal Service	103LTS5	302369
Cuba	Multilateral	28 Jun 29	Postal Service	103LTS249	302371
Cuba	Multilateral	28 Jun 29	Postal Service	103LTS429	302374
Cuba	Multilateral	28 Jun 29	Postal Service	102LTS245	302368
Cuba	Multilateral	27 Jul 29	Other Military	118LTS343	302734
Cuba	Multilateral	27 Jul 29	Other Military	118LTS303	302733
Cuba	Multilateral	14 Sep 29	UN Charter	165LTS353	303822
Cuba	Multilateral	12 Apr 30	Admin Cooperation	179LTS89	304137
Cuba	Multilateral	12 Apr 30	Milit Servic/Citiz	178LTS227	304117
Cuba	Multilateral	12 Apr 30	Admin Cooperation	179LTS115	304138
Cuba	Multilateral	17 Apr 30	Extradition	126LTS201	302883
Cuba	Multilateral	23 Oct 30	Water Transport	125LTS95	302849
Cuba	Multilateral	23 Oct 30	Water Transport	112LTS21	302603
Cuba	Multilateral	13 Jul 31	Other HEW	139LTS301	303219
Cuba	Multilateral	10 Nov 31	Postal Service	131LTS389	303024
Cuba	Multilateral	10 Nov 31	Postal Service	131LTS327	303023
Cuba	Multilateral	09 Dec 32	Telecommunications	151LTS5	303479
Cuba	Multilateral	11 Mar 33	Water Transport	135LTS301	303119
Cuba	Multilateral	10 Oct 33	General Amity	163LTS393	303781
Cuba	Multilateral	26 Dec 33	Extradition	165LTS45	303803
Cuba	Multilateral	26 Dec 33	Recognition	165LTS19	303802
Cuba	Multilateral	20 Mar 34	Postal Service	176LTS55	304054
Cuba	Multilateral	20 Mar 34	Postal Service	174LTS171	304048
Cuba	Multilateral	20 Mar 34	Postal Service	175LTS363	304052
Cuba	Multilateral	20 Mar 34	Postal Service	175LTS73	304050
Cuba	Multilateral	20 Mar 34	Postal Service	175LTS5	304049
Cuba	Multilateral	20 Mar 34	Postal Service	175LTS269	304051
Cuba	Multilateral	20 Mar 34	Finance	176LTS9	304053
Cuba	Multilateral	02 Jun 34	General Trade	192LTS9	304458
Cuba	Multilateral	02 Jun 34	Patents/Copyrights	192LTS17	304459
Cuba	Multilateral	15 Jul 34	Mostfavored Nation	165LTS9	303801
Cuba	Multilateral	15 Apr 35	Culture	167LTS289	303874
Cuba	Multilateral	26 Jun 36	Other HEW	198LTS299	304648
Cuba	Multilateral	23 Dec 36	Admin Cooperation	201LTS295	304721
Cuba	Multilateral	23 Dec 36	Dispute Settlement	195LTS229	304548
Cuba	Multilateral	23 Dec 36	Culture	188LTS125	304355
Cuba	Multilateral	23 Dec 36	Culture	188LTS151	304356
Cuba	Multilateral	23 Dec 36	Peace/Disarmament	188LTS9	304350
Cuba	Multilateral	23 Dec 36	Dispute Settlement	188LTS53	304352
Cuba	Multilateral	23 Dec 36	Land Transport	188LTS99	304354
Cuba	Multilateral	23 Dec 36	General Amity	188LTS31	304351
Cuba	Multilateral	23 Dec 36	Dispute Settlement	188LTS75	304353
Cuba	Multilateral	31 Mar 37	Commodity Trade	189LTS359	304394
Cuba	Multilateral	03 Dec 38	Education	200LTS249	304694

PARTY ONE	PARTY TWO	DATE	TOPIC	CITATION	NUMBER
Cuba	Multilateral	23 May 39	Postal Service	202LTS159	304742
Cuba	Multilateral	01 Jan 42	General Military	204LTS381	304817
Cuba	Netherlands	31 Dec 13	Consul/Citizenship	14LTS29	300366
Cuba	Portugal	06 Sep 38	General Trade	195LTS443	304565
Cuba	Spain	15 Jul 27	General Trade	120LTS251	302770
Cuba	UK Great Britain	01 Dec 28	Postal Service	85LTS149	301929
Cuba	UK Great Britain	19 Feb 37	General Trade	192LTS301	304480
Cuba	USA (United States)	02 Mar 04	Territory Boundary	127LTS143	302915
Cuba	USA (United States)	18 Nov 25	Extradition	61LTS363	301446
Cuba	USA (United States)	04 Mar 26	Admin Cooperation	61LTS369	301447
Cuba	USA (United States)	11 Mar 26	Admin Cooperation	61LTS383	301448
Cuba	USA (United States)	22 Apr 26	Consul/Citizenship	60LTS371	301421
Cuba	USA (United States)	29 May 34	General Amity	150LTS95	303456
Cuba	USA (United States)	24 Aug 34	General Trade	153LTS369	303533
Cuba	USA (United States)	12 May 38	Admin Cooperation	191LTS19	304432
Cuba	USA (United States)	18 Dec 39	General Trade	202LTS71	304736
Curacao	Barbados	10 Oct 33	Postal Service	145LTS245	303357
Curacao	British Guiana	16 Jul 42	Postal Service	205LTS13	304823
Curacao	Multilateral	30 Jun 20	Patents/Copyrights	1LTS59	300008
Curacao	Multilateral	26 Sep 27	Dispute Settlement	92LTS301	302096
Curacao	Multilateral	08 Nov 27	General Trade	97LTS391	302238
Curacao	Multilateral	25 Nov 27	Telecommunications	84LTS97	301905
Curacao	Multilateral	07 Jun 30	Finance	143LTS337	303315
Curacao	Multilateral	07 Jun 30	Finance	143LTS257	303313
Curacao	Multilateral	07 Jun 30	Finance	143LTS317	303314
Curacao	Multilateral	30 Mar 31	Land Transport	150LTS247	303459
Curacao	Multilateral	09 Dec 32	Telecommunications	151LTS5	303479
Curacao	Trinidad/Tobago	23 Apr 42	Postal Service	204LTS335	304812
Curacao Surinam	Multilateral	20 Mar 34	Postal Service	175LTS5	304049
Curacao Surinam	Multilateral	20 Mar 34	Postal Service	175LTS73	304050
Curacao Surinam	Multilateral	20 Mar 34	Finance	176LTS9	304053
Curacao Surinam	Multilateral	20 Mar 34	Postal Service	175LTS269	304051
Curacao Surinam	Multilateral	23 May 39	Postal Service	202LTS159	304742
Cyprus	Multilateral	30 Jun 20	Patents/Copyrights	1LTS59	300008
Cyprus	Multilateral	31 Mar 22	Humanitarian	9LTS415	300269
Cyprus	Multilateral	09 Dec 23	Water Transport	58LTS284	301379
Cyprus	Multilateral	25 Aug 24	Water Transport	120LTS155	302764
Cyprus	Multilateral	01 Dec 24	Sanitation	78LTS351	301794
Cyprus	Multilateral	25 Nov 27	Telecommunications	84LTS97	301905
Cyprus	Multilateral	20 Apr 29	Admin Cooperation	112LTS371	302623
Cyprus	Multilateral	20 Apr 29	Admin Cooperation	112LTS395	302624
Cyprus	Multilateral	28 Oct 33	Refugees	159LTS199	303663
Cyprus	Multilateral	23 Sep 36	Gen Communications	186LTS301	304319
Cyprus	Multilateral	10 Feb 38	Refugees	192LTS59	304461
Cyrenaica	Multilateral	05 Jun 12	Telecommunications	1LTS135	300013
Cyrenaica	Multilateral	29 Oct 25	Telecommunications	57LTS201	301365
Cyrenaica	Multilateral	29 Oct 25	Telecommunications	57LTS201	301365
Cyrenaica	Multilateral	25 Nov 27	Telecommunications	84LTS97	301905
Cyrenaica	Multilateral	16 Apr 29	Specific Resources	126LTS305	302891
Cyrenaica	Multilateral	09 Dec 32	Telecommunications	151LTS5	303479
Czechoslovakia	Afghanistan	13 Oct 37	General Amity	191LTS9	304431
Czechoslovakia	Albania	19 Jan 26	General Trade	64LTS349	301507
Czechoslovakia	Albania	09 Apr 34	General Trade	158LTS59	303626
Czechoslovakia	Albania	14 Apr 34	Extradition	188LTS255	304362
Czechoslovakia	Argentina	31 Mar 32	Non-ILO Labor	155LTS379	303589
Czechoslovakia	Australia	19 Aug 36	General Trade	177LTS245	304093
Czechoslovakia	Austria	07 Jun 20	Consul/Citizenship	3LTS189	300098
Czechoslovakia	Austria	02 Aug 20	Finance	32LTS365	300826
Czechoslovakia	Austria	23 Aug 20	Health/Educ/Welfare	3LTS229	300099
Czechoslovakia	Austria	10 Mar 21	Territory Boundary	9LTS333	300267
Czechoslovakia	Austria	04 May 21	General Economic	15LTS13	300388
Czechoslovakia	Austria	16 Dec 21	General Amity	9LTS247	300257
Czechoslovakia	Austria	17 Dec 21	Finance	22LTS401	300570
Czechoslovakia	Austria	11 Feb 22	Taxation	152LTS175	303492
Czechoslovakia	Austria	18 Feb 22	Taxation	14LTS129	300371

PARTY ONE	PARTY TWO	DATE	TOPIC	CITATION	NUMBER
Czechoslovakia	Austria	18 Jan 23	Visas	88LTS237	302000
Czechoslovakia	Austria	30 Nov 23	Non-ILO Labor	126LTS171	302880
Czechoslovakia	Austria	29 Mar 24	Non-ILO Labor	94LTS75	302139
Czechoslovakia	Austria	29 Mar 24	Non-ILO Labor	94LTS103	302140
Czechoslovakia	Austria	15 Jun 24	Non-ILO Labor	94LTS149	302142
Czechoslovakia	Austria	15 Jun 24	Non-ILO Labor	94LTS131	302141
Czechoslovakia	Austria	15 Jun 24	Non-ILO Labor	94LTS165	302143
Czechoslovakia	Austria	12 Jul 24	Finance	50LTS111	301199
Czechoslovakia	Austria	27 Nov 24	General Economic	42LTS201	301041
Czechoslovakia	Austria	22 Dec 24	Non-ILO Labor	94LTS179	302144
Czechoslovakia	Austria	17 Jan 25	Non-ILO Labor	94LTS245	302146
Czechoslovakia	Austria	17 Jan 25	Non-ILO Labor	94LTS185	302145
Czechoslovakia	Austria	14 May 25	Finance	50LTS39	301198
Czechoslovakia	Austria	29 May 25	Non-ILO Labor	98LTS91	302242
Czechoslovakia	Austria	07 Dec 25	Admin Cooperation	86LTS7	301947
Czechoslovakia	Austria	05 Mar 26	General Amity	51LTS349	301240
Czechoslovakia	Austria	12 Jul 26	Taxation	86LTS383	301951
Czechoslovakia	Austria	12 Jul 26	Admin Cooperation	86LTS395	301952
Czechoslovakia	Austria	15 Feb 27	Air Transport	73LTS349	301724
Czechoslovakia	Austria	15 Feb 27	Air Transport	73LTS381	301725
Czechoslovakia	Austria	21 Jul 27	General Trade	81LTS7	301842
Czechoslovakia	Austria	30 Mar 28	Visas	73LTS87	301709
Czechoslovakia	Austria	12 Dec 28	Territory Boundary	108LTS9	302501
Czechoslovakia	Austria	12 Dec 28	Territory Boundary	107LTS137	302474
Czechoslovakia	Austria	03 Feb 29	Non-ILO Labor	102LTS191	302362
Czechoslovakia	Austria	03 Feb 29	Non-ILO Labor	101LTS285	302329
Czechoslovakia	Austria	12 Sep 30	Admin Cooperation	107LTS341	302489
Czechoslovakia	Austria	22 Jul 31	General Trade	128LTS59	302938
Czechoslovakia	Austria	18 Jan 33	Non-ILO Labor	142LTS41	303278
Czechoslovakia	Austria	02 Apr 36	General Economic	180LTS51	304173
Czechoslovakia	Bel-Lux Econ Union	28 Dec 25	General Economic	58LTS189	301372
Czechoslovakia	Belgium	19 Jul 27	Admin Cooperation	73LTS307	301721
Czechoslovakia	Belgium	19 Jul 27	Extradition	73LTS283	301720
Czechoslovakia	Belgium	26 Jun 28	Visas	80LTS9	301819
Czechoslovakia	Belgium	29 Apr 29	Dispute Settlement	110LTS113	302556
Czechoslovakia	Belgium	16 Oct 37	Visas	184LTS73	304243
Czechoslovakia	Brazil	27 Nov 31	General Trade	136LTS453	303144
Czechoslovakia	Brazil	22 Jul 36	General Trade	188LTS275	304363
Czechoslovakia	Bulgaria	06 Sep 25	Health/Educ/Welfare	50LTS253	301208
Czechoslovakia	Bulgaria	16 Oct 25	General Economic	56LTS265	301334
Czechoslovakia	Bulgaria	15 May 26	Admin Cooperation	60LTS203	301413
Czechoslovakia	Bulgaria	15 May 26	Extradition	60LTS169	301412
Czechoslovakia	Bulgaria	29 Aug 33	General Economic	148LTS15	303402
Czechoslovakia	Canada	15 Mar 28	General Trade	82LTS147	301865
Czechoslovakia	Chile	18 Sep 30	General Trade	140LTS161	303233
Czechoslovakia	China	12 Feb 30	General Economic	110LTS285	302561
Czechoslovakia	Denmark	16 Jan 22	Finance	14LTS267	300378
Czechoslovakia	Denmark	31 Jan 24	General Trade	23LTS139	300585
Czechoslovakia	Denmark	02 Jun 24	Education	57LTS115	301357
Czechoslovakia	Denmark	19 May 25	General Amity	36LTS113	300908
Czechoslovakia	Denmark	24 Jul 25	Visas	37LTS97	300948
Czechoslovakia	Denmark	30 Nov 26	Dispute Settlement	67LTS105	301541
Czechoslovakia	Denmark	21 Jun 29	Visas	91LTS351	302075
Czechoslovakia	Denmark	07 Oct 31	Extradition	127LTS103	302911
Czechoslovakia	Denmark	04 Jul 32	Customs	143LTS251	303312
Czechoslovakia	Estonia	17 Jul 26	Admin Cooperation	69LTS385	301620
Czechoslovakia	Estonia	17 Jul 26	Extradition	63LTS255	301495
Czechoslovakia	Estonia	20 Jul 27	General Trade	77LTS341	301776
Czechoslovakia	Estonia	09 Jul 29	Dispute Settlement	101LTS423	302341
Czechoslovakia	Finland	02 Mar 27	General Economic	66LTS385	301532
Czechoslovakia	Finland	26 Apr 28	Visas	80LTS335	301838
Czechoslovakia	Finland	02 Oct 29	Dispute Settlement	115LTS155	302684
Czechoslovakia	Finland	22 May 34	General Economic	153LTS17	303502
Czechoslovakia	Finland	28 Jan 36	General Economic	166LTS259	303841
Czechoslovakia	Finland	21 Mar 36	Admin Cooperation	179LTS295	304156

PARTY ONE	PARTY TWO	DATE	TOPIC	CITATION	NUMBER
Czechoslovakia	Finland	17 Apr 37	General Economic	179LTS317	304159
Czechoslovakia	France	20 Mar 20	Visas	3LTS139	300095
Czechoslovakia	France	07 Oct 22	Admin Cooperation	47LTS365	301141
Czechoslovakia	France	25 Jan 24	General Amity	23LTS163	300588
Czechoslovakia	France	18 Aug 24	General Trade	44LTS21	301080
Czechoslovakia	France	26 May 25	Air Transport	150LTS43	303452
Czechoslovakia	France	16 Oct 25	Peace/Disarmament	54LTS359	301298
Czechoslovakia	France	03 Jun 27	Consul/Citizenship	131LTS177	303009
Czechoslovakia	France	07 May 28	Admin Cooperation	114LTS171	302663
Czechoslovakia	France	07 May 28	Extradition	114LTS117	302660
Czechoslovakia	France	02 Jul 28	General Trade	99LTS105	302272
Czechoslovakia	France	03 Oct 30	Health/Educ/Welfare	125LTS59	302846
Czechoslovakia	Germany	29 Jun 20	General Economic	17LTS69	300430
Czechoslovakia	Germany	29 Jun 20	Consul/Citizenship	20LTS85	300509
Czechoslovakia	Germany	29 Jun 20	General Economic	17LTS139	300431
Czechoslovakia	Germany	03 Feb 21	Territory Boundary	5LTS246	300132
Czechoslovakia	Germany	31 Dec 21	Taxation	17LTS401	300447
Czechoslovakia	Germany	20 Jan 22	Admin Cooperation	26LTS201	300648
Czechoslovakia	Germany	22 Feb 22	IGO Operations	26LTS249	300650
Czechoslovakia	Germany	18 Mar 22	Taxation	17LTS453	300448
Czechoslovakia	Germany	12 Apr 22	Non-ILO Labor	22LTS329	300562
Czechoslovakia	Germany	08 May 22	Extradition	23LTS171	300589
Czechoslovakia	Germany	02 May 23	Admin Cooperation	31LTS0	300793
Czechoslovakia	Germany	15 Aug 23	Admin Cooperation	27LTS94	300670
Czechoslovakia	Germany	04 Mar 24	Land Transport	41LTS243	301018
Czechoslovakia	Germany	15 Dec 24	Non-ILO Labor	52LTS31	301248
Czechoslovakia	Germany	15 Dec 24	Non-ILO Labor	52LTS41	301249
Czechoslovakia	Germany	06 Feb 25	Admin Cooperation	46LTS165	301118
Czechoslovakia	Germany	16 Oct 25	General Military	54LTS341	301296
Czechoslovakia	Germany	22 Jan 27	Air Transport	89LTS261	302020
Czechoslovakia	Germany	22 Jan 27	Air Transport	89LTS231	302019
Czechoslovakia	Germany	25 Mar 27	Land Transport	75LTS353	301758
Czechoslovakia	Germany	22 Mar 28	Territory Boundary	93LTS235	302113
Czechoslovakia	Germany	27 Mar 28	Visas	90LTS151	302032
Czechoslovakia	Germany	11 May 28	Non-ILO Labor	81LTS441	301854
Czechoslovakia	Germany	05 Jun 28	Admin Cooperation	177LTS19	302700
Czechoslovakia	Germany	20 Mar 29	Territory Boundary	109LTS219	302541
Czechoslovakia	Germany	22 Dec 29	Customs	110LTS417	302573
Czechoslovakia	Germany	31 Jan 30	Territory Boundary	145LTS51	303345
Czechoslovakia	Germany	27 Jun 30	Customs	112LTS169	302614
Czechoslovakia	Germany	21 Mar 31	Non-ILO Labor	143LTS177	303308
Czechoslovakia	Germany	20 Apr 31	Patents/Copyrights	141LTS307	303271
Czechoslovakia	Germany	29 Apr 31	Air Transport	133LTS359	303073
Czechoslovakia	Germany	29 Apr 31	Air Transport	133LTS347	303072
Czechoslovakia	Germany	25 Jul 31	Land Transport	187LTS279	304344
Czechoslovakia	Germany	19 Sep 32	Health/Educ/Welfare	137LTS453	303175
Czechoslovakia	Germany	26 Jun 35	Commodity Trade	173LTS385	304029
Czechoslovakia	Germany	27 Sep 35	Territory Boundary	182LTS267	304217
Czechoslovakia	Germany	30 Dec 35	Customs	173LTS333	304023
Czechoslovakia	Great Britain	09 Aug 25	Postal Service	38LTS231	300980
Czechoslovakia	Greece	10 Jan 23	General Trade	21LTS217	300544
Czechoslovakia	Greece	08 Apr 25	General Trade	38LTS291	300984
Czechoslovakia	Greece	07 Apr 27	Admin Cooperation	88LTS187	301997
Czechoslovakia	Greece	07 Apr 27	Admin Cooperation	88LTS211	301998
Czechoslovakia	Greece	07 Apr 27	Extradition	88LTS219	301999
Czechoslovakia	Greece	08 Jun 29	General Amity	108LTS255	302512
Czechoslovakia	Greece	30 Jul 32	General Trade	156LTS159	303599
Czechoslovakia	Guatemala	20 Sep 36	General Trade	185LTS269	304293
Czechoslovakia	Hungary	08 Mar 23	Land Transport	48LTS257	301167
Czechoslovakia	Hungary	13 Jul 23	Taxation	35LTS237	300898
Czechoslovakia	Hungary	13 Jul 23	Claims and Debts	35LTS271	300900
Czechoslovakia	Hungary	13 Jul 23	Claims and Debts	35LTS253	300899
Czechoslovakia	Hungary	13 Jul 23	Taxation	36LTS53	300903
Czechoslovakia	Hungary	13 Jul 23	Claims and Debts	36LTS41	300902
Czechoslovakia	Hungary	13 Jul 23	Claims and Debts	36LTS13	300901

PARTY ONE	PARTY TWO	DATE	TOPIC	CITATION	NUMBER
Czechoslovakia	Hungary	09 Feb 24	Postal Service	30LTS325	300772
Czechoslovakia	Hungary	09 Feb 24	Specific Resources	30LTS335	300773
Czechoslovakia	Hungary	08 Mar 24	Claims and Debts	36LTS61	300904
Czechoslovakia	Hungary	30 Sep 26	Territory Boundary	57LTS87	301356
Czechoslovakia	Hungary	31 May 27	General Transport	65LTS61	301520
Czechoslovakia	Hungary	03 Jun 27	Admin Cooperation	67LTS31	301538
Czechoslovakia	Hungary	26 May 28	Claims and Debts	101LTS265	302328
Czechoslovakia	Hungary	14 Nov 28	Water Transport	142LTS227	303295
Czechoslovakia	Hungary	14 Nov 28	Territory Boundary	110LTS425	302574
Czechoslovakia	Hungary	08 Jun 34	Specific Resources	172LTS61	303979
Czechoslovakia	Hungary	14 Jun 35	General Trade	171LTS401	303976
Czechoslovakia	Hungary	15 Jun 36	General Economic	179LTS73	304135
Czechoslovakia	Hungary	24 Aug 37	Specific Resources	189LTS403	304397
Czechoslovakia	Iceland	08 May 24	General Economic	46LTS419	301125
Czechoslovakia	Iceland	25 Jun 29	Visas	91LTS359	302076
Czechoslovakia	Italy	23 Mar 21	General Trade	32LTS183	300815
Czechoslovakia	Italy	23 Mar 21	Finance	32LTS261	300817
Czechoslovakia	Italy	23 Mar 21	Water Transport	32LTS241	300816
Czechoslovakia	Italy	06 Apr 22	Admin Cooperation	55LTS189	301314
Czechoslovakia	Italy	06 Apr 22	Extradition	55LTS171	301313
Czechoslovakia	Italy	06 Apr 22	Admin Cooperation	55LTS207	301315
Czechoslovakia	Italy	01 Mar 24	Taxation	36LTS229	300925
Czechoslovakia	Italy	01 Mar 24	Consul/Citizenship	34LTS55	300867
Czechoslovakia	Italy	05 Jul 24	General Amity	26LTS21	300637
Czechoslovakia	Italy	15 Nov 24	Land Transport	92LTS91	302081
Czechoslovakia	Italy	04 May 26	Other Economic	61LTS257	301438
Czechoslovakia	Italy	28 Mar 31	Culture	125LTS347	302863
Czechoslovakia	Italy	23 May 31	Admin Cooperation	126LTS185	302881
Czechoslovakia	Italy	28 Apr 32	Air Transport	136LTS267	303129
Czechoslovakia	Italy	27 Nov 33	General Economic	153LTS351	303531
Czechoslovakia	Italy	31 Mar 37	General Trade	193LTS165	304492
Czechoslovakia	Italy	10 May 37	Air Transport	190LTS397	304430
Czechoslovakia	Japan	30 Oct 25	General Trade	58LTS263	301377
Czechoslovakia	Latvia	07 Oct 22	General Trade	20LTS379	300528
Czechoslovakia	Latvia	07 Aug 24	Sanitation	38LTS123	300970
Czechoslovakia	Latvia	06 Jul 26	Extradition	62LTS229	301465
Czechoslovakia	Latvia	24 Dec 29	Visas	99LTS9	302263
Czechoslovakia	Latvia	11 Oct 33	Dispute Settlement	155LTS195	303577
Czechoslovakia	Lithuania	08 Mar 30	Dispute Settlement	115LTS61	302677
Czechoslovakia	Lithuania	24 Apr 31	Admin Cooperation	126LTS279	302890
Czechoslovakia	Lithuania	24 Apr 31	Extradition	126LTS261	302889
Czechoslovakia	Luxembourg	18 Sep 29	Dispute Settlement	107LTS49	302467
Czechoslovakia	Luxembourg	01 Dec 34	Extradition	168LTS287	303906
Czechoslovakia	Monaco	22 Dec 34	Extradition	171LTS27	303949
Czechoslovakia	Multilateral	09 Sep 86*	Patents/Copyrights	123LTS233	302816
Czechoslovakia	Multilateral	18 Mar 04	Humanitarian	1LTS83	300011
Czechoslovakia	Multilateral	13 Nov 08	General Ad Hoc	1LTS217	300015
Czechoslovakia	Multilateral	05 Jun 12	Telecommunications	1LTS135	300013
Czechoslovakia	Multilateral	20 Mar 14	Patents/Copyrights	1LTS243	300016
Czechoslovakia	Multilateral	10 Sep 19	General Trade	7LTS331	300200
Czechoslovakia	Multilateral	10 Sep 19	Reparations	2LTS44	300045
Czechoslovakia	Multilateral	10 Sep 19	General Economic	2LTS35	300044
Czechoslovakia	Multilateral	10 Sep 19	Reparations	2LTS29	300043
Czechoslovakia	Multilateral	01 May 20	Air Transport	11LTS173	300297
Czechoslovakia	Multilateral	04 Jun 20	Peace/Disarmament	6LTS187	300152
Czechoslovakia	Multilateral	21 Jun 20	Health/Educ/Welfare	8LTS65	300207
Czechoslovakia	Multilateral	30 Jun 20	Patents/Copyrights	1LTS59	300008
Czechoslovakia	Multilateral	16 Dec 20	General IGO	6LTS379	300170
Czechoslovakia	Multilateral	20 Apr 21	Water Transport	7LTS35	300172
Czechoslovakia	Multilateral	20 Apr 21	Land Transport	7LTS11	300171
Czechoslovakia	Multilateral	20 Apr 21	Water Transport	7LTS65	300173
Czechoslovakia	Multilateral	20 Apr 21	Water Transport	7LTS73	300174
Czechoslovakia	Multilateral	23 Jul 21	Water Transport	26LTS173	300647
Czechoslovakia	Multilateral	05 Aug 21	Admin Cooperation	27LTS349	300695
Czechoslovakia	Multilateral	05 Oct 21	IGO Establishment	51LTS361	301241

PARTY ONE	PARTY TWO	DATE	TOPIC	CITATION	NUMBER
Czechoslovakia	Multilateral	05 Oct 21	Admin Cooperation	29LTS73	300734
Czechoslovakia	Multilateral	05 Oct 21	Admin Cooperation	29LTS79	300735
Czechoslovakia	Multilateral	05 Oct 21	Admin Cooperation	29LTS67	300733
Czechoslovakia	Multilateral	06 Oct 21	General Economic	17LTS45	300427
Czechoslovakia	Multilateral	27 Jan 22	Visas	9LTS291	300262
Czechoslovakia	Multilateral	22 Feb 22	Water Transport	26LTS219	300649
Czechoslovakia	Multilateral	31 Mar 22	Humanitarian	9LTS415	300269
Czechoslovakia	Multilateral	06 Apr 22	Admin Cooperation	123LTS277	302818
Czechoslovakia	Multilateral	06 Apr 22	Milit Assistance	20LTS11	300501
Czechoslovakia	Multilateral	05 Jul 22	Reparations	13LTS237	300355
Czechoslovakia	Multilateral	04 Oct 22	Territory Boundary	12LTS385	300334
Czechoslovakia	Multilateral	04 Oct 22	Territory Boundary	12LTS391	300335
Czechoslovakia	Multilateral	27 Jan 23	Water Transport	26LTS253	300651
Czechoslovakia	Multilateral	24 Sep 23	Dispute Settlement	27LTS157	300678
Czechoslovakia	Multilateral	03 Nov 23	Customs	30LTS371	300775
Czechoslovakia	Multilateral	30 Nov 23	Non-ILO Labor	102LTS153	302360
Czechoslovakia	Multilateral	30 Nov 23	Non-ILO Labor	102LTS183	302361
Czechoslovakia	Multilateral	09 Dec 23	Water Transport	58LTS284	301379
Czechoslovakia	Multilateral	09 Dec 23	General Economic	58LTS315	301380
Czechoslovakia	Multilateral	09 Dec 23	Land Transport	47LTS55	301129
Czechoslovakia	Multilateral	25 Jan 24	Sanitation	57LTS135	301360
Czechoslovakia	Multilateral	14 Mar 24	Finance	25LTS423	300633
Czechoslovakia	Multilateral	31 Mar 24	Sanitation	27LTS211	300685
Czechoslovakia	Multilateral	28 Aug 24	Postal Service	41LTS97	301008
Czechoslovakia	Multilateral	28 Aug 24	Postal Service	41LTS9	301006
Czechoslovakia	Multilateral	28 Aug 24	Postal Service	41LTS55	301007
Czechoslovakia	Multilateral	28 Aug 24	Postal Service	40LTS437	301005
Czechoslovakia	Multilateral	28 Aug 24	Postal Service	40LTS19	301002
Czechoslovakia	Multilateral	28 Aug 24	Postal Service	40LTS307	301004
Czechoslovakia	Multilateral	28 Aug 24	Postal Service	40LTS249	301003
Czechoslovakia	Multilateral	23 Oct 24	General Transport	77LTS367	301778
Czechoslovakia	Multilateral	23 Oct 24	Land Transport	78LTS17	301779
Czechoslovakia	Multilateral	19 Feb 25	Admin Cooperation	81LTS317	301845
Czechoslovakia	Multilateral	17 Jun 25	Peace/Disarmament	94LTS65	302138
Czechoslovakia	Multilateral	29 Oct 25	Telecommunications	57LTS201	301365
Czechoslovakia	Multilateral	06 Nov 25	Patents/Copyrights	74LTS289	301743
Czechoslovakia	Multilateral	06 Nov 25	Patents/Copyrights	74LTS327	301745
Czechoslovakia	Multilateral	06 Nov 25	Other Economic	74LTS319	301744
Czechoslovakia	Multilateral	27 Nov 25	Water Transport	67LTS63	301539
Czechoslovakia	Multilateral	24 Apr 26	Land Transport	108LTS123	302505
Czechoslovakia	Multilateral	21 Jun 26	Sanitation	78LTS229	301793
Czechoslovakia	Multilateral	25 Sep 26	ILO Labor	60LTS253	301414
Czechoslovakia	Multilateral	22 Jan 27	Telecommunications	68LTS149	301578
Czechoslovakia	Multilateral	25 Feb 27	Telecommunications	78LTS123	301783
Czechoslovakia	Multilateral	08 Mar 27	Telecommunications	78LTS134	301784
Czechoslovakia	Multilateral	12 Jul 27	Direct Aid	135LTS247	303115
Czechoslovakia	Multilateral	10 Sep 27	Postal Service	75LTS39	301750
Czechoslovakia	Multilateral	10 Sep 27	Postal Service	75LTS7	301749
Czechoslovakia	Multilateral	26 Sep 27	Dispute Settlement	92LTS301	302096
Czechoslovakia	Multilateral	29 Oct 27	Scientific Project	127LTS27	302903
Czechoslovakia	Multilateral	08 Nov 27	General Trade	97LTS391	302238
Czechoslovakia	Multilateral	25 Nov 27	Telecommunications	84LTS97	301905
Czechoslovakia	Multilateral	23 Apr 28	Telecommunications	78LTS197	301790
Czechoslovakia	Multilateral	11 Jul 28	Commodity Trade	95LTS357	302184
Czechoslovakia	Multilateral	11 Jul 28	Commodity Trade	95LTS373	302185
Czechoslovakia	Multilateral	27 Aug 28	General Military	94LTS57	302137
Czechoslovakia	Multilateral	30 Oct 28	Non-ILO Labor	130LTS405	302999
Czechoslovakia	Multilateral	30 Oct 28	Dispute Settlement	87LTS103	301963
Czechoslovakia	Multilateral	14 Dec 28	General Economic	110LTS171	302560
Czechoslovakia	Multilateral	20 Apr 29	Admin Cooperation	112LTS371	302623
Czechoslovakia	Multilateral	20 Apr 29	Admin Cooperation	112LTS395	302624
Czechoslovakia	Multilateral	21 May 29	Dispute Settlement	96LTS311	302210
Czechoslovakia	Multilateral	28 Jun 29	Postal Service	103LTS5	302369
Czechoslovakia	Multilateral	28 Jun 29	Postal Service	103LTS321	302372
Czechoslovakia	Multilateral	28 Jun 29	Postal Service	103LTS71	302370

PARTY ONE	PARTY TWO	DATE	TOPIC	CITATION	NUMBER
Czechoslovakia	Multilateral	28 Jun 29	Postal Service	103LTS249	302371
Czechoslovakia	Multilateral	28 Jun 29	Postal Service	102LTS245	302368
Czechoslovakia	Multilateral	28 Jun 29	Postal Service	103LTS429	302374
Czechoslovakia	Multilateral	28 Jun 29	Postal Service	103LTS377	302373
Czechoslovakia	Multilateral	27 Jul 29	Other Military	118LTS343	302734
Czechoslovakia	Multilateral	27 Jul 29	Other Military	118LTS303	302733
Czechoslovakia	Multilateral	14 Sep 29	UN Charter	165LTS353	303822
Czechoslovakia	Multilateral	10 Oct 29	Telecommunications	98LTS375	302257
Czechoslovakia	Multilateral	12 Oct 29	General Transport	137LTS11	303145
Czechoslovakia	Multilateral	29 Oct 29	Telecommunications	99LTS85	302270
Czechoslovakia	Multilateral	09 Nov 29	Land Transport	125LTS205	302855
Czechoslovakia	Multilateral	20 Jan 30	Reparations	113LTS389	302650
Czechoslovakia	Multilateral	20 Jan 30	Reparations	104LTS243	302394
Czechoslovakia	Multilateral	20 Jan 30	Finance	104LTS413	302395
Czechoslovakia	Multilateral	20 Jan 30	Finance	104LTS433	302397
Czechoslovakia	Multilateral	12 Apr 30	Admin Cooperation	179LTS89	304137
Czechoslovakia	Multilateral	12 Apr 30	Admin Cooperation	179LTS115	304138
Czechoslovakia	Multilateral	28 Apr 30	Claims and Debts	121LTS69	302785
Czechoslovakia	Multilateral	07 Jun 30	Finance	143LTS257	303313
Czechoslovakia	Multilateral	07 Jun 30	Finance	143LTS317	303314
Czechoslovakia	Multilateral	07 Jun 30	Finance	143LTS337	303315
Czechoslovakia	Multilateral	31 Oct 30	Dispute Settlement	120LTS9	302760
Czechoslovakia	Multilateral	19 Mar 31	Finance	143LTS407	303317
Czechoslovakia	Multilateral	19 Mar 31	Admin Cooperation	143LTS7	303301
Czechoslovakia	Multilateral	19 Mar 31	Finance	143LTS355	303316
Czechoslovakia	Multilateral	27 Mar 31	ICJ Option Clause	167LTS341	303877
Czechoslovakia	Multilateral	28 Mar 31	Customs	119LTS47	302739
Czechoslovakia	Multilateral	30 Mar 31	Land Transport	150LTS247	303459
Czechoslovakia	Multilateral	13 Jul 31	Other HEW	139LTS301	303219
Czechoslovakia	Multilateral	21 Aug 31	Other Economic	127LTS95	302910
Czechoslovakia	Multilateral	24 Sep 31	Specific Resources	155LTS349	303586
Czechoslovakia	Multilateral	15 Jul 32	Direct Aid	135LTS285	303118
Czechoslovakia	Multilateral	02 Sep 32	Land Transport	154LTS123	303543
Czechoslovakia	Multilateral	09 Dec 32	Telecommunications	151LTS5	303479
Czechoslovakia	Multilateral	16 Feb 33	Admin Cooperation	139LTS233	303213
Czechoslovakia	Multilateral	11 Mar 33	Water Transport	135LTS301	303119
Czechoslovakia	Multilateral	29 May 33	Admin Cooperation	192LTS289	304479
Czechoslovakia	Multilateral	19 Jun 33	Gen Communications	154LTS133	303544
Czechoslovakia	Multilateral	04 Jul 33	Peace/Disarmament	148LTS211	303414
Czechoslovakia	Multilateral	25 Aug 33	Commodity Trade	141LTS71	303262
Czechoslovakia	Multilateral	10 Oct 33	General Amity	163LTS393	303781
Czechoslovakia	Multilateral	11 Oct 33	Consul/Citizenship	150LTS431	303476
Czechoslovakia	Multilateral	28 Oct 33	Refugees	159LTS199	303663
Czechoslovakia	Multilateral	23 Nov 33	Land Transport	192LTS389	304484
Czechoslovakia	Multilateral	23 Nov 33	Land Transport	192LTS327	304483
Czechoslovakia	Multilateral	20 Mar 34	Postal Service	175LTS269	304051
Czechoslovakia	Multilateral	20 Mar 34	Postal Service	176LTS55	304054
Czechoslovakia	Multilateral	20 Mar 34	Postal Service	175LTS363	304052
Czechoslovakia	Multilateral	20 Mar 34	Postal Service	175LTS73	304050
Czechoslovakia	Multilateral	20 Mar 34	Postal Service	174LTS171	304048
Czechoslovakia	Multilateral	20 Mar 34	Finance	176LTS9	304053
Czechoslovakia	Multilateral	20 Mar 34	Postal Service	175LTS5	304049
Czechoslovakia	Multilateral	26 Apr 34	Admin Cooperation	164LTS63	303789
Czechoslovakia	Multilateral	02 Jun 34	General Trade	192LTS9	304458
Czechoslovakia	Multilateral	02 Jun 34	Patents/Copyrights	205LTS179	304834
Czechoslovakia	Multilateral	02 Jun 34	Patents/Copyrights	192LTS17	304459
Czechoslovakia	Multilateral	19 Jun 34	Admin Cooperation	154LTS381	303564
Czechoslovakia	Multilateral	25 Jul 34	Other HEW	177LTS59	304080
Czechoslovakia	Multilateral	20 Feb 35	Sanitation	193LTS37	304486
Czechoslovakia	Multilateral	20 Feb 35	Sanitation	193LTS59	304487
Czechoslovakia	Multilateral	20 Feb 35	Sanitation	186LTS173	304310
Czechoslovakia	Multilateral	26 Jun 36	Other HEW	198LTS299	304648
Czechoslovakia	Multilateral	23 Sep 36	Gen Communications	186LTS301	304319
Czechoslovakia	Multilateral	06 Nov 36	General Military	173LTS353	304025
Czechoslovakia	Multilateral	10 Feb 37	General Transport	189LTS313	304391

PARTY ONE	PARTY TWO	DATE	TOPIC	CITATION	NUMBER
Czechoslovakia	Multilateral	31 Mar 37	Commodity Trade	189LTS359	304394
Czechoslovakia	Multilateral	31 Oct 38	Sanitation	198LTS205	304642
Czechoslovakia	Multilateral	27 Jan 39	Loans and Credits	196LTS287	304591
Czechoslovakia	Multilateral	01 Jan 42	General Military	204LTS381	304817
Czechoslovakia	Multilateral	02 Jun 42	Patents/Copyrights	205LTS163	304833
Czechoslovakia	Netherlands	17 Oct 24	General Trade	31LTS93	300786
Czechoslovakia	Netherlands	14 Sep 29	Dispute Settlement	107LTS201	302477
Czechoslovakia	Netherlands	11 Aug 31	Land Transport	127LTS347	302928
Czechoslovakia	Netherlands	04 Dec 31	Extradition	129LTS343	302969
Czechoslovakia	Netherlands	18 Jul 33	Land Transport	152LTS265	303499
Czechoslovakia	Netherlands	25 May 37	Education	180LTS43	304172
Czechoslovakia	Norway	02 Oct 23	General Trade	20LTS355	300526
Czechoslovakia	Norway	09 Sep 29	Dispute Settlement	101LTS355	302336
Czechoslovakia	Norway	11 Oct 29	Visas	96LTS211	302202
Czechoslovakia	Persia	30 Apr 29	General Economic	110LTS357	302567
Czechoslovakia	Persia	29 Oct 30	General Amity	121LTS53	302783
Czechoslovakia	Persia	29 Oct 30	Privil/Immunities	121LTS59	302784
Czechoslovakia	Poland	23 Sep 22	Scientific Project	50LTS321	301216
Czechoslovakia	Poland	06 Mar 25	Admin Cooperation	46LTS201	301120
Czechoslovakia	Poland	07 Apr 25	General Trade	56LTS285	301337
Czechoslovakia	Poland	23 Apr 25	Taxation	44LTS309	301091
Czechoslovakia	Poland	23 Apr 25	Taxation	44LTS271	301089
Czechoslovakia	Poland	23 Apr 25	Taxation	44LTS285	301090
Czechoslovakia	Poland	23 Apr 25	Dispute Settlement	48LTS383	301171
Czechoslovakia	Poland	23 Apr 25	Admin Cooperation	48LTS287	301170
Czechoslovakia	Poland	30 May 25	Territory Boundary	48LTS397	301172
Czechoslovakia	Poland	30 May 25	General Transport	50LTS243	301207
Czechoslovakia	Poland	05 Sep 25	Sanitation	58LTS143	301370
Czechoslovakia	Poland	15 Apr 26	Air Transport	67LTS305	301554
Czechoslovakia	Poland	21 Apr 26	Sanitation	58LTS9	301367
Czechoslovakia	Poland	08 Feb 27	Admin Cooperation	70LTS289	301640
Czechoslovakia	Poland	08 Feb 27	Admin Cooperation	70LTS299	301641
Czechoslovakia	Poland	08 Feb 27	Admin Cooperation	70LTS275	301639
Czechoslovakia	Poland	08 Feb 27	Admin Cooperation	70LTS261	301638
Czechoslovakia	Poland	14 Apr 27	Admin Cooperation	82LTS157	301867
Czechoslovakia	Poland	30 May 27	Land Transport	98LTS233	302251
Czechoslovakia	Poland	18 Feb 28	Specific Resources	119LTS385	302758
Czechoslovakia	Poland	18 Feb 28	Specific Resources	100LTS273	302301
Czechoslovakia	Poland	22 May 28	Water Transport	82LTS171	301868
Czechoslovakia	Poland	21 Dec 29	General Amity	115LTS201	302687
Czechoslovakia	Poland	18 Jun 30	Land Transport	137LTS137	303151
Czechoslovakia	Poland	17 Feb 33	Land Transport	143LTS167	303307
Czechoslovakia	Poland	25 Jan 34	Admin Cooperation	177LTS139	304088
Czechoslovakia	Poland	10 Feb 34	General Trade	183LTS213	304238
Czechoslovakia	Poland	10 Feb 34	Admin Cooperation	178LTS159	304111
Czechoslovakia	Portugal	23 Nov 27	Extradition	124LTS7	302829
Czechoslovakia	Portugal	23 Nov 27	Dispute Settlement	123LTS403	302827
Czechoslovakia	Portugal	23 Nov 27	Dispute Settlement	123LTS417	302828
Czechoslovakia	Romania	23 Apr 21	General Economic	15LTS235	300397
Czechoslovakia	Romania	23 Apr 21	General Amity	6LTS215	300155
Czechoslovakia	Romania	14 Oct 22	Admin Cooperation	25LTS163	300604
Czechoslovakia	Romania	07 May 23	General Amity	18LTS81	300455
Czechoslovakia	Romania	01 Oct 24	Sanitation	51LTS71	301223
Czechoslovakia	Romania	16 Apr 25	Territory Boundary	46LTS427	301126
Czechoslovakia	Romania	07 May 25	Extradition	54LTS51	301273
Czechoslovakia	Romania	07 May 25	Admin Cooperation	54LTS17	301272
Czechoslovakia	Romania	13 Jun 26	General Military	54LTS253	301288
Czechoslovakia	Romania	21 May 29	General Amity	96LTS307	302209
Czechoslovakia	Romania	20 Jun 30	Air Transport	150LTS63	303453
Czechoslovakia	Romania	27 Jun 30	General Economic	119LTS73	302742
Czechoslovakia	Romania	15 Jul 30	Territory Boundary	164LTS157	303793
Czechoslovakia	Romania	05 Dec 30	Claims and Debts	167LTS221	303868
Czechoslovakia	Romania	05 Dec 30	Claims and Debts	167LTS231	303869
Czechoslovakia	Romania	05 Dec 30	Claims and Debts	167LTS205	303867
Czechoslovakia	Romania	22 Dec 30	Territory Boundary	167LTS243	303870

PARTY ONE	PARTY TWO	DATE	TOPIC	CITATION	NUMBER
Czechoslovakia	Romania	22 Dec 30	Claims and Debts	167LTS263	303872
Czechoslovakia	Romania	22 Dec 30	Customs	168LTS209	303900
Czechoslovakia	Romania	22 Dec 30	Territory Boundary	167LTS257	303871
Czechoslovakia	Romania	20 Jun 34	Taxation	168LTS241	303901
Czechoslovakia	Romania	20 Jun 34	Taxation	168LTS249	303902
Czechoslovakia	Romania	20 Jun 34	Admin Cooperation	168LTS257	303903
Czechoslovakia	Serb/Croat/Slovene	14 Aug 20	General Amity	6LTS209	300154
Czechoslovakia	Serb/Croat/Slovene	18 Oct 20	General Economic	17LTS19	300424
Czechoslovakia	Serb/Croat/Slovene	31 Aug 22	General Amity	13LTS231	300354
Czechoslovakia	Serb/Croat/Slovene	17 Mar 23	Admin Cooperation	30LTS185	300768
Czechoslovakia	Serb/Croat/Slovene	19 Sep 28	Admin Cooperation	87LTS309	301976
Czechoslovakia	Serb/Croat/Slovene	29 Sep 28	Claims and Debts	96LTS421	302215
Czechoslovakia	Serb/Croat/Slovene	07 Nov 28	Consul/Citizenship	98LTS297	302252
Czechoslovakia	Serb/Croat/Slovene	07 Nov 28	Claims and Debts	95LTS101	302169
Czechoslovakia	Serb/Croat/Slovene	14 Nov 28	General Economic	97LTS9	302216
Czechoslovakia	Serb/Croat/Slovene	21 May 29	General Amity	94LTS53	302136
Czechoslovakia	South Africa	27 Jan 37	General Trade	189LTS97	304377
Czechoslovakia	Spain	19 Jul 25	General Economic	60LTS329	301419
Czechoslovakia	Spain	26 Oct 27	Extradition	121LTS271	302791
Czechoslovakia	Spain	26 Oct 27	Privil/Immunities	121LTS287	302792
Czechoslovakia	Spain	26 Oct 27	Privil/Immunities	121LTS311	302793
Czechoslovakia	Spain	13 Aug 28	Dispute Settlement	121LTS321	302794
Czechoslovakia	Spain	16 Nov 28	Dispute Settlement	100LTS313	302303
Czechoslovakia	Spain	13 Dec 28	General Trade	98LTS65	302240
Czechoslovakia	Spain	29 Jun 32	Non-ILO Labor	166LTS355	303851
Czechoslovakia	Sweden	07 Sep 21	Humanitarian	7LTS97	300177
Czechoslovakia	Sweden	18 Apr 25	General Amity	36LTS289	300929
Czechoslovakia	Sweden	02 Jan 26	Dispute Settlement	48LTS173	301159
Czechoslovakia	Sweden	17 Nov 31	Extradition	134LTS135	303088
Czechoslovakia	Sweden	23 Jul 36	Non-ILO Labor	171LTS111	303954
Czechoslovakia	Switzerland	30 Sep 25	General Trade	58LTS279	301378
Czechoslovakia	Switzerland	21 Dec 26	Admin Cooperation	86LTS443	301956
Czechoslovakia	Switzerland	21 Dec 26	Admin Cooperation	68LTS393	301594
Czechoslovakia	Switzerland	16 Feb 27	General Trade	64LTS7	301501
Czechoslovakia	Switzerland	20 Sep 29	Dispute Settlement	102LTS123	302357
Czechoslovakia	Turkey	11 Oct 24	General Amity	38LTS317	300987
Czechoslovakia	Turkey	31 May 27	Admin Cooperation	75LTS79	301753
Czechoslovakia	Turkey	31 May 27	General Trade	71LTS335	301674
Czechoslovakia	Turkey	22 Aug 30	Admin Cooperation	138LTS311	303195
Czechoslovakia	Turkey	22 Aug 30	Extradition	138LTS375	303196
Czechoslovakia	Turkey	17 Mar 31	Dispute Settlement	133LTS151	303065
Czechoslovakia	UK Great Britain	04 Aug 21	Sanitation	16LTS157	300406
Czechoslovakia	UK Great Britain	31 Jan 23	Customs	20LTS53	300506
Czechoslovakia	UK Great Britain	14 Jul 23	General Trade	29LTS377	300748
Czechoslovakia	UK Great Britain	01 Feb 26	Customs	49LTS175	301181
Czechoslovakia	UK Great Britain	04 Jun 26	Extradition	59LTS269	301397
Czechoslovakia	UK Great Britain	11 Jun 26	Admin Cooperation	48LTS425	301173
Czechoslovakia	UK Great Britain	15 Feb 35	Admin Cooperation	161LTS389	303727
Czechoslovakia	UK Great Britain	04 Mar 35	Consul/Citizenship	160LTS283	303698
Czechoslovakia	UK Great Britain	05 Aug 42	General Amity	204LTS377	304816
Czechoslovakia	United Arab Rep	16 Mar 30	General Economic	107LTS179	302475
Czechoslovakia	USA (United States)	05 Dec 24	General Economic	56LTS271	301335
Czechoslovakia	USA (United States)	02 Jul 25	Extradition	50LTS143	301200
Czechoslovakia	USA (United States)	16 Jul 28	Consul/Citizenship	96LTS301	302208
Czechoslovakia	USA (United States)	16 Aug 28	Dispute Settlement	89LTS219	302017
Czechoslovakia	USA (United States)	16 Aug 28	Dispute Settlement	89LTS225	302018
Czechoslovakia	USA (United States)	29 Mar 35	General Trade	159LTS155	303659
Czechoslovakia	USA (United States)	29 Apr 35	Extradition	162LTS83	303736
Czechoslovakia	USA (United States)	07 Mar 38	General Trade	200LTS87	304687
Czechoslovakia	USA (United States)	18 May 38	Customs	199LTS305	304680
Czechoslovakia	USSR (Soviet Union)	25 Mar 35	Patents/Copyrights	161LTS309	303719
Czechoslovakia	USSR (Soviet Union)	25 Mar 35	General Economic	161LTS257	303718
Czechoslovakia	USSR (Soviet Union)	16 May 35	General Amity	159LTS347	303677
Czechoslovakia	USSR (Soviet Union)	08 Jun 35	Postal Service	167LTS181	303865
Czechoslovakia	USSR (Soviet Union)	16 Nov 35	Consul/Citizenship	169LTS143	303918

PARTY ONE	PARTY TWO	DATE	TOPIC	CITATION	NUMBER
Czechoslovakia	Yugoslavia	30 Mar 31	General Economic	125LTS273	302861
Czechoslovakia	Yugoslavia	08 Jun 32	Finance	139LTS45	303203
Czechoslovakia	Yugoslavia	24 Feb 36	Taxation	187LTS185	304338
Czechoslovakia	Yugoslavia	10 Nov 36	General Trade	186LTS191	304311
Dahomey	Multilateral	25 Sep 26	ILO Labor	60LTS253	301414
Dahomey	Multilateral	20 Apr 29	Admin Cooperation	112LTS371	302623
Dahomey	Multilateral	11 Oct 33	Consul/Citizenship	150LTS431	303476
Danube Commission	Multilateral	28 Jun 32	Admin Cooperation	140LTS191	303237
Danzig	Finland	08 Jun 31	Visas	120LTS291	302772
Danzig	Multilateral	09 Sep 86*	Patents/Copyrights	123LTS233	302816
Danzig	Multilateral	13 Nov 08	General Ad Hoc	1LTS217	300015
Danzig	Multilateral	12 Jan 12	Sanitation	4LTS281	300112
Danzig	Multilateral	23 Jan 12	Sanitation	8LTS187	300222
Danzig	Multilateral	05 Jun 12	Telecommunications	1LTS135	300013
Danzig	Multilateral	20 Mar 14	Patents/Copyrights	1LTS243	300016
Danzig	Multilateral	30 Jun 20	Patents/Copyrights	1LTS59	300008
Danzig	Multilateral	20 Apr 21	Water Transport	7LTS73	300174
Danzig	Multilateral	20 Apr 21	Land Transport	7LTS11	300171
Danzig	Multilateral	24 Sep 23	Dispute Settlement	27LTS157	300678
Danzig	Multilateral	09 Dec 23	General Economic	58LTS315	301380
Danzig	Multilateral	09 Dec 23	Land Transport	47LTS55	301129
Danzig	Multilateral	09 Dec 23	Non-IBRD Project	36LTS76	300905
Danzig	Multilateral	31 Mar 24	Sanitation	27LTS211	300685
Danzig	Multilateral	28 Aug 24	Postal Service	40LTS307	301004
Danzig	Multilateral	28 Aug 24	Postal Service	40LTS437	301005
Danzig	Multilateral	28 Aug 24	Postal Service	41LTS55	301007
Danzig	Multilateral	28 Aug 24	Postal Service	41LTS9	301006
Danzig	Multilateral	28 Aug 24	Postal Service	40LTS19	301002
Danzig	Multilateral	28 Aug 24	Postal Service	41LTS97	301008
Danzig	Multilateral	28 Aug 24	Postal Service	40LTS249	301003
Danzig	Multilateral	23 Oct 24	General Transport	77LTS367	301778
Danzig	Multilateral	23 Oct 24	Land Transport	78LTS17	301779
Danzig	Multilateral	19 Feb 25	Admin Cooperation	81LTS317	301845
Danzig	Multilateral	19 Aug 25	Customs	42LTS73	301033
Danzig	Multilateral	29 Oct 25	Telecommunications	57LTS201	301365
Danzig	Multilateral	06 Nov 25	Other Economic	74LTS319	301744
Danzig	Multilateral	06 Nov 25	Patents/Copyrights	74LTS289	301743
Danzig	Multilateral	06 Nov 25	Patents/Copyrights	74LTS327	301745
Danzig	Multilateral	06 Nov 25	Other Economic	74LTS341	301746
Danzig	Multilateral	31 Dec 25	Territory Boundary	79LTS167	301809
Danzig	Multilateral	24 Apr 26	Land Transport	108LTS123	302505
Danzig	Multilateral	24 Apr 26	Land Transport	97LTS83	302220
Danzig	Multilateral	21 Jun 26	Sanitation	78LTS229	301793
Danzig	Multilateral	12 Jul 27	Direct Aid	135LTS247	303115
Danzig	Multilateral	10 Sep 27	Postal Service	75LTS7	301749
Danzig	Multilateral	10 Sep 27	Postal Service	75LTS39	301750
Danzig	Multilateral	26 Sep 27	Dispute Settlement	92LTS301	302096
Danzig	Multilateral	25 Nov 27	Telecommunications	84LTS97	301905
Danzig	Multilateral	22 May 28	Telecommunications	85LTS99	301925
Danzig	Multilateral	27 Aug 28	General Military	94LTS57	302137
Danzig	Multilateral	20 Apr 29	Admin Cooperation	112LTS371	302623
Danzig	Multilateral	31 May 29	Water Transport	136LTS81	303127
Danzig	Multilateral	14 Jun 29	Visas	94LTS275	302148
Danzig	Multilateral	28 Jun 29	Postal Service	103LTS321	302372
Danzig	Multilateral	28 Jun 29	Postal Service	103LTS249	302371
Danzig	Multilateral	28 Jun 29	Postal Service	103LTS71	302370
Danzig	Multilateral	28 Jun 29	Postal Service	103LTS429	302374
Danzig	Multilateral	28 Jun 29	Postal Service	103LTS5	302369
Danzig	Multilateral	28 Jun 29	Postal Service	102LTS245	302368
Danzig	Multilateral	28 Jun 29	Postal Service	103LTS377	302373
Danzig	Multilateral	17 Dec 29	Specific Resources	115LTS93	302679
Danzig	Multilateral	12 Apr 30	Admin Cooperation	179LTS89	304137
Danzig	Multilateral	12 Apr 30	Admin Cooperation	179LTS115	304138
Danzig	Multilateral	07 Jun 30	Finance	143LTS257	303313
Danzig	Multilateral	07 Jun 30	Finance	143LTS317	303314
Danzig	Multilateral	07 Jun 30	Finance	143LTS337	303315
Danzig	Multilateral	23 Oct 30	Water Transport	125LTS95	302849
Danzig	Multilateral	23 Oct 30	Water Transport	112LTS21	302603
Danzig	Multilateral	19 Mar 31	Admin Cooperation	143LTS7	303301
Danzig	Multilateral	19 Mar 31	Finance	143LTS407	303317
Danzig	Multilateral	19 Mar 31	Finance	143LTS355	303316
Danzig	Multilateral	30 Mar 31	Land Transport	150LTS247	303459
Danzig	Multilateral	30 Mar 31	Taxation	138LTS149	303185
Danzig	Multilateral	13 Jul 31	Other HEW	139LTS301	303219
Danzig	Multilateral	15 Oct 31	Water Transport	125LTS83	302847
Danzig	Multilateral	15 Oct 31	Water Transport	125LTS89	302848
Danzig	Multilateral	02 Sep 32	Land Transport	154LTS123	303543
Danzig	Multilateral	09 Dec 32	Telecommunications	151LTS5	303479
Danzig	Multilateral	11 Mar 33	Water Transport	135LTS301	303119
Danzig	Multilateral	19 Jun 33	Gen Communications	154LTS133	303544
Danzig	Multilateral	11 Oct 33	Consul/Citizenship	150LTS431	303476
Danzig	Multilateral	23 Nov 33	Land Transport	192LTS389	304484
Danzig	Multilateral	23 Nov 33	Land Transport	192LTS327	304483
Danzig	Multilateral	20 Mar 34	Postal Service	175LTS73	304050
Danzig	Multilateral	20 Mar 34	Postal Service	174LTS171	304048
Danzig	Multilateral	20 Mar 34	Postal Service	175LTS269	304051
Danzig	Multilateral	20 Mar 34	Postal Service	176LTS55	304054
Danzig	Multilateral	02 Jun 34	Patents/Copyrights	205LTS179	304834
Danzig	Multilateral	15 Sep 36	Scientific Project	178LTS439	304126
Danzig	Multilateral	23 May 39	Postal Service	202LTS159	304742
Danzig	Norway	07 Apr 30	Visas	100LTS391	302308
Danzig	Poland	09 Nov 20	Territory Boundary	6LTS189	300153
Danzig	Poland	24 Oct 21	Recognition	116LTS5	302699
Danzig	UK Great Britain	13 Jan 37	Postal Service	178LTS87	304109
Denmark	Argentina	16 Nov 27	Non-ILO Labor	165LTS177	303809
Denmark	Argentina	03 May 28	Sanitation	168LTS309	303907
Denmark	Austria	30 Jun 23	General Trade	18LTS189	300463
Denmark	Austria	30 Jun 23	General Trade	18LTS195	300464
Denmark	Austria	19 Dec 25	Education	57LTS121	301358
Denmark	Austria	11 Jun 27	Visas	68LTS87	301572
Denmark	Austria	06 Apr 28	General Trade	85LTS423	301943
Denmark	Austria	05 Aug 32	Air Transport	132LTS165	303036
Denmark	Belgium	28 Jun 23	Air Transport	20LTS59	300507
Denmark	Belgium	25 Oct 26	Extradition	58LTS259	301376
Denmark	Belgium	13 Mar 27	Dispute Settlement	67LTS117	301542
Denmark	Belgium	12 Dec 28	Taxation	107LTS363	302492
Denmark	Belgium	14 Mar 32	Extradition	139LTS39	303202
Denmark	Belgium	27 Jul 34	Health/Educ/Welfare	150LTS351	303467
Denmark	Belgium	22 May 35	Admin Cooperation	159LTS255	303669
Denmark	Belgium	16 Sep 37	Visas	197LTS67	304606
Denmark	Bolivia	09 Nov 31	General Economic	147LTS27	303387
Denmark	Brazil	29 Apr 29	Admin Cooperation	89LTS295	302024
Denmark	Brazil	30 Nov 31	Customs	128LTS29	302934
Denmark	Brazil	05 Aug 32	Health/Educ/Welfare	132LTS211	303039
Denmark	Brazil	30 Jul 36	General Trade	194LTS81	304510
Denmark	Bulgaria	11 Jul 22	Mostfavored Nation	12LTS225	300314
Denmark	Bulgaria	07 Dec 35	Dispute Settlement	182LTS183	304211
Denmark	Canada	18 Jun 29	Taxation	95LTS81	302167
Denmark	Chile	23 Dec 31	Dispute Settlement	145LTS77	303346
Denmark	Chile	22 Aug 34	Patents/Copyrights	154LTS181	303546
Denmark	China	12 Dec 28	General Amity	91LTS207	302062
Denmark	Colombia	21 Jun 29	General Economic	125LTS113	302850
Denmark	Czechoslovakia	16 Jan 22	Finance	14LTS267	300378
Denmark	Czechoslovakia	31 Jan 24	General Trade	23LTS139	300585
Denmark	Czechoslovakia	02 Jun 24	Education	57LTS115	301357
Denmark	Czechoslovakia	19 May 25	General Amity	36LTS113	300908
Denmark	Czechoslovakia	24 Jul 25	Visas	37LTS97	300948
Denmark	Czechoslovakia	30 Nov 26	Dispute Settlement	67LTS105	301541
Denmark	Czechoslovakia	21 Jun 29	Visas	91LTS351	302075
Denmark	Czechoslovakia	07 Oct 31	Extradition	127LTS103	302911

PARTY ONE	PARTY TWO	DATE	TOPIC	CITATION	NUMBER
Denmark	Czechoslovakia	04 Jul 32	Customs	143LTS251	303312
Denmark	Estonia	07 Apr 22	Water Transport	14LTS243	300375
Denmark	Estonia	27 Jul 23	Patents/Copyrights	19LTS259	300500
Denmark	Estonia	27 Jul 23	Patents/Copyrights	19LTS253	300499
Denmark	Estonia	07 Sep 23	General Trade	23LTS73	300577
Denmark	Estonia	18 Dec 26	Dispute Settlement	63LTS363	301500
Denmark	Estonia	09 May 27	Admin Cooperation	72LTS25	301687
Denmark	Estonia	12 Dec 29	Admin Cooperation	98LTS341	302254
Denmark	Estonia	13 May 30	Extradition	106LTS159	302443
Denmark	Estonia	16 Jan 31	Water Transport	112LTS215	302615
Denmark	Estonia	01 Nov 34	Admin Cooperation	154LTS175	303545
Denmark	Finland	27 Jul 20	Telecommunications	19LTS71	300484
Denmark	Finland	22 May 22	Postal Service	9LTS435	300270
Denmark	Finland	12 Feb 23	Customs	18LTS71	300454
Denmark	Finland	12 Feb 23	Extradition	18LTS33	300452
Denmark	Finland	21 Apr 23	Milit Servic/Citiz	17LTS57	300428
Denmark	Finland	03 Aug 23	General Trade	21LTS269	300547
Denmark	Finland	30 Nov 23	Non-ILO Labor	22LTS427	300571
Denmark	Finland	27 Jun 24	Dispute Settlement	33LTS131	300839
Denmark	Finland	31 Jul 24	Postal Service	29LTS183	300741
Denmark	Finland	04 Jun 25	Water Transport	37LTS24	300946
Denmark	Finland	19 Oct 25	Taxation	47LTS259	301140
Denmark	Finland	30 Jan 26	Dispute Settlement	51LTS367	301242
Denmark	Finland	14 May 30	Postal Service	105LTS455	302433
Denmark	Finland	30 Jun 30	Land Transport	105LTS179	302411
Denmark	Finland	09 Jul 31	Water Transport	123LTS393	302826
Denmark	Finland	12 Dec 31	Taxation	112LTS29	302604
Denmark	Finland	18 Jul 35	Admin Cooperation	161LTS205	303712
Denmark	Finland	02 Dec 37	Taxation	187LTS379	304345
Denmark	France	25 Feb 25	Consul/Citizenship	33LTS277	300852
Denmark	France	19 Oct 25	Mostfavored Nation	38LTS325	300988
Denmark	France	05 Jul 26	Dispute Settlement	71LTS455	301684
Denmark	France	23 Jan 28	Admin Cooperation	71LTS267	301667
Denmark	France	14 Jan 30	Education	100LTS327	302304
Denmark	France	28 Feb 30	General Economic	101LTS17	302316
Denmark	France	01 Aug 30	Air Transport	108LTS115	302504
Denmark	France	31 Jul 34	General Economic	150LTS381	303471
Denmark	France	28 Jan 35	Non-ILO Labor	158LTS11	303619
Denmark	France	21 Sep 35	Admin Cooperation	162LTS383	303751
Denmark	Germany	30 Aug 20	Telecommunications	14LTS257	300377
Denmark	Germany	12 Jul 21	Visas	26LTS151	300645
Denmark	Germany	12 Jul 21	Visas	26LTS163	300646
Denmark	Germany	10 Apr 22	Water Transport	44LTS389	301095
Denmark	Germany	10 Apr 22	Territory Boundary	29LTS9	300730
Denmark	Germany	10 Apr 22	Territory Boundary	10LTS73	300274
Denmark	Germany	25 Apr 22	Air Transport	18LTS227	300466
Denmark	Germany	31 Mar 23	Extradition	17LTS181	300436
Denmark	Germany	29 Nov 24	Admin Cooperation	31LTS131	300790
Denmark	Germany	18 Apr 25	Water Transport	37LTS103	300949
Denmark	Germany	20 Mar 26	Visas	53LTS377	301267
Denmark	Germany	20 Mar 26	General Trade	57LTS131	301359
Denmark	Germany	20 Mar 26	Customs	51LTS317	301237
Denmark	Germany	12 Apr 26	Customs	48LTS237	301165
Denmark	Germany	01 May 26	Visas	107LTS229	302480
Denmark	Germany	28 Oct 26	Milit Servic/Citiz	57LTS185	301363
Denmark	Germany	23 Feb 27	Dispute Settlement	61LTS325	301444
Denmark	Germany	08 Nov 27	Customs	70LTS83	301625
Denmark	Germany	14 Feb 28	Taxation	71LTS285	301669
Denmark	Germany	14 Oct 29	Water Transport	98LTS211	302248
Denmark	Germany	03 Jul 30	General Transport	105LTS427	302430
Denmark	Germany	23 Jun 31	Extradition	119LTS321	302753
Denmark	Germany	06 Jan 32	Admin Cooperation	126LTS333	302892
Denmark	Germany	19 Jul 33	Non-ILO Labor	170LTS385	303947
Denmark	Germany	15 Dec 33	Culture	171LTS9	303948
Denmark	Germany	13 Jan 34	Taxation	144LTS379	303340
Denmark	Germany	01 Mar 34	General Trade	150LTS31	303451
Denmark	Germany	24 Jan 35	General Trade	160LTS155	303689
Denmark	Germany	25 May 35	Territory Boundary	159LTS389	303680
Denmark	Germany	09 Jan 36	Land Transport	166LTS135	303835
Denmark	Germany	30 Jan 36	Commodity Trade	174LTS155	304046
Denmark	Germany	17 Jun 36	Admin Cooperation	171LTS163	303958
Denmark	Germany	23 Dec 36	Commodity Trade	174LTS165	304047
Denmark	Germany	27 Nov 37	General Trade	183LTS175	304234
Denmark	Germany	11 Nov 38	General Trade	193LTS79	304488
Denmark	Germany	31 May 39	General Amity	197LTS37	304603
Denmark	Germany	22 Dec 39	Commodity Trade	199LTS87	304669
Denmark	Great Britain	11 Jun 29	Water Transport	93LTS401	302128
Denmark	Greece	10 Dec 24	General Economic	31LTS227	300798
Denmark	Greece	29 Sep 27	Mostfavored Nation	62LTS219	301464
Denmark	Greece	22 Aug 28	General Economic	94LTS263	302147
Denmark	Greece	13 Apr 33	Dispute Settlement	150LTS465	303478
Denmark	Haiti	05 Apr 28	Dispute Settlement	99LTS19	302264
Denmark	Haiti	21 Oct 37	General Trade	190LTS231	304422
Denmark	Hungary	04 Jun 25	General Amity	36LTS119	300909
Denmark	Iceland	26 Jun 20	Postal Service	12LTS323	300324
Denmark	Iceland	27 Aug 21	Postal Service	12LTS345	300325
Denmark	Iceland	09 Oct 22	Humanitarian	14LTS13	300364
Denmark	Iceland	30 Sep 24	Water Transport	32LTS355	300825
Denmark	Iceland	11 Aug 27	Taxation	75LTS345	301757
Denmark	Iceland	13 Oct 27	Non-ILO Labor	67LTS411	301562
Denmark	Iceland	30 Nov 27	Postal Service	71LTS43	301653
Denmark	Iceland	27 Jun 30	Dispute Settlement	118LTS121	302717
Denmark	Iceland	11 Jul 31	Taxation	141LTS323	303273
Denmark	India	16 Dec 30	Postal Service	114LTS73	302656
Denmark	India	08 Aug 32	Water Transport	140LTS369	303246
Denmark	Irish Free State	25 Apr 34	Taxation	149LTS31	303430
Denmark	Italy	26 Oct 27	Consul/Citizenship	68LTS229	301586
Denmark	Italy	11 Dec 29	Extradition	97LTS373	302235
Denmark	Italy	03 Feb 31	Admin Cooperation	113LTS45	302634
Denmark	Japan	22 May 22	Water Transport	14LTS247	300376
Denmark	Japan	05 Jun 26	Water Transport	55LTS219	301317
Denmark	Japan	15 Oct 27	Taxation	71LTS75	301655
Denmark	Japan	23 Jul 36	Admin Cooperation	171LTS279	303964
Denmark	Latvia	03 Apr 24	General Trade	33LTS393	300860
Denmark	Latvia	09 Jan 29	General Trade	86LTS37	301948
Denmark	Latvia	28 Feb 30	Dispute Settlement	113LTS27	302632
Denmark	Latvia	28 Aug 30	Extradition	113LTS169	302644
Denmark	Latvia	14 Feb 35	Admin Cooperation	158LTS21	303621
Denmark	Lithuania	18 Jul 23	General Trade	20LTS197	300518
Denmark	Lithuania	11 Dec 26	Dispute Settlement	67LTS333	301555
Denmark	Lithuania	21 Jun 30	General Economic	114LTS151	302662
Denmark	Lithuania	17 Jan 34	Patents/Copyrights	149LTS43	303432
Denmark	Lithuania	20 Dec 34	Admin Cooperation	162LTS347	303748
Denmark	Lithuania	20 Dec 34	Admin Cooperation	155LTS237	303579
Denmark	Luxembourg	23 Feb 32	Admin Cooperation	127LTS211	302920
Denmark	Malaya	23 Oct 34	Postal Service	155LTS141	303575
Denmark	Multilateral	09 Sep 86*	Patents/Copyrights	123LTS233	302816
Denmark	Multilateral	18 Mar 04	Humanitarian	1LTS83	300011
Denmark	Multilateral	13 Nov 08	General Ad Hoc	1LTS217	300015
Denmark	Multilateral	12 Jan 12	Sanitation	4LTS281	300112
Denmark	Multilateral	05 Jun 12	Telecommunications	1LTS135	300013
Denmark	Multilateral	20 Mar 14	Patents/Copyrights	1LTS243	300016
Denmark	Multilateral	18 Jan 20	Admin Cooperation	12LTS321	300323
Denmark	Multilateral	09 Feb 20	Territory Boundary	2LTS7	300041
Denmark	Multilateral	01 May 20	Air Transport	11LTS173	300297
Denmark	Multilateral	11 May 20	Finance	1LTS15	300001
Denmark	Multilateral	21 Jun 20	Health/Educ/Welfare	8LTS65	300207
Denmark	Multilateral	30 Jun 20	Patents/Copyrights	1LTS59	300008
Denmark	Multilateral	05 Jul 20	Dispute Settlement	2LTS241	300070
Denmark	Multilateral	16 Dec 20	General IGO	6LTS379	300170

PARTY ONE	PARTY TWO	DATE	TOPIC	CITATION	NUMBER
Denmark	Multilateral	29 Dec 20	Telecommunications	13LTS281	300359
Denmark	Multilateral	20 Apr 21	Water Transport	7LTS65	300173
Denmark	Multilateral	20 Apr 21	Water Transport	7LTS35	300172
Denmark	Multilateral	20 Apr 21	Land Transport	7LTS11	300171
Denmark	Multilateral	20 Apr 21	Water Transport	7LTS73	300174
Denmark	Multilateral	05 Aug 21	Admin Cooperation	27LTS349	300695
Denmark	Multilateral	05 Oct 21	IGO Establishment	51LTS361	301241
Denmark	Multilateral	05 Oct 21	Admin Cooperation	29LTS79	300735
Denmark	Multilateral	05 Oct 21	Admin Cooperation	29LTS73	300734
Denmark	Multilateral	05 Oct 21	Admin Cooperation	29LTS67	300733
Denmark	Multilateral	06 Oct 21	General Economic	17LTS45	300427
Denmark	Multilateral	20 Oct 21	Peace/Disarmament	9LTS211	300255
Denmark	Multilateral	06 Feb 22	Customs	38LTS267	300981
Denmark	Multilateral	06 Feb 22	General Trade	38LTS277	300982
Denmark	Multilateral	31 Mar 22	Humanitarian	9LTS415	300269
Denmark	Multilateral	05 Jul 22	Reparations	13LTS237	300355
Denmark	Multilateral	18 Aug 22	Telecommunications	13LTS289	300360
Denmark	Multilateral	11 Jul 23	Admin Cooperation	18LTS85	300456
Denmark	Multilateral	24 Sep 23	Dispute Settlement	27LTS157	300678
Denmark	Multilateral	03 Nov 23	Customs	30LTS371	300775
Denmark	Multilateral	09 Dec 23	Water Transport	58LTS284	301379
Denmark	Multilateral	09 Dec 23	Non-IBRD Project	36LTS76	300905
Denmark	Multilateral	09 Dec 23	General Economic	58LTS315	301380
Denmark	Multilateral	09 Dec 23	Land Transport	47LTS55	301129
Denmark	Multilateral	25 Jan 24	Sanitation	57LTS135	301360
Denmark	Multilateral	22 Mar 24	Finance	25LTS171	300605
Denmark	Multilateral	31 Mar 24	Sanitation	27LTS211	300685
Denmark	Multilateral	04 Jul 24	Admin Cooperation	51LTS227	301231
Denmark	Multilateral	26 Jul 24	Postal Service	30LTS271	300771
Denmark	Multilateral	25 Aug 24	Water Transport	120LTS123	302763
Denmark	Multilateral	28 Aug 24	Postal Service	41LTS55	301007
Denmark	Multilateral	28 Aug 24	Postal Service	41LTS97	301008
Denmark	Multilateral	28 Aug 24	Postal Service	40LTS249	301003
Denmark	Multilateral	28 Aug 24	Postal Service	41LTS9	301006
Denmark	Multilateral	28 Aug 24	Postal Service	40LTS19	301002
Denmark	Multilateral	28 Aug 24	Postal Service	40LTS437	301005
Denmark	Multilateral	28 Aug 24	Postal Service	40LTS307	301004
Denmark	Multilateral	23 Oct 24	Land Transport	78LTS17	301779
Denmark	Multilateral	23 Oct 24	General Transport	77LTS367	301778
Denmark	Multilateral	01 Dec 24	Sanitation	78LTS351	301794
Denmark	Multilateral	19 Feb 25	Admin Cooperation	81LTS317	301845
Denmark	Multilateral	17 Jun 25	Peace/Disarmament	94LTS65	302138
Denmark	Multilateral	19 Aug 25	Customs	42LTS73	301033
Denmark	Multilateral	29 Oct 25	Telecommunications	57LTS201	301365
Denmark	Multilateral	06 Nov 25	Patents/Copyrights	74LTS289	301743
Denmark	Multilateral	31 Dec 25	Territory Boundary	79LTS167	301809
Denmark	Multilateral	28 Jan 26	Water Transport	51LTS9	301219
Denmark	Multilateral	10 Apr 26	Water Transport	176LTS199	304062
Denmark	Multilateral	10 Apr 26	Water Transport	120LTS187	302765
Denmark	Multilateral	24 Apr 26	Land Transport	108LTS123	302505
Denmark	Multilateral	12 May 26	Refugees	89LTS47	302004
Denmark	Multilateral	21 Jun 26	Sanitation	78LTS229	301793
Denmark	Multilateral	25 Sep 26	ILO Labor	60LTS253	301414
Denmark	Multilateral	01 Nov 26	Telecommunications	78LTS109	301782
Denmark	Multilateral	24 Feb 27	Telecommunications	68LTS159	301579
Denmark	Multilateral	10 Sep 27	Postal Service	75LTS39	301750
Denmark	Multilateral	10 Sep 27	Postal Service	75LTS7	301749
Denmark	Multilateral	26 Sep 27	Dispute Settlement	92LTS301	302096
Denmark	Multilateral	08 Nov 27	General Trade	97LTS391	302238
Denmark	Multilateral	25 Nov 27	Telecommunications	84LTS97	301905
Denmark	Multilateral	11 Jul 28	Commodity Trade	95LTS357	302184
Denmark	Multilateral	11 Jul 28	Commodity Trade	95LTS373	302185
Denmark	Multilateral	27 Aug 28	General Military	94LTS57	302137
Denmark	Multilateral	12 Sep 28	Telecommunications	104LTS43	302377
Denmark	Multilateral	26 Sep 28	Dispute Settlement	93LTS343	302123

PARTY ONE	PARTY TWO	DATE	TOPIC	CITATION	NUMBER
Denmark	Multilateral	25 Oct 28	Consul/Citizenship	84LTS7	301901
Denmark	Multilateral	30 Oct 28	Dispute Settlement	87LTS103	301963
Denmark	Multilateral	22 Nov 28	Culture	111LTS343	302598
Denmark	Multilateral	14 Dec 28	General Economic	110LTS171	302560
Denmark	Multilateral	22 Dec 28	Telecommunications	104LTS103	302381
Denmark	Multilateral	16 Jan 29	Telecommunications	87LTS155	301967
Denmark	Multilateral	20 Apr 29	Admin Cooperation	112LTS371	302623
Denmark	Multilateral	31 May 29	Water Transport	136LTS81	303127
Denmark	Multilateral	28 Jun 29	Postal Service	103LTS71	302370
Denmark	Multilateral	28 Jun 29	Postal Service	103LTS321	302372
Denmark	Multilateral	28 Jun 29	Postal Service	103LTS5	302369
Denmark	Multilateral	28 Jun 29	Postal Service	103LTS429	302374
Denmark	Multilateral	28 Jun 29	Postal Service	103LTS377	302373
Denmark	Multilateral	28 Jun 29	Postal Service	103LTS249	302371
Denmark	Multilateral	28 Jun 29	Postal Service	102LTS245	302368
Denmark	Multilateral	27 Jul 29	Other Military	118LTS343	302734
Denmark	Multilateral	27 Jul 29	Other Military	118LTS303	302733
Denmark	Multilateral	20 Aug 29	Sanitation	98LTS125	302243
Denmark	Multilateral	30 Aug 29	Telecommunications	96LTS129	302195
Denmark	Multilateral	14 Sep 29	UN Charter	165LTS353	303822
Denmark	Multilateral	12 Oct 29	General Transport	137LTS11	303145
Denmark	Multilateral	18 Nov 29	Telecommunications	99LTS415	302287
Denmark	Multilateral	17 Dec 29	Specific Resources	115LTS93	302679
Denmark	Multilateral	25 Feb 30	Telecommunications	101LTS343	302335
Denmark	Multilateral	12 Apr 30	Admin Cooperation	179LTS115	304138
Denmark	Multilateral	12 Apr 30	Admin Cooperation	179LTS89	304137
Denmark	Multilateral	12 Apr 30	Milit Servic/Citiz	178LTS227	304117
Denmark	Multilateral	14 May 30	Postal Service	105LTS353	302428
Denmark	Multilateral	07 Jun 30	Finance	143LTS317	303314
Denmark	Multilateral	07 Jun 30	Finance	143LTS337	303315
Denmark	Multilateral	07 Jun 30	Finance	143LTS257	303313
Denmark	Multilateral	01 Aug 30	Health/Educ/Welfare	128LTS9	302932
Denmark	Multilateral	23 Oct 30	Water Transport	112LTS21	302603
Denmark	Multilateral	22 Dec 30	General Trade	126LTS341	302893
Denmark	Multilateral	06 Feb 31	Admin Cooperation	126LTS121	302877
Denmark	Multilateral	10 Feb 31	Admin Cooperation	126LTS41	302870
Denmark	Multilateral	19 Mar 31	Finance	143LTS355	303316
Denmark	Multilateral	19 Mar 31	Admin Cooperation	143LTS7	303301
Denmark	Multilateral	19 Mar 31	Finance	143LTS407	303317
Denmark	Multilateral	27 Mar 31	ICJ Option Clause	167LTS341	303877
Denmark	Multilateral	28 Mar 31	Customs	119LTS47	302739
Denmark	Multilateral	30 Mar 31	Land Transport	150LTS247	303459
Denmark	Multilateral	30 Mar 31	Taxation	138LTS149	303185
Denmark	Multilateral	06 May 31	Telecommunications	120LTS217	302767
Denmark	Multilateral	13 Jul 31	Other HEW	139LTS301	303219
Denmark	Multilateral	24 Sep 31	Specific Resources	155LTS349	303586
Denmark	Multilateral	15 Oct 31	Water Transport	125LTS83	302847
Denmark	Multilateral	16 Mar 32	Admin Cooperation	139LTS165	303209
Denmark	Multilateral	02 Sep 32	Land Transport	154LTS123	303543
Denmark	Multilateral	09 Dec 32	Telecommunications	151LTS5	303479
Denmark	Multilateral	13 Dec 32	Territory Boundary	139LTS189	303210
Denmark	Multilateral	11 Mar 33	Water Transport	135LTS301	303119
Denmark	Multilateral	29 May 33	Admin Cooperation	192LTS289	304479
Denmark	Multilateral	19 Jun 33	Gen Communications	154LTS133	303544
Denmark	Multilateral	11 Oct 33	Education	155LTS331	303585
Denmark	Multilateral	28 Oct 33	Refugees	159LTS199	303663
Denmark	Multilateral	07 Nov 33	Finance	155LTS115	303574
Denmark	Multilateral	23 Nov 33	Land Transport	192LTS327	304483
Denmark	Multilateral	23 Nov 33	Land Transport	192LTS389	304484
Denmark	Multilateral	20 Mar 34	Finance	176LTS9	304053
Denmark	Multilateral	20 Mar 34	Postal Service	175LTS363	304052
Denmark	Multilateral	20 Mar 34	Postal Service	175LTS5	304049
Denmark	Multilateral	20 Mar 34	Postal Service	176LTS55	304054
Denmark	Multilateral	20 Mar 34	Postal Service	174LTS171	304048
Denmark	Multilateral	20 Mar 34	Postal Service	175LTS269	304051

PARTY ONE	PARTY TWO	DATE	TOPIC	CITATION	NUMBER
Denmark	Multilateral	20 Mar 34	Postal Service	175LTS73	304050
Denmark	Multilateral	26 Apr 34	Admin Cooperation	164LTS63	303789
Denmark	Multilateral	02 Jun 34	Patents/Copyrights	192LTS17	304459
Denmark	Multilateral	25 Jul 34	Other HEW	177LTS59	304080
Denmark	Multilateral	19 Nov 34	Admin Cooperation	164LTS243	303797
Denmark	Multilateral	22 Dec 34	Visas	183LTS145	304230
Denmark	Multilateral	22 Dec 34	Admin Cooperation	183LTS153	304231
Denmark	Multilateral	31 Dec 34	Postal Service	158LTS111	303630
Denmark	Multilateral	26 Jun 36	Other HEW	198LTS299	304648
Denmark	Multilateral	04 Jul 36	Refugees	171LTS75	303952
Denmark	Multilateral	15 Sep 36	Scientific Project	178LTS439	304126
Denmark	Multilateral	23 Sep 36	Gen Communications	186LTS301	304319
Denmark	Multilateral	06 Nov 36	General Military	173LTS353	304025
Denmark	Multilateral	10 Feb 37	General Transport	189LTS313	304391
Denmark	Multilateral	11 Feb 37	Telecommunications	186LTS55	304303
Denmark	Multilateral	03 Mar 37	Admin Cooperation	182LTS127	304205
Denmark	Multilateral	06 Mar 37	Gen Communications	186LTS109	304305
Denmark	Multilateral	31 Mar 37	Commodity Trade	189LTS359	304394
Denmark	Multilateral	08 May 37	Privil/Immunities	182LTS37	304202
Denmark	Multilateral	28 May 37	General Trade	180LTS5	304170
Denmark	Multilateral	21 Jul 37	Admin Cooperation	184LTS271	304250
Denmark	Multilateral	06 Sep 37	Specific Resources	186LTS419	304326
Denmark	Multilateral	15 Sep 37	Gen Communications	186LTS135	304307
Denmark	Multilateral	23 Sep 37	Postal Service	190LTS299	304427
Denmark	Multilateral	02 Oct 37	Education	182LTS263	304216
Denmark	Multilateral	23 Dec 37	Gen Communications	186LTS99	304304
Denmark	Multilateral	10 Feb 38	Refugees	192LTS59	304461
Denmark	Multilateral	11 May 38	General Trade	189LTS237	304386
Denmark	Multilateral	27 May 38	Other Military	188LTS293	304365
Denmark	Multilateral	12 Sep 38	Culture	198LTS111	304630
Denmark	Multilateral	31 Oct 38	Sanitation	198LTS205	304642
Denmark	Multilateral	03 Dec 38	Education	200LTS249	304694
Denmark	Multilateral	23 May 39	Postal Service	202LTS159	304742
Denmark	Netherlands	23 Jul 26	Air Transport	66LTS133	301528
Denmark	Netherlands	23 Oct 26	Non-ILO Labor	72LTS13	301686
Denmark	Netherlands	19 Feb 27	Admin Cooperation	60LTS271	301415
Denmark	Netherlands	08 Nov 30	Taxation	109LTS115	302531
Denmark	Netherlands	15 Jul 31	Land Transport	127LTS329	302926
Denmark	Netherlands	18 Jul 33	Land Transport	152LTS253	303497
Denmark	Netherlands	29 Jul 37	Customs	192LTS137	304467
Denmark	Netherlands	24 Mar 38	Taxation	190LTS225	304421
Denmark	Norway	21 Jul 21	Telecommunications	13LTS357	300362
Denmark	Norway	27 Jul 21	Air Transport	9LTS23	300241
Denmark	Norway	30 Nov 23	Admin Cooperation	22LTS121	300555
Denmark	Norway	27 Jun 24	Dispute Settlement	33LTS173	300842
Denmark	Norway	09 Jul 24	Territory Boundary	27LTS203	300684
Denmark	Norway	15 Jan 26	Dispute Settlement	60LTS311	301418
Denmark	Norway	15 Dec 26	Non-ILO Labor	59LTS255	301396
Denmark	Norway	30 Nov 28	Admin Cooperation	82LTS223	301873
Denmark	Norway	21 Jan 29	Telecommunications	104LTS119	302382
Denmark	Norway	06 Nov 30	Admin Cooperation	109LTS283	302545
Denmark	Norway	05 Aug 31	Taxation	121LTS9	302779
Denmark	Norway	04 Dec 31	Admin Cooperation	128LTS37	302935
Denmark	Norway	08 Jul 33	Water Transport	140LTS149	303232
Denmark	Norway	11 Nov 33	Consul/Citizenship	143LTS25	303302
Denmark	Norway	21 Apr 34	Customs	148LTS331	303419
Denmark	Norway	23 Feb 35	Admin Cooperation	158LTS31	303622
Denmark	Norway	30 Dec 38	General Economic	195LTS121	304540
Denmark	Norway	18 Jun 39	Patents/Copyrights	197LTS227	304615
Denmark	Norway	29 Aug 39	Customs	198LTS231	304644
Denmark	Persia	08 Sep 28	General Amity	82LTS57	301859
Denmark	Persia	20 Feb 34	General Amity	158LTS299	303640
Denmark	Poland	14 Jul 23	Milit Servic/Citiz	19LTS65	300483
Denmark	Poland	22 Mar 24	General Trade	31LTS13	300778
Denmark	Poland	16 Dec 24	Air Transport	32LTS409	300829
Denmark	Poland	23 Apr 26	Dispute Settlement	61LTS245	301437
Denmark	Poland	26 Oct 31	Visas	125LTS337	302862
Denmark	Poland	25 Jan 33	Admin Cooperation	136LTS421	303141
Denmark	Poland	01 May 34	Customs	154LTS221	303548
Denmark	Portugal	09 Apr 23	General Economic	17LTS63	300429
Denmark	Portugal	07 Sep 25	Water Transport	55LTS215	301316
Denmark	Portugal	18 Jun 35	Extradition	163LTS51	303760
Denmark	Romania	08 May 23	General Economic	17LTS31	300425
Denmark	Romania	28 Aug 30	Mostfavored Nation	108LTS165	302506
Denmark	Siam	01 Mar 26	General Economic	47LTS103	301131
Denmark	Siam	05 Nov 37	General Amity	188LTS187	304358
Denmark	Spain	02 Jan 28	General Trade	71LTS271	301668
Denmark	Spain	14 Mar 28	Dispute Settlement	74LTS93	301735
Denmark	Spain	15 Apr 31	Admin Cooperation	115LTS233	302688
Denmark	Spain	10 Oct 34	Extradition	153LTS345	303530
Denmark	Spain	17 Aug 35	General Trade	163LTS307	303773
Denmark	Sweden	26 Jan 20	Water Transport	14LTS273	300379
Denmark	Sweden	08 Jun 21	Telecommunications	14LTS195	300374
Denmark	Sweden	07 Nov 22	Air Transport	14LTS95	300370
Denmark	Sweden	13 Jul 23	Admin Cooperation	18LTS131	300460
Denmark	Sweden	13 Jul 23	Admin Cooperation	18LTS143	300461
Denmark	Sweden	28 Apr 24	Customs	27LTS355	300696
Denmark	Sweden	27 Jun 24	Dispute Settlement	33LTS149	300840
Denmark	Sweden	28 Nov 24	Water Transport	32LTS41	300804
Denmark	Sweden	21 Nov 25	Water Transport	42LTS55	301032
Denmark	Sweden	21 Nov 25	General Trade	42LTS139	301037
Denmark	Sweden	14 Jan 26	Dispute Settlement	51LTS251	301235
Denmark	Sweden	03 Feb 27	Admin Cooperation	109LTS205	302540
Denmark	Sweden	08 Mar 27	Visas	63LTS315	301498
Denmark	Sweden	13 Dec 28	Telecommunications	104LTS55	302378
Denmark	Sweden	28 Feb 29	Telecommunications	104LTS69	302379
Denmark	Sweden	26 Apr 30	Land Transport	101LTS319	302333
Denmark	Sweden	03 Sep 30	Water Transport	106LTS397	302458
Denmark	Sweden	09 Oct 31	Specific Resources	126LTS255	302888
Denmark	Sweden	30 Jan 32	Territory Boundary	127LTS57	302906
Denmark	Sweden	06 May 32	Taxation	130LTS161	302989
Denmark	Sweden	23 Dec 32	Water Transport	136LTS37	303123
Denmark	Sweden	31 Dec 32	Territory Boundary	139LTS205	303211
Denmark	Sweden	16 Aug 33	Consul/Citizenship	164LTS55	303788
Denmark	Sweden	04 Mar 35	Admin Cooperation	158LTS39	303623
Denmark	Sweden	25 Jun 35	Sanitation	160LTS185	303692
Denmark	Sweden	28 Oct 35	Admin Cooperation	166LTS299	303845
Denmark	Sweden	20 Nov 36	Non-ILO Labor	173LTS207	304014
Denmark	Sweden	30 Mar 37	Gen Communications	186LTS117	304306
Denmark	Sweden	10 Jun 38	Admin Cooperation	188LTS461	304371
Denmark	Sweden	30 Dec 38	General Economic	195LTS413	304561
Denmark	Switzerland	30 May 24	General Economic	25LTS415	300632
Denmark	Switzerland	06 Jun 24	Dispute Settlement	34LTS175	300873
Denmark	Switzerland	25 Aug 26	General Amity	69LTS313	301613
Denmark	Turkey	26 Jan 25	General Amity	36LTS317	300931
Denmark	Turkey	22 Mar 26	General Economic	48LTS231	301164
Denmark	Turkey	19 Sep 26	General Economic	56LTS259	301333
Denmark	Turkey	24 Sep 27	Mostfavored Nation	61LTS287	301439
Denmark	Turkey	31 May 30	General Economic	119LTS165	302744
Denmark	Turkey	08 Mar 32	Dispute Settlement	143LTS223	303310
Denmark	UK Great Britain	20 Aug 20	Postal Service	5LTS129	300122
Denmark	UK Great Britain	23 Dec 20	Air Transport	2LTS249	300071
Denmark	UK Great Britain	01 Jun 21	Admin Cooperation	5LTS161	300125
Denmark	UK Great Britain	12 Jul 21	Admin Cooperation	8LTS397	300238
Denmark	UK Great Britain	14 Jul 21	Consul/Citizenship	6LTS181	300151
Denmark	UK Great Britain	01 May 22	Dispute Settlement	12LTS11	300301
Denmark	UK Great Britain	25 Apr 23	Postal Service	22LTS157	300557
Denmark	UK Great Britain	18 Dec 24	Taxation	32LTS89	300808
Denmark	UK Great Britain	18 Dec 24	Admin Cooperation	32LTS287	300819
Denmark	UK Great Britain	04 Jun 25	Consul/Citizenship	36LTS131	300911

PARTY ONE	PARTY TWO	DATE	TOPIC	CITATION	NUMBER
Denmark	UK Great Britain	02 Jun 26	Non-ILO Labor	61LTS353	301445
Denmark	UK Great Britain	04 Jun 26	Dispute Settlement	61LTS185	301432
Denmark	UK Great Britain	29 Nov 32	Admin Cooperation	139LTS9	303201
Denmark	UK Great Britain	24 Apr 33	General Trade	139LTS127	303208
Denmark	UK Great Britain	15 Oct 35	Extradition	169LTS337	303922
Denmark	UK Great Britain	24 Mar 37	Water Transport	178LTS319	304120
Denmark	UK Great Britain	14 Sep 39	Refugees	198LTS141	304634
Denmark	United Arab Rep	07 May 30	General Economic	102LTS137	302358
Denmark	USA (United States)	08 Jun 22	Postal Service	11LTS311	300298
Denmark	USA (United States)	05 Dec 22	Taxation	113LTS381	302649
Denmark	USA (United States)	29 May 24	Sanitation	27LTS361	300697
Denmark	USA (United States)	14 Jun 28	Dispute Settlement	88LTS173	301995
Denmark	USA (United States)	16 Jan 32	Water Transport	127LTS127	302913
Denmark	USA (United States)	28 Dec 32	Postal Service	140LTS453	303255
Denmark	USA (United States)	11 Nov 33	Postal Service	145LTS113	303349
Denmark	USA (United States)	24 Mar 34	Air Transport	149LTS493	303449
Denmark	USA (United States)	24 Mar 34	Air Transport	149LTS485	303448
Denmark	USA (United States)	24 Mar 34	Air Transport	149LTS471	303447
Denmark	USA (United States)	06 May 36	Extradition	172LTS203	303991
Denmark	USA (United States)	09 Apr 41	General Military	204LTS135	304792
Denmark	USSR (Soviet Union)	23 Apr 23	General Amity	18LTS15	300450
Denmark	USSR (Soviet Union)	18 Jun 24	General Trade	27LTS149	300677
Denmark	USSR (Soviet Union)	29 Jun 25	Water Transport	36LTS251	300926
Denmark	USSR (Soviet Union)	23 Dec 27	Patents/Copyrights	70LTS245	301636
Denmark	USSR (Soviet Union)	29 Jun 36	Postal Service	174LTS93	304040
Denmark	Venezuela	19 Dec 33	Dispute Settlement	158LTS249	303635
Denmark	Yugoslavia	14 Dec 35	Dispute Settlement	184LTS99	304245
Dominican Republic	Haiti	20 Jan 29	Peace/Disarmament	105LTS215	302414
Dominican Republic	Haiti	21 Jan 29	Territory Boundary	105LTS193	302413
Dominican Republic	Haiti	27 Feb 35	Territory Boundary	171LTS89	303953
Dominican Republic	Haiti	31 Jan 38	Territory Boundary	187LTS169	304336
Dominican Republic	Multilateral	20 Aug 10	Patents/Copyrights	155LTS179	303576
Dominican Republic	Multilateral	23 Jan 12	Sanitation	8LTS187	300222
Dominican Republic	Multilateral	23 Jan 12	Sanitation	8LTS187	300222
Dominican Republic	Multilateral	16 Dec 20	General IGO	6LTS379	300170
Dominican Republic	Multilateral	15 Sep 21	Postal Service	30LTS141	300767
Dominican Republic	Multilateral	28 Apr 23	Patents/Copyrights	33LTS47	300832
Dominican Republic	Multilateral	03 May 23	General Trade	33LTS81	300833
Dominican Republic	Multilateral	03 May 23	Customs	33LTS11	300830
Dominican Republic	Multilateral	03 May 23	General Amity	33LTS25	300831
Dominican Republic	Multilateral	28 Aug 24	Postal Service	40LTS307	301004
Dominican Republic	Multilateral	28 Aug 24	Postal Service	40LTS19	301002
Dominican Republic	Multilateral	14 Nov 24	Sanitation	86LTS43	301949
Dominican Republic	Multilateral	19 Feb 25	Admin Cooperation	81LTS317	301845
Dominican Republic	Multilateral	06 Nov 25	Patents/Copyrights	74LTS289	301743
Dominican Republic	Multilateral	21 Jun 26	Sanitation	78LTS229	301793
Dominican Republic	Multilateral	26 Sep 27	Dispute Settlement	92LTS301	302096
Dominican Republic	Multilateral	29 Oct 27	Scientific Project	127LTS27	302903
Dominican Republic	Multilateral	25 Nov 27	Telecommunications	84LTS97	301905
Dominican Republic	Multilateral	18 Feb 28	Patents/Copyrights	132LTS275	303044
Dominican Republic	Multilateral	20 Feb 28	Consul/Citizenship	155LTS289	303582
Dominican Republic	Multilateral	20 Feb 28	Consul/Citizenship	155LTS259	303581
Dominican Republic	Multilateral	20 Feb 28	General Amity	135LTS187	303111
Dominican Republic	Multilateral	20 Feb 28	Air Transport	129LTS223	302963
Dominican Republic	Multilateral	20 Feb 28	Privil/Immunities	132LTS301	303045
Dominican Republic	Multilateral	20 Feb 28	Admin Cooperation	134LTS45	303082
Dominican Republic	Multilateral	20 Feb 28	Consul/Citizenship	132LTS323	303046
Dominican Republic	Multilateral	20 Feb 28	Other Ad Hoc	86LTS111	301950
Dominican Republic	Multilateral	27 Aug 28	General Military	94LTS57	302137
Dominican Republic	Multilateral	22 Nov 28	Culture	111LTS343	302598
Dominican Republic	Multilateral	05 Jan 29	Dispute Settlement	130LTS135	302988
Dominican Republic	Multilateral	05 Jan 29	Dispute Settlement	100LTS399	302309
Dominican Republic	Multilateral	20 Feb 29	Patents/Copyrights	124LTS357	302840
Dominican Republic	Multilateral	31 May 29	Water Transport	136LTS81	303127
Dominican Republic	Multilateral	28 Jun 29	Postal Service	103LTS429	302374

PARTY ONE	PARTY TWO	DATE	TOPIC	CITATION	NUMBER
Dominican Republic	Multilateral	28 Jun 29	Postal Service	103LTS71	302370
Dominican Republic	Multilateral	28 Jun 29	Postal Service	103LTS321	302372
Dominican Republic	Multilateral	28 Jun 29	Postal Service	103LTS377	302373
Dominican Republic	Multilateral	28 Jun 29	Postal Service	103LTS249	302371
Dominican Republic	Multilateral	28 Jun 29	Postal Service	103LTS5	302369
Dominican Republic	Multilateral	28 Jun 29	Postal Service	102LTS245	302368
Dominican Republic	Multilateral	27 Jul 29	Other Military	118LTS303	302733
Dominican Republic	Multilateral	27 Jul 29	Other Military	118LTS343	302734
Dominican Republic	Multilateral	14 Sep 29	UN Charter	165LTS353	303822
Dominican Republic	Multilateral	13 Jul 31	Other HEW	139LTS301	303219
Dominican Republic	Multilateral	10 Nov 31	Postal Service	131LTS327	303023
Dominican Republic	Multilateral	10 Nov 31	Postal Service	131LTS389	303024
Dominican Republic	Multilateral	10 Nov 31	Postal Service	131LTS447	303025
Dominican Republic	Multilateral	09 Dec 32	Telecommunications	151LTS5	303479
Dominican Republic	Multilateral	11 Mar 33	Water Transport	135LTS301	303119
Dominican Republic	Multilateral	10 Oct 33	General Amity	163LTS393	303781
Dominican Republic	Multilateral	26 Dec 33	Recognition	165LTS19	303802
Dominican Republic	Multilateral	26 Dec 33	Extradition	165LTS45	303803
Dominican Republic	Multilateral	20 Mar 34	Postal Service	175LTS5	304049
Dominican Republic	Multilateral	20 Mar 34	Finance	176LTS9	304053
Dominican Republic	Multilateral	20 Mar 34	Postal Service	175LTS363	304052
Dominican Republic	Multilateral	20 Mar 34	Postal Service	175LTS269	304051
Dominican Republic	Multilateral	20 Mar 34	Postal Service	176LTS55	304054
Dominican Republic	Multilateral	20 Mar 34	Postal Service	175LTS73	304050
Dominican Republic	Multilateral	20 Mar 34	Postal Service	174LTS171	304048
Dominican Republic	Multilateral	15 Apr 35	Culture	167LTS289	303874
Dominican Republic	Multilateral	23 Sep 36	Gen Communications	186LTS301	304319
Dominican Republic	Multilateral	23 Dec 36	Admin Cooperation	201LTS295	304721
Dominican Republic	Multilateral	23 Dec 36	Culture	188LTS125	304355
Dominican Republic	Multilateral	23 Dec 36	Dispute Settlement	188LTS53	304352
Dominican Republic	Multilateral	23 Dec 36	Dispute Settlement	195LTS229	304548
Dominican Republic	Multilateral	23 Dec 36	General Amity	188LTS31	304351
Dominican Republic	Multilateral	23 Dec 36	Culture	188LTS151	304356
Dominican Republic	Multilateral	23 Dec 36	Dispute Settlement	188LTS75	304353
Dominican Republic	Multilateral	23 Dec 36	Land Transport	188LTS99	304354
Dominican Republic	Multilateral	23 Dec 36	Peace/Disarmament	188LTS9	304350
Dominican Republic	Multilateral	02 Oct 37	Education	182LTS263	304216
Dominican Republic	Multilateral	31 Oct 38	Sanitation	198LTS205	304642
Dominican Republic	Multilateral	03 Dec 38	Education	200LTS249	304694
Dominican Republic	Multilateral	23 May 39	Postal Service	202LTS159	304742
Dominican Republic	Multilateral	01 Jan 42	General Military	204LTS381	304817
Dominican Republic	Newfoundland	16 Mar 40	General Trade	203LTS141	304757
Dominican Republic	USA (United States)	12 Jun 24	Admin Cooperation	48LTS91	301153
Dominican Republic	USA (United States)	19 Jul 26	Customs	54LTS145	301282
Dominican Republic	USA (United States)	24 Sep 40	Customs	204LTS203	304801
Dutch East Indies	Multilateral	18 Mar 04	Humanitarian	1LTS83	300011
Dutch East Indies	Multilateral	28 Aug 24	Postal Service	41LTS9	301006
Dutch East Indies	Multilateral	29 Oct 25	Telecommunications	57LTS201	301365
Dutch East Indies	Multilateral	25 Nov 27	Telecommunications	84LTS97	301905
Dutch East Indies	Multilateral	16 Apr 29	Specific Resources	126LTS305	302891
Dutch East Indies	Multilateral	11 Mar 33	Water Transport	135LTS301	303119
Dutch East Indies	Multilateral	20 Mar 34	Postal Service	175LTS5	304049
Dutch Indies	Australia	19 Sep 33	Postal Service	144LTS335	303337
Dutch Indies	India	28 Nov 35	Postal Service	168LTS147	303896
Dutch Indies	Malaya	30 Oct 34	Postal Service	157LTS127	303608
Dutch Indies	Malaya	26 Feb 35	Postal Service	160LTS191	303693
Dutch Indies	Multilateral	28 Aug 24	Postal Service	40LTS437	301005
Dutch Indies	Multilateral	28 Aug 24	Postal Service	40LTS307	301004
Dutch Indies	Multilateral	28 Aug 24	Postal Service	41LTS55	301007
Dutch Indies	Multilateral	24 Apr 26	Land Transport	108LTS123	302505
Dutch Indies	Multilateral	26 Sep 27	Dispute Settlement	92LTS301	302096
Dutch Indies	Multilateral	14 Dec 28	General Economic	110LTS171	302560
Dutch Indies	Multilateral	28 Jun 29	Postal Service	103LTS377	302373
Dutch Indies	Multilateral	28 Jun 29	Postal Service	102LTS245	302368
Dutch Indies	Multilateral	28 Jun 29	Postal Service	103LTS71	302370

PARTY ONE	PARTY TWO	DATE	TOPIC	CITATION	NUMBER
Dutch Indies	Multilateral	07 Jun 30	Finance	143LTS337	303315
Dutch Indies	Multilateral	07 Jun 30	Finance	143LTS257	303313
Dutch Indies	Multilateral	07 Jun 30	Finance	143LTS317	303314
Dutch Indies	Multilateral	30 Mar 31	Land Transport	150LTS247	303459
Dutch Indies	Multilateral	09 Dec 32	Telecommunications	151LTS5	303479
Dutch Indies	Multilateral	20 Mar 34	Postal Service	175LTS73	304050
Dutch Indies	Multilateral	20 Mar 34	Postal Service	175LTS363	304052
Dutch Indies	Multilateral	20 Mar 34	Postal Service	175LTS5	304049
Dutch Indies	Multilateral	20 Mar 34	Postal Service	174LTS171	304048
Dutch Indies	Multilateral	20 Mar 34	Postal Service	175LTS269	304051
Dutch Indies	Multilateral	20 Mar 34	Finance	176LTS9	304053
Dutch Indies	Multilateral	23 May 39	Postal Service	202LTS159	304742
Dutch Indies	UK Great Britain	17 Jun 33	Postal Service	144LTS47	303320
Dutch Indies	USA (United States)	04 Oct 34	Postal Service	158LTS395	303646
Ecuador	Belgium	05 Dec 29	Visas	97LTS385	302237
Ecuador	Belgium	06 Jun 33	Extradition	159LTS249	303668
Ecuador	Germany	28 Apr 28	Visas	90LTS163	302033
Ecuador	Multilateral	20 Aug 10	Patents/Copyrights	155LTS179	303576
Ecuador	Multilateral	12 Jan 12	Sanitation	4LTS281	300112
Ecuador	Multilateral	23 Jan 12	Sanitation	8LTS187	300222
Ecuador	Multilateral	05 Jun 12	Telecommunications	1LTS135	300013
Ecuador	Multilateral	10 Sep 19	General Trade	7LTS331	300200
Ecuador	Multilateral	01 May 20	Air Transport	11LTS173	300297
Ecuador	Multilateral	15 Sep 21	Postal Service	30LTS141	300767
Ecuador	Multilateral	28 Apr 23	Patents/Copyrights	33LTS47	300832
Ecuador	Multilateral	03 May 23	General Amity	33LTS25	300831
Ecuador	Multilateral	03 May 23	Customs	33LTS11	300830
Ecuador	Multilateral	03 May 23	General Trade	33LTS81	300833
Ecuador	Multilateral	28 Aug 24	Postal Service	40LTS307	301004
Ecuador	Multilateral	28 Aug 24	Postal Service	40LTS19	301002
Ecuador	Multilateral	29 Oct 25	Telecommunications	57LTS201	301365
Ecuador	Multilateral	21 Jun 26	Sanitation	78LTS229	301793
Ecuador	Multilateral	12 Jul 27	Direct Aid	135LTS247	303115
Ecuador	Multilateral	18 Feb 28	Patents/Copyrights	132LTS275	303044
Ecuador	Multilateral	20 Feb 28	Admin Cooperation	134LTS45	303082
Ecuador	Multilateral	20 Feb 28	Other Ad Hoc	86LTS111	301950
Ecuador	Multilateral	20 Feb 28	Air Transport	129LTS223	302963
Ecuador	Multilateral	20 Feb 28	Consul/Citizenship	132LTS323	303046
Ecuador	Multilateral	20 Feb 28	General Amity	135LTS187	303111
Ecuador	Multilateral	20 Feb 28	Privil/Immunities	132LTS301	303045
Ecuador	Multilateral	20 Feb 28	Consul/Citizenship	155LTS259	303581
Ecuador	Multilateral	20 Feb 28	Consul/Citizenship	155LTS289	303582
Ecuador	Multilateral	27 Aug 28	General Military	94LTS57	302137
Ecuador	Multilateral	05 Jan 29	Dispute Settlement	130LTS135	302988
Ecuador	Multilateral	05 Jan 29	Dispute Settlement	100LTS399	302309
Ecuador	Multilateral	20 Feb 29	Patents/Copyrights	124LTS357	302840
Ecuador	Multilateral	20 Apr 29	Admin Cooperation	112LTS371	302623
Ecuador	Multilateral	28 Jun 29	Postal Service	103LTS71	302370
Ecuador	Multilateral	28 Jun 29	Postal Service	102LTS245	302368
Ecuador	Multilateral	07 Jun 30	Finance	143LTS257	303313
Ecuador	Multilateral	07 Jun 30	Finance	143LTS337	303315
Ecuador	Multilateral	07 Jun 30	Finance	143LTS317	303314
Ecuador	Multilateral	19 Mar 31	Finance	143LTS407	303317
Ecuador	Multilateral	19 Mar 31	Admin Cooperation	143LTS7	303301
Ecuador	Multilateral	19 Mar 31	Finance	143LTS355	303316
Ecuador	Multilateral	13 Jul 31	Other HEW	139LTS301	303219
Ecuador	Multilateral	24 Sep 31	Specific Resources	155LTS349	303586
Ecuador	Multilateral	10 Nov 31	Postal Service	131LTS327	303023
Ecuador	Multilateral	10 Nov 31	Postal Service	131LTS447	303025
Ecuador	Multilateral	10 Nov 31	Postal Service	131LTS389	303024
Ecuador	Multilateral	09 Dec 32	Telecommunications	151LTS5	303479
Ecuador	Multilateral	11 Mar 33	Water Transport	135LTS301	303119
Ecuador	Multilateral	10 Oct 33	General Amity	163LTS393	303781
Ecuador	Multilateral	26 Dec 33	Recognition	165LTS19	303802
Ecuador	Multilateral	26 Dec 33	Extradition	165LTS45	303803

PARTY ONE	PARTY TWO	DATE	TOPIC	CITATION	NUMBER
Ecuador	Multilateral	20 Mar 34	Postal Service	174LTS171	304048
Ecuador	Multilateral	20 Mar 34	Postal Service	175LTS73	304050
Ecuador	Multilateral	04 Jun 34	Extradition	184LTS437	304264
Ecuador	Multilateral	15 Apr 35	Culture	167LTS289	303874
Ecuador	Multilateral	26 Jun 36	Other HEW	198LTS299	304648
Ecuador	Multilateral	23 Dec 36	Culture	188LTS125	304355
Ecuador	Multilateral	23 Dec 36	Dispute Settlement	188LTS53	304352
Ecuador	Multilateral	23 Dec 36	Land Transport	188LTS99	304354
Ecuador	Multilateral	23 Dec 36	General Amity	188LTS31	304351
Ecuador	Multilateral	23 Dec 36	Dispute Settlement	188LTS75	304353
Ecuador	Multilateral	23 Dec 36	Peace/Disarmament	188LTS9	304350
Ecuador	Multilateral	23 Dec 36	Dispute Settlement	195LTS229	304548
Ecuador	Multilateral	23 Dec 36	Culture	188LTS151	304356
Ecuador	Multilateral	03 Dec 38	Education	200LTS249	304694
Ecuador	Multilateral	23 May 39	Postal Service	202LTS159	304742
Ecuador	Netherlands	27 May 37	General Trade	194LTS179	304521
Ecuador	Peru	21 Jun 24	Territory Boundary	27LTS345	300694
Ecuador	Peru	06 Jul 36	Territory Boundary	173LTS359	304026
Ecuador	Sweden	11 Nov 38	Water Transport	195LTS347	304554
Ecuador	UK Great Britain	05 Jan 29	Consul/Citizenship	90LTS369	302048
Ecuador	USA (United States)	12 Jun 36	General Trade	170LTS377	303946
Ecuador	USA (United States)	06 Aug 38	General Trade	193LTS85	304489
Ecuador	USA (United States)	22 Sep 39	Extradition	204LTS169	304796
Ecuador	USA (United States)	12 Dec 40	Military Mission	203LTS305	304771
Ecuador	USA (United States)	12 Dec 40	Military Mission	203LTS327	304773
El Salvador	Belgium	31 Aug 33	Extradition	145LTS129	303350
El Salvador	France	25 Aug 24	Admin Cooperation	93LTS365	302124
El Salvador	Germany	19 Feb 29	Visas	99LTS317	302274
El Salvador	Guatemala	09 Apr 38	Territory Boundary	189LTS275	304390
El Salvador	Multilateral	20 Aug 10	Patents/Copyrights	155LTS179	303576
El Salvador	Multilateral	12 Jan 12	Sanitation	4LTS281	300112
El Salvador	Multilateral	23 Jan 12	Sanitation	8LTS187	300222
El Salvador	Multilateral	16 Dec 20	General IGO	6LTS379	300170
El Salvador	Multilateral	19 Jan 21	Recognition	5LTS9	300113
El Salvador	Multilateral	15 Sep 21	Postal Service	30LTS141	300767
El Salvador	Multilateral	28 Apr 23	Patents/Copyrights	33LTS47	300832
El Salvador	Multilateral	03 May 23	General Trade	33LTS81	300833
El Salvador	Multilateral	03 May 23	Customs	33LTS11	300830
El Salvador	Multilateral	03 May 23	General Amity	33LTS25	300831
El Salvador	Multilateral	24 Sep 23	Dispute Settlement	27LTS157	300678
El Salvador	Multilateral	09 Dec 23	Water Transport	58LTS284	301379
El Salvador	Multilateral	09 Dec 23	Land Transport	47LTS55	301129
El Salvador	Multilateral	31 Mar 24	Sanitation	27LTS211	300685
El Salvador	Multilateral	28 Aug 24	Postal Service	40LTS307	301004
El Salvador	Multilateral	28 Aug 24	Postal Service	40LTS249	301003
El Salvador	Multilateral	28 Aug 24	Postal Service	40LTS19	301002
El Salvador	Multilateral	14 Nov 24	Sanitation	86LTS43	301949
El Salvador	Multilateral	19 Feb 25	Admin Cooperation	81LTS317	301845
El Salvador	Multilateral	17 Jun 25	Peace/Disarmament	94LTS65	302138
El Salvador	Multilateral	21 Jun 26	Sanitation	78LTS229	301793
El Salvador	Multilateral	25 Nov 27	Telecommunications	84LTS97	301905
El Salvador	Multilateral	18 Feb 28	Patents/Copyrights	132LTS275	303044
El Salvador	Multilateral	20 Feb 28	Consul/Citizenship	155LTS259	303581
El Salvador	Multilateral	20 Feb 28	Consul/Citizenship	155LTS289	303582
El Salvador	Multilateral	20 Feb 28	Other Ad Hoc	86LTS111	301950
El Salvador	Multilateral	20 Feb 28	Air Transport	129LTS223	302963
El Salvador	Multilateral	20 Feb 28	Privil/Immunities	132LTS301	303045
El Salvador	Multilateral	20 Feb 28	Consul/Citizenship	132LTS323	303046
El Salvador	Multilateral	20 Feb 28	General Amity	135LTS187	303111
El Salvador	Multilateral	20 Feb 28	Admin Cooperation	134LTS45	303082
El Salvador	Multilateral	05 Jan 29	Dispute Settlement	130LTS135	302988
El Salvador	Multilateral	05 Jan 29	Dispute Settlement	100LTS399	302309
El Salvador	Multilateral	28 Jun 29	Postal Service	102LTS245	302368
El Salvador	Multilateral	28 Jun 29	Postal Service	103LTS71	302370
El Salvador	Multilateral	27 Jul 29	Other Military	118LTS303	302733

PARTY ONE	PARTY TWO	DATE	TOPIC	CITATION	NUMBER
El Salvador	Multilateral	27 Jul 29	Other Military	118LTS343	302734
El Salvador	Multilateral	14 Sep 29	UN Charter	165LTS353	303822
El Salvador	Multilateral	12 Apr 30	Milit Servic/Citiz	178LTS227	304117
El Salvador	Multilateral	12 Apr 30	Admin Cooperation	179LTS89	304137
El Salvador	Multilateral	12 Apr 30	Admin Cooperation	179LTS115	304138
El Salvador	Multilateral	13 Jul 31	Other HEW	139LTS301	303219
El Salvador	Multilateral	10 Nov 31	Postal Service	131LTS447	303025
El Salvador	Multilateral	10 Nov 31	Postal Service	131LTS327	303023
El Salvador	Multilateral	10 Nov 31	Postal Service	131LTS389	303024
El Salvador	Multilateral	09 Dec 32	Telecommunications	151LTS5	303479
El Salvador	Multilateral	29 May 33	Admin Cooperation	192LTS289	304479
El Salvador	Multilateral	10 Oct 33	General Amity	163LTS393	303781
El Salvador	Multilateral	26 Dec 33	Recognition	165LTS19	303802
El Salvador	Multilateral	26 Dec 33	Extradition	165LTS45	303803
El Salvador	Multilateral	20 Mar 34	Postal Service	175LTS73	304050
El Salvador	Multilateral	20 Mar 34	Postal Service	175LTS269	304051
El Salvador	Multilateral	15 Apr 35	Culture	167LTS289	303874
El Salvador	Multilateral	23 Sep 36	Gen Communications	186LTS301	304319
El Salvador	Multilateral	06 Nov 36	General Military	173LTS353	304025
El Salvador	Multilateral	23 Dec 36	General Amity	188LTS31	304351
El Salvador	Multilateral	23 Dec 36	Land Transport	188LTS99	304354
El Salvador	Multilateral	23 Dec 36	Dispute Settlement	188LTS75	304353
El Salvador	Multilateral	23 Dec 36	Peace/Disarmament	188LTS9	304350
El Salvador	Multilateral	23 Dec 36	Culture	188LTS125	304355
El Salvador	Multilateral	23 Dec 36	Dispute Settlement	188LTS53	304352
El Salvador	Multilateral	23 Dec 36	Culture	188LTS151	304356
El Salvador	Multilateral	23 Dec 36	Dispute Settlement	195LTS229	304548
El Salvador	Multilateral	23 Dec 36	Admin Cooperation	201LTS295	304721
El Salvador	Multilateral	08 Dec 38	Gen Communications	202LTS49	304734
El Salvador	Multilateral	23 May 39	Postal Service	202LTS159	304742
El Salvador	Multilateral	01 Jan 42	General Military	204LTS381	304817
El Salvador	Norway	21 Nov 38	General Trade	198LTS157	304636
El Salvador	Spain	15 Jun 35	Culture	165LTS321	303818
El Salvador	Sweden	23 Jun 36	Mostfavored Nation	171LTS291	303966
El Salvador	UK Great Britain	07 Jan 28	General Trade	80LTS231	301828
El Salvador	UK Great Britain	14 Sep 32	General Trade	128LTS417	302945
El Salvador	Uruguay	07 Nov 24	Dispute Settlement	108LTS103	302502
El Salvador	USA (United States)	05 Sep 30	General Amity	134LTS207	303093
El Salvador	USA (United States)	19 Feb 37	General Trade	179LTS219	304150
Eritrea	Multilateral	21 Jun 20	Health/Educ/Welfare	8LTS65	300207
Eritrea	Multilateral	29 Oct 25	Telecommunications	57LTS201	301365
Eritrea	Multilateral	06 Nov 25	Patents/Copyrights	74LTS327	301745
Eritrea	Multilateral	06 Nov 25	Patents/Copyrights	74LTS289	301743
Eritrea	Multilateral	25 Nov 27	Telecommunications	84LTS97	301905
Eritrea	Multilateral	16 Apr 29	Specific Resources	126LTS305	302891
Eritrea	Multilateral	09 Dec 32	Telecommunications	151LTS5	303479
Estonia	Afghanistan	06 Dec 30	General Amity	137LTS445	303174
Estonia	Austria	15 Oct 26	Consul/Citizenship	93LTS137	302106
Estonia	Austria	15 Oct 26	Extradition	74LTS213	301739
Estonia	Austria	11 Dec 28	General Trade	92LTS229	302091
Estonia	Austria	22 Mar 29	Visas	89LTS301	302025
Estonia	Bel-Lux Econ Union	28 Sep 26	General Economic	62LTS433	301475
Estonia	Bel-Lux Econ Union	19 Jun 35	Finance	170LTS243	303940
Estonia	Bel-Lux Econ Union	13 Jan 38	General Trade	185LTS63	304275
Estonia	Belgium	28 Sep 26	Water Transport	60LTS9	301401
Estonia	Belgium	11 Nov 26	Extradition	65LTS405	301523
Estonia	Belgium	08 Feb 27	Consul/Citizenship	74LTS227	301740
Estonia	Belgium	24 Apr 31	Customs	119LTS371	302756
Estonia	Brazil	30 Sep 32	General Trade	134LTS247	303095
Estonia	Bulgaria	11 Feb 28	General Trade	79LTS43	301803
Estonia	China	21 Dec 37	General Amity	194LTS123	304516
Estonia	Czechoslovakia	17 Jul 26	Admin Cooperation	69LTS385	301620
Estonia	Czechoslovakia	17 Jul 26	Extradition	63LTS255	301495
Estonia	Czechoslovakia	20 Jul 27	General Trade	77LTS341	301776
Estonia	Czechoslovakia	09 Jul 29	Dispute Settlement	101LTS423	302341

PARTY ONE	PARTY TWO	DATE	TOPIC	CITATION	NUMBER
Estonia	Denmark	07 Apr 22	Water Transport	14LTS243	300375
Estonia	Denmark	27 Jul 23	Patents/Copyrights	19LTS253	300499
Estonia	Denmark	27 Jul 23	Patents/Copyrights	19LTS259	300500
Estonia	Denmark	07 Sep 23	General Trade	23LTS73	300577
Estonia	Denmark	18 Dec 26	Dispute Settlement	63LTS363	301500
Estonia	Denmark	09 May 27	Admin Cooperation	72LTS25	301687
Estonia	Denmark	12 Dec 29	Admin Cooperation	98LTS341	302254
Estonia	Denmark	13 May 30	Extradition	106LTS159	302443
Estonia	Denmark	16 Jan 31	Water Transport	112LTS215	302615
Estonia	Denmark	01 Nov 34	Admin Cooperation	154LTS175	303545
Estonia	Finland	29 Oct 21	Telecommunications	13LTS167	300350
Estonia	Finland	29 Oct 21	Telecommunications	13LTS159	300349
Estonia	Finland	29 Oct 21	General Trade	13LTS59	300348
Estonia	Finland	28 Nov 22	Telecommunications	19LTS213	300494
Estonia	Finland	18 Mar 24	Admin Cooperation	32LTS119	300811
Estonia	Finland	02 Jan 25	Extradition	43LTS11	301044
Estonia	Finland	20 Apr 25	Telecommunications	51LTS31	301220
Estonia	Finland	10 Dec 25	Non-ILO Labor	50LTS335	301217
Estonia	Finland	17 May 27	Visas	66LTS411	301534
Estonia	Finland	20 Aug 28	Postal Service	85LTS195	301930
Estonia	Finland	12 Jul 30	Other Economic	111LTS321	302596
Estonia	Finland	11 Apr 31	General Economic	124LTS217	302835
Estonia	Finland	17 Jul 31	Water Transport	126LTS93	302873
Estonia	Finland	16 May 33	Claims and Debts	141LTS19	303257
Estonia	Finland	05 Jul 34	General Economic	153LTS167	303516
Estonia	Finland	03 Apr 36	General Economic	168LTS111	303891
Estonia	Finland	16 Apr 36	Telecommunications	171LTS55	303950
Estonia	Finland	12 Sep 36	Air Transport	172LTS345	303999
Estonia	Finland	18 Dec 36	Postal Service	178LTS41	304105
Estonia	Finland	02 Sep 37	General Economic	183LTS93	304229
Estonia	Finland	01 Dec 37	Education	187LTS413	304347
Estonia	Finland	14 Jan 38	Admin Cooperation	185LTS53	304274
Estonia	France	07 Jan 22	General Trade	62LTS9	301452
Estonia	France	15 Mar 29	General Trade	89LTS381	302029
Estonia	France	07 Oct 29	Commodity Trade	104LTS193	302389
Estonia	France	26 Mar 32	Claims and Debts	128LTS51	302937
Estonia	France	27 Apr 33	General Trade	141LTS43	303260
Estonia	France	27 Jul 33	General Trade	141LTS65	303261
Estonia	France	22 Feb 36	General Economic	168LTS105	303890
Estonia	France	16 Oct 37	Finance	183LTS37	304226
Estonia	France	16 Oct 37	General Trade	183LTS41	304227
Estonia	Germany	28 Dec 22	Water Transport	41LTS147	301010
Estonia	Germany	27 Jun 23	General Amity	41LTS155	301012
Estonia	Germany	27 Jun 23	General Trade	41LTS161	301013
Estonia	Germany	09 Jan 25	Extradition	42LTS13	301028
Estonia	Germany	13 Mar 25	Consul/Citizenship	51LTS263	301236
Estonia	Germany	10 Aug 25	Dispute Settlement	63LTS111	301484
Estonia	Germany	25 Nov 25	Admin Cooperation	54LTS79	301275
Estonia	Germany	05 Apr 27	Sanitation	64LTS355	301508
Estonia	Germany	07 Dec 28	General Economic	99LTS259	302273
Estonia	Germany	30 Apr 29	Visas	99LTS325	302275
Estonia	Germany	29 Mar 34	General Trade	148LTS251	303416
Estonia	Germany	24 Oct 37	Finance	184LTS81	304244
Estonia	Germany	24 Oct 37	General Economic	182LTS201	304212
Estonia	Germany	23 Dec 37	Air Transport	189LTS333	304393
Estonia	Germany	07 Jun 39	General Amity	198LTS49	304622
Estonia	Great Britain	12 Oct 26	Postal Service	60LTS387	301422
Estonia	Greece	04 Jan 27	General Economic	69LTS33	301598
Estonia	Greece	25 Nov 37	Finance	184LTS427	304263
Estonia	Hungary	19 Oct 22	General Trade	30LTS347	300774
Estonia	Hungary	01 Nov 23	General Trade	62LTS47	301453
Estonia	Hungary	29 Apr 29	General Economic	96LTS23	302189
Estonia	Hungary	27 Nov 29	Dispute Settlement	106LTS331	302454
Estonia	Hungary	08 Aug 34	Extradition	167LTS153	303863
Estonia	Hungary	13 Oct 37	Education	189LTS433	304400

PARTY ONE	PARTY TWO	DATE	TOPIC	CITATION	NUMBER
Estonia	Hungary	02 Dec 37	General Trade	184LTS395	304259
Estonia	Hungary	19 Jan 38	Visas	185LTS363	304300
Estonia	Iceland	07 Sep 23	General Trade	23LTS131	300584
Estonia	Iceland	30 May 31	Water Transport	119LTS69	302741
Estonia	Italy	01 Jul 28	General Economic	87LTS277	301974
Estonia	Italy	10 Aug 35	Extradition	185LTS287	304295
Estonia	Italy	06 Oct 36	Finance	172LTS189	303989
Estonia	Japan	21 Jun 34	General Economic	150LTS423	303475
Estonia	Latvia	22 Mar 20	Dispute Settlement	2LTS187	300066
Estonia	Latvia	19 Oct 20	Territory Boundary	17LTS189	300437
Estonia	Latvia	12 Jul 21	Extradition	37LTS423	300964
Estonia	Latvia	12 Jul 21	Consul/Citizenship	11LTS87	300291
Estonia	Latvia	24 Jun 22	Sanitation	38LTS57	300967
Estonia	Latvia	31 Oct 23	Water Transport	25LTS321	300621
Estonia	Latvia	01 Nov 23	Territory Boundary	61LTS315	301443
Estonia	Latvia	01 Nov 23	Territory Boundary	25LTS345	300623
Estonia	Latvia	01 Nov 23	Claims and Debts	25LTS341	300622
Estonia	Latvia	01 Nov 23	Other Economic	25LTS354	300624
Estonia	Latvia	01 Nov 23	General Amity	23LTS81	300578
Estonia	Latvia	10 Jan 24	Visas	38LTS103	300968
Estonia	Latvia	02 Apr 24	Land Transport	38LTS113	300969
Estonia	Latvia	28 Oct 25	Specific Resources	54LTS231	301286
Estonia	Latvia	11 Nov 25	Admin Cooperation	42LTS93	301034
Estonia	Latvia	02 Feb 26	Land Transport	64LTS413	301514
Estonia	Latvia	05 Feb 26	Specific Resources	64LTS361	301509
Estonia	Latvia	03 Mar 26	Humanitarian	63LTS13	301476
Estonia	Latvia	28 May 26	Taxation	159LTS291	303672
Estonia	Latvia	05 Feb 27	Customs	62LTS319	301470
Estonia	Latvia	22 Jul 27	Admin Cooperation	73LTS333	301723
Estonia	Latvia	25 Mar 28	General Economic	72LTS195	301692
Estonia	Latvia	15 May 28	Visas	74LTS281	301742
Estonia	Latvia	19 Oct 28	Admin Cooperation	97LTS359	302233
Estonia	Latvia	20 Dec 29	Telecommunications	106LTS173	302444
Estonia	Latvia	05 Sep 30	Territory Boundary	112LTS219	302616
Estonia	Latvia	28 Feb 31	Water Transport	114LTS379	302667
Estonia	Latvia	16 May 31	Taxation	123LTS61	302805
Estonia	Latvia	03 Jun 31	Mostfavored Nation	120LTS235	302769
Estonia	Latvia	14 Nov 32	General Trade	136LTS295	303132
Estonia	Latvia	17 Feb 34	Taxation	159LTS299	303673
Estonia	Latvia	17 Feb 34	General Amity	150LTS103	303457
Estonia	Latvia	17 Feb 34	Education	150LTS299	303463
Estonia	Latvia	17 Feb 34	Sanitation	150LTS391	303472
Estonia	Latvia	10 Apr 35	Finance	159LTS103	303652
Estonia	Latvia	14 Nov 35	Admin Cooperation	166LTS83	303832
Estonia	Latvia	07 Dec 35	General Economic	169LTS101	303915
Estonia	Latvia	07 Dec 35	General Economic	169LTS119	303916
Estonia	Latvia	10 Dec 35	Territory Boundary	168LTS83	303888
Estonia	Latvia	06 Oct 36	Territory Boundary	172LTS221	303994
Estonia	Latvia	10 Feb 37	Admin Cooperation	176LTS287	304067
Estonia	Latvia	10 Feb 37	General Economic	176LTS296	304068
Estonia	Latvia	11 Jan 39	Taxation	194LTS103	304512
Estonia	Latvia	26 May 39	General Trade	198LTS99	304628
Estonia	Lithuania	12 Jul 21	Extradition	43LTS179	301054
Estonia	Lithuania	12 Jul 21	Consul/Citizenship	11LTS99	300292
Estonia	Lithuania	21 May 24	General Transport	62LTS55	301454
Estonia	Lithuania	15 Jan 31	General Economic	114LTS141	302661
Estonia	Lithuania	17 May 33	General Trade	141LTS29	303258
Estonia	Lithuania	13 Jan 34	General Economic	148LTS337	303420
Estonia	Lithuania	10 Dec 35	Patents/Copyrights	168LTS101	303889
Estonia	Lithuania	03 Dec 38	Taxation	193LTS217	304498
Estonia	Mexico	28 Jan 37	General Amity	185LTS39	304272
Estonia	Multilateral	09 Sep 86*	Patents/Copyrights	123LTS233	302816
Estonia	Multilateral	18 Mar 04	Humanitarian	1LTS83	300011
Estonia	Multilateral	23 Jan 12	Sanitation	8LTS187	300222
Estonia	Multilateral	05 Jun 12	Telecommunications	1LTS135	300013

PARTY ONE	PARTY TWO	DATE	TOPIC	CITATION	NUMBER
Estonia	Multilateral	21 Jun 20	Health/Educ/Welfare	8LTS65	300207
Estonia	Multilateral	30 Jun 20	Patents/Copyrights	1LTS59	300008
Estonia	Multilateral	16 Dec 20	General IGO	6LTS379	300170
Estonia	Multilateral	20 Apr 21	Land Transport	7LTS11	300171
Estonia	Multilateral	20 Apr 21	Water Transport	7LTS35	300172
Estonia	Multilateral	20 Apr 21	Water Transport	7LTS73	300174
Estonia	Multilateral	12 Jul 21	Admin Cooperation	37LTS433	300965
Estonia	Multilateral	12 Jul 21	Postal Service	11LTS111	300293
Estonia	Multilateral	05 Aug 21	Admin Cooperation	27LTS349	300695
Estonia	Multilateral	05 Oct 21	IGO Establishment	51LTS361	301241
Estonia	Multilateral	05 Oct 21	Admin Cooperation	29LTS73	300734
Estonia	Multilateral	05 Oct 21	Admin Cooperation	29LTS67	300733
Estonia	Multilateral	05 Oct 21	Admin Cooperation	29LTS79	300735
Estonia	Multilateral	20 Oct 21	Peace/Disarmament	9LTS211	300255
Estonia	Multilateral	17 Mar 22	Dispute Settlement	11LTS167	300296
Estonia	Multilateral	31 Mar 22	Humanitarian	9LTS415	300269
Estonia	Multilateral	24 Sep 23	Dispute Settlement	27LTS157	300678
Estonia	Multilateral	03 Nov 23	Customs	30LTS371	300775
Estonia	Multilateral	09 Dec 23	Water Transport	58LTS284	301379
Estonia	Multilateral	09 Dec 23	Land Transport	47LTS55	301129
Estonia	Multilateral	25 Aug 24	Water Transport	120LTS155	302764
Estonia	Multilateral	25 Aug 24	Water Transport	120LTS123	302763
Estonia	Multilateral	28 Aug 24	Postal Service	40LTS437	301005
Estonia	Multilateral	28 Aug 24	Postal Service	40LTS249	301003
Estonia	Multilateral	28 Aug 24	Postal Service	40LTS19	301002
Estonia	Multilateral	28 Aug 24	Postal Service	41LTS97	301008
Estonia	Multilateral	28 Aug 24	Postal Service	40LTS307	301004
Estonia	Multilateral	23 Oct 24	General Transport	77LTS367	301778
Estonia	Multilateral	23 Oct 24	Land Transport	78LTS17	301779
Estonia	Multilateral	17 Jan 25	Dispute Settlement	38LTS357	300991
Estonia	Multilateral	17 Jun 25	Peace/Disarmament	94LTS65	302138
Estonia	Multilateral	19 Aug 25	Customs	42LTS73	301033
Estonia	Multilateral	29 Oct 25	Land Transport	66LTS147	301529
Estonia	Multilateral	29 Oct 25	Telecommunications	57LTS201	301365
Estonia	Multilateral	06 Nov 25	Patents/Copyrights	74LTS289	301743
Estonia	Multilateral	31 Dec 25	Territory Boundary	79LTS167	301809
Estonia	Multilateral	10 Apr 26	Water Transport	176LTS199	304062
Estonia	Multilateral	10 Apr 26	Water Transport	120LTS187	302765
Estonia	Multilateral	24 Apr 26	Land Transport	108LTS123	302505
Estonia	Multilateral	12 May 26	Refugees	89LTS47	302004
Estonia	Multilateral	25 Sep 26	ILO Labor	60LTS253	301414
Estonia	Multilateral	15 Jun 27	Telecommunications	69LTS375	301619
Estonia	Multilateral	10 Sep 27	Postal Service	75LTS39	301750
Estonia	Multilateral	10 Sep 27	Postal Service	75LTS7	301749
Estonia	Multilateral	26 Sep 27	Dispute Settlement	92LTS301	302096
Estonia	Multilateral	08 Nov 27	General Trade	97LTS391	302238
Estonia	Multilateral	25 Nov 27	Telecommunications	84LTS97	301905
Estonia	Multilateral	30 Jun 28	Refugees	89LTS53	302005
Estonia	Multilateral	30 Jun 28	Refugees	89LTS63	302006
Estonia	Multilateral	27 Aug 28	General Amity	89LTS369	302028
Estonia	Multilateral	27 Aug 28	General Military	94LTS57	302137
Estonia	Multilateral	26 Sep 28	Dispute Settlement	93LTS343	302123
Estonia	Multilateral	20 Apr 29	Admin Cooperation	112LTS371	302623
Estonia	Multilateral	08 May 29	Telecommunications	91LTS337	302074
Estonia	Multilateral	28 Jun 29	Postal Service	103LTS377	302373
Estonia	Multilateral	28 Jun 29	Postal Service	103LTS249	302371
Estonia	Multilateral	28 Jun 29	Postal Service	103LTS5	302369
Estonia	Multilateral	28 Jun 29	Postal Service	103LTS321	302372
Estonia	Multilateral	28 Jun 29	Postal Service	103LTS71	302370
Estonia	Multilateral	28 Jun 29	Postal Service	103LTS429	302374
Estonia	Multilateral	28 Jun 29	Postal Service	102LTS245	302368
Estonia	Multilateral	27 Jul 29	Other Military	118LTS343	302734
Estonia	Multilateral	27 Jul 29	Other Military	118LTS303	302733
Estonia	Multilateral	30 Aug 29	Telecommunications	96LTS117	302194
Estonia	Multilateral	30 Aug 29	Telecommunications	96LTS129	302195

PARTY ONE	PARTY TWO	DATE	TOPIC	CITATION	NUMBER
Estonia	Multilateral	14 Sep 29	UN Charter	165LTS353	303822
Estonia	Multilateral	12 Oct 29	General Transport	137LTS11	303145
Estonia	Multilateral	28 Oct 29	Telecommunications	97LTS71	302219
Estonia	Multilateral	14 Jan 30	Telecommunications	99LTS343	302278
Estonia	Multilateral	25 Feb 30	Telecommunications	101LTS343	302335
Estonia	Multilateral	12 Apr 30	Admin Cooperation	179LTS89	304137
Estonia	Multilateral	12 Apr 30	Admin Cooperation	179LTS115	304138
Estonia	Multilateral	23 Oct 30	Water Transport	125LTS95	302849
Estonia	Multilateral	23 Oct 30	Water Transport	112LTS21	302603
Estonia	Multilateral	27 Mar 31	ICJ Option Clause	167LTS341	303877
Estonia	Multilateral	13 Jul 31	Other HEW	139LTS301	303219
Estonia	Multilateral	11 Dec 31	Commodity Trade	170LTS251	303941
Estonia	Multilateral	02 Sep 32	Land Transport	154LTS123	303543
Estonia	Multilateral	09 Dec 32	Telecommunications	151LTS5	303479
Estonia	Multilateral	19 Jun 33	Gen Communications	154LTS133	303544
Estonia	Multilateral	03 Jul 33	Peace/Disarmament	147LTS67	303391
Estonia	Multilateral	11 Oct 33	Education	155LTS331	303585
Estonia	Multilateral	23 Nov 33	Land Transport	192LTS389	304484
Estonia	Multilateral	23 Nov 33	Land Transport	192LTS327	304483
Estonia	Multilateral	20 Mar 34	Finance	176LTS9	304053
Estonia	Multilateral	20 Mar 34	Postal Service	175LTS73	304050
Estonia	Multilateral	20 Mar 34	Postal Service	176LTS55	304054
Estonia	Multilateral	20 Mar 34	Postal Service	175LTS363	304052
Estonia	Multilateral	20 Mar 34	Postal Service	174LTS171	304048
Estonia	Multilateral	20 Mar 34	Postal Service	175LTS269	304051
Estonia	Multilateral	20 Mar 34	Postal Service	175LTS5	304049
Estonia	Multilateral	12 Sep 34	General Amity	154LTS93	303540
Estonia	Multilateral	22 Dec 34	Admin Cooperation	183LTS153	304231
Estonia	Multilateral	22 Dec 34	Visas	183LTS145	304230
Estonia	Multilateral	14 Nov 35	Admin Cooperation	166LTS87	303833
Estonia	Multilateral	14 Nov 35	Admin Cooperation	166LTS75	303831
Estonia	Multilateral	26 Jun 36	Other HEW	198LTS299	304648
Estonia	Multilateral	15 Sep 36	Scientific Project	178LTS439	304126
Estonia	Multilateral	23 Sep 36	Gen Communications	186LTS301	304319
Estonia	Multilateral	06 Nov 36	General Military	173LTS353	304025
Estonia	Multilateral	02 Oct 37	Education	182LTS263	304216
Estonia	Multilateral	09 Apr 38	Admin Cooperation	191LTS119	304441
Estonia	Multilateral	09 Apr 38	Admin Cooperation	191LTS165	304442
Estonia	Multilateral	23 May 39	Postal Service	202LTS159	304742
Estonia	Netherlands	22 Jul 24	General Economic	48LTS199	301162
Estonia	Netherlands	01 Sep 30	Other Economic	111LTS395	302600
Estonia	Netherlands	08 Mar 33	Extradition	146LTS319	303382
Estonia	Netherlands	22 Nov 38	Customs	195LTS133	304542
Estonia	Netherlands	22 Nov 38	General Trade	193LTS209	304497
Estonia	Norway	28 Jul 26	General Economic	43LTS25	301045
Estonia	Norway	03 Apr 30	Extradition	106LTS147	302442
Estonia	Norway	31 Jan 31	Visas	113LTS39	302633
Estonia	Other Unilat Decla	10 Dec 26	Finance	62LTS277	301467
Estonia	Persia	03 Oct 31	General Amity	137LTS183	303155
Estonia	Poland	11 Jan 24	Consul/Citizenship	47LTS129	301132
Estonia	Poland	19 Feb 27	General Economic	115LTS177	302686
Estonia	Poland	20 May 31	Admin Cooperation	144LTS327	303336
Estonia	Poland	26 Sep 33	Sanitation	150LTS309	303464
Estonia	Poland	27 Mar 35	Customs	159LTS97	303651
Estonia	Portugal	22 Aug 29	General Trade	98LTS225	302250
Estonia	Romania	30 Aug 30	Mostfavored Nation	114LTS59	302654
Estonia	Serb/Croat/Slovene	01 Feb 28	General Economic	106LTS139	302441
Estonia	Spain	23 Jun 32	Admin Cooperation	143LTS31	303303
Estonia	Spain	08 May 35	Finance	159LTS381	303679
Estonia	Spain	08 May 35	General Trade	159LTS363	303678
Estonia	Sweden	07 Jul 23	General Trade	20LTS189	300517
Estonia	Sweden	27 Nov 23	Admin Cooperation	57LTS83	301355
Estonia	Sweden	07 Jul 24	Water Transport	73LTS27	301702
Estonia	Sweden	30 Aug 24	Admin Cooperation	31LTS217	300797
Estonia	Sweden	29 May 25	Dispute Settlement	46LTS289	301123
Estonia	Sweden	11 Jun 28	Admin Cooperation	81LTS277	301843
Estonia	Sweden	23 Jun 28	Water Transport	87LTS253	301972
Estonia	Sweden	23 Apr 29	Admin Cooperation	89LTS277	302022
Estonia	Sweden	20 Jan 30	Extradition	106LTS279	302451
Estonia	Sweden	04 Apr 30	Patents/Copyrights	101LTS51	302318
Estonia	Sweden	07 Dec 34	Commodity Trade	154LTS319	303558
Estonia	Sweden	26 Mar 35	Finance	158LTS239	303634
Estonia	Sweden	20 May 35	Air Transport	162LTS371	303750
Estonia	Sweden	21 Dec 35	Commodity Trade	164LTS293	303798
Estonia	Sweden	16 Jan 37	Postal Service	178LTS49	304106
Estonia	Sweden	08 Feb 37	Commodity Trade	176LTS193	304061
Estonia	Sweden	18 Feb 38	Commodity Trade	185LTS237	304287
Estonia	Sweden	30 Jan 39	Commodity Trade	194LTS131	304517
Estonia	Switzerland	14 Oct 25	General Economic	49LTS421	301195
Estonia	Switzerland	29 Oct 26	Admin Cooperation	63LTS23	301477
Estonia	Switzerland	12 Nov 38	General Trade	194LTS17	304503
Estonia	Turkey	01 Dec 24	General Amity	70LTS77	301624
Estonia	Turkey	12 Mar 28	General Trade	86LTS453	301957
Estonia	Turkey	14 Sep 29	General Trade	97LTS365	302234
Estonia	Turkey	16 Sep 29	General Economic	117LTS377	302704
Estonia	Turkey	13 Mar 35	Finance	159LTS87	303650
Estonia	Turkey	06 Jun 37	Finance	179LTS159	304143
Estonia	Turkey	06 Jun 37	General Trade	179LTS151	304142
Estonia	UK Great Britain	20 Jul 20	Mostfavored Nation	1LTS295	300025
Estonia	UK Great Britain	25 Apr 21	General Economic	5LTS173	300127
Estonia	UK Great Britain	22 May 22	Admin Cooperation	13LTS33	300344
Estonia	UK Great Britain	18 Jan 26	General Economic	48LTS209	301163
Estonia	UK Great Britain	15 Mar 26	Telecommunications	50LTS219	301204
Estonia	UK Great Britain	03 May 26	General Trade	59LTS41	301388
Estonia	UK Great Britain	24 Jun 26	Water Transport	57LTS65	301352
Estonia	UK Great Britain	22 Dec 31	Claims and Debts	131LTS323	303022
Estonia	UK Great Britain	22 Dec 31	Admin Cooperation	132LTS231	303041
Estonia	UK Great Britain	15 Jul 33	General Economic	141LTS33	303259
Estonia	UK Great Britain	11 Jul 34	General Economic	152LTS131	303491
Estonia	UK Great Britain	14 Dec 37	Postal Service	187LTS223	304343
Estonia	Ukrainian SSR	25 Nov 21	Consul/Citizenship	11LTS143	300295
Estonia	Ukrainian SSR	25 Nov 21	Dispute Settlement	11LTS121	300294
Estonia	USA (United States)	08 Nov 23	Extradition	43LTS277	301063
Estonia	USA (United States)	02 Mar 25	General Economic	43LTS289	301064
Estonia	USA (United States)	28 Oct 25	Claims and Debts	62LTS63	301455
Estonia	USA (United States)	23 Dec 25	General Amity	50LTS13	301197
Estonia	USA (United States)	30 Nov 26	General Transport	62LTS313	301469
Estonia	USA (United States)	27 Aug 29	Dispute Settlement	102LTS239	302367
Estonia	USA (United States)	27 Aug 29	Dispute Settlement	102LTS233	302366
Estonia	USA (United States)	10 Oct 34	Extradition	159LTS149	303658
Estonia	USA (United States)	06 Dec 38	Admin Cooperation	198LTS361	304655
Estonia	USSR (Soviet Union)	02 Feb 20	Peace/Disarmament	11LTS29	300289
Estonia	USSR (Soviet Union)	25 Jan 21	Postal Service	11LTS73	300290
Estonia	USSR (Soviet Union)	04 Mar 26	General Transport	62LTS77	301456
Estonia	USSR (Soviet Union)	08 Aug 27	Dispute Settlement	70LTS401	301648
Estonia	USSR (Soviet Union)	03 Mar 28	Patents/Copyrights	80LTS401	301840
Estonia	USSR (Soviet Union)	17 May 29	General Economic	94LTS323	302152
Estonia	USSR (Soviet Union)	20 Jan 30	Dispute Settlement	102LTS225	302365
Estonia	USSR (Soviet Union)	04 May 32	General Amity	131LTS297	303020
Estonia	USSR (Soviet Union)	16 Jun 32	Consul/Citizenship	131LTS309	303021
Estonia	USSR (Soviet Union)	04 Apr 34	General Amity	150LTS87	303455
Estonia	USSR (Soviet Union)	28 Sep 39	General Military	198LTS223	304643
Ethiopia	Greece	18 Feb 22	General Economic	15LTS267	300399
Ethiopia	Greece	23 Mar 31	General Amity	153LTS127	303512
Ethiopia	Multilateral	28 Jun 29	Postal Service	103LTS377	302373
Ethiopia	Multilateral	28 Jun 29	Postal Service	103LTS321	302372
Ethiopia	Multilateral	28 Jun 29	Postal Service	103LTS429	302374
Ethiopia	Multilateral	14 Sep 29	UN Charter	165LTS353	303822
Ethiopia	Multilateral	09 Dec 32	Telecommunications	151LTS5	303479
Ethiopia	Multilateral	20 Mar 34	Postal Service	174LTS171	304048

PARTY ONE	PARTY TWO	DATE	TOPIC	CITATION	NUMBER
Ethiopia	Multilateral	20 Mar 34	Postal Service	176LTS55	304054
Ethiopia	Multilateral	20 Mar 34	Postal Service	175LTS363	304052
Ethiopia	Multilateral	20 Mar 34	Postal Service	175LTS73	304050
Ethiopia	Multilateral	20 Mar 34	Postal Service	175LTS5	304049
Ethiopia	Multilateral	20 Mar 34	Postal Service	175LTS269	304051
Ethiopia	Multilateral	20 Mar 34	Finance	176LTS9	304053
Ethiopia	Other Unilat Decla	27 Sep 23	UN Charter	25LTS180	300606
Ethiopia	Switzerland	24 May 33	General Amity	153LTS63	303508
Falkland Islands	Multilateral	30 Jun 20	Patents/Copyrights	1LTS59	300008
Falkland Islands	Multilateral	31 Mar 22	Humanitarian	9LTS415	300269
Falkland Islands	Multilateral	25 Aug 24	Water Transport	120LTS155	302764
Falkland Islands	Multilateral	01 Dec 24	Sanitation	78LTS351	301794
Falkland Islands	Multilateral	26 Sep 27	Dispute Settlement	92LTS301	302096
Falkland Islands	Multilateral	25 Nov 27	Telecommunications	84LTS97	301905
Falkland Islands	Multilateral	28 Oct 33	Refugees	159LTS199	303663
Falkland Islands	Multilateral	23 Sep 36	Gen Communications	186LTS301	304319
Falkland Islands	Multilateral	10 Feb 38	Refugees	192LTS59	304461
Fed of Malaya	Multilateral	20 Apr 21	Water Transport	7LTS65	300173
Fed of Malaya	Multilateral	28 Oct 33	Refugees	159LTS199	303663
Fed of Malaya	Multilateral	10 Feb 38	Refugees	192LTS59	304461
Fed Rhod/Nyasaland	Multilateral	02 Jun 34	Patents/Copyrights	192LTS17	304459
Fiji Islands	Multilateral	30 Jun 20	Patents/Copyrights	1LTS59	300008
Fiji Islands	Multilateral	31 Mar 22	Humanitarian	9LTS415	300269
Fiji Islands	Multilateral	25 Aug 24	Water Transport	120LTS155	302764
Fiji Islands	Multilateral	01 Dec 24	Sanitation	78LTS351	301794
Fiji Islands	Multilateral	25 Nov 27	Telecommunications	84LTS97	301905
Fiji Islands	Multilateral	30 Mar 31	Taxation	138LTS149	303185
Fiji Islands	Multilateral	12 Apr 33	Sanitation	161LTS65	303706
Fiji Islands	Multilateral	28 Oct 33	Refugees	159LTS199	303663
Fiji Islands	Multilateral	23 Sep 36	Gen Communications	186LTS301	304319
Fiji Islands	Multilateral	10 Feb 38	Refugees	192LTS59	304461
Fiji Islands	USA (United States)	10 Jan 39	Postal Service	196LTS185	304581
Finland	Afghanistan	17 Jul 28	General Amity	112LTS9	302601
Finland	Argentina	03 Nov 31	Customs	126LTS101	302874
Finland	Austria	21 Jul 27	Visas	66LTS419	301535
Finland	Austria	08 Aug 27	General Trade	70LTS349	301645
Finland	Austria	22 Oct 28	Extradition	89LTS69	302007
Finland	Belgium	04 Mar 27	Dispute Settlement	69LTS361	301618
Finland	Belgium	23 Jan 28	Extradition	74LTS353	301747
Finland	Belgium	01 Jun 28	Visas	77LTS327	301774
Finland	Belgium	19 Feb 29	Taxation	111LTS31	302577
Finland	Belgium	03 Jun 32	Extradition	132LTS269	303043
Finland	Brazil	26 Nov 31	General Trade	126LTS239	302886
Finland	Bulgaria	22 Mar 35	Mostfavored Nation	159LTS123	303654
Finland	Bulgaria	27 Oct 36	General Trade	179LTS309	304158
Finland	Bulgaria	27 Oct 36	Finance	173LTS201	304013
Finland	Canada	18 Dec 25	Postal Service	47LTS319	301137
Finland	Chile	01 Mar 35	Mostfavored Nation	159LTS113	303653
Finland	China	29 Oct 26	General Amity	67LTS345	301556
Finland	Czechoslovakia	02 Mar 27	General Economic	66LTS385	301532
Finland	Czechoslovakia	26 Apr 28	Visas	80LTS335	301838
Finland	Czechoslovakia	02 Oct 29	Dispute Settlement	115LTS155	302684
Finland	Czechoslovakia	22 May 34	General Economic	153LTS17	303502
Finland	Czechoslovakia	28 Jan 36	General Economic	166LTS259	303841
Finland	Czechoslovakia	21 Mar 36	Admin Cooperation	179LTS295	304156
Finland	Czechoslovakia	17 Apr 37	General Economic	179LTS317	304159
Finland	Danzig	08 Jun 31	Visas	120LTS291	302772
Finland	Denmark	27 Jul 20	Telecommunications	19LTS71	300484
Finland	Denmark	22 May 22	Postal Service	9LTS435	300270
Finland	Denmark	12 Feb 23	Extradition	18LTS33	300452
Finland	Denmark	12 Feb 23	Customs	18LTS71	300454
Finland	Denmark	21 Apr 23	Milit Servic/Citiz	17LTS57	300428
Finland	Denmark	03 Aug 23	General Trade	21LTS269	300547
Finland	Denmark	30 Nov 23	Non-ILO Labor	22LTS427	300571
Finland	Denmark	27 Jun 24	Dispute Settlement	33LTS131	300839

PARTY ONE	PARTY TWO	DATE	TOPIC	CITATION	NUMBER
Finland	Denmark	31 Jul 24	Postal Service	29LTS183	300741
Finland	Denmark	04 Jun 25	Water Transport	37LTS24	300946
Finland	Denmark	19 Oct 25	Taxation	47LTS259	301140
Finland	Denmark	30 Jan 26	Dispute Settlement	51LTS367	301242
Finland	Denmark	14 May 30	Postal Service	105LTS455	302433
Finland	Denmark	30 Jun 30	Land Transport	105LTS179	302411
Finland	Denmark	09 Jul 31	Water Transport	123LTS393	302826
Finland	Denmark	12 Dec 31	Taxation	112LTS29	302604
Finland	Denmark	18 Jul 35	Admin Cooperation	161LTS205	303712
Finland	Denmark	02 Dec 37	Taxation	187LTS379	304345
Finland	Estonia	29 Oct 21	Telecommunications	13LTS167	300350
Finland	Estonia	29 Oct 21	General Trade	13LTS59	300348
Finland	Estonia	29 Oct 21	Telecommunications	13LTS159	300349
Finland	Estonia	28 Nov 22	Telecommunications	19LTS213	300494
Finland	Estonia	18 Mar 24	Admin Cooperation	32LTS119	300811
Finland	Estonia	02 Jan 25	Extradition	43LTS11	301044
Finland	Estonia	20 Apr 25	Telecommunications	51LTS31	301220
Finland	Estonia	10 Dec 25	Non-ILO Labor	50LTS335	301217
Finland	Estonia	17 May 27	Visas	66LTS411	301534
Finland	Estonia	20 Aug 28	Postal Service	85LTS195	301930
Finland	Estonia	12 Jul 30	Other Economic	111LTS321	302596
Finland	Estonia	11 Apr 31	General Economic	124LTS217	302835
Finland	Estonia	17 Jul 31	Water Transport	126LTS93	302873
Finland	Estonia	16 May 33	Claims and Debts	141LTS19	303257
Finland	Estonia	05 Jul 34	General Economic	153LTS167	303516
Finland	Estonia	03 Apr 36	General Economic	168LTS111	303891
Finland	Estonia	16 Apr 36	Telecommunications	171LTS55	303950
Finland	Estonia	12 Sep 36	Air Transport	172LTS345	303999
Finland	Estonia	18 Dec 36	Postal Service	178LTS41	304105
Finland	Estonia	02 Sep 37	General Economic	183LTS93	304229
Finland	Estonia	01 Dec 37	Education	187LTS413	304347
Finland	Estonia	14 Jan 38	Admin Cooperation	185LTS53	304274
Finland	France	13 Jul 21	General Trade	29LTS445	300755
Finland	France	20 Jan 27	Admin Cooperation	66LTS381	301531
Finland	France	28 Apr 30	Dispute Settlement	139LTS381	303222
Finland	France	24 Apr 31	Water Transport	126LTS85	302872
Finland	France	02 Jun 34	Commodity Trade	153LTS23	303503
Finland	France	26 May 37	Non-ILO Labor	179LTS327	304160
Finland	Germany	20 Feb 22	Extradition	19LTS81	300486
Finland	Germany	21 Apr 22	General Economic	19LTS87	300487
Finland	Germany	14 Nov 24	Postal Service	32LTS137	300813
Finland	Germany	02 Feb 25	Claims and Debts	33LTS127	300838
Finland	Germany	14 Mar 25	Dispute Settlement	43LTS347	301070
Finland	Germany	26 Jun 26	General Economic	56LTS203	301332
Finland	Germany	14 May 27	Visas	66LTS403	301533
Finland	Germany	18 Jun 27	Non-ILO Labor	71LTS361	301675
Finland	Germany	28 Aug 30	General Trade	111LTS327	302597
Finland	Germany	24 Mar 34	General Economic	149LTS343	303442
Finland	Germany	25 Sep 34	General Trade	154LTS9	303534
Finland	Germany	02 Oct 34	Finance	154LTS17	303535
Finland	Germany	22 Dec 34	General Trade	155LTS317	303583
Finland	Germany	29 May 35	Finance	160LTS69	303683
Finland	Germany	25 Sep 35	Taxation	173LTS11	304001
Finland	Germany	25 Sep 35	Taxation	172LTS359	304000
Finland	Great Britain	18 Nov 25	Taxation	42LTS445	301042
Finland	Great Britain	14 Dec 25	Air Transport	47LTS403	301144
Finland	Greece	22 Jun 26	General Economic	56LTS197	301331
Finland	Greece	18 Dec 26	General Trade	70LTS89	301626
Finland	Greece	27 Jul 34	Claims and Debts	153LTS41	303505
Finland	Greece	17 Nov 37	General Economic	188LTS207	304359
Finland	Hungary	20 Apr 26	General Economic	48LTS119	301154
Finland	Hungary	12 Dec 28	Admin Cooperation	96LTS67	302191
Finland	Hungary	07 Nov 33	Commodity Trade	142LTS179	303290
Finland	Hungary	03 Apr 36	Visas	172LTS167	303987
Finland	Hungary	22 Oct 37	Education	190LTS281	304426

PARTY ONE	PARTY TWO	DATE	TOPIC	CITATION	NUMBER
Finland	Hungary	27 Mar 39	Visas	195LTS425	304563
Finland	Iceland	28 May 24	General Trade	27LTS117	300676
Finland	Iceland	07 Mar 25	Patents/Copyrights	34LTS169	300872
Finland	Iceland	27 Jun 30	Dispute Settlement	167LTS271	303873
Finland	Italy	22 Oct 24	General Trade	32LTS149	300814
Finland	Italy	12 May 28	Visas	77LTS334	301775
Finland	Italy	21 Aug 28	Dispute Settlement	89LTS25	302002
Finland	Italy	21 Aug 28	Admin Cooperation	84LTS265	301906
Finland	Italy	10 Jul 29	Extradition	111LTS295	302593
Finland	Italy	15 Aug 29	Admin Cooperation	99LTS363	302280
Finland	Italy	18 Oct 29	Visas	97LTS65	302218
Finland	Italy	28 Sep 36	Finance	172LTS155	303986
Finland	Japan	07 Jun 24	General Economic	58LTS379	301383
Finland	Japan	25 Feb 28	Visas	71LTS467	301685
Finland	Latvia	07 Jun 24	Admin Cooperation	58LTS375	301382
Finland	Latvia	07 Jun 24	Extradition	38LTS343	300990
Finland	Latvia	23 Aug 24	General Trade	37LTS383	300962
Finland	Latvia	14 May 27	Visas	63LTS97	301482
Finland	Latvia	29 Apr 32	Water Transport	133LTS71	303057
Finland	Latvia	28 Mar 36	Finance	171LTS155	303957
Finland	Latvia	28 May 37	Postal Service	179LTS333	304161
Finland	Latvia	11 Apr 40	Finance	201LTS389	304727
Finland	Lithuania	06 Oct 28	General Trade	82LTS71	301861
Finland	Lithuania	19 Jun 34	Patents/Copyrights	153LTS49	303506
Finland	Lithuania	12 Apr 38	Finance	194LTS9	304501
Finland	Mexico	02 Oct 36	General Amity	179LTS303	304157
Finland	Multilateral	09 Sep 86*	Patents/Copyrights	123LTS233	302816
Finland	Multilateral	23 Jan 12	Sanitation	8LTS187	300222
Finland	Multilateral	10 Sep 19	General Trade	7LTS331	300200
Finland	Multilateral	01 May 20	Air Transport	11LTS173	300297
Finland	Multilateral	21 Jun 20	Health/Educ/Welfare	8LTS65	300207
Finland	Multilateral	30 Jun 20	Patents/Copyrights	1LTS59	300008
Finland	Multilateral	16 Dec 20	General IGO	6LTS379	300170
Finland	Multilateral	20 Apr 21	Water Transport	7LTS73	300174
Finland	Multilateral	20 Apr 21	Water Transport	7LTS65	300173
Finland	Multilateral	20 Apr 21	Land Transport	7LTS11	300171
Finland	Multilateral	20 Apr 21	Water Transport	7LTS35	300172
Finland	Multilateral	05 Aug 21	Admin Cooperation	27LTS349	300695
Finland	Multilateral	19 Sep 21	Telecommunications	15LTS191	300392
Finland	Multilateral	05 Oct 21	IGO Establishment	51LTS361	301241
Finland	Multilateral	05 Oct 21	Admin Cooperation	29LTS67	300733
Finland	Multilateral	05 Oct 21	Admin Cooperation	29LTS73	300734
Finland	Multilateral	05 Oct 21	Admin Cooperation	29LTS79	300735
Finland	Multilateral	06 Oct 21	General Economic	17LTS45	300427
Finland	Multilateral	20 Oct 21	Peace/Disarmament	9LTS211	300255
Finland	Multilateral	17 Mar 22	Dispute Settlement	11LTS167	300296
Finland	Multilateral	11 Jul 23	Admin Cooperation	18LTS85	300456
Finland	Multilateral	24 Sep 23	Dispute Settlement	27LTS157	300678
Finland	Multilateral	03 Nov 23	Customs	30LTS371	300775
Finland	Multilateral	09 Dec 23	Land Transport	47LTS55	301129
Finland	Multilateral	25 Jan 24	Sanitation	57LTS135	301360
Finland	Multilateral	12 Mar 24	General Trade	24LTS17	300595
Finland	Multilateral	31 Mar 24	Sanitation	27LTS211	300685
Finland	Multilateral	28 Aug 24	Postal Service	40LTS437	301005
Finland	Multilateral	28 Aug 24	Postal Service	40LTS249	301003
Finland	Multilateral	28 Aug 24	Postal Service	40LTS19	301002
Finland	Multilateral	28 Aug 24	Postal Service	41LTS97	301008
Finland	Multilateral	28 Aug 24	Postal Service	40LTS307	301004
Finland	Multilateral	23 Oct 24	General Transport	77LTS367	301778
Finland	Multilateral	23 Oct 24	Land Transport	78LTS17	301779
Finland	Multilateral	01 Dec 24	Sanitation	78LTS351	301794
Finland	Multilateral	17 Jan 25	Dispute Settlement	38LTS357	300991
Finland	Multilateral	19 Feb 25	Admin Cooperation	81LTS317	301845
Finland	Multilateral	17 Jun 25	Peace/Disarmament	94LTS65	302138
Finland	Multilateral	19 Aug 25	Customs	42LTS73	301033

PARTY ONE	PARTY TWO	DATE	TOPIC	CITATION	NUMBER
Finland	Multilateral	29 Oct 25	Telecommunications	57LTS201	301365
Finland	Multilateral	06 Nov 25	Patents/Copyrights	74LTS289	301743
Finland	Multilateral	27 Nov 25	Water Transport	67LTS63	301539
Finland	Multilateral	31 Dec 25	Territory Boundary	79LTS167	301809
Finland	Multilateral	28 Jan 26	Water Transport	51LTS9	301219
Finland	Multilateral	24 Apr 26	Land Transport	108LTS123	302505
Finland	Multilateral	12 May 26	Refugees	89LTS47	302004
Finland	Multilateral	21 Jun 26	Sanitation	78LTS229	301793
Finland	Multilateral	25 Sep 26	ILO Labor	60LTS253	301414
Finland	Multilateral	15 Jun 27	Telecommunications	69LTS375	301619
Finland	Multilateral	12 Jul 27	Direct Aid	135LTS247	303115
Finland	Multilateral	10 Sep 27	Postal Service	75LTS39	301750
Finland	Multilateral	10 Sep 27	Postal Service	75LTS7	301749
Finland	Multilateral	26 Sep 27	Dispute Settlement	92LTS301	302096
Finland	Multilateral	08 Nov 27	General Trade	97LTS391	302238
Finland	Multilateral	25 Nov 27	Telecommunications	84LTS97	301905
Finland	Multilateral	11 Jul 28	Commodity Trade	95LTS373	302185
Finland	Multilateral	11 Jul 28	Commodity Trade	95LTS357	302184
Finland	Multilateral	27 Aug 28	General Military	94LTS57	302137
Finland	Multilateral	25 Oct 28	Consul/Citizenship	84LTS7	301901
Finland	Multilateral	30 Nov 28	Telecommunications	87LTS119	301965
Finland	Multilateral	14 Dec 28	General Economic	110LTS171	302560
Finland	Multilateral	14 Jan 29	Telecommunications	87LTS169	301968
Finland	Multilateral	16 Jan 29	Telecommunications	87LTS155	301967
Finland	Multilateral	16 Apr 29	Specific Resources	126LTS305	302891
Finland	Multilateral	20 Apr 29	Admin Cooperation	112LTS371	302623
Finland	Multilateral	20 Apr 29	Admin Cooperation	112LTS395	302624
Finland	Multilateral	08 May 29	Telecommunications	91LTS337	302074
Finland	Multilateral	31 May 29	Water Transport	136LTS81	303127
Finland	Multilateral	14 Jun 29	Visas	94LTS275	302148
Finland	Multilateral	28 Jun 29	Postal Service	103LTS377	302373
Finland	Multilateral	28 Jun 29	Postal Service	103LTS5	302369
Finland	Multilateral	28 Jun 29	Postal Service	103LTS429	302374
Finland	Multilateral	28 Jun 29	Postal Service	103LTS249	302371
Finland	Multilateral	28 Jun 29	Postal Service	102LTS245	302368
Finland	Multilateral	28 Jun 29	Postal Service	103LTS71	302370
Finland	Multilateral	27 Jul 29	Other Military	118LTS303	302733
Finland	Multilateral	27 Jul 29	Other Military	118LTS343	302734
Finland	Multilateral	20 Aug 29	Sanitation	98LTS125	302243
Finland	Multilateral	30 Aug 29	Telecommunications	96LTS129	302195
Finland	Multilateral	30 Aug 29	Telecommunications	96LTS117	302194
Finland	Multilateral	07 Sep 29	Telecommunications	98LTS345	302255
Finland	Multilateral	14 Sep 29	UN Charter	165LTS353	303822
Finland	Multilateral	25 Sep 29	Telecommunications	98LTS361	302256
Finland	Multilateral	26 Sep 29	Telecommunications	98LTS395	302259
Finland	Multilateral	30 Sep 29	Postal Service	99LTS71	302269
Finland	Multilateral	30 Sep 29	Telecommunications	98LTS183	302246
Finland	Multilateral	01 Oct 29	Telecommunications	98LTS197	302247
Finland	Multilateral	08 Oct 29	Telecommunications	98LTS409	302260
Finland	Multilateral	10 Oct 29	Telecommunications	98LTS375	302257
Finland	Multilateral	12 Oct 29	General Transport	137LTS11	303145
Finland	Multilateral	28 Oct 29	Telecommunications	97LTS71	302219
Finland	Multilateral	29 Oct 29	Telecommunications	99LTS85	302270
Finland	Multilateral	14 Jan 30	Telecommunications	99LTS343	302278
Finland	Multilateral	25 Feb 30	Telecommunications	101LTS343	302335
Finland	Multilateral	10 Apr 30	Telecommunications	101LTS465	302345
Finland	Multilateral	07 Jun 30	Finance	143LTS337	303315
Finland	Multilateral	07 Jun 30	Finance	143LTS257	303313
Finland	Multilateral	07 Jun 30	Finance	143LTS317	303314
Finland	Multilateral	23 Oct 30	Water Transport	125LTS95	302849
Finland	Multilateral	23 Oct 30	Water Transport	112LTS321	302603
Finland	Multilateral	22 Dec 30	General Trade	126LTS341	302893
Finland	Multilateral	06 Feb 31	Admin Cooperation	126LTS121	302877
Finland	Multilateral	10 Feb 31	Admin Cooperation	126LTS41	302870
Finland	Multilateral	19 Mar 31	Admin Cooperation	143LTS7	303301

PARTY ONE	PARTY TWO	DATE	TOPIC	CITATION	NUMBER
Finland	Multilateral	19 Mar 31	Finance	143LTS407	303317
Finland	Multilateral	19 Mar 31	Finance	143LTS355	303316
Finland	Multilateral	27 Mar 31	ICJ Option Clause	167LTS341	303877
Finland	Multilateral	30 Mar 31	Taxation	138LTS149	303185
Finland	Multilateral	06 May 31	Telecommunications	120LTS217	302767
Finland	Multilateral	13 Jul 31	Other HEW	139LTS301	303219
Finland	Multilateral	24 Sep 31	Specific Resources	155LTS349	303586
Finland	Multilateral	11 Dec 31	Commodity Trade	170LTS251	303941
Finland	Multilateral	16 Mar 32	Admin Cooperation	139LTS165	303209
Finland	Multilateral	02 Sep 32	Land Transport	154LTS123	303543
Finland	Multilateral	09 Dec 32	Telecommunications	151LTS5	303479
Finland	Multilateral	11 Mar 33	Water Transport	135LTS301	303119
Finland	Multilateral	03 Jul 33	Peace/Disarmament	147LTS67	303391
Finland	Multilateral	10 Oct 33	General Amity	163LTS393	303781
Finland	Multilateral	11 Oct 33	Education	155LTS331	303585
Finland	Multilateral	07 Nov 33	Finance	155LTS115	303574
Finland	Multilateral	23 Nov 33	Land Transport	192LTS327	304483
Finland	Multilateral	23 Nov 33	Land Transport	192LTS389	304484
Finland	Multilateral	20 Mar 34	Postal Service	175LTS269	304051
Finland	Multilateral	20 Mar 34	Postal Service	175LTS73	304050
Finland	Multilateral	20 Mar 34	Postal Service	175LTS5	304049
Finland	Multilateral	20 Mar 34	Finance	176LTS9	304053
Finland	Multilateral	20 Mar 34	Postal Service	176LTS55	304054
Finland	Multilateral	20 Mar 34	Postal Service	174LTS171	304048
Finland	Multilateral	26 Apr 34	Admin Cooperation	164LTS63	303789
Finland	Multilateral	02 Jun 34	Patents/Copyrights	192LTS17	304459
Finland	Multilateral	19 Nov 34	Admin Cooperation	164LTS243	303797
Finland	Multilateral	31 Dec 34	Postal Service	158LTS111	303630
Finland	Multilateral	15 Sep 36	Scientific Project	178LTS439	304126
Finland	Multilateral	23 Sep 36	Gen Communications	186LTS301	304319
Finland	Multilateral	06 Nov 36	General Military	173LTS353	304025
Finland	Multilateral	11 Feb 37	Telecommunications	186LTS55	304303
Finland	Multilateral	03 Mar 37	Admin Cooperation	182LTS127	304205
Finland	Multilateral	31 Mar 37	Commodity Trade	189LTS359	304394
Finland	Multilateral	28 May 37	General Trade	180LTS5	304170
Finland	Multilateral	15 Sep 37	Gen Communications	186LTS135	304307
Finland	Multilateral	23 Sep 37	Postal Service	190LTS299	304427
Finland	Multilateral	02 Oct 37	Education	182LTS263	304216
Finland	Multilateral	23 Dec 37	Gen Communications	186LTS99	304304
Finland	Multilateral	11 May 38	General Trade	189LTS237	304386
Finland	Multilateral	27 May 38	Other Military	188LTS293	304365
Finland	Multilateral	03 Dec 38	Education	200LTS249	304694
Finland	Multilateral	23 May 39	Postal Service	202LTS159	304742
Finland	Netherlands	01 Nov 23	General Trade	23LTS33	300574
Finland	Netherlands	09 Mar 25	Consul/Citizenship	47LTS431	301148
Finland	Netherlands	07 May 28	Visas	74LTS367	301748
Finland	Netherlands	09 Jun 28	Dispute Settlement	87LTS321	301978
Finland	Netherlands	21 Feb 33	Extradition	139LTS365	303221
Finland	Netherlands	22 May 33	Water Transport	140LTS279	303243
Finland	Netherlands	25 Aug 36	General Trade	172LTS151	303985
Finland	Netherlands	20 Dec 38	Customs	194LTS55	304506
Finland	Norway	14 Jul 20	Specific Resources	1LTS317	300027
Finland	Norway	16 Jul 21	Admin Cooperation	19LTS77	300485
Finland	Norway	03 Mar 22	Specif Goods/Equip	14LTS157	300372
Finland	Norway	23 May 22	Postal Service	14LTS323	300382
Finland	Norway	07 Sep 22	Telecommunications	12LTS357	300328
Finland	Norway	28 Apr 23	Admin Cooperation	19LTS225	300496
Finland	Norway	28 Apr 24	Visas	30LTS35	300757
Finland	Norway	28 Apr 24	Territory Boundary	30LTS49	300758
Finland	Norway	27 Jun 24	Dispute Settlement	29LTS403	300751
Finland	Norway	11 Oct 24	Postal Service	32LTS123	300812
Finland	Norway	14 Feb 25	Specific Resources	49LTS379	301193
Finland	Norway	14 Feb 25	Specific Resources	49LTS391	301194
Finland	Norway	10 Nov 25	Dispute Settlement	43LTS381	301071
Finland	Norway	19 Dec 25	Water Transport	56LTS183	301330

PARTY ONE	PARTY TWO	DATE	TOPIC	CITATION	NUMBER
Finland	Norway	03 Feb 26	Dispute Settlement	60LTS353	301420
Finland	Norway	30 Sep 27	Customs	67LTS359	301557
Finland	Norway	23 Oct 28	Water Transport	85LTS211	301932
Finland	Norway	24 Nov 28	Visas	82LTS215	301872
Finland	Norway	14 May 30	Postal Service	105LTS399	302429
Finland	Norway	11 Nov 30	General Trade	130LTS17	302980
Finland	Norway	20 Nov 30	Land Transport	110LTS313	302563
Finland	Norway	05 Nov 35	Territory Boundary	169LTS33	303913
Finland	Norway	21 Jul 37	General Trade	191LTS75	304435
Finland	Norway	21 Apr 38	Specific Resources	188LTS231	304361
Finland	Norway	21 Apr 38	Specific Resources	188LTS215	304360
Finland	Norway	28 Dec 39	General Economic	199LTS71	304667
Finland	Persia	18 Nov 34	Mostfavored Nation	158LTS315	303641
Finland	Poland	10 Nov 23	General Trade	29LTS229	300744
Finland	Poland	15 May 30	Visas	111LTS309	302594
Finland	Poland	20 Mar 31	Admin Cooperation	140LTS405	303250
Finland	Poland	19 Dec 31	Non-ILO Labor	131LTS193	303010
Finland	Poland	30 Jun 34	Customs	153LTS29	303504
Finland	Poland	16 Jul 36	General Trade	172LTS143	303984
Finland	Poland	14 Feb 38	Education	194LTS175	304520
Finland	Portugal	08 Mar 30	General Economic	105LTS441	302431
Finland	Romania	28 Aug 30	Mostfavored Nation	118LTS193	302723
Finland	Romania	03 Dec 35	Finance	165LTS287	303815
Finland	Romania	16 Nov 36	Visas	179LTS377	304164
Finland	Serb/Croat/Slovene	29 Jan 29	General Trade	96LTS77	302192
Finland	South Africa	14 Feb 38	Visas	190LTS211	304419
Finland	Spain	16 Jul 25	General Trade	47LTS271	301135
Finland	Spain	31 May 28	Dispute Settlement	82LTS229	301874
Finland	Sweden	10 May 20	Dispute Settlement	2LTS141	300058
Finland	Sweden	29 Jul 21	Humanitarian	6LTS353	300168
Finland	Sweden	22 May 22	Postal Service	14LTS297	300381
Finland	Sweden	26 May 23	Water Transport	18LTS57	300453
Finland	Sweden	11 Sep 23	ILO Labor	20LTS79	300508
Finland	Sweden	12 Oct 23	Water Transport	21LTS147	300538
Finland	Sweden	29 Nov 23	Extradition	23LTS41	300575
Finland	Sweden	10 Jan 24	Admin Cooperation	24LTS167	300558
Finland	Sweden	27 Jun 24	Dispute Settlement	29LTS19	300731
Finland	Sweden	28 Jun 24	Land Transport	28LTS327	300718
Finland	Sweden	26 Jul 24	Postal Service	29LTS167	300740
Finland	Sweden	22 Dec 24	Water Transport	73LTS33	301703
Finland	Sweden	09 May 25	Territory Boundary	47LTS283	301136
Finland	Sweden	29 Jan 26	Dispute Settlement	49LTS367	301192
Finland	Sweden	01 Apr 27	Water Transport	62LTS89	301458
Finland	Sweden	10 May 27	Specific Resources	70LTS201	301634
Finland	Sweden	14 Dec 27	General Trade	72LTS29	301688
Finland	Sweden	09 Mar 28	Visas	72LTS429	301699
Finland	Sweden	10 Jul 28	Telecommunications	87LTS131	301966
Finland	Sweden	14 May 30	Postal Service	106LTS9	302434
Finland	Sweden	17 Jul 30	Land Transport	105LTS343	302427
Finland	Sweden	16 Mar 31	Taxation	118LTS71	302714
Finland	Sweden	29 Dec 33	General Trade	149LTS23	303429
Finland	Sweden	05 Sep 34	Commodity Trade	154LTS239	303550
Finland	Sweden	18 Dec 35	Admin Cooperation	165LTS347	303821
Finland	Sweden	09 Jan 38	Admin Cooperation	195LTS157	304545
Finland	Sweden	16 Dec 39	Water Transport	199LTS43	304662
Finland	Switzerland	24 Jun 27	Mostfavored Nation	68LTS103	301574
Finland	Switzerland	14 Oct 27	Visas	71LTS205	301663
Finland	Switzerland	16 Nov 27	Dispute Settlement	77LTS93	301765
Finland	Switzerland	22 May 29	Visas	91LTS305	302069
Finland	Switzerland	22 May 29	Visas	91LTS311	302070
Finland	Switzerland	07 May 36	Consul/Citizenship	166LTS35	303827
Finland	Turkey	09 Dec 24	General Amity	59LTS287	301398
Finland	Turkey	02 Jun 26	General Trade	70LTS329	301644
Finland	Turkey	19 Oct 26	General Economic	58LTS393	301384
Finland	Turkey	12 Oct 29	General Economic	96LTS239	302205

PARTY ONE	PARTY TWO	DATE	TOPIC	CITATION	NUMBER
Finland	Turkey	19 Dec 33	General Trade	149LTS333	303441
Finland	Turkey	06 Jun 35	General Trade	160LTS165	303690
Finland	Turkey	20 Jun 36	General Trade	172LTS125	303982
Finland	Turkey	20 Jun 36	Finance	172LTS135	303983
Finland	UK Great Britain	10 Jun 21	Sanitation	16LTS133	300403
Finland	UK Great Britain	14 Dec 23	General Trade	29LTS129	300739
Finland	UK Great Britain	14 Dec 23	Non-ILO Labor	23LTS125	300583
Finland	UK Great Britain	30 May 24	Extradition	34LTS79	300868
Finland	UK Great Britain	21 Jun 24	Water Transport	28LTS511	300726
Finland	UK Great Britain	12 Dec 24	Postal Service	34LTS123	300870
Finland	UK Great Britain	30 Sep 32	Dispute Settlement	135LTS9	303101
Finland	UK Great Britain	11 Aug 33	Admin Cooperation	149LTS131	303437
Finland	UK Great Britain	29 Sep 33	General Trade	149LTS167	303438
Finland	UK Great Britain	13 Oct 33	Commodity Trade	142LTS187	303291
Finland	UK Great Britain	04 Nov 33	Postal Service	149LTS285	303440
Finland	UK Great Britain	21 Feb 35	Taxation	158LTS323	303642
Finland	UK Great Britain	03 May 35	Water Transport	159LTS129	303655
Finland	UK Great Britain	14 Apr 37	Commodity Trade	179LTS289	304155
Finland	United Arab Rep	13 Jun 30	Mostfavored Nation	111LTS315	302595
Finland	USA (United States)	21 Jul 22	Postal Service	13LTS243	300356
Finland	USA (United States)	26 Jun 24	Postal Service	30LTS9	300756
Finland	USA (United States)	01 Aug 24	Extradition	34LTS103	300869
Finland	USA (United States)	02 May 25	General Economic	47LTS351	301139
Finland	USA (United States)	21 Dec 25	Customs	47LTS345	301138
Finland	USA (United States)	07 Jun 28	Dispute Settlement	87LTS15	301959
Finland	USA (United States)	07 Jun 28	Dispute Settlement	87LTS9	301958
Finland	USA (United States)	13 Feb 34	General Amity	152LTS45	303484
Finland	USA (United States)	17 May 34	Extradition	152LTS83	303485
Finland	USA (United States)	18 May 36	General Trade	172LTS97	303981
Finland	USA (United States)	30 Dec 38	Admin Cooperation	195LTS417	304562
Finland	USA (United States)	27 Jan 39	Milit Servic/Citiz	201LTS187	304713
Finland	USSR (Soviet Union)	14 Oct 20	Peace/Disarmament	3LTS5	300091
Finland	USSR (Soviet Union)	14 Dec 21	Land Transport	16LTS221	300414
Finland	USSR (Soviet Union)	01 Jun 22	Territory Boundary	16LTS319	300415
Finland	USSR (Soviet Union)	13 Jun 22	Telecommunications	16LTS349	300416
Finland	USSR (Soviet Union)	22 Jun 22	Postal Service	16LTS361	300417
Finland	USSR (Soviet Union)	07 Jul 22	Peace/Disarmament	19LTS99	300488
Finland	USSR (Soviet Union)	12 Aug 22	Refugees	19LTS105	300489
Finland	USSR (Soviet Union)	20 Sep 22	Specific Resources	19LTS143	300490
Finland	USSR (Soviet Union)	21 Oct 22	Specific Resources	29LTS197	300742
Finland	USSR (Soviet Union)	28 Oct 22	Specific Resources	29LTS211	300743
Finland	USSR (Soviet Union)	28 Oct 22	Water Transport	19LTS183	300492
Finland	USSR (Soviet Union)	28 Oct 22	General Transport	19LTS199	300493
Finland	USSR (Soviet Union)	28 Oct 22	Water Transport	19LTS153	300491
Finland	USSR (Soviet Union)	21 Feb 23	Customs	19LTS219	300495
Finland	USSR (Soviet Union)	05 Jun 23	Water Transport	18LTS203	300465
Finland	USSR (Soviet Union)	28 Jul 23	Admin Cooperation	32LTS101	300810
Finland	USSR (Soviet Union)	18 Jun 24	Admin Cooperation	47LTS241	301134
Finland	USSR (Soviet Union)	18 Jun 24	Land Transport	47LTS153	301133
Finland	USSR (Soviet Union)	18 Jun 24	Telecommunications	29LTS265	300745
Finland	USSR (Soviet Union)	18 Jun 24	Telecommunications	29LTS295	300746
Finland	USSR (Soviet Union)	18 Jun 24	Postal Service	29LTS313	300747
Finland	USSR (Soviet Union)	20 Feb 25	Postal Service	34LTS153	300871
Finland	USSR (Soviet Union)	29 Mar 27	General Transport	71LTS11	301651
Finland	USSR (Soviet Union)	17 Mar 28	Water Transport	80LTS151	301824
Finland	USSR (Soviet Union)	24 Sep 28	Territory Boundary	82LTS63	301860
Finland	USSR (Soviet Union)	13 Apr 29	Customs	96LTS93	302193
Finland	USSR (Soviet Union)	07 Oct 29	Postal Service	96LTS349	302212
Finland	USSR (Soviet Union)	21 Jan 32	General Amity	157LTS393	303613
Finland	USSR (Soviet Union)	22 Jan 32	Dispute Settlement	157LTS401	303614
Finland	USSR (Soviet Union)	04 Jul 33	Territory Boundary	149LTS83	303436
Finland	USSR (Soviet Union)	15 Oct 33	Territory Boundary	149LTS243	303439
Finland	USSR (Soviet Union)	07 Apr 34	General Amity	155LTS325	303584
Finland	USSR (Soviet Union)	25 May 34	Specific Resources	155LTS207	303578
Fr Equatorial Afri	Belgian Colonies	04 May 22	Telecommunications	148LTS61	303403

PARTY ONE	PARTY TWO	DATE	TOPIC	CITATION	NUMBER
Fr Equatorial Afri	Multilateral	24 Apr 26	Land Transport	108LTS123	302505
Fr Equatorial Afri	Multilateral	24 Apr 26	Land Transport	97LTS83	302220
Fr Equatorial Afri	Multilateral	21 Jun 26	Sanitation	78LTS229	301793
Fr Equatorial Afri	Multilateral	23 Oct 30	Water Transport	125LTS95	302849
France	Afghanistan	28 Apr 22	Consul/Citizenship	105LTS147	302408
France	Afghanistan	09 Sep 22	Education	105LTS153	302409
France	Albania	15 Feb 28	Consul/Citizenship	107LTS307	302487
France	Argentina	26 Jun 27	Milit Servic/Citiz	62LTS85	301457
France	Australia	30 May 34	Postal Service	165LTS81	303804
France	Australia	27 Nov 36	General Trade	177LTS301	304095
France	Austria	03 Aug 20	Claims and Debts	5LTS355	300141
France	Austria	07 Feb 21	General Military	4LTS251	300108
France	Austria	11 Aug 24	General Trade	44LTS7	301079
France	Austria	04 Mar 25	Admin Cooperation	75LTS97	301755
France	Austria	04 Mar 25	Admin Cooperation	44LTS205	301084
France	Austria	16 May 28	General Trade	88LTS21	301986
France	Austria	29 Dec 32	Commodity Trade	147LTS101	303394
France	Bel-Lux Econ Union	04 Apr 25	General Trade	44LTS213	301085
France	Bel-Lux Econ Union	23 Feb 28	General Trade	72LTS61	301689
France	Bel-Lux Econ Union	28 Mar 29	General Trade	96LTS41	302190
France	Bel-Lux Econ Union	16 Jul 35	Territory Boundary	162LTS19	303731
France	Belgium	24 Jul 20	Reparations	1LTS311	300026
France	Belgium	07 Sep 20	General Military	2LTS127	300056
France	Belgium	14 Feb 21	Admin Cooperation	12LTS245	300317
France	Belgium	04 Oct 21	Milit Servic/Citiz	8LTS157	300219
France	Belgium	30 Nov 21	Humanitarian	27LTS173	300680
France	Belgium	24 Dec 24	Non-ILO Labor	78LTS367	301795
France	Belgium	24 Jun 26	Extradition	94LTS349	302153
France	Belgium	11 Apr 27	Land Transport	143LTS215	303309
France	Belgium	21 May 27	Non-ILO Labor	105LTS125	302407
France	Belgium	21 May 27	Non-ILO Labor	95LTS283	302180
France	Belgium	06 Oct 27	Admin Cooperation	69LTS49	301599
France	Belgium	23 May 28	Sanitation	88LTS145	301993
France	Belgium	30 May 28	Education	95LTS195	302173
France	Belgium	30 Jun 28	IGO Operations	93LTS377	302126
France	Belgium	04 Jul 28	Visas	85LTS205	301931
France	Belgium	12 Sep 28	Consul/Citizenship	123LTS91	302808
France	Belgium	12 Sep 28	Milit Servic/Citiz	123LTS97	302809
France	Belgium	01 Jul 29	Non-ILO Labor	93LTS371	302125
France	Belgium	07 Oct 29	Taxation	111LTS43	302579
France	Belgium	07 Nov 29	Reparations	134LTS257	303096
France	Belgium	23 May 30	Telecommunications	119LTS33	302738
France	Belgium	23 Aug 30	Non-ILO Labor	166LTS11	303825
France	Belgium	30 Mar 31	Non-ILO Labor	126LTS195	302882
France	Belgium	15 Apr 31	Territory Boundary	119LTS161	302743
France	Belgium	16 May 31	Taxation	141LTS333	303274
France	Belgium	29 Jul 31	Sanitation	127LTS85	302909
France	Belgium	07 Sep 31	Non-ILO Labor	134LTS65	303083
France	Belgium	17 Nov 31	Reparations	152LTS121	303490
France	Belgium	23 Dec 31	Taxation	137LTS277	303162
France	Belgium	18 Jun 32	Taxation	137LTS289	303163
France	Belgium	28 Jul 34	Visas	152LTS27	303481
France	Belgium	09 May 35	Territory Boundary	162LTS437	303755
France	Belgium	25 Aug 35	Extradition	161LTS369	303725
France	Belgium	30 Dec 35	General Trade	166LTS25	303826
France	Belgium	16 Jul 36	Admin Cooperation	171LTS287	303965
France	Belgium	07 Jul 37	Admin Cooperation	181LTS111	304182
France	Belgium	02 Oct 37	Water Transport	184LTS65	304242
France	Belgium	06 Mar 39	Non-ILO Labor	195LTS353	304555
France	Brazil	27 Aug 27	Dispute Settlement	75LTS91	301754
France	Bulgaria	22 Oct 25	General Trade	44LTS257	301087
France	Bulgaria	06 Jul 36	Finance	171LTS269	303963
France	Burma	26 Jan 39	Postal Service	201LTS9	304701
France	Canada	19 Sep 07	Customs	1LTS95	300012
France	Canada	29 Jan 21	General Trade	8LTS105	300212

PARTY ONE	PARTY TWO	DATE	TOPIC	CITATION	NUMBER
France	Canada	15 Dec 22	General Trade	21LTS38	300532
France	Chile	24 Feb 27	Dispute Settlement	69LTS277	301610
France	Chile	22 May 31	Customs	124LTS31	302831
France	Chile	19 Nov 37	Admin Cooperation	185LTS261	304291
France	China	23 Dec 28	Customs	92LTS267	302095
France	China	16 May 30	General Amity	162LTS99	303738
France	Cuba	06 Nov 29	General Economic	114LTS345	302665
France	Czechoslovakia	20 Mar 20	Visas	3LTS139	300095
France	Czechoslovakia	07 Oct 22	Admin Cooperation	47LTS365	301141
France	Czechoslovakia	25 Jan 24	General Amity	23LTS163	300588
France	Czechoslovakia	18 Aug 24	General Trade	44LTS21	301080
France	Czechoslovakia	26 May 25	Air Transport	150LTS43	303452
France	Czechoslovakia	16 Oct 25	Peace/Disarmament	54LTS359	301298
France	Czechoslovakia	03 Jun 27	Consul/Citizenship	131LTS177	303009
France	Czechoslovakia	07 May 28	Admin Cooperation	114LTS171	302663
France	Czechoslovakia	07 May 28	Extradition	114LTS117	302660
France	Czechoslovakia	02 Jul 28	General Trade	99LTS105	302272
France	Czechoslovakia	03 Oct 30	Health/Educ/Welfare	125LTS59	302846
France	Denmark	25 Feb 25	Consul/Citizenship	33LTS277	300852
France	Denmark	19 Oct 25	Mostfavored Nation	38LTS325	300988
France	Denmark	05 Jul 26	Dispute Settlement	71LTS455	301684
France	Denmark	23 Jan 28	Admin Cooperation	71LTS267	301667
France	Denmark	14 Jan 30	Education	100LTS327	302304
France	Denmark	28 Feb 30	General Economic	101LTS17	302316
France	Denmark	01 Aug 30	Air Transport	108LTS115	302504
France	Denmark	31 Jul 34	General Economic	150LTS381	303471
France	Denmark	28 Jan 35	Non-ILO Labor	158LTS11	303619
France	Denmark	21 Sep 35	Admin Cooperation	162LTS383	303751
France	El Salvador	25 Aug 24	Admin Cooperation	93LTS365	302124
France	Estonia	07 Jan 22	General Trade	62LTS9	301452
France	Estonia	15 Mar 29	General Trade	89LTS381	302029
France	Estonia	07 Oct 29	Commodity Trade	104LTS193	302389
France	Estonia	26 Mar 32	Claims and Debts	128LTS51	302937
France	Estonia	27 Apr 33	General Trade	141LTS43	303260
France	Estonia	27 Jul 33	General Trade	141LTS65	303261
France	Estonia	22 Feb 36	General Economic	168LTS105	303890
France	Estonia	16 Oct 37	Finance	183LTS37	304226
France	Estonia	16 Oct 37	General Trade	183LTS41	304227
France	Finland	13 Jul 21	General Trade	29LTS445	300755
France	Finland	20 Jan 27	Admin Cooperation	66LTS381	301531
France	Finland	28 Apr 30	Dispute Settlement	139LTS381	303222
France	Finland	24 Apr 31	Water Transport	126LTS85	302872
France	Finland	02 Jun 34	Commodity Trade	153LTS23	303503
France	Finland	26 May 37	Non-ILO Labor	179LTS327	304160
France	Germany	01 Mar 20	Admin Cooperation	1LTS367	300030
France	Germany	03 Mar 20	Non-ILO Labor	8LTS45	300205
France	Germany	25 Mar 20	Claims and Debts	1LTS347	300029
France	Germany	05 May 20	Dispute Settlement	8LTS55	300206
France	Germany	19 May 20	Customs	1LTS383	300031
France	Germany	30 Jun 20	Dispute Settlement	8LTS79	300208
France	Germany	01 Jul 20	Territory Boundary	8LTS87	300209
France	Germany	17 Nov 20	Peace/Disarmament	8LTS99	300211
France	Germany	13 Apr 25	Admin Cooperation	109LTS295	302546
France	Germany	14 Aug 25	Territory Boundary	75LTS103	301756
France	Germany	16 Oct 25	General Military	54LTS315	301294
France	Germany	12 Feb 26	General Economic	48LTS153	301157
France	Germany	04 Jun 26	Admin Cooperation	53LTS423	301270
France	Germany	28 Jun 26	Extradition	53LTS435	301271
France	Germany	05 Aug 26	General Trade	73LTS105	301711
France	Germany	22 Dec 26	Territory Boundary	77LTS141	301768
France	Germany	16 Feb 27	Commodity Trade	62LTS155	301463
France	Germany	31 Mar 27	General Economic	66LTS7	301524
France	Germany	30 Jun 27	General Trade	73LTS243	301717
France	Germany	17 Aug 27	General Trade	76LTS5	301761
France	Germany	05 Oct 27	Admin Cooperation	77LTS7	301762
France	Germany	23 Feb 28	General Trade	79LTS247	301815
France	Germany	16 Mar 28	Customs	79LTS121	301805
France	Germany	25 Apr 29	Land Transport	109LTS333	302548
France	Germany	20 Nov 29	Admin Cooperation	99LTS339	302277
France	Germany	31 Dec 29	Reparations	106LTS93	302438
France	Great Britain	02 Feb 26	General Amity	56LTS79	301324
France	Great Britain	15 Mar 26	Postal Service	47LTS415	301146
France	Great Britain	14 Sep 27	Admin Cooperation	69LTS269	301609
France	Greece	20 Apr 20	General Aid	3LTS93	300093
France	Greece	27 Aug 21	General Military	8LTS137	300214
France	Greece	21 Feb 24	General Economic	43LTS481	301077
France	Greece	11 Mar 29	General Economic	95LTS401	302187
France	Greece	23 May 31	General Trade	125LTS415	302867
France	Greece	05 Jun 31	Air Transport	31LTS201	303011
France	Greece	11 Oct 37	Admin Cooperation	185LTS253	304289
France	Greece	19 Dec 38	Education	196LTS99	304572
France	Hungary	31 Jan 21	Claims and Debts	15LTS221	300396
France	Hungary	13 Oct 25	General Trade	67LTS255	301553
France	Hungary	13 Oct 25	General Economic	48LTS9	301150
France	Hungary	21 Dec 29	General Trade	132LTS189	303038
France	Hungary	25 Sep 31	General Trade	132LTS171	303037
France	Hungary	03 Mar 33	General Trade	140LTS177	303235
France	Hungary	07 Apr 33	Admin Cooperation	162LTS463	303756
France	Hungary	23 Jul 35	Air Transport	173LTS243	304016
France	Hungary	18 Nov 37	Admin Cooperation	185LTS257	304290
France	India	12 May 23	Territory Boundary	25LTS381	300627
France	India	19 Jun 26	Territory Boundary	57LTS35	301350
France	India	06 Jun 29	Admin Cooperation	95LTS61	302164
France	India	07 Mar 31	Postal Service	119LTS269	302750
France	India	09 May 32	Admin Cooperation	132LTS37	303029
France	India	28 Dec 32	Commodity Trade	140LTS36	303226
France	India	31 May 35	Admin Cooperation	163LTS287	303770
France	India	04 Jan 36	Commodity Trade	170LTS97	303930
France	India	01 May 36	Postal Service	178LTS57	304107
France	India	18 Dec 36	Sanitation	178LTS399	304122
France	India	22 Mar 39	Commodity Trade	197LTS273	304619
France	India	28 Jan 41	General Trade	204LTS323	304811
France	Italy	30 Sep 19	ILO Labor	5LTS279	300133
France	Italy	19 Feb 20	Non-ILO Labor	8LTS41	300204
France	Italy	27 Aug 20	Commodity Trade	8LTS95	300210
France	Italy	12 Sep 20	Telecommunications	1LTS397	300033
France	Italy	10 Jan 24	Customs	43LTS431	301076
France	Italy	10 Apr 24	General Trade	43LTS485	301078
France	Italy	29 May 26	General Trade	62LTS347	301473
France	Italy	29 May 26	Commodity Trade	62LTS425	301474
France	Italy	26 Jan 27	Customs	79LTS49	301804
France	Italy	07 Mar 28	General Trade	72LTS213	301694
France	Italy	10 Mar 29	Air Transport	93LTS319	302120
France	Italy	03 Jun 30	Admin Cooperation	153LTS135	303513
France	Italy	16 Jun 30	Taxation	144LTS115	303323
France	Italy	08 Jul 30	Territory Boundary	137LTS93	303148
France	Italy	13 Feb 31	Land Transport	139LTS109	303206
France	Italy	26 Dec 31	Patents/Copyrights	133LTS45	303055
France	Italy	03 Oct 32	Taxation	153LTS55	303507
France	Japan	30 Aug 27	General Economic	68LTS235	301587
France	Latvia	29 Oct 24	Extradition	93LTS265	302115
France	Latvia	30 Oct 24	General Trade	37LTS399	300963
France	Latvia	20 Jan 30	Consul/Citizenship	169LTS125	303917
France	Latvia	08 Mar 32	Claims and Debts	128LTS43	302936
France	Luxembourg	16 Jan 26	Taxation	48LTS149	301156
France	Luxembourg	20 Oct 27	Dispute Settlement	106LTS457	302462
France	Luxembourg	21 Feb 29	Extradition	123LTS387	302825
France	Luxembourg	31 Mar 30	Privil/Immunities	122LTS29	302797
France	Luxembourg	30 Jul 37	Admin Cooperation	181LTS107	304181
France	Malaya	31 Aug 35	Postal Service	165LTS215	303811

PARTY ONE	PARTY TWO	DATE	TOPIC	CITATION	NUMBER
France	Mexico	25 Sep 24	Claims and Debts	79LTS417	301818
France	Mexico	10 Nov 28	General Trade	86LTS423	301953
France	Monaco	26 May 25	Admin Cooperation	44LTS249	301086
France	Morocco	21 Jun 38	Admin Cooperation	189LTS423	304398
France	Multilateral	09 Sep 86*	Patents/Copyrights	123LTS233	302816
France	Multilateral	18 Mar 04	Humanitarian	1LTS83	300011
France	Multilateral	13 Nov 08	General Ad Hoc	1LTS217	300015
France	Multilateral	12 Jan 12	Sanitation	4LTS281	300112
France	Multilateral	23 Jan 12	Sanitation	8LTS187	300222
France	Multilateral	05 Jun 12	Telecommunications	1LTS135	300013
France	Multilateral	20 Mar 14	Patents/Copyrights	1LTS243	300016
France	Multilateral	21 Apr 14	Sanitation	5LTS394	300144
France	Multilateral	10 Sep 19	Health/Educ/Welfare	8LTS11	300201
France	Multilateral	10 Sep 19	Reparations	2LTS29	300043
France	Multilateral	10 Sep 19	Reparations	2LTS21	300042
France	Multilateral	10 Sep 19	Reparations	2LTS44	300045
France	Multilateral	10 Sep 19	General Economic	2LTS35	300044
France	Multilateral	10 Sep 19	Admin Cooperation	8LTS25	300202
France	Multilateral	10 Sep 19	General Trade	7LTS331	300200
France	Multilateral	09 Dec 19	Territory Boundary	5LTS335	300140
France	Multilateral	09 Feb 20	Territory Boundary	2LTS7	300041
France	Multilateral	25 Mar 20	Finance	1LTS45	300006
France	Multilateral	24 Apr 20	General Economic	136LTS381	303135
France	Multilateral	01 May 20	Air Transport	11LTS173	300297
France	Multilateral	04 Jun 20	Peace/Disarmament	6LTS187	300152
France	Multilateral	21 Jun 20	Health/Educ/Welfare	8LTS65	300207
France	Multilateral	30 Jun 20	Patents/Copyrights	1LTS59	300008
France	Multilateral	05 Jul 20	Dispute Settlement	2LTS241	300070
France	Multilateral	05 Aug 20	Territory Boundary	2LTS49	300046
France	Multilateral	10 Aug 20	Consul/Citizenship	28LTS223	300711
France	Multilateral	10 Aug 20	Territory Boundary	28LTS225	300710
France	Multilateral	31 Oct 20	Sanitation	164LTS85	303790
France	Multilateral	16 Dec 20	General IGO	6LTS379	300170
France	Multilateral	20 Apr 21	Land Transport	7LTS11	300171
France	Multilateral	20 Apr 21	Water Transport	7LTS35	300172
France	Multilateral	20 Apr 21	Water Transport	7LTS73	300174
France	Multilateral	05 May 21	Peace/Disarmament	12LTS419	300338
France	Multilateral	10 Jun 21	Customs	8LTS297	300227
France	Multilateral	20 Jul 21	General Military	8LTS115	300213
France	Multilateral	23 Jul 21	Water Transport	26LTS173	300647
France	Multilateral	05 Aug 21	Admin Cooperation	27LTS349	300695
France	Multilateral	03 Sep 21	Postal Service	8LTS147	300216
France	Multilateral	03 Sep 21	Postal Service	8LTS151	300217
France	Multilateral	05 Oct 21	IGO Establishment	51LTS361	301241
France	Multilateral	05 Oct 21	Admin Cooperation	29LTS73	300734
France	Multilateral	05 Oct 21	Admin Cooperation	29LTS79	300735
France	Multilateral	05 Oct 21	Admin Cooperation	29LTS67	300733
France	Multilateral	06 Oct 21	General Economic	17LTS45	300427
France	Multilateral	20 Oct 21	Peace/Disarmament	9LTS211	300255
France	Multilateral	09 Nov 21	Territory Boundary	12LTS381	300333
France	Multilateral	13 Dec 21	Territory Boundary	25LTS184	300607
France	Multilateral	06 Feb 22	General Trade	38LTS277	300982
France	Multilateral	06 Feb 22	Customs	38LTS267	300981
France	Multilateral	06 Feb 22	Admin Cooperation	25LTS195	300608
France	Multilateral	06 Feb 22	Peace/Disarmament	25LTS201	300609
France	Multilateral	22 Feb 22	Water Transport	26LTS219	300649
France	Multilateral	10 May 22	Water Transport	26LTS265	300652
France	Multilateral	05 Jul 22	Reparations	13LTS237	300355
France	Multilateral	04 Oct 22	Territory Boundary	12LTS385	300334
France	Multilateral	04 Oct 22	Territory Boundary	12LTS391	300335
France	Multilateral	02 Nov 22	Peace/Disarmament	149LTS35	303431
France	Multilateral	14 Dec 22	Water Transport	36LTS457	300943
France	Multilateral	27 Jan 23	Water Transport	26LTS253	300651
France	Multilateral	05 Feb 23	Telecommunications	28LTS409	300720
France	Multilateral	15 Mar 23	Territory Boundary	15LTS259	300398

PARTY ONE	PARTY TWO	DATE	TOPIC	CITATION	NUMBER
France	Multilateral	29 Mar 23	Admin Cooperation	20LTS111	300510
France	Multilateral	24 Jul 23	General Amity	36LTS145	300913
France	Multilateral	24 Jul 23	Taxation	36LTS175	300918
France	Multilateral	24 Jul 23	Consul/Citizenship	36LTS167	300917
France	Multilateral	24 Jul 23	General Trade	28LTS203	300707
France	Multilateral	24 Jul 23	Water Transport	28LTS115	300702
France	Multilateral	24 Jul 23	Admin Cooperation	28LTS283	300714
France	Multilateral	24 Jul 23	Admin Cooperation	28LTS197	300706
France	Multilateral	24 Jul 23	Peace/Disarmament	28LTS11	300701
France	Multilateral	24 Jul 23	Consul/Citizenship	28LTS221	300709
France	Multilateral	24 Jul 23	General Trade	28LTS151	300704
France	Multilateral	24 Jul 23	Territory Boundary	28LTS139	300703
France	Multilateral	24 Jul 23	Territory Boundary	28LTS215	300708
France	Multilateral	24 Jul 23	Admin Cooperation	36LTS201	300922
France	Multilateral	24 Jul 23	General Trade	28LTS171	300705
France	Multilateral	24 Jul 23	Water Transport	36LTS187	300920
France	Multilateral	24 Jul 23	Recognition	36LTS179	300919
France	Multilateral	29 Sep 23	Refugees	20LTS41	300504
France	Multilateral	03 Nov 23	Customs	30LTS371	300775
France	Multilateral	23 Nov 23	Reparations	28LTS273	300713
France	Multilateral	23 Nov 23	Claims and Debts	28LTS267	300712
France	Multilateral	09 Dec 23	General Economic	58LTS315	301380
France	Multilateral	09 Dec 23	Water Transport	58LTS284	301379
France	Multilateral	09 Dec 23	Land Transport	47LTS55	301129
France	Multilateral	09 Dec 23	Non-IBRD Project	36LTS76	300905
France	Multilateral	18 Dec 23	Territory Boundary	28LTS541	300729
France	Multilateral	08 Jan 24	Dispute Settlement	23LTS63	300576
France	Multilateral	25 Jan 24	Sanitation	57LTS135	301360
France	Multilateral	07 Feb 24	Water Transport	25LTS265	300614
France	Multilateral	14 Mar 24	Finance	25LTS423	300633
France	Multilateral	28 Mar 24	Finance	31LTS53	300781
France	Multilateral	28 Mar 24	Finance	31LTS46	300780
France	Multilateral	31 Mar 24	Sanitation	27LTS211	300685
France	Multilateral	08 May 24	Territory Boundary	29LTS85	300736
France	Multilateral	04 Jul 24	Admin Cooperation	51LTS227	301231
France	Multilateral	16 Aug 24	Taxation	41LTS429	301024
France	Multilateral	25 Aug 24	Water Transport	120LTS123	302763
France	Multilateral	25 Aug 24	Water Transport	120LTS155	302764
France	Multilateral	28 Aug 24	Postal Service	41LTS97	301008
France	Multilateral	28 Aug 24	Postal Service	40LTS437	301005
France	Multilateral	28 Aug 24	Postal Service	40LTS249	301003
France	Multilateral	28 Aug 24	Postal Service	40LTS307	301004
France	Multilateral	28 Aug 24	Postal Service	41LTS55	301007
France	Multilateral	28 Aug 24	Postal Service	40LTS19	301002
France	Multilateral	30 Aug 24	Admin Cooperation	30LTS75	300760
France	Multilateral	30 Aug 24	General Economic	30LTS63	300759
France	Multilateral	30 Aug 24	Admin Cooperation	30LTS79	300761
France	Multilateral	30 Aug 24	Reparations	30LTS97	300762
France	Multilateral	25 Sep 24	Admin Cooperation	30LTS421	300777
France	Multilateral	23 Oct 24	General Transport	77LTS367	301778
France	Multilateral	23 Oct 24	Land Transport	78LTS17	301779
France	Multilateral	29 Nov 24	General IGO	80LTS293	301835
France	Multilateral	01 Dec 24	Sanitation	78LTS351	301794
France	Multilateral	11 Feb 25	Sanitation	51LTS337	301239
France	Multilateral	19 Feb 25	Admin Cooperation	81LTS317	301845
France	Multilateral	00 Apr 25	Water Transport	37LTS21	300945
France	Multilateral	23 Apr 25	Water Transport	37LTS9	300944
France	Multilateral	05 May 25	Finance	55LTS225	301318
France	Multilateral	17 Jun 25	Peace/Disarmament	94LTS65	302138
France	Multilateral	16 Oct 25	Peace/Disarmament	54LTS289	301292
France	Multilateral	29 Oct 25	Telecommunications	57LTS201	301365
France	Multilateral	06 Nov 25	Patents/Copyrights	74LTS289	301743
France	Multilateral	06 Nov 25	Other Economic	74LTS341	301746
France	Multilateral	06 Nov 25	Other Economic	74LTS319	301744
France	Multilateral	06 Nov 25	Patents/Copyrights	74LTS327	301745

PARTY ONE	PARTY TWO	DATE	TOPIC	CITATION	NUMBER
France	Multilateral	27 Nov 25	Water Transport	67LTS63	301539
France	Multilateral	00 Apr 26	Water Transport	57LTS437	301366
France	Multilateral	10 Apr 26	Water Transport	176LTS199	304062
France	Multilateral	10 Apr 26	Water Transport	120LTS187	302765
France	Multilateral	24 Apr 26	Land Transport	108LTS123	302505
France	Multilateral	24 Apr 26	Land Transport	97LTS83	302220
France	Multilateral	12 May 26	Refugees	89LTS47	302004
France	Multilateral	22 May 26	Air Transport	58LTS331	301381
France	Multilateral	21 Jun 26	Sanitation	78LTS229	301793
France	Multilateral	14 Sep 26	Non-ILO Labor	77LTS149	301769
France	Multilateral	18 Sep 26	General IGO	59LTS237	301393
France	Multilateral	25 Sep 26	ILO Labor	60LTS253	301414
France	Multilateral	13 Nov 26	Territory Boundary	77LTS171	301770
France	Multilateral	13 Nov 26	Territory Boundary	77LTS199	301771
France	Multilateral	13 Nov 26	Territory Boundary	77LTS217	301772
France	Multilateral	13 Nov 26	Territory Boundary	77LTS249	301773
France	Multilateral	31 Mar 27	Air Transport	66LTS59	301525
France	Multilateral	02 May 27	Telecommunications	68LTS189	301582
France	Multilateral	19 May 27	Air Transport	68LTS407	301595
France	Multilateral	12 Jul 27	Direct Aid	135LTS247	303115
France	Multilateral	16 Aug 27	Telecommunications	78LTS141	301785
France	Multilateral	10 Sep 27	Postal Service	75LTS7	301749
France	Multilateral	10 Sep 27	Postal Service	75LTS39	301750
France	Multilateral	26 Sep 27	Dispute Settlement	92LTS301	302096
France	Multilateral	27 Oct 27	Air Transport	148LTS265	303417
France	Multilateral	29 Oct 27	Scientific Project	127LTS27	302903
France	Multilateral	08 Nov 27	General Trade	97LTS391	302238
France	Multilateral	25 Nov 27	Telecommunications	84LTS97	301905
France	Multilateral	08 Dec 27	Loans and Credits	70LTS73	301623
France	Multilateral	08 Mar 28	Telecommunications	80LTS241	301829
France	Multilateral	30 Jun 28	Refugees	89LTS53	302005
France	Multilateral	30 Jun 28	Refugees	89LTS63	302006
France	Multilateral	11 Jul 28	Commodity Trade	95LTS373	302185
France	Multilateral	11 Jul 28	Commodity Trade	95LTS357	302184
France	Multilateral	15 Jul 28	Patents/Copyrights	79LTS133	301806
France	Multilateral	25 Jul 28	General Amity	87LTS211	301971
France	Multilateral	27 Aug 28	General Military	94LTS57	302137
France	Multilateral	26 Sep 28	Dispute Settlement	93LTS343	302123
France	Multilateral	30 Oct 28	Dispute Settlement	87LTS103	301963
France	Multilateral	22 Nov 28	Culture	111LTS343	302598
France	Multilateral	14 Dec 28	General Economic	110LTS171	302560
France	Multilateral	20 Dec 28	Specific Resources	86LTS429	301954
France	Multilateral	02 Feb 29	Telecommunications	92LTS353	302100
France	Multilateral	16 Apr 29	Specific Resources	126LTS305	302891
France	Multilateral	20 Apr 29	Admin Cooperation	112LTS371	302623
France	Multilateral	31 May 29	Water Transport	136LTS81	303127
France	Multilateral	14 Jun 29	Visas	94LTS275	302148
France	Multilateral	28 Jun 29	Postal Service	102LTS245	302368
France	Multilateral	28 Jun 29	Postal Service	103LTS249	302371
France	Multilateral	28 Jun 29	Postal Service	103LTS377	302373
France	Multilateral	28 Jun 29	Postal Service	103LTS429	302374
France	Multilateral	28 Jun 29	Postal Service	103LTS71	302370
France	Multilateral	28 Jun 29	Postal Service	103LTS5	302369
France	Multilateral	28 Jun 29	Postal Service	103LTS321	302372
France	Multilateral	27 Jul 29	Other Military	118LTS343	302734
France	Multilateral	27 Jul 29	Other Military	118LTS303	302733
France	Multilateral	20 Aug 29	Sanitation	98LTS125	302243
France	Multilateral	30 Aug 29	Consul/Citizenship	104LTS473	302399
France	Multilateral	30 Aug 29	General Amity	104LTS487	302400
France	Multilateral	07 Sep 29	Telecommunications	98LTS345	302255
France	Multilateral	14 Sep 29	UN Charter	165LTS353	303822
France	Multilateral	12 Oct 29	General Transport	137LTS11	303145
France	Multilateral	18 Dec 29	Admin Cooperation	104LTS27	302376
France	Multilateral	20 Jan 30	Reparations	104LTS421	302396
France	Multilateral	20 Jan 30	Finance	104LTS433	302397

PARTY ONE	PARTY TWO	DATE	TOPIC	CITATION	NUMBER
France	Multilateral	20 Jan 30	Reparations	104LTS243	302394
France	Multilateral	20 Jan 30	Finance	104LTS413	302395
France	Multilateral	20 Jan 30	Reparations	112LTS361	302622
France	Multilateral	20 Jan 30	Reparations	113LTS389	302650
France	Multilateral	24 Jan 30	Peace/Disarmament	106LTS85	302437
France	Multilateral	17 Feb 30	Dispute Settlement	102LTS87	302354
France	Multilateral	12 Apr 30	Milit Servic/Citiz	178LTS227	304117
France	Multilateral	12 Apr 30	Admin Cooperation	179LTS115	304138
France	Multilateral	12 Apr 30	Admin Cooperation	179LTS89	304137
France	Multilateral	22 Apr 30	Peace/Disarmament	112LTS65	302608
France	Multilateral	28 Apr 30	Claims and Debts	121LTS69	302785
France	Multilateral	07 Jun 30	Finance	143LTS257	303313
France	Multilateral	07 Jun 30	Finance	143LTS337	303315
France	Multilateral	07 Jun 30	Finance	143LTS317	303314
France	Multilateral	10 Jun 30	Loans and Credits	112LTS237	302618
France	Multilateral	01 Aug 30	Health/Educ/Welfare	128LTS9	302932
France	Multilateral	23 Oct 30	Water Transport	125LTS95	302849
France	Multilateral	23 Oct 30	Water Transport	112LTS21	302603
France	Multilateral	19 Mar 31	Finance	143LTS355	303316
France	Multilateral	19 Mar 31	Admin Cooperation	143LTS7	303301
France	Multilateral	19 Mar 31	Finance	143LTS407	303317
France	Multilateral	28 Mar 31	Customs	119LTS47	302739
France	Multilateral	30 Mar 31	Land Transport	150LTS247	303459
France	Multilateral	30 Jun 31	Scientific Project	149LTS63	303434
France	Multilateral	13 Jul 31	Other HEW	139LTS301	303219
France	Multilateral	21 Aug 31	Other Ad Hoc	185LTS45	304273
France	Multilateral	21 Aug 31	Other Economic	127LTS95	302910
France	Multilateral	24 Sep 31	Specific Resources	155LTS349	303586
France	Multilateral	27 Nov 31	Sanitation	177LTS373	304100
France	Multilateral	11 Dec 31	Commodity Trade	170LTS251	303941
France	Multilateral	15 Jul 32	Direct Aid	135LTS285	303118
France	Multilateral	02 Sep 32	Land Transport	154LTS123	303543
France	Multilateral	09 Dec 32	Telecommunications	151LTS5	303479
France	Multilateral	11 Mar 33	Water Transport	135LTS301	303119
France	Multilateral	12 Apr 33	Sanitation	161LTS65	303706
France	Multilateral	29 May 33	Admin Cooperation	192LTS289	304479
France	Multilateral	19 Jun 33	Gen Communications	154LTS133	303544
France	Multilateral	29 Jul 33	Extradition	142LTS165	303288
France	Multilateral	25 Aug 33	Commodity Trade	141LTS71	303262
France	Multilateral	11 Oct 33	Education	155LTS331	303585
France	Multilateral	11 Oct 33	Consul/Citizenship	150LTS431	303476
France	Multilateral	28 Oct 33	Refugees	159LTS199	303663
France	Multilateral	08 Nov 33	Specific Resources	172LTS241	303995
France	Multilateral	23 Nov 33	Land Transport	192LTS389	304484
France	Multilateral	23 Nov 33	Land Transport	192LTS327	304483
France	Multilateral	20 Mar 34	Postal Service	174LTS171	304048
France	Multilateral	20 Mar 34	Postal Service	175LTS363	304052
France	Multilateral	20 Mar 34	Postal Service	175LTS5	304049
France	Multilateral	20 Mar 34	Finance	176LTS9	304053
France	Multilateral	20 Mar 34	Postal Service	176LTS55	304054
France	Multilateral	20 Mar 34	Postal Service	175LTS73	304050
France	Multilateral	20 Mar 34	Postal Service	175LTS269	304051
France	Multilateral	26 Apr 34	Admin Cooperation	164LTS63	303789
France	Multilateral	07 May 34	Commodity Trade	171LTS203	303961
France	Multilateral	02 Jun 34	General Trade	192LTS9	304458
France	Multilateral	02 Jun 34	Patents/Copyrights	205LTS179	304834
France	Multilateral	02 Jun 34	Patents/Copyrights	192LTS17	304459
France	Multilateral	12 Jun 34	Milit Installation	155LTS367	303587
France	Multilateral	25 Jul 34	Other HEW	177LTS59	304080
France	Multilateral	22 Dec 34	Visas	183LTS145	304230
France	Multilateral	20 Feb 35	Sanitation	193LTS59	304487
France	Multilateral	20 Feb 35	Sanitation	193LTS37	304486
France	Multilateral	20 Feb 35	Sanitation	186LTS173	304310
France	Multilateral	25 Mar 36	Peace/Disarmament	184LTS115	304246
France	Multilateral	26 Jun 36	Other HEW	198LTS299	304648

PARTY ONE	PARTY TWO	DATE	TOPIC	CITATION	NUMBER
France	Multilateral	04 Jul 36	Refugees	171LTS75	303952
France	Multilateral	20 Jul 36	Territory Boundary	173LTS213	304015
France	Multilateral	30 Jul 36	IGO Status/Immunit	197LTS31	304602
France	Multilateral	23 Sep 36	Gen Communications	186LTS301	304319
France	Multilateral	06 Nov 36	General Military	173LTS353	304025
France	Multilateral	10 Feb 37	General Transport	189LTS313	304391
France	Multilateral	31 Mar 37	Commodity Trade	189LTS359	304394
France	Multilateral	08 May 37	Privil/Immunities	182LTS37	304202
France	Multilateral	14 Sep 37	General Military	181LTS137	304184
France	Multilateral	17 Sep 37	Milit Installation	181LTS150	304185
France	Multilateral	10 Feb 38	Refugees	192LTS59	304461
France	Multilateral	15 Jul 38	Visas	195LTS73	304536
France	Multilateral	18 Aug 38	Admin Cooperation	196LTS113	304574
France	Multilateral	12 Sep 38	Culture	198LTS111	304630
France	Multilateral	25 Oct 38	Air Transport	192LTS323	304482
France	Multilateral	31 Oct 38	Sanitation	198LTS205	304642
France	Multilateral	03 Dec 38	Education	200LTS249	304694
France	Multilateral	28 Dec 38	Other Military	196LTS221	304585
France	Multilateral	27 Jan 39	Loans and Credits	196LTS287	304591
France	Multilateral	03 Apr 39	Water Transport	195LTS471	304566
France	Multilateral	23 Apr 39	Land Transport	104LTS87	302380
France	Multilateral	23 May 39	Postal Service	202LTS159	304742
France	Multilateral	07 Sep 39	Loans and Credits	198LTS357	304654
France	Multilateral	19 Oct 39	General Military	200LTS167	304689
France	Multilateral	02 Jun 42	Patents/Copyrights	205LTS163	304833
France	Netherlands	16 Sep 20	General Transport	12LTS213	300312
France	Netherlands	16 Apr 21	General Aid	11LTS341	300300
France	Netherlands	02 Jul 23	Air Transport	20LTS131	300512
France	Netherlands	07 Feb 24	Gen Communications	25LTS265	300615
France	Netherlands	10 Mar 28	Dispute Settlement	102LTS109	302356
France	Netherlands	28 Feb 30	Taxation	101LTS303	302331
France	Netherlands	29 Oct 30	Education	125LTS29	302843
France	Netherlands	19 Oct 35	Taxation	166LTS67	303830
France	Netherlands	25 May 36	Visas	173LTS187	304011
France	Netherlands	15 Jul 38	Air Transport	192LTS151	304469
France	Norway	23 Apr 21	Commodity Trade	14LTS375	300386
France	Norway	01 Oct 23	Admin Cooperation	33LTS237	300847
France	Norway	11 Jun 26	Patents/Copyrights	50LTS315	301215
France	Norway	12 Apr 27	Commodity Trade	178LTS199	304114
France	Norway	21 Nov 27	Education	70LTS167	301632
France	Norway	02 Jun 30	Taxation	102LTS27	302350
France	Norway	19 Nov 34	Commodity Trade	178LTS217	304115
France	Norway	27 Mar 37	Commodity Trade	178LTS221	304116
France	Norway	28 Feb 39	Admin Cooperation	195LTS165	304546
France	Palestine	19 Jun 36	Postal Service	172LTS17	303977
France	Panama	16 Aug 22	Consul/Citizenship	43LTS423	301075
France	Panama	15 Aug 24	Customs	93LTS425	302130
France	Persia	18 Oct 27	Scientific Project	112LTS267	302619
France	Persia	11 May 28	General Amity	82LTS43	301858
France	Persia	10 May 29	General Amity	150LTS329	303465
France	Poland	03 Sep 19	Visas	1LTS337	300028
France	Poland	17 Feb 21	General Amity	18LTS11	300449
France	Poland	06 Feb 22	General Economic	43LTS415	301074
France	Poland	06 Feb 22	Admin Cooperation	43LTS399	301073
France	Poland	09 Dec 24	General Trade	44LTS127	301081
France	Poland	16 Oct 25	Peace/Disarmament	54LTS353	301297
France	Poland	30 Dec 25	Admin Cooperation	95LTS233	302177
France	Poland	30 Dec 25	Admin Cooperation	48LTS139	301155
France	Poland	30 Dec 25	Extradition	95LTS217	302176
France	Poland	30 Dec 25	Consul/Citizenship	73LTS265	301719
France	Poland	20 Jan 30	Claims and Debts	126LTS117	302876
France	Poland	02 Aug 30	Air Transport	114LTS93	302657
France	Poland	24 Apr 31	Sanitation	130LTS417	303000
France	Portugal	08 Jun 20	Customs	1LTS393	300032
France	Portugal	04 Mar 25	General Economic	44LTS197	301083

PARTY ONE	PARTY TWO	DATE	TOPIC	CITATION	NUMBER
France	Portugal	06 Jul 28	Dispute Settlement	126LTS27	302869
France	Romania	10 Jun 26	General Amity	58LTS225	301373
France	Romania	10 Jun 26	Dispute Settlement	58LTS233	301374
France	Romania	27 Aug 30	Consul/Citizenship	158LTS379	303644
France	Romania	31 Mar 39	Education	199LTS213	304676
France	Romania	31 Mar 39	Finance	199LTS219	304677
France	Saar	30 Jul 20	Extradition	27LTS241	300687
France	Saar	05 Jul 22	Taxation	27LTS265	300689
France	Saar	30 Nov 22	Customs	27LTS283	300691
France	Saar	15 Jan 25	Customs	44LTS181	301082
France	Saar	27 May 26	Non-ILO Labor	55LTS157	301312
France	Saar	14 Apr 27	Land Transport	70LTS115	301628
France	Saar	14 Dec 27	Dispute Settlement	70LTS155	301630
France	Saar	14 Dec 27	Admin Cooperation	70LTS163	301631
France	Saar	12 Nov 28	Finance	85LTS451	301945
France	San Marino	30 Apr 26	Extradition	89LTS9	302001
France	Serb/Croat/Slovene	11 Nov 27	Dispute Settlement	68LTS381	301593
France	Serb/Croat/Slovene	11 Nov 27	General Amity	68LTS373	301592
France	Siam	14 Feb 25	General Amity	43LTS189	301055
France	Siam	07 Dec 37	General Amity	201LTS113	304708
France	Siam	09 Dec 37	General Trade	201LTS145	304709
France	South Africa	11 Feb 35	General Trade	189LTS17	304372
France	South Africa	27 Aug 35	General Trade	189LTS41	304374
France	Spain	16 Feb 24	Admin Cooperation	25LTS409	300631
France	Spain	03 Aug 25	General Trade	38LTS371	300992
France	Spain	22 Mar 28	Air Transport	73LTS63	301707
France	Spain	12 Jun 28	Territory Boundary	136LTS289	303131
France	Spain	16 Jul 28	Postal Service	135LTS149	303110
France	Spain	07 Mar 32	Military Mission	148LTS385	303424
France	Spain	21 Dec 35	General Economic	167LTS9	303856
France	Spain	30 Dec 35	Commodity Trade	172LTS217	303993
France	Spain	10 Jul 39	Dispute Settlement	148LTS369	303423
France	Sweden	25 Nov 20	General Transport	2LTS183	300065
France	Sweden	09 Nov 21	Humanitarian	7LTS303	300197
France	Sweden	19 Jul 26	Consul/Citizenship	54LTS283	301291
France	Sweden	03 Mar 28	Dispute Settlement	95LTS89	302168
France	Sweden	25 Jan 30	Taxation	99LTS99	302271
France	Sweden	13 Mar 33	General Trade	142LTS131	303285
France	Sweden	09 Jun 34	Education	154LTS101	303541
France	Sweden	22 Mar 35	General Trade	158LTS287	303639
France	Sweden	18 Jan 36	Customs	167LTS197	303866
France	Sweden	04 Dec 36	Taxation	184LTS35	304241
France	Sweden	24 Dec 36	Taxation	181LTS315	304198
France	Sweden	17 Feb 37	General Trade	176LTS267	304065
France	Sweden	30 Jun 37	Admin Cooperation	179LTS203	304148
France	Sweden	31 Jan 38	General Trade	185LTS223	304286
France	Sweden	18 Apr 39	Dispute Settlement	198LTS131	304632
France	Sweden	05 May 39	Taxation	198LTS201	304641
France	Switzerland	11 Jun 14	General Amity	12LTS361	300329
France	Switzerland	09 Dec 19	Air Transport	1LTS29	300004
France	Switzerland	24 Jan 22	Telecommunications	12LTS371	300331
France	Switzerland	20 Mar 22	Customs	12LTS377	300332
France	Switzerland	06 Apr 25	Dispute Settlement	147LTS89	303393
France	Switzerland	27 Aug 26	Admin Cooperation	71LTS63	301654
France	Switzerland	27 Aug 26	Admin Cooperation	59LTS231	301392
France	Switzerland	21 Jan 28	General Trade	72LTS275	301698
France	Switzerland	08 Jul 29	General Economic	114LTS189	302664
France	Switzerland	09 Sep 31	Non-ILO Labor	142LTS205	303293
France	Switzerland	09 Jun 33	Other HEW	181LTS275	304194
France	Switzerland	04 Oct 36	Admin Cooperation	195LTS287	304550
France	Switzerland	29 Jan 37	Land Transport	195LTS291	304551
France	Switzerland	13 Oct 37	Taxation	194LTS191	304522
France	Switzerland	03 Dec 37	Admin Cooperation	185LTS265	304292
France	Switzerland	31 Jan 38	Territory Boundary	195LTS313	304553
France	Turkey	30 May 26	General Amity	54LTS195	301285

PARTY ONE	PARTY TWO	DATE	TOPIC	CITATION	NUMBER
France	Turkey	31 Jul 26	General Amity	54LTS177	301284
France	Turkey	01 Nov 27	Visas	92LTS249	302092
France	Turkey	29 Aug 29	General Economic	123LTS193	302815
France	Turkey	27 Oct 32	Land Transport	136LTS23	303121
France	Turkey	15 Jun 37	General Trade	179LTS195	304147
France	UK Great Britain	16 Apr 02	Customs	1LTS79	300010
France	UK Great Britain	06 Aug 14	Admin Cooperation	10LTS333	300278
France	UK Great Britain	10 Jan 20	Claims and Debts	1LTS249	300017
France	UK Great Britain	10 Jan 20	Telecommunications	5LTS53	300117
France	UK Great Britain	24 Apr 20	Specific Resources	1LTS281	300022
France	UK Great Britain	26 Apr 20	Admin Cooperation	1LTS287	300023
France	UK Great Britain	20 Oct 20	Air Transport	2LTS323	300085
France	UK Great Britain	23 Dec 20	Territory Boundary	22LTS353	300564
France	UK Great Britain	29 Jun 21	Reparations	6LTS23	300146
France	UK Great Britain	09 Jul 21	Non-ILO Labor	6LTS341	300166
France	UK Great Britain	03 Sep 21	Postal Service	8LTS153	300218
France	UK Great Britain	10 Oct 21	Air Transport	9LTS181	300250
France	UK Great Britain	30 Jan 22	Air Transport	12LTS449	300341
France	UK Great Britain	02 Feb 22	Admin Cooperation	10LTS448	300284
France	UK Great Britain	22 Feb 22	Non-ILO Labor	9LTS198	300253
France	UK Great Britain	26 Dec 22	Other Ad Hoc	16LTS213	300413
France	UK Great Britain	07 Mar 23	Territory Boundary	22LTS363	300565
France	UK Great Britain	24 May 23	Consul/Citizenship	18LTS305	300472
France	UK Great Britain	24 Jul 23	Peace/Disarmament	36LTS207	300923
France	UK Great Britain	29 Sep 23	Admin Cooperation	20LTS183	300516
France	UK Great Britain	29 Sep 23	Specific Resources	21LTS137	300536
France	UK Great Britain	10 Oct 23	Postal Service	22LTS381	300567
France	UK Great Britain	13 Nov 23	Extradition	21LTS131	300535
France	UK Great Britain	27 Dec 23	Visas	24LTS131	300600
France	UK Great Britain	21 Jan 24	Territory Boundary	28LTS461	300723
France	UK Great Britain	28 Jan 25	Visas	33LTS335	300856
France	UK Great Britain	17 Apr 25	Postal Service	36LTS429	300939
France	UK Great Britain	12 Jul 26	Reparations	98LTS155	302244
France	UK Great Britain	23 May 27	Telecommunications	67LTS227	301550
France	UK Great Britain	16 May 28	Non-ILO Labor	80LTS257	301832
France	UK Great Britain	12 Jun 28	Postal Service	85LTS109	301926
France	UK Great Britain	23 Sep 28	Postal Service	87LTS29	301961
France	UK Great Britain	06 Mar 29	Postal Service	90LTS391	302050
France	UK Great Britain	06 May 29	Territory Boundary	93LTS27	302102
France	UK Great Britain	15 May 29	Postal Service	134LTS263	303097
France	UK Great Britain	25 May 29	Admin Cooperation	95LTS55	302163
France	UK Great Britain	02 Aug 29	Reparations	100LTS459	302314
France	UK Great Britain	24 Mar 30	Telecommunications	105LTS227	302415
France	UK Great Britain	04 Sep 30	Finance	109LTS31	302526
France	UK Great Britain	17 Nov 31	Postal Service	134LTS299	303098
France	UK Great Britain	27 Nov 31	Postal Service	132LTS25	303028
France	UK Great Britain	28 Nov 31	Postal Service	127LTS195	302919
France	UK Great Britain	15 Dec 31	Admin Cooperation	129LTS445	302976
France	UK Great Britain	28 Dec 31	Postal Service	133LTS79	303058
France	UK Great Britain	22 Aug 32	Postal Service	136LTS313	303133
France	UK Great Britain	01 Oct 32	Taxation	135LTS25	303102
France	UK Great Britain	18 Jan 34	Admin Cooperation	171LTS183	303960
France	UK Great Britain	08 May 34	General Economic	154LTS367	303562
France	UK Great Britain	31 Jan 35	Admin Cooperation	160LTS275	303697
France	UK Great Britain	09 Apr 35	Taxation	199LTS49	304663
France	UK Great Britain	16 Jul 35	Postal Service	168LTS179	303898
France	UK Great Britain	15 Apr 36	Admin Cooperation	203LTS123	304755
France	UK Great Britain	03 Apr 37	Admin Cooperation	179LTS265	304154
France	UK Great Britain	24 Apr 37	Other Military	178LTS186	304112
France	UK Great Britain	23 Jul 37	Customs	184LTS279	304251
France	UK Great Britain	29 Jul 37	Privil/Immunities	184LTS351	304257
France	UK Great Britain	14 Oct 37	General Trade	184LTS457	304266
France	UK Great Britain	19 Aug 38	Postal Service	192LTS189	304471
France	UK Great Britain	26 Oct 38	Postal Service	194LTS371	304530
France	UK Great Britain	08 Nov 38	Customs	196LTS215	304584
France	UK Great Britain	13 Sep 39	Telecommunications	201LTS369	304724
France	UK Great Britain	08 Oct 39	Admin Cooperation	201LTS59	304703
France	UK Great Britain	18 Jan 40	Territory Boundary	201LTS375	304725
France	United Arab Rep	13 Jun 30	Health/Educ/Welfare	106LTS39	302435
France	United Arab Rep	03 Aug 40	Claims and Debts	202LTS121	304740
France	USA (United States)	03 Sep 21	Postal Service	8LTS145	300215
France	USA (United States)	13 Feb 23	Territory Boundary	26LTS53	300640
France	USA (United States)	13 Feb 23	Territory Boundary	26LTS69	300641
France	USA (United States)	19 Jul 23	Dispute Settlement	25LTS405	300630
France	USA (United States)	30 Jun 24	Admin Cooperation	61LTS415	301451
France	USA (United States)	29 Apr 26	Claims and Debts	100LTS27	302292
France	USA (United States)	08 Jul 27	Taxation	114LTS413	302669
France	USA (United States)	29 Aug 27	Other Military	68LTS253	301589
France	USA (United States)	06 Feb 28	Dispute Settlement	91LTS323	302072
France	USA (United States)	15 Jan 29	Extradition	92LTS259	302093
France	USA (United States)	27 Apr 32	Taxation	164LTS211	303795
France	USA (United States)	04 Mar 33	Admin Cooperation	138LTS349	303198
France	USA (United States)	08 Oct 34	Postal Service	157LTS21	303603
France	USA (United States)	30 Dec 35	Postal Service	171LTS117	303955
France	USA (United States)	23 Apr 36	Extradition	172LTS197	303990
France	USA (United States)	06 May 36	General Trade	199LTS259	304679
France	USA (United States)	12 Dec 36	Customs	176LTS403	304076
France	USA (United States)	18 Feb 37	Customs	184LTS479	304269
France	USA (United States)	14 Jan 38	Visas	191LTS213	304445
France	USA (United States)	15 Jul 39	Air Transport	199LTS355	304683
France	USA (United States)	15 Jul 39	Air Transport	199LTS207	304675
France	USSR (Soviet Union)	29 Nov 32	General Amity	157LTS411	303615
France	USSR (Soviet Union)	29 Nov 32	Dispute Settlement	157LTS421	303616
France	USSR (Soviet Union)	11 Jan 34	Customs	167LTS349	303878
France	USSR (Soviet Union)	02 May 35	General Amity	167LTS395	303881
France	USSR (Soviet Union)	09 Mar 36	Postal Service	179LTS131	304140
France	USSR (Soviet Union)	11 Aug 36	Admin Cooperation	176LTS365	304073
France	Yugoslavia	20 Jan 30	Reparations	104LTS171	302386
France	Yugoslavia	20 Jan 30	Claims and Debts	104LTS177	302387
France	Yugoslavia	07 Nov 31	Commodity Trade	144LTS281	303331
France	Yugoslavia	29 Jul 32	Education	144LTS313	303334
France	Yugoslavia	28 Oct 32	General Amity	135LTS281	303117
France	Yugoslavia	12 Oct 37	General Amity	182LTS149	304206
French India	Multilateral	24 Apr 26	Land Transport	108LTS123	302505
French India	Multilateral	23 Oct 30	Water Transport	125LTS95	302849
French Morocco	Multilateral	31 Oct 20	Sanitation	164LTS85	303790
French Morocco	Multilateral	20 Mar 34	Postal Service	175LTS73	304050
French Morocco	Multilateral	20 Mar 34	Postal Service	175LTS363	304052
French Morocco	Multilateral	20 Mar 34	Postal Service	175LTS269	304051
French Morocco	Multilateral	20 Mar 34	Postal Service	176LTS55	304054
French Morocco	Multilateral	20 Mar 34	Postal Service	175LTS5	304049
French Morocco	Multilateral	20 Mar 34	Finance	176LTS9	304053
French Morocco	Multilateral	02 Jun 34	Patents/Copyrights	205LTS179	304834
French Morocco	Multilateral	02 Jun 42	Patents/Copyrights	205LTS163	304833
French Settlements	Multilateral	05 Jun 12	Telecommunications	1LTS135	300013
French Somaliland	Multilateral	05 Jun 12	Telecommunications	1LTS135	300013
French Somaliland	Multilateral	29 Oct 25	Telecommunications	57LTS201	301365
French Somaliland	Multilateral	24 Apr 26	Land Transport	108LTS123	302505
French Somaliland	Multilateral	24 Apr 26	Land Transport	97LTS83	302220
French Somaliland	Multilateral	23 Oct 30	Water Transport	125LTS95	302849
French Togoland	Multilateral	28 Jun 29	Postal Service	103LTS5	302369
French Togoland	Multilateral	28 Jun 29	Postal Service	103LTS71	302370
French Togoland	Multilateral	28 Jun 29	Postal Service	103LTS249	302371
French Togoland	Multilateral	28 Jun 29	Postal Service	102LTS245	302368
French Togoland	Multilateral	23 Oct 30	Water Transport	125LTS95	302849
French West Africa	Multilateral	21 Jun 20	Health/Educ/Welfare	8LTS65	300207
French West Africa	Multilateral	31 Oct 20	Sanitation	164LTS85	303790
French West Africa	Multilateral	24 Apr 26	Land Transport	108LTS123	302505
French West Africa	Multilateral	24 Apr 26	Land Transport	97LTS83	302220
French West Africa	Multilateral	21 Jun 26	Sanitation	78LTS229	301793

PARTY ONE	PARTY TWO	DATE	TOPIC	CITATION	NUMBER
French West Africa	Multilateral	25 Nov 27	Telecommunications	84LTS97	301905
French West Africa	Multilateral	23 Oct 30	Water Transport	125LTS95	302849
French West Africa	Multilateral	31 Mar 37	Commodity Trade	189LTS359	304394
Gabon	Multilateral	20 Apr 29	Admin Cooperation	112LTS395	302624
Gabon	Multilateral	20 Apr 29	Admin Cooperation	112LTS371	302623
Gambia	Multilateral	18 Mar 04	Humanitarian	1LTS83	300011
Gambia	Multilateral	30 Jun 20	Patents/Copyrights	1LTS59	300008
Gambia	Multilateral	31 Mar 22	Humanitarian	9LTS415	300269
Gambia	Multilateral	25 Aug 24	Water Transport	120LTS155	302764
Gambia	Multilateral	01 Dec 24	Sanitation	78LTS351	301794
Gambia	Multilateral	25 Nov 27	Telecommunications	84LTS97	301905
Gambia	Multilateral	28 Oct 33	Refugees	159LTS199	303663
Gambia	Multilateral	23 Sep 36	Gen Communications	186LTS301	304319
Gambia	Multilateral	10 Feb 38	Refugees	192LTS59	304461
Germany	Afghanistan	03 Mar 26	General Amity	62LTS115	301460
Germany	Allied Powers	17 Dec 20	Territory Boundary	12LTS39	300306
Germany	Allied Powers	28 Oct 24	General Military	41LTS461	301025
Germany	Australia	31 May 26	Postal Service	60LTS121	301409
Germany	Austria	01 Sep 20	General Economic	4LTS201	300107
Germany	Austria	01 Sep 20	Finance	2LTS132	300057
Germany	Austria	11 Aug 21	Non-ILO Labor	29LTS429	300753
Germany	Austria	17 Aug 21	Claims and Debts	19LTS237	300497
Germany	Austria	23 May 22	Taxation	26LTS405	300660
Germany	Austria	28 May 22	Taxation	26LTS445	300661
Germany	Austria	21 Jun 23	Admin Cooperation	27LTS88	300669
Germany	Austria	21 Jun 23	Admin Cooperation	27LTS57	300668
Germany	Austria	18 Feb 24	Non-ILO Labor	29LTS435	300754
Germany	Austria	30 Apr 24	Admin Cooperation	46LTS175	301119
Germany	Austria	12 Jul 24	General Trade	41LTS287	301022
Germany	Austria	19 May 25	Air Transport	52LTS121	301253
Germany	Austria	03 Oct 25	Customs	52LTS171	301255
Germany	Austria	08 Jan 26	Admin Cooperation	62LTS95	301459
Germany	Austria	21 May 26	General Economic	53LTS397	301269
Germany	Austria	05 Feb 27	Territory Boundary	73LTS205	301714
Germany	Austria	05 Feb 27	Admin Cooperation	73LTS227	301715
Germany	Austria	29 Feb 28	Non-ILO Labor	79LTS405	301816
Germany	Austria	17 Jan 30	Reparations	107LTS325	302488
Germany	Austria	05 Feb 30	Non-ILO Labor	119LTS201	302746
Germany	Austria	15 Feb 30	Patents/Copyrights	109LTS501	302552
Germany	Austria	12 Apr 30	Customs	115LTS333	302694
Germany	Austria	12 Apr 30	Privil/Immunities	115LTS297	302693
Germany	Austria	12 Apr 30	General Transport	115LTS277	302692
Germany	Austria	01 Aug 30	Admin Cooperation	115LTS465	302695
Germany	Austria	07 Dec 32	Extradition	137LTS69	303147
Germany	Austria	26 Aug 36	Visas	171LTS357	303972
Germany	Bel-Lux Econ Union	05 Sep 34	General Trade	154LTS187	303547
Germany	Belgium	23 Apr 20	Admin Cooperation	12LTS29	300305
Germany	Belgium	09 Jul 20	Peace/Disarmament	12LTS45	300307
Germany	Belgium	11 Sep 22	General Amity	41LTS141	301009
Germany	Belgium	18 Apr 25	Admin Cooperation	42LTS49	301031
Germany	Belgium	03 Oct 25	Visas	38LTS285	300983
Germany	Belgium	16 Oct 25	General Military	54LTS303	301293
Germany	Belgium	29 May 26	Air Transport	127LTS149	302916
Germany	Belgium	01 Jul 26	General Transport	62LTS127	301461
Germany	Belgium	09 Jul 27	Admin Cooperation	75LTS367	301759
Germany	Belgium	13 Jul 29	Finance	104LTS201	302390
Germany	Belgium	13 Jul 29	Consul/Citizenship	104LTS211	302391
Germany	Belgium	07 Nov 29	Territory Boundary	121LTS327	302795
Germany	Belgium	16 Jan 30	Admin Cooperation	104LTS223	302392
Germany	Belgium	20 Jun 30	Land Transport	110LTS107	302555
Germany	Belgium	16 Jul 31	Non-ILO Labor	145LTS137	303351
Germany	Belgium	21 Dec 34	Taxation	162LTS9	303730
Germany	Belgium	10 May 35	Territory Boundary	182LTS323	304220
Germany	Belgium	10 May 35	Territory Boundary	182LTS335	304221
Germany	Belgium	10 May 35	Territory Boundary	165LTS169	303808

PARTY ONE	PARTY TWO	DATE	TOPIC	CITATION	NUMBER
Germany	Belgium	10 May 35	Territory Boundary	165LTS143	303807
Germany	Benelux Econ Union	04 Apr 25	General Trade	37LTS203	300957
Germany	Benelux Econ Union	15 Jul 26	Visas	63LTS137	301485
Germany	Bolivia	20 Jul 21	General Amity	10LTS301	300275
Germany	Bolivia	12 Mar 24	General Amity	73LTS95	301710
Germany	Bolivia	20 Feb 25	General Trade	42LTS43	301030
Germany	Brazil	22 Oct 31	General Trade	136LTS443	303143
Germany	Brazil	14 Jun 33	Admin Cooperation	178LTS19	304102
Germany	Bulgaria	19 Feb 21	Other Economic	6LTS227	300157
Germany	Bulgaria	22 Dec 26	Admin Cooperation	64LTS77	301502
Germany	Bulgaria	04 Jun 29	Consul/Citizenship	106LTS49	302436
Germany	Bulgaria	24 Jun 32	General Economic	147LTS211	303400
Germany	Canada	17 Jan 30	Reparations	109LTS473	302550
Germany	Canada	17 Apr 30	Taxation	101LTS245	302326
Germany	Canada	22 Oct 36	Finance	173LTS311	304021
Germany	Ceylon (Sri Lanka)	02 May 27	Postal Service	69LTS203	301606
Germany	Chile	18 Apr 28	Sanitation	79LTS411	301817
Germany	China	20 May 21	Peace/Disarmament	9LTS271	300261
Germany	China	31 Dec 24	Customs	42LTS7	301027
Germany	China	17 Aug 28	General Trade	91LTS93	302057
Germany	China	20 Dec 28	Customs	90LTS337	302047
Germany	Cuba	14 Jun 28	Postal Service	124LTS47	302832
Germany	Czechoslovakia	29 Jun 20	Consul/Citizenship	20LTS85	300509
Germany	Czechoslovakia	29 Jun 20	General Economic	17LTS69	300430
Germany	Czechoslovakia	29 Jun 20	General Economic	17LTS139	300431
Germany	Czechoslovakia	03 Feb 21	Territory Boundary	5LTS246	300132
Germany	Czechoslovakia	31 Dec 21	Taxation	17LTS401	300447
Germany	Czechoslovakia	20 Jan 22	Admin Cooperation	26LTS201	300648
Germany	Czechoslovakia	22 Feb 22	IGO Operations	26LTS249	300650
Germany	Czechoslovakia	18 Mar 22	Taxation	17LTS453	300448
Germany	Czechoslovakia	12 Apr 22	Non-ILO Labor	22LTS329	300562
Germany	Czechoslovakia	08 May 22	Extradition	23LTS171	300589
Germany	Czechoslovakia	02 May 23	Admin Cooperation	31LTS0	300793
Germany	Czechoslovakia	15 Aug 23	Admin Cooperation	27LTS94	300670
Germany	Czechoslovakia	04 Mar 24	Land Transport	41LTS243	301018
Germany	Czechoslovakia	15 Dec 24	Non-ILO Labor	52LTS41	301249
Germany	Czechoslovakia	15 Dec 24	Non-ILO Labor	52LTS31	301248
Germany	Czechoslovakia	06 Feb 25	Admin Cooperation	46LTS165	301118
Germany	Czechoslovakia	16 Oct 25	General Military	54LTS341	301296
Germany	Czechoslovakia	22 Jan 27	Air Transport	89LTS261	302020
Germany	Czechoslovakia	22 Jan 27	Air Transport	89LTS231	302019
Germany	Czechoslovakia	25 Mar 27	Land Transport	75LTS353	301758
Germany	Czechoslovakia	22 Mar 28	Territory Boundary	93LTS235	302113
Germany	Czechoslovakia	27 Mar 28	Visas	90LTS151	302032
Germany	Czechoslovakia	11 May 28	Non-ILO Labor	81LTS441	301854
Germany	Czechoslovakia	05 Jun 28	Admin Cooperation	177LTS19	302700
Germany	Czechoslovakia	20 Mar 29	Territory Boundary	109LTS219	302541
Germany	Czechoslovakia	22 Dec 29	Customs	110LTS417	302573
Germany	Czechoslovakia	31 Jan 30	Territory Boundary	145LTS51	303345
Germany	Czechoslovakia	27 Jun 30	Customs	112LTS169	302614
Germany	Czechoslovakia	21 Mar 31	Non-ILO Labor	143LTS177	303308
Germany	Czechoslovakia	20 Apr 31	Patents/Copyrights	141LTS307	303271
Germany	Czechoslovakia	29 Apr 31	Air Transport	133LTS359	303073
Germany	Czechoslovakia	29 Apr 31	Air Transport	133LTS347	303072
Germany	Czechoslovakia	25 Jul 31	Land Transport	187LTS279	304344
Germany	Czechoslovakia	19 Sep 32	Health/Educ/Welfare	137LTS453	303175
Germany	Czechoslovakia	26 Jun 35	Commodity Trade	173LTS385	304029
Germany	Czechoslovakia	27 Sep 35	Territory Boundary	182LTS267	304217
Germany	Czechoslovakia	30 Dec 35	Customs	173LTS333	304023
Germany	Denmark	30 Aug 20	Telecommunications	14LTS257	300377
Germany	Denmark	12 Jul 21	Visas	26LTS163	300646
Germany	Denmark	12 Jul 21	Visas	26LTS151	300645
Germany	Denmark	10 Apr 22	Water Transport	44LTS389	301095
Germany	Denmark	10 Apr 22	Territory Boundary	29LTS9	300730
Germany	Denmark	10 Apr 22	Territory Boundary	10LTS73	300274

PARTY ONE	PARTY TWO	DATE	TOPIC	CITATION	NUMBER
Germany	Denmark	25 Apr 22	Air Transport	18LTS227	300466
Germany	Denmark	31 Mar 23	Extradition	17LTS181	300436
Germany	Denmark	29 Nov 24	Admin Cooperation	31LTS131	300790
Germany	Denmark	18 Apr 25	Water Transport	37LTS103	300949
Germany	Denmark	20 Mar 26	General Trade	57LTS131	301359
Germany	Denmark	20 Mar 26	Visas	53LTS377	301267
Germany	Denmark	20 Mar 26	Customs	51LTS317	301237
Germany	Denmark	12 Apr 26	Customs	48LTS237	301165
Germany	Denmark	01 May 26	Visas	107LTS229	302480
Germany	Denmark	28 Oct 26	Milit Servic/Citiz	57LTS185	301363
Germany	Denmark	23 Feb 27	Dispute Settlement	61LTS325	301444
Germany	Denmark	08 Nov 27	Customs	70LTS83	301625
Germany	Denmark	14 Feb 28	Taxation	71LTS285	301669
Germany	Denmark	14 Oct 29	Water Transport	98LTS211	302248
Germany	Denmark	03 Jul 30	General Transport	105LTS427	302430
Germany	Denmark	23 Jun 31	Extradition	119LTS321	302753
Germany	Denmark	06 Jan 32	Admin Cooperation	126LTS333	302892
Germany	Denmark	19 Jul 33	Non-ILO Labor	170LTS385	303947
Germany	Denmark	15 Dec 33	Culture	171LTS9	303948
Germany	Denmark	13 Jan 34	Taxation	144LTS379	303340
Germany	Denmark	01 Mar 34	General Trade	150LTS31	303451
Germany	Denmark	24 Jan 35	General Trade	160LTS155	303689
Germany	Denmark	25 May 35	Territory Boundary	159LTS389	303680
Germany	Denmark	09 Jan 36	Land Transport	166LTS135	303835
Germany	Denmark	30 Jan 36	Commodity Trade	174LTS155	304046
Germany	Denmark	17 Jun 36	Admin Cooperation	171LTS163	303958
Germany	Denmark	23 Dec 36	Commodity Trade	174LTS165	304047
Germany	Denmark	27 Nov 37	General Trade	183LTS175	304234
Germany	Denmark	11 Nov 38	General Trade	193LTS79	304488
Germany	Denmark	31 May 39	General Amity	197LTS37	304603
Germany	Denmark	22 Dec 39	Commodity Trade	199LTS87	304669
Germany	Ecuador	28 Apr 28	Visas	90LTS163	302033
Germany	El Salvador	19 Feb 29	Visas	99LTS317	302274
Germany	Estonia	28 Dec 22	Water Transport	41LTS147	301010
Germany	Estonia	27 Jun 23	General Amity	41LTS155	301012
Germany	Estonia	27 Jun 23	General Trade	41LTS161	301013
Germany	Estonia	09 Jan 25	Extradition	42LTS13	301028
Germany	Estonia	13 Mar 25	Consul/Citizenship	51LTS263	301236
Germany	Estonia	10 Aug 25	Dispute Settlement	63LTS111	301484
Germany	Estonia	25 Nov 25	Admin Cooperation	54LTS79	301275
Germany	Estonia	05 Apr 27	Sanitation	64LTS355	301508
Germany	Estonia	07 Dec 28	General Economic	99LTS259	302273
Germany	Estonia	30 Apr 29	Visas	99LTS325	302275
Germany	Estonia	29 Mar 34	General Trade	148LTS251	303416
Germany	Estonia	24 Oct 37	Finance	184LTS81	304244
Germany	Estonia	24 Oct 37	General Economic	182LTS201	304212
Germany	Estonia	23 Dec 37	Air Transport	189LTS333	304393
Germany	Estonia	07 Jun 39	General Amity	198LTS49	304622
Germany	Finland	20 Feb 22	Extradition	19LTS81	300486
Germany	Finland	21 Apr 22	General Economic	19LTS87	300487
Germany	Finland	14 Nov 24	Postal Service	32LTS137	300813
Germany	Finland	02 Feb 25	Claims and Debts	33LTS127	300838
Germany	Finland	14 Mar 25	Dispute Settlement	43LTS347	301070
Germany	Finland	26 Jun 26	General Economic	56LTS203	301332
Germany	Finland	14 May 27	Visas	66LTS403	301533
Germany	Finland	18 Jun 27	Non-ILO Labor	71LTS361	301675
Germany	Finland	28 Aug 30	General Trade	111LTS327	302597
Germany	Finland	24 Mar 34	General Economic	149LTS343	303442
Germany	Finland	25 Sep 34	General Trade	154LTS9	303534
Germany	Finland	02 Oct 34	Finance	154LTS17	303535
Germany	Finland	22 Dec 34	General Trade	155LTS317	303583
Germany	Finland	29 May 35	Finance	160LTS69	303683
Germany	Finland	25 Sep 35	Taxation	173LTS11	304001
Germany	Finland	25 Sep 35	Taxation	172LTS359	304000
Germany	France	01 Mar 20	Admin Cooperation	1LTS367	300030
Germany	France	03 Mar 20	Non-ILO Labor	8LTS45	300205
Germany	France	25 Mar 20	Claims and Debts	1LTS347	300029
Germany	France	05 May 20	Dispute Settlement	8LTS55	300206
Germany	France	19 May 20	Customs	1LTS383	300031
Germany	France	30 Jun 20	Dispute Settlement	8LTS79	300208
Germany	France	01 Jul 20	Territory Boundary	8LTS87	300209
Germany	France	17 Nov 20	Peace/Disarmament	8LTS99	300211
Germany	France	13 Apr 25	Admin Cooperation	109LTS295	302546
Germany	France	14 Aug 25	Territory Boundary	75LTS103	301756
Germany	France	16 Oct 25	General Military	54LTS315	301294
Germany	France	12 Feb 26	General Economic	48LTS153	301157
Germany	France	04 Jun 26	Admin Cooperation	53LTS423	301270
Germany	France	28 Jun 26	Extradition	53LTS435	301271
Germany	France	05 Aug 26	General Trade	73LTS105	301711
Germany	France	22 Dec 26	Territory Boundary	77LTS141	301768
Germany	France	16 Feb 27	Commodity Trade	62LTS155	301463
Germany	France	31 Mar 27	General Economic	66LTS7	301524
Germany	France	30 Jun 27	General Trade	73LTS243	301717
Germany	France	17 Aug 27	General Trade	76LTS5	301761
Germany	France	05 Oct 27	Admin Cooperation	77LTS7	301762
Germany	France	23 Feb 28	General Trade	79LTS247	301815
Germany	France	16 Mar 28	Customs	79LTS121	301805
Germany	France	25 Apr 29	Land Transport	109LTS333	302548
Germany	France	20 Nov 29	Admin Cooperation	99LTS339	302277
Germany	France	31 Dec 29	Reparations	106LTS93	302438
Germany	Great Britain	30 Jul 25	Reparations	38LTS181	300974
Germany	Great Britain	13 Aug 25	Reparations	38LTS185	300975
Germany	Great Britain	15 Nov 28	Visas	90LTS213	302040
Germany	Great Britain	17 Jan 28	Taxation	71LTS193	301661
Germany	Greece	20 Jan 97*	Water Transport	2LTS107	300053
Germany	Greece	12 Mar 07	Extradition	2LTS111	300054
Germany	Greece	01 Dec 10	Claims and Debts	2LTS123	300055
Germany	Greece	21 Mar 24	Patents/Copyrights	30LTS257	300769
Germany	Greece	15 May 25	General Trade	40LTS6	301001
Germany	Greece	24 Mar 28	General Economic	90LTS9	302031
Germany	Greece	10 Nov 31	Dispute Settlement	133LTS385	303076
Germany	Greece	09 Nov 36	Air Transport	182LTS9	304201
Germany	Greece	24 Sep 37	General Economic	190LTS51	304404
Germany	Greece	14 Apr 38	Admin Cooperation	198LTS389	304657
Germany	Greece	11 May 38	Admin Cooperation	197LTS75	304608
Germany	Greece	01 Oct 38	General Economic	197LTS233	304616
Germany	Guatemala	04 Oct 24	General Economic	52LTS19	301246
Germany	Haiti	15 Oct 24	Finance	52LTS27	301247
Germany	Haiti	10 Mar 30	General Trade	119LTS231	302747
Germany	Hedjaz	26 Apr 29	General Amity	115LTS265	302690
Germany	Honduras	21 Sep 29	Visas	133LTS311	303070
Germany	Hungary	08 May 20	Reparations	2LTS79	300050
Germany	Hungary	01 Jun 20	General Economic	7LTS207	300187
Germany	Hungary	06 Nov 23	Taxation	45LTS279	301104
Germany	Hungary	06 Nov 23	Taxation	45LTS253	301103
Germany	Hungary	26 Nov 23	Taxation	45LTS309	301105
Germany	Hungary	01 May 24	Extradition	41LTS282	301021
Germany	Hungary	18 Jul 31	General Trade	150LTS111	303458
Germany	Hungary	26 Oct 31	Extradition	133LTS369	303074
Germany	Hungary	22 Jul 33	General Economic	171LTS313	303969
Germany	Hungary	21 Feb 34	General Economic	171LTS327	303970
Germany	Hungary	28 May 36	Culture	178LTS445	304127
Germany	Iceland	12 Feb 23	Patents/Copyrights	27LTS405	300700
Germany	Iraq	04 Aug 35	Mostfavored Nation	171LTS65	303951
Germany	Irish Free State	29 Dec 24	Postal Service	56LTS341	301341
Germany	Irish Free State	12 May 30	General Economic	131LTS153	303008
Germany	Italy	21 Jun 25	Admin Cooperation	68LTS11	301565
Germany	Italy	31 Oct 25	Taxation	53LTS245	301261
Germany	Italy	31 Oct 25	General Economic	52LTS179	301256
Germany	Italy	29 Dec 26	Dispute Settlement	78LTS383	301797

PARTY ONE	PARTY TWO	DATE	TOPIC	CITATION	NUMBER
Germany	Italy	20 May 27	Air Transport	79LTS179	301810
Germany	Italy	01 Sep 27	Peace/Disarmament	67LTS425	301564
Germany	Latvia	09 Jul 26	Sanitation	63LTS321	301499
Germany	Latvia	13 Apr 28	Water Transport	73LTS46	301705
Germany	Latvia	02 Jun 28	Visas	75LTS69	301752
Germany	Latvia	18 Jul 34	Extradition	154LTS69	303537
Germany	Latvia	04 Dec 35	General Trade	166LTS93	303834
Germany	Latvia	31 Oct 37	Finance	189LTS139	304382
Germany	Latvia	07 Jun 39	General Amity	198LTS105	304629
Germany	Latvia	30 Oct 39	Refugees	200LTS213	304693
Germany	Lithuania	31 May 23	Reparations	51LTS381	301243
Germany	Lithuania	01 Jun 23	General Economic	51LTS387	301244
Germany	Lithuania	10 Feb 25	Admin Cooperation	42LTS17	301029
Germany	Lithuania	16 Jul 25	General Trade	85LTS357	301939
Germany	Lithuania	29 Jan 28	Non-ILO Labor	89LTS83	302008
Germany	Lithuania	29 Jan 28	Territory Boundary	89LTS97	302009
Germany	Lithuania	29 Jan 28	Territory Boundary	89LTS338	302027
Germany	Lithuania	29 Jan 28	Dispute Settlement	90LTS233	302042
Germany	Lithuania	29 Jan 28	Specific Resources	89LTS309	302026
Germany	Lithuania	30 Oct 28	General Economic	89LTS127	302010
Germany	Lithuania	30 Oct 28	Consul/Citizenship	90LTS255	302043
Germany	Lithuania	30 Oct 28	Admin Cooperation	91LTS365	302077
Germany	Lithuania	26 Jan 29	Non-ILO Labor	89LTS181	302012
Germany	Lithuania	09 Nov 31	Non-ILO Labor	133LTS379	303075
Germany	Lithuania	20 Nov 31	Sanitation	133LTS391	303077
Germany	Lithuania	19 Mar 31	Privil/Immunities	125LTS265	302860
Germany	Luxembourg	28 Jun 28	Refugees	90LTS183	302036
Germany	Luxembourg	11 Sep 29	Dispute Settlement	118LTS97	302715
Germany	Malaya	17 Dec 36	Postal Service	178LTS484	304129
Germany	Mexico	16 Mar 25	Reparations	52LTS93	301251
Germany	Mexico	20 Dec 27	Claims and Debts	79LTS229	301812
Germany	Multilateral	09 Sep 86*	Patents/Copyrights	123LTS233	302816
Germany	Multilateral	18 Mar 04	Humanitarian	1LTS83	300011
Germany	Multilateral	13 Nov 08	General Ad Hoc	1LTS217	300015
Germany	Multilateral	12 Jan 12	Sanitation	4LTS281	300112
Germany	Multilateral	23 Jan 12	Sanitation	8LTS187	300222
Germany	Multilateral	05 Jun 12	Telecommunications	1LTS135	300013
Germany	Multilateral	20 Mar 14	Patents/Copyrights	1LTS243	300016
Germany	Multilateral	30 Jun 20	Patents/Copyrights	1LTS59	300008
Germany	Multilateral	20 Apr 21	Water Transport	7LTS73	300174
Germany	Multilateral	20 Apr 21	Land Transport	7LTS11	300171
Germany	Multilateral	10 Jun 21	Customs	8LTS297	300227
Germany	Multilateral	23 Jul 21	Water Transport	26LTS173	300647
Germany	Multilateral	06 Oct 21	General Economic	17LTS45	300427
Germany	Multilateral	20 Oct 21	Peace/Disarmament	9LTS211	300255
Germany	Multilateral	22 Feb 22	Water Transport	26LTS219	300649
Germany	Multilateral	31 Mar 22	Humanitarian	9LTS415	300269
Germany	Multilateral	10 May 22	Water Transport	26LTS265	300652
Germany	Multilateral	15 Jun 22	Dispute Settlement	21LTS463	300551
Germany	Multilateral	05 Jul 22	Reparations	13LTS237	300355
Germany	Multilateral	14 Dec 22	Water Transport	36LTS457	300943
Germany	Multilateral	27 Jan 23	Water Transport	26LTS253	300651
Germany	Multilateral	24 Sep 23	Dispute Settlement	27LTS157	300678
Germany	Multilateral	03 Nov 23	Customs	30LTS371	300775
Germany	Multilateral	28 Nov 23	Admin Cooperation	51LTS221	301230
Germany	Multilateral	28 Nov 23	Admin Cooperation	51LTS233	301232
Germany	Multilateral	28 Nov 23	Admin Cooperation	51LTS209	301228
Germany	Multilateral	28 Nov 23	Admin Cooperation	51LTS239	301233
Germany	Multilateral	28 Nov 23	Admin Cooperation	51LTS215	301229
Germany	Multilateral	09 Dec 23	Water Transport	58LTS284	301379
Germany	Multilateral	09 Dec 23	Land Transport	47LTS55	301129
Germany	Multilateral	08 Jan 24	Dispute Settlement	23LTS63	300576
Germany	Multilateral	07 Feb 24	Water Transport	25LTS265	300614
Germany	Multilateral	31 Mar 24	Sanitation	27LTS211	300685
Germany	Multilateral	04 Jul 24	Admin Cooperation	51LTS227	301231

PARTY ONE	PARTY TWO	DATE	TOPIC	CITATION	NUMBER
Germany	Multilateral	16 Aug 24	Taxation	41LTS429	301024
Germany	Multilateral	25 Aug 24	Water Transport	120LTS155	302764
Germany	Multilateral	28 Aug 24	Postal Service	40LTS19	301002
Germany	Multilateral	28 Aug 24	Postal Service	40LTS307	301004
Germany	Multilateral	28 Aug 24	Postal Service	41LTS97	301008
Germany	Multilateral	28 Aug 24	Postal Service	40LTS249	301003
Germany	Multilateral	28 Aug 24	Postal Service	40LTS437	301005
Germany	Multilateral	28 Aug 24	Postal Service	41LTS9	301006
Germany	Multilateral	30 Aug 24	Admin Cooperation	30LTS79	300761
Germany	Multilateral	30 Aug 24	Admin Cooperation	30LTS75	300760
Germany	Multilateral	30 Aug 24	General Economic	30LTS63	300759
Germany	Multilateral	23 Oct 24	Land Transport	78LTS17	301779
Germany	Multilateral	23 Oct 24	General Transport	77LTS367	301778
Germany	Multilateral	19 Feb 25	Admin Cooperation	81LTS317	301845
Germany	Multilateral	00 Apr 25	Water Transport	37LTS21	300945
Germany	Multilateral	23 Apr 25	Water Transport	37LTS9	300944
Germany	Multilateral	05 May 25	Finance	55LTS225	301318
Germany	Multilateral	17 Jun 25	Peace/Disarmament	94LTS65	302138
Germany	Multilateral	19 Aug 25	Customs	42LTS73	301033
Germany	Multilateral	16 Oct 25	Peace/Disarmament	54LTS289	301292
Germany	Multilateral	29 Oct 25	Telecommunications	57LTS201	301365
Germany	Multilateral	06 Nov 25	Other Economic	74LTS341	301746
Germany	Multilateral	06 Nov 25	Patents/Copyrights	74LTS289	301743
Germany	Multilateral	06 Nov 25	Patents/Copyrights	74LTS327	301745
Germany	Multilateral	06 Nov 25	Other Economic	74LTS319	301744
Germany	Multilateral	27 Nov 25	Water Transport	67LTS63	301539
Germany	Multilateral	31 Dec 25	Territory Boundary	79LTS167	301809
Germany	Multilateral	00 Apr 26	Water Transport	57LTS437	301366
Germany	Multilateral	10 Apr 26	Water Transport	176LTS199	304062
Germany	Multilateral	10 Apr 26	Water Transport	120LTS187	302765
Germany	Multilateral	24 Apr 26	Land Transport	108LTS123	302505
Germany	Multilateral	12 May 26	Refugees	89LTS47	302004
Germany	Multilateral	22 May 26	Air Transport	58LTS331	301381
Germany	Multilateral	21 Jun 26	Sanitation	78LTS229	301793
Germany	Multilateral	14 Sep 26	Non-ILO Labor	77LTS149	301769
Germany	Multilateral	25 Sep 26	ILO Labor	60LTS253	301414
Germany	Multilateral	30 Oct 26	Telecommunications	61LTS65	301426
Germany	Multilateral	01 Nov 26	Telecommunications	78LTS109	301782
Germany	Multilateral	13 Nov 26	Territory Boundary	77LTS171	301770
Germany	Multilateral	13 Nov 26	Territory Boundary	77LTS199	301771
Germany	Multilateral	13 Nov 26	Territory Boundary	77LTS249	301773
Germany	Multilateral	13 Nov 26	Territory Boundary	77LTS217	301772
Germany	Multilateral	22 Jan 27	Telecommunications	68LTS129	301576
Germany	Multilateral	22 Jan 27	Telecommunications	68LTS149	301578
Germany	Multilateral	24 Jan 27	General Ad Hoc	70LTS453	301650
Germany	Multilateral	19 Feb 27	Telecommunications	68LTS139	301577
Germany	Multilateral	24 Feb 27	Telecommunications	68LTS159	301579
Germany	Multilateral	25 Feb 27	Telecommunications	78LTS123	301783
Germany	Multilateral	08 Mar 27	Telecommunications	78LTS134	301784
Germany	Multilateral	12 Jul 27	Direct Aid	135LTS247	303115
Germany	Multilateral	16 Aug 27	Telecommunications	78LTS141	301785
Germany	Multilateral	10 Sep 27	Postal Service	75LTS39	301750
Germany	Multilateral	10 Sep 27	Postal Service	75LTS7	301749
Germany	Multilateral	26 Sep 27	Dispute Settlement	92LTS301	302096
Germany	Multilateral	08 Nov 27	General Trade	97LTS391	302238
Germany	Multilateral	11 Nov 27	Telecommunications	78LTS153	301786
Germany	Multilateral	21 Nov 27	Telecommunications	78LTS163	301787
Germany	Multilateral	25 Nov 27	Telecommunications	84LTS97	301905
Germany	Multilateral	07 Jan 28	Telecommunications	78LTS187	301789
Germany	Multilateral	10 Mar 28	Telecommunications	132LTS405	303049
Germany	Multilateral	19 Mar 28	Telecommunications	78LTS177	301788
Germany	Multilateral	23 Apr 28	Telecommunications	78LTS197	301790
Germany	Multilateral	25 Apr 28	Telecommunications	78LTS207	301791
Germany	Multilateral	01 May 28	Telecommunications	132LTS415	303050
Germany	Multilateral	22 May 28	Telecommunications	85LTS99	301925

PARTY ONE	PARTY TWO	DATE	TOPIC	CITATION	NUMBER
Germany	Multilateral	09 Jun 28	Telecommunications	78LTS219	301792
Germany	Multilateral	30 Jun 28	Refugees	89LTS53	302005
Germany	Multilateral	30 Jun 28	Refugees	89LTS63	302006
Germany	Multilateral	11 Jul 28	Commodity Trade	95LTS373	302185
Germany	Multilateral	11 Jul 28	Commodity Trade	95LTS357	302184
Germany	Multilateral	15 Jul 28	Patents/Copyrights	79LTS133	301806
Germany	Multilateral	27 Aug 28	General Military	94LTS57	302137
Germany	Multilateral	12 Sep 28	Telecommunications	104LTS43	302377
Germany	Multilateral	30 Oct 28	Dispute Settlement	87LTS103	301963
Germany	Multilateral	22 Nov 28	Culture	111LTS343	302598
Germany	Multilateral	30 Nov 28	Telecommunications	87LTS119	301965
Germany	Multilateral	05 Jan 29	Telecommunications	132LTS425	303051
Germany	Multilateral	20 Apr 29	Admin Cooperation	112LTS371	302623
Germany	Multilateral	31 May 29	Water Transport	136LTS81	303127
Germany	Multilateral	14 Jun 29	Visas	94LTS275	302148
Germany	Multilateral	28 Jun 29	Postal Service	103LTS5	302369
Germany	Multilateral	28 Jun 29	Postal Service	103LTS249	302371
Germany	Multilateral	28 Jun 29	Postal Service	103LTS377	302373
Germany	Multilateral	28 Jun 29	Postal Service	103LTS321	302372
Germany	Multilateral	28 Jun 29	Postal Service	103LTS429	302374
Germany	Multilateral	28 Jun 29	Postal Service	103LTS71	302370
Germany	Multilateral	28 Jun 29	Postal Service	102LTS245	302368
Germany	Multilateral	27 Jul 29	Other Military	118LTS303	302733
Germany	Multilateral	27 Jul 29	Other Military	118LTS343	302734
Germany	Multilateral	30 Aug 29	General Amity	104LTS487	302400
Germany	Multilateral	30 Aug 29	Consul/Citizenship	104LTS473	302399
Germany	Multilateral	07 Sep 29	Telecommunications	98LTS345	302255
Germany	Multilateral	14 Sep 29	UN Charter	165LTS353	303822
Germany	Multilateral	25 Sep 29	Telecommunications	98LTS361	302256
Germany	Multilateral	26 Sep 29	Telecommunications	98LTS395	302259
Germany	Multilateral	30 Sep 29	Telecommunications	98LTS183	302246
Germany	Multilateral	30 Sep 29	Postal Service	99LTS71	302269
Germany	Multilateral	01 Oct 29	Telecommunications	98LTS197	302247
Germany	Multilateral	08 Oct 29	Telecommunications	98LTS409	302260
Germany	Multilateral	10 Oct 29	Telecommunications	98LTS375	302257
Germany	Multilateral	12 Oct 29	General Transport	137LTS11	303145
Germany	Multilateral	29 Oct 29	Telecommunications	99LTS85	302270
Germany	Multilateral	18 Nov 29	Telecommunications	99LTS415	302287
Germany	Multilateral	17 Dec 29	Specific Resources	115LTS93	302679
Germany	Multilateral	18 Dec 29	Admin Cooperation	104LTS27	302376
Germany	Multilateral	20 Jan 30	Other Economic	104LTS441	302398
Germany	Multilateral	20 Jan 30	Reparations	104LTS243	302394
Germany	Multilateral	20 Jan 30	Reparations	104LTS421	302396
Germany	Multilateral	24 Jan 30	Peace/Disarmament	106LTS85	302437
Germany	Multilateral	10 Apr 30	Telecommunications	101LTS465	302345
Germany	Multilateral	12 Apr 30	Admin Cooperation	179LTS89	304137
Germany	Multilateral	12 Apr 30	Milit Servic/Citiz	178LTS227	304117
Germany	Multilateral	07 Jun 30	Finance	143LTS257	303313
Germany	Multilateral	07 Jun 30	Finance	143LTS317	303314
Germany	Multilateral	07 Jun 30	Finance	143LTS337	303315
Germany	Multilateral	10 Jun 30	Loans and Credits	112LTS237	302618
Germany	Multilateral	26 Jun 30	Telecommunications	133LTS9	303052
Germany	Multilateral	28 Aug 30	Telecommunications	133LTS21	303053
Germany	Multilateral	23 Oct 30	Water Transport	125LTS95	302849
Germany	Multilateral	23 Oct 30	Water Transport	112LTS21	302603
Germany	Multilateral	19 Mar 31	Finance	143LTS407	303317
Germany	Multilateral	19 Mar 31	Admin Cooperation	143LTS7	303301
Germany	Multilateral	19 Mar 31	Finance	143LTS355	303316
Germany	Multilateral	28 Mar 31	Customs	119LTS47	302739
Germany	Multilateral	30 Mar 31	Land Transport	150LTS247	303459
Germany	Multilateral	13 Jul 31	Other HEW	139LTS301	303219
Germany	Multilateral	24 Sep 31	Specific Resources	155LTS349	303586
Germany	Multilateral	11 Dec 31	Commodity Trade	170LTS251	303941
Germany	Multilateral	02 Sep 32	Land Transport	154LTS123	303543
Germany	Multilateral	09 Dec 32	Telecommunications	151LTS5	303479

PARTY ONE	PARTY TWO	DATE	TOPIC	CITATION	NUMBER
Germany	Multilateral	11 Mar 33	Water Transport	135LTS301	303119
Germany	Multilateral	12 Apr 33	Sanitation	161LTS65	303706
Germany	Multilateral	29 May 33	Admin Cooperation	192LTS289	304479
Germany	Multilateral	19 Jun 33	Gen Communications	154LTS133	303544
Germany	Multilateral	25 Aug 33	Commodity Trade	141LTS71	303262
Germany	Multilateral	11 Oct 33	Education	155LTS331	303585
Germany	Multilateral	11 Oct 33	Consul/Citizenship	150LTS431	303476
Germany	Multilateral	23 Nov 33	Land Transport	192LTS389	304484
Germany	Multilateral	23 Nov 33	Land Transport	192LTS327	304483
Germany	Multilateral	20 Mar 34	Postal Service	175LTS73	304050
Germany	Multilateral	20 Mar 34	Postal Service	176LTS55	304054
Germany	Multilateral	20 Mar 34	Finance	176LTS9	304053
Germany	Multilateral	20 Mar 34	Postal Service	174LTS171	304048
Germany	Multilateral	20 Mar 34	Postal Service	175LTS269	304051
Germany	Multilateral	20 Mar 34	Postal Service	175LTS363	304052
Germany	Multilateral	20 Mar 34	Postal Service	175LTS5	304049
Germany	Multilateral	26 Apr 34	Admin Cooperation	164LTS63	303789
Germany	Multilateral	02 Jun 34	Patents/Copyrights	205LTS179	304834
Germany	Multilateral	02 Jun 34	General Trade	192LTS9	304458
Germany	Multilateral	02 Jun 34	Patents/Copyrights	192LTS17	304459
Germany	Multilateral	19 Jun 34	Admin Cooperation	154LTS381	303564
Germany	Multilateral	25 Jul 34	Other HEW	177LTS59	304080
Germany	Multilateral	15 Sep 36	Scientific Project	178LTS439	304126
Germany	Multilateral	06 Nov 36	General Military	173LTS353	304025
Germany	Multilateral	10 Feb 37	General Transport	189LTS313	304391
Germany	Multilateral	31 Mar 37	Commodity Trade	189LTS359	304394
Germany	Multilateral	08 Jun 37	Specific Resources	190LTS79	304406
Germany	Multilateral	24 Jun 38	Specific Resources	196LTS131	304575
Germany	Multilateral	27 Jun 38	Visas	191LTS199	304443
Germany	Multilateral	18 Aug 38	Admin Cooperation	196LTS113	304574
Germany	Multilateral	31 Oct 38	Sanitation	198LTS205	304642
Germany	Multilateral	23 Apr 39	Land Transport	104LTS87	302380
Germany	Multilateral	06 May 39	Finance	198LTS81	304626
Germany	Multilateral	02 Jun 42	Patents/Copyrights	205LTS163	304833
Germany	Netherlands	11 May 20	Loans and Credits	3LTS153	300097
Germany	Netherlands	05 Jul 21	Territory Boundary	13LTS41	300346
Germany	Netherlands	23 May 23	Customs	25LTS275	300617
Germany	Netherlands	03 Jun 23	Water Transport	28LTS297	300716
Germany	Netherlands	27 Mar 24	Customs	25LTS289	300618
Germany	Netherlands	26 Nov 25	Customs	57LTS159	301362
Germany	Netherlands	26 Nov 25	General Economic	57LTS147	301361
Germany	Netherlands	24 Mar 26	Telecommunications	51LTS245	301234
Germany	Netherlands	20 May 26	Dispute Settlement	66LTS103	301527
Germany	Netherlands	03 Nov 26	Telecommunications	68LTS111	301575
Germany	Netherlands	28 Apr 28	Customs	95LTS333	302183
Germany	Netherlands	17 Aug 28	Air Transport	93LTS409	302129
Germany	Netherlands	11 Jun 31	Land Transport	120LTS413	302778
Germany	Netherlands	27 Apr 33	Customs	145LTS155	303353
Germany	Netherlands	28 Jun 33	Land Transport	152LTS209	303495
Germany	Netherlands	06 Jun 34	Customs	174LTS44	304035
Germany	Netherlands	06 Jun 34	General Trade	174LTS33	304034
Germany	Netherlands	05 Dec 34	Finance	160LTS109	303686
Germany	Netherlands	23 Dec 36	Finance	179LTS359	304163
Germany	Netherlands	30 Apr 37	Customs	187LTS215	304342
Germany	Netherlands	30 Jun 37	General Trade	189LTS373	304395
Germany	Netherlands	18 Dec 37	Finance	190LTS29	304403
Germany	Netherlands	25 May 38	Finance	192LTS143	304468
Germany	Netherlands	17 May 39	Territory Boundary	199LTS239	304678
Germany	New Zealand	17 Jan 30	Reparations	109LTS485	302551
Germany	Nicaragua	06 Mar 24	General Economic	41LTS264	301019
Germany	Nicaragua	30 Mar 28	Visas	93LTS123	302104
Germany	Norway	11 Apr 25	Customs	52LTS115	301252
Germany	Norway	15 Jun 26	Telecommunications	51LTS329	301238
Germany	Norway	27 Apr 27	Customs	69LTS57	301600
Germany	Norway	17 Jan 28	Visas	70LTS251	301637

PARTY ONE	PARTY TWO	DATE	TOPIC	CITATION	NUMBER
Germany	Norway	23 Jan 29	Air Transport	93LTS197	302110
Germany	Norway	30 May 30	Customs	107LTS129	302473
Germany	Norway	09 Jan 33	Finance	137LTS395	303168
Germany	Norway	03 Mar 33	Visas	138LTS179	303186
Germany	Norway	06 Sep 34	Finance	161LTS187	303711
Germany	Norway	19 Jul 35	Land Transport	161LTS375	303726
Germany	Norway	27 Feb 37	Finance	178LTS427	304125
Germany	Panama	21 Nov 27	General Economic	115LTS239	302689
Germany	Paraguay	26 Feb 27	Mostfavored Nation	73LTS235	301716
Germany	Persia	15 May 28	Privil/Immunities	107LTS389	302495
Germany	Persia	17 Feb 29	General Economic	111LTS263	302591
Germany	Persia	17 Feb 29	General Amity	111LTS19	302576
Germany	Persia	17 Feb 29	Privil/Immunities	111LTS241	302590
Germany	Persia	24 Feb 30	Patents/Copyrights	113LTS15	302630
Germany	Poland	09 Jan 20	Admin Cooperation	9LTS77	300245
Germany	Poland	20 Sep 20	Admin Cooperation	9LTS103	300246
Germany	Poland	02 Nov 20	Reparations	2LTS277	300081
Germany	Poland	23 Nov 20	Reparations	2LTS295	300082
Germany	Poland	08 Dec 20	Consul/Citizenship	7LTS323	300199
Germany	Poland	20 Jan 21	Territory Boundary	6LTS221	300156
Germany	Poland	12 Feb 21	Reparations	9LTS149	300247
Germany	Poland	10 Apr 21	Customs	6LTS233	300158
Germany	Poland	21 Apr 21	General Transport	12LTS61	300308
Germany	Poland	06 Jun 21	Specific Property	34LTS185	300874
Germany	Poland	24 Feb 22	Admin Cooperation	26LTS479	300664
Germany	Poland	24 Feb 22	Admin Cooperation	27LTS15	300665
Germany	Poland	12 Apr 22	Territory Boundary	21LTS327	300548
Germany	Poland	29 Apr 22	Admin Cooperation	21LTS391	300549
Germany	Poland	15 May 22	Visas	10LTS37	300273
Germany	Poland	15 May 22	Postal Service	10LTS8	300272
Germany	Poland	03 Jun 22	Territory Boundary	9LTS465	300271
Germany	Poland	15 Jun 22	Territory Boundary	34LTS201	300875
Germany	Poland	15 Jun 22	Specific Resources	21LTS433	300550
Germany	Poland	18 Jun 22	Specific Property	34LTS235	300876
Germany	Poland	21 Jun 22	Dispute Settlement	22LTS7	300552
Germany	Poland	23 Jun 22	Specific Resources	22LTS25	300553
Germany	Poland	24 Jun 22	Water Transport	26LTS271	300653
Germany	Poland	15 Jul 22	General Transport	26LTS353	300654
Germany	Poland	01 Aug 22	Specific Property	34LTS253	300877
Germany	Poland	25 Aug 22	Non-ILO Labor	22LTS63	300554
Germany	Poland	26 Aug 22	Admin Cooperation	26LTS365	300656
Germany	Poland	14 Sep 22	Admin Cooperation	34LTS265	300878
Germany	Poland	18 Dec 22	Admin Cooperation	26LTS395	300658
Germany	Poland	18 Dec 22	Finance	34LTS283	300879
Germany	Poland	18 Dec 22	Sanitation	34LTS301	300880
Germany	Poland	27 Jan 23	Admin Cooperation	26LTS461	300663
Germany	Poland	21 Mar 23	Taxation	34LTS315	300881
Germany	Poland	02 May 23	Admin Cooperation	27LTS51	300667
Germany	Poland	04 Jun 23	Health/Educ/Welfare	34LTS329	300882
Germany	Poland	14 Jun 23	Admin Cooperation	34LTS343	300883
Germany	Poland	23 Jun 23	Specific Property	67LTS9	301537
Germany	Poland	10 Jul 23	General Transport	34LTS349	300884
Germany	Poland	14 Jul 23	Admin Cooperation	26LTS399	300659
Germany	Poland	11 Jan 24	General Economic	41LTS187	301014
Germany	Poland	12 Jan 24	Specific Resources	65LTS47	301519
Germany	Poland	23 Feb 24	Territory Boundary	41LTS197	301015
Germany	Poland	23 Feb 24	Land Transport	49LTS355	301191
Germany	Poland	05 Mar 24	Admin Cooperation	49LTS181	301182
Germany	Poland	05 Mar 24	Admin Cooperation	49LTS251	301184
Germany	Poland	07 Mar 24	Admin Cooperation	52LTS7	301245
Germany	Poland	30 Aug 24	Consul/Citizenship	32LTS331	300824
Germany	Poland	30 Dec 24	Specific Property	52LTS51	301250
Germany	Poland	14 Mar 25	Territory Boundary	95LTS239	302178
Germany	Poland	03 Oct 25	Admin Cooperation	50LTS189	301201
Germany	Poland	16 Oct 25	General Military	54LTS327	301295

PARTY ONE	PARTY TWO	DATE	TOPIC	CITATION	NUMBER
Germany	Poland	02 Dec 25	Territory Boundary	70LTS427	301649
Germany	Poland	16 Dec 25	Admin Cooperation	46LTS139	301117
Germany	Poland	27 Jan 26	Territory Boundary	64LTS113	301504
Germany	Poland	27 Mar 26	Land Transport	64LTS249	301506
Germany	Poland	16 Jun 26	Land Transport	65LTS379	301522
Germany	Poland	21 Jun 26	Territory Boundary	72LTS203	301693
Germany	Poland	19 Aug 26	Admin Cooperation	64LTS420	301515
Germany	Poland	27 Oct 26	Admin Cooperation	108LTS275	302513
Germany	Poland	22 Dec 26	Culture	68LTS263	301590
Germany	Poland	16 Feb 27	Territory Boundary	71LTS369	301676
Germany	Poland	26 Mar 27	Land Transport	64LTS177	301505
Germany	Poland	11 Apr 27	Territory Boundary	69LTS419	301621
Germany	Poland	14 Jul 27	Non-ILO Labor	73LTS251	301718
Germany	Poland	24 Nov 27	Non-ILO Labor	92LTS19	302080
Germany	Poland	07 Dec 27	Specific Property	92LTS203	302088
Germany	Poland	10 Dec 27	Specific Resources	120LTS299	302773
Germany	Poland	05 Jul 28	Peace/Disarmament	113LTS189	302646
Germany	Poland	14 Dec 28	Finance	113LTS367	302648
Germany	Poland	14 Dec 28	Finance	113LTS311	302647
Germany	Poland	28 Aug 29	Air Transport	146LTS333	303383
Germany	Poland	31 Oct 29	Claims and Debts	124LTS345	302838
Germany	Poland	21 Nov 30	Land Transport	139LTS351	303220
Germany	Poland	11 Jun 31	Non-ILO Labor	141LTS91	303263
Germany	Poland	01 Dec 31	Dispute Settlement	141LTS315	303272
Germany	Poland	15 Dec 31	Admin Cooperation	142LTS249	303298
Germany	Poland	22 Dec 31	Visas	144LTS191	303329
Germany	Portugal	28 Apr 23	General Trade	32LTS385	300827
Germany	Portugal	20 Mar 26	General Economic	53LTS361	301266
Germany	Portugal	21 Jul 27	Admin Cooperation	75LTS375	301760
Germany	Portugal	08 Apr 29	Admin Cooperation	93LTS253	302114
Germany	Romania	10 Nov 28	Dispute Settlement	91LTS101	302058
Germany	Romania	28 Feb 29	Visas	97LTS61	302217
Germany	Romania	18 Jun 30	Mostfavored Nation	110LTS95	302554
Germany	Romania	03 Oct 37	Air Transport	190LTS369	304429
Germany	Romania	03 Mar 39	Admin Cooperation	201LTS381	304726
Germany	Romania	23 Mar 39	Other Economic	199LTS77	304668
Germany	Saar	03 Jun 21	General Ad Hoc	5LTS189	300129
Germany	Saar	26 Aug 22	Admin Cooperation	27LTS249	300688
Germany	Saar	13 Nov 22	Health/Educ/Welfare	27LTS273	300690
Germany	Saar	17 Jan 23	Land Transport	27LTS290	300692
Germany	Saar	21 Apr 23	Non-ILO Labor	27LTS295	300693
Germany	Saar	20 Sep 24	Admin Cooperation	30LTS121	300765
Germany	Saar	28 Feb 25	Land Transport	33LTS123	300837
Germany	Saar	21 Dec 25	Admin Cooperation	55LTS349	301319
Germany	Saar	23 Nov 26	Admin Cooperation	70LTS105	301627
Germany	Saar	13 Oct 27	Non-ILO Labor	70LTS121	301629
Germany	Serb/Croat/Slovene	06 Oct 27	General Trade	77LTS19	301763
Germany	Serb/Croat/Slovene	15 Dec 28	Non-ILO Labor	95LTS149	302171
Germany	Serb/Croat/Slovene	15 Dec 28	Non-ILO Labor	95LTS113	302170
Germany	Siam	28 Feb 24	General Economic	32LTS399	300828
Germany	Siam	07 Apr 28	General Amity	85LTS337	301938
Germany	Siam	06 Jul 29	Visas	99LTS333	302276
Germany	Siam	30 Dec 37	General Amity	188LTS401	304368
Germany	South Africa	23 Oct 23	Milit Servic/Citiz	28LTS417	300721
Germany	South Africa	01 Sep 28	General Economic	95LTS289	302181
Germany	South Africa	12 May 30	Patents/Copyrights	123LTS301	302821
Germany	South Africa	16 Mar 37	Admin Cooperation	189LTS107	304378
Germany	Spain	15 Jan 23	General Economic	26LTS455	300662
Germany	Spain	25 Jul 24	General Trade	41LTS363	301023
Germany	Spain	18 Nov 25	General Economic	53LTS309	301263
Germany	Spain	07 May 26	General Economic	53LTS321	301264
Germany	Spain	09 Dec 27	Air Transport	79LTS203	301811
Germany	Spain	09 Feb 29	Visas	89LTS369	302038
Germany	Spain	06 Jul 32	Reparations	148LTS391	303425
Germany	Spain	11 Dec 34	Air Transport	166LTS311	303846

PARTY ONE	PARTY TWO	DATE	TOPIC	CITATION	NUMBER
Germany	Spain	21 Dec 34	General Economic	165LTS307	303817
Germany	Spain	07 Jan 35	Air Transport	166LTS363	303852
Germany	Spain	30 Sep 35	Air Transport	163LTS327	303775
Germany	Sweden	02 May 11	General Economic	2LTS59	300047
Germany	Sweden	16 Dec 20	General Economic	2LTS263	300072
Germany	Sweden	19 Jan 23	Admin Cooperation	41LTS151	301011
Germany	Sweden	29 Aug 24	Dispute Settlement	42LTS111	301036
Germany	Sweden	29 May 25	Air Transport	46LTS121	301116
Germany	Sweden	31 Dec 25	Taxation	43LTS219	301056
Germany	Sweden	14 May 26	General Economic	51LTS99	301225
Germany	Sweden	25 Apr 28	Taxation	81LTS281	301844
Germany	Sweden	01 Jun 32	Water Transport	129LTS471	302979
Germany	Sweden	28 Aug 34	Finance	154LTS249	303551
Germany	Sweden	28 Aug 34	Finance	154LTS267	303552
Germany	Sweden	28 Aug 34	Claims and Debts	154LTS273	303553
Germany	Sweden	22 Dec 34	Claims and Debts	156LTS151	303598
Germany	Sweden	22 Dec 34	Finance	156LTS127	303596
Germany	Sweden	22 Dec 34	Finance	156LTS145	303597
Germany	Sweden	13 Mar 35	Sanitation	158LTS233	303633
Germany	Sweden	14 May 35	Taxation	163LTS425	303784
Germany	Sweden	14 May 35	Taxation	163LTS459	303785
Germany	Sweden	19 Jul 35	Loans and Credits	161LTS35	303704
Germany	Sweden	31 Jan 36	Claims and Debts	168LTS19	303884
Germany	Sweden	31 Jan 36	Finance	168LTS13	303883
Germany	Sweden	19 May 36	Admin Cooperation	182LTS395	304224
Germany	Sweden	28 Oct 38	Claims and Debts	196LTS81	304570
Germany	Sweden	28 Oct 38	Claims and Debts	196LTS91	304571
Germany	Switzerland	15 Mar 20	Customs	12LTS19	300303
Germany	Switzerland	09 Jul 20	Commodity Trade	12LTS25	300304
Germany	Switzerland	14 Sep 20	Air Transport	2LTS331	300087
Germany	Switzerland	06 Dec 20	Finance	2LTS343	300088
Germany	Switzerland	29 Oct 21	Finance	13LTS193	300351
Germany	Switzerland	03 Dec 21	Dispute Settlement	12LTS271	300320
Germany	Switzerland	24 Mar 23	Taxation	27LTS41	300666
Germany	Switzerland	25 Mar 23	Finance	18LTS273	300470
Germany	Switzerland	17 Nov 24	General Trade	41LTS473	301026
Germany	Switzerland	12 Oct 25	Extradition	53LTS241	301260
Germany	Switzerland	06 Nov 25	Customs	53LTS283	301262
Germany	Switzerland	14 Jul 26	General Trade	59LTS87	301391
Germany	Switzerland	04 Feb 28	Non-ILO Labor	79LTS241	301814
Germany	Switzerland	23 Apr 29	General Trade	96LTS257	302206
Germany	Switzerland	28 May 29	Territory Boundary	104LTS19	302375
Germany	Switzerland	02 Nov 29	Admin Cooperation	109LTS273	302544
Germany	Switzerland	15 Jul 31	Taxation	144LTS389	303341
Germany	Switzerland	21 Sep 38	Territory Boundary	196LTS365	304595
Germany	Turkey	03 Mar 24	General Amity	41LTS237	301017
Germany	Turkey	13 Dec 25	General Economic	53LTS355	301265
Germany	Turkey	12 Jan 27	Admin Cooperation	73LTS187	301713
Germany	Turkey	12 Jan 27	General Trade	73LTS133	301712
Germany	Turkey	16 May 29	Dispute Settlement	109LTS451	302549
Germany	Turkey	28 May 29	Admin Cooperation	133LTS235	303068
Germany	Turkey	28 May 29	Consul/Citizenship	133LTS257	303069
Germany	Turkey	27 May 30	General Economic	110LTS9	302553
Germany	Turkey	03 Sep 30	Extradition	133LTS321	303071
Germany	UK Great Britain	25 Jun 20	Admin Cooperation	5LTS303	300135
Germany	UK Great Britain	31 Dec 20	Peace/Disarmament	8LTS241	300223
Germany	UK Great Britain	18 Jun 21	Sanitation	16LTS139	300404
Germany	UK Great Britain	23 Nov 21	Peace/Disarmament	8LTS381	300237
Germany	UK Great Britain	05 Apr 23	Reparations	17LTS173	300435
Germany	UK Great Britain	05 Jan 24	Claims and Debts	36LTS365	300935
Germany	UK Great Britain	03 Apr 25	Reparations	33LTS383	300859
Germany	UK Great Britain	13 Aug 25	General Economic	43LTS89	301050
Germany	UK Great Britain	19 Oct 26	Gen Communications	67LTS203	301547
Germany	UK Great Britain	29 Jun 27	Air Transport	71LTS165	301659

PARTY ONE	PARTY TWO	DATE	TOPIC	CITATION	NUMBER
Germany	UK Great Britain	20 Mar 28	Admin Cooperation	90LTS287	302044
Germany	UK Great Britain	26 Jul 28	Specific Property	85LTS135	301928
Germany	UK Great Britain	17 Jul 29	Postal Service	100LTS439	302313
Germany	UK Great Britain	28 Dec 29	Admin Cooperation	102LTS49	302352
Germany	UK Great Britain	09 May 30	Milit Occupation	105LTS271	302419
Germany	UK Great Britain	26 Jul 32	Dispute Settlement	133LTS99	303060
Germany	UK Great Britain	27 Jul 32	Admin Cooperation	134LTS311	303099
Germany	UK Great Britain	29 Oct 32	Postal Service	138LTS69	303182
Germany	UK Great Britain	03 May 33	General Trade	140LTS139	303231
Germany	UK Great Britain	07 Jul 33	Commodity Trade	145LTS237	303356
Germany	UK Great Britain	10 Aug 34	Finance	155LTS53	303568
Germany	UK Great Britain	18 Sep 34	Air Transport	155LTS243	303580
Germany	UK Great Britain	01 Nov 34	Finance	163LTS79	303762
Germany	UK Great Britain	03 Jun 35	General Amity	163LTS415	303782
Germany	UK Great Britain	07 Jun 35	Water Transport	163LTS293	303771
Germany	UK Great Britain	18 Jun 35	General Military	161LTS9	303701
Germany	UK Great Britain	02 Dec 36	Postal Service	178LTS329	304121
Germany	UK Great Britain	17 Jul 37	Peace/Disarmament	187LTS43	304332
Germany	UK Great Britain	10 Nov 37	Taxation	186LTS277	304316
Germany	UK Great Britain	01 Jul 38	Finance	194LTS245	304526
Germany	UK Great Britain	01 Jul 38	Finance	194LTS235	304525
Germany	UK Great Britain	13 Aug 38	Finance	194LTS257	304527
Germany	UK Great Britain	10 Sep 38	Recognition	194LTS313	304528
Germany	UK Great Britain	16 Jun 39	General Trade	197LTS277	304620
Germany	United Arab Rep	25 Mar 30	Mostfavored Nation	115LTS271	302691
Germany	Uruguay	26 Oct 28	Visas	90LTS205	302039
Germany	USA (United States)	25 Aug 21	Peace/Disarmament	12LTS191	300310
Germany	USA (United States)	10 Aug 22	Admin Cooperation	26LTS357	300655
Germany	USA (United States)	19 May 24	Customs	41LTS271	301020
Germany	USA (United States)	20 Mar 25	Taxation	119LTS185	302745
Germany	USA (United States)	21 May 25	General Economic	52LTS133	301254
Germany	USA (United States)	14 Feb 28	Admin Cooperation	79LTS235	301813
Germany	USA (United States)	05 May 28	Dispute Settlement	90LTS171	302034
Germany	USA (United States)	05 May 28	Dispute Settlement	90LTS177	302035
Germany	USA (United States)	23 Jun 30	Reparations	106LTS121	302440
Germany	USA (United States)	12 Jul 30	Extradition	119LTS247	302748
Germany	USA (United States)	16 Dec 31	Water Transport	129LTS129	302957
Germany	USA (United States)	31 May 32	Air Transport	133LTS427	303079
Germany	USA (United States)	31 May 32	Air Transport	133LTS409	303078
Germany	USA (United States)	16 Mar 39	Postal Service	198LTS237	304645
Germany	USSR (Soviet Union)	19 Apr 20	Reparations	2LTS63	300048
Germany	USSR (Soviet Union)	07 Jul 20	Reparations	2LTS85	300051
Germany	USSR (Soviet Union)	06 May 21	Reparations	12LTS177	300309
Germany	USSR (Soviet Union)	06 May 21	Reparations	6LTS267	300159
Germany	USSR (Soviet Union)	16 Apr 22	General Amity	19LTS247	300498
Germany	USSR (Soviet Union)	05 Nov 22	Admin Cooperation	26LTS387	300657
Germany	USSR (Soviet Union)	12 Oct 25	Other Ad Hoc	53LTS7	301257
Germany	USSR (Soviet Union)	12 Oct 25	Admin Cooperation	53LTS227	301259
Germany	USSR (Soviet Union)	12 Oct 25	Consul/Citizenship	53LTS163	301258
Germany	USSR (Soviet Union)	24 Apr 26	General Amity	53LTS387	301268
Germany	USSR (Soviet Union)	25 Jan 29	Dispute Settlement	90LTS219	302041
Germany	USSR (Soviet Union)	16 Apr 29	Water Transport	109LTS327	302547
Germany	USSR (Soviet Union)	24 Jun 31	Admin Cooperation	157LTS383	303612
Germany	USSR (Soviet Union)	07 Mar 35	Postal Service	169LTS7	303911
Germany	Yugoslavia	29 Jul 33	Mostfavored Nation	149LTS77	303435
Ghana	Multilateral	31 Mar 22	Humanitarian	9LTS415	300269
Ghana	Multilateral	25 Sep 26	ILO Labor	60LTS253	301414
Ghana	Multilateral	20 Apr 29	Admin Cooperation	112LTS395	302624
Ghana	Multilateral	20 Apr 29	Admin Cooperation	112LTS371	302623
Ghana	Multilateral	11 Mar 33	Water Transport	135LTS301	303119
Gibralter	Multilateral	30 Jun 20	Patents/Copyrights	1LTS59	300008
Gibralter	Multilateral	31 Mar 22	Humanitarian	9LTS415	300269
Gibralter	Multilateral	25 Aug 24	Water Transport	120LTS155	302764
Gibralter	Multilateral	01 Dec 24	Sanitation	78LTS351	301794

PARTY ONE	PARTY TWO	DATE	TOPIC	CITATION	NUMBER
Gibralter	Multilateral	24 Apr 26	Land Transport	108LTS123	302505
Gibralter	Multilateral	26 Sep 27	Dispute Settlement	92LTS301	302096
Gibralter	Multilateral	25 Nov 27	Telecommunications	84LTS97	301905
Gibralter	Multilateral	23 Sep 36	Gen Communications	186LTS301	304319
Gibralter	USA (United States)	05 Jan 37	Postal Service	177LTS21	304078
Gilbert Islands	Multilateral	18 Mar 04	Humanitarian	1LTS83	300011
Gilbert Islands	Multilateral	30 Jun 20	Patents/Copyrights	1LTS59	300008
Gilbert Islands	Multilateral	31 Mar 22	Humanitarian	9LTS415	300269
Gilbert Islands	Multilateral	25 Aug 24	Water Transport	120LTS155	302764
Gilbert Islands	Multilateral	01 Dec 24	Sanitation	78LTS351	301794
Gilbert Islands	Multilateral	25 Nov 27	Telecommunications	84LTS97	301905
Gilbert Islands	Multilateral	12 Apr 33	Sanitation	161LTS65	303706
Gilbert Islands	Multilateral	28 Oct 33	Refugees	159LTS199	303663
Gilbert Islands	Multilateral	23 Sep 36	Gen Communications	186LTS301	304319
Gilbert Islands	Multilateral	10 Feb 38	Refugees	192LTS59	304461
Gold Coast	Multilateral	30 Jun 20	Patents/Copyrights	1LTS59	300008
Gold Coast	Multilateral	31 Mar 22	Humanitarian	9LTS415	300269
Gold Coast	Multilateral	25 Aug 24	Water Transport	120LTS155	302764
Gold Coast	Multilateral	26 Sep 27	Dispute Settlement	92LTS301	302096
Gold Coast	Multilateral	25 Nov 27	Telecommunications	84LTS97	301905
Gold Coast	Multilateral	28 Oct 33	Refugees	159LTS199	303663
Gold Coast	Multilateral	23 Sep 36	Gen Communications	186LTS301	304319
Gold Coast	Multilateral	10 Feb 38	Refugees	192LTS59	304461
Gold Coast	Togo	07 Oct 33	Telecommunications	144LTS95	303321
Great Britain	Austria	18 Jul 27	Visas	68LTS97	301573
Great Britain	Austria	13 Apr 28	Patents/Copyrights	80LTS247	301830
Great Britain	Belgium	21 Dec 28	Admin Cooperation	85LTS415	301942
Great Britain	Bulgaria	07 May 25	Postal Service	38LTS153	300973
Great Britain	Czechoslovakia	09 Aug 25	Postal Service	38LTS231	300980
Great Britain	Denmark	11 Jun 29	Water Transport	93LTS401	302128
Great Britain	Estonia	12 Oct 26	Postal Service	60LTS387	301422
Great Britain	Finland	18 Nov 25	Taxation	42LTS445	301042
Great Britain	Finland	14 Dec 25	Air Transport	47LTS403	301144
Great Britain	France	02 Feb 26	General Amity	56LTS79	301324
Great Britain	France	15 Mar 26	Postal Service	47LTS415	301146
Great Britain	France	14 Sep 27	Admin Cooperation	69LTS269	301609
Great Britain	Germany	30 Jul 25	Reparations	38LTS181	300974
Great Britain	Germany	13 Aug 25	Reparations	38LTS185	300975
Great Britain	Germany	15 Nov 28	Visas	90LTS213	302040
Great Britain	Germany		Taxation	71LTS193	301661
Great Britain	Iraq	13 Jan 26	Territory Boundary	47LTS419	301147
Great Britain	Irish Free State	03 Dec 25	Admin Cooperation	44LTS263	301088
Great Britain	Italy	10 Sep 26	Land Transport	57LTS77	301354
Great Britain	Japan	30 Jul 25	General Economic	65LTS29	301517
Great Britain	Latvia	16 Jul 24	Extradition	37LTS369	300961
Great Britain	Latvia	13 Aug 25	Milit Assistance	56LTS177	301329
Great Britain	Latvia	16 Nov 27	Customs	71LTS185	301660
Great Britain	Lithuania	18 Aug 25	Postal Service	43LTS135	301051
Great Britain	Multilateral	23 Jan 12	Sanitation	8LTS187	300222
Great Britain	Multilateral	01 May 20	Air Transport	11LTS173	300297
Great Britain	Multilateral	21 Jun 20	Health/Educ/Welfare	8LTS65	300207
Great Britain	Multilateral	06 Oct 21	General Economic	17LTS45	300427
Great Britain	Multilateral	14 Dec 22	Water Transport	36LTS457	300943
Great Britain	Multilateral	24 Jul 23	Admin Cooperation	36LTS201	300922
Great Britain	Multilateral	24 Jul 23	Consul/Citizenship	36LTS167	300917
Great Britain	Multilateral	24 Jul 23	Recognition	36LTS179	300919
Great Britain	Multilateral	24 Jul 23	Water Transport	36LTS187	300920
Great Britain	Multilateral	24 Jul 23	Taxation	36LTS175	300918
Great Britain	Multilateral	29 Sep 23	Refugees	20LTS41	300504
Great Britain	Multilateral	09 Dec 23	General Economic	58LTS315	301380
Great Britain	Multilateral	09 Dec 23	Water Transport	58LTS284	301379
Great Britain	Multilateral	25 Jan 24	Sanitation	57LTS135	301360
Great Britain	Multilateral	28 Mar 24	Finance	31LTS53	300781
Great Britain	Multilateral	22 May 24	General Trade	35LTS175	300895
Great Britain	Multilateral	28 Aug 24	Postal Service	40LTS19	301002

PARTY ONE	PARTY TWO	DATE	TOPIC	CITATION	NUMBER
Great Britain	Multilateral	28 Aug 24	Postal Service	40LTS249	301003
Great Britain	Multilateral	30 Aug 24	Reparations	30LTS97	300762
Great Britain	Multilateral	25 Sep 24	Admin Cooperation	30LTS421	300777
Great Britain	Multilateral	00 Apr 25	Water Transport	37LTS21	300945
Great Britain	Multilateral	23 Apr 25	Water Transport	37LTS9	300944
Great Britain	Multilateral	16 Oct 25	Peace/Disarmament	54LTS289	301292
Great Britain	Multilateral	29 Oct 25	Telecommunications	57LTS201	301365
Great Britain	Multilateral	00 Apr 26	Water Transport	57LTS437	301366
Great Britain	Multilateral	10 Apr 26	Water Transport	176LTS199	304062
Great Britain	Multilateral	12 May 26	Refugees	89LTS47	302004
Great Britain	Multilateral	18 Sep 26	General IGO	59LTS237	301393
Great Britain	Multilateral	30 Oct 26	Telecommunications	61LTS65	301426
Great Britain	Multilateral	10 Sep 27	Postal Service	75LTS39	301750
Great Britain	Multilateral	10 Sep 27	Postal Service	75LTS7	301749
Great Britain	Multilateral	08 Nov 27	General Trade	97LTS391	302238
Great Britain	Multilateral	25 Nov 27	Telecommunications	84LTS97	301905
Great Britain	Multilateral	25 Jul 28	General Amity	87LTS211	301971
Great Britain	Multilateral	30 Oct 28	Dispute Settlement	87LTS103	301963
Great Britain	Multilateral	28 Jun 29	Postal Service	103LTS5	302369
Great Britain	Multilateral	13 Jul 31	Other HEW	139LTS301	303219
Great Britain	Multilateral	11 Oct 33	Education	155LTS331	303585
Great Britain	Multilateral	19 Jun 34	Admin Cooperation	154LTS381	303564
Great Britain	Multilateral	22 Dec 34	Visas	183LTS145	304230
Great Britain	Multilateral	23 Apr 39	Land Transport	104LTS87	302380
Great Britain	Muscat and Oman	11 Feb 26	General Economic	57LTS13	301347
Great Britain	Nejd	02 Nov 25	Territory Boundary	60LTS419	301423
Great Britain	Netherlands	27 Apr 26	Telecommunications	50LTS295	301212
Great Britain	Portugal	30 Aug 24	Postal Service	38LTS217	300979
Great Britain	Portugal	29 Aug 25	Admin Cooperation	38LTS213	300978
Great Britain	Portugal	27 Jan 27	Water Transport	71LTS199	301662
Great Britain	Serb/Croat/Slovene	09 Aug 27	Reparations	69LTS255	301607
Great Britain	Spain	08 Sep 27	Patents/Copyrights	69LTS263	301608
Great Britain	USA (United States)	25 Sep 25	Telecommunications	69LTS179	301603
Great Britain	USA (United States)	01 Oct 25	Telecommunications	69LTS187	301604
Greece		24 Jul 23	Consul/Citizenship	36LTS153	300914
Greece		15 Sep 27	Loans and Credits	70LTS9	301622
Greece	Albania	25 Jun 26	Extradition	83LTS305	301898
Greece	Albania	13 Oct 26	General Trade	83LTS325	301899
Greece	Albania	13 Oct 26	Consul/Citizenship	83LTS361	301900
Greece	Austria	12 Jun 56*	Specif Goods/Equip	2LTS157	300061
Greece	Austria	28 Mar 74*	Extradition	2LTS169	300063
Greece	Austria	16 Sep 04	Claims and Debts	2LTS161	300062
Greece	Austria	27 May 24	Patents/Copyrights	27LTS99	300671
Greece	Austria	18 Apr 25	General Trade	38LTS311	300986
Greece	Austria	27 Dec 29	Claims and Debts	100LTS423	302311
Greece	Austria	26 Jun 30	Dispute Settlement	119LTS353	302755
Greece	Austria	15 Sep 33	General Trade	161LTS251	303717
Greece	Austria-Hungary	21 Dec 04	Extradition	2LTS173	300064
Greece	Bel-Lux Econ Union	22 Nov 27	Milit Assistance	69LTS341	301616
Greece	Belgium	25 Jun 29	Dispute Settlement	113LTS117	302640
Greece	Belgium	04 Aug 33	Extradition	153LTS325	303528
Greece	Belgium	01 Aug 34	Water Transport	153LTS273	303521
Greece	Belgium	09 Sep 37	Visas	197LTS63	304605
Greece	British Empire	26 Nov 25	General Trade	63LTS167	301488
Greece	Bulgaria	27 Nov 19	Consul/Citizenship	1LTS67	300009
Greece	Bulgaria	28 Feb 27	Mostfavored Nation	68LTS59	301568
Greece	Bulgaria	09 Dec 27	Finance	87LTS199	301970
Greece	Bulgaria	21 Feb 29	Extradition	106LTS443	302461
Greece	Bulgaria	16 Sep 38	General Trade	195LTS27	304534
Greece	Canada	30 Sep 29	Taxation	96LTS159	302198
Greece	China	30 Sep 29	General Amity	123LTS127	302811
Greece	Czechoslovakia	10 Jan 23	General Trade	21LTS217	300544
Greece	Czechoslovakia	08 Apr 25	General Trade	38LTS291	300984
Greece	Czechoslovakia	07 Apr 27	Extradition	88LTS219	301999
Greece	Czechoslovakia	07 Apr 27	Admin Cooperation	88LTS211	301998

PARTY ONE	PARTY TWO	DATE	TOPIC	CITATION	NUMBER
Greece	Czechoslovakia	07 Apr 27	Admin Cooperation	88LTS187	301997
Greece	Czechoslovakia	08 Jun 29	General Amity	108LTS255	302512
Greece	Czechoslovakia	30 Jul 32	General Trade	156LTS159	303599
Greece	Denmark	10 Dec 24	General Economic	31LTS227	300798
Greece	Denmark	29 Sep 27	Mostfavored Nation	62LTS219	301464
Greece	Denmark	22 Aug 28	General Economic	94LTS263	302147
Greece	Denmark	13 Apr 33	Dispute Settlement	150LTS465	303478
Greece	Estonia	04 Jan 27	General Economic	69LTS33	301598
Greece	Estonia	25 Nov 37	Finance	184LTS427	304263
Greece	Ethiopia	18 Feb 22	General Economic	15LTS267	300399
Greece	Ethiopia	23 Mar 31	General Amity	153LTS127	303512
Greece	Finland	22 Jun 26	General Economic	56LTS197	301331
Greece	Finland	18 Dec 26	General Trade	70LTS89	301626
Greece	Finland	27 Jul 34	Claims and Debts	153LTS41	303505
Greece	Finland	17 Nov 37	General Economic	188LTS207	304359
Greece	France	20 Apr 20	General Aid	3LTS93	300093
Greece	France	27 Aug 21	General Military	8LTS137	300214
Greece	France	21 Feb 24	General Economic	43LTS481	301077
Greece	France	11 Mar 29	General Economic	95LTS401	302187
Greece	France	23 May 31	General Trade	125LTS415	302867
Greece	France	05 Jun 31	Air Transport	31LTS201	303011
Greece	France	11 Oct 37	Admin Cooperation	185LTS253	304289
Greece	France	19 Dec 38	Education	196LTS99	304572
Greece	Germany	20 Jan 97*	Water Transport	2LTS107	300053
Greece	Germany	12 Mar 07	Extradition	2LTS111	300054
Greece	Germany	01 Dec 10	Claims and Debts	2LTS123	300055
Greece	Germany	21 Mar 24	Patents/Copyrights	30LTS257	300769
Greece	Germany	15 May 25	General Trade	40LTS6	301001
Greece	Germany	24 Mar 28	General Economic	90LTS9	302031
Greece	Germany	10 Nov 31	Dispute Settlement	133LTS385	303076
Greece	Germany	09 Nov 36	Air Transport	182LTS9	304201
Greece	Germany	24 Sep 37	General Economic	190LTS51	304404
Greece	Germany	14 Apr 38	Admin Cooperation	198LTS389	304657
Greece	Germany	11 May 38	Admin Cooperation	197LTS75	304608
Greece	Germany	01 Oct 38	General Economic	197LTS233	304616
Greece	Hungary	04 Jun 25	General Trade	39LTS139	300998
Greece	Hungary	28 Jun 28	Water Transport	82LTS209	301871
Greece	Hungary	05 May 30	Dispute Settlement	118LTS293	302732
Greece	Hungary	03 Jun 30	General Trade	122LTS37	302798
Greece	Hungary	06 Apr 38	Admin Cooperation	188LTS455	304370
Greece	Iceland	28 Jan 30	Mostfavored Nation	118LTS285	302731
Greece	Irish Free State	15 May 30	General Trade	136LTS33	303122
Greece	Italy	24 Oct 26	General Trade	63LTS51	301480
Greece	Italy	24 Nov 26	Specific Resources	63LTS91	301481
Greece	Italy	23 Sep 28	Dispute Settlement	108LTS219	302510
Greece	Italy	15 Jan 32	Taxation	137LTS397	303169
Greece	Italy	30 Jun 36	Air Transport	185LTS93	304277
Greece	Latvia	25 Feb 27	General Trade	71LTS25	301652
Greece	Latvia	15 Jan 38	General Trade	195LTS19	304533
Greece	Lithuania	01 Dec 37	General Trade	193LTS185	304495
Greece	Luxembourg	01 Sep 37	Extradition	193LTS151	304491
Greece	Mexico	17 Mar 38	General Amity	198LTS325	304649
Greece	Multilateral	09 Sep 86*	Patents/Copyrights	123LTS233	302816
Greece	Multilateral	12 Jan 12	Sanitation	4LTS281	300112
Greece	Multilateral	05 Jun 12	Telecommunications	1LTS135	300013
Greece	Multilateral	20 Mar 14	Patents/Copyrights	1LTS243	300016
Greece	Multilateral	10 Sep 19	General Trade	7LTS331	300200
Greece	Multilateral	10 Sep 19	General Economic	2LTS35	300044
Greece	Multilateral	10 Sep 19	Reparations	2LTS29	300043
Greece	Multilateral	10 Sep 19	Reparations	2LTS21	300042
Greece	Multilateral	25 Mar 20	Finance	1LTS45	300006
Greece	Multilateral	01 May 20	Air Transport	11LTS173	300297
Greece	Multilateral	21 Jun 20	Health/Educ/Welfare	8LTS65	300207
Greece	Multilateral	10 Aug 20	Consul/Citizenship	28LTS223	300711
Greece	Multilateral	10 Aug 20	Territory Boundary	28LTS225	300710

PARTY ONE	PARTY TWO	DATE	TOPIC	CITATION	NUMBER
Greece	Multilateral	31 Oct 20	Sanitation	164LTS85	303790
Greece	Multilateral	16 Dec 20	General IGO	6LTS379	300170
Greece	Multilateral	20 Apr 21	Land Transport	7LTS11	300171
Greece	Multilateral	20 Apr 21	Water Transport	7LTS65	300173
Greece	Multilateral	20 Apr 21	Water Transport	7LTS73	300174
Greece	Multilateral	20 Apr 21	Water Transport	7LTS35	300172
Greece	Multilateral	10 Jun 21	Customs	8LTS297	300227
Greece	Multilateral	23 Jul 21	Water Transport	26LTS173	300647
Greece	Multilateral	05 Aug 21	Admin Cooperation	27LTS349	300695
Greece	Multilateral	05 Oct 21	IGO Establishment	51LTS361	301241
Greece	Multilateral	05 Oct 21	Admin Cooperation	29LTS67	300733
Greece	Multilateral	05 Oct 21	Admin Cooperation	29LTS79	300735
Greece	Multilateral	05 Oct 21	Admin Cooperation	29LTS73	300734
Greece	Multilateral	31 Mar 22	Humanitarian	9LTS415	300269
Greece	Multilateral	05 Jul 22	Reparations	13LTS237	300355
Greece	Multilateral	02 Nov 22	Peace/Disarmament	149LTS35	303431
Greece	Multilateral	24 Jul 23	General Amity	36LTS145	300913
Greece	Multilateral	24 Jul 23	Peace/Disarmament	28LTS11	300701
Greece	Multilateral	24 Jul 23	Territory Boundary	28LTS215	300708
Greece	Multilateral	24 Jul 23	Admin Cooperation	28LTS197	300706
Greece	Multilateral	24 Jul 23	Admin Cooperation	28LTS283	300714
Greece	Multilateral	24 Jul 23	General Trade	28LTS151	300704
Greece	Multilateral	24 Jul 23	Consul/Citizenship	28LTS221	300709
Greece	Multilateral	24 Jul 23	Water Transport	28LTS115	300702
Greece	Multilateral	24 Jul 23	General Trade	28LTS171	300705
Greece	Multilateral	24 Jul 23	General Trade	28LTS203	300707
Greece	Multilateral	24 Jul 23	Territory Boundary	28LTS139	300703
Greece	Multilateral	24 Sep 23	Dispute Settlement	27LTS157	300678
Greece	Multilateral	03 Nov 23	Customs	30LTS371	300775
Greece	Multilateral	23 Nov 23	Claims and Debts	28LTS267	300712
Greece	Multilateral	09 Dec 23	Land Transport	47LTS55	301129
Greece	Multilateral	09 Dec 23	Non-IBRD Project	36LTS76	300905
Greece	Multilateral	09 Dec 23	Water Transport	58LTS284	301379
Greece	Multilateral	09 Dec 23	General Economic	58LTS315	301380
Greece	Multilateral	25 Jan 24	Sanitation	57LTS135	301360
Greece	Multilateral	31 Mar 24	Sanitation	27LTS211	300685
Greece	Multilateral	16 Aug 24	Taxation	41LTS429	301024
Greece	Multilateral	28 Aug 24	Postal Service	41LTS55	301007
Greece	Multilateral	28 Aug 24	Postal Service	40LTS307	301004
Greece	Multilateral	28 Aug 24	Postal Service	40LTS249	301003
Greece	Multilateral	28 Aug 24	Postal Service	40LTS19	301002
Greece	Multilateral	28 Aug 24	Postal Service	41LTS97	301008
Greece	Multilateral	28 Aug 24	Postal Service	40LTS437	301005
Greece	Multilateral	30 Aug 24	Admin Cooperation	30LTS79	300761
Greece	Multilateral	30 Aug 24	Admin Cooperation	30LTS75	300760
Greece	Multilateral	30 Aug 24	General Economic	30LTS63	300759
Greece	Multilateral	23 Oct 24	Land Transport	78LTS17	301779
Greece	Multilateral	23 Oct 24	General Transport	77LTS367	301778
Greece	Multilateral	29 Nov 24	General IGO	80LTS293	301835
Greece	Multilateral	01 Dec 24	Sanitation	78LTS351	301794
Greece	Multilateral	19 Feb 25	Admin Cooperation	81LTS317	301845
Greece	Multilateral	17 Jun 25	Peace/Disarmament	94LTS65	302138
Greece	Multilateral	29 Oct 25	Telecommunications	57LTS201	301365
Greece	Multilateral	27 Nov 25	Water Transport	67LTS63	301539
Greece	Multilateral	24 Apr 26	Land Transport	108LTS123	302505
Greece	Multilateral	12 May 26	Refugees	89LTS47	302004
Greece	Multilateral	21 Jun 26	Sanitation	78LTS229	301793
Greece	Multilateral	25 Sep 26	ILO Labor	60LTS253	301414
Greece	Multilateral	12 Jul 27	Direct Aid	135LTS247	303115
Greece	Multilateral	26 Sep 27	Dispute Settlement	92LTS301	302096
Greece	Multilateral	29 Oct 27	Scientific Project	127LTS27	302903
Greece	Multilateral	25 Nov 27	Telecommunications	84LTS97	301905
Greece	Multilateral	30 Jun 28	Refugees	89LTS53	302005
Greece	Multilateral	27 Aug 28	General Military	94LTS57	302137
Greece	Multilateral	22 Nov 28	Culture	111LTS343	302598

PARTY ONE	PARTY TWO	DATE	TOPIC	CITATION	NUMBER
Greece	Multilateral	14 Dec 28	General Economic	110LTS171	302560
Greece	Multilateral	20 Apr 29	Admin Cooperation	112LTS371	302623
Greece	Multilateral	20 Apr 29	Admin Cooperation	112LTS395	302624
Greece	Multilateral	31 May 29	Water Transport	136LTS81	303127
Greece	Multilateral	14 Jun 29	Visas	94LTS275	302148
Greece	Multilateral	28 Jun 29	Postal Service	103LTS249	302371
Greece	Multilateral	28 Jun 29	Postal Service	103LTS377	302373
Greece	Multilateral	28 Jun 29	Postal Service	103LTS5	302369
Greece	Multilateral	28 Jun 29	Postal Service	103LTS429	302374
Greece	Multilateral	28 Jun 29	Postal Service	103LTS321	302372
Greece	Multilateral	28 Jun 29	Postal Service	102LTS245	302368
Greece	Multilateral	28 Jun 29	Postal Service	103LTS71	302370
Greece	Multilateral	27 Jul 29	Other Military	118LTS303	302733
Greece	Multilateral	27 Jul 29	Other Military	118LTS343	302734
Greece	Multilateral	20 Aug 29	Sanitation	98LTS125	302243
Greece	Multilateral	14 Sep 29	UN Charter	165LTS353	303822
Greece	Multilateral	12 Oct 29	General Transport	137LTS11	303145
Greece	Multilateral	20 Jan 30	Reparations	104LTS243	302394
Greece	Multilateral	20 Jan 30	Reparations	104LTS421	302396
Greece	Multilateral	20 Jan 30	Reparations	112LTS361	302622
Greece	Multilateral	20 Jan 30	Reparations	113LTS389	302650
Greece	Multilateral	20 Jan 30	Finance	104LTS413	302395
Greece	Multilateral	20 Jan 30	Finance	104LTS433	302397
Greece	Multilateral	12 Apr 30	Admin Cooperation	179LTS89	304137
Greece	Multilateral	12 Apr 30	Admin Cooperation	179LTS115	304138
Greece	Multilateral	12 Apr 30	Milit Servic/Citiz	178LTS227	304117
Greece	Multilateral	28 Apr 30	Claims and Debts	121LTS69	302785
Greece	Multilateral	07 Jun 30	Finance	143LTS317	303314
Greece	Multilateral	07 Jun 30	Finance	143LTS257	303313
Greece	Multilateral	01 Aug 30	Health/Educ/Welfare	128LTS9	302932
Greece	Multilateral	23 Oct 30	Water Transport	125LTS95	302849
Greece	Multilateral	23 Oct 30	Water Transport	112LTS21	302603
Greece	Multilateral	19 Mar 31	Finance	143LTS355	303316
Greece	Multilateral	19 Mar 31	Finance	143LTS407	303317
Greece	Multilateral	19 Mar 31	Admin Cooperation	143LTS7	303301
Greece	Multilateral	28 Mar 31	Customs	119LTS47	302739
Greece	Multilateral	30 Mar 31	Taxation	138LTS149	303185
Greece	Multilateral	13 Jul 31	Other HEW	139LTS301	303219
Greece	Multilateral	24 Sep 31	Specific Resources	155LTS349	303586
Greece	Multilateral	11 Dec 31	Commodity Trade	170LTS251	303941
Greece	Multilateral	02 Sep 32	Land Transport	154LTS123	303543
Greece	Multilateral	09 Dec 32	Telecommunications	151LTS5	303479
Greece	Multilateral	11 Mar 33	Water Transport	135LTS301	303119
Greece	Multilateral	12 Apr 33	Sanitation	161LTS65	303706
Greece	Multilateral	25 Aug 33	Commodity Trade	141LTS71	303262
Greece	Multilateral	10 Oct 33	General Amity	163LTS393	303781
Greece	Multilateral	11 Oct 33	Education	155LTS331	303585
Greece	Multilateral	11 Oct 33	Consul/Citizenship	150LTS431	303476
Greece	Multilateral	23 Nov 33	Land Transport	192LTS327	304483
Greece	Multilateral	23 Nov 33	Land Transport	192LTS389	304484
Greece	Multilateral	09 Feb 34	General Military	153LTS153	303514
Greece	Multilateral	20 Mar 34	Postal Service	175LTS5	304049
Greece	Multilateral	20 Mar 34	Postal Service	176LTS55	304054
Greece	Multilateral	20 Mar 34	Postal Service	174LTS171	304048
Greece	Multilateral	20 Mar 34	Postal Service	175LTS363	304052
Greece	Multilateral	20 Mar 34	Postal Service	175LTS269	304051
Greece	Multilateral	20 Mar 34	Finance	176LTS9	304053
Greece	Multilateral	20 Mar 34	Postal Service	175LTS73	304050
Greece	Multilateral	26 Apr 34	Admin Cooperation	164LTS63	303789
Greece	Multilateral	19 Jun 34	Admin Cooperation	154LTS381	303564
Greece	Multilateral	15 Jul 34	Mostfavored Nation	165LTS9	303801
Greece	Multilateral	25 Jul 34	Other HEW	177LTS59	304080
Greece	Multilateral	22 Dec 34	Admin Cooperation	183LTS153	304231
Greece	Multilateral	22 Dec 34	Visas	183LTS145	304230
Greece	Multilateral	20 Feb 35	Sanitation	193LTS59	304487

PARTY ONE	PARTY TWO	DATE	TOPIC	CITATION	NUMBER
Greece	Multilateral	20 Feb 35	Sanitation	193LTS37	304486
Greece	Multilateral	20 Feb 35	Sanitation	186LTS173	304310
Greece	Multilateral	26 Jun 36	Other HEW	198LTS299	304648
Greece	Multilateral	20 Jul 36	Territory Boundary	173LTS213	304015
Greece	Multilateral	30 Jul 36	IGO Status/Immunit	197LTS31	304602
Greece	Multilateral	23 Sep 36	Gen Communications	186LTS301	304319
Greece	Multilateral	06 Nov 36	General Military	173LTS353	304025
Greece	Multilateral	31 Mar 37	Commodity Trade	189LTS359	304394
Greece	Multilateral	08 May 37	Privil/Immunities	182LTS37	304202
Greece	Multilateral	14 Sep 37	General Military	181LTS137	304184
Greece	Multilateral	17 Sep 37	Milit Installation	181LTS150	304185
Greece	Multilateral	02 Oct 37	Education	182LTS263	304216
Greece	Multilateral	15 Apr 38	Visas	200LTS285	304698
Greece	Multilateral	12 Sep 38	Culture	198LTS111	304630
Greece	Multilateral	31 Oct 38	Sanitation	198LTS205	304642
Greece	Multilateral	03 Dec 38	Education	200LTS249	304694
Greece	Multilateral	23 May 39	Postal Service	202LTS159	304742
Greece	Multilateral	01 Jan 42	General Military	204LTS381	304817
Greece	Netherlands	12 May 26	General Trade	61LTS295	301440
Greece	Netherlands	05 Dec 30	Taxation	117LTS357	302702
Greece	New Zealand	16 Nov 26	General Trade	85LTS43	301921
Greece	Norway	10 Dec 24	General Economic	31LTS231	300799
Greece	Norway	29 Jun 27	General Trade	82LTS187	301869
Greece	Norway	15 Aug 31	General Economic	123LTS271	302817
Greece	Norway	28 Feb 38	General Trade	186LTS159	304308
Greece	Norway	28 Feb 38	Finance	186LTS165	304309
Greece	Other Unilat Decla	29 Sep 23	Refugees	20LTS29	300503
Greece	Other Unilat Decla	19 Sep 24	Refugees	30LTS413	300776
Greece	Other Unilat Decla	29 Sep 24	Consul/Citizenship	29LTS123	300738
Greece	Other Unilat Decla	14 Jan 30	Refugees	108LTS349	302518
Greece	Palestine	28 Mar 36	Postal Service	170LTS145	303932
Greece	Persia	24 May 29	Mostfavored Nation	121LTS221	302788
Greece	Poland	17 Apr 25	General Trade	38LTS301	300985
Greece	Poland	10 Apr 30	General Economic	120LTS369	302775
Greece	Poland	10 Apr 30	Admin Cooperation	123LTS165	302813
Greece	Poland	22 Apr 31	Air Transport	129LTS313	302966
Greece	Poland	04 Jan 32	Dispute Settlement	131LTS229	303014
Greece	Poland	05 Oct 36	Air Transport	181LTS29	304174
Greece	Poland	11 Mar 38	General Economic	194LTS13	304502
Greece	Poland	30 Sep 38	Air Transport	196LTS387	304599
Greece	Portugal	15 Aug 38	General Trade	201LTS201	304707
Greece	Romania	28 Mar 27	Mostfavored Nation	68LTS67	301569
Greece	Romania	21 Mar 28	General Military	108LTS187	302508
Greece	Romania	11 Aug 31	Recognition	130LTS69	302982
Greece	Romania	11 Aug 31	Health/Educ/Welfare	130LTS79	302983
Greece	Romania	11 Aug 31	General Economic	130LTS33	302981
Greece	Romania	11 Aug 31	Education	130LTS93	302984
Greece	Romania	12 Jun 33	Air Transport	150LTS357	303468
Greece	Serb/Croat/Slovene	10 May 23	Land Transport	25LTS441	300635
Greece	Serb/Croat/Slovene	02 Nov 27	General Economic	91LTS137	302060
Greece	Serb/Croat/Slovene	27 Mar 29	Dispute Settlement	108LTS201	302509
Greece	Spain	06 Mar 19	Claims and Debts	3LTS81	300092
Greece	Spain	23 Sep 26	Consul/Citizenship	91LTS121	302059
Greece	Spain	23 Jan 30	Dispute Settlement	139LTS93	303205
Greece	Spain	11 Jul 32	Finance	148LTS397	303426
Greece	Sweden	10 Sep 26	General Trade	63LTS37	301479
Greece	Sweden	18 Oct 29	Admin Cooperation	95LTS201	302174
Greece	Sweden	19 Nov 31	Taxation	126LTS411	302899
Greece	Sweden	17 Jan 35	General Trade	157LTS9	303601
Greece	Sweden	11 Jan 36	Finance	165LTS299	303816
Greece	Sweden	31 Dec 36	Finance	174LTS87	304039
Greece	Sweden	01 Feb 38	General Trade	185LTS217	304285
Greece	Sweden	01 May 39	General Trade	196LTS205	304582
Greece	Switzerland	21 Sep 25	Dispute Settlement	87LTS187	301969
Greece	Switzerland	29 Nov 26	General Trade	63LTS27	301478

PARTY ONE	PARTY TWO	DATE	TOPIC	CITATION	NUMBER
Greece	Switzerland	01 Dec 27	Admin Cooperation	84LTS271	301907
Greece	Switzerland	30 Mar 38	Admin Cooperation	185LTS245	304288
Greece	Turkey	30 Jan 23	Consul/Citizenship	32LTS75	300807
Greece	Turkey	30 Jan 23	Consul/Citizenship	36LTS137	300912
Greece	Turkey	10 Jun 30	Refugees	108LTS233	302511
Greece	Turkey	30 Oct 30	Dispute Settlement	125LTS9	302841
Greece	Turkey	30 Oct 30	General Economic	125LTS371	302866
Greece	Turkey	14 Sep 33	General Amity	156LTS165	303600
Greece	Turkey	15 Jan 37	Admin Cooperation	202LTS107	304739
Greece	Turkey	25 Nov 37	Land Transport	195LTS137	304543
Greece	Turkey	27 Apr 38	General Amity	193LTS175	304493
Greece	Turkey	07 Mar 39	Extradition	201LTS239	304717
Greece	UK Great Britain	22 Sep 20	Admin Cooperation	2LTS367	300090
Greece	UK Great Britain	27 Jul 21	Visas	6LTS347	300167
Greece	UK Great Britain	27 Aug 21	Other Military	8LTS332	300233
Greece	UK Great Britain	10 Nov 21	Sanitation	16LTS165	300407
Greece	UK Great Britain	03 Feb 22	Reparations	9LTS191	300252
Greece	UK Great Britain	10 Dec 24	General Economic	36LTS441	300941
Greece	UK Great Britain	30 Nov 25	Reparations	50LTS273	301210
Greece	UK Great Britain	01 Dec 26	Water Transport	61LTS109	301428
Greece	UK Great Britain	17 Feb 27	Claims and Debts	90LTS379	302049
Greece	UK Great Britain	09 Apr 27	Claims and Debts	67LTS217	301549
Greece	UK Great Britain	13 May 27	General Economic	61LTS15	301425
Greece	UK Great Britain	21 Jun 29	Finance	94LTS33	302134
Greece	UK Great Britain	31 Jul 29	Taxation	95LTS67	302165
Greece	UK Great Britain	17 Apr 31	Air Transport	129LTS287	302965
Greece	UK Great Britain	21 Apr 33	Visas	140LTS133	303230
Greece	UK Great Britain	21 Jan 36	Admin Cooperation	168LTS171	303897
Greece	UK Great Britain	27 Feb 36	Admin Cooperation	185LTS113	304278
Greece	UK Great Britain	17 Sep 36	Taxation	176LTS183	304060
Greece	UK Great Britain	30 May 39	Air Transport	202LTS7	304732
Greece	United Arab Rep	10 Apr 26	Mostfavored Nation	61LTS305	301441
Greece	USA (United States)	25 Apr 28	Commodity Trade	91LTS231	302064
Greece	USA (United States)	10 Jun 29	Taxation	98LTS81	302241
Greece	USA (United States)	19 Jun 30	Dispute Settlement	136LTS399	303138
Greece	USA (United States)	19 Jun 30	Dispute Settlement	136LTS393	303137
Greece	USA (United States)	06 May 31	Extradition	138LTS293	303194
Greece	USA (United States)	21 Nov 36	Privil/Immunities	183LTS169	304233
Greece	USA (United States)	15 Nov 38	General Trade	195LTS145	304544
Greece	Yugoslavia	22 Jul 33	Air Transport	161LTS219	303714
Grenada	Multilateral	30 Jun 20	Patents/Copyrights	1LTS59	300008
Grenada	Multilateral	31 Mar 22	Humanitarian	9LTS415	300269
Grenada	Multilateral	25 Aug 24	Water Transport	120LTS155	302764
Grenada	Multilateral	01 Dec 24	Sanitation	78LTS351	301794
Guadeloupe	Multilateral	05 Jun 12	Telecommunications	1LTS135	300013
Guadeloupe	Multilateral	24 Apr 26	Land Transport	108LTS123	302505
Guadeloupe	Multilateral	24 Apr 26	Land Transport	97LTS83	302220
Guadeloupe	Multilateral	23 Oct 30	Water Transport	125LTS95	302849
Guatemala	Bel-Lux Econ Union	07 Nov 24	General Economic	69LTS17	301596
Guatemala	Belgium	26 Apr 34	Extradition	161LTS415	303729
Guatemala	Canada	28 Sep 37	General Trade	194LTS65	304508
Guatemala	Czechoslovakia	20 Sep 36	General Trade	185LTS269	304293
Guatemala	El Salvador	09 Apr 38	Territory Boundary	189LTS275	304390
Guatemala	Germany	04 Oct 24	General Economic	52LTS19	301246
Guatemala	Honduras	16 Jul 30	Dispute Settlement	137LTS231	303159
Guatemala	Italy	15 Sep 26	General Trade	70LTS175	301633
Guatemala	Multilateral	20 Aug 10	Patents/Copyrights	155LTS179	303576
Guatemala	Multilateral	12 Jan 12	Sanitation	4LTS281	300112
Guatemala	Multilateral	05 Jun 12	Telecommunications	1LTS135	300013
Guatemala	Multilateral	10 Sep 19	General Trade	7LTS331	300200
Guatemala	Multilateral	01 May 20	Air Transport	11LTS173	300297
Guatemala	Multilateral	21 Jun 20	Health/Educ/Welfare	8LTS65	300207
Guatemala	Multilateral	19 Jan 21	Recognition	5LTS9	300113
Guatemala	Multilateral	20 Apr 21	Land Transport	7LTS11	300171
Guatemala	Multilateral	20 Apr 21	Water Transport	7LTS73	300174
Guatemala	Multilateral	20 Apr 21	Water Transport	7LTS35	300172
Guatemala	Multilateral	15 Sep 21	Postal Service	30LTS141	300767
Guatemala	Multilateral	28 Apr 23	Patents/Copyrights	33LTS47	300832
Guatemala	Multilateral	03 May 23	Customs	33LTS11	300830
Guatemala	Multilateral	03 May 23	General Trade	33LTS81	300833
Guatemala	Multilateral	03 May 23	General Amity	33LTS25	300831
Guatemala	Multilateral	25 Jan 24	Sanitation	57LTS135	301360
Guatemala	Multilateral	31 Mar 24	Sanitation	27LTS211	300685
Guatemala	Multilateral	28 Aug 24	Postal Service	40LTS307	301004
Guatemala	Multilateral	28 Aug 24	Postal Service	40LTS19	301002
Guatemala	Multilateral	28 Aug 24	Postal Service	40LTS249	301003
Guatemala	Multilateral	14 Nov 24	Sanitation	86LTS43	301949
Guatemala	Multilateral	24 Apr 26	Land Transport	108LTS123	302505
Guatemala	Multilateral	24 Apr 26	Land Transport	97LTS83	302220
Guatemala	Multilateral	21 Jun 26	Sanitation	78LTS229	301793
Guatemala	Multilateral	12 Jul 27	Direct Aid	135LTS247	303115
Guatemala	Multilateral	25 Nov 27	Telecommunications	84LTS97	301905
Guatemala	Multilateral	18 Feb 28	Patents/Copyrights	132LTS275	303044
Guatemala	Multilateral	20 Feb 28	Consul/Citizenship	155LTS289	303582
Guatemala	Multilateral	20 Feb 28	General Amity	135LTS187	303111
Guatemala	Multilateral	20 Feb 28	Admin Cooperation	134LTS45	303082
Guatemala	Multilateral	20 Feb 28	Consul/Citizenship	132LTS323	303046
Guatemala	Multilateral	20 Feb 28	Air Transport	129LTS223	302963
Guatemala	Multilateral	20 Feb 28	Privil/Immunities	132LTS301	303045
Guatemala	Multilateral	20 Feb 28	Other Ad Hoc	86LTS111	301950
Guatemala	Multilateral	27 Aug 28	General Military	94LTS57	302137
Guatemala	Multilateral	22 Nov 28	Culture	111LTS343	302598
Guatemala	Multilateral	05 Jan 29	Dispute Settlement	130LTS135	302988
Guatemala	Multilateral	05 Jan 29	Dispute Settlement	100LTS399	302309
Guatemala	Multilateral	20 Feb 29	Patents/Copyrights	124LTS357	302840
Guatemala	Multilateral	28 Jun 29	Postal Service	103LTS71	302370
Guatemala	Multilateral	28 Jun 29	Postal Service	102LTS245	302368
Guatemala	Multilateral	14 Sep 29	UN Charter	165LTS353	303822
Guatemala	Multilateral	13 Jul 31	Other HEW	139LTS301	303219
Guatemala	Multilateral	10 Nov 31	Postal Service	131LTS389	303024
Guatemala	Multilateral	10 Nov 31	Postal Service	131LTS447	303025
Guatemala	Multilateral	10 Nov 31	Postal Service	131LTS327	303023
Guatemala	Multilateral	09 Dec 32	Telecommunications	151LTS5	303479
Guatemala	Multilateral	29 May 33	Admin Cooperation	192LTS289	304479
Guatemala	Multilateral	10 Oct 33	General Amity	163LTS393	303781
Guatemala	Multilateral	26 Dec 33	Recognition	165LTS19	303802
Guatemala	Multilateral	26 Dec 33	Extradition	165LTS45	303803
Guatemala	Multilateral	20 Mar 34	Postal Service	174LTS171	304048
Guatemala	Multilateral	15 Jul 34	Mostfavored Nation	165LTS9	303801
Guatemala	Multilateral	15 Apr 35	Culture	167LTS289	303874
Guatemala	Multilateral	26 Jun 36	Other HEW	198LTS299	304648
Guatemala	Multilateral	23 Sep 36	Gen Communications	186LTS301	304319
Guatemala	Multilateral	06 Nov 36	General Military	173LTS353	304025
Guatemala	Multilateral	23 Dec 36	Admin Cooperation	201LTS295	304721
Guatemala	Multilateral	23 Dec 36	Dispute Settlement	195LTS229	304548
Guatemala	Multilateral	23 Dec 36	Dispute Settlement	188LTS75	304353
Guatemala	Multilateral	23 Dec 36	Peace/Disarmament	188LTS9	304350
Guatemala	Multilateral	23 Dec 36	Culture	188LTS125	304355
Guatemala	Multilateral	23 Dec 36	Dispute Settlement	188LTS53	304352
Guatemala	Multilateral	23 Dec 36	Culture	188LTS151	304356
Guatemala	Multilateral	23 Dec 36	Land Transport	188LTS99	304354
Guatemala	Multilateral	23 Dec 36	General Amity	188LTS31	304351
Guatemala	Multilateral	03 Dec 38	Education	200LTS249	304694
Guatemala	Multilateral	08 Dec 38	Gen Communications	202LTS49	304734
Guatemala	Multilateral	23 May 39	Postal Service	202LTS159	304742
Guatemala	Multilateral	01 Jan 42	General Military	204LTS381	304817
Guatemala	Netherlands	12 May 27	General Trade	85LTS323	301937
Guatemala	Nicaragua	10 Sep 24	General Trade	130LTS127	302987
Guatemala	Norway	20 Dec 38	General Trade	198LTS117	304631
Guatemala	Spain	14 Aug 35	Mass Media	166LTS381	303854

PARTY ONE	PARTY TWO	DATE	TOPIC	CITATION	NUMBER
Guatemala	Sweden	11 Jul 36	Mostfavored Nation	171LTS299	303967
Guatemala	UK Great Britain	22 Feb 28	General Economic	97LTS229	302226
Guatemala	UK Great Britain	06 Jun 31	Privil/Immunities	132LTS15	303027
Guatemala	UK Great Britain	26 Aug 31	Territory Boundary	128LTS427	302946
Guatemala	USA (United States)	24 Apr 36	General Trade	170LTS345	303945
Guatemala	USA (United States)	28 Mar 39	Military Mission	199LTS181	304671
Guatemala	USA (United States)	20 Feb 40	Extradition	204LTS111	304789
Guatemala	USA (United States)	27 May 41	Milit Assistance	204LTS185	304799
Guernsey Island	Multilateral	30 Jun 20	Patents/Copyrights	1LTS59	300008
Guinea	Multilateral	25 Sep 26	ILO Labor	60LTS253	301414
Guinea	Multilateral	23 Oct 30	Water Transport	125LTS95	302849
Guyana	Multilateral	24 Apr 26	Land Transport	108LTS123	302505
Guyana	Multilateral	24 Apr 26	Land Transport	97LTS83	302220
Haiti	Canada	23 Apr 37	General Trade	194LTS59	304507
Haiti	Denmark	05 Apr 28	Dispute Settlement	99LTS19	302264
Haiti	Denmark	21 Oct 37	General Trade	190LTS231	304422
Haiti	Dominican Republic	20 Jan 29	Peace/Disarmament	105LTS215	302414
Haiti	Dominican Republic	21 Jan 29	Territory Boundary	105LTS193	302413
Haiti	Dominican Republic	27 Feb 35	Territory Boundary	171LTS89	303953
Haiti	Dominican Republic	31 Jan 38	Territory Boundary	187LTS169	304336
Haiti	Germany	15 Oct 24	Finance	52LTS27	301247
Haiti	Germany	10 Mar 30	General Trade	119LTS231	302747
Haiti	Italy	03 Jan 27	General Trade	71LTS405	301678
Haiti	Jamaica	07 Dec 36	Postal Service	178LTS65	304108
Haiti	Multilateral	13 Nov 08	General Ad Hoc	1LTS217	300015
Haiti	Multilateral	20 Aug 10	Patents/Copyrights	155LTS179	303576
Haiti	Multilateral	12 Jan 12	Sanitation	4LTS281	300112
Haiti	Multilateral	20 Mar 14	Patents/Copyrights	1LTS243	300016
Haiti	Multilateral	10 Sep 19	General Trade	7LTS331	300200
Haiti	Multilateral	01 May 20	Air Transport	11LTS173	300297
Haiti	Multilateral	21 Jun 20	Health/Educ/Welfare	8LTS65	300207
Haiti	Multilateral	16 Dec 20	General IGO	6LTS379	300170
Haiti	Multilateral	05 Aug 21	Admin Cooperation	27LTS349	300695
Haiti	Multilateral	05 Oct 21	Admin Cooperation	29LTS73	300734
Haiti	Multilateral	05 Oct 21	Admin Cooperation	29LTS67	300733
Haiti	Multilateral	05 Oct 21	IGO Establishment	51LTS361	301241
Haiti	Multilateral	05 Oct 21	Admin Cooperation	29LTS79	300735
Haiti	Multilateral	28 Apr 23	Patents/Copyrights	33LTS47	300832
Haiti	Multilateral	03 May 23	General Amity	33LTS25	300831
Haiti	Multilateral	03 May 23	Customs	33LTS11	300830
Haiti	Multilateral	03 May 23	General Trade	33LTS81	300833
Haiti	Multilateral	31 Mar 24	Sanitation	27LTS211	300685
Haiti	Multilateral	28 Aug 24	Postal Service	40LTS307	301004
Haiti	Multilateral	28 Aug 24	Postal Service	40LTS19	301002
Haiti	Multilateral	28 Aug 24	Postal Service	40LTS249	301003
Haiti	Multilateral	14 Nov 24	Sanitation	86LTS43	301949
Haiti	Multilateral	19 Feb 25	Admin Cooperation	81LTS317	301845
Haiti	Multilateral	21 Jun 26	Sanitation	78LTS229	301793
Haiti	Multilateral	25 Sep 26	ILO Labor	60LTS253	301414
Haiti	Multilateral	25 Nov 27	Telecommunications	84LTS97	301905
Haiti	Multilateral	18 Feb 28	Patents/Copyrights	132LTS275	303044
Haiti	Multilateral	20 Feb 28	Consul/Citizenship	155LTS259	303581
Haiti	Multilateral	20 Feb 28	Consul/Citizenship	155LTS289	303582
Haiti	Multilateral	20 Feb 28	Admin Cooperation	134LTS45	303082
Haiti	Multilateral	20 Feb 28	Other Ad Hoc	86LTS111	301950
Haiti	Multilateral	20 Feb 28	Privil/Immunities	132LTS301	303045
Haiti	Multilateral	20 Feb 28	Consul/Citizenship	132LTS323	303046
Haiti	Multilateral	20 Feb 28	General Amity	135LTS187	303111
Haiti	Multilateral	20 Feb 28	Air Transport	129LTS223	302963
Haiti	Multilateral	27 Aug 28	General Military	94LTS57	302137
Haiti	Multilateral	22 Nov 28	Culture	111LTS343	302598
Haiti	Multilateral	05 Jan 29	Dispute Settlement	130LTS135	302988
Haiti	Multilateral	05 Jan 29	Dispute Settlement	100LTS399	302309
Haiti	Multilateral	20 Feb 29	Patents/Copyrights	124LTS357	302840
Haiti	Multilateral	16 Apr 29	Specific Resources	126LTS305	302891

PARTY ONE	PARTY TWO	DATE	TOPIC	CITATION	NUMBER
Haiti	Multilateral	31 May 29	Water Transport	136LTS81	303127
Haiti	Multilateral	28 Jun 29	Postal Service	102LTS245	302368
Haiti	Multilateral	28 Jun 29	Postal Service	103LTS71	302370
Haiti	Multilateral	28 Jun 29	Postal Service	103LTS5	302369
Haiti	Multilateral	14 Sep 29	UN Charter	165LTS353	303822
Haiti	Multilateral	13 Jul 31	Other HEW	139LTS301	303219
Haiti	Multilateral	10 Nov 31	Postal Service	131LTS447	303025
Haiti	Multilateral	10 Nov 31	Postal Service	131LTS327	303023
Haiti	Multilateral	10 Nov 31	Postal Service	131LTS389	303024
Haiti	Multilateral	10 Oct 33	General Amity	163LTS393	303781
Haiti	Multilateral	26 Dec 33	Extradition	165LTS45	303803
Haiti	Multilateral	26 Dec 33	Recognition	165LTS19	303802
Haiti	Multilateral	20 Mar 34	Finance	176LTS9	304053
Haiti	Multilateral	20 Mar 34	Postal Service	175LTS269	304051
Haiti	Multilateral	20 Mar 34	Postal Service	176LTS55	304054
Haiti	Multilateral	20 Mar 34	Postal Service	175LTS5	304049
Haiti	Multilateral	20 Mar 34	Postal Service	175LTS363	304052
Haiti	Multilateral	20 Mar 34	Postal Service	175LTS73	304050
Haiti	Multilateral	02 Jun 34	Patents/Copyrights	192LTS17	304459
Haiti	Multilateral	15 Apr 35	Culture	167LTS289	303874
Haiti	Multilateral	26 Jun 36	Other HEW	198LTS299	304648
Haiti	Multilateral	06 Nov 36	General Military	173LTS353	304025
Haiti	Multilateral	23 Dec 36	Dispute Settlement	195LTS229	304548
Haiti	Multilateral	23 Dec 36	Admin Cooperation	201LTS295	304721
Haiti	Multilateral	23 Dec 36	Culture	188LTS125	304355
Haiti	Multilateral	23 Dec 36	Culture	188LTS151	304356
Haiti	Multilateral	23 Dec 36	Land Transport	188LTS99	304354
Haiti	Multilateral	23 Dec 36	Dispute Settlement	188LTS75	304353
Haiti	Multilateral	23 Dec 36	General Amity	188LTS31	304351
Haiti	Multilateral	23 Dec 36	Dispute Settlement	188LTS53	304352
Haiti	Multilateral	23 Dec 36	Peace/Disarmament	188LTS9	304350
Haiti	Multilateral	31 Oct 38	Sanitation	198LTS205	304642
Haiti	Multilateral	03 Dec 38	Education	200LTS249	304694
Haiti	Multilateral	23 May 39	Postal Service	202LTS159	304742
Haiti	Multilateral	01 Jan 42	General Military	204LTS381	304817
Haiti	Netherlands	07 Sep 26	General Trade	71LTS219	301665
Haiti	UK Great Britain	16 Nov 22	Sanitation	16LTS173	300408
Haiti	UK Great Britain	13 Feb 28	Postal Service	85LTS63	301923
Haiti	UK Great Britain	25 Feb 28	General Trade	85LTS91	301924
Haiti	USA (United States)	05 Aug 31	Admin Cooperation	125LTS241	302857
Haiti	USA (United States)	07 Aug 33	Status of Forces	146LTS305	303381
Haiti	USA (United States)	24 Jul 34	Status of Forces	153LTS285	303523
Haiti	USA (United States)	28 Mar 35	General Trade	161LTS157	303709
Haiti	USA (United States)	13 Jan 38	Finance	187LTS201	304340
Haiti	USA (United States)	01 Jul 38	Finance	192LTS89	304463
Haiti	USA (United States)	18 Jul 39	Finance	198LTS329	304650
Haiti	USA (United States)	27 Sep 40	Finance	203LTS257	304767
Haiti	USA (United States)	13 Feb 41	Finance	203LTS363	304778
Hedjaz	British Empire	20 May 27	General Amity	71LTS131	301658
Hedjaz	Germany	26 Apr 29	General Amity	115LTS265	302690
Hedjaz	Multilateral	10 Sep 19	General Trade	7LTS331	300200
Hedjaz	Multilateral	01 May 20	Air Transport	11LTS173	300297
Hedjaz	Multilateral	21 Jun 26	Sanitation	78LTS229	301793
Hedjaz	Multilateral	18 Dec 26	Telecommunications	63LTS185	301489
Hedjaz	Multilateral	27 Aug 28	General Military	94LTS57	302137
Hedjaz	Multilateral	28 Jun 29	Postal Service	103LTS5	302369
Hedjaz	Multilateral	28 Jun 29	Postal Service	103LTS377	302373
Hedjaz	Multilateral	28 Jun 29	Postal Service	103LTS429	302374
Hedjaz	Multilateral	28 Jun 29	Postal Service	103LTS321	302372
Hedjaz	Multilateral	28 Jun 29	Postal Service	103LTS249	302371
Hedjaz	Multilateral	28 Jun 29	Postal Service	102LTS245	302368
Hedjaz	Multilateral	28 Jun 29	Postal Service	103LTS71	302370
Hedjaz	Multilateral	13 Jul 31	Other HEW	139LTS301	303219
Hedjaz	Persia	24 Aug 29	General Amity	106LTS269	302450
Honduras	Belgium	17 Jun 33	Extradition	167LTS69	303857

PARTY ONE	PARTY TWO	DATE	TOPIC	CITATION	NUMBER
Honduras	Germany	21 Sep 29	Visas	133LTS311	303070
Honduras	Guatemala	16 Jul 30	Dispute Settlement	137LTS231	303159
Honduras	Multilateral	20 Aug 10	Patents/Copyrights	155LTS179	303576
Honduras	Multilateral	12 Jan 12	Sanitation	4LTS281	300112
Honduras	Multilateral	05 Jun 12	Telecommunications	1LTS135	300013
Honduras	Multilateral	01 May 20	Air Transport	11LTS173	300297
Honduras	Multilateral	19 Jan 21	Recognition	5LTS9	300113
Honduras	Multilateral	28 Apr 23	Patents/Copyrights	33LTS47	300832
Honduras	Multilateral	03 May 23	General Trade	33LTS81	300833
Honduras	Multilateral	03 May 23	Customs	33LTS11	300830
Honduras	Multilateral	03 May 23	General Amity	33LTS25	300831
Honduras	Multilateral	31 Mar 24	Sanitation	27LTS211	300685
Honduras	Multilateral	28 Aug 24	Postal Service	41LTS97	301008
Honduras	Multilateral	28 Aug 24	Postal Service	40LTS307	301004
Honduras	Multilateral	28 Aug 24	Postal Service	40LTS249	301003
Honduras	Multilateral	14 Nov 24	Sanitation	86LTS43	301949
Honduras	Multilateral	21 Jun 26	Sanitation	78LTS229	301793
Honduras	Multilateral	25 Nov 27	Telecommunications	84LTS97	301905
Honduras	Multilateral	18 Feb 28	Patents/Copyrights	132LTS275	303044
Honduras	Multilateral	20 Feb 28	Consul/Citizenship	155LTS289	303582
Honduras	Multilateral	20 Feb 28	Consul/Citizenship	155LTS259	303581
Honduras	Multilateral	20 Feb 28	Privil/Immunities	132LTS301	303045
Honduras	Multilateral	20 Feb 28	Other Ad Hoc	86LTS111	301950
Honduras	Multilateral	20 Feb 28	General Amity	135LTS187	303111
Honduras	Multilateral	20 Feb 28	Consul/Citizenship	132LTS323	303046
Honduras	Multilateral	20 Feb 28	Air Transport	129LTS223	302963
Honduras	Multilateral	20 Feb 28	Admin Cooperation	134LTS45	303082
Honduras	Multilateral	27 Aug 28	General Military	94LTS57	302137
Honduras	Multilateral	05 Jan 29	Dispute Settlement	130LTS135	302988
Honduras	Multilateral	05 Jan 29	Dispute Settlement	100LTS399	302309
Honduras	Multilateral	20 Feb 29	Patents/Copyrights	124LTS357	302840
Honduras	Multilateral	28 Jun 29	Postal Service	103LTS249	302371
Honduras	Multilateral	28 Jun 29	Postal Service	103LTS377	302373
Honduras	Multilateral	28 Jun 29	Postal Service	103LTS321	302372
Honduras	Multilateral	28 Jun 29	Postal Service	103LTS5	302369
Honduras	Multilateral	28 Jun 29	Postal Service	102LTS245	302368
Honduras	Multilateral	28 Jun 29	Postal Service	103LTS429	302374
Honduras	Multilateral	28 Jun 29	Postal Service	103LTS71	302370
Honduras	Multilateral	13 Jul 31	Other HEW	139LTS301	303219
Honduras	Multilateral	10 Nov 31	Postal Service	131LTS447	303025
Honduras	Multilateral	10 Nov 31	Postal Service	131LTS389	303024
Honduras	Multilateral	10 Nov 31	Postal Service	131LTS327	303023
Honduras	Multilateral	09 Dec 32	Telecommunications	151LTS5	303479
Honduras	Multilateral	11 Mar 33	Water Transport	135LTS301	303119
Honduras	Multilateral	10 Oct 33	General Amity	163LTS393	303781
Honduras	Multilateral	26 Dec 33	Extradition	165LTS45	303803
Honduras	Multilateral	26 Dec 33	Recognition	165LTS19	303802
Honduras	Multilateral	20 Mar 34	Postal Service	175LTS363	304052
Honduras	Multilateral	20 Mar 34	Postal Service	175LTS269	304051
Honduras	Multilateral	20 Mar 34	Postal Service	175LTS73	304050
Honduras	Multilateral	20 Mar 34	Finance	176LTS9	304053
Honduras	Multilateral	20 Mar 34	Postal Service	174LTS171	304048
Honduras	Multilateral	20 Mar 34	Postal Service	176LTS55	304054
Honduras	Multilateral	20 Mar 34	Postal Service	175LTS5	304049
Honduras	Multilateral	15 Apr 35	Culture	167LTS289	303874
Honduras	Multilateral	26 Jun 36	Other HEW	198LTS299	304648
Honduras	Multilateral	23 Dec 36	Admin Cooperation	201LTS295	304721
Honduras	Multilateral	23 Dec 36	Dispute Settlement	195LTS229	304548
Honduras	Multilateral	23 Dec 36	Dispute Settlement	188LTS53	304352
Honduras	Multilateral	23 Dec 36	Culture	188LTS125	304355
Honduras	Multilateral	23 Dec 36	Peace/Disarmament	188LTS9	304350
Honduras	Multilateral	23 Dec 36	Dispute Settlement	188LTS75	304353
Honduras	Multilateral	23 Dec 36	Land Transport	188LTS99	304354
Honduras	Multilateral	23 Dec 36	General Amity	188LTS31	304351
Honduras	Multilateral	23 Dec 36	Culture	188LTS151	304356

PARTY ONE	PARTY TWO	DATE	TOPIC	CITATION	NUMBER
Honduras	Multilateral	08 Dec 38	Gen Communications	202LTS49	304734
Honduras	Multilateral	23 May 39	Postal Service	202LTS159	304742
Honduras	Multilateral	01 Jan 42	General Military	204LTS381	304817
Honduras	Nicaragua	30 Jan 30	General Trade	142LTS241	303297
Honduras	UK Great Britain	23 Apr 35	Postal Service	163LTS199	303768
Honduras	USA (United States)	18 Dec 35	Customs	167LTS313	303876
Honduras	USA (United States)	12 Dec 40	Admin Cooperation	203LTS341	304774
Hong Kong	Multilateral	31 Mar 22	Humanitarian	9LTS415	300269
Hong Kong	Multilateral	24 Sep 23	Dispute Settlement	27LTS157	300678
Hong Kong	Multilateral	25 Aug 24	Water Transport	120LTS155	302764
Hong Kong	Multilateral	26 Sep 27	Dispute Settlement	92LTS301	302096
Hong Kong	Multilateral	25 Nov 27	Telecommunications	84LTS97	301905
Hong Kong	Multilateral	28 Oct 33	Refugees	159LTS199	303663
Hong Kong	Multilateral	23 Sep 36	Gen Communications	186LTS301	304319
Hong Kong	Multilateral	10 Feb 38	Refugees	192LTS59	304461
Hungary	Albania	02 Jun 28	Water Transport	82LTS201	301870
Hungary	Austria	08 Oct 21	General Economic	16LTS19	300402
Hungary	Austria	13 Oct 21	Territory Boundary	9LTS203	300254
Hungary	Austria	08 Feb 22	General Economic	55LTS367	301320
Hungary	Austria	10 Apr 23	Dispute Settlement	18LTS93	300457
Hungary	Austria	30 Sep 24	Consul/Citizenship	42LTS177	301040
Hungary	Austria	08 Nov 24	Taxation	45LTS21	301097
Hungary	Austria	08 Nov 24	Taxation	44LTS407	301096
Hungary	Austria	10 May 26	General Trade	56LTS39	301321
Hungary	Austria	14 Jul 26	Visas	61LTS123	301430
Hungary	Austria	14 Jul 26	Visas	61LTS159	301431
Hungary	Austria	11 Mar 27	Admin Cooperation	80LTS67	301823
Hungary	Austria	14 Jun 28	General Trade	79LTS17	301802
Hungary	Austria	25 Jun 28	Admin Cooperation	100LTS85	302296
Hungary	Austria	11 Apr 30	Visas	101LTS309	302332
Hungary	Austria	03 Jun 30	Land Transport	122LTS69	302799
Hungary	Austria	26 Jan 31	General Amity	123LTS171	302814
Hungary	Austria	30 Jun 31	General Trade	122LTS123	302800
Hungary	Austria	27 Nov 32	Culture	162LTS387	303752
Hungary	Austria	27 Nov 32	Culture	162LTS395	303753
Hungary	Austria	21 Dec 32	General Economic	169LTS161	303919
Hungary	Austria	12 Jan 34	Admin Cooperation	162LTS419	303754
Hungary	Austria	04 Mar 35	Education	163LTS33	303759
Hungary	Bel-Lux Econ Union	26 Mar 32	Finance	136LTS405	303139
Hungary	Bel-Lux Econ Union	24 May 33	Claims and Debts	140LTS169	303234
Hungary	Belgium	05 Dec 25	Admin Cooperation	43LTS173	301053
Hungary	Belgium	30 Sep 26	Claims and Debts	97LTS215	302225
Hungary	Brazil	24 Dec 31	Mostfavored Nation	147LTS51	303389
Hungary	Brazil	30 Jul 36	General Trade	177LTS53	304079
Hungary	Bulgaria	03 Sep 21	Mostfavored Nation	7LTS229	300188
Hungary	Bulgaria	10 Sep 26	General Economic	69LTS333	301615
Hungary	Bulgaria	05 Jan 29	Health/Educ/Welfare	118LTS279	302730
Hungary	Bulgaria	17 May 29	Extradition	92LTS197	302087
Hungary	Bulgaria	22 Jul 29	Dispute Settlement	101LTS41	302317
Hungary	Bulgaria	12 Jun 34	Finance	160LTS73	303684
Hungary	Czechoslovakia	08 Mar 23	Land Transport	48LTS257	301167
Hungary	Czechoslovakia	13 Jul 23	Taxation	35LTS237	300898
Hungary	Czechoslovakia	13 Jul 23	Claims and Debts	35LTS271	300900
Hungary	Czechoslovakia	13 Jul 23	Claims and Debts	36LTS41	300902
Hungary	Czechoslovakia	13 Jul 23	Taxation	36LTS53	300903
Hungary	Czechoslovakia	13 Jul 23	Claims and Debts	35LTS253	300899
Hungary	Czechoslovakia	13 Jul 23	Claims and Debts	36LTS13	300901
Hungary	Czechoslovakia	09 Feb 24	Postal Service	30LTS325	300772
Hungary	Czechoslovakia	09 Feb 24	Specific Resources	30LTS335	300773
Hungary	Czechoslovakia	08 Mar 24	Claims and Debts	36LTS61	300904
Hungary	Czechoslovakia	30 Sep 26	Territory Boundary	57LTS87	301356
Hungary	Czechoslovakia	31 May 27	General Transport	65LTS61	301520
Hungary	Czechoslovakia	03 Jun 27	Admin Cooperation	67LTS31	301538
Hungary	Czechoslovakia	26 May 28	Claims and Debts	101LTS265	302328
Hungary	Czechoslovakia	14 Nov 28	Water Transport	142LTS227	303295

PARTY ONE	PARTY TWO	DATE	TOPIC	CITATION	NUMBER
Hungary	Czechoslovakia	14 Nov 28	Territory Boundary	110LTS425	302574
Hungary	Czechoslovakia	08 Jun 34	Specific Resources	172LTS61	303979
Hungary	Czechoslovakia	14 Jun 35	General Trade	171LTS401	303976
Hungary	Czechoslovakia	15 Jun 36	General Economic	179LTS73	304135
Hungary	Czechoslovakia	24 Aug 37	Specific Resources	189LTS403	304397
Hungary	Denmark	04 Jun 25	General Amity	36LTS119	300909
Hungary	Estonia	19 Oct 22	General Trade	30LTS347	300774
Hungary	Estonia	01 Nov 23	General Trade	62LTS47	301453
Hungary	Estonia	29 Apr 29	General Economic	96LTS23	302189
Hungary	Estonia	27 Nov 29	Dispute Settlement	106LTS331	302454
Hungary	Estonia	08 Aug 34	Extradition	167LTS153	303863
Hungary	Estonia	13 Oct 37	Education	189LTS433	304400
Hungary	Estonia	02 Dec 37	General Trade	184LTS395	304259
Hungary	Estonia	19 Jan 38	Visas	185LTS363	304300
Hungary	Finland	20 Apr 26	General Economic	48LTS119	301154
Hungary	Finland	12 Dec 28	Admin Cooperation	96LTS67	302191
Hungary	Finland	07 Nov 33	Commodity Trade	142LTS179	303290
Hungary	Finland	03 Apr 36	Visas	172LTS167	303987
Hungary	Finland	22 Oct 37	Education	190LTS281	304426
Hungary	Finland	27 Mar 39	Visas	195LTS425	304563
Hungary	France	31 Jan 21	Claims and Debts	15LTS221	300396
Hungary	France	13 Oct 25	General Trade	67LTS255	301553
Hungary	France	13 Oct 25	General Economic	48LTS9	301150
Hungary	France	21 Dec 29	General Trade	132LTS189	303038
Hungary	France	25 Sep 31	General Trade	132LTS171	303037
Hungary	France	03 Mar 33	General Trade	140LTS177	303235
Hungary	France	07 Apr 33	Admin Cooperation	162LTS463	303756
Hungary	France	23 Jul 35	Air Transport	173LTS243	304016
Hungary	France	18 Nov 37	Admin Cooperation	185LTS257	304290
Hungary	Germany	08 May 20	Reparations	2LTS79	300050
Hungary	Germany	01 Jun 20	General Economic	7LTS207	300187
Hungary	Germany	06 Nov 23	Taxation	45LTS253	301103
Hungary	Germany	06 Nov 23	Taxation	45LTS279	301104
Hungary	Germany	26 Nov 23	Taxation	45LTS309	301105
Hungary	Germany	01 May 24	Extradition	41LTS282	301021
Hungary	Germany	18 Jul 31	General Trade	150LTS111	303458
Hungary	Germany	26 Oct 31	Extradition	133LTS369	303074
Hungary	Germany	22 Jul 33	General Economic	171LTS313	303969
Hungary	Germany	21 Feb 34	General Economic	171LTS327	303970
Hungary	Germany	28 May 36	Culture	178LTS445	304127
Hungary	Greece	04 Jun 25	General Trade	39LTS139	300998
Hungary	Greece	28 Jun 28	Water Transport	82LTS209	301871
Hungary	Greece	05 May 30	Dispute Settlement	118LTS293	302732
Hungary	Greece	03 Jun 30	General Trade	122LTS37	302798
Hungary	Greece	06 Apr 38	Admin Cooperation	188LTS455	304370
Hungary	Iran	18 Dec 37	General Trade	189LTS243	304387
Hungary	Italy	27 Mar 24	Postal Service	55LTS103	301307
Hungary	Italy	27 Mar 24	Finance	45LTS241	301102
Hungary	Italy	27 Mar 24	Finance	45LTS83	301100
Hungary	Italy	27 Mar 24	Finance	45LTS65	301099
Hungary	Italy	27 Mar 24	Finance	45LTS229	301101
Hungary	Italy	27 Mar 24	Telecommunications	55LTS109	301308
Hungary	Italy	20 Jul 25	Admin Cooperation	45LTS39	301098
Hungary	Italy	25 Nov 25	Taxation	74LTS251	301741
Hungary	Italy	30 Mar 26	Finance	54LTS85	301276
Hungary	Italy	15 Mar 27	Claims and Debts	68LTS221	301585
Hungary	Italy	05 Apr 27	General Amity	67LTS399	301561
Hungary	Italy	21 May 27	Finance	74LTS19	301727
Hungary	Italy	21 May 27	Finance	74LTS33	301729
Hungary	Italy	21 May 27	Claims and Debts	74LTS27	301728
Hungary	Italy	25 Jul 27	Water Transport	74LTS53	301731
Hungary	Italy	25 Jul 27	Other Ad Hoc	74LTS77	301733
Hungary	Italy	25 Jul 27	Customs	74LTS67	301732
Hungary	Italy	10 Dec 27	Dispute Settlement	78LTS403	301798
Hungary	Italy	04 Jul 28	Sanitation	92LTS169	302084

PARTY ONE	PARTY TWO	DATE	TOPIC	CITATION	NUMBER
Hungary	Italy	04 Jul 28	General Economic	92LTS117	302083
Hungary	Italy	07 May 30	Visas	101LTS445	302343
Hungary	Italy	05 Jul 32	Air Transport	144LTS257	303330
Hungary	Italy	12 Nov 32	Claims and Debts	142LTS109	303282
Hungary	Italy	12 Nov 32	Claims and Debts	142LTS115	303283
Hungary	Italy	12 Nov 32	Claims and Debts	142LTS87	303279
Hungary	Italy	12 Nov 32	Dispute Settlement	142LTS95	303280
Hungary	Italy	12 Nov 32	Finance	142LTS101	303281
Hungary	Italy	18 Nov 34	Water Transport	166LTS263	303842
Hungary	Italy	16 Feb 35	Culture	163LTS15	303758
Hungary	Italy	04 Jul 36	Commodity Trade	181LTS331	304199
Hungary	Italy	09 Mar 37	Water Transport	184LTS297	304254
Hungary	Japan	23 Jan 29	General Trade	91LTS317	302071
Hungary	Latvia	19 Nov 23	General Trade	37LTS341	300959
Hungary	Latvia	04 May 30	Admin Cooperation	101LTS449	302344
Hungary	Latvia	13 Aug 30	Dispute Settlement	117LTS395	302705
Hungary	Latvia	16 Nov 37	Finance	183LTS205	304237
Hungary	Latvia	25 Mar 38	Visas	188LTS447	304369
Hungary	Lithuania	23 Oct 28	General Trade	84LTS281	301908
Hungary	Lithuania	16 May 29	General Economic	96LTS333	302211
Hungary	Lithuania	12 Nov 37	Finance	183LTS197	304236
Hungary	Multilateral	09 Sep 86*	Patents/Copyrights	123LTS233	302816
Hungary	Multilateral	13 Nov 08	General Ad Hoc	1LTS217	300015
Hungary	Multilateral	05 Jun 12	Telecommunications	1LTS135	300013
Hungary	Multilateral	20 Mar 14	Patents/Copyrights	1LTS243	300016
Hungary	Multilateral	04 Jun 20	Peace/Disarmament	6LTS187	300152
Hungary	Multilateral	30 Jun 20	Patents/Copyrights	1LTS59	300008
Hungary	Multilateral	31 Oct 20	Sanitation	164LTS85	303790
Hungary	Multilateral	16 Dec 20	General IGO	6LTS379	300170
Hungary	Multilateral	23 Jul 21	Water Transport	26LTS173	300647
Hungary	Multilateral	05 Aug 21	Admin Cooperation	27LTS349	300695
Hungary	Multilateral	05 Oct 21	IGO Establishment	51LTS361	301241
Hungary	Multilateral	05 Oct 21	Admin Cooperation	29LTS73	300734
Hungary	Multilateral	05 Oct 21	Admin Cooperation	29LTS67	300733
Hungary	Multilateral	05 Oct 21	Admin Cooperation	29LTS79	300735
Hungary	Multilateral	06 Oct 21	General Economic	17LTS45	300427
Hungary	Multilateral	27 Jan 22	Visas	9LTS291	300262
Hungary	Multilateral	31 Mar 22	Humanitarian	9LTS415	300269
Hungary	Multilateral	05 Jul 22	Reparations	13LTS237	300355
Hungary	Multilateral	29 Mar 23	Land Transport	23LTS378	300594
Hungary	Multilateral	29 Mar 23	Land Transport	23LTS256	300593
Hungary	Multilateral	03 Nov 23	Customs	30LTS371	300775
Hungary	Multilateral	28 Nov 23	Admin Cooperation	51LTS239	301233
Hungary	Multilateral	28 Nov 23	Admin Cooperation	51LTS215	301229
Hungary	Multilateral	28 Nov 23	Admin Cooperation	51LTS209	301228
Hungary	Multilateral	28 Nov 23	Admin Cooperation	51LTS221	301230
Hungary	Multilateral	09 Dec 23	Land Transport	47LTS55	301129
Hungary	Multilateral	09 Dec 23	Non-IBRD Project	36LTS76	300905
Hungary	Multilateral	09 Dec 23	General Economic	58LTS315	301380
Hungary	Multilateral	09 Dec 23	Water Transport	58LTS284	301379
Hungary	Multilateral	25 Jan 24	Sanitation	57LTS135	301360
Hungary	Multilateral	14 Mar 24	Finance	25LTS423	300633
Hungary	Multilateral	31 Mar 24	Sanitation	27LTS211	300685
Hungary	Multilateral	04 Jul 24	Admin Cooperation	51LTS227	301231
Hungary	Multilateral	25 Aug 24	Water Transport	120LTS123	302763
Hungary	Multilateral	25 Aug 24	Water Transport	120LTS155	302764
Hungary	Multilateral	28 Aug 24	Postal Service	41LTS97	301008
Hungary	Multilateral	28 Aug 24	Postal Service	40LTS19	301002
Hungary	Multilateral	28 Aug 24	Postal Service	40LTS249	301003
Hungary	Multilateral	28 Aug 24	Postal Service	40LTS437	301005
Hungary	Multilateral	28 Aug 24	Postal Service	40LTS307	301004
Hungary	Multilateral	28 Aug 24	Postal Service	41LTS55	301007
Hungary	Multilateral	30 Sep 24	Mostfavored Nation	30LTS135	300766
Hungary	Multilateral	23 Oct 24	General Transport	77LTS367	301778
Hungary	Multilateral	23 Oct 24	Land Transport	78LTS17	301779

PARTY ONE	PARTY TWO	DATE	TOPIC	CITATION	NUMBER
Hungary	Multilateral	26 Nov 24	Finance	48LTS69	301151
Hungary	Multilateral	29 Nov 24	General IGO	80LTS293	301835
Hungary	Multilateral	19 Feb 25	Admin Cooperation	81LTS317	301845
Hungary	Multilateral	29 Oct 25	Telecommunications	57LTS201	301365
Hungary	Multilateral	06 Nov 25	Patents/Copyrights	74LTS289	301743
Hungary	Multilateral	06 Nov 25	Patents/Copyrights	74LTS327	301745
Hungary	Multilateral	06 Nov 25	Other Economic	74LTS319	301744
Hungary	Multilateral	27 Nov 25	Water Transport	67LTS63	301539
Hungary	Multilateral	10 Apr 26	Water Transport	176LTS199	304062
Hungary	Multilateral	10 Apr 26	Water Transport	120LTS187	302765
Hungary	Multilateral	24 Apr 26	Land Transport	108LTS123	302505
Hungary	Multilateral	24 Apr 26	Land Transport	97LTS83	302220
Hungary	Multilateral	12 May 26	Refugees	89LTS47	302004
Hungary	Multilateral	21 Jun 26	Sanitation	78LTS229	301793
Hungary	Multilateral	25 Sep 26	ILO Labor	60LTS253	301414
Hungary	Multilateral	19 May 27	Air Transport	68LTS407	301595
Hungary	Multilateral	12 Jul 27	Direct Aid	135LTS247	303115
Hungary	Multilateral	10 Sep 27	Postal Service	75LTS7	301749
Hungary	Multilateral	10 Sep 27	Postal Service	75LTS39	301750
Hungary	Multilateral	08 Nov 27	General Trade	97LTS391	302238
Hungary	Multilateral	25 Nov 27	Telecommunications	84LTS97	301905
Hungary	Multilateral	10 Mar 28	Telecommunications	132LTS405	303049
Hungary	Multilateral	11 Jul 28	Commodity Trade	95LTS373	302185
Hungary	Multilateral	11 Jul 28	Commodity Trade	95LTS357	302184
Hungary	Multilateral	15 Jul 28	Patents/Copyrights	79LTS133	301806
Hungary	Multilateral	27 Aug 28	General Military	94LTS57	302137
Hungary	Multilateral	22 Nov 28	Culture	111LTS343	302598
Hungary	Multilateral	16 Apr 29	Specific Resources	126LTS305	302891
Hungary	Multilateral	20 Apr 29	Admin Cooperation	112LTS371	302623
Hungary	Multilateral	31 May 29	Water Transport	136LTS81	303127
Hungary	Multilateral	14 Jun 29	Visas	94LTS275	302148
Hungary	Multilateral	28 Jun 29	Postal Service	103LTS71	302370
Hungary	Multilateral	28 Jun 29	Postal Service	103LTS321	302372
Hungary	Multilateral	28 Jun 29	Postal Service	103LTS429	302374
Hungary	Multilateral	28 Jun 29	Postal Service	103LTS5	302369
Hungary	Multilateral	28 Jun 29	Postal Service	102LTS245	302368
Hungary	Multilateral	28 Jun 29	Postal Service	103LTS249	302371
Hungary	Multilateral	28 Jun 29	Postal Service	103LTS377	302373
Hungary	Multilateral	27 Jul 29	Other Military	118LTS303	302733
Hungary	Multilateral	27 Jul 29	Other Military	118LTS343	302734
Hungary	Multilateral	14 Sep 29	UN Charter	165LTS353	303822
Hungary	Multilateral	12 Oct 29	General Transport	137LTS11	303145
Hungary	Multilateral	29 Oct 29	Telecommunications	99LTS85	302270
Hungary	Multilateral	12 Apr 30	Admin Cooperation	179LTS89	304137
Hungary	Multilateral	28 Apr 30	Claims and Debts	121LTS69	302785
Hungary	Multilateral	07 Jun 30	Finance	143LTS317	303314
Hungary	Multilateral	07 Jun 30	Finance	143LTS337	303315
Hungary	Multilateral	07 Jun 30	Finance	143LTS257	303313
Hungary	Multilateral	01 Jul 30	Claims and Debts	121LTS153	302786
Hungary	Multilateral	31 Oct 30	Dispute Settlement	120LTS9	302760
Hungary	Multilateral	19 Mar 31	Finance	143LTS355	303316
Hungary	Multilateral	19 Mar 31	Finance	143LTS407	303317
Hungary	Multilateral	19 Mar 31	Admin Cooperation	143LTS7	303301
Hungary	Multilateral	27 Mar 31	ICJ Option Clause	167LTS341	303877
Hungary	Multilateral	28 Mar 31	Customs	119LTS47	302739
Hungary	Multilateral	30 Mar 31	Land Transport	150LTS247	303459
Hungary	Multilateral	13 Jul 31	Other HEW	139LTS301	303219
Hungary	Multilateral	21 Aug 31	Other Ad Hoc	185LTS45	304273
Hungary	Multilateral	02 Sep 32	Land Transport	154LTS123	303543
Hungary	Multilateral	09 Dec 32	Telecommunications	151LTS5	303479
Hungary	Multilateral	11 Mar 33	Water Transport	135LTS301	303119
Hungary	Multilateral	29 May 33	Admin Cooperation	192LTS289	304479
Hungary	Multilateral	25 Aug 33	Commodity Trade	141LTS71	303262
Hungary	Multilateral	11 Oct 33	Consul/Citizenship	150LTS431	303476
Hungary	Multilateral	11 Oct 33	Education	155LTS331	303585

PARTY ONE	PARTY TWO	DATE	TOPIC	CITATION	NUMBER
Hungary	Multilateral	23 Nov 33	Land Transport	192LTS389	304484
Hungary	Multilateral	23 Nov 33	Land Transport	192LTS327	304483
Hungary	Multilateral	17 Mar 34	General Amity	154LTS281	303554
Hungary	Multilateral	17 Mar 34	General Economic	154LTS287	303555
Hungary	Multilateral	20 Mar 34	Postal Service	175LTS363	304052
Hungary	Multilateral	20 Mar 34	Postal Service	175LTS269	304051
Hungary	Multilateral	20 Mar 34	Finance	176LTS9	304053
Hungary	Multilateral	20 Mar 34	Postal Service	175LTS73	304050
Hungary	Multilateral	20 Mar 34	Postal Service	174LTS171	304048
Hungary	Multilateral	20 Mar 34	Postal Service	176LTS55	304054
Hungary	Multilateral	20 Mar 34	Postal Service	175LTS5	304049
Hungary	Multilateral	26 Apr 34	Admin Cooperation	164LTS63	303789
Hungary	Multilateral	02 Jun 34	Patents/Copyrights	205LTS179	304834
Hungary	Multilateral	02 Jun 34	Patents/Copyrights	192LTS17	304459
Hungary	Multilateral	19 Jun 34	Admin Cooperation	154LTS381	303564
Hungary	Multilateral	26 Jun 36	Other HEW	198LTS299	304648
Hungary	Multilateral	06 Nov 36	General Military	173LTS353	304025
Hungary	Multilateral	12 Sep 38	Culture	198LTS111	304630
Hungary	Multilateral	31 Oct 38	Sanitation	198LTS205	304642
Hungary	Multilateral	03 Dec 38	Education	200LTS249	304694
Hungary	Multilateral	02 Jun 42	Patents/Copyrights	205LTS163	304833
Hungary	Netherlands	09 Dec 24	General Trade	47LTS91	301130
Hungary	Netherlands	26 Jun 31	Land Transport	127LTS217	302921
Hungary	Netherlands	08 Jun 35	Air Transport	171LTS385	303975
Hungary	Norway	16 Sep 24	General Trade	33LTS103	300835
Hungary	Norway	01 Feb 29	Customs	86LTS435	301955
Hungary	Norway	04 Jul 34	Customs	152LTS115	303489
Hungary	Norway	16 Nov 37	Visas	183LTS81	304228
Hungary	Norway	18 Feb 38	Visas	185LTS357	304299
Hungary	Norway	05 Jul 38	Admin Cooperation	189LTS427	304399
Hungary	Other Unilat Decla	12 Nov 21	Admin Cooperation	14LTS385	300387
Hungary	Other Unilat Decla	14 Mar 24	Finance	25LTS427	300634
Hungary	Persia	19 Jun 29	Mostfavored Nation	107LTS355	302491
Hungary	Poland	26 Mar 25	Privil/Immunities	37LTS151	300954
Hungary	Poland	22 Jul 25	Admin Cooperation	48LTS167	301158
Hungary	Poland	16 Nov 25	Dispute Settlement	43LTS265	301061
Hungary	Poland	12 May 28	Taxation	123LTS15	302802
Hungary	Poland	12 May 28	Taxation	123LTS47	302804
Hungary	Poland	30 Nov 28	Dispute Settlement	100LTS67	302294
Hungary	Poland	04 Nov 31	Patents/Copyrights	134LTS199	303092
Hungary	Poland	09 Jul 32	Admin Cooperation	140LTS429	303253
Hungary	Poland	09 Jul 32	Admin Cooperation	142LTS239	303296
Hungary	Poland	21 Oct 34	Education	163LTS9	303757
Hungary	Poland	24 Apr 36	Consul/Citizenship	185LTS303	304296
Hungary	Poland	24 Apr 36	Extradition	181LTS115	304183
Hungary	Portugal	14 Nov 29	General Trade	105LTS287	302421
Hungary	Romania	27 Dec 23	Dispute Settlement	21LTS263	300546
Hungary	Romania	14 Apr 24	Specific Resources	46LTS41	301113
Hungary	Romania	16 Apr 24	Finance	46LTS7	301111
Hungary	Romania	16 Apr 24	Territory Boundary	46LTS27	301112
Hungary	Romania	16 Apr 24	Admin Cooperation	45LTS325	301106
Hungary	Romania	16 Apr 24	Admin Cooperation	46LTS113	301115
Hungary	Romania	16 Apr 24	Admin Cooperation	45LTS341	301107
Hungary	Romania	16 Apr 24	General Economic	46LTS95	301114
Hungary	Romania	16 Apr 24	Extradition	42LTS145	301038
Hungary	Romania	16 Apr 24	Finance	45LTS403	301110
Hungary	Romania	16 Apr 24	Admin Cooperation	45LTS349	301108
Hungary	Romania	16 Apr 24	Admin Cooperation	42LTS165	301039
Hungary	Romania	16 Apr 24	Finance	45LTS355	301109
Hungary	Romania	28 May 24	Admin Cooperation	27LTS117	300674
Hungary	Romania	17 Nov 26	Land Transport	61LTS207	301435
Hungary	Romania	10 Aug 30	General Economic	107LTS185	302476
Hungary	Romania	12 Aug 31	General Trade	186LTS325	304321
Hungary	Romania	19 Oct 39	Land Transport	201LTS415	304729
Hungary	Romania	19 Oct 39	Land Transport	201LTS395	304728

PARTY ONE	PARTY TWO	DATE	TOPIC	CITATION	NUMBER
Hungary	Romania	19 Oct 39	Territory Boundary	201LTS419	304731
Hungary	Romania	19 Oct 39	General Transport	201LTS419	304730
Hungary	Serb/Croat/Slovene	20 Mar 23	Refugees	16LTS447	300422
Hungary	Serb/Croat/Slovene	14 Dec 24	Admin Cooperation	39LTS91	300997
Hungary	Serb/Croat/Slovene	24 Jul 26	Admin Cooperation	97LTS165	302223
Hungary	Serb/Croat/Slovene	22 Feb 28	Admin Cooperation	181LTS229	304192
Hungary	Serb/Croat/Slovene	22 Feb 28	Claims and Debts	100LTS345	302306
Hungary	Serb/Croat/Slovene	22 Feb 28	Taxation	100LTS331	302305
Hungary	Serb/Croat/Slovene	22 Feb 28	Sanitation	113LTS49	302635
Hungary	Serb/Croat/Slovene	22 Feb 28	Extradition	104LTS151	302385
Hungary	Serb/Croat/Slovene	22 Feb 28	Health/Educ/Welfare	110LTS411	302572
Hungary	Serb/Croat/Slovene	22 Feb 28	Territory Boundary	88LTS111	301991
Hungary	Serb/Croat/Slovene	22 Feb 28	Non-ILO Labor	88LTS125	301992
Hungary	Serb/Croat/Slovene	22 Feb 28	Finance	87LTS331	301979
Hungary	Serb/Croat/Slovene	22 Feb 28	Consul/Citizenship	87LTS361	301982
Hungary	Serb/Croat/Slovene	19 Nov 28	General Trade	97LTS101	302222
Hungary	Spain	17 Jun 25	General Economic	60LTS69	301406
Hungary	Spain	28 Feb 29	General Trade	94LTS313	302151
Hungary	Spain	10 Jun 29	Dispute Settlement	101LTS251	302327
Hungary	Spain	28 Aug 30	Visas	110LTS307	302562
Hungary	Spain	19 Sep 31	Visas	124LTS353	302839
Hungary	Sweden	26 Feb 23	Admin Cooperation	17LTS35	300426
Hungary	Sweden	08 Nov 28	General Economic	89LTS283	302023
Hungary	Sweden	17 Jun 36	Taxation	184LTS11	304239
Hungary	Sweden	17 Jun 36	Taxation	184LTS25	304240
Hungary	Switzerland	22 Mar 21	General Economic	7LTS235	300189
Hungary	Switzerland	18 Jun 24	Dispute Settlement	34LTS387	300887
Hungary	Switzerland	18 Jun 35	Air Transport	174LTS7	304033
Hungary	Turkey	18 Dec 23	General Amity	43LTS271	301062
Hungary	Turkey	20 Dec 26	General Trade	72LTS255	301697
Hungary	Turkey	20 Dec 26	Consul/Citizenship	72LTS245	301696
Hungary	Turkey	05 Jan 29	Dispute Settlement	100LTS137	302300
Hungary	Turkey	21 May 30	General Economic	109LTS153	302534
Hungary	Turkey	21 May 30	Mostfavored Nation	105LTS117	302406
Hungary	UK Great Britain	30 Oct 21	General Military	8LTS375	300236
Hungary	UK Great Britain	20 Dec 21	Reparations	10LTS437	300283
Hungary	UK Great Britain	11 Dec 23	Finance	23LTS119	300582
Hungary	UK Great Britain	17 Oct 25	Finance	47LTS373	301142
Hungary	UK Great Britain	28 Dec 25	Postal Service	49LTS125	301179
Hungary	UK Great Britain	23 Jul 26	General Trade	67LTS183	301546
Hungary	UK Great Britain	10 Jun 32	Postal Service	132LTS53	303031
Hungary	UK Great Britain	31 Jan 35	Dispute Settlement	160LTS271	303696
Hungary	UK Great Britain	25 Sep 35	Admin Cooperation	170LTS51	303928
Hungary	UK Great Britain	18 Sep 36	Extradition	181LTS337	304200
Hungary	UK Great Britain	22 Mar 37	Air Transport	190LTS59	304405
Hungary	United Arab Rep	16 Feb 27	General Trade	80LTS61	301822
Hungary	United Arab Rep	12 Jun 30	General Economic	106LTS437	302460
Hungary	USA (United States)	29 Aug 21	General Amity	48LTS191	301161
Hungary	USA (United States)	04 Sep 26	Admin Cooperation	58LTS111	301369
Hungary	USA (United States)	26 Jan 29	Dispute Settlement	96LTS207	302201
Hungary	USA (United States)	26 Jan 29	Dispute Settlement	96LTS173	302200
Hungary	Yugoslavia	11 Nov 29	Admin Cooperation	111LTS197	302587
Hungary	Yugoslavia	27 Apr 30	Dispute Settlement	113LTS153	302642
Hungary	Yugoslavia	27 Aug 30	Dispute Settlement	113LTS163	302643
Hungary	Yugoslavia	30 Jan 31	Dispute Settlement	120LTS105	302761
Hungary	Yugoslavia	15 May 33	General Trade	144LTS321	303335
Hungary	Yugoslavia	17 Dec 36	Finance	196LTS143	304577
Hungary	Yugoslavia	17 Dec 36	General Trade	196LTS137	304576
Iceland	Austria	06 Apr 28	General Trade	87LTS343	301980
Iceland	Belgium	21 Dec 28	Taxation	107LTS369	302493
Iceland	Bolivia	09 Nov 31	Mostfavored Nation	147LTS43	303388
Iceland	Brazil	30 Nov 31	Customs	128LTS369	302942
Iceland	Czechoslovakia	08 May 24	General Economic	46LTS419	301125
Iceland	Czechoslovakia	25 Jun 29	Visas	91LTS359	302076
Iceland	Denmark	26 Jun 20	Postal Service	12LTS323	300324

PARTY ONE	PARTY TWO	DATE	TOPIC	CITATION	NUMBER
Iceland	Denmark	27 Aug 21	Postal Service	12LTS345	300325
Iceland	Denmark	09 Oct 22	Humanitarian	14LTS13	300364
Iceland	Denmark	30 Sep 24	Water Transport	32LTS355	300825
Iceland	Denmark	11 Aug 27	Taxation	75LTS345	301757
Iceland	Denmark	13 Oct 27	Non-ILO Labor	67LTS411	301562
Iceland	Denmark	30 Nov 27	Postal Service	71LTS43	301653
Iceland	Denmark	27 Jun 30	Dispute Settlement	118LTS121	302717
Iceland	Denmark	11 Jul 31	Taxation	141LTS323	303273
Iceland	Estonia	07 Sep 23	General Trade	23LTS131	300584
Iceland	Estonia	30 May 31	Water Transport	119LTS69	302741
Iceland	Finland	28 May 24	General Trade	27LTS117	300676
Iceland	Finland	07 Mar 25	Patents/Copyrights	34LTS169	300872
Iceland	Finland	27 Jun 30	Dispute Settlement	167LTS271	303873
Iceland	Germany	12 Feb 23	Patents/Copyrights	27LTS405	300700
Iceland	Greece	28 Jan 30	Mostfavored Nation	118LTS285	302731
Iceland	Latvia	03 Nov 24	General Economic	43LTS339	301069
Iceland	Lithuania	18 Jul 23	General Trade	20LTS329	300523
Iceland	Lithuania	21 Jun 30	General Economic	119LTS403	302759
Iceland	Multilateral	18 Mar 04	Humanitarian	1LTS83	300011
Iceland	Multilateral	05 Jun 12	Telecommunications	1LTS135	300013
Iceland	Multilateral	28 Aug 24	Postal Service	41LTS55	301007
Iceland	Multilateral	28 Aug 24	Postal Service	40LTS307	301004
Iceland	Multilateral	28 Aug 24	Postal Service	40LTS19	301002
Iceland	Multilateral	28 Aug 24	Postal Service	40LTS249	301003
Iceland	Multilateral	28 Aug 24	Postal Service	40LTS437	301005
Iceland	Multilateral	01 Dec 24	Sanitation	78LTS351	301794
Iceland	Multilateral	29 Oct 25	Telecommunications	57LTS201	301365
Iceland	Multilateral	28 Jan 26	Water Transport	51LTS9	301219
Iceland	Multilateral	24 Apr 26	Land Transport	108LTS123	302505
Iceland	Multilateral	25 Nov 27	Telecommunications	84LTS97	301905
Iceland	Multilateral	27 Aug 28	General Military	94LTS57	302137
Iceland	Multilateral	31 May 29	Water Transport	136LTS81	303127
Iceland	Multilateral	28 Jun 29	Postal Service	103LTS5	302369
Iceland	Multilateral	28 Jun 29	Postal Service	103LTS249	302371
Iceland	Multilateral	28 Jun 29	Postal Service	103LTS71	302370
Iceland	Multilateral	28 Jun 29	Postal Service	103LTS377	302373
Iceland	Multilateral	28 Jun 29	Postal Service	102LTS245	302368
Iceland	Multilateral	20 Aug 29	Sanitation	98LTS125	302243
Iceland	Multilateral	12 Apr 30	Admin Cooperation	179LTS89	304137
Iceland	Multilateral	06 Feb 31	Admin Cooperation	126LTS121	302877
Iceland	Multilateral	10 Feb 31	Admin Cooperation	126LTS41	302870
Iceland	Multilateral	06 May 31	Telecommunications	120LTS217	302767
Iceland	Multilateral	15 Oct 31	Water Transport	125LTS89	302848
Iceland	Multilateral	16 Mar 32	Admin Cooperation	139LTS165	303209
Iceland	Multilateral	09 Dec 32	Telecommunications	151LTS5	303479
Iceland	Multilateral	11 Mar 33	Water Transport	135LTS301	303119
Iceland	Multilateral	19 Jun 33	Gen Communications	154LTS133	303544
Iceland	Multilateral	07 Nov 33	Finance	155LTS115	303574
Iceland	Multilateral	20 Mar 34	Postal Service	175LTS269	304051
Iceland	Multilateral	20 Mar 34	Postal Service	175LTS5	304049
Iceland	Multilateral	20 Mar 34	Postal Service	175LTS73	304050
Iceland	Multilateral	20 Mar 34	Finance	176LTS9	304053
Iceland	Multilateral	20 Mar 34	Postal Service	174LTS171	304048
Iceland	Multilateral	19 Nov 34	Admin Cooperation	164LTS243	303797
Iceland	Multilateral	31 Dec 34	Postal Service	158LTS111	303630
Iceland	Multilateral	11 Feb 37	Telecommunications	186LTS55	304303
Iceland	Multilateral	03 Mar 37	Admin Cooperation	182LTS127	304205
Iceland	Multilateral	15 Sep 37	Gen Communications	186LTS135	304307
Iceland	Multilateral	23 Sep 37	Postal Service	190LTS299	304427
Iceland	Multilateral	02 Oct 37	Education	182LTS263	304216
Iceland	Multilateral	27 May 38	Other Military	188LTS293	304365
Iceland	Multilateral	23 May 39	Postal Service	202LTS159	304742
Iceland	Norway	17 Aug 22	Postal Service	14LTS9	300363
Iceland	Norway	10 Aug 23	Postal Service	20LTS363	300527
Iceland	Norway	31 May 30	Non-ILO Labor	108LTS339	302517

PARTY ONE	PARTY TWO	DATE	TOPIC	CITATION	NUMBER
Iceland	Norway	27 Jun 30	Dispute Settlement	126LTS417	302900
Iceland	Norway	27 Feb 39	Specific Resources	196LTS377	304598
Iceland	Poland	22 Mar 24	General Trade	31LTS35	300779
Iceland	Poland	14 Apr 26	Consul/Citizenship	48LTS279	301169
Iceland	Romania	08 May 31	General Economic	127LTS11	302901
Iceland	Spain	26 Aug 29	Dispute Settlement	104LTS183	302388
Iceland	Sweden	23 Mar 21	Patents/Copyrights	4LTS137	300105
Iceland	Sweden	10 Mar 28	Water Transport	71LTS315	301672
Iceland	Sweden	27 Jun 30	Dispute Settlement	127LTS67	302907
Iceland	Sweden	31 Oct 30	Non-ILO Labor	109LTS171	302535
Iceland	Sweden	08 Sep 37	Taxation	187LTS405	304346
Iceland	UK Great Britain	13 Oct 21	Postal Service	8LTS337	300234
Iceland	UK Great Britain	12 Dec 21	Admin Cooperation	12LTS351	300326
Iceland	UK Great Britain	01 May 22	Dispute Settlement	12LTS15	300302
Iceland	UK Great Britain	04 Jun 26	Dispute Settlement	61LTS189	301433
Iceland	UK Great Britain	27 Apr 28	Taxation	80LTS253	301831
Iceland	UK Great Britain	19 May 33	General Trade	144LTS33	303319
Iceland	UK Great Britain	03 Nov 33	Postal Service	145LTS269	303358
Iceland	UK Great Britain	25 Oct 38	Extradition	198LTS147	304635
Iceland	USA (United States)		Dispute Settlement	108LTS109	302503
Iceland	USA (United States)	16 Jan 32	Water Transport	127LTS135	302914
Iceland	USA (United States)	31 Oct 38	Postal Service	194LTS149	304519
Iceland	USSR (Soviet Union)	25 May 27	General Trade	63LTS105	301483
ILO (Labor Org)	United Arab Rep	19 Jun 36	IGO Operations	177LTS343	304096
India	Brazil	21 Jul 32	General Trade	133LTS93	303059
India	China	13 Jun 34	Postal Service	157LTS77	303606
India	Denmark	16 Dec 30	Postal Service	114LTS73	302656
India	Denmark	08 Aug 32	Water Transport	140LTS369	303246
India	Dutch Indies	28 Nov 35	Postal Service	168LTS147	303896
India	France	12 May 23	Territory Boundary	25LTS381	300627
India	France	19 Jun 26	Territory Boundary	57LTS35	301350
India	France	06 Jun 29	Admin Cooperation	95LTS61	302164
India	France	07 Mar 31	Postal Service	119LTS269	302750
India	France	09 May 32	Admin Cooperation	132LTS37	303029
India	France	28 Dec 32	Commodity Trade	140LTS36	303226
India	France	31 May 35	Admin Cooperation	163LTS287	303770
India	France	04 Jan 36	Commodity Trade	170LTS97	303930
India	France	01 May 36	Postal Service	178LTS57	304107
India	France	18 Dec 36	Sanitation	178LTS399	304122
India	France	22 Mar 39	Commodity Trade	197LTS273	304619
India	France	28 Jan 41	General Trade	204LTS323	304811
India	Indochina	20 Mar 26	General Trade	57LTS19	301348
India	Indochina	01 Mar 38	Admin Cooperation	194LTS231	304524
India	Iraq	20 Oct 21	Postal Service	69LTS139	301601
India	Iraq	02 Apr 22	Postal Service	69LTS157	301602
India	Iraq	08 Feb 23	Postal Service	85LTS37	301920
India	Iraq	30 Aug 26	Postal Service	69LTS193	301605
India	Iraq	13 Mar 33	Postal Service	140LTS43	303227
India	Iraq	31 Mar 33	Postal Service	140LTS63	303228
India	Irish Free State	04 Apr 26	Postal Service	56LTS415	301344
India	Japan	12 Jul 34	General Trade	155LTS31	303566
India	Multilateral	09 Sep 86*	Patents/Copyrights	123LTS233	302816
India	Multilateral	18 Mar 04	Humanitarian	1LTS83	300011
India	Multilateral	05 Jun 12	Telecommunications	1LTS135	300013
India	Multilateral	10 Sep 19	Health/Educ/Welfare	8LTS11	300201
India	Multilateral	10 Sep 19	General Trade	7LTS331	300200
India	Multilateral	09 Feb 20	Territory Boundary	2LTS7	300041
India	Multilateral	01 May 20	Air Transport	11LTS173	300297
India	Multilateral	21 Jun 20	Health/Educ/Welfare	8LTS65	300207
India	Multilateral	30 Jun 20	Patents/Copyrights	1LTS59	300008
India	Multilateral	10 Aug 20	Territory Boundary	28LTS225	300710
India	Multilateral	10 Aug 20	Consul/Citizenship	28LTS223	300711
India	Multilateral	16 Dec 20	General IGO	6LTS379	300170
India	Multilateral	20 Apr 21	Water Transport	7LTS65	300173
India	Multilateral	20 Apr 21	Water Transport	7LTS73	300174

PARTY ONE	PARTY TWO	DATE	TOPIC	CITATION	NUMBER
India	Multilateral	20 Apr 21	Water Transport	7LTS35	300172
India	Multilateral	20 Apr 21	Land Transport	7LTS11	300171
India	Multilateral	05 Aug 21	Admin Cooperation	27LTS349	300695
India	Multilateral	05 Oct 21	IGO Establishment	51LTS361	301241
India	Multilateral	05 Oct 21	Admin Cooperation	29LTS73	300734
India	Multilateral	05 Oct 21	Admin Cooperation	29LTS67	300733
India	Multilateral	05 Oct 21	Admin Cooperation	29LTS79	300735
India	Multilateral	06 Feb 22	Customs	38LTS267	300981
India	Multilateral	06 Feb 22	General Trade	38LTS277	300982
India	Multilateral	31 Mar 22	Humanitarian	9LTS415	300269
India	Multilateral	02 Nov 22	Peace/Disarmament	149LTS35	303431
India	Multilateral	24 Sep 23	Dispute Settlement	27LTS157	300678
India	Multilateral	03 Nov 23	Customs	30LTS371	300775
India	Multilateral	09 Dec 23	Land Transport	47LTS55	301129
India	Multilateral	31 Mar 24	Sanitation	27LTS211	300685
India	Multilateral	16 Aug 24	Taxation	41LTS429	301024
India	Multilateral	28 Aug 24	Postal Service	40LTS307	301004
India	Multilateral	28 Aug 24	Postal Service	40LTS19	301002
India	Multilateral	28 Aug 24	Postal Service	40LTS249	301003
India	Multilateral	30 Aug 24	Admin Cooperation	30LTS75	300760
India	Multilateral	30 Aug 24	Admin Cooperation	30LTS79	300761
India	Multilateral	19 Feb 25	Admin Cooperation	81LTS317	301845
India	Multilateral	17 Jun 25	Peace/Disarmament	94LTS65	302138
India	Multilateral	29 Oct 25	Telecommunications	57LTS201	301365
India	Multilateral	24 Apr 26	Land Transport	108LTS123	302505
India	Multilateral	24 Apr 26	Land Transport	97LTS83	302220
India	Multilateral	12 May 26	Refugees	89LTS47	302004
India	Multilateral	21 Jun 26	Sanitation	78LTS229	301793
India	Multilateral	25 Sep 26	ILO Labor	60LTS253	301414
India	Multilateral	12 Jul 27	Direct Aid	135LTS247	303115
India	Multilateral	26 Sep 27	Dispute Settlement	92LTS301	302096
India	Multilateral	08 Nov 27	General Trade	97LTS391	302238
India	Multilateral	25 Nov 27	Telecommunications	84LTS97	301905
India	Multilateral	27 Aug 28	General Military	94LTS57	302137
India	Multilateral	26 Sep 28	Dispute Settlement	93LTS343	302123
India	Multilateral	14 Dec 28	General Economic	110LTS171	302560
India	Multilateral	20 Apr 29	Admin Cooperation	112LTS371	302623
India	Multilateral	31 May 29	Water Transport	136LTS81	303127
India	Multilateral	28 Jun 29	Postal Service	102LTS245	302368
India	Multilateral	28 Jun 29	Postal Service	103LTS71	302370
India	Multilateral	28 Jun 29	Postal Service	103LTS5	302369
India	Multilateral	27 Jul 29	Other Military	118LTS343	302734
India	Multilateral	27 Jul 29	Other Military	118LTS303	302733
India	Multilateral	14 Sep 29	UN Charter	165LTS353	303822
India	Multilateral	20 Jan 30	Reparations	112LTS361	302622
India	Multilateral	20 Jan 30	Finance	104LTS433	302397
India	Multilateral	20 Jan 30	Finance	104LTS413	302395
India	Multilateral	20 Jan 30	Reparations	113LTS389	302650
India	Multilateral	20 Jan 30	Reparations	104LTS243	302394
India	Multilateral	15 Mar 30	Finance	113LTS395	302651
India	Multilateral	12 Apr 30	Milit Servic/Citiz	178LTS227	304117
India	Multilateral	12 Apr 30	Admin Cooperation	179LTS89	304137
India	Multilateral	12 Apr 30	Admin Cooperation	179LTS115	304138
India	Multilateral	22 Apr 30	Peace/Disarmament	112LTS65	302608
India	Multilateral	28 Apr 30	Claims and Debts	121LTS69	302785
India	Multilateral	10 Jun 30	Loans and Credits	112LTS237	302618
India	Multilateral	01 Jul 30	Claims and Debts	121LTS153	302786
India	Multilateral	01 Aug 30	Health/Educ/Welfare	128LTS9	302932
India	Multilateral	23 Oct 30	Water Transport	112LTS21	302603
India	Multilateral	13 Apr 31	Air Transport	119LTS275	302751
India	Multilateral	16 May 31	Air Transport	136LTS245	303128
India	Multilateral	13 Jul 31	Other HEW	139LTS301	303219
India	Multilateral	24 Sep 31	Specific Resources	155LTS349	303586
India	Multilateral	27 Nov 31	Sanitation	177LTS373	304100
India	Multilateral	20 Jan 32	Extradition	141LTS267	303269

PARTY ONE	PARTY TWO	DATE	TOPIC	CITATION	NUMBER
India	Multilateral	17 Feb 32	Telecommunications	138LTS61	303181
India	Multilateral	14 Mar 32	Territory Boundary	131LTS135	303006
India	Multilateral	11 Mar 33	Water Transport	135LTS301	303119
India	Multilateral	29 May 33	Admin Cooperation	192LTS289	304479
India	Multilateral	22 Jul 33	Specific Resources	153LTS107	303511
India	Multilateral	29 Jul 33	Extradition	142LTS165	303288
India	Multilateral	11 Oct 33	Education	155LTS331	303585
India	Multilateral	08 Nov 33	Specific Resources	172LTS241	303995
India	Multilateral	03 Feb 34	Territory Boundary	154LTS349	303560
India	Multilateral	20 Mar 34	Postal Service	175LTS73	304050
India	Multilateral	20 Mar 34	Postal Service	175LTS5	304049
India	Multilateral	16 Apr 34	Water Transport	163LTS185	303767
India	Multilateral	07 May 34	Commodity Trade	171LTS203	303961
India	Multilateral	01 Jun 34	Territory Boundary	154LTS373	303563
India	Multilateral	07 Dec 34	Air Transport	158LTS91	303629
India	Multilateral	15 Mar 35	Other Military	170LTS9	303926
India	Multilateral	09 Apr 35	Territory Boundary	163LTS177	303766
India	Multilateral	20 Dec 35	Other Military	167LTS141	303862
India	Multilateral	25 Mar 36	Peace/Disarmament	184LTS115	304246
India	Multilateral	26 Jun 36	Other HEW	198LTS299	304648
India	Multilateral	30 Jul 36	IGO Status/Immunit	197LTS31	304602
India	Multilateral	23 Sep 36	Gen Communications	186LTS301	304319
India	Multilateral	06 Nov 36	General Military	173LTS353	304025
India	Multilateral	08 May 37	Privil/Immunities	182LTS37	304202
India	Multilateral	02 Jun 37	Specific Property	184LTS445	304265
India	Multilateral	21 Jul 37	Admin Cooperation	184LTS271	304250
India	Multilateral	11 Oct 37	Air Transport	182LTS173	304210
India	Multilateral	03 Dec 37	Air Transport	186LTS293	304318
India	Multilateral	29 Apr 38	Visas	190LTS115	304410
India	Multilateral	17 May 38	Visas	192LTS319	304481
India	Multilateral	30 May 38	Visas	191LTS299	304451
India	Multilateral	15 Jul 38	Visas	195LTS73	304536
India	Multilateral	12 Sep 38	Culture	198LTS111	304630
India	Multilateral	31 Oct 38	Sanitation	198LTS205	304642
India	Multilateral	05 Feb 39	General Amity	196LTS303	304592
India	Multilateral	23 May 39	Postal Service	202LTS159	304742
India	Multilateral	21 Aug 39	Visas	198LTS343	304652
India	Multilateral	08 Jan 40	Visas	203LTS133	304756
India	Multilateral	01 Jan 42	General Military	204LTS381	304817
India	Nepal	23 Dec 36	Postal Service	178LTS405	304123
India	Poland	18 May 31	General Trade	131LTS9	303001
India	Saudi Arabia	09 Nov 31	Postal Service	157LTS35	303604
India	Siam	11 Sep 24	General Economic	31LTS115	300788
India	Turkey	03 Sep 30	Mostfavored Nation	109LTS25	302525
Indochina	Australia	20 May 36	Visas	170LTS221	303937
Indochina	India	20 Mar 26	General Trade	57LTS19	301348
Indochina	India	01 Mar 38	Admin Cooperation	194LTS231	304524
Indochina	Malaya	07 Sep 34	Postal Service	155LTS73	303569
Indochina	Malaya	08 Oct 34	Postal Service	157LTS95	303607
Indochina	Multilateral	21 Jun 20	Health/Educ/Welfare	8LTS65	300207
Indochina	Multilateral	31 Oct 20	Sanitation	164LTS85	303790
Indochina	Multilateral	28 Aug 24	Postal Service	40LTS249	301003
Indochina	Multilateral	28 Aug 24	Postal Service	40LTS19	301002
Indochina	Multilateral	29 Oct 25	Telecommunications	57LTS201	301365
Indochina	Multilateral	24 Apr 26	Land Transport	108LTS123	302505
Indochina	Multilateral	24 Apr 26	Land Transport	97LTS83	302220
Indochina	Multilateral	21 Jun 26	Sanitation	78LTS229	301793
Indochina	Multilateral	25 Nov 27	Telecommunications	84LTS97	301905
Indochina	Multilateral	28 Jun 29	Postal Service	103LTS5	302369
Indochina	Multilateral	28 Jun 29	Postal Service	103LTS249	302371
Indochina	Multilateral	28 Jun 29	Postal Service	103LTS71	302370
Indochina	Multilateral	28 Jun 29	Postal Service	102LTS245	302368
Indochina	Multilateral	23 Oct 30	Water Transport	125LTS95	302849
Indochina	Multilateral	20 Mar 34	Postal Service	175LTS73	304050
Indochina	Multilateral	20 Mar 34	Postal Service	175LTS269	304051

PARTY ONE	PARTY TWO	DATE	TOPIC	CITATION	NUMBER
Indochina	Multilateral	20 Mar 34	Postal Service	175LTS5	304049
Indochina	Siam	14 Jul 27	Consul/Citizenship	69LTS327	301614
Indonesia	Multilateral	27 Jul 29	Other Military	118LTS343	302734
Indonesia	Multilateral	27 Jul 29	Other Military	118LTS303	302733
Indonesia	Multilateral	11 Mar 33	Water Transport	135LTS301	303119
Inter-Allied Com	Multilateral	15 Jun 22	Dispute Settlement	21LTS463	300551
Iran	Hungary	18 Dec 37	General Trade	189LTS243	304387
Iran	Iraq	04 Jul 37	Territory Boundary	190LTS241	304423
Iran	Iraq	18 Jul 37	General Amity	190LTS259	304424
Iran	Iraq	24 Jul 37	Dispute Settlement	190LTS269	304425
Iran	Multilateral	16 Dec 20	General IGO	6LTS379	300170
Iran	Multilateral	09 Dec 32	Telecommunications	151LTS5	303479
Iran	Multilateral	11 Oct 33	Education	155LTS331	303585
Iran	Multilateral	11 Oct 33	Consul/Citizenship	150LTS431	303476
Iran	Multilateral	06 Nov 36	General Military	173LTS353	304025
Iran	Multilateral	08 Jul 37	General Amity	190LTS21	304402
Iran	Multilateral	02 Oct 37	Education	182LTS263	304216
Iran	Multilateral	23 May 39	Postal Service	202LTS159	304742
Iran	USSR (Soviet Union)	27 Aug 35	General Trade	176LTS299	304069
Iran	USSR (Soviet Union)	27 Aug 35	Health/Educ/Welfare	176LTS335	304070
Iran	USSR (Soviet Union)	27 Aug 35	Sanitation	176LTS349	304072
Iran	USSR (Soviet Union)	27 Aug 35	Health/Educ/Welfare	176LTS344	304071
Iraq	Afghanistan	20 Dec 32	General Amity	155LTS375	303588
Iraq	Germany	04 Aug 35	Mostfavored Nation	171LTS65	303951
Iraq	Great Britain	13 Jan 26	Territory Boundary	47LTS419	301147
Iraq	India	20 Oct 21	Postal Service	69LTS139	301601
Iraq	India	02 Apr 22	Postal Service	69LTS157	301602
Iraq	India	08 Feb 23	Postal Service	85LTS37	301920
Iraq	India	30 Aug 26	Postal Service	69LTS193	301605
Iraq	India	13 Mar 33	Postal Service	140LTS43	303227
Iraq	India	31 Mar 33	Postal Service	140LTS63	303228
Iraq	Iran	04 Jul 37	Territory Boundary	190LTS241	304423
Iraq	Iran	18 Jul 37	General Amity	190LTS259	304424
Iraq	Iran	24 Jul 37	Dispute Settlement	190LTS269	304425
Iraq	Multilateral	23 Jan 12	Sanitation	8LTS187	300222
Iraq	Multilateral	24 Apr 20	General Economic	136LTS381	303135
Iraq	Multilateral	30 Jun 20	Patents/Copyrights	1LTS59	300008
Iraq	Multilateral	16 Dec 20	General IGO	6LTS379	300170
Iraq	Multilateral	20 Apr 21	Land Transport	7LTS11	300171
Iraq	Multilateral	03 Nov 23	Customs	30LTS371	300775
Iraq	Multilateral	09 Dec 23	General Economic	58LTS315	301380
Iraq	Multilateral	01 Dec 24	Sanitation	78LTS351	301794
Iraq	Multilateral	19 Feb 25	Admin Cooperation	81LTS317	301845
Iraq	Multilateral	09 Jun 25	Customs	49LTS9	301174
Iraq	Multilateral	17 Jun 25	Peace/Disarmament	94LTS65	302138
Iraq	Multilateral	24 Apr 26	Land Transport	108LTS123	302505
Iraq	Multilateral	20 May 26	Health/Educ/Welfare	109LTS121	302532
Iraq	Multilateral	12 Jul 27	Direct Aid	135LTS247	303115
Iraq	Multilateral	28 Jul 27	Territory Boundary	64LTS379	301511
Iraq	Multilateral	25 Nov 27	Telecommunications	84LTS97	301905
Iraq	Multilateral	27 Aug 28	General Military	94LTS57	302137
Iraq	Multilateral	20 Apr 29	Admin Cooperation	112LTS395	302624
Iraq	Multilateral	20 Apr 29	Admin Cooperation	112LTS371	302623
Iraq	Multilateral	28 Jun 29	Postal Service	102LTS245	302368
Iraq	Multilateral	28 Jun 29	Postal Service	103LTS5	302369
Iraq	Multilateral	27 Jul 29	Other Military	118LTS303	302733
Iraq	Multilateral	09 Jan 30	Admin Cooperation	115LTS473	302696
Iraq	Multilateral	23 Oct 30	Water Transport	112LTS21	302603
Iraq	Multilateral	13 Jul 31	Other HEW	139LTS301	303219
Iraq	Multilateral	12 Apr 33	Sanitation	161LTS65	303706
Iraq	Multilateral	20 Mar 34	Postal Service	175LTS73	304050
Iraq	Multilateral	20 Mar 34	Postal Service	175LTS5	304049
Iraq	Multilateral	20 Mar 34	Postal Service	174LTS171	304048
Iraq	Multilateral	20 Feb 35	Sanitation	186LTS173	304310
Iraq	Multilateral	15 Mar 35	Other Military	170LTS9	303926

PARTY ONE	PARTY TWO	DATE	TOPIC	CITATION	NUMBER
Iraq	Multilateral	06 Nov 36	General Military	173LTS353	304025
Iraq	Multilateral	08 Jul 37	General Amity	190LTS21	304402
Iraq	Multilateral	12 Sep 38	Culture	198LTS111	304630
Iraq	Multilateral	23 May 39	Postal Service	202LTS159	304742
Iraq	Norway	14 Mar 33	Mostfavored Nation	138LTS23	303177
Iraq	Palestine	04 Aug 27	Postal Service	80LTS211	301826
Iraq	Saudi Arabia	02 Apr 36	General Amity	174LTS131	304044
Iraq	Sweden	03 Nov 35	Mostfavored Nation	163LTS419	303783
Iraq	Turkey	09 Jan 32	Recognition	139LTS263	303217
Iraq	Turkey	09 Jan 32	Extradition	139LTS273	303218
Iraq	Turkey	10 Jan 32	Mostfavored Nation	152LTS17	303480
Iraq	UK Great Britain	16 Jan 22	General Economic	12LTS431	300340
Iraq	UK Great Britain	30 Apr 23	General Amity	35LTS13	300890
Iraq	UK Great Britain	25 Mar 24	General Military	35LTS103	300892
Iraq	UK Great Britain	25 Mar 24	Finance	35LTS145	300894
Iraq	UK Great Britain	25 Mar 24	Consul/Citizenship	35LTS35	300891
Iraq	UK Great Britain	25 Mar 24	Admin Cooperation	35LTS131	300893
Iraq	UK Great Britain	30 Jun 30	General Military	132LTS363	303048
Iraq	UK Great Britain	19 Aug 30	Finance	118LTS231	302727
Iraq	UK Great Britain	04 Mar 31	Privil/Immunities	123LTS77	302807
Iraq	UK Great Britain	02 May 32	Extradition	141LTS277	303270
Iraq	UK Great Britain	25 Jul 35	Admin Cooperation	176LTS229	304064
Iraq	UK Great Britain	31 Mar 36	Land Transport	172LTS175	303988
Iraq	UK Great Britain	14 Dec 36	Customs	177LTS221	304091
Iraq	United Arab Rep	16 May 38	General Trade	190LTS177	304415
Iraq	USA (United States)	07 Jun 34	Extradition	170LTS267	303942
Iraq	USA (United States)	03 Dec 38	General Trade	203LTS107	304753
Ireland	Multilateral	13 Mar 21	Admin Cooperation	8LTS327	300232
Ireland	Multilateral	20 Jul 21	General Military	8LTS115	300213
Ireland	Multilateral	03 Sep 21	Postal Service	8LTS147	300216
Ireland	Multilateral	03 Sep 21	Postal Service	8LTS151	300217
Ireland	Multilateral	21 Sep 21	Humanitarian	7LTS127	300181
Ireland	Multilateral	24 Sep 23	Dispute Settlement	27LTS157	300678
Ireland	Multilateral	31 Mar 24	Sanitation	27LTS211	300685
Ireland	Multilateral	28 Aug 24	Postal Service	40LTS19	301002
Ireland	Multilateral	01 Dec 24	Sanitation	78LTS351	301794
Ireland	Multilateral	19 Feb 25	Admin Cooperation	81LTS317	301845
Ireland	Multilateral	26 Sep 27	Dispute Settlement	92LTS301	302096
Ireland	Multilateral	26 Sep 28	Dispute Settlement	93LTS343	302123
Ireland	Multilateral	31 May 29	Water Transport	136LTS81	303127
Ireland	Multilateral	30 Mar 31	Taxation	138LTS149	303185
Ireland	Multilateral	24 Sep 31	Specific Resources	155LTS349	303586
Ireland	Multilateral	11 Mar 33	Water Transport	135LTS301	303119
Ireland	Multilateral	25 Aug 33	Commodity Trade	141LTS71	303262
Ireland	Multilateral	11 Oct 33	Consul/Citizenship	150LTS431	303476
Ireland	Multilateral	20 Mar 34	Postal Service	175LTS5	304049
Ireland	Multilateral	02 Jun 34	General Trade	192LTS9	304458
Ireland	Multilateral	02 Jun 34	Patents/Copyrights	192LTS17	304459
Ireland	Multilateral	12 Jun 34	Milit Installation	155LTS367	303587
Ireland	Multilateral	23 Sep 36	Gen Communications	186LTS301	304319
Ireland	Multilateral	24 Jun 38	Specific Resources	196LTS131	304575
Ireland	Multilateral	12 Sep 38	Culture	198LTS111	304630
Ireland	Multilateral	31 Oct 38	Sanitation	198LTS205	304642
Ireland	Multilateral	23 May 39	Postal Service	202LTS159	304742
Ireland	UK Great Britain	06 Dec 21	Dispute Settlement	26LTS9	300636
Ireland	USA (United States)	04 Nov 37	Air Transport	185LTS71	304276
Irish Free State	Belgium	24 Sep 29	Postal Service	102LTS213	302364
Irish Free State	Brazil	16 Oct 31	Mostfavored Nation	134LTS75	303084
Irish Free State	Canada	12 Oct 23	Postal Service	56LTS291	301338
Irish Free State	Canada	12 Nov 24	Postal Service	56LTS333	301340
Irish Free State	Denmark	25 Apr 34	Taxation	149LTS31	303430
Irish Free State	Germany	29 Dec 24	Postal Service	56LTS341	301341
Irish Free State	Germany	12 May 30	General Economic	131LTS153	303008
Irish Free State	Great Britain	03 Dec 25	Admin Cooperation	44LTS263	301088
Irish Free State	Greece	15 May 30	General Trade	136LTS33	303122

PARTY ONE	PARTY TWO	DATE	TOPIC	CITATION	NUMBER
Irish Free State	India	04 Apr 26	Postal Service	56LTS415	301344
Irish Free State	Italy	10 May 30	Water Transport	132LTS147	303034
Irish Free State	Multilateral	05 Jun 12	Telecommunications	1LTS135	300013
Irish Free State	Multilateral	01 May 20	Air Transport	11LTS173	300297
Irish Free State	Multilateral	16 Dec 20	General IGO	6LTS379	300170
Irish Free State	Multilateral	31 Mar 22	Humanitarian	9LTS415	300269
Irish Free State	Multilateral	28 Aug 24	Postal Service	40LTS249	301003
Irish Free State	Multilateral	19 Feb 25	Admin Cooperation	81LTS317	301845
Irish Free State	Multilateral	17 Jun 25	Peace/Disarmament	94LTS65	302138
Irish Free State	Multilateral	29 Oct 25	Telecommunications	57LTS201	301365
Irish Free State	Multilateral	06 Nov 25	Patents/Copyrights	74LTS289	301743
Irish Free State	Multilateral	24 Apr 26	Land Transport	108LTS123	302505
Irish Free State	Multilateral	12 May 26	Refugees	89LTS47	302004
Irish Free State	Multilateral	25 Nov 27	Telecommunications	84LTS97	301905
Irish Free State	Multilateral	27 Aug 28	General Military	94LTS57	302137
Irish Free State	Multilateral	14 Dec 28	General Economic	110LTS171	302560
Irish Free State	Multilateral	20 Dec 28	Specific Resources	86LTS429	301954
Irish Free State	Multilateral	31 May 29	Water Transport	136LTS81	303127
Irish Free State	Multilateral	28 Jun 29	Postal Service	103LTS5	302369
Irish Free State	Multilateral	28 Jun 29	Postal Service	102LTS245	302368
Irish Free State	Multilateral	27 Jul 29	Other Military	118LTS343	302734
Irish Free State	Multilateral	27 Jul 29	Other Military	118LTS303	302733
Irish Free State	Multilateral	14 Sep 29	UN Charter	165LTS353	303822
Irish Free State	Multilateral	12 Oct 29	General Transport	137LTS11	303145
Irish Free State	Multilateral	12 Apr 30	Milit Servic/Citiz	178LTS227	304117
Irish Free State	Multilateral	12 Apr 30	Admin Cooperation	179LTS115	304138
Irish Free State	Multilateral	12 Apr 30	Admin Cooperation	179LTS89	304137
Irish Free State	Multilateral	22 Apr 30	Peace/Disarmament	112LTS65	302608
Irish Free State	Multilateral	28 Mar 31	Customs	119LTS47	302739
Irish Free State	Multilateral	30 Mar 31	Taxation	138LTS149	303185
Irish Free State	Multilateral	13 Jul 31	Other HEW	139LTS301	303219
Irish Free State	Multilateral	10 Dec 31	Water Transport	129LTS177	302961
Irish Free State	Multilateral	09 Dec 32	Telecommunications	151LTS5	303479
Irish Free State	Multilateral	12 Apr 33	Sanitation	161LTS65	303706
Irish Free State	Multilateral	19 Jun 33	Gen Communications	154LTS133	303544
Irish Free State	Multilateral	11 Oct 33	Education	155LTS331	303585
Irish Free State	Multilateral	20 Mar 34	Postal Service	174LTS171	304048
Irish Free State	Multilateral	12 Jun 34	Milit Installation	155LTS367	303587
Irish Free State	Multilateral	19 Jun 34	Admin Cooperation	154LTS381	303564
Irish Free State	Multilateral	06 Nov 36	General Military	173LTS353	304025
Irish Free State	Multilateral	08 May 37	Privil/Immunities	182LTS37	304202
Irish Free State	Multilateral	08 Jun 37	Specific Resources	190LTS79	304406
Irish Free State	New Zealand	30 Apr 25	Postal Service	56LTS373	301342
Irish Free State	Norway	21 Oct 30	Taxation	109LTS177	302536
Irish Free State	Portugal	29 Oct 29	General Economic	131LTS145	303007
Irish Free State	South Africa	01 Oct 25	Postal Service	56LTS389	301343
Irish Free State	Spain	04 Apr 35	General Trade	166LTS391	303855
Irish Free State	Spain	14 Jan 36	Consul/Citizenship	168LTS201	303899
Irish Free State	Sweden	08 Oct 31	Taxation	125LTS23	302842
Irish Free State	Switzerland	03 Nov 30	Non-ILO Labor	132LTS159	303035
Irish Free State	United Arab Rep	28 Jul 30	Mostfavored Nation	137LTS421	303172
Irish Free State	USA (United States)	31 Dec 23	Postal Service	56LTS303	301339
Irish Free State	USA (United States)	10 May 26	Postal Service	56LTS433	301345
Irish Free State	USA (United States)	18 Nov 31	Water Transport	131LTS279	303018
Isle of Man	Multilateral	30 Jun 20	Patents/Copyrights	1LTS59	300008
Israel	Multilateral	24 Sep 23	Dispute Settlement	27LTS157	300678
Israel	Multilateral	03 Nov 23	Customs	30LTS371	300775
Israel	Multilateral	25 Sep 26	ILO Labor	60LTS253	301414
Israel	Multilateral	26 Sep 27	Dispute Settlement	92LTS301	302096
Israel	Multilateral	20 Apr 29	Admin Cooperation	112LTS395	302624
Israel	Multilateral	20 Apr 29	Admin Cooperation	112LTS371	302623
Israel	Multilateral	31 May 29	Water Transport	136LTS81	303127
Israel	Multilateral	11 Mar 33	Water Transport	135LTS301	303119
It Aegean Colonies	Multilateral	09 Dec 32	Telecommunications	151LTS5	303479
Italian Colonies	Multilateral	28 Aug 24	Postal Service	41LTS97	301008

PARTY ONE	PARTY TWO	DATE	TOPIC	CITATION	NUMBER
Italian Colonies	Multilateral	28 Aug 24	Postal Service	41LTS55	301007
Italian Colonies	Multilateral	28 Jun 29	Postal Service	102LTS245	302368
Italian Somaliland	Multilateral	29 Oct 25	Telecommunications	57LTS201	301365
Italian Somaliland	Multilateral	25 Nov 27	Telecommunications	84LTS97	301905
Italian Somaliland	Multilateral	16 Apr 29	Specific Resources	126LTS305	302891
Italian Somaliland	Multilateral	09 Dec 32	Telecommunications	151LTS5	303479
Italy	Abyssinia	02 Aug 28	Land Transport	94LTS423	302159
Italy	Abyssinia	02 Aug 28	General Amity	94LTS413	302158
Italy	Albania	04 Dec 22	Telecommunications	15LTS213	300395
Italy	Albania	05 Dec 22	Postal Service	15LTS203	300394
Italy	Albania	29 Feb 24	Consul/Citizenship	44LTS343	301093
Italy	Albania	29 Feb 24	General Trade	44LTS331	301092
Italy	Albania	06 Mar 25	General Economic	44LTS359	301094
Italy	Albania	27 Nov 26	General Amity	60LTS15	301402
Italy	Albania	19 Mar 36	Finance	173LTS51	304002
Italy	Albania	19 Mar 36	Sanitation	173LTS107	304007
Italy	Albania	19 Mar 36	Finance	173LTS63	304003
Italy	Albania	19 Mar 36	Loans and Credits	173LTS83	304005
Italy	Albania	19 Mar 36	Loans and Credits	173LTS73	304004
Italy	Albania	19 Mar 36	General Trade	173LTS131	304008
Italy	Albania	19 Mar 36	Water Transport	173LTS93	304006
Italy	Argentina	26 Mar 20	Non-ILO Labor	15LTS271	300400
Italy	Australia	22 Jun 34	Postal Service	165LTS107	303806
Italy	Austria	16 Jul 23	General Trade	27LTS383	300699
Italy	Austria	29 Mar 24	Non-ILO Labor	84LTS293	301910
Italy	Austria	29 Mar 24	Other HEW	84LTS321	301911
Italy	Austria	18 Jun 24	Finance	84LTS381	301914
Italy	Austria	18 Jun 24	Non-ILO Labor	84LTS349	301912
Italy	Austria	18 Jun 24	Non-ILO Labor	84LTS367	301913
Italy	Austria	27 Sep 24	Non-ILO Labor	84LTS409	301916
Italy	Austria	27 Sep 24	Non-ILO Labor	84LTS397	301915
Italy	Austria	17 Jan 25	Non-ILO Labor	84LTS419	301917
Italy	Austria	17 Jan 25	Non-ILO Labor	85LTS9	301918
Italy	Austria	17 Jan 25	Non-ILO Labor	85LTS19	301919
Italy	Austria	22 Dec 27	General Economic	91LTS283	302068
Italy	Austria	30 Dec 27	General Economic	87LTS109	301964
Italy	Austria	11 May 28	Air Transport	100LTS375	302307
Italy	Austria	11 May 28	Air Transport	100LTS41	302293
Italy	Austria	22 Feb 29	Territory Boundary	89LTS271	302021
Italy	Austria	06 Feb 30	Dispute Settlement	105LTS97	302405
Italy	Austria	06 Jun 30	Visas	105LTS329	302425
Italy	Austria	07 May 31	General Trade	132LTS9	303026
Italy	Austria	19 Nov 31	Extradition	126LTS163	302879
Italy	Austria	17 Mar 34	General Economic	154LTS297	303556
Italy	Bel-Lux Econ Union	30 Jun 37	Finance	182LTS106	304203
Italy	Bel-Lux Econ Union	30 Jun 37	General Trade	197LTS23	304601
Italy	Belgium	28 Jan 29	Extradition	92LTS263	302094
Italy	Belgium	11 Jul 31	Taxation	136LTS9	303120
Italy	Belgium	07 Feb 34	Consul/Citizenship	147LTS107	303395
Italy	Belgium	04 May 35	Air Transport	159LTS165	303660
Italy	Belgium	02 Dec 35	Extradition	172LTS209	303992
Italy	Belgium	01 May 37	Visas	198LTS73	304624
Italy	Brazil	08 Oct 21	Non-ILO Labor	16LTS9	300401
Italy	Brazil	08 Feb 30	Visas	101LTS57	302319
Italy	Brazil	28 Nov 31	Mostfavored Nation	131LTS273	303017
Italy	Brazil	28 Nov 31	Extradition	132LTS345	303047
Italy	Bulgaria	20 May 31	Mostfavored Nation	129LTS371	302971
Italy	Bulgaria	20 May 31	Patents/Copyrights	129LTS361	302970
Italy	Canada	04 Jan 23	General Economic	25LTS375	300626
Italy	Chile	10 Nov 27	Postal Service	69LTS289	301611
Italy	China	27 Nov 28	General Amity	93LTS173	302109
Italy	Czechoslovakia	23 Mar 21	Finance	32LTS261	300817
Italy	Czechoslovakia	23 Mar 21	General Trade	32LTS183	300815
Italy	Czechoslovakia	23 Mar 21	Water Transport	32LTS241	300816
Italy	Czechoslovakia	06 Apr 22	Admin Cooperation	55LTS207	301315

PARTY ONE	PARTY TWO	DATE	TOPIC	CITATION	NUMBER
Italy	Czechoslovakia	06 Apr 22	Extradition	55LTS171	301313
Italy	Czechoslovakia	06 Apr 22	Admin Cooperation	55LTS189	301314
Italy	Czechoslovakia	01 Mar 24	Consul/Citizenship	34LTS55	300867
Italy	Czechoslovakia	01 Mar 24	Taxation	36LTS229	300925
Italy	Czechoslovakia	05 Jul 24	General Amity	26LTS21	300637
Italy	Czechoslovakia	15 Nov 24	Land Transport	92LTS91	302081
Italy	Czechoslovakia	04 May 26	Other Economic	61LTS257	301438
Italy	Czechoslovakia	28 Mar 31	Culture	125LTS347	302863
Italy	Czechoslovakia	23 May 31	Admin Cooperation	126LTS185	302881
Italy	Czechoslovakia	28 Apr 32	Air Transport	136LTS267	303129
Italy	Czechoslovakia	27 Nov 33	General Economic	153LTS351	303531
Italy	Czechoslovakia	31 Mar 37	General Trade	193LTS165	304492
Italy	Czechoslovakia	10 May 37	Air Transport	190LTS397	304430
Italy	Denmark	26 Oct 27	Consul/Citizenship	68LTS229	301586
Italy	Denmark	11 Dec 29	Extradition	97LTS373	302235
Italy	Denmark	03 Feb 31	Admin Cooperation	113LTS45	302634
Italy	Estonia	01 Jul 28	General Economic	87LTS277	301974
Italy	Estonia	10 Aug 35	Extradition	185LTS287	304295
Italy	Estonia	06 Oct 36	Finance	172LTS189	303989
Italy	Finland	22 Oct 24	General Trade	32LTS149	300814
Italy	Finland	12 May 28	Visas	77LTS334	301775
Italy	Finland	21 Aug 28	Admin Cooperation	84LTS265	301906
Italy	Finland	21 Aug 28	Dispute Settlement	89LTS25	302002
Italy	Finland	10 Jul 29	Extradition	111LTS295	302593
Italy	Finland	15 Aug 29	Admin Cooperation	99LTS363	302280
Italy	Finland	18 Oct 29	Visas	97LTS65	302218
Italy	Finland	28 Sep 36	Finance	172LTS155	303986
Italy	France	30 Sep 19	ILO Labor	5LTS279	300133
Italy	France	19 Feb 20	Non-ILO Labor	8LTS41	300204
Italy	France	27 Aug 20	Commodity Trade	8LTS95	300210
Italy	France	12 Sep 20	Telecommunications	1LTS397	300033
Italy	France	10 Jan 24	Customs	43LTS431	301076
Italy	France	10 Apr 24	General Trade	43LTS485	301078
Italy	France	29 May 26	General Trade	62LTS347	301473
Italy	France	29 May 26	Commodity Trade	62LTS425	301474
Italy	France	26 Jan 27	Customs	79LTS49	301804
Italy	France	07 Mar 28	General Trade	72LTS213	301694
Italy	France	10 Mar 29	Air Transport	93LTS319	302120
Italy	France	03 Jun 30	Admin Cooperation	153LTS135	303513
Italy	France	16 Jun 30	Taxation	144LTS115	303323
Italy	France	08 Jul 30	Territory Boundary	137LTS93	303148
Italy	France	13 Feb 31	Land Transport	139LTS109	303206
Italy	France	26 Dec 31	Patents/Copyrights	133LTS45	303055
Italy	France	03 Oct 32	Taxation	153LTS55	303507
Italy	Germany	21 Jun 25	Admin Cooperation	68LTS11	301565
Italy	Germany	31 Oct 25	General Economic	52LTS179	301256
Italy	Germany	31 Oct 25	Taxation	53LTS245	301261
Italy	Germany	29 Dec 26	Dispute Settlement	78LTS383	301797
Italy	Germany	20 May 27	Air Transport	79LTS179	301810
Italy	Germany	01 Sep 27	Peace/Disarmament	67LTS425	301564
Italy	Germany	23 Mar 28	Admin Cooperation	93LTS165	302108
Italy	Germany	27 Aug 28	Visas	90LTS191	302037
Italy	Germany	20 Jan 30	Peace/Disarmament	106LTS109	302439
Italy	Germany	25 Feb 30	Scientific Project	118LTS49	302713
Italy	Great Britain	10 Sep 26	Land Transport	57LTS77	301354
Italy	Greece	24 Oct 26	General Trade	63LTS51	301480
Italy	Greece	24 Nov 26	Specific Resources	63LTS91	301481
Italy	Greece	23 Sep 28	Dispute Settlement	108LTS219	302510
Italy	Greece	15 Jan 32	Taxation	137LTS397	303169
Italy	Greece	30 Jun 36	Air Transport	185LTS93	304277
Italy	Guatemala	15 Sep 26	General Trade	70LTS175	301633
Italy	Haiti	03 Jan 27	General Trade	71LTS405	301678
Italy	Hungary	27 Mar 24	Telecommunications	55LTS109	301308
Italy	Hungary	27 Mar 24	Postal Service	55LTS103	301307
Italy	Hungary	27 Mar 24	Finance	45LTS65	301099

PARTY ONE	PARTY TWO	DATE	TOPIC	CITATION	NUMBER
Italy	Hungary	27 Mar 24	Finance	45LTS83	301100
Italy	Hungary	27 Mar 24	Finance	45LTS241	301102
Italy	Hungary	27 Mar 24	Finance	45LTS229	301101
Italy	Hungary	20 Jul 25	Admin Cooperation	45LTS39	301098
Italy	Hungary	25 Nov 25	Taxation	74LTS251	301741
Italy	Hungary	30 Mar 26	Finance	54LTS85	301276
Italy	Hungary	15 Mar 27	Claims and Debts	68LTS221	301585
Italy	Hungary	05 Apr 27	General Amity	67LTS399	301561
Italy	Hungary	21 May 27	Finance	74LTS19	301727
Italy	Hungary	21 May 27	Finance	74LTS33	301729
Italy	Hungary	21 May 27	Claims and Debts	74LTS27	301728
Italy	Hungary	25 Jul 27	Customs	74LTS67	301732
Italy	Hungary	25 Jul 27	Other Ad Hoc	74LTS77	301733
Italy	Hungary	25 Jul 27	Water Transport	74LTS53	301731
Italy	Hungary	10 Dec 27	Dispute Settlement	78LTS403	301798
Italy	Hungary	04 Jul 28	Sanitation	92LTS169	302084
Italy	Hungary	04 Jul 28	General Economic	92LTS117	302083
Italy	Hungary	07 May 30	Visas	101LTS445	302343
Italy	Hungary	05 Jul 32	Air Transport	144LTS257	303330
Italy	Hungary	12 Nov 32	Claims and Debts	142LTS87	303279
Italy	Hungary	12 Nov 32	Finance	142LTS101	303281
Italy	Hungary	12 Nov 32	Claims and Debts	142LTS115	303283
Italy	Hungary	12 Nov 32	Claims and Debts	142LTS109	303282
Italy	Hungary	12 Nov 32	Dispute Settlement	142LTS95	303280
Italy	Hungary	18 Nov 34	Water Transport	166LTS263	303842
Italy	Hungary	16 Feb 35	Culture	163LTS15	303758
Italy	Hungary	04 Jul 36	Commodity Trade	181LTS331	304199
Italy	Hungary	09 Mar 37	Water Transport	184LTS297	304254
Italy	Irish Free State	10 May 30	Water Transport	132LTS147	303034
Italy	Latvia	25 Jul 25	General Economic	60LTS91	301407
Italy	Latvia	12 Jun 26	Visas	51LTS65	301222
Italy	Latvia	28 Apr 31	Dispute Settlement	126LTS399	302898
Italy	Latvia	11 May 32	Consul/Citizenship	150LTS9	303450
Italy	Latvia	05 Feb 37	General Trade	178LTS33	304104
Italy	Latvia	05 Feb 37	Finance	178LTS25	304103
Italy	Lithuania	17 Sep 27	Dispute Settlement	72LTS439	301700
Italy	Lithuania	17 Sep 27	General Trade	73LTS9	301701
Italy	Luxembourg	15 Apr 32	Dispute Settlement	142LTS119	303284
Italy	Malaya	09 Mar 35	Postal Service	163LTS113	303764
Italy	Multilateral	09 Sep 86*	Patents/Copyrights	123LTS233	302816
Italy	Multilateral	18 Mar 04	Humanitarian	1LTS83	300011
Italy	Multilateral	13 Nov 08	General Ad Hoc	1LTS217	300015
Italy	Multilateral	12 Jan 12	Sanitation	4LTS281	300112
Italy	Multilateral	23 Jan 12	Sanitation	8LTS187	300222
Italy	Multilateral	05 Jun 12	Telecommunications	1LTS135	300013
Italy	Multilateral	20 Mar 14	Patents/Copyrights	1LTS243	300016
Italy	Multilateral	21 Apr 14	Sanitation	5LTS394	300144
Italy	Multilateral	10 Sep 19	General Trade	7LTS331	300200
Italy	Multilateral	10 Sep 19	Admin Cooperation	8LTS25	300202
Italy	Multilateral	10 Sep 19	Reparations	2LTS21	300042
Italy	Multilateral	10 Sep 19	General Economic	2LTS35	300044
Italy	Multilateral	10 Sep 19	Reparations	2LTS29	300043
Italy	Multilateral	10 Sep 19	Health/Educ/Welfare	8LTS11	300201
Italy	Multilateral	10 Sep 19	Reparations	2LTS44	300045
Italy	Multilateral	09 Dec 19	Territory Boundary	5LTS335	300140
Italy	Multilateral	09 Feb 20	Territory Boundary	2LTS7	300041
Italy	Multilateral	25 Mar 20	Finance	1LTS45	300006
Italy	Multilateral	01 May 20	Air Transport	11LTS173	300297
Italy	Multilateral	04 Jun 20	Peace/Disarmament	6LTS187	300152
Italy	Multilateral	21 Jun 20	Health/Educ/Welfare	8LTS65	300207
Italy	Multilateral	30 Jun 20	Patents/Copyrights	1LTS59	300008
Italy	Multilateral	05 Jul 20	Dispute Settlement	2LTS241	300070
Italy	Multilateral	05 Aug 20	Territory Boundary	2LTS49	300046
Italy	Multilateral	10 Aug 20	Territory Boundary	28LTS225	300710
Italy	Multilateral	10 Aug 20	Consul/Citizenship	28LTS223	300711
Italy	Multilateral	31 Oct 20	Sanitation	164LTS85	303790
Italy	Multilateral	16 Dec 20	General IGO	6LTS379	300170
Italy	Multilateral	20 Apr 21	Water Transport	7LTS73	300174
Italy	Multilateral	20 Apr 21	Land Transport	7LTS11	300171
Italy	Multilateral	20 Apr 21	Water Transport	7LTS35	300172
Italy	Multilateral	05 May 21	Peace/Disarmament	12LTS419	300338
Italy	Multilateral	10 Jun 21	Customs	8LTS297	300227
Italy	Multilateral	23 Jul 21	Water Transport	26LTS173	300647
Italy	Multilateral	05 Aug 21	Admin Cooperation	27LTS349	300695
Italy	Multilateral	05 Oct 21	IGO Establishment	51LTS361	301241
Italy	Multilateral	05 Oct 21	Admin Cooperation	29LTS79	300735
Italy	Multilateral	05 Oct 21	Admin Cooperation	29LTS73	300734
Italy	Multilateral	05 Oct 21	Admin Cooperation	29LTS67	300733
Italy	Multilateral	06 Oct 21	General Economic	17LTS45	300427
Italy	Multilateral	20 Oct 21	Peace/Disarmament	9LTS211	300255
Italy	Multilateral	09 Nov 21	Territory Boundary	12LTS381	300333
Italy	Multilateral	27 Jan 22	Visas	9LTS291	300262
Italy	Multilateral	06 Feb 22	General Trade	38LTS277	300982
Italy	Multilateral	06 Feb 22	Customs	38LTS267	300981
Italy	Multilateral	06 Feb 22	Peace/Disarmament	25LTS201	300609
Italy	Multilateral	22 Feb 22	Water Transport	26LTS219	300649
Italy	Multilateral	31 Mar 22	Humanitarian	9LTS415	300269
Italy	Multilateral	06 Apr 22	Admin Cooperation	123LTS277	302818
Italy	Multilateral	06 Apr 22	Milit Assistance	20LTS11	300501
Italy	Multilateral	04 Oct 22	Territory Boundary	12LTS391	300335
Italy	Multilateral	04 Oct 22	Territory Boundary	12LTS385	300334
Italy	Multilateral	14 Dec 22	Water Transport	36LTS457	300943
Italy	Multilateral	27 Jan 23	Water Transport	26LTS253	300651
Italy	Multilateral	15 Mar 23	Territory Boundary	15LTS259	300398
Italy	Multilateral	29 Mar 23	Land Transport	23LTS378	300594
Italy	Multilateral	29 Mar 23	Admin Cooperation	20LTS111	300510
Italy	Multilateral	29 Mar 23	Land Transport	23LTS256	300593
Italy	Multilateral	24 Jul 23	General Trade	28LTS151	300704
Italy	Multilateral	24 Jul 23	Territory Boundary	28LTS215	300708
Italy	Multilateral	24 Jul 23	Territory Boundary	28LTS139	300703
Italy	Multilateral	24 Jul 23	Admin Cooperation	28LTS197	300706
Italy	Multilateral	24 Jul 23	Peace/Disarmament	28LTS11	300701
Italy	Multilateral	24 Jul 23	Water Transport	28LTS115	300702
Italy	Multilateral	24 Jul 23	General Trade	28LTS203	300707
Italy	Multilateral	24 Jul 23	General Trade	28LTS171	300705
Italy	Multilateral	24 Jul 23	Consul/Citizenship	28LTS221	300709
Italy	Multilateral	24 Jul 23	Recognition	36LTS179	300919
Italy	Multilateral	24 Jul 23	Admin Cooperation	28LTS283	300714
Italy	Multilateral	24 Jul 23	General Amity	36LTS145	300913
Italy	Multilateral	24 Jul 23	Water Transport	36LTS187	300920
Italy	Multilateral	24 Jul 23	Taxation	36LTS175	300918
Italy	Multilateral	24 Jul 23	Consul/Citizenship	36LTS167	300917
Italy	Multilateral	24 Sep 23	Dispute Settlement	27LTS157	300678
Italy	Multilateral	29 Sep 23	Refugees	20LTS41	300504
Italy	Multilateral	03 Nov 23	Customs	30LTS371	300775
Italy	Multilateral	23 Nov 23	Reparations	28LTS273	300713
Italy	Multilateral	23 Nov 23	Claims and Debts	28LTS267	300712
Italy	Multilateral	28 Nov 23	Admin Cooperation	51LTS239	301233
Italy	Multilateral	28 Nov 23	Admin Cooperation	51LTS215	301229
Italy	Multilateral	28 Nov 23	Admin Cooperation	51LTS209	301228
Italy	Multilateral	28 Nov 23	Admin Cooperation	51LTS221	301230
Italy	Multilateral	28 Nov 23	Admin Cooperation	51LTS233	301232
Italy	Multilateral	30 Nov 23	Non-ILO Labor	102LTS183	302361
Italy	Multilateral	30 Nov 23	Non-ILO Labor	102LTS153	302360
Italy	Multilateral	09 Dec 23	General Economic	58LTS315	301380
Italy	Multilateral	09 Dec 23	Non-IBRD Project	36LTS76	300905
Italy	Multilateral	09 Dec 23	Water Transport	58LTS284	301379
Italy	Multilateral	09 Dec 23	Land Transport	47LTS55	301129
Italy	Multilateral	25 Jan 24	Sanitation	57LTS135	301360
Italy	Multilateral	07 Feb 24	Water Transport	25LTS265	300614

PARTY ONE	PARTY TWO	DATE	TOPIC	CITATION	NUMBER
Italy	Multilateral	14 Mar 24	Finance	25LTS423	300633
Italy	Multilateral	28 Mar 24	Finance	31LTS53	300781
Italy	Multilateral	28 Mar 24	Finance	31LTS46	300780
Italy	Multilateral	31 Mar 24	Sanitation	27LTS211	300685
Italy	Multilateral	08 May 24	Territory Boundary	29LTS85	300736
Italy	Multilateral	04 Jul 24	Admin Cooperation	51LTS227	301231
Italy	Multilateral	16 Aug 24	Taxation	41LTS429	301024
Italy	Multilateral	25 Aug 24	Water Transport	120LTS123	302763
Italy	Multilateral	25 Aug 24	Water Transport	120LTS155	302764
Italy	Multilateral	28 Aug 24	Postal Service	41LTS55	301007
Italy	Multilateral	28 Aug 24	Postal Service	40LTS19	301002
Italy	Multilateral	28 Aug 24	Postal Service	40LTS437	301005
Italy	Multilateral	28 Aug 24	Postal Service	40LTS249	301003
Italy	Multilateral	28 Aug 24	Postal Service	41LTS97	301008
Italy	Multilateral	28 Aug 24	Postal Service	40LTS307	301004
Italy	Multilateral	30 Aug 24	Reparations	30LTS97	300762
Italy	Multilateral	30 Aug 24	Admin Cooperation	30LTS75	300760
Italy	Multilateral	30 Aug 24	General Economic	30LTS63	300759
Italy	Multilateral	30 Aug 24	Admin Cooperation	30LTS79	300761
Italy	Multilateral	25 Sep 24	Admin Cooperation	30LTS421	300777
Italy	Multilateral	23 Oct 24	Land Transport	78LTS17	301779
Italy	Multilateral	23 Oct 24	General Transport	77LTS367	301778
Italy	Multilateral	29 Nov 24	General IGO	80LTS293	301835
Italy	Multilateral	01 Dec 24	Sanitation	78LTS351	301794
Italy	Multilateral	19 Feb 25	Admin Cooperation	81LTS317	301845
Italy	Multilateral	00 Apr 25	Water Transport	37LTS21	300945
Italy	Multilateral	23 Apr 25	Water Transport	37LTS9	300944
Italy	Multilateral	05 May 25	Finance	55LTS225	301318
Italy	Multilateral	17 Jun 25	Peace/Disarmament	94LTS65	302138
Italy	Multilateral	16 Oct 25	Peace/Disarmament	54LTS289	301292
Italy	Multilateral	29 Oct 25	Telecommunications	57LTS201	301365
Italy	Multilateral	06 Nov 25	Patents/Copyrights	74LTS327	301745
Italy	Multilateral	06 Nov 25	Patents/Copyrights	74LTS289	301743
Italy	Multilateral	27 Nov 25	Water Transport	67LTS63	301539
Italy	Multilateral	00 Apr 26	Water Transport	57LTS437	301366
Italy	Multilateral	10 Apr 26	Water Transport	176LTS199	304062
Italy	Multilateral	10 Apr 26	Water Transport	120LTS187	302765
Italy	Multilateral	24 Apr 26	Land Transport	108LTS123	302505
Italy	Multilateral	24 Apr 26	Land Transport	97LTS83	302220
Italy	Multilateral	22 May 26	Air Transport	58LTS331	301381
Italy	Multilateral	21 Jun 26	Sanitation	78LTS229	301793
Italy	Multilateral	18 Sep 26	General IGO	59LTS237	301393
Italy	Multilateral	25 Sep 26	ILO Labor	60LTS253	301414
Italy	Multilateral	31 Mar 27	Air Transport	66LTS59	301525
Italy	Multilateral	19 May 27	Air Transport	68LTS407	301595
Italy	Multilateral	12 Jul 27	Direct Aid	135LTS247	303115
Italy	Multilateral	26 Sep 27	Dispute Settlement	92LTS301	302096
Italy	Multilateral	27 Oct 27	Air Transport	148LTS265	303417
Italy	Multilateral	08 Nov 27	General Trade	97LTS391	302238
Italy	Multilateral	25 Nov 27	Telecommunications	84LTS97	301905
Italy	Multilateral	08 Dec 27	Loans and Credits	70LTS73	301623
Italy	Multilateral	01 May 28	Telecommunications	132LTS415	303050
Italy	Multilateral	11 Jul 28	Commodity Trade	95LTS357	302184
Italy	Multilateral	11 Jul 28	Commodity Trade	95LTS373	302185
Italy	Multilateral	15 Jul 28	Patents/Copyrights	79LTS133	301806
Italy	Multilateral	25 Jul 28	General Amity	87LTS211	301971
Italy	Multilateral	27 Aug 28	General Military	94LTS57	302137
Italy	Multilateral	26 Sep 28	Dispute Settlement	93LTS343	302123
Italy	Multilateral	22 Nov 28	Culture	111LTS343	302598
Italy	Multilateral	14 Dec 28	General Economic	110LTS171	302560
Italy	Multilateral	16 Apr 29	Specific Resources	126LTS305	302891
Italy	Multilateral	20 Apr 29	Admin Cooperation	112LTS371	302623
Italy	Multilateral	31 May 29	Water Transport	136LTS81	303127
Italy	Multilateral	14 Jun 29	Visas	94LTS275	302148
Italy	Multilateral	28 Jun 29	Postal Service	103LTS377	302373
Italy	Multilateral	28 Jun 29	Postal Service	103LTS71	302370
Italy	Multilateral	28 Jun 29	Postal Service	103LTS249	302371
Italy	Multilateral	28 Jun 29	Postal Service	102LTS245	302368
Italy	Multilateral	28 Jun 29	Postal Service	103LTS429	302374
Italy	Multilateral	28 Jun 29	Postal Service	103LTS321	302372
Italy	Multilateral	28 Jun 29	Postal Service	103LTS5	302369
Italy	Multilateral	27 Jul 29	Other Military	118LTS303	302733
Italy	Multilateral	27 Jul 29	Other Military	118LTS343	302734
Italy	Multilateral	20 Aug 29	Sanitation	98LTS125	302243
Italy	Multilateral	30 Aug 29	General Amity	104LTS487	302400
Italy	Multilateral	14 Sep 29	UN Charter	165LTS353	303822
Italy	Multilateral	12 Oct 29	General Transport	137LTS11	303145
Italy	Multilateral	18 Nov 29	Telecommunications	99LTS415	302287
Italy	Multilateral	20 Jan 30	Reparations	112LTS361	302622
Italy	Multilateral	20 Jan 30	Reparations	104LTS421	302396
Italy	Multilateral	20 Jan 30	Reparations	104LTS243	302394
Italy	Multilateral	20 Jan 30	Other Economic	104LTS441	302398
Italy	Multilateral	20 Jan 30	Finance	104LTS413	302395
Italy	Multilateral	20 Jan 30	Reparations	113LTS389	302650
Italy	Multilateral	20 Jan 30	Finance	104LTS433	302397
Italy	Multilateral	12 Apr 30	Admin Cooperation	179LTS89	304137
Italy	Multilateral	22 Apr 30	Peace/Disarmament	112LTS65	302608
Italy	Multilateral	28 Apr 30	Claims and Debts	121LTS69	302785
Italy	Multilateral	07 Jun 30	Finance	143LTS257	303313
Italy	Multilateral	07 Jun 30	Finance	143LTS337	303315
Italy	Multilateral	07 Jun 30	Finance	143LTS317	303314
Italy	Multilateral	10 Jun 30	Loans and Credits	112LTS237	302618
Italy	Multilateral	01 Aug 30	Health/Educ/Welfare	128LTS9	302932
Italy	Multilateral	19 Mar 31	Finance	143LTS407	303317
Italy	Multilateral	19 Mar 31	Finance	143LTS355	303316
Italy	Multilateral	19 Mar 31	Admin Cooperation	143LTS7	303301
Italy	Multilateral	27 Mar 31	ICJ Option Clause	167LTS341	303877
Italy	Multilateral	28 Mar 31	Customs	119LTS47	302739
Italy	Multilateral	30 Mar 31	Taxation	138LTS149	303185
Italy	Multilateral	30 Mar 31	Land Transport	150LTS247	303459
Italy	Multilateral	13 Apr 31	Air Transport	119LTS275	302751
Italy	Multilateral	16 May 31	Air Transport	136LTS245	303128
Italy	Multilateral	13 Jul 31	Other HEW	139LTS301	303219
Italy	Multilateral	21 Aug 31	Other Ad Hoc	185LTS45	304273
Italy	Multilateral	21 Aug 31	Other Economic	127LTS95	302910
Italy	Multilateral	24 Sep 31	Specific Resources	155LTS349	303586
Italy	Multilateral	11 Dec 31	Commodity Trade	170LTS251	303941
Italy	Multilateral	15 Jul 32	Direct Aid	135LTS285	303118
Italy	Multilateral	02 Sep 32	Land Transport	154LTS123	303543
Italy	Multilateral	09 Dec 32	Telecommunications	151LTS5	303479
Italy	Multilateral	11 Mar 33	Water Transport	135LTS301	303119
Italy	Multilateral	12 Apr 33	Sanitation	161LTS65	303706
Italy	Multilateral	29 May 33	Admin Cooperation	192LTS289	304479
Italy	Multilateral	19 Jun 33	Gen Communications	154LTS133	303544
Italy	Multilateral	25 Aug 33	Commodity Trade	141LTS71	303262
Italy	Multilateral	10 Oct 33	General Amity	163LTS393	303781
Italy	Multilateral	11 Oct 33	Education	155LTS331	303585
Italy	Multilateral	28 Oct 33	Refugees	159LTS199	303663
Italy	Multilateral	08 Nov 33	Specific Resources	172LTS241	303995
Italy	Multilateral	23 Nov 33	Land Transport	192LTS327	304483
Italy	Multilateral	23 Nov 33	Land Transport	192LTS389	304484
Italy	Multilateral	17 Mar 34	General Amity	154LTS281	303554
Italy	Multilateral	17 Mar 34	General Economic	154LTS287	303555
Italy	Multilateral	20 Mar 34	Postal Service	174LTS171	304048
Italy	Multilateral	20 Mar 34	Postal Service	176LTS55	304054
Italy	Multilateral	20 Mar 34	Postal Service	175LTS5	304049
Italy	Multilateral	20 Mar 34	Postal Service	175LTS73	304050
Italy	Multilateral	20 Mar 34	Finance	176LTS9	304053
Italy	Multilateral	20 Mar 34	Postal Service	175LTS269	304051
Italy	Multilateral	20 Mar 34	Postal Service	175LTS363	304052

PARTY ONE	PARTY TWO	DATE	TOPIC	CITATION	NUMBER
Italy	Multilateral	26 Apr 34	Admin Cooperation	164LTS63	303789
Italy	Multilateral	02 Jun 34	Patents/Copyrights	205LTS179	304834
Italy	Multilateral	02 Jun 34	Patents/Copyrights	192LTS17	304459
Italy	Multilateral	12 Jun 34	Milit Installation	155LTS367	303587
Italy	Multilateral	19 Jun 34	Admin Cooperation	154LTS381	303564
Italy	Multilateral	20 Jul 34	Territory Boundary	155LTS45	303567
Italy	Multilateral	25 Jul 34	Other HEW	177LTS59	304080
Italy	Multilateral	07 Dec 34	Air Transport	158LTS91	303629
Italy	Multilateral	20 Feb 35	Sanitation	186LTS173	304310
Italy	Multilateral	20 Feb 35	Sanitation	193LTS37	304486
Italy	Multilateral	20 Feb 35	Sanitation	193LTS59	304487
Italy	Multilateral	25 Mar 36	Peace/Disarmament	184LTS115	304246
Italy	Multilateral	30 Jul 36	IGO Status/Immunit	197LTS31	304602
Italy	Multilateral	06 Nov 36	General Military	173LTS353	304025
Italy	Multilateral	10 Feb 37	General Transport	189LTS313	304391
Italy	Multilateral	31 Mar 37	Commodity Trade	189LTS359	304394
Italy	Multilateral	08 May 37	Privil/Immunities	182LTS37	304202
Italy	Multilateral	16 Apr 38	Peace/Disarmament	195LTS103	304538
Italy	Multilateral	18 Aug 38	Admin Cooperation	196LTS113	304574
Italy	Multilateral	31 Oct 38	Sanitation	198LTS205	304642
Italy	Multilateral	23 Apr 39	Land Transport	104LTS87	302380
Italy	Multilateral	02 Jun 42	Patents/Copyrights	205LTS163	304833
Italy	Netherlands	11 Oct 20	Land Transport	18LTS253	300468
Italy	Netherlands	28 Jun 27	Water Transport	68LTS203	301583
Italy	Netherlands	01 Jul 31	General Transport	127LTS235	302923
Italy	Netherlands	03 Oct 31	Air Transport	126LTS109	302875
Italy	Netherlands	06 Jul 33	Land Transport	152LTS247	303496
Italy	Netherlands	01 Mar 34	General Trade	163LTS367	303779
Italy	Netherlands	29 Jul 35	Finance	165LTS329	303819
Italy	Netherlands	01 Jan 37	Finance	178LTS415	304124
Italy	Netherlands	26 Feb 38	Air Transport	194LTS75	304509
Italy	Norway	10 Jun 29	Dispute Settlement	105LTS161	302410
Italy	Norway	31 Jul 30	Other Economic	118LTS113	302716
Italy	Norway	02 Jul 35	General Trade	162LTS317	303744
Italy	Norway	02 Jul 35	Finance	162LTS323	303745
Italy	Norway	25 Aug 36	Finance	171LTS377	303974
Italy	Norway	31 Mar 37	Customs	177LTS349	304097
Italy	Norway	31 Mar 37	Finance	177LTS367	304099
Italy	Norway	31 Mar 37	Finance	177LTS355	304098
Italy	Norway	21 Jun 38	General Trade	190LTS193	304417
Italy	Palestine	06 Dec 32	Postal Service	139LTS59	303204
Italy	Panama	16 Oct 29	General Economic	138LTS355	303199
Italy	Panama	07 Aug 30	Extradition	140LTS241	303240
Italy	Persia	24 Jul 28	General Amity	95LTS269	302179
Italy	Persia	05 Sep 29	General Amity	141LTS185	303264
Italy	Poland	12 May 22	General Trade	59LTS293	301399
Italy	Poland	22 Jul 25	General Economic	54LTS101	301278
Italy	Poland	20 Jan 30	Claims and Debts	127LTS41	302904
Italy	Poland	22 Jul 30	Sanitation	121LTS17	302780
Italy	Poland	12 Dec 31	Admin Cooperation	140LTS421	303252
Italy	Poland	30 Oct 33	Loans and Credits	145LTS103	303348
Italy	Portugal	18 Dec 26	Finance	93LTS313	302119
Italy	Romania	16 Sep 26	General Amity	67LTS393	301560
Italy	Romania	25 Feb 30	Sanitation	106LTS423	302459
Italy	Romania	25 Feb 30	Other Economic	106LTS231	302447
Italy	Romania	25 Feb 30	General Economic	106LTS179	302445
Italy	Romania	25 Feb 30	Peace/Disarmament	106LTS225	302446
Italy	Serb/Croat/Slovene	12 Nov 20	Territory Boundary	18LTS387	300477
Italy	Serb/Croat/Slovene	14 Sep 21	Specific Resources	19LTS14	300482
Italy	Serb/Croat/Slovene	06 Apr 22	Admin Cooperation	123LTS289	302819
Italy	Serb/Croat/Slovene	06 Apr 22	Dispute Settlement	118LTS199	302724
Italy	Serb/Croat/Slovene	06 Apr 22	Extradition	118LTS221	302726
Italy	Serb/Croat/Slovene	06 Apr 22	Privil/Immunities	118LTS207	302725
Italy	Serb/Croat/Slovene	23 Oct 22	Customs	18LTS441	300480
Italy	Serb/Croat/Slovene	23 Oct 22	Customs	18LTS413	300479

PARTY ONE	PARTY TWO	DATE	TOPIC	CITATION	NUMBER
Italy	Serb/Croat/Slovene	23 Oct 22	Territory Boundary	18LTS461	300481
Italy	Serb/Croat/Slovene	23 Oct 22	General Economic	18LTS405	300478
Italy	Serb/Croat/Slovene	27 Jan 24	Admin Cooperation	83LTS87	301886
Italy	Serb/Croat/Slovene	27 Jan 24	Visas	83LTS139	301887
Italy	Serb/Croat/Slovene	27 Jan 24	General Amity	24LTS31	300596
Italy	Serb/Croat/Slovene	14 Jul 24	General Trade	82LTS257	301876
Italy	Serb/Croat/Slovene	14 Jul 24	Land Transport	82LTS327	301877
Italy	Serb/Croat/Slovene	14 Jul 24	Land Transport	82LTS349	301878
Italy	Serb/Croat/Slovene	12 Aug 24	Sanitation	83LTS19	301884
Italy	Serb/Croat/Slovene	12 Aug 24	Admin Cooperation	82LTS355	301879
Italy	Serb/Croat/Slovene	12 Aug 24	Territory Boundary	82LTS423	301882
Italy	Serb/Croat/Slovene	12 Aug 24	Customs	82LTS391	301880
Italy	Serb/Croat/Slovene	12 Aug 24	Telecommunications	82LTS401	301881
Italy	Serb/Croat/Slovene	21 Aug 24	Consul/Citizenship	82LTS445	301883
Italy	Serb/Croat/Slovene	20 Jul 25	Admin Cooperation	83LTS241	301889
Italy	Serb/Croat/Slovene	20 Jul 25	Visas	83LTS287	301896
Italy	Serb/Croat/Slovene	20 Jul 25	General Transport	83LTS33	301885
Italy	Serb/Croat/Slovene	20 Jul 25	Other Ad Hoc	83LTS259	301892
Italy	Serb/Croat/Slovene	20 Jul 25	Consul/Citizenship	83LTS159	301888
Italy	Serb/Croat/Slovene	20 Jul 25	Visas	83LTS253	301891
Italy	Serb/Croat/Slovene	20 Jul 25	Visas	83LTS277	301895
Italy	Serb/Croat/Slovene	20 Jul 25	Consul/Citizenship	83LTS265	301893
Italy	Serb/Croat/Slovene	20 Jul 25	Land Transport	83LTS247	301890
Italy	Serb/Croat/Slovene	20 Jul 25	Consul/Citizenship	83LTS271	301894
Italy	Serb/Croat/Slovene	20 Jul 25	Telecommunications	83LTS295	301897
Italy	Serb/Croat/Slovene	16 Sep 29	Territory Boundary	101LTS127	302322
Italy	Siam	09 May 26	General Economic	61LTS215	301436
Italy	Siam	03 Dec 37	General Amity	189LTS255	304389
Italy	South Africa	19 Jul 33	Postal Service	146LTS369	303385
Italy	South Africa	21 May 35	General Trade	189LTS31	304373
Italy	Spain	15 Nov 23	General Trade	39LTS49	300996
Italy	Spain	25 Nov 25	Refugees	60LTS59	301405
Italy	Spain	07 Aug 26	General Amity	67LTS365	301558
Italy	Spain	15 Aug 27	Air Transport	94LTS361	302155
Italy	Spain	28 Nov 27	Finance	82LTS27	301857
Italy	Spain	03 Oct 28	Air Transport	94LTS387	302156
Italy	Spain	30 Jul 32	Status of Forces	149LTS9	303427
Italy	Spain	01 Oct 35	Consul/Citizenship	163LTS345	303777
Italy	Sweden	04 Jun 21	Land Transport	6LTS47	300148
Italy	Sweden	22 Feb 29	Customs	87LTS265	301973
Italy	Sweden	24 Jun 35	Finance	161LTS27	303703
Italy	Sweden	24 Jun 35	General Trade	161LTS21	303702
Italy	Sweden	01 Dec 36	Finance	173LTS279	304019
Italy	Sweden	01 Dec 36	Finance	173LTS269	304018
Italy	Sweden	01 Dec 36	General Trade	173LTS257	304017
Italy	Switzerland	12 Nov 18	Land Transport	25LTS369	300625
Italy	Switzerland	24 Sep 21	General Transport	12LTS367	300330
Italy	Switzerland	27 Jan 23	General Trade	25LTS21	300603
Italy	Switzerland	22 Oct 23	Water Transport	65LTS301	301521
Italy	Switzerland	20 Sep 24	Admin Cooperation	33LTS91	300834
Italy	Switzerland	03 Jan 33	Admin Cooperation	142LTS17	303276
Italy	Switzerland	20 Sep 34	Dispute Settlement	158LTS17	303620
Italy	Turkey	24 Jul 23	Admin Cooperation	36LTS195	300921
Italy	Turkey	30 May 28	Dispute Settlement	95LTS183	302172
Italy	Turkey	09 Sep 29	Consul/Citizenship	129LTS195	302962
Italy	Turkey	04 Jan 32	Territory Boundary	138LTS243	303191
Italy	UK Great Britain	01 Jun 21	Reparations	6LTS323	300163
Italy	UK Great Britain	11 May 22	Other Military	11LTS23	300288
Italy	UK Great Britain	14 Aug 23	Admin Cooperation	21LTS127	300534
Italy	UK Great Britain	19 May 24	Territory Boundary	28LTS497	300725
Italy	UK Great Britain	15 Jul 24	Territory Boundary	36LTS379	300936
Italy	UK Great Britain	21 May 25	Health/Educ/Welfare	43LTS75	301048
Italy	UK Great Britain	15 Jun 25	Water Transport	38LTS189	300976
Italy	UK Great Britain	20 Dec 25	Admin Cooperation	50LTS281	301211
Italy	UK Great Britain	20 Dec 25	Postal Service	49LTS79	301178

PARTY ONE	PARTY TWO	DATE	TOPIC	CITATION	NUMBER
Italy	UK Great Britain	29 Jan 26	Extradition	47LTS409	301145
Italy	UK Great Britain	24 Jun 26	Patents/Copyrights	57LTS71	301353
Italy	UK Great Britain	25 Jan 29	Admin Cooperation	95LTS39	302162
Italy	UK Great Britain	28 Aug 30	Postal Service	111LTS91	302583
Italy	UK Great Britain	02 Sep 30	Reparations	140LTS19	303225
Italy	UK Great Britain	17 Dec 30	Admin Cooperation	131LTS79	303004
Italy	UK Great Britain	24 Aug 32	Postal Service	136LTS331	303134
Italy	UK Great Britain	26 Nov 32	Admin Cooperation	136LTS385	303136
Italy	UK Great Britain	22 Nov 33	Territory Boundary	145LTS337	303359
Italy	UK Great Britain	17 Sep 34	Air Transport	155LTS85	303570
Italy	UK Great Britain	18 Mar 35	General Trade	160LTS289	303699
Italy	UK Great Britain	06 Nov 36	Finance	177LTS183	304090
Italy	UK Great Britain	06 Nov 36	Customs	177LTS169	304089
Italy	UK Great Britain	02 Jan 37	Water Transport	177LTS241	304092
Italy	UK Great Britain	14 Dec 37	Air Transport	185LTS199	304283
Italy	UK Great Britain	18 Mar 38	General Trade	187LTS139	304334
Italy	UK Great Britain	18 Mar 38	General Trade	187LTS149	304335
Italy	UK Great Britain	16 Apr 38	Peace/Disarmament	195LTS79	304537
Italy	USA (United States)	05 May 26	Taxation	113LTS21	302631
Italy	USA (United States)	19 Apr 28	Dispute Settlement	113LTS183	302645
Italy	USA (United States)	17 Aug 31	Water Transport	137LTS175	303154
Italy	USA (United States)	23 Sep 31	General Amity	134LTS191	303091
Italy	USA (United States)	14 Oct 31	Air Transport	137LTS209	303157
Italy	USA (United States)	01 Jun 32	General Transport	140LTS273	303242
Italy	USA (United States)	16 Dec 37	General Trade	187LTS15	304329
Italy	USSR (Soviet Union)	06 May 33	Customs	158LTS51	303625
Italy	USSR (Soviet Union)	02 Sep 33	General Amity	148LTS319	303418
Italy	Venezuela	23 Aug 30	Extradition	128LTS377	302943
Italy	Yemen	02 Sep 26	General Amity	67LTS383	301559
Italy	Yugoslavia	25 Apr 32	General Economic	153LTS305	303526
Italy	Yugoslavia	16 Jun 33	General Economic	153LTS317	303527
Ivory Coast	Multilateral	09 Dec 23	Water Transport	58LTS284	301379
Ivory Coast	Multilateral	25 Sep 26	ILO Labor	60LTS253	301414
Ivory Coast	Multilateral	20 Apr 29	Admin Cooperation	112LTS395	302624
Ivory Coast	Multilateral	20 Apr 29	Admin Cooperation	112LTS371	302623
Ivory Coast	Multilateral	11 Oct 33	Consul/Citizenship	150LTS431	303476
Jamaica	Haiti	07 Dec 36	Postal Service	178LTS65	304108
Jamaica	Multilateral	31 Mar 22	Humanitarian	9LTS415	300269
Jamaica	Multilateral	25 Aug 24	Water Transport	120LTS155	302764
Jamaica	Multilateral	01 Dec 24	Sanitation	78LTS351	301794
Jamaica	Multilateral	26 Sep 27	Dispute Settlement	92LTS301	302096
Jamaica	Multilateral	25 Nov 27	Telecommunications	84LTS97	301905
Jamaica	Multilateral	12 Apr 30	Admin Cooperation	179LTS115	304138
Jamaica	Multilateral	07 Jun 30	Finance	143LTS337	303315
Jamaica	Multilateral	19 Mar 31	Admin Cooperation	143LTS7	303301
Jamaica	Multilateral	23 Sep 36	Gen Communications	186LTS301	304319
Japan	Abyssinia	15 Nov 30	General Trade	133LTS135	303063
Japan	Afghanistan	19 Nov 30	General Amity	121LTS237	302789
Japan	Albania	20 Jun 30	General Trade	123LTS295	302820
Japan	Austria	02 Oct 23	General Trade	22LTS349	300563
Japan	Austria	06 Jul 28	Visas	81LTS425	301851
Japan	Austria	16 Aug 30	General Economic	126LTS351	302894
Japan	Bel-Lux Econ Union	27 Jun 25	Water Transport	36LTS95	300907
Japan	Belgium	28 Aug 34	Health/Educ/Welfare	155LTS395	303591
Japan	British Empire	30 Nov 22	Water Transport	16LTS207	300412
Japan	Canada	21 Sep 29	Taxation	96LTS143	302196
Japan	China	04 Feb 22	Dispute Settlement	10LTS309	300277
Japan	China	28 Mar 22	Reparations	13LTS213	300353
Japan	China	01 Dec 22	Territory Boundary	22LTS179	300559
Japan	China	05 Dec 22	Land Transport	22LTS293	300560
Japan	China	08 Dec 22	Postal Service	20LTS233	300520
Japan	China	08 Dec 22	Postal Service	20LTS253	300521
Japan	China	08 Dec 22	Postal Service	20LTS289	300522
Japan	China	08 Dec 22	Postal Service	20LTS205	300519
Japan	China	06 May 30	Customs	106LTS295	302452

PARTY ONE	PARTY TWO	DATE	TOPIC	CITATION	NUMBER
Japan	Cuba	21 Dec 29	Mostfavored Nation	111LTS13	302575
Japan	Czechoslovakia	30 Oct 25	General Trade	58LTS263	301377
Japan	Denmark	22 May 22	Water Transport	14LTS247	300376
Japan	Denmark	05 Jun 26	Water Transport	55LTS219	301317
Japan	Denmark	15 Oct 27	Taxation	71LTS75	301655
Japan	Denmark	23 Jul 36	Admin Cooperation	171LTS279	303964
Japan	Estonia	21 Jun 34	General Economic	150LTS423	303475
Japan	Finland	07 Jun 24	General Economic	58LTS379	301383
Japan	Finland	25 Feb 28	Visas	71LTS467	301685
Japan	France	30 Aug 27	General Economic	68LTS235	301587
Japan	Germany	12 Sep 24	Admin Cooperation	59LTS17	301387
Japan	Germany	20 Jul 27	General Trade	74LTS107	301736
Japan	Great Britain	30 Jul 25	General Economic	65LTS29	301517
Japan	Hungary	23 Jan 29	General Trade	91LTS317	302071
Japan	India	12 Jul 34	General Trade	155LTS31	303566
Japan	Latvia	04 Jul 25	General Trade	80LTS305	301836
Japan	Lithuania	02 May 30	General Economic	126LTS369	302895
Japan	Mexico	08 Oct 24	General Amity	36LTS259	300927
Japan	Multilateral	09 Sep 86*	Patents/Copyrights	123LTS233	302816
Japan	Multilateral	18 Mar 04	Humanitarian	1LTS83	300011
Japan	Multilateral	13 Nov 08	General Ad Hoc	1LTS217	300015
Japan	Multilateral	23 Jan 12	Sanitation	8LTS187	300222
Japan	Multilateral	05 Jun 12	Telecommunications	1LTS135	300013
Japan	Multilateral	20 Mar 14	Patents/Copyrights	1LTS243	300016
Japan	Multilateral	21 Apr 14	Sanitation	5LTS394	300144
Japan	Multilateral	10 Sep 19	Admin Cooperation	8LTS25	300202
Japan	Multilateral	10 Sep 19	Reparations	2LTS44	300045
Japan	Multilateral	10 Sep 19	General Economic	2LTS35	300044
Japan	Multilateral	10 Sep 19	Health/Educ/Welfare	8LTS11	300201
Japan	Multilateral	10 Sep 19	General Trade	7LTS331	300200
Japan	Multilateral	10 Sep 19	Reparations	2LTS29	300043
Japan	Multilateral	10 Sep 19	Reparations	2LTS21	300042
Japan	Multilateral	09 Dec 19	Territory Boundary	5LTS335	300140
Japan	Multilateral	09 Feb 20	Territory Boundary	2LTS7	300041
Japan	Multilateral	01 May 20	Air Transport	11LTS173	300297
Japan	Multilateral	04 Jun 20	Peace/Disarmament	6LTS187	300152
Japan	Multilateral	21 Jun 20	Health/Educ/Welfare	8LTS65	300207
Japan	Multilateral	30 Jun 20	Patents/Copyrights	1LTS59	300008
Japan	Multilateral	05 Jul 20	Dispute Settlement	2LTS241	300070
Japan	Multilateral	05 Aug 20	Territory Boundary	2LTS49	300046
Japan	Multilateral	10 Aug 20	Territory Boundary	28LTS225	300710
Japan	Multilateral	10 Aug 20	Consul/Citizenship	28LTS223	300711
Japan	Multilateral	16 Dec 20	General IGO	6LTS379	300170
Japan	Multilateral	20 Apr 21	Water Transport	7LTS73	300174
Japan	Multilateral	20 Apr 21	Land Transport	7LTS11	300171
Japan	Multilateral	05 May 21	Peace/Disarmament	12LTS419	300338
Japan	Multilateral	05 Aug 21	Admin Cooperation	27LTS349	300695
Japan	Multilateral	05 Oct 21	Admin Cooperation	29LTS73	300734
Japan	Multilateral	05 Oct 21	IGO Establishment	51LTS361	301241
Japan	Multilateral	05 Oct 21	Admin Cooperation	29LTS67	300733
Japan	Multilateral	05 Oct 21	Admin Cooperation	29LTS79	300735
Japan	Multilateral	06 Oct 21	General Economic	17LTS45	300427
Japan	Multilateral	09 Nov 21	Tзrritory Boundary	12LTS381	300333
Japan	Multilateral	13 Dec 21	Territory Boundary	25LTS184	300607
Japan	Multilateral	06 Feb 22	Admin Cooperation	25LTS195	300608
Japan	Multilateral	06 Feb 22	Peace/Disarmament	25LTS201	300609
Japan	Multilateral	06 Feb 22	General Trade	38LTS277	300982
Japan	Multilateral	06 Feb 22	Customs	38LTS267	300981
Japan	Multilateral	31 Mar 22	Humanitarian	9LTS415	300269
Japan	Multilateral	02 Nov 22	Peace/Disarmament	149LTS35	303431
Japan	Multilateral	15 Mar 23	Territory Boundary	15LTS259	300398
Japan	Multilateral	24 Jul 23	General Amity	36LTS145	300913
Japan	Multilateral	24 Jul 23	Peace/Disarmament	28LTS11	300701
Japan	Multilateral	24 Jul 23	Territory Boundary	28LTS215	300708
Japan	Multilateral	24 Jul 23	Water Transport	28LTS115	300702

PARTY ONE	PARTY TWO	DATE	TOPIC	CITATION	NUMBER
Japan	Multilateral	24 Jul 23	General Trade	28LTS171	300705
Japan	Multilateral	24 Jul 23	Territory Boundary	28LTS139	300703
Japan	Multilateral	24 Jul 23	Consul/Citizenship	28LTS221	300709
Japan	Multilateral	24 Jul 23	General Trade	28LTS151	300704
Japan	Multilateral	24 Jul 23	Admin Cooperation	28LTS197	300706
Japan	Multilateral	24 Sep 23	Dispute Settlement	27LTS157	300678
Japan	Multilateral	03 Nov 23	Customs	30LTS371	300775
Japan	Multilateral	23 Nov 23	Reparations	28LTS273	300713
Japan	Multilateral	09 Dec 23	Land Transport	47LTS55	301129
Japan	Multilateral	09 Dec 23	Water Transport	58LTS284	301379
Japan	Multilateral	31 Mar 24	Sanitation	27LTS211	300685
Japan	Multilateral	08 May 24	Territory Boundary	29LTS85	300736
Japan	Multilateral	16 Aug 24	Taxation	41LTS429	301024
Japan	Multilateral	25 Aug 24	Water Transport	120LTS155	302764
Japan	Multilateral	25 Aug 24	Water Transport	120LTS123	302763
Japan	Multilateral	28 Aug 24	Postal Service	40LTS437	301005
Japan	Multilateral	28 Aug 24	Postal Service	40LTS249	301003
Japan	Multilateral	28 Aug 24	Postal Service	40LTS19	301002
Japan	Multilateral	28 Aug 24	Postal Service	40LTS307	301004
Japan	Multilateral	30 Aug 24	Reparations	30LTS97	300762
Japan	Multilateral	30 Aug 24	Admin Cooperation	30LTS79	300761
Japan	Multilateral	30 Aug 24	Admin Cooperation	30LTS75	300760
Japan	Multilateral	11 Feb 25	Sanitation	51LTS337	301239
Japan	Multilateral	19 Feb 25	Admin Cooperation	81LTS317	301845
Japan	Multilateral	05 May 25	Finance	55LTS225	301318
Japan	Multilateral	17 Jun 25	Peace/Disarmament	94LTS65	302138
Japan	Multilateral	29 Oct 25	Telecommunications	57LTS201	301365
Japan	Multilateral	06 Nov 25	Patents/Copyrights	74LTS289	301743
Japan	Multilateral	10 Apr 26	Water Transport	120LTS187	302765
Japan	Multilateral	22 May 26	Air Transport	58LTS331	301381
Japan	Multilateral	21 Jun 26	Sanitation	78LTS229	301793
Japan	Multilateral	31 Mar 27	Air Transport	66LTS59	301525
Japan	Multilateral	19 May 27	Air Transport	68LTS407	301595
Japan	Multilateral	26 Sep 27	Dispute Settlement	92LTS301	302096
Japan	Multilateral	27 Oct 27	Air Transport	148LTS265	303417
Japan	Multilateral	08 Nov 27	General Trade	97LTS391	302238
Japan	Multilateral	25 Nov 27	Telecommunications	84LTS97	301905
Japan	Multilateral	27 Aug 28	General Military	94LTS57	302137
Japan	Multilateral	22 Nov 28	Culture	111LTS343	302598
Japan	Multilateral	14 Dec 28	General Economic	110LTS171	302560
Japan	Multilateral	20 Apr 29	Admin Cooperation	112LTS371	302623
Japan	Multilateral	31 May 29	Water Transport	136LTS81	303127
Japan	Multilateral	28 Jun 29	Postal Service	102LTS245	302368
Japan	Multilateral	28 Jun 29	Postal Service	103LTS249	302371
Japan	Multilateral	28 Jun 29	Postal Service	103LTS5	302369
Japan	Multilateral	28 Jun 29	Postal Service	103LTS321	302372
Japan	Multilateral	28 Jun 29	Postal Service	103LTS71	302370
Japan	Multilateral	27 Jul 29	Other Military	118LTS303	302733
Japan	Multilateral	27 Jul 29	Other Military	118LTS343	302734
Japan	Multilateral	14 Sep 29	UN Charter	165LTS353	303822
Japan	Multilateral	12 Oct 29	General Transport	137LTS11	303145
Japan	Multilateral	20 Jan 30	Reparations	113LTS389	302650
Japan	Multilateral	20 Jan 30	Finance	104LTS433	302397
Japan	Multilateral	20 Jan 30	Other Economic	104LTS441	302398
Japan	Multilateral	20 Jan 30	Reparations	104LTS243	302394
Japan	Multilateral	20 Jan 30	Finance	104LTS413	302395
Japan	Multilateral	12 Apr 30	Admin Cooperation	179LTS89	304137
Japan	Multilateral	12 Apr 30	Admin Cooperation	179LTS115	304138
Japan	Multilateral	22 Apr 30	Peace/Disarmament	112LTS65	302608
Japan	Multilateral	28 Apr 30	Claims and Debts	121LTS69	302785
Japan	Multilateral	07 Jun 30	Finance	143LTS317	303314
Japan	Multilateral	07 Jun 30	Finance	143LTS337	303315
Japan	Multilateral	07 Jun 30	Finance	143LTS257	303313
Japan	Multilateral	10 Jun 30	Loans and Credits	112LTS237	302618
Japan	Multilateral	01 Aug 30	Health/Educ/Welfare	128LTS9	302932

PARTY ONE	PARTY TWO	DATE	TOPIC	CITATION	NUMBER
Japan	Multilateral	19 Mar 31	Finance	143LTS407	303317
Japan	Multilateral	19 Mar 31	Admin Cooperation	143LTS7	303301
Japan	Multilateral	19 Mar 31	Finance	143LTS355	303316
Japan	Multilateral	13 Jul 31	Other HEW	139LTS301	303219
Japan	Multilateral	27 Nov 31	Sanitation	177LTS373	304100
Japan	Multilateral	09 Dec 32	Telecommunications	151LTS5	303479
Japan	Multilateral	11 Mar 33	Water Transport	135LTS301	303119
Japan	Multilateral	20 Mar 34	Postal Service	175LTS363	304052
Japan	Multilateral	20 Mar 34	Postal Service	175LTS5	304049
Japan	Multilateral	20 Mar 34	Postal Service	174LTS171	304048
Japan	Multilateral	20 Mar 34	Postal Service	175LTS73	304050
Japan	Multilateral	20 Mar 34	Postal Service	175LTS269	304051
Japan	Multilateral	02 Jun 34	Patents/Copyrights	192LTS17	304459
Japan	Multilateral	02 Jun 34	General Trade	192LTS9	304458
Japan	Multilateral	26 Jun 36	Other HEW	198LTS299	304648
Japan	Multilateral	20 Jul 36	Territory Boundary	173LTS213	304015
Japan	Multilateral	30 Jul 36	IGO Status/Immunit	197LTS31	304602
Japan	Multilateral	06 Nov 36	General Military	173LTS353	304025
Japan	Multilateral	31 Mar 37	Commodity Trade	189LTS359	304394
Japan	Multilateral	31 Oct 38	Sanitation	198LTS205	304642
Japan	Multilateral	23 Apr 39	Land Transport	104LTS87	302380
Japan	Multilateral	23 May 39	Postal Service	202LTS159	304742
Japan	Netherlands	12 Oct 21	Water Transport	12LTS239	300316
Japan	Netherlands	26 Jan 33	Taxation	138LTS185	303187
Japan	Netherlands	19 Apr 33	Dispute Settlement	163LTS351	303778
Japan	New Zealand	24 Jul 28	General Trade	85LTS129	301927
Japan	Norway	06 Nov 23	Admin Cooperation	33LTS265	300850
Japan	Norway	29 Mar 28	Visas	73LTS81	301708
Japan	Norway	23 Dec 31	Taxation	127LTS21	302902
Japan	Paraguay	30 Nov 20	General Economic	6LTS367	300169
Japan	Persia	30 Mar 29	Privil/Immunities	107LTS427	302499
Japan	Peru	30 Sep 24	General Amity	102LTS33	302351
Japan	Poland	07 Dec 22	General Trade	32LTS61	300806
Japan	Portugal	23 Mar 32	General Economic	128LTS363	302941
Japan	Romania	22 Oct 30	Mostfavored Nation	112LTS15	302602
Japan	Serb/Croat/Slovene	16 Nov 23	General Economic	42LTS99	301035
Japan	Siam	09 Mar 24	General Trade	31LTS187	300795
Japan	Siam	08 Dec 37	General Amity	188LTS375	304367
Japan	South Africa	16 Oct 30	Visas	126LTS17	302868
Japan	Spain	05 Aug 29	Mostfavored Nation	113LTS9	302629
Japan	Strait Settlements	18 Jul 24	General Transport	31LTS109	300787
Japan	Sweden	01 May 23	Admin Cooperation	17LTS391	300446
Japan	Switzerland	26 Dec 24	Dispute Settlement	43LTS393	301072
Japan	Thailand	30 Nov 39	Air Transport	200LTS197	304691
Japan	Thailand	12 Jun 40	General Amity	204LTS131	304791
Japan	Turkey	31 Jul 29	Mostfavored Nation	111LTS289	302592
Japan	UK Great Britain	12 Nov 19	Reparations	6LTS333	300164
Japan	UK Great Britain	08 Jul 20	Admin Cooperation	1LTS23	300002
Japan	UK Great Britain	21 Jan 24	Admin Cooperation	25LTS11	300601
Japan	UK Great Britain	14 Jul 24	General Economic	28LTS537	300728
Japan	UK Great Britain	28 Jul 25	Postal Service	49LTS73	301177
Japan	UK Great Britain	10 Aug 29	Taxation	95LTS73	302166
Japan	UK Great Britain	20 Aug 29	Postal Service	107LTS243	302481
Japan	UK Great Britain	25 Mar 37	Milit Installation	181LTS289	304196
Japan	UK Great Britain	22 Mar 40	Admin Cooperation	203LTS194	304760
Japan	United Arab Rep	19 Mar 30	Mostfavored Nation	111LTS223	302588
Japan	USA (United States)	11 Feb 22	Territory Boundary	12LTS201	300311
Japan	USA (United States)	23 Aug 23	Admin Cooperation	30LTS263	300770
Japan	USA (United States)	31 May 28	Customs	101LTS63	302320
Japan	USA (United States)	25 Mar 37	Specific Property	181LTS217	304191
Japan	USA (United States)	20 Jun 38	Postal Service	191LTS43	304434
Japan	USSR (Soviet Union)	20 Jan 25	General Amity	34LTS31	300866
Japan	USSR (Soviet Union)	23 Jan 28	Specific Resources	80LTS341	301839
Japan	USSR (Soviet Union)	23 Nov 31	Postal Service	132LTS133	303033
Jersey Island	Multilateral	30 Jun 20	Patents/Copyrights	1LTS59	300008

PARTY ONE	PARTY TWO	DATE	TOPIC	CITATION	NUMBER
Jordan	Multilateral	23 Jan 12	Sanitation	8LTS187	300222
Kenya	Multilateral	30 Jun 20	Patents/Copyrights	1LTS59	300008
Kenya	Multilateral	31 Mar 22	Humanitarian	9LTS415	300269
Kenya	Multilateral	25 Aug 24	Water Transport	120LTS155	302764
Kenya	Multilateral	26 Sep 27	Dispute Settlement	92LTS301	302096
Kenya	Multilateral	25 Nov 27	Telecommunications	84LTS97	301905
Kenya	Multilateral	30 Mar 31	Taxation	138LTS149	303185
Kenya	Multilateral	28 Oct 33	Refugees	159LTS199	303663
Kenya	Multilateral	30 Oct 35	Telecommunications	189LTS51	304375
Kenya	Multilateral	30 Oct 35	Postal Service	189LTS85	304376
Kenya	Multilateral	23 Sep 36	Gen Communications	186LTS301	304319
Kenya	Multilateral	10 Feb 38	Refugees	192LTS59	304461
Kenya	Multilateral	02 Jun 38	Postal Service	192LTS157	304470
Kenya	Multilateral	02 Jan 39	Postal Service	196LTS235	304587
Korea, South	Multilateral	11 Mar 33	Water Transport	135LTS301	303119
Kuwait	Multilateral	11 Mar 33	Water Transport	135LTS301	303119
Laos	Multilateral	20 Apr 21	Land Transport	7LTS11	300171
Laos	Multilateral	12 Oct 29	General Transport	137LTS11	303145
Laos	Multilateral	23 Sep 36	Gen Communications	186LTS301	304319
Latvia	Afghanistan	16 Feb 28	General Amity	78LTS99	301781
Latvia	Austria	09 Aug 24	General Economic	65LTS7	301516
Latvia	Austria	30 Jun 27	Visas	66LTS97	301526
Latvia	Austria	05 Jan 32	Extradition	133LTS59	303056
Latvia	Bel-Lux Econ Union	22 Feb 36	General Trade	171LTS147	303956
Latvia	Bel-Lux Econ Union	31 Jan 39	General Economic	195LTS401	304559
Latvia	Belgium	11 Dec 26	Extradition	63LTS299	301497
Latvia	Brazil	21 Sep 32	General Trade	137LTS61	303146
Latvia	Bulgaria	22 Jun 28	General Trade	97LTS379	302236
Latvia	Bulgaria	17 May 38	General Trade	189LTS249	304388
Latvia	China	25 Jun 36	General Amity	176LTS275	304066
Latvia	Czechoslovakia	07 Oct 22	General Trade	20LTS379	300528
Latvia	Czechoslovakia	07 Aug 24	Sanitation	38LTS123	300970
Latvia	Czechoslovakia	06 Jul 26	Extradition	62LTS229	301465
Latvia	Czechoslovakia	24 Dec 29	Visas	99LTS9	302263
Latvia	Czechoslovakia	11 Oct 33	Dispute Settlement	155LTS195	303577
Latvia	Denmark	03 Apr 24	General Trade	33LTS393	300860
Latvia	Denmark	09 Jan 29	General Trade	86LTS37	301948
Latvia	Denmark	28 Feb 30	Dispute Settlement	113LTS27	302632
Latvia	Denmark	28 Aug 30	Extradition	113LTS169	302644
Latvia	Denmark	14 Feb 35	Admin Cooperation	158LTS21	303621
Latvia	Estonia	22 Mar 20	Dispute Settlement	2LTS187	300066
Latvia	Estonia	19 Oct 20	Territory Boundary	17LTS189	300437
Latvia	Estonia	12 Jul 21	Extradition	37LTS423	300964
Latvia	Estonia	12 Jul 21	Consul/Citizenship	11LTS87	300291
Latvia	Estonia	24 Jun 22	Sanitation	38LTS57	300967
Latvia	Estonia	31 Oct 23	Water Transport	25LTS321	300621
Latvia	Estonia	01 Nov 23	Territory Boundary	61LTS315	301443
Latvia	Estonia	01 Nov 23	Claims and Debts	25LTS341	300622
Latvia	Estonia	01 Nov 23	Other Economic	25LTS354	300624
Latvia	Estonia	01 Nov 23	General Amity	23LTS81	300578
Latvia	Estonia	01 Nov 23	Territory Boundary	25LTS345	300623
Latvia	Estonia	10 Jan 24	Visas	38LTS103	300968
Latvia	Estonia	02 Apr 24	Land Transport	38LTS113	300969
Latvia	Estonia	28 Oct 25	Specific Resources	54LTS231	301286
Latvia	Estonia	11 Nov 25	Admin Cooperation	42LTS93	301034
Latvia	Estonia	02 Feb 26	Land Transport	64LTS413	301514
Latvia	Estonia	05 Feb 26	Specific Resources	64LTS361	301509
Latvia	Estonia	03 Mar 26	Humanitarian	63LTS13	301476
Latvia	Estonia	28 May 26	Taxation	159LTS291	303672
Latvia	Estonia	05 Feb 27	Customs	62LTS319	301470
Latvia	Estonia	22 Jul 27	Admin Cooperation	73LTS333	301723
Latvia	Estonia	25 Mar 28	General Economic	72LTS195	301692
Latvia	Estonia	15 May 28	Visas	74LTS281	301742
Latvia	Estonia	19 Oct 28	Admin Cooperation	97LTS359	302233
Latvia	Estonia	20 Dec 29	Telecommunications	106LTS173	302444

PARTY ONE	PARTY TWO	DATE	TOPIC	CITATION	NUMBER
Latvia	Estonia	05 Sep 30	Territory Boundary	112LTS219	302616
Latvia	Estonia	28 Feb 31	Water Transport	114LTS379	302667
Latvia	Estonia	16 May 31	Taxation	123LTS61	302805
Latvia	Estonia	03 Jun 31	Mostfavored Nation	120LTS235	302769
Latvia	Estonia	14 Nov 32	General Trade	136LTS295	303132
Latvia	Estonia	17 Feb 34	Education	150LTS299	303463
Latvia	Estonia	17 Feb 34	Taxation	159LTS299	303673
Latvia	Estonia	17 Feb 34	Sanitation	150LTS391	303472
Latvia	Estonia	17 Feb 34	General Amity	150LTS103	303457
Latvia	Estonia	10 Apr 35	Finance	159LTS103	303652
Latvia	Estonia	14 Nov 35	Admin Cooperation	166LTS83	303832
Latvia	Estonia	07 Dec 35	General Economic	169LTS119	303916
Latvia	Estonia	07 Dec 35	General Economic	169LTS101	303915
Latvia	Estonia	10 Dec 35	Territory Boundary	168LTS83	303888
Latvia	Estonia	06 Oct 36	Territory Boundary	172LTS221	303994
Latvia	Estonia	10 Feb 37	Admin Cooperation	176LTS287	304067
Latvia	Estonia	10 Feb 37	General Economic	176LTS296	304068
Latvia	Estonia	11 Jan 39	Taxation	194LTS103	304512
Latvia	Estonia	26 May 39	General Trade	198LTS99	304628
Latvia	Finland	07 Jun 24	Admin Cooperation	58LTS375	301382
Latvia	Finland	07 Jun 24	Extradition	38LTS343	300990
Latvia	Finland	23 Aug 24	General Trade	37LTS383	300962
Latvia	Finland	14 May 27	Visas	63LTS97	301482
Latvia	Finland	29 Apr 32	Water Transport	133LTS71	303057
Latvia	Finland	28 Mar 36	Finance	171LTS155	303957
Latvia	Finland	28 May 37	Postal Service	179LTS333	304161
Latvia	Finland	11 Apr 40	Finance	201LTS389	304727
Latvia	France	29 Oct 24	Extradition	93LTS265	302115
Latvia	France	30 Oct 24	General Trade	37LTS399	300963
Latvia	France	20 Jan 30	Consul/Citizenship	169LTS125	303917
Latvia	France	08 Mar 32	Claims and Debts	128LTS43	302936
Latvia	Germany	20 Apr 20	Reparations	2LTS71	300049
Latvia	Germany	15 Jul 20	Dispute Settlement	2LTS91	300052
Latvia	Germany	24 Feb 24	Admin Cooperation	41LTS231	301016
Latvia	Germany	28 Jun 26	General Economic	58LTS403	301385
Latvia	Germany	09 Jul 26	Sanitation	63LTS321	301499
Latvia	Germany	13 Apr 28	Water Transport	73LTS46	301705
Latvia	Germany	02 Jun 28	Visas	75LTS69	301752
Latvia	Germany	18 Jul 34	Extradition	154LTS69	303537
Latvia	Germany	04 Dec 35	General Trade	166LTS93	303834
Latvia	Germany	31 Oct 37	Finance	189LTS139	304382
Latvia	Germany	07 Jun 39	General Amity	198LTS105	304629
Latvia	Germany	30 Oct 39	Refugees	200LTS213	304693
Latvia	Great Britain	16 Jul 24	Extradition	37LTS369	300961
Latvia	Great Britain	13 Aug 25	Milit Assistance	56LTS177	301329
Latvia	Great Britain	16 Nov 27	Customs	71LTS185	301660
Latvia	Greece	25 Feb 27	General Trade	71LTS25	301652
Latvia	Greece	15 Jan 38	General Trade	195LTS19	304533
Latvia	Hungary	19 Nov 23	General Trade	37LTS341	300959
Latvia	Hungary	04 May 30	Admin Cooperation	101LTS449	302344
Latvia	Hungary	13 Aug 30	Dispute Settlement	117LTS395	302705
Latvia	Hungary	16 Nov 37	Finance	183LTS205	304237
Latvia	Hungary	25 Mar 38	Visas	188LTS447	304369
Latvia	Iceland	03 Nov 24	General Economic	43LTS339	301069
Latvia	Italy	25 Jul 25	General Economic	60LTS91	301407
Latvia	Italy	12 Jun 26	Visas	51LTS65	301222
Latvia	Italy	28 Apr 31	Dispute Settlement	126LTS399	302898
Latvia	Italy	11 May 32	Consul/Citizenship	150LTS9	303450
Latvia	Italy	05 Feb 37	General Trade	178LTS33	304104
Latvia	Italy	05 Feb 37	Finance	178LTS25	304103
Latvia	Japan	04 Jul 25	General Trade	80LTS305	301836
Latvia	Lithuania	28 Sep 20	Dispute Settlement	2LTS234	300068
Latvia	Lithuania	13 May 21	Territory Boundary	17LTS211	300438
Latvia	Lithuania	14 May 21	Consul/Citizenship	17LTS233	300439
Latvia	Lithuania	12 Jul 21	Extradition	25LTS311	300620

PARTY ONE	PARTY TWO	DATE	TOPIC	CITATION	NUMBER
Latvia	Lithuania	12 Jul 21	Consul/Citizenship	25LTS299	300619
Latvia	Lithuania	21 May 24	Health/Educ/Welfare	37LTS363	300960
Latvia	Lithuania	18 Oct 24	Territory Boundary	56LTS157	301327
Latvia	Lithuania	24 Nov 30	General Economic	112LTS417	302627
Latvia	Lithuania	24 Nov 30	Dispute Settlement	112LTS405	302626
Latvia	Lithuania	25 Jan 31	Admin Cooperation	118LTS157	302721
Latvia	Lithuania	25 Jan 31	Territory Boundary	118LTS143	302719
Latvia	Lithuania	25 Jan 31	Territory Boundary	118LTS175	302722
Latvia	Lithuania	25 Jan 31	Education	118LTS151	302720
Latvia	Lithuania	25 Jan 31	Education	118LTS135	302718
Latvia	Lithuania	01 Dec 33	General Economic	148LTS97	303407
Latvia	Lithuania	01 Dec 33	Visas	148LTS87	303406
Latvia	Lithuania	10 Apr 35	Finance	159LTS321	303675
Latvia	Lithuania	10 Apr 35	General Trade	159LTS305	303674
Latvia	Multilateral	23 Jan 12	Sanitation	8LTS187	300222
Latvia	Multilateral	05 Jun 12	Telecommunications	1LTS135	300013
Latvia	Multilateral	16 Dec 20	General IGO	6LTS379	300170
Latvia	Multilateral	20 Apr 21	Water Transport	7LTS73	300174
Latvia	Multilateral	20 Apr 21	Land Transport	7LTS11	300171
Latvia	Multilateral	12 Jul 21	Admin Cooperation	37LTS433	300965
Latvia	Multilateral	12 Jul 21	Postal Service	11LTS111	300293
Latvia	Multilateral	05 Aug 21	Admin Cooperation	27LTS349	300695
Latvia	Multilateral	05 Oct 21	IGO Establishment	51LTS361	301241
Latvia	Multilateral	05 Oct 21	Admin Cooperation	29LTS73	300734
Latvia	Multilateral	05 Oct 21	Admin Cooperation	29LTS67	300733
Latvia	Multilateral	05 Oct 21	Admin Cooperation	29LTS79	300735
Latvia	Multilateral	20 Oct 21	Peace/Disarmament	9LTS211	300255
Latvia	Multilateral	17 Mar 22	Dispute Settlement	11LTS167	300296
Latvia	Multilateral	31 Mar 22	Humanitarian	9LTS415	300269
Latvia	Multilateral	24 Sep 23	Dispute Settlement	27LTS157	300678
Latvia	Multilateral	03 Nov 23	Customs	30LTS371	300775
Latvia	Multilateral	09 Dec 23	Land Transport	47LTS55	301129
Latvia	Multilateral	31 Mar 24	Sanitation	27LTS211	300685
Latvia	Multilateral	25 Aug 24	Water Transport	120LTS123	302763
Latvia	Multilateral	28 Aug 24	Postal Service	40LTS249	301003
Latvia	Multilateral	28 Aug 24	Postal Service	40LTS437	301005
Latvia	Multilateral	28 Aug 24	Postal Service	40LTS19	301002
Latvia	Multilateral	28 Aug 24	Postal Service	41LTS97	301008
Latvia	Multilateral	28 Aug 24	Postal Service	41LTS55	301007
Latvia	Multilateral	28 Aug 24	Postal Service	40LTS307	301004
Latvia	Multilateral	28 Aug 24	Postal Service	41LTS9	301006
Latvia	Multilateral	23 Oct 24	Land Transport	78LTS17	301779
Latvia	Multilateral	23 Oct 24	General Transport	77LTS367	301778
Latvia	Multilateral	17 Jan 25	Dispute Settlement	38LTS357	300991
Latvia	Multilateral	19 Feb 25	Admin Cooperation	81LTS317	301845
Latvia	Multilateral	17 Jun 25	Peace/Disarmament	94LTS65	302138
Latvia	Multilateral	19 Aug 25	Customs	42LTS73	301033
Latvia	Multilateral	29 Oct 25	Land Transport	66LTS147	301529
Latvia	Multilateral	29 Oct 25	Telecommunications	57LTS201	301365
Latvia	Multilateral	31 Dec 25	Territory Boundary	79LTS167	301809
Latvia	Multilateral	10 Apr 26	Water Transport	120LTS187	302765
Latvia	Multilateral	24 Apr 26	Land Transport	108LTS123	302505
Latvia	Multilateral	12 May 26	Refugees	89LTS47	302004
Latvia	Multilateral	25 Sep 26	ILO Labor	60LTS253	301414
Latvia	Multilateral	15 Jun 27	Telecommunications	69LTS375	301619
Latvia	Multilateral	12 Jul 27	Direct Aid	135LTS247	303115
Latvia	Multilateral	10 Sep 27	Postal Service	75LTS7	301749
Latvia	Multilateral	10 Sep 27	Postal Service	75LTS39	301750
Latvia	Multilateral	08 Nov 27	General Trade	97LTS391	302238
Latvia	Multilateral	30 Jun 28	Refugees	89LTS53	302005
Latvia	Multilateral	30 Jun 28	Refugees	89LTS63	302006
Latvia	Multilateral	27 Aug 28	General Military	94LTS57	302137
Latvia	Multilateral	27 Aug 28	General Amity	89LTS369	302028
Latvia	Multilateral	26 Sep 28	Dispute Settlement	93LTS343	302123
Latvia	Multilateral	14 Dec 28	General Economic	110LTS171	302560
Latvia	Multilateral	20 Apr 29	Admin Cooperation	112LTS395	302624
Latvia	Multilateral	20 Apr 29	Admin Cooperation	112LTS371	302623
Latvia	Multilateral	08 May 29	Telecommunications	91LTS337	302074
Latvia	Multilateral	28 Jun 29	Postal Service	103LTS429	302374
Latvia	Multilateral	28 Jun 29	Postal Service	103LTS5	302369
Latvia	Multilateral	28 Jun 29	Postal Service	103LTS321	302372
Latvia	Multilateral	28 Jun 29	Postal Service	103LTS377	302373
Latvia	Multilateral	28 Jun 29	Postal Service	102LTS245	302368
Latvia	Multilateral	28 Jun 29	Postal Service	103LTS249	302371
Latvia	Multilateral	28 Jun 29	Postal Service	103LTS71	302370
Latvia	Multilateral	27 Jul 29	Other Military	118LTS343	302734
Latvia	Multilateral	27 Jul 29	Other Military	118LTS303	302733
Latvia	Multilateral	20 Aug 29	Sanitation	98LTS125	302243
Latvia	Multilateral	14 Sep 29	UN Charter	165LTS353	303822
Latvia	Multilateral	12 Oct 29	General Transport	137LTS11	303145
Latvia	Multilateral	28 Oct 29	Telecommunications	97LTS71	302219
Latvia	Multilateral	14 Jan 30	Telecommunications	99LTS343	302278
Latvia	Multilateral	25 Feb 30	Telecommunications	101LTS343	302335
Latvia	Multilateral	12 Apr 30	Admin Cooperation	179LTS89	304137
Latvia	Multilateral	12 Apr 30	Admin Cooperation	179LTS115	304138
Latvia	Multilateral	26 Jun 30	Telecommunications	133LTS9	303052
Latvia	Multilateral	23 Oct 30	Water Transport	112LTS21	302603
Latvia	Multilateral	23 Oct 30	Water Transport	125LTS95	302849
Latvia	Multilateral	30 Mar 31	Land Transport	150LTS247	303459
Latvia	Multilateral	30 Mar 31	Taxation	138LTS149	303185
Latvia	Multilateral	13 Jul 31	Other HEW	139LTS301	303219
Latvia	Multilateral	24 Sep 31	Specific Resources	155LTS349	303586
Latvia	Multilateral	02 Sep 32	Land Transport	154LTS123	303543
Latvia	Multilateral	09 Dec 32	Telecommunications	151LTS5	303479
Latvia	Multilateral	11 Mar 33	Water Transport	135LTS301	303119
Latvia	Multilateral	19 Jun 33	Gen Communications	154LTS133	303544
Latvia	Multilateral	03 Jul 33	Peace/Disarmament	147LTS67	303391
Latvia	Multilateral	11 Oct 33	Education	155LTS331	303585
Latvia	Multilateral	11 Oct 33	Consul/Citizenship	150LTS431	303476
Latvia	Multilateral	23 Nov 33	Land Transport	192LTS389	304484
Latvia	Multilateral	23 Nov 33	Land Transport	192LTS327	304483
Latvia	Multilateral	20 Mar 34	Postal Service	176LTS55	304054
Latvia	Multilateral	20 Mar 34	Postal Service	175LTS363	304052
Latvia	Multilateral	20 Mar 34	Postal Service	175LTS73	304050
Latvia	Multilateral	20 Mar 34	Postal Service	175LTS269	304051
Latvia	Multilateral	20 Mar 34	Postal Service	174LTS171	304048
Latvia	Multilateral	20 Mar 34	Finance	176LTS9	304053
Latvia	Multilateral	20 Mar 34	Postal Service	175LTS5	304049
Latvia	Multilateral	19 Jun 34	Admin Cooperation	154LTS381	303564
Latvia	Multilateral	12 Sep 34	General Amity	154LTS93	303540
Latvia	Multilateral	22 Dec 34	Visas	183LTS145	304230
Latvia	Multilateral	20 Feb 35	Sanitation	193LTS59	304487
Latvia	Multilateral	20 Feb 35	Sanitation	193LTS37	304486
Latvia	Multilateral	20 Feb 35	Sanitation	186LTS173	304310
Latvia	Multilateral	14 Nov 35	Admin Cooperation	166LTS75	303831
Latvia	Multilateral	14 Nov 35	Admin Cooperation	166LTS87	303833
Latvia	Multilateral	15 Sep 36	Scientific Project	178LTS439	304126
Latvia	Multilateral	23 Sep 36	Gen Communications	186LTS301	304319
Latvia	Multilateral	06 Nov 36	General Military	173LTS353	304025
Latvia	Multilateral	09 Apr 38	Admin Cooperation	191LTS165	304442
Latvia	Multilateral	09 Apr 38	Admin Cooperation	191LTS119	304441
Latvia	Multilateral	12 Sep 38	Culture	198LTS111	304630
Latvia	Multilateral	03 Dec 38	Education	200LTS249	304694
Latvia	Multilateral	23 May 39	Postal Service	202LTS159	304742
Latvia	Netherlands	02 Jul 24	General Trade	37LTS121	300951
Latvia	Netherlands	27 Jan 30	Extradition	117LTS343	302701
Latvia	Netherlands	15 Dec 31	Water Transport	133LTS107	303061
Latvia	Norway	14 Aug 24	General Amity	36LTS211	300924
Latvia	Norway	10 Jun 25	Water Transport	36LTS91	300906
Latvia	Norway	12 Sep 27	Extradition	71LTS303	301671

PARTY ONE	PARTY TWO	DATE	TOPIC	CITATION	NUMBER
Latvia	Norway	10 Feb 30	Visas	100LTS79	302295
Latvia	Norway	28 Jun 34	Visas	152LTS107	303488
Latvia	Persia	15 Jan 29	General Amity	162LTS299	303742
Latvia	Poland	07 Jul 22	Sanitation	37LTS317	300958
Latvia	Poland	03 Jan 24	Consul/Citizenship	42LTS451	301043
Latvia	Poland	22 Aug 27	Mostfavored Nation	115LTS121	302681
Latvia	Poland	12 Feb 29	General Economic	115LTS135	302683
Latvia	Poland	12 Feb 29	Land Transport	101LTS75	302321
Latvia	Poland	18 Aug 32	Admin Cooperation	140LTS443	303254
Latvia	Poland	20 Dec 34	Non-ILO Labor	162LTS361	303749
Latvia	Poland	16 Nov 37	Sanitation	197LTS43	304604
Latvia	Poland	05 Mar 38	Customs	192LTS283	304478
Latvia	Poland	16 Jun 38	Air Transport	196LTS105	304573
Latvia	Poland	29 Oct 38	Non-ILO Labor	195LTS169	304547
Latvia	Portugal	15 Jun 29	General Economic	98LTS447	302262
Latvia	Romania	23 Oct 30	Mostfavored Nation	118LTS33	302711
Latvia	Romania	22 Mar 38	General Trade	187LTS439	304349
Latvia	Serb/Croat/Slovene	18 Oct 29	General Economic	96LTS229	302204
Latvia	Spain	08 Mar 30	Extradition	113LTS135	302641
Latvia	Sweden	15 Nov 24	Admin Cooperation	56LTS173	301328
Latvia	Sweden	22 Dec 24	General Amity	36LTS283	300928
Latvia	Sweden	28 Mar 25	Dispute Settlement	37LTS131	300952
Latvia	Sweden	30 Mar 28	Water Transport	73LTS39	301704
Latvia	Sweden	21 Jun 28	Admin Cooperation	88LTS107	301990
Latvia	Sweden	12 Jan 29	Admin Cooperation	85LTS403	301940
Latvia	Sweden	11 Jan 30	Land Transport	109LTS193	302539
Latvia	Sweden	30 Jan 30	Extradition	110LTS139	302558
Latvia	Sweden	26 Mar 35	Finance	158LTS269	303637
Latvia	Sweden	30 Dec 36	Postal Service	174LTS147	304045
Latvia	Sweden	15 Apr 39	General Trade	196LTS373	304597
Latvia	Switzerland	04 Dec 24	General Trade	34LTS405	300889
Latvia	Turkey	03 Jan 25	General Amity	59LTS81	301390
Latvia	Turkey	28 May 28	General Economic	94LTS295	302150
Latvia	Turkey	12 Jan 38	General Trade	201LTS229	304716
Latvia	UK Great Britain	17 Oct 22	Finance	16LTS397	300419
Latvia	UK Great Britain	22 Jun 23	General Trade	20LTS395	300529
Latvia	UK Great Britain	24 Jun 27	Water Transport	67LTS245	301552
Latvia	UK Great Britain	24 Jul 30	Admin Cooperation	107LTS301	302486
Latvia	UK Great Britain	06 Jul 33	General Trade	142LTS217	303294
Latvia	UK Great Britain	17 Jul 34	General Trade	154LTS25	303536
Latvia	UK Great Britain	23 Aug 39	Admin Cooperation	201LTS37	304702
Latvia	Ukrainian SSR	03 Aug 21	Refugees	17LTS295	300441
Latvia	Ukrainian SSR	03 Aug 21	Refugees	17LTS317	300442
Latvia	USA (United States)	14 Oct 22	Postal Service	38LTS331	300989
Latvia	USA (United States)	16 Oct 23	Extradition	27LTS371	300698
Latvia	USA (United States)	01 Feb 26	General Economic	55LTS33	301302
Latvia	USA (United States)	20 Apr 28	General Amity	80LTS35	301821
Latvia	USA (United States)	14 Jan 30	Dispute Settlement	105LTS301	302422
Latvia	USA (United States)	14 Jan 30	Dispute Settlement	105LTS307	302423
Latvia	USA (United States)	10 Oct 34	Extradition	158LTS263	303636
Latvia	USSR (Soviet Union)	11 Aug 20	Peace/Disarmament	2LTS195	300067
Latvia	USSR (Soviet Union)	20 Oct 21	Dispute Settlement	54LTS155	301283
Latvia	USSR (Soviet Union)	06 Nov 21	Refugees	17LTS251	300440
Latvia	USSR (Soviet Union)	24 Jun 22	Sanitation	38LTS9	300966
Latvia	USSR (Soviet Union)	19 Mar 25	Water Transport	38LTS141	300971
Latvia	USSR (Soviet Union)	02 Jun 27	General Economic	68LTS321	301591
Latvia	USSR (Soviet Union)	10 Oct 27	Dispute Settlement	84LTS47	301903
Latvia	USSR (Soviet Union)	05 Feb 32	General Amity	148LTS113	303408
Latvia	USSR (Soviet Union)	18 Jun 32	Dispute Settlement	148LTS129	303409
Latvia	USSR (Soviet Union)	04 Dec 33	General Economic	148LTS177	303411
Latvia	USSR (Soviet Union)	04 Dec 33	General Trade	148LTS145	303410
Latvia	USSR (Soviet Union)	21 Jun 37	General Economic	189LTS131	304381
Latvia	USSR (Soviet Union)	05 Oct 39	General Military	198LTS381	304656
Latvia	Vatican/Holy See	30 May 22	General Amity	17LTS365	300443
Latvia	Vatican/Holy See	25 Jan 38	Education	186LTS319	304320

PARTY ONE	PARTY TWO	DATE	TOPIC	CITATION	NUMBER
Lebanon	Multilateral	09 Sep 86*	Patents/Copyrights	123LTS233	302816
Lebanon	Multilateral	03 Nov 23	Customs	30LTS371	300775
Lebanon	Multilateral	09 Jun 25	Customs	49LTS9	301174
Lebanon	Multilateral	29 Oct 25	Telecommunications	57LTS201	301365
Lebanon	Multilateral	25 Sep 26	ILO Labor	60LTS253	301414
Lebanon	Multilateral	25 Nov 27	Telecommunications	84LTS97	301905
Lebanon	Multilateral	09 Dec 32	Telecommunications	151LTS5	303479
Lebanon	Multilateral	12 Apr 33	Sanitation	161LTS65	303706
Lebanon	Multilateral	19 Jun 33	Gen Communications	154LTS133	303544
Lebanon	Multilateral	02 Jun 34	Patents/Copyrights	192LTS17	304459
Lebanon	Multilateral	02 Jun 34	General Trade	192LTS9	304458
Leeward Islands	Multilateral	09 Sep 86*	Patents/Copyrights	123LTS233	302816
Leeward Islands	Multilateral	30 Jun 20	Patents/Copyrights	1LTS59	300008
Leeward Islands	Multilateral	31 Mar 22	Humanitarian	9LTS415	300269
Leeward Islands	Multilateral	25 Aug 24	Water Transport	120LTS155	302764
Leeward Islands	Multilateral	01 Dec 24	Sanitation	78LTS351	301794
Leeward Islands	Multilateral	25 Nov 27	Telecommunications	84LTS97	301905
Leeward Islands	Multilateral	28 Oct 33	Refugees	159LTS199	303663
Leeward Islands	Multilateral	23 Sep 36	Gen Communications	186LTS301	304319
Leeward Islands	Multilateral	10 Feb 38	Refugees	192LTS59	304461
Levant	Multilateral	20 Mar 34	Postal Service	175LTS269	304051
Levant	Multilateral	20 Mar 34	Postal Service	175LTS73	304050
Levant	Multilateral	20 Mar 34	Postal Service	175LTS5	304049
Levant	Multilateral	23 May 39	Postal Service	202LTS159	304742
Liberia	Monaco	28 Oct 26	Extradition	68LTS241	301588
Liberia	Multilateral	13 Nov 08	General Ad Hoc	1LTS217	300015
Liberia	Multilateral	20 Mar 14	Patents/Copyrights	1LTS243	300016
Liberia	Multilateral	01 May 20	Air Transport	11LTS173	300297
Liberia	Multilateral	16 Dec 20	General IGO	6LTS379	300170
Liberia	Multilateral	05 Aug 21	Admin Cooperation	27LTS349	300695
Liberia	Multilateral	05 Oct 21	Admin Cooperation	29LTS79	300735
Liberia	Multilateral	05 Oct 21	Admin Cooperation	29LTS73	300734
Liberia	Multilateral	05 Oct 21	IGO Establishment	51LTS361	301241
Liberia	Multilateral	05 Oct 21	Admin Cooperation	29LTS67	300733
Liberia	Multilateral	28 Aug 24	Postal Service	40LTS307	301004
Liberia	Multilateral	28 Aug 24	Postal Service	40LTS437	301005
Liberia	Multilateral	28 Aug 24	Postal Service	40LTS19	301002
Liberia	Multilateral	28 Aug 24	Postal Service	40LTS249	301003
Liberia	Multilateral	17 Jun 25	Peace/Disarmament	94LTS65	302138
Liberia	Multilateral	21 Jun 26	Sanitation	78LTS229	301793
Liberia	Multilateral	25 Sep 26	ILO Labor	60LTS253	301414
Liberia	Multilateral	25 Nov 27	Telecommunications	84LTS97	301905
Liberia	Multilateral	27 Aug 28	General Military	94LTS57	302137
Liberia	Multilateral	31 May 29	Water Transport	136LTS81	303127
Liberia	Multilateral	28 Jun 29	Postal Service	103LTS5	302369
Liberia	Multilateral	28 Jun 29	Postal Service	103LTS249	302371
Liberia	Multilateral	28 Jun 29	Postal Service	103LTS71	302370
Liberia	Multilateral	28 Jun 29	Postal Service	102LTS245	302368
Liberia	Multilateral	14 Sep 29	UN Charter	165LTS353	303822
Liberia	Multilateral	13 Jul 31	Other HEW	139LTS301	303219
Liberia	Multilateral	09 Dec 32	Telecommunications	151LTS5	303479
Liberia	Multilateral	11 Mar 33	Water Transport	135LTS301	303119
Liberia	Multilateral	12 Apr 33	Sanitation	161LTS65	303706
Liberia	Multilateral	20 Mar 34	Postal Service	176LTS55	304054
Liberia	Multilateral	20 Mar 34	Postal Service	175LTS269	304051
Liberia	Multilateral	20 Mar 34	Postal Service	175LTS73	304050
Liberia	Multilateral	23 May 39	Postal Service	202LTS159	304742
Liberia	UK Great Britain	10 Apr 13	Water Transport	1LTS205	300014
Liberia	UK Great Britain	25 Jun 17	General Ad Hoc	5LTS39	300115
Liberia	UK Great Britain	17 Jan 30	Territory Boundary	101LTS395	302338
Liberia	USA (United States)	10 Feb 26	Dispute Settlement	56LTS279	301336
Liberia	USA (United States)	01 Nov 37	Extradition	201LTS151	304710
Liberia	USA (United States)	08 Aug 38	General Amity	201LTS163	304711
Liberia	USA (United States)	07 Oct 38	Consul/Citizenship	201LTS183	304712
Liberia	USA (United States)	14 Jun 39	Air Transport	202LTS93	304737

PARTY ONE	PARTY TWO	DATE	TOPIC	CITATION	NUMBER
Liberia	USA (United States)	21 Aug 39	Dispute Settlement	204LTS165	304795
Libya	Multilateral	06 Nov 25	Patents/Copyrights	74LTS289	301743
Libya	Multilateral	06 Nov 25	Patents/Copyrights	74LTS327	301745
Liechtenstein	Belgium	05 Aug 36	Extradition	185LTS33	304302
Liechtenstein	Multilateral	09 Sep 86*	Patents/Copyrights	123LTS233	302816
Liechtenstein	Multilateral	13 Nov 08	General Ad Hoc	1LTS217	300015
Liechtenstein	Multilateral	23 Jan 12	Sanitation	8LTS187	300222
Liechtenstein	Multilateral	16 Dec 20	General IGO	6LTS379	300170
Liechtenstein	Multilateral	24 Sep 23	Dispute Settlement	27LTS157	300678
Liechtenstein	Multilateral	06 Nov 25	Patents/Copyrights	74LTS289	301743
Liechtenstein	Multilateral	06 Nov 25	Patents/Copyrights	74LTS327	301745
Liechtenstein	Multilateral	06 Nov 25	Other Economic	74LTS319	301744
Liechtenstein	Multilateral	06 Nov 25	Other Economic	74LTS341	301746
Liechtenstein	Multilateral	12 Oct 29	General Transport	137LTS11	303145
Liechtenstein	Multilateral	02 Sep 32	Land Transport	154LTS123	303543
Liechtenstein	Multilateral	23 Nov 33	Land Transport	192LTS389	304484
Liechtenstein	Multilateral	23 Nov 33	Land Transport	192LTS327	304483
Liechtenstein	Multilateral	02 Jun 34	General Trade	192LTS9	304458
Liechtenstein	Multilateral	02 Jun 34	Patents/Copyrights	192LTS17	304459
Liechtenstein	Multilateral	02 Jun 42	Patents/Copyrights	205LTS163	304833
Liechtenstein	Switzerland	10 Nov 20	Postal Service	2LTS305	300084
Liechtenstein	Switzerland	29 Mar 23	Customs	21LTS231	300545
Liechtenstein	USA (United States)	20 May 36	Extradition	183LTS181	304235
Lithuania	Afghanistan	09 Dec 30	General Amity	138LTS29	303178
Lithuania	Argentina	20 Oct 32	Non-ILO Labor	154LTS113	303542
Lithuania	Belgium	17 May 27	Extradition	77LTS123	301767
Lithuania	Belgium	24 Sep 30	Dispute Settlement	129LTS399	302974
Lithuania	Belgium	12 Dec 30	Admin Cooperation	135LTS231	303114
Lithuania	Belgium	21 Jul 31	Patents/Copyrights	137LTS225	303158
Lithuania	Belgium	16 Jun 32	Extradition	137LTS439	303173
Lithuania	Belgium	20 Sep 34	Water Transport	153LTS289	303524
Lithuania	Brazil	28 Sep 37	General Trade	186LTS403	304324
Lithuania	Czechoslovakia	08 Mar 30	Dispute Settlement	115LTS61	302677
Lithuania	Czechoslovakia	24 Apr 31	Admin Cooperation	126LTS279	302890
Lithuania	Czechoslovakia	24 Apr 31	Extradition	126LTS261	302889
Lithuania	Denmark	18 Jul 23	General Trade	20LTS197	300518
Lithuania	Denmark	11 Dec 26	Dispute Settlement	67LTS333	301555
Lithuania	Denmark	21 Jun 30	General Economic	114LTS151	302662
Lithuania	Denmark	17 Jan 34	Patents/Copyrights	149LTS43	303432
Lithuania	Denmark	20 Dec 34	Admin Cooperation	155LTS237	303579
Lithuania	Denmark	20 Dec 34	Admin Cooperation	162LTS347	303748
Lithuania	Estonia	12 Jul 21	Extradition	43LTS179	301054
Lithuania	Estonia	12 Jul 21	Consul/Citizenship	11LTS99	300292
Lithuania	Estonia	21 May 24	General Transport	62LTS55	301454
Lithuania	Estonia	15 Jan 31	General Economic	114LTS141	302661
Lithuania	Estonia	17 May 33	General Trade	141LTS29	303258
Lithuania	Estonia	13 Jan 34	General Economic	148LTS337	303420
Lithuania	Estonia	10 Dec 35	Patents/Copyrights	168LTS101	303889
Lithuania	Estonia	03 Dec 38	Taxation	193LTS217	304498
Lithuania	Finland	06 Oct 28	General Trade	82LTS71	301861
Lithuania	Finland	19 Jun 34	Patents/Copyrights	153LTS49	303506
Lithuania	Finland	12 Apr 38	Finance	194LTS9	304501
Lithuania	Germany	31 May 23	Reparations	51LTS381	301243
Lithuania	Germany	01 Jun 23	General Economic	51LTS387	301244
Lithuania	Germany	10 Feb 25	Admin Cooperation	42LTS17	301029
Lithuania	Germany	16 Jul 25	General Trade	85LTS357	301939
Lithuania	Germany	29 Jan 28	Specific Resources	89LTS309	302026
Lithuania	Germany	29 Jan 28	Territory Boundary	89LTS338	302027
Lithuania	Germany	29 Jan 28	Dispute Settlement	90LTS233	302042
Lithuania	Germany	29 Jan 28	Territory Boundary	89LTS97	302009
Lithuania	Germany	29 Jan 28	Non-ILO Labor	89LTS83	302008
Lithuania	Germany	30 Oct 28	General Economic	89LTS127	302010
Lithuania	Germany	30 Oct 28	Admin Cooperation	91LTS365	302077
Lithuania	Germany	30 Oct 28	Consul/Citizenship	90LTS255	302043
Lithuania	Germany	26 Jan 29	Non-ILO Labor	89LTS181	302012

PARTY ONE	PARTY TWO	DATE	TOPIC	CITATION	NUMBER
Lithuania	Germany	09 Nov 31	Non-ILO Labor	133LTS379	303075
Lithuania	Germany	20 Nov 31	Sanitation	133LTS391	303077
Lithuania	Germany	19 Mar 31	Privil/Immunities	125LTS265	302860
Lithuania	Great Britain	18 Aug 25	Postal Service	43LTS135	301051
Lithuania	Greece	01 Dec 37	General Trade	193LTS185	304495
Lithuania	Hungary	23 Oct 28	General Trade	84LTS281	301908
Lithuania	Hungary	16 May 29	General Economic	96LTS333	302211
Lithuania	Hungary	12 Nov 37	Finance	183LTS197	304236
Lithuania	Iceland	18 Jul 23	General Trade	20LTS329	300523
Lithuania	Iceland	21 Jun 30	General Economic	119LTS403	302759
Lithuania	Italy	17 Sep 27	General Trade	73LTS9	301701
Lithuania	Italy	17 Sep 27	Dispute Settlement	72LTS439	301700
Lithuania	Japan	02 May 30	General Economic	126LTS369	302895
Lithuania	Latvia	28 Sep 20	Dispute Settlement	2LTS234	300068
Lithuania	Latvia	13 May 21	Territory Boundary	17LTS211	300438
Lithuania	Latvia	14 May 21	Consul/Citizenship	17LTS233	300439
Lithuania	Latvia	12 Jul 21	Consul/Citizenship	25LTS299	300619
Lithuania	Latvia	12 Jul 21	Extradition	25LTS311	300620
Lithuania	Latvia	21 May 24	Health/Educ/Welfare	37LTS363	300960
Lithuania	Latvia	18 Oct 24	Territory Boundary	56LTS157	301327
Lithuania	Latvia	24 Nov 30	General Economic	112LTS417	302627
Lithuania	Latvia	24 Nov 30	Dispute Settlement	112LTS405	302626
Lithuania	Latvia	25 Jan 31	Territory Boundary	118LTS175	302722
Lithuania	Latvia	25 Jan 31	Education	118LTS151	302720
Lithuania	Latvia	25 Jan 31	Territory Boundary	118LTS143	302719
Lithuania	Latvia	25 Jan 31	Admin Cooperation	118LTS157	302721
Lithuania	Latvia	25 Jan 31	Education	118LTS135	302718
Lithuania	Latvia	01 Dec 33	General Economic	148LTS97	303407
Lithuania	Latvia	01 Dec 33	Visas	148LTS87	303406
Lithuania	Latvia	10 Apr 35	Finance	159LTS321	303675
Lithuania	Latvia	10 Apr 35	General Trade	159LTS305	303674
Lithuania	Multilateral	23 Jan 12	Sanitation	8LTS187	300222
Lithuania	Multilateral	05 Jun 12	Telecommunications	1LTS135	300013
Lithuania	Multilateral	16 Dec 20	General IGO	6LTS379	300170
Lithuania	Multilateral	20 Apr 21	Water Transport	7LTS73	300174
Lithuania	Multilateral	20 Apr 21	Water Transport	7LTS35	300172
Lithuania	Multilateral	20 Apr 21	Land Transport	7LTS11	300171
Lithuania	Multilateral	12 Jul 21	Admin Cooperation	37LTS433	300965
Lithuania	Multilateral	12 Jul 21	Postal Service	11LTS111	300293
Lithuania	Multilateral	05 Aug 21	Admin Cooperation	27LTS349	300695
Lithuania	Multilateral	05 Oct 21	IGO Establishment	51LTS361	301241
Lithuania	Multilateral	05 Oct 21	Admin Cooperation	29LTS79	300735
Lithuania	Multilateral	05 Oct 21	Admin Cooperation	29LTS73	300734
Lithuania	Multilateral	05 Oct 21	Admin Cooperation	29LTS67	300733
Lithuania	Multilateral	31 Mar 22	Humanitarian	9LTS415	300269
Lithuania	Multilateral	05 Jul 22	Reparations	13LTS237	300355
Lithuania	Multilateral	24 Sep 23	Dispute Settlement	27LTS157	300678
Lithuania	Multilateral	03 Nov 23	Customs	30LTS371	300775
Lithuania	Multilateral	09 Dec 23	Land Transport	47LTS55	301129
Lithuania	Multilateral	09 Dec 23	Water Transport	58LTS284	301379
Lithuania	Multilateral	09 Dec 23	General Economic	58LTS315	301380
Lithuania	Multilateral	09 Dec 23	Non-IBRD Project	36LTS76	300905
Lithuania	Multilateral	31 Mar 24	Sanitation	27LTS211	300685
Lithuania	Multilateral	08 May 24	Territory Boundary	29LTS85	300736
Lithuania	Multilateral	28 Aug 24	Postal Service	40LTS19	301002
Lithuania	Multilateral	28 Aug 24	Postal Service	40LTS307	301004
Lithuania	Multilateral	28 Aug 24	Postal Service	40LTS437	301005
Lithuania	Multilateral	28 Aug 24	Postal Service	41LTS9	301006
Lithuania	Multilateral	28 Aug 24	Postal Service	41LTS55	301007
Lithuania	Multilateral	28 Aug 24	Postal Service	40LTS249	301003
Lithuania	Multilateral	23 Oct 24	General Transport	77LTS367	301778
Lithuania	Multilateral	23 Oct 24	Land Transport	78LTS17	301779
Lithuania	Multilateral	19 Feb 25	Admin Cooperation	81LTS317	301845
Lithuania	Multilateral	17 Jun 25	Peace/Disarmament	94LTS65	302138
Lithuania	Multilateral	19 Aug 25	Customs	42LTS73	301033

PARTY ONE	PARTY TWO	DATE	TOPIC	CITATION	NUMBER
Lithuania	Multilateral	29 Oct 25	Telecommunications	57LTS201	301365
Lithuania	Multilateral	31 Dec 25	Territory Boundary	79LTS167	301809
Lithuania	Multilateral	24 Apr 26	Land Transport	108LTS123	302505
Lithuania	Multilateral	21 Jun 26	Sanitation	78LTS229	301793
Lithuania	Multilateral	25 Sep 26	ILO Labor	60LTS253	301414
Lithuania	Multilateral	27 Aug 28	General Military	94LTS57	302137
Lithuania	Multilateral	14 Dec 28	General Economic	110LTS171	302560
Lithuania	Multilateral	05 Jan 29	Telecommunications	132LTS425	303051
Lithuania	Multilateral	28 Jun 29	Postal Service	103LTS429	302374
Lithuania	Multilateral	28 Jun 29	Postal Service	103LTS321	302372
Lithuania	Multilateral	28 Jun 29	Postal Service	103LTS5	302369
Lithuania	Multilateral	28 Jun 29	Postal Service	103LTS71	302370
Lithuania	Multilateral	28 Jun 29	Postal Service	103LTS377	302373
Lithuania	Multilateral	28 Jun 29	Postal Service	103LTS249	302371
Lithuania	Multilateral	28 Jun 29	Postal Service	102LTS245	302368
Lithuania	Multilateral	27 Jul 29	Other Military	118LTS343	302734
Lithuania	Multilateral	27 Jul 29	Other Military	118LTS303	302733
Lithuania	Multilateral	14 Sep 29	UN Charter	165LTS353	303822
Lithuania	Multilateral	14 Jan 30	Telecommunications	99LTS343	302278
Lithuania	Multilateral	26 Jun 30	Telecommunications	133LTS9	303052
Lithuania	Multilateral	13 Jul 31	Other HEW	139LTS301	303219
Lithuania	Multilateral	09 Dec 32	Telecommunications	151LTS5	303479
Lithuania	Multilateral	29 May 33	Admin Cooperation	192LTS289	304479
Lithuania	Multilateral	11 Oct 33	Consul/Citizenship	150LTS431	303476
Lithuania	Multilateral	12 Sep 34	General Amity	154LTS93	303540
Lithuania	Multilateral	22 Dec 34	Visas	183LTS145	304230
Lithuania	Multilateral	14 Nov 35	Admin Cooperation	166LTS87	303833
Lithuania	Multilateral	14 Nov 35	Admin Cooperation	166LTS75	303831
Lithuania	Multilateral	15 Sep 36	Scientific Project	178LTS439	304126
Lithuania	Multilateral	23 Sep 36	Gen Communications	186LTS301	304319
Lithuania	Multilateral	06 Nov 36	General Military	173LTS353	304025
Lithuania	Multilateral	09 Apr 38	Admin Cooperation	191LTS165	304442
Lithuania	Multilateral	09 Apr 38	Admin Cooperation	191LTS119	304441
Lithuania	Multilateral	03 Dec 38	Education	200LTS249	304694
Lithuania	Multilateral	23 May 39	Postal Service	202LTS159	304742
Lithuania	Netherlands	10 Jun 24	General Trade	34LTS373	300885
Lithuania	Netherlands	01 Dec 33	Extradition	150LTS337	303466
Lithuania	Norway	21 Dec 23	General Trade	32LTS55	300805
Lithuania	Norway	14 Nov 30	Land Transport	109LTS187	302538
Lithuania	Other Unilat Decla	12 May 22	Admin Cooperation	22LTS393	300569
Lithuania	Persia	13 Jan 30	General Amity	131LTS221	303013
Lithuania	Poland	07 Oct 20	Territory Boundary	8LTS173	300221
Lithuania	Poland	29 Nov 20	Peace/Disarmament	9LTS63	300243
Lithuania	Poland	07 Nov 28	Visas	89LTS171	302011
Lithuania	Poland	14 May 38	Water Transport	191LTS373	304456
Lithuania	Poland	22 May 38	Postal Service	191LTS359	304455
Lithuania	Poland	25 May 38	Land Transport	191LTS391	304457
Lithuania	Poland	23 Jul 38	Land Transport	192LTS83	304462
Lithuania	Portugal	12 Apr 32	General Trade	129LTS135	302958
Lithuania	Spain	07 Sep 35	Visas	163LTS321	303774
Lithuania	Sweden	17 Feb 24	General Trade	23LTS153	300587
Lithuania	Sweden	11 Jun 25	Dispute Settlement	57LTS191	301364
Lithuania	Sweden	04 Jan 29	Admin Cooperation	92LTS191	302086
Lithuania	Sweden	16 Oct 31	Patents/Copyrights	126LTS233	302885
Lithuania	Sweden	01 Jul 37	Customs	179LTS251	304152
Lithuania	Sweden	17 May 38	Postal Service	192LTS237	304474
Lithuania	Turkey	17 Sep 30	General Amity	125LTS249	302858
Lithuania	UK Great Britain	06 May 22	General Economic	13LTS25	300343
Lithuania	UK Great Britain	18 May 26	Extradition	61LTS401	301450
Lithuania	UK Great Britain	10 Dec 29	General Economic	99LTS47	302266
Lithuania	UK Great Britain	24 Apr 34	Admin Cooperation	169LTS373	303925
Lithuania	UK Great Britain	06 Jul 34	General Trade	155LTS9	303565
Lithuania	USA (United States)	09 Apr 24	Extradition	51LTS191	301226
Lithuania	USA (United States)	23 Dec 25	Customs	54LTS377	301300
Lithuania	USA (United States)	14 Nov 28	Dispute Settlement	100LTS117	302298

PARTY ONE	PARTY TWO	DATE	TOPIC	CITATION	NUMBER
Lithuania	USA (United States)	14 Nov 28	Dispute Settlement	100LTS111	302297
Lithuania	USA (United States)	17 May 34	Extradition	157LTS441	303618
Lithuania	USA (United States)	28 Jun 34	Postal Service	153LTS295	303525
Lithuania	USA (United States)	18 Oct 37	Milit Servic/Citiz	191LTS351	304454
Lithuania	USA (United States)	28 Dec 39	Postal Service	202LTS381	304743
Lithuania	USSR (Soviet Union)	12 Jul 20	Peace/Disarmament	3LTS106	300094
Lithuania	USSR (Soviet Union)	28 Sep 26	Peace/Disarmament	60LTS145	301410
Lithuania	USSR (Soviet Union)	17 Sep 30	General Amity	125LTS255	302859
Lithuania	USSR (Soviet Union)	05 Jul 33	Peace/Disarmament	148LTS79	303405
Lithuania	USSR (Soviet Union)	04 Apr 34	Peace/Disarmament	186LTS267	304315
Luxembourg	Austria	30 Jan 30	Admin Cooperation	99LTS357	302279
Luxembourg	Austria	07 Mar 30	Visas	101LTS237	302325
Luxembourg	Belgium	25 Jul 21	General Economic	9LTS223	300256
Luxembourg	Belgium	27 Dec 21	Telecommunications	12LTS253	300318
Luxembourg	Belgium	17 Jul 23	Humanitarian	27LTS235	300686
Luxembourg	Belgium	24 Aug 26	Extradition	61LTS311	301442
Luxembourg	Belgium	20 Oct 26	Non-ILO Labor	78LTS375	301796
Luxembourg	Belgium	17 Oct 27	Dispute Settlement	124LTS203	302834
Luxembourg	Belgium	13 Apr 28	Admin Cooperation	72LTS237	301695
Luxembourg	Belgium	26 Apr 28	Admin Cooperation	93LTS159	302107
Luxembourg	Belgium	18 May 28	Postal Service	89LTS207	302015
Luxembourg	Belgium	18 May 28	Postal Service	89LTS213	302016
Luxembourg	Belgium	18 May 29	Customs	119LTS377	302757
Luxembourg	Belgium	09 Mar 31	Taxation	137LTS267	303161
Luxembourg	Belgium	31 May 33	Consul/Citizenship	141LTS9	303256
Luxembourg	Belgium	23 May 35	General Trade	161LTS335	303722
Luxembourg	Belgium	23 May 35	Direct Aid	161LTS327	303721
Luxembourg	Belgium	23 May 35	Taxation	161LTS347	303723
Luxembourg	Belgium	22 Jul 38	Territory Boundary	191LTS113	304440
Luxembourg	Belgium	04 Mar 39	Admin Cooperation	197LTS141	304610
Luxembourg	Czechoslovakia	18 Sep 29	Dispute Settlement	107LTS49	302467
Luxembourg	Czechoslovakia	01 Dec 34	Extradition	168LTS287	303906
Luxembourg	Denmark	23 Feb 32	Admin Cooperation	127LTS211	302920
Luxembourg	France	16 Jan 26	Taxation	48LTS149	301156
Luxembourg	France	20 Oct 27	Dispute Settlement	106LTS457	302462
Luxembourg	France	21 Feb 29	Extradition	123LTS387	302825
Luxembourg	France	31 Mar 30	Privil/Immunities	122LTS29	302797
Luxembourg	France	30 Jul 37	Admin Cooperation	181LTS107	304181
Luxembourg	Germany	28 Jun 28	Refugees	90LTS183	302036
Luxembourg	Germany	11 Sep 29	Dispute Settlement	118LTS97	302715
Luxembourg	Greece	01 Sep 37	Extradition	193LTS151	304491
Luxembourg	Italy	15 Apr 32	Dispute Settlement	142LTS119	303284
Luxembourg	Multilateral	09 Sep 86*	Patents/Copyrights	123LTS233	302816
Luxembourg	Multilateral	18 Mar 04	Humanitarian	1LTS83	300011
Luxembourg	Multilateral	13 Nov 08	General Ad Hoc	1LTS217	300015
Luxembourg	Multilateral	12 Jan 12	Sanitation	4LTS281	300112
Luxembourg	Multilateral	23 Jan 12	Sanitation	8LTS187	300222
Luxembourg	Multilateral	20 Mar 14	Patents/Copyrights	1LTS243	300016
Luxembourg	Multilateral	21 Jun 20	Health/Educ/Welfare	8LTS65	300207
Luxembourg	Multilateral	30 Jun 20	Patents/Copyrights	1LTS59	300008
Luxembourg	Multilateral	16 Dec 20	General IGO	6LTS379	300170
Luxembourg	Multilateral	20 Apr 21	Water Transport	7LTS35	300172
Luxembourg	Multilateral	20 Apr 21	Land Transport	7LTS11	300171
Luxembourg	Multilateral	31 Mar 22	Humanitarian	9LTS415	300269
Luxembourg	Multilateral	30 Dec 22	General Trade	21LTS183	300542
Luxembourg	Multilateral	24 Sep 23	Dispute Settlement	27LTS157	300678
Luxembourg	Multilateral	03 Nov 23	Customs	30LTS371	300775
Luxembourg	Multilateral	28 Nov 23	Admin Cooperation	51LTS215	301229
Luxembourg	Multilateral	28 Nov 23	Admin Cooperation	51LTS209	301228
Luxembourg	Multilateral	28 Nov 23	Admin Cooperation	51LTS221	301230
Luxembourg	Multilateral	14 Dec 23	General Trade	29LTS37	300732
Luxembourg	Multilateral	25 Jan 24	Sanitation	57LTS135	301360
Luxembourg	Multilateral	12 Mar 24	General Trade	24LTS17	300595
Luxembourg	Multilateral	31 Mar 24	Sanitation	27LTS211	300685
Luxembourg	Multilateral	04 Jul 24	Admin Cooperation	51LTS227	301231

PARTY ONE	PARTY TWO	DATE	TOPIC	CITATION	NUMBER
Luxembourg	Multilateral	28 Aug 24	Postal Service	40LTS249	301003
Luxembourg	Multilateral	28 Aug 24	Postal Service	40LTS19	301002
Luxembourg	Multilateral	28 Aug 24	Postal Service	41LTS97	301008
Luxembourg	Multilateral	28 Aug 24	Postal Service	40LTS307	301004
Luxembourg	Multilateral	28 Aug 24	Postal Service	40LTS437	301005
Luxembourg	Multilateral	28 Aug 24	Postal Service	41LTS55	301007
Luxembourg	Multilateral	28 Aug 24	Postal Service	41LTS9	301006
Luxembourg	Multilateral	30 Sep 24	Mostfavored Nation	30LTS135	300766
Luxembourg	Multilateral	23 Oct 24	Land Transport	78LTS17	301779
Luxembourg	Multilateral	23 Oct 24	General Transport	77LTS367	301778
Luxembourg	Multilateral	29 Nov 24	General IGO	80LTS293	301835
Luxembourg	Multilateral	12 Dec 24	Gen Communications	37LTS113	300950
Luxembourg	Multilateral	19 Feb 25	Admin Cooperation	81LTS317	301845
Luxembourg	Multilateral	17 Jun 25	Peace/Disarmament	94LTS65	302138
Luxembourg	Multilateral	29 Oct 25	Telecommunications	57LTS201	301365
Luxembourg	Multilateral	24 Apr 26	Land Transport	97LTS83	302220
Luxembourg	Multilateral	24 Apr 26	Land Transport	108LTS123	302505
Luxembourg	Multilateral	12 May 26	Refugees	89LTS47	302004
Luxembourg	Multilateral	21 Jun 26	Sanitation	78LTS229	301793
Luxembourg	Multilateral	18 Mar 27	Telecommunications	68LTS179	301581
Luxembourg	Multilateral	12 Jul 27	Direct Aid	135LTS247	303115
Luxembourg	Multilateral	26 Sep 27	Dispute Settlement	92LTS301	302096
Luxembourg	Multilateral	29 Oct 27	Scientific Project	127LTS27	302903
Luxembourg	Multilateral	08 Nov 27	General Trade	97LTS391	302238
Luxembourg	Multilateral	11 Jul 28	Commodity Trade	95LTS373	302185
Luxembourg	Multilateral	11 Jul 28	Commodity Trade	95LTS357	302184
Luxembourg	Multilateral	27 Aug 28	General Military	94LTS57	302137
Luxembourg	Multilateral	12 Sep 28	Telecommunications	104LTS43	302377
Luxembourg	Multilateral	27 Nov 28	Telecommunications	92LTS321	302098
Luxembourg	Multilateral	16 Apr 29	Specific Resources	126LTS305	302891
Luxembourg	Multilateral	20 Apr 29	Admin Cooperation	112LTS371	302623
Luxembourg	Multilateral	28 Jun 29	Postal Service	103LTS249	302371
Luxembourg	Multilateral	28 Jun 29	Postal Service	103LTS5	302369
Luxembourg	Multilateral	28 Jun 29	Postal Service	102LTS245	302368
Luxembourg	Multilateral	28 Jun 29	Postal Service	103LTS321	302372
Luxembourg	Multilateral	28 Jun 29	Postal Service	103LTS377	302373
Luxembourg	Multilateral	28 Jun 29	Postal Service	103LTS429	302374
Luxembourg	Multilateral	28 Jun 29	Postal Service	103LTS71	302370
Luxembourg	Multilateral	27 Jul 29	Other Military	118LTS343	302734
Luxembourg	Multilateral	27 Jul 29	Other Military	118LTS303	302733
Luxembourg	Multilateral	14 Sep 29	UN Charter	165LTS353	303822
Luxembourg	Multilateral	25 Sep 29	Telecommunications	98LTS361	302256
Luxembourg	Multilateral	12 Oct 29	General Transport	137LTS11	303145
Luxembourg	Multilateral	12 Apr 30	Admin Cooperation	179LTS89	304137
Luxembourg	Multilateral	12 Apr 30	Milit Servic/Citiz	178LTS227	304117
Luxembourg	Multilateral	12 Apr 30	Admin Cooperation	179LTS115	304138
Luxembourg	Multilateral	07 Jun 30	Finance	143LTS337	303315
Luxembourg	Multilateral	07 Jun 30	Finance	143LTS257	303313
Luxembourg	Multilateral	07 Jun 30	Finance	143LTS317	303314
Luxembourg	Multilateral	19 Mar 31	Admin Cooperation	143LTS7	303301
Luxembourg	Multilateral	19 Mar 31	Finance	143LTS407	303317
Luxembourg	Multilateral	19 Mar 31	Finance	143LTS355	303316
Luxembourg	Multilateral	27 Mar 31	ICJ Option Clause	167LTS341	303877
Luxembourg	Multilateral	28 Mar 31	Customs	119LTS47	302739
Luxembourg	Multilateral	30 Mar 31	Land Transport	150LTS247	303459
Luxembourg	Multilateral	30 Mar 31	Taxation	138LTS149	303185
Luxembourg	Multilateral	13 Jul 31	Other HEW	139LTS301	303219
Luxembourg	Multilateral	02 Sep 32	Land Transport	154LTS123	303543
Luxembourg	Multilateral	09 Dec 32	Telecommunications	151LTS5	303479
Luxembourg	Multilateral	23 Nov 33	Land Transport	192LTS327	304483
Luxembourg	Multilateral	23 Nov 33	Land Transport	192LTS389	304484
Luxembourg	Multilateral	20 Mar 34	Finance	176LTS9	304053
Luxembourg	Multilateral	20 Mar 34	Postal Service	175LTS269	304051
Luxembourg	Multilateral	20 Mar 34	Postal Service	175LTS363	304052
Luxembourg	Multilateral	20 Mar 34	Postal Service	175LTS73	304050

PARTY ONE	PARTY TWO	DATE	TOPIC	CITATION	NUMBER
Luxembourg	Multilateral	20 Mar 34	Postal Service	176LTS55	304054
Luxembourg	Multilateral	20 Mar 34	Postal Service	175LTS5	304049
Luxembourg	Multilateral	02 Jun 34	Patents/Copyrights	192LTS17	304459
Luxembourg	Multilateral	23 Sep 36	Gen Communications	186LTS301	304319
Luxembourg	Multilateral	23 Jan 37	Extradition	191LTS219	304446
Luxembourg	Multilateral	31 Mar 37	Commodity Trade	189LTS359	304394
Luxembourg	Multilateral	28 May 37	General Trade	180LTS5	304170
Luxembourg	Multilateral	11 May 38	General Trade	189LTS237	304386
Luxembourg	Multilateral	27 Jun 38	Visas	191LTS199	304443
Luxembourg	Multilateral	31 Oct 38	Sanitation	198LTS205	304642
Luxembourg	Multilateral	03 Dec 38	Education	200LTS249	304694
Luxembourg	Multilateral	06 May 39	Finance	198LTS81	304626
Luxembourg	Multilateral	23 May 39	Postal Service	202LTS159	304742
Luxembourg	Multilateral	01 Jan 42	General Military	204LTS381	304817
Luxembourg	Multilateral	02 Jun 42	Patents/Copyrights	205LTS163	304833
Luxembourg	Netherlands	17 Sep 29	Dispute Settlement	107LTS35	302466
Luxembourg	Netherlands	01 Apr 36	Non-ILO Labor	179LTS11	304130
Luxembourg	Norway	12 Sep 27	Visas	68LTS37	301566
Luxembourg	Norway	12 Feb 32	Dispute Settlement	142LTS29	303277
Luxembourg	Poland	29 Oct 28	Dispute Settlement	111LTS71	302581
Luxembourg	Poland	10 Apr 31	Admin Cooperation	140LTS411	303251
Luxembourg	Portugal	15 Aug 29	Dispute Settlement	115LTS77	302678
Luxembourg	Romania	22 Jan 30	Dispute Settlement	110LTS151	302559
Luxembourg	Spain	21 Jun 28	Dispute Settlement	109LTS137	302533
Luxembourg	Sweden	11 Apr 23	Admin Cooperation	16LTS453	300423
Luxembourg	Switzerland	16 Sep 29	Dispute Settlement	107LTS23	302465
Luxembourg	UK Great Britain	08 Sep 23	Postal Service	35LTS203	300896
Luxembourg	USA (United States)	06 Apr 29	Dispute Settlement	106LTS469	302463
Luxembourg	USA (United States)	06 Apr 29	Dispute Settlement	106LTS475	302464
Luxembourg	USA (United States)	24 Apr 35	Extradition	168LTS129	303893
Madagascar	Multilateral	21 Jun 20	Health/Educ/Welfare	8LTS65	300207
Madagascar	Multilateral	31 Oct 20	Sanitation	164LTS85	303790
Madagascar	Multilateral	09 Dec 23	Water Transport	58LTS284	301379
Madagascar	Multilateral	29 Oct 25	Telecommunications	57LTS201	301365
Madagascar	Multilateral	24 Apr 26	Land Transport	108LTS123	302505
Madagascar	Multilateral	24 Apr 26	Land Transport	97LTS83	302220
Madagascar	Multilateral	25 Nov 27	Telecommunications	84LTS97	301905
Madagascar	Multilateral	23 Oct 30	Water Transport	125LTS95	302849
Malawi	Multilateral	09 Dec 23	Land Transport	47LTS55	301129
Malawi	Multilateral	20 Apr 29	Admin Cooperation	112LTS395	302624
Malawi	Multilateral	20 Apr 29	Admin Cooperation	112LTS371	302623
Malawi	Multilateral	12 Apr 30	Admin Cooperation	179LTS115	304138
Malawi	Multilateral	19 Mar 31	Finance	143LTS355	303316
Malay States	Australia	24 Jan 21	Postal Service	23LTS209	300590
Malay States	Multilateral	09 Sep 86*	Patents/Copyrights	123LTS233	302816
Malay States	Multilateral	20 Apr 21	Water Transport	7LTS35	300172
Malay States	Multilateral	20 Apr 21	Land Transport	7LTS11	300171
Malay States	Multilateral	25 Aug 24	Water Transport	120LTS155	302764
Malay States	Multilateral	12 Oct 29	General Transport	137LTS11	303145
Malay States	Multilateral	30 Mar 31	Taxation	138LTS149	303185
Malay States	Multilateral	23 Sep 36	Gen Communications	186LTS301	304319
Malaya	China	30 Mar 35	Postal Service	163LTS159	303765
Malaya	China	12 Feb 36	Postal Service	170LTS19	303927
Malaya	Denmark	23 Oct 34	Postal Service	155LTS141	303575
Malaya	Dutch Indies	30 Oct 34	Postal Service	157LTS127	303608
Malaya	Dutch Indies	26 Feb 35	Postal Service	160LTS191	303693
Malaya	France	31 Aug 35	Postal Service	165LTS215	303811
Malaya	Germany	17 Dec 36	Postal Service	178LTS484	304129
Malaya	Indochina	07 Sep 34	Postal Service	155LTS73	303569
Malaya	Indochina	08 Oct 34	Postal Service	157LTS95	303607
Malaya	Italy	09 Mar 35	Postal Service	163LTS113	303764
Malaya	Netherlands	16 Mar 37	Postal Service	184LTS181	304248
Malaya	Siam	15 Sep 37	Postal Service	191LTS225	304447
Malaya	Siam	16 Sep 37	Postal Service	191LTS265	304448
Malaya	United Arab Rep	29 Feb 36	Postal Service	170LTS103	303931

PARTY ONE	PARTY TWO	DATE	TOPIC	CITATION	NUMBER
Malaya	USA (United States)	11 Dec 34	Postal Service	156LTS101	303595
Malaya	USA (United States)	22 Mar 35	Postal Service	161LTS41	303705
Malayan Union	Multilateral	20 Apr 21	Water Transport	7LTS65	300173
Malayan Union	Multilateral	28 Oct 33	Refugees	159LTS199	303663
Malayan Union	Multilateral	10 Feb 38	Refugees	192LTS59	304461
Malaysia	Multilateral	09 Dec 23	Water Transport	58LTS284	301379
Malaysia	Multilateral	25 Nov 27	Telecommunications	84LTS97	301905
Malaysia	Multilateral	28 Jun 29	Postal Service	103LTS5	302369
Malta	Multilateral	09 Sep 86*	Patents/Copyrights	123LTS233	302816
Malta	Multilateral	20 Apr 21	Water Transport	7LTS73	300174
Malta	Multilateral	31 Mar 22	Humanitarian	9LTS415	300269
Malta	Multilateral	24 Apr 26	Land Transport	108LTS123	302505
Malta	Multilateral	25 Nov 27	Telecommunications	84LTS97	301905
Malta	Multilateral	23 Sep 36	Gen Communications	186LTS301	304319
Martinique	Barbados	21 Oct 39	Postal Service	201LTS65	304704
Martinique	Multilateral	05 Jun 12	Telecommunications	1LTS135	300013
Martinique	Multilateral	24 Apr 26	Land Transport	108LTS123	302505
Martinique	Multilateral	24 Apr 26	Land Transport	97LTS83	302220
Martinique	Multilateral	23 Oct 30	Water Transport	125LTS95	302849
Martinique	St. Lucia	25 Aug 34	Postal Service	165LTS183	303810
Mauritania	Multilateral	30 Jun 20	Patents/Copyrights	1LTS59	300008
Mauritania	Multilateral	12 Apr 30	Milit Servic/Citiz	178LTS227	304117
Mauritius	Multilateral	31 Mar 22	Humanitarian	9LTS415	300269
Mauritius	Multilateral	25 Aug 24	Water Transport	120LTS155	302764
Mauritius	Multilateral	01 Dec 24	Sanitation	78LTS351	301794
Mauritius	Multilateral	24 Apr 26	Land Transport	108LTS123	302505
Mauritius	Multilateral	26 Sep 27	Dispute Settlement	92LTS301	302096
Mauritius	Multilateral	25 Nov 27	Telecommunications	84LTS97	301905
Mauritius	Multilateral	28 Oct 33	Refugees	159LTS199	303663
Mauritius	Multilateral	23 Sep 36	Gen Communications	186LTS301	304319
Mauritius	Multilateral	10 Feb 38	Refugees	192LTS59	304461
Mexico	Belgium	22 Sep 38	Extradition	198LTS399	304658
Mexico	Brazil	07 Dec 31	General Trade	139LTS247	303215
Mexico	Brazil	18 Dec 33	Education	186LTS395	304323
Mexico	British Honduras	25 Mar 25	Postal Service	43LTS61	301047
Mexico	Bulgaria	05 Nov 36	General Amity	187LTS37	304331
Mexico	China	26 Sep 21	General Amity	13LTS201	300352
Mexico	Cuba	29 Jun 28	Telecommunications	124LTS189	302833
Mexico	Estonia	28 Jan 37	General Amity	185LTS39	304272
Mexico	Finland	02 Oct 36	General Amity	179LTS303	304157
Mexico	France	25 Sep 24	Claims and Debts	79LTS417	301818
Mexico	France	10 Nov 28	General Trade	86LTS423	301953
Mexico	Germany	16 Mar 25	Reparations	52LTS93	301251
Mexico	Germany	20 Dec 27	Claims and Debts	79LTS229	301812
Mexico	Greece	17 Mar 38	General Amity	198LTS325	304649
Mexico	Japan	08 Oct 24	General Amity	36LTS259	300927
Mexico	Multilateral	20 Aug 10	Patents/Copyrights	155LTS179	303576
Mexico	Multilateral	12 Jan 12	Sanitation	4LTS281	300112
Mexico	Multilateral	23 Jan 12	Sanitation	8LTS187	300222
Mexico	Multilateral	05 Jun 12	Telecommunications	1LTS135	300013
Mexico	Multilateral	31 Oct 20	Sanitation	164LTS85	303790
Mexico	Multilateral	20 Apr 21	Water Transport	7LTS73	300174
Mexico	Multilateral	15 Sep 21	Postal Service	30LTS141	300767
Mexico	Multilateral	06 Oct 21	General Economic	17LTS45	300427
Mexico	Multilateral	31 Mar 22	Humanitarian	9LTS415	300269
Mexico	Multilateral	05 Jul 22	Reparations	13LTS237	300355
Mexico	Multilateral	02 Nov 22	Peace/Disarmament	149LTS35	303431
Mexico	Multilateral	03 May 23	General Amity	33LTS25	300831
Mexico	Multilateral	09 Dec 23	Water Transport	58LTS284	301379
Mexico	Multilateral	25 Jan 24	Sanitation	57LTS135	301360
Mexico	Multilateral	31 Mar 24	Sanitation	27LTS211	300685
Mexico	Multilateral	28 Aug 24	Postal Service	40LTS19	301002
Mexico	Multilateral	14 Nov 24	Sanitation	86LTS43	301949
Mexico	Multilateral	17 Jun 25	Peace/Disarmament	94LTS65	302138
Mexico	Multilateral	06 Nov 25	Patents/Copyrights	74LTS327	301745

PARTY ONE	PARTY TWO	DATE	TOPIC	CITATION	NUMBER
Mexico	Multilateral	06 Nov 25	Patents/Copyrights	74LTS289	301743
Mexico	Multilateral	10 Apr 26	Water Transport	176LTS199	304062
Mexico	Multilateral	10 Apr 26	Water Transport	120LTS187	302765
Mexico	Multilateral	24 Apr 26	Land Transport	108LTS123	302505
Mexico	Multilateral	24 Apr 26	Land Transport	97LTS83	302220
Mexico	Multilateral	21 Jun 26	Sanitation	78LTS229	301793
Mexico	Multilateral	29 Oct 27	Scientific Project	127LTS27	302903
Mexico	Multilateral	25 Nov 27	Telecommunications	84LTS97	301905
Mexico	Multilateral	18 Feb 28	Patents/Copyrights	132LTS275	303044
Mexico	Multilateral	20 Feb 28	Consul/Citizenship	155LTS259	303581
Mexico	Multilateral	20 Feb 28	Consul/Citizenship	155LTS289	303582
Mexico	Multilateral	20 Feb 28	Privil/Immunities	132LTS301	303045
Mexico	Multilateral	20 Feb 28	Air Transport	129LTS223	302963
Mexico	Multilateral	20 Feb 28	General Amity	135LTS187	303111
Mexico	Multilateral	20 Feb 28	Admin Cooperation	134LTS45	303082
Mexico	Multilateral	20 Feb 28	Consul/Citizenship	132LTS323	303046
Mexico	Multilateral	20 Feb 28	Other Ad Hoc	86LTS111	301950
Mexico	Multilateral	27 Aug 28	General Military	94LTS57	302137
Mexico	Multilateral	05 Jan 29	Dispute Settlement	130LTS135	302988
Mexico	Multilateral	05 Jan 29	Dispute Settlement	100LTS399	302309
Mexico	Multilateral	20 Feb 29	Patents/Copyrights	124LTS357	302840
Mexico	Multilateral	28 Jun 29	Postal Service	102LTS245	302368
Mexico	Multilateral	27 Jul 29	Other Military	118LTS343	302734
Mexico	Multilateral	27 Jul 29	Other Military	118LTS303	302733
Mexico	Multilateral	12 Oct 29	General Transport	137LTS11	303145
Mexico	Multilateral	12 Apr 30	Milit Servic/Citiz	178LTS227	304117
Mexico	Multilateral	12 Apr 30	Admin Cooperation	179LTS89	304137
Mexico	Multilateral	12 Apr 30	Admin Cooperation	179LTS115	304138
Mexico	Multilateral	01 Aug 30	Health/Educ/Welfare	128LTS9	302932
Mexico	Multilateral	19 Mar 31	Finance	143LTS355	303316
Mexico	Multilateral	19 Mar 31	Finance	143LTS407	303317
Mexico	Multilateral	19 Mar 31	Admin Cooperation	143LTS7	303301
Mexico	Multilateral	13 Jul 31	Other HEW	139LTS301	303219
Mexico	Multilateral	24 Sep 31	Specific Resources	155LTS349	303586
Mexico	Multilateral	10 Nov 31	Postal Service	131LTS327	303023
Mexico	Multilateral	10 Nov 31	Postal Service	131LTS389	303024
Mexico	Multilateral	10 Nov 31	Postal Service	131LTS447	303025
Mexico	Multilateral	09 Dec 32	Telecommunications	151LTS5	303479
Mexico	Multilateral	11 Mar 33	Water Transport	135LTS301	303119
Mexico	Multilateral	22 Jul 33	Specific Resources	153LTS107	303511
Mexico	Multilateral	10 Oct 33	General Amity	163LTS393	303781
Mexico	Multilateral	11 Oct 33	Consul/Citizenship	150LTS431	303476
Mexico	Multilateral	26 Dec 33	Recognition	165LTS19	303802
Mexico	Multilateral	26 Dec 33	Extradition	165LTS45	303803
Mexico	Multilateral	20 Mar 34	Postal Service	174LTS171	304048
Mexico	Multilateral	02 Jun 34	Patents/Copyrights	205LTS179	304834
Mexico	Multilateral	02 Jun 34	Patents/Copyrights	192LTS17	304459
Mexico	Multilateral	19 Jun 34	Admin Cooperation	154LTS381	303564
Mexico	Multilateral	15 Apr 35	Culture	167LTS289	303874
Mexico	Multilateral	26 Jun 36	Other HEW	198LTS299	304648
Mexico	Multilateral	23 Sep 36	Gen Communications	186LTS301	304319
Mexico	Multilateral	06 Nov 36	General Military	173LTS353	304025
Mexico	Multilateral	23 Dec 36	Land Transport	188LTS99	304354
Mexico	Multilateral	23 Dec 36	Dispute Settlement	188LTS53	304352
Mexico	Multilateral	23 Dec 36	Admin Cooperation	201LTS295	304721
Mexico	Multilateral	23 Dec 36	Culture	188LTS125	304355
Mexico	Multilateral	23 Dec 36	Peace/Disarmament	188LTS9	304350
Mexico	Multilateral	23 Dec 36	General Amity	188LTS31	304351
Mexico	Multilateral	23 Dec 36	Culture	188LTS151	304356
Mexico	Multilateral	23 Dec 36	Dispute Settlement	195LTS229	304548
Mexico	Multilateral	23 Dec 36	Dispute Settlement	188LTS75	304353
Mexico	Multilateral	08 Jun 37	Specific Resources	190LTS79	304406
Mexico	Multilateral	31 Oct 38	Sanitation	198LTS205	304642
Mexico	Multilateral	03 Dec 38	Education	200LTS249	304694
Mexico	Multilateral	23 May 39	Postal Service	202LTS159	304742

PARTY ONE	PARTY TWO	DATE	TOPIC	CITATION	NUMBER
Mexico	Multilateral	01 Jan 42	General Military	204LTS381	304817
Mexico	Multilateral	02 Jun 42	Patents/Copyrights	205LTS163	304833
Mexico	Norway	01 Oct 23	Admin Cooperation	33LTS255	300849
Mexico	Norway	14 Jun 29	Postal Service	99LTS381	302283
Mexico	Panama	09 Jun 28	Consul/Citizenship	141LTS191	303265
Mexico	Panama	23 Oct 28	Extradition	194LTS137	304518
Mexico	Spain	31 Mar 24	Patents/Copyrights	43LTS297	301065
Mexico	Sweden	17 Oct 22	Humanitarian	15LTS179	300391
Mexico	Sweden	14 Sep 31	Postal Service	192LTS195	304472
Mexico	UK Great Britain	17 May 22	Admin Cooperation	14LTS83	300368
Mexico	UK Great Britain	19 Nov 26	Claims and Debts	85LTS51	301922
Mexico	UK Great Britain	24 Oct 28	Postal Service	87LTS63	301962
Mexico	UK Great Britain	05 Dec 30	Claims and Debts	119LTS261	302749
Mexico	UK Great Britain	18 Jul 43	Milit Servic/Citiz	205LTS115	304828
Mexico	USA (United States)	18 Jun 32	Claims and Debts	158LTS67	303627
Mexico	USA (United States)	24 Apr 34	Claims and Debts	156LTS81	303593
Mexico	USA (United States)	24 Apr 34	Claims and Debts	149LTS49	303433
Mexico	USA (United States)	13 Jun 35	Water Transport	168LTS135	303894
Mexico	USA (United States)	07 Feb 36	Admin Cooperation	178LTS309	304119
Mexico	USA (United States)	06 Oct 36	Admin Cooperation	180LTS33	304171
Mexico	USA (United States)	24 Sep 37	Admin Cooperation	185LTS23	304270
Mexico	USA (United States)	29 Aug 38	Admin Cooperation	195LTS359	304556
Mexico	USA (United States)	18 Apr 39	Specific Property	201LTS201	304714
Mexico	USA (United States)	16 Aug 39	Extradition	294LTS159	304794
Mexico	USA (United States)	28 Aug 40	Gen Communications	203LTS357	304777
Mexico	USA (United States)	01 Apr 41	Air Transport	204LTS179	304798
Monaco	Austria	07 Feb 36	Visas	167LTS389	303880
Monaco	Belgium	28 May 32	Claims and Debts	136LTS415	303140
Monaco	Belgium	16 Dec 37	Extradition	187LTS195	304339
Monaco	Czechoslovakia	22 Dec 34	Extradition	171LTS27	303949
Monaco	France	26 May 25	Admin Cooperation	44LTS249	301086
Monaco	Liberia	28 Oct 26	Extradition	68LTS241	301588
Monaco	Multilateral	09 Sep 86*	Patents/Copyrights	123LTS233	302816
Monaco	Multilateral	18 Mar 04	Humanitarian	1LTS83	300011
Monaco	Multilateral	13 Nov 08	General Ad Hoc	1LTS217	300015
Monaco	Multilateral	12 Jan 12	Sanitation	4LTS281	300112
Monaco	Multilateral	23 Jan 12	Sanitation	8LTS187	300222
Monaco	Multilateral	05 Jun 12	Telecommunications	1LTS135	300013
Monaco	Multilateral	20 Mar 14	Patents/Copyrights	1LTS243	300016
Monaco	Multilateral	21 Jun 20	Health/Educ/Welfare	8LTS65	300207
Monaco	Multilateral	30 Jun 20	Patents/Copyrights	1LTS59	300008
Monaco	Multilateral	16 Dec 20	General IGO	6LTS379	300170
Monaco	Multilateral	31 Mar 22	Humanitarian	9LTS415	300269
Monaco	Multilateral	25 Jan 24	Sanitation	57LTS135	301360
Monaco	Multilateral	31 Mar 24	Sanitation	27LTS211	300685
Monaco	Multilateral	01 Dec 24	Sanitation	78LTS351	301794
Monaco	Multilateral	19 Feb 25	Admin Cooperation	81LTS317	301845
Monaco	Multilateral	24 Apr 26	Land Transport	108LTS123	302505
Monaco	Multilateral	24 Apr 26	Land Transport	97LTS83	302220
Monaco	Multilateral	21 Jun 26	Sanitation	78LTS229	301793
Monaco	Multilateral	12 Jul 27	Direct Aid	135LTS247	303115
Monaco	Multilateral	29 Oct 27	Scientific Project	127LTS27	302903
Monaco	Multilateral	20 Apr 29	Admin Cooperation	112LTS371	302623
Monaco	Multilateral	12 Apr 30	Admin Cooperation	179LTS89	304137
Monaco	Multilateral	07 Jun 30	Finance	143LTS337	303315
Monaco	Multilateral	07 Jun 30	Finance	143LTS317	303314
Monaco	Multilateral	07 Jun 30	Finance	143LTS257	303313
Monaco	Multilateral	01 Aug 30	Health/Educ/Welfare	128LTS9	302932
Monaco	Multilateral	23 Oct 30	Water Transport	125LTS95	302849
Monaco	Multilateral	23 Oct 30	Water Transport	112LTS21	302603
Monaco	Multilateral	27 Nov 30	Extradition	121LTS39	302781
Monaco	Multilateral	19 Mar 31	Admin Cooperation	143LTS7	303301
Monaco	Multilateral	19 Mar 31	Finance	143LTS355	303316
Monaco	Multilateral	19 Mar 31	Finance	143LTS407	303317
Monaco	Multilateral	30 Mar 31	Land Transport	150LTS247	303459

PARTY ONE	PARTY TWO	DATE	TOPIC	CITATION	NUMBER
Monaco	Multilateral	13 Jul 31	Other HEW	139LTS301	303219
Monaco	Multilateral	24 Sep 31	Specific Resources	155LTS349	303586
Monaco	Multilateral	12 Apr 33	Sanitation	161LTS65	303706
Monaco	Multilateral	11 Oct 33	Education	155LTS331	303585
Monaco	Multilateral	11 Oct 33	Consul/Citizenship	150LTS431	303476
Monaco	Multilateral	02 Jun 34	General Trade	192LTS9	304458
Monaco	Multilateral	26 Jun 36	Other HEW	198LTS299	304648
Monaco	Multilateral	12 Sep 38	Culture	198LTS111	304630
Monaco	Multilateral	31 Oct 38	Sanitation	198LTS205	304642
Monaco	Multilateral	03 Dec 38	Education	200LTS249	304694
Monaco	USA (United States)	15 Feb 39	Extradition	202LTS61	304735
Montenegro	Multilateral	12 Jan 12	Sanitation	4LTS281	300112
Montserrat	Multilateral	09 Sep 86*	Patents/Copyrights	123LTS233	302816
Montserrat	Multilateral	26 Sep 27	Dispute Settlement	92LTS301	302096
Morocco	France	21 Jun 38	Admin Cooperation	189LTS423	304398
Morocco	Multilateral	09 Sep 86*	Patents/Copyrights	123LTS233	302816
Morocco	Multilateral	18 Mar 04	Humanitarian	1LTS83	300011
Morocco	Multilateral	13 Nov 08	General Ad Hoc	1LTS217	300015
Morocco	Multilateral	05 Jun 12	Telecommunications	1LTS135	300013
Morocco	Multilateral	21 Jun 20	Health/Educ/Welfare	8LTS65	300207
Morocco	Multilateral	30 Jun 20	Patents/Copyrights	1LTS59	300008
Morocco	Multilateral	25 Jan 24	Sanitation	57LTS135	301360
Morocco	Multilateral	31 Mar 24	Sanitation	27LTS211	300685
Morocco	Multilateral	28 Aug 24	Postal Service	41LTS97	301008
Morocco	Multilateral	28 Aug 24	Postal Service	41LTS9	301006
Morocco	Multilateral	28 Aug 24	Postal Service	40LTS437	301005
Morocco	Multilateral	28 Aug 24	Postal Service	40LTS307	301004
Morocco	Multilateral	28 Aug 24	Postal Service	41LTS55	301007
Morocco	Multilateral	28 Aug 24	Postal Service	40LTS19	301002
Morocco	Multilateral	28 Aug 24	Postal Service	40LTS249	301003
Morocco	Multilateral	01 Dec 24	Sanitation	78LTS351	301794
Morocco	Multilateral	29 Oct 25	Telecommunications	57LTS201	301365
Morocco	Multilateral	24 Apr 26	Land Transport	108LTS123	302505
Morocco	Multilateral	24 Apr 26	Land Transport	97LTS83	302220
Morocco	Multilateral	21 Jun 26	Sanitation	78LTS229	301793
Morocco	Multilateral	10 Sep 27	Postal Service	75LTS7	301749
Morocco	Multilateral	10 Sep 27	Postal Service	75LTS39	301750
Morocco	Multilateral	29 Oct 27	Scientific Project	127LTS27	302903
Morocco	Multilateral	25 Nov 27	Telecommunications	84LTS97	301905
Morocco	Multilateral	22 Nov 28	Culture	111LTS343	302598
Morocco	Multilateral	16 Apr 29	Specific Resources	126LTS305	302891
Morocco	Multilateral	28 Jun 29	Postal Service	103LTS321	302372
Morocco	Multilateral	28 Jun 29	Postal Service	103LTS377	302373
Morocco	Multilateral	28 Jun 29	Postal Service	103LTS249	302371
Morocco	Multilateral	28 Jun 29	Postal Service	103LTS5	302369
Morocco	Multilateral	28 Jun 29	Postal Service	102LTS245	302368
Morocco	Multilateral	28 Jun 29	Postal Service	103LTS71	302370
Morocco	Multilateral	28 Jun 29	Postal Service	103LTS429	302374
Morocco	Multilateral	01 Aug 30	Health/Educ/Welfare	128LTS9	302932
Morocco	Multilateral	23 Oct 30	Water Transport	125LTS95	302849
Morocco	Multilateral	23 Oct 30	Water Transport	112LTS21	302603
Morocco	Multilateral	09 Dec 32	Telecommunications	151LTS5	303479
Morocco	Multilateral	12 Apr 33	Sanitation	161LTS65	303706
Morocco	Multilateral	19 Jun 33	Gen Communications	154LTS133	303544
Morocco	Multilateral	20 Mar 34	Postal Service	174LTS171	304048
Morocco	Multilateral	02 Jun 34	Patents/Copyrights	205LTS179	304834
Morocco	Multilateral	02 Jun 34	General Trade	192LTS9	304458
Morocco	Multilateral	02 Jun 34	Patents/Copyrights	192LTS17	304459
Morocco	Multilateral	23 May 39	Postal Service	202LTS159	304742
Mozambique	Multilateral	29 Oct 25	Telecommunications	57LTS201	301365
Mozambique	Multilateral	30 Oct 35	Postal Service	189LTS85	304376
Mozambique	Multilateral	30 Oct 35	Telecommunications	189LTS51	304375
Muscat and Oman	Great Britain	11 Feb 26	General Economic	57LTS13	301347
Muscat and Oman	Multilateral	10 Sep 19	General Trade	7LTS331	300200
Muscat and Oman	Multilateral	05 Feb 39	General Amity	196LTS303	304592

PARTY ONE	PARTY TWO	DATE	TOPIC	CITATION	NUMBER
Muscat and Oman	UK Great Britain	11 Feb 20	Water Transport	5LTS59	300118
Muscat and Oman	UK Great Britain	11 Feb 21	General Economic	8LTS261	300224
Muscat and Oman	UK Great Britain	11 Feb 22	General Economic	10LTS459	300285
Muscat and Oman	UK Great Britain	11 Feb 23	General Amity	17LTS163	300433
Muscat and Oman	UK Great Britain	11 Feb 24	Admin Cooperation	25LTS387	300628
Muscat and Oman	UK Great Britain	11 Feb 25	General Amity	35LTS233	300897
Muscat and Oman	UK Great Britain	11 Feb 27	General Amity	64LTS398	301512
Nauru	Australia	27 Oct 21	Postal Service	23LTS229	300591
Nejd	Great Britain	02 Nov 25	Territory Boundary	60LTS419	301423
Nepal	India	23 Dec 36	Postal Service	178LTS405	304123
Nepal	Multilateral	20 Apr 21	Land Transport	7LTS11	300171
Nepal	Multilateral	06 Nov 36	General Military	173LTS353	304025
Nepal	UK Great Britain	21 Dec 23	General Amity	36LTS357	300934
Netherlands	Abyssinia	30 Sep 26	General Trade	78LTS89	301780
Netherlands	Argentina	31 Jan 34	Mostfavored Nation	148LTS355	303421
Netherlands	Argentina	31 Jan 34	Finance	148LTS361	303422
Netherlands	Argentina	05 Feb 37	Finance	179LTS383	304165
Netherlands	Argentina	06 Sep 38	Visas	194LTS409	304531
Netherlands	Australia	30 May 23	Postal Service	22LTS129	300556
Netherlands	Australia	14 Sep 36	Territory Boundary	173LTS325	304022
Netherlands	Austria	01 Dec 21	Extradition	9LTS167	300248
Netherlands	Austria	06 Nov 22	Consul/Citizenship	17LTS375	300444
Netherlands	Austria	05 Sep 23	General Trade	20LTS147	300514
Netherlands	Austria	04 Aug 26	Customs	59LTS243	301394
Netherlands	Austria	01 Mar 27	Visas	68LTS75	301570
Netherlands	Austria	28 Mar 29	General Economic	109LTS39	302527
Netherlands	Austria	31 Dec 29	Air Transport	111LTS177	302586
Netherlands	Austria	26 Jun 31	Land Transport	127LTS225	302922
Netherlands	Austria	28 Jun 33	Land Transport	152LTS193	303493
Netherlands	Austria	02 Apr 37	Customs	179LTS81	304136
Netherlands	Belgium	31 May 89*	Extradition	137LTS261	303160
Netherlands	Belgium	08 Mar 20	Telecommunications	1LTS25	300003
Netherlands	Belgium	06 Oct 20	Land Transport	18LTS247	300467
Netherlands	Belgium	09 Feb 21	Non-ILO Labor	11LTS333	300299
Netherlands	Belgium	15 Oct 21	Postal Service	12LTS233	300315
Netherlands	Belgium	08 Jul 22	Air Transport	13LTS273	300358
Netherlands	Belgium	14 Jul 23	Water Transport	20LTS119	300511
Netherlands	Belgium	02 May 24	Admin Cooperation	27LTS113	300673
Netherlands	Belgium	28 Aug 25	Dispute Settlement	93LTS431	302131
Netherlands	Belgium	05 Mar 26	Postal Service	50LTS213	301203
Netherlands	Belgium	28 Feb 27	Telecommunications	68LTS169	301580
Netherlands	Belgium	24 Mar 27	Sanitation	84LTS34	301902
Netherlands	Belgium	25 Oct 27	Extradition	69LTS29	301597
Netherlands	Belgium	26 Oct 27	Education	89LTS37	302003
Netherlands	Belgium	16 Apr 28	Admin Cooperation	75LTS61	301751
Netherlands	Belgium	27 Mar 29	Finance	89LTS201	302014
Netherlands	Belgium	28 May 29	Sanitation	89LTS191	302013
Netherlands	Belgium	16 Oct 31	Admin Cooperation	137LTS411	303171
Netherlands	Belgium	22 Oct 31	Customs	125LTS367	302865
Netherlands	Belgium	29 Dec 31	General Trade	127LTS163	302917
Netherlands	Belgium	04 Aug 32	Postal Service	134LTS117	303086
Netherlands	Belgium	20 Feb 33	Taxation	164LTS223	303796
Netherlands	Belgium	20 Feb 33	Non-ILO Labor	165LTS383	303824
Netherlands	Belgium	01 Aug 34	Telecommunications	153LTS267	303520
Netherlands	Belgium	06 Apr 35	Water Transport	160LTS137	303687
Netherlands	Belgium	15 May 36	Humanitarian	179LTS41	304131
Netherlands	Belgium	13 Jul 36	Postal Service	177LTS93	304083
Netherlands	Belgium	26 Mar 37	Customs	179LTS52	304132
Netherlands	Belgium	09 Jun 37	Consul/Citizenship	181LTS153	304186
Netherlands	Belgium	31 Dec 37	Land Transport	189LTS387	304396
Netherlands	Belgium	07 Feb 38	Admin Cooperation	187LTS9	304328
Netherlands	Belgium	30 Apr 38	Taxation	190LTS199	304418
Netherlands	Belgium	17 Dec 38	Water Transport	198LTS177	304638
Netherlands	Bolivia	30 May 29	General Trade	133LTS113	303062
Netherlands	Brazil	16 Sep 30	Mostfavored Nation	125LTS197	302854
Netherlands	Brazil	22 Sep 31	Territory Boundary	130LTS113	302986
Netherlands	Brazil	15 Mar 37	Finance	179LTS405	304167
Netherlands	Brazil	15 Mar 37	General Trade	179LTS395	304166
Netherlands	Bulgaria	13 Nov 20	Customs	7LTS107	300178
Netherlands	Bulgaria	09 Mar 22	Customs	9LTS265	300260
Netherlands	Bulgaria	23 Sep 35	Finance	166LTS51	303829
Netherlands	Canada	11 Jul 24	General Trade	39LTS45	300995
Netherlands	Canada	23 Sep 29	Taxation	96LTS151	302197
Netherlands	Chile	04 Nov 13	Consul/Citizenship	84LTS79	301904
Netherlands	Chile	17 Dec 31	Mostfavored Nation	127LTS79	302908
Netherlands	Chile	01 Jun 34	Claims and Debts	154LTS325	303559
Netherlands	Chile	30 Dec 36	General Trade	177LTS87	304082
Netherlands	Chile	05 May 37	General Trade	182LTS385	304223
Netherlands	China	19 Dec 28	Customs	111LTS161	302585
Netherlands	Cuba	31 Dec 13	Consul/Citizenship	14LTS29	300366
Netherlands	Czechoslovakia	17 Oct 24	General Trade	31LTS93	300786
Netherlands	Czechoslovakia	14 Sep 29	Dispute Settlement	107LTS201	302477
Netherlands	Czechoslovakia	11 Aug 31	Land Transport	127LTS347	302928
Netherlands	Czechoslovakia	04 Dec 31	Extradition	129LTS343	302969
Netherlands	Czechoslovakia	18 Jul 33	Land Transport	152LTS265	303499
Netherlands	Czechoslovakia	25 May 37	Education	180LTS43	304172
Netherlands	Denmark	23 Jul 26	Air Transport	66LTS133	301528
Netherlands	Denmark	23 Oct 26	Non-ILO Labor	72LTS13	301686
Netherlands	Denmark	19 Feb 27	Admin Cooperation	60LTS271	301415
Netherlands	Denmark	08 Nov 30	Taxation	109LTS115	302531
Netherlands	Denmark	15 Jul 31	Land Transport	127LTS329	302926
Netherlands	Denmark	18 Jul 33	Land Transport	152LTS253	303497
Netherlands	Denmark	29 Jul 37	Customs	192LTS137	304467
Netherlands	Denmark	24 Mar 38	Taxation	190LTS225	304421
Netherlands	Ecuador	27 May 37	General Trade	194LTS179	304521
Netherlands	Estonia	22 Jul 24	General Economic	48LTS199	301162
Netherlands	Estonia	01 Sep 30	Other Economic	111LTS395	302600
Netherlands	Estonia	08 Mar 33	Extradition	146LTS319	303382
Netherlands	Estonia	22 Nov 38	Customs	195LTS133	304542
Netherlands	Estonia	22 Nov 38	General Trade	193LTS209	304497
Netherlands	Finland	01 Nov 23	General Trade	23LTS33	300574
Netherlands	Finland	09 Mar 25	Consul/Citizenship	47LTS431	301148
Netherlands	Finland	07 May 28	Visas	74LTS367	301748
Netherlands	Finland	09 Jun 28	Dispute Settlement	87LTS321	301978
Netherlands	Finland	21 Feb 33	Extradition	139LTS365	303221
Netherlands	Finland	22 May 33	Water Transport	140LTS279	303243
Netherlands	Finland	25 Aug 36	General Trade	172LTS151	303985
Netherlands	Finland	20 Dec 38	Customs	194LTS55	304506
Netherlands	France	16 Sep 20	General Transport	12LTS213	300312
Netherlands	France	16 Apr 21	General Aid	11LTS341	300300
Netherlands	France	02 Jul 23	Air Transport	20LTS131	300512
Netherlands	France	07 Feb 24	Gen Communications	25LTS265	300615
Netherlands	France	10 Mar 28	Dispute Settlement	102LTS109	302356
Netherlands	France	28 Feb 30	Taxation	101LTS303	302331
Netherlands	France	29 Oct 30	Education	125LTS29	302843
Netherlands	France	19 Oct 35	Taxation	166LTS67	303830
Netherlands	France	25 May 36	Visas	173LTS187	304011
Netherlands	France	15 Jul 38	Air Transport	192LTS151	304469
Netherlands	Germany	11 May 20	Loans and Credits	3LTS153	300097
Netherlands	Germany	05 Jul 21	Territory Boundary	13LTS41	300346
Netherlands	Germany	23 May 23	Customs	25LTS275	300617
Netherlands	Germany	03 Jun 23	Water Transport	28LTS297	300716
Netherlands	Germany	27 Mar 24	Customs	25LTS289	300618
Netherlands	Germany	26 Nov 25	Customs	57LTS159	301362
Netherlands	Germany	26 Nov 25	General Economic	57LTS147	301361
Netherlands	Germany	24 Mar 26	Telecommunications	51LTS245	301234
Netherlands	Germany	20 May 26	Dispute Settlement	66LTS103	301527
Netherlands	Germany	03 Nov 26	Telecommunications	68LTS111	301575
Netherlands	Germany	28 Apr 28	Customs	95LTS333	302183
Netherlands	Germany	17 Aug 28	Air Transport	93LTS409	302129

PARTY ONE	PARTY TWO	DATE	TOPIC	CITATION	NUMBER
Netherlands	Germany	11 Jun 31	Land Transport	120LTS413	302778
Netherlands	Germany	27 Apr 33	Customs	145LTS155	303353
Netherlands	Germany	28 Jun 33	Land Transport	152LTS209	303495
Netherlands	Germany	06 Jun 34	General Trade	174LTS33	304034
Netherlands	Germany	06 Jun 34	Customs	174LTS44	304035
Netherlands	Germany	05 Dec 34	Finance	160LTS109	303686
Netherlands	Germany	23 Dec 36	Finance	179LTS359	304163
Netherlands	Germany	30 Apr 37	Customs	187LTS215	304342
Netherlands	Germany	30 Jun 37	General Trade	189LTS373	304395
Netherlands	Germany	18 Dec 37	Finance	190LTS29	304403
Netherlands	Germany	25 May 38	Finance	192LTS143	304468
Netherlands	Germany	17 May 39	Territory Boundary	199LTS239	304678
Netherlands	Great Britain	27 Apr 26	Telecommunications	50LTS295	301212
Netherlands	Greece	12 May 26	General Trade	61LTS295	301440
Netherlands	Greece	05 Dec 30	Taxation	117LTS357	302702
Netherlands	Guatemala	12 May 27	General Trade	85LTS323	301937
Netherlands	Haiti	07 Sep 26	General Trade	71LTS219	301665
Netherlands	Hungary	09 Dec 24	General Trade	47LTS91	301130
Netherlands	Hungary	26 Jun 31	Land Transport	127LTS217	302921
Netherlands	Hungary	08 Jun 35	Air Transport	171LTS385	303975
Netherlands	Italy	11 Oct 20	Land Transport	18LTS253	300468
Netherlands	Italy	28 Jun 27	Water Transport	68LTS203	301583
Netherlands	Italy	01 Jul 31	General Transport	127LTS235	302923
Netherlands	Italy	03 Oct 31	Air Transport	126LTS109	302875
Netherlands	Italy	06 Jul 33	Land Transport	152LTS247	303496
Netherlands	Italy	01 Mar 34	General Trade	163LTS367	303779
Netherlands	Italy	29 Jul 35	Finance	165LTS329	303819
Netherlands	Italy	01 Jan 37	Finance	178LTS415	304124
Netherlands	Italy	26 Feb 38	Air Transport	194LTS75	304509
Netherlands	Japan	12 Oct 21	Water Transport	12LTS239	300316
Netherlands	Japan	26 Jan 33	Taxation	138LTS185	303187
Netherlands	Japan	19 Apr 33	Dispute Settlement	163LTS351	303778
Netherlands	Latvia	02 Jul 24	General Trade	37LTS121	300951
Netherlands	Latvia	27 Jan 30	Extradition	117LTS343	302701
Netherlands	Latvia	15 Dec 31	Water Transport	133LTS107	303061
Netherlands	Lithuania	10 Jun 24	General Trade	34LTS373	300885
Netherlands	Lithuania	01 Dec 33	Extradition	150LTS337	303466
Netherlands	Luxembourg	17 Sep 29	Dispute Settlement	107LTS35	302466
Netherlands	Luxembourg	01 Apr 36	Non-ILO Labor	179LTS11	304130
Netherlands	Malaya	16 Mar 37	Postal Service	184LTS181	304248
Netherlands	Multilateral	09 Sep 86*	Patents/Copyrights	123LTS233	302816
Netherlands	Multilateral	18 Mar 04	Humanitarian	1LTS83	300011
Netherlands	Multilateral	13 Nov 08	General Ad Hoc	1LTS217	300015
Netherlands	Multilateral	12 Jan 12	Sanitation	4LTS281	300112
Netherlands	Multilateral	23 Jan 12	Sanitation	8LTS187	300222
Netherlands	Multilateral	05 Jun 12	Telecommunications	1LTS135	300013
Netherlands	Multilateral	20 Mar 14	Patents/Copyrights	1LTS243	300016
Netherlands	Multilateral	01 May 20	Air Transport	11LTS173	300297
Netherlands	Multilateral	21 Jun 20	Health/Educ/Welfare	8LTS65	300207
Netherlands	Multilateral	30 Jun 20	Patents/Copyrights	1LTS59	300008
Netherlands	Multilateral	16 Dec 20	General IGO	6LTS379	300170
Netherlands	Multilateral	20 Apr 21	Water Transport	7LTS73	300174
Netherlands	Multilateral	20 Apr 21	Land Transport	7LTS11	300171
Netherlands	Multilateral	05 Aug 21	Admin Cooperation	27LTS349	300695
Netherlands	Multilateral	05 Oct 21	IGO Establishment	51LTS361	301241
Netherlands	Multilateral	05 Oct 21	Admin Cooperation	29LTS79	300735
Netherlands	Multilateral	05 Oct 21	Admin Cooperation	29LTS73	300734
Netherlands	Multilateral	05 Oct 21	Admin Cooperation	29LTS67	300733
Netherlands	Multilateral	06 Oct 21	General Economic	17LTS45	300427
Netherlands	Multilateral	06 Feb 22	General Trade	38LTS277	300982
Netherlands	Multilateral	06 Feb 22	Customs	38LTS267	300981
Netherlands	Multilateral	31 Mar 22	Humanitarian	9LTS415	300269
Netherlands	Multilateral	04 Oct 22	Territory Boundary	12LTS391	300335
Netherlands	Multilateral	14 Dec 22	Water Transport	36LTS457	300943
Netherlands	Multilateral	29 Mar 23	Admin Cooperation	20LTS111	300510

PARTY ONE	PARTY TWO	DATE	TOPIC	CITATION	NUMBER
Netherlands	Multilateral	24 Sep 23	Dispute Settlement	27LTS157	300678
Netherlands	Multilateral	03 Nov 23	Customs	30LTS371	300775
Netherlands	Multilateral	28 Nov 23	Admin Cooperation	51LTS233	301232
Netherlands	Multilateral	28 Nov 23	Admin Cooperation	51LTS215	301229
Netherlands	Multilateral	28 Nov 23	Admin Cooperation	51LTS221	301230
Netherlands	Multilateral	28 Nov 23	Admin Cooperation	51LTS209	301228
Netherlands	Multilateral	28 Nov 23	Admin Cooperation	51LTS239	301233
Netherlands	Multilateral	09 Dec 23	Land Transport	47LTS55	301129
Netherlands	Multilateral	09 Dec 23	Water Transport	58LTS284	301379
Netherlands	Multilateral	18 Dec 23	Territory Boundary	28LTS541	300729
Netherlands	Multilateral	25 Jan 24	Sanitation	57LTS135	301360
Netherlands	Multilateral	07 Feb 24	Water Transport	25LTS265	300614
Netherlands	Multilateral	31 Mar 24	Sanitation	27LTS211	300685
Netherlands	Multilateral	04 Jul 24	Admin Cooperation	51LTS227	301231
Netherlands	Multilateral	28 Aug 24	Postal Service	40LTS19	301002
Netherlands	Multilateral	28 Aug 24	Postal Service	40LTS437	301005
Netherlands	Multilateral	28 Aug 24	Postal Service	40LTS249	301003
Netherlands	Multilateral	28 Aug 24	Postal Service	41LTS55	301007
Netherlands	Multilateral	28 Aug 24	Postal Service	40LTS307	301004
Netherlands	Multilateral	28 Aug 24	Postal Service	41LTS97	301008
Netherlands	Multilateral	28 Aug 24	Postal Service	41LTS9	301006
Netherlands	Multilateral	23 Oct 24	General Transport	77LTS367	301778
Netherlands	Multilateral	23 Oct 24	Land Transport	78LTS17	301779
Netherlands	Multilateral	01 Dec 24	Sanitation	78LTS351	301794
Netherlands	Multilateral	12 Dec 24	Gen Communications	37LTS113	300950
Netherlands	Multilateral	11 Feb 25	Sanitation	51LTS337	301239
Netherlands	Multilateral	19 Feb 25	Admin Cooperation	81LTS317	301845
Netherlands	Multilateral	00 Apr 25	Water Transport	37LTS21	300945
Netherlands	Multilateral	23 Apr 25	Water Transport	37LTS9	300944
Netherlands	Multilateral	17 Jun 25	Peace/Disarmament	94LTS65	302138
Netherlands	Multilateral	29 Oct 25	Telecommunications	57LTS201	301365
Netherlands	Multilateral	06 Nov 25	Other Economic	74LTS341	301746
Netherlands	Multilateral	06 Nov 25	Patents/Copyrights	74LTS327	301745
Netherlands	Multilateral	06 Nov 25	Patents/Copyrights	74LTS289	301743
Netherlands	Multilateral	27 Nov 25	Water Transport	67LTS63	301539
Netherlands	Multilateral	00 Apr 26	Water Transport	57LTS437	301366
Netherlands	Multilateral	10 Apr 26	Water Transport	176LTS199	304062
Netherlands	Multilateral	10 Apr 26	Water Transport	120LTS187	302765
Netherlands	Multilateral	24 Apr 26	Land Transport	108LTS123	302505
Netherlands	Multilateral	21 Jun 26	Sanitation	78LTS229	301793
Netherlands	Multilateral	25 Sep 26	ILO Labor	60LTS253	301414
Netherlands	Multilateral	30 Oct 26	Telecommunications	61LTS65	301426
Netherlands	Multilateral	22 Jan 27	Telecommunications	68LTS149	301578
Netherlands	Multilateral	22 Jan 27	Telecommunications	68LTS129	301576
Netherlands	Multilateral	19 Feb 27	Telecommunications	68LTS139	301577
Netherlands	Multilateral	24 Feb 27	Telecommunications	68LTS159	301579
Netherlands	Multilateral	18 Mar 27	Telecommunications	68LTS179	301581
Netherlands	Multilateral	02 May 27	Telecommunications	68LTS189	301582
Netherlands	Multilateral	10 Sep 27	Postal Service	75LTS39	301750
Netherlands	Multilateral	10 Sep 27	Postal Service	75LTS7	301749
Netherlands	Multilateral	26 Sep 27	Dispute Settlement	92LTS301	302096
Netherlands	Multilateral	08 Nov 27	General Trade	97LTS391	302238
Netherlands	Multilateral	25 Nov 27	Telecommunications	84LTS97	301905
Netherlands	Multilateral	07 Jan 28	Telecommunications	78LTS187	301789
Netherlands	Multilateral	10 Mar 28	Telecommunications	132LTS405	303049
Netherlands	Multilateral	01 May 28	Telecommunications	132LTS415	303050
Netherlands	Multilateral	22 May 28	Telecommunications	85LTS99	301925
Netherlands	Multilateral	09 Jun 28	Telecommunications	78LTS219	301792
Netherlands	Multilateral	11 Jul 28	Commodity Trade	95LTS373	302185
Netherlands	Multilateral	11 Jul 28	Commodity Trade	95LTS357	302184
Netherlands	Multilateral	25 Jul 28	General Amity	87LTS211	301971
Netherlands	Multilateral	27 Aug 28	General Military	94LTS57	302137
Netherlands	Multilateral	22 Nov 28	Culture	111LTS343	302598
Netherlands	Multilateral	14 Dec 28	General Economic	110LTS171	302560
Netherlands	Multilateral	05 Jan 29	Telecommunications	132LTS425	303051

PARTY ONE	PARTY TWO	DATE	TOPIC	CITATION	NUMBER
Netherlands	Multilateral	16 Apr 29	Specific Resources	126LTS305	302891
Netherlands	Multilateral	20 Apr 29	Admin Cooperation	112LTS371	302623
Netherlands	Multilateral	31 May 29	Water Transport	136LTS81	303127
Netherlands	Multilateral	14 Jun 29	Visas	94LTS275	302148
Netherlands	Multilateral	28 Jun 29	Postal Service	103LTS5	302369
Netherlands	Multilateral	28 Jun 29	Postal Service	103LTS321	302372
Netherlands	Multilateral	28 Jun 29	Postal Service	103LTS71	302370
Netherlands	Multilateral	28 Jun 29	Postal Service	103LTS377	302373
Netherlands	Multilateral	28 Jun 29	Postal Service	102LTS245	302368
Netherlands	Multilateral	28 Jun 29	Postal Service	103LTS429	302374
Netherlands	Multilateral	28 Jun 29	Postal Service	103LTS249	302371
Netherlands	Multilateral	27 Jul 29	Other Military	118LTS303	302733
Netherlands	Multilateral	27 Jul 29	Other Military	118LTS343	302734
Netherlands	Multilateral	20 Aug 29	Sanitation	98LTS125	302243
Netherlands	Multilateral	14 Sep 29	UN Charter	165LTS353	303822
Netherlands	Multilateral	30 Sep 29	Telecommunications	98LTS183	302246
Netherlands	Multilateral	12 Oct 29	General Transport	137LTS11	303145
Netherlands	Multilateral	17 Feb 30	Dispute Settlement	102LTS87	302354
Netherlands	Multilateral	10 Apr 30	Telecommunications	101LTS465	302345
Netherlands	Multilateral	12 Apr 30	Admin Cooperation	179LTS89	304137
Netherlands	Multilateral	12 Apr 30	Milit Servic/Citiz	178LTS227	304117
Netherlands	Multilateral	12 Apr 30	Admin Cooperation	179LTS115	304138
Netherlands	Multilateral	07 Jun 30	Finance	143LTS337	303315
Netherlands	Multilateral	07 Jun 30	Finance	143LTS257	303313
Netherlands	Multilateral	07 Jun 30	Finance	143LTS317	303314
Netherlands	Multilateral	26 Jun 30	Telecommunications	133LTS9	303052
Netherlands	Multilateral	28 Aug 30	Telecommunications	133LTS21	303053
Netherlands	Multilateral	23 Oct 30	Water Transport	125LTS95	302849
Netherlands	Multilateral	23 Oct 30	Water Transport	112LTS21	302603
Netherlands	Multilateral	22 Dec 30	General Trade	126LTS341	302893
Netherlands	Multilateral	19 Mar 31	Finance	143LTS355	303316
Netherlands	Multilateral	19 Mar 31	Finance	143LTS407	303317
Netherlands	Multilateral	19 Mar 31	Admin Cooperation	143LTS7	303301
Netherlands	Multilateral	27 Mar 31	ICJ Option Clause	167LTS341	303877
Netherlands	Multilateral	28 Mar 31	Customs	119LTS47	302739
Netherlands	Multilateral	30 Mar 31	Land Transport	150LTS247	303459
Netherlands	Multilateral	30 Mar 31	Taxation	138LTS149	303185
Netherlands	Multilateral	13 Jul 31	Other HEW	139LTS301	303219
Netherlands	Multilateral	24 Sep 31	Specific Resources	155LTS349	303586
Netherlands	Multilateral	27 Nov 31	Sanitation	177LTS373	304100
Netherlands	Multilateral	11 Dec 31	Commodity Trade	170LTS251	303941
Netherlands	Multilateral	15 Jul 32	Direct Aid	135LTS285	303118
Netherlands	Multilateral	02 Sep 32	Land Transport	154LTS123	303543
Netherlands	Multilateral	09 Dec 32	Telecommunications	151LTS5	303479
Netherlands	Multilateral	11 Mar 33	Water Transport	135LTS301	303119
Netherlands	Multilateral	12 Apr 33	Sanitation	161LTS65	303706
Netherlands	Multilateral	29 May 33	Admin Cooperation	192LTS289	304479
Netherlands	Multilateral	11 Oct 33	Consul/Citizenship	150LTS431	303476
Netherlands	Multilateral	23 Nov 33	Land Transport	192LTS327	304483
Netherlands	Multilateral	23 Nov 33	Land Transport	192LTS389	304484
Netherlands	Multilateral	20 Mar 34	Finance	176LTS9	304053
Netherlands	Multilateral	20 Mar 34	Postal Service	174LTS171	304048
Netherlands	Multilateral	20 Mar 34	Postal Service	175LTS5	304049
Netherlands	Multilateral	20 Mar 34	Postal Service	175LTS269	304051
Netherlands	Multilateral	20 Mar 34	Postal Service	175LTS73	304050
Netherlands	Multilateral	20 Mar 34	Postal Service	175LTS363	304052
Netherlands	Multilateral	20 Mar 34	Postal Service	176LTS55	304054
Netherlands	Multilateral	26 Apr 34	Admin Cooperation	164LTS63	303789
Netherlands	Multilateral	07 May 34	Commodity Trade	171LTS203	303961
Netherlands	Multilateral	02 Jun 34	Patents/Copyrights	192LTS17	304459
Netherlands	Multilateral	12 Jun 34	Milit Installation	155LTS367	303587
Netherlands	Multilateral	19 Jun 34	Admin Cooperation	154LTS381	303564
Netherlands	Multilateral	22 Dec 34	Admin Cooperation	183LTS153	304231
Netherlands	Multilateral	22 Dec 34	Visas	183LTS145	304230
Netherlands	Multilateral	20 Feb 35	Sanitation	193LTS37	304486
Netherlands	Multilateral	20 Feb 35	Sanitation	193LTS59	304487
Netherlands	Multilateral	20 Feb 35	Sanitation	186LTS173	304310
Netherlands	Multilateral	26 Jun 36	Other HEW	198LTS299	304648
Netherlands	Multilateral	04 Jul 36	Refugees	171LTS75	303952
Netherlands	Multilateral	30 Jul 36	IGO Status/Immunit	197LTS31	304602
Netherlands	Multilateral	23 Sep 36	Gen Communications	186LTS301	304319
Netherlands	Multilateral	06 Nov 36	General Military	173LTS353	304025
Netherlands	Multilateral	10 Feb 37	General Transport	189LTS313	304391
Netherlands	Multilateral	31 Mar 37	Commodity Trade	189LTS359	304394
Netherlands	Multilateral	08 May 37	Privil/Immunities	182LTS37	304202
Netherlands	Multilateral	28 May 37	General Trade	180LTS5	304170
Netherlands	Multilateral	08 Jun 37	Specific Resources	190LTS79	304406
Netherlands	Multilateral	02 Oct 37	Education	182LTS263	304216
Netherlands	Multilateral	10 Feb 38	Refugees	192LTS59	304461
Netherlands	Multilateral	11 May 38	General Trade	189LTS237	304386
Netherlands	Multilateral	24 Jun 38	Specific Resources	196LTS131	304575
Netherlands	Multilateral	31 Oct 38	Sanitation	198LTS205	304642
Netherlands	Multilateral	03 Dec 38	Education	200LTS249	304694
Netherlands	Multilateral	03 Apr 39	Water Transport	195LTS471	304566
Netherlands	Multilateral	23 May 39	Postal Service	202LTS159	304742
Netherlands	Multilateral	21 Aug 39	Visas	198LTS343	304652
Netherlands	Multilateral	01 Jan 42	General Military	204LTS381	304817
Netherlands	Multilateral	02 Jun 42	Patents/Copyrights	205LTS163	304833
Netherlands	Multilateral	09 Sep 42	Commodity Trade	205LTS137	304831
Netherlands	New Zealand	14 Jan 38	General Trade	185LTS329	304297
Netherlands	Norway	08 Jan 25	Air Transport	46LTS279	301122
Netherlands	Norway	09 Jan 25	Non-ILO Labor	48LTS247	301166
Netherlands	Norway	21 Sep 26	Admin Cooperation	56LTS89	301325
Netherlands	Norway	11 Jan 29	Taxation	85LTS409	301941
Netherlands	Norway	15 Jul 31	Land Transport	127LTS313	302924
Netherlands	Norway	23 Mar 33	Dispute Settlement	146LTS291	303380
Netherlands	Norway	18 Jul 33	Land Transport	152LTS259	303498
Netherlands	Norway	28 Oct 38	Visas	193LTS223	304499
Netherlands	Persia	20 Jun 28	General Amity	81LTS431	301852
Netherlands	Persia	12 Mar 30	General Amity	111LTS387	302599
Netherlands	Poland	30 May 24	General Trade	34LTS9	300865
Netherlands	Poland	04 Sep 25	Air Transport	58LTS179	301371
Netherlands	Poland	12 Apr 30	Dispute Settlement	113LTS65	302636
Netherlands	Poland	24 Dec 31	Admin Cooperation	131LTS269	303016
Netherlands	Poland	28 Jun 33	Land Transport	152LTS201	303494
Netherlands	Poland	11 Dec 33	General Trade	163LTS381	303780
Netherlands	Poland	09 Apr 36	Customs	177LTS71	304081
Netherlands	Portugal	22 Aug 23	General Trade	20LTS139	300513
Netherlands	Portugal	27 Feb 24	General Trade	27LTS105	300672
Netherlands	Portugal	27 Aug 24	General Trade	31LTS235	300800
Netherlands	Portugal	27 Jun 28	Admin Cooperation	81LTS437	301853
Netherlands	Romania	20 Feb 22	General Transport	12LTS219	300313
Netherlands	Romania	19 Dec 22	General Economic	14LTS191	300373
Netherlands	Romania	22 Jan 30	Dispute Settlement	112LTS121	302611
Netherlands	Romania	29 Aug 30	Mostfavored Nation	108LTS177	302507
Netherlands	Romania	20 Jul 31	Land Transport	127LTS425	302929
Netherlands	Romania	28 Aug 36	Finance	182LTS363	304222
Netherlands	Romania	10 Oct 38	Finance	195LTS9	304532
Netherlands	Serb/Croat/Slovene	15 Jun 23	Land Transport	20LTS337	300524
Netherlands	Siam	08 Jun 25	General Economic	56LTS57	301323
Netherlands	Siam	27 Oct 28	Dispute Settlement	93LTS131	302105
Netherlands	Siam	01 Feb 38	General Amity	193LTS13	304485
Netherlands	South Africa	10 Sep 29	Postal Service	98LTS423	302261
Netherlands	South Africa	29 Jun 32	Postal Service	133LTS33	303054
Netherlands	South Africa	20 Feb 35	General Trade	160LTS143	303688
Netherlands	Spain	24 Mar 21	General Economic	7LTS115	300179
Netherlands	Spain	24 Jun 21	General Economic	7LTS121	300180
Netherlands	Spain	05 Jan 22	General Economic	9LTS257	300259
Netherlands	Spain	27 Mar 29	Admin Cooperation	101LTS479	302346
Netherlands	Spain	14 Feb 30	Air Transport	137LTS149	303152

PARTY ONE	PARTY TWO	DATE	TOPIC	CITATION	NUMBER
Netherlands	Spain	30 Mar 31	Dispute Settlement	137LTS161	303153
Netherlands	Spain	16 Jun 34	General Economic	168LTS29	303885
Netherlands	Sweden	21 Nov 25	Air Transport	55LTS79	301305
Netherlands	Sweden	21 May 27	Dispute Settlement	79LTS147	301807
Netherlands	Sweden	24 Dec 27	Water Transport	71LTS391	301677
Netherlands	Sweden	30 Dec 27	Admin Cooperation	70LTS365	301646
Netherlands	Sweden	15 Jul 31	Land Transport	127LTS321	302925
Netherlands	Sweden	29 Nov 33	Land Transport	153LTS11	303501
Netherlands	Sweden	21 Mar 35	Taxation	148LTS451	303648
Netherlands	Switzerland	18 May 25	Air Transport	54LTS365	301299
Netherlands	Switzerland	12 Dec 25	Dispute Settlement	63LTS289	301496
Netherlands	Switzerland	27 Aug 28	Admin Cooperation	82LTS153	301866
Netherlands	Switzerland	15 Oct 36	Air Transport	177LTS101	304084
Netherlands	Switzerland	27 Jan 37	Non-ILO Labor	186LTS433	304327
Netherlands	Switzerland	01 Jul 39	Customs	198LTS195	304640
Netherlands	Turkey	16 Aug 24	Admin Cooperation	39LTS148	300999
Netherlands	Turkey	11 Aug 26	General Economic	48LTS271	301168
Netherlands	Turkey	25 Jul 28	General Economic	93LTS279	302116
Netherlands	Turkey	21 Nov 29	General Trade	99LTS397	302284
Netherlands	Turkey	16 Apr 32	Dispute Settlement	143LTS237	303311
Netherlands	Turkey	17 Feb 37	Finance	182LTS221	304213
Netherlands	UK Great Britain	13 Apr 20	Extradition	1LTS275	300021
Netherlands	UK Great Britain	01 Jul 20	Dispute Settlement	1LTS291	300024
Netherlands	UK Great Britain	18 Jan 21	Telecommunications	5LTS157	300124
Netherlands	UK Great Britain	02 Jun 22	Postal Service	13LTS263	300357
Netherlands	UK Great Britain	18 Jan 23	Postal Service	18LTS257	300469
Netherlands	UK Great Britain	23 Jan 23	Postal Service	16LTS425	300420
Netherlands	UK Great Britain	30 Apr 23	Postal Service	20LTS343	300525
Netherlands	UK Great Britain	11 Jul 23	Air Transport	33LTS111	300836
Netherlands	UK Great Britain	06 Sep 23	Postal Service	22LTS433	300572
Netherlands	UK Great Britain	28 Sep 23	Sanitation	23LTS113	300581
Netherlands	UK Great Britain	02 Oct 23	Postal Service	23LTS9	300573
Netherlands	UK Great Britain	12 Jul 25	Admin Cooperation	38LTS207	300977
Netherlands	UK Great Britain	30 Dec 25	Postal Service	61LTS9	301424
Netherlands	UK Great Britain	20 May 26	Taxation	50LTS309	301214
Netherlands	UK Great Britain	14 Aug 26	Sanitation	57LTS41	301351
Netherlands	UK Great Britain	11 Mar 27	Telecommunications	64LTS403	301513
Netherlands	UK Great Britain	14 Nov 27	Postal Service	71LTS227	301666
Netherlands	UK Great Britain	26 Mar 28	Territory Boundary	108LTS331	302516
Netherlands	UK Great Britain	22 Mar 29	Reparations	90LTS421	302052
Netherlands	UK Great Britain	04 May 29	Postal Service	93LTS9	302101
Netherlands	UK Great Britain	10 Feb 30	Postal Service	102LTS67	302353
Netherlands	UK Great Britain	05 May 30	Air Transport	105LTS261	302417
Netherlands	UK Great Britain	03 Jun 30	Postal Service	111LTS85	302582
Netherlands	UK Great Britain	01 Jan 31	Postal Service	115LTS509	302698
Netherlands	UK Great Britain	09 Apr 31	Education	125LTS41	302844
Netherlands	UK Great Britain	04 Jan 32	Postal Service	128LTS307	302939
Netherlands	UK Great Britain	04 Jan 32	Postal Service	128LTS347	302940
Netherlands	UK Great Britain	31 May 32	Admin Cooperation	140LTS287	303244
Netherlands	UK Great Britain	13 Aug 32	Postal Service	134LTS317	303100
Netherlands	UK Great Britain	30 Jul 34	General Trade	154LTS305	303557
Netherlands	UK Great Britain	06 Jun 35	Taxation	169LTS359	303924
Netherlands	UK Great Britain	07 Nov 35	Water Transport	165LTS337	303820
Netherlands	UK Great Britain	18 Dec 35	General Trade	165LTS255	303812
Netherlands	UK Great Britain	30 Dec 35	Customs	165LTS263	303813
Netherlands	UK Great Britain	27 Aug 36	Air Transport	172LTS53	303978
Netherlands	UK Great Britain	04 Aug 39	Gen Communications	198LTS349	304653
Netherlands	United Arab Rep	17 Mar 30	Mostfavored Nation	105LTS91	302404
Netherlands	Uruguay	29 Jan 34	General Economic	166LTS43	303828
Netherlands	USA (United States)	18 Dec 13	Dispute Settlement	74LTS157	301737
Netherlands	USA (United States)	03 Apr 23	Patents/Copyrights	21LTS175	300541
Netherlands	USA (United States)	13 Feb 24	Admin Cooperation	25LTS269	300616
Netherlands	USA (United States)	15 Feb 24	Postal Service	31LTS61	300783
Netherlands	USA (United States)	21 Aug 24	Sanitation	33LTS433	300863
Netherlands	USA (United States)	23 Jan 25	Territory Boundary	33LTS445	300864

PARTY ONE	PARTY TWO	DATE	TOPIC	CITATION	NUMBER
Netherlands	USA (United States)	19 Jan 26	Postal Service	50LTS199	301202
Netherlands	USA (United States)	27 Nov 26	Taxation	112LTS433	302628
Netherlands	USA (United States)	30 Dec 27	Finance	72LTS179	301691
Netherlands	USA (United States)	13 Jan 30	Dispute Settlement	107LTS69	302468
Netherlands	USA (United States)	09 Jul 30	Postal Service	125LTS123	302851
Netherlands	USA (United States)	16 Sep 30	Postal Service	125LTS173	302853
Netherlands	USA (United States)	16 Sep 30	Postal Service	125LTS147	302852
Netherlands	USA (United States)	20 Dec 35	General Trade	178LTS239	304118
Netherlands	USA (United States)	20 Sep 37	Postal Service	184LTS319	304256
Netherlands	USA (United States)	18 Feb 38	Dispute Settlement	192LTS49	304460
Netherlands	Venezuela	11 May 20	General Amity	7LTS85	300176
Netherlands	Venezuela	05 Apr 33	Dispute Settlement	144LTS353	303338
Netherlands	Yemen	12 Mar 33	General Amity	146LTS359	303384
Netherlands	Yugoslavia	28 May 30	General Economic	129LTS73	302951
Netherlands	Yugoslavia	11 Mar 31	Dispute Settlement	129LTS89	302952
Netherlands	Yugoslavia	15 Jul 31	Land Transport	127LTS337	302927
Netherlands	Yugoslavia	18 Jul 33	Land Transport	152LTS273	303500
New Caledonia	Multilateral	05 Jun 12	Telecommunications	1LTS135	300013
New Caledonia	Multilateral	29 Oct 25	Telecommunications	57LTS201	301365
New Caledonia	Multilateral	24 Apr 26	Land Transport	108LTS123	302505
New Caledonia	Multilateral	24 Apr 26	Land Transport	97LTS83	302220
New Caledonia	Multilateral	23 Oct 30	Water Transport	125LTS95	302849
New Guinea	Multilateral	06 Nov 25	Patents/Copyrights	74LTS289	301743
New Hebrides Is	Multilateral	25 Nov 27	Telecommunications	84LTS97	301905
New Hebrides Is	Multilateral	07 Jun 30	Finance	143LTS337	303315
New Hebrides Is	Multilateral	19 Mar 31	Admin Cooperation	143LTS7	303301
New Hebrides Is	Multilateral	09 Dec 32	Telecommunications	151LTS5	303479
New Hebrides Is	Multilateral	23 Sep 36	Gen Communications	186LTS301	304319
New Zealand	Bel-Lux Econ Union	05 Dec 33	Mostfavored Nation	149LTS435	303445
New Zealand	Germany	17 Jan 30	Reparations	109LTS485	302551
New Zealand	Greece	16 Nov 26	General Trade	85LTS43	301921
New Zealand	Irish Free State	30 Apr 25	Postal Service	56LTS373	301342
New Zealand	Japan	24 Jul 28	General Trade	85LTS129	301927
New Zealand	Multilateral	09 Sep 86*	Patents/Copyrights	123LTS233	302816
New Zealand	Multilateral	18 Mar 04	Humanitarian	1LTS83	300011
New Zealand	Multilateral	12 Jan 12	Sanitation	4LTS281	300112
New Zealand	Multilateral	05 Jun 12	Telecommunications	1LTS135	300013
New Zealand	Multilateral	10 Sep 19	Health/Educ/Welfare	8LTS11	300201
New Zealand	Multilateral	10 Sep 19	General Trade	7LTS331	300200
New Zealand	Multilateral	09 Feb 20	Territory Boundary	2LTS7	300041
New Zealand	Multilateral	01 May 20	Air Transport	11LTS173	300297
New Zealand	Multilateral	21 Jun 20	Health/Educ/Welfare	8LTS65	300207
New Zealand	Multilateral	30 Jun 20	Patents/Copyrights	1LTS59	300008
New Zealand	Multilateral	10 Aug 20	Territory Boundary	28LTS225	300710
New Zealand	Multilateral	10 Aug 20	Consul/Citizenship	28LTS223	300711
New Zealand	Multilateral	16 Dec 20	General IGO	6LTS379	300170
New Zealand	Multilateral	19 Jan 21	Recognition	5LTS9	300113
New Zealand	Multilateral	20 Apr 21	Water Transport	7LTS65	300173
New Zealand	Multilateral	20 Apr 21	Water Transport	7LTS73	300174
New Zealand	Multilateral	20 Apr 21	Water Transport	7LTS35	300172
New Zealand	Multilateral	20 Apr 21	Land Transport	7LTS11	300171
New Zealand	Multilateral	05 Aug 21	Admin Cooperation	27LTS349	300695
New Zealand	Multilateral	05 Oct 21	IGO Establishment	51LTS361	301241
New Zealand	Multilateral	05 Oct 21	Admin Cooperation	29LTS67	300733
New Zealand	Multilateral	05 Oct 21	Admin Cooperation	29LTS73	300734
New Zealand	Multilateral	05 Oct 21	Admin Cooperation	29LTS79	300735
New Zealand	Multilateral	06 Feb 22	Customs	38LTS267	300981
New Zealand	Multilateral	06 Feb 22	General Trade	38LTS277	300982
New Zealand	Multilateral	31 Mar 22	Humanitarian	9LTS415	300269
New Zealand	Multilateral	02 Nov 22	Peace/Disarmament	149LTS35	303431
New Zealand	Multilateral	03 Nov 23	Customs	30LTS371	300775
New Zealand	Multilateral	09 Dec 23	Land Transport	47LTS55	301129
New Zealand	Multilateral	31 Mar 24	Sanitation	27LTS211	300685
New Zealand	Multilateral	16 Aug 24	Taxation	41LTS429	301024
New Zealand	Multilateral	28 Aug 24	Postal Service	40LTS249	301003

PARTY ONE	PARTY TWO	DATE	TOPIC	CITATION	NUMBER
New Zealand	Multilateral	28 Aug 24	Postal Service	40LTS19	301002
New Zealand	Multilateral	30 Aug 24	Admin Cooperation	30LTS75	300760
New Zealand	Multilateral	30 Aug 24	Admin Cooperation	30LTS79	300761
New Zealand	Multilateral	01 Dec 24	Sanitation	78LTS351	301794
New Zealand	Multilateral	19 Feb 25	Admin Cooperation	81LTS317	301845
New Zealand	Multilateral	17 Jun 25	Peace/Disarmament	94LTS65	302138
New Zealand	Multilateral	29 Oct 25	Telecommunications	57LTS201	301365
New Zealand	Multilateral	06 Nov 25	Patents/Copyrights	74LTS289	301743
New Zealand	Multilateral	06 Nov 25	Other Economic	74LTS319	301744
New Zealand	Multilateral	21 Jun 26	Sanitation	78LTS229	301793
New Zealand	Multilateral	25 Sep 26	ILO Labor	60LTS253	301414
New Zealand	Multilateral	12 Jul 27	Direct Aid	135LTS247	303115
New Zealand	Multilateral	26 Sep 27	Dispute Settlement	92LTS301	302096
New Zealand	Multilateral	25 Nov 27	Telecommunications	84LTS97	301905
New Zealand	Multilateral	27 Aug 28	General Military	94LTS57	302137
New Zealand	Multilateral	26 Sep 28	Dispute Settlement	93LTS343	302123
New Zealand	Multilateral	31 May 29	Water Transport	136LTS81	303127
New Zealand	Multilateral	28 Jun 29	Postal Service	103LTS5	302369
New Zealand	Multilateral	28 Jun 29	Postal Service	102LTS245	302368
New Zealand	Multilateral	27 Jul 29	Other Military	118LTS303	302733
New Zealand	Multilateral	27 Jul 29	Other Military	118LTS343	302734
New Zealand	Multilateral	14 Sep 29	UN Charter	165LTS353	303822
New Zealand	Multilateral	20 Jan 30	Reparations	112LTS361	302622
New Zealand	Multilateral	20 Jan 30	Reparations	113LTS389	302650
New Zealand	Multilateral	20 Jan 30	Reparations	104LTS243	302394
New Zealand	Multilateral	20 Jan 30	Finance	104LTS433	302397
New Zealand	Multilateral	20 Jan 30	Finance	104LTS413	302395
New Zealand	Multilateral	15 Mar 30	Finance	113LTS395	302651
New Zealand	Multilateral	17 Apr 30	Extradition	126LTS201	302883
New Zealand	Multilateral	22 Apr 30	Peace/Disarmament	112LTS65	302608
New Zealand	Multilateral	28 Apr 30	Claims and Debts	121LTS69	302785
New Zealand	Multilateral	10 Jun 30	Loans and Credits	112LTS237	302618
New Zealand	Multilateral	01 Jul 30	Claims and Debts	121LTS153	302786
New Zealand	Multilateral	27 Nov 30	Extradition	121LTS39	302781
New Zealand	Multilateral	13 Apr 31	Air Transport	119LTS275	302751
New Zealand	Multilateral	24 Sep 31	Specific Resources	155LTS349	303586
New Zealand	Multilateral	10 Dec 31	Water Transport	129LTS177	302961
New Zealand	Multilateral	20 Jan 32	Extradition	141LTS267	303269
New Zealand	Multilateral	09 Dec 32	Telecommunications	151LTS5	303479
New Zealand	Multilateral	11 Mar 33	Water Transport	135LTS301	303119
New Zealand	Multilateral	12 Apr 33	Sanitation	161LTS65	303706
New Zealand	Multilateral	30 Sep 33	Extradition	205LTS155	304832
New Zealand	Multilateral	20 Mar 34	Postal Service	174LTS171	304048
New Zealand	Multilateral	20 Mar 34	Postal Service	175LTS5	304049
New Zealand	Multilateral	16 Apr 34	Water Transport	163LTS185	303767
New Zealand	Multilateral	02 Jun 34	Patents/Copyrights	192LTS17	304459
New Zealand	Multilateral	04 Jun 34	Extradition	184LTS437	304264
New Zealand	Multilateral	19 Jun 34	Admin Cooperation	154LTS381	303564
New Zealand	Multilateral	22 Dec 34	Visas	183LTS145	304230
New Zealand	Multilateral	22 Dec 34	Admin Cooperation	183LTS153	304231
New Zealand	Multilateral	15 Mar 35	Other Military	170LTS9	303926
New Zealand	Multilateral	20 Dec 35	Other Military	167LTS141	303862
New Zealand	Multilateral	25 Mar 36	Peace/Disarmament	184LTS115	304246
New Zealand	Multilateral	27 May 36	Admin Cooperation	203LTS367	304779
New Zealand	Multilateral	30 Jul 36	IGO Status/Immunit	197LTS31	304602
New Zealand	Multilateral	23 Sep 36	Gen Communications	186LTS301	304319
New Zealand	Multilateral	06 Nov 36	General Military	173LTS353	304025
New Zealand	Multilateral	23 Jan 37	Extradition	191LTS219	304446
New Zealand	Multilateral	31 Mar 37	Commodity Trade	189LTS359	304394
New Zealand	Multilateral	08 May 37	Privil/Immunities	182LTS37	304202
New Zealand	Multilateral	02 Jun 37	Specific Property	184LTS445	304265
New Zealand	Multilateral	08 Jun 37	Specific Resources	190LTS79	304406
New Zealand	Multilateral	21 Jul 37	Admin Cooperation	184LTS271	304250
New Zealand	Multilateral	11 Oct 37	Air Transport	182LTS173	304210
New Zealand	Multilateral	29 Apr 38	Visas	190LTS115	304410

PARTY ONE	PARTY TWO	DATE	TOPIC	CITATION	NUMBER
New Zealand	Multilateral	17 May 38	Visas	192LTS319	304481
New Zealand	Multilateral	30 May 38	Visas	191LTS299	304451
New Zealand	Multilateral	24 Jun 38	Specific Resources	196LTS131	304575
New Zealand	Multilateral	25 Oct 38	Air Transport	192LTS323	304482
New Zealand	Multilateral	28 Dec 38	Other Military	196LTS221	304585
New Zealand	Multilateral	23 May 39	Postal Service	202LTS159	304742
New Zealand	Multilateral	21 Aug 39	Visas	198LTS343	304652
New Zealand	Multilateral	08 Jan 40	Visas	203LTS133	304756
New Zealand	Multilateral	01 Jan 42	General Military	204LTS381	304817
New Zealand	Netherlands	14 Jan 38	General Trade	185LTS329	304297
New Zealand	Norway	27 Oct 33	Mostfavored Nation	149LTS429	303444
New Zealand	Sweden	24 May 35	General Economic	159LTS143	303657
New Zealand	Switzerland	05 May 38	General Trade	189LTS167	304384
New Zealand	USA (United States)	28 Feb 40	Admin Cooperation	203LTS11	304746
New Zealand	USA (United States)	06 Sep 40	General Amity	204LTS253	304805
Newfoundland	Dominican Republic	16 Mar 40	General Trade	203LTS141	304757
Newfoundland	Multilateral	09 Sep 86*	Patents/Copyrights	123LTS233	302816
Newfoundland	Multilateral	18 Mar 04	Humanitarian	1LTS83	300011
Newfoundland	Multilateral	12 Jan 12	Sanitation	4LTS281	300112
Newfoundland	Multilateral	05 Jun 12	Telecommunications	1LTS135	300013
Newfoundland	Multilateral	30 Jun 20	Patents/Copyrights	1LTS59	300008
Newfoundland	Multilateral	24 Sep 23	Dispute Settlement	27LTS157	300678
Newfoundland	Multilateral	31 Mar 24	Sanitation	27LTS211	300685
Newfoundland	Multilateral	28 Aug 24	Postal Service	40LTS19	301002
Newfoundland	Multilateral	24 Apr 26	Land Transport	108LTS123	302505
Newfoundland	Multilateral	26 Sep 27	Dispute Settlement	92LTS301	302096
Newfoundland	Multilateral	12 Oct 29	General Transport	137LTS11	303145
Newfoundland	Multilateral	07 Jun 30	Finance	143LTS337	303315
Newfoundland	Multilateral	30 Mar 31	Taxation	138LTS149	303185
Newfoundland	Multilateral	13 Jul 31	Other HEW	139LTS301	303219
Newfoundland	Multilateral	10 Dec 31	Water Transport	129LTS177	302961
Nicaragua	Belgium	13 Jul 33	Extradition	161LTS361	303724
Nicaragua	Colombia	25 Mar 29	Extradition	132LTS255	303042
Nicaragua	Colombia	05 May 30	Territory Boundary	105LTS337	302426
Nicaragua	Germany	06 Mar 24	General Economic	41LTS264	301019
Nicaragua	Germany	30 Mar 28	Visas	93LTS123	302104
Nicaragua	Guatemala	10 Sep 24	General Trade	130LTS127	302987
Nicaragua	Honduras	30 Jan 30	General Trade	142LTS241	303297
Nicaragua	Multilateral	20 Aug 10	Patents/Copyrights	155LTS179	303576
Nicaragua	Multilateral	10 Sep 19	Reparations	2LTS21	300042
Nicaragua	Multilateral	10 Sep 19	General Trade	7LTS331	300200
Nicaragua	Multilateral	10 Sep 19	General Economic	2LTS35	300044
Nicaragua	Multilateral	10 Sep 19	Reparations	2LTS44	300045
Nicaragua	Multilateral	10 Sep 19	Reparations	2LTS29	300043
Nicaragua	Multilateral	01 May 20	Air Transport	11LTS173	300297
Nicaragua	Multilateral	16 Dec 20	General IGO	6LTS379	300170
Nicaragua	Multilateral	15 Sep 21	Postal Service	30LTS141	300767
Nicaragua	Multilateral	31 Mar 22	Humanitarian	9LTS415	300269
Nicaragua	Multilateral	28 Apr 23	Patents/Copyrights	33LTS47	300832
Nicaragua	Multilateral	03 May 23	General Trade	33LTS81	300833
Nicaragua	Multilateral	03 May 23	General Amity	33LTS25	300831
Nicaragua	Multilateral	03 May 23	Customs	33LTS11	300830
Nicaragua	Multilateral	28 Aug 24	Postal Service	40LTS249	301003
Nicaragua	Multilateral	28 Aug 24	Postal Service	40LTS437	301005
Nicaragua	Multilateral	28 Aug 24	Postal Service	40LTS19	301002
Nicaragua	Multilateral	28 Aug 24	Postal Service	40LTS307	301004
Nicaragua	Multilateral	19 Feb 25	Admin Cooperation	81LTS317	301845
Nicaragua	Multilateral	17 Jun 25	Peace/Disarmament	94LTS65	302138
Nicaragua	Multilateral	25 Sep 26	ILO Labor	60LTS253	301414
Nicaragua	Multilateral	12 Jul 27	Direct Aid	135LTS247	303115
Nicaragua	Multilateral	26 Sep 27	Dispute Settlement	92LTS301	302096
Nicaragua	Multilateral	25 Nov 27	Telecommunications	84LTS97	301905
Nicaragua	Multilateral	18 Feb 28	Patents/Copyrights	132LTS275	303044
Nicaragua	Multilateral	20 Feb 28	Consul/Citizenship	155LTS289	303582
Nicaragua	Multilateral	20 Feb 28	Consul/Citizenship	155LTS259	303581

PARTY ONE	PARTY TWO	DATE	TOPIC	CITATION	NUMBER
Nicaragua	Multilateral	20 Feb 28	Admin Cooperation	134LTS45	303082
Nicaragua	Multilateral	20 Feb 28	Other Ad Hoc	86LTS111	301950
Nicaragua	Multilateral	20 Feb 28	Consul/Citizenship	132LTS323	303046
Nicaragua	Multilateral	20 Feb 28	Air Transport	129LTS223	302963
Nicaragua	Multilateral	20 Feb 28	Privil/Immunities	132LTS301	303045
Nicaragua	Multilateral	20 Feb 28	General Amity	135LTS187	303111
Nicaragua	Multilateral	27 Aug 28	General Military	94LTS57	302137
Nicaragua	Multilateral	05 Jan 29	Dispute Settlement	130LTS135	302988
Nicaragua	Multilateral	05 Jan 29	Dispute Settlement	100LTS399	302309
Nicaragua	Multilateral	20 Feb 29	Patents/Copyrights	124LTS357	302840
Nicaragua	Multilateral	28 Jun 29	Postal Service	103LTS249	302371
Nicaragua	Multilateral	28 Jun 29	Postal Service	103LTS5	302369
Nicaragua	Multilateral	28 Jun 29	Postal Service	103LTS71	302370
Nicaragua	Multilateral	28 Jun 29	Postal Service	102LTS245	302368
Nicaragua	Multilateral	27 Jul 29	Other Military	118LTS303	302733
Nicaragua	Multilateral	27 Jul 29	Other Military	118LTS343	302734
Nicaragua	Multilateral	14 Sep 29	UN Charter	165LTS353	303822
Nicaragua	Multilateral	19 Mar 31	Admin Cooperation	143LTS7	303301
Nicaragua	Multilateral	19 Mar 31	Finance	143LTS355	303316
Nicaragua	Multilateral	19 Mar 31	Finance	143LTS407	303317
Nicaragua	Multilateral	13 Jul 31	Other HEW	139LTS301	303219
Nicaragua	Multilateral	24 Sep 31	Specific Resources	155LTS349	303586
Nicaragua	Multilateral	10 Nov 31	Postal Service	131LTS389	303024
Nicaragua	Multilateral	10 Nov 31	Postal Service	131LTS327	303023
Nicaragua	Multilateral	10 Nov 31	Postal Service	131LTS447	303025
Nicaragua	Multilateral	09 Dec 32	Telecommunications	151LTS5	303479
Nicaragua	Multilateral	11 Mar 33	Water Transport	135LTS301	303119
Nicaragua	Multilateral	10 Oct 33	General Amity	163LTS393	303781
Nicaragua	Multilateral	11 Oct 33	Education	155LTS331	303585
Nicaragua	Multilateral	26 Dec 33	Extradition	165LTS45	303803
Nicaragua	Multilateral	26 Dec 33	Recognition	165LTS19	303802
Nicaragua	Multilateral	20 Mar 34	Postal Service	174LTS171	304048
Nicaragua	Multilateral	20 Mar 34	Postal Service	175LTS73	304050
Nicaragua	Multilateral	20 Mar 34	Postal Service	175LTS5	304049
Nicaragua	Multilateral	20 Mar 34	Postal Service	175LTS269	304051
Nicaragua	Multilateral	15 Jul 34	Mostfavored Nation	165LTS9	303801
Nicaragua	Multilateral	15 Apr 35	Culture	167LTS289	303874
Nicaragua	Multilateral	23 Dec 36	Admin Cooperation	201LTS295	304721
Nicaragua	Multilateral	23 Dec 36	Culture	188LTS125	304355
Nicaragua	Multilateral	23 Dec 36	Peace/Disarmament	188LTS9	304350
Nicaragua	Multilateral	23 Dec 36	General Amity	188LTS31	304351
Nicaragua	Multilateral	23 Dec 36	Land Transport	188LTS99	304354
Nicaragua	Multilateral	23 Dec 36	Culture	188LTS151	304356
Nicaragua	Multilateral	23 Dec 36	Dispute Settlement	188LTS53	304352
Nicaragua	Multilateral	23 Dec 36	Dispute Settlement	188LTS75	304353
Nicaragua	Multilateral	23 Dec 36	Dispute Settlement	195LTS229	304548
Nicaragua	Multilateral	08 Dec 38	Gen Communications	202LTS49	304734
Nicaragua	Multilateral	23 May 39	Postal Service	202LTS159	304742
Nicaragua	Multilateral	01 Jan 42	General Military	204LTS381	304817
Nicaragua	Spain	20 Nov 34	Patents/Copyrights	166LTS143	303836
Nicaragua	Spain	06 Nov 35	Mass Media	166LTS317	303847
Nicaragua	USA (United States)	11 Mar 36	Customs	173LTS141	304009
Nicaragua	USA (United States)	14 Apr 38	Taxation	192LTS275	304477
Nicaragua	USA (United States)	22 May 39	Military Mission	199LTS189	304672
Nicaragua	USA (United States)	19 Feb 40	Admin Cooperation	203LTS47	304749
Nicaragua	USA (United States)	22 May 41	Milit Assistance	204LTS283	304809
Niger	Multilateral	03 Nov 23	Customs	30LTS371	300775
Niger	Multilateral	25 Sep 26	ILO Labor	60LTS253	301414
Nigeria	Multilateral	25 Aug 24	Water Transport	120LTS155	302764
Nigeria	Multilateral	25 Nov 27	Telecommunications	84LTS97	301905
Nigeria	Multilateral	28 Oct 33	Refugees	159LTS199	303663
Nigeria	Multilateral	23 Sep 36	Gen Communications	186LTS301	304319
Nigeria	Multilateral	10 Feb 38	Refugees	192LTS59	304461
Nigeria	Spanish Colonies	09 Dec 42	Non-ILO Labor	205LTS41	304825
Norfolk Islands	Multilateral	05 Jun 12	Telecommunications	1LTS135	300013

PARTY ONE	PARTY TWO	DATE	TOPIC	CITATION	NUMBER
Norfolk Islands	Multilateral	12 Apr 33	Sanitation	161LTS65	303706
North Borneo	Multilateral	25 Aug 24	Water Transport	120LTS155	302764
North Borneo	Multilateral	25 Nov 27	Telecommunications	84LTS97	301905
North Borneo	Multilateral	12 Oct 29	General Transport	137LTS11	303145
North Borneo	Multilateral	23 Sep 36	Gen Communications	186LTS301	304319
Northern Rhodesia	Multilateral	31 Mar 22	Humanitarian	9LTS415	300269
Northern Rhodesia	Multilateral	26 Sep 27	Dispute Settlement	92LTS301	302096
Northern Rhodesia	Multilateral	25 Nov 27	Telecommunications	84LTS97	301905
Northern Rhodesia	Multilateral	30 Mar 31	Taxation	138LTS149	303185
Northern Rhodesia	Multilateral	12 Apr 33	Sanitation	161LTS65	303706
Northern Rhodesia	Multilateral	30 Oct 35	Postal Service	189LTS85	304376
Northern Rhodesia	Multilateral	30 Oct 35	Telecommunications	189LTS51	304375
Northern Rhodesia	Multilateral	23 Sep 36	Gen Communications	186LTS301	304319
Northern Rhodesia	South Africa	02 Oct 31	Customs	129LTS115	302955
Northern Rhodesia	South Africa	26 Sep 32	Visas	135LTS225	303113
Norway	Argentina	07 Oct 24	Admin Cooperation	33LTS191	300843
Norway	Australia	13 Dec 27	Non-ILO Labor	69LTS307	301612
Norway	Austria	20 Jun 24	Admin Cooperation	27LTS123	300675
Norway	Austria	03 Dec 24	General Trade	31LTS151	300792
Norway	Austria	06 Dec 24	Consul/Citizenship	31LTS179	300794
Norway	Austria	17 Dec 25	Extradition	48LTS77	301152
Norway	Austria	08 Feb 28	Visas	71LTS211	301664
Norway	Austria	01 Oct 30	Extradition	119LTS15	302737
Norway	Austria	03 Sep 32	Finance	137LTS403	303170
Norway	Belgium	29 Oct 28	Taxation	107LTS75	302469
Norway	Belgium	20 Jul 34	Consul/Citizenship	150LTS369	303469
Norway	Belgium	17 Dec 36	Taxation	178LTS153	304110
Norway	Belgium	10 Mar 37	Customs	178LTS12	304101
Norway	Brazil	31 Dec 31	General Trade	126LTS385	302896
Norway	Brazil	27 Jul 36	General Trade	176LTS125	304056
Norway	Bulgaria	02 Oct 24	General Trade	30LTS103	300763
Norway	Bulgaria	26 Nov 31	Dispute Settlement	134LTS27	303081
Norway	Bulgaria	05 Dec 32	Patents/Copyrights	136LTS281	303130
Norway	Canada	30 Apr 26	Postal Service	51LTS203	301227
Norway	Canada	02 May 29	Taxation	91LTS329	302073
Norway	Canada	13 Mar 33	Postal Service	141LTS211	303266
Norway	Chile	27 Jul 23	Admin Cooperation	33LTS249	300848
Norway	Chile	09 Feb 27	General Trade	80LTS325	301837
Norway	Chile	27 Jan 36	Dispute Settlement	179LTS433	304169
Norway	China	12 Nov 28	Customs	87LTS381	301983
Norway	China	23 Apr 31	Privil/Immunities	119LTS9	302736
Norway	Czechoslovakia	02 Oct 23	General Trade	20LTS355	300526
Norway	Czechoslovakia	09 Sep 29	Dispute Settlement	101LTS355	302336
Norway	Czechoslovakia	11 Oct 29	Visas	96LTS211	302202
Norway	Danzig	07 Apr 30	Visas	100LTS391	302308
Norway	Denmark	21 Jul 21	Telecommunications	13LTS357	300362
Norway	Denmark	27 Jul 21	Air Transport	9LTS23	300241
Norway	Denmark	30 Nov 23	Admin Cooperation	22LTS121	300555
Norway	Denmark	27 Jun 24	Dispute Settlement	33LTS173	300842
Norway	Denmark	09 Jul 24	Territory Boundary	27LTS203	300684
Norway	Denmark	15 Jan 26	Dispute Settlement	60LTS311	301418
Norway	Denmark	15 Dec 26	Non-ILO Labor	59LTS255	301396
Norway	Denmark	30 Nov 28	Admin Cooperation	82LTS223	301873
Norway	Denmark	21 Jan 29	Telecommunications	104LTS119	302382
Norway	Denmark	06 Nov 30	Admin Cooperation	109LTS283	302545
Norway	Denmark	05 Aug 31	Taxation	121LTS9	302779
Norway	Denmark	04 Dec 31	Admin Cooperation	128LTS37	302935
Norway	Denmark	08 Jul 33	Water Transport	140LTS149	303232
Norway	Denmark	11 Nov 33	Consul/Citizenship	143LTS25	303302
Norway	Denmark	21 Apr 34	Customs	148LTS331	303419
Norway	Denmark	23 Feb 35	Admin Cooperation	158LTS31	303622
Norway	Denmark	30 Dec 38	General Economic	195LTS121	304540
Norway	Denmark	18 Jun 39	Patents/Copyrights	197LTS227	304615
Norway	Denmark	29 Aug 39	Customs	198LTS231	304644
Norway	El Salvador	21 Nov 38	General Trade	198LTS157	304636

PARTY ONE	PARTY TWO	DATE	TOPIC	CITATION	NUMBER
Norway	Estonia	28 Jul 26	General Economic	43LTS25	301045
Norway	Estonia	03 Apr 30	Extradition	106LTS147	302442
Norway	Estonia	31 Jan 31	Visas	113LTS39	302633
Norway	Finland	14 Jul 20	Specific Resources	1LTS317	300027
Norway	Finland	16 Jul 21	Admin Cooperation	19LTS77	300485
Norway	Finland	03 Mar 22	Specif Goods/Equip	14LTS157	300372
Norway	Finland	23 May 22	Postal Service	14LTS323	300382
Norway	Finland	07 Sep 22	Telecommunications	12LTS357	300328
Norway	Finland	28 Apr 23	Admin Cooperation	19LTS225	300496
Norway	Finland	28 Apr 24	Visas	30LTS35	300757
Norway	Finland	28 Apr 24	Territory Boundary	30LTS49	300758
Norway	Finland	27 Jun 24	Dispute Settlement	29LTS403	300751
Norway	Finland	11 Oct 24	Postal Service	32LTS123	300812
Norway	Finland	14 Feb 25	Specific Resources	49LTS379	301193
Norway	Finland	14 Feb 25	Specific Resources	49LTS391	301194
Norway	Finland	10 Nov 25	Dispute Settlement	43LTS381	301071
Norway	Finland	19 Dec 25	Water Transport	56LTS183	301330
Norway	Finland	03 Feb 26	Dispute Settlement	60LTS353	301420
Norway	Finland	30 Sep 27	Customs	67LTS359	301557
Norway	Finland	23 Oct 28	Water Transport	85LTS211	301932
Norway	Finland	24 Nov 28	Visas	82LTS215	301872
Norway	Finland	14 May 30	Postal Service	105LTS399	302429
Norway	Finland	11 Nov 30	General Trade	130LTS17	302980
Norway	Finland	20 Nov 30	Land Transport	110LTS313	302563
Norway	Finland	05 Nov 35	Territory Boundary	169LTS33	303913
Norway	Finland	21 Jul 37	General Trade	191LTS75	304435
Norway	Finland	21 Apr 38	Specific Resources	188LTS231	304361
Norway	Finland	21 Apr 38	Specific Resources	188LTS215	304360
Norway	Finland	28 Dec 39	General Economic	199LTS71	304667
Norway	France	23 Apr 21	Commodity Trade	14LTS375	300386
Norway	France	01 Oct 23	Admin Cooperation	33LTS237	300847
Norway	France	11 Jun 26	Patents/Copyrights	50LTS315	301215
Norway	France	12 Apr 27	Commodity Trade	178LTS199	304114
Norway	France	21 Nov 27	Education	70LTS167	301632
Norway	France	02 Jun 30	Taxation	102LTS27	302350
Norway	France	19 Nov 34	Commodity Trade	178LTS217	304115
Norway	France	27 Mar 37	Commodity Trade	178LTS221	304116
Norway	France	28 Feb 39	Admin Cooperation	195LTS165	304546
Norway	Germany	11 Apr 25	Customs	52LTS115	301252
Norway	Germany	15 Jun 26	Telecommunications	51LTS329	301238
Norway	Germany	27 Apr 27	Customs	69LTS57	301600
Norway	Germany	17 Jan 28	Visas	70LTS251	301637
Norway	Germany	23 Jan 29	Air Transport	93LTS197	302110
Norway	Germany	30 May 30	Customs	107LTS129	302473
Norway	Germany	09 Jan 33	Finance	137LTS395	303168
Norway	Germany	03 Mar 33	Visas	138LTS179	303186
Norway	Germany	06 Sep 34	Finance	161LTS187	303711
Norway	Germany	19 Jul 35	Land Transport	161LTS375	303726
Norway	Germany	27 Feb 37	Finance	178LTS427	304125
Norway	Greece	10 Dec 24	General Economic	31LTS231	300799
Norway	Greece	29 Jun 27	General Trade	82LTS187	301869
Norway	Greece	15 Aug 31	General Economic	123LTS271	302817
Norway	Greece	28 Feb 38	Finance	186LTS165	304309
Norway	Greece	28 Feb 38	General Trade	186LTS159	304308
Norway	Guatemala	20 Dec 38	General Trade	198LTS117	304631
Norway	Hungary	16 Sep 24	General Trade	33LTS103	300835
Norway	Hungary	01 Feb 29	Customs	86LTS435	301955
Norway	Hungary	04 Jul 34	Customs	152LTS115	303489
Norway	Hungary	16 Nov 37	Visas	183LTS81	304228
Norway	Hungary	18 Feb 38	Visas	185LTS357	304299
Norway	Hungary	05 Jul 38	Admin Cooperation	189LTS427	304399
Norway	Iceland	17 Aug 22	Postal Service	14LTS9	300363
Norway	Iceland	10 Aug 23	Postal Service	20LTS363	300527
Norway	Iceland	31 May 30	Non-ILO Labor	108LTS339	302517
Norway	Iceland	27 Jun 30	Dispute Settlement	126LTS417	302900

PARTY ONE	PARTY TWO	DATE	TOPIC	CITATION	NUMBER
Norway	Iceland	27 Feb 39	Specific Resources	196LTS377	304598
Norway	Iraq	14 Mar 33	Mostfavored Nation	138LTS23	303177
Norway	Irish Free State	21 Oct 30	Taxation	109LTS177	302536
Norway	Italy	10 Jun 29	Dispute Settlement	105LTS161	302410
Norway	Italy	31 Jul 30	Other Economic	118LTS113	302716
Norway	Italy	02 Jul 35	Finance	162LTS323	303745
Norway	Italy	02 Jul 35	General Trade	162LTS317	303744
Norway	Italy	25 Aug 36	Finance	171LTS377	303974
Norway	Italy	31 Mar 37	Finance	177LTS367	304099
Norway	Italy	31 Mar 37	Finance	177LTS355	304098
Norway	Italy	31 Mar 37	Customs	177LTS349	304097
Norway	Italy	21 Jun 38	General Trade	190LTS193	304417
Norway	Japan	06 Nov 23	Admin Cooperation	33LTS265	300850
Norway	Japan	29 Mar 28	Visas	73LTS81	301708
Norway	Japan	23 Dec 31	Taxation	127LTS21	302902
Norway	Latvia	14 Aug 24	General Amity	36LTS211	300924
Norway	Latvia	10 Jun 25	Water Transport	36LTS91	300906
Norway	Latvia	12 Sep 27	Extradition	71LTS303	301671
Norway	Latvia	10 Feb 30	Visas	100LTS79	302295
Norway	Latvia	28 Jun 34	Visas	152LTS107	303488
Norway	Lithuania	21 Dec 23	General Trade	32LTS55	300805
Norway	Lithuania	14 Nov 30	Land Transport	109LTS187	302538
Norway	Luxembourg	12 Sep 27	Visas	68LTS37	301566
Norway	Luxembourg	12 Feb 32	Dispute Settlement	142LTS29	303277
Norway	Mexico	01 Oct 23	Admin Cooperation	33LTS255	300849
Norway	Mexico	14 Jun 29	Postal Service	99LTS381	302283
Norway	Multilateral	09 Sep 86*	Patents/Copyrights	123LTS233	302816
Norway	Multilateral	18 Mar 04	Humanitarian	1LTS83	300011
Norway	Multilateral	13 Nov 08	General Ad Hoc	1LTS217	300015
Norway	Multilateral	12 Jan 12	Sanitation	4LTS281	300112
Norway	Multilateral	05 Jun 12	Telecommunications	1LTS135	300013
Norway	Multilateral	20 Mar 14	Patents/Copyrights	1LTS243	300016
Norway	Multilateral	18 Jan 20	Admin Cooperation	12LTS321	300323
Norway	Multilateral	09 Feb 20	Territory Boundary	2LTS7	300041
Norway	Multilateral	01 May 20	Air Transport	11LTS173	300297
Norway	Multilateral	11 May 20	Finance	1LTS15	300001
Norway	Multilateral	21 Jun 20	Health/Educ/Welfare	8LTS65	300207
Norway	Multilateral	30 Jun 20	Patents/Copyrights	1LTS59	300008
Norway	Multilateral	16 Dec 20	General IGO	6LTS379	300170
Norway	Multilateral	29 Dec 20	Telecommunications	13LTS281	300359
Norway	Multilateral	20 Apr 21	Water Transport	7LTS65	300173
Norway	Multilateral	20 Apr 21	Land Transport	7LTS11	300171
Norway	Multilateral	20 Apr 21	Water Transport	7LTS73	300174
Norway	Multilateral	20 Apr 21	Water Transport	7LTS35	300172
Norway	Multilateral	05 Aug 21	Admin Cooperation	27LTS349	300695
Norway	Multilateral	19 Sep 21	Telecommunications	15LTS191	300392
Norway	Multilateral	05 Oct 21	IGO Establishment	51LTS361	301241
Norway	Multilateral	05 Oct 21	Admin Cooperation	29LTS67	300733
Norway	Multilateral	05 Oct 21	Admin Cooperation	29LTS73	300734
Norway	Multilateral	05 Oct 21	Admin Cooperation	29LTS79	300735
Norway	Multilateral	06 Oct 21	General Economic	17LTS45	300427
Norway	Multilateral	06 Feb 22	General Trade	38LTS277	300982
Norway	Multilateral	06 Feb 22	Customs	38LTS267	300981
Norway	Multilateral	31 Mar 22	Humanitarian	9LTS415	300269
Norway	Multilateral	18 Aug 22	Telecommunications	13LTS289	300360
Norway	Multilateral	02 Nov 22	Peace/Disarmament	149LTS35	303431
Norway	Multilateral	11 Jul 23	Admin Cooperation	18LTS85	300456
Norway	Multilateral	24 Sep 23	Dispute Settlement	27LTS157	300678
Norway	Multilateral	03 Nov 23	Customs	30LTS371	300775
Norway	Multilateral	09 Dec 23	Water Transport	58LTS284	301379
Norway	Multilateral	09 Dec 23	Land Transport	47LTS55	301129
Norway	Multilateral	08 Jan 24	Dispute Settlement	23LTS63	300576
Norway	Multilateral	22 Mar 24	Finance	25LTS171	300605
Norway	Multilateral	04 Jul 24	Admin Cooperation	51LTS227	301231
Norway	Multilateral	26 Jul 24	Postal Service	30LTS271	300771

PARTY ONE	PARTY TWO	DATE	TOPIC	CITATION	NUMBER
Norway	Multilateral	25 Aug 24	Water Transport	120LTS123	302763
Norway	Multilateral	28 Aug 24	Postal Service	40LTS437	301005
Norway	Multilateral	28 Aug 24	Postal Service	41LTS9	301006
Norway	Multilateral	28 Aug 24	Postal Service	41LTS55	301007
Norway	Multilateral	28 Aug 24	Postal Service	41LTS97	301008
Norway	Multilateral	28 Aug 24	Postal Service	40LTS19	301002
Norway	Multilateral	28 Aug 24	Postal Service	40LTS249	301003
Norway	Multilateral	28 Aug 24	Postal Service	40LTS307	301004
Norway	Multilateral	23 Oct 24	Land Transport	78LTS17	301779
Norway	Multilateral	23 Oct 24	General Transport	77LTS367	301778
Norway	Multilateral	19 Feb 25	Admin Cooperation	81LTS317	301845
Norway	Multilateral	17 Jun 25	Peace/Disarmament	94LTS65	302138
Norway	Multilateral	19 Aug 25	Customs	42LTS73	301033
Norway	Multilateral	29 Oct 25	Telecommunications	57LTS201	301365
Norway	Multilateral	06 Nov 25	Patents/Copyrights	74LTS289	301743
Norway	Multilateral	28 Jan 26	Water Transport	51LTS9	301219
Norway	Multilateral	10 Apr 26	Water Transport	176LTS199	304062
Norway	Multilateral	10 Apr 26	Water Transport	120LTS187	302765
Norway	Multilateral	24 Apr 26	Land Transport	108LTS123	302505
Norway	Multilateral	12 May 26	Refugees	89LTS47	302004
Norway	Multilateral	21 Jun 26	Sanitation	78LTS229	301793
Norway	Multilateral	25 Sep 26	ILO Labor	60LTS253	301414
Norway	Multilateral	01 Nov 26	Telecommunications	78LTS109	301782
Norway	Multilateral	08 Nov 27	General Trade	97LTS391	302238
Norway	Multilateral	11 Nov 27	Telecommunications	78LTS153	301786
Norway	Multilateral	21 Nov 27	Telecommunications	78LTS163	301787
Norway	Multilateral	25 Nov 27	Telecommunications	84LTS97	301905
Norway	Multilateral	19 Mar 28	Telecommunications	78LTS177	301788
Norway	Multilateral	23 Apr 28	Telecommunications	78LTS197	301790
Norway	Multilateral	09 Jun 28	Telecommunications	78LTS219	301792
Norway	Multilateral	11 Jul 28	Commodity Trade	95LTS357	302184
Norway	Multilateral	11 Jul 28	Commodity Trade	95LTS373	302185
Norway	Multilateral	27 Aug 28	General Military	94LTS57	302137
Norway	Multilateral	26 Sep 28	Dispute Settlement	93LTS343	302123
Norway	Multilateral	25 Oct 28	Consul/Citizenship	84LTS7	301901
Norway	Multilateral	22 Dec 28	Telecommunications	104LTS103	302381
Norway	Multilateral	14 Jan 29	Telecommunications	87LTS169	301968
Norway	Multilateral	20 Apr 29	Admin Cooperation	112LTS371	302623
Norway	Multilateral	31 May 29	Water Transport	136LTS81	303127
Norway	Multilateral	28 Jun 29	Postal Service	103LTS429	302374
Norway	Multilateral	28 Jun 29	Postal Service	103LTS377	302373
Norway	Multilateral	28 Jun 29	Postal Service	103LTS249	302371
Norway	Multilateral	28 Jun 29	Postal Service	103LTS5	302369
Norway	Multilateral	28 Jun 29	Postal Service	103LTS71	302370
Norway	Multilateral	28 Jun 29	Postal Service	102LTS245	302368
Norway	Multilateral	27 Jul 29	Other Military	118LTS303	302733
Norway	Multilateral	27 Jul 29	Other Military	118LTS343	302734
Norway	Multilateral	20 Aug 29	Sanitation	98LTS125	302243
Norway	Multilateral	14 Sep 29	UN Charter	165LTS353	303822
Norway	Multilateral	12 Oct 29	General Transport	137LTS11	303145
Norway	Multilateral	17 Feb 30	Dispute Settlement	102LTS87	302354
Norway	Multilateral	12 Apr 30	Admin Cooperation	179LTS89	304137
Norway	Multilateral	14 May 30	Postal Service	105LTS353	302428
Norway	Multilateral	07 Jun 30	Finance	143LTS317	303314
Norway	Multilateral	07 Jun 30	Finance	143LTS257	303313
Norway	Multilateral	07 Jun 30	Finance	143LTS337	303315
Norway	Multilateral	22 Dec 30	General Trade	126LTS341	302893
Norway	Multilateral	06 Feb 31	Admin Cooperation	126LTS121	302877
Norway	Multilateral	10 Feb 31	Admin Cooperation	126LTS41	302870
Norway	Multilateral	19 Mar 31	Finance	143LTS407	303317
Norway	Multilateral	19 Mar 31	Finance	143LTS355	303316
Norway	Multilateral	19 Mar 31	Admin Cooperation	143LTS7	303301
Norway	Multilateral	27 Mar 31	ICJ Option Clause	167LTS341	303877
Norway	Multilateral	28 Mar 31	Customs	119LTS47	302739
Norway	Multilateral	06 May 31	Telecommunications	120LTS217	302767

PARTY ONE	PARTY TWO	DATE	TOPIC	CITATION	NUMBER
Norway	Multilateral	30 Jun 31	Scientific Project	149LTS63	303434
Norway	Multilateral	24 Sep 31	Specific Resources	155LTS349	303586
Norway	Multilateral	11 Dec 31	Commodity Trade	170LTS251	303941
Norway	Multilateral	16 Mar 32	Admin Cooperation	139LTS165	303209
Norway	Multilateral	02 Sep 32	Land Transport	154LTS123	303543
Norway	Multilateral	09 Dec 32	Telecommunications	151LTS5	303479
Norway	Multilateral	13 Dec 32	Territory Boundary	139LTS189	303210
Norway	Multilateral	11 Mar 33	Water Transport	135LTS301	303119
Norway	Multilateral	29 May 33	Admin Cooperation	192LTS289	304479
Norway	Multilateral	19 Jun 33	Gen Communications	154LTS133	303544
Norway	Multilateral	11 Oct 33	Education	155LTS331	303585
Norway	Multilateral	11 Oct 33	Consul/Citizenship	150LTS431	303476
Norway	Multilateral	28 Oct 33	Refugees	159LTS199	303663
Norway	Multilateral	07 Nov 33	Finance	155LTS115	303574
Norway	Multilateral	23 Nov 33	Land Transport	192LTS389	304484
Norway	Multilateral	23 Nov 33	Land Transport	192LTS327	304483
Norway	Multilateral	20 Mar 34	Finance	176LTS9	304053
Norway	Multilateral	20 Mar 34	Postal Service	174LTS171	304048
Norway	Multilateral	20 Mar 34	Postal Service	175LTS269	304051
Norway	Multilateral	20 Mar 34	Postal Service	176LTS55	304054
Norway	Multilateral	20 Mar 34	Postal Service	175LTS5	304049
Norway	Multilateral	20 Mar 34	Postal Service	175LTS73	304050
Norway	Multilateral	26 Apr 34	Admin Cooperation	164LTS63	303789
Norway	Multilateral	02 Jun 34	Patents/Copyrights	192LTS17	304459
Norway	Multilateral	19 Nov 34	Admin Cooperation	164LTS243	303797
Norway	Multilateral	22 Dec 34	Visas	183LTS145	304230
Norway	Multilateral	31 Dec 34	Postal Service	158LTS111	303630
Norway	Multilateral	04 Jul 36	Refugees	171LTS75	303952
Norway	Multilateral	23 Sep 36	Gen Communications	186LTS301	304319
Norway	Multilateral	06 Nov 36	General Military	173LTS353	304025
Norway	Multilateral	11 Feb 37	Telecommunications	186LTS55	304303
Norway	Multilateral	06 Mar 37	Gen Communications	186LTS109	304305
Norway	Multilateral	31 Mar 37	Commodity Trade	189LTS359	304394
Norway	Multilateral	08 May 37	Privil/Immunities	182LTS37	304202
Norway	Multilateral	28 May 37	General Trade	180LTS5	304170
Norway	Multilateral	08 Jun 37	Specific Resources	190LTS79	304406
Norway	Multilateral	06 Sep 37	Specific Resources	186LTS419	304326
Norway	Multilateral	15 Sep 37	Gen Communications	186LTS135	304307
Norway	Multilateral	23 Sep 37	Postal Service	190LTS299	304427
Norway	Multilateral	02 Oct 37	Education	182LTS263	304216
Norway	Multilateral	11 Oct 37	Air Transport	182LTS173	304210
Norway	Multilateral	10 Feb 38	Refugees	192LTS59	304461
Norway	Multilateral	11 May 38	General Trade	189LTS237	304386
Norway	Multilateral	27 May 38	Other Military	188LTS293	304365
Norway	Multilateral	24 Jun 38	Specific Resources	196LTS131	304575
Norway	Multilateral	12 Sep 38	Culture	198LTS111	304630
Norway	Multilateral	03 Dec 38	Education	200LTS249	304694
Norway	Multilateral	23 May 39	Postal Service	202LTS159	304742
Norway	Multilateral	01 Jan 42	General Military	204LTS381	304817
Norway	Netherlands	08 Jan 25	Air Transport	46LTS279	301122
Norway	Netherlands	09 Jan 25	Non-ILO Labor	48LTS247	301166
Norway	Netherlands	21 Sep 26	Admin Cooperation	56LTS89	301325
Norway	Netherlands	11 Jan 29	Taxation	85LTS409	301941
Norway	Netherlands	15 Jul 31	Land Transport	127LTS313	302924
Norway	Netherlands	23 Mar 33	Dispute Settlement	146LTS291	303380
Norway	Netherlands	18 Jul 33	Land Transport	152LTS259	303498
Norway	Netherlands	28 Oct 38	Visas	193LTS223	304499
Norway	New Zealand	27 Oct 33	Mostfavored Nation	149LTS429	303444
Norway	Persia	10 May 29	Privil/Immunities	107LTS403	302497
Norway	Persia	08 May 30	General Economic	134LTS153	303089
Norway	Poland	22 Dec 26	General Economic	66LTS359	301530
Norway	Poland	26 Apr 28	General Economic	88LTS179	301996
Norway	Poland	09 Dec 29	Dispute Settlement	101LTS325	302334
Norway	Poland	14 Mar 36	General Trade	171LTS371	303973
Norway	Poland	18 Jun 37	Customs	190LTS187	304416

PARTY ONE	PARTY TWO	DATE	TOPIC	CITATION	NUMBER
Norway	Portugal	14 Oct 20	Water Transport	2LTS237	300069
Norway	Portugal	11 Apr 23	General Trade	16LTS379	300418
Norway	Portugal	21 Oct 24	Admin Cooperation	30LTS117	300764
Norway	Portugal	30 Nov 27	Water Transport	69LTS355	301617
Norway	Portugal	07 Feb 29	Water Transport	104LTS137	302383
Norway	Portugal	26 Jul 30	Dispute Settlement	134LTS123	303087
Norway	Portugal	13 Nov 31	General Economic	129LTS455	302977
Norway	Portugal	04 Sep 34	General Trade	161LTS211	303713
Norway	Romania	01 Oct 24	General Trade	29LTS397	300750
Norway	Romania	21 Jun 30	General Economic	120LTS113	302762
Norway	Romania	10 Dec 36	Finance	174LTS59	304037
Norway	Siam	16 Jul 26	General Economic	60LTS35	301404
Norway	Siam	15 Nov 37	General Amity	186LTS9	304301
Norway	South Africa	25 Jan 27	Postal Service	60LTS277	301416
Norway	Spain	22 Nov 20	General Trade	2LTS359	300089
Norway	Spain	01 Dec 21	General Economic	9LTS69	300244
Norway	Spain	04 Apr 22	General Economic	9LTS253	300258
Norway	Spain	06 May 22	General Trade	9LTS329	300266
Norway	Spain	12 Jun 22	General Economic	10LTS305	300276
Norway	Spain	07 Oct 23	General Trade	59LTS47	301389
Norway	Spain	27 Dec 28	Dispute Settlement	97LTS339	302231
Norway	Spain	13 Jun 36	General Trade	170LTS199	303935
Norway	Spain	13 Jun 36	Finance	170LTS207	303936
Norway	Spain	26 Jul 39	General Trade	198LTS87	304627
Norway	Sweden	29 Mar 22	Telecommunications	13LTS311	300361
Norway	Sweden	05 May 22	Humanitarian	15LTS165	300390
Norway	Sweden	26 May 23	Air Transport	18LTS155	300462
Norway	Sweden	27 Jun 24	Dispute Settlement	28LTS309	300717
Norway	Sweden	22 Dec 24	Admin Cooperation	32LTS13	300802
Norway	Sweden	23 Oct 25	Dispute Settlement	39LTS153	301000
Norway	Sweden	25 Nov 25	Dispute Settlement	60LTS295	301417
Norway	Sweden	09 Mar 27	Privil/Immunities	62LTS341	301472
Norway	Sweden	19 Nov 27	Land Transport	68LTS209	301584
Norway	Sweden	11 May 29	Water Transport	120LTS263	302771
Norway	Sweden	26 Jul 29	Admin Cooperation	94LTS287	302149
Norway	Sweden	18 Dec 29	Customs	98LTS389	302258
Norway	Sweden	08 Aug 31	Land Transport	123LTS67	302806
Norway	Sweden	10 Mar 33	Water Transport	138LTS17	303176
Norway	Sweden	22 Aug 33	Consul/Citizenship	141LTS217	303267
Norway	Sweden	09 Oct 33	Customs	142LTS171	303289
Norway	Sweden	14 Jun 37	Taxation	179LTS245	304151
Norway	Sweden	20 Apr 38	Specific Property	189LTS153	304383
Norway	Sweden	30 Dec 38	General Economic	195LTS127	304541
Norway	Switzerland	15 Apr 24	General Economic	27LTS168	300679
Norway	Switzerland	21 Aug 25	Dispute Settlement	51LTS89	301224
Norway	Turkey	02 May 26	General Amity	56LTS51	301322
Norway	Turkey	11 Aug 26	General Economic	47LTS441	301149
Norway	Turkey	16 Mar 31	General Economic	138LTS41	303180
Norway	Turkey	16 Jan 33	Dispute Settlement	161LTS173	303710
Norway	Turkey	08 Jun 36	General Trade	170LTS227	303938
Norway	Turkey	08 Jun 36	Finance	170LTS235	303939
Norway	UK Great Britain	06 Jul 20	Postal Service	5LTS107	300121
Norway	UK Great Britain	22 Apr 21	Admin Cooperation	5LTS33	300114
Norway	UK Great Britain	15 Jul 21	Air Transport	6LTS307	300162
Norway	UK Great Britain	16 Dec 21	Sanitation	16LTS187	300409
Norway	UK Great Britain	22 Feb 23	Air Transport	15LTS159	300389
Norway	UK Great Britain	05 Jun 24	Admin Cooperation	27LTS195	300683
Norway	UK Great Britain	18 Dec 24	Taxation	32LTS9	300801
Norway	UK Great Britain	13 May 25	Admin Cooperation	36LTS435	300940
Norway	UK Great Britain	18 Nov 30	Recognition	112LTS97	302609
Norway	UK Great Britain	30 Jan 31	Privil/Immunities	123LTS343	302823
Norway	UK Great Britain	15 May 33	General Trade	145LTS187	303355
Norway	UK Great Britain	05 Nov 34	Claims and Debts	154LTS231	303549
Norway	UK Great Britain	18 Nov 36	Water Transport	173LTS193	304012
Norway	UK Great Britain	21 Dec 38	Taxation	201LTS357	304723

PARTY ONE	PARTY TWO	DATE	TOPIC	CITATION	NUMBER
Norway	UK Great Britain	02 Dec 39	Commodity Trade	201LTS97	304706
Norway	United Arab Rep	27 May 30	Commodity Trade	105LTS449	302432
Norway	Uruguay	04 Apr 36	General Trade	176LTS115	304055
Norway	USA (United States)	11 Feb 21	Postal Service	5LTS217	300130
Norway	USA (United States)	30 Jun 21	Dispute Settlement	14LTS19	300365
Norway	USA (United States)	26 Nov 23	Dispute Settlement	23LTS249	300592
Norway	USA (United States)	24 May 24	Customs	26LTS43	300639
Norway	USA (United States)	24 Mar 25	Taxation	67LTS417	301563
Norway	USA (United States)	20 Feb 29	Dispute Settlement	91LTS413	302079
Norway	USA (United States)	25 Feb 29	General Amity	134LTS81	303085
Norway	USA (United States)	30 Mar 29	Postal Service	91LTS383	302078
Norway	USA (United States)	23 Jul 29	Visas	93LTS223	302111
Norway	USA (United States)	01 Nov 30	Milit Servic/Citiz	112LTS399	302625
Norway	USA (United States)	20 Jan 32	Customs	126LTS393	302897
Norway	USA (United States)	16 Oct 33	Air Transport	145LTS43	303344
Norway	USA (United States)	16 Oct 33	Air Transport	145LTS31	303343
Norway	USA (United States)	16 Oct 33	Air Transport	145LTS9	303342
Norway	USA (United States)	09 Nov 34	Postal Service	156LTS33	303592
Norway	USA (United States)	01 Feb 38	Extradition	191LTS83	304436
Norway	USA (United States)	11 Jul 42	General Military	204LTS415	304821
Norway	USSR (Soviet Union)	02 Sep 21	Consul/Citizenship	7LTS293	300196
Norway	USSR (Soviet Union)	15 Dec 25	General Economic	47LTS9	301127
Norway	USSR (Soviet Union)	09 Apr 26	Water Transport	48LTS185	301160
Norway	USSR (Soviet Union)	16 Jan 28	Consul/Citizenship	70LTS239	301635
Norway	USSR (Soviet Union)	24 Feb 28	Admin Cooperation	79LTS9	301801
Norway	Venezuela	13 May 35	Dispute Settlement	167LTS407	303882
Norway	Venezuela	18 Feb 38	General Trade	187LTS205	304341
Nyasaland	Multilateral	30 Jun 20	Patents/Copyrights	1LTS59	300008
Nyasaland	Multilateral	31 Mar 22	Humanitarian	9LTS415	300269
Nyasaland	Multilateral	25 Nov 27	Telecommunications	84LTS97	301905
Nyasaland	Multilateral	30 Mar 31	Taxation	138LTS149	303185
Nyasaland	Multilateral	28 Oct 33	Refugees	159LTS199	303663
Nyasaland	Multilateral	30 Oct 35	Telecommunications	189LTS51	304375
Nyasaland	Multilateral	30 Oct 35	Postal Service	189LTS85	304376
Nyasaland	Multilateral	23 Sep 36	Gen Communications	186LTS301	304319
Nyasaland	Multilateral	10 Feb 38	Refugees	192LTS59	304461
Oceania	Multilateral	24 Apr 26	Land Transport	108LTS123	302505
Oceania	Multilateral	24 Apr 26	Land Transport	97LTS83	302220
Oceania	Multilateral	23 Oct 30	Water Transport	125LTS95	302849
Pakistan	Multilateral	31 May 29	Water Transport	136LTS81	303127
Pakistan	Multilateral	12 Apr 30	Admin Cooperation	179LTS89	304137
Pakistan	Multilateral	12 Apr 30	Admin Cooperation	179LTS115	304138
Palestine	France	19 Jun 36	Postal Service	172LTS17	303977
Palestine	Greece	28 Mar 36	Postal Service	170LTS145	303932
Palestine	Iraq	04 Aug 27	Postal Service	80LTS211	301826
Palestine	Italy	06 Dec 32	Postal Service	139LTS59	303204
Palestine	Multilateral	18 Mar 04	Humanitarian	1LTS83	300011
Palestine	Multilateral	30 Jun 20	Patents/Copyrights	1LTS59	300008
Palestine	Multilateral	20 Apr 21	Water Transport	7LTS65	300173
Palestine	Multilateral	20 Apr 21	Water Transport	7LTS35	300172
Palestine	Multilateral	31 Mar 22	Humanitarian	9LTS415	300269
Palestine	Multilateral	25 Aug 24	Water Transport	120LTS155	302764
Palestine	Multilateral	06 Nov 25	Patents/Copyrights	74LTS289	301743
Palestine	Multilateral	06 Nov 25	Other Economic	74LTS319	301744
Palestine	Multilateral	24 Apr 26	Land Transport	108LTS123	302505
Palestine	Multilateral	20 May 26	Health/Educ/Welfare	109LTS121	302532
Palestine	Multilateral	26 Sep 27	Dispute Settlement	92LTS301	302096
Palestine	Multilateral	25 Nov 27	Telecommunications	84LTS97	301905
Palestine	Multilateral	30 Mar 31	Taxation	138LTS149	303185
Palestine	Multilateral	19 Jun 33	Gen Communications	154LTS133	303544
Palestine	Multilateral	23 Sep 36	Gen Communications	186LTS301	304319
Palestine	Switzerland	15 May 29	Postal Service	95LTS395	302186
Palestine	UK Great Britain	23 Jan 22	General Economic	13LTS9	300342
Palestine	United Arab Rep	07 Aug 22	Extradition	36LTS343	300933
Palestine	United Arab Rep	21 Jun 28	General Trade	80LTS277	301833

PARTY ONE	PARTY TWO	DATE	TOPIC	CITATION	NUMBER
Palestine	United Arab Rep	12 Jan 29	Dispute Settlement	94LTS9	302132
Panama	Austria	05 Mar 30	Visas	101LTS293	302330
Panama	Colombia	20 Aug 24	Territory Boundary	33LTS167	300841
Panama	Colombia	24 Dec 27	Extradition	87LTS409	301985
Panama	Colombia	17 Jun 38	Territory Boundary	193LTS231	304500
Panama	France	16 Aug 22	Consul/Citizenship	43LTS423	301075
Panama	France	15 Aug 24	Customs	93LTS425	302130
Panama	Germany	21 Nov 27	General Economic	115LTS239	302689
Panama	Italy	16 Oct 29	General Economic	138LTS355	303199
Panama	Italy	07 Aug 30	Extradition	140LTS241	303240
Panama	Mexico	09 Jun 28	Consul/Citizenship	141LTS191	303265
Panama	Mexico	23 Oct 28	Extradition	194LTS137	304518
Panama	Multilateral	20 Aug 10	Patents/Copyrights	155LTS179	303576
Panama	Multilateral	12 Jan 12	Sanitation	4LTS281	300112
Panama	Multilateral	05 Jun 12	Telecommunications	1LTS135	300013
Panama	Multilateral	10 Sep 19	Reparations	2LTS44	300045
Panama	Multilateral	10 Sep 19	Reparations	2LTS21	300042
Panama	Multilateral	10 Sep 19	General Trade	7LTS331	300200
Panama	Multilateral	10 Sep 19	General Economic	2LTS35	300044
Panama	Multilateral	10 Sep 19	Reparations	2LTS29	300043
Panama	Multilateral	01 May 20	Air Transport	11LTS173	300297
Panama	Multilateral	21 Jun 20	Health/Educ/Welfare	8LTS65	300207
Panama	Multilateral	16 Dec 20	General IGO	6LTS379	300170
Panama	Multilateral	20 Apr 21	Land Transport	7LTS11	300171
Panama	Multilateral	20 Apr 21	Water Transport	7LTS73	300174
Panama	Multilateral	20 Apr 21	Water Transport	7LTS35	300172
Panama	Multilateral	05 Aug 21	Admin Cooperation	27LTS349	300695
Panama	Multilateral	15 Sep 21	Postal Service	30LTS141	300767
Panama	Multilateral	05 Oct 21	Admin Cooperation	29LTS73	300734
Panama	Multilateral	05 Oct 21	Admin Cooperation	29LTS67	300733
Panama	Multilateral	05 Oct 21	IGO Establishment	51LTS361	301241
Panama	Multilateral	05 Oct 21	Admin Cooperation	29LTS79	300735
Panama	Multilateral	31 Mar 22	Humanitarian	9LTS415	300269
Panama	Multilateral	28 Apr 23	Patents/Copyrights	33LTS47	300832
Panama	Multilateral	03 May 23	General Trade	33LTS81	300833
Panama	Multilateral	03 May 23	General Amity	33LTS25	300831
Panama	Multilateral	03 May 23	Customs	33LTS11	300830
Panama	Multilateral	09 Dec 23	Water Transport	58LTS284	301379
Panama	Multilateral	31 Mar 24	Sanitation	27LTS211	300685
Panama	Multilateral	28 Aug 24	Postal Service	40LTS437	301005
Panama	Multilateral	28 Aug 24	Postal Service	40LTS249	301003
Panama	Multilateral	28 Aug 24	Postal Service	40LTS307	301004
Panama	Multilateral	28 Aug 24	Postal Service	40LTS19	301002
Panama	Multilateral	14 Nov 24	Sanitation	86LTS43	301949
Panama	Multilateral	17 Jun 25	Peace/Disarmament	94LTS65	302138
Panama	Multilateral	25 Sep 26	ILO Labor	60LTS253	301414
Panama	Multilateral	25 Nov 27	Telecommunications	84LTS97	301905
Panama	Multilateral	18 Feb 28	Patents/Copyrights	132LTS275	303044
Panama	Multilateral	20 Feb 28	Privil/Immunities	132LTS301	303045
Panama	Multilateral	20 Feb 28	Consul/Citizenship	132LTS323	303046
Panama	Multilateral	20 Feb 28	Consul/Citizenship	155LTS289	303582
Panama	Multilateral	20 Feb 28	Consul/Citizenship	155LTS259	303581
Panama	Multilateral	20 Feb 28	Admin Cooperation	134LTS45	303082
Panama	Multilateral	20 Feb 28	Other Ad Hoc	86LTS111	301950
Panama	Multilateral	20 Feb 28	Air Transport	129LTS223	302963
Panama	Multilateral	20 Feb 28	General Amity	135LTS187	303111
Panama	Multilateral	27 Aug 28	General Military	94LTS57	302137
Panama	Multilateral	05 Jan 29	Dispute Settlement	130LTS135	302988
Panama	Multilateral	05 Jan 29	Dispute Settlement	100LTS399	302309
Panama	Multilateral	20 Feb 29	Patents/Copyrights	124LTS357	302840
Panama	Multilateral	20 Apr 29	Admin Cooperation	112LTS395	302624
Panama	Multilateral	20 Apr 29	Admin Cooperation	112LTS371	302623
Panama	Multilateral	31 May 29	Water Transport	136LTS81	303127
Panama	Multilateral	28 Jun 29	Postal Service	103LTS249	302371
Panama	Multilateral	28 Jun 29	Postal Service	103LTS5	302369

PARTY ONE	PARTY TWO	DATE	TOPIC	CITATION	NUMBER
Panama	Multilateral	28 Jun 29	Postal Service	103LTS71	302370
Panama	Multilateral	28 Jun 29	Postal Service	102LTS245	302368
Panama	Multilateral	14 Sep 29	UN Charter	165LTS353	303822
Panama	Multilateral	13 Jul 31	Other HEW	139LTS301	303219
Panama	Multilateral	10 Nov 31	Postal Service	131LTS447	303025
Panama	Multilateral	10 Nov 31	Postal Service	131LTS327	303023
Panama	Multilateral	10 Nov 31	Postal Service	131LTS389	303024
Panama	Multilateral	09 Dec 32	Telecommunications	151LTS5	303479
Panama	Multilateral	11 Mar 33	Water Transport	135LTS301	303119
Panama	Multilateral	10 Oct 33	General Amity	163LTS393	303781
Panama	Multilateral	11 Oct 33	Education	155LTS331	303585
Panama	Multilateral	11 Oct 33	Consul/Citizenship	150LTS431	303476
Panama	Multilateral	26 Dec 33	Recognition	165LTS19	303802
Panama	Multilateral	26 Dec 33	Extradition	165LTS45	303803
Panama	Multilateral	20 Mar 34	Postal Service	175LTS73	304050
Panama	Multilateral	20 Mar 34	Postal Service	174LTS171	304048
Panama	Multilateral	20 Mar 34	Postal Service	175LTS5	304049
Panama	Multilateral	20 Mar 34	Postal Service	175LTS269	304051
Panama	Multilateral	15 Jul 34	Mostfavored Nation	165LTS9	303801
Panama	Multilateral	15 Apr 35	Culture	167LTS289	303874
Panama	Multilateral	26 Jun 36	Other HEW	198LTS299	304648
Panama	Multilateral	06 Nov 36	General Military	173LTS353	304025
Panama	Multilateral	23 Dec 36	Admin Cooperation	201LTS295	304721
Panama	Multilateral	23 Dec 36	Dispute Settlement	188LTS75	304353
Panama	Multilateral	23 Dec 36	Culture	188LTS151	304356
Panama	Multilateral	23 Dec 36	General Amity	188LTS31	304351
Panama	Multilateral	23 Dec 36	Land Transport	188LTS99	304354
Panama	Multilateral	23 Dec 36	Dispute Settlement	188LTS53	304352
Panama	Multilateral	23 Dec 36	Peace/Disarmament	188LTS9	304350
Panama	Multilateral	23 Dec 36	Culture	188LTS125	304355
Panama	Multilateral	23 Dec 36	Dispute Settlement	195LTS229	304548
Panama	Multilateral	08 Dec 38	Gen Communications	202LTS49	304734
Panama	Multilateral	23 May 39	Postal Service	202LTS159	304742
Panama	Multilateral	01 Jan 42	General Military	204LTS381	304817
Panama	Spain	22 Sep 30	Dispute Settlement	162LTS309	303743
Panama	UK Great Britain	25 Sep 28	General Economic	90LTS311	302045
Panama	UK Great Britain	26 Sep 28	Consul/Citizenship	90LTS327	302046
Panama	USA (United States)	06 Jun 24	Commodity Trade	138LTS397	303200
Panama	USA (United States)	17 Dec 32	Finance	138LTS119	303183
Panama	USA (United States)	02 Mar 36	Specific Property	200LTS17	304686
Panama	USA (United States)	02 Mar 36	Land Transport	200LTS205	304692
Panama	USA (United States)	17 Aug 37	Water Transport	182LTS159	304208
Panama	USA (United States)	25 Aug 39	General Amity	199LTS317	304681
Panama	USA (United States)	04 Jan 40	Land Transport	202LTS421	304744
Papua	Multilateral	05 Jun 12	Telecommunications	1LTS135	300013
Papua	Multilateral	06 Nov 25	Patents/Copyrights	74LTS289	301743
Papua	Multilateral	12 Apr 33	Sanitation	161LTS65	303706
Paraguay	Belgium	20 Jan 26	Extradition	97LTS197	302224
Paraguay	Brazil	24 Feb 22	Extradition	138LTS211	303189
Paraguay	Brazil	09 Dec 31	Territory Boundary	136LTS427	303142
Paraguay	Germany	26 Feb 27	Mostfavored Nation	73LTS235	301716
Paraguay	Japan	30 Nov 20	General Economic	6LTS367	300169
Paraguay	Multilateral	20 Aug 10	Patents/Copyrights	155LTS179	303576
Paraguay	Multilateral	23 Jan 12	Sanitation	8LTS187	300222
Paraguay	Multilateral	21 Apr 14	Sanitation	5LTS394	300144
Paraguay	Multilateral	29 Feb 20	Admin Cooperation	127LTS433	302930
Paraguay	Multilateral	16 Dec 20	General IGO	6LTS379	300170
Paraguay	Multilateral	05 Aug 21	Admin Cooperation	27LTS349	300695
Paraguay	Multilateral	15 Sep 21	Postal Service	30LTS141	300767
Paraguay	Multilateral	05 Oct 21	IGO Establishment	51LTS361	301241
Paraguay	Multilateral	05 Oct 21	Admin Cooperation	29LTS67	300733
Paraguay	Multilateral	05 Oct 21	Admin Cooperation	29LTS79	300735
Paraguay	Multilateral	05 Oct 21	Admin Cooperation	29LTS73	300734
Paraguay	Multilateral	02 Nov 22	Peace/Disarmament	149LTS35	303431
Paraguay	Multilateral	28 Apr 23	Patents/Copyrights	33LTS47	300832

PARTY ONE	PARTY TWO	DATE	TOPIC	CITATION	NUMBER
Paraguay	Multilateral	03 May 23	General Amity	33LTS25	300831
Paraguay	Multilateral	03 May 23	General Trade	33LTS81	300833
Paraguay	Multilateral	03 May 23	Customs	33LTS11	300830
Paraguay	Multilateral	24 Sep 23	Dispute Settlement	27LTS157	300678
Paraguay	Multilateral	03 Nov 23	Customs	30LTS371	300775
Paraguay	Multilateral	31 Mar 24	Sanitation	27LTS211	300685
Paraguay	Multilateral	28 Aug 24	Postal Service	40LTS249	301003
Paraguay	Multilateral	28 Aug 24	Postal Service	40LTS437	301005
Paraguay	Multilateral	28 Aug 24	Postal Service	40LTS307	301004
Paraguay	Multilateral	28 Aug 24	Postal Service	40LTS19	301002
Paraguay	Multilateral	14 Nov 24	Sanitation	86LTS43	301949
Paraguay	Multilateral	19 Feb 25	Admin Cooperation	81LTS317	301845
Paraguay	Multilateral	21 Jun 26	Sanitation	78LTS229	301793
Paraguay	Multilateral	29 Oct 27	Scientific Project	127LTS27	302903
Paraguay	Multilateral	25 Nov 27	Telecommunications	84LTS97	301905
Paraguay	Multilateral	18 Feb 28	Patents/Copyrights	132LTS275	303044
Paraguay	Multilateral	20 Feb 28	Other Ad Hoc	86LTS111	301950
Paraguay	Multilateral	20 Feb 28	Privil/Immunities	132LTS301	303045
Paraguay	Multilateral	20 Feb 28	Consul/Citizenship	132LTS323	303046
Paraguay	Multilateral	20 Feb 28	General Amity	135LTS187	303111
Paraguay	Multilateral	20 Feb 28	Admin Cooperation	134LTS45	303082
Paraguay	Multilateral	20 Feb 28	Consul/Citizenship	155LTS259	303581
Paraguay	Multilateral	20 Feb 28	Consul/Citizenship	155LTS289	303582
Paraguay	Multilateral	27 Aug 28	General Military	94LTS57	302137
Paraguay	Multilateral	05 Jan 29	Dispute Settlement	130LTS135	302988
Paraguay	Multilateral	05 Jan 29	Dispute Settlement	100LTS399	302309
Paraguay	Multilateral	20 Feb 29	Patents/Copyrights	124LTS357	302840
Paraguay	Multilateral	16 Apr 29	Specific Resources	126LTS305	302891
Paraguay	Multilateral	28 Jun 29	Postal Service	103LTS249	302371
Paraguay	Multilateral	28 Jun 29	Postal Service	103LTS377	302373
Paraguay	Multilateral	28 Jun 29	Postal Service	103LTS321	302372
Paraguay	Multilateral	28 Jun 29	Postal Service	103LTS429	302374
Paraguay	Multilateral	28 Jun 29	Postal Service	103LTS5	302369
Paraguay	Multilateral	28 Jun 29	Postal Service	103LTS71	302370
Paraguay	Multilateral	28 Jun 29	Postal Service	102LTS245	302368
Paraguay	Multilateral	14 Sep 29	UN Charter	165LTS353	303822
Paraguay	Multilateral	13 Jul 31	Other HEW	139LTS301	303219
Paraguay	Multilateral	10 Nov 31	Postal Service	131LTS327	303023
Paraguay	Multilateral	10 Nov 31	Postal Service	131LTS447	303025
Paraguay	Multilateral	10 Nov 31	Postal Service	131LTS389	303024
Paraguay	Multilateral	11 Mar 33	Water Transport	135LTS301	303119
Paraguay	Multilateral	30 Sep 33	Extradition	205LTS155	304832
Paraguay	Multilateral	10 Oct 33	General Amity	163LTS393	303781
Paraguay	Multilateral	26 Dec 33	Recognition	165LTS19	303802
Paraguay	Multilateral	26 Dec 33	Extradition	165LTS45	303803
Paraguay	Multilateral	20 Mar 34	Finance	176LTS9	304053
Paraguay	Multilateral	20 Mar 34	Postal Service	176LTS55	304054
Paraguay	Multilateral	20 Mar 34	Postal Service	175LTS269	304051
Paraguay	Multilateral	20 Mar 34	Postal Service	175LTS5	304049
Paraguay	Multilateral	20 Mar 34	Postal Service	174LTS171	304048
Paraguay	Multilateral	20 Mar 34	Postal Service	175LTS363	304052
Paraguay	Multilateral	20 Mar 34	Postal Service	175LTS73	304050
Paraguay	Multilateral	19 Jun 34	Admin Cooperation	154LTS381	303564
Paraguay	Multilateral	15 Apr 35	Culture	167LTS289	303874
Paraguay	Multilateral	23 Dec 36	Admin Cooperation	201LTS295	304721
Paraguay	Multilateral	23 Dec 36	General Amity	188LTS31	304351
Paraguay	Multilateral	23 Dec 36	Land Transport	188LTS99	304354
Paraguay	Multilateral	23 Dec 36	Dispute Settlement	188LTS75	304353
Paraguay	Multilateral	23 Dec 36	Dispute Settlement	188LTS53	304352
Paraguay	Multilateral	23 Dec 36	Culture	188LTS151	304356
Paraguay	Multilateral	23 Dec 36	Dispute Settlement	195LTS229	304548
Paraguay	Multilateral	23 Dec 36	Peace/Disarmament	188LTS9	304350
Paraguay	Multilateral	23 Dec 36	Culture	188LTS125	304355
Paraguay	Multilateral	03 Dec 38	Education	200LTS249	304694
Paraguay	Multilateral	23 May 39	Postal Service	202LTS159	304742

PARTY ONE	PARTY TWO	DATE	TOPIC	CITATION	NUMBER
Paraguay	Spain	08 Jul 25	Patents/Copyrights	138LTS225	303190
Paraguay	UK Great Britain	16 Jul 28	General Economic	108LTS365	302519
Paraguay	Uruguay	28 Feb 15	Admin Cooperation	15LTS195	300393
Persia	Afghanistan	22 Jun 21	General Amity	33LTS285	300853
Persia	Afghanistan	27 Nov 27	General Military	107LTS433	302500
Persia	Afghanistan	26 Jun 28	Admin Cooperation	106LTS321	302453
Persia	Austria	17 Jun 28	Dispute Settlement	112LTS101	302610
Persia	Bel-Lux Econ Union	09 May 29	General Economic	110LTS377	302569
Persia	Belgium	15 May 28	General Amity	94LTS447	302160
Persia	Belgium	09 May 29	Privil/Immunities	110LTS391	302570
Persia	Belgium	23 May 29	General Amity	110LTS369	302568
Persia	China	01 Jun 20	General Amity	9LTS17	300240
Persia	Czechoslovakia	30 Apr 29	General Economic	110LTS357	302567
Persia	Czechoslovakia	29 Oct 30	Privil/Immunities	121LTS59	302784
Persia	Czechoslovakia	29 Oct 30	General Amity	121LTS53	302783
Persia	Denmark	08 Sep 28	General Amity	82LTS57	301859
Persia	Denmark	20 Feb 34	General Amity	158LTS299	303640
Persia	Estonia	03 Oct 31	General Amity	137LTS183	303155
Persia	Finland	18 Nov 34	Mostfavored Nation	158LTS315	303641
Persia	France	18 Oct 27	Scientific Project	112LTS267	302619
Persia	France	11 May 28	General Amity	82LTS43	301858
Persia	France	10 May 29	General Amity	150LTS329	303465
Persia	Germany	15 May 28	Privil/Immunities	107LTS389	302495
Persia	Germany	17 Feb 29	Privil/Immunities	111LTS241	302590
Persia	Germany	17 Feb 29	General Amity	111LTS19	302576
Persia	Germany	17 Feb 29	General Economic	111LTS263	302591
Persia	Germany	24 Feb 30	Patents/Copyrights	113LTS15	302630
Persia	Greece	24 May 29	Mostfavored Nation	121LTS221	302788
Persia	Hedjaz	24 Aug 29	General Amity	106LTS269	302450
Persia	Hungary	19 Jun 29	Mostfavored Nation	107LTS355	302491
Persia	Italy	24 Jul 28	General Amity	95LTS269	302179
Persia	Italy	05 Sep 29	General Amity	141LTS185	303264
Persia	Japan	30 Mar 29	Privil/Immunities	107LTS427	302499
Persia	Latvia	15 Jan 29	General Amity	162LTS299	303742
Persia	Lithuania	13 Jan 30	General Amity	131LTS221	303013
Persia	Multilateral	12 Jan 12	Sanitation	4LTS281	300112
Persia	Multilateral	23 Jan 12	Sanitation	8LTS187	300222
Persia	Multilateral	05 Jun 12	Telecommunications	1LTS135	300013
Persia	Multilateral	10 Sep 19	General Trade	7LTS331	300200
Persia	Multilateral	01 May 20	Air Transport	11LTS173	300297
Persia	Multilateral	16 Dec 20	General IGO	6LTS379	300170
Persia	Multilateral	20 Apr 21	Water Transport	7LTS73	300174
Persia	Multilateral	20 Apr 21	Land Transport	7LTS11	300171
Persia	Multilateral	05 Aug 21	Admin Cooperation	27LTS349	300695
Persia	Multilateral	05 Oct 21	IGO Establishment	51LTS361	301241
Persia	Multilateral	05 Oct 21	Admin Cooperation	29LTS73	300734
Persia	Multilateral	31 Mar 22	Humanitarian	9LTS415	300269
Persia	Multilateral	03 Nov 23	Customs	30LTS371	300775
Persia	Multilateral	31 Mar 24	Sanitation	27LTS211	300685
Persia	Multilateral	28 Aug 24	Postal Service	40LTS249	301003
Persia	Multilateral	28 Aug 24	Postal Service	40LTS19	301002
Persia	Multilateral	28 Aug 24	Postal Service	40LTS307	301004
Persia	Multilateral	19 Feb 25	Admin Cooperation	81LTS317	301845
Persia	Multilateral	17 Jun 25	Peace/Disarmament	94LTS65	302138
Persia	Multilateral	29 Oct 25	Telecommunications	57LTS201	301365
Persia	Multilateral	24 Apr 26	Land Transport	108LTS123	302505
Persia	Multilateral	21 Jun 26	Sanitation	78LTS229	301793
Persia	Multilateral	25 Sep 26	ILO Labor	60LTS253	301414
Persia	Multilateral	12 Jul 27	Direct Aid	135LTS247	303115
Persia	Multilateral	10 Sep 27	Postal Service	75LTS39	301750
Persia	Multilateral	10 Sep 27	Postal Service	75LTS7	301749
Persia	Multilateral	25 Nov 27	Telecommunications	84LTS97	301905
Persia	Multilateral	27 Aug 28	General Military	94LTS57	302137
Persia	Multilateral	28 Jun 29	Postal Service	103LTS249	302371
Persia	Multilateral	28 Jun 29	Postal Service	103LTS71	302370

PARTY ONE	PARTY TWO	DATE	TOPIC	CITATION	NUMBER
Persia	Multilateral	28 Jun 29	Postal Service	102LTS245	302368
Persia	Multilateral	28 Jun 29	Postal Service	103LTS5	302369
Persia	Multilateral	27 Jul 29	Other Military	118LTS343	302734
Persia	Multilateral	27 Jul 29	Other Military	118LTS303	302733
Persia	Multilateral	14 Sep 29	UN Charter	165LTS353	303822
Persia	Multilateral	13 Jul 31	Other HEW	139LTS301	303219
Persia	Multilateral	17 Feb 32	Telecommunications	138LTS61	303181
Persia	Multilateral	09 Dec 32	Telecommunications	151LTS5	303479
Persia	Multilateral	03 Jul 33	Peace/Disarmament	147LTS67	303391
Persia	Multilateral	20 Mar 34	Postal Service	174LTS171	304048
Persia	Multilateral	20 Mar 34	Postal Service	175LTS73	304050
Persia	Multilateral	20 Mar 34	Postal Service	175LTS269	304051
Persia	Multilateral	20 Mar 34	Postal Service	175LTS5	304049
Persia	Multilateral	19 Jun 34	Admin Cooperation	154LTS381	303564
Persia	Netherlands	20 Jun 28	General Amity	81LTS431	301852
Persia	Netherlands	12 Mar 30	General Amity	111LTS387	302599
Persia	Norway	10 May 29	Privil/Immunities	107LTS403	302497
Persia	Norway	08 May 30	General Economic	134LTS153	303089
Persia	Poland	19 Mar 27	General Amity	109LTS87	302529
Persia	Poland	19 Mar 27	General Economic	109LTS53	302528
Persia	Russ Fed Sov Rep	25 Apr 23	Postal Service	110LTS323	302564
Persia	Russ Fed Sov Rep	27 Apr 23	Telecommunications	110LTS333	302565
Persia	Sweden	09 Aug 28	General Amity	80LTS407	301841
Persia	Sweden	10 May 29	General Amity	102LTS9	302349
Persia	Sweden	27 May 29	General Amity	105LTS279	302420
Persia	Switzerland	28 Aug 28	Privil/Immunities	107LTS397	302496
Persia	Switzerland	25 Apr 34	Consul/Citizenship	160LTS173	303691
Persia	Switzerland	25 Apr 34	General Amity	159LTS235	303666
Persia	Turkey	15 Jun 28	General Amity	106LTS247	302449
Persia	UK Great Britain	21 Mar 20	General Trade	4LTS47	300102
Persia	United Arab Rep	28 Nov 28	General Amity	93LTS381	302127
Persia	United Arab Rep	17 Jun 30	Mostfavored Nation	107LTS349	302490
Persia	USA (United States)	11 Jul 28	Privil/Immunities	107LTS375	302494
Persia	USSR (Soviet Union)	26 Feb 21	General Amity	9LTS383	300268
Persia	USSR (Soviet Union)	01 Oct 27	Admin Cooperation	112LTS275	302620
Persia	USSR (Soviet Union)	01 Oct 27	Specific Resources	112LTS297	302621
Persia	USSR (Soviet Union)	31 May 28	Admin Cooperation	110LTS343	302566
Persia	USSR (Soviet Union)	10 Mar 29	Customs	107LTS419	302498
Persia	USSR (Soviet Union)	02 Aug 29	Postal Service	109LTS99	302530
Peru	Brazil	31 Dec 28	Gen Communications	127LTS455	302931
Peru	Chile	20 Jul 22	Dispute Settlement	21LTS141	300537
Peru	Chile	03 Jun 29	Dispute Settlement	94LTS401	302157
Peru	Chile	29 Apr 30	Admin Cooperation	112LTS133	302612
Peru	Colombia	24 Mar 22	Territory Boundary	74LTS9	301726
Peru	Colombia	25 May 33	Admin Cooperation	138LTS251	303192
Peru	Colombia	24 May 34	General Amity	164LTS21	303786
Peru	Ecuador	21 Jun 24	Territory Boundary	27LTS345	300694
Peru	Ecuador	06 Jul 36	Territory Boundary	173LTS359	304026
Peru	Japan	30 Sep 24	General Amity	102LTS33	302351
Peru	Multilateral	20 Aug 10	Patents/Copyrights	155LTS179	303576
Peru	Multilateral	05 Jun 12	Telecommunications	1LTS135	300013
Peru	Multilateral	10 Sep 19	General Trade	7LTS331	300200
Peru	Multilateral	29 Feb 20	Admin Cooperation	127LTS433	302930
Peru	Multilateral	01 May 20	Air Transport	11LTS173	300297
Peru	Multilateral	21 Jun 20	Health/Educ/Welfare	8LTS65	300207
Peru	Multilateral	16 Dec 20	General IGO	6LTS379	300170
Peru	Multilateral	20 Apr 21	Water Transport	7LTS73	300174
Peru	Multilateral	15 Sep 21	Postal Service	30LTS141	300767
Peru	Multilateral	06 Oct 21	General Economic	17LTS45	300427
Peru	Multilateral	31 Mar 22	Humanitarian	9LTS415	300269
Peru	Multilateral	03 May 23	General Amity	33LTS25	300831
Peru	Multilateral	25 Jan 24	Sanitation	57LTS135	301360
Peru	Multilateral	31 Mar 24	Sanitation	27LTS211	300685
Peru	Multilateral	25 Aug 24	Water Transport	120LTS123	302763
Peru	Multilateral	28 Aug 24	Postal Service	40LTS307	301004

PARTY ONE	PARTY TWO	DATE	TOPIC	CITATION	NUMBER
Peru	Multilateral	28 Aug 24	Postal Service	40LTS19	301002
Peru	Multilateral	28 Aug 24	Postal Service	40LTS249	301003
Peru	Multilateral	28 Aug 24	Postal Service	40LTS437	301005
Peru	Multilateral	14 Nov 24	Sanitation	86LTS43	301949
Peru	Multilateral	01 Dec 24	Sanitation	78LTS351	301794
Peru	Multilateral	10 Apr 26	Water Transport	120LTS187	302765
Peru	Multilateral	24 Apr 26	Land Transport	108LTS123	302505
Peru	Multilateral	24 Apr 26	Land Transport	97LTS83	302220
Peru	Multilateral	21 Jun 26	Sanitation	78LTS229	301793
Peru	Multilateral	12 Jul 27	Direct Aid	135LTS247	303115
Peru	Multilateral	29 Oct 27	Scientific Project	127LTS27	302903
Peru	Multilateral	25 Nov 27	Telecommunications	84LTS97	301905
Peru	Multilateral	18 Feb 28	Patents/Copyrights	132LTS275	303044
Peru	Multilateral	20 Feb 28	Consul/Citizenship	155LTS289	303582
Peru	Multilateral	20 Feb 28	Other Ad Hoc	86LTS111	301950
Peru	Multilateral	20 Feb 28	Privil/Immunities	132LTS301	303045
Peru	Multilateral	20 Feb 28	Admin Cooperation	134LTS45	303082
Peru	Multilateral	20 Feb 28	General Amity	135LTS187	303111
Peru	Multilateral	20 Feb 28	Air Transport	129LTS223	302963
Peru	Multilateral	20 Feb 28	Consul/Citizenship	155LTS259	303581
Peru	Multilateral	20 Feb 28	Consul/Citizenship	132LTS323	303046
Peru	Multilateral	27 Aug 28	General Military	94LTS57	302137
Peru	Multilateral	26 Sep 28	Dispute Settlement	93LTS343	302123
Peru	Multilateral	22 Nov 28	Culture	111LTS343	302598
Peru	Multilateral	05 Jan 29	Dispute Settlement	130LTS135	302988
Peru	Multilateral	05 Jan 29	Dispute Settlement	100LTS399	302309
Peru	Multilateral	20 Feb 29	Patents/Copyrights	124LTS357	302840
Peru	Multilateral	28 Jun 29	Postal Service	103LTS71	302370
Peru	Multilateral	28 Jun 29	Postal Service	103LTS249	302371
Peru	Multilateral	28 Jun 29	Postal Service	102LTS245	302368
Peru	Multilateral	27 Jul 29	Other Military	118LTS303	302733
Peru	Multilateral	14 Sep 29	UN Charter	165LTS353	303822
Peru	Multilateral	12 Apr 30	Admin Cooperation	179LTS115	304138
Peru	Multilateral	12 Apr 30	Admin Cooperation	179LTS89	304137
Peru	Multilateral	12 Apr 30	Milit Servic/Citiz	178LTS227	304117
Peru	Multilateral	07 Jun 30	Finance	143LTS317	303314
Peru	Multilateral	07 Jun 30	Finance	143LTS257	303313
Peru	Multilateral	07 Jun 30	Finance	143LTS337	303315
Peru	Multilateral	13 Jul 31	Other HEW	139LTS301	303219
Peru	Multilateral	10 Nov 31	Postal Service	131LTS389	303024
Peru	Multilateral	10 Nov 31	Postal Service	131LTS447	303025
Peru	Multilateral	10 Nov 31	Postal Service	131LTS327	303023
Peru	Multilateral	09 Dec 32	Telecommunications	151LTS5	303479
Peru	Multilateral	11 Mar 33	Water Transport	135LTS301	303119
Peru	Multilateral	22 Jul 33	Specific Resources	153LTS107	303511
Peru	Multilateral	10 Oct 33	General Amity	163LTS393	303781
Peru	Multilateral	26 Dec 33	Extradition	165LTS45	303803
Peru	Multilateral	26 Dec 33	Recognition	165LTS19	303802
Peru	Multilateral	20 Mar 34	Postal Service	175LTS269	304051
Peru	Multilateral	20 Mar 34	Postal Service	174LTS171	304048
Peru	Multilateral	20 Mar 34	Postal Service	175LTS73	304050
Peru	Multilateral	19 Jun 34	Admin Cooperation	154LTS381	303564
Peru	Multilateral	15 Apr 35	Culture	167LTS289	303874
Peru	Multilateral	06 Nov 36	General Military	173LTS353	304025
Peru	Multilateral	23 Dec 36	Dispute Settlement	188LTS75	304353
Peru	Multilateral	23 Dec 36	Dispute Settlement	188LTS53	304352
Peru	Multilateral	23 Dec 36	Peace/Disarmament	188LTS9	304350
Peru	Multilateral	23 Dec 36	Dispute Settlement	195LTS229	304548
Peru	Multilateral	23 Dec 36	Land Transport	188LTS99	304354
Peru	Multilateral	23 Dec 36	General Amity	188LTS31	304351
Peru	Multilateral	23 Dec 36	Culture	188LTS125	304355
Peru	Multilateral	23 Dec 36	Admin Cooperation	201LTS295	304721
Peru	Multilateral	23 Dec 36	Culture	188LTS151	304356
Peru	Multilateral	03 Dec 38	Education	200LTS249	304694
Peru	Multilateral	23 May 39	Postal Service	202LTS159	304742

PARTY ONE	PARTY TWO	DATE	TOPIC	CITATION	NUMBER
Peru	Spain	05 Mar 36	Mass Media	169LTS331	303921
Peru	UK Great Britain	27 Aug 21	Specific Resources	7LTS289	300195
Peru	UK Great Britain	02 Mar 22	Specific Resources	10LTS463	300286
Peru	UK Great Britain	31 Dec 28	Consul/Citizenship	100LTS431	302312
Peru	Uruguay	18 Jul 17	Dispute Settlement	14LTS359	300384
Peru	USA (United States)	21 May 21	Claims and Debts	6LTS171	300150
Peru	USA (United States)	23 May 34	Gen Communications	152LTS99	303487
Peru	USA (United States)	16 Oct 36	Admin Cooperation	181LTS161	304187
Peru	USA (United States)	31 Jul 40	Military Mission	203LTS75	304751
Peru	USA (United States)	31 Jul 40	Military Mission	203LTS91	304752
Peru	USA (United States)	15 Apr 41	Milit Assistance	204LTS117	304790
Peru	Venezuela	14 Mar 23	Admin Cooperation	20LTS45	300505
Philippines	Multilateral	31 May 29	Water Transport	136LTS81	303127
Philippines	Multilateral	28 Jun 29	Postal Service	102LTS245	302368
Philippines	Multilateral	11 Mar 33	Water Transport	135LTS301	303119
Philippines	Multilateral	20 Mar 34	Postal Service	174LTS171	304048
Philippines	Multilateral	23 May 39	Postal Service	202LTS159	304742
Philippines	Multilateral	01 Jan 42	General Military	204LTS381	304817
Poland	Afghanistan	03 Nov 27	General Amity	74LTS83	301734
Poland	Allied Powers	01 Apr 22	Reparations	9LTS325	300265
Poland	Austria	09 Jan 20	General Economic	7LTS163	300185
Poland	Austria	23 Sep 21	General Economic	7LTS181	300186
Poland	Austria	25 Sep 22	General Trade	59LTS307	301400
Poland	Austria	13 Nov 23	Dispute Settlement	34LTS399	300888
Poland	Austria	19 Mar 24	Admin Cooperation	56LTS95	301326
Poland	Austria	29 Mar 24	Non-ILO Labor	130LTS223	302992
Poland	Austria	29 Mar 24	Non-ILO Labor	130LTS251	302993
Poland	Austria	18 Jun 24	Non-ILO Labor	130LTS309	302996
Poland	Austria	18 Jun 24	Non-ILO Labor	130LTS293	302995
Poland	Austria	18 Jun 24	Non-ILO Labor	130LTS279	302994
Poland	Austria	17 Jan 25	Non-ILO Labor	130LTS327	302997
Poland	Austria	17 Jan 25	Non-ILO Labor	130LTS387	302998
Poland	Austria	05 May 25	Air Transport	46LTS269	301121
Poland	Austria	16 Apr 26	Dispute Settlement	62LTS329	301471
Poland	Austria	24 Nov 26	Customs	77LTS359	301777
Poland	Austria	24 Feb 28	Claims and Debts	81LTS417	301850
Poland	Austria	20 Jan 30	Claims and Debts	133LTS223	303067
Poland	Austria	10 Apr 30	Air Transport	108LTS289	302514
Poland	Austria	22 Apr 32	Taxation	143LTS45	303304
Poland	Austria	26 Oct 32	Admin Cooperation	138LTS193	303188
Poland	Bel-Lux Econ Union	10 Jun 33	General Trade	144LTS137	303324
Poland	Bel-Lux Econ Union	02 Mar 36	General Economic	168LTS67	303887
Poland	Belgium	30 Dec 22	Finance	21LTS201	300543
Poland	Belgium	01 Sep 25	Admin Cooperation	54LTS69	301274
Poland	Belgium	12 Jun 28	Consul/Citizenship	123LTS25	302803
Poland	Belgium	18 Dec 30	Health/Educ/Welfare	134LTS177	303090
Poland	Belgium	13 May 31	Extradition	131LTS109	303005
Poland	Brazil	03 Feb 32	Mostfavored Nation	147LTS113	303396
Poland	Brazil	15 Oct 32	Admin Cooperation	176LTS373	304074
Poland	Brazil	27 Jan 33	Dispute Settlement	142LTS255	303299
Poland	Bulgaria	29 Apr 25	General Economic	60LTS103	301408
Poland	Bulgaria	31 Dec 29	Dispute Settlement	113LTS89	302638
Poland	Bulgaria	07 Apr 31	Air Transport	127LTS45	302905
Poland	Bulgaria	22 Dec 34	Consul/Citizenship	159LTS265	303671
Poland	Bulgaria	08 Apr 35	Education	161LTS319	303720
Poland	Canada	03 Jul 35	General Trade	172LTS69	303980
Poland	Chile	19 Oct 29	Dispute Settlement	113LTS79	302637
Poland	China	18 Sep 29	General Economic	120LTS331	302774
Poland	Czechoslovakia	23 Sep 22	Scientific Project	50LTS321	301216
Poland	Czechoslovakia	06 Mar 25	Admin Cooperation	46LTS201	301120
Poland	Czechoslovakia	07 Apr 25	General Trade	56LTS285	301337
Poland	Czechoslovakia	23 Apr 25	Dispute Settlement	48LTS383	301171
Poland	Czechoslovakia	23 Apr 25	Taxation	44LTS309	301091
Poland	Czechoslovakia	23 Apr 25	Taxation	44LTS271	301089
Poland	Czechoslovakia	23 Apr 25	Admin Cooperation	48LTS287	301170

PARTY ONE	PARTY TWO	DATE	TOPIC	CITATION	NUMBER
Poland	Czechoslovakia	23 Apr 25	Taxation	44LTS285	301090
Poland	Czechoslovakia	30 May 25	General Transport	50LTS243	301207
Poland	Czechoslovakia	30 May 25	Territory Boundary	48LTS397	301172
Poland	Czechoslovakia	05 Sep 25	Sanitation	58LTS143	301370
Poland	Czechoslovakia	15 Apr 26	Air Transport	67LTS305	301554
Poland	Czechoslovakia	21 Apr 26	Sanitation	58LTS9	301367
Poland	Czechoslovakia	08 Feb 27	Admin Cooperation	70LTS289	301640
Poland	Czechoslovakia	08 Feb 27	Admin Cooperation	70LTS275	301639
Poland	Czechoslovakia	08 Feb 27	Admin Cooperation	70LTS261	301638
Poland	Czechoslovakia	08 Feb 27	Admin Cooperation	70LTS299	301641
Poland	Czechoslovakia	14 Apr 27	Admin Cooperation	82LTS157	301867
Poland	Czechoslovakia	30 May 27	Land Transport	98LTS233	302251
Poland	Czechoslovakia	18 Feb 28	Specific Resources	119LTS385	302758
Poland	Czechoslovakia	18 Feb 28	Specific Resources	100LTS273	302301
Poland	Czechoslovakia	22 May 28	Water Transport	82LTS171	301868
Poland	Czechoslovakia	21 Dec 29	General Amity	115LTS201	302687
Poland	Czechoslovakia	18 Jun 30	Land Transport	137LTS137	303151
Poland	Czechoslovakia	17 Feb 33	Land Transport	143LTS167	303307
Poland	Czechoslovakia	25 Jan 34	Admin Cooperation	177LTS139	304088
Poland	Czechoslovakia	10 Feb 34	General Trade	183LTS213	304238
Poland	Czechoslovakia	10 Feb 34	Admin Cooperation	178LTS159	304111
Poland	Danzig	09 Nov 20	Territory Boundary	6LTS189	300153
Poland	Danzig	24 Oct 21	Recognition	116LTS5	302699
Poland	Denmark	14 Jul 23	Milit Servic/Citiz	19LTS65	300483
Poland	Denmark	22 Mar 24	General Trade	31LTS13	300778
Poland	Denmark	16 Dec 24	Air Transport	32LTS409	300829
Poland	Denmark	23 Apr 26	Dispute Settlement	61LTS245	301437
Poland	Denmark	26 Oct 31	Visas	125LTS337	302862
Poland	Denmark	25 Jan 33	Admin Cooperation	136LTS421	303141
Poland	Denmark	01 May 34	Customs	154LTS221	303548
Poland	Estonia	11 Jan 24	Consul/Citizenship	47LTS129	301132
Poland	Estonia	19 Feb 27	General Economic	115LTS177	302686
Poland	Estonia	20 May 31	Admin Cooperation	144LTS327	303336
Poland	Estonia	26 Sep 33	Sanitation	150LTS309	303464
Poland	Estonia	27 Mar 35	Customs	159LTS97	303651
Poland	Finland	10 Nov 23	General Trade	29LTS229	300744
Poland	Finland	15 May 30	Visas	111LTS309	302594
Poland	Finland	20 Mar 31	Admin Cooperation	140LTS405	303250
Poland	Finland	19 Dec 31	Non-ILO Labor	131LTS193	303010
Poland	Finland	30 Jun 34	Customs	153LTS29	303504
Poland	Finland	16 Jul 36	General Trade	172LTS143	303984
Poland	Finland	14 Feb 38	Education	194LTS175	304520
Poland	France	03 Sep 19	Visas	1LTS337	300028
Poland	France	17 Feb 21	General Amity	18LTS11	300449
Poland	France	06 Feb 22	General Economic	43LTS415	301074
Poland	France	06 Feb 22	Admin Cooperation	43LTS399	301073
Poland	France	09 Dec 24	General Trade	44LTS127	301081
Poland	France	16 Oct 25	Peace/Disarmament	54LTS353	301297
Poland	France	30 Dec 25	Consul/Citizenship	73LTS265	301719
Poland	France	30 Dec 25	Admin Cooperation	48LTS139	301155
Poland	France	30 Dec 25	Admin Cooperation	95LTS233	302177
Poland	France	30 Dec 25	Extradition	95LTS217	302176
Poland	France	20 Jan 30	Claims and Debts	126LTS117	302876
Poland	France	02 Aug 30	Air Transport	114LTS93	302657
Poland	France	24 Apr 31	Sanitation	130LTS417	303000
Poland	Germany	09 Jan 20	Admin Cooperation	9LTS77	300245
Poland	Germany	20 Sep 20	Admin Cooperation	9LTS103	300246
Poland	Germany	02 Nov 20	Reparations	2LTS277	300081
Poland	Germany	23 Nov 20	Reparations	2LTS295	300082
Poland	Germany	08 Dec 20	Consul/Citizenship	7LTS323	300199
Poland	Germany	20 Jan 21	Territory Boundary	6LTS221	300156
Poland	Germany	12 Feb 21	Reparations	9LTS149	300247
Poland	Germany	10 Apr 21	Customs	6LTS233	300158
Poland	Germany	21 Apr 21	General Transport	12LTS61	300308
Poland	Germany	06 Jun 21	Specific Property	34LTS185	300874

PARTY ONE	PARTY TWO	DATE	TOPIC	CITATION	NUMBER
Poland	Germany	24 Feb 22	Admin Cooperation	27LTS15	300665
Poland	Germany	24 Feb 22	Admin Cooperation	26LTS479	300664
Poland	Germany	12 Apr 22	Territory Boundary	21LTS327	300548
Poland	Germany	29 Apr 22	Admin Cooperation	21LTS391	300549
Poland	Germany	15 May 22	Visas	10LTS37	300273
Poland	Germany	15 May 22	Postal Service	10LTS8	300272
Poland	Germany	03 Jun 22	Territory Boundary	9LTS465	300271
Poland	Germany	15 Jun 22	Territory Boundary	34LTS201	300875
Poland	Germany	15 Jun 22	Specific Resources	21LTS433	300550
Poland	Germany	18 Jun 22	Specific Property	34LTS235	300876
Poland	Germany	21 Jun 22	Dispute Settlement	22LTS7	300552
Poland	Germany	23 Jun 22	Specific Resources	22LTS25	300553
Poland	Germany	24 Jun 22	Water Transport	26LTS271	300653
Poland	Germany	15 Jul 22	General Transport	26LTS353	300654
Poland	Germany	01 Aug 22	Specific Property	34LTS253	300877
Poland	Germany	25 Aug 22	Non-ILO Labor	22LTS63	300554
Poland	Germany	26 Aug 22	Admin Cooperation	26LTS365	300656
Poland	Germany	14 Sep 22	Admin Cooperation	34LTS265	300878
Poland	Germany	18 Dec 22	Sanitation	34LTS301	300880
Poland	Germany	18 Dec 22	Finance	34LTS283	300879
Poland	Germany	18 Dec 22	Admin Cooperation	26LTS395	300658
Poland	Germany	27 Jan 23	Admin Cooperation	26LTS461	300663
Poland	Germany	21 Mar 23	Taxation	34LTS315	300881
Poland	Germany	02 May 23	Admin Cooperation	27LTS51	300667
Poland	Germany	04 Jun 23	Health/Educ/Welfare	34LTS329	300882
Poland	Germany	14 Jun 23	Admin Cooperation	34LTS343	300883
Poland	Germany	23 Jun 23	Specific Property	67LTS9	301537
Poland	Germany	10 Jul 23	General Transport	34LTS349	300884
Poland	Germany	14 Jul 23	Admin Cooperation	26LTS399	300659
Poland	Germany	11 Jan 24	General Economic	41LTS187	301014
Poland	Germany	12 Jan 24	Specific Resources	65LTS47	301519
Poland	Germany	23 Feb 24	Land Transport	49LTS355	301191
Poland	Germany	23 Feb 24	Territory Boundary	41LTS197	301015
Poland	Germany	05 Mar 24	Admin Cooperation	49LTS181	301182
Poland	Germany	05 Mar 24	Admin Cooperation	49LTS251	301184
Poland	Germany	07 Mar 24	Admin Cooperation	52LTS7	301245
Poland	Germany	30 Aug 24	Consul/Citizenship	32LTS331	300824
Poland	Germany	30 Dec 24	Specific Property	52LTS51	301250
Poland	Germany	14 Mar 25	Territory Boundary	95LTS239	302178
Poland	Germany	03 Oct 25	Admin Cooperation	50LTS189	301201
Poland	Germany	16 Oct 25	General Military	54LTS327	301295
Poland	Germany	02 Dec 25	Territory Boundary	70LTS427	301649
Poland	Germany	16 Dec 25	Admin Cooperation	46LTS139	301117
Poland	Germany	27 Jan 26	Territory Boundary	64LTS113	301504
Poland	Germany	27 Mar 26	Land Transport	64LTS249	301506
Poland	Germany	16 Jun 26	Land Transport	65LTS379	301522
Poland	Germany	21 Jun 26	Territory Boundary	72LTS203	301693
Poland	Germany	19 Aug 26	Admin Cooperation	64LTS420	301515
Poland	Germany	27 Oct 26	Admin Cooperation	108LTS275	302513
Poland	Germany	22 Dec 26	Culture	68LTS263	301590
Poland	Germany	16 Feb 27	Territory Boundary	71LTS369	301676
Poland	Germany	26 Mar 27	Land Transport	64LTS177	301505
Poland	Germany	11 Apr 27	Territory Boundary	69LTS419	301621
Poland	Germany	14 Jul 27	Non-ILO Labor	73LTS251	301718
Poland	Germany	24 Nov 27	Non-ILO Labor	92LTS19	302080
Poland	Germany	07 Dec 27	Specific Property	92LTS203	302088
Poland	Germany	10 Dec 27	Specific Resources	120LTS299	302773
Poland	Germany	05 Jul 28	Peace/Disarmament	113LTS189	302646
Poland	Germany	14 Dec 28	Finance	113LTS367	302648
Poland	Germany	14 Dec 28	Finance	113LTS311	302647
Poland	Germany	28 Aug 29	Air Transport	146LTS333	303383
Poland	Germany	31 Oct 29	Claims and Debts	124LTS345	302838
Poland	Germany	21 Nov 30	Land Transport	139LTS351	303220
Poland	Germany	11 Jun 31	Non-ILO Labor	141LTS91	303263
Poland	Germany	01 Dec 31	Dispute Settlement	141LTS315	303272

PARTY ONE	PARTY TWO	DATE	TOPIC	CITATION	NUMBER
Poland	Germany	15 Dec 31	Admin Cooperation	142LTS249	303298
Poland	Germany	22 Dec 31	Visas	144LTS191	303329
Poland	Greece	17 Apr 25	General Trade	38LTS301	300985
Poland	Greece	10 Apr 30	General Economic	120LTS369	302775
Poland	Greece	10 Apr 30	Admin Cooperation	123LTS165	302813
Poland	Greece	22 Apr 31	Air Transport	129LTS313	302966
Poland	Greece	04 Jan 32	Dispute Settlement	131LTS229	303014
Poland	Greece	05 Oct 36	Air Transport	181LTS29	304174
Poland	Greece	11 Mar 38	General Economic	194LTS13	304502
Poland	Greece	30 Sep 38	Air Transport	196LTS387	304599
Poland	Hungary	26 Mar 25	Privil/Immunities	37LTS151	300954
Poland	Hungary	22 Jul 25	Admin Cooperation	48LTS167	301158
Poland	Hungary	16 Nov 25	Dispute Settlement	43LTS265	301061
Poland	Hungary	12 May 28	Taxation	123LTS47	302804
Poland	Hungary	12 May 28	Taxation	123LTS15	302802
Poland	Hungary	30 Nov 28	Dispute Settlement	100LTS67	302294
Poland	Hungary	04 Nov 31	Patents/Copyrights	134LTS199	303092
Poland	Hungary	09 Jul 32	Admin Cooperation	140LTS429	303253
Poland	Hungary	09 Jul 32	Admin Cooperation	142LTS239	303296
Poland	Hungary	21 Oct 34	Education	163LTS9	303757
Poland	Hungary	24 Apr 36	Consul/Citizenship	185LTS303	304296
Poland	Hungary	24 Apr 36	Extradition	181LTS115	304183
Poland	Iceland	22 Mar 24	General Trade	31LTS35	300779
Poland	Iceland	14 Apr 26	Consul/Citizenship	48LTS279	301169
Poland	India	18 May 31	General Trade	131LTS9	303001
Poland	Italy	12 May 22	General Trade	59LTS293	301399
Poland	Ita'y	22 Jul 25	General Economic	54LTS101	301278
Poland	Italy	20 Jan 30	Claims and Debts	127LTS41	302904
Poland	Italy	22 Jul 30	Sanitation	121LTS17	302780
Poland	Italy	12 Dec 31	Admin Cooperation	140LTS421	303252
Poland	Italy	30 Oct 33	Loans and Credits	145LTS103	303348
Poland	Japan	07 Dec 22	General Trade	32LTS61	300806
Poland	Latvia	07 Jul 22	Sanitation	37LTS317	300958
Poland	Latvia	03 Jan 24	Consul/Citizenship	42LTS451	301043
Poland	Latvia	22 Aug 27	Mostfavored Nation	115LTS121	302681
Poland	Latvia	12 Feb 29	General Economic	115LTS135	302683
Poland	Latvia	12 Feb 29	Land Transport	101LTS75	302321
Poland	Latvia	18 Aug 32	Admin Cooperation	140LTS443	303254
Poland	Latvia	20 Dec 34	Non-ILO Labor	162LTS361	303749
Poland	Latvia	16 Nov 37	Sanitation	197LTS43	304604
Poland	Latvia	05 Mar 38	Customs	192LTS283	304478
Poland	Latvia	16 Jun 38	Air Transport	196LTS105	304573
Poland	Latvia	29 Oct 38	Non-ILO Labor	195LTS169	304547
Poland	Lithuania	07 Oct 20	Territory Boundary	8LTS173	300221
Poland	Lithuania	29 Nov 20	Peace/Disarmament	9LTS63	300243
Poland	Lithuania	07 Nov 28	Visas	89LTS171	302011
Poland	Lithuania	14 May 38	Water Transport	191LTS373	304456
Poland	Lithuania	22 May 38	Postal Service	191LTS359	304455
Poland	Lithuania	25 May 38	Land Transport	191LTS391	304457
Poland	Lithuania	23 Jul 38	Land Transport	192LTS83	304462
Poland	Luxembourg	29 Oct 28	Dispute Settlement	111LTS71	302581
Poland	Luxembourg	10 Apr 31	Admin Cooperation	140LTS411	303251
Poland	Multilateral	09 Sep 86*	Patents/Copyrights	123LTS233	302816
Poland	Multilateral	18 Mar 04	Humanitarian	1LTS83	300011
Poland	Multilateral	13 Nov 08	General Ad Hoc	1LTS217	300015
Poland	Multilateral	12 Jan 12	Sanitation	4LTS281	300112
Poland	Multilateral	05 Jun 12	Telecommunications	1LTS135	300013
Poland	Multilateral	10 Sep 19	Reparations	2LTS29	300043
Poland	Multilateral	10 Sep 19	Reparations	2LTS21	300042
Poland	Multilateral	10 Sep 19	Reparations	2LTS44	300045
Poland	Multilateral	10 Sep 19	General Economic	2LTS35	300044
Poland	Multilateral	10 Sep 19	General Trade	7LTS331	300200
Poland	Multilateral	01 May 20	Air Transport	11LTS173	300297
Poland	Multilateral	21 Jun 20	Health/Educ/Welfare	8LTS65	300207
Poland	Multilateral	30 Jun 20	Patents/Copyrights	1LTS59	300008

PARTY ONE	PARTY TWO	DATE	TOPIC	CITATION	NUMBER
Poland	Multilateral	16 Dec 20	General IGO	6LTS379	300170
Poland	Multilateral	20 Apr 21	Water Transport	7LTS73	300174
Poland	Multilateral	20 Apr 21	Land Transport	7LTS11	300171
Poland	Multilateral	20 Apr 21	Water Transport	7LTS35	300172
Poland	Multilateral	05 Aug 21	Admin Cooperation	27LTS349	300695
Poland	Multilateral	05 Oct 21	IGO Establishment	51LTS361	301241
Poland	Multilateral	05 Oct 21	Admin Cooperation	29LTS79	300735
Poland	Multilateral	05 Oct 21	Admin Cooperation	29LTS67	300733
Poland	Multilateral	05 Oct 21	Admin Cooperation	29LTS73	300734
Poland	Multilateral	06 Oct 21	General Economic	17LTS45	300427
Poland	Multilateral	20 Oct 21	Peace/Disarmament	9LTS211	300255
Poland	Multilateral	27 Jan 22	Visas	9LTS291	300262
Poland	Multilateral	17 Mar 22	Dispute Settlement	11LTS167	300296
Poland	Multilateral	31 Mar 22	Humanitarian	9LTS415	300269
Poland	Multilateral	06 Apr 22	Admin Cooperation	123LTS277	302818
Poland	Multilateral	06 Apr 22	Milit Assistance	20LTS11	300501
Poland	Multilateral	15 Jun 22	Dispute Settlement	21LTS463	300551
Poland	Multilateral	05 Jul 22	Reparations	13LTS237	300355
Poland	Multilateral	02 Nov 22	Peace/Disarmament	149LTS35	303431
Poland	Multilateral	30 Dec 22	General Trade	21LTS183	300542
Poland	Multilateral	24 May 23	Postal Service	50LTS341	301218
Poland	Multilateral	24 Sep 23	Dispute Settlement	27LTS157	300678
Poland	Multilateral	03 Nov 23	Customs	30LTS371	300775
Poland	Multilateral	30 Nov 23	Non-ILO Labor	102LTS153	302360
Poland	Multilateral	09 Dec 23	Non-IBRD Project	36LTS76	300905
Poland	Multilateral	09 Dec 23	General Economic	58LTS315	301380
Poland	Multilateral	09 Dec 23	Land Transport	47LTS55	301129
Poland	Multilateral	25 Jan 24	Sanitation	57LTS135	301360
Poland	Multilateral	31 Mar 24	Sanitation	27LTS211	300685
Poland	Multilateral	25 Aug 24	Water Transport	120LTS155	302764
Poland	Multilateral	25 Aug 24	Water Transport	120LTS123	302763
Poland	Multilateral	28 Aug 24	Postal Service	40LTS307	301004
Poland	Multilateral	28 Aug 24	Postal Service	41LTS9	301006
Poland	Multilateral	28 Aug 24	Postal Service	40LTS249	301003
Poland	Multilateral	28 Aug 24	Postal Service	40LTS437	301005
Poland	Multilateral	28 Aug 24	Postal Service	40LTS19	301002
Poland	Multilateral	28 Aug 24	Postal Service	41LTS97	301008
Poland	Multilateral	28 Aug 24	Postal Service	41LTS55	301007
Poland	Multilateral	23 Oct 24	Land Transport	78LTS17	301779
Poland	Multilateral	23 Oct 24	General Transport	77LTS367	301778
Poland	Multilateral	01 Dec 24	Sanitation	78LTS351	301794
Poland	Multilateral	17 Jan 25	Dispute Settlement	38LTS357	300991
Poland	Multilateral	19 Feb 25	Admin Cooperation	81LTS317	301845
Poland	Multilateral	17 Jun 25	Peace/Disarmament	94LTS65	302138
Poland	Multilateral	19 Aug 25	Customs	42LTS73	301033
Poland	Multilateral	29 Oct 25	Telecommunications	57LTS201	301365
Poland	Multilateral	06 Nov 25	Patents/Copyrights	74LTS289	301743
Poland	Multilateral	06 Nov 25	Other Economic	74LTS319	301744
Poland	Multilateral	27 Nov 25	Water Transport	67LTS63	301539
Poland	Multilateral	31 Dec 25	Territory Boundary	79LTS167	301809
Poland	Multilateral	10 Apr 26	Water Transport	176LTS199	304062
Poland	Multilateral	10 Apr 26	Water Transport	120LTS187	302765
Poland	Multilateral	24 Apr 26	Land Transport	108LTS123	302505
Poland	Multilateral	24 Apr 26	Land Transport	97LTS83	302220
Poland	Multilateral	12 May 26	Refugees	89LTS47	302004
Poland	Multilateral	21 Jun 26	Sanitation	78LTS229	301793
Poland	Multilateral	25 Sep 26	ILO Labor	60LTS253	301414
Poland	Multilateral	24 Jan 27	General Ad Hoc	70LTS453	301650
Poland	Multilateral	12 Jul 27	Direct Aid	135LTS247	303115
Poland	Multilateral	10 Sep 27	Postal Service	75LTS7	301749
Poland	Multilateral	10 Sep 27	Postal Service	75LTS39	301750
Poland	Multilateral	29 Oct 27	Scientific Project	127LTS27	302903
Poland	Multilateral	08 Nov 27	General Trade	97LTS391	302238
Poland	Multilateral	25 Nov 27	Telecommunications	84LTS97	301905
Poland	Multilateral	30 Jun 28	Refugees	89LTS63	302006

PARTY ONE	PARTY TWO	DATE	TOPIC	CITATION	NUMBER
Poland	Multilateral	30 Jun 28	Refugees	89LTS53	302005
Poland	Multilateral	11 Jul 28	Commodity Trade	95LTS357	302184
Poland	Multilateral	11 Jul 28	Commodity Trade	95LTS373	302185
Poland	Multilateral	27 Aug 28	General Military	94LTS57	302137
Poland	Multilateral	27 Aug 28	General Amity	89LTS369	302028
Poland	Multilateral	30 Oct 28	Non-ILO Labor	130LTS405	302999
Poland	Multilateral	30 Oct 28	Dispute Settlement	87LTS103	301963
Poland	Multilateral	22 Nov 28	Culture	111LTS343	302598
Poland	Multilateral	14 Dec 28	General Economic	110LTS171	302560
Poland	Multilateral	20 Apr 29	Admin Cooperation	112LTS395	302624
Poland	Multilateral	20 Apr 29	Admin Cooperation	112LTS371	302623
Poland	Multilateral	31 May 29	Water Transport	136LTS81	303127
Poland	Multilateral	14 Jun 29	Visas	94LTS275	302148
Poland	Multilateral	28 Jun 29	Postal Service	103LTS71	302370
Poland	Multilateral	28 Jun 29	Postal Service	103LTS321	302372
Poland	Multilateral	28 Jun 29	Postal Service	102LTS245	302368
Poland	Multilateral	28 Jun 29	Postal Service	103LTS377	302373
Poland	Multilateral	28 Jun 29	Postal Service	103LTS5	302369
Poland	Multilateral	28 Jun 29	Postal Service	103LTS429	302374
Poland	Multilateral	28 Jun 29	Postal Service	103LTS249	302371
Poland	Multilateral	27 Jul 29	Other Military	118LTS303	302733
Poland	Multilateral	27 Jul 29	Other Military	118LTS343	302734
Poland	Multilateral	14 Sep 29	UN Charter	165LTS353	303822
Poland	Multilateral	01 Oct 29	Telecommunications	98LTS197	302247
Poland	Multilateral	12 Oct 29	General Transport	137LTS11	303145
Poland	Multilateral	09 Nov 29	Land Transport	125LTS205	302855
Poland	Multilateral	17 Dec 29	Specific Resources	115LTS93	302679
Poland	Multilateral	20 Jan 30	Finance	104LTS413	302395
Poland	Multilateral	20 Jan 30	Finance	104LTS433	302397
Poland	Multilateral	20 Jan 30	Reparations	113LTS389	302650
Poland	Multilateral	20 Jan 30	Reparations	104LTS243	302394
Poland	Multilateral	12 Apr 30	Admin Cooperation	179LTS89	304137
Poland	Multilateral	12 Apr 30	Admin Cooperation	179LTS115	304138
Poland	Multilateral	28 Apr 30	Claims and Debts	121LTS69	302785
Poland	Multilateral	07 Jun 30	Finance	143LTS257	303313
Poland	Multilateral	07 Jun 30	Finance	143LTS317	303314
Poland	Multilateral	07 Jun 30	Finance	143LTS337	303315
Poland	Multilateral	28 Aug 30	Telecommunications	133LTS21	303053
Poland	Multilateral	23 Oct 30	Water Transport	125LTS95	302849
Poland	Multilateral	23 Oct 30	Water Transport	112LTS21	302603
Poland	Multilateral	31 Oct 30	Dispute Settlement	120LTS9	302760
Poland	Multilateral	19 Mar 31	Finance	143LTS407	303317
Poland	Multilateral	19 Mar 31	Admin Cooperation	143LTS7	303301
Poland	Multilateral	19 Mar 31	Finance	143LTS355	303316
Poland	Multilateral	28 Mar 31	Customs	119LTS47	302739
Poland	Multilateral	30 Mar 31	Land Transport	150LTS247	303459
Poland	Multilateral	30 Mar 31	Taxation	138LTS149	303185
Poland	Multilateral	13 Jul 31	Other HEW	139LTS301	303219
Poland	Multilateral	24 Sep 31	Specific Resources	155LTS349	303586
Poland	Multilateral	15 Oct 31	Water Transport	125LTS83	302847
Poland	Multilateral	15 Oct 31	Water Transport	125LTS89	302848
Poland	Multilateral	02 Sep 32	Land Transport	154LTS123	303543
Poland	Multilateral	09 Dec 32	Telecommunications	151LTS5	303479
Poland	Multilateral	11 Mar 33	Water Transport	135LTS301	303119
Poland	Multilateral	12 Apr 33	Sanitation	161LTS65	303706
Poland	Multilateral	29 May 33	Admin Cooperation	192LTS289	304479
Poland	Multilateral	03 Jul 33	Peace/Disarmament	147LTS67	303391
Poland	Multilateral	25 Aug 33	Commodity Trade	141LTS71	303262
Poland	Multilateral	11 Oct 33	Education	155LTS331	303585
Poland	Multilateral	11 Oct 33	Consul/Citizenship	150LTS431	303476
Poland	Multilateral	23 Nov 33	Land Transport	192LTS327	304483
Poland	Multilateral	23 Nov 33	Land Transport	192LTS389	304484
Poland	Multilateral	20 Mar 34	Postal Service	176LTS55	304054
Poland	Multilateral	20 Mar 34	Postal Service	174LTS171	304048
Poland	Multilateral	20 Mar 34	Postal Service	175LTS363	304052

PARTY ONE	PARTY TWO	DATE	TOPIC	CITATION	NUMBER
Poland	Multilateral	20 Mar 34	Postal Service	175LTS5	304049
Poland	Multilateral	20 Mar 34	Postal Service	175LTS73	304050
Poland	Multilateral	20 Mar 34	Finance	176LTS9	304053
Poland	Multilateral	20 Mar 34	Postal Service	175LTS269	304051
Poland	Multilateral	16 Apr 34	Water Transport	163LTS185	303767
Poland	Multilateral	02 Jun 34	General Trade	192LTS9	304458
Poland	Multilateral	02 Jun 34	Patents/Copyrights	192LTS17	304459
Poland	Multilateral	19 Jun 34	Admin Cooperation	154LTS381	303564
Poland	Multilateral	20 Feb 35	Sanitation	193LTS59	304487
Poland	Multilateral	20 Feb 35	Sanitation	193LTS37	304486
Poland	Multilateral	20 Feb 35	Sanitation	186LTS173	304310
Poland	Multilateral	26 Jun 36	Other HEW	198LTS299	304648
Poland	Multilateral	30 Jul 36	IGO Status/Immunit	197LTS31	304602
Poland	Multilateral	15 Sep 36	Scientific Project	178LTS439	304126
Poland	Multilateral	06 Nov 36	General Military	173LTS353	304025
Poland	Multilateral	31 Mar 37	Commodity Trade	189LTS359	304394
Poland	Multilateral	12 Sep 38	Culture	198LTS111	304630
Poland	Multilateral	31 Oct 38	Sanitation	198LTS205	304642
Poland	Multilateral	03 Dec 38	Education	200LTS249	304694
Poland	Multilateral	23 May 39	Postal Service	202LTS159	304742
Poland	Multilateral	07 Sep 39	Loans and Credits	198LTS357	304654
Poland	Multilateral	01 Jan 42	General Military	204LTS381	304817
Poland	Netherlands	30 May 24	General Trade	34LTS9	300865
Poland	Netherlands	04 Sep 25	Air Transport	58LTS179	301371
Poland	Netherlands	12 Apr 30	Dispute Settlement	113LTS65	302636
Poland	Netherlands	24 Dec 31	Admin Cooperation	131LTS269	303016
Poland	Netherlands	28 Jun 33	Land Transport	152LTS201	303494
Poland	Netherlands	11 Dec 33	General Trade	163LTS381	303780
Poland	Netherlands	09 Apr 36	Customs	177LTS71	304081
Poland	Norway	22 Dec 26	General Economic	66LTS359	301530
Poland	Norway	26 Apr 28	General Economic	88LTS179	301996
Poland	Norway	09 Dec 29	Dispute Settlement	101LTS325	302334
Poland	Norway	14 Mar 36	General Trade	171LTS371	303973
Poland	Norway	18 Jun 37	Customs	190LTS187	304416
Poland	Persia	19 Mar 27	General Economic	109LTS53	302528
Poland	Persia	19 Mar 27	General Amity	109LTS87	302529
Poland	Portugal	28 Dec 29	General Economic	117LTS363	302703
Poland	Portugal	27 Aug 30	Water Transport	115LTS127	302682
Poland	Romania	03 Mar 21	General Amity	7LTS77	300175
Poland	Romania	24 Jul 23	Sanitation	18LTS103	300458
Poland	Romania	26 Mar 26	Peace/Disarmament	60LTS161	301411
Poland	Romania	29 Nov 28	Admin Cooperation	96LTS15	302188
Poland	Romania	30 Mar 29	Land Transport	123LTS147	302812
Poland	Romania	24 May 29	Territory Boundary	124LTS333	302836
Poland	Romania	24 May 29	Territory Boundary	124LTS339	302837
Poland	Romania	24 Oct 29	Dispute Settlement	100LTS299	302302
Poland	Romania	30 Oct 29	Land Transport	121LTS243	302790
Poland	Romania	30 Oct 29	Land Transport	121LTS167	302787
Poland	Romania	07 Dec 29	Admin Cooperation	119LTS283	302752
Poland	Romania	17 Dec 29	Consul/Citizenship	119LTS333	302754
Poland	Romania	19 Dec 29	Admin Cooperation	130LTS205	302991
Poland	Romania	26 Mar 30	Extradition	153LTS87	303510
Poland	Romania	09 May 30	Air Transport	112LTS225	302617
Poland	Romania	23 Jun 30	General Economic	133LTS163	303066
Poland	Romania	15 Jan 31	Admin Cooperation	115LTS171	302685
Poland	Romania	02 May 31	Air Transport	152LTS33	303482
Poland	Romania	17 May 35	Territory Boundary	173LTS363	304027
Poland	Romania	17 May 35	Territory Boundary	173LTS373	304028
Poland	Romania	27 Nov 36	Other HEW	178LTS191	304113
Poland	Romania	24 May 37	Finance	190LTS361	304428
Poland	Romania	09 Feb 38	General Economic	197LTS71	304607
Poland	Serb/Croat/Slovene	04 May 23	Admin Cooperation	85LTS455	301946
Poland	Serb/Croat/Slovene	05 Apr 24	General Economic	49LTS265	301185
Poland	Serb/Croat/Slovene	18 Sep 26	General Amity	78LTS413	301799
Poland	Serb/Croat/Slovene	18 Sep 26	Dispute Settlement	78LTS419	301800

PARTY ONE	PARTY TWO	DATE	TOPIC	CITATION	NUMBER
Poland	Serb/Croat/Slovene	06 Mar 27	Consul/Citizenship	126LTS67	302871
Poland	Spain	03 Dec 28	Dispute Settlement	101LTS501	302348
Poland	Spain	14 Dec 34	General Economic	168LTS315	303908
Poland	Sweden	27 Dec 21	Humanitarian	8LTS163	300220
Poland	Sweden	02 Dec 24	General Amity	36LTS299	300930
Poland	Sweden	01 Oct 25	Air Transport	54LTS113	301279
Poland	Sweden	03 Nov 25	Dispute Settlement	62LTS263	301466
Poland	Sweden	25 Jan 28	Admin Cooperation	140LTS385	303248
Poland	Sweden	22 Sep 28	Admin Cooperation	140LTS391	303249
Poland	Sweden	30 Aug 30	Extradition	129LTS383	302973
Poland	Sweden	16 May 31	Commodity Trade	120LTS223	302768
Poland	Sweden	21 Oct 33	General Trade	150LTS73	303454
Poland	Sweden	03 Jul 36	General Trade	171LTS307	303968
Poland	Sweden	13 Sep 37	Non-ILO Labor	187LTS431	304348
Poland	Switzerland	26 Jun 22	General Economic	12LTS305	300322
Poland	Switzerland	07 Mar 25	Dispute Settlement	50LTS261	301209
Poland	Switzerland	03 Feb 34	General Trade	160LTS83	303685
Poland	Switzerland	19 Nov 37	Extradition	195LTS297	304552
Poland	Turkey	09 May 23	Sanitation	49LTS315	301187
Poland	Turkey	23 Jul 23	General Amity	49LTS323	301188
Poland	Turkey	23 Jul 23	General Economic	49LTS329	301189
Poland	Turkey	23 Jul 23	Admin Cooperation	49LTS345	301190
Poland	Turkey	29 Aug 31	Consul/Citizenship	144LTS367	303339
Poland	UK Great Britain	26 Nov 23	Water Transport	28LTS428	300722
Poland	UK Great Britain	13 Aug 24	Air Transport	31LTS213	300796
Poland	UK Great Britain	04 Oct 29	Postal Service	97LTS261	302227
Poland	UK Great Britain	20 Jan 30	Claims and Debts	126LTS159	302878
Poland	UK Great Britain	26 Aug 31	Admin Cooperation	131LTS19	303002
Poland	UK Great Britain	11 Jan 32	Extradition	148LTS221	303415
Poland	UK Great Britain	26 Oct 33	General Economic	158LTS73	303628
Poland	UK Great Britain	27 Feb 35	General Trade	162LTS181	303740
Poland	UK Great Britain	10 Sep 37	Customs	184LTS289	304253
Poland	UK Great Britain	14 Oct 37	Customs	191LTS279	304449
Poland	UK Great Britain	27 Apr 38	Peace/Disarmament	195LTS39	304535
Poland	UK Great Britain	05 Oct 38	Postal Service	194LTS321	304529
Poland	UK Great Britain	25 Aug 39	General Military	199LTS57	304665
Poland	UK Great Britain	25 Nov 39	General Military	199LTS65	304666
Poland	United Arab Rep	22 Apr 30	Mostfavored Nation	118LTS413	302735
Poland	USA (United States)	10 Feb 25	General Trade	37LTS141	300953
Poland	USA (United States)	14 Nov 26	Finance	58LTS97	301368
Poland	USA (United States)	22 Nov 27	Extradition	92LTS101	302082
Poland	USA (United States)	16 Aug 28	Dispute Settlement	99LTS401	302285
Poland	USA (United States)	16 Aug 28	Dispute Settlement	99LTS409	302286
Poland	USA (United States)	19 Jun 30	Commodity Trade	108LTS223	302515
Poland	USA (United States)	15 Jun 31	General Amity	139LTS395	303223
Poland	USA (United States)	17 Apr 34	Patents/Copyrights	150LTS403	303473
Poland	USA (United States)	05 Oct 34	Water Transport	156LTS91	303594
Poland	USA (United States)	05 Apr 35	Extradition	170LTS287	303943
Poland	USSR (Soviet Union)	12 Oct 20	Peace/Disarmament	4LTS7	300101
Poland	USSR (Soviet Union)	24 Feb 21	Refugees	4LTS141	300106
Poland	USSR (Soviet Union)	18 Mar 21	Peace/Disarmament	6LTS51	300149
Poland	USSR (Soviet Union)	07 Feb 23	Sanitation	49LTS285	301186
Poland	USSR (Soviet Union)	24 Apr 24	Visas	37LTS33	300947
Poland	USSR (Soviet Union)	05 May 24	Admin Cooperation	157LTS431	303617
Poland	USSR (Soviet Union)	18 Jul 24	Consul/Citizenship	49LTS201	301183
Poland	USSR (Soviet Union)	10 Apr 32	Territory Boundary	141LTS349	303275
Poland	USSR (Soviet Union)	25 Jul 32	General Military	136LTS41	303124
Poland	USSR (Soviet Union)	22 Nov 32	Dispute Settlement	136LTS55	303125
Poland	USSR (Soviet Union)	03 Jun 33	Dispute Settlement	142LTS265	303300
Poland	USSR (Soviet Union)	26 Jul 34	General Transport	164LTS301	303799
Poland	USSR (Soviet Union)	31 Mar 36	Water Transport	186LTS211	304313
Poland	USSR (Soviet Union)	31 Mar 36	Admin Cooperation	186LTS203	304312
Poland	Yugoslavia	02 Dec 31	Education	139LTS119	303207
Portug Colonies	Multilateral	28 Aug 24	Postal Service	41LTS97	301008
Portug Colonies	Multilateral	28 Aug 24	Postal Service	41LTS55	301007

PARTY ONE	PARTY TWO	DATE	TOPIC	CITATION	NUMBER
Portug West Africa	Multilateral	25 Nov 27	Telecommunications	84LTS97	301905
Portugal	Austria	18 Dec 25	General Economic	54LTS91	301277
Portugal	Austria	28 Mar 27	Visas	68LTS81	301571
Portugal	Bel-Lux Econ Union	06 Jan 27	General Trade	91LTS239	302065
Portugal	Belgium	22 Jan 20	Customs	3LTS149	300096
Portugal	Belgium	27 Feb 25	Water Transport	91LTS201	302061
Portugal	Belgium	09 Jul 27	Dispute Settlement	74LTS39	301730
Portugal	Belgium	19 Jul 27	Sanitation	71LTS419	301680
Portugal	Belgium	20 Jul 27	General Economic	71LTS431	301681
Portugal	Belgium	21 Jul 27	Water Transport	71LTS439	301682
Portugal	Belgium	22 Jul 27	Territory Boundary	71LTS449	301683
Portugal	Belgium	28 Mar 28	Admin Cooperation	92LTS185	302085
Portugal	Brazil	26 Sep 22	Patents/Copyrights	25LTS229	300610
Portugal	Brazil	26 Aug 33	General Trade	179LTS63	304134
Portugal	China	19 Dec 28	General Economic	107LTS93	302471
Portugal	Cuba	06 Sep 38	General Trade	195LTS443	304565
Portugal	Czechoslovakia	23 Nov 27	Dispute Settlement	123LTS417	302828
Portugal	Czechoslovakia	23 Nov 27	Extradition	124LTS7	302829
Portugal	Czechoslovakia	23 Nov 27	Dispute Settlement	123LTS403	302827
Portugal	Denmark	09 Apr 23	General Economic	17LTS63	300429
Portugal	Denmark	07 Sep 25	Water Transport	55LTS215	301316
Portugal	Denmark	18 Jun 35	Extradition	163LTS51	303760
Portugal	Estonia	22 Aug 29	General Trade	98LTS225	302250
Portugal	Finland	08 Mar 30	General Economic	105LTS441	302431
Portugal	France	08 Jun 20	Customs	1LTS393	300032
Portugal	France	04 Mar 25	General Economic	44LTS197	301083
Portugal	France	06 Jul 28	Dispute Settlement	126LTS27	302869
Portugal	Germany	28 Apr 23	General Trade	32LTS385	300827
Portugal	Germany	20 Mar 26	General Economic	53LTS361	301266
Portugal	Germany	21 Jul 27	Admin Cooperation	75LTS375	301760
Portugal	Germany	08 Apr 29	Admin Cooperation	93LTS253	302114
Portugal	Great Britain	30 Aug 24	Postal Service	38LTS217	300979
Portugal	Great Britain	29 Aug 25	Admin Cooperation	38LTS213	300978
Portugal	Great Britain	27 Jan 27	Water Transport	71LTS199	301662
Portugal	Greece	15 Aug 38	General Trade	201LTS201	304707
Portugal	Hungary	14 Nov 29	General Trade	105LTS287	302421
Portugal	Irish Free State	29 Oct 29	General Economic	131LTS145	303007
Portugal	Italy	18 Dec 26	Finance	93LTS313	302119
Portugal	Japan	23 Mar 32	General Economic	128LTS363	302941
Portugal	Latvia	15 Jun 29	General Economic	98LTS447	302262
Portugal	Lithuania	12 Apr 32	General Trade	129LTS135	302958
Portugal	Luxembourg	15 Aug 29	Dispute Settlement	115LTS77	302678
Portugal	Multilateral	09 Sep 86*	Patents/Copyrights	123LTS233	302816
Portugal	Multilateral	18 Mar 04	Humanitarian	1LTS83	300011
Portugal	Multilateral	13 Nov 08	General Ad Hoc	1LTS217	300015
Portugal	Multilateral	12 Jan 12	Sanitation	4LTS281	300112
Portugal	Multilateral	23 Jan 12	Sanitation	8LTS187	300222
Portugal	Multilateral	05 Jun 12	Telecommunications	1LTS135	300013
Portugal	Multilateral	20 Mar 14	Patents/Copyrights	1LTS243	300016
Portugal	Multilateral	10 Sep 19	Reparations	2LTS29	300043
Portugal	Multilateral	10 Sep 19	Admin Cooperation	8LTS25	300202
Portugal	Multilateral	10 Sep 19	General Trade	7LTS331	300200
Portugal	Multilateral	10 Sep 19	General Economic	2LTS35	300044
Portugal	Multilateral	10 Sep 19	Health/Educ/Welfare	8LTS11	300201
Portugal	Multilateral	10 Sep 19	Reparations	2LTS44	300045
Portugal	Multilateral	01 May 20	Air Transport	11LTS173	300297
Portugal	Multilateral	21 Jun 20	Health/Educ/Welfare	8LTS65	300207
Portugal	Multilateral	30 Jun 20	Patents/Copyrights	1LTS59	300008
Portugal	Multilateral	16 Dec 20	General IGO	6LTS379	300170
Portugal	Multilateral	20 Apr 21	Water Transport	7LTS65	300173
Portugal	Multilateral	20 Apr 21	Water Transport	7LTS73	300174
Portugal	Multilateral	20 Apr 21	Water Transport	7LTS35	300172
Portugal	Multilateral	20 Apr 21	Land Transport	7LTS11	300171
Portugal	Multilateral	05 Oct 21	Admin Cooperation	29LTS79	300735
Portugal	Multilateral	05 Oct 21	Admin Cooperation	29LTS73	300734

PARTY ONE	PARTY TWO	DATE	TOPIC	CITATION	NUMBER
Portugal	Multilateral	05 Oct 21	Admin Cooperation	29LTS67	300733
Portugal	Multilateral	06 Oct 21	General Economic	17LTS45	300427
Portugal	Multilateral	06 Feb 22	General Trade	38LTS277	300982
Portugal	Multilateral	06 Feb 22	Customs	38LTS267	300981
Portugal	Multilateral	31 Mar 22	Humanitarian	9LTS415	300269
Portugal	Multilateral	05 Jul 22	Reparations	13LTS237	300355
Portugal	Multilateral	24 Jul 23	Admin Cooperation	28LTS197	300706
Portugal	Multilateral	24 Sep 23	Dispute Settlement	27LTS157	300678
Portugal	Multilateral	03 Nov 23	Customs	30LTS371	300775
Portugal	Multilateral	28 Nov 23	Admin Cooperation	51LTS239	301233
Portugal	Multilateral	28 Nov 23	Admin Cooperation	51LTS221	301230
Portugal	Multilateral	28 Nov 23	Admin Cooperation	51LTS209	301228
Portugal	Multilateral	28 Nov 23	Admin Cooperation	51LTS233	301232
Portugal	Multilateral	28 Nov 23	Admin Cooperation	51LTS215	301229
Portugal	Multilateral	09 Dec 23	Land Transport	47LTS55	301129
Portugal	Multilateral	25 Jan 24	Sanitation	57LTS135	301360
Portugal	Multilateral	31 Mar 24	Sanitation	27LTS211	300685
Portugal	Multilateral	04 Jul 24	Admin Cooperation	51LTS227	301231
Portugal	Multilateral	16 Aug 24	Taxation	41LTS429	301024
Portugal	Multilateral	25 Aug 24	Water Transport	120LTS123	302763
Portugal	Multilateral	28 Aug 24	Postal Service	40LTS437	301005
Portugal	Multilateral	28 Aug 24	Postal Service	41LTS97	301008
Portugal	Multilateral	28 Aug 24	Postal Service	41LTS9	301006
Portugal	Multilateral	28 Aug 24	Postal Service	41LTS55	301007
Portugal	Multilateral	28 Aug 24	Postal Service	40LTS19	301002
Portugal	Multilateral	28 Aug 24	Postal Service	40LTS307	301004
Portugal	Multilateral	28 Aug 24	Postal Service	40LTS249	301003
Portugal	Multilateral	30 Aug 24	Admin Cooperation	30LTS75	300760
Portugal	Multilateral	30 Aug 24	Admin Cooperation	30LTS79	300761
Portugal	Multilateral	23 Oct 24	Land Transport	78LTS17	301779
Portugal	Multilateral	23 Oct 24	General Transport	77LTS367	301778
Portugal	Multilateral	29 Nov 24	General IGO	80LTS293	301835
Portugal	Multilateral	11 Feb 25	Sanitation	51LTS337	301239
Portugal	Multilateral	19 Feb 25	Admin Cooperation	81LTS317	301845
Portugal	Multilateral	17 Jun 25	Peace/Disarmament	94LTS65	302138
Portugal	Multilateral	29 Oct 25	Telecommunications	57LTS201	301365
Portugal	Multilateral	06 Nov 25	Other Economic	74LTS319	301744
Portugal	Multilateral	06 Nov 25	Other Economic	74LTS341	301746
Portugal	Multilateral	06 Nov 25	Patents/Copyrights	74LTS289	301743
Portugal	Multilateral	06 Nov 25	Patents/Copyrights	74LTS327	301745
Portugal	Multilateral	10 Apr 26	Water Transport	176LTS199	304062
Portugal	Multilateral	24 Apr 26	Land Transport	108LTS123	302505
Portugal	Multilateral	24 Apr 26	Land Transport	97LTS83	302220
Portugal	Multilateral	21 Jun 26	Sanitation	78LTS229	301793
Portugal	Multilateral	25 Sep 26	ILO Labor	60LTS253	301414
Portugal	Multilateral	12 Jul 27	Direct Aid	135LTS247	303115
Portugal	Multilateral	26 Sep 27	Dispute Settlement	92LTS301	302096
Portugal	Multilateral	29 Oct 27	Scientific Project	127LTS27	302903
Portugal	Multilateral	08 Nov 27	General Trade	97LTS391	302238
Portugal	Multilateral	25 Nov 27	Telecommunications	84LTS97	301905
Portugal	Multilateral	27 Aug 28	General Military	94LTS57	302137
Portugal	Multilateral	22 Nov 28	Culture	111LTS343	302598
Portugal	Multilateral	14 Dec 28	General Economic	110LTS171	302560
Portugal	Multilateral	16 Apr 29	Specific Resources	126LTS305	302891
Portugal	Multilateral	20 Apr 29	Admin Cooperation	112LTS395	302624
Portugal	Multilateral	20 Apr 29	Admin Cooperation	112LTS371	302623
Portugal	Multilateral	31 May 29	Water Transport	136LTS81	303127
Portugal	Multilateral	28 Jun 29	Postal Service	103LTS429	302374
Portugal	Multilateral	28 Jun 29	Postal Service	103LTS249	302371
Portugal	Multilateral	28 Jun 29	Postal Service	103LTS321	302372
Portugal	Multilateral	28 Jun 29	Postal Service	103LTS5	302369
Portugal	Multilateral	28 Jun 29	Postal Service	103LTS71	302370
Portugal	Multilateral	28 Jun 29	Postal Service	103LTS377	302373
Portugal	Multilateral	28 Jun 29	Postal Service	102LTS245	302368
Portugal	Multilateral	27 Jul 29	Other Military	118LTS343	302734

PARTY ONE	PARTY TWO	DATE	TOPIC	CITATION	NUMBER
Portugal	Multilateral	27 Jul 29	Other Military	118LTS303	302733
Portugal	Multilateral	14 Sep 29	UN Charter	165LTS353	303822
Portugal	Multilateral	20 Jan 30	Reparations	113LTS389	302650
Portugal	Multilateral	20 Jan 30	Finance	104LTS433	302397
Portugal	Multilateral	20 Jan 30	Reparations	104LTS421	302396
Portugal	Multilateral	20 Jan 30	Reparations	104LTS243	302394
Portugal	Multilateral	20 Jan 30	Finance	104LTS413	302395
Portugal	Multilateral	12 Apr 30	Milit Servic/Citiz	178LTS227	304117
Portugal	Multilateral	12 Apr 30	Admin Cooperation	179LTS115	304138
Portugal	Multilateral	12 Apr 30	Admin Cooperation	179LTS89	304137
Portugal	Multilateral	28 Apr 30	Claims and Debts	121LTS69	302785
Portugal	Multilateral	07 Jun 30	Finance	143LTS337	303315
Portugal	Multilateral	07 Jun 30	Finance	143LTS257	303313
Portugal	Multilateral	07 Jun 30	Finance	143LTS317	303314
Portugal	Multilateral	10 Jun 30	Loans and Credits	112LTS237	302618
Portugal	Multilateral	23 Oct 30	Water Transport	125LTS95	302849
Portugal	Multilateral	23 Oct 30	Water Transport	112LTS21	302603
Portugal	Multilateral	19 Mar 31	Finance	143LTS355	303316
Portugal	Multilateral	19 Mar 31	Admin Cooperation	143LTS7	303301
Portugal	Multilateral	19 Mar 31	Finance	143LTS407	303317
Portugal	Multilateral	27 Mar 31	ICJ Option Clause	167LTS341	303877
Portugal	Multilateral	28 Mar 31	Customs	119LTS47	302739
Portugal	Multilateral	30 Mar 31	Land Transport	150LTS247	303459
Portugal	Multilateral	30 Mar 31	Taxation	138LTS149	303185
Portugal	Multilateral	13 Jul 31	Other HEW	139LTS301	303219
Portugal	Multilateral	27 Nov 31	Sanitation	177LTS373	304100
Portugal	Multilateral	20 Jan 32	Extradition	141LTS267	303269
Portugal	Multilateral	09 Dec 32	Telecommunications	151LTS5	303479
Portugal	Multilateral	11 Mar 33	Water Transport	135LTS301	303119
Portugal	Multilateral	19 Jun 33	Gen Communications	154LTS133	303544
Portugal	Multilateral	10 Oct 33	General Amity	163LTS393	303781
Portugal	Multilateral	11 Oct 33	Consul/Citizenship	150LTS431	303476
Portugal	Multilateral	08 Nov 33	Specific Resources	172LTS241	303995
Portugal	Multilateral	23 Nov 33	Land Transport	192LTS327	304483
Portugal	Multilateral	23 Nov 33	Land Transport	192LTS389	304484
Portugal	Multilateral	20 Mar 34	Postal Service	175LTS269	304051
Portugal	Multilateral	20 Mar 34	Postal Service	175LTS363	304052
Portugal	Multilateral	20 Mar 34	Finance	176LTS9	304053
Portugal	Multilateral	20 Mar 34	Postal Service	176LTS55	304054
Portugal	Multilateral	20 Mar 34	Postal Service	175LTS5	304049
Portugal	Multilateral	20 Mar 34	Postal Service	175LTS73	304050
Portugal	Multilateral	20 Mar 34	Postal Service	174LTS171	304048
Portugal	Multilateral	02 Jun 34	Patents/Copyrights	205LTS179	304834
Portugal	Multilateral	02 Jun 34	General Trade	192LTS9	304458
Portugal	Multilateral	02 Jun 34	Patents/Copyrights	192LTS17	304459
Portugal	Multilateral	12 Jun 34	Milit Installation	155LTS367	303587
Portugal	Multilateral	25 Jul 34	Other HEW	177LTS59	304080
Portugal	Multilateral	26 Jun 36	Other HEW	198LTS299	304648
Portugal	Multilateral	30 Jul 36	IGO Status/Immunit	197LTS31	304602
Portugal	Multilateral	08 May 37	Privil/Immunities	182LTS37	304202
Portugal	Multilateral	31 Oct 38	Sanitation	198LTS205	304642
Portugal	Multilateral	03 Dec 38	Education	200LTS249	304694
Portugal	Multilateral	23 May 39	Postal Service	202LTS159	304742
Portugal	Multilateral	08 Jan 40	Visas	203LTS133	304756
Portugal	Multilateral	02 Jun 42	Patents/Copyrights	205LTS163	304833
Portugal	Netherlands	22 Aug 23	General Trade	20LTS139	300513
Portugal	Netherlands	27 Feb 24	General Trade	27LTS105	300672
Portugal	Netherlands	27 Aug 24	General Trade	31LTS235	300800
Portugal	Netherlands	27 Jun 28	Admin Cooperation	81LTS437	301853
Portugal	Norway	14 Oct 20	Water Transport	2LTS237	300069
Portugal	Norway	11 Apr 23	General Trade	16LTS379	300418
Portugal	Norway	21 Oct 24	Admin Cooperation	30LTS117	300764
Portugal	Norway	30 Nov 27	Water Transport	69LTS355	301617
Portugal	Norway	07 Feb 29	Water Transport	104LTS137	302383
Portugal	Norway	26 Jul 30	Dispute Settlement	134LTS123	303087

PARTY ONE	PARTY TWO	DATE	TOPIC	CITATION	NUMBER
Portugal	Norway	13 Nov 31	General Economic	129LTS455	302977
Portugal	Norway	04 Sep 34	General Trade	161LTS211	303713
Portugal	Poland	28 Dec 29	General Economic	117LTS363	302703
Portugal	Poland	27 Aug 30	Water Transport	115LTS127	302682
Portugal	Romania	05 Dec 30	General Economic	114LTS369	302666
Portugal	Siam	14 Aug 25	General Economic	55LTS57	301304
Portugal	Siam	02 Jul 38	General Amity	200LTS149	304688
Portugal	South Africa	22 Jun 26	Territory Boundary	70LTS305	301642
Portugal	South Africa	01 Jul 26	General Ad Hoc	70LTS315	301643
Portugal	South Africa	06 Oct 27	Territory Boundary	81LTS359	301846
Portugal	South Africa	11 Sep 28	Non-ILO Labor	98LTS9	302239
Portugal	South Africa	29 Apr 31	Territory Boundary	129LTS157	302960
Portugal	South Africa	18 Jun 37	Air Transport	189LTS121	304380
Portugal	Spain	26 Mar 23	Postal Service	18LTS349	300475
Portugal	Spain	26 Mar 23	Postal Service	18LTS373	300476
Portugal	Spain	29 Jul 26	Territory Boundary	82LTS95	301863
Portugal	Spain	11 Aug 27	Admin Cooperation	82LTS113	301864
Portugal	Spain	18 Jan 28	Dispute Settlement	77LTS105	301766
Portugal	Sweden	20 Sep 21	Humanitarian	7LTS143	300183
Portugal	Sweden	17 May 27	Admin Cooperation	64LTS373	301510
Portugal	Sweden	03 Jan 29	Water Transport	87LTS313	301977
Portugal	Sweden	06 Dec 32	Dispute Settlement	145LTS91	303347
Portugal	Sweden	19 Oct 34	General Trade	154LTS77	303538
Portugal	Switzerland	17 Oct 28	Dispute Settlement	96LTS287	302207
Portugal	UK Great Britain	07 Apr 20	Non-ILO Labor	5LTS297	300134
Portugal	UK Great Britain	06 May 20	Territory Boundary	4LTS93	300103
Portugal	UK Great Britain	09 Dec 20	Dispute Settlement	7LTS257	300192
Portugal	UK Great Britain	10 Jan 21	Extradition	7LTS271	300194
Portugal	UK Great Britain	10 Jan 21	Extradition	7LTS264	300193
Portugal	UK Great Britain	06 May 21	Air Transport	5LTS179	300128
Portugal	UK Great Britain	04 Feb 22	Health/Educ/Welfare	9LTS187	300251
Portugal	UK Great Britain	31 Mar 23	Admin Cooperation	18LTS29	300451
Portugal	UK Great Britain	19 May 25	Consul/Citizenship	36LTS125	300910
Portugal	UK Great Britain	03 Nov 25	Territory Boundary	47LTS379	301143
Portugal	UK Great Britain	20 May 26	Water Transport	50LTS303	301213
Portugal	UK Great Britain	31 Dec 26	Claims and Debts	61LTS115	301429
Portugal	UK Great Britain	06 Nov 27	Territory Boundary	80LTS219	301827
Portugal	UK Great Britain	18 Feb 30	General Trade	108LTS393	302522
Portugal	UK Great Britain	14 Jun 30	Postal Service	107LTS275	302484
Portugal	UK Great Britain	27 Jun 30	Postal Service	107LTS281	302485
Portugal	UK Great Britain	09 Aug 31	Admin Cooperation	129LTS417	302975
Portugal	UK Great Britain	14 Oct 33	General Trade	144LTS107	303322
Portugal	UK Great Britain	24 Oct 35	Air Transport	167LTS133	303861
Portugal	UK Great Britain	24 Mar 37	Postal Service	185LTS175	304281
Portugal	UK Great Britain	24 Mar 37	Postal Service	185LTS151	304280
Portugal	UK Great Britain	24 Mar 37	Postal Service	185LTS143	304279
Portugal	UK Great Britain	28 Dec 37	Territory Boundary	185LTS205	304284
Portugal	UK Great Britain	11 May 38	General Trade	191LTS285	304450
Portugal	UK Great Britain	25 Jan 39	Air Transport	196LTS281	304590
Portugal	UK Great Britain	29 Oct 40	Territory Boundary	204LTS261	304807
Portugal	USA (United States)	14 Sep 20	Dispute Settlement	7LTS253	300191
Portugal	USA (United States)	05 Sep 23	Dispute Settlement	50LTS239	301206
Portugal	USA (United States)	01 Mar 29	Dispute Settlement	99LTS375	302282
Prussia	Multilateral	12 Jan 12	Sanitation	4LTS281	300112
Reunion	Multilateral	24 Apr 26	Land Transport	108LTS123	302505
Reunion	Multilateral	24 Apr 26	Land Transport	97LTS83	302220
Reunion	Multilateral	23 Oct 30	Water Transport	125LTS95	302849
Rhine Navigation	Multilateral	00 Apr 26	Water Transport	57LTS437	301366
Rhine Navigation	Other Unilat Decla	25 Feb 21	Water Transport	12LTS355	300327
Rhine Navigation	Other Unilat Decla	16 Dec 21	Water Transport	13LTS53	300347
Rhine Navigation	Other Unilat Decla	10 Sep 26	Specific Property	62LTS141	301462
Rhine Navigation	Other Unilat Decla	08 Nov 30	Admin Cooperation	118LTS275	302729
Romania		28 Jan 33	Tech Assistance	138LTS271	303193
Romania		21 Jun 34	Finance	168LTS265	303904
Romania	Albania	03 Nov 30	Mostfavored Nation	118LTS39	302712

PARTY ONE	PARTY TWO	DATE	TOPIC	CITATION	NUMBER
Romania	Austria	26 Jul 24	Claims and Debts	85LTS223	301933
Romania	Austria	26 Jul 24	Finance	85LTS243	301934
Romania	Austria	30 Aug 30	Mostfavored Nation	118LTS17	302709
Romania	Austria	10 Oct 34	Admin Cooperation	158LTS281	303638
Romania	Bel-Lux Econ Union	28 Aug 30	Mostfavored Nation	107LTS221	302479
Romania	Bel-Lux Econ Union	24 Aug 37	Finance	193LTS189	304496
Romania	Belgium	08 Jul 30	Dispute Settlement	128LTS403	302944
Romania	Brazil	16 Dec 31	General Trade	139LTS255	303216
Romania	Bulgaria	19 Apr 24	Admin Cooperation	33LTS209	300845
Romania	Bulgaria	19 Apr 24	Extradition	33LTS221	300846
Romania	Bulgaria	27 Sep 30	Mostfavored Nation	118LTS27	302710
Romania	Bulgaria	26 Jul 35	Land Transport	198LTS9	304621
Romania	Bulgaria	22 May 37	Air Transport	188LTS173	304357
Romania	Bulgaria	20 Jul 37	Water Transport	202LTS33	304733
Romania	Czechoslovakia	23 Apr 21	General Economic	15LTS235	300397
Romania	Czechoslovakia	23 Apr 21	General Amity	6LTS215	300155
Romania	Czechoslovakia	14 Oct 22	Admin Cooperation	25LTS163	300604
Romania	Czechoslovakia	07 May 23	General Amity	18LTS81	300455
Romania	Czechoslovakia	01 Oct 24	Sanitation	51LTS71	301223
Romania	Czechoslovakia	16 Apr 25	Territory Boundary	46LTS427	301126
Romania	Czechoslovakia	07 May 25	Extradition	54LTS51	301273
Romania	Czechoslovakia	07 May 25	Admin Cooperation	54LTS17	301272
Romania	Czechoslovakia	13 Jun 26	General Military	54LTS253	301288
Romania	Czechoslovakia	21 May 29	General Amity	96LTS307	302209
Romania	Czechoslovakia	20 Jun 30	Air Transport	150LTS63	303453
Romania	Czechoslovakia	27 Jun 30	General Economic	119LTS73	302742
Romania	Czechoslovakia	15 Jul 30	Territory Boundary	164LTS157	303793
Romania	Czechoslovakia	05 Dec 30	Claims and Debts	167LTS231	303869
Romania	Czechoslovakia	05 Dec 30	Claims and Debts	167LTS205	303867
Romania	Czechoslovakia	05 Dec 30	Claims and Debts	167LTS221	303868
Romania	Czechoslovakia	22 Dec 30	Territory Boundary	167LTS243	303870
Romania	Czechoslovakia	22 Dec 30	Territory Boundary	167LTS257	303871
Romania	Czechoslovakia	22 Dec 30	Claims and Debts	167LTS263	303872
Romania	Czechoslovakia	22 Dec 30	Customs	168LTS209	303900
Romania	Czechoslovakia	20 Jun 34	Taxation	168LTS249	303902
Romania	Czechoslovakia	20 Jun 34	Taxation	168LTS241	303901
Romania	Czechoslovakia	20 Jun 34	Admin Cooperation	168LTS257	303903
Romania	Denmark	08 May 23	General Economic	17LTS31	300425
Romania	Denmark	28 Aug 30	Mostfavored Nation	108LTS165	302506
Romania	Estonia	30 Aug 30	Mostfavored Nation	114LTS59	302654
Romania	Finland	28 Aug 30	Mostfavored Nation	118LTS193	302723
Romania	Finland	03 Dec 35	Finance	165LTS287	303815
Romania	Finland	16 Nov 36	Visas	179LTS377	304164
Romania	France	10 Jun 26	General Amity	58LTS225	301373
Romania	France	10 Jun 26	Dispute Settlement	58LTS233	301374
Romania	France	27 Aug 30	Consul/Citizenship	158LTS379	303644
Romania	France	31 Mar 39	Education	199LTS213	304676
Romania	France	31 Mar 39	Finance	199LTS219	304677
Romania	Germany	10 Nov 28	Dispute Settlement	91LTS101	302058
Romania	Germany	28 Feb 29	Visas	97LTS61	302217
Romania	Germany	18 Jun 30	Mostfavored Nation	110LTS95	302554
Romania	Germany	03 Oct 37	Air Transport	190LTS369	304429
Romania	Germany	03 Mar 39	Admin Cooperation	201LTS381	304726
Romania	Germany	23 Mar 39	Other Economic	199LTS77	304668
Romania	Greece	28 Mar 27	Mostfavored Nation	68LTS67	301569
Romania	Greece	21 Mar 28	General Military	108LTS187	302508
Romania	Greece	11 Aug 31	General Economic	130LTS33	302981
Romania	Greece	11 Aug 31	Education	130LTS93	302984
Romania	Greece	11 Aug 31	Recognition	130LTS69	302982
Romania	Greece	11 Aug 31	Health/Educ/Welfare	130LTS79	302983
Romania	Greece	12 Jun 33	Air Transport	150LTS357	303468
Romania	Hungary	27 Dec 23	Dispute Settlement	21LTS263	300546
Romania	Hungary	14 Apr 24	Specific Resources	46LTS41	301113
Romania	Hungary	16 Apr 24	Admin Cooperation	42LTS165	301039
Romania	Hungary	16 Apr 24	Finance	46LTS7	301111
Romania	Hungary	16 Apr 24	General Economic	46LTS95	301114
Romania	Hungary	16 Apr 24	Admin Cooperation	45LTS349	301108
Romania	Hungary	16 Apr 24	Finance	45LTS355	301109
Romania	Hungary	16 Apr 24	Territory Boundary	46LTS27	301112
Romania	Hungary	16 Apr 24	Extradition	42LTS145	301038
Romania	Hungary	16 Apr 24	Admin Cooperation	45LTS341	301107
Romania	Hungary	16 Apr 24	Admin Cooperation	46LTS113	301115
Romania	Hungary	16 Apr 24	Admin Cooperation	45LTS325	301106
Romania	Hungary	16 Apr 24	Finance	45LTS403	301110
Romania	Hungary	28 May 24	Admin Cooperation	27LTS117	300674
Romania	Hungary	17 Nov 26	Land Transport	61LTS207	301435
Romania	Hungary	10 Aug 30	General Economic	107LTS185	302476
Romania	Hungary	12 Aug 31	General Trade	186LTS325	304321
Romania	Hungary	19 Oct 39	Land Transport	201LTS395	304728
Romania	Hungary	19 Oct 39	General Transport	201LTS419	304730
Romania	Hungary	19 Oct 39	Territory Boundary	201LTS419	304731
Romania	Hungary	19 Oct 39	Land Transport	201LTS415	304729
Romania	Iceland	08 May 31	General Economic	127LTS11	302901
Romania	Italy	16 Sep 26	General Amity	67LTS393	301560
Romania	Italy	25 Feb 30	Other Economic	106LTS231	302447
Romania	Italy	25 Feb 30	Sanitation	106LTS423	302459
Romania	Italy	25 Feb 30	Peace/Disarmament	106LTS225	302446
Romania	Italy	25 Feb 30	General Economic	106LTS179	302445
Romania	Japan	22 Oct 30	Mostfavored Nation	112LTS15	302602
Romania	Latvia	23 Oct 30	Mostfavored Nation	118LTS33	302711
Romania	Latvia	22 Mar 38	General Trade	187LTS439	304349
Romania	Luxembourg	22 Jan 30	Dispute Settlement	110LTS151	302559
Romania	Multilateral	09 Sep 86*	Patents/Copyrights	123LTS233	302816
Romania	Multilateral	12 Jan 12	Sanitation	4LTS281	300112
Romania	Multilateral	05 Jun 12	Telecommunications	1LTS135	300013
Romania	Multilateral	21 Apr 14	Sanitation	5LTS394	300144
Romania	Multilateral	10 Sep 19	General Economic	2LTS35	300044
Romania	Multilateral	10 Sep 19	General Trade	7LTS331	300200
Romania	Multilateral	09 Dec 19	Territory Boundary	5LTS335	300140
Romania	Multilateral	01 May 20	Air Transport	11LTS173	300297
Romania	Multilateral	21 Jun 20	Health/Educ/Welfare	8LTS65	300207
Romania	Multilateral	30 Jun 20	Patents/Copyrights	1LTS59	300008
Romania	Multilateral	16 Dec 20	General IGO	6LTS379	300170
Romania	Multilateral	20 Apr 21	Land Transport	7LTS11	300171
Romania	Multilateral	20 Apr 21	Water Transport	7LTS73	300174
Romania	Multilateral	23 Jul 21	Water Transport	26LTS173	300647
Romania	Multilateral	05 Aug 21	Admin Cooperation	27LTS349	300695
Romania	Multilateral	05 Oct 21	Admin Cooperation	29LTS67	300733
Romania	Multilateral	05 Oct 21	Admin Cooperation	29LTS79	300735
Romania	Multilateral	05 Oct 21	Admin Cooperation	29LTS73	300734
Romania	Multilateral	06 Oct 21	General Economic	17LTS45	300427
Romania	Multilateral	27 Jan 22	Visas	9LTS291	300262
Romania	Multilateral	31 Mar 22	Humanitarian	9LTS415	300269
Romania	Multilateral	06 Apr 22	Admin Cooperation	123LTS277	302818
Romania	Multilateral	06 Apr 22	Milit Assistance	20LTS11	300501
Romania	Multilateral	05 Jul 22	Reparations	13LTS237	300355
Romania	Multilateral	24 Jul 23	General Amity	36LTS145	300913
Romania	Multilateral	24 Jul 23	General Trade	28LTS151	300704
Romania	Multilateral	24 Jul 23	Territory Boundary	28LTS139	300703
Romania	Multilateral	24 Jul 23	Peace/Disarmament	28LTS11	300701
Romania	Multilateral	24 Jul 23	General Trade	28LTS203	300707
Romania	Multilateral	24 Jul 23	Water Transport	28LTS115	300702
Romania	Multilateral	24 Jul 23	Admin Cooperation	28LTS197	300706
Romania	Multilateral	24 Sep 23	Dispute Settlement	27LTS157	300678
Romania	Multilateral	03 Nov 23	Customs	30LTS371	300775
Romania	Multilateral	23 Nov 23	Reparations	28LTS273	300713
Romania	Multilateral	28 Nov 23	Admin Cooperation	51LTS239	301233
Romania	Multilateral	28 Nov 23	Admin Cooperation	51LTS233	301232
Romania	Multilateral	28 Nov 23	Admin Cooperation	51LTS209	301228
Romania	Multilateral	28 Nov 23	Admin Cooperation	51LTS221	301230

PARTY ONE	PARTY TWO	DATE	TOPIC	CITATION	NUMBER
Romania	Multilateral	28 Nov 23	Admin Cooperation	51LTS215	301229
Romania	Multilateral	30 Nov 23	Non-ILO Labor	102LTS153	302360
Romania	Multilateral	30 Nov 23	Non-ILO Labor	102LTS183	302361
Romania	Multilateral	09 Dec 23	Land Transport	47LTS55	301129
Romania	Multilateral	25 Jan 24	Sanitation	57LTS135	301360
Romania	Multilateral	14 Mar 24	Finance	25LTS423	300633
Romania	Multilateral	31 Mar 24	Sanitation	27LTS211	300685
Romania	Multilateral	04 Jul 24	Admin Cooperation	51LTS227	301231
Romania	Multilateral	16 Aug 24	Taxation	41LTS429	301024
Romania	Multilateral	25 Aug 24	Water Transport	120LTS123	302763
Romania	Multilateral	28 Aug 24	Postal Service	40LTS19	301002
Romania	Multilateral	28 Aug 24	Postal Service	41LTS55	301007
Romania	Multilateral	28 Aug 24	Postal Service	41LTS97	301008
Romania	Multilateral	28 Aug 24	Postal Service	40LTS437	301005
Romania	Multilateral	28 Aug 24	Postal Service	40LTS249	301003
Romania	Multilateral	28 Aug 24	Postal Service	40LTS307	301004
Romania	Multilateral	28 Aug 24	Postal Service	41LTS9	301006
Romania	Multilateral	30 Aug 24	Admin Cooperation	30LTS75	300760
Romania	Multilateral	30 Aug 24	Admin Cooperation	30LTS79	300761
Romania	Multilateral	23 Oct 24	Land Transport	78LTS17	301779
Romania	Multilateral	23 Oct 24	General Transport	77LTS367	301778
Romania	Multilateral	01 Dec 24	Sanitation	78LTS351	301794
Romania	Multilateral	19 Feb 25	Admin Cooperation	81LTS317	301845
Romania	Multilateral	17 Jun 25	Peace/Disarmament	94LTS65	302138
Romania	Multilateral	29 Oct 25	Telecommunications	57LTS201	301365
Romania	Multilateral	27 Nov 25	Water Transport	67LTS63	301539
Romania	Multilateral	10 Apr 26	Water Transport	176LTS199	304062
Romania	Multilateral	10 Apr 26	Water Transport	120LTS187	302765
Romania	Multilateral	24 Apr 26	Land Transport	108LTS123	302505
Romania	Multilateral	24 Apr 26	Land Transport	97LTS83	302220
Romania	Multilateral	12 May 26	Refugees	89LTS47	302004
Romania	Multilateral	21 Jun 26	Sanitation	78LTS229	301793
Romania	Multilateral	18 Sep 26	General IGO	59LTS237	301393
Romania	Multilateral	25 Sep 26	ILO Labor	60LTS253	301414
Romania	Multilateral	12 Jul 27	Direct Aid	135LTS247	303115
Romania	Multilateral	26 Sep 27	Dispute Settlement	92LTS301	302096
Romania	Multilateral	29 Oct 27	Scientific Project	127LTS27	302903
Romania	Multilateral	08 Nov 27	General Trade	97LTS391	302238
Romania	Multilateral	25 Nov 27	Telecommunications	84LTS97	301905
Romania	Multilateral	30 Jun 28	Refugees	89LTS63	302006
Romania	Multilateral	30 Jun 28	Refugees	89LTS53	302005
Romania	Multilateral	11 Jul 28	Commodity Trade	95LTS373	302185
Romania	Multilateral	11 Jul 28	Commodity Trade	95LTS357	302184
Romania	Multilateral	27 Aug 28	General Military	94LTS57	302137
Romania	Multilateral	27 Aug 28	General Amity	89LTS369	302028
Romania	Multilateral	22 Nov 28	Culture	111LTS343	302598
Romania	Multilateral	14 Dec 28	General Economic	110LTS171	302560
Romania	Multilateral	16 Apr 29	Specific Resources	126LTS305	302891
Romania	Multilateral	20 Apr 29	Admin Cooperation	112LTS371	302623
Romania	Multilateral	20 Apr 29	Admin Cooperation	112LTS395	302624
Romania	Multilateral	21 May 29	Dispute Settlement	96LTS311	302210
Romania	Multilateral	31 May 29	Water Transport	136LTS81	303127
Romania	Multilateral	14 Jun 29	Visas	94LTS275	302148
Romania	Multilateral	28 Jun 29	Postal Service	103LTS429	302374
Romania	Multilateral	28 Jun 29	Postal Service	103LTS377	302373
Romania	Multilateral	28 Jun 29	Postal Service	103LTS249	302371
Romania	Multilateral	28 Jun 29	Postal Service	102LTS245	302368
Romania	Multilateral	28 Jun 29	Postal Service	103LTS71	302370
Romania	Multilateral	28 Jun 29	Postal Service	103LTS5	302369
Romania	Multilateral	27 Jul 29	Other Military	118LTS343	302734
Romania	Multilateral	27 Jul 29	Other Military	118LTS303	302733
Romania	Multilateral	20 Aug 29	Sanitation	98LTS125	302243
Romania	Multilateral	14 Sep 29	UN Charter	165LTS353	303822
Romania	Multilateral	12 Oct 29	General Transport	137LTS11	303145
Romania	Multilateral	09 Nov 29	Land Transport	125LTS205	302855
Romania	Multilateral	20 Jan 30	Reparations	113LTS389	302650
Romania	Multilateral	20 Jan 30	Reparations	104LTS243	302394
Romania	Multilateral	20 Jan 30	Reparations	112LTS361	302622
Romania	Multilateral	20 Jan 30	Finance	104LTS433	302397
Romania	Multilateral	20 Jan 30	Reparations	104LTS421	302396
Romania	Multilateral	20 Jan 30	Finance	104LTS413	302395
Romania	Multilateral	28 Apr 30	Claims and Debts	121LTS69	302785
Romania	Multilateral	23 Oct 30	Water Transport	125LTS95	302849
Romania	Multilateral	23 Oct 30	Water Transport	112LTS21	302603
Romania	Multilateral	31 Oct 30	Dispute Settlement	120LTS9	302760
Romania	Multilateral	19 Mar 31	Finance	143LTS355	303316
Romania	Multilateral	19 Mar 31	Finance	143LTS407	303317
Romania	Multilateral	19 Mar 31	Admin Cooperation	143LTS7	303301
Romania	Multilateral	27 Mar 31	ICJ Option Clause	167LTS341	303877
Romania	Multilateral	30 Mar 31	Taxation	138LTS149	303185
Romania	Multilateral	30 Mar 31	Land Transport	150LTS247	303459
Romania	Multilateral	13 Jul 31	Other HEW	139LTS301	303219
Romania	Multilateral	21 Aug 31	Other Economic	127LTS95	302910
Romania	Multilateral	24 Sep 31	Specific Resources	155LTS349	303586
Romania	Multilateral	28 Jun 32	Admin Cooperation	140LTS191	303237
Romania	Multilateral	02 Sep 32	Land Transport	154LTS123	303543
Romania	Multilateral	09 Dec 32	Telecommunications	151LTS5	303479
Romania	Multilateral	16 Feb 33	Admin Cooperation	139LTS233	303213
Romania	Multilateral	11 Mar 33	Water Transport	135LTS301	303119
Romania	Multilateral	12 Apr 33	Sanitation	161LTS65	303706
Romania	Multilateral	29 May 33	Admin Cooperation	192LTS289	304479
Romania	Multilateral	19 Jun 33	Gen Communications	154LTS133	303544
Romania	Multilateral	03 Jul 33	Peace/Disarmament	147LTS67	303391
Romania	Multilateral	04 Jul 33	Peace/Disarmament	148LTS211	303414
Romania	Multilateral	25 Aug 33	Commodity Trade	141LTS71	303262
Romania	Multilateral	10 Oct 33	General Amity	163LTS393	303781
Romania	Multilateral	11 Oct 33	Education	155LTS331	303585
Romania	Multilateral	11 Oct 33	Consul/Citizenship	150LTS431	303476
Romania	Multilateral	23 Nov 33	Land Transport	192LTS389	304484
Romania	Multilateral	23 Nov 33	Land Transport	192LTS327	304483
Romania	Multilateral	09 Feb 34	General Military	153LTS153	303514
Romania	Multilateral	20 Mar 34	Postal Service	176LTS55	304054
Romania	Multilateral	20 Mar 34	Postal Service	175LTS269	304051
Romania	Multilateral	20 Mar 34	Postal Service	175LTS363	304052
Romania	Multilateral	20 Mar 34	Postal Service	174LTS171	304048
Romania	Multilateral	20 Mar 34	Postal Service	175LTS5	304049
Romania	Multilateral	20 Mar 34	Finance	176LTS9	304053
Romania	Multilateral	20 Mar 34	Postal Service	175LTS73	304050
Romania	Multilateral	25 Jul 34	Other HEW	177LTS59	304080
Romania	Multilateral	22 Dec 34	Visas	183LTS145	304230
Romania	Multilateral	20 Feb 35	Sanitation	193LTS59	304487
Romania	Multilateral	20 Feb 35	Sanitation	193LTS37	304486
Romania	Multilateral	20 Feb 35	Sanitation	186LTS173	304310
Romania	Multilateral	26 Jun 36	Other HEW	198LTS299	304648
Romania	Multilateral	20 Jul 36	Territory Boundary	173LTS213	304015
Romania	Multilateral	30 Jul 36	IGO Status/Immunit	197LTS31	304602
Romania	Multilateral	23 Sep 36	Gen Communications	186LTS301	304319
Romania	Multilateral	31 Mar 37	Commodity Trade	189LTS359	304394
Romania	Multilateral	14 Sep 37	General Military	181LTS137	304184
Romania	Multilateral	17 Sep 37	Milit Installation	181LTS150	304185
Romania	Multilateral	15 Apr 38	Visas	200LTS285	304698
Romania	Multilateral	18 Aug 38	Admin Cooperation	196LTS113	304574
Romania	Multilateral	31 Oct 38	Sanitation	198LTS205	304642
Romania	Multilateral	03 Dec 38	Education	200LTS249	304694
Romania	Multilateral	23 May 39	Postal Service	202LTS159	304742
Romania	Netherlands	20 Feb 22	General Transport	12LTS219	300313
Romania	Netherlands	19 Dec 22	General Economic	14LTS191	300373
Romania	Netherlands	22 Jan 30	Dispute Settlement	112LTS121	302611
Romania	Netherlands	29 Aug 30	Mostfavored Nation	108LTS177	302507
Romania	Netherlands	20 Jul 31	Land Transport	127LTS425	302929

PARTY ONE	PARTY TWO	DATE	TOPIC	CITATION	NUMBER
Romania	Netherlands	28 Aug 36	Finance	182LTS363	304222
Romania	Netherlands	10 Oct 38	Finance	195LTS9	304532
Romania	Norway	01 Oct 24	General Trade	29LTS397	300750
Romania	Norway	21 Jun 30	General Economic	120LTS113	302762
Romania	Norway	10 Dec 36	Finance	174LTS59	304037
Romania	Poland	03 Mar 21	General Amity	7LTS77	300175
Romania	Poland	24 Jul 23	Sanitation	18LTS103	300458
Romania	Poland	26 Mar 26	Peace/Disarmament	60LTS161	301411
Romania	Poland	29 Nov 28	Admin Cooperation	96LTS15	302188
Romania	Poland	30 Mar 29	Land Transport	123LTS147	302812
Romania	Poland	24 May 29	Territory Boundary	124LTS339	302837
Romania	Poland	24 May 29	Territory Boundary	124LTS333	302836
Romania	Poland	24 Oct 29	Dispute Settlement	100LTS299	302302
Romania	Poland	30 Oct 29	Land Transport	121LTS167	302787
Romania	Poland	30 Oct 29	Land Transport	121LTS243	302790
Romania	Poland	07 Dec 29	Admin Cooperation	119LTS283	302752
Romania	Poland	17 Dec 29	Consul/Citizenship	119LTS333	302754
Romania	Poland	19 Dec 29	Admin Cooperation	130LTS205	302991
Romania	Poland	26 Mar 30	Extradition	153LTS87	303510
Romania	Poland	09 May 30	Air Transport	112LTS225	302617
Romania	Poland	23 Jun 30	General Economic	133LTS163	303066
Romania	Poland	15 Jan 31	Admin Cooperation	115LTS171	302685
Romania	Poland	02 May 31	Air Transport	152LTS33	303482
Romania	Poland	17 May 35	Territory Boundary	173LTS363	304027
Romania	Poland	17 May 35	Territory Boundary	173LTS373	304028
Romania	Poland	27 Nov 36	Other HEW	178LTS191	304113
Romania	Poland	24 May 37	Finance	190LTS361	304428
Romania	Poland	09 Feb 38	General Economic	197LTS71	304607
Romania	Portugal	05 Dec 30	General Economic	114LTS369	302666
Romania	Serb/Croat/Slovene	13 Jun 26	General Military	54LTS257	301289
Romania	Serb/Croat/Slovene	04 Jun 27	Territory Boundary	158LTS443	303647
Romania	Serb/Croat/Slovene	21 May 29	General Amity	98LTS221	302249
Romania	Spain	20 Jun 30	Mostfavored Nation	117LTS411	302707
Romania	Spain	21 Mar 34	General Trade	159LTS171	303661
Romania	Sweden	21 Apr 21	Other Economic	4LTS265	300110
Romania	Sweden	25 Nov 21	General Economic	7LTS247	300190
Romania	Sweden	18 Dec 22	General Economic	14LTS353	300383
Romania	Sweden	21 Mar 31	General Economic	106LTS237	302448
Romania	Sweden	07 Oct 31	General Economic	131LTS51	303003
Romania	Switzerland	03 Feb 26	Dispute Settlement	55LTS91	301306
Romania	Switzerland	25 Aug 30	Mostfavored Nation	118LTS9	302708
Romania	Switzerland	16 Jan 33	General Trade	153LTS359	303532
Romania	Switzerland	19 Jul 38	Consul/Citizenship	152LTS89	303486
Romania	Switzerland	02 Nov 39	Finance	200LTS289	304699
Romania	Turkey	11 Jun 29	General Economic	112LTS139	302613
Romania	Turkey	17 Oct 33	Dispute Settlement	165LTS273	303814
Romania	Turkey	04 Sep 36	Visas	195LTS429	304564
Romania	UK Great Britain	22 Jan 20	Commodity Trade	1LTS257	300018
Romania	UK Great Britain	21 Apr 21	Peace/Disarmament	8LTS293	300226
Romania	UK Great Britain	24 May 23	General Trade	18LTS301	300471
Romania	UK Great Britain	02 Apr 30	Postal Service	105LTS235	302416
Romania	UK Great Britain	06 Aug 30	General Economic	123LTS307	302822
Romania	UK Great Britain	25 Sep 33	Consul/Citizenship	149LTS425	303443
Romania	UK Great Britain	14 Jun 35	Consul/Citizenship	163LTS301	303772
Romania	UK Great Britain	02 May 36	Finance	184LTS145	304247
Romania	UK Great Britain	06 Dec 37	Admin Cooperation	184LTS467	304267
Romania	UK Great Britain	02 Sep 38	Finance	191LTS313	304453
Romania	UK Great Britain	11 May 39	General Trade	196LTS351	304594
Romania	UK Great Britain	06 Jun 40	Finance	203LTS197	304761
Romania	United Arab Rep	16 Apr 30	Mostfavored Nation	117LTS405	302706
Romania	USA (United States)	26 Feb 26	Mostfavored Nation	51LTS59	301221
Romania	USA (United States)	21 Mar 29	Dispute Settlement	105LTS79	302402
Romania	USA (United States)	21 Mar 29	Dispute Settlement	105LTS85	302403
Romania	USA (United States)	20 Aug 30	Mostfavored Nation	115LTS115	302680
Romania	USA (United States)	16 Nov 36	Extradition	181LTS178	304188

PARTY ONE	PARTY TWO	DATE	TOPIC	CITATION	NUMBER
Romania	USA (United States)	10 Aug 37	Postal Service	183LTS7	304225
Romania	USA (United States)	30 Apr 39	Visas	203LTS349	304775
Romania	Vatican/Holy See	30 May 32	Admin Cooperation	201LTS257	304719
Romania	Yugoslavia	19 Jun 30	Territory Boundary	140LTS229	303238
Romania	Yugoslavia	24 Jun 30	Admin Cooperation	140LTS235	303239
Romania	Yugoslavia	27 Jun 30	General Military	107LTS215	302478
Romania	Yugoslavia	04 Aug 30	General Economic	107LTS253	302482
Romania	Yugoslavia	14 Dec 31	Finance	135LTS99	303106
Romania	Yugoslavia	14 Dec 31	Water Transport	135LTS71	303104
Romania	Yugoslavia	14 Dec 31	Water Transport	135LTS31	303103
Romania	Yugoslavia	14 Dec 31	Water Transport	135LTS133	303108
Romania	Yugoslavia	14 Dec 31	Water Transport	135LTS143	303109
Romania	Yugoslavia	14 Dec 31	Water Transport	135LTS117	303107
Romania	Yugoslavia	14 Dec 31	Finance	135LTS89	303105
Romania	Yugoslavia	30 Jan 33	Taxation	146LTS99	303362
Romania	Yugoslavia	30 Jan 33	Extradition	146LTS81	303361
Romania	Yugoslavia	30 Jan 33	Extradition	146LTS113	303363
Romania	Yugoslavia	30 Jan 33	Admin Cooperation	146LTS121	303364
Romania	Yugoslavia	30 Jan 33	Claims and Debts	146LTS129	303365
Romania	Yugoslavia	30 Jan 33	Culture	146LTS183	303371
Romania	Yugoslavia	30 Jan 33	Consul/Citizenship	146LTS173	303369
Romania	Yugoslavia	30 Jan 33	Territory Boundary	146LTS139	303366
Romania	Yugoslavia	30 Jan 33	Non-ILO Labor	146LTS151	303367
Romania	Yugoslavia	30 Jan 33	Visas	146LTS179	303370
Romania	Yugoslavia	30 Jan 33	Admin Cooperation	146LTS165	303368
Romania	Yugoslavia	10 Feb 33	Territory Boundary	174LTS115	304042
Romania	Yugoslavia	10 Mar 33	Sanitation	146LTS209	303372
Romania	Yugoslavia	10 Mar 33	Finance	146LTS263	303376
Romania	Yugoslavia	10 Mar 33	Territory Boundary	146LTS245	303374
Romania	Yugoslavia	10 Mar 33	Education	146LTS231	303373
Romania	Yugoslavia	10 Mar 33	Land Transport	146LTS271	303377
Romania	Yugoslavia	10 Mar 33	Non-ILO Labor	146LTS255	303375
Romania	Yugoslavia	11 Mar 33	Claims and Debts	146LTS285	303379
Romania	Yugoslavia	11 Mar 33	Territory Boundary	146LTS277	303378
Romania	Yugoslavia	13 Mar 35	Consul/Citizenship	179LTS57	304133
Romania	Yugoslavia	13 May 37	Territory Boundary	197LTS101	304609
Romania	Yugoslavia	13 May 37	Sanitation	197LTS161	304612
Romania	Yugoslavia	13 May 37	Consul/Citizenship	197LTS145	304611
Ruanda-Urundi	Belgian Colonies	06 Aug 35	Admin Cooperation	164LTS49	303787
Ruanda-Urundi	Multilateral	23 Jan 12	Sanitation	8LTS187	300222
Ruanda-Urundi	Multilateral	19 Feb 25	Admin Cooperation	81LTS317	301845
Ruanda-Urundi	Multilateral	13 Jul 31	Other HEW	139LTS301	303219
Ruanda-Urundi	Multilateral	02 Jan 39	Postal Service	196LTS235	304587
Russ Fed Sov Rep	Multilateral	24 May 23	Postal Service	50LTS341	301218
Russ Fed Sov Rep	Persia	25 Apr 23	Postal Service	110LTS323	302564
Russ Fed Sov Rep	Persia	27 Apr 23	Telecommunications	110LTS333	302565
Russia	Multilateral	18 Mar 04	Humanitarian	1LTS83	300011
Russia	Multilateral	12 Jan 12	Sanitation	4LTS281	300112
Rwanda	Multilateral	23 Jan 12	Sanitation	8LTS187	300222
Rwanda	Multilateral	20 Apr 21	Land Transport	7LTS11	300171
Rwanda	Multilateral	20 Apr 21	Water Transport	7LTS73	300174
Saar	France	30 Jul 20	Extradition	27LTS241	300687
Saar	France	05 Jul 22	Taxation	27LTS265	300689
Saar	France	30 Nov 22	Customs	27LTS283	300691
Saar	France	15 Jan 25	Customs	44LTS181	301082
Saar	France	27 May 26	Non-ILO Labor	55LTS157	301312
Saar	France	14 Apr 27	Land Transport	70LTS115	301628
Saar	France	14 Dec 27	Dispute Settlement	70LTS155	301630
Saar	France	14 Dec 27	Admin Cooperation	70LTS163	301631
Saar	France	12 Nov 28	Finance	85LTS451	301945
Saar	Germany	03 Jun 21	General Ad Hoc	5LTS189	300129
Saar	Germany	26 Aug 22	Admin Cooperation	27LTS249	300688
Saar	Germany	13 Nov 22	Health/Educ/Welfare	27LTS273	300690
Saar	Germany	17 Jan 23	Land Transport	27LTS290	300692
Saar	Germany	21 Apr 23	Non-ILO Labor	27LTS295	300693

PARTY ONE	PARTY TWO	DATE	TOPIC	CITATION	NUMBER
Saar	Germany	20 Sep 24	Admin Cooperation	30LTS121	300765
Saar	Germany	28 Feb 25	Land Transport	33LTS123	300837
Saar	Germany	21 Dec 25	Admin Cooperation	55LTS349	301319
Saar	Germany	23 Nov 26	Admin Cooperation	70LTS105	301627
Saar	Germany	13 Oct 27	Non-ILO Labor	70LTS121	301629
Saar	Multilateral	01 May 20	Air Transport	11LTS173	300297
Saar	Multilateral	28 Aug 24	Postal Service	40LTS437	301005
Saar	Multilateral	28 Aug 24	Postal Service	40LTS19	301002
Saar	Multilateral	28 Aug 24	Postal Service	41LTS97	301008
Saar	Multilateral	28 Aug 24	Postal Service	41LTS55	301007
Saar	Multilateral	28 Aug 24	Postal Service	40LTS249	301003
Saar	Multilateral	28 Aug 24	Postal Service	40LTS307	301004
Saar	Multilateral	28 Aug 24	Postal Service	41LTS9	301006
Saar	Multilateral	23 Oct 24	General Transport	77LTS367	301778
Saar	Multilateral	23 Oct 24	Land Transport	78LTS17	301779
Saar	Multilateral	29 Oct 25	Telecommunications	57LTS201	301365
Saar	Multilateral	24 Apr 26	Land Transport	108LTS123	302505
Saar	Multilateral	24 Apr 26	Land Transport	97LTS83	302220
Saar	Multilateral	14 Sep 26	Non-ILO Labor	77LTS149	301769
Saar	Multilateral	13 Nov 26	Territory Boundary	77LTS217	301772
Saar	Multilateral	13 Nov 26	Territory Boundary	77LTS199	301771
Saar	Multilateral	13 Nov 26	Territory Boundary	77LTS171	301770
Saar	Multilateral	13 Nov 26	Territory Boundary	77LTS249	301773
Saar	Multilateral	02 Feb 29	Telecommunications	92LTS353	302100
Saar	Multilateral	14 Jun 29	Visas	94LTS275	302148
Saar	Multilateral	28 Jun 29	Postal Service	103LTS377	302373
Saar	Multilateral	28 Jun 29	Postal Service	103LTS321	302372
Saar	Multilateral	28 Jun 29	Postal Service	103LTS5	302369
Saar	Multilateral	28 Jun 29	Postal Service	103LTS71	302370
Saar	Multilateral	28 Jun 29	Postal Service	102LTS245	302368
Saar	Multilateral	28 Jun 29	Postal Service	103LTS429	302374
Saar	Multilateral	28 Jun 29	Postal Service	103LTS249	302371
Saar	Multilateral	02 Sep 32	Land Transport	154LTS123	303543
Saar	Multilateral	23 Nov 33	Land Transport	192LTS327	304483
Saar	Multilateral	23 Nov 33	Land Transport	192LTS389	304484
Saar	Switzerland	15 Aug 28	Air Transport	81LTS373	301847
San Marino	France	30 Apr 26	Extradition	89LTS9	302001
San Marino	Multilateral	05 Jun 12	Telecommunications	1LTS135	300013
San Marino	Multilateral	28 Aug 24	Postal Service	41LTS97	301008
San Marino	Multilateral	28 Aug 24	Postal Service	41LTS55	301007
San Marino	Multilateral	28 Aug 24	Postal Service	40LTS307	301004
San Marino	Multilateral	28 Aug 24	Postal Service	41LTS9	301006
San Marino	Multilateral	28 Aug 24	Postal Service	40LTS437	301005
San Marino	Multilateral	28 Aug 24	Postal Service	40LTS249	301003
San Marino	Multilateral	28 Aug 24	Postal Service	40LTS19	301002
San Marino	Multilateral	19 Feb 25	Admin Cooperation	81LTS317	301845
San Marino	Multilateral	21 Jun 26	Sanitation	78LTS229	301793
San Marino	Multilateral	12 Jul 27	Direct Aid	135LTS247	303115
San Marino	Multilateral	25 Nov 27	Telecommunications	84LTS97	301905
San Marino	Multilateral	28 Jun 29	Postal Service	103LTS249	302371
San Marino	Multilateral	28 Jun 29	Postal Service	103LTS429	302374
San Marino	Multilateral	28 Jun 29	Postal Service	103LTS71	302370
San Marino	Multilateral	28 Jun 29	Postal Service	103LTS377	302373
San Marino	Multilateral	28 Jun 29	Postal Service	103LTS321	302372
San Marino	Multilateral	28 Jun 29	Postal Service	103LTS5	302369
San Marino	Multilateral	28 Jun 29	Postal Service	102LTS245	302368
San Marino	Multilateral	27 Jul 29	Other Military	118LTS303	302733
San Marino	Multilateral	13 Jul 31	Other HEW	139LTS301	303219
San Marino	Multilateral	29 May 33	Admin Cooperation	192LTS289	304479
San Marino	Multilateral	20 Mar 34	Postal Service	176LTS55	304054
San Marino	Multilateral	20 Mar 34	Postal Service	174LTS171	304048
San Marino	Multilateral	20 Mar 34	Finance	176LTS9	304053
San Marino	Multilateral	20 Mar 34	Postal Service	175LTS5	304049
San Marino	Multilateral	20 Mar 34	Postal Service	175LTS363	304052
San Marino	Multilateral	20 Mar 34	Postal Service	175LTS73	304050

PARTY ONE	PARTY TWO	DATE	TOPIC	CITATION	NUMBER
San Marino	Multilateral	20 Mar 34	Postal Service	175LTS269	304051
San Marino	USA (United States)	10 Oct 34	Extradition	161LTS149	303708
Sarawak	Multilateral	18 Mar 04	Humanitarian	1LTS83	300011
Sarawak	Multilateral	05 Jun 12	Telecommunications	1LTS135	300013
Sarawak	Multilateral	30 Jun 20	Patents/Copyrights	1LTS59	300008
Sarawak	Multilateral	31 Mar 22	Humanitarian	9LTS415	300269
Sarawak	Multilateral	25 Nov 27	Telecommunications	84LTS97	301905
Sarawak	Multilateral	12 Oct 29	General Transport	137LTS11	303145
Sarawak	Multilateral	23 Sep 36	Gen Communications	186LTS301	304319
Saudi Arabia	India	09 Nov 31	Postal Service	157LTS35	303604
Saudi Arabia	Iraq	02 Apr 36	General Amity	174LTS131	304044
Saudi Arabia	Multilateral	23 Jan 12	Sanitation	8LTS187	300222
Saudi Arabia	Multilateral	13 Jul 31	Other HEW	139LTS301	303219
Saudi Arabia	Multilateral	20 Mar 34	Postal Service	176LTS55	304054
Saudi Arabia	Multilateral	20 Mar 34	Postal Service	175LTS269	304051
Saudi Arabia	Multilateral	20 Mar 34	Postal Service	175LTS363	304052
Saudi Arabia	Multilateral	20 Mar 34	Postal Service	174LTS171	304048
Saudi Arabia	Multilateral	20 Mar 34	Postal Service	175LTS5	304049
Saudi Arabia	Multilateral	20 Mar 34	Postal Service	175LTS73	304050
Saudi Arabia	Multilateral	20 Mar 34	Finance	176LTS9	304053
Saudi Arabia	Multilateral	06 Nov 36	General Military	173LTS353	304025
Saudi Arabia	UK Great Britain	17 Nov 35	Customs	170LTS87	303929
Senegal	Multilateral	29 Oct 25	Telecommunications	57LTS201	301365
Senegal	Multilateral	25 Sep 26	ILO Labor	60LTS253	301414
Senegal	Multilateral	20 Apr 29	Admin Cooperation	112LTS395	302624
Senegal	Multilateral	20 Apr 29	Admin Cooperation	112LTS371	302623
Senegal	Multilateral	11 Oct 33	Consul/Citizenship	150LTS431	303476
Serb/Croat/Slovene		12 Aug 27	Claims and Debts	101LTS485	302347
Serb/Croat/Slovene	Albania	22 Jun 26	Extradition	91LTS81	302056
Serb/Croat/Slovene	Albania	22 Jun 26	Consul/Citizenship	91LTS55	302055
Serb/Croat/Slovene	Albania	22 Jun 26	General Economic	91LTS9	302054
Serb/Croat/Slovene	Albania	11 Aug 29	Territory Boundary	101LTS439	302342
Serb/Croat/Slovene	Argentina	13 Mar 35	Non-ILO Labor	158LTS189	303631
Serb/Croat/Slovene	Austria	29 Mar 24	Land Transport	114LTS421	302670
Serb/Croat/Slovene	Austria	29 Mar 24	Non-ILO Labor	114LTS451	302671
Serb/Croat/Slovene	Austria	18 Jun 24	Non-ILO Labor	115LTS9	302673
Serb/Croat/Slovene	Austria	18 Jun 24	Non-ILO Labor	114LTS481	302672
Serb/Croat/Slovene	Austria	18 Jun 24	Non-ILO Labor	115LTS25	302674
Serb/Croat/Slovene	Austria	27 Jun 24	Non-ILO Labor	115LTS49	302676
Serb/Croat/Slovene	Austria	27 Jun 24	Non-ILO Labor	115LTS39	302675
Serb/Croat/Slovene	Austria	17 Jan 25	Health/Educ/Welfare	128LTS453	302949
Serb/Croat/Slovene	Austria	17 Jan 25	Health/Educ/Welfare	128LTS445	302948
Serb/Croat/Slovene	Austria	01 May 28	Admin Cooperation	96LTS373	302214
Serb/Croat/Slovene	Austria	06 Jun 28	Non-ILO Labor	129LTS11	302950
Serb/Croat/Slovene	Austria	09 Jul 28	General Trade	85LTS265	301936
Serb/Croat/Slovene	Bel-Lux Econ Union	16 Dec 26	General Trade	70LTS371	301647
Serb/Croat/Slovene	Bulgaria	26 Nov 23	Extradition	26LTS119	300643
Serb/Croat/Slovene	Bulgaria	26 Nov 23	Reparations	21LTS153	300539
Serb/Croat/Slovene	Bulgaria	26 Nov 23	Reparations	21LTS163	300540
Serb/Croat/Slovene	Bulgaria	26 Nov 23	Admin Cooperation	26LTS85	300642
Serb/Croat/Slovene	Bulgaria	26 Nov 23	Humanitarian	26LTS141	300644
Serb/Croat/Slovene	Czechoslovakia	14 Aug 20	General Amity	6LTS209	300154
Serb/Croat/Slovene	Czechoslovakia	18 Oct 20	General Economic	17LTS19	300424
Serb/Croat/Slovene	Czechoslovakia	31 Aug 22	General Amity	13LTS231	300354
Serb/Croat/Slovene	Czechoslovakia	17 Mar 23	Admin Cooperation	30LTS185	300768
Serb/Croat/Slovene	Czechoslovakia	19 Sep 28	Admin Cooperation	87LTS309	301976
Serb/Croat/Slovene	Czechoslovakia	29 Sep 28	Claims and Debts	96LTS421	302215
Serb/Croat/Slovene	Czechoslovakia	07 Nov 28	Claims and Debts	95LTS101	302169
Serb/Croat/Slovene	Czechoslovakia	07 Nov 28	Consul/Citizenship	98LTS297	302252
Serb/Croat/Slovene	Czechoslovakia	14 Nov 28	General Economic	97LTS9	302216
Serb/Croat/Slovene	Czechoslovakia	21 May 29	General Amity	94LTS53	302136
Serb/Croat/Slovene	Estonia	01 Feb 28	General Economic	106LTS139	302441
Serb/Croat/Slovene	Finland	29 Jan 29	General Trade	96LTS77	302192
Serb/Croat/Slovene	France	11 Nov 27	Dispute Settlement	68LTS381	301593
Serb/Croat/Slovene	France	11 Nov 27	General Amity	68LTS373	301592

PARTY ONE	PARTY TWO	DATE	TOPIC	CITATION	NUMBER
Serb/Croat/Slovene	Germany	06 Oct 27	General Trade	77LTS19	301763
Serb/Croat/Slovene	Germany	15 Dec 28	Non-ILO Labor	95LTS113	302170
Serb/Croat/Slovene	Germany	15 Dec 28	Non-ILO Labor	95LTS149	302171
Serb/Croat/Slovene	Great Britain	09 Aug 27	Reparations	69LTS255	301607
Serb/Croat/Slovene	Greece	10 May 23	Land Transport	25LTS441	300635
Serb/Croat/Slovene	Greece	02 Nov 27	General Economic	91LTS137	302060
Serb/Croat/Slovene	Greece	27 Mar 29	Dispute Settlement	108LTS201	302509
Serb/Croat/Slovene	Hungary	20 Mar 23	Refugees	16LTS447	300422
Serb/Croat/Slovene	Hungary	14 Dec 24	Admin Cooperation	39LTS91	300997
Serb/Croat/Slovene	Hungary	24 Jul 26	Admin Cooperation	97LTS165	302223
Serb/Croat/Slovene	Hungary	22 Feb 28	Health/Educ/Welfare	110LTS411	302572
Serb/Croat/Slovene	Hungary	22 Feb 28	Admin Cooperation	181LTS229	304192
Serb/Croat/Slovene	Hungary	22 Feb 28	Claims and Debts	100LTS345	302306
Serb/Croat/Slovene	Hungary	22 Feb 28	Taxation	100LTS331	302305
Serb/Croat/Slovene	Hungary	22 Feb 28	Sanitation	113LTS49	302635
Serb/Croat/Slovene	Hungary	22 Feb 28	Extradition	104LTS151	302385
Serb/Croat/Slovene	Hungary	22 Feb 28	Finance	87LTS331	301979
Serb/Croat/Slovene	Hungary	22 Feb 28	Non-ILO Labor	88LTS125	301992
Serb/Croat/Slovene	Hungary	22 Feb 28	Territory Boundary	88LTS111	301991
Serb/Croat/Slovene	Hungary	22 Feb 28	Consul/Citizenship	87LTS361	301982
Serb/Croat/Slovene	Hungary	19 Nov 28	General Trade	97LTS101	302222
Serb/Croat/Slovene	Italy	12 Nov 20	Territory Boundary	18LTS387	300477
Serb/Croat/Slovene	Italy	14 Sep 21	Specific Resources	19LTS14	300482
Serb/Croat/Slovene	Italy	06 Apr 22	Admin Cooperation	123LTS289	302819
Serb/Croat/Slovene	Italy	06 Apr 22	Privil/Immunities	118LTS207	302725
Serb/Croat/Slovene	Italy	06 Apr 22	Dispute Settlement	118LTS199	302724
Serb/Croat/Slovene	Italy	06 Apr 22	Extradition	118LTS221	302726
Serb/Croat/Slovene	Italy	23 Oct 22	Territory Boundary	18LTS461	300481
Serb/Croat/Slovene	Italy	23 Oct 22	General Economic	18LTS405	300478
Serb/Croat/Slovene	Italy	23 Oct 22	Customs	18LTS413	300479
Serb/Croat/Slovene	Italy	23 Oct 22	Customs	18LTS441	300480
Serb/Croat/Slovene	Italy	27 Jan 24	Visas	83LTS139	301887
Serb/Croat/Slovene	Italy	27 Jan 24	Admin Cooperation	83LTS87	301886
Serb/Croat/Slovene	Italy	27 Jan 24	General Amity	24LTS31	300596
Serb/Croat/Slovene	Italy	14 Jul 24	General Trade	82LTS257	301876
Serb/Croat/Slovene	Italy	14 Jul 24	Land Transport	82LTS327	301877
Serb/Croat/Slovene	Italy	14 Jul 24	Land Transport	82LTS349	301878
Serb/Croat/Slovene	Italy	12 Aug 24	Telecommunications	82LTS401	301881
Serb/Croat/Slovene	Italy	12 Aug 24	Territory Boundary	82LTS423	301882
Serb/Croat/Slovene	Italy	12 Aug 24	Sanitation	83LTS19	301884
Serb/Croat/Slovene	Italy	12 Aug 24	Customs	82LTS391	301880
Serb/Croat/Slovene	Italy	12 Aug 24	Admin Cooperation	82LTS355	301879
Serb/Croat/Slovene	Italy	21 Aug 24	Consul/Citizenship	82LTS445	301883
Serb/Croat/Slovene	Italy	20 Jul 25	Consul/Citizenship	83LTS159	301888
Serb/Croat/Slovene	Italy	20 Jul 25	Visas	83LTS253	301891
Serb/Croat/Slovene	Italy	20 Jul 25	General Transport	83LTS33	301885
Serb/Croat/Slovene	Italy	20 Jul 25	Telecommunications	83LTS295	301897
Serb/Croat/Slovene	Italy	20 Jul 25	Land Transport	83LTS247	301890
Serb/Croat/Slovene	Italy	20 Jul 25	Other Ad Hoc	83LTS259	301892
Serb/Croat/Slovene	Italy	20 Jul 25	Consul/Citizenship	83LTS271	301894
Serb/Croat/Slovene	Italy	20 Jul 25	Visas	83LTS277	301895
Serb/Croat/Slovene	Italy	20 Jul 25	Consul/Citizenship	83LTS265	301893
Serb/Croat/Slovene	Italy	20 Jul 25	Visas	83LTS287	301896
Serb/Croat/Slovene	Italy	20 Jul 25	Admin Cooperation	83LTS241	301889
Serb/Croat/Slovene	Italy	16 Sep 29	Territory Boundary	101LTS127	302322
Serb/Croat/Slovene	Japan	16 Nov 23	General Economic	42LTS99	301035
Serb/Croat/Slovene	Latvia	18 Oct 29	General Economic	96LTS229	302204
Serb/Croat/Slovene	Multilateral	12 Jan 12	Sanitation	4LTS281	300112
Serb/Croat/Slovene	Multilateral	05 Jun 12	Telecommunications	1LTS135	300013
Serb/Croat/Slovene	Multilateral	10 Sep 19	General Economic	2LTS35	300044
Serb/Croat/Slovene	Multilateral	10 Sep 19	General Trade	7LTS331	300200
Serb/Croat/Slovene	Multilateral	10 Sep 19	Reparations	2LTS21	300042
Serb/Croat/Slovene	Multilateral	01 May 20	Air Transport	11LTS173	300297
Serb/Croat/Slovene	Multilateral	21 Jun 20	Health/Educ/Welfare	8LTS65	300207
Serb/Croat/Slovene	Multilateral	30 Jun 20	Patents/Copyrights	1LTS59	300008
Serb/Croat/Slovene	Multilateral	31 Oct 20	Sanitation	164LTS85	303790
Serb/Croat/Slovene	Multilateral	16 Dec 20	General IGO	6LTS379	300170
Serb/Croat/Slovene	Multilateral	20 Apr 21	Land Transport	7LTS11	300171
Serb/Croat/Slovene	Multilateral	20 Apr 21	Water Transport	7LTS73	300174
Serb/Croat/Slovene	Multilateral	23 Jul 21	Water Transport	26LTS173	300647
Serb/Croat/Slovene	Multilateral	06 Oct 21	General Economic	17LTS45	300427
Serb/Croat/Slovene	Multilateral	27 Jan 22	Visas	9LTS291	300262
Serb/Croat/Slovene	Multilateral	06 Apr 22	Admin Cooperation	123LTS277	302818
Serb/Croat/Slovene	Multilateral	06 Apr 22	Milit Assistance	20LTS11	300501
Serb/Croat/Slovene	Multilateral	05 Jul 22	Reparations	13LTS237	300355
Serb/Croat/Slovene	Multilateral	02 Nov 22	Peace/Disarmament	149LTS35	303431
Serb/Croat/Slovene	Multilateral	29 Mar 23	Land Transport	23LTS378	300594
Serb/Croat/Slovene	Multilateral	29 Mar 23	Land Transport	23LTS256	300593
Serb/Croat/Slovene	Multilateral	24 Jul 23	General Trade	28LTS203	300707
Serb/Croat/Slovene	Multilateral	24 Jul 23	Territory Boundary	28LTS139	300703
Serb/Croat/Slovene	Multilateral	24 Jul 23	Admin Cooperation	28LTS197	300706
Serb/Croat/Slovene	Multilateral	24 Jul 23	Water Transport	28LTS115	300702
Serb/Croat/Slovene	Multilateral	24 Jul 23	Peace/Disarmament	28LTS11	300701
Serb/Croat/Slovene	Multilateral	24 Jul 23	General Trade	28LTS151	300704
Serb/Croat/Slovene	Multilateral	03 Nov 23	Customs	30LTS371	300775
Serb/Croat/Slovene	Multilateral	30 Nov 23	Non-ILO Labor	102LTS153	302360
Serb/Croat/Slovene	Multilateral	30 Nov 23	Non-ILO Labor	102LTS183	302361
Serb/Croat/Slovene	Multilateral	09 Dec 23	Land Transport	47LTS55	301129
Serb/Croat/Slovene	Multilateral	09 Dec 23	Water Transport	58LTS284	301379
Serb/Croat/Slovene	Multilateral	09 Dec 23	General Economic	58LTS315	301380
Serb/Croat/Slovene	Multilateral	09 Dec 23	Non-IBRD Project	36LTS76	300905
Serb/Croat/Slovene	Multilateral	14 Mar 24	Finance	25LTS423	300633
Serb/Croat/Slovene	Multilateral	31 Mar 24	Sanitation	27LTS211	300685
Serb/Croat/Slovene	Multilateral	16 Aug 24	Taxation	41LTS429	301024
Serb/Croat/Slovene	Multilateral	25 Aug 24	Water Transport	120LTS155	302764
Serb/Croat/Slovene	Multilateral	25 Aug 24	Water Transport	120LTS123	302763
Serb/Croat/Slovene	Multilateral	28 Aug 24	Postal Service	41LTS97	301008
Serb/Croat/Slovene	Multilateral	28 Aug 24	Postal Service	41LTS9	301006
Serb/Croat/Slovene	Multilateral	28 Aug 24	Postal Service	40LTS307	301004
Serb/Croat/Slovene	Multilateral	28 Aug 24	Postal Service	40LTS249	301003
Serb/Croat/Slovene	Multilateral	28 Aug 24	Postal Service	40LTS437	301005
Serb/Croat/Slovene	Multilateral	28 Aug 24	Postal Service	41LTS55	301007
Serb/Croat/Slovene	Multilateral	28 Aug 24	Postal Service	40LTS19	301002
Serb/Croat/Slovene	Multilateral	30 Aug 24	Admin Cooperation	30LTS75	300760
Serb/Croat/Slovene	Multilateral	30 Aug 24	Admin Cooperation	30LTS79	300761
Serb/Croat/Slovene	Multilateral	30 Aug 24	Reparations	30LTS97	300762
Serb/Croat/Slovene	Multilateral	23 Oct 24	Land Transport	78LTS17	301779
Serb/Croat/Slovene	Multilateral	23 Oct 24	General Transport	77LTS367	301778
Serb/Croat/Slovene	Multilateral	19 Feb 25	Admin Cooperation	81LTS317	301845
Serb/Croat/Slovene	Multilateral	17 Jun 25	Peace/Disarmament	94LTS65	302138
Serb/Croat/Slovene	Multilateral	29 Oct 25	Telecommunications	57LTS201	301365
Serb/Croat/Slovene	Multilateral	06 Nov 25	Patents/Copyrights	74LTS289	301743
Serb/Croat/Slovene	Multilateral	06 Nov 25	Patents/Copyrights	74LTS327	301745
Serb/Croat/Slovene	Multilateral	27 Nov 25	Water Transport	67LTS63	301539
Serb/Croat/Slovene	Multilateral	10 Apr 26	Water Transport	176LTS199	304062
Serb/Croat/Slovene	Multilateral	10 Apr 26	Water Transport	120LTS187	302765
Serb/Croat/Slovene	Multilateral	24 Apr 26	Land Transport	108LTS123	302505
Serb/Croat/Slovene	Multilateral	24 Apr 26	Land Transport	97LTS83	302220
Serb/Croat/Slovene	Multilateral	12 May 26	Refugees	89LTS47	302004
Serb/Croat/Slovene	Multilateral	21 Jun 26	Sanitation	78LTS229	301793
Serb/Croat/Slovene	Multilateral	25 Sep 26	ILO Labor	60LTS253	301414
Serb/Croat/Slovene	Multilateral	29 Oct 27	Scientific Project	127LTS27	302903
Serb/Croat/Slovene	Multilateral	08 Nov 27	General Trade	97LTS391	302238
Serb/Croat/Slovene	Multilateral	25 Nov 27	Telecommunications	84LTS97	301905
Serb/Croat/Slovene	Multilateral	30 Jun 28	Refugees	89LTS53	302005
Serb/Croat/Slovene	Multilateral	11 Jul 28	Commodity Trade	95LTS373	302185
Serb/Croat/Slovene	Multilateral	27 Aug 28	General Military	94LTS57	302137
Serb/Croat/Slovene	Multilateral	14 Dec 28	General Economic	110LTS171	302560
Serb/Croat/Slovene	Multilateral	16 Apr 29	Specific Resources	126LTS305	302891
Serb/Croat/Slovene	Multilateral	20 Apr 29	Admin Cooperation	112LTS371	302623

PARTY ONE	PARTY TWO	DATE	TOPIC	CITATION	NUMBER
Serb/Croat/Slovene	Multilateral	20 Apr 29	Admin Cooperation	112LTS395	302624
Serb/Croat/Slovene	Multilateral	21 May 29	Dispute Settlement	96LTS311	302210
Serb/Croat/Slovene	Multilateral	28 Jun 29	Postal Service	103LTS429	302374
Serb/Croat/Slovene	Multilateral	28 Jun 29	Postal Service	103LTS5	302369
Serb/Croat/Slovene	Multilateral	28 Jun 29	Postal Service	103LTS71	302370
Serb/Croat/Slovene	Multilateral	28 Jun 29	Postal Service	103LTS321	302372
Serb/Croat/Slovene	Multilateral	28 Jun 29	Postal Service	102LTS245	302368
Serb/Croat/Slovene	Multilateral	28 Jun 29	Postal Service	103LTS249	302371
Serb/Croat/Slovene	Multilateral	28 Jun 29	Postal Service	103LTS377	302373
Serb/Croat/Slovene	Multilateral	27 Jul 29	Other Military	118LTS303	302733
Serb/Croat/Slovene	Multilateral	27 Jul 29	Other Military	118LTS343	302734
Serb/Croat/Slovene	Multilateral	20 Aug 29	Sanitation	98LTS125	302243
Serb/Croat/Slovene	Multilateral	14 Sep 29	UN Charter	165LTS353	303822
Serb/Croat/Slovene	Multilateral	31 Oct 30	Dispute Settlement	120LTS9	302760
Serb/Croat/Slovene	Netherlands	15 Jun 23	Land Transport	20LTS337	300524
Serb/Croat/Slovene	Poland	04 May 23	Admin Cooperation	85LTS455	301946
Serb/Croat/Slovene	Poland	05 Apr 24	General Economic	49LTS265	301185
Serb/Croat/Slovene	Poland	18 Sep 26	Dispute Settlement	78LTS419	301800
Serb/Croat/Slovene	Poland	18 Sep 26	General Amity	78LTS413	301799
Serb/Croat/Slovene	Poland	06 Mar 27	Consul/Citizenship	126LTS67	302871
Serb/Croat/Slovene	Romania	13 Jun 26	General Military	54LTS257	301289
Serb/Croat/Slovene	Romania	04 Jun 27	Territory Boundary	158LTS443	303647
Serb/Croat/Slovene	Romania	21 May 29	General Amity	98LTS221	302249
Serb/Croat/Slovene	Spain	27 Sep 29	General Economic	98LTS319	302253
Serb/Croat/Slovene	UK Great Britain	29 Jul 21	Reparations	10LTS411	300280
Serb/Croat/Slovene	UK Great Britain	18 Jun 26	General Economic	57LTS23	301349
Serb/Croat/Slovene	UK Great Britain	12 May 27	General Trade	80LTS165	301825
Serb/Croat/Slovene	United Arab Rep	15 May 27	General Trade	96LTS367	302213
Serb/Croat/Slovene	USA (United States)	21 Jan 29	Dispute Settlement	93LTS307	302118
Serb/Croat/Slovene	USA (United States)	21 Jan 29	Dispute Settlement	93LTS301	302117
Seychelles	Multilateral	30 Jun 20	Patents/Copyrights	1LTS59	300008
Seychelles	Multilateral	31 Mar 22	Humanitarian	9LTS415	300269
Seychelles	Multilateral	25 Aug 24	Water Transport	120LTS155	302764
Seychelles	Multilateral	01 Dec 24	Sanitation	78LTS351	301794
Seychelles	Multilateral	25 Nov 27	Telecommunications	84LTS97	301905
Seychelles	Multilateral	23 Sep 36	Gen Communications	186LTS301	304319
Shereefian	Belgium	24 Jul 30	Non-ILO Labor	138LTS35	303179
Siam	Bel-Lux Econ Union	13 Jul 26	General Economic	62LTS287	301468
Siam	Bel-Lux Econ Union	05 Nov 37	General Amity	190LTS151	304413
Siam	Belgium	14 Jan 37	Extradition	179LTS419	304168
Siam	Belgium	05 Nov 37	Privil/Immunities	190LTS163	304414
Siam	Burma	14 Feb 39	Postal Service	197LTS255	304618
Siam	Denmark	01 Mar 26	General Economic	47LTS103	301131
Siam	Denmark	05 Nov 37	General Amity	188LTS187	304358
Siam	France	14 Feb 25	General Amity	43LTS189	301055
Siam	France	07 Dec 37	General Amity	201LTS113	304708
Siam	France	09 Dec 37	General Trade	201LTS145	304709
Siam	Germany	28 Feb 24	General Economic	32LTS399	300828
Siam	Germany	07 Apr 28	General Amity	85LTS337	301938
Siam	Germany	06 Jul 29	Visas	99LTS333	302276
Siam	Germany	30 Dec 37	General Amity	188LTS401	304368
Siam	India	11 Sep 24	General Economic	31LTS115	300788
Siam	Indochina	14 Jul 27	Consul/Citizenship	69LTS327	301614
Siam	Italy	09 May 26	General Economic	61LTS215	301436
Siam	Italy	03 Dec 37	General Amity	189LTS255	304389
Siam	Japan	09 Mar 24	General Trade	31LTS187	300795
Siam	Japan	08 Dec 37	General Amity	188LTS375	304367
Siam	Malaya	15 Sep 37	Postal Service	191LTS225	304447
Siam	Malaya	16 Sep 37	Postal Service	191LTS265	304448
Siam	Multilateral	18 Mar 04	Humanitarian	1LTS83	300011
Siam	Multilateral	13 Nov 08	General Ad Hoc	1LTS217	300015
Siam	Multilateral	12 Jan 12	Sanitation	4LTS281	300112
Siam	Multilateral	23 Jan 12	Sanitation	8LTS187	300222
Siam	Multilateral	05 Jun 12	Telecommunications	1LTS135	300013
Siam	Multilateral	20 Mar 14	Patents/Copyrights	1LTS243	300016

PARTY ONE	PARTY TWO	DATE	TOPIC	CITATION	NUMBER
Siam	Multilateral	10 Sep 19	Reparations	2LTS44	300045
Siam	Multilateral	10 Sep 19	General Economic	2LTS35	300044
Siam	Multilateral	10 Sep 19	Reparations	2LTS29	300043
Siam	Multilateral	10 Sep 19	General Trade	7LTS331	300200
Siam	Multilateral	01 May 20	Air Transport	11LTS173	300297
Siam	Multilateral	04 Jun 20	Peace/Disarmament	6LTS187	300152
Siam	Multilateral	21 Jun 20	Health/Educ/Welfare	8LTS65	300207
Siam	Multilateral	30 Jun 20	Patents/Copyrights	1LTS59	300008
Siam	Multilateral	16 Dec 20	General IGO	6LTS379	300170
Siam	Multilateral	20 Apr 21	Water Transport	7LTS73	300174
Siam	Multilateral	10 Jun 21	Customs	8LTS297	300227
Siam	Multilateral	05 Aug 21	Admin Cooperation	27LTS349	300695
Siam	Multilateral	05 Oct 21	IGO Establishment	51LTS361	301241
Siam	Multilateral	05 Oct 21	Admin Cooperation	29LTS79	300735
Siam	Multilateral	05 Oct 21	Admin Cooperation	29LTS67	300733
Siam	Multilateral	05 Oct 21	Admin Cooperation	29LTS73	300734
Siam	Multilateral	06 Oct 21	General Economic	17LTS45	300427
Siam	Multilateral	31 Mar 22	Humanitarian	9LTS415	300269
Siam	Multilateral	02 Nov 22	Peace/Disarmament	149LTS35	303431
Siam	Multilateral	24 Sep 23	Dispute Settlement	27LTS157	300678
Siam	Multilateral	03 Nov 23	Customs	30LTS371	300775
Siam	Multilateral	09 Dec 23	Land Transport	47LTS55	301129
Siam	Multilateral	09 Dec 23	Water Transport	58LTS284	301379
Siam	Multilateral	09 Dec 23	Non-IBRD Project	36LTS76	300905
Siam	Multilateral	25 Jan 24	Sanitation	57LTS135	301360
Siam	Multilateral	31 Mar 24	Sanitation	27LTS211	300685
Siam	Multilateral	28 Aug 24	Postal Service	40LTS437	301005
Siam	Multilateral	28 Aug 24	Postal Service	40LTS307	301004
Siam	Multilateral	28 Aug 24	Postal Service	40LTS19	301002
Siam	Multilateral	28 Aug 24	Postal Service	40LTS249	301003
Siam	Multilateral	11 Feb 25	Sanitation	51LTS337	301239
Siam	Multilateral	19 Feb 25	Admin Cooperation	81LTS317	301845
Siam	Multilateral	17 Jun 25	Peace/Disarmament	94LTS65	302138
Siam	Multilateral	29 Oct 25	Telecommunications	57LTS201	301365
Siam	Multilateral	24 Apr 26	Land Transport	108LTS123	302505
Siam	Multilateral	26 Sep 27	Dispute Settlement	92LTS301	302096
Siam	Multilateral	08 Nov 27	General Trade	97LTS391	302238
Siam	Multilateral	25 Nov 27	Telecommunications	84LTS97	301905
Siam	Multilateral	27 Aug 28	General Military	94LTS57	302137
Siam	Multilateral	28 Jun 29	Postal Service	103LTS429	302374
Siam	Multilateral	28 Jun 29	Postal Service	103LTS377	302373
Siam	Multilateral	28 Jun 29	Postal Service	103LTS249	302371
Siam	Multilateral	28 Jun 29	Postal Service	103LTS71	302370
Siam	Multilateral	28 Jun 29	Postal Service	103LTS5	302369
Siam	Multilateral	28 Jun 29	Postal Service	102LTS245	302368
Siam	Multilateral	27 Jul 29	Other Military	118LTS343	302734
Siam	Multilateral	27 Jul 29	Other Military	118LTS303	302733
Siam	Multilateral	14 Sep 29	UN Charter	165LTS353	303822
Siam	Multilateral	13 Jul 31	Other HEW	139LTS301	303219
Siam	Multilateral	27 Nov 31	Sanitation	177LTS373	304100
Siam	Multilateral	14 Mar 32	Territory Boundary	131LTS135	303006
Siam	Multilateral	11 Mar 33	Water Transport	135LTS301	303119
Siam	Multilateral	07 May 34	Commodity Trade	171LTS203	303961
Siam	Multilateral	01 Jun 34	Territory Boundary	154LTS373	303563
Siam	Multilateral	06 Nov 36	General Military	173LTS353	304025
Siam	Multilateral	03 Dec 37	Air Transport	186LTS293	304318
Siam	Multilateral	03 Dec 38	Education	200LTS249	304694
Siam	Multilateral	23 May 39	Postal Service	202LTS159	304742
Siam	Netherlands	08 Jun 25	General Economic	56LTS57	301323
Siam	Netherlands	27 Oct 28	Dispute Settlement	93LTS131	302105
Siam	Netherlands	01 Feb 38	General Amity	193LTS13	304485
Siam	Norway	16 Jul 26	General Economic	60LTS35	301404
Siam	Norway	15 Nov 37	General Amity	186LTS9	304301
Siam	Portugal	14 Aug 25	General Economic	55LTS57	301304
Siam	Portugal	02 Jul 38	General Amity	200LTS149	304688

PARTY ONE	PARTY TWO	DATE	TOPIC	CITATION	NUMBER
Siam	Spain	03 Aug 25	General Economic	55LTS39	301303
Siam	Strait Settlements	12 Jan 26	Postal Service	49LTS161	301180
Siam	Sweden	19 Dec 25	General Economic	58LTS429	301386
Siam	Sweden	05 Nov 37	Privil/Immunities	182LTS257	304215
Siam	Sweden	08 Nov 37	General Amity	185LTS337	304298
Siam	Switzerland	28 May 31	General Trade	125LTS357	302864
Siam	Switzerland	04 Nov 37	General Amity	190LTS137	304412
Siam	UK Great Britain	20 Dec 21	Peace/Disarmament	10LTS421	300282
Siam	UK Great Britain	15 Sep 25	Admin Cooperation	49LTS29	301175
Siam	UK Great Britain	15 Sep 25	General Economic	49LTS51	301176
Siam	UK Great Britain	25 Nov 25	Dispute Settlement	63LTS161	301487
Siam	UK Great Britain	21 Feb 28	Water Transport	87LTS21	301960
Siam	UK Great Britain	20 Mar 30	Postal Service	106LTS363	302456
Siam	UK Great Britain	31 Mar 37	Admin Cooperation	179LTS257	304153
Siam	UK Great Britain	23 Nov 37	General Trade	188LTS333	304366
Siam	USA (United States)	16 Dec 20	Admin Cooperation	6LTS291	300161
Siam	USA (United States)	30 Dec 22	Extradition	25LTS394	300629
Siam	USA (United States)	13 Nov 37	General Amity	192LTS247	304476
Sierra Leone	Multilateral	30 Jun 20	Patents/Copyrights	1LTS59	300008
Sierra Leone	Multilateral	25 Aug 24	Water Transport	120LTS155	302764
Sierra Leone	Multilateral	25 Nov 27	Telecommunications	84LTS97	301905
Sierra Leone	Multilateral	30 Sep 29	Postal Service	99LTS71	302269
Sierra Leone	Multilateral	28 Oct 33	Refugees	159LTS199	303663
Sierra Leone	Multilateral	23 Sep 36	Gen Communications	186LTS301	304319
Sierra Leone	Multilateral	10 Feb 38	Refugees	192LTS59	304461
Singapore	Multilateral	03 Nov 23	Customs	30LTS371	300775
Slovakia	Multilateral	27 Jul 29	Other Military	118LTS343	302734
Slovakia	Multilateral	27 Jul 29	Other Military	118LTS303	302733
Solomon Islands	Multilateral	18 Mar 04	Humanitarian	1LTS83	300011
Solomon Islands	Multilateral	30 Jun 20	Patents/Copyrights	1LTS59	300008
Solomon Islands	Multilateral	31 Mar 22	Humanitarian	9LTS415	300269
Solomon Islands	Multilateral	25 Nov 27	Telecommunications	84LTS97	301905
Somalia	Multilateral	21 Jun 20	Health/Educ/Welfare	8LTS65	300207
Somalia	Multilateral	25 Aug 24	Water Transport	120LTS155	302764
Somalia	Multilateral	25 Nov 27	Telecommunications	84LTS97	301905
Somalia	Multilateral	07 Jun 30	Finance	143LTS337	303315
Somalia	Multilateral	19 Mar 31	Admin Cooperation	143LTS7	303301
Somalia	Multilateral	28 Oct 33	Refugees	159LTS199	303663
Somalia	Multilateral	23 Sep 36	Gen Communications	186LTS301	304319
Somalia	Multilateral	10 Feb 38	Refugees	192LTS59	304461
South Africa	Bel-Lux Econ Union	13 Jul 37	General Trade	182LTS247	304214
South Africa	Belgium	04 Feb 32	Admin Cooperation	127LTS121	302912
South Africa	Brazil	11 Apr 32	Mostfavored Nation	135LTS219	303112
South Africa	Brazil	18 Apr 39	General Trade	198LTS289	304646
South Africa	Czechoslovakia	27 Jan 37	General Trade	189LTS97	304377
South Africa	Finland	14 Feb 38	Visas	190LTS211	304419
South Africa	France	11 Feb 35	General Trade	189LTS17	304372
South Africa	France	27 Aug 35	General Trade	189LTS41	304374
South Africa	Germany	23 Oct 23	Milit Servic/Citiz	28LTS417	300721
South Africa	Germany	01 Sep 28	General Economic	95LTS289	302181
South Africa	Germany	12 May 30	Patents/Copyrights	123LTS301	302821
South Africa	Germany	16 Mar 37	Admin Cooperation	189LTS107	304378
South Africa	Irish Free State	01 Oct 25	Postal Service	56LTS389	301343
South Africa	Italy	19 Jul 33	Postal Service	146LTS369	303385
South Africa	Italy	21 May 35	General Trade	189LTS31	304373
South Africa	Japan	16 Oct 30	Visas	126LTS17	302868
South Africa	Multilateral	13 Nov 08	General Ad Hoc	1LTS217	300015
South Africa	Multilateral	05 Jun 12	Telecommunications	1LTS135	300013
South Africa	Multilateral	10 Sep 19	Health/Educ/Welfare	8LTS11	300201
South Africa	Multilateral	10 Sep 19	General Trade	7LTS331	300200
South Africa	Multilateral	09 Feb 20	Territory Boundary	2LTS7	300041
South Africa	Multilateral	01 May 20	Air Transport	11LTS173	300297
South Africa	Multilateral	21 Jun 20	Health/Educ/Welfare	8LTS65	300207
South Africa	Multilateral	30 Jun 20	Patents/Copyrights	1LTS59	300008
South Africa	Multilateral	10 Aug 20	Territory Boundary	28LTS225	300710
South Africa	Multilateral	10 Aug 20	Consul/Citizenship	28LTS223	300711
South Africa	Multilateral	16 Dec 20	General IGO	6LTS379	300170
South Africa	Multilateral	20 Apr 21	Water Transport	7LTS73	300174
South Africa	Multilateral	05 Aug 21	Admin Cooperation	27LTS349	300695
South Africa	Multilateral	05 Oct 21	Admin Cooperation	29LTS67	300733
South Africa	Multilateral	05 Oct 21	Admin Cooperation	29LTS79	300735
South Africa	Multilateral	05 Oct 21	IGO Establishment	51LTS361	301241
South Africa	Multilateral	05 Oct 21	Admin Cooperation	29LTS73	300734
South Africa	Multilateral	06 Feb 22	General Trade	38LTS277	300982
South Africa	Multilateral	06 Feb 22	Customs	38LTS267	300981
South Africa	Multilateral	31 Mar 22	Humanitarian	9LTS415	300269
South Africa	Multilateral	02 Nov 22	Peace/Disarmament	149LTS35	303431
South Africa	Multilateral	03 Nov 23	Customs	30LTS371	300775
South Africa	Multilateral	31 Mar 24	Sanitation	27LTS211	300685
South Africa	Multilateral	16 Aug 24	Taxation	41LTS429	301024
South Africa	Multilateral	28 Aug 24	Postal Service	40LTS19	301002
South Africa	Multilateral	30 Aug 24	Admin Cooperation	30LTS79	300761
South Africa	Multilateral	30 Aug 24	Admin Cooperation	30LTS75	300760
South Africa	Multilateral	19 Feb 25	Admin Cooperation	81LTS317	301845
South Africa	Multilateral	17 Jun 25	Peace/Disarmament	94LTS65	302138
South Africa	Multilateral	29 Oct 25	Telecommunications	57LTS201	301365
South Africa	Multilateral	12 May 26	Refugees	89LTS47	302004
South Africa	Multilateral	21 Jun 26	Sanitation	78LTS229	301793
South Africa	Multilateral	25 Sep 26	ILO Labor	60LTS253	301414
South Africa	Multilateral	25 Nov 27	Telecommunications	84LTS97	301905
South Africa	Multilateral	27 Aug 28	General Military	94LTS57	302137
South Africa	Multilateral	14 Dec 28	General Economic	110LTS171	302560
South Africa	Multilateral	20 Apr 29	Admin Cooperation	112LTS371	302623
South Africa	Multilateral	31 May 29	Water Transport	136LTS81	303127
South Africa	Multilateral	28 Jun 29	Postal Service	102LTS245	302368
South Africa	Multilateral	27 Jul 29	Other Military	118LTS343	302734
South Africa	Multilateral	27 Jul 29	Other Military	118LTS303	302733
South Africa	Multilateral	14 Sep 29	UN Charter	165LTS353	303822
South Africa	Multilateral	12 Oct 29	General Transport	137LTS11	303145
South Africa	Multilateral	20 Jan 30	Reparations	112LTS361	302622
South Africa	Multilateral	20 Jan 30	Finance	104LTS413	302395
South Africa	Multilateral	20 Jan 30	Finance	104LTS433	302397
South Africa	Multilateral	20 Jan 30	Reparations	104LTS243	302394
South Africa	Multilateral	20 Jan 30	Reparations	113LTS389	302650
South Africa	Multilateral	12 Apr 30	Admin Cooperation	179LTS115	304138
South Africa	Multilateral	12 Apr 30	Admin Cooperation	179LTS89	304137
South Africa	Multilateral	17 Apr 30	Extradition	126LTS201	302883
South Africa	Multilateral	22 Apr 30	Peace/Disarmament	112LTS65	302608
South Africa	Multilateral	28 Apr 30	Claims and Debts	121LTS69	302785
South Africa	Multilateral	10 Jun 30	Loans and Credits	112LTS237	302618
South Africa	Multilateral	23 Oct 30	Water Transport	125LTS95	302849
South Africa	Multilateral	27 Nov 30	Extradition	121LTS39	302781
South Africa	Multilateral	13 Apr 31	Air Transport	119LTS275	302751
South Africa	Multilateral	13 Jul 31	Other HEW	139LTS301	303219
South Africa	Multilateral	24 Sep 31	Specific Resources	155LTS349	303586
South Africa	Multilateral	10 Dec 31	Water Transport	129LTS177	302961
South Africa	Multilateral	20 Jan 32	Extradition	141LTS267	303269
South Africa	Multilateral	09 Dec 32	Telecommunications	151LTS5	303479
South Africa	Multilateral	11 Mar 33	Water Transport	135LTS301	303119
South Africa	Multilateral	12 Apr 33	Sanitation	161LTS65	303706
South Africa	Multilateral	30 Sep 33	Extradition	205LTS155	304832
South Africa	Multilateral	11 Oct 33	Education	155LTS331	303585
South Africa	Multilateral	11 Oct 33	Consul/Citizenship	150LTS431	303476
South Africa	Multilateral	08 Nov 33	Specific Resources	172LTS241	303995
South Africa	Multilateral	20 Mar 34	Postal Service	174LTS171	304048
South Africa	Multilateral	04 Jun 34	Extradition	184LTS437	304264
South Africa	Multilateral	19 Jun 34	Admin Cooperation	154LTS381	303564
South Africa	Multilateral	25 Jul 34	Other HEW	177LTS59	304080
South Africa	Multilateral	22 Dec 34	Visas	183LTS145	304230
South Africa	Multilateral	22 Dec 34	Admin Cooperation	183LTS153	304231

PARTY ONE	PARTY TWO	DATE	TOPIC	CITATION	NUMBER
South Africa	Multilateral	15 Mar 35	Other Military	170LTS9	303926
South Africa	Multilateral	30 Oct 35	Postal Service	189LTS85	304376
South Africa	Multilateral	30 Oct 35	Telecommunications	189LTS51	304375
South Africa	Multilateral	20 Dec 35	Other Military	167LTS141	303862
South Africa	Multilateral	30 Jul 36	IGO Status/Immunit	197LTS31	304602
South Africa	Multilateral	23 Sep 36	Gen Communications	186LTS301	304319
South Africa	Multilateral	06 Nov 36	General Military	173LTS353	304025
South Africa	Multilateral	31 Mar 37	Commodity Trade	189LTS359	304394
South Africa	Multilateral	08 May 37	Privil/Immunities	182LTS37	304202
South Africa	Multilateral	02 Jun 37	Specific Property	184LTS445	304265
South Africa	Multilateral	08 Jun 37	Specific Resources	190LTS79	304406
South Africa	Multilateral	02 Oct 37	Education	182LTS263	304216
South Africa	Multilateral	24 Jun 38	Specific Resources	196LTS131	304575
South Africa	Multilateral	12 Sep 38	Culture	198LTS111	304630
South Africa	Multilateral	03 Dec 38	Education	200LTS249	304694
South Africa	Multilateral	23 May 39	Postal Service	202LTS159	304742
South Africa	Multilateral	01 Jan 42	General Military	204LTS381	304817
South Africa	Netherlands	10 Sep 29	Postal Service	98LTS423	302261
South Africa	Netherlands	29 Jun 32	Postal Service	133LTS33	303054
South Africa	Netherlands	20 Feb 35	General Trade	160LTS143	303688
South Africa	Northern Rhodesia	02 Oct 31	Customs	129LTS115	302955
South Africa	Northern Rhodesia	26 Sep 32	Visas	135LTS225	303113
South Africa	Norway	25 Jan 27	Postal Service	60LTS277	301416
South Africa	Portugal	22 Jun 26	Territory Boundary	70LTS305	301642
South Africa	Portugal	01 Jul 26	General Ad Hoc	70LTS315	301643
South Africa	Portugal	06 Oct 27	Territory Boundary	81LTS359	301846
South Africa	Portugal	11 Sep 28	Non-ILO Labor	98LTS9	302239
South Africa	Portugal	29 Apr 31	Territory Boundary	129LTS157	302960
South Africa	Portugal	18 Jun 37	Air Transport	189LTS121	304380
South Africa	Southern Rhodesia	19 Aug 31	Customs	129LTS103	302953
South Africa	Southern Rhodesia	21 Apr 32	Taxation	142LTS197	303292
South Africa	Swaziland	19 Aug 31	Customs	129LTS109	302954
South Africa	Swaziland	16 Mar 32	Taxation	129LTS377	302972
South Africa	United Arab Rep	31 May 39	General Trade	198LTS295	304647
South Africa	USA (United States)	01 Dec 31	Air Transport	129LTS121	302956
South Africa	USA (United States)	20 Sep 33	Air Transport	148LTS189	303412
South Africa	USA (United States)	20 Sep 33	Air Transport	148LTS203	303413
South Africa	USA (United States)	24 Mar 37	Visas	189LTS113	304379
South Africa	USA (United States)	02 Apr 40	General Amity	204LTS79	304786
Southern Rhodesia	Multilateral	30 Jun 20	Patents/Copyrights	1LTS59	300008
Southern Rhodesia	Multilateral	31 Mar 22	Humanitarian	9LTS415	300269
Southern Rhodesia	Multilateral	24 Sep 23	Dispute Settlement	27LTS157	300678
Southern Rhodesia	Multilateral	31 Mar 24	Sanitation	27LTS211	300685
Southern Rhodesia	Multilateral	22 May 24	General Trade	35LTS175	300895
Southern Rhodesia	Multilateral	28 Aug 24	Postal Service	40LTS19	301002
Southern Rhodesia	Multilateral	29 Oct 25	Telecommunications	57LTS201	301365
Southern Rhodesia	Multilateral	30 Mar 31	Taxation	138LTS149	303185
Southern Rhodesia	Multilateral	13 Jul 31	Other HEW	139LTS301	303219
Southern Rhodesia	Multilateral	30 Oct 35	Postal Service	189LTS85	304376
Southern Rhodesia	Multilateral	30 Oct 35	Telecommunications	189LTS51	304375
Southern Rhodesia	Multilateral	23 Sep 36	Gen Communications	186LTS301	304319
Southern Rhodesia	Multilateral	12 Sep 38	Culture	198LTS111	304630
Southern Rhodesia	South Africa	19 Aug 31	Customs	129LTS103	302953
Southern Rhodesia	South Africa	21 Apr 32	Taxation	142LTS197	303292
Southwest Africa	Multilateral	13 Nov 08	General Ad Hoc	1LTS217	300015
Southwest Africa	Multilateral	20 Mar 14	Patents/Copyrights	1LTS243	300016
Southwest Africa	Multilateral	30 Oct 35	Telecommunications	189LTS51	304375
Southwest Africa	Multilateral	30 Oct 35	Postal Service	189LTS85	304376
Spain	Argentina	17 Feb 35	Extradition	166LTS375	303853
Spain	Austria	03 Feb 25	General Economic	43LTS313	301067
Spain	Austria	11 Jun 28	Dispute Settlement	87LTS393	301984
Spain	Austria	23 Aug 29	Visas	97LTS353	302232
Spain	Bel-Lux Econ Union	15 Dec 28	General Trade	84LTS287	301909
Spain	Bel-Lux Econ Union	04 Apr 36	Finance	168LTS339	303909
Spain	Belgium	19 Jul 27	Dispute Settlement	80LTS17	301820

PARTY ONE	PARTY TWO	DATE	TOPIC	CITATION	NUMBER
Spain	Belgium	31 Jan 30	Taxation	99LTS369	302281
Spain	Belgium	27 Feb 32	Air Transport	137LTS111	303149
Spain	Belgium	27 Feb 32	Air Transport	137LTS129	303150
Spain	Bolivia	13 Mar 36	Patents/Copyrights	170LTS179	303933
Spain	Brazil	08 Apr 09	Dispute Settlement	88LTS86	301987
Spain	Bulgaria	17 Jul 30	Extradition	114LTS41	302653
Spain	Bulgaria	26 Jun 31	Dispute Settlement	166LTS341	303850
Spain	Bulgaria	19 Nov 34	Finance	166LTS277	303843
Spain	Canada	11 Apr 25	General Economic	43LTS333	301068
Spain	Chile	28 May 27	Dispute Settlement	71LTS329	301673
Spain	Chile	18 Feb 36	Mass Media	169LTS321	303920
Spain	Colombia	19 Jul 29	Dispute Settlement	114LTS105	302658
Spain	Colombia	30 Sep 35	Education	163LTS337	303776
Spain	Costa Rica	21 Mar 30	Milit Servic/Citiz	168LTS61	303886
Spain	Cuba	15 Jul 27	General Trade	120LTS251	302770
Spain	Czechoslovakia	19 Jul 25	General Economic	60LTS329	301419
Spain	Czechoslovakia	26 Oct 27	Privil/Immunities	121LTS287	302792
Spain	Czechoslovakia	26 Oct 27	Privil/Immunities	121LTS311	302793
Spain	Czechoslovakia	26 Oct 27	Extradition	121LTS271	302791
Spain	Czechoslovakia	13 Aug 28	Dispute Settlement	121LTS321	302794
Spain	Czechoslovakia	16 Nov 28	Dispute Settlement	100LTS313	302303
Spain	Czechoslovakia	13 Dec 28	General Trade	98LTS65	302240
Spain	Czechoslovakia	29 Jun 32	Non-ILO Labor	166LTS355	303851
Spain	Denmark	02 Jan 28	General Trade	71LTS271	301668
Spain	Denmark	14 Mar 28	Dispute Settlement	74LTS93	301735
Spain	Denmark	15 Apr 31	Admin Cooperation	115LTS233	302688
Spain	Denmark	10 Oct 34	Extradition	153LTS345	303530
Spain	Denmark	17 Aug 35	General Trade	163LTS307	303773
Spain	El Salvador	15 Jun 35	Culture	165LTS321	303818
Spain	Estonia	23 Jun 32	Admin Cooperation	143LTS31	303303
Spain	Estonia	08 May 35	General Trade	159LTS363	303678
Spain	Estonia	08 May 35	Finance	159LTS381	303679
Spain	Finland	16 Jul 25	General Trade	47LTS271	301135
Spain	Finland	31 May 28	Dispute Settlement	82LTS229	301874
Spain	France	16 Feb 24	Admin Cooperation	25LTS409	300631
Spain	France	03 Aug 25	General Trade	38LTS371	300992
Spain	France	22 Mar 28	Air Transport	73LTS63	301707
Spain	France	12 Jun 28	Territory Boundary	136LTS289	303131
Spain	France	16 Jul 28	Postal Service	135LTS149	303110
Spain	France	07 Mar 32	Military Mission	148LTS385	303424
Spain	France	21 Dec 35	General Economic	167LTS9	303856
Spain	France	30 Dec 35	Commodity Trade	172LTS217	303993
Spain	France	10 Jul 39	Dispute Settlement	148LTS369	303423
Spain	Germany	15 Jan 23	General Economic	26LTS455	300662
Spain	Germany	25 Jul 24	General Trade	41LTS363	301023
Spain	Germany	18 Nov 25	General Economic	53LTS309	301263
Spain	Germany	07 May 26	General Economic	53LTS321	301264
Spain	Germany	09 Dec 27	Air Transport	79LTS203	301811
Spain	Germany	09 Feb 29	Visas	89LTS369	302038
Spain	Germany	06 Jul 32	Reparations	148LTS391	303425
Spain	Germany	11 Dec 34	Air Transport	166LTS311	303846
Spain	Germany	21 Dec 34	General Economic	165LTS307	303817
Spain	Germany	07 Jan 35	Air Transport	166LTS363	303852
Spain	Germany	30 Sep 35	Air Transport	163LTS327	303775
Spain	Great Britain	08 Sep 27	Patents/Copyrights	69LTS263	301608
Spain	Greece	06 Mar 19	Claims and Debts	3LTS81	300092
Spain	Greece	23 Sep 26	Consul/Citizenship	91LTS121	302059
Spain	Greece	23 Jan 30	Dispute Settlement	139LTS93	303205
Spain	Greece	11 Jul 32	Finance	148LTS397	303426
Spain	Guatemala	14 Aug 35	Mass Media	166LTS381	303854
Spain	Hungary	17 Jun 25	General Economic	60LTS69	301406
Spain	Hungary	28 Feb 29	General Trade	94LTS313	302151
Spain	Hungary	10 Jun 29	Dispute Settlement	101LTS251	302327
Spain	Hungary	28 Aug 30	Visas	110LTS307	302562
Spain	Hungary	19 Sep 31	Visas	124LTS353	302839

PARTY ONE	PARTY TWO	DATE	TOPIC	CITATION	NUMBER
Spain	Iceland	26 Aug 29	Dispute Settlement	104LTS183	302388
Spain	Irish Free State	04 Apr 35	General Trade	166LTS391	303855
Spain	Irish Free State	14 Jan 36	Consul/Citizenship	168LTS201	303899
Spain	Italy	15 Nov 23	General Trade	39LTS49	300996
Spain	Italy	25 Nov 25	Refugees	60LTS59	301405
Spain	Italy	07 Aug 26	General Amity	67LTS365	301558
Spain	Italy	15 Aug 27	Air Transport	94LTS361	302155
Spain	Italy	28 Nov 27	Finance	82LTS27	301857
Spain	Italy	03 Oct 28	Air Transport	94LTS387	302156
Spain	Italy	30 Jul 32	Status of Forces	149LTS9	303427
Spain	Italy	01 Oct 35	Consul/Citizenship	163LTS345	303777
Spain	Japan	05 Aug 29	Mostfavored Nation	113LTS9	302629
Spain	Latvia	08 Mar 30	Extradition	113LTS135	302641
Spain	Lithuania	07 Sep 35	Visas	163LTS321	303774
Spain	Luxembourg	21 Jun 28	Dispute Settlement	109LTS137	302533
Spain	Mexico	31 Mar 24	Patents/Copyrights	43LTS297	301065
Spain	Multilateral	09 Sep 86*	Patents/Copyrights	123LTS233	302816
Spain	Multilateral	18 Mar 04	Humanitarian	1LTS83	300011
Spain	Multilateral	13 Nov 08	General Ad Hoc	1LTS217	300015
Spain	Multilateral	12 Jan 12	Sanitation	4LTS281	300112
Spain	Multilateral	05 Jun 12	Telecommunications	1LTS135	300013
Spain	Multilateral	20 Mar 14	Patents/Copyrights	1LTS243	300016
Spain	Multilateral	21 Jun 20	Health/Educ/Welfare	8LTS65	300207
Spain	Multilateral	30 Jun 20	Patents/Copyrights	1LTS59	300008
Spain	Multilateral	31 Oct 20	Sanitation	164LTS85	303790
Spain	Multilateral	16 Dec 20	General IGO	6LTS379	300170
Spain	Multilateral	20 Apr 21	Water Transport	7LTS35	300172
Spain	Multilateral	20 Apr 21	Water Transport	7LTS65	300173
Spain	Multilateral	20 Apr 21	Land Transport	7LTS11	300171
Spain	Multilateral	20 Apr 21	Water Transport	7LTS73	300174
Spain	Multilateral	05 Aug 21	Admin Cooperation	27LTS349	300695
Spain	Multilateral	15 Sep 21	Postal Service	30LTS141	300767
Spain	Multilateral	05 Oct 21	Admin Cooperation	29LTS73	300734
Spain	Multilateral	05 Oct 21	Admin Cooperation	29LTS67	300733
Spain	Multilateral	05 Oct 21	Admin Cooperation	29LTS79	300735
Spain	Multilateral	06 Oct 21	General Economic	17LTS45	300427
Spain	Multilateral	31 Mar 22	Humanitarian	9LTS415	300269
Spain	Multilateral	05 Jul 22	Reparations	13LTS237	300355
Spain	Multilateral	04 Oct 22	Territory Boundary	12LTS385	300334
Spain	Multilateral	24 Sep 23	Dispute Settlement	27LTS157	300678
Spain	Multilateral	03 Nov 23	Customs	30LTS371	300775
Spain	Multilateral	28 Nov 23	Admin Cooperation	51LTS221	301230
Spain	Multilateral	09 Dec 23	Land Transport	47LTS55	301129
Spain	Multilateral	09 Dec 23	General Economic	58LTS315	301380
Spain	Multilateral	09 Dec 23	Water Transport	58LTS284	301379
Spain	Multilateral	18 Dec 23	Territory Boundary	28LTS541	300729
Spain	Multilateral	25 Jan 24	Sanitation	57LTS135	301360
Spain	Multilateral	31 Mar 24	Sanitation	27LTS211	300685
Spain	Multilateral	04 Jul 24	Admin Cooperation	51LTS227	301231
Spain	Multilateral	25 Aug 24	Water Transport	120LTS123	302763
Spain	Multilateral	25 Aug 24	Water Transport	120LTS155	302764
Spain	Multilateral	28 Aug 24	Postal Service	41LTS9	301006
Spain	Multilateral	28 Aug 24	Postal Service	40LTS249	301003
Spain	Multilateral	28 Aug 24	Postal Service	40LTS19	301002
Spain	Multilateral	28 Aug 24	Postal Service	40LTS437	301005
Spain	Multilateral	28 Aug 24	Postal Service	41LTS55	301007
Spain	Multilateral	28 Aug 24	Postal Service	41LTS97	301008
Spain	Multilateral	28 Aug 24	Postal Service	40LTS307	301004
Spain	Multilateral	23 Oct 24	General Transport	77LTS367	301778
Spain	Multilateral	23 Oct 24	Land Transport	78LTS17	301779
Spain	Multilateral	29 Nov 24	General IGO	80LTS293	301835
Spain	Multilateral	19 Feb 25	Admin Cooperation	81LTS317	301845
Spain	Multilateral	17 Jun 25	Peace/Disarmament	94LTS65	302138
Spain	Multilateral	29 Oct 25	Telecommunications	57LTS201	301365
Spain	Multilateral	06 Nov 25	Patents/Copyrights	74LTS289	301743

PARTY ONE	PARTY TWO	DATE	TOPIC	CITATION	NUMBER
Spain	Multilateral	06 Nov 25	Other Economic	74LTS341	301746
Spain	Multilateral	06 Nov 25	Patents/Copyrights	74LTS327	301745
Spain	Multilateral	06 Nov 25	Other Economic	74LTS319	301744
Spain	Multilateral	27 Nov 25	Water Transport	67LTS63	301539
Spain	Multilateral	10 Apr 26	Water Transport	176LTS199	304062
Spain	Multilateral	10 Apr 26	Water Transport	120LTS187	302765
Spain	Multilateral	24 Apr 26	Land Transport	108LTS123	302505
Spain	Multilateral	24 Apr 26	Land Transport	97LTS83	302220
Spain	Multilateral	21 Jun 26	Sanitation	78LTS229	301793
Spain	Multilateral	25 Sep 26	ILO Labor	60LTS253	301414
Spain	Multilateral	12 Jul 27	Direct Aid	135LTS247	303115
Spain	Multilateral	26 Sep 27	Dispute Settlement	92LTS301	302096
Spain	Multilateral	25 Nov 27	Telecommunications	84LTS97	301905
Spain	Multilateral	15 Jul 28	Patents/Copyrights	79LTS133	301806
Spain	Multilateral	25 Jul 28	General Amity	87LTS211	301971
Spain	Multilateral	27 Aug 28	General Military	94LTS57	302137
Spain	Multilateral	26 Sep 28	Dispute Settlement	93LTS343	302123
Spain	Multilateral	22 Nov 28	Culture	111LTS343	302598
Spain	Multilateral	16 Apr 29	Specific Resources	126LTS305	302891
Spain	Multilateral	20 Apr 29	Admin Cooperation	112LTS371	302623
Spain	Multilateral	20 Apr 29	Admin Cooperation	112LTS395	302624
Spain	Multilateral	31 May 29	Water Transport	136LTS81	303127
Spain	Multilateral	14 Jun 29	Visas	94LTS275	302148
Spain	Multilateral	28 Jun 29	Postal Service	103LTS377	302373
Spain	Multilateral	28 Jun 29	Postal Service	103LTS321	302372
Spain	Multilateral	28 Jun 29	Postal Service	102LTS245	302368
Spain	Multilateral	28 Jun 29	Postal Service	103LTS249	302371
Spain	Multilateral	28 Jun 29	Postal Service	103LTS71	302370
Spain	Multilateral	28 Jun 29	Postal Service	103LTS429	302374
Spain	Multilateral	28 Jun 29	Postal Service	103LTS5	302369
Spain	Multilateral	27 Jul 29	Other Military	118LTS303	302733
Spain	Multilateral	27 Jul 29	Other Military	118LTS343	302734
Spain	Multilateral	14 Sep 29	UN Charter	165LTS353	303822
Spain	Multilateral	12 Oct 29	General Transport	137LTS11	303145
Spain	Multilateral	12 Apr 30	Admin Cooperation	179LTS115	304138
Spain	Multilateral	12 Apr 30	Milit Servic/Citiz	178LTS227	304117
Spain	Multilateral	12 Apr 30	Admin Cooperation	179LTS89	304137
Spain	Multilateral	07 Jun 30	Finance	143LTS257	303313
Spain	Multilateral	07 Jun 30	Finance	143LTS337	303315
Spain	Multilateral	07 Jun 30	Finance	143LTS317	303314
Spain	Multilateral	23 Oct 30	Water Transport	125LTS95	302849
Spain	Multilateral	23 Oct 30	Water Transport	112LTS21	302603
Spain	Multilateral	19 Mar 31	Finance	143LTS407	303317
Spain	Multilateral	19 Mar 31	Admin Cooperation	143LTS7	303301
Spain	Multilateral	19 Mar 31	Finance	143LTS355	303316
Spain	Multilateral	27 Mar 31	ICJ Option Clause	167LTS341	303877
Spain	Multilateral	28 Mar 31	Customs	119LTS47	302739
Spain	Multilateral	30 Mar 31	Land Transport	150LTS247	303459
Spain	Multilateral	30 Mar 31	Taxation	138LTS149	303185
Spain	Multilateral	13 Jul 31	Other HEW	139LTS301	303219
Spain	Multilateral	24 Sep 31	Specific Resources	155LTS349	303586
Spain	Multilateral	10 Nov 31	Postal Service	131LTS447	303025
Spain	Multilateral	10 Nov 31	Postal Service	131LTS389	303024
Spain	Multilateral	10 Nov 31	Postal Service	131LTS327	303023
Spain	Multilateral	11 Dec 31	Commodity Trade	170LTS251	303941
Spain	Multilateral	02 Sep 32	Land Transport	154LTS123	303543
Spain	Multilateral	09 Dec 32	Telecommunications	151LTS5	303479
Spain	Multilateral	11 Mar 33	Water Transport	135LTS301	303119
Spain	Multilateral	12 Apr 33	Sanitation	161LTS65	303706
Spain	Multilateral	29 May 33	Admin Cooperation	192LTS289	304479
Spain	Multilateral	19 Jun 33	Gen Communications	154LTS133	303544
Spain	Multilateral	22 Jul 33	Specific Resources	153LTS107	303511
Spain	Multilateral	25 Aug 33	Commodity Trade	141LTS71	303262
Spain	Multilateral	10 Oct 33	General Amity	163LTS393	303781
Spain	Multilateral	11 Oct 33	Consul/Citizenship	150LTS431	303476

PARTY ONE	PARTY TWO	DATE	TOPIC	CITATION	NUMBER
Spain	Multilateral	08 Nov 33	Specific Resources	172LTS241	303995
Spain	Multilateral	23 Nov 33	Land Transport	192LTS389	304484
Spain	Multilateral	23 Nov 33	Land Transport	192LTS327	304483
Spain	Multilateral	20 Mar 34	Finance	176LTS9	304053
Spain	Multilateral	20 Mar 34	Postal Service	176LTS55	304054
Spain	Multilateral	20 Mar 34	Postal Service	175LTS73	304050
Spain	Multilateral	20 Mar 34	Postal Service	175LTS5	304049
Spain	Multilateral	20 Mar 34	Postal Service	174LTS171	304048
Spain	Multilateral	20 Mar 34	Postal Service	175LTS269	304051
Spain	Multilateral	20 Mar 34	Postal Service	175LTS363	304052
Spain	Multilateral	02 Jun 34	Patents/Copyrights	192LTS17	304459
Spain	Multilateral	02 Jun 34	General Trade	192LTS9	304458
Spain	Multilateral	12 Jun 34	Milit Installation	155LTS367	303587
Spain	Multilateral	19 Jun 34	Admin Cooperation	154LTS381	303564
Spain	Multilateral	25 Jul 34	Other HEW	177LTS59	304080
Spain	Multilateral	20 Feb 35	Sanitation	193LTS59	304487
Spain	Multilateral	20 Feb 35	Sanitation	193LTS37	304486
Spain	Multilateral	20 Feb 35	Sanitation	186LTS173	304310
Spain	Multilateral	26 Jun 36	Other HEW	198LTS299	304648
Spain	Multilateral	04 Jul 36	Refugees	171LTS75	303952
Spain	Multilateral	23 Sep 36	Gen Communications	186LTS301	304319
Spain	Multilateral	08 May 37	Privil/Immunities	182LTS37	304202
Spain	Multilateral	10 Feb 38	Refugees	192LTS59	304461
Spain	Multilateral	03 Dec 38	Education	200LTS249	304694
Spain	Multilateral	02 Jun 42	Patents/Copyrights	205LTS163	304833
Spain	Netherlands	24 Mar 21	General Economic	7LTS115	300179
Spain	Netherlands	24 Jun 21	General Economic	7LTS121	300180
Spain	Netherlands	05 Jan 22	General Economic	9LTS257	300259
Spain	Netherlands	27 Mar 29	Admin Cooperation	101LTS479	302346
Spain	Netherlands	14 Feb 30	Air Transport	137LTS149	303152
Spain	Netherlands	30 Mar 31	Dispute Settlement	137LTS161	303153
Spain	Netherlands	16 Jun 34	General Economic	168LTS29	303885
Spain	Nicaragua	20 Nov 34	Patents/Copyrights	166LTS143	303836
Spain	Nicaragua	06 Nov 35	Mass Media	166LTS317	303847
Spain	Norway	22 Nov 20	General Trade	2LTS359	300089
Spain	Norway	01 Dec 21	General Economic	9LTS69	300244
Spain	Norway	04 Apr 22	General Economic	9LTS253	300258
Spain	Norway	06 May 22	General Trade	9LTS329	300266
Spain	Norway	12 Jun 22	General Economic	10LTS305	300276
Spain	Norway	07 Oct 23	General Trade	59LTS47	301389
Spain	Norway	27 Dec 28	Dispute Settlement	97LTS339	302231
Spain	Norway	13 Jun 36	General Trade	170LTS199	303935
Spain	Norway	13 Jun 36	Finance	170LTS207	303936
Spain	Norway	26 Jul 39	General Trade	198LTS87	304627
Spain	Panama	22 Sep 30	Dispute Settlement	162LTS309	303743
Spain	Paraguay	08 Jul 25	Patents/Copyrights	138LTS225	303190
Spain	Peru	05 Mar 36	Mass Media	169LTS331	303921
Spain	Poland	03 Dec 28	Dispute Settlement	101LTS501	302348
Spain	Poland	14 Dec 34	General Economic	168LTS315	303908
Spain	Portugal	26 Mar 23	Postal Service	18LTS349	300475
Spain	Portugal	26 Mar 23	Postal Service	18LTS373	300476
Spain	Portugal	29 Jul 26	Territory Boundary	82LTS95	301863
Spain	Portugal	11 Aug 27	Admin Cooperation	82LTS113	301864
Spain	Portugal	18 Jan 28	Dispute Settlement	77LTS105	301766
Spain	Romania	20 Jun 30	Mostfavored Nation	117LTS411	302707
Spain	Romania	21 Mar 34	General Trade	159LTS171	303661
Spain	Serb/Croat/Slovene	27 Sep 29	General Economic	98LTS319	302253
Spain	Siam	03 Aug 25	General Economic	55LTS39	301303
Spain	Sweden	18 Dec 20	General Trade	2LTS267	300073
Spain	Sweden	18 Mar 21	Other Economic	4LTS259	300109
Spain	Sweden	19 Jun 21	Mostfavored Nation	5LTS387	300143
Spain	Sweden	29 Dec 21	Customs	9LTS58	300242
Spain	Sweden	04 May 25	General Trade	36LTS323	300932
Spain	Sweden	26 Apr 28	Dispute Settlement	77LTS77	301764
Spain	Sweden	02 Jan 29	Admin Cooperation	94LTS353	302154

PARTY ONE	PARTY TWO	DATE	TOPIC	CITATION	NUMBER
Spain	Sweden	08 Apr 32	Air Transport	138LTS135	303184
Spain	Sweden	23 Aug 35	General Trade	162LTS331	303746
Spain	Switzerland	20 Apr 26	Dispute Settlement	60LTS23	301403
Spain	Switzerland	04 Aug 26	Admin Cooperation	65LTS39	301518
Spain	Switzerland	30 Oct 35	Patents/Copyrights	166LTS157	303837
Spain	Turkey	27 Sep 24	General Amity	43LTS307	301066
Spain	Turkey	19 May 34	General Trade	149LTS15	303428
Spain	Turkey	31 Dec 35	General Trade	166LTS163	303838
Spain	UK Great Britain	31 Oct 22	Water Transport	28LTS339	300719
Spain	UK Great Britain	09 Feb 24	Admin Cooperation	25LTS17	300602
Spain	UK Great Britain	27 Jun 24	General Trade	28LTS523	300727
Spain	UK Great Britain	19 Oct 26	Postal Service	61LTS79	301427
Spain	UK Great Britain	30 Jul 27	General Trade	63LTS189	301490
Spain	UK Great Britain	27 Jun 29	Admin Cooperation	101LTS375	302337
Spain	UK Great Britain	26 May 32	Water Transport	132LTS43	303030
Spain	UK Great Britain	06 Jan 36	Finance	166LTS283	303844
Spain	UK Great Britain	18 Mar 40	Finance	203LTS157	304759
Spain	UK Great Britain	18 Mar 40	Loans and Credits	203LTS149	304758
Spain	UK Great Britain	07 Apr 41	Loans and Credits	204LTS75	304785
Spain	Uruguay	23 Mar 22	Dispute Settlement	63LTS233	301493
Spain	Uruguay	02 Jan 35	General Trade	164LTS95	303791
Spain	USA (United States)	15 Sep 14	Dispute Settlement	89LTS427	302030
Spain	USA (United States)	10 Feb 26	Admin Cooperation	67LTS131	301543
Spain	USA (United States)	20 Jun 29	Claims and Debts	120LTS401	302776
Spain	USA (United States)	10 Jun 30	Taxation	120LTS407	302777
Spain	Yugoslavia	15 May 36	General Economic	170LTS185	303934
Spanish Colonies	Multilateral	28 Aug 24	Postal Service	41LTS9	301006
Spanish Colonies	Multilateral	28 Aug 24	Postal Service	40LTS437	301005
Spanish Colonies	Multilateral	28 Aug 24	Postal Service	40LTS249	301003
Spanish Colonies	Multilateral	28 Aug 24	Postal Service	41LTS97	301008
Spanish Colonies	Multilateral	28 Aug 24	Postal Service	41LTS55	301007
Spanish Colonies	Multilateral	28 Jun 29	Postal Service	102LTS245	302368
Spanish Colonies	Multilateral	20 Mar 34	Postal Service	176LTS55	304054
Spanish Colonies	Multilateral	20 Mar 34	Postal Service	175LTS363	304052
Spanish Colonies	Multilateral	20 Mar 34	Postal Service	175LTS73	304050
Spanish Colonies	Multilateral	20 Mar 34	Postal Service	175LTS269	304051
Spanish Colonies	Multilateral	20 Mar 34	Postal Service	175LTS5	304049
Spanish Colonies	Multilateral	20 Mar 34	Finance	176LTS9	304053
Spanish Colonies	Nigeria	09 Dec 42	Non-ILO Labor	205LTS41	304825
Spanish Guinea	Multilateral	25 Nov 27	Telecommunications	84LTS97	301905
Spanish Morroco	Multilateral	31 Oct 20	Sanitation	164LTS85	303790
Spanish Morroco	Multilateral	28 Aug 24	Postal Service	40LTS19	301002
Spanish Morroco	Multilateral	28 Aug 24	Postal Service	40LTS307	301004
Spanish Morroco	Multilateral	28 Aug 24	Postal Service	41LTS55	301007
Spanish Morroco	Multilateral	28 Aug 24	Postal Service	40LTS437	301005
Spanish Morroco	Multilateral	28 Aug 24	Postal Service	41LTS97	301008
Spanish Morroco	Multilateral	28 Aug 24	Postal Service	41LTS9	301006
Spanish Morroco	Multilateral	06 Nov 25	Patents/Copyrights	74LTS289	301743
Spanish Morroco	Multilateral	06 Nov 25	Other Economic	74LTS319	301744
Spanish Morroco	Multilateral	06 Nov 25	Other Economic	74LTS341	301746
Spanish Morroco	Multilateral	06 Nov 25	Patents/Copyrights	74LTS327	301745
Spanish Morroco	Multilateral	28 Jun 29	Postal Service	103LTS429	302374
Spanish Morroco	Multilateral	28 Jun 29	Postal Service	103LTS321	302372
Spanish Morroco	Multilateral	28 Jun 29	Postal Service	102LTS245	302368
Spanish Morroco	Multilateral	28 Jun 29	Postal Service	103LTS71	302370
Spanish Morroco	Multilateral	28 Jun 29	Postal Service	103LTS5	302369
Spanish Morroco	Multilateral	09 Dec 32	Telecommunications	151LTS5	303479
Spanish Morroco	Multilateral	20 Mar 34	Postal Service	175LTS269	304051
Spanish Morroco	Multilateral	20 Mar 34	Postal Service	175LTS5	304049
Spanish Morroco	Multilateral	20 Mar 34	Postal Service	174LTS171	304048
Spanish Morroco	Multilateral	20 Mar 34	Postal Service	176LTS55	304054
Spanish Morroco	Multilateral	20 Mar 34	Finance	176LTS9	304053
Spanish Morroco	Multilateral	20 Mar 34	Postal Service	175LTS73	304050
Spanish Morroco	Multilateral	20 Mar 34	Postal Service	175LTS363	304052
St. Christopher	Multilateral	26 Sep 27	Dispute Settlement	92LTS301	302096

PARTY ONE	PARTY TWO	DATE	TOPIC	CITATION	NUMBER
St. Helena	Multilateral	25 Nov 27	Telecommunications	84LTS97	301905
St. Helena	Multilateral	30 Mar 31	Taxation	138LTS149	303185
St. Helena	Multilateral	28 Oct 33	Refugees	159LTS199	303663
St. Helena	Multilateral	23 Sep 36	Gen Communications	186LTS301	304319
St. Helena	Multilateral	10 Feb 38	Refugees	192LTS59	304461
St. Lucia	Martinique	25 Aug 34	Postal Service	165LTS183	303810
St. Lucia	Multilateral	30 Jun 20	Patents/Copyrights	1LTS59	300008
St. Lucia	Multilateral	31 Mar 22	Humanitarian	9LTS415	300269
St. Lucia	Multilateral	25 Aug 24	Water Transport	120LTS155	302764
St. Lucia	Multilateral	01 Dec 24	Sanitation	78LTS351	301794
St. Pierre	Multilateral	23 Oct 30	Water Transport	125LTS95	302849
St. Vincent	Multilateral	30 Jun 20	Patents/Copyrights	1LTS59	300008
St. Vincent	Multilateral	31 Mar 22	Humanitarian	9LTS415	300269
St. Vincent	Multilateral	25 Aug 24	Water Transport	120LTS155	302764
St. Vincent	Multilateral	01 Dec 24	Sanitation	78LTS351	301794
Strait Settlements	China	16 Jan 25	Postal Service	36LTS395	300937
Strait Settlements	Japan	18 Jul 24	General Transport	31LTS109	300787
Strait Settlements	Multilateral	30 Jun 20	Patents/Copyrights	1LTS59	300008
Strait Settlements	Multilateral	31 Mar 22	Humanitarian	9LTS415	300269
Strait Settlements	Multilateral	25 Aug 24	Water Transport	120LTS155	302764
Strait Settlements	Multilateral	01 Dec 24	Sanitation	78LTS351	301794
Strait Settlements	Multilateral	30 Mar 31	Taxation	138LTS149	303185
Strait Settlements	Multilateral	28 Oct 33	Refugees	159LTS199	303663
Strait Settlements	Multilateral	23 Sep 36	Gen Communications	186LTS301	304319
Strait Settlements	Multilateral	10 Feb 38	Refugees	192LTS59	304461
Strait Settlements	Siam	12 Jan 26	Postal Service	49LTS161	301180
Sudan	Multilateral	31 Mar 22	Humanitarian	9LTS415	300269
Sudan	Multilateral	19 Feb 25	Admin Cooperation	81LTS317	301845
Sudan	Multilateral	21 Jun 26	Sanitation	78LTS229	301793
Sudan	Multilateral	25 Sep 26	ILO Labor	60LTS253	301414
Sudan	Multilateral	18 Dec 26	Telecommunications	63LTS185	301489
Sudan	Multilateral	12 Jul 27	Direct Aid	135LTS247	303115
Sudan	Multilateral	13 Jul 31	Other HEW	139LTS301	303219
Sudan	Multilateral	24 Sep 31	Specific Resources	155LTS349	303586
Sudan	Multilateral	12 Apr 33	Sanitation	161LTS65	303706
Sudan	Multilateral	11 Oct 33	Consul/Citizenship	150LTS431	303476
Sudan	Multilateral	08 Nov 33	Specific Resources	172LTS241	303995
Surinam	Multilateral	30 Jun 20	Patents/Copyrights	1LTS59	300008
Surinam	Multilateral	26 Sep 27	Dispute Settlement	92LTS301	302096
Surinam	Multilateral	25 Nov 27	Telecommunications	84LTS97	301905
Surinam	Multilateral	30 Mar 31	Land Transport	150LTS247	303459
Surinam	Multilateral	09 Dec 32	Telecommunications	151LTS5	303479
Surinam	UK Great Britain	15 Mar 38	Postal Service	189LTS183	304385
Swaziland	Multilateral	25 Nov 27	Telecommunications	84LTS97	301905
Swaziland	Multilateral	28 Oct 33	Refugees	159LTS199	303663
Swaziland	Multilateral	30 Oct 35	Postal Service	189LTS85	304376
Swaziland	Multilateral	30 Oct 35	Telecommunications	189LTS51	304375
Swaziland	Multilateral	23 Sep 36	Gen Communications	186LTS301	304319
Swaziland	Multilateral	10 Feb 38	Refugees	192LTS59	304461
Swaziland	South Africa	19 Aug 31	Customs	129LTS109	302954
Swaziland	South Africa	16 Mar 32	Taxation	129LTS377	302972
Sweden	Argentina	14 May 28	Non-ILO Labor	155LTS109	303573
Sweden	Austria	04 Oct 22	Humanitarian	9LTS317	300264
Sweden	Austria	10 Nov 24	General Economic	31LTS57	300782
Sweden	Austria	06 Mar 26	Admin Cooperation	47LTS39	301128
Sweden	Austria	28 May 26	Dispute Settlement	61LTS193	301434
Sweden	Austria	20 Dec 27	Visas	71LTS293	301670
Sweden	Austria	24 Mar 30	Extradition	105LTS313	302424
Sweden	Austria	15 Jan 37	Non-ILO Labor	174LTS125	304043
Sweden	Belgium	03 Jan 21	Land Transport	2LTS301	300083
Sweden	Belgium	25 Oct 22	Admin Cooperation	18LTS121	300459
Sweden	Belgium	30 Apr 26	Dispute Settlement	67LTS91	301540
Sweden	Belgium	13 May 29	Taxation	111LTS37	302578
Sweden	Belgium	22 Sep 34	Water Transport	153LTS261	303519
Sweden	Belgium	15 Jun 37	Visas	198LTS77	304625

PARTY ONE	PARTY TWO	DATE	TOPIC	CITATION	NUMBER
Sweden	Brazil	16 Oct 31	Mostfavored Nation	125LTS51	302845
Sweden	Brazil	27 Jan 32	Admin Cooperation	177LTS119	304086
Sweden	Bulgaria	14 Apr 21	Mostfavored Nation	5LTS240	300131
Sweden	Bulgaria	30 Sep 21	General Economic	7LTS137	300182
Sweden	Bulgaria	31 Dec 23	General Trade	22LTS323	300561
Sweden	Bulgaria	07 Dec 36	General Trade	173LTS393	304030
Sweden	Canada	21 Nov 29	Taxation	97LTS331	302230
Sweden	Chile	26 Mar 20	Dispute Settlement	4LTS271	300111
Sweden	Chile	08 Mar 33	Claims and Debts	142LTS147	303286
Sweden	Chile	21 Oct 36	Patents/Copyrights	174LTS109	304041
Sweden	Chile	30 Oct 36	General Trade	188LTS283	304364
Sweden	China	20 Dec 28	Customs	107LTS81	302470
Sweden	Colombia	13 Sep 27	Dispute Settlement	132LTS123	303032
Sweden	Colombia	09 Mar 28	General Trade	85LTS443	301944
Sweden	Czechoslovakia	07 Sep 21	Humanitarian	7LTS97	300177
Sweden	Czechoslovakia	18 Apr 25	General Amity	36LTS289	300929
Sweden	Czechoslovakia	02 Jan 26	Dispute Settlement	48LTS173	301159
Sweden	Czechoslovakia	17 Nov 31	Extradition	134LTS135	303088
Sweden	Czechoslovakia	23 Jul 36	Non-ILO Labor	171LTS111	303954
Sweden	Denmark	26 Jan 20	Water Transport	14LTS273	300379
Sweden	Denmark	08 Jun 21	Telecommunications	14LTS195	300374
Sweden	Denmark	07 Nov 22	Air Transport	14LTS95	300370
Sweden	Denmark	13 Jul 23	Admin Cooperation	18LTS143	300461
Sweden	Denmark	13 Jul 23	Admin Cooperation	18LTS131	300460
Sweden	Denmark	28 Apr 24	Customs	27LTS355	300696
Sweden	Denmark	27 Jun 24	Dispute Settlement	33LTS149	300840
Sweden	Denmark	28 Nov 24	Water Transport	32LTS41	300804
Sweden	Denmark	21 Nov 25	General Trade	42LTS139	301037
Sweden	Denmark	21 Nov 25	Water Transport	42LTS55	301032
Sweden	Denmark	14 Jan 26	Dispute Settlement	51LTS251	301235
Sweden	Denmark	03 Feb 27	Admin Cooperation	109LTS205	302540
Sweden	Denmark	08 Mar 27	Visas	63LTS315	301498
Sweden	Denmark	13 Dec 28	Telecommunications	104LTS55	302378
Sweden	Denmark	28 Feb 29	Telecommunications	104LTS69	302379
Sweden	Denmark	26 Apr 30	Land Transport	101LTS319	302333
Sweden	Denmark	03 Sep 30	Water Transport	106LTS397	302458
Sweden	Denmark	09 Oct 31	Specific Resources	126LTS255	302888
Sweden	Denmark	30 Jan 32	Territory Boundary	127LTS57	302906
Sweden	Denmark	06 May 32	Taxation	130LTS161	302989
Sweden	Denmark	23 Dec 32	Water Transport	136LTS37	303123
Sweden	Denmark	31 Dec 32	Territory Boundary	139LTS205	303211
Sweden	Denmark	16 Aug 33	Consul/Citizenship	164LTS55	303788
Sweden	Denmark	04 Mar 35	Admin Cooperation	158LTS39	303623
Sweden	Denmark	25 Jun 35	Sanitation	160LTS185	303692
Sweden	Denmark	28 Oct 35	Admin Cooperation	166LTS299	303845
Sweden	Denmark	20 Nov 36	Non-ILO Labor	173LTS207	304014
Sweden	Denmark	30 Mar 37	Gen Communications	186LTS117	304306
Sweden	Denmark	10 Jun 38	Admin Cooperation	188LTS461	304371
Sweden	Denmark	30 Dec 38	General Economic	195LTS413	304561
Sweden	Ecuador	11 Nov 38	Water Transport	195LTS347	304554
Sweden	El Salvador	23 Jun 36	Mostfavored Nation	171LTS291	303966
Sweden	Estonia	07 Jul 23	General Trade	20LTS189	300517
Sweden	Estonia	27 Nov 23	Admin Cooperation	57LTS83	301355
Sweden	Estonia	07 Jul 24	Water Transport	73LTS27	301702
Sweden	Estonia	30 Aug 24	Admin Cooperation	31LTS217	300797
Sweden	Estonia	29 May 25	Dispute Settlement	46LTS289	301123
Sweden	Estonia	11 Jun 28	Admin Cooperation	81LTS277	301843
Sweden	Estonia	23 Jun 28	Water Transport	87LTS253	301972
Sweden	Estonia	23 Apr 29	Admin Cooperation	89LTS277	302022
Sweden	Estonia	20 Jan 30	Extradition	106LTS279	302451
Sweden	Estonia	04 Apr 30	Patents/Copyrights	101LTS51	302318
Sweden	Estonia	07 Dec 34	Commodity Trade	154LTS319	303558
Sweden	Estonia	26 Mar 35	Finance	158LTS239	303634
Sweden	Estonia	20 May 35	Air Transport	162LTS371	303750
Sweden	Estonia	21 Dec 35	Commodity Trade	164LTS293	303798

PARTY ONE	PARTY TWO	DATE	TOPIC	CITATION	NUMBER
Sweden	Estonia	16 Jan 37	Postal Service	178LTS49	304106
Sweden	Estonia	08 Feb 37	Commodity Trade	176LTS193	304061
Sweden	Estonia	18 Feb 38	Commodity Trade	185LTS237	304287
Sweden	Estonia	30 Jan 39	Commodity Trade	194LTS131	304517
Sweden	Finland	10 May 20	Dispute Settlement	2LTS141	300058
Sweden	Finland	29 Jul 21	Humanitarian	6LTS353	300168
Sweden	Finland	22 May 22	Postal Service	14LTS297	300381
Sweden	Finland	26 May 23	Water Transport	18LTS57	300453
Sweden	Finland	11 Sep 23	ILO Labor	20LTS79	300508
Sweden	Finland	12 Oct 23	Water Transport	21LTS147	300538
Sweden	Finland	29 Nov 23	Extradition	23LTS41	300575
Sweden	Finland	10 Jan 24	Admin Cooperation	24LTS167	300558
Sweden	Finland	27 Jun 24	Dispute Settlement	29LTS19	300731
Sweden	Finland	28 Jun 24	Land Transport	28LTS327	300718
Sweden	Finland	26 Jul 24	Postal Service	29LTS167	300740
Sweden	Finland	22 Dec 24	Water Transport	73LTS33	301703
Sweden	Finland	09 May 25	Territory Boundary	47LTS283	301136
Sweden	Finland	29 Jan 26	Dispute Settlement	49LTS367	301192
Sweden	Finland	01 Apr 27	Water Transport	62LTS89	301458
Sweden	Finland	10 May 27	Specific Resources	70LTS201	301634
Sweden	Finland	14 Dec 27	General Trade	72LTS29	301688
Sweden	Finland	09 Mar 28	Visas	72LTS429	301699
Sweden	Finland	10 Jul 28	Telecommunications	87LTS131	301966
Sweden	Finland	14 May 30	Postal Service	106LTS9	302434
Sweden	Finland	17 Jul 30	Land Transport	105LTS343	302427
Sweden	Finland	16 Mar 31	Taxation	118LTS71	302714
Sweden	Finland	29 Dec 33	General Trade	149LTS23	303429
Sweden	Finland	05 Sep 34	Commodity Trade	154LTS239	303550
Sweden	Finland	18 Dec 35	Admin Cooperation	165LTS347	303821
Sweden	Finland	09 Jan 38	Admin Cooperation	195LTS157	304545
Sweden	Finland	16 Dec 39	Water Transport	199LTS43	304662
Sweden	France	25 Nov 20	General Transport	2LTS183	300065
Sweden	France	09 Nov 21	Humanitarian	7LTS303	300197
Sweden	France	19 Jul 26	Consul/Citizenship	54LTS283	301291
Sweden	France	03 Mar 28	Dispute Settlement	95LTS89	302168
Sweden	France	25 Jan 30	Taxation	99LTS99	302271
Sweden	France	13 Mar 33	General Trade	142LTS131	303285
Sweden	France	09 Jun 34	Education	154LTS101	303541
Sweden	France	22 Mar 35	General Trade	158LTS287	303639
Sweden	France	18 Jan 36	Customs	167LTS197	303866
Sweden	France	04 Dec 36	Taxation	184LTS35	304241
Sweden	France	24 Dec 36	Taxation	181LTS315	304198
Sweden	France	17 Feb 37	General Trade	176LTS267	304065
Sweden	France	30 Jun 37	Admin Cooperation	179LTS203	304148
Sweden	France	31 Jan 38	General Trade	185LTS223	304286
Sweden	France	18 Apr 39	Dispute Settlement	198LTS131	304632
Sweden	France	05 May 39	Taxation	198LTS201	304641
Sweden	Germany	02 May 11	General Economic	2LTS59	300047
Sweden	Germany	16 Dec 20	General Economic	2LTS263	300072
Sweden	Germany	19 Jan 23	Admin Cooperation	41LTS151	301011
Sweden	Germany	29 Aug 24	Dispute Settlement	42LTS111	301036
Sweden	Germany	29 May 25	Air Transport	46LTS121	301116
Sweden	Germany	31 Dec 25	Taxation	43LTS219	301056
Sweden	Germany	14 May 26	General Economic	51LTS99	301225
Sweden	Germany	25 Apr 28	Taxation	81LTS281	301844
Sweden	Germany	01 Jun 32	Water Transport	129LTS471	302979
Sweden	Germany	28 Aug 34	Finance	154LTS267	303552
Sweden	Germany	28 Aug 34	Finance	154LTS249	303551
Sweden	Germany	28 Aug 34	Claims and Debts	154LTS273	303553
Sweden	Germany	22 Dec 34	Finance	156LTS145	303597
Sweden	Germany	22 Dec 34	Claims and Debts	156LTS151	303598
Sweden	Germany	22 Dec 34	Finance	156LTS127	303596
Sweden	Germany	13 Mar 35	Sanitation	158LTS233	303633
Sweden	Germany	14 May 35	Taxation	163LTS425	303784
Sweden	Germany	14 May 35	Taxation	163LTS459	303785

PARTY ONE	PARTY TWO	DATE	TOPIC	CITATION	NUMBER
Sweden	Germany	19 Jul 35	Loans and Credits	161LTS35	303704
Sweden	Germany	31 Jan 36	Claims and Debts	168LTS19	303884
Sweden	Germany	31 Jan 36	Finance	168LTS13	303883
Sweden	Germany	19 May 36	Admin Cooperation	182LTS395	304224
Sweden	Germany	28 Oct 38	Claims and Debts	196LTS91	304571
Sweden	Germany	28 Oct 38	Claims and Debts	196LTS81	304570
Sweden	Greece	10 Sep 26	General Trade	63LTS37	301479
Sweden	Greece	18 Oct 29	Admin Cooperation	95LTS201	302174
Sweden	Greece	19 Nov 31	Taxation	126LTS411	302899
Sweden	Greece	17 Jan 35	General Trade	157LTS9	303601
Sweden	Greece	11 Jan 36	Finance	165LTS299	303816
Sweden	Greece	31 Dec 36	Finance	174LTS87	304039
Sweden	Greece	01 Feb 38	General Trade	185LTS217	304285
Sweden	Greece	01 May 39	General Trade	196LTS205	304582
Sweden	Guatemala	11 Jul 36	Mostfavored Nation	171LTS299	303967
Sweden	Hungary	26 Feb 23	Admin Cooperation	17LTS35	300426
Sweden	Hungary	08 Nov 28	General Economic	89LTS283	302023
Sweden	Hungary	17 Jun 36	Taxation	184LTS25	304240
Sweden	Hungary	17 Jun 36	Taxation	184LTS11	304239
Sweden	Iceland	23 Mar 21	Patents/Copyrights	4LTS137	300105
Sweden	Iceland	10 Mar 28	Water Transport	71LTS315	301672
Sweden	Iceland	27 Jun 30	Dispute Settlement	127LTS67	302907
Sweden	Iceland	31 Oct 30	Non-ILO Labor	109LTS171	302535
Sweden	Iceland	08 Sep 37	Taxation	187LTS405	304346
Sweden	Iraq	03 Nov 35	Mostfavored Nation	163LTS419	303783
Sweden	Irish Free State	08 Oct 31	Taxation	125LTS23	302842
Sweden	Italy	04 Jun 21	Land Transport	6LTS47	300148
Sweden	Italy	22 Feb 29	Customs	87LTS265	301973
Sweden	Italy	24 Jun 35	General Trade	161LTS21	303702
Sweden	Italy	24 Jun 35	Finance	161LTS27	303703
Sweden	Italy	01 Dec 36	General Trade	173LTS257	304017
Sweden	Italy	01 Dec 36	Finance	173LTS279	304019
Sweden	Italy	01 Dec 36	Finance	173LTS269	304018
Sweden	Japan	01 May 23	Admin Cooperation	17LTS391	300446
Sweden	Latvia	15 Nov 24	Admin Cooperation	56LTS173	301328
Sweden	Latvia	22 Dec 24	General Amity	36LTS283	300928
Sweden	Latvia	28 Mar 25	Dispute Settlement	37LTS131	300952
Sweden	Latvia	30 Mar 28	Water Transport	73LTS39	301704
Sweden	Latvia	21 Jun 28	Admin Cooperation	88LTS107	301990
Sweden	Latvia	12 Jan 29	Admin Cooperation	85LTS403	301940
Sweden	Latvia	11 Jan 30	Land Transport	109LTS193	302539
Sweden	Latvia	30 Jan 30	Extradition	110LTS139	302558
Sweden	Latvia	26 Mar 35	Finance	158LTS269	303637
Sweden	Latvia	30 Dec 36	Postal Service	174LTS147	304045
Sweden	Latvia	15 Apr 39	General Trade	196LTS373	304597
Sweden	Lithuania	17 Feb 24	General Trade	23LTS153	300587
Sweden	Lithuania	11 Jun 25	Dispute Settlement	57LTS191	301364
Sweden	Lithuania	04 Jan 29	Admin Cooperation	92LTS191	302086
Sweden	Lithuania	16 Oct 31	Patents/Copyrights	126LTS233	302885
Sweden	Lithuania	01 Jul 37	Customs	179LTS251	304152
Sweden	Lithuania	17 May 38	Postal Service	192LTS237	304474
Sweden	Luxembourg	11 Apr 23	Admin Cooperation	16LTS453	300423
Sweden	Mexico	17 Oct 22	Humanitarian	15LTS179	300391
Sweden	Mexico	14 Sep 31	Postal Service	192LTS195	304472
Sweden	Multilateral	09 Sep 86*	Patents/Copyrights	123LTS233	302816
Sweden	Multilateral	18 Mar 04	Humanitarian	1LTS83	300011
Sweden	Multilateral	13 Nov 08	General Ad Hoc	1LTS217	300015
Sweden	Multilateral	12 Jan 12	Sanitation	4LTS281	300112
Sweden	Multilateral	05 Jun 12	Telecommunications	1LTS135	300013
Sweden	Multilateral	20 Mar 14	Patents/Copyrights	1LTS243	300016
Sweden	Multilateral	18 Jan 20	Admin Cooperation	12LTS321	300323
Sweden	Multilateral	09 Feb 20	Territory Boundary	2LTS7	300041
Sweden	Multilateral	01 May 20	Air Transport	11LTS173	300297
Sweden	Multilateral	11 May 20	Finance	1LTS15	300001
Sweden	Multilateral	21 Jun 20	Health/Educ/Welfare	8LTS65	300207

PARTY ONE	PARTY TWO	DATE	TOPIC	CITATION	NUMBER
Sweden	Multilateral	30 Jun 20	Patents/Copyrights	1LTS59	300008
Sweden	Multilateral	16 Dec 20	General IGO	6LTS379	300170
Sweden	Multilateral	29 Dec 20	Telecommunications	13LTS281	300359
Sweden	Multilateral	19 Jan 21	Recognition	5LTS9	300113
Sweden	Multilateral	20 Apr 21	Water Transport	7LTS73	300174
Sweden	Multilateral	20 Apr 21	Land Transport	7LTS11	300171
Sweden	Multilateral	20 Apr 21	Water Transport	7LTS35	300172
Sweden	Multilateral	20 Apr 21	Water Transport	7LTS65	300173
Sweden	Multilateral	05 Aug 21	Admin Cooperation	27LTS349	300695
Sweden	Multilateral	21 Sep 21	Humanitarian	7LTS127	300181
Sweden	Multilateral	05 Oct 21	IGO Establishment	51LTS361	301241
Sweden	Multilateral	05 Oct 21	Admin Cooperation	29LTS79	300735
Sweden	Multilateral	05 Oct 21	Admin Cooperation	29LTS67	300733
Sweden	Multilateral	05 Oct 21	Admin Cooperation	29LTS73	300734
Sweden	Multilateral	06 Oct 21	General Economic	17LTS45	300427
Sweden	Multilateral	20 Oct 21	Peace/Disarmament	9LTS211	300255
Sweden	Multilateral	06 Feb 22	Customs	38LTS267	300981
Sweden	Multilateral	06 Feb 22	General Trade	38LTS277	300982
Sweden	Multilateral	31 Mar 22	Humanitarian	9LTS415	300269
Sweden	Multilateral	18 Aug 22	Telecommunications	13LTS289	300360
Sweden	Multilateral	04 Oct 22	Territory Boundary	12LTS391	300335
Sweden	Multilateral	11 Jul 23	Admin Cooperation	18LTS85	300456
Sweden	Multilateral	24 Sep 23	Dispute Settlement	27LTS157	300678
Sweden	Multilateral	03 Nov 23	Customs	30LTS371	300775
Sweden	Multilateral	28 Nov 23	Admin Cooperation	51LTS221	301230
Sweden	Multilateral	28 Nov 23	Admin Cooperation	51LTS233	301232
Sweden	Multilateral	28 Nov 23	Admin Cooperation	51LTS239	301233
Sweden	Multilateral	28 Nov 23	Admin Cooperation	51LTS215	301229
Sweden	Multilateral	28 Nov 23	Admin Cooperation	51LTS209	301228
Sweden	Multilateral	09 Dec 23	Water Transport	58LTS284	301379
Sweden	Multilateral	09 Dec 23	Land Transport	47LTS55	301129
Sweden	Multilateral	25 Jan 24	Sanitation	57LTS135	301360
Sweden	Multilateral	22 Mar 24	Finance	25LTS171	300605
Sweden	Multilateral	04 Jul 24	Admin Cooperation	51LTS227	301231
Sweden	Multilateral	26 Jul 24	Postal Service	30LTS271	300771
Sweden	Multilateral	25 Aug 24	Water Transport	120LTS123	302763
Sweden	Multilateral	28 Aug 24	Postal Service	40LTS437	301005
Sweden	Multilateral	28 Aug 24	Postal Service	41LTS9	301006
Sweden	Multilateral	28 Aug 24	Postal Service	40LTS249	301003
Sweden	Multilateral	28 Aug 24	Postal Service	40LTS307	301004
Sweden	Multilateral	28 Aug 24	Postal Service	41LTS55	301007
Sweden	Multilateral	28 Aug 24	Postal Service	40LTS19	301002
Sweden	Multilateral	28 Aug 24	Postal Service	41LTS97	301008
Sweden	Multilateral	23 Oct 24	General Transport	77LTS367	301778
Sweden	Multilateral	23 Oct 24	Land Transport	78LTS17	301779
Sweden	Multilateral	01 Dec 24	Sanitation	78LTS351	301794
Sweden	Multilateral	19 Feb 25	Admin Cooperation	81LTS317	301845
Sweden	Multilateral	17 Jun 25	Peace/Disarmament	94LTS65	302138
Sweden	Multilateral	19 Aug 25	Customs	42LTS73	301033
Sweden	Multilateral	29 Oct 25	Telecommunications	57LTS201	301365
Sweden	Multilateral	06 Nov 25	Patents/Copyrights	74LTS289	301743
Sweden	Multilateral	06 Nov 25	Other Economic	74LTS319	301744
Sweden	Multilateral	31 Dec 25	Territory Boundary	79LTS167	301809
Sweden	Multilateral	28 Jan 26	Water Transport	51LTS9	301219
Sweden	Multilateral	10 Apr 26	Water Transport	176LTS199	304062
Sweden	Multilateral	10 Apr 26	Water Transport	120LTS187	302765
Sweden	Multilateral	24 Apr 26	Land Transport	108LTS123	302505
Sweden	Multilateral	12 May 26	Refugees	89LTS47	302004
Sweden	Multilateral	25 Sep 26	ILO Labor	60LTS253	301414
Sweden	Multilateral	01 Nov 26	Telecommunications	78LTS109	301782
Sweden	Multilateral	25 Feb 27	Telecommunications	78LTS123	301783
Sweden	Multilateral	08 Mar 27	Telecommunications	78LTS134	301784
Sweden	Multilateral	16 Aug 27	Telecommunications	78LTS141	301785
Sweden	Multilateral	10 Sep 27	Postal Service	75LTS7	301749
Sweden	Multilateral	10 Sep 27	Postal Service	75LTS39	301750

PARTY ONE	PARTY TWO	DATE	TOPIC	CITATION	NUMBER
Sweden	Multilateral	26 Sep 27	Dispute Settlement	92LTS301	302096
Sweden	Multilateral	08 Nov 27	General Trade	97LTS391	302238
Sweden	Multilateral	11 Nov 27	Telecommunications	78LTS153	301786
Sweden	Multilateral	21 Nov 27	Telecommunications	78LTS163	301787
Sweden	Multilateral	25 Nov 27	Telecommunications	84LTS97	301905
Sweden	Multilateral	07 Jan 28	Telecommunications	78LTS187	301789
Sweden	Multilateral	19 Mar 28	Telecommunications	78LTS177	301788
Sweden	Multilateral	23 Apr 28	Telecommunications	78LTS197	301790
Sweden	Multilateral	25 Apr 28	Telecommunications	78LTS207	301791
Sweden	Multilateral	09 Jun 28	Telecommunications	78LTS219	301792
Sweden	Multilateral	11 Jul 28	Commodity Trade	95LTS373	302185
Sweden	Multilateral	11 Jul 28	Commodity Trade	95LTS357	302184
Sweden	Multilateral	27 Aug 28	General Military	94LTS57	302137
Sweden	Multilateral	26 Sep 28	Dispute Settlement	93LTS343	302123
Sweden	Multilateral	25 Oct 28	Consul/Citizenship	84LTS7	301901
Sweden	Multilateral	30 Oct 28	Dispute Settlement	87LTS103	301963
Sweden	Multilateral	22 Nov 28	Culture	111LTS343	302598
Sweden	Multilateral	30 Nov 28	Telecommunications	87LTS119	301965
Sweden	Multilateral	14 Dec 28	General Economic	110LTS171	302560
Sweden	Multilateral	22 Dec 28	Telecommunications	104LTS103	302381
Sweden	Multilateral	14 Jan 29	Telecommunications	87LTS169	301968
Sweden	Multilateral	16 Jan 29	Telecommunications	87LTS155	301967
Sweden	Multilateral	08 May 29	Telecommunications	91LTS337	302074
Sweden	Multilateral	31 May 29	Water Transport	136LTS81	303127
Sweden	Multilateral	28 Jun 29	Postal Service	102LTS245	302368
Sweden	Multilateral	28 Jun 29	Postal Service	103LTS71	302370
Sweden	Multilateral	28 Jun 29	Postal Service	103LTS5	302369
Sweden	Multilateral	28 Jun 29	Postal Service	103LTS321	302372
Sweden	Multilateral	28 Jun 29	Postal Service	103LTS249	302371
Sweden	Multilateral	28 Jun 29	Postal Service	103LTS377	302373
Sweden	Multilateral	28 Jun 29	Postal Service	103LTS429	302374
Sweden	Multilateral	27 Jul 29	Other Military	118LTS303	302733
Sweden	Multilateral	27 Jul 29	Other Military	118LTS343	302734
Sweden	Multilateral	20 Aug 29	Sanitation	98LTS125	302243
Sweden	Multilateral	30 Aug 29	Telecommunications	96LTS117	302194
Sweden	Multilateral	30 Aug 29	Telecommunications	96LTS129	302195
Sweden	Multilateral	07 Sep 29	Telecommunications	98LTS345	302255
Sweden	Multilateral	14 Sep 29	UN Charter	165LTS353	303822
Sweden	Multilateral	25 Sep 29	Telecommunications	98LTS361	302256
Sweden	Multilateral	26 Sep 29	Telecommunications	98LTS395	302259
Sweden	Multilateral	30 Sep 29	Telecommunications	98LTS183	302246
Sweden	Multilateral	30 Sep 29	Postal Service	99LTS71	302269
Sweden	Multilateral	01 Oct 29	Telecommunications	98LTS197	302247
Sweden	Multilateral	08 Oct 29	Telecommunications	98LTS409	302260
Sweden	Multilateral	10 Oct 29	Telecommunications	98LTS375	302257
Sweden	Multilateral	12 Oct 29	General Transport	137LTS11	303145
Sweden	Multilateral	29 Oct 29	Telecommunications	99LTS85	302270
Sweden	Multilateral	17 Dec 29	Specific Resources	115LTS93	302679
Sweden	Multilateral	25 Feb 30	Telecommunications	101LTS343	302335
Sweden	Multilateral	10 Apr 30	Telecommunications	101LTS465	302345
Sweden	Multilateral	12 Apr 30	Milit Servic/Citiz	178LTS227	304117
Sweden	Multilateral	12 Apr 30	Admin Cooperation	179LTS89	304137
Sweden	Multilateral	14 May 30	Postal Service	105LTS353	302428
Sweden	Multilateral	07 Jun 30	Finance	143LTS317	303314
Sweden	Multilateral	07 Jun 30	Finance	143LTS337	303315
Sweden	Multilateral	07 Jun 30	Finance	143LTS257	303313
Sweden	Multilateral	23 Oct 30	Water Transport	125LTS95	302849
Sweden	Multilateral	23 Oct 30	Water Transport	112LTS21	302603
Sweden	Multilateral	22 Dec 30	General Trade	126LTS341	302893
Sweden	Multilateral	06 Feb 31	Admin Cooperation	126LTS121	302877
Sweden	Multilateral	10 Feb 31	Admin Cooperation	126LTS41	302870
Sweden	Multilateral	19 Mar 31	Admin Cooperation	143LTS7	303301
Sweden	Multilateral	19 Mar 31	Finance	143LTS407	303317
Sweden	Multilateral	19 Mar 31	Finance	143LTS355	303316
Sweden	Multilateral	27 Mar 31	ICJ Option Clause	167LTS341	303877

PARTY ONE	PARTY TWO	DATE	TOPIC	CITATION	NUMBER
Sweden	Multilateral	28 Mar 31	Customs	119LTS47	302739
Sweden	Multilateral	30 Mar 31	Land Transport	150LTS247	303459
Sweden	Multilateral	30 Mar 31	Taxation	138LTS149	303185
Sweden	Multilateral	06 May 31	Telecommunications	120LTS217	302767
Sweden	Multilateral	13 Jul 31	Other HEW	139LTS301	303219
Sweden	Multilateral	16 Mar 32	Admin Cooperation	139LTS165	303209
Sweden	Multilateral	02 Sep 32	Land Transport	154LTS123	303543
Sweden	Multilateral	09 Dec 32	Telecommunications	151LTS5	303479
Sweden	Multilateral	13 Dec 32	Territory Boundary	139LTS189	303210
Sweden	Multilateral	11 Mar 33	Water Transport	135LTS301	303119
Sweden	Multilateral	12 Apr 33	Sanitation	161LTS65	303706
Sweden	Multilateral	25 Aug 33	Commodity Trade	141LTS71	303262
Sweden	Multilateral	11 Oct 33	Education	155LTS331	303585
Sweden	Multilateral	11 Oct 33	Consul/Citizenship	150LTS431	303476
Sweden	Multilateral	07 Nov 33	Finance	155LTS115	303574
Sweden	Multilateral	23 Nov 33	Land Transport	192LTS389	304484
Sweden	Multilateral	23 Nov 33	Land Transport	192LTS327	304483
Sweden	Multilateral	20 Mar 34	Postal Service	175LTS269	304051
Sweden	Multilateral	20 Mar 34	Postal Service	175LTS363	304052
Sweden	Multilateral	20 Mar 34	Postal Service	175LTS5	304049
Sweden	Multilateral	20 Mar 34	Finance	176LTS9	304053
Sweden	Multilateral	20 Mar 34	Postal Service	176LTS55	304054
Sweden	Multilateral	20 Mar 34	Postal Service	174LTS171	304048
Sweden	Multilateral	20 Mar 34	Postal Service	175LTS73	304050
Sweden	Multilateral	26 Apr 34	Admin Cooperation	164LTS63	303789
Sweden	Multilateral	02 Jun 34	General Trade	192LTS9	304458
Sweden	Multilateral	02 Jun 34	Patents/Copyrights	192LTS17	304459
Sweden	Multilateral	19 Nov 34	Admin Cooperation	164LTS243	303797
Sweden	Multilateral	22 Dec 34	Visas	183LTS145	304230
Sweden	Multilateral	22 Dec 34	Admin Cooperation	183LTS153	304231
Sweden	Multilateral	31 Dec 34	Postal Service	158LTS111	303630
Sweden	Multilateral	15 Sep 36	Scientific Project	178LTS439	304126
Sweden	Multilateral	23 Sep 36	Gen Communications	186LTS301	304319
Sweden	Multilateral	06 Nov 36	General Military	173LTS353	304025
Sweden	Multilateral	11 Feb 37	Telecommunications	186LTS55	304303
Sweden	Multilateral	03 Mar 37	Admin Cooperation	182LTS127	304205
Sweden	Multilateral	06 Mar 37	Gen Communications	186LTS109	304305
Sweden	Multilateral	31 Mar 37	Commodity Trade	189LTS359	304394
Sweden	Multilateral	08 May 37	Privil/Immunities	182LTS37	304202
Sweden	Multilateral	28 May 37	General Trade	180LTS5	304170
Sweden	Multilateral	06 Sep 37	Specific Resources	186LTS419	304326
Sweden	Multilateral	15 Sep 37	Gen Communications	186LTS135	304307
Sweden	Multilateral	23 Sep 37	Postal Service	190LTS299	304427
Sweden	Multilateral	02 Oct 37	Education	182LTS263	304216
Sweden	Multilateral	23 Dec 37	Gen Communications	186LTS99	304304
Sweden	Multilateral	11 May 38	General Trade	189LTS237	304386
Sweden	Multilateral	27 May 38	Other Military	188LTS293	304365
Sweden	Multilateral	30 May 38	Visas	191LTS299	304451
Sweden	Multilateral	12 Sep 38	Culture	198LTS111	304630
Sweden	Multilateral	31 Oct 38	Sanitation	198LTS205	304642
Sweden	Multilateral	23 May 39	Postal Service	202LTS159	304742
Sweden	Netherlands	21 Nov 25	Air Transport	55LTS79	301305
Sweden	Netherlands	21 May 27	Dispute Settlement	79LTS147	301807
Sweden	Netherlands	24 Dec 27	Water Transport	71LTS391	301677
Sweden	Netherlands	30 Dec 27	Admin Cooperation	70LTS365	301646
Sweden	Netherlands	15 Jul 31	Land Transport	127LTS321	302925
Sweden	Netherlands	29 Nov 33	Land Transport	153LTS11	303501
Sweden	Netherlands	21 Mar 35	Taxation	148LTS451	303648
Sweden	New Zealand	24 May 35	General Economic	159LTS143	303657
Sweden	Norway	29 Mar 22	Telecommunications	13LTS311	300361
Sweden	Norway	05 May 22	Humanitarian	15LTS165	300390
Sweden	Norway	26 May 23	Air Transport	18LTS155	300462
Sweden	Norway	27 Jun 24	Dispute Settlement	28LTS309	300717
Sweden	Norway	22 Dec 24	Admin Cooperation	32LTS13	300802
Sweden	Norway	23 Oct 25	Dispute Settlement	39LTS153	301000

PARTY ONE	PARTY TWO	DATE	TOPIC	CITATION	NUMBER
Sweden	Norway	25 Nov 25	Dispute Settlement	60LTS295	301417
Sweden	Norway	09 Mar 27	Privil/Immunities	62LTS341	301472
Sweden	Norway	19 Nov 27	Land Transport	68LTS209	301584
Sweden	Norway	11 May 29	Water Transport	120LTS263	302771
Sweden	Norway	26 Jul 29	Admin Cooperation	94LTS287	302149
Sweden	Norway	18 Dec 29	Customs	98LTS389	302258
Sweden	Norway	08 Aug 31	Land Transport	123LTS67	302806
Sweden	Norway	10 Mar 33	Water Transport	138LTS17	303176
Sweden	Norway	22 Aug 33	Consul/Citizenship	141LTS217	303267
Sweden	Norway	09 Oct 33	Customs	142LTS171	303289
Sweden	Norway	14 Jun 37	Taxation	179LTS245	304151
Sweden	Norway	20 Apr 38	Specific Property	189LTS153	304383
Sweden	Norway	30 Dec 38	General Economic	195LTS127	304541
Sweden	Persia	09 Aug 28	General Amity	80LTS407	301841
Sweden	Persia	10 May 29	General Amity	102LTS9	302349
Sweden	Persia	27 May 29	General Amity	105LTS279	302420
Sweden	Poland	27 Dec 21	Humanitarian	8LTS163	300220
Sweden	Poland	02 Dec 24	General Amity	36LTS299	300930
Sweden	Poland	01 Oct 25	Air Transport	54LTS113	301279
Sweden	Poland	03 Nov 25	Dispute Settlement	62LTS263	301466
Sweden	Poland	25 Jan 28	Admin Cooperation	140LTS385	303248
Sweden	Poland	22 Sep 28	Admin Cooperation	140LTS391	303249
Sweden	Poland	30 Aug 30	Extradition	129LTS383	302973
Sweden	Poland	16 May 31	Commodity Trade	120LTS223	302768
Sweden	Poland	21 Oct 33	General Trade	150LTS73	303454
Sweden	Poland	03 Jul 36	General Trade	171LTS307	303968
Sweden	Poland	13 Sep 37	Non-ILO Labor	187LTS431	304348
Sweden	Portugal	20 Sep 21	Humanitarian	7LTS143	300183
Sweden	Portugal	17 May 27	Admin Cooperation	64LTS373	301510
Sweden	Portugal	03 Jan 29	Water Transport	87LTS313	301977
Sweden	Portugal	06 Dec 32	Dispute Settlement	145LTS91	303347
Sweden	Portugal	19 Oct 34	General Trade	154LTS77	303538
Sweden	Romania	21 Apr 21	Other Economic	4LTS265	300110
Sweden	Romania	25 Nov 21	General Economic	7LTS247	300190
Sweden	Romania	18 Dec 22	General Economic	14LTS353	300383
Sweden	Romania	21 Mar 31	General Economic	106LTS237	302448
Sweden	Romania	07 Oct 31	General Economic	131LTS51	303003
Sweden	Siam	19 Dec 25	General Economic	58LTS429	301386
Sweden	Siam	05 Nov 37	Privil/Immunities	182LTS257	304215
Sweden	Siam	08 Nov 37	General Amity	185LTS337	304298
Sweden	Spain	18 Dec 20	General Trade	2LTS267	300073
Sweden	Spain	18 Mar 21	Other Economic	4LTS259	300109
Sweden	Spain	19 Jun 21	Mostfavored Nation	5LTS387	300143
Sweden	Spain	29 Dec 21	Customs	9LTS58	300242
Sweden	Spain	04 May 25	General Trade	36LTS323	300932
Sweden	Spain	26 Apr 28	Dispute Settlement	77LTS77	301764
Sweden	Spain	02 Jan 29	Admin Cooperation	94LTS353	302154
Sweden	Spain	08 Apr 32	Air Transport	138LTS135	303184
Sweden	Spain	23 Aug 35	General Trade	162LTS331	303746
Sweden	Switzerland	29 Nov 21	Humanitarian	7LTS313	300198
Sweden	Switzerland	01 Jan 22	Visas	9LTS11	300239
Sweden	Switzerland	20 Mar 24	General Trade	25LTS243	300612
Sweden	Switzerland	02 Jun 24	Admin Cooperation	33LTS199	300844
Sweden	Switzerland	15 Jan 36	Admin Cooperation	169LTS347	303923
Sweden	Switzerland	25 Jul 36	Non-ILO Labor	171LTS177	303959
Sweden	Turkey	31 May 24	General Amity	38LTS148	300972
Sweden	Turkey	04 Feb 28	General Trade	88LTS155	301994
Sweden	Turkey	24 Sep 28	General Trade	82LTS9	301855
Sweden	Turkey	29 Sep 29	General Economic	119LTS53	302740
Sweden	Turkey	19 Oct 29	General Trade	96LTS221	302203
Sweden	Turkey	24 Apr 32	Privil/Immunities	129LTS325	302967
Sweden	Turkey	19 Jun 34	Claims and Debts	150LTS413	303474
Sweden	Turkey	27 Feb 36	Finance	167LTS83	303859
Sweden	Turkey	27 Feb 36	General Trade	167LTS75	303858
Sweden	Turkey	14 Dec 36	Finance	174LTS51	304036

PARTY ONE	PARTY TWO	DATE	TOPIC	CITATION	NUMBER
Sweden	Turkey	31 Dec 37	General Trade	184LTS399	304260
Sweden	Turkey	31 Dec 37	Finance	184LTS409	304261
Sweden	Turkey	31 Dec 37	General Trade	184LTS417	304262
Sweden	Turkey	20 Jan 39	General Trade	194LTS119	304515
Sweden	Turkey	20 Jan 39	Finance	194LTS113	304514
Sweden	Turkey	20 Jan 39	General Trade	194LTS107	304513
Sweden	Turkey	29 Feb 40	Finance	200LTS273	304696
Sweden	Turkey	29 Feb 40	General Trade	200LTS281	304697
Sweden	Turkey	29 Feb 40	General Trade	200LTS267	304695
Sweden	UK Great Britain	03 Mar 20	Postal Service	5LTS63	300119
Sweden	UK Great Britain	16 Feb 21	Air Transport	3LTS233	300100
Sweden	UK Great Britain	08 Jul 21	Claims and Debts	5LTS329	300139
Sweden	UK Great Britain	29 Aug 21	Other HEW	6LTS285	300160
Sweden	UK Great Britain	27 Oct 23	Admin Cooperation	22LTS387	300568
Sweden	UK Great Britain	05 Mar 24	Air Transport	23LTS149	300586
Sweden	UK Great Britain	09 Oct 24	Admin Cooperation	34LTS381	300886
Sweden	UK Great Britain	19 Dec 24	Taxation	32LTS291	300820
Sweden	UK Great Britain	28 Aug 30	Admin Cooperation	114LTS9	302652
Sweden	UK Great Britain	06 Jul 31	Taxation	120LTS211	302766
Sweden	UK Great Britain	15 May 33	General Trade	140LTS317	303245
Sweden	UK Great Britain	20 Oct 34	Water Transport	154LTS85	303539
Sweden	UK Great Britain	30 Apr 36	Water Transport	168LTS121	303892
Sweden	United Arab Rep	07 Jun 30	General Economic	102LTS207	302363
Sweden	Uruguay	24 Feb 23	Dispute Settlement	63LTS239	301494
Sweden	Uruguay	13 Aug 36	General Trade	183LTS161	304232
Sweden	USA (United States)	27 Feb 20	Patents/Copyrights	2LTS147	300059
Sweden	USA (United States)	29 Jun 20	Consul/Citizenship	2LTS153	300060
Sweden	USA (United States)	28 May 21	Water Transport	6LTS41	300147
Sweden	USA (United States)	17 Apr 22	Postal Service	14LTS281	300380
Sweden	USA (United States)	22 May 24	Customs	29LTS421	300752
Sweden	USA (United States)	24 Jun 24	Dispute Settlement	33LTS273	300851
Sweden	USA (United States)	27 Oct 28	Dispute Settlement	91LTS225	302063
Sweden	USA (United States)	29 Oct 30	Water Transport	109LTS181	302537
Sweden	USA (United States)	17 Dec 30	Dispute Settlement	125LTS233	302856
Sweden	USA (United States)	01 Jun 32	Water Transport	131LTS213	303012
Sweden	USA (United States)	11 Jul 32	Postal Service	192LTS205	304473
Sweden	USA (United States)	31 Jan 33	Status of Forces	159LTS261	303670
Sweden	USA (United States)	09 Sep 33	Air Transport	144LTS171	303327
Sweden	USA (United States)	09 Sep 33	Air Transport	144LTS183	303328
Sweden	USA (United States)	09 Sep 33	Air Transport	144LTS153	303326
Sweden	USA (United States)	17 May 34	Extradition	150LTS375	303470
Sweden	USA (United States)	25 May 35	General Trade	161LTS109	303707
Sweden	USA (United States)	31 Mar 38	Taxation	189LTS327	304392
Sweden	USA (United States)	23 Mar 39	Taxation	199LTS17	304661
Sweden	USA (United States)	30 Jun 39	Admin Cooperation	199LTS203	304674
Sweden	USA (United States)	05 Oct 39	Visas	203LTS353	304776
Sweden	USSR (Soviet Union)	15 Mar 24	General Trade	25LTS251	300613
Sweden	USSR (Soviet Union)	12 Sep 24	Postal Service	31LTS75	300784
Sweden	USSR (Soviet Union)	21 Jul 26	Patents/Copyrights	57LTS9	301346
Sweden	USSR (Soviet Union)	08 Oct 27	Admin Cooperation	71LTS411	301679
Sweden	Yugoslavia	14 May 37	General Trade	194LTS21	304504
Sweden	Yugoslavia	14 May 37	General Trade	179LTS147	304141
Switzerland	Afghanistan	17 Feb 28	General Amity	73LTS323	301722
Switzerland	Albania	10 Jun 29	General Trade	104LTS145	302384
Switzerland	Australia	22 Nov 38	General Trade	194LTS35	304505
Switzerland	Austria	11 Oct 24	Dispute Settlement	33LTS423	300862
Switzerland	Austria	19 Nov 24	Water Transport	39LTS26	300994
Switzerland	Austria	06 Jan 26	General Economic	46LTS299	301124
Switzerland	Austria	15 Mar 27	Admin Cooperation	87LTS351	301981
Switzerland	Austria	24 Oct 27	Taxation	85LTS253	301935
Switzerland	Austria	21 Nov 36	Land Transport	179LTS341	304162
Switzerland	Bel-Lux Econ Union	26 Aug 29	General Economic	105LTS9	302401
Switzerland	Belgium	13 Jun 22	Air Transport	12LTS295	300321
Switzerland	Belgium	05 Feb 27	Dispute Settlement	68LTS45	301567
Switzerland	Belgium	30 Aug 35	Taxation	162LTS293	303741

PARTY ONE	PARTY TWO	DATE	TOPIC	CITATION	NUMBER
Switzerland	Belgium	14 May 38	Extradition	190LTS217	304420
Switzerland	Brazil	23 Jun 24	Dispute Settlement	33LTS415	300861
Switzerland	Brazil	29 Oct 30	General Trade	140LTS265	303241
Switzerland	Brazil	23 Jul 32	Extradition	145LTS167	303354
Switzerland	China	12 Apr 27	Sanitation	66LTS427	301536
Switzerland	Colombia	20 Aug 27	Dispute Settlement	111LTS229	302589
Switzerland	Czechoslovakia	30 Sep 25	General Trade	58LTS279	301378
Switzerland	Czechoslovakia	21 Dec 26	Admin Cooperation	86LTS443	301956
Switzerland	Czechoslovakia	21 Dec 26	Admin Cooperation	68LTS393	301594
Switzerland	Czechoslovakia	16 Feb 27	General Trade	64LTS7	301501
Switzerland	Czechoslovakia	20 Sep 29	Dispute Settlement	102LTS123	302357
Switzerland	Denmark	30 May 24	General Economic	25LTS415	300632
Switzerland	Denmark	06 Jun 24	Dispute Settlement	34LTS175	300873
Switzerland	Denmark	25 Aug 26	General Amity	69LTS313	301613
Switzerland	Estonia	14 Oct 25	General Economic	49LTS421	301195
Switzerland	Estonia	29 Oct 26	Admin Cooperation	63LTS23	301477
Switzerland	Estonia	12 Nov 38	General Trade	194LTS17	304503
Switzerland	Ethiopia	24 May 33	General Amity	153LTS63	303508
Switzerland	Finland	24 Jun 27	Mostfavored Nation	68LTS103	301574
Switzerland	Finland	14 Oct 27	Visas	71LTS205	301663
Switzerland	Finland	16 Nov 27	Dispute Settlement	77LTS93	301765
Switzerland	Finland	22 May 29	Visas	91LTS305	302069
Switzerland	Finland	22 May 29	Visas	91LTS311	302070
Switzerland	Finland	07 May 36	Consul/Citizenship	166LTS35	303827
Switzerland	France	11 Jun 14	General Amity	12LTS361	300329
Switzerland	France	09 Dec 19	Air Transport	1LTS29	300004
Switzerland	France	24 Jan 22	Telecommunications	12LTS371	300331
Switzerland	France	20 Mar 22	Customs	12LTS377	300332
Switzerland	France	06 Apr 25	Dispute Settlement	147LTS89	303393
Switzerland	France	27 Aug 26	Admin Cooperation	71LTS63	301654
Switzerland	France	27 Aug 26	Admin Cooperation	59LTS231	301392
Switzerland	France	21 Jan 28	General Trade	72LTS275	301698
Switzerland	France	08 Jul 29	General Economic	114LTS189	302664
Switzerland	France	09 Sep 31	Non-ILO Labor	142LTS205	303293
Switzerland	France	09 Jun 33	Other HEW	181LTS275	304194
Switzerland	France	04 Oct 36	Admin Cooperation	195LTS287	304550
Switzerland	France	29 Jan 37	Land Transport	195LTS291	304551
Switzerland	France	13 Oct 37	Taxation	194LTS191	304522
Switzerland	France	03 Dec 37	Admin Cooperation	185LTS265	304292
Switzerland	France	31 Jan 38	Territory Boundary	195LTS313	304553
Switzerland	Germany	15 Mar 20	Customs	12LTS19	300303
Switzerland	Germany	09 Jul 20	Commodity Trade	12LTS25	300304
Switzerland	Germany	14 Sep 20	Air Transport	2LTS331	300087
Switzerland	Germany	06 Dec 20	Finance	2LTS343	300088
Switzerland	Germany	29 Oct 21	Finance	13LTS193	300351
Switzerland	Germany	03 Dec 21	Dispute Settlement	12LTS271	300320
Switzerland	Germany	24 Mar 23	Taxation	27LTS41	300666
Switzerland	Germany	25 Mar 23	Finance	18LTS273	300470
Switzerland	Germany	17 Nov 24	General Trade	41LTS473	301026
Switzerland	Germany	12 Oct 25	Extradition	53LTS241	301260
Switzerland	Germany	06 Nov 25	Customs	53LTS283	301262
Switzerland	Germany	14 Jul 26	General Trade	59LTS87	301391
Switzerland	Germany	04 Feb 28	Non-ILO Labor	79LTS241	301814
Switzerland	Germany	23 Apr 29	General Trade	96LTS257	302206
Switzerland	Germany	28 May 29	Territory Boundary	104LTS19	302375
Switzerland	Germany	02 Nov 29	Admin Cooperation	109LTS273	302544
Switzerland	Germany	15 Jul 31	Taxation	144LTS389	303341
Switzerland	Germany	21 Sep 38	Territory Boundary	196LTS365	304595
Switzerland	Greece	21 Sep 25	Dispute Settlement	87LTS187	301969
Switzerland	Greece	29 Nov 26	General Trade	63LTS27	301478
Switzerland	Greece	01 Dec 27	Admin Cooperation	84LTS271	301907
Switzerland	Greece	30 Mar 38	Admin Cooperation	185LTS245	304288
Switzerland	Hungary	22 Mar 21	General Economic	7LTS235	300189
Switzerland	Hungary	18 Jun 24	Dispute Settlement	34LTS387	300887
Switzerland	Hungary	18 Jun 35	Air Transport	174LTS7	304033

PARTY ONE	PARTY TWO	DATE	TOPIC	CITATION	NUMBER
Switzerland	Irish Free State	03 Nov 30	Non-ILO Labor	132LTS159	303035
Switzerland	Italy	12 Nov 18	Land Transport	25LTS369	300625
Switzerland	Italy	24 Sep 21	General Transport	12LTS367	300330
Switzerland	Italy	27 Jan 23	General Trade	25LTS21	300603
Switzerland	Italy	22 Oct 23	Water Transport	65LTS301	301521
Switzerland	Italy	20 Sep 24	Admin Cooperation	33LTS91	300834
Switzerland	Italy	03 Jan 33	Admin Cooperation	142LTS17	303276
Switzerland	Italy	20 Sep 34	Dispute Settlement	158LTS17	303620
Switzerland	Japan	26 Dec 24	Dispute Settlement	43LTS393	301072
Switzerland	Latvia	04 Dec 24	General Trade	34LTS405	300889
Switzerland	Liechtenstein	10 Nov 20	Postal Service	2LTS305	300084
Switzerland	Liechtenstein	29 Mar 23	Customs	21LTS231	300545
Switzerland	Luxembourg	16 Sep 29	Dispute Settlement	107LTS23	302465
Switzerland	Multilateral	09 Sep 86*	Patents/Copyrights	123LTS233	302816
Switzerland	Multilateral	18 Mar 04	Humanitarian	1LTS83	300011
Switzerland	Multilateral	13 Nov 08	General Ad Hoc	1LTS217	300015
Switzerland	Multilateral	12 Jan 12	Sanitation	4LTS281	300112
Switzerland	Multilateral	23 Jan 12	Sanitation	8LTS187	300222
Switzerland	Multilateral	05 Jun 12	Telecommunications	1LTS135	300013
Switzerland	Multilateral	20 Mar 14	Patents/Copyrights	1LTS243	300016
Switzerland	Multilateral	25 Mar 20	Finance	1LTS45	300006
Switzerland	Multilateral	21 Jun 20	Health/Educ/Welfare	8LTS65	300207
Switzerland	Multilateral	30 Jun 20	Patents/Copyrights	1LTS59	300008
Switzerland	Multilateral	16 Dec 20	General IGO	6LTS379	300170
Switzerland	Multilateral	20 Apr 21	Land Transport	7LTS11	300171
Switzerland	Multilateral	20 Apr 21	Water Transport	7LTS73	300174
Switzerland	Multilateral	05 Aug 21	Admin Cooperation	27LTS349	300695
Switzerland	Multilateral	05 Oct 21	IGO Establishment	51LTS361	301241
Switzerland	Multilateral	05 Oct 21	Admin Cooperation	29LTS73	300734
Switzerland	Multilateral	05 Oct 21	Admin Cooperation	29LTS79	300735
Switzerland	Multilateral	05 Oct 21	Admin Cooperation	29LTS67	300733
Switzerland	Multilateral	06 Oct 21	General Economic	17LTS45	300427
Switzerland	Multilateral	31 Mar 22	Humanitarian	9LTS415	300269
Switzerland	Multilateral	10 May 22	Water Transport	26LTS265	300652
Switzerland	Multilateral	05 Jul 22	Reparations	13LTS237	300355
Switzerland	Multilateral	14 Dec 22	Water Transport	36LTS457	300943
Switzerland	Multilateral	05 Feb 23	Telecommunications	28LTS409	300720
Switzerland	Multilateral	24 Sep 23	Dispute Settlement	27LTS157	300678
Switzerland	Multilateral	03 Nov 23	Customs	30LTS371	300775
Switzerland	Multilateral	28 Nov 23	Admin Cooperation	51LTS209	301228
Switzerland	Multilateral	28 Nov 23	Admin Cooperation	51LTS215	301229
Switzerland	Multilateral	28 Nov 23	Admin Cooperation	51LTS221	301230
Switzerland	Multilateral	09 Dec 23	Water Transport	58LTS284	301379
Switzerland	Multilateral	09 Dec 23	Land Transport	47LTS55	301129
Switzerland	Multilateral	25 Jan 24	Sanitation	57LTS135	301360
Switzerland	Multilateral	07 Feb 24	Water Transport	25LTS265	300614
Switzerland	Multilateral	31 Mar 24	Sanitation	27LTS211	300685
Switzerland	Multilateral	04 Jul 24	Admin Cooperation	51LTS227	301231
Switzerland	Multilateral	25 Aug 24	Water Transport	120LTS155	302764
Switzerland	Multilateral	28 Aug 24	Postal Service	40LTS249	301003
Switzerland	Multilateral	28 Aug 24	Postal Service	40LTS19	301002
Switzerland	Multilateral	28 Aug 24	Postal Service	40LTS307	301004
Switzerland	Multilateral	28 Aug 24	Postal Service	41LTS97	301008
Switzerland	Multilateral	28 Aug 24	Postal Service	40LTS437	301005
Switzerland	Multilateral	28 Aug 24	Postal Service	41LTS55	301007
Switzerland	Multilateral	23 Oct 24	Land Transport	78LTS17	301779
Switzerland	Multilateral	23 Oct 24	General Transport	77LTS367	301778
Switzerland	Multilateral	19 Feb 25	Admin Cooperation	81LTS317	301845
Switzerland	Multilateral	00 Apr 25	Water Transport	37LTS21	300945
Switzerland	Multilateral	23 Apr 25	Water Transport	37LTS9	300944
Switzerland	Multilateral	17 Jun 25	Peace/Disarmament	94LTS65	302138
Switzerland	Multilateral	29 Oct 25	Telecommunications	57LTS201	301365
Switzerland	Multilateral	06 Nov 25	Other Economic	74LTS341	301746
Switzerland	Multilateral	06 Nov 25	Patents/Copyrights	74LTS327	301745
Switzerland	Multilateral	06 Nov 25	Other Economic	74LTS319	301744

PARTY ONE	PARTY TWO	DATE	TOPIC	CITATION	NUMBER
Switzerland	Multilateral	06 Nov 25	Patents/Copyrights	74LTS289	301743
Switzerland	Multilateral	27 Nov 25	Water Transport	67LTS63	301539
Switzerland	Multilateral	00 Apr 26	Water Transport	57LTS437	301366
Switzerland	Multilateral	24 Apr 26	Land Transport	108LTS123	302505
Switzerland	Multilateral	24 Apr 26	Land Transport	97LTS83	302220
Switzerland	Multilateral	12 May 26	Refugees	89LTS47	302004
Switzerland	Multilateral	21 Jun 26	Sanitation	78LTS229	301793
Switzerland	Multilateral	25 Sep 26	ILO Labor	60LTS253	301414
Switzerland	Multilateral	19 Feb 27	Telecommunications	68LTS139	301577
Switzerland	Multilateral	12 Jul 27	Direct Aid	135LTS247	303115
Switzerland	Multilateral	10 Sep 27	Postal Service	75LTS39	301750
Switzerland	Multilateral	10 Sep 27	Postal Service	75LTS7	301749
Switzerland	Multilateral	08 Nov 27	General Trade	97LTS391	302238
Switzerland	Multilateral	11 Nov 27	Telecommunications	78LTS153	301786
Switzerland	Multilateral	25 Nov 27	Telecommunications	84LTS97	301905
Switzerland	Multilateral	08 Mar 28	Telecommunications	80LTS241	301829
Switzerland	Multilateral	01 May 28	Telecommunications	132LTS415	303050
Switzerland	Multilateral	30 Jun 28	Refugees	89LTS63	302006
Switzerland	Multilateral	30 Jun 28	Refugees	89LTS53	302005
Switzerland	Multilateral	11 Jul 28	Commodity Trade	95LTS373	302185
Switzerland	Multilateral	11 Jul 28	Commodity Trade	95LTS357	302184
Switzerland	Multilateral	27 Aug 28	General Military	94LTS57	302137
Switzerland	Multilateral	22 Nov 28	Culture	111LTS343	302598
Switzerland	Multilateral	14 Dec 28	General Economic	110LTS171	302560
Switzerland	Multilateral	16 Apr 29	Specific Resources	126LTS305	302891
Switzerland	Multilateral	20 Apr 29	Admin Cooperation	112LTS371	302623
Switzerland	Multilateral	14 Jun 29	Visas	94LTS275	302148
Switzerland	Multilateral	28 Jun 29	Postal Service	103LTS71	302370
Switzerland	Multilateral	28 Jun 29	Postal Service	102LTS245	302368
Switzerland	Multilateral	28 Jun 29	Postal Service	103LTS321	302372
Switzerland	Multilateral	28 Jun 29	Postal Service	103LTS249	302371
Switzerland	Multilateral	28 Jun 29	Postal Service	103LTS377	302373
Switzerland	Multilateral	28 Jun 29	Postal Service	103LTS429	302374
Switzerland	Multilateral	28 Jun 29	Postal Service	103LTS5	302369
Switzerland	Multilateral	27 Jul 29	Other Military	118LTS303	302733
Switzerland	Multilateral	27 Jul 29	Other Military	118LTS343	302734
Switzerland	Multilateral	20 Aug 29	Sanitation	98LTS125	302243
Switzerland	Multilateral	14 Sep 29	UN Charter	165LTS353	303822
Switzerland	Multilateral	08 Oct 29	Telecommunications	98LTS409	302260
Switzerland	Multilateral	12 Oct 29	General Transport	137LTS11	303145
Switzerland	Multilateral	18 Nov 29	Telecommunications	99LTS415	302287
Switzerland	Multilateral	18 Dec 29	Admin Cooperation	104LTS27	302376
Switzerland	Multilateral	20 Jan 30	Other Economic	104LTS441	302398
Switzerland	Multilateral	12 Apr 30	Admin Cooperation	179LTS89	304137
Switzerland	Multilateral	07 Jun 30	Finance	143LTS337	303315
Switzerland	Multilateral	07 Jun 30	Finance	143LTS317	303314
Switzerland	Multilateral	07 Jun 30	Finance	143LTS257	303313
Switzerland	Multilateral	19 Mar 31	Finance	143LTS355	303316
Switzerland	Multilateral	19 Mar 31	Finance	143LTS407	303317
Switzerland	Multilateral	19 Mar 31	Admin Cooperation	143LTS7	303301
Switzerland	Multilateral	27 Mar 31	ICJ Option Clause	167LTS341	303877
Switzerland	Multilateral	28 Mar 31	Customs	119LTS47	302739
Switzerland	Multilateral	30 Mar 31	Land Transport	150LTS247	303459
Switzerland	Multilateral	30 Mar 31	Taxation	138LTS149	303185
Switzerland	Multilateral	13 Jul 31	Other HEW	139LTS301	303219
Switzerland	Multilateral	21 Aug 31	Other Ad Hoc	185LTS45	304273
Switzerland	Multilateral	21 Aug 31	Other Economic	127LTS95	302910
Switzerland	Multilateral	24 Sep 31	Specific Resources	155LTS349	303586
Switzerland	Multilateral	11 Dec 31	Commodity Trade	170LTS251	303941
Switzerland	Multilateral	02 Sep 32	Land Transport	154LTS123	303543
Switzerland	Multilateral	09 Dec 32	Telecommunications	151LTS5	303479
Switzerland	Multilateral	11 Mar 33	Water Transport	135LTS301	303119
Switzerland	Multilateral	29 May 33	Admin Cooperation	192LTS289	304479
Switzerland	Multilateral	19 Jun 33	Gen Communications	154LTS133	303544
Switzerland	Multilateral	25 Aug 33	Commodity Trade	141LTS71	303262

PARTY ONE	PARTY TWO	DATE	TOPIC	CITATION	NUMBER
Switzerland	Multilateral	11 Oct 33	Education	155LTS331	303585
Switzerland	Multilateral	11 Oct 33	Consul/Citizenship	150LTS431	303476
Switzerland	Multilateral	23 Nov 33	Land Transport	192LTS389	304484
Switzerland	Multilateral	23 Nov 33	Land Transport	192LTS327	304483
Switzerland	Multilateral	20 Mar 34	Postal Service	175LTS363	304052
Switzerland	Multilateral	20 Mar 34	Postal Service	175LTS73	304050
Switzerland	Multilateral	20 Mar 34	Postal Service	175LTS269	304051
Switzerland	Multilateral	20 Mar 34	Finance	176LTS9	304053
Switzerland	Multilateral	20 Mar 34	Postal Service	176LTS55	304054
Switzerland	Multilateral	20 Mar 34	Postal Service	175LTS5	304049
Switzerland	Multilateral	20 Mar 34	Postal Service	174LTS171	304048
Switzerland	Multilateral	26 Apr 34	Admin Cooperation	164LTS63	303789
Switzerland	Multilateral	02 Jun 34	Patents/Copyrights	205LTS179	304834
Switzerland	Multilateral	02 Jun 34	Patents/Copyrights	192LTS17	304459
Switzerland	Multilateral	02 Jun 34	General Trade	192LTS9	304458
Switzerland	Multilateral	20 Feb 35	Sanitation	193LTS59	304487
Switzerland	Multilateral	20 Feb 35	Sanitation	193LTS37	304486
Switzerland	Multilateral	20 Feb 35	Sanitation	186LTS173	304310
Switzerland	Multilateral	26 Jun 36	Other HEW	198LTS299	304648
Switzerland	Multilateral	04 Jul 36	Refugees	171LTS75	303952
Switzerland	Multilateral	30 Jul 36	IGO Status/Immunit	197LTS31	304602
Switzerland	Multilateral	23 Sep 36	Gen Communications	186LTS301	304319
Switzerland	Multilateral	06 Nov 36	General Military	173LTS353	304025
Switzerland	Multilateral	10 Feb 37	General Transport	189LTS313	304391
Switzerland	Multilateral	31 Mar 37	Commodity Trade	189LTS359	304394
Switzerland	Multilateral	17 May 38	Visas	192LTS319	304481
Switzerland	Multilateral	12 Sep 38	Culture	198LTS111	304630
Switzerland	Multilateral	31 Oct 38	Sanitation	198LTS205	304642
Switzerland	Multilateral	03 Dec 38	Education	200LTS249	304694
Switzerland	Multilateral	23 May 39	Postal Service	202LTS159	304742
Switzerland	Multilateral	02 Jun 42	Patents/Copyrights	205LTS163	304833
Switzerland	Netherlands	18 May 25	Air Transport	54LTS365	301299
Switzerland	Netherlands	12 Dec 25	Dispute Settlement	63LTS289	301496
Switzerland	Netherlands	27 Aug 28	Admin Cooperation	82LTS153	301866
Switzerland	Netherlands	15 Oct 36	Air Transport	177LTS101	304084
Switzerland	Netherlands	27 Jan 37	Non-ILO Labor	186LTS433	304327
Switzerland	Netherlands	01 Jul 39	Customs	198LTS195	304640
Switzerland	New Zealand	05 May 38	General Trade	189LTS167	304384
Switzerland	Norway	15 Apr 24	General Economic	27LTS168	300679
Switzerland	Norway	21 Aug 25	Dispute Settlement	51LTS89	301224
Switzerland	Palestine	15 May 29	Postal Service	95LTS395	302186
Switzerland	Persia	28 Aug 28	Privil/Immunities	107LTS397	302496
Switzerland	Persia	25 Apr 34	General Amity	159LTS235	303666
Switzerland	Persia	25 Apr 34	Consul/Citizenship	160LTS173	303691
Switzerland	Poland	26 Jun 22	General Economic	12LTS305	300322
Switzerland	Poland	07 Mar 25	Dispute Settlement	50LTS261	301209
Switzerland	Poland	03 Feb 34	General Trade	160LTS83	303685
Switzerland	Poland	19 Nov 37	Extradition	195LTS297	304552
Switzerland	Portugal	17 Oct 28	Dispute Settlement	96LTS287	302207
Switzerland	Romania	03 Feb 26	Dispute Settlement	55LTS91	301306
Switzerland	Romania	25 Aug 30	Mostfavored Nation	118LTS9	302708
Switzerland	Romania	16 Jan 33	General Trade	153LTS359	303532
Switzerland	Romania	19 Jul 38	Consul/Citizenship	152LTS89	303486
Switzerland	Romania	02 Nov 39	Finance	200LTS289	304699
Switzerland	Saar	15 Aug 28	Air Transport	81LTS373	301847
Switzerland	Siam	28 May 31	General Trade	125LTS357	302864
Switzerland	Siam	04 Nov 37	General Amity	190LTS137	304412
Switzerland	Spain	20 Apr 26	Dispute Settlement	60LTS23	301403
Switzerland	Spain	04 Aug 26	Admin Cooperation	65LTS39	301518
Switzerland	Spain	30 Oct 35	Patents/Copyrights	166LTS157	303837
Switzerland	Sweden	29 Nov 21	Humanitarian	7LTS313	300198
Switzerland	Sweden	01 Jan 22	Visas	9LTS11	300239
Switzerland	Sweden	20 Mar 24	General Trade	25LTS243	300612
Switzerland	Sweden	02 Jun 24	Admin Cooperation	33LTS199	300844
Switzerland	Sweden	15 Jan 36	Admin Cooperation	169LTS347	303923
Switzerland	Sweden	25 Jul 36	Non-ILO Labor	171LTS177	303959
Switzerland	Turkey	19 Sep 25	General Amity	61LTS395	301449
Switzerland	Turkey	04 May 27	General Trade	67LTS141	301544
Switzerland	Turkey	07 Aug 27	Admin Cooperation	73LTS51	301706
Switzerland	Turkey	09 Dec 28	Dispute Settlement	159LTS219	303664
Switzerland	Turkey	13 Dec 30	Privil/Immunities	129LTS331	302968
Switzerland	Turkey	13 Dec 30	General Trade	129LTS267	302964
Switzerland	Turkey	01 Jun 33	Admin Cooperation	159LTS187	303662
Switzerland	Turkey	01 Jun 33	Dispute Settlement	159LTS229	303665
Switzerland	Turkey	01 Jun 33	Extradition	159LTS329	303676
Switzerland	UK Great Britain	06 Nov 19	Air Transport	1LTS37	300005
Switzerland	UK Great Britain	28 Feb 20	Postal Service	6LTS9	300145
Switzerland	UK Great Britain	02 Jul 20	Extradition	1LTS53	300007
Switzerland	UK Great Britain	26 Apr 24	General Economic	27LTS189	300682
Switzerland	UK Great Britain	09 Nov 29	Non-ILO Labor	100LTS21	302291
Switzerland	UK Great Britain	10 Dec 29	Postal Service	99LTS53	302267
Switzerland	UK Great Britain	17 Oct 31	Taxation	131LTS245	303015
Switzerland	UK Great Britain	19 Dec 34	Extradition	163LTS103	303763
Switzerland	UK Great Britain	25 May 35	Postal Service	163LTS239	303769
Switzerland	UK Great Britain	03 Dec 37	Admin Cooperation	194LTS223	304523
Switzerland	UK Great Britain	26 Jul 38	Customs	191LTS307	304452
Switzerland	United Arab Rep	07 Jun 34	General Amity	159LTS137	303656
Switzerland	Uruguay	26 Nov 26	Extradition	63LTS207	301491
Switzerland	USA (United States)	16 Feb 31	Dispute Settlement	129LTS465	302978
Switzerland	USA (United States)	10 Jan 35	Extradition	159LTS243	303667
Switzerland	USA (United States)	09 Jan 36	General Trade	171LTS231	303962
Switzerland	USA (United States)	11 Nov 37	Milit Servic/Citiz	193LTS183	304494
Switzerland	USA (United States)	31 Jan 40	Extradition	204LTS175	304797
Switzerland	Yugoslavia	27 Apr 32	Other Economic	131LTS285	303019
Switzerland	Yugoslavia	27 Jun 38	General Trade	196LTS27	304568
Syria	Multilateral	09 Sep 86*	Patents/Copyrights	123LTS233	302816
Syria	Multilateral	03 Nov 23	Customs	30LTS371	300775
Syria	Multilateral	09 Jun 25	Customs	49LTS9	301174
Syria	Multilateral	29 Oct 25	Telecommunications	57LTS201	301365
Syria	Multilateral	06 Nov 25	Other Economic	74LTS341	301746
Syria	Multilateral	06 Nov 25	Other Economic	74LTS319	301744
Syria	Multilateral	06 Nov 25	Patents/Copyrights	74LTS289	301743
Syria	Multilateral	20 May 26	Health/Educ/Welfare	109LTS121	302532
Syria	Multilateral	21 Jun 26	Sanitation	78LTS229	301793
Syria	Multilateral	25 Sep 26	ILO Labor	60LTS253	301414
Syria	Multilateral	25 Nov 27	Telecommunications	84LTS97	301905
Syria	Multilateral	09 Dec 32	Telecommunications	151LTS5	303479
Syria	Multilateral	12 Apr 33	Sanitation	161LTS65	303706
Syria	Multilateral	19 Jun 33	Gen Communications	154LTS133	303544
Syria	Multilateral	02 Jun 34	Patents/Copyrights	192LTS17	304459
Syria	Multilateral	02 Jun 34	General Trade	192LTS9	304458
Tanganyika	Belgian Colonies	10 Jul 22	Telecommunications	148LTS71	303404
Tanganyika	Multilateral	18 Mar 04	Humanitarian	1LTS83	300011
Tanganyika	Multilateral	05 Jun 12	Telecommunications	1LTS135	300013
Tanganyika	Multilateral	30 Jun 20	Patents/Copyrights	1LTS59	300008
Tanganyika	Multilateral	31 Mar 22	Humanitarian	9LTS415	300269
Tanganyika	Multilateral	25 Aug 24	Water Transport	120LTS155	302764
Tanganyika	Multilateral	26 Sep 27	Dispute Settlement	92LTS301	302096
Tanganyika	Multilateral	25 Nov 27	Telecommunications	84LTS97	301905
Tanganyika	Multilateral	28 Jun 29	Postal Service	103LTS5	302369
Tanganyika	Multilateral	30 Mar 31	Taxation	138LTS149	303185
Tanganyika	Multilateral	08 Nov 33	Specific Resources	172LTS241	303995
Tanganyika	Multilateral	30 Oct 35	Postal Service	189LTS85	304376
Tanganyika	Multilateral	30 Oct 35	Telecommunications	189LTS51	304375
Tanganyika	Multilateral	23 Sep 36	Gen Communications	186LTS301	304319
Tanganyika	Multilateral	02 Jan 39	Postal Service	196LTS235	304587
Tanganyika	United Arab Rep	25 Feb 25	Postal Service	36LTS409	300938
Tangier	Multilateral	24 Apr 26	Land Transport	108LTS123	302505
Tangier	Multilateral	24 Apr 26	Land Transport	97LTS83	302220
Tangier	Multilateral	02 Jun 34	Patents/Copyrights	205LTS179	304834

PARTY ONE	PARTY TWO	DATE	TOPIC	CITATION	NUMBER
Tangier	Multilateral	02 Jun 42	Patents/Copyrights	205LTS163	304833
Tanzania	Multilateral	30 Oct 35	Postal Service	189LTS85	304376
Tanzania	Multilateral	30 Oct 35	Telecommunications	189LTS51	304375
Thailand	Japan	30 Nov 39	Air Transport	200LTS197	304691
Thailand	Japan	12 Jun 40	General Amity	204LTS131	304791
Thailand	Multilateral	16 Dec 20	General IGO	6LTS379	300170
Thailand	Multilateral	20 Apr 29	Admin Cooperation	112LTS371	302623
Thailand	UK Great Britain	12 Jun 40	General Amity	203LTS421	304782
Thailand	UK Great Britain	10 Dec 40	Territory Boundary	203LTS433	304783
Togo	Gold Coast	07 Oct 33	Telecommunications	144LTS95	303321
Togo	Multilateral	24 Apr 26	Land Transport	97LTS83	302220
Togo	Multilateral	24 Apr 26	Land Transport	108LTS123	302505
Togo	Multilateral	25 Sep 26	ILO Labor	60LTS253	301414
Tonga	Multilateral	05 Jun 12	Telecommunications	1LTS135	300013
Tonga	Multilateral	25 Aug 24	Water Transport	120LTS155	302764
Tonga	Multilateral	25 Nov 27	Telecommunications	84LTS97	301905
Tonga	Multilateral	28 Jun 29	Postal Service	102LTS245	302368
Tonga	Multilateral	12 Oct 29	General Transport	137LTS11	303145
Tonga	Multilateral	12 Apr 33	Sanitation	161LTS65	303706
Tonga	Multilateral	20 Mar 34	Postal Service	175LTS5	304049
Tonga	Multilateral	23 Sep 36	Gen Communications	186LTS301	304319
Transjordan	Multilateral	23 Jan 12	Sanitation	8LTS187	300222
Transjordan	Multilateral	20 May 26	Health/Educ/Welfare	109LTS121	302532
Transjordan	Multilateral	12 Oct 29	General Transport	137LTS11	303145
Transjordan	Multilateral	30 Mar 31	Taxation	138LTS149	303185
Transjordan	Multilateral	23 Sep 36	Gen Communications	186LTS301	304319
Trinidad	Multilateral	30 Jun 20	Patents/Copyrights	1LTS59	300008
Trinidad	Multilateral	31 Mar 22	Humanitarian	9LTS415	300269
Trinidad	Multilateral	01 Dec 24	Sanitation	78LTS351	301794
Trinidad	Multilateral	30 Mar 31	Taxation	138LTS149	303185
Trinidad/Tobago	Curacao	23 Apr 42	Postal Service	204LTS335	304812
Trinidad/Tobago	Multilateral	31 Mar 22	Humanitarian	9LTS415	300269
Trinidad/Tobago	Multilateral	25 Aug 24	Water Transport	120LTS155	302764
Trinidad/Tobago	Multilateral	06 Nov 25	Other Economic	74LTS319	301744
Trinidad/Tobago	Multilateral	06 Nov 25	Patents/Copyrights	74LTS289	301743
Trinidad/Tobago	Multilateral	25 Nov 27	Telecommunications	84LTS97	301905
Trinidad/Tobago	Multilateral	28 Oct 33	Refugees	159LTS199	303663
Trinidad/Tobago	Multilateral	23 Sep 36	Gen Communications	186LTS301	304319
Trinidad/Tobago	Multilateral	10 Feb 38	Refugees	192LTS59	304461
Tripoli	Multilateral	05 Jun 12	Telecommunications	1LTS135	300013
Tripoli	Multilateral	21 Jun 20	Health/Educ/Welfare	8LTS65	300207
Tripoli	Multilateral	29 Oct 25	Telecommunications	57LTS201	301365
Tripoli	Multilateral	25 Nov 27	Telecommunications	84LTS97	301905
Tripoli	Multilateral	16 Apr 29	Specific Resources	126LTS305	302891
Tripoli	Multilateral	09 Dec 32	Telecommunications	151LTS5	303479
Tunis	Multilateral	28 Aug 24	Postal Service	41LTS55	301007
Tunis	Multilateral	28 Aug 24	Postal Service	41LTS97	301008
Tunisia	Multilateral	09 Sep 86*	Patents/Copyrights	123LTS233	302816
Tunisia	Multilateral	18 Mar 04	Humanitarian	1LTS83	300011
Tunisia	Multilateral	13 Nov 08	General Ad Hoc	1LTS217	300015
Tunisia	Multilateral	20 Mar 14	Patents/Copyrights	1LTS243	300016
Tunisia	Multilateral	21 Jun 20	Health/Educ/Welfare	8LTS65	300207
Tunisia	Multilateral	30 Jun 20	Patents/Copyrights	1LTS59	300008
Tunisia	Multilateral	31 Oct 20	Sanitation	164LTS85	303790
Tunisia	Multilateral	25 Jan 24	Sanitation	57LTS135	301360
Tunisia	Multilateral	28 Aug 24	Postal Service	40LTS19	301002
Tunisia	Multilateral	28 Aug 24	Postal Service	40LTS307	301004
Tunisia	Multilateral	28 Aug 24	Postal Service	40LTS437	301005
Tunisia	Multilateral	28 Aug 24	Postal Service	40LTS249	301003
Tunisia	Multilateral	28 Aug 24	Postal Service	41LTS9	301006
Tunisia	Multilateral	29 Nov 24	General IGO	80LTS293	301835
Tunisia	Multilateral	01 Dec 24	Sanitation	78LTS351	301794
Tunisia	Multilateral	29 Oct 25	Telecommunications	57LTS201	301365
Tunisia	Multilateral	06 Nov 25	Other Economic	74LTS319	301744
Tunisia	Multilateral	06 Nov 25	Patents/Copyrights	74LTS327	301745

PARTY ONE	PARTY TWO	DATE	TOPIC	CITATION	NUMBER
Tunisia	Multilateral	06 Nov 25	Patents/Copyrights	74LTS289	301743
Tunisia	Multilateral	06 Nov 25	Other Economic	74LTS341	301746
Tunisia	Multilateral	24 Apr 26	Land Transport	108LTS123	302505
Tunisia	Multilateral	24 Apr 26	Land Transport	97LTS83	302220
Tunisia	Multilateral	21 Jun 26	Sanitation	78LTS229	301793
Tunisia	Multilateral	29 Oct 27	Scientific Project	127LTS27	302903
Tunisia	Multilateral	25 Nov 27	Telecommunications	84LTS97	301905
Tunisia	Multilateral	22 Nov 28	Culture	111LTS343	302598
Tunisia	Multilateral	16 Apr 29	Specific Resources	126LTS305	302891
Tunisia	Multilateral	28 Jun 29	Postal Service	103LTS429	302374
Tunisia	Multilateral	28 Jun 29	Postal Service	102LTS245	302368
Tunisia	Multilateral	28 Jun 29	Postal Service	103LTS5	302369
Tunisia	Multilateral	28 Jun 29	Postal Service	103LTS377	302373
Tunisia	Multilateral	28 Jun 29	Postal Service	103LTS71	302370
Tunisia	Multilateral	28 Jun 29	Postal Service	103LTS321	302372
Tunisia	Multilateral	28 Jun 29	Postal Service	103LTS249	302371
Tunisia	Multilateral	01 Aug 30	Health/Educ/Welfare	128LTS9	302932
Tunisia	Multilateral	23 Oct 30	Water Transport	125LTS95	302849
Tunisia	Multilateral	23 Oct 30	Water Transport	112LTS21	302603
Tunisia	Multilateral	09 Dec 32	Telecommunications	151LTS5	303479
Tunisia	Multilateral	12 Apr 33	Sanitation	161LTS65	303706
Tunisia	Multilateral	19 Jun 33	Gen Communications	154LTS133	303544
Tunisia	Multilateral	20 Mar 34	Postal Service	176LTS55	304054
Tunisia	Multilateral	20 Mar 34	Postal Service	174LTS171	304048
Tunisia	Multilateral	20 Mar 34	Postal Service	175LTS269	304051
Tunisia	Multilateral	20 Mar 34	Postal Service	175LTS363	304052
Tunisia	Multilateral	20 Mar 34	Postal Service	175LTS5	304049
Tunisia	Multilateral	20 Mar 34	Finance	176LTS9	304053
Tunisia	Multilateral	20 Mar 34	Postal Service	175LTS73	304050
Tunisia	Multilateral	26 Apr 34	Admin Cooperation	164LTS63	303789
Tunisia	Multilateral	02 Jun 34	Patents/Copyrights	192LTS17	304459
Tunisia	Multilateral	02 Jun 34	Patents/Copyrights	205LTS179	304834
Tunisia	Multilateral	02 Jun 34	General Trade	192LTS9	304458
Tunisia	Multilateral	31 Mar 37	Commodity Trade	189LTS359	304394
Tunisia	Multilateral	23 May 39	Postal Service	202LTS159	304742
Tunisia	Multilateral	02 Jun 42	Patents/Copyrights	205LTS163	304833
Turkey		24 Jul 23	Admin Cooperation	36LTS161	300916
Turkey		24 Jul 23	Sanitation	36LTS157	300915
Turkey	Austria	28 Jan 24	General Trade	32LTS313	300823
Turkey	Austria	28 Jan 24	Consul/Citizenship	32LTS303	300822
Turkey	Austria	28 Jan 24	General Amity	32LTS297	300821
Turkey	Austria	14 Sep 32	Admin Cooperation	135LTS275	303116
Turkey	Bel-Lux Econ Union	28 Aug 27	General Trade	82LTS77	301862
Turkey	Bel-Lux Econ Union	24 May 34	Mostfavored Nation	150LTS269	303460
Turkey	Bel-Lux Econ Union	31 May 34	General Trade	150LTS289	303462
Turkey	Bel-Lux Econ Union	31 May 34	Claims and Debts	150LTS277	303461
Turkey	Belgium	27 May 30	General Economic	111LTS49	302580
Turkey	Belgium	09 Feb 38	Extradition	198LTS181	304639
Turkey	Bulgaria	27 Dec 24	Admin Cooperation	54LTS135	301281
Turkey	Bulgaria	18 Oct 25	General Amity	54LTS125	301280
Turkey	Bulgaria	12 Feb 28	General Trade	81LTS383	301848
Turkey	Bulgaria	06 Mar 29	Dispute Settlement	114LTS399	302668
Turkey	Bulgaria	23 Dec 29	Extradition	122LTS17	302796
Turkey	Bulgaria	21 Dec 33	General Trade	148LTS9	303401
Turkey	Chile	30 Jan 26	General Amity	59LTS249	301395
Turkey	China	04 Apr 34	Consul/Citizenship	153LTS161	303515
Turkey	Czechoslovakia	11 Oct 24	General Amity	38LTS317	300987
Turkey	Czechoslovakia	31 May 27	Admin Cooperation	75LTS79	301753
Turkey	Czechoslovakia	31 May 27	General Trade	71LTS335	301674
Turkey	Czechoslovakia	22 Aug 30	Admin Cooperation	138LTS311	303195
Turkey	Czechoslovakia	22 Aug 30	Extradition	138LTS375	303196
Turkey	Czechoslovakia	17 Mar 31	Dispute Settlement	133LTS151	303065
Turkey	Denmark	26 Jan 25	General Amity	36LTS317	300931
Turkey	Denmark	22 Mar 26	General Economic	48LTS231	301164
Turkey	Denmark	19 Sep 26	General Economic	56LTS259	301333

PARTY ONE	PARTY TWO	DATE	TOPIC	CITATION	NUMBER
Turkey	Denmark	24 Sep 27	Mostfavored Nation	61LTS287	301439
Turkey	Denmark	31 May 30	General Economic	119LTS165	302744
Turkey	Denmark	08 Mar 32	Dispute Settlement	143LTS223	303310
Turkey	Estonia	01 Dec 24	General Amity	70LTS77	301624
Turkey	Estonia	12 Mar 28	General Trade	86LTS453	301957
Turkey	Estonia	14 Sep 29	General Trade	97LTS365	302234
Turkey	Estonia	16 Sep 29	General Economic	117LTS377	302704
Turkey	Estonia	13 Mar 35	Finance	159LTS87	303650
Turkey	Estonia	06 Jun 37	Finance	179LTS159	304143
Turkey	Estonia	06 Jun 37	General Trade	179LTS151	304142
Turkey	Finland	09 Dec 24	General Amity	59LTS287	301398
Turkey	Finland	02 Jun 26	General Trade	70LTS329	301644
Turkey	Finland	19 Oct 26	General Economic	58LTS393	301384
Turkey	Finland	12 Oct 29	General Economic	96LTS239	302205
Turkey	Finland	19 Dec 33	General Trade	149LTS333	303441
Turkey	Finland	06 Jun 35	General Trade	160LTS165	303690
Turkey	Finland	20 Jun 36	Finance	172LTS135	303983
Turkey	Finland	20 Jun 36	General Trade	172LTS125	303982
Turkey	France	30 May 26	General Amity	54LTS195	301285
Turkey	France	31 Jul 26	General Amity	54LTS177	301284
Turkey	France	01 Nov 27	Visas	92LTS249	302092
Turkey	France	29 Aug 29	General Economic	123LTS193	302815
Turkey	France	27 Oct 32	Land Transport	136LTS23	303121
Turkey	France	15 Jun 37	General Trade	179LTS195	304147
Turkey	Germany	03 Mar 24	General Amity	41LTS237	301017
Turkey	Germany	13 Dec 25	General Economic	53LTS355	301265
Turkey	Germany	12 Jan 27	Admin Cooperation	73LTS187	301713
Turkey	Germany	12 Jan 27	General Trade	73LTS133	301712
Turkey	Germany	16 May 29	Dispute Settlement	109LTS451	302549
Turkey	Germany	28 May 29	Consul/Citizenship	133LTS257	303069
Turkey	Germany	28 May 29	Admin Cooperation	133LTS235	303068
Turkey	Germany	27 May 30	General Economic	110LTS9	302553
Turkey	Germany	03 Sep 30	Extradition	133LTS321	303071
Turkey	Greece	30 Jan 23	Consul/Citizenship	36LTS137	300912
Turkey	Greece	30 Jan 23	Consul/Citizenship	32LTS75	300807
Turkey	Greece	10 Jun 30	Refugees	108LTS233	302511
Turkey	Greece	30 Oct 30	General Economic	125LTS371	302866
Turkey	Greece	30 Oct 30	Dispute Settlement	125LTS9	302841
Turkey	Greece	14 Sep 33	General Amity	156LTS165	303600
Turkey	Greece	15 Jan 37	Admin Cooperation	202LTS107	304739
Turkey	Greece	25 Nov 37	Land Transport	195LTS137	304543
Turkey	Greece	27 Apr 38	General Amity	193LTS175	304493
Turkey	Greece	07 Mar 39	Extradition	201LTS239	304717
Turkey	Hungary	18 Dec 23	General Amity	43LTS271	301062
Turkey	Hungary	20 Dec 26	Consul/Citizenship	72LTS245	301696
Turkey	Hungary	20 Dec 26	General Trade	72LTS255	301697
Turkey	Hungary	05 Jan 29	Dispute Settlement	100LTS137	302300
Turkey	Hungary	21 May 30	Mostfavored Nation	105LTS117	302406
Turkey	Hungary	21 May 30	General Economic	109LTS153	302534
Turkey	India	03 Sep 30	Mostfavored Nation	109LTS25	302525
Turkey	Iraq	09 Jan 32	Extradition	139LTS273	303218
Turkey	Iraq	09 Jan 32	Recognition	139LTS263	303217
Turkey	Iraq	10 Jan 32	Mostfavored Nation	152LTS17	303480
Turkey	Italy	24 Jul 23	Admin Cooperation	36LTS195	300921
Turkey	Italy	30 May 28	Dispute Settlement	95LTS183	302172
Turkey	Italy	09 Sep 29	Consul/Citizenship	129LTS195	302962
Turkey	Italy	04 Jan 32	Territory Boundary	138LTS243	303191
Turkey	Japan	31 Jul 29	Mostfavored Nation	111LTS289	302592
Turkey	Latvia	03 Jan 25	General Amity	59LTS81	301390
Turkey	Latvia	28 May 28	General Economic	94LTS295	302150
Turkey	Latvia	12 Jan 38	General Trade	201LTS229	304716
Turkey	Lithuania	17 Sep 30	General Amity	125LTS249	302858
Turkey	Multilateral	12 Jan 12	Sanitation	4LTS281	300112
Turkey	Multilateral	23 Jan 12	Sanitation	8LTS187	300222
Turkey	Multilateral	05 Jun 12	Telecommunications	1LTS135	300013

PARTY ONE	PARTY TWO	DATE	TOPIC	CITATION	NUMBER
Turkey	Multilateral	20 Apr 21	Land Transport	7LTS11	300171
Turkey	Multilateral	20 Apr 21	Water Transport	7LTS65	300173
Turkey	Multilateral	20 Apr 21	Water Transport	7LTS73	300174
Turkey	Multilateral	20 Apr 21	Water Transport	7LTS35	300172
Turkey	Multilateral	24 Jul 23	Consul/Citizenship	36LTS167	300917
Turkey	Multilateral	24 Jul 23	Peace/Disarmament	28LTS11	300701
Turkey	Multilateral	24 Jul 23	Admin Cooperation	28LTS283	300714
Turkey	Multilateral	24 Jul 23	Taxation	36LTS175	300918
Turkey	Multilateral	24 Jul 23	Territory Boundary	28LTS139	300703
Turkey	Multilateral	24 Jul 23	Water Transport	36LTS187	300920
Turkey	Multilateral	24 Jul 23	General Amity	36LTS145	300913
Turkey	Multilateral	24 Jul 23	Recognition	36LTS179	300919
Turkey	Multilateral	24 Jul 23	Admin Cooperation	36LTS201	300922
Turkey	Multilateral	24 Jul 23	Admin Cooperation	28LTS197	300706
Turkey	Multilateral	24 Jul 23	General Trade	28LTS203	300707
Turkey	Multilateral	24 Jul 23	General Trade	28LTS151	300704
Turkey	Multilateral	24 Jul 23	Water Transport	28LTS115	300702
Turkey	Multilateral	24 Jul 23	Territory Boundary	28LTS215	300708
Turkey	Multilateral	24 Jul 23	General Trade	28LTS171	300705
Turkey	Multilateral	31 Mar 24	Sanitation	27LTS211	300685
Turkey	Multilateral	28 Aug 24	Postal Service	41LTS9	301006
Turkey	Multilateral	28 Aug 24	Postal Service	40LTS437	301005
Turkey	Multilateral	28 Aug 24	Postal Service	41LTS97	301008
Turkey	Multilateral	28 Aug 24	Postal Service	40LTS249	301003
Turkey	Multilateral	28 Aug 24	Postal Service	40LTS307	301004
Turkey	Multilateral	28 Aug 24	Postal Service	40LTS19	301002
Turkey	Multilateral	19 Feb 25	Admin Cooperation	81LTS317	301845
Turkey	Multilateral	17 Jun 25	Peace/Disarmament	94LTS65	302138
Turkey	Multilateral	29 Oct 25	Telecommunications	57LTS201	301365
Turkey	Multilateral	24 Apr 26	Land Transport	108LTS123	302505
Turkey	Multilateral	20 May 26	Health/Educ/Welfare	109LTS121	302532
Turkey	Multilateral	21 Jun 26	Sanitation	78LTS229	301793
Turkey	Multilateral	25 Sep 26	ILO Labor	60LTS253	301414
Turkey	Multilateral	12 Jul 27	Direct Aid	135LTS247	303115
Turkey	Multilateral	28 Jul 27	Territory Boundary	64LTS379	301511
Turkey	Multilateral	29 Oct 27	Scientific Project	127LTS27	302903
Turkey	Multilateral	08 Nov 27	General Trade	97LTS391	302238
Turkey	Multilateral	25 Nov 27	Telecommunications	84LTS97	301905
Turkey	Multilateral	11 Jul 28	Commodity Trade	95LTS357	302184
Turkey	Multilateral	11 Jul 28	Commodity Trade	95LTS373	302185
Turkey	Multilateral	27 Aug 28	General Military	94LTS57	302137
Turkey	Multilateral	31 May 29	Water Transport	136LTS81	303127
Turkey	Multilateral	28 Jun 29	Postal Service	103LTS429	302374
Turkey	Multilateral	28 Jun 29	Postal Service	103LTS5	302369
Turkey	Multilateral	28 Jun 29	Postal Service	103LTS377	302373
Turkey	Multilateral	28 Jun 29	Postal Service	103LTS249	302371
Turkey	Multilateral	28 Jun 29	Postal Service	102LTS245	302368
Turkey	Multilateral	28 Jun 29	Postal Service	103LTS71	302370
Turkey	Multilateral	27 Jul 29	Other Military	118LTS343	302734
Turkey	Multilateral	27 Jul 29	Other Military	118LTS303	302733
Turkey	Multilateral	07 Jun 30	Finance	143LTS337	303315
Turkey	Multilateral	07 Jun 30	Finance	143LTS317	303314
Turkey	Multilateral	07 Jun 30	Finance	143LTS257	303313
Turkey	Multilateral	01 Aug 30	Health/Educ/Welfare	128LTS9	302932
Turkey	Multilateral	19 Mar 31	Admin Cooperation	143LTS7	303301
Turkey	Multilateral	19 Mar 31	Finance	143LTS355	303316
Turkey	Multilateral	19 Mar 31	Finance	143LTS407	303317
Turkey	Multilateral	28 Mar 31	Customs	119LTS47	302739
Turkey	Multilateral	30 Mar 31	Land Transport	150LTS247	303459
Turkey	Multilateral	30 Mar 31	Taxation	138LTS149	303185
Turkey	Multilateral	13 Jul 31	Other HEW	139LTS301	303219
Turkey	Multilateral	24 Sep 31	Specific Resources	155LTS349	303586
Turkey	Multilateral	02 Sep 32	Land Transport	154LTS123	303543
Turkey	Multilateral	09 Dec 32	Telecommunications	151LTS5	303479
Turkey	Multilateral	11 Mar 33	Water Transport	135LTS301	303119

PARTY ONE	PARTY TWO	DATE	TOPIC	CITATION	NUMBER
Turkey	Multilateral	12 Apr 33	Sanitation	161LTS65	303706
Turkey	Multilateral	29 May 33	Admin Cooperation	192LTS289	304479
Turkey	Multilateral	19 Jun 33	Gen Communications	154LTS133	303544
Turkey	Multilateral	03 Jul 33	Peace/Disarmament	147LTS67	303391
Turkey	Multilateral	04 Jul 33	Peace/Disarmament	148LTS211	303414
Turkey	Multilateral	10 Oct 33	General Amity	163LTS393	303781
Turkey	Multilateral	11 Oct 33	Consul/Citizenship	150LTS431	303476
Turkey	Multilateral	23 Nov 33	Land Transport	192LTS327	304483
Turkey	Multilateral	23 Nov 33	Land Transport	192LTS389	304484
Turkey	Multilateral	09 Feb 34	General Military	153LTS153	303514
Turkey	Multilateral	20 Mar 34	Finance	176LTS9	304053
Turkey	Multilateral	20 Mar 34	Postal Service	174LTS171	304048
Turkey	Multilateral	20 Mar 34	Postal Service	175LTS269	304051
Turkey	Multilateral	20 Mar 34	Postal Service	175LTS5	304049
Turkey	Multilateral	20 Mar 34	Postal Service	175LTS73	304050
Turkey	Multilateral	20 Mar 34	Postal Service	176LTS55	304054
Turkey	Multilateral	02 Jun 34	Patents/Copyrights	192LTS17	304459
Turkey	Multilateral	02 Jun 34	Patents/Copyrights	205LTS179	304834
Turkey	Multilateral	02 Jun 34	General Trade	192LTS9	304458
Turkey	Multilateral	25 Jul 34	Other HEW	177LTS59	304080
Turkey	Multilateral	20 Feb 35	Sanitation	186LTS173	304310
Turkey	Multilateral	20 Feb 35	Sanitation	193LTS37	304486
Turkey	Multilateral	20 Feb 35	Sanitation	193LTS59	304487
Turkey	Multilateral	26 Jun 36	Other HEW	198LTS299	304648
Turkey	Multilateral	20 Jul 36	Territory Boundary	173LTS213	304015
Turkey	Multilateral	23 Sep 36	Gen Communications	186LTS301	304319
Turkey	Multilateral	06 Nov 36	General Military	173LTS353	304025
Turkey	Multilateral	10 Feb 37	General Transport	189LTS313	304391
Turkey	Multilateral	08 Jul 37	General Amity	190LTS21	304402
Turkey	Multilateral	14 Sep 37	General Military	181LTS137	304184
Turkey	Multilateral	17 Sep 37	Milit Installation	181LTS150	304185
Turkey	Multilateral	15 Apr 38	Visas	200LTS285	304698
Turkey	Multilateral	23 May 39	Postal Service	202LTS159	304742
Turkey	Multilateral	19 Oct 39	General Military	200LTS167	304689
Turkey	Multilateral	02 Jun 42	Patents/Copyrights	205LTS163	304833
Turkey	Netherlands	16 Aug 24	Admin Cooperation	39LTS148	300999
Turkey	Netherlands	11 Aug 26	General Economic	48LTS271	301168
Turkey	Netherlands	25 Jul 28	General Economic	93LTS279	302116
Turkey	Netherlands	21 Nov 29	General Trade	99LTS397	302284
Turkey	Netherlands	16 Apr 32	Dispute Settlement	143LTS237	303311
Turkey	Netherlands	17 Feb 37	Finance	182LTS221	304213
Turkey	Norway	02 May 26	General Amity	56LTS51	301322
Turkey	Norway	11 Aug 26	General Economic	47LTS441	301149
Turkey	Norway	16 Mar 31	General Economic	138LTS41	303180
Turkey	Norway	16 Jan 33	Dispute Settlement	161LTS173	303710
Turkey	Norway	08 Jun 36	Finance	170LTS235	303939
Turkey	Norway	08 Jun 36	General Trade	170LTS227	303938
Turkey	Persia	15 Jun 28	General Amity	106LTS247	302449
Turkey	Poland	09 May 23	Sanitation	49LTS315	301187
Turkey	Poland	23 Jul 23	General Amity	49LTS323	301188
Turkey	Poland	23 Jul 23	Admin Cooperation	49LTS345	301190
Turkey	Poland	23 Jul 23	General Economic	49LTS329	301189
Turkey	Poland	29 Aug 31	Consul/Citizenship	144LTS367	303339
Turkey	Romania	11 Jun 29	General Economic	112LTS139	302613
Turkey	Romania	17 Oct 33	Dispute Settlement	165LTS273	303814
Turkey	Romania	04 Sep 36	Visas	195LTS429	304564
Turkey	Spain	27 Sep 24	General Amity	43LTS307	301066
Turkey	Spain	19 May 34	General Trade	149LTS15	303428
Turkey	Spain	31 Dec 35	General Trade	166LTS163	303838
Turkey	Sweden	31 May 24	General Amity	38LTS148	300972
Turkey	Sweden	04 Feb 28	General Trade	88LTS155	301994
Turkey	Sweden	24 Sep 28	General Trade	82LTS9	301855
Turkey	Sweden	29 Sep 29	General Economic	119LTS53	302740
Turkey	Sweden	19 Oct 29	General Trade	96LTS221	302203
Turkey	Sweden	24 Apr 32	Privil/Immunities	129LTS325	302967

PARTY ONE	PARTY TWO	DATE	TOPIC	CITATION	NUMBER
Turkey	Sweden	19 Jun 34	Claims and Debts	150LTS413	303474
Turkey	Sweden	27 Feb 36	Finance	167LTS83	303859
Turkey	Sweden	27 Feb 36	General Trade	167LTS75	303858
Turkey	Sweden	14 Dec 36	Finance	174LTS51	304036
Turkey	Sweden	31 Dec 37	General Trade	184LTS399	304260
Turkey	Sweden	31 Dec 37	General Trade	184LTS417	304262
Turkey	Sweden	31 Dec 37	Finance	184LTS409	304261
Turkey	Sweden	20 Jan 39	General Trade	194LTS119	304515
Turkey	Sweden	20 Jan 39	General Trade	194LTS107	304513
Turkey	Sweden	20 Jan 39	Finance	194LTS113	304514
Turkey	Sweden	29 Feb 40	Finance	200LTS273	304696
Turkey	Sweden	29 Feb 40	General Trade	200LTS281	304697
Turkey	Sweden	29 Feb 40	General Trade	200LTS267	304695
Turkey	Switzerland	19 Sep 25	General Amity	61LTS395	301449
Turkey	Switzerland	04 May 27	General Trade	67LTS141	301544
Turkey	Switzerland	07 Aug 27	Admin Cooperation	73LTS51	301706
Turkey	Switzerland	09 Dec 28	Dispute Settlement	159LTS219	303664
Turkey	Switzerland	13 Dec 30	General Trade	129LTS267	302964
Turkey	Switzerland	13 Dec 30	Privil/Immunities	129LTS331	302968
Turkey	Switzerland	01 Jun 33	Extradition	159LTS329	303676
Turkey	Switzerland	01 Jun 33	Dispute Settlement	159LTS229	303665
Turkey	Switzerland	01 Jun 33	Admin Cooperation	159LTS187	303662
Turkey	UK Great Britain	15 Jan 29	General Economic	108LTS385	302521
Turkey	UK Great Britain	25 Sep 29	General Trade	94LTS41	302135
Turkey	UK Great Britain	01 Mar 30	General Economic	108LTS407	302523
Turkey	UK Great Britain	28 Nov 31	Admin Cooperation	141LTS225	303268
Turkey	UK Great Britain	04 Jun 35	General Trade	167LTS91	303860
Turkey	UK Great Britain	02 Sep 36	General Trade	172LTS289	303998
Turkey	UK Great Britain	27 May 38	General Trade	190LTS121	304411
Turkey	UK Great Britain	27 May 38	Milit Assistance	199LTS9	304660
Turkey	UK Great Britain	10 Feb 39	Admin Cooperation	204LTS257	304806
Turkey	UK Great Britain	22 Nov 39	General Trade	201LTS93	304705
Turkey	UK Great Britain	03 Feb 40	General Trade	203LTS399	304781
Turkey	United Arab Rep	07 Apr 37	General Amity	191LTS89	304437
Turkey	United Arab Rep	07 Apr 37	Consul/Citizenship	191LTS105	304439
Turkey	United Arab Rep	07 Apr 37	Privil/Immunities	191LTS95	304438
Turkey	USA (United States)	06 Aug 23	Extradition	153LTS71	303509
Turkey	USA (United States)	28 Oct 31	Admin Cooperation	138LTS345	303197
Turkey	USA (United States)	25 Oct 34	Claims and Debts	158LTS389	303645
Turkey	USA (United States)	02 Jul 35	Postal Service	164LTS125	303792
Turkey	USA (United States)	01 Apr 39	General Trade	202LTS129	304741
Turkey	USSR (Soviet Union)	17 Dec 25	General Amity	157LTS353	303610
Turkey	USSR (Soviet Union)	07 Nov 35	General Amity	179LTS127	304139
Turkey	Yugoslavia	14 Apr 32	Commodity Trade	144LTS291	303332
Turkey	Yugoslavia	27 Nov 33	Dispute Settlement	161LTS229	303715
Turkey	Yugoslavia	28 Nov 33	Claims and Debts	161LTS245	303716
Turkey	Yugoslavia	03 Jul 34	Admin Cooperation	179LTS207	304149
Turkey	Yugoslavia	17 Dec 34	Sanitation	178LTS471	304128
Uganda	Multilateral	18 Mar 04	Humanitarian	1LTS83	300011
Uganda	Multilateral	30 Jun 20	Patents/Copyrights	1LTS59	300008
Uganda	Multilateral	31 Mar 22	Humanitarian	9LTS415	300269
Uganda	Multilateral	24 Sep 23	Dispute Settlement	27LTS157	300678
Uganda	Multilateral	26 Sep 27	Dispute Settlement	92LTS301	302096
Uganda	Multilateral	25 Nov 27	Telecommunications	84LTS97	301905
Uganda	Multilateral	20 Apr 29	Admin Cooperation	112LTS371	302623
Uganda	Multilateral	07 Jun 30	Finance	143LTS337	303315
Uganda	Multilateral	30 Mar 31	Taxation	138LTS149	303185
Uganda	Multilateral	28 Oct 33	Refugees	159LTS199	303663
Uganda	Multilateral	30 Oct 35	Telecommunications	189LTS51	304375
Uganda	Multilateral	30 Oct 35	Postal Service	189LTS85	304376
Uganda	Multilateral	23 Sep 36	Gen Communications	186LTS301	304319
Uganda	Multilateral	10 Feb 38	Refugees	192LTS59	304461
Uganda	Multilateral	02 Jun 38	Postal Service	192LTS157	304470
Uganda	Multilateral	02 Jan 39	Postal Service	196LTS235	304587
UK Great Britain		07 Jun 37	General Trade	185LTS185	304282

PARTY ONE	PARTY TWO	DATE	TOPIC	CITATION	NUMBER
UK Great Britain	Afghanistan	22 Nov 21	General Amity	14LTS47	300367
UK Great Britain	Afghanistan	05 Jun 23	General Trade	21LTS89	300533
UK Great Britain	Afghanistan	06 May 30	Admin Cooperation	105LTS265	302418
UK Great Britain	Albania	10 Jun 25	General Economic	43LTS81	301049
UK Great Britain	Albania	22 Jul 26	Admin Cooperation	67LTS165	301545
UK Great Britain	Argentina	07 Apr 12	Postal Service	6LTS337	300165
UK Great Britain	Argentina	29 Jul 21	Admin Cooperation	8LTS315	300229
UK Great Britain	Argentina	15 Nov 29	Non-ILO Labor	160LTS257	303694
UK Great Britain	Argentina	01 May 33	General Trade	143LTS67	303305
UK Great Britain	Argentina	28 Jun 37	Commodity Trade	196LTS263	304588
UK Great Britain	Austria	22 Sep 20	Admin Cooperation	5LTS309	300136
UK Great Britain	Austria	14 Jul 21	Sanitation	16LTS151	300405
UK Great Britain	Austria	02 Oct 22	Reparations	12LTS413	300337
UK Great Britain	Austria	28 Mar 23	Customs	17LTS385	300445
UK Great Britain	Austria	31 Mar 31	Admin Cooperation	127LTS167	302918
UK Great Britain	Austria	14 Jul 31	Dispute Settlement	123LTS383	302824
UK Great Britain	Austria	16 Jul 32	Air Transport	144LTS9	303318
UK Great Britain	Austria	27 Jul 33	Patents/Copyrights	142LTS157	303287
UK Great Britain	Austria	15 Dec 33	Postal Service	146LTS9	303360
UK Great Britain	Austria	29 Oct 34	Extradition	165LTS373	303823
UK Great Britain	Belgium	05 Oct 20	Postal Service	5LTS147	300123
UK Great Britain	Belgium	15 Mar 21	Land Transport	5LTS319	300138
UK Great Britain	Belgium	20 Jul 21	Reparations	8LTS301	300228
UK Great Britain	Belgium	21 Jun 22	Admin Cooperation	24LTS91	300597
UK Great Britain	Belgium	28 Mar 23	Reparations	16LTS439	300421
UK Great Britain	Belgium	08 Aug 23	Extradition	22LTS375	300566
UK Great Britain	Belgium	29 Jul 24	Telecommunications	29LTS389	300749
UK Great Britain	Belgium	18 Feb 25	Postal Service	33LTS341	300857
UK Great Britain	Belgium	18 Feb 25	Postal Service	33LTS361	300858
UK Great Britain	Belgium	26 Feb 25	Telecommunications	71LTS83	301656
UK Great Britain	Belgium	11 May 26	Postal Service	71LTS97	301657
UK Great Britain	Belgium	17 May 26	Territory Boundary	54LTS239	301287
UK Great Britain	Belgium	09 Apr 27	Telecommunications	67LTS209	301548
UK Great Britain	Belgium	03 May 27	Territory Boundary	140LTS71	303229
UK Great Britain	Belgium	06 May 27	Admin Cooperation	63LTS153	301486
UK Great Britain	Belgium	04 Nov 32	Admin Cooperation	153LTS251	303518
UK Great Britain	Belgium	13 Apr 34	Dispute Settlement	154LTS361	303561
UK Great Britain	Belgium	02 May 34	Admin Cooperation	173LTS291	304020
UK Great Britain	Belgium	22 Nov 34	Territory Boundary	190LTS95	304407
UK Great Britain	Belgium	22 Nov 34	Specific Resources	190LTS99	304408
UK Great Britain	Belgium	01 Jun 37	Taxation	196LTS209	304583
UK Great Britain	Belgium	29 Jul 38	Postal Service	201LTS317	304722
UK Great Britain	Belgium	19 Jun 39	Admin Cooperation	198LTS171	304637
UK Great Britain	Belgium	04 Jun 42	Commodity Trade	204LTS363	304814
UK Great Britain	Bolivia	05 Apr 20	General Trade	1LTS271	300020
UK Great Britain	Bolivia	11 Aug 21	Admin Cooperation	8LTS323	300231
UK Great Britain	Bolivia	14 Mar 21	Patents/Copyrights	5LTS315	300137
UK Great Britain	Bolivia	18 Jan 29	Postal Service	95LTS9	302161
UK Great Britain	Brazil	04 Apr 19	General Amity	5LTS45	300116
UK Great Britain	Brazil	01 Mar 21	Postal Service	8LTS265	300225
UK Great Britain	Brazil	16 Jul 21	Admin Cooperation	10LTS407	300279
UK Great Britain	Brazil	22 Apr 27	Territory Boundary	92LTS311	302097
UK Great Britain	Brazil	21 Feb 30	Consul/Citizenship	101LTS11	302315
UK Great Britain	Brazil	18 Mar 30	Territory Boundary	101LTS401	302339
UK Great Britain	Brazil	11 Sep 31	Mostfavored Nation	130LTS103	302985
UK Great Britain	Brazil	01 Nov 32	Territory Boundary	177LTS127	304087
UK Great Britain	Brazil	27 Mar 35	Finance	160LTS311	303700
UK Great Britain	Brazil	10 Aug 36	General Economic	172LTS283	303997
UK Great Britain	Brazil	10 Aug 36	Mostfavored Nation	172LTS273	303996
UK Great Britain	Bulgaria	05 Apr 22	Sanitation	16LTS191	300410
UK Great Britain	Bulgaria	12 Nov 25	General Trade	43LTS165	301052
UK Great Britain	Bulgaria	17 Jun 27	Dispute Settlement	67LTS239	301551
UK Great Britain	Bulgaria	24 Nov 38	General Military	195LTS117	304539
UK Great Britain	Chile	12 Apr 22	Admin Cooperation	11LTS17	300287
UK Great Britain	Chile	15 Oct 31	Mostfavored Nation	128LTS439	302947

PARTY ONE	PARTY TWO	DATE	TOPIC	CITATION	NUMBER
UK Great Britain	Chile	26 Nov 37	General Trade	186LTS285	304317
UK Great Britain	Chile	09 Jan 39	General Trade	196LTS277	304589
UK Great Britain	Chile	17 Jun 42	General Trade	204LTS371	304815
UK Great Britain	Chile	28 Jun 43	General Trade	205LTS109	304827
UK Great Britain	China	26 Apr 20	Postal Service	5LTS83	300120
UK Great Britain	China	07 Jan 24	Postal Service	24LTS115	300599
UK Great Britain	China	23 May 24	Postal Service	28LTS481	300724
UK Great Britain	China	26 Nov 24	Admin Cooperation	32LTS281	300818
UK Great Britain	China	31 Oct 29	Admin Cooperation	99LTS441	302289
UK Great Britain	China	09 Nov 29	Claims and Debts	99LTS453	302290
UK Great Britain	China	18 Apr 30	Recognition	112LTS49	302607
UK Great Britain	China	17 Sep 30	Admin Cooperation	111LTS153	302584
UK Great Britain	China	22 Sep 30	Reparations	115LTS493	302697
UK Great Britain	China	28 Apr 32	Postal Service	137LTS319	303165
UK Great Britain	China	27 Oct 34	Taxation	160LTS265	303695
UK Great Britain	China	17 Jul 36	Postal Service	173LTS343	304024
UK Great Britain	China	24 Jan 39	Air Transport	199LTS53	304664
UK Great Britain	China	11 Jan 43	Privil/Immunities	205LTS67	304826
UK Great Britain	Colombia	27 Sep 21	Admin Cooperation	10LTS417	300281
UK Great Britain	Colombia	08 Mar 23	Sanitation	17LTS167	300434
UK Great Britain	Colombia	02 Dec 29	Extradition	110LTS401	302571
UK Great Britain	Colombia	30 Dec 38	General Economic	196LTS231	304586
UK Great Britain	Costa Rica	12 Jan 22	Claims and Debts	17LTS151	300432
UK Great Britain	Costa Rica	25 Apr 23	General Trade	20LTS19	300502
UK Great Britain	Costa Rica	29 Sep 24	Postal Service	31LTS121	300789
UK Great Britain	Costa Rica	27 Dec 28	General Economic	108LTS375	302520
UK Great Britain	Cuba	01 Dec 28	Postal Service	85LTS149	301929
UK Great Britain	Cuba	19 Feb 37	General Trade	192LTS301	304480
UK Great Britain	Czechoslovakia	04 Aug 21	Sanitation	16LTS157	300406
UK Great Britain	Czechoslovakia	31 Jan 23	Customs	20LTS53	300506
UK Great Britain	Czechoslovakia	14 Jul 23	General Trade	29LTS377	300748
UK Great Britain	Czechoslovakia	01 Feb 26	Customs	49LTS175	301181
UK Great Britain	Czechoslovakia	04 Jun 26	Extradition	59LTS269	301397
UK Great Britain	Czechoslovakia	11 Jun 26	Admin Cooperation	48LTS425	301173
UK Great Britain	Czechoslovakia	15 Feb 35	Admin Cooperation	161LTS389	303727
UK Great Britain	Czechoslovakia	04 Mar 35	Consul/Citizenship	160LTS283	303698
UK Great Britain	Czechoslovakia	05 Aug 42	General Amity	204LTS377	304816
UK Great Britain	Danzig	13 Jan 37	Postal Service	178LTS87	304109
UK Great Britain	Denmark	20 Aug 20	Postal Service	5LTS129	300122
UK Great Britain	Denmark	23 Dec 20	Air Transport	2LTS249	300071
UK Great Britain	Denmark	01 Jun 21	Admin Cooperation	5LTS161	300125
UK Great Britain	Denmark	12 Jul 21	Admin Cooperation	8LTS397	300238
UK Great Britain	Denmark	14 Jul 21	Consul/Citizenship	6LTS181	300151
UK Great Britain	Denmark	01 May 22	Dispute Settlement	12LTS11	300301
UK Great Britain	Denmark	25 Apr 23	Postal Service	22LTS157	300557
UK Great Britain	Denmark	18 Dec 24	Taxation	32LTS89	300808
UK Great Britain	Denmark	18 Dec 24	Admin Cooperation	32LTS287	300819
UK Great Britain	Denmark	04 Jun 25	Consul/Citizenship	36LTS131	300911
UK Great Britain	Denmark	02 Jun 26	Non-ILO Labor	61LTS353	301445
UK Great Britain	Denmark	04 Jun 26	Dispute Settlement	61LTS185	301432
UK Great Britain	Denmark	29 Nov 32	Admin Cooperation	139LTS9	303201
UK Great Britain	Denmark	24 Apr 33	General Trade	139LTS127	303208
UK Great Britain	Denmark	15 Oct 35	Extradition	169LTS337	303922
UK Great Britain	Denmark	24 Mar 37	Water Transport	178LTS319	304120
UK Great Britain	Denmark	14 Sep 39	Refugees	198LTS141	304634
UK Great Britain	Dutch Indies	17 Jun 33	Postal Service	144LTS47	303320
UK Great Britain	Ecuador	05 Jan 29	Consul/Citizenship	90LTS369	302048
UK Great Britain	El Salvador	07 Jan 28	General Trade	80LTS231	301828
UK Great Britain	El Salvador	14 Sep 32	General Trade	128LTS417	302945
UK Great Britain	Estonia	20 Jul 20	Mostfavored Nation	1LTS295	300025
UK Great Britain	Estonia	25 Apr 21	General Economic	5LTS173	300127
UK Great Britain	Estonia	22 May 22	Admin Cooperation	13LTS33	300344
UK Great Britain	Estonia	18 Jan 26	General Economic	48LTS209	301163
UK Great Britain	Estonia	15 Mar 26	Telecommunications	50LTS219	301204
UK Great Britain	Estonia	03 May 26	General Trade	59LTS41	301388

PARTY ONE	PARTY TWO	DATE	TOPIC	CITATION	NUMBER
UK Great Britain	Estonia	24 Jun 26	Water Transport	57LTS65	301352
UK Great Britain	Estonia	22 Dec 31	Admin Cooperation	132LTS231	303041
UK Great Britain	Estonia	22 Dec 31	Claims and Debts	131LTS323	303022
UK Great Britain	Estonia	15 Jul 33	General Economic	141LTS33	303259
UK Great Britain	Estonia	11 Jul 34	General Economic	152LTS131	303491
UK Great Britain	Estonia	14 Dec 37	Postal Service	187LTS223	304343
UK Great Britain	Finland	10 Jun 21	Sanitation	16LTS133	300403
UK Great Britain	Finland	14 Dec 23	General Trade	29LTS129	300739
UK Great Britain	Finland	14 Dec 23	Non-ILO Labor	23LTS125	300583
UK Great Britain	Finland	30 May 24	Extradition	34LTS79	300868
UK Great Britain	Finland	21 Jun 24	Water Transport	28LTS511	300726
UK Great Britain	Finland	12 Dec 24	Postal Service	34LTS123	300870
UK Great Britain	Finland	30 Sep 32	Dispute Settlement	135LTS9	303101
UK Great Britain	Finland	11 Aug 33	Admin Cooperation	149LTS131	303437
UK Great Britain	Finland	29 Sep 33	General Trade	149LTS167	303438
UK Great Britain	Finland	13 Oct 33	Commodity Trade	142LTS187	303291
UK Great Britain	Finland	04 Nov 33	Postal Service	149LTS285	303440
UK Great Britain	Finland	21 Feb 35	Taxation	158LTS323	303642
UK Great Britain	Finland	03 May 35	Water Transport	159LTS129	303655
UK Great Britain	Finland	14 Apr 37	Commodity Trade	179LTS289	304155
UK Great Britain	France	16 Apr 02	Customs	1LTS79	300010
UK Great Britain	France	06 Aug 14	Admin Cooperation	10LTS333	300278
UK Great Britain	France	10 Jan 20	Claims and Debts	1LTS249	300017
UK Great Britain	France	10 Jan 20	Telecommunications	5LTS53	300117
UK Great Britain	France	24 Apr 20	Specific Resources	1LTS281	300022
UK Great Britain	France	26 Apr 20	Admin Cooperation	1LTS287	300023
UK Great Britain	France	20 Oct 20	Air Transport	2LTS323	300085
UK Great Britain	France	23 Dec 20	Territory Boundary	22LTS353	300564
UK Great Britain	France	29 Jun 21	Reparations	6LTS23	300146
UK Great Britain	France	09 Jul 21	Non-ILO Labor	6LTS341	300166
UK Great Britain	France	03 Sep 21	Postal Service	8LTS153	300218
UK Great Britain	France	10 Oct 21	Air Transport	9LTS181	300250
UK Great Britain	France	30 Jan 22	Air Transport	12LTS449	300341
UK Great Britain	France	02 Feb 22	Admin Cooperation	10LTS448	300284
UK Great Britain	France	22 Feb 22	Non-ILO Labor	9LTS198	300253
UK Great Britain	France	26 Dec 22	Other Ad Hoc	16LTS213	300413
UK Great Britain	France	07 Mar 23	Territory Boundary	22LTS363	300565
UK Great Britain	France	24 May 23	Consul/Citizenship	18LTS305	300472
UK Great Britain	France	24 Jul 23	Peace/Disarmament	36LTS207	300923
UK Great Britain	France	29 Sep 23	Admin Cooperation	20LTS183	300516
UK Great Britain	France	29 Sep 23	Specific Resources	21LTS137	300536
UK Great Britain	France	10 Oct 23	Postal Service	22LTS381	300567
UK Great Britain	France	13 Nov 23	Extradition	21LTS131	300535
UK Great Britain	France	27 Dec 23	Visas	24LTS131	300600
UK Great Britain	France	21 Jan 24	Territory Boundary	28LTS461	300723
UK Great Britain	France	28 Jan 25	Visas	33LTS335	300856
UK Great Britain	France	17 Apr 25	Postal Service	36LTS429	300939
UK Great Britain	France	12 Jul 26	Reparations	98LTS155	302244
UK Great Britain	France	23 May 27	Telecommunications	67LTS227	301550
UK Great Britain	France	16 May 28	Non-ILO Labor	80LTS257	301832
UK Great Britain	France	12 Jun 28	Postal Service	85LTS109	301926
UK Great Britain	France	23 Sep 28	Postal Service	87LTS29	301961
UK Great Britain	France	06 Mar 29	Postal Service	90LTS391	302050
UK Great Britain	France	06 May 29	Territory Boundary	93LTS27	302102
UK Great Britain	France	15 May 29	Postal Service	134LTS263	303097
UK Great Britain	France	25 May 29	Admin Cooperation	95LTS55	302163
UK Great Britain	France	02 Aug 29	Reparations	100LTS459	302314
UK Great Britain	France	24 Mar 30	Telecommunications	105LTS227	302415
UK Great Britain	France	04 Sep 30	Finance	109LTS31	302526
UK Great Britain	France	17 Nov 31	Postal Service	134LTS299	303098
UK Great Britain	France	27 Nov 31	Postal Service	132LTS25	303028
UK Great Britain	France	28 Nov 31	Postal Service	127LTS195	302919
UK Great Britain	France	15 Dec 31	Admin Cooperation	129LTS445	302976
UK Great Britain	France	28 Dec 31	Postal Service	133LTS79	303058
UK Great Britain	France	22 Aug 32	Postal Service	136LTS313	303133

PARTY ONE	PARTY TWO	DATE	TOPIC	CITATION	NUMBER
UK Great Britain	France	01 Oct 32	Taxation	135LTS25	303102
UK Great Britain	France	18 Jan 34	Admin Cooperation	171LTS183	303960
UK Great Britain	France	08 May 34	General Economic	154LTS367	303562
UK Great Britain	France	31 Jan 35	Admin Cooperation	160LTS275	303697
UK Great Britain	France	09 Apr 35	Taxation	199LTS49	304663
UK Great Britain	France	16 Jul 35	Postal Service	168LTS179	303898
UK Great Britain	France	15 Apr 36	Admin Cooperation	203LTS123	304755
UK Great Britain	France	03 Apr 37	Admin Cooperation	179LTS265	304154
UK Great Britain	France	24 Apr 37	Other Military	178LTS186	304112
UK Great Britain	France	23 Jul 37	Customs	184LTS279	304251
UK Great Britain	France	29 Jul 37	Privil/Immunities	184LTS351	304257
UK Great Britain	France	14 Oct 37	General Trade	184LTS457	304266
UK Great Britain	France	19 Aug 38	Postal Service	192LTS189	304471
UK Great Britain	France	26 Oct 38	Postal Service	194LTS371	304530
UK Great Britain	France	08 Nov 38	Customs	196LTS215	304584
UK Great Britain	France	13 Sep 39	Telecommunications	201LTS369	304724
UK Great Britain	France	08 Oct 39	Admin Cooperation	201LTS59	304703
UK Great Britain	France	18 Jan 40	Territory Boundary	201LTS375	304725
UK Great Britain	Germany	25 Jun 20	Admin Cooperation	5LTS303	300135
UK Great Britain	Germany	31 Dec 20	Peace/Disarmament	8LTS241	300223
UK Great Britain	Germany	18 Jun 21	Sanitation	16LTS139	300404
UK Great Britain	Germany	23 Nov 21	Peace/Disarmament	8LTS381	300237
UK Great Britain	Germany	05 Apr 23	Reparations	17LTS173	300435
UK Great Britain	Germany	05 Jan 24	Claims and Debts	36LTS365	300935
UK Great Britain	Germany	03 Apr 25	Reparations	33LTS383	300859
UK Great Britain	Germany	13 Aug 25	General Economic	43LTS89	301050
UK Great Britain	Germany	19 Oct 26	Gen Communications	67LTS203	301547
UK Great Britain	Germany	29 Jun 27	Air Transport	71LTS165	301659
UK Great Britain	Germany	20 Mar 28	Admin Cooperation	90LTS287	302044
UK Great Britain	Germany	26 Jul 28	Specific Property	85LTS135	301928
UK Great Britain	Germany	17 Jul 29	Postal Service	100LTS439	302313
UK Great Britain	Germany	28 Dec 29	Admin Cooperation	102LTS49	302352
UK Great Britain	Germany	09 May 30	Milit Occupation	105LTS271	302419
UK Great Britain	Germany	26 Jul 32	Dispute Settlement	133LTS99	303060
UK Great Britain	Germany	27 Jul 32	Admin Cooperation	134LTS311	303099
UK Great Britain	Germany	29 Oct 32	Postal Service	138LTS69	303182
UK Great Britain	Germany	03 May 33	General Trade	140LTS139	303231
UK Great Britain	Germany	07 Jul 33	Commodity Trade	145LTS237	303356
UK Great Britain	Germany	10 Aug 34	Finance	155LTS53	303568
UK Great Britain	Germany	18 Sep 34	Air Transport	155LTS243	303580
UK Great Britain	Germany	01 Nov 34	Finance	163LTS79	303762
UK Great Britain	Germany	03 Jun 35	General Amity	163LTS415	303782
UK Great Britain	Germany	07 Jun 35	Water Transport	163LTS293	303771
UK Great Britain	Germany	18 Jun 35	General Military	161LTS9	303701
UK Great Britain	Germany	02 Dec 36	Postal Service	178LTS329	304121
UK Great Britain	Germany	17 Jul 37	Peace/Disarmament	187LTS43	304332
UK Great Britain	Germany	10 Nov 37	Taxation	186LTS277	304316
UK Great Britain	Germany	01 Jul 38	Finance	194LTS245	304526
UK Great Britain	Germany	01 Jul 38	Finance	194LTS235	304525
UK Great Britain	Germany	13 Aug 38	Finance	194LTS257	304527
UK Great Britain	Germany	10 Sep 38	Recognition	194LTS313	304528
UK Great Britain	Germany	16 Jun 39	General Trade	197LTS277	304620
UK Great Britain	Greece	22 Sep 20	Admin Cooperation	2LTS367	300090
UK Great Britain	Greece	27 Jul 21	Visas	6LTS347	300167
UK Great Britain	Greece	27 Aug 21	Other Military	8LTS332	300233
UK Great Britain	Greece	10 Nov 21	Sanitation	16LTS165	300407
UK Great Britain	Greece	03 Feb 22	Reparations	9LTS191	300252
UK Great Britain	Greece	10 Dec 24	General Economic	36LTS441	300941
UK Great Britain	Greece	30 Nov 25	Reparations	50LTS273	301210
UK Great Britain	Greece	01 Dec 26	Water Transport	61LTS109	301428
UK Great Britain	Greece	17 Feb 27	Claims and Debts	90LTS379	302049
UK Great Britain	Greece	09 Apr 27	Claims and Debts	67LTS217	301549
UK Great Britain	Greece	13 May 27	General Economic	61LTS15	301425
UK Great Britain	Greece	21 Jun 29	Finance	94LTS33	302134
UK Great Britain	Greece	31 Jul 29	Taxation	95LTS67	302165

PARTY ONE	PARTY TWO	DATE	TOPIC	CITATION	NUMBER
UK Great Britain	Greece	17 Apr 31	Air Transport	129LTS287	302965
UK Great Britain	Greece	21 Apr 33	Visas	140LTS133	303230
UK Great Britain	Greece	21 Jan 36	Admin Cooperation	168LTS171	303897
UK Great Britain	Greece	27 Feb 36	Admin Cooperation	185LTS113	304278
UK Great Britain	Greece	17 Sep 36	Taxation	176LTS183	304060
UK Great Britain	Greece	30 May 39	Air Transport	202LTS7	304732
UK Great Britain	Guatemala	22 Feb 28	General Economic	97LTS229	302226
UK Great Britain	Guatemala	06 Jun 31	Privil/Immunities	132LTS15	303027
UK Great Britain	Guatemala	26 Aug 31	Territory Boundary	128LTS427	302946
UK Great Britain	Haiti	16 Nov 22	Sanitation	16LTS173	300408
UK Great Britain	Haiti	13 Feb 28	Postal Service	85LTS63	301923
UK Great Britain	Haiti	25 Feb 28	General Trade	85LTS91	301924
UK Great Britain	Honduras	23 Apr 35	Postal Service	163LTS199	303768
UK Great Britain	Hungary	30 Oct 21	General Military	8LTS375	300236
UK Great Britain	Hungary	20 Dec 21	Reparations	10LTS437	300283
UK Great Britain	Hungary	11 Dec 23	Finance	23LTS119	300582
UK Great Britain	Hungary	17 Oct 25	Finance	47LTS373	301142
UK Great Britain	Hungary	28 Dec 25	Postal Service	49LTS125	301179
UK Great Britain	Hungary	23 Jul 26	General Trade	67LTS183	301546
UK Great Britain	Hungary	10 Jun 32	Postal Service	132LTS53	303031
UK Great Britain	Hungary	31 Jan 35	Dispute Settlement	160LTS271	303696
UK Great Britain	Hungary	25 Sep 35	Admin Cooperation	170LTS51	303928
UK Great Britain	Hungary	18 Sep 36	Extradition	181LTS337	304200
UK Great Britain	Hungary	22 Mar 37	Air Transport	190LTS59	304405
UK Great Britain	Iceland	13 Oct 21	Postal Service	8LTS337	300234
UK Great Britain	Iceland	12 Dec 21	Admin Cooperation	12LTS351	300326
UK Great Britain	Iceland	01 May 22	Dispute Settlement	12LTS15	300302
UK Great Britain	Iceland	04 Jun 26	Dispute Settlement	61LTS189	301433
UK Great Britain	Iceland	27 Apr 28	Taxation	80LTS253	301831
UK Great Britain	Iceland	19 May 33	General Trade	144LTS33	303319
UK Great Britain	Iceland	03 Nov 33	Postal Service	145LTS269	303358
UK Great Britain	Iceland	25 Oct 38	Extradition	198LTS147	304635
UK Great Britain	Iraq	16 Jan 22	General Economic	12LTS431	300340
UK Great Britain	Iraq	30 Apr 23	General Amity	35LTS13	300890
UK Great Britain	Iraq	25 Mar 24	Consul/Citizenship	35LTS35	300891
UK Great Britain	Iraq	25 Mar 24	Finance	35LTS145	300894
UK Great Britain	Iraq	25 Mar 24	Admin Cooperation	35LTS131	300893
UK Great Britain	Iraq	25 Mar 24	General Military	35LTS103	300892
UK Great Britain	Iraq	30 Jun 30	General Military	132LTS363	303048
UK Great Britain	Iraq	19 Aug 30	Finance	118LTS231	302727
UK Great Britain	Iraq	04 Mar 31	Privil/Immunities	123LTS77	302807
UK Great Britain	Iraq	02 May 32	Extradition	141LTS277	303270
UK Great Britain	Iraq	25 Jul 35	Admin Cooperation	176LTS229	304064
UK Great Britain	Iraq	31 Mar 36	Land Transport	172LTS175	303988
UK Great Britain	Iraq	14 Dec 36	Customs	177LTS221	304091
UK Great Britain	Ireland	06 Dec 21	Dispute Settlement	26LTS9	300636
UK Great Britain	Italy	01 Jun 21	Reparations	6LTS323	300163
UK Great Britain	Italy	11 May 22	Other Military	11LTS23	300288
UK Great Britain	Italy	14 Aug 23	Admin Cooperation	21LTS127	300534
UK Great Britain	Italy	19 May 24	Territory Boundary	28LTS497	300725
UK Great Britain	Italy	15 Jul 24	Territory Boundary	36LTS379	300936
UK Great Britain	Italy	21 May 25	Health/Educ/Welfare	43LTS75	301048
UK Great Britain	Italy	15 Jun 25	Water Transport	38LTS189	300976
UK Great Britain	Italy	20 Dec 25	Admin Cooperation	50LTS281	301211
UK Great Britain	Italy	20 Dec 25	Postal Service	49LTS79	301178
UK Great Britain	Italy	29 Jan 26	Extradition	47LTS409	301145
UK Great Britain	Italy	24 Jun 26	Patents/Copyrights	57LTS71	301353
UK Great Britain	Italy	25 Jan 29	Admin Cooperation	95LTS39	302162
UK Great Britain	Italy	28 Aug 30	Postal Service	111LTS91	302583
UK Great Britain	Italy	02 Sep 30	Reparations	140LTS19	303225
UK Great Britain	Italy	17 Dec 30	Admin Cooperation	131LTS79	303004
UK Great Britain	Italy	24 Aug 32	Postal Service	136LTS331	303134
UK Great Britain	Italy	26 Nov 32	Admin Cooperation	136LTS385	303136
UK Great Britain	Italy	22 Nov 33	Territory Boundary	145LTS337	303359
UK Great Britain	Italy	17 Sep 34	Air Transport	155LTS85	303570

PARTY ONE	PARTY TWO	DATE	TOPIC	CITATION	NUMBER
UK Great Britain	Italy	18 Mar 35	General Trade	160LTS289	303699
UK Great Britain	Italy	06 Nov 36	Finance	177LTS183	304090
UK Great Britain	Italy	06 Nov 36	Customs	177LTS169	304089
UK Great Britain	Italy	02 Jan 37	Water Transport	177LTS241	304092
UK Great Britain	Italy	14 Dec 37	Air Transport	185LTS199	304283
UK Great Britain	Italy	18 Mar 38	General Trade	187LTS149	304335
UK Great Britain	Italy	18 Mar 38	General Trade	187LTS139	304334
UK Great Britain	Italy	16 Apr 38	Peace/Disarmament	195LTS79	304537
UK Great Britain	Japan	12 Nov 19	Reparations	6LTS333	300164
UK Great Britain	Japan	08 Jul 20	Admin Cooperation	1LTS23	300002
UK Great Britain	Japan	21 Jan 24	Admin Cooperation	25LTS11	300601
UK Great Britain	Japan	14 Jul 24	General Economic	28LTS537	300728
UK Great Britain	Japan	28 Jul 25	Postal Service	49LTS73	301177
UK Great Britain	Japan	10 Aug 29	Taxation	95LTS73	302166
UK Great Britain	Japan	20 Aug 29	Postal Service	107LTS243	302481
UK Great Britain	Japan	25 Mar 37	Milit Installation	181LTS289	304196
UK Great Britain	Japan	22 Mar 40	Admin Cooperation	203LTS194	304760
UK Great Britain	Latvia	17 Oct 22	Finance	16LTS397	300419
UK Great Britain	Latvia	22 Jun 23	General Trade	20LTS395	300529
UK Great Britain	Latvia	24 Jun 27	Water Transport	67LTS245	301552
UK Great Britain	Latvia	24 Jul 30	Admin Cooperation	107LTS301	302486
UK Great Britain	Latvia	06 Jul 33	General Trade	142LTS217	303294
UK Great Britain	Latvia	17 Jul 34	General Trade	154LTS25	303536
UK Great Britain	Latvia	23 Aug 39	Admin Cooperation	201LTS37	304702
UK Great Britain	Liberia	10 Apr 13	Water Transport	1LTS205	300014
UK Great Britain	Liberia	25 Jun 17	General Ad Hoc	5LTS39	300115
UK Great Britain	Liberia	17 Jan 30	Territory Boundary	101LTS395	302338
UK Great Britain	Lithuania	06 May 22	General Economic	13LTS25	300343
UK Great Britain	Lithuania	18 May 26	Extradition	61LTS401	301450
UK Great Britain	Lithuania	10 Dec 29	General Economic	99LTS47	302266
UK Great Britain	Lithuania	24 Apr 34	Admin Cooperation	169LTS373	303925
UK Great Britain	Lithuania	06 Jul 34	General Trade	155LTS9	303565
UK Great Britain	Luxembourg	08 Sep 23	Postal Service	35LTS203	300896
UK Great Britain	Mexico	17 May 22	Admin Cooperation	14LTS83	300368
UK Great Britain	Mexico	19 Nov 26	Claims and Debts	85LTS51	301922
UK Great Britain	Mexico	24 Oct 28	Postal Service	87LTS63	301962
UK Great Britain	Mexico	05 Dec 30	Claims and Debts	119LTS261	302749
UK Great Britain	Mexico	18 Jul 43	Milit Servic/Citiz	205LTS115	304828
UK Great Britain	Multilateral	09 Sep 86*	Patents/Copyrights	123LTS233	302816
UK Great Britain	Multilateral	18 Mar 04	Humanitarian	1LTS83	300011
UK Great Britain	Multilateral	13 Nov 08	General Ad Hoc	1LTS217	300015
UK Great Britain	Multilateral	12 Jan 12	Sanitation	4LTS281	300112
UK Great Britain	Multilateral	23 Jan 12	Sanitation	8LTS187	300222
UK Great Britain	Multilateral	05 Jun 12	Telecommunications	1LTS135	300013
UK Great Britain	Multilateral	20 Mar 14	Patents/Copyrights	1LTS243	300016
UK Great Britain	Multilateral	10 Sep 19	General Trade	7LTS331	300200
UK Great Britain	Multilateral	10 Sep 19	Health/Educ/Welfare	8LTS11	300201
UK Great Britain	Multilateral	09 Feb 20	Territory Boundary	2LTS7	300041
UK Great Britain	Multilateral	24 Apr 20	General Economic	136LTS381	303135
UK Great Britain	Multilateral	21 Jun 20	Health/Educ/Welfare	8LTS65	300207
UK Great Britain	Multilateral	30 Jun 20	Patents/Copyrights	1LTS59	300008
UK Great Britain	Multilateral	16 Dec 20	General IGO	6LTS379	300170
UK Great Britain	Multilateral	13 Mar 21	Admin Cooperation	8LTS327	300232
UK Great Britain	Multilateral	20 Apr 21	Water Transport	7LTS73	300174
UK Great Britain	Multilateral	20 Apr 21	Land Transport	7LTS11	300171
UK Great Britain	Multilateral	20 Apr 21	Water Transport	7LTS35	300172
UK Great Britain	Multilateral	20 Apr 21	Water Transport	7LTS65	300173
UK Great Britain	Multilateral	05 May 21	Peace/Disarmament	12LTS419	300338
UK Great Britain	Multilateral	10 Jun 21	Customs	8LTS297	300227
UK Great Britain	Multilateral	20 Jul 21	General Military	8LTS115	300213
UK Great Britain	Multilateral	23 Jul 21	Water Transport	26LTS173	300647
UK Great Britain	Multilateral	03 Sep 21	Postal Service	8LTS147	300216
UK Great Britain	Multilateral	03 Sep 21	Postal Service	8LTS151	300217
UK Great Britain	Multilateral	21 Sep 21	Humanitarian	7LTS127	300181
UK Great Britain	Multilateral	06 Oct 21	General Economic	17LTS45	300427

PARTY ONE	PARTY TWO	DATE	TOPIC	CITATION	NUMBER
UK Great Britain	Multilateral	22 Feb 22	Water Transport	26LTS219	300649
UK Great Britain	Multilateral	31 Mar 22	Humanitarian	9LTS415	300269
UK Great Britain	Multilateral	05 Jul 22	Reparations	13LTS237	300355
UK Great Britain	Multilateral	04 Oct 22	Territory Boundary	12LTS391	300335
UK Great Britain	Multilateral	04 Oct 22	Territory Boundary	12LTS385	300334
UK Great Britain	Multilateral	27 Jan 23	Water Transport	26LTS253	300651
UK Great Britain	Multilateral	05 Feb 23	Telecommunications	28LTS409	300720
UK Great Britain	Multilateral	29 Mar 23	Admin Cooperation	20LTS111	300510
UK Great Britain	Multilateral	03 Nov 23	Customs	30LTS371	300775
UK Great Britain	Multilateral	18 Dec 23	Territory Boundary	28LTS541	300729
UK Great Britain	Multilateral	08 Jan 24	Dispute Settlement	23LTS63	300576
UK Great Britain	Multilateral	07 Feb 24	Water Transport	25LTS265	300614
UK Great Britain	Multilateral	14 Mar 24	Finance	25LTS423	300633
UK Great Britain	Multilateral	28 Mar 24	Finance	31LTS46	300780
UK Great Britain	Multilateral	31 Mar 24	Sanitation	27LTS211	300685
UK Great Britain	Multilateral	22 May 24	General Trade	35LTS175	300895
UK Great Britain	Multilateral	25 Aug 24	Water Transport	120LTS155	302764
UK Great Britain	Multilateral	25 Aug 24	Water Transport	120LTS123	302763
UK Great Britain	Multilateral	30 Aug 24	Admin Cooperation	30LTS79	300761
UK Great Britain	Multilateral	30 Aug 24	Admin Cooperation	30LTS75	300760
UK Great Britain	Multilateral	01 Dec 24	Sanitation	78LTS351	301794
UK Great Britain	Multilateral	11 Feb 25	Sanitation	51LTS337	301239
UK Great Britain	Multilateral	19 Feb 25	Admin Cooperation	81LTS317	301845
UK Great Britain	Multilateral	06 Nov 25	Other Economic	74LTS319	301744
UK Great Britain	Multilateral	06 Nov 25	Patents/Copyrights	74LTS289	301743
UK Great Britain	Multilateral	27 Nov 25	Water Transport	67LTS63	301539
UK Great Britain	Multilateral	10 Apr 26	Water Transport	176LTS199	304062
UK Great Britain	Multilateral	10 Apr 26	Water Transport	120LTS187	302765
UK Great Britain	Multilateral	24 Apr 26	Land Transport	108LTS123	302505
UK Great Britain	Multilateral	25 Sep 26	ILO Labor	60LTS253	301414
UK Great Britain	Multilateral	12 Jul 27	Direct Aid	135LTS247	303115
UK Great Britain	Multilateral	28 Jul 27	Territory Boundary	64LTS379	301511
UK Great Britain	Multilateral	26 Sep 27	Dispute Settlement	92LTS301	302096
UK Great Britain	Multilateral	27 Oct 27	Air Transport	148LTS265	303417
UK Great Britain	Multilateral	08 Nov 27	General Trade	97LTS391	302238
UK Great Britain	Multilateral	08 Dec 27	Loans and Credits	70LTS73	301623
UK Great Britain	Multilateral	08 Mar 28	Telecommunications	80LTS241	301829
UK Great Britain	Multilateral	22 May 28	Telecommunications	85LTS99	301925
UK Great Britain	Multilateral	11 Jul 28	Commodity Trade	95LTS357	302184
UK Great Britain	Multilateral	11 Jul 28	Commodity Trade	95LTS373	302185
UK Great Britain	Multilateral	27 Aug 28	General Military	94LTS57	302137
UK Great Britain	Multilateral	26 Sep 28	Dispute Settlement	93LTS343	302123
UK Great Britain	Multilateral	22 Nov 28	Culture	111LTS343	302598
UK Great Britain	Multilateral	27 Nov 28	Telecommunications	92LTS321	302098
UK Great Britain	Multilateral	14 Dec 28	General Economic	110LTS171	302560
UK Great Britain	Multilateral	20 Dec 28	Specific Resources	86LTS429	301954
UK Great Britain	Multilateral	02 Feb 29	Telecommunications	92LTS353	302100
UK Great Britain	Multilateral	20 Apr 29	Admin Cooperation	112LTS371	302623
UK Great Britain	Multilateral	31 May 29	Water Transport	136LTS81	303127
UK Great Britain	Multilateral	14 Jun 29	Visas	94LTS275	302148
UK Great Britain	Multilateral	28 Jun 29	Postal Service	103LTS5	302369
UK Great Britain	Multilateral	28 Jun 29	Postal Service	102LTS245	302368
UK Great Britain	Multilateral	27 Jul 29	Other Military	118LTS303	302733
UK Great Britain	Multilateral	27 Jul 29	Other Military	118LTS343	302734
UK Great Britain	Multilateral	30 Aug 29	General Amity	104LTS487	302400
UK Great Britain	Multilateral	30 Aug 29	Consul/Citizenship	104LTS473	302399
UK Great Britain	Multilateral	12 Oct 29	General Transport	137LTS11	303145
UK Great Britain	Multilateral	09 Jan 30	Admin Cooperation	115LTS473	302696
UK Great Britain	Multilateral	20 Jan 30	Reparations	112LTS361	302622
UK Great Britain	Multilateral	20 Jan 30	Reparations	104LTS421	302396
UK Great Britain	Multilateral	20 Jan 30	Reparations	104LTS243	302394
UK Great Britain	Multilateral	20 Jan 30	Finance	104LTS433	302397
UK Great Britain	Multilateral	20 Jan 30	Finance	104LTS413	302395
UK Great Britain	Multilateral	20 Jan 30	Reparations	113LTS389	302650
UK Great Britain	Multilateral	20 Jan 30	Other Economic	104LTS441	302398

PARTY ONE	PARTY TWO	DATE	TOPIC	CITATION	NUMBER
UK Great Britain	Multilateral	17 Feb 30	Dispute Settlement	102LTS87	302354
UK Great Britain	Multilateral	15 Mar 30	Finance	113LTS395	302651
UK Great Britain	Multilateral	10 Apr 30	Telecommunications	101LTS465	302345
UK Great Britain	Multilateral	12 Apr 30	Admin Cooperation	179LTS89	304137
UK Great Britain	Multilateral	12 Apr 30	Milit Servic/Citiz	178LTS227	304117
UK Great Britain	Multilateral	12 Apr 30	Admin Cooperation	179LTS115	304138
UK Great Britain	Multilateral	17 Apr 30	Extradition	126LTS201	302883
UK Great Britain	Multilateral	22 Apr 30	Peace/Disarmament	112LTS65	302608
UK Great Britain	Multilateral	28 Apr 30	Claims and Debts	121LTS69	302785
UK Great Britain	Multilateral	07 Jun 30	Finance	143LTS337	303315
UK Great Britain	Multilateral	10 Jun 30	Loans and Credits	112LTS237	302618
UK Great Britain	Multilateral	01 Jul 30	Claims and Debts	121LTS153	302786
UK Great Britain	Multilateral	01 Aug 30	Health/Educ/Welfare	128LTS9	302932
UK Great Britain	Multilateral	23 Oct 30	Water Transport	112LTS21	302603
UK Great Britain	Multilateral	27 Nov 30	Extradition	121LTS39	302781
UK Great Britain	Multilateral	19 Mar 31	Admin Cooperation	143LTS7	303301
UK Great Britain	Multilateral	28 Mar 31	Customs	119LTS47	302739
UK Great Britain	Multilateral	30 Mar 31	Taxation	138LTS149	303185
UK Great Britain	Multilateral	13 Apr 31	Air Transport	119LTS275	302751
UK Great Britain	Multilateral	16 May 31	Air Transport	136LTS245	303128
UK Great Britain	Multilateral	13 Jul 31	Other HEW	139LTS301	303219
UK Great Britain	Multilateral	21 Aug 31	Other Ad Hoc	185LTS45	304273
UK Great Britain	Multilateral	21 Aug 31	Other Economic	127LTS95	302910
UK Great Britain	Multilateral	24 Sep 31	Specific Resources	155LTS349	303586
UK Great Britain	Multilateral	27 Nov 31	Sanitation	177LTS373	304100
UK Great Britain	Multilateral	10 Dec 31	Water Transport	129LTS177	302961
UK Great Britain	Multilateral	20 Jan 32	Extradition	141LTS267	303269
UK Great Britain	Multilateral	17 Feb 32	Telecommunications	138LTS61	303181
UK Great Britain	Multilateral	14 Mar 32	Territory Boundary	131LTS135	303006
UK Great Britain	Multilateral	15 Jul 32	Direct Aid	135LTS285	303118
UK Great Britain	Multilateral	09 Dec 32	Telecommunications	151LTS5	303479
UK Great Britain	Multilateral	11 Mar 33	Water Transport	135LTS301	303119
UK Great Britain	Multilateral	12 Apr 33	Sanitation	161LTS65	303706
UK Great Britain	Multilateral	29 May 33	Admin Cooperation	192LTS289	304479
UK Great Britain	Multilateral	19 Jun 33	Gen Communications	154LTS133	303544
UK Great Britain	Multilateral	29 Jul 33	Extradition	142LTS165	303288
UK Great Britain	Multilateral	25 Aug 33	Commodity Trade	141LTS71	303262
UK Great Britain	Multilateral	30 Sep 33	Extradition	205LTS155	304832
UK Great Britain	Multilateral	11 Oct 33	Education	155LTS331	303585
UK Great Britain	Multilateral	11 Oct 33	Consul/Citizenship	150LTS431	303476
UK Great Britain	Multilateral	08 Nov 33	Specific Resources	172LTS241	303995
UK Great Britain	Multilateral	03 Feb 34	Territory Boundary	154LTS349	303560
UK Great Britain	Multilateral	20 Mar 34	Postal Service	175LTS5	304049
UK Great Britain	Multilateral	20 Mar 34	Postal Service	174LTS171	304048
UK Great Britain	Multilateral	16 Apr 34	Water Transport	163LTS185	303767
UK Great Britain	Multilateral	07 May 34	Commodity Trade	171LTS203	303961
UK Great Britain	Multilateral	01 Jun 34	Territory Boundary	154LTS373	303563
UK Great Britain	Multilateral	02 Jun 34	General Trade	192LTS9	304458
UK Great Britain	Multilateral	02 Jun 34	Patents/Copyrights	192LTS17	304459
UK Great Britain	Multilateral	04 Jun 34	Extradition	184LTS437	304264
UK Great Britain	Multilateral	12 Jun 34	Milit Installation	155LTS367	303587
UK Great Britain	Multilateral	19 Jun 34	Admin Cooperation	154LTS381	303564
UK Great Britain	Multilateral	20 Jul 34	Territory Boundary	155LTS45	303567
UK Great Britain	Multilateral	25 Jul 34	Other HEW	177LTS59	304080
UK Great Britain	Multilateral	07 Dec 34	Air Transport	158LTS91	303629
UK Great Britain	Multilateral	22 Dec 34	Visas	183LTS145	304230
UK Great Britain	Multilateral	22 Dec 34	Admin Cooperation	183LTS153	304231
UK Great Britain	Multilateral	15 Mar 35	Other Military	170LTS9	303926
UK Great Britain	Multilateral	09 Apr 35	Territory Boundary	163LTS177	303766
UK Great Britain	Multilateral	20 Dec 35	Other Military	167LTS141	303862
UK Great Britain	Multilateral	25 Mar 36	Peace/Disarmament	184LTS115	304246
UK Great Britain	Multilateral	27 May 36	Admin Cooperation	203LTS367	304779
UK Great Britain	Multilateral	26 Jun 36	Other HEW	198LTS299	304648
UK Great Britain	Multilateral	04 Jul 36	Refugees	171LTS75	303952
UK Great Britain	Multilateral	20 Jul 36	Territory Boundary	173LTS213	304015

PARTY ONE	PARTY TWO	DATE	TOPIC	CITATION	NUMBER
UK Great Britain	Multilateral	30 Jul 36	IGO Status/Immunit	197LTS31	304602
UK Great Britain	Multilateral	23 Sep 36	Gen Communications	186LTS301	304319
UK Great Britain	Multilateral	06 Nov 36	General Military	173LTS353	304025
UK Great Britain	Multilateral	23 Jan 37	Extradition	191LTS219	304446
UK Great Britain	Multilateral	31 Mar 37	Commodity Trade	189LTS359	304394
UK Great Britain	Multilateral	08 May 37	Privil/Immunities	182LTS37	304202
UK Great Britain	Multilateral	02 Jun 37	Specific Property	184LTS445	304265
UK Great Britain	Multilateral	08 Jun 37	Specific Resources	190LTS79	304406
UK Great Britain	Multilateral	21 Jul 37	Admin Cooperation	184LTS271	304250
UK Great Britain	Multilateral	14 Sep 37	General Military	181LTS137	304184
UK Great Britain	Multilateral	17 Sep 37	Milit Installation	181LTS150	304185
UK Great Britain	Multilateral	11 Oct 37	Air Transport	182LTS173	304210
UK Great Britain	Multilateral	03 Dec 37	Air Transport	186LTS293	304318
UK Great Britain	Multilateral	10 Feb 38	Refugees	192LTS59	304461
UK Great Britain	Multilateral	16 Apr 38	Peace/Disarmament	195LTS103	304538
UK Great Britain	Multilateral	29 Apr 38	Visas	190LTS115	304410
UK Great Britain	Multilateral	17 May 38	Visas	192LTS319	304481
UK Great Britain	Multilateral	30 May 38	Visas	191LTS299	304451
UK Great Britain	Multilateral	24 Jun 38	Specific Resources	196LTS131	304575
UK Great Britain	Multilateral	15 Jul 38	Visas	195LTS73	304536
UK Great Britain	Multilateral	18 Aug 38	Admin Cooperation	196LTS113	304574
UK Great Britain	Multilateral	12 Sep 38	Culture	198LTS111	304630
UK Great Britain	Multilateral	25 Oct 38	Air Transport	192LTS323	304482
UK Great Britain	Multilateral	31 Oct 38	Sanitation	198LTS205	304642
UK Great Britain	Multilateral	28 Dec 38	Other Military	196LTS221	304585
UK Great Britain	Multilateral	27 Jan 39	Loans and Credits	196LTS287	304591
UK Great Britain	Multilateral	05 Feb 39	General Amity	196LTS303	304592
UK Great Britain	Multilateral	23 May 39	Postal Service	202LTS159	304742
UK Great Britain	Multilateral	21 Aug 39	Visas	198LTS343	304652
UK Great Britain	Multilateral	07 Sep 39	Loans and Credits	198LTS357	304654
UK Great Britain	Multilateral	19 Oct 39	General Military	200LTS167	304689
UK Great Britain	Multilateral	08 Jan 40	Visas	203LTS133	304756
UK Great Britain	Multilateral	01 Jan 42	General Military	204LTS381	304817
UK Great Britain	Multilateral	09 Sep 42	Commodity Trade	205LTS137	304831
UK Great Britain	Muscat and Oman	11 Feb 20	Water Transport	5LTS59	300118
UK Great Britain	Muscat and Oman	11 Feb 21	General Economic	8LTS261	300224
UK Great Britain	Muscat and Oman	11 Feb 22	General Economic	10LTS459	300285
UK Great Britain	Muscat and Oman	11 Feb 23	General Amity	17LTS163	300433
UK Great Britain	Muscat and Oman	11 Feb 24	Admin Cooperation	25LTS387	300628
UK Great Britain	Muscat and Oman	11 Feb 25	General Amity	35LTS233	300897
UK Great Britain	Muscat and Oman	11 Feb 27	General Amity	64LTS398	301512
UK Great Britain	Nepal	21 Dec 23	General Amity	36LTS357	300934
UK Great Britain	Netherlands	13 Apr 20	Extradition	1LTS275	300021
UK Great Britain	Netherlands	01 Jul 20	Dispute Settlement	1LTS291	300024
UK Great Britain	Netherlands	18 Jan 21	Telecommunications	5LTS157	300124
UK Great Britain	Netherlands	02 Jun 22	Postal Service	13LTS263	300357
UK Great Britain	Netherlands	18 Jan 23	Postal Service	18LTS257	300469
UK Great Britain	Netherlands	23 Jan 23	Postal Service	16LTS425	300420
UK Great Britain	Netherlands	30 Apr 23	Postal Service	20LTS343	300525
UK Great Britain	Netherlands	11 Jul 23	Air Transport	33LTS111	300836
UK Great Britain	Netherlands	06 Sep 23	Postal Service	22LTS433	300572
UK Great Britain	Netherlands	28 Sep 23	Sanitation	23LTS113	300581
UK Great Britain	Netherlands	02 Oct 23	Postal Service	23LTS9	300573
UK Great Britain	Netherlands	12 Jul 25	Admin Cooperation	38LTS207	300977
UK Great Britain	Netherlands	30 Dec 25	Postal Service	61LTS9	301424
UK Great Britain	Netherlands	20 May 26	Taxation	50LTS309	301214
UK Great Britain	Netherlands	14 Aug 26	Sanitation	57LTS41	301351
UK Great Britain	Netherlands	11 Mar 27	Telecommunications	64LTS403	301513
UK Great Britain	Netherlands	14 Nov 27	Postal Service	71LTS227	301666
UK Great Britain	Netherlands	26 Mar 28	Territory Boundary	108LTS331	302516
UK Great Britain	Netherlands	22 Mar 29	Reparations	90LTS421	302052
UK Great Britain	Netherlands	04 May 29	Postal Service	93LTS9	302101
UK Great Britain	Netherlands	10 Feb 30	Postal Service	102LTS67	302353
UK Great Britain	Netherlands	05 May 30	Air Transport	105LTS261	302417
UK Great Britain	Netherlands	03 Jun 30	Postal Service	111LTS85	302582

PARTY ONE	PARTY TWO	DATE	TOPIC	CITATION	NUMBER
UK Great Britain	Netherlands	01 Jan 31	Postal Service	115LTS509	302698
UK Great Britain	Netherlands	09 Apr 31	Education	125LTS41	302844
UK Great Britain	Netherlands	04 Jan 32	Postal Service	128LTS347	302940
UK Great Britain	Netherlands	04 Jan 32	Postal Service	128LTS307	302939
UK Great Britain	Netherlands	31 May 32	Admin Cooperation	140LTS287	303244
UK Great Britain	Netherlands	13 Aug 32	Postal Service	134LTS317	303100
UK Great Britain	Netherlands	30 Jul 34	General Trade	154LTS305	303557
UK Great Britain	Netherlands	06 Jun 35	Taxation	169LTS359	303924
UK Great Britain	Netherlands	07 Nov 35	Water Transport	165LTS337	303820
UK Great Britain	Netherlands	18 Dec 35	General Trade	165LTS255	303812
UK Great Britain	Netherlands	30 Dec 35	Customs	165LTS263	303813
UK Great Britain	Netherlands	27 Aug 36	Air Transport	172LTS53	303978
UK Great Britain	Netherlands	04 Aug 39	Gen Communications	198LTS349	304653
UK Great Britain	Norway	06 Jul 20	Postal Service	5LTS107	300121
UK Great Britain	Norway	22 Apr 21	Admin Cooperation	5LTS33	300114
UK Great Britain	Norway	15 Jul 21	Air Transport	6LTS307	300162
UK Great Britain	Norway	16 Dec 21	Sanitation	16LTS187	300409
UK Great Britain	Norway	22 Feb 23	Air Transport	15LTS159	300389
UK Great Britain	Norway	05 Jun 24	Admin Cooperation	27LTS195	300683
UK Great Britain	Norway	18 Dec 24	Taxation	32LTS9	300801
UK Great Britain	Norway	13 May 25	Admin Cooperation	36LTS435	300940
UK Great Britain	Norway	18 Nov 30	Recognition	112LTS97	302609
UK Great Britain	Norway	30 Jan 31	Privil/Immunities	123LTS343	302823
UK Great Britain	Norway	15 May 33	General Trade	145LTS187	303355
UK Great Britain	Norway	05 Nov 34	Claims and Debts	154LTS231	303549
UK Great Britain	Norway	18 Nov 36	Water Transport	173LTS193	304012
UK Great Britain	Norway	21 Dec 38	Taxation	201LTS357	304723
UK Great Britain	Norway	02 Dec 39	Commodity Trade	201LTS97	304706
UK Great Britain	Palestine	23 Jan 22	General Economic	13LTS9	300342
UK Great Britain	Panama	25 Sep 28	General Economic	90LTS311	302045
UK Great Britain	Panama	26 Sep 28	Consul/Citizenship	90LTS327	302046
UK Great Britain	Paraguay	16 Jul 28	General Economic	108LTS365	302519
UK Great Britain	Persia	21 Mar 20	General Trade	4LTS47	300102
UK Great Britain	Peru	27 Aug 21	Specific Resources	7LTS289	300195
UK Great Britain	Peru	02 Mar 22	Specific Resources	10LTS463	300286
UK Great Britain	Peru	31 Dec 28	Consul/Citizenship	100LTS431	302312
UK Great Britain	Poland	26 Nov 23	Water Transport	28LTS428	300722
UK Great Britain	Poland	13 Aug 24	Air Transport	31LTS213	300796
UK Great Britain	Poland	04 Oct 29	Postal Service	97LTS261	302227
UK Great Britain	Poland	20 Jan 30	Claims and Debts	126LTS159	302878
UK Great Britain	Poland	26 Aug 31	Admin Cooperation	131LTS19	303002
UK Great Britain	Poland	11 Jan 32	Extradition	148LTS221	303415
UK Great Britain	Poland	26 Oct 33	General Economic	158LTS73	303628
UK Great Britain	Poland	27 Feb 35	General Trade	162LTS181	303740
UK Great Britain	Poland	10 Sep 37	Customs	184LTS289	304253
UK Great Britain	Poland	14 Oct 37	Customs	191LTS279	304449
UK Great Britain	Poland	27 Apr 38	Peace/Disarmament	195LTS39	304535
UK Great Britain	Poland	05 Oct 38	Postal Service	194LTS321	304529
UK Great Britain	Poland	25 Aug 39	General Military	199LTS57	304665
UK Great Britain	Poland	25 Nov 39	General Military	199LTS65	304666
UK Great Britain	Portugal	07 Apr 20	Non-ILO Labor	5LTS297	300134
UK Great Britain	Portugal	06 May 20	Territory Boundary	4LTS93	300103
UK Great Britain	Portugal	09 Dec 20	Dispute Settlement	7LTS257	300192
UK Great Britain	Portugal	10 Jan 21	Extradition	7LTS264	300193
UK Great Britain	Portugal	10 Jan 21	Extradition	7LTS271	300194
UK Great Britain	Portugal	06 May 21	Air Transport	5LTS179	300128
UK Great Britain	Portugal	04 Feb 22	Health/Educ/Welfare	9LTS187	300251
UK Great Britain	Portugal	31 Mar 23	Admin Cooperation	18LTS29	300451
UK Great Britain	Portugal	19 May 25	Consul/Citizenship	36LTS125	300910
UK Great Britain	Portugal	03 Nov 25	Territory Boundary	47LTS379	301143
UK Great Britain	Portugal	20 May 26	Water Transport	50LTS303	301213
UK Great Britain	Portugal	31 Dec 26	Claims and Debts	61LTS115	301429
UK Great Britain	Portugal	06 Nov 27	Territory Boundary	80LTS219	301827
UK Great Britain	Portugal	18 Feb 30	General Trade	108LTS393	302522
UK Great Britain	Portugal	14 Jun 30	Postal Service	107LTS275	302484

PARTY ONE	PARTY TWO	DATE	TOPIC	CITATION	NUMBER
UK Great Britain	Portugal	27 Jun 30	Postal Service	107LTS281	302485
UK Great Britain	Portugal	09 Aug 31	Admin Cooperation	129LTS417	302975
UK Great Britain	Portugal	14 Oct 33	General Trade	144LTS107	303322
UK Great Britain	Portugal	24 Oct 35	Air Transport	167LTS133	303861
UK Great Britain	Portugal	24 Mar 37	Postal Service	185LTS151	304280
UK Great Britain	Portugal	24 Mar 37	Postal Service	185LTS175	304281
UK Great Britain	Portugal	24 Mar 37	Postal Service	185LTS143	304279
UK Great Britain	Portugal	28 Dec 37	Territory Boundary	185LTS205	304284
UK Great Britain	Portugal	11 May 38	General Trade	191LTS285	304450
UK Great Britain	Portugal	25 Jan 39	Air Transport	196LTS281	304590
UK Great Britain	Portugal	29 Oct 40	Territory Boundary	204LTS261	304807
UK Great Britain	Romania	22 Jan 20	Commodity Trade	1LTS257	300018
UK Great Britain	Romania	21 Apr 21	Peace/Disarmament	8LTS293	300226
UK Great Britain	Romania	24 May 23	General Trade	18LTS301	300471
UK Great Britain	Romania	02 Apr 30	Postal Service	105LTS235	302416
UK Great Britain	Romania	06 Aug 30	General Economic	123LTS307	302822
UK Great Britain	Romania	25 Sep 33	Consul/Citizenship	149LTS425	303443
UK Great Britain	Romania	14 Jun 35	Consul/Citizenship	163LTS301	303772
UK Great Britain	Romania	02 May 36	Finance	184LTS145	304247
UK Great Britain	Romania	06 Dec 37	Admin Cooperation	184LTS467	304267
UK Great Britain	Romania	02 Sep 38	Finance	191LTS313	304453
UK Great Britain	Romania	11 May 39	General Trade	196LTS351	304594
UK Great Britain	Romania	06 Jun 40	Finance	203LTS197	304761
UK Great Britain	Saudi Arabia	17 Nov 35	Customs	170LTS87	303929
UK Great Britain	Serb/Croat/Slovene	29 Jul 21	Reparations	10LTS411	300280
UK Great Britain	Serb/Croat/Slovene	18 Jun 26	General Economic	57LTS23	301349
UK Great Britain	Serb/Croat/Slovene	12 May 27	General Trade	80LTS165	301825
UK Great Britain	Siam	20 Dec 21	Peace/Disarmament	10LTS421	300282
UK Great Britain	Siam	15 Sep 25	Admin Cooperation	49LTS29	301175
UK Great Britain	Siam	15 Sep 25	General Economic	49LTS51	301176
UK Great Britain	Siam	25 Nov 25	Dispute Settlement	63LTS161	301487
UK Great Britain	Siam	21 Feb 28	Water Transport	87LTS21	301960
UK Great Britain	Siam	20 Mar 30	Postal Service	106LTS363	302456
UK Great Britain	Siam	31 Mar 37	Admin Cooperation	179LTS257	304153
UK Great Britain	Siam	23 Nov 37	General Trade	188LTS333	304366
UK Great Britain	Spain	31 Oct 22	Water Transport	28LTS339	300719
UK Great Britain	Spain	09 Feb 24	Admin Cooperation	25LTS17	300602
UK Great Britain	Spain	27 Jun 24	General Trade	28LTS523	300727
UK Great Britain	Spain	19 Oct 26	Postal Service	61LTS79	301427
UK Great Britain	Spain	30 Jul 27	General Trade	63LTS189	301490
UK Great Britain	Spain	27 Jun 29	Admin Cooperation	101LTS375	302337
UK Great Britain	Spain	26 May 32	Water Transport	132LTS43	303030
UK Great Britain	Spain	06 Jan 36	Finance	166LTS283	303844
UK Great Britain	Spain	18 Mar 40	Finance	203LTS157	304759
UK Great Britain	Spain	18 Mar 40	Loans and Credits	203LTS149	304758
UK Great Britain	Spain	07 Apr 41	Loans and Credits	204LTS75	304785
UK Great Britain	Surinam	15 Mar 38	Postal Service	189LTS183	304385
UK Great Britain	Sweden	03 Mar 20	Postal Service	5LTS63	300119
UK Great Britain	Sweden	16 Feb 21	Air Transport	3LTS233	300100
UK Great Britain	Sweden	08 Jul 21	Claims and Debts	5LTS329	300139
UK Great Britain	Sweden	29 Aug 21	Other HEW	6LTS285	300160
UK Great Britain	Sweden	27 Oct 23	Admin Cooperation	22LTS387	300568
UK Great Britain	Sweden	05 Mar 24	Air Transport	23LTS149	300586
UK Great Britain	Sweden	09 Oct 24	Admin Cooperation	34LTS381	300886
UK Great Britain	Sweden	19 Dec 24	Taxation	32LTS291	300820
UK Great Britain	Sweden	28 Aug 30	Admin Cooperation	114LTS9	302652
UK Great Britain	Sweden	06 Jul 31	Taxation	120LTS211	302766
UK Great Britain	Sweden	15 May 33	General Trade	140LTS317	303245
UK Great Britain	Sweden	20 Oct 34	Water Transport	154LTS85	303539
UK Great Britain	Sweden	30 Apr 36	Water Transport	168LTS121	303892
UK Great Britain	Switzerland	06 Nov 19	Air Transport	1LTS37	300005
UK Great Britain	Switzerland	28 Feb 20	Postal Service	6LTS9	300145
UK Great Britain	Switzerland	02 Jul 20	Extradition	1LTS53	300007
UK Great Britain	Switzerland	26 Apr 24	General Economic	27LTS189	300682
UK Great Britain	Switzerland	09 Nov 29	Non-ILO Labor	100LTS21	302291

PARTY ONE	PARTY TWO	DATE	TOPIC	CITATION	NUMBER
UK Great Britain	Switzerland	10 Dec 29	Postal Service	99LTS53	302267
UK Great Britain	Switzerland	17 Oct 31	Taxation	131LTS245	303015
UK Great Britain	Switzerland	19 Dec 34	Extradition	163LTS103	303763
UK Great Britain	Switzerland	25 May 35	Postal Service	163LTS239	303769
UK Great Britain	Switzerland	03 Dec 37	Admin Cooperation	194LTS223	304523
UK Great Britain	Switzerland	26 Jul 38	Customs	191LTS307	304452
UK Great Britain	Thailand	12 Jun 40	General Amity	203LTS421	304782
UK Great Britain	Thailand	10 Dec 40	Territory Boundary	203LTS433	304783
UK Great Britain	Turkey	15 Jan 29	General Economic	108LTS385	302521
UK Great Britain	Turkey	25 Sep 29	General Trade	94LTS41	302135
UK Great Britain	Turkey	01 Mar 30	General Economic	108LTS407	302523
UK Great Britain	Turkey	28 Nov 31	Admin Cooperation	141LTS225	303268
UK Great Britain	Turkey	04 Jun 35	General Trade	167LTS91	303860
UK Great Britain	Turkey	02 Sep 36	General Trade	172LTS289	303998
UK Great Britain	Turkey	27 May 38	Milit Assistance	199LTS9	304660
UK Great Britain	Turkey	27 May 38	General Trade	190LTS121	304411
UK Great Britain	Turkey	10 Feb 39	Admin Cooperation	204LTS257	304806
UK Great Britain	Turkey	22 Nov 39	General Trade	201LTS93	304705
UK Great Britain	Turkey	03 Feb 40	General Trade	203LTS399	304781
UK Great Britain	United Arab Rep	05 Jul 23	Other Ad Hoc	18LTS311	300473
UK Great Britain	United Arab Rep	18 Jul 23	Admin Cooperation	18LTS323	300474
UK Great Britain	United Arab Rep	17 Mar 29	Loans and Credits	90LTS413	302051
UK Great Britain	United Arab Rep	07 May 29	Specific Resources	93LTS43	302103
UK Great Britain	United Arab Rep	07 Jun 30	General Trade	107LTS267	302483
UK Great Britain	United Arab Rep	12 Aug 36	Telecommunications	182LTS311	304218
UK Great Britain	United Arab Rep	18 Aug 36	General Trade	176LTS177	304059
UK Great Britain	United Arab Rep	26 Aug 36	Status of Forces	173LTS433	304032
UK Great Britain	United Arab Rep	26 Aug 36	General Military	173LTS401	304031
UK Great Britain	United Arab Rep	09 Sep 36	Admin Cooperation	182LTS317	304219
UK Great Britain	United Arab Rep	21 Oct 37	Privil/Immunities	184LTS285	304252
UK Great Britain	United Arab Rep	20 Feb 39	Water Transport	195LTS407	304560
UK Great Britain	United Arab Rep	17 Apr 40	Claims and Debts	201LTS253	304718
UK Great Britain	United Arab Rep	17 Jul 40	Claims and Debts	202LTS97	304738
UK Great Britain	United Arab Rep	26 May 41	General Trade	204LTS147	304793
UK Great Britain	Uruguay	08 Aug 21	Admin Cooperation	8LTS319	300230
UK Great Britain	Uruguay	19 Oct 22	Sanitation	16LTS201	300411
UK Great Britain	Uruguay	26 Jun 35	General Trade	176LTS153	304058
UK Great Britain	USA (United States)	05 Oct 21	General Economic	8LTS371	300235
UK Great Britain	USA (United States)	21 Oct 21	Claims and Debts	12LTS425	300339
UK Great Britain	USA (United States)	22 Apr 22	Postal Service	20LTS415	300530
UK Great Britain	USA (United States)	15 May 22	Extradition	14LTS89	300369
UK Great Britain	USA (United States)	28 Dec 22	Postal Service	21LTS9	300531
UK Great Britain	USA (United States)	23 Jun 23	Dispute Settlement	23LTS87	300579
UK Great Britain	USA (United States)	30 Aug 23	Postal Service	24LTS103	300598
UK Great Britain	USA (United States)	08 Dec 23	Postal Service	23LTS93	300580
UK Great Britain	USA (United States)	23 Jan 24	Sanitation	27LTS181	300681
UK Great Britain	USA (United States)	27 Oct 24	Postal Service	33LTS315	300855
UK Great Britain	USA (United States)	03 Dec 24	Consul/Citizenship	43LTS41	301046
UK Great Britain	USA (United States)	10 Feb 25	Admin Cooperation	55LTS119	301309
UK Great Britain	USA (United States)	10 Feb 25	Admin Cooperation	55LTS133	301310
UK Great Britain	USA (United States)	10 Feb 25	Admin Cooperation	55LTS145	301311
UK Great Britain	USA (United States)	16 Mar 25	Taxation	113LTS105	302639
UK Great Britain	USA (United States)	23 Feb 27	Admin Cooperation	82LTS17	301856
UK Great Britain	USA (United States)	19 May 27	Finance	64LTS101	301503
UK Great Britain	USA (United States)	02 Apr 29	Postal Service	94LTS17	302133
UK Great Britain	USA (United States)	06 Apr 29	Water Transport	99LTS27	302265
UK Great Britain	USA (United States)	04 Jul 29	Postal Service	92LTS329	302099
UK Great Britain	USA (United States)	11 Jul 29	Postal Service	98LTS161	302245
UK Great Britain	USA (United States)	02 Jan 30	Territory Boundary	137LTS297	303164
UK Great Britain	USA (United States)	16 Apr 30	Postal Service	109LTS9	302524
UK Great Britain	USA (United States)	22 Dec 31	Extradition	163LTS59	303761
UK Great Britain	USA (United States)	17 Sep 34	Air Transport	153LTS331	303529
UK Great Britain	USA (United States)	05 Apr 35	Air Transport	162LTS59	303734
UK Great Britain	USA (United States)	05 Apr 35	Air Transport	162LTS39	303733
UK Great Britain	USA (United States)	17 Nov 38	General Trade	200LTS293	304700

PARTY ONE	PARTY TWO	DATE	TOPIC	CITATION	NUMBER
UK Great Britain	USA (United States)	06 Apr 39	Territory Boundary	196LTS343	304593
UK Great Britain	USA (United States)	23 Jun 39	Commodity Trade	198LTS333	304651
UK Great Britain	USA (United States)	02 Sep 40	Milit Assistance	203LTS201	304762
UK Great Britain	USA (United States)	09 Dec 40	General Military	203LTS319	304772
UK Great Britain	USA (United States)	27 Mar 41	Milit Installation	204LTS15	304784
UK Great Britain	USA (United States)	23 Feb 42	Milit Assistance	204LTS389	304818
UK Great Britain	USA (United States)	24 Aug 42	Patents/Copyrights	204LTS403	304820
UK Great Britain	USA (United States)	03 Sep 42	Milit Assistance	204LTS395	304819
UK Great Britain	USA (United States)	04 Dec 42	Water Transport	295LTS33	304824
UK Great Britain	USSR (Soviet Union)	12 Feb 20	General Military	1LTS263	300019
UK Great Britain	USSR (Soviet Union)	16 Mar 21	General Trade	4LTS127	300104
UK Great Britain	USSR (Soviet Union)	06 Dec 21	Telecommunications	31LTS85	300785
UK Great Britain	USSR (Soviet Union)	03 Jul 22	General Trade	13LTS37	300345
UK Great Britain	USSR (Soviet Union)	21 Dec 29	Consul/Citizenship	99LTS61	302268
UK Great Britain	USSR (Soviet Union)	22 May 30	Specific Resources	102LTS103	302355
UK Great Britain	USSR (Soviet Union)	16 Sep 30	General Trade	101LTS409	302340
UK Great Britain	USSR (Soviet Union)	16 Feb 34	Mostfavored Nation	149LTS445	303446
UK Great Britain	USSR (Soviet Union)	19 Apr 34	Postal Service	158LTS331	303643
UK Great Britain	USSR (Soviet Union)	17 Jul 37	Peace/Disarmament	187LTS93	304333
UK Great Britain	USSR (Soviet Union)	12 Jul 41	General Military	204LTS277	304808
UK Great Britain	USSR (Soviet Union)	26 May 42	General Military	204LTS353	304813
UK Great Britain	Venezuela	22 Mar 21	Claims and Debts	5LTS169	300126
UK Great Britain	Venezuela	26 Feb 42	Territory Boundary	205LTS121	304829
UK Great Britain	Venezuela	26 Feb 42	Territory Boundary	205LTS131	304830
UK Great Britain	Yemen	11 Feb 34	General Amity	157LTS63	303605
UK Great Britain	Yugoslavia	23 Oct 31	Postal Service	126LTS209	302884
UK Great Britain	Yugoslavia	27 Feb 36	Admin Cooperation	181LTS241	304193
UK Great Britain	Yugoslavia	27 Nov 36	General Trade	181LTS281	304195
UK Great Britain	Yugoslavia	07 Jun 37	Postal Service	184LTS229	304249
Ukrainian SSR	Estonia	25 Nov 21	Consul/Citizenship	11LTS143	300295
Ukrainian SSR	Estonia	25 Nov 21	Dispute Settlement	11LTS121	300294
Ukrainian SSR	Latvia	03 Aug 21	Refugees	17LTS317	300442
Ukrainian SSR	Latvia	03 Aug 21	Refugees	17LTS295	300441
Ukrainian SSR	Multilateral	24 May 23	Postal Service	50LTS341	301218
United Arab Rep	Aden	03 Nov 38	Postal Service	197LTS241	304617
United Arab Rep	Aden	25 Aug 40	Postal Service	204LTS297	304810
United Arab Rep	Australia	08 Jun 34	Postal Service	165LTS95	303805
United Arab Rep	Austria	07 Mar 30	General Economic	100LTS417	302310
United Arab Rep	Austria	13 Oct 34	Admin Cooperation	153LTS279	303522
United Arab Rep	Belgium	20 May 37	Taxation	182LTS153	304207
United Arab Rep	Burma	30 Sep 38	Postal Service	203LTS373	304780
United Arab Rep	Chile	05 Mar 30	Mostfavored Nation	124LTS25	302830
United Arab Rep	Czechoslovakia	16 Mar 30	General Economic	107LTS179	302475
United Arab Rep	Denmark	07 May 30	General Economic	102LTS137	302358
United Arab Rep	Finland	13 Jun 30	Mostfavored Nation	111LTS315	302595
United Arab Rep	France	13 Jun 30	Health/Educ/Welfare	106LTS39	302435
United Arab Rep	France	03 Aug 40	Claims and Debts	202LTS121	304740
United Arab Rep	Germany	25 Mar 30	Mostfavored Nation	115LTS271	302691
United Arab Rep	Greece	10 Apr 26	Mostfavored Nation	61LTS305	301441
United Arab Rep	Hungary	16 Feb 27	General Trade	80LTS61	301822
United Arab Rep	Hungary	12 Jun 30	General Economic	106LTS437	302460
United Arab Rep	ILO (Labor Org)	19 Jun 36	IGO Operations	177LTS343	304096
United Arab Rep	Iraq	16 May 38	General Trade	190LTS177	304415
United Arab Rep	Irish Free State	28 Jul 30	Mostfavored Nation	137LTS421	303172
United Arab Rep	Japan	19 Mar 30	Mostfavored Nation	111LTS223	302588
United Arab Rep	Malaya	29 Feb 36	Postal Service	170LTS103	303931
United Arab Rep	Multilateral	12 Jan 12	Sanitation	4LTS281	300112
United Arab Rep	Multilateral	23 Jan 12	Sanitation	8LTS187	300222
United Arab Rep	Multilateral	05 Jun 12	Telecommunications	1LTS135	300013
United Arab Rep	Multilateral	31 Oct 20	Sanitation	164LTS85	303790
United Arab Rep	Multilateral	16 Dec 20	General IGO	6LTS379	300170
United Arab Rep	Multilateral	31 Mar 22	Humanitarian	9LTS415	300269
United Arab Rep	Multilateral	03 Nov 23	Customs	30LTS371	300775
United Arab Rep	Multilateral	09 Dec 23	General Economic	58LTS315	301380
United Arab Rep	Multilateral	09 Dec 23	Non-IBRD Project	36LTS76	300905

PARTY ONE	PARTY TWO	DATE	TOPIC	CITATION	NUMBER
United Arab Rep	Multilateral	25 Jan 24	Sanitation	57LTS135	301360
United Arab Rep	Multilateral	31 Mar 24	Sanitation	27LTS211	300685
United Arab Rep	Multilateral	25 Aug 24	Water Transport	120LTS155	302764
United Arab Rep	Multilateral	28 Aug 24	Postal Service	41LTS97	301008
United Arab Rep	Multilateral	28 Aug 24	Postal Service	41LTS55	301007
United Arab Rep	Multilateral	28 Aug 24	Postal Service	40LTS307	301004
United Arab Rep	Multilateral	28 Aug 24	Postal Service	40LTS437	301005
United Arab Rep	Multilateral	28 Aug 24	Postal Service	41LTS9	301006
United Arab Rep	Multilateral	28 Aug 24	Postal Service	40LTS249	301003
United Arab Rep	Multilateral	28 Aug 24	Postal Service	40LTS19	301002
United Arab Rep	Multilateral	19 Feb 25	Admin Cooperation	81LTS317	301845
United Arab Rep	Multilateral	17 Jun 25	Peace/Disarmament	94LTS65	302138
United Arab Rep	Multilateral	29 Oct 25	Telecommunications	57LTS201	301365
United Arab Rep	Multilateral	24 Apr 26	Land Transport	108LTS123	302505
United Arab Rep	Multilateral	24 Apr 26	Land Transport	97LTS83	302220
United Arab Rep	Multilateral	21 Jun 26	Sanitation	78LTS229	301793
United Arab Rep	Multilateral	12 Jul 27	Direct Aid	135LTS247	303115
United Arab Rep	Multilateral	08 Nov 27	General Trade	97LTS391	302238
United Arab Rep	Multilateral	25 Nov 27	Telecommunications	84LTS97	301905
United Arab Rep	Multilateral	27 Aug 28	General Military	94LTS57	302137
United Arab Rep	Multilateral	14 Dec 28	General Economic	110LTS171	302560
United Arab Rep	Multilateral	16 Apr 29	Specific Resources	126LTS305	302891
United Arab Rep	Multilateral	20 Apr 29	Admin Cooperation	112LTS371	302623
United Arab Rep	Multilateral	31 May 29	Water Transport	136LTS81	303127
United Arab Rep	Multilateral	28 Jun 29	Postal Service	103LTS71	302370
United Arab Rep	Multilateral	28 Jun 29	Postal Service	103LTS377	302373
United Arab Rep	Multilateral	28 Jun 29	Postal Service	103LTS429	302374
United Arab Rep	Multilateral	28 Jun 29	Postal Service	102LTS245	302368
United Arab Rep	Multilateral	28 Jun 29	Postal Service	103LTS249	302371
United Arab Rep	Multilateral	28 Jun 29	Postal Service	103LTS5	302369
United Arab Rep	Multilateral	27 Jul 29	Other Military	118LTS303	302733
United Arab Rep	Multilateral	27 Jul 29	Other Military	118LTS343	302734
United Arab Rep	Multilateral	20 Aug 29	Sanitation	98LTS125	302243
United Arab Rep	Multilateral	12 Oct 29	General Transport	137LTS11	303145
United Arab Rep	Multilateral	12 Apr 30	Milit Servic/Citiz	178LTS227	304117
United Arab Rep	Multilateral	12 Apr 30	Admin Cooperation	179LTS89	304137
United Arab Rep	Multilateral	12 Apr 30	Admin Cooperation	179LTS115	304138
United Arab Rep	Multilateral	30 Mar 31	Taxation	138LTS149	303185
United Arab Rep	Multilateral	30 Jun 31	Scientific Project	149LTS63	303434
United Arab Rep	Multilateral	13 Jul 31	Other HEW	139LTS301	303219
United Arab Rep	Multilateral	24 Sep 31	Specific Resources	155LTS349	303586
United Arab Rep	Multilateral	09 Dec 32	Telecommunications	151LTS5	303479
United Arab Rep	Multilateral	11 Mar 33	Water Transport	135LTS301	303119
United Arab Rep	Multilateral	12 Apr 33	Sanitation	161LTS65	303706
United Arab Rep	Multilateral	19 Jun 33	Gen Communications	154LTS133	303544
United Arab Rep	Multilateral	11 Oct 33	Education	155LTS331	303585
United Arab Rep	Multilateral	28 Oct 33	Refugees	159LTS199	303663
United Arab Rep	Multilateral	08 Nov 33	Specific Resources	172LTS241	303995
United Arab Rep	Multilateral	20 Mar 34	Finance	176LTS9	304053
United Arab Rep	Multilateral	20 Mar 34	Postal Service	175LTS73	304050
United Arab Rep	Multilateral	20 Mar 34	Postal Service	174LTS171	304048
United Arab Rep	Multilateral	20 Mar 34	Postal Service	175LTS5	304049
United Arab Rep	Multilateral	20 Mar 34	Postal Service	176LTS55	304054
United Arab Rep	Multilateral	20 Mar 34	Postal Service	175LTS269	304051
United Arab Rep	Multilateral	19 Jun 34	Admin Cooperation	154LTS381	303564
United Arab Rep	Multilateral	20 Jul 34	Territory Boundary	155LTS45	303567
United Arab Rep	Multilateral	25 Jul 34	Other HEW	177LTS59	304080
United Arab Rep	Multilateral	26 Jun 36	Other HEW	198LTS299	304648
United Arab Rep	Multilateral	23 Sep 36	Gen Communications	186LTS301	304319
United Arab Rep	Multilateral	06 Nov 36	General Military	173LTS353	304025
United Arab Rep	Multilateral	10 Feb 37	General Transport	189LTS313	304391
United Arab Rep	Multilateral	08 May 37	Privil/Immunities	182LTS37	304202
United Arab Rep	Multilateral	02 Jun 37	Specific Property	184LTS445	304265
United Arab Rep	Multilateral	14 Sep 37	General Military	181LTS137	304184
United Arab Rep	Multilateral	17 Sep 37	Milit Installation	181LTS150	304185

PARTY ONE	PARTY TWO	DATE	TOPIC	CITATION	NUMBER
United Arab Rep	Multilateral	02 Oct 37	Education	182LTS263	304216
United Arab Rep	Multilateral	16 Apr 38	Peace/Disarmament	195LTS103	304538
United Arab Rep	Multilateral	02 Jun 38	Postal Service	192LTS157	304470
United Arab Rep	Multilateral	12 Sep 38	Culture	198LTS111	304630
United Arab Rep	Multilateral	31 Oct 38	Sanitation	198LTS205	304642
United Arab Rep	Multilateral	03 Dec 38	Education	200LTS249	304694
United Arab Rep	Multilateral	23 May 39	Postal Service	202LTS159	304742
United Arab Rep	Netherlands	17 Mar 30	Mostfavored Nation	105LTS91	302404
United Arab Rep	Norway	27 May 30	Commodity Trade	105LTS449	302432
United Arab Rep	Palestine	07 Aug 22	Extradition	36LTS343	300933
United Arab Rep	Palestine	21 Jun 28	General Trade	80LTS277	301833
United Arab Rep	Palestine	12 Jan 29	Dispute Settlement	94LTS9	302132
United Arab Rep	Persia	28 Nov 28	General Amity	93LTS381	302127
United Arab Rep	Persia	17 Jun 30	Mostfavored Nation	107LTS349	302490
United Arab Rep	Poland	22 Apr 30	Mostfavored Nation	118LTS413	302735
United Arab Rep	Romania	16 Apr 30	Mostfavored Nation	117LTS405	302706
United Arab Rep	Serb/Croat/Slovene	15 May 27	General Trade	96LTS367	302213
United Arab Rep	South Africa	31 May 39	General Trade	198LTS295	304647
United Arab Rep	Sweden	07 Jun 30	General Economic	102LTS207	302363
United Arab Rep	Switzerland	07 Jun 34	General Amity	159LTS137	303656
United Arab Rep	Tanganyika	25 Feb 25	Postal Service	36LTS409	300938
United Arab Rep	Turkey	07 Apr 37	Privil/Immunities	191LTS95	304438
United Arab Rep	Turkey	07 Apr 37	Consul/Citizenship	191LTS105	304439
United Arab Rep	Turkey	07 Apr 37	General Amity	191LTS89	304437
United Arab Rep	UK Great Britain	05 Jul 23	Other Ad Hoc	18LTS311	300473
United Arab Rep	UK Great Britain	18 Jul 23	Admin Cooperation	18LTS323	300474
United Arab Rep	UK Great Britain	17 Mar 29	Loans and Credits	90LTS413	302051
United Arab Rep	UK Great Britain	07 May 29	Specific Resources	93LTS43	302103
United Arab Rep	UK Great Britain	07 Jun 30	General Trade	107LTS267	302483
United Arab Rep	UK Great Britain	12 Aug 36	Telecommunications	182LTS311	304218
United Arab Rep	UK Great Britain	18 Aug 36	General Trade	176LTS177	304059
United Arab Rep	UK Great Britain	26 Aug 36	General Military	173LTS401	304031
United Arab Rep	UK Great Britain	26 Aug 36	Status of Forces	173LTS433	304032
United Arab Rep	UK Great Britain	09 Sep 36	Admin Cooperation	182LTS317	304219
United Arab Rep	UK Great Britain	21 Oct 37	Privil/Immunities	184LTS285	304252
United Arab Rep	UK Great Britain	20 Feb 39	Water Transport	195LTS407	304560
United Arab Rep	UK Great Britain	17 Apr 40	Claims and Debts	201LTS253	304718
United Arab Rep	UK Great Britain	17 Jul 40	Claims and Debts	202LTS97	304738
United Arab Rep	UK Great Britain	26 May 41	General Trade	204LTS147	304793
United Arab Rep	USA (United States)	13 Nov 39	Postal Service	198LTS419	304659
United Arab Rep	USA (United States)	02 Mar 43	Status of Forces	204LTS425	304822
United Arab Rep	Yugoslavia	13 Mar 30	Mostfavored Nation	110LTS133	302557
Upper Volta	Multilateral	09 Dec 23	Water Transport	58LTS284	301379
Upper Volta	Multilateral	20 Apr 29	Admin Cooperation	112LTS371	302623
Uruguay	Argentina	11 Apr 18	Territory Boundary	14LTS367	300385
Uruguay	Austria	25 May 29	Visas	93LTS229	302112
Uruguay	Bel-Lux Econ Union	22 Feb 37	General Trade	196LTS391	304600
Uruguay	Brazil	01 Aug 21	Education	177LTS109	304085
Uruguay	Brazil	07 Dec 21	Extradition	63LTS223	301492
Uruguay	Brazil	25 Aug 33	General Trade	176LTS381	304075
Uruguay	Brazil	20 Dec 33	Visas	181LTS55	304177
Uruguay	Brazil	20 Dec 33	Customs	181LTS45	304176
Uruguay	Brazil	20 Dec 33	Culture	181LTS35	304175
Uruguay	Brazil	20 Dec 33	Territory Boundary	181LTS69	304178
Uruguay	Brazil	20 Dec 33	Admin Cooperation	181LTS91	304179
Uruguay	El Salvador	07 Nov 24	Dispute Settlement	108LTS103	302502
Uruguay	Germany	26 Oct 28	Visas	90LTS205	302039
Uruguay	Multilateral	18 Mar 04	Humanitarian	1LTS83	300011
Uruguay	Multilateral	20 Aug 10	Patents/Copyrights	155LTS179	303576
Uruguay	Multilateral	12 Jan 12	Sanitation	4LTS281	300112
Uruguay	Multilateral	05 Jun 12	Telecommunications	1LTS135	300013
Uruguay	Multilateral	21 Apr 14	Sanitation	5LTS394	300144
Uruguay	Multilateral	29 Feb 20	Admin Cooperation	127LTS433	302930
Uruguay	Multilateral	01 May 20	Air Transport	11LTS173	300297
Uruguay	Multilateral	21 Jun 20	Health/Educ/Welfare	8LTS65	300207
Uruguay	Multilateral	30 Jun 20	Patents/Copyrights	1LTS59	300008
Uruguay	Multilateral	31 Oct 20	Sanitation	164LTS85	303790
Uruguay	Multilateral	16 Dec 20	General IGO	6LTS379	300170
Uruguay	Multilateral	20 Apr 21	Water Transport	7LTS73	300174
Uruguay	Multilateral	20 Apr 21	Land Transport	7LTS11	300171
Uruguay	Multilateral	20 Apr 21	Water Transport	7LTS35	300172
Uruguay	Multilateral	15 Sep 21	Postal Service	30LTS141	300767
Uruguay	Multilateral	05 Oct 21	Admin Cooperation	29LTS67	300733
Uruguay	Multilateral	05 Oct 21	Admin Cooperation	29LTS73	300734
Uruguay	Multilateral	05 Oct 21	Admin Cooperation	29LTS79	300735
Uruguay	Multilateral	06 Oct 21	General Economic	17LTS45	300427
Uruguay	Multilateral	31 Mar 22	Humanitarian	9LTS415	300269
Uruguay	Multilateral	05 Jul 22	Reparations	13LTS237	300355
Uruguay	Multilateral	28 Apr 23	Patents/Copyrights	33LTS47	300832
Uruguay	Multilateral	03 May 23	Customs	33LTS11	300830
Uruguay	Multilateral	03 May 23	General Amity	33LTS25	300831
Uruguay	Multilateral	03 May 23	General Trade	33LTS81	300833
Uruguay	Multilateral	24 Sep 23	Dispute Settlement	27LTS157	300678
Uruguay	Multilateral	03 Nov 23	Customs	30LTS371	300775
Uruguay	Multilateral	09 Dec 23	Land Transport	47LTS55	301129
Uruguay	Multilateral	09 Dec 23	Non-IBRD Project	36LTS76	300905
Uruguay	Multilateral	09 Dec 23	Water Transport	58LTS284	301379
Uruguay	Multilateral	09 Dec 23	General Economic	58LTS315	301380
Uruguay	Multilateral	31 Mar 24	Sanitation	27LTS211	300685
Uruguay	Multilateral	28 Aug 24	Postal Service	40LTS307	301004
Uruguay	Multilateral	28 Aug 24	Postal Service	41LTS97	301008
Uruguay	Multilateral	28 Aug 24	Postal Service	40LTS19	301002
Uruguay	Multilateral	28 Aug 24	Postal Service	40LTS437	301005
Uruguay	Multilateral	14 Nov 24	Sanitation	86LTS43	301949
Uruguay	Multilateral	19 Feb 25	Admin Cooperation	81LTS317	301845
Uruguay	Multilateral	17 Jun 25	Peace/Disarmament	94LTS65	302138
Uruguay	Multilateral	29 Oct 25	Telecommunications	57LTS201	301365
Uruguay	Multilateral	24 Apr 26	Land Transport	108LTS123	302505
Uruguay	Multilateral	24 Apr 26	Land Transport	97LTS83	302220
Uruguay	Multilateral	21 Jun 26	Sanitation	78LTS229	301793
Uruguay	Multilateral	25 Sep 26	ILO Labor	60LTS253	301414
Uruguay	Multilateral	12 Jul 27	Direct Aid	135LTS247	303115
Uruguay	Multilateral	25 Nov 27	Telecommunications	84LTS97	301905
Uruguay	Multilateral	18 Feb 28	Patents/Copyrights	132LTS275	303044
Uruguay	Multilateral	20 Feb 28	Air Transport	129LTS223	302963
Uruguay	Multilateral	20 Feb 28	Other Ad Hoc	86LTS111	301950
Uruguay	Multilateral	20 Feb 28	Admin Cooperation	134LTS45	303082
Uruguay	Multilateral	20 Feb 28	Privil/Immunities	132LTS301	303045
Uruguay	Multilateral	20 Feb 28	General Amity	135LTS187	303111
Uruguay	Multilateral	20 Feb 28	Consul/Citizenship	132LTS323	303046
Uruguay	Multilateral	20 Feb 28	Consul/Citizenship	155LTS289	303582
Uruguay	Multilateral	20 Feb 28	Consul/Citizenship	155LTS259	303581
Uruguay	Multilateral	05 Jan 29	Dispute Settlement	130LTS135	302988
Uruguay	Multilateral	05 Jan 29	Dispute Settlement	100LTS399	302309
Uruguay	Multilateral	20 Feb 29	Patents/Copyrights	124LTS357	302840
Uruguay	Multilateral	16 Apr 29	Specific Resources	126LTS305	302891
Uruguay	Multilateral	28 Jun 29	Postal Service	102LTS245	302368
Uruguay	Multilateral	28 Jun 29	Postal Service	103LTS429	302374
Uruguay	Multilateral	28 Jun 29	Postal Service	103LTS249	302371
Uruguay	Multilateral	28 Jun 29	Postal Service	103LTS71	302370
Uruguay	Multilateral	27 Jul 29	Other Military	118LTS303	302733
Uruguay	Multilateral	27 Jul 29	Other Military	118LTS343	302734
Uruguay	Multilateral	14 Sep 29	UN Charter	165LTS353	303822
Uruguay	Multilateral	12 Apr 30	Milit Servic/Citiz	178LTS227	304117
Uruguay	Multilateral	12 Apr 30	Admin Cooperation	179LTS89	304137
Uruguay	Multilateral	12 Apr 30	Admin Cooperation	179LTS115	304138
Uruguay	Multilateral	01 Aug 30	Health/Educ/Welfare	128LTS9	302932
Uruguay	Multilateral	13 Jul 31	Other HEW	139LTS301	303219
Uruguay	Multilateral	10 Nov 31	Postal Service	131LTS327	303023
Uruguay	Multilateral	10 Nov 31	Postal Service	131LTS389	303024

PARTY ONE	PARTY TWO	DATE	TOPIC	CITATION	NUMBER
Uruguay	Multilateral	10 Nov 31	Postal Service	131LTS447	303025
Uruguay	Multilateral	09 Dec 32	Telecommunications	151LTS5	303479
Uruguay	Multilateral	11 Mar 33	Water Transport	135LTS301	303119
Uruguay	Multilateral	10 Oct 33	General Amity	163LTS393	303781
Uruguay	Multilateral	11 Oct 33	Education	155LTS331	303585
Uruguay	Multilateral	26 Dec 33	Recognition	165LTS19	303802
Uruguay	Multilateral	26 Dec 33	Extradition	165LTS45	303803
Uruguay	Multilateral	20 Mar 34	Postal Service	175LTS269	304051
Uruguay	Multilateral	20 Mar 34	Postal Service	175LTS73	304050
Uruguay	Multilateral	20 Mar 34	Postal Service	176LTS55	304054
Uruguay	Multilateral	20 Mar 34	Postal Service	174LTS171	304048
Uruguay	Multilateral	15 Apr 35	Culture	167LTS289	303874
Uruguay	Multilateral	26 Jun 36	Other HEW	198LTS299	304648
Uruguay	Multilateral	23 Sep 36	Gen Communications	186LTS301	304319
Uruguay	Multilateral	23 Dec 36	General Amity	188LTS31	304351
Uruguay	Multilateral	23 Dec 36	Dispute Settlement	188LTS75	304353
Uruguay	Multilateral	23 Dec 36	Dispute Settlement	188LTS53	304352
Uruguay	Multilateral	23 Dec 36	Land Transport	188LTS99	304354
Uruguay	Multilateral	23 Dec 36	Peace/Disarmament	188LTS9	304350
Uruguay	Multilateral	23 Dec 36	Culture	188LTS151	304356
Uruguay	Multilateral	23 Dec 36	Culture	188LTS125	304355
Uruguay	Multilateral	23 Dec 36	Admin Cooperation	201LTS295	304721
Uruguay	Multilateral	23 Dec 36	Dispute Settlement	195LTS229	304548
Uruguay	Multilateral	31 Mar 37	Commodity Trade	189LTS359	304394
Uruguay	Multilateral	03 Dec 38	Education	200LTS249	304694
Uruguay	Multilateral	23 May 39	Postal Service	202LTS159	304742
Uruguay	Netherlands	29 Jan 34	General Economic	166LTS43	303828
Uruguay	Norway	04 Apr 36	General Trade	176LTS115	304055
Uruguay	Paraguay	28 Feb 15	Admin Cooperation	15LTS195	300393
Uruguay	Peru	18 Jul 17	Dispute Settlement	14LTS359	300384
Uruguay	Spain	23 Mar 22	Dispute Settlement	63LTS233	301493
Uruguay	Spain	02 Jan 35	General Trade	164LTS95	303791
Uruguay	Sweden	24 Feb 23	Dispute Settlement	63LTS239	301494
Uruguay	Sweden	13 Aug 36	General Trade	183LTS161	304232
Uruguay	Switzerland	26 Nov 26	Extradition	63LTS207	301491
Uruguay	UK Great Britain	08 Aug 21	Admin Cooperation	8LTS319	300230
Uruguay	UK Great Britain	19 Oct 22	Sanitation	16LTS201	300411
Uruguay	UK Great Britain	26 Jun 35	General Trade	176LTS153	304058
Uruguay	Venezuela	28 Feb 23	Admin Cooperation	36LTS451	300942
USA (United States)	Afghanistan	26 Mar 36	General Amity	168LTS143	303895
USA (United States)	Albania	22 Oct 28	Dispute Settlement	92LTS217	302089
USA (United States)	Albania	22 Oct 28	Dispute Settlement	92LTS223	302090
USA (United States)	Albania	05 Apr 32	Consul/Citizenship	162LTS31	303732
USA (United States)	Albania	01 Mar 33	Extradition	166LTS195	303839
USA (United States)	Argentina	03 Sep 34	Patents/Copyrights	160LTS57	303682
USA (United States)	Argentina	08 Apr 39	Postal Service	198LTS55	304623
USA (United States)	Argentina	12 Sep 39	Military Mission	201LTS213	304715
USA (United States)	Argentina	17 Oct 39	Admin Cooperation	201LTS273	304720
USA (United States)	Argentina	29 Jun 40	Milit Assistance	203LTS57	304750
USA (United States)	Australia	06 Sep 40	General Amity	204LTS245	304803
USA (United States)	Austria	24 Aug 21	General Amity	7LTS155	300184
USA (United States)	Austria	19 Jun 28	Consul/Citizenship	118LTS241	302728
USA (United States)	Austria	16 Aug 28	Dispute Settlement	88LTS101	301989
USA (United States)	Austria	16 Aug 28	Dispute Settlement	88LTS95	301988
USA (United States)	Austria	30 Jan 30	Extradition	106LTS379	302457
USA (United States)	Austria	19 May 34	Extradition	153LTS247	303517
USA (United States)	Bahamas	21 Dec 36	Postal Service	176LTS411	304077
USA (United States)	Barbados	13 Sep 39	Postal Service	199LTS375	304685
USA (United States)	Bel-Lux Econ Union	27 Feb 35	General Trade	160LTS27	303681
USA (United States)	Belgium	30 Mar 22	General Transport	12LTS259	300319
USA (United States)	Belgium	21 Jan 24	Territory Boundary	31LTS137	300791
USA (United States)	Belgium	18 Nov 25	Extradition	50LTS225	301205
USA (United States)	Belgium	09 Dec 25	Other Ad Hoc	72LTS171	301690
USA (United States)	Belgium	20 Mar 29	Dispute Settlement	109LTS261	302542
USA (United States)	Belgium	20 Mar 29	Dispute Settlement	109LTS267	302543

PARTY ONE	PARTY TWO	DATE	TOPIC	CITATION	NUMBER
USA (United States)	Belgium	04 Oct 29	Other Military	105LTS189	302412
USA (United States)	Belgium	19 Apr 32	Water Transport	134LTS19	303080
USA (United States)	Belgium	22 Oct 32	Air Transport	137LTS389	303167
USA (United States)	Belgium	20 Jun 35	Extradition	164LTS205	303794
USA (United States)	Belgium	28 Jan 36	Taxation	166LTS333	303849
USA (United States)	Belgium	15 Jan 39	Postal Service	199LTS321	304682
USA (United States)	Brazil	10 May 34	Military Mission	150LTS445	303477
USA (United States)	Brazil	02 Feb 35	General Trade	166LTS211	303840
USA (United States)	Brazil	27 May 36	Military Mission	171LTS343	303971
USA (United States)	Brazil	12 Nov 36	Military Mission	176LTS133	304057
USA (United States)	Brazil	17 Dec 37	Visas	186LTS413	304325
USA (United States)	Brazil	12 Nov 38	Military Mission	195LTS375	304557
USA (United States)	Brazil	24 Jun 40	Admin Cooperation	203LTS227	304766
USA (United States)	Brazil	11 Oct 40	Privil/Immunities	203LTS261	304768
USA (United States)	Brazil	17 Jan 41	Military Mission	204LTS97	304788
USA (United States)	British Empire	15 Nov 23	Postal Service	33LTS304	300854
USA (United States)	British Guiana	06 Sep 38	Postal Service	193LTS117	304490
USA (United States)	Bulgaria	23 Nov 23	Consul/Citizenship	25LTS238	300611
USA (United States)	Bulgaria	19 Mar 24	Extradition	26LTS27	300638
USA (United States)	Bulgaria	21 Jan 29	Dispute Settlement	93LTS331	302121
USA (United States)	Bulgaria	21 Jan 29	Dispute Settlement	93LTS337	302122
USA (United States)	Bulgaria	18 Aug 32	Mostfavored Nation	136LTS73	303126
USA (United States)	Bulgaria	08 Jun 34	Extradition	161LTS409	303728
USA (United States)	Bulgaria	05 Jan 38	Admin Cooperation	191LTS207	304444
USA (United States)	Canada	02 Mar 23	Specific Resources	32LTS93	300809
USA (United States)	Canada	06 Jun 24	Customs	43LTS225	301057
USA (United States)	Canada	08 Jan 25	Extradition	43LTS233	301058
USA (United States)	Canada	24 Feb 25	Territory Boundary	43LTS251	301060
USA (United States)	Canada	24 Feb 25	Territory Boundary	43LTS239	301059
USA (United States)	Canada	17 Sep 28	Taxation	95LTS209	302175
USA (United States)	Canada	12 Jan 29	Telecommunications	102LTS143	302359
USA (United States)	Canada	22 Oct 29	Air Transport	97LTS321	302229
USA (United States)	Canada	23 Oct 29	Sanitation	96LTS167	302199
USA (United States)	Canada	09 May 30	Specific Resources	121LTS45	302782
USA (United States)	Canada	09 Dec 33	Water Transport	152LTS39	303483
USA (United States)	Canada	15 Apr 35	Dispute Settlement	162LTS73	303735
USA (United States)	Canada	15 Nov 35	General Trade	168LTS355	303910
USA (United States)	Canada	30 Dec 36	Taxation	184LTS473	304268
USA (United States)	Canada	29 Jan 37	Specific Resources	181LTS209	304190
USA (United States)	Canada	09 Oct 37	Admin Cooperation	185LTS33	304271
USA (United States)	Canada	07 Jan 38	Specific Resources	184LTS305	304255
USA (United States)	Canada	24 Jan 38	Admin Cooperation	187LTS27	304330
USA (United States)	Canada	28 Jul 38	Admin Cooperation	192LTS125	304466
USA (United States)	Canada	28 Jul 38	Air Transport	192LTS94	304464
USA (United States)	Canada	28 Jul 38	Admin Cooperation	192LTS115	304465
USA (United States)	Canada	15 Sep 38	Specific Resources	203LTS207	304763
USA (United States)	Canada	17 Nov 38	General Trade	199LTS91	304670
USA (United States)	Canada	20 Dec 38	Telecommunications	196LTS171	304580
USA (United States)	Canada	20 Feb 39	Gen Communications	197LTS181	304613
USA (United States)	Canada	22 Jun 39	Other Military	199LTS197	304673
USA (United States)	Canada	18 Aug 39	Air Transport	199LTS367	304684
USA (United States)	Canada	30 Dec 39	General Trade	203LTS211	304764
USA (United States)	Canada	29 Feb 40	Admin Cooperation	203LTS119	304754
USA (United States)	Canada	04 Mar 40	Admin Cooperation	202LTS429	304745
USA (United States)	Canada	18 Jun 40	Finance	203LTS41	304748
USA (United States)	Canada	06 Sep 40	General Amity	204LTS249	304804
USA (United States)	Canada	07 Nov 40	Specific Resources	203LTS267	304769
USA (United States)	Canada	02 Dec 40	Air Transport	203LTS219	304765
USA (United States)	Canada	20 May 41	Specific Resources	204LTS199	304800
USA (United States)	Chile	27 May 30	Other Economic	133LTS141	303064
USA (United States)	Chile	28 Sep 31	General Trade	144LTS147	303325
USA (United States)	Chile	17 Aug 34	Gen Communications	157LTS15	303602
USA (United States)	Chile	27 Oct 37	Admin Cooperation	186LTS219	304314
USA (United States)	Chile	01 Feb 38	General Trade	190LTS9	304401
USA (United States)	Chile	24 Feb 39	General Trade	197LTS217	304614

PARTY ONE	PARTY TWO	DATE	TOPIC	CITATION	NUMBER
USA (United States)	Chile	23 Apr 40	Military Mission	203LTS29	304747
USA (United States)	China	25 Jul 28	Customs	107LTS121	302472
USA (United States)	China	27 Jun 30	Dispute Settlement	140LTS184	303236
USA (United States)	Colombia	06 Apr 14	Dispute Settlement	9LTS302	300263
USA (United States)	Colombia	13 Sep 35	General Trade	170LTS293	303944
USA (United States)	Colombia	11 Jan 36	Postal Service	169LTS79	303914
USA (United States)	Colombia	23 Nov 38	Military Mission	196LTS147	304578
USA (United States)	Colombia	23 Nov 38	Military Mission	196LTS157	304579
USA (United States)	Colombia	07 Feb 39	Postal Service	196LTS53	304569
USA (United States)	Costa Rica	28 Nov 36	General Trade	181LTS183	304189
USA (United States)	Costa Rica	14 Jul 41	Military Mission	204LTS231	304802
USA (United States)	Cuba	02 Mar 04	Territory Boundary	127LTS143	302915
USA (United States)	Cuba	18 Nov 25	Extradition	61LTS363	301446
USA (United States)	Cuba	04 Mar 26	Admin Cooperation	61LTS369	301447
USA (United States)	Cuba	11 Mar 26	Admin Cooperation	61LTS383	301448
USA (United States)	Cuba	22 Apr 26	Consul/Citizenship	60LTS371	301421
USA (United States)	Cuba	29 May 34	General Amity	150LTS95	303456
USA (United States)	Cuba	24 Aug 34	General Trade	153LTS369	303533
USA (United States)	Cuba	12 May 38	Admin Cooperation	191LTS19	304432
USA (United States)	Cuba	18 Dec 39	General Trade	202LTS71	304736
USA (United States)	Czechoslovakia	05 Dec 24	General Economic	56LTS271	301335
USA (United States)	Czechoslovakia	02 Jul 25	Extradition	50LTS143	301200
USA (United States)	Czechoslovakia	16 Jul 28	Consul/Citizenship	96LTS301	302208
USA (United States)	Czechoslovakia	16 Aug 28	Dispute Settlement	89LTS225	302018
USA (United States)	Czechoslovakia	16 Aug 28	Dispute Settlement	89LTS219	302017
USA (United States)	Czechoslovakia	29 Mar 35	General Trade	159LTS155	303659
USA (United States)	Czechoslovakia	29 Apr 35	Extradition	162LTS83	303736
USA (United States)	Czechoslovakia	07 Mar 38	General Trade	200LTS87	304687
USA (United States)	Czechoslovakia	18 May 38	Customs	199LTS305	304680
USA (United States)	Denmark	08 Jun 22	Postal Service	11LTS311	300298
USA (United States)	Denmark	05 Dec 22	Taxation	113LTS381	302649
USA (United States)	Denmark	29 May 24	Sanitation	27LTS361	300697
USA (United States)	Denmark	14 Jun 28	Dispute Settlement	88LTS173	301995
USA (United States)	Denmark	16 Jan 32	Water Transport	127LTS127	302913
USA (United States)	Denmark	28 Dec 32	Postal Service	140LTS453	303255
USA (United States)	Denmark	11 Nov 33	Postal Service	145LTS113	303349
USA (United States)	Denmark	24 Mar 34	Air Transport	149LTS485	303448
USA (United States)	Denmark	24 Mar 34	Air Transport	149LTS493	303449
USA (United States)	Denmark	24 Mar 34	Air Transport	149LTS471	303447
USA (United States)	Denmark	06 May 36	Extradition	172LTS203	303991
USA (United States)	Denmark	09 Apr 41	General Military	204LTS135	304792
USA (United States)	Dominican Republic	12 Jun 24	Admin Cooperation	48LTS91	301153
USA (United States)	Dominican Republic	19 Jul 26	Customs	54LTS145	301282
USA (United States)	Dominican Republic	24 Sep 40	Customs	204LTS203	304801
USA (United States)	Dutch Indies	04 Oct 34	Postal Service	158LTS395	303646
USA (United States)	Ecuador	12 Jun 36	General Trade	170LTS377	303946
USA (United States)	Ecuador	06 Aug 38	General Trade	193LTS85	304489
USA (United States)	Ecuador	22 Sep 39	Extradition	204LTS169	304796
USA (United States)	Ecuador	12 Dec 40	Military Mission	203LTS327	304773
USA (United States)	Ecuador	12 Dec 40	Military Mission	203LTS305	304771
USA (United States)	El Salvador	05 Sep 30	General Amity	134LTS207	303093
USA (United States)	El Salvador	19 Feb 37	General Trade	179LTS219	304150
USA (United States)	Estonia	08 Nov 23	Extradition	43LTS277	301063
USA (United States)	Estonia	02 Mar 25	General Economic	43LTS289	301064
USA (United States)	Estonia	28 Oct 25	Claims and Debts	62LTS63	301455
USA (United States)	Estonia	23 Dec 25	General Amity	50LTS13	301197
USA (United States)	Estonia	30 Nov 26	General Transport	62LTS313	301469
USA (United States)	Estonia	27 Aug 29	Dispute Settlement	102LTS239	302367
USA (United States)	Estonia	27 Aug 29	Dispute Settlement	102LTS233	302366
USA (United States)	Estonia	10 Oct 34	Extradition	159LTS149	303658
USA (United States)	Estonia	06 Dec 38	Admin Cooperation	198LTS361	304655
USA (United States)	Fiji Islands	10 Jan 39	Postal Service	196LTS185	304581
USA (United States)	Finland	21 Jul 22	Postal Service	13LTS243	300356
USA (United States)	Finland	26 Jun 24	Postal Service	30LTS9	300756
USA (United States)	Finland	01 Aug 24	Extradition	34LTS103	300869

PARTY ONE	PARTY TWO	DATE	TOPIC	CITATION	NUMBER
USA (United States)	Finland	02 May 25	General Economic	47LTS351	301139
USA (United States)	Finland	21 Dec 25	Customs	47LTS345	301138
USA (United States)	Finland	07 Jun 28	Dispute Settlement	87LTS9	301958
USA (United States)	Finland	07 Jun 28	Dispute Settlement	87LTS15	301959
USA (United States)	Finland	13 Feb 34	General Amity	152LTS45	303484
USA (United States)	Finland	17 May 34	Extradition	152LTS83	303485
USA (United States)	Finland	18 May 36	General Trade	172LTS97	303981
USA (United States)	Finland	30 Dec 38	Admin Cooperation	195LTS417	304562
USA (United States)	Finland	27 Jan 39	Milit Servic/Citiz	201LTS187	304713
USA (United States)	France	03 Sep 21	Postal Service	8LTS145	300215
USA (United States)	France	13 Feb 23	Territory Boundary	26LTS53	300640
USA (United States)	France	13 Feb 23	Territory Boundary	26LTS69	300641
USA (United States)	France	19 Jul 23	Dispute Settlement	25LTS405	300630
USA (United States)	France	30 Jun 24	Admin Cooperation	61LTS415	301451
USA (United States)	France	29 Apr 26	Claims and Debts	100LTS27	302292
USA (United States)	France	08 Jul 27	Taxation	114LTS413	302669
USA (United States)	France	29 Aug 27	Other Military	68LTS253	301589
USA (United States)	France	06 Feb 28	Dispute Settlement	91LTS323	302072
USA (United States)	France	15 Jan 29	Extradition	92LTS259	302093
USA (United States)	France	27 Apr 32	Taxation	164LTS211	303795
USA (United States)	France	04 Mar 33	Admin Cooperation	138LTS349	303198
USA (United States)	France	08 Oct 34	Postal Service	157LTS21	303603
USA (United States)	France	30 Dec 35	Postal Service	171LTS117	303955
USA (United States)	France	23 Apr 36	Extradition	172LTS197	303990
USA (United States)	France	06 May 36	General Trade	199LTS259	304679
USA (United States)	France	12 Dec 36	Customs	176LTS403	304076
USA (United States)	France	18 Feb 37	Customs	184LTS479	304269
USA (United States)	France	14 Jan 38	Visas	191LTS213	304445
USA (United States)	France	15 Jul 39	Air Transport	199LTS207	304675
USA (United States)	France	15 Jul 39	Air Transport	199LTS355	304683
USA (United States)	Germany	25 Aug 21	Peace/Disarmament	12LTS191	300310
USA (United States)	Germany	10 Aug 22	Admin Cooperation	26LTS357	300655
USA (United States)	Germany	19 May 24	Customs	41LTS271	301020
USA (United States)	Germany	20 Mar 25	Taxation	119LTS185	302745
USA (United States)	Germany	21 May 25	General Economic	52LTS133	301254
USA (United States)	Germany	14 Feb 28	Admin Cooperation	79LTS235	301813
USA (United States)	Germany	05 May 28	Dispute Settlement	90LTS177	302035
USA (United States)	Germany	05 May 28	Dispute Settlement	90LTS171	302034
USA (United States)	Germany	23 Jun 30	Reparations	106LTS121	302440
USA (United States)	Germany	12 Jul 30	Extradition	119LTS247	302748
USA (United States)	Germany	16 Dec 31	Water Transport	129LTS129	302957
USA (United States)	Germany	31 May 32	Air Transport	133LTS409	303078
USA (United States)	Germany	31 May 32	Air Transport	133LTS427	303079
USA (United States)	Germany	16 Mar 39	Postal Service	198LTS237	304645
USA (United States)	Gibralter	05 Jan 37	Postal Service	177LTS21	304078
USA (United States)	Great Britain	25 Sep 25	Telecommunications	69LTS179	301603
USA (United States)	Great Britain	01 Oct 25	Telecommunications	69LTS187	301604
USA (United States)	Greece	25 Apr 28	Commodity Trade	91LTS231	302064
USA (United States)	Greece	10 Jun 29	Taxation	98LTS81	302241
USA (United States)	Greece	19 Jun 30	Dispute Settlement	136LTS399	303138
USA (United States)	Greece	19 Jun 30	Dispute Settlement	136LTS393	303137
USA (United States)	Greece	06 May 31	Extradition	138LTS293	303194
USA (United States)	Greece	21 Nov 36	Privil/Immunities	183LTS169	304233
USA (United States)	Greece	15 Nov 38	General Trade	195LTS145	304544
USA (United States)	Guatemala	24 Apr 36	General Trade	170LTS345	303945
USA (United States)	Guatemala	28 Mar 39	Military Mission	199LTS181	304671
USA (United States)	Guatemala	20 Feb 40	Extradition	204LTS111	304789
USA (United States)	Guatemala	27 May 41	Milit Assistance	204LTS185	304799
USA (United States)	Haiti	05 Aug 31	Admin Cooperation	125LTS241	302857
USA (United States)	Haiti	07 Aug 33	Status of Forces	146LTS305	303381
USA (United States)	Haiti	24 Jul 34	Status of Forces	153LTS285	303523
USA (United States)	Haiti	28 Mar 35	General Trade	161LTS157	303709
USA (United States)	Haiti	13 Jan 38	Finance	187LTS201	304340
USA (United States)	Haiti	01 Jul 38	Finance	192LTS89	304463
USA (United States)	Haiti	18 Jul 39	Finance	198LTS329	304650

PARTY ONE	PARTY TWO	DATE	TOPIC	CITATION	NUMBER
USA (United States)	Haiti	27 Sep 40	Finance	203LTS257	304767
USA (United States)	Haiti	13 Feb 41	Finance	203LTS363	304778
USA (United States)	Honduras	18 Dec 35	Customs	167LTS313	303876
USA (United States)	Honduras	12 Dec 40	Admin Cooperation	203LTS341	304774
USA (United States)	Hungary	29 Aug 21	General Amity	48LTS191	301161
USA (United States)	Hungary	04 Sep 26	Admin Cooperation	58LTS111	301369
USA (United States)	Hungary	26 Jan 29	Dispute Settlement	96LTS207	302201
USA (United States)	Hungary	26 Jan 29	Dispute Settlement	96LTS173	302200
USA (United States)	Iceland	15 May 30	Dispute Settlement	108LTS109	302503
USA (United States)	Iceland	16 Jan 32	Water Transport	127LTS135	302914
USA (United States)	Iceland	31 Oct 38	Postal Service	194LTS149	304519
USA (United States)	Iraq	07 Jun 34	Extradition	170LTS267	303942
USA (United States)	Iraq	03 Dec 38	General Trade	203LTS107	304753
USA (United States)	Ireland	04 Nov 37	Air Transport	185LTS71	304276
USA (United States)	Irish Free State	31 Dec 23	Postal Service	56LTS303	301339
USA (United States)	Irish Free State	10 May 26	Postal Service	56LTS433	301345
USA (United States)	Irish Free State	18 Nov 31	Water Transport	131LTS279	303018
USA (United States)	Italy	05 May 26	Taxation	113LTS21	302631
USA (United States)	Italy	19 Apr 28	Dispute Settlement	113LTS183	302645
USA (United States)	Italy	17 Aug 31	Water Transport	137LTS175	303154
USA (United States)	Italy	23 Sep 31	General Amity	134LTS191	303091
USA (United States)	Italy	14 Oct 31	Air Transport	137LTS209	303157
USA (United States)	Italy	01 Jun 32	General Transport	140LTS273	303242
USA (United States)	Italy	16 Dec 37	General Trade	187LTS15	304329
USA (United States)	Japan	11 Feb 22	Territory Boundary	12LTS201	300311
USA (United States)	Japan	23 Aug 23	Admin Cooperation	30LTS263	300770
USA (United States)	Japan	31 May 28	Customs	101LTS63	302320
USA (United States)	Japan	25 Mar 37	Specific Property	181LTS217	304191
USA (United States)	Japan	20 Jun 38	Postal Service	191LTS43	304434
USA (United States)	Latvia	14 Oct 22	Postal Service	38LTS331	300989
USA (United States)	Latvia	16 Oct 23	Extradition	27LTS371	300698
USA (United States)	Latvia	01 Feb 26	General Economic	55LTS33	301302
USA (United States)	Latvia	20 Apr 28	General Amity	80LTS35	301821
USA (United States)	Latvia	14 Jan 30	Dispute Settlement	105LTS301	302422
USA (United States)	Latvia	14 Jan 30	Dispute Settlement	105LTS307	302423
USA (United States)	Latvia	10 Oct 34	Extradition	158LTS263	303636
USA (United States)	Liberia	10 Feb 26	Dispute Settlement	56LTS279	301336
USA (United States)	Liberia	01 Nov 37	Extradition	201LTS151	304710
USA (United States)	Liberia	08 Aug 38	General Amity	201LTS163	304711
USA (United States)	Liberia	07 Oct 38	Consul/Citizenship	201LTS183	304712
USA (United States)	Liberia	14 Jun 39	Air Transport	202LTS93	304737
USA (United States)	Liberia	21 Aug 39	Dispute Settlement	204LTS165	304795
USA (United States)	Liechtenstein	20 May 36	Extradition	183LTS181	304235
USA (United States)	Lithuania	09 Apr 24	Extradition	51LTS191	301226
USA (United States)	Lithuania	23 Dec 25	Customs	54LTS377	301300
USA (United States)	Lithuania	14 Nov 28	Dispute Settlement	100LTS117	302298
USA (United States)	Lithuania	14 Nov 28	Dispute Settlement	100LTS111	302297
USA (United States)	Lithuania	17 May 34	Extradition	157LTS441	303618
USA (United States)	Lithuania	28 Jun 34	Postal Service	153LTS295	303525
USA (United States)	Lithuania	18 Oct 37	Milit Servic/Citiz	191LTS351	304454
USA (United States)	Lithuania	28 Dec 39	Postal Service	202LTS381	304743
USA (United States)	Luxembourg	06 Apr 29	Dispute Settlement	106LTS475	302464
USA (United States)	Luxembourg	06 Apr 29	Dispute Settlement	106LTS469	302463
USA (United States)	Luxembourg	24 Apr 35	Extradition	168LTS129	303893
USA (United States)	Malaya	11 Dec 34	Postal Service	156LTS101	303595
USA (United States)	Malaya	22 Mar 35	Postal Service	161LTS41	303705
USA (United States)	Mexico	18 Jun 32	Claims and Debts	158LTS67	303627
USA (United States)	Mexico	24 Apr 34	Claims and Debts	156LTS81	303593
USA (United States)	Mexico	24 Apr 34	Claims and Debts	149LTS49	303433
USA (United States)	Mexico	13 Jun 35	Water Transport	168LTS135	303894
USA (United States)	Mexico	07 Feb 36	Admin Cooperation	178LTS309	304119
USA (United States)	Mexico	06 Oct 36	Admin Cooperation	180LTS33	304171
USA (United States)	Mexico	24 Sep 37	Admin Cooperation	185LTS23	304270
USA (United States)	Mexico	29 Aug 38	Admin Cooperation	195LTS359	304556
USA (United States)	Mexico	18 Apr 39	Specific Property	201LTS201	304714

PARTY ONE	PARTY TWO	DATE	TOPIC	CITATION	NUMBER
USA (United States)	Mexico	16 Aug 39	Extradition	294LTS159	304794
USA (United States)	Mexico	28 Aug 40	Gen Communications	203LTS357	304777
USA (United States)	Mexico	01 Apr 41	Air Transport	204LTS179	304798
USA (United States)	Monaco	15 Feb 39	Extradition	202LTS61	304735
USA (United States)	Multilateral	18 Mar 04	Humanitarian	1LTS83	300011
USA (United States)	Multilateral	20 Aug 10	Patents/Copyrights	155LTS179	303576
USA (United States)	Multilateral	12 Jan 12	Sanitation	4LTS281	300112
USA (United States)	Multilateral	23 Jan 12	Sanitation	8LTS187	300222
USA (United States)	Multilateral	05 Jun 12	Telecommunications	1LTS135	300013
USA (United States)	Multilateral	21 Apr 14	Sanitation	5LTS394	300144
USA (United States)	Multilateral	10 Sep 19	General Trade	7LTS331	300200
USA (United States)	Multilateral	10 Sep 19	Health/Educ/Welfare	8LTS11	300201
USA (United States)	Multilateral	10 Sep 19	Reparations	2LTS44	300045
USA (United States)	Multilateral	10 Sep 19	Reparations	2LTS21	300042
USA (United States)	Multilateral	10 Sep 19	Admin Cooperation	8LTS25	300202
USA (United States)	Multilateral	10 Sep 19	General Economic	2LTS35	300044
USA (United States)	Multilateral	10 Sep 19	Reparations	2LTS29	300043
USA (United States)	Multilateral	09 Dec 19	Territory Boundary	5LTS335	300140
USA (United States)	Multilateral	09 Feb 20	Territory Boundary	2LTS7	300041
USA (United States)	Multilateral	01 May 20	Air Transport	11LTS173	300297
USA (United States)	Multilateral	05 Jul 20	Dispute Settlement	2LTS241	300070
USA (United States)	Multilateral	05 Aug 20	Territory Boundary	2LTS49	300046
USA (United States)	Multilateral	16 Dec 20	General IGO	6LTS379	300170
USA (United States)	Multilateral	15 Sep 21	Postal Service	30LTS141	300767
USA (United States)	Multilateral	06 Oct 21	General Economic	17LTS45	300427
USA (United States)	Multilateral	13 Dec 21	Territory Boundary	25LTS184	300607
USA (United States)	Multilateral	06 Feb 22	Customs	38LTS267	300981
USA (United States)	Multilateral	06 Feb 22	General Trade	38LTS277	300982
USA (United States)	Multilateral	06 Feb 22	Peace/Disarmament	25LTS201	300609
USA (United States)	Multilateral	06 Feb 22	Admin Cooperation	25LTS195	300608
USA (United States)	Multilateral	28 Apr 23	Patents/Copyrights	33LTS47	300832
USA (United States)	Multilateral	03 May 23	General Amity	33LTS25	300831
USA (United States)	Multilateral	03 May 23	General Trade	33LTS81	300833
USA (United States)	Multilateral	03 May 23	Customs	33LTS11	300830
USA (United States)	Multilateral	25 Aug 24	Water Transport	120LTS155	302764
USA (United States)	Multilateral	28 Aug 24	Postal Service	40LTS19	301002
USA (United States)	Multilateral	14 Nov 24	Sanitation	86LTS43	301949
USA (United States)	Multilateral	26 Nov 24	Finance	48LTS69	301151
USA (United States)	Multilateral	17 Jun 25	Peace/Disarmament	94LTS65	302138
USA (United States)	Multilateral	06 Nov 25	Patents/Copyrights	74LTS289	301743
USA (United States)	Multilateral	06 Nov 25	Patents/Copyrights	74LTS327	301745
USA (United States)	Multilateral	21 Jun 26	Sanitation	78LTS229	301793
USA (United States)	Multilateral	08 Nov 27	General Trade	97LTS391	302238
USA (United States)	Multilateral	25 Nov 27	Telecommunications	84LTS97	301905
USA (United States)	Multilateral	18 Feb 28	Patents/Copyrights	132LTS275	303044
USA (United States)	Multilateral	20 Feb 28	Admin Cooperation	134LTS45	303082
USA (United States)	Multilateral	20 Feb 28	Consul/Citizenship	132LTS323	303046
USA (United States)	Multilateral	20 Feb 28	Consul/Citizenship	155LTS289	303582
USA (United States)	Multilateral	20 Feb 28	Consul/Citizenship	155LTS259	303581
USA (United States)	Multilateral	20 Feb 28	Air Transport	129LTS223	302963
USA (United States)	Multilateral	20 Feb 28	Other Ad Hoc	86LTS111	301950
USA (United States)	Multilateral	20 Feb 28	General Amity	135LTS187	303111
USA (United States)	Multilateral	20 Feb 28	Privil/Immunities	132LTS301	303045
USA (United States)	Multilateral	27 Aug 28	General Military	94LTS57	302137
USA (United States)	Multilateral	05 Jan 29	Dispute Settlement	130LTS135	302988
USA (United States)	Multilateral	05 Jan 29	Dispute Settlement	100LTS399	302309
USA (United States)	Multilateral	20 Feb 29	Patents/Copyrights	124LTS357	302840
USA (United States)	Multilateral	28 Feb 29	Telecommunications	97LTS301	302228
USA (United States)	Multilateral	20 Apr 29	Admin Cooperation	112LTS371	302623
USA (United States)	Multilateral	31 May 29	Water Transport	136LTS81	303127
USA (United States)	Multilateral	28 Jun 29	Postal Service	102LTS245	302368
USA (United States)	Multilateral	27 Jul 29	Other Military	118LTS343	302734
USA (United States)	Multilateral	27 Jul 29	Other Military	118LTS303	302733
USA (United States)	Multilateral	14 Sep 29	UN Charter	165LTS353	303822
USA (United States)	Multilateral	09 Jan 30	Admin Cooperation	115LTS473	302696

PARTY ONE	PARTY TWO	DATE	TOPIC	CITATION	NUMBER
USA (United States)	Multilateral	17 Feb 30	Dispute Settlement	102LTS87	302354
USA (United States)	Multilateral	12 Apr 30	Milit Servic/Citiz	178LTS227	304117
USA (United States)	Multilateral	22 Apr 30	Peace/Disarmament	112LTS65	302608
USA (United States)	Multilateral	13 Jul 31	Other HEW	139LTS301	303219
USA (United States)	Multilateral	24 Sep 31	Specific Resources	155LTS349	303586
USA (United States)	Multilateral	10 Nov 31	Postal Service	131LTS327	303023
USA (United States)	Multilateral	10 Nov 31	Postal Service	131LTS447	303025
USA (United States)	Multilateral	10 Nov 31	Postal Service	131LTS389	303024
USA (United States)	Multilateral	09 Dec 32	Telecommunications	151LTS5	303479
USA (United States)	Multilateral	11 Mar 33	Water Transport	135LTS301	303119
USA (United States)	Multilateral	12 Apr 33	Sanitation	161LTS65	303706
USA (United States)	Multilateral	29 May 33	Admin Cooperation	192LTS289	304479
USA (United States)	Multilateral	22 Jul 33	Specific Resources	153LTS107	303511
USA (United States)	Multilateral	25 Aug 33	Commodity Trade	141LTS71	303262
USA (United States)	Multilateral	10 Oct 33	General Amity	163LTS393	303781
USA (United States)	Multilateral	11 Oct 33	Education	155LTS331	303585
USA (United States)	Multilateral	26 Dec 33	Recognition	165LTS19	303802
USA (United States)	Multilateral	26 Dec 33	Extradition	165LTS45	303803
USA (United States)	Multilateral	20 Mar 34	Postal Service	174LTS171	304048
USA (United States)	Multilateral	02 Jun 34	Patents/Copyrights	192LTS17	304459
USA (United States)	Multilateral	19 Jun 34	Admin Cooperation	154LTS381	303564
USA (United States)	Multilateral	15 Jul 34	Mostfavored Nation	165LTS9	303801
USA (United States)	Multilateral	15 Apr 35	Culture	167LTS289	303874
USA (United States)	Multilateral	25 Mar 36	Peace/Disarmament	184LTS115	304246
USA (United States)	Multilateral	27 May 36	Admin Cooperation	203LTS367	304779
USA (United States)	Multilateral	06 Nov 36	General Military	173LTS353	304025
USA (United States)	Multilateral	23 Dec 36	Admin Cooperation	201LTS295	304721
USA (United States)	Multilateral	23 Dec 36	Dispute Settlement	195LTS229	304548
USA (United States)	Multilateral	23 Dec 36	General Amity	188LTS31	304351
USA (United States)	Multilateral	23 Dec 36	Dispute Settlement	188LTS75	304353
USA (United States)	Multilateral	23 Dec 36	Culture	188LTS125	304355
USA (United States)	Multilateral	23 Dec 36	Dispute Settlement	188LTS53	304352
USA (United States)	Multilateral	23 Dec 36	Peace/Disarmament	188LTS9	304350
USA (United States)	Multilateral	23 Dec 36	Culture	188LTS151	304356
USA (United States)	Multilateral	23 Dec 36	Land Transport	188LTS99	304354
USA (United States)	Multilateral	08 May 37	Privil/Immunities	182LTS37	304202
USA (United States)	Multilateral	08 Jun 37	Specific Resources	190LTS79	304406
USA (United States)	Multilateral	24 Jun 38	Specific Resources	196LTS131	304575
USA (United States)	Multilateral	12 Sep 38	Culture	198LTS111	304630
USA (United States)	Multilateral	31 Oct 38	Sanitation	198LTS205	304642
USA (United States)	Multilateral	08 Dec 38	Gen Communications	202LTS49	304734
USA (United States)	Multilateral	23 May 39	Postal Service	202LTS159	304742
USA (United States)	Multilateral	01 Jan 42	General Military	204LTS381	304817
USA (United States)	Netherlands	18 Dec 13	Dispute Settlement	74LTS157	301737
USA (United States)	Netherlands	03 Apr 23	Patents/Copyrights	21LTS175	300541
USA (United States)	Netherlands	13 Feb 24	Admin Cooperation	25LTS269	300616
USA (United States)	Netherlands	15 Feb 24	Postal Service	31LTS61	300783
USA (United States)	Netherlands	21 Aug 24	Sanitation	33LTS433	300863
USA (United States)	Netherlands	23 Jan 25	Territory Boundary	33LTS445	300864
USA (United States)	Netherlands	19 Jan 26	Postal Service	50LTS199	301202
USA (United States)	Netherlands	27 Nov 26	Taxation	112LTS433	302628
USA (United States)	Netherlands	30 Dec 27	Finance	72LTS179	301691
USA (United States)	Netherlands	13 Jan 30	Dispute Settlement	107LTS69	302468
USA (United States)	Netherlands	09 Jul 30	Postal Service	125LTS123	302851
USA (United States)	Netherlands	16 Sep 30	Postal Service	125LTS147	302852
USA (United States)	Netherlands	16 Sep 30	Postal Service	125LTS173	302853
USA (United States)	Netherlands	20 Dec 35	General Trade	178LTS239	304118
USA (United States)	Netherlands	20 Sep 37	Postal Service	184LTS319	304256
USA (United States)	Netherlands	18 Feb 38	Dispute Settlement	192LTS49	304460
USA (United States)	New Zealand	28 Feb 40	Admin Cooperation	203LTS11	304746
USA (United States)	New Zealand	06 Sep 40	General Amity	204LTS253	304805
USA (United States)	Nicaragua	11 Mar 36	Customs	173LTS141	304009
USA (United States)	Nicaragua	14 Apr 38	Taxation	192LTS275	304477
USA (United States)	Nicaragua	22 May 39	Military Mission	199LTS189	304672
USA (United States)	Nicaragua	19 Feb 40	Admin Cooperation	203LTS47	304749

PARTY ONE	PARTY TWO	DATE	TOPIC	CITATION	NUMBER
USA (United States)	Nicaragua	22 May 41	Milit Assistance	204LTS283	304809
USA (United States)	Norway	11 Feb 21	Postal Service	5LTS217	300130
USA (United States)	Norway	30 Jun 21	Dispute Settlement	14LTS19	300365
USA (United States)	Norway	26 Nov 23	Dispute Settlement	23LTS249	300592
USA (United States)	Norway	24 May 24	Customs	26LTS43	300639
USA (United States)	Norway	24 Mar 25	Taxation	67LTS417	301563
USA (United States)	Norway	20 Feb 29	Dispute Settlement	91LTS413	302079
USA (United States)	Norway	25 Feb 29	General Amity	134LTS81	303085
USA (United States)	Norway	30 Mar 29	Postal Service	91LTS383	302078
USA (United States)	Norway	23 Jul 29	Visas	93LTS223	302111
USA (United States)	Norway	01 Nov 30	Milit Servic/Citiz	112LTS399	302625
USA (United States)	Norway	20 Jan 32	Customs	126LTS393	302897
USA (United States)	Norway	16 Oct 33	Air Transport	145LTS43	303344
USA (United States)	Norway	16 Oct 33	Air Transport	145LTS31	303343
USA (United States)	Norway	16 Oct 33	Air Transport	145LTS9	303342
USA (United States)	Norway	09 Nov 34	Postal Service	156LTS33	303592
USA (United States)	Norway	01 Feb 38	Extradition	191LTS83	304436
USA (United States)	Norway	11 Jul 42	General Military	204LTS415	304821
USA (United States)	Other Unilat Decla	20 Aug 34	Non-ILO Labor	158LTS45	303624
USA (United States)	Panama	06 Jun 24	Commodity Trade	138LTS397	303200
USA (United States)	Panama	17 Dec 32	Finance	138LTS119	303183
USA (United States)	Panama	02 Mar 36	Specific Property	200LTS17	304686
USA (United States)	Panama	02 Mar 36	Land Transport	200LTS205	304692
USA (United States)	Panama	17 Aug 37	Water Transport	182LTS159	304208
USA (United States)	Panama	25 Aug 39	General Amity	199LTS317	304681
USA (United States)	Panama	04 Jan 40	Land Transport	202LTS421	304744
USA (United States)	Persia	11 Jul 28	Privil/Immunities	107LTS375	302494
USA (United States)	Peru	21 May 21	Claims and Debts	6LTS171	300150
USA (United States)	Peru	23 May 34	Gen Communications	152LTS99	303487
USA (United States)	Peru	16 Oct 36	Admin Cooperation	181LTS161	304187
USA (United States)	Peru	31 Jul 40	Military Mission	203LTS91	304752
USA (United States)	Peru	31 Jul 40	Military Mission	203LTS75	304751
USA (United States)	Peru	15 Apr 41	Milit Assistance	204LTS117	304790
USA (United States)	Poland	10 Feb 25	General Trade	37LTS141	300953
USA (United States)	Poland	14 Nov 26	Finance	58LTS97	301368
USA (United States)	Poland	22 Nov 27	Extradition	92LTS101	302082
USA (United States)	Poland	16 Aug 28	Dispute Settlement	99LTS409	302286
USA (United States)	Poland	16 Aug 28	Dispute Settlement	99LTS401	302285
USA (United States)	Poland	19 Jun 30	Commodity Trade	108LTS223	302515
USA (United States)	Poland	15 Jun 31	General Amity	139LTS395	303223
USA (United States)	Poland	17 Apr 34	Patents/Copyrights	150LTS403	303473
USA (United States)	Poland	05 Oct 34	Water Transport	156LTS91	303594
USA (United States)	Poland	05 Apr 35	Extradition	170LTS287	303943
USA (United States)	Portugal	14 Sep 20	Dispute Settlement	7LTS253	300191
USA (United States)	Portugal	05 Sep 23	Dispute Settlement	50LTS239	301206
USA (United States)	Portugal	01 Mar 29	Dispute Settlement	99LTS375	302282
USA (United States)	Romania	26 Feb 26	Mostfavored Nation	51LTS59	301221
USA (United States)	Romania	21 Mar 29	Dispute Settlement	105LTS79	302402
USA (United States)	Romania	21 Mar 29	Dispute Settlement	105LTS85	302403
USA (United States)	Romania	20 Aug 30	Mostfavored Nation	115LTS115	302680
USA (United States)	Romania	16 Nov 36	Extradition	181LTS178	304188
USA (United States)	Romania	10 Aug 37	Postal Service	183LTS7	304225
USA (United States)	Romania	30 Apr 39	Visas	203LTS349	304775
USA (United States)	San Marino	10 Oct 34	Extradition	161LTS149	303708
USA (United States)	Serb/Croat/Slovene	21 Jan 29	Dispute Settlement	93LTS301	302117
USA (United States)	Serb/Croat/Slovene	21 Jan 29	Dispute Settlement	93LTS307	302118
USA (United States)	Siam	16 Dec 20	Admin Cooperation	6LTS291	300161
USA (United States)	Siam	30 Dec 22	Extradition	25LTS394	300629
USA (United States)	Siam	13 Nov 37	General Amity	192LTS247	304476
USA (United States)	South Africa	01 Dec 31	Air Transport	129LTS121	302956
USA (United States)	South Africa	20 Sep 33	Air Transport	148LTS203	303413
USA (United States)	South Africa	20 Sep 33	Air Transport	148LTS189	303412
USA (United States)	South Africa	24 Mar 37	Visas	189LTS113	304379
USA (United States)	South Africa	02 Apr 40	General Amity	204LTS79	304786
USA (United States)	Spain	15 Sep 14	Dispute Settlement	89LTS427	302030

PARTY ONE	PARTY TWO	DATE	TOPIC	CITATION	NUMBER
USA (United States)	Spain	10 Feb 26	Admin Cooperation	67LTS131	301543
USA (United States)	Spain	20 Jun 29	Claims and Debts	120LTS401	302776
USA (United States)	Spain	10 Jun 30	Taxation	120LTS407	302777
USA (United States)	Sweden	27 Feb 20	Patents/Copyrights	2LTS147	300059
USA (United States)	Sweden	29 Jun 20	Consul/Citizenship	2LTS153	300060
USA (United States)	Sweden	28 May 21	Water Transport	6LTS41	300147
USA (United States)	Sweden	17 Apr 22	Postal Service	14LTS281	300380
USA (United States)	Sweden	22 May 24	Customs	29LTS421	300752
USA (United States)	Sweden	24 Jun 24	Dispute Settlement	33LTS273	300851
USA (United States)	Sweden	27 Oct 28	Dispute Settlement	91LTS225	302063
USA (United States)	Sweden	29 Oct 30	Water Transport	109LTS181	302537
USA (United States)	Sweden	17 Dec 30	Dispute Settlement	125LTS233	302856
USA (United States)	Sweden	01 Jun 32	Water Transport	131LTS213	303012
USA (United States)	Sweden	11 Jul 32	Postal Service	192LTS205	304473
USA (United States)	Sweden	31 Jan 33	Status of Forces	159LTS261	303670
USA (United States)	Sweden	09 Sep 33	Air Transport	144LTS171	303327
USA (United States)	Sweden	09 Sep 33	Air Transport	144LTS153	303326
USA (United States)	Sweden	09 Sep 33	Air Transport	144LTS183	303328
USA (United States)	Sweden	17 May 34	Extradition	150LTS375	303470
USA (United States)	Sweden	25 May 35	General Trade	161LTS109	303707
USA (United States)	Sweden	31 Mar 38	Taxation	189LTS327	304392
USA (United States)	Sweden	23 Mar 39	Taxation	199LTS17	304661
USA (United States)	Sweden	30 Jun 39	Admin Cooperation	199LTS203	304674
USA (United States)	Sweden	05 Oct 39	Visas	203LTS353	304776
USA (United States)	Switzerland	16 Feb 31	Dispute Settlement	129LTS465	302978
USA (United States)	Switzerland	10 Jan 35	Extradition	159LTS243	303667
USA (United States)	Switzerland	09 Jan 36	General Trade	171LTS231	303962
USA (United States)	Switzerland	11 Nov 37	Milit Servic/Citiz	193LTS183	304494
USA (United States)	Switzerland	31 Jan 40	Extradition	204LTS175	304797
USA (United States)	Turkey	06 Aug 23	Extradition	153LTS71	303509
USA (United States)	Turkey	28 Oct 31	Admin Cooperation	138LTS345	303197
USA (United States)	Turkey	25 Oct 34	Claims and Debts	158LTS389	303645
USA (United States)	Turkey	02 Jul 35	Postal Service	164LTS125	303792
USA (United States)	Turkey	01 Apr 39	General Trade	202LTS129	304741
USA (United States)	UK Great Britain	05 Oct 21	General Economic	8LTS371	300235
USA (United States)	UK Great Britain	21 Oct 21	Claims and Debts	12LTS425	300339
USA (United States)	UK Great Britain	22 Apr 22	Postal Service	20LTS415	300530
USA (United States)	UK Great Britain	15 May 22	Extradition	14LTS89	300369
USA (United States)	UK Great Britain	28 Dec 22	Postal Service	21LTS9	300531
USA (United States)	UK Great Britain	23 Jun 23	Dispute Settlement	23LTS87	300579
USA (United States)	UK Great Britain	30 Aug 23	Postal Service	24LTS103	300598
USA (United States)	UK Great Britain	08 Dec 23	Postal Service	23LTS93	300580
USA (United States)	UK Great Britain	23 Jan 24	Sanitation	27LTS181	300681
USA (United States)	UK Great Britain	27 Oct 24	Postal Service	33LTS315	300855
USA (United States)	UK Great Britain	03 Dec 24	Consul/Citizenship	43LTS41	301046
USA (United States)	UK Great Britain	10 Feb 25	Admin Cooperation	55LTS119	301309
USA (United States)	UK Great Britain	10 Feb 25	Admin Cooperation	55LTS133	301310
USA (United States)	UK Great Britain	10 Feb 25	Admin Cooperation	55LTS145	301311
USA (United States)	UK Great Britain	16 Mar 25	Taxation	113LTS105	302639
USA (United States)	UK Great Britain	23 Feb 27	Admin Cooperation	82LTS17	301856
USA (United States)	UK Great Britain	19 May 27	Finance	64LTS101	301503
USA (United States)	UK Great Britain	02 Apr 29	Postal Service	94LTS17	302133
USA (United States)	UK Great Britain	06 Apr 29	Water Transport	99LTS27	302265
USA (United States)	UK Great Britain	04 Jul 29	Postal Service	92LTS329	302099
USA (United States)	UK Great Britain	11 Jul 29	Postal Service	98LTS161	302245
USA (United States)	UK Great Britain	02 Jan 30	Territory Boundary	137LTS297	303164
USA (United States)	UK Great Britain	16 Apr 30	Postal Service	109LTS9	302524
USA (United States)	UK Great Britain	22 Dec 31	Extradition	163LTS59	303761
USA (United States)	UK Great Britain	17 Sep 34	Air Transport	153LTS331	303529
USA (United States)	UK Great Britain	05 Apr 35	Air Transport	162LTS39	303733
USA (United States)	UK Great Britain	05 Apr 35	Air Transport	162LTS59	303734
USA (United States)	UK Great Britain	17 Nov 38	General Trade	200LTS293	304700
USA (United States)	UK Great Britain	06 Apr 39	Territory Boundary	196LTS343	304593
USA (United States)	UK Great Britain	23 Jun 39	Commodity Trade	198LTS333	304651
USA (United States)	UK Great Britain	02 Sep 40	Milit Assistance	203LTS201	304762

PARTY ONE	PARTY TWO	DATE	TOPIC	CITATION	NUMBER
USA (United States)	UK Great Britain	09 Dec 40	General Military	203LTS319	304772
USA (United States)	UK Great Britain	27 Mar 41	Milit Installation	204LTS15	304784
USA (United States)	UK Great Britain	23 Feb 42	Milit Assistance	204LTS389	304818
USA (United States)	UK Great Britain	24 Aug 42	Patents/Copyrights	204LTS403	304820
USA (United States)	UK Great Britain	03 Sep 42	Milit Assistance	204LTS395	304819
USA (United States)	UK Great Britain	04 Dec 42	Water Transport	295LTS33	304824
USA (United States)	United Arab Rep	13 Nov 39	Postal Service	198LTS419	304659
USA (United States)	United Arab Rep	02 Mar 43	Status of Forces	204LTS425	304822
USA (United States)	USSR (Soviet Union)	15 Jul 35	General Trade	162LTS91	303737
USA (United States)	USSR (Soviet Union)	22 Nov 35	Admin Cooperation	167LTS303	303875
USA (United States)	USSR (Soviet Union)	04 Aug 37	General Trade	182LTS113	304204
USA (United States)	Venezuela	21 Jan 22	Extradition	49LTS435	301196
USA (United States)	Venezuela	12 May 38	General Trade	191LTS35	304433
USA (United States)	Venezuela	09 May 39	General Trade	198LTS135	304633
USA (United States)	Venezuela	06 Nov 39	General Trade	203LTS273	304770
USA (United States)	Venezuela	24 Mar 41	Military Mission	204LTS83	304787
USA (United States)	Windward Islands	21 Jun 35	Postal Service	162LTS157	303739
USA (United States)	Yugoslavia	20 Jun 38	Postal Service	195LTS259	304549
USSR (Soviet Union)	Afghanistan	24 Jun 31	General Amity	157LTS371	303611
USSR (Soviet Union)	Afghanistan	06 May 35	Sanitation	164LTS335	303800
USSR (Soviet Union)	Austria	08 Sep 23	Consul/Citizenship	20LTS153	300515
USSR (Soviet Union)	Bel-Lux Econ Union	05 Sep 35	General Trade	173LTS169	304010
USSR (Soviet Union)	Bulgaria	10 Jul 35	Postal Service	168LTS275	303905
USSR (Soviet Union)	China	31 May 24	General Amity	37LTS175	300955
USSR (Soviet Union)	China	31 May 24	Land Transport	37LTS193	300956
USSR (Soviet Union)	China	21 Aug 37	General Amity	181LTS101	304180
USSR (Soviet Union)	Czechoslovakia	25 Mar 35	Patents/Copyrights	161LTS309	303719
USSR (Soviet Union)	Czechoslovakia	25 Mar 35	General Economic	161LTS257	303718
USSR (Soviet Union)	Czechoslovakia	16 May 35	General Amity	159LTS347	303677
USSR (Soviet Union)	Czechoslovakia	08 Jun 35	Postal Service	167LTS181	303865
USSR (Soviet Union)	Czechoslovakia	16 Nov 35	Consul/Citizenship	169LTS143	303918
USSR (Soviet Union)	Denmark	23 Apr 23	General Amity	18LTS15	300450
USSR (Soviet Union)	Denmark	18 Jun 24	General Trade	27LTS149	300677
USSR (Soviet Union)	Denmark	29 Jun 25	Water Transport	36LTS251	300926
USSR (Soviet Union)	Denmark	23 Dec 27	Patents/Copyrights	70LTS245	301636
USSR (Soviet Union)	Denmark	29 Jun 36	Postal Service	174LTS93	304040
USSR (Soviet Union)	Estonia	02 Feb 20	Peace/Disarmament	11LTS29	300289
USSR (Soviet Union)	Estonia	25 Jan 21	Postal Service	11LTS73	300290
USSR (Soviet Union)	Estonia	04 Mar 26	General Transport	62LTS77	301456
USSR (Soviet Union)	Estonia	08 Aug 27	Dispute Settlement	70LTS401	301648
USSR (Soviet Union)	Estonia	03 Mar 28	Patents/Copyrights	80LTS401	301840
USSR (Soviet Union)	Estonia	17 May 29	General Economic	94LTS323	302152
USSR (Soviet Union)	Estonia	20 Jan 30	Dispute Settlement	102LTS225	302365
USSR (Soviet Union)	Estonia	04 May 32	General Amity	131LTS297	303020
USSR (Soviet Union)	Estonia	16 Jun 32	Consul/Citizenship	131LTS309	303021
USSR (Soviet Union)	Estonia	04 Apr 34	General Amity	150LTS87	303455
USSR (Soviet Union)	Estonia	28 Sep 39	General Military	198LTS223	304643
USSR (Soviet Union)	Finland	14 Oct 20	Peace/Disarmament	3LTS5	300091
USSR (Soviet Union)	Finland	14 Dec 21	Land Transport	16LTS221	300414
USSR (Soviet Union)	Finland	01 Jun 22	Territory Boundary	16LTS319	300415
USSR (Soviet Union)	Finland	13 Jun 22	Telecommunications	16LTS349	300416
USSR (Soviet Union)	Finland	22 Jun 22	Postal Service	16LTS361	300417
USSR (Soviet Union)	Finland	07 Jul 22	Peace/Disarmament	19LTS99	300488
USSR (Soviet Union)	Finland	12 Aug 22	Refugees	19LTS105	300489
USSR (Soviet Union)	Finland	20 Sep 22	Specific Resources	19LTS143	300490
USSR (Soviet Union)	Finland	21 Oct 22	Specific Resources	29LTS197	300742
USSR (Soviet Union)	Finland	28 Oct 22	Specific Resources	29LTS211	300743
USSR (Soviet Union)	Finland	28 Oct 22	General Transport	19LTS199	300493
USSR (Soviet Union)	Finland	28 Oct 22	Water Transport	19LTS183	300492
USSR (Soviet Union)	Finland	28 Oct 22	Water Transport	19LTS153	300491
USSR (Soviet Union)	Finland	21 Feb 23	Customs	19LTS219	300495
USSR (Soviet Union)	Finland	05 Jun 23	Water Transport	18LTS203	300465
USSR (Soviet Union)	Finland	28 Jul 23	Admin Cooperation	32LTS101	300810
USSR (Soviet Union)	Finland	18 Jun 24	Admin Cooperation	47LTS241	301134
USSR (Soviet Union)	Finland	18 Jun 24	Land Transport	47LTS153	301133

PARTY ONE	PARTY TWO	DATE	TOPIC	CITATION	NUMBER
USSR (Soviet Union)	Finland	18 Jun 24	Telecommunications	29LTS295	300746
USSR (Soviet Union)	Finland	18 Jun 24	Postal Service	29LTS313	300747
USSR (Soviet Union)	Finland	18 Jun 24	Telecommunications	29LTS265	300745
USSR (Soviet Union)	Finland	20 Feb 25	Postal Service	34LTS153	300871
USSR (Soviet Union)	Finland	29 Mar 27	General Transport	71LTS11	301651
USSR (Soviet Union)	Finland	17 Mar 28	Water Transport	80LTS151	301824
USSR (Soviet Union)	Finland	24 Sep 28	Territory Boundary	82LTS63	301860
USSR (Soviet Union)	Finland	13 Apr 29	Customs	96LTS93	302193
USSR (Soviet Union)	Finland	07 Oct 29	Postal Service	96LTS349	302212
USSR (Soviet Union)	Finland	21 Jan 32	General Amity	157LTS393	303613
USSR (Soviet Union)	Finland	22 Jan 32	Dispute Settlement	157LTS401	303614
USSR (Soviet Union)	Finland	04 Jul 33	Territory Boundary	149LTS83	303436
USSR (Soviet Union)	Finland	15 Oct 33	Territory Boundary	149LTS243	303439
USSR (Soviet Union)	Finland	07 Apr 34	General Amity	155LTS325	303584
USSR (Soviet Union)	Finland	25 May 34	Specific Resources	155LTS207	303578
USSR (Soviet Union)	France	29 Nov 32	General Amity	157LTS411	303615
USSR (Soviet Union)	France	29 Nov 32	Dispute Settlement	157LTS421	303616
USSR (Soviet Union)	France	11 Jan 34	Customs	167LTS349	303878
USSR (Soviet Union)	France	02 May 35	General Amity	167LTS395	303881
USSR (Soviet Union)	France	09 Mar 36	Postal Service	179LTS131	304140
USSR (Soviet Union)	France	11 Aug 36	Admin Cooperation	176LTS365	304073
USSR (Soviet Union)	Germany	19 Apr 20	Reparations	2LTS63	300048
USSR (Soviet Union)	Germany	07 Jul 20	Reparations	2LTS85	300051
USSR (Soviet Union)	Germany	06 May 21	Reparations	12LTS177	300309
USSR (Soviet Union)	Germany	06 May 21	Reparations	6LTS267	300159
USSR (Soviet Union)	Germany	16 Apr 22	General Amity	19LTS247	300498
USSR (Soviet Union)	Germany	05 Nov 22	Admin Cooperation	26LTS387	300657
USSR (Soviet Union)	Germany	12 Oct 25	Other Ad Hoc	53LTS7	301257
USSR (Soviet Union)	Germany	12 Oct 25	Admin Cooperation	53LTS227	301259
USSR (Soviet Union)	Germany	12 Oct 25	Consul/Citizenship	53LTS163	301258
USSR (Soviet Union)	Germany	24 Apr 26	General Amity	53LTS387	301268
USSR (Soviet Union)	Germany	25 Jan 29	Dispute Settlement	90LTS219	302041
USSR (Soviet Union)	Germany	16 Apr 29	Water Transport	109LTS327	302547
USSR (Soviet Union)	Germany	24 Jun 31	Admin Cooperation	157LTS383	303612
USSR (Soviet Union)	Germany	07 Mar 35	Postal Service	169LTS7	303911
USSR (Soviet Union)	Iceland	25 May 27	General Trade	63LTS105	301483
USSR (Soviet Union)	Iran	27 Aug 35	Health/Educ/Welfare	176LTS335	304070
USSR (Soviet Union)	Iran	27 Aug 35	Health/Educ/Welfare	176LTS344	304071
USSR (Soviet Union)	Iran	27 Aug 35	General Trade	176LTS299	304069
USSR (Soviet Union)	Iran	27 Aug 35	Sanitation	176LTS349	304072
USSR (Soviet Union)	Italy	06 May 33	Customs	158LTS51	303625
USSR (Soviet Union)	Italy	02 Sep 33	General Amity	148LTS319	303418
USSR (Soviet Union)	Japan	20 Jan 25	General Amity	34LTS31	300866
USSR (Soviet Union)	Japan	23 Jan 28	Specific Resources	80LTS341	301839
USSR (Soviet Union)	Japan	23 Nov 31	Postal Service	132LTS133	303033
USSR (Soviet Union)	Latvia	11 Aug 20	Peace/Disarmament	2LTS195	300067
USSR (Soviet Union)	Latvia	20 Oct 21	Dispute Settlement	54LTS155	301283
USSR (Soviet Union)	Latvia	06 Nov 21	Refugees	17LTS251	300440
USSR (Soviet Union)	Latvia	24 Jun 22	Sanitation	38LTS9	300966
USSR (Soviet Union)	Latvia	19 Mar 25	Water Transport	38LTS141	300971
USSR (Soviet Union)	Latvia	02 Jun 27	General Economic	68LTS321	301591
USSR (Soviet Union)	Latvia	10 Oct 27	Dispute Settlement	84LTS47	301903
USSR (Soviet Union)	Latvia	05 Feb 32	General Amity	148LTS113	303408
USSR (Soviet Union)	Latvia	18 Jun 32	Dispute Settlement	148LTS129	303409
USSR (Soviet Union)	Latvia	04 Dec 33	General Economic	148LTS177	303411
USSR (Soviet Union)	Latvia	04 Dec 33	General Trade	148LTS145	303410
USSR (Soviet Union)	Latvia	21 Jun 37	General Economic	189LTS131	304381
USSR (Soviet Union)	Latvia	05 Oct 39	General Military	198LTS381	304656
USSR (Soviet Union)	Lithuania	12 Jul 20	Peace/Disarmament	3LTS106	300094
USSR (Soviet Union)	Lithuania	28 Sep 26	Peace/Disarmament	60LTS145	301410
USSR (Soviet Union)	Lithuania	17 Sep 30	General Amity	125LTS255	302859
USSR (Soviet Union)	Lithuania	05 Jul 33	Peace/Disarmament	148LTS79	303405
USSR (Soviet Union)	Lithuania	04 Apr 34	Peace/Disarmament	186LTS267	304315
USSR (Soviet Union)	Multilateral	18 Mar 04	Humanitarian	1LTS83	300011
USSR (Soviet Union)	Multilateral	12 Jan 12	Sanitation	4LTS281	300112

PARTY ONE	PARTY TWO	DATE	TOPIC	CITATION	NUMBER
USSR (Soviet Union)	Multilateral	23 Jan 12	Sanitation	8LTS187	300222
USSR (Soviet Union)	Multilateral	05 Jun 12	Telecommunications	1LTS135	300013
USSR (Soviet Union)	Multilateral	30 Jun 20	Patents/Copyrights	1LTS59	300008
USSR (Soviet Union)	Multilateral	19 Sep 21	Telecommunications	15LTS191	300392
USSR (Soviet Union)	Multilateral	06 Oct 21	General Economic	17LTS45	300427
USSR (Soviet Union)	Multilateral	31 Mar 22	Humanitarian	9LTS415	300269
USSR (Soviet Union)	Multilateral	24 May 23	Postal Service	50LTS341	301218
USSR (Soviet Union)	Multilateral	24 Jul 23	Water Transport	28LTS115	300702
USSR (Soviet Union)	Multilateral	31 Mar 24	Sanitation	27LTS211	300685
USSR (Soviet Union)	Multilateral	28 Aug 24	Postal Service	40LTS249	301003
USSR (Soviet Union)	Multilateral	28 Aug 24	Postal Service	40LTS19	301002
USSR (Soviet Union)	Multilateral	28 Aug 24	Postal Service	40LTS307	301004
USSR (Soviet Union)	Multilateral	28 Aug 24	Postal Service	40LTS437	301005
USSR (Soviet Union)	Multilateral	19 Feb 25	Admin Cooperation	81LTS317	301845
USSR (Soviet Union)	Multilateral	17 Jun 25	Peace/Disarmament	94LTS65	302138
USSR (Soviet Union)	Multilateral	19 Aug 25	Customs	42LTS73	301033
USSR (Soviet Union)	Multilateral	29 Oct 25	Land Transport	66LTS147	301529
USSR (Soviet Union)	Multilateral	29 Oct 25	Telecommunications	57LTS201	301365
USSR (Soviet Union)	Multilateral	27 Nov 25	Water Transport	67LTS63	301539
USSR (Soviet Union)	Multilateral	31 Dec 25	Territory Boundary	79LTS167	301809
USSR (Soviet Union)	Multilateral	24 Apr 26	Land Transport	108LTS123	302505
USSR (Soviet Union)	Multilateral	21 Jun 26	Sanitation	78LTS229	301793
USSR (Soviet Union)	Multilateral	10 Sep 27	Postal Service	75LTS39	301750
USSR (Soviet Union)	Multilateral	10 Sep 27	Postal Service	75LTS7	301749
USSR (Soviet Union)	Multilateral	29 Oct 27	Scientific Project	127LTS27	302903
USSR (Soviet Union)	Multilateral	27 Aug 28	General Amity	89LTS369	302028
USSR (Soviet Union)	Multilateral	27 Aug 28	General Military	94LTS57	302137
USSR (Soviet Union)	Multilateral	22 Nov 28	Culture	111LTS343	302598
USSR (Soviet Union)	Multilateral	20 Apr 29	Admin Cooperation	112LTS371	302623
USSR (Soviet Union)	Multilateral	31 May 29	Water Transport	136LTS81	303127
USSR (Soviet Union)	Multilateral	28 Jun 29	Postal Service	102LTS245	302368
USSR (Soviet Union)	Multilateral	28 Jun 29	Postal Service	103LTS5	302369
USSR (Soviet Union)	Multilateral	12 Oct 29	General Transport	137LTS11	303145
USSR (Soviet Union)	Multilateral	01 Aug 30	Health/Educ/Welfare	128LTS9	302932
USSR (Soviet Union)	Multilateral	23 Oct 30	Water Transport	125LTS95	302849
USSR (Soviet Union)	Multilateral	23 Oct 30	Water Transport	112LTS21	302603
USSR (Soviet Union)	Multilateral	28 Mar 31	Customs	119LTS47	302739
USSR (Soviet Union)	Multilateral	30 Mar 31	Land Transport	150LTS247	303459
USSR (Soviet Union)	Multilateral	30 Mar 31	Taxation	138LTS149	303185
USSR (Soviet Union)	Multilateral	13 Jul 31	Other HEW	139LTS301	303219
USSR (Soviet Union)	Multilateral	09 Dec 32	Telecommunications	151LTS5	303479
USSR (Soviet Union)	Multilateral	11 Mar 33	Water Transport	135LTS301	303119
USSR (Soviet Union)	Multilateral	19 Jun 33	Gen Communications	154LTS133	303544
USSR (Soviet Union)	Multilateral	03 Jul 33	Peace/Disarmament	147LTS67	303391
USSR (Soviet Union)	Multilateral	04 Jul 33	Peace/Disarmament	148LTS211	303414
USSR (Soviet Union)	Multilateral	25 Aug 33	Commodity Trade	141LTS71	303262
USSR (Soviet Union)	Multilateral	11 Oct 33	Consul/Citizenship	150LTS431	303476
USSR (Soviet Union)	Multilateral	20 Mar 34	Postal Service	175LTS5	304049
USSR (Soviet Union)	Multilateral	20 Mar 34	Postal Service	174LTS171	304048
USSR (Soviet Union)	Multilateral	25 Jul 34	Other HEW	177LTS59	304080
USSR (Soviet Union)	Multilateral	22 Dec 34	Visas	183LTS145	304230
USSR (Soviet Union)	Multilateral	22 Dec 34	Admin Cooperation	183LTS153	304231
USSR (Soviet Union)	Multilateral	20 Feb 35	Sanitation	186LTS173	304310
USSR (Soviet Union)	Multilateral	20 Feb 35	Sanitation	193LTS59	304487
USSR (Soviet Union)	Multilateral	20 Feb 35	Sanitation	193LTS37	304486
USSR (Soviet Union)	Multilateral	26 Jun 36	Other HEW	198LTS299	304648
USSR (Soviet Union)	Multilateral	20 Jul 36	Territory Boundary	173LTS213	304015
USSR (Soviet Union)	Multilateral	15 Sep 36	Scientific Project	178LTS439	304126
USSR (Soviet Union)	Multilateral	23 Sep 36	Gen Communications	186LTS301	304319
USSR (Soviet Union)	Multilateral	06 Nov 36	General Military	173LTS353	304025
USSR (Soviet Union)	Multilateral	31 Mar 37	Commodity Trade	189LTS359	304394
USSR (Soviet Union)	Multilateral	14 Sep 37	General Military	181LTS137	304184
USSR (Soviet Union)	Multilateral	17 Sep 37	Milit Installation	181LTS150	304185
USSR (Soviet Union)	Multilateral	23 May 39	Postal Service	202LTS159	304742
USSR (Soviet Union)	Multilateral	01 Jan 42	General Military	204LTS381	304817

PARTY ONE	PARTY TWO	DATE	TOPIC	CITATION	NUMBER
USSR (Soviet Union)	Norway	02 Sep 21	Consul/Citizenship	7LTS293	300196
USSR (Soviet Union)	Norway	15 Dec 25	General Economic	47LTS9	301127
USSR (Soviet Union)	Norway	09 Apr 26	Water Transport	48LTS185	301160
USSR (Soviet Union)	Norway	16 Jan 28	Consul/Citizenship	70LTS239	301635
USSR (Soviet Union)	Norway	24 Feb 28	Admin Cooperation	79LTS9	301801
USSR (Soviet Union)	Persia	26 Feb 21	General Amity	9LTS383	300268
USSR (Soviet Union)	Persia	01 Oct 27	Specific Resources	112LTS297	302621
USSR (Soviet Union)	Persia	01 Oct 27	Admin Cooperation	112LTS275	302620
USSR (Soviet Union)	Persia	31 May 28	Admin Cooperation	110LTS343	302566
USSR (Soviet Union)	Persia	10 Mar 29	Customs	107LTS419	302498
USSR (Soviet Union)	Persia	02 Aug 29	Postal Service	109LTS99	302530
USSR (Soviet Union)	Poland	12 Oct 20	Peace/Disarmament	4LTS7	300101
USSR (Soviet Union)	Poland	24 Feb 21	Refugees	4LTS141	300106
USSR (Soviet Union)	Poland	18 Mar 21	Peace/Disarmament	6LTS51	300149
USSR (Soviet Union)	Poland	07 Feb 23	Sanitation	49LTS285	301186
USSR (Soviet Union)	Poland	24 Apr 24	Visas	37LTS33	300947
USSR (Soviet Union)	Poland	05 May 24	Admin Cooperation	157LTS431	303617
USSR (Soviet Union)	Poland	18 Jul 24	Consul/Citizenship	49LTS201	301183
USSR (Soviet Union)	Poland	10 Apr 32	Territory Boundary	141LTS349	303275
USSR (Soviet Union)	Poland	25 Jul 32	General Military	136LTS41	303124
USSR (Soviet Union)	Poland	22 Nov 32	Dispute Settlement	136LTS55	303125
USSR (Soviet Union)	Poland	03 Jun 33	Dispute Settlement	142LTS265	303300
USSR (Soviet Union)	Poland	26 Jul 34	General Transport	164LTS301	303799
USSR (Soviet Union)	Poland	31 Mar 36	Admin Cooperation	186LTS203	304312
USSR (Soviet Union)	Poland	31 Mar 36	Water Transport	186LTS211	304313
USSR (Soviet Union)	Sweden	15 Mar 24	General Trade	25LTS251	300613
USSR (Soviet Union)	Sweden	12 Sep 24	Postal Service	31LTS75	300784
USSR (Soviet Union)	Sweden	21 Jul 26	Patents/Copyrights	57LTS9	301346
USSR (Soviet Union)	Sweden	08 Oct 27	Admin Cooperation	71LTS411	301679
USSR (Soviet Union)	Turkey	17 Dec 25	General Amity	157LTS353	303610
USSR (Soviet Union)	Turkey	07 Nov 35	General Amity	179LTS127	304139
USSR (Soviet Union)	UK Great Britain	12 Feb 20	General Military	1LTS263	300019
USSR (Soviet Union)	UK Great Britain	16 Mar 21	General Trade	4LTS127	300104
USSR (Soviet Union)	UK Great Britain	06 Dec 21	Telecommunications	31LTS85	300785
USSR (Soviet Union)	UK Great Britain	03 Jul 22	General Trade	13LTS37	300345
USSR (Soviet Union)	UK Great Britain	21 Dec 29	Consul/Citizenship	99LTS61	302268
USSR (Soviet Union)	UK Great Britain	22 May 30	Specific Resources	102LTS103	302355
USSR (Soviet Union)	UK Great Britain	16 Sep 30	General Trade	101LTS409	302340
USSR (Soviet Union)	UK Great Britain	16 Feb 34	Mostfavored Nation	149LTS445	303446
USSR (Soviet Union)	UK Great Britain	19 Apr 34	Postal Service	158LTS331	303643
USSR (Soviet Union)	UK Great Britain	17 Jul 37	Peace/Disarmament	187LTS93	304333
USSR (Soviet Union)	UK Great Britain	12 Jul 41	General Military	204LTS277	304808
USSR (Soviet Union)	UK Great Britain	26 May 42	General Military	204LTS353	304813
USSR (Soviet Union)	USA (United States)	15 Jul 35	General Trade	162LTS91	303737
USSR (Soviet Union)	USA (United States)	22 Nov 35	Admin Cooperation	167LTS303	303875
USSR (Soviet Union)	USA (United States)	04 Aug 37	General Trade	182LTS113	304204
Vatican/Holy See	Austria	23 Mar 35	Visas	167LTS385	303879
Vatican/Holy See	Colombia	05 May 28	Consul/Citizenship	79LTS157	301808
Vatican/Holy See	Latvia	30 May 22	General Amity	17LTS365	300443
Vatican/Holy See	Latvia	25 Jan 38	Education	186LTS319	304320
Vatican/Holy See	Multilateral	25 Nov 27	Telecommunications	84LTS97	301905
Vatican/Holy See	Multilateral	20 Apr 29	Admin Cooperation	112LTS371	302623
Vatican/Holy See	Multilateral	28 Jun 29	Postal Service	103LTS321	302372
Vatican/Holy See	Multilateral	28 Jun 29	Postal Service	103LTS5	302369
Vatican/Holy See	Multilateral	28 Jun 29	Postal Service	102LTS245	302368
Vatican/Holy See	Multilateral	28 Jun 29	Postal Service	103LTS249	302371
Vatican/Holy See	Multilateral	28 Jun 29	Postal Service	103LTS377	302373
Vatican/Holy See	Multilateral	28 Jun 29	Postal Service	103LTS71	302370
Vatican/Holy See	Multilateral	28 Jun 29	Postal Service	103LTS429	302374
Vatican/Holy See	Multilateral	09 Dec 32	Telecommunications	151LTS5	303479
Vatican/Holy See	Multilateral	19 Jun 33	Gen Communications	154LTS133	303544
Vatican/Holy See	Multilateral	20 Mar 34	Postal Service	175LTS269	304051
Vatican/Holy See	Multilateral	20 Mar 34	Finance	176LTS9	304053
Vatican/Holy See	Multilateral	20 Mar 34	Postal Service	174LTS171	304048
Vatican/Holy See	Multilateral	20 Mar 34	Postal Service	175LTS73	304050

PARTY ONE	PARTY TWO	DATE	TOPIC	CITATION	NUMBER
Vatican/Holy See	Multilateral	20 Mar 34	Postal Service	175LTS363	304052
Vatican/Holy See	Multilateral	20 Mar 34	Postal Service	176LTS55	304054
Vatican/Holy See	Multilateral	20 Mar 34	Postal Service	175LTS5	304049
Vatican/Holy See	Multilateral	06 Nov 36	General Military	173LTS353	304025
Vatican/Holy See	Multilateral	23 May 39	Postal Service	202LTS159	304742
Vatican/Holy See	Romania	30 May 32	Admin Cooperation	201LTS257	304719
Venezuela	Argentina	22 Jul 11	Dispute Settlement	28LTS287	300715
Venezuela	Brazil	13 Apr 26	General Amity	80LTS283	301834
Venezuela	Brazil	07 Nov 29	Territory Boundary	99LTS427	302288
Venezuela	Colombia	20 Jul 25	General Transport	39LTS15	300993
Venezuela	Denmark	19 Dec 33	Dispute Settlement	158LTS249	303635
Venezuela	Italy	23 Aug 30	Extradition	128LTS377	302943
Venezuela	Multilateral	20 Aug 10	Patents/Copyrights	155LTS179	303576
Venezuela	Multilateral	05 Jun 12	Telecommunications	1LTS135	300013
Venezuela	Multilateral	10 Sep 19	General Trade	7LTS331	300200
Venezuela	Multilateral	16 Dec 20	General IGO	6LTS379	300170
Venezuela	Multilateral	13 Mar 21	Admin Cooperation	8LTS327	300232
Venezuela	Multilateral	05 Aug 21	Admin Cooperation	27LTS349	300695
Venezuela	Multilateral	15 Sep 21	Postal Service	30LTS141	300767
Venezuela	Multilateral	05 Oct 21	IGO Establishment	51LTS361	301241
Venezuela	Multilateral	05 Oct 21	Admin Cooperation	29LTS79	300735
Venezuela	Multilateral	05 Oct 21	Admin Cooperation	29LTS67	300733
Venezuela	Multilateral	05 Oct 21	Admin Cooperation	29LTS73	300734
Venezuela	Multilateral	28 Apr 23	Patents/Copyrights	33LTS47	300832
Venezuela	Multilateral	03 May 23	General Amity	33LTS25	300831
Venezuela	Multilateral	03 May 23	Customs	33LTS11	300830
Venezuela	Multilateral	03 May 23	General Trade	33LTS81	300833
Venezuela	Multilateral	28 Aug 24	Postal Service	40LTS19	301002
Venezuela	Multilateral	28 Aug 24	Postal Service	41LTS9	301006
Venezuela	Multilateral	28 Aug 24	Postal Service	40LTS249	301003
Venezuela	Multilateral	28 Aug 24	Postal Service	40LTS307	301004
Venezuela	Multilateral	28 Aug 24	Postal Service	41LTS97	301008
Venezuela	Multilateral	28 Aug 24	Postal Service	40LTS437	301005
Venezuela	Multilateral	28 Aug 24	Postal Service	41LTS55	301007
Venezuela	Multilateral	14 Nov 24	Sanitation	86LTS43	301949
Venezuela	Multilateral	19 Feb 25	Admin Cooperation	81LTS317	301845
Venezuela	Multilateral	17 Jun 25	Peace/Disarmament	94LTS65	302138
Venezuela	Multilateral	29 Oct 25	Telecommunications	57LTS201	301365
Venezuela	Multilateral	21 Jun 26	Sanitation	78LTS229	301793
Venezuela	Multilateral	12 Jul 27	Direct Aid	135LTS247	303115
Venezuela	Multilateral	25 Nov 27	Telecommunications	84LTS97	301905
Venezuela	Multilateral	18 Feb 28	Patents/Copyrights	132LTS275	303044
Venezuela	Multilateral	20 Feb 28	Air Transport	129LTS223	302963
Venezuela	Multilateral	20 Feb 28	Consul/Citizenship	132LTS323	303046
Venezuela	Multilateral	20 Feb 28	Other Ad Hoc	86LTS111	301950
Venezuela	Multilateral	20 Feb 28	Admin Cooperation	134LTS45	303082
Venezuela	Multilateral	20 Feb 28	General Amity	135LTS187	303111
Venezuela	Multilateral	20 Feb 28	Consul/Citizenship	155LTS259	303581
Venezuela	Multilateral	20 Feb 28	Privil/Immunities	132LTS301	303045
Venezuela	Multilateral	20 Feb 28	Consul/Citizenship	155LTS289	303582
Venezuela	Multilateral	27 Aug 28	General Military	94LTS57	302137
Venezuela	Multilateral	05 Jan 29	Dispute Settlement	130LTS135	302988
Venezuela	Multilateral	05 Jan 29	Dispute Settlement	100LTS399	302309
Venezuela	Multilateral	20 Feb 29	Patents/Copyrights	124LTS357	302840
Venezuela	Multilateral	28 Jun 29	Postal Service	103LTS71	302370
Venezuela	Multilateral	28 Jun 29	Postal Service	103LTS5	302369
Venezuela	Multilateral	28 Jun 29	Postal Service	103LTS249	302371
Venezuela	Multilateral	28 Jun 29	Postal Service	103LTS429	302374
Venezuela	Multilateral	28 Jun 29	Postal Service	103LTS321	302372
Venezuela	Multilateral	28 Jun 29	Postal Service	103LTS377	302373
Venezuela	Multilateral	28 Jun 29	Postal Service	102LTS245	302368
Venezuela	Multilateral	27 Jul 29	Other Military	118LTS343	302734
Venezuela	Multilateral	27 Jul 29	Other Military	118LTS303	302733
Venezuela	Multilateral	14 Sep 29	UN Charter	165LTS353	303822
Venezuela	Multilateral	12 Oct 29	General Transport	137LTS11	303145

PARTY ONE	PARTY TWO	DATE	TOPIC	CITATION	NUMBER
Venezuela	Multilateral	13 Jul 31	Other HEW	139LTS301	303219
Venezuela	Multilateral	10 Nov 31	Postal Service	131LTS447	303025
Venezuela	Multilateral	10 Nov 31	Postal Service	131LTS327	303023
Venezuela	Multilateral	10 Nov 31	Postal Service	131LTS389	303024
Venezuela	Multilateral	09 Dec 32	Telecommunications	151LTS5	303479
Venezuela	Multilateral	11 Mar 33	Water Transport	135LTS301	303119
Venezuela	Multilateral	10 Oct 33	General Amity	163LTS393	303781
Venezuela	Multilateral	26 Dec 33	Recognition	165LTS19	303802
Venezuela	Multilateral	20 Mar 34	Postal Service	175LTS73	304050
Venezuela	Multilateral	20 Mar 34	Postal Service	175LTS363	304052
Venezuela	Multilateral	20 Mar 34	Postal Service	176LTS55	304054
Venezuela	Multilateral	20 Mar 34	Postal Service	175LTS5	304049
Venezuela	Multilateral	20 Mar 34	Postal Service	175LTS269	304051
Venezuela	Multilateral	20 Mar 34	Postal Service	174LTS171	304048
Venezuela	Multilateral	20 Mar 34	Finance	176LTS9	304053
Venezuela	Multilateral	19 Jun 34	Admin Cooperation	154LTS381	303564
Venezuela	Multilateral	15 Apr 35	Culture	167LTS289	303874
Venezuela	Multilateral	26 Jun 36	Other HEW	198LTS299	304648
Venezuela	Multilateral	23 Dec 36	Admin Cooperation	201LTS295	304721
Venezuela	Multilateral	23 Dec 36	Dispute Settlement	195LTS229	304548
Venezuela	Multilateral	23 Dec 36	Peace/Disarmament	188LTS9	304350
Venezuela	Multilateral	23 Dec 36	Dispute Settlement	188LTS75	304353
Venezuela	Multilateral	23 Dec 36	Culture	188LTS151	304356
Venezuela	Multilateral	23 Dec 36	Dispute Settlement	188LTS53	304352
Venezuela	Multilateral	23 Dec 36	General Amity	188LTS31	304351
Venezuela	Multilateral	23 Dec 36	Culture	188LTS125	304355
Venezuela	Multilateral	23 Dec 36	Land Transport	188LTS99	304354
Venezuela	Multilateral	31 Oct 38	Sanitation	198LTS205	304642
Venezuela	Multilateral	03 Dec 38	Education	200LTS249	304694
Venezuela	Multilateral	23 May 39	Postal Service	202LTS159	304742
Venezuela	Netherlands	11 May 20	General Amity	7LTS85	300176
Venezuela	Netherlands	05 Apr 33	Dispute Settlement	144LTS353	303338
Venezuela	Norway	13 May 35	Dispute Settlement	167LTS407	303882
Venezuela	Norway	18 Feb 38	General Trade	187LTS205	304341
Venezuela	Peru	14 Mar 23	Admin Cooperation	20LTS45	300505
Venezuela	UK Great Britain	22 Mar 21	Claims and Debts	5LTS169	300126
Venezuela	UK Great Britain	26 Feb 42	Territory Boundary	205LTS121	304829
Venezuela	UK Great Britain	26 Feb 42	Territory Boundary	205LTS131	304830
Venezuela	Uruguay	28 Feb 23	Admin Cooperation	36LTS451	300942
Venezuela	USA (United States)	21 Jan 22	Extradition	49LTS435	301196
Venezuela	USA (United States)	12 May 38	General Trade	191LTS35	304433
Venezuela	USA (United States)	09 May 39	General Trade	198LTS135	304633
Venezuela	USA (United States)	06 Nov 39	General Trade	203LTS273	304770
Venezuela	USA (United States)	24 Mar 41	Military Mission	204LTS83	304787
Vietnam	Multilateral	31 May 29	Water Transport	136LTS81	303127
Vietnam, South	Multilateral	20 Apr 29	Admin Cooperation	112LTS371	302623
Virgin Islands	Multilateral	26 Sep 27	Dispute Settlement	92LTS301	302096
Western Samoa	Multilateral	06 Nov 25	Patents/Copyrights	74LTS289	301743
Windward Islands	Multilateral	25 Aug 24	Water Transport	120LTS155	302764
Windward Islands	Multilateral	26 Sep 27	Dispute Settlement	92LTS301	302096
Windward Islands	Multilateral	25 Nov 27	Telecommunications	84LTS97	301905
Windward Islands	Multilateral	30 Mar 31	Taxation	138LTS149	303185
Windward Islands	Multilateral	28 Oct 33	Refugees	159LTS199	303663
Windward Islands	Multilateral	23 Sep 36	Gen Communications	186LTS301	304319
Windward Islands	Multilateral	10 Feb 38	Refugees	192LTS59	304461
Windward Islands	USA (United States)	21 Jun 35	Postal Service	162LTS157	303739
Yemen	Italy	02 Sep 26	General Amity	67LTS383	301559
Yemen	Multilateral	20 Mar 34	Postal Service	176LTS55	304054
Yemen	Multilateral	20 Mar 34	Postal Service	175LTS73	304050
Yemen	Multilateral	20 Mar 34	Postal Service	175LTS269	304051
Yemen	Multilateral	20 Mar 34	Finance	176LTS9	304053
Yemen	Multilateral	20 Mar 34	Postal Service	175LTS5	304049
Yemen	Multilateral	20 Mar 34	Postal Service	175LTS363	304052
Yemen	Netherlands	12 Mar 33	General Amity	146LTS359	303384
Yemen	UK Great Britain	11 Feb 34	General Amity	157LTS63	303605

PARTY ONE	PARTY TWO	DATE	TOPIC	CITATION	NUMBER
Yugoslavia	Albania	05 May 34	General Economic	187LTS179	304337
Yugoslavia	Albania	08 May 34	General Economic	159LTS9	303649
Yugoslavia	Austria	21 Jul 31	Non-ILO Labor	147LTS123	303397
Yugoslavia	Austria	09 Mar 32	General Trade	157LTS145	303609
Yugoslavia	Austria	20 Apr 32	Claims and Debts	132LTS217	303040
Yugoslavia	Austria	14 Oct 32	Air Transport	147LTS173	303398
Yugoslavia	Austria	09 Aug 33	General Trade	158LTS195	303632
Yugoslavia	Bel-Lux Econ Union	07 Aug 32	Finance	139LTS223	303212
Yugoslavia	Bel-Lux Econ Union	21 Feb 33	Claims and Debts	147LTS203	303399
Yugoslavia	Bel-Lux Econ Union	26 Nov 37	Finance	196LTS19	304567
Yugoslavia	Belgium	25 Mar 30	Dispute Settlement	106LTS343	302455
Yugoslavia	Belgium	29 Feb 36	Admin Cooperation	184LTS379	304258
Yugoslavia	Brazil	16 May 32	Mostfavored Nation	144LTS303	303333
Yugoslavia	Bulgaria	26 Sep 29	Territory Boundary	101LTS217	302324
Yugoslavia	Bulgaria	14 Feb 30	Claims and Debts	101LTS135	302323
Yugoslavia	Bulgaria	09 Nov 35	Territory Boundary	194LTS89	304511
Yugoslavia	Bulgaria	24 Jan 37	General Amity	176LTS221	304063
Yugoslavia	Czechoslovakia	30 Mar 31	General Economic	125LTS273	302861
Yugoslavia	Czechoslovakia	08 Jun 32	Finance	139LTS45	303203
Yugoslavia	Czechoslovakia	24 Feb 36	Taxation	187LTS185	304338
Yugoslavia	Czechoslovakia	10 Nov 36	General Trade	186LTS191	304311
Yugoslavia	Denmark	14 Dec 35	Dispute Settlement	184LTS99	304245
Yugoslavia	France	20 Jan 30	Claims and Debts	104LTS177	302387
Yugoslavia	France	20 Jan 30	Reparations	104LTS171	302386
Yugoslavia	France	07 Nov 31	Commodity Trade	144LTS281	303331
Yugoslavia	France	29 Jul 32	Education	144LTS313	303334
Yugoslavia	France	28 Oct 32	General Amity	135LTS281	303117
Yugoslavia	France	12 Oct 37	General Amity	182LTS149	304206
Yugoslavia	Germany	29 Jul 33	Mostfavored Nation	149LTS77	303435
Yugoslavia	Greece	22 Jul 33	Air Transport	161LTS219	303714
Yugoslavia	Hungary	11 Nov 29	Admin Cooperation	111LTS197	302587
Yugoslavia	Hungary	27 Apr 30	Dispute Settlement	113LTS153	302642
Yugoslavia	Hungary	27 Aug 30	Dispute Settlement	113LTS163	302643
Yugoslavia	Hungary	30 Jan 31	Dispute Settlement	120LTS105	302761
Yugoslavia	Hungary	15 May 33	General Trade	144LTS321	303335
Yugoslavia	Hungary	17 Dec 36	General Trade	196LTS137	304576
Yugoslavia	Hungary	17 Dec 36	Finance	196LTS143	304577
Yugoslavia	Italy	25 Apr 32	General Economic	153LTS305	303526
Yugoslavia	Italy	16 Jun 33	General Economic	153LTS317	303527
Yugoslavia	Multilateral	09 Sep 86*	Patents/Copyrights	123LTS233	302816
Yugoslavia	Multilateral	18 Mar 04	Humanitarian	1LTS83	300011
Yugoslavia	Multilateral	01 May 20	Air Transport	11LTS173	300297
Yugoslavia	Multilateral	30 Jun 20	Patents/Copyrights	1LTS59	300008
Yugoslavia	Multilateral	16 Dec 20	General IGO	6LTS379	300170
Yugoslavia	Multilateral	23 Jul 21	Water Transport	26LTS173	300647
Yugoslavia	Multilateral	05 Aug 21	Admin Cooperation	27LTS349	300695
Yugoslavia	Multilateral	05 Oct 21	IGO Establishment	51LTS361	301241
Yugoslavia	Multilateral	05 Oct 21	Admin Cooperation	29LTS79	300735
Yugoslavia	Multilateral	05 Oct 21	Admin Cooperation	29LTS73	300734
Yugoslavia	Multilateral	05 Oct 21	Admin Cooperation	29LTS67	300733
Yugoslavia	Multilateral	06 Oct 21	General Economic	17LTS45	300427
Yugoslavia	Multilateral	24 Sep 23	Dispute Settlement	27LTS157	300678
Yugoslavia	Multilateral	09 Dec 23	Water Transport	58LTS284	301379
Yugoslavia	Multilateral	24 Apr 26	Land Transport	108LTS123	302505
Yugoslavia	Multilateral	21 Jun 26	Sanitation	78LTS229	301793
Yugoslavia	Multilateral	12 Jul 27	Direct Aid	135LTS247	303115
Yugoslavia	Multilateral	29 Oct 27	Scientific Project	127LTS27	302903
Yugoslavia	Multilateral	25 Nov 27	Telecommunications	84LTS97	301905
Yugoslavia	Multilateral	11 Jul 28	Commodity Trade	95LTS357	302184
Yugoslavia	Multilateral	22 Nov 28	Culture	111LTS343	302598
Yugoslavia	Multilateral	20 Apr 29	Admin Cooperation	112LTS371	302623
Yugoslavia	Multilateral	31 May 29	Water Transport	136LTS81	303127
Yugoslavia	Multilateral	28 Jun 29	Postal Service	102LTS245	302368
Yugoslavia	Multilateral	27 Jul 29	Other Military	118LTS303	302733
Yugoslavia	Multilateral	27 Jul 29	Other Military	118LTS343	302734

PARTY ONE	PARTY TWO	DATE	TOPIC	CITATION	NUMBER
Yugoslavia	Multilateral	12 Oct 29	General Transport	137LTS11	303145
Yugoslavia	Multilateral	20 Jan 30	Reparations	104LTS421	302396
Yugoslavia	Multilateral	20 Jan 30	Finance	104LTS433	302397
Yugoslavia	Multilateral	20 Jan 30	Reparations	112LTS361	302622
Yugoslavia	Multilateral	20 Jan 30	Finance	104LTS413	302395
Yugoslavia	Multilateral	20 Jan 30	Reparations	113LTS389	302650
Yugoslavia	Multilateral	20 Jan 30	Reparations	104LTS243	302394
Yugoslavia	Multilateral	12 Apr 30	Admin Cooperation	179LTS89	304137
Yugoslavia	Multilateral	12 Apr 30	Admin Cooperation	179LTS115	304138
Yugoslavia	Multilateral	28 Apr 30	Claims and Debts	121LTS69	302785
Yugoslavia	Multilateral	07 Jun 30	Finance	143LTS317	303314
Yugoslavia	Multilateral	07 Jun 30	Finance	143LTS257	303313
Yugoslavia	Multilateral	07 Jun 30	Finance	143LTS337	303315
Yugoslavia	Multilateral	10 Jun 30	Loans and Credits	112LTS237	302618
Yugoslavia	Multilateral	01 Aug 30	Health/Educ/Welfare	128LTS9	302932
Yugoslavia	Multilateral	23 Oct 30	Water Transport	125LTS95	302849
Yugoslavia	Multilateral	23 Oct 30	Water Transport	112LTS21	302603
Yugoslavia	Multilateral	19 Mar 31	Finance	143LTS355	303316
Yugoslavia	Multilateral	19 Mar 31	Admin Cooperation	143LTS7	303301
Yugoslavia	Multilateral	19 Mar 31	Finance	143LTS407	303317
Yugoslavia	Multilateral	27 Mar 31	ICJ Option Clause	167LTS341	303877
Yugoslavia	Multilateral	28 Mar 31	Customs	119LTS47	302739
Yugoslavia	Multilateral	30 Mar 31	Land Transport	150LTS247	303459
Yugoslavia	Multilateral	30 Mar 31	Taxation	138LTS149	303185
Yugoslavia	Multilateral	30 Jun 31	Scientific Project	149LTS63	303434
Yugoslavia	Multilateral	21 Aug 31	Other Economic	127LTS95	302910
Yugoslavia	Multilateral	24 Sep 31	Specific Resources	155LTS349	303586
Yugoslavia	Multilateral	28 Jun 32	Admin Cooperation	140LTS191	303237
Yugoslavia	Multilateral	02 Sep 32	Land Transport	154LTS123	303543
Yugoslavia	Multilateral	09 Dec 32	Telecommunications	151LTS5	303479
Yugoslavia	Multilateral	16 Feb 33	Admin Cooperation	139LTS233	303213
Yugoslavia	Multilateral	11 Mar 33	Water Transport	135LTS301	303119
Yugoslavia	Multilateral	29 May 33	Admin Cooperation	192LTS289	304479
Yugoslavia	Multilateral	19 Jun 33	Gen Communications	154LTS133	303544
Yugoslavia	Multilateral	04 Jul 33	Peace/Disarmament	148LTS211	303414
Yugoslavia	Multilateral	25 Aug 33	Commodity Trade	141LTS71	303262
Yugoslavia	Multilateral	10 Oct 33	General Amity	163LTS393	303781
Yugoslavia	Multilateral	11 Oct 33	Consul/Citizenship	150LTS431	303476
Yugoslavia	Multilateral	23 Nov 33	Land Transport	192LTS389	304484
Yugoslavia	Multilateral	23 Nov 33	Land Transport	192LTS327	304483
Yugoslavia	Multilateral	09 Feb 34	General Military	153LTS153	303514
Yugoslavia	Multilateral	20 Mar 34	Postal Service	175LTS5	304049
Yugoslavia	Multilateral	20 Mar 34	Finance	176LTS9	304053
Yugoslavia	Multilateral	20 Mar 34	Postal Service	175LTS363	304052
Yugoslavia	Multilateral	20 Mar 34	Postal Service	175LTS73	304050
Yugoslavia	Multilateral	20 Mar 34	Postal Service	176LTS55	304054
Yugoslavia	Multilateral	20 Mar 34	Postal Service	174LTS171	304048
Yugoslavia	Multilateral	20 Mar 34	Postal Service	175LTS269	304051
Yugoslavia	Multilateral	26 Apr 34	Admin Cooperation	164LTS63	303789
Yugoslavia	Multilateral	02 Jun 34	Patents/Copyrights	205LTS179	304834
Yugoslavia	Multilateral	02 Jun 34	Patents/Copyrights	192LTS17	304459
Yugoslavia	Multilateral	25 Jul 34	Other HEW	177LTS59	304080
Yugoslavia	Multilateral	22 Dec 34	Visas	183LTS145	304230
Yugoslavia	Multilateral	20 Jul 36	Territory Boundary	173LTS213	304015
Yugoslavia	Multilateral	30 Jul 36	IGO Status/Immunit	197LTS31	304602
Yugoslavia	Multilateral	06 Nov 36	General Military	173LTS353	304025
Yugoslavia	Multilateral	31 Mar 37	Commodity Trade	189LTS359	304394
Yugoslavia	Multilateral	14 Sep 37	General Military	181LTS137	304184
Yugoslavia	Multilateral	17 Sep 37	Milit Installation	181LTS150	304185
Yugoslavia	Multilateral	15 Apr 38	Visas	200LTS285	304698
Yugoslavia	Multilateral	31 Oct 38	Sanitation	198LTS205	304642
Yugoslavia	Multilateral	03 Dec 38	Education	200LTS249	304694
Yugoslavia	Multilateral	23 May 39	Postal Service	202LTS159	304742
Yugoslavia	Multilateral	01 Jan 42	General Military	204LTS381	304817
Yugoslavia	Multilateral	02 Jun 42	Patents/Copyrights	205LTS163	304833

PARTY ONE	PARTY TWO	DATE	TOPIC	CITATION	NUMBER
Yugoslavia	Netherlands	28 May 30	General Economic	129LTS73	302951
Yugoslavia	Netherlands	11 Mar 31	Dispute Settlement	129LTS89	302952
Yugoslavia	Netherlands	15 Jul 31	Land Transport	127LTS337	302927
Yugoslavia	Netherlands	18 Jul 33	Land Transport	152LTS273	303500
Yugoslavia	Poland	02 Dec 31	Education	139LTS119	303207
Yugoslavia	Romania	19 Jun 30	Territory Boundary	140LTS229	303238
Yugoslavia	Romania	24 Jun 30	Admin Cooperation	140LTS235	303239
Yugoslavia	Romania	27 Jun 30	General Military	107LTS215	302478
Yugoslavia	Romania	04 Aug 30	General Economic	107LTS253	302482
Yugoslavia	Romania	14 Dec 31	Water Transport	135LTS31	303103
Yugoslavia	Romania	14 Dec 31	Water Transport	135LTS133	303108
Yugoslavia	Romania	14 Dec 31	Finance	135LTS89	303105
Yugoslavia	Romania	14 Dec 31	Water Transport	135LTS71	303104
Yugoslavia	Romania	14 Dec 31	Water Transport	135LTS117	303107
Yugoslavia	Romania	14 Dec 31	Finance	135LTS99	303106
Yugoslavia	Romania	14 Dec 31	Water Transport	135LTS143	303109
Yugoslavia	Romania	30 Jan 33	Non-ILO Labor	146LTS151	303367
Yugoslavia	Romania	30 Jan 33	Admin Cooperation	146LTS165	303368
Yugoslavia	Romania	30 Jan 33	Culture	146LTS183	303371
Yugoslavia	Romania	30 Jan 33	Visas	146LTS179	303370
Yugoslavia	Romania	30 Jan 33	Admin Cooperation	146LTS121	303364
Yugoslavia	Romania	30 Jan 33	Extradition	146LTS113	303363
Yugoslavia	Romania	30 Jan 33	Extradition	146LTS81	303361
Yugoslavia	Romania	30 Jan 33	Consul/Citizenship	146LTS173	303369
Yugoslavia	Romania	30 Jan 33	Taxation	146LTS99	303362
Yugoslavia	Romania	30 Jan 33	Territory Boundary	146LTS139	303366
Yugoslavia	Romania	30 Jan 33	Claims and Debts	146LTS129	303365
Yugoslavia	Romania	10 Feb 33	Territory Boundary	174LTS115	304042
Yugoslavia	Romania	10 Mar 33	Sanitation	146LTS209	303372
Yugoslavia	Romania	10 Mar 33	Territory Boundary	146LTS245	303374
Yugoslavia	Romania	10 Mar 33	Non-ILO Labor	146LTS255	303375
Yugoslavia	Romania	10 Mar 33	Land Transport	146LTS271	303377
Yugoslavia	Romania	10 Mar 33	Education	146LTS231	303373
Yugoslavia	Romania	10 Mar 33	Finance	146LTS263	303376
Yugoslavia	Romania	11 Mar 33	Territory Boundary	146LTS277	303378
Yugoslavia	Romania	11 Mar 33	Claims and Debts	146LTS285	303379
Yugoslavia	Romania	13 Mar 35	Consul/Citizenship	179LTS57	304133
Yugoslavia	Romania	13 May 37	Sanitation	197LTS161	304612
Yugoslavia	Romania	13 May 37	Territory Boundary	197LTS101	304609
Yugoslavia	Romania	13 May 37	Consul/Citizenship	197LTS145	304611
Yugoslavia	Spain	15 May 36	General Economic	170LTS185	303934
Yugoslavia	Sweden	14 May 37	General Trade	194LTS21	304504
Yugoslavia	Sweden	14 May 37	General Trade	179LTS147	304141
Yugoslavia	Switzerland	27 Apr 32	Other Economic	131LTS285	303019
Yugoslavia	Switzerland	27 Jun 38	General Trade	196LTS27	304568
Yugoslavia	Turkey	14 Apr 32	Commodity Trade	144LTS291	303332
Yugoslavia	Turkey	27 Nov 33	Dispute Settlement	161LTS229	303715
Yugoslavia	Turkey	28 Nov 33	Claims and Debts	161LTS245	303716
Yugoslavia	Turkey	03 Jul 34	Admin Cooperation	179LTS207	304149
Yugoslavia	Turkey	17 Dec 34	Sanitation	178LTS471	304128
Yugoslavia	UK Great Britain	23 Oct 31	Postal Service	126LTS209	302884
Yugoslavia	UK Great Britain	27 Feb 36	Admin Cooperation	181LTS241	304193
Yugoslavia	UK Great Britain	27 Nov 36	General Trade	181LTS281	304195
Yugoslavia	UK Great Britain	07 Jun 37	Postal Service	184LTS229	304249
Yugoslavia	United Arab Rep	13 Mar 30	Mostfavored Nation	110LTS133	302557
Yugoslavia	USA (United States)	20 Jun 38	Postal Service	195LTS259	304549
Zanzibar	Multilateral	18 Mar 04	Humanitarian	1LTS83	300011
Zanzibar	Multilateral	05 Jun 12	Telecommunications	1LTS135	300013
Zanzibar	Multilateral	30 Jun 20	Patents/Copyrights	1LTS59	300008
Zanzibar	Multilateral	31 Mar 22	Humanitarian	9LTS415	300269
Zanzibar	Multilateral	25 Aug 24	Water Transport	120LTS155	302764
Zanzibar	Multilateral	26 Sep 27	Dispute Settlement	92LTS301	302096
Zanzibar	Multilateral	25 Nov 27	Telecommunications	84LTS97	301905
Zanzibar	Multilateral	30 Mar 31	Taxation	138LTS149	303185
Zanzibar	Multilateral	23 Sep 36	Gen Communications	186LTS301	304319
Zanzibar	Multilateral	10 Feb 38	Refugees	192LTS59	304461

United Nations Treaty Series
National Treaty Collections

PARTY ONE	PARTY TWO	DATE	TOPIC	CITATION	NUMBER
Afghanistan	Accept UN Charter	19 Nov 46	UN Charter	1UNTS39	100007
Afghanistan	Austria	21 Jul 58	Air Transport	0UNTS0	109236
Afghanistan	Bulgaria	29 Jun 63	Culture	0UNTS0	109873
Afghanistan	China People's Rep	28 Jul 57	General Economic	57CCJC72	410437
Afghanistan	China People's Rep	26 Aug 60	General Amity	60CCJC88	410716
Afghanistan	China People's Rep	22 Nov 63	Territory Boundary	63CCJC136	411033
Afghanistan	China People's Rep	24 Mar 65	Culture	65CCJC41	411046
Afghanistan	China People's Rep	24 Mar 65	Direct Aid	65CCJC40	411045
Afghanistan	China People's Rep	24 Mar 65	Territory Boundary	65CCJC39	411044
Afghanistan	China People's Rep	06 Nov 65	General Trade	65CCJC136	411042
Afghanistan	China People's Rep	24 May 66	Culture	66CCJC37	411047
Afghanistan	China People's Rep	29 Jul 66	General Economic	66CCJC73	411048
Afghanistan	China People's Rep	28 Dec 66	General Trade	66CCJC105	411049
Afghanistan	Czechoslovakia	28 May 60	Air Transport	497UNTS129	107266
Afghanistan	Czechoslovakia	23 Apr 61	Culture	437UNTS25	106297
Afghanistan	Denmark	24 May 67	Air Transport	0UNTS0	109951
Afghanistan	France	06 Jan 59	General Aid	61FRRT40	415001
Afghanistan	France	15 May 61	Air Transport	62FRRT4	415002
Afghanistan	France	21 Aug 66	Health/Educ/Welfare	67FRJO801	416003
Afghanistan	Germany, West	31 Jan 58	Direct Aid	58WGBB83	425002
Afghanistan	Germany, West	31 Jan 58	General Economic	58WBGA83	424001
Afghanistan	Germany, West	22 Jul 59	Air Transport	464UNTS177	106715
Afghanistan	Germany, West	18 Apr 61	Culture	63WGBB1069	425003
Afghanistan	IAEA (Atom Energy)	24 Sep 65	Atomic Energy	556UNTS101	108121
Afghanistan	IBRD (World Bank)	22 Nov 66	IBRD Project	632UNTS171	109019
Afghanistan	IBRD (World Bank)	26 Jun 69	IBRD Project	0UNTS0	110649
Afghanistan	IDA (Devel Assoc)	23 Nov 64	Non-IBRD Project	567UNTS155	108255
Afghanistan	India	14 Dec 49	Telecommunications	53UNTS95	100774
Afghanistan	India	04 Jan 50	General Amity	81UNTS75	101064
Afghanistan	India	04 Apr 50	General Trade	167UNTS105	102201
Afghanistan	Iran	30 Jun 48	Territory Boundary	0IRTB1	433001
Afghanistan	Iran	26 Jun 56	Admin Cooperation	0IRTB2	433002
Afghanistan	Iran	01 Feb 62	General Transport	0IRTB2	433005
Afghanistan	Iran	31 Oct 63	Finance	0IRTB2	433004
Afghanistan	Iran	31 Oct 63	General Trade	0IRTB2	433003
Afghanistan	Iran	02 Nov 63	Telecommunications	0IRTB2	433006
Afghanistan	Iran	31 Dec 63	Taxation	0IRTB3	433008
Afghanistan	Iran	11 Jan 69	Telecommunications	0IRTB3	433007
Afghanistan	Italy	30 Jan 59	Air Transport	61ITDI347	436001
Afghanistan	Italy	10 Dec 60	Tech Assistance	63ITGU9	435002
Afghanistan	Japan	15 Mar 61	Education	450UNTS373	106480
Afghanistan	Japan	27 Nov 68	Loans and Credits	69JJS3	442257
Afghanistan	Japan	04 Oct 69	Direct Aid	69JJS11	442249
Afghanistan	Multilateral	02 Aug 44	Scientific Project	67UNTS221	200221
Afghanistan	Multilateral	07 Dec 44	Air Transport	84UNTS389	200252
Afghanistan	Multilateral	07 Dec 44	Air Transport	171UNTS345	200501
Afghanistan	Multilateral	07 Dec 44	Air Transport	171UNTS387	200502
Afghanistan	Multilateral	07 Dec 44	IGO Establishment	15UNTS295	200102

PARTY ONE	PARTY TWO	DATE	TOPIC	CITATION	NUMBER
Afghanistan	Multilateral	11 Dec 46	Sanitation	12UNTS179	100186
Afghanistan	Multilateral	27 May 47	Air Transport	418UNTS161	106021
Afghanistan	Multilateral	12 Nov 47	Admin Cooperation	53UNTS49	100772
Afghanistan	Multilateral	12 Nov 47	Admin Cooperation	53UNTS39	100771
Afghanistan	Multilateral	12 Nov 47	Admin Cooperation	46UNTS169	100709
Afghanistan	Multilateral	12 Nov 47	Admin Cooperation	53UNTS13	100770
Afghanistan	Multilateral	12 Nov 47	Admin Cooperation	46UNTS201	100710
Afghanistan	Multilateral	24 Jul 48	Sanitation	66UNTS25	100847
Afghanistan	Multilateral	19 Nov 48	Sanitation	44UNTS277	100688
Afghanistan	Multilateral	09 Dec 48	Humanitarian	78UNTS277	101021
Afghanistan	Multilateral	15 Jul 49	Health/Educ/Welfare	197UNTS3	102631
Afghanistan	Multilateral	12 Aug 49	Humanitarian	75UNTS287	100973
Afghanistan	Multilateral	12 Aug 49	Humanitarian	75UNTS85	100971
Afghanistan	Multilateral	12 Aug 49	Humanitarian	75UNTS31	100970
Afghanistan	Multilateral	12 Aug 49	General Military	75UNTS135	100972
Afghanistan	Multilateral	22 Nov 50	Culture	131UNTS25	101734
Afghanistan	Multilateral	07 Dec 50	Admin Cooperation	212UNTS17	102861
Afghanistan	Multilateral	25 May 51	Status of Forces	175UNTS215	102303
Afghanistan	Multilateral	23 Jan 52	Tech Assistance	127UNTS269	101708
Afghanistan	Multilateral	11 Jul 52	IGO Establishment	169UNTS3	102220
Afghanistan	Multilateral	11 Jul 52	Postal Service	170UNTS63	102222
Afghanistan	Multilateral	07 Dec 53	Admin Cooperation	182UNTS51	102422
Afghanistan	Multilateral	14 Jun 54	Air Transport	320UNTS209	104643
Afghanistan	Multilateral	14 Jun 54	Air Transport	320UNTS217	104644
Afghanistan	Multilateral	25 May 55	IGO Establishment	264UNTS117	103791
Afghanistan	Multilateral	10 May 56	Tech Assistance	243UNTS103	103449
Afghanistan	Multilateral	26 Oct 56	IGO Establishment	276UNTS3	103988
Afghanistan	Multilateral	03 Oct 57	Postal Service	365UNTS3	105213
Afghanistan	Multilateral	03 Oct 57	Postal Service	364UNTS3	105211
Afghanistan	Multilateral	29 Apr 58	Specific Resources	559UNTS285	108164
Afghanistan	Multilateral	29 Apr 58	Territory Boundary	516UNTS205	107477
Afghanistan	Multilateral	29 Apr 58	Territory Boundary	499UNTS311	107302
Afghanistan	Multilateral	29 Apr 58	Water Transport	450UNTS11	106465
Afghanistan	Multilateral	26 Jan 60	IGO Establishment	439UNTS249	106333
Afghanistan	Multilateral	30 Mar 61	Sanitation	520UNTS151	107515
Afghanistan	Multilateral	18 Apr 61	Consul/Citizenship	500UNTS95	107310
Afghanistan	Multilateral	05 Aug 63	Sanitation	480UNTS43	106964
Afghanistan	Multilateral	03 Dec 63	IGO Establishment	529UNTS217	107663
Afghanistan	Multilateral	10 Jul 64	Postal Service	612UNTS3	108847
Afghanistan	Multilateral	10 Jul 64	Postal Service	611UNTS105	108845
Afghanistan	Multilateral	10 Jul 64	Postal Service	611UNTS7	108844
Afghanistan	Multilateral	23 Feb 65	IGO Operations	527UNTS120	107622
Afghanistan	Multilateral	18 Mar 65	Dispute Settlement	575UNTS159	108359
Afghanistan	Multilateral	08 Jul 65	General Trade	597UNTS3	108641
Afghanistan	Multilateral	04 Dec 65	IGO Establishment	571UNTS123	108303
Afghanistan	Multilateral	27 Jan 67	Scientific Project	610UNTS205	108843
Afghanistan	Multilateral	01 Jul 68	Peace/Disarmament	0UNTS0	110485
Afghanistan	Netherlands	26 Jul 39	General Amity	32UNTS381	200177

PARTY ONE	PARTY TWO	DATE	TOPIC	CITATION	NUMBER
Afghanistan	Pakistan	13 Jun 57	Air Transport	327UNTS51	104717
Afghanistan	Poland	19 Sep 60	Tech Assistance	60PZUM116	458079
Afghanistan	Poland	27 Jun 62	Air Transport	62PZUM57	458096
Afghanistan	Poland	25 Jun 66	Culture	72PDZU373	457137
Afghanistan	Spain	28 Oct 57	General Amity	58SPBO2507	460001
Afghanistan	Sweden	22 Oct 40	General Amity	191UNTS349	200516
Afghanistan	Switzerland	27 Sep 61	Air Transport	63SWRO874	462089
Afghanistan	Turkey	08 Feb 58	Air Transport	464UNTS39	106711
Afghanistan	Turkey	07 Nov 59	Culture	64TURG601	466034
Afghanistan	UK Great Britain	19 Apr 65	Culture	633UNTS45	109033
Afghanistan	UN Special Fund	21 Feb 60	Direct Aid	351UNTS93	105019
Afghanistan	UNESCO (Educ/Cult)	08 Dec 48	Education	46UNTS3	100697
Afghanistan	UNICEF (Children)	04 Jul 50	IGO Operations	71UNTS3	100906
Afghanistan	UNICEF (Children)	22 Oct 70	IGO Operations	0UNTS0	110797
Afghanistan	United Nations	24 Nov 59	Tech Assistance	397UNTS187	105705
Afghanistan	United Nations	28 Apr 64	Education	494UNTS77	107227
Afghanistan	USA (United States)	29 Feb 44	Admin Cooperation	106UNTS247	200344
Afghanistan	USA (United States)	07 Feb 51	Tech Assistance	132UNTS265	101766
Afghanistan	USA (United States)	30 Jun 53	Tech Assistance	215UNTS3	102908
Afghanistan	USA (United States)	20 Mar 54	Direct Aid	229UNTS7	103156
Afghanistan	USA (United States)	29 May 54	Direct Aid	234UNTS3	103268
Afghanistan	USA (United States)	23 Jun 56	Direct Aid	271UNTS295	103921
Afghanistan	USA (United States)	09 Jun 57	Admin Cooperation	307UNTS97	104445
Afghanistan	USA (United States)	26 Jun 58	Culture	321UNTS67	104654
Afghanistan	USA (United States)	15 Feb 61	Mass Media	406UNTS235	105852
Afghanistan	USA (United States)	11 Sep 62	General Aid	461UNTS169	106661
Afghanistan	USA (United States)	20 Aug 63	Education	488UNTS41	107118
Afghanistan	USA (United States)	22 May 65	US Agri Commod Aid	579UNTS29	108396
Afghanistan	USA (United States)	20 Dec 66	US Agri Commod Aid	0UNTS0	109699
Afghanistan	USA (United States)	19 Jul 67	US Agri Commod Aid	0UNTS0	109909
Afghanistan	USA (United States)	02 Jul 68	US Agri Commod Aid	0UNTS0	110148
Afghanistan	USSR (Soviet Union)	13 Jun 46	Territory Boundary	31UNTS147	100476
Afghanistan	USSR (Soviet Union)	13 Apr 47	Telecommunications	0SUST231	468001
Afghanistan	USSR (Soviet Union)	17 Jul 50	General Economic	0SUST276	468002
Afghanistan	USSR (Soviet Union)	27 Jan 54	Loans and Credits	0SUST306	468003
Afghanistan	USSR (Soviet Union)	28 Jun 55	General Transport	240UNTS253	103407
Afghanistan	USSR (Soviet Union)	18 Dec 55	Admin Cooperation	259UNTS101	103684
Afghanistan	USSR (Soviet Union)	28 Jan 56	Loans and Credits	0SUST347	468005
Afghanistan	USSR (Soviet Union)	24 Mar 56	Air Transport	0SUST351	468006
Afghanistan	USSR (Soviet Union)	18 Jan 58	Admin Cooperation	7SUGG102	469486
Afghanistan	USSR (Soviet Union)	18 Jan 58	Visas	321UNTS77	104655
Afghanistan	USSR (Soviet Union)	25 Jun 58	Specific Resources	7SUGG114	469515
Afghanistan	USSR (Soviet Union)	04 Feb 59	Telecommunications	8SUGG136	469556
Afghanistan	USSR (Soviet Union)	28 May 59	General Aid	8SUGG145	469576
Afghanistan	USSR (Soviet Union)	18 Jul 59	Non-IBRD Project	8SUGG149	469591
Afghanistan	USSR (Soviet Union)	19 Jan 60	General Aid	9SUGG121	469623
Afghanistan	USSR (Soviet Union)	18 Feb 60	Education	9SUGG126	469631
Afghanistan	USSR (Soviet Union)	04 Mar 60	Culture	9SUGG129	469638
Afghanistan	USSR (Soviet Union)	25 May 60	Non-IBRD Project	9SUGG136	469662
Afghanistan	USSR (Soviet Union)	12 Aug 60	General Trade	9SUGG144	469682
Afghanistan	USSR (Soviet Union)	13 Nov 60	Tech Assistance	9SUGG151	469708
Afghanistan	USSR (Soviet Union)	16 Oct 61	General Aid	10SUGG143	469800
Afghanistan	USSR (Soviet Union)	13 Jan 62	General Trade	11SUGG130	469816
Afghanistan	USSR (Soviet Union)	11 Apr 62	Tech Assistance	11SUGG137	469832
Afghanistan	USSR (Soviet Union)	17 May 62	General Aid	11SUGG140	469839
Afghanistan	USSR (Soviet Union)	06 Feb 68	Tech Assistance	0UNTS0	110279
Afghanistan	WHO (World Health)	04 Dec 49	Direct Aid	102UNTS117	101414
Afghanistan	WHO (World Health)	18 Dec 58	Tech Assistance	324UNTS121	104681
African Coffee Org	France	19 Apr 66	IGO Status/Immunit	67FRJO1903	416507
African Coffee Org	France	14 Apr 67	IGO Establishment	0UNTS0	110312
African Devel Bank	UN Special Fund	09 Oct 68	Non-IBRD Project	0UNTS0	200641
African Insur Org	France	08 Feb 67	IGO Status/Immunit	67FRJO212	416509
Afromalagasy Coffee	France	14 Apr 67	IGO Status/Immunit	69FRJO2204	416510
Afromalagasy Org	ILO (Labor Org)	30 May 63	IGO Operations	467UNTS482	200602
AID (Int Devel)	IBRD (World Bank)	03 Jan 67	Direct Aid	619UNTS321	200635
AID (Int Devel)	Multilateral	26 May 64	IBRD Project	541UNTS271	200613
Albania	Accept UN Charter	02 Dec 48	UN Charter	223UNTS23	103043
Albania	Austria	27 Jul 61	General Economic	407UNTS37	105858
Albania	China People's Rep	14 Oct 54	Culture	54CCJC71	410178
Albania	China People's Rep	14 Oct 54	Scientific Project	54CCJC70	410177
Albania	China People's Rep	03 Dec 54	General Economic	54CCJC79	410186
Albania	China People's Rep	03 Dec 54	Loans and Credits	54CCJC80	410187
Albania	China People's Rep	28 Sep 55	Mass Media	55CCJC66	410258
Albania	China People's Rep	13 Mar 56	General Economic	56CCJC40	410324
Albania	China People's Rep	08 Mar 57	General Economic	57CCJC25	410407
Albania	China People's Rep	31 May 57	Gen Communications	57CCJC54	410425
Albania	China People's Rep	12 Mar 58	General Economic	58CCJC25	410500
Albania	China People's Rep	16 Jan 59	General Trade	59CCJC6	410570
Albania	China People's Rep	16 Jan 59	Loans and Credits	59CCJC7	410571
Albania	China People's Rep	16 Jan 59	General Economic	59CCJC8	410572
Albania	China People's Rep	11 Jul 59	Mass Media	59CCJC89	410632
Albania	China People's Rep	15 Mar 60	General Economic	60CCJC41	410686
Albania	China People's Rep	02 Feb 61	General Trade	61CCJC17	410755
Albania	China People's Rep	02 Feb 61	General Amity	61CCJC16	410754
Albania	China People's Rep	02 Feb 61	Loans and Credits	61CCJC18	410756
Albania	China People's Rep	18 Feb 63	Sanitation	63CCJC14	410948
Albania	China People's Rep	06 Dec 63	General Economic	63CCJC144	411039
Albania	China People's Rep	02 Jan 64	Sanitation	64CCJC3	411050
Albania	China People's Rep	05 Mar 64	Health/Educ/Welfare	64CCJC34	411051
Albania	China People's Rep	12 Mar 65	Culture	65CCJC26	411070
Albania	China People's Rep	22 Mar 65	General Transport	65CCJC34	411071
Albania	China People's Rep	08 Jun 65	General Economic	65CCJC77	411055
Albania	China People's Rep	08 Jun 65	General Economic	65CCJC76	411054
Albania	China People's Rep	08 Jun 65	Loans and Credits	65CCJC75	411053
Albania	China People's Rep	06 Oct 65	Tech Assistance	65CCJC131	411056
Albania	China People's Rep	12 Nov 65	General Trade	65CCJC140	411072
Albania	China People's Rep	04 May 66	Water Transport	66CCJC27	411057
Albania	China People's Rep	24 May 66	Scientific Project	66CCJC38	411073
Albania	China People's Rep	20 Oct 66	Loans and Credits	66CCJC86	411074
Albania	China People's Rep	21 Nov 66	General Economic	66CCJC96	411075
Albania	China People's Rep	30 Nov 66	Tech Assistance	66CCJC102	411076
Albania	China People's Rep	24 Apr 67	Culture	67CCJC14	411077
Albania	China People's Rep	28 May 67	Water Transport	67CCJC22	411078
Albania	China People's Rep	23 Jun 67	Direct Aid	67CCJC23	411079
Albania	Cuba	16 Jan 61	General Trade	448UNTS67	106425
Albania	Czechoslovakia	16 Jan 59	Consul/Citizenship	363UNTS165	105207
Albania	Czechoslovakia	16 Jan 59	Admin Cooperation	363UNTS195	105208
Albania	France	14 Dec 63	General Amity	65FRRT41	415004
Albania	France	10 Feb 69	General Trade	69FRMD2402	417005
Albania	Germany, East	27 Mar 51	General Trade	1EGDA474	419006
Albania	Germany, East	26 Feb 52	Tech Assistance	4EGDA547	419007
Albania	Germany, East	31 Jul 53	Culture	4EGDA548	419008
Albania	Germany, East	26 Oct 53	Tech Assistance	1EGDA474	419009
Albania	Germany, East	05 Nov 53	Consul/Citizenship	1EGDA478	419010
Albania	Germany, East	28 Mar 55	Consul/Citizenship	2EGDA477	419011
Albania	Germany, East	15 Feb 56	Tech Assistance	3EGDA596	419012
Albania	Germany, East	22 Feb 57	Tech Assistance	5EGDA284	419013
Albania	Germany, East	05 Jun 57	Postal Service	5EGDA285	419014
Albania	Germany, East	05 Jun 57	Telecommunications	5EGDA292	419015
Albania	Germany, East	17 Aug 57	Sanitation	5EGDA302	419016
Albania	Germany, East	11 Jan 59	Admin Cooperation	7EGDA283	419018
Albania	Germany, East	11 Jan 59	Consul/Citizenship	7EGDA275	419017
Albania	Germany, East	08 Oct 59	General Economic	7EGDA311	419019
Albania	Germany, East	21 Jan 60	Air Transport	8EGDA310	419020
Albania	Germany, East	25 Apr 60	Finance	8EGDA316	419021
Albania	Germany, East	11 Jan 61	General Trade	9EGDA309	419022
Albania	Germany, East	13 Jan 61	Sanitation	9EGDA310	419023
Albania	Germany, East	23 Jul 65	Water Transport	51EGDZ340	420024
Albania	Germany, East	01 Mar 66	General Trade	51EGDZ355	420025
Albania	Hungary	12 Jan 60	Admin Cooperation	520UNTS3	107511

PARTY ONE	PARTY TWO	DATE	TOPIC	CITATION	NUMBER
Albania	Italy	22 Jun 57	Admin Cooperation	59ITDI216	436004
Albania	Italy	22 Jun 57	Other Military	59ITDI216	436005
Albania	Italy	22 Jun 57	Peace/Disarmament	57ITGU263	435003
Albania	Italy	26 May 58	Finance	362UNTS259	105191
Albania	Italy	11 Jun 58	Water Transport	58ITGU244	435006
Albania	Italy	21 Apr 62	Air Transport	63ITDI273	436007
Albania	Italy	19 Dec 64	General Trade	65ITDI115	436008
Albania	Multilateral	02 Aug 44	Scientific Project	67UNTS221	200221
Albania	Multilateral	14 Jan 46	Reparations	555UNTS69	108105
Albania	Multilateral	22 Jul 46	IGO Establishment	14UNTS185	100221
Albania	Multilateral	22 Jul 46	IGO Establishment	9UNTS3	100125
Albania	Multilateral	11 Dec 46	Sanitation	12UNTS179	100186
Albania	Multilateral	10 Feb 47	Peace/Disarmament	49UNTS3	100747
Albania	Multilateral	02 Oct 47	Telecommunications	193UNTS188	102616
Albania	Multilateral	12 Nov 47	Admin Cooperation	53UNTS13	100770
Albania	Multilateral	12 Nov 47	Admin Cooperation	46UNTS201	100710
Albania	Multilateral	12 Nov 47	Admin Cooperation	46UNTS169	100709
Albania	Multilateral	12 Nov 47	Admin Cooperation	53UNTS39	100771
Albania	Multilateral	24 Jul 48	Sanitation	66UNTS25	100847
Albania	Multilateral	19 Nov 48	Sanitation	44UNTS277	100688
Albania	Multilateral	09 Dec 48	Humanitarian	78UNTS277	101021
Albania	Multilateral	12 Aug 49	Humanitarian	75UNTS31	100970
Albania	Multilateral	12 Aug 49	General Military	75UNTS135	100972
Albania	Multilateral	12 Aug 49	Humanitarian	75UNTS85	100971
Albania	Multilateral	12 Aug 49	Humanitarian	75UNTS287	100973
Albania	Multilateral	21 Mar 50	Admin Cooperation	96UNTS271	101342
Albania	Multilateral	07 Dec 50	Admin Cooperation	212UNTS17	102861
Albania	Multilateral	11 Jul 52	Postal Service	170UNTS269	102223
Albania	Multilateral	11 Jul 52	Postal Service	170UNTS63	102222
Albania	Multilateral	11 Jul 52	Postal Service	171UNTS89	102225
Albania	Multilateral	11 Jul 52	IGO Establishment	169UNTS3	102220
Albania	Multilateral	11 Jul 52	Postal Service	171UNTS143	102226
Albania	Multilateral	11 Jul 52	Postal Service	171UNTS3	102224
Albania	Multilateral	11 Jul 52	Postal Service	170UNTS3	102221
Albania	Multilateral	14 May 54	Culture	249UNTS215	103511
Albania	Multilateral	14 May 55	General Amity	219UNTS3	102962
Albania	Multilateral	26 Mar 56	IGO Establishment	259UNTS125	103686
Albania	Multilateral	26 Oct 56	IGO Establishment	276UNTS3	103988
Albania	Multilateral	20 Feb 57	Consul/Citizenship	309UNTS65	104468
Albania	Multilateral	03 Oct 57	Postal Service	366UNTS87	105216
Albania	Multilateral	03 Oct 57	Postal Service	365UNTS207	105214
Albania	Multilateral	03 Oct 57	Postal Service	366UNTS255	105219
Albania	Multilateral	03 Oct 57	Postal Service	366UNTS141	105217
Albania	Multilateral	03 Oct 57	Postal Service	364UNTS3	105211
Albania	Multilateral	03 Oct 57	Postal Service	364UNTS331	105212
Albania	Multilateral	03 Oct 57	Postal Service	366UNTS3	105215
Albania	Multilateral	03 Oct 57	Postal Service	365UNTS3	105213
Albania	Multilateral	29 Apr 58	Territory Boundary	499UNTS311	107302
Albania	Multilateral	14 Dec 59	Sanitation	422UNTS33	106067
Albania	Multilateral	14 Dec 59	IGO Status/Immunit	368UNTS237	105244
Albania	Multilateral	14 Dec 59	Sanitation	422UNTS57	106068
Albania	Multilateral	14 Dec 59	IGO Establishment	368UNTS253	105245
Albania	Multilateral	14 Dec 60	Education	429UNTS93	106193
Albania	Multilateral	18 Apr 61	Consul/Citizenship	500UNTS95	107310
Albania	Multilateral	24 Apr 63	Consul/Citizenship	596UNTS261	108638
Albania	Multilateral	10 Jul 64	Postal Service	612UNTS233	108848
Albania	Multilateral	10 Jul 64	Postal Service	612UNTS3	108847
Albania	Multilateral	10 Jul 64	Postal Service	613UNTS3	108851
Albania	Multilateral	10 Jul 64	Postal Service	612UNTS361	108849
Albania	Multilateral	10 Jul 64	Postal Service	613UNTS3	108850
Albania	Multilateral	10 Jul 64	Postal Service	611UNTS387	108846
Albania	Multilateral	10 Jul 64	Postal Service	611UNTS105	108845
Albania	Multilateral	10 Jul 64	Postal Service	613UNTS193	108852
Albania	Multilateral	10 Jul 64	Postal Service	611UNTS7	108844
Albania	Poland	02 Dec 50	Culture	260UNTS131	103707

PARTY ONE	PARTY TWO	DATE	TOPIC	CITATION	NUMBER
Albania	Poland	25 Jan 51	Scientific Project	260UNTS217	103710
Albania	Poland	08 Jul 57	Air Transport	57PZUM74	458051
Albania	Romania	14 Feb 53	Culture	342UNTS107	104903
Albania	Romania	03 May 61	Non-ILO Labor	592UNTS21	108567
Albania	UNICEF (Children)	20 Nov 47	IGO Operations	65UNTS163	200208
Albania	USSR (Soviet Union)	10 Nov 45	Consul/Citizenship	0SUST201	471019
Albania	USSR (Soviet Union)	26 Jul 47	General Economic	0SUST235	468007
Albania	USSR (Soviet Union)	03 Sep 48	General Trade	0SUST252	471026
Albania	USSR (Soviet Union)	03 Sep 48	Loans and Credits	0SUST252	471027
Albania	USSR (Soviet Union)	10 Apr 49	General Economic	0SUST258	468008
Albania	USSR (Soviet Union)	27 Jun 50	Mass Media	0SUST275	468009
Albania	USSR (Soviet Union)	17 Feb 51	Loans and Credits	0SUST280	468010
Albania	USSR (Soviet Union)	19 Apr 52	Tech Assistance	0SUST286	468011
Albania	USSR (Soviet Union)	05 Jul 52	Education	0SUST288	468012
Albania	USSR (Soviet Union)	27 Aug 55	Sanitation	0SUST334	468013
Albania	USSR (Soviet Union)	03 May 56	Culture	259UNTS391	103699
Albania	USSR (Soviet Union)	17 Apr 57	General Amity	0SUST381	468014
Albania	USSR (Soviet Union)	18 Sep 57	Consul/Citizenship	307UNTS251	104454
Albania	USSR (Soviet Union)	18 Sep 57	Consul/Citizenship	307UNTS265	104455
Albania	USSR (Soviet Union)	26 Oct 57	Mass Media	16SUGG122	469948
Albania	USSR (Soviet Union)	22 Nov 57	General Aid	0SUST392	468017
Albania	USSR (Soviet Union)	15 Feb 58	General Trade	7SUGG105	469497
Albania	USSR (Soviet Union)	15 Feb 58	General Economic	313UNTS261	104536
Albania	USSR (Soviet Union)	30 Jun 58	Admin Cooperation	328UNTS3	104729
Albania	USSR (Soviet Union)	06 Feb 59	General Trade	8SUGG136	469557
Albania	USSR (Soviet Union)	03 Apr 59	General Economic	8SUGG141	469570
Albania	USSR (Soviet Union)	03 Jul 59	Tech Assistance	8SUGG148	469585
Albania	USSR (Soviet Union)	03 Jul 59	Non-IBRD Project	8SUGG148	469587
Albania	USSR (Soviet Union)	03 Jul 59	Culture	8SUGG148	469584
Albania	USSR (Soviet Union)	03 Jul 59	Non-IBRD Project	8SUGG148	469586
Albania	USSR (Soviet Union)	25 Jan 60	General Trade	9SUGG122	469626
Albania	USSR (Soviet Union)	19 Jul 60	Tech Assistance	9SUGG142	469676
Albania	USSR (Soviet Union)	31 Aug 60	Tech Assistance	9SUGG146	469689
Albania	USSR (Soviet Union)	04 Jan 61	General Economic	10SUGG117	469732
Albania	Yugoslavia	23 Mar 44	General Military	1UNTS81	100015
Albania	Yugoslavia	01 Jul 46	General Economic	111UNTS3	101517
Albania	Yugoslavia	01 Jul 46	Loans and Credits	111UNTS81	101518
Albania	Yugoslavia	11 Jul 46	Air Transport	4UNTS407	100058
Albania	Yugoslavia	03 Oct 46	General Trade	111UNTS227	101537
Albania	Yugoslavia	03 Oct 46	Loans and Credits	111UNTS87	101519
Albania	Yugoslavia	28 Nov 46	Land Transport	111UNTS139	101526
Albania	Yugoslavia	28 Nov 46	Finance	111UNTS171	101530
Albania	Yugoslavia	28 Nov 46	Finance	111UNTS143	101527
Albania	Yugoslavia	28 Nov 46	Non-IBRD Project	111UNTS93	101520
Albania	Yugoslavia	28 Nov 46	Non-IBRD Project	111UNTS151	101528
Albania	Yugoslavia	28 Nov 46	Non-IBRD Project	111UNTS113	101523
Albania	Yugoslavia	28 Nov 46	Non-IBRD Project	111UNTS109	101522
Albania	Yugoslavia	28 Nov 46	Non-IBRD Project	111UNTS123	101524
Albania	Yugoslavia	28 Nov 46	Non-IBRD Project	111UNTS127	101525
Albania	Yugoslavia	28 Nov 46	Non-IBRD Project	111UNTS105	101521
Albania	Yugoslavia	28 Nov 46	Non-ILO Labor	111UNTS163	101529
Albania	Yugoslavia	12 Jun 47	Loans and Credits	111UNTS189	101533
Albania	Yugoslavia	12 Jun 47	Finance	111UNTS195	101534
Albania	Yugoslavia	12 Jun 47	Direct Aid	111UNTS177	101531
Albania	Yugoslavia	12 Jun 47	Dispute Settlement	111UNTS183	101532
Albania	Yugoslavia	12 Jun 47	IGO Establishment	111UNTS201	101535
Albania	Yugoslavia	22 Jun 47	General Trade	111UNTS207	101536
Albania	Yugoslavia	09 Jul 47	Culture	33UNTS91	100516
Albania	Yugoslavia	23 Nov 56	Air Transport	386UNTS73	105539
Albania	Yugoslavia	23 Nov 56	Air Transport	363UNTS123	105204
Albania	Yugoslavia	20 May 57	Sanitation	363UNTS99	105203
Albania	Yugoslavia	29 Aug 57	Postal Service	391UNTS167	105622
Albania	Yugoslavia	29 Aug 57	Postal Service	391UNTS127	105621
Albania	Yugoslavia	28 Apr 58	Consul/Citizenship	386UNTS103	105540
Albania	Yugoslavia	29 Dec 59	General Trade	396UNTS63	105693

PARTY ONE	PARTY TWO	DATE	TOPIC	CITATION	NUMBER
Algeria	Accept UN Charter	30 Sep 62	UN Charter	442UNTS37	106336
Algeria	Belgium	27 Feb 68	Non-ILO Labor	0UNTS0	110110
Algeria	Belgium	08 Jan 70	Tech Assistance	0UNTS0	110313
Algeria	Belgium	08 Jan 70	Non-ILO Labor	0UNTS0	110314
Algeria	Benelux Econ Union	18 Mar 70	General Economic	0UNTS0	110773
Algeria	China People's Rep	11 Sep 63	Culture	63CCJC106	411009
Algeria	China People's Rep	11 Oct 63	Loans and Credits	63CCJC116	411017
Algeria	China People's Rep	14 Apr 64	Mass Media	64CCJC48	411060
Algeria	China People's Rep	19 Sep 64	General Trade	64CCJC118	411063
Algeria	China People's Rep	19 Sep 64	Finance	64CCJC119	411064
Algeria	China People's Rep	25 Dec 64	Scientific Project	64CCJC187	411068
Algeria	China People's Rep	14 Jan 65	Commodity Trade	65CCJC6	411069
Algeria	China People's Rep	03 Jun 65	Culture	65CCJC72	411052
Algeria	Czechoslovakia	09 Mar 64	Air Transport	601UNTS247	108700
Algeria	Czechoslovakia	14 May 64	Culture	538UNTS301	107817
Algeria	France	16 Dec 44	Non-ILO Labor	0UNTS0	110350
Algeria	France	19 Mar 62	Recognition	62FRJO2003	416006
Algeria	France	03 Jul 62	Recognition	507UNTS25	107395
Algeria	France	28 Aug 62	Specific Resources	62FRRT27	415007
Algeria	France	07 Sep 62	Education	0UNTS0	110819
Algeria	France	24 Sep 62	Tech Assistance	62FRRT30	415008
Algeria	France	24 Sep 62	Tech Assistance	0UNTS0	109507
Algeria	France	17 Dec 62	Tech Assistance	63FRRT8	415009
Algeria	France	31 Dec 62	Tech Assistance	63FRRT13	415010
Algeria	France	16 Jan 63	Direct Aid	63FRRT11	415011
Algeria	France	19 Jan 63	Finance	63FRRT17	415012
Algeria	France	23 Jan 63	Mass Media	63FRRT12	415013
Algeria	France	18 Feb 63	Air Transport	563UNTS263	108214
Algeria	France	19 Apr 63	Tech Assistance	64FRRT20	415014
Algeria	France	22 Apr 63	Education	0UNTS0	110349
Algeria	France	11 Jun 63	Tech Assistance	64FRRT21	415015
Algeria	France	11 Jun 63	Education	0UNTS0	110820
Algeria	France	23 Oct 63	Health/Educ/Welfare	64FRRT24	415016
Algeria	France	27 Aug 64	Extradition	65FRRT72	415017
Algeria	France	16 Dec 64	Extradition	65FRRT4	415018
Algeria	France	19 Jan 65	Non-ILO Labor	65FRJO1905	416020
Algeria	France	19 Jan 65	Non-ILO Labor	65FRRT50	415019
Algeria	France	28 Jul 65	Non-IBRD Project	65FRRT107	415021
Algeria	France	28 Jul 65	Tech Assistance	0UNTS0	110609
Algeria	France	29 Jul 65	Specific Resources	65FRRT106	415022
Algeria	France	29 Jul 65	Non-IBRD Project	0UNTS0	110610
Algeria	France	08 Apr 66	Health/Educ/Welfare	66FRRT34	415023
Algeria	France	08 Apr 66	Tech Assistance	0UNTS0	109508
Algeria	France	23 Dec 66	Health/Educ/Welfare	67FRJO3003	416024
Algeria	France	20 Jun 67	General Ad Hoc	68FRJO1008	416030
Algeria	France	26 Jun 67	Health/Educ/Welfare	67FRJO2809	416025
Algeria	France	08 Jul 67	Non-IBRD Project	69FRJO2006	416026
Algeria	France	08 Jul 67	Education	0UNTS0	110351
Algeria	France	20 Jul 67	Water Transport	67FRJO2510	416027
Algeria	France	01 Oct 67	Non-IBRD Project	70FRJO1004	416031
Algeria	France	26 Dec 67	Air Transport	69FRJO1101	416028
Algeria	France	26 Dec 67	Admin Cooperation	0UNTS0	109509
Algeria	France	16 Mar 68	Tech Assistance	69FRJO2006	416029
Algeria	France	16 Mar 68	Scientific Project	0UNTS0	110821
Algeria	France	02 Aug 68	Scientific Project	0UNTS0	110474
Algeria	France	01 Oct 68	Education	0UNTS0	110477
Algeria	France	27 Dec 68	Non-ILO Labor	69FRJO2203	416032
Algeria	France	27 Dec 68	Privil/Immunities	0UNTS0	109640
Algeria	France	27 Nov 69	Tech Assistance	0UNTS0	110478
Algeria	Germany, East	24 Jun 66	Education	44EGDZ362	420026
Algeria	Germany, East	12 Dec 66	General Trade	41EGDZ374	420027
Algeria	Germany, East	21 Dec 66	Culture	41EGDZ374	420028
Algeria	Germany, East	21 Dec 66	Air Transport	41EGDZ374	420029
Algeria	Germany, West	03 Oct 64	Finance	65WBGA116	424004
Algeria	Germany, West	17 Dec 64	Tech Assistance	65WBGA100	424005

PARTY ONE	PARTY TWO	DATE	TOPIC	CITATION	NUMBER
Algeria	IBRD (World Bank)	14 May 64	IBRD Project	522UNTS265	107552
Algeria	ILO (Labor Org)	06 Apr 67	IGO Establishment	595UNTS99	108614
Algeria	Iran	08 Aug 68	Culture	0IRTB5	433010
Algeria	Italy	12 Jan 55	Admin Cooperation	57ITGU87	435009
Algeria	Italy	03 Jun 65	Air Transport	67ITGU137	435010
Algeria	Ivory Coast	16 Feb 67	Air Transport	0UNTS0	109245
Algeria	Mali	22 Jul 63	Air Transport	564UNTS29	108219
Algeria	Morocco	30 Apr 63	Air Transport	564UNTS3	108217
Algeria	Morocco	15 Jan 69	General Amity	0UNTS0	110095
Algeria	Multilateral	07 Dec 44	IGO Establishment	15UNTS295	200102
Algeria	Multilateral	11 Dec 46	Sanitation	12UNTS179	100186
Algeria	Multilateral	12 Nov 47	Admin Cooperation	53UNTS39	100771
Algeria	Multilateral	12 Nov 47	Admin Cooperation	53UNTS49	100772
Algeria	Multilateral	06 Mar 48	Water Transport	289UNTS3	104214
Algeria	Multilateral	10 Jun 48	Humanitarian	164UNTS113	102163
Algeria	Multilateral	19 Jun 48	Air Transport	310UNTS151	104492
Algeria	Multilateral	09 Dec 48	Humanitarian	78UNTS277	101021
Algeria	Multilateral	04 May 49	Admin Cooperation	92UNTS19	101257
Algeria	Multilateral	04 May 49	Admin Cooperation	98UNTS101	101358
Algeria	Multilateral	18 Jun 49	ILO Labor	605UNTS295	108768
Algeria	Multilateral	24 Sep 49	IGO Establishment	126UNTS237	101691
Algeria	Multilateral	21 Mar 50	Admin Cooperation	96UNTS271	101342
Algeria	Multilateral	07 Dec 50	Admin Cooperation	212UNTS17	102861
Algeria	Multilateral	02 Jul 51	Refugees	189UNTS137	102545
Algeria	Multilateral	10 May 52	Admin Cooperation	439UNTS217	106331
Algeria	Multilateral	11 Jul 52	Postal Service	170UNTS269	102223
Algeria	Multilateral	11 Jul 52	Postal Service	171UNTS143	102226
Algeria	Multilateral	11 Jul 52	Postal Service	171UNTS3	102224
Algeria	Multilateral	11 Jul 52	Postal Service	171UNTS89	102225
Algeria	Multilateral	11 Jul 52	IGO Establishment	169UNTS3	102220
Algeria	Multilateral	11 Jul 52	Postal Service	170UNTS3	102221
Algeria	Multilateral	11 Jul 52	Postal Service	170UNTS63	102222
Algeria	Multilateral	07 Oct 52	Admin Cooperation	310UNTS181	104493
Algeria	Multilateral	12 May 54	Admin Cooperation	327UNTS3	104714
Algeria	Multilateral	28 Sep 54	Refugees	360UNTS117	105158
Algeria	Multilateral	18 May 56	Customs	327UNTS123	104721
Algeria	Multilateral	18 May 56	Customs	338UNTS103	104834
Algeria	Multilateral	18 May 56	Customs	319UNTS21	104630
Algeria	Multilateral	03 Oct 57	Postal Service	365UNTS207	105214
Algeria	Multilateral	03 Oct 57	Postal Service	365UNTS3	105213
Algeria	Multilateral	03 Oct 57	Postal Service	366UNTS3	105215
Algeria	Multilateral	03 Oct 57	Postal Service	366UNTS255	105219
Algeria	Multilateral	03 Oct 57	Postal Service	366UNTS141	105217
Algeria	Multilateral	03 Oct 57	Postal Service	364UNTS3	105211
Algeria	Multilateral	03 Oct 57	Postal Service	366UNTS87	105216
Algeria	Multilateral	03 Oct 57	Postal Service	364UNTS331	105212
Algeria	Multilateral	26 Jan 60	IGO Establishment	439UNTS249	106333
Algeria	Multilateral	17 Jun 60	Humanitarian	536UNTS27	107794
Algeria	Multilateral	18 Apr 61	Consul/Citizenship	500UNTS95	107310
Algeria	Multilateral	15 Nov 62	Tech Assistance	448UNTS50	106424
Algeria	Multilateral	20 Apr 63	IGO Establishment	495UNTS3	107239
Algeria	Multilateral	25 May 63	IGO Establishment	479UNTS39	106947
Algeria	Multilateral	04 Aug 63	IGO Establishment	510UNTS3	107408
Algeria	Multilateral	05 Aug 63	Sanitation	480UNTS43	106964
Algeria	Multilateral	10 Jul 64	Postal Service	611UNTS387	108846
Algeria	Multilateral	10 Jul 64	Postal Service	613UNTS3	108850
Algeria	Multilateral	10 Jul 64	Postal Service	611UNTS105	108845
Algeria	Multilateral	10 Jul 64	Postal Service	612UNTS233	108848
Algeria	Multilateral	10 Jul 64	Postal Service	612UNTS361	108849
Algeria	Multilateral	10 Jul 64	Postal Service	613UNTS193	108852
Algeria	Multilateral	10 Jul 64	Postal Service	613UNTS127	108853
Algeria	Multilateral	10 Jul 64	Postal Service	613UNTS3	108851
Algeria	Multilateral	10 Jul 64	Postal Service	612UNTS3	108847
Algeria	Multilateral	10 Jul 64	Postal Service	611UNTS7	108844
Algeria	Multilateral	20 Aug 64	Telecommunications	514UNTS25	107441

PARTY ONE	PARTY TWO	DATE	TOPIC	CITATION	NUMBER
Algeria	Multilateral	09 Mar 65	Water Transport	591UNTS265	108564
Algeria	Multilateral	28 Jun 67	ILO Labor	0UNTS0	110355
Algeria	Multilateral	11 Jun 68	Scientific Project	0UNTS0	109884
Algeria	Poland	26 Jan 63	Tech Assistance	63PZUM11	458100
Algeria	Poland	22 Jul 64	Culture	64PDZU71	457114
Algeria	Poland	06 Feb 65	Air Transport	64PZUM9	458117
Algeria	Tunisia	01 Sep 63	Air Transport	601UNTS275	108701
Algeria	UN Special Fund	15 Nov 62	Tech Assistance	452UNTS243	106512
Algeria	UNICEF (Children)	20 Nov 62	Direct Aid	453UNTS151	106522
Algeria	United Nations	23 Sep 64	IGO Operations	510UNTS217	107416
Algeria	USA (United States)	23 Feb 66	Direct Aid	592UNTS117	108571
Algeria	USSR (Soviet Union)	23 Mar 62	Recognition	11SUGG136	469828
Algeria	WHO (World Health)	20 Dec 62	Tech Assistance	463UNTS135	106698
Allied Milit Occup	Multilateral	19 Sep 47	Finance	30UNTS269	100462
Allied Milit Occup	Multilateral	19 Sep 47	General Trade	30UNTS249	100461
Allied Milit Occup	Multilateral	05 Oct 47	Finance	34UNTS23	100525
Allied Milit Occup	Multilateral	10 Aug 49	Finance	45UNTS3	100689
Allied Milit Occup	Norway	17 Feb 49	Milit Occupation	30UNTS137	100451
Allied Milit Occup	Norway	16 Sep 49	General Trade	53UNTS3	100769
Andorra	Multilateral	06 Sep 52	Patents/Copyrights	216UNTS132	102937
Andorra	Multilateral	14 May 54	Culture	249UNTS215	103511
Anglo-Egypt Sudan	Fr Equatorial Afri	02 Nov 39	Telecommunications	2UNTS209	200012
Anguilla	Multilateral	01 Jul 68	Peace/Disarmament	0UNTS0	110485
Antigua	Multilateral	01 Jul 68	Peace/Disarmament	0UNTS0	110485
Antigua	Multilateral	24 Dec 68	Commodity Trade	0UNTS0	109369
Antigua	Multilateral	18 Oct 69	IGO Establishment	0UNTS0	110232
Arab League	ILO (Labor Org)	26 May 58	IGO Operations	302UNTS343	200549
Argentina	Austria	17 Jun 60	Visas	60ABGB215	403001
Argentina	Belgium	25 Jul 49	Taxation	46UNTS103	100703
Argentina	Belgium	09 May 59	Visas	340UNTS53	104858
Argentina	Belgium	11 Jun 63	Milit Servic/Citiz	635UNTS135	109077
Argentina	Belgium	05 Nov 65	Culture	635UNTS229	109086
Argentina	Bolivia	07 Sep 60	Land Transport	0UNTS0	109516
Argentina	Bolivia	09 Dec 60	General Trade	0UNTS0	109549
Argentina	Bolivia	02 Aug 63	Claims and Debts	0UNTS0	109517
Argentina	Bolivia	15 Jun 66	Finance	0UNTS0	109518
Argentina	Bolivia	19 Dec 66	Air Transport	0UNTS0	110180
Argentina	Bolivia	19 Dec 66	Education	636UNTS83	109093
Argentina	Bolivia	19 Dec 66	Telecommunications	636UNTS89	109094
Argentina	Bolivia	19 Dec 66	Tech Assistance	636UNTS75	109092
Argentina	Bolivia	26 Oct 67	Land Transport	0UNTS0	109550
Argentina	Bolivia	18 Apr 68	Commodity Trade	0UNTS0	109551
Argentina	Bolivia	09 Jul 68	Telecommunications	0UNTS0	109552
Argentina	Bolivia	05 Aug 68	Specific Resources	0UNTS0	109553
Argentina	Bolivia	11 Dec 68	General Trade	0UNTS0	109554
Argentina	Brazil	27 Dec 27	Territory Boundary	51UNTS271	200193
Argentina	Brazil	23 Jan 40	Admin Cooperation	51UNTS281	200194
Argentina	Brazil	02 Jun 48	Air Transport	0UNTS0	109515
Argentina	Brazil	19 Sep 58	Tech Assistance	374UNTS57	105329
Argentina	Brazil	22 Dec 58	Water Transport	0UNTS0	109545
Argentina	Brazil	26 Nov 59	Visas	374UNTS51	105328
Argentina	Brazil	26 Nov 59	General Trade	374UNTS31	105325
Argentina	Brazil	26 Nov 59	General Trade	374UNTS39	105326
Argentina	Brazil	26 Nov 59	General Trade	374UNTS45	105327
Argentina	Brazil	06 Jul 61	Postal Service	0UNTS0	109410
Argentina	Brazil	15 Nov 61	Extradition	0UNTS0	109424
Argentina	Brazil	15 Nov 61	Admin Cooperation	0UNTS0	109546
Argentina	Brazil	23 Apr 65	IGO Establishment	0UNTS0	109411
Argentina	Brazil	25 Jan 68	Culture	0UNTS0	109547
Argentina	Brazil	27 Sep 68	Water Transport	0UNTS0	109420
Argentina	Brazil	24 Jan 69	Telecommunications	0UNTS0	109548
Argentina	Canada	06 Aug 49	Taxation	231UNTS43	103202
Argentina	Chile	14 Dec 48	Air Transport	635UNTS21	109071
Argentina	Chile	29 Dec 61	Territory Boundary	635UNTS111	109075
Argentina	Chile	06 Nov 67	Taxation	636UNTS111	109097

PARTY ONE	PARTY TWO	DATE	TOPIC	CITATION	NUMBER
Argentina	Chile	31 Jul 68	Land Transport	0UNTS0	109570
Argentina	Colombia	12 Sep 64	Visas	635UNTS149	109079
Argentina	Colombia	15 Sep 67	Taxation	0UNTS0	109529
Argentina	Colombia	09 Apr 68	General Military	0UNTS0	109566
Argentina	Colombia	27 Mar 69	Culture	0UNTS0	109568
Argentina	Colombia	27 Mar 69	Visas	0UNTS0	109567
Argentina	Costa Rica	23 Nov 64	Culture	635UNTS213	109084
Argentina	Denmark	18 Mar 48	Air Transport	94UNTS175	101311
Argentina	Denmark	14 Dec 48	General Economic	74UNTS41	100956
Argentina	Denmark	15 Dec 48	Taxation	67UNTS71	100866
Argentina	Denmark	25 Nov 57	General Economic	299UNTS83	104308
Argentina	Denmark	28 Nov 62	Milit Servic/Citiz	455UNTS429	106554
Argentina	Dominican Republic	09 Sep 67	Culture	0UNTS0	110412
Argentina	Dominican Republic	12 Sep 67	Culture	0UNTS0	109560
Argentina	Finland	08 May 63	Milit Servic/Citiz	482UNTS309	107000
Argentina	France	25 Nov 57	Finance	57FRMD1112	417052
Argentina	France	25 Nov 57	General Trade	57FRMD1112	417053
Argentina	France	17 Jan 63	Culture	65FRRT44	415054
Argentina	France	03 Oct 64	Culture	635UNTS155	109080
Argentina	France	03 Oct 64	Culture	0UNTS0	109555
Argentina	France	21 Mar 69	Culture	0UNTS0	110187
Argentina	France	21 Mar 69	Scientific Project	69FRJO1609	416055
Argentina	Germany, West	26 Oct 51	General Trade	51WBGA227	424006
Argentina	Germany, West	25 Nov 57	General Trade	58WBGA6	424007
Argentina	Germany, West	20 Sep 60	Air Transport	61WGBB1045	425008
Argentina	Germany, West	01 Mar 66	Tech Assistance	635UNTS247	109087
Argentina	Germany, West	13 Jul 66	Taxation	636UNTS3	109091
Argentina	Germany, West	21 Mar 68	Admin Cooperation	0UNTS0	109563
Argentina	Germany, West	29 Aug 68	Tech Assistance	0UNTS0	109564
Argentina	Germany, West	04 Dec 68	Loans and Credits	69WBGA39	424009
Argentina	Germany, West	04 Dec 68	Direct Aid	0UNTS0	109569
Argentina	Germany, West	23 Dec 68	Tech Assistance	0UNTS0	109565
Argentina	Germany, West	31 Mar 69	Scientific Project	0UNTS0	110188
Argentina	Germany, West	31 Mar 69	Scientific Project	70WGBB5	425010
Argentina	Germany, West	19 May 69	Non-IBRD Project	0UNTS0	110190
Argentina	Germany, West	23 Oct 69	Non-IBRD Project	0UNTS0	110195
Argentina	Germany, West	23 Oct 69	Non-IBRD Project	70WBGA6	424011
Argentina	Germany, West	03 Feb 70	Loans and Credits	70WBGA82	424012
Argentina	Germany, West	21 May 71	Water Transport	71WGBB2655	425013
Argentina	Greece	21 Mar 50	Taxation	187UNTS213	102514
Argentina	Guatemala	30 Oct 64	Culture	601UNTS175	108695
Argentina	Honduras	26 Nov 64	Culture	0UNTS0	109557
Argentina	Hungary	06 Nov 67	General Trade	0UNTS0	109561
Argentina	IAEA (Atom Energy)	02 Dec 64	Atomic Energy	525UNTS29	107582
Argentina	IAEA (Atom Energy)	03 Jun 69	Atomic Energy	0UNTS0	109947
Argentina	IBRD (World Bank)	30 Jun 61	IBRD Project	445UNTS85	106379
Argentina	IBRD (World Bank)	19 Jan 62	IBRD Project	446UNTS305	106407
Argentina	IBRD (World Bank)	31 Jul 67	IBRD Project	633UNTS289	109042
Argentina	IBRD (World Bank)	25 Jan 68	IBRD Project	639UNTS187	109150
Argentina	IBRD (World Bank)	19 Dec 68	IBRD Project	0UNTS0	109631
Argentina	IBRD (World Bank)	24 Jun 69	IBRD Project	0UNTS0	110290
Argentina	IBRD (World Bank)	14 Nov 69	IBRD Project	0UNTS0	110675
Argentina	ILO (Labor Org)	06 Apr 70	IGO Operations	0UNTS0	110430
Argentina	India	26 Mar 66	General Trade	601UNTS201	108697
Argentina	India	04 Sep 68	Visas	0UNTS0	109571
Argentina	Iran	12 May 65	Culture	0IRTB11	433019
Argentina	Ireland	25 Jun 65	Visas	0UNTS0	109523
Argentina	Israel	23 May 57	Culture	280UNTS199	104059
Argentina	Italy	16 Apr 47	Sanitation	61ITMA451	437011
Argentina	Italy	26 Jan 48	Health/Educ/Welfare	1ITMA82	437012
Argentina	Italy	18 Feb 48	Air Transport	48ITGU179	435013
Argentina	Italy	12 Apr 49	Taxation	52ITGU22	435014
Argentina	Italy	25 Jun 52	Health/Educ/Welfare	52ITDI223	436015
Argentina	Italy	05 Dec 52	Mass Media	52ITDI225	436016
Argentina	Italy	23 May 56	Claims and Debts	267UNTS255	103846

PARTY ONE	PARTY TWO	DATE	TOPIC	CITATION	NUMBER
Argentina	Italy	25 Nov 57	General Economic	305UNTS275	104424
Argentina	Italy	25 Nov 57	Health/Educ/Welfare	58ITGU120	435017
Argentina	Italy	19 Nov 59	Visas	61ITDI245	436018
Argentina	Italy	21 Jan 60	General Economic	62ITDI313	436019
Argentina	Italy	14 Jun 60	Atomic Energy	62ITDI314	436020
Argentina	Italy	01 Aug 60	Taxation	63ITGU9	435021
Argentina	Italy	12 Apr 61	Non-ILO Labor	0UNTS0	109522
Argentina	Italy	12 Apr 61	Culture	63ITGU86	435022
Argentina	Italy	12 Apr 61	Loans and Credits	62ITDI490	436024
Argentina	Italy	12 Apr 61	Non-ILO Labor	63ITGU8	435023
Argentina	Italy	21 Feb 68	Visas	0UNTS0	109562
Argentina	Japan	20 Dec 61	Sanitation	0JGJI1460	441109
Argentina	Japan	20 Dec 61	Health/Educ/Welfare	0JGJI1504	441112
Argentina	Japan	20 Dec 61	Sanitation	0JGJI1462	441111
Argentina	Japan	20 Dec 61	Sanitation	451UNTS77	106486
Argentina	Japan	20 Dec 61	Taxation	451UNTS91	106487
Argentina	Japan	20 Dec 61	Visas	451UNTS71	106485
Argentina	Japan	20 Dec 61	General Amity	613UNTS323	108859
Argentina	Japan	20 Dec 61	General Amity	67JHZ9	439038
Argentina	Japan	20 Dec 61	Commodity Trade	0JGJI1461	441110
Argentina	Japan	15 Oct 65	Finance	0JGJI1613	441142
Argentina	Korea, South	08 Jul 68	Culture	0UNTS0	110186
Argentina	Mexico	26 Jan 60	Culture	635UNTS79	109073
Argentina	Morocco	10 Nov 64	Culture	0UNTS0	110179
Argentina	Multilateral	30 Jul 40	Admin Cooperation	161UNTS253	200488
Argentina	Multilateral	12 Oct 40	Specific Resources	161UNTS193	200485
Argentina	Multilateral	22 Apr 42	Commodity Trade	8UNTS237	200044
Argentina	Multilateral	02 Aug 44	Scientific Project	67UNTS221	200221
Argentina	Multilateral	07 Dec 44	Air Transport	84UNTS389	200252
Argentina	Multilateral	07 Dec 44	IGO Establishment	15UNTS295	200102
Argentina	Multilateral	16 Nov 45	IGO Establishment	4UNTS275	100052
Argentina	Multilateral	03 Jun 46	Commodity Trade	7UNTS331	100109
Argentina	Multilateral	22 Jul 46	IGO Establishment	14UNTS185	100221
Argentina	Multilateral	22 Jul 46	IGO Establishment	9UNTS3	100125
Argentina	Multilateral	15 Oct 46	Refugees	11UNTS73	100150
Argentina	Multilateral	02 Dec 46	Specific Resources	161UNTS72	102124
Argentina	Multilateral	11 Dec 46	Sanitation	12UNTS179	100186
Argentina	Multilateral	15 Dec 46	IGO Establishment	18UNTS3	100283
Argentina	Multilateral	27 May 47	Air Transport	418UNTS161	106021
Argentina	Multilateral	02 Sep 47	General Military	21UNTS77	100324
Argentina	Multilateral	02 Oct 47	Telecommunications	193UNTS188	102616
Argentina	Multilateral	11 Oct 47	IGO Establishment	77UNTS143	100998
Argentina	Multilateral	12 Nov 47	Admin Cooperation	46UNTS169	100709
Argentina	Multilateral	06 Mar 48	Water Transport	289UNTS3	104214
Argentina	Multilateral	30 Apr 48	IGO Establishment	119UNTS3	101609
Argentina	Multilateral	30 Apr 48	Dispute Settlement	30UNTS55	100449
Argentina	Multilateral	10 Jun 48	Humanitarian	191UNTS3	102576
Argentina	Multilateral	10 Jun 48	Humanitarian	164UNTS113	102163
Argentina	Multilateral	19 Jun 48	Air Transport	310UNTS151	104492
Argentina	Multilateral	24 Jul 48	Sanitation	66UNTS25	100847
Argentina	Multilateral	19 Nov 48	Sanitation	44UNTS277	100688
Argentina	Multilateral	09 Jul 49	Telecommunications	168UNTS143	102218
Argentina	Multilateral	12 Aug 49	Humanitarian	75UNTS31	100970
Argentina	Multilateral	12 Aug 49	General Military	75UNTS135	100972
Argentina	Multilateral	12 Aug 49	Humanitarian	75UNTS85	100971
Argentina	Multilateral	12 Aug 49	Humanitarian	75UNTS287	100973
Argentina	Multilateral	16 Dec 49	Admin Cooperation	72UNTS3	100924
Argentina	Multilateral	21 Mar 50	Admin Cooperation	96UNTS271	101342
Argentina	Multilateral	25 May 51	Status of Forces	175UNTS215	102303
Argentina	Multilateral	02 Jul 51	Refugees	189UNTS137	102545
Argentina	Multilateral	08 Sep 51	Peace/Disarmament	136UNTS45	101832
Argentina	Multilateral	06 Dec 51	IGO Establishment	425UNTS61	106119
Argentina	Multilateral	06 Dec 51	Admin Cooperation	150UNTS67	101963
Argentina	Multilateral	10 May 52	Taxation	439UNTS233	106332
Argentina	Multilateral	10 May 52	Admin Cooperation	439UNTS217	106331

PARTY ONE	PARTY TWO	DATE	TOPIC	CITATION	NUMBER
Argentina	Multilateral	12 Jun 52	Dispute Settlement	138UNTS183	101869
Argentina	Multilateral	11 Jul 52	Postal Service	171UNTS191	102227
Argentina	Multilateral	11 Jul 52	Postal Service	170UNTS63	102222
Argentina	Multilateral	11 Jul 52	Postal Service	170UNTS269	102223
Argentina	Multilateral	11 Jul 52	Postal Service	171UNTS3	102224
Argentina	Multilateral	11 Jul 52	Postal Service	170UNTS3	102221
Argentina	Multilateral	11 Jul 52	Postal Service	171UNTS89	102225
Argentina	Multilateral	11 Jul 52	IGO Establishment	169UNTS3	102220
Argentina	Multilateral	11 Jul 52	Postal Service	171UNTS143	102226
Argentina	Multilateral	06 Sep 52	Patents/Copyrights	216UNTS132	102937
Argentina	Multilateral	07 Oct 52	Admin Cooperation	310UNTS181	104493
Argentina	Multilateral	27 Feb 53	Claims and Debts	333UNTS3	104764
Argentina	Multilateral	31 Mar 53	Mass Media	435UNTS191	106280
Argentina	Multilateral	31 Mar 53	Privil/Immunities	193UNTS136	102613
Argentina	Multilateral	11 May 53	Sanitation	456UNTS3	106555
Argentina	Multilateral	19 Oct 53	IGO Establishment	207UNTS189	102807
Argentina	Multilateral	04 Jun 54	Customs	282UNTS249	104101
Argentina	Multilateral	04 Jun 54	Customs	276UNTS191	103992
Argentina	Multilateral	14 Jun 54	Air Transport	320UNTS209	104643
Argentina	Multilateral	14 Jun 54	Air Transport	320UNTS217	104644
Argentina	Multilateral	01 May 55	Admin Cooperation	0UNTS0	110416
Argentina	Multilateral	25 May 55	IGO Establishment	264UNTS117	103791
Argentina	Multilateral	25 Apr 56	Commodity Trade	270UNTS103	103896
Argentina	Multilateral	12 Jun 56	Tech Assistance	243UNTS187	103453
Argentina	Multilateral	26 Oct 56	IGO Establishment	276UNTS3	103988
Argentina	Multilateral	20 Feb 57	Consul/Citizenship	309UNTS65	104468
Argentina	Multilateral	01 May 57	Admin Cooperation	284UNTS201	104138
Argentina	Multilateral	03 Oct 57	Postal Service	366UNTS141	105217
Argentina	Multilateral	03 Oct 57	Postal Service	366UNTS3	105215
Argentina	Multilateral	03 Oct 57	Postal Service	364UNTS3	105211
Argentina	Multilateral	03 Oct 57	Postal Service	365UNTS3	105213
Argentina	Multilateral	03 Oct 57	Postal Service	364UNTS331	105212
Argentina	Multilateral	03 Oct 57	Postal Service	365UNTS207	105214
Argentina	Multilateral	03 Oct 57	Postal Service	366UNTS87	105216
Argentina	Multilateral	03 Oct 57	Postal Service	366UNTS255	105219
Argentina	Multilateral	29 Apr 58	Territory Boundary	499UNTS311	107302
Argentina	Multilateral	29 Apr 58	Territory Boundary	516UNTS205	107477
Argentina	Multilateral	29 Apr 58	Specific Resources	559UNTS285	108164
Argentina	Multilateral	29 Apr 58	Water Transport	450UNTS11	106465
Argentina	Multilateral	10 Jun 58	Admin Cooperation	330UNTS3	104739
Argentina	Multilateral	01 Dec 58	Commodity Trade	385UNTS137	105534
Argentina	Multilateral	06 Apr 59	Commodity Trade	349UNTS167	105013
Argentina	Multilateral	08 Apr 59	IGO Establishment	389UNTS69	105593
Argentina	Multilateral	19 Nov 59	IGO Operations	410UNTS156	105902
Argentina	Multilateral	01 Dec 59	Territory Boundary	402UNTS71	105778
Argentina	Multilateral	26 Jan 60	IGO Establishment	439UNTS249	106333
Argentina	Multilateral	17 Jun 60	Humanitarian	536UNTS27	107794
Argentina	Multilateral	28 Jul 60	IGO Establishment	485UNTS3	107042
Argentina	Multilateral	14 Dec 60	Education	429UNTS93	106193
Argentina	Multilateral	30 Mar 61	Sanitation	520UNTS151	107515
Argentina	Multilateral	18 Apr 61	Consul/Citizenship	500UNTS223	107311
Argentina	Multilateral	18 Apr 61	Consul/Citizenship	500UNTS95	107310
Argentina	Multilateral	21 Jun 61	IGO Establishment	514UNTS209	107449
Argentina	Multilateral	26 Oct 61	Patents/Copyrights	496UNTS43	107247
Argentina	Multilateral	26 Mar 62	IGO Establishment	539UNTS67	107825
Argentina	Multilateral	15 May 62	Commodity Trade	444UNTS3	106367
Argentina	Multilateral	28 Sep 62	IGO Establishment	469UNTS169	106791
Argentina	Multilateral	20 Apr 63	IGO Establishment	495UNTS3	107239
Argentina	Multilateral	24 Apr 63	Consul/Citizenship	596UNTS487	108640
Argentina	Multilateral	24 Apr 63	Consul/Citizenship	596UNTS261	108638
Argentina	Multilateral	05 Aug 63	Sanitation	480UNTS43	106964
Argentina	Multilateral	10 Jul 64	Postal Service	613UNTS193	108852
Argentina	Multilateral	10 Jul 64	Postal Service	613UNTS3	108851
Argentina	Multilateral	10 Jul 64	Postal Service	611UNTS105	108845
Argentina	Multilateral	10 Jul 64	Postal Service	611UNTS7	108844

PARTY ONE	PARTY TWO	DATE	TOPIC	CITATION	NUMBER
Argentina	Multilateral	10 Jul 64	Postal Service	612UNTS361	108849
Argentina	Multilateral	10 Jul 64	Postal Service	612UNTS3	108847
Argentina	Multilateral	10 Jul 64	Postal Service	613UNTS3	108850
Argentina	Multilateral	10 Jul 64	Postal Service	611UNTS387	108846
Argentina	Multilateral	10 Jul 64	Postal Service	612UNTS233	108848
Argentina	Multilateral	02 Dec 64	Scientific Project	572UNTS229	108317
Argentina	Multilateral	02 Dec 64	Atomic Energy	525UNTS51	107583
Argentina	Multilateral	09 Mar 65	Water Transport	591UNTS265	108564
Argentina	Multilateral	08 Jul 65	General Trade	597UNTS3	108641
Argentina	Multilateral	30 Dec 65	Atomic Energy	557UNTS3	108126
Argentina	Multilateral	05 Apr 66	Water Transport	640UNTS133	109159
Argentina	Multilateral	27 Jan 67	Scientific Project	610UNTS205	108843
Argentina	Multilateral	03 May 67	IGO Operations	0UNTS0	110764
Argentina	Multilateral	22 Apr 68	Scientific Project	0UNTS0	109574
Argentina	Multilateral	24 Dec 68	Commodity Trade	0UNTS0	109369
Argentina	Netherlands	29 Oct 48	Air Transport	95UNTS21	101316
Argentina	Netherlands	15 Jan 49	Taxation	46UNTS241	100713
Argentina	Netherlands	06 May 54	General Economic	54NET175	447046
Argentina	Nicaragua	25 Nov 64	Culture	0UNTS0	109556
Argentina	Norway	18 Mar 48	Air Transport	2NORT475	451001
Argentina	Norway	09 Nov 48	Taxation	2NORT488	451002
Argentina	Norway	09 Sep 49	Finance	42UNTS125	100646
Argentina	Norway	10 Mar 61	Milit Servic/Citiz	3NORT826	451003
Argentina	Norway	06 Sep 61	Visas	3NORT842	451004
Argentina	Panama	21 Nov 64	Culture	635UNTS205	109083
Argentina	Paraguay	23 Jan 58	Scientific Project	0UNTS0	109294
Argentina	Paraguay	07 Feb 64	Air Transport	634UNTS127	109057
Argentina	Paraguay	21 Oct 64	Specific Property	635UNTS177	109081
Argentina	Paraguay	21 Oct 64	Specific Property	635UNTS189	109082
Argentina	Paraguay	23 Jan 67	Water Transport	634UNTS181	109060
Argentina	Paraguay	23 Jan 67	General Trade	634UNTS193	109061
Argentina	Paraguay	14 Jul 67	Culture	0UNTS0	110181
Argentina	Paraguay	20 Jul 67	Atomic Energy	0UNTS0	110182
Argentina	Paraguay	20 Jul 67	Tech Assistance	0UNTS0	110183
Argentina	Paraguay	15 Jul 69	Territory Boundary	0UNTS0	110193
Argentina	Peru	25 May 68	Atomic Energy	0UNTS0	110184
Argentina	Philippines	12 Feb 60	General Amity	535UNTS293	107785
Argentina	Poland	29 Oct 52	General Economic	53PZUM67	458007
Argentina	Portugal	20 May 66	Non-ILO Labor	635UNTS301	109090
Argentina	Romania	05 Nov 68	Culture	0UNTS0	109573
Argentina	Romania	03 Apr 69	General Trade	0UNTS0	110189
Argentina	Spain	01 Mar 47	Air Transport	47SPBO2004	460031
Argentina	Spain	18 Oct 48	Culture	48SPBO3110	460033
Argentina	Spain	18 Oct 48	Culture	48SPBO3110	460035
Argentina	Spain	18 Oct 48	Milit Servic/Citiz	48SPBO3110	460032
Argentina	Spain	18 Oct 48	Health/Educ/Welfare	48SPBO3110	460034
Argentina	Spain	22 Apr 60	Mass Media	61SPBO2109	460037
Argentina	Spain	08 Jul 60	Health/Educ/Welfare	60SPBO508	460036
Argentina	Spain	12 Oct 65	Visas	635UNTS221	109085
Argentina	Spain	10 Nov 65	Culture	0UNTS0	109559
Argentina	Spain	28 May 66	Non-ILO Labor	0UNTS0	109525
Argentina	Spain	28 Aug 69	Culture	0UNTS0	110194
Argentina	Sweden	31 Jul 45	General Trade	45SOFM119	461012
Argentina	Sweden	20 Nov 48	Taxation	197UNTS47	102633
Argentina	Sweden	23 Nov 48	General Economic	49SOFM571	461094
Argentina	Sweden	16 Jan 59	Milit Servic/Citiz	427UNTS327	106163
Argentina	Sweden	12 Jun 59	Culture	427UNTS337	106164
Argentina	Switzerland	13 Jan 50	Taxation	50SWRO584	462042
Argentina	Switzerland	25 Jan 56	Air Transport	559UNTS121	108157
Argentina	Switzerland	25 Nov 57	General Economic	58SWRO38	462120
Argentina	Switzerland	05 Sep 68	Loans and Credits	0UNTS0	109572
Argentina	Taiwan	10 Feb 47	General Amity	486UNTS143	107077
Argentina	Taiwan	19 Mar 66	Culture	635UNTS281	109089
Argentina	Thailand	10 Dec 61	General Trade	422UNTS87	106070
Argentina	Turkey	19 Aug 65	Culture	0UNTS0	109558

PARTY ONE	PARTY TWO	DATE	TOPIC	CITATION	NUMBER
Argentina	UK Great Britain	17 Apr 46	Air Transport	164UNTS53	102159
Argentina	UK Great Britain	17 Sep 46	General Economic	88UNTS47	101185
Argentina	UK Great Britain	19 Mar 47	General Trade	11UNTS195	100157
Argentina	UK Great Britain	14 Mar 49	Taxation	83UNTS193	101108
Argentina	UK Great Britain	27 Jun 49	General Economic	83UNTS217	101110
Argentina	UK Great Britain	31 Mar 55	General Economic	210UNTS223	102840
Argentina	UK Great Britain	30 Jun 56	General Economic	269UNTS235	103884
Argentina	UK Great Britain	31 Oct 56	Finance	269UNTS229	103883
Argentina	UK Great Britain	25 Nov 57	Claims and Debts	313UNTS95	104531
Argentina	UK Great Britain	19 Jun 61	Culture	470UNTS71	106797
Argentina	UK Great Britain	05 Jun 63	Loans and Credits	482UNTS353	107004
Argentina	UK Great Britain	12 Sep 63	Milit Servic/Citiz	601UNTS213	108698
Argentina	UK Great Britain	15 Apr 64	Commodity Trade	515UNTS3	107450
Argentina	UK Great Britain	12 Jan 65	Air Transport	597UNTS177	108645
Argentina	UK Great Britain	15 Sep 66	Loans and Credits	603UNTS151	108732
Argentina	UK Great Britain	17 Feb 67	Visas	617UNTS193	108913
Argentina	UN Special Fund	04 Dec 59	Direct Aid	345UNTS263	104972
Argentina	UNICEF (Children)	19 Nov 57	Direct Aid	300UNTS229	104338
Argentina	United Arab Rep	21 Jun 65	Commodity Trade	634UNTS177	109059
Argentina	United Arab Rep	21 Jun 65	General Economic	634UNTS161	109058
Argentina	Uruguay	30 Dec 46	Specific Resources	0UNTS0	109540
Argentina	Uruguay	27 Apr 57	Non-ILO Labor	635UNTS69	109072
Argentina	Uruguay	23 Nov 60	Non-IBRD Project	0UNTS0	109519
Argentina	Uruguay	07 Apr 61	Territory Boundary	635UNTS91	109074
Argentina	Uruguay	04 Sep 63	General Economic	0UNTS0	109541
Argentina	Uruguay	12 Feb 66	Non-IBRD Project	0UNTS0	109520
Argentina	Uruguay	07 Mar 66	General Trade	635UNTS275	109088
Argentina	Uruguay	12 Feb 67	Water Transport	635UNTS125	109076
Argentina	Uruguay	30 May 67	Non-IBRD Project	0UNTS0	109521
Argentina	Uruguay	08 Jul 68	Non-IBRD Project	0UNTS0	109542
Argentina	Uruguay	08 Jul 68	Visas	0UNTS0	109544
Argentina	Uruguay	08 Jul 68	Territory Boundary	0UNTS0	110185
Argentina	Uruguay	16 Oct 68	Territory Boundary	0UNTS0	109543
Argentina	Uruguay	27 Jun 69	Commodity Trade	0UNTS0	110191
Argentina	Uruguay	18 Sep 69	Commodity Trade	0UNTS0	110192
Argentina	USA (United States)	15 Apr 41	Visas	103UNTS307	200321
Argentina	USA (United States)	14 Oct 41	General Trade	119UNTS193	200384
Argentina	USA (United States)	02 Sep 43	Military Mission	9UNTS363	200052
Argentina	USA (United States)	09 May 45	Commodity Trade	139UNTS227	200453
Argentina	USA (United States)	19 Sep 46	Commodity Trade	7UNTS131	100095
Argentina	USA (United States)	06 Oct 48	Military Mission	80UNTS91	101046
Argentina	USA (United States)	20 Jul 50	Taxation	89UNTS63	101209
Argentina	USA (United States)	08 Jan 51	Milit Assistance	165UNTS89	102170
Argentina	USA (United States)	25 Apr 55	US Agri Commod Aid	251UNTS283	103546
Argentina	USA (United States)	29 Jul 55	Atomic Energy	235UNTS121	103298
Argentina	USA (United States)	21 Dec 55	Commodity Trade	240UNTS329	103411
Argentina	USA (United States)	03 Oct 56	Military Mission	279UNTS13	104032
Argentina	USA (United States)	05 Nov 56	Education	277UNTS143	104004
Argentina	USA (United States)	03 Jun 57	Tech Assistance	291UNTS61	104244
Argentina	USA (United States)	28 Apr 58	Status of Forces	315UNTS211	104570
Argentina	USA (United States)	12 Jun 59	US Agri Commod Aid	347UNTS59	104990
Argentina	USA (United States)	22 Dec 59	Admin Cooperation	411UNTS42	105912
Argentina	USA (United States)	01 Apr 60	Milit Assistance	371UNTS245	105281
Argentina	USA (United States)	23 May 60	Atomic Energy	377UNTS3	105392
Argentina	USA (United States)	02 Aug 60	Military Mission	384UNTS105	105514
Argentina	USA (United States)	16 Mar 62	Scientific Project	454UNTS3	106535
Argentina	USA (United States)	22 Jun 62	Atomic Energy	458UNTS97	106594
Argentina	USA (United States)	24 Jul 63	General Trade	487UNTS183	107103
Argentina	USA (United States)	21 Aug 63	Education	488UNTS61	107119
Argentina	USA (United States)	30 Nov 63	Scientific Project	505UNTS131	107369
Argentina	USA (United States)	10 May 64	Milit Assistance	527UNTS77	107618
Argentina	USA (United States)	08 Aug 66	Admin Cooperation	606UNTS209	108786
Argentina	USA (United States)	31 Mar 67	Gen Communications	636UNTS95	109095
Argentina	USA (United States)	31 Mar 67	Gen Communications	636UNTS103	109096
Argentina	USA (United States)	25 Jun 69	Atomic Energy	0UNTS0	110336

PARTY ONE	PARTY TWO	DATE	TOPIC	CITATION	NUMBER
Argentina	USA (United States)	05 May 70	General Military	0UNTS0	110779
Argentina	USSR (Soviet Union)	05 Jun 46	General Amity	0SUST212	468018
Argentina	USSR (Soviet Union)	05 Aug 53	General Economic	221UNTS99	103004
Argentina	USSR (Soviet Union)	03 Jun 54	Culture	0SUST316	468019
Argentina	USSR (Soviet Union)	19 May 55	General Trade	0SUST328	468020
Argentina	USSR (Soviet Union)	27 Oct 58	Loans and Credits	7SUGG122	469537
Argentina	USSR (Soviet Union)	27 May 60	Loans and Credits	9SUGG137	469663
Argentina	Vatican/Holy See	10 Oct 66	Consul/Citizenship	601UNTS187	108696
Argentina	Yugoslavia	21 Mar 64	Claims and Debts	635UNTS153	109078
Argentina	Yugoslavia	09 Jun 65	General Trade	601UNTS3	108684
Ascension Island	USA (United States)	22 Jun 67	Air Transport	0UNTS0	110021
Asian Devel Bank	Denmark	05 Feb 69	Loans and Credits	0UNTS0	109702
Asian Devel Bank	Denmark	01 Apr 69	Loans and Credits	0UNTS0	109877
Asian Devel Bank	Multilateral	04 Dec 65	IGO Establishment	571UNTS123	108303
Asian Devel Bank	Philippines	22 Dec 66	IGO Establishment	615UNTS375	108887
Asian Devel Bank	Vietnam, South	16 Dec 70	Loans and Credits	0VKNG381	496095
Asian Productivity	ILO (Labor Org)	27 Oct 64	IGO Operations	516UNTS367	200610
Asian Productivity	Japan	05 Apr 67	IGO Status/Immunit	67JHZ7	439008
Australia	Austria	19 Jul 48	Direct Aid	22UNTS25	100328
Australia	Austria	17 Nov 51	Admin Cooperation	133UNTS137	101785
Australia	Austria	20 Dec 54	Postal Service	205UNTS157	102775
Australia	Austria	15 Mar 56	Visas	241UNTS331	103441
Australia	Austria	18 Dec 59	Reparations	348UNTS201	105001
Australia	Austria	22 Mar 67	Air Transport	67ABGB152	403002
Australia	Austria	22 Mar 67	Air Transport	0UNTS0	109246
Australia	Austria	05 Jul 67	Other Military	636UNTS117	109098
Australia	Belgium	09 Dec 48	Claims and Debts	25UNTS159	100361
Australia	Belgium	25 Jul 51	Visas	108UNTS303	101482
Australia	Belgium	26 Mar 54	General Trade	198UNTS305	102673
Australia	Brazil	15 Aug 69	Visas	0UNTS0	110177
Australia	Bulgaria	22 Jun 66	General Trade	607UNTS69	108796
Australia	Canada	11 Jun 46	Air Transport	10UNTS47	100142
Australia	Canada	01 Oct 57	Taxation	392UNTS41	105638
Australia	Canada	04 Aug 59	Atomic Energy	391UNTS191	105623
Australia	Canada	12 Feb 60	General Trade	369UNTS89	105253
Australia	Ceylon (Sri Lanka)	12 Jan 50	Air Transport	53UNTS295	100789
Australia	Ceylon (Sri Lanka)	07 Nov 53	Admin Cooperation	191UNTS249	102585
Australia	Czechoslovakia	01 Apr 55	Postal Service	213UNTS199	102888
Australia	Denmark	08 Oct 48	Claims and Debts	22UNTS43	100330
Australia	Denmark	01 May 52	Visas	152UNTS3	102006
Australia	Eur Space Vehicle	13 Jul 65	IGO Operations	543UNTS183	107902
Australia	FAO (Food Agri)	07 Jul 52	Tech Assistance	184UNTS209	102449
Australia	FAO (Food Agri)	08 Jul 57	Tech Assistance	277UNTS315	104015
Australia	Fed of Malaya	26 Aug 58	General Trade	325UNTS253	104703
Australia	Fed of Malaya	29 Sep 59	Air Transport	357UNTS29	105104
Australia	Fed of Malaya	26 Nov 62	Specif Goods/Equip	453UNTS161	106523
Australia	Fed Rhod/Nyasaland	30 Jun 55	General Trade	226UNTS215	103115
Australia	Finland	07 Jan 49	Admin Cooperation	189UNTS227	102547
Australia	Finland	04 Jan 51	Claims and Debts	80UNTS27	101042
Australia	Finland	21 Feb 61	Visas	390UNTS61	105602
Australia	Finland	31 Jul 63	Admin Cooperation	478UNTS363	106942
Australia	France	28 Jul 47	Reparations	97UNTS271	101353
Australia	France	28 Sep 51	Reparations	161UNTS185	102128
Australia	France	27 Dec 55	Admin Cooperation	241UNTS325	103440
Australia	France	13 Apr 65	Air Transport	601UNTS293	108702
Australia	France	08 Nov 67	Scientific Project	0UNTS0	109668
Australia	France	27 Mar 70	Taxation	0UNTS0	110802
Australia	Germany, West	29 Aug 52	Non-ILO Labor	184UNTS147	102446
Australia	Germany, West	17 Dec 52	Visas	188UNTS267	102530
Australia	Germany, West	05 Mar 56	Other Military	328UNTS241	104737
Australia	Germany, West	22 May 57	Air Transport	357UNTS45	105105
Australia	Germany, West	27 Aug 58	Non-ILO Labor	320UNTS303	104649
Australia	Germany, West	14 Oct 59	General Trade	345UNTS35	104957
Australia	Germany, West	19 Mar 62	Postal Service	488UNTS203	107130
Australia	Germany, West	21 Apr 65	Claims and Debts	598UNTS25	108654

PARTY ONE	PARTY TWO	DATE	TOPIC	CITATION	NUMBER
Australia	Germany, West	21 Jun 65	Visas	542UNTS53	107879
Australia	Germany, West	08 Jul 65	Postal Service	543UNTS305	107907
Australia	Greece	16 Jun 48	Claims and Debts	18UNTS211	100290
Australia	Greece	01 Jul 48	Direct Aid	22UNTS33	100329
Australia	Greece	23 May 52	Visas	223UNTS17	103042
Australia	Greece	24 May 54	Visas	193UNTS175	102614
Australia	Greece	24 May 54	Postal Service	191UNTS255	102586
Australia	Greece	15 Mar 56	Consul/Citizenship	241UNTS313	103438
Australia	Hungary	01 Jul 48	Direct Aid	22UNTS3	100325
Australia	Hungary	07 Jan 49	Admin Cooperation	189UNTS233	102548
Australia	Hungary	10 Feb 55	Postal Service	207UNTS173	102806
Australia	Hungary	05 Dec 67	General Trade	638UNTS209	109137
Australia	IBRD (World Bank)	14 Nov 50	IBRD Project	156UNTS147	102041
Australia	IBRD (World Bank)	08 Jul 52	IBRD Project	159UNTS295	102092
Australia	IBRD (World Bank)	02 Mar 54	IBRD Project	191UNTS103	102579
Australia	IBRD (World Bank)	18 Mar 55	IBRD Project	220UNTS131	102998
Australia	IBRD (World Bank)	15 Nov 56	IBRD Project	288UNTS117	104201
Australia	IBRD (World Bank)	03 Dec 56	IBRD Project	288UNTS99	104200
Australia	IBRD (World Bank)	23 Jan 62	IBRD Project	430UNTS3	106201
Australia	IBRD (World Bank)	28 Jun 68	IBRD Project	0UNTS0	109483
Australia	Iceland	13 Nov 52	General Trade	161UNTS59	102122
Australia	Iceland	29 Apr 69	Visas	0UNTS0	110176
Australia	ICJ Option Clause	06 Feb 54	ICJ Option Clause	186UNTS77	102484
Australia	IDA (Devel Assoc)	21 Jan 69	Non-IBRD Project	0UNTS0	110486
Australia	IDA (Devel Assoc)	30 Jan 70	Non-IBRD Project	0UNTS0	110654
Australia	India	11 Jul 49	Air Transport	35UNTS83	100552
Australia	India	23 Jan 63	Patents/Copyrights	456UNTS185	106556
Australia	India	03 Dec 63	Milit Assistance	486UNTS279	107082
Australia	Indonesia	17 Dec 59	General Trade	354UNTS109	105058
Australia	Indonesia	14 Jun 68	Culture	0UNTS0	110173
Australia	Indonesia	07 Mar 69	Air Transport	0UNTS0	109735
Australia	Ireland	30 Dec 57	Air Transport	497UNTS29	107260
Australia	Israel	06 Sep 51	Mostfavored Nation	188UNTS303	102534
Australia	Israel	18 Jun 54	Postal Service	220UNTS29	102985
Australia	Israel	14 Apr 64	Visas	496UNTS233	107255
Australia	Italy	08 Jul 48	Direct Aid	22UNTS11	100326
Australia	Italy	02 Aug 48	Air Transport	28UNTS165	100424
Australia	Italy	07 Jan 49	Admin Cooperation	189UNTS239	102549
Australia	Italy	29 Mar 51	Non-ILO Labor	131UNTS187	101741
Australia	Italy	19 Jun 51	Visas	184UNTS185	102447
Australia	Italy	20 Dec 51	Peace/Disarmament	190UNTS223	102566
Australia	Italy	24 May 52	Reparations	161UNTS65	102123
Australia	Italy	27 Aug 53	Other Military	225UNTS47	103086
Australia	Italy	12 Feb 59	Commodity Trade	328UNTS133	104732
Australia	Italy	10 Nov 60	Air Transport	497UNTS247	107271
Australia	Italy	31 Jan 64	Non-ILO Labor	488UNTS197	107129
Australia	Japan	27 Apr 53	Admin Cooperation	193UNTS78	102612
Australia	Japan	24 May 54	Specif Claim/Waive	191UNTS125	102580
Australia	Japan	19 Jan 56	Air Transport	311UNTS291	104507
Australia	Japan	06 Jul 57	General Trade	318UNTS381	104627
Australia	Japan	07 Feb 61	Postal Service	450UNTS343	106478
Australia	Japan	01 Mar 62	Postal Service	517UNTS81	107483
Australia	Japan	07 Aug 62	Atomic Energy	435UNTS261	106283
Australia	Japan	27 Nov 68	Specific Resources	0UNTS0	110174
Australia	Japan	27 Nov 68	Specific Resources	69JHZ8	439025
Australia	Japan	10 Jan 69	Visas	69JJS35	442229
Australia	Japan	20 Mar 69	Taxation	70JHZ7	439028
Australia	Korea, South	21 Sep 65	General Trade	548UNTS163	107977
Australia	Laos	24 Dec 63	Finance	503UNTS315	107350
Australia	Luxembourg	05 Sep 51	Visas	109UNTS31	101487
Australia	Malaysia	21 Jun 65	Humanitarian	542UNTS75	107880
Australia	Malta	28 Apr 65	Non-ILO Labor	548UNTS203	107979
Australia	Mexico	13 Jan 67	Visas	607UNTS77	108797
Australia	Monaco	07 Jul 59	Visas	354UNTS105	105057
Australia	Multilateral	22 Apr 42	Commodity Trade	8UNTS237	200044

PARTY ONE	PARTY TWO	DATE	TOPIC	CITATION	NUMBER
Australia	Multilateral	19 Apr 44	Scientific Project	89UNTS279	200257
Australia	Multilateral	02 Aug 44	Scientific Project	67UNTS221	200221
Australia	Multilateral	07 Dec 44	IGO Establishment	15UNTS295	200102
Australia	Multilateral	07 Dec 44	Air Transport	171UNTS345	200501
Australia	Multilateral	07 Dec 44	Air Transport	84UNTS389	200252
Australia	Multilateral	15 Dec 44	Sanitation	17UNTS305	200110
Australia	Multilateral	15 Dec 44	Sanitation	16UNTS247	200106
Australia	Multilateral	08 Aug 45	General Military	82UNTS279	200251
Australia	Multilateral	02 Sep 45	Peace/Disarmament	139UNTS387	200465
Australia	Multilateral	16 Nov 45	IGO Establishment	4UNTS275	100052
Australia	Multilateral	04 Dec 45	Telecommunications	9UNTS101	100128
Australia	Multilateral	14 Jan 46	Reparations	555UNTS69	108105
Australia	Multilateral	23 Apr 46	Sanitation	16UNTS179	100257
Australia	Multilateral	23 Apr 46	Sanitation	17UNTS3	100265
Australia	Multilateral	03 Jun 46	Commodity Trade	7UNTS331	100109
Australia	Multilateral	22 Jul 46	IGO Establishment	14UNTS185	100221
Australia	Multilateral	22 Jul 46	IGO Establishment	9UNTS3	100125
Australia	Multilateral	27 Jul 46	Patents/Copyrights	90UNTS229	101238
Australia	Multilateral	30 Oct 46	IGO Establishment	11UNTS107	100151
Australia	Multilateral	02 Dec 46	Specific Resources	161UNTS72	102124
Australia	Multilateral	07 Dec 46	Commodity Trade	157UNTS103	102050
Australia	Multilateral	11 Dec 46	Sanitation	12UNTS179	100186
Australia	Multilateral	15 Dec 46	IGO Establishment	18UNTS3	100283
Australia	Multilateral	06 Feb 47	IGO Establishment	97UNTS227	101352
Australia	Multilateral	10 Feb 47	Peace/Disarmament	42UNTS3	100645
Australia	Multilateral	10 Feb 47	Peace/Disarmament	41UNTS21	100643
Australia	Multilateral	10 Feb 47	Peace/Disarmament	49UNTS3	100747
Australia	Multilateral	10 Feb 47	Peace/Disarmament	41UNTS135	100644
Australia	Multilateral	10 Feb 47	Peace/Disarmament	48UNTS203	100746
Australia	Multilateral	03 Mar 47	Humanitarian	11UNTS43	100148
Australia	Multilateral	04 Aug 47	Air Transport	28UNTS41	100418
Australia	Multilateral	02 Oct 47	Telecommunications	193UNTS188	102616
Australia	Multilateral	11 Oct 47	IGO Establishment	77UNTS143	100998
Australia	Multilateral	12 Nov 47	Admin Cooperation	53UNTS13	100770
Australia	Multilateral	12 Nov 47	Admin Cooperation	53UNTS49	100772
Australia	Multilateral	12 Nov 47	Admin Cooperation	46UNTS169	100709
Australia	Multilateral	12 Nov 47	Admin Cooperation	46UNTS201	100710
Australia	Multilateral	12 Nov 47	Admin Cooperation	53UNTS39	100771
Australia	Multilateral	06 Mar 48	Water Transport	289UNTS3	104214
Australia	Multilateral	11 May 48	Telecommunications	500UNTS267	107313
Australia	Multilateral	10 Jun 48	Humanitarian	191UNTS3	102576
Australia	Multilateral	10 Jun 48	Humanitarian	164UNTS113	102163
Australia	Multilateral	19 Jun 48	Air Transport	310UNTS151	104492
Australia	Multilateral	26 Jun 48	Culture	331UNTS217	104757
Australia	Multilateral	24 Jul 48	Sanitation	66UNTS25	100847
Australia	Multilateral	19 Oct 48	Specif Claim/Waive	84UNTS201	101130
Australia	Multilateral	15 Nov 48	IGO Establishment	120UNTS59	101615
Australia	Multilateral	19 Nov 48	Sanitation	44UNTS277	100688
Australia	Multilateral	29 Nov 48	IGO Establishment	120UNTS13	101613
Australia	Multilateral	09 Dec 48	Scientific Project	20UNTS229	100318
Australia	Multilateral	09 Dec 48	Scientific Project	73UNTS39	100942
Australia	Multilateral	09 Dec 48	Humanitarian	78UNTS277	101021
Australia	Multilateral	23 Mar 49	Commodity Trade	203UNTS179	102746
Australia	Multilateral	04 May 49	Admin Cooperation	30UNTS23	100446
Australia	Multilateral	04 May 49	Admin Cooperation	47UNTS159	100728
Australia	Multilateral	04 May 49	Admin Cooperation	98UNTS101	101358
Australia	Multilateral	04 May 49	Admin Cooperation	92UNTS19	101257
Australia	Multilateral	04 May 49	Admin Cooperation	30UNTS3	100445
Australia	Multilateral	12 Aug 49	General Military	75UNTS135	100972
Australia	Multilateral	12 Aug 49	Humanitarian	75UNTS287	100973
Australia	Multilateral	12 Aug 49	Humanitarian	75UNTS31	100970
Australia	Multilateral	12 Aug 49	Humanitarian	75UNTS85	100971
Australia	Multilateral	12 Aug 49	IGO Establishment	87UNTS131	101169
Australia	Multilateral	15 Sep 49	Air Transport	53UNTS235	100783
Australia	Multilateral	27 Oct 49	Air Transport	53UNTS241	100784

PARTY ONE	PARTY TWO	DATE	TOPIC	CITATION	NUMBER
Australia	Multilateral	16 Dec 49	Admin Cooperation	72UNTS3	100924
Australia	Multilateral	28 Jun 50	Loans and Credits	87UNTS153	101170
Australia	Multilateral	07 Dec 50	Admin Cooperation	212UNTS17	102861
Australia	Multilateral	02 Jul 51	Refugees	189UNTS137	102545
Australia	Multilateral	10 Jul 51	Other Military	108UNTS287	101481
Australia	Multilateral	29 Jul 51	Other Military	117UNTS85	101585
Australia	Multilateral	01 Sep 51	General Military	131UNTS83	101736
Australia	Multilateral	08 Sep 51	Peace/Disarmament	136UNTS45	101832
Australia	Multilateral	08 Sep 51	General Military	136UNTS165	101833
Australia	Multilateral	31 Oct 51	Other Military	172UNTS193	102247
Australia	Multilateral	06 Dec 51	Admin Cooperation	150UNTS67	101963
Australia	Multilateral	20 May 52	Sanitation	219UNTS55	102966
Australia	Multilateral	08 Jun 52	Other Military	210UNTS317	102843
Australia	Multilateral	12 Jun 52	Dispute Settlement	138UNTS183	101869
Australia	Multilateral	11 Jul 52	IGO Establishment	169UNTS3	102220
Australia	Multilateral	06 Sep 52	Patents/Copyrights	216UNTS132	102937
Australia	Multilateral	07 Oct 52	Admin Cooperation	310UNTS181	104493
Australia	Multilateral	27 Feb 53	Claims and Debts	333UNTS3	104764
Australia	Multilateral	11 May 53	Sanitation	456UNTS3	106555
Australia	Multilateral	27 Aug 53	Other Military	213UNTS137	102884
Australia	Multilateral	01 Oct 53	Commodity Trade	258UNTS153	103677
Australia	Multilateral	19 Oct 53	IGO Establishment	207UNTS189	102807
Australia	Multilateral	26 Oct 53	Status of Forces	207UNTS237	102809
Australia	Multilateral	07 Dec 53	Admin Cooperation	182UNTS51	102422
Australia	Multilateral	11 Dec 53	Education	218UNTS125	102954
Australia	Multilateral	19 Feb 54	Status of Forces	214UNTS51	102899
Australia	Multilateral	22 Feb 54	Other Military	188UNTS273	102531
Australia	Multilateral	25 Feb 54	Air Transport	215UNTS249	102922
Australia	Multilateral	01 Mar 54	Commodity Trade	256UNTS31	103622
Australia	Multilateral	12 May 54	Admin Cooperation	327UNTS3	104714
Australia	Multilateral	14 May 54	Culture	249UNTS215	103511
Australia	Multilateral	14 Jun 54	Air Transport	320UNTS217	104644
Australia	Multilateral	14 Jun 54	Air Transport	320UNTS209	104643
Australia	Multilateral	24 Aug 54	Other Military	247UNTS213	103471
Australia	Multilateral	08 Sep 54	Milit Assistance	209UNTS23	102819
Australia	Multilateral	28 Sep 54	Reparations	207UNTS293	102812
Australia	Multilateral	19 Dec 54	Patents/Copyrights	218UNTS51	102953
Australia	Multilateral	15 May 55	Recognition	217UNTS223	102949
Australia	Multilateral	25 May 55	IGO Establishment	264UNTS117	103791
Australia	Multilateral	28 Sep 55	Air Transport	478UNTS371	106943
Australia	Multilateral	12 Oct 55	IGO Establishment	560UNTS3	108165
Australia	Multilateral	05 Mar 56	Other Military	326UNTS169	104711
Australia	Multilateral	05 Mar 56	Other Military	326UNTS181	104712
Australia	Multilateral	25 Apr 56	Commodity Trade	270UNTS103	103896
Australia	Multilateral	18 May 56	Customs	338UNTS103	104834
Australia	Multilateral	20 Jun 56	Admin Cooperation	268UNTS3	103850
Australia	Multilateral	07 Sep 56	Humanitarian	266UNTS3	103822
Australia	Multilateral	25 Sep 56	Air Transport	334UNTS89	104767
Australia	Multilateral	25 Sep 56	Air Transport	334UNTS13	104766
Australia	Multilateral	26 Oct 56	IGO Establishment	276UNTS3	103988
Australia	Multilateral	20 Feb 57	Consul/Citizenship	309UNTS65	104468
Australia	Multilateral	15 Jun 57	General Trade	550UNTS45	108008
Australia	Multilateral	03 Oct 57	Postal Service	364UNTS3	105211
Australia	Multilateral	15 Jan 58	Customs	383UNTS229	105503
Australia	Multilateral	29 Apr 58	Territory Boundary	516UNTS205	107477
Australia	Multilateral	29 Apr 58	Specific Resources	559UNTS285	108164
Australia	Multilateral	29 Apr 58	Dispute Settlement	450UNTS169	106466
Australia	Multilateral	29 Apr 58	Water Transport	450UNTS11	106465
Australia	Multilateral	29 Apr 58	Territory Boundary	499UNTS311	107302
Australia	Multilateral	01 Dec 58	Commodity Trade	385UNTS137	105534
Australia	Multilateral	06 Apr 59	Commodity Trade	349UNTS167	105013
Australia	Multilateral	01 Dec 59	Territory Boundary	402UNTS71	105778
Australia	Multilateral	26 Jan 60	IGO Establishment	439UNTS249	106333
Australia	Multilateral	17 Jun 60	Humanitarian	536UNTS27	107794
Australia	Multilateral	01 Sep 60	Commodity Trade	403UNTS3	105792

PARTY ONE	PARTY TWO	DATE	TOPIC	CITATION	NUMBER
Australia	Multilateral	19 Sep 60	IBRD Project	444UNTS259	106371
Australia	Multilateral	26 Nov 60	Taxation	500UNTS25	107304
Australia	Multilateral	23 Jan 61	Postal Service	530UNTS141	107679
Australia	Multilateral	30 Mar 61	Sanitation	520UNTS151	107515
Australia	Multilateral	18 Apr 61	Dispute Settlement	500UNTS243	107312
Australia	Multilateral	18 Apr 61	Consul/Citizenship	500UNTS95	107310
Australia	Multilateral	08 Jun 61	Customs	473UNTS187	106863
Australia	Multilateral	08 Jun 61	Customs	473UNTS153	106862
Australia	Multilateral	21 Jun 61	IGO Establishment	514UNTS209	107449
Australia	Multilateral	18 Sep 61	Air Transport	500UNTS31	107305
Australia	Multilateral	06 Dec 61	Customs	473UNTS219	106864
Australia	Multilateral	29 Mar 62	IGO Establishment	507UNTS177	107401
Australia	Multilateral	09 May 62	IGO Establishment	453UNTS299	106531
Australia	Multilateral	15 May 62	Commodity Trade	444UNTS3	106367
Australia	Multilateral	10 Sep 62	Other Military	502UNTS3	107323
Australia	Multilateral	28 Sep 62	IGO Establishment	469UNTS169	106791
Australia	Multilateral	16 Oct 62	Postal Service	470UNTS291	106814
Australia	Multilateral	16 Oct 62	Postal Service	470UNTS336	106816
Australia	Multilateral	16 Oct 62	Postal Service	470UNTS321	106815
Australia	Multilateral	24 Apr 63	Consul/Citizenship	596UNTS261	108638
Australia	Multilateral	09 Jun 63	General Economic	538UNTS309	107818
Australia	Multilateral	05 Aug 63	Sanitation	480UNTS43	106964
Australia	Multilateral	06 May 64	IGO Operations	514UNTS71	107442
Australia	Multilateral	20 Jun 64	General Economic	539UNTS3	107819
Australia	Multilateral	10 Jul 64	Postal Service	611UNTS105	108845
Australia	Multilateral	10 Jul 64	Postal Service	612UNTS361	108849
Australia	Multilateral	10 Jul 64	Postal Service	612UNTS3	108847
Australia	Multilateral	10 Jul 64	Postal Service	611UNTS7	108844
Australia	Multilateral	20 Aug 64	Telecommunications	514UNTS25	107441
Australia	Multilateral	01 Dec 64	Water Transport	550UNTS133	108012
Australia	Multilateral	26 Nov 65	Recognition	598UNTS81	108655
Australia	Multilateral	04 Dec 65	IGO Establishment	571UNTS123	108303
Australia	Multilateral	31 Dec 65	Specific Resources	616UNTS317	108904
Australia	Multilateral	30 Mar 66	Scientific Project	593UNTS261	108588
Australia	Multilateral	05 Apr 66	Water Transport	640UNTS133	109159
Australia	Multilateral	04 May 66	IBRD Project	575UNTS49	108354
Australia	Multilateral	27 Jan 67	Scientific Project	610UNTS205	108843
Australia	Multilateral	03 May 67	IGO Operations	0UNTS0	110764
Australia	Multilateral	30 Jun 67	Commodity Trade	0UNTS0	109864
Australia	Multilateral	06 Nov 67	Other Military	640UNTS87	109155
Australia	Multilateral	18 Mar 68	Commodity Trade	0UNTS0	109262
Australia	Multilateral	11 Jun 68	Scientific Project	0UNTS0	109884
Australia	Multilateral	01 Aug 68	Culture	0UNTS0	109368
Australia	Multilateral	24 Sep 68	Air Transport	0UNTS0	110612
Australia	Multilateral	28 Sep 68	Tech Assistance	0UNTS0	109296
Australia	Multilateral	24 Dec 68	Commodity Trade	0UNTS0	109369
Australia	Multilateral	27 Jan 69	Telecommunications	0UNTS0	109664
Australia	Multilateral	11 Jun 69	Scientific Project	0UNTS0	110100
Australia	Multilateral	12 Jan 70	Commodity Trade	0UNTS0	110603
Australia	Netherlands	24 Jan 47	Finance	10UNTS77	100144
Australia	Netherlands	12 Aug 49	Reparations	34UNTS213	100539
Australia	Netherlands	26 Apr 50	Claims and Debts	54UNTS83	100796
Australia	Netherlands	20 Feb 51	Visas	97UNTS283	101354
Australia	Netherlands	22 Feb 51	Non-ILO Labor	128UNTS115	101717
Australia	Netherlands	25 Sep 51	Air Transport	128UNTS63	101713
Australia	Netherlands	22 Oct 53	Postal Service	184UNTS193	102448
Australia	Netherlands	01 Aug 56	Non-ILO Labor	280UNTS3	104047
Australia	Netherlands	29 Nov 56	Air Transport	302UNTS141	104356
Australia	Netherlands	09 Oct 57	Dispute Settlement	312UNTS225	104520
Australia	Netherlands	23 Jul 58	Postal Service	328UNTS227	104736
Australia	Netherlands	01 Jun 65	Consul/Citizenship	560UNTS85	108170
Australia	New Zealand	21 Jan 44	General Amity	18UNTS357	200113
Australia	New Zealand	15 Apr 49	Non-ILO Labor	34UNTS225	100540
Australia	New Zealand	26 Nov 49	Territory Boundary	198UNTS161	102662
Australia	New Zealand	30 Sep 58	Territory Boundary	340UNTS61	104859

PARTY ONE	PARTY TWO	DATE	TOPIC	CITATION	NUMBER
Australia	New Zealand	12 May 60	Taxation	369UNTS119	105254
Australia	New Zealand	25 Jul 61	Air Transport	523UNTS271	107561
Australia	New Zealand	29 Apr 63	Customs	483UNTS241	107017
Australia	New Zealand	31 Aug 65	General Trade	554UNTS169	108101
Australia	Norway	24 Mar 47	Claims and Debts	18UNTS185	100288
Australia	Norway	19 Oct 51	Visas	128UNTS109	101716
Australia	Norway	04 Jan 68	Water Transport	3NORT999	451005
Australia	Pakistan	03 Jun 49	Air Transport	35UNTS23	100549
Australia	Pakistan	16 Jan 52	Postal Service	151UNTS281	102001
Australia	Philippines	01 Sep 49	Postal Service	46UNTS215	100711
Australia	Philippines	14 Apr 50	Air Transport	127UNTS281	101709
Australia	Philippines	23 Feb 60	Visas	358UNTS139	105131
Australia	Philippines	16 Jun 65	General Trade	541UNTS31	107858
Australia	Poland	03 Jun 48	Direct Aid	16UNTS189	100258
Australia	Poland	25 Nov 54	Postal Service	521UNTS281	107526
Australia	Poland	30 Dec 58	Privil/Immunities	58PZUM122	458063
Australia	Poland	20 Jun 66	General Trade	638UNTS201	109136
Australia	Portugal	29 Mar 63	Visas	468UNTS313	106778
Australia	Romania	07 Jan 49	Admin Cooperation	189UNTS263	102550
Australia	Romania	18 May 67	General Trade	642UNTS25	109162
Australia	Singapore	03 Nov 67	Air Transport	0UNTS0	110167
Australia	Singapore	27 Jun 68	Health/Educ/Welfare	0UNTS0	109669
Australia	Singapore	11 Feb 69	Taxation	0UNTS0	110175
Australia	South Africa	04 Nov 55	Air Transport	232UNTS143	103234
Australia	South Africa	26 Sep 58	Air Transport	335UNTS121	104780
Australia	Spain	27 Sep 61	Visas	426UNTS159	106135
Australia	State/IGO Group	21 May 68	Tech Assistance	636UNTS326	109108
Australia	Sweden	16 Sep 46	General Trade	10UNTS63	100143
Australia	Sweden	22 Sep 50	General Trade	50SOFM1075	461131
Australia	Sweden	26 Sep 51	Visas	109UNTS39	101488
Australia	Sweden	25 May 53	General Trade	53SOFM1099	461194
Australia	Switzerland	21 May 59	Taxation	341UNTS283	104891
Australia	Taiwan	22 Mar 55	Postal Service	209UNTS3	102818
Australia	Taiwan	29 Jul 55	Patents/Copyrights	213UNTS193	102887
Australia	Taiwan	22 Apr 68	General Trade	0UNTS0	109734
Australia	Thailand	26 Oct 53	Air Transport	255UNTS117	103607
Australia	Thailand	20 Dec 56	Admin Cooperation	265UNTS149	103810
Australia	Thailand	28 Jul 59	Customs	339UNTS91	104847
Australia	Thailand	26 Feb 60	Air Transport	392UNTS255	105647
Australia	Turkey	10 Apr 56	Visas	247UNTS139	103462
Australia	Turkey	05 Oct 67	Visas	0UNTS0	109457
Australia	UK Great Britain	29 Oct 46	Taxation	17UNTS181	100276
Australia	UK Great Britain	28 Apr 50	Air Transport	95UNTS249	101324
Australia	UK Great Britain	19 Dec 50	Territory Boundary	93UNTS81	101292
Australia	UK Great Britain	08 Jun 53	Non-ILO Labor	201UNTS187	102718
Australia	UK Great Britain	26 Feb 57	General Trade	265UNTS197	103813
Australia	UK Great Britain	01 Apr 57	Non-ILO Labor	271UNTS235	103918
Australia	UK Great Britain	29 Jan 58	Non-ILO Labor	292UNTS233	104275
Australia	UK Great Britain	07 Feb 58	Air Transport	335UNTS23	104776
Australia	UK Great Britain	14 Nov 61	Air Transport	466UNTS35	106735
Australia	UK Great Britain	28 May 62	Admin Cooperation	434UNTS219	106264
Australia	UK Great Britain	16 Aug 62	Non-ILO Labor	439UNTS163	106328
Australia	UK Great Britain	06 Dec 62	Postal Service	457UNTS145	106584
Australia	UK Great Britain	06 Jun 63	Sanitation	472UNTS157	106838
Australia	UK Great Britain	23 Sep 63	Postal Service	483UNTS39	107006
Australia	UK Great Britain	15 Apr 64	Commodity Trade	515UNTS23	107451
Australia	UK Great Britain	07 Dec 67	Taxation	0UNTS0	109458
Australia	UK Great Britain	03 Oct 68	Finance	0UNTS0	109821
Australia	UK Great Britain	16 Oct 68	Scientific Project	0UNTS0	109459
Australia	UN Special Fund	30 Sep 64	Scientific Project	510UNTS277	107419
Australia	UN Special Fund	06 Feb 67	IGO Operations	590UNTS3	108543
Australia	UNICEF (Children)	21 Dec 67	IGO Operations	614UNTS83	108864
Australia	United Arab Rep	14 Jun 52	Air Transport	173UNTS241	102269
Australia	United Nations	13 May 63	Education	463UNTS187	106702
Australia	United Nations	25 Feb 66	IGO Operations	557UNTS85	108129

PARTY ONE	PARTY TWO	DATE	TOPIC	CITATION	NUMBER
Australia	USA (United States)	03 Sep 42	Milit Assistance	24UNTS195	200143
Australia	USA (United States)	30 Sep 42	Milit Servic/Citiz	13UNTS125	200074
Australia	USA (United States)	10 May 44	Reparations	106UNTS237	200343
Australia	USA (United States)	08 Mar 45	Claims and Debts	121UNTS205	200400
Australia	USA (United States)	07 Jun 46	Milit Assistance	4UNTS237	100048
Australia	USA (United States)	03 Dec 46	Air Transport	7UNTS201	100100
Australia	USA (United States)	10 Mar 47	Air Transport	10UNTS89	100145
Australia	USA (United States)	26 Nov 49	Reparations	45UNTS133	100695
Australia	USA (United States)	29 Dec 49	Patents/Copyrights	71UNTS45	100909
Australia	USA (United States)	10 Feb 50	Visas	51UNTS167	100763
Australia	USA (United States)	20 Feb 51	Milit Assistance	132UNTS297	101769
Australia	USA (United States)	16 Nov 51	Tech Assistance	168UNTS75	102214
Australia	USA (United States)	27 May 52	Postal Service	178UNTS113	102338
Australia	USA (United States)	14 May 53	Taxation	205UNTS237	102778
Australia	USA (United States)	14 May 53	Taxation	205UNTS277	102780
Australia	USA (United States)	14 May 53	Taxation	205UNTS253	102779
Australia	USA (United States)	20 Aug 55	Visas	268UNTS133	103855
Australia	USA (United States)	22 Jun 56	Atomic Energy	283UNTS275	104123
Australia	USA (United States)	31 Dec 56	Milit Assistance	266UNTS89	103823
Australia	USA (United States)	12 Jul 57	Milit Assistance	290UNTS139	104233
Australia	USA (United States)	24 Jan 58	Patents/Copyrights	307UNTS105	104446
Australia	USA (United States)	25 Feb 58	Tech Assistance	317UNTS153	104601
Australia	USA (United States)	20 Jun 58	Postal Service	336UNTS97	104802
Australia	USA (United States)	19 Aug 59	Visas	388UNTS183	105578
Australia	USA (United States)	20 Nov 59	Air Transport	349UNTS293	105015
Australia	USA (United States)	26 Feb 60	Specific Property	354UNTS95	105056
Australia	USA (United States)	23 Aug 60	General Military	388UNTS237	105581
Australia	USA (United States)	09 May 61	Scientific Project	409UNTS203	105886
Australia	USA (United States)	22 May 61	Scientific Project	419UNTS3	106026
Australia	USA (United States)	05 Jun 61	Scientific Project	409UNTS279	105892
Australia	USA (United States)	09 May 63	Milit Installation	475UNTS331	106897
Australia	USA (United States)	09 May 63	Status of Forces	469UNTS55	106784
Australia	USA (United States)	03 Jan 64	Gen Communications	505UNTS159	107371
Australia	USA (United States)	05 Feb 64	Status of Forces	511UNTS103	107430
Australia	USA (United States)	17 Feb 64	Commodity Trade	511UNTS17	107422
Australia	USA (United States)	17 Aug 64	Scientific Project	530UNTS209	107683
Australia	USA (United States)	28 Aug 64	Education	510UNTS201	107415
Australia	USA (United States)	25 Jun 65	Gen Communications	541UNTS155	107868
Australia	USA (United States)	09 Dec 66	Scientific Project	607UNTS83	108798
Australia	USA (United States)	13 Jan 69	Scientific Project	0UNTS0	110262
Australia	USA (United States)	13 Jan 69	Scientific Project	0UNTS0	109460
Australia	USA (United States)	10 Nov 69	General Military	0UNTS0	110479
Australia	USA (United States)	30 Jan 70	General Trade	0UNTS0	110618
Australia	USA (United States)	25 Mar 70	Gen Communications	0UNTS0	110693
Australia	USA (United States)	22 May 70	General Military	0UNTS0	110661
Australia	USSR (Soviet Union)	15 Jul 47	Consul/Citizenship	0SUST234	468021
Australia	USSR (Soviet Union)	13 Mar 59	Consul/Citizenship	8SUGG139	469564
Australia	USSR (Soviet Union)	29 Jun 60	Postal Service	392UNTS131	105641
Australia	USSR (Soviet Union)	15 Oct 65	General Trade	553UNTS239	108092
Australia	Vietnam, South	04 Oct 54	Admin Cooperation	0VKNG81	496022
Australia	Vietnam, South	04 Oct 54	Admin Cooperation	201UNTS349	102723
Australia	Yugoslavia	09 Jul 48	Direct Aid	22UNTS17	100327
Australia	Yugoslavia	22 Feb 50	Claims and Debts	51UNTS201	100766
Australia	Yugoslavia	19 Nov 53	Admin Cooperation	191UNTS241	102584
Australia	Yugoslavia	28 Feb 56	Postal Service	243UNTS53	103446
Australia	Yugoslavia	12 Feb 70	Non-ILO Labor	0UNTS0	110660
Austria	Accept UN Charter	06 Aug 52	UN Charter	223UNTS27	103044
Austria	Afghanistan	21 Jul 58	Air Transport	0UNTS0	109236
Austria	Albania	27 Jul 61	General Economic	407UNTS37	105858
Austria	Argentina	17 Jun 60	Visas	60ABGB215	403001
Austria	Australia	19 Jul 48	Direct Aid	22UNTS25	100328
Austria	Australia	17 Nov 51	Admin Cooperation	133UNTS137	101785
Austria	Australia	20 Dec 54	Postal Service	205UNTS157	102775
Austria	Australia	15 Mar 56	Visas	241UNTS331	103441
Austria	Australia	18 Dec 59	Reparations	348UNTS201	105001

PARTY ONE	PARTY TWO	DATE	TOPIC	CITATION	NUMBER
Austria	Australia	22 Mar 67	Air Transport	67ABGB152	403002
Austria	Australia	22 Mar 67	Air Transport	0UNTS0	109246
Austria	Australia	05 Jul 67	Other Military	636UNTS117	109098
Austria	Belgium	05 Nov 49	Extradition	48UNTS107	100739
Austria	Belgium	22 Dec 49	Admin Cooperation	46UNTS233	100712
Austria	Belgium	16 Mar 51	Visas	88UNTS357	101203
Austria	Belgium	11 Oct 51	Visas	110UNTS45	101500
Austria	Belgium	17 Oct 52	Culture	162UNTS183	102135
Austria	Belgium	07 Jan 55	Air Transport	380UNTS219	105458
Austria	Belgium	20 Jan 56	Non-ILO Labor	248UNTS3	103481
Austria	Belgium	25 Oct 57	Admin Cooperation	372UNTS177	105297
Austria	Belgium	20 Jun 58	Land Transport	312UNTS95	104513
Austria	Belgium	22 Apr 59	Extradition	356UNTS309	105102
Austria	Belgium	16 Jun 59	Admin Cooperation	419UNTS45	106029
Austria	Belgium	14 Nov 63	Specific Property	544UNTS97	107912
Austria	Belgium	20 Jan 64	Land Transport	509UNTS275	107406
Austria	Belgium	11 Jun 64	Taxation	521UNTS157	107518
Austria	Belgium	10 Feb 70	Land Transport	0UNTS0	110539
Austria	Belgium	10 Feb 70	Land Transport	70ABGB70	403005
Austria	Bolivia	03 Aug 60	Visas	60ABGB216	403006
Austria	Brazil	04 Jul 56	Finance	57ABGB47	403008
Austria	Brazil	04 Jul 56	General Economic	57ABGB46	403007
Austria	Brazil	07 Dec 59	Visas	67ABGB332	403009
Austria	Brazil	21 Dec 65	Admin Cooperation	595UNTS299	108624
Austria	Brazil	22 Aug 67	Visas	0UNTS0	109528
Austria	Bulgaria	10 Mar 55	Water Transport	56ABGB140	403010
Austria	Bulgaria	12 Sep 58	Air Transport	353UNTS3	105036
Austria	Bulgaria	05 Apr 63	General Trade	480UNTS3	106963
Austria	Bulgaria	02 May 63	Finance	535UNTS143	107778
Austria	Bulgaria	12 Jul 65	Sanitation	587UNTS51	108510
Austria	Bulgaria	12 Jul 65	Visas	587UNTS45	108509
Austria	Bulgaria	21 Apr 67	Visas	603UNTS121	108729
Austria	Bulgaria	20 Oct 67	Admin Cooperation	0UNTS0	110601
Austria	Bulgaria	27 Oct 67	Customs	68ABGB23	403011
Austria	Bulgaria	06 May 68	Tech Assistance	0UNTS0	109875
Austria	Bulgaria	09 May 68	Customs	68ABGB404	403012
Austria	Bulgaria	27 May 68	Scientific Project	72ABGB86	403013
Austria	Bulgaria	17 Apr 70	Culture	70ABGB204	403014
Austria	Bulgaria	08 Jul 70	Land Transport	70ABGB279	403015
Austria	Bulgaria	13 Oct 71	Finance	71ABGB442	403016
Austria	Bulgaria	22 Feb 72	Admin Cooperation	72ABGB113	403017
Austria	Canada	18 Jan 52	Admin Cooperation	236UNTS245	103327
Austria	Canada	19 Jun 56	Visas	305UNTS51	104412
Austria	Canada	11 May 67	Extradition	69ABGB324	403018
Austria	Canada	28 Feb 68	Other Military	636UNTS141	109101
Austria	Chile	25 Oct 54	Visas	55ABGB173	403019
Austria	China People's Rep	13 Sep 56	General Trade	56CCJC99	410362
Austria	China People's Rep	07 Dec 64	General Economic	64CCJC175	411080
Austria	Costa Rica	30 Apr 68	Visas	0UNTS0	109324
Austria	Costa Rica	15 Jul 68	Visas	68ABGB344	403020
Austria	Costa Rica	17 Sep 69	Telecommunications	69ABGB357	403021
Austria	Cyprus	14 Dec 67	Visas	636UNTS267	109104
Austria	Czechoslovakia	29 Oct 48	Water Transport	56ABGB74	403022
Austria	Czechoslovakia	30 Mar 50	Sanitation	495UNTS85	107240
Austria	Czechoslovakia	23 Jan 60	Scientific Project	495UNTS99	107241
Austria	Czechoslovakia	23 Jan 60	Specific Resources	495UNTS125	107242
Austria	Czechoslovakia	14 Sep 60	Commodity Trade	495UNTS143	107243
Austria	Czechoslovakia	17 Jan 61	Customs	61ABGB222	403023
Austria	Czechoslovakia	10 Nov 61	Admin Cooperation	455UNTS337	106550
Austria	Czechoslovakia	13 Feb 62	Education	455UNTS381	106551
Austria	Czechoslovakia	01 Mar 62	Air Transport	62ABGB319	403024
Austria	Czechoslovakia	22 Sep 62	Land Transport	495UNTS157	107244
Austria	Czechoslovakia	08 Mar 63	General Economic	495UNTS219	107245
Austria	Czechoslovakia	03 Jan 67	Visas	67ABGB348	403025
Austria	Czechoslovakia	30 Jun 67	Customs	67ABGB299	403026

PARTY ONE	PARTY TWO	DATE	TOPIC	CITATION	NUMBER
Austria	Czechoslovakia	19 Oct 67	Land Transport	634UNTS19	109048
Austria	Czechoslovakia	07 Dec 67	Water Transport	0UNTS0	110475
Austria	Czechoslovakia	07 Dec 67	Specific Resources	70ABGB106	403027
Austria	Czechoslovakia	14 Dec 67	Visas	634UNTS51	109050
Austria	Czechoslovakia	02 Jul 69	General Trade	70ABGB129	403028
Austria	Czechoslovakia	16 Dec 70	Customs	71ABGB84	403029
Austria	Czechoslovakia	12 Sep 71	General Economic	72ABGB24	403030
Austria	Czechoslovakia	22 Oct 71	Finance	71ABGB496	403031
Austria	Denmark	29 Nov 48	General Trade	74UNTS243	100967
Austria	Denmark	29 Nov 48	Finance	74UNTS257	100968
Austria	Denmark	02 Dec 49	Air Transport	53UNTS281	100788
Austria	Denmark	23 Feb 50	General Trade	74UNTS269	100969
Austria	Denmark	27 Mar 54	Visas	55ABGB192	403032
Austria	Denmark	07 Sep 54	Non-ILO Labor	201UNTS39	102709
Austria	Denmark	14 Nov 59	Commodity Trade	630UNTS29	108962
Austria	Denmark	23 Oct 61	Taxation	425UNTS115	106122
Austria	Denmark	17 Jul 63	Consul/Citizenship	479UNTS263	106958
Austria	Denmark	09 Dec 63	Admin Cooperation	520UNTS133	107514
Austria	Dominican Republic	21 Feb 68	Visas	68ABGB109	403033
Austria	Dominican Republic	21 Feb 68	Visas	0UNTS0	109215
Austria	ECSC (Coal/Steel)	26 Jul 57	Land Transport	58ABGB63	403141
Austria	Ecuador	07 Feb 68	Visas	68ABGB108	403034
Austria	Ecuador	07 Feb 68	Visas	0UNTS0	109212
Austria	Ecuador	28 Mar 69	General Trade	71ABGB121	403035
Austria	EEC (Econ Commnty)	26 Jun 69	General Trade	70ABGB128	403041
Austria	EEC (Econ Commnty)	04 Nov 70	Commodity Trade	71ABGB156	403042
Austria	EEC (Econ Commnty)	04 Nov 70	Commodity Trade	71ABGB157	403043
Austria	El Salvador	23 Mar 60	General Trade	390UNTS3	105599
Austria	El Salvador	21 Jun 60	Visas	60ABGB189	403161
Austria	El Salvador	03 Oct 63	Visas	64ABGB34	403162
Austria	Eurocontrol	31 Mar 71	Air Transport	72ABGB56	403044
Austria	Finland	05 Nov 54	Visas	56ABGB47	403045
Austria	Finland	01 Feb 62	Non-ILO Labor	425UNTS33	106116
Austria	Finland	08 Oct 63	Taxation	490UNTS255	107160
Austria	Finland	23 Jul 64	Taxation	65ABGB117	403046
Austria	Finland	09 Dec 65	Education	0UNTS0	109462
Austria	Finland	09 Dec 65	Admin Cooperation	69ABGB3	403047
Austria	Finland	21 Feb 66	Claims and Debts	597UNTS273	108651
Austria	Finland	04 Jun 69	Air Transport	0UNTS0	109886
Austria	Finland	04 Jun 69	Air Transport	69ABGB257	403048
Austria	Finland	21 Sep 70	Taxation	72ABGB110	403049
Austria	France	15 Mar 47	Culture	12UNTS109	100182
Austria	France	31 Aug 55	Non-ILO Labor	55ABGB208	403050
Austria	France	26 Jun 58	Admin Cooperation	60FRRT19	415056
Austria	France	01 Oct 59	Patents/Copyrights	60FRRT21	415057
Austria	France	08 Oct 59	Taxation	453UNTS95	106521
Austria	France	30 Nov 62	Visas	463UNTS173	106701
Austria	France	12 Jul 63	Air Transport	499UNTS91	107294
Austria	France	19 Jul 63	Culture	65FRRT43	415058
Austria	France	05 May 64	Patents/Copyrights	64FRRT46	415059
Austria	France	14 Oct 64	Land Transport	64ABGB324	403054
Austria	France	15 Jul 66	Admin Cooperation	604UNTS265	108755
Austria	France	15 Jul 66	Admin Cooperation	634UNTS3	109047
Austria	France	12 Jan 68	Scientific Project	0UNTS0	109531
Austria	France	12 Mar 68	Scientific Project	69FRJO1001	416060
Austria	France	04 Jul 69	Land Transport	69ABGB335	403055
Austria	France	30 Oct 70	Taxation	72ABGB147	403056
Austria	France	05 Jul 71	Telecommunications	71ABGB325	403057
Austria	Germany, West	21 Apr 51	Non-ILO Labor	52WGBB317	425523
Austria	Germany, West	19 May 51	Non-ILO Labor	52WGBB612	425524
Austria	Germany, West	23 Nov 51	Non-ILO Labor	59WBGA13	424526
Austria	Germany, West	23 Nov 51	Non-ILO Labor	53ABGB10	403060
Austria	Germany, West	23 Nov 51	Non-ILO Labor	52WGBB609	425525
Austria	Germany, West	11 Jul 53	Non-ILO Labor	54ABGB250	403059
Austria	Germany, West	31 Oct 53	Non-ILO Labor	55ABGB248	403058

PARTY ONE	PARTY TWO	DATE	TOPIC	CITATION	NUMBER
Austria	Germany, West	31 Oct 53	Non-ILO Labor	55ABGB74	403061
Austria	Germany, West	06 Apr 54	Visas	55ABGB247	403062
Austria	Germany, West	13 May 54	General Trade	54WBGA99	424527
Austria	Germany, West	14 Sep 54	Admin Cooperation	57ABGB245	403063
Austria	Germany, West	15 Sep 54	Visas	55WBGA148	424528
Austria	Germany, West	04 Oct 54	Admin Cooperation	55WGBB833	425531
Austria	Germany, West	04 Oct 54	Taxation	55WGBB755	425530
Austria	Germany, West	04 Oct 54	Taxation	55WGBB749	425529
Austria	Germany, West	10 May 55	Visas	55WBGA103	424532
Austria	Germany, West	14 Sep 55	Visas	57WGBB585	425534
Austria	Germany, West	14 Sep 55	Visas	57WGBB589	425535
Austria	Germany, West	14 Sep 55	Privil/Immunities	57WGBB596	425538
Austria	Germany, West	14 Sep 55	Visas	57WGBB594	425537
Austria	Germany, West	14 Sep 55	Privil/Immunities	57WGBB592	425536
Austria	Germany, West	14 Sep 55	Customs	57WGBB581	421533
Austria	Germany, West	28 Oct 55	Visas	57WGBB598	425539
Austria	Germany, West	25 Mar 57	Specific Resources	58ABGB197	403003
Austria	Germany, West	31 May 57	Visas	57ABGB192	403064
Austria	Germany, West	15 Jun 57	Finance	58WGBB129	425540
Austria	Germany, West	09 Jul 57	Admin Cooperation	57ABGB198	403065
Austria	Germany, West	22 Sep 58	Extradition	60WGBB1341	425541
Austria	Germany, West	22 Sep 58	Admin Cooperation	60WGBB1341	425542
Austria	Germany, West	10 Oct 58	Admin Cooperation	58WBGA228	424543
Austria	Germany, West	16 Jan 59	Specific Property	59WBGA51	424544
Austria	Germany, West	06 Jun 59	Admin Cooperation	60WGBB1245	425546
Austria	Germany, West	06 Jun 59	Admin Cooperation	59WGBB1523	425545
Austria	Germany, West	18 Jan 61	Customs	62WGBB933	425547
Austria	Germany, West	19 Jul 61	Extradition	61WBGA169	424548
Austria	Germany, West	19 Jul 61	Visas	414UNTS211	105974
Austria	Germany, West	27 Nov 61	Refugees	62WGBB1041	425549
Austria	Germany, West	06 Sep 62	Visas	63WGBB1279	425550
Austria	Germany, West	07 May 63	Health/Educ/Welfare	64WGBB220	425551
Austria	Germany, West	12 Sep 63	Visas	63ABGB296	403004
Austria	Germany, West	15 Mar 65	Air Transport	66WGBB126	425552
Austria	Germany, West	15 Mar 65	Air Transport	0UNTS0	109478
Austria	Germany, West	17 Jan 66	Health/Educ/Welfare	0UNTS0	110163
Austria	Germany, West	17 Jan 66	Health/Educ/Welfare	69WGBB1	425553
Austria	Germany, West	17 Feb 66	Land Transport	615UNTS3	108876
Austria	Germany, West	17 Feb 66	Land Transport	614UNTS263	108875
Austria	Germany, West	27 Sep 66	Commodity Trade	66WBGA235	424554
Austria	Germany, West	17 Oct 66	Admin Cooperation	67WGBB2318	425555
Austria	Germany, West	22 Dec 66	Non-ILO Labor	69WGBB1233	425556
Austria	Germany, West	22 Dec 66	Non-ILO Labor	0UNTS0	110090
Austria	Germany, West	31 May 67	Visas	70WGBB697	425557
Austria	Germany, West	07 Aug 67	Patents/Copyrights	68WGBB5	425558
Austria	Germany, West	23 Oct 68	Customs	68ABGB409	403066
Austria	Germany, West	23 Oct 68	Customs	68ABGB410	403067
Austria	Germany, West	25 Oct 68	Health/Educ/Welfare	69ABGB259	403068
Austria	Germany, West	13 Nov 68	General Transport	69WGBB1457	425559
Austria	Germany, West	07 Feb 69	Health/Educ/Welfare	70ABGB210	403069
Austria	Germany, West	31 Mar 69	Admin Cooperation	70ABGB340	403070
Austria	Germany, West	18 Nov 69	Taxation	70WGBB1370	425560
Austria	Germany, West	11 Mar 70	Visas	70ABGB130	403071
Austria	Germany, West	06 Jul 70	Visas	70ABGB285	403072
Austria	Germany, West	11 Sep 70	Admin Cooperation	71WGBB1001	425561
Austria	Germany, West	25 Jan 71	Visas	71ABGB98	403074
Austria	Germany, West	25 Jan 71	Visas	71ABGB97	403073
Austria	Germany, West	25 Jan 71	Visas	71ABGB99	403075
Austria	Germany, West	25 Jan 71	Visas	71ABGB102	403078
Austria	Germany, West	25 Jan 71	Visas	71ABGB100	403076
Austria	Germany, West	25 Jan 71	Visas	71ABGB101	403077
Austria	Germany, West	05 Jul 72	Visas	72ABGB308	403079
Austria	Germany, West	05 Jul 72	Visas	72ABGB311	403082
Austria	Germany, West	05 Jul 72	Visas	72ABGB310	403081
Austria	Germany, West	05 Jul 72	Visas	72ABGB309	403080

PARTY ONE	PARTY TWO	DATE	TOPIC	CITATION	NUMBER
Austria	Germany, West	05 Jul 72	Visas	72ABGB312	403083
Austria	Greece	11 May 50	General Trade	184UNTS217	102450
Austria	Greece	22 Mar 52	General Economic	187UNTS255	102517
Austria	Greece	20 Sep 52	General Trade	187UNTS191	102512
Austria	Greece	12 Aug 53	Visas	53ABGB158	403084
Austria	Greece	15 Jan 62	Air Transport	498UNTS3	107275
Austria	Greece	06 Dec 65	Admin Cooperation	71ABGB2	403085
Austria	Greece	04 Mar 70	Land Transport	71ABGB83	403086
Austria	Greece	22 Sep 70	Taxation	72ABGB39	403087
Austria	Guatemala	18 Mar 60	General Trade	379UNTS89	105435
Austria	Hungary	18 May 55	Water Transport	55ABGB195	403088
Austria	Hungary	09 Apr 56	Specific Resources	438UNTS123	106315
Austria	Hungary	17 Jul 59	Air Transport	60ABGB76	403089
Austria	Hungary	17 Jul 59	Air Transport	0UNTS0	109237
Austria	Hungary	17 Jan 61	Customs	61ABGB42	403091
Austria	Hungary	09 Jul 63	Sanitation	482UNTS29	106989
Austria	Hungary	31 Oct 64	Finance	605UNTS3	108758
Austria	Hungary	31 Oct 64	Visas	545UNTS241	107937
Austria	Hungary	31 Oct 64	Claims and Debts	605UNTS77	108760
Austria	Hungary	31 Oct 64	Visas	545UNTS223	107936
Austria	Hungary	31 Oct 64	Claims and Debts	605UNTS63	108759
Austria	Hungary	11 Nov 64	Sanitation	576UNTS163	108368
Austria	Hungary	09 Apr 65	Admin Cooperation	638UNTS135	109133
Austria	Hungary	09 Apr 65	Visas	564UNTS179	108228
Austria	Hungary	09 Apr 65	Recognition	638UNTS105	109132
Austria	Hungary	09 Apr 65	Visas	638UNTS53	109131
Austria	Hungary	31 Oct 67	Claims and Debts	67ABGB293	403092
Austria	Hungary	08 Jun 68	Customs	68ABGB293	403093
Austria	Hungary	27 Nov 68	Customs	69ABGB261	403094
Austria	Hungary	29 Apr 69	Visas	69ABGB167	403095
Austria	Hungary	28 May 69	Health/Educ/Welfare	72ABGB111	403096
Austria	Hungary	28 Apr 71	Visas	71ABGB203	403097
Austria	Hungary	05 May 71	Air Transport	71ABGB403	403090
Austria	Hungary	17 May 71	Visas	71ABGB252	403098
Austria	Hungary	28 Oct 71	Finance	71ABGB421	403099
Austria	IAEA (Atom Energy)	11 Dec 57	Atomic Energy	339UNTS110	104849
Austria	IAEA (Atom Energy)	21 Jun 63	Atomic Energy	490UNTS351	107164
Austria	IBRD (World Bank)	08 Nov 54	IBRD Project	216UNTS305	200528
Austria	IBRD (World Bank)	14 Jun 55	IBRD Project	221UNTS375	200531
Austria	IBRD (World Bank)	21 Sep 56	IBRD Project	259UNTS43	103682
Austria	IBRD (World Bank)	21 Sep 56	IBRD Project	259UNTS17	103681
Austria	IBRD (World Bank)	10 Oct 57	IBRD Project	301UNTS95	104343
Austria	IBRD (World Bank)	28 Apr 58	IBRD Project	359UNTS145	105142
Austria	IBRD (World Bank)	02 Dec 58	IBRD Project	340UNTS3	104856
Austria	IBRD (World Bank)	25 Sep 59	IBRD Project	355UNTS223	105079
Austria	IBRD (World Bank)	15 Jun 62	IBRD Project	447UNTS127	106414
Austria	ICAO (Civil Aviat)	01 Apr 71	IGO Operations	71ABGB152	403101
Austria	India	24 Sep 63	Taxation	545UNTS199	107935
Austria	India	10 Jul 68	Other Military	0UNTS0	109227
Austria	India	10 Jul 68	Other Military	68ABGB326	403100
Austria	Iran	09 Sep 59	General Amity	66ABGB45	403103
Austria	Iran	05 Mar 70	General Amity	70ABGB111	403104
Austria	Iraq	21 Nov 70	Air Transport	71ABGB270	403102
Austria	Ireland	06 Oct 50	General Trade	557UNTS173	108133
Austria	Ireland	24 May 66	Taxation	636UNTS149	109102
Austria	Ireland	10 Dec 70	Visas	70ABGB428	403105
Austria	Israel	17 Nov 55	Air Transport	232UNTS153	103235
Austria	Israel	17 Jan 56	Air Transport	59ABGB162	403106
Austria	Israel	25 Nov 57	Visas	314UNTS81	104542
Austria	Israel	10 Oct 61	Extradition	448UNTS161	106430
Austria	Israel	22 Aug 63	Air Transport	63ABGB260	403107
Austria	Israel	06 Jun 66	Admin Cooperation	0UNTS0	109346
Austria	Israel	06 Jun 66	Admin Cooperation	0UNTS0	109347
Austria	Israel	06 Jun 66	Admin Cooperation	68ABGB349	403108
Austria	Israel	06 Jun 66	Admin Cooperation	68ABGB348	403109

PARTY ONE	PARTY TWO	DATE	TOPIC	CITATION	NUMBER
Austria	Israel	03 Apr 67	Gen Communications	630UNTS301	108976
Austria	Israel	22 Nov 68	Visas	68ABGB438	403110
Austria	Israel	22 Nov 68	Visas	0UNTS0	109388
Austria	Israel	29 Jan 70	Taxation	71ABGB85	403111
Austria	Italy	05 Sep 46	Peace/Disarmament	47ITGU295	435027
Austria	Italy	09 Nov 48	Land Transport	51ITGU71	435029
Austria	Italy	09 Nov 48	Land Transport	50ITGU44	435028
Austria	Italy	12 May 49	General Trade	51ITGU201	435030
Austria	Italy	19 May 49	General Trade	50ITGU137	435031
Austria	Italy	04 Oct 50	Finance	50ABGB220	403112
Austria	Italy	30 Dec 50	Non-ILO Labor	54ITGU278	435032
Austria	Italy	02 Aug 51	Visas	51ABGB253	403113
Austria	Italy	02 Aug 51	General Trade	53ITGU78	435033
Austria	Italy	01 Feb 52	Patents/Copyrights	53ABGB130	403114
Austria	Italy	01 Feb 52	Patents/Copyrights	54ITGU143	435034
Austria	Italy	01 Feb 52	Admin Cooperation	54ABGB235	403254
Austria	Italy	14 Mar 52	Culture	54ABGB270	403115
Austria	Italy	14 Mar 52	Admin Cooperation	56ABGB87	403116
Austria	Italy	14 Mar 53	Culture	54ITGU215	435035
Austria	Italy	10 Jul 54	Admin Cooperation	55ITGU75	435036
Austria	Italy	16 Jul 54	Admin Cooperation	67ITGU3	435037
Austria	Italy	05 Feb 55	Specific Resources	56ABGB42	403117
Austria	Italy	22 Oct 55	Specific Property	260UNTS327	103716
Austria	Italy	28 Dec 55	Visas	260UNTS345	103718
Austria	Italy	23 Jan 56	Air Transport	393UNTS97	105653
Austria	Italy	07 May 56	Finance	284UNTS351	104147
Austria	Italy	09 May 56	Education	267UNTS227	103845
Austria	Italy	12 Jul 56	Non-ILO Labor	378UNTS249	105426
Austria	Italy	19 Nov 56	Admin Cooperation	284UNTS293	104143
Austria	Italy	22 Apr 63	Visas	491UNTS53	107173
Austria	Italy	24 Oct 63	Mass Media	65ITGU152	435039
Austria	Italy	02 Aug 65	Air Transport	66ITDI118	436040
Austria	Italy	21 Apr 67	Admin Cooperation	72ABGB15	403118
Austria	Italy	24 Apr 68	Culture	68ABGB197	403119
Austria	Jamaica	25 Aug 70	Visas	70ABGB306	403120
Austria	Japan	16 Nov 55	Recognition	0JGJI1280	441087
Austria	Japan	20 Mar 58	Visas	324UNTS205	104686
Austria	Japan	20 Dec 61	Taxation	517UNTS155	107485
Austria	Japan	30 Apr 65	General Trade	0JGJI1598	441137
Austria	Japan	04 Nov 66	General Trade	66JJS1	442182
Austria	Japan	24 Dec 68	General Trade	68JJS1	442225
Austria	Korea, South	29 Jun 70	Visas	70ABGB242	403121
Austria	Korea, South	01 Sep 71	General Trade	71ABGB398	403122
Austria	Liechtenstein	01 Apr 55	Admin Cooperation	56ABGB212	403124
Austria	Liechtenstein	01 Apr 55	Admin Cooperation	56ABGB213	403123
Austria	Liechtenstein	07 Dec 55	Taxation	56ABGB214	403126
Austria	Liechtenstein	17 Mar 60	Territory Boundary	60ABGB228	403128
Austria	Liechtenstein	02 Sep 63	Visas	65ABGB11	403129
Austria	Liechtenstein	01 Jun 66	Admin Cooperation	68ABGB99	403125
Austria	Liechtenstein	24 Oct 67	Visas	68ABGB21	403130
Austria	Liechtenstein	26 Sep 68	Non-ILO Labor	69ABGB72	403131
Austria	Liechtenstein	26 Sep 68	Non-ILO Labor	0UNTS0	109492
Austria	Liechtenstein	30 Oct 68	Non-ILO Labor	69ABGB73	403132
Austria	Liechtenstein	05 Nov 69	Taxation	71ABGB24	403133
Austria	Liechtenstein	06 Nov 69	Taxation	0UNTS0	110323
Austria	Liechtenstein	06 Nov 69	Taxation	69ABGB479	403134
Austria	Liechtenstein	12 Oct 71	Taxation	71ABGB493	403135
Austria	Luxembourg	13 Oct 52	Air Transport	192UNTS291	102606
Austria	Luxembourg	12 Sep 58	Non-ILO Labor	59ABGB27	403136
Austria	Luxembourg	18 Oct 62	Taxation	496UNTS97	107248
Austria	Luxembourg	10 Apr 64	Taxation	64ABGB143	403137
Austria	Luxembourg	16 Jul 71	Land Transport	71ABGB404	403138
Austria	Malta	21 Dec 66	Visas	595UNTS307	108625
Austria	Mexico	06 Jun 58	Visas	59ABGB44	403139
Austria	Monaco	04 Jun 54	Visas	55ABGB215	403140

PARTY ONE	PARTY TWO	DATE	TOPIC	CITATION	NUMBER
Austria	Mongolia	15 Jul 63	General Trade	496UNTS171	107251
Austria	Multilateral	02 Aug 44	Scientific Project	67UNTS221	200221
Austria	Multilateral	22 Jul 46	IGO Establishment	9UNTS3	100125
Austria	Multilateral	22 Jul 46	IGO Establishment	14UNTS185	100221
Austria	Multilateral	11 Dec 46	Sanitation	12UNTS179	100186
Austria	Multilateral	06 Feb 47	IGO Establishment	97UNTS227	101352
Austria	Multilateral	03 Mar 47	Humanitarian	11UNTS43	100148
Austria	Multilateral	02 Oct 47	Telecommunications	193UNTS188	102616
Austria	Multilateral	11 Oct 47	IGO Establishment	77UNTS143	100998
Austria	Multilateral	04 Nov 47	Reparations	93UNTS61	101288
Austria	Multilateral	12 Nov 47	Admin Cooperation	53UNTS13	100770
Austria	Multilateral	12 Nov 47	Admin Cooperation	46UNTS201	100710
Austria	Multilateral	12 Nov 47	Admin Cooperation	53UNTS39	100771
Austria	Multilateral	12 Nov 47	Admin Cooperation	53UNTS49	100772
Austria	Multilateral	12 Nov 47	Admin Cooperation	46UNTS169	100709
Austria	Multilateral	10 May 48	Culture	289UNTS111	104215
Austria	Multilateral	26 Jun 48	Culture	331UNTS217	104757
Austria	Multilateral	24 Jul 48	Sanitation	66UNTS25	100847
Austria	Multilateral	18 Aug 48	Water Transport	33UNTS181	100518
Austria	Multilateral	09 Dec 48	Scientific Project	73UNTS39	100942
Austria	Multilateral	09 Dec 48	Scientific Project	20UNTS229	100318
Austria	Multilateral	09 Dec 48	Humanitarian	78UNTS277	101021
Austria	Multilateral	23 Mar 49	Commodity Trade	203UNTS179	102746
Austria	Multilateral	04 May 49	Admin Cooperation	98UNTS101	101358
Austria	Multilateral	04 May 49	Admin Cooperation	47UNTS159	100728
Austria	Multilateral	04 May 49	Admin Cooperation	92UNTS19	101257
Austria	Multilateral	04 May 49	Admin Cooperation	30UNTS3	100445
Austria	Multilateral	04 May 49	Admin Cooperation	30UNTS23	100446
Austria	Multilateral	05 May 49	IGO Establishment	87UNTS103	101168
Austria	Multilateral	16 Jun 49	Land Transport	45UNTS149	100696
Austria	Multilateral	12 Aug 49	General Military	75UNTS135	100972
Austria	Multilateral	12 Aug 49	Humanitarian	75UNTS31	100970
Austria	Multilateral	12 Aug 49	Humanitarian	75UNTS287	100973
Austria	Multilateral	12 Aug 49	Humanitarian	75UNTS85	100971
Austria	Multilateral	02 Sep 49	IGO Status/Immunit	250UNTS12	103515
Austria	Multilateral	19 Sep 49	Land Transport	125UNTS3	101671
Austria	Multilateral	16 Dec 49	Admin Cooperation	72UNTS3	100924
Austria	Multilateral	13 May 50	Land Transport	128UNTS171	101719
Austria	Multilateral	16 Sep 50	General Transport	92UNTS91	101264
Austria	Multilateral	18 Oct 50	Specific Resources	638UNTS185	109134
Austria	Multilateral	04 Nov 50	Humanitarian	213UNTS221	102889
Austria	Multilateral	22 Nov 50	Culture	131UNTS25	101734
Austria	Multilateral	07 Dec 50	Admin Cooperation	212UNTS17	102861
Austria	Multilateral	15 Dec 50	Customs	171UNTS305	102234
Austria	Multilateral	15 Dec 50	Customs	347UNTS127	104994
Austria	Multilateral	15 Dec 50	IGO Operations	160UNTS267	102111
Austria	Multilateral	15 Dec 50	Customs	157UNTS129	102052
Austria	Multilateral	25 May 51	Status of Forces	175UNTS215	102303
Austria	Multilateral	02 Jul 51	Refugees	189UNTS137	102545
Austria	Multilateral	09 Oct 51	IGO Establishment	220UNTS121	102997
Austria	Multilateral	06 Dec 51	Admin Cooperation	150UNTS67	101963
Austria	Multilateral	11 Jul 52	Postal Service	170UNTS269	102223
Austria	Multilateral	11 Jul 52	Postal Service	171UNTS89	102225
Austria	Multilateral	11 Jul 52	Postal Service	171UNTS143	102226
Austria	Multilateral	11 Jul 52	Postal Service	171UNTS3	102224
Austria	Multilateral	11 Jul 52	Postal Service	171UNTS191	102227
Austria	Multilateral	11 Jul 52	IGO Establishment	169UNTS3	102220
Austria	Multilateral	11 Jul 52	Postal Service	170UNTS63	102222
Austria	Multilateral	11 Jul 52	Postal Service	170UNTS3	102221
Austria	Multilateral	06 Sep 52	Patents/Copyrights	216UNTS132	102937
Austria	Multilateral	27 Feb 53	Claims and Debts	333UNTS3	104764
Austria	Multilateral	01 Jul 53	IGO Establishment	200UNTS149	102701
Austria	Multilateral	17 Oct 53	General Transport	184UNTS42	102438
Austria	Multilateral	19 Oct 53	IGO Establishment	207UNTS189	102807
Austria	Multilateral	07 Dec 53	Admin Cooperation	182UNTS51	102422
Austria	Multilateral	11 Dec 53	Sanitation	191UNTS285	102588
Austria	Multilateral	01 Mar 54	Commodity Trade	256UNTS31	103622
Austria	Multilateral	01 Mar 54	Admin Cooperation	286UNTS265	104173
Austria	Multilateral	14 May 54	Culture	249UNTS215	103511
Austria	Multilateral	04 Jun 54	Customs	276UNTS191	103992
Austria	Multilateral	04 Jun 54	Customs	282UNTS249	104101
Austria	Multilateral	14 Jun 54	Air Transport	320UNTS209	104643
Austria	Multilateral	14 Jun 54	Air Transport	320UNTS217	104644
Austria	Multilateral	19 Dec 54	Culture	218UNTS139	102955
Austria	Multilateral	01 May 55	Admin Cooperation	0UNTS0	110416
Austria	Multilateral	10 May 55	Claims and Debts	273UNTS121	103948
Austria	Multilateral	15 May 55	Recognition	217UNTS223	102949
Austria	Multilateral	25 May 55	IGO Establishment	264UNTS117	103791
Austria	Multilateral	21 Sep 55	Other Military	269UNTS241	103885
Austria	Multilateral	12 Oct 55	IGO Establishment	560UNTS3	108165
Austria	Multilateral	20 Oct 55	IGO Establishment	378UNTS159	105425
Austria	Multilateral	13 Dec 55	Humanitarian	250UNTS3	103514
Austria	Multilateral	13 Dec 55	IGO Operations	529UNTS141	107660
Austria	Multilateral	01 Mar 56	Customs	343UNTS129	104923
Austria	Multilateral	25 Apr 56	Commodity Trade	270UNTS103	103896
Austria	Multilateral	30 Apr 56	Air Transport	310UNTS229	104494
Austria	Multilateral	18 May 56	Land Transport	339UNTS3	104844
Austria	Multilateral	18 May 56	Customs	327UNTS123	104721
Austria	Multilateral	18 May 56	Customs	319UNTS21	104630
Austria	Multilateral	18 May 56	Customs	338UNTS103	104834
Austria	Multilateral	19 May 56	Land Transport	399UNTS189	105742
Austria	Multilateral	20 Jun 56	Admin Cooperation	268UNTS3	103850
Austria	Multilateral	24 Oct 56	Admin Cooperation	510UNTS161	107412
Austria	Multilateral	26 Oct 56	IGO Establishment	276UNTS3	103988
Austria	Multilateral	14 Dec 56	Taxation	436UNTS131	106293
Austria	Multilateral	14 Dec 56	Taxation	436UNTS115	106292
Austria	Multilateral	15 Dec 56	Education	278UNTS73	104023
Austria	Multilateral	20 Feb 57	Consul/Citizenship	309UNTS65	104468
Austria	Multilateral	29 Apr 57	Dispute Settlement	320UNTS243	104646
Austria	Multilateral	15 Jun 57	Patents/Copyrights	583UNTS3	108470
Austria	Multilateral	26 Jul 57	Land Transport	386UNTS3	105535
Austria	Multilateral	30 Sep 57	General Transport	619UNTS77	108940
Austria	Multilateral	03 Oct 57	Postal Service	364UNTS3	105211
Austria	Multilateral	03 Oct 57	Postal Service	366UNTS87	105216
Austria	Multilateral	03 Oct 57	Postal Service	366UNTS141	105217
Austria	Multilateral	03 Oct 57	Postal Service	366UNTS3	105215
Austria	Multilateral	03 Oct 57	Postal Service	365UNTS3	105213
Austria	Multilateral	03 Oct 57	Postal Service	365UNTS207	105214
Austria	Multilateral	03 Oct 57	Postal Service	366UNTS255	105219
Austria	Multilateral	03 Oct 57	Postal Service	364UNTS331	105212
Austria	Multilateral	13 Dec 57	Extradition	359UNTS273	105146
Austria	Multilateral	13 Dec 57	Visas	315UNTS139	104565
Austria	Multilateral	15 Apr 58	Health/Educ/Welfare	539UNTS27	107822
Austria	Multilateral	29 Apr 58	Territory Boundary	516UNTS205	107477
Austria	Multilateral	29 Apr 58	Water Transport	450UNTS11	106465
Austria	Multilateral	29 Apr 58	Dispute Settlement	450UNTS169	106466
Austria	Multilateral	15 Dec 58	Mass Media	546UNTS235	107950
Austria	Multilateral	15 Dec 58	Sanitation	351UNTS159	105022
Austria	Multilateral	15 Jan 59	Customs	348UNTS13	104996
Austria	Multilateral	06 Apr 59	Commodity Trade	349UNTS167	105013
Austria	Multilateral	20 Apr 59	Admin Cooperation	472UNTS185	106841
Austria	Multilateral	11 May 59	Claims and Debts	527UNTS145	107623
Austria	Multilateral	19 Nov 59	IGO Operations	410UNTS156	105902
Austria	Multilateral	14 Dec 59	Admin Cooperation	444UNTS193	106369
Austria	Multilateral	04 Jan 60	IGO Establishment	370UNTS3	105266
Austria	Multilateral	26 Jan 60	IGO Establishment	439UNTS249	106333
Austria	Multilateral	15 Mar 60	Water Transport	572UNTS133	108310
Austria	Multilateral	22 Apr 60	Air Transport	418UNTS211	106023
Austria	Multilateral	28 Apr 60	Health/Educ/Welfare	376UNTS111	105377
Austria	Multilateral	17 Jun 60	Humanitarian	536UNTS27	107794

PARTY ONE	PARTY TWO	DATE	TOPIC	CITATION	NUMBER
Austria	Multilateral	28 Jul 60	IGO Status/Immunit	394UNTS37	105667
Austria	Multilateral	01 Sep 60	Commodity Trade	403UNTS3	105792
Austria	Multilateral	06 Oct 60	Customs	473UNTS131	106861
Austria	Multilateral	01 Dec 60	Scientific Project	414UNTS110	105970
Austria	Multilateral	09 Dec 60	Customs	429UNTS211	106200
Austria	Multilateral	27 Mar 61	IGO Establishment	420UNTS109	106043
Austria	Multilateral	30 Mar 61	Sanitation	520UNTS151	107515
Austria	Multilateral	18 Apr 61	Dispute Settlement	500UNTS243	107312
Austria	Multilateral	18 Apr 61	Consul/Citizenship	500UNTS95	107310
Austria	Multilateral	21 Apr 61	IGO Establishment	484UNTS349	107041
Austria	Multilateral	08 Jun 61	Customs	473UNTS187	106863
Austria	Multilateral	08 Jun 61	Customs	473UNTS153	106862
Austria	Multilateral	21 Jun 61	IGO Establishment	514UNTS209	107449
Austria	Multilateral	05 Oct 61	Dispute Settlement	510UNTS175	107413
Austria	Multilateral	05 Oct 61	Patents/Copyrights	527UNTS181	107625
Austria	Multilateral	18 Oct 61	IGO Establishment	529UNTS89	107659
Austria	Multilateral	26 Oct 61	Patents/Copyrights	496UNTS43	107247
Austria	Multilateral	06 Dec 61	Customs	473UNTS219	106864
Austria	Multilateral	15 May 62	Commodity Trade	444UNTS3	106367
Austria	Multilateral	28 Sep 62	IGO Establishment	469UNTS169	106791
Austria	Multilateral	08 Dec 62	Finance	510UNTS235	107418
Austria	Multilateral	17 Dec 62	Admin Cooperation	590UNTS81	108548
Austria	Multilateral	17 Dec 62	Sanitation	486UNTS119	107076
Austria	Multilateral	17 Dec 62	General Economic	523UNTS93	107555
Austria	Multilateral	24 Apr 63	Consul/Citizenship	596UNTS487	108640
Austria	Multilateral	24 Apr 63	Consul/Citizenship	596UNTS261	108638
Austria	Multilateral	06 May 63	Consul/Citizenship	634UNTS221	109065
Austria	Multilateral	05 Aug 63	Sanitation	480UNTS43	106964
Austria	Multilateral	02 Sep 63	General Transport	548UNTS129	107974
Austria	Multilateral	09 Nov 63	Direct Aid	489UNTS209	107141
Austria	Multilateral	09 Mar 64	Specific Resources	581UNTS57	108432
Austria	Multilateral	10 Jul 64	Postal Service	612UNTS361	108849
Austria	Multilateral	10 Jul 64	Postal Service	612UNTS3	108847
Austria	Multilateral	10 Jul 64	Postal Service	611UNTS387	108846
Austria	Multilateral	10 Jul 64	Postal Service	613UNTS3	108850
Austria	Multilateral	10 Jul 64	Postal Service	613UNTS3	108851
Austria	Multilateral	10 Jul 64	Postal Service	613UNTS193	108852
Austria	Multilateral	10 Jul 64	Postal Service	611UNTS105	108845
Austria	Multilateral	10 Jul 64	Postal Service	611UNTS7	108844
Austria	Multilateral	10 Jul 64	Postal Service	612UNTS233	108848
Austria	Multilateral	28 Jul 64	IGO Operations	555UNTS183	108113
Austria	Multilateral	15 Feb 65	Refugees	546UNTS277	107952
Austria	Multilateral	15 Feb 65	Visas	547UNTS3	107953
Austria	Multilateral	18 Mar 65	Dispute Settlement	575UNTS159	108359
Austria	Multilateral	08 Jul 65	General Trade	597UNTS3	108641
Austria	Multilateral	04 Dec 65	IGO Establishment	571UNTS123	108303
Austria	Multilateral	31 Dec 65	Specific Resources	616UNTS317	108904
Austria	Multilateral	30 Apr 66	Specific Resources	620UNTS191	108956
Austria	Multilateral	27 Jan 67	Scientific Project	610UNTS205	108843
Austria	Multilateral	09 Mar 67	Other Military	603UNTS135	108730
Austria	Multilateral	29 Jun 67	Non-ILO Labor	0UNTS0	110030
Austria	Multilateral	01 Jul 68	Peace/Disarmament	0UNTS0	110485
Austria	Netherlands	22 Jan 48	Air Transport	17UNTS99	100270
Austria	Netherlands	22 Mar 51	General Transport	51NET59	447018
Austria	Netherlands	22 Mar 51	Finance	51NET60	447019
Austria	Netherlands	24 May 51	Visas	51NET88	447024
Austria	Netherlands	24 May 51	Visas	52ABGB26	403142
Austria	Netherlands	17 Nov 54	Non-ILO Labor	292UNTS45	104266
Austria	Netherlands	18 Feb 55	Finance	55NET95	447053
Austria	Netherlands	03 May 58	Admin Cooperation	342UNTS3	104895
Austria	Netherlands	30 May 58	Visas	458UNTS147	106598
Austria	Netherlands	19 Mar 59	Admin Cooperation	485UNTS117	107048
Austria	Netherlands	29 Apr 59	Finance	486UNTS373	107087
Austria	Netherlands	06 May 59	Land Transport	485UNTS175	107055
Austria	Netherlands	06 May 59	Land Transport	485UNTS153	107054

PARTY ONE	PARTY TWO	DATE	TOPIC	CITATION	NUMBER
Austria	Netherlands	30 Sep 59	Specific Property	507UNTS111	107397
Austria	Netherlands	16 Oct 59	Admin Cooperation	458UNTS173	106600
Austria	Netherlands	06 Feb 63	Admin Cooperation	570UNTS101	108290
Austria	Netherlands	23 Jul 64	Admin Cooperation	544UNTS265	107921
Austria	Netherlands	02 Feb 70	Land Transport	70ABGB86	403143
Austria	Netherlands	01 Sep 70	Taxation	71ABGB191	403144
Austria	New Zealand	10 Jun 52	Admin Cooperation	171UNTS263	102229
Austria	New Zealand	14 May 58	Visas	317UNTS117	104598
Austria	Norway	14 Apr 47	Finance	15UNTS211	100235
Austria	Norway	14 Apr 47	General Trade	31UNTS21	100466
Austria	Norway	27 Nov 48	General Trade	2NORT490	451221
Austria	Norway	28 Jan 49	General Trade	30UNTS145	100452
Austria	Norway	02 Dec 49	Air Transport	72UNTS230	100936
Austria	Norway	23 Apr 54	Visas	2NORT626	451222
Austria	Norway	18 Mar 55	Finance	2NORT650	451223
Austria	Norway	12 Dec 56	Patents/Copyrights	3NORT701	451224
Austria	Norway	07 Jul 58	Admin Cooperation	3NORT750	451225
Austria	Norway	25 Feb 60	Taxation	60ABGB205	403145
Austria	Norway	25 Feb 60	Taxation	376UNTS155	105380
Austria	Norway	24 May 63	Visas	3NORT888	451226
Austria	Norway	16 Dec 70	Taxation	71ABGB414	403146
Austria	Pakistan	24 Dec 56	General Trade	316UNTS83	104579
Austria	Pakistan	16 Aug 57	Visas	306UNTS3	104429
Austria	Pakistan	10 Jan 68	Other Military	636UNTS133	109100
Austria	Pakistan	06 Jul 70	Taxation	71ABGB297	403147
Austria	Pakistan	28 May 71	Air Transport	71ABGB296	403148
Austria	Paraguay	17 Jan 69	Visas	69ABGB92	403149
Austria	Peru	25 Jul 59	Visas	59ABGB242	403150
Austria	Petrol Export Org	24 Jun 65	IGO Operations	589UNTS135	108540
Austria	Poland	08 Feb 56	Air Transport	334UNTS221	104770
Austria	Poland	21 Jun 63	Air Transport	63ABGB294	403151
Austria	Poland	25 Oct 63	Land Transport	63PZUM67	458106
Austria	Poland	11 Dec 63	Admin Cooperation	63PZUM76	458108
Austria	Poland	05 Feb 68	Taxation	0UNTS0	109213
Austria	Poland	05 Feb 68	Taxation	68ABGB123	403152
Austria	Poland	09 Jun 70	General Amity	70ABGB278	403153
Austria	Poland	09 Sep 71	General Economic	71ABGB495	403154
Austria	Portugal	14 Dec 54	Visas	55ABGB175	403155
Austria	Portugal	29 Dec 70	Taxation	72ABGB85	403156
Austria	Romania	11 May 55	Water Transport	342UNTS119	104904
Austria	Romania	10 Jul 58	Air Transport	353UNTS155	105041
Austria	Romania	21 Jul 61	General Trade	421UNTS161	106057
Austria	Romania	03 Jul 63	Claims and Debts	588UNTS3	108516
Austria	Romania	27 May 64	Land Transport	588UNTS29	108517
Austria	Romania	18 Dec 64	Sanitation	65ABGB34	403157
Austria	Romania	17 Nov 65	Admin Cooperation	0UNTS0	109625
Austria	Romania	17 Nov 65	Visas	564UNTS185	108229
Austria	Romania	28 Apr 68	Customs	0UNTS0	109377
Austria	Romania	17 Dec 68	Visas	0UNTS0	109468
Austria	Romania	17 Dec 68	Visas	69ABGB39	403158
Austria	Romania	24 Sep 70	General Trade	70ABGB328	403159
Austria	Romania	02 Oct 70	Customs	70ABGB338	403160
Austria	San Marino	30 May 72	Visas	72ABGB259	403163
Austria	Singapore	13 Jan 69	Admin Cooperation	0UNTS0	110409
Austria	Singapore	13 Jan 69	Admin Cooperation	69ABGB435	403164
Austria	South Africa	11 Jun 57	Visas	272UNTS229	103941
Austria	South Africa	26 Sep 57	Postal Service	287UNTS3	104176
Austria	South Africa	31 Aug 62	Visas	443UNTS65	106359
Austria	South Africa	08 Nov 67	Other Military	636UNTS125	109099
Austria	South Africa	26 Mar 69	Air Transport	0UNTS0	110471
Austria	Spain	21 Mar 56	Finance	56SPBO2404	460040
Austria	Spain	21 Mar 56	General Trade	56SPBO2404	460039
Austria	Spain	09 Nov 56	Visas	56ABGB241	403165
Austria	Spain	28 Mar 57	General Trade	57SPBO2004	460041
Austria	Spain	10 Jun 59	Visas	59ABGB223	403166

PARTY ONE	PARTY TWO	DATE	TOPIC	CITATION	NUMBER
Austria	Spain	04 Aug 59	Culture	61ABGB256	403167
Austria	Spain	17 Jun 60	General Trade	390UNTS17	105600
Austria	Spain	19 Feb 62	Air Transport	0UNTS0	109238
Austria	Spain	19 Feb 62	Air Transport	62SPB02910	460042
Austria	Spain	02 May 62	Non-ILO Labor	62SPB0606	460043
Austria	Spain	15 Jul 64	Non-ILO Labor	589UNTS169	108541
Austria	Spain	14 Oct 64	Non-ILO Labor	66ABGB9	403168
Austria	Spain	24 Mar 66	Land Transport	590UNTS203	108555
Austria	Spain	20 Dec 66	Taxation	636UNTS197	109103
Austria	Spain	23 Oct 69	Non-ILO Labor	70ABGB358	403169
Austria	Spain	09 Feb 70	Culture	70ABGB87	403170
Austria	Spain	14 May 70	Non-ILO Labor	70ABGB358	403171
Austria	Spain	14 Mar 72	Admin Cooperation	72ABGB249	403172
Austria	Sweden	02 Dec 49	Air Transport	108UNTS3	101465
Austria	Sweden	02 Mar 50	General Trade	50SOFM59	461100
Austria	Sweden	31 Oct 50	Non-ILO Labor	197UNTS311	102645
Austria	Sweden	23 May 51	Finance	51SOFM251	461144
Austria	Sweden	23 May 51	General Trade	51SOFM243	461143
Austria	Sweden	29 May 51	General Amity	197UNTS431	102650
Austria	Sweden	19 Jul 51	Taxation	198UNTS9	102652
Austria	Sweden	01 Aug 51	Taxation	198UNTS13	102653
Austria	Sweden	29 Apr 52	General Trade	52SOFM235	461166
Austria	Sweden	01 Jun 53	General Trade	53SOFM699	461184
Austria	Sweden	09 Apr 54	Visas	55ABGB193	403173
Austria	Sweden	17 Oct 55	Taxation	262UNTS283	103756
Austria	Sweden	03 Nov 55	Non-ILO Labor	262UNTS289	103757
Austria	Sweden	14 Aug 56	Taxation	262UNTS355	103760
Austria	Sweden	10 Apr 57	Admin Cooperation	427UNTS343	106165
Austria	Sweden	18 Feb 58	Land Transport	427UNTS349	106166
Austria	Sweden	19 Feb 58	Land Transport	427UNTS211	106155
Austria	Sweden	18 Jun 58	Visas	59ABGB30	403174
Austria	Sweden	14 May 59	Taxation	428UNTS3	106167
Austria	Sweden	22 Feb 60	Taxation	60ABGB143	403175
Austria	Sweden	21 Nov 62	Taxation	63ABGB212	403176
Austria	Sweden	06 Apr 70	Taxation	70ABGB341	403177
Austria	Sweden	14 Mar 72	Taxation	72ABGB298	403178
Austria	Switzerland	30 Apr 47	Sanitation	48SWRO192	462104
Austria	Switzerland	30 Apr 47	Customs	48SWRO197	462073
Austria	Switzerland	30 Apr 47	Land Transport	48SWRO183	462068
Austria	Switzerland	30 Apr 47	Customs	48SWRO204	462011
Austria	Switzerland	19 Dec 49	Air Transport	254UNTS287	103597
Austria	Switzerland	30 May 50	Land Transport	50SWRO781	462069
Austria	Switzerland	15 Jul 50	Non-ILO Labor	51SWRO787	462093
Austria	Switzerland	15 Jul 50	Non-ILO Labor	51ABGB232	403179
Austria	Switzerland	14 Sep 50	Admin Cooperation	51SWRO639	462010
Austria	Switzerland	14 Sep 50	Visas	51SWRO642	462013
Austria	Switzerland	17 May 52	Admin Cooperation	52SWRO529	462030
Austria	Switzerland	12 Nov 53	Taxation	54SWRO1109	462043
Austria	Switzerland	09 Dec 53	Admin Cooperation	54ABGB164	403181
Austria	Switzerland	08 Apr 54	Taxation	54SWRO1125	462044
Austria	Switzerland	10 Apr 54	Specific Resources	55SWRO741	462035
Austria	Switzerland	13 Jul 54	Finance	55ABGB42	403184
Austria	Switzerland	15 Sep 54	General Economic	54SWRO1005	462122
Austria	Switzerland	05 Jan 55	Extradition	55SWRO61	462009
Austria	Switzerland	19 Mar 56	Non-ILO Labor	56SWRO663	462012
Austria	Switzerland	01 Jun 57	Visas	57ABGB159	403185
Austria	Switzerland	22 Jul 57	Land Transport	57ABGB268	403186
Austria	Switzerland	22 Jul 57	Land Transport	57SWRO906	462076
Austria	Switzerland	16 Dec 57	Claims and Debts	58SWRO239	462121
Austria	Switzerland	22 Oct 58	Land Transport	59SWRO329	462080
Austria	Switzerland	22 Dec 58	Land Transport	59ABGB123	403187
Austria	Switzerland	06 Apr 59	Taxation	59ABGB196	403182
Austria	Switzerland	16 Dec 60	Admin Cooperation	62SWRO270	462029
Austria	Switzerland	06 Apr 62	Admin Cooperation	62SWRO1659	462024
Austria	Switzerland	26 Apr 62	Admin Cooperation	62ABGB320	403189

PARTY ONE	PARTY TWO	DATE	TOPIC	CITATION	NUMBER
Austria	Switzerland	02 Sep 63	Visas	548UNTS91	107973
Austria	Switzerland	20 Feb 65	Non-ILO Labor	66ABGB41	403180
Austria	Switzerland	20 Feb 65	Non-ILO Labor	66ABGB41	403190
Austria	Switzerland	29 Dec 66	Taxation	67ABGB355	403183
Austria	Switzerland	23 Aug 67	Tech Assistance	67ABGB333	403191
Austria	Switzerland	24 Oct 67	Visas	68ABGB21	403192
Austria	Switzerland	15 Nov 67	Non-ILO Labor	69ABGB4	403193
Austria	Switzerland	15 Nov 67	Non-ILO Labor	0UNTS0	109434
Austria	Switzerland	29 Dec 67	Admin Cooperation	68ABGB84	403188
Austria	Switzerland	26 Aug 68	Admin Cooperation	0UNTS0	110354
Austria	Switzerland	01 Oct 68	Non-ILO Labor	69ABGB5	403194
Austria	Thailand	30 Sep 64	General Trade	527UNTS239	107628
Austria	Thailand	25 Apr 66	Admin Cooperation	66ABGB135	403195
Austria	Tunisia	28 Jun 65	Visas	65ABGB254	403197
Austria	Tunisia	28 Jun 65	Admin Cooperation	65ABGB255	403196
Austria	Tunisia	30 Dec 65	Tech Assistance	589UNTS119	108539
Austria	Tunisia	17 Oct 66	Air Transport	67ABGB251	403198
Austria	Turkey	08 Aug 49	Mostfavored Nation	49ABGB234	403199
Austria	Turkey	07 Apr 54	Visas	55ABGB194	403200
Austria	Turkey	09 Oct 54	General Aid	56TURG404	466100
Austria	Turkey	19 Oct 56	Visas	56TURG2710	466010
Austria	Turkey	06 Apr 57	Admin Cooperation	58TURG2602	466032
Austria	Turkey	30 Dec 63	Direct Aid	64TURG903	466101
Austria	Turkey	15 May 64	Non-ILO Labor	515UNTS109	107457
Austria	Turkey	12 Oct 66	Non-ILO Labor	69ABGB338	403201
Austria	Turkey	08 Feb 68	Customs	68ABGB280	403202
Austria	Turkey	07 Nov 69	Land Transport	70ABGB274	403203
Austria	UK Great Britain	23 Dec 46	General Aid	88UNTS93	101186
Austria	UK Great Britain	28 Apr 47	Reparations	93UNTS53	101287
Austria	UK Great Britain	26 Jan 50	Finance	97UNTS183	101350
Austria	UK Great Britain	31 Jan 51	Finance	88UNTS107	101187
Austria	UK Great Britain	28 Jun 51	Admin Cooperation	117UNTS99	101586
Austria	UK Great Britain	30 Jun 52	Reparations	138UNTS153	101867
Austria	UK Great Britain	12 Dec 52	Culture	172UNTS9	102237
Austria	UK Great Britain	31 May 54	Claims and Debts	54ABGB259	403213
Austria	UK Great Britain	09 Jul 54	Finance	201UNTS277	102720
Austria	UK Great Britain	14 Oct 54	Claims and Debts	204UNTS87	102751
Austria	UK Great Britain	15 May 55	Claims and Debts	344UNTS9	104940
Austria	UK Great Britain	09 Jul 56	Non-ILO Labor	310UNTS61	104487
Austria	UK Great Britain	20 Jul 56	Taxation	269UNTS147	103880
Austria	UK Great Britain	27 Oct 56	Air Transport	264UNTS67	103789
Austria	UK Great Britain	14 Mar 59	Claims and Debts	343UNTS263	104930
Austria	UK Great Britain	24 Jun 60	Consul/Citizenship	502UNTS79	107327
Austria	UK Great Britain	14 Jul 61	Admin Cooperation	453UNTS267	106530
Austria	UK Great Britain	09 Jan 63	Extradition	0UNTS0	110806
Austria	UK Great Britain	01 Mar 67	Air Transport	67ABGB119	403214
Austria	UK Great Britain	09 Mar 67	Other Military	67ABGB192	403216
Austria	UK Great Britain	03 Apr 68	Visas	0UNTS0	109214
Austria	UK Great Britain	15 Jan 69	Extradition	70ABGB169	403215
Austria	UK Great Britain	30 Apr 69	Taxation	70ABGB390	403250
Austria	UK Great Britain	29 May 69	Land Transport	70ABGB39	403218
Austria	UK Great Britain	09 Jun 69	Visas	69ABGB260	403217
Austria	UK Great Britain	27 May 70	Visas	70ABGB167	403219
Austria	UK Great Britain	12 Jul 71	Visas	71ABGB278	403220
Austria	UNESCO (Educ/Cult)	04 Nov 63	IGO Establishment	63ABGB337	403204
Austria	UNICEF (Children)	07 Nov 47	IGO Operations	68UNTS252	200237
Austria	United Arab Rep	16 Oct 62	Taxation	491UNTS63	107174
Austria	United Nations	27 Feb 61	IGO Status/Immunit	394UNTS27	105666
Austria	United Nations	29 Jan 63	Consul/Citizenship	452UNTS261	106513
Austria	United Nations	11 Jun 64	IGO Status/Immunit	500UNTS85	107309
Austria	United Nations	24 Feb 66	IGO Operations	557UNTS129	108131
Austria	United Nations	13 Apr 67	IGO Establishment	600UNTS93	108679
Austria	United Nations	12 Mar 68	IGO Operations	632UNTS131	109015
Austria	United Nations	25 May 68	IGO Operations	637UNTS0	109117
Austria	United Nations	25 May 68	IGO Operations	637UNTS0	109118

PARTY ONE	PARTY TWO	DATE	TOPIC	CITATION	NUMBER
Austria	United Nations	24 Sep 68	IGO Operations	68ABGB377	403249
Austria	United Nations	24 Sep 68	IGO Operations	0UNTS0	109253
Austria	United Nations	22 Sep 70	IGO Operations	70ABGB318	403252
Austria	United Nations	15 Dec 70	Non-ILO Labor	71ABGB424	403253
Austria	UNRRA (Relief)	05 Apr 46	Direct Aid	46ABGB116	403205
Austria	Uruguay	06 Jul 61	Visas	63ABGB223	403206
Austria	USA (United States)	21 Jun 47	Milit Occupation	67UNTS99	100869
Austria	USA (United States)	21 Jun 47	Reparations	67UNTS89	100868
Austria	USA (United States)	25 Jun 47	Direct Aid	22UNTS141	100334
Austria	USA (United States)	08 Oct 47	Air Transport	25UNTS3	100354
Austria	USA (United States)	02 Jan 48	Direct Aid	34UNTS141	100534
Austria	USA (United States)	02 Jul 48	Milit Occupation	25UNTS53	100357
Austria	USA (United States)	02 Jul 48	Direct Aid	21UNTS29	100323
Austria	USA (United States)	11 Feb 49	Direct Aid	79UNTS113	101035
Austria	USA (United States)	23 Mar 49	Admin Cooperation	43UNTS127	100667
Austria	USA (United States)	12 Jul 49	Visas	84UNTS291	101138
Austria	USA (United States)	06 Jun 50	Education	92UNTS201	101273
Austria	USA (United States)	15 May 51	Direct Aid	139UNTS79	101876
Austria	USA (United States)	05 Jan 52	Milit Assistance	179UNTS73	102355
Austria	USA (United States)	16 Feb 52	Direct Aid	177UNTS299	102329
Austria	USA (United States)	14 Jun 55	US Agri Commod Aid	258UNTS37	103668
Austria	USA (United States)	26 Sep 55	Specific Property	272UNTS31	103930
Austria	USA (United States)	07 Feb 56	US Agri Commod Aid	272UNTS117	103933
Austria	USA (United States)	08 Jun 56	Atomic Energy	253UNTS139	103581
Austria	USA (United States)	25 Oct 56	Taxation	299UNTS123	104310
Austria	USA (United States)	21 Nov 56	Claims and Debts	290UNTS181	104237
Austria	USA (United States)	10 May 57	Direct Aid	283UNTS33	104104
Austria	USA (United States)	10 May 57	US Agri Commod Aid	283UNTS15	104103
Austria	USA (United States)	09 Aug 57	Milit Assistance	288UNTS299	104211
Austria	USA (United States)	30 Jan 59	Claims and Debts	511UNTS145	107432
Austria	USA (United States)	30 Apr 59	Air Transport	343UNTS41	104920
Austria	USA (United States)	22 May 59	Reparations	347UNTS3	104988
Austria	USA (United States)	22 Jul 59	Atomic Energy	368UNTS199	105242
Austria	USA (United States)	15 Jun 60	Patents/Copyrights	376UNTS267	105383
Austria	USA (United States)	29 Mar 61	Direct Aid	459UNTS45	106612
Austria	USA (United States)	03 Oct 61	Direct Aid	426UNTS187	106137
Austria	USA (United States)	25 Jun 63	Education	479UNTS223	106956
Austria	USA (United States)	23 Jun 66	Air Transport	601UNTS51	108687
Austria	USA (United States)	04 Jul 67	Taxation	0UNTS0	109981
Austria	USA (United States)	21 Nov 67	Gen Communications	634UNTS43	109049
Austria	USA (United States)	11 Jul 69	Atomic Energy	0UNTS0	110431
Austria	USSR (Soviet Union)	29 Apr 45	Recognition	0SUST176	471015
Austria	USSR (Soviet Union)	24 Oct 45	Consul/Citizenship	0SUST200	468050
Austria	USSR (Soviet Union)	16 Jul 46	Claims and Debts	0SUST215	468049
Austria	USSR (Soviet Union)	17 Jul 53	Specif Goods/Equip	0SUST297	468051
Austria	USSR (Soviet Union)	30 Jul 53	Milit Occupation	0SUST298	468052
Austria	USSR (Soviet Union)	15 Apr 55	General Ad Hoc	0SUST325	468053
Austria	USSR (Soviet Union)	15 May 55	Recognition	0SUST328	468054
Austria	USSR (Soviet Union)	31 Aug 55	Specific Property	0SUST335	468055
Austria	USSR (Soviet Union)	17 Oct 55	General Economic	240UNTS289	103409
Austria	USSR (Soviet Union)	17 Oct 55	Finance	0UNTS0	109255
Austria	USSR (Soviet Union)	17 Oct 55	Non-IBRD Project	0UNTS0	109254
Austria	USSR (Soviet Union)	17 Oct 55	Finance	56ABGB86	403221
Austria	USSR (Soviet Union)	09 Nov 55	Air Transport	255UNTS247	103613
Austria	USSR (Soviet Union)	06 Dec 55	General Amity	0SUST444	468058
Austria	USSR (Soviet Union)	28 Dec 55	Postal Service	0SUST345	468059
Austria	USSR (Soviet Union)	27 Apr 57	General Amity	0SUST382	468060
Austria	USSR (Soviet Union)	14 Jun 57	Water Transport	285UNTS169	104152
Austria	USSR (Soviet Union)	28 Feb 59	Consul/Citizenship	356UNTS39	105091
Austria	USSR (Soviet Union)	06 Jun 59	Air Transport	8SUGG147	469581
Austria	USSR (Soviet Union)	13 Dec 60	General Trade	9SUGG154	469722
Austria	USSR (Soviet Union)	22 Mar 68	Culture	0UNTS0	110281
Austria	USSR (Soviet Union)	02 Jul 68	Air Transport	68ABGB295	403222
Austria	USSR (Soviet Union)	15 Jan 70	Air Transport	70ABGB109	403223
Austria	USSR (Soviet Union)	11 Mar 70	Admin Cooperation	72ABGB112	403224

PARTY ONE	PARTY TWO	DATE	TOPIC	CITATION	NUMBER
Austria	USSR (Soviet Union)	05 Aug 70	General Economic	70ABGB317	403225
Austria	Vatican/Holy See	23 Jun 60	Admin Cooperation	60ABGB196	403209
Austria	Vatican/Holy See	23 Jun 60	Claims and Debts	60ABGB195	403207
Austria	Vatican/Holy See	09 Jul 62	Education	62ABGB273	403210
Austria	Vatican/Holy See	07 Jul 64	Admin Cooperation	64ABGB227	403211
Austria	Vatican/Holy See	07 Oct 68	Admin Cooperation	68ABGB417	403212
Austria	Vatican/Holy See	29 Sep 69	Claims and Debts	70ABGB107	403208
Austria	WHO (World Health)	10 Jan 52	Tech Assistance	131UNTS295	200438
Austria	Yugoslavia	19 Mar 53	Visas	467UNTS293	106767
Austria	Yugoslavia	19 Mar 53	Visas	467UNTS323	106768
Austria	Yugoslavia	11 Nov 53	Air Transport	363UNTS149	105206
Austria	Yugoslavia	25 May 54	Specific Resources	227UNTS111	103135
Austria	Yugoslavia	02 Nov 54	Patents/Copyrights	55ABGB199	403229
Austria	Yugoslavia	10 Nov 54	Water Transport	56ABGB118	403230
Austria	Yugoslavia	27 Nov 54	Specific Resources	396UNTS75	105694
Austria	Yugoslavia	16 Dec 54	Territory Boundary	56ABGB119	403231
Austria	Yugoslavia	16 Dec 54	Admin Cooperation	55ABGB224	403232
Austria	Yugoslavia	18 Jan 55	Mass Media	378UNTS31	105416
Austria	Yugoslavia	15 Jun 56	Sanitation	396UNTS117	105695
Austria	Yugoslavia	19 Mar 58	Territory Boundary	58ABGB144	403233
Austria	Yugoslavia	14 Mar 59	Admin Cooperation	59ABGB163	403234
Austria	Yugoslavia	18 Mar 60	Consul/Citizenship	68ABGB378	403251
Austria	Yugoslavia	18 Mar 60	Admin Cooperation	61ABGB115	403235
Austria	Yugoslavia	18 Mar 60	Visas	60ABGB232	403226
Austria	Yugoslavia	18 Mar 60	Admin Cooperation	60ABGB265	403255
Austria	Yugoslavia	23 Mar 61	Land Transport	61ABGB223	403236
Austria	Yugoslavia	30 Jun 61	Admin Cooperation	443UNTS51	106358
Austria	Yugoslavia	10 Oct 61	Admin Cooperation	62ABGB310	403237
Austria	Yugoslavia	11 Dec 62	Land Transport	546UNTS3	107938
Austria	Yugoslavia	18 Jul 63	Visas	63ABGB244	403227
Austria	Yugoslavia	08 Apr 64	Territory Boundary	66ABGB229	403238
Austria	Yugoslavia	20 May 64	Extradition	514UNTS3	107439
Austria	Yugoslavia	27 Nov 64	Visas	64ABGB325	403228
Austria	Yugoslavia	28 Jun 65	Visas	66ABGB23	403240
Austria	Yugoslavia	28 Sep 65	Customs	66ABGB239	403239
Austria	Yugoslavia	19 Nov 65	Non-ILO Labor	591UNTS3	108556
Austria	Yugoslavia	19 Nov 65	Non-ILO Labor	587UNTS239	108512
Austria	Yugoslavia	17 Dec 65	Non-ILO Labor	66ABGB290	403241
Austria	Yugoslavia	20 Dec 65	Visas	573UNTS165	108329
Austria	Yugoslavia	10 Oct 66	Visas	595UNTS273	108622
Austria	Yugoslavia	08 Apr 67	Visas	0UNTS0	109216
Austria	Yugoslavia	26 Apr 67	Visas	67ABGB177	403243
Austria	Yugoslavia	26 Apr 67	Admin Cooperation	603UNTS143	108731
Austria	Yugoslavia	28 Apr 67	Visas	68ABGB173	403244
Austria	Yugoslavia	28 Jul 67	Visas	68ABGB379	403245
Austria	Yugoslavia	22 Apr 68	Customs	68ABGB400	403246
Austria	Yugoslavia	12 Jul 68	Visas	68ABGB345	403247
Austria	Yugoslavia	05 Mar 69	Visas	70ABGB82	403242
Austria	Yugoslavia	03 Apr 70	Visas	70ABGB141	403248
Bahamas	Multilateral	18 Oct 69	IGO Establishment	0UNTS0	110232
Bank Int Settlement	Germany, West	29 Nov 65	Claims and Debts	66WGBB209	425742
Bank Int Settlement	Multilateral	13 May 48	Reparations	140UNTS187	101888
Barbados	Denmark	27 Oct 69	Air Transport	0UNTS0	110394
Barbados	Germany, West	06 Nov 69	Visas	70WBGA8	424460
Barbados	Israel	18 Jun 69	Visas	0UNTS0	110387
Barbados	Multilateral	09 Mar 64	Specific Resources	581UNTS57	108432
Barbados	Multilateral	10 Jul 64	Postal Service	611UNTS105	108845
Barbados	Multilateral	10 Jul 64	Postal Service	611UNTS7	108844
Barbados	Multilateral	10 Jul 64	Postal Service	611UNTS387	108846
Barbados	Multilateral	10 Jul 64	Postal Service	612UNTS3	108847
Barbados	Multilateral	03 Mar 67	Tech Assistance	594UNTS96	108597
Barbados	Multilateral	22 Apr 68	Scientific Project	0UNTS0	109574
Barbados	Multilateral	24 Dec 68	Commodity Trade	0UNTS0	109369
Barbados	Multilateral	27 Jan 69	Telecommunications	0UNTS0	109664
Barbados	Multilateral	18 Oct 69	IGO Establishment	0UNTS0	110232

PARTY ONE	PARTY TWO	DATE	TOPIC	CITATION	NUMBER
Barbados	Multilateral	26 Sep 70	IGO Operations	0UNTS0	110768
Barbados	UK Great Britain	25 Sep 68	Finance	0UNTS0	109802
Barbados	UN Special Fund	03 Mar 67	Tech Assistance	594UNTS91	108596
Barbados	UNICEF (Children)	30 Mar 68	IGO Operations	637UNTS0	109123
Barbados	USA (United States)	11 Mar 68	Finance	0UNTS0	110007
Barbados	USA (United States)	09 Jul 68	Scientific Project	0UNTS0	110068
Barbados	USA (United States)	12 Sep 68	Gen Communications	0UNTS0	110075
Barbados	WHO (World Health)	18 Jul 67	Tech Assistance	603UNTS87	108726
Bel-Lux Econ Union	Bulgaria	14 Jun 66	General Economic	601UNTS167	108694
Bel-Lux Econ Union	Czechoslovakia	10 Oct 67	Tech Assistance	0UNTS0	109362
Bel-Lux Econ Union	Morocco	28 Apr 65	General Economic	620UNTS171	108954
Bel-Lux Econ Union	Multilateral	12 Feb 49	Customs	189UNTS33	102541
Bel-Lux Econ Union	Multilateral	16 Jun 49	Land Transport	45UNTS149	100696
Bel-Lux Econ Union	Multilateral	25 Apr 56	Commodity Trade	270UNTS103	103896
Bel-Lux Econ Union	Multilateral	18 Jun 58	Finance	386UNTS355	105553
Bel-Lux Econ Union	Multilateral	18 Jun 58	General Trade	386UNTS345	105552
Bel-Lux Econ Union	Multilateral	01 Dec 58	Commodity Trade	385UNTS137	105534
Bel-Lux Econ Union	Multilateral	08 Oct 60	General Trade	450UNTS309	106476
Bel-Lux Econ Union	Multilateral	30 Apr 63	General Trade	570UNTS23	108285
Bel-Lux Econ Union	Romania	16 Sep 68	Tech Assistance	0UNTS0	110212
Bel-Lux Econ Union	Romania	16 Sep 68	General Economic	0UNTS0	110042
Belgian Colonies	Multilateral	02 Oct 47	Telecommunications	193UNTS188	102616
Belgian Colonies	Multilateral	11 Jul 52	Postal Service	170UNTS3	102221
Belgian Colonies	Multilateral	11 Jul 52	IGO Establishment	169UNTS3	102220
Belgian Colonies	Multilateral	11 Jul 52	Postal Service	170UNTS63	102222
Belgian Colonies	Multilateral	04 Jun 54	Customs	282UNTS249	104101
Belgian Colonies	Multilateral	03 Oct 57	Postal Service	364UNTS3	105211
Belgian Colonies	Multilateral	03 Oct 57	Postal Service	365UNTS3	105213
Belgian Colonies	Multilateral	31 Dec 65	Specific Resources	616UNTS317	108904
Belgium	Algeria	27 Feb 68	Non-ILO Labor	0UNTS0	110110
Belgium	Algeria	08 Jan 70	Non-ILO Labor	0UNTS0	110314
Belgium	Algeria	08 Jan 70	Tech Assistance	0UNTS0	110313
Belgium	Argentina	25 Jul 49	Taxation	46UNTS103	100703
Belgium	Argentina	09 May 59	Visas	340UNTS53	104858
Belgium	Argentina	11 Jun 63	Milit Servic/Citiz	635UNTS135	109077
Belgium	Argentina	05 Nov 65	Culture	635UNTS229	109086
Belgium	Australia	09 Dec 48	Claims and Debts	25UNTS159	100361
Belgium	Australia	25 Jul 51	Visas	108UNTS303	101482
Belgium	Australia	26 Mar 54	General Trade	198UNTS305	102673
Belgium	Austria	05 Nov 49	Extradition	48UNTS107	100739
Belgium	Austria	22 Dec 49	Admin Cooperation	46UNTS233	100712
Belgium	Austria	16 Mar 51	Visas	88UNTS357	101203
Belgium	Austria	11 Oct 51	Visas	110UNTS45	101500
Belgium	Austria	17 Oct 52	Culture	162UNTS183	102135
Belgium	Austria	07 Jan 55	Air Transport	380UNTS219	105458
Belgium	Austria	20 Jan 56	Non-ILO Labor	248UNTS3	103481
Belgium	Austria	25 Oct 57	Admin Cooperation	372UNTS177.	105297
Belgium	Austria	20 Jun 58	Land Transport	312UNTS95	104513
Belgium	Austria	22 Apr 59	Extradition	356UNTS309	105102
Belgium	Austria	16 Jun 59	Admin Cooperation	419UNTS45	106029
Belgium	Austria	14 Nov 63	Specific Property	544UNTS97	107912
Belgium	Austria	20 Jan 64	Land Transport	509UNTS275	107406
Belgium	Austria	11 Jun 64	Taxation	521UNTS157	107518
Belgium	Austria	10 Feb 70	Land Transport	70ABGB70	403005
Belgium	Austria	10 Feb 70	Land Transport	0UNTS0	110539
Belgium	Bolivia	26 Apr 49	Finance	34UNTS103	100530
Belgium	Bolivia	30 Sep 61	Visas	425UNTS53	106118
Belgium	Brazil	14 Jun 41	Extradition	272UNTS157	103936
Belgium	Brazil	08 May 51	Consul/Citizenship	91UNTS75	101242
Belgium	Brazil	11 Aug 51	Consul/Citizenship	104UNTS17	101431
Belgium	Brazil	10 Jan 55	Admin Cooperation	272UNTS181	103937
Belgium	Brazil	27 Feb 57	Visas	265UNTS189	103812
Belgium	Brazil	06 Jan 60	Culture	531UNTS149	107701
Belgium	Bulgaria	14 May 57	Air Transport	317UNTS81	104596
Belgium	Bulgaria	14 Jun 66	Other HEW	607UNTS183	108806

PARTY ONE	PARTY TWO	DATE	TOPIC	CITATION	NUMBER
Belgium	Bulgaria	17 May 67	Culture	631UNTS215	108995
Belgium	Bulgaria	31 Jul 69	Land Transport	0UNTS0	109870
Belgium	Burma	17 Aug 60	Air Transport	540UNTS185	107850
Belgium	Canada	25 Oct 45	Finance	230UNTS127	103180
Belgium	Canada	13 Jul 46	Reparations	230UNTS159	103181
Belgium	Canada	30 Aug 49	Air Transport	53UNTS221	100782
Belgium	Canada	16 Nov 49	Reparations	51UNTS3	100748
Belgium	Canada	19 Nov 49	Visas	150UNTS231	101977
Belgium	Canada	30 Mar 53	Status of Forces	181UNTS95	102401
Belgium	Canada	08 May 67	Culture	637UNTS0	109119
Belgium	Chile	11 Feb 47	Patents/Copyrights	76UNTS107	100983
Belgium	Chile	23 Aug 49	General Economic	46UNTS163	100708
Belgium	Chile	09 Oct 56	Visas	257UNTS227	103658
Belgium	Chile	07 Apr 61	Visas	410UNTS255	105909
Belgium	Colombia	24 May 57	Visas	274UNTS245	103969
Belgium	Colombia	27 Aug 62	Visas	449UNTS199	106461
Belgium	Congo (Zaire)	15 Nov 60	Finance	394UNTS79	105670
Belgium	Congo (Zaire)	06 Feb 65	Finance	540UNTS275	107853
Belgium	Congo (Zaire)	06 Feb 65	Claims and Debts	540UNTS227	107852
Belgium	Cuba	16 Dec 53	Visas	185UNTS285	102475
Belgium	Cyprus	08 Jun 63	Air Transport	601UNTS311	108703
Belgium	Czechoslovakia	16 May 45	Refugees	19UNTS251	200119
Belgium	Czechoslovakia	06 Mar 47	Culture	34UNTS77	100528
Belgium	Czechoslovakia	19 Mar 47	Claims and Debts	23UNTS35	100341
Belgium	Czechoslovakia	03 Jul 48	General Trade	77UNTS137	100997
Belgium	Czechoslovakia	14 Nov 49	Visas	46UNTS319	100718
Belgium	Czechoslovakia	02 May 51	Taxation	109UNTS3	101483
Belgium	Czechoslovakia	08 Aug 56	Visas	257UNTS215	103656
Belgium	Czechoslovakia	12 Mar 57	Air Transport	312UNTS75	104512
Belgium	Czechoslovakia	17 Apr 68	Land Transport	0UNTS0	109539
Belgium	Denmark	08 Apr 46	Claims and Debts	4UNTS429	100059
Belgium	Denmark	28 Jan 47	Visas	18UNTS221	100291
Belgium	Denmark	30 Dec 48	Dispute Settlement	25UNTS173	100362
Belgium	Denmark	31 May 49	Visas	32UNTS337	100506
Belgium	Denmark	13 Dec 49	Admin Cooperation	173UNTS193	102266
Belgium	Denmark	31 Dec 57	Culture	305UNTS247	104422
Belgium	Denmark	23 Oct 61	Taxation	425UNTS181	106123
Belgium	Denmark	20 Sep 65	Taxation	549UNTS63	107990
Belgium	Denmark	04 Feb 66	Land Transport	561UNTS233	108187
Belgium	Denmark	29 Jun 67	Specific Resources	606UNTS113	108780
Belgium	Ecuador	20 Mar 58	Visas	304UNTS207	104397
Belgium	Ecuador	10 Jan 63	Visas	457UNTS153	106585
Belgium	Eur Space Vehicle	29 Sep 69	IGO Operations	0UNTS0	110203
Belgium	Fed of Malaya	19 Jul 60	Visas	379UNTS391	105445
Belgium	Finland	09 Feb 50	Visas	51UNTS77	100753
Belgium	Finland	20 Mar 51	Non-ILO Labor	110UNTS27	101498
Belgium	Finland	11 Feb 54	Taxation	211UNTS63	102848
Belgium	Finland	15 Nov 68	Land Transport	0UNTS0	109673
Belgium	France	30 Mar 45	Water Transport	20UNTS297	200122
Belgium	France	30 Mar 45	Visas	21UNTS325	200132
Belgium	France	21 May 45	Visas	23UNTS215	200133
Belgium	France	30 Oct 45	Reparations	19UNTS87	100306
Belgium	France	22 Feb 46	Culture	68UNTS157	100892
Belgium	France	17 Apr 46	Land Transport	49FRJO1509	416276
Belgium	France	09 Jan 47	Admin Cooperation	36UNTS145	100568
Belgium	France	17 Jan 48	Non-ILO Labor	36UNTS233	100570
Belgium	France	13 Apr 48	Territory Boundary	31UNTS409	100483
Belgium	France	23 Apr 48	Territory Boundary	19UNTS95	100307
Belgium	France	28 Oct 48	Visas	25UNTS151	100360
Belgium	France	08 Jan 49	Non-ILO Labor	36UNTS151	100569
Belgium	France	18 Feb 49	Claims and Debts	31UNTS173	100478
Belgium	France	12 Apr 49	Visas	30UNTS45	100447
Belgium	France	29 Aug 49	Milit Servic/Citiz	93UNTS87	101293
Belgium	France	07 Sep 49	Loans and Credits	123UNTS13	101651
Belgium	France	30 Dec 49	Taxation	46UNTS111	100704

PARTY ONE	PARTY TWO	DATE	TOPIC	CITATION	NUMBER
Belgium	France	14 Mar 50	Visas	65UNTS139	100842
Belgium	France	26 Sep 50	Visas	79UNTS3	101026
Belgium	France	21 Mar 52	Land Transport	137UNTS249	101856
Belgium	France	30 Jun 52	General Transport	137UNTS259	101857
Belgium	France	29 Nov 52	Visas	160UNTS261	102110
Belgium	France	30 Jan 53	Visas	188UNTS141	102525
Belgium	France	27 Feb 53	Non-ILO Labor	164UNTS49	102158
Belgium	France	11 Mar 53	Reparations	191UNTS329	102590
Belgium	France	07 Jun 54	Admin Cooperation	69FRJO2006	416061
Belgium	France	09 Jun 54	Visas	0UNTS0	110703
Belgium	France	15 Oct 54	Admin Cooperation	218UNTS19	102951
Belgium	France	12 Nov 54	Reparations	306UNTS85	104434
Belgium	France	10 Dec 55	Taxation	231UNTS101	103211
Belgium	France	01 Mar 56	Admin Cooperation	337UNTS53	104815
Belgium	France	18 Jul 56	Non-ILO Labor	248UNTS121	103491
Belgium	France	15 Feb 57	Refugees	267UNTS3	103834
Belgium	France	06 Sep 57	Specific Resources	59FRRT39	415062
Belgium	France	20 Sep 57	Postal Service	57FRJO1910	416063
Belgium	France	12 Nov 57	Non-ILO Labor	328UNTS167	104734
Belgium	France	31 May 58	Patents/Copyrights	60FRRT20	415064
Belgium	France	03 Sep 58	Health/Educ/Welfare	58FRJO1910	416065
Belgium	France	20 Sep 58	Reparations	376UNTS331	105387
Belgium	France	20 Jan 59	Taxation	361UNTS155	105178
Belgium	France	07 Jul 61	Taxation	406UNTS157	105846
Belgium	France	30 Mar 62	Visas	502UNTS297	107335
Belgium	France	20 Sep 62	Culture	65FRRT34	415066
Belgium	France	12 Oct 62	Milit Servic/Citiz	64FRRT61	415067
Belgium	France	10 Mar 64	Taxation	557UNTS13	108127
Belgium	France	24 Mar 64	Non-ILO Labor	64FRJO51	416068
Belgium	France	23 Sep 66	Atomic Energy	588UNTS227	108528
Belgium	France	31 May 67	Admin Cooperation	67FRJO408	416069
Belgium	France	17 Oct 67	Culture	68FRJO1008	416070
Belgium	France	19 Dec 67	Admin Cooperation	68FRJO2801	416071
Belgium	France	20 Sep 68	Admin Cooperation	68FRJO2211	416072
Belgium	France	02 Dec 68	Admin Cooperation	69FRJO2006	416073
Belgium	France	06 Jun 69	Admin Cooperation	69FRJO2009	416074
Belgium	Germany, West	18 Jan 52	Visas	243UNTS3	103443
Belgium	Germany, West	18 Jan 52	Education	124UNTS9	101663
Belgium	Germany, West	01 Feb 52	Land Transport	52WGBB437	425019
Belgium	Germany, West	01 Apr 52	Visas	132UNTS45	101750
Belgium	Germany, West	14 Aug 52	Admin Cooperation	139UNTS29	101873
Belgium	Germany, West	14 Nov 52	Visas	160UNTS217	102108
Belgium	Germany, West	06 Dec 52	Visas	152UNTS11	102007
Belgium	Germany, West	23 Dec 52	Claims and Debts	186UNTS69	102483
Belgium	Germany, West	20 Mar 53	Customs	53WGBB534	425020
Belgium	Germany, West	20 May 53	Admin Cooperation	180UNTS3	102370
Belgium	Germany, West	19 Dec 53	Visas	185UNTS277	102474
Belgium	Germany, West	03 Mar 54	Admin Cooperation	188UNTS259	102529
Belgium	Germany, West	30 Mar 54	Admin Cooperation	190UNTS63	102558
Belgium	Germany, West	01 Apr 54	Admin Cooperation	190UNTS43	102556
Belgium	Germany, West	03 Apr 54	Admin Cooperation	190UNTS247	102568
Belgium	Germany, West	15 Apr 54	Admin Cooperation	190UNTS253	102569
Belgium	Germany, West	28 May 54	Other Military	54WBGA128	424021
Belgium	Germany, West	28 May 54	Non-ILO Labor	249UNTS387	103512
Belgium	Germany, West	03 Nov 54	Admin Cooperation	201UNTS359	102724
Belgium	Germany, West	23 Nov 54	Admin Cooperation	202UNTS109	102726
Belgium	Germany, West	14 Apr 56	Air Transport	344UNTS103	104945
Belgium	Germany, West	15 May 56	Visas	58WGBB190	425022
Belgium	Germany, West	26 Jul 56	Visas	249UNTS187	103508
Belgium	Germany, West	24 Sep 56	Territory Boundary	314UNTS195	104549
Belgium	Germany, West	24 Sep 56	Culture	263UNTS31	103766
Belgium	Germany, West	09 Jul 57	General Military	59WGBB409	425023
Belgium	Germany, West	07 Dec 57	Non-ILO Labor	64WGBB170	425025
Belgium	Germany, West	07 Dec 57	Non-ILO Labor	63WGBB404	425024
Belgium	Germany, West	17 Jan 58	Extradition	328UNTS173	104735

PARTY ONE	PARTY TWO	DATE	TOPIC	CITATION	NUMBER
Belgium	Germany, West	30 Jun 58	Admin Cooperation	387UNTS245	105566
Belgium	Germany, West	25 Apr 59	Admin Cooperation	59WGBB1524	425026
Belgium	Germany, West	03 Aug 59	Admin Cooperation	61WGBB1183	425027
Belgium	Germany, West	01 Jun 60	Admin Cooperation	60WBGA150	424028
Belgium	Germany, West	28 Sep 60	Specif Claim/Waive	61WGBB2640	425029
Belgium	Germany, West	12 Jul 62	Non-ILO Labor	63WBGA48	424030
Belgium	Germany, West	21 Sep 62	Reparations	502UNTS63	107326
Belgium	Germany, West	01 Feb 63	General Military	63WBGA171	424031
Belgium	Germany, West	30 Dec 63	Admin Cooperation	64WBGA78	424032
Belgium	Germany, West	27 Jul 64	Commodity Trade	67WBGA236	424033
Belgium	Germany, West	06 Oct 64	Non-ILO Labor	65WBGA157	424034
Belgium	Germany, West	17 Dec 64	Land Transport	631UNTS229	108996
Belgium	Germany, West	17 Dec 64	Taxation	66WGBB1508	425035
Belgium	Germany, West	20 Jul 65	Non-ILO Labor	67WGBB813	425036
Belgium	Germany, West	11 Apr 67	Taxation	69WGBB17	425037
Belgium	Germany, West	11 Apr 67	Taxation	0UNTS0	110109
Belgium	Germany, West	14 Apr 67	Admin Cooperation	67WGBB2545	425038
Belgium	Germany, West	29 Jan 69	Non-ILO Labor	71WGBB857	425039
Belgium	Germany, West	07 Mar 69	Admin Cooperation	69WGBB1147	425040
Belgium	Germany, West	24 Dec 69	Specific Resources	70WGBB1205	425041
Belgium	Germany, West	04 May 70	General Military	70WBGA85	424042
Belgium	Greece	27 Dec 48	General Trade	77UNTS265	101004
Belgium	Greece	27 Dec 48	Finance	77UNTS293	101005
Belgium	Greece	21 Jun 49	Air Transport	137UNTS215	101854
Belgium	Greece	24 Apr 52	Finance	166UNTS261	102191
Belgium	Greece	05 Aug 53	Visas	173UNTS53	102260
Belgium	Greece	23 Jun 54	Taxation	199UNTS43	102676
Belgium	Greece	09 Dec 54	Culture	257UNTS243	103660
Belgium	Greece	16 Dec 54	Claims and Debts	223UNTS73	103056
Belgium	Greece	01 Apr 58	Non-ILO Labor	388UNTS93	105574
Belgium	Greece	24 May 68	Taxation	0UNTS0	110552
Belgium	Greece	16 Jul 69	General Transport	0UNTS0	109869
Belgium	Hungary	01 Jun 57	Air Transport	291UNTS17	104242
Belgium	Hungary	11 Feb 65	Culture	544UNTS3	107908
Belgium	Hungary	20 Mar 67	Land Transport	601UNTS37	108686
Belgium	IBRD (World Bank)	01 Mar 49	IBRD Project	154UNTS133	102029
Belgium	IBRD (World Bank)	13 Sep 51	IBRD Project	158UNTS349	102071
Belgium	IBRD (World Bank)	13 Sep 51	IBRD Project	158UNTS323	102070
Belgium	IBRD (World Bank)	14 Dec 54	IBRD Project	210UNTS113	102837
Belgium	IBRD (World Bank)	26 Jun 57	IBRD Project	322UNTS301	104661
Belgium	IBRD (World Bank)	10 Sep 57	IBRD Project	286UNTS291	104174
Belgium	IBRD (World Bank)	27 Nov 57	IBRD Project	292UNTS175	104273
Belgium	IBRD (World Bank)	30 Mar 60	IBRD Project	379UNTS161	105439
Belgium	IBRD (World Bank)	30 Mar 60	IBRD Project	379UNTS129	105438
Belgium	IBRD (World Bank)	30 Mar 60	IBRD Project	379UNTS103	105437
Belgium	Iceland	10 Dec 52	Patents/Copyrights	158UNTS445	102078
Belgium	Iceland	09 Jul 70	Taxation	0UNTS0	110607
Belgium	ICJ Option Clause	10 Jun 48	ICJ Option Clause	16UNTS203	100260
Belgium	ICJ Option Clause	03 Apr 58	ICJ Option Clause	302UNTS251	104364
Belgium	India	04 Aug 47	Reparations	76UNTS23	100976
Belgium	India	16 Jul 62	Admin Cooperation	453UNTS259	106529
Belgium	India	26 Mar 70	Scientific Project	0UNTS0	110551
Belgium	Iran	14 Apr 58	Air Transport	381UNTS309	105473
Belgium	Iran	14 May 60	Culture	522UNTS249	107551
Belgium	Iran	19 Nov 64	Visas	0IRTB14	433022
Belgium	Iran	01 Sep 65	Taxation	0IRTB14	433021
Belgium	Iran	12 Mar 70	Health/Educ/Welfare	0IRTB14	433023
Belgium	Iraq	05 Jul 50	Claims and Debts	68UNTS165	100893
Belgium	Ireland	25 Mar 47	Visas	18UNTS227	100292
Belgium	Ireland	16 Apr 48	Visas	26UNTS159	100386
Belgium	Ireland	30 Jun 54	Air Transport	212UNTS255	102876
Belgium	Ireland	10 Sep 55	Air Transport	255UNTS235	103612
Belgium	Ireland	23 Sep 60	Commodity Trade	557UNTS180	108134
Belgium	Ireland	04 Dec 67	Taxation	0UNTS0	110594
Belgium	Israel	30 Jun 52	Air Transport	183UNTS263	102435

PARTY ONE	PARTY TWO	DATE	TOPIC	CITATION	NUMBER
Belgium	Israel	29 May 53	Admin Cooperation	219UNTS197	102975
Belgium	Israel	08 Feb 54	Extradition	188UNTS251	102528
Belgium	Israel	22 Jun 54	Visas	196UNTS245	102627
Belgium	Israel	14 Dec 54	Admin Cooperation	220UNTS49	102987
Belgium	Israel	15 Apr 55	Visas	211UNTS43	102845
Belgium	Israel	26 Mar 56	Extradition	260UNTS3	103702
Belgium	Israel	26 Apr 66	Admin Cooperation	566UNTS187	108243
Belgium	Israel	23 Mar 67	Culture	630UNTS275	108974
Belgium	Israel	25 Sep 68	Consul/Citizenship	0UNTS0	109359
Belgium	Italy	23 Jun 46	Non-ILO Labor	19UNTS65	100305
Belgium	Italy	09 Feb 48	Non-ILO Labor	71UNTS143	100915
Belgium	Italy	30 Apr 48	Non-ILO Labor	36UNTS305	100571
Belgium	Italy	29 Nov 48	Culture	41UNTS3	100641
Belgium	Italy	01 Jan 49	Visas	26UNTS151	100385
Belgium	Italy	30 Dec 49	Visas	51UNTS83	100754
Belgium	Italy	20 Oct 50	Non-ILO Labor	50ITGU296	435041
Belgium	Italy	24 Oct 50	Admin Cooperation	110UNTS39	101499
Belgium	Italy	19 Jan 51	Non-ILO Labor	51ITGU46	435043
Belgium	Italy	19 Jan 51	Non-ILO Labor	51ITGU45	435042
Belgium	Italy	24 Jan 52	Peace/Disarmament	53ITGU51	435046
Belgium	Italy	10 May 52	Non-ILO Labor	54ITGU244	435044
Belgium	Italy	25 Jun 52	Visas	137UNTS239	101855
Belgium	Italy	01 Aug 52	Non-ILO Labor	54ITGU185	435045
Belgium	Italy	22 Sep 52	Customs	157UNTS121	102051
Belgium	Italy	06 Aug 53	Non-ILO Labor	54ITGU123	435047
Belgium	Italy	12 Jul 54	Finance	288UNTS59	104198
Belgium	Italy	09 Dec 57	Non-ILO Labor	58ITGU9	435048
Belgium	Italy	10 Dec 57	Non-ILO Labor	58ITGU19	435049
Belgium	Italy	11 Dec 57	Health/Educ/Welfare	59ITDI245	436050
Belgium	Italy	28 Oct 61	Culture	429UNTS199	106199
Belgium	Italy	06 Apr 62	Admin Cooperation	490UNTS317	107161
Belgium	Italy	21 Feb 64	Health/Educ/Welfare	65ITDI119	436051
Belgium	Italy	23 Apr 65	Privil/Immunities	66ITGU165	435052
Belgium	Ivory Coast	12 Feb 62	Visas	429UNTS193	106198
Belgium	Japan	29 Aug 50	General Trade	76UNTS113	100984
Belgium	Japan	29 Aug 50	General Trade	82UNTS147	101089
Belgium	Japan	11 Jul 56	Visas	248UNTS129	103492
Belgium	Japan	18 Mar 58	Admin Cooperation	303UNTS149	104378
Belgium	Japan	30 Apr 58	Finance	303UNTS109	104373
Belgium	Japan	20 Jun 59	Air Transport	411UNTS3	105911
Belgium	Japan	28 Mar 68	Taxation	0UNTS0	110513
Belgium	Japan	28 Mar 68	Taxation	70JHZ4	439021
Belgium	Jordan	19 Oct 60	Air Transport	479UNTS277	106959
Belgium	Lebanon	24 Dec 53	Extradition	539UNTS321	107842
Belgium	Lebanon	24 Dec 53	Air Transport	219UNTS153	102972
Belgium	Luxembourg	28 Apr 45	Visas	41UNTS265	200181
Belgium	Luxembourg	14 May 45	Refugees	19UNTS243	200118
Belgium	Luxembourg	25 Mar 48	Taxation	18UNTS323	100300
Belgium	Luxembourg	27 Mar 48	Culture	178UNTS265	102343
Belgium	Luxembourg	24 Aug 48	Extradition	117UNTS131	101589
Belgium	Luxembourg	09 Oct 48	Taxation	123UNTS29	101652
Belgium	Luxembourg	14 Jan 49	Direct Aid	36UNTS339	100572
Belgium	Luxembourg	25 Feb 49	Admin Cooperation	47UNTS3	100719
Belgium	Luxembourg	07 Jun 49	Postal Service	34UNTS117	100531
Belgium	Luxembourg	15 Jul 49	Visas	41UNTS13	100642
Belgium	Luxembourg	03 Dec 49	Non-ILO Labor	91UNTS31	101241
Belgium	Luxembourg	06 Apr 50	Visas	65UNTS147	100843
Belgium	Luxembourg	12 Sep 50	Customs	110UNTS21	101497
Belgium	Luxembourg	07 Feb 52	Taxation	147UNTS3	101924
Belgium	Luxembourg	26 Sep 52	Reparations	141UNTS111	101910
Belgium	Luxembourg	04 Apr 55	Refugees	211UNTS57	102847
Belgium	Luxembourg	28 Mar 58	General Trade	303UNTS101	104372
Belgium	Luxembourg	29 Nov 61	Visas	486UNTS37	107071
Belgium	Luxembourg	30 Aug 62	Taxation	485UNTS313	107062
Belgium	Luxembourg	29 Jan 63	Direct Aid	0UNTS0	110432

PARTY ONE	PARTY TWO	DATE	TOPIC	CITATION	NUMBER
Belgium	Luxembourg	29 Jan 63	IGO Establishment	547UNTS39	107955
Belgium	Luxembourg	14 Jan 65	Claims and Debts	620UNTS3	108949
Belgium	Luxembourg	11 Mar 65	Taxation	540UNTS297	107854
Belgium	Luxembourg	30 Sep 65	Consul/Citizenship	590UNTS35	108545
Belgium	Luxembourg	22 Feb 67	Culture	639UNTS3	109140
Belgium	Luxembourg	07 Feb 68	Finance	0UNTS0	110811
Belgium	Mexico	16 Sep 50	General Trade	188UNTS119	102523
Belgium	Mexico	18 Mar 58	Visas	301UNTS291	104348
Belgium	Mexico	19 Nov 64	Culture	546UNTS217	107949
Belgium	Monaco	05 Jun 48	Admin Cooperation	18UNTS245	100294
Belgium	Monaco	06 Feb 50	Visas	51UNTS93	100755
Belgium	Morocco	20 Jan 58	Air Transport	288UNTS3	104192
Belgium	Morocco	12 Apr 58	Visas	303UNTS141	104377
Belgium	Morocco	27 Feb 59	Extradition	390UNTS275	105611
Belgium	Multilateral	12 May 40	Scientific Project	101UNTS91	101405
Belgium	Multilateral	27 Mar 41	Military Mission	67UNTS231	200222
Belgium	Multilateral	21 Oct 43	Finance	2UNTS281	200021
Belgium	Multilateral	19 Apr 44	Scientific Project	89UNTS279	200257
Belgium	Multilateral	02 Aug 44	Scientific Project	67UNTS221	200221
Belgium	Multilateral	07 Dec 44	Air Transport	171UNTS345	200501
Belgium	Multilateral	07 Dec 44	IGO Establishment	15UNTS295	200102
Belgium	Multilateral	07 Dec 44	Air Transport	84UNTS389	200252
Belgium	Multilateral	15 Dec 44	Sanitation	16UNTS247	200106
Belgium	Multilateral	15 Dec 44	Sanitation	17UNTS305	200110
Belgium	Multilateral	20 Mar 45	General Economic	2UNTS299	200022
Belgium	Multilateral	08 Aug 45	General Military	82UNTS279	200251
Belgium	Multilateral	27 Sep 45	IGO Establishment	5UNTS327	200035
Belgium	Multilateral	16 Nov 45	IGO Establishment	4UNTS275	100052
Belgium	Multilateral	04 Jan 46	IGO Establishment	6UNTS35	100066
Belgium	Multilateral	14 Jan 46	Reparations	555UNTS69	108105
Belgium	Multilateral	05 Apr 46	Specific Resources	231UNTS199	103221
Belgium	Multilateral	17 Apr 46	Land Transport	27UNTS103	100402
Belgium	Multilateral	23 Apr 46	Sanitation	17UNTS3	100265
Belgium	Multilateral	23 Apr 46	Sanitation	16UNTS179	100257
Belgium	Multilateral	22 Jul 46	IGO Establishment	9UNTS3	100125
Belgium	Multilateral	22 Jul 46	IGO Establishment	14UNTS185	100221
Belgium	Multilateral	27 Jul 46	Patents/Copyrights	90UNTS229	101238
Belgium	Multilateral	15 Oct 46	Refugees	11UNTS73	100150
Belgium	Multilateral	30 Oct 46	IGO Establishment	11UNTS107	100151
Belgium	Multilateral	11 Dec 46	Sanitation	12UNTS179	100186
Belgium	Multilateral	15 Dec 46	IGO Establishment	18UNTS3	100283
Belgium	Multilateral	08 Feb 47	Patents/Copyrights	14UNTS287	100222
Belgium	Multilateral	10 Feb 47	Peace/Disarmament	49UNTS3	100747
Belgium	Multilateral	06 Jun 47	Patents/Copyrights	46UNTS249	100714
Belgium	Multilateral	10 Jun 47	Water Transport	208UNTS3	102814
Belgium	Multilateral	02 Oct 47	Telecommunications	193UNTS188	102616
Belgium	Multilateral	11 Oct 47	IGO Establishment	77UNTS143	100998
Belgium	Multilateral	12 Nov 47	Admin Cooperation	53UNTS49	100772
Belgium	Multilateral	12 Nov 47	Admin Cooperation	46UNTS201	100710
Belgium	Multilateral	12 Nov 47	Admin Cooperation	53UNTS13	100770
Belgium	Multilateral	12 Nov 47	Admin Cooperation	53UNTS39	100771
Belgium	Multilateral	12 Nov 47	Admin Cooperation	46UNTS169	100709
Belgium	Multilateral	18 Nov 47	Finance	17UNTS89	100269
Belgium	Multilateral	22 Dec 47	Customs	32UNTS143	100496
Belgium	Multilateral	06 Mar 48	Water Transport	289UNTS3	104214
Belgium	Multilateral	17 Mar 48	General Military	19UNTS51	100304
Belgium	Multilateral	10 May 48	Culture	289UNTS111	104215
Belgium	Multilateral	10 Jun 48	Humanitarian	164UNTS113	102163
Belgium	Multilateral	10 Jun 48	Humanitarian	191UNTS3	102576
Belgium	Multilateral	19 Jun 48	Air Transport	310UNTS151	104492
Belgium	Multilateral	26 Jun 48	Culture	331UNTS217	104757
Belgium	Multilateral	24 Jul 48	Sanitation	66UNTS25	100847
Belgium	Multilateral	14 Sep 48	Milit Occupation	18UNTS267	100296
Belgium	Multilateral	17 Sep 48	Telecommunications	97UNTS31	101345
Belgium	Multilateral	08 Oct 48	Education	19UNTS113	100308

PARTY ONE	PARTY TWO	DATE	TOPIC	CITATION	NUMBER
Belgium	Multilateral	19 Nov 48	Sanitation	44UNTS277	100688
Belgium	Multilateral	09 Dec 48	Scientific Project	73UNTS39	100942
Belgium	Multilateral	09 Dec 48	Humanitarian	78UNTS277	101021
Belgium	Multilateral	12 Feb 49	Customs	189UNTS33	102541
Belgium	Multilateral	22 Feb 49	Sanitation	93UNTS129	101296
Belgium	Multilateral	23 Mar 49	Commodity Trade	203UNTS179	102746
Belgium	Multilateral	04 Apr 49	General Military	34UNTS243	100541
Belgium	Multilateral	28 Apr 49	IGO Establishment	83UNTS105	101105
Belgium	Multilateral	04 May 49	Admin Cooperation	30UNTS3	100445
Belgium	Multilateral	04 May 49	Admin Cooperation	92UNTS19	101257
Belgium	Multilateral	04 May 49	Admin Cooperation	30UNTS23	100446
Belgium	Multilateral	04 May 49	Admin Cooperation	47UNTS159	100728
Belgium	Multilateral	05 May 49	IGO Establishment	87UNTS103	101168
Belgium	Multilateral	18 Jun 49	ILO Labor	605UNTS295	108768
Belgium	Multilateral	12 Aug 49	Humanitarian	75UNTS85	100971
Belgium	Multilateral	12 Aug 49	Humanitarian	75UNTS31	100970
Belgium	Multilateral	12 Aug 49	General Military	75UNTS135	100972
Belgium	Multilateral	12 Aug 49	Humanitarian	75UNTS287	100973
Belgium	Multilateral	02 Sep 49	IGO Status/Immunit	250UNTS12	103515
Belgium	Multilateral	19 Sep 49	Land Transport	125UNTS3	101671
Belgium	Multilateral	07 Nov 49	Non-ILO Labor	132UNTS31	101749
Belgium	Multilateral	07 Nov 49	Sanitation	132UNTS3	101748
Belgium	Multilateral	16 Dec 49	Admin Cooperation	72UNTS3	100924
Belgium	Multilateral	18 Feb 50	Customs	123UNTS45	101654
Belgium	Multilateral	21 Mar 50	Admin Cooperation	96UNTS271	101342
Belgium	Multilateral	06 Apr 50	Admin Cooperation	119UNTS99	101610
Belgium	Multilateral	08 Apr 50	IGO Establishment	66UNTS285	100860
Belgium	Multilateral	08 Apr 50	Specif Goods/Equip	68UNTS99	100889
Belgium	Multilateral	17 Apr 50	Visas	131UNTS99	101738
Belgium	Multilateral	17 Apr 50	Non-ILO Labor	126UNTS285	101694
Belgium	Multilateral	13 May 50	Land Transport	128UNTS171	101719
Belgium	Multilateral	27 Jul 50	Non-ILO Labor	166UNTS73	102186
Belgium	Multilateral	16 Sep 50	General Transport	92UNTS91	101264
Belgium	Multilateral	18 Oct 50	Specific Resources	638UNTS185	109134
Belgium	Multilateral	04 Nov 50	Humanitarian	213UNTS221	102889
Belgium	Multilateral	22 Nov 50	Culture	131UNTS25	101734
Belgium	Multilateral	07 Dec 50	Admin Cooperation	212UNTS17	102861
Belgium	Multilateral	15 Dec 50	IGO Operations	160UNTS267	102111
Belgium	Multilateral	15 Dec 50	Customs	157UNTS129	102052
Belgium	Multilateral	15 Dec 50	Customs	171UNTS305	102234
Belgium	Multilateral	15 Dec 50	Customs	347UNTS127	104994
Belgium	Multilateral	18 Apr 51	IGO Establishment	261UNTS140	103729
Belgium	Multilateral	25 May 51	Status of Forces	175UNTS215	102303
Belgium	Multilateral	19 Jun 51	Status of Forces	199UNTS67	102678
Belgium	Multilateral	02 Jul 51	Refugees	189UNTS137	102545
Belgium	Multilateral	29 Jul 51	Other Military	117UNTS85	101585
Belgium	Multilateral	08 Sep 51	Peace/Disarmament	136UNTS45	101832
Belgium	Multilateral	08 Sep 51	General Military	136UNTS165	101833
Belgium	Multilateral	20 Sep 51	IGO Status/Immunit	200UNTS3	102691
Belgium	Multilateral	09 Oct 51	IGO Establishment	220UNTS121	102997
Belgium	Multilateral	06 Dec 51	Admin Cooperation	150UNTS67	101963
Belgium	Multilateral	06 Dec 51	IGO Establishment	425UNTS61	106119
Belgium	Multilateral	10 Jan 52	Visas	163UNTS3	102138
Belgium	Multilateral	10 Jan 52	Visas	163UNTS27	102139
Belgium	Multilateral	04 Feb 52	General Economic	124UNTS3	101662
Belgium	Multilateral	15 Feb 52	Scientific Project	132UNTS51	101751
Belgium	Multilateral	16 Apr 52	General Economic	139UNTS35	101874
Belgium	Multilateral	10 May 52	Taxation	439UNTS233	106332
Belgium	Multilateral	10 May 52	Admin Cooperation	439UNTS217	106331
Belgium	Multilateral	10 May 52	Admin Cooperation	439UNTS193	106330
Belgium	Multilateral	15 May 52	Sanitation	0UNTS0	110476
Belgium	Multilateral	20 May 52	Sanitation	219UNTS55	102966
Belgium	Multilateral	12 Jun 52	Dispute Settlement	138UNTS183	101869
Belgium	Multilateral	11 Jul 52	Postal Service	170UNTS63	102222
Belgium	Multilateral	11 Jul 52	Postal Service	171UNTS89	102225

PARTY ONE	PARTY TWO	DATE	TOPIC	CITATION	NUMBER
Belgium	Multilateral	11 Jul 52	Postal Service	171UNTS3	102224
Belgium	Multilateral	11 Jul 52	Postal Service	170UNTS3	102221
Belgium	Multilateral	11 Jul 52	IGO Establishment	169UNTS3	102220
Belgium	Multilateral	11 Jul 52	Postal Service	170UNTS269	102223
Belgium	Multilateral	11 Jul 52	Postal Service	171UNTS191	102227
Belgium	Multilateral	11 Jul 52	Postal Service	171UNTS143	102226
Belgium	Multilateral	05 Sep 52	Taxation	256UNTS3	103619
Belgium	Multilateral	05 Sep 52	Customs	247UNTS329	103479
Belgium	Multilateral	06 Sep 52	Patents/Copyrights	216UNTS132	102937
Belgium	Multilateral	07 Oct 52	Admin Cooperation	310UNTS181	104493
Belgium	Multilateral	07 Nov 52	General Trade	221UNTS255	103010
Belgium	Multilateral	10 Nov 52	Admin Cooperation	214UNTS265	102904
Belgium	Multilateral	27 Feb 53	Claims and Debts	333UNTS3	104764
Belgium	Multilateral	31 Mar 53	Privil/Immunities	193UNTS136	102613
Belgium	Multilateral	11 May 53	Sanitation	456UNTS3	106555
Belgium	Multilateral	01 Jul 53	IGO Establishment	200UNTS149	102701
Belgium	Multilateral	24 Jul 53	General Amity	250UNTS108	103520
Belgium	Multilateral	01 Oct 53	Commodity Trade	258UNTS153	103677
Belgium	Multilateral	17 Oct 53	General Transport	184UNTS42	102438
Belgium	Multilateral	26 Oct 53	Status of Forces	207UNTS237	102809
Belgium	Multilateral	07 Dec 53	Admin Cooperation	182UNTS51	102422
Belgium	Multilateral	09 Dec 53	General Economic	249UNTS197	103509
Belgium	Multilateral	11 Dec 53	Education	218UNTS125	102954
Belgium	Multilateral	11 Dec 53	Sanitation	191UNTS285	102588
Belgium	Multilateral	11 Dec 53	Patents/Copyrights	218UNTS27	102952
Belgium	Multilateral	11 Dec 53	Non-ILO Labor	218UNTS153	102956
Belgium	Multilateral	11 Dec 53	Non-ILO Labor	218UNTS255	102958
Belgium	Multilateral	11 Dec 53	Non-ILO Labor	218UNTS211	102957
Belgium	Multilateral	18 Jan 54	IGO Establishment	330UNTS121	104743
Belgium	Multilateral	25 Feb 54	Air Transport	215UNTS249	102922
Belgium	Multilateral	01 Mar 54	Admin Cooperation	286UNTS265	104173
Belgium	Multilateral	01 Mar 54	Commodity Trade	256UNTS31	103622
Belgium	Multilateral	12 May 54	Admin Cooperation	327UNTS3	104714
Belgium	Multilateral	14 May 54	Culture	249UNTS215	103511
Belgium	Multilateral	21 May 54	Non-ILO Labor	345UNTS285	104973
Belgium	Multilateral	04 Jun 54	Customs	282UNTS249	104101
Belgium	Multilateral	04 Jun 54	Customs	276UNTS191	103992
Belgium	Multilateral	14 Jun 54	Air Transport	320UNTS217	104644
Belgium	Multilateral	14 Jun 54	Air Transport	320UNTS209	104643
Belgium	Multilateral	08 Jul 54	Finance	287UNTS27	104178
Belgium	Multilateral	29 Jul 54	Sanitation	249UNTS45	103500
Belgium	Multilateral	28 Sep 54	Refugees	360UNTS117	105158
Belgium	Multilateral	23 Oct 54	Status of Forces	334UNTS3	104765
Belgium	Multilateral	29 Nov 54	General Trade	287UNTS209	104187
Belgium	Multilateral	19 Dec 54	Culture	218UNTS139	102955
Belgium	Multilateral	19 Dec 54	Patents/Copyrights	218UNTS51	102953
Belgium	Multilateral	21 Dec 54	General Amity	258UNTS322	103678
Belgium	Multilateral	06 Apr 55	General Amity	261UNTS55	103725
Belgium	Multilateral	25 May 55	IGO Establishment	264UNTS117	103791
Belgium	Multilateral	03 Jun 55	Specific Resources	310UNTS145	104491
Belgium	Multilateral	06 Jun 55	IGO Establishment	219UNTS79	102968
Belgium	Multilateral	22 Jun 55	Atomic Energy	249UNTS3	103498
Belgium	Multilateral	28 Sep 55	Air Transport	478UNTS371	106943
Belgium	Multilateral	12 Oct 55	IGO Establishment	560UNTS3	108165
Belgium	Multilateral	20 Oct 55	IGO Establishment	378UNTS159	105425
Belgium	Multilateral	05 Nov 55	IGO Establishment	250UNTS201	103524
Belgium	Multilateral	13 Dec 55	IGO Operations	529UNTS141	107660
Belgium	Multilateral	13 Dec 55	Humanitarian	250UNTS3	103514
Belgium	Multilateral	21 Dec 55	General Trade	292UNTS63	104267
Belgium	Multilateral	04 Jan 56	Scientific Project	256UNTS171	103627
Belgium	Multilateral	01 Mar 56	Customs	343UNTS129	104923
Belgium	Multilateral	25 Apr 56	Commodity Trade	270UNTS103	103896
Belgium	Multilateral	30 Apr 56	Air Transport	310UNTS229	104494
Belgium	Multilateral	18 May 56	Land Transport	339UNTS3	104844
Belgium	Multilateral	18 May 56	Customs	319UNTS21	104630

PARTY ONE	PARTY TWO	DATE	TOPIC	CITATION	NUMBER
Belgium	Multilateral	18 May 56	Customs	327UNTS123	104721
Belgium	Multilateral	18 May 56	Customs	338UNTS103	104834
Belgium	Multilateral	19 May 56	Land Transport	399UNTS189	105742
Belgium	Multilateral	07 Jun 56	Non-ILO Labor	381UNTS145	105470
Belgium	Multilateral	06 Jul 56	Admin Cooperation	312UNTS109	104514
Belgium	Multilateral	09 Jul 56	Non-ILO Labor	314UNTS3	104539
Belgium	Multilateral	16 Aug 56	General Trade	287UNTS223	104188
Belgium	Multilateral	07 Sep 56	Humanitarian	266UNTS3	103822
Belgium	Multilateral	25 Sep 56	Air Transport	334UNTS89	104767
Belgium	Multilateral	25 Sep 56	Air Transport	334UNTS13	104766
Belgium	Multilateral	26 Oct 56	IGO Establishment	276UNTS3	103988
Belgium	Multilateral	29 Oct 56	Territory Boundary	263UNTS165	103772
Belgium	Multilateral	15 Dec 56	Education	278UNTS73	104023
Belgium	Multilateral	25 Mar 57	IGO Establishment	294UNTS2	104300
Belgium	Multilateral	25 Mar 57	IGO Status/Immunit	294UNTS411	104302
Belgium	Multilateral	25 Mar 57	IGO Establishment	294UNTS259	104301
Belgium	Multilateral	12 Apr 57	Education	443UNTS128	106362
Belgium	Multilateral	29 Apr 57	Dispute Settlement	320UNTS243	104646
Belgium	Multilateral	15 Jun 57	Patents/Copyrights	583UNTS3	108470
Belgium	Multilateral	15 Jun 57	General Trade	550UNTS45	108008
Belgium	Multilateral	27 Jun 57	General Economic	284UNTS139	104133
Belgium	Multilateral	26 Jul 57	Land Transport	386UNTS3	105535
Belgium	Multilateral	27 Sep 57	Admin Cooperation	299UNTS211	104314
Belgium	Multilateral	30 Sep 57	General Transport	619UNTS77	108940
Belgium	Multilateral	03 Oct 57	Postal Service	366UNTS193	105218
Belgium	Multilateral	03 Oct 57	Postal Service	366UNTS255	105219
Belgium	Multilateral	03 Oct 57	Postal Service	364UNTS3	105211
Belgium	Multilateral	03 Oct 57	Postal Service	365UNTS3	105213
Belgium	Multilateral	03 Oct 57	Postal Service	366UNTS87	105216
Belgium	Multilateral	03 Oct 57	Postal Service	365UNTS207	105214
Belgium	Multilateral	03 Oct 57	Postal Service	366UNTS141	105217
Belgium	Multilateral	03 Oct 57	Postal Service	364UNTS331	105212
Belgium	Multilateral	03 Oct 57	Postal Service	366UNTS3	105215
Belgium	Multilateral	23 Nov 57	Refugees	506UNTS125	107384
Belgium	Multilateral	25 Nov 57	General Trade	403UNTS169	105795
Belgium	Multilateral	13 Dec 57	Land Transport	372UNTS159	105296
Belgium	Multilateral	13 Dec 57	Visas	315UNTS139	104565
Belgium	Multilateral	13 Dec 57	Extradition	359UNTS273	105146
Belgium	Multilateral	15 Jan 58	Customs	383UNTS229	105503
Belgium	Multilateral	03 Feb 58	IGO Establishment	381UNTS165	105471
Belgium	Multilateral	20 Mar 58	Admin Cooperation	335UNTS211	104789
Belgium	Multilateral	31 Mar 58	Specific Property	320UNTS103	104639
Belgium	Multilateral	03 Apr 58	Commodity Trade	336UNTS177	104806
Belgium	Multilateral	15 Apr 58	Health/Educ/Welfare	539UNTS27	107822
Belgium	Multilateral	10 Jun 58	Admin Cooperation	330UNTS3	104739
Belgium	Multilateral	18 Jun 58	Finance	386UNTS355	105553
Belgium	Multilateral	18 Jun 58	General Trade	386UNTS345	105552
Belgium	Multilateral	25 Jul 58	Customs	352UNTS3	105035
Belgium	Multilateral	15 Dec 58	Mass Media	546UNTS235	107950
Belgium	Multilateral	15 Dec 58	Sanitation	351UNTS159	105022
Belgium	Multilateral	15 Jan 59	Customs	348UNTS13	104996
Belgium	Multilateral	24 Jan 59	IGO Establishment	486UNTS157	107078
Belgium	Multilateral	30 Jan 59	General Trade	0UNTS0	109234
Belgium	Multilateral	06 Apr 59	Commodity Trade	349UNTS167	105013
Belgium	Multilateral	20 Apr 59	Admin Cooperation	472UNTS185	106841
Belgium	Multilateral	20 Apr 59	Visas	376UNTS85	105375
Belgium	Multilateral	11 May 59	Claims and Debts	527UNTS145	107623
Belgium	Multilateral	03 Aug 59	Status of Forces	481UNTS262	106986
Belgium	Multilateral	19 Nov 59	IGO Operations	410UNTS156	105902
Belgium	Multilateral	01 Dec 59	Territory Boundary	402UNTS71	105778
Belgium	Multilateral	14 Dec 59	Admin Cooperation	444UNTS193	106369
Belgium	Multilateral	26 Jan 60	IGO Establishment	439UNTS249	106333
Belgium	Multilateral	15 Mar 60	Water Transport	572UNTS133	108310
Belgium	Multilateral	11 Apr 60	Visas	374UNTS3	105323
Belgium	Multilateral	15 Apr 60	Finance	470UNTS239	106811

PARTY ONE	PARTY TWO	DATE	TOPIC	CITATION	NUMBER
Belgium	Multilateral	22 Apr 60	Air Transport	418UNTS211	106023
Belgium	Multilateral	28 Apr 60	Health/Educ/Welfare	376UNTS111	105377
Belgium	Multilateral	17 Jun 60	Humanitarian	536UNTS27	107794
Belgium	Multilateral	22 Jun 60	Mass Media	546UNTS247	107951
Belgium	Multilateral	01 Sep 60	Commodity Trade	403UNTS3	105792
Belgium	Multilateral	21 Sep 60	Patents/Copyrights	394UNTS3	105664
Belgium	Multilateral	06 Oct 60	Customs	473UNTS131	106861
Belgium	Multilateral	08 Oct 60	General Trade	450UNTS309	106476
Belgium	Multilateral	01 Dec 60	Scientific Project	414UNTS110	105970
Belgium	Multilateral	09 Dec 60	Customs	429UNTS211	106200
Belgium	Multilateral	13 Dec 60	Air Transport	523UNTS117	107557
Belgium	Multilateral	13 Feb 61	ILO Labor	0UNTS0	110306
Belgium	Multilateral	16 Mar 61	General Trade	638UNTS235	109139
Belgium	Multilateral	30 Mar 61	Sanitation	520UNTS151	107515
Belgium	Multilateral	18 Apr 61	Consul/Citizenship	500UNTS95	107310
Belgium	Multilateral	18 Apr 61	Consul/Citizenship	500UNTS223	107311
Belgium	Multilateral	18 Apr 61	Dispute Settlement	500UNTS243	107312
Belgium	Multilateral	21 Apr 61	IGO Establishment	484UNTS349	107041
Belgium	Multilateral	08 Jun 61	Customs	473UNTS187	106863
Belgium	Multilateral	08 Jun 61	Customs	473UNTS153	106862
Belgium	Multilateral	21 Jun 61	IGO Establishment	514UNTS209	107449
Belgium	Multilateral	18 Oct 61	IGO Establishment	529UNTS89	107659
Belgium	Multilateral	26 Oct 61	Patents/Copyrights	496UNTS43	107247
Belgium	Multilateral	06 Dec 61	Customs	473UNTS219	106864
Belgium	Multilateral	16 Dec 61	Visas	544UNTS19	107909
Belgium	Multilateral	07 Mar 62	Commodity Trade	445UNTS199	106388
Belgium	Multilateral	07 Mar 62	Commodity Trade	445UNTS205	106389
Belgium	Multilateral	19 Mar 62	Patents/Copyrights	0UNTS0	110108
Belgium	Multilateral	29 Mar 62	IGO Establishment	507UNTS177	107401
Belgium	Multilateral	09 May 62	IGO Establishment	453UNTS299	106531
Belgium	Multilateral	14 May 62	Scientific Project	544UNTS39	107910
Belgium	Multilateral	14 May 62	Sanitation	544UNTS81	107911
Belgium	Multilateral	15 May 62	Commodity Trade	444UNTS3	106367
Belgium	Multilateral	14 Jun 62	IGO Establishment	528UNTS33	107634
Belgium	Multilateral	27 Jun 62	Extradition	616UNTS79	108893
Belgium	Multilateral	27 Jun 62	Atomic Energy	463UNTS3	106688
Belgium	Multilateral	27 Jun 62	Atomic Energy	463UNTS11	106689
Belgium	Multilateral	14 Sep 62	Visas	443UNTS73	106360
Belgium	Multilateral	28 Sep 62	IGO Establishment	469UNTS169	106791
Belgium	Multilateral	05 Oct 62	IGO Establishment	502UNTS225	107333
Belgium	Multilateral	29 Nov 62	Visas	457UNTS63	106577
Belgium	Multilateral	17 Dec 62	Sanitation	486UNTS119	107076
Belgium	Multilateral	17 Dec 62	General Economic	523UNTS93	107555
Belgium	Multilateral	17 Dec 62	Admin Cooperation	590UNTS81	108548
Belgium	Multilateral	02 Apr 63	Commodity Trade	475UNTS121	106889
Belgium	Multilateral	20 Apr 63	IGO Establishment	495UNTS3	107239
Belgium	Multilateral	24 Apr 63	Consul/Citizenship	596UNTS487	108640
Belgium	Multilateral	24 Apr 63	Consul/Citizenship	596UNTS261	108638
Belgium	Multilateral	06 May 63	Consul/Citizenship	634UNTS221	109065
Belgium	Multilateral	19 Jun 63	Visas	482UNTS19	106988
Belgium	Multilateral	05 Aug 63	Sanitation	480UNTS43	106964
Belgium	Multilateral	13 Aug 63	General Trade	592UNTS139	108572
Belgium	Multilateral	14 Nov 63	Finance	619UNTS299	108948
Belgium	Multilateral	10 Feb 64	Visas	496UNTS151	107249
Belgium	Multilateral	15 Feb 64	Milit Installation	533UNTS98	107736
Belgium	Multilateral	09 Mar 64	Specific Resources	581UNTS89	108434
Belgium	Multilateral	09 Mar 64	Specific Resources	581UNTS83	108433
Belgium	Multilateral	09 Mar 64	Specific Resources	581UNTS57	108432
Belgium	Multilateral	16 Apr 64	Visas	548UNTS27	107967
Belgium	Multilateral	14 May 64	Refugees	528UNTS23	107633
Belgium	Multilateral	14 May 64	Visas	528UNTS3	107631
Belgium	Multilateral	14 May 64	Refugees	528UNTS13	107632
Belgium	Multilateral	25 May 64	Taxation	620UNTS149	108953
Belgium	Multilateral	18 Jun 64	Atomic Energy	542UNTS145	107886
Belgium	Multilateral	10 Jul 64	Postal Service	611UNTS105	108845

PARTY ONE	PARTY TWO	DATE	TOPIC	CITATION	NUMBER
Belgium	Multilateral	10 Jul 64	Postal Service	611UNTS387	108846
Belgium	Multilateral	10 Jul 64	Postal Service	612UNTS3	108847
Belgium	Multilateral	10 Jul 64	Postal Service	612UNTS361	108849
Belgium	Multilateral	10 Jul 64	Postal Service	613UNTS3	108850
Belgium	Multilateral	10 Jul 64	Postal Service	613UNTS3	108851
Belgium	Multilateral	10 Jul 64	Postal Service	613UNTS193	108852
Belgium	Multilateral	10 Jul 64	Postal Service	612UNTS233	108848
Belgium	Multilateral	10 Jul 64	Postal Service	611UNTS7	108844
Belgium	Multilateral	10 Jul 64	Postal Service	613UNTS127	108853
Belgium	Multilateral	20 Aug 64	Telecommunications	514UNTS25	107441
Belgium	Multilateral	12 Sep 64	Specific Resources	0UNTS0	109344
Belgium	Multilateral	15 Sep 64	General Trade	510UNTS147	107411
Belgium	Multilateral	19 Nov 64	Visas	523UNTS3	107553
Belgium	Multilateral	27 Nov 64	Visas	548UNTS47	107968
Belgium	Multilateral	01 Dec 64	Water Transport	550UNTS133	108012
Belgium	Multilateral	22 Jan 65	Gen Communications	634UNTS239	109066
Belgium	Multilateral	15 Feb 65	Visas	547UNTS3	107953
Belgium	Multilateral	15 Feb 65	Refugees	546UNTS277	107952
Belgium	Multilateral	09 Mar 65	Water Transport	591UNTS265	108564
Belgium	Multilateral	18 Mar 65	Dispute Settlement	575UNTS159	108359
Belgium	Multilateral	25 Apr 65	Finance	0UNTS0	110810
Belgium	Multilateral	08 Jul 65	General Trade	597UNTS3	108641
Belgium	Multilateral	16 Jul 65	General Trade	600UNTS49	108675
Belgium	Multilateral	08 Sep 65	Visas	578UNTS3	108382
Belgium	Multilateral	04 Dec 65	IGO Establishment	571UNTS123	108303
Belgium	Multilateral	31 Dec 65	Specific Resources	616UNTS317	108904
Belgium	Multilateral	05 Apr 66	Water Transport	640UNTS133	109159
Belgium	Multilateral	17 May 66	Visas	571UNTS89	108302
Belgium	Multilateral	12 Jul 66	Visas	578UNTS23	108384
Belgium	Multilateral	26 Apr 67	General Trade	0UNTS0	109890
Belgium	Multilateral	20 Jun 67	Visas	607UNTS97	108799
Belgium	Multilateral	22 Aug 67	General Trade	0UNTS0	110687
Belgium	Multilateral	15 Nov 67	General Trade	0UNTS0	109703
Belgium	Multilateral	18 Mar 68	Commodity Trade	0UNTS0	109262
Belgium	Multilateral	27 Mar 68	Visas	0UNTS0	109293
Belgium	Multilateral	24 Sep 68	Air Transport	0UNTS0	110612
Belgium	Multilateral	10 Dec 68	Visas	0UNTS0	109387
Belgium	Multilateral	07 Feb 69	Status of Forces	0UNTS0	110586
Belgium	Multilateral	09 Jun 69	Specific Resources	0UNTS0	110099
Belgium	Multilateral	12 Jun 69	Visas	0UNTS0	110305
Belgium	Multilateral	17 Jul 69	Visas	0UNTS0	109729
Belgium	Multilateral	03 Dec 69	Visas	0UNTS0	110526
Belgium	Multilateral	12 Jan 70	Commodity Trade	0UNTS0	110603
Belgium	Multilateral	28 Apr 70	Visas	0UNTS0	110805
Belgium	Multilateral	04 May 70	Visas	0UNTS0	110579
Belgium	Netherlands	02 Jan 45	Refugees	19UNTS259	200120
Belgium	Netherlands	16 May 46	Culture	17UNTS13	100266
Belgium	Netherlands	24 May 46	Finance	31UNTS169	100477
Belgium	Netherlands	12 Oct 46	Claims and Debts	23UNTS179	100347
Belgium	Netherlands	25 Mar 47	Postal Service	18UNTS309	100299
Belgium	Netherlands	28 Apr 47	Visas	37UNTS199	100577
Belgium	Netherlands	29 Aug 47	Non-ILO Labor	36UNTS349	100573
Belgium	Netherlands	13 Apr 48	Customs	32UNTS153	100497
Belgium	Netherlands	25 Sep 48	Taxation	123UNTS81	101655
Belgium	Netherlands	11 Oct 48	Finance	26UNTS95	100379
Belgium	Netherlands	13 May 49	Customs	65UNTS133	100841
Belgium	Netherlands	20 Aug 49	Visas	46UNTS133	100706
Belgium	Netherlands	07 Sep 49	Loans and Credits	117UNTS3	101581
Belgium	Netherlands	17 Feb 50	Water Transport	51UNTS101	100756
Belgium	Netherlands	29 Mar 50	Visas	68UNTS45	100883
Belgium	Netherlands	23 Oct 50	Territory Boundary	136UNTS31	101831
Belgium	Netherlands	25 Nov 50	Non-ILO Labor	51NET15	447016
Belgium	Netherlands	15 Mar 51	Reparations	93UNTS97	101294
Belgium	Netherlands	21 Apr 51	Non-ILO Labor	51NET64	447022
Belgium	Netherlands	14 Jun 51	Reparations	101UNTS3	101397
Belgium	Netherlands	15 Jun 51	Claims and Debts	51NET106	447026
Belgium	Netherlands	14 Nov 51	Admin Cooperation	123UNTS91	101656
Belgium	Netherlands	26 Mar 53	Visas	165UNTS297	102180
Belgium	Netherlands	29 Apr 53	Admin Cooperation	173UNTS61	102261
Belgium	Netherlands	27 Jan 54	Non-ILO Labor	54NET46	447045
Belgium	Netherlands	09 Jun 54	Milit Servic/Citiz	216UNTS121	102936
Belgium	Netherlands	28 Jun 54	Territory Boundary	272UNTS235	103942
Belgium	Netherlands	10 Sep 54	Customs	54NET153	447050
Belgium	Netherlands	13 Jan 55	Visas	210UNTS63	102834
Belgium	Netherlands	16 Feb 55	Refugees	211UNTS49	102846
Belgium	Netherlands	07 Mar 57	Dispute Settlement	282UNTS241	104100
Belgium	Netherlands	23 Oct 57	Water Transport	0UNTS0	109725
Belgium	Netherlands	24 Oct 57	Water Transport	489UNTS11	107132
Belgium	Netherlands	24 Oct 57	Water Transport	292UNTS199	104274
Belgium	Netherlands	24 Oct 57	Water Transport	489UNTS3	107131
Belgium	Netherlands	03 Feb 58	Territory Boundary	381UNTS305	105472
Belgium	Netherlands	04 Feb 58	Extradition	330UNTS83	104740
Belgium	Netherlands	28 Apr 59	Finance	485UNTS123	107049
Belgium	Netherlands	20 Jan 60	Admin Cooperation	373UNTS3	105310
Belgium	Netherlands	20 Jun 60	Specific Property	423UNTS19	106084
Belgium	Netherlands	24 Feb 61	Admin Cooperation	474UNTS161	106880
Belgium	Netherlands	24 Feb 61	Water Transport	474UNTS167	106881
Belgium	Netherlands	13 May 63	Territory Boundary	540UNTS3	107843
Belgium	Netherlands	06 Jan 64	Reparations	531UNTS119	107698
Belgium	Netherlands	27 Apr 65	Specific Resources	596UNTS235	108636
Belgium	Netherlands	21 Mar 68	Non-ILO Labor	0UNTS0	109363
Belgium	Netherlands	12 Dec 68	Water Transport	0UNTS0	109793
Belgium	Netherlands	04 Feb 69	Non-ILO Labor	0UNTS0	109714
Belgium	New Zealand	01 Nov 51	Visas	118UNTS169	101605
Belgium	New Zealand	01 Sep 53	Air Transport	192UNTS283	102605
Belgium	Norway	23 Oct 45	Finance	16UNTS311	200107
Belgium	Norway	23 Oct 45	Claims and Debts	183UNTS337	200510
Belgium	Norway	21 Feb 46	Finance	31UNTS199	100479
Belgium	Norway	21 Feb 46	General Trade	31UNTS435	100485
Belgium	Norway	15 Jul 47	Visas	33UNTS25	100511
Belgium	Norway	20 Feb 48	Culture	32UNTS39	100487
Belgium	Norway	08 Mar 49	General Trade	29UNTS83	100435
Belgium	Norway	21 Jan 52	Claims and Debts	123UNTS39	101653
Belgium	Norway	24 Mar 54	Sanitation	219UNTS73	102967
Belgium	Norway	28 May 57	General Trade	3NORT0	451006
Belgium	Norway	30 Jun 67	Taxation	3NORT999	451007
Belgium	Norway	30 Jun 67	Taxation	0UNTS0	110020
Belgium	Pakistan	20 Feb 52	Extradition	133UNTS199	101790
Belgium	Pakistan	15 Mar 52	General Trade	316UNTS65	104578
Belgium	Pakistan	19 Oct 56	Visas	257UNTS221	103657
Belgium	Pakistan	04 Jul 58	Air Transport	387UNTS305	105569
Belgium	Pakistan	14 Nov 63	Culture	535UNTS393	107792
Belgium	Paraguay	21 Nov 60	Visas	387UNTS237	105565
Belgium	Peru	03 May 57	Visas	274UNTS251	103970
Belgium	Peru	22 Jan 65	Tech Assistance	0UNTS0	110565
Belgium	Philippines	05 Feb 57	Patents/Copyrights	269UNTS49	103872
Belgium	Philippines	17 Feb 60	Visas	356UNTS303	105101
Belgium	Poland	24 Mar 47	Non-ILO Labor	18UNTS279	100297
Belgium	Poland	17 Oct 56	Air Transport	356UNTS279	105100
Belgium	Poland	14 Nov 63	Claims and Debts	66PZUM85	458107
Belgium	Poland	09 Dec 63	Culture	514UNTS195	107448
Belgium	Poland	26 Nov 65	Non-ILO Labor	620UNTS13	108950
Belgium	Poland	07 Dec 65	Atomic Energy	65PZUM77	458127
Belgium	Poland	30 Oct 68	Land Transport	0UNTS0	109597
Belgium	Portugal	07 Jan 46	Finance	19UNTS159	100310
Belgium	Portugal	22 Oct 46	Air Transport	34UNTS49	100527
Belgium	Portugal	01 Mar 49	Finance	32UNTS49	100488
Belgium	Portugal	03 Jul 51	Visas	101UNTS17	101398
Belgium	Portugal	30 Jul 55	Culture	250UNTS213	103525
Belgium	Romania	04 Dec 56	Air Transport	317UNTS161	104602

PARTY ONE	PARTY TWO	DATE	TOPIC	CITATION	NUMBER
Belgium	Romania	12 Oct 62	Sanitation	502UNTS31	107325
Belgium	Romania	13 Nov 63	Culture	520UNTS119	107513
Belgium	Romania	22 Sep 67	Land Transport	637UNTS0	109109
Belgium	Romania	25 Oct 69	Visas	0UNTS0	110557
Belgium	Rwanda	13 Oct 62	Tech Assistance	456UNTS425	106568
Belgium	Rwanda	13 Oct 62	Tech Assistance	456UNTS431	106569
Belgium	Rwanda	07 Aug 70	Admin Cooperation	0UNTS0	110834
Belgium	San Marino	14 Dec 49	Visas	51UNTS107	100757
Belgium	San Marino	22 Apr 55	Non-ILO Labor	253UNTS41	103574
Belgium	South Africa	04 Jul 47	Claims and Debts	47UNTS9	100720
Belgium	South Africa	01 Jun 54	Culture	201UNTS25	102708
Belgium	South Africa	13 Sep 54	Air Transport	201UNTS15	102707
Belgium	South Africa	11 Jun 57	Taxation	292UNTS165	104272
Belgium	South Africa	28 Apr 58	Visas	303UNTS131	104375
Belgium	South Africa	11 Jun 58	Air Transport	335UNTS63	104778
Belgium	South Africa	25 May 65	Non-ILO Labor	0UNTS0	110762
Belgium	South Africa	13 Nov 67	Air Transport	0UNTS0	110168
Belgium	Spain	24 Jan 47	Admin Cooperation	19UNTS3	100301
Belgium	Spain	04 Jan 52	Visas	121UNTS25	101622
Belgium	Spain	10 Mar 52	Air Transport	178UNTS243	102342
Belgium	Spain	27 Jan 55	General Economic	55SPBO2302	460044
Belgium	Spain	22 Jun 55	Finance	55SPBO908	460045
Belgium	Spain	30 Jan 56	General Economic	56SPBO803	460046
Belgium	Spain	25 Apr 56	Finance	56SPBO2405	460047
Belgium	Spain	30 Jul 56	Finance	56SPBO610	460048
Belgium	Spain	07 Aug 56	General Trade	56SPBO3108	460049
Belgium	Spain	28 Nov 56	Non-ILO Labor	58SPBO2705	460051
Belgium	Spain	28 Nov 56	Non-ILO Labor	58SPBO2605	460050
Belgium	Spain	28 Nov 56	Non-ILO Labor	308UNTS239	104464
Belgium	Spain	28 Nov 56	Non-ILO Labor	308UNTS285	104465
Belgium	Spain	28 Nov 56	Non-ILO Labor	58SPBO2705	460052
Belgium	Spain	26 Jul 57	Finance	57SPBO2208	460053
Belgium	Spain	10 Sep 57	Non-ILO Labor	58SPBO3005	460054
Belgium	Spain	27 Oct 58	Culture	327UNTS107	104720
Belgium	Spain	27 May 59	Visas	340UNTS81	104860
Belgium	Spain	11 Sep 59	Visas	345UNTS29	104956
Belgium	Spain	19 Jul 66	Land Transport	575UNTS3	108352
Belgium	Sweden	30 May 45	General Trade	45SOFM99	461007
Belgium	Sweden	30 May 45	Finance	45SOFM100	461008
Belgium	Sweden	30 Dec 46	General Trade	47SOFM23	461038
Belgium	Sweden	30 Dec 46	Claims and Debts	23UNTS197	100348
Belgium	Sweden	20 Mar 47	Visas	34UNTS3	100522
Belgium	Sweden	16 Dec 48	Visas	26UNTS3	100372
Belgium	Sweden	14 Feb 49	Finance	49SOFM87	461076
Belgium	Sweden	21 Feb 49	Air Transport	95UNTS73	101317
Belgium	Sweden	29 Dec 50	Finance	50SOFM900	461118
Belgium	Sweden	18 Sep 51	Non-ILO Labor	133UNTS187	101789
Belgium	Sweden	21 Apr 52	Air Transport	166UNTS9	102183
Belgium	Sweden	01 Apr 53	Taxation	185UNTS225	102473
Belgium	Sweden	20 Nov 53	General Trade	53SOFM1057	461191
Belgium	Sweden	18 Jan 56	Taxation	293UNTS23	104283
Belgium	Sweden	20 Nov 56	Taxation	281UNTS239	104081
Belgium	Sweden	08 May 58	Land Transport	312UNTS145	104516
Belgium	Sweden	18 May 59	Admin Cooperation	341UNTS277	104890
Belgium	Sweden	11 Jan 65	Education	533UNTS157	107741
Belgium	Sweden	02 Jul 65	Taxation	0UNTS0	109367
Belgium	Sweden	20 Mar 67	Land Transport	0UNTS0	109795
Belgium	Switzerland	03 Jul 47	Visas	29UNTS277	100444
Belgium	Switzerland	01 Sep 48	Visas	23UNTS139	100344
Belgium	Switzerland	21 Mar 49	Admin Cooperation	34UNTS17	100524
Belgium	Switzerland	28 Jul 50	Visas	71UNTS91	100911
Belgium	Switzerland	17 Jun 52	Non-ILO Labor	180UNTS23	102373
Belgium	Switzerland	05 Jan 56	Reparations	228UNTS159	103149
Belgium	Switzerland	21 Jun 57	General Trade	57SWRO521	462162
Belgium	Switzerland	05 Dec 57	Taxation	293UNTS317	104299

PARTY ONE	PARTY TWO	DATE	TOPIC	CITATION	NUMBER
Belgium	Switzerland	29 Apr 59	Admin Cooperation	443UNTS35	106356
Belgium	Switzerland	24 Mar 60	Air Transport	416UNTS81	105996
Belgium	Taiwan	20 Oct 43	Privil/Immunities	14UNTS376	200095
Belgium	Taiwan	13 Jan 54	Milit Assistance	223UNTS111	103059
Belgium	Thailand	02 Dec 59	Visas	351UNTS89	105018
Belgium	Tunisia	13 Oct 60	Visas	421UNTS71	106052
Belgium	Tunisia	21 Dec 62	Culture	482UNTS3	106987
Belgium	Tunisia	15 Jul 64	Tech Assistance	560UNTS65	108169
Belgium	Tunisia	15 Jul 64	General Economic	561UNTS297	108190
Belgium	Tunisia	15 Jul 64	Tech Assistance	560UNTS57	108168
Belgium	Tunisia	07 Aug 69	Education	0UNTS0	109974
Belgium	Tunisia	07 Aug 69	Non-ILO Labor	0UNTS0	109973
Belgium	Turkey	12 Mar 47	Finance	33UNTS43	100513
Belgium	Turkey	12 Mar 47	Mostfavored Nation	37UNTS221	100579
Belgium	Turkey	12 Mar 47	General Trade	37UNTS215	100578
Belgium	Turkey	25 Feb 48	Visas	18UNTS237	100293
Belgium	Turkey	25 Mar 48	General Economic	48TURG2906	466044
Belgium	Turkey	02 Dec 48	General Economic	50TURG3001	466045
Belgium	Turkey	16 Oct 52	Visas	149UNTS289	101958
Belgium	Turkey	15 Apr 55	General Economic	58TURG2903	466046
Belgium	Turkey	02 Jan 56	Visas	228UNTS203	103152
Belgium	Turkey	25 Oct 56	Air Transport	380UNTS3	105447
Belgium	Turkey	28 Nov 58	Loans and Credits	64TURG909	466102
Belgium	Turkey	29 Dec 58	Culture	357UNTS195	105118
Belgium	Turkey	23 Sep 63	Direct Aid	566UNTS195	108244
Belgium	Turkey	04 Jul 66	Non-ILO Labor	0UNTS0	109397
Belgium	UK Great Britain	16 May 44	Admin Cooperation	90UNTS283	200266
Belgium	UK Great Britain	22 Aug 44	Direct Aid	90UNTS295	200267
Belgium	UK Great Britain	05 Oct 44	Finance	5UNTS227	200031
Belgium	UK Great Britain	25 Jun 45	Reparations	90UNTS307	200268
Belgium	UK Great Britain	11 Mar 46	Status of Forces	26UNTS167	100387
Belgium	UK Great Britain	17 Apr 46	Health/Educ/Welfare	6UNTS177	100075
Belgium	UK Great Britain	16 Jan 47	Milit Installation	54UNTS97	100797
Belgium	UK Great Britain	05 Feb 47	Visas	11UNTS261	100164
Belgium	UK Great Britain	14 Nov 47	Finance	25UNTS269	100367
Belgium	UK Great Britain	07 Jun 48	Reparations	20UNTS33	100313
Belgium	UK Great Britain	29 Dec 48	Visas	27UNTS135	100404
Belgium	UK Great Britain	14 Apr 49	Visas	65UNTS117	100840
Belgium	UK Great Britain	07 Sep 49	Loans and Credits	106UNTS61	101457
Belgium	UK Great Britain	23 Dec 49	Status of Forces	99UNTS61	101371
Belgium	UK Great Britain	15 Mar 50	Patents/Copyrights	76UNTS85	100981
Belgium	UK Great Britain	06 Apr 51	Specific Property	110UNTS3	101496
Belgium	UK Great Britain	08 May 51	Air Transport	158UNTS451	102079
Belgium	UK Great Britain	30 Jun 52	Milit Assistance	199UNTS113	102679
Belgium	UK Great Britain	12 Nov 52	Status of Forces	180UNTS15	102372
Belgium	UK Great Britain	27 Mar 53	Taxation	188UNTS153	102526
Belgium	UK Great Britain	10 Sep 53	Admin Cooperation	183UNTS203	102429
Belgium	UK Great Britain	04 Jan 54	Sanitation	247UNTS47	103459
Belgium	UK Great Britain	09 Jul 54	Finance	201UNTS299	102721
Belgium	UK Great Britain	05 Nov 54	Visas	209UNTS69	102822
Belgium	UK Great Britain	10 Nov 55	Status of Forces	331UNTS209	104756
Belgium	UK Great Britain	18 Nov 55	Atomic Energy	222UNTS327	103038
Belgium	UK Great Britain	20 May 57	Non-ILO Labor	303UNTS53	104371
Belgium	UK Great Britain	03 Oct 57	Reparations	394UNTS69	105669
Belgium	UK Great Britain	23 Apr 59	Finance	343UNTS271	104931
Belgium	UK Great Britain	01 Apr 60	Visas	361UNTS135	105177
Belgium	UK Great Britain	21 Feb 61	Visas	398UNTS229	105724
Belgium	UK Great Britain	08 Mar 61	Consul/Citizenship	523UNTS17	107554
Belgium	UK Great Britain	29 Aug 67	Taxation	0UNTS0	110540
Belgium	UK Great Britain	11 Dec 68	Land Transport	0UNTS0	109586
Belgium	UNICEF (Children)	17 Jun 52	Direct Aid	171UNTS249	102228
Belgium	United Arab Rep	01 Jul 47	Claims and Debts	34UNTS93	100529
Belgium	United Arab Rep	19 Sep 49	Air Transport	137UNTS189	101853
Belgium	United Arab Rep	28 Nov 49	Culture	76UNTS91	100982
Belgium	United Arab Rep	31 Oct 56	Taxation	257UNTS235	103659

PARTY ONE	PARTY TWO	DATE	TOPIC	CITATION	NUMBER
Belgium	United Arab Rep	30 Mar 66	Claims and Debts	632UNTS237	109026
Belgium	United Arab Rep	17 May 67	Culture	0UNTS0	109501
Belgium	United Nations	20 Mar 64	Milit Installation	533UNTS83	107734
Belgium	United Nations	20 Feb 65	Finance	535UNTS191	107779
Belgium	United Nations	20 Feb 65	Claims and Debts	535UNTS197	107780
Belgium	USA (United States)	16 Jun 42	Milit Assistance	105UNTS159	200329
Belgium	USA (United States)	16 Oct 42	Milit Servic/Citiz	13UNTS211	200080
Belgium	USA (United States)	30 Jan 43	Milit Assistance	13UNTS371	200084
Belgium	USA (United States)	04 Aug 43	Status of Forces	109UNTS149	200356
Belgium	USA (United States)	17 Apr 45	Milit Assistance	139UNTS253	200454
Belgium	USA (United States)	19 Apr 45	Milit Installation	139UNTS179	200455
Belgium	USA (United States)	05 Apr 46	Air Transport	4UNTS125	100041
Belgium	USA (United States)	11 Jul 46	Mostfavored Nation	13UNTS43	100200
Belgium	USA (United States)	24 Sep 46	Claims and Debts	132UNTS80	101753
Belgium	USA (United States)	23 Jan 47	Visas	47UNTS23	100721
Belgium	USA (United States)	03 Feb 47	Visas	84UNTS255	101134
Belgium	USA (United States)	23 Jul 47	Other Military	33UNTS33	100512
Belgium	USA (United States)	30 Oct 47	General Economic	125UNTS103	101672
Belgium	USA (United States)	02 Jul 48	Direct Aid	19UNTS127	100309
Belgium	USA (United States)	02 Jul 48	Mostfavored Nation	27UNTS43	100397
Belgium	USA (United States)	26 Oct 48	Visas	84UNTS265	101135
Belgium	USA (United States)	28 Oct 48	Taxation	173UNTS67	102262
Belgium	USA (United States)	27 Jan 50	Milit Assistance	51UNTS213	100767
Belgium	USA (United States)	16 Mar 51	Reparations	93UNTS109	101295
Belgium	USA (United States)	07 Jan 52	Milit Assistance	179UNTS81	102356
Belgium	USA (United States)	07 Apr 52	Taxation	205UNTS3	102765
Belgium	USA (United States)	12 May 52	Finance	179UNTS15	102352
Belgium	USA (United States)	18 Jun 53	Milit Assistance	222UNTS3	103019
Belgium	USA (United States)	18 Jul 53	Taxation	180UNTS9	102371
Belgium	USA (United States)	02 Sep 53	Milit Assistance	200UNTS127	102700
Belgium	USA (United States)	17 Nov 53	Milit Assistance	251UNTS105	103536
Belgium	USA (United States)	12 Oct 54	Patents/Copyrights	202UNTS289	102735
Belgium	USA (United States)	23 Nov 54	Tech Assistance	235UNTS19	103292
Belgium	USA (United States)	15 Jun 55	Atomic Energy	235UNTS133	103299
Belgium	USA (United States)	15 Jul 55	Milit Assistance	223UNTS3	103040
Belgium	USA (United States)	31 Aug 55	Milit Assistance	223UNTS111	103041
Belgium	USA (United States)	03 Dec 57	Air Transport	303UNTS45	104370
Belgium	USA (United States)	27 Nov 59	Other Military	366UNTS331	105221
Belgium	USA (United States)	22 Apr 60	Milit Assistance	372UNTS277	105304
Belgium	USA (United States)	18 May 60	Patents/Copyrights	373UNTS31	105313
Belgium	USA (United States)	21 Feb 61	General Amity	480UNTS149	106967
Belgium	USA (United States)	17 May 62	Milit Assistance	461UNTS3	106647
Belgium	USA (United States)	23 May 62	Visas	434UNTS133	106260
Belgium	USA (United States)	19 Apr 63	Water Transport	493UNTS83	107209
Belgium	USA (United States)	19 Apr 63	Gen Communications	476UNTS29	106900
Belgium	USA (United States)	14 Nov 63	Extradition	522UNTS237	107549
Belgium	USA (United States)	18 Jun 65	Gen Communications	549UNTS95	107992
Belgium	USSR (Soviet Union)	13 Mar 45	Refugees	19UNTS235	200117
Belgium	USSR (Soviet Union)	27 Nov 45	Admin Cooperation	0SUST212	468022
Belgium	USSR (Soviet Union)	10 Nov 47	Finance	18UNTS299	100298
Belgium	USSR (Soviet Union)	18 Feb 48	Finance	0SUST245	468025
Belgium	USSR (Soviet Union)	18 Feb 48	General Trade	0SUST244	468024
Belgium	USSR (Soviet Union)	30 Jun 48	Finance	16SUGG64	469885
Belgium	USSR (Soviet Union)	02 Dec 49	Finance	16SUGG66	469894
Belgium	USSR (Soviet Union)	14 Nov 50	General Trade	0SUST278	468026
Belgium	USSR (Soviet Union)	02 Nov 56	General Amity	0SUST371	468023
Belgium	USSR (Soviet Union)	05 Jun 58	Air Transport	345UNTS145	104965
Belgium	Venezuela	15 May 63	Culture	470UNTS259	106812
Belgium	Vietnam, South	29 May 53	General Trade	0VKNG56	496012
Belgium	Yugoslavia	01 Nov 54	Non-ILO Labor	251UNTS123	103538
Belgium	Yugoslavia	05 Feb 57	Culture	276UNTS143	103990
Belgium	Yugoslavia	31 Oct 61	Sanitation	426UNTS165	106136
Benelux Econ Union	Algeria	18 Mar 70	General Economic	0UNTS0	110773
Benelux Econ Union	Japan	22 Jul 66	General Trade	66JJS31	442172
Benelux Econ Union	Japan	22 Oct 69	Commodity Trade	69JJS45	442250

PARTY ONE	PARTY TWO	DATE	TOPIC	CITATION	NUMBER
Benelux Econ Union	Multilateral	08 Oct 60	General Trade	450UNTS309	106476
Benelux Econ Union	Multilateral	13 Aug 63	General Trade	592UNTS139	108572
Benelux Econ Union	Poland	17 Feb 65	General Economic	547UNTS165	107956
Benelux Econ Union	Portugal	24 May 67	Visas	601UNTS153	108693
Bolivia	Argentina	07 Sep 60	Land Transport	0UNTS0	109516
Bolivia	Argentina	09 Dec 60	General Trade	0UNTS0	109549
Bolivia	Argentina	02 Aug 63	Claims and Debts	0UNTS0	109517
Bolivia	Argentina	15 Jun 66	Finance	0UNTS0	109518
Bolivia	Argentina	19 Dec 66	Tech Assistance	636UNTS75	109092
Bolivia	Argentina	19 Dec 66	Education	636UNTS83	109093
Bolivia	Argentina	19 Dec 66	Air Transport	0UNTS0	110180
Bolivia	Argentina	19 Dec 66	Telecommunications	636UNTS89	109094
Bolivia	Argentina	26 Oct 67	Land Transport	0UNTS0	109550
Bolivia	Argentina	18 Apr 68	Commodity Trade	0UNTS0	109551
Bolivia	Argentina	09 Jul 68	Telecommunications	0UNTS0	109552
Bolivia	Argentina	05 Aug 68	Specific Resources	0UNTS0	109553
Bolivia	Argentina	11 Dec 68	General Trade	0UNTS0	109554
Bolivia	Austria	03 Aug 60	Visas	60ABGB216	403006
Bolivia	Belgium	26 Apr 49	Finance	34UNTS103	100530
Bolivia	Belgium	30 Sep 61	Visas	425UNTS53	106118
Bolivia	Brazil	25 Feb 38	Extradition	54UNTS333	200205
Bolivia	Brazil	25 Feb 38	Specific Resources	51UNTS245	200192
Bolivia	Brazil	25 Feb 38	Land Transport	88UNTS379	200254
Bolivia	Canada	31 May 63	Gen Communications	529UNTS37	107654
Bolivia	Denmark	19 Jun 70	Finance	0UNTS0	110795
Bolivia	France	26 May 66	Health/Educ/Welfare	68FRJO1606	416075
Bolivia	Germany, West	04 Aug 66	Culture	70WGBB977	425047
Bolivia	Germany, West	15 Nov 68	Air Transport	70WGBB1197	425048
Bolivia	Germany, West	05 Aug 69	Loans and Credits	69WBGA204	424049
Bolivia	ICJ Option Clause	05 Jul 48	ICJ Option Clause	16UNTS207	100261
Bolivia	IDA (Devel Assoc)	24 Jul 64	Non-IBRD Project	534UNTS171	107762
Bolivia	IDA (Devel Assoc)	24 Jul 64	Non-IBRD Project	534UNTS203	107763
Bolivia	IDA (Devel Assoc)	26 May 67	Non-IBRD Project	618UNTS159	108927
Bolivia	IDA (Devel Assoc)	28 Apr 69	Non-IBRD Project	0UNTS0	110235
Bolivia	IDA (Devel Assoc)	13 Jan 70	Non-IBRD Project	0UNTS0	110652
Bolivia	Italy	31 Jan 53	Culture	281UNTS181	104079
Bolivia	Italy	06 Dec 60	Visas	62ITDI317	436053
Bolivia	Japan	02 Aug 56	Health/Educ/Welfare	0JGJI1299	441096
Bolivia	Mexico	12 Apr 62	Culture	66MEXD1708	444001
Bolivia	Multilateral	17 Feb 40	Privil/Immunities	161UNTS229	200487
Bolivia	Multilateral	30 Jul 40	Admin Cooperation	161UNTS253	200488
Bolivia	Multilateral	12 Oct 40	Specific Resources	161UNTS193	200485
Bolivia	Multilateral	15 Jan 44	IGO Establishment	161UNTS281	200489
Bolivia	Multilateral	02 Aug 44	Scientific Project	67UNTS221	200221
Bolivia	Multilateral	07 Dec 44	Air Transport	84UNTS389	200252
Bolivia	Multilateral	07 Dec 44	Air Transport	171UNTS345	200501
Bolivia	Multilateral	07 Dec 44	Air Transport	171UNTS387	200502
Bolivia	Multilateral	07 Dec 44	IGO Establishment	15UNTS295	200102
Bolivia	Multilateral	15 Dec 44	Sanitation	16UNTS247	200106
Bolivia	Multilateral	16 Nov 45	IGO Establishment	4UNTS275	100052
Bolivia	Multilateral	27 Dec 45	IGO Establishment	2UNTS39	100020
Bolivia	Multilateral	22 Jul 46	IGO Establishment	9UNTS3	100125
Bolivia	Multilateral	22 Jul 46	IGO Establishment	14UNTS185	100221
Bolivia	Multilateral	27 Jul 46	Patents/Copyrights	90UNTS229	101238
Bolivia	Multilateral	11 Dec 46	Sanitation	12UNTS179	100186
Bolivia	Multilateral	15 Dec 46	IGO Establishment	18UNTS3	100283
Bolivia	Multilateral	02 Sep 47	General Military	21UNTS77	100324
Bolivia	Multilateral	30 Apr 48	IGO Establishment	119UNTS3	101609
Bolivia	Multilateral	30 Apr 48	Dispute Settlement	30UNTS55	100449
Bolivia	Multilateral	24 Jul 48	Sanitation	66UNTS25	100847
Bolivia	Multilateral	19 Nov 48	Sanitation	44UNTS277	100688
Bolivia	Multilateral	09 Dec 48	Humanitarian	78UNTS277	101021
Bolivia	Multilateral	23 Mar 49	Commodity Trade	203UNTS179	102746
Bolivia	Multilateral	09 Jul 49	Telecommunications	168UNTS143	102218
Bolivia	Multilateral	12 Aug 49	General Military	75UNTS135	100972

PARTY ONE	PARTY TWO	DATE	TOPIC	CITATION	NUMBER
Bolivia	Multilateral	12 Aug 49	Humanitarian	75UNTS31	100970
Bolivia	Multilateral	12 Aug 49	Humanitarian	75UNTS287	100973
Bolivia	Multilateral	12 Aug 49	Humanitarian	75UNTS85	100971
Bolivia	Multilateral	06 Apr 50	Admin Cooperation	119UNTS99	101610
Bolivia	Multilateral	22 Nov 50	Culture	131UNTS25	101734
Bolivia	Multilateral	25 May 51	Status of Forces	175UNTS215	102303
Bolivia	Multilateral	08 Sep 51	Peace/Disarmament	136UNTS45	101832
Bolivia	Multilateral	01 Oct 51	Tech Assistance	104UNTS249	101446
Bolivia	Multilateral	06 Dec 51	Admin Cooperation	150UNTS67	101963
Bolivia	Multilateral	11 Jul 52	Postal Service	170UNTS3	102221
Bolivia	Multilateral	11 Jul 52	Postal Service	170UNTS63	102222
Bolivia	Multilateral	11 Jul 52	Postal Service	171UNTS143	102226
Bolivia	Multilateral	11 Jul 52	IGO Establishment	169UNTS3	102220
Bolivia	Multilateral	11 Jul 52	Postal Service	170UNTS269	102223
Bolivia	Multilateral	11 Jul 52	Postal Service	171UNTS89	102225
Bolivia	Multilateral	11 Jul 52	Postal Service	171UNTS3	102224
Bolivia	Multilateral	31 Mar 53	Privil/Immunities	193UNTS136	102613
Bolivia	Multilateral	01 Mar 54	Commodity Trade	256UNTS31	103622
Bolivia	Multilateral	14 Jun 54	Air Transport	320UNTS217	104644
Bolivia	Multilateral	14 Jun 54	Air Transport	320UNTS209	104643
Bolivia	Multilateral	25 May 55	IGO Establishment	264UNTS117	103791
Bolivia	Multilateral	25 Apr 56	Commodity Trade	270UNTS103	103896
Bolivia	Multilateral	20 Jun 56	Admin Cooperation	268UNTS3	103850
Bolivia	Multilateral	26 Oct 56	IGO Establishment	276UNTS3	103988
Bolivia	Multilateral	01 Mar 57	Tech Assistance	264UNTS94	103790
Bolivia	Multilateral	03 Oct 57	Postal Service	366UNTS3	105215
Bolivia	Multilateral	03 Oct 57	Postal Service	364UNTS3	105211
Bolivia	Multilateral	03 Oct 57	Postal Service	366UNTS141	105217
Bolivia	Multilateral	03 Oct 57	Postal Service	364UNTS331	105212
Bolivia	Multilateral	03 Oct 57	Postal Service	365UNTS3	105213
Bolivia	Multilateral	03 Oct 57	Postal Service	366UNTS255	105219
Bolivia	Multilateral	03 Oct 57	Postal Service	365UNTS207	105214
Bolivia	Multilateral	03 Oct 57	Postal Service	366UNTS87	105216
Bolivia	Multilateral	29 Apr 58	Dispute Settlement	450UNTS169	106466
Bolivia	Multilateral	29 Apr 58	Water Transport	450UNTS11	106465
Bolivia	Multilateral	29 Apr 58	Specific Resources	559UNTS285	108164
Bolivia	Multilateral	29 Apr 58	Territory Boundary	499UNTS311	107302
Bolivia	Multilateral	29 Apr 58	Territory Boundary	516UNTS205	107477
Bolivia	Multilateral	01 Dec 58	Commodity Trade	385UNTS137	105534
Bolivia	Multilateral	08 Apr 59	IGO Establishment	389UNTS69	105593
Bolivia	Multilateral	26 Jan 60	IGO Establishment	439UNTS249	106333
Bolivia	Multilateral	28 Jul 60	IGO Establishment	485UNTS3	107042
Bolivia	Multilateral	01 Sep 60	Commodity Trade	403UNTS3	105792
Bolivia	Multilateral	26 Mar 62	IGO Establishment	539UNTS67	107825
Bolivia	Multilateral	28 Sep 62	IGO Establishment	469UNTS169	106791
Bolivia	Multilateral	24 Apr 63	Consul/Citizenship	596UNTS261	108638
Bolivia	Multilateral	05 Aug 63	Sanitation	480UNTS43	106964
Bolivia	Multilateral	10 Jul 64	Postal Service	613UNTS193	108852
Bolivia	Multilateral	10 Jul 64	Postal Service	612UNTS361	108849
Bolivia	Multilateral	10 Jul 64	Postal Service	611UNTS7	108844
Bolivia	Multilateral	10 Jul 64	Postal Service	612UNTS3	108847
Bolivia	Multilateral	10 Jul 64	Postal Service	613UNTS3	108850
Bolivia	Multilateral	10 Jul 64	Postal Service	613UNTS3	108851
Bolivia	Multilateral	10 Jul 64	Postal Service	612UNTS233	108848
Bolivia	Multilateral	10 Jul 64	Postal Service	611UNTS387	108846
Bolivia	Multilateral	10 Jul 64	Postal Service	611UNTS105	108845
Bolivia	Multilateral	12 May 65	IGO Operations	534UNTS390	107769
Bolivia	Multilateral	08 Jul 65	General Trade	597UNTS3	108641
Bolivia	Multilateral	31 Dec 65	Specific Resources	616UNTS317	108904
Bolivia	Multilateral	14 Feb 67	General Military	634UNTS281	109068
Bolivia	Multilateral	18 Mar 68	Commodity Trade	0UNTS0	109262
Bolivia	Netherlands	30 Sep 61	Visas	487UNTS105	107097
Bolivia	Netherlands	31 Mar 69	Non-ILO Labor	0UNTS0	110749
Bolivia	Norway	19 Jul 61	Visas	3NORT838	451008
Bolivia	Philippines	22 Feb 63	Visas	490UNTS231	107156
Bolivia	Spain	12 Oct 61	Consul/Citizenship	64SPBO1406	460055
Bolivia	Taiwan	29 Jul 66	Admin Cooperation	0UNTS0	110434
Bolivia	UK Great Britain	18 Mar 60	Visas	374UNTS199	105335
Bolivia	UN Special Fund	09 Feb 60	Direct Aid	351UNTS203	105024
Bolivia	UNICEF (Children)	03 Feb 50	Tech Assistance	65UNTS82	100835
Bolivia	United Nations	01 Oct 51	Tech Assistance	104UNTS263	101447
Bolivia	United Nations	14 Dec 60	Tech Assistance	382UNTS283	105489
Bolivia	USA (United States)	04 Sep 41	Military Mission	8UNTS345	200046
Bolivia	USA (United States)	31 Jan 42	Admin Cooperation	101UNTS137	200290
Bolivia	USA (United States)	16 Jul 42	Sanitation	13UNTS101	200072
Bolivia	USA (United States)	11 Aug 42	Military Mission	9UNTS309	200049
Bolivia	USA (United States)	07 Sep 44	Education	162UNTS315	200494
Bolivia	USA (United States)	10 Jun 46	Mostfavored Nation	13UNTS19	100197
Bolivia	USA (United States)	16 May 47	Tech Assistance	168UNTS89	102215
Bolivia	USA (United States)	03 Nov 47	Air Transport	51UNTS33	100750
Bolivia	USA (United States)	14 Jul 48	Sanitation	136UNTS238	101838
Bolivia	USA (United States)	29 Sep 48	Air Transport	505UNTS139	107370
Bolivia	USA (United States)	16 May 49	Education	162UNTS3	102129
Bolivia	USA (United States)	30 Mar 50	Military Mission	241UNTS77	103425
Bolivia	USA (United States)	22 Nov 50	Education	152UNTS17	102008
Bolivia	USA (United States)	14 Mar 51	Tech Assistance	132UNTS319	101771
Bolivia	USA (United States)	18 Jun 52	Tech Assistance	199UNTS211	102686
Bolivia	USA (United States)	06 Nov 53	Direct Aid	222UNTS41	103021
Bolivia	USA (United States)	15 Jan 54	Tech Assistance	229UNTS213	103168
Bolivia	USA (United States)	16 Jun 54	Direct Aid	234UNTS35	103271
Bolivia	USA (United States)	03 Aug 55	Non-IBRD Project	264UNTS225	103795
Bolivia	USA (United States)	09 Sep 55	Military Mission	256UNTS239	103633
Bolivia	USA (United States)	23 Sep 55	Claims and Debts	256UNTS275	103637
Bolivia	USA (United States)	10 Mar 56	Mass Media	270UNTS199	103897
Bolivia	USA (United States)	30 Jun 56	Military Mission	271UNTS243	103919
Bolivia	USA (United States)	30 Jun 56	Military Mission	271UNTS269	103920
Bolivia	USA (United States)	07 Jun 57	US Agri Commod Aid	291UNTS77	104245
Bolivia	USA (United States)	22 Apr 58	Milit Assistance	317UNTS209	104605
Bolivia	USA (United States)	09 Feb 61	Milit Assistance	405UNTS113	105827
Bolivia	USA (United States)	07 Apr 61	US Agri Commod Aid	433UNTS3	106227
Bolivia	USA (United States)	23 Oct 61	Telecommunications	424UNTS93	106101
Bolivia	USA (United States)	15 Nov 61	US Agri Commod Aid	456UNTS192	106557
Bolivia	USA (United States)	12 Feb 62	US Agri Commod Aid	451UNTS281	106499
Bolivia	USA (United States)	26 Apr 62	Milit Assistance	461UNTS105	106654
Bolivia	USA (United States)	19 Jun 62	General Aid	458UNTS239	106606
Bolivia	USA (United States)	17 Dec 62	US Agri Commod Aid	469UNTS121	106788
Bolivia	USA (United States)	04 Feb 63	US Agri Commod Aid	473UNTS65	106856
Bolivia	USA (United States)	25 Mar 64	US Agri Commod Aid	532UNTS3	107710
Bolivia	USA (United States)	16 Mar 65	Gen Communications	542UNTS209	107891
Bolivia	USA (United States)	12 May 65	US Agri Commod Aid	564UNTS143	108226
Bolivia	USA (United States)	17 Aug 65	US Agri Commod Aid	587UNTS289	108514
Bolivia	USA (United States)	22 Apr 66	US Agri Commod Aid	578UNTS73	108388
Bolivia	USA (United States)	16 Jan 68	US Agri Commod Aid	0UNTS0	110064
Bolivia	USA (United States)	16 Jan 68	US Agri Commod Aid	0UNTS0	110065
Bolivia	USA (United States)	07 Mar 69	US Agri Commod Aid	0UNTS0	110153
Bolivia	USA (United States)	07 Mar 69	US Agri Commod Aid	0UNTS0	110154
Bolivia	USSR (Soviet Union)	18 Apr 45	Consul/Citizenship	0SUST176	471014
Bolivia	WHO (World Health)	07 Feb 51	Sanitation	104UNTS167	101438
Botswana	Accept UN Charter	30 Sep 66	UN Charter	575UNTS151	108357
Botswana	ICJ Option Clause	14 Jan 70	ICJ Option Clause	0UNTS0	110359
Botswana	Multilateral	28 Sep 54	Refugees	360UNTS117	105158
Botswana	Multilateral	26 Jan 60	IGO Establishment	439UNTS249	106333
Botswana	Multilateral	18 Apr 61	Consul/Citizenship	500UNTS223	107311
Botswana	Multilateral	18 Apr 61	Dispute Settlement	500UNTS243	107312
Botswana	Multilateral	10 Jul 64	Postal Service	612UNTS3	108847
Botswana	Multilateral	30 Sep 66	IGO Operations	576UNTS8	108361
Botswana	Multilateral	31 Jan 67	Refugees	606UNTS267	108791
Botswana	Multilateral	12 Oct 67	Direct Aid	607UNTS20	108793
Botswana	Multilateral	12 Oct 67	Direct Aid	607UNTS2	108792
Botswana	Multilateral	22 Apr 68	Scientific Project	0UNTS0	109574

PARTY ONE	PARTY TWO	DATE	TOPIC	CITATION	NUMBER
Botswana	Multilateral	01 Jul 68	Peace/Disarmament	0UNTS0	110485
Botswana	Multilateral	27 Jan 69	Telecommunications	0UNTS0	109664
Botswana	UK Great Britain	30 Sep 66	Status of Forces	597UNTS211	108646
Botswana	UK Great Britain	30 Sep 66	Consul/Citizenship	633UNTS339	109044
Botswana	UK Great Britain	09 Oct 68	Military Mission	0UNTS0	109711
Botswana	UK Great Britain	01 Sep 69	Finance	0UNTS0	110240
Botswana	UK Great Britain	06 Apr 70	Taxation	0UNTS0	110808
Botswana	UN Special Fund	30 Sep 66	IGO Operations	576UNTS3	108360
Botswana	UN Special Fund	12 Oct 67	Direct Aid	607UNTS37	108794
Botswana	UNICEF (Children)	25 Jun 68	IGO Operations	639UNTS61	109144
Botswana	United Nations	30 Sep 66	Tech Assistance	576UNTS17	108362
Botswana	USA (United States)	30 Sep 66	Admin Cooperation	0UNTS0	109682
Botswana	USA (United States)	12 Jan 68	Finance	0UNTS0	109997
Brazil	Argentina	27 Dec 27	Territory Boundary	51UNTS271	200193
Brazil	Argentina	23 Jan 40	Admin Cooperation	51UNTS281	200194
Brazil	Argentina	02 Jun 48	Air Transport	0UNTS0	109515
Brazil	Argentina	19 Sep 58	Tech Assistance	374UNTS57	105329
Brazil	Argentina	22 Dec 58	Water Transport	0UNTS0	109545
Brazil	Argentina	26 Nov 59	Visas	374UNTS51	105328
Brazil	Argentina	26 Nov 59	General Trade	374UNTS39	105326
Brazil	Argentina	26 Nov 59	General Trade	374UNTS31	105325
Brazil	Argentina	26 Nov 59	General Trade	374UNTS45	105327
Brazil	Argentina	06 Jul 61	Postal Service	0UNTS0	109410
Brazil	Argentina	15 Nov 61	Extradition	0UNTS0	109424
Brazil	Argentina	15 Nov 61	Admin Cooperation	0UNTS0	109546
Brazil	Argentina	23 Apr 65	IGO Establishment	0UNTS0	109411
Brazil	Argentina	25 Jan 68	Culture	0UNTS0	109547
Brazil	Argentina	27 Sep 68	Water Transport	0UNTS0	109420
Brazil	Argentina	24 Jan 69	Telecommunications	0UNTS0	109548
Brazil	Australia	15 Aug 69	Visas	0UNTS0	110177
Brazil	Austria	04 Jul 56	Finance	57ABGB47	403008
Brazil	Austria	04 Jul 56	General Economic	57ABGB46	403007
Brazil	Austria	07 Dec 59	Visas	67ABGB332	403009
Brazil	Austria	21 Dec 65	Admin Cooperation	595UNTS299	108624
Brazil	Austria	22 Aug 67	Visas	0UNTS0	109528
Brazil	Belgium	14 Jun 41	Extradition	272UNTS157	103936
Brazil	Belgium	08 May 51	Consul/Citizenship	91UNTS75	101242
Brazil	Belgium	11 Aug 51	Consul/Citizenship	104UNTS17	101431
Brazil	Belgium	10 Jan 55	Admin Cooperation	272UNTS181	103937
Brazil	Belgium	27 Feb 57	Visas	265UNTS189	103812
Brazil	Belgium	06 Jan 60	Culture	531UNTS149	107701
Brazil	Bolivia	25 Feb 38	Land Transport	88UNTS379	200254
Brazil	Bolivia	25 Feb 38	Extradition	54UNTS333	200205
Brazil	Bolivia	25 Feb 38	Specific Resources	51UNTS245	200192
Brazil	Bulgaria	30 Nov 66	Finance	0UNTS0	109874
Brazil	Canada	17 Oct 41	General Trade	67UNTS263	200224
Brazil	Canada	24 May 44	Culture	65UNTS265	200215
Brazil	Chile	18 Nov 41	Culture	67UNTS279	200225
Brazil	Chile	18 Mar 66	Mass Media	0UNTS0	109418
Brazil	Colombia	28 May 58	Tech Assistance	369UNTS141	105255
Brazil	Colombia	02 Aug 62	Visas	0UNTS0	109422
Brazil	Costa Rica	19 Nov 64	Culture	0UNTS0	109429
Brazil	Denmark	14 Nov 47	Air Transport	47UNTS39	100722
Brazil	Denmark	25 Feb 66	Tech Assistance	590UNTS95	108549
Brazil	Denmark	08 Jul 66	Loans and Credits	581UNTS95	108435
Brazil	Dominican Republic	09 Dec 42	Culture	65UNTS217	200213
Brazil	Dominican Republic	09 Apr 45	Culture	67UNTS293	200226
Brazil	Ecuador	24 May 44	Culture	73UNTS223	200242
Brazil	Ecuador	31 May 47	Consul/Citizenship	72UNTS25	100925
Brazil	Ecuador	04 May 53	General Trade	369UNTS37	105249
Brazil	Ecuador	05 Mar 58	General Economic	369UNTS43	105250
Brazil	Ecuador	19 May 65	Visas	0UNTS0	109419
Brazil	El Salvador	30 Nov 65	Culture	0UNTS0	109430
Brazil	France	27 Jan 40	Air Transport	72UNTS77	100929
Brazil	France	06 Dec 46	Culture	0UNTS0	110228

PARTY ONE	PARTY TWO	DATE	TOPIC	CITATION	NUMBER
Brazil	France	06 Dec 48	Culture	60FRRT58	415076
Brazil	France	04 May 56	Finance	323UNTS339	104675
Brazil	France	23 Aug 56	General Economic	56FRMD1009	417077
Brazil	France	22 Jan 63	Tech Assistance	69FRJO2005	416078
Brazil	France	22 Jan 63	Privil/Immunities	0UNTS0	110229
Brazil	France	26 Oct 65	Finance	66FRRT10	415079
Brazil	France	29 Oct 65	Air Transport	67FRJO1105	416080
Brazil	France	16 Jan 67	Tech Assistance	69FRJO2704	416081
Brazil	France	16 Jan 67	Tech Assistance	0UNTS0	110230
Brazil	France	20 Jun 68	Specific Property	69FRJO1903	416082
Brazil	France	20 Jun 68	Scientific Project	0UNTS0	110231
Brazil	France	06 Feb 69	Culture	69FRJO506	416083
Brazil	France	06 Feb 69	Culture	0UNTS0	110555
Brazil	France	21 Mar 69	Specific Property	69FRJO1609	416084
Brazil	Germany, West	17 Aug 50	General Trade	51WGBB11	425050
Brazil	Germany, West	04 Sep 53	Patents/Copyrights	54WGBB533	425051
Brazil	Germany, West	04 Sep 53	Claims and Debts	50WBGA212	424052
Brazil	Germany, West	01 Jul 55	General Trade	55WBGA141	424053
Brazil	Germany, West	15 May 57	Admin Cooperation	58WBGA91	424054
Brazil	Germany, West	29 Aug 57	Air Transport	59WGBB73	425055
Brazil	Germany, West	30 Nov 63	Consul/Citizenship	0UNTS0	109423
Brazil	Germany, West	30 Nov 63	Finance	0UNTS0	109425
Brazil	Germany, West	30 Nov 63	Water Transport	0UNTS0	109426
Brazil	Germany, West	30 Nov 63	Tech Assistance	64WBGA49	424056
Brazil	Germany, West	30 Nov 63	Consul/Citizenship	65WGBB1565	425057
Brazil	Germany, West	30 Nov 63	Tech Assistance	0UNTS0	109421
Brazil	Germany, West	09 Apr 69	Loans and Credits	69WBGA106	424058
Brazil	Germany, West	30 May 69	Loans and Credits	69WBGA138	424059
Brazil	Germany, West	09 Jun 69	Culture	71WGBB117	425061
Brazil	Germany, West	09 Jun 69	Scientific Project	69WBGA2118	424060
Brazil	Germany, West	02 Oct 70	Loans and Credits	70WBGA232	424062
Brazil	Germany, West	23 Apr 71	Loans and Credits	71WBGA109	424063
Brazil	Greece	30 Jul 60	General Trade	607UNTS245	108808
Brazil	IBRD (World Bank)	27 Jan 49	IBRD Project	153UNTS264	102026
Brazil	IBRD (World Bank)	26 May 50	IBRD Project	301UNTS165	104345
Brazil	IBRD (World Bank)	27 Jun 52	IBRD Project	190UNTS115	102561
Brazil	IBRD (World Bank)	27 Jun 52	IBRD Project	190UNTS85	102560
Brazil	IBRD (World Bank)	30 Apr 53	IBRD Project	190UNTS133	102562
Brazil	IBRD (World Bank)	17 Jul 53	IBRD Project	190UNTS149	102563
Brazil	IBRD (World Bank)	18 Dec 53	IBRD Project	301UNTS229	104346
Brazil	IBRD (World Bank)	18 Dec 53	IBRD Project	190UNTS179	102564
Brazil	IBRD (World Bank)	24 Feb 54	IBRD Project	301UNTS249	104347
Brazil	IBRD (World Bank)	22 Jan 58	IBRD Project	323UNTS99	104666
Brazil	IBRD (World Bank)	03 Oct 58	IBRD Project	337UNTS177	104823
Brazil	IBRD (World Bank)	17 Jun 59	IBRD Project	377UNTS111	105398
Brazil	IBRD (World Bank)	26 Feb 65	IBRD Project	567UNTS91	108253
Brazil	IBRD (World Bank)	26 Feb 65	IBRD Project	553UNTS3	108065
Brazil	IBRD (World Bank)	15 Mar 66	IBRD Project	599UNTS52	108664
Brazil	IBRD (World Bank)	19 Dec 66	IBRD Project	599UNTS107	108665
Brazil	IBRD (World Bank)	19 Dec 66	IBRD Project	599UNTS149	108666
Brazil	IBRD (World Bank)	19 Dec 66	IBRD Project	599UNTS177	108667
Brazil	IBRD (World Bank)	19 Dec 66	IBRD Project	599UNTS205	108668
Brazil	IBRD (World Bank)	23 Sep 67	IBRD Project	620UNTS77	108951
Brazil	IBRD (World Bank)	26 Jan 68	IBRD Project	0UNTS0	109613
Brazil	IBRD (World Bank)	23 Oct 68	IBRD Project	0UNTS0	109628
Brazil	IBRD (World Bank)	23 Oct 68	IBRD Project	0UNTS0	109629
Brazil	IBRD (World Bank)	23 Oct 68	IBRD Project	0UNTS0	110119
Brazil	IBRD (World Bank)	16 Feb 70	IBRD Project	0UNTS0	110826
Brazil	ICJ Option Clause	12 Feb 48	ICJ Option Clause	15UNTS221	100237
Brazil	Iran	22 Nov 57	Culture	0IRTB15	433024
Brazil	Israel	24 Jun 59	Culture	515UNTS151	107458
Brazil	Israel	27 Jan 67	Commodity Trade	0UNTS0	109845
Brazil	Italy	08 Oct 49	Peace/Disarmament	50ITGU195	435054
Brazil	Italy	12 Oct 49	General Amity	1ITMA365	437055
Brazil	Italy	05 Jul 50	General Economic	51ITGU38	435057

PARTY ONE	PARTY TWO	DATE	TOPIC	CITATION	NUMBER
Brazil	Italy	05 Jul 50	General Economic	51ITGU36	435056
Brazil	Italy	25 Jan 51	Air Transport	52ITGU169	435058
Brazil	Italy	24 Nov 54	Dispute Settlement	284UNTS325	104146
Brazil	Italy	04 Oct 57	Taxation	62ITGU240	435059
Brazil	Italy	08 Jan 58	Reparations	362UNTS273	105192
Brazil	Italy	06 Sep 58	Culture	62ITGU153	435062
Brazil	Italy	06 Sep 58	Milit Servic/Citiz	60ITGU215	435060
Brazil	Italy	06 Sep 58	Atomic Energy	60ITGU96	435061
Brazil	Italy	21 Apr 60	Visas	62ITDI319	436063
Brazil	Italy	28 Nov 60	Consul/Citizenship	62ITDI468	436064
Brazil	Italy	09 Dec 60	Health/Educ/Welfare	63ITGU109	435065
Brazil	Italy	06 Sep 63	Patents/Copyrights	64ITDI240	436066
Brazil	Italy	18 Apr 64	Mass Media	65ITDI120	436067
Brazil	Japan	14 Dec 56	Air Transport	0JGJI1485	441101
Brazil	Japan	14 Nov 60	Consul/Citizenship	518UNTS29	107491
Brazil	Japan	23 Jan 61	Culture	569UNTS81	108281
Brazil	Japan	28 Mar 62	Education	451UNTS125	106489
Brazil	Japan	19 Feb 65	Finance	0JGJI1585	441130
Brazil	Japan	26 Mar 65	Finance	0JGJI1587	441133
Brazil	Japan	07 Oct 66	Loans and Credits	68JJS39	442178
Brazil	Japan	24 Jan 67	Taxation	67JHZ12	439005
Brazil	Japan	24 Jan 67	Taxation	0UNTS0	109716
Brazil	Japan	23 Jun 67	Customs	67JJS93	442195
Brazil	Korea, South	07 Feb 66	Culture	0UNTS0	109524
Brazil	Mexico	20 Jan 60	Culture	65MEXD2306	444002
Brazil	Mexico	17 Oct 66	Air Transport	71MEXD903	444003
Brazil	Multilateral	17 Feb 40	Privil/Immunities	161UNTS229	200487
Brazil	Multilateral	30 Jul 40	Admin Cooperation	161UNTS253	200488
Brazil	Multilateral	12 Oct 40	Specific Resources	161UNTS193	200485
Brazil	Multilateral	28 Nov 40	Commodity Trade	139UNTS159	200452
Brazil	Multilateral	27 Mar 41	Military Mission	67UNTS231	200222
Brazil	Multilateral	21 Dec 43	Commodity Trade	65UNTS231	200214
Brazil	Multilateral	02 Aug 44	Scientific Project	67UNTS221	200221
Brazil	Multilateral	07 Dec 44	Air Transport	171UNTS345	200501
Brazil	Multilateral	07 Dec 44	IGO Establishment	15UNTS295	200102
Brazil	Multilateral	16 Nov 45	IGO Establishment	4UNTS275	100052
Brazil	Multilateral	27 Dec 45	IGO Establishment	2UNTS39	100020
Brazil	Multilateral	22 Jul 46	IGO Establishment	14UNTS185	100221
Brazil	Multilateral	22 Jul 46	IGO Establishment	9UNTS3	100125
Brazil	Multilateral	03 Sep 46	Commodity Trade	139UNTS3	101872
Brazil	Multilateral	15 Oct 46	Refugees	11UNTS73	100150
Brazil	Multilateral	02 Dec 46	Specific Resources	161UNTS72	102124
Brazil	Multilateral	11 Dec 46	Sanitation	12UNTS179	100186
Brazil	Multilateral	15 Dec 46	IGO Establishment	18UNTS3	100283
Brazil	Multilateral	23 Dec 46	Commodity Trade	126UNTS47	101681
Brazil	Multilateral	08 Feb 47	Patents/Copyrights	14UNTS287	100222
Brazil	Multilateral	10 Feb 47	Peace/Disarmament	49UNTS3	100747
Brazil	Multilateral	27 May 47	Air Transport	418UNTS161	106021
Brazil	Multilateral	02 Sep 47	General Military	21UNTS77	100324
Brazil	Multilateral	02 Oct 47	Telecommunications	193UNTS188	102616
Brazil	Multilateral	11 Oct 47	IGO Establishment	77UNTS143	100998
Brazil	Multilateral	12 Nov 47	Admin Cooperation	53UNTS13	100770
Brazil	Multilateral	12 Nov 47	Admin Cooperation	53UNTS49	100772
Brazil	Multilateral	12 Nov 47	Admin Cooperation	46UNTS169	100709
Brazil	Multilateral	12 Nov 47	Admin Cooperation	46UNTS201	100710
Brazil	Multilateral	12 Nov 47	Admin Cooperation	53UNTS39	100771
Brazil	Multilateral	06 Mar 48	Water Transport	289UNTS3	104214
Brazil	Multilateral	30 Apr 48	Dispute Settlement	30UNTS55	100449
Brazil	Multilateral	30 Apr 48	IGO Establishment	119UNTS3	101609
Brazil	Multilateral	10 Jun 48	Humanitarian	191UNTS3	102576
Brazil	Multilateral	10 Jun 48	Humanitarian	164UNTS113	102163
Brazil	Multilateral	19 Jun 48	Air Transport	310UNTS151	104492
Brazil	Multilateral	26 Jun 48	Culture	331UNTS217	104757
Brazil	Multilateral	24 Jul 48	Sanitation	66UNTS25	100847
Brazil	Multilateral	14 Sep 48	Milit Occupation	18UNTS267	100296

PARTY ONE	PARTY TWO	DATE	TOPIC	CITATION	NUMBER
Brazil	Multilateral	19 Nov 48	Sanitation	44UNTS277	100688
Brazil	Multilateral	29 Nov 48	IGO Establishment	120UNTS13	101613
Brazil	Multilateral	09 Dec 48	Humanitarian	78UNTS277	101021
Brazil	Multilateral	23 Mar 49	Commodity Trade	203UNTS179	102746
Brazil	Multilateral	04 May 49	Admin Cooperation	30UNTS3	100445
Brazil	Multilateral	04 May 49	Admin Cooperation	30UNTS23	100446
Brazil	Multilateral	18 Jun 49	ILO Labor	605UNTS295	108768
Brazil	Multilateral	09 Jul 49	Telecommunications	168UNTS143	102218
Brazil	Multilateral	15 Jul 49	Health/Educ/Welfare	197UNTS3	102631
Brazil	Multilateral	12 Aug 49	Humanitarian	75UNTS31	100970
Brazil	Multilateral	12 Aug 49	Humanitarian	75UNTS85	100971
Brazil	Multilateral	12 Aug 49	General Military	75UNTS135	100972
Brazil	Multilateral	12 Aug 49	Humanitarian	75UNTS287	100973
Brazil	Multilateral	16 Dec 49	Admin Cooperation	72UNTS3	100924
Brazil	Multilateral	21 Mar 50	Admin Cooperation	96UNTS271	101342
Brazil	Multilateral	06 Apr 50	Admin Cooperation	119UNTS99	101610
Brazil	Multilateral	07 Dec 50	Admin Cooperation	212UNTS17	102861
Brazil	Multilateral	25 May 51	Status of Forces	175UNTS215	102303
Brazil	Multilateral	02 Jul 51	Refugees	189UNTS137	102545
Brazil	Multilateral	08 Sep 51	Peace/Disarmament	136UNTS45	101832
Brazil	Multilateral	06 Dec 51	Admin Cooperation	150UNTS67	101963
Brazil	Multilateral	10 May 52	Admin Cooperation	439UNTS217	106331
Brazil	Multilateral	10 May 52	Admin Cooperation	439UNTS193	106330
Brazil	Multilateral	10 May 52	Taxation	439UNTS233	106332
Brazil	Multilateral	11 Jul 52	Postal Service	170UNTS63	102222
Brazil	Multilateral	11 Jul 52	IGO Establishment	169UNTS3	102220
Brazil	Multilateral	11 Jul 52	Postal Service	170UNTS3	102221
Brazil	Multilateral	06 Sep 52	Patents/Copyrights	216UNTS132	102937
Brazil	Multilateral	07 Oct 52	Admin Cooperation	310UNTS181	104493
Brazil	Multilateral	31 Mar 53	Privil/Immunities	193UNTS136	102613
Brazil	Multilateral	11 May 53	Sanitation	456UNTS3	106555
Brazil	Multilateral	14 May 54	Culture	249UNTS215	103511
Brazil	Multilateral	14 Jun 54	Air Transport	320UNTS209	104643
Brazil	Multilateral	14 Jun 54	Air Transport	320UNTS217	104644
Brazil	Multilateral	28 Sep 54	Refugees	360UNTS117	105158
Brazil	Multilateral	15 May 55	Recognition	217UNTS223	102949
Brazil	Multilateral	25 May 55	IGO Establishment	264UNTS117	103791
Brazil	Multilateral	28 Sep 55	Air Transport	478UNTS371	106943
Brazil	Multilateral	25 Apr 56	Commodity Trade	270UNTS103	103896
Brazil	Multilateral	20 Jun 56	Admin Cooperation	268UNTS3	103850
Brazil	Multilateral	26 Oct 56	IGO Establishment	276UNTS3	103988
Brazil	Multilateral	20 Feb 57	Consul/Citizenship	309UNTS65	104468
Brazil	Multilateral	01 May 57	Admin Cooperation	284UNTS201	104138
Brazil	Multilateral	03 Oct 57	Postal Service	365UNTS3	105213
Brazil	Multilateral	03 Oct 57	Postal Service	364UNTS331	105212
Brazil	Multilateral	03 Oct 57	Postal Service	364UNTS3	105211
Brazil	Multilateral	01 Dec 58	Commodity Trade	385UNTS137	105534
Brazil	Multilateral	03 Dec 58	Admin Cooperation	416UNTS51	105995
Brazil	Multilateral	06 Apr 59	Commodity Trade	349UNTS167	105013
Brazil	Multilateral	08 Apr 59	IGO Establishment	389UNTS69	105593
Brazil	Multilateral	18 Nov 59	IGO Establishment	390UNTS227	105610
Brazil	Multilateral	26 Jan 60	IGO Establishment	439UNTS249	106333
Brazil	Multilateral	17 Jun 60	Humanitarian	536UNTS27	107794
Brazil	Multilateral	14 Dec 60	Education	429UNTS93	106193
Brazil	Multilateral	30 Mar 61	Sanitation	520UNTS151	107515
Brazil	Multilateral	18 Apr 61	Consul/Citizenship	500UNTS95	107310
Brazil	Multilateral	26 Oct 61	Patents/Copyrights	496UNTS43	107247
Brazil	Multilateral	26 Mar 62	IGO Establishment	539UNTS67	107825
Brazil	Multilateral	15 May 62	Commodity Trade	444UNTS3	106367
Brazil	Multilateral	28 Sep 62	IGO Establishment	469UNTS169	106791
Brazil	Multilateral	24 Apr 63	Consul/Citizenship	596UNTS261	108638
Brazil	Multilateral	05 Aug 63	Sanitation	480UNTS43	106964
Brazil	Multilateral	10 Jul 64	Postal Service	611UNTS387	108846
Brazil	Multilateral	10 Jul 64	Postal Service	611UNTS105	108845
Brazil	Multilateral	10 Jul 64	Postal Service	612UNTS3	108847

PARTY ONE	PARTY TWO	DATE	TOPIC	CITATION	NUMBER
Brazil	Multilateral	10 Jul 64	Postal Service	611UNTS7	108844
Brazil	Multilateral	09 Mar 65	Water Transport	591UNTS265	108564
Brazil	Multilateral	08 Jul 65	General Trade	597UNTS3	108641
Brazil	Multilateral	05 Apr 66	Water Transport	640UNTS133	109159
Brazil	Multilateral	14 May 66	Specific Resources	0UNTS0	109587
Brazil	Multilateral	27 Jan 67	Scientific Project	610UNTS205	108843
Brazil	Multilateral	14 Feb 67	General Military	634UNTS281	109068
Brazil	Multilateral	03 May 67	IGO Operations	0UNTS0	110764
Brazil	Multilateral	18 Mar 68	Commodity Trade	0UNTS0	109262
Brazil	Multilateral	24 Dec 68	Commodity Trade	0UNTS0	109369
Brazil	Netherlands	06 Nov 47	Air Transport	53UNTS59	100773
Brazil	Netherlands	15 Dec 50	Non-ILO Labor	123UNTS101	101657
Brazil	Netherlands	29 Nov 55	General Economic	56NET96	447059
Brazil	Netherlands	16 Mar 59	Admin Cooperation	499UNTS219	107300
Brazil	Netherlands	12 Oct 66	Culture	643UNTS271	109197
Brazil	Norway	14 Nov 47	Air Transport	44UNTS163	100684
Brazil	Norway	27 May 52	Consul/Citizenship	2NORT583	451009
Brazil	Norway	19 Dec 56	Patents/Copyrights	3NORT705	451010
Brazil	Norway	29 May 59	Visas	3NORT772	451011
Brazil	Norway	11 Aug 61	Finance	3NORT839	451012
Brazil	Norway	20 Oct 67	Taxation	3NORT1005	451013
Brazil	Norway	30 Oct 67	Taxation	0UNTS0	110602
Brazil	Paraguay	14 Apr 41	Commodity Trade	54UNTS269	200199
Brazil	Paraguay	14 Jun 41	Culture	54UNTS249	200197
Brazil	Paraguay	14 Jun 41	Visas	88UNTS401	200255
Brazil	Paraguay	14 Jun 41	Land Transport	54UNTS289	200201
Brazil	Paraguay	14 Jun 41	IGO Establishment	54UNTS303	200202
Brazil	Paraguay	14 Jun 41	Admin Cooperation	54UNTS279	200200
Brazil	Paraguay	14 Jun 41	Finance	54UNTS313	200203
Brazil	Paraguay	14 Jun 41	Culture	54UNTS235	200196
Brazil	Paraguay	14 Jun 41	Specific Property	54UNTS259	200198
Brazil	Paraguay	14 Jun 41	IGO Establishment	54UNTS323	200204
Brazil	Paraguay	08 Oct 42	Telecommunications	65UNTS191	200211
Brazil	Paraguay	11 Aug 44	Land Transport	67UNTS303	200227
Brazil	Poland	24 Oct 52	General Economic	53PZUM59	458006
Brazil	Poland	19 Oct 61	Culture	552UNTS75	108050
Brazil	Poland	25 May 68	Water Transport	68PZUM88	458158
Brazil	Portugal	30 Apr 42	Postal Service	65UNTS183	200210
Brazil	Portugal	10 Dec 46	Air Transport	200UNTS67	102695
Brazil	Spain	28 Nov 49	Air Transport	215UNTS303	102923
Brazil	Spain	30 Dec 54	General Economic	55SPBO2201	460056
Brazil	Spain	30 Sep 57	General Economic	57SPBO1810	460057
Brazil	Spain	25 Jun 60	Culture	65SPBO907	460058
Brazil	Spain	25 Jun 60	Culture	0UNTS0	109427
Brazil	Spain	13 Oct 60	Visas	0UNTS0	109416
Brazil	Spain	27 Dec 60	Health/Educ/Welfare	64SPBO508	460061
Brazil	Spain	27 Dec 60	Health/Educ/Welfare	64SPBO508	460059
Brazil	Spain	27 Dec 60	Health/Educ/Welfare	64SPBO508	460060
Brazil	Spain	27 Dec 60	Visas	0UNTS0	109428
Brazil	Spain	11 Aug 64	Health/Educ/Welfare	0UNTS0	109417
Brazil	Spain	12 Aug 65	Visas	0UNTS0	109486
Brazil	Sweden	14 Nov 47	Air Transport	94UNTS139	101310
Brazil	Sweden	29 Apr 55	Patents/Copyrights	228UNTS115	103145
Brazil	Switzerland	10 Aug 48	Air Transport	94UNTS269	101314
Brazil	Switzerland	22 Jun 56	Taxation	56SWRO1087	462045
Brazil	Taiwan	20 Aug 43	General Amity	14UNTS365	200094
Brazil	Taiwan	27 Mar 46	Culture	0CTRC43	413001
Brazil	Taiwan	28 Dec 62	General Trade	500UNTS61	107307
Brazil	Turkey	21 Sep 50	Air Transport	150UNTS299	101981
Brazil	UK Great Britain	15 Mar 40	Territory Boundary	5UNTS71	200029
Brazil	UK Great Britain	27 May 44	Milit Servic/Citiz	2UNTS235	200016
Brazil	UK Great Britain	31 Oct 46	Air Transport	11UNTS115	100152
Brazil	UK Great Britain	21 May 48	Finance	66UNTS121	100851
Brazil	UK Great Britain	03 Aug 49	General Trade	86UNTS113	101154
Brazil	UK Great Britain	18 Sep 50	General Trade	88UNTS115	101188
Brazil	UK Great Britain	01 Oct 53	Claims and Debts	183UNTS207	102430
Brazil	UK Great Britain	05 Apr 55	Milit Servic/Citiz	403UNTS139	105793
Brazil	UK Great Britain	21 Jul 61	Loans and Credits	414UNTS26	105962
Brazil	UK Great Britain	14 Oct 64	Loans and Credits	539UNTS289	107840
Brazil	UK Great Britain	29 Dec 67	Taxation	643UNTS217	109193
Brazil	UK Great Britain	18 Jan 68	Tech Assistance	0UNTS0	109472
Brazil	UN Special Fund	16 Sep 60	Tech Assistance	375UNTS3	105351
Brazil	UNICEF (Children)	09 Jun 50	IGO Operations	66UNTS75	100848
Brazil	UNICEF (Children)	28 Mar 66	IGO Operations	607UNTS235	108807
Brazil	United Nations	04 Aug 52	Tech Assistance	135UNTS185	101820
Brazil	United Nations	13 Aug 57	Milit Assistance	274UNTS199	103966
Brazil	United Nations	24 Mar 66	IGO Establishment	560UNTS47	108167
Brazil	UNRRA (Relief)	12 Oct 44	IGO Establishment	67UNTS321	200228
Brazil	Uruguay	08 Jan 42	Admin Cooperation	54UNTS359	200206
Brazil	Uruguay	18 May 42	Telecommunications	54UNTS369	200207
Brazil	Uruguay	22 Nov 44	Specif Goods/Equip	65UNTS289	200217
Brazil	Uruguay	16 Dec 44	Admin Cooperation	65UNTS305	200218
Brazil	USA (United States)	03 Mar 42	Tech Assistance	105UNTS99	200325
Brazil	USA (United States)	03 Mar 42	Tech Assistance	105UNTS91	200324
Brazil	USA (United States)	14 Mar 42	Sanitation	102UNTS195	200302
Brazil	USA (United States)	07 May 42	Military Mission	6UNTS377	200040
Brazil	USA (United States)	17 Jul 42	Sanitation	102UNTS203	200303
Brazil	USA (United States)	03 Sep 42	Non-IBRD Project	13UNTS109	200073
Brazil	USA (United States)	10 Feb 43	Sanitation	102UNTS217	200304
Brazil	USA (United States)	24 May 43	Status of Forces	28UNTS385	200162
Brazil	USA (United States)	25 Nov 43	Sanitation	102UNTS227	200305
Brazil	USA (United States)	29 Sep 44	Military Mission	65UNTS271	200216
Brazil	USA (United States)	15 Feb 46	Education	162UNTS21	102130
Brazil	USA (United States)	05 Apr 46	Education	12UNTS131	100183
Brazil	USA (United States)	28 Jun 46	Milit Assistance	6UNTS327	100085
Brazil	USA (United States)	06 Sep 46	Air Transport	54UNTS197	100805
Brazil	USA (United States)	17 Sep 46	Military Mission	7UNTS49	100091
Brazil	USA (United States)	02 Feb 48	Status of Forces	67UNTS109	100870
Brazil	USA (United States)	30 Jun 48	General Trade	125UNTS111	101673
Brazil	USA (United States)	29 Jul 48	Military Mission	80UNTS111	101047
Brazil	USA (United States)	26 Nov 48	Scientific Project	88UNTS3	101180
Brazil	USA (United States)	30 Dec 48	Sanitation	102UNTS3	101406
Brazil	USA (United States)	31 Aug 49	Sanitation	102UNTS13	101407
Brazil	USA (United States)	23 May 50	Admin Cooperation	151UNTS141	101989
Brazil	USA (United States)	16 Aug 50	Tech Assistance	140UNTS223	101890
Brazil	USA (United States)	19 Dec 50	Direct Aid	140UNTS365	101899
Brazil	USA (United States)	19 Dec 50	Tech Assistance	141UNTS3	101900
Brazil	USA (United States)	27 Dec 50	Sanitation	147UNTS33	101926
Brazil	USA (United States)	04 Jan 51	Milit Assistance	165UNTS97	102171
Brazil	USA (United States)	29 Jun 51	Tech Assistance	184UNTS303	102455
Brazil	USA (United States)	24 Jul 51	Direct Aid	134UNTS195	101799
Brazil	USA (United States)	15 Mar 52	Milit Assistance	199UNTS221	102687
Brazil	USA (United States)	02 Jun 52	Scientific Project	181UNTS109	102403
Brazil	USA (United States)	30 Jun 52	Tech Assistance	185UNTS79	102460
Brazil	USA (United States)	30 May 53	Tech Assistance	460UNTS89	106633
Brazil	USA (United States)	26 Jun 53	Direct Aid	336UNTS241	104808
Brazil	USA (United States)	30 Jun 54	Non-IBRD Project	237UNTS137	103341
Brazil	USA (United States)	20 Aug 54	Commodity Trade	410UNTS79	105898
Brazil	USA (United States)	03 Aug 55	Atomic Energy	235UNTS159	103300
Brazil	USA (United States)	03 Aug 55	Scientific Project	270UNTS71	103893
Brazil	USA (United States)	20 Sep 55	Military Mission	257UNTS349	103665
Brazil	USA (United States)	16 Nov 55	Commodity Trade	239UNTS207	103381
Brazil	USA (United States)	31 Dec 56	US Agri Commod Aid	266UNTS151	103829
Brazil	USA (United States)	16 Jan 57	Milit Assistance	266UNTS99	103824
Brazil	USA (United States)	21 Jan 57	Milit Installation	278UNTS97	104025
Brazil	USA (United States)	02 Apr 57	Patents/Copyrights	290UNTS119	104231
Brazil	USA (United States)	05 Nov 57	Education	303UNTS3	104368
Brazil	USA (United States)	19 Oct 59	Milit Assistance	372UNTS131	105293
Brazil	USA (United States)	27 Feb 60	Direct Aid	384UNTS131	105515
Brazil	USA (United States)	13 Jan 61	Extradition	532UNTS177	107718

PARTY ONE	PARTY TWO	DATE	TOPIC	CITATION	NUMBER
Brazil	USA (United States)	17 Mar 61	Atomic Energy	406UNTS241	105853
Brazil	USA (United States)	04 May 61	US Agri Commod Aid	433UNTS91	106233
Brazil	USA (United States)	27 Oct 61	Telecommunications	433UNTS113	106234
Brazil	USA (United States)	11 Nov 61	Direct Aid	433UNTS199	106243
Brazil	USA (United States)	15 Mar 62	US Agri Commod Aid	456UNTS209	106558
Brazil	USA (United States)	13 Apr 62	Non-IBRD Project	445UNTS227	106391
Brazil	USA (United States)	19 Apr 62	General Trade	456UNTS255	106560
Brazil	USA (United States)	29 Mar 63	Scientific Project	476UNTS67	106904
Brazil	USA (United States)	11 Sep 63	US Agri Commod Aid	493UNTS267	107220
Brazil	USA (United States)	30 Jan 64	Milit Assistance	511UNTS77	107428
Brazil	USA (United States)	06 Feb 65	Direct Aid	0UNTS0	110324
Brazil	USA (United States)	26 May 65	Visas	549UNTS125	107995
Brazil	USA (United States)	01 Jun 65	Gen Communications	546UNTS195	107946
Brazil	USA (United States)	08 Jul 65	Atomic Energy	0UNTS0	109603
Brazil	USA (United States)	23 Apr 66	US Agri Commod Aid	607UNTS117	108801
Brazil	USA (United States)	19 Oct 66	Education	0UNTS0	109685
Brazil	USA (United States)	27 Jan 67	Milit Installation	0UNTS0	109844
Brazil	USA (United States)	28 Jun 67	Water Transport	0UNTS0	109775
Brazil	USA (United States)	28 Jun 67	Water Transport	0UNTS0	109774
Brazil	USA (United States)	12 Mar 68	Scientific Project	0UNTS0	110138
Brazil	USA (United States)	10 Sep 68	Scientific Project	0UNTS0	110074
Brazil	USA (United States)	20 Sep 68	Gen Communications	0UNTS0	110078
Brazil	USSR (Soviet Union)	02 Apr 45	Consul/Citizenship	0SUST437	468027
Brazil	USSR (Soviet Union)	09 Dec 59	General Economic	8SUGG160	469615
Brazil	USSR (Soviet Union)	27 May 61	General Trade	10SUGG131	469771
Brazil	USSR (Soviet Union)	27 May 61	General Trade	10SUGG131	469770
Brazil	USSR (Soviet Union)	27 May 61	Loans and Credits	10SUGG131	469769
Brazil	USSR (Soviet Union)	23 Nov 61	Consul/Citizenship	10SUGG145	469806
Brazil	USSR (Soviet Union)	20 Apr 63	General Trade	0UNTS0	109256
Brazil	USSR (Soviet Union)	20 Apr 63	General Trade	0UNTS0	109257
Brazil	Venezuela	30 Mar 40	Dispute Settlement	51UNTS291	200195
Brazil	Venezuela	22 Oct 42	Culture	65UNTS203	200212
Brazil	Venezuela	30 Jan 46	Consul/Citizenship	65UNTS107	100839
Brazil	WHO (World Health)	12 Jun 52	Scientific Project	151UNTS333	102003
Brazil	WHO (World Health)	04 Feb 54	Tech Assistance	233UNTS49	103250
British Guiana	USA (United States)	29 May 65	Loans and Credits	605UNTS87	108761
British Honduras	Multilateral	24 Dec 68	Commodity Trade	0UNTS0	109369
British Honduras	Multilateral	18 Oct 69	IGO Establishment	0UNTS0	110232
British Occup Germ	Multilateral	20 Jan 47	Water Transport	87UNTS247	101176
British Occup Germ	Multilateral	19 Sep 47	General Trade	30UNTS249	100461
British Occup Germ	Multilateral	19 Sep 47	Finance	30UNTS269	100462
British Occup Germ	Multilateral	05 Oct 47	Finance	34UNTS23	100525
British Occup Germ	Multilateral	14 Jul 48	Mostfavored Nation	31UNTS123	100473
British Occup Germ	Multilateral	14 Jul 48	Direct Aid	23UNTS3	100340
British Occup Germ	Multilateral	16 Dec 48	Direct Aid	79UNTS85	101033
British Occup Germ	Multilateral	16 Mar 49	Finance	29UNTS95	100436
British Occup Germ	Multilateral	08 Apr 49	Milit Occupation	140UNTS196	101889
British Occup Germ	Multilateral	14 Apr 49	Milit Occupation	141UNTS281	101919
British Occup Germ	Multilateral	05 Aug 49	Finance	88UNTS229	101195
British Occup Germ	Multilateral	10 Aug 49	Finance	45UNTS3	100689
Brunei	Multilateral	04 Aug 63	IGO Establishment	510UNTS3	107408
Bulgaria	Accept UN Charter	09 Oct 48	UN Charter	223UNTS31	103045
Bulgaria	Afghanistan	29 Jun 63	Culture	0UNTS0	109873
Bulgaria	Australia	22 Jun 66	General Trade	607UNTS69	108796
Bulgaria	Austria	10 Mar 55	Water Transport	56ABGB140	403010
Bulgaria	Austria	12 Sep 58	Air Transport	353UNTS3	105036
Bulgaria	Austria	05 Apr 63	General Trade	480UNTS3	106963
Bulgaria	Austria	02 May 63	Finance	535UNTS143	107778
Bulgaria	Austria	12 Jul 65	Visas	587UNTS45	108509
Bulgaria	Austria	12 Jul 65	Sanitation	587UNTS51	108510
Bulgaria	Austria	21 Apr 67	Visas	603UNTS121	108729
Bulgaria	Austria	20 Oct 67	Admin Cooperation	0UNTS0	110601
Bulgaria	Austria	27 Oct 67	Customs	68ABGB23	403011
Bulgaria	Austria	06 May 68	Tech Assistance	0UNTS0	109875
Bulgaria	Austria	09 May 68	Customs	68ABGB404	403012

PARTY ONE	PARTY TWO	DATE	TOPIC	CITATION	NUMBER
Bulgaria	Austria	27 May 68	Scientific Project	72ABGB86	403013
Bulgaria	Austria	17 Apr 70	Culture	70ABGB204	403014
Bulgaria	Austria	08 Jul 70	Land Transport	70ABGB279	403015
Bulgaria	Austria	13 Oct 71	Finance	71ABGB442	403016
Bulgaria	Austria	22 Feb 72	Admin Cooperation	72ABGB113	403017
Bulgaria	Bel-Lux Econ Union	14 Jun 66	General Economic	601UNTS167	108694
Bulgaria	Belgium	14 May 57	Air Transport	317UNTS81	104596
Bulgaria	Belgium	14 Jun 66	Other HEW	607UNTS183	108806
Bulgaria	Belgium	17 May 67	Culture	631UNTS215	108995
Bulgaria	Belgium	31 Jul 69	Land Transport	0UNTS0	109870
Bulgaria	Brazil	30 Nov 66	Finance	0UNTS0	109874
Bulgaria	Ceylon (Sri Lanka)	19 Jun 56	General Trade	315UNTS23	104556
Bulgaria	Ceylon (Sri Lanka)	19 Jun 56	Finance	315UNTS33	104557
Bulgaria	China People's Rep	14 Jul 52	Culture	52CCJC35	410070
Bulgaria	China People's Rep	21 Jul 52	General Economic	52CCJC40	410071
Bulgaria	China People's Rep	03 Dec 52	General Economic	52CCJC60	410084
Bulgaria	China People's Rep	15 Oct 53	Mass Media	53CCJC60	410123
Bulgaria	China People's Rep	25 Mar 54	General Economic	54CCJC8	410135
Bulgaria	China People's Rep	27 Jan 55	General Economic	55CCJC6	410212
Bulgaria	China People's Rep	23 Mar 55	Scientific Project	55CCJC18	410222
Bulgaria	China People's Rep	11 Jul 55	Sanitation	55CCJC50	410243
Bulgaria	China People's Rep	14 Sep 55	Gen Communications	55CCJC64	410256
Bulgaria	China People's Rep	21 Jan 56	General Economic	56CCJC13	410302
Bulgaria	China People's Rep	28 Jan 57	General Economic	57CCJC13	410398
Bulgaria	China People's Rep	13 Mar 58	General Economic	58CCJC27	410501
Bulgaria	China People's Rep	18 Dec 58	General Economic	58CCJC108	410561
Bulgaria	China People's Rep	23 Apr 59	Scientific Project	59CCJC69	410617
Bulgaria	China People's Rep	06 Aug 59	Mass Media	59CCJC90	410633
Bulgaria	China People's Rep	15 Mar 60	General Trade	60CCJC45	410689
Bulgaria	China People's Rep	08 Mar 61	General Trade	61CCJC34	410766
Bulgaria	China People's Rep	30 Mar 62	General Economic	62CCJC31	410879
Bulgaria	China People's Rep	05 Mar 63	General Economic	63CCJC31	410959
Bulgaria	China People's Rep	14 Apr 64	General Economic	64CCJC46	411084
Bulgaria	China People's Rep	12 Dec 64	General Economic	64CCJC180	411088
Bulgaria	China People's Rep	13 May 65	Culture	65CCJC65	411090
Bulgaria	China People's Rep	09 Nov 65	Scientific Project	65CCJC137	411081
Bulgaria	China People's Rep	16 Mar 66	General Economic	66CCJC7	411091
Bulgaria	China People's Rep	01 Jul 66	Culture	66CCJC62	411082
Bulgaria	China People's Rep	31 Jan 67	General Economic	67CCJC3	411092
Bulgaria	China People's Rep	27 Feb 67	Scientific Project	67CCJC9	411093
Bulgaria	COMECON (Econ Aid)	30 Mar 63	IGO Operations	506UNTS257	107389
Bulgaria	Cuba	31 May 65	Air Transport	0UNTS0	110298
Bulgaria	Cuba	31 May 65	Visas	0UNTS0	110299
Bulgaria	Cyprus	08 May 65	Air Transport	0UNTS0	109957
Bulgaria	Czechoslovakia	20 Jun 47	Education	46UNTS15	100698
Bulgaria	Czechoslovakia	05 Mar 48	Admin Cooperation	26UNTS115	100382
Bulgaria	Czechoslovakia	13 Apr 54	Admin Cooperation	501UNTS3	107314
Bulgaria	Czechoslovakia	25 Jan 57	Non-ILO Labor	501UNTS149	107316
Bulgaria	Czechoslovakia	03 Jun 57	Sanitation	292UNTS3	104261
Bulgaria	Czechoslovakia	27 May 59	Consul/Citizenship	360UNTS335	105167
Bulgaria	Czechoslovakia	19 Sep 59	Sanitation	355UNTS77	105074
Bulgaria	Czechoslovakia	22 May 65	Culture	545UNTS65	107925
Bulgaria	Czechoslovakia	04 Jun 65	Visas	0UNTS0	110515
Bulgaria	Czechoslovakia	26 Apr 68	General Amity	0UNTS0	110344
Bulgaria	Denmark	09 May 47	Finance	74UNTS139	100960
Bulgaria	Denmark	09 May 47	General Trade	74UNTS131	100959
Bulgaria	Denmark	28 May 58	Air Transport	312UNTS235	104521
Bulgaria	Denmark	02 Sep 67	Visas	631UNTS71	108987
Bulgaria	Denmark	02 Sep 67	General Economic	0UNTS0	109726
Bulgaria	Denmark	25 Oct 68	Land Transport	0UNTS0	109876
Bulgaria	Finland	14 Dec 67	Visas	0UNTS0	109969
Bulgaria	Finland	19 Mar 68	Sanitation	0UNTS0	109970
Bulgaria	Finland	14 Nov 69	Scientific Project	0UNTS0	110550
Bulgaria	Finland	19 Mar 70	Air Transport	0UNTS0	110611
Bulgaria	France	07 Mar 50	Admin Cooperation	50FRJO1607	416085

PARTY ONE	PARTY TWO	DATE	TOPIC	CITATION	NUMBER
Bulgaria	France	28 Jul 55	Finance	59FRRT4	415086
Bulgaria	France	04 Aug 65	Air Transport	0UNTS0	109958
Bulgaria	France	04 Aug 65	Air Transport	65FRRT81	415087
Bulgaria	France	15 Oct 66	Culture	67FRJO204	416089
Bulgaria	France	15 Oct 66	Tech Assistance	67FRJO204	416088
Bulgaria	France	30 Jan 68	Sanitation	68FRJO1808	416090
Bulgaria	France	10 Jul 68	General Economic	0UNTS0	110731
Bulgaria	France	10 Jul 68	General Economic	69FRJO3007	416091
Bulgaria	France	22 Jul 68	Consul/Citizenship	0UNTS0	110732
Bulgaria	France	27 Mar 69	Water Transport	69FRJO1906	416092
Bulgaria	France	27 Mar 69	Land Transport	0UNTS0	110556
Bulgaria	Germany, East	19 Jun 50	Health/Educ/Welfare	4EGDA459	419031
Bulgaria	Germany, East	25 Sep 50	Finance	4EGDA462	419032
Bulgaria	Germany, East	25 Sep 50	Culture	4EGDA465	419033
Bulgaria	Germany, East	30 Jan 51	Postal Service	4EGDA468	419034
Bulgaria	Germany, East	30 Jan 51	Postal Service	4EGDA472	419035
Bulgaria	Germany, East	30 Jan 51	Telecommunications	4EGDA477	419036
Bulgaria	Germany, East	15 May 53	Mass Media	4EGDA482	419037
Bulgaria	Germany, East	17 Oct 53	Commodity Trade	1EGDA467	419038
Bulgaria	Germany, East	23 Oct 53	Consul/Citizenship	1EGDA468	419039
Bulgaria	Germany, East	04 Feb 55	General Transport	58EGDZ172	420040
Bulgaria	Germany, East	05 Feb 55	Culture	58EGDZ172	420041
Bulgaria	Germany, East	14 Apr 55	General Economic	2EGDA462	419043
Bulgaria	Germany, East	29 Apr 55	Finance	4EGDA486	419044
Bulgaria	Germany, East	26 May 55	General Economic	3EGDA545	419045
Bulgaria	Germany, East	17 Jun 55	Sanitation	4EGDA490	419046
Bulgaria	Germany, East	30 Jul 55	Air Transport	4EGDA495	419047
Bulgaria	Germany, East	22 Aug 55	General Economic	3EGDA546	419048
Bulgaria	Germany, East	22 Sep 55	General Economic	58EGDZ172	420049
Bulgaria	Germany, East	17 Oct 55	Commodity Trade	58EGDZ172	420050
Bulgaria	Germany, East	05 Jul 56	Sanitation	5EGDA311	419051
Bulgaria	Germany, East	10 Jan 57	Patents/Copyrights	5EGDA790	419052
Bulgaria	Germany, East	27 Apr 57	General Economic	58EGDZ172	420053
Bulgaria	Germany, East	10 Jan 58	Finance	6EGDA216	419054
Bulgaria	Germany, East	27 Jan 58	Admin Cooperation	6EGDA221	419055
Bulgaria	Germany, East	20 Feb 58	Health/Educ/Welfare	6EGDA250	419056
Bulgaria	Germany, East	18 Apr 58	Health/Educ/Welfare	6EGDA278	419058
Bulgaria	Germany, East	18 Apr 58	Consul/Citizenship	6EGDA270	419057
Bulgaria	Germany, East	18 Apr 58	Sanitation	6EGDA282	419059
Bulgaria	Germany, East	25 Sep 58	Commodity Trade	6EGDA519	419060
Bulgaria	Germany, East	20 Mar 59	General Economic	7EGDA319	419061
Bulgaria	Germany, East	16 Jul 59	General Economic	7EGDA320	419062
Bulgaria	Germany, East	11 Apr 60	General Trade	8EGDA325	419063
Bulgaria	Germany, East	10 Oct 61	Education	9EGDA319	419064
Bulgaria	Germany, East	14 Dec 61	General Economic	9EGDA325	419065
Bulgaria	Germany, East	11 Sep 62	Air Transport	10EGDA368	419066
Bulgaria	Germany, East	15 Jul 63	Tech Assistance	11EGDA610	419067
Bulgaria	Germany, East	19 Mar 65	Health/Educ/Welfare	50EGDZ332	420068
Bulgaria	Germany, East	21 Aug 65	Consul/Citizenship	43EGDZ342	420069
Bulgaria	Germany, East	20 Dec 65	General Trade	59EGDZ350	420070
Bulgaria	Germany, East	15 Oct 66	Finance	34EGDZ370	420071
Bulgaria	Germany, East	25 Oct 66	Land Transport	36EGDZ370	420072
Bulgaria	Germany, East	07 Sep 67	General Amity	631UNTS81	108988
Bulgaria	Germany, East	15 Apr 69	Gen Communications	0UNTS0	110838
Bulgaria	Germany, West	20 Feb 50	Health/Educ/Welfare	0UNTS0	109871
Bulgaria	Germany, West	18 Apr 58	Consul/Citizenship	0UNTS0	109872
Bulgaria	Germany, West	06 Mar 64	General Trade	64WBGA148	424064
Bulgaria	Germany, West	07 Jul 64	General Trade	64WGBB781	425065
Bulgaria	Germany, West	12 Feb 71	General Trade	71WBGA69	424066
Bulgaria	Greece	05 Dec 53	Finance	225UNTS145	103096
Bulgaria	Greece	05 Dec 53	General Trade	225UNTS135	103095
Bulgaria	Greece	19 Apr 56	Sanitation	594UNTS131	108600
Bulgaria	Greece	09 Jul 64	Air Transport	0UNTS0	110297
Bulgaria	Greece	09 Jul 64	Postal Service	0UNTS0	110294
Bulgaria	Greece	09 Jul 64	Land Transport	0UNTS0	110295

PARTY ONE	PARTY TWO	DATE	TOPIC	CITATION	NUMBER
Bulgaria	Greece	09 Jul 64	Visas	0UNTS0	110296
Bulgaria	Hungary	16 Jul 48	General Amity	477UNTS169	106921
Bulgaria	Hungary	13 Mar 58	Sanitation	438UNTS191	106317
Bulgaria	Hungary	13 Mar 58	Sanitation	438UNTS173	106316
Bulgaria	Hungary	27 Jun 58	Culture	438UNTS235	106318
Bulgaria	Hungary	03 Apr 59	Sanitation	438UNTS269	106319
Bulgaria	Hungary	30 Jun 61	Admin Cooperation	438UNTS287	106320
Bulgaria	Hungary	19 Aug 65	Culture	577UNTS67	108373
Bulgaria	Hungary	16 May 66	Admin Cooperation	0UNTS0	110417
Bulgaria	Hungary	22 Jan 69	Visas	0UNTS0	110837
Bulgaria	Hungary	10 Jul 69	General Amity	0UNTS0	110111
Bulgaria	Iceland	10 Apr 68	Visas	0UNTS0	110304
Bulgaria	India	20 Feb 63	Culture	0UNTS0	109955
Bulgaria	Iran	09 Feb 67	General Trade	0IRTB16	433026
Bulgaria	Iran	09 Feb 67	General Economic	0IRTB16	433028
Bulgaria	Iran	09 Feb 67	Finance	0IRTB16	433027
Bulgaria	Iran	26 Nov 67	Culture	0IRTB16	433025
Bulgaria	Iraq	15 Nov 66	Air Transport	0UNTS0	109965
Bulgaria	Italy	19 Dec 50	Customs	52ITGU224	435068
Bulgaria	Italy	25 Feb 58	Finance	362UNTS279	105193
Bulgaria	Italy	25 Feb 58	General Trade	362UNTS291	105194
Bulgaria	Italy	30 May 63	Tech Assistance	64ITDI344	436069
Bulgaria	Italy	10 Dec 65	Water Transport	66ITDI121	436071
Bulgaria	Italy	10 Dec 65	General Trade	66ITDI120	436070
Bulgaria	Italy	20 Sep 66	General Economic	0UNTS0	109964
Bulgaria	Italy	29 Jul 67	Mass Media	631UNTS33	108985
Bulgaria	Italy	11 Jan 68	Land Transport	0UNTS0	110303
Bulgaria	Japan	28 Mar 67	General Trade	67JJS103	442190
Bulgaria	Japan	15 Mar 68	Visas	68JJS3	442211
Bulgaria	Japan	28 Feb 70	General Economic	70JHZ8	439035
Bulgaria	Lebanon	17 Feb 67	Air Transport	0UNTS0	110538
Bulgaria	Mongolia	18 Oct 66	Visas	0UNTS0	110301
Bulgaria	Mongolia	21 Jul 67	General Amity	610UNTS0	108839
Bulgaria	Mongolia	27 Nov 68	Admin Cooperation	0UNTS0	109885
Bulgaria	Mongolia	27 Nov 68	Admin Cooperation	0UNTS0	109633
Bulgaria	Multilateral	27 Mar 41	Military Mission	67UNTS231	200222
Bulgaria	Multilateral	02 Aug 44	Scientific Project	67UNTS221	200221
Bulgaria	Multilateral	28 Oct 44	Peace/Disarmament	123UNTS223	200414
Bulgaria	Multilateral	22 Jul 46	IGO Establishment	9UNTS3	100125
Bulgaria	Multilateral	22 Jul 46	IGO Establishment	14UNTS185	100221
Bulgaria	Multilateral	10 Feb 47	Peace/Disarmament	41UNTS21	100643
Bulgaria	Multilateral	02 Oct 47	Telecommunications	193UNTS188	102616
Bulgaria	Multilateral	06 Mar 48	Water Transport	289UNTS3	104214
Bulgaria	Multilateral	10 Jun 48	Humanitarian	164UNTS113	102163
Bulgaria	Multilateral	24 Jul 48	Sanitation	66UNTS25	100847
Bulgaria	Multilateral	18 Aug 48	Water Transport	33UNTS181	100518
Bulgaria	Multilateral	09 Dec 48	Humanitarian	78UNTS277	101021
Bulgaria	Multilateral	12 Aug 49	Humanitarian	75UNTS287	100973
Bulgaria	Multilateral	12 Aug 49	Humanitarian	75UNTS85	100971
Bulgaria	Multilateral	12 Aug 49	Humanitarian	75UNTS31	100970
Bulgaria	Multilateral	12 Aug 49	General Military	75UNTS135	100972
Bulgaria	Multilateral	16 Sep 50	General Transport	92UNTS91	101264
Bulgaria	Multilateral	18 Oct 50	Specific Resources	638UNTS185	109134
Bulgaria	Multilateral	22 Nov 50	Culture	131UNTS25	101734
Bulgaria	Multilateral	11 Jul 52	Postal Service	171UNTS191	102227
Bulgaria	Multilateral	11 Jul 52	Postal Service	170UNTS63	102222
Bulgaria	Multilateral	11 Jul 52	Postal Service	170UNTS269	102223
Bulgaria	Multilateral	11 Jul 52	Postal Service	170UNTS3	102221
Bulgaria	Multilateral	11 Jul 52	IGO Establishment	169UNTS3	102220
Bulgaria	Multilateral	31 Mar 53	Privil/Immunities	193UNTS136	102613
Bulgaria	Multilateral	14 May 54	Culture	249UNTS215	103511
Bulgaria	Multilateral	14 May 55	General Amity	219UNTS3	102962
Bulgaria	Multilateral	12 Oct 55	IGO Establishment	560UNTS3	108165
Bulgaria	Multilateral	26 Mar 56	IGO Establishment	259UNTS125	103686
Bulgaria	Multilateral	18 May 56	Customs	327UNTS123	104721

PARTY ONE	PARTY TWO	DATE	TOPIC	CITATION	NUMBER
Bulgaria	Multilateral	18 May 56	Customs	338UNTS103	104834
Bulgaria	Multilateral	19 May 56	Land Transport	399UNTS189	105742
Bulgaria	Multilateral	11 Sep 56	Humanitarian	266UNTS221	103832
Bulgaria	Multilateral	26 Oct 56	IGO Establishment	276UNTS3	103988
Bulgaria	Multilateral	20 Feb 57	Consul/Citizenship	309UNTS65	104468
Bulgaria	Multilateral	03 Oct 57	Postal Service	365UNTS3	105213
Bulgaria	Multilateral	03 Oct 57	Postal Service	366UNTS255	105219
Bulgaria	Multilateral	03 Oct 57	Postal Service	364UNTS3	105211
Bulgaria	Multilateral	03 Oct 57	Postal Service	365UNTS207	105214
Bulgaria	Multilateral	03 Oct 57	Postal Service	364UNTS331	105212
Bulgaria	Multilateral	13 Dec 57	Land Transport	372UNTS159	105296
Bulgaria	Multilateral	29 Jan 58	Specific Resources	339UNTS23	104845
Bulgaria	Multilateral	29 Apr 58	Territory Boundary	516UNTS205	107477
Bulgaria	Multilateral	29 Apr 58	Water Transport	450UNTS11	106465
Bulgaria	Multilateral	29 Apr 58	Territory Boundary	499UNTS311	107302
Bulgaria	Multilateral	10 Jun 58	Admin Cooperation	330UNTS3	104739
Bulgaria	Multilateral	03 Dec 58	Admin Cooperation	416UNTS51	105995
Bulgaria	Multilateral	03 Dec 58	Admin Cooperation	398UNTS9	105715
Bulgaria	Multilateral	15 Jan 59	Customs	348UNTS13	104996
Bulgaria	Multilateral	07 Jul 59	Specific Resources	377UNTS203	105402
Bulgaria	Multilateral	14 Dec 59	Land Transport	422UNTS75	106069
Bulgaria	Multilateral	14 Dec 59	Sanitation	422UNTS57	106068
Bulgaria	Multilateral	14 Dec 59	IGO Establishment	368UNTS253	105245
Bulgaria	Multilateral	14 Dec 59	Sanitation	422UNTS33	106067
Bulgaria	Multilateral	14 Dec 59	IGO Status/Immunit	368UNTS237	105244
Bulgaria	Multilateral	17 Jun 60	Humanitarian	536UNTS27	107794
Bulgaria	Multilateral	29 Jul 60	Water Transport	392UNTS69	105640
Bulgaria	Multilateral	09 Dec 60	Customs	429UNTS211	106200
Bulgaria	Multilateral	14 Dec 60	Education	429UNTS93	106193
Bulgaria	Multilateral	30 Mar 61	Sanitation	520UNTS151	107515
Bulgaria	Multilateral	18 Apr 61	Consul/Citizenship	500UNTS95	107310
Bulgaria	Multilateral	21 Apr 61	IGO Establishment	484UNTS349	107041
Bulgaria	Multilateral	08 Jun 61	Customs	473UNTS153	106862
Bulgaria	Multilateral	08 Jun 61	Customs	473UNTS187	106863
Bulgaria	Multilateral	06 Dec 61	Customs	473UNTS219	106864
Bulgaria	Multilateral	15 Dec 61	Admin Cooperation	424UNTS43	106098
Bulgaria	Multilateral	25 Jul 62	Specific Property	506UNTS177	107387
Bulgaria	Multilateral	28 Jul 62	Specific Resources	460UNTS219	106642
Bulgaria	Multilateral	05 Aug 63	Sanitation	480UNTS43	106964
Bulgaria	Multilateral	23 Oct 63	IGO Establishment	506UNTS197	107388
Bulgaria	Multilateral	10 Jul 64	Postal Service	613UNTS193	108852
Bulgaria	Multilateral	10 Jul 64	Postal Service	611UNTS7	108844
Bulgaria	Multilateral	10 Jul 64	Postal Service	611UNTS387	108846
Bulgaria	Multilateral	10 Jul 64	Postal Service	612UNTS3	108847
Bulgaria	Multilateral	10 Jul 64	Postal Service	612UNTS233	108848
Bulgaria	Multilateral	10 Jul 64	Postal Service	611UNTS105	108845
Bulgaria	Multilateral	25 Apr 65	Finance	0UNTS0	110810
Bulgaria	Multilateral	16 Jul 65	General Trade	600UNTS49	108675
Bulgaria	Multilateral	18 Nov 65	Customs	609UNTS115	108830
Bulgaria	Multilateral	05 Apr 66	Water Transport	640UNTS133	109159
Bulgaria	Multilateral	09 Sep 66	IGO Status/Immunit	0UNTS0	109343
Bulgaria	Multilateral	27 Jan 67	Scientific Project	610UNTS205	108843
Bulgaria	Multilateral	20 Jun 67	Tech Assistance	0UNTS0	109290
Bulgaria	Multilateral	22 Apr 68	Scientific Project	0UNTS0	109574
Bulgaria	Multilateral	01 Jul 68	Peace/Disarmament	0UNTS0	110485
Bulgaria	Multilateral	24 Sep 68	Air Transport	0UNTS0	110612
Bulgaria	Multilateral	26 Nov 68	Humanitarian	0UNTS0	110823
Bulgaria	Netherlands	07 Feb 58	Air Transport	335UNTS45	104777
Bulgaria	Netherlands	07 Jul 61	Finance	489UNTS21	107133
Bulgaria	New Zealand	03 Nov 67	General Trade	0UNTS0	109207
Bulgaria	Norway	19 Jun 58	Air Transport	3NORT746	451014
Bulgaria	Norway	28 Oct 67	Visas	3NORT1007	451015
Bulgaria	Norway	28 Oct 67	Visas	0UNTS0	110302
Bulgaria	Norway	15 Nov 68	General Trade	3NORT0	451016
Bulgaria	Poland	28 Jun 47	Culture	15UNTS123	100230

PARTY ONE	PARTY TWO	DATE	TOPIC	CITATION	NUMBER
Bulgaria	Poland	29 May 48	General Military	26UNTS213	100389
Bulgaria	Poland	30 May 48	General Trade	37UNTS3	100574
Bulgaria	Poland	16 May 49	Air Transport	84UNTS313	101140
Bulgaria	Poland	26 Sep 49	Sanitation	260UNTS249	103712
Bulgaria	Poland	26 Sep 49	Sanitation	260UNTS227	103711
Bulgaria	Poland	19 Oct 53	Gen Communications	53PZUM117	458013
Bulgaria	Poland	30 Dec 58	General Economic	58PZUM124	458064
Bulgaria	Poland	20 Jun 59	Customs	59PZUM78	458068
Bulgaria	Poland	12 Jul 61	Admin Cooperation	436UNTS147	106294
Bulgaria	Poland	19 Sep 61	Consul/Citizenship	483UNTS249	107018
Bulgaria	Poland	04 Dec 61	Admin Cooperation	484UNTS3	107019
Bulgaria	Poland	03 Oct 64	Land Transport	64PZUM48	458115
Bulgaria	Poland	08 Jun 65	Visas	0UNTS0	110300
Bulgaria	Poland	08 Jun 65	Visas	65PZUM44	458122
Bulgaria	Poland	07 Apr 66	Culture	66PZUM14	458131
Bulgaria	Poland	03 Oct 66	Culture	618UNTS3	108921
Bulgaria	Poland	06 Apr 67	General Amity	617UNTS327	108920
Bulgaria	Poland	06 Dec 68	Sanitation	70PDZU13	457162
Bulgaria	Poland	07 Feb 72	Consul/Citizenship	72PDZU401	457178
Bulgaria	Romania	29 Sep 50	Scientific Project	342UNTS141	104905
Bulgaria	Romania	22 Jul 54	Sanitation	362UNTS101	105184
Bulgaria	Romania	03 Dec 58	Admin Cooperation	417UNTS133	106007
Bulgaria	Romania	23 Apr 59	Consul/Citizenship	387UNTS81	105559
Bulgaria	Romania	21 Sep 59	Consul/Citizenship	387UNTS61	105558
Bulgaria	Romania	14 Mar 60	Admin Cooperation	472UNTS279	106844
Bulgaria	Romania	15 Jun 67	Visas	634UNTS57	109051
Bulgaria	Romania	22 Aug 67	Visas	631UNTS49	108986
Bulgaria	Singapore	05 May 66	General Trade	631UNTS165	108993
Bulgaria	Sudan	06 Mar 67	Scientific Project	0UNTS0	109966
Bulgaria	Sweden	22 Sep 47	Finance	47SOFM508	461051
Bulgaria	Sweden	22 Sep 47	General Trade	47SOFM499	461050
Bulgaria	Sweden	11 Oct 49	General Trade	49SOFM519	461090
Bulgaria	Sweden	17 Apr 57	Air Transport	464UNTS3	106709
Bulgaria	Sweden	19 Oct 67	Education	0UNTS0	109968
Bulgaria	Switzerland	26 Nov 54	General Economic	54SWRO1171	462123
Bulgaria	Syria	28 Jun 62	Culture	0UNTS0	109954
Bulgaria	Syria	13 Dec 64	Air Transport	0UNTS0	109956
Bulgaria	Syria	08 Nov 65	Scientific Project	0UNTS0	109959
Bulgaria	Syria	12 Jun 66	Visas	0UNTS0	109961
Bulgaria	Tanzania	15 Jul 66	Scientific Project	0UNTS0	109962
Bulgaria	Tunisia	29 Apr 69	Water Transport	0UNTS0	110839
Bulgaria	Turkey	07 Jun 4€	General Trade	46TURG2112	466048
Bulgaria	Turkey	05 Dec 46	General Economic	47TURG2802	466049
Bulgaria	Turkey	07 Sep 49	General Economic	50TURG1001	466050
Bulgaria	Turkey	23 Feb 55	General Economic	56TURG202	466047
Bulgaria	Turkey	18 Apr 66	Air Transport	631UNTS263	108999
Bulgaria	Turkey	30 May 67	Sanitation	0UNTS0	109967
Bulgaria	Turkey	30 May 67	Sanitation	631UNTS19	108984
Bulgaria	Turkey	15 Dec 67	Land Transport	0UNTS0	110836
Bulgaria	UK Great Britain	13 Mar 48	Postal Service	104UNTS25	101432
Bulgaria	UK Great Britain	22 Sep 55	Finance	222UNTS349	103039
Bulgaria	UK Great Britain	13 Mar 68	Sanitation	0UNTS0	109585
Bulgaria	UK Great Britain	13 Mar 68	Consul/Citizenship	0UNTS0	109708
Bulgaria	UK Great Britain	28 Feb 69	Scientific Project	0UNTS0	109789
Bulgaria	UK Great Britain	27 Apr 70	General Trade	0UNTS0	110787
Bulgaria	UK Great Britain	28 May 70	Air Transport	0UNTS0	110788
Bulgaria	UN Special Fund	26 May 66	General Aid	563UNTS71	108205
Bulgaria	UNICEF (Children)	23 Aug 47	IGO Operations	68UNTS223	200232
Bulgaria	UNICEF (Children)	10 Mar 66	IGO Operations	559UNTS13	108152
Bulgaria	United Arab Rep	09 Jul 59	Air Transport	411UNTS187	105920
Bulgaria	United Arab Rep	17 Nov 65	Visas	0UNTS0	109960
Bulgaria	United Arab Rep	29 Aug 66	Sanitation	0UNTS0	109963
Bulgaria	United Arab Rep	29 Aug 66	Sanitation	630UNTS325	108980
Bulgaria	United Arab Rep	12 Feb 67	Gen Communications	630UNTS353	108981
Bulgaria	United Arab Rep	12 Feb 67	Telecommunications	630UNTS363	108982

PARTY ONE	PARTY TWO	DATE	TOPIC	CITATION	NUMBER
Bulgaria	United Arab Rep	24 May 69	Water Transport	0UNTS0	110566
Bulgaria	USA (United States)	08 Mar 48	Admin Cooperation	29UNTS101	100437
Bulgaria	USA (United States)	02 Jul 63	Claims and Debts	479UNTS245	106957
Bulgaria	USSR (Soviet Union)	14 Mar 45	General Trade	0SUST175	468028
Bulgaria	USSR (Soviet Union)	16 Aug 45	Consul/Citizenship	0SUST193	471018
Bulgaria	USSR (Soviet Union)	10 Feb 47	Peace/Disarmament	0SUST226	468029
Bulgaria	USSR (Soviet Union)	05 Jul 47	General Economic	0SUST233	468030
Bulgaria	USSR (Soviet Union)	23 Aug 47	Loans and Credits	0SUST236	471022
Bulgaria	USSR (Soviet Union)	17 Dec 47	Postal Service	0SUST241	468032
Bulgaria	USSR (Soviet Union)	17 Dec 47	Gen Communications	0SUST241	468031
Bulgaria	USSR (Soviet Union)	18 Mar 48	General Military	48UNTS135	100741
Bulgaria	USSR (Soviet Union)	01 Apr 48	General Trade	0SUST247	471025
Bulgaria	USSR (Soviet Union)	01 Apr 48	General Economic	217UNTS97	102946
Bulgaria	USSR (Soviet Union)	09 Aug 48	Loans and Credits	0SUST251	468035
Bulgaria	USSR (Soviet Union)	18 Feb 50	Tech Assistance	0SUST271	468036
Bulgaria	USSR (Soviet Union)	24 May 50	Admin Cooperation	0SUST274	468037
Bulgaria	USSR (Soviet Union)	25 Aug 50	Sanitation	221UNTS57	103002
Bulgaria	USSR (Soviet Union)	07 Mar 51	Education	0SUST285	468040
Bulgaria	USSR (Soviet Union)	10 Apr 51	Scientific Project	0SUST281	468039
Bulgaria	USSR (Soviet Union)	09 Oct 54	Specific Property	0SUST317	468041
Bulgaria	USSR (Soviet Union)	26 Nov 55	Specific Property	0SUST342	468042
Bulgaria	USSR (Soviet Union)	03 Feb 56	General Aid	0SUST348	468043
Bulgaria	USSR (Soviet Union)	28 Apr 56	Culture	259UNTS363	103697
Bulgaria	USSR (Soviet Union)	22 Nov 56	Mass Media	16SUGG74	469930
Bulgaria	USSR (Soviet Union)	20 Feb 57	General Economic	0SUST378	468045
Bulgaria	USSR (Soviet Union)	19 Nov 57	General Trade	0SUST391	468046
Bulgaria	USSR (Soviet Union)	12 Dec 57	Consul/Citizenship	302UNTS3	104351
Bulgaria	USSR (Soviet Union)	12 Dec 57	Admin Cooperation	317UNTS217	104606
Bulgaria	USSR (Soviet Union)	12 Dec 57	Consul/Citizenship	302UNTS21	104352
Bulgaria	USSR (Soviet Union)	18 Jan 58	Claims and Debts	7SUGG102	469487
Bulgaria	USSR (Soviet Union)	26 Apr 58	General Trade	7SUGG111	469508
Bulgaria	USSR (Soviet Union)	26 Apr 58	Commodity Trade	7SUGG111	469507
Bulgaria	USSR (Soviet Union)	19 Jul 58	Tech Assistance	7SUGG116	469521
Bulgaria	USSR (Soviet Union)	26 Dec 58	Non-IBRD Project	7SUGG130	469546
Bulgaria	USSR (Soviet Union)	26 Dec 58	Non-IBRD Project	7SUGG130	469547
Bulgaria	USSR (Soviet Union)	04 Nov 59	Tech Assistance	8SUGG156	469608
Bulgaria	USSR (Soviet Union)	04 Nov 59	General Trade	8SUGG156	469607
Bulgaria	USSR (Soviet Union)	11 Dec 59	Non-ILO Labor	368UNTS287	105246
Bulgaria	USSR (Soviet Union)	20 Jan 60	Tech Assistance	9SUGG22	469624
Bulgaria	USSR (Soviet Union)	28 Jun 60	Tech Assistance	9SUGG140	469669
Bulgaria	USSR (Soviet Union)	22 Jul 60	Tech Assistance	9SUGG143	469678
Bulgaria	USSR (Soviet Union)	22 Sep 60	Education	16SUGG129	469982
Bulgaria	USSR (Soviet Union)	08 Oct 60	Tech Assistance	9SUGG149	469703
Bulgaria	USSR (Soviet Union)	29 Nov 60	Tech Assistance	9SUGG152	469716
Bulgaria	USSR (Soviet Union)	30 Nov 60	Tech Assistance	9SUGG153	469718
Bulgaria	USSR (Soviet Union)	30 Nov 60	General Aid	9SUGG153	469717
Bulgaria	USSR (Soviet Union)	31 Dec 60	Loans and Credits	9SUGG158	469730
Bulgaria	USSR (Soviet Union)	18 Jan 61	General Trade	10SUGG118	469737
Bulgaria	USSR (Soviet Union)	18 Feb 61	Tech Assistance	10SUGG122	469742
Bulgaria	USSR (Soviet Union)	29 Sep 61	Tech Assistance	10SUGG142	469795
Bulgaria	USSR (Soviet Union)	20 Jun 62	General Trade	11SUGG144	469844
Bulgaria	USSR (Soviet Union)	20 Jun 62	Commodity Trade	11SUGG144	469845
Bulgaria	USSR (Soviet Union)	25 Dec 62	Mass Media	11SUGG160	469879
Bulgaria	USSR (Soviet Union)	06 Jul 66	Consul/Citizenship	596UNTS177	108632
Bulgaria	USSR (Soviet Union)	27 Apr 67	Atomic Energy	631UNTS3	108983
Bulgaria	USSR (Soviet Union)	12 May 67	General Amity	631UNTS239	108997
Bulgaria	Yemen	08 Apr 64	Culture	0UNTS0	110293
Bulgaria	Yemen	08 Apr 64	General Amity	0UNTS0	110292
Bulgaria	Yugoslavia	22 Aug 47	Finance	111UNTS241	101538
Bulgaria	Yugoslavia	20 Feb 54	Territory Boundary	397UNTS13	105700
Bulgaria	Yugoslavia	22 Apr 54	Dispute Settlement	397UNTS43	105701
Bulgaria	Yugoslavia	02 Nov 54	Patents/Copyrights	375UNTS333	105371
Bulgaria	Yugoslavia	16 Mar 55	General Economic	397UNTS83	105702
Bulgaria	Yugoslavia	17 Jun 55	Sanitation	375UNTS287	105370
Bulgaria	Yugoslavia	01 Oct 55	Air Transport	396UNTS223	105698
Bulgaria	Yugoslavia	15 Nov 55	Consul/Citizenship	396UNTS179	105696
Bulgaria	Yugoslavia	15 Nov 55	General Transport	396UNTS191	105697
Bulgaria	Yugoslavia	11 Dec 55	Sanitation	378UNTS49	105417
Bulgaria	Yugoslavia	10 Feb 56	Scientific Project	349UNTS21	105007
Bulgaria	Yugoslavia	23 Mar 56	Admin Cooperation	367UNTS213	105230
Bulgaria	Yugoslavia	04 Apr 56	Air Transport	391UNTS47	105616
Bulgaria	Yugoslavia	22 May 56	Visas	367UNTS119	105229
Bulgaria	Yugoslavia	16 Jun 56	Territory Boundary	375UNTS235	105368
Bulgaria	Yugoslavia	16 Jun 56	Territory Boundary	391UNTS3	105613
Bulgaria	Yugoslavia	24 Dec 56	Culture	397UNTS3	105699
Bulgaria	Yugoslavia	19 Apr 57	Water Transport	349UNTS3	105006
Bulgaria	Yugoslavia	04 Jun 57	Sanitation	349UNTS35	105008
Bulgaria	Yugoslavia	17 Jun 57	Territory Boundary	375UNTS249	105369
Bulgaria	Yugoslavia	18 Dec 57	Non-ILO Labor	376UNTS3	105372
Bulgaria	Yugoslavia	21 Mar 58	Land Transport	386UNTS119	105541
Bulgaria	Yugoslavia	21 Mar 58	Land Transport	349UNTS61	105009
Bulgaria	Yugoslavia	21 Mar 58	Customs	376UNTS53	105373
Bulgaria	Yugoslavia	04 Apr 58	Water Transport	367UNTS89	105228
Burma	Accept UN Charter	17 Mar 48	UN Charter	15UNTS3	100225
Burma	Belgium	17 Aug 60	Air Transport	540UNTS185	107850
Burma	Ceylon (Sri Lanka)	29 Jun 50	Air Transport	73UNTS3	100940
Burma	China People's Rep	22 Apr 54	Finance	54CCJC19	410142
Burma	China People's Rep	22 Apr 54	General Trade	54CCJC18	410141
Burma	China People's Rep	03 Nov 54	Commodity Trade	54CCJC77	410184
Burma	China People's Rep	08 Nov 55	Air Transport	55CCJC77	410265
Burma	China People's Rep	08 Nov 55	Air Transport	55CCJC78	410266
Burma	China People's Rep	08 Nov 55	Consul/Citizenship	55CCJC79	410267
Burma	China People's Rep	08 Nov 55	Air Transport	306UNTS11	104430
Burma	China People's Rep	29 Dec 55	Commodity Trade	55CCJC107	410288
Burma	China People's Rep	01 Nov 57	Postal Service	57CCJC105	410460
Burma	China People's Rep	01 Nov 57	Postal Service	57CCJC104	410459
Burma	China People's Rep	31 Jan 58	Telecommunications	58CCJC15	410492
Burma	China People's Rep	21 Feb 58	General Trade	58CCJC21	410496
Burma	China People's Rep	28 Jan 60	Territory Boundary	60CCJC8	410659
Burma	China People's Rep	28 Jan 60	General Amity	60CCJC7	410658
Burma	China People's Rep	01 Oct 60	Territory Boundary	60CCJC98	410721
Burma	China People's Rep	01 Oct 60	Territory Boundary	60CCJC99	410722
Burma	China People's Rep	09 Jan 61	Finance	61CCJC3	410746
Burma	China People's Rep	09 Jan 61	Direct Aid	61CCJC2	410745
Burma	China People's Rep	27 Jan 61	General Trade	61CCJC6	410749
Burma	China People's Rep	13 Oct 61	Territory Boundary	61CCJC135	410838
Burma	China People's Rep	28 Aug 63	Admin Cooperation	63CCJC100	411004
Burma	China People's Rep	26 Jan 65	Commodity Trade	65CCJC9	411089
Burma	Czechoslovakia	15 Dec 65	Air Transport	602UNTS71	108707
Burma	Denmark	30 Jul 51	Air Transport	108UNTS167	101472
Burma	Germany, East	26 Aug 60	Consul/Citizenship	45EGDZ255	420074
Burma	Germany, East	14 Mar 61	Water Transport	9EGDA459	419075
Burma	Germany, East	08 Jan 66	General Economic	51EGDZ351	420076
Burma	Germany, West	12 Jul 62	Direct Aid	62WBGA161	424043
Burma	Germany, West	11 Nov 67	Loans and Credits	68WBGA15	424044
Burma	Germany, West	09 May 70	Loans and Credits	70WBGA145	424045
Burma	Germany, West	18 Sep 70	Loans and Credits	70WBGA220	424046
Burma	IAEA (Atom Energy)	11 Oct 67	Atomic Energy	630UNTS49	108964
Burma	IBRD (World Bank)	04 May 56	IBRD Project	253UNTS209	103585
Burma	IBRD (World Bank)	04 May 56	IBRD Project	253UNTS179	103584
Burma	IBRD (World Bank)	16 Jan 61	IBRD Project	400UNTS73	105749
Burma	India	07 Jul 51	General Amity	149UNTS35	101949
Burma	India	29 Sep 51	General Trade	132UNTS71	101752
Burma	India	12 Mar 57	Finance	312UNTS131	104515
Burma	Israel	05 Mar 56	Direct Aid	280UNTS209	104060
Burma	Japan	05 Nov 54	Peace/Disarmament	251UNTS201	103542
Burma	Japan	05 Nov 54	Reparations	251UNTS215	103543
Burma	Japan	18 Oct 55	Admin Cooperation	0JGJI1254	441146
Burma	Japan	20 Jun 56	Admin Cooperation	306UNTS61	104431
Burma	Japan	29 Mar 63	General Aid	518UNTS3	107490

PARTY ONE	PARTY TWO	DATE	TOPIC	CITATION	NUMBER
Burma	Japan	15 Feb 69	Loans and Credits	69JJS69	442233
Burma	Multilateral	27 May 47	Air Transport	418UNTS161	106021
Burma	Multilateral	02 Oct 47	Telecommunications	193UNTS188	102616
Burma	Multilateral	11 Oct 47	IGO Establishment	77UNTS143	100998
Burma	Multilateral	12 Nov 47	Admin Cooperation	46UNTS201	100710
Burma	Multilateral	12 Nov 47	Admin Cooperation	53UNTS39	100771
Burma	Multilateral	12 Nov 47	Admin Cooperation	46UNTS169	100709
Burma	Multilateral	24 Jul 48	Sanitation	66UNTS25	100847
Burma	Multilateral	15 Nov 48	IGO Establishment	120UNTS59	101615
Burma	Multilateral	19 Nov 48	Sanitation	44UNTS277	100688
Burma	Multilateral	29 Nov 48	IGO Establishment	120UNTS13	101613
Burma	Multilateral	09 Dec 48	Scientific Project	20UNTS229	100318
Burma	Multilateral	09 Dec 48	Humanitarian	78UNTS277	101021
Burma	Multilateral	06 Apr 50	Admin Cooperation	119UNTS99	101610
Burma	Multilateral	28 Jun 50	Loans and Credits	87UNTS153	101170
Burma	Multilateral	07 Dec 50	Admin Cooperation	212UNTS17	102861
Burma	Multilateral	05 Mar 51	Tech Assistance	81UNTS261	101075
Burma	Multilateral	06 Dec 51	Admin Cooperation	150UNTS67	101963
Burma	Multilateral	10 May 52	Taxation	439UNTS233	106332
Burma	Multilateral	11 Jul 52	IGO Establishment	169UNTS3	102220
Burma	Multilateral	11 Jul 52	Postal Service	170UNTS3	102221
Burma	Multilateral	07 Dec 53	Admin Cooperation	182UNTS51	102422
Burma	Multilateral	20 Apr 54	Tech Assistance	189UNTS11	102539
Burma	Multilateral	14 May 54	Culture	249UNTS215	103511
Burma	Multilateral	14 Jun 54	Air Transport	320UNTS217	104644
Burma	Multilateral	25 May 55	IGO Establishment	264UNTS117	103791
Burma	Multilateral	26 Oct 56	IGO Establishment	276UNTS3	103988
Burma	Multilateral	03 Oct 57	Postal Service	364UNTS331	105212
Burma	Multilateral	03 Oct 57	Postal Service	364UNTS3	105211
Burma	Multilateral	26 Jan 60	IGO Establishment	439UNTS249	106333
Burma	Multilateral	17 Jun 60	Humanitarian	536UNTS27	107794
Burma	Multilateral	30 Mar 61	Sanitation	520UNTS151	107515
Burma	Multilateral	23 Jul 62	Recognition	456UNTS302	106564
Burma	Multilateral	02 Apr 63	Commodity Trade	475UNTS121	106889
Burma	Multilateral	05 Aug 63	Sanitation	480UNTS43	106964
Burma	Multilateral	10 Jul 64	Postal Service	611UNTS7	108844
Burma	Multilateral	10 Jul 64	Postal Service	612UNTS3	108847
Burma	Multilateral	10 Jul 64	Postal Service	611UNTS387	108846
Burma	Multilateral	10 Jul 64	Postal Service	611UNTS105	108845
Burma	Multilateral	27 Jan 67	Scientific Project	610UNTS205	108843
Burma	Netherlands	06 Sep 51	Air Transport	108UNTS187	101473
Burma	Norway	22 Jun 53	Air Transport	174UNTS49	102277
Burma	Pakistan	18 Nov 47	Air Transport	35UNTS321	100562
Burma	Pakistan	22 Jun 48	Postal Service	91UNTS197	101252
Burma	Pakistan	25 Jun 52	General Amity	173UNTS41	102259
Burma	Philippines	15 Aug 52	Air Transport	200UNTS97	102696
Burma	Sweden	14 Sep 50	Air Transport	96UNTS45	101330
Burma	Sweden	06 Mar 56	General Trade	369UNTS275	105261
Burma	Switzerland	31 Oct 60	Air Transport	465UNTS97	106723
Burma	Thailand	15 Oct 56	General Amity	277UNTS87	104000
Burma	Thailand	08 Jun 60	Visas	372UNTS321	105308
Burma	Thailand	17 May 63	Visas	468UNTS319	106779
Burma	Thailand	15 Aug 69	Air Transport	0UNTS0	109978
Burma	UK Great Britain	17 Oct 47	Recognition	70UNTS183	100904
Burma	UK Great Britain	12 Oct 48	Finance	71UNTS255	100923
Burma	UK Great Britain	13 Mar 50	Taxation	131UNTS53	101735
Burma	UK Great Britain	25 Oct 52	Air Transport	150UNTS237	101978
Burma	UK Great Britain	18 Jun 56	Commodity Trade	256UNTS125	103623
Burma	UK Great Britain	20 Jan 59	Commodity Trade	343UNTS201	104926
Burma	UK Great Britain	06 Feb 59	Commodity Trade	343UNTS223	104927
Burma	UK Great Britain	02 Apr 63	Commodity Trade	475UNTS139	106890
Burma	UN Special Fund	03 Jan 61	Direct Aid	387UNTS219	105564
Burma	UNICEF (Children)	22 Apr 50	IGO Operations	68UNTS96	100888
Burma	United Nations	15 Dec 58	Tech Assistance	319UNTS3	104629
Burma	USA (United States)	28 Feb 47	Direct Aid	25UNTS27	100355

PARTY ONE	PARTY TWO	DATE	TOPIC	CITATION	NUMBER
Burma	USA (United States)	05 Apr 48	Admin Cooperation	73UNTS73	100945
Burma	USA (United States)	28 Sep 49	Air Transport	55UNTS3	100806
Burma	USA (United States)	13 Sep 50	Direct Aid	92UNTS361	101280
Burma	USA (United States)	06 Nov 50	Milit Assistance	122UNTS81	101638
Burma	USA (United States)	09 Feb 52	Milit Assistance	179UNTS91	102357
Burma	USA (United States)	24 Oct 52	Tech Assistance	222UNTS55	103022
Burma	USA (United States)	30 Jun 56	Tech Assistance	281UNTS65	104070
Burma	USA (United States)	23 Oct 56	Mass Media	282UNTS37	104091
Burma	USA (United States)	04 Dec 56	US Agri Commod Aid	268UNTS189	103858
Burma	USA (United States)	21 Mar 57	Direct Aid	300UNTS11	104327
Burma	USA (United States)	27 May 58	US Agri Commod Aid	315UNTS197	104569
Burma	USA (United States)	24 Jun 58	Milit Assistance	335UNTS193	104786
Burma	USA (United States)	25 Aug 58	Commodity Trade	336UNTS3	104795
Burma	USA (United States)	24 Jun 59	Direct Aid	358UNTS91	105127
Burma	USA (United States)	09 Nov 62	US Agri Commod Aid	461UNTS113	106655
Burma	USA (United States)	01 Jun 66	Loans and Credits	580UNTS253	108428
Burma	USSR (Soviet Union)	18 Feb 48	Consul/Citizenship	0SUST245	468061
Burma	USSR (Soviet Union)	01 Jul 55	General Trade	0SUST331	468062
Burma	USSR (Soviet Union)	01 Apr 56	Commodity Trade	0SUST352	468063
Burma	USSR (Soviet Union)	30 Sep 57	Specif Goods/Equip	16SUGG121	469946
Burma	USSR (Soviet Union)	04 May 60	Direct Aid	9SUGG134	469653
Burma	USSR (Soviet Union)	19 Feb 62	Direct Aid	11SUGG133	469821
Burma	USSR (Soviet Union)	30 Aug 62	Non-IBRD Project	11SUGG150	469857
Burma	WHO (World Health)	13 Jun 51	Sanitation	117UNTS115	101588
Burma	WHO (World Health)	09 Jul 51	Sanitation	104UNTS187	101440
Burma	WHO (World Health)	09 Jul 51	Sanitation	102UNTS131	101416
Burma	WHO (World Health)	09 Jul 51	Sanitation	107UNTS9	101463
Burma	WHO (World Health)	09 Jul 51	Sanitation	104UNTS175	101439
Burma	WHO (World Health)	17 Jul 51	Tech Assistance	102UNTS127	101415
Burma	WHO (World Health)	18 Feb 52	Scientific Project	127UNTS43	101698
Burma	WHO (World Health)	09 Jun 52	Sanitation	134UNTS273	101806
Burma	WHO (World Health)	20 Sep 57	Tech Assistance	282UNTS113	104096
Burma	Yugoslavia	29 Jun 53	General Trade	378UNTS83	105418
Burma	Yugoslavia	14 Jun 55	Direct Aid	378UNTS93	105419
Burma	Yugoslavia	07 Mar 56	Direct Aid	378UNTS99	105420
Burma	Yugoslavia	07 Mar 56	Commodity Trade	386UNTS207	105542
Burma	Yugoslavia	07 Mar 56	Tech Assistance	386UNTS235	105543
Burundi	Accept UN Charter	04 Jul 62	UN Charter	437UNTS149	106303
Burundi	China People's Rep	22 Oct 64	General Economic	64CCJC148	411086
Burundi	France	11 Feb 63	Health/Educ/Welfare	65FRRT18	415093
Burundi	France	07 Oct 69	Milit Assistance	0UNTS0	110534
Burundi	Germany, West	31 Mar 65	Tech Assistance	65WBGA142	424067
Burundi	Germany, West	23 Dec 65	Loans and Credits	66WBGA88	424068
Burundi	Germany, West	21 Nov 68	Loans and Credits	69WBGA14	424069
Burundi	IDA (Devel Assoc)	31 Mar 66	Loans and Credits	569UNTS3	108277
Burundi	IDA (Devel Assoc)	11 Apr 69	Non-IBRD Project	0UNTS0	110218
Burundi	Multilateral	22 Feb 49	Sanitation	93UNTS129	101296
Burundi	Multilateral	02 Jul 51	Refugees	189UNTS137	102545
Burundi	Multilateral	26 Jan 60	IGO Establishment	439UNTS249	106333
Burundi	Multilateral	18 Apr 61	Consul/Citizenship	500UNTS95	107310
Burundi	Multilateral	28 Sep 62	IGO Establishment	469UNTS169	106791
Burundi	Multilateral	05 Feb 63	Tech Assistance	453UNTS36	106518
Burundi	Multilateral	25 May 63	IGO Establishment	479UNTS39	106947
Burundi	Multilateral	04 Aug 63	IGO Establishment	510UNTS3	107408
Burundi	Multilateral	05 Aug 63	Sanitation	480UNTS43	106964
Burundi	Multilateral	10 Jul 64	Postal Service	611UNTS387	108846
Burundi	Multilateral	10 Jul 64	Postal Service	613UNTS3	108850
Burundi	Multilateral	10 Jul 64	Postal Service	612UNTS233	108848
Burundi	Multilateral	10 Jul 64	Postal Service	612UNTS361	108849
Burundi	Multilateral	10 Jul 64	Postal Service	612UNTS3	108847
Burundi	Multilateral	10 Jul 64	Postal Service	611UNTS105	108845
Burundi	Multilateral	10 Jul 64	Postal Service	611UNTS7	108844
Burundi	Multilateral	09 Mar 65	Water Transport	591UNTS265	108564
Burundi	Multilateral	08 Jul 65	General Trade	597UNTS3	108641
Burundi	Multilateral	18 Mar 68	Commodity Trade	0UNTS0	109262

PARTY ONE	PARTY TWO	DATE	TOPIC	CITATION	NUMBER
Burundi	Multilateral	24 Feb 70	Non-IBRD Project	0UNTS0	110623
Burundi	UN Special Fund	22 Aug 63	Direct Aid	476UNTS49	106903
Burundi	UNICEF (Children)	08 Jan 64	IGO Operations	485UNTS45	107045
Burundi	United Nations	29 Dec 62	Tech Assistance	450UNTS279	106474
Burundi	USA (United States)	06 May 69	Finance	0UNTS0	110799
Burundi	USSR (Soviet Union)	30 Jun 62	Recognition	11SUGG145	469848
Burundi	USSR (Soviet Union)	01 Oct 62	Consul/Citizenship	11SUGG154	469866
Burundi	WHO (World Health)	08 Aug 63	Tech Assistance	477UNTS346	106928
Burundi	WHO (World Health)	30 Aug 63	IGO Operations	490UNTS423	107169
Byelorussia	Multilateral	02 Aug 44	Scientific Project	67UNTS221	200221
Byelorussia	Multilateral	22 Jul 46	IGO Establishment	9UNTS3	100125
Byelorussia	Multilateral	22 Jul 46	IGO Establishment	14UNTS185	100221
Byelorussia	Multilateral	11 Dec 46	Sanitation	12UNTS179	100186
Byelorussia	Multilateral	10 Feb 47	Peace/Disarmament	41UNTS21	100643
Byelorussia	Multilateral	10 Feb 47	Peace/Disarmament	48UNTS203	100746
Byelorussia	Multilateral	10 Feb 47	Peace/Disarmament	49UNTS3	100747
Byelorussia	Multilateral	10 Feb 47	Peace/Disarmament	42UNTS3	100645
Byelorussia	Multilateral	10 Feb 47	Peace/Disarmament	41UNTS135	100644
Byelorussia	Multilateral	02 Oct 47	Telecommunications	193UNTS188	102616
Byelorussia	Multilateral	11 Oct 47	IGO Establishment	77UNTS143	100998
Byelorussia	Multilateral	24 Jul 48	Sanitation	66UNTS25	100847
Byelorussia	Multilateral	19 Nov 48	Sanitation	44UNTS277	100688
Byelorussia	Multilateral	09 Dec 48	Humanitarian	78UNTS277	101021
Byelorussia	Multilateral	12 Aug 49	Humanitarian	75UNTS287	100973
Byelorussia	Multilateral	12 Aug 49	Humanitarian	75UNTS31	100970
Byelorussia	Multilateral	12 Aug 49	General Military	75UNTS135	100972
Byelorussia	Multilateral	12 Aug 49	Humanitarian	75UNTS85	100971
Byelorussia	Multilateral	07 Dec 50	Admin Cooperation	212UNTS17	102861
Byelorussia	Multilateral	11 Jul 52	Postal Service	170UNTS3	102221
Byelorussia	Multilateral	11 Jul 52	IGO Establishment	169UNTS3	102220
Byelorussia	Multilateral	31 Mar 53	Privil/Immunities	193UNTS136	102613
Byelorussia	Multilateral	14 May 54	Culture	249UNTS215	103511
Byelorussia	Multilateral	28 Sep 55	Air Transport	478UNTS371	106943
Byelorussia	Multilateral	20 Jun 56	Admin Cooperation	268UNTS3	103850
Byelorussia	Multilateral	07 Sep 56	Humanitarian	266UNTS3	103822
Byelorussia	Multilateral	26 Oct 56	IGO Establishment	276UNTS3	103988
Byelorussia	Multilateral	20 Feb 57	Consul/Citizenship	309UNTS65	104468
Byelorussia	Multilateral	03 Oct 57	Postal Service	365UNTS3	105213
Byelorussia	Multilateral	03 Oct 57	Postal Service	364UNTS331	105212
Byelorussia	Multilateral	03 Oct 57	Postal Service	364UNTS3	105211
Byelorussia	Multilateral	29 Apr 58	Water Transport	450UNTS11	106465
Byelorussia	Multilateral	29 Apr 58	Territory Boundary	499UNTS311	107302
Byelorussia	Multilateral	10 Jun 58	Admin Cooperation	330UNTS3	104739
Byelorussia	Multilateral	03 Dec 58	Admin Cooperation	398UNTS9	105715
Byelorussia	Multilateral	03 Dec 58	Admin Cooperation	416UNTS51	105995
Byelorussia	Multilateral	14 Dec 60	Education	429UNTS93	106193
Byelorussia	Multilateral	30 Mar 61	Sanitation	520UNTS151	107515
Byelorussia	Multilateral	18 Apr 61	Consul/Citizenship	500UNTS95	107310
Byelorussia	Multilateral	21 Apr 61	IGO Establishment	484UNTS349	107041
Byelorussia	Multilateral	05 Aug 63	Sanitation	480UNTS43	106964
Byelorussia	Multilateral	10 Jul 64	Postal Service	611UNTS387	108846
Byelorussia	Multilateral	10 Jul 64	Postal Service	611UNTS7	108844
Byelorussia	Multilateral	10 Jul 64	Postal Service	612UNTS3	108847
Byelorussia	Multilateral	10 Jul 64	Postal Service	611UNTS105	108845
Byelorussia	Multilateral	08 Jul 65	General Trade	597UNTS3	108641
Byelorussia	Multilateral	22 Apr 68	Scientific Project	0UNTS0	109574
Byelorussia	Multilateral	26 Nov 68	Humanitarian	0UNTS0	110823
Cambodia	Accept UN Charter	15 Jun 52	UN Charter	223UNTS35	103046
Cambodia	China People's Rep	24 Apr 56	General Trade	56CCJC54	410333
Cambodia	China People's Rep	24 Apr 56	General Trade	56CCJC55	410334
Cambodia	China People's Rep	21 Jun 56	Direct Aid	56CCJC76	410345
Cambodia	China People's Rep	21 Nov 59	Customs	59CCJC104	410645
Cambodia	China People's Rep	19 Dec 60	General Amity	60CCJC129	410741
Cambodia	China People's Rep	23 May 62	Admin Cooperation	62CCJC50	410892
Cambodia	China People's Rep	25 Nov 63	Air Transport	63CCJC138	411034

PARTY ONE	PARTY TWO	DATE	TOPIC	CITATION	NUMBER
Cambodia	China People's Rep	26 Nov 63	Air Transport	63CCJC141	411037
Cambodia	China People's Rep	22 Mar 65	Health/Educ/Welfare	65CCJC35	411127
Cambodia	China People's Rep	16 Sep 65	Mass Media	65CCJC119	411135
Cambodia	China People's Rep	31 Mar 66	Health/Educ/Welfare	66CCJC12	411140
Cambodia	China People's Rep	29 Apr 66	General Economic	66CCJC22	411142
Cambodia	Czechoslovakia	27 Nov 60	Culture	410UNTS263	105910
Cambodia	Czechoslovakia	27 Nov 60	General Amity	412UNTS179	105931
Cambodia	Denmark	20 Nov 69	Loans and Credits	0UNTS0	110353
Cambodia	France	08 Nov 49	Recognition	53FRJO1403	416094
Cambodia	France	29 Aug 53	Recognition	59FRRT7	415095
Cambodia	France	09 Sep 53	Admin Cooperation	59FRRT7	415096
Cambodia	France	15 Jan 64	Air Transport	64FRRT14	415097
Cambodia	France	04 Jul 64	General Aid	67FRJO2107	416098
Cambodia	Germany, East	29 Aug 60	Tech Assistance	8EGDA371	419167
Cambodia	Germany, East	29 Aug 60	Finance	8EGDA372	419166
Cambodia	Germany, East	29 Aug 60	General Trade	8EGDA371	419165
Cambodia	Germany, East	02 Feb 64	Health/Educ/Welfare	12EGDA826	419168
Cambodia	ICJ Option Clause	17 Jul 52	UN Charter	137UNTS11	101844
Cambodia	ICJ Option Clause	09 Sep 57	ICJ Option Clause	277UNTS77	103998
Cambodia	Japan	09 Dec 55	General Amity	0JGJI1301	441089
Cambodia	Japan	02 Mar 59	General Economic	341UNTS163	104882
Cambodia	Japan	16 May 59	General Economic	0JGJI1401	441149
Cambodia	Japan	30 Sep 66	Tech Assistance	66JJS53	442177
Cambodia	Japan	02 Nov 68	Tech Assistance	68JJS49	442221
Cambodia	Japan	21 Mar 69	Direct Aid	69JJS75	442237
Cambodia	Japan	21 Mar 69	Non-IBRD Project	0UNTS0	110577
Cambodia	Japan	01 Aug 69	Non-IBRD Project	69JHZ8	439030
Cambodia	Multilateral	07 Dec 44	IGO Establishment	15UNTS295	200102
Cambodia	Multilateral	11 Dec 46	Sanitation	12UNTS179	100186
Cambodia	Multilateral	12 Nov 47	Admin Cooperation	46UNTS201	100710
Cambodia	Multilateral	06 Mar 48	Water Transport	289UNTS3	104214
Cambodia	Multilateral	10 Jun 48	Humanitarian	164UNTS113	102163
Cambodia	Multilateral	24 Jul 48	Sanitation	66UNTS25	100847
Cambodia	Multilateral	15 Nov 48	IGO Establishment	120UNTS59	101615
Cambodia	Multilateral	29 Nov 48	IGO Establishment	120UNTS13	101613
Cambodia	Multilateral	09 Dec 48	Humanitarian	78UNTS277	101021
Cambodia	Multilateral	04 May 49	Admin Cooperation	47UNTS159	100728
Cambodia	Multilateral	15 Jul 49	Health/Educ/Welfare	197UNTS3	102631
Cambodia	Multilateral	06 Apr 50	Admin Cooperation	119UNTS99	101610
Cambodia	Multilateral	22 Nov 50	Culture	131UNTS25	101734
Cambodia	Multilateral	23 Dec 50	Tech Assistance	185UNTS3	102456
Cambodia	Multilateral	25 May 51	Status of Forces	175UNTS215	102303
Cambodia	Multilateral	08 Sep 51	General Military	136UNTS165	101833
Cambodia	Multilateral	08 Sep 51	Peace/Disarmament	136UNTS45	101832
Cambodia	Multilateral	06 Dec 51	Admin Cooperation	150UNTS67	101963
Cambodia	Multilateral	10 May 52	Taxation	439UNTS233	106332
Cambodia	Multilateral	10 May 52	Admin Cooperation	439UNTS193	106330
Cambodia	Multilateral	10 May 52	Admin Cooperation	439UNTS217	106331
Cambodia	Multilateral	12 Jun 52	Dispute Settlement	138UNTS183	101869
Cambodia	Multilateral	11 Jul 52	Postal Service	171UNTS143	102226
Cambodia	Multilateral	11 Jul 52	Postal Service	170UNTS3	102221
Cambodia	Multilateral	11 Jul 52	Postal Service	170UNTS63	102222
Cambodia	Multilateral	11 Jul 52	IGO Establishment	169UNTS3	102220
Cambodia	Multilateral	11 Jul 52	Postal Service	171UNTS89	102225
Cambodia	Multilateral	11 Jul 52	Postal Service	170UNTS269	102223
Cambodia	Multilateral	06 Sep 52	Patents/Copyrights	216UNTS132	102937
Cambodia	Multilateral	27 Feb 53	Claims and Debts	333UNTS3	104764
Cambodia	Multilateral	11 May 53	Sanitation	456UNTS3	106555
Cambodia	Multilateral	14 May 54	Culture	249UNTS215	103511
Cambodia	Multilateral	04 Jun 54	Customs	276UNTS191	103992
Cambodia	Multilateral	04 Jun 54	Customs	282UNTS249	104101
Cambodia	Multilateral	18 May 56	Land Transport	339UNTS3	104844
Cambodia	Multilateral	18 May 56	Customs	327UNTS123	104721
Cambodia	Multilateral	05 Oct 56	Tech Assistance	251UNTS267	103545
Cambodia	Multilateral	26 Oct 56	IGO Establishment	276UNTS3	103988

PARTY ONE	PARTY TWO	DATE	TOPIC	CITATION	NUMBER
Cambodia	Multilateral	03 Oct 57	Postal Service	364UNTS331	105212
Cambodia	Multilateral	03 Oct 57	Postal Service	366UNTS87	105216
Cambodia	Multilateral	03 Oct 57	Postal Service	366UNTS255	105219
Cambodia	Multilateral	03 Oct 57	Postal Service	365UNTS3	105213
Cambodia	Multilateral	03 Oct 57	Postal Service	366UNTS141	105217
Cambodia	Multilateral	03 Oct 57	Postal Service	365UNTS207	105214
Cambodia	Multilateral	03 Oct 57	Postal Service	364UNTS3	105211
Cambodia	Multilateral	29 Apr 58	Water Transport	450UNTS11	106465
Cambodia	Multilateral	29 Apr 58	Territory Boundary	499UNTS311	107302
Cambodia	Multilateral	29 Apr 58	Territory Boundary	516UNTS205	107477
Cambodia	Multilateral	29 Apr 58	Specific Resources	559UNTS285	108164
Cambodia	Multilateral	10 Jun 58	Admin Cooperation	330UNTS3	104739
Cambodia	Multilateral	06 Oct 60	Customs	473UNTS131	106861
Cambodia	Multilateral	26 Nov 60	Taxation	500UNTS25	107304
Cambodia	Multilateral	30 Mar 61	Sanitation	520UNTS151	107515
Cambodia	Multilateral	18 Apr 61	Consul/Citizenship	500UNTS95	107310
Cambodia	Multilateral	18 Apr 61	Consul/Citizenship	500UNTS223	107311
Cambodia	Multilateral	18 Apr 61	Dispute Settlement	500UNTS243	107312
Cambodia	Multilateral	08 Jun 61	Customs	473UNTS187	106863
Cambodia	Multilateral	26 Oct 61	Patents/Copyrights	496UNTS43	107247
Cambodia	Multilateral	23 Jul 62	Recognition	456UNTS302	106564
Cambodia	Multilateral	19 Oct 63	Direct Aid	523UNTS249	107559
Cambodia	Multilateral	10 Jul 64	Postal Service	611UNTS387	108846
Cambodia	Multilateral	10 Jul 64	Postal Service	612UNTS233	108848
Cambodia	Multilateral	10 Jul 64	Postal Service	611UNTS105	108845
Cambodia	Multilateral	10 Jul 64	Postal Service	613UNTS193	108852
Cambodia	Multilateral	10 Jul 64	Postal Service	611UNTS7	108844
Cambodia	Multilateral	10 Jul 64	Postal Service	613UNTS3	108851
Cambodia	Multilateral	10 Jul 64	Postal Service	613UNTS3	108850
Cambodia	Multilateral	10 Jul 64	Postal Service	612UNTS3	108847
Cambodia	Multilateral	04 Dec 65	IGO Establishment	571UNTS123	108303
Cambodia	Multilateral	28 Sep 68	Tech Assistance	0UNTS0	109296
Cambodia	Netherlands	04 Jul 69	Non-IBRD Project	0UNTS0	110391
Cambodia	Poland	17 Dec 57	Tech Assistance	57PZUM130	458058
Cambodia	Singapore	25 Nov 69	General Economic	0UNTS0	110561
Cambodia	Thailand	15 Dec 60	Extradition	382UNTS315	105492
Cambodia	Thailand	15 Dec 60	Mass Media	382UNTS301	105490
Cambodia	Thailand	15 Dec 60	Extradition	382UNTS321	105493
Cambodia	Thailand	15 Dec 60	Admin Cooperation	382UNTS307	105491
Cambodia	UK Great Britain	09 Jul 69	Loans and Credits	0UNTS0	110117
Cambodia	UN Special Fund	24 Nov 60	Direct Aid	382UNTS255	105487
Cambodia	UNICEF (Children)	28 Apr 56	Direct Aid	136UNTS341	200446
Cambodia	UNICEF (Children)	25 Jun 56	Direct Aid	249UNTS153	103505
Cambodia	United Nations	24 Jun 53	Tech Assistance	168UNTS309	200500
Cambodia	United Nations	30 Nov 60	Tech Assistance	383UNTS147	105500
Cambodia	USA (United States)	08 Sep 51	Direct Aid	174UNTS115	102282
Cambodia	USA (United States)	28 Dec 51	Milit Assistance	179UNTS97	102358
Cambodia	USA (United States)	16 May 55	Milit Assistance	263UNTS273	103777
Cambodia	USA (United States)	17 Oct 57	Scientific Project	299UNTS203	104313
Cambodia	USA (United States)	15 Jul 60	Admin Cooperation	380UNTS129	105453
Cambodia	USSR (Soviet Union)	13 May 56	Consul/Citizenship	16SUGG70	469915
Cambodia	USSR (Soviet Union)	07 Jul 56	Direct Aid	0SUST363	468064
Cambodia	USSR (Soviet Union)	31 May 57	Finance	0SUST384	468067
Cambodia	USSR (Soviet Union)	31 May 57	General Trade	0SUST384	468065
Cambodia	USSR (Soviet Union)	31 May 57	Health/Educ/Welfare	0SUST384	468066
Cambodia	USSR (Soviet Union)	12 Sep 58	Non-IBRD Project	7SUGG121	469531
Cambodia	USSR (Soviet Union)	10 May 60	Direct Aid	9SUGG135	469657
Cambodia	USSR (Soviet Union)	10 May 60	Direct Aid	9SUGG165	469658
Cambodia	USSR (Soviet Union)	24 Jun 61	Non-IBRD Project	10SUGG136	469781
Cambodia	Vietnam, South	29 Dec 54	Water Transport	0VKNG85	496023
Cambodia	Vietnam, South	22 Aug 55	Finance	0VKNG100	496032
Cambodia	Vietnam, South	27 May 70	General Economic	0VKNG333	496085
Cambodia	Vietnam, South	27 May 70	Consul/Citizenship	0VKNG334	496086
Cambodia	Vietnam, South	27 May 70	Consul/Citizenship	0VKNG332	496084
Cambodia	Vietnam, South	22 Jan 71	General Amity	0VKNG370	496093
Cambodia	Vietnam, South	04 Jun 71	Customs	0VKNG382	496096
Cambodia	Vietnam, South	04 Jun 71	Visas	0VKNG383	496097
Cambodia	WHO (World Health)	31 May 51	Tech Assistance	102UNTS279	200307
Cambodia	WHO (World Health)	19 May 60	Tech Assistance	372UNTS193	105298
Cameroon	Accept UN Charter	13 Jan 60	UN Charter	375UNTS79	105354
Cameroon	Denmark	08 Oct 62	General Trade	0UNTS0	110770
Cameroon	France	13 Nov 60	Military Mission	0UNTS0	110641
Cameroon	France	13 Nov 60	General Amity	61FRRT29	415099
Cameroon	France	13 Nov 60	General Economic	0UNTS0	110639
Cameroon	France	13 Nov 60	Air Transport	0UNTS0	110642
Cameroon	France	13 Nov 60	Admin Cooperation	0UNTS0	110637
Cameroon	France	13 Nov 60	Admin Cooperation	0UNTS0	110643
Cameroon	France	13 Nov 60	Military Mission	0UNTS0	110640
Cameroon	France	13 Nov 60	General Economic	0UNTS0	110638
Cameroon	France	13 Nov 60	Consul/Citizenship	0UNTS0	110635
Cameroon	France	13 Nov 60	Culture	0UNTS0	110636
Cameroon	France	13 Nov 60	General Amity	0UNTS0	110634
Cameroon	France	16 Jun 61	Air Transport	412UNTS148	105929
Cameroon	France	16 Jan 63	Customs	63FRRT15	415101
Cameroon	France	16 Jan 63	Education	63FRRT53	415100
Cameroon	France	05 May 63	Mass Media	65FRRT48	415102
Cameroon	France	10 Aug 63	Specific Property	64FRRT71	415103
Cameroon	France	10 Jul 65	Taxation	0UNTS0	109433
Cameroon	France	10 Jul 65	Finance	68FRJO2703	416104
Cameroon	Germany, West	05 Mar 56	Other Military	68WBGA203	424348
Cameroon	Germany, West	11 Dec 57	Atomic Energy	58WBGA46	424349
Cameroon	Germany, West	03 Aug 59	General Military	61WGBB1183	425350
Cameroon	Germany, West	08 Mar 62	General Trade	62WBGA126	424342
Cameroon	Germany, West	08 Mar 62	Water Transport	62WBGA126	424343
Cameroon	Germany, West	29 Jun 62	Claims and Debts	63WGBB911	425344
Cameroon	Germany, West	29 Jun 62	Direct Aid	62WBGA172	424345
Cameroon	Germany, West	03 May 63	Loans and Credits	63WBGA115	424346
Cameroon	Germany, West	28 Aug 64	General Military	64WBGA195	424351
Cameroon	Germany, West	22 Oct 64	Air Transport	66WGBB109	425347
Cameroon	Germany, West	08 Jul 69	Scientific Project	70WGBB97	425352
Cameroon	Germany, West	23 Oct 69	Admin Cooperation	70WGBB846	425353
Cameroon	Germany, West	19 Dec 69	Non-ILO Labor	70WGBB253	425354
Cameroon	Greece	29 Oct 62	General Trade	538UNTS185	107815
Cameroon	IBRD (World Bank)	28 Mar 67	IBRD Project	618UNTS89	108925
Cameroon	IBRD (World Bank)	15 Apr 69	IBRD Project	0UNTS0	110171
Cameroon	IBRD (World Bank)	02 Jun 69	IBRD Project	0UNTS0	110122
Cameroon	IBRD (World Bank)	27 Mar 70	IBRD Project	0UNTS0	110681
Cameroon	IDA (Devel Assoc)	28 Mar 67	Non-IBRD Project	618UNTS133	108926
Cameroon	IDA (Devel Assoc)	29 Jan 68	Non-IBRD Project	0UNTS0	109325
Cameroon	IDA (Devel Assoc)	23 Sep 69	Non-IBRD Project	0UNTS0	110580
Cameroon	IDA (Devel Assoc)	27 Mar 70	Non-IBRD Project	0UNTS0	110682
Cameroon	ILO (Labor Org)	07 May 67	IGO Operations	596UNTS209	108634
Cameroon	Israel	24 Oct 62	Culture	449UNTS15	106447
Cameroon	Israel	24 Oct 62	General Aid	449UNTS3	106446
Cameroon	Israel	09 Aug 63	Air Transport	499UNTS121	107295
Cameroon	Mali	17 Mar 64	Air Transport	524UNTS61	107566
Cameroon	Multilateral	07 Dec 44	Air Transport	84UNTS389	200252
Cameroon	Multilateral	07 Dec 44	IGO Establishment	15UNTS295	200102
Cameroon	Multilateral	11 Dec 46	Sanitation	12UNTS179	100186
Cameroon	Multilateral	06 Mar 48	Water Transport	289UNTS3	104214
Cameroon	Multilateral	24 Jul 48	Sanitation	66UNTS25	100847
Cameroon	Multilateral	04 May 49	Admin Cooperation	98UNTS101	101358
Cameroon	Multilateral	04 May 49	Admin Cooperation	92UNTS19	101257
Cameroon	Multilateral	22 Nov 50	Culture	131UNTS25	101734
Cameroon	Multilateral	02 Jul 51	Refugees	189UNTS137	102545
Cameroon	Multilateral	11 May 53	Sanitation	456UNTS3	106555
Cameroon	Multilateral	18 Jan 54	IGO Establishment	330UNTS121	104743
Cameroon	Multilateral	14 May 54	Culture	249UNTS215	103511
Cameroon	Multilateral	14 Jun 54	Air Transport	320UNTS217	104644
Cameroon	Multilateral	14 Jun 54	Air Transport	320UNTS209	104643

PARTY ONE	PARTY TWO	DATE	TOPIC	CITATION	NUMBER
Cameroon	Multilateral	29 Jul 54	Sanitation	249UNTS45	103500
Cameroon	Multilateral	28 Sep 55	Air Transport	478UNTS371	106943
Cameroon	Multilateral	18 May 56	Customs	338UNTS103	104834
Cameroon	Multilateral	26 Jan 60	IGO Establishment	439UNTS249	106333
Cameroon	Multilateral	17 Jun 60	Humanitarian	536UNTS27	107794
Cameroon	Multilateral	30 Mar 61	Sanitation	520UNTS151	107515
Cameroon	Multilateral	21 Jun 61	IGO Establishment	514UNTS209	107449
Cameroon	Multilateral	29 Aug 62	Tech Assistance	443UNTS280	106366
Cameroon	Multilateral	14 Sep 62	Visas	443UNTS73	106360
Cameroon	Multilateral	28 Sep 62	IGO Establishment	469UNTS169	106791
Cameroon	Multilateral	24 Apr 63	Consul/Citizenship	596UNTS261	108638
Cameroon	Multilateral	24 Apr 63	Consul/Citizenship	596UNTS487	108640
Cameroon	Multilateral	25 May 63	IGO Establishment	479UNTS39	106947
Cameroon	Multilateral	04 Aug 63	IGO Establishment	510UNTS3	107408
Cameroon	Multilateral	05 Aug 63	Sanitation	480UNTS43	106964
Cameroon	Multilateral	26 Oct 63	Water Transport	587UNTS9	108506
Cameroon	Multilateral	09 Nov 63	Direct Aid	489UNTS209	107141
Cameroon	Multilateral	10 Jul 64	Postal Service	613UNTS3	108850
Cameroon	Multilateral	10 Jul 64	Postal Service	613UNTS193	108852
Cameroon	Multilateral	10 Jul 64	Postal Service	613UNTS3	108851
Cameroon	Multilateral	10 Jul 64	Postal Service	613UNTS127	108853
Cameroon	Multilateral	10 Jul 64	Postal Service	612UNTS361	108849
Cameroon	Multilateral	10 Jul 64	Postal Service	611UNTS105	108845
Cameroon	Multilateral	10 Jul 64	Postal Service	612UNTS233	108848
Cameroon	Multilateral	10 Jul 64	Postal Service	611UNTS7	108844
Cameroon	Multilateral	10 Jul 64	Postal Service	612UNTS3	108847
Cameroon	Multilateral	10 Jul 64	Postal Service	611UNTS387	108846
Cameroon	Multilateral	25 Nov 64	Water Transport	587UNTS19	108507
Cameroon	Multilateral	18 Mar 65	Dispute Settlement	575UNTS159	108359
Cameroon	Multilateral	08 Jul 65	General Trade	597UNTS3	108641
Cameroon	Multilateral	31 Dec 65	Specific Resources	616UNTS317	108904
Cameroon	Multilateral	27 May 66	IGO Establishment	637UNTSO	109121
Cameroon	Multilateral	31 Jan 67	Refugees	606UNTS267	108791
Cameroon	Multilateral	18 Mar 68	Commodity Trade	OUNTSO	109262
Cameroon	Multilateral	22 Apr 68	Scientific Project	OUNTSO	109574
Cameroon	Multilateral	01 Jul 68	Peace/Disarmament	OUNTSO	110485
Cameroon	Multilateral	24 Sep 68	Air Transport	OUNTSO	110612
Cameroon	Netherlands	18 Dec 63	General Aid	521UNTS303	107527
Cameroon	Netherlands	06 Jul 65	Tech Assistance	571UNTS75	108300
Cameroon	Netherlands	06 Jul 65	Tech Assistance	571UNTS63	108299
Cameroon	Poland	26 Apr 63	Tech Assistance	63PZUM27	458101
Cameroon	Poland	26 Apr 63	Culture	63PZUM31	458102
Cameroon	Switzerland	28 Jan 63	General Economic	64SWRO400	462124
Cameroon	UK Great Britain	29 Jul 63	General Economic	478UNTS148	106935
Cameroon	UK Great Britain	20 Aug 63	Culture	539UNTS233	107834
Cameroon	UK Great Britain	16 Jun 67	Loans and Credits	618UNTS329	108933
Cameroon	UN Special Fund	13 Jun 61	Direct Aid	397UNTS297	105713
Cameroon	UNICEF (Children)	12 Aug 61	Direct Aid	402UNTS235	105788
Cameroon	United Nations	29 Aug 62	Tech Assistance	442UNTS3	106334
Cameroon	USA (United States)	26 May 61	General Aid	413UNTS195	105953
Cameroon	USA (United States)	10 Sep 62	Tech Assistance	461UNTS177	106662
Cameroon	USA (United States)	07 Mar 67	Finance	OUNTSO	109855
Cameroon	USSR (Soviet Union)	24 Sep 62	General Trade	OUNTSO	109580
Cameroon	USSR (Soviet Union)	24 Sep 62	General Trade	11SUGG153	469862
Cameroon	USSR (Soviet Union)	24 Sep 62	General Trade	11SUGG153	469863
Cameroon	WHO (World Health)	08 Dec 62	Tech Assistance	451UNTS215	106496
Canada	Argentina	06 Aug 49	Taxation	231UNTS43	103202
Canada	Australia	11 Jun 46	Air Transport	10UNTS47	100142
Canada	Australia	01 Oct 57	Taxation	392UNTS41	105638
Canada	Australia	04 Aug 59	Atomic Energy	391UNTS191	105623
Canada	Australia	12 Feb 60	General Trade	369UNTS89	105253
Canada	Austria	18 Jan 52	Admin Cooperation	236UNTS245	103327
Canada	Austria	19 Jun 56	Visas	305UNTS51	104412
Canada	Austria	11 May 67	Extradition	69ABGB324	403018
Canada	Austria	28 Feb 68	Other Military	636UNTS141	109101

PARTY ONE	PARTY TWO	DATE	TOPIC	CITATION	NUMBER
Canada	Belgium	25 Oct 45	Finance	230UNTS127	103180
Canada	Belgium	13 Jul 46	Reparations	230UNTS159	103181
Canada	Belgium	30 Aug 49	Air Transport	53UNTS221	100782
Canada	Belgium	16 Nov 49	Reparations	51UNTS3	100748
Canada	Belgium	19 Nov 49	Visas	150UNTS231	101977
Canada	Belgium	30 Mar 53	Status of Forces	181UNTS95	102401
Canada	Belgium	08 May 67	Culture	637UNTSO	109119
Canada	Bolivia	31 May 63	Gen Communications	529UNTS37	107654
Canada	Brazil	17 Oct 41	General Trade	67UNTS263	200224
Canada	Brazil	24 May 44	Culture	65UNTS265	200215
Canada	Ceylon (Sri Lanka)	24 Apr 51	Visas	248UNTS101	103488
Canada	Ceylon (Sri Lanka)	11 Jul 52	General Aid	391UNTS245	105630
Canada	Ceylon (Sri Lanka)	05 Nov 58	Loans and Credits	391UNTS225	105627
Canada	Chile	14 Oct 62	Gen Communications	528UNTS273	107648
Canada	Costa Rica	18 Nov 50	General Economic	231UNTS25	103200
Canada	Czechoslovakia	01 Mar 45	Finance	45UNTS283	200185
Canada	Czechoslovakia	28 Jun 46	Finance	43UNTS81	100662
Canada	Czechoslovakia	20 Mar 69	Air Transport	OUNTSO	110470
Canada	Denmark	14 Oct 49	Visas	46UNTS97	100702
Canada	Denmark	13 Dec 49	Air Transport	72UNTS247	100937
Canada	Denmark	25 Mar 50	Reparations	230UNTS343	103193
Canada	Denmark	30 Sep 55	Taxation	258UNTS115	103675
Canada	Denmark	17 Apr 57	Milit Assistance	316UNTS207	104586
Canada	Denmark	28 Nov 63	Air Transport	496UNTS223	107254
Canada	Denmark	15 Oct 64	Water Transport	525UNTS227	107595
Canada	Denmark	25 Jul 68	Admin Cooperation	OUNTSO	109701
Canada	Ecuador	10 Nov 50	General Economic	231UNTS15	103199
Canada	El Salvador	11 Mar 63	Gen Communications	529UNTS25	107652
Canada	Ethiopia	03 Jun 55	General Economic	247UNTS157	103465
Canada	Euratom	06 Oct 59	Scientific Project	475UNTS187	106894
Canada	Fed Rhod/Nyasaland	06 Feb 58	General Trade	392UNTS27	105636
Canada	Finland	17 Nov 48	General Trade	231UNTS75	103207
Canada	Finland	09 Jan 56	Visas	305UNTS33	104410
Canada	Finland	09 Dec 58	Visas	323UNTS331	104674
Canada	Finland	28 Mar 59	Taxation	355UNTS3	105072
Canada	Finland	05 Jun 63	Water Transport	472UNTS345	106846
Canada	France	12 May 33	Admin Cooperation	253UNTS285	200545
Canada	France	22 Mar 46	Reparations	230UNTS165	103182
Canada	France	09 Apr 46	Finance	43UNTS43	100660
Canada	France	05 May 47	Reparations	231UNTS81	103208
Canada	France	08 Sep 47	Taxation	253UNTS259	103587
Canada	France	05 May 48	Reparations	231UNTS87	103209
Canada	France	17 Apr 50	Visas	230UNTS365	103196
Canada	France	01 Aug 50	Air Transport	73UNTS21	100941
Canada	France	26 Jan 51	Claims and Debts	233UNTS65	103251
Canada	France	16 Mar 51	Taxation	236UNTS267	103330
Canada	France	16 Mar 51	Taxation	236UNTS297	103331
Canada	France	04 Jul 51	Reparations	233UNTS101	103253
Canada	France	04 Sep 56	Other Military	305UNTS79	104415
Canada	France	04 Oct 56	Non-ILO Labor	305UNTS65	104414
Canada	France	25 May 62	Other Military	470UNTS163	106808
Canada	France	11 Oct 63	Mass Media	529UNTS71	107657
Canada	France	15 Jan 64	Education	65FRRT37	415105
Canada	France	27 Feb 65	Education	65FRRT40	415106
Canada	France	17 Nov 65	Culture	66FRJO1401	416107
Canada	France	24 Nov 65	Culture	66FRJO1401	416108
Canada	France	03 Apr 69	Sanitation	OUNTSO	110532
Canada	France	03 Apr 69	Sanitation	69FRJO2512	416109
Canada	Germany, West	15 Apr 53	Visas	236UNTS323	103333
Canada	Germany, West	30 Oct 53	Admin Cooperation	236UNTS317	103332
Canada	Germany, West	04 Jun 56	Taxation	316UNTS231	104589
Canada	Germany, West	10 Dec 56	Milit Assistance	392UNTS3	105633
Canada	Germany, West	04 Sep 59	Air Transport	411UNTS260	105922
Canada	Ghana	08 Jan 62	Military Mission	528UNTS221	107645
Canada	Greece	28 Jul 47	Customs	43UNTS111	100665

PARTY ONE	PARTY TWO	DATE	TOPIC	CITATION	NUMBER
Canada	Greece	01 Jul 57	Visas	316UNTS201	104585
Canada	Greece	30 Sep 59	Visas	470UNTS87	106798
Canada	Greece	18 Jul 62	General Military	528UNTS265	107647
Canada	Honduras	11 Jul 56	Mostfavored Nation	305UNTS39	104411
Canada	Hungary	08 Mar 56	Commodity Trade	305UNTS27	104409
Canada	IAEA (Atom Energy)	24 Mar 59	Atomic Energy	339UNTS315	104851
Canada	ICAO (Civil Aviat)	14 Apr 51	IGO Status/Immunit	96UNTS155	101335
Canada	Iceland	17 Oct 62	Visas	528UNTS281	107649
Canada	ICJ Option Clause	07 Apr 70	ICJ Option Clause	0UNTS0	110415
Canada	India	26 Jan 51	Visas	248UNTS89	103486
Canada	India	10 Sep 51	General Aid	391UNTS237	105629
Canada	India	12 Jun 53	Admin Cooperation	248UNTS113	103490
Canada	India	30 Aug 56	Patents/Copyrights	305UNTS59	104413
Canada	India	20 Feb 58	Loans and Credits	391UNTS231	105628
Canada	India	22 Oct 58	Finance	392UNTS21	105635
Canada	India	14 May 63	Loans and Credits	529UNTS31	107653
Canada	India	16 Dec 63	Atomic Energy	529UNTS45	107655
Canada	Iran	10 Mar 61	Visas	470UNTS139	106805
Canada	Ireland	20 Aug 32	General Trade	0UNTS0	200645
Canada	Ireland	08 Aug 47	Air Transport	28UNTS47	100419
Canada	Ireland	28 Oct 54	Taxation	305UNTS3	104407
Canada	Ireland	28 Oct 54	Taxation	304UNTS317	104406
Canada	Ireland	21 Dec 67	General Trade	0UNTS0	109448
Canada	Israel	02 Aug 55	Visas	226UNTS265	103121
Canada	Israel	12 Sep 66	Telecommunications	581UNTS167	108440
Canada	Israel	30 Nov 66	Taxation	630UNTS267	108973
Canada	Israel	10 Mar 67	Extradition	0UNTS0	110380
Canada	Israel	05 Apr 67	Gen Communications	0UNTS0	109350
Canada	Italy	28 Apr 48	General Economic	231UNTS69	103206
Canada	Italy	30 May 50	Culture	53ITDI80	436072
Canada	Italy	20 Sep 51	Reparations	236UNTS251	103328
Canada	Italy	10 Oct 52	Visas	233UNTS137	103258
Canada	Italy	12 Feb 54	Culture	55ITGU53	435074
Canada	Italy	02 Feb 60	Air Transport	62ITGU22	435075
Canada	Italy	18 Dec 61	Specific Resources	470UNTS153	106807
Canada	Italy	18 Sep 63	Specific Resources	64ITDI245	436076
Canada	Jamaica	16 Jul 65	Milit Assistance	548UNTS265	107982
Canada	Japan	31 Mar 54	General Trade	236UNTS329	103334
Canada	Japan	12 Jan 55	Air Transport	311UNTS167	104503
Canada	Japan	13 Jun 55	Visas	247UNTS151	103464
Canada	Japan	20 Mar 56	Postal Service	517UNTS33	107482
Canada	Japan	02 Jul 59	Atomic Energy	383UNTS243	105504
Canada	Japan	05 Sep 61	Reparations	451UNTS47	106483
Canada	Japan	05 Sep 64	Visas	0JGJI1558	441122
Canada	Japan	05 Sep 64	Taxation	569UNTS99	108282
Canada	Luxembourg	26 Nov 49	Visas	231UNTS51	103203
Canada	Mexico	08 Feb 46	General Trade	230UNTS183	103183
Canada	Mexico	27 Jul 53	Air Transport	192UNTS255	102604
Canada	Mexico	21 Dec 61	Air Transport	64MEXD607	444004
Canada	Mexico	30 Jul 62	Gen Communications	528UNTS257	107646
Canada	Monaco	20 Mar 52	Visas	233UNTS123	103256
Canada	Multilateral	12 May 40	Scientific Project	101UNTS91	101405
Canada	Multilateral	22 Apr 42	Commodity Trade	8UNTS237	200044
Canada	Multilateral	26 Mar 43	Specif Goods/Equip	13UNTS427	200089
Canada	Multilateral	19 Apr 44	Scientific Project	89UNTS279	200257
Canada	Multilateral	02 Aug 44	Scientific Project	67UNTS221	200221
Canada	Multilateral	08 Oct 44	Reparations	45UNTS311	200187
Canada	Multilateral	07 Dec 44	Air Transport	84UNTS389	200252
Canada	Multilateral	07 Dec 44	IGO Establishment	15UNTS295	200102
Canada	Multilateral	07 Dec 44	Air Transport	171UNTS345	200501
Canada	Multilateral	15 Dec 44	Sanitation	16UNTS247	200106
Canada	Multilateral	15 Dec 44	Sanitation	17UNTS305	200110
Canada	Multilateral	02 Sep 45	Peace/Disarmament	139UNTS387	200465
Canada	Multilateral	15 Nov 45	Atomic Energy	3UNTS123	100026
Canada	Multilateral	16 Nov 45	IGO Establishment	4UNTS275	100052

PARTY ONE	PARTY TWO	DATE	TOPIC	CITATION	NUMBER
Canada	Multilateral	04 Dec 45	Telecommunications	9UNTS101	100128
Canada	Multilateral	27 Dec 45	IGO Establishment	2UNTS39	100020
Canada	Multilateral	14 Jan 46	Reparations	555UNTS69	108105
Canada	Multilateral	31 Mar 46	Milit Installation	17UNTS159	100274
Canada	Multilateral	23 Apr 46	Sanitation	17UNTS3	100265
Canada	Multilateral	23 Apr 46	Sanitation	16UNTS179	100257
Canada	Multilateral	03 Jun 46	Commodity Trade	7UNTS331	100109
Canada	Multilateral	22 Jul 46	IGO Establishment	14UNTS185	100221
Canada	Multilateral	22 Jul 46	IGO Establishment	9UNTS3	100125
Canada	Multilateral	27 Jul 46	Patents/Copyrights	90UNTS229	101238
Canada	Multilateral	30 Oct 46	IGO Establishment	11UNTS107	100151
Canada	Multilateral	02 Dec 46	Specific Resources	161UNTS72	102124
Canada	Multilateral	11 Dec 46	Sanitation	12UNTS179	100186
Canada	Multilateral	15 Dec 46	IGO Establishment	18UNTS3	100283
Canada	Multilateral	10 Feb 47	Peace/Disarmament	42UNTS3	100645
Canada	Multilateral	10 Feb 47	Peace/Disarmament	49UNTS3	100747
Canada	Multilateral	10 Feb 47	Peace/Disarmament	48UNTS203	100746
Canada	Multilateral	10 Feb 47	Peace/Disarmament	41UNTS135	100644
Canada	Multilateral	03 Mar 47	Humanitarian	11UNTS43	100148
Canada	Multilateral	27 May 47	Air Transport	418UNTS161	106021
Canada	Multilateral	29 Sep 47	Peace/Disarmament	45UNTS125	100694
Canada	Multilateral	02 Oct 47	Telecommunications	193UNTS188	102616
Canada	Multilateral	11 Oct 47	IGO Establishment	77UNTS143	100998
Canada	Multilateral	12 Nov 47	Admin Cooperation	46UNTS169	100709
Canada	Multilateral	12 Nov 47	Admin Cooperation	53UNTS13	100770
Canada	Multilateral	12 Nov 47	Admin Cooperation	53UNTS39	100771
Canada	Multilateral	12 Nov 47	Admin Cooperation	46UNTS201	100710
Canada	Multilateral	06 Mar 48	Water Transport	289UNTS3	104214
Canada	Multilateral	10 May 48	Culture	289UNTS111	104215
Canada	Multilateral	11 May 48	Telecommunications	500UNTS267	107313
Canada	Multilateral	10 Jun 48	Humanitarian	164UNTS113	102163
Canada	Multilateral	10 Jun 48	Humanitarian	191UNTS3	102576
Canada	Multilateral	26 Jun 48	Culture	331UNTS217	104757
Canada	Multilateral	24 Jul 48	Sanitation	66UNTS25	100847
Canada	Multilateral	14 Sep 48	Milit Occupation	18UNTS267	100296
Canada	Multilateral	19 Nov 48	Sanitation	44UNTS277	100688
Canada	Multilateral	09 Dec 48	Humanitarian	78UNTS277	101021
Canada	Multilateral	09 Dec 48	Scientific Project	73UNTS39	100942
Canada	Multilateral	09 Dec 48	Scientific Project	20UNTS229	100318
Canada	Multilateral	08 Feb 49	Specific Resources	157UNTS157	102053
Canada	Multilateral	23 Mar 49	Commodity Trade	203UNTS179	102746
Canada	Multilateral	04 Apr 49	General Military	34UNTS243	100541
Canada	Multilateral	04 May 49	Admin Cooperation	92UNTS19	101257
Canada	Multilateral	04 May 49	Admin Cooperation	47UNTS159	100728
Canada	Multilateral	04 May 49	Admin Cooperation	98UNTS101	101358
Canada	Multilateral	04 May 49	Admin Cooperation	30UNTS23	100446
Canada	Multilateral	04 May 49	Admin Cooperation	30UNTS3	100445
Canada	Multilateral	09 Jul 49	Telecommunications	168UNTS143	102218
Canada	Multilateral	15 Jul 49	Health/Educ/Welfare	197UNTS3	102631
Canada	Multilateral	12 Aug 49	Humanitarian	75UNTS287	100973
Canada	Multilateral	12 Aug 49	Humanitarian	75UNTS31	100970
Canada	Multilateral	12 Aug 49	Humanitarian	75UNTS85	100971
Canada	Multilateral	12 Aug 49	IGO Establishment	87UNTS131	101169
Canada	Multilateral	12 Aug 49	General Military	75UNTS135	100972
Canada	Multilateral	16 Dec 49	Admin Cooperation	72UNTS3	100924
Canada	Multilateral	06 Apr 50	Admin Cooperation	119UNTS99	101610
Canada	Multilateral	07 Dec 50	Admin Cooperation	212UNTS17	102861
Canada	Multilateral	25 May 51	Status of Forces	175UNTS215	102303
Canada	Multilateral	19 Jun 51	Status of Forces	199UNTS67	102678
Canada	Multilateral	10 Jul 51	Other Military	108UNTS287	101481
Canada	Multilateral	29 Jul 51	Other Military	117UNTS85	101585
Canada	Multilateral	08 Sep 51	Peace/Disarmament	136UNTS45	101832
Canada	Multilateral	08 Sep 51	General Military	136UNTS165	101833
Canada	Multilateral	20 Sep 51	IGO Status/Immunit	200UNTS3	102691
Canada	Multilateral	31 Oct 51	Other Military	172UNTS193	102247

PARTY ONE	PARTY TWO	DATE	TOPIC	CITATION	NUMBER
Canada	Multilateral	06 Dec 51	Admin Cooperation	150UNTS67	101963
Canada	Multilateral	01 Mar 52	Specific Resources	168UNTS9	102210
Canada	Multilateral	09 May 52	Specific Resources	205UNTS65	102770
Canada	Multilateral	08 Jun 52	Other Military	210UNTS317	102843
Canada	Multilateral	12 Jun 52	Dispute Settlement	138UNTS183	101869
Canada	Multilateral	11 Jul 52	IGO Establishment	169UNTS3	102220
Canada	Multilateral	06 Sep 52	Patents/Copyrights	216UNTS132	102937
Canada	Multilateral	07 Oct 52	Admin Cooperation	310UNTS181	104493
Canada	Multilateral	27 Feb 53	Claims and Debts	333UNTS3	104764
Canada	Multilateral	31 Mar 53	Privil/Immunities	193UNTS136	102613
Canada	Multilateral	11 May 53	Sanitation	456UNTS3	106555
Canada	Multilateral	27 Aug 53	Other Military	213UNTS137	102884
Canada	Multilateral	01 Oct 53	Commodity Trade	258UNTS153	103677
Canada	Multilateral	19 Oct 53	IGO Establishment	207UNTS189	102807
Canada	Multilateral	26 Oct 53	Status of Forces	207UNTS237	102809
Canada	Multilateral	07 Dec 53	Admin Cooperation	182UNTS51	102422
Canada	Multilateral	19 Feb 54	Status of Forces	214UNTS51	102899
Canada	Multilateral	22 Feb 54	Other Military	188UNTS273	102531
Canada	Multilateral	25 Feb 54	Air Transport	215UNTS249	102922
Canada	Multilateral	01 Mar 54	Commodity Trade	256UNTS31	103622
Canada	Multilateral	12 May 54	Admin Cooperation	327UNTS3	104714
Canada	Multilateral	04 Jun 54	Customs	282UNTS249	104101
Canada	Multilateral	04 Jun 54	Customs	276UNTS191	103992
Canada	Multilateral	14 Jun 54	Air Transport	320UNTS209	104643
Canada	Multilateral	14 Jun 54	Air Transport	320UNTS217	104644
Canada	Multilateral	23 Oct 54	Status of Forces	334UNTS3	104765
Canada	Multilateral	25 May 55	IGO Establishment	264UNTS117	103791
Canada	Multilateral	22 Jun 55	Atomic Energy	249UNTS3	103498
Canada	Multilateral	21 Sep 55	Other Military	269UNTS241	103885
Canada	Multilateral	28 Sep 55	Air Transport	478UNTS371	106943
Canada	Multilateral	04 Jan 56	Scientific Project	256UNTS171	103627
Canada	Multilateral	05 Mar 56	Other Military	326UNTS169	104711
Canada	Multilateral	05 Mar 56	Other Military	326UNTS181	104712
Canada	Multilateral	25 Apr 56	Commodity Trade	270UNTS103	103896
Canada	Multilateral	07 Sep 56	Humanitarian	266UNTS3	103822
Canada	Multilateral	24 Sep 56	Patents/Copyrights	253UNTS171	103583
Canada	Multilateral	25 Sep 56	Air Transport	334UNTS89	104767
Canada	Multilateral	25 Sep 56	Air Transport	334UNTS13	104766
Canada	Multilateral	26 Oct 56	IGO Establishment	276UNTS3	103988
Canada	Multilateral	09 Feb 57	Specific Resources	314UNTS105	104546
Canada	Multilateral	20 Feb 57	Consul/Citizenship	309UNTS65	104468
Canada	Multilateral	03 Oct 57	Postal Service	364UNTS3	105211
Canada	Multilateral	29 Apr 58	Specific Resources	559UNTS285	108164
Canada	Multilateral	29 Apr 58	Territory Boundary	499UNTS311	107302
Canada	Multilateral	29 Apr 58	Territory Boundary	516UNTS205	107477
Canada	Multilateral	29 Apr 58	Water Transport	450UNTS11	106465
Canada	Multilateral	29 Apr 58	Dispute Settlement	450UNTS169	106466
Canada	Multilateral	01 Dec 58	Commodity Trade	385UNTS137	105534
Canada	Multilateral	06 Apr 59	Commodity Trade	349UNTS167	105013
Canada	Multilateral	03 Aug 59	Status of Forces	481UNTS262	106986
Canada	Multilateral	19 Nov 59	IGO Operations	410UNTS156	105902
Canada	Multilateral	26 Jan 60	IGO Establishment	439UNTS249	106333
Canada	Multilateral	17 Jun 60	Humanitarian	536UNTS27	107794
Canada	Multilateral	01 Sep 60	Commodity Trade	403UNTS3	105792
Canada	Multilateral	19 Sep 60	IBRD Project	444UNTS259	106371
Canada	Multilateral	21 Sep 60	Patents/Copyrights	394UNTS3	105664
Canada	Multilateral	30 Mar 61	Sanitation	520UNTS151	107515
Canada	Multilateral	18 Apr 61	Consul/Citizenship	500UNTS95	107310
Canada	Multilateral	21 Jun 61	IGO Establishment	514UNTS209	107449
Canada	Multilateral	15 May 62	Commodity Trade	444UNTS3	106367
Canada	Multilateral	23 Jul 62	Recognition	456UNTS302	106564
Canada	Multilateral	10 Sep 62	Other Military	502UNTS3	107323
Canada	Multilateral	28 Sep 62	IGO Establishment	469UNTS169	106791
Canada	Multilateral	05 Aug 63	Sanitation	480UNTS43	106964
Canada	Multilateral	18 Jun 64	Atomic Energy	542UNTS145	107886

PARTY ONE	PARTY TWO	DATE	TOPIC	CITATION	NUMBER
Canada	Multilateral	10 Jul 64	Postal Service	611UNTS105	108845
Canada	Multilateral	10 Jul 64	Postal Service	611UNTS7	108844
Canada	Multilateral	20 Aug 64	Telecommunications	514UNTS25	107441
Canada	Multilateral	12 Sep 64	Specific Resources	0UNTS0	109344
Canada	Multilateral	09 Mar 65	Water Transport	591UNTS265	108564
Canada	Multilateral	04 Dec 65	IGO Establishment	571UNTS123	108303
Canada	Multilateral	31 Dec 65	Specific Resources	616UNTS317	108904
Canada	Multilateral	05 Apr 66	Water Transport	640UNTS133	109159
Canada	Multilateral	04 May 66	IBRD Project	575UNTS49	108354
Canada	Multilateral	14 May 66	Specific Resources	0UNTS0	109587
Canada	Multilateral	20 Jun 66	Scientific Project	572UNTS263	108318
Canada	Multilateral	27 Jan 67	Scientific Project	610UNTS205	108843
Canada	Multilateral	03 May 67	IGO Operations	0UNTS0	110764
Canada	Multilateral	30 Jun 67	Commodity Trade	0UNTS0	109864
Canada	Multilateral	06 Nov 67	Other Military	640UNTS87	109155
Canada	Multilateral	18 Mar 68	Commodity Trade	0UNTS0	109262
Canada	Multilateral	01 Jul 68	Peace/Disarmament	0UNTS0	110485
Canada	Multilateral	24 Sep 68	Air Transport	0UNTS0	110612
Canada	Multilateral	28 Sep 68	Tech Assistance	0UNTS0	109296
Canada	Multilateral	24 Dec 68	Commodity Trade	0UNTS0	109369
Canada	Multilateral	27 Jan 69	Telecommunications	0UNTS0	109664
Canada	Multilateral	07 Feb 69	Status of Forces	0UNTS0	110586
Canada	Multilateral	17 Oct 69	Atomic Energy	0UNTS0	110518
Canada	Multilateral	18 Oct 69	IGO Establishment	0UNTS0	110232
Canada	Multilateral	12 Jan 70	Commodity Trade	0UNTS0	110603
Canada	Multilateral	24 Feb 70	Non-IBRD Project	0UNTS0	110623
Canada	Netherlands	05 Feb 46	Finance	43UNTS3	100658
Canada	Netherlands	05 Feb 46	General Trade	230UNTS199	103184
Canada	Netherlands	30 Dec 46	Reparations	230UNTS205	103185
Canada	Netherlands	02 Jun 48	Air Transport	32UNTS215	100499
Canada	Netherlands	28 Oct 48	Reparations	231UNTS95	103210
Canada	Netherlands	09 May 49	Reparations	46UNTS263	100715
Canada	Netherlands	14 Dec 49	Visas	230UNTS337	103192
Canada	Netherlands	10 Apr 52	Reparations	233UNTS129	103257
Canada	Netherlands	02 Apr 57	Taxation	285UNTS193	104153
Canada	Netherlands	13 Apr 57	Milit Assistance	316UNTS223	104588
Canada	New Zealand	12 Mar 48	Taxation	231UNTS219	103222
Canada	New Zealand	16 Aug 50	Air Transport	77UNTS239	101002
Canada	Newfoundland	29 Jul 46	Air Transport	17UNTS169	100275
Canada	Nicaragua	19 Dec 46	General Trade	236UNTS229	103326
Canada	Nigeria	03 Jul 63	Milit Assistance	529UNTS57	107656
Canada	Norway	25 Jun 45	Finance	45UNTS297	200186
Canada	Norway	06 Jun 46	Finance	43UNTS67	100661
Canada	Norway	14 Feb 50	Air Transport	53UNTS329	100790
Canada	Norway	13 Mar 50	Visas	90UNTS181	101235
Canada	Norway	18 Mar 50	Reparations	230UNTS349	103194
Canada	Norway	06 Jul 54	Privil/Immunities	2NORT637	451017
Canada	Norway	20 Dec 55	Milit Assistance	305UNTS17	104408
Canada	Norway	17 Apr 57	Milit Assistance	316UNTS215	104587
Canada	Norway	25 Apr 60	Milit Installation	470UNTS109	106801
Canada	Norway	24 May 60	Milit Installation	470UNTS125	106803
Canada	Norway	23 Nov 66	Taxation	604UNTS295	108757
Canada	Norway	26 Apr 68	Specific Resources	3NORT0	451018
Canada	Norway	08 Oct 68	Gen Communications	3NORT0	451019
Canada	Pakistan	10 Sep 51	Direct Aid	122UNTS21	101632
Canada	Pakistan	23 Oct 51	Visas	248UNTS95	103487
Canada	Pakistan	15 Jan 58	Patents/Copyrights	392UNTS35	105637
Canada	Pakistan	14 May 59	Atomic Energy	426UNTS129	106133
Canada	Pakistan	21 Dec 60	Air Transport	465UNTS115	106724
Canada	Peru	18 Feb 54	Air Transport	411UNTS64	105915
Canada	Poland	05 Nov 63	Commodity Trade	529UNTS81	107658
Canada	Portugal	25 Apr 47	Air Transport	94UNTS87	101308
Canada	Portugal	28 May 54	General Trade	391UNTS253	105631
Canada	Portugal	24 Jan 58	Visas	392UNTS15	105634
Canada	San Marino	16 Oct 62	Visas	529UNTS3	107650

PARTY ONE	PARTY TWO	DATE	TOPIC	CITATION	NUMBER
Canada	South Africa	26 Nov 51	Taxation	248UNTS107	103489
Canada	South Africa	04 Aug 54	Postal Service	261UNTS3	103722
Canada	South Africa	21 Mar 55	Commodity Trade	213UNTS291	102892
Canada	South Africa	28 Sep 56	Taxation	299UNTS3	104303
Canada	South Africa	28 Sep 56	Taxation	299UNTS17	104304
Canada	Spain	29 Jan 52	Claims and Debts	233UNTS117	103255
Canada	Spain	26 May 54	General Trade	391UNTS273	105632
Canada	Spain	18 Dec 59	Visas	470UNTS117	106802
Canada	Spain	08 Sep 64	Atomic Energy	65SPBO2505	460062
Canada	Sweden	12 Apr 45	Air Transport	45SOFM65	461001
Canada	Sweden	27 Jun 47	Air Transport	27UNTS313	100414
Canada	Sweden	30 Jun 49	Visas	231UNTS37	103201
Canada	Sweden	06 Apr 51	Taxation	197UNTS393	102648
Canada	Sweden	11 Sep 62	Atomic Energy	529UNTS9	107651
Canada	Switzerland	14 Jul 47	Admin Cooperation	43UNTS103	100664
Canada	Switzerland	10 Jan 58	Air Transport	464UNTS21	106710
Canada	Switzerland	06 Mar 58	Atomic Energy	58SWRO724	462040
Canada	Switzerland	23 Jun 58	Admin Cooperation	391UNTS213	105625
Canada	Switzerland	22 Sep 59	Taxation	470UNTS101	106800
Canada	Taiwan	22 Mar 44	Milit Assistance	14UNTS397	200096
Canada	Taiwan	14 Apr 44	Privil/Immunities	14UNTS408	200097
Canada	Taiwan	07 Feb 46	Finance	43UNTS23	100659
Canada	Taiwan	26 Sep 46	General Trade	14UNTS167	100219
Canada	Taiwan	28 May 47	Direct Aid	0CTRC63	413017
Canada	Thailand	27 Apr 69	General Economic	0UNTS0	109675
Canada	Turkey	15 Mar 48	General Economic	231UNTS63	103205
Canada	Turkey	28 Feb 49	Visas	231UNTS57	103204
Canada	Turkey	09 Feb 51	Visas	233UNTS95	103252
Canada	Turkey	21 Aug 56	Visas	305UNTS89	104416
Canada	UK Great Britain	21 Dec 45	Air Transport	27UNTS155	100405
Canada	UK Great Britain	06 Mar 46	Reparations	20UNTS3	100311
Canada	UK Great Britain	06 Mar 46	Finance	20UNTS13	100312
Canada	UK Great Britain	05 Jun 46	Taxation	86UNTS3	101147
Canada	UK Great Britain	05 Jun 46	Taxation	27UNTS207	100408
Canada	UK Great Britain	17 Jul 47	Air Transport	28UNTS3	100416
Canada	UK Great Britain	19 Aug 49	Air Transport	44UNTS223	100686
Canada	UK Great Britain	19 Oct 54	Milit Assistance	214UNTS309	102906
Canada	UK Great Britain	09 Jan 56	Status of Forces	331UNTS192	104755
Canada	UK Great Britain	21 Jun 56	Postal Service	381UNTS111	105467
Canada	UK Great Britain	20 Oct 56	Postal Service	381UNTS99	105466
Canada	UK Great Britain	16 Nov 56	Postal Service	412UNTS166	105930
Canada	UK Great Britain	18 Oct 58	General Aid	392UNTS61	105639
Canada	UK Great Britain	10 Dec 59	Non-ILO Labor	379UNTS201	105440
Canada	UK Great Britain	05 Aug 60	Milit Installation	470UNTS133	106804
Canada	UK Great Britain	15 Apr 64	Commodity Trade	515UNTS39	107452
Canada	UK Great Britain	11 Sep 64	Status of Forces	522UNTS99	107538
Canada	UK Great Britain	06 Dec 65	Taxation	572UNTS161	108311
Canada	UK Great Britain	13 Dec 66	Non-ILO Labor	0UNTS0	109274
Canada	United Arab Rep	03 Dec 52	Mostfavored Nation	233UNTS145	103259
Canada	United Nations	27 Aug 48	Humanitarian	47UNTS167	100729
Canada	United Nations	29 Jul 57	Milit Assistance	274UNTS47	103957
Canada	United Nations	21 Feb 66	IGO Operations	555UNTS119	108107
Canada	USA (United States)	10 Jun 39	Milit Assistance	149UNTS332	200476
Canada	USA (United States)	29 May 40	Status of Forces	119UNTS285	200385
Canada	USA (United States)	13 Dec 40	General Trade	117UNTS173	200368
Canada	USA (United States)	27 Jun 41	IGO Establishment	103UNTS205	200315
Canada	USA (United States)	10 Nov 41	Specific Resources	23UNTS275	200134
Canada	USA (United States)	27 Nov 41	Specific Resources	103UNTS193	200314
Canada	USA (United States)	04 Mar 42	Taxation	124UNTS271	200426
Canada	USA (United States)	12 Mar 42	Non-ILO Labor	119UNTS295	200386
Canada	USA (United States)	18 Mar 42	Land Transport	101UNTS205	200294
Canada	USA (United States)	20 Mar 42	Milit Servic/Citiz	105UNTS169	200330
Canada	USA (United States)	08 Apr 42	Milit Servic/Citiz	105UNTS179	200331
Canada	USA (United States)	09 May 42	Land Transport	101UNTS215	200295
Canada	USA (United States)	27 Jun 42	Other Military	99UNTS223	200276

PARTY ONE	PARTY TWO	DATE	TOPIC	CITATION	NUMBER
Canada	USA (United States)	15 Aug 42	Other Military	99UNTS233	200277
Canada	USA (United States)	10 Sep 42	Land Transport	101UNTS221	200296
Canada	USA (United States)	04 Nov 42	Non-ILO Labor	24UNTS217	200146
Canada	USA (United States)	09 Nov 42	General Trade	101UNTS233	200298
Canada	USA (United States)	30 Nov 42	Reparations	119UNTS305	200387
Canada	USA (United States)	07 Dec 42	Land Transport	101UNTS227	200297
Canada	USA (United States)	19 Dec 42	Commodity Trade	26UNTS363	200156
Canada	USA (United States)	28 Dec 42	Other Military	99UNTS241	200278
Canada	USA (United States)	27 Jan 43	Milit Installation	101UNTS257	200300
Canada	USA (United States)	23 Feb 43	Land Transport	101UNTS243	200299
Canada	USA (United States)	04 Mar 43	Air Transport	13UNTS411	200087
Canada	USA (United States)	13 Mar 43	Other Military	99UNTS249	200279
Canada	USA (United States)	10 Apr 43	Territory Boundary	21UNTS237	200126
Canada	USA (United States)	26 May 43	Privil/Immunities	7UNTS345	200043
Canada	USA (United States)	19 Jul 43	Land Transport	29UNTS289	200167
Canada	USA (United States)	09 Aug 43	Milit Installation	29UNTS295	200168
Canada	USA (United States)	13 Aug 43	Admin Cooperation	109UNTS135	200355
Canada	USA (United States)	17 Jan 44	Mass Media	109UNTS199	200360
Canada	USA (United States)	03 Mar 44	Specific Resources	109UNTS191	200359
Canada	USA (United States)	23 Mar 44	Claims and Debts	125UNTS345	200432
Canada	USA (United States)	07 Jun 44	Specific Property	99UNTS259	200280
Canada	USA (United States)	08 Jun 44	Taxation	124UNTS297	200427
Canada	USA (United States)	27 Jun 44	Milit Installation	101UNTS273	200301
Canada	USA (United States)	05 Aug 44	Specific Resources	121UNTS299	200408
Canada	USA (United States)	13 Feb 45	Status of Forces	200UNTS219	200519
Canada	USA (United States)	17 Feb 45	Air Transport	122UNTS261	200409
Canada	USA (United States)	26 Feb 45	Other Military	99UNTS273	200281
Canada	USA (United States)	15 May 45	Peace/Disarmament	125UNTS353	200433
Canada	USA (United States)	06 Sep 45	Other Military	99UNTS281	200282
Canada	USA (United States)	03 Mar 46	Specific Property	6UNTS279	100081
Canada	USA (United States)	30 Mar 46	Milit Installation	7UNTS15	100089
Canada	USA (United States)	27 Sep 46	Patents/Copyrights	21UNTS3	100320
Canada	USA (United States)	15 Nov 46	Specif Claim/Waive	7UNTS141	100096
Canada	USA (United States)	06 Dec 46	Milit Assistance	149UNTS3	101945
Canada	USA (United States)	09 Jan 47	Specific Property	11UNTS341	100173
Canada	USA (United States)	06 Mar 47	Specific Resources	11UNTS325	100172
Canada	USA (United States)	18 Mar 47	Commodity Trade	117UNTS79	101584
Canada	USA (United States)	12 Apr 47	Air Transport	122UNTS229	101648
Canada	USA (United States)	19 May 47	Non-ILO Labor	43UNTS97	100663
Canada	USA (United States)	20 Aug 47	Telecommunications	27UNTS3	100392
Canada	USA (United States)	15 Oct 47	Telecommunications	82UNTS53	101085
Canada	USA (United States)	30 Oct 47	General Economic	27UNTS19	100394
Canada	USA (United States)	26 Dec 47	Commodity Trade	27UNTS29	100395
Canada	USA (United States)	31 Mar 48	Specific Property	81UNTS285	101077
Canada	USA (United States)	01 Apr 48	Telecommunications	82UNTS99	101086
Canada	USA (United States)	30 Apr 48	Sanitation	77UNTS191	100999
Canada	USA (United States)	23 Nov 48	Commodity Trade	81UNTS295	101078
Canada	USA (United States)	31 Jan 49	Humanitarian	43UNTS119	100666
Canada	USA (United States)	14 Mar 49	Reparations	82UNTS3	101079
Canada	USA (United States)	12 Apr 49	Milit Assistance	206UNTS241	102789
Canada	USA (United States)	04 Jun 49	Air Transport	122UNTS237	101649
Canada	USA (United States)	04 Jun 49	Air Transport	200UNTS201	102704
Canada	USA (United States)	24 Jan 50	Specif Claim/Waive	151UNTS171	101992
Canada	USA (United States)	27 Feb 50	Specific Resources	132UNTS223	101762
Canada	USA (United States)	24 Mar 50	Customs	200UNTS211	102705
Canada	USA (United States)	12 Jun 50	Taxation	127UNTS67	101700
Canada	USA (United States)	12 Jun 50	Taxation	127UNTS57	101699
Canada	USA (United States)	22 Jun 50	Scientific Project	70UNTS115	100900
Canada	USA (United States)	26 Oct 50	Direct Aid	132UNTS247	101764
Canada	USA (United States)	08 Feb 51	Telecommunications	207UNTS17	102797
Canada	USA (United States)	27 Mar 51	Milit Assistance	132UNTS333	101772
Canada	USA (United States)	18 Apr 51	Milit Assistance	134UNTS205	101800
Canada	USA (United States)	01 Aug 51	Milit Installation	233UNTS109	103254
Canada	USA (United States)	11 Sep 51	Non-ILO Labor	206UNTS311	102793
Canada	USA (United States)	26 Oct 51	Extradition	206UNTS319	102794

PARTY ONE	PARTY TWO	DATE	TOPIC	CITATION	NUMBER
Canada	USA (United States)	21 Feb 52	Humanitarian	205UNTS293	102781
Canada	USA (United States)	19 Mar 52	Status of Forces	174UNTS267	102291
Canada	USA (United States)	30 Apr 52	Milit Installation	235UNTS269	103308
Canada	USA (United States)	23 Jun 52	Telecommunications	207UNTS25	102798
Canada	USA (United States)	30 Jun 52	Water Transport	234UNTS199	103283
Canada	USA (United States)	08 Nov 52	Gen Communications	207UNTS3	102796
Canada	USA (United States)	05 Dec 52	Milit Installation	206UNTS11	102783
Canada	USA (United States)	02 Mar 53	Specific Resources	222UNTS77	103024
Canada	USA (United States)	17 Mar 53	Telecommunications	236UNTS259	103329
Canada	USA (United States)	30 Jun 53	Specific Property	206UNTS93	102786
Canada	USA (United States)	30 Jun 53	General Military	215UNTS103	102914
Canada	USA (United States)	12 Nov 53	IGO Establishment	234UNTS97	103274
Canada	USA (United States)	12 Nov 53	General Economic	223UNTS139	103062
Canada	USA (United States)	03 May 54	Milit Assistance	221UNTS339	103015
Canada	USA (United States)	10 Sep 54	Specific Resources	238UNTS97	103355
Canada	USA (United States)	05 May 55	Milit Installation	241UNTS179	103433
Canada	USA (United States)	08 Jun 55	Customs	247UNTS163	103466
Canada	USA (United States)	13 Jun 55	Specif Goods/Equip	268UNTS87	103851
Canada	USA (United States)	15 Jun 55	Milit Assistance	235UNTS201	103302
Canada	USA (United States)	15 Jun 55	Atomic Energy	235UNTS176	103301
Canada	USA (United States)	15 Jun 55	Specif Goods/Equip	268UNTS101	103852
Canada	USA (United States)	21 Jul 55	Milit Assistance	269UNTS53	103873
Canada	USA (United States)	22 Sep 55	Specif Goods/Equip	256UNTS227	103632
Canada	USA (United States)	26 Jan 56	Status of Forces	241UNTS115	103428
Canada	USA (United States)	19 Apr 56	Milit Installation	274UNTS3	103955
Canada	USA (United States)	23 Apr 56	Non-ILO Labor	300UNTS29	104329
Canada	USA (United States)	24 Oct 56	Specif Goods/Equip	281UNTS281	104084
Canada	USA (United States)	28 Dec 56	Specific Resources	290UNTS103	104229
Canada	USA (United States)	17 Jan 57	Specif Goods/Equip	266UNTS109	103825
Canada	USA (United States)	26 Feb 57	Water Transport	279UNTS179	104039
Canada	USA (United States)	09 Apr 57	Water Transport	283UNTS217	104119
Canada	USA (United States)	12 May 58	General Military	316UNTS151	104582
Canada	USA (United States)	20 Jun 58	Milit Assistance	317UNTS37	104592
Canada	USA (United States)	02 Sep 58	General Military	335UNTS249	104792
Canada	USA (United States)	31 Oct 58	Non-ILO Labor	391UNTS219	105626
Canada	USA (United States)	07 Jan 59	Specific Property	391UNTS207	105624
Canada	USA (United States)	27 Feb 59	Specific Resources	341UNTS3	104873
Canada	USA (United States)	09 Mar 59	Territory Boundary	340UNTS295	104872
Canada	USA (United States)	13 Apr 59	Specific Property	342UNTS43	104899
Canada	USA (United States)	01 May 59	Specific Property	343UNTS27	104919
Canada	USA (United States)	22 May 59	Milit Assistance	354UNTS63	105054
Canada	USA (United States)	13 Jul 59	Milit Assistance	353UNTS237	105045
Canada	USA (United States)	31 Mar 60	Specif Goods/Equip	400UNTS315	105755
Canada	USA (United States)	14 Jun 60	Scientific Project	377UNTS365	105413
Canada	USA (United States)	24 Aug 60	Scientific Project	388UNTS225	105580
Canada	USA (United States)	31 Aug 60	Milit Assistance	393UNTS247	105659
Canada	USA (United States)	13 Jan 61	Postal Service	410UNTS62	105897
Canada	USA (United States)	17 Jan 61	Specific Resources	542UNTS224	107894
Canada	USA (United States)	17 Feb 61	Taxation	445UNTS143	106383
Canada	USA (United States)	05 May 61	Admin Cooperation	419UNTS9	106027
Canada	USA (United States)	12 Jun 61	Milit Assistance	410UNTS21	105894
Canada	USA (United States)	01 Sep 61	Claims and Debts	421UNTS199	106058
Canada	USA (United States)	23 Sep 61	Milit Installation	421UNTS79	106053
Canada	USA (United States)	27 Sep 61	Milit Assistance	421UNTS85	106054
Canada	USA (United States)	17 Oct 61	Water Transport	424UNTS101	106102
Canada	USA (United States)	17 Oct 61	Specific Property	426UNTS201	106138
Canada	USA (United States)	07 Mar 62	General Trade	436UNTS3	106286
Canada	USA (United States)	19 Apr 62	Specific Property	445UNTS265	106394
Canada	USA (United States)	13 Jul 62	Water Transport	460UNTS83	106632
Canada	USA (United States)	24 Oct 62	Telecommunications	462UNTS67	106672
Canada	USA (United States)	28 Dec 62	Scientific Project	471UNTS13	106818
Canada	USA (United States)	23 Aug 63	Telecommunications	494UNTS13	107222
Canada	USA (United States)	15 Nov 63	Other Military	493UNTS67	107207
Canada	USA (United States)	27 Dec 63	Air Transport	494UNTS21	107223
Canada	USA (United States)	22 Jan 64	Specific Property	530UNTS89	107674

PARTY ONE	PARTY TWO	DATE	TOPIC	CITATION	NUMBER
Canada	USA (United States)	06 Mar 64	Specific Property	524UNTS255	107577
Canada	USA (United States)	06 May 64	Scientific Project	524UNTS173	107572
Canada	USA (United States)	25 May 64	Milit Installation	526UNTS251	107609
Canada	USA (United States)	16 Sep 64	Gen Communications	530UNTS267	107687
Canada	USA (United States)	16 Jan 65	Commodity Trade	606UNTS31	108772
Canada	USA (United States)	25 Mar 65	Dispute Settlement	607UNTS141	108802
Canada	USA (United States)	12 May 65	Milit Installation	545UNTS169	107933
Canada	USA (United States)	08 Jun 65	Gen Communications	546UNTS201	107947
Canada	USA (United States)	11 Jun 65	Scientific Project	564UNTS83	108222
Canada	USA (United States)	29 Jun 65	Scientific Project	549UNTS273	108003
Canada	USA (United States)	01 Dec 65	Milit Installation	574UNTS37	108340
Canada	USA (United States)	17 Dec 65	General Trade	574UNTS49	108341
Canada	USA (United States)	17 Jan 66	Air Transport	586UNTS151	108502
Canada	USA (United States)	09 Jun 66	Non-IBRD Project	580UNTS263	108429
Canada	USA (United States)	10 Jun 66	Water Transport	639UNTS13	109141
Canada	USA (United States)	15 Jun 66	Milit Installation	594UNTS83	108595
Canada	USA (United States)	30 Sep 66	Milit Installation	616UNTS193	108896
Canada	USA (United States)	06 Oct 66	Scientific Project	0UNTS0	109607
Canada	USA (United States)	13 Apr 67	Water Transport	0UNTS0	109759
Canada	USA (United States)	05 May 67	Non-ILO Labor	0UNTS0	109764
Canada	USA (United States)	12 Jun 67	Gen Communications	0UNTS0	109772
Canada	USA (United States)	08 Aug 67	Scientific Project	0UNTS0	109913
Canada	USA (United States)	11 Aug 67	Scientific Project	0UNTS0	109914
Canada	USA (United States)	25 Sep 67	Commodity Trade	0UNTS0	110503
Canada	USA (United States)	25 Oct 67	Scientific Project	0UNTS0	110052
Canada	USA (United States)	30 Jan 69	Sanitation	0UNTS0	110265
Canada	USA (United States)	21 Mar 69	Other Ad Hoc	0UNTS0	110271
Canada	USA (United States)	21 Mar 69	Other Ad Hoc	0UNTS0	110270
Canada	USA (United States)	31 Jul 69	Water Transport	0UNTS0	110341
Canada	USA (United States)	29 Jan 70	Specific Resources	0UNTS0	110800
Canada	USA (United States)	25 Jun 70	Scientific Project	0UNTS0	110817
Canada	USSR (Soviet Union)	29 Sep 50	Claims and Debts	230UNTS371	103197
Canada	USSR (Soviet Union)	24 Jun 55	Postal Service	16SUGG68	469906
Canada	USSR (Soviet Union)	29 Feb 56	General Trade	252UNTS165	103566
Canada	USSR (Soviet Union)	15 Jan 59	Consul/Citizenship	8SUGG133	469551
Canada	USSR (Soviet Union)	23 Dec 59	Visas	16SUGG127	469968
Canada	Venezuela	11 Oct 50	General Economic	231UNTS3	103198
Canada	Venezuela	08 Oct 59	Visas	470UNTS93	106799
Canada	Venezuela	22 Nov 61	Telecommunications	470UNTS148	106806
Canada	Vietnam, South	18 Sep 59	Direct Aid	0VKNG146	496042
Canada	Vietnam, South	25 Sep 61	Direct Aid	0VKNG172	496052
Canada	Yugoslavia	29 Mar 50	Reparations	230UNTS357	103195
Cayman Island	Multilateral	18 Oct 69	IGO Establishment	0UNTS0	110232
Central Afri Power	Multilateral	30 Dec 63	IBRD Project	551UNTS75	108035
Central Afri Rep	Accept UN Charter	13 Aug 60	UN Charter	375UNTS115	105363
Central Afri Rep	China People's Rep	29 Sep 64	Culture	64CCJC129	411117
Central Afri Rep	China People's Rep	29 Sep 64	General Economic	64CCJC130	411118
Central Afri Rep	China People's Rep	29 Sep 64	Direct Aid	64CCJC128	411116
Central Afri Rep	China People's Rep	14 Jan 65	Direct Aid	65CCJC7	411125
Central Afri Rep	France	12 Jul 60	Recognition	60FRRT50	415110
Central Afri Rep	France	13 Aug 60	General Amity	60FRRT76	415111
Central Afri Rep	France	26 Aug 61	Specific Property	63FRRT19	415112
Central Afri Rep	France	27 Mar 63	Customs	63FRRT43	415113
Central Afri Rep	France	18 Jan 65	Admin Cooperation	67FRJO1905	416114
Central Afri Rep	Germany, West	29 Dec 62	Direct Aid	63WBGA210	424731
Central Afri Rep	Germany, West	29 Dec 62	General Economic	63WBGA210	424730
Central Afri Rep	Germany, West	02 Oct 64	Loans and Credits	64WBGA234	424732
Central Afri Rep	Germany, West	23 Aug 65	Claims and Debts	67WGBB1657	425733
Central Afri Rep	Germany, West	31 Jan 67	Loans and Credits	67WBGA73	424734
Central Afri Rep	Germany, West	22 May 69	Loans and Credits	69WBGA148	424735
Central Afri Rep	Israel	14 Feb 62	Visas	484UNTS143	107022
Central Afri Rep	Israel	13 Jun 62	Tech Assistance	448UNTS265	106439
Central Afri Rep	Japan	15 Oct 68	General Economic	68JJS57	442219
Central Afri Rep	Multilateral	07 Dec 44	IGO Establishment	15UNTS295	200102
Central Afri Rep	Multilateral	11 Dec 46	Sanitation	12UNTS179	100186

PARTY ONE	PARTY TWO	DATE	TOPIC	CITATION	NUMBER
Central Afri Rep	Multilateral	27 May 47	Air Transport	418UNTS161	106021
Central Afri Rep	Multilateral	24 Jul 48	Sanitation	66UNTS25	100847
Central Afri Rep	Multilateral	04 May 49	Admin Cooperation	98UNTS101	101358
Central Afri Rep	Multilateral	04 May 49	Admin Cooperation	92UNTS19	101257
Central Afri Rep	Multilateral	02 Jul 51	Refugees	189UNTS137	102545
Central Afri Rep	Multilateral	31 Mar 53	Privil/Immunities	193UNTS136	102613
Central Afri Rep	Multilateral	11 May 53	Sanitation	456UNTS3	106555
Central Afri Rep	Multilateral	18 Jan 54	IGO Establishment	330UNTS121	104743
Central Afri Rep	Multilateral	14 Jun 54	Air Transport	320UNTS217	104644
Central Afri Rep	Multilateral	14 Jun 54	Air Transport	320UNTS209	104643
Central Afri Rep	Multilateral	29 Jul 54	Sanitation	249UNTS45	103500
Central Afri Rep	Multilateral	20 Jun 56	Admin Cooperation	268UNTS3	103850
Central Afri Rep	Multilateral	29 Apr 58	Water Transport	450UNTS11	106465
Central Afri Rep	Multilateral	10 Jun 58	Admin Cooperation	330UNTS3	104739
Central Afri Rep	Multilateral	26 Jan 60	IGO Establishment	439UNTS249	106333
Central Afri Rep	Multilateral	06 Oct 60	Customs	473UNTS131	106861
Central Afri Rep	Multilateral	14 Dec 60	Education	429UNTS93	106193
Central Afri Rep	Multilateral	18 Apr 61	Dispute Settlement	500UNTS243	107312
Central Afri Rep	Multilateral	18 Apr 61	Consul/Citizenship	500UNTS223	107311
Central Afri Rep	Multilateral	18 Apr 61	Consul/Citizenship	500UNTS95	107310
Central Afri Rep	Multilateral	08 Jun 61	Customs	473UNTS153	106862
Central Afri Rep	Multilateral	08 Jun 61	Customs	473UNTS187	106863
Central Afri Rep	Multilateral	21 Jun 61	IGO Establishment	514UNTS209	107449
Central Afri Rep	Multilateral	22 Jun 62	ILO Labor	494UNTS249	107237
Central Afri Rep	Multilateral	28 Jun 62	ILO Labor	494UNTS271	107238
Central Afri Rep	Multilateral	28 Sep 62	IGO Establishment	469UNTS169	106791
Central Afri Rep	Multilateral	24 Apr 63	Consul/Citizenship	596UNTS487	108640
Central Afri Rep	Multilateral	24 Apr 63	Consul/Citizenship	596UNTS261	108638
Central Afri Rep	Multilateral	25 May 63	IGO Establishment	479UNTS39	106947
Central Afri Rep	Multilateral	04 Aug 63	IGO Establishment	510UNTS3	107408
Central Afri Rep	Multilateral	30 Oct 63	Tech Assistance	480UNTS180	106968
Central Afri Rep	Multilateral	10 Jul 64	Postal Service	612UNTS361	108849
Central Afri Rep	Multilateral	10 Jul 64	Postal Service	612UNTS233	108848
Central Afri Rep	Multilateral	10 Jul 64	Postal Service	611UNTS387	108846
Central Afri Rep	Multilateral	10 Jul 64	Postal Service	613UNTS3	108851
Central Afri Rep	Multilateral	10 Jul 64	Postal Service	613UNTS3	108850
Central Afri Rep	Multilateral	10 Jul 64	Postal Service	613UNTS127	108853
Central Afri Rep	Multilateral	10 Jul 64	Postal Service	611UNTS105	108845
Central Afri Rep	Multilateral	10 Jul 64	Postal Service	611UNTS7	108844
Central Afri Rep	Multilateral	18 Mar 65	Dispute Settlement	575UNTS159	108359
Central Afri Rep	Multilateral	08 Jul 65	General Trade	597UNTS3	108641
Central Afri Rep	Multilateral	27 May 66	IGO Establishment	637UNTS0	109121
Central Afri Rep	Multilateral	31 Jan 67	Refugees	606UNTS267	108791
Central Afri Rep	Multilateral	18 Mar 68	Commodity Trade	0UNTS0	109262
Central Afri Rep	Multilateral	03 Mar 69	Commodity Trade	0UNTS0	110233
Central Afri Rep	Romania	13 Sep 68	Tech Assistance	0UNTS0	110209
Central Afri Rep	Romania	13 Sep 68	General Trade	0UNTS0	110208
Central Afri Rep	UN Special Fund	30 Oct 63	Direct Aid	481UNTS247	106985
Central Afri Rep	UNICEF (Children)	21 Aug 61	Direct Aid	413UNTS48	105939
Central Afri Rep	USA (United States)	10 Feb 63	Direct Aid	473UNTS83	106857
Central Afri Rep	USA (United States)	31 Dec 64	Claims and Debts	542UNTS29	107877
Central Afri Rep	USA (United States)	24 Nov 66	Direct Aid	0UNTS0	109690
Central Afri Rep	USSR (Soviet Union)	07 Dec 60	Consul/Citizenship	9SUGG154	469721
Central Afri Rep	WHO (World Health)	13 Feb 61	Tech Assistance	394UNTS149	105675
Central Am Bank	Germany, West	22 Jul 70	Loans and Credits	70WBGA149	424749
CERN (Nuc Resrch)	France	13 Sep 65	Atomic Energy	0UNTS0	109862
CERN (Nuc Resrch)	France	13 Sep 65	IGO Status/Immunit	69FRJO1004	416514
CERN (Nuc Resrch)	Switzerland	11 Jun 55	IGO Status/Immunit	249UNTS405	200544
Ceylon (Sri Lanka)	Accept UN Charter	16 Jun 48	UN Charter	223UNTS39	103047
Ceylon (Sri Lanka)	Australia	12 Jan 50	Air Transport	53UNTS295	100789
Ceylon (Sri Lanka)	Australia	07 Nov 53	Admin Cooperation	191UNTS249	102585
Ceylon (Sri Lanka)	Bulgaria	19 Jun 56	General Trade	315UNTS23	104556
Ceylon (Sri Lanka)	Bulgaria	19 Jun 56	Finance	315UNTS33	104557
Ceylon (Sri Lanka)	Burma	29 Jun 50	Air Transport	73UNTS3	100940
Ceylon (Sri Lanka)	Canada	24 Apr 51	Visas	248UNTS101	103488

PARTY ONE	PARTY TWO	DATE	TOPIC	CITATION	NUMBER
Ceylon (Sri Lanka)	Canada	11 Jul 52	General Aid	391UNTS245	105630
Ceylon (Sri Lanka)	Canada	05 Nov 58	Loans and Credits	391UNTS225	105627
Ceylon (Sri Lanka)	China People's Rep	04 Oct 52	General Trade	52CCJC55	410079
Ceylon (Sri Lanka)	China People's Rep	18 Dec 52	Commodity Trade	52CCJC62	410085
Ceylon (Sri Lanka)	China People's Rep	12 Oct 55	Commodity Trade	55CCJC68	410260
Ceylon (Sri Lanka)	China People's Rep	29 Dec 56	Commodity Trade	56CCJC146	410392
Ceylon (Sri Lanka)	China People's Rep	19 Sep 57	Customs	57CCJC84	410445
Ceylon (Sri Lanka)	China People's Rep	19 Sep 57	General Economic	337UNTS137	104821
Ceylon (Sri Lanka)	China People's Rep	19 Sep 57	Direct Aid	337UNTS169	104822
Ceylon (Sri Lanka)	China People's Rep	19 Sep 57	General Trade	57CCJC85	410446
Ceylon (Sri Lanka)	China People's Rep	19 Sep 57	General Trade	57CCJC86	410447
Ceylon (Sri Lanka)	China People's Rep	19 Sep 57	Direct Aid	57CCJC87	410448
Ceylon (Sri Lanka)	China People's Rep	19 Sep 57	General Economic	57CCJC83	410444
Ceylon (Sri Lanka)	China People's Rep	17 Sep 58	Loans and Credits	58CCJC83	410540
Ceylon (Sri Lanka)	China People's Rep	26 Mar 59	Air Transport	59CCJC57	410608
Ceylon (Sri Lanka)	China People's Rep	13 Jun 59	General Trade	59CCJC83	410626
Ceylon (Sri Lanka)	China People's Rep	13 Jun 59	Commodity Trade	59CCJC84	410627
Ceylon (Sri Lanka)	China People's Rep	04 Apr 61	General Trade	61CCJC47	410777
Ceylon (Sri Lanka)	China People's Rep	07 Oct 61	General Trade	61CCJC132	410836
Ceylon (Sri Lanka)	China People's Rep	07 Feb 62	Admin Cooperation	62CCJC18	410867
Ceylon (Sri Lanka)	China People's Rep	03 Oct 62	Direct Aid	62CCJC94	410920
Ceylon (Sri Lanka)	China People's Rep	03 Oct 62	General Economic	62CCJC93	410919
Ceylon (Sri Lanka)	China People's Rep	03 Oct 62	General Trade	62CCJC95	410921
Ceylon (Sri Lanka)	China People's Rep	25 Jul 63	Water Transport	63CCJC92	410999
Ceylon (Sri Lanka)	China People's Rep	10 Oct 63	General Trade	63CCJC114	411015
Ceylon (Sri Lanka)	China People's Rep	24 Oct 64	General Trade	64CCJC150	411119
Ceylon (Sri Lanka)	China People's Rep	15 Mar 65	Direct Aid	65CCJC27	411126
Ceylon (Sri Lanka)	China People's Rep	13 Jul 65	Direct Aid	65CCJC91	411133
Ceylon (Sri Lanka)	China People's Rep	12 Oct 65	General Trade	65CCJC132	411136
Ceylon (Sri Lanka)	China People's Rep	01 Dec 65	Commodity Trade	65CCJC147	411102
Ceylon (Sri Lanka)	China People's Rep	29 Nov 66	Commodity Trade	66CCJC101	411148
Ceylon (Sri Lanka)	China People's Rep	29 Nov 66	General Trade	66CCJC100	411147
Ceylon (Sri Lanka)	Denmark	29 May 59	Air Transport	348UNTS225	105002
Ceylon (Sri Lanka)	Denmark	16 Feb 63	Taxation	486UNTS285	107083
Ceylon (Sri Lanka)	Denmark	28 Dec 68	Loans and Credits	0UNTS0	109490
Ceylon (Sri Lanka)	Finland	08 Jan 64	Water Transport	492UNTS285	107198
Ceylon (Sri Lanka)	Germany, East	22 Feb 65	General Economic	51EGDZ330	420077
Ceylon (Sri Lanka)	Germany, West	22 Nov 52	General Trade	55WGBB189	425070
Ceylon (Sri Lanka)	Germany, West	01 Apr 55	General Trade	369UNTS57	105251
Ceylon (Sri Lanka)	Germany, West	04 Jul 62	Taxation	64WGBB789	425071
Ceylon (Sri Lanka)	Germany, West	08 Nov 63	Loans and Credits	66WGBB909	425072
Ceylon (Sri Lanka)	Germany, West	30 Jun 66	Loans and Credits	66WBGA160	424073
Ceylon (Sri Lanka)	Germany, West	20 Aug 66	Loans and Credits	66WBGA212	424074
Ceylon (Sri Lanka)	Germany, West	30 Sep 67	Loans and Credits	68WBGA15	424075
Ceylon (Sri Lanka)	Germany, West	20 Jun 68	Loans and Credits	68WBGA170	424076
Ceylon (Sri Lanka)	Germany, West	03 Aug 69	Loans and Credits	69WBGA199	424077
Ceylon (Sri Lanka)	Hungary	04 Jun 56	General Trade	315UNTS13	104555
Ceylon (Sri Lanka)	IBRD (World Bank)	09 Jul 54	IBRD Project	198UNTS313	200517
Ceylon (Sri Lanka)	IBRD (World Bank)	17 Sep 58	IBRD Project	323UNTS51	104664
Ceylon (Sri Lanka)	IBRD (World Bank)	06 Jun 61	IBRD Project	414UNTS349	105978
Ceylon (Sri Lanka)	IBRD (World Bank)	24 Aug 67	IBRD Project	632UNTS217	109025
Ceylon (Sri Lanka)	IBRD (World Bank)	22 Nov 67	IBRD Project	639UNTS221	109151
Ceylon (Sri Lanka)	IBRD (World Bank)	12 Nov 68	IBRD Project	0UNTS0	109623
Ceylon (Sri Lanka)	IBRD (World Bank)	18 Jul 69	IBRD Project	0UNTS0	110484
Ceylon (Sri Lanka)	IBRD (World Bank)	28 Jul 69	IBRD Project	0UNTS0	110483
Ceylon (Sri Lanka)	ICJ Option Clause	23 Apr 52	UN Charter	137UNTS7	101843
Ceylon (Sri Lanka)	IDA (Devel Assoc)	19 Jun 68	Non-IBRD Project	0UNTS0	109622
Ceylon (Sri Lanka)	IDA (Devel Assoc)	12 Nov 68	Non-IBRD Project	0UNTS0	109624
Ceylon (Sri Lanka)	IDA (Devel Assoc)	13 Nov 69	Non-IBRD Project	0UNTS0	110582
Ceylon (Sri Lanka)	ILO (Labor Org)	24 Jan 51	Tech Assistance	117UNTS355	200380
Ceylon (Sri Lanka)	ILO (Labor Org)	06 Apr 51	Tech Assistance	100UNTS235	200286
Ceylon (Sri Lanka)	ILO (Labor Org)	21 Nov 62	IGO Operations	449UNTS263	106463
Ceylon (Sri Lanka)	India	12 Aug 46	Postal Service	196UNTS209	102626
Ceylon (Sri Lanka)	India	21 Dec 48	Air Transport	28UNTS223	100427
Ceylon (Sri Lanka)	India	30 Apr 51	General Trade	196UNTS199	102625

PARTY ONE	PARTY TWO	DATE	TOPIC	CITATION	NUMBER
Ceylon (Sri Lanka)	India	10 Sep 56	Taxation	315UNTS59	104560
Ceylon (Sri Lanka)	India	13 Jan 58	Commodity Trade	315UNTS107	104562
Ceylon (Sri Lanka)	Ireland	20 Nov 53	General Economic	345UNTS189	104967
Ceylon (Sri Lanka)	Italy	23 Apr 57	General Trade	337UNTS115	104820
Ceylon (Sri Lanka)	Italy	01 Jun 59	Air Transport	63ITDI14	436083
Ceylon (Sri Lanka)	Japan	06 Sep 52	General Economic	314UNTS279	104552
Ceylon (Sri Lanka)	Japan	20 Mar 61	Education	450UNTS385	106481
Ceylon (Sri Lanka)	Japan	09 Sep 66	Loans and Credits	66JJS89	442175
Ceylon (Sri Lanka)	Japan	22 Sep 67	Loans and Credits	67JJS119	442202
Ceylon (Sri Lanka)	Japan	12 Dec 67	Taxation	0UNTS0	109721
Ceylon (Sri Lanka)	Japan	12 Dec 67	Taxation	68JHZ9	439015
Ceylon (Sri Lanka)	Japan	03 Sep 68	Loans and Credits	68JJS113	442218
Ceylon (Sri Lanka)	Japan	27 Dec 68	Loans and Credits	68JJS121	442227
Ceylon (Sri Lanka)	Japan	24 Oct 69	Loans and Credits	69JJS117	442254
Ceylon (Sri Lanka)	Japan	02 Nov 69	Direct Aid	69JJS125	442256
Ceylon (Sri Lanka)	Multilateral	11 Dec 46	Sanitation	12UNTS179	100186
Ceylon (Sri Lanka)	Multilateral	27 May 47	Air Transport	418UNTS161	106021
Ceylon (Sri Lanka)	Multilateral	12 Nov 47	Admin Cooperation	46UNTS201	100710
Ceylon (Sri Lanka)	Multilateral	11 May 48	Telecommunications	500UNTS267	107313
Ceylon (Sri Lanka)	Multilateral	24 Jul 48	Sanitation	66UNTS25	100847
Ceylon (Sri Lanka)	Multilateral	14 Sep 48	Milit Occupation	18UNTS267	100296
Ceylon (Sri Lanka)	Multilateral	15 Nov 48	IGO Establishment	120UNTS59	101615
Ceylon (Sri Lanka)	Multilateral	19 Nov 48	Sanitation	44UNTS277	100688
Ceylon (Sri Lanka)	Multilateral	29 Nov 48	IGO Establishment	120UNTS13	101613
Ceylon (Sri Lanka)	Multilateral	09 Dec 48	Humanitarian	78UNTS277	101021
Ceylon (Sri Lanka)	Multilateral	23 Mar 49	Commodity Trade	203UNTS179	102746
Ceylon (Sri Lanka)	Multilateral	04 May 49	Admin Cooperation	92UNTS19	101257
Ceylon (Sri Lanka)	Multilateral	04 May 49	Admin Cooperation	98UNTS101	101358
Ceylon (Sri Lanka)	Multilateral	04 May 49	Admin Cooperation	30UNTS23	100446
Ceylon (Sri Lanka)	Multilateral	04 May 49	Admin Cooperation	30UNTS3	100445
Ceylon (Sri Lanka)	Multilateral	04 May 49	Admin Cooperation	47UNTS159	100728
Ceylon (Sri Lanka)	Multilateral	12 Aug 49	IGO Establishment	87UNTS131	101169
Ceylon (Sri Lanka)	Multilateral	12 Aug 49	Humanitarian	75UNTS85	100971
Ceylon (Sri Lanka)	Multilateral	12 Aug 49	Humanitarian	75UNTS31	100970
Ceylon (Sri Lanka)	Multilateral	12 Aug 49	General Military	75UNTS135	100972
Ceylon (Sri Lanka)	Multilateral	21 Mar 50	Admin Cooperation	96UNTS271	101342
Ceylon (Sri Lanka)	Multilateral	28 Jun 50	Loans and Credits	87UNTS153	101170
Ceylon (Sri Lanka)	Multilateral	22 Nov 50	Culture	131UNTS25	101734
Ceylon (Sri Lanka)	Multilateral	07 Dec 50	Admin Cooperation	212UNTS17	102861
Ceylon (Sri Lanka)	Multilateral	25 May 51	Status of Forces	175UNTS215	102303
Ceylon (Sri Lanka)	Multilateral	18 Jul 51	Direct Aid	102UNTS291	200308
Ceylon (Sri Lanka)	Multilateral	08 Sep 51	Peace/Disarmament	136UNTS45	101832
Ceylon (Sri Lanka)	Multilateral	08 Sep 51	General Military	136UNTS165	101833
Ceylon (Sri Lanka)	Multilateral	06 Dec 51	Admin Cooperation	150UNTS67	101963
Ceylon (Sri Lanka)	Multilateral	06 Dec 51	IGO Establishment	425UNTS61	106119
Ceylon (Sri Lanka)	Multilateral	18 Feb 52	Tech Assistance	126UNTS319	200434
Ceylon (Sri Lanka)	Multilateral	12 Jun 52	Dispute Settlement	138UNTS183	101869
Ceylon (Sri Lanka)	Multilateral	11 Jul 52	IGO Establishment	169UNTS3	102220
Ceylon (Sri Lanka)	Multilateral	11 Jul 52	Postal Service	170UNTS3	102221
Ceylon (Sri Lanka)	Multilateral	07 Oct 52	Admin Cooperation	310UNTS181	104493
Ceylon (Sri Lanka)	Multilateral	07 Nov 52	General Trade	221UNTS255	103010
Ceylon (Sri Lanka)	Multilateral	27 Feb 53	Claims and Debts	333UNTS3	104764
Ceylon (Sri Lanka)	Multilateral	11 May 53	Sanitation	456UNTS3	106555
Ceylon (Sri Lanka)	Multilateral	12 May 54	Admin Cooperation	327UNTS3	104714
Ceylon (Sri Lanka)	Multilateral	04 Jun 54	Customs	282UNTS249	104101
Ceylon (Sri Lanka)	Multilateral	04 Jun 54	Customs	276UNTS191	103992
Ceylon (Sri Lanka)	Multilateral	14 Jun 54	Air Transport	320UNTS217	104644
Ceylon (Sri Lanka)	Multilateral	14 Jun 54	Air Transport	320UNTS209	104643
Ceylon (Sri Lanka)	Multilateral	16 Dec 54	Tech Assistance	204UNTS323	200523
Ceylon (Sri Lanka)	Multilateral	25 May 55	IGO Establishment	264UNTS117	103791
Ceylon (Sri Lanka)	Multilateral	20 Jun 56	Admin Cooperation	268UNTS3	103850
Ceylon (Sri Lanka)	Multilateral	26 Oct 56	IGO Establishment	276UNTS3	103988
Ceylon (Sri Lanka)	Multilateral	20 Feb 57	Consul/Citizenship	309UNTS65	104468
Ceylon (Sri Lanka)	Multilateral	03 Oct 57	Postal Service	364UNTS3	105211
Ceylon (Sri Lanka)	Multilateral	03 Oct 57	Postal Service	364UNTS331	105212

PARTY ONE	PARTY TWO	DATE	TOPIC	CITATION	NUMBER
Ceylon (Sri Lanka)	Multilateral	03 Oct 57	Postal Service	365UNTS3	105213
Ceylon (Sri Lanka)	Multilateral	29 Apr 58	Water Transport	450UNTS11	106465
Ceylon (Sri Lanka)	Multilateral	29 Apr 58	Dispute Settlement	450UNTS169	106466
Ceylon (Sri Lanka)	Multilateral	29 Apr 58	Territory Boundary	499UNTS311	107302
Ceylon (Sri Lanka)	Multilateral	29 Apr 58	Territory Boundary	516UNTS205	107477
Ceylon (Sri Lanka)	Multilateral	29 Apr 58	Specific Resources	559UNTS285	108164
Ceylon (Sri Lanka)	Multilateral	10 Jun 58	Admin Cooperation	330UNTS3	104739
Ceylon (Sri Lanka)	Multilateral	03 Dec 58	Admin Cooperation	398UNTS9	105715
Ceylon (Sri Lanka)	Multilateral	26 Jan 60	IGO Establishment	439UNTS249	106333
Ceylon (Sri Lanka)	Multilateral	30 Mar 61	Sanitation	520UNTS151	107515
Ceylon (Sri Lanka)	Multilateral	18 Apr 61	Consul/Citizenship	500UNTS95	107310
Ceylon (Sri Lanka)	Multilateral	21 Jun 61	IGO Establishment	514UNTS209	107449
Ceylon (Sri Lanka)	Multilateral	10 Dec 62	Culture	521UNTS231	107525
Ceylon (Sri Lanka)	Multilateral	05 Aug 63	Sanitation	480UNTS43	106964
Ceylon (Sri Lanka)	Multilateral	10 Jul 64	Postal Service	612UNTS3	108847
Ceylon (Sri Lanka)	Multilateral	10 Jul 64	Postal Service	611UNTS387	108846
Ceylon (Sri Lanka)	Multilateral	10 Jul 64	Postal Service	611UNTS105	108845
Ceylon (Sri Lanka)	Multilateral	10 Jul 64	Postal Service	611UNTS7	108844
Ceylon (Sri Lanka)	Multilateral	20 Aug 64	Telecommunications	514UNTS25	107441
Ceylon (Sri Lanka)	Multilateral	18 Mar 65	Dispute Settlement	575UNTS159	108359
Ceylon (Sri Lanka)	Multilateral	04 Dec 65	IGO Establishment	571UNTS123	108303
Ceylon (Sri Lanka)	Multilateral	10 Jun 67	Direct Aid	602UNTS212	108714
Ceylon (Sri Lanka)	Multilateral	12 Dec 68	IGO Establishment	0UNTS0	109733
Ceylon (Sri Lanka)	Multilateral	27 Jan 69	Telecommunications	0UNTS0	109664
Ceylon (Sri Lanka)	Netherlands	14 Sep 53	Air Transport	193UNTS21	102608
Ceylon (Sri Lanka)	Norway	29 May 59	Air Transport	411UNTS165	105919
Ceylon (Sri Lanka)	Norway	11 Jun 64	Taxation	559UNTS23	108153
Ceylon (Sri Lanka)	Pakistan	15 Dec 48	Postal Service	91UNTS303	101255
Ceylon (Sri Lanka)	Pakistan	03 Jan 49	Air Transport	28UNTS247	100428
Ceylon (Sri Lanka)	Pakistan	23 May 55	General Trade	286UNTS15	104159
Ceylon (Sri Lanka)	Romania	16 Mar 56	General Trade	315UNTS41	104558
Ceylon (Sri Lanka)	Romania	16 Mar 56	Finance	315UNTS51	104559
Ceylon (Sri Lanka)	Spain	22 Jul 55	General Trade	56SPBO2310	460063
Ceylon (Sri Lanka)	Sweden	18 May 57	Taxation	315UNTS85	104561
Ceylon (Sri Lanka)	Sweden	22 May 58	Tech Assistance	428UNTS65	106168
Ceylon (Sri Lanka)	Sweden	29 May 59	Air Transport	464UNTS109	106713
Ceylon (Sri Lanka)	Thailand	24 Feb 50	Air Transport	72UNTS261	100938
Ceylon (Sri Lanka)	UK Great Britain	11 Nov 47	Milit Assistance	86UNTS19	101148
Ceylon (Sri Lanka)	UK Great Britain	11 Nov 47	Consul/Citizenship	86UNTS25	101149
Ceylon (Sri Lanka)	UK Great Britain	11 Nov 47	Admin Cooperation	86UNTS31	101150
Ceylon (Sri Lanka)	UK Great Britain	30 Apr 48	Finance	182UNTS2	102421
Ceylon (Sri Lanka)	UK Great Britain	28 Feb 49	Gen Communications	314UNTS269	104551
Ceylon (Sri Lanka)	UK Great Britain	05 Aug 49	Air Transport	35UNTS137	100554
Ceylon (Sri Lanka)	UK Great Britain	26 Jul 50	Taxation	337UNTS77	104818
Ceylon (Sri Lanka)	UK Great Britain	07 Jun 57	Milit Installation	280UNTS107	104055
Ceylon (Sri Lanka)	UK Great Britain	18 Sep 68	Finance	0UNTS0	109798
Ceylon (Sri Lanka)	UN Special Fund	03 May 61	Direct Aid	395UNTS217	105687
Ceylon (Sri Lanka)	UNICEF (Children)	07 Jun 50	IGO Operations	68UNTS256	200239
Ceylon (Sri Lanka)	UNICEF (Children)	27 Jan 69	IGO Operations	0UNTS0	109394
Ceylon (Sri Lanka)	United Arab Rep	26 Sep 50	Air Transport	192UNTS53	102595
Ceylon (Sri Lanka)	United Arab Rep	17 Nov 54	General Trade	315UNTS3	104554
Ceylon (Sri Lanka)	United Nations	21 Jan 52	Tech Assistance	118UNTS281	200382
Ceylon (Sri Lanka)	United Nations	04 Dec 61	Tech Assistance	415UNTS236	105987
Ceylon (Sri Lanka)	USA (United States)	31 Jan 49	Admin Cooperation	88UNTS21	101181
Ceylon (Sri Lanka)	USA (United States)	07 Nov 50	Tech Assistance	92UNTS125	101265
Ceylon (Sri Lanka)	USA (United States)	14 May 51	Gen Communications	141UNTS159	101913
Ceylon (Sri Lanka)	USA (United States)	17 Nov 52	Education	180UNTS207	102386
Ceylon (Sri Lanka)	USA (United States)	23 Aug 54	Mass Media	314UNTS297	104553
Ceylon (Sri Lanka)	USA (United States)	18 Jul 55	Postal Service	281UNTS295	104086
Ceylon (Sri Lanka)	USA (United States)	28 Apr 56	Direct Aid	274UNTS35	103956
Ceylon (Sri Lanka)	USA (United States)	07 Sep 56	Visas	280UNTS35	104048
Ceylon (Sri Lanka)	USA (United States)	02 Nov 56	Milit Assistance	282UNTS93	104094
Ceylon (Sri Lanka)	USA (United States)	18 Jun 58	US Agri Commod Aid	316UNTS15	104574
Ceylon (Sri Lanka)	USA (United States)	13 Mar 59	US Agri Commod Aid	342UNTS51	104900
Ceylon (Sri Lanka)	USA (United States)	30 Sep 60	US Agri Commod Aid	389UNTS221	105594

PARTY ONE	PARTY TWO	DATE	TOPIC	CITATION	NUMBER
Ceylon (Sri Lanka)	USA (United States)	19 Jul 62	US Agri Commod Aid	454UNTS31	106538
Ceylon (Sri Lanka)	USA (United States)	21 Nov 62	General Aid	462UNTS237	106683
Ceylon (Sri Lanka)	USA (United States)	29 Aug 64	Education	531UNTS93	107695
Ceylon (Sri Lanka)	USA (United States)	23 Feb 66	Finance	586UNTS91	108498
Ceylon (Sri Lanka)	USA (United States)	12 Mar 66	US Agri Commod Aid	579UNTS117	108403
Ceylon (Sri Lanka)	USA (United States)	24 Oct 67	US Agri Commod Aid	0UNTS0	109984
Ceylon (Sri Lanka)	USA (United States)	21 Jun 68	US Agri Commod Aid	0UNTS0	110327
Ceylon (Sri Lanka)	USA (United States)	19 Feb 69	US Agri Commod Aid	0UNTS0	110152
Ceylon (Sri Lanka)	USSR (Soviet Union)	06 Dec 56	Consul/Citizenship	16SUGG74	469931
Ceylon (Sri Lanka)	USSR (Soviet Union)	15 Jan 58	Culture	305UNTS235	104421
Ceylon (Sri Lanka)	USSR (Soviet Union)	08 Feb 58	General Trade	16SUGG124	469955
Ceylon (Sri Lanka)	USSR (Soviet Union)	08 Feb 58	Finance	0UNTS0	110491
Ceylon (Sri Lanka)	USSR (Soviet Union)	08 Feb 58	General Trade	7SUGG105	469496
Ceylon (Sri Lanka)	USSR (Soviet Union)	08 Feb 58	General Trade	348UNTS159	104999
Ceylon (Sri Lanka)	USSR (Soviet Union)	22 Feb 62	General Trade	11SUGG133	469822
Ceylon (Sri Lanka)	USSR (Soviet Union)	12 Jun 62	General Aid	11SUGG143	469841
Ceylon (Sri Lanka)	USSR (Soviet Union)	09 Aug 62	General Aid	11SUGG149	469854
Ceylon (Sri Lanka)	USSR (Soviet Union)	22 Sep 62	Non-IBRD Project	11SUGG153	469861
Ceylon (Sri Lanka)	USSR (Soviet Union)	14 Nov 62	Water Transport	11SUGG156	469872
Ceylon (Sri Lanka)	USSR (Soviet Union)	25 Feb 70	General Economic	0UNTS0	110361
Ceylon (Sri Lanka)	WHO (World Health)	17 Feb 50	Direct Aid	102UNTS309	200309
Ceylon (Sri Lanka)	WHO (World Health)	04 Mar 52	Direct Aid	128UNTS281	200437
Ceylon (Sri Lanka)	WHO (World Health)	26 Mar 52	Sanitation	134UNTS341	200442
Ceylon (Sri Lanka)	WHO (World Health)	21 Nov 52	Sanitation	161UNTS315	200490
Ceylon (Sri Lanka)	WHO (World Health)	21 Dec 59	Tech Assistance	349UNTS109	105011
Ceylon (Sri Lanka)	Yugoslavia	30 Jul 53	General Trade	337UNTS103	104819
Ceylon (Sri Lanka)	Yugoslavia	05 May 59	Scientific Project	391UNTS101	105618
Chad	Accept UN Charter	12 Aug 60	UN Charter	375UNTS107	105361
Chad	Denmark	31 Jul 69	Loans and Credits	0UNTS0	110201
Chad	France	12 Jul 60	Recognition	60FRRT50	415426
Chad	France	11 Aug 60	General Amity	60FRRT76	415427
Chad	France	25 Oct 61	Specific Property	63FRRT23	415428
Chad	France	08 Jan 63	Air Transport	63FRRT31	415430
Chad	France	29 Mar 63	Customs	63FRRT43	415429
Chad	France	17 Aug 63	Direct Aid	64FRRT16	415431
Chad	France	19 May 64	General Aid	0UNTS0	109441
Chad	France	19 May 64	Non-ILO Labor	68FRJO1112	416432
Chad	France	19 May 64	Culture	0UNTS0	109442
Chad	France	19 May 64	Culture	68FRJO1112	416434
Chad	France	19 May 64	IGO Establishment	0UNTS0	109440
Chad	France	19 May 64	Milit Assistance	0UNTS0	109443
Chad	France	19 May 64	Milit Assistance	68FRJO1112	416435
Chad	Germany, West	31 May 63	General Economic	63WBGA224	424670
Chad	Germany, West	31 May 63	Tech Assistance	63WBGA224	424671
Chad	Germany, West	07 May 65	Loans and Credits	65WBGA135	424672
Chad	Germany, West	11 Apr 67	Claims and Debts	68WGBB221	425673
Chad	Germany, West	10 Apr 68	Loans and Credits	68WBGA152	424674
Chad	Germany, West	18 Apr 69	Loans and Credits	69WBGA143	424675
Chad	IDA (Devel Assoc)	14 Aug 68	Non-IBRD Project	0UNTS0	109641
Chad	IDA (Devel Assoc)	29 Aug 68	Non-IBRD Project	0UNTS0	109642
Chad	Israel	07 Oct 64	Tech Assistance	630UNTS175	108969
Chad	Italy	04 Jun 64	General Aid	65ITDI216	436084
Chad	Japan	24 Nov 64	General Trade	0JGJI1591	441126
Chad	Multilateral	07 Dec 44	IGO Establishment	15UNTS295	200102
Chad	Multilateral	27 May 47	Air Transport	418UNTS161	106021
Chad	Multilateral	24 Jul 48	Sanitation	66UNTS25	100847
Chad	Multilateral	18 Jan 54	IGO Establishment	330UNTS121	104743
Chad	Multilateral	14 Jun 54	Air Transport	320UNTS209	104643
Chad	Multilateral	14 Jun 54	Air Transport	320UNTS217	104644
Chad	Multilateral	29 Jul 54	Sanitation	249UNTS45	103500
Chad	Multilateral	26 Jan 60	IGO Establishment	439UNTS249	106333
Chad	Multilateral	30 Mar 61	Sanitation	520UNTS151	107515
Chad	Multilateral	21 Jun 61	IGO Establishment	514UNTS209	107449
Chad	Multilateral	25 May 62	IGO Establishment	486UNTS103	107075
Chad	Multilateral	06 Dec 62	Tech Assistance	450UNTS240	106471

PARTY ONE	PARTY TWO	DATE	TOPIC	CITATION	NUMBER
Chad	Multilateral	25 May 63	IGO Establishment	479UNTS39	106947
Chad	Multilateral	05 Aug 63	Sanitation	480UNTS43	106964
Chad	Multilateral	26 Oct 63	Water Transport	587UNTS9	108506
Chad	Multilateral	10 Jul 64	Postal Service	612UNTS233	108848
Chad	Multilateral	10 Jul 64	Postal Service	613UNTS3	108850
Chad	Multilateral	10 Jul 64	Postal Service	613UNTS3	108851
Chad	Multilateral	10 Jul 64	Postal Service	611UNTS7	108844
Chad	Multilateral	10 Jul 64	Postal Service	611UNTS387	108846
Chad	Multilateral	10 Jul 64	Postal Service	612UNTS361	108849
Chad	Multilateral	10 Jul 64	Postal Service	611UNTS105	108845
Chad	Multilateral	10 Jul 64	Postal Service	612UNTS3	108847
Chad	Multilateral	25 Nov 64	Water Transport	587UNTS19	108507
Chad	Multilateral	18 Mar 65	Dispute Settlement	575UNTS159	108359
Chad	Multilateral	08 Jul 65	General Trade	597UNTS3	108641
Chad	Multilateral	27 May 66	IGO Establishment	637UNTS0	109121
Chad	Multilateral	11 Jun 68	Scientific Project	0UNTS0	109884
Chad	Multilateral	24 Sep 68	Air Transport	0UNTS0	110612
Chad	State/IGO Group	17 Feb 68	Direct Aid	0UNTS0	109658
Chad	UN Special Fund	23 Jan 61	Direct Aid	390UNTS69	105603
Chad	UNICEF (Children)	26 Aug 61	Direct Aid	422UNTS231	106077
Chad	USA (United States)	12 May 65	Finance	546UNTS183	107944
Chad	USA (United States)	31 Aug 66	Direct Aid	606UNTS47	108773
Chad	USSR (Soviet Union)	22 Jun 67	Mostfavored Nation	643UNTS121	109188
Chad	Vietnam, South	02 Jul 71	Consul/Citizenship	0VKNG387	496099
Chad	WHO (World Health)	03 Feb 61	Tech Assistance	394UNTS161	105676
Chile	Argentina	14 Dec 48	Air Transport	635UNTS21	109071
Chile	Argentina	29 Dec 61	Territory Boundary	635UNTS111	109075
Chile	Argentina	06 Nov 67	Taxation	636UNTS111	109097
Chile	Argentina	31 Jul 68	Land Transport	0UNTS0	109570
Chile	Austria	25 Oct 54	Visas	55ABGB173	403019
Chile	Belgium	11 Feb 47	Patents/Copyrights	76UNTS107	100983
Chile	Belgium	23 Aug 49	General Economic	46UNTS163	100708
Chile	Belgium	09 Oct 56	Visas	257UNTS227	103658
Chile	Belgium	07 Apr 61	Visas	410UNTS255	105909
Chile	Brazil	18 Nov 41	Culture	67UNTS279	200225
Chile	Brazil	18 Mar 66	Mass Media	0UNTS0	109418
Chile	Canada	14 Oct 62	Gen Communications	528UNTS273	107648
Chile	Denmark	27 Oct 52	Air Transport	271UNTS93	103911
Chile	Denmark	22 Oct 53	Milit Servic/Citiz	348UNTS261	105004
Chile	Denmark	15 Dec 67	Scientific Project	643UNTS293	109199
Chile	Denmark	27 Jan 70	Non-IBRD Project	0UNTS0	110558
Chile	France	23 Nov 55	Culture	60FRRT61	415115
Chile	France	14 Sep 62	Tech Assistance	65FRRT17	415116
Chile	Germany, East	05 Dec 66	Culture	34EGDZ373	420078
Chile	Germany, West	02 Feb 51	General Trade	52WGBB325	425078
Chile	Germany, West	06 Sep 52	Customs	53WGBB292	425079
Chile	Germany, West	03 Nov 53	Customs	54WGBB631	425080
Chile	Germany, West	29 Jun 56	Customs	58WGBB108	425081
Chile	Germany, West	02 Nov 56	General Economic	56WBGA230	424082
Chile	Germany, West	20 Nov 56	Culture	59WGBB549	425083
Chile	Germany, West	10 Nov 61	Admin Cooperation	62WBGA35	424084
Chile	Germany, West	13 Sep 62	Admin Cooperation	63WBGA13	424085
Chile	Germany, West	30 Mar 64	Air Transport	65WGBB79	425086
Chile	Germany, West	30 Apr 64	Air Transport	0UNTS0	109476
Chile	Germany, West	18 Oct 68	Loans and Credits	69WBGA146	424088
Chile	Germany, West	18 Oct 68	General Aid	70WBGA64	424087
Chile	Germany, West	28 Aug 70	Scientific Project	71WGBB106	425089
Chile	IAEA (Atom Energy)	19 Dec 69	Atomic Energy	0UNTS0	110521
Chile	IBRD (World Bank)	23 Mar 49	IBRD Project	153UNTS141	102019
Chile	IBRD (World Bank)	23 Mar 49	IBRD Project	153UNTS61	102018
Chile	IBRD (World Bank)	10 Oct 51	IBRD Project	158UNTS369	102072
Chile	IBRD (World Bank)	10 Sep 53	IBRD Project	188UNTS25	102520
Chile	IBRD (World Bank)	01 Nov 56	IBRD Project	261UNTS27	103724
Chile	IBRD (World Bank)	24 Jul 57	IBRD Project	282UNTS189	104099
Chile	IBRD (World Bank)	24 Jul 57	IBRD Project	282UNTS139	104098

PARTY ONE	PARTY TWO	DATE	TOPIC	CITATION	NUMBER
Chile	IBRD (World Bank)	28 Apr 58	IBRD Project	359UNTS89	105140
Chile	IBRD (World Bank)	28 Jun 61	IBRD Project	426UNTS33	106129
Chile	IBRD (World Bank)	18 Dec 63	IBRD Project	504UNTS29	107352
Chile	IBRD (World Bank)	18 Dec 63	IBRD Project	504UNTS3	107351
Chile	IBRD (World Bank)	12 Feb 65	IBRD Project	537UNTS35	107796
Chile	IBRD (World Bank)	06 Oct 65	IBRD Project	567UNTS293	108261
Chile	IBRD (World Bank)	23 Dec 66	IBRD Project	595UNTS141	108618
Chile	IBRD (World Bank)	19 Sep 68	IBRD Project	0UNTS0	109590
Chile	IBRD (World Bank)	23 Apr 70	IBRD Project	0UNTS0	110827
Chile	IDA (Devel Assoc)	28 Jun 61	Loans and Credits	426UNTS89	106131
Chile	ILO (Labor Org)	23 Jul 52	Tech Assistance	178UNTS323	102348
Chile	Israel	29 Dec 65	Scientific Project	0UNTS0	110375
Chile	Italy	24 Mar 49	General Amity	1ITMA525	437085
Chile	Italy	01 Dec 49	Health/Educ/Welfare	1ITMA526	437086
Chile	Italy	04 Jun 56	Milit Servic/Citiz	362UNTS309	105195
Chile	Italy	02 Aug 60	General Aid	62ITDI320	436087
Chile	Italy	30 Jun 65	Claims and Debts	66ITDI127	436088
Chile	Italy	30 Jun 65	Water Transport	66ITDI229	436089
Chile	Japan	31 Aug 65	Finance	0JGJI1610	441141
Chile	Japan	22 Oct 69	Visas	69JJS133	442252
Chile	Mexico	28 Jan 60	Culture	63MEXD3010	444012
Chile	Multilateral	25 Jun 36	Privil/Immunities	161UNTS217	200486
Chile	Multilateral	30 Jul 40	Admin Cooperation	161UNTS253	200488
Chile	Multilateral	12 Oct 40	Specific Resources	161UNTS193	200485
Chile	Multilateral	15 Jan 44	IGO Establishment	161UNTS281	200489
Chile	Multilateral	02 Aug 44	Scientific Project	67UNTS221	200221
Chile	Multilateral	07 Dec 44	Air Transport	171UNTS345	200501
Chile	Multilateral	07 Dec 44	Air Transport	84UNTS389	200252
Chile	Multilateral	07 Dec 44	IGO Establishment	15UNTS295	200102
Chile	Multilateral	16 Nov 45	IGO Establishment	4UNTS275	100052
Chile	Multilateral	27 Dec 45	IGO Establishment	2UNTS39	100020
Chile	Multilateral	22 Jul 46	IGO Establishment	9UNTS3	100125
Chile	Multilateral	22 Jul 46	IGO Establishment	14UNTS185	100221
Chile	Multilateral	27 Jul 46	Patents/Copyrights	90UNTS229	101238
Chile	Multilateral	15 Oct 46	Refugees	11UNTS73	100150
Chile	Multilateral	30 Oct 46	IGO Establishment	11UNTS107	100151
Chile	Multilateral	02 Dec 46	Specific Resources	161UNTS72	102124
Chile	Multilateral	11 Dec 46	Sanitation	12UNTS179	100186
Chile	Multilateral	02 Sep 47	General Military	21UNTS77	100324
Chile	Multilateral	02 Oct 47	Telecommunications	193UNTS188	102616
Chile	Multilateral	11 Oct 47	IGO Establishment	77UNTS143	100998
Chile	Multilateral	06 Mar 48	Water Transport	289UNTS3	104214
Chile	Multilateral	30 Apr 48	Dispute Settlement	30UNTS55	100449
Chile	Multilateral	30 Apr 48	IGO Establishment	119UNTS3	101609
Chile	Multilateral	10 Jun 48	Humanitarian	191UNTS3	102576
Chile	Multilateral	10 Jun 48	Humanitarian	164UNTS113	102163
Chile	Multilateral	19 Jun 48	Air Transport	310UNTS151	104492
Chile	Multilateral	24 Jul 48	Sanitation	66UNTS25	100847
Chile	Multilateral	19 Nov 48	Sanitation	44UNTS277	100688
Chile	Multilateral	09 Dec 48	Humanitarian	78UNTS277	101021
Chile	Multilateral	04 May 49	Admin Cooperation	98UNTS101	101358
Chile	Multilateral	04 May 49	Admin Cooperation	92UNTS19	101257
Chile	Multilateral	09 Jul 49	Telecommunications	168UNTS143	102218
Chile	Multilateral	12 Aug 49	General Military	75UNTS135	100972
Chile	Multilateral	12 Aug 49	Humanitarian	75UNTS287	100973
Chile	Multilateral	12 Aug 49	Humanitarian	75UNTS31	100970
Chile	Multilateral	12 Aug 49	Humanitarian	75UNTS85	100971
Chile	Multilateral	16 Dec 49	Admin Cooperation	72UNTS3	100924
Chile	Multilateral	08 Sep 51	Peace/Disarmament	136UNTS45	101832
Chile	Multilateral	06 Dec 51	Admin Cooperation	150UNTS67	101963
Chile	Multilateral	12 Jun 52	Dispute Settlement	138UNTS183	101869
Chile	Multilateral	11 Jul 52	Postal Service	170UNTS3	102221
Chile	Multilateral	11 Jul 52	IGO Establishment	169UNTS3	102220
Chile	Multilateral	11 Jul 52	Postal Service	171UNTS89	102225
Chile	Multilateral	11 Jul 52	Postal Service	171UNTS191	102227

PARTY ONE	PARTY TWO	DATE	TOPIC	CITATION	NUMBER
Chile	Multilateral	11 Jul 52	Postal Service	170UNTS269	102223
Chile	Multilateral	11 Jul 52	Postal Service	170UNTS63	102222
Chile	Multilateral	11 Jul 52	Postal Service	171UNTS3	102224
Chile	Multilateral	11 Jul 52	Postal Service	171UNTS143	102226
Chile	Multilateral	21 Aug 52	Tech Assistance	141UNTS129	101912
Chile	Multilateral	06 Sep 52	Patents/Copyrights	216UNTS132	102937
Chile	Multilateral	27 Feb 53	Claims and Debts	333UNTS3	104764
Chile	Multilateral	31 Mar 53	Mass Media	435UNTS191	106280
Chile	Multilateral	31 Mar 53	Privil/Immunities	193UNTS136	102613
Chile	Multilateral	11 May 53	Sanitation	456UNTS3	106555
Chile	Multilateral	19 Oct 53	IGO Establishment	207UNTS189	102807
Chile	Multilateral	01 May 55	Admin Cooperation	0UNTS0	110416
Chile	Multilateral	25 May 55	IGO Establishment	264UNTS117	103791
Chile	Multilateral	20 Jun 56	Admin Cooperation	268UNTS3	103850
Chile	Multilateral	26 Oct 56	IGO Establishment	276UNTS3	103988
Chile	Multilateral	15 Jan 57	Tech Assistance	376UNTS122	105378
Chile	Multilateral	20 Feb 57	Consul/Citizenship	309UNTS65	104468
Chile	Multilateral	03 Oct 57	Postal Service	364UNTS3	105211
Chile	Multilateral	03 Oct 57	Postal Service	366UNTS193	105218
Chile	Multilateral	03 Oct 57	Postal Service	366UNTS255	105219
Chile	Multilateral	03 Oct 57	Postal Service	366UNTS3	105215
Chile	Multilateral	03 Oct 57	Postal Service	366UNTS141	105217
Chile	Multilateral	03 Oct 57	Postal Service	364UNTS331	105212
Chile	Multilateral	03 Oct 57	Postal Service	365UNTS3	105213
Chile	Multilateral	03 Oct 57	Postal Service	365UNTS207	105214
Chile	Multilateral	29 Apr 58	Territory Boundary	499UNTS311	107302
Chile	Multilateral	29 Apr 58	Water Transport	450UNTS11	106465
Chile	Multilateral	08 Apr 59	IGO Establishment	389UNTS69	105593
Chile	Multilateral	18 Nov 59	IGO Establishment	390UNTS227	105610
Chile	Multilateral	01 Dec 59	Territory Boundary	402UNTS71	105778
Chile	Multilateral	26 Jan 60	IGO Establishment	439UNTS249	106333
Chile	Multilateral	28 Jul 60	IGO Establishment	485UNTS3	107042
Chile	Multilateral	30 Mar 61	Sanitation	520UNTS151	107515
Chile	Multilateral	18 Apr 61	Consul/Citizenship	500UNTS95	107310
Chile	Multilateral	26 Oct 61	Patents/Copyrights	496UNTS43	107247
Chile	Multilateral	26 Mar 62	IGO Establishment	539UNTS67	107825
Chile	Multilateral	28 Sep 62	IGO Establishment	469UNTS169	106791
Chile	Multilateral	10 Dec 62	Culture	521UNTS231	107525
Chile	Multilateral	06 Mar 63	Tech Assistance	455UNTS386	106552
Chile	Multilateral	24 Apr 63	Consul/Citizenship	596UNTS487	108640
Chile	Multilateral	24 Apr 63	Consul/Citizenship	596UNTS261	108638
Chile	Multilateral	05 Aug 63	Sanitation	480UNTS43	106964
Chile	Multilateral	10 Jul 64	Postal Service	611UNTS387	108846
Chile	Multilateral	10 Jul 64	Postal Service	613UNTS127	108853
Chile	Multilateral	10 Jul 64	Postal Service	612UNTS361	108849
Chile	Multilateral	10 Jul 64	Postal Service	613UNTS3	108851
Chile	Multilateral	10 Jul 64	Postal Service	611UNTS7	108844
Chile	Multilateral	10 Jul 64	Postal Service	612UNTS3	108847
Chile	Multilateral	10 Jul 64	Postal Service	611UNTS105	108845
Chile	Multilateral	10 Jul 64	Postal Service	612UNTS233	108848
Chile	Multilateral	10 Jul 64	Postal Service	613UNTS193	108852
Chile	Multilateral	10 Jul 64	Postal Service	613UNTS3	108850
Chile	Multilateral	13 Jul 64	ILO Labor	569UNTS65	108279
Chile	Multilateral	08 Jul 65	General Trade	597UNTS3	108641
Chile	Multilateral	27 Jan 67	Scientific Project	610UNTS205	108843
Chile	Multilateral	14 Feb 67	General Military	634UNTS281	109068
Chile	Multilateral	19 Dec 69	Atomic Energy	0UNTS0	110520
Chile	Netherlands	18 Jun 54	Visas	292UNTS37	104265
Chile	Netherlands	07 Apr 61	Visas	453UNTS239	106527
Chile	Netherlands	28 May 62	Admin Cooperation	0UNTS0	110029
Chile	Netherlands	13 Jul 62	Air Transport	466UNTS109	106740
Chile	Norway	27 Oct 52	Air Transport	2NORT592	451020
Chile	Norway	16 Mar 53	Visas	167UNTS13	102198
Chile	Norway	05 Feb 62	Claims and Debts	3NORT849	451021
Chile	Spain	09 Aug 50	General Economic	54SPBO1308	460073

PARTY ONE	PARTY TWO	DATE	TOPIC	CITATION	NUMBER
Chile	Spain	24 May 58	Health/Educ/Welfare	58SPBO1411	460074
Chile	Spain	23 Jun 58	Health/Educ/Welfare	58SPBO1411	460075
Chile	Spain	07 Jun 61	Health/Educ/Welfare	65SPBO1911	460076
Chile	Sweden	27 Oct 52	Air Transport	311UNTS63	104499
Chile	Switzerland	17 Jun 55	General Trade	55SWRO705	462125
Chile	Switzerland	24 Nov 61	Loans and Credits	62SWRO77	462107
Chile	UK Great Britain	01 Jul 44	General Trade	2UNTS243	200017
Chile	UK Great Britain	25 Jun 46	General Trade	91UNTS137	101246
Chile	UK Great Britain	16 Sep 47	Air Transport	133UNTS143	101786
Chile	UK Great Britain	27 Oct 47	Milit Servic/Citiz	82UNTS209	101094
Chile	UK Great Britain	24 Jun 48	Finance	77UNTS113	100995
Chile	UK Great Britain	31 Jul 54	Milit Servic/Citiz	618UNTS353	108934
Chile	UK Great Britain	21 Oct 60	Loans and Credits	385UNTS15	105525
Chile	UK Great Britain	09 May 61	Visas	414UNTS37	105963
Chile	UK Great Britain	23 Nov 65	Loans and Credits	560UNTS215	108176
Chile	UK Great Britain	07 Oct 66	Tech Assistance	603UNTS167	108733
Chile	UK Great Britain	18 Nov 68	Atomic Energy	0UNTS0	110236
Chile	UN Special Fund	22 Jan 60	Direct Aid	351UNTS115	105020
Chile	UNICEF (Children)	03 Mar 50	Direct Aid	126UNTS119	101685
Chile	UNICEF (Children)	30 Nov 65	IGO Operations	596UNTS215	108635
Chile	United Nations	16 Feb 53	IGO Operations	314UNTS49	104541
Chile	USA (United States)	14 Apr 43	Military Mission	9UNTS331	200050
Chile	USA (United States)	11 May 43	Sanitation	139UNTS295	200456
Chile	USA (United States)	24 May 45	Military Mission	121UNTS219	200401
Chile	USA (United States)	11 Jun 45	Milit Servic/Citiz	121UNTS291	200407
Chile	USA (United States)	30 Jul 45	General Trade	6UNTS409	200042
Chile	USA (United States)	30 Jul 46	General Trade	7UNTS41	100090
Chile	USA (United States)	10 May 47	Air Transport	55UNTS21	100807
Chile	USA (United States)	21 Jan 49	Sanitation	160UNTS185	102107
Chile	USA (United States)	09 Apr 49	Customs	122UNTS169	101646
Chile	USA (United States)	12 May 50	Consul/Citizenship	177UNTS103	102312
Chile	USA (United States)	29 Aug 50	Visas	122UNTS43	101634
Chile	USA (United States)	04 Jan 51	Milit Assistance	165UNTS105	102172
Chile	USA (United States)	16 Jan 51	Direct Aid	157UNTS3	102043
Chile	USA (United States)	16 Jan 51	Education	147UNTS11	101925
Chile	USA (United States)	16 Jan 51	Tech Assistance	151UNTS147	101990
Chile	USA (United States)	15 Feb 51	Military Mission	133UNTS95	101783
Chile	USA (United States)	15 Feb 51	Military Mission	133UNTS117	101784
Chile	USA (United States)	09 Apr 52	Milit Assistance	186UNTS53	102482
Chile	USA (United States)	30 Jun 52	Tech Assistance	199UNTS241	102688
Chile	USA (United States)	27 Jun 53	Tech Assistance	229UNTS53	103160
Chile	USA (United States)	27 Jun 53	Tech Assistance	229UNTS193	103167
Chile	USA (United States)	30 Dec 53	Tech Assistance	236UNTS41	103315
Chile	USA (United States)	10 May 54	Customs	247UNTS299	103477
Chile	USA (United States)	28 Jun 54	Tech Assistance	233UNTS3	103246
Chile	USA (United States)	14 Jan 55	Mass Media	238UNTS191	103362
Chile	USA (United States)	27 Jan 55	US Agri Commod Aid	262UNTS3	103735
Chile	USA (United States)	31 Mar 55	Education	262UNTS19	103736
Chile	USA (United States)	05 Apr 55	Direct Aid	250UNTS253	103527
Chile	USA (United States)	08 Aug 55	Atomic Energy	235UNTS209	103303
Chile	USA (United States)	13 Mar 56	US Agri Commod Aid	275UNTS49	103975
Chile	USA (United States)	20 Apr 56	Atomic Energy	293UNTS277	104295
Chile	USA (United States)	15 Nov 56	Military Mission	282UNTS3	104089
Chile	USA (United States)	01 Mar 57	Non-ILO Labor	283UNTS127	104112
Chile	USA (United States)	19 Feb 59	Specific Property	343UNTS17	104918
Chile	USA (United States)	19 Feb 60	Atomic Energy	371UNTS255	105282
Chile	USA (United States)	28 Mar 60	Scientific Project	401UNTS105	105765
Chile	USA (United States)	02 Jun 60	US Agri Commod Aid	377UNTS11	105393
Chile	USA (United States)	29 Jun 60	Direct Aid	377UNTS355	105411
Chile	USA (United States)	16 Jul 60	Milit Assistance	393UNTS271	105661
Chile	USA (United States)	29 Jul 60	Admin Cooperation	405UNTS127	105829
Chile	USA (United States)	28 Oct 60	Direct Aid	401UNTS177	105770
Chile	USA (United States)	08 Nov 60	US Agri Commod Aid	405UNTS85	105825
Chile	USA (United States)	03 Aug 61	Direct Aid	433UNTS21	106228
Chile	USA (United States)	12 Aug 61	Scientific Project	421UNTS209	106059

PARTY ONE	PARTY TWO	DATE	TOPIC	CITATION	NUMBER
Chile	USA (United States)	07 Aug 62	US Agri Commod Aid	461UNTS61	106652
Chile	USA (United States)	04 Oct 62	Tech Assistance	461UNTS129	106656
Chile	USA (United States)	27 Oct 64	Military Mission	532UNTS347	107727
Chile	USA (United States)	27 Jul 65	US Agri Commod Aid	574UNTS83	108342
Chile	USA (United States)	30 Nov 67	Gen Communications	0UNTS0	110058
Chile	USA (United States)	29 Dec 67	US Agri Commod Aid	0UNTS0	109992
Chile	USA (United States)	29 Apr 69	Commodity Trade	0UNTS0	110273
Chile	WHO (World Health)	31 May 52	Sanitation	136UNTS323	101841
Chile	WHO (World Health)	11 Jul 52	Tech Assistance	137UNTS27	101846
Chile	WHO (World Health)	24 Oct 52	Sanitation	151UNTS339	102004
Chile	WHO (World Health)	04 Nov 52	Sanitation	150UNTS119	101966
China	IBRD (World Bank)	14 Jun 67	IGO Operations	615UNTS243	108882
China	Multilateral	02 Sep 45	Peace/Disarmament	139UNTS387	200465
China	Multilateral	27 Dec 45	IGO Establishment	2UNTS39	100020
China	Multilateral	11 Oct 47	IGO Establishment	77UNTS143	100998
China	Multilateral	12 Nov 47	Admin Cooperation	46UNTS201	100710
China	Multilateral	06 Mar 48	Water Transport	289UNTS3	104214
China	Multilateral	18 Jun 49	ILO Labor	605UNTS295	108768
China	Multilateral	03 Oct 57	Postal Service	365UNTS3	105213
China	Multilateral	03 Oct 57	Postal Service	366UNTS87	105216
China	Multilateral	03 Oct 57	Postal Service	364UNTS3	105211
China	Multilateral	03 Oct 57	Postal Service	365UNTS207	105214
China	Multilateral	03 Oct 57	Postal Service	366UNTS255	105219
China	Multilateral	03 Oct 57	Postal Service	364UNTS331	105212
China	Multilateral	24 Apr 63	Consul/Citizenship	596UNTS261	108638
China	Multilateral	10 Jul 64	Postal Service	613UNTS193	108852
China	Multilateral	10 Jul 64	Postal Service	613UNTS3	108850
China	Multilateral	23 Jun 65	General IGO	614UNTS239	108873
China	USA (United States)	31 Aug 65	Status of Forces	572UNTS3	108308
China People's Rep	Afghanistan	28 Jul 57	General Economic	57CCJC72	410437
China People's Rep	Afghanistan	26 Aug 60	General Amity	60CCJC88	410716
China People's Rep	Afghanistan	22 Nov 63	Territory Boundary	63CCJC136	411033
China People's Rep	Afghanistan	24 Mar 65	Territory Boundary	65CCJC39	411044
China People's Rep	Afghanistan	24 Mar 65	Direct Aid	65CCJC40	411045
China People's Rep	Afghanistan	24 Mar 65	Culture	65CCJC41	411046
China People's Rep	Afghanistan	06 Nov 65	General Trade	65CCJC136	411042
China People's Rep	Afghanistan	24 May 66	Culture	66CCJC37	411047
China People's Rep	Afghanistan	29 Jul 66	General Economic	66CCJC73	411048
China People's Rep	Afghanistan	28 Dec 66	General Trade	66CCJC105	411049
China People's Rep	Albania	14 Oct 54	Culture	54CCJC71	410178
China People's Rep	Albania	14 Oct 54	Scientific Project	54CCJC70	410177
China People's Rep	Albania	03 Dec 54	General Economic	54CCJC79	410186
China People's Rep	Albania	03 Dec 54	Loans and Credits	54CCJC80	410187
China People's Rep	Albania	28 Sep 55	Mass Media	55CCJC66	410258
China People's Rep	Albania	13 Mar 56	General Economic	56CCJC40	410324
China People's Rep	Albania	08 Mar 57	General Economic	57CCJC25	410407
China People's Rep	Albania	31 May 57	Gen Communications	57CCJC54	410425
China People's Rep	Albania	12 Mar 58	General Economic	58CCJC25	410500
China People's Rep	Albania	16 Jan 59	Loans and Credits	59CCJC7	410571
China People's Rep	Albania	16 Jan 59	General Trade	59CCJC6	410570
China People's Rep	Albania	16 Jan 59	General Economic	59CCJC8	410572
China People's Rep	Albania	11 Jul 59	Mass Media	59CCJC89	410632
China People's Rep	Albania	15 Mar 60	General Economic	60CCJC41	410686
China People's Rep	Albania	02 Feb 61	General Trade	61CCJC17	410755
China People's Rep	Albania	02 Feb 61	General Amity	61CCJC16	410754
China People's Rep	Albania	02 Feb 61	Loans and Credits	61CCJC18	410756
China People's Rep	Albania	18 Feb 63	Sanitation	63CCJC14	410948
China People's Rep	Albania	06 Dec 63	General Economic	63CCJC144	411039
China People's Rep	Albania	02 Jan 64	Sanitation	64CCJC3	411050
China People's Rep	Albania	05 Mar 64	Health/Educ/Welfare	64CCJC34	411051
China People's Rep	Albania	12 Mar 65	Culture	65CCJC26	411070
China People's Rep	Albania	22 Mar 65	General Transport	65CCJC34	411071
China People's Rep	Albania	08 Jun 65	Loans and Credits	65CCJC75	411053
China People's Rep	Albania	08 Jun 65	General Economic	65CCJC77	411055
China People's Rep	Albania	08 Jun 65	General Economic	65CCJC76	411054

PARTY ONE	PARTY TWO	DATE	TOPIC	CITATION	NUMBER
China People's Rep	Albania	06 Oct 65	Tech Assistance	65CCJC131	411056
China People's Rep	Albania	12 Nov 65	General Trade	65CCJC140	411072
China People's Rep	Albania	04 May 66	Water Transport	66CCJC27	411057
China People's Rep	Albania	24 May 66	Scientific Project	66CCJC38	411073
China People's Rep	Albania	20 Oct 66	Loans and Credits	66CCJC86	411074
China People's Rep	Albania	21 Nov 66	General Economic	66CCJC96	411075
China People's Rep	Albania	30 Nov 66	Tech Assistance	66CCJC102	411076
China People's Rep	Albania	24 Apr 67	Culture	67CCJC14	411077
China People's Rep	Albania	28 May 67	Water Transport	67CCJC22	411078
China People's Rep	Albania	23 Jun 67	Direct Aid	67CCJC23	411079
China People's Rep	Algeria	11 Sep 63	Culture	63CCJC106	411009
China People's Rep	Algeria	11 Oct 63	Loans and Credits	63CCJC116	411017
China People's Rep	Algeria	14 Apr 64	Mass Media	64CCJC48	411060
China People's Rep	Algeria	19 Sep 64	General Trade	64CCJC118	411063
China People's Rep	Algeria	19 Sep 64	Finance	64CCJC119	411064
China People's Rep	Algeria	25 Dec 64	Scientific Project	64CCJC187	411068
China People's Rep	Algeria	14 Jan 65	Commodity Trade	65CCJC6	411069
China People's Rep	Algeria	03 Jun 65	Culture	65CCJC72	411052
China People's Rep	Austria	13 Sep 56	General Trade	56CCJC99	410362
China People's Rep	Austria	07 Dec 64	General Economic	64CCJC175	411080
China People's Rep	Bulgaria	14 Jul 52	Culture	52CCJC35	410070
China People's Rep	Bulgaria	21 Jul 52	General Economic	52CCJC40	410071
China People's Rep	Bulgaria	03 Dec 52	General Economic	52CCJC60	410084
China People's Rep	Bulgaria	15 Oct 53	Mass Media	53CCJC60	410123
China People's Rep	Bulgaria	25 Mar 54	General Economic	54CCJC8	410135
China People's Rep	Bulgaria	27 Jan 55	General Economic	55CCJC6	410212
China People's Rep	Bulgaria	23 Mar 55	Scientific Project	55CCJC18	410222
China People's Rep	Bulgaria	11 Jul 55	Sanitation	55CCJC50	410243
China People's Rep	Bulgaria	14 Sep 55	Gen Communications	55CCJC64	410256
China People's Rep	Bulgaria	21 Jan 56	General Economic	56CCJC13	410302
China People's Rep	Bulgaria	28 Jan 57	General Economic	57CCJC13	410398
China People's Rep	Bulgaria	13 Mar 58	General Economic	58CCJC27	410501
China People's Rep	Bulgaria	18 Dec 58	General Economic	58CCJC108	410561
China People's Rep	Bulgaria	23 Apr 59	Scientific Project	59CCJC69	410617
China People's Rep	Bulgaria	06 Aug 59	Mass Media	59CCJC90	410633
China People's Rep	Bulgaria	15 Mar 60	General Trade	60CCJC45	410689
China People's Rep	Bulgaria	08 Mar 61	General Trade	61CCJC34	410766
China People's Rep	Bulgaria	30 Mar 62	General Economic	62CCJC31	410879
China People's Rep	Bulgaria	05 Mar 63	General Economic	63CCJC31	410959
China People's Rep	Bulgaria	14 Apr 64	General Economic	64CCJC46	411084
China People's Rep	Bulgaria	12 Dec 64	General Economic	64CCJC180	411088
China People's Rep	Bulgaria	13 May 65	Culture	65CCJC65	411090
China People's Rep	Bulgaria	09 Nov 65	Scientific Project	65CCJC137	411081
China People's Rep	Bulgaria	16 Mar 66	General Economic	66CCJC7	411091
China People's Rep	Bulgaria	01 Jul 66	Culture	66CCJC62	411082
China People's Rep	Bulgaria	31 Jan 67	General Economic	67CCJC3	411092
China People's Rep	Bulgaria	27 Feb 67	Scientific Project	67CCJC9	411093
China People's Rep	Burma	22 Apr 54	Finance	54CCJC19	410142
China People's Rep	Burma	22 Apr 54	General Trade	54CCJC18	410141
China People's Rep	Burma	03 Nov 54	Commodity Trade	54CCJC77	410184
China People's Rep	Burma	08 Nov 55	Air Transport	55CCJC78	410266
China People's Rep	Burma	08 Nov 55	Air Transport	306UNTS11	104430
China People's Rep	Burma	08 Nov 55	Consul/Citizenship	55CCJC79	410267
China People's Rep	Burma	08 Nov 55	Air Transport	55CCJC77	410265
China People's Rep	Burma	29 Dec 55	Commodity Trade	55CCJC107	410288
China People's Rep	Burma	01 Nov 57	Postal Service	57CCJC105	410460
China People's Rep	Burma	01 Nov 57	Postal Service	57CCJC104	410459
China People's Rep	Burma	31 Jan 58	Telecommunications	58CCJC15	410492
China People's Rep	Burma	21 Feb 58	General Trade	58CCJC21	410496
China People's Rep	Burma	28 Jan 60	General Amity	60CCJC7	410658
China People's Rep	Burma	28 Jan 60	Territory Boundary	60CCJC8	410659
China People's Rep	Burma	01 Oct 60	Territory Boundary	60CCJC98	410721
China People's Rep	Burma	01 Oct 60	Territory Boundary	60CCJC99	410722
China People's Rep	Burma	09 Jan 61	Direct Aid	61CCJC2	410745
China People's Rep	Burma	09 Jan 61	Finance	61CCJC3	410746

PARTY ONE	PARTY TWO	DATE	TOPIC	CITATION	NUMBER
China People's Rep	Burma	27 Jan 61	General Trade	61CCJC6	410749
China People's Rep	Burma	13 Oct 61	Territory Boundary	61CCJC135	410838
China People's Rep	Burma	28 Aug 63	Admin Cooperation	63CCJC100	411004
China People's Rep	Burma	26 Jan 65	Commodity Trade	65CCJC9	411089
China People's Rep	Burundi	22 Oct 64	General Economic	64CCJC148	411086
China People's Rep	Cambodia	24 Apr 56	General Trade	56CCJC54	410333
China People's Rep	Cambodia	24 Apr 56	General Trade	56CCJC55	410334
China People's Rep	Cambodia	21 Jun 56	Direct Aid	56CCJC76	410345
China People's Rep	Cambodia	21 Nov 59	Customs	59CCJC104	410645
China People's Rep	Cambodia	19 Dec 60	General Amity	60CCJC129	410741
China People's Rep	Cambodia	23 May 62	Admin Cooperation	62CCJC50	410892
China People's Rep	Cambodia	25 Nov 63	Air Transport	63CCJC138	411034
China People's Rep	Cambodia	26 Nov 63	Air Transport	63CCJC141	411037
China People's Rep	Cambodia	22 Mar 65	Health/Educ/Welfare	65CCJC35	411127
China People's Rep	Cambodia	16 Sep 65	Mass Media	65CCJC119	411135
China People's Rep	Cambodia	31 Mar 66	Health/Educ/Welfare	66CCJC12	411140
China People's Rep	Cambodia	29 Apr 66	General Economic	66CCJC22	411142
China People's Rep	Central Afri Rep	29 Sep 64	Culture	64CCJC129	411117
China People's Rep	Central Afri Rep	29 Sep 64	General Economic	64CCJC130	411118
China People's Rep	Central Afri Rep	29 Sep 64	Direct Aid	64CCJC128	411116
China People's Rep	Central Afri Rep	14 Jan 65	Direct Aid	65CCJC7	411125
China People's Rep	Ceylon (Sri Lanka)	04 Oct 52	General Trade	52CCJC55	410079
China People's Rep	Ceylon (Sri Lanka)	18 Dec 52	Commodity Trade	52CCJC62	410085
China People's Rep	Ceylon (Sri Lanka)	12 Oct 55	Commodity Trade	55CCJC68	410260
China People's Rep	Ceylon (Sri Lanka)	29 Dec 56	Commodity Trade	56CCJC146	410392
China People's Rep	Ceylon (Sri Lanka)	19 Sep 57	Direct Aid	57CCJC87	410448
China People's Rep	Ceylon (Sri Lanka)	19 Sep 57	General Trade	57CCJC85	410446
China People's Rep	Ceylon (Sri Lanka)	19 Sep 57	Direct Aid	337UNTS169	104822
China People's Rep	Ceylon (Sri Lanka)	19 Sep 57	Customs	57CCJC84	410445
China People's Rep	Ceylon (Sri Lanka)	19 Sep 57	General Economic	337UNTS137	104821
China People's Rep	Ceylon (Sri Lanka)	19 Sep 57	General Trade	57CCJC86	410447
China People's Rep	Ceylon (Sri Lanka)		General Economic	57CCJC83	410444
China People's Rep	Ceylon (Sri Lanka)	17 Sep 58	Loans and Credits	58CCJC83	410540
China People's Rep	Ceylon (Sri Lanka)	26 Mar 59	Air Transport	59CCJC57	410608
China People's Rep	Ceylon (Sri Lanka)	13 Jun 59	Commodity Trade	59CCJC84	410627
China People's Rep	Ceylon (Sri Lanka)	13 Jun 59	General Trade	59CCJC83	410626
China People's Rep	Ceylon (Sri Lanka)	04 Apr 61	General Trade	61CCJC47	410777
China People's Rep	Ceylon (Sri Lanka)	07 Oct 61	General Trade	61CCJC132	410836
China People's Rep	Ceylon (Sri Lanka)	07 Feb 62	Admin Cooperation	62CCJC18	410867
China People's Rep	Ceylon (Sri Lanka)	03 Oct 62	General Economic	62CCJC93	410919
China People's Rep	Ceylon (Sri Lanka)	03 Oct 62	Direct Aid	62CCJC94	410920
China People's Rep	Ceylon (Sri Lanka)	03 Oct 62	General Trade	62CCJC95	410921
China People's Rep	Ceylon (Sri Lanka)	25 Jul 63	Water Transport	63CCJC92	410999
China People's Rep	Ceylon (Sri Lanka)	10 Oct 63	General Trade	63CCJC114	411015
China People's Rep	Ceylon (Sri Lanka)	24 Oct 64	General Trade	64CCJC150	411119
China People's Rep	Ceylon (Sri Lanka)	15 Mar 65	Direct Aid	65CCJC27	411126
China People's Rep	Ceylon (Sri Lanka)	13 Jul 65	Direct Aid	65CCJC91	411133
China People's Rep	Ceylon (Sri Lanka)	12 Oct 65	General Trade	65CCJC132	411136
China People's Rep	Ceylon (Sri Lanka)	01 Dec 65	Commodity Trade	65CCJC147	411102
China People's Rep	Ceylon (Sri Lanka)	29 Nov 66	General Trade	66CCJC100	411147
China People's Rep	Ceylon (Sri Lanka)	29 Nov 66	Commodity Trade	66CCJC101	411148
China People's Rep	Congo (Brazzaville)	23 Jul 64	General Economic	64CCJC100	411113
China People's Rep	Congo (Brazzaville)	02 Oct 64	Water Transport	64CCJC136	411096
China People's Rep	Congo (Brazzaville)	02 Oct 64	General Amity	64CCJC135	411095
China People's Rep	Congo (Brazzaville)	06 Feb 65	Direct Aid	65CCJC14	411100
China People's Rep	Congo (Brazzaville)	12 May 65	Mass Media	65CCJC64	411129
China People's Rep	Congo (Brazzaville)	13 Jun 65	Direct Aid	65CCJC83	411131
China People's Rep	Congo (Brazzaville)	13 Aug 65	Culture	65CCJC106	411134
China People's Rep	Congo (Brazzaville)	14 Apr 66	Culture	66CCJC16	411141
China People's Rep	Cuba	23 Jul 60	Culture	60CCJC83	410714
China People's Rep	Cuba	23 Jul 60	General Economic	60CCJC81	410712
China People's Rep	Cuba	23 Jul 60	Tech Assistance	60CCJC82	410713
China People's Rep	Cuba	30 Nov 60	Direct Aid	60CCJC122	410737
China People's Rep	Cuba	08 Mar 61	Finance	61CCJC32	410764
China People's Rep	Cuba	21 Oct 61	Telecommunications	61CCJC143	410842

PARTY ONE	PARTY TWO	DATE	TOPIC	CITATION	NUMBER
China People's Rep	Cuba	21 Oct 61	Postal Service	61CCJC144	410843
China People's Rep	Cuba	27 Jan 62	Mass Media	62CCJC15	410864
China People's Rep	Cuba	25 Jun 63	Scientific Project	63CCJC83	410992
China People's Rep	Cuba	15 Jan 64	General Economic	64CCJC9	411106
China People's Rep	Cuba	11 Aug 64	General Economic	64CCJC108	411114
China People's Rep	Cuba	31 Dec 64	General Trade	64CCJC189	411124
China People's Rep	Cuba	21 May 65	Tech Assistance	65CCJC68	411130
China People's Rep	Cuba	29 Dec 65	Culture	65CCJC161	411139
China People's Rep	Cuba	26 May 66	General Trade	66CCJC39	411144
China People's Rep	Cuba	27 May 66	Scientific Project	66CCJC40	411145
China People's Rep	Cuba	06 Jul 66	Tech Assistance	66CCJC67	411104
China People's Rep	Cuba	21 Mar 67	General Trade	67CCJC11	411149
China People's Rep	Czechoslovakia	14 Jun 50	General Trade	50CCJC22	410017
China People's Rep	Czechoslovakia	21 Jun 51	General Trade	51CCJC19	410040
China People's Rep	Czechoslovakia	06 May 52	Telecommunications	52CCJC18	410063
China People's Rep	Czechoslovakia	06 May 52	Postal Service	52CCJC17	410062
China People's Rep	Czechoslovakia	06 May 52	Scientific Project	52CCJC19	410064
China People's Rep	Czechoslovakia	24 May 52	Culture	52CCJC20	410065
China People's Rep	Czechoslovakia	07 May 53	Telecommunications	53CCJC24	410101
China People's Rep	Czechoslovakia	07 May 53	General Trade	53CCJC22	410100
China People's Rep	Czechoslovakia	18 Aug 53	Sanitation	53CCJC48	410114
China People's Rep	Czechoslovakia	27 Apr 54	General Economic	54CCJC20	410143
China People's Rep	Czechoslovakia	06 Apr 55	General Trade	55CCJC22	410225
China People's Rep	Czechoslovakia	06 Apr 55	General Economic	55CCJC21	410224
China People's Rep	Czechoslovakia	11 Nov 55	General Economic	55CCJC81	410269
China People's Rep	Czechoslovakia	03 Dec 55	Scientific Project	55CCJC94	410279
China People's Rep	Czechoslovakia	06 Mar 57	General Economic	57CCJC22	410404
China People's Rep	Czechoslovakia	27 Mar 57	Sanitation	57CCJC31	410411
China People's Rep	Czechoslovakia	27 Mar 57	General Amity	57CCJC29	410409
China People's Rep	Czechoslovakia	27 Mar 57	Culture	57CCJC30	410410
China People's Rep	Czechoslovakia	16 Apr 58	General Economic	58CCJC51	410517
China People's Rep	Czechoslovakia	03 Mar 59	Scientific Project	59CCJC41	410595
China People's Rep	Czechoslovakia	12 Mar 59	General Economic	59CCJC48	410601
China People's Rep	Czechoslovakia	30 Apr 59	Mass Media	59CCJC73	410620
China People's Rep	Czechoslovakia	02 Feb 60	General Economic	60CCJC10	410661
China People's Rep	Czechoslovakia	07 May 60	Consul/Citizenship	60CCJC61	410700
China People's Rep	Czechoslovakia	07 May 60	Consul/Citizenship	402UNTS209	105787
China People's Rep	Czechoslovakia	20 Oct 61	General Trade	61CCJC141	410841
China People's Rep	Czechoslovakia	07 Mar 62	Finance	62CCJC22	410871
China People's Rep	Czechoslovakia	17 Jul 62	General Economic	62CCJC64	410901
China People's Rep	Czechoslovakia	30 Sep 62	Scientific Project	62CCJC90	410918
China People's Rep	Czechoslovakia	19 Apr 63	General Economic	63CCJC44	410969
China People's Rep	Czechoslovakia	20 Nov 63	Finance	63CCJC135	411032
China People's Rep	Czechoslovakia	24 Mar 65	Scientific Project	65CCJC42	411128
China People's Rep	Czechoslovakia	08 Apr 65	General Economic	65CCJC53	411101
China People's Rep	Czechoslovakia	18 Jun 65	Culture	65CCJC84	411132
China People's Rep	Czechoslovakia	26 Oct 65	Scientific Project	65CCJC133	411137
China People's Rep	Czechoslovakia	23 Dec 65	Scientific Project	65CCJC160	411138
China People's Rep	Czechoslovakia	04 Feb 66	General Economic	66CCJC3	411103
China People's Rep	Czechoslovakia	11 May 66	Culture	66CCJC32	411143
China People's Rep	Czechoslovakia	28 Oct 66	Scientific Project	66CCJC90	411146
China People's Rep	Denmark	01 Dec 57	Mostfavored Nation	57CCJC112	410466
China People's Rep	Denmark	01 Dec 57	General Economic	57CCJC111	410465
China People's Rep	Denmark	01 Dec 57	General Economic	309UNTS241	104475
China People's Rep	Denmark	12 Apr 58	Patents/Copyrights	58CCJC49	410515
China People's Rep	Denmark	23 Sep 61	Taxation	61CCJC126	410831
China People's Rep	Denmark	23 Sep 61	Taxation	446UNTS3	106397
China People's Rep	Finland	05 Jun 53	Finance	53CCJC32	410106
China People's Rep	Finland	05 Jun 53	General Trade	53CCJC30	410105
China People's Rep	Finland	17 Jun 54	General Trade	54CCJC36	410156
China People's Rep	Finland	21 Jun 54	General Trade	54CCJC37	410157
China People's Rep	Finland	08 Aug 55	General Trade	55CCJC54	410247
China People's Rep	Finland	31 Mar 56	Mostfavored Nation	56CCJC44	410326
China People's Rep	Finland	31 Jul 56	General Trade	56CCJC91	410355
China People's Rep	Finland	18 Dec 57	General Trade	57CCJC119	410472

PARTY ONE	PARTY TWO	DATE	TOPIC	CITATION	NUMBER
China People's Rep	Finland	15 May 59	General Trade	59CCJC76	410622
China People's Rep	Finland	16 Dec 59	General Trade	59CCJC111	410650
China People's Rep	Finland	11 Apr 61	General Trade	61CCJC55	410784
China People's Rep	Finland	29 Mar 62	General Trade	62CCJC30	410878
China People's Rep	Finland	29 May 63	General Trade	63CCJC68	410983
China People's Rep	Finland	28 Oct 63	General Trade	63CCJC126	411025
China People's Rep	Finland	24 Mar 65	General Trade	65CCJC43	411152
China People's Rep	Finland	23 Nov 65	General Trade	65CCJC145	411153
China People's Rep	Finland	26 Jan 67	Patents/Copyrights	67CCJC2	411155
China People's Rep	Finland	25 Apr 67	General Trade	67CCJC16	411156
China People's Rep	France	05 Jun 53	General Trade	53CCJC33	410107
China People's Rep	France	19 Feb 56	Finance	56CCJC34	410318
China People's Rep	France	19 Feb 56	Finance	56CCJC33	410317
China People's Rep	France	01 Oct 65	Culture	65CCJC126	411150
China People's Rep	France	01 Jun 66	Air Transport	66CCJC43	411151
China People's Rep	France	01 Jun 66	Air Transport	66FRRT23	415117
China People's Rep	France	25 Jul 66	Air Transport	66CCJC71	411154
China People's Rep	France	22 Sep 66	Air Transport	68FRJO2801	416118
China People's Rep	Germany, East	10 Oct 50	General Economic	50CCJC27	410022
China People's Rep	Germany, East	09 Oct 51	Culture	51CCJC23	410043
China People's Rep	Germany, East	09 Oct 51	Culture	4EGDA73	419080
China People's Rep	Germany, East	12 Oct 51	Postal Service	4EGDA73	419081
China People's Rep	Germany, East	12 Oct 51	Postal Service	51CCJC24	410044
China People's Rep	Germany, East	12 Oct 51	Telecommunications	4EGDA81	419082
China People's Rep	Germany, East	21 Oct 51	Telecommunications	51CCJC25	410045
China People's Rep	Germany, East	28 May 52	General Economic	52CCJC23	410068
China People's Rep	Germany, East	30 Apr 53	General Economic	53CCJC20	410099
China People's Rep	Germany, East	05 Oct 53	Consul/Citizenship	1EGDA327	419083
China People's Rep	Germany, East	30 Oct 53	Health/Educ/Welfare	4EGDA85	419084
China People's Rep	Germany, East	30 Oct 53	Scientific Project	53CCJC63	410125
China People's Rep	Germany, East	28 Nov 53	Culture	53CCJC67	410127
China People's Rep	Germany, East	30 Mar 54	General Economic	54CCJC12	410138
China People's Rep	Germany, East	08 Jun 54	Mass Media	4EGDA86	419085
China People's Rep	Germany, East	10 Jun 54	Mass Media	54CCJC35	410155
China People's Rep	Germany, East	23 Jun 54	Scientific Project	54CCJC38	410158
China People's Rep	Germany, East	23 Jun 54	Health/Educ/Welfare	2EGDA368	419086
China People's Rep	Germany, East	27 Dec 54	Education	2EGDA407	419087
China People's Rep	Germany, East	27 Dec 54	Education	54CCJC95	410199
China People's Rep	Germany, East	24 Apr 55	General Economic	55CCJC30	410231
China People's Rep	Germany, East	20 Aug 55	Scientific Project	55CCJC57	410250
China People's Rep	Germany, East	16 Sep 55	General Trade	55CCJC65	410257
China People's Rep	Germany, East	20 Nov 55	General Economic	55CCJC84	410271
China People's Rep	Germany, East	25 Dec 55	General Amity	4EGDA95	419089
China People's Rep	Germany, East	25 Dec 55	Sanitation	4EGDA100	419091
China People's Rep	Germany, East	25 Dec 55	General Amity	55CCJC102	410284
China People's Rep	Germany, East	25 Dec 55	Culture	4EGDA98	419090
China People's Rep	Germany, East	25 Dec 55	Culture	55CCJC103	410285
China People's Rep	Germany, East	25 Dec 55	Sanitation	55CCJC104	410286
China People's Rep	Germany, East	22 May 56	General Trade	56CCJC67	410338
China People's Rep	Germany, East	05 Apr 57	General Economic	57CCJC36	410415
China People's Rep	Germany, East	26 Sep 57	Commodity Trade	5EGDA332	419092
China People's Rep	Germany, East	16 Dec 57	Sanitation	57CCJC118	410471
China People's Rep	Germany, East	16 Dec 57	Sanitation	5EGDA333	419093
China People's Rep	Germany, East	27 Mar 58	Finance	58CCJC34	410506
China People's Rep	Germany, East	23 Apr 58	General Economic	58CCJC58	410522
China People's Rep	Germany, East	09 Oct 58	Commodity Trade	18EGDZ198	420094
China People's Rep	Germany, East	27 Jan 59	Consul/Citizenship	59CCJC19	410579
China People's Rep	Germany, East	27 Jan 59	Consul/Citizenship	7EGDA335	419095
China People's Rep	Germany, East	05 Feb 59	General Economic	59CCJC22	410582
China People's Rep	Germany, East	17 Mar 59	Scientific Project	59CCJC51	410603
China People's Rep	Germany, East	25 Apr 59	Mass Media	59CCJC70	410618
China People's Rep	Germany, East	25 Apr 59	Mass Media	59CCJC71	410619
China People's Rep	Germany, East	18 Jan 60	General Amity	60CCJC2	410656
China People's Rep	Germany, East	18 Jan 60	General Economic	8EGDA333	419096
China People's Rep	Germany, East	23 Mar 60	General Trade	60CCJC49	410692

PARTY ONE	PARTY TWO	DATE	TOPIC	CITATION	NUMBER
China People's Rep	Germany, East	15 May 61	General Economic	61CCJC76	410797
China People's Rep	Germany, East	15 Jun 61	Finance	61CCJC84	410801
China People's Rep	Germany, East	04 Aug 62	General Economic	62CCJC77	410910
China People's Rep	Germany, East	07 Jun 63	Culture	63CCJC70	410984
China People's Rep	Germany, East	22 Jun 63	General Economic	63CCJC80	410991
China People's Rep	Germany, East	16 Jan 64	Health/Educ/Welfare	12EGDA726	419097
China People's Rep	Germany, East	01 Aug 64	General Economic	64CCJC106	411160
China People's Rep	Germany, East	19 Feb 65	General Economic	65CCJC20	411179
China People's Rep	Germany, East	03 May 65	Culture	65CCJC59	411164
China People's Rep	Germany, East	15 Jul 65	Education	48EGDZ339	420098
China People's Rep	Germany, East	15 Jul 65	Education	65CCJC94	411181
China People's Rep	Germany, East	22 Nov 65	Scientific Project	65CCJC146	411184
China People's Rep	Germany, East	25 Mar 66	General Economic	66CCJC10	411185
China People's Rep	Germany, East	04 Jul 66	Scientific Project	66CCJC65	411170
China People's Rep	Germany, East	22 Jul 66	Culture	66CCJC70	411187
China People's Rep	Germany, East	14 Apr 67	General Economic	67CCJC13	411192
China People's Rep	Germany, West	27 Sep 57	General Trade	57CCJC91	410451
China People's Rep	Germany, West	27 Sep 57	General Trade	57CCJC90	410450
China People's Rep	Germany, West	27 Sep 57	Dispute Settlement	57CCJC92	410452
China People's Rep	Ghana	18 Aug 61	Culture	61CCJC111	410820
China People's Rep	Ghana	18 Aug 61	Milit Assistance	61CCJC110	410819
China People's Rep	Ghana	18 Aug 61	General Amity	61CCJC108	410817
China People's Rep	Ghana	18 Aug 61	General Aid	61CCJC109	410818
China People's Rep	Ghana	26 Mar 63	Water Transport	63CCJC36	410963
China People's Rep	Ghana	05 Feb 64	General Trade	64CCJC24	411158
China People's Rep	Ghana	03 Dec 64	General Trade	64CCJC174	411163
China People's Rep	Ghana	19 May 65	Scientific Project	65CCJC67	411180
China People's Rep	Ghana	05 Aug 65	Milit Assistance	65CCJC154	411166
China People's Rep	Guinea	07 Oct 59	Culture	29CCJC595	410637
China People's Rep	Guinea	13 Sep 60	Direct Aid	60CCJC94	410718
China People's Rep	Guinea	13 Sep 60	General Trade	60CCJC95	410719
China People's Rep	Guinea	13 Sep 60	General Amity	60CCJC93	410717
China People's Rep	Guinea	07 Jan 64	General Trade	64CCJC4	411157
China People's Rep	Guinea	05 Aug 64	Mass Media	64CCJC107	411161
China People's Rep	Guinea	05 Jun 65	Culture	65CCJC74	411165
China People's Rep	Guinea	14 Sep 65	Telecommunications	65CCJC115	411183
China People's Rep	Guinea	14 Sep 65	Postal Service	65CCJC114	411182
China People's Rep	Guinea	02 Oct 65	Culture	65CCJC127	411167
China People's Rep	Guinea	01 Feb 66	General Trade	66CCJC2	411168
China People's Rep	Guinea	30 Apr 66	Culture	66CCJC24	411186
China People's Rep	Guinea	02 Jun 66	Scientific Project	66CCJC46	411169
China People's Rep	Guinea	16 Nov 66	Direct Aid	66CCJC93	411189
China People's Rep	Guinea	16 Nov 66	Loans and Credits	66CCJC94	411190
China People's Rep	Guinea	16 Nov 66	General Economic	66CCJC92	411188
China People's Rep	Guinea	16 Nov 66	General Trade	66CCJC95	411191
China People's Rep	Hungary	22 Jan 51	General Economic	51CCJC3	410026
China People's Rep	Hungary	12 Jul 51	Culture	51CCJC21	410041
China People's Rep	Hungary	30 Mar 53	General Economic	53CCJC17	410098
China People's Rep	Hungary	16 Jul 53	Telecommunications	53CCJC41	410113
China People's Rep	Hungary	16 Jul 53	Postal Service	53CCJC40	410112
China People's Rep	Hungary	03 Oct 53	Scientific Project	53CCJC56	410119
China People's Rep	Hungary	15 Oct 53	Mass Media	53CCJC57	410120
China People's Rep	Hungary	28 Dec 54	Sanitation	54CCJC96	410200
China People's Rep	Hungary	26 Apr 55	General Economic	55CCJC32	410232
China People's Rep	Hungary	27 Jan 56	General Economic	56CCJC15	410303
China People's Rep	Hungary	08 Jun 57	General Economic	57CCJC65	410432
China People's Rep	Hungary	21 Mar 58	General Economic	58CCJC30	410504
China People's Rep	Hungary	17 May 58	Scientific Project	58CCJC62	410526
China People's Rep	Hungary	17 Mar 59	General Economic	59CCJC49	410602
China People's Rep	Hungary	06 Apr 59	Mass Media	59CCJC62	410611
China People's Rep	Hungary	06 May 59	General Amity	59CCJC75	410621
China People's Rep	Hungary	28 Feb 60	General Economic	60CCJC29	410677
China People's Rep	Hungary	15 Jul 61	General Economic	61CCJC102	410813
China People's Rep	Hungary	15 Jul 61	Finance	61CCJC100	410812
China People's Rep	Hungary	30 Mar 62	General Economic	62CCJC33	410880

PARTY ONE	PARTY TWO	DATE	TOPIC	CITATION	NUMBER
China People's Rep	Hungary	10 Apr 63	General Economic	63CCJC42	410968
China People's Rep	Hungary	31 Jan 64	Mass Media	64CCJC20	411195
China People's Rep	Hungary	28 Mar 64	General Economic	64CCJC42	411197
China People's Rep	Hungary	26 Mar 65	General Economic	65CCJC46	411198
China People's Rep	Hungary	28 May 65	Scientific Project	65CCJC71	411199
China People's Rep	Hungary	05 Jun 65	Culture	65CCJC73	411193
China People's Rep	Hungary	20 Feb 66	General Economic	66CCJC5	411200
China People's Rep	Hungary	20 Jul 66	Culture	66CCJC69	411201
China People's Rep	Hungary	09 Aug 66	Scientific Project	66CCJC76	411194
China People's Rep	Hungary	22 Jun 67	General Economic	67CCJC25	411202
China People's Rep	India	29 Apr 54	Specif Claim/Waive	54CCJC23	410145
China People's Rep	India	29 Apr 54	General Economic	54CCJC22	410144
China People's Rep	India	29 Apr 54	General Trade	299UNTS57	104307
China People's Rep	India	14 Oct 54	General Trade	54CCJC74	410181
China People's Rep	India	14 Oct 54	General Trade	54CCJC72	410179
China People's Rep	India	14 Oct 54	Privil/Immunities	54CCJC73	410180
China People's Rep	India	01 Apr 55	Specific Property	55CCJC20	410223
China People's Rep	Indonesia	30 Nov 53	General Trade	53CCJC68	410128
China People's Rep	Indonesia	01 Sep 54	Finance	54CCJC55	410169
China People's Rep	Indonesia	01 Sep 54	General Trade	54CCJC54	410168
China People's Rep	Indonesia	22 Apr 55	Consul/Citizenship	55CCJC28	410230
China People's Rep	Indonesia	03 Nov 56	Direct Aid	56CCJC129	410379
China People's Rep	Indonesia	03 Nov 56	General Trade	56CCJC126	410377
China People's Rep	Indonesia	03 Nov 56	Finance	56CCJC128	410378
China People's Rep	Indonesia	01 Apr 61	General Amity	61CCJC43	410774
China People's Rep	Indonesia	01 Apr 61	Culture	61CCJC44	410775
China People's Rep	Indonesia	11 Oct 61	General Aid	61CCJC134	410837
China People's Rep	Indonesia	01 Nov 62	Scientific Project	62CCJC98	410924
China People's Rep	Indonesia	06 Nov 64	Air Transport	64CCJC161	411203
China People's Rep	Indonesia	12 Jan 65	Visas	65CCJC4	411209
China People's Rep	Indonesia	28 Jan 65	Direct Aid	65CCJC11	411210
China People's Rep	Indonesia	28 Jan 65	Loans and Credits	65CCJC12	411211
China People's Rep	Indonesia	16 Mar 65	Tech Assistance	65CCJC28	411212
China People's Rep	Indonesia	24 Jul 65	Water Transport	65CCJC100	411213
China People's Rep	Indonesia	14 Sep 65	Non-IBRD Project	65CCJC117	411214
China People's Rep	Indonesia	30 Sep 65	General Trade	65CCJC123	411216
China People's Rep	Indonesia	30 Sep 65	Finance	65CCJC124	411217
China People's Rep	Indonesia	30 Sep 65	Direct Aid	65CCJC122	411215
China People's Rep	Iraq	03 Jan 59	General Economic	59CCJC2	410566
China People's Rep	Iraq	03 Jan 59	General Trade	59CCJC3	410567
China People's Rep	Iraq	04 Apr 59	Culture	59CCJC61	410610
China People's Rep	Iraq	18 Oct 61	General Trade	61CCJC140	410840
China People's Rep	Iraq	23 Sep 64	General Trade	64CCJC123	411207
China People's Rep	Iraq	04 Jun 66	Culture	66CCJC48	411204
China People's Rep	Iraq	04 Jun 66	Mass Media	66CCJC49	411205
China People's Rep	Japan	15 Apr 55	Territory Boundary	55CCJC25	410227
China People's Rep	Japan	15 Apr 55	Specif Claim/Waive	55CCJC26	410228
China People's Rep	Japan	15 Apr 55	Specific Resources	55CCJC24	410226
China People's Rep	Japan	04 May 55	General Trade	55CCJC36	410234
China People's Rep	Japan	27 Nov 55	Culture	55CCJC90	410275
China People's Rep	Japan	05 Mar 58	General Trade	58CCJC24	410499
China People's Rep	Japan	09 Nov 62	General Trade	62CCJC103	410928
China People's Rep	Japan	27 Dec 62	General Trade	62CCJC118	410939
China People's Rep	Japan	09 Nov 63	Dispute Settlement	63CCJC131	411030
China People's Rep	Japan	09 Nov 63	Specific Resources	63CCJC129	411028
China People's Rep	Japan	09 Nov 63	General Ad Hoc	63CCJC130	411029
China People's Rep	Japan	05 Aug 65	Specific Resources	65CCJC104	411218
China People's Rep	Japan	17 Dec 65	Specific Resources	65CCJC156	411219
China People's Rep	Kenya	10 May 64	Direct Aid	64CCJC64	411229
China People's Rep	Korea, North	25 Dec 49	Postal Service	49CCJC1	410383
China People's Rep	Korea, North	25 Dec 49	Telecommunications	49CCJC3	410384
China People's Rep	Korea, North	25 Dec 49	Telecommunications	49CCJC4	410385
China People's Rep	Korea, North	18 Aug 50	General Trade	50CCJC25	410020
China People's Rep	Korea, North	23 Nov 53	Health/Educ/Welfare	53CCJC66	410126
China People's Rep	Korea, North	30 Mar 54	Postal Service	54CCJC11	410137

PARTY ONE	PARTY TWO	DATE	TOPIC	CITATION	NUMBER
China People's Rep	Korea, North	30 Jun 54	General Trade	54CCJC41	410159
China People's Rep	Korea, North	14 Jan 56	Specific Resources	56CCJC10	410299
China People's Rep	Korea, North	30 May 56	Culture	56CCJC68	410339
China People's Rep	Korea, North	13 Aug 56	Mass Media	56CCJC92	410356
China People's Rep	Korea, North	02 Sep 56	Specific Resources	56CCJC97	410360
China People's Rep	Korea, North	10 Apr 57	Sanitation	57CCJC40	410418
China People's Rep	Korea, North	07 Jun 57	Telecommunications	57CCJC60	410428
China People's Rep	Korea, North	07 Jun 57	Postal Service	57CCJC59	410427
China People's Rep	Korea, North	31 Dec 57	Scientific Project	57CCJC129	410479
China People's Rep	Korea, North	31 Dec 57	Scientific Project	57CCJC130	410480
China People's Rep	Korea, North	21 Jan 58	General Trade	58CCJC10	410488
China People's Rep	Korea, North	27 Sep 58	Specif Goods/Equip	58CCJC88	410545
China People's Rep	Korea, North	19 Nov 58	General Trade	58CCJC99	410554
China People's Rep	Korea, North	18 Feb 59	Air Transport	59CCJC34	410589
China People's Rep	Korea, North	21 Feb 59	Culture	59CCJC38	410592
China People's Rep	Korea, North	29 Feb 60	General Trade	60CCJC31	410678
China People's Rep	Korea, North	23 May 60	Water Transport	60CCJC66	410702
China People's Rep	Korea, North	11 Jul 61	General Amity	61CCJC96	410809
China People's Rep	Korea, North	08 Jan 62	General Trade	62CCJC1	410854
China People's Rep	Korea, North	05 Nov 62	General Amity	62CCJC100	410925
China People's Rep	Korea, North	14 Oct 63	General Trade	63CCJC118	411019
China People's Rep	Korea, North	24 Sep 64	General Trade	64CCJC126	411232
China People's Rep	Korea, North	27 Dec 64	Mass Media	64CCJC188	411237
China People's Rep	Korea, North	18 Jun 65	Commodity Trade	65CCJC85	411238
China People's Rep	Korea, North	30 Jul 65	Culture	65CCJC102	411239
China People's Rep	Korea, North	01 Nov 65	Scientific Project	65CCJC135	411221
China People's Rep	Korea, North	09 Nov 65	Sanitation	65CCJC138	411222
China People's Rep	Korea, North	18 Nov 65	Land Transport	65CCJC144	411240
China People's Rep	Korea, North	02 Dec 65	Water Transport	65CCJC150	411223
China People's Rep	Korea, North	14 Dec 65	General Trade	65CCJC154	411241
China People's Rep	Korea, North	25 Feb 66	Culture	66CCJC6	411242
China People's Rep	Korea, North	01 Jun 66	Sanitation	66CCJC44	411224
China People's Rep	Korea, North	05 Jul 66	Tech Assistance	66CCJC66	411225
China People's Rep	Korea, North	30 Jul 66	Direct Aid	66CCJC74	411243
China People's Rep	Korea, North	03 Dec 66	General Trade	66CCJC103	411226
China People's Rep	Korea, North	30 Dec 66	Mass Media	66CCJC106	411244
China People's Rep	Lebanon	31 Dec 55	General Trade	55CCJC111	410292
China People's Rep	Lebanon	31 Dec 55	General Trade	55CCJC112	410293
China People's Rep	Lebanon	31 Dec 55	General Trade	55CCJC110	410291
China People's Rep	Malagasy	13 Aug 66	Tech Assistance	66CCJC77	411264
China People's Rep	Mali	28 Feb 61	General Trade	61CCJC27	410761
China People's Rep	Mali	22 Sep 61	General Aid	61CCJC125	410830
China People's Rep	Mali	15 May 63	Culture	63CCJC58	410976
China People's Rep	Mali	31 Aug 63	Mass Media	63CCJC103	411007
China People's Rep	Mali	03 Nov 64	General Amity	64CCJC157	411246
China People's Rep	Mali	17 Mar 65	Direct Aid	65CCJC30	411257
China People's Rep	Mali	17 Apr 65	Culture	65CCJC54	411259
China People's Rep	Mali	15 Jul 65	Specific Property	65CCJC95	411260
China People's Rep	Mali	13 May 66	Culture	66CCJC33	411262
China People's Rep	Mali	09 Jun 66	Loans and Credits	66CCJC51	411250
China People's Rep	Mali	14 Aug 67	Direct Aid	67CCJC30	411269
China People's Rep	Mauritania	16 Feb 67	Direct Aid	67CCJC6	411267
China People's Rep	Mauritania	16 Feb 67	Culture	67CCJC7	411268
China People's Rep	Mauritania	16 Feb 67	General Trade	67CCJC5	411266
China People's Rep	Mongolia	04 Oct 52	Health/Educ/Welfare	52CCJC54	410078
China People's Rep	Mongolia	16 Jan 53	Telecommunications	53CCJC3	410088
China People's Rep	Mongolia	16 Jan 53	Postal Service	53CCJC2	410087
China People's Rep	Mongolia	07 Apr 54	General Economic	54CCJC14	410139
China People's Rep	Mongolia	16 Dec 54	General Trade	54CCJC85	410190
China People's Rep	Mongolia	21 Dec 55	Mass Media	55CCJC98	410282
China People's Rep	Mongolia	07 Feb 56	General Trade	56CCJC20	410307
China People's Rep	Mongolia	25 Feb 56	Postal Service	56CCJC37	410321
China People's Rep	Mongolia	29 Aug 56	Direct Aid	56CCJC96	410359
China People's Rep	Mongolia	22 Dec 56	General Trade	56CCJC141	410390
China People's Rep	Mongolia	17 Jan 58	Air Transport	58CCJC6	410484

PARTY ONE	PARTY TWO	DATE	TOPIC	CITATION	NUMBER
China People's Rep	Mongolia	24 Jan 58	Air Transport	58CCJC13	410490
China People's Rep	Mongolia	28 Jan 58	General Trade	58CCJC14	410491
China People's Rep	Mongolia	21 Feb 58	Culture	58CCJC19	410494
China People's Rep	Mongolia	30 Jan 59	General Trade	59CCJC21	410581
China People's Rep	Mongolia	23 Feb 60	General Trade	60CCJC23	410673
China People's Rep	Mongolia	06 May 60	Mass Media	60CCJC60	410699
China People's Rep	Mongolia	31 May 60	General Amity	60CCJC72	410705
China People's Rep	Mongolia	31 May 60	Tech Assistance	60CCJC74	410707
China People's Rep	Mongolia	26 Apr 61	General Trade	61CCJC70	410793
China People's Rep	Mongolia	26 Apr 61	General Amity	61CCJC69	410792
China People's Rep	Mongolia	25 Feb 62	General Trade	62CCJC20	410869
China People's Rep	Mongolia	26 Dec 62	Territory Boundary	62CCJC117	410938
China People's Rep	Mongolia	18 Mar 63	General Trade	63CCJC34	410961
China People's Rep	Mongolia	20 Jan 64	General Trade	64CCJC13	411252
China People's Rep	Mongolia	30 Jun 64	Territory Boundary	64CCJC90	411255
China People's Rep	Mongolia	24 Mar 65	General Trade	65CCJC38	411258
China People's Rep	Mongolia	09 Jun 65	Culture	65CCJC80	411249
China People's Rep	Mongolia	28 Mar 66	General Trade	66CCJC11	411261
China People's Rep	Mongolia	30 May 66	Tech Assistance	66CCJC42	411263
China People's Rep	Mongolia	29 Sep 66	Culture	66CCJC82	411265
China People's Rep	Morocco	27 Oct 61	Finance	61CCJC145	410844
China People's Rep	Morocco	30 Mar 63	General Trade	63CCJC39	410966
China People's Rep	Multilateral	26 Mar 56	IGO Establishment	259UNTS125	103686
China People's Rep	Nepal	20 Sep 56	Consul/Citizenship	56CCJC106	410367
China People's Rep	Nepal	20 Sep 56	Consul/Citizenship	56CCJC105	410366
China People's Rep	Nepal	20 Sep 56	General Amity	56CCJC104	410365
China People's Rep	Nepal	07 Oct 56	Finance	56CCJC112	410369
China People's Rep	Nepal	07 Oct 56	Finance	56CCJC113	410370
China People's Rep	Nepal	07 Oct 56	Direct Aid	56CCJC111	410368
China People's Rep	Nepal	21 Mar 60	Direct Aid	60CCJC48	410691
China People's Rep	Nepal	21 Mar 60	Territory Boundary	60CCJC47	410690
China People's Rep	Nepal	28 Apr 60	General Amity	60CCJC58	410698
China People's Rep	Nepal	05 Oct 61	Territory Boundary	61CCJC128	410832
China People's Rep	Nepal	15 Oct 61	Non-IBRD Project	61CCJC138	410839
China People's Rep	Nepal	14 Aug 62	Consul/Citizenship	62CCJC79	410911
China People's Rep	Nepal	20 Jan 63	Territory Boundary	63CCJC10	410947
China People's Rep	Nepal	11 Oct 64	Culture	64CCJC147	411276
China People's Rep	Nepal	21 Jan 65	Postal Service	65CCJC8	411277
China People's Rep	Nepal	29 Aug 65	Non-IBRD Project	65CCJC109	411278
China People's Rep	Nepal	03 Sep 65	Culture	65CCJC111	411272
China People's Rep	Nepal	02 May 66	General Trade	66CCJC26	411273
China People's Rep	Nepal	18 Oct 66	Direct Aid	66CCJC85	411280
China People's Rep	Nepal	21 Dec 66	Direct Aid	66CCJC104	411281
China People's Rep	Nepal	14 Mar 67	Direct Aid	67CCJC10	411282
China People's Rep	Nepal	25 May 67	Non-IBRD Project	67CCJC20	411283
China People's Rep	Nepal	28 May 67	Non-IBRD Project	67CCJC21	411284
China People's Rep	Norway	04 Jun 58	General Economic	3NORT742	451022
China People's Rep	Norway	04 Jun 58	General Economic	58CCJC65	410527
China People's Rep	Norway	04 Apr 61	Visas	61CCJC45	410776
China People's Rep	Norway	04 Apr 61	Visas	3NORT829	451023
China People's Rep	Norway	18 Jun 63	Culture	3NORT890	451024
China People's Rep	Norway	18 Jun 63	Culture	63CCJC76	410987
China People's Rep	Norway	30 Apr 66	Culture	66CCJC23	411279
China People's Rep	Norway	02 Dec 67	Consul/Citizenship	3NORT1008	451025
China People's Rep	Pakistan	14 Mar 53	Commodity Trade	53CCJC11	410094
China People's Rep	Pakistan	19 Mar 56	Direct Aid	56CCJC41	410325
China People's Rep	Pakistan	03 Jun 58	Commodity Trade	58CCJC64	410431
China People's Rep	Pakistan	04 Oct 58	Mostfavored Nation	58CCJC89	410546
China People's Rep	Pakistan	02 Mar 63	Territory Boundary	63CCJC28	410957
China People's Rep	Pakistan	29 Aug 63	Air Transport	63CCJC101	411005
China People's Rep	Pakistan	18 Feb 65	Direct Aid	65CCJC19	411295
China People's Rep	Pakistan	26 Mar 65	Culture	65CCJC45	411298
China People's Rep	Pakistan	26 Mar 65	Territory Boundary	65CCJC44	411297
China People's Rep	Pakistan	01 Nov 65	Direct Aid	65CCJC134	411288
China People's Rep	Pakistan	01 Jun 66	Culture	66CCJC45	411289

PARTY ONE	PARTY TWO	DATE	TOPIC	CITATION	NUMBER
China People's Rep	Pakistan	23 Jun 66	Direct Aid	66CCJC56	411303
China People's Rep	Pakistan	04 Jul 66	General Trade	66CCJC64	411290
China People's Rep	Pakistan	21 Oct 66	Water Transport	66CCJC87	411305
China People's Rep	Pakistan	17 Jan 67	Direct Aid	67CCJC1	411306
China People's Rep	Pakistan	14 Sep 67	Culture	67CCJC34	411308
China People's Rep	Poland	29 Jan 51	General Economic	51CCJC4	410027
China People's Rep	Poland	29 Jan 51	Postal Service	51CCJC6	410029
China People's Rep	Poland	29 Jan 51	Telecommunications	51CCJC5	410028
China People's Rep	Poland	29 Jan 51	Water Transport	51CCJC7	410030
China People's Rep	Poland	03 Apr 51	Culture	304UNTS187	104396
China People's Rep	Poland	03 Apr 51	Culture	51CCJC12	410033
China People's Rep	Poland	25 May 53	General Economic	53CCJC27	410103
China People's Rep	Poland	15 Oct 53	Mass Media	53PZUM115	458012
China People's Rep	Poland	15 Oct 53	Mass Media	53CCJC58	410121
China People's Rep	Poland	19 Feb 54	General Economic	54CCJC5	410133
China People's Rep	Poland	20 Jul 54	Scientific Project	54PZUM50	458019
China People's Rep	Poland	20 Jul 54	Scientific Project	54CCJC47	410164
China People's Rep	Poland	21 Mar 55	General Economic	55CCJC16	410221
China People's Rep	Poland	21 Dec 55	General Trade	55CCJC99	410283
China People's Rep	Poland	24 Feb 56	Gen Communications	56CCJC35	410319
China People's Rep	Poland	25 Feb 56	Postal Service	56PZUM109	458040
China People's Rep	Poland	25 Feb 56	Gen Communications	56CCJC36	410320
China People's Rep	Poland	23 Apr 56	Scientific Project	56CCJC53	410332
China People's Rep	Poland	14 Jul 56	Education	56CCJC86	410351
China People's Rep	Poland	01 Apr 57	General Trade	57CCJC34	410414
China People's Rep	Poland	29 Oct 57	Sanitation	57CCJC102	410457
China People's Rep	Poland	07 Apr 58	General Trade	58CCJC47	410514
China People's Rep	Poland	14 Feb 59	General Trade	59CCJC26	410585
China People's Rep	Poland	06 Mar 59	General Trade	59CCJC43	410597
China People's Rep	Poland	15 Apr 59	Mass Media	59CCJC66	410615
China People's Rep	Poland	15 May 61	Finance	61CCJC75	410796
China People's Rep	Poland	10 Jul 61	General Trade	61CCJC95	410808
China People's Rep	Poland	16 Mar 65	General Economic	65CCJC29	411296
China People's Rep	Poland	26 Apr 65	Scientific Project	65CCJC56	411299
China People's Rep	Poland	05 May 65	Culture	65CCJC62	411287
China People's Rep	Poland	15 Dec 65	Scientific Project	65CCJC155	411300
China People's Rep	Poland	22 Mar 66	General Economic	66CCJC9	411301
China People's Rep	Poland	20 Jun 66	Scientific Project	66CCJC54	411302
China People's Rep	Poland	24 Jun 66	Culture	66CCJC57	411304
China People's Rep	Poland	30 Jun 67	General Economic	67CCJC26	411307
China People's Rep	Romania	12 Dec 51	Culture	51CCJC27	410047
China People's Rep	Romania	30 Jul 52	General Economic	52CCJC42	410072
China People's Rep	Romania	09 Jan 53	Scientific Project	53CCJC1	410086
China People's Rep	Romania	19 Jan 53	General Trade	53CCJC4	410089
China People's Rep	Romania	15 Oct 53	Mass Media	53CCJC59	410122
China People's Rep	Romania	19 Apr 54	General Economic	54CCJC16	410140
China People's Rep	Romania	20 Jan 55	General Economic	55CCJC3	410210
China People's Rep	Romania	30 Jul 55	Gen Communications	55CCJC53	410246
China People's Rep	Romania	03 Jan 56	General Economic	56CCJC2	410295
China People's Rep	Romania	19 Apr 57	General Economic	57CCJC46	410422
China People's Rep	Romania	30 Mar 58	General Economic	58CCJC36	410508
China People's Rep	Romania	22 Mar 59	General Economic	59CCJC55	410607
China People's Rep	Romania	13 Apr 59	Scientific Project	59CCJC64	410613
China People's Rep	Romania	15 Mar 60	General Economic	60CCJC39	410685
China People's Rep	Romania	07 Jul 61	General Economic	61CCJC93	410807
China People's Rep	Romania	29 May 62	General Economic	62CCJC52	410893
China People's Rep	Romania	08 Apr 63	General Economic	63CCJC40	410967
China People's Rep	Romania	08 Jun 63	Scientific Project	63CCJC71	410985
China People's Rep	Romania	06 Jul 63	Scientific Project	63CCJC86	410994
China People's Rep	Romania	27 Dec 63	General Economic	63CCJC151	411041
China People's Rep	Romania	03 Oct 64	Mass Media	64CCJC140	411310
China People's Rep	Romania	15 May 65	Scientific Project	65CCJC66	411314
China People's Rep	Romania	27 May 65	Culture	65CCJC70	411315
China People's Rep	Romania	27 May 65	Culture	592UNTS3	108566
China People's Rep	Romania	01 Dec 65	Scientific Project	65CCJC149	411312

PARTY ONE	PARTY TWO	DATE	TOPIC	CITATION	NUMBER
China People's Rep	Romania	21 Dec 65	General Trade	65CCJC159	411316
China People's Rep	Romania	11 Feb 66	Culture	66CCJC4	411317
China People's Rep	Romania	31 Jul 66	Scientific Project	66CCJC75	411318
China People's Rep	Romania	14 Feb 67	General Economic	67CCJC4	411319
China People's Rep	Somalia	10 Jan 63	Culture	63CCJC6	410943
China People's Rep	Somalia	15 May 63	General Economic	63CCJC61	410979
China People's Rep	Somalia	17 Aug 65	Culture	65CCJC107	411324
China People's Rep	Somalia	11 Jun 66	Culture	66CCJC53	411326
China People's Rep	Somalia	23 Oct 66	Non-ILO Labor	66CCJC88	411328
China People's Rep	Somalia	19 Aug 67	Culture	67CCJC32	411330
China People's Rep	Sudan	12 Apr 56	General Trade	56CCJC50	410330
China People's Rep	Sudan	23 May 62	General Trade	62CCJC49	410891
China People's Rep	Sudan	27 Jul 66	General Trade	66CCJC72	411327
China People's Rep	Sweden	24 Jun 55	Consul/Citizenship	228UNTS153	103148
China People's Rep	Sweden	24 Jun 55	Consul/Citizenship	55CCJC45	410239
China People's Rep	Sweden	08 Apr 57	Patents/Copyrights	57CCJC38	410416
China People's Rep	Sweden	08 Apr 57	Patents/Copyrights	428UNTS267	106179
China People's Rep	Sweden	08 Nov 57	General Trade	57CCJC108	410462
China People's Rep	Switzerland	14 Apr 57	Patents/Copyrights	57CCJC23	410405
China People's Rep	Syria	30 Nov 55	Finance	55CCJC93	410278
China People's Rep	Syria	30 Nov 55	General Trade	55CCJC92	410277
China People's Rep	Syria	12 Jun 56	Culture	56CCJC72	410342
China People's Rep	Syria	12 Jun 56	Culture	56CCJC71	410341
China People's Rep	Syria	03 Jul 57	General Trade	57CCJC69	410434
China People's Rep	Syria	21 Feb 63	General Trade	63CCJC15	410949
China People's Rep	Syria	21 Feb 63	Direct Aid	63CCJC17	410951
China People's Rep	Syria	21 Feb 63	Finance	63CCJC16	410950
China People's Rep	Syria	18 Mar 65	Culture	65CCJC31	411323
China People's Rep	Syria	06 Oct 65	Mass Media	65CCJC130	411322
China People's Rep	Syria	20 Apr 66	Culture	66CCJC19	411325
China People's Rep	Syria	13 Apr 67	Tech Assistance	67CCJC12	411329
China People's Rep	Tanganyika	13 Dec 62	Culture	62CCJC114	410935
China People's Rep	Tanzania	16 Jun 64	Direct Aid	64CCJC85	411335
China People's Rep	Tanzania	05 Jan 65	Tech Assistance	65CCJC3	411332
China People's Rep	Tanzania	05 Jan 65	Direct Aid	65CCJC2	411331
China People's Rep	Tanzania	10 Feb 65	General Trade	65CCJC16	411337
China People's Rep	Tanzania	10 Feb 65	General Trade	65CCJC15	411336
China People's Rep	Tanzania	20 Feb 65	General Amity	65CCJC21	411338
China People's Rep	Tanzania	22 Apr 66	Water Transport	66CCJC21	411339
China People's Rep	Tanzania	07 May 66	Culture	66CCJC29	411333
China People's Rep	Tanzania	08 Jun 66	General Economic	66CCJC50	411334
China People's Rep	Tanzania	10 Oct 66	Direct Aid	66CCJC83	411340
China People's Rep	Tunisia	25 Sep 58	General Trade	58CCJC84	410541
China People's Rep	Uganda	21 Apr 65	Direct Aid	65CCJC55	411353
China People's Rep	UK Great Britain	06 Jul 53	General Trade	53CCJC39	410111
China People's Rep	UK Great Britain	20 Sep 53	Reparations	53CCJC54	410118
China People's Rep	UK Great Britain	01 Jun 56	Patents/Copyrights	56CCJC69	410340
China People's Rep	United Arab Rep	22 Aug 55	General Trade	55CCJC58	410251
China People's Rep	United Arab Rep	22 Aug 55	General Trade	55CCJC59	410252
China People's Rep	United Arab Rep	15 Apr 56	Culture	56CCJC51	410331
China People's Rep	United Arab Rep	20 May 56	Culture	56CCJC66	410337
China People's Rep	United Arab Rep	22 Oct 56	General Trade	56CCJC117	410371
China People's Rep	United Arab Rep	22 Oct 56	Finance	56CCJC118	410372
China People's Rep	United Arab Rep	21 Dec 57	General Trade	57CCJC122	410474
China People's Rep	United Arab Rep	25 Aug 58	Postal Service	58CCJC81	410538
China People's Rep	United Arab Rep	15 Dec 58	Finance	58CCJC105	410558
China People's Rep	United Arab Rep	15 Dec 58	General Trade	58CCJC106	410559
China People's Rep	United Arab Rep	15 Dec 58	General Trade	58CCJC104	410557
China People's Rep	United Arab Rep	05 Feb 61	General Trade	61CCJC23	410758
China People's Rep	United Arab Rep	17 Mar 62	Finance	62CCJC25	410874
China People's Rep	United Arab Rep	17 Mar 62	General Trade	62CCJC24	410873
China People's Rep	United Arab Rep	17 Mar 62	General Trade	62CCJC26	410875
China People's Rep	United Arab Rep	05 Jan 63	Telecommunications	63CCJC2	410942
China People's Rep	United Arab Rep	14 Jul 63	General Trade	63CCJC88	410995
China People's Rep	United Arab Rep	22 Dec 64	General Trade	64CCJC186	411351

PARTY ONE	PARTY TWO	DATE	TOPIC	CITATION	NUMBER
China People's Rep	United Arab Rep	22 Dec 64	Direct Aid	64CCJC184	411350
China People's Rep	United Arab Rep	13 Jan 65	Tech Assistance	65CCJC5	411352
China People's Rep	United Arab Rep	02 May 65	Air Transport	65CCJC58	411341
China People's Rep	United Arab Rep	04 May 66	General Trade	66CCJC28	411343
China People's Rep	United Arab Rep	07 May 66	Culture	66CCJC30	411344
China People's Rep	United Arab Rep	25 May 67	General Trade	67CCJC19	411360
China People's Rep	USA (United States)	10 Sep 55	Extradition	55CCJC63	410255
China People's Rep	USSR (Soviet Union)	02 Oct 49	Consul/Citizenship	0SUST263	468068
China People's Rep	USSR (Soviet Union)	07 Feb 50	Postal Service	0SUST268	468069
China People's Rep	USSR (Soviet Union)	07 Feb 50	Gen Communications	50CCJC2	410002
China People's Rep	USSR (Soviet Union)	07 Feb 50	Gen Communications	50CCJC1	410386
China People's Rep	USSR (Soviet Union)	07 Feb 50	Telecommunications	0SUST268	468070
China People's Rep	USSR (Soviet Union)	14 Feb 50	Specific Property	0SUST270	468071
China People's Rep	USSR (Soviet Union)	14 Feb 50	Consul/Citizenship	50CCJC5	410004
China People's Rep	USSR (Soviet Union)	14 Feb 50	Milit Installation	0SUST270	468072
China People's Rep	USSR (Soviet Union)	14 Feb 50	Loans and Credits	226UNTS21	103104
China People's Rep	USSR (Soviet Union)	14 Feb 50	General Amity	226UNTS3	103103
China People's Rep	USSR (Soviet Union)	14 Feb 50	Privil/Immunities	226UNTS31	103105
China People's Rep	USSR (Soviet Union)	14 Feb 50	Loans and Credits	50CCJC6	410005
China People's Rep	USSR (Soviet Union)	14 Feb 50	General Amity	50CCJC4	410003
China People's Rep	USSR (Soviet Union)	27 Mar 50	Specific Property	0SUST272	468074
China People's Rep	USSR (Soviet Union)	27 Mar 50	Specific Property	0SUST272	468075
China People's Rep	USSR (Soviet Union)	27 Mar 50	Specific Property	0SUST272	468073
China People's Rep	USSR (Soviet Union)	27 Mar 50	Specif Goods/Equip	50CCJC15	410011
China People's Rep	USSR (Soviet Union)	27 Mar 50	Specif Goods/Equip	50CCJC14	410010
China People's Rep	USSR (Soviet Union)	27 Mar 50	Privil/Immunities	0SUST272	468076
China People's Rep	USSR (Soviet Union)	27 Mar 50	Non-ILO Labor	50CCJC16	410012
China People's Rep	USSR (Soviet Union)	27 Mar 50	Specif Goods/Equip	50CCJC13	410009
China People's Rep	USSR (Soviet Union)	19 Apr 50	General Trade	50CCJC18	410014
China People's Rep	USSR (Soviet Union)	19 Apr 50	General Trade	0SUST273	468077
China People's Rep	USSR (Soviet Union)	19 Apr 50	General Trade	50CCJC17	410013
China People's Rep	USSR (Soviet Union)	19 Apr 50	General Aid	50CCJC20	410015
China People's Rep	USSR (Soviet Union)	28 Aug 50	Specific Property	50CCJC26	410021
China People's Rep	USSR (Soviet Union)	25 Oct 50	Privil/Immunities	0SUST278	468078
China People's Rep	USSR (Soviet Union)	02 Jan 51	Water Transport	0SUST279	468079
China People's Rep	USSR (Soviet Union)	02 Jan 51	Water Transport	51CCJC1	410024
China People's Rep	USSR (Soviet Union)	14 Mar 51	Land Transport	0SUST280	468080
China People's Rep	USSR (Soviet Union)	15 Jun 51	General Trade	51CCJC17	410038
China People's Rep	USSR (Soviet Union)	28 Jul 51	Specific Property	0SUST282	468081
China People's Rep	USSR (Soviet Union)	06 Dec 51	Education	0SUST283	468082
China People's Rep	USSR (Soviet Union)	06 Dec 51	Tech Assistance	51CCJC26	410046
China People's Rep	USSR (Soviet Union)	12 Apr 52	General Trade	52CCJC5	410050
China People's Rep	USSR (Soviet Union)	09 Aug 52	Education	0SUST289	468083
China People's Rep	USSR (Soviet Union)	09 Aug 52	Education	52CCJC45	410073
China People's Rep	USSR (Soviet Union)	15 Sep 52	Specific Property	0SUST290	468084
China People's Rep	USSR (Soviet Union)	15 Sep 52	Milit Installation	52CCJC49	410076
China People's Rep	USSR (Soviet Union)	15 Sep 52	Milit Installation	226UNTS45	103106
China People's Rep	USSR (Soviet Union)	19 Sep 57	Direct Aid	53CCJC29	410104
China People's Rep	USSR (Soviet Union)	21 Mar 53	General Trade	53CCJC13	410095
China People's Rep	USSR (Soviet Union)	21 Mar 53	Direct Aid	0SUST294	468085
China People's Rep	USSR (Soviet Union)	21 Aug 54	Mass Media	54CCJC51	410166
China People's Rep	USSR (Soviet Union)	21 Aug 54	Mass Media	0SUST315	468086
China People's Rep	USSR (Soviet Union)	12 Oct 54	Tech Assistance	0SUST318	468091
China People's Rep	USSR (Soviet Union)	12 Oct 54	General Amity	226UNTS57	103108
China People's Rep	USSR (Soviet Union)	12 Oct 54	Milit Installation	226UNTS51	103107
China People's Rep	USSR (Soviet Union)	12 Oct 54	General Ad Hoc	0SUST318	468089
China People's Rep	USSR (Soviet Union)	12 Oct 54	Scientific Project	54CCJC65	410174
China People's Rep	USSR (Soviet Union)	12 Oct 54	Specific Property	0SUST317	468087
China People's Rep	USSR (Soviet Union)	12 Oct 54	Health/Educ/Welfare	0SUST318	468088
China People's Rep	USSR (Soviet Union)	12 Oct 54	Loans and Credits	0SUST318	468090
China People's Rep	USSR (Soviet Union)	12 Oct 54	General Amity	226UNTS69	103109
China People's Rep	USSR (Soviet Union)	30 Dec 54	Air Transport	54CCJC99	410202
China People's Rep	USSR (Soviet Union)	30 Dec 54	Air Transport	0SUST321	468092
China People's Rep	USSR (Soviet Union)	12 Feb 55	General Trade	16SUGG68	469904
China People's Rep	USSR (Soviet Union)	12 Feb 55	General Trade	55CCJC10	410215

PARTY ONE	PARTY TWO	DATE	TOPIC	CITATION	NUMBER
China People's Rep	USSR (Soviet Union)	16 Aug 55	Sanitation	55CCJC56	410249
China People's Rep	USSR (Soviet Union)	16 Aug 55	Sanitation	0SUST334	468093
China People's Rep	USSR (Soviet Union)	27 Dec 55	General Trade	16SUGG70	469911
China People's Rep	USSR (Soviet Union)	27 Dec 55	General Trade	55CCJC105	410287
China People's Rep	USSR (Soviet Union)	07 Apr 56	Direct Aid	0SUST353	468094
China People's Rep	USSR (Soviet Union)	07 Apr 56	Direct Aid	0SUST353	468095
China People's Rep	USSR (Soviet Union)	14 Jun 56	General Trade	56CCJC73	410343
China People's Rep	USSR (Soviet Union)	14 Jun 56	Commodity Trade	16SUGG71	469918
China People's Rep	USSR (Soviet Union)	05 Jul 56	Culture	56CCJC84	410349
China People's Rep	USSR (Soviet Union)	05 Jul 56	Culture	263UNTS129	103770
China People's Rep	USSR (Soviet Union)	18 Aug 56	Scientific Project	0SUST366	468096
China People's Rep	USSR (Soviet Union)	18 Sep 56	Specif Goods/Equip	16SUGG73	469927
China People's Rep	USSR (Soviet Union)	24 Dec 56	Scientific Project	56CCJC143	410391
China People's Rep	USSR (Soviet Union)	15 Feb 57	Gen Communications	57CCJC17	410399
China People's Rep	USSR (Soviet Union)	27 Mar 57	Specific Property	16SUGG119	469935
China People's Rep	USSR (Soviet Union)	10 Apr 57	General Trade	57CCJC39	410417
China People's Rep	USSR (Soviet Union)	15 Oct 57	Atomic Energy	16SUGG122	469947
China People's Rep	USSR (Soviet Union)	11 Dec 57	Scientific Project	57CCJC114	410468
China People's Rep	USSR (Soviet Union)	21 Dec 57	Visas	305UNTS213	104420
China People's Rep	USSR (Soviet Union)	21 Dec 57	Water Transport	57CCJC120	410473
China People's Rep	USSR (Soviet Union)	28 Dec 57	Tech Assistance	16SUGG124	469953
China People's Rep	USSR (Soviet Union)	28 Dec 57	Education	16SUGG124	469954
China People's Rep	USSR (Soviet Union)	18 Jan 58	Scientific Project	7SUGG102	469488
China People's Rep	USSR (Soviet Union)	23 Apr 58	General Trade	58CCJC56	410520
China People's Rep	USSR (Soviet Union)	23 Apr 58	General Trade	58CCJC57	410521
China People's Rep	USSR (Soviet Union)	23 Apr 58	General Economic	313UNTS135	104534
China People's Rep	USSR (Soviet Union)	08 Aug 58	Tech Assistance	7SUGG118	469522
China People's Rep	USSR (Soviet Union)	17 Jan 59	General Trade	16SUGG126	469963
China People's Rep	USSR (Soviet Union)	07 Feb 59	Direct Aid	59CCJC24	410583
China People's Rep	USSR (Soviet Union)	07 Feb 59	Tech Assistance	8SUGG136	469558
China People's Rep	USSR (Soviet Union)	01 Jun 59	Scientific Project	59CCJC81	410625
China People's Rep	USSR (Soviet Union)	23 Jun 59	Consul/Citizenship	356UNTS83	105092
China People's Rep	USSR (Soviet Union)	23 Jun 59	Consul/Citizenship	59CCJC86	410629
China People's Rep	USSR (Soviet Union)	29 Jan 60	Specific Resources	60CCJC9	410660
China People's Rep	USSR (Soviet Union)	29 Jan 60	Specific Resources	16SUGG127	469970
China People's Rep	USSR (Soviet Union)	28 May 60	Visas	16SUGG128	469976
China People's Rep	USSR (Soviet Union)	20 Mar 61	Finance	61CCJC38	410770
China People's Rep	USSR (Soviet Union)	07 Apr 61	Direct Aid	10SUGG127	469761
China People's Rep	USSR (Soviet Union)	07 Apr 61	Finance	10SUGG127	469760
China People's Rep	USSR (Soviet Union)	25 May 61	Mass Media	61CCJC79	410799
China People's Rep	USSR (Soviet Union)	19 Jun 61	General Economic	10SUGG136	469778
China People's Rep	USSR (Soviet Union)	19 Jun 61	Scientific Project	10SUGG136	469779
China People's Rep	USSR (Soviet Union)	19 Jun 61	Tech Assistance	16SUGG131	469994
China People's Rep	USSR (Soviet Union)	19 Jun 61	General Aid	16SUGG131	469995
China People's Rep	USSR (Soviet Union)	19 Jun 61	Scientific Project	61CCJC87	410803
China People's Rep	USSR (Soviet Union)	21 Jun 61	Scientific Project	61CCJC88	410804
China People's Rep	USSR (Soviet Union)	29 Apr 65	General Trade	65CCJC57	411354
China People's Rep	USSR (Soviet Union)	25 May 65	Culture	65CCJC69	411355
China People's Rep	USSR (Soviet Union)	12 Jun 65	Scientific Project	65CCJC82	411356
China People's Rep	USSR (Soviet Union)	18 Nov 65	Scientific Project	65CCJC143	411357
China People's Rep	USSR (Soviet Union)	04 Apr 66	Air Transport	66CCJC14	411342
China People's Rep	USSR (Soviet Union)	19 Apr 66	General Trade	66CCJC18	411358
China People's Rep	USSR (Soviet Union)	27 Jun 66	Culture	66CCJC59	411359
China People's Rep	USSR (Soviet Union)	06 Nov 66	Scientific Project	66CCJC91	411345
China People's Rep	USSR (Soviet Union)	27 Jul 67	General Trade	67CCJC27	411361
China People's Rep	Vietnam, North	25 Aug 53	General Trade	53CCJC51	410116
China People's Rep	Vietnam, North	07 Jul 54	General Trade	54CCJC44	410161
China People's Rep	Vietnam, North	24 Dec 54	Postal Service	54CCJC86	410191
China People's Rep	Vietnam, North	24 Dec 54	Telecommunications	54CCJC88	410192
China People's Rep	Vietnam, North	24 Dec 54	Direct Aid	54CCJC90	410194
China People's Rep	Vietnam, North	25 May 55	Land Transport	55CCJC38	410235
China People's Rep	Vietnam, North	07 Jul 55	General Trade	55CCJC48	410241
China People's Rep	Vietnam, North	07 Jul 55	General Trade	55CCJC49	410242
China People's Rep	Vietnam, North	07 Jul 55	Culture	55CCJC47	410240
China People's Rep	Vietnam, North	05 Apr 56	Air Transport	56CCJC45	410327

PARTY ONE	PARTY TWO	DATE	TOPIC	CITATION	NUMBER
China People's Rep	Vietnam, North	18 Jun 56	General Trade	56CCJC74	410344
China People's Rep	Vietnam, North	20 Dec 56	Water Transport	56CCJC139	410388
China People's Rep	Vietnam, North	31 Jul 57	General Economic	57CCJC73	410438
China People's Rep	Vietnam, North	31 Jul 57	General Trade	57CCJC75	410440
China People's Rep	Vietnam, North	15 Mar 58	Mass Media	58CCJC28	410502
China People's Rep	Vietnam, North	31 Mar 58	General Economic	58CCJC38	410509
China People's Rep	Vietnam, North	08 Dec 58	Land Transport	58CCJC102	410556
China People's Rep	Vietnam, North	16 Jan 59	Culture	59CCJC11	410573
China People's Rep	Vietnam, North	18 Feb 59	General Economic	59CCJC28	410587
China People's Rep	Vietnam, North	20 Jun 59	Finance	59CCJC85	410628
China People's Rep	Vietnam, North	27 Jun 59	Scientific Project	59CCJC87	410630
China People's Rep	Vietnam, North	07 Mar 60	General Economic	60CCJC36	410682
China People's Rep	Vietnam, North	28 Nov 60	Scientific Project	60CCJC118	410735
China People's Rep	Vietnam, North	31 Jan 61	Land Transport	61CCJC12	410753
China People's Rep	Vietnam, North	05 Dec 62	General Amity	62CCJC108	410931
China People's Rep	Vietnam, North	05 Dec 62	General Economic	62CCJC109	410932
China People's Rep	Vietnam, North	09 Mar 64	Land Transport	64CCJC36	411363
China People's Rep	Vietnam, North	29 Jul 64	Postal Service	64CCJC102	411370
China People's Rep	Vietnam, North	29 Jul 64	Telecommunications	64CCJC103	411371
China People's Rep	Vietnam, North	31 Jul 64	Sanitation	64CCJC105	411372
China People's Rep	Vietnam, North	12 Sep 64	Air Transport	64CCJC116	411374
China People's Rep	Vietnam, North	19 Jun 65	Culture	65CCJC86	411376
China People's Rep	Vietnam, North	13 Jul 65	Direct Aid	65CCJC90	411377
China People's Rep	Vietnam, North	16 Sep 65	Sanitation	65CCJC118	411378
China People's Rep	Vietnam, North	13 Nov 65	Scientific Project	65CCJC142	411379
China People's Rep	Vietnam, North	03 Dec 65	Tech Assistance	65CCJC151	411364
China People's Rep	Vietnam, North	05 Dec 65	Loans and Credits	65CCJC152	411365
China People's Rep	Vietnam, North	05 Dec 65	General Trade	65CCJC153	411366
China People's Rep	Vietnam, North	21 Mar 66	Land Transport	66CCJC8	411380
China People's Rep	Vietnam, North	22 Apr 66	Tech Assistance	66CCJC20	411381
China People's Rep	Vietnam, North	28 May 66	Culture	66CCJC41	411382
China People's Rep	Vietnam, North	02 Jul 66	Direct Aid	66CCJC63	411367
China People's Rep	Vietnam, North	21 Aug 66	Scientific Project	66CCJC78	411383
China People's Rep	Vietnam, North	29 Aug 66	Direct Aid	66CCJC81	411384
China People's Rep	Vietnam, North	12 Oct 66	Sanitation	66CCJC84	411385
China People's Rep	Vietnam, North	23 Nov 66	General Economic	66CCJC99	411386
China People's Rep	Vietnam, North	25 Apr 67	Culture	67CCJC15	411387
China People's Rep	Vietnam, North	03 Aug 67	Direct Aid	67CCJC28	411368
China People's Rep	Vietnam, North	05 Aug 67	Direct Aid	67CCJC29	411369
China People's Rep	Yemen	12 Jan 58	Health/Educ/Welfare	58CCJC5	410483
China People's Rep	Yemen	12 Jan 58	General Amity	58CCJC3	410481
China People's Rep	Yemen	12 Jan 58	General Trade	58CCJC4	410482
China People's Rep	Yemen	09 Jun 64	Culture	64CCJC80	411390
China People's Rep	Yemen	09 Jun 64	General Amity	64CCJC78	411388
China People's Rep	Yemen	23 Mar 65	Direct Aid	65CCJC37	411393
China People's Rep	Yemen	03 May 65	Culture	65CCJC60	411391
China People's Rep	Yemen	23 May 66	Culture	66CCJC36	411395
China People's Rep	Yugoslavia	14 Feb 56	Telecommunications	56CCJC24	410310
China People's Rep	Yugoslavia	14 Feb 56	Postal Service	56CCJC23	410309
China People's Rep	Yugoslavia	17 Feb 56	Dispute Settlement	56CCJC26	410312
China People's Rep	Yugoslavia	17 Feb 56	Finance	56CCJC27	410313
China People's Rep	Yugoslavia	17 Feb 56	Dispute Settlement	56CCJC28	410314
China People's Rep	Yugoslavia	17 Feb 56	Dispute Settlement	56CCJC30	410316
China People's Rep	Yugoslavia	17 Feb 56	General Trade	56CCJC25	410311
China People's Rep	Yugoslavia	17 Feb 56	Scientific Project	56CCJC29	410315
China People's Rep	Yugoslavia	04 Jan 57	General Transport	57CCJC2	410394
China People's Rep	Yugoslavia	04 Jan 57	General Trade	57CCJC1	410393
China People's Rep	Yugoslavia	07 Jun 57	Culture	57CCJC62	410429
China People's Rep	Yugoslavia	01 Nov 57	Scientific Project	57CCJC103	410458
China People's Rep	Yugoslavia	27 Dec 57	Scientific Project	57CCJC125	410475
China People's Rep	Yugoslavia	29 Mar 58	Culture	58CCJC35	410507
China People's Rep	Yugoslavia	18 Mar 59	General Trade	59CCJC53	410605
China People's Rep	Yugoslavia	25 Mar 60	General Trade	60CCJC52	410694
China People's Rep	Yugoslavia	15 Jul 61	General Trade	61CCJC103	410814
China People's Rep	Yugoslavia	28 Jun 62	General Trade	62CCJC60	410898

PARTY ONE	PARTY TWO	DATE	TOPIC	CITATION	NUMBER
China People's Rep	Yugoslavia	05 Nov 63	General Trade	63CCJC128	411027
China People's Rep	Yugoslavia	11 Jun 64	General Trade	64CCJC82	411392
China People's Rep	Yugoslavia	11 May 65	General Trade	65CCJC63	411394
China People's Rep	Yugoslavia	10 Jun 66	General Trade	66CCJC52	411396
China People's Rep	Zambia	22 Aug 66	Culture	66CCJC80	411397
China People's Rep	Zambia	28 Apr 67	General Trade	67CCJC18	411398
Colombia	Argentina	12 Sep 64	Visas	635UNTS149	109079
Colombia	Argentina	15 Sep 67	Taxation	0UNTS0	109529
Colombia	Argentina	09 Apr 68	General Military	0UNTS0	109566
Colombia	Argentina	27 Mar 69	Culture	0UNTS0	109568
Colombia	Argentina	27 Mar 69	Visas	0UNTS0	109567
Colombia	Belgium	24 May 57	Visas	274UNTS245	103969
Colombia	Belgium	27 Aug 62	Visas	449UNTS199	106461
Colombia	Brazil	28 May 58	Tech Assistance	369UNTS141	105255
Colombia	Brazil	02 Aug 62	Visas	0UNTS0	109422
Colombia	Denmark	26 Jan 51	Finance	87UNTS161	101171
Colombia	Denmark	10 May 68	Loans and Credits	0UNTS0	110482
Colombia	France	28 Apr 53	Patents/Copyrights	62FRRT16	415119
Colombia	France	18 Sep 63	Tech Assistance	65FRRT19	415120
Colombia	Germany, West	19 May 54	Patents/Copyrights	54WBGA184	424367
Colombia	Germany, West	09 Nov 57	General Trade	58WBGA49	424368
Colombia	Germany, West	11 May 59	Patents/Copyrights	61WGBB13	425369
Colombia	Germany, West	11 Oct 60	Culture	65WGBB1948	425370
Colombia	Germany, West	04 Aug 62	Claims and Debts	64WGBB257	425371
Colombia	Germany, West	02 Mar 65	Tech Assistance	65WBGA140	424372
Colombia	Germany, West	11 Jun 65	Loans and Credits	66WBGA238	424374
Colombia	Germany, West	11 Jun 65	Claims and Debts	67WGBB1552	425373
Colombia	Germany, West	10 Sep 65	Taxation	67WGBB762	425375
Colombia	Germany, West	25 Nov 68	Air Transport	70WGBB673	425376
Colombia	Germany, West	27 Jan 70	Loans and Credits	70WBGA74	424377
Colombia	Germany, West	10 Dec 70	Loans and Credits	71WBGA58	424378
Colombia	IBRD (World Bank)	19 Aug 49	IBRD Project	154UNTS329	102032
Colombia	IBRD (World Bank)	02 Nov 50	IBRD Project	158UNTS59	102062
Colombia	IBRD (World Bank)	28 Dec 50	IBRD Project	158UNTS87	102063
Colombia	IBRD (World Bank)	10 Apr 51	IBRD Project	158UNTS155	102066
Colombia	IBRD (World Bank)	13 Oct 51	IBRD Project	159UNTS75	102084
Colombia	IBRD (World Bank)	26 Aug 52	IBRD Project	159UNTS339	102094
Colombia	IBRD (World Bank)	10 Sep 53	IBRD Project	203UNTS3	102738
Colombia	IBRD (World Bank)	29 Dec 54	IBRD Project	211UNTS135	102851
Colombia	IBRD (World Bank)	24 Mar 55	IBRD Project	212UNTS217	102874
Colombia	IBRD (World Bank)	15 Jun 55	IBRD Project	248UNTS161	103494
Colombia	IBRD (World Bank)	06 Jun 56	IBRD Project	248UNTS139	103493
Colombia	IBRD (World Bank)	15 Dec 58	IBRD Project	354UNTS233	105065
Colombia	IBRD (World Bank)	30 Jan 59	IBRD Project	337UNTS327	104828
Colombia	IBRD (World Bank)	20 May 59	IBRD Project	344UNTS251	104953
Colombia	IBRD (World Bank)	20 Jan 60	IBRD Project	375UNTS49	105353
Colombia	IBRD (World Bank)	10 May 60	IBRD Project	379UNTS218	105441
Colombia	IBRD (World Bank)	20 Sep 60	IBRD Project	390UNTS173	105608
Colombia	IBRD (World Bank)	12 May 61	IBRD Project	415UNTS172	105985
Colombia	IBRD (World Bank)	28 Aug 61	IBRD Project	416UNTS23	105993
Colombia	IBRD (World Bank)	23 May 62	IBRD Project	447UNTS39	106411
Colombia	IBRD (World Bank)	03 Jun 63	IBRD Project	490UNTS199	107155
Colombia	IBRD (World Bank)	21 Jun 63	IBRD Project	482UNTS159	106994
Colombia	IBRD (World Bank)	28 Jun 63	IBRD Project	489UNTS113	107137
Colombia	IBRD (World Bank)	16 Jul 63	IBRD Project	482UNTS256	106998
Colombia	IBRD (World Bank)	07 Feb 64	IBRD Project	516UNTS99	107473
Colombia	IBRD (World Bank)	16 May 66	Loans and Credits	608UNTS249	108819
Colombia	IBRD (World Bank)	31 May 66	Loans and Credits	608UNTS279	108820
Colombia	IBRD (World Bank)	15 Jun 67	Gen Communications	615UNTS47	108877
Colombia	IBRD (World Bank)	29 Jun 67	IBRD Project	619UNTS99	108941
Colombia	IBRD (World Bank)	22 May 68	IBRD Project	0UNTS0	109614
Colombia	IBRD (World Bank)	03 Jun 68	IBRD Project	0UNTS0	109334
Colombia	IBRD (World Bank)	03 Jun 68	IBRD Project	0UNTS0	109333
Colombia	IBRD (World Bank)	25 Jul 68	IBRD Project	0UNTS0	109484
Colombia	IBRD (World Bank)	27 Jul 68	IBRD Project	0UNTS0	109485

PARTY ONE	PARTY TWO	DATE	TOPIC	CITATION	NUMBER
Colombia	IBRD (World Bank)	31 Jul 68	IBRD Project	0UNTS0	109512
Colombia	IBRD (World Bank)	02 Dec 68	IBRD Project	0UNTS0	109592
Colombia	IBRD (World Bank)	27 Jun 69	IBRD Project	0UNTS0	110104
Colombia	IBRD (World Bank)	27 Jun 69	IBRD Project	0UNTS0	110500
Colombia	IDA (Devel Assoc)	28 Aug 61	Loans and Credits	416UNTS3	105992
Colombia	Israel	21 Dec 62	Visas	484UNTS149	107023
Colombia	Israel	15 Jan 65	Tech Assistance	581UNTS173	108441
Colombia	Israel	12 Jul 66	Visas	581UNTS181	108442
Colombia	Italy	27 Aug 49	General Amity	1ITMA551	437091
Colombia	Italy	19 Jun 52	General Trade	53ITGU77	435092
Colombia	Italy	20 Dec 55	Specif Goods/Equip	260UNTS315	103714
Colombia	Italy	25 May 62	Visas	63ITDI279	436093
Colombia	Multilateral	17 Feb 40	Privil/Immunities	161UNTS229	200487
Colombia	Multilateral	30 Jul 40	Admin Cooperation	161UNTS253	200488
Colombia	Multilateral	12 Oct 40	Specific Resources	161UNTS193	200485
Colombia	Multilateral	28 Nov 40	Commodity Trade	139UNTS159	200452
Colombia	Multilateral	15 Jan 44	IGO Establishment	161UNTS281	200489
Colombia	Multilateral	02 Aug 44	Scientific Project	67UNTS221	200221
Colombia	Multilateral	07 Dec 44	Air Transport	171UNTS345	200501
Colombia	Multilateral	07 Dec 44	IGO Establishment	15UNTS295	200102
Colombia	Multilateral	16 Nov 45	IGO Establishment	4UNTS275	100052
Colombia	Multilateral	27 Dec 45	IGO Establishment	2UNTS39	100020
Colombia	Multilateral	22 Jul 46	IGO Establishment	9UNTS3	100125
Colombia	Multilateral	22 Jul 46	IGO Establishment	14UNTS185	100221
Colombia	Multilateral	03 Sep 46	Commodity Trade	139UNTS3	101872
Colombia	Multilateral	11 Dec 46	Sanitation	12UNTS179	100186
Colombia	Multilateral	02 Sep 47	General Military	21UNTS77	100324
Colombia	Multilateral	02 Oct 47	Telecommunications	193UNTS188	102616
Colombia	Multilateral	11 Oct 47	IGO Establishment	77UNTS143	100998
Colombia	Multilateral	06 Mar 48	Water Transport	289UNTS3	104214
Colombia	Multilateral	30 Apr 48	IGO Establishment	119UNTS3	101609
Colombia	Multilateral	30 Apr 48	Dispute Settlement	30UNTS55	100449
Colombia	Multilateral	19 Jun 48	Air Transport	310UNTS151	104492
Colombia	Multilateral	24 Jul 48	Sanitation	66UNTS25	100847
Colombia	Multilateral	19 Nov 48	Sanitation	44UNTS277	100688
Colombia	Multilateral	29 Nov 48	IGO Establishment	120UNTS13	101613
Colombia	Multilateral	09 Dec 48	Humanitarian	78UNTS277	101021
Colombia	Multilateral	23 Mar 49	Commodity Trade	203UNTS179	102746
Colombia	Multilateral	09 Jul 49	Telecommunications	168UNTS143	102218
Colombia	Multilateral	12 Aug 49	General Military	75UNTS135	100972
Colombia	Multilateral	12 Aug 49	Humanitarian	75UNTS287	100973
Colombia	Multilateral	12 Aug 49	Humanitarian	75UNTS31	100970
Colombia	Multilateral	12 Aug 49	Humanitarian	75UNTS85	100971
Colombia	Multilateral	16 Dec 49	Admin Cooperation	72UNTS3	100924
Colombia	Multilateral	22 Nov 50	Culture	131UNTS25	101734
Colombia	Multilateral	24 Nov 50	Tech Assistance	81UNTS188	101072
Colombia	Multilateral	02 Jul 51	Refugees	189UNTS137	102545
Colombia	Multilateral	08 Sep 51	Peace/Disarmament	136UNTS45	101832
Colombia	Multilateral	06 Dec 51	Admin Cooperation	150UNTS67	101963
Colombia	Multilateral	11 Jul 52	Postal Service	171UNTS143	102226
Colombia	Multilateral	11 Jul 52	Postal Service	170UNTS269	102223
Colombia	Multilateral	11 Jul 52	Postal Service	170UNTS3	102221
Colombia	Multilateral	11 Jul 52	Postal Service	171UNTS89	102225
Colombia	Multilateral	11 Jul 52	IGO Establishment	169UNTS3	102220
Colombia	Multilateral	11 Jul 52	Postal Service	171UNTS3	102224
Colombia	Multilateral	11 Jul 52	Postal Service	170UNTS63	102222
Colombia	Multilateral	28 Sep 54	Refugees	360UNTS117	105158
Colombia	Multilateral	25 May 55	IGO Establishment	264UNTS117	103791
Colombia	Multilateral	20 Jun 56	Admin Cooperation	268UNTS3	103850
Colombia	Multilateral	26 Oct 56	IGO Establishment	276UNTS3	103988
Colombia	Multilateral	20 Feb 57	Consul/Citizenship	309UNTS65	104468
Colombia	Multilateral	03 Oct 57	Postal Service	365UNTS207	105214
Colombia	Multilateral	03 Oct 57	Postal Service	366UNTS255	105219
Colombia	Multilateral	03 Oct 57	Postal Service	366UNTS141	105217
Colombia	Multilateral	03 Oct 57	Postal Service	366UNTS3	105215

PARTY ONE	PARTY TWO	DATE	TOPIC	CITATION	NUMBER
Colombia	Multilateral	03 Oct 57	Postal Service	366UNTS87	105216
Colombia	Multilateral	03 Oct 57	Postal Service	364UNTS331	105212
Colombia	Multilateral	03 Oct 57	Postal Service	364UNTS3	105211
Colombia	Multilateral	03 Oct 57	Postal Service	365UNTS3	105213
Colombia	Multilateral	29 Apr 58	Water Transport	450UNTS11	106465
Colombia	Multilateral	29 Apr 58	Dispute Settlement	450UNTS169	106466
Colombia	Multilateral	29 Apr 58	Specific Resources	559UNTS285	108164
Colombia	Multilateral	29 Apr 58	Territory Boundary	499UNTS311	107302
Colombia	Multilateral	29 Apr 58	Territory Boundary	516UNTS205	107477
Colombia	Multilateral	01 Dec 58	Commodity Trade	385UNTS137	105534
Colombia	Multilateral	08 Apr 59	IGO Establishment	389UNTS69	105593
Colombia	Multilateral	26 Jan 60	IGO Establishment	439UNTS249	106333
Colombia	Multilateral	28 Jul 60	IGO Establishment	485UNTS3	107042
Colombia	Multilateral	18 Apr 61	Dispute Settlement	500UNTS243	107312
Colombia	Multilateral	18 Apr 61	Consul/Citizenship	500UNTS95	107310
Colombia	Multilateral	28 Aug 61	IBRD Project	416UNTS45	105994
Colombia	Multilateral	26 Mar 62	IGO Establishment	539UNTS67	107825
Colombia	Multilateral	28 Sep 62	IGO Establishment	469UNTS169	106791
Colombia	Multilateral	24 Apr 63	Consul/Citizenship	596UNTS487	108640
Colombia	Multilateral	24 Apr 63	Consul/Citizenship	596UNTS261	108638
Colombia	Multilateral	05 Aug 63	Sanitation	480UNTS43	106964
Colombia	Multilateral	10 Jul 64	Postal Service	613UNTS3	108851
Colombia	Multilateral	10 Jul 64	Postal Service	612UNTS3	108847
Colombia	Multilateral	10 Jul 64	Postal Service	613UNTS193	108852
Colombia	Multilateral	10 Jul 64	Postal Service	611UNTS387	108846
Colombia	Multilateral	10 Jul 64	Postal Service	611UNTS105	108845
Colombia	Multilateral	10 Jul 64	Postal Service	612UNTS233	108848
Colombia	Multilateral	10 Jul 64	Postal Service	612UNTS361	108849
Colombia	Multilateral	10 Jul 64	Postal Service	613UNTS3	108850
Colombia	Multilateral	10 Jul 64	Postal Service	613UNTS127	108853
Colombia	Multilateral	10 Jul 64	Postal Service	611UNTS7	108844
Colombia	Multilateral	20 Aug 64	Telecommunications	514UNTS25	107441
Colombia	Multilateral	14 Feb 67	General Military	634UNTS281	109068
Colombia	Multilateral	18 Mar 68	Commodity Trade	0UNTS0	109262
Colombia	Multilateral	24 Sep 68	Air Transport	0UNTS0	110612
Colombia	Multilateral	24 Dec 68	Commodity Trade	0UNTS0	109369
Colombia	Netherlands	03 Aug 62	Visas	485UNTS225	107058
Colombia	Netherlands	06 Jul 64	General Aid	543UNTS289	107906
Colombia	Netherlands	19 Jul 66	Tech Assistance	591UNTS201	108558
Colombia	Norway	01 Oct 59	Visas	3NORT785	451026
Colombia	Portugal	09 Mar 51	Air Transport	108UNTS87	101469
Colombia	Spain	11 Dec 51	Air Transport	216UNTS73	102933
Colombia	Spain	01 Apr 53	Culture	65SPBO1201	460064
Colombia	Spain	10 Nov 55	Telecommunications	56SPBO1704	460065
Colombia	Sweden	27 Jan 53	General Trade	53SOFM1	461180
Colombia	Switzerland	15 Jan 59	Milit Servic/Citiz	63SWRO143	462005
Colombia	UK Great Britain	16 Oct 47	Air Transport	160UNTS297	102115
Colombia	UK Great Britain	13 Dec 49	Finance	88UNTS133	101189
Colombia	UK Great Britain	26 May 61	Visas	414UNTS85	105967
Colombia	UN Special Fund	04 Feb 60	Direct Aid	355UNTS257	105080
Colombia	UNICEF (Children)	15 Mar 50	Tech Assistance	65UNTS104	100838
Colombia	United Nations	17 Jul 52	Tech Assistance	135UNTS61	101815
Colombia	United Nations	27 Aug 63	Education	481UNTS3	106975
Colombia	USA (United States)	09 Sep 40	Extradition	125UNTS239	200428
Colombia	USA (United States)	19 Feb 42	Military Mission	117UNTS185	200369
Colombia	USA (United States)	29 May 42	Military Mission	8UNTS365	200047
Colombia	USA (United States)	23 Oct 42	Sanitation	105UNTS109	200326
Colombia	USA (United States)	05 Nov 42	Military Mission	24UNTS227	200147
Colombia	USA (United States)	29 Mar 43	Milit Installation	124UNTS139	200416
Colombia	USA (United States)	12 Feb 44	Milit Servic/Citiz	109UNTS287	200365
Colombia	USA (United States)	17 Apr 45	Customs	139UNTS303	200457
Colombia	USA (United States)	03 Dec 45	Military Mission	107UNTS3	101462
Colombia	USA (United States)	19 Feb 46	Sanitation	166UNTS104	102187
Colombia	USA (United States)	14 Oct 46	Military Mission	7UNTS97	100093
Colombia	USA (United States)	22 Dec 47	Air Transport	51UNTS45	100751

PARTY ONE	PARTY TWO	DATE	TOPIC	CITATION	NUMBER
Colombia	USA (United States)	21 Feb 49	Military Mission	44UNTS83	100680
Colombia	USA (United States)	21 Feb 49	Military Mission	92UNTS227	101275
Colombia	USA (United States)	26 Jul 49	Admin Cooperation	73UNTS106	100949
Colombia	USA (United States)	12 Oct 49	General Trade	133UNTS15	101774
Colombia	USA (United States)	24 Nov 50	Scientific Project	133UNTS49	101779
Colombia	USA (United States)	09 Mar 51	Tech Assistance	141UNTS15	101901
Colombia	USA (United States)	12 Jan 52	Education	168UNTS109	102216
Colombia	USA (United States)	17 Apr 52	Milit Assistance	174UNTS215	102287
Colombia	USA (United States)	09 Jun 53	Tech Assistance	213UNTS3	102877
Colombia	USA (United States)	22 May 54	Visas	354UNTS21	105050
Colombia	USA (United States)	30 Jun 54	Non-IBRD Project	237UNTS263	103351
Colombia	USA (United States)	14 Jun 55	Non-IBRD Project	256UNTS211	103630
Colombia	USA (United States)	23 Jun 55	US Agri Commod Aid	263UNTS337	103781
Colombia	USA (United States)	19 Jul 55	Atomic Energy	235UNTS233	103305
Colombia	USA (United States)	16 Sep 55	Military Mission	256UNTS221	103631
Colombia	USA (United States)	18 Nov 55	Claims and Debts	239UNTS173	103377
Colombia	USA (United States)	28 Nov 55	Non-IBRD Project	241UNTS39	103422
Colombia	USA (United States)	20 Dec 55	US Agri Commod Aid	241UNTS25	103421
Colombia	USA (United States)	14 Mar 56	Scientific Project	271UNTS303	103922
Colombia	USA (United States)	27 Mar 56	Air Transport	273UNTS235	103954
Colombia	USA (United States)	24 Oct 56	Air Transport	476UNTS77	106905
Colombia	USA (United States)	09 Jan 57	Education	462UNTS151	106676
Colombia	USA (United States)	16 Apr 57	US Agri Commod Aid	283UNTS245	104121
Colombia	USA (United States)	14 Mar 58	US Agri Commod Aid	308UNTS115	104459
Colombia	USA (United States)	08 May 59	Direct Aid	344UNTS193	104950
Colombia	USA (United States)	06 Oct 59	US Agri Commod Aid	358UNTS145	105132
Colombia	USA (United States)	11 Jan 60	Tech Assistance	371UNTS37	105268
Colombia	USA (United States)	07 Apr 60	Milit Assistance	372UNTS27	105285
Colombia	USA (United States)	03 Apr 61	Milit Assistance	407UNTS3	105856
Colombia	USA (United States)	04 Apr 61	Direct Aid	405UNTS55	105822
Colombia	USA (United States)	01 Aug 61	Taxation	433UNTS123	106235
Colombia	USA (United States)	09 Apr 62	Scientific Project	476UNTS9	106899
Colombia	USA (United States)	15 May 62	General Trade	445UNTS279	106396
Colombia	USA (United States)	23 Jul 62	General Aid	458UNTS123	106595
Colombia	USA (United States)	05 Oct 62	Finance	459UNTS191	106621
Colombia	USA (United States)	27 Mar 63	US Agri Commod Aid	489UNTS289	107145
Colombia	USA (United States)	29 Nov 63	Gen Communications	494UNTS49	107225
Colombia	USA (United States)	13 May 64	Scientific Project	530UNTS77	107673
Colombia	USA (United States)	08 Oct 64	US Agri Commod Aid	579UNTS3	108395
Colombia	USA (United States)	09 Jun 65	Commodity Trade	549UNTS3	107985
Colombia	USA (United States)	28 Oct 65	Telecommunications	574UNTS109	108343
Colombia	USA (United States)	10 Mar 66	US Agri Commod Aid	0UNTS0	109604
Colombia	USA (United States)	25 Oct 66	Tech Assistance	0UNTS0	109687
Colombia	USA (United States)	10 May 68	Customs	0UNTS0	110016
Colombia	USA (United States)	31 May 68	US Agri Commod Aid	0UNTS0	110067
Colombia	USA (United States)	18 Sep 68	Commodity Trade	0UNTS0	110077
Colombia	USA (United States)	19 Dec 68	Scientific Project	0UNTS0	110257
Colombia	WHO (World Health)	05 Jan 51	Sanitation	102UNTS139	101417
Colombia	WHO (World Health)	04 May 51	Tech Assistance	110UNTS83	101503
Colombia	WHO (World Health)	18 Sep 51	Tech Assistance	109UNTS45	101489
COMECON (Econ Aid)	Bulgaria	30 Mar 63	IGO Operations	506UNTS257	107389
COMECON (Econ Aid)	Czechoslovakia	20 Jul 62	IGO Operations	506UNTS345	107393
COMECON (Econ Aid)	Hungary	28 Feb 63	IGO Operations	506UNTS281	107390
COMECON (Econ Aid)	Poland	22 Feb 63	IGO Operations	506UNTS303	107391
COMECON (Econ Aid)	USSR (Soviet Union)	07 Dec 61	IGO Operations	506UNTS325	107392
Congo (Brazzaville)	Accept UN Charter	12 Aug 60	UN Charter	375UNTS111	105362
Congo (Brazzaville)	China People's Rep	23 Jul 64	General Economic	64CCJC100	411113
Congo (Brazzaville)	China People's Rep	02 Oct 64	Water Transport	64CCJC136	411096
Congo (Brazzaville)	China People's Rep	02 Oct 64	General Amity	64CCJC135	411095
Congo (Brazzaville)	China People's Rep	06 Feb 65	Direct Aid	65CCJC14	411100
Congo (Brazzaville)	China People's Rep	12 May 65	Mass Media	65CCJC64	411129
Congo (Brazzaville)	China People's Rep	13 Jun 65	Direct Aid	65CCJC83	411131
Congo (Brazzaville)	China People's Rep	13 Aug 65	Culture	65CCJC106	411134
Congo (Brazzaville)	China People's Rep	14 Apr 66	Culture	66CCJC16	411141
Congo (Brazzaville)	Czechoslovakia	29 Nov 66	Culture	635UNTS3	109069

PARTY ONE	PARTY TWO	DATE	TOPIC	CITATION	NUMBER
Congo (Brazzaville)	Denmark	27 Feb 67	Air Transport	600UNTS189	108681
Congo (Brazzaville)	France	12 Jul 60	Recognition	60FRRT50	415121
Congo (Brazzaville)	France	15 Aug 60	General Military	60FRRT76	415122
Congo (Brazzaville)	France	02 May 62	Air Transport	63FRRT25	415123
Congo (Brazzaville)	France	18 May 62	Admin Cooperation	65FRRT9	415124
Congo (Brazzaville)	France	27 Mar 63	Customs	63FRRT43	415125
Congo (Brazzaville)	France	09 Jun 66	Direct Aid	66FRJO6051	416126
Congo (Brazzaville)	France	13 Nov 67	Taxation	0UNTS0	110315
Congo (Brazzaville)	France	13 Nov 67	Finance	70FRJO307	416127
Congo (Brazzaville)	Germany, East	06 May 65	General Aid	43EGDZ335	420169
Congo (Brazzaville)	Germany, West	30 Oct 62	General Transport	63WBGA59	424380
Congo (Brazzaville)	Germany, West	30 Oct 62	General Economic	63WBGA59	424379
Congo (Brazzaville)	Germany, West	30 Oct 62	Tech Assistance	63WBGA59	424381
Congo (Brazzaville)	Germany, West	13 Sep 65	Claims and Debts	67WGBB1733	425382
Congo (Brazzaville)	Germany, West	27 Oct 65	Loans and Credits	66WBGA4	424383
Congo (Brazzaville)	IBRD (World Bank)	30 Jun 59	IBRD Project	452UNTS123	106506
Congo (Brazzaville)	IBRD (World Bank)	09 Jan 67	IBRD Project	598UNTS161	108659
Congo (Brazzaville)	IBRD (World Bank)	10 May 67	IBRD Project	632UNTS185	109021
Congo (Brazzaville)	Multilateral	07 Dec 44	IGO Establishment	15UNTS295	200102
Congo (Brazzaville)	Multilateral	11 Dec 46	Sanitation	12UNTS179	100186
Congo (Brazzaville)	Multilateral	27 May 47	Air Transport	418UNTS161	106021
Congo (Brazzaville)	Multilateral	24 Jul 48	Sanitation	66UNTS25	100847
Congo (Brazzaville)	Multilateral	04 May 49	Admin Cooperation	92UNTS19	101257
Congo (Brazzaville)	Multilateral	04 May 49	Admin Cooperation	98UNTS101	101358
Congo (Brazzaville)	Multilateral	15 Jul 49	Health/Educ/Welfare	197UNTS3	102631
Congo (Brazzaville)	Multilateral	22 Nov 50	Culture	131UNTS25	101734
Congo (Brazzaville)	Multilateral	02 Jul 51	Refugees	189UNTS137	102545
Congo (Brazzaville)	Multilateral	31 Mar 53	Privil/Immunities	193UNTS136	102613
Congo (Brazzaville)	Multilateral	11 May 53	Sanitation	456UNTS3	106555
Congo (Brazzaville)	Multilateral	18 Jan 54	IGO Establishment	330UNTS121	104743
Congo (Brazzaville)	Multilateral	14 Jun 54	Air Transport	320UNTS217	104644
Congo (Brazzaville)	Multilateral	14 Jun 54	Air Transport	320UNTS209	104643
Congo (Brazzaville)	Multilateral	29 Jul 54	Sanitation	249UNTS45	103500
Congo (Brazzaville)	Multilateral	28 Sep 55	Air Transport	478UNTS371	106943
Congo (Brazzaville)	Multilateral	26 Jan 60	IGO Establishment	439UNTS249	106333
Congo (Brazzaville)	Multilateral	30 Mar 61	Sanitation	520UNTS151	107515
Congo (Brazzaville)	Multilateral	18 Apr 61	Consul/Citizenship	500UNTS95	107310
Congo (Brazzaville)	Multilateral	21 Jun 61	IGO Establishment	514UNTS209	107449
Congo (Brazzaville)	Multilateral	26 Oct 61	Patents/Copyrights	496UNTS43	107247
Congo (Brazzaville)	Multilateral	28 Jun 62	ILO Labor	494UNTS271	107238
Congo (Brazzaville)	Multilateral	24 Apr 63	Consul/Citizenship	596UNTS261	108638
Congo (Brazzaville)	Multilateral	24 Apr 63	Consul/Citizenship	596UNTS487	108640
Congo (Brazzaville)	Multilateral	25 May 63	IGO Establishment	479UNTS39	106947
Congo (Brazzaville)	Multilateral	04 Aug 63	IGO Establishment	510UNTS3	107408
Congo (Brazzaville)	Multilateral	07 Nov 63	Tech Assistance	480UNTS232	106971
Congo (Brazzaville)	Multilateral	10 Jul 64	Postal Service	611UNTS387	108846
Congo (Brazzaville)	Multilateral	10 Jul 64	Postal Service	611UNTS105	108845
Congo (Brazzaville)	Multilateral	10 Jul 64	Postal Service	612UNTS3	108847
Congo (Brazzaville)	Multilateral	10 Jul 64	Postal Service	611UNTS7	108844
Congo (Brazzaville)	Multilateral	10 Jul 64	Postal Service	613UNTS3	108851
Congo (Brazzaville)	Multilateral	10 Jul 64	Postal Service	612UNTS361	108849
Congo (Brazzaville)	Multilateral	10 Jul 64	Postal Service	613UNTS3	108850
Congo (Brazzaville)	Multilateral	10 Jul 64	Postal Service	612UNTS233	108848
Congo (Brazzaville)	Multilateral	18 Mar 65	Dispute Settlement	575UNTS159	108359
Congo (Brazzaville)	Multilateral	05 Jul 65	General Aid	563UNTS104	108207
Congo (Brazzaville)	Multilateral	08 Jul 65	General Trade	597UNTS3	108641
Congo (Brazzaville)	Multilateral	27 Jan 67	Scientific Project	610UNTS205	108843
Congo (Brazzaville)	Multilateral	18 Mar 68	Commodity Trade	0UNTS0	109262
Congo (Brazzaville)	Switzerland	18 Oct 62	General Economic	64SWRO635	462126
Congo (Brazzaville)	UN Special Fund	09 Nov 61	Direct Aid	413UNTS58	105940
Congo (Brazzaville)	UNICEF (Children)	09 Apr 62	Direct Aid	431UNTS65	106210
Congo (Brazzaville)	United Nations	13 Mar 68	IGO Operations	632UNTS161	109018
Congo (Brazzaville)	USA (United States)	05 Aug 61	Admin Cooperation	603UNTS19	108720
Congo (Brazzaville)	USA (United States)	01 Sep 62	Claims and Debts	459UNTS117	106616
Congo (Brazzaville)	USA (United States)	14 May 69	Commodity Trade	0UNTS0	110274

PARTY ONE	PARTY TWO	DATE	TOPIC	CITATION	NUMBER
Congo (Brazzaville)	WHO (World Health)	12 Dec 60	Tech Assistance	399UNTS105	105737
Congo (Zaire)	Accept UN Charter	31 Oct 61	UN Charter	418UNTS157	106020
Congo (Zaire)	Belgium	15 Nov 60	Finance	394UNTS79	105670
Congo (Zaire)	Belgium	06 Feb 65	Claims and Debts	540UNTS227	107852
Congo (Zaire)	Belgium	06 Feb 65	Finance	540UNTS275	107853
Congo (Zaire)	Denmark	25 May 68	Tech Assistance	0UNTS0	109289
Congo (Zaire)	France	17 Jul 63	Non-ILO Labor	67FRJO1511	416128
Congo (Zaire)	France	17 Dec 63	Health/Educ/Welfare	67FRJO1511	416129
Congo (Zaire)	Germany, West	23 Nov 64	Loans and Credits	65WBGA38	424384
Congo (Zaire)	Germany, West	23 Jun 65	Loans and Credits	65WBGA170	424385
Congo (Zaire)	Germany, West	07 Mar 67	Loans and Credits	67WBGA98	424386
Congo (Zaire)	Germany, West	18 Mar 69	Loans and Credits	69WBGA84	424387
Congo (Zaire)	Germany, West	18 Mar 69	Claims and Debts	70WGBB509	425388
Congo (Zaire)	IAEA (Atom Energy)	27 Jun 62	Direct Aid	463UNTS31	106691
Congo (Zaire)	IDA (Devel Assoc)	26 May 69	Loans and Credits	0UNTS0	110285
Congo (Zaire)	IDA (Devel Assoc)	09 Jun 69	Non-IBRD Project	0UNTS0	110588
Congo (Zaire)	IDA (Devel Assoc)	28 May 70	Non-IBRD Project	0UNTS0	110659
Congo (Zaire)	Israel	14 Apr 64	Visas	552UNTS305	108062
Congo (Zaire)	Italy	07 Dec 62	Air Transport	66ITGU211	435094
Congo (Zaire)	Multilateral	07 Dec 44	IGO Establishment	15UNTS295	200102
Congo (Zaire)	Multilateral	11 Dec 46	Sanitation	12UNTS179	100186
Congo (Zaire)	Multilateral	12 Nov 47	Admin Cooperation	46UNTS201	100710
Congo (Zaire)	Multilateral	09 Dec 48	Humanitarian	78UNTS277	101021
Congo (Zaire)	Multilateral	04 May 49	Admin Cooperation	47UNTS159	100728
Congo (Zaire)	Multilateral	22 Nov 50	Culture	131UNTS25	101734
Congo (Zaire)	Multilateral	02 Jul 51	Refugees	189UNTS137	102545
Congo (Zaire)	Multilateral	07 Nov 52	General Trade	221UNTS255	103010
Congo (Zaire)	Multilateral	11 May 53	Sanitation	456UNTS3	106555
Congo (Zaire)	Multilateral	18 Jan 54	IGO Establishment	330UNTS121	104743
Congo (Zaire)	Multilateral	14 Jun 54	Air Transport	320UNTS209	104643
Congo (Zaire)	Multilateral	14 Jun 54	Air Transport	320UNTS217	104644
Congo (Zaire)	Multilateral	29 Jul 54	Sanitation	249UNTS45	103500
Congo (Zaire)	Multilateral	03 Oct 57	Postal Service	365UNTS3	105213
Congo (Zaire)	Multilateral	26 Jan 60	IGO Establishment	439UNTS249	106333
Congo (Zaire)	Multilateral	01 Sep 60	Commodity Trade	403UNTS3	105792
Congo (Zaire)	Multilateral	30 Mar 61	Sanitation	520UNTS151	107515
Congo (Zaire)	Multilateral	18 Apr 61	Dispute Settlement	500UNTS243	107312
Congo (Zaire)	Multilateral	18 Apr 61	Consul/Citizenship	500UNTS95	107310
Congo (Zaire)	Multilateral	22 Jun 62	ILO Labor	494UNTS249	107237
Congo (Zaire)	Multilateral	27 Jun 62	Atomic Energy	463UNTS3	106688
Congo (Zaire)	Multilateral	27 Jun 62	Atomic Energy	463UNTS17	106690
Congo (Zaire)	Multilateral	27 Jun 62	Atomic Energy	463UNTS11	106689
Congo (Zaire)	Multilateral	28 Sep 62	IGO Establishment	469UNTS169	106791
Congo (Zaire)	Multilateral	02 Apr 63	Commodity Trade	475UNTS121	106889
Congo (Zaire)	Multilateral	24 Apr 63	Consul/Citizenship	596UNTS487	108640
Congo (Zaire)	Multilateral	24 Apr 63	Consul/Citizenship	596UNTS261	108638
Congo (Zaire)	Multilateral	25 May 63	IGO Establishment	479UNTS39	106947
Congo (Zaire)	Multilateral	04 Aug 63	IGO Establishment	510UNTS3	107408
Congo (Zaire)	Multilateral	05 Aug 63	Sanitation	480UNTS43	106964
Congo (Zaire)	Multilateral	15 Feb 64	Milit Installation	533UNTS98	107736
Congo (Zaire)	Multilateral	10 Jul 64	Postal Service	611UNTS105	108845
Congo (Zaire)	Multilateral	10 Jul 64	Postal Service	611UNTS387	108846
Congo (Zaire)	Multilateral	10 Jul 64	Postal Service	611UNTS7	108844
Congo (Zaire)	Multilateral	10 Jul 64	Postal Service	612UNTS361	108849
Congo (Zaire)	Multilateral	10 Jul 64	Postal Service	612UNTS233	108848
Congo (Zaire)	Multilateral	10 Jul 64	Postal Service	612UNTS3	108847
Congo (Zaire)	Multilateral	10 Jul 64	Postal Service	613UNTS3	108850
Congo (Zaire)	Multilateral	31 Dec 65	Specific Resources	616UNTS317	108904
Congo (Zaire)	Multilateral	05 Apr 66	Water Transport	640UNTS133	109159
Congo (Zaire)	Multilateral	27 May 66	IGO Establishment	637UNTS0	109121
Congo (Zaire)	Multilateral	06 Aug 66	Tech Assistance	570UNTS178	108294
Congo (Zaire)	Multilateral	18 Mar 68	Commodity Trade	0UNTS0	109262
Congo (Zaire)	Netherlands	03 Feb 69	Air Transport	0UNTS0	110469
Congo (Zaire)	Switzerland	29 Jun 59	Taxation	59SWRO639	462046
Congo (Zaire)	UK Great Britain	03 Jan 64	Loans and Credits	534UNTS417	107770

PARTY ONE	PARTY TWO	DATE	TOPIC	CITATION	NUMBER
Congo (Zaire)	UN Special Fund	26 Jul 63	Direct Aid	474UNTS137	106878
Congo (Zaire)	United Nations	23 Aug 60	Direct Aid	373UNTS327	200576
Congo (Zaire)	United Nations	12 Jun 61	General Aid	494UNTS205	107234
Congo (Zaire)	United Nations	27 Nov 61	IGO Status/Immunit	414UNTS229	105975
Congo (Zaire)	United Nations	02 Mar 64	Milit Installation	533UNTS93	107735
Congo (Zaire)	USA (United States)	18 Nov 61	US Agri Commod Aid	433UNTS207	106244
Congo (Zaire)	USA (United States)	17 Nov 62	Finance	474UNTS41	106870
Congo (Zaire)	USA (United States)	23 Feb 63	US Agri Commod Aid	493UNTS3	107203
Congo (Zaire)	USA (United States)	23 Feb 63	US Agri Commod Aid	493UNTS17	107204
Congo (Zaire)	USA (United States)	19 Jul 63	Milit Installation	511UNTS47	107425
Congo (Zaire)	USA (United States)	28 Apr 64	US Agri Commod Aid	526UNTS55	107600
Congo (Zaire)	USA (United States)	09 Dec 64	US Agri Commod Aid	531UNTS249	107707
Congo (Zaire)	USA (United States)	19 Jul 65	Direct Aid	593UNTS215	108586
Congo (Zaire)	USA (United States)	03 Oct 66	US Agri Commod Aid	0UNTS0	109683
Congo (Zaire)	USA (United States)	15 Mar 67	US Agri Commod Aid	0UNTS0	109897
Congo (Zaire)	USA (United States)	11 Dec 67	US Agri Commod Aid	0UNTS0	110059
Congo (Zaire)	USA (United States)	12 Aug 68	US Agri Commod Aid	0UNTS0	110150
Congo (Zaire)	USA (United States)	21 Oct 69	US Agri Commod Aid	0UNTS0	110450
Congo (Zaire)	USSR (Soviet Union)	07 Jul 60	Recognition	16SUGG128	469978
Congo (Zaire)	USSR (Soviet Union)	07 Jul 60	Consul/Citizenship	9SUGG141	469671
Congo (Zaire)	USSR (Soviet Union)	26 May 64	General Trade	0UNTS0	109582
Costa Rica	Argentina	23 Nov 64	Culture	635UNTS213	109084
Costa Rica	Austria	30 Apr 68	Visas	0UNTS0	109324
Costa Rica	Austria	15 Jul 68	Visas	68ABGB344	403020
Costa Rica	Austria	17 Sep 69	Telecommunications	69ABGB357	403021
Costa Rica	Brazil	19 Nov 64	Culture	0UNTS0	109429
Costa Rica	Canada	18 Nov 50	General Economic	231UNTS25	103200
Costa Rica	Denmark	26 Sep 56	General Economic	341UNTS305	104893
Costa Rica	Dominican Republic	09 Oct 67	Culture	0UNTS0	110413
Costa Rica	France	30 Apr 53	General Trade	54FRJO1902	416134
Costa Rica	France	02 Jun 55	General Amity	55FRRT9002	415135
Costa Rica	France	18 Jun 64	Telecommunications	65FRRT32	415136
Costa Rica	France	30 Nov 67	Education	68FRJO206	416137
Costa Rica	France	30 Nov 67	Education	0UNTS0	110668
Costa Rica	France	30 May 69	Culture	0UNTS0	110741
Costa Rica	France	23 Sep 69	Education	0UNTS0	110669
Costa Rica	Germany, West	23 Jul 65	Tech Assistance	66WBGA66	424090
Costa Rica	Germany, West	19 Jul 68	Loans and Credits	68WBGA185	424091
Costa Rica	Guatemala	20 Dec 55	General Economic	280UNTS121	104056
Costa Rica	IBRD (World Bank)	18 Sep 56	IBRD Project	260UNTS369	103721
Costa Rica	IBRD (World Bank)	11 Feb 59	IBRD Project	337UNTS245	104825
Costa Rica	IBRD (World Bank)	04 May 60	IBRD Project	390UNTS201	105609
Costa Rica	IBRD (World Bank)	03 Feb 61	IBRD Project	414UNTS314	105977
Costa Rica	IBRD (World Bank)	06 Sep 61	IBRD Project	446UNTS345	106408
Costa Rica	IBRD (World Bank)	13 Oct 61	IBRD Project	430UNTS27	106202
Costa Rica	IBRD (World Bank)	10 Jul 63	IBRD Project	482UNTS69	106991
Costa Rica	IBRD (World Bank)	05 Jun 68	IBRD Project	0UNTS0	109365
Costa Rica	IBRD (World Bank)	10 Jul 69	IBRD Project	0UNTS0	110487
Costa Rica	IBRD (World Bank)	10 Jul 69	IBRD Project	0UNTS0	110488
Costa Rica	IBRD (World Bank)	02 Apr 70	IBRD Project	0UNTS0	110683
Costa Rica	IDA (Devel Assoc)	13 Oct 61	Non-IBRD Project	431UNTS3	106204
Costa Rica	ILO (Labor Org)	09 May 69	IGO Establishment	0UNTS0	110307
Costa Rica	Israel	01 Sep 61	Visas	448UNTS247	106436
Costa Rica	Israel	31 Jul 62	Education	484UNTS155	107024
Costa Rica	Israel	06 Apr 68	Visas	0UNTS0	109355
Costa Rica	Italy	20 Feb 53	General Trade	54ITGU198	435098
Costa Rica	Mexico	04 Feb 46	General Trade	50MEXD1810	444007
Costa Rica	Mexico	19 Jan 66	Culture	67MEXD2511	444009
Costa Rica	Mexico	19 Jan 66	Tech Assistance	67MEXD2511	444008
Costa Rica	Mexico	08 Sep 66	Air Transport	70MEXD304	444010
Costa Rica	Multilateral	30 Jul 40	Admin Cooperation	161UNTS253	200488
Costa Rica	Multilateral	12 Oct 40	Specific Resources	161UNTS193	200485
Costa Rica	Multilateral	28 Nov 40	Commodity Trade	139UNTS159	200452
Costa Rica	Multilateral	15 Jan 44	IGO Establishment	161UNTS281	200489
Costa Rica	Multilateral	02 Aug 44	Scientific Project	67UNTS221	200221

PARTY ONE	PARTY TWO	DATE	TOPIC	CITATION	NUMBER
Costa Rica	Multilateral	07 Dec 44	Air Transport	84UNTS389	200252
Costa Rica	Multilateral	07 Dec 44	Air Transport	171UNTS387	200502
Costa Rica	Multilateral	07 Dec 44	Air Transport	171UNTS345	200501
Costa Rica	Multilateral	07 Dec 44	IGO Establishment	15UNTS295	200102
Costa Rica	Multilateral	27 Dec 45	IGO Establishment	2UNTS39	100020
Costa Rica	Multilateral	22 Jul 46	IGO Establishment	14UNTS185	100221
Costa Rica	Multilateral	22 Jul 46	IGO Establishment	9UNTS3	100125
Costa Rica	Multilateral	03 Sep 46	Commodity Trade	139UNTS3	101872
Costa Rica	Multilateral	11 Dec 46	Sanitation	12UNTS179	100186
Costa Rica	Multilateral	27 May 47	Air Transport	418UNTS161	106021
Costa Rica	Multilateral	02 Sep 47	General Military	21UNTS77	100324
Costa Rica	Multilateral	30 Apr 48	IGO Establishment	119UNTS3	101609
Costa Rica	Multilateral	30 Apr 48	Dispute Settlement	30UNTS55	100449
Costa Rica	Multilateral	24 Jul 48	Sanitation	66UNTS25	100847
Costa Rica	Multilateral	19 Nov 48	Sanitation	44UNTS277	100688
Costa Rica	Multilateral	09 Dec 48	Humanitarian	78UNTS277	101021
Costa Rica	Multilateral	23 Mar 49	Commodity Trade	203UNTS179	102746
Costa Rica	Multilateral	09 Jul 49	Telecommunications	168UNTS143	102218
Costa Rica	Multilateral	28 Mar 51	Tech Assistance	181UNTS61	102399
Costa Rica	Multilateral	25 May 51	Status of Forces	175UNTS215	102303
Costa Rica	Multilateral	01 Jun 51	Tech Assistance	118UNTS57	101596
Costa Rica	Multilateral	08 Sep 51	Peace/Disarmament	136UNTS45	101832
Costa Rica	Multilateral	14 Oct 51	IGO Establishment	122UNTS3	101631
Costa Rica	Multilateral	06 Dec 51	Admin Cooperation	150UNTS67	101963
Costa Rica	Multilateral	10 May 52	Taxation	439UNTS233	106332
Costa Rica	Multilateral	10 May 52	Admin Cooperation	439UNTS217	106331
Costa Rica	Multilateral	10 May 52	Admin Cooperation	439UNTS193	106330
Costa Rica	Multilateral	11 Jul 52	Postal Service	170UNTS63	102222
Costa Rica	Multilateral	11 Jul 52	IGO Establishment	169UNTS3	102220
Costa Rica	Multilateral	06 Sep 52	Patents/Copyrights	216UNTS132	102937
Costa Rica	Multilateral	31 Mar 53	Privil/Immunities	193UNTS136	102613
Costa Rica	Multilateral	11 May 53	Sanitation	456UNTS3	106555
Costa Rica	Multilateral	04 Jun 54	Customs	276UNTS191	103992
Costa Rica	Multilateral	04 Jun 54	Customs	282UNTS249	104101
Costa Rica	Multilateral	14 Jun 54	Air Transport	320UNTS217	104644
Costa Rica	Multilateral	14 Jun 54	Air Transport	320UNTS209	104643
Costa Rica	Multilateral	28 Sep 54	Refugees	360UNTS117	105158
Costa Rica	Multilateral	25 May 55	IGO Establishment	264UNTS117	103791
Costa Rica	Multilateral	25 Apr 56	Commodity Trade	270UNTS103	103896
Costa Rica	Multilateral	26 Oct 56	IGO Establishment	276UNTS3	103988
Costa Rica	Multilateral	08 Nov 56	Commodity Trade	470UNTS171	106809
Costa Rica	Multilateral	22 Feb 57	Tech Assistance	274UNTS93	103960
Costa Rica	Multilateral	01 May 57	Admin Cooperation	284UNTS201	104138
Costa Rica	Multilateral	03 Oct 57	Postal Service	364UNTS3	105211
Costa Rica	Multilateral	03 Oct 57	Postal Service	365UNTS3	105213
Costa Rica	Multilateral	29 Apr 58	Dispute Settlement	450UNTS169	106466
Costa Rica	Multilateral	29 Apr 58	Water Transport	450UNTS11	106465
Costa Rica	Multilateral	29 Apr 58	Territory Boundary	516UNTS205	107477
Costa Rica	Multilateral	29 Apr 58	Specific Resources	559UNTS285	108164
Costa Rica	Multilateral	29 Apr 58	Territory Boundary	499UNTS311	107302
Costa Rica	Multilateral	10 Jun 58	Land Transport	454UNTS115	106540
Costa Rica	Multilateral	10 Jun 58	Land Transport	454UNTS211	106541
Costa Rica	Multilateral	10 Jun 58	General Economic	454UNTS47	106539
Costa Rica	Multilateral	10 Jun 58	Admin Cooperation	330UNTS3	104739
Costa Rica	Multilateral	01 Dec 58	Commodity Trade	385UNTS137	105534
Costa Rica	Multilateral	06 Apr 59	Commodity Trade	349UNTS167	105013
Costa Rica	Multilateral	08 Apr 59	IGO Establishment	389UNTS69	105593
Costa Rica	Multilateral	01 Sep 59	Customs	454UNTS289	106542
Costa Rica	Multilateral	18 Nov 59	IGO Establishment	390UNTS227	105610
Costa Rica	Multilateral	03 Dec 59	Tech Assistance	345UNTS251	104971
Costa Rica	Multilateral	26 Jan 60	IGO Establishment	439UNTS249	106333
Costa Rica	Multilateral	26 Feb 60	Air Transport	418UNTS171	106022
Costa Rica	Multilateral	28 Jul 60	IGO Establishment	485UNTS3	107042
Costa Rica	Multilateral	13 Dec 60	IGO Establishment	455UNTS204	106544
Costa Rica	Multilateral	14 Dec 60	Education	429UNTS93	106193

PARTY ONE	PARTY TWO	DATE	TOPIC	CITATION	NUMBER
Costa Rica	Multilateral	30 Mar 61	Sanitation	520UNTS151	107515
Costa Rica	Multilateral	18 Apr 61	Dispute Settlement	500UNTS243	107312
Costa Rica	Multilateral	18 Apr 61	Consul/Citizenship	500UNTS95	107310
Costa Rica	Multilateral	21 Jun 61	IGO Establishment	514UNTS209	107449
Costa Rica	Multilateral	22 Jun 62	ILO Labor	494UNTS249	107237
Costa Rica	Multilateral	28 Sep 62	IGO Establishment	469UNTS169	106791
Costa Rica	Multilateral	12 Dec 62	IGO Establishment	552UNTS15	108048
Costa Rica	Multilateral	24 Apr 63	Consul/Citizenship	596UNTS261	108638
Costa Rica	Multilateral	05 Aug 63	Sanitation	480UNTS43	106964
Costa Rica	Multilateral	27 Aug 63	Tech Assistance	511UNTS210	107435
Costa Rica	Multilateral	21 Oct 63	Tech Assistance	480UNTS197	106969
Costa Rica	Multilateral	14 Dec 63	IGO Establishment	507UNTS149	107399
Costa Rica	Multilateral	10 Jul 64	Postal Service	611UNTS387	108846
Costa Rica	Multilateral	10 Jul 64	Postal Service	611UNTS7	108844
Costa Rica	Multilateral	10 Jul 64	Postal Service	611UNTS105	108845
Costa Rica	Multilateral	10 Jul 64	Postal Service	612UNTS233	108848
Costa Rica	Multilateral	10 Jul 64	Postal Service	612UNTS3	108847
Costa Rica	Multilateral	13 Jul 64	ILO Labor	569UNTS65	108279
Costa Rica	Multilateral	14 Feb 67	General Military	634UNTS281	109068
Costa Rica	Multilateral	13 Apr 67	IGO Operations	595UNTS60	108612
Costa Rica	Multilateral	18 Mar 68	Commodity Trade	0UNTS0	109262
Costa Rica	Multilateral	01 Jun 68	General Trade	0UNTS0	110835
Costa Rica	Multilateral	01 Jul 68	Peace/Disarmament	0UNTS0	110485
Costa Rica	Multilateral	24 Sep 68	Air Transport	0UNTS0	110612
Costa Rica	Norway	15 Oct 52	General Trade	2NORT590	451027
Costa Rica	Norway	21 Oct 59	Visas	3NORT785	451028
Costa Rica	Norway	06 Jan 60	Visas	3NORT785	451029
Costa Rica	Spain	09 Jan 53	General Amity	54SPBO303	460066
Costa Rica	Spain	08 Jun 64	Consul/Citizenship	65SPBO2506	460067
Costa Rica	Taiwan	05 May 44	General Amity	14UNTS427	200098
Costa Rica	Taiwan	10 Apr 58	Culture	315UNTS165	104567
Costa Rica	UK Great Britain	19 Nov 68	Visas	0UNTS0	109661
Costa Rica	UN Special Fund	10 Jan 61	Direct Aid	389UNTS253	105597
Costa Rica	UNICEF (Children)	14 Jan 50	Tech Assistance	65UNTS70	100830
Costa Rica	United Nations	27 Feb 53	Tech Assistance	161UNTS45	102121
Costa Rica	USA (United States)	18 Jun 41	Specific Resources	103UNTS173	200313
Costa Rica	USA (United States)	16 Jan 42	Land Transport	23UNTS285	200135
Costa Rica	USA (United States)	03 Apr 43	Specif Goods/Equip	13UNTS463	200090
Costa Rica	USA (United States)	29 May 44	Non-ILO Labor	124UNTS155	200417
Costa Rica	USA (United States)	10 Dec 45	Military Mission	3UNTS157	100029
Costa Rica	USA (United States)	12 Jan 48	Consul/Citizenship	70UNTS27	100896
Costa Rica	USA (United States)	27 Feb 48	Direct Aid	135UNTS74	101816
Costa Rica	USA (United States)	31 May 49	IGO Establishment	80UNTS3	101041
Costa Rica	USA (United States)	04 Apr 50	General Trade	132UNTS177	101759
Costa Rica	USA (United States)	02 Dec 50	Admin Cooperation	133UNTS61	101780
Costa Rica	USA (United States)	11 Jan 51	Tech Assistance	92UNTS179	101270
Costa Rica	USA (United States)	17 Jan 51	Land Transport	134UNTS215	101801
Costa Rica	USA (United States)	13 Feb 51	Sanitation	141UNTS169	101914
Costa Rica	USA (United States)	11 Sep 51	Air Transport	234UNTS255	103288
Costa Rica	USA (United States)	25 Feb 52	Status of Forces	174UNTS233	102288
Costa Rica	USA (United States)	30 Jun 54	Tech Assistance	235UNTS35	103294
Costa Rica	USA (United States)	26 Feb 55	Claims and Debts	252UNTS129	103562
Costa Rica	USA (United States)	18 May 56	Atomic Energy	404UNTS237	105814
Costa Rica	USA (United States)	19 Oct 56	Gen Communications	278UNTS65	104022
Costa Rica	USA (United States)	22 Dec 61	General Aid	460UNTS277	106646
Costa Rica	USA (United States)	18 Jun 62	Milit Assistance	461UNTS155	106659
Costa Rica	USA (United States)	23 Nov 62	General Aid	541UNTS67	107861
Costa Rica	USA (United States)	24 Aug 64	Gen Communications	531UNTS107	107696
Costa Rica	USA (United States)	22 Nov 68	Finance	0UNTS0	110445
Costa Rica	USA (United States)	01 Oct 69	Commodity Trade	0UNTS0	110507
Costa Rica	USA (United States)	06 Mar 70	Commodity Trade	0UNTS0	110627
Costa Rica	WHO (World Health)	13 Apr 51	Sanitation	103UNTS3	101419
Costa Rica	WHO (World Health)	14 Jun 51	Sanitation	102UNTS151	101418
Costa Rica	WHO (World Health)	23 Jan 52	Sanitation	135UNTS265	101826
Council of Europe	France	02 Sep 49	IGO Status/Immunit	249UNTS207	103510

PARTY ONE	PARTY TWO	DATE	TOPIC	CITATION	NUMBER
Council of Europe	France	21 Dec 59	Non-ILO Labor	60FRRT34	415500
Council of Europe	ILO (Labor Org)	23 Nov 51	IGO Operations	126UNTS331	200435
Council of Europe	ILO (Labor Org)	08 Dec 60	IGO Operations	389UNTS291	200579
Council of Europe	Multilateral	05 May 49	IGO Establishment	87UNTS103	101168
Council of Europe	Multilateral	11 Dec 53	Education	218UNTS125	102954
Council of Europe	Multilateral	20 Apr 59	Visas	376UNTS85	105375
Cuba	Albania	16 Jan 61	General Trade	448UNTS67	106425
Cuba	Belgium	16 Dec 53	Visas	185UNTS285	102475
Cuba	Bulgaria	31 May 65	Visas	0UNTS0	110299
Cuba	Bulgaria	31 May 65	Air Transport	0UNTS0	110298
Cuba	China People's Rep	23 Jul 60	Culture	60CCJC83	410714
Cuba	China People's Rep	23 Jul 60	General Economic	60CCJC81	410712
Cuba	China People's Rep	23 Jul 60	Tech Assistance	60CCJC82	410713
Cuba	China People's Rep	30 Nov 60	Direct Aid	60CCJC122	410737
Cuba	China People's Rep	08 Mar 61	Finance	61CCJC32	410764
Cuba	China People's Rep	21 Oct 61	Postal Service	61CCJC144	410843
Cuba	China People's Rep	21 Oct 61	Telecommunications	61CCJC143	410842
Cuba	China People's Rep	27 Jan 62	Mass Media	62CCJC15	410864
Cuba	China People's Rep	25 Jun 63	Scientific Project	63CCJC83	410992
Cuba	China People's Rep	15 Jan 64	General Economic	64CCJC9	411106
Cuba	China People's Rep	11 Aug 64	General Economic	64CCJC108	411114
Cuba	China People's Rep	31 Dec 64	General Trade	64CCJC189	411124
Cuba	China People's Rep	21 May 65	Tech Assistance	65CCJC68	411130
Cuba	China People's Rep	29 Dec 65	Culture	65CCJC161	411139
Cuba	China People's Rep	26 May 66	General Trade	66CCJC39	411144
Cuba	China People's Rep	27 May 66	Scientific Project	66CCJC40	411145
Cuba	China People's Rep	06 Jul 66	Tech Assistance	66CCJC67	411104
Cuba	China People's Rep	21 Mar 67	General Trade	67CCJC11	411149
Cuba	Czechoslovakia	10 Jun 60	General Trade	447UNTS75	106412
Cuba	Czechoslovakia	22 Dec 60	Culture	426UNTS145	106134
Cuba	Czechoslovakia	04 Mar 61	Air Transport	465UNTS209	106728
Cuba	Czechoslovakia	05 Apr 61	Sanitation	442UNTS201	106350
Cuba	Czechoslovakia	03 Jun 64	Sanitation	527UNTS205	107626
Cuba	France	17 Jan 51	Claims and Debts	52FRJO2609	416143
Cuba	France	16 Mar 67	Claims and Debts	46FRJO7041	416144
Cuba	Germany, East	29 Feb 60	Consul/Citizenship	8EGDA394	419184
Cuba	Germany, East	17 Dec 60	Tech Assistance	8EGDA397	419185
Cuba	Germany, East	29 Mar 61	Culture	448UNTS81	106426
Cuba	Germany, East	04 Oct 62	Mass Media	10EGDA407	419186
Cuba	Germany, East	13 Feb 63	General Trade	11EGDA585	419187
Cuba	Germany, East	11 May 63	Mass Media	11EGDA414	419188
Cuba	Germany, East	03 Sep 63	Loans and Credits	11EGDA615	419189
Cuba	Germany, East	26 Apr 64	General Aid	12EGDA837	419190
Cuba	Germany, East	20 Jul 64	Loans and Credits	12EGDA1149	419191
Cuba	Germany, East	05 Oct 64	Sanitation	12EGDA841	419192
Cuba	Germany, East	29 Oct 64	Commodity Trade	12EGDA1166	419193
Cuba	Germany, East	15 Mar 65	Education	49EGDZ332	420194
Cuba	Germany, East	01 Jun 66	Gen Communications	41EGDZ361	420195
Cuba	Germany, West	07 Jul 51	General Trade	52WGBB958	425399
Cuba	Germany, West	11 May 53	General Economic	55WGBB1055	425400
Cuba	Germany, West	22 Mar 54	Patents/Copyrights	54WGBB1112	425401
Cuba	Germany, West	23 May 57	Postal Service	61WGBB441	425402
Cuba	ILO (Labor Org)	21 Apr 51	Tech Assistance	99UNTS205	101382
Cuba	Italy	30 Jun 47	Peace/Disarmament	47ITGU300	435099
Cuba	Italy	19 Sep 49	General Amity	1ITMA616	437100
Cuba	Italy	18 May 64	Loans and Credits	65ITDI219	436101
Cuba	Japan	22 Apr 60	General Trade	442UNTS261	106354
Cuba	Korea, North	29 Aug 60	Consul/Citizenship	469UNTS163	106790
Cuba	Korea, North	29 Aug 60	Culture	473UNTS117	106860
Cuba	Multilateral	30 Jul 40	Admin Cooperation	161UNTS253	200488
Cuba	Multilateral	12 Oct 40	Specific Resources	161UNTS193	200485
Cuba	Multilateral	28 Nov 40	Commodity Trade	139UNTS159	200452
Cuba	Multilateral	15 Jan 44	IGO Establishment	161UNTS281	200489
Cuba	Multilateral	02 Aug 44	Scientific Project	67UNTS221	200221
Cuba	Multilateral	07 Dec 44	Air Transport	84UNTS389	200252

PARTY ONE	PARTY TWO	DATE	TOPIC	CITATION	NUMBER
Cuba	Multilateral	07 Dec 44	Air Transport	171UNTS387	200502
Cuba	Multilateral	07 Dec 44	Air Transport	171UNTS345	200501
Cuba	Multilateral	07 Dec 44	IGO Establishment	15UNTS295	200102
Cuba	Multilateral	15 Dec 44	Sanitation	17UNTS305	200110
Cuba	Multilateral	15 Dec 44	Sanitation	16UNTS247	200106
Cuba	Multilateral	16 Nov 45	IGO Establishment	4UNTS275	100052
Cuba	Multilateral	27 Dec 45	IGO Establishment	2UNTS39	100020
Cuba	Multilateral	22 Jul 46	IGO Establishment	14UNTS185	100221
Cuba	Multilateral	22 Jul 46	IGO Establishment	9UNTS3	100125
Cuba	Multilateral	27 Jul 46	Patents/Copyrights	90UNTS229	101238
Cuba	Multilateral	03 Sep 46	Commodity Trade	139UNTS3	101872
Cuba	Multilateral	11 Dec 46	Sanitation	12UNTS179	100186
Cuba	Multilateral	27 May 47	Air Transport	418UNTS161	106021
Cuba	Multilateral	02 Sep 47	General Military	21UNTS77	100324
Cuba	Multilateral	02 Oct 47	Telecommunications	193UNTS188	102616
Cuba	Multilateral	11 Oct 47	IGO Establishment	77UNTS143	100998
Cuba	Multilateral	06 Mar 48	Water Transport	289UNTS3	104214
Cuba	Multilateral	30 Apr 48	IGO Establishment	119UNTS3	101609
Cuba	Multilateral	30 Apr 48	Dispute Settlement	30UNTS55	100449
Cuba	Multilateral	10 Jun 48	Humanitarian	164UNTS113	102163
Cuba	Multilateral	10 Jun 48	Humanitarian	191UNTS3	102576
Cuba	Multilateral	19 Jun 48	Air Transport	310UNTS151	104492
Cuba	Multilateral	29 Nov 48	IGO Establishment	120UNTS13	101613
Cuba	Multilateral	09 Dec 48	Humanitarian	78UNTS277	101021
Cuba	Multilateral	23 Mar 49	Commodity Trade	203UNTS179	102746
Cuba	Multilateral	04 May 49	Admin Cooperation	92UNTS19	101257
Cuba	Multilateral	04 May 49	Admin Cooperation	98UNTS101	101358
Cuba	Multilateral	04 May 49	Admin Cooperation	30UNTS23	100446
Cuba	Multilateral	04 May 49	Admin Cooperation	30UNTS3	100445
Cuba	Multilateral	18 Jun 49	ILO Labor	605UNTS295	108768
Cuba	Multilateral	09 Jul 49	Telecommunications	168UNTS143	102218
Cuba	Multilateral	12 Aug 49	Humanitarian	75UNTS287	100973
Cuba	Multilateral	12 Aug 49	Humanitarian	75UNTS31	100970
Cuba	Multilateral	12 Aug 49	General Military	75UNTS135	100972
Cuba	Multilateral	12 Aug 49	Humanitarian	75UNTS85	100971
Cuba	Multilateral	21 Mar 50	Admin Cooperation	96UNTS271	101342
Cuba	Multilateral	06 Apr 50	Admin Cooperation	119UNTS99	101610
Cuba	Multilateral	22 Nov 50	Culture	131UNTS25	101734
Cuba	Multilateral	07 Dec 50	Admin Cooperation	212UNTS17	102861
Cuba	Multilateral	25 May 51	Status of Forces	175UNTS215	102303
Cuba	Multilateral	08 Sep 51	Peace/Disarmament	136UNTS45	101832
Cuba	Multilateral	06 Dec 51	Admin Cooperation	150UNTS67	101963
Cuba	Multilateral	06 Dec 51	IGO Establishment	425UNTS61	106119
Cuba	Multilateral	12 Jun 52	Dispute Settlement	138UNTS183	101869
Cuba	Multilateral	19 Jun 52	Tech Assistance	133UNTS165	101787
Cuba	Multilateral	11 Jul 52	Postal Service	171UNTS143	102226
Cuba	Multilateral	11 Jul 52	Postal Service	170UNTS269	102223
Cuba	Multilateral	11 Jul 52	Postal Service	171UNTS89	102225
Cuba	Multilateral	11 Jul 52	Postal Service	170UNTS3	102221
Cuba	Multilateral	11 Jul 52	Postal Service	170UNTS63	102222
Cuba	Multilateral	11 Jul 52	IGO Establishment	169UNTS3	102220
Cuba	Multilateral	11 Jul 52	Postal Service	171UNTS3	102224
Cuba	Multilateral	06 Sep 52	Patents/Copyrights	216UNTS132	102937
Cuba	Multilateral	31 Mar 53	Mass Media	435UNTS191	106280
Cuba	Multilateral	31 Mar 53	Privil/Immunities	193UNTS136	102613
Cuba	Multilateral	11 May 53	Sanitation	456UNTS3	106555
Cuba	Multilateral	01 Oct 53	Commodity Trade	258UNTS153	103677
Cuba	Multilateral	07 Dec 53	Admin Cooperation	182UNTS51	102422
Cuba	Multilateral	14 May 54	Culture	249UNTS215	103511
Cuba	Multilateral	04 Jun 54	Customs	282UNTS249	104101
Cuba	Multilateral	04 Jun 54	Customs	276UNTS191	103992
Cuba	Multilateral	14 Jun 54	Air Transport	320UNTS209	104643
Cuba	Multilateral	14 Jun 54	Air Transport	320UNTS217	104644
Cuba	Multilateral	25 May 55	IGO Establishment	264UNTS117	103791
Cuba	Multilateral	12 Oct 55	IGO Establishment	560UNTS3	108165

PARTY ONE	PARTY TWO	DATE	TOPIC	CITATION	NUMBER
Cuba	Multilateral	25 Apr 56	Commodity Trade	270UNTS103	103896
Cuba	Multilateral	18 May 56	Customs	327UNTS123	104721
Cuba	Multilateral	18 May 56	Customs	338UNTS103	104834
Cuba	Multilateral	20 Jun 56	Admin Cooperation	268UNTS3	103850
Cuba	Multilateral	07 Sep 56	Humanitarian	266UNTS3	103822
Cuba	Multilateral	26 Oct 56	IGO Establishment	276UNTS3	103988
Cuba	Multilateral	14 Dec 56	Taxation	436UNTS131	106293
Cuba	Multilateral	14 Dec 56	Taxation	436UNTS115	106292
Cuba	Multilateral	20 Feb 57	Consul/Citizenship	309UNTS65	104468
Cuba	Multilateral	01 May 57	Admin Cooperation	284UNTS201	104138
Cuba	Multilateral	03 Oct 57	Postal Service	366UNTS141	105217
Cuba	Multilateral	03 Oct 57	Postal Service	364UNTS3	105211
Cuba	Multilateral	03 Oct 57	Postal Service	366UNTS87	105216
Cuba	Multilateral	03 Oct 57	Postal Service	366UNTS255	105219
Cuba	Multilateral	03 Oct 57	Postal Service	364UNTS331	105212
Cuba	Multilateral	03 Oct 57	Postal Service	366UNTS3	105215
Cuba	Multilateral	03 Oct 57	Postal Service	365UNTS207	105214
Cuba	Multilateral	03 Oct 57	Postal Service	365UNTS3	105213
Cuba	Multilateral	29 Apr 58	Dispute Settlement	450UNTS169	106466
Cuba	Multilateral	29 Apr 58	Specific Resources	559UNTS285	108164
Cuba	Multilateral	29 Apr 58	Territory Boundary	499UNTS311	107302
Cuba	Multilateral	29 Apr 58	Territory Boundary	516UNTS205	107477
Cuba	Multilateral	29 Apr 58	Water Transport	450UNTS11	106465
Cuba	Multilateral	01 Dec 58	Commodity Trade	385UNTS137	105534
Cuba	Multilateral	03 Dec 58	Admin Cooperation	416UNTS51	105995
Cuba	Multilateral	03 Dec 58	Admin Cooperation	398UNTS9	105715
Cuba	Multilateral	06 Apr 59	Commodity Trade	349UNTS167	105013
Cuba	Multilateral	18 Nov 59	IGO Establishment	390UNTS227	105610
Cuba	Multilateral	14 Dec 59	Sanitation	422UNTS57	106068
Cuba	Multilateral	17 Jun 60	Humanitarian	536UNTS27	107794
Cuba	Multilateral	06 Oct 60	Customs	473UNTS131	106861
Cuba	Multilateral	09 Dec 60	Customs	429UNTS211	106200
Cuba	Multilateral	14 Dec 60	Education	429UNTS93	106193
Cuba	Multilateral	30 Mar 61	Sanitation	520UNTS151	107515
Cuba	Multilateral	18 Apr 61	Consul/Citizenship	500UNTS95	107310
Cuba	Multilateral	21 Apr 61	IGO Establishment	484UNTS349	107041
Cuba	Multilateral	08 Jun 61	Customs	473UNTS187	106863
Cuba	Multilateral	08 Jun 61	Customs	473UNTS153	106862
Cuba	Multilateral	21 Jun 61	IGO Establishment	514UNTS209	107449
Cuba	Multilateral	06 Dec 61	Customs	473UNTS219	106864
Cuba	Multilateral	26 Mar 62	IGO Establishment	539UNTS67	107825
Cuba	Multilateral	15 May 62	Commodity Trade	444UNTS3	106367
Cuba	Multilateral	28 Sep 62	IGO Establishment	469UNTS169	106791
Cuba	Multilateral	10 Dec 62	Culture	521UNTS231	107525
Cuba	Multilateral	24 Apr 63	Consul/Citizenship	596UNTS261	108638
Cuba	Multilateral	09 Nov 63	Direct Aid	489UNTS209	107141
Cuba	Multilateral	10 Jul 64	Postal Service	612UNTS3	108847
Cuba	Multilateral	10 Jul 64	Postal Service	613UNTS3	108850
Cuba	Multilateral	10 Jul 64	Postal Service	611UNTS387	108846
Cuba	Multilateral	10 Jul 64	Postal Service	613UNTS193	108852
Cuba	Multilateral	10 Jul 64	Postal Service	611UNTS105	108845
Cuba	Multilateral	10 Jul 64	Postal Service	611UNTS7	108844
Cuba	Multilateral	10 Jul 64	Postal Service	612UNTS361	108849
Cuba	Multilateral	10 Jul 64	Postal Service	612UNTS233	108848
Cuba	Multilateral	10 Jul 64	Postal Service	613UNTS3	108851
Cuba	Multilateral	05 Apr 66	Water Transport	640UNTS133	109159
Cuba	Multilateral	03 May 67	IGO Operations	0UNTS0	110764
Cuba	Multilateral	24 Dec 68	Commodity Trade	0UNTS0	109369
Cuba	Norway	06 Mar 53	Visas	2NORT599	451030
Cuba	Philippines	03 Sep 52	General Amity	3PTS3	465030
Cuba	Poland	01 Jul 60	Tech Assistance	60PZUM71	458077
Cuba	Poland	06 Mar 61	Culture	484UNTS123	107020
Cuba	Poland	12 Oct 62	Mass Media	62PZUM93	458098
Cuba	Portugal	26 Jun 51	Air Transport	192UNTS115	102598
Cuba	Romania	28 Oct 60	Culture	457UNTS9	106574

PARTY ONE	PARTY TWO	DATE	TOPIC	CITATION	NUMBER
Cuba	Spain	19 Jun 51	Air Transport	53SPBO2504	460068
Cuba	Spain	18 Aug 53	General Economic	54SPBO408	460069
Cuba	Spain	06 Jul 54	General Economic	56SPBO1702	460070
Cuba	Spain	21 Jul 55	General Economic	55SPBO1508	460071
Cuba	Spain	14 Aug 56	General Economic	56SPBO609	460072
Cuba	Switzerland	30 Mar 54	General Trade	54SWRO537	462128
Cuba	Taiwan	12 Nov 42	General Amity	10UNTS243	200065
Cuba	UK Great Britain	02 Dec 46	Admin Cooperation	11UNTS161	100154
Cuba	UK Great Britain	19 Mar 48	Air Transport	175UNTS23	102294
Cuba	UK Great Britain	02 Mar 51	Visas	88UNTS191	101190
Cuba	UK Great Britain	10 Aug 51	General Trade	108UNTS243	101478
Cuba	UK Great Britain	18 Dec 53	General Trade	186UNTS157	102490
Cuba	UN Special Fund	10 Mar 61	Direct Aid	390UNTS35	105601
Cuba	UNICEF (Children)	11 Feb 60	Direct Aid	349UNTS277	105014
Cuba	USA (United States)	16 May 32	Consul/Citizenship	234UNTS283	200537
Cuba	USA (United States)	23 Dec 41	General Trade	119UNTS313	200388
Cuba	USA (United States)	01 Feb 43	Milit Servic/Citiz	13UNTS379	200085
Cuba	USA (United States)	30 Oct 47	General Economic	119UNTS163	101611
Cuba	USA (United States)	27 Jan 48	Scientific Project	67UNTS3	100862
Cuba	USA (United States)	21 Feb 49	Status of Forces	231UNTS108	103212
Cuba	USA (United States)	22 Dec 50	Military Mission	122UNTS97	101640
Cuba	USA (United States)	20 Jun 51	Tech Assistance	148UNTS3	101931
Cuba	USA (United States)	28 Aug 51	Military Mission	140UNTS239	101891
Cuba	USA (United States)	28 Aug 51	Military Mission	134UNTS225	101802
Cuba	USA (United States)	17 Dec 51	Visas	152UNTS87	102012
Cuba	USA (United States)	18 Dec 51	General Military	165UNTS3	102164
Cuba	USA (United States)	27 Feb 52	Gen Communications	168UNTS3	102209
Cuba	USA (United States)	07 Mar 52	Milit Assistance	165UNTS11	102165
Cuba	USA (United States)	26 May 53	Air Transport	224UNTS75	103070
Cuba	USA (United States)	26 Nov 53	Air Transport	205UNTS213	102777
Cuba	USA (United States)	03 Aug 55	Military Mission	265UNTS41	103805
Cuba	USA (United States)	10 Jan 56	Milit Assistance	240UNTS101	103398
Cuba	USA (United States)	26 Jun 56	Atomic Energy	293UNTS257	104294
Cuba	USA (United States)	04 Feb 57	Admin Cooperation	302UNTS273	104366
Cuba	USA (United States)	15 Aug 58	Specific Resources	358UNTS63	105124
Cuba	USA (United States)	06 Nov 65	Refugees	601UNTS81	108688
Cuba	USSR (Soviet Union)	13 Feb 60	General Economic	369UNTS17	105248
Cuba	USSR (Soviet Union)	13 Feb 60	Claims and Debts	369UNTS3	105247
Cuba	USSR (Soviet Union)	20 Feb 60	General Trade	9SUGG126	469632
Cuba	USSR (Soviet Union)	08 May 60	Consul/Citizenship	9SUGG135	469656
Cuba	USSR (Soviet Union)	18 Jun 60	General Trade	9SUGG139	469666
Cuba	USSR (Soviet Union)	18 Jun 60	Finance	9SUGG139	469667
Cuba	USSR (Soviet Union)	16 Nov 60	Tech Assistance	9SUGG152	469713
Cuba	USSR (Soviet Union)	16 Nov 60	Education	9SUGG152	469714
Cuba	USSR (Soviet Union)	12 Dec 60	Culture	421UNTS3	106048
Cuba	USSR (Soviet Union)	19 Dec 60	General Aid	9SUGG155	469723
Cuba	USSR (Soviet Union)	19 Dec 60	Education	9SUGG155	469724
Cuba	USSR (Soviet Union)	01 Jun 61	Tech Assistance	10SUGG132	469773
Cuba	USSR (Soviet Union)	11 Oct 61	Tech Assistance	10SUGG143	469799
Cuba	USSR (Soviet Union)	08 May 62	Direct Aid	11SUGG139	469836
Cuba	USSR (Soviet Union)	14 May 62	General Trade	11SUGG140	469838
Cuba	USSR (Soviet Union)	17 Jul 62	Air Transport	11SUGG147	469850
Cuba	USSR (Soviet Union)	17 Jul 62	Air Transport	0UNTS0	110123
Cuba	USSR (Soviet Union)	03 Aug 62	Tech Assistance	16SUGG134	470010
Cuba	USSR (Soviet Union)	04 Aug 62	Education	11SUGG149	469852
Cuba	USSR (Soviet Union)	30 Aug 62	Non-IBRD Project	11SUGG150	469858
Cuba	USSR (Soviet Union)	25 Sep 62	Specific Resources	11SUGG153	469864
Cuba	USSR (Soviet Union)	25 Sep 62	Non-IBRD Project	11SUGG153	469865
Cuba	USSR (Soviet Union)	26 Sep 62	Specific Resources	16SUGG134	470011
Cuba	USSR (Soviet Union)	17 Feb 65	Finance	0UNTS0	109830
Cuba	USSR (Soviet Union)	17 Feb 65	General Trade	0UNTS0	109583
Customs Coop Coun	Multilateral	01 Mar 56	Customs	343UNTS129	104923
Customs Coop Coun	Multilateral	11 Jun 68	Scientific Project	0UNTS0	109884
Cyprus	Accept UN Charter	29 May 61	UN Charter	397UNTS283	105711
Cyprus	Austria	14 Dec 67	Visas	636UNTS267	109104

PARTY ONE	PARTY TWO	DATE	TOPIC	CITATION	NUMBER
Cyprus	Belgium	08 Jun 63	Air Transport	601UNTS311	108703
Cyprus	Bulgaria	08 May 65	Air Transport	0UNTS0	109957
Cyprus	Denmark	27 Apr 63	Air Transport	529UNTS255	107664
Cyprus	France	29 Oct 69	Culture	0UNTS0	110461
Cyprus	Germany, East	07 Nov 64	General Economic	12EGDA1107	419498
Cyprus	Germany, East	12 Feb 66	General Economic	52EGDZ353	420499
Cyprus	Germany, East	04 Aug 66	Sanitation	50EGDZ365	420500
Cyprus	Germany, West	30 Oct 61	General Economic	62WBGA3	424737
Cyprus	Germany, West	30 Oct 61	Tech Assistance	62WBGA3	424738
Cyprus	Germany, West	30 Oct 61	General Trade	62WBGA3	424736
Cyprus	Germany, West	30 May 67	Commodity Trade	69WBGA2	424739
Cyprus	Germany, West	18 Oct 67	Air Transport	69WGBB981	425740
Cyprus	Germany, West	24 Jun 70	Loans and Credits	70WBGA163	424741
Cyprus	Greece	23 Nov 61	Air Transport	497UNTS311	107274
Cyprus	Greece	23 Aug 62	General Trade	609UNTS15	108825
Cyprus	Greece	30 Mar 68	Taxation	0UNTS0	109465
Cyprus	Hungary	02 Jun 64	Air Transport	602UNTS3	108704
Cyprus	IBRD (World Bank)	17 Apr 63	IBRD Project	476UNTS185	106909
Cyprus	IBRD (World Bank)	16 May 67	Loans and Credits	617UNTS21	108906
Cyprus	IBRD (World Bank)	30 Jun 69	IBRD Project	0UNTS0	110309
Cyprus	IBRD (World Bank)	24 Dec 69	IBRD Project	0UNTS0	110676
Cyprus	Israel	17 Aug 61	Visas	484UNTS169	107025
Cyprus	Multilateral	07 Dec 44	Air Transport	84UNTS389	200252
Cyprus	Multilateral	07 Dec 44	IGO Establishment	15UNTS295	200102
Cyprus	Multilateral	11 Dec 46	Sanitation	12UNTS179	100186
Cyprus	Multilateral	12 Nov 47	Admin Cooperation	46UNTS201	100710
Cyprus	Multilateral	11 May 48	Telecommunications	500UNTS267	107313
Cyprus	Multilateral	24 Jul 48	Sanitation	66UNTS25	100847
Cyprus	Multilateral	04 May 49	Admin Cooperation	98UNTS101	101358
Cyprus	Multilateral	04 May 49	Admin Cooperation	92UNTS19	101257
Cyprus	Multilateral	04 May 49	Admin Cooperation	47UNTS159	100728
Cyprus	Multilateral	05 May 49	IGO Establishment	87UNTS103	101168
Cyprus	Multilateral	02 Sep 49	IGO Status/Immunit	250UNTS12	103515
Cyprus	Multilateral	24 Sep 49	IGO Establishment	126UNTS237	101691
Cyprus	Multilateral	22 Nov 50	Culture	131UNTS25	101734
Cyprus	Multilateral	02 Jul 51	Refugees	189UNTS137	102545
Cyprus	Multilateral	07 Nov 52	General Trade	221UNTS255	103010
Cyprus	Multilateral	31 Mar 53	Privil/Immunities	193UNTS136	102613
Cyprus	Multilateral	25 May 55	IGO Establishment	264UNTS117	103791
Cyprus	Multilateral	26 Jan 60	IGO Establishment	439UNTS249	106333
Cyprus	Multilateral	17 Jun 60	Humanitarian	536UNTS27	107794
Cyprus	Multilateral	16 Aug 60	General Amity	397UNTS287	105712
Cyprus	Multilateral	16 Aug 60	Recognition	382UNTS3	105475
Cyprus	Multilateral	16 Aug 60	Recognition	382UNTS8	105476
Cyprus	Multilateral	21 Jun 61	IGO Establishment	514UNTS209	107449
Cyprus	Multilateral	18 Oct 61	IGO Establishment	529UNTS89	107659
Cyprus	Multilateral	18 Apr 62	Tech Assistance	463UNTS44	106692
Cyprus	Multilateral	29 Nov 62	Visas	457UNTS63	106577
Cyprus	Multilateral	05 Aug 63	Sanitation	480UNTS43	106964
Cyprus	Multilateral	10 Jul 64	Postal Service	611UNTS387	108846
Cyprus	Multilateral	10 Jul 64	Postal Service	611UNTS105	108845
Cyprus	Multilateral	10 Jul 64	Postal Service	612UNTS3	108847
Cyprus	Multilateral	10 Jul 64	Postal Service	611UNTS7	108844
Cyprus	Multilateral	13 Jul 64	ILO Labor	569UNTS65	108279
Cyprus	Multilateral	05 Mar 65	IGO Operations	527UNTS221	107627
Cyprus	Multilateral	18 Mar 65	Dispute Settlement	575UNTS159	108359
Cyprus	Multilateral	23 Jun 65	General IGO	614UNTS239	108873
Cyprus	Multilateral	31 Jan 67	Refugees	606UNTS267	108791
Cyprus	Multilateral	29 Jun 67	Non-ILO Labor	0UNTS0	110030
Cyprus	Multilateral	18 Mar 68	Commodity Trade	0UNTS0	109262
Cyprus	Multilateral	07 Jun 68	Admin Cooperation	0UNTS0	110346
Cyprus	Multilateral	01 Jul 68	Peace/Disarmament	0UNTS0	110485
Cyprus	Multilateral	27 Jan 69	Telecommunications	0UNTS0	109664
Cyprus	Netherlands	18 Apr 69	Air Transport	0UNTS0	110472
Cyprus	Norway	18 May 55	Taxation	2NORT553	451031

PARTY ONE	PARTY TWO	DATE	TOPIC	CITATION	NUMBER
Cyprus	Norway	25 May 62	Visas	3NORT857	451032
Cyprus	Norway	05 Mar 63	Air Transport	563UNTS305	108216
Cyprus	Syria	22 Dec 64	Air Transport	602UNTS25	108705
Cyprus	UK Great Britain	16 Aug 60	Customs	382UNTS215	105482
Cyprus	UK Great Britain	16 Aug 60	Specific Property	382UNTS207	105481
Cyprus	UK Great Britain	16 Aug 60	Privil/Immunities	382UNTS225	105483
Cyprus	UK Great Britain	16 Aug 60	Specific Property	382UNTS177	105477
Cyprus	UK Great Britain	16 Aug 60	Consul/Citizenship	382UNTS247	105486
Cyprus	UK Great Britain	16 Aug 60	Dispute Settlement	382UNTS183	105478
Cyprus	UK Great Britain	16 Aug 60	Specific Property	382UNTS201	105480
Cyprus	UK Great Britain	16 Aug 60	Claims and Debts	382UNTS239	105485
Cyprus	UK Great Britain	16 Aug 60	Direct Aid	382UNTS231	105484
Cyprus	UK Great Britain	16 Aug 60	Specific Property	382UNTS189	105479
Cyprus	UK Great Britain	02 Jul 64	Commodity Trade	522UNTS129	107540
Cyprus	UK Great Britain	07 Mar 68	Taxation	0UNTS0	109342
Cyprus	UK Great Britain	11 Mar 68	Military Mission	0UNTS0	109285
Cyprus	UK Great Britain	21 Sep 68	Finance	0UNTS0	109808
Cyprus	UK Great Britain	06 Oct 69	Non-ILO Labor	0UNTS0	110426
Cyprus	UN Special Fund	24 Feb 61	Direct Aid	389UNTS3	105588
Cyprus	UNICEF (Children)	19 Apr 61	Direct Aid	394UNTS185	105678
Cyprus	United Nations	15 Jun 61	Tech Assistance	398UNTS39	105716
Cyprus	United Nations	30 Mar 64	IGO Status/Immunit	492UNTS261	107194
Cyprus	United Nations	31 Mar 64	IGO Status/Immunit	492UNTS57	107187
Cyprus	USA (United States)	08 Dec 60	Direct Aid	405UNTS145	105831
Cyprus	USA (United States)	29 Jun 61	General Aid	411UNTS56	105914
Cyprus	USA (United States)	15 Jan 62	Commodity Trade	435UNTS15	106267
Cyprus	USA (United States)	18 Jan 62	Education	435UNTS3	106266
Cyprus	USA (United States)	02 Mar 62	Direct Aid	445UNTS189	106386
Cyprus	USA (United States)	23 Aug 62	General Aid	461UNTS147	106658
Cyprus	USA (United States)	11 Jan 63	Visas	471UNTS127	106827
Cyprus	USA (United States)	23 Apr 63	Telecommunications	487UNTS291	107111
Cyprus	USA (United States)	29 May 63	Finance	487UNTS283	107110
Cyprus	USA (United States)	18 Jun 63	US Agri Commod Aid	479UNTS191	106953
Cyprus	USSR (Soviet Union)	18 Aug 60	Recognition	16SUGG128	469981
Cyprus	USSR (Soviet Union)	13 Nov 60	Consul/Citizenship	9SUGG151	469709
Cyprus	USSR (Soviet Union)	22 Dec 61	General Trade	0UNTS0	109828
Cyprus	USSR (Soviet Union)	22 Dec 61	General Economic	10SUGG147	469813
Cyprus	USSR (Soviet Union)	29 Feb 64	Air Transport	602UNTS45	108706
Cyprus	USSR (Soviet Union)	22 Feb 65	General Trade	0UNTS0	109584
Cyprus	WHO (World Health)	07 Oct 67	Direct Aid	608UNTS327	108821
Czechoslovakia	Afghanistan	28 May 60	Air Transport	497UNTS129	107266
Czechoslovakia	Afghanistan	23 Apr 61	Culture	437UNTS25	106297
Czechoslovakia	Albania	16 Jan 59	Consul/Citizenship	363UNTS165	105207
Czechoslovakia	Albania	16 Jan 59	Admin Cooperation	363UNTS195	105208
Czechoslovakia	Algeria	09 Mar 64	Air Transport	601UNTS247	108700
Czechoslovakia	Algeria	14 May 64	Culture	538UNTS301	107817
Czechoslovakia	Australia	01 Apr 55	Postal Service	213UNTS199	102888
Czechoslovakia	Austria	29 Oct 48	Water Transport	56ABGB74	403022
Czechoslovakia	Austria	30 Mar 50	Sanitation	495UNTS85	107240
Czechoslovakia	Austria	23 Jan 60	Specific Resources	495UNTS125	107242
Czechoslovakia	Austria	23 Jan 60	Scientific Project	495UNTS99	107241
Czechoslovakia	Austria	14 Sep 60	Commodity Trade	495UNTS143	107243
Czechoslovakia	Austria	17 Jan 61	Customs	61ABGB222	403023
Czechoslovakia	Austria	10 Nov 61	Admin Cooperation	455UNTS337	106550
Czechoslovakia	Austria	13 Feb 62	Education	455UNTS381	106551
Czechoslovakia	Austria	01 Mar 62	Air Transport	62ABGB319	403024
Czechoslovakia	Austria	22 Sep 62	Land Transport	495UNTS157	107244
Czechoslovakia	Austria	08 Mar 63	General Economic	495UNTS219	107245
Czechoslovakia	Austria	03 Jan 67	Visas	67ABGB348	403025
Czechoslovakia	Austria	30 Jun 67	Customs	67ABGB299	403026
Czechoslovakia	Austria	19 Oct 67	Land Transport	634UNTS19	109048
Czechoslovakia	Austria	07 Dec 67	Water Transport	0UNTS0	110475
Czechoslovakia	Austria	07 Dec 67	Specific Resources	70ABGB106	403027
Czechoslovakia	Austria	14 Dec 67	Visas	634UNTS51	109050
Czechoslovakia	Austria	02 Jul 69	General Trade	70ABGB129	403028

PARTY ONE	PARTY TWO	DATE	TOPIC	CITATION	NUMBER
Czechoslovakia	Austria	16 Dec 70	Customs	71ABGB84	403029
Czechoslovakia	Austria	12 Sep 71	General Economic	72ABGB24	403030
Czechoslovakia	Austria	22 Oct 71	Finance	71ABGB496	403031
Czechoslovakia	Bel-Lux Econ Union	10 Oct 67	Tech Assistance	0UNTS0	109362
Czechoslovakia	Belgium	16 May 45	Refugees	19UNTS251	200119
Czechoslovakia	Belgium	06 Mar 47	Culture	34UNTS77	100528
Czechoslovakia	Belgium	19 Mar 47	Claims and Debts	23UNTS35	100341
Czechoslovakia	Belgium	03 Jul 48	General Trade	77UNTS137	100997
Czechoslovakia	Belgium	14 Nov 49	Visas	46UNTS319	100718
Czechoslovakia	Belgium	02 May 51	Taxation	109UNTS3	101483
Czechoslovakia	Belgium	08 Aug 56	Visas	257UNTS215	103656
Czechoslovakia	Belgium	12 Mar 57	Air Transport	312UNTS75	104512
Czechoslovakia	Belgium	17 Apr 68	Land Transport	0UNTS0	109539
Czechoslovakia	Bulgaria	20 Jun 47	Education	46UNTS15	100698
Czechoslovakia	Bulgaria	05 Mar 48	Admin Cooperation	26UNTS115	100382
Czechoslovakia	Bulgaria	13 Apr 54	Admin Cooperation	501UNTS3	107314
Czechoslovakia	Bulgaria	25 Jan 57	Non-ILO Labor	501UNTS149	107316
Czechoslovakia	Bulgaria	03 Jun 57	Sanitation	292UNTS3	104261
Czechoslovakia	Bulgaria	27 May 59	Consul/Citizenship	360UNTS335	105167
Czechoslovakia	Bulgaria	19 Sep 59	Sanitation	355UNTS77	105074
Czechoslovakia	Bulgaria	22 May 65	Culture	545UNTS65	107925
Czechoslovakia	Bulgaria	04 Jun 65	Visas	0UNTS0	110515
Czechoslovakia	Bulgaria	26 Apr 68	General Amity	0UNTS0	110344
Czechoslovakia	Burma	15 Dec 65	Air Transport	602UNTS71	108707
Czechoslovakia	Cambodia	27 Nov 60	Culture	410UNTS263	105910
Czechoslovakia	Cambodia	27 Nov 60	General Amity	412UNTS179	105931
Czechoslovakia	Canada	01 Mar 45	Finance	45UNTS283	200185
Czechoslovakia	Canada	28 Jun 46	Finance	43UNTS81	100662
Czechoslovakia	Canada	20 Mar 69	Air Transport	0UNTS0	110470
Czechoslovakia	China People's Rep	14 Jun 50	General Trade	50CCJC22	410017
Czechoslovakia	China People's Rep	21 Jun 51	General Trade	51CCJC19	410040
Czechoslovakia	China People's Rep	06 May 52	Postal Service	52CCJC17	410062
Czechoslovakia	China People's Rep	06 May 52	Scientific Project	52CCJC19	410064
Czechoslovakia	China People's Rep	06 May 52	Telecommunications	52CCJC18	410063
Czechoslovakia	China People's Rep	24 May 52	Culture	52CCJC20	410065
Czechoslovakia	China People's Rep	07 May 53	General Trade	53CCJC22	410100
Czechoslovakia	China People's Rep	07 May 53	Telecommunications	53CCJC24	410101
Czechoslovakia	China People's Rep	18 Aug 53	Sanitation	53CCJC48	410114
Czechoslovakia	China People's Rep	27 Apr 54	General Economic	54CCJC20	410143
Czechoslovakia	China People's Rep	06 Apr 55	General Economic	55CCJC21	410224
Czechoslovakia	China People's Rep	06 Apr 55	General Trade	55CCJC22	410225
Czechoslovakia	China People's Rep	11 Nov 55	General Economic	55CCJC81	410269
Czechoslovakia	China People's Rep	03 Dec 55	Scientific Project	55CCJC94	410279
Czechoslovakia	China People's Rep	06 Mar 57	General Economic	57CCJC22	410404
Czechoslovakia	China People's Rep	27 Mar 57	Culture	57CCJC30	410410
Czechoslovakia	China People's Rep	27 Mar 57	General Amity	57CCJC29	410409
Czechoslovakia	China People's Rep	27 Mar 57	Sanitation	57CCJC31	410411
Czechoslovakia	China People's Rep	16 Apr 58	General Economic	58CCJC51	410517
Czechoslovakia	China People's Rep	03 Mar 59	Scientific Project	59CCJC41	410595
Czechoslovakia	China People's Rep	12 Mar 59	General Economic	59CCJC48	410601
Czechoslovakia	China People's Rep	30 Apr 59	Mass Media	59CCJC73	410620
Czechoslovakia	China People's Rep	02 Feb 60	General Economic	60CCJC10	410661
Czechoslovakia	China People's Rep	07 May 60	Consul/Citizenship	402UNTS209	105787
Czechoslovakia	China People's Rep	07 May 60	Consul/Citizenship	60CCJC61	410700
Czechoslovakia	China People's Rep	20 Oct 61	General Trade	61CCJC141	410841
Czechoslovakia	China People's Rep	07 Mar 62	Finance	62CCJC22	410871
Czechoslovakia	China People's Rep	17 Jul 62	General Economic	62CCJC64	410901
Czechoslovakia	China People's Rep	30 Sep 62	Scientific Project	62CCJC90	410918
Czechoslovakia	China People's Rep	19 Apr 63	General Economic	63CCJC44	410969
Czechoslovakia	China People's Rep	20 Nov 63	Finance	63CCJC135	411032
Czechoslovakia	China People's Rep	24 Mar 65	Scientific Project	65CCJC42	411128
Czechoslovakia	China People's Rep	08 Apr 65	General Economic	65CCJC53	411101
Czechoslovakia	China People's Rep	18 Jun 65	Culture	65CCJC84	411132
Czechoslovakia	China People's Rep	26 Oct 65	Scientific Project	65CCJC133	411137
Czechoslovakia	China People's Rep	23 Dec 65	Scientific Project	65CCJC160	411138

PARTY ONE	PARTY TWO	DATE	TOPIC	CITATION	NUMBER
Czechoslovakia	China People's Rep	04 Feb 66	General Economic	66CCJC3	411103
Czechoslovakia	China People's Rep	11 May 66	Culture	66CCJC32	411143
Czechoslovakia	China People's Rep	28 Oct 66	Scientific Project	66CCJC90	411146
Czechoslovakia	COMECON (Econ Aid)	20 Jul 62	IGO Operations	506UNTS345	107393
Czechoslovakia	Congo (Brazzaville)	29 Nov 66	Culture	635UNTS3	109069
Czechoslovakia	Cuba	10 Jun 60	General Trade	447UNTS75	106412
Czechoslovakia	Cuba	22 Dec 60	Culture	426UNTS145	106134
Czechoslovakia	Cuba	04 Mar 61	Air Transport	465UNTS209	106728
Czechoslovakia	Cuba	05 Apr 61	Sanitation	442UNTS201	106350
Czechoslovakia	Cuba	03 Jun 64	Sanitation	527UNTS205	107626
Czechoslovakia	Denmark	14 May 47	Air Transport	27UNTS297	100413
Czechoslovakia	Denmark	17 Dec 49	Finance	74UNTS159	100962
Czechoslovakia	Denmark	17 Dec 49	General Trade	74UNTS147	100961
Czechoslovakia	Denmark	04 Apr 52	General Trade	133UNTS245	101792
Czechoslovakia	Denmark	23 Apr 53	General Trade	174UNTS95	102280
Czechoslovakia	Denmark	23 Apr 53	Finance	174UNTS107	102281
Czechoslovakia	Denmark	25 Oct 62	Taxation	456UNTS457	106571
Czechoslovakia	Denmark	21 Jan 69	Land Transport	0UNTS0	109469
Czechoslovakia	Ethiopia	11 Dec 59	General Amity	386UNTS51	105537
Czechoslovakia	Ethiopia	11 Dec 59	Scientific Project	386UNTS45	105536
Czechoslovakia	Ethiopia	11 Dec 59	Culture	399UNTS93	105736
Czechoslovakia	Finland	13 Jul 49	Air Transport	53UNTS153	100779
Czechoslovakia	France	08 Dec 45	Education	46UNTS77	100701
Czechoslovakia	France	20 Nov 46	Reparations	48FRJO1501	416436
Czechoslovakia	France	01 Dec 47	Reparations	50FRJO0	416437
Czechoslovakia	France	06 Aug 48	Claims and Debts	48FRMD1908	417439
Czechoslovakia	France	06 Aug 48	Taxation	49FRJO2207	416438
Czechoslovakia	France	12 Oct 48	Non-ILO Labor	45UNTS81	100693
Czechoslovakia	France	02 Jun 50	Claims and Debts	63FRRT51	415440
Czechoslovakia	France	16 Jan 64	Dispute Settlement	64FRRT15	415441
Czechoslovakia	France	26 Sep 64	Culture	0UNTS0	110726
Czechoslovakia	France	29 Jun 65	Tech Assistance	66FRJO2502	416443
Czechoslovakia	France	29 Jun 65	General Trade	65FRMD2807	417442
Czechoslovakia	France	29 Jun 65	Scientific Project	0UNTS0	110727
Czechoslovakia	France	30 May 67	Sanitation	68FRJO1101	416444
Czechoslovakia	France	26 Oct 67	Culture	68FRJO2109	416445
Czechoslovakia	France	03 Mar 68	Culture	68FRJO1709	416446
Czechoslovakia	France	06 Mar 68	Mass Media	0UNTS0	109379
Czechoslovakia	France	21 Sep 68	General Transport	69FRJO2006	416447
Czechoslovakia	France	21 Sep 68	Land Transport	0UNTS0	110347
Czechoslovakia	Germany, East	23 Jun 50	Finance	4EGDA250	419327
Czechoslovakia	Germany, East	23 Jun 50	Finance	1EGDA376	419326
Czechoslovakia	Germany, East	23 Jun 50	Culture	4EGDA252	419328
Czechoslovakia	Germany, East	23 Jun 50	General Amity	504UNTS163	107357
Czechoslovakia	Germany, East	23 Jun 50	Scientific Project	4EGDA248	419325
Czechoslovakia	Germany, East	12 Jul 50	Sanitation	4EGDA255	419329
Czechoslovakia	Germany, East	25 Aug 50	Postal Service	4EGDA259	419330
Czechoslovakia	Germany, East	25 Aug 50	Postal Service	4EGDA263	419331
Czechoslovakia	Germany, East	25 Aug 50	Telecommunications	4EGDA267	419332
Czechoslovakia	Germany, East	30 Dec 50	Visas	4EGDA272	419333
Czechoslovakia	Germany, East	01 Dec 51	General Economic	1EGDA393	419334
Czechoslovakia	Germany, East	19 Feb 53	Culture	4EGDA282	419335
Czechoslovakia	Germany, East	20 Mar 53	General Trade	1EGDA421	419336
Czechoslovakia	Germany, East	01 Apr 53	Finance	4EGDA288	419337
Czechoslovakia	Germany, East	03 Oct 53	Land Transport	4EGDA194	419338
Czechoslovakia	Germany, East	13 Oct 53	Consul/Citizenship	1EGDA422	419339
Czechoslovakia	Germany, East	17 Feb 54	Sanitation	4EGDA302	419340
Czechoslovakia	Germany, East	21 Jul 54	General Economic	2EGDA442	419341
Czechoslovakia	Germany, East	15 Oct 54	Water Transport	4EGDA308	419342
Czechoslovakia	Germany, East	28 Jan 55	Mass Media	4EGDA320	419343
Czechoslovakia	Germany, East	31 Mar 55	Postal Service	4EGDA267	419344
Czechoslovakia	Germany, East	20 Jun 55	General Economic	3EGDA511	419345
Czechoslovakia	Germany, East	08 Aug 55	Air Transport	4EGDA325	419346
Czechoslovakia	Germany, East	30 Aug 55	Sanitation	504UNTS279	107361
Czechoslovakia	Germany, East	24 Oct 55	Land Transport	504UNTS173	107358

PARTY ONE	PARTY TWO	DATE	TOPIC	CITATION	NUMBER
Czechoslovakia	Germany, East	14 Nov 55	Specific Resources	4EGDA345	419347
Czechoslovakia	Germany, East	23 Nov 55	Scientific Project	3EGDA516	419348
Czechoslovakia	Germany, East	25 Apr 56	Land Transport	4EGDA359	419349
Czechoslovakia	Germany, East	04 May 56	Consul/Citizenship	4EGDA366	419350
Czechoslovakia	Germany, East	24 Aug 56	Customs	5EGDA486	419351
Czechoslovakia	Germany, East	31 Aug 56	Finance	5EGDA491	419352
Czechoslovakia	Germany, East	11 Sep 56	Consul/Citizenship	5EGDA506	419353
Czechoslovakia	Germany, East	11 Sep 56	Health/Educ/Welfare	5EGDA539	419356
Czechoslovakia	Germany, East	11 Sep 56	Admin Cooperation	5EGDA511	419355
Czechoslovakia	Germany, East	11 Sep 56	General Economic	5EGDA507	419354
Czechoslovakia	Germany, East	06 Oct 56	Humanitarian	501UNTS109	107315
Czechoslovakia	Germany, East	21 Dec 56	Scientific Project	5EGDA554	419357
Czechoslovakia	Germany, East	29 Jan 57	Culture	5EGDA557	419358
Czechoslovakia	Germany, East	24 May 57	Consul/Citizenship	292UNTS327	104279
Czechoslovakia	Germany, East	20 Dec 57	IGO Establishment	5EGDA580	419359
Czechoslovakia	Germany, East	26 Jun 58	Patents/Copyrights	504UNTS221	107359
Czechoslovakia	Germany, East	29 Jan 59	General Economic	7EGDA447	419360
Czechoslovakia	Germany, East	12 Sep 59	General Aid	7EGDA449	419361
Czechoslovakia	Germany, East	18 Sep 59	Customs	363UNTS287	105209
Czechoslovakia	Germany, East	25 Nov 59	General Economic	374UNTS101	105331
Czechoslovakia	Germany, East	01 Jun 60	General Trade	8EGDA438	419362
Czechoslovakia	Germany, East	16 Jun 60	General Economic	415UNTS248	105988
Czechoslovakia	Germany, East	08 Nov 60	Admin Cooperation	424UNTS71	106100
Czechoslovakia	Germany, East	26 Nov 60	Specific Property	8EGDA452	419363
Czechoslovakia	Germany, East	15 Dec 60	Finance	8EGDA457	419364
Czechoslovakia	Germany, East	09 Dec 61	Specific Property	9EGDA395	419365
Czechoslovakia	Germany, East	28 Nov 62	Specific Resources	52EGDZ276	420366
Czechoslovakia	Germany, East	27 Jun 63	Health/Educ/Welfare	11EGDA647	419367
Czechoslovakia	Germany, East	09 Dec 63	Air Transport	11EGDA501	419368
Czechoslovakia	Germany, East	06 Oct 64	Culture	545UNTS113	107927
Czechoslovakia	Germany, East	21 Dec 65	General Trade	59EGDZ350	420369
Czechoslovakia	Germany, East	16 Feb 66	Finance	51EGDZ354	420370
Czechoslovakia	Germany, East	20 Jul 66	Admin Cooperation	45EGDZ364	420371
Czechoslovakia	Germany, East	17 Mar 67	General Amity	609UNTS187	108831
Czechoslovakia	Germany, West	03 Aug 67	General Economic	68WBGA61	424676
Czechoslovakia	Germany, West	17 Dec 70	General Economic	71WBGA1	424677
Czechoslovakia	Ghana	23 Nov 60	Tech Assistance	431UNTS85	106212
Czechoslovakia	Ghana	23 Nov 60	Culture	431UNTS91	106213
Czechoslovakia	Ghana	02 Aug 61	Air Transport	465UNTS249	106730
Czechoslovakia	Greece	30 Jul 47	Finance	185UNTS115	102463
Czechoslovakia	Greece	30 Jul 47	Claims and Debts	185UNTS143	102465
Czechoslovakia	Greece	30 Jul 47	Reparations	185UNTS149	102466
Czechoslovakia	Greece	30 Jul 47	General Trade	185UNTS133	102464
Czechoslovakia	Greece	01 Feb 54	General Trade	225UNTS77	103091
Czechoslovakia	Greece	01 Feb 54	Finance	225UNTS95	103092
Czechoslovakia	Guinea	30 Nov 59	Culture	386UNTS63	105538
Czechoslovakia	Guinea	16 Dec 61	Air Transport	559UNTS49	108154
Czechoslovakia	Hungary	27 Feb 49	Admin Cooperation	26UNTS119	100383
Czechoslovakia	Hungary	16 Apr 49	General Amity	477UNTS183	106922
Czechoslovakia	Hungary	16 Apr 54	Specific Resources	504UNTS231	107360
Czechoslovakia	Hungary	28 Apr 55	Sanitation	477UNTS197	106923
Czechoslovakia	Hungary	13 Oct 56	Territory Boundary	300UNTS177	104337
Czechoslovakia	Hungary	13 Oct 56	Territory Boundary	300UNTS125	104336
Czechoslovakia	Hungary	12 Mar 58	Sanitation	408UNTS178	105870
Czechoslovakia	Hungary	08 May 58	Customs	407UNTS92	105862
Czechoslovakia	Hungary	27 Jun 58	Consul/Citizenship	477UNTS321	106927
Czechoslovakia	Hungary	30 Jan 59	Non-ILO Labor	351UNTS3	105016
Czechoslovakia	Hungary	27 Mar 59	Consul/Citizenship	351UNTS57	105017
Czechoslovakia	Hungary	04 Nov 60	Consul/Citizenship	397UNTS227	105708
Czechoslovakia	Hungary	24 Feb 61	Culture	422UNTS15	106066
Czechoslovakia	Hungary	02 Nov 61	Admin Cooperation	438UNTS3	106313
Czechoslovakia	Hungary	16 Oct 62	Visas	479UNTS301	106961
Czechoslovakia	Hungary	22 Oct 63	Land Transport	514UNTS95	107444
Czechoslovakia	Hungary	20 Dec 63	General Economic	538UNTS127	107812
Czechoslovakia	Hungary	17 Oct 64	Land Transport	545UNTS21	107924

PARTY ONE	PARTY TWO	DATE	TOPIC	CITATION	NUMBER
Czechoslovakia	Hungary	27 Feb 68	IGO Establishment	640UNTS49	109154
Czechoslovakia	Hungary	14 Jun 68	General Amity	0UNTS0	109645
Czechoslovakia	India	07 Jul 59	Culture	359UNTS259	105145
Czechoslovakia	India	19 Sep 60	Air Transport	465UNTS67	106722
Czechoslovakia	Indonesia	29 May 61	General Amity	479UNTS337	106962
Czechoslovakia	Iran	29 Jan 66	General Economic	0IRTB66	433106
Czechoslovakia	Iran	26 May 67	Culture	0IRTB66	433105
Czechoslovakia	Iran	12 Mar 69	General Economic	0IRTB66	433107
Czechoslovakia	Iran	12 Mar 69	General Trade	0IRTB66	433108
Czechoslovakia	Iran	12 Mar 69	Finance	0IRTB67	433109
Czechoslovakia	Iraq	11 Mar 60	Air Transport	464UNTS267	106718
Czechoslovakia	Ireland	29 Jan 47	Air Transport	27UNTS267	100411
Czechoslovakia	Italy	02 Jul 47	Mostfavored Nation	48ITGU167	435077
Czechoslovakia	Italy	25 Feb 48	Admin Cooperation	26UNTS103	100380
Czechoslovakia	Italy	05 May 58	Finance	58ITGU129	435078
Czechoslovakia	Italy	22 Sep 60	Finance	62ITDI470	436079
Czechoslovakia	Italy	02 Oct 62	Admin Cooperation	63ITDI277	436080
Czechoslovakia	Italy	27 Mar 65	Tech Assistance	66ITDI123	436081
Czechoslovakia	Italy	15 Jul 65	General Trade	66ITDI124	436082
Czechoslovakia	Japan	13 Feb 57	General Amity	300UNTS119	104335
Czechoslovakia	Japan	15 Dec 59	General Trade	383UNTS277	105505
Czechoslovakia	Korea, North	04 Jun 59	Sanitation	338UNTS291	104842
Czechoslovakia	Mali	27 Nov 61	Air Transport	466UNTS41	106736
Czechoslovakia	Mexico	09 Aug 68	Culture	71MEXD903	444011
Czechoslovakia	Mongolia	08 Apr 57	General Amity	501UNTS171	107317
Czechoslovakia	Mongolia	08 Nov 63	Consul/Citizenship	503UNTS125	107341
Czechoslovakia	Mongolia	21 Oct 64	Sanitation	545UNTS91	107926
Czechoslovakia	Mongolia	09 Dec 66	Sanitation	637UNTS0	109124
Czechoslovakia	Mongolia	31 Mar 68	Sanitation	0UNTS0	109279
Czechoslovakia	Morocco	08 Jun 61	Air Transport	497UNTS275	107272
Czechoslovakia	Multilateral	27 Mar 41	Military Mission	67UNTS231	200222
Czechoslovakia	Multilateral	02 Aug 44	Scientific Project	67UNTS221	200221
Czechoslovakia	Multilateral	07 Dec 44	Air Transport	84UNTS389	200252
Czechoslovakia	Multilateral	07 Dec 44	IGO Establishment	15UNTS295	200102
Czechoslovakia	Multilateral	07 Dec 44	Air Transport	171UNTS345	200501
Czechoslovakia	Multilateral	15 Dec 44	Sanitation	17UNTS305	200110
Czechoslovakia	Multilateral	08 Aug 45	General Military	82UNTS279	200251
Czechoslovakia	Multilateral	27 Sep 45	IGO Establishment	5UNTS327	200035
Czechoslovakia	Multilateral	16 Nov 45	IGO Establishment	4UNTS275	100052
Czechoslovakia	Multilateral	27 Dec 45	IGO Establishment	2UNTS39	100020
Czechoslovakia	Multilateral	04 Jan 46	IGO Establishment	6UNTS35	100066
Czechoslovakia	Multilateral	14 Jan 46	Reparations	555UNTS69	108105
Czechoslovakia	Multilateral	22 Jul 46	IGO Establishment	14UNTS185	100221
Czechoslovakia	Multilateral	22 Jul 46	IGO Establishment	9UNTS3	100125
Czechoslovakia	Multilateral	27 Jul 46	Patents/Copyrights	90UNTS229	101238
Czechoslovakia	Multilateral	11 Dec 46	Sanitation	12UNTS179	100186
Czechoslovakia	Multilateral	08 Feb 47	Patents/Copyrights	14UNTS287	100222
Czechoslovakia	Multilateral	10 Feb 47	Peace/Disarmament	41UNTS21	100643
Czechoslovakia	Multilateral	10 Feb 47	Peace/Disarmament	48UNTS203	100746
Czechoslovakia	Multilateral	10 Feb 47	Peace/Disarmament	42UNTS3	100645
Czechoslovakia	Multilateral	10 Feb 47	Peace/Disarmament	41UNTS135	100644
Czechoslovakia	Multilateral	10 Feb 47	Peace/Disarmament	49UNTS3	100747
Czechoslovakia	Multilateral	27 May 47	Air Transport	418UNTS161	106021
Czechoslovakia	Multilateral	02 Oct 47	Telecommunications	193UNTS188	102616
Czechoslovakia	Multilateral	11 Oct 47	IGO Establishment	77UNTS143	100998
Czechoslovakia	Multilateral	12 Nov 47	Admin Cooperation	46UNTS201	100710
Czechoslovakia	Multilateral	12 Nov 47	Admin Cooperation	53UNTS39	100771
Czechoslovakia	Multilateral	12 Nov 47	Admin Cooperation	46UNTS169	100709
Czechoslovakia	Multilateral	12 Nov 47	Admin Cooperation	53UNTS13	100770
Czechoslovakia	Multilateral	12 Nov 47	Admin Cooperation	53UNTS49	100772
Czechoslovakia	Multilateral	06 Mar 48	Water Transport	289UNTS3	104214
Czechoslovakia	Multilateral	10 Jun 48	Humanitarian	191UNTS3	102576
Czechoslovakia	Multilateral	10 Jun 48	Humanitarian	164UNTS113	102163
Czechoslovakia	Multilateral	26 Jun 48	Culture	331UNTS217	104757
Czechoslovakia	Multilateral	24 Jul 48	Sanitation	66UNTS25	100847

PARTY ONE	PARTY TWO	DATE	TOPIC	CITATION	NUMBER
Czechoslovakia	Multilateral	18 Aug 48	Water Transport	33UNTS181	100518
Czechoslovakia	Multilateral	19 Nov 48	Sanitation	44UNTS277	100688
Czechoslovakia	Multilateral	09 Dec 48	Humanitarian	78UNTS277	101021
Czechoslovakia	Multilateral	04 May 49	Admin Cooperation	47UNTS159	100728
Czechoslovakia	Multilateral	04 May 49	Admin Cooperation	92UNTS19	101257
Czechoslovakia	Multilateral	04 May 49	Admin Cooperation	98UNTS101	101358
Czechoslovakia	Multilateral	04 May 49	Admin Cooperation	30UNTS23	100446
Czechoslovakia	Multilateral	04 May 49	Admin Cooperation	30UNTS3	100445
Czechoslovakia	Multilateral	16 Jun 49	Land Transport	45UNTS149	100696
Czechoslovakia	Multilateral	12 Aug 49	Humanitarian	75UNTS287	100973
Czechoslovakia	Multilateral	12 Aug 49	Humanitarian	75UNTS31	100970
Czechoslovakia	Multilateral	12 Aug 49	General Military	75UNTS135	100972
Czechoslovakia	Multilateral	12 Aug 49	Humanitarian	75UNTS85	100971
Czechoslovakia	Multilateral	19 Sep 49	Land Transport	125UNTS3	101671
Czechoslovakia	Multilateral	21 Mar 50	Admin Cooperation	96UNTS271	101342
Czechoslovakia	Multilateral	11 Jul 52	IGO Establishment	169UNTS3	102220
Czechoslovakia	Multilateral	11 Jul 52	Postal Service	170UNTS269	102223
Czechoslovakia	Multilateral	11 Jul 52	Postal Service	170UNTS63	102222
Czechoslovakia	Multilateral	11 Jul 52	Postal Service	170UNTS3	102221
Czechoslovakia	Multilateral	11 Jul 52	Postal Service	171UNTS89	102225
Czechoslovakia	Multilateral	31 Mar 53	Privil/Immunities	193UNTS136	102613
Czechoslovakia	Multilateral	01 Oct 53	Commodity Trade	258UNTS153	103677
Czechoslovakia	Multilateral	14 May 54	Culture	249UNTS215	103511
Czechoslovakia	Multilateral	14 Jun 54	Air Transport	320UNTS209	104643
Czechoslovakia	Multilateral	14 Jun 54	Air Transport	320UNTS217	104644
Czechoslovakia	Multilateral	14 May 55	General Amity	219UNTS3	102962
Czechoslovakia	Multilateral	15 May 55	Recognition	217UNTS223	102949
Czechoslovakia	Multilateral	28 Sep 55	Air Transport	478UNTS371	106943
Czechoslovakia	Multilateral	12 Oct 55	IGO Establishment	560UNTS3	108165
Czechoslovakia	Multilateral	26 Mar 56	IGO Establishment	259UNTS125	103686
Czechoslovakia	Multilateral	18 May 56	Customs	338UNTS103	104834
Czechoslovakia	Multilateral	18 May 56	Land Transport	339UNTS3	104844
Czechoslovakia	Multilateral	07 Sep 56	Humanitarian	266UNTS3	103822
Czechoslovakia	Multilateral	26 Oct 56	IGO Establishment	276UNTS3	103988
Czechoslovakia	Multilateral	14 Dec 56	Taxation	436UNTS115	106292
Czechoslovakia	Multilateral	14 Dec 56	Taxation	436UNTS131	106293
Czechoslovakia	Multilateral	20 Feb 57	Consul/Citizenship	309UNTS65	104468
Czechoslovakia	Multilateral	15 Jun 57	General Trade	550UNTS45	108008
Czechoslovakia	Multilateral	15 Jun 57	Patents/Copyrights	583UNTS3	108470
Czechoslovakia	Multilateral	03 Oct 57	Postal Service	364UNTS3	105211
Czechoslovakia	Multilateral	03 Oct 57	Postal Service	366UNTS87	105216
Czechoslovakia	Multilateral	03 Oct 57	Postal Service	364UNTS331	105212
Czechoslovakia	Multilateral	03 Oct 57	Postal Service	365UNTS3	105213
Czechoslovakia	Multilateral	03 Oct 57	Postal Service	365UNTS207	105214
Czechoslovakia	Multilateral	13 Dec 57	Land Transport	372UNTS159	105296
Czechoslovakia	Multilateral	20 Mar 58	Admin Cooperation	335UNTS211	104789
Czechoslovakia	Multilateral	29 Apr 58	Territory Boundary	516UNTS205	107477
Czechoslovakia	Multilateral	29 Apr 58	Water Transport	450UNTS11	106465
Czechoslovakia	Multilateral	29 Apr 58	Territory Boundary	499UNTS311	107302
Czechoslovakia	Multilateral	10 Jun 58	Admin Cooperation	330UNTS3	104739
Czechoslovakia	Multilateral	01 Dec 58	Commodity Trade	385UNTS137	105534
Czechoslovakia	Multilateral	03 Dec 58	Admin Cooperation	398UNTS9	105715
Czechoslovakia	Multilateral	03 Dec 58	Admin Cooperation	416UNTS51	105995
Czechoslovakia	Multilateral	15 Jan 59	Customs	348UNTS13	104996
Czechoslovakia	Multilateral	14 Dec 59	Sanitation	422UNTS57	106068
Czechoslovakia	Multilateral	14 Dec 59	Land Transport	422UNTS75	106069
Czechoslovakia	Multilateral	14 Dec 59	Sanitation	422UNTS33	106067
Czechoslovakia	Multilateral	14 Dec 59	IGO Status/Immunit	368UNTS237	105244
Czechoslovakia	Multilateral	14 Dec 59	IGO Establishment	368UNTS253	105245
Czechoslovakia	Multilateral	06 Oct 60	Customs	473UNTS131	106861
Czechoslovakia	Multilateral	09 Dec 60	Customs	429UNTS211	106200
Czechoslovakia	Multilateral	14 Dec 60	Education	429UNTS93	106193
Czechoslovakia	Multilateral	30 Mar 61	Sanitation	520UNTS151	107515
Czechoslovakia	Multilateral	18 Apr 61	Consul/Citizenship	500UNTS95	107310
Czechoslovakia	Multilateral	21 Apr 61	IGO Establishment	484UNTS349	107041

PARTY ONE	PARTY TWO	DATE	TOPIC	CITATION	NUMBER
Czechoslovakia	Multilateral	08 Jun 61	Customs	473UNTS153	106862
Czechoslovakia	Multilateral	08 Jun 61	Customs	473UNTS187	106863
Czechoslovakia	Multilateral	21 Jun 61	IGO Establishment	514UNTS209	107449
Czechoslovakia	Multilateral	26 Oct 61	Patents/Copyrights	496UNTS43	107247
Czechoslovakia	Multilateral	06 Dec 61	Customs	473UNTS219	106864
Czechoslovakia	Multilateral	15 Dec 61	Admin Cooperation	424UNTS43	106098
Czechoslovakia	Multilateral	25 Jul 62	Specific Property	506UNTS177	107387
Czechoslovakia	Multilateral	10 Dec 62	Culture	521UNTS231	107525
Czechoslovakia	Multilateral	24 Apr 63	Consul/Citizenship	596UNTS261	108638
Czechoslovakia	Multilateral	05 Aug 63	Sanitation	480UNTS43	106964
Czechoslovakia	Multilateral	23 Oct 63	IGO Establishment	506UNTS197	107388
Czechoslovakia	Multilateral	10 Jul 64	Postal Service	613UNTS3	108850
Czechoslovakia	Multilateral	10 Jul 64	Postal Service	612UNTS233	108848
Czechoslovakia	Multilateral	10 Jul 64	Postal Service	611UNTS387	108846
Czechoslovakia	Multilateral	10 Jul 64	Postal Service	611UNTS105	108845
Czechoslovakia	Multilateral	10 Jul 64	Postal Service	612UNTS3	108847
Czechoslovakia	Multilateral	10 Jul 64	Postal Service	611UNTS7	108844
Czechoslovakia	Multilateral	15 Jul 64	IGO Establishment	610UNTS143	108840
Czechoslovakia	Multilateral	09 Mar 65	Water Transport	591UNTS265	108564
Czechoslovakia	Multilateral	08 Jul 65	General Trade	597UNTS3	108641
Czechoslovakia	Multilateral	18 Nov 65	Customs	609UNTS115	108830
Czechoslovakia	Multilateral	31 Dec 65	Specific Resources	616UNTS317	108904
Czechoslovakia	Multilateral	09 Sep 66	IGO Status/Immunit	0UNTS0	109343
Czechoslovakia	Multilateral	27 Jan 67	Scientific Project	610UNTS205	108843
Czechoslovakia	Multilateral	15 Nov 67	General Trade	0UNTS0	109703
Czechoslovakia	Multilateral	18 Mar 68	Commodity Trade	0UNTS0	109262
Czechoslovakia	Multilateral	22 Apr 68	Scientific Project	0UNTS0	109574
Czechoslovakia	Multilateral	01 Jul 68	Peace/Disarmament	0UNTS0	110485
Czechoslovakia	Multilateral	26 Nov 68	Humanitarian	0UNTS0	110823
Czechoslovakia	Multilateral	24 Dec 68	Commodity Trade	0UNTS0	109369
Czechoslovakia	Netherlands	15 Nov 46	Finance	51NET162	447003
Czechoslovakia	Netherlands	01 Sep 47	Air Transport	32UNTS129	100495
Czechoslovakia	Netherlands	24 Jun 48	General Trade	51NET49	447008
Czechoslovakia	Netherlands	07 Jul 49	General Trade	51NET163	447011
Czechoslovakia	Netherlands	11 Jun 64	Claims and Debts	556UNTS89	108120
Czechoslovakia	Netherlands	15 Nov 67	Land Transport	0UNTS0	109223
Czechoslovakia	New Zealand	08 Aug 47	Claims and Debts	18UNTS161	100285
Czechoslovakia	New Zealand	22 Jan 48	Commodity Trade	16UNTS229	100264
Czechoslovakia	Norway	13 Dec 45	Finance	17UNTS261	100280
Czechoslovakia	Norway	20 Mar 47	General Trade	30UNTS223	100460
Czechoslovakia	Norway	09 Jun 54	Claims and Debts	2NORT636	451033
Czechoslovakia	Norway	25 Oct 62	Taxation	498UNTS335	107287
Czechoslovakia	Norway	03 Dec 68	Air Transport	3NORTO	451034
Czechoslovakia	Norway	03 Dec 68	General Trade	3NORTO	451035
Czechoslovakia	Poland	24 Jan 46	Air Transport	25UNTS181	100363
Czechoslovakia	Poland	12 Feb 46	Reparations	25UNTS207	100364
Czechoslovakia	Poland	10 Mar 47	General Military	25UNTS231	100365
Czechoslovakia	Poland	04 Apr 47	General Economic	85UNTS62	101146
Czechoslovakia	Poland	04 Jul 47	General Economic	50PDZU93	457002
Czechoslovakia	Poland	04 Jul 47	Culture	25UNTS249	100366
Czechoslovakia	Poland	05 Apr 48	Non-ILO Labor	31UNTS355	100482
Czechoslovakia	Poland	05 Apr 48	Admin Cooperation	31UNTS325	100481
Czechoslovakia	Poland	12 Nov 48	Land Transport	84UNTS347	101141
Czechoslovakia	Poland	21 Jan 49	Admin Cooperation	31UNTS205	100480
Czechoslovakia	Poland	22 Jan 49	Sanitation	85UNTS3	101142
Czechoslovakia	Poland	02 Jul 49	Land Transport	260UNTS179	103709
Czechoslovakia	Poland	02 Jul 49	Land Transport	260UNTS149	103708
Czechoslovakia	Poland	17 Nov 50	Sanitation	530UNTS195	107682
Czechoslovakia	Poland	20 Dec 52	General Economic	53PZUM77	458008
Czechoslovakia	Poland	00 Feb 54	Mass Media	54PZUM11	458014
Czechoslovakia	Poland	29 May 54	Postal Service	54PZUM34	458018
Czechoslovakia	Poland	06 Sep 55	Visas	55PZUM23	458024
Czechoslovakia	Poland	23 Sep 55	Territory Boundary	55PZUM27	458025
Czechoslovakia	Poland	30 Sep 55	Non-ILO Labor	55PZUM33	458026
Czechoslovakia	Poland	13 Jan 56	Gen Communications	265UNTS157	103811

PARTY ONE	PARTY TWO	DATE	TOPIC	CITATION	NUMBER
Czechoslovakia	Poland	13 Jan 56	Land Transport	56PZUM30	458034
Czechoslovakia	Poland	13 Jan 56	Water Transport	56PZUM25	458033
Czechoslovakia	Poland	07 May 57	General Economic	57PZUM69	458050
Czechoslovakia	Poland	31 Jan 58	Land Transport	431UNTS99	106214
Czechoslovakia	Poland	21 Mar 58	Specific Resources	538UNTS89	107811
Czechoslovakia	Poland	27 Mar 58	Culture	58PZUM61	458060
Czechoslovakia	Poland	29 Mar 58	Reparations	340UNTS199	104865
Czechoslovakia	Poland	13 Jun 58	Territory Boundary	354UNTS221	105064
Czechoslovakia	Poland	25 Nov 58	Customs	372UNTS205	105299
Czechoslovakia	Poland	08 Apr 59	Sanitation	59PZUM60	458066
Czechoslovakia	Poland	04 Jul 59	Visas	363UNTS333	105210
Czechoslovakia	Poland	16 Dec 59	Admin Cooperation	372UNTS223	105300
Czechoslovakia	Poland	02 Apr 60	General Economic	60PZUM16	458073
Czechoslovakia	Poland	17 May 60	Consul/Citizenship	424UNTS3	106096
Czechoslovakia	Poland	10 Sep 60	General Economic	60PZUM110	458078
Czechoslovakia	Poland	14 Nov 60	Sanitation	413UNTS4	105938
Czechoslovakia	Poland	04 Jul 61	Admin Cooperation	436UNTS189	106295
Czechoslovakia	Poland	29 Sep 62	Specific Property	62PZUM81	458097
Czechoslovakia	Poland	16 Nov 62	Land Transport	526UNTS3	107597
Czechoslovakia	Poland	27 Apr 63	Mass Media	63PZUM39	458104
Czechoslovakia	Poland	27 Apr 63	Mass Media	63PZUM34	458103
Czechoslovakia	Poland	17 May 65	Consul/Citizenship	572UNTS181	108312
Czechoslovakia	Poland	17 May 65	Consul/Citizenship	66PDZU135	457121
Czechoslovakia	Poland	29 Jul 65	Dispute Settlement	572UNTS203	108313
Czechoslovakia	Poland	23 Sep 65	Admin Cooperation	72PDZU237	457138
Czechoslovakia	Poland	22 Jan 66	Culture	588UNTS175	108524
Czechoslovakia	Poland	01 Mar 67	General Amity	632UNTS255	109027
Czechoslovakia	Poland	08 Apr 67	Land Transport	72PDZU240	457143
Czechoslovakia	Poland	26 Apr 67	Education	610UNTS0	108832
Czechoslovakia	Poland	02 Dec 67	Admin Cooperation	71PDZU117	457150
Czechoslovakia	Romania	05 Sep 47	Education	46UNTS37	100699
Czechoslovakia	Romania	01 Mar 48	Admin Cooperation	26UNTS109	100381
Czechoslovakia	Romania	31 Jul 52	Sanitation	362UNTS123	105185
Czechoslovakia	Romania	02 May 57	Health/Educ/Welfare	387UNTS167	105562
Czechoslovakia	Romania	25 Mar 58	Sanitation	339UNTS77	104846
Czechoslovakia	Romania	25 Oct 58	Culture	338UNTS301	104843
Czechoslovakia	Romania	25 Oct 58	Admin Cooperation	417UNTS37	106006
Czechoslovakia	Romania	21 May 60	Consul/Citizenship	397UNTS245	105709
Czechoslovakia	Romania	16 Dec 63	General Trade	527UNTS285	107630
Czechoslovakia	Romania	17 Nov 67	Sanitation	0UNTS0	109280
Czechoslovakia	Romania	06 Dec 67	Land Transport	0UNTS0	109537
Czechoslovakia	Romania	16 Aug 68	General Amity	0UNTS0	110392
Czechoslovakia	Romania	23 Nov 68	Culture	0UNTS0	110211
Czechoslovakia	Senegal	20 Jun 62	Air Transport	498UNTS145	107280
Czechoslovakia	Somalia	04 Jun 61	Tech Assistance	480UNTS261	106973
Czechoslovakia	Somalia	04 Jun 61	Culture	479UNTS291	106960
Czechoslovakia	Sweden	23 Oct 45	Admin Cooperation	46SOFM313	461036
Czechoslovakia	Sweden	15 Nov 45	Air Transport	45SOFM71	461005
Czechoslovakia	Sweden	17 Nov 45	General Trade	45SOFM137	461015
Czechoslovakia	Sweden	17 Nov 45	Finance	45SOFM138	461016
Czechoslovakia	Sweden	29 Jul 46	Finance	46SOFM255	461032
Czechoslovakia	Sweden	29 Jul 46	General Trade	46SOFM253	461031
Czechoslovakia	Sweden	22 Oct 46	Admin Cooperation	200UNTS31	102692
Czechoslovakia	Sweden	10 Mar 47	General Trade	47SOFM571	461055
Czechoslovakia	Sweden	15 Mar 47	Claims and Debts	47SOFM572	461056
Czechoslovakia	Sweden	15 Oct 47	Air Transport	44UNTS149	100683
Czechoslovakia	Sweden	30 Oct 47	General Trade	47SOFM485	461048
Czechoslovakia	Sweden	30 Oct 47	Finance	47SOFM494	461049
Czechoslovakia	Sweden	01 Feb 49	Finance	49SOFM76	461074
Czechoslovakia	Sweden	01 Feb 49	General Trade	49SOFM63	461073
Czechoslovakia	Sweden	30 Mar 50	General Trade	50SOFM95	461104
Czechoslovakia	Sweden	30 Mar 50	Finance	50SOFM116	461105
Czechoslovakia	Sweden	16 Mar 51	General Trade	51SOFM125	461138
Czechoslovakia	Sweden	14 Mar 52	General Trade	52SOFM83	461157
Czechoslovakia	Sweden	25 Oct 62	Air Transport	498UNTS343	107288

PARTY ONE	PARTY TWO	DATE	TOPIC	CITATION	NUMBER
Czechoslovakia	Switzerland	10 Sep 47	Air Transport	35UNTS275	100559
Czechoslovakia	Switzerland	22 Dec 49	General Economic	50SWRO15	462158
Czechoslovakia	Switzerland	24 Nov 53	General Trade	54SWRO745	462157
Czechoslovakia	Switzerland	04 Jun 59	Non-ILO Labor	349UNTS121	105012
Czechoslovakia	Switzerland	26 Apr 60	Taxation	60SWRO538	462063
Czechoslovakia	Syria	18 Jun 57	Culture	303UNTS119	104374
Czechoslovakia	Tunisia	06 Apr 63	Culture	555UNTS111	108106
Czechoslovakia	Turkey	05 Mar 47	Air Transport	14UNTS101	100214
Czechoslovakia	UK Great Britain	01 Nov 45	Finance	5UNTS15	100062
Czechoslovakia	UK Great Britain	19 Feb 47	Milit Installation	9UNTS173	100131
Czechoslovakia	UK Great Britain	16 Jun 47	Education	46UNTS61	100700
Czechoslovakia	UK Great Britain	03 Mar 49	Other Military	83UNTS95	101104
Czechoslovakia	UK Great Britain	18 Aug 49	Finance	86UNTS129	101155
Czechoslovakia	UK Great Britain	28 Sep 49	General Economic	86UNTS141	101156
Czechoslovakia	UK Great Britain	28 Sep 49	Claims and Debts	86UNTS175	101158
Czechoslovakia	UK Great Britain	28 Sep 49	Reparations	86UNTS161	101157
Czechoslovakia	UK Great Britain	15 Jan 60	Air Transport	374UNTS207	105336
Czechoslovakia	UK Great Britain	26 Mar 68	Scientific Project	0UNTS0	109278
Czechoslovakia	UN Special Fund	13 Jul 67	Non-IBRD Project	606UNTS71	108776
Czechoslovakia	UNICEF (Children)	03 Oct 47	Tech Assistance	65UNTS26	100816
Czechoslovakia	United Arab Rep	06 May 57	Tech Assistance	292UNTS317	104278
Czechoslovakia	United Arab Rep	30 Jun 57	Air Transport	411UNTS126	105917
Czechoslovakia	United Arab Rep	19 Oct 57	Culture	530UNTS181	107681
Czechoslovakia	United Arab Rep	07 Feb 59	General Economic	372UNTS243	105301
Czechoslovakia	United Arab Rep	26 Nov 64	Sanitation	545UNTS11	107923
Czechoslovakia	United Nations	07 Oct 48	Humanitarian	47UNTS185	100730
Czechoslovakia	USA (United States)	11 Jul 42	Milit Assistance	90UNTS257	200263
Czechoslovakia	USA (United States)	21 Oct 43	Milit Servic/Citiz	29UNTS369	200172
Czechoslovakia	USA (United States)	03 Jan 46	Air Transport	6UNTS309	100084
Czechoslovakia	USA (United States)	14 Nov 46	General Trade	7UNTS119	100094
Czechoslovakia	USA (United States)	25 Jul 47	Reparations	90UNTS19	101223
Czechoslovakia	USA (United States)	16 Sep 48	Milit Assistance	90UNTS35	101224
Czechoslovakia	USA (United States)	29 Sep 50	Postal Service	290UNTS3	104227
Czechoslovakia	USA (United States)	21 Dec 62	Visas	469UNTS115	106787
Czechoslovakia	USA (United States)	28 Aug 67	Consul/Citizenship	0UNTS0	110443
Czechoslovakia	USA (United States)	28 Feb 69	Air Transport	0UNTS0	110269
Czechoslovakia	USA (United States)	29 Aug 69	General Trade	0UNTS0	110406
Czechoslovakia	USSR (Soviet Union)	31 Mar 45	General Military	16SUGG62	469881
Czechoslovakia	USSR (Soviet Union)	31 Mar 45	Claims and Debts	16SUGG61	469880
Czechoslovakia	USSR (Soviet Union)	14 Apr 45	Milit Installation	16SUGG62	469882
Czechoslovakia	USSR (Soviet Union)	29 Jun 45	Territory Boundary	504UNTS299	200607
Czechoslovakia	USSR (Soviet Union)	22 Oct 45	Postal Service	0SUST200	468099
Czechoslovakia	USSR (Soviet Union)	12 Apr 46	Claims and Debts	0SUST210	468101
Czechoslovakia	USSR (Soviet Union)	12 Apr 46	General Trade	0SUST210	468100
Czechoslovakia	USSR (Soviet Union)	10 Jul 46	Consul/Citizenship	0SUST214	468102
Czechoslovakia	USSR (Soviet Union)	25 Jul 46	Air Transport	27UNTS231	100409
Czechoslovakia	USSR (Soviet Union)	12 Jul 47	General Trade	0SUST234	468103
Czechoslovakia	USSR (Soviet Union)	28 Nov 47	Sanitation	216UNTS285	102941
Czechoslovakia	USSR (Soviet Union)	11 Dec 47	Loans and Credits	0SUST240	471023
Czechoslovakia	USSR (Soviet Union)	11 Dec 47	General Economic	0SUST240	471024
Czechoslovakia	USSR (Soviet Union)	11 Dec 47	General Economic	217UNTS35	102943
Czechoslovakia	USSR (Soviet Union)	11 Dec 47	Scientific Project	0SUST240	468104
Czechoslovakia	USSR (Soviet Union)	09 Feb 48	General Trade	0SUST244	468105
Czechoslovakia	USSR (Soviet Union)	15 Dec 48	General Economic	0SUST255	468106
Czechoslovakia	USSR (Soviet Union)	03 Nov 49	Mass Media	16SUGG65	469892
Czechoslovakia	USSR (Soviet Union)	03 Nov 50	General Economic	0SUST278	468107
Czechoslovakia	USSR (Soviet Union)	08 Aug 51	Postal Service	0SUST282	468108
Czechoslovakia	USSR (Soviet Union)	11 Apr 52	Education	0SUST286	468109
Czechoslovakia	USSR (Soviet Union)	23 Apr 55	Atomic Energy	0SUST326	468110
Czechoslovakia	USSR (Soviet Union)	28 Apr 55	Specific Resources	16SUGG68	469905
Czechoslovakia	USSR (Soviet Union)	01 Jun 56	Culture	259UNTS341	103696
Czechoslovakia	USSR (Soviet Union)	30 Nov 56	Territory Boundary	266UNTS243	103833
Czechoslovakia	USSR (Soviet Union)	14 Jan 57	General Trade	0SUST376	468111
Czechoslovakia	USSR (Soviet Union)	25 Jan 57	Mass Media	16SUGG118	469932
Czechoslovakia	USSR (Soviet Union)	01 Mar 57	Specif Goods/Equip	16SUGG119	469933

PARTY ONE	PARTY TWO	DATE	TOPIC	CITATION	NUMBER
Czechoslovakia	USSR (Soviet Union)	06 Jul 57	Claims and Debts	0SUST385	468112
Czechoslovakia	USSR (Soviet Union)	31 Aug 57	Admin Cooperation	308UNTS3	104456
Czechoslovakia	USSR (Soviet Union)	05 Oct 57	Consul/Citizenship	320UNTS111	104640
Czechoslovakia	USSR (Soviet Union)	05 Oct 57	Consul/Citizenship	320UNTS129	104641
Czechoslovakia	USSR (Soviet Union)	04 Dec 57	Sanitation	313UNTS291	104537
Czechoslovakia	USSR (Soviet Union)	01 Apr 58	Customs	7SUGG108	469502
Czechoslovakia	USSR (Soviet Union)	30 Jun 58	Claims and Debts	7SUGG115	469517
Czechoslovakia	USSR (Soviet Union)	05 Sep 58	Scientific Project	7SUGG120	469526
Czechoslovakia	USSR (Soviet Union)	05 Sep 58	Scientific Project	7SUGG120	469527
Czechoslovakia	USSR (Soviet Union)	14 Oct 58	Commodity Trade	7SUGG122	469535
Czechoslovakia	USSR (Soviet Union)	07 Jan 59	Non-IBRD Project	8SUGG133	469550
Czechoslovakia	USSR (Soviet Union)	17 Jan 59	General Trade	8SUGG134	469552
Czechoslovakia	USSR (Soviet Union)	02 Dec 59	Non-ILO Labor	374UNTS63	105330
Czechoslovakia	USSR (Soviet Union)	20 Jan 60	General Trade	9SUGG122	469625
Czechoslovakia	USSR (Soviet Union)	07 Mar 60	Tech Assistance	9SUGG129	469639
Czechoslovakia	USSR (Soviet Union)	31 Mar 60	Non-IBRD Project	9SUGG132	469647
Czechoslovakia	USSR (Soviet Union)	28 Apr 60	General Trade	9SUGG134	469651
Czechoslovakia	USSR (Soviet Union)	12 May 60	Tech Assistance	9SUGG135	469659
Czechoslovakia	USSR (Soviet Union)	21 Feb 61	Scientific Project	10SUGG122	469743
Czechoslovakia	USSR (Soviet Union)	28 Jun 61	Non-IBRD Project	10SUGG136	469782
Czechoslovakia	USSR (Soviet Union)	21 Aug 61	Non-IBRD Project	10SUGG140	469793
Czechoslovakia	USSR (Soviet Union)	21 Dec 61	Non-IBRD Project	10SUGG147	469811
Czechoslovakia	USSR (Soviet Union)	17 Apr 62	Atomic Energy	11SUGG138	469833
Czechoslovakia	USSR (Soviet Union)	27 Nov 63	General Amity	496UNTS161	107250
Czechoslovakia	USSR (Soviet Union)	17 Sep 65	Visas	549UNTS221	108001
Czechoslovakia	USSR (Soviet Union)	23 Apr 66	Culture	566UNTS159	108242
Czechoslovakia	USSR (Soviet Union)	03 Feb 67	Land Transport	617UNTS267	108917
Czechoslovakia	USSR (Soviet Union)	23 Nov 67	Gen Communications	0UNTS0	109224
Czechoslovakia	USSR (Soviet Union)	06 May 70	General Amity	0UNTS0	110560
Czechoslovakia	Vietnam, North	14 Jan 63	Consul/Citizenship	501UNTS181	107318
Czechoslovakia	Yemen	02 Apr 68	General Amity	0UNTS0	110172
Czechoslovakia	Yugoslavia	09 May 46	General Military	1UNTS67	100014
Czechoslovakia	Yugoslavia	25 Feb 47	General Trade	112UNTS3	101539
Czechoslovakia	Yugoslavia	27 Apr 47	Culture	33UNTS49	100514
Czechoslovakia	Yugoslavia	04 Sep 47	Claims and Debts	112UNTS91	101540
Czechoslovakia	Yugoslavia	14 Mar 48	Air Transport	28UNTS81	100421
Czechoslovakia	Yugoslavia	10 Apr 48	General Economic	112UNTS101	101541
Czechoslovakia	Yugoslavia	24 May 48	Finance	112UNTS225	101545
Czechoslovakia	Yugoslavia	24 May 48	Specif Goods/Equip	112UNTS215	101544
Czechoslovakia	Yugoslavia	24 May 48	Finance	112UNTS183	101543
Czechoslovakia	Yugoslavia	24 May 48	General Trade	112UNTS111	101542
Czechoslovakia	Yugoslavia	01 Mar 49	General Trade	113UNTS3	101547
Czechoslovakia	Yugoslavia	01 Mar 49	Finance	112UNTS241	101546
Czechoslovakia	Yugoslavia	11 Feb 56	Admin Cooperation	397UNTS135	105703
Czechoslovakia	Yugoslavia	16 Jun 56	Health/Educ/Welfare	552UNTS325	108064
Czechoslovakia	Yugoslavia	03 Jul 56	General Economic	397UNTS165	105704
Czechoslovakia	Yugoslavia	29 Jan 57	Culture	300UNTS249	104339
Czechoslovakia	Yugoslavia	22 May 57	Non-ILO Labor	391UNTS57	105617
Czechoslovakia	Yugoslavia	22 May 57	Non-ILO Labor	391UNTS33	105615
Czechoslovakia	Yugoslavia	11 Jun 57	Sanitation	504UNTS107	107355
Czechoslovakia	Yugoslavia	22 Oct 62	Land Transport	480UNTS267	106974
Czechoslovakia	Yugoslavia	24 Jun 63	Consul/Citizenship	496UNTS3	107246
Czechoslovakia	Yugoslavia	05 Oct 63	Sanitation	504UNTS151	107356
Czechoslovakia	Yugoslavia	20 Jan 64	Admin Cooperation	538UNTS197	107816
Czechoslovakia	Yugoslavia	14 Mar 64	Visas	544UNTS147	107917
Czechoslovakia	Yugoslavia	08 Oct 64	Visas	544UNTS129	107916
Czechoslovakia	Yugoslavia	17 May 67	Customs	617UNTS305	108918
Dahomey	Accept UN Charter	02 Aug 60	UN Charter	375UNTS91	105357
Dahomey	Denmark	15 Apr 69	Loans and Credits	0UNTS0	110200
Dahomey	France	11 Jul 60	Recognition	60FRRT52	415145
Dahomey	France	24 Apr 61	General Amity	62FRRT8	415146
Dahomey	France	28 Mar 62	Customs	63FRRT30	415147
Dahomey	France	10 Apr 62	Claims and Debts	62FRRT38	415148
Dahomey	France	09 Dec 63	Air Transport	64FRRT13	415149
Dahomey	France	21 Oct 65	Finance	67FRRT905	415150

PARTY ONE	PARTY TWO	DATE	TOPIC	CITATION	NUMBER
Dahomey	Germany, West	19 Jun 61	Water Transport	61WBGA196	424094
Dahomey	Germany, West	19 Jun 61	General Economic	61WBGA196	424093
Dahomey	Germany, West	19 Jun 61	General Economic	64WBGA196	424092
Dahomey	Germany, West	15 Jul 63	Loans and Credits	63WBGA192	424095
Dahomey	Germany, West	23 Jul 70	Loans and Credits	70WBGA215	424096
Dahomey	IDA (Devel Assoc)	05 Mar 69	Non-IBRD Project	0UNTS0	110216
Dahomey	Israel	28 Sep 61	Tech Assistance	448UNTS151	106429
Dahomey	Israel	18 Dec 61	Visas	448UNTS259	106438
Dahomey	Italy	10 Mar 65	Tech Assistance	66ITDI175	436102
Dahomey	Multilateral	07 Dec 44	Air Transport	84UNTS389	200252
Dahomey	Multilateral	07 Dec 44	IGO Establishment	15UNTS295	200102
Dahomey	Multilateral	11 Dec 46	Sanitation	12UNTS179	100186
Dahomey	Multilateral	24 Jul 48	Sanitation	66UNTS25	100847
Dahomey	Multilateral	04 May 49	Admin Cooperation	92UNTS19	101257
Dahomey	Multilateral	04 May 49	Admin Cooperation	98UNTS101	101358
Dahomey	Multilateral	02 Jul 51	Refugees	189UNTS137	102545
Dahomey	Multilateral	18 Jan 54	IGO Establishment	330UNTS121	104743
Dahomey	Multilateral	28 Sep 55	Air Transport	478UNTS371	106943
Dahomey	Multilateral	26 Jan 60	IGO Establishment	439UNTS249	106333
Dahomey	Multilateral	14 Dec 60	Education	429UNTS93	106193
Dahomey	Multilateral	30 Mar 61	Sanitation	520UNTS151	107515
Dahomey	Multilateral	21 Jun 61	IGO Establishment	514UNTS209	107449
Dahomey	Multilateral	17 Jan 62	Tech Assistance	419UNTS294	106033
Dahomey	Multilateral	25 May 62	IGO Establishment	486UNTS103	107075
Dahomey	Multilateral	10 Dec 62	Culture	521UNTS231	107525
Dahomey	Multilateral	24 Apr 63	Consul/Citizenship	596UNTS487	108640
Dahomey	Multilateral	24 Apr 63	Consul/Citizenship	596UNTS261	108638
Dahomey	Multilateral	25 May 63	IGO Establishment	479UNTS39	106947
Dahomey	Multilateral	04 Aug 63	IGO Establishment	510UNTS3	107408
Dahomey	Multilateral	05 Aug 63	Sanitation	480UNTS43	106964
Dahomey	Multilateral	26 Oct 63	Water Transport	587UNTS9	108506
Dahomey	Multilateral	10 Jul 64	Postal Service	613UNTS193	108852
Dahomey	Multilateral	10 Jul 64	Postal Service	612UNTS233	108848
Dahomey	Multilateral	10 Jul 64	Postal Service	613UNTS3	108851
Dahomey	Multilateral	10 Jul 64	Postal Service	611UNTS387	108846
Dahomey	Multilateral	10 Jul 64	Postal Service	612UNTS3	108847
Dahomey	Multilateral	10 Jul 64	Postal Service	613UNTS127	108853
Dahomey	Multilateral	10 Jul 64	Postal Service	611UNTS105	108845
Dahomey	Multilateral	10 Jul 64	Postal Service	611UNTS7	108844
Dahomey	Multilateral	10 Jul 64	Postal Service	612UNTS361	108849
Dahomey	Multilateral	25 Nov 64	Water Transport	587UNTS19	108507
Dahomey	Multilateral	18 Mar 65	Dispute Settlement	575UNTS159	108359
Dahomey	Multilateral	27 May 66	IGO Establishment	637UNTS0	109121
Dahomey	Multilateral	04 May 67	IGO Establishment	595UNTS287	108623
Dahomey	Multilateral	20 Jul 67	General Economic	0UNTS0	109259
Dahomey	Multilateral	22 Sep 67	Non-IBRD Project	0UNTS0	109258
Dahomey	Multilateral	18 Mar 68	Commodity Trade	0UNTS0	109262
Dahomey	Multilateral	11 Jun 68	Scientific Project	0UNTS0	109884
Dahomey	Poland	05 Mar 65	Culture	66PDZU395	457118
Dahomey	State/IGO Group	14 Mar 70	IGO Operations	0UNTS0	110457
Dahomey	UN Special Fund	28 Mar 62	Tech Assistance	424UNTS55	106099
Dahomey	UNICEF (Children)	28 Aug 63	IGO Operations	507UNTS101	107396
Dahomey	United Nations	15 Apr 69	IGO Operations	0UNTS0	110170
Dahomey	USA (United States)	27 May 61	General Aid	445UNTS23	106373
Dahomey	USA (United States)	13 Jun 62	Milit Assistance	458UNTS219	106603
Dahomey	USA (United States)	31 Dec 64	US Agri Commod Aid	541UNTS117	107865
Dahomey	USA (United States)	13 Mar 65	Claims and Debts	549UNTS43	107987
Dahomey	USA (United States)	03 Jul 67	Direct Aid	0UNTS0	109907
Dahomey	USSR (Soviet Union)	04 Jun 62	Consul/Citizenship	11SUGG141	469840
Dahomey	USSR (Soviet Union)	20 Mar 63	Culture	528UNTS181	107641
Dahomey	USSR (Soviet Union)	10 Jul 63	General Trade	528UNTS167	107640
Dahomey	WHO (World Health)	07 Dec 60	Tech Assistance	387UNTS277	105567
Danube Commission	Multilateral	08 Dec 62	Finance	510UNTS235	107418
Denmark	Afghanistan	24 May 67	Air Transport	0UNTS0	109951
Denmark	Argentina	18 Mar 48	Air Transport	94UNTS175	101311

PARTY ONE	PARTY TWO	DATE	TOPIC	CITATION	NUMBER
Denmark	Argentina	14 Dec 48	General Economic	74UNTS41	100956
Denmark	Argentina	15 Dec 48	Taxation	67UNTS71	100866
Denmark	Argentina	25 Nov 57	General Economic	299UNTS83	104308
Denmark	Argentina	28 Nov 62	Milit Servic/Citiz	455UNTS429	106554
Denmark	Asian Devel Bank	05 Feb 69	Loans and Credits	0UNTS0	109702
Denmark	Asian Devel Bank	01 Apr 69	Loans and Credits	0UNTS0	109877
Denmark	Australia	08 Oct 48	Claims and Debts	22UNTS43	100330
Denmark	Australia	01 May 52	Visas	152UNTS3	102006
Denmark	Austria	29 Nov 48	Finance	74UNTS257	100968
Denmark	Austria	29 Nov 48	General Trade	74UNTS243	100967
Denmark	Austria	02 Dec 49	Air Transport	53UNTS281	100788
Denmark	Austria	23 Feb 50	General Trade	74UNTS269	100969
Denmark	Austria	27 Mar 54	Visas	55ABGB192	403032
Denmark	Austria	07 Sep 54	Non-ILO Labor	201UNTS39	102709
Denmark	Austria	14 Nov 59	Commodity Trade	630UNTS29	108962
Denmark	Austria	23 Oct 61	Taxation	425UNTS115	106122
Denmark	Austria	17 Jul 63	Consul/Citizenship	479UNTS263	106958
Denmark	Austria	09 Dec 63	Admin Cooperation	520UNTS133	107514
Denmark	Barbados	27 Oct 69	Air Transport	0UNTS0	110394
Denmark	Belgium	08 Apr 46	Claims and Debts	4UNTS429	100059
Denmark	Belgium	28 Jan 47	Visas	18UNTS221	100291
Denmark	Belgium	30 Dec 48	Dispute Settlement	25UNTS173	100362
Denmark	Belgium	31 May 49	Visas	32UNTS337	100506
Denmark	Belgium	13 Dec 49	Admin Cooperation	173UNTS193	102266
Denmark	Belgium	31 Dec 57	Culture	305UNTS247	104422
Denmark	Belgium	23 Oct 61	Taxation	425UNTS181	106123
Denmark	Belgium	20 Sep 65	Taxation	549UNTS63	107990
Denmark	Belgium	04 Feb 66	Land Transport	561UNTS233	108187
Denmark	Belgium	29 Jun 67	Specific Resources	606UNTS113	108780
Denmark	Bolivia	19 Jun 70	Finance	0UNTS0	110795
Denmark	Brazil	14 Nov 47	Air Transport	47UNTS39	100722
Denmark	Brazil	25 Feb 66	Tech Assistance	590UNTS95	108549
Denmark	Brazil	08 Jul 66	Loans and Credits	581UNTS95	108435
Denmark	Bulgaria	09 May 47	Finance	74UNTS139	100960
Denmark	Bulgaria	09 May 47	General Trade	74UNTS131	100959
Denmark	Bulgaria	28 May 58	Air Transport	312UNTS235	104521
Denmark	Bulgaria	02 Sep 67	Visas	631UNTS71	108987
Denmark	Bulgaria	02 Sep 67	General Economic	0UNTS0	109726
Denmark	Bulgaria	25 Oct 68	Land Transport	0UNTS0	109876
Denmark	Burma	30 Jul 51	Air Transport	108UNTS167	101472
Denmark	Cambodia	20 Nov 69	Loans and Credits	0UNTS0	110353
Denmark	Cameroon	08 Oct 62	General Trade	0UNTS0	110770
Denmark	Canada	14 Oct 49	Visas	46UNTS97	100702
Denmark	Canada	13 Dec 49	Air Transport	72UNTS247	100937
Denmark	Canada	25 Mar 50	Reparations	230UNTS343	103193
Denmark	Canada	30 Sep 55	Taxation	258UNTS115	103675
Denmark	Canada	17 Apr 57	Milit Assistance	316UNTS207	104586
Denmark	Canada	28 Nov 63	Air Transport	496UNTS223	107254
Denmark	Canada	15 Oct 64	Water Transport	525UNTS227	107595
Denmark	Canada	25 Jul 68	Admin Cooperation	0UNTS0	109701
Denmark	Ceylon (Sri Lanka)	29 May 59	Air Transport	348UNTS225	105002
Denmark	Ceylon (Sri Lanka)	16 Feb 63	Taxation	486UNTS285	107083
Denmark	Ceylon (Sri Lanka)	28 Dec 68	Loans and Credits	0UNTS0	109490
Denmark	Chad	31 Jul 69	Loans and Credits	0UNTS0	110201
Denmark	Chile	27 Oct 52	Air Transport	271UNTS93	103911
Denmark	Chile	22 Oct 53	Milit Servic/Citiz	348UNTS261	105004
Denmark	Chile	15 Dec 67	Scientific Project	643UNTS293	109199
Denmark	Chile	27 Jan 70	Non-IBRD Project	0UNTS0	110558
Denmark	China People's Rep	01 Dec 57	General Economic	57CCJC111	410465
Denmark	China People's Rep	01 Dec 57	General Economic	309UNTS241	104475
Denmark	China People's Rep	01 Dec 57	Mostfavored Nation	57CCJC112	410466
Denmark	China People's Rep	12 Apr 58	Patents/Copyrights	58CCJC49	410515
Denmark	China People's Rep	23 Sep 61	Taxation	446UNTS3	106397
Denmark	China People's Rep	23 Sep 61	Taxation	61CCJC126	410831
Denmark	Colombia	26 Jan 51	Finance	87UNTS161	101171

PARTY ONE	PARTY TWO	DATE	TOPIC	CITATION	NUMBER
Denmark	Colombia	10 May 68	Loans and Credits	0UNTS0	110482
Denmark	Congo (Brazzaville)	27 Feb 67	Air Transport	600UNTS189	108681
Denmark	Congo (Zaire)	25 May 68	Tech Assistance	0UNTS0	109289
Denmark	Costa Rica	26 Sep 56	General Economic	341UNTS305	104893
Denmark	Cyprus	27 Apr 63	Air Transport	529UNTS255	107664
Denmark	Czechoslovakia	14 May 47	Air Transport	27UNTS297	100413
Denmark	Czechoslovakia	17 Dec 49	Finance	74UNTS159	100962
Denmark	Czechoslovakia	17 Dec 49	General Trade	74UNTS147	100961
Denmark	Czechoslovakia	04 Apr 52	General Trade	133UNTS245	101792
Denmark	Czechoslovakia	23 Apr 53	Finance	174UNTS107	102281
Denmark	Czechoslovakia	23 Apr 53	General Trade	174UNTS95	102280
Denmark	Czechoslovakia	25 Oct 62	Taxation	456UNTS457	106571
Denmark	Czechoslovakia	21 Jan 69	Land Transport	0UNTS0	109469
Denmark	Dahomey	15 Apr 69	Loans and Credits	0UNTS0	110200
Denmark	EEC (Econ Commnty)	30 Jun 67	General Trade	0UNTS0	109745
Denmark	EEC (Econ Commnty)	30 Jun 67	General Trade	0UNTS0	109748
Denmark	EEC (Econ Commnty)	30 Jun 67	General Trade	0UNTS0	109746
Denmark	EEC (Econ Commnty)	30 Jun 67	General Trade	0UNTS0	109747
Denmark	El Salvador	09 Jul 58	General Economic	341UNTS289	104892
Denmark	Finland	22 Mar 49	Finance	33UNTS247	100520
Denmark	Finland	26 Aug 49	Air Transport	53UNTS191	100781
Denmark	Finland	21 Dec 49	Visas	46UNTS125	100705
Denmark	Finland	08 Jul 50	General Trade	73UNTS191	100953
Denmark	Finland	24 Sep 53	Dispute Settlement	188UNTS283	102532
Denmark	Finland	18 Jul 55	Taxation	250UNTS149	103521
Denmark	Finland	18 Jul 55	Taxation	250UNTS167	103522
Denmark	Finland	15 Sep 56	General Transport	254UNTS3	103589
Denmark	Finland	27 Mar 61	Commodity Trade	630UNTS3	108961
Denmark	Finland	07 Apr 64	Taxation	525UNTS89	107586
Denmark	France	04 Jan 46	Air Transport	27UNTS169	100406
Denmark	France	16 Jul 47	Patents/Copyrights	12UNTS3	100177
Denmark	France	22 Jun 49	Milit Servic/Citiz	48UNTS3	100737
Denmark	France	30 Jun 51	Non-ILO Labor	151UNTS241	102000
Denmark	France	08 Feb 57	Taxation	58FRRT27	415151
Denmark	France	29 May 59	General Trade	59FRMD1706	417152
Denmark	France	17 Sep 59	Taxation	410UNTS141	105901
Denmark	France	06 Jun 63	Milit Servic/Citiz	600UNTS213	108682
Denmark	France	14 Jun 66	General Trade	66FRMD2076	417153
Denmark	France	15 Feb 67	Culture	604UNTS247	108754
Denmark	France	25 Jul 69	Land Transport	0UNTS0	110033
Denmark	Germany, West	15 Dec 49	Finance	51UNTS11	100749
Denmark	Germany, West	15 Feb 52	Land Transport	61WBGA58	424097
Denmark	Germany, West	26 Feb 53	Claims and Debts	178UNTS3	102332
Denmark	Germany, West	14 Aug 53	Non-ILO Labor	202UNTS3	102725
Denmark	Germany, West	31 May 54	Extradition	200UNTS53	102694
Denmark	Germany, West	30 Jun 56	Visas	258UNTS65	103671
Denmark	Germany, West	29 Jan 57	Air Transport	302UNTS75	104354
Denmark	Germany, West	07 Jun 57	General Military	59WGBB409	425098
Denmark	Germany, West	29 May 58	Specific Resources	0UNTS0	109731
Denmark	Germany, West	29 May 58	Specific Resources	59WGBB1072	425099
Denmark	Germany, West	22 Dec 58	General Trade	59WBGA37	424100
Denmark	Germany, West	01 Aug 59	Non-ILO Labor	60WGBB2109	425101
Denmark	Germany, West	24 Aug 59	Specif Claim/Waive	60WGBB1333	425102
Denmark	Germany, West	10 Nov 60	Consul/Citizenship	431UNTS21	106205
Denmark	Germany, West	12 Sep 61	Non-ILO Labor	516UNTS283	107478
Denmark	Germany, West	30 Jan 62	Taxation	63WGBB1311	425103
Denmark	Germany, West	03 Oct 62	Other Military	450UNTS291	106475
Denmark	Germany, West	10 Jun 63	Admin Cooperation	477UNTS405	106930
Denmark	Germany, West	06 Jan 65	Admin Cooperation	528UNTS201	107643
Denmark	Germany, West	09 Jun 65	Territory Boundary	605UNTS95	108762
Denmark	Germany, West	09 Jun 65	Water Transport	581UNTS141	108439
Denmark	Germany, West	09 Jun 65	Territory Boundary	570UNTS91	108289
Denmark	Germany, West	02 Feb 67	Dispute Settlement	606UNTS97	108778
Denmark	Germany, West	30 Mar 67	Customs	69WGBB937	425104
Denmark	Germany, West	30 Mar 67	Customs	0UNTS0	109975

PARTY ONE	PARTY TWO	DATE	TOPIC	CITATION	NUMBER
Denmark	Germany, West	30 Nov 67	Specific Resources	632UNTS153	109017
Denmark	Germany, West	11 Jun 71	Status of Forces	71WGBB1092	425105
Denmark	Ghana	09 Aug 67	Loans and Credits	610UNTS0	108842
Denmark	Greece	14 Nov 47	Air Transport	35UNTS295	100560
Denmark	Greece	25 Feb 49	General Trade	78UNTS325	101022
Denmark	Greece	25 Feb 49	Finance	78UNTS335	101023
Denmark	Greece	15 Sep 52	General Trade	187UNTS207	102513
Denmark	Greece	19 Oct 53	General Trade	225UNTS9	103082
Denmark	Greece	29 Aug 55	General Trade	230UNTS25	103174
Denmark	Greece	04 Sep 56	General Trade	256UNTS319	103643
Denmark	Greece	04 Mar 61	Taxation	534UNTS157	107760
Denmark	Greece	26 Sep 63	General Trade	534UNTS43	107752
Denmark	Guatemala	04 Mar 48	General Economic	96UNTS223	101339
Denmark	Hungary	28 Feb 48	Finance	85UNTS35	101144
Denmark	Hungary	10 Feb 51	General Trade	85UNTS49	101145
Denmark	Hungary	17 Jul 58	Air Transport	344UNTS281	104954
Denmark	Hungary	20 Oct 69	Scientific Project	0UNTS0	110525
Denmark	IBRD (World Bank)	22 Aug 47	IBRD Project	152UNTS223	102016
Denmark	IBRD (World Bank)	04 Feb 59	IBRD Project	328UNTS143	104733
Denmark	IBRD (World Bank)	24 Jul 63	IBRD Project	481UNTS171	106982
Denmark	ICAO (Civil Aviat)	09 Sep 49	Air Transport	53UNTS341	100791
Denmark	Iceland	14 May 48	Non-ILO Labor	23UNTS163	100346
Denmark	Iceland	22 Mar 50	Air Transport	72UNTS273	100939
Denmark	Iceland	10 Oct 55	Taxation	230UNTS3	103171
Denmark	Iceland	01 Aug 61	Specific Resources	425UNTS191	106124
Denmark	ICJ Option Clause	10 Dec 46	ICJ Option Clause	1UNTS45	100010
Denmark	ICJ Option Clause	10 Dec 56	ICJ Option Clause	257UNTS35	103646
Denmark	India	20 Dec 46	Reparations	7UNTS309	100107
Denmark	India	16 Sep 59	Taxation	405UNTS13	105820
Denmark	India	15 May 63	Direct Aid	616UNTS23	108889
Denmark	India	15 May 63	Tech Assistance	616UNTS49	108891
Denmark	India	15 May 63	Direct Aid	616UNTS39	108890
Denmark	India	12 Jul 63	Loans and Credits	616UNTS3	108888
Denmark	India	06 Feb 65	Water Transport	531UNTS23	107690
Denmark	India	01 Sep 67	Direct Aid	616UNTS69	108892
Denmark	India	25 Mar 68	Direct Aid	0UNTS0	109229
Denmark	India	29 Apr 68	Direct Aid	0UNTS0	109230
Denmark	India	10 Jun 68	Sanitation	0UNTS0	109219
Denmark	India	08 May 69	General Aid	0UNTS0	109887
Denmark	India	30 Sep 69	Non-IBRD Project	0UNTS0	110541
Denmark	India	16 Feb 70	Tech Assistance	0UNTS0	110697
Denmark	Indonesia	30 Jan 68	General Economic	0UNTS0	110352
Denmark	Indonesia	22 Oct 69	Loans and Credits	0UNTS0	110393
Denmark	Int Coun Expl Sea	24 Jul 68	IGO Status/Immunit	0UNTS0	109413
Denmark	Iran	18 Jun 51	Air Transport	255UNTS3	103602
Denmark	Iran	16 Sep 56	Taxation	0IRTB19	433030
Denmark	Iran	14 Jun 66	Tech Assistance	597UNTS283	108652
Denmark	Iran	23 Jun 67	Visas	0IRTB19	433031
Denmark	Iran	02 Nov 67	Loans and Credits	638UNTS217	109138
Denmark	Iraq	18 Nov 51	Air Transport	232UNTS25	103227
Denmark	Ireland	13 May 47	Visas	553UNTS37	108066
Denmark	Ireland	18 Nov 47	Air Transport	35UNTS309	100561
Denmark	Ireland	18 Oct 54	Taxation	218UNTS295	102959
Denmark	Ireland	04 Feb 64	Taxation	525UNTS233	107596
Denmark	Israel	14 Nov 52	General Economic	160UNTS275	102112
Denmark	Israel	14 Nov 52	General Trade	160UNTS279	102113
Denmark	Israel	14 Nov 52	Finance	160UNTS289	102114
Denmark	Israel	04 Apr 55	Taxation	213UNTS283	102891
Denmark	Israel	29 Apr 55	Visas	220UNTS87	102992
Denmark	Israel	23 Feb 66	Visas	581UNTS187	108443
Denmark	Israel	27 Jun 66	Taxation	581UNTS227	108448
Denmark	Israel	14 Feb 67	Admin Cooperation	620UNTS211	108957
Denmark	Italy	01 Jul 50	Patents/Copyrights	133UNTS181	101788
Denmark	Italy	04 Oct 50	Finance	78UNTS353	101025
Denmark	Italy	04 Oct 50	General Trade	78UNTS341	101024

PARTY ONE	PARTY TWO	DATE	TOPIC	CITATION	NUMBER
Denmark	Italy	24 Oct 51	General Trade	118UNTS91	101598
Denmark	Italy	28 Oct 52	General Trade	167UNTS125	102202
Denmark	Italy	10 Apr 54	General Trade	196UNTS175	102623
Denmark	Italy	15 Jul 54	Milit Servic/Citiz	250UNTS43	103516
Denmark	Italy	12 May 56	General Trade	260UNTS357	103720
Denmark	Italy	26 Oct 56	Culture	267UNTS261	103847
Denmark	Italy	12 Jul 57	General Trade	291UNTS169	104251
Denmark	Italy	18 Jul 63	Privil/Immunities	64ITDI252	436103
Denmark	Italy	10 Mar 66	Taxation	0UNTS0	109217
Denmark	Italy	10 Mar 66	Taxation	643UNTS349	109201
Denmark	Ivory Coast	07 Jun 66	Air Transport	595UNTS313	108626
Denmark	Ivory Coast	23 Nov 66	General Trade	0UNTS0	110554
Denmark	Ivory Coast	23 Dec 68	Loans and Credits	0UNTS0	110178
Denmark	Jamaica	25 Mar 69	Visas	0UNTS0	109940
Denmark	Japan	29 Feb 52	Consul/Citizenship	126UNTS139	101686
Denmark	Japan	28 Apr 52	Air Transport	166UNTS3	102182
Denmark	Japan	26 Feb 53	Air Transport	173UNTS329	102273
Denmark	Japan	21 Oct 53	Patents/Copyrights	0JGJI1171	441076
Denmark	Japan	31 May 54	Patents/Copyrights	0JGJI1173	441079
Denmark	Japan	20 Jul 56	Visas	0JGJI1296	441095
Denmark	Japan	10 Mar 59	Taxation	341UNTS55	104878
Denmark	Japan	25 May 59	Reparations	341UNTS157	104881
Denmark	Japan	03 Feb 68	Taxation	0UNTS0	109405
Denmark	Japan	03 Feb 68	Taxation	68JHZ7	439016
Denmark	Jordan	07 Dec 61	Air Transport	631UNTS333	109003
Denmark	Jordan	28 Jun 66	Loans and Credits	574UNTS3	108338
Denmark	Kenya	26 Jun 64	Education	573UNTS107	108325
Denmark	Kenya	26 Jun 68	Loans and Credits	0UNTS0	109210
Denmark	Kenya	28 Jun 68	Direct Aid	0UNTS0	109393
Denmark	Korea, South	04 Dec 69	Loans and Credits	0UNTS0	110396
Denmark	Lebanon	21 Oct 55	Air Transport	248UNTS17	103482
Denmark	Lebanon	29 Mar 67	Taxation	602UNTS251	108717
Denmark	Luxembourg	21 May 46	Claims and Debts	4UNTS435	100060
Denmark	Luxembourg	10 Jun 58	Air Transport	356UNTS193	105096
Denmark	Madagascar	10 Dec 65	General Trade	0UNTS0	110553
Denmark	Malawi	01 Sep 66	Loans and Credits	586UNTS3	108493
Denmark	Malawi	03 Sep 68	Education	0UNTS0	109414
Denmark	Malawi	16 Dec 68	Loans and Credits	0UNTS0	109461
Denmark	Malaysia	26 Mar 65	Air Transport	540UNTS205	107851
Denmark	Malaysia	14 Dec 67	Air Transport	614UNTS26	108862
Denmark	Malaysia	29 Feb 68	Loans and Credits	640UNTS29	109153
Denmark	Malta	30 Dec 65	Visas	561UNTS199	108182
Denmark	Malta	06 May 69	Air Transport	0UNTS0	109931
Denmark	Mexico	12 Jul 54	Patents/Copyrights	55MEXD2608	444013
Denmark	Mexico	04 Feb 70	Air Transport	71MEXD503	444014
Denmark	Morocco	22 Apr 68	Tech Assistance	0UNTS0	109218
Denmark	Morocco	05 Nov 68	Loans and Credits	0UNTS0	109415
Denmark	Multilateral	12 May 40	Scientific Project	101UNTS91	101405
Denmark	Multilateral	27 Mar 41	Military Mission	67UNTS231	200222
Denmark	Multilateral	02 Aug 44	Scientific Project	67UNTS221	200221
Denmark	Multilateral	07 Dec 44	Air Transport	171UNTS345	200501
Denmark	Multilateral	07 Dec 44	IGO Establishment	15UNTS295	200102
Denmark	Multilateral	07 Dec 44	Air Transport	171UNTS387	200502
Denmark	Multilateral	07 Dec 44	Air Transport	84UNTS389	200252
Denmark	Multilateral	15 Dec 44	Sanitation	17UNTS305	200110
Denmark	Multilateral	08 Aug 45	General Military	82UNTS279	200251
Denmark	Multilateral	27 Sep 45	IGO Establishment	5UNTS327	200035
Denmark	Multilateral	16 Nov 45	IGO Establishment	4UNTS275	100052
Denmark	Multilateral	04 Jan 46	IGO Establishment	6UNTS35	100066
Denmark	Multilateral	14 Jan 46	Reparations	555UNTS69	108105
Denmark	Multilateral	05 Apr 46	Specific Resources	231UNTS199	103221
Denmark	Multilateral	23 Apr 46	Sanitation	17UNTS3	100265
Denmark	Multilateral	22 Jul 46	IGO Establishment	14UNTS185	100221
Denmark	Multilateral	22 Jul 46	IGO Establishment	9UNTS3	100125
Denmark	Multilateral	27 Jul 46	Patents/Copyrights	90UNTS229	101238

PARTY ONE	PARTY TWO	DATE	TOPIC	CITATION	NUMBER
Denmark	Multilateral	15 Oct 46	Refugees	11UNTS73	100150
Denmark	Multilateral	30 Oct 46	IGO Establishment	11UNTS107	100151
Denmark	Multilateral	02 Dec 46	Specific Resources	161UNTS72	102124
Denmark	Multilateral	11 Dec 46	Sanitation	12UNTS179	100186
Denmark	Multilateral	15 Dec 46	IGO Establishment	18UNTS3	100283
Denmark	Multilateral	08 Feb 47	Patents/Copyrights	14UNTS287	100222
Denmark	Multilateral	03 Mar 47	Humanitarian	11UNTS43	100148
Denmark	Multilateral	10 Jun 47	Water Transport	208UNTS3	102814
Denmark	Multilateral	02 Oct 47	Telecommunications	193UNTS188	102616
Denmark	Multilateral	05 Oct 47	Finance	34UNTS23	100525
Denmark	Multilateral	11 Oct 47	IGO Establishment	77UNTS143	100998
Denmark	Multilateral	12 Nov 47	Admin Cooperation	53UNTS13	100770
Denmark	Multilateral	12 Nov 47	Admin Cooperation	46UNTS201	100710
Denmark	Multilateral	12 Nov 47	Admin Cooperation	53UNTS39	100771
Denmark	Multilateral	12 Nov 47	Admin Cooperation	46UNTS169	100709
Denmark	Multilateral	08 Mar 48	Admin Cooperation	27UNTS117	100403
Denmark	Multilateral	10 May 48	Culture	289UNTS111	104215
Denmark	Multilateral	10 Jun 48	Humanitarian	191UNTS3	102576
Denmark	Multilateral	10 Jun 48	Humanitarian	164UNTS113	102163
Denmark	Multilateral	19 Jun 48	Air Transport	310UNTS151	104492
Denmark	Multilateral	26 Jun 48	Culture	331UNTS217	104757
Denmark	Multilateral	24 Jul 48	Sanitation	66UNTS25	100847
Denmark	Multilateral	14 Sep 48	Milit Occupation	18UNTS267	100296
Denmark	Multilateral	17 Sep 48	Telecommunications	97UNTS31	101345
Denmark	Multilateral	19 Nov 48	Sanitation	44UNTS277	100688
Denmark	Multilateral	09 Dec 48	Scientific Project	20UNTS229	100318
Denmark	Multilateral	09 Dec 48	Humanitarian	78UNTS277	101021
Denmark	Multilateral	09 Dec 48	Scientific Project	73UNTS39	100942
Denmark	Multilateral	08 Feb 49	Specific Resources	157UNTS157	102053
Denmark	Multilateral	23 Mar 49	Commodity Trade	203UNTS179	102746
Denmark	Multilateral	04 Apr 49	General Military	34UNTS243	100541
Denmark	Multilateral	04 May 49	Admin Cooperation	30UNTS23	100446
Denmark	Multilateral	04 May 49	Admin Cooperation	30UNTS3	100445
Denmark	Multilateral	04 May 49	Admin Cooperation	47UNTS159	100728
Denmark	Multilateral	04 May 49	Admin Cooperation	98UNTS101	101358
Denmark	Multilateral	04 May 49	Admin Cooperation	92UNTS19	101257
Denmark	Multilateral	05 May 49	IGO Establishment	87UNTS103	101168
Denmark	Multilateral	16 Jun 49	Land Transport	45UNTS149	100696
Denmark	Multilateral	15 Jul 49	Health/Educ/Welfare	197UNTS3	102631
Denmark	Multilateral	10 Aug 49	Finance	45UNTS3	100689
Denmark	Multilateral	12 Aug 49	Humanitarian	75UNTS287	100973
Denmark	Multilateral	12 Aug 49	Humanitarian	75UNTS31	100970
Denmark	Multilateral	12 Aug 49	General Military	75UNTS135	100972
Denmark	Multilateral	12 Aug 49	Humanitarian	75UNTS85	100971
Denmark	Multilateral	27 Aug 49	Non-ILO Labor	47UNTS127	100727
Denmark	Multilateral	02 Sep 49	IGO Status/Immunit	250UNTS12	103515
Denmark	Multilateral	19 Sep 49	Land Transport	125UNTS3	101671
Denmark	Multilateral	16 Dec 49	Admin Cooperation	72UNTS3	100924
Denmark	Multilateral	21 Mar 50	Admin Cooperation	96UNTS271	101342
Denmark	Multilateral	06 Apr 50	Admin Cooperation	119UNTS99	101610
Denmark	Multilateral	13 May 50	Land Transport	128UNTS171	101719
Denmark	Multilateral	31 May 50	General Trade	74UNTS95	100957
Denmark	Multilateral	04 Nov 50	Humanitarian	213UNTS221	102889
Denmark	Multilateral	22 Nov 50	Culture	131UNTS25	101734
Denmark	Multilateral	07 Dec 50	Admin Cooperation	212UNTS17	102861
Denmark	Multilateral	15 Dec 50	Customs	347UNTS127	104994
Denmark	Multilateral	15 Dec 50	Customs	171UNTS305	102234
Denmark	Multilateral	15 Dec 50	IGO Operations	160UNTS267	102111
Denmark	Multilateral	15 Dec 50	Customs	157UNTS129	102052
Denmark	Multilateral	21 Dec 50	Admin Cooperation	90UNTS3	101222
Denmark	Multilateral	09 Jan 51	Humanitarian	197UNTS341	102647
Denmark	Multilateral	25 May 51	Status of Forces	175UNTS215	102303
Denmark	Multilateral	19 Jun 51	Status of Forces	199UNTS67	102678
Denmark	Multilateral	02 Jul 51	Refugees	189UNTS137	102545
Denmark	Multilateral	20 Sep 51	IGO Status/Immunit	200UNTS3	102691
Denmark	Multilateral	09 Oct 51	IGO Establishment	220UNTS121	102997
Denmark	Multilateral	06 Dec 51	Admin Cooperation	150UNTS67	101963
Denmark	Multilateral	20 Dec 51	Air Transport	163UNTS309	102152
Denmark	Multilateral	20 Dec 51	Air Transport	163UNTS293	102151
Denmark	Multilateral	15 Feb 52	Scientific Project	132UNTS51	101751
Denmark	Multilateral	07 Mar 52	Specific Resources	175UNTS205	102302
Denmark	Multilateral	10 May 52	Admin Cooperation	439UNTS217	106331
Denmark	Multilateral	10 May 52	Taxation	439UNTS233	106332
Denmark	Multilateral	20 May 52	Sanitation	219UNTS55	102966
Denmark	Multilateral	11 Jul 52	Postal Service	171UNTS191	102227
Denmark	Multilateral	11 Jul 52	IGO Establishment	169UNTS3	102220
Denmark	Multilateral	11 Jul 52	Postal Service	171UNTS89	102225
Denmark	Multilateral	11 Jul 52	Postal Service	171UNTS143	102226
Denmark	Multilateral	11 Jul 52	Postal Service	170UNTS63	102222
Denmark	Multilateral	11 Jul 52	Postal Service	170UNTS269	102223
Denmark	Multilateral	11 Jul 52	Postal Service	171UNTS3	102224
Denmark	Multilateral	11 Jul 52	Postal Service	170UNTS3	102221
Denmark	Multilateral	14 Jul 52	Consul/Citizenship	198UNTS47	102656
Denmark	Multilateral	14 Jul 52	Visas	198UNTS37	102655
Denmark	Multilateral	06 Sep 52	Patents/Copyrights	216UNTS132	102937
Denmark	Multilateral	07 Oct 52	Admin Cooperation	310UNTS181	104493
Denmark	Multilateral	07 Nov 52	General Trade	221UNTS255	103010
Denmark	Multilateral	27 Feb 53	Claims and Debts	333UNTS3	104764
Denmark	Multilateral	23 Mar 53	Admin Cooperation	202UNTS241	102732
Denmark	Multilateral	31 Mar 53	Privil/Immunities	193UNTS136	102613
Denmark	Multilateral	01 Apr 53	Non-ILO Labor	227UNTS169	103138
Denmark	Multilateral	11 May 53	Sanitation	456UNTS3	106555
Denmark	Multilateral	01 Jul 53	IGO Establishment	200UNTS149	102701
Denmark	Multilateral	20 Jul 53	Non-ILO Labor	228UNTS3	103141
Denmark	Multilateral	20 Jul 53	Non-ILO Labor	227UNTS217	103140
Denmark	Multilateral	20 Jul 53	Non-ILO Labor	228UNTS41	103142
Denmark	Multilateral	01 Oct 53	Commodity Trade	258UNTS153	103677
Denmark	Multilateral	17 Oct 53	General Transport	184UNTS42	102438
Denmark	Multilateral	19 Oct 53	IGO Establishment	207UNTS189	102807
Denmark	Multilateral	07 Dec 53	Admin Cooperation	182UNTS51	102422
Denmark	Multilateral	11 Dec 53	Patents/Copyrights	218UNTS27	102952
Denmark	Multilateral	11 Dec 53	Non-ILO Labor	218UNTS211	102957
Denmark	Multilateral	11 Dec 53	Non-ILO Labor	218UNTS153	102956
Denmark	Multilateral	11 Dec 53	Non-ILO Labor	218UNTS255	102958
Denmark	Multilateral	11 Dec 53	Education	218UNTS125	102954
Denmark	Multilateral	11 Dec 53	Sanitation	191UNTS285	102588
Denmark	Multilateral	22 Feb 54	Other Military	188UNTS273	102531
Denmark	Multilateral	25 Feb 54	Air Transport	215UNTS249	102922
Denmark	Multilateral	01 Mar 54	Commodity Trade	256UNTS31	103622
Denmark	Multilateral	01 Mar 54	Admin Cooperation	286UNTS265	104173
Denmark	Multilateral	12 May 54	Admin Cooperation	327UNTS3	104714
Denmark	Multilateral	14 May 54	Culture	249UNTS215	103511
Denmark	Multilateral	22 May 54	Non-ILO Labor	199UNTS3	102674
Denmark	Multilateral	22 May 54	Visas	199UNTS29	102675
Denmark	Multilateral	04 Jun 54	Customs	282UNTS249	104101
Denmark	Multilateral	04 Jun 54	Customs	276UNTS191	103992
Denmark	Multilateral	14 Jun 54	Air Transport	320UNTS217	104644
Denmark	Multilateral	14 Jun 54	Air Transport	320UNTS209	104643
Denmark	Multilateral	28 Sep 54	Refugees	360UNTS117	105158
Denmark	Multilateral	23 Oct 54	Status of Forces	334UNTS3	104765
Denmark	Multilateral	19 Dec 54	Patents/Copyrights	218UNTS51	102953
Denmark	Multilateral	19 Dec 54	Culture	218UNTS139	102955
Denmark	Multilateral	12 Mar 55	Land Transport	211UNTS3	102844
Denmark	Multilateral	19 Mar 55	Sanitation	228UNTS95	103144
Denmark	Multilateral	25 May 55	IGO Establishment	264UNTS117	103791
Denmark	Multilateral	03 Jun 55	Specific Resources	310UNTS145	104491
Denmark	Multilateral	22 Jun 55	Atomic Energy	249UNTS3	103498
Denmark	Multilateral	15 Sep 55	Non-ILO Labor	254UNTS55	103593
Denmark	Multilateral	28 Sep 55	Air Transport	478UNTS371	106943
Denmark	Multilateral	29 Sep 55	Air Transport	222UNTS313	103037

PARTY ONE	PARTY TWO	DATE	TOPIC	CITATION	NUMBER
Denmark	Multilateral	12 Oct 55	IGO Establishment	560UNTS3	108165
Denmark	Multilateral	20 Oct 55	IGO Establishment	378UNTS159	105425
Denmark	Multilateral	13 Dec 55	Humanitarian	250UNTS3	103514
Denmark	Multilateral	13 Dec 55	IGO Operations	529UNTS141	107660
Denmark	Multilateral	04 Jan 56	Scientific Project	256UNTS171	103627
Denmark	Multilateral	01 Mar 56	Customs	343UNTS129	104923
Denmark	Multilateral	03 Mar 56	Milit Servic/Citiz	243UNTS169	103452
Denmark	Multilateral	13 Mar 56	Humanitarian	427UNTS245	106158
Denmark	Multilateral	25 Apr 56	Commodity Trade	270UNTS103	103896
Denmark	Multilateral	30 Apr 56	Air Transport	310UNTS229	104494
Denmark	Multilateral	18 May 56	Customs	338UNTS103	104834
Denmark	Multilateral	18 May 56	Customs	327UNTS123	104721
Denmark	Multilateral	18 May 56	Customs	319UNTS21	104630
Denmark	Multilateral	19 May 56	Land Transport	399UNTS189	105742
Denmark	Multilateral	20 Jun 56	Admin Cooperation	268UNTS3	103850
Denmark	Multilateral	07 Sep 56	Humanitarian	266UNTS3	103822
Denmark	Multilateral	15 Sep 56	Admin Cooperation	254UNTS45	103592
Denmark	Multilateral	25 Sep 56	Air Transport	334UNTS89	104767
Denmark	Multilateral	25 Sep 56	Air Transport	334UNTS13	104766
Denmark	Multilateral	26 Oct 56	IGO Establishment	276UNTS3	103988
Denmark	Multilateral	15 Dec 56	Education	278UNTS73	104023
Denmark	Multilateral	19 Dec 56	Non-ILO Labor	427UNTS93	106148
Denmark	Multilateral	21 Dec 56	Humanitarian	427UNTS81	106147
Denmark	Multilateral	20 Feb 57	Consul/Citizenship	309UNTS65	104468
Denmark	Multilateral	29 Apr 57	Dispute Settlement	320UNTS243	104646
Denmark	Multilateral	15 Jun 57	General Trade	550UNTS45	108008
Denmark	Multilateral	12 Jul 57	Visas	322UNTS245	104660
Denmark	Multilateral	03 Oct 57	Postal Service	366UNTS87	105216
Denmark	Multilateral	03 Oct 57	Postal Service	365UNTS207	105214
Denmark	Multilateral	03 Oct 57	Postal Service	366UNTS141	105217
Denmark	Multilateral	03 Oct 57	Postal Service	364UNTS331	105212
Denmark	Multilateral	03 Oct 57	Postal Service	365UNTS3	105213
Denmark	Multilateral	03 Oct 57	Postal Service	364UNTS3	105211
Denmark	Multilateral	03 Oct 57	Postal Service	366UNTS3	105215
Denmark	Multilateral	03 Oct 57	Postal Service	366UNTS255	105219
Denmark	Multilateral	23 Nov 57	Refugees	506UNTS125	107384
Denmark	Multilateral	13 Dec 57	Extradition	359UNTS273	105146
Denmark	Multilateral	15 Jan 58	Customs	383UNTS229	105503
Denmark	Multilateral	15 Apr 58	Health/Educ/Welfare	539UNTS27	107822
Denmark	Multilateral	29 Apr 58	Specific Resources	559UNTS285	108164
Denmark	Multilateral	29 Apr 58	Territory Boundary	499UNTS311	107302
Denmark	Multilateral	29 Apr 58	Territory Boundary	516UNTS205	107477
Denmark	Multilateral	29 Apr 58	Dispute Settlement	450UNTS169	106466
Denmark	Multilateral	29 Apr 58	Water Transport	450UNTS11	106465
Denmark	Multilateral	26 Jun 58	Admin Cooperation	324UNTS97	104679
Denmark	Multilateral	05 Nov 58	Land Transport	428UNTS73	106169
Denmark	Multilateral	01 Dec 58	Commodity Trade	385UNTS137	105534
Denmark	Multilateral	03 Dec 58	Admin Cooperation	416UNTS51	105995
Denmark	Multilateral	03 Dec 58	Admin Cooperation	398UNTS9	105715
Denmark	Multilateral	15 Dec 58	Sanitation	351UNTS159	105022
Denmark	Multilateral	15 Dec 58	Mass Media	546UNTS235	107950
Denmark	Multilateral	15 Jan 59	Customs	348UNTS13	104996
Denmark	Multilateral	24 Jan 59	IGO Establishment	486UNTS157	107078
Denmark	Multilateral	06 Apr 59	Commodity Trade	349UNTS167	105013
Denmark	Multilateral	20 Apr 59	Land Transport	0UNTS0	110345
Denmark	Multilateral	20 Apr 59	Admin Cooperation	472UNTS185	106841
Denmark	Multilateral	20 Apr 59	Visas	376UNTS85	105375
Denmark	Multilateral	11 May 59	Claims and Debts	527UNTS145	107623
Denmark	Multilateral	20 Aug 59	Air Transport	376UNTS99	105376
Denmark	Multilateral	08 Sep 59	Non-ILO Labor	383UNTS203	105502
Denmark	Multilateral	01 Dec 59	Territory Boundary	402UNTS71	105778
Denmark	Multilateral	14 Dec 59	Admin Cooperation	444UNTS193	106369
Denmark	Multilateral	04 Jan 60	IGO Establishment	370UNTS3	105266
Denmark	Multilateral	26 Jan 60	IGO Establishment	439UNTS249	106333
Denmark	Multilateral	22 Apr 60	Air Transport	418UNTS211	106023
Denmark	Multilateral	28 Apr 60	Health/Educ/Welfare	376UNTS111	105377
Denmark	Multilateral	17 Jun 60	Humanitarian	536UNTS27	107794
Denmark	Multilateral	22 Jun 60	Mass Media	546UNTS247	107951
Denmark	Multilateral	28 Jul 60	IGO Status/Immunit	394UNTS37	105667
Denmark	Multilateral	01 Sep 60	Commodity Trade	403UNTS3	105792
Denmark	Multilateral	21 Sep 60	Patents/Copyrights	394UNTS3	105664
Denmark	Multilateral	06 Oct 60	Customs	473UNTS131	106861
Denmark	Multilateral	01 Dec 60	Scientific Project	414UNTS110	105970
Denmark	Multilateral	09 Dec 60	Customs	429UNTS211	106200
Denmark	Multilateral	14 Dec 60	Education	429UNTS93	106193
Denmark	Multilateral	27 Mar 61	IGO Establishment	420UNTS109	106043
Denmark	Multilateral	30 Mar 61	Sanitation	520UNTS151	107515
Denmark	Multilateral	18 Apr 61	Consul/Citizenship	500UNTS223	107311
Denmark	Multilateral	18 Apr 61	Consul/Citizenship	500UNTS95	107310
Denmark	Multilateral	18 Apr 61	Dispute Settlement	500UNTS243	107312
Denmark	Multilateral	21 Apr 61	IGO Establishment	484UNTS349	107041
Denmark	Multilateral	08 Jun 61	Customs	473UNTS187	106863
Denmark	Multilateral	08 Jun 61	Customs	473UNTS153	106862
Denmark	Multilateral	21 Jun 61	IGO Establishment	514UNTS209	107449
Denmark	Multilateral	05 Oct 61	Dispute Settlement	510UNTS175	107413
Denmark	Multilateral	18 Oct 61	IGO Establishment	529UNTS89	107659
Denmark	Multilateral	26 Oct 61	Patents/Copyrights	496UNTS43	107247
Denmark	Multilateral	06 Dec 61	Customs	473UNTS219	106864
Denmark	Multilateral	16 Dec 61	Visas	544UNTS19	107909
Denmark	Multilateral	20 Dec 61	Water Transport	419UNTS79	106031
Denmark	Multilateral	20 Feb 62	Water Transport	597UNTS159	108644
Denmark	Multilateral	23 Mar 62	Admin Cooperation	470UNTS25	106793
Denmark	Multilateral	23 Mar 62	General Amity	434UNTS145	106262
Denmark	Multilateral	14 May 62	Sanitation	544UNTS81	107911
Denmark	Multilateral	14 May 62	Scientific Project	544UNTS39	107910
Denmark	Multilateral	14 Jun 62	IGO Establishment	528UNTS33	107634
Denmark	Multilateral	18 Sep 62	Water Transport	442UNTS215	106351
Denmark	Multilateral	28 Sep 62	IGO Establishment	469UNTS169	106791
Denmark	Multilateral	10 Dec 62	Culture	521UNTS231	107525
Denmark	Multilateral	17 Dec 62	Sanitation	486UNTS119	107076
Denmark	Multilateral	15 Jan 63	Tech Assistance	456UNTS409	106567
Denmark	Multilateral	24 Apr 63	Consul/Citizenship	596UNTS261	108638
Denmark	Multilateral	24 Apr 63	Consul/Citizenship	596UNTS487	108640
Denmark	Multilateral	05 Aug 63	Sanitation	480UNTS43	106964
Denmark	Multilateral	14 Sep 63	Air Transport	0UNTS0	110106
Denmark	Multilateral	14 Sep 63	Telecommunications	488UNTS121	107123
Denmark	Multilateral	17 Oct 63	Atomic Energy	525UNTS75	107585
Denmark	Multilateral	09 Mar 64	Specific Resources	581UNTS57	108432
Denmark	Multilateral	18 Jun 64	Atomic Energy	542UNTS145	107886
Denmark	Multilateral	10 Jul 64	Postal Service	612UNTS233	108848
Denmark	Multilateral	10 Jul 64	Postal Service	613UNTS3	108850
Denmark	Multilateral	10 Jul 64	Postal Service	613UNTS3	108851
Denmark	Multilateral	10 Jul 64	Postal Service	613UNTS193	108852
Denmark	Multilateral	10 Jul 64	Postal Service	612UNTS361	108849
Denmark	Multilateral	10 Jul 64	Postal Service	611UNTS387	108846
Denmark	Multilateral	10 Jul 64	Postal Service	612UNTS3	108847
Denmark	Multilateral	10 Jul 64	Postal Service	611UNTS7	108844
Denmark	Multilateral	10 Jul 64	Postal Service	611UNTS105	108845
Denmark	Multilateral	20 Aug 64	Telecommunications	514UNTS25	107441
Denmark	Multilateral	12 Sep 64	Specific Resources	0UNTS0	109344
Denmark	Multilateral	15 Sep 64	General Trade	510UNTS147	107411
Denmark	Multilateral	01 Dec 64	Water Transport	550UNTS133	108012
Denmark	Multilateral	22 Jan 65	Gen Communications	634UNTS239	109066
Denmark	Multilateral	09 Mar 65	Water Transport	591UNTS265	108564
Denmark	Multilateral	18 Mar 65	Dispute Settlement	575UNTS159	108359
Denmark	Multilateral	23 Jun 65	Atomic Energy	548UNTS241	107981
Denmark	Multilateral	03 Dec 65	Admin Cooperation	572UNTS105	108309
Denmark	Multilateral	04 Dec 65	IGO Establishment	571UNTS123	108303
Denmark	Multilateral	31 Dec 65	Specific Resources	616UNTS317	108904
Denmark	Multilateral	04 May 66	IBRD Project	575UNTS49	108354

PARTY ONE	PARTY TWO	DATE	TOPIC	CITATION	NUMBER
Denmark	Multilateral	03 Oct 66	Culture	610UNTS169	108841
Denmark	Multilateral	19 Dec 66	Specific Resources	605UNTS313	108769
Denmark	Multilateral	31 Jan 67	Refugees	606UNTS267	108791
Denmark	Multilateral	02 Feb 67	Dispute Settlement	606UNTS89	108777
Denmark	Multilateral	24 Feb 67	Health/Educ/Welfare	596UNTS133	108631
Denmark	Multilateral	17 Apr 67	Consul/Citizenship	0UNTS0	110377
Denmark	Multilateral	24 Apr 67	Humanitarian	634UNTS255	109067
Denmark	Multilateral	25 Oct 67	Scientific Project	0UNTS0	110322
Denmark	Multilateral	08 Dec 67	Specific Resources	620UNTS225	108959
Denmark	Multilateral	18 Mar 68	Commodity Trade	0UNTS0	109262
Denmark	Multilateral	22 Apr 68	Scientific Project	0UNTS0	109574
Denmark	Multilateral	11 Jun 68	Scientific Project	0UNTS0	109884
Denmark	Multilateral	01 Jul 68	Peace/Disarmament	0UNTS0	110485
Denmark	Multilateral	05 Dec 68	Scientific Project	0UNTS0	109952
Denmark	Multilateral	24 Dec 68	Commodity Trade	0UNTS0	109369
Denmark	Multilateral	15 Jan 69	Consul/Citizenship	0UNTS0	109491
Denmark	Multilateral	09 Jun 69	Specific Resources	0UNTS0	110099
Denmark	Multilateral	12 Dec 69	General Economic	0UNTS0	110755
Denmark	Multilateral	12 Jan 70	Commodity Trade	0UNTS0	110603
Denmark	Netherlands	31 Jan 46	Finance	3UNTS3	100021
Denmark	Netherlands	03 May 46	General Trade	52NET139	447001
Denmark	Netherlands	08 May 52	Reparations	131UNTS91	101737
Denmark	Netherlands	31 Jan 56	Finance	286UNTS255	104172
Denmark	Netherlands	20 Feb 57	Taxation	287UNTS41	104179
Denmark	Netherlands	13 Nov 57	Land Transport	306UNTS67	104432
Denmark	Netherlands	30 Apr 59	Finance	487UNTS23	107092
Denmark	Netherlands	06 Jun 63	Patents/Copyrights	484UNTS137	107021
Denmark	Netherlands	31 Mar 66	Territory Boundary	604UNTS209	108751
Denmark	Netherlands	20 Jun 67	Non-ILO Labor	619UNTS67	108939
Denmark	Netherlands	30 May 68	Specific Resources	0UNTS0	109233
Denmark	New Zealand	18 Sep 46	Claims and Debts	10UNTS39	100141
Denmark	New Zealand	13 Dec 48	Visas	92UNTS65	101261
Denmark	Nigeria	08 Sep 66	Air Transport	591UNTS177	108557
Denmark	Norway	07 Aug 45	Telecommunications	10UNTS203	200062
Denmark	Norway	10 Oct 45	Visas	104UNTS335	200323
Denmark	Norway	30 Mar 46	General Trade	29UNTS163	100438
Denmark	Norway	08 Jul 46	Territory Boundary	7UNTS247	100103
Denmark	Norway	30 Dec 46	Taxation	8UNTS21	100111
Denmark	Norway	15 Apr 47	Finance	12UNTS323	100191
Denmark	Norway	09 Jul 47	Territory Boundary	7UNTS321	100108
Denmark	Norway	21 Jan 48	Non-ILO Labor	14UNTS307	100223
Denmark	Norway	21 Apr 48	Finance	18UNTS139	100284
Denmark	Norway	18 Jan 51	Non-ILO Labor	82UNTS153	101090
Denmark	Norway	14 Jan 52	Claims and Debts	120UNTS119	101618
Denmark	Norway	23 May 56	Taxation	271UNTS49	103909
Denmark	Norway	23 May 56	Taxation	271UNTS75	103910
Denmark	Norway	15 Sep 56	General Transport	259UNTS3	103680
Denmark	Norway	22 Feb 57	Taxation	286UNTS127	104164
Denmark	Norway	31 Oct 58	Privil/Immunities	3NORT752	451036
Denmark	Norway	05 Sep 62	Water Transport	3NORT863	451037
Denmark	Norway	11 May 63	General Trade	613UNTS271	108856
Denmark	Norway	12 Sep 63	General Trade	613UNTS289	108857
Denmark	Norway	08 Dec 65	Territory Boundary	634UNTS71	109052
Denmark	Norway	19 Dec 66	Specific Resources	606UNTS3	108770
Denmark	Norway	23 Dec 66	General Trade	613UNTS265	108855
Denmark	Norway	20 Apr 67	Specific Resources	604UNTS103	108747
Denmark	Norway	26 Apr 68	Specific Resources	3NORT0	451038
Denmark	Norway	26 Apr 68	Specific Resources	0UNTS0	109211
Denmark	Norway	28 Apr 69	Admin Cooperation	0UNTS0	110578
Denmark	Pakistan	09 Nov 49	Air Transport	44UNTS255	100687
Denmark	Pakistan	30 Aug 54	Visas	203UNTS59	102740
Denmark	Pakistan	10 Apr 57	Air Transport	302UNTS53	104353
Denmark	Pakistan	05 Sep 59	Admin Cooperation	354UNTS377	105071
Denmark	Pakistan	04 Sep 61	Taxation	455UNTS305	106549
Denmark	Pakistan	12 Dec 64	Tech Assistance	636UNTS313	109107

PARTY ONE	PARTY TWO	DATE	TOPIC	CITATION	NUMBER
Denmark	Pakistan	01 Jun 67	Water Transport	620UNTS217	108958
Denmark	Pakistan	21 Oct 67	Tech Assistance	632UNTS105	109012
Denmark	Pakistan	05 Sep 68	Tech Assistance	0UNTS0	109396
Denmark	Paraguay	18 May 57	Finance	286UNTS117	104163
Denmark	Paraguay	03 May 67	General Trade	608UNTS55	108812
Denmark	Peru	10 Jun 57	General Economic	406UNTS63	105839
Denmark	Peru	22 Jun 60	Air Transport	439UNTS113	106326
Denmark	Peru	30 Dec 64	Tech Assistance	595UNTS47	108611
Denmark	Peru	20 Jun 67	Loans and Credits	0UNTS0	109446
Denmark	Philippines	20 Oct 54	Air Transport	216UNTS3	102927
Denmark	Philippines	21 Apr 59	Visas	3PTS827	465040
Denmark	Philippines	20 Dec 66	Visas	591UNTS259	108563
Denmark	Philippines	08 May 69	Air Transport	0UNTS0	109866
Denmark	Poland	14 Dec 48	Finance	81UNTS33	101060
Denmark	Poland	12 May 49	Claims and Debts	87UNTS179	101172
Denmark	Poland	07 Dec 49	Commodity Trade	81UNTS21	101059
Denmark	Poland	01 Oct 50	General Economic	81UNTS43	101061
Denmark	Poland	09 Jun 52	General Trade	135UNTS209	101822
Denmark	Poland	09 Jun 52	Finance	135UNTS221	101823
Denmark	Poland	26 Feb 53	Claims and Debts	186UNTS301	102496
Denmark	Poland	08 Jun 60	Culture	424UNTS37	106097
Denmark	Poland	17 Jan 61	Air Transport	412UNTS111	105927
Denmark	Poland	15 Nov 67	General Economic	643UNTS383	109203
Denmark	Poland	26 Feb 68	Water Transport	643UNTS371	109202
Denmark	Poland	01 Jun 71	Specific Property	72PDZU33	457172
Denmark	Portugal	15 Dec 47	Air Transport	35UNTS329	100563
Denmark	Portugal	08 Apr 49	General Trade	74UNTS209	100964
Denmark	Portugal	08 Apr 49	Finance	74UNTS221	100965
Denmark	Portugal	02 Jun 50	General Trade	74UNTS229	100966
Denmark	Portugal	05 Jun 51	General Trade	101UNTS61	101402
Denmark	Portugal	29 Aug 52	General Trade	149UNTS49	101950
Denmark	Portugal	20 Feb 65	Commodity Trade	639UNTS43	109143
Denmark	Romania	25 Jun 58	Air Transport	345UNTS231	104970
Denmark	Romania	29 Aug 67	General Economic	0UNTS0	109404
Denmark	Romania	29 Aug 67	Land Transport	0UNTS0	109231
Denmark	Romania	29 Aug 67	Culture	642UNTS357	109183
Denmark	Senegal	11 Apr 62	General Trade	0UNTS0	110769
Denmark	Senegal	03 Aug 68	Loans and Credits	0UNTS0	109282
Denmark	Singapore	20 Dec 66	Air Transport	593UNTS125	108580
Denmark	Singapore	07 Mar 69	Taxation	0UNTS0	110771
Denmark	South Africa	14 Oct 46	Claims and Debts	10UNTS29	100140
Denmark	South Africa	30 Nov 50	Taxation	84UNTS51	101118
Denmark	South Africa	30 Apr 53	Air Transport	174UNTS19	102275
Denmark	South Africa	28 Mar 58	Air Transport	300UNTS107	104334
Denmark	Spain	12 Jul 50	Finance	71UNTS129	100913
Denmark	Spain	12 Jul 50	General Trade	71UNTS135	100914
Denmark	Spain	03 Jul 51	General Trade	101UNTS51	101401
Denmark	Spain	28 Jul 52	Commodity Trade	135UNTS255	101825
Denmark	Spain	01 Jul 57	General Trade	57SPBO1009	460078
Denmark	Spain	15 Jul 57	General Trade	57SPBO1009	460079
Denmark	Spain	05 May 65	Air Transport	543UNTS255	107905
Denmark	Sudan	11 May 59	Air Transport	445UNTS105	106380
Denmark	Sweden	18 Nov 46	Non-ILO Labor	7UNTS251	100104
Denmark	Sweden	12 Dec 46	General Trade	47SOFM573	461057
Denmark	Sweden	14 Nov 47	General Trade	47SOFM513	461054
Denmark	Sweden	23 Dec 47	Non-ILO Labor	14UNTS3	100207
Denmark	Sweden	23 Dec 47	Non-ILO Labor	47SOFM635	461061
Denmark	Sweden	08 Feb 49	General Trade	49SOFM1	461071
Denmark	Sweden	08 Feb 49	Finance	33UNTS227	100519
Denmark	Sweden	17 Jun 49	Commodity Trade	49SOFM307	461084
Denmark	Sweden	08 Mar 50	General Trade	50SOFM89	461102
Denmark	Sweden	08 Mar 50	Finance	50SOFM93	461103
Denmark	Sweden	16 Aug 50	Commodity Trade	50SOFM943	461122
Denmark	Sweden	10 Feb 51	General Trade	51SOFM94	461134
Denmark	Sweden	10 Feb 51	Finance	51SOFM104	461135

PARTY ONE	PARTY TWO	DATE	TOPIC	CITATION	NUMBER
Denmark	Sweden	11 Feb 53	General Trade	53SOFM5	461181
Denmark	Sweden	27 Oct 53	Taxation	198UNTS71	102658
Denmark	Sweden	27 Oct 53	Taxation	198UNTS129	102660
Denmark	Sweden	27 Oct 53	Taxation	198UNTS111	102659
Denmark	Sweden	30 Sep 54	Patents/Copyrights	262UNTS199	103745
Denmark	Sweden	28 Oct 54	Sanitation	262UNTS211	103747
Denmark	Sweden	07 Dec 55	Admin Cooperation	262UNTS235	103749
Denmark	Sweden	15 Sep 56	General Transport	263UNTS3	103764
Denmark	Sweden	21 Jul 58	Taxation	320UNTS163	104642
Denmark	Sweden	04 Jan 60	General Trade	376UNTS375	105390
Denmark	Sweden	05 Dec 67	Specific Resources	631UNTS257	108998
Denmark	Sweden	11 Sep 70	General Military	0UNTS0	110840
Denmark	Switzerland	21 Feb 48	Non-ILO Labor	14UNTS321	100224
Denmark	Switzerland	06 Apr 50	General Trade	87UNTS197	101173
Denmark	Switzerland	22 Jun 50	Air Transport	96UNTS3	101328
Denmark	Switzerland	20 Jan 51	Finance	87UNTS223	101174
Denmark	Switzerland	15 Sep 51	General Trade	110UNTS55	101501
Denmark	Switzerland	21 May 54	Non-ILO Labor	55SWRO290	462094
Denmark	Switzerland	14 Jan 57	Taxation	286UNTS85	104161
Denmark	Switzerland	14 Jan 57	Taxation	286UNTS27	104160
Denmark	Switzerland	21 Dec 59	Commodity Trade	633UNTS351	109045
Denmark	Switzerland	14 Aug 63	Land Transport	63SWRO797	462081
Denmark	Syria	20 Oct 55	Air Transport	250UNTS61	103518
Denmark	Syria	28 Dec 65	Tech Assistance	588UNTS163	108523
Denmark	Taiwan	20 May 46	Privil/Immunities	12UNTS59	100180
Denmark	Tanganyika	04 Aug 64	Taxation	544UNTS117	107914
Denmark	Tanganyika	04 Aug 64	Dispute Settlement	544UNTS123	107915
Denmark	Tanzania	05 Apr 67	Scientific Project	604UNTS19	108740
Denmark	Tanzania	05 Apr 67	Tech Assistance	603UNTS111	108728
Denmark	Tanzania	01 Nov 67	Loans and Credits	619UNTS47	108938
Denmark	Tanzania	27 May 69	Education	0UNTS0	110763
Denmark	Thailand	23 Nov 49	Air Transport	53UNTS255	100786
Denmark	Thailand	25 Jan 65	Tech Assistance	530UNTS173	107680
Denmark	Thailand	01 Jun 65	Taxation	551UNTS157	108040
Denmark	Thailand	16 Oct 68	Scientific Project	0UNTS0	109463
Denmark	Thailand	16 Jun 69	Scientific Project	0UNTS0	109794
Denmark	Thailand	18 Nov 69	Admin Cooperation	0UNTS0	110765
Denmark	Thailand	18 Nov 69	Culture	0UNTS0	110766
Denmark	Trinidad/Tobago	02 Nov 69	Air Transport	0UNTS0	110395
Denmark	Tunisia	14 Apr 59	Air Transport	340UNTS273	104870
Denmark	Tunisia	07 Jun 68	Loans and Credits	0UNTS0	109407
Denmark	Tunisia	10 Jun 69	Loans and Credits	0UNTS0	110772
Denmark	Turkey	30 Jun 47	Air Transport	32UNTS301	100504
Denmark	Turkey	15 Dec 48	General Trade	76UNTS17	100975
Denmark	Turkey	15 Dec 48	Finance	76UNTS3	100974
Denmark	Turkey	17 Dec 58	Direct Aid	64TURG909	466103
Denmark	Turkey	06 Mar 70	Finance	0UNTS0	110542
Denmark	Uganda	01 Apr 68	Loans and Credits	0UNTS0	109209
Denmark	Uganda	03 Jul 68	Tech Assistance	0UNTS0	109466
Denmark	Uganda	03 Jul 68	Direct Aid	0UNTS0	109305
Denmark	Uganda	03 Jul 68	Non-IBRD Project	0UNTS0	109467
Denmark	Uganda	20 Jun 69	Education	0UNTS0	109932
Denmark	UK Great Britain	16 Aug 45	Finance	5UNTS251	200033
Denmark	UK Great Britain	24 Oct 45	Milit Assistance	93UNTS143	101297
Denmark	UK Great Britain	06 Dec 45	Finance	5UNTS3	100061
Denmark	UK Great Britain	16 Aug 46	Milit Installation	9UNTS163	100130
Denmark	UK Great Britain	20 Jan 47	Telecommunications	118UNTS73	101597
Denmark	UK Great Britain	20 Mar 47	Visas	11UNTS285	100168
Denmark	UK Great Britain	22 Apr 47	Milit Occupation	8UNTS3	100110
Denmark	UK Great Britain	19 Aug 47	Reparations	9UNTS277	100137
Denmark	UK Great Britain	01 Dec 47	Reparations	93UNTS151	101298
Denmark	UK Great Britain	04 Mar 48	Milit Assistance	77UNTS57	100992
Denmark	UK Great Britain	11 Nov 48	Finance	25UNTS333	100371
Denmark	UK Great Britain	13 Aug 49	General Trade	68UNTS105	100890
Denmark	UK Great Britain	27 Mar 50	Taxation	68UNTS117	100891
Denmark	UK Great Britain	19 Oct 50	Finance	79UNTS25	101028
Denmark	UK Great Britain	23 Jun 52	Air Transport	151UNTS3	101982
Denmark	UK Great Britain	15 Dec 53	Non-ILO Labor	196UNTS105	102620
Denmark	UK Great Britain	23 Jul 54	Specific Resources	213UNTS313	102894
Denmark	UK Great Britain	20 Jan 55	Milit Servic/Citiz	210UNTS303	102842
Denmark	UK Great Britain	27 Feb 56	Commodity Trade	252UNTS83	103558
Denmark	UK Great Britain	09 Jul 56	Non-ILO Labor	264UNTS45	103787
Denmark	UK Great Britain	08 Oct 56	Consul/Citizenship	331UNTS181	104754
Denmark	UK Great Britain	18 Nov 57	General Trade	403UNTS153	105794
Denmark	UK Great Britain	28 Apr 59	Finance	343UNTS257	104929
Denmark	UK Great Britain	27 Aug 59	Non-ILO Labor	360UNTS11	105153
Denmark	UK Great Britain	08 Apr 60	Customs	374UNTS233	105337
Denmark	UK Great Britain	20 May 60	Atomic Energy	374UNTS245	105338
Denmark	UK Great Britain	10 May 61	Visas	414UNTS17	105961
Denmark	UK Great Britain	15 Nov 61	Dispute Settlement	420UNTS67	106041
Denmark	UK Great Britain	27 Jun 62	Consul/Citizenship	562UNTS75	108197
Denmark	UK Great Britain	30 Jun 64	Water Transport	539UNTS203	107833
Denmark	UK Great Britain	16 Sep 64	Commodity Trade	534UNTS427	107771
Denmark	UK Great Britain	03 Mar 66	Territory Boundary	592UNTS207	108574
Denmark	United Arab Rep	14 Mar 50	Air Transport	95UNTS197	101322
Denmark	United Arab Rep	01 Dec 58	Taxation	337UNTS69	104817
Denmark	United Arab Rep	12 Jan 65	Sanitation	0UNTS0	109732
Denmark	United Arab Rep	12 Apr 69	Loans and Credits	0UNTS0	109953
Denmark	United Arab Rep	24 Nov 69	Direct Aid	0UNTS0	110456
Denmark	United Nations	16 Jul 57	Milit Assistance	274UNTS81	103959
Denmark	United Nations	21 Feb 66	IGO Operations	555UNTS151	108108
Denmark	Uruguay	04 Mar 53	General Economic	250UNTS51	103517
Denmark	Uruguay	09 Sep 53	Finance	256UNTS149	103625
Denmark	Uruguay	04 Jun 57	Finance	286UNTS107	104162
Denmark	USA (United States)	16 Dec 44	Air Transport	10UNTS213	200063
Denmark	USA (United States)	21 Mar 46	Air Transport	3UNTS301	100038
Denmark	USA (United States)	10 Sep 46	Mostfavored Nation	13UNTS75	100204
Denmark	USA (United States)	01 Oct 46	Air Transport	42UNTS219	100650
Denmark	USA (United States)	09 Jun 47	Visas	132UNTS145	101755
Denmark	USA (United States)	06 May 48	Taxation	26UNTS55	100377
Denmark	USA (United States)	29 Jun 48	Direct Aid	22UNTS217	100338
Denmark	USA (United States)	29 Jun 48	Mostfavored Nation	27UNTS35	100396
Denmark	USA (United States)	01 Aug 49	Admin Cooperation	79UNTS147	101038
Denmark	USA (United States)	27 Jan 50	Milit Assistance	48UNTS115	100740
Denmark	USA (United States)	27 Apr 51	General Military	94UNTS35	101305
Denmark	USA (United States)	23 Aug 51	Education	147UNTS49	101928
Denmark	USA (United States)	01 Oct 51	General Amity	421UNTS105	106056
Denmark	USA (United States)	16 Nov 51	Milit Assistance	180UNTS275	102391
Denmark	USA (United States)	08 Jan 52	Milit Assistance	179UNTS65	102354
Denmark	USA (United States)	04 Feb 52	Patents/Copyrights	157UNTS25	102044
Denmark	USA (United States)	04 Apr 52	Telecommunications	177UNTS13	102305
Denmark	USA (United States)	07 Apr 52	Milit Assistance	177UNTS257	102324
Denmark	USA (United States)	08 Aug 52	Direct Aid	181UNTS249	102414
Denmark	USA (United States)	15 Oct 53	Patents/Copyrights	215UNTS111	102915
Denmark	USA (United States)	08 Jun 54	Milit Assistance	307UNTS133	104448
Denmark	USA (United States)	06 Aug 54	Air Transport	222UNTS235	103030
Denmark	USA (United States)	15 Dec 54	Air Transport	213UNTS273	102890
Denmark	USA (United States)	25 Jul 55	Atomic Energy	235UNTS245	103306
Denmark	USA (United States)	12 Dec 56	Status of Forces	304UNTS311	104405
Denmark	USA (United States)	28 Aug 58	Reparations	335UNTS133	104781
Denmark	USA (United States)	08 May 59	Milit Assistance	344UNTS185	104949
Denmark	USA (United States)	19 Feb 60	Patents/Copyrights	354UNTS151	105061
Denmark	USA (United States)	12 Apr 60	Milit Assistance	373UNTS9	105311
Denmark	USA (United States)	07 Jul 60	Air Transport	380UNTS39	105449
Denmark	USA (United States)	02 Dec 60	Milit Installation	402UNTS245	105789
Denmark	USA (United States)	05 Mar 62	General Economic	446UNTS9	106398
Denmark	USA (United States)	28 May 62	Education	450UNTS215	106469
Denmark	USA (United States)	02 Jul 64	Water Transport	529UNTS277	107665
Denmark	USSR (Soviet Union)	16 May 45	Consul/Citizenship	0SUST178	468115
Denmark	USSR (Soviet Union)	08 Jul 46	General Trade	0SUST214	468116

PARTY ONE	PARTY TWO	DATE	TOPIC	CITATION	NUMBER
Denmark	USSR (Soviet Union)	08 Aug 46	Telecommunications	0SUST217	468117
Denmark	USSR (Soviet Union)	17 Aug 46	General Economic	8UNTS201	100124
Denmark	USSR (Soviet Union)	17 Aug 46	Dispute Settlement	0SUST217	468118
Denmark	USSR (Soviet Union)	17 Aug 46	Finance	16SUGG63	469884
Denmark	USSR (Soviet Union)	17 Jul 53	General Trade	175UNTS3	102292
Denmark	USSR (Soviet Union)	18 Aug 55	Consul/Citizenship	16SUGG69	469908
Denmark	USSR (Soviet Union)	17 Sep 55	Consul/Citizenship	0SUST336	468119
Denmark	USSR (Soviet Union)	06 Mar 56	Health/Educ/Welfare	0SUST350	468120
Denmark	USSR (Soviet Union)	31 Mar 56	Air Transport	259UNTS169	103689
Denmark	USSR (Soviet Union)	14 May 56	General Trade	271UNTS125	103912
Denmark	USSR (Soviet Union)	30 May 59	Finance	8SUGG146	469578
Denmark	USSR (Soviet Union)	10 May 60	Taxation	16SUGG127	469975
Denmark	USSR (Soviet Union)	20 Jul 60	Consul/Citizenship	16SUGG128	469979
Denmark	USSR (Soviet Union)	11 Sep 62	Culture	458UNTS3	106589
Denmark	USSR (Soviet Union)	27 Feb 64	Specif Claim/Waive	509UNTS285	107407
Denmark	USSR (Soviet Union)	17 Jul 70	Scientific Project	0UNTS0	110784
Denmark	WHO (World Health)	14 Feb 51	Sanitation	104UNTS243	101445
Denmark	WHO (World Health)	05 Nov 51	Sanitation	110UNTS253	101514
Denmark	WHO (World Health)	30 Nov 51	Scientific Project	118UNTS3	101592
Denmark	WHO (World Health)	26 Mar 52	Scientific Project	134UNTS285	101807
Denmark	WHO (World Health)	29 Jun 55	IGO Status/Immunit	247UNTS168	103467
Denmark	WHO (World Health)	03 Sep 56	Sanitation	258UNTS103	103674
Denmark	Yugoslavia	28 Jun 47	General Economic	78UNTS242	101020
Denmark	Yugoslavia	27 Jan 54	Admin Cooperation	193UNTS181	102615
Denmark	Yugoslavia	13 Jul 59	Specif Claim/Waive	386UNTS251	105545
Denmark	Yugoslavia	11 Feb 64	Air Transport	511UNTS241	107437
Denmark	Yugoslavia	11 Apr 68	Taxation	0UNTS0	109406
Denmark	Yugoslavia	13 May 68	Land Transport	0UNTS0	109727
Denmark	Zambia	12 Dec 65	Tech Assistance	574UNTS21	108339
Denmark	Zambia	17 Oct 67	Tech Assistance	620UNTS239	108960
Denmark	Zambia	18 Oct 67	Loans and Credits	637UNTS0	109116
Denmark	Zambia	11 Jul 68	Tech Assistance	0UNTS0	110794
Denmark	Zambia	11 Jul 68	Direct Aid	0UNTS0	109306
Dominican Republic	Argentina	09 Sep 67	Culture	0UNTS0	110412
Dominican Republic	Argentina	12 Sep 67	Culture	0UNTS0	109560
Dominican Republic	Austria	21 Feb 68	Visas	0UNTS0	109215
Dominican Republic	Austria	21 Feb 68	Visas	68ABGB109	403033
Dominican Republic	Brazil	09 Dec 42	Culture	65UNTS217	200213
Dominican Republic	Brazil	09 Apr 45	Culture	67UNTS293	200226
Dominican Republic	Costa Rica	09 Oct 67	Culture	0UNTS0	110413
Dominican Republic	Germany, West	23 Dec 57	General Amity	59WGBB1468	425106
Dominican Republic	IBRD (World Bank)	10 Dec 69	IBRD Project	0UNTS0	110689
Dominican Republic	ILO (Labor Org)	18 Jun 51	Tech Assistance	100UNTS3	101383
Dominican Republic	Israel	25 Dec 63	Tech Assistance	550UNTS221	108018
Dominican Republic	Israel	02 May 68	Visas	0UNTS0	109357
Dominican Republic	Italy	27 Sep 49	Peace/Disarmament	51ITGU15	435104
Dominican Republic	Italy	18 Feb 54	General Trade	55ITGU124	435105
Dominican Republic	Japan	20 Mar 57	Visas	318UNTS245	104619
Dominican Republic	Multilateral	25 Jun 36	Privil/Immunities	161UNTS217	200486
Dominican Republic	Multilateral	30 Jul 40	Admin Cooperation	161UNTS253	200488
Dominican Republic	Multilateral	12 Oct 40	Specific Resources	161UNTS193	200485
Dominican Republic	Multilateral	28 Nov 40	Commodity Trade	139UNTS159	200452
Dominican Republic	Multilateral	27 Mar 41	Military Mission	67UNTS231	200222
Dominican Republic	Multilateral	15 Jan 44	IGO Establishment	161UNTS281	200489
Dominican Republic	Multilateral	19 Apr 44	Scientific Project	89UNTS279	200257
Dominican Republic	Multilateral	02 Aug 44	Scientific Project	67UNTS221	200221
Dominican Republic	Multilateral	07 Dec 44	Air Transport	171UNTS345	200501
Dominican Republic	Multilateral	07 Dec 44	IGO Establishment	15UNTS295	200102
Dominican Republic	Multilateral	07 Dec 44	Air Transport	171UNTS387	200502
Dominican Republic	Multilateral	15 Dec 44	Sanitation	17UNTS305	200110
Dominican Republic	Multilateral	15 Dec 44	Sanitation	16UNTS247	200106
Dominican Republic	Multilateral	16 Nov 45	IGO Establishment	4UNTS275	100052
Dominican Republic	Multilateral	27 Dec 45	IGO Establishment	2UNTS39	100020
Dominican Republic	Multilateral	23 Apr 46	Sanitation	17UNTS3	100265
Dominican Republic	Multilateral	23 Apr 46	Sanitation	16UNTS179	100257

PARTY ONE	PARTY TWO	DATE	TOPIC	CITATION	NUMBER
Dominican Republic	Multilateral	22 Jul 46	IGO Establishment	9UNTS3	100125
Dominican Republic	Multilateral	22 Jul 46	IGO Establishment	14UNTS185	100221
Dominican Republic	Multilateral	27 Jul 46	Patents/Copyrights	90UNTS229	101238
Dominican Republic	Multilateral	03 Sep 46	Commodity Trade	139UNTS3	101872
Dominican Republic	Multilateral	15 Oct 46	Refugees	11UNTS73	100150
Dominican Republic	Multilateral	11 Dec 46	Sanitation	12UNTS179	100186
Dominican Republic	Multilateral	15 Dec 46	IGO Establishment	18UNTS3	100283
Dominican Republic	Multilateral	08 Feb 47	Patents/Copyrights	14UNTS287	100222
Dominican Republic	Multilateral	27 May 47	Air Transport	418UNTS161	106021
Dominican Republic	Multilateral	02 Sep 47	General Military	21UNTS77	100324
Dominican Republic	Multilateral	02 Oct 47	Telecommunications	193UNTS188	102616
Dominican Republic	Multilateral	11 Oct 47	IGO Establishment	77UNTS143	100998
Dominican Republic	Multilateral	06 Mar 48	Water Transport	289UNTS3	104214
Dominican Republic	Multilateral	30 Apr 48	IGO Establishment	119UNTS3	101609
Dominican Republic	Multilateral	30 Apr 48	Dispute Settlement	30UNTS55	100449
Dominican Republic	Multilateral	10 Jun 48	Humanitarian	164UNTS113	102163
Dominican Republic	Multilateral	19 Jun 48	Air Transport	310UNTS151	104492
Dominican Republic	Multilateral	24 Jul 48	Sanitation	66UNTS25	100847
Dominican Republic	Multilateral	14 Sep 48	Milit Occupation	18UNTS267	100296
Dominican Republic	Multilateral	19 Nov 48	Sanitation	44UNTS277	100688
Dominican Republic	Multilateral	29 Nov 48	IGO Establishment	120UNTS13	101613
Dominican Republic	Multilateral	09 Dec 48	Humanitarian	78UNTS277	101021
Dominican Republic	Multilateral	23 Mar 49	Commodity Trade	203UNTS179	102746
Dominican Republic	Multilateral	09 Jul 49	Telecommunications	168UNTS143	102218
Dominican Republic	Multilateral	15 Jul 49	Health/Educ/Welfare	197UNTS3	102631
Dominican Republic	Multilateral	19 Sep 49	Land Transport	125UNTS3	101671
Dominican Republic	Multilateral	16 Dec 49	Admin Cooperation	72UNTS3	100924
Dominican Republic	Multilateral	22 Nov 50	Culture	131UNTS25	101734
Dominican Republic	Multilateral	25 May 51	Status of Forces	175UNTS215	102303
Dominican Republic	Multilateral	08 Sep 51	General Military	136UNTS165	101833
Dominican Republic	Multilateral	08 Sep 51	Peace/Disarmament	136UNTS45	101832
Dominican Republic	Multilateral	06 Dec 51	Admin Cooperation	150UNTS67	101963
Dominican Republic	Multilateral	12 Jun 52	Dispute Settlement	138UNTS183	101869
Dominican Republic	Multilateral	11 Jul 52	Postal Service	171UNTS3	102224
Dominican Republic	Multilateral	11 Jul 52	Postal Service	171UNTS89	102225
Dominican Republic	Multilateral	11 Jul 52	Postal Service	170UNTS63	102222
Dominican Republic	Multilateral	11 Jul 52	IGO Establishment	169UNTS3	102220
Dominican Republic	Multilateral	11 Jul 52	Postal Service	171UNTS143	102226
Dominican Republic	Multilateral	11 Jul 52	Postal Service	170UNTS3	102221
Dominican Republic	Multilateral	11 Jul 52	Postal Service	170UNTS269	102223
Dominican Republic	Multilateral	07 Oct 52	Admin Cooperation	310UNTS181	104493
Dominican Republic	Multilateral	31 Mar 53	Privil/Immunities	193UNTS136	102613
Dominican Republic	Multilateral	11 May 53	Sanitation	456UNTS3	106555
Dominican Republic	Multilateral	01 Oct 53	Commodity Trade	258UNTS153	103677
Dominican Republic	Multilateral	12 May 54	Admin Cooperation	327UNTS3	104714
Dominican Republic	Multilateral	14 May 54	Culture	249UNTS215	103511
Dominican Republic	Multilateral	04 Jun 54	Customs	282UNTS249	104101
Dominican Republic	Multilateral	04 Jun 54	Customs	276UNTS191	103992
Dominican Republic	Multilateral	14 Jun 54	Air Transport	320UNTS217	104644
Dominican Republic	Multilateral	14 Jun 54	Air Transport	320UNTS209	104643
Dominican Republic	Multilateral	25 May 55	IGO Establishment	264UNTS117	103791
Dominican Republic	Multilateral	12 Oct 55	IGO Establishment	560UNTS3	108165
Dominican Republic	Multilateral	25 Apr 56	Commodity Trade	270UNTS103	103896
Dominican Republic	Multilateral	20 Jun 56	Admin Cooperation	268UNTS3	103850
Dominican Republic	Multilateral	05 Oct 56	Tech Assistance	251UNTS245	103544
Dominican Republic	Multilateral	26 Oct 56	IGO Establishment	276UNTS3	103988
Dominican Republic	Multilateral	20 Feb 57	Consul/Citizenship	309UNTS65	104468
Dominican Republic	Multilateral	01 May 57	Admin Cooperation	284UNTS201	104138
Dominican Republic	Multilateral	03 Oct 57	Postal Service	365UNTS3	105213
Dominican Republic	Multilateral	03 Oct 57	Postal Service	364UNTS331	105212
Dominican Republic	Multilateral	03 Oct 57	Postal Service	364UNTS3	105211
Dominican Republic	Multilateral	03 Oct 57	Postal Service	366UNTS141	105217
Dominican Republic	Multilateral	03 Oct 57	Postal Service	366UNTS255	105219
Dominican Republic	Multilateral	03 Oct 57	Postal Service	366UNTS87	105216
Dominican Republic	Multilateral	29 Apr 58	Specific Resources	559UNTS285	108164

PARTY ONE	PARTY TWO	DATE	TOPIC	CITATION	NUMBER
Dominican Republic	Multilateral	29 Apr 58	Territory Boundary	516UNTS205	107477
Dominican Republic	Multilateral	29 Apr 58	Dispute Settlement	450UNTS169	106466
Dominican Republic	Multilateral	29 Apr 58	Territory Boundary	499UNTS311	107302
Dominican Republic	Multilateral	29 Apr 58	Water Transport	450UNTS11	106465
Dominican Republic	Multilateral	01 Dec 58	Commodity Trade	385UNTS137	105534
Dominican Republic	Multilateral	06 Apr 59	Commodity Trade	349UNTS167	105013
Dominican Republic	Multilateral	08 Apr 59	IGO Establishment	389UNTS69	105593
Dominican Republic	Multilateral	18 Nov 59	IGO Establishment	390UNTS227	105610
Dominican Republic	Multilateral	26 Jan 60	IGO Establishment	439UNTS249	106333
Dominican Republic	Multilateral	17 Jun 60	Humanitarian	536UNTS27	107794
Dominican Republic	Multilateral	30 Mar 61	Sanitation	520UNTS151	107515
Dominican Republic	Multilateral	18 Apr 61	Dispute Settlement	500UNTS243	107312
Dominican Republic	Multilateral	18 Apr 61	Consul/Citizenship	500UNTS95	107310
Dominican Republic	Multilateral	18 Apr 61	Consul/Citizenship	500UNTS223	107311
Dominican Republic	Multilateral	08 Jun 61	Customs	473UNTS187	106863
Dominican Republic	Multilateral	21 Jun 61	IGO Establishment	514UNTS209	107449
Dominican Republic	Multilateral	15 May 62	Commodity Trade	444UNTS3	106367
Dominican Republic	Multilateral	28 Sep 62	IGO Establishment	469UNTS169	106791
Dominican Republic	Multilateral	10 Dec 62	Culture	521UNTS231	107525
Dominican Republic	Multilateral	20 Apr 63	IGO Establishment	495UNTS3	107239
Dominican Republic	Multilateral	24 Apr 63	Consul/Citizenship	596UNTS487	108640
Dominican Republic	Multilateral	24 Apr 63	Consul/Citizenship	596UNTS261	108638
Dominican Republic	Multilateral	05 Aug 63	Sanitation	480UNTS43	106964
Dominican Republic	Multilateral	20 Feb 64	Tech Assistance	491UNTS30	107172
Dominican Republic	Multilateral	20 Feb 64	Tech Assistance	491UNTS30	107172
Dominican Republic	Multilateral	10 Jul 64	Postal Service	612UNTS3	108847
Dominican Republic	Multilateral	10 Jul 64	Postal Service	613UNTS3	108850
Dominican Republic	Multilateral	10 Jul 64	Postal Service	613UNTS193	108852
Dominican Republic	Multilateral	10 Jul 64	Postal Service	613UNTS3	108851
Dominican Republic	Multilateral	10 Jul 64	Postal Service	611UNTS7	108844
Dominican Republic	Multilateral	10 Jul 64	Postal Service	611UNTS105	108845
Dominican Republic	Multilateral	09 Mar 65	Water Transport	591UNTS265	108564
Dominican Republic	Multilateral	05 Apr 66	Water Transport	640UNTS133	109159
Dominican Republic	Multilateral	14 Feb 67	General Military	634UNTS281	109068
Dominican Republic	Multilateral	18 Mar 68	Commodity Trade	OUNTSO	109262
Dominican Republic	Multilateral	01 Jul 68	Peace/Disarmament	OUNTSO	110485
Dominican Republic	Multilateral	24 Dec 68	Commodity Trade	OUNTSO	109369
Dominican Republic	Multilateral	18 Oct 69	IGO Establishment	OUNTSO	110232
Dominican Republic	Norway	27 Oct 59	Visas	3NORT786	451039
Dominican Republic	Norway	28 Apr 60	Visas	3NORT786	451040
Dominican Republic	Philippines	02 Nov 52	General Amity	543UNTS175	107901
Dominican Republic	Spain	10 Nov 52	General Amity	53SPBO309	460080
Dominican Republic	Spain	27 Jan 53	Culture	53SPBO112	460081
Dominican Republic	Spain	14 Jan 54	General Trade	54SPBO1808	460082
Dominican Republic	Spain	01 Feb 56	Health/Educ/Welfare	57SPBO2901	460083
Dominican Republic	Spain	01 May 67	Admin Cooperation	OUNTSO	110410
Dominican Republic	Spain	15 Mar 68	Consul/Citizenship	OUNTSO	110411
Dominican Republic	Taiwan	11 May 40	General Amity	10UNTS285	200067
Dominican Republic	Turkey	28 Nov 51	General Amity	52TURG605	466001
Dominican Republic	UK Great Britain	26 Nov 51	Milit Installation	133UNTS205	101791
Dominican Republic	UK Great Britain	09 Aug 56	Consul/Citizenship	252UNTS127	103561
Dominican Republic	UK Great Britain	20 Jun 67	Visas	619UNTS3	108935
Dominican Republic	UN Special Fund	06 Jun 62	Direct Aid	429UNTS169	106197
Dominican Republic	UNICEF (Children)	15 Feb 52	Humanitarian	121UNTS43	101625
Dominican Republic	United Nations	19 Nov 53	Tech Assistance	180UNTS45	102374
Dominican Republic	United Nations	05 Aug 63	IGO Status/Immunit	472UNTS353	106847
Dominican Republic	USA (United States)	14 Nov 42	Customs	24UNTS233	200148
Dominican Republic	USA (United States)	10 Dec 42	Admin Cooperation	24UNTS257	200151
Dominican Republic	USA (United States)	25 Jan 43	Military Mission	13UNTS399	200083
Dominican Republic	USA (United States)	10 Jun 43	Specific Resources	21UNTS277	200129
Dominican Republic	USA (United States)	07 Jul 43	Sanitation	28UNTS419	200165
Dominican Republic	USA (United States)	19 Oct 43	Non-ILO Labor	21UNTS295	200130
Dominican Republic	USA (United States)	11 Feb 44	Milit Assistance	109UNTS251	200363
Dominican Republic	USA (United States)	13 Oct 45	Education	149UNTS361	200477
Dominican Republic	USA (United States)	07 Oct 46	Mostfavored Nation	13UNTS91	100206

PARTY ONE	PARTY TWO	DATE	TOPIC	CITATION	NUMBER
Dominican Republic	USA (United States)	19 Jul 49	Air Transport	51UNTS145	100762
Dominican Republic	USA (United States)	23 Jan 50	Consul/Citizenship	236UNTS3	103312
Dominican Republic	USA (United States)	11 Aug 50	Status of Forces	92UNTS329	101278
Dominican Republic	USA (United States)	20 Feb 51	Tech Assistance	132UNTS305	101770
Dominican Republic	USA (United States)	16 Mar 51	Education	148UNTS15	101932
Dominican Republic	USA (United States)	26 Nov 51	Milit Installation	150UNTS227	101976
Dominican Republic	USA (United States)	07 Jan 52	Direct Aid	174UNTS243	102289
Dominican Republic	USA (United States)	06 Mar 53	Milit Assistance	199UNTS267	102689
Dominican Republic	USA (United States)	22 Apr 55	Milit Assistance	239UNTS325	103389
Dominican Republic	USA (United States)	30 Jun 55	Non-IBRD Project	257UNTS313	103664
Dominican Republic	USA (United States)	16 Dec 55	Visas	241UNTS101	103427
Dominican Republic	USA (United States)	15 Jun 56	Atomic Energy	265UNTS227	103815
Dominican Republic	USA (United States)	11 Aug 56	Scientific Project	263UNTS181	103773
Dominican Republic	USA (United States)	07 Dec 56	Military Mission	263UNTS193	103774
Dominican Republic	USA (United States)	09 Mar 57	Gen Communications	279UNTS249	104044
Dominican Republic	USA (United States)	11 Jan 62	General Aid	433UNTS133	106236
Dominican Republic	USA (United States)	08 Mar 62	Milit Assistance	527UNTS29	107615
Dominican Republic	USA (United States)	02 May 62	Direct Aid	442UNTS107	106342
Dominican Republic	USA (United States)	02 May 62	Claims and Debts	442UNTS99	106341
Dominican Republic	USA (United States)	25 Oct 62	Scientific Project	459UNTS247	106627
Dominican Republic	USA (United States)	30 Nov 62	US Agri Commod Aid	471UNTS25	106819
Dominican Republic	USA (United States)	22 Apr 63	Telecommunications	487UNTS169	107101
Dominican Republic	USA (United States)	13 Aug 63	US Agri Commod Aid	492UNTS327	107202
Dominican Republic	USA (United States)	28 Aug 64	Scientific Project	531UNTS35	107691
Dominican Republic	USA (United States)	02 Feb 65	Gen Communications	542UNTS117	107884
Dominican Republic	USA (United States)	18 Mar 65	US Agri Commod Aid	542UNTS215	107892
Dominican Republic	USA (United States)	21 Jul 66	Scientific Project	OUNTSO	109680
Dominican Republic	USA (United States)	01 Apr 68	General Aid	OUNTSO	110249
Dominican Republic	USA (United States)	10 May 68	US Agri Commod Aid	OUNTSO	110326
Dominican Republic	USA (United States)	11 Jun 68	General Aid	OUNTSO	110250
Dominican Republic	USA (United States)	28 Mar 69	General Aid	OUNTSO	110251
Dominican Republic	USA (United States)	11 Apr 69	Scientific Project	OUNTSO	110159
Dominican Republic	USA (United States)	09 Mar 70	Commodity Trade	OUNTSO	110691
Dominican Republic	USA (United States)	31 Mar 70	US Agri Commod Aid	OUNTSO	110632
Dominican Republic	USSR (Soviet Union)	08 Mar 45	Consul/Citizenship	OSUST174	468121
Dominican Republic	WHO (World Health)	15 Feb 52	Sanitation	134UNTS291	101808
Dominican Republic	WHO (World Health)	10 Oct 52	Sanitation	150UNTS133	101967
Dutch East Indies	Multilateral	02 Oct 47	Telecommunications	193UNTS188	102616
East Afri Service	IBRD (World Bank)	29 Sep 65	IBRD Project	568UNTS327	200623
East Afri Service	IBRD (World Bank)	17 Feb 67	IBRD Project	599UNTS335	200629
East Afri Service	Multilateral	04 Mar 66	US Agri Commod Aid	578UNTS57	108387
East Afri Service	United Nations	27 Nov 65	Health/Educ/Welfare	550UNTS375	200616
ECSC (Coal/Steel)	Austria	26 Jul 57	Land Transport	58ABGB63	403141
ECSC (Coal/Steel)	ILO (Labor Org)	16 Jul 53	IGO Operations	412UNTS273	200591
ECSC (Coal/Steel)	Multilateral	18 Apr 51	IGO Establishment	261UNTS140	103729
ECSC (Coal/Steel)	Multilateral	21 Dec 54	General Amity	258UNTS322	103678
ECSC (Coal/Steel)	Multilateral	06 Apr 55	General Amity	261UNTS55	103725
ECSC (Coal/Steel)	Multilateral	26 Jul 57	Land Transport	386UNTS3	105535
ECSC (Coal/Steel)	Multilateral	25 Nov 57	General Trade	403UNTS169	105795
ECSC (Coal/Steel)	USA (United States)	23 Apr 54	Loans and Credits	229UNTS229	103170
Ecuador	Austria	07 Feb 68	Visas	OUNTSO	109212
Ecuador	Austria	07 Feb 68	Visas	68ABGB108	403034
Ecuador	Austria	28 Mar 69	General Trade	71ABGB121	403035
Ecuador	Belgium	20 Mar 58	Visas	304UNTS207	104397
Ecuador	Belgium	10 Jan 63	Visas	457UNTS153	106585
Ecuador	Brazil	24 May 44	Culture	73UNTS223	200242
Ecuador	Brazil	31 May 47	Consul/Citizenship	72UNTS25	100925
Ecuador	Brazil	04 May 53	General Trade	369UNTS37	105249
Ecuador	Brazil	05 Mar 58	General Economic	369UNTS43	105250
Ecuador	Brazil	19 May 65	Visas	OUNTSO	109419
Ecuador	Canada	10 Nov 50	General Economic	231UNTS15	103199
Ecuador	France	25 Oct 49	Finance	49FRMD2411	417154
Ecuador	France	20 Mar 59	General Trade	59FRRT42	415155
Ecuador	France	13 Apr 59	Tech Assistance	65FRRT16	415156
Ecuador	France	03 Feb 64	Air Transport	64FRRT38	415157

PARTY ONE	PARTY TWO	DATE	TOPIC	CITATION	NUMBER
Ecuador	France	02 Sep 65	Visas	65FRRT89	415158
Ecuador	France	17 Feb 66	Tech Assistance	66FRJO2206	416159
Ecuador	France	05 Jul 66	Culture	66FRJO2011	416160
Ecuador	Germany, West	01 Aug 53	Patents/Copyrights	53WBGA192	424109
Ecuador	Germany, West	01 Aug 53	General Trade	54WGBB712	425107
Ecuador	Germany, West	01 Aug 53	General Trade	53WBGA192	424108
Ecuador	Germany, West	13 May 54	Visas	57WBGA193	424110
Ecuador	Germany, West	21 Jul 58	Admin Cooperation	58WBGA218	424111
Ecuador	Germany, West	20 Sep 62	Air Transport	498UNTS199	107283
Ecuador	Germany, West	08 Nov 63	Finance	64WBGA41	424112
Ecuador	Germany, West	28 Jun 65	Claims and Debts	66WGBB825	425114
Ecuador	Germany, West	28 Jun 65	Loans and Credits	65WBGA185	424113
Ecuador	Germany, West	12 Jul 67	Visas	67WBGA166	424115
Ecuador	Germany, West	10 Apr 68	Education	68WBGA148	424116
Ecuador	Germany, West	13 Mar 69	Culture	70WGBB1025	425117
Ecuador	Germany, West	14 Aug 69	Loans and Credits	69WBGA232	424118
Ecuador	Germany, West	24 Apr 70	Loans and Credits	70WBGA135	424119
Ecuador	IBRD (World Bank)	10 Feb 54	IBRD Project	209UNTS261	102830
Ecuador	IBRD (World Bank)	26 Mar 56	IBRD Project	292UNTS391	104277
Ecuador	IBRD (World Bank)	20 Sep 57	IBRD Project	289UNTS237	104221
Ecuador	IBRD (World Bank)	20 Sep 57	IBRD Project	293UNTS135	104291
Ecuador	IBRD (World Bank)	09 Oct 58	IBRD Project	337UNTS299	104827
Ecuador	IBRD (World Bank)	26 May 64	IBRD Project	534UNTS113	107758
Ecuador	IBRD (World Bank)	05 Sep 68	IBRD Project	0UNTS0	110112
Ecuador	IDA (Devel Assoc)	26 May 64	Non-IBRD Project	534UNTS93	107757
Ecuador	IDA (Devel Assoc)	27 Jun 68	Non-IBRD Project	0UNTS0	109321
Ecuador	IDA (Devel Assoc)	20 Jan 70	Non-IBRD Project	0UNTS0	110653
Ecuador	ILO (Labor Org)	19 Apr 51	Tech Assistance	100UNTS77	101389
Ecuador	Israel	20 Jun 66	Visas	581UNTS265	108449
Ecuador	Israel	09 Aug 67	Visas	630UNTS319	108979
Ecuador	Italy	24 Aug 49	General Amity	72UNTS35	100926
Ecuador	Italy	07 Mar 52	Education	55ITGU80	435107
Ecuador	Italy	16 Apr 64	Visas	65ITDI127	436108
Ecuador	Mexico	10 Aug 48	Culture	52MEXD2810	444015
Ecuador	Multilateral	25 Jun 36	Privil/Immunities	161UNTS217	200486
Ecuador	Multilateral	30 Jul 40	Admin Cooperation	161UNTS253	200488
Ecuador	Multilateral	12 Oct 40	Specific Resources	161UNTS193	200485
Ecuador	Multilateral	28 Nov 40	Commodity Trade	139UNTS159	200452
Ecuador	Multilateral	15 Jan 44	IGO Establishment	161UNTS281	200489
Ecuador	Multilateral	19 Apr 44	Scientific Project	89UNTS279	200257
Ecuador	Multilateral	02 Aug 44	Scientific Project	67UNTS221	200221
Ecuador	Multilateral	07 Dec 44	Air Transport	171UNTS387	200502
Ecuador	Multilateral	07 Dec 44	Air Transport	171UNTS345	200501
Ecuador	Multilateral	07 Dec 44	IGO Establishment	15UNTS295	200102
Ecuador	Multilateral	07 Dec 44	Air Transport	84UNTS389	200252
Ecuador	Multilateral	15 Dec 44	Sanitation	16UNTS247	200106
Ecuador	Multilateral	15 Dec 44	Sanitation	17UNTS305	200110
Ecuador	Multilateral	16 Nov 45	IGO Establishment	4UNTS275	100052
Ecuador	Multilateral	27 Dec 45	IGO Establishment	2UNTS39	100020
Ecuador	Multilateral	23 Apr 46	Sanitation	17UNTS3	100265
Ecuador	Multilateral	23 Apr 46	Sanitation	16UNTS179	100257
Ecuador	Multilateral	22 Jul 46	IGO Establishment	9UNTS3	100125
Ecuador	Multilateral	22 Jul 46	IGO Establishment	14UNTS185	100221
Ecuador	Multilateral	27 Jul 46	Patents/Copyrights	90UNTS229	101238
Ecuador	Multilateral	03 Sep 46	Commodity Trade	139UNTS3	101872
Ecuador	Multilateral	15 Oct 46	Refugees	11UNTS73	100150
Ecuador	Multilateral	11 Dec 46	Sanitation	12UNTS179	100186
Ecuador	Multilateral	02 Sep 47	General Military	21UNTS77	100324
Ecuador	Multilateral	02 Oct 47	Telecommunications	193UNTS188	102616
Ecuador	Multilateral	11 Oct 47	IGO Establishment	77UNTS143	100998
Ecuador	Multilateral	06 Mar 48	Water Transport	289UNTS3	104214
Ecuador	Multilateral	30 Apr 48	Dispute Settlement	30UNTS55	100449
Ecuador	Multilateral	30 Apr 48	IGO Establishment	119UNTS3	101609
Ecuador	Multilateral	19 Jun 48	Air Transport	310UNTS151	104492
Ecuador	Multilateral	24 Jul 48	Sanitation	66UNTS25	100847

PARTY ONE	PARTY TWO	DATE	TOPIC	CITATION	NUMBER
Ecuador	Multilateral	19 Nov 48	Sanitation	44UNTS277	100688
Ecuador	Multilateral	29 Nov 48	IGO Establishment	120UNTS13	101613
Ecuador	Multilateral	09 Dec 48	Humanitarian	78UNTS277	101021
Ecuador	Multilateral	23 Mar 49	Commodity Trade	203UNTS179	102746
Ecuador	Multilateral	09 Jul 49	Telecommunications	168UNTS143	102218
Ecuador	Multilateral	15 Jul 49	Health/Educ/Welfare	197UNTS3	102631
Ecuador	Multilateral	12 Aug 49	Humanitarian	75UNTS85	100971
Ecuador	Multilateral	12 Aug 49	General Military	75UNTS135	100972
Ecuador	Multilateral	12 Aug 49	Humanitarian	75UNTS31	100970
Ecuador	Multilateral	12 Aug 49	Humanitarian	75UNTS287	100973
Ecuador	Multilateral	19 Sep 49	Land Transport	125UNTS3	101671
Ecuador	Multilateral	21 Mar 50	Admin Cooperation	96UNTS271	101342
Ecuador	Multilateral	06 Apr 50	Admin Cooperation	119UNTS99	101610
Ecuador	Multilateral	22 Nov 50	Culture	131UNTS25	101734
Ecuador	Multilateral	07 Dec 50	Admin Cooperation	212UNTS17	102861
Ecuador	Multilateral	25 May 51	Status of Forces	175UNTS215	102303
Ecuador	Multilateral	02 Jul 51	Refugees	189UNTS137	102545
Ecuador	Multilateral	08 Sep 51	Peace/Disarmament	136UNTS45	101832
Ecuador	Multilateral	06 Dec 51	IGO Establishment	425UNTS61	106119
Ecuador	Multilateral	06 Dec 51	Admin Cooperation	150UNTS67	101963
Ecuador	Multilateral	11 Jul 52	IGO Establishment	169UNTS3	102220
Ecuador	Multilateral	11 Jul 52	Postal Service	170UNTS63	102222
Ecuador	Multilateral	07 Oct 52	Admin Cooperation	310UNTS181	104493
Ecuador	Multilateral	31 Mar 53	Mass Media	435UNTS191	106280
Ecuador	Multilateral	31 Mar 53	Privil/Immunities	193UNTS136	102613
Ecuador	Multilateral	11 May 53	Sanitation	456UNTS3	106555
Ecuador	Multilateral	07 Dec 53	Admin Cooperation	182UNTS51	102422
Ecuador	Multilateral	01 Mar 54	Commodity Trade	256UNTS31	103622
Ecuador	Multilateral	14 May 54	Culture	249UNTS215	103511
Ecuador	Multilateral	04 Jun 54	Customs	282UNTS249	104101
Ecuador	Multilateral	04 Jun 54	Customs	276UNTS191	103992
Ecuador	Multilateral	28 Sep 54	Refugees	360UNTS117	105158
Ecuador	Multilateral	25 May 55	IGO Establishment	264UNTS117	103791
Ecuador	Multilateral	10 Feb 56	Tech Assistance	228UNTS167	103150
Ecuador	Multilateral	25 Apr 56	Commodity Trade	270UNTS103	103896
Ecuador	Multilateral	20 Jun 56	Admin Cooperation	268UNTS3	103850
Ecuador	Multilateral	26 Oct 56	IGO Establishment	276UNTS3	103988
Ecuador	Multilateral	20 Feb 57	Consul/Citizenship	309UNTS65	104468
Ecuador	Multilateral	03 Oct 57	Postal Service	365UNTS3	105213
Ecuador	Multilateral	03 Oct 57	Postal Service	364UNTS3	105211
Ecuador	Multilateral	29 Apr 58	Territory Boundary	499UNTS311	107302
Ecuador	Multilateral	10 Jun 58	Admin Cooperation	330UNTS3	104739
Ecuador	Multilateral	01 Dec 58	Commodity Trade	385UNTS137	105534
Ecuador	Multilateral	03 Dec 58	Admin Cooperation	416UNTS51	105995
Ecuador	Multilateral	03 Dec 58	Admin Cooperation	398UNTS9	105715
Ecuador	Multilateral	08 Apr 59	IGO Establishment	389UNTS69	105593
Ecuador	Multilateral	18 Nov 59	IGO Establishment	390UNTS227	105610
Ecuador	Multilateral	26 Jan 60	IGO Establishment	439UNTS249	106333
Ecuador	Multilateral	28 Jul 60	IGO Establishment	485UNTS3	107042
Ecuador	Multilateral	30 Mar 61	Sanitation	520UNTS151	107515
Ecuador	Multilateral	18 Apr 61	Dispute Settlement	500UNTS243	107312
Ecuador	Multilateral	18 Apr 61	Consul/Citizenship	500UNTS95	107310
Ecuador	Multilateral	26 Oct 61	Patents/Copyrights	496UNTS43	107247
Ecuador	Multilateral	26 Mar 62	IGO Establishment	539UNTS67	107825
Ecuador	Multilateral	28 Sep 62	IGO Establishment	469UNTS169	106791
Ecuador	Multilateral	24 Apr 63	Consul/Citizenship	596UNTS261	108638
Ecuador	Multilateral	05 Aug 63	Sanitation	480UNTS43	106964
Ecuador	Multilateral	26 May 64	IBRD Project	541UNTS271	200613
Ecuador	Multilateral	10 Jul 64	Postal Service	613UNTS193	108852
Ecuador	Multilateral	10 Jul 64	Postal Service	612UNTS3	108847
Ecuador	Multilateral	10 Jul 64	Postal Service	611UNTS7	108844
Ecuador	Multilateral	10 Jul 64	Postal Service	611UNTS105	108845
Ecuador	Multilateral	09 Mar 65	Water Transport	591UNTS265	108564
Ecuador	Multilateral	05 Apr 66	Water Transport	640UNTS133	109159
Ecuador	Multilateral	27 Jan 67	Scientific Project	610UNTS205	108843

PARTY ONE	PARTY TWO	DATE	TOPIC	CITATION	NUMBER
Ecuador	Multilateral	31 Jan 67	Refugees	606UNTS267	108791
Ecuador	Multilateral	14 Feb 67	General Military	634UNTS281	109068
Ecuador	Multilateral	28 Jun 67	ILO Labor	0UNTS0	110355
Ecuador	Multilateral	18 Mar 68	Commodity Trade	0UNTS0	109262
Ecuador	Multilateral	22 Apr 68	Scientific Project	0UNTS0	109574
Ecuador	Multilateral	01 Jul 68	Peace/Disarmament	0UNTS0	110485
Ecuador	Netherlands	14 Dec 54	Air Transport	232UNTS115	103233
Ecuador	Netherlands	21 Jan 63	Visas	514UNTS87	107443
Ecuador	Netherlands	14 Jan 65	Health/Educ/Welfare	551UNTS129	108038
Ecuador	Norway	15 Jan 51	General Trade	2NORT548	451041
Ecuador	Norway	29 Jan 64	Visas	3NORT899	451042
Ecuador	Other Party Combin	19 Jun 67	IGO Operations	615UNTS75	108878
Ecuador	Philippines	24 Mar 48	General Amity	1PTS695	465014
Ecuador	Romania	10 Oct 67	General Trade	642UNTS33	109163
Ecuador	Spain	05 May 53	Culture	54SPBO3001	460084
Ecuador	Spain	12 Jul 54	Finance	55SPBO1909	460086
Ecuador	Spain	12 Jul 54	General Trade	55SPBO1909	460085
Ecuador	Spain	06 Dec 54	Culture	56SPBO706	460088
Ecuador	Spain	09 Jun 55	General Economic	55SPBO3009	460087
Ecuador	Spain	01 Apr 60	Non-ILO Labor	62SPBO2310	460089
Ecuador	Spain	04 Mar 64	Consul/Citizenship	65SPBO1301	460090
Ecuador	Switzerland	08 Oct 57	General Trade	59SWRO194	462130
Ecuador	Taiwan	06 Jan 46	General Amity	7UNTS233	100102
Ecuador	Taiwan	12 Jun 59	Culture	387UNTS3	105554
Ecuador	Taiwan	17 Jun 64	General Trade	533UNTS141	107740
Ecuador	Taiwan	23 Oct 64	General Trade	543UNTS241	107904
Ecuador	UK Great Britain	13 Sep 63	Visas	490UNTS19	107152
Ecuador	UK Great Britain	15 Nov 69	Loans and Credits	0UNTS0	110600
Ecuador	UN Special Fund	10 Nov 59	Direct Aid	345UNTS3	104955
Ecuador	UNICEF (Children)	12 Oct 49	Tech Assistance	65UNTS62	100827
Ecuador	United Nations	16 Jun 53	Tech Assistance	166UNTS289	102194
Ecuador	United Nations	26 Nov 62	Tech Assistance	445UNTS3	106372
Ecuador	USA (United States)	24 Feb 42	Sanitation	26UNTS379	200157
Ecuador	USA (United States)	02 Mar 42	General Trade	105UNTS195	200332
Ecuador	USA (United States)	29 Oct 42	Scientific Project	89UNTS301	200259
Ecuador	USA (United States)	13 Sep 43	Military Mission	29UNTS349	200171
Ecuador	USA (United States)	29 Jun 44	Military Mission	80UNTS283	200250
Ecuador	USA (United States)	22 Jan 45	Education	24UNTS273	200152
Ecuador	USA (United States)	05 Apr 45	Milit Servic/Citiz	121UNTS265	200404
Ecuador	USA (United States)	11 Jun 46	Status of Forces	167UNTS135	102203
Ecuador	USA (United States)	08 Jan 47	Air Transport	22UNTS119	100333
Ecuador	USA (United States)	21 Jun 47	Sanitation	26UNTS275	100391
Ecuador	USA (United States)	27 Oct 47	Air Transport	44UNTS45	100677
Ecuador	USA (United States)	29 Oct 47	Admin Cooperation	21UNTS21	100322
Ecuador	USA (United States)	14 Nov 47	Education	149UNTS297	101959
Ecuador	USA (United States)	14 May 48	Scientific Project	89UNTS71	101210
Ecuador	USA (United States)	21 Sep 48	Military Mission	80UNTS127	101048
Ecuador	USA (United States)	04 Feb 49	Military Mission	80UNTS137	101049
Ecuador	USA (United States)	17 May 49	Military Mission	66UNTS3	100845
Ecuador	USA (United States)	03 May 51	Tech Assistance	141UNTS27	101902
Ecuador	USA (United States)	20 Feb 52	Milit Assistance	177UNTS43	102308
Ecuador	USA (United States)	17 Mar 52	Telecommunications	177UNTS115	102313
Ecuador	USA (United States)	29 May 52	Tech Assistance	185UNTS203	102471
Ecuador	USA (United States)	30 Jun 54	Tech Assistance	236UNTS163	103323
Ecuador	USA (United States)	29 Mar 55	Claims and Debts	261UNTS343	103732
Ecuador	USA (United States)	08 Jul 55	Milit Assistance	265UNTS49	103806
Ecuador	USA (United States)	24 Aug 55	Military Mission	256UNTS299	103640
Ecuador	USA (United States)	06 Sep 55	Direct Aid	256UNTS187	103628
Ecuador	USA (United States)	07 Oct 55	US Agri Commod Aid	256UNTS197	103629
Ecuador	USA (United States)	19 Jul 56	Milit Assistance	372UNTS149	105295
Ecuador	USA (United States)	31 Oct 56	Education	283UNTS151	104114
Ecuador	USA (United States)	15 Feb 57	US Agri Commod Aid	279UNTS155	104037
Ecuador	USA (United States)	24 Apr 57	Scientific Project	284UNTS3	104124
Ecuador	USA (United States)	31 May 57	Atomic Energy	304UNTS61	104391
Ecuador	USA (United States)	06 Nov 57	Consul/Citizenship	307UNTS49	104441

PARTY ONE	PARTY TWO	DATE	TOPIC	CITATION	NUMBER
Ecuador	USA (United States)	27 Jun 58	Direct Aid	317UNTS51	104593
Ecuador	USA (United States)	30 Jun 58	US Agri Commod Aid	336UNTS11	104796
Ecuador	USA (United States)	11 Feb 60	Milit Assistance	372UNTS141	105294
Ecuador	USA (United States)	24 Feb 60	Tech Assistance	371UNTS55	105270
Ecuador	USA (United States)	27 Sep 60	US Agri Commod Aid	401UNTS115	105766
Ecuador	USA (United States)	03 Apr 61	US Agri Commod Aid	409UNTS140	105882
Ecuador	USA (United States)	17 Jun 61	Direct Aid	411UNTS49	105913
Ecuador	USA (United States)	17 Apr 62	General Aid	442UNTS69	106339
Ecuador	USA (United States)	03 Aug 62	General Aid	460UNTS133	106636
Ecuador	USA (United States)	07 Jan 63	Visas	477UNTS101	106917
Ecuador	USA (United States)	05 Apr 63	US Agri Commod Aid	477UNTS135	106919
Ecuador	USA (United States)	20 Sep 63	Education	488UNTS147	107125
Ecuador	USA (United States)	26 Mar 65	Gen Communications	542UNTS237	107893
Ecuador	USA (United States)	25 Jun 65	US Agri Commod Aid	549UNTS23	107986
Ecuador	USA (United States)	20 Aug 68	Scientific Project	0UNTS0	110504
Ecuador	USA (United States)	30 Jun 69	US Agri Commod Aid	0UNTS0	110690
Ecuador	USSR (Soviet Union)	16 Jun 45	Consul/Citizenship	0SUST180	468122
Ecuador	WHO (World Health)	16 Oct 51	Tech Assistance	110UNTS263	101515
EEC (Econ Commnty)	Austria	26 Jun 69	General Trade	70ABGB128	403041
EEC (Econ Commnty)	Austria	04 Nov 70	Commodity Trade	71ABGB156	403042
EEC (Econ Commnty)	Austria	04 Nov 70	Commodity Trade	71ABGB157	403043
EEC (Econ Commnty)	Denmark	30 Jun 67	General Trade	0UNTS0	109747
EEC (Econ Commnty)	Denmark	30 Jun 67	General Trade	0UNTS0	109748
EEC (Econ Commnty)	Denmark	30 Jun 67	General Trade	0UNTS0	109746
EEC (Econ Commnty)	Denmark	30 Jun 67	General Trade	0UNTS0	109745
EEC (Econ Commnty)	ILO (Labor Org)	07 Jul 58	IGO Operations	312UNTS387	200551
EEC (Econ Commnty)	Iran	14 Oct 63	General Trade	0IRTB85	433138
EEC (Econ Commnty)	Japan	30 Jun 67	General Trade	68JHZ5	439011
EEC (Econ Commnty)	Multilateral	07 Mar 62	Commodity Trade	445UNTS205	106389
EEC (Econ Commnty)	Multilateral	07 Mar 62	Commodity Trade	445UNTS199	106388
EEC (Econ Commnty)	Multilateral	29 Mar 65	Non-IBRD Project	540UNTS145	107848
EEC (Econ Commnty)	Multilateral	29 Apr 65	Non-IBRD Project	586UNTS123	108500
EEC (Econ Commnty)	Multilateral	12 Jan 70	Commodity Trade	0UNTS0	110603
EEC (Econ Commnty)	Turkey	12 Sep 63	Other Economic	64TURG1202	466005
EEC (Econ Commnty)	USA (United States)	07 Mar 62	General Economic	446UNTS81	106405
EEC (Econ Commnty)	USA (United States)	07 Mar 62	General Trade	445UNTS195	106387
EEC (Econ Commnty)	USA (United States)	07 Mar 62	General Trade	436UNTS49	106288
EFTA (Free Trade)	Switzerland	10 Aug 61	IGO Status/Immunit	61SWRO763	462193
El Salvador	Austria	23 Mar 60	General Trade	390UNTS3	105599
El Salvador	Austria	21 Jun 60	Visas	60ABGB189	403161
El Salvador	Austria	03 Oct 63	Visas	64ABGB34	403162
El Salvador	Brazil	30 Nov 65	Culture	0UNTS0	109430
El Salvador	Canada	11 Mar 63	Gen Communications	529UNTS25	107652
El Salvador	Denmark	09 Jul 58	General Economic	341UNTS289	104892
El Salvador	France	23 Mar 53	General Trade	54FRJO1902	416386
El Salvador	France	19 Feb 64	Telecommunications	65FRRT38	415387
El Salvador	Germany, West	31 Oct 52	Mostfavored Nation	54WGBB49	425128
El Salvador	Germany, West	24 Sep 63	Tech Assistance	64WBGA198	424129
El Salvador	Germany, West	19 Sep 66	Loans and Credits	67WBGA42	424130
El Salvador	Guatemala	14 Dec 51	General Economic	131UNTS131	101740
El Salvador	IBRD (World Bank)	14 Dec 49	IBRD Project	155UNTS43	102035
El Salvador	IBRD (World Bank)	12 Oct 54	IBRD Project	203UNTS37	102739
El Salvador	IBRD (World Bank)	07 Jan 59	IBRD Project	346UNTS51	104977
El Salvador	IBRD (World Bank)	20 Feb 59	IBRD Project	362UNTS75	105183
El Salvador	IBRD (World Bank)	29 Jul 60	IBRD Project	390UNTS101	105605
El Salvador	IBRD (World Bank)	19 Jun 63	IBRD Project	481UNTS59	106978
El Salvador	IBRD (World Bank)	01 Oct 63	IBRD Project	517UNTS3	107481
El Salvador	IBRD (World Bank)	07 Dec 67	Loans and Credits	0UNTS0	109299
El Salvador	IBRD (World Bank)	11 Jun 69	IBRD Project	0UNTS0	110288
El Salvador	IDA (Devel Assoc)	02 Nov 62	Non-IBRD Project	468UNTS331	106780
El Salvador	Israel	14 Nov 58	Culture	345UNTS67	104959
El Salvador	Israel	05 Sep 60	Visas	413UNTS73	105941
El Salvador	Israel	04 Oct 61	Visas	448UNTS253	106437
El Salvador	Italy	30 Mar 53	General Trade	53ITDI410	436106
El Salvador	Japan	19 Jul 63	General Economic	518UNTS135	107494

PARTY ONE	PARTY TWO	DATE	TOPIC	CITATION	NUMBER
El Salvador	Japan	26 Jul 68	Direct Aid	68JJS165	442217
El Salvador	Mexico	14 Dec 50	General Trade	52MEXD605	444016
El Salvador	Mexico	13 Jan 66	Culture	67MEXD1711	444017
El Salvador	Mexico	23 Jun 66	Tech Assistance	68MEXD1403	444018
El Salvador	Multilateral	25 Jun 36	Privil/Immunities	161UNTS217	200486
El Salvador	Multilateral	17 Feb 40	Privil/Immunities	161UNTS229	200487
El Salvador	Multilateral	30 Jul 40	Admin Cooperation	161UNTS253	200488
El Salvador	Multilateral	12 Oct 40	Specific Resources	161UNTS193	200485
El Salvador	Multilateral	28 Nov 40	Commodity Trade	139UNTS159	200452
El Salvador	Multilateral	27 Mar 41	Military Mission	67UNTS231	200222
El Salvador	Multilateral	15 Jan 44	IGO Establishment	161UNTS281	200489
El Salvador	Multilateral	02 Aug 44	Scientific Project	67UNTS221	200221
El Salvador	Multilateral	07 Dec 44	Air Transport	171UNTS345	200501
El Salvador	Multilateral	07 Dec 44	Air Transport	171UNTS387	200502
El Salvador	Multilateral	07 Dec 44	Air Transport	84UNTS389	200252
El Salvador	Multilateral	07 Dec 44	IGO Establishment	15UNTS295	200102
El Salvador	Multilateral	22 Jul 46	IGO Establishment	14UNTS185	100221
El Salvador	Multilateral	22 Jul 46	IGO Establishment	9UNTS3	100125
El Salvador	Multilateral	27 Jul 46	Patents/Copyrights	90UNTS229	101238
El Salvador	Multilateral	03 Sep 46	Commodity Trade	139UNTS3	101872
El Salvador	Multilateral	27 May 47	Air Transport	418UNTS161	106021
El Salvador	Multilateral	02 Sep 47	General Military	21UNTS77	100324
El Salvador	Multilateral	02 Oct 47	Telecommunications	193UNTS188	102616
El Salvador	Multilateral	30 Apr 48	IGO Establishment	119UNTS3	101609
El Salvador	Multilateral	30 Apr 48	Dispute Settlement	30UNTS55	100449
El Salvador	Multilateral	19 Jun 48	Air Transport	310UNTS151	104492
El Salvador	Multilateral	24 Jul 48	Sanitation	66UNTS25	100847
El Salvador	Multilateral	19 Nov 48	Sanitation	44UNTS277	100688
El Salvador	Multilateral	09 Dec 48	Humanitarian	78UNTS277	101021
El Salvador	Multilateral	23 Mar 49	Commodity Trade	203UNTS179	102746
El Salvador	Multilateral	04 May 49	Admin Cooperation	30UNTS3	100445
El Salvador	Multilateral	15 Jul 49	Health/Educ/Welfare	197UNTS3	102631
El Salvador	Multilateral	12 Aug 49	Humanitarian	75UNTS85	100971
El Salvador	Multilateral	12 Aug 49	Humanitarian	75UNTS287	100973
El Salvador	Multilateral	12 Aug 49	General Military	75UNTS135	100972
El Salvador	Multilateral	12 Aug 49	Humanitarian	75UNTS31	100970
El Salvador	Multilateral	22 Nov 50	Culture	131UNTS25	101734
El Salvador	Multilateral	15 Feb 51	Tech Assistance	81UNTS245	101074
El Salvador	Multilateral	25 May 51	Status of Forces	175UNTS215	102303
El Salvador	Multilateral	01 Jun 51	Tech Assistance	118UNTS57	101596
El Salvador	Multilateral	08 Sep 51	Peace/Disarmament	136UNTS45	101832
El Salvador	Multilateral	14 Oct 51	IGO Establishment	122UNTS3	101631
El Salvador	Multilateral	06 Dec 51	Admin Cooperation	150UNTS67	101963
El Salvador	Multilateral	11 Jul 52	Postal Service	170UNTS63	102222
El Salvador	Multilateral	11 Jul 52	IGO Establishment	169UNTS3	102220
El Salvador	Multilateral	11 Jul 52	Postal Service	170UNTS269	102223
El Salvador	Multilateral	06 Sep 52	Patents/Copyrights	216UNTS132	102937
El Salvador	Multilateral	31 Mar 53	Mass Media	435UNTS191	106280
El Salvador	Multilateral	31 Mar 53	Privil/Immunities	193UNTS136	102613
El Salvador	Multilateral	11 May 53	Sanitation	456UNTS3	106555
El Salvador	Multilateral	14 May 54	Culture	249UNTS215	103511
El Salvador	Multilateral	28 Sep 54	Refugees	360UNTS117	105158
El Salvador	Multilateral	25 May 55	IGO Establishment	264UNTS117	103791
El Salvador	Multilateral	28 Sep 55	Air Transport	478UNTS371	106943
El Salvador	Multilateral	25 Apr 56	Commodity Trade	270UNTS103	103896
El Salvador	Multilateral	20 Jun 56	Admin Cooperation	268UNTS3	103850
El Salvador	Multilateral	07 Sep 56	Humanitarian	266UNTS3	103822
El Salvador	Multilateral	26 Oct 56	IGO Establishment	276UNTS3	103988
El Salvador	Multilateral	08 Nov 56	Commodity Trade	470UNTS171	106809
El Salvador	Multilateral	22 Feb 57	Tech Assistance	274UNTS93	103960
El Salvador	Multilateral	01 May 57	Admin Cooperation	284UNTS201	104138
El Salvador	Multilateral	03 Oct 57	Postal Service	365UNTS3	105213
El Salvador	Multilateral	03 Oct 57	Postal Service	365UNTS207	105214
El Salvador	Multilateral	03 Oct 57	Postal Service	364UNTS331	105212
El Salvador	Multilateral	10 Jun 58	Land Transport	454UNTS211	106541

PARTY ONE	PARTY TWO	DATE	TOPIC	CITATION	NUMBER
El Salvador	Multilateral	10 Jun 58	Land Transport	454UNTS115	106540
El Salvador	Multilateral	10 Jun 58	Admin Cooperation	330UNTS3	104739
El Salvador	Multilateral	10 Jun 58	General Economic	454UNTS47	106539
El Salvador	Multilateral	06 Apr 59	Commodity Trade	349UNTS167	105013
El Salvador	Multilateral	08 Apr 59	IGO Establishment	389UNTS69	105593
El Salvador	Multilateral	01 Sep 59	Customs	454UNTS289	106542
El Salvador	Multilateral	03 Dec 59	Tech Assistance	345UNTS251	104971
El Salvador	Multilateral	26 Jan 60	IGO Establishment	439UNTS249	106333
El Salvador	Multilateral	06 Feb 60	General Economic	383UNTS3	105494
El Salvador	Multilateral	26 Feb 60	Air Transport	418UNTS171	106022
El Salvador	Multilateral	28 Jul 60	IGO Establishment	485UNTS3	107042
El Salvador	Multilateral	13 Dec 60	IGO Establishment	455UNTS204	106544
El Salvador	Multilateral	13 Dec 60	General Economic	455UNTS3	106543
El Salvador	Multilateral	30 Mar 61	Sanitation	520UNTS151	107515
El Salvador	Multilateral	18 Apr 61	Consul/Citizenship	500UNTS95	107310
El Salvador	Multilateral	21 Jun 61	IGO Establishment	514UNTS209	107449
El Salvador	Multilateral	28 Sep 62	IGO Establishment	469UNTS169	106791
El Salvador	Multilateral	12 Dec 62	IGO Establishment	552UNTS15	108048
El Salvador	Multilateral	31 Jul 63	Tech Assistance	472UNTS220	106842
El Salvador	Multilateral	05 Aug 63	Sanitation	480UNTS43	106964
El Salvador	Multilateral	21 Oct 63	Tech Assistance	480UNTS197	106969
El Salvador	Multilateral	10 Jul 64	Postal Service	611UNTS7	108844
El Salvador	Multilateral	10 Jul 64	Postal Service	611UNTS387	108846
El Salvador	Multilateral	10 Jul 64	Postal Service	611UNTS105	108845
El Salvador	Multilateral	10 Jul 64	Postal Service	612UNTS233	108848
El Salvador	Multilateral	10 Jul 64	Postal Service	612UNTS3	108847
El Salvador	Multilateral	05 Apr 66	Water Transport	640UNTS133	109159
El Salvador	Multilateral	14 Feb 67	General Military	634UNTS281	109068
El Salvador	Multilateral	18 Mar 68	Commodity Trade	0UNTS0	109262
El Salvador	Multilateral	01 Jun 68	General Trade	0UNTS0	110835
El Salvador	Norway	21 Oct 59	Visas	3NORT786	451138
El Salvador	Spain	19 Feb 52	General Amity	52SPBO1611	460091
El Salvador	Spain	02 Dec 52	General Trade	53SPBO511	460092
El Salvador	Spain	02 Dec 52	Finance	53SPBO511	460093
El Salvador	Spain	06 Nov 53	Consul/Citizenship	54SPBO508	460094
El Salvador	State/IGO Group	22 Oct 70	Tech Assistance	0UNTS0	110796
El Salvador	Switzerland	11 Feb 54	General Trade	54SWRO687	462154
El Salvador	Taiwan	09 Dec 54	General Amity	214UNTS217	102900
El Salvador	Taiwan	27 Nov 61	Culture	437UNTS161	106306
El Salvador	UK Great Britain	16 Dec 43	General Trade	2UNTS221	200014
El Salvador	UK Great Britain	16 Dec 46	General Trade	6UNTS131	100072
El Salvador	UK Great Britain	20 Aug 62	Visas	453UNTS309	106532
El Salvador	UK Great Britain	20 Jun 67	Tech Assistance	0UNTS0	109471
El Salvador	UN Special Fund	24 Oct 60	Direct Aid	377UNTS171	105400
El Salvador	UNICEF (Children)	18 Jan 50	Tech Assistance	65UNTS78	100833
El Salvador	USA (United States)	27 Nov 41	Admin Cooperation	120UNTS161	200389
El Salvador	USA (United States)	13 Feb 42	Land Transport	23UNTS293	200136
El Salvador	USA (United States)	05 May 42	Sanitation	21UNTS215	200124
El Salvador	USA (United States)	24 Nov 42	Military Mission	24UNTS241	200149
El Salvador	USA (United States)	02 Dec 42	Scientific Project	122UNTS277	200410
El Salvador	USA (United States)	25 Mar 43	Military Mission	13UNTS419	200088
El Salvador	USA (United States)	21 May 43	Military Mission	9UNTS341	200051
El Salvador	USA (United States)	31 May 43	Milit Servic/Citiz	105UNTS205	200333
El Salvador	USA (United States)	09 Jun 45	Education	149UNTS379	200478
El Salvador	USA (United States)	19 Aug 47	Military Mission	51UNTS57	100752
El Salvador	USA (United States)	23 Sep 48	Sanitation	181UNTS101	102402
El Salvador	USA (United States)	27 Jul 49	Sanitation	180UNTS219	102387
El Salvador	USA (United States)	13 Dec 50	Sanitation	166UNTS149	102188
El Salvador	USA (United States)	19 Mar 51	Land Transport	134UNTS245	101803
El Salvador	USA (United States)	18 Apr 51	Tech Assistance	141UNTS37	101903
El Salvador	USA (United States)	11 May 51	Direct Aid	141UNTS191	101915
El Salvador	USA (United States)	19 Jul 51	Tech Assistance	140UNTS259	101892
El Salvador	USA (United States)	23 Jul 51	Direct Aid	138UNTS127	101865
El Salvador	USA (United States)	23 Oct 51	Direct Aid	137UNTS43	101847
El Salvador	USA (United States)	12 Dec 51	Education	132UNTS287	101768

PARTY ONE	PARTY TWO	DATE	TOPIC	CITATION	NUMBER
El Salvador	USA (United States)	07 Jan 52	Tech Assistance	198UNTS231	102667
El Salvador	USA (United States)	04 Apr 52	Tech Assistance	177UNTS219	102320
El Salvador	USA (United States)	14 May 53	Direct Aid	234UNTS71	103273
El Salvador	USA (United States)	21 May 53	Military Mission	213UNTS15	102878
El Salvador	USA (United States)	15 Dec 53	Visas	236UNTS25	103314
El Salvador	USA (United States)	16 Jul 54	Non-IBRD Project	237UNTS237	103350
El Salvador	USA (United States)	31 Aug 54	Non-IBRD Project	237UNTS49	103336
El Salvador	USA (United States)	23 Sep 54	Military Mission	237UNTS91	103338
El Salvador	USA (United States)	21 Mar 55	Non-IBRD Project	250UNTS261	103528
El Salvador	USA (United States)	08 Aug 55	Non-IBRD Project	264UNTS301	103801
El Salvador	USA (United States)	21 Nov 57	Military Mission	303UNTS19	104369
El Salvador	USA (United States)	09 May 58	Visas	316UNTS29	104575
El Salvador	USA (United States)	29 Jan 60	Claims and Debts	372UNTS3	105283
El Salvador	USA (United States)	21 Aug 61	US Agri Commod Aid	418UNTS35	106015
El Salvador	USA (United States)	20 Nov 61	Direct Aid	433UNTS221	106245
El Salvador	USA (United States)	19 Dec 61	General Aid	445UNTS175	106385
El Salvador	USA (United States)	05 Apr 62	Telecommunications	442UNTS41	106337
El Salvador	USA (United States)	13 Apr 62	Milit Assistance	451UNTS307	106500
El Salvador	USA (United States)	15 May 62	General Trade	452UNTS49	106503
El Salvador	USA (United States)	07 May 63	US Agri Commod Aid	476UNTS35	106901
El Salvador	USA (United States)	05 Jun 67	Gen Communications	0UNTS0	109902
El Salvador	WHO (World Health)	21 Apr 50	Sanitation	103UNTS13	101420
El Salvador	WHO (World Health)	02 Jan 51	Sanitation	103UNTS29	101421
Ethiopia	Canada	03 Jun 55	General Economic	247UNTS157	103465
Ethiopia	Czechoslovakia	11 Dec 59	General Amity	386UNTS51	105537
Ethiopia	Czechoslovakia	11 Dec 59	Culture	399UNTS93	105736
Ethiopia	Czechoslovakia	11 Dec 59	Scientific Project	386UNTS45	105536
Ethiopia	Finland	25 Nov 68	Tech Assistance	0UNTS0	109674
Ethiopia	France	12 Nov 59	Specific Property	381UNTS3	105465
Ethiopia	France	12 Nov 59	Land Transport	60FRRT30	415183
Ethiopia	France	27 Aug 66	Health/Educ/Welfare	67FRJO3103	416184
Ethiopia	France	27 Aug 66	Education	67FRJO3103	416185
Ethiopia	France	27 Aug 66	Culture	67FRJO3103	416186
Ethiopia	France	27 Aug 66	Culture	0UNTS0	110646
Ethiopia	France	27 Aug 66	Culture	0UNTS0	110645
Ethiopia	France	27 Aug 66	Culture	0UNTS0	110644
Ethiopia	France	28 Mar 69	Health/Educ/Welfare	69FRJO2412	416187
Ethiopia	France	28 Mar 69	Education	0UNTS0	110647
Ethiopia	France	10 Jul 69	Tech Assistance	0UNTS0	110318
Ethiopia	Germany, West	16 Apr 58	Air Transport	59WGBB1065	425014
Ethiopia	Germany, West	21 Apr 64	Claims and Debts	65WGBB1521	425015
Ethiopia	Germany, West	21 Apr 64	Air Transport	68WBGA38	424018
Ethiopia	Germany, West	21 Apr 64	Water Transport	68WBGA38	424017
Ethiopia	Germany, West	21 Apr 64	General Economic	68WBGA38	424016
Ethiopia	Greece	20 Jan 54	Air Transport	222UNTS281	103035
Ethiopia	Greece	31 Jul 54	Culture	241UNTS319	103439
Ethiopia	Greece	22 Jun 59	General Economic	534UNTS147	107759
Ethiopia	Greece	07 Nov 62	Taxation	550UNTS179	108014
Ethiopia	Greece	07 Nov 62	Taxation	550UNTS189	108015
Ethiopia	Hungary	25 May 65	Health/Educ/Welfare	577UNTS193	108377
Ethiopia	IBRD (World Bank)	13 Sep 50	IBRD Project	157UNTS233	102056
Ethiopia	IBRD (World Bank)	13 Sep 50	IBRD Project	157UNTS213	102055
Ethiopia	IBRD (World Bank)	19 Feb 51	IBRD Project	186UNTS101	102486
Ethiopia	IBRD (World Bank)	28 Jan 57	IBRD Project	286UNTS307	104175
Ethiopia	IBRD (World Bank)	22 Nov 61	IBRD Project	426UNTS255	106142
Ethiopia	IBRD (World Bank)	31 May 62	IBRD Project	467UNTS237	106765
Ethiopia	IBRD (World Bank)	08 May 64	IBRD Project	505UNTS51	107364
Ethiopia	IBRD (World Bank)	28 Dec 65	IBRD Project	567UNTS229	108258
Ethiopia	IBRD (World Bank)	09 May 69	IBRD Project	0UNTS0	110219
Ethiopia	ICAO (Civil Aviat)	02 Feb 51	Tech Assistance	96UNTS123	101333
Ethiopia	IDA (Devel Assoc)	27 Feb 63	Non-IBRD Project	478UNTS289	106939
Ethiopia	IDA (Devel Assoc)	16 Feb 66	Loans and Credits	569UNTS43	108278
Ethiopia	IDA (Devel Assoc)	26 Nov 69	Non-IBRD Project	0UNTS0	110583
Ethiopia	ILO (Labor Org)	10 Dec 64	IGO Establishment	521UNTS217	107524
Ethiopia	India	07 Jun 49	Air Transport	35UNTS13	100548

PARTY ONE	PARTY TWO	DATE	TOPIC	CITATION	NUMBER
Ethiopia	Iran	06 Jun 68	General Amity	0IRTB28	433039
Ethiopia	Italy	05 Mar 56	Reparations	267UNTS189	103844
Ethiopia	Japan	19 Dec 57	General Amity	325UNTS91	104695
Ethiopia	Japan	18 Aug 67	General Trade	68JJS175	442199
Ethiopia	Multilateral	02 Aug 44	Scientific Project	67UNTS221	200221
Ethiopia	Multilateral	07 Dec 44	Air Transport	84UNTS389	200252
Ethiopia	Multilateral	07 Dec 44	IGO Establishment	15UNTS295	200102
Ethiopia	Multilateral	07 Dec 44	Air Transport	171UNTS387	200502
Ethiopia	Multilateral	07 Dec 44	Air Transport	171UNTS345	200501
Ethiopia	Multilateral	08 Aug 45	General Military	82UNTS279	200251
Ethiopia	Multilateral	27 Dec 45	IGO Establishment	2UNTS39	100020
Ethiopia	Multilateral	22 Jul 46	IGO Establishment	14UNTS185	100221
Ethiopia	Multilateral	22 Jul 46	IGO Establishment	9UNTS3	100125
Ethiopia	Multilateral	27 Jul 46	Patents/Copyrights	90UNTS229	101238
Ethiopia	Multilateral	11 Dec 46	Sanitation	12UNTS179	100186
Ethiopia	Multilateral	10 Feb 47	Peace/Disarmament	49UNTS3	100747
Ethiopia	Multilateral	02 Oct 47	Telecommunications	193UNTS188	102616
Ethiopia	Multilateral	24 Jul 48	Sanitation	66UNTS25	100847
Ethiopia	Multilateral	19 Nov 48	Sanitation	44UNTS277	100688
Ethiopia	Multilateral	09 Dec 48	Humanitarian	78UNTS277	101021
Ethiopia	Multilateral	12 Aug 49	General Military	75UNTS135	100972
Ethiopia	Multilateral	12 Aug 49	Humanitarian	75UNTS287	100973
Ethiopia	Multilateral	12 Aug 49	Humanitarian	75UNTS85	100971
Ethiopia	Multilateral	12 Aug 49	Humanitarian	75UNTS31	100970
Ethiopia	Multilateral	06 Apr 50	Admin Cooperation	119UNTS99	101610
Ethiopia	Multilateral	25 May 51	Status of Forces	175UNTS215	102303
Ethiopia	Multilateral	08 Sep 51	General Military	136UNTS165	101833
Ethiopia	Multilateral	08 Sep 51	Peace/Disarmament	136UNTS45	101832
Ethiopia	Multilateral	11 Jul 52	IGO Establishment	169UNTS3	102220
Ethiopia	Multilateral	11 Jul 52	Postal Service	170UNTS63	102222
Ethiopia	Multilateral	31 Mar 53	Privil/Immunities	193UNTS136	102613
Ethiopia	Multilateral	31 Mar 53	Mass Media	435UNTS191	106280
Ethiopia	Multilateral	14 Jun 54	Air Transport	320UNTS217	104644
Ethiopia	Multilateral	14 Jun 54	Air Transport	320UNTS209	104643
Ethiopia	Multilateral	25 May 55	IGO Establishment	264UNTS117	103791
Ethiopia	Multilateral	26 Oct 56	IGO Establishment	276UNTS3	103988
Ethiopia	Multilateral	03 Oct 57	Postal Service	365UNTS3	105213
Ethiopia	Multilateral	03 Oct 57	Postal Service	364UNTS3	105211
Ethiopia	Multilateral	15 Mar 58	Tech Assistance	292UNTS273	104276
Ethiopia	Multilateral	26 Jan 60	IGO Establishment	439UNTS249	106333
Ethiopia	Multilateral	21 Jun 61	IGO Establishment	514UNTS209	107449
Ethiopia	Multilateral	25 May 63	IGO Establishment	479UNTS39	106947
Ethiopia	Multilateral	04 Aug 63	IGO Establishment	510UNTS3	107408
Ethiopia	Multilateral	05 Aug 63	Sanitation	480UNTS43	106964
Ethiopia	Multilateral	10 Jul 64	Postal Service	612UNTS3	108847
Ethiopia	Multilateral	10 Jul 64	Postal Service	611UNTS105	108845
Ethiopia	Multilateral	10 Jul 64	Postal Service	611UNTS7	108844
Ethiopia	Multilateral	20 Aug 64	Telecommunications	514UNTS25	107441
Ethiopia	Multilateral	18 Mar 65	Dispute Settlement	575UNTS159	108359
Ethiopia	Multilateral	12 Nov 65	IGO Operations	550UNTS160	108013
Ethiopia	Multilateral	06 Nov 67	Other Military	640UNTS87	109155
Ethiopia	Multilateral	18 Mar 68	Commodity Trade	0UNTS0	109262
Ethiopia	Multilateral	01 Jul 68	Peace/Disarmament	0UNTS0	110485
Ethiopia	Netherlands	28 Oct 64	Tech Assistance	541UNTS235	107872
Ethiopia	Pakistan	01 Jan 48	Air Transport	35UNTS3	100547
Ethiopia	Pakistan	29 Aug 52	Air Transport	150UNTS257	101979
Ethiopia	Poland	01 Dec 65	Tech Assistance	65PZUM71	458126
Ethiopia	Sweden	13 Oct 54	Tech Assistance	202UNTS273	102734
Ethiopia	Sweden	16 Mar 57	Tech Assistance	304UNTS214	104398
Ethiopia	UK Great Britain	19 Dec 44	General Amity	93UNTS303	200272
Ethiopia	UK Great Britain	29 Sep 47	Territory Boundary	82UNTS191	101092
Ethiopia	UK Great Britain	03 Jul 52	Status of Forces	151UNTS207	101996
Ethiopia	UK Great Britain	29 Aug 52	Trusteeship	190UNTS329	102573
Ethiopia	UK Great Britain	06 Sep 52	Finance	149UNTS57	101951
Ethiopia	UK Great Britain	29 Nov 54	Status of Forces	207UNTS283	102811

PARTY ONE	PARTY TWO	DATE	TOPIC	CITATION	NUMBER
Ethiopia	UK Great Britain	12 Aug 55	Territory Boundary	227UNTS3	103127
Ethiopia	UK Great Britain	07 Jul 58	Air Transport	331UNTS3	104749
Ethiopia	UK Great Britain	13 Feb 69	Admin Cooperation	0UNTS0	109788
Ethiopia	UN Special Fund	13 Jul 60	Tech Assistance	368UNTS159	105240
Ethiopia	UNICEF (Children)	27 Apr 53	Direct Aid	213UNTS169	102885
Ethiopia	UNICEF (Children)	01 Apr 63	IGO Operations	457UNTS103	106579
Ethiopia	United Nations	22 Jun 53	Tech Assistance	172UNTS93	102241
Ethiopia	United Nations	18 Jun 58	IGO Operations	317UNTS101	104597
Ethiopia	United Nations	13 Jul 60	Tech Assistance	368UNTS143	105239
Ethiopia	United Nations	14 Jun 61	Direct Aid	406UNTS81	105840
Ethiopia	USA (United States)	09 Aug 43	Milit Installation	29UNTS303	200169
Ethiopia	USA (United States)	04 Jul 46	Mostfavored Nation	13UNTS27	100198
Ethiopia	USA (United States)	20 May 49	Milit Assistance	89UNTS99	101211
Ethiopia	USA (United States)	02 May 51	Direct Aid	139UNTS85	101877
Ethiopia	USA (United States)	16 Jun 51	Tech Assistance	148UNTS39	101933
Ethiopia	USA (United States)	07 Sep 51	General Amity	206UNTS41	102785
Ethiopia	USA (United States)	15 May 52	Education	180UNTS227	102388
Ethiopia	USA (United States)	13 Jun 52	Milit Assistance	205UNTS17	102766
Ethiopia	USA (United States)	18 Jun 52	Tech Assistance	181UNTS207	102410
Ethiopia	USA (United States)	24 Jun 52	Tech Assistance	181UNTS215	102411
Ethiopia	USA (United States)	05 Nov 52	Sanitation	184UNTS139	102445
Ethiopia	USA (United States)	07 Nov 52	Tech Assistance	184UNTS285	102453
Ethiopia	USA (United States)	29 Apr 53	Sanitation	224UNTS121	103073
Ethiopia	USA (United States)	22 May 53	Milit Installation	191UNTS59	102577
Ethiopia	USA (United States)	22 May 53	Milit Assistance	207UNTS127	102803
Ethiopia	USA (United States)	25 Jun 53	Tech Assistance	212UNTS175	102869
Ethiopia	USA (United States)	30 Jun 53	Direct Aid	212UNTS135	102865
Ethiopia	USA (United States)	21 Apr 54	Tech Assistance	232UNTS299	103244
Ethiopia	USA (United States)	01 Jun 54	Direct Aid	232UNTS311	103245
Ethiopia	USA (United States)	12 Jun 54	Tech Assistance	234UNTS25	103270
Ethiopia	USA (United States)	25 Apr 57	Direct Aid	283UNTS205	104118
Ethiopia	USA (United States)	26 Dec 57	Milit Assistance	307UNTS71	104443
Ethiopia	USA (United States)	06 Dec 61	Education	433UNTS231	106246
Ethiopia	USA (United States)	23 May 62	General Aid	456UNTS293	106563
Ethiopia	USA (United States)	03 Aug 62	Claims and Debts	459UNTS79	106613
Ethiopia	USA (United States)	13 Aug 62	US Agri Commod Aid	459UNTS31	106611
Ethiopia	USA (United States)	25 Jan 63	Scientific Project	473UNTS27	106851
Ethiopia	USA (United States)	11 Jun 63	US Agri Commod Aid	487UNTS269	107109
Ethiopia	USA (United States)	25 Nov 64	Mass Media	532UNTS125	107715
Ethiopia	USA (United States)	17 Aug 65	US Agri Commod Aid	564UNTS119	108224
Ethiopia	USA (United States)	14 Dec 65	US Agri Commod Aid	574UNTS115	108344
Ethiopia	USA (United States)	30 Dec 65	Milit Installation	574UNTS129	108345
Ethiopia	USA (United States)	15 Jun 67	Postal Service	0UNTS0	109905
Ethiopia	USSR (Soviet Union)	18 May 56	Consul/Citizenship	16SUGG71	469917
Ethiopia	USSR (Soviet Union)	02 Jun 56	Consul/Citizenship	0SUST357	468131
Ethiopia	USSR (Soviet Union)	11 Jul 59	General Trade	8SUGG149	469588
Ethiopia	USSR (Soviet Union)	11 Jul 59	General Trade	0UNTS0	110494
Ethiopia	USSR (Soviet Union)	12 Jul 59	Culture	8SUGG149	469590
Ethiopia	USSR (Soviet Union)	12 Jul 59	General Aid	8SUGG149	469589
Ethiopia	USSR (Soviet Union)	08 Mar 60	Non-IBRD Project	9SUGG129	469640
Ethiopia	USSR (Soviet Union)	25 Mar 60	Tech Assistance	9SUGG131	469645
Ethiopia	USSR (Soviet Union)	13 Jan 61	Culture	421UNTS13	106049
Ethiopia	USSR (Soviet Union)	29 Aug 62	Non-IBRD Project	11SUGG150	469856
Ethiopia	WHO (World Health)	02 Jul 51	Tech Assistance	103UNTS39	101422
Ethiopia	WHO (World Health)	17 Feb 56	Tech Assistance	243UNTS91	103448
Ethiopia	WHO (World Health)	11 Jan 62	Tech Assistance	423UNTS99	106087
Ethiopia	WHO (World Health)	27 Jan 65	IGO Operations	541UNTS135	107866
Ethiopia	Yugoslavia	21 Aug 53	General Economic	378UNTS105	105421
Ethiopia	Yugoslavia	06 Jun 59	Loans and Credits	386UNTS243	105544
Eur Foot Mouth Dis	Multilateral	11 Dec 53	Sanitation	191UNTS285	102588
Eur Plant Protect	France	30 Jun 64	IGO Status/Immunit	65FRRT74	415501
Eur Space Research	France	10 Aug 64	IGO Operations	528UNTS135	107637
Eur Space Research	France	08 Oct 65	Non-ILO Labor	66FRRT19	415505
Eur Space Research	Germany, West	08 Sep 67	IGO Establishment	69WGBB92	425747
Eur Space Research	Italy	23 May 64	IGO Operations	528UNTS75	107635

PARTY ONE	PARTY TWO	DATE	TOPIC	CITATION	NUMBER
Eur Space Research	Norway	21 Sep 65	IGO Operations	579UNTS251	108413
Eur Space Research	Norway	31 Jan 66	Specific Property	580UNTS3	108414
Eur Space Research	Sweden	29 Jul 64	IGO Operations	528UNTS81	107636
Eur Space Research	UK Great Britain	24 Nov 67	Gen Communications	638UNTS17	109129
Eur Space Research	UK Great Britain	30 Jan 69	Scientific Project	0UNTS0	109665
Eur Space Research	UK Great Britain	19 Dec 69	Scientific Project	0UNTS0	110442
Eur Space Research	USA (United States)	28 Nov 66	Scientific Project	0UNTS0	109691
Eur Space Vehicle	Australia	13 Jul 65	IGO Operations	543UNTS183	107902
Eur Space Vehicle	Belgium	29 Sep 69	IGO Operations	0UNTS0	110203
Eur Space Vehicle	France	11 Mar 65	Scientific Project	66FRRT21	415504
Eur Space Vehicle	France	11 Jun 68	Gen Communications	0UNTS0	110028
Eur Space Vehicle	France	11 Jun 68	Specific Property	69FRJO1903	416512
Eur Space Vehicle	Germany, West	26 Jan 70	IGO Operations	70WGBB185	425743
Eur Space Vehicle	Multilateral	06 May 64	IGO Operations	514UNTS71	107442
Euratom	Canada	06 Oct 59	Scientific Project	475UNTS187	106894
Euratom	ILO (Labor Org)	26 Jan 61	IGO Operations	390UNTS323	200580
Euratom	Netherlands	25 Jul 61	Scientific Project	462UNTS263	106686
Euratom	Netherlands	25 Jul 61	IGO Status/Immunit	462UNTS313	106687
Euratom	UK Great Britain	04 Feb 59	Atomic Energy	331UNTS125	104752
Euratom	UK Great Britain	11 Jul 66	Taxation	639UNTS99	109147
Euratom	USA (United States)	29 May 58	Atomic Energy	335UNTS161	104783
Euratom	USA (United States)	08 Nov 58	Atomic Energy	338UNTS135	104835
Eurocontrol	Austria	31 Mar 71	Air Transport	72ABGB56	403044
Eurocontrol	Germany, West	08 Sep 70	Admin Cooperation	71WGBB1153	425748
Export-Import Bank	Japan	06 Jul 55	Loans and Credits	0JGJI1234	441145
Export-Import Bank	Japan	10 Aug 56	Loans and Credits	0JGJI1300	441147
FAO (Food Agri)	Australia	07 Jul 52	Tech Assistance	184UNTS209	102449
FAO (Food Agri)	Australia	08 Jul 57	Tech Assistance	277UNTS315	104015
FAO (Food Agri)	IAEA (Atom Energy)	01 Oct 58	IGO Operations	361UNTS211	200571
FAO (Food Agri)	ILO (Labor Org)	11 Sep 47	IGO Operations	18UNTS335	200111
FAO (Food Agri)	IMCO (Maritime Org)	11 Jul 66	IGO Operations	575UNTS238	200627
FAO (Food Agri)	Japan	22 Jan 69	Direct Aid	69JJS561	442231
FAO (Food Agri)	Multilateral	29 Nov 48	IGO Establishment	120UNTS13	101613
FAO (Food Agri)	Multilateral	02 Nov 50	Tech Assistance	81UNTS160	101071
FAO (Food Agri)	Multilateral	24 Nov 50	Tech Assistance	81UNTS188	101072
FAO (Food Agri)	Multilateral	15 Dec 50	Tech Assistance	76UNTS120	100985
FAO (Food Agri)	Multilateral	18 Jan 51	Tech Assistance	81UNTS233	101073
FAO (Food Agri)	Multilateral	15 Feb 51	Tech Assistance	81UNTS245	101074
FAO (Food Agri)	Multilateral	05 Mar 51	Tech Assistance	81UNTS261	101075
FAO (Food Agri)	Multilateral	20 Mar 51	IGO Operations	82UNTS172	101091
FAO (Food Agri)	Multilateral	01 Jun 51	Tech Assistance	118UNTS57	101596
FAO (Food Agri)	Multilateral	25 Jun 51	Tech Assistance	92UNTS27	101258
FAO (Food Agri)	Multilateral	28 Jun 51	Tech Assistance	118UNTS154	101604
FAO (Food Agri)	Multilateral	27 Jul 51	Tech Assistance	97UNTS291	200273
FAO (Food Agri)	Multilateral	04 Aug 51	Sanitation	104UNTS197	101441
FAO (Food Agri)	Multilateral	05 Sep 51	Tech Assistance	173UNTS15	102256
FAO (Food Agri)	Multilateral	01 Oct 51	Tech Assistance	104UNTS249	101446
FAO (Food Agri)	Multilateral	24 Dec 51	Tech Assistance	118UNTS290	200383
FAO (Food Agri)	Multilateral	18 Feb 52	Tech Assistance	126UNTS319	200434
FAO (Food Agri)	Multilateral	11 Apr 52	Tech Assistance	173UNTS2	102255
FAO (Food Agri)	Multilateral	22 May 52	Tech Assistance	131UNTS115	101739
FAO (Food Agri)	Multilateral	19 Jun 52	Tech Assistance	133UNTS165	101787
FAO (Food Agri)	Multilateral	15 Oct 52	Tech Assistance	141UNTS96	101909
FAO (Food Agri)	Multilateral	20 Apr 54	Tech Assistance	189UNTS11	102539
FAO (Food Agri)	Multilateral	31 May 54	Tech Assistance	192UNTS20	102592
FAO (Food Agri)	Multilateral	01 Jun 54	Tech Assistance	200UNTS235	200520
FAO (Food Agri)	Multilateral	30 Jun 54	Tech Assistance	193UNTS67	102611
FAO (Food Agri)	Multilateral	19 Aug 54	Tech Assistance	201UNTS51	102710
FAO (Food Agri)	Multilateral	06 Oct 54	Tech Assistance	201UNTS75	102711
FAO (Food Agri)	Multilateral	27 Oct 54	Tech Assistance	201UNTS95	102712
FAO (Food Agri)	Multilateral	29 Oct 54	Tech Assistance	201UNTS115	102713
FAO (Food Agri)	Multilateral	16 Dec 54	Tech Assistance	204UNTS323	200523
FAO (Food Agri)	Multilateral	04 Apr 55	Tech Assistance	208UNTS239	102816
FAO (Food Agri)	Multilateral	04 Jul 55	Tech Assistance	214UNTS10	102897
FAO (Food Agri)	Multilateral	13 Dec 55	Tech Assistance	407UNTS8	105857

PARTY ONE	PARTY TWO	DATE	TOPIC	CITATION	NUMBER
FAO (Food Agri)	Multilateral	02 Feb 56	Tech Assistance	227UNTS153	103137
FAO (Food Agri)	Multilateral	10 Feb 56	Tech Assistance	228UNTS167	103150
FAO (Food Agri)	Multilateral	10 Feb 56	Tech Assistance	228UNTS189	103151
FAO (Food Agri)	Multilateral	30 Mar 56	IGO Operations	604UNTS114	108748
FAO (Food Agri)	Multilateral	10 May 56	Tech Assistance	243UNTS103	103449
FAO (Food Agri)	Multilateral	31 May 56	Tech Assistance	251UNTS181	103541
FAO (Food Agri)	Multilateral	08 Jun 56	Tech Assistance	247UNTS366	200541
FAO (Food Agri)	Multilateral	12 Jun 56	Tech Assistance	243UNTS187	103453
FAO (Food Agri)	Multilateral	14 Jun 56	Tech Assistance	265UNTS125	103809
FAO (Food Agri)	Multilateral	26 Jun 56	Tech Assistance	321UNTS2	104650
FAO (Food Agri)	Multilateral	26 Jun 56	Tech Assistance	253UNTS12	103573
FAO (Food Agri)	Multilateral	02 Jul 56	Tech Assistance	248UNTS37	103484
FAO (Food Agri)	Multilateral	02 Jul 56	Tech Assistance	540UNTS110	107846
FAO (Food Agri)	Multilateral	31 Aug 56	Tech Assistance	249UNTS158	103506
FAO (Food Agri)	Multilateral	05 Oct 56	Tech Assistance	251UNTS267	103545
FAO (Food Agri)	Multilateral	05 Oct 56	Tech Assistance	251UNTS245	103544
FAO (Food Agri)	Multilateral	21 Nov 56	Tech Assistance	253UNTS266	103588
FAO (Food Agri)	Multilateral	15 Jan 57	Tech Assistance	376UNTS122	105378
FAO (Food Agri)	Multilateral	23 Jan 57	Tech Assistance	259UNTS426	103701
FAO (Food Agri)	Multilateral	17 Feb 57	Tech Assistance	271UNTS2	103907
FAO (Food Agri)	Multilateral	01 Mar 57	Tech Assistance	264UNTS94	103790
FAO (Food Agri)	Multilateral	28 Mar 57	Tech Assistance	271UNTS30	103908
FAO (Food Agri)	Multilateral	09 Apr 57	Tech Assistance	274UNTS172	103965
FAO (Food Agri)	Multilateral	24 May 57	Tech Assistance	268UNTS270	103861
FAO (Food Agri)	Multilateral	30 Jun 57	Tech Assistance	286UNTS171	104165
FAO (Food Agri)	Multilateral	09 Jul 57	Tech Assistance	274UNTS300	103972
FAO (Food Agri)	Multilateral	05 Nov 57	Tech Assistance	285UNTS301	104155
FAO (Food Agri)	Multilateral	15 Mar 58	Tech Assistance	292UNTS273	104276
FAO (Food Agri)	Multilateral	19 Jun 58	Tech Assistance	306UNTS236	200550
FAO (Food Agri)	Multilateral	09 Oct 59	Tech Assistance	376UNTS382	105391
FAO (Food Agri)	Multilateral	18 Nov 59	IGO Establishment	390UNTS227	105610
FAO (Food Agri)	Multilateral	03 Dec 59	Tech Assistance	348UNTS246	105003
FAO (Food Agri)	Multilateral	12 Apr 60	Tech Assistance	359UNTS323	105150
FAO (Food Agri)	Multilateral	04 Jun 60	Tech Assistance	360UNTS208	105159
FAO (Food Agri)	Multilateral	19 Jun 60	IGO Operations	537UNTS214	107803
FAO (Food Agri)	Multilateral	08 Jul 60	Tech Assistance	366UNTS310	105220
FAO (Food Agri)	Multilateral	28 Jan 61	Tech Assistance	387UNTS202	105563
FAO (Food Agri)	Multilateral	20 Sep 61	Tech Assistance	407UNTS52	105859
FAO (Food Agri)	Multilateral	16 Oct 61	Tech Assistance	410UNTS242	105908
FAO (Food Agri)	Multilateral	07 Nov 61	Tech Assistance	412UNTS258	105937
FAO (Food Agri)	Multilateral	27 Dec 61	Tech Assistance	425UNTS83	106120
FAO (Food Agri)	Multilateral	17 Jan 62	Tech Assistance	419UNTS294	106033
FAO (Food Agri)	Multilateral	20 Jan 62	Tech Assistance	429UNTS230	200596
FAO (Food Agri)	Multilateral	13 Feb 62	Tech Assistance	422UNTS288	200594
FAO (Food Agri)	Multilateral	21 Feb 62	Tech Assistance	423UNTS151	106091
FAO (Food Agri)	Multilateral	01 Mar 62	Tech Assistance	423UNTS122	106089
FAO (Food Agri)	Multilateral	10 Apr 62	Tech Assistance	429UNTS78	106192
FAO (Food Agri)	Multilateral	18 Apr 62	Tech Assistance	463UNTS44	106692
FAO (Food Agri)	Multilateral	17 May 62	Tech Assistance	429UNTS46	106189
FAO (Food Agri)	Multilateral	12 Aug 62	Tech Assistance	443UNTS266	106365
FAO (Food Agri)	Multilateral	29 Aug 62	Tech Assistance	443UNTS280	106366
FAO (Food Agri)	Multilateral	11 Sep 62	Tech Assistance	455UNTS402	106553
FAO (Food Agri)	Multilateral	14 Sep 62	Visas	443UNTS73	106360
FAO (Food Agri)	Multilateral	15 Nov 62	Tech Assistance	448UNTS50	106424
FAO (Food Agri)	Multilateral	06 Dec 62	Tech Assistance	450UNTS240	106471
FAO (Food Agri)	Multilateral	12 Dec 62	Tech Assistance	457UNTS72	106578
FAO (Food Agri)	Multilateral	21 Jan 63	Tech Assistance	453UNTS20	106517
FAO (Food Agri)	Multilateral	05 Feb 63	Tech Assistance	453UNTS36	106518
FAO (Food Agri)	Multilateral	14 Feb 63	Tech Assistance	453UNTS168	106524
FAO (Food Agri)	Multilateral	06 Mar 63	Tech Assistance	455UNTS386	106552
FAO (Food Agri)	Multilateral	18 Apr 63	Tech Assistance	463UNTS121	106697
FAO (Food Agri)	Multilateral	06 May 63	Tech Assistance	463UNTS78	106694
FAO (Food Agri)	Multilateral	09 May 63	Tech Assistance	463UNTS159	106700
FAO (Food Agri)	Multilateral	22 May 63	Tech Assistance	483UNTS72	107007
FAO (Food Agri)	Multilateral	24 May 63	Tech Assistance	466UNTS346	106754
FAO (Food Agri)	Multilateral	24 May 63	Tech Assistance	470UNTS208	106810
FAO (Food Agri)	Multilateral	23 Jul 63	Tech Assistance	471UNTS158	106831
FAO (Food Agri)	Multilateral	31 Jul 63	Tech Assistance	472UNTS220	106842
FAO (Food Agri)	Multilateral	27 Aug 63	Tech Assistance	511UNTS210	107435
FAO (Food Agri)	Multilateral	10 Sep 63	Tech Assistance	480UNTS100	106965
FAO (Food Agri)	Multilateral	30 Oct 63	Tech Assistance	480UNTS180	106968
FAO (Food Agri)	Multilateral	07 Nov 63	Tech Assistance	480UNTS232	106971
FAO (Food Agri)	Multilateral	08 Nov 63	Tech Assistance	482UNTS286	106999
FAO (Food Agri)	Multilateral	03 Dec 63	IGO Establishment	529UNTS217	107663
FAO (Food Agri)	Multilateral	28 Jan 64	Tech Assistance	502UNTS321	107336
FAO (Food Agri)	Multilateral	20 Feb 64	Tech Assistance	491UNTS30	107172
FAO (Food Agri)	Multilateral	23 Jun 64	Tech Assistance	506UNTS108	107383
FAO (Food Agri)	Multilateral	28 Jun 64	Tech Assistance	519UNTS14	107499
FAO (Food Agri)	Multilateral	03 Aug 64	Tech Assistance	503UNTS239	107347
FAO (Food Agri)	Multilateral	24 Oct 64	Tech Assistance	514UNTS220	200608
FAO (Food Agri)	Multilateral	11 Nov 64	Tech Assistance	515UNTS94	107456
FAO (Food Agri)	Multilateral	11 Dec 64	IGO Operations	547UNTS297	107964
FAO (Food Agri)	Multilateral	15 Dec 64	Tech Assistance	522UNTS20	107533
FAO (Food Agri)	Multilateral	27 Jan 65	Tech Assistance	523UNTS102	107556
FAO (Food Agri)	Multilateral	02 Feb 65	Tech Assistance	523UNTS256	107560
FAO (Food Agri)	Multilateral	12 Feb 65	Tech Assistance	525UNTS148	107587
FAO (Food Agri)	Multilateral	23 Feb 65	IGO Operations	527UNTS120	107622
FAO (Food Agri)	Multilateral	05 Mar 65	IGO Operations	527UNTS221	107627
FAO (Food Agri)	Multilateral	08 Apr 65	IGO Operations	533UNTS66	107733
FAO (Food Agri)	Multilateral	26 Apr 65	IGO Operations	533UNTS50	107732
FAO (Food Agri)	Multilateral	12 May 65	IGO Operations	534UNTS390	107769
FAO (Food Agri)	Multilateral	14 May 65	IGO Operations	550UNTS310	108026
FAO (Food Agri)	Multilateral	25 May 65	IGO Operations	535UNTS374	107791
FAO (Food Agri)	Multilateral	02 Jun 65	Tech Assistance	537UNTS348	200611
FAO (Food Agri)	Multilateral	02 Jun 65	Tech Assistance	551UNTS2	108030
FAO (Food Agri)	Multilateral	05 Jul 65	General Aid	563UNTS104	108207
FAO (Food Agri)	Multilateral	20 Jul 65	IGO Operations	541UNTS12	107857
FAO (Food Agri)	Multilateral	13 Sep 65	IGO Operations	547UNTS248	107961
FAO (Food Agri)	Multilateral	13 Sep 65	Tech Assistance	547UNTS264	107962
FAO (Food Agri)	Multilateral	21 Sep 65	IGO Operations	547UNTS280	107963
FAO (Food Agri)	Multilateral	21 Oct 65	Tech Assistance	547UNTS216	107959
FAO (Food Agri)	Multilateral	12 Nov 65	IGO Operations	550UNTS160	108013
FAO (Food Agri)	Multilateral	31 Dec 65	Recognition	552UNTS292	108060
FAO (Food Agri)	Multilateral	12 May 66	General Aid	563UNTS54	108204
FAO (Food Agri)	Multilateral	06 Aug 66	Tech Assistance	570UNTS178	108294
FAO (Food Agri)	Multilateral	22 Aug 66	Tech Assistance	571UNTS298	200624
FAO (Food Agri)	Multilateral	23 Sep 66	IGO Operations	573UNTS132	108327
FAO (Food Agri)	Multilateral	23 Sep 66	General Aid	573UNTS148	108328
FAO (Food Agri)	Multilateral	30 Sep 66	IGO Operations	576UNTS8	108361
FAO (Food Agri)	Multilateral	17 Nov 66	IGO Operations	580UNTS22	108417
FAO (Food Agri)	Multilateral	25 Jan 67	IGO Operations	588UNTS212	108527
FAO (Food Agri)	Multilateral	27 Feb 67	IGO Operations	590UNTS156	108552
FAO (Food Agri)	Multilateral	13 Apr 67	IGO Operations	595UNTS60	108612
FAO (Food Agri)	Multilateral	19 Apr 67	Tech Assistance	595UNTS120	108617
FAO (Food Agri)	Multilateral	10 Jun 67	Direct Aid	602UNTS212	108714
FAO (Food Agri)	Multilateral	14 Jun 67	Direct Aid	603UNTS2	108719
FAO (Food Agri)	Multilateral	20 Jun 67	Tech Assistance	0UNTS0	109290
FAO (Food Agri)	Multilateral	21 Jun 67	Tech Assistance	598UNTS2	108653
FAO (Food Agri)	Multilateral	12 Oct 67	Direct Aid	607UNTS2	108792
FAO (Food Agri)	Multilateral	12 Oct 67	Direct Aid	607UNTS20	108793
FAO (Food Agri)	Multilateral	27 Oct 67	General Aid	608UNTS37	108811
FAO (Food Agri)	Multilateral	14 Nov 67	Admin Cooperation	614UNTS2	108860
FAO (Food Agri)	Multilateral	18 Jun 69	IGO Operations	0UNTS0	109740
FAO (Food Agri)	Multilateral	18 Jun 69	IGO Operations	0UNTS0	109741
FAO (Food Agri)	Multilateral	24 Jun 69	IGO Operations	0UNTS0	109743
FAO (Food Agri)	Multilateral	26 Sep 70	IGO Operations	0UNTS0	110768
FAO (Food Agri)	Philippines	03 Apr 52	Tech Assistance	2PTS785	465073
FAO (Food Agri)	Philippines	30 Oct 52	Tech Assistance	3PTS36	465075
FAO (Food Agri)	Philippines	14 Nov 52	Tech Assistance	3PTS49	465078
FAO (Food Agri)	Philippines	25 Jun 53	Tech Assistance	3PTS165	465081

PARTY ONE	PARTY TWO	DATE	TOPIC	CITATION	NUMBER
FAO (Food Agri)	Turkey	14 Apr 51	Tech Assistance	51TURG407	466134
FAO (Food Agri)	UK Great Britain	24 Apr 58	IGO Operations	642UNTS245	109177
FAO (Food Agri)	UK Great Britain	20 Feb 61	IGO Operations	642UNTS253	109178
FAO (Food Agri)	UK Great Britain	13 Jul 67	IGO Operations	642UNTS263	109179
FAO (Food Agri)	UN Special Fund	28 Sep 59	IGO Operations	341UNTS353	200562
FAO (Food Agri)	UNESCO (Educ/Cult)	23 Aug 48	IGO Operations	18UNTS345	200112
FAO (Food Agri)	UNESCO (Educ/Cult)	09 Feb 49	IGO Operations	43UNTS315	200182
FAO (Food Agri)	United Nations	03 Feb 47	IGO Operations	1UNTS207	200010
FAO (Food Agri)	United Nations	02 Aug 50	IGO Operations	139UNTS407	200467
FAO (Food Agri)	USA (United States)	29 Mar 62	IGO Operations	454UNTS13	106536
FAO (Food Agri)	USA (United States)	26 May 67	Direct Aid	0UNTS0	109901
FAO (Food Agri)	Vietnam, South	28 Jan 53	Tech Assistance	0VKNG52	496010
FAO (Food Agri)	WHO (World Health)	17 Jul 48	IGO Operations	76UNTS171	200244
Fed of Malaya	Accept UN Charter	31 Aug 57	UN Charter	277UNTS3	103995
Fed of Malaya	Australia	26 Aug 58	General Trade	325UNTS253	104703
Fed of Malaya	Australia	29 Sep 59	Air Transport	357UNTS29	105104
Fed of Malaya	Australia	26 Nov 62	Specif Goods/Equip	453UNTS161	106523
Fed of Malaya	Belgium	19 Jul 60	Visas	379UNTS391	105445
Fed of Malaya	IBRD (World Bank)	22 Sep 58	IBRD Project	323UNTS71	104665
Fed of Malaya	Japan	10 May 60	General Trade	383UNTS293	105506
Fed of Malaya	Multilateral	07 Dec 44	IGO Establishment	15UNTS295	200102
Fed of Malaya	Multilateral	07 Dec 44	Air Transport	84UNTS389	200252
Fed of Malaya	Multilateral	11 Dec 46	Sanitation	12UNTS179	100186
Fed of Malaya	Multilateral	27 May 47	Air Transport	418UNTS161	106021
Fed of Malaya	Multilateral	12 Nov 47	Admin Cooperation	46UNTS201	100710
Fed of Malaya	Multilateral	11 May 48	Telecommunications	500UNTS267	107313
Fed of Malaya	Multilateral	24 Jul 48	Sanitation	66UNTS25	100847
Fed of Malaya	Multilateral	15 Nov 48	IGO Establishment	120UNTS59	101615
Fed of Malaya	Multilateral	29 Nov 48	IGO Establishment	120UNTS13	101613
Fed of Malaya	Multilateral	04 May 49	Admin Cooperation	47UNTS159	100728
Fed of Malaya	Multilateral	06 Dec 51	Admin Cooperation	150UNTS67	101963
Fed of Malaya	Multilateral	07 Nov 52	General Trade	221UNTS255	103010
Fed of Malaya	Multilateral	14 May 54	Culture	249UNTS215	103511
Fed of Malaya	Multilateral	14 Jun 54	Air Transport	320UNTS217	104644
Fed of Malaya	Multilateral	14 Jun 54	Air Transport	320UNTS209	104643
Fed of Malaya	Multilateral	25 May 55	IGO Establishment	264UNTS117	103791
Fed of Malaya	Multilateral	20 Feb 57	Consul/Citizenship	309UNTS65	104468
Fed of Malaya	Multilateral	03 Oct 57	Postal Service	364UNTS3	105211
Fed of Malaya	Multilateral	03 Oct 57	Postal Service	364UNTS331	105212
Fed of Malaya	Multilateral	29 Apr 58	Dispute Settlement	450UNTS169	106466
Fed of Malaya	Multilateral	26 Jan 60	IGO Establishment	439UNTS249	106333
Fed of Malaya	Multilateral	01 Sep 60	Commodity Trade	403UNTS3	105792
Fed of Malaya	Multilateral	21 Jun 61	IGO Establishment	514UNTS209	107449
Fed of Malaya	Multilateral	01 Mar 62	Tech Assistance	423UNTS122	106089
Fed of Malaya	Multilateral	16 Oct 62	Postal Service	470UNTS321	106815
Fed of Malaya	Multilateral	16 Oct 62	Postal Service	470UNTS336	106816
Fed of Malaya	Multilateral	16 Oct 62	Postal Service	470UNTS291	106814
Fed of Malaya	Multilateral	31 Jul 63	General Amity	550UNTS343	108029
Fed of Malaya	Multilateral	05 Aug 63	Sanitation	480UNTS43	106964
Fed of Malaya	UK Great Britain	12 Sep 57	Recognition	279UNTS287	104046
Fed of Malaya	UK Great Britain	12 Oct 57	Milit Assistance	285UNTS59	104149
Fed of Malaya	UK Great Britain	18 Oct 57	Air Transport	335UNTS3	104775
Fed of Malaya	UK Great Britain	04 Mar 58	Admin Cooperation	314UNTS253	104550
Fed of Malaya	UK Great Britain	08 Nov 58	Recognition	327UNTS301	104728
Fed of Malaya	UK Great Britain	01 May 59	Loans and Credits	345UNTS57	104958
Fed of Malaya	UK Great Britain	27 Jul 59	Non-ILO Labor	374UNTS21	105324
Fed of Malaya	UK Great Britain	07 Jun 60	Scientific Project	375UNTS141	105365
Fed of Malaya	UK Great Britain	11 Sep 63	Admin Cooperation	0UNTS0	110761
Fed of Malaya	UN Special Fund	25 Jul 61	Direct Aid	401UNTS159	105769
Fed of Malaya	United Nations	29 May 58	Tech Assistance	330UNTS109	104742
Fed of Malaya	USA (United States)	09 Jul 58	Milit Assistance	336UNTS79	104799
Fed of Malaya	USA (United States)	21 Apr 59	Admin Cooperation	343UNTS3	104916
Fed of Malaya	USA (United States)	22 May 59	Tech Assistance	346UNTS263	104985
Fed of Malaya	USA (United States)	04 Sep 61	Direct Aid	421UNTS215	106060
Fed of Malaya	WHO (World Health)	25 Nov 60	Tech Assistance	387UNTS37	105556

PARTY ONE	PARTY TWO	DATE	TOPIC	CITATION	NUMBER
Fed Rhod/Nyasaland	Australia	30 Jun 55	General Trade	226UNTS215	103115
Fed Rhod/Nyasaland	Canada	06 Feb 58	General Trade	392UNTS27	105636
Fed Rhod/Nyasaland	IBRD (World Bank)	21 Jun 56	IBRD Project	285UNTS317	104156
Fed Rhod/Nyasaland	Multilateral	11 May 48	Telecommunications	500UNTS267	107313
Fed Rhod/Nyasaland	Multilateral	07 Nov 52	General Trade	221UNTS255	103010
Fed Rhod/Nyasaland	Multilateral	18 Jan 54	IGO Establishment	330UNTS121	104743
Fed Rhod/Nyasaland	Multilateral	29 Jul 54	Sanitation	249UNTS45	103500
Fed Rhod/Nyasaland	Multilateral	02 Oct 54	IBRD Project	201UNTS179	102717
Fed Rhod/Nyasaland	Multilateral	02 Oct 54	IBRD Project	201UNTS171	102716
Fed Rhod/Nyasaland	Multilateral	06 Apr 59	Commodity Trade	349UNTS167	105013
Fed Rhod/Nyasaland	Multilateral	15 May 62	Commodity Trade	444UNTS3	106367
Fed Rhod/Nyasaland	Netherlands	02 Nov 55	Non-ILO Labor	263UNTS381	103784
Fed Rhod/Nyasaland	Norway	18 Jun 66	Taxation	580UNTS9	108415
Fed Rhod/Nyasaland	Portugal	29 Nov 58	General Trade	354UNTS137	105060
Fed Rhod/Nyasaland	South Africa	28 Jun 53	General Trade	267UNTS270	103848
Fed Rhod/Nyasaland	South Africa	22 May 56	Taxation	254UNTS227	103595
Fed Rhod/Nyasaland	South Africa	30 May 56	Air Transport	255UNTS317	103615
Fed Rhod/Nyasaland	South Africa	11 Oct 58	Non-ILO Labor	373UNTS75	105315
Fed Rhod/Nyasaland	South Africa	16 May 60	General Trade	376UNTS217	105381
Fed Rhod/Nyasaland	South Africa	19 Nov 62	Extradition	458UNTS59	106592
Fiji Islands	Accept UN Charter	10 Oct 70	UN Charter	0UNTS0	110789
Fiji Islands	Multilateral	07 Nov 64	Sanitation	548UNTS3	107965
Fiji Islands	Multilateral	24 Dec 68	Commodity Trade	0UNTS0	109369
Fiji Islands	State/IGO Group	13 Oct 70	General Aid	0UNTS0	110791
Fiji Islands	State/IGO Group	30 Oct 70	Tech Assistance	0UNTS0	110790
Fiji Islands	UN Special Fund	13 Oct 70	IGO Operations	0UNTS0	110792
Finland	Argentina	08 May 63	Milit Servic/Citiz	482UNTS309	107000
Finland	Australia	07 Jan 49	Admin Cooperation	189UNTS227	102547
Finland	Australia	04 Jan 51	Claims and Debts	80UNTS27	101042
Finland	Australia	21 Feb 61	Visas	390UNTS61	105602
Finland	Australia	31 Jul 63	Admin Cooperation	478UNTS363	106942
Finland	Austria	05 Nov 54	Visas	56ABGB47	403045
Finland	Austria	01 Feb 62	Non-ILO Labor	425UNTS33	106116
Finland	Austria	08 Oct 63	Taxation	490UNTS255	107160
Finland	Austria	23 Jul 64	Taxation	65ABGB117	403046
Finland	Austria	09 Dec 65	Admin Cooperation	69ABGB3	403047
Finland	Austria	09 Dec 65	Education	0UNTS0	109462
Finland	Austria	21 Feb 66	Claims and Debts	597UNTS273	108651
Finland	Austria	04 Jun 69	Air Transport	69ABGB257	403048
Finland	Austria	04 Jun 69	Air Transport	0UNTS0	109886
Finland	Austria	21 Sep 70	Taxation	72ABGB110	403049
Finland	Belgium	09 Feb 50	Visas	51UNTS77	100753
Finland	Belgium	20 Mar 51	Non-ILO Labor	110UNTS27	101498
Finland	Belgium	11 Feb 54	Taxation	211UNTS63	102848
Finland	Belgium	15 Nov 68	Land Transport	0UNTS0	109673
Finland	Bulgaria	14 Dec 67	Visas	0UNTS0	109969
Finland	Bulgaria	19 Mar 68	Sanitation	0UNTS0	109970
Finland	Bulgaria	14 Nov 69	Scientific Project	0UNTS0	110550
Finland	Bulgaria	19 Mar 70	Air Transport	0UNTS0	110611
Finland	Canada	17 Nov 48	General Trade	231UNTS75	103207
Finland	Canada	09 Jan 56	Visas	305UNTS33	104410
Finland	Canada	09 Dec 58	Visas	323UNTS331	104674
Finland	Canada	28 Mar 59	Taxation	355UNTS3	105072
Finland	Canada	05 Jun 63	Water Transport	472UNTS345	106846
Finland	Ceylon (Sri Lanka)	08 Jan 64	Water Transport	492UNTS285	107198
Finland	China People's Rep	05 Jun 53	Finance	53CCJC32	410106
Finland	China People's Rep	05 Jun 53	General Trade	53CCJC30	410105
Finland	China People's Rep	17 Jun 54	General Trade	54CCJC36	410156
Finland	China People's Rep	21 Jun 54	General Trade	54CCJC37	410157
Finland	China People's Rep	08 Aug 55	General Trade	55CCJC54	410247
Finland	China People's Rep	31 Mar 56	Mostfavored Nation	56CCJC44	410326
Finland	China People's Rep	31 Jul 56	General Trade	56CCJC91	410355
Finland	China People's Rep	18 Dec 57	General Trade	57CCJC119	410472
Finland	China People's Rep	15 May 59	General Trade	59CCJC76	410622
Finland	China People's Rep	16 Dec 59	General Trade	59CCJC111	410650

PARTY ONE	PARTY TWO	DATE	TOPIC	CITATION	NUMBER
Finland	China People's Rep	11 Apr 61	General Trade	61CCJC55	410784
Finland	China People's Rep	29 Mar 62	General Trade	62CCJC30	410878
Finland	China People's Rep	29 May 63	General Trade	63CCJC68	410983
Finland	China People's Rep	28 Oct 63	General Trade	63CCJC126	411025
Finland	China People's Rep	24 Mar 65	General Trade	65CCJC43	411152
Finland	China People's Rep	23 Nov 65	General Trade	65CCJC145	411153
Finland	China People's Rep	26 Jan 67	Patents/Copyrights	67CCJC2	411155
Finland	China People's Rep	25 Apr 67	General Trade	67CCJC16	411156
Finland	Czechoslovakia	13 Jul 49	Air Transport	53UNTS153	100779
Finland	Denmark	22 Mar 49	Finance	33UNTS247	100520
Finland	Denmark	26 Aug 49	Air Transport	53UNTS191	100781
Finland	Denmark	21 Dec 49	Visas	46UNTS125	100705
Finland	Denmark	08 Jul 50	General Trade	73UNTS191	100953
Finland	Denmark	24 Sep 53	Dispute Settlement	188UNTS283	102532
Finland	Denmark	18 Jul 55	Taxation	250UNTS149	103521
Finland	Denmark	18 Jul 55	Taxation	250UNTS167	103522
Finland	Denmark	15 Sep 56	General Transport	254UNTS3	103589
Finland	Denmark	27 Mar 61	Commodity Trade	630UNTS3	108961
Finland	Denmark	07 Apr 64	Taxation	525UNTS89	107586
Finland	Ethiopia	25 Nov 68	Tech Assistance	0UNTS0	109674
Finland	France	15 Apr 50	Education	50FRJO206	416188
Finland	France	25 Aug 58	Taxation	59FRRT28	415190
Finland	France	25 Aug 58	Taxation	59FRRT28	415189
Finland	France	12 Oct 62	Air Transport	498UNTS299	107285
Finland	France	27 Oct 67	General Transport	643UNTS75	109185
Finland	France	31 Mar 69	Taxation	0UNTS0	110035
Finland	Germany, East	15 Oct 49	General Trade	1EGDA498	419099
Finland	Germany, East	25 Jan 56	Finance	3EGDA646	419100
Finland	Germany, East	10 Mar 57	General Economic	5EGDA790	419101
Finland	Germany, East	09 Feb 59	Finance	7EGDA356	419102
Finland	Germany, East	25 Feb 59	Finance	7EGDA357	419103
Finland	Germany, East	23 Aug 66	Sanitation	40EGDZ366	420104
Finland	Germany, West	16 Apr 52	General Economic	52WBGA81	424131
Finland	Germany, West	25 Sep 62	Land Transport	62WBGA217	424132
Finland	Germany, West	03 Dec 69	General Economic	70WBGA31	424133
Finland	Greece	24 Mar 49	Finance	78UNTS13	101009
Finland	Greece	24 Mar 49	General Trade	78UNTS3	101008
Finland	Hungary	10 Jun 59	Culture	439UNTS3	106321
Finland	Hungary	13 Feb 62	Air Transport	463UNTS61	106693
Finland	Hungary	10 Nov 67	Land Transport	643UNTS95	109186
Finland	Hungary	01 Oct 69	General Economic	0UNTS0	110481
Finland	Hungary	01 Oct 69	Visas	0UNTS0	110358
Finland	IAEA (Atom Energy)	30 Dec 60	Atomic Energy	395UNTS257	105690
Finland	IAEA (Atom Energy)	02 Jul 63	Atomic Energy	490UNTS403	107167
Finland	IAEA (Atom Energy)	30 Jul 63	Atomic Energy	490UNTS413	107168
Finland	IAEA (Atom Energy)	27 Jan 64	Scientific Project	501UNTS213	107319
Finland	IBRD (World Bank)	01 Aug 49	IBRD Project	156UNTS289	200480
Finland	IBRD (World Bank)	17 Oct 49	IBRD Project	156UNTS355	200481
Finland	IBRD (World Bank)	30 Apr 52	IBRD Project	159UNTS408	200483
Finland	IBRD (World Bank)	24 Mar 55	IBRD Project	211UNTS305	200525
Finland	IBRD (World Bank)	22 May 56	IBRD Project	248UNTS57	103485
Finland	IBRD (World Bank)	16 Mar 59	IBRD Project	337UNTS269	104826
Finland	IBRD (World Bank)	09 Aug 61	IBRD Project	415UNTS204	105986
Finland	IBRD (World Bank)	15 Aug 62	IBRD Project	467UNTS177	106763
Finland	IBRD (World Bank)	18 Sep 63	IBRD Project	491UNTS345	107183
Finland	IBRD (World Bank)	10 Jul 64	IBRD Project	516UNTS125	107474
Finland	IBRD (World Bank)	30 Jun 65	IBRD Project	550UNTS63	108009
Finland	IBRD (World Bank)	27 Apr 66	IBRD Project	568UNTS107	108266
Finland	IBRD (World Bank)	24 Jan 69	IBRD Project	0UNTS0	109596
Finland	Iceland	10 Mar 60	Air Transport	497UNTS95	107264
Finland	ICJ Option Clause	26 Feb 54	Dispute Settlement	189UNTS223	102546
Finland	ICJ Option Clause	25 Jun 58	ICJ Option Clause	303UNTS137	104376
Finland	India	14 Jun 57	Tech Assistance	277UNTS327	104016
Finland	India	23 Jun 61	Taxation	421UNTS49	106051
Finland	Iran	25 Apr 69	Visas	0IRTB29	433040

PARTY ONE	PARTY TWO	DATE	TOPIC	CITATION	NUMBER
Finland	Ireland	06 Jan 51	General Trade	558UNTS120	108140
Finland	Ireland	01 Feb 55	Visas	553UNTS45	108067
Finland	Ireland	15 Sep 65	Taxation	0UNTS0	109372
Finland	Ireland	15 Sep 65	Water Transport	604UNTS199	108750
Finland	Ireland	21 Apr 69	Taxation	0UNTS0	110818
Finland	Israel	16 Nov 55	Visas	257UNTS39	103647
Finland	Israel	21 Jan 65	Taxation	581UNTS275	108450
Finland	Israel	23 Feb 66	Visas	581UNTS219	108447
Finland	Italy	10 Apr 52	Consul/Citizenship	52ITDI295	436109
Finland	Italy	17 Dec 57	Finance	291UNTS133	104248
Finland	Italy	18 Feb 61	Non-ILO Labor	434UNTS199	106263
Finland	Japan	22 Dec 58	Visas	341UNTS41	104876
Finland	Luxembourg	15 Aug 61	Air Transport	541UNTS45	107859
Finland	Malta	08 Dec 65	Visas	561UNTS205	108183
Finland	Multilateral	27 Mar 41	Military Mission	67UNTS231	200222
Finland	Multilateral	02 Aug 44	Scientific Project	67UNTS221	200221
Finland	Multilateral	07 Dec 44	IGO Establishment	15UNTS295	200102
Finland	Multilateral	22 Jul 46	IGO Establishment	9UNTS3	100125
Finland	Multilateral	22 Jul 46	IGO Establishment	14UNTS185	100221
Finland	Multilateral	11 Dec 46	Sanitation	12UNTS179	100186
Finland	Multilateral	08 Feb 47	Patents/Copyrights	14UNTS287	100222
Finland	Multilateral	10 Feb 47	Peace/Disarmament	48UNTS203	100746
Finland	Multilateral	10 Jun 47	Water Transport	208UNTS3	102814
Finland	Multilateral	02 Oct 47	Telecommunications	193UNTS188	102616
Finland	Multilateral	11 Oct 47	IGO Establishment	77UNTS143	100998
Finland	Multilateral	12 Nov 47	Admin Cooperation	53UNTS49	100772
Finland	Multilateral	12 Nov 47	Admin Cooperation	53UNTS13	100770
Finland	Multilateral	12 Nov 47	Admin Cooperation	46UNTS201	100710
Finland	Multilateral	12 Nov 47	Admin Cooperation	46UNTS169	100709
Finland	Multilateral	12 Nov 47	Admin Cooperation	53UNTS39	100771
Finland	Multilateral	06 Mar 48	Water Transport	289UNTS3	104214
Finland	Multilateral	10 May 48	Culture	289UNTS111	104215
Finland	Multilateral	10 Jun 48	Humanitarian	191UNTS3	102576
Finland	Multilateral	10 Jun 48	Humanitarian	164UNTS113	102163
Finland	Multilateral	26 Jun 48	Culture	331UNTS217	104757
Finland	Multilateral	24 Jul 48	Sanitation	66UNTS25	100847
Finland	Multilateral	19 Nov 48	Sanitation	44UNTS277	100688
Finland	Multilateral	09 Dec 48	Scientific Project	73UNTS39	100942
Finland	Multilateral	09 Dec 48	Humanitarian	78UNTS277	101021
Finland	Multilateral	09 Dec 48	Scientific Project	20UNTS229	100318
Finland	Multilateral	04 May 49	Admin Cooperation	98UNTS101	101358
Finland	Multilateral	04 May 49	Admin Cooperation	30UNTS23	100446
Finland	Multilateral	04 May 49	Admin Cooperation	30UNTS3	100445
Finland	Multilateral	04 May 49	Admin Cooperation	92UNTS19	101257
Finland	Multilateral	04 May 49	Admin Cooperation	47UNTS159	100728
Finland	Multilateral	18 Jun 49	ILO Labor	605UNTS295	108768
Finland	Multilateral	12 Aug 49	Humanitarian	75UNTS287	100973
Finland	Multilateral	12 Aug 49	Humanitarian	75UNTS31	100970
Finland	Multilateral	12 Aug 49	General Military	75UNTS135	100972
Finland	Multilateral	12 Aug 49	Humanitarian	75UNTS85	100971
Finland	Multilateral	27 Aug 49	Non-ILO Labor	47UNTS127	100727
Finland	Multilateral	16 Dec 49	Admin Cooperation	72UNTS3	100924
Finland	Multilateral	13 May 50	Land Transport	128UNTS171	101719
Finland	Multilateral	16 Sep 50	General Transport	92UNTS91	101264
Finland	Multilateral	22 Nov 50	Culture	131UNTS25	101734
Finland	Multilateral	07 Dec 50	Admin Cooperation	212UNTS17	102861
Finland	Multilateral	09 Jan 51	Humanitarian	197UNTS341	102647
Finland	Multilateral	25 May 51	Status of Forces	175UNTS215	102303
Finland	Multilateral	02 Jul 51	Refugees	189UNTS137	102545
Finland	Multilateral	28 Aug 51	Non-ILO Labor	198UNTS17	102654
Finland	Multilateral	06 Dec 51	Admin Cooperation	150UNTS67	101963
Finland	Multilateral	20 May 52	Sanitation	219UNTS55	102966
Finland	Multilateral	11 Jul 52	IGO Establishment	169UNTS3	102220
Finland	Multilateral	11 Jul 52	Postal Service	170UNTS269	102223
Finland	Multilateral	11 Jul 52	Postal Service	171UNTS3	102224

PARTY ONE	PARTY TWO	DATE	TOPIC	CITATION	NUMBER
Finland	Multilateral	11 Jul 52	Postal Service	170UNTS3	102221
Finland	Multilateral	11 Jul 52	Postal Service	170UNTS63	102222
Finland	Multilateral	11 Jul 52	Postal Service	171UNTS89	102225
Finland	Multilateral	11 Jul 52	Postal Service	171UNTS143	102226
Finland	Multilateral	14 Jul 52	Visas	198UNTS37	102655
Finland	Multilateral	14 Jul 52	Consul/Citizenship	198UNTS47	102656
Finland	Multilateral	06 Sep 52	Patents/Copyrights	216UNTS132	102937
Finland	Multilateral	07 Nov 52	General Trade	221UNTS255	103010
Finland	Multilateral	07 Feb 53	Territory Boundary	173UNTS143	102264
Finland	Multilateral	27 Feb 53	Claims and Debts	333UNTS3	104764
Finland	Multilateral	23 Mar 53	Admin Cooperation	202UNTS241	102732
Finland	Multilateral	31 Mar 53	Privil/Immunities	193UNTS136	102613
Finland	Multilateral	01 Apr 53	Non-ILO Labor	227UNTS169	103138
Finland	Multilateral	20 Jul 53	Non-ILO Labor	228UNTS3	103141
Finland	Multilateral	20 Jul 53	Non-ILO Labor	228UNTS41	103142
Finland	Multilateral	07 Dec 53	Admin Cooperation	182UNTS51	102422
Finland	Multilateral	01 Mar 54	Admin Cooperation	286UNTS265	104173
Finland	Multilateral	12 May 54	Admin Cooperation	327UNTS3	104714
Finland	Multilateral	22 May 54	Non-ILO Labor	199UNTS3	102674
Finland	Multilateral	22 May 54	Visas	199UNTS29	102675
Finland	Multilateral	14 Jun 54	Air Transport	320UNTS217	104644
Finland	Multilateral	14 Jun 54	Air Transport	320UNTS209	104643
Finland	Multilateral	28 Sep 54	Refugees	360UNTS117	105158
Finland	Multilateral	19 Mar 55	Sanitation	228UNTS95	103144
Finland	Multilateral	25 May 55	IGO Establishment	264UNTS117	103791
Finland	Multilateral	15 Sep 55	Non-ILO Labor	254UNTS55	103593
Finland	Multilateral	12 Oct 55	IGO Establishment	560UNTS3	108165
Finland	Multilateral	24 Feb 56	Specific Resources	243UNTS147	103451
Finland	Multilateral	30 Apr 56	Air Transport	310UNTS229	104494
Finland	Multilateral	18 May 56	Customs	319UNTS21	104630
Finland	Multilateral	18 May 56	Customs	338UNTS103	104834
Finland	Multilateral	18 May 56	Land Transport	339UNTS3	104844
Finland	Multilateral	20 Jun 56	Admin Cooperation	268UNTS3	103850
Finland	Multilateral	15 Sep 56	Admin Cooperation	254UNTS45	103592
Finland	Multilateral	20 Feb 57	Consul/Citizenship	309UNTS65	104468
Finland	Multilateral	12 Jul 57	Visas	322UNTS245	104660
Finland	Multilateral	03 Oct 57	Postal Service	365UNTS3	105213
Finland	Multilateral	03 Oct 57	Postal Service	364UNTS3	105211
Finland	Multilateral	03 Oct 57	Postal Service	366UNTS87	105216
Finland	Multilateral	03 Oct 57	Postal Service	366UNTS141	105217
Finland	Multilateral	03 Oct 57	Postal Service	366UNTS255	105219
Finland	Multilateral	03 Oct 57	Postal Service	364UNTS331	105212
Finland	Multilateral	03 Oct 57	Postal Service	366UNTS3	105215
Finland	Multilateral	03 Oct 57	Postal Service	365UNTS207	105214
Finland	Multilateral	29 Apr 58	Water Transport	450UNTS11	106465
Finland	Multilateral	29 Apr 58	Dispute Settlement	450UNTS169	106466
Finland	Multilateral	29 Apr 58	Territory Boundary	516UNTS205	107477
Finland	Multilateral	29 Apr 58	Territory Boundary	499UNTS311	107302
Finland	Multilateral	29 Apr 58	Specific Resources	559UNTS285	108164
Finland	Multilateral	10 Jun 58	Admin Cooperation	330UNTS3	104739
Finland	Multilateral	05 Nov 58	Land Transport	428UNTS73	106169
Finland	Multilateral	29 Apr 59	Specific Property	346UNTS167	104980
Finland	Multilateral	08 Sep 59	Non-ILO Labor	383UNTS203	105502
Finland	Multilateral	26 Jan 60	IGO Establishment	439UNTS249	106333
Finland	Multilateral	22 Apr 60	Air Transport	418UNTS211	106023
Finland	Multilateral	17 Jun 60	Humanitarian	536UNTS27	107794
Finland	Multilateral	28 Jul 60	IGO Status/Immunit	394UNTS37	105667
Finland	Multilateral	06 Oct 60	Customs	473UNTS131	106861
Finland	Multilateral	09 Dec 60	Customs	429UNTS211	106200
Finland	Multilateral	30 Dec 60	Atomic Energy	395UNTS241	105689
Finland	Multilateral	27 Mar 61	IGO Establishment	420UNTS109	106043
Finland	Multilateral	30 Mar 61	Sanitation	520UNTS151	107515
Finland	Multilateral	18 Apr 61	Consul/Citizenship	500UNTS223	107311
Finland	Multilateral	18 Apr 61	Dispute Settlement	500UNTS243	107312
Finland	Multilateral	18 Apr 61	Consul/Citizenship	500UNTS95	107310
Finland	Multilateral	21 Apr 61	IGO Establishment	484UNTS349	107041
Finland	Multilateral	08 Jun 61	Customs	473UNTS153	106862
Finland	Multilateral	08 Jun 61	Customs	473UNTS187	106863
Finland	Multilateral	21 Jun 61	IGO Establishment	514UNTS209	107449
Finland	Multilateral	05 Oct 61	Dispute Settlement	510UNTS175	107413
Finland	Multilateral	05 Oct 61	Patents/Copyrights	527UNTS181	107625
Finland	Multilateral	26 Oct 61	Patents/Copyrights	496UNTS43	107247
Finland	Multilateral	06 Dec 61	Customs	473UNTS219	106864
Finland	Multilateral	20 Dec 61	Water Transport	419UNTS79	106031
Finland	Multilateral	23 Mar 62	Admin Cooperation	470UNTS25	106793
Finland	Multilateral	23 Mar 62	General Amity	434UNTS145	106262
Finland	Multilateral	18 Sep 62	Water Transport	442UNTS215	106351
Finland	Multilateral	10 Dec 62	Culture	521UNTS231	107525
Finland	Multilateral	15 Jan 63	Tech Assistance	456UNTS409	106567
Finland	Multilateral	24 Apr 63	Consul/Citizenship	596UNTS487	108640
Finland	Multilateral	24 Apr 63	Consul/Citizenship	596UNTS261	108638
Finland	Multilateral	05 Aug 63	Sanitation	480UNTS43	106964
Finland	Multilateral	17 Oct 63	Atomic Energy	525UNTS75	107585
Finland	Multilateral	10 Jul 64	Postal Service	613UNTS127	108853
Finland	Multilateral	10 Jul 64	Postal Service	612UNTS233	108848
Finland	Multilateral	10 Jul 64	Postal Service	612UNTS361	108849
Finland	Multilateral	10 Jul 64	Postal Service	613UNTS3	108850
Finland	Multilateral	10 Jul 64	Postal Service	611UNTS387	108846
Finland	Multilateral	10 Jul 64	Postal Service	612UNTS3	108847
Finland	Multilateral	10 Jul 64	Postal Service	613UNTS193	108852
Finland	Multilateral	10 Jul 64	Postal Service	611UNTS7	108844
Finland	Multilateral	10 Jul 64	Postal Service	611UNTS105	108845
Finland	Multilateral	13 Jul 64	ILO Labor	569UNTS65	108279
Finland	Multilateral	12 Sep 64	Specific Resources	0UNTS0	109344
Finland	Multilateral	15 Sep 64	General Trade	510UNTS147	107411
Finland	Multilateral	01 Dec 64	Water Transport	550UNTS133	108012
Finland	Multilateral	09 Mar 65	Water Transport	591UNTS265	108564
Finland	Multilateral	18 Mar 65	Dispute Settlement	575UNTS159	108359
Finland	Multilateral	23 Jun 65	General IGO	614UNTS239	108873
Finland	Multilateral	03 Dec 65	Admin Cooperation	572UNTS105	108309
Finland	Multilateral	04 Dec 65	IGO Establishment	571UNTS123	108303
Finland	Multilateral	05 Apr 66	Water Transport	640UNTS133	109159
Finland	Multilateral	08 Jul 66	Atomic Energy	572UNTS283	108319
Finland	Multilateral	03 Oct 66	Culture	610UNTS169	108841
Finland	Multilateral	31 Jan 67	Refugees	606UNTS267	108791
Finland	Multilateral	24 Feb 67	Health/Educ/Welfare	596UNTS133	108631
Finland	Multilateral	17 Apr 67	Consul/Citizenship	0UNTS0	110377
Finland	Multilateral	03 May 67	IGO Operations	0UNTS0	110764
Finland	Multilateral	10 Jul 67	Air Transport	0UNTS0	109971
Finland	Multilateral	05 Nov 67	Atomic Energy	630UNTS77	108967
Finland	Multilateral	08 Dec 67	Specific Resources	620UNTS225	108959
Finland	Multilateral	18 Mar 68	Commodity Trade	0UNTS0	109262
Finland	Multilateral	01 Jul 68	Peace/Disarmament	0UNTS0	110485
Finland	Multilateral	05 Dec 68	Scientific Project	0UNTS0	109952
Finland	Multilateral	15 Jan 69	Consul/Citizenship	0UNTS0	109491
Finland	Multilateral	27 Nov 69	Atomic Energy	0UNTS0	110519
Finland	Multilateral	12 Dec 69	General Economic	0UNTS0	110755
Finland	Netherlands	25 Feb 49	Air Transport	53UNTS123	100777
Finland	Netherlands	30 May 51	General Trade	51NET83	447025
Finland	Netherlands	11 Jul 51	Non-ILO Labor	51NET113	447029
Finland	Netherlands	24 Jul 52	Visas	52NET106	447035
Finland	Netherlands	29 Mar 54	Taxation	252UNTS185	103567
Finland	Netherlands	29 Mar 54	Taxation	252UNTS239	103568
Finland	Netherlands	29 Jun 55	Finance	55NET91	447055
Finland	New Zealand	12 Nov 62	Water Transport	485UNTS331	107064
Finland	Norway	27 Nov 45	Finance	17UNTS247	100279
Finland	Norway	15 Nov 47	General Trade	29UNTS179	100439
Finland	Norway	10 Sep 48	Specific Resources	32UNTS3	100486
Finland	Norway	13 Jun 49	Commodity Trade	34UNTS9	100523
Finland	Norway	24 Aug 49	Air Transport	53UNTS167	100780

PARTY ONE	PARTY TWO	DATE	TOPIC	CITATION	NUMBER
Finland	Norway	30 Dec 49	Visas	90UNTS175	101234
Finland	Norway	25 Apr 51	Specific Resources	2NORT551	451048
Finland	Norway	16 Jan 52	General Ad Hoc	2NORT578	451049
Finland	Norway	18 Mar 52	Specific Resources	188UNTS187	102527
Finland	Norway	20 May 53	Specific Resources	173UNTS163	102265
Finland	Norway	22 Sep 53	Milit Servic/Citiz	183UNTS245	102433
Finland	Norway	29 Mar 54	Taxation	2NORT625	451053
Finland	Norway	29 Mar 54	Taxation	2NORT624	451052
Finland	Norway	29 Mar 54	Taxation	2NORT623	451051
Finland	Norway	15 Sep 56	Admin Cooperation	254UNTS17	103590
Finland	Norway	28 Jun 57	Non-IBRD Project	272UNTS191	103938
Finland	Norway	21 Jan 59	Non-ILO Labor	325UNTS295	104705
Finland	Norway	15 Nov 60	Specific Resources	383UNTS159	105501
Finland	Norway	29 Jun 61	Extradition	2NORT241	451055
Finland	Norway	09 Jun 64	Specific Resources	503UNTS205	107345
Finland	Norway	10 Dec 68	Territory Boundary	0UNTS0	109977
Finland	Norway	10 Dec 68	Customs	3NORT0	451056
Finland	Pakistan	11 Dec 67	Water Transport	631UNTS99	108989
Finland	Poland	10 Jun 63	Air Transport	503UNTS179	107343
Finland	Poland	18 Dec 63	Non-ILO Labor	486UNTS57	107072
Finland	Poland	18 Oct 69	Land Transport	0UNTS0	110463
Finland	Romania	01 Apr 68	Land Transport	0UNTS0	109392
Finland	Romania	25 Sep 69	General Economic	0UNTS0	110398
Finland	South Africa	15 Nov 48	Admin Cooperation	225UNTS59	103088
Finland	South Africa	24 Mar 54	Admin Cooperation	230UNTS121	103179
Finland	South Africa	05 Dec 56	Visas	258UNTS59	103670
Finland	South Africa	12 Jun 64	Water Transport	505UNTS107	107367
Finland	Spain	21 May 56	General Trade	56SPBO906	460099
Finland	Spain	21 May 56	Finance	56SPBO906	460100
Finland	Spain	25 May 57	General Trade	57SPBO2007	460279
Finland	Spain	10 May 58	General Trade	58SPBO2405	460278
Finland	Spain	15 Nov 67	Taxation	0UNTS0	109375
Finland	Sweden	10 Mar 43	Taxation	198UNTS333	200518
Finland	Sweden	17 Aug 45	General Trade	45SOFM124	461013
Finland	Sweden	17 Feb 49	Specific Resources	197UNTS123	102636
Finland	Sweden	18 Mar 49	General Trade	49SOFM137	461078
Finland	Sweden	26 Apr 49	Air Transport	95UNTS83	101318
Finland	Sweden	17 Nov 49	Claims and Debts	50SOFM849	461116
Finland	Sweden	21 Dec 49	Taxation	197UNTS243	102642
Finland	Sweden	31 Mar 50	Taxation	197UNTS285	102643
Finland	Sweden	01 Apr 50	General Economic	50SOFM169	461109
Finland	Sweden	29 Dec 50	Taxation	197UNTS333	102646
Finland	Sweden	16 Mar 51	General Economic	51SOFM109	461136
Finland	Sweden	15 Jun 51	Visas	198UNTS3	102651
Finland	Sweden	09 Apr 52	General Trade	52SOFM203	461164
Finland	Sweden	09 Apr 53	Dispute Settlement	198UNTS61	102657
Finland	Sweden	07 Jul 56	General Transport	258UNTS83	103672
Finland	Sweden	15 Sep 56	Admin Cooperation	254UNTS31	103591
Finland	Sweden	22 Sep 58	Water Transport	428UNTS119	106170
Finland	Sweden	16 Oct 58	Culture	428UNTS125	106171
Finland	Sweden	13 Apr 60	Culture	428UNTS131	106172
Finland	Sweden	21 Nov 60	Territory Boundary	383UNTS125	105498
Finland	Sweden	18 Feb 61	Visas	428UNTS145	106173
Finland	Sweden	05 Nov 62	Customs	455UNTS289	106548
Finland	Sweden	29 Jun 63	Land Transport	477UNTS21	106912
Finland	Sweden	07 Oct 68	General Ad Hoc	0UNTS0	109376
Finland	Sweden	15 Oct 68	Atomic Energy	0UNTS0	110798
Finland	Switzerland	15 Oct 55	Finance	55SWRO1014	462134
Finland	Switzerland	15 Oct 55	General Trade	55SWRO1017	462135
Finland	Switzerland	27 Dec 56	Taxation	277UNTS7	103996
Finland	Switzerland	27 Dec 56	Taxation	277UNTS59	103997
Finland	Switzerland	17 Jun 57	Taxation	57SWRO756	462048
Finland	Switzerland	07 Jan 59	Air Transport	353UNTS173	105042
Finland	Tanzania	01 Jun 68	Non-ILO Labor	0UNTS0	109791
Finland	Turkey	15 May 46	General Economic	46TURG2312	466052

PARTY ONE	PARTY TWO	DATE	TOPIC	CITATION	NUMBER
Finland	Turkey	12 Jun 48	Finance	49TURG1902	466053
Finland	Turkey	12 Jun 48	General Trade	49TURG1902	466054
Finland	Turkey	27 Oct 53	General Trade	55TURG702	466055
Finland	Turkey	29 Sep 54	Visas	59TURG1006	466012
Finland	Turkey	13 May 60	General Trade	60TURG1908	466056
Finland	Turkey	13 May 60	Finance	60TURG1908	466057
Finland	UK Great Britain	12 Mar 48	Admin Cooperation	104UNTS29	101433
Finland	UK Great Britain	28 Dec 49	Peace/Disarmament	86UNTS191	101159
Finland	UK Great Britain	07 Jul 50	Finance	138UNTS171	101868
Finland	UK Great Britain	12 Dec 51	Taxation	172UNTS45	102239
Finland	UK Great Britain	16 Nov 54	Visas	204UNTS177	102756
Finland	UK Great Britain	28 Jul 59	Non-ILO Labor	355UNTS31	105073
Finland	UK Great Britain	05 May 61	Visas	414UNTS101	105969
Finland	UK Great Britain	09 Jun 61	Visas	414UNTS53	105965
Finland	UK Great Britain	05 Dec 61	Admin Cooperation	424UNTS217	106110
Finland	UK Great Britain	12 Sep 64	Commodity Trade	535UNTS13	107773
Finland	UK Great Britain	25 Mar 65	Air Transport	539UNTS103	107826
Finland	UK Great Britain	24 May 68	Atomic Energy	0UNTS0	109575
Finland	UK Great Britain	17 Jul 69	Taxation	0UNTS0	110321
Finland	UNICEF (Children)	23 Aug 47	IGO Operations	68UNTS224	200233
Finland	United Arab Rep	01 Apr 65	Taxation	562UNTS3	108193
Finland	United Nations	20 May 48	Humanitarian	47UNTS319	200189
Finland	United Nations	27 Jun 57	Status of Forces	271UNTS135	103913
Finland	United Nations	21 Feb 66	IGO Operations	555UNTS157	108109
Finland	United Nations	16 Jan 67	Education	588UNTS153	108522
Finland	USA (United States)	07 Jan 47	Taxation	15UNTS273	100243
Finland	USA (United States)	29 Mar 49	Air Transport	55UNTS59	100808
Finland	USA (United States)	01 Nov 49	Claims and Debts	68UNTS11	100880
Finland	USA (United States)	18 Jan 50	General Economic	92UNTS197	101272
Finland	USA (United States)	16 Nov 51	Patents/Copyrights	140UNTS273	101893
Finland	USA (United States)	03 Mar 52	Taxation	177UNTS141	102316
Finland	USA (United States)	03 Mar 52	Taxation	177UNTS163	102317
Finland	USA (United States)	02 Jul 52	Education	165UNTS203	102177
Finland	USA (United States)	04 Dec 52	General Amity	205UNTS149	102774
Finland	USA (United States)	06 May 55	US Agri Commod Aid	251UNTS3	103529
Finland	USA (United States)	14 Dec 55	Visas	335UNTS263	104794
Finland	USA (United States)	10 May 57	US Agri Commod Aid	283UNTS43	104105
Finland	USA (United States)	21 Feb 58	US Agri Commod Aid	304UNTS253	104401
Finland	USA (United States)	15 Aug 58	Visas	314UNTS43	104540
Finland	USA (United States)	30 Dec 58	US Agri Commod Aid	340UNTS259	104869
Finland	USA (United States)	22 Jul 59	Admin Cooperation	354UNTS39	105051
Finland	USA (United States)	23 Mar 60	US Agri Commod Aid	371UNTS117	105274
Finland	USA (United States)	16 Jun 61	Claims and Debts	413UNTS211	105955
Finland	USA (United States)	04 Aug 61	US Agri Commod Aid	418UNTS19	106014
Finland	USA (United States)	05 Mar 62	General Economic	446UNTS19	106399
Finland	USA (United States)	03 Nov 65	Air Transport	573UNTS175	108330
Finland	USA (United States)	27 Dec 67	Gen Communications	0UNTS0	109991
Finland	USA (United States)	08 Apr 70	Atomic Energy	0UNTS0	110767
Finland	USSR (Soviet Union)	28 Oct 22	Specific Resources	67UNTS157	100874
Finland	USSR (Soviet Union)	28 Oct 22	Specific Resources	67UNTS153	100873
Finland	USSR (Soviet Union)	11 Oct 40	Territory Boundary	67UNTS139	100872
Finland	USSR (Soviet Union)	31 Jan 45	General Trade	0SUST170	468132
Finland	USSR (Soviet Union)	08 May 45	General Trade	0SUST177	471016
Finland	USSR (Soviet Union)	06 Aug 45	Consul/Citizenship	0SUST188	471017
Finland	USSR (Soviet Union)	26 Oct 45	Territory Boundary	0SUST200	468133
Finland	USSR (Soviet Union)	31 Dec 45	Reparations	0SUST205	471020
Finland	USSR (Soviet Union)	30 Apr 46	Specific Property	0SUST211	468134
Finland	USSR (Soviet Union)	19 Aug 46	Telecommunications	0SUST217	468135
Finland	USSR (Soviet Union)	19 Aug 46	Postal Service	0SUST217	468137
Finland	USSR (Soviet Union)	05 Dec 46	General Economic	0SUST222	468136
Finland	USSR (Soviet Union)	03 Feb 47	Specific Property	0SUST226	468140
Finland	USSR (Soviet Union)	03 Feb 47	Specific Property	0SUST225	468139
Finland	USSR (Soviet Union)	03 Feb 47	Finance	0SUST225	468138
Finland	USSR (Soviet Union)	03 Feb 47	Territory Boundary	216UNTS231	102939
Finland	USSR (Soviet Union)	24 Apr 47	Specific Resources	0SUST231	468141

PARTY ONE	PARTY TWO	DATE	TOPIC	CITATION	NUMBER
Finland	USSR (Soviet Union)	24 May 47	Specific Property	0SUST232	468142
Finland	USSR (Soviet Union)	01 Dec 47	General Trade	217UNTS3	102942
Finland	USSR (Soviet Union)	07 Dec 47	Territory Boundary	0SUST239	468143
Finland	USSR (Soviet Union)	19 Dec 47	Land Transport	0SUST242	468144
Finland	USSR (Soviet Union)	16 Mar 48	Admin Cooperation	0SUST246	468145
Finland	USSR (Soviet Union)	06 Apr 48	General Military	48UNTS149	100742
Finland	USSR (Soviet Union)	19 Jun 48	Dispute Settlement	0SUST249	468146
Finland	USSR (Soviet Union)	28 Jul 48	Reparations	16SUGG64	469886
Finland	USSR (Soviet Union)	09 Dec 48	Territory Boundary	217UNTS135	102947
Finland	USSR (Soviet Union)	17 Dec 48	General Trade	0SUST256	471029
Finland	USSR (Soviet Union)	13 Jun 50	General Trade	0SUST275	468147
Finland	USSR (Soviet Union)	06 Feb 54	Loans and Credits	221UNTS143	103006
Finland	USSR (Soviet Union)	29 Apr 54	Specific Resources	0SUST311	468148
Finland	USSR (Soviet Union)	17 Jul 54	General Trade	240UNTS173	103403
Finland	USSR (Soviet Union)	24 Jan 55	Loans and Credits	240UNTS243	103406
Finland	USSR (Soviet Union)	19 Sep 55	Milit Installation	226UNTS187	103113
Finland	USSR (Soviet Union)	19 Oct 55	Air Transport	353UNTS185	105043
Finland	USSR (Soviet Union)	14 Sep 56	Land Transport	255UNTS365	103618
Finland	USSR (Soviet Union)	07 Dec 56	Humanitarian	258UNTS89	103673
Finland	USSR (Soviet Union)	26 Jun 58	Commodity Trade	7SUGG114	469516
Finland	USSR (Soviet Union)	21 Feb 59	Specific Resources	338UNTS3	104830
Finland	USSR (Soviet Union)	29 Apr 59	Specif Claim/Waive	346UNTS209	104981
Finland	USSR (Soviet Union)	22 Oct 59	General Trade	8SUGG155	469606
Finland	USSR (Soviet Union)	22 Dec 59	Loans and Credits	8SUGG163	469617
Finland	USSR (Soviet Union)	27 May 60	Culture	379UNTS381	105444
Finland	USSR (Soviet Union)	23 Jun 60	Territory Boundary	379UNTS277	105443
Finland	USSR (Soviet Union)	24 Nov 60	Customs	9SUGG152	469715
Finland	USSR (Soviet Union)	03 Feb 61	Specific Property	10SUGG120	469740
Finland	USSR (Soviet Union)	01 Apr 61	Customs	10SUGG127	469757
Finland	USSR (Soviet Union)	06 Apr 61	Tech Assistance	10SUGG127	469758
Finland	USSR (Soviet Union)	27 Sep 62	Territory Boundary	479UNTS99	106949
Finland	USSR (Soviet Union)	24 Apr 64	Territory Boundary	537UNTS231	107804
Finland	USSR (Soviet Union)	20 May 65	Territory Boundary	566UNTS31	108238
Finland	USSR (Soviet Union)	04 Jun 65	Specific Resources	560UNTS169	108173
Finland	USSR (Soviet Union)	24 Jan 66	Consul/Citizenship	576UNTS35	108364
Finland	USSR (Soviet Union)	05 May 67	Specific Resources	640UNTS111	109157
Finland	USSR (Soviet Union)	07 Mar 68	General Transport	643UNTS107	109187
Finland	USSR (Soviet Union)	18 Oct 68	Land Transport	0UNTS0	109609
Finland	USSR (Soviet Union)	14 May 69	Atomic Energy	0UNTS0	110040
Finland	USSR (Soviet Union)	30 May 69	Education	0UNTS0	110041
Finland	USSR (Soviet Union)	13 Jun 69	Specific Resources	0UNTS0	110606
Finland	WHO (World Health)	07 Mar 52	Tech Assistance	128UNTS269	200436
Finland	Zambia	29 Aug 70	Tech Assistance	0UNTS0	110841
Fr Equatorial Afri	Anglo-Egypt Sudan	02 Nov 39	Telecommunications	2UNTS209	200012
France	Afghanistan	06 Jan 59	General Aid	61FRRT40	415001
France	Afghanistan	15 May 61	Air Transport	62FRRT4	415002
France	Afghanistan	21 Aug 66	Health/Educ/Welfare	67FRJO801	416003
France	African Coffee Org	19 Apr 66	IGO Status/Immunit	67FRJO1903	416507
France	African Coffee Org	14 Apr 67	IGO Establishment	0UNTS0	110312
France	African Insur Org	08 Feb 67	IGO Status/Immunit	67FRJO212	416509
France	Afromalagasy Coffee	14 Apr 67	IGO Status/Immunit	69FRJO2204	416510
France	Albania	14 Dec 63	General Amity	65FRRT41	415004
France	Albania	10 Feb 69	General Trade	69FRMD2402	417005
France	Algeria	16 Dec 44	Non-ILO Labor	0UNTS0	110350
France	Algeria	19 Mar 62	Recognition	62FRJO2003	416006
France	Algeria	03 Jul 62	Recognition	507UNTS25	107395
France	Algeria	28 Aug 62	Specific Resources	62FRRT27	415007
France	Algeria	07 Sep 62	Education	0UNTS0	110819
France	Algeria	24 Sep 62	Tech Assistance	62FRRT30	415008
France	Algeria	24 Sep 62	Tech Assistance	0UNTS0	109507
France	Algeria	17 Dec 62	Tech Assistance	63FRRT8	415009
France	Algeria	31 Dec 62	Tech Assistance	63FRRT13	415010
France	Algeria	16 Jan 63	Direct Aid	63FRRT11	415011
France	Algeria	19 Jan 63	Finance	63FRRT17	415012
France	Algeria	23 Jan 63	Mass Media	63FRRT12	415013

PARTY ONE	PARTY TWO	DATE	TOPIC	CITATION	NUMBER
France	Algeria	18 Feb 63	Air Transport	563UNTS263	108214
France	Algeria	19 Apr 63	Tech Assistance	64FRRT20	415014
France	Algeria	22 Apr 63	Education	0UNTS0	110349
France	Algeria	11 Jun 63	Tech Assistance	64FRRT21	415015
France	Algeria	11 Jun 63	Education	0UNTS0	110820
France	Algeria	23 Oct 63	Health/Educ/Welfare	64FRRT24	415016
France	Algeria	27 Aug 64	Extradition	65FRRT72	415017
France	Algeria	16 Dec 64	Extradition	65FRRT4	415018
France	Algeria	19 Jan 65	Non-ILO Labor	65FRJO1905	416020
France	Algeria	19 Jan 65	Non-ILO Labor	65FRRT50	415019
France	Algeria	28 Jul 65	Non-IBRD Project	65FRRT107	415021
France	Algeria	28 Jul 65	Tech Assistance	0UNTS0	110609
France	Algeria	29 Jul 65	Specific Resources	65FRRT106	415022
France	Algeria	29 Jul 65	Non-IBRD Project	0UNTS0	110610
France	Algeria	08 Apr 66	Tech Assistance	0UNTS0	109508
France	Algeria	08 Apr 66	Health/Educ/Welfare	66FRRT34	415023
France	Algeria	23 Dec 66	Health/Educ/Welfare	67FRJO3003	416024
France	Algeria	20 Jun 67	General Ad Hoc	68FRJO1008	416030
France	Algeria	26 Jun 67	Health/Educ/Welfare	67FRJO2809	416025
France	Algeria	08 Jul 67	Non-IBRD Project	69FRJO2006	416026
France	Algeria	08 Jul 67	Education	0UNTS0	110351
France	Algeria	20 Jul 67	Water Transport	67FRJO2510	416027
France	Algeria	01 Oct 67	Non-IBRD Project	70FRJO1004	416031
France	Algeria	26 Dec 67	Air Transport	69FRJO1101	416028
France	Algeria	26 Dec 67	Admin Cooperation	0UNTS0	109509
France	Algeria	16 Mar 68	Scientific Project	0UNTS0	110821
France	Algeria	16 Mar 68	Tech Assistance	69FRJO2006	416029
France	Algeria	02 Aug 68	Scientific Project	0UNTS0	110474
France	Algeria	01 Oct 68	Education	0UNTS0	110477
France	Algeria	27 Dec 68	Privil/Immunities	0UNTS0	109640
France	Algeria	27 Dec 68	Non-ILO Labor	69FRJO2203	416032
France	Algeria	27 Nov 69	Tech Assistance	0UNTS0	110478
France	Argentina	25 Nov 57	Finance	57FRMD1112	417052
France	Argentina	25 Nov 57	General Trade	57FRMD1112	417053
France	Argentina	17 Jan 63	Culture	65FRRT44	415054
France	Argentina	03 Oct 64	Culture	0UNTS0	109555
France	Argentina	03 Oct 64	Culture	635UNTS155	109080
France	Argentina	21 Mar 69	Culture	0UNTS0	110187
France	Argentina	21 Mar 69	Scientific Project	69FRJO1609	416055
France	Australia	28 Jul 47	Reparations	97UNTS271	101353
France	Australia	28 Sep 51	Reparations	161UNTS185	102128
France	Australia	27 Dec 55	Admin Cooperation	241UNTS325	103440
France	Australia	13 Apr 65	Air Transport	601UNTS293	108702
France	Australia	08 Nov 67	Scientific Project	0UNTS0	109668
France	Australia	27 Mar 70	Taxation	0UNTS0	110802
France	Austria	15 Mar 47	Culture	12UNTS109	100182
France	Austria	31 Aug 55	Non-ILO Labor	55ABGB208	403050
France	Austria	26 Jun 58	Admin Cooperation	60FRRT19	415056
France	Austria	01 Oct 59	Patents/Copyrights	60FRRT21	415057
France	Austria	08 Oct 59	Taxation	453UNTS95	106521
France	Austria	30 Nov 62	Visas	463UNTS173	106701
France	Austria	12 Jul 63	Air Transport	499UNTS91	107294
France	Austria	19 Jul 63	Culture	65FRRT43	415058
France	Austria	05 May 64	Patents/Copyrights	64FRRT46	415059
France	Austria	14 Oct 64	Land Transport	64ABGB324	403054
France	Austria	15 Jul 66	Admin Cooperation	634UNTS3	109047
France	Austria	15 Jul 66	Admin Cooperation	604UNTS265	108755
France	Austria	12 Jan 68	Scientific Project	0UNTS0	109531
France	Austria	12 Mar 68	Scientific Project	69FRJO1001	416060
France	Austria	04 Jul 69	Land Transport	69ABGB335	403055
France	Austria	30 Oct 70	Taxation	72ABGB147	403056
France	Austria	05 Jul 71	Telecommunications	71ABGB325	403057
France	Belgium	30 Mar 45	Water Transport	20UNTS297	200122
France	Belgium	30 Mar 45	Visas	21UNTS325	200132
France	Belgium	21 May 45	Visas	23UNTS215	200133

PARTY ONE	PARTY TWO	DATE	TOPIC	CITATION	NUMBER
France	Belgium	30 Oct 45	Reparations	19UNTS87	100306
France	Belgium	22 Feb 46	Culture	68UNTS157	100892
France	Belgium	17 Apr 46	Land Transport	49FRJO1509	416276
France	Belgium	09 Jan 47	Admin Cooperation	36UNTS145	100568
France	Belgium	17 Jan 48	Non-ILO Labor	36UNTS233	100570
France	Belgium	13 Apr 48	Territory Boundary	31UNTS409	100483
France	Belgium	23 Apr 48	Territory Boundary	19UNTS95	100307
France	Belgium	28 Oct 48	Visas	25UNTS151	100360
France	Belgium	08 Jan 49	Non-ILO Labor	36UNTS151	100569
France	Belgium	18 Feb 49	Claims and Debts	31UNTS173	100478
France	Belgium	12 Apr 49	Visas	30UNTS45	100447
France	Belgium	29 Aug 49	Milit Servic/Citiz	93UNTS87	101293
France	Belgium	07 Sep 49	Loans and Credits	123UNTS13	101651
France	Belgium	30 Dec 49	Taxation	46UNTS111	100704
France	Belgium	14 Mar 50	Visas	65UNTS139	100842
France	Belgium	26 Sep 50	Visas	79UNTS3	101026
France	Belgium	21 Mar 52	Land Transport	137UNTS249	101856
France	Belgium	30 Jun 52	General Transport	137UNTS259	101857
France	Belgium	29 Nov 52	Visas	160UNTS261	102110
France	Belgium	30 Jan 53	Visas	188UNTS141	102525
France	Belgium	27 Feb 53	Non-ILO Labor	164UNTS49	102158
France	Belgium	11 Mar 53	Reparations	191UNTS329	102590
France	Belgium	07 Jun 54	Admin Cooperation	69FRJO2006	416061
France	Belgium	09 Jun 54	Visas	0UNTS0	110703
France	Belgium	15 Oct 54	Admin Cooperation	218UNTS19	102951
France	Belgium	12 Nov 54	Reparations	306UNTS85	104434
France	Belgium	10 Dec 55	Taxation	231UNTS101	103211
France	Belgium	01 Mar 56	Admin Cooperation	337UNTS53	104815
France	Belgium	18 Jul 56	Non-ILO Labor	248UNTS121	103491
France	Belgium	15 Feb 57	Refugees	267UNTS3	103834
France	Belgium	06 Sep 57	Specific Resources	59FRRT39	415062
France	Belgium	20 Sep 57	Postal Service	57FRJO1910	416063
France	Belgium	12 Nov 57	Non-ILO Labor	328UNTS167	104734
France	Belgium	31 May 58	Patents/Copyrights	60FRRT20	415064
France	Belgium	03 Sep 58	Health/Educ/Welfare	58FRJO1910	416065
France	Belgium	20 Sep 58	Reparations	376UNTS331	105387
France	Belgium	20 Jan 59	Taxation	361UNTS155	105178
France	Belgium	07 Jul 61	Taxation	406UNTS157	105846
France	Belgium	30 Mar 62	Visas	502UNTS297	107335
France	Belgium	20 Sep 62	Culture	65FRRT34	415066
France	Belgium	12 Oct 62	Milit Servic/Citiz	64FRRT61	415067
France	Belgium	10 Mar 64	Taxation	557UNTS13	108127
France	Belgium	24 Mar 64	Non-ILO Labor	64FRJO51	416068
France	Belgium	23 Sep 66	Atomic Energy	588UNTS227	108528
France	Belgium	31 May 67	Admin Cooperation	67FRJO408	416069
France	Belgium	17 Oct 67	Culture	68FRJO1008	416070
France	Belgium	19 Dec 67	Admin Cooperation	68FRJO2801	416071
France	Belgium	20 Sep 68	Admin Cooperation	68FRJO2211	416072
France	Belgium	02 Dec 68	Admin Cooperation	69FRJO2006	416073
France	Belgium	06 Jun 69	Admin Cooperation	69FRJO2009	416074
France	Bolivia	26 May 66	Health/Educ/Welfare	68FRJO1606	416075
France	Brazil	27 Jan 40	Air Transport	72UNTS77	100929
France	Brazil	06 Dec 46	Culture	0UNTS0	110228
France	Brazil	06 Dec 48	Culture	60FRRT58	415076
France	Brazil	04 May 56	Finance	323UNTS339	104675
France	Brazil	23 Aug 56	General Economic	56FRMD1009	417077
France	Brazil	22 Jan 63	Tech Assistance	69FRJO2005	416078
France	Brazil	22 Jan 63	Privil/Immunities	0UNTS0	110229
France	Brazil	26 Oct 65	Finance	66FRRT10	415079
France	Brazil	29 Oct 65	Air Transport	67FRJO1105	416080
France	Brazil	16 Jan 67	Tech Assistance	69FRJO2704	416081
France	Brazil	16 Jan 67	Tech Assistance	0UNTS0	110230
France	Brazil	20 Jun 68	Scientific Project	0UNTS0	110231
France	Brazil	20 Jun 68	Specific Property	69FRJO1903	416082
France	Brazil	06 Feb 69	Culture	69FRJO506	416083

PARTY ONE	PARTY TWO	DATE	TOPIC	CITATION	NUMBER
France	Brazil	06 Feb 69	Culture	0UNTS0	110555
France	Brazil	21 Mar 69	Specific Property	69FRJO1609	416084
France	Bulgaria	07 Mar 50	Admin Cooperation	50FRJO1607	416085
France	Bulgaria	28 Jul 55	Finance	59FRRT4	415086
France	Bulgaria	04 Aug 65	Air Transport	65FRRT81	415087
France	Bulgaria	04 Aug 65	Air Transport	0UNTS0	109958
France	Bulgaria	15 Oct 66	Culture	67FRJO204	416089
France	Bulgaria	15 Oct 66	Tech Assistance	67FRJO204	416088
France	Bulgaria	30 Jan 68	Sanitation	68FRJO1808	416090
France	Bulgaria	10 Jul 68	General Economic	69FRJO3007	416091
France	Bulgaria	10 Jul 68	General Economic	0UNTS0	110731
France	Bulgaria	22 Jul 68	Consul/Citizenship	0UNTS0	110732
France	Bulgaria	27 Mar 69	Water Transport	69FRJO1906	416092
France	Bulgaria	27 Mar 69	Land Transport	0UNTS0	110556
France	Burundi	11 Feb 63	Health/Educ/Welfare	65FRRT18	415093
France	Burundi	07 Oct 69	Milit Assistance	0UNTS0	110534
France	Cambodia	08 Nov 49	Recognition	53FRJO1403	416094
France	Cambodia	29 Aug 53	Recognition	59FRRT7	415095
France	Cambodia	09 Sep 53	Admin Cooperation	59FRRT7	415096
France	Cambodia	15 Jan 64	Air Transport	64FRRT14	415097
France	Cambodia	04 Jul 64	General Aid	67FRJO2107	416098
France	Cameroon	13 Nov 60	Military Mission	0UNTS0	110640
France	Cameroon	13 Nov 60	General Economic	0UNTS0	110639
France	Cameroon	13 Nov 60	Admin Cooperation	0UNTS0	110637
France	Cameroon	13 Nov 60	General Amity	61FRRT29	415099
France	Cameroon	13 Nov 60	Consul/Citizenship	0UNTS0	110635
France	Cameroon	13 Nov 60	Culture	0UNTS0	110636
France	Cameroon	13 Nov 60	Admin Cooperation	0UNTS0	110643
France	Cameroon	13 Nov 60	General Economic	0UNTS0	110638
France	Cameroon	13 Nov 60	General Amity	0UNTS0	110634
France	Cameroon	13 Nov 60	Military Mission	0UNTS0	110641
France	Cameroon	13 Nov 60	Air Transport	0UNTS0	110642
France	Cameroon	16 Jun 61	Air Transport	412UNTS148	105929
France	Cameroon	16 Jan 63	Education	63FRRT53	415100
France	Cameroon	16 Jan 63	Customs	63FRRT15	415101
France	Cameroon	05 May 63	Mass Media	65FRRT48	415102
France	Cameroon	10 Aug 63	Specific Property	64FRRT71	415103
France	Cameroon	10 Jul 65	Finance	68FRJO2703	416104
France	Cameroon	10 Jul 65	Taxation	0UNTS0	109433
France	Canada	12 May 33	Admin Cooperation	253UNTS285	200545
France	Canada	22 Mar 46	Reparations	230UNTS165	103182
France	Canada	09 Apr 46	Finance	43UNTS43	100660
France	Canada	05 May 47	Reparations	231UNTS81	103208
France	Canada	08 Sep 47	Taxation	253UNTS259	103587
France	Canada	05 May 48	Reparations	231UNTS87	103209
France	Canada	17 Apr 50	Visas	230UNTS365	103196
France	Canada	01 Aug 50	Air Transport	73UNTS21	100941
France	Canada	26 Jan 51	Claims and Debts	233UNTS65	103251
France	Canada	16 Mar 51	Taxation	236UNTS267	103330
France	Canada	16 Mar 51	Taxation	236UNTS297	103331
France	Canada	04 Jul 51	Reparations	233UNTS101	103253
France	Canada	04 Sep 56	Other Military	305UNTS79	104415
France	Canada	04 Oct 56	Non-ILO Labor	305UNTS65	104414
France	Canada	25 May 62	Other Military	470UNTS163	106808
France	Canada	11 Oct 63	Mass Media	529UNTS71	107657
France	Canada	15 Jan 64	Education	65FRRT37	415105
France	Canada	27 Feb 65	Education	65FRRT40	415106
France	Canada	17 Nov 65	Culture	66FRJO1401	416107
France	Canada	24 Nov 65	Culture	66FRJO1401	416108
France	Canada	03 Apr 69	Sanitation	69FRJO2512	416109
France	Canada	03 Apr 69	Sanitation	0UNTS0	110532
France	Central Afri Rep	12 Jul 60	Recognition	60FRRT50	415110
France	Central Afri Rep	13 Aug 60	General Amity	60FRRT76	415111
France	Central Afri Rep	26 Aug 61	Specific Property	63FRRT19	415112
France	Central Afri Rep	27 Mar 63	Customs	63FRRT43	415113

PARTY ONE	PARTY TWO	DATE	TOPIC	CITATION	NUMBER
France	Central Afri Rep	18 Jan 65	Admin Cooperation	67FRJO1905	416114
France	CERN (Nuc Resrch)	13 Sep 65	Atomic Energy	0UNTS0	109862
France	CERN (Nuc Resrch)	13 Sep 65	IGO Status/Immunit	69FRJO1004	416514
France	Chad	12 Jul 60	Recognition	60FRRT50	415426
France	Chad	11 Aug 60	General Amity	60FRRT76	415427
France	Chad	25 Oct 61	Specific Property	63FRRT23	415428
France	Chad	08 Jan 63	Air Transport	63FRRT31	415430
France	Chad	29 Mar 63	Customs	63FRRT43	415429
France	Chad	17 Aug 63	Direct Aid	64FRRT16	415431
France	Chad	19 May 64	Culture	68FRJO1112	416434
France	Chad	19 May 64	Culture	0UNTS0	109442
France	Chad	19 May 64	Milit Assistance	0UNTS0	109443
France	Chad	19 May 64	General Aid	0UNTS0	109441
France	Chad	19 May 64	Milit Assistance	68FRJO1112	416435
France	Chad	19 May 64	Non-ILO Labor	68FRJO1112	416432
France	Chad	19 May 64	IGO Establishment	0UNTS0	109440
France	Chile	23 Nov 55	Culture	60FRRT61	415115
France	Chile	14 Sep 62	Tech Assistance	65FRRT17	415116
France	China People's Rep	05 Jun 53	General Trade	53CCJC33	410107
France	China People's Rep	19 Feb 56	Finance	56CCJC34	410318
France	China People's Rep	19 Feb 56	Finance	56CCJC33	410317
France	China People's Rep	01 Oct 65	Culture	65CCJC126	411150
France	China People's Rep	01 Jun 66	Air Transport	66CCJC43	411151
France	China People's Rep	01 Jun 66	Air Transport	66FRRT23	415117
France	China People's Rep	25 Jul 66	Air Transport	66CCJC71	411154
France	China People's Rep	22 Sep 66	Air Transport	68FRJO2801	416118
France	Colombia	28 Apr 53	Patents/Copyrights	62FRRT16	415119
France	Colombia	18 Sep 63	Tech Assistance	65FRRT19	415120
France	Congo (Brazzaville)	12 Jul 60	Recognition	60FRRT50	415121
France	Congo (Brazzaville)	15 Aug 60	General Military	60FRRT76	415122
France	Congo (Brazzaville)	02 May 62	Air Transport	63FRRT25	415123
France	Congo (Brazzaville)	18 May 62	Admin Cooperation	65FRRT9	415124
France	Congo (Brazzaville)	27 Mar 63	Customs	63FRRT43	415125
France	Congo (Brazzaville)	09 Jun 66	Direct Aid	66FRJO6051	416126
France	Congo (Brazzaville)	13 Nov 67	Taxation	0UNTS0	110315
France	Congo (Brazzaville)	13 Nov 67	Finance	70FRJO307	416127
France	Congo (Zaire)	17 Jul 63	Non-ILO Labor	67FRJO1511	416128
France	Congo (Zaire)	17 Dec 63	Health/Educ/Welfare	67FRJO1511	416129
France	Costa Rica	30 Apr 53	General Trade	54FRJO1902	416134
France	Costa Rica	02 Jun 55	General Amity	55FRRT9002	415135
France	Costa Rica	18 Jun 64	Telecommunications	65FRRT32	415136
France	Costa Rica	30 Nov 67	Education	68FRJO206	416137
France	Costa Rica	30 Nov 67	Education	0UNTS0	110668
France	Costa Rica	30 May 69	Culture	0UNTS0	110741
France	Costa Rica	23 Sep 69	Education	0UNTS0	110669
France	Council of Europe	02 Sep 49	IGO Status/Immunit	249UNTS207	103510
France	Council of Europe	21 Dec 59	Non-ILO Labor	60FRRT34	415500
France	Cuba	17 Jan 51	Claims and Debts	52FRJO2609	416143
France	Cuba	16 Mar 67	Claims and Debts	46FRJO7041	416144
France	Cyprus	29 Oct 69	Culture	0UNTS0	110461
France	Czechoslovakia	08 Dec 45	Education	46UNTS77	100701
France	Czechoslovakia	20 Nov 46	Reparations	48FRJO1501	416436
France	Czechoslovakia	01 Dec 47	Reparations	50FRJO0	416437
France	Czechoslovakia	06 Aug 48	Taxation	49FRJO2207	416438
France	Czechoslovakia	06 Aug 48	Claims and Debts	48FRMD1908	417439
France	Czechoslovakia	12 Oct 48	Non-ILO Labor	45UNTS81	100693
France	Czechoslovakia	02 Jun 50	Claims and Debts	63FRRT51	415440
France	Czechoslovakia	16 Jan 64	Dispute Settlement	64FRRT15	415441
France	Czechoslovakia	26 Sep 64	Culture	0UNTS0	110726
France	Czechoslovakia	29 Jun 65	Tech Assistance	66FRJO2502	416443
France	Czechoslovakia	29 Jun 65	General Trade	65FRMD2807	417442
France	Czechoslovakia	29 Jun 65	Scientific Project	0UNTS0	110727
France	Czechoslovakia	30 May 67	Sanitation	68FRJO1101	416444
France	Czechoslovakia	26 Oct 67	Culture	68FRJO2109	416445
France	Czechoslovakia	03 Mar 68	Culture	68FRJO1709	416446

PARTY ONE	PARTY TWO	DATE	TOPIC	CITATION	NUMBER
France	Czechoslovakia	06 Mar 68	Mass Media	0UNTS0	109379
France	Czechoslovakia	21 Sep 68	General Transport	69FRJO2006	416447
France	Czechoslovakia	21 Sep 68	Land Transport	0UNTS0	110347
France	Dahomey	11 Jul 60	Recognition	60FRRT52	415145
France	Dahomey	24 Apr 61	General Amity	62FRRT8	415146
France	Dahomey	28 Mar 62	Customs	63FRRT30	415147
France	Dahomey	10 Apr 62	Claims and Debts	62FRRT38	415148
France	Dahomey	09 Dec 63	Air Transport	64FRRT13	415149
France	Dahomey	21 Oct 65	Finance	67FRRT905	415150
France	Denmark	04 Jan 46	Air Transport	27UNTS169	100406
France	Denmark	16 Jul 47	Patents/Copyrights	12UNTS3	100177
France	Denmark	22 Jun 49	Milit Servic/Citiz	48UNTS3	100737
France	Denmark	30 Jun 51	Non-ILO Labor	151UNTS241	102000
France	Denmark	08 Feb 57	Taxation	58FRRT27	415151
France	Denmark	29 May 59	General Trade	59FRMD1706	417152
France	Denmark	17 Sep 59	Taxation	410UNTS141	105901
France	Denmark	06 Jun 63	Milit Servic/Citiz	600UNTS213	108682
France	Denmark	14 Jun 66	General Trade	66FRMD2076	417153
France	Denmark	15 Feb 67	Culture	604UNTS247	108754
France	Denmark	25 Jul 69	Land Transport	0UNTS0	110033
France	Ecuador	25 Oct 49	Finance	49FRMD2411	417154
France	Ecuador	20 Mar 59	General Trade	59FRRT42	415155
France	Ecuador	13 Apr 59	Tech Assistance	65FRRT16	415156
France	Ecuador	03 Feb 64	Air Transport	64FRRT38	415157
France	Ecuador	02 Sep 65	Visas	65FRRT89	415158
France	Ecuador	17 Feb 66	Tech Assistance	66FRJO2206	416159
France	Ecuador	05 Jul 66	Culture	66FRJO2011	416160
France	El Salvador	23 Mar 53	General Trade	54FRJO1902	416386
France	El Salvador	19 Feb 64	Telecommunications	65FRRT38	415387
France	Ethiopia	12 Nov 59	Land Transport	60FRRT30	415183
France	Ethiopia	12 Nov 59	Specific Property	381UNTS3	105465
France	Ethiopia	27 Aug 66	Culture	0UNTS0	110644
France	Ethiopia	27 Aug 66	Education	67FRJO3103	416185
France	Ethiopia	27 Aug 66	Culture	0UNTS0	110645
France	Ethiopia	27 Aug 66	Health/Educ/Welfare	67FRJO3103	416184
France	Ethiopia	27 Aug 66	Culture	67FRJO3103	416186
France	Ethiopia	27 Aug 66	Culture	0UNTS0	110646
France	Ethiopia	28 Mar 69	Health/Educ/Welfare	69FRJO2412	416187
France	Ethiopia	28 Mar 69	Education	0UNTS0	110647
France	Ethiopia	10 Jul 69	Tech Assistance	0UNTS0	110318
France	Eur Plant Protect	30 Jun 64	IGO Status/Immunit	65FRRT74	415501
France	Eur Space Research	10 Aug 64	IGO Operations	528UNTS135	107637
France	Eur Space Research	08 Oct 65	Non-ILO Labor	66FRRT19	415505
France	Eur Space Vehicle	11 Mar 65	Scientific Project	66FRRT21	415504
France	Eur Space Vehicle	11 Jun 68	Gen Communications	0UNTS0	110028
France	Eur Space Vehicle	11 Jun 68	Specific Property	69FRJO1903	416512
France	Finland	15 Apr 50	Education	50FRJO206	416188
France	Finland	25 Aug 58	Taxation	59FRRT28	415189
France	Finland	25 Aug 58	Taxation	59FRRT28	415190
France	Finland	12 Oct 62	Air Transport	498UNTS299	107285
France	Finland	27 Oct 67	General Transport	643UNTS75	109185
France	Finland	31 Mar 69	Taxation	0UNTS0	110035
France	Gabon	15 Jul 60	Recognition	60FRRT51	415191
France	Gabon	17 Aug 60	General Amity	60FRRT77	415192
France	Gabon	06 Jun 61	Specific Property	63FRRT20	415193
France	Gabon	28 Sep 62	Customs	62FRRT39	415194
France	Gabon	23 Jul 63	Admin Cooperation	65FRRT26	415195
France	Gabon	02 Dec 63	Air Transport	64FRRT9	415196
France	Gabon	21 Apr 66	Finance	69FRJO2404	416197
France	Gabon	22 Apr 66	Taxation	0UNTS0	109647
France	Gabon	03 Apr 68	General Economic	0UNTS0	110529
France	Germany, West	10 Jul 50	Non-ILO Labor	51WGBB177	425134
France	Germany, West	10 Jul 50	Visas	51WGBB87	425135
France	Germany, West	10 Jul 50	Education	51FRJO706	416033
France	Germany, West	10 Jul 50	Non-ILO Labor	51WGBB69	425137

PARTY ONE	PARTY TWO	DATE	TOPIC	CITATION	NUMBER
France	Germany, West	10 Jul 50	Non-ILO Labor	51WGBB98	425136
France	Germany, West	19 Nov 51	Extradition	53WGBB151	425138
France	Germany, West	27 Feb 53	Specif Claim/Waive	53WGBB508	425139
France	Germany, West	31 Aug 54	Admin Cooperation	54FRJO1909	416034
France	Germany, West	23 Oct 54	Culture	55WGBB885	425142
France	Germany, West	23 Oct 54	Extradition	57WBGA225	424141
France	Germany, West	23 Oct 54	Territory Boundary	55WGBB295	425140
France	Germany, West	23 Oct 54	Other Military	58WBGA64	424143
France	Germany, West	27 Nov 54	Visas	55WBGA34	424144
France	Germany, West	16 Dec 54	Visas	55WBGA41	424145
France	Germany, West	24 Jun 55	Commodity Trade	55WBGA159	424146
France	Germany, West	04 Oct 55	Air Transport	353UNTS203	105044
France	Germany, West	27 Oct 56	Territory Boundary	56WGBB1587	425147
France	Germany, West	27 Oct 56	Specific Resources	56WGBB1863	425148
France	Germany, West	27 Oct 56	General Amity	57WGBB1661	425149
France	Germany, West	08 Dec 56	Land Transport	58WBGA4	424150
France	Germany, West	14 Jan 57	Visas	57WBGA137	424151
France	Germany, West	07 Jun 57	General Military	59WGBB409	425152
France	Germany, West	31 Mar 58	Specific Property	59WGBB189	425153
France	Germany, West	18 Apr 58	Visas	60WGBB1533	425154
France	Germany, West	18 Apr 58	General Transport	0UNTS0	110714
France	Germany, West	22 Aug 58	Finance	58FRRT28	415047
France	Germany, West	30 Jun 59	Visas	59WGBB389	425155
France	Germany, West	21 Jul 59	Taxation	61WGBB397	425156
France	Germany, West	03 Aug 59	Dispute Settlement	61WGBB1183	425157
France	Germany, West	27 Oct 59	Visas	61WBGA11	424158
France	Germany, West	22 Jan 60	Extradition	60WBGA63	424159
France	Germany, West	08 Mar 60	Patents/Copyrights	61WGBB22	425160
France	Germany, West	08 Mar 60	Patents/Copyrights	0UNTS0	110715
France	Germany, West	22 Apr 60	Admin Cooperation	60WGBB2325	425181
France	Germany, West	15 Jul 60	Specif Claim/Waive	61WGBB1029	425182
France	Germany, West	06 May 61	Admin Cooperation	61WGBB1040	425183
France	Germany, West	13 Jun 61	Visas	66WBGA245	424184
France	Germany, West	27 Jul 61	Claims and Debts	63FRJO33	416039
France	Germany, West	28 Sep 61	General Military	63WBGA171	424185
France	Germany, West	27 Nov 61	Admin Cooperation	62WGBB705	425186
France	Germany, West	20 Dec 61	IGO Establishment	62WGBB1106	425187
France	Germany, West	19 Jan 62	Admin Cooperation	62FRJO13	416040
France	Germany, West	2(Apr 62	Admin Cooperation	62FRRT23	415041
France	Germany, West	12 Jul 62	Non-ILO Labor	63WBGA75	424188
France	Germany, West	19 Dec 62	Postal Service	62FRJO2812	416042
France	Germany, West	22 Jan 63	General Amity	63WGBB405	425189
France	Germany, West	27 Jun 63	Non-ILO Labor	63WBGA231	424190
France	Germany, West	05 Jul 63	Health/Educ/Welfare	63WGBB1612	425191
France	Germany, West	13 Aug 63	Admin Cooperation	63FRRT69	415043
France	Germany, West	20 Dec 63	Non-ILO Labor	64WGBB702	425193
France	Germany, West	20 Dec 63	Non-ILO Labor	65WGBB1287	425192
France	Germany, West	15 Jan 64	Admin Cooperation	70WGBB1	425194
France	Germany, West	27 Feb 64	Visas	64WBGA238	424195
France	Germany, West	18 Jan 65	Admin Cooperation	67WBGA10	424196
France	Germany, West	16 Mar 65	Non-ILO Labor	65WBGA157	424197
France	Germany, West	22 Mar 65	Culture	65FRRT79	415045
France	Germany, West	25 Mar 65	Status of Forces	69FRJO1810	416044
France	Germany, West	19 Apr 66	Other Military	66WBGA161	424199
France	Germany, West	11 Jun 66	Admin Cooperation	66WBGA192	424198
France	Germany, West	27 Jun 66	Culture	66FRRT24	415046
France	Germany, West	19 Jan 67	Atomic Energy	67WGBB2430	425200
France	Germany, West	06 Jun 67	Telecommunications	69WGBB84	425201
France	Germany, West	04 Jul 69	Specific Resources	70WGBB726	425202
France	Germany, West	03 Nov 69	Taxation	70WGBB1317	425203
France	Germany, West	02 Feb 71	Admin Cooperation	71WGBB2434	425204
France	Greece	24 Apr 46	Finance	91UNTS83	101243
France	Greece	05 May 47	Air Transport	76UNTS61	100980
France	Greece	06 Aug 49	General Trade	91UNTS95	101244
France	Greece	09 Dec 50	Taxation	166UNTS315	102196

PARTY ONE	PARTY TWO	DATE	TOPIC	CITATION	NUMBER
France	Greece	03 Sep 51	Mostfavored Nation	187UNTS113	102505
France	Greece	31 Jul 52	General Trade	187UNTS169	102510
France	Greece	23 Dec 52	General Trade	187UNTS175	102511
France	Greece	08 Feb 54	Status of Forces	225UNTS107	103093
France	Greece	08 Feb 54	Status of Forces	225UNTS121	103094
France	Greece	13 May 54	Non-ILO Labor	222UNTS299	103036
France	Greece	30 Jun 54	Non-ILO Labor	257UNTS83	103651
France	Greece	22 Jul 54	General Trade	225UNTS199	103099
France	Greece	28 Jun 55	General Trade	225UNTS219	103100
France	Greece	25 Jun 56	General Trade	251UNTS167	103540
France	Greece	19 Apr 58	Non-ILO Labor	59FRRT14	415204
France	Greece	25 Jul 60	General Aid	533UNTS227	107745
France	Greece	21 Aug 63	Taxation	533UNTS235	107746
France	Greece	14 Dec 65	Loans and Credits	67FRJO1005	416205
France	Greece	09 Apr 69	Land Transport	0UNTS0	110738
France	Greece	09 Apr 69	Land Transport	69FRJO3007	416206
France	Guatemala	26 Sep 50	Culture	60FRRT82	415207
France	Guinea	29 Jul 61	Culture	62FRRT17	415208
France	Guinea	21 Mar 62	Air Transport	63FRRT59	415209
France	Guinea	22 May 63	General Trade	63FRRT62	415211
France	Guinea	22 May 63	Tech Assistance	63FRRT61	415210
France	Haiti	08 Apr 52	Education	52FRJO2404	416212
France	Haiti	15 Jun 65	Air Transport	67FRJO1205	416213
France	Honduras	15 Aug 55	Consul/Citizenship	60FRRT29	415219
France	Honduras	13 Jan 68	Culture	0UNTS0	109530
France	Honduras	13 Jan 68	Health/Educ/Welfare	69FRJO1101	416220
France	Hungary	12 Jun 50	Claims and Debts	52FRJO2509	416221
France	Hungary	02 May 60	Air Transport	60FRRT63	415222
France	Hungary	14 May 65	Claims and Debts	65FRRT68	415223
France	Hungary	15 Feb 66	General Trade	66FRMD2602	417224
France	Hungary	28 Jul 66	Scientific Project	67FRJO201	416226
France	Hungary	28 Jul 66	Consul/Citizenship	67FRJO2210	416225
France	Hungary	28 Jul 66	Culture	67FRJO204	416227
France	Hungary	08 Oct 66	Land Transport	67FRJO3003	416228
France	Hungary	19 Mar 68	Admin Cooperation	0UNTS0	109532
France	IBRD (World Bank)	09 May 47	IBRD Project	152UNTS111	102014
France	IBRD (World Bank)	10 Jun 54	IBRD Project	210UNTS89	102836
France	IBRD (World Bank)	26 Aug 55	IBRD Project	247UNTS305	103478
France	IBRD (World Bank)	30 Jun 59	IBRD Project	452UNTS67	106505
France	IBRD (World Bank)	10 Dec 59	IBRD Project	380UNTS319	105464
France	IBRD (World Bank)	17 Mar 60	IBRD Project	452UNTS147	106508
France	ICAO (Civil Aviat)	14 Mar 47	IGO Status/Immunit	94UNTS59	101306
France	ICJ Option Clause	18 Feb 47	ICJ Option Clause	26UNTS91	100378
France	ICJ Option Clause	10 Jul 59	ICJ Option Clause	337UNTS65	104816
France	ICJ Option Clause	16 May 66	ICJ Option Clause	562UNTS299	108196
France	IDA (Devel Assoc)	05 Mar 69	Non-IBRD Project	0UNTS0	110217
France	India	16 Jul 47	Air Transport	27UNTS325	100415
France	India	02 Feb 51	Territory Boundary	203UNTS155	102744
France	India	21 Oct 54	Specific Property	62FRRT33	415229
France	India	28 May 56	Specific Property	62FRRT33	415230
France	India	07 Jun 66	Health/Educ/Welfare	66FRRT32	415231
France	India	31 Jul 67	Air Transport	69FRJO709	416232
France	India	26 Mar 69	Taxation	70FRJO2803	416233
France	India	26 Mar 69	Taxation	0UNTS0	110735
France	Indonesia	24 Nov 67	Air Transport	68FRJO3103	416234
France	Indonesia	03 Apr 69	Atomic Energy	69FRJO2707	416235
France	Indonesia	03 Apr 69	Atomic Energy	0UNTS0	110736
France	Indonesia	20 Sep 69	Culture	0UNTS0	110737
France	Int Exhibit Bureau	11 Jan 65	IGO Status/Immunit	66FRRT36	415513
France	Int Org Metrology	01 Sep 64	IGO Status/Immunit	65FRRT76	415502
France	Int Wine Office	20 Jan 65	IGO Status/Immunit	66FRRT35	415503
France	Iran	30 Aug 56	Taxation	0IRTB30	433041
France	Iran	12 May 59	General Trade	0IRTB31	433042
France	Iran	21 Apr 60	Air Transport	86FRRT5009	415238
France	Iran	24 Jun 64	Water Transport	69FRJO511	416240

PARTY ONE	PARTY TWO	DATE	TOPIC	CITATION	NUMBER
France	Iran	24 Jun 64	Extradition	67FRJO3003	416239
France	Iran	24 Jun 64	Consul/Citizenship	0UNTS0	110722
France	Iran	03 Feb 66	Visas	66FRRT14	415241
France	Iran	27 Dec 67	Tech Assistance	69FRJO1304	416242
France	Iraq	19 May 66	Air Transport	67FRJO1901	416236
France	Iraq	25 Sep 67	General Trade	69FRJO1408	416237
France	Iraq	25 Sep 67	General Trade	0UNTS0	110822
France	Iraq	24 Apr 69	Culture	0UNTS0	110739
France	Iraq	19 Jun 69	Tech Assistance	0UNTS0	110740
France	Ireland	16 May 46	Air Transport	44UNTS105	100681
France	Ireland	22 Apr 47	Visas	553UNTS51	108068
France	Ireland	06 May 48	General Trade	558UNTS170	108141
France	Ireland	21 Nov 49	Non-ILO Labor	553UNTS59	108069
France	Ireland	07 Jun 55	General Trade	558UNTS217	108142
France	Ireland	04 Nov 67	Culture	68FRJO2402	416243
France	Ireland	04 Nov 67	Culture	0UNTS0	109291
France	Israel	03 Jun 51	Extradition	219UNTS215	102977
France	Israel	24 Jan 52	Taxation	220UNTS55	102988
France	Israel	29 Apr 52	Air Transport	189UNTS55	102542
France	Israel	15 Sep 52	Customs	220UNTS65	102989
France	Israel	10 Jul 53	General Economic	53FRMD2307	417244
France	Israel	01 Mar 58	Visas	314UNTS87	104543
France	Israel	12 Nov 58	Admin Cooperation	345UNTS79	104960
France	Israel	19 May 59	Admin Cooperation	377UNTS231	105403
France	Israel	30 Jun 59	Milit Servic/Citiz	448UNTS107	106428
France	Israel	30 Nov 59	Culture	377UNTS237	105404
France	Israel	07 Jul 60	Visas	413UNTS79	105942
France	Israel	20 Aug 63	Taxation	515UNTS173	107460
France	Israel	20 Dec 63	Customs	515UNTS165	107459
France	Israel	17 Dec 65	Non-ILO Labor	581UNTS311	108451
France	Israel	17 Dec 65	Non-ILO Labor	582UNTS3	108452
France	Israel	28 Nov 69	Visas	0UNTS0	110388
France	Italy	29 Nov 47	Peace/Disarmament	48ITGU38	435110
France	Italy	09 Feb 48	Education	50FRJO702	416245
France	Italy	31 Mar 48	Non-ILO Labor	49ITGU157	435111
France	Italy	29 May 48	Patents/Copyrights	49ITGU247	435112
France	Italy	29 May 48	Patents/Copyrights	49ITGU250	435113
France	Italy	03 Feb 49	Air Transport	53ITGU91	435114
France	Italy	30 May 49	Peace/Disarmament	50ITGU89	435115
France	Italy	26 Sep 49	Patents/Copyrights	52ITGU124	435116
France	Italy	04 Nov 49	Culture	52ITGU213	435117
France	Italy	07 Mar 50	Gen Communications	53ITGU296	435118
France	Italy	14 Mar 50	Patents/Copyrights	52ITGU127	435119
France	Italy	20 Jun 50	Other Military	52ITGU203	435121
France	Italy	04 Oct 50	Non-ILO Labor	50ITGU240	435122
France	Italy	29 Jan 51	Land Transport	52ITGU287	435123
France	Italy	29 Jan 51	Sanitation	52ITGU24	435125
France	Italy	29 Jan 51	Visas	52ITGU10	435124
France	Italy	02 Feb 51	General Trade	52ITGU68	435126
France	Italy	21 Mar 51	Health/Educ/Welfare	53ITGU22	435127
France	Italy	21 Mar 51	Non-ILO Labor	53ITGU22	435129
France	Italy	21 Mar 51	Non-ILO Labor	53ITGU22	435128
France	Italy	23 Aug 51	Consul/Citizenship	291UNTS143	104249
France	Italy	22 Mar 52	Consul/Citizenship	52ITDI336	436131
France	Italy	05 Apr 52	Patents/Copyrights	52ITGU127	435132
France	Italy	02 Dec 52	Claims and Debts	53ITGU51	435133
France	Italy	14 Mar 53	Land Transport	284UNTS221	104140
France	Italy	29 Jul 53	Peace/Disarmament	53ITDI289	436134
France	Italy	28 Dec 53	Milit Servic/Citiz	267UNTS89	103836
France	Italy	08 Jan 55	Patents/Copyrights	57ITGU137	435137
France	Italy	08 Jan 55	Patents/Copyrights	57ITGU68	435138
France	Italy	12 Jan 55	Consul/Citizenship	58ITGU99	435139
France	Italy	12 Jan 55	Admin Cooperation	57ITGU87	435140
France	Italy	12 Jan 55	Specific Resources	56ITGU13	435141
France	Italy	14 Feb 56	Culture	57ITGU139	435142

PARTY ONE	PARTY TWO	DATE	TOPIC	CITATION	NUMBER
France	Italy	03 Mar 56	Non-ILO Labor	267UNTS181	103843
France	Italy	06 Apr 56	Admin Cooperation	60FRRT15	415246
France	Italy	28 Dec 56	Non-ILO Labor	291UNTS203	104255
France	Italy	11 Jan 57	Non-ILO Labor	59ITDI264	436144
France	Italy	27 Feb 57	Non-ILO Labor	59ITDI264	436145
France	Italy	28 Feb 57	Visas	291UNTS191	104253
France	Italy	29 Jul 57	Patents/Copyrights	291UNTS163	104250
France	Italy	01 Aug 57	Non-ILO Labor	302UNTS221	104360
France	Italy	19 Sep 57	Non-ILO Labor	302UNTS225	104361
France	Italy	08 Nov 57	Mass Media	305UNTS393	104427
France	Italy	25 Jan 58	Non-ILO Labor	58ITGU123	435146
France	Italy	27 Mar 58	Non-ILO Labor	305UNTS409	104428
France	Italy	27 Mar 58	Visas	305UNTS387	104426
France	Italy	29 Oct 58	Taxation	68FRJO1403	416247
France	Italy	30 Oct 58	Visas	363UNTS3	105196
France	Italy	21 Oct 59	General Economic	61ITDI264	436147
France	Italy	06 Feb 60	Non-ILO Labor	62ITDI325	436151
France	Italy	01 Jun 60	General Military	62ITDI325	436152
France	Italy	14 Sep 60	General Ad Hoc	61ITDI213	436153
France	Italy	18 Dec 61	Culture	62ITDI506	436154
France	Italy	17 Jul 63	Non-ILO Labor	64ITDI254	436156
France	Italy	17 Jul 63	Non-ILO Labor	64ITDI253	436155
France	Italy	11 Oct 63	Land Transport	65ITGU181	435157
France	Italy	28 Apr 64	Patents/Copyrights	69FRJO2704	416248
France	Italy	28 Apr 64	Territory Boundary	65ITDI128	436158
France	Italy	02 Jun 64	Finance	634UNTS117	109056
France	Italy	25 Mar 65	Land Transport	65ITGU193	435159
France	Italy	16 Jul 65	Visas	65FRRT71	415249
France	Italy	29 Oct 65	Taxation	0UNTS0	109445
France	Italy	01 Mar 66	Admin Cooperation	67FRJO1108	416250
France	Italy	03 Jun 66	Visas	66FRRT30	415251
France	Italy	01 Aug 66	Culture	66FRRT40	415252
France	Italy	01 Aug 66	Mass Media	0UNTS0	110728
France	Italy	16 Feb 70	Mass Media	0UNTS0	110729
France	Ivory Coast	11 Jul 60	Recognition	60FRRT52	415138
France	Ivory Coast	24 Apr 61	General Amity	62FRRT8	415139
France	Ivory Coast	24 Apr 61	Culture	0UNTS0	110718
France	Ivory Coast	24 Apr 61	Admin Cooperation	0UNTS0	110717
France	Ivory Coast	26 Oct 61	Customs	62FRRT37	415140
France	Ivory Coast	19 Oct 62	Air Transport	498UNTS317	107286
France	Ivory Coast	06 Apr 66	Finance	69FRJO2201	416141
France	Ivory Coast	07 May 66	Claims and Debts	66FRJO2011	416142
France	Ivory Coast	21 Feb 70	Visas	0UNTS0	110536
France	Jamaica	24 Sep 68	Visas	69FRJO2810	416253
France	Jamaica	24 Sep 68	Visas	0UNTS0	109336
France	Japan	11 Jun 52	Admin Cooperation	0JGJI1021	441144
France	Japan	25 Apr 53	Admin Cooperation	187UNTS41	102500
France	Japan	12 May 53	Culture	53FRJO610	416254
France	Japan	18 Nov 55	Visas	0JGJI1263	441088
France	Japan	17 Jan 56	Air Transport	255UNTS275	103614
France	Japan	27 Mar 57	Specif Claim/Waive	318UNTS233	104617
France	Japan	21 Dec 62	Taxation	0JGJI1502	441115
France	Japan	14 May 63	General Economic	518UNTS111	107493
France	Japan	27 Nov 64	Taxation	65FRRT75	415255
France	Japan	27 Nov 64	Taxation	569UNTS157	108283
France	Japan	23 Jul 65	Atomic Energy	0JGJI1604	441139
France	Japan	30 Mar 68	General Trade	68JJS187	442212
France	Japan	30 Sep 69	Commodity Trade	69JJS155	442248
France	Jordan	16 Jun 65	Health/Educ/Welfare	65FRRT86	415256
France	Jordan	30 Apr 66	Air Transport	66FRJO2606	416257
France	Kenya	28 Jul 64	Air Transport	65FRJO2511	416258
France	Korea, South	01 Feb 61	Patents/Copyrights	61FRRT11	415130
France	Korea, South	26 Apr 63	Patents/Copyrights	64FRRT2	415131
France	Korea, South	28 Dec 65	Health/Educ/Welfare	68FRJO1909	416132
France	Korea, South	11 Feb 67	Visas	67FRJO1204	416133

PARTY ONE	PARTY TWO	DATE	TOPIC	CITATION	NUMBER
France	Kuwait	18 Sep 69	Culture	0UNTS0	110742
France	Laos	22 Oct 53	Admin Cooperation	59FRRT7	415259
France	Laos	16 Nov 56	Admin Cooperation	60FRRT22	415260
France	Lebanon	24 Jan 48	Finance	173UNTS99	102263
France	Lebanon	24 Jul 62	Taxation	64FRRT6	415261
France	Liberia	13 Jan 66	Air Transport	68FRJO1904	416262
France	Libya	10 Aug 55	General Amity	57FRJO704	416263
France	Libya	26 Dec 56	Territory Boundary	300UNTS263	104340
France	Luxembourg	30 Mar 49	Milit Servic/Citiz	50FRJO1003	416264
France	Luxembourg	27 Jun 49	Education	49FRJO2510	416265
France	Luxembourg	12 Nov 49	Non-ILO Labor	50FRJO110	416266
France	Luxembourg	29 Apr 52	Customs	55FRJO601	416267
France	Luxembourg	08 Feb 54	Culture	55FRJO1603	416268
France	Luxembourg	23 Jul 56	Admin Cooperation	60FRRT45	415269
France	Luxembourg	01 Apr 58	Taxation	60FRRT18	415270
France	Luxembourg	25 Jul 58	Postal Service	58FRJO2507	416271
France	Luxembourg	29 Mar 62	Air Transport	563UNTS227	108212
France	Luxembourg	10 Dec 62	Humanitarian	63FRRT9	415272
France	Luxembourg	16 Jul 63	Territory Boundary	68FRJO1101	416273
France	Luxembourg	21 May 64	Territory Boundary	0UNTS0	110527
France	Luxembourg	03 Jun 64	Non-ILO Labor	67FRJO2412	416274
France	Luxembourg	16 Jul 64	Territory Boundary	0UNTS0	109225
France	Luxembourg	31 Aug 65	Health/Educ/Welfare	68FRJO1910	416275
France	Malagasy	02 Apr 60	Recognition	60FRRT38	415278
France	Malagasy	27 Jun 60	General Amity	60FRRT46	415279
France	Malagasy	18 Oct 61	Specific Property	63FRRT21	415280
France	Malagasy	23 May 62	Customs	62FRRT40	415281
France	Malagasy	29 Sep 62	General Economic	65FRRT69	415282
France	Malagasy	25 Apr 63	Consul/Citizenship	65FRRT83	415283
France	Malagasy	06 Jul 63	Claims and Debts	63FRRT81	415284
France	Malagasy	19 Jun 64	Visas	64FRRT69	415285
France	Malagasy	08 May 67	Non-ILO Labor	68FRJO708	416286
France	Malagasy	22 May 68	Tech Assistance	68FRJO2211	416287
France	Malaysia	22 May 67	Air Transport	67FRJO508	416277
France	Mali	22 Aug 61	Claims and Debts	63FRRT27	415288
France	Mali	09 Mar 62	General Amity	64FRRT49	415289
France	Mali	08 Mar 63	Visas	63FRRT42	415290
France	Mali	11 Mar 65	Non-ILO Labor	67FRJO3008	416291
France	Mali	15 Feb 67	Finance	67FRJO2706	416292
France	Malta	14 Feb 68	Culture	68FRRT60	415293
France	Malta	24 Mar 69	Visas	0UNTS0	110734
France	Malta	27 Mar 69	Visas	69FRRT50	415294
France	Mauritania	19 Oct 60	Recognition	60FRRT75	415311
France	Mauritania	19 Jun 61	General Amity	62FRRT9	415312
France	Mauritania	10 May 63	Specific Property	63FRRT72	415313
France	Mauritania	29 May 63	Direct Aid	65FRRT99	415314
France	Mauritania	15 Jul 63	Visas	64FRRT8	415315
France	Mauritania	24 Oct 63	Air Transport	64FRRT10	415316
France	Mauritania	07 Feb 64	Consul/Citizenship	66FRJO1901	416317
France	Mauritania	16 Nov 64	Education	65FRRT91	415318
France	Mauritania	22 Jul 65	Non-ILO Labor	67FRJO1202	416319
France	Mauritania	22 Jul 65	Non-ILO Labor	0UNTS0	109329
France	Mauritania	15 Nov 67	Finance	69FRJO2704	416320
France	Mauritania	15 Nov 67	Taxation	0UNTS0	110244
France	Mauritania	17 Feb 68	Scientific Project	68FRJO706	416321
France	Mauritius	19 May 69	General Trade	69FRMD3107	417310
France	Mexico	11 Dec 50	Patents/Copyrights	51FRJO1111	416322
France	Mexico	29 Nov 51	General Trade	53FRJO2905	416323
France	Mexico	17 Apr 52	Air Transport	163UNTS321	102153
France	Mexico	22 Apr 65	Tech Assistance	63FRRT13	415324
France	Monaco	14 Apr 45	Finance	45FRJO106	416325
France	Monaco	14 Apr 45	Finance	45FRJO106	416326
France	Monaco	14 Apr 45	Admin Cooperation	45FRJO106	416327
France	Monaco	26 Oct 46	Reparations	60FRJO44	416328
France	Monaco	16 Jun 47	Consul/Citizenship	47FRJO2106	416329

PARTY ONE	PARTY TWO	DATE	TOPIC	CITATION	NUMBER
France	Monaco	01 Apr 50	Taxation	53FRJO1006	416330
France	Monaco	13 Sep 50	Claims and Debts	54FRJO2706	416331
France	Monaco	13 Nov 52	Claims and Debts	54FRJO508	416332
France	Monaco	18 May 63	Finance	63FRRT66	415333
France	Monaco	18 May 63	Taxation	0UNTS0	109438
France	Monaco	18 May 63	Non-ILO Labor	0UNTS0	110719
France	Monaco	15 Oct 63	Admin Cooperation	63FRRT77	415334
France	Monaco	31 Aug 64	Visas	64FRRT66	415335
France	Monaco	09 Dec 66	Finance	0UNTS0	109439
France	Monaco	18 May 67	Culture	0UNTS0	110662
France	Monaco	26 Sep 68	General Economic	70FRJO1601	416336
France	Monaco	26 Sep 68	Non-ILO Labor	0UNTS0	110720
France	Monaco	23 Jan 70	Education	0UNTS0	110664
France	Monaco	23 Jan 70	Culture	0UNTS0	110663
France	Monaco	16 Apr 70	Admin Cooperation	0UNTS0	110721
France	Mongolia	31 Jan 68	Culture	68FRJO1010	416337
France	Morocco	06 Feb 57	Admin Cooperation	60FRRT11	415295
France	Morocco	06 Feb 57	Admin Cooperation	0UNTS0	109933
France	Morocco	05 Oct 57	Admin Cooperation	0UNTS0	110712
France	Morocco	05 Oct 57	Admin Cooperation	60FRRT4	415296
France	Morocco	05 Oct 57	Admin Cooperation	0UNTS0	110713
France	Morocco	25 Oct 57	Air Transport	559UNTS95	108156
France	Morocco	14 May 60	Non-IBRD Project	60FRRT40	415297
France	Morocco	20 Sep 60	Health/Educ/Welfare	60FRRT80	415298
France	Morocco	10 Mar 61	Air Transport	61FRRT52	415299
France	Morocco	21 Jun 61	Customs	61FRRT38	415300
France	Morocco	23 Jul 63	Non-ILO Labor	0UNTS0	109934
France	Morocco	17 Oct 64	Non-ILO Labor	0UNTS0	109935
France	Morocco	09 Jul 65	Non-ILO Labor	67FRJO605	416309
France	Morocco	09 Jul 65	Non-ILO Labor	0UNTS0	109936
France	Multilateral	12 May 40	Scientific Project	101UNTS91	101405
France	Multilateral	27 Mar 41	Military Mission	67UNTS231	200222
France	Multilateral	19 Apr 44	Scientific Project	89UNTS279	200257
France	Multilateral	02 Aug 44	Scientific Project	67UNTS221	200221
France	Multilateral	14 Nov 44	Milit Occupation	236UNTS359	200539
France	Multilateral	07 Dec 44	Air Transport	84UNTS389	200252
France	Multilateral	07 Dec 44	Air Transport	171UNTS345	200501
France	Multilateral	07 Dec 44	IGO Establishment	15UNTS295	200102
France	Multilateral	15 Dec 44	Sanitation	16UNTS247	200106
France	Multilateral	15 Dec 44	Sanitation	17UNTS305	200110
France	Multilateral	20 Mar 45	General Economic	2UNTS299	200022
France	Multilateral	05 Jun 45	Milit Occupation	68UNTS189	200230
France	Multilateral	09 Jul 45	Milit Occupation	160UNTS359	200484
France	Multilateral	26 Jul 45	Milit Occupation	227UNTS297	200533
France	Multilateral	08 Aug 45	General Military	82UNTS279	200251
France	Multilateral	02 Sep 45	Peace/Disarmament	139UNTS387	200465
France	Multilateral	27 Sep 45	IGO Establishment	5UNTS327	200035
France	Multilateral	16 Nov 45	IGO Establishment	4UNTS275	100052
France	Multilateral	27 Dec 45	IGO Establishment	2UNTS39	100020
France	Multilateral	04 Jan 46	IGO Establishment	6UNTS35	100066
France	Multilateral	14 Jan 46	Reparations	555UNTS69	108105
France	Multilateral	05 Apr 46	Specific Resources	231UNTS199	103221
France	Multilateral	17 Apr 46	Land Transport	27UNTS103	100402
France	Multilateral	23 Apr 46	Sanitation	17UNTS3	100265
France	Multilateral	23 Apr 46	Sanitation	16UNTS179	100257
France	Multilateral	28 Jun 46	Milit Occupation	138UNTS85	101862
France	Multilateral	18 Jul 46	Reparations	125UNTS119	101674
France	Multilateral	22 Jul 46	IGO Establishment	9UNTS3	100125
France	Multilateral	22 Jul 46	IGO Establishment	14UNTS185	100221
France	Multilateral	27 Jul 46	Patents/Copyrights	90UNTS229	101238
France	Multilateral	15 Oct 46	Refugees	11UNTS73	100150
France	Multilateral	30 Oct 46	IGO Establishment	11UNTS107	100151
France	Multilateral	30 Oct 46	IGO Establishment	27UNTS77	100401
France	Multilateral	02 Dec 46	Specific Resources	161UNTS72	102124
France	Multilateral	11 Dec 46	Sanitation	12UNTS179	100186

PARTY ONE	PARTY TWO	DATE	TOPIC	CITATION	NUMBER
France	Multilateral	15 Dec 46	IGO Establishment	18UNTS3	100283
France	Multilateral	06 Feb 47	IGO Establishment	97UNTS227	101352
France	Multilateral	08 Feb 47	Patents/Copyrights	14UNTS287	100222
France	Multilateral	10 Feb 47	Peace/Disarmament	49UNTS3	100747
France	Multilateral	10 Feb 47	Reparations	140UNTS111	101886
France	Multilateral	03 Mar 47	Humanitarian	11UNTS43	100148
France	Multilateral	06 Jun 47	Patents/Copyrights	46UNTS249	100714
France	Multilateral	10 Jun 47	Water Transport	208UNTS3	102814
France	Multilateral	14 Aug 47	Reparations	138UNTS111	101863
France	Multilateral	02 Oct 47	Telecommunications	193UNTS188	102616
France	Multilateral	11 Oct 47	IGO Establishment	77UNTS143	100998
France	Multilateral	04 Nov 47	Reparations	93UNTS61	101288
France	Multilateral	18 Nov 47	Finance	17UNTS89	100269
France	Multilateral	16 Dec 47	Reparations	82UNTS237	101096
France	Multilateral	06 Mar 48	Water Transport	289UNTS3	104214
France	Multilateral	17 Mar 48	General Military	19UNTS51	100304
France	Multilateral	10 May 48	Culture	289UNTS111	104215
France	Multilateral	10 May 48	Reparations	140UNTS129	101887
France	Multilateral	13 May 48	Reparations	140UNTS187	101888
France	Multilateral	10 Jun 48	Humanitarian	164UNTS113	102163
France	Multilateral	10 Jun 48	Humanitarian	191UNTS3	102576
France	Multilateral	19 Jun 48	Air Transport	310UNTS151	104492
France	Multilateral	26 Jun 48	Culture	331UNTS217	104757
France	Multilateral	24 Jul 48	Sanitation	66UNTS25	100847
France	Multilateral	14 Sep 48	Milit Occupation	18UNTS267	100296
France	Multilateral	17 Sep 48	Telecommunications	97UNTS31	101345
France	Multilateral	19 Oct 48	Specif Claim/Waive	84UNTS201	101130
France	Multilateral	15 Nov 48	IGO Establishment	120UNTS59	101615
France	Multilateral	19 Nov 48	Sanitation	44UNTS277	100688
France	Multilateral	29 Nov 48	IGO Establishment	120UNTS13	101613
France	Multilateral	09 Dec 48	Scientific Project	73UNTS39	100942
France	Multilateral	09 Dec 48	Scientific Project	20UNTS229	100318
France	Multilateral	09 Dec 48	Humanitarian	78UNTS277	101021
France	Multilateral	08 Feb 49	Specific Resources	157UNTS157	102053
France	Multilateral	23 Mar 49	Commodity Trade	203UNTS179	102746
France	Multilateral	31 Mar 49	Reparations	122UNTS57	101636
France	Multilateral	04 Apr 49	General Military	34UNTS243	100541
France	Multilateral	08 Apr 49	Milit Occupation	140UNTS196	101889
France	Multilateral	28 Apr 49	IGO Establishment	83UNTS105	101105
France	Multilateral	04 May 49	Admin Cooperation	47UNTS159	100728
France	Multilateral	04 May 49	Admin Cooperation	92UNTS19	101257
France	Multilateral	04 May 49	Milit Occupation	138UNTS123	101864
France	Multilateral	04 May 49	Admin Cooperation	98UNTS101	101358
France	Multilateral	05 May 49	IGO Establishment	87UNTS103	101168
France	Multilateral	16 Jun 49	Land Transport	45UNTS149	100696
France	Multilateral	18 Jun 49	ILO Labor	605UNTS295	108768
France	Multilateral	20 Jun 49	IGO Establishment	128UNTS141	101718
France	Multilateral	22 Jul 49	General Trade	557UNTS211	108135
France	Multilateral	12 Aug 49	Humanitarian	75UNTS85	100971
France	Multilateral	12 Aug 49	Humanitarian	75UNTS31	100970
France	Multilateral	12 Aug 49	Humanitarian	75UNTS287	100973
France	Multilateral	12 Aug 49	General Military	75UNTS135	100972
France	Multilateral	02 Sep 49	IGO Status/Immunit	250UNTS12	103515
France	Multilateral	19 Sep 49	Land Transport	125UNTS3	101671
France	Multilateral	24 Sep 49	IGO Establishment	126UNTS237	101691
France	Multilateral	07 Nov 49	Non-ILO Labor	132UNTS31	101749
France	Multilateral	07 Nov 49	Sanitation	132UNTS3	101748
France	Multilateral	22 Nov 49	Recognition	185UNTS307	102477
France	Multilateral	16 Dec 49	Admin Cooperation	72UNTS3	100924
France	Multilateral	21 Mar 50	Admin Cooperation	96UNTS271	101342
France	Multilateral	06 Apr 50	Admin Cooperation	119UNTS99	101610
France	Multilateral	08 Apr 50	Specif Goods/Equip	68UNTS99	100889
France	Multilateral	08 Apr 50	IGO Establishment	66UNTS285	100860
France	Multilateral	17 Apr 50	Visas	131UNTS99	101738
France	Multilateral	17 Apr 50	Non-ILO Labor	126UNTS285	101694

PARTY ONE	PARTY TWO	DATE	TOPIC	CITATION	NUMBER
France	Multilateral	13 May 50	Land Transport	128UNTS171	101719
France	Multilateral	27 Jul 50	Non-ILO Labor	166UNTS73	102186
France	Multilateral	16 Sep 50	General Transport	92UNTS91	101264
France	Multilateral	18 Oct 50	Specific Resources	638UNTS185	109134
France	Multilateral	04 Nov 50	Humanitarian	213UNTS221	102889
France	Multilateral	22 Nov 50	Culture	131UNTS25	101734
France	Multilateral	29 Nov 50	Patents/Copyrights	88UNTS221	101194
France	Multilateral	07 Dec 50	Admin Cooperation	212UNTS17	102861
France	Multilateral	15 Dec 50	Customs	171UNTS305	102234
France	Multilateral	15 Dec 50	IGO Operations	160UNTS267	102111
France	Multilateral	15 Dec 50	Customs	157UNTS129	102052
France	Multilateral	15 Dec 50	Customs	347UNTS127	104994
France	Multilateral	23 Dec 50	Tech Assistance	185UNTS3	102456
France	Multilateral	06 Mar 51	Milit Assistance	138UNTS67	101860
France	Multilateral	06 Mar 51	Claims and Debts	106UNTS141	101461
France	Multilateral	20 Mar 51	IGO Operations	82UNTS172	101091
France	Multilateral	03 Apr 51	Milit Occupation	141UNTS303	101920
France	Multilateral	18 Apr 51	IGO Establishment	261UNTS140	103729
France	Multilateral	25 Apr 51	Reparations	91UNTS21	101240
France	Multilateral	25 May 51	Status of Forces	175UNTS215	102303
France	Multilateral	15 Jun 51	Tech Assistance	148UNTS67	101936
France	Multilateral	19 Jun 51	Status of Forces	199UNTS67	102678
France	Multilateral	02 Jul 51	Refugees	189UNTS137	102545
France	Multilateral	08 Sep 51	General Military	136UNTS165	101833
France	Multilateral	08 Sep 51	Peace/Disarmament	136UNTS45	101832
France	Multilateral	20 Sep 51	IGO Status/Immunit	200UNTS3	102691
France	Multilateral	09 Oct 51	IGO Establishment	220UNTS121	102997
France	Multilateral	31 Oct 51	Other Military	172UNTS193	102247
France	Multilateral	06 Dec 51	IGO Establishment	425UNTS61	106119
France	Multilateral	06 Dec 51	Admin Cooperation	150UNTS67	101963
France	Multilateral	10 Jan 52	Visas	163UNTS3	102138
France	Multilateral	10 Jan 52	Visas	163UNTS27	102139
France	Multilateral	15 Feb 52	Scientific Project	132UNTS51	101751
France	Multilateral	10 May 52	Taxation	439UNTS233	106332
France	Multilateral	10 May 52	Admin Cooperation	439UNTS193	106330
France	Multilateral	10 May 52	Admin Cooperation	439UNTS217	106331
France	Multilateral	15 May 52	Sanitation	0UNTS0	110476
France	Multilateral	20 May 52	Sanitation	219UNTS55	102966
France	Multilateral	12 Jun 52	Dispute Settlement	138UNTS183	101869
France	Multilateral	11 Jul 52	Postal Service	170UNTS3	102221
France	Multilateral	11 Jul 52	Postal Service	170UNTS269	102223
France	Multilateral	11 Jul 52	Postal Service	171UNTS3	102224
France	Multilateral	11 Jul 52	Postal Service	171UNTS191	102227
France	Multilateral	11 Jul 52	Postal Service	170UNTS63	102222
France	Multilateral	11 Jul 52	Postal Service	171UNTS143	102226
France	Multilateral	11 Jul 52	IGO Establishment	169UNTS3	102220
France	Multilateral	11 Jul 52	Postal Service	171UNTS89	102225
France	Multilateral	28 Aug 52	Claims and Debts	175UNTS69	102296
France	Multilateral	06 Sep 52	Patents/Copyrights	216UNTS132	102937
France	Multilateral	07 Oct 52	Admin Cooperation	310UNTS181	104493
France	Multilateral	10 Nov 52	Admin Cooperation	214UNTS265	102904
France	Multilateral	27 Feb 53	Claims and Debts	333UNTS3	104764
France	Multilateral	31 Mar 53	Mass Media	435UNTS191	106280
France	Multilateral	31 Mar 53	Privil/Immunities	193UNTS136	102613
France	Multilateral	30 Apr 53	Admin Cooperation	175UNTS89	102297
France	Multilateral	11 May 53	Sanitation	456UNTS3	106555
France	Multilateral	01 Jul 53	IGO Establishment	200UNTS149	102701
France	Multilateral	01 Oct 53	Commodity Trade	258UNTS153	103677
France	Multilateral	17 Oct 53	General Transport	184UNTS42	102438
France	Multilateral	26 Oct 53	Status of Forces	207UNTS237	102809
France	Multilateral	07 Dec 53	Admin Cooperation	182UNTS51	102422
France	Multilateral	11 Dec 53	Non-ILO Labor	218UNTS255	102958
France	Multilateral	11 Dec 53	Education	218UNTS125	102954
France	Multilateral	11 Dec 53	Non-ILO Labor	218UNTS153	102956
France	Multilateral	11 Dec 53	Patents/Copyrights	218UNTS27	102952

PARTY ONE	PARTY TWO	DATE	TOPIC	CITATION	NUMBER
France	Multilateral	11 Dec 53	Non-ILO Labor	218UNTS211	102957
France	Multilateral	18 Jan 54	IGO Establishment	330UNTS121	104743
France	Multilateral	19 Feb 54	Status of Forces	214UNTS51	102899
France	Multilateral	25 Feb 54	Air Transport	215UNTS249	102922
France	Multilateral	01 Mar 54	Commodity Trade	256UNTS31	103622
France	Multilateral	01 Mar 54	Admin Cooperation	286UNTS265	104173
France	Multilateral	12 May 54	Admin Cooperation	327UNTS3	104714
France	Multilateral	14 May 54	Culture	249UNTS215	103511
France	Multilateral	21 May 54	Non-ILO Labor	345UNTS285	104973
France	Multilateral	31 May 54	Tech Assistance	192UNTS20	102592
France	Multilateral	04 Jun 54	Customs	282UNTS249	104101
France	Multilateral	04 Jun 54	Customs	276UNTS191	103992
France	Multilateral	14 Jun 54	Air Transport	320UNTS217	104644
France	Multilateral	14 Jun 54	Air Transport	320UNTS209	104643
France	Multilateral	30 Jun 54	Admin Cooperation	204UNTS99	102752
France	Multilateral	29 Jul 54	Sanitation	249UNTS45	103500
France	Multilateral	08 Sep 54	Milit Assistance	209UNTS23	102819
France	Multilateral	28 Sep 54	Refugees	360UNTS117	105158
France	Multilateral	23 Oct 54	Status of Forces	332UNTS3	104760
France	Multilateral	23 Oct 54	Milit Occupation	331UNTS253	104758
France	Multilateral	23 Oct 54	Status of Forces	332UNTS387	104763
France	Multilateral	23 Oct 54	Milit Occupation	332UNTS157	104761
France	Multilateral	23 Oct 54	Reparations	332UNTS219	104762
France	Multilateral	23 Oct 54	Status of Forces	334UNTS3	104765
France	Multilateral	23 Oct 54	Milit Occupation	331UNTS327	104759
France	Multilateral	01 Dec 54	Admin Cooperation	210UNTS197	102839
France	Multilateral	19 Dec 54	Culture	218UNTS139	102955
France	Multilateral	19 Dec 54	Patents/Copyrights	218UNTS51	102953
France	Multilateral	21 Dec 54	General Amity	258UNTS322	103678
France	Multilateral	06 Apr 55	General Amity	261UNTS55	103725
France	Multilateral	01 May 55	Admin Cooperation	0UNTS0	110416
France	Multilateral	15 May 55	Recognition	217UNTS223	102949
France	Multilateral	25 May 55	IGO Establishment	264UNTS117	103791
France	Multilateral	03 Jun 55	Specific Resources	310UNTS145	104491
France	Multilateral	06 Jun 55	IGO Establishment	219UNTS79	102968
France	Multilateral	22 Jun 55	Atomic Energy	249UNTS3	103498
France	Multilateral	28 Sep 55	Air Transport	478UNTS371	106943
France	Multilateral	12 Oct 55	IGO Establishment	560UNTS3	108165
France	Multilateral	20 Oct 55	IGO Establishment	378UNTS159	105425
France	Multilateral	13 Dec 55	IGO Operations	529UNTS141	107660
France	Multilateral	13 Dec 55	Humanitarian	250UNTS3	103514
France	Multilateral	04 Jan 56	Scientific Project	256UNTS171	103627
France	Multilateral	01 Mar 56	Customs	343UNTS129	104923
France	Multilateral	05 Mar 56	Other Military	326UNTS169	104711
France	Multilateral	25 Apr 56	Commodity Trade	270UNTS103	103896
France	Multilateral	30 Apr 56	Air Transport	310UNTS229	104494
France	Multilateral	18 May 56	Customs	319UNTS21	104630
France	Multilateral	18 May 56	Land Transport	339UNTS3	104844
France	Multilateral	18 May 56	Customs	338UNTS103	104834
France	Multilateral	18 May 56	Customs	327UNTS123	104721
France	Multilateral	19 May 56	Land Transport	399UNTS189	105742
France	Multilateral	20 Jun 56	Admin Cooperation	268UNTS3	103850
France	Multilateral	05 Jul 56	Patents/Copyrights	258UNTS371	103679
France	Multilateral	09 Jul 56	Non-ILO Labor	314UNTS3	104539
France	Multilateral	13 Jul 56	Dispute Settlement	281UNTS3	104066
France	Multilateral	07 Sep 56	Humanitarian	266UNTS3	103822
France	Multilateral	25 Sep 56	Air Transport	334UNTS13	104766
France	Multilateral	25 Sep 56	Air Transport	334UNTS89	104767
France	Multilateral	24 Oct 56	Admin Cooperation	510UNTS161	107412
France	Multilateral	26 Oct 56	IGO Establishment	276UNTS3	103988
France	Multilateral	29 Oct 56	Territory Boundary	263UNTS165	103772
France	Multilateral	15 Dec 56	Education	278UNTS73	104023
France	Multilateral	31 Jan 57	Claims and Debts	278UNTS105	104026
France	Multilateral	25 Mar 57	IGO Establishment	294UNTS2	104300
France	Multilateral	25 Mar 57	IGO Status/Immunit	294UNTS411	104302

PARTY ONE	PARTY TWO	DATE	TOPIC	CITATION	NUMBER
France	Multilateral	25 Mar 57	IGO Establishment	294UNTS259	104301
France	Multilateral	29 Mar 57	Claims and Debts	283UNTS137	104113
France	Multilateral	12 Apr 57	Education	443UNTS128	106362
France	Multilateral	29 Apr 57	Dispute Settlement	320UNTS243	104646
France	Multilateral	15 Jun 57	Patents/Copyrights	583UNTS3	108470
France	Multilateral	15 Jun 57	General Trade	550UNTS45	108008
France	Multilateral	01 Jul 57	Culture	0UNTS0	110418
France	Multilateral	26 Jul 57	Land Transport	386UNTS3	105535
France	Multilateral	27 Sep 57	Admin Cooperation	299UNTS211	104314
France	Multilateral	30 Sep 57	General Transport	619UNTS77	108940
France	Multilateral	03 Oct 57	Postal Service	365UNTS207	105214
France	Multilateral	03 Oct 57	Postal Service	365UNTS3	105213
France	Multilateral	03 Oct 57	Postal Service	364UNTS331	105212
France	Multilateral	03 Oct 57	Postal Service	366UNTS255	105219
France	Multilateral	03 Oct 57	Postal Service	366UNTS141	105217
France	Multilateral	03 Oct 57	Postal Service	364UNTS3	105211
France	Multilateral	03 Oct 57	Postal Service	366UNTS87	105216
France	Multilateral	03 Oct 57	Postal Service	366UNTS193	105218
France	Multilateral	03 Oct 57	Postal Service	366UNTS3	105215
France	Multilateral	23 Nov 57	Refugees	506UNTS125	107384
France	Multilateral	25 Nov 57	General Trade	403UNTS169	105795
France	Multilateral	13 Dec 57	Visas	315UNTS139	104565
France	Multilateral	13 Dec 57	Land Transport	372UNTS159	105296
France	Multilateral	13 Dec 57	Extradition	359UNTS273	105146
France	Multilateral	15 Jan 58	Customs	383UNTS229	105503
France	Multilateral	20 Mar 58	Admin Cooperation	335UNTS211	104789
France	Multilateral	31 Mar 58	Specific Property	320UNTS103	104639
France	Multilateral	03 Apr 58	Commodity Trade	336UNTS177	104806
France	Multilateral	03 Apr 58	Commodity Trade	302UNTS121	104355
France	Multilateral	15 Apr 58	Health/Educ/Welfare	539UNTS27	107822
France	Multilateral	29 Apr 58	Specific Resources	559UNTS285	108164
France	Multilateral	29 Apr 58	Dispute Settlement	450UNTS169	106466
France	Multilateral	29 Apr 58	Water Transport	450UNTS11	106465
France	Multilateral	29 Apr 58	Territory Boundary	499UNTS311	107302
France	Multilateral	10 Jun 58	Admin Cooperation	330UNTS3	104739
France	Multilateral	27 Oct 58	Reparations	351UNTS303	105031
France	Multilateral	01 Dec 58	Commodity Trade	385UNTS137	105534
France	Multilateral	03 Dec 58	Admin Cooperation	416UNTS51	105995
France	Multilateral	03 Dec 58	Admin Cooperation	398UNTS9	105715
France	Multilateral	15 Dec 58	Mass Media	546UNTS235	107950
France	Multilateral	15 Dec 58	Sanitation	351UNTS159	105022
France	Multilateral	15 Jan 59	Customs	348UNTS13	104996
France	Multilateral	24 Jan 59	IGO Establishment	486UNTS157	107078
France	Multilateral	06 Apr 59	Commodity Trade	349UNTS167	105013
France	Multilateral	20 Apr 59	Visas	376UNTS85	105375
France	Multilateral	20 Apr 59	Admin Cooperation	472UNTS185	106841
France	Multilateral	11 May 59	Claims and Debts	527UNTS145	107623
France	Multilateral	03 Aug 59	Status of Forces	481UNTS262	106986
France	Multilateral	18 Nov 59	IGO Establishment	390UNTS227	105610
France	Multilateral	19 Nov 59	IGO Operations	410UNTS156	105902
France	Multilateral	01 Dec 59	Territory Boundary	402UNTS71	105778
France	Multilateral	14 Dec 59	Admin Cooperation	444UNTS193	106369
France	Multilateral	26 Jan 60	IGO Establishment	439UNTS249	106333
France	Multilateral	15 Mar 60	Water Transport	572UNTS133	108310
France	Multilateral	22 Apr 60	Air Transport	418UNTS211	106023
France	Multilateral	28 Apr 60	Health/Educ/Welfare	376UNTS111	105377
France	Multilateral	17 Jun 60	Humanitarian	536UNTS27	107794
France	Multilateral	21 Jun 60	IGO Establishment	418UNTS109	106019
France	Multilateral	22 Jun 60	Mass Media	546UNTS247	107951
France	Multilateral	01 Sep 60	Commodity Trade	403UNTS3	105792
France	Multilateral	21 Sep 60	Patents/Copyrights	394UNTS3	105664
France	Multilateral	06 Oct 60	Customs	473UNTS131	106861
France	Multilateral	01 Dec 60	Scientific Project	414UNTS110	105970
France	Multilateral	09 Dec 60	Customs	429UNTS211	106200
France	Multilateral	13 Dec 60	Air Transport	523UNTS117	107557

PARTY ONE	PARTY TWO	DATE	TOPIC	CITATION	NUMBER
France	Multilateral	14 Dec 60	Education	429UNTS93	106193
France	Multilateral	13 Feb 61	ILO Labor	0UNTS0	110306
France	Multilateral	18 Apr 61	Dispute Settlement	500UNTS243	107312
France	Multilateral	18 Apr 61	Consul/Citizenship	500UNTS95	107310
France	Multilateral	21 Apr 61	IGO Establishment	484UNTS349	107041
France	Multilateral	08 Jun 61	Customs	473UNTS153	106862
France	Multilateral	08 Jun 61	Customs	473UNTS187	106863
France	Multilateral	21 Jun 61	IGO Establishment	514UNTS209	107449
France	Multilateral	18 Sep 61	Air Transport	500UNTS31	107305
France	Multilateral	05 Oct 61	Patents/Copyrights	527UNTS181	107625
France	Multilateral	05 Oct 61	Dispute Settlement	510UNTS175	107413
France	Multilateral	18 Oct 61	IGO Establishment	529UNTS89	107659
France	Multilateral	26 Oct 61	Patents/Copyrights	496UNTS43	107247
France	Multilateral	06 Dec 61	Customs	473UNTS219	106864
France	Multilateral	16 Dec 61	Visas	544UNTS19	107909
France	Multilateral	07 Mar 62	Commodity Trade	445UNTS199	106388
France	Multilateral	07 Mar 62	Commodity Trade	445UNTS205	106389
France	Multilateral	29 Mar 62	IGO Establishment	507UNTS177	107401
France	Multilateral	09 May 62	IGO Establishment	453UNTS299	106531
France	Multilateral	14 May 62	Scientific Project	544UNTS39	107910
France	Multilateral	15 May 62	Commodity Trade	444UNTS3	106367
France	Multilateral	14 Jun 62	IGO Establishment	528UNTS33	107634
France	Multilateral	23 Jul 62	Recognition	456UNTS302	106564
France	Multilateral	28 Sep 62	IGO Establishment	469UNTS169	106791
France	Multilateral	05 Oct 62	IGO Establishment	502UNTS225	107333
France	Multilateral	10 Dec 62	Culture	521UNTS231	107525
France	Multilateral	17 Dec 62	Sanitation	486UNTS119	107076
France	Multilateral	17 Dec 62	General Economic	523UNTS93	107555
France	Multilateral	17 Dec 62	Admin Cooperation	590UNTS81	108548
France	Multilateral	20 Apr 63	IGO Establishment	495UNTS3	107239
France	Multilateral	24 Apr 63	Consul/Citizenship	596UNTS261	108638
France	Multilateral	24 Apr 63	Consul/Citizenship	596UNTS487	108640
France	Multilateral	06 May 63	Consul/Citizenship	634UNTS221	109065
France	Multilateral	09 Nov 63	Direct Aid	489UNTS209	107141
France	Multilateral	09 Mar 64	Specific Resources	581UNTS89	108434
France	Multilateral	09 Mar 64	Specific Resources	581UNTS57	108432
France	Multilateral	09 Mar 64	Specific Resources	581UNTS83	108433
France	Multilateral	16 Apr 64	Visas	548UNTS27	107967
France	Multilateral	18 Jun 64	Atomic Energy	542UNTS145	107886
France	Multilateral	10 Jul 64	Postal Service	613UNTS127	108853
France	Multilateral	10 Jul 64	Postal Service	611UNTS7	108844
France	Multilateral	10 Jul 64	Postal Service	611UNTS105	108845
France	Multilateral	10 Jul 64	Postal Service	612UNTS3	108847
France	Multilateral	10 Jul 64	Postal Service	612UNTS361	108849
France	Multilateral	10 Jul 64	Postal Service	612UNTS233	108848
France	Multilateral	10 Jul 64	Postal Service	611UNTS387	108846
France	Multilateral	10 Jul 64	Postal Service	613UNTS3	108850
France	Multilateral	10 Jul 64	Postal Service	613UNTS3	108851
France	Multilateral	10 Jul 64	Postal Service	613UNTS193	108852
France	Multilateral	20 Aug 64	Telecommunications	514UNTS25	107441
France	Multilateral	12 Sep 64	Specific Resources	0UNTS0	109344
France	Multilateral	15 Sep 64	General Trade	510UNTS147	107411
France	Multilateral	22 Jan 65	Gen Communications	634UNTS239	109066
France	Multilateral	09 Mar 65	Water Transport	591UNTS265	108564
France	Multilateral	18 Mar 65	Dispute Settlement	575UNTS159	108359
France	Multilateral	08 Jul 65	General Trade	597UNTS3	108641
France	Multilateral	31 Dec 65	Specific Resources	616UNTS317	108904
France	Multilateral	05 Apr 66	Water Transport	640UNTS133	109159
France	Multilateral	28 Apr 66	Non-ILO Labor	604UNTS219	108752
France	Multilateral	14 May 66	Specific Resources	0UNTS0	109587
France	Multilateral	27 Jan 67	Scientific Project	610UNTS205	108843
France	Multilateral	24 Apr 67	Humanitarian	634UNTS255	109067
France	Multilateral	03 May 67	IGO Operations	0UNTS0	110764
France	Multilateral	10 Jul 67	Air Transport	0UNTS0	109971
France	Multilateral	18 Mar 68	Commodity Trade	0UNTS0	109262

PARTY ONE	PARTY TWO	DATE	TOPIC	CITATION	NUMBER
France	Multilateral	11 Jun 68	Scientific Project	0UNTS0	109884
France	Multilateral	24 Sep 68	Air Transport	0UNTS0	110612
France	Multilateral	28 Sep 68	Tech Assistance	0UNTS0	109296
France	Multilateral	03 Mar 69	Commodity Trade	0UNTS0	110233
France	Multilateral	09 Jun 69	Specific Resources	0UNTS0	110099
France	Multilateral	12 Jan 70	Commodity Trade	0UNTS0	110603
France	Multilateral	13 Apr 70	Education	0UNTS0	110793
France	Netherlands	14 Jun 40	Finance	2UNTS263	200019
France	Netherlands	27 Mar 46	Visas	247UNTS3	103456
France	Netherlands	09 Apr 46	Finance	3UNTS57	100024
France	Netherlands	19 Nov 46	Culture	32UNTS101	100493
France	Netherlands	02 Dec 47	Finance	63FRRT76	415356
France	Netherlands	02 Jan 48	Visas	70UNTS105	100899
France	Netherlands	02 Jun 48	Non-ILO Labor	204UNTS275	102762
France	Netherlands	02 Jun 48	Education	50FRJO1002	416357
France	Netherlands	20 Jul 49	Mostfavored Nation	204UNTS287	102763
France	Netherlands	03 Aug 49	General Trade	51NET40	447012
France	Netherlands	30 Dec 49	Taxation	203UNTS133	102743
France	Netherlands	30 Dec 49	Taxation	203UNTS85	102742
France	Netherlands	07 Jan 50	Non-ILO Labor	120UNTS25	101614
France	Netherlands	03 Jul 51	Finance	63FRRT76	415358
France	Netherlands	07 Feb 52	General Trade	54NET90	447032
France	Netherlands	20 Jun 53	Land Transport	187UNTS97	102503
France	Netherlands	27 Nov 53	Reparations	302UNTS245	104363
France	Netherlands	30 Apr 54	Reparations	202UNTS115	102727
France	Netherlands	09 Jul 54	Finance	287UNTS169	104183
France	Netherlands	15 Dec 54	Reparations	288UNTS37	104195
France	Netherlands	15 Feb 57	Refugees	286UNTS243	104170
France	Netherlands	21 May 57	Visas	299UNTS43	104305
France	Netherlands	29 Apr 59	Finance	486UNTS379	107088
France	New Zealand	02 Jul 47	Commodity Trade	16UNTS219	100263
France	New Zealand	22 Nov 47	Visas	15UNTS29	100228
France	New Zealand	15 Nov 49	Air Transport	53UNTS247	100785
France	New Zealand	13 Jan 50	Reparations	150UNTS151	101969
France	New Zealand	27 Feb 64	Air Transport	499UNTS191	107298
France	New Zealand	09 Nov 67	Air Transport	68FRJO103	416347
France	Nicaragua	22 Dec 66	Health/Educ/Welfare	68FRJO1105	416338
France	Niger	11 Jul 60	Recognition	60FRRT52	415339
France	Niger	24 Apr 61	General Amity	62FRRT8	415340
France	Niger	28 May 62	Air Transport	63FRRT1	415341
France	Niger	29 Nov 62	Customs	63FRRT28	415342
France	Niger	01 Jun 65	Finance	66FRRT48	415343
France	Niger	23 Sep 65	Extradition	65FRRT90	415344
France	Niger	25 Feb 67	Mass Media	68FRJO204	416345
France	Niger	25 Feb 67	Mass Media	0UNTS0	109261
France	Niger	16 Feb 70	Visas	0UNTS0	110535
France	Norway	06 Mar 46	Finance	15UNTS13	100227
France	Norway	26 Mar 46	General Trade	31UNTS69	100468
France	Norway	30 Jun 47	Visas	104UNTS313	101449
France	Norway	15 Jul 47	Specific Property	15UNTS5	100226
France	Norway	11 Jun 48	General Trade	31UNTS83	100469
France	Norway	05 Jul 48	General Trade	30UNTS281	100463
France	Norway	09 Feb 49	General Economic	29UNTS13	100431
France	Norway	06 Nov 51	Education	2NORT572	451057
France	Norway	22 Sep 53	Taxation	2NORT607	451058
France	Norway	04 Dec 53	Culture	2NORT611	451059
France	Norway	30 Sep 54	Non-ILO Labor	2NORT641	451060
France	Norway	06 Dec 54	Milit Servic/Citiz	202UNTS313	102737
France	Norway	20 Nov 56	Patents/Copyrights	3NORT699	451061
France	Norway	02 Apr 60	General Trade	60FRMD904	417346
France	Norway	24 May 63	Visas	3NORT886	451062
France	Norway	16 Jul 64	Patents/Copyrights	510UNTS229	107417
France	OECD (Econ Coop)	05 Mar 59	Non-ILO Labor	59FRRT40	415499
France	OECD (Econ Coop)	26 Jan 66	Non-ILO Labor	66FRRT12	415506
France	Pakistan	31 Jul 50	Air Transport	96UNTS23	101329

PARTY ONE	PARTY TWO	DATE	TOPIC	CITATION	NUMBER
France	Pakistan	17 Feb 58	General Trade	58FRMD2202	417349
France	Pakistan	27 Aug 64	Visas	64FRMD67	417350
France	Pakistan	22 Jul 66	Taxation	69FRMD25	417351
France	Pakistan	22 Jul 66	Taxation	0UNTS0	109648
France	Pakistan	22 Oct 69	Water Transport	0UNTS0	110633
France	Panama	10 Jul 53	Consul/Citizenship	58FRRT19	415352
France	Paraguay	11 Sep 56	General Trade	58FRRT18	415353
France	Paraguay	05 Apr 63	Visas	63FRRT50	415354
France	Paraguay	10 Dec 63	Health/Educ/Welfare	65FRRT15	415355
France	Peru	23 Apr 59	Air Transport	61FRRT19	415359
France	Philippines	26 Jun 47	General Amity	1PTS427	465008
France	Philippines	08 Mar 63	Visas	569UNTS77	108280
France	Philippines	29 Oct 68	Air Transport	0UNTS0	109972
France	Philippines	21 May 70	Visas	0UNTS0	110744
France	Poland	11 Feb 47	Reparations	12UNTS287	100189
France	Poland	19 Feb 47	Scientific Project	47PDZU1044	457001
France	Poland	19 May 47	Education	12UNTS95	100181
France	Poland	19 Mar 48	Claims and Debts	51FRJO1111	416360
France	Poland	09 Jun 48	Non-ILO Labor	32UNTS251	100503
France	Poland	17 Aug 48	Non-ILO Labor	0UNTS0	110700
France	Poland	07 Sep 51	Claims and Debts	57FRJO708	416361
France	Poland	12 Nov 59	Taxation	59PZUM106	458071
France	Poland	25 Jun 60	Air Transport	60PZUM53	458075
France	Poland	25 Jun 60	Air Transport	61FRRT20	415362
France	Poland	25 May 61	Non-ILO Labor	61PZUM118	458083
France	Poland	25 May 61	Non-ILO Labor	0UNTS0	110701
France	Poland	15 Jun 61	Consul/Citizenship	61PZUM127	458085
France	Poland	22 Oct 65	General Trade	65FRMD611	417363
France	Poland	28 Apr 66	Non-ILO Labor	66PZUM76	458133
France	Poland	28 Apr 66	Non-ILO Labor	0UNTS0	110702
France	Poland	20 May 66	Scientific Project	66PZUM79	458135
France	Poland	20 May 66	Tech Assistance	67FRJO404	416364
France	Poland	20 May 66	Culture	67FRJO204	416365
France	Poland	22 May 66	Culture	66PZUM70	458136
France	Poland	05 Apr 67	Admin Cooperation	0UNTS0	109510
France	Poland	05 Apr 67	Admin Cooperation	69PDZU29	457142
France	Poland	05 Apr 67	Consul/Citizenship	69FRJO2202	416366
France	Poland	05 Apr 67	Admin Cooperation	0UNTS0	109636
France	Poland	03 Mar 68	Land Transport	68PZUM65	458153
France	Poland	03 Mar 68	General Transport	68FRJO308	416367
France	Portugal	30 Apr 46	Air Transport	35UNTS197	100556
France	Portugal	16 Nov 57	Non-ILO Labor	59FRRT16	415368
France	Portugal	30 Oct 58	Non-ILO Labor	59FRRT16	415369
France	Portugal	31 Dec 63	Non-ILO Labor	64FRRT12	415370
France	Portugal	16 Oct 64	Education	64FRRT68	415371
France	Portugal	26 Jan 65	Admin Cooperation	65FRRT25	415372
France	Portugal	11 Sep 67	Non-ILO Labor	67FRJO2910	416373
France	Refrigeration Inst	05 Jul 66	IGO Status/Immunit	67FRJO1203	416508
France	Romania	09 Feb 59	Finance	59FRJO1903	416374
France	Romania	18 May 62	Air Transport	498UNTS115	107279
France	Romania	31 Jul 64	Tech Assistance	64FRRT64	415375
France	Romania	31 Jul 64	Education	0UNTS0	110723
France	Romania	11 Jan 65	Culture	65FRRT46	415376
France	Romania	11 Jan 65	Culture	0UNTS0	110528
France	Romania	08 Feb 65	General Economic	65FRMD1302	417377
France	Romania	14 Mar 66	Land Transport	604UNTS33	108741
France	Romania	22 Apr 66	Culture	66FRRT38	415378
France	Romania	13 Feb 67	Sanitation	67FRJO508	416379
France	Romania	26 Jun 67	Culture	642UNTS181	109173
France	Romania	18 May 68	Consul/Citizenship	0UNTS0	110724
France	Romania	17 Jan 69	Admin Cooperation	0UNTS0	110725
France	Romania	12 Mar 69	Sanitation	69FRJO609	416380
France	Romania	12 Mar 69	Sanitation	0UNTS0	110531
France	Romania	25 Jun 69	Culture	0UNTS0	110533
France	Rwanda	04 Dec 62	General Amity	65FRRT20	415381

PARTY ONE	PARTY TWO	DATE	TOPIC	CITATION	NUMBER
France	San Marino	12 Jul 49	Non-ILO Labor	51FRJO203	416382
France	San Marino	15 Jan 54	Consul/Citizenship	56FRJO106	416383
France	San Marino	21 May 65	Non-ILO Labor	65FRRT58	415384
France	San Marino	25 May 67	Admin Cooperation	69FRJO1503	416385
France	San Marino	25 May 67	Admin Cooperation	0UNTS0	109527
France	Saudi Arabia	07 Jul 63	Health/Educ/Welfare	65FRRT21	415051
France	Senegal	22 Jun 60	General Amity	60FRRT47	415388
France	Senegal	19 Sep 60	Admin Cooperation	61FRRT22	415389
France	Senegal	14 Jun 62	Admin Cooperation	65FRRT28	415390
France	Senegal	15 Jun 62	Air Transport	524UNTS3	107563
France	Senegal	18 Sep 62	Specific Property	63FRRT22	415391
France	Senegal	13 Oct 62	Customs	63FRRT55	415392
France	Senegal	16 Feb 63	Consul/Citizenship	65FRRT51	415393
France	Senegal	24 Apr 63	Claims and Debts	65FRRT7	415394
France	Senegal	21 Jan 64	Education	64FRRT25	415396
France	Senegal	21 Jan 64	Visas	64FRRT32	415395
France	Senegal	15 May 64	Education	66FRJO1601	416397
France	Senegal	05 Mar 65	Non-ILO Labor	67FRJO3110	416398
France	Senegal	03 May 65	General Economic	0UNTS0	109489
France	Sierra Leone	19 Oct 64	Health/Educ/Welfare	65FRRT30	415399
France	Sierra Leone	18 Jul 67	Air Transport	67FRJO1410	416400
France	Singapore	29 Jun 67	Air Transport	67FRJO1110	416401
France	South Africa	18 Apr 47	Reparations	225UNTS35	103085
France	South Africa	05 May 54	Air Transport	215UNTS401	102926
France	South Africa	17 Sep 54	Air Transport	216UNTS29	102930
France	South Africa	22 Nov 54	Taxation	219UNTS35	102963
France	South Africa	06 Jan 64	Scientific Project	601UNTS229	108699
France	South Africa	27 Mar 68	Scientific Project	643UNTS343	109200
France	Spain	29 Apr 48	Air Transport	48SPBO1605	460101
France	Spain	23 Aug 48	Air Transport	28UNTS173	100425
France	Spain	24 Sep 52	Territory Boundary	54SPBO1230	460102
France	Spain	15 May 53	Admin Cooperation	55SPBO1508	460103
France	Spain	19 Nov 54	General Trade	55SPBO1301	460104
France	Spain	17 Dec 54	Mass Media	55SPBO2101	460105
France	Spain	17 Feb 55	Specific Resources	55SPBO1503	460106
France	Spain	15 Mar 55	General Trade	55SPBO304	460107
France	Spain	31 Mar 55	General Trade	55SPBO105	460108
France	Spain	31 Mar 55	Mass Media	55SPBO105	460109
France	Spain	13 May 55	Customs	55FRJO2408	416161
France	Spain	25 Nov 55	General Trade	56SPBO202	460110
France	Spain	28 Mar 56	General Trade	56SPBO2704	460111
France	Spain	02 Jun 56	Mass Media	56SPBO2406	460112
France	Spain	01 Dec 56	General Trade	57SPBO301	460113
France	Spain	17 May 57	General Trade	57SPBO606	460114
France	Spain	21 Jun 57	Patents/Copyrights	51FRJO1108	416162
France	Spain	25 Jun 57	Patents/Copyrights	58SPBO2203	460115
France	Spain	27 Jun 57	Non-ILO Labor	59SPBO3003	460276
France	Spain	27 Jun 57	Non-ILO Labor	0UNTS0	110704
France	Spain	27 Jun 57	Non-ILO Labor	57SPBO1409	460118
France	Spain	27 Jun 57	Non-ILO Labor	57SPBO1409	460117
France	Spain	27 Jun 57	Non-ILO Labor	59SPBO1104	460277
France	Spain	27 Jun 57	Non-ILO Labor	59SPBO3003	460116
France	Spain	19 Nov 57	General Economic	58SPBO301	460119
France	Spain	29 Nov 57	Non-ILO Labor	57SPBO3112	460120
France	Spain	04 Dec 57	General Trade	58SPBO301	460121
France	Spain	28 Mar 58	Non-ILO Labor	58SPBO1504	460122
France	Spain	28 Mar 58	Non-ILO Labor	58SPBO2204	460123
France	Spain	19 Apr 58	General Trade	58SPBO805	460124
France	Spain	14 Jul 59	Specific Resources	65SPBO202	460125
France	Spain	14 Jul 59	Sanitation	60SPBO305	460126
France	Spain	14 Jul 59	Visas	60SPBO404	460128
France	Spain	14 Jul 59	Health/Educ/Welfare	60SPBO404	460127
France	Spain	20 Oct 59	Non-ILO Labor	60SPBO2603	460129
France	Spain	11 Apr 60	Non-ILO Labor	60SPBO2007	460130
France	Spain	25 Jan 61	Non-ILO Labor	61SPBO2802	460131

PARTY ONE	PARTY TWO	DATE	TOPIC	CITATION	NUMBER
France	Spain	25 Jan 61	Non-ILO Labor	62SPBO2103	460132
France	Spain	17 Apr 61	Admin Cooperation	61SPBO2505	460133
France	Spain	30 May 61	Customs	63SPBO1009	460134
France	Spain	15 Jun 61	Admin Cooperation	61FRRT42	415163
France	Spain	04 Oct 61	Non-ILO Labor	62SPBO401	460135
France	Spain	14 Dec 61	Non-ILO Labor	62SPBO2002	460137
France	Spain	14 Dec 61	Non-ILO Labor	62SPBO1902	460136
France	Spain	30 Mar 62	General Transport	62SPBO2311	460139
France	Spain	30 Mar 62	Admin Cooperation	62SPBO1711	460140
France	Spain	30 Mar 62	General Transport	62SPBO1911	460138
France	Spain	12 Apr 62	Non-ILO Labor	62SPBO3107	460141
France	Spain	30 May 62	Customs	63FRRT68	415164
France	Spain	17 Jul 62	Culture	66FRRT17	415165
France	Spain	02 Nov 62	Non-ILO Labor	63SPBO403	460142
France	Spain	23 Nov 62	Non-ILO Labor	63SPBO202	460143
France	Spain	08 Jan 63	Taxation	64SPBO701	460144
France	Spain	08 Jul 63	Non-ILO Labor	63SPBO1312	460145
France	Spain	08 Jul 63	Non-ILO Labor	OUNTSO	110705
France	Spain	29 Jul 63	Specific Resources	64SPBO108	460146
France	Spain	11 Oct 63	Non-ILO Labor	63SPBO1612	460147
France	Spain	15 Nov 63	Loans and Credits	64SPBO1403	460148
France	Spain	23 May 64	General Trade	64FRRT48	415166
France	Spain	04 Jun 64	Scientific Project	65SPBO1805	460149
France	Spain	03 Jul 64	Non-ILO Labor	64SPBO1509	460151
France	Spain	11 Jul 64	General Ad Hoc	67FRJO2502	416167
France	Spain	11 Jul 64	Specific Property	OUNTSO	110374
France	Spain	29 Aug 64	Non-ILO Labor	65SPBO302	460150
France	Spain	29 Aug 64	Non-ILO Labor	65SPBO1602	460152
France	Spain	29 Aug 64	Non-ILO Labor	64SPBO112	460153
France	Spain	29 Aug 64	Non-ILO Labor	OUNTSO	110706
France	Spain	01 Jun 65	Non-ILO Labor	65SPBO2906	460154
France	Spain	07 Jul 65	Admin Cooperation	66FRRT16	415168
France	Spain	22 Jul 66	Admin Cooperation	67FRJO408	416169
France	Spain	20 Mar 67	Specific Resources	67FRJO408	416170
France	Spain	20 Mar 67	Specific Resources	OUNTSO	110234
France	Spain	03 May 67	Admin Cooperation	67FRJO1108	416171
France	Spain	15 Jun 67	Visas	67FRJO608	416172
France	Spain	20 Jun 67	Visas	67FRJO608	416173
France	Spain	15 Mar 68	Admin Cooperation	70FRJO2503	416174
France	Spain	02 Aug 68	Non-ILO Labor	69FRJO1809	416175
France	Spain	07 Feb 69	Culture	OUNTSO	110707
France	Spain	11 Mar 69	Specific Resources	69FRJO909	416176
France	Spain	09 Apr 69	Milit Servic/Citiz	OUNTSO	110709
France	Spain	09 Apr 69	Admin Cooperation	OUNTSO	110708
France	Spain	28 May 69	Admin Cooperation	OUNTSO	110710
France	Spain	30 May 69	Specific Resources	76FRJO9070	416177
France	Spain	17 Jun 69	General Ad Hoc	64FRJO1010	416178
France	Spain	28 Jul 69	Non-ILO Labor	OUNTSO	110711
France	Sudan	22 Dec 69	Culture	OUNTSO	110743
France	Sweden	21 Jun 45	Finance	45SOFM107	461010
France	Sweden	21 Jun 45	General Trade	45SOFM105	461009
France	Sweden	16 Aug 45	Air Transport	45SOFM69	461003
France	Sweden	28 Jun 46	General Trade	46SOFM201	461026
France	Sweden	28 Jun 46	Finance	46SOFM203	461027
France	Sweden	02 Aug 46	Air Transport	27UNTS251	100410
France	Sweden	31 Oct 47	General Trade	47SOFM455	461045
France	Sweden	31 Oct 47	Finance	47SOFM480	461046
France	Sweden	03 Mar 49	General Trade	49SOFM97	461077
France	Sweden	08 Apr 49	Taxation	197UNTS183	102638
France	Sweden	08 Apr 49	Taxation	197UNTS177	102637
France	Sweden	30 Jun 49	General Trade	49SOFM484	461088
France	Sweden	17 Dec 49	General Trade	49SOFM584	461095
France	Sweden	31 Oct 50	General Trade	50SOFM981	461124
France	Sweden	02 Dec 50	Non-ILO Labor	50SOFM1061	461129
France	Sweden	11 Apr 51	General Trade	51SOFM203	461141

PARTY ONE	PARTY TWO	DATE	TOPIC	CITATION	NUMBER
France	Sweden	16 Nov 51	General Trade	51SOFM411	461151
France	Sweden	29 Nov 52	General Trade	52SOFM545	461177
France	Sweden	24 Apr 53	General Trade	53SOFM577	461183
France	Sweden	07 Nov 53	General Trade	53SOFM1023	461188
France	Sweden	16 Feb 54	General Transport	228UNTS137	103147
France	Sweden	05 Nov 54	Taxation	262UNTS229	103748
France	Sweden	05 Mar 55	Consul/Citizenship	427UNTS133	106150
France	Sweden	07 Mar 56	Admin Cooperation	369UNTS155	105256
France	Sweden	07 Mar 56	Admin Cooperation	369UNTS171	105257
France	Sweden	10 May 57	Admin Cooperation	427UNTS127	106149
France	Sweden	13 Oct 65	Culture	65FRRT103	415402
France	Sweden	16 Dec 68	General Transport	69FRJO2702	416403
France	Sweden	16 Dec 68	Land Transport	OUNTSO	109865
France	Switzerland	29 Jun 46	Refugees	47FRJO2905	416404
France	Switzerland	01 Aug 46	Non-ILO Labor	11SWRS623	463018
France	Switzerland	01 Aug 46	Non-ILO Labor	11SWRS615	463015
France	Switzerland	01 Aug 46	Non-ILO Labor	11SWRS621	463016
France	Switzerland	01 Aug 46	Customs	12SWRS656	463071
France	Switzerland	27 Apr 48	Non-ILO Labor	51SWRO1019	462017
France	Switzerland	15 Jun 48	Specific Resources	66FRRT33	415405
France	Switzerland	04 Jul 49	Specific Property	50SWRO1334	462088
France	Switzerland	09 Jul 49	Non-ILO Labor	50SWRO1164	462096
France	Switzerland	21 Nov 49	Claims and Debts	49SWRO1953	462168
France	Switzerland	20 Nov 51	Land Transport	52SWRO623	462083
France	Switzerland	25 Feb 53	Territory Boundary	60SWRO1546	462174
France	Switzerland	25 Feb 53	Territory Boundary	57SWRO884	462002
France	Switzerland	31 Dec 53	Taxation	55SWRO138	462050
France	Switzerland	31 Dec 53	Taxation	55SWRO132	462051
France	Switzerland	31 Dec 53	Taxation	55SWRO115	462049
France	Switzerland	11 May 54	Land Transport	54SWRO1148	462077
France	Switzerland	29 Oct 55	General Trade	55SWRO1092	462136
France	Switzerland	25 Apr 56	Specific Property	58SWRO135	462004
France	Switzerland	25 Apr 56	Specific Property	58SWRO135	462087
France	Switzerland	14 Oct 57	Visas	58FRRT4	415406
France	Switzerland	04 Dec 57	Specific Resources	58SWRO49	462106
France	Switzerland	01 Aug 58	Milit Servic/Citiz	59SWRO223	462006
France	Switzerland	24 Sep 58	Non-ILO Labor	62SWRO1016	462102
France	Switzerland	16 Oct 58	Land Transport	58SWRO1087	462084
France	Switzerland	16 Apr 59	Non-ILO Labor	61SWRO24	462101
France	Switzerland	03 Dec 59	Specific Resources	60SWRO1548	462033
France	Switzerland	03 Dec 59	Specific Resources	60SWRO1552	462034
France	Switzerland	03 Dec 59	Territory Boundary	60SWRO1550	462003
France	Switzerland	03 Dec 59	Territory Boundary	60SWRO1555	462175
France	Switzerland	03 Dec 59	Territory Boundary	60SWRO1554	462173
France	Switzerland	12 Apr 60	Refugees	60FRRT41	415407
France	Switzerland	28 Sep 60	Customs	61SWRO574	462074
France	Switzerland	28 Sep 60	General Transport	OUNTSO	110716
France	Switzerland	17 Sep 62	Customs	62SWRO1657	462070
France	Switzerland	16 Nov 62	Specific Resources	63SWRO961	462039
France	Switzerland	28 Feb 63	Visas	63FRRT34	415408
France	Switzerland	28 Feb 63	Visas	63FRRT37	415409
France	Switzerland	04 Apr 63	Claims and Debts	63FRRT45	415410
France	Switzerland	23 Aug 63	Territory Boundary	64SWRO1272	462001
France	Switzerland	23 Aug 63	Specific Property	64SWRO1255	462032
France	Switzerland	19 Sep 63	Finance	63FRRT83	415411
France	Switzerland	27 May 64	Non-ILO Labor	64FRRT42	415412
France	Switzerland	28 Sep 64	Admin Cooperation	64FRRT63	415413
France	Switzerland	10 Mar 65	Admin Cooperation	67FRJO604	416414
France	Switzerland	30 Jun 65	Admin Cooperation	65FRRT78	415415
France	Switzerland	24 Jul 65	General Transport	65FRRT80	415416
France	Switzerland	24 Jul 65	Land Transport	65FRRT80	415417
France	Switzerland	13 Sep 65	IGO Status/Immunit	69FRJO1004	416418
France	Switzerland	13 Sep 65	Atomic Energy	OUNTSO	109863
France	Switzerland	12 May 66	Visas	66FRJO2406	416419
France	Switzerland	09 Sep 66	Taxation	67FRJO1010	416420

PARTY ONE	PARTY TWO	DATE	TOPIC	CITATION	NUMBER
France	Switzerland	16 Jun 67	Admin Cooperation	67FRJO1108	416421
France	Switzerland	19 Jul 67	Admin Cooperation	67FRJO1108	416422
France	Syria	07 Feb 49	Finance	50FRJO1003	416423
France	Syria	07 Jan 66	Air Transport	67FRJO404	416424
France	Taiwan	18 Aug 45	Territory Boundary	14UNTS477	200101
France	Taiwan	28 Feb 46	Privil/Immunities	14UNTS113	100215
France	Taiwan	28 Feb 46	Milit Occupation	14UNTS151	100217
France	Taiwan	28 Feb 46	General Amity	14UNTS137	100216
France	Taiwan	14 Dec 46	Air Transport	0CTRC160	413002
France	Taiwan	28 Jun 47	Air Transport	0CTRC165	413018
France	Taiwan	10 May 48	Air Transport	0CTRC169	413019
France	Taiwan	30 Apr 49	Air Transport	0CTRC172	413020
France	Taiwan	12 May 54	General Trade	0CTRC174	413003
France	Taiwan	12 May 54	Finance	0CTRC178	413004
France	Taiwan	15 Apr 55	General Economic	0CTRC183	413021
France	Taiwan	21 Oct 55	Telecommunications	0CTRC186	413005
France	Taiwan	24 May 58	Patents/Copyrights	0CTRC10	413006
France	Tanzania	28 Apr 64	Air Transport	65FRRT97	415425
France	Thailand	17 Nov 46	Admin Cooperation	47FRJO1503	416448
France	Thailand	17 Nov 46	Reparations	344UNTS59	104943
France	Thailand	26 Feb 60	Air Transport	392UNTS279	105648
France	Togo	09 Apr 62	Direct Aid	62FRRT41	415449
France	Togo	10 Jul 63	General Amity	64FRRT39	415450
France	Togo	10 Jul 63	General Military	0UNTS0	110365
France	Togo	10 Jul 63	Admin Cooperation	0UNTS0	110370
France	Togo	10 Jul 63	Tech Assistance	0UNTS0	110369
France	Togo	10 Jul 63	Consul/Citizenship	0UNTS0	110366
France	Togo	10 Jul 63	General Economic	0UNTS0	110371
France	Togo	10 Jul 63	Admin Cooperation	0UNTS0	110367
France	Togo	10 Jul 63	Culture	0UNTS0	110368
France	Togo	10 Jul 63	Finance	0UNTS0	110372
France	Togo	30 Apr 68	Claims and Debts	69FRJO2006	416451
France	Togo	30 Apr 68	Territory Boundary	0UNTS0	110373
France	Togo	03 Feb 69	Scientific Project	0UNTS0	110670
France	Togo	25 Feb 70	Visas	0UNTS0	110537
France	Trinidad/Tobago	12 Oct 64	Air Transport	535UNTS25	107774
France	Tunisia	16 Apr 53	Health/Educ/Welfare	53FRJO2407	416452
France	Tunisia	03 Jun 55	General Amity	55FRJO609	416453
France	Tunisia	09 Mar 57	General Amity	58FRRT8	415454
France	Tunisia	27 Oct 58	Water Transport	60FRRT17	415455
France	Tunisia	15 Apr 59	Health/Educ/Welfare	59FRRT47	415456
France	Tunisia	20 May 61	Air Transport	65FRRT53	415457
France	Tunisia	08 Jan 63	Health/Educ/Welfare	63FRRT10	415458
France	Tunisia	31 Jan 63	Customs	63FRRT32	415459
France	Tunisia	09 Aug 63	Claims and Debts	65FRRT77	415461
France	Tunisia	09 Aug 63	Education	63FRRT70	415460
France	Tunisia	29 Jan 64	Visas	64FRRT26	415463
France	Tunisia	29 Jan 64	Visas	64FRRT30	415462
France	Tunisia	17 Dec 65	Non-ILO Labor	66FRRT37	415464
France	Tunisia	17 Dec 65	Non-ILO Labor	0UNTS0	110665
France	Tunisia	20 Mar 68	Non-ILO Labor	0UNTS0	110730
France	Tunisia	14 Feb 69	Culture	0UNTS0	110316
France	Tunisia	17 Feb 69	Culture	69FRJO110	416465
France	Tunisia	05 Jun 69	Tech Assistance	0UNTS0	110317
France	Tunisia	05 Jun 69	Tech Assistance	69FRJO2109	416466
France	Tunisia	20 Mar 70	Finance	0UNTS0	110666
France	Turkey	31 Aug 46	General Economic	47FRJO310	416467
France	Turkey	12 Oct 46	Air Transport	14UNTS33	100209
France	Turkey	21 Oct 46	General Trade	48TURG2302	466060
France	Turkey	22 Dec 50	Non-ILO Labor	98UNTS11	101356
France	Turkey	17 Jun 52	Culture	60FRRT2	415515
France	Turkey	18 Jan 54	Claims and Debts	54TURG1003	466104
France	Turkey	19 Jan 54	Commodity Trade	55TURG3105	466062
France	Turkey	06 Apr 57	General Economic	58TURG407	466063
France	Turkey	08 Apr 61	Commodity Trade	61TURG1109	466064

PARTY ONE	PARTY TWO	DATE	TOPIC	CITATION	NUMBER
France	Turkey	08 Jan 65	Non-ILO Labor	65FRRT57	415468
France	Uganda	28 Apr 64	Air Transport	65FRRT95	415348
France	UK Great Britain	27 Mar 45	Finance	98UNTS227	200274
France	UK Great Britain	29 Aug 45	Patents/Copyrights	11UNTS397	200069
France	UK Great Britain	31 Aug 45	IGO Establishment	98UNTS249	200275
France	UK Great Britain	04 Dec 45	Milit Installation	9UNTS121	100129
France	UK Great Britain	26 Jan 46	Reparations	91UNTS183	101251
France	UK Great Britain	28 Feb 46	Air Transport	27UNTS173	100407
France	UK Great Britain	29 Apr 46	Finance	98UNTS123	101360
France	UK Great Britain	03 Dec 46	Finance	54UNTS117	100798
France	UK Great Britain	03 Dec 46	Reparations	54UNTS127	100799
France	UK Great Britain	14 Dec 46	Taxation	105UNTS27	101452
France	UK Great Britain	27 Dec 46	Visas	11UNTS255	100163
France	UK Great Britain	04 Mar 47	General Amity	9UNTS187	100132
France	UK Great Britain	18 Jun 47	Air Transport	9UNTS203	100134
France	UK Great Britain	13 Aug 47	Non-ILO Labor	91UNTS169	101249
France	UK Great Britain	02 Mar 48	Culture	77UNTS33	100990
France	UK Great Britain	19 Apr 48	Status of Forces	83UNTS201	101109
France	UK Great Britain	11 Jun 48	Non-ILO Labor	66UNTS151	100852
France	UK Great Britain	12 Jul 48	Postal Service	90UNTS83	101230
France	UK Great Britain	15 Jul 48	Claims and Debts	71UNTS215	100920
France	UK Great Britain	21 Dec 49	Milit Servic/Citiz	264UNTS37	103786
France	UK Great Britain	23 Jan 50	Reparations	97UNTS149	101348
France	UK Great Britain	28 Jan 50	Non-ILO Labor	97UNTS155	101349
France	UK Great Britain	06 Oct 50	Air Transport	96UNTS63	101331
France	UK Great Britain	14 Dec 50	Taxation	51FRJO2108	416198
France	UK Great Britain	29 Dec 50	Dispute Settlement	118UNTS149	101603
France	UK Great Britain	24 Jan 51	Postal Service	90UNTS193	101237
France	UK Great Britain	30 Jan 51	Privil/Immunities	121UNTS97	101629
France	UK Great Britain	30 Jan 51	Specific Resources	51FRJO2010	416199
France	UK Great Britain	17 Feb 51	Finance	88UNTS199	101191
France	UK Great Britain	11 Apr 51	Claims and Debts	106UNTS3	101456
France	UK Great Britain	20 Apr 51	Air Transport	106UNTS81	101458
France	UK Great Britain	20 Aug 51	Finance	108UNTS263	101479
France	UK Great Britain	31 Dec 51	Consul/Citizenship	330UNTS145	104744
France	UK Great Britain	10 Nov 52	Admin Cooperation	214UNTS255	102903
France	UK Great Britain	13 Apr 53	Admin Cooperation	172UNTS173	102245
France	UK Great Britain	14 Oct 53	Admin Cooperation	186UNTS151	102489
France	UK Great Britain	10 Jul 56	Non-ILO Labor	326UNTS23	104708
France	UK Great Britain	28 Nov 58	Taxation	351UNTS263	105027
France	UK Great Britain	26 Jan 59	Admin Cooperation	330UNTS207	104745
France	UK Great Britain	26 Jan 59	Admin Cooperation	330UNTS213	104746
France	UK Great Britain	05 Mar 59	Finance	343UNTS277	104932
France	UK Great Britain	14 Feb 61	Visas	398UNTS267	105729
France	UK Great Britain	29 Nov 62	Scientific Project	453UNTS325	106534
France	UK Great Britain	17 Apr 63	Admin Cooperation	474UNTS295	106886
France	UK Great Britain	21 Jun 63	Taxation	540UNTS311	107855
France	UK Great Britain	05 Nov 63	Taxation	539UNTS277	107838
France	UK Great Britain	10 Apr 64	Specific Resources	0UNTS0	109272
France	UK Great Britain	03 Jun 64	General Ad Hoc	65FRRT92	415200
France	UK Great Britain	03 Jun 64	Scientific Project	539UNTS253	107836
France	UK Great Britain	25 Feb 65	Non-ILO Labor	543UNTS157	107899
France	UK Great Britain	21 Sep 65	Culture	561UNTS3	108177
France	UK Great Britain	19 Nov 65	Non-ILO Labor	561UNTS19	108178
France	UK Great Britain	19 Nov 65	Non-ILO Labor	65FRRT105	415201
France	UK Great Britain	14 Feb 67	Non-ILO Labor	0UNTS0	109493
France	UK Great Britain	15 Feb 67	Admin Cooperation	606UNTS119	108781
France	UK Great Britain	22 Nov 67	Gen Communications	643UNTS225	109194
France	UK Great Britain	22 May 68	Taxation	0UNTS0	110422
France	UK Great Britain	22 May 68	Finance	69FRJO2511	416202
France	UK Great Britain	13 Sep 68	Culture	69FRJO1001	416203
France	UK Great Britain	28 Mar 69	Land Transport	0UNTS0	110599
France	UK Great Britain	28 May 69	Taxation	0UNTS0	110423
France	UK Great Britain	19 May 70	Consul/Citizenship	0UNTS0	110809
France	UN Special Fund	17 Mar 60	Direct Aid	354UNTS119	105059

PARTY ONE	PARTY TWO	DATE	TOPIC	CITATION	NUMBER
France	UNESCO (Educ/Cult)	25 Jun 54	Specific Property	55FRJO1208	416497
France	UNESCO (Educ/Cult)	02 Jul 54	IGO Status/Immunit	357UNTS3	105103
France	UNICEF (Children)	19 Feb 48	IGO Operations	68UNTS75	100885
France	United Arab Rep	08 Aug 50	Air Transport	127UNTS293	101710
France	United Arab Rep	22 Aug 58	General Amity	0UNTS0	110511
France	United Arab Rep	05 Nov 64	Claims and Debts	64FRRT73	415048
France	United Arab Rep	28 Jul 66	Admin Cooperation	67FRJO810	416049
France	United Arab Rep	28 Jul 66	Visas	0UNTS0	110512
France	United Arab Rep	19 Mar 68	Health/Educ/Welfare	69FRJO3005	416050
France	United Arab Rep	19 Mar 68	Culture	0UNTS0	110101
France	United Arab Rep	19 Mar 68	Education	0UNTS0	110102
France	United Arab Rep	05 Sep 68	Taxation	0UNTS0	110801
France	United Nations	10 Mar 48	Humanitarian	47UNTS203	100731
France	United Nations	17 Aug 51	IGO Operations	122UNTS191	101647
France	Upper Volta	11 Jul 60	Recognition	60FRRT52	415214
France	Upper Volta	24 Apr 61	General Amity	62FRRT8	415215
France	Upper Volta	31 Mar 62	Customs	62FRRT42	415216
France	Upper Volta	29 May 62	Air Transport	63FRRT2	415217
France	Upper Volta	11 Aug 65	Finance	67FRJO106	416218
France	Upper Volta	30 May 70	Visas	0UNTS0	110745
France	Uruguay	09 May 60	Finance	60FRRT43	415478
France	USA (United States)	25 Jul 39	Taxation	125UNTS259	200429
France	USA (United States)	03 Sep 42	Milit Assistance	24UNTS177	200141
France	USA (United States)	25 Sep 43	Direct Aid	76UNTS183	200245
France	USA (United States)	25 Aug 44	Milit Occupation	138UNTS247	200449
France	USA (United States)	20 Feb 45	IGO Status/Immunit	76UNTS223	200248
France	USA (United States)	20 Feb 45	Direct Aid	76UNTS193	200246
France	USA (United States)	28 Feb 45	IGO Status/Immunit	76UNTS213	200247
France	USA (United States)	14 Aug 45	Admin Cooperation	73UNTS237	200243
France	USA (United States)	08 Nov 45	General Trade	76UNTS151	100986
France	USA (United States)	29 Dec 45	Air Transport	139UNTS105	101878
France	USA (United States)	07 Feb 46	Commodity Trade	3UNTS239	100034
France	USA (United States)	27 Mar 46	Air Transport	139UNTS114	101879
France	USA (United States)	28 May 46	Status of Forces	84UNTS121	101123
France	USA (United States)	28 May 46	Milit Assistance	84UNTS59	101119
France	USA (United States)	28 May 46	General Economic	84UNTS167	101127
France	USA (United States)	28 May 46	Reparations	84UNTS113	101122
France	USA (United States)	28 May 46	Reparations	84UNTS93	101121
France	USA (United States)	28 May 46	Mass Media	84UNTS161	101126
France	USA (United States)	28 May 46	Milit Assistance	84UNTS79	101120
France	USA (United States)	28 May 46	General Trade	84UNTS151	101125
France	USA (United States)	28 May 46	Status of Forces	84UNTS141	101124
France	USA (United States)	18 Jun 46	Air Transport	42UNTS183	100647
France	USA (United States)	18 Jul 46	Reparations	125UNTS165	101675
France	USA (United States)	18 Oct 46	Taxation	140UNTS23	101882
France	USA (United States)	10 Dec 46	Visas	15UNTS265	100242
France	USA (United States)	11 Mar 47	Humanitarian	151UNTS159	101991
France	USA (United States)	27 Mar 47	Patents/Copyrights	16UNTS65	100249
France	USA (United States)	04 Apr 47	Patents/Copyrights	24UNTS133	100353
France	USA (United States)	19 Apr 47	General Trade	132UNTS135	101754
France	USA (United States)	16 Sep 47	Visas	84UNTS19	101115
France	USA (United States)	01 Oct 47	Other Military	148UNTS303	101940
France	USA (United States)	25 Oct 47	Non-ILO Labor	89UNTS111	101212
France	USA (United States)	30 Oct 47	General Economic	125UNTS171	101676
France	USA (United States)	02 Jan 48	Direct Aid	31UNTS97	100470
France	USA (United States)	25 Feb 48	Milit Servic/Citiz	67UNTS33	100864
France	USA (United States)	27 Feb 48	Reparations	84UNTS207	101131
France	USA (United States)	28 Jun 48	Mostfavored Nation	31UNTS115	100472
France	USA (United States)	28 Jun 48	Direct Aid	19UNTS9	100302
France	USA (United States)	09 Jul 48	Mostfavored Nation	32UNTS93	100492
France	USA (United States)	09 Jul 48	Direct Aid	24UNTS103	100352
France	USA (United States)	16 Sep 48	Culture	84UNTS185	101129
France	USA (United States)	19 Oct 48	Air Transport	98UNTS3	101355
France	USA (United States)	22 Oct 48	Education	84UNTS173	101128
France	USA (United States)	27 Nov 48	Scientific Project	168UNTS119	102217

PARTY ONE	PARTY TWO	DATE	TOPIC	CITATION	NUMBER
France	USA (United States)	23 Dec 48	Direct Aid	67UNTS171	100876
France	USA (United States)	07 Feb 49	Direct Aid	67UNTS189	100877
France	USA (United States)	14 Mar 49	Claims and Debts	84UNTS225	101132
France	USA (United States)	14 Mar 49	Claims and Debts	84UNTS237	101133
France	USA (United States)	31 Mar 49	Visas	84UNTS283	101137
France	USA (United States)	27 Jan 50	Milit Assistance	80UNTS171	101051
France	USA (United States)	27 Feb 51	Milit Installation	0UNTS0	109598
France	USA (United States)	05 Jan 52	Milit Assistance	181UNTS177	102408
France	USA (United States)	02 Feb 52	Reparations	247UNTS223	103472
France	USA (United States)	13 Mar 52	Milit Assistance	177UNTS21	102306
France	USA (United States)	13 Jun 52	Taxation	181UNTS3	102393
France	USA (United States)	22 Jul 52	Direct Aid	181UNTS319	102420
France	USA (United States)	04 Oct 52	Milit Installation	0UNTS0	109599
France	USA (United States)	17 Jun 53	Milit Installation	0UNTS0	109600
France	USA (United States)	30 Jun 53	Milit Installation	0UNTS0	109601
France	USA (United States)	02 Sep 53	Milit Assistance	224UNTS153	103075
France	USA (United States)	31 May 54	Milit Assistance	236UNTS141	103321
France	USA (United States)	01 Jul 55	Other Military	270UNTS19	103888
France	USA (United States)	11 Aug 55	US Agri Commod Aid	251UNTS15	103530
France	USA (United States)	23 Sep 55	Milit Assistance	270UNTS341	103904
France	USA (United States)	19 Mar 56	Other Military	275UNTS37	103974
France	USA (United States)	23 Mar 56	Specific Property	278UNTS131	104029
France	USA (United States)	19 Jun 56	Atomic Energy	281UNTS341	104087
France	USA (United States)	22 Jun 56	Taxation	291UNTS101	104246
France	USA (United States)	06 Sep 56	Milit Installation	335UNTS173	104784
France	USA (United States)	08 Nov 56	Direct Aid	280UNTS189	104058
France	USA (United States)	14 Dec 56	Air Transport	266UNTS117	103826
France	USA (United States)	12 Mar 57	Patents/Copyrights	279UNTS275	104045
France	USA (United States)	23 Sep 57	Tech Assistance	293UNTS297	104297
France	USA (United States)	27 Dec 57	US Agri Commod Aid	307UNTS79	104444
France	USA (United States)	30 Jan 58	Specif Claim/Waive	304UNTS9	104388
France	USA (United States)	28 Feb 58	US Agri Commod Aid	366UNTS343	105222
France	USA (United States)	08 Dec 58	Milit Installation	0UNTS0	109602
France	USA (United States)	21 Mar 59	US Agri Commod Aid	342UNTS71	104901
France	USA (United States)	07 May 59	Milit Assistance	354UNTS83	105055
France	USA (United States)	10 Jul 59	Patents/Copyrights	62FRRT12	415179
France	USA (United States)	25 Nov 59	Admin Cooperation	401UNTS75	105764
France	USA (United States)	19 Sep 60	Milit Assistance	400UNTS21	105745
France	USA (United States)	04 Nov 60	US Agri Commod Aid	400UNTS323	105756
France	USA (United States)	31 Mar 61	Scientific Project	409UNTS136	105881
France	USA (United States)	27 Jul 61	Milit Assistance	433UNTS29	106229
France	USA (United States)	21 Sep 61	Visas	433UNTS243	106247
France	USA (United States)	22 Jan 63	Dispute Settlement	473UNTS3	106849
France	USA (United States)	01 Aug 63	Taxation	527UNTS89	107619
France	USA (United States)	07 May 65	Education	573UNTS183	108331
France	USA (United States)	05 May 66	Admin Cooperation	593UNTS279	108589
France	USA (United States)	17 Jun 66	Scientific Project	601UNTS113	108690
France	USA (United States)	18 Jul 66	Consul/Citizenship	0UNTS0	110044
France	USA (United States)	18 Jul 66	Consul/Citizenship	68FRRT7	415180
France	USA (United States)	24 Mar 67	Specific Property	0UNTS0	109858
France	USA (United States)	28 Jul 67	Taxation	68FRJO1210	416181
France	USA (United States)	28 Jul 67	Taxation	0UNTS0	110325
France	USA (United States)	24 May 68	Non-ILO Labor	69FRJO607	416182
France	USSR (Soviet Union)	29 Jun 45	Refugees	0SUST181	468150
France	USSR (Soviet Union)	29 Dec 45	General Trade	0SUST205	468151
France	USSR (Soviet Union)	06 Apr 46	Commodity Trade	0SUST209	471021
France	USSR (Soviet Union)	03 Sep 51	General Trade	221UNTS79	103003
France	USSR (Soviet Union)	15 Jul 53	General Trade	0UNTS0	110492
France	USSR (Soviet Union)	29 Jun 54	Air Transport	0SUST313	468155
France	USSR (Soviet Union)	31 Mar 56	General Trade	0SUST351	468156
France	USSR (Soviet Union)	31 Mar 56	Culture	0SUST355	468157
France	USSR (Soviet Union)	23 Jul 56	Culture	65FRRT52	415469
France	USSR (Soviet Union)	11 Feb 57	General Trade	0SUST377	468158
France	USSR (Soviet Union)	14 Nov 58	General Trade	7SUGG125	469540
France	USSR (Soviet Union)	14 Nov 58	General Trade	7SUGG125	469541

PARTY ONE	PARTY TWO	DATE	TOPIC	CITATION	NUMBER
France	USSR (Soviet Union)	02 Apr 60	Finance	9SUGG132	469649
France	USSR (Soviet Union)	02 Apr 60	Finance	0UNTS0	110493
France	USSR (Soviet Union)	12 Jul 60	Culture	9SUGG142	469675
France	USSR (Soviet Union)	24 Jan 63	Finance	63FRMD1302	417470
France	USSR (Soviet Union)	30 Oct 64	General Trade	64FRMD411	417471
France	USSR (Soviet Union)	22 Mar 65	Mass Media	65FRRT60	415472
France	USSR (Soviet Union)	30 Jun 66	Scientific Project	589UNTS99	108537
France	USSR (Soviet Union)	30 Jun 66	Culture	589UNTS109	108538
France	USSR (Soviet Union)	08 Dec 66	Consul/Citizenship	69FRJO1610	416473
France	USSR (Soviet Union)	08 Dec 66	Consul/Citizenship	0UNTS0	110363
France	USSR (Soviet Union)	08 Dec 66	Consul/Citizenship	0UNTS0	110031
France	USSR (Soviet Union)	14 Mar 67	Patents/Copyrights	68FRJO2103	416474
France	USSR (Soviet Union)	14 Mar 67	Taxation	0UNTS0	109330
France	USSR (Soviet Union)	20 Apr 67	Water Transport	67FRJO2709	416475
France	USSR (Soviet Union)	08 Jul 67	Culture	68FRJO1603	416476
France	USSR (Soviet Union)	08 Jul 67	Mass Media	0UNTS0	109378
France	USSR (Soviet Union)	09 Jan 69	Health/Educ/Welfare	0UNTS0	110733
France	USSR (Soviet Union)	09 Jan 69	Health/Educ/Welfare	69FRJO3007	416477
France	USSR (Soviet Union)	13 Oct 69	Other Military	0UNTS0	110319
France	USSR (Soviet Union)	24 Oct 69	Scientific Project	0UNTS0	110460
France	Venezuela	26 Jul 50	General Economic	50FRMD2408	417479
France	Vietnam, South	30 May 50	Education	0VKNG9	496001
France	Vietnam, South	15 Jun 50	Education	0VKNG10	496002
France	Vietnam, South	16 Jun 50	Water Transport	0VKNG11	496003
France	Vietnam, South	17 Jun 50	IGO Establishment	0VKNG13	496004
France	Vietnam, South	12 Mar 51	Specific Property	0VKNG25	496005
France	Vietnam, South	08 Feb 52	Education	0VKNG41	496006
France	Vietnam, South	26 May 52	Land Transport	0VKNG45	496007
France	Vietnam, South	07 Jun 52	Education	0VKNG47	496008
France	Vietnam, South	09 May 53	General Military	0VKNG53	496011
France	Vietnam, South	09 Jul 53	Education	0VKNG59	496013
France	Vietnam, South	19 Oct 53	Admin Cooperation	0VKNG62	496014
France	Vietnam, South	05 Apr 54	Admin Cooperation	0VKNG67	496018
France	Vietnam, South	04 Jun 54	General Amity	0VKNG68	496019
France	Vietnam, South	20 Jul 54	Peace/Disarmament	0VKNG72	496020
France	Vietnam, South	16 Sep 54	Recognition	59FRRT7	415480
France	Vietnam, South	30 Dec 54	General Economic	0VKNG85	496024
France	Vietnam, South	30 Dec 54	Status of Forces	0VKNG85	496025
France	Vietnam, South	11 May 55	Education	0VKNG91	496027
France	Vietnam, South	15 May 55	Status of Forces	0VKNG92	496028
France	Vietnam, South	13 Jun 55	Milit Installation	0VKNG94	496029
France	Vietnam, South	20 Jun 55	Air Transport	0VKNG95	496030
France	Vietnam, South	16 Aug 55	Consul/Citizenship	59FRRT7	415481
France	Vietnam, South	17 Aug 55	Finance	0VKNG98	496031
France	Vietnam, South	05 Apr 56	Mass Media	0VKNG104	496033
France	Vietnam, South	14 Jul 56	Consul/Citizenship	0VKNG109	496034
France	Vietnam, South	28 Jul 56	Air Transport	0VKNG110	496035
France	Vietnam, South	10 Sep 58	Finance	0VKNG130	496037
France	Vietnam, South	29 Sep 59	Scientific Project	0VKNG151	496043
France	Vietnam, South	14 Nov 59	General Economic	0VKNG153	496044
France	Vietnam, South	24 Mar 60	General Economic	0VKNG153	496045
France	Vietnam, South	24 Mar 60	Claims and Debts	0UNTS0	110473
France	Vietnam, South	24 Mar 60	Specific Property	70FRJO2203	416482
France	Vietnam, South	28 Jan 61	Atomic Energy	0VKNG159	496047
France	Vietnam, South	11 Feb 61	Culture	0VKNG160	496048
France	Vietnam, South	10 Aug 61	Tech Assistance	0VKNG170	496050
France	Vietnam, South	22 Nov 62	Education	0VKNG184	496054
France	Vietnam, South	15 May 63	Admin Cooperation	0VKNG190	496056
France	Vietnam, South	22 May 63	Specific Property	0VKNG191	496057
France	WEU (West Europe)	09 Jun 58	Non-ILO Labor	58FRRT32	415498
France	WEU (West Europe)	30 Nov 67	Non-ILO Labor	68FRJO506	416511
France	WHO (World Health)	23 Jul 52	IGO Status/Immunit	209UNTS231	102829
France	WHO (World Health)	02 Apr 53	Tech Assistance	174UNTS83	102279
France	WHO (World Health)	30 Apr 53	Tech Assistance	174UNTS71	102278
France	WHO (World Health)	14 Mar 67	IGO Operations	0UNTS0	110667

PARTY ONE	PARTY TWO	DATE	TOPIC	CITATION	NUMBER
France	Yugoslavia	05 Jan 50	Non-ILO Labor	0UNTS0	109502
France	Yugoslavia	05 Jan 50	Non-ILO Labor	51FRJO2404	416483
France	Yugoslavia	14 Apr 51	Claims and Debts	53FRJO3107	416484
France	Yugoslavia	02 Aug 58	Claims and Debts	59FRRT11	415485
France	Yugoslavia	12 Jul 63	Claims and Debts	64FRRT31	415486
France	Yugoslavia	25 Jan 64	General Trade	64FRMD102	417487
France	Yugoslavia	19 Jun 64	Culture	65FRRT31	415488
France	Yugoslavia	17 Oct 64	General Transport	65FRRT88	415489
France	Yugoslavia	25 Jan 65	Non-ILO Labor	65FRRT82	415490
France	Yugoslavia	08 Feb 66	Health/Educ/Welfare	67FRJO1802	416492
France	Yugoslavia	08 Feb 66	Sanitation	0UNTS0	109503
France	Yugoslavia	08 Feb 66	Sanitation	67FRJO102	416491
France	Yugoslavia	27 Jun 66	Tech Assistance	67FRJO504	416493
France	Yugoslavia	23 Mar 67	Air Transport	67FRJO410	416494
France	Yugoslavia	15 Jan 69	Visas	69FRJO2205	416496
France	Yugoslavia	15 Jan 69	Scientific Project	0UNTS0	110530
France	Yugoslavia	15 Jan 69	General Economic	69FRJO2811	416495
France	Yugoslavia	05 Mar 70	Non-ILO Labor	0UNTS0	110803
French Occup Germ	Multilateral	05 Oct 47	Finance	34UNTS23	100525
French Occup Germ	Multilateral	16 Mar 49	Finance	29UNTS95	100436
French Occup Germ	Multilateral	08 Apr 49	Milit Occupation	140UNTS196	101889
French Occup Germ	Multilateral	14 Apr 49	Milit Occupation	141UNTS281	101919
French Occup Germ	Multilateral	05 Aug 49	Finance	88UNTS229	101195
French Occup Germ	Multilateral	10 Aug 49	Finance	45UNTS3	100689
Gabon	Accept UN Charter	02 Nov 60	UN Charter	379UNTS99	105436
Gabon	France	15 Jul 60	Recognition	60FRRT51	415191
Gabon	France	17 Aug 60	General Amity	60FRRT77	415192
Gabon	France	06 Jun 61	Specific Property	63FRRT20	415193
Gabon	France	28 Sep 62	Customs	62FRRT39	415194
Gabon	France	23 Jul 63	Admin Cooperation	65FRRT26	415195
Gabon	France	02 Dec 63	Air Transport	64FRRT9	415196
Gabon	France	21 Apr 66	Finance	69FRJO2404	416197
Gabon	France	22 Apr 66	Taxation	0UNTS0	109647
Gabon	France	03 Apr 68	General Economic	0UNTS0	110529
Gabon	Germany, West	11 Jul 62	General Transport	63WBGA58	424207
Gabon	Germany, West	11 Jul 62	General Economic	63WBGA58	424205
Gabon	Germany, West	11 Jul 62	Direct Aid	63WBGA58	424206
Gabon	Germany, West	31 Oct 63	Loans and Credits	64WBGA155	424208
Gabon	Germany, West	10 Jan 67	Loans and Credits	67WBGA63	424209
Gabon	Germany, West	27 Nov 68	Loans and Credits	69WBGA27	424210
Gabon	Germany, West	16 May 69	Claims and Debts	70WGBB657	425211
Gabon	Germany, West	05 Nov 70	Loans and Credits	70WBGA235	424212
Gabon	IBRD (World Bank)	30 Jun 59	IBRD Project	452UNTS135	106507
Gabon	IBRD (World Bank)	10 Jul 64	IBRD Project	537UNTS63	107797
Gabon	IBRD (World Bank)	07 Jul 68	IBRD Project	0UNTS0	109361
Gabon	IBRD (World Bank)	10 Jan 69	IBRD Project	0UNTS0	109654
Gabon	Israel	15 May 62	General Amity	484UNTS181	107027
Gabon	Israel	15 May 62	Tech Assistance	448UNTS211	106433
Gabon	Israel	10 Oct 62	Visas	484UNTS175	107026
Gabon	Multilateral	07 Dec 44	IGO Establishment	15UNTS295	200102
Gabon	Multilateral	24 Jul 48	Sanitation	66UNTS25	100847
Gabon	Multilateral	22 Nov 50	Culture	131UNTS25	101734
Gabon	Multilateral	02 Jul 51	Refugees	189UNTS137	102545
Gabon	Multilateral	18 Jan 54	IGO Establishment	330UNTS121	104743
Gabon	Multilateral	14 May 54	Culture	249UNTS215	103511
Gabon	Multilateral	29 Jul 54	Sanitation	249UNTS45	103500
Gabon	Multilateral	26 Jan 60	IGO Establishment	439UNTS249	106333
Gabon	Multilateral	18 Apr 61	Dispute Settlement	500UNTS243	107312
Gabon	Multilateral	18 Apr 61	Consul/Citizenship	500UNTS223	107311
Gabon	Multilateral	18 Apr 61	Consul/Citizenship	500UNTS95	107310
Gabon	Multilateral	21 Feb 62	Tech Assistance	423UNTS151	106091
Gabon	Multilateral	28 Sep 62	IGO Establishment	469UNTS169	106791
Gabon	Multilateral	24 Apr 63	Consul/Citizenship	596UNTS261	108638
Gabon	Multilateral	24 Apr 63	Consul/Citizenship	596UNTS487	108640
Gabon	Multilateral	25 May 63	IGO Establishment	479UNTS39	106947

PARTY ONE	PARTY TWO	DATE	TOPIC	CITATION	NUMBER
Gabon	Multilateral	05 Aug 63	Sanitation	480UNTS43	106964
Gabon	Multilateral	10 Jul 64	Postal Service	611UNTS387	108846
Gabon	Multilateral	10 Jul 64	Postal Service	612UNTS3	108847
Gabon	Multilateral	10 Jul 64	Postal Service	613UNTS3	108850
Gabon	Multilateral	10 Jul 64	Postal Service	612UNTS361	108849
Gabon	Multilateral	10 Jul 64	Postal Service	613UNTS3	108851
Gabon	Multilateral	10 Jul 64	Postal Service	612UNTS233	108848
Gabon	Multilateral	10 Jul 64	Postal Service	611UNTS105	108845
Gabon	Multilateral	10 Jul 64	Postal Service	611UNTS7	108844
Gabon	Multilateral	18 Mar 65	Dispute Settlement	575UNTS159	108359
Gabon	Multilateral	23 Jun 65	General IGO	614UNTS239	108873
Gabon	Multilateral	27 May 66	IGO Establishment	637UNTS0	109121
Gabon	Multilateral	18 Mar 68	Commodity Trade	0UNTS0	109262
Gabon	Multilateral	22 Apr 68	Scientific Project	0UNTS0	109574
Gabon	Multilateral	11 Jun 68	Scientific Project	0UNTS0	109884
Gabon	Multilateral	24 Sep 68	Air Transport	0UNTS0	110612
Gabon	UN Special Fund	02 Feb 61	Direct Aid	387UNTS289	105568
Gabon	UNICEF (Children)	02 Nov 61	Direct Aid	422UNTS241	106078
Gabon	United Nations	11 Jan 63	IGO Operations	450UNTS257	106472
Gabon	USA (United States)	04 Oct 62	General Aid	459UNTS185	106620
Gabon	USA (United States)	10 Apr 63	Finance	474UNTS113	106876
Gabon	WHO (World Health)	27 Apr 61	Tech Assistance	397UNTS215	105707
Gambia	Accept UN Charter	18 Feb 65	UN Charter	545UNTS143	107928
Gambia	Germany, West	02 Nov 67	Visas	68WBGA80	424213
Gambia	ICJ Option Clause	14 Jun 66	ICJ Option Clause	565UNTS21	108232
Gambia	Israel	11 Jul 66	Visas	582UNTS11	108453
Gambia	Italy	09 Dec 65	Visas	66ITDI131	436161
Gambia	Multilateral	02 Jul 51	Refugees	189UNTS137	102545
Gambia	Multilateral	26 Jan 60	IGO Establishment	439UNTS249	106333
Gambia	Multilateral	02 Jun 65	Tech Assistance	537UNTS348	200611
Gambia	Multilateral	02 Jun 65	Tech Assistance	551UNTS2	108030
Gambia	Multilateral	31 Jan 67	Refugees	606UNTS267	108791
Gambia	Multilateral	27 Mar 68	Visas	0UNTS0	109293
Gambia	Multilateral	22 Apr 68	Scientific Project	0UNTS0	109574
Gambia	Multilateral	27 Jan 69	Telecommunications	0UNTS0	109664
Gambia	Norway	18 May 55	Taxation	2NORT553	451063
Gambia	Norway	28 Oct 65	Visas	3NORT948	451064
Gambia	Senegal	19 Apr 67	General Amity	640UNTS101	109156
Gambia	UK Great Britain	05 Jun 65	Admin Cooperation	551UNTS193	108041
Gambia	UK Great Britain	20 Jun 66	Recognition	573UNTS203	108333
Gambia	UK Great Britain	01 Apr 68	Taxation	0UNTS0	109709
Gambia	UK Great Britain	19 Sep 68	Finance	0UNTS0	109799
Gambia	UN Special Fund	09 Jun 65	IGO Operations	538UNTS321	200612
Gambia	UN Special Fund	25 Mar 70	Tech Assistance	0UNTS0	110397
Gambia	UNICEF (Children)	29 May 65	IGO Operations	547UNTS29	107954
Gambia	USA (United States)	05 Dec 66	Direct Aid	0UNTS0	109693
Gambia	USA (United States)	04 Nov 67	Finance	0UNTS0	110055
Germany, East	Albania	27 Mar 51	General Trade	1EGDA474	419006
Germany, East	Albania	26 Feb 52	Tech Assistance	4EGDA547	419007
Germany, East	Albania	31 Jul 53	Culture	4EGDA548	419008
Germany, East	Albania	26 Oct 53	Tech Assistance	1EGDA474	419009
Germany, East	Albania	05 Nov 53	Consul/Citizenship	1EGDA478	419010
Germany, East	Albania	28 Mar 55	Consul/Citizenship	2EGDA477	419011
Germany, East	Albania	15 Feb 56	Tech Assistance	3EGDA596	419012
Germany, East	Albania	22 Feb 57	Tech Assistance	5EGDA284	419013
Germany, East	Albania	05 Jun 57	Postal Service	5EGDA285	419014
Germany, East	Albania	05 Jun 57	Telecommunications	5EGDA292	419015
Germany, East	Albania	17 Aug 57	Sanitation	5EGDA302	419016
Germany, East	Albania	11 Jan 59	Consul/Citizenship	7EGDA275	419017
Germany, East	Albania	11 Jan 59	Admin Cooperation	7EGDA283	419018
Germany, East	Albania	08 Oct 59	General Economic	7EGDA311	419019
Germany, East	Albania	21 Jan 60	Air Transport	8EGDA310	419020
Germany, East	Albania	25 Apr 60	Finance	8EGDA316	419021
Germany, East	Albania	11 Jan 61	General Trade	9EGDA309	419022
Germany, East	Albania	13 Jan 61	Sanitation	9EGDA310	419023

PARTY ONE	PARTY TWO	DATE	TOPIC	CITATION	NUMBER
Germany, East	Albania	23 Jul 65	Water Transport	51EGDZ340	420024
Germany, East	Albania	01 Mar 66	General Trade	51EGDZ355	420025
Germany, East	Algeria	24 Jun 66	Education	44EGDZ362	420026
Germany, East	Algeria	12 Dec 66	General Trade	41EGDZ374	420027
Germany, East	Algeria	21 Dec 66	Air Transport	41EGDZ374	420029
Germany, East	Algeria	21 Dec 66	Culture	41EGDZ374	420028
Germany, East	Bulgaria	19 Jun 50	Health/Educ/Welfare	4EGDA459	419031
Germany, East	Bulgaria	25 Sep 50	Finance	4EGDA462	419032
Germany, East	Bulgaria	25 Sep 50	Culture	4EGDA465	419033
Germany, East	Bulgaria	30 Jan 51	Postal Service	4EGDA472	419035
Germany, East	Bulgaria	30 Jan 51	Postal Service	4EGDA468	419034
Germany, East	Bulgaria	30 Jan 51	Telecommunications	4EGDA477	419036
Germany, East	Bulgaria	15 May 53	Mass Media	4EGDA482	419037
Germany, East	Bulgaria	17 Oct 53	Commodity Trade	1EGDA467	419038
Germany, East	Bulgaria	23 Oct 53	Consul/Citizenship	1EGDA468	419039
Germany, East	Bulgaria	04 Feb 55	General Transport	58EGDZ172	420040
Germany, East	Bulgaria	05 Feb 55	Culture	58EGDZ172	420041
Germany, East	Bulgaria	14 Apr 55	General Economic	2EGDA462	419043
Germany, East	Bulgaria	29 Apr 55	Finance	4EGDA486	419044
Germany, East	Bulgaria	26 May 55	General Economic	3EGDA545	419045
Germany, East	Bulgaria	17 Jun 55	Sanitation	4EGDA490	419046
Germany, East	Bulgaria	30 Jul 55	Air Transport	4EGDA495	419047
Germany, East	Bulgaria	22 Aug 55	General Economic	3EGDA546	419048
Germany, East	Bulgaria	22 Sep 55	General Economic	58EGDZ172	420049
Germany, East	Bulgaria	17 Oct 55	Commodity Trade	58EGDZ172	420050
Germany, East	Bulgaria	05 Jul 56	Sanitation	5EGDA311	419051
Germany, East	Bulgaria	10 Jan 57	Patents/Copyrights	5EGDA790	419052
Germany, East	Bulgaria	27 Apr 57	General Economic	58EGDZ172	420053
Germany, East	Bulgaria	10 Jan 58	Finance	6EGDA216	419054
Germany, East	Bulgaria	27 Jan 58	Admin Cooperation	6EGDA221	419055
Germany, East	Bulgaria	20 Feb 58	Health/Educ/Welfare	6EGDA250	419056
Germany, East	Bulgaria	18 Apr 58	Sanitation	6EGDA282	419059
Germany, East	Bulgaria	18 Apr 58	Consul/Citizenship	6EGDA270	419057
Germany, East	Bulgaria	18 Apr 58	Health/Educ/Welfare	6EGDA278	419058
Germany, East	Bulgaria	25 Sep 58	Commodity Trade	6EGDA519	419060
Germany, East	Bulgaria	20 Mar 59	General Economic	7EGDA319	419061
Germany, East	Bulgaria	16 Jul 59	General Economic	7EGDA320	419062
Germany, East	Bulgaria	11 Apr 60	General Trade	8EGDA325	419063
Germany, East	Bulgaria	10 Oct 61	Education	9EGDA319	419064
Germany, East	Bulgaria	14 Dec 61	General Economic	9EGDA325	419065
Germany, East	Bulgaria	11 Sep 62	Air Transport	10EGDA368	419066
Germany, East	Bulgaria	15 Jul 63	Tech Assistance	11EGDA610	419067
Germany, East	Bulgaria	19 Mar 65	Health/Educ/Welfare	50EGDZ332	420068
Germany, East	Bulgaria	21 Aug 65	Consul/Citizenship	43EGDZ342	420069
Germany, East	Bulgaria	20 Dec 65	General Trade	59EGDZ350	420070
Germany, East	Bulgaria	15 Oct 66	Finance	34EGDZ370	420071
Germany, East	Bulgaria	25 Oct 66	Land Transport	36EGDZ370	420072
Germany, East	Bulgaria	07 Sep 67	General Amity	631UNTS81	108988
Germany, East	Bulgaria	15 Apr 69	Gen Communications	0UNTS0	110838
Germany, East	Burma	26 Aug 60	Consul/Citizenship	45EGDZ255	420074
Germany, East	Burma	14 Mar 61	Water Transport	9EGDA459	419075
Germany, East	Burma	08 Jan 66	General Economic	51EGDZ351	420076
Germany, East	Cambodia	29 Aug 60	Tech Assistance	8EGDA371	419167
Germany, East	Cambodia	29 Aug 60	Finance	8EGDA372	419166
Germany, East	Cambodia	29 Aug 60	General Trade	8EGDA371	419165
Germany, East	Cambodia	02 Feb 64	Health/Educ/Welfare	12EGDA826	419168
Germany, East	Ceylon (Sri Lanka)	22 Feb 65	General Economic	51EGDZ330	420077
Germany, East	Chile	05 Dec 66	Culture	34EGDZ373	420078
Germany, East	China People's Rep	10 Oct 50	General Economic	50CCJC27	410022
Germany, East	China People's Rep	09 Oct 51	Culture	51CCJC23	410043
Germany, East	China People's Rep	09 Oct 51	Culture	4EGDA73	419080
Germany, East	China People's Rep	12 Oct 51	Telecommunications	4EGDA81	419082
Germany, East	China People's Rep	12 Oct 51	Postal Service	4EGDA73	419081
Germany, East	China People's Rep	12 Oct 51	Postal Service	51CCJC24	410044
Germany, East	China People's Rep	21 Oct 51	Telecommunications	51CCJC25	410045

PARTY ONE	PARTY TWO	DATE	TOPIC	CITATION	NUMBER
Germany, East	China People's Rep	28 May 52	General Economic	52CCJC23	410068
Germany, East	China People's Rep	30 Apr 53	General Economic	53CCJC20	410099
Germany, East	China People's Rep	05 Oct 53	Consul/Citizenship	1EGDA327	419083
Germany, East	China People's Rep	30 Oct 53	Scientific Project	53CCJC63	410125
Germany, East	China People's Rep	30 Oct 53	Health/Educ/Welfare	4EGDA85	419084
Germany, East	China People's Rep	28 Nov 53	Culture	53CCJC67	410127
Germany, East	China People's Rep	30 Mar 54	General Economic	54CCJC12	410138
Germany, East	China People's Rep	08 Jun 54	Mass Media	4EGDA86	419085
Germany, East	China People's Rep	10 Jun 54	Mass Media	54CCJC35	410155
Germany, East	China People's Rep	23 Jun 54	Health/Educ/Welfare	2EGDA368	419086
Germany, East	China People's Rep	23 Jun 54	Scientific Project	54CCJC38	410158
Germany, East	China People's Rep	27 Dec 54	Education	54CCJC95	410199
Germany, East	China People's Rep	27 Dec 54	Education	2EGDA407	419087
Germany, East	China People's Rep	24 Apr 55	General Economic	55CCJC30	410231
Germany, East	China People's Rep	20 Aug 55	Scientific Project	55CCJC57	410250
Germany, East	China People's Rep	16 Sep 55	General Trade	55CCJC65	410257
Germany, East	China People's Rep	20 Nov 55	General Economic	55CCJC84	410271
Germany, East	China People's Rep	25 Dec 55	Sanitation	4EGDA100	419091
Germany, East	China People's Rep	25 Dec 55	General Amity	4EGDA95	419089
Germany, East	China People's Rep	25 Dec 55	Culture	4EGDA98	419090
Germany, East	China People's Rep	25 Dec 55	General Amity	55CCJC102	410284
Germany, East	China People's Rep	25 Dec 55	Culture	55CCJC103	410285
Germany, East	China People's Rep	25 Dec 55	Sanitation	55CCJC104	410286
Germany, East	China People's Rep	22 May 56	General Trade	56CCJC67	410338
Germany, East	China People's Rep	05 Apr 57	General Economic	57CCJC36	410415
Germany, East	China People's Rep	26 Sep 57	Commodity Trade	5EGDA332	419092
Germany, East	China People's Rep	16 Dec 57	Sanitation	5EGDA333	419093
Germany, East	China People's Rep	16 Dec 57	Sanitation	57CCJC118	410471
Germany, East	China People's Rep	27 Mar 58	Finance	58CCJC34	410506
Germany, East	China People's Rep	23 Apr 58	General Economic	58CCJC58	410522
Germany, East	China People's Rep	09 Oct 58	Commodity Trade	18EGDZ198	420094
Germany, East	China People's Rep	27 Jan 59	Consul/Citizenship	59CCJC19	410579
Germany, East	China People's Rep	27 Jan 59	Consul/Citizenship	7EGDA335	419095
Germany, East	China People's Rep	05 Feb 59	General Economic	59CCJC22	410582
Germany, East	China People's Rep	17 Mar 59	Scientific Project	59CCJC51	410603
Germany, East	China People's Rep	25 Apr 59	Mass Media	59CCJC70	410618
Germany, East	China People's Rep	25 Apr 59	Mass Media	59CCJC71	410619
Germany, East	China People's Rep	18 Jan 60	General Economic	8EGDA333	419096
Germany, East	China People's Rep	18 Jan 60	General Amity	60CCJC2	410656
Germany, East	China People's Rep	23 Mar 60	General Trade	60CCJC49	410692
Germany, East	China People's Rep	15 May 61	General Economic	61CCJC76	410797
Germany, East	China People's Rep	15 Jun 61	Finance	61CCJC84	410801
Germany, East	China People's Rep	04 Aug 62	General Economic	62CCJC77	410910
Germany, East	China People's Rep	07 Jun 63	Culture	63CCJC70	410984
Germany, East	China People's Rep	22 Jun 63	General Economic	63CCJC80	410991
Germany, East	China People's Rep	16 Jan 64	Health/Educ/Welfare	12EGDA726	419097
Germany, East	China People's Rep	01 Aug 64	General Economic	64CCJC106	411160
Germany, East	China People's Rep	19 Feb 65	General Economic	65CCJC20	411179
Germany, East	China People's Rep	03 May 65	Culture	65CCJC59	411164
Germany, East	China People's Rep	15 Jul 65	Education	48EGDZ339	420098
Germany, East	China People's Rep	15 Jul 65	Education	65CCJC94	411181
Germany, East	China People's Rep	22 Nov 65	Scientific Project	65CCJC146	411184
Germany, East	China People's Rep	25 Mar 66	General Economic	66CCJC10	411185
Germany, East	China People's Rep	04 Jul 66	Scientific Project	66CCJC65	411170
Germany, East	China People's Rep	22 Jul 66	Culture	66CCJC70	411187
Germany, East	China People's Rep	14 Apr 67	General Economic	67CCJC13	411192
Germany, East	Congo (Brazzaville)	06 May 65	General Aid	43EGDZ335	420169
Germany, East	Cuba	29 Feb 60	Consul/Citizenship	8EGDA394	419184
Germany, East	Cuba	17 Dec 60	Tech Assistance	8EGDA397	419185
Germany, East	Cuba	29 Mar 61	Culture	448UNTS81	106426
Germany, East	Cuba	04 Oct 62	Mass Media	10EGDA407	419186
Germany, East	Cuba	13 Feb 63	General Trade	11EGDA585	419187
Germany, East	Cuba	11 May 63	Mass Media	11EGDA414	419188
Germany, East	Cuba	03 Sep 63	Loans and Credits	11EGDA615	419189
Germany, East	Cuba	26 Apr 64	General Aid	12EGDA837	419190

PARTY ONE	PARTY TWO	DATE	TOPIC	CITATION	NUMBER
Germany, East	Cuba	20 Jul 64	Loans and Credits	12EGDA1149	419191
Germany, East	Cuba	05 Oct 64	Sanitation	12EGDA841	419192
Germany, East	Cuba	29 Oct 64	Commodity Trade	12EGDA1166	419193
Germany, East	Cuba	15 Mar 65	Education	49EGDZ332	420194
Germany, East	Cuba	01 Jun 66	Gen Communications	41EGDZ361	420195
Germany, East	Cyprus	07 Nov 64	General Economic	12EGDA1107	419498
Germany, East	Cyprus	12 Feb 66	General Economic	52EGDZ353	420499
Germany, East	Cyprus	04 Aug 66	Sanitation	50EGDZ365	420500
Germany, East	Czechoslovakia	23 Jun 50	Culture	4EGDA252	419328
Germany, East	Czechoslovakia	23 Jun 50	Finance	4EGDA250	419327
Germany, East	Czechoslovakia	23 Jun 50	Finance	1EGDA376	419326
Germany, East	Czechoslovakia	23 Jun 50	Scientific Project	4EGDA248	419325
Germany, East	Czechoslovakia	23 Jun 50	General Amity	504UNTS163	107357
Germany, East	Czechoslovakia	12 Jul 50	Sanitation	4EGDA255	419329
Germany, East	Czechoslovakia	25 Aug 50	Telecommunications	4EGDA267	419332
Germany, East	Czechoslovakia	25 Aug 50	Postal Service	4EGDA263	419331
Germany, East	Czechoslovakia	25 Aug 50	Postal Service	4EGDA259	419330
Germany, East	Czechoslovakia	30 Dec 50	Visas	4EGDA272	419333
Germany, East	Czechoslovakia	01 Dec 51	General Economic	1EGDA393	419334
Germany, East	Czechoslovakia	19 Feb 53	Culture	4EGDA282	419335
Germany, East	Czechoslovakia	20 Mar 53	General Trade	1EGDA421	419336
Germany, East	Czechoslovakia	01 Apr 53	Finance	4EGDA288	419337
Germany, East	Czechoslovakia	03 Oct 53	Land Transport	4EGDA194	419338
Germany, East	Czechoslovakia	13 Oct 53	Consul/Citizenship	1EGDA422	419339
Germany, East	Czechoslovakia	17 Feb 54	Sanitation	4EGDA302	419340
Germany, East	Czechoslovakia	21 Jul 54	General Economic	2EGDA442	419341
Germany, East	Czechoslovakia	15 Oct 54	Water Transport	4EGDA308	419342
Germany, East	Czechoslovakia	28 Jan 55	Mass Media	4EGDA320	419343
Germany, East	Czechoslovakia	31 Mar 55	Postal Service	4EGDA267	419344
Germany, East	Czechoslovakia	20 Jun 55	General Economic	3EGDA511	419345
Germany, East	Czechoslovakia	08 Aug 55	Air Transport	4EGDA325	419346
Germany, East	Czechoslovakia	30 Aug 55	Sanitation	504UNTS279	107361
Germany, East	Czechoslovakia	24 Oct 55	Land Transport	504UNTS173	107358
Germany, East	Czechoslovakia	14 Nov 55	Specific Resources	4EGDA345	419347
Germany, East	Czechoslovakia	23 Nov 55	Scientific Project	3EGDA516	419348
Germany, East	Czechoslovakia	25 Apr 56	Land Transport	4EGDA359	419349
Germany, East	Czechoslovakia	04 May 56	Consul/Citizenship	4EGDA366	419350
Germany, East	Czechoslovakia	24 Aug 56	Customs	5EGDA486	419351
Germany, East	Czechoslovakia	31 Aug 56	Finance	5EGDA491	419352
Germany, East	Czechoslovakia	11 Sep 56	General Economic	5EGDA507	419354
Germany, East	Czechoslovakia	11 Sep 56	Health/Educ/Welfare	5EGDA539	419356
Germany, East	Czechoslovakia	11 Sep 56	Consul/Citizenship	5EGDA506	419353
Germany, East	Czechoslovakia	11 Sep 56	Admin Cooperation	5EGDA511	419355
Germany, East	Czechoslovakia	06 Oct 56	Humanitarian	501UNTS109	107315
Germany, East	Czechoslovakia	21 Dec 56	Scientific Project	5EGDA554	419357
Germany, East	Czechoslovakia	29 Jan 57	Culture	5EGDA557	419358
Germany, East	Czechoslovakia	24 May 57	Consul/Citizenship	292UNTS327	104279
Germany, East	Czechoslovakia	20 Dec 57	IGO Establishment	5EGDA580	419359
Germany, East	Czechoslovakia	26 Jun 58	Patents/Copyrights	504UNTS221	107359
Germany, East	Czechoslovakia	29 Jan 59	General Economic	7EGDA447	419360
Germany, East	Czechoslovakia	12 Sep 59	General Aid	7EGDA449	419361
Germany, East	Czechoslovakia	18 Sep 59	Customs	363UNTS287	105209
Germany, East	Czechoslovakia	25 Nov 59	General Economic	374UNTS101	105331
Germany, East	Czechoslovakia	01 Jun 60	General Trade	8EGDA438	419362
Germany, East	Czechoslovakia	16 Jun 60	General Economic	415UNTS248	105988
Germany, East	Czechoslovakia	08 Nov 60	Admin Cooperation	424UNTS71	106100
Germany, East	Czechoslovakia	26 Nov 60	Specific Property	8EGDA452	419363
Germany, East	Czechoslovakia	15 Dec 60	Finance	8EGDA457	419364
Germany, East	Czechoslovakia	09 Dec 61	Specific Property	9EGDA395	419365
Germany, East	Czechoslovakia	28 Nov 62	Specific Resources	52EGDZ276	420366
Germany, East	Czechoslovakia	27 Jun 63	Health/Educ/Welfare	11EGDA647	419367
Germany, East	Czechoslovakia	09 Dec 63	Air Transport	11EGDA501	419368
Germany, East	Czechoslovakia	06 Oct 64	Culture	545UNTS113	107927
Germany, East	Czechoslovakia	21 Dec 65	General Trade	59EGDZ350	420369
Germany, East	Czechoslovakia	16 Feb 66	Finance	51EGDZ354	420370

PARTY ONE	PARTY TWO	DATE	TOPIC	CITATION	NUMBER
Germany, East	Czechoslovakia	20 Jul 66	Admin Cooperation	45EGDZ364	420371
Germany, East	Czechoslovakia	17 Mar 67	General Amity	609UNTS187	108831
Germany, East	Finland	15 Oct 49	General Trade	1EGDA498	419099
Germany, East	Finland	25 Jan 56	Finance	3EGDA646	419100
Germany, East	Finland	10 Mar 57	General Economic	5EGDA790	419101
Germany, East	Finland	09 Feb 59	Finance	7EGDA356	419102
Germany, East	Finland	25 Feb 59	Finance	7EGDA357	419103
Germany, East	Finland	23 Aug 66	Sanitation	40EGDZ366	420104
Germany, East	Ghana	25 Feb 59	Consul/Citizenship	7EGDA363	419105
Germany, East	Ghana	08 Jul 61	General Trade	9EGDA338	419106
Germany, East	Ghana	19 Oct 61	General Trade	9EGDA333	419107
Germany, East	Ghana	19 Oct 61	Finance	9EGDA338	419108
Germany, East	Ghana	19 Oct 61	Culture	9EGDA344	419110
Germany, East	Ghana	19 Oct 61	Tech Assistance	9EGDA342	419109
Germany, East	Ghana	14 May 64	Non-ILO Labor	12EGDA740	419111
Germany, East	Ghana	14 May 64	Education	12EGDA746	419112
Germany, East	Ghana	24 Jul 65	Tech Assistance	51EGDZ340	420113
Germany, East	Guinea	17 Nov 58	General Economic	6EGDA309	419115
Germany, East	Guinea	17 Nov 58	Culture	6EGDA309	419116
Germany, East	Guinea	17 Nov 58	Consul/Citizenship	6EGDA309	419114
Germany, East	Guinea	03 Mar 59	General Trade	7EGDA365	419117
Germany, East	Guinea	10 Jan 60	General Economic	8EGDA345	419118
Germany, East	Guinea	11 Feb 63	General Economic	11EGDA584	419119
Germany, East	Guinea	29 May 64	Education	12EGDA765	419121
Germany, East	Guinea	29 May 64	Non-ILO Labor	12EGDA759	419120
Germany, East	Guinea	09 Aug 65	General Economic	52EGDZ341	420122
Germany, East	Guinea	10 Dec 65	General Economic	51EGDZ349	420123
Germany, East	Hungary	19 Oct 49	General Economic	1EGDA426	419431
Germany, East	Hungary	24 Jun 50	Scientific Project	4EGDA378	419432
Germany, East	Hungary	24 Jun 50	General Trade	1EGDA428	419434
Germany, East	Hungary	24 Jun 50	Finance	4EGDA380	419433
Germany, East	Hungary	24 Jun 50	Culture	4EGDA382	419435
Germany, East	Hungary	03 Mar 51	Mass Media	4EGDA384	419436
Germany, East	Hungary	01 Aug 51	Finance	1EGDA438	419437
Germany, East	Hungary	07 Mar 52	General Trade	1EGDA439	419438
Germany, East	Hungary	25 Mar 52	Postal Service	4EGDA387	419439
Germany, East	Hungary	25 Mar 52	Postal Service	4EGDA390	419440
Germany, East	Hungary	26 Mar 52	Telecommunications	4EGDA394	419441
Germany, East	Hungary	17 Oct 53	Consul/Citizenship	1EGDA446	419442
Germany, East	Hungary	23 Oct 54	General Economic	2EGDA448	419443
Germany, East	Hungary	10 Sep 55	Air Transport	407UNTS132	105863
Germany, East	Hungary	23 Sep 55	Mass Media	4EGDA405	419444
Germany, East	Hungary	10 Nov 55	Other Military	3EGDA527	419445
Germany, East	Hungary	01 Dec 55	Mass Media	4EGDA410	419446
Germany, East	Hungary	12 Dec 55	General Economic	3EGDA528	419447
Germany, East	Hungary	30 Jan 56	General Economic	3EGDA530	419448
Germany, East	Hungary	06 Jul 56	Health/Educ/Welfare	5EGDA582	419449
Germany, East	Hungary	05 Oct 56	Finance	5EGDA583	419450
Germany, East	Hungary	29 Jun 57	Patents/Copyrights	5EGDA792	419451
Germany, East	Hungary	03 Jul 57	Consul/Citizenship	407UNTS186	105865
Germany, East	Hungary	25 Oct 57	Sanitation	408UNTS156	105869
Germany, East	Hungary	30 Oct 57	Admin Cooperation	408UNTS4	105867
Germany, East	Hungary	13 Nov 57	Sanitation	407UNTS216	105866
Germany, East	Hungary	14 Jun 58	Sanitation	407UNTS78	105861
Germany, East	Hungary	14 Oct 58	General Trade	6EGDA422	419452
Germany, East	Hungary	14 Oct 58	General Economic	6EGDA422	419453
Germany, East	Hungary	19 Dec 59	Health/Educ/Welfare	7EGDA490	419454
Germany, East	Hungary	19 Dec 59	Health/Educ/Welfare	409UNTS4	105874
Germany, East	Hungary	12 Jan 60	Patents/Copyrights	409UNTS22	105875
Germany, East	Hungary	30 Jan 60	Health/Educ/Welfare	408UNTS230	105873
Germany, East	Hungary	08 Apr 60	General Trade	8EGDA478	419455
Germany, East	Hungary	27 Apr 60	Specif Goods/Equip	8EGDA479	419456
Germany, East	Hungary	09 Jul 60	Mass Media	8EGDA480	419457
Germany, East	Hungary	26 Apr 61	General Economic	9EGDA402	419458
Germany, East	Hungary	11 May 62	Education	10EGDA497	419459

PARTY ONE	PARTY TWO	DATE	TOPIC	CITATION	NUMBER
Germany, East	Hungary	05 Sep 63	Non-ILO Labor	11EGDA648	419460
Germany, East	Hungary	18 Sep 63	Visas	11EGDA619	419461
Germany, East	Hungary	18 Jan 65	General Economic	51EGDZ328	420462
Germany, East	Hungary	15 Dec 65	General Trade	52EGDZ349	420463
Germany, East	Hungary	19 Feb 66	Scientific Project	51EGDZ354	420464
Germany, East	Hungary	11 Mar 66	Specific Property	51EGDZ355	420465
Germany, East	Hungary	01 Aug 66	Land Transport	49EGDZ365	420466
Germany, East	Hungary	03 Oct 66	Mass Media	45EGDZ369	420467
Germany, East	Hungary	18 May 67	General Amity	617UNTS3	108905
Germany, East	Hungary	30 May 67	Admin Cooperation	38EGDZ384	420468
Germany, East	Hungary	24 Jun 67	Admin Cooperation	42EGDZ386	420469
Germany, East	Hungary	07 Jul 67	Health/Educ/Welfare	48EGDZ387	420470
Germany, East	India	16 Oct 54	General Economic	2EGDA521	419125
Germany, East	India	16 Oct 54	Tech Assistance	2EGDA521	419126
Germany, East	India	08 Oct 56	General Trade	5EGDA342	419127
Germany, East	India	18 Dec 59	General Economic	7EGDA367	419128
Germany, East	India	23 Nov 63	Water Transport	11EGDA388	419129
Germany, East	India	20 Feb 64	Culture	12EGDA1128	419130
Germany, East	India	12 Sep 64	General Economic	12EGDA771	419131
Germany, East	Indonesia	12 Dec 56	General Trade	5EGDA344	419132
Germany, East	Indonesia	16 Feb 61	General Trade	9EGDA350	419133
Germany, East	Indonesia	16 Feb 61	Health/Educ/Welfare	9EGDA350	419134
Germany, East	Indonesia	16 Feb 61	Commodity Trade	9EGDA351	419135
Germany, East	Indonesia	16 Feb 61	Water Transport	9EGDA351	419136
Germany, East	Iraq	26 Oct 58	General Trade	6EGDA314	419138
Germany, East	Iraq	26 Oct 58	Consul/Citizenship	6EGDA314	419137
Germany, East	Iraq	01 Apr 59	Health/Educ/Welfare	7EGDA370	419139
Germany, East	Iraq	24 May 62	Consul/Citizenship	10EGDA384	419140
Germany, East	Iraq	22 Oct 66	Air Transport	36EGDZ370	420141
Germany, East	Korea, North	30 Dec 54	Finance	4EGDA505	419171
Germany, East	Korea, North	27 Jan 55	Tech Assistance	4EGDA507	419172
Germany, East	Korea, North	01 Dec 55	Postal Service	4EGDA508	419173
Germany, East	Korea, North	01 Dec 55	Telecommunications	4EGDA516	419174
Germany, East	Korea, North	12 Jun 56	Mass Media	1EGDA534	419176
Germany, East	Korea, North	12 Jun 56	Health/Educ/Welfare	4EGDA532	419175
Germany, East	Korea, North	22 Feb 57	General Trade	5EGDA355	419177
Germany, East	Korea, North	12 Mar 57	Tech Assistance	5EGDA355	419178
Germany, East	Korea, North	18 Apr 58	Health/Educ/Welfare	6EGDA323	419179
Germany, East	Korea, North	07 Dec 59	Education	7EGDA384	419180
Germany, East	Korea, North	03 Jun 60	Consul/Citizenship	8EGDA381	419181
Germany, East	Korea, North	29 Dec 61	General Economic	10EGDA399	419182
Germany, East	Korea, North	27 Jul 65	Sanitation	52EGDZ340	420183
Germany, East	Lebanon	20 May 63	General Economic	11EGDA603	419196
Germany, East	Mali	01 Apr 61	Consul/Citizenship	9EGDA462	419197
Germany, East	Mali	17 Apr 61	Finance	9EGDA372	419198
Germany, East	Mali	30 Sep 63	Tech Assistance	11EGDA424	419199
Germany, East	Mali	03 Jun 64	Health/Educ/Welfare	12EGDA844	419200
Germany, East	Mali	03 Jun 64	Education	12EGDA849	419201
Germany, East	Mali	17 May 65	Mass Media	50EGDZ336	420202
Germany, East	Mali	30 May 65	Tech Assistance	51EGDZ336	420203
Germany, East	Mali	12 Nov 65	Tech Assistance	44EGDZ347	420204
Germany, East	Mali	08 Jun 66	Air Transport	42EGDZ361	420205
Germany, East	Mali	17 Sep 66	Mass Media	34EGDZ368	420206
Germany, East	Mongolia	16 Oct 53	Consul/Citizenship	1EGDA482	419211
Germany, East	Mongolia	18 Jul 55	Mass Media	4EGDA559	419212
Germany, East	Mongolia	17 Oct 55	Consul/Citizenship	3EGDA600	419213
Germany, East	Mongolia	22 Aug 57	General Amity	521UNTS351	107530
Germany, East	Mongolia	22 Aug 57	Health/Educ/Welfare	5EGDA363	419214
Germany, East	Mongolia	30 Oct 57	Finance	5EGDA366	419215
Germany, East	Mongolia	06 Nov 57	General Trade	5EGDA370	419216
Germany, East	Mongolia	01 Jul 58	Health/Educ/Welfare	6EGDA518	419217
Germany, East	Mongolia	11 Apr 59	Tech Assistance	7EGDA399	419218
Germany, East	Mongolia	12 Jun 59	Telecommunications	7EGDA399	419220
Germany, East	Mongolia	12 Jun 59	Postal Service	7EGDA392	419219
Germany, East	Mongolia	07 Jan 63	Consul/Citizenship	11EGDA430	419221

PARTY ONE	PARTY TWO	DATE	TOPIC	CITATION	NUMBER
Germany, East	Mongolia	26 Aug 64	Tech Assistance	12EGDA1153	419222
Germany, East	Mongolia	28 May 65	Education	51EGDZ336	420223
Germany, East	Mongolia	11 Aug 65	Sanitation	52EGDZ341	420224
Germany, East	Mongolia	19 Mar 66	Tech Assistance	51EGDZ356	420225
Germany, East	Mongolia	12 Sep 68	General Amity	0UNTS0	109453
Germany, East	Mongolia	30 Apr 69	Admin Cooperation	0UNTS0	110320
Germany, East	Morocco	08 Aug 60	Finance	8EGDA401	419207
Germany, East	Morocco	31 Jul 64	General Trade	12EGDA856	419208
Germany, East	Morocco	31 Jul 64	Finance	12EGDA859	419209
Germany, East	Multilateral	14 May 55	General Amity	219UNTS3	102962
Germany, East	Multilateral	28 Sep 55	Air Transport	478UNTS371	106943
Germany, East	Multilateral	26 Mar 56	IGO Establishment	259UNTS125	103686
Germany, East	Multilateral	15 Jun 57	Patents/Copyrights	583UNTS3	108470
Germany, East	Multilateral	15 Apr 58	Health/Educ/Welfare	539UNTS27	107822
Germany, East	Multilateral	14 Dec 59	Land Transport	422UNTS75	106069
Germany, East	Multilateral	14 Dec 59	Sanitation	422UNTS33	106067
Germany, East	Multilateral	14 Dec 59	Sanitation	422UNTS57	106068
Germany, East	Multilateral	14 Dec 59	IGO Establishment	368UNTS253	105245
Germany, East	Multilateral	14 Dec 59	IGO Status/Immunit	368UNTS237	105244
Germany, East	Multilateral	15 Dec 61	Admin Cooperation	424UNTS43	106098
Germany, East	Multilateral	25 Jul 62	Specific Property	506UNTS177	107387
Germany, East	Multilateral	07 Jun 63	Water Transport	472UNTS95	106837
Germany, East	Multilateral	05 Aug 63	Sanitation	480UNTS43	106964
Germany, East	Multilateral	23 Oct 63	IGO Establishment	506UNTS197	107388
Germany, East	Multilateral	18 Nov 65	Customs	609UNTS115	108830
Germany, East	Multilateral	09 Sep 66	IGO Status/Immunit	0UNTS0	109343
Germany, East	Multilateral	27 Jan 67	Scientific Project	610UNTS205	108843
Germany, East	Multilateral	01 Jul 68	Peace/Disarmament	0UNTS0	110485
Germany, East	Poland	06 Jun 50	Culture	4EGDA118	419230
Germany, East	Poland	06 Jun 50	Finance	4EGDA115	419228
Germany, East	Poland	06 Jun 50	General Economic	4EGDA114	419229
Germany, East	Poland	06 Jun 50	Territory Boundary	4EGDA113	419227
Germany, East	Poland	23 Jun 50	Sanitation	304UNTS91	104393
Germany, East	Poland	06 Jul 50	Telecommunications	4EGDA128	419232
Germany, East	Poland	06 Jul 50	Territory Boundary	319UNTS93	104631
Germany, East	Poland	19 Jan 51	Territory Boundary	4EGDA130	419233
Germany, East	Poland	03 Feb 51	Postal Service	4EGDA137	419234
Germany, East	Poland	03 Feb 51	Telecommunications	4EGDA144	419235
Germany, East	Poland	08 Jan 52	Culture	304UNTS113	104394
Germany, East	Poland	18 Jan 52	Finance	4EGDA153	419236
Germany, East	Poland	06 Feb 52	Water Transport	304UNTS131	104395
Germany, East	Poland	06 Oct 53	Consul/Citizenship	53PZUM113	458011
Germany, East	Poland	06 Oct 53	Consul/Citizenship	1EGDA370	419237
Germany, East	Poland	19 Dec 53	Culture	4EGDA171	419238
Germany, East	Poland	27 May 54	Water Transport	4EGDA193	419240
Germany, East	Poland	27 May 54	Water Transport	4EGDA175	419239
Germany, East	Poland	27 May 54	Water Transport	54PZUM22	458017
Germany, East	Poland	27 May 54	Water Transport	54PZUM16	458016
Germany, East	Poland	02 Aug 54	Specific Resources	54PZUM53	458020
Germany, East	Poland	02 Aug 54	Specific Resources	2EGDA426	419241
Germany, East	Poland	05 Nov 54	Land Transport	4EGDA204	419242
Germany, East	Poland	21 Feb 55	General Economic	2EGDA431	419244
Germany, East	Poland	28 May 55	Postal Service	3EGDA458	419245
Germany, East	Poland	20 Jun 55	Air Transport	55PZUM13	458022
Germany, East	Poland	20 Jun 55	Air Transport	4EGDA224	419246
Germany, East	Poland	09 Jul 55	Sanitation	55PZUM19	458023
Germany, East	Poland	09 Jul 55	Sanitation	4EGDA230	419247
Germany, East	Poland	07 Oct 55	Sanitation	55PZUM41	458027
Germany, East	Poland	07 Oct 55	Sanitation	4EGDA234	419248
Germany, East	Poland	12 Jan 56	Water Transport	4EGDA237	419249
Germany, East	Poland	12 Jan 56	Water Transport	56PZUM11	458032
Germany, East	Poland	27 Jan 56	Scientific Project	3EGDA504	419250
Germany, East	Poland	31 Jan 56	Water Transport	3EGDA504	419251
Germany, East	Poland	01 Feb 57	Admin Cooperation	319UNTS115	104632
Germany, East	Poland	17 Apr 57	Specific Resources	5EGDA407	419252
Germany, East	Poland	13 Jul 57	Health/Educ/Welfare	319UNTS229	104634
Germany, East	Poland	05 Sep 57	Customs	57PZUM94	458053
Germany, East	Poland	05 Sep 57	Customs	5EGDA433	419253
Germany, East	Poland	17 Sep 57	Atomic Energy	5EGDA438	419254
Germany, East	Poland	17 Sep 57	Atomic Energy	57PZUM99	458054
Germany, East	Poland	16 Nov 57	General Economic	5EGDA440	419255
Germany, East	Poland	25 Nov 57	Consul/Citizenship	340UNTS99	104862
Germany, East	Poland	03 Dec 57	General Economic	5EGDA794	419256
Germany, East	Poland	14 Mar 58	Health/Educ/Welfare	6EGDA332	419257
Germany, East	Poland	24 Oct 58	General Economic	6EGDA332	419259
Germany, East	Poland	24 Oct 58	Commodity Trade	6EGDA332	419258
Germany, East	Poland	06 May 59	Culture	7EGDA409	419260
Germany, East	Poland	08 May 59	Culture	59PZUM64	458067
Germany, East	Poland	27 May 59	Commodity Trade	7EGDA568	419261
Germany, East	Poland	23 Sep 59	Visas	7EGDA416	419262
Germany, East	Poland	23 Sep 59	Land Transport	59PZUM90	458069
Germany, East	Poland	10 Nov 59	Specific Resources	59PZUM100	458070
Germany, East	Poland	10 Nov 59	Specific Resources	7EGDA426	419263
Germany, East	Poland	09 Jan 60	Water Transport	8EGDA414	419264
Germany, East	Poland	09 Jan 60	Water Transport	8EGDA419	419265
Germany, East	Poland	22 Apr 60	General Economic	60PZUM20	458074
Germany, East	Poland	22 Apr 60	General Economic	8EGDA423	419266
Germany, East	Poland	18 Jan 61	Specific Property	9EGDA379	419267
Germany, East	Poland	13 May 61	Admin Cooperation	9EGDA469	419268
Germany, East	Poland	09 May 62	Visas	10EGDA575	419269
Germany, East	Poland	17 Mar 63	Non-ILO Labor	11EGDA589	419270
Germany, East	Poland	30 Dec 63	Air Transport	11EGDA416	419271
Germany, East	Poland	14 Mar 64	Visas	64PZUM16	458110
Germany, East	Poland	07 Jun 64	Visas	12EGDA1144	419272
Germany, East	Poland	06 Oct 64	Culture	552UNTS89	108051
Germany, East	Poland	11 Mar 65	Specific Resources	52EGDZ331	420273
Germany, East	Poland	12 May 65	Specific Property	44EGDZ335	420274
Germany, East	Poland	04 Nov 65	Education	65PZUM65	458125
Germany, East	Poland	30 Dec 65	General Economic	60EGDZ350	420275
Germany, East	Poland	05 Mar 66	Commodity Trade	51EGDZ355	420276
Germany, East	Poland	15 Mar 67	General Amity	618UNTS21	108922
Germany, East	Poland	05 May 67	Scientific Project	48EGDZ383	420277
Germany, East	Poland	29 Oct 67	Territory Boundary	69PDZU217	457160
Germany, East	Poland	15 May 69	Water Transport	70PDZU96	457163
Germany, East	Poland	28 Oct 69	Admin Cooperation	70PDZU221	457165
Germany, East	Poland	16 Jul 71	Gen Communications	72PDZU41	457174
Germany, East	Poland	25 Nov 71	Visas	71PDZU357	457177
Germany, East	Poland	25 Nov 71	Admin Cooperation	72PDZU48	457176
Germany, East	Romania	22 Sep 50	Scientific Project	4EGDA419	419279
Germany, East	Romania	22 Sep 50	Finance	4EGDA420	419280
Germany, East	Romania	22 Sep 50	Culture	4EGDA422	419281
Germany, East	Romania	06 Nov 50	General Trade	1EGDA453	419282
Germany, East	Romania	23 Jan 52	General Trade	1EGDA454	419283
Germany, East	Romania	12 Sep 52	General Economic	1EGDA455	419284
Germany, East	Romania	31 Oct 52	Postal Service	4EGDA425	419285
Germany, East	Romania	31 Oct 52	Telecommunications	4EGDA431	419286
Germany, East	Romania	17 Oct 53	Consul/Citizenship	1EGDA457	419287
Germany, East	Romania	21 Dec 53	Mass Media	4EGDA437	419288
Germany, East	Romania	03 Jun 55	Scientific Project	3EGDA577	419290
Germany, East	Romania	28 Jul 55	Air Transport	342UNTS207	104909
Germany, East	Romania	05 Aug 55	Sanitation	342UNTS229	104910
Germany, East	Romania	21 Dec 55	Finance	4EGDA451	419291
Germany, East	Romania	08 Dec 56	Sanitation	362UNTS189	105188
Germany, East	Romania	28 Apr 57	Sanitation	5EGDA479	419293
Germany, East	Romania	28 Apr 57	Health/Educ/Welfare	5EGDA468	419292
Germany, East	Romania	15 Jul 58	Consul/Citizenship	387UNTS133	105561
Germany, East	Romania	15 Jul 58	Admin Cooperation	395UNTS3	105681
Germany, East	Romania	15 Jul 58	Health/Educ/Welfare	387UNTS115	105560
Germany, East	Romania	16 Mar 59	General Economic	7EGDA432	419294
Germany, East	Romania	18 Mar 59	Mass Media	7EGDA438	419295

PARTY ONE	PARTY TWO	DATE	TOPIC	CITATION	NUMBER
Germany, East	Romania	12 Nov 59	Atomic Energy	7EGDA443	419296
Germany, East	Romania	17 Feb 61	General Trade	9EGDA388	419297
Germany, East	Romania	02 Mar 61	Scientific Project	9EGDA389	419298
Germany, East	Romania	18 Dec 62	IGO Establishment	51EGDZ278	420299
Germany, East	Romania	12 Jun 63	Non-ILO Labor	11EGDA605	419300
Germany, East	Romania	20 Nov 63	Air Transport	11EGDA478	419301
Germany, East	Romania	19 Dec 63	Education	11EGDA638	419302
Germany, East	Romania	15 Jun 65	Visas	44EGDZ337	420303
Germany, East	Romania	22 Jan 66	General Trade	40EGDZ352	420304
Germany, East	Romania	07 Jul 66	Mass Media	48EGDZ363	420305
Germany, East	Sudan	10 Jun 55	Finance	3EGDA660	419308
Germany, East	Sudan	03 Mar 60	Scientific Project	46EGDZ364	420309
Germany, East	Sweden	24 Jan 49	General Trade	49SOFM13	461072
Germany, East	Sweden	19 Jul 49	General Economic	49SOFM251	461082
Germany, East	Syria	07 Nov 55	Consul/Citizenship	3EGDA668	419310
Germany, East	Syria	27 Nov 55	General Economic	3EGDA668	419311
Germany, East	Syria	08 Jul 56	Culture	5EGDA485	419312
Germany, East	Syria	03 Sep 57	General Trade	5EGDA485	419313
Germany, East	Syria	27 Jan 58	Mass Media	6EGDA515	419314
Germany, East	Syria	06 Jun 65	Air Transport	43EGDZ337	420315
Germany, East	Syria	02 Aug 65	Finance	51EGDZ341	420318
Germany, East	Syria	02 Aug 65	Tech Assistance	51EGDZ341	420317
Germany, East	Syria	02 Aug 65	Water Transport	51EGDZ341	420319
Germany, East	Syria	02 Aug 65	General Trade	51EGDZ341	420316
Germany, East	Syria	17 Oct 65	General Economic	52EGDZ356	420320
Germany, East	Syria	23 Apr 66	Mass Media	47EGDZ358	420321
Germany, East	Syria	30 Aug 66	General Economic	42EGDZ366	420322
Germany, East	Syria	14 Sep 66	Culture	37EGDZ367	420323
Germany, East	Syria	30 Oct 66	Tech Assistance	37EGDZ370	420324
Germany, East	Tanzania	17 May 64	General Amity	12EGDA1139	419485
Germany, East	Tunisia	26 May 61	Mass Media	9EGDA400	419372
Germany, East	Tunisia	28 Feb 62	Finance	10EGDA566	419373
Germany, East	Tunisia	27 Nov 64	General Trade	12EGDA1171	419374
Germany, East	Tunisia	27 Nov 64	Finance	12EGDA903	419375
Germany, East	United Arab Rep	10 Nov 55	General Trade	3EGDA621	419001
Germany, East	United Arab Rep	12 Nov 55	Consul/Citizenship	3EGDA624	419002
Germany, East	United Arab Rep	06 Aug 56	Mass Media	5EGDA278	419003
Germany, East	United Arab Rep	07 Sep 57	Consul/Citizenship	5EGDA281	419004
Germany, East	United Arab Rep	07 Sep 57	General Economic	5EGDA280	419005
Germany, East	United Arab Rep	27 Mar 58	Water Transport	6EGDA474	419471
Germany, East	United Arab Rep	29 Aug 58	Tech Assistance	6EGDA484	419473
Germany, East	United Arab Rep	29 Aug 58	General Aid	6EGDA484	419472
Germany, East	United Arab Rep	27 Nov 58	Specific Property	6EGDA521	419474
Germany, East	United Arab Rep	13 Dec 58	General Trade	8EGDA559	419476
Germany, East	United Arab Rep	13 Dec 58	Finance	6EGDA485	419475
Germany, East	United Arab Rep	02 Aug 62	Mass Media	10EGDA547	419477
Germany, East	United Arab Rep	16 Dec 62	General Trade	10EGDA620	419478
Germany, East	United Arab Rep	06 May 65	Tech Assistance	43EGDZ335	420479
Germany, East	United Arab Rep	20 May 65	Air Transport	52EGDZ329	420480
Germany, East	United Arab Rep	11 Feb 66	Water Transport	52EGDZ353	420481
Germany, East	United Arab Rep	03 May 66	General Economic	33EGDZ359	420483
Germany, East	United Arab Rep	03 May 66	General Economic	33EGDZ359	420482
Germany, East	United Arab Rep	02 Aug 66	Sanitation	49EGDZ365	420484
Germany, East	USSR (Soviet Union)	19 Nov 49	Consul/Citizenship	1EGDA329	419376
Germany, East	USSR (Soviet Union)	12 Apr 50	General Economic	1EGDA245	419377
Germany, East	USSR (Soviet Union)	15 May 50	Reparations	OSUST274	468160
Germany, East	USSR (Soviet Union)	19 May 50	Claims and Debts	OSUST274	468161
Germany, East	USSR (Soviet Union)	01 Jul 50	Postal Service	4EGDA11	419378
Germany, East	USSR (Soviet Union)	01 Jul 50	Postal Service	4EGDA16	419379
Germany, East	USSR (Soviet Union)	01 Jul 50	Telecommunications	4EGDA27	419380
Germany, East	USSR (Soviet Union)	27 Sep 51	Scientific Project	4EGDA33	419382
Germany, East	USSR (Soviet Union)	27 Sep 51	General Trade	1EGDA256	419381
Germany, East	USSR (Soviet Union)	12 May 52	Education	4EGDA428	419383
Germany, East	USSR (Soviet Union)	13 Jan 53	Mass Media	4EGDA34	419384
Germany, East	USSR (Soviet Union)	20 Jul 53	Direct Aid	1EGDA273	419385

PARTY ONE	PARTY TWO	DATE	TOPIC	CITATION	NUMBER
Germany, East	USSR (Soviet Union)	22 Aug 53	Consul/Citizenship	1EGDA286	419386
Germany, East	USSR (Soviet Union)	22 Aug 53	Other Military	1EGDA286	419387
Germany, East	USSR (Soviet Union)	22 Aug 53	Reparations	221UNTS129	103005
Germany, East	USSR (Soviet Union)	31 Dec 53	Specif Goods/Equip	1EGDA299	419388
Germany, East	USSR (Soviet Union)	30 Apr 54	Specif Goods/Equip	4EGDA41	419389
Germany, East	USSR (Soviet Union)	30 Sep 54	Finance	4EGDA42	419391
Germany, East	USSR (Soviet Union)	30 Sep 54	Consul/Citizenship	2EGDA275	419390
Germany, East	USSR (Soviet Union)	27 Apr 55	Specific Property	2EGDA337	419392
Germany, East	USSR (Soviet Union)	28 Apr 55	Atomic Energy	OSUST327	468162
Germany, East	USSR (Soviet Union)	30 Jun 55	Specif Goods/Equip	3EGDA205	419393
Germany, East	USSR (Soviet Union)	01 Jul 55	Culture	2EGDA206	419394
Germany, East	USSR (Soviet Union)	25 Aug 55	Claims and Debts	OSUST334	468163
Germany, East	USSR (Soviet Union)	03 Sep 55	Scientific Project	3EGDA242	419395
Germany, East	USSR (Soviet Union)	20 Sep 55	Admin Cooperation	OSUST338	468164
Germany, East	USSR (Soviet Union)	20 Sep 55	General Amity	226UNTS201	103114
Germany, East	USSR (Soviet Union)	18 Oct 55	Air Transport	3EGDA327	419397
Germany, East	USSR (Soviet Union)	27 Nov 55	Specif Goods/Equip	4EGDA51	419398
Germany, East	USSR (Soviet Union)	23 Dec 55	Commodity Trade	3EGDA353	419399
Germany, East	USSR (Soviet Union)	26 Apr 56	Health/Educ/Welfare	259UNTS279	103692
Germany, East	USSR (Soviet Union)	30 May 56	Sanitation	263UNTS143	103771
Germany, East	USSR (Soviet Union)	18 Jun 56	Air Transport	4EGDA61	419400
Germany, East	USSR (Soviet Union)	17 Jul 56	Milit Occupation	5EGDA645	419401
Germany, East	USSR (Soviet Union)	12 Oct 56	Mass Media	OSUST369	468165
Germany, East	USSR (Soviet Union)	12 Oct 56	Mass Media	OSUST369	468166
Germany, East	USSR (Soviet Union)	26 Feb 57	Specific Property	5EGDA686	419402
Germany, East	USSR (Soviet Union)	12 Mar 57	Status of Forces	285UNTS105	104150
Germany, East	USSR (Soviet Union)	04 Apr 57	Specif Goods/Equip	16SUGG119	469936
Germany, East	USSR (Soviet Union)	10 May 57	Consul/Citizenship	285UNTS135	104151
Germany, East	USSR (Soviet Union)	25 May 57	General Economic	5EGDA697	419403
Germany, East	USSR (Soviet Union)	02 Aug 57	Status of Forces	5EGDA699	419404
Germany, East	USSR (Soviet Union)	27 Sep 57	General Economic	5EGDA730	419405
Germany, East	USSR (Soviet Union)	27 Sep 57	General Economic	292UNTS75	104268
Germany, East	USSR (Soviet Union)	28 Nov 57	Admin Cooperation	305UNTS113	104419
Germany, East	USSR (Soviet Union)	27 Dec 57	Admin Cooperation	OSUST395	468169
Germany, East	USSR (Soviet Union)	21 Feb 58	Education	6EGDA425	419407
Germany, East	USSR (Soviet Union)	21 Feb 58	Specific Property	6EGDA429	419406
Germany, East	USSR (Soviet Union)	25 Feb 58	General Economic	6EGDA431	419408
Germany, East	USSR (Soviet Union)	24 Jun 58	Milit Occupation	6EGDA447	419409
Germany, East	USSR (Soviet Union)	08 Sep 58	Specif Goods/Equip	6EGDA452	419410
Germany, East	USSR (Soviet Union)	21 Oct 58	Sanitation	6EGDA457	419411
Germany, East	USSR (Soviet Union)	21 Oct 58	Sanitation	16SUGG125	469961
Germany, East	USSR (Soviet Union)	22 Oct 58	Tech Assistance	6EGDA521	419412
Germany, East	USSR (Soviet Union)	22 Dec 58	Scientific Project	7SUGG129	469545
Germany, East	USSR (Soviet Union)	21 Nov 59	General Trade	7EGDA531	419414
Germany, East	USSR (Soviet Union)	01 Mar 60	Tech Assistance	8EGDA538	419415
Germany, East	USSR (Soviet Union)	24 May 60	Non-ILO Labor	392UNTS205	105645
Germany, East	USSR (Soviet Union)	29 Jul 60	Specif Goods/Equip	8EGDA577	419416
Germany, East	USSR (Soviet Union)	30 Aug 60	Education	9SUGG146	469688
Germany, East	USSR (Soviet Union)	27 Sep 60	Tech Assistance	9SUGG148	469695
Germany, East	USSR (Soviet Union)	31 Dec 60	General Economic	9SUGG159	469731
Germany, East	USSR (Soviet Union)	30 May 61	General Economic	9EGDA418	419417
Germany, East	USSR (Soviet Union)	10 Nov 61	Tech Assistance	10SUGG145	469804
Germany, East	USSR (Soviet Union)	28 Dec 61	Atomic Energy	9EGDA442	419418
Germany, East	USSR (Soviet Union)	05 Mar 62	Loans and Credits	10EGDA504	419419
Germany, East	USSR (Soviet Union)	03 May 62	Tech Assistance	10EGDA574	419420
Germany, East	USSR (Soviet Union)	08 Aug 62	Scientific Project	10EGDA521	419421
Germany, East	USSR (Soviet Union)	11 Mar 63	Commodity Trade	11EGDA588	419422
Germany, East	USSR (Soviet Union)	18 Jul 63	Tech Assistance	11EGDA611	419423
Germany, East	USSR (Soviet Union)	05 May 64	Tech Assistance	12EGDA1137	419424
Germany, East	USSR (Soviet Union)	12 Jun 64	General Amity	553UNTS249	108093
Germany, East	USSR (Soviet Union)	01 Oct 64	Health/Educ/Welfare	12EGDA1077	419425
Germany, East	USSR (Soviet Union)	14 Jul 65	Atomic Energy	48EGDZ339	420426
Germany, East	USSR (Soviet Union)	03 Dec 65	General Trade	61EGDZ349	420427
Germany, East	USSR (Soviet Union)	16 Mar 66	IGO Establishment	51EGDZ356	420428
Germany, East	USSR (Soviet Union)	01 Jun 66	Land Transport	41EGDZ361	420429

PARTY ONE	PARTY TWO	DATE	TOPIC	CITATION	NUMBER
Germany, East	USSR (Soviet Union)	01 Sep 66	Air Transport	34EGDZ367	420430
Germany, East	Vietnam, North	14 Mar 56	Tech Assistance	4EGDA567	419486
Germany, East	Vietnam, North	15 Jun 56	Finance	3EGDA612	419487
Germany, East	Vietnam, North	31 Jul 57	Culture	5EGDA780	419488
Germany, East	Vietnam, North	14 May 58	Telecommunications	6EGDA505	419490
Germany, East	Vietnam, North	14 May 58	Postal Service	6EGDA494	419489
Germany, East	Vietnam, North	01 Dec 58	General Economic	7EGDA559	419491
Germany, East	Vietnam, North	07 Mar 59	General Economic	7EGDA541	419492
Germany, East	Vietnam, North	09 Oct 59	Consul/Citizenship	7EGDA547	419493
Germany, East	Vietnam, North	09 Feb 61	General Economic	9EGDA448	419494
Germany, East	Vietnam, North	04 Nov 65	Education	43EGDZ347	420495
Germany, East	Vietnam, North	10 Oct 66	Loans and Credits	46EGDZ369	420496
Germany, East	Vietnam, North	10 Oct 66	Education	46EGDZ369	420497
Germany, East	Yemen	28 Oct 63	Consul/Citizenship	11EGDA627	419143
Germany, East	Yugoslavia	10 Oct 57	Consul/Citizenship	5EGDA348	419144
Germany, East	Yugoslavia	19 Oct 57	Finance	5EGDA352	419146
Germany, East	Yugoslavia	19 Oct 57	General Trade	5EGDA352	419145
Germany, East	Yugoslavia	06 Feb 60	Air Transport	8EGDA354	419147
Germany, East	Yugoslavia	02 Dec 60	General Economic	8EGDA364	419148
Germany, East	Yugoslavia	27 Jul 61	General Economic	9EGDA484	419149
Germany, East	Yugoslavia	22 May 63	General Ad Hoc	11EGDA603	419150
Germany, East	Yugoslavia	20 Jul 63	General Trade	51EGDZ292	420151
Germany, East	Yugoslavia	28 Sep 63	Humanitarian	11EGDA620	419153
Germany, East	Yugoslavia	28 Sep 63	General Economic	11EGDA620	419152
Germany, East	Yugoslavia	19 Dec 63	Sanitation	11EGDA395	419154
Germany, East	Yugoslavia	12 Feb 64	Consul/Citizenship	12EGDA792	419155
Germany, East	Yugoslavia	15 May 64	IGO Establishment	12EGDA806	419156
Germany, East	Yugoslavia	10 Jul 64	Health/Educ/Welfare	12EGDA815	419157
Germany, East	Yugoslavia	22 Mar 65	Sanitation	50EGDZ332	420158
Germany, East	Yugoslavia	31 Aug 65	Sanitation	44EGDZ342	420159
Germany, East	Yugoslavia	22 Apr 66	Gen Communications	47EGDZ358	420160
Germany, East	Yugoslavia	20 May 66	Admin Cooperation	45EGDZ360	420161
Germany, East	Yugoslavia	18 Sep 66	Land Transport	34EGDZ368	420162
Germany, East	Yugoslavia	01 Oct 66	Consul/Citizenship	46EGDZ369	420163
Germany, East	Yugoslavia	03 Jun 67	Scientific Project	42EGDZ385	420164
Germany, East	Zanzibar	17 May 64	General Aid	12EGDA1139	419306
Germany, East	Zanzibar	27 Jun 64	Tech Assistance	12EGDA1146	419307
Germany, West	Afghanistan	31 Jan 58	Direct Aid	58WGBB83	425002
Germany, West	Afghanistan	31 Jan 58	General Economic	58WBGA83	424001
Germany, West	Afghanistan	22 Jul 59	Air Transport	464UNTS177	106715
Germany, West	Afghanistan	18 Apr 61	Culture	63WGBB1069	425003
Germany, West	Algeria	03 Oct 64	Finance	65WBGA116	424004
Germany, West	Algeria	17 Dec 64	Tech Assistance	65WBGA100	424005
Germany, West	Argentina	26 Oct 51	General Trade	51WBGA227	424006
Germany, West	Argentina	25 Nov 57	General Trade	58WBGA6	424007
Germany, West	Argentina	20 Sep 60	Air Transport	61WGBB1045	425008
Germany, West	Argentina	01 Mar 66	Tech Assistance	635UNTS247	109087
Germany, West	Argentina	13 Jul 66	Taxation	636UNTS3	109091
Germany, West	Argentina	21 Mar 68	Admin Cooperation	0UNTS0	109563
Germany, West	Argentina	29 Aug 68	Tech Assistance	0UNTS0	109564
Germany, West	Argentina	04 Dec 68	Loans and Credits	69WBGA39	424009
Germany, West	Argentina	04 Dec 68	Direct Aid	0UNTS0	109569
Germany, West	Argentina	23 Dec 68	Tech Assistance	0UNTS0	109565
Germany, West	Argentina	31 Mar 69	Scientific Project	0UNTS0	110188
Germany, West	Argentina	31 Mar 69	Scientific Project	70WGBB5	425010
Germany, West	Argentina	19 May 69	Non-IBRD Project	0UNTS0	110190
Germany, West	Argentina	23 Oct 69	Non-IBRD Project	70WBGA6	424011
Germany, West	Argentina	23 Oct 69	Non-IBRD Project	0UNTS0	110195
Germany, West	Argentina	03 Feb 70	Loans and Credits	70WBGA82	424012
Germany, West	Argentina	21 May 71	Water Transport	71WGBB2655	425013
Germany, West	Australia	29 Aug 52	Non-ILO Labor	184UNTS147	102446
Germany, West	Australia	17 Dec 52	Visas	188UNTS267	102530
Germany, West	Australia	05 Mar 56	Other Military	328UNTS241	104737
Germany, West	Australia	22 May 57	Air Transport	357UNTS45	105105
Germany, West	Australia	27 Aug 58	Non-ILO Labor	320UNTS303	104649

PARTY ONE	PARTY TWO	DATE	TOPIC	CITATION	NUMBER
Germany, West	Australia	14 Oct 59	General Trade	345UNTS35	104957
Germany, West	Australia	19 Mar 62	Postal Service	488UNTS203	107130
Germany, West	Australia	21 Apr 65	Claims and Debts	598UNTS25	108654
Germany, West	Australia	21 Jun 65	Visas	542UNTS53	107879
Germany, West	Australia	08 Jul 65	Postal Service	543UNTS305	107907
Germany, West	Austria	21 Apr 51	Non-ILO Labor	52WGBB317	425523
Germany, West	Austria	19 May 51	Non-ILO Labor	52WGBB612	425524
Germany, West	Austria	23 Nov 51	Non-ILO Labor	52WGBB609	425525
Germany, West	Austria	23 Nov 51	Non-ILO Labor	53ABGB10	403060
Germany, West	Austria	23 Nov 51	Non-ILO Labor	59WBGA13	424526
Germany, West	Austria	11 Jul 53	Non-ILO Labor	54ABGB250	403059
Germany, West	Austria	31 Oct 53	Non-ILO Labor	55ABGB248	403058
Germany, West	Austria	31 Oct 53	Non-ILO Labor	55ABGB74	403061
Germany, West	Austria	06 Apr 54	Visas	55ABGB247	403062
Germany, West	Austria	13 May 54	General Trade	54WBGA99	424527
Germany, West	Austria	14 Sep 54	Admin Cooperation	57ABGB245	403063
Germany, West	Austria	15 Sep 54	Visas	55WBGA148	424528
Germany, West	Austria	04 Oct 54	Admin Cooperation	55WGBB833	425531
Germany, West	Austria	04 Oct 54	Taxation	55WGBB749	425529
Germany, West	Austria	04 Oct 54	Taxation	55WGBB755	425530
Germany, West	Austria	10 May 55	Visas	55WBGA103	424532
Germany, West	Austria	14 Sep 55	Visas	57WGBB585	425534
Germany, West	Austria	14 Sep 55	Customs	57WGBB581	421533
Germany, West	Austria	14 Sep 55	Visas	57WGBB594	425537
Germany, West	Austria	14 Sep 55	Privil/Immunities	57WGBB592	425536
Germany, West	Austria	14 Sep 55	Privil/Immunities	57WGBB596	425538
Germany, West	Austria	14 Sep 55	Visas	57WGBB589	425535
Germany, West	Austria	28 Oct 55	Visas	57WGBB598	425539
Germany, West	Austria	25 Mar 57	Specific Resources	58ABGB197	403003
Germany, West	Austria	31 May 57	Visas	57ABGB192	403064
Germany, West	Austria	15 Jun 57	Finance	58WGBB129	425540
Germany, West	Austria	09 Jul 57	Admin Cooperation	57ABGB198	403065
Germany, West	Austria	22 Sep 58	Extradition	60WGBB1341	425541
Germany, West	Austria	22 Sep 58	Admin Cooperation	60WGBB1341	425542
Germany, West	Austria	10 Oct 58	Admin Cooperation	58WBGA228	424543
Germany, West	Austria	16 Jan 59	Specific Property	59WBGA51	424544
Germany, West	Austria	06 Jun 59	Admin Cooperation	59WGBB1523	425545
Germany, West	Austria	06 Jun 59	Admin Cooperation	60WGBB1245	425546
Germany, West	Austria	18 Jan 61	Customs	62WGBB933	425547
Germany, West	Austria	19 Jul 61	Visas	414UNTS211	105974
Germany, West	Austria	19 Jul 61	Extradition	61WBGA169	424548
Germany, West	Austria	27 Nov 61	Refugees	62WGBB1041	425549
Germany, West	Austria	06 Sep 62	Visas	63WGBB1279	425550
Germany, West	Austria	07 May 63	Health/Educ/Welfare	64WGBB220	425551
Germany, West	Austria	12 Sep 63	Visas	63ABGB296	403004
Germany, West	Austria	15 Mar 65	Air Transport	66WGBB126	425552
Germany, West	Austria	15 Mar 65	Air Transport	0UNTS0	109478
Germany, West	Austria	17 Jan 66	Health/Educ/Welfare	0UNTS0	110163
Germany, West	Austria	17 Jan 66	Health/Educ/Welfare	69WGBB1	425553
Germany, West	Austria	17 Feb 66	Land Transport	614UNTS263	108875
Germany, West	Austria	17 Feb 66	Land Transport	615UNTS3	108876
Germany, West	Austria	27 Sep 66	Commodity Trade	66WBGA235	424554
Germany, West	Austria	17 Oct 66	Admin Cooperation	67WGBB2318	425555
Germany, West	Austria	22 Dec 66	Non-ILO Labor	69WGBB1233	425556
Germany, West	Austria	22 Dec 66	Non-ILO Labor	0UNTS0	110090
Germany, West	Austria	31 May 67	Visas	70WGBB697	425557
Germany, West	Austria	07 Aug 67	Patents/Copyrights	68WGBB5	425558
Germany, West	Austria	23 Oct 68	Customs	68ABGB410	403067
Germany, West	Austria	23 Oct 68	Customs	68ABGB409	403066
Germany, West	Austria	25 Oct 68	Health/Educ/Welfare	69ABGB259	403068
Germany, West	Austria	13 Nov 68	General Transport	69WGBB1457	425559
Germany, West	Austria	07 Feb 69	Health/Educ/Welfare	70ABGB210	403069
Germany, West	Austria	31 Mar 69	Admin Cooperation	70ABGB340	403070
Germany, West	Austria	18 Nov 69	Taxation	70WGBB1370	425560
Germany, West	Austria	11 Mar 70	Visas	70ABGB130	403071

PARTY ONE	PARTY TWO	DATE	TOPIC	CITATION	NUMBER
Germany, West	Austria	06 Jul 70	Visas	70ABGB285	403072
Germany, West	Austria	11 Sep 70	Admin Cooperation	71WGBB1001	425561
Germany, West	Austria	25 Jan 71	Visas	71ABGB100	403076
Germany, West	Austria	25 Jan 71	Visas	71ABGB99	403075
Germany, West	Austria	25 Jan 71	Visas	71ABGB97	403073
Germany, West	Austria	25 Jan 71	Visas	71ABGB98	403074
Germany, West	Austria	25 Jan 71	Visas	71ABGB102	403078
Germany, West	Austria	25 Jan 71	Visas	71ABGB101	403077
Germany, West	Austria	05 Jul 72	Visas	72ABGB308	403079
Germany, West	Austria	05 Jul 72	Visas	72ABGB309	403080
Germany, West	Austria	05 Jul 72	Visas	72ABGB311	403082
Germany, West	Austria	05 Jul 72	Visas	72ABGB310	403081
Germany, West	Austria	05 Jul 72	Visas	72ABGB312	403083
Germany, West	Bank Int Settlement	29 Nov 65	Claims and Debts	66WGBB209	425742
Germany, West	Barbados	06 Nov 69	Visas	70WBGA8	424460
Germany, West	Belgium	18 Jan 52	Visas	243UNTS3	103443
Germany, West	Belgium	18 Jan 52	Education	124UNTS9	101663
Germany, West	Belgium	01 Feb 52	Land Transport	52WGBB437	425019
Germany, West	Belgium	01 Apr 52	Visas	132UNTS45	101750
Germany, West	Belgium	14 Aug 52	Admin Cooperation	139UNTS29	101873
Germany, West	Belgium	14 Nov 52	Visas	160UNTS217	102108
Germany, West	Belgium	06 Dec 52	Visas	152UNTS11	102007
Germany, West	Belgium	23 Dec 52	Claims and Debts	186UNTS69	102483
Germany, West	Belgium	20 Mar 53	Customs	53WGBB534	425020
Germany, West	Belgium	20 May 53	Admin Cooperation	180UNTS3	102370
Germany, West	Belgium	19 Dec 53	Visas	185UNTS277	102474
Germany, West	Belgium	03 Mar 54	Admin Cooperation	188UNTS259	102529
Germany, West	Belgium	30 Mar 54	Admin Cooperation	190UNTS63	102558
Germany, West	Belgium	01 Apr 54	Admin Cooperation	190UNTS43	102556
Germany, West	Belgium	03 Apr 54	Admin Cooperation	190UNTS247	102568
Germany, West	Belgium	15 Apr 54	Admin Cooperation	190UNTS253	102569
Germany, West	Belgium	28 May 54	Non-ILO Labor	249UNTS387	103512
Germany, West	Belgium	28 May 54	Other Military	54WBGA128	424021
Germany, West	Belgium	03 Nov 54	Admin Cooperation	201UNTS359	102724
Germany, West	Belgium	23 Nov 54	Admin Cooperation	202UNTS109	102726
Germany, West	Belgium	14 Apr 56	Air Transport	344UNTS103	104945
Germany, West	Belgium	15 May 56	Visas	58WGBB190	425022
Germany, West	Belgium	26 Jul 56	Visas	249UNTS187	103508
Germany, West	Belgium	24 Sep 56	Territory Boundary	314UNTS195	104549
Germany, West	Belgium	24 Sep 56	Culture	263UNTS31	103766
Germany, West	Belgium	09 Jul 57	General Military	59WGBB409	425023
Germany, West	Belgium	07 Dec 57	Non-ILO Labor	64WGBB170	425025
Germany, West	Belgium	07 Dec 57	Non-ILO Labor	63WGBB404	425024
Germany, West	Belgium	17 Jan 58	Extradition	328UNTS173	104735
Germany, West	Belgium	30 Jun 58	Admin Cooperation	387UNTS245	105566
Germany, West	Belgium	25 Apr 59	Admin Cooperation	59WGBB1524	425026
Germany, West	Belgium	03 Aug 59	Admin Cooperation	61WGBB1183	425027
Germany, West	Belgium	01 Jun 60	Admin Cooperation	60WBGA150	424028
Germany, West	Belgium	28 Sep 60	Specif Claim/Waive	61WGBB2640	425029
Germany, West	Belgium	12 Jul 62	Non-ILO Labor	63WBGA48	424030
Germany, West	Belgium	21 Sep 62	Reparations	502UNTS63	107326
Germany, West	Belgium	01 Feb 63	General Military	63WBGA171	424031
Germany, West	Belgium	30 Dec 63	Admin Cooperation	64WBGA78	424032
Germany, West	Belgium	27 Jul 64	Commodity Trade	67WBGA236	424033
Germany, West	Belgium	06 Oct 64	Non-ILO Labor	65WBGA157	424034
Germany, West	Belgium	17 Dec 64	Land Transport	631UNTS229	108996
Germany, West	Belgium	17 Dec 64	Taxation	66WGBB1508	425035
Germany, West	Belgium	20 Jul 65	Non-ILO Labor	67WGBB813	425036
Germany, West	Belgium	11 Apr 67	Taxation	69WGBB17	425037
Germany, West	Belgium	11 Apr 67	Taxation	0UNTS0	110109
Germany, West	Belgium	14 Apr 67	Admin Cooperation	67WGBB2545	425038
Germany, West	Belgium	29 Jan 69	Non-ILO Labor	71WGBB857	425039
Germany, West	Belgium	07 Mar 69	Admin Cooperation	69WGBB1147	425040
Germany, West	Belgium	24 Dec 69	Specific Resources	70WGBB1205	425041
Germany, West	Belgium	04 May 70	General Military	70WBGA85	424042

PARTY ONE	PARTY TWO	DATE	TOPIC	CITATION	NUMBER
Germany, West	Bolivia	04 Aug 66	Culture	70WGBB977	425047
Germany, West	Bolivia	15 Nov 68	Air Transport	70WGBB1197	425048
Germany, West	Bolivia	05 Aug 69	Loans and Credits	69WBGA204	424049
Germany, West	Brazil	17 Aug 50	General Trade	51WGBB11	425050
Germany, West	Brazil	04 Sep 53	Patents/Copyrights	54WGBB533	425051
Germany, West	Brazil	04 Sep 53	Claims and Debts	50WBGA212	424052
Germany, West	Brazil	01 Jul 55	General Trade	55WBGA141	424053
Germany, West	Brazil	15 May 57	Admin Cooperation	58WBGA91	424054
Germany, West	Brazil	29 Aug 57	Air Transport	59WGBB73	425055
Germany, West	Brazil	30 Nov 63	Consul/Citizenship	65WGBB1565	425057
Germany, West	Brazil	30 Nov 63	Water Transport	0UNTS0	109426
Germany, West	Brazil	30 Nov 63	Tech Assistance	64WBGA49	424056
Germany, West	Brazil	30 Nov 63	Consul/Citizenship	0UNTS0	109423
Germany, West	Brazil	30 Nov 63	Finance	0UNTS0	109425
Germany, West	Brazil	30 Nov 63	Tech Assistance	0UNTS0	109421
Germany, West	Brazil	09 Apr 69	Loans and Credits	69WBGA106	424058
Germany, West	Brazil	30 May 69	Loans and Credits	69WBGA138	424059
Germany, West	Brazil	09 Jun 69	Culture	71WGBB117	425061
Germany, West	Brazil	09 Jun 69	Scientific Project	69WBGA2118	424060
Germany, West	Brazil	02 Oct 70	Loans and Credits	70WBGA232	424062
Germany, West	Brazil	23 Apr 71	Loans and Credits	71WBGA109	424063
Germany, West	Bulgaria	20 Feb 50	Health/Educ/Welfare	0UNTS0	109871
Germany, West	Bulgaria	18 Apr 58	Consul/Citizenship	0UNTS0	109872
Germany, West	Bulgaria	06 Mar 64	General Trade	64WBGA148	424064
Germany, West	Bulgaria	07 Jul 64	General Trade	64WGBB781	425065
Germany, West	Bulgaria	12 Feb 71	General Trade	71WBGA69	424066
Germany, West	Burma	12 Jul 62	Direct Aid	62WBGA161	424043
Germany, West	Burma	11 Nov 67	Loans and Credits	68WBGA15	424044
Germany, West	Burma	09 May 70	Loans and Credits	70WBGA145	424045
Germany, West	Burma	18 Sep 70	Loans and Credits	70WBGA220	424046
Germany, West	Burundi	31 Mar 65	Tech Assistance	65WBGA142	424067
Germany, West	Burundi	23 Dec 65	Loans and Credits	66WBGA88	424068
Germany, West	Burundi	21 Nov 68	Loans and Credits	69WBGA14	424069
Germany, West	Cameroon	05 Mar 56	Other Military	68WBGA203	424348
Germany, West	Cameroon	11 Dec 57	Atomic Energy	58WBGA46	424349
Germany, West	Cameroon	03 Aug 59	General Military	61WGBB1183	425350
Germany, West	Cameroon	08 Mar 62	Water Transport	62WBGA126	424343
Germany, West	Cameroon	08 Mar 62	General Trade	62WBGA126	424342
Germany, West	Cameroon	29 Jun 62	Claims and Debts	63WGBB911	425344
Germany, West	Cameroon	29 Jun 62	Direct Aid	62WBGA172	424345
Germany, West	Cameroon	03 May 63	Loans and Credits	63WBGA115	424346
Germany, West	Cameroon	28 Aug 64	General Military	64WBGA195	424351
Germany, West	Cameroon	22 Oct 64	Air Transport	66WGBB109	425347
Germany, West	Cameroon	08 Jul 69	Scientific Project	70WGBB97	425352
Germany, West	Cameroon	23 Oct 69	Admin Cooperation	70WGBB846	425353
Germany, West	Cameroon	19 Dec 69	Non-ILO Labor	70WGBB253	425354
Germany, West	Canada	15 Apr 53	Visas	236UNTS323	103333
Germany, West	Canada	30 Oct 53	Admin Cooperation	236UNTS317	103332
Germany, West	Canada	04 Jun 56	Taxation	316UNTS231	104589
Germany, West	Canada	10 Dec 56	Milit Assistance	392UNTS3	105633
Germany, West	Canada	04 Sep 59	Air Transport	411UNTS260	105922
Germany, West	Central Afri Rep	29 Dec 62	General Economic	63WBGA210	424730
Germany, West	Central Afri Rep	29 Dec 62	Direct Aid	63WBGA210	424731
Germany, West	Central Afri Rep	02 Oct 64	Loans and Credits	64WBGA234	424732
Germany, West	Central Afri Rep	23 Aug 65	Claims and Debts	67WGBB1657	425733
Germany, West	Central Afri Rep	31 Jan 67	Loans and Credits	67WBGA73	424734
Germany, West	Central Afri Rep	22 May 69	Loans and Credits	69WBGA148	424735
Germany, West	Central Am Bank	22 Jul 70	Loans and Credits	70WBGA149	424749
Germany, West	Ceylon (Sri Lanka)	22 Nov 52	General Trade	55WGBB189	425070
Germany, West	Ceylon (Sri Lanka)	01 Apr 55	General Trade	369UNTS57	105251
Germany, West	Ceylon (Sri Lanka)	04 Jul 62	Taxation	64WGBB789	425071
Germany, West	Ceylon (Sri Lanka)	08 Nov 63	Loans and Credits	66WGBB909	425072
Germany, West	Ceylon (Sri Lanka)	30 Jun 66	Loans and Credits	66WBGA160	424073
Germany, West	Ceylon (Sri Lanka)	20 Aug 66	Loans and Credits	66WBGA212	424074
Germany, West	Ceylon (Sri Lanka)	30 Sep 67	Loans and Credits	68WBGA15	424075

PARTY ONE	PARTY TWO	DATE	TOPIC	CITATION	NUMBER
Germany, West	Ceylon (Sri Lanka)	20 Jun 68	Loans and Credits	68WBGA170	424076
Germany, West	Ceylon (Sri Lanka)	03 Aug 69	Loans and Credits	69WBGA199	424077
Germany, West	Chad	31 May 63	Tech Assistance	63WBGA224	424671
Germany, West	Chad	31 May 63	General Economic	63WBGA224	424670
Germany, West	Chad	07 May 65	Loans and Credits	65WBGA135	424672
Germany, West	Chad	11 Apr 67	Claims and Debts	68WGBB221	425673
Germany, West	Chad	10 Apr 68	Loans and Credits	68WBGA152	424674
Germany, West	Chad	18 Apr 69	Loans and Credits	69WBGA143	424675
Germany, West	Chile	02 Feb 51	General Trade	52WGBB325	425078
Germany, West	Chile	06 Sep 52	Customs	53WGBB292	425079
Germany, West	Chile	03 Nov 53	Customs	54WGBB631	425080
Germany, West	Chile	29 Jun 56	Customs	58WGBB108	425081
Germany, West	Chile	02 Nov 56	General Economic	56WBGA230	424082
Germany, West	Chile	20 Nov 56	Culture	59WGBB549	425083
Germany, West	Chile	10 Nov 61	Admin Cooperation	62WBGA35	424084
Germany, West	Chile	13 Sep 62	Admin Cooperation	63WBGA13	424085
Germany, West	Chile	30 Mar 64	Air Transport	65WGBB79	425086
Germany, West	Chile	30 Apr 64	Air Transport	0UNTS0	109476
Germany, West	Chile	18 Oct 68	General Aid	70WBGA64	424087
Germany, West	Chile	18 Oct 68	Loans and Credits	69WBGA146	424088
Germany, West	Chile	28 Aug 70	Scientific Project	71WGBB106	425089
Germany, West	China People's Rep	27 Sep 57	Dispute Settlement	57CCJC92	410452
Germany, West	China People's Rep	27 Sep 57	General Trade	57CCJC91	410451
Germany, West	China People's Rep	27 Sep 57	General Trade	57CCJC90	410450
Germany, West	Colombia	19 May 54	Patents/Copyrights	54WBGA184	424367
Germany, West	Colombia	09 Nov 57	General Trade	58WBGA49	424368
Germany, West	Colombia	11 May 59	Patents/Copyrights	61WGBB13	425369
Germany, West	Colombia	11 Oct 60	Culture	65WGBB1948	425370
Germany, West	Colombia	04 Aug 62	Claims and Debts	64WGBB257	425371
Germany, West	Colombia	02 Mar 65	Tech Assistance	65WBGA140	424372
Germany, West	Colombia	11 Jun 65	Claims and Debts	67WGBB1552	425373
Germany, West	Colombia	11 Jun 65	Loans and Credits	66WBGA238	424374
Germany, West	Colombia	10 Sep 65	Taxation	67WGBB762	425375
Germany, West	Colombia	25 Nov 68	Air Transport	70WGBB673	425376
Germany, West	Colombia	27 Jan 70	Loans and Credits	70WBGA74	424377
Germany, West	Colombia	10 Dec 70	Loans and Credits	71WBGA58	424378
Germany, West	Congo (Brazzaville)	30 Oct 62	General Economic	63WBGA59	424379
Germany, West	Congo (Brazzaville)	30 Oct 62	General Transport	63WBGA59	424380
Germany, West	Congo (Brazzaville)	30 Oct 62	Tech Assistance	63WBGA59	424381
Germany, West	Congo (Brazzaville)	13 Sep 65	Claims and Debts	67WGBB1733	425382
Germany, West	Congo (Brazzaville)	27 Oct 65	Loans and Credits	66WBGA4	424383
Germany, West	Congo (Zaire)	23 Nov 64	Loans and Credits	65WBGA38	424384
Germany, West	Congo (Zaire)	23 Jun 65	Loans and Credits	65WBGA170	424385
Germany, West	Congo (Zaire)	07 Mar 67	Loans and Credits	67WBGA98	424386
Germany, West	Congo (Zaire)	18 Mar 69	Claims and Debts	70WGBB509	425388
Germany, West	Congo (Zaire)	18 Mar 69	Loans and Credits	69WBGA84	424387
Germany, West	Costa Rica	23 Jul 65	Tech Assistance	66WBGA66	424090
Germany, West	Costa Rica	19 Jul 68	Loans and Credits	68WBGA185	424091
Germany, West	Cuba	07 Jul 51	General Trade	52WGBB958	425399
Germany, West	Cuba	11 May 53	General Economic	55WGBB1055	425400
Germany, West	Cuba	22 Mar 54	Patents/Copyrights	54WGBB1112	425401
Germany, West	Cuba	23 May 57	Postal Service	61WGBB441	425402
Germany, West	Cyprus	30 Oct 61	General Economic	62WBGA3	424737
Germany, West	Cyprus	30 Oct 61	General Trade	62WBGA3	424736
Germany, West	Cyprus	30 Oct 61	Tech Assistance	62WBGA3	424738
Germany, West	Cyprus	30 May 67	Commodity Trade	69WBGA2	424739
Germany, West	Cyprus	18 Oct 67	Air Transport	69WGBB981	425740
Germany, West	Cyprus	24 Jun 70	Loans and Credits	70WBGA163	424741
Germany, West	Czechoslovakia	03 Aug 67	General Economic	68WBGA61	424676
Germany, West	Czechoslovakia	17 Dec 70	General Economic	71WBGA1	424677
Germany, West	Dahomey	19 Jun 61	General Economic	64WBGA196	424092
Germany, West	Dahomey	19 Jun 61	Water Transport	61WBGA196	424094
Germany, West	Dahomey	19 Jun 61	General Economic	61WBGA196	424093
Germany, West	Dahomey	15 Jul 63	Loans and Credits	63WBGA192	424095
Germany, West	Dahomey	23 Jul 70	Loans and Credits	70WBGA215	424096
Germany, West	Denmark	15 Dec 49	Finance	51UNTS11	100749
Germany, West	Denmark	15 Feb 52	Land Transport	61WBGA58	424097
Germany, West	Denmark	26 Feb 53	Claims and Debts	178UNTS3	102332
Germany, West	Denmark	14 Aug 53	Non-ILO Labor	202UNTS3	102725
Germany, West	Denmark	31 May 54	Extradition	200UNTS53	102694
Germany, West	Denmark	30 Jun 56	Visas	258UNTS65	103671
Germany, West	Denmark	29 Jan 57	Air Transport	302UNTS75	104354
Germany, West	Denmark	07 Jun 57	General Military	59WGBB409	425098
Germany, West	Denmark	29 May 58	Specific Resources	59WGBB1072	425099
Germany, West	Denmark	29 May 58	Specific Resources	0UNTS0	109731
Germany, West	Denmark	22 Dec 58	General Trade	59WBGA37	424100
Germany, West	Denmark	01 Aug 59	Non-ILO Labor	60WGBB2109	425101
Germany, West	Denmark	24 Aug 59	Specif Claim/Waive	60WGBB1333	425102
Germany, West	Denmark	10 Nov 60	Consul/Citizenship	431UNTS21	106205
Germany, West	Denmark	12 Sep 61	Non-ILO Labor	516UNTS283	107478
Germany, West	Denmark	30 Jan 62	Taxation	63WGBB1311	425103
Germany, West	Denmark	03 Oct 62	Other Military	450UNTS291	106475
Germany, West	Denmark	10 Jun 63	Admin Cooperation	477UNTS405	106930
Germany, West	Denmark	06 Jan 65	Admin Cooperation	528UNTS201	107643
Germany, West	Denmark	09 Jun 65	Territory Boundary	605UNTS95	108762
Germany, West	Denmark	09 Jun 65	Water Transport	581UNTS141	108439
Germany, West	Denmark	09 Jun 65	Territory Boundary	570UNTS91	108289
Germany, West	Denmark	02 Feb 67	Dispute Settlement	606UNTS97	108778
Germany, West	Denmark	30 Mar 67	Customs	0UNTS0	109975
Germany, West	Denmark	30 Mar 67	Customs	69WGBB937	425104
Germany, West	Denmark	30 Nov 67	Specific Resources	632UNTS153	109017
Germany, West	Denmark	11 Jun 71	Status of Forces	71WGBB1092	425105
Germany, West	Dominican Republic	23 Dec 57	General Amity	59WGBB1468	425106
Germany, West	Ecuador	01 Aug 53	General Trade	54WGBB712	425107
Germany, West	Ecuador	01 Aug 53	General Trade	53WBGA192	424108
Germany, West	Ecuador	01 Aug 53	Patents/Copyrights	53WBGA192	424109
Germany, West	Ecuador	13 May 54	Visas	57WBGA193	424110
Germany, West	Ecuador	21 Jul 58	Admin Cooperation	58WBGA218	424111
Germany, West	Ecuador	20 Sep 62	Air Transport	498UNTS199	107283
Germany, West	Ecuador	08 Nov 63	Finance	64WBGA41	424112
Germany, West	Ecuador	28 Jun 65	Loans and Credits	65WBGA185	424113
Germany, West	Ecuador	28 Jun 65	Claims and Debts	66WGBB825	425114
Germany, West	Ecuador	12 Jul 67	Visas	67WBGA166	424115
Germany, West	Ecuador	10 Apr 68	Education	68WBGA148	424116
Germany, West	Ecuador	13 Mar 69	Culture	70WGBB1025	425117
Germany, West	Ecuador	14 Aug 69	Loans and Credits	69WBGA232	424118
Germany, West	Ecuador	24 Apr 70	Loans and Credits	70WBGA135	424119
Germany, West	El Salvador	31 Oct 52	Mostfavored Nation	54WGBB49	425128
Germany, West	El Salvador	24 Sep 63	Tech Assistance	64WBGA198	424129
Germany, West	El Salvador	19 Sep 66	Loans and Credits	67WBGA42	424130
Germany, West	Ethiopia	16 Apr 58	Air Transport	59WGBB1065	425014
Germany, West	Ethiopia	21 Apr 64	General Economic	68WBGA38	424016
Germany, West	Ethiopia	21 Apr 64	Water Transport	68WBGA38	424017
Germany, West	Ethiopia	21 Apr 64	Air Transport	68WBGA38	424018
Germany, West	Ethiopia	21 Apr 64	Claims and Debts	65WGBB1521	425015
Germany, West	Eur Space Research	08 Sep 67	IGO Establishment	69WGBB92	425747
Germany, West	Eur Space Vehicle	26 Jan 70	IGO Operations	70WGBB185	425743
Germany, West	Eurocontrol	08 Sep 70	Admin Cooperation	71WGBB1153	425748
Germany, West	Finland	16 Apr 52	General Economic	52WBGA81	424131
Germany, West	Finland	25 Sep 62	Land Transport	62WBGA217	424132
Germany, West	Finland	03 Dec 69	General Economic	70WBGA31	424133
Germany, West	France	10 Jul 50	Non-ILO Labor	51WGBB69	425137
Germany, West	France	10 Jul 50	Non-ILO Labor	51WGBB98	425136
Germany, West	France	10 Jul 50	Visas	51WGBB87	425135
Germany, West	France	10 Jul 50	Education	51FRJO706	416033
Germany, West	France	10 Jul 50	Non-ILO Labor	51WGBB177	425134
Germany, West	France	19 Nov 51	Extradition	53WGBB151	425138
Germany, West	France	27 Feb 53	Specif Claim/Waive	53WGBB508	425139
Germany, West	France	31 Aug 54	Admin Cooperation	54FRJO1909	416034
Germany, West	France	23 Oct 54	Culture	55WGBB885	425142

PARTY ONE	PARTY TWO	DATE	TOPIC	CITATION	NUMBER
Germany, West	France	23 Oct 54	Territory Boundary	55WGBB295	425140
Germany, West	France	23 Oct 54	Extradition	57WBGA225	424141
Germany, West	France	23 Oct 54	Other Military	58WBGA64	424143
Germany, West	France	27 Nov 54	Visas	55WBGA34	424144
Germany, West	France	16 Dec 54	Visas	55WBGA41	424145
Germany, West	France	24 Jun 55	Commodity Trade	55WBGA159	424146
Germany, West	France	04 Oct 55	Air Transport	353UNTS203	105044
Germany, West	France	27 Oct 56	General Amity	57WGBB1661	425149
Germany, West	France	27 Oct 56	Specific Resources	56WGBB1863	425148
Germany, West	France	27 Oct 56	Territory Boundary	56WGBB1587	425147
Germany, West	France	08 Dec 56	Land Transport	58WBGA4	424150
Germany, West	France	14 Jan 57	Visas	57WBGA137	424151
Germany, West	France	07 Jun 57	General Military	59WGBB409	425152
Germany, West	France	31 Mar 58	Specific Property	59WGBB189	425153
Germany, West	France	18 Apr 58	Visas	60WGBB1533	425154
Germany, West	France	18 Apr 58	General Transport	0UNTS0	110714
Germany, West	France	22 Aug 58	Finance	58FRRT28	415047
Germany, West	France	30 Jun 59	Visas	59WGBB389	425155
Germany, West	France	21 Jul 59	Taxation	61WGBB397	425156
Germany, West	France	03 Aug 59	Dispute Settlement	61WGBB1183	425157
Germany, West	France	27 Oct 59	Visas	61WBGA11	424158
Germany, West	France	22 Jan 60	Extradition	60WBGA63	424159
Germany, West	France	08 Mar 60	Patents/Copyrights	61WGBB22	425160
Germany, West	France	08 Mar 60	Patents/Copyrights	0UNTS0	110715
Germany, West	France	22 Apr 60	Admin Cooperation	60WGBB2325	425181
Germany, West	France	15 Jul 60	Specif Claim/Waive	61WGBB1029	425182
Germany, West	France	06 May 61	Admin Cooperation	61WGBB1040	425183
Germany, West	France	13 Jun 61	Visas	66WBGA245	424184
Germany, West	France	27 Jul 61	Claims and Debts	63FRJO33	416039
Germany, West	France	28 Sep 61	General Military	63WBGA171	424185
Germany, West	France	27 Nov 61	Admin Cooperation	62WGBB705	425186
Germany, West	France	20 Dec 61	IGO Establishment	62WGBB1106	425187
Germany, West	France	19 Jan 62	Admin Cooperation	62FRJO13	416040
Germany, West	France	27 Apr 62	Admin Cooperation	62FRRT23	415041
Germany, West	France	12 Jul 62	Non-ILO Labor	63WBGA75	424188
Germany, West	France	19 Dec 62	Postal Service	62FRJO2812	416042
Germany, West	France	22 Jan 63	General Amity	63WGBB405	425189
Germany, West	France	27 Jun 63	Non-ILO Labor	63WBGA231	424190
Germany, West	France	05 Jul 63	Health/Educ/Welfare	63WGBB1612	425191
Germany, West	France	13 Aug 63	Admin Cooperation	63FRRT69	415043
Germany, West	France	20 Dec 63	Non-ILO Labor	64WGBB702	425193
Germany, West	France	20 Dec 63	Non-ILO Labor	65WGBB1287	425192
Germany, West	France	15 Jan 64	Admin Cooperation	70WGBB1	425194
Germany, West	France	27 Feb 64	Visas	64WBGA238	424195
Germany, West	France	18 Jan 65	Admin Cooperation	67WBGA10	424196
Germany, West	France	16 Mar 65	Non-ILO Labor	65WBGA157	424197
Germany, West	France	22 Mar 65	Culture	65FRRT79	415045
Germany, West	France	25 Mar 65	Status of Forces	69FRJO1810	416044
Germany, West	France	19 Apr 66	Other Military	66WBGA161	424199
Germany, West	France	11 Jun 66	Admin Cooperation	66WBGA192	424198
Germany, West	France	27 Jun 66	Culture	66FRRT24	415046
Germany, West	France	19 Jan 67	Atomic Energy	67WGBB2430	425200
Germany, West	France	06 Jun 67	Telecommunications	69WGBB84	425201
Germany, West	France	04 Jul 69	Specific Resources	70WGBB726	425202
Germany, West	France	03 Nov 69	Taxation	70WGBB1317	425203
Germany, West	France	02 Feb 71	Admin Cooperation	71WGBB2434	425204
Germany, West	Gabon	11 Jul 62	General Economic	63WBGA58	424205
Germany, West	Gabon	11 Jul 62	Direct Aid	63WBGA58	424206
Germany, West	Gabon	11 Jul 62	General Transport	63WBGA58	424207
Germany, West	Gabon	31 Oct 63	Loans and Credits	64WBGA155	424208
Germany, West	Gabon	10 Jan 67	Loans and Credits	67WBGA63	424209
Germany, West	Gabon	27 Nov 68	Loans and Credits	69WBGA27	424210
Germany, West	Gabon	16 May 69	Claims and Debts	70WGBB657	425211
Germany, West	Gabon	05 Nov 70	Loans and Credits	70WBGA235	424212
Germany, West	Gambia	02 Nov 67	Visas	68WBGA80	424213

PARTY ONE	PARTY TWO	DATE	TOPIC	CITATION	NUMBER
Germany, West	Ghana	21 Dec 59	General Trade	60WBGA241	424215
Germany, West	Ghana	21 Dec 59	Direct Aid	60WBGA196	424214
Germany, West	Ghana	15 May 63	Water Transport	63WBGA131	424217
Germany, West	Ghana	15 May 63	Air Transport	63WBGA131	424218
Germany, West	Ghana	15 May 63	Loans and Credits	63WBGA131	424216
Germany, West	Ghana	06 Apr 66	Loans and Credits	66WBGA131	424219
Germany, West	Ghana	10 Jun 66	Extradition	67WGBB1743	425220
Germany, West	Ghana	19 May 67	Loans and Credits	68WGBB1251	425221
Germany, West	Ghana	01 Sep 67	Loans and Credits	67WBGA193	424222
Germany, West	Ghana	30 Mar 68	Tech Assistance	68WBGA147	424223
Germany, West	Ghana	07 May 68	Loans and Credits	68WBGA130	424224
Germany, West	Ghana	06 Aug 68	Air Transport	69WGBB1553	425225
Germany, West	Ghana	11 Jul 69	Loans and Credits	69WBGA176	424226
Germany, West	Ghana	08 Dec 70	Loans and Credits	71WBGA64	424227
Germany, West	Greece	16 Mar 49	Finance	77UNTS327	101007
Germany, West	Greece	16 Mar 49	General Trade	77UNTS307	101006
Germany, West	Greece	12 Feb 51	General Trade	198UNTS193	102665
Germany, West	Greece	28 Jul 52	General Trade	182UNTS85	102424
Germany, West	Greece	11 Nov 53	General Economic	53WBGA228	424228
Germany, West	Greece	21 Sep 55	Admin Cooperation	55WBGA203	424229
Germany, West	Greece	17 May 56	Culture	57WGBB501	425230
Germany, West	Greece	27 Nov 58	General Economic	59WBGA3	424231
Germany, West	Greece	18 Feb 60	Non-ILO Labor	60WBGA173	424232
Germany, West	Greece	18 Mar 60	Specif Claim/Waive	61WGBB1596	425233
Germany, West	Greece	18 Mar 60	General Economic	62WGBB1505	425234
Germany, West	Greece	30 Mar 60	Non-ILO Labor	61WBGA25	424235
Germany, West	Greece	27 Mar 61	Claims and Debts	63WGBB216	425236
Germany, West	Greece	25 Apr 61	Non-ILO Labor	63WGBB678	425237
Germany, West	Greece	31 May 61	Non-ILO Labor	62WGBB1109	425238
Germany, West	Greece	04 Nov 61	Admin Cooperation	63WGBB109	425239
Germany, West	Greece	08 Mar 62	Land Transport	533UNTS269	107747
Germany, West	Greece	07 Jun 63	Air Transport	544UNTS193	107919
Germany, West	Greece	26 Sep 63	Other Military	550UNTS203	108017
Germany, West	Greece	16 Apr 64	Other Economic	609UNTS27	108826
Germany, West	Greece	18 Apr 66	Taxation	67WGBB852	425240
Germany, West	Greece	18 Apr 66	Taxation	0UNTS0	109395
Germany, West	Guatemala	24 Apr 66	Tech Assistance	67WBGA39	424241
Germany, West	Guinea	18 Mar 59	Direct Aid	59WBGA77	424242
Germany, West	Guinea	09 Mar 61	Water Transport	61WBGA160	424243
Germany, West	Guinea	19 Apr 62	Claims and Debts	64WGBB145	425244
Germany, West	Guinea	19 Apr 62	Loans and Credits	62WBGA134	424246
Germany, West	Guinea	19 Apr 62	Air Transport	62WBGA134	424247
Germany, West	Guinea	19 Apr 62	General Economic	62WBGA134	424245
Germany, West	Guinea	10 Jul 64	Commodity Trade	64WBGA195	424248
Germany, West	Guinea	03 Jun 65	Loans and Credits	65WBGA136	424249
Germany, West	Honduras	18 Apr 64	Tech Assistance	66WBGA33	424250
Germany, West	Hungary	27 Jul 57	Commodity Trade	57WBGA164	424704
Germany, West	Hungary	10 Nov 63	General Economic	64WBGA14	424705
Germany, West	Hungary	27 Oct 70	General Economic	70WBGA218	424706
Germany, West	Iceland	19 Dec 50	General Amity	51WGBB153	425279
Germany, West	Iceland	19 Dec 50	Patents/Copyrights	56WGBB899	425278
Germany, West	Iceland	20 May 54	General Trade	54WBGA124	424280
Germany, West	Iceland	14 Sep 56	Visas	57WBGA192	424281
Germany, West	Iceland	12 Aug 59	Air Transport	411UNTS224	105921
Germany, West	Iceland	19 Jul 61	Specific Resources	409UNTS47	105877
Germany, West	India	19 Mar 52	General Trade	52WBGA83	424251
Germany, West	India	31 Mar 55	General Trade	55WBGA174	424252
Germany, West	India	05 Mar 56	Other Military	68WBGA202	424253
Germany, West	India	07 Aug 58	Education	58WBGA178	424254
Germany, West	India	18 Mar 59	Taxation	60WGBB1828	425255
Germany, West	India	31 May 63	Air Transport	64WGBB677	425256
Germany, West	India	15 Oct 64	Claims and Debts	64WBGA235	424257
Germany, West	India	15 Jun 66	Water Transport	66WBGA190	424258
Germany, West	India	24 Jul 68	Customs	69WGBB1012	425259
Germany, West	India	20 Mar 69	Culture	69WGBB1713	425260

PARTY ONE	PARTY TWO	DATE	TOPIC	CITATION	NUMBER
Germany, West	Indonesia	22 Apr 53	General Trade	53WBGA163	424261
Germany, West	Indonesia	29 Aug 57	Direct Aid	57WBGA228	424262
Germany, West	Indonesia	17 May 68	Loans and Credits	68WBGA139	424263
Germany, West	Indonesia	08 Nov 68	Loans and Credits	70WGBB492	425264
Germany, West	Indonesia	08 May 69	Loans and Credits	69WBGA189	424265
Germany, West	Indonesia	23 Oct 69	Loans and Credits	70WBGA28	424266
Germany, West	Indonesia	04 Dec 69	Air Transport	71WGBB192	425267
Germany, West	Indonesia	27 Aug 70	Loans and Credits	70WBGA226	424268
Germany, West	Iran	04 Nov 54	Direct Aid	56WGBB2091	425271
Germany, West	Iran	07 Apr 57	Taxation	0IRTB7	433011
Germany, West	Iran	22 Dec 59	Admin Cooperation	61WGBB105	425272
Germany, West	Iran	04 Feb 60	Non-IBRD Project	0IRTB8	433013
Germany, West	Iran	16 Apr 60	Non-IBRD Project	0IRTB9	433014
Germany, West	Iran	01 Jul 61	Air Transport	0UNTS0	110465
Germany, West	Iran	01 Jul 61	Air Transport	63WGBB1086	425273
Germany, West	Iran	11 Nov 65	Loans and Credits	67WGBB2549	425274
Germany, West	Iran	22 Apr 68	Loans and Credits	68WBGA112	424275
Germany, West	Iran	04 May 68	Taxation	0IRTB7	433012
Germany, West	Iran	08 Sep 68	Loans and Credits	69WBGA216	424276
Germany, West	Iran	07 Nov 68	Tech Assistance	0IRTB9	433015
Germany, West	Iran	20 Dec 68	Taxation	69WGBB2133	425277
Germany, West	Iran	27 Nov 69	Non-IBRD Project	0IRTB9	433016
Germany, West	Iraq	07 Oct 51	General Trade	53WGBB543	425269
Germany, West	Iraq	07 Nov 58	Admin Cooperation	59WBGA93	424270
Germany, West	Ireland	12 Jul 50	General Trade	557UNTS221	108136
Germany, West	Ireland	23 Jul 51	General Trade	558UNTS3	108137
Germany, West	Ireland	26 Sep 52	General Trade	558UNTS27	108138
Germany, West	Ireland	02 Dec 53	General Trade	558UNTS38	108139
Germany, West	Ireland	12 Jun 56	Air Transport	353UNTS121	105040
Germany, West	Ireland	11 May 60	Non-ILO Labor	553UNTS69	108070
Germany, West	Ireland	17 Oct 62	Taxation	604UNTS135	108749
Germany, West	Ireland	13 May 64	Other Military	553UNTS87	108071
Germany, West	Israel	10 Sep 52	Consul/Citizenship	345UNTS91	104961
Germany, West	Israel	10 Sep 52	Reparations	162UNTS205	102137
Germany, West	Israel	01 Jun 62	Specific Property	448UNTS227	106435
Germany, West	Israel	09 Jul 62	Taxation	630UNTS87	108968
Germany, West	Israel	12 May 66	Direct Aid	66WBGA111	424282
Germany, West	Israel	12 Sep 66	Education	582UNTS17	108454
Germany, West	Israel	19 Sep 66	Admin Cooperation	67WGBB719	425283
Germany, West	Israel	25 Feb 68	Admin Cooperation	69WBGA94	424284
Germany, West	Israel	18 Jul 68	Direct Aid	68WBGA165	424285
Germany, West	Israel	31 Mar 69	Admin Cooperation	0UNTS0	110384
Germany, West	Italy	26 Oct 51	Non-ILO Labor	53ITGU90	435162
Germany, West	Italy	30 Apr 52	Patents/Copyrights	52WGBB975	425286
Germany, West	Italy	05 May 53	Non-ILO Labor	54WGBB485	425287
Germany, West	Italy	05 May 53	Non-ILO Labor	53WBGA134	424288
Germany, West	Italy	05 May 53	Non-ILO Labor	267UNTS9	103835
Germany, West	Italy	12 Nov 53	Patents/Copyrights	56WGBB1883	425289
Germany, West	Italy	20 Apr 54	Admin Cooperation	55WGBB108	425290
Germany, West	Italy	28 Jun 54	Loans and Credits	288UNTS83	104199
Germany, West	Italy	18 Oct 55	Commodity Trade	56WBGA17	424291
Germany, West	Italy	22 Dec 55	Other Military	57WGBB1277	425292
Germany, West	Italy	08 Feb 56	Culture	58WGBB77	425293
Germany, West	Italy	19 Apr 56	General Trade	281UNTS195	104080
Germany, West	Italy	04 Jul 57	General Transport	64WBGA97	424294
Germany, West	Italy	12 Jul 57	Finance	291UNTS181	104252
Germany, West	Italy	21 Nov 57	General Amity	59WGBB949	425295
Germany, West	Italy	17 Apr 59	Status of Forces	60WGBB1961	425296
Germany, West	Italy	02 Jun 61	Specif Claim/Waive	63WGBB791	425297
Germany, West	Italy	02 Jun 61	Claims and Debts	63WGBB668	425298
Germany, West	Italy	12 Jul 61	Privil/Immunities	65WGBB843	425299
Germany, West	Italy	12 Jul 62	Non-ILO Labor	63WBGA75	424300
Germany, West	Italy	27 Jun 63	Non-ILO Labor	63WBGA231	424301
Germany, West	Italy	23 Jul 63	Patents/Copyrights	65WGBB156	425302
Germany, West	Italy	27 Feb 64	Non-ILO Labor	65ITDI129	436177

PARTY ONE	PARTY TWO	DATE	TOPIC	CITATION	NUMBER
Germany, West	Italy	20 Dec 64	Dispute Settlement	66ITGU214	435178
Germany, West	Italy	23 Feb 65	Non-ILO Labor	65WBGA63	424303
Germany, West	Italy	27 Jul 66	Commodity Trade	67WBGA81	424304
Germany, West	Italy	19 Oct 67	Specif Claim/Waive	67WGBB1997	425305
Germany, West	Italy	17 Sep 68	Taxation	70WGBB723	425307
Germany, West	Italy	05 Nov 68	Non-ILO Labor	70WGBB797	425308
Germany, West	Italy	17 Jul 69	Admin Cooperation	69WBGA197	424309
Germany, West	Ivory Coast	18 Dec 61	General Economic	62WBGA58	424120
Germany, West	Ivory Coast	18 Dec 61	Direct Aid	62WBGA58	424121
Germany, West	Ivory Coast	18 Dec 61	Water Transport	62WBGA58	424122
Germany, West	Ivory Coast	03 Sep 63	Loans and Credits	63WBGA210	424123
Germany, West	Ivory Coast	27 Oct 66	Claims and Debts	68WBGA61	424124
Germany, West	Ivory Coast	11 Jun 68	Loans and Credits	68WGBB167	425125
Germany, West	Ivory Coast	17 Jun 68	Loans and Credits	68WBGA153	424126
Germany, West	Ivory Coast	05 May 70	Loans and Credits	70WBGA145	424127
Germany, West	Jamaica	07 Oct 64	Air Transport	514UNTS187	107447
Germany, West	Jamaica	16 Dec 64	Tech Assistance	531UNTS129	107699
Germany, West	Jamaica	03 Feb 65	Scientific Project	531UNTS143	107700
Germany, West	Japan	08 Aug 52	Admin Cooperation	0JGJI4507	441071
Germany, West	Japan	08 May 53	Patents/Copyrights	0JGJI1172	441073
Germany, West	Japan	24 May 54	Admin Cooperation	0JGJI4508	441080
Germany, West	Japan	18 Jun 55	Visas	0JGJI1262	441085
Germany, West	Japan	02 Nov 56	Non-ILO Labor	0JGJI1325	441099
Germany, West	Japan	14 Feb 57	Culture	318UNTS361	104626
Germany, West	Japan	27 Jun 57	Admin Cooperation	318UNTS335	104624
Germany, West	Japan	26 Jul 57	Visas	0JGJI1262	441102
Germany, West	Japan	01 Jul 60	General Trade	60WBGA156	424750
Germany, West	Japan	18 Jan 61	Air Transport	465UNTS173	106727
Germany, West	Japan	08 Apr 64	General Trade	65JAIL234	440164
Germany, West	Japan	05 Oct 64	Taxation	0JGJI1559	441123
Germany, West	Japan	22 Apr 66	Taxation	68JAIL201	440069
Germany, West	Japan	22 Apr 66	Taxation	0UNTS0	109715
Germany, West	Japan	27 Dec 67	General Trade	68JAIL169	440206
Germany, West	Japan	27 Dec 67	Water Transport	68WBGA43	424751
Germany, West	Japan	22 Oct 69	Commodity Trade	69JJS169	442251
Germany, West	Jordan	14 Mar 67	Loans and Credits	67WBGA90	424314
Germany, West	Jordan	24 Oct 67	Loans and Credits	68WBGA42	424315
Germany, West	Jordan	25 Jul 68	Loans and Credits	68WBGA199	424316
Germany, West	Jordan	29 Jan 70	Air Transport	71WGBB1080	425318
Germany, West	Jordan	29 Jan 70	Loans and Credits	70WBGA54	424317
Germany, West	Kenya	04 Dec 64	General Economic	66WBGA165	424356
Germany, West	Kenya	04 Dec 64	Loans and Credits	66WBGA165	424358
Germany, West	Kenya	04 Dec 64	Tech Assistance	66WBGA165	424357
Germany, West	Kenya	04 Dec 64	Claims and Debts	66WGBB899	425355
Germany, West	Kenya	08 Dec 66	Loans and Credits	67WBGA52	424359
Germany, West	Kenya	30 Nov 67	Loans and Credits	68WBGA47	424360
Germany, West	Kenya	08 Aug 68	Visas	68WBGA184	424361
Germany, West	Kenya	11 Apr 69	Loans and Credits	69WBGA115	424362
Germany, West	Kenya	13 Mar 70	Loans and Credits	70WBGA98	424363
Germany, West	Kenya	20 Jun 70	Admin Cooperation	71WGBB924	425364
Germany, West	Kenya	01 Jul 70	Loans and Credits	70WBGA151	424365
Germany, West	Kenya	13 May 71	Loans and Credits	71WBGA114	424366
Germany, West	Korea, South	22 Sep 61	Visas	62WBGA8	424389
Germany, West	Korea, South	16 Dec 63	Non-ILO Labor	64WGBB143	425390
Germany, West	Korea, South	04 Feb 64	Claims and Debts	66WGBB841	425391
Germany, West	Korea, South	07 Dec 64	Loans and Credits	65WBGA29	424393
Germany, West	Korea, South	08 Apr 65	General Trade	65WBGA29	424394
Germany, West	Korea, South	09 Apr 65	Water Transport	71WGBB1259	425395
Germany, West	Korea, South	18 Feb 70	Non-ILO Labor	70WBGA99	424396
Germany, West	Korea, South	21 May 71	Loans and Credits	71WBGA142	424397
Germany, West	Korea, South	02 Jun 71	Non-ILO Labor	71WGBB927	425398
Germany, West	Lebanon	16 Nov 51	Mostfavored Nation	53WGBB540	425403
Germany, West	Lebanon	08 Mar 55	Patents/Copyrights	55WGBB897	425404
Germany, West	Lebanon	12 Jun 56	Admin Cooperation	57WBGA173	424405
Germany, West	Lebanon	15 Mar 61	Air Transport	62WGBB184	425406

PARTY ONE	PARTY TWO	DATE	TOPIC	CITATION	NUMBER
Germany, West	Lebanon	21 May 65	General Economic	67WGBB1673	425407
Germany, West	Liberia	17 Nov 59	Direct Aid	60WBGA69	424408
Germany, West	Liberia	12 Dec 61	Claims and Debts	67WGBB1537	425409
Germany, West	Liberia	12 Dec 61	General Transport	62WBGA46	424410
Germany, West	Liberia	12 Dec 61	Direct Aid	62WBGA46	424411
Germany, West	Liberia	05 Dec 66	Loans and Credits	67WBGA40	424412
Germany, West	Liberia	27 May 70	Specific Property	71WGBB953	425413
Germany, West	Libya	08 Jul 60	Direct Aid	61WBGA21	424414
Germany, West	Liechtenstein	30 Jan 53	Claims and Debts	54WGBB522	425415
Germany, West	Liechtenstein	29 May 58	Admin Cooperation	59WBGA73	424416
Germany, West	Luxembourg	30 Apr 52	General Transport	61WBGA173	424417
Germany, West	Luxembourg	09 Dec 53	Extradition	63WBGA47	424418
Germany, West	Luxembourg	25 Jul 56	Visas	51WBGA114	424419
Germany, West	Luxembourg	13 May 57	Sanitation	60WBGA180	424420
Germany, West	Luxembourg	01 Dec 57	Non-ILO Labor	60WGBB2305	425421
Germany, West	Luxembourg	28 Aug 58	Taxation	59WGBB1269	425422
Germany, West	Luxembourg	11 Jul 59	Admin Cooperation	60WGBB2077	425423
Germany, West	Luxembourg	14 Feb 60	Non-ILO Labor	63WGBB385	425424
Germany, West	Luxembourg	14 Jul 60	Non-ILO Labor	63WGBB397	425425
Germany, West	Luxembourg	31 May 61	Consul/Citizenship	61WBGA141	424426
Germany, West	Luxembourg	31 May 61	Admin Cooperation	62WBGA23	424427
Germany, West	Luxembourg	05 Jul 61	Air Transport	62WGBB195	425428
Germany, West	Luxembourg	16 Feb 62	Visas	63WGBB141	425429
Germany, West	Luxembourg	12 Jul 62	Non-ILO Labor	63WBGA75	424430
Germany, West	Luxembourg	07 Dec 62	Admin Cooperation	64WGBB193	425431
Germany, West	Luxembourg	27 Jun 63	Non-ILO Labor	63WBGA231	424432
Germany, West	Luxembourg	06 Oct 64	Non-ILO Labor	65WBGA157	424433
Germany, West	Luxembourg	09 Dec 65	Visas	67WGBB909	425434
Germany, West	Luxembourg	17 May 66	Extradition	66WBGA131	424435
Germany, West	Luxembourg	28 Feb 67	Specif Claim/Waive	67WGBB1694	425436
Germany, West	Luxembourg	09 Dec 69	Non-ILO Labor	71WGBB40	425437
Germany, West	Malagasy	06 Jun 62	General Economic	62WBGA153	424438
Germany, West	Malagasy	06 Jun 62	Water Transport	62WBGA153	424440
Germany, West	Malagasy	06 Jun 62	Direct Aid	62WBGA153	424439
Germany, West	Malagasy	21 Sep 62	Claims and Debts	65WGBB369	425441
Germany, West	Malagasy	10 Mar 66	Loans and Credits	66WBGA151	424442
Germany, West	Malagasy	18 Jul 68	Loans and Credits	68WBGA175	424443
Germany, West	Malawi	30 Jul 56	Consul/Citizenship	57WGBB284	425444
Germany, West	Malawi	25 Sep 64	Loans and Credits	65WBGA67	424445
Germany, West	Malawi	08 Aug 66	Loans and Credits	66WBGA188	424446
Germany, West	Malawi	22 Apr 68	Loans and Credits	68WBGA129	424447
Germany, West	Malawi	04 Sep 68	Loans and Credits	68WBGA215	424448
Germany, West	Malawi	07 Oct 70	Loans and Credits	70WBGA221	424449
Germany, West	Malaysia	22 Dec 60	Claims and Debts	62WGBB1064	425450
Germany, West	Malaysia	09 Dec 63	Loans and Credits	64WBGA13	424451
Germany, West	Malaysia	08 Nov 65	Loans and Credits	65WBGA242	424452
Germany, West	Malaysia	23 Jul 68	Air Transport	70WGBB681	425453
Germany, West	Malaysia	18 Mar 69	Loans and Credits	69WBGA99	424454
Germany, West	Malaysia	11 Feb 71	Loans and Credits	71WBGA82	424455
Germany, West	Mali	14 Feb 62	Loans and Credits	62WBGA75	424456
Germany, West	Mali	06 May 66	Loans and Credits	66WBGA124	424457
Germany, West	Mali	21 Nov 69	Loans and Credits	70WBGA15	424458
Germany, West	Mali	13 Mar 71	Loans and Credits	71WBGA86	424459
Germany, West	Malta	29 Feb 64	General Trade	64WBGA87	424461
Germany, West	Malta	09 May 68	Water Transport	68WBGA119	424462
Germany, West	Mauritania	02 Oct 67	Loans and Credits	56WBGA91	424475
Germany, West	Mauritius	20 Nov 69	Visas	70WBGA84	424476
Germany, West	Mexico	04 Nov 54	Patents/Copyrights	55WGBB903	425477
Germany, West	Mexico	18 Dec 56	Admin Cooperation	57WGBB500	425478
Germany, West	Mexico	19 Nov 59	Visas	60WBGA101	424479
Germany, West	Mexico	08 Mar 67	Air Transport	69WGBB193	425480
Germany, West	Monaco	14 May 59	Visas	60WBGA85	424481
Germany, West	Monaco	21 May 62	Extradition	64WGBB1297	425482
Germany, West	Monaco	21 May 62	Admin Cooperation	64WGBB1297	425483
Germany, West	Morocco	17 Jul 58	Admin Cooperation	59WGBB118	425463

PARTY ONE	PARTY TWO	DATE	TOPIC	CITATION	NUMBER
Germany, West	Morocco	15 Apr 61	General Trade	61WBGA150	424464
Germany, West	Morocco	31 Aug 61	Claims and Debts	67WGBB1641	425465
Germany, West	Morocco	12 Oct 61	Air Transport	523UNTS289	107562
Germany, West	Morocco	21 May 63	Non-ILO Labor	71WGBB1365	425466
Germany, West	Morocco	13 Sep 66	Loans and Credits	66WBGA207	424467
Germany, West	Morocco	24 Nov 66	Water Transport	67WBGA49	424469
Germany, West	Morocco	24 Nov 66	Loans and Credits	67WBGA49	424468
Germany, West	Morocco	24 Nov 66	General Economic	67WBGA49	424470
Germany, West	Morocco	22 Jun 68	Loans and Credits	68WBGA154	424471
Germany, West	Morocco	19 Jun 69	Loans and Credits	69WBGA165	424472
Germany, West	Morocco	02 Jul 70	Loans and Credits	70WBGA165	424473
Germany, West	Morocco	10 Jun 71	Loans and Credits	71WBGA151	424474
Germany, West	Multilateral	07 Dec 44	Air Transport	84UNTS389	200252
Germany, West	Multilateral	07 Dec 44	IGO Establishment	15UNTS295	200102
Germany, West	Multilateral	05 Apr 46	Specific Resources	231UNTS199	103221
Germany, West	Multilateral	15 Oct 46	Refugees	11UNTS73	100150
Germany, West	Multilateral	11 Dec 46	Sanitation	12UNTS179	100186
Germany, West	Multilateral	20 Jan 47	Water Transport	87UNTS247	101176
Germany, West	Multilateral	06 Mar 48	Water Transport	289UNTS3	104214
Germany, West	Multilateral	17 Mar 48	General Military	19UNTS51	100304
Germany, West	Multilateral	10 May 48	Culture	289UNTS111	104215
Germany, West	Multilateral	10 Jun 48	Humanitarian	191UNTS3	102576
Germany, West	Multilateral	10 Jun 48	Humanitarian	164UNTS113	102163
Germany, West	Multilateral	19 Jun 48	Air Transport	310UNTS151	104492
Germany, West	Multilateral	14 Jul 48	Direct Aid	23UNTS3	100340
Germany, West	Multilateral	14 Jul 48	Mostfavored Nation	31UNTS123	100473
Germany, West	Multilateral	24 Jul 48	Sanitation	66UNTS25	100847
Germany, West	Multilateral	09 Dec 48	Humanitarian	78UNTS277	101021
Germany, West	Multilateral	16 Dec 48	Direct Aid	79UNTS85	101033
Germany, West	Multilateral	08 Feb 49	Specific Resources	157UNTS157	102053
Germany, West	Multilateral	23 Mar 49	Commodity Trade	203UNTS179	102746
Germany, West	Multilateral	05 May 49	IGO Establishment	87UNTS103	101168
Germany, West	Multilateral	02 Sep 49	IGO Status/Immunit	250UNTS12	103515
Germany, West	Multilateral	22 Nov 49	Recognition	185UNTS307	102477
Germany, West	Multilateral	16 Dec 49	Admin Cooperation	72UNTS3	100924
Germany, West	Multilateral	06 Apr 50	Admin Cooperation	119UNTS99	101610
Germany, West	Multilateral	17 Apr 50	Visas	131UNTS99	101738
Germany, West	Multilateral	17 Apr 50	Non-ILO Labor	126UNTS285	101694
Germany, West	Multilateral	27 Jul 50	Non-ILO Labor	166UNTS73	102186
Germany, West	Multilateral	16 Sep 50	General Transport	92UNTS91	101264
Germany, West	Multilateral	04 Nov 50	Humanitarian	213UNTS221	102889
Germany, West	Multilateral	22 Nov 50	Culture	131UNTS25	101734
Germany, West	Multilateral	15 Dec 50	Customs	347UNTS127	104994
Germany, West	Multilateral	15 Dec 50	IGO Operations	160UNTS267	102111
Germany, West	Multilateral	15 Dec 50	Customs	171UNTS305	102234
Germany, West	Multilateral	15 Dec 50	Customs	157UNTS129	102052
Germany, West	Multilateral	06 Mar 51	Milit Assistance	138UNTS67	101860
Germany, West	Multilateral	06 Mar 51	Claims and Debts	106UNTS141	101461
Germany, West	Multilateral	18 Apr 51	IGO Establishment	261UNTS140	103729
Germany, West	Multilateral	19 Jun 51	Status of Forces	199UNTS67	102678
Germany, West	Multilateral	02 Jul 51	Refugees	189UNTS137	102545
Germany, West	Multilateral	20 Sep 51	IGO Status/Immunit	200UNTS3	102691
Germany, West	Multilateral	06 Dec 51	Admin Cooperation	150UNTS67	101963
Germany, West	Multilateral	15 Feb 52	Scientific Project	132UNTS51	101751
Germany, West	Multilateral	10 May 52	Taxation	439UNTS233	106332
Germany, West	Multilateral	10 May 52	Admin Cooperation	439UNTS217	106331
Germany, West	Multilateral	10 May 52	Admin Cooperation	439UNTS193	106330
Germany, West	Multilateral	20 May 52	Sanitation	219UNTS55	102966
Germany, West	Multilateral	11 Jul 52	Postal Service	170UNTS3	102221
Germany, West	Multilateral	11 Jul 52	Postal Service	171UNTS143	102226
Germany, West	Multilateral	11 Jul 52	Postal Service	170UNTS63	102222
Germany, West	Multilateral	11 Jul 52	Postal Service	171UNTS191	102227
Germany, West	Multilateral	11 Jul 52	Postal Service	171UNTS89	102225
Germany, West	Multilateral	11 Jul 52	Postal Service	171UNTS3	102224
Germany, West	Multilateral	06 Sep 52	Patents/Copyrights	216UNTS132	102937

PARTY ONE	PARTY TWO	DATE	TOPIC	CITATION	NUMBER
Germany, West	Multilateral	07 Nov 52	General Trade	221UNTS255	103010
Germany, West	Multilateral	27 Feb 53	Claims and Debts	333UNTS3	104764
Germany, West	Multilateral	30 Apr 53	Admin Cooperation	175UNTS89	102297
Germany, West	Multilateral	11 May 53	Sanitation	456UNTS3	106555
Germany, West	Multilateral	01 Jul 53	IGO Establishment	200UNTS149	102701
Germany, West	Multilateral	01 Oct 53	Commodity Trade	258UNTS153	103677
Germany, West	Multilateral	17 Oct 53	General Transport	184UNTS42	102438
Germany, West	Multilateral	19 Oct 53	IGO Establishment	207UNTS189	102807
Germany, West	Multilateral	11 Dec 53	Education	218UNTS125	102954
Germany, West	Multilateral	11 Dec 53	Non-ILO Labor	218UNTS255	102958
Germany, West	Multilateral	11 Dec 53	Non-ILO Labor	218UNTS211	102957
Germany, West	Multilateral	11 Dec 53	Patents/Copyrights	218UNTS27	102952
Germany, West	Multilateral	11 Dec 53	Non-ILO Labor	218UNTS153	102956
Germany, West	Multilateral	25 Feb 54	Air Transport	215UNTS249	102922
Germany, West	Multilateral	01 Mar 54	Admin Cooperation	286UNTS265	104173
Germany, West	Multilateral	12 May 54	Admin Cooperation	327UNTS3	104714
Germany, West	Multilateral	14 May 54	Culture	249UNTS215	103511
Germany, West	Multilateral	21 May 54	Non-ILO Labor	345UNTS285	104973
Germany, West	Multilateral	04 Jun 54	Customs	282UNTS249	104101
Germany, West	Multilateral	04 Jun 54	Customs	276UNTS191	103992
Germany, West	Multilateral	14 Jun 54	Air Transport	320UNTS217	104644
Germany, West	Multilateral	14 Jun 54	Air Transport	320UNTS209	104643
Germany, West	Multilateral	28 Sep 54	Refugees	360UNTS117	105158
Germany, West	Multilateral	23 Oct 54	Status of Forces	332UNTS3	104760
Germany, West	Multilateral	23 Oct 54	Status of Forces	332UNTS387	104763
Germany, West	Multilateral	23 Oct 54	Milit Occupation	331UNTS253	104758
Germany, West	Multilateral	23 Oct 54	Reparations	332UNTS219	104762
Germany, West	Multilateral	23 Oct 54	Milit Occupation	331UNTS327	104759
Germany, West	Multilateral	23 Oct 54	Milit Occupation	332UNTS157	104761
Germany, West	Multilateral	23 Oct 54	Status of Forces	334UNTS3	104765
Germany, West	Multilateral	01 Dec 54	Admin Cooperation	210UNTS197	102839
Germany, West	Multilateral	19 Dec 54	Culture	218UNTS139	102955
Germany, West	Multilateral	19 Dec 54	Patents/Copyrights	218UNTS51	102953
Germany, West	Multilateral	21 Dec 54	General Amity	258UNTS322	103678
Germany, West	Multilateral	06 Apr 55	General Amity	261UNTS55	103725
Germany, West	Multilateral	01 May 55	Admin Cooperation	0UNTS0	110416
Germany, West	Multilateral	25 May 55	IGO Establishment	264UNTS117	103791
Germany, West	Multilateral	03 Jun 55	Specific Resources	310UNTS145	104491
Germany, West	Multilateral	06 Jun 55	IGO Establishment	219UNTS79	102968
Germany, West	Multilateral	22 Jun 55	Atomic Energy	249UNTS3	103498
Germany, West	Multilateral	28 Sep 55	Air Transport	478UNTS371	106943
Germany, West	Multilateral	12 Oct 55	IGO Establishment	560UNTS3	108165
Germany, West	Multilateral	20 Oct 55	IGO Establishment	378UNTS159	105425
Germany, West	Multilateral	13 Dec 55	IGO Operations	529UNTS141	107660
Germany, West	Multilateral	13 Dec 55	Humanitarian	250UNTS3	103514
Germany, West	Multilateral	04 Jan 56	Scientific Project	256UNTS171	103627
Germany, West	Multilateral	01 Mar 56	Customs	343UNTS129	104923
Germany, West	Multilateral	05 Mar 56	Other Military	326UNTS181	104712
Germany, West	Multilateral	05 Mar 56	Other Military	326UNTS169	104711
Germany, West	Multilateral	25 Apr 56	Commodity Trade	270UNTS103	103896
Germany, West	Multilateral	30 Apr 56	Air Transport	310UNTS229	104494
Germany, West	Multilateral	18 May 56	Customs	338UNTS103	104834
Germany, West	Multilateral	18 May 56	Customs	327UNTS123	104721
Germany, West	Multilateral	18 May 56	Land Transport	339UNTS3	104844
Germany, West	Multilateral	18 May 56	Customs	319UNTS21	104630
Germany, West	Multilateral	19 May 56	Land Transport	399UNTS189	105742
Germany, West	Multilateral	20 Jun 56	Admin Cooperation	268UNTS3	103850
Germany, West	Multilateral	09 Jul 56	Non-ILO Labor	314UNTS3	104539
Germany, West	Multilateral	13 Jul 56	Dispute Settlement	281UNTS3	104066
Germany, West	Multilateral	07 Sep 56	Humanitarian	266UNTS3	103822
Germany, West	Multilateral	25 Sep 56	Air Transport	334UNTS89	104767
Germany, West	Multilateral	25 Sep 56	Air Transport	334UNTS13	104766
Germany, West	Multilateral	24 Oct 56	Admin Cooperation	510UNTS161	107412
Germany, West	Multilateral	26 Oct 56	IGO Establishment	276UNTS3	103988
Germany, West	Multilateral	15 Dec 56	Education	278UNTS73	104023

PARTY ONE	PARTY TWO	DATE	TOPIC	CITATION	NUMBER
Germany, West	Multilateral	25 Mar 57	IGO Status/Immunit	294UNTS411	104302
Germany, West	Multilateral	25 Mar 57	IGO Establishment	294UNTS2	104300
Germany, West	Multilateral	25 Mar 57	IGO Establishment	294UNTS259	104301
Germany, West	Multilateral	12 Apr 57	Education	443UNTS128	106362
Germany, West	Multilateral	29 Apr 57	Dispute Settlement	320UNTS243	104646
Germany, West	Multilateral	15 Jun 57	General Trade	550UNTS45	108008
Germany, West	Multilateral	15 Jun 57	Patents/Copyrights	583UNTS3	108470
Germany, West	Multilateral	26 Jul 57	Land Transport	386UNTS3	105535
Germany, West	Multilateral	30 Sep 57	General Transport	619UNTS77	108940
Germany, West	Multilateral	03 Oct 57	Postal Service	366UNTS255	105219
Germany, West	Multilateral	03 Oct 57	Postal Service	365UNTS3	105213
Germany, West	Multilateral	03 Oct 57	Postal Service	365UNTS207	105214
Germany, West	Multilateral	03 Oct 57	Postal Service	364UNTS3	105211
Germany, West	Multilateral	03 Oct 57	Postal Service	364UNTS331	105212
Germany, West	Multilateral	03 Oct 57	Postal Service	366UNTS141	105217
Germany, West	Multilateral	03 Oct 57	Postal Service	366UNTS87	105216
Germany, West	Multilateral	03 Oct 57	Postal Service	366UNTS193	105218
Germany, West	Multilateral	03 Oct 57	Postal Service	366UNTS3	105215
Germany, West	Multilateral	23 Nov 57	Refugees	506UNTS125	107384
Germany, West	Multilateral	25 Nov 57	General Trade	403UNTS169	105795
Germany, West	Multilateral	13 Dec 57	Land Transport	372UNTS159	105296
Germany, West	Multilateral	13 Dec 57	Visas	315UNTS139	104565
Germany, West	Multilateral	13 Dec 57	Extradition	359UNTS273	105146
Germany, West	Multilateral	15 Jan 58	Customs	383UNTS229	105503
Germany, West	Multilateral	20 Mar 58	Admin Cooperation	335UNTS211	104789
Germany, West	Multilateral	29 Apr 58	Dispute Settlement	450UNTS169	106466
Germany, West	Multilateral	29 Apr 58	Territory Boundary	499UNTS311	107302
Germany, West	Multilateral	29 Apr 58	Water Transport	450UNTS11	106465
Germany, West	Multilateral	10 Jun 58	Admin Cooperation	330UNTS3	104739
Germany, West	Multilateral	01 Dec 58	Commodity Trade	385UNTS137	105534
Germany, West	Multilateral	15 Dec 58	Sanitation	351UNTS159	105022
Germany, West	Multilateral	15 Jan 59	Customs	348UNTS13	104996
Germany, West	Multilateral	24 Jan 59	IGO Establishment	486UNTS157	107078
Germany, West	Multilateral	06 Apr 59	Commodity Trade	349UNTS167	105013
Germany, West	Multilateral	20 Apr 59	Land Transport	0UNTS0	110345
Germany, West	Multilateral	20 Apr 59	Admin Cooperation	472UNTS185	106841
Germany, West	Multilateral	20 Apr 59	Visas	376UNTS85	105375
Germany, West	Multilateral	11 May 59	Claims and Debts	527UNTS145	107623
Germany, West	Multilateral	03 Aug 59	Status of Forces	481UNTS262	106986
Germany, West	Multilateral	19 Nov 59	IGO Operations	410UNTS156	105902
Germany, West	Multilateral	26 Jan 60	IGO Establishment	439UNTS249	106333
Germany, West	Multilateral	15 Mar 60	Water Transport	572UNTS133	108310
Germany, West	Multilateral	22 Apr 60	Air Transport	418UNTS211	106023
Germany, West	Multilateral	28 Apr 60	Health/Educ/Welfare	376UNTS111	105377
Germany, West	Multilateral	17 Jun 60	Humanitarian	536UNTS27	107794
Germany, West	Multilateral	22 Jun 60	Mass Media	546UNTS247	107951
Germany, West	Multilateral	19 Sep 60	IBRD Project	444UNTS259	106371
Germany, West	Multilateral	21 Sep 60	Patents/Copyrights	394UNTS3	105664
Germany, West	Multilateral	06 Oct 60	Customs	473UNTS131	106861
Germany, West	Multilateral	01 Dec 60	Scientific Project	414UNTS110	105970
Germany, West	Multilateral	09 Dec 60	Customs	429UNTS211	106200
Germany, West	Multilateral	13 Dec 60	Air Transport	523UNTS117	107557
Germany, West	Multilateral	14 Dec 60	Education	429UNTS93	106193
Germany, West	Multilateral	13 Feb 61	ILO Labor	0UNTS0	110306
Germany, West	Multilateral	30 Mar 61	Sanitation	520UNTS151	107515
Germany, West	Multilateral	18 Apr 61	Consul/Citizenship	500UNTS95	107310
Germany, West	Multilateral	18 Apr 61	Consul/Citizenship	500UNTS223	107311
Germany, West	Multilateral	18 Apr 61	Dispute Settlement	500UNTS243	107312
Germany, West	Multilateral	21 Apr 61	IGO Establishment	484UNTS349	107041
Germany, West	Multilateral	08 Jun 61	Customs	473UNTS187	106863
Germany, West	Multilateral	08 Jun 61	Customs	473UNTS153	106862
Germany, West	Multilateral	21 Jun 61	IGO Establishment	514UNTS209	107449
Germany, West	Multilateral	18 Sep 61	Air Transport	500UNTS31	107305
Germany, West	Multilateral	05 Oct 61	Patents/Copyrights	527UNTS181	107625
Germany, West	Multilateral	05 Oct 61	Dispute Settlement	510UNTS175	107413

PARTY ONE	PARTY TWO	DATE	TOPIC	CITATION	NUMBER
Germany, West	Multilateral	18 Oct 61	IGO Establishment	529UNTS89	107659
Germany, West	Multilateral	26 Oct 61	Patents/Copyrights	496UNTS43	107247
Germany, West	Multilateral	06 Dec 61	Customs	473UNTS219	106864
Germany, West	Multilateral	20 Feb 62	Water Transport	597UNTS159	108644
Germany, West	Multilateral	07 Mar 62	Commodity Trade	445UNTS205	106389
Germany, West	Multilateral	07 Mar 62	Commodity Trade	445UNTS199	106388
Germany, West	Multilateral	29 Mar 62	IGO Establishment	507UNTS177	107401
Germany, West	Multilateral	09 May 62	IGO Establishment	453UNTS299	106531
Germany, West	Multilateral	14 May 62	Sanitation	544UNTS81	107911
Germany, West	Multilateral	14 May 62	Scientific Project	544UNTS39	107910
Germany, West	Multilateral	15 May 62	Commodity Trade	444UNTS3	106367
Germany, West	Multilateral	14 Jun 62	IGO Establishment	528UNTS33	107634
Germany, West	Multilateral	28 Jul 62	Specific Resources	460UNTS219	106642
Germany, West	Multilateral	28 Sep 62	IGO Establishment	469UNTS169	106791
Germany, West	Multilateral	05 Oct 62	IGO Establishment	502UNTS225	107333
Germany, West	Multilateral	17 Dec 62	Admin Cooperation	590UNTS81	108548
Germany, West	Multilateral	17 Dec 62	General Economic	523UNTS93	107555
Germany, West	Multilateral	17 Dec 62	Sanitation	486UNTS119	107076
Germany, West	Multilateral	24 Apr 63	Consul/Citizenship	596UNTS261	108638
Germany, West	Multilateral	24 Apr 63	Consul/Citizenship	596UNTS487	108640
Germany, West	Multilateral	07 Jun 63	Water Transport	472UNTS95	106837
Germany, West	Multilateral	05 Aug 63	Sanitation	480UNTS43	106964
Germany, West	Multilateral	09 Mar 64	Specific Resources	581UNTS83	108433
Germany, West	Multilateral	09 Mar 64	Specific Resources	581UNTS89	108434
Germany, West	Multilateral	09 Mar 64	Specific Resources	581UNTS57	108432
Germany, West	Multilateral	18 Jun 64	Atomic Energy	542UNTS145	107886
Germany, West	Multilateral	10 Jul 64	Postal Service	612UNTS361	108849
Germany, West	Multilateral	10 Jul 64	Postal Service	611UNTS7	108844
Germany, West	Multilateral	10 Jul 64	Postal Service	611UNTS105	108845
Germany, West	Multilateral	10 Jul 64	Postal Service	613UNTS193	108852
Germany, West	Multilateral	10 Jul 64	Postal Service	611UNTS387	108846
Germany, West	Multilateral	10 Jul 64	Postal Service	612UNTS3	108847
Germany, West	Multilateral	10 Jul 64	Postal Service	612UNTS233	108848
Germany, West	Multilateral	10 Jul 64	Postal Service	613UNTS3	108850
Germany, West	Multilateral	10 Jul 64	Postal Service	613UNTS127	108853
Germany, West	Multilateral	10 Jul 64	Postal Service	613UNTS3	108851
Germany, West	Multilateral	20 Aug 64	Telecommunications	514UNTS25	107441
Germany, West	Multilateral	12 Sep 64	Specific Resources	0UNTS0	109344
Germany, West	Multilateral	01 Dec 64	Water Transport	550UNTS133	108012
Germany, West	Multilateral	22 Jan 65	Gen Communications	634UNTS239	109066
Germany, West	Multilateral	09 Mar 65	Water Transport	591UNTS265	108564
Germany, West	Multilateral	18 Mar 65	Dispute Settlement	575UNTS159	108359
Germany, West	Multilateral	08 Jul 65	General Trade	597UNTS3	108641
Germany, West	Multilateral	18 Nov 65	Customs	609UNTS115	108830
Germany, West	Multilateral	04 Dec 65	IGO Establishment	571UNTS123	108303
Germany, West	Multilateral	31 Dec 65	Specific Resources	616UNTS317	108904
Germany, West	Multilateral	05 Apr 66	Water Transport	640UNTS133	109159
Germany, West	Multilateral	30 Apr 66	Specific Resources	620UNTS191	108956
Germany, West	Multilateral	17 May 66	Visas	571UNTS89	108302
Germany, West	Multilateral	02 Feb 67	Dispute Settlement	606UNTS89	108777
Germany, West	Multilateral	24 Apr 67	Humanitarian	634UNTS255	109067
Germany, West	Multilateral	18 Mar 68	Commodity Trade	0UNTS0	109262
Germany, West	Multilateral	22 Apr 68	Scientific Project	0UNTS0	109574
Germany, West	Multilateral	11 Jun 68	Scientific Project	0UNTS0	109884
Germany, West	Multilateral	24 Sep 68	Air Transport	0UNTS0	110612
Germany, West	Multilateral	28 Sep 68	Tech Assistance	0UNTS0	109296
Germany, West	Multilateral	07 Feb 69	Status of Forces	0UNTS0	110587
Germany, West	Multilateral	07 Feb 69	Status of Forces	0UNTS0	110586
Germany, West	Multilateral	09 Jun 69	Specific Resources	0UNTS0	110099
Germany, West	Multilateral	12 Jan 70	Commodity Trade	0UNTS0	110603
Germany, West	Multilateral	13 Apr 70	Education	0UNTS0	110793
Germany, West	NATO (North Atlan)	13 Mar 67	Military Mission	69WGBB1997	425744
Germany, West	Nepal	06 Oct 67	Scientific Project	68WGBB81	425484
Germany, West	Netherlands	14 Dec 50	Water Transport	87UNTS257	101177
Germany, West	Netherlands	29 Mar 51	Non-ILO Labor	149UNTS71	101952

PARTY ONE	PARTY TWO	DATE	TOPIC	CITATION	NUMBER
Germany, West	Netherlands	29 Jun 51	General Trade	51NET119	447028
Germany, West	Netherlands	18 Jan 52	Specific Property	179UNTS147	102364
Germany, West	Netherlands	31 Jan 52	Admin Cooperation	492UNTS295	107199
Germany, West	Netherlands	19 May 52	Reparations	134UNTS3	101794
Germany, West	Netherlands	20 Jun 52	Reparations	136UNTS221	101836
Germany, West	Netherlands	13 Mar 53	Visas	293UNTS123	104289
Germany, West	Netherlands	17 Mar 53	Visas	293UNTS129	104290
Germany, West	Netherlands	10 Oct 53	Visas	293UNTS115	104288
Germany, West	Netherlands	13 Aug 54	Admin Cooperation	492UNTS305	107200
Germany, West	Netherlands	11 Oct 54	Other Military	291UNTS9	104241
Germany, West	Netherlands	29 Oct 54	Non-ILO Labor	237UNTS3	103335
Germany, West	Netherlands	20 Sep 56	Specific Property	509UNTS269	107405
Germany, West	Netherlands	28 Sep 56	Air Transport	327UNTS185	104722
Germany, West	Netherlands	31 Oct 56	Admin Cooperation	287UNTS21	104177
Germany, West	Netherlands	01 Dec 56	Extradition	276UNTS127	103989
Germany, West	Netherlands	29 Jan 57	Status of Forces	314UNTS173	104548
Germany, West	Netherlands	10 Jul 57	Status of Forces	339UNTS97	104848
Germany, West	Netherlands	28 Jan 58	Specif Goods/Equip	453UNTS183	106525
Germany, West	Netherlands	30 Jan 58	Humanitarian	315UNTS117	104563
Germany, West	Netherlands	09 Apr 58	Visas	335UNTS237	104791
Germany, West	Netherlands	16 Apr 58	Sanitation	486UNTS331	107084
Germany, West	Netherlands	30 May 58	Visas	570UNTS127	108291
Germany, West	Netherlands	30 Jun 58	Non-ILO Labor	315UNTS179	104568
Germany, West	Netherlands	10 Oct 58	Visas	486UNTS345	107085
Germany, West	Netherlands	30 Apr 59	Finance	485UNTS141	107052
Germany, West	Netherlands	16 Jun 59	Taxation	593UNTS3	108576
Germany, West	Netherlands	08 Apr 60	Territory Boundary	508UNTS14	107404
Germany, West	Netherlands	03 Jun 60	Visas	487UNTS37	107094
Germany, West	Netherlands	09 Mar 61	Admin Cooperation	485UNTS185	107056
Germany, West	Netherlands	27 Apr 61	Culture	487UNTS77	107095
Germany, West	Netherlands	16 May 61	General Military	64WBGA168	424487
Germany, West	Netherlands	18 Jul 61	Sanitation	487UNTS95	107096
Germany, West	Netherlands	03 Aug 61	Admin Cooperation	492UNTS321	107201
Germany, West	Netherlands	12 Jul 62	Non-ILO Labor	63WBGA75	424488
Germany, West	Netherlands	30 Aug 62	Admin Cooperation	500UNTS3	107303
Germany, West	Netherlands	30 Aug 62	Admin Cooperation	547UNTS173	107957
Germany, West	Netherlands	27 Jun 63	Non-ILO Labor	63WBGA231	424489
Germany, West	Netherlands	27 May 64	Non-ILO Labor	64WBGA237	424490
Germany, West	Netherlands	06 Oct 64	Non-ILO Labor	65WBGA157	424491
Germany, West	Netherlands	01 Dec 64	Territory Boundary	550UNTS123	108011
Germany, West	Netherlands	14 Sep 65	Status of Forces	65WBGA203	424492
Germany, West	Netherlands	22 Sep 66	Land Transport	0UNTS0	109226
Germany, West	Netherlands	02 Feb 67	Dispute Settlement	606UNTS105	108779
Germany, West	Netherlands	14 Mar 68	Status of Forces	68WBGA81	424493
Germany, West	Netherlands	15 Mar 68	Admin Cooperation	68WBGA106	424494
Germany, West	Netherlands	28 Oct 68	Specific Property	69WGBB1121	425495
Germany, West	Netherlands	20 Dec 68	Admin Cooperation	69WGBB609	425496
Germany, West	Netherlands	21 Jan 69	Non-ILO Labor	0UNTS0	110751
Germany, West	Netherlands	21 Jan 69	Non-ILO Labor	70WGBB277	425497
Germany, West	Netherlands	03 Sep 69	Non-ILO Labor	71WGBB37	425498
Germany, West	Netherlands	22 Sep 70	Land Transport	70WGBB1056	425500
Germany, West	Netherlands	22 Sep 70	Land Transport	70WGBB1056	425499
Germany, West	Netherlands	18 Dec 70	Specific Property	71WGBB122	425501
Germany, West	New Zealand	30 Mar 55	Admin Cooperation	271UNTS207	103916
Germany, West	New Zealand	10 Jun 55	Visas	380UNTS307	105462
Germany, West	New Zealand	05 Mar 56	Other Military	402UNTS103	105779
Germany, West	New Zealand	20 Apr 59	General Trade	402UNTS125	105782
Germany, West	Nicaragua	08 Apr 65	Tech Assistance	65WBGA169	424485
Germany, West	Nicaragua	09 Oct 68	Loans and Credits	69WBGA11	424486
Germany, West	Niger	14 Jun 61	General Economic	61WBGA195	424502
Germany, West	Niger	14 Jun 61	Direct Aid	61WBGA195	424503
Germany, West	Niger	30 Jun 64	Loans and Credits	65WBGA14	424504
Germany, West	Niger	29 Oct 64	Claims and Debts	65WGBB1402	425505
Germany, West	Niger	18 Mar 68	Loans and Credits	68WBGA108	424506
Germany, West	Niger	19 Jul 69	Loans and Credits	69WBGA193	424507

PARTY ONE	PARTY TWO	DATE	TOPIC	CITATION	NUMBER
Germany, West	Nigeria	25 Mar 63	Loans and Credits	64WBGA5	424509
Germany, West	Nigeria	25 Mar 63	General Transport	64WBGA5	424511
Germany, West	Nigeria	25 Mar 63	Tech Assistance	64WBGA5	424510
Germany, West	Nigeria	25 Mar 63	General Trade	64WBGA5	424508
Germany, West	Nigeria	31 Jul 69	Loans and Credits	69WBGA193	424512
Germany, West	Nigeria	12 Feb 71	Loans and Credits	71WBGA102	424513
Germany, West	Nigeria	13 May 71	Loans and Credits	71WBGA115	424514
Germany, West	Norway	20 Dec 50	General Trade	2NORT545	451183
Germany, West	Norway	07 May 51	Claims and Debts	92UNTS51	101260
Germany, West	Norway	15 Feb 52	Land Transport	61WBGA58	424516
Germany, West	Norway	30 Dec 53	Customs	2NORT618	451184
Germany, West	Norway	25 May 54	Visas	2NORT633	451185
Germany, West	Norway	27 Jul 54	Privil/Immunities	2NORT639	451186
Germany, West	Norway	18 Mar 55	Extradition	209UNTS309	102832
Germany, West	Norway	29 May 56	Culture	3NORT688	451187
Germany, West	Norway	29 Jan 57	Air Transport	353UNTS39	105037
Germany, West	Norway	30 Oct 57	Milit Installation	3NORT728	451188
Germany, West	Norway	18 Nov 58	Taxation	357UNTS205	105119
Germany, West	Norway	07 Aug 59	Reparations	358UNTS185	105136
Germany, West	Norway	17 Dec 60	Milit Installation	3NORT822	451189
Germany, West	Norway	24 May 63	Visas	3NORT887	451190
Germany, West	Norway	30 Nov 63	Milit Installation	3NORT896	451191
Germany, West	Norway	04 Sep 64	Customs	3NORT923	451192
Germany, West	Norway	06 Sep 65	General Aid	3NORT946	451193
Germany, West	Norway	29 Oct 68	Gen Communications	3NORTO	451194
Germany, West	Norway	09 Sep 71	Admin Cooperation	71WGBB1266	425520
Germany, West	Pakistan	04 Mar 50	General Trade	50WGBB717	425562
Germany, West	Pakistan	05 Mar 56	Other Military	68WBGA203	424563
Germany, West	Pakistan	09 Mar 57	General Trade	52WBGA132	424564
Germany, West	Pakistan	07 Aug 58	Taxation	60WGBB1799	425565
Germany, West	Pakistan	25 Nov 59	General Economic	457UNTS22	106575
Germany, West	Pakistan	20 Jul 60	Air Transport	465UNTS41	106721
Germany, West	Pakistan	09 Nov 61	Culture	63WGBB43	425566
Germany, West	Panama	09 Feb 60	Admin Cooperation	60WBGA169	424567
Germany, West	Panama	30 Sep 64	Tech Assistance	65WBGA7	424568
Germany, West	Panama	31 Jul 67	Visas	67WBGA171	424569
Germany, West	Panama	05 Jul 68	Air Transport	69WGBB1560	425570
Germany, West	Paraguay	25 Jul 55	Finance	55WBGA187	424572
Germany, West	Paraguay	25 Jul 55	General Trade	55WBGA187	424571
Germany, West	Paraguay	30 Jul 55	Mostfavored Nation	57WGBB1273	425573
Germany, West	Paraguay	11 Nov 69	Loans and Credits	70WBGA41	424574
Germany, West	Paraguay	29 Apr 71	Loans and Credits	71WBGA114	424575
Germany, West	Peru	20 Jul 51	General Trade	52WGBB333	425576
Germany, West	Peru	20 Dec 56	Admin Cooperation	61WBGA200	424577
Germany, West	Peru	30 Apr 62	Air Transport	63WGBB373	425578
Germany, West	Peru	30 Apr 62	Air Transport	0UNTS0	110466
Germany, West	Peru	20 Nov 64	Culture	66WGBB76	425579
Germany, West	Peru	21 Jul 65	Tech Assistance	69WBGA126	424580
Germany, West	Philippines	25 Apr 55	General Trade	3PTS417	465035
Germany, West	Philippines	09 Mar 62	Visas	449UNTS35	106450
Germany, West	Philippines	05 Feb 63	Tech Assistance	4PTS639	465049
Germany, West	Philippines	28 Feb 64	General Trade	4PTS831	465057
Germany, West	Philippines	29 Feb 64	Direct Aid	4PTS835	465058
Germany, West	Philippines	03 Mar 64	Water Transport	4PTS841	465060
Germany, West	Philippines	03 Mar 64	General Amity	64WBGA89	424781
Germany, West	Philippines	03 Mar 64	Admin Cooperation	64WBGA89	424581
Germany, West	Philippines	03 Mar 64	Visas	4PTS839	465059
Germany, West	Philippines	03 Mar 64	General Economic	4PTS843	465061
Germany, West	Philippines	30 Apr 68	Visas	68WBGA135	424582
Germany, West	Philippines	30 Apr 68	Visas	68WBGA135	424782
Germany, West	Philippines	27 May 71	Loans and Credits	71WBGA158	424783
Germany, West	Philippines	27 May 71	Loans and Credits	71WBGA158	424583
Germany, West	Poland	16 Nov 56	General Economic	57WBGA1	424584
Germany, West	Poland	07 Mar 63	General Economic	63WBGA64	424585
Germany, West	Poland	11 Sep 69	Land Transport	69WBGA191	424586

PARTY ONE	PARTY TWO	DATE	TOPIC	CITATION	NUMBER
Germany, West	Poland	15 Oct 70	General Economic	70WBGA211	424587
Germany, West	Poland	07 Dec 70	Territory Boundary	72PDZU229	457169
Germany, West	Portugal	24 Aug 50	General Economic	50WBGA164	424588
Germany, West	Portugal	26 Sep 51	Customs	52WGBB505	425589
Germany, West	Portugal	21 Mar 58	Air Transport	464UNTS71	106712
Germany, West	Portugal	03 Apr 58	Patents/Copyrights	59WGBB264	425591
Germany, West	Portugal	03 Apr 58	Finance	59WGBB264	425592
Germany, West	Portugal	03 Jun 58	Claims and Debts	59WGBB264	425590
Germany, West	Portugal	30 May 59	General Economic	59WBGA131	424593
Germany, West	Portugal	13 May 61	Admin Cooperation	61WBGA125	424594
Germany, West	Portugal	17 Mar 64	Non-ILO Labor	64WBGA104	424595
Germany, West	Portugal	15 Jun 64	Extradition	67WGBB2345	425596
Germany, West	Portugal	06 Nov 64	Non-ILO Labor	68WGBB473	425597
Germany, West	Portugal	22 Oct 65	Culture	67WGBB721	425598
Germany, West	Romania	24 Dec 63	General Trade	64WBGA57	424604
Germany, West	Romania	03 Aug 67	General Economic	642UNTS47	109164
Germany, West	Romania	16 Jul 68	Land Transport	0UNTS0	110207
Germany, West	Romania	10 Jun 69	Tech Assistance	69WBGA72	424605
Germany, West	Romania	12 Oct 70	Land Transport	70WGBB1217	425606
Germany, West	Rwanda	25 Apr 64	Loans and Credits	64WBGA243	424600
Germany, West	Rwanda	16 Feb 65	Tech Assistance	65WBGA90	424601
Germany, West	Rwanda	18 May 67	Claims and Debts	68WGBB1260	425602
Germany, West	Rwanda	08 Apr 71	Loans and Credits	71WBGA112	424603
Germany, West	San Marino	08 Oct 68	Visas	69WGBB203	425612
Germany, West	Senegal	27 Jun 61	Direct Aid	61WBGA194	424619
Germany, West	Senegal	27 Jun 61	Water Transport	61WBGA171	424620
Germany, West	Senegal	24 Jan 64	Claims and Debts	65WGBB1391	425621
Germany, West	Senegal	29 Oct 64	Air Transport	0UNTS0	110467
Germany, West	Senegal	29 Oct 64	Air Transport	66WGBB118	425622
Germany, West	Senegal	13 Feb 68	Loans and Credits	68WBGA78	424623
Germany, West	Senegal	23 Sep 68	Culture	70WGBB1224	425624
Germany, West	Senegal	20 Nov 68	Loans and Credits	69WBGA28	424625
Germany, West	Senegal	17 Apr 69	Admin Cooperation	71WGBB1309	425626
Germany, West	Senegal	28 Sep 70	Loans and Credits	70WBGA214	424627
Germany, West	Sierra Leone	13 Sep 63	Tech Assistance	63WBGA222	424629
Germany, West	Sierra Leone	13 Sep 63	General Economic	63WBGA222	424628
Germany, West	Sierra Leone	13 Sep 63	Loans and Credits	63WBGA222	424630
Germany, West	Sierra Leone	13 Sep 63	Water Transport	63WBGA222	424631
Germany, West	Sierra Leone	08 Apr 65	Claims and Debts	66WGBB861	425632
Germany, West	Sierra Leone	05 Sep 67	Loans and Credits	67WBGA214	424633
Germany, West	Sierra Leone	15 Dec 70	Loans and Credits	71WBGA64	424634
Germany, West	Singapore	15 Feb 69	Air Transport	71WGBB184	425643
Germany, West	Somalia	19 Jan 62	General Trade	62WBGA113	424635
Germany, West	Somalia	19 Jan 62	General Transport	62WBGA113	424637
Germany, West	Somalia	19 Jan 62	Direct Aid	62WBGA113	424636
Germany, West	Somalia	19 Jan 62	Loans and Credits	62WBGA113	424638
Germany, West	Somalia	30 Nov 67	Loans and Credits	68WBGA77	424639
Germany, West	Somalia	06 Jun 68	Loans and Credits	68WBGA149	424640
Germany, West	Somalia	28 Nov 68	Loans and Credits	69WBGA157	424641
Germany, West	Somalia	20 Jan 70	Loans and Credits	70WBGA48	424642
Germany, West	South Africa	28 Aug 51	General Economic	51WBGA216	424645
Germany, West	South Africa	05 Mar 56	Other Military	68WBGA205	424646
Germany, West	South Africa	28 Sep 56	Taxation	327UNTS83	104718
Germany, West	South Africa	11 Jun 62	Culture	64WGBB13	425647
Germany, West	Spain	25 Jan 52	Non-ILO Labor	53SPBO1616	460002
Germany, West	Spain	10 Dec 54	Culture	56SPBO2503	460003
Germany, West	Spain	16 May 55	General Trade	55SPBO2106	460006
Germany, West	Spain	16 May 55	Finance	55SPBO2106	460007
Germany, West	Spain	03 May 56	Mass Media	56SPBO706	460005
Germany, West	Spain	03 May 56	Mass Media	56SPBO706	460004
Germany, West	Spain	18 May 56	General Trade	56SPBO307	460008
Germany, West	Spain	18 May 56	Finance	56SPBO307	460009
Germany, West	Spain	27 May 57	General Trade	57SPBO1007	460010
Germany, West	Spain	08 Apr 58	Finance	59SPBO2606	460012
Germany, West	Spain	08 Apr 58	Patents/Copyrights	59SPBO2606	460016

PARTY ONE	PARTY TWO	DATE	TOPIC	CITATION	NUMBER
Germany, West	Spain	08 Apr 58	Specif Goods/Equip	59SPBO2606	460014
Germany, West	Spain	08 Apr 58	Finance	59SPBO2606	460019
Germany, West	Spain	08 Apr 58	Claims and Debts	59SPBO2606	460011
Germany, West	Spain	08 Apr 58	Finance	59SPBO2606	460013
Germany, West	Spain	08 Apr 58	Finance	59SPBO2606	460017
Germany, West	Spain	08 Apr 58	Finance	59SPBO2606	460018
Germany, West	Spain	08 Apr 58	Patents/Copyrights	59SPBO2606	460020
Germany, West	Spain	08 Apr 58	Finance	59SPBO2606	460015
Germany, West	Spain	29 Oct 59	Non-ILO Labor	61SPBO2312	460024
Germany, West	Spain	29 Oct 59	Non-ILO Labor	61SPBO1110	460023
Germany, West	Spain	29 Oct 59	Non-ILO Labor	61SPBO1110	460021
Germany, West	Spain	29 Oct 59	Non-ILO Labor	61SPBO1110	460022
Germany, West	Spain	29 Mar 60	Non-ILO Labor	60SPBO505	460025
Germany, West	Spain	28 Apr 60	Air Transport	465UNTS3	106720
Germany, West	Spain	24 Oct 60	Non-ILO Labor	61SPBO710	460026
Germany, West	Spain	09 May 61	General Economic	61SPBO2905	460027
Germany, West	Spain	29 May 62	Humanitarian	65SPBO706	460028
Germany, West	Spain	27 Apr 63	Scientific Project	63SPBO2205	460029
Germany, West	Spain	15 May 64	Non-ILO Labor	65SPBO1907	460030
Germany, West	Sudan	07 Feb 63	Claims and Debts	66WGBB889	425648
Germany, West	Sudan	07 Feb 63	Tech Assistance	64WBGA6	424649
Germany, West	Sweden	05 Oct 47	Finance	47SOFM651	461062
Germany, West	Sweden	14 Jan 49	Finance	49SOFM84	461075
Germany, West	Sweden	25 May 49	Finance	49SOFM457	461087
Germany, West	Sweden	04 Sep 50	Finance	50SOFM196	461112
Germany, West	Sweden	04 Sep 50	General Trade	50SOFM181	461111
Germany, West	Sweden	26 Jan 51	General Trade	51WBGA23	424613
Germany, West	Sweden	02 Feb 51	Patents/Copyrights	51WGBB105	425614
Germany, West	Sweden	15 May 53	Non-ILO Labor	227UNTS195	103139
Germany, West	Sweden	31 May 54	Extradition	200UNTS39	102693
Germany, West	Sweden	05 Aug 55	Land Transport	262UNTS265	103754
Germany, West	Sweden	17 Jan 56	Reparations	262UNTS301	103758
Germany, West	Sweden	22 Mar 56	Claims and Debts	262UNTS361	103761
Germany, West	Sweden	22 Mar 56	Reparations	262UNTS401	103762
Germany, West	Sweden	22 Mar 56	Patents/Copyrights	262UNTS423	103763
Germany, West	Sweden	29 Jan 57	Air Transport	393UNTS113	105654
Germany, West	Sweden	13 Feb 57	Admin Cooperation	428UNTS149	106174
Germany, West	Sweden	29 Aug 58	Admin Cooperation	59WGBB401	425615
Germany, West	Sweden	17 Apr 59	Taxation	428UNTS155	106175
Germany, West	Sweden	07 Jun 60	Admin Cooperation	60WGBB2299	425616
Germany, West	Sweden	03 Aug 64	Specif Claim/Waive	64WGBB1402	425617
Germany, West	Sweden	21 Sep 66	Other Military	66WBGA213	424618
Germany, West	Switzerland	24 Oct 50	Non-ILO Labor	51SWRO937	462092
Germany, West	Switzerland	02 Nov 50	Patents/Copyrights	51WGBB63	425752
Germany, West	Switzerland	20 Dec 51	Customs	52SWRO367	462114
Germany, West	Switzerland	25 Jan 52	Land Transport	53SWRO4	462067
Germany, West	Switzerland	14 Jul 52	Non-ILO Labor	53SWRO423	462103
Germany, West	Switzerland	19 Jul 52	Claims and Debts	53SWRO413	462026
Germany, West	Switzerland	26 Aug 52	Finance	53SWRO134	462116
Germany, West	Switzerland	26 Aug 52	Claims and Debts	53SWRO119	462115
Germany, West	Switzerland	26 Aug 52	Claims and Debts	53WGBB703	425753
Germany, West	Switzerland	08 Oct 52	Admin Cooperation	53WGBB519	425754
Germany, West	Switzerland	27 Feb 53	Claims and Debts	54SWRO3	462118
Germany, West	Switzerland	11 Jul 53	Claims and Debts	53SWRO936	462117
Germany, West	Switzerland	17 Dec 53	Land Transport	54SWRO449	462079
Germany, West	Switzerland	25 Oct 54	Extradition	55SWRO25	462007
Germany, West	Switzerland	02 Dec 54	General Trade	54SWRO1291	462112
Germany, West	Switzerland	28 Dec 54	Extradition	55WBGA19	424755
Germany, West	Switzerland	02 Feb 55	Non-ILO Labor	55WBGA48	424756
Germany, West	Switzerland	02 Feb 55	Non-ILO Labor	55SWRO315	462008
Germany, West	Switzerland	06 Dec 55	Admin Cooperation	57SWRO821	462025
Germany, West	Switzerland	02 May 56	Air Transport	559UNTS157	108158
Germany, West	Switzerland	06 Jun 56	Admin Cooperation	60SWRO617	462023
Germany, West	Switzerland	16 Jul 56	Finance	57SWRO399	462113
Germany, West	Switzerland	21 Jul 56	Visas	57WBGA107	424757

PARTY ONE	PARTY TWO	DATE	TOPIC	CITATION	NUMBER
Germany, West	Switzerland	01 Nov 57	Specific Resources	59SWRO369	462105
Germany, West	Switzerland	05 Feb 58	Land Transport	60SWRO1639	462065
Germany, West	Switzerland	05 Feb 58	Land Transport	60SWRO1671	462066
Germany, West	Switzerland	21 Nov 58	Customs	60WGBB941	425758
Germany, West	Switzerland	01 Jun 61	Customs	64SWRO387	462072
Germany, West	Switzerland	29 Jun 61	Claims and Debts	62SWRO1311	462167
Germany, West	Switzerland	25 Feb 64	Non-ILO Labor	65WGBB1293	425759
Germany, West	Switzerland	23 Nov 64	Territory Boundary	67WGBB2029	425761
Germany, West	Switzerland	23 Nov 64	Territory Boundary	67WGBB2040	425760
Germany, West	Switzerland	29 Apr 65	Humanitarian	67WGBB773	425762
Germany, West	Switzerland	25 May 66	Territory Boundary	67WBGA165	424763
Germany, West	Switzerland	07 Mar 67	Patents/Copyrights	69WGBB138	425764
Germany, West	Switzerland	26 Mar 69	Admin Cooperation	69WBGA142	424765
Germany, West	Switzerland	26 May 69	Admin Cooperation	71WGBB90	425766
Germany, West	Switzerland	21 May 70	Visas	70WGBB745	425767
Germany, West	Syria	25 Jun 62	Tech Assistance	489UNTS71	107135
Germany, West	Syria	22 Aug 63	Direct Aid	64WBGA79	424650
Germany, West	Tanzania	06 Sep 62	Tech Assistance	62WBGA225	424652
Germany, West	Tanzania	06 Sep 62	General Economic	62WBGA225	424651
Germany, West	Tanzania	11 Sep 62	Water Transport	62WBGA225	424654
Germany, West	Tanzania	11 Sep 62	Loans and Credits	62WBGA225	424653
Germany, West	Tanzania	30 Jan 65	Claims and Debts	66WGBB873	425655
Germany, West	Tanzania	06 Feb 71	Loans and Credits	71WBGA114	424656
Germany, West	Thailand	09 Oct 56	Direct Aid	258UNTS143	103676
Germany, West	Thailand	13 Dec 61	Claims and Debts	541UNTS181	107870
Germany, West	Thailand	05 Mar 62	Air Transport	563UNTS165	108210
Germany, West	Thailand	02 Apr 64	Tech Assistance	503UNTS3	107338
Germany, West	Thailand	28 Oct 64	Non-IBRD Project	521UNTS311	107528
Germany, West	Thailand	28 Oct 64	Loans and Credits	521UNTS333	107529
Germany, West	Thailand	23 Dec 64	Non-IBRD Project	525UNTS193	107591
Germany, West	Thailand	23 Dec 64	Scientific Project	525UNTS177	107589
Germany, West	Thailand	23 Dec 64	Tech Assistance	525UNTS185	107590
Germany, West	Thailand	23 Dec 64	Sanitation	525UNTS201	107592
Germany, West	Thailand	10 Jul 67	Taxation	68WGBB589	425657
Germany, West	Thailand	29 Mar 68	Direct Aid	637UNTSO	109122
Germany, West	Thailand	08 Oct 68	Loans and Credits	68WBGA234	424658
Germany, West	Thailand	08 Oct 68	Loans and Credits	OUNTSO	109637
Germany, West	Thailand	04 Dec 68	Loans and Credits	OUNTSO	109638
Germany, West	Togo	20 Jul 60	Direct Aid	60WBGA243	424660
Germany, West	Togo	20 Jul 60	Water Transport	60WBGA237	424659
Germany, West	Togo	16 May 61	Claims and Debts	64WGBB154	425661
Germany, West	Togo	09 Jul 63	Loans and Credits	63WBGA199	424662
Germany, West	Togo	25 Mar 66	Non-IBRD Project	66WBGA111	424663
Germany, West	Togo	03 Feb 67	Loans and Credits	67WBGA136	424664
Germany, West	Togo	31 Jul 67	Loans and Credits	67WBGA218	424665
Germany, West	Togo	28 Aug 68	Tech Assistance	68WBGA219	424666
Germany, West	Togo	18 Jun 70	Loans and Credits	70WBGA196	424667
Germany, West	Togo	20 Mar 71	Loans and Credits	71WBGA115	424668
Germany, West	Togo	27 May 71	Loans and Credits	71WBGA114	424669
Germany, West	Tunisia	29 Jan 60	General Trade	60WBGA107	424678
Germany, West	Tunisia	20 Dec 63	Claims and Debts	65WGBB1377	425679
Germany, West	Tunisia	20 Dec 63	Loans and Credits	64WBGA73	424680
Germany, West	Tunisia	20 Apr 65	Tech Assistance	65WBGA123	424681
Germany, West	Tunisia	14 Jul 65	Loans and Credits	65WBGA182	424682
Germany, West	Tunisia	18 Oct 65	Non-ILO Labor	66WBGA57	424683
Germany, West	Tunisia	28 Mar 66	Other Military	66WBGA90	424684
Germany, West	Tunisia	03 Jun 66	Loans and Credits	66WBGA148	424685
Germany, West	Tunisia	19 Jul 66	Admin Cooperation	69WGBB889	425688
Germany, West	Tunisia	19 Jul 66	Culture	67WGBB1210	425687
Germany, West	Tunisia	19 Jul 66	Extradition	69WGBB1157	425689
Germany, West	Tunisia	19 Jul 66	Water Transport	67WBGA66	424686
Germany, West	Tunisia	02 Jun 67	Loans and Credits	67WBGA128	424690
Germany, West	Tunisia	28 May 68	Loans and Credits	68WBGA156	424691
Germany, West	Tunisia	24 Apr 69	Loans and Credits	69WBGA144	424692
Germany, West	Tunisia	26 May 69	Air Transport	71WGBB177	425693

PARTY ONE	PARTY TWO	DATE	TOPIC	CITATION	NUMBER
Germany, West	Tunisia	23 Apr 70	Finance	70WBGA126	424694
Germany, West	Tunisia	23 Apr 70	Tech Assistance	70WBGA196	424695
Germany, West	Tunisia	07 May 71	Finance	71WBGA116	424696
Germany, West	Turkey	19 Apr 48	General Trade	49TURG1902	466065
Germany, West	Turkey	18 Dec 48	General Economic	50TURG1001	466140
Germany, West	Turkey	15 Jan 49	General Economic	49TURG2812	466066
Germany, West	Turkey	14 Nov 49	Mostfavored Nation	50TURG1002	466029
Germany, West	Turkey	16 Feb 52	General Trade	53TURG202	466028
Germany, West	Turkey	16 Feb 52	Extradition	52TURG305	466006
Germany, West	Turkey	16 Feb 52	General Economic	52TURG305	466067
Germany, West	Turkey	16 Feb 52	Admin Cooperation	52TURG1602	466033
Germany, West	Turkey	16 Feb 52	Customs	52WGBB616	425768
Germany, West	Turkey	16 Feb 52	Finance	52WBGA50	424769
Germany, West	Turkey	06 Aug 53	Commodity Trade	54TURG2203	466043
Germany, West	Turkey	08 May 57	Culture	58WBGA336	424770
Germany, West	Turkey	05 Jul 57	Air Transport	62WGBB2376	425771
Germany, West	Turkey	05 Jul 57	Air Transport	0UNTS0	110464
Germany, West	Turkey	07 May 58	Culture	58TURG1505	466036
Germany, West	Turkey	27 Nov 58	Direct Aid	64TURG909	466106
Germany, West	Turkey	26 Jun 59	Claims and Debts	60WGBB2365	425772
Germany, West	Turkey	19 Apr 60	Direct Aid	60TURG2208	466107
Germany, West	Turkey	06 Jun 61	Loans and Credits	61TURG1907	466108
Germany, West	Turkey	20 Jun 62	Loans and Credits	65WGBB1193	425774
Germany, West	Turkey	11 Sep 62	Visas	62WBGA217	424775
Germany, West	Turkey	30 Apr 64	Health/Educ/Welfare	65WGBB1169	425776
Germany, West	Turkey	30 Sep 64	Non-ILO Labor	68WBGA22	424773
Germany, West	Turkey	08 Dec 65	Admin Cooperation	67WGBB1692	425777
Germany, West	Turkey	03 Jun 69	Loans and Credits	69WBGA133	424778
Germany, West	Turkey	16 Jun 70	Loans and Credits	70WBGA135	424779
Germany, West	Turkey	03 Dec 71	Loans and Credits	71WBGA242	424780
Germany, West	Uganda	17 Mar 64	General Trade	67WBGA89	424698
Germany, West	Uganda	17 Mar 64	Water Transport	66WBGA167	424697
Germany, West	Uganda	20 Mar 64	Loans and Credits	66WBGA167	424699
Germany, West	Uganda	20 Mar 64	Tech Assistance	66WBGA167	424700
Germany, West	Uganda	29 Nov 66	Claims and Debts	68WGBB449	425701
Germany, West	Uganda	19 Oct 67	Loans and Credits	68WBGA224	424702
Germany, West	Uganda	15 Jan 69	Loans and Credits	69WBGA123	424703
Germany, West	UK Great Britain	09 Dec 50	Finance	88UNTS247	101196
Germany, West	UK Great Britain	09 Sep 52	Milit Installation	151UNTS215	101997
Germany, West	UK Great Britain	27 Feb 53	Claims and Debts	330UNTS217	104747
Germany, West	UK Great Britain	22 May 53	Finance	172UNTS179	102246
Germany, West	UK Great Britain	10 Jul 54	Finance	199UNTS135	102680
Germany, West	UK Great Britain	18 Oct 54	Taxation	218UNTS301	102960
Germany, West	UK Great Britain	22 Jul 55	Air Transport	269UNTS223	103882
Germany, West	UK Great Britain	22 Jul 55	Air Transport	269UNTS189	103881
Germany, West	UK Great Britain	30 Jul 56	Consul/Citizenship	330UNTS233	104748
Germany, West	UK Great Britain	31 Jul 56	Atomic Energy	252UNTS93	103559
Germany, West	UK Great Britain	11 Apr 57	Status of Forces	331UNTS173	104753
Germany, West	UK Great Britain	07 Jun 57	Milit Assistance	398UNTS275	105730
Germany, West	UK Great Britain	18 Apr 58	Culture	343UNTS241	104928
Germany, West	UK Great Britain	03 Oct 58	Milit Assistance	398UNTS293	105731
Germany, West	UK Great Britain	10 Apr 59	Claims and Debts	343UNTS295	104935
Germany, West	UK Great Britain	03 Aug 59	Dispute Settlement	502UNTS197	107331
Germany, West	UK Great Britain	16 Oct 59	Other Military	385UNTS21	105526
Germany, West	UK Great Britain	28 Jan 60	Reparations	420UNTS29	106038
Germany, West	UK Great Britain	23 Feb 60	Extradition	385UNTS39	105527
Germany, West	UK Great Britain	09 Mar 60	Admin Cooperation	403UNTS253	105796
Germany, West	UK Great Britain	20 Apr 60	Non-ILO Labor	449UNTS77	106453
Germany, West	UK Great Britain	20 Apr 60	Non-ILO Labor	413UNTS236	105958
Germany, West	UK Great Britain	20 Jun 60	Visas	385UNTS55	105528
Germany, West	UK Great Britain	14 Jul 60	Admin Cooperation	414UNTS144	105972
Germany, West	UK Great Britain	20 Feb 61	Visas	398UNTS249	105727
Germany, West	UK Great Britain	02 May 61	Admin Cooperation	414UNTS3	105959
Germany, West	UK Great Britain	12 Jul 61	Status of Forces	424UNTS211	106109
Germany, West	UK Great Britain	26 Sep 61	Milit Assistance	424UNTS201	106108

PARTY ONE	PARTY TWO	DATE	TOPIC	CITATION	NUMBER
Germany, West	UK Great Britain	06 Jun 62	Status of Forces	437UNTS39	106298
Germany, West	UK Great Britain	20 Sep 62	Admin Cooperation	453UNTS317	106533
Germany, West	UK Great Britain	09 Jun 64	Reparations	539UNTS187	107831
Germany, West	UK Great Britain	27 Jul 64	Status of Forces	539UNTS243	107835
Germany, West	UK Great Britain	26 Nov 64	Taxation	603UNTS183	108734
Germany, West	UK Great Britain	11 Jan 67	Commodity Trade	67WBGA22	424716
Germany, West	UK Great Britain	31 Mar 67	Commodity Trade	67WBGA83	424717
Germany, West	UK Great Britain	05 May 67	Finance	613UNTS313	108858
Germany, West	UK Great Britain	02 Jun 67	Land Transport	67WBGA135	424718
Germany, West	UK Great Britain	20 Jul 67	General Trade	67WBGA176	424719
Germany, West	UK Great Britain	11 Apr 68	Finance	0UNTS0	109288
Germany, West	UK Great Britain	19 May 69	Finance	0UNTS0	110025
Germany, West	UK Great Britain	01 Sep 69	Finance	0UNTS0	110241
Germany, West	UNESCO (Educ/Cult)	06 May 69	IGO Operations	69WBGA207	424745
Germany, West	United Arab Rep	21 Apr 51	General Trade	52WGBB525	425710
Germany, West	United Arab Rep	31 Jul 54	Customs	55WGBB857	425711
Germany, West	United Arab Rep	18 Feb 56	General Trade	56WBGA110	424712
Germany, West	United Arab Rep	22 Feb 56	Other Military	57WBGA48	424713
Germany, West	United Arab Rep	11 Nov 59	Culture	60WGBB2351	425714
Germany, West	United Arab Rep	17 Nov 59	Taxation	61WGBB420	425715
Germany, West	United Arab Rep	16 Feb 60	Air Transport	464UNTS233	106717
Germany, West	United Nations	28 Jun 62	IGO Operations	434UNTS249	200597
Germany, West	Upper Volta	08 Jun 61	General Economic	61WBGA193	424521
Germany, West	Upper Volta	08 Jun 61	Direct Aid	61WBGA193	424522
Germany, West	Uruguay	18 Apr 53	General Trade	54WGBB51	425707
Germany, West	Uruguay	18 Apr 53	General Trade	53WBGA94	424708
Germany, West	Uruguay	31 Aug 57	Air Transport	59WGBB80	425709
Germany, West	USA (United States)	30 Mar 42	Humanitarian	105UNTS219	200334
Germany, West	USA (United States)	15 Dec 49	Direct Aid	92UNTS269	101277
Germany, West	USA (United States)	07 Jun 51	Direct Aid	238UNTS161	103360
Germany, West	USA (United States)	19 Sep 51	General Trade	180UNTS161	102381
Germany, West	USA (United States)	28 Dec 51	Milit Assistance	181UNTS45	102397
Germany, West	USA (United States)	11 Jun 52	Mass Media	273UNTS105	103947
Germany, West	USA (United States)	18 Jul 52	Education	165UNTS167	102175
Germany, West	USA (United States)	09 Jan 53	Visas	212UNTS3	102859
Germany, West	USA (United States)	27 Feb 53	Claims and Debts	224UNTS31	103068
Germany, West	USA (United States)	27 Feb 53	Claims and Debts	224UNTS13	103067
Germany, West	USA (United States)	27 Feb 53	Claims and Debts	223UNTS167	103065
Germany, West	USA (United States)	27 Feb 53	Claims and Debts	205UNTS103	102771
Germany, West	USA (United States)	30 Mar 53	Reparations	235UNTS285	103310
Germany, West	USA (United States)	01 Apr 53	Claims and Debts	224UNTS3	103066
Germany, West	USA (United States)	09 Apr 53	Culture	204UNTS79	102750
Germany, West	USA (United States)	02 Jun 53	General Amity	231UNTS151	103214
Germany, West	USA (United States)	03 Jun 53	General Amity	253UNTS89	103578
Germany, West	USA (United States)	20 Aug 53	Milit Assistance	224UNTS49	103069
Germany, West	USA (United States)	23 Nov 53	Milit Installation	224UNTS107	103071
Germany, West	USA (United States)	12 Feb 54	Milit Assistance	223UNTS153	103064
Germany, West	USA (United States)	22 Jul 54	Taxation	221UNTS351	103016
Germany, West	USA (United States)	22 Jul 54	Taxation	239UNTS3	103369
Germany, West	USA (United States)	17 Aug 54	Direct Aid	233UNTS31	103248
Germany, West	USA (United States)	28 Aug 54	Milit Installation	299UNTS377	104325
Germany, West	USA (United States)	15 Oct 54	Milit Assistance	239UNTS135	103375
Germany, West	USA (United States)	27 Oct 54	Admin Cooperation	234UNTS131	103278
Germany, West	USA (United States)	29 Oct 54	General Amity	273UNTS3	103943
Germany, West	USA (United States)	18 Feb 55	Milit Assistance	247UNTS257	103474
Germany, West	USA (United States)	04 Apr 55	Milit Assistance	279UNTS73	104034
Germany, West	USA (United States)	14 Apr 55	General Military	263UNTS351	103782
Germany, West	USA (United States)	06 Jun 55	Humanitarian	315UNTS155	104566
Germany, West	USA (United States)	30 Jun 55	Milit Assistance	240UNTS47	103393
Germany, West	USA (United States)	30 Jun 55	Milit Assistance	240UNTS69	103394
Germany, West	USA (United States)	07 Jul 55	Air Transport	275UNTS3	103973
Germany, West	USA (United States)	02 Aug 55	Specif Goods/Equip	268UNTS121	103854
Germany, West	USA (United States)	23 Dec 55	US Agri Commod Aid	240UNTS79	103395
Germany, West	USA (United States)	04 Jan 56	General Military	268UNTS143	103856
Germany, West	USA (United States)	13 Feb 56	Atomic Energy	253UNTS119	103580

PARTY ONE	PARTY TWO	DATE	TOPIC	CITATION	NUMBER
Germany, West	USA (United States)	02 Mar 56	Claims and Debts	273UNTS209	103952
Germany, West	USA (United States)	07 Mar 56	Sanitation	271UNTS361	103926
Germany, West	USA (United States)	18 Apr 56	Admin Cooperation	271UNTS319	103923
Germany, West	USA (United States)	26 Apr 56	Culture	283UNTS267	104122
Germany, West	USA (United States)	27 Jul 56	Admin Cooperation	278UNTS3	104017
Germany, West	USA (United States)	08 Oct 56	Milit Assistance	278UNTS9	104018
Germany, West	USA (United States)	12 Dec 56	Milit Assistance	280UNTS63	104051
Germany, West	USA (United States)	12 Dec 56	Milit Assistance	280UNTS71	104052
Germany, West	USA (United States)	11 Apr 57	Admin Cooperation	283UNTS233	104120
Germany, West	USA (United States)	01 May 57	Milit Assistance	284UNTS85	104131
Germany, West	USA (United States)	07 Jun 57	Milit Assistance	346UNTS241	104984
Germany, West	USA (United States)	28 Jun 57	Atomic Energy	288UNTS339	104213
Germany, West	USA (United States)	03 Jul 57	Atomic Energy	288UNTS305	104212
Germany, West	USA (United States)	10 Dec 57	Milit Assistance	307UNTS59	104442
Germany, West	USA (United States)	11 Dec 58	Air Transport	337UNTS31	104813
Germany, West	USA (United States)	20 Mar 59	Claims and Debts	341UNTS15	104874
Germany, West	USA (United States)	05 May 59	Atomic Energy	355UNTS307	105083
Germany, West	USA (United States)	03 Aug 59	Status of Forces	490UNTS28	107153
Germany, West	USA (United States)	01 Oct 59	Air Transport	358UNTS129	105130
Germany, West	USA (United States)	16 Mar 60	Specific Property	371UNTS101	105272
Germany, West	USA (United States)	27 May 60	Milit Assistance	377UNTS45	105395
Germany, West	USA (United States)	16 Aug 60	Claims and Debts	418UNTS235	106024
Germany, West	USA (United States)	03 Jan 61	Admin Cooperation	416UNTS93	105997
Germany, West	USA (United States)	29 Sep 61	Scientific Project	424UNTS113	106103
Germany, West	USA (United States)	25 May 62	Milit Assistance	458UNTS259	106608
Germany, West	USA (United States)	20 Nov 62	Education	505UNTS263	107377
Germany, West	USA (United States)	29 Nov 62	Water Transport	460UNTS169	106639
Germany, West	USA (United States)	14 Mar 63	Status of Forces	474UNTS71	106872
Germany, West	USA (United States)	17 Mar 64	Education	64WBGA113	424720
Germany, West	USA (United States)	18 Dec 65	Status of Forces	579UNTS193	108407
Germany, West	USA (United States)	25 Mar 66	Commodity Trade	66WBGA144	424721
Germany, West	USA (United States)	30 Jun 66	Gen Communications	601UNTS107	108689
Germany, West	USA (United States)	16 Dec 66	Culture	0UNTSO	109694
Germany, West	USA (United States)	23 Dec 66	Education	68WBGA21	424722
Germany, West	USA (United States)	29 Dec 66	General Aid	0UNTSO	109839
Germany, West	USA (United States)	16 Mar 67	Commodity Trade	67WBGA150	424723
Germany, West	USA (United States)	12 Jul 67	Patents/Copyrights	0UNTSO	109908
Germany, West	USA (United States)	24 Oct 67	Status of Forces	67WBGA213	424724
Germany, West	USA (United States)	27 Feb 68	Admin Cooperation	0UNTSO	110134
Germany, West	USA (United States)	24 Jun 69	Specific Property	69WBGA156	424725
Germany, West	USA (United States)	11 Sep 70	Non-ILO Labor	70WGBB2778	425726
Germany, West	USA (United States)	03 Dec 70	Milit Installation	71WGBB407	425727
Germany, West	USSR (Soviet Union)	13 Sep 55	Consul/Citizenship	0SUST334	468159
Germany, West	USSR (Soviet Union)	05 Aug 57	Admin Cooperation	16SUGG121	469945
Germany, West	USSR (Soviet Union)	25 Apr 58	Consul/Citizenship	338UNTS49	104832
Germany, West	USSR (Soviet Union)	25 Apr 58	General Economic	346UNTS71	104978
Germany, West	USSR (Soviet Union)	25 Mar 59	Scientific Project	8SUGG141	469568
Germany, West	USSR (Soviet Union)	30 May 59	Health/Educ/Welfare	8SUGG146	469579
Germany, West	USSR (Soviet Union)	31 Dec 60	General Economic	61WBGA12	424644
Germany, West	Vietnam, South	10 Dec 53	General Trade	0VKNG66	496017
Germany, West	Vietnam, South	27 May 59	Education	0VKNG141	496040
Germany, West	Vietnam, South	10 Aug 61	Tech Assistance	0VKNG171	496051
Germany, West	Vietnam, South	19 Jul 63	Direct Aid	0VKNG192	496058
Germany, West	Vietnam, South	04 Dec 63	Loans and Credits	0VKNG194	496059
Germany, West	Vietnam, South	28 Mar 66	Specif Goods/Equip	66WGBB322	425728
Germany, West	Vietnam, South	28 Jun 66	Direct Aid	0VKNG237	496063
Germany, West	Vietnam, South	30 Mar 67	Humanitarian	67WGBB2105	425729
Germany, West	Yemen	21 Apr 53	General Amity	54WGBB573	425310
Germany, West	Yemen	28 Nov 69	Loans and Credits	70WBGA37	424311
Germany, West	Yemen	28 Sep 70	Loans and Credits	70WBGA226	424312
Germany, West	Yemen	03 Jun 71	Loans and Credits	71WBGA146	424313
Germany, West	Yugoslavia	12 Oct 36	Non-ILO Labor	69WGBB1473	425336
Germany, West	Yugoslavia	12 Oct 36	Non-ILO Labor	56WGBB9437	425333
Germany, West	Yugoslavia	11 Jun 52	General Trade	52WBGA169	424319
Germany, West	Yugoslavia	18 Dec 53	Admin Cooperation	55WBGA36	424320
Germany, West	Yugoslavia	26 Jun 54	Water Transport	59WGBB735	425321
Germany, West	Yugoslavia	21 Jul 54	Patents/Copyrights	55WGBB89	425322
Germany, West	Yugoslavia	14 May 55	Extradition	57WBGA146	424323
Germany, West	Yugoslavia	10 Mar 56	General Economic	56WGBB967	425325
Germany, West	Yugoslavia	10 Mar 56	Non-ILO Labor	58WGBB168	425324
Germany, West	Yugoslavia	10 Mar 56	Specif Claim/Waive	57WBGA9	424328
Germany, West	Yugoslavia	10 Mar 56	Claims and Debts	57WBGA9	424327
Germany, West	Yugoslavia	10 Mar 56	General Economic	57WBGA9	424326
Germany, West	Yugoslavia	17 Jul 56	Customs	59WGBB735	425329
Germany, West	Yugoslavia	17 Jul 56	Finance	56WBGA160	424330
Germany, West	Yugoslavia	10 Apr 57	Air Transport	463UNTS269	106708
Germany, West	Yugoslavia	19 Jul 57	Commodity Trade	57WBGA183	424331
Germany, West	Yugoslavia	16 Jul 64	Direct Aid	65WBGA17	424333
Germany, West	Yugoslavia	16 Jul 64	Visas	64WBGA192	424332
Germany, West	Yugoslavia	12 Oct 68	Non-ILO Labor	69WGBB1107	425337
Germany, West	Yugoslavia	23 Oct 68	Visas	69WBGA59	424338
Germany, West	Yugoslavia	10 Feb 69	General Economic	69WBGA145	424339
Germany, West	Yugoslavia	28 Jul 69	Consul/Citizenship	70WGBB1191	425340
Germany, West	Yugoslavia	28 Jul 69	Health/Educ/Welfare	70WGBB1375	425341
Germany, West	Zambia	10 Dec 66	Claims and Debts	68WGBB33	425610
Germany, West	Zambia	10 Dec 66	Tech Assistance	67WBGA51	424609
Germany, West	Zambia	10 Dec 66	General Economic	67WBGA51	424607
Germany, West	Zambia	10 Dec 66	Loans and Credits	67WBGA51	424608
Germany, West	Zambia	11 Apr 68	Tech Assistance	68WBGA147	424611
Ghana	Accept UN Charter	01 Mar 57	IGO Establishment	261UNTS113	103727
Ghana	Canada	08 Jan 62	Military Mission	528UNTS221	107645
Ghana	China People's Rep	18 Aug 61	Milit Assistance	61CCJC110	410819
Ghana	China People's Rep	18 Aug 61	Culture	61CCJC111	410820
Ghana	China People's Rep	18 Aug 61	General Amity	61CCJC108	410817
Ghana	China People's Rep	18 Aug 61	General Aid	61CCJC109	410818
Ghana	China People's Rep	26 Mar 63	Water Transport	63CCJC36	410963
Ghana	China People's Rep	05 Feb 64	General Trade	64CCJC24	411158
Ghana	China People's Rep	03 Dec 64	General Trade	64CCJC174	411163
Ghana	China People's Rep	19 May 65	Scientific Project	65CCJC67	411180
Ghana	China People's Rep	05 Aug 65	Milit Assistance	65CCJC154	411166
Ghana	Czechoslovakia	23 Nov 60	Tech Assistance	431UNTS85	106212
Ghana	Czechoslovakia	23 Nov 60	Culture	431UNTS91	106213
Ghana	Czechoslovakia	02 Aug 61	Air Transport	465UNTS249	106730
Ghana	Denmark	09 Aug 67	Loans and Credits	610UNTSO	108842
Ghana	Germany, East	25 Feb 59	Consul/Citizenship	7EGDA363	419105
Ghana	Germany, East	08 Jul 61	General Trade	9EGDA338	419106
Ghana	Germany, East	19 Oct 61	Finance	9EGDA338	419108
Ghana	Germany, East	19 Oct 61	General Trade	9EGDA333	419107
Ghana	Germany, East	19 Oct 61	Tech Assistance	9EGDA342	419109
Ghana	Germany, East	19 Oct 61	Culture	9EGDA344	419110
Ghana	Germany, East	14 May 64	Non-ILO Labor	12EGDA740	419111
Ghana	Germany, East	14 May 64	Education	12EGDA746	419112
Ghana	Germany, East	24 Jul 65	Tech Assistance	51EGDZ340	420113
Ghana	Germany, West	21 Dec 59	Direct Aid	60WBGA196	424214
Ghana	Germany, West	21 Dec 59	General Trade	60WBGA241	424215
Ghana	Germany, West	15 May 63	Water Transport	63WBGA131	424217
Ghana	Germany, West	15 May 63	Loans and Credits	63WBGA131	424216
Ghana	Germany, West	15 May 63	Air Transport	63WBGA131	424218
Ghana	Germany, West	06 Apr 66	Loans and Credits	66WBGA131	424219
Ghana	Germany, West	10 Jun 66	Extradition	67WGBB1743	425220
Ghana	Germany, West	19 May 67	Loans and Credits	68WGBB1251	425221
Ghana	Germany, West	01 Sep 67	Loans and Credits	67WBGA193	424222
Ghana	Germany, West	30 Mar 68	Tech Assistance	68WBGA147	424223
Ghana	Germany, West	07 May 68	Loans and Credits	68WBGA130	424224
Ghana	Germany, West	06 Aug 68	Air Transport	69WGBB1553	425225
Ghana	Germany, West	11 Jul 69	Loans and Credits	69WBGA176	424226
Ghana	Germany, West	08 Dec 70	Loans and Credits	71WBGA64	424227
Ghana	Hungary	27 Apr 61	Culture	439UNTS17	106322
Ghana	IBRD (World Bank)	08 Feb 62	IBRD Project	449UNTS207	106462
Ghana	IBRD (World Bank)	23 Jun 69	IBRD Project	0UNTSO	110107

PARTY ONE	PARTY TWO	DATE	TOPIC	CITATION	NUMBER
Ghana	IDA (Devel Assoc)	14 Jun 68	Non-IBRD Project	0UNTS0	109303
Ghana	IDA (Devel Assoc)	29 Jul 69	Loans and Credits	0UNTS0	110291
Ghana	IDA (Devel Assoc)	28 Aug 69	Non-IBRD Project	0UNTS0	110573
Ghana	IDA (Devel Assoc)	25 Sep 69	Non-IBRD Project	0UNTS0	110591
Ghana	Israel	25 May 62	Tech Assistance	515UNTS237	107461
Ghana	Israel	30 Nov 64	Tech Assistance	550UNTS231	108019
Ghana	Italy	20 Jun 63	Air Transport	65ITGU193	435180
Ghana	Japan	24 Sep 62	Direct Aid	0JGJI1501	441114
Ghana	Japan	23 May 63	Education	0JGJI1506	441116
Ghana	Japan	22 May 67	Education	67JJS193	442189
Ghana	Malawi	04 May 65	Air Transport	541UNTS163	107869
Ghana	Mali	09 Jan 63	Air Transport	466UNTS165	106742
Ghana	Multilateral	07 Dec 44	IGO Establishment	15UNTS295	200102
Ghana	Multilateral	11 Dec 46	Sanitation	12UNTS179	100186
Ghana	Multilateral	12 Nov 47	Admin Cooperation	46UNTS201	100710
Ghana	Multilateral	06 Mar 48	Water Transport	289UNTS3	104214
Ghana	Multilateral	11 May 48	Telecommunications	500UNTS267	107313
Ghana	Multilateral	10 Jun 48	Humanitarian	191UNTS3	102576
Ghana	Multilateral	10 Jun 48	Humanitarian	164UNTS113	102163
Ghana	Multilateral	24 Jul 48	Sanitation	66UNTS25	100847
Ghana	Multilateral	09 Dec 48	Scientific Project	73UNTS39	100942
Ghana	Multilateral	09 Dec 48	Humanitarian	78UNTS277	101021
Ghana	Multilateral	04 May 49	Admin Cooperation	92UNTS19	101257
Ghana	Multilateral	04 May 49	Admin Cooperation	47UNTS159	100728
Ghana	Multilateral	04 May 49	Admin Cooperation	98UNTS101	101358
Ghana	Multilateral	15 Jul 49	Health/Educ/Welfare	197UNTS3	102631
Ghana	Multilateral	22 Nov 50	Culture	131UNTS25	101734
Ghana	Multilateral	02 Jul 51	Refugees	189UNTS137	102545
Ghana	Multilateral	06 Dec 51	IGO Establishment	425UNTS61	106119
Ghana	Multilateral	07 Nov 52	General Trade	221UNTS255	103010
Ghana	Multilateral	31 Mar 53	Privil/Immunities	193UNTS136	102613
Ghana	Multilateral	18 Jan 54	IGO Establishment	330UNTS121	104743
Ghana	Multilateral	12 May 54	Admin Cooperation	327UNTS3	104714
Ghana	Multilateral	14 May 54	Culture	249UNTS215	103511
Ghana	Multilateral	14 Jun 54	Air Transport	320UNTS217	104644
Ghana	Multilateral	14 Jun 54	Air Transport	320UNTS209	104643
Ghana	Multilateral	29 Jul 54	Sanitation	249UNTS45	103500
Ghana	Multilateral	25 May 55	IGO Establishment	264UNTS117	103791
Ghana	Multilateral	18 May 56	Land Transport	339UNTS3	104844
Ghana	Multilateral	14 Dec 56	Taxation	436UNTS115	106292
Ghana	Multilateral	14 Dec 56	Taxation	436UNTS131	106293
Ghana	Multilateral	24 May 57	Tech Assistance	268UNTS270	103861
Ghana	Multilateral	03 Oct 57	Postal Service	364UNTS3	105211
Ghana	Multilateral	13 Dec 57	Land Transport	372UNTS159	105296
Ghana	Multilateral	29 Apr 58	Territory Boundary	516UNTS205	107477
Ghana	Multilateral	29 Apr 58	Specific Resources	559UNTS285	108164
Ghana	Multilateral	29 Apr 58	Territory Boundary	499UNTS311	107302
Ghana	Multilateral	29 Apr 58	Water Transport	450UNTS11	106465
Ghana	Multilateral	29 Apr 58	Dispute Settlement	450UNTS169	106466
Ghana	Multilateral	01 Dec 58	Commodity Trade	385UNTS137	105534
Ghana	Multilateral	03 Dec 58	Admin Cooperation	416UNTS51	105995
Ghana	Multilateral	03 Dec 58	Admin Cooperation	398UNTS9	105715
Ghana	Multilateral	26 Jan 60	IGO Establishment	439UNTS249	106333
Ghana	Multilateral	17 Jun 60	Humanitarian	536UNTS27	107794
Ghana	Multilateral	30 Mar 61	Sanitation	520UNTS151	107515
Ghana	Multilateral	18 Apr 61	Consul/Citizenship	500UNTS95	107310
Ghana	Multilateral	18 Apr 61	Dispute Settlement	500UNTS243	107312
Ghana	Multilateral	18 Apr 61	Consul/Citizenship	500UNTS223	107311
Ghana	Multilateral	21 Jun 61	IGO Establishment	514UNTS209	107449
Ghana	Multilateral	25 May 62	IGO Establishment	486UNTS103	107075
Ghana	Multilateral	22 Jun 62	ILO Labor	494UNTS249	107237
Ghana	Multilateral	24 Apr 63	Consul/Citizenship	596UNTS487	108640
Ghana	Multilateral	24 Apr 63	Consul/Citizenship	596UNTS261	108638
Ghana	Multilateral	25 May 63	IGO Establishment	479UNTS39	106947
Ghana	Multilateral	04 Aug 63	IGO Establishment	510UNTS3	107408

PARTY ONE	PARTY TWO	DATE	TOPIC	CITATION	NUMBER
Ghana	Multilateral	05 Aug 63	Sanitation	480UNTS43	106964
Ghana	Multilateral	10 Jul 64	Postal Service	612UNTS233	108848
Ghana	Multilateral	10 Jul 64	Postal Service	611UNTS105	108845
Ghana	Multilateral	10 Jul 64	Postal Service	611UNTS7	108844
Ghana	Multilateral	10 Jul 64	Postal Service	612UNTS3	108847
Ghana	Multilateral	10 Jul 64	Postal Service	611UNTS387	108846
Ghana	Multilateral	09 Mar 65	Water Transport	591UNTS265	108564
Ghana	Multilateral	18 Mar 65	Dispute Settlement	575UNTS159	108359
Ghana	Multilateral	05 Apr 66	Water Transport	640UNTS133	109159
Ghana	Multilateral	14 May 66	Specific Resources	0UNTS0	109587
Ghana	Multilateral	31 Jan 67	Refugees	606UNTS267	108791
Ghana	Multilateral	04 May 67	IGO Establishment	595UNTS287	108623
Ghana	Multilateral	18 Mar 68	Commodity Trade	0UNTS0	109262
Ghana	Multilateral	11 Jun 68	Scientific Project	0UNTS0	109884
Ghana	Multilateral	01 Jul 68	Peace/Disarmament	0UNTS0	110485
Ghana	Multilateral	27 Jan 69	Telecommunications	0UNTS0	109664
Ghana	Netherlands	30 Jul 60	Air Transport	412UNTS51	105925
Ghana	Netherlands	28 Dec 67	Education	0UNTS0	110747
Ghana	Norway	29 Jun 68	Tech Assistance	3NORTO	451065
Ghana	Poland	17 Jan 61	Culture	572UNTS209	108314
Ghana	Poland	19 Apr 61	Tech Assistance	61PZUM94	458082
Ghana	Poland	17 Jan 64	Culture	65PDZU393	457109
Ghana	Romania	30 Sep 61	Air Transport	467UNTS443	106769
Ghana	Romania	30 Sep 61	Culture	457UNTS3	106573
Ghana	Romania	23 Nov 66	Loans and Credits	642UNTS79	109166
Ghana	Romania	23 Nov 66	General Trade	642UNTS63	109165
Ghana	Switzerland	17 May 61	Air Transport	559UNTS193	108159
Ghana	Switzerland	06 Dec 63	Taxation	64SWRO426	462052
Ghana	Tunisia	11 Dec 62	Air Transport	563UNTS243	108213
Ghana	UK Great Britain	25 Nov 57	Recognition	287UNTS233	104189
Ghana	UK Great Britain	24 Sep 58	Air Transport	411UNTS146	105918
Ghana	UK Great Britain	17 Apr 59	Status of Forces	337UNTS353	104829
Ghana	UK Great Britain	04 Jun 60	Admin Cooperation	377UNTS197	105401
Ghana	UK Great Britain	05 Jul 60	Admin Cooperation	402UNTS17	105774
Ghana	UK Great Britain	27 Feb 67	Claims and Debts	606UNTS133	108783
Ghana	UK Great Britain	21 Sep 68	Finance	0UNTS0	109807
Ghana	UK Great Britain	17 Dec 68	Claims and Debts	0UNTS0	109712
Ghana	UN Special Fund	12 Aug 59	Direct Aid	338UNTS203	104836
Ghana	UNICEF (Children)	12 Aug 58	Direct Aid	309UNTS103	104469
Ghana	United Arab Rep	29 Aug 60	Air Transport	412UNTS71	105926
Ghana	United Nations	27 Feb 59	Tech Assistance	324UNTS133	104682
Ghana	United Nations	29 Aug 61	Tech Assistance	406UNTS117	105843
Ghana	United Nations	08 Apr 67	IGO Operations	594UNTS149	108601
Ghana	United Nations	19 Sep 68	IGO Operations	0UNTS0	109250
Ghana	USA (United States)	03 Jun 57	Tech Assistance	284UNTS63	104129
Ghana	USA (United States)	12 Feb 58	Admin Cooperation	442UNTS175	106348
Ghana	USA (United States)	30 Sep 58	Admin Cooperation	336UNTS169	104805
Ghana	USA (United States)	09 Apr 59	Customs	342UNTS21	104897
Ghana	USA (United States)	19 Jul 61	Direct Aid	416UNTS167	106002
Ghana	USA (United States)	03 Jan 62	Scientific Project	433UNTS147	106237
Ghana	USA (United States)	24 Jan 62	Education	435UNTS23	106268
Ghana	USA (United States)	01 Apr 66	US Agri Commod Aid	579UNTS157	108405
Ghana	USA (United States)	03 Mar 67	US Agri Commod Aid	0UNTS0	109854
Ghana	USA (United States)	24 Oct 67	US Agri Commod Aid	0UNTS0	109985
Ghana	USA (United States)	03 Jan 68	US Agri Commod Aid	0UNTS0	109986
Ghana	USA (United States)	10 Dec 68	General Aid	0UNTS0	110254
Ghana	USA (United States)	09 Jun 69	General Aid	0UNTS0	110255
Ghana	USA (United States)	22 Jun 70	Commodity Trade	0UNTS0	110782
Ghana	USSR (Soviet Union)	14 Jan 58	Consul/Citizenship	7SUGG102	469485
Ghana	USSR (Soviet Union)	10 Jun 59	General Trade	8SUGG147	469582
Ghana	USSR (Soviet Union)	04 Aug 60	General Aid	399UNTS61	105734
Ghana	USSR (Soviet Union)	04 Aug 60	General Trade	421UNTS27	106050
Ghana	USSR (Soviet Union)	25 Aug 60	Culture	9SUGG145	469686
Ghana	USSR (Soviet Union)	01 Feb 61	Specif Goods/Equip	10SUGG120	469739
Ghana	USSR (Soviet Union)	28 Feb 61	Atomic Energy	10SUGG124	469748

PARTY ONE	PARTY TWO	DATE	TOPIC	CITATION	NUMBER
Ghana	USSR (Soviet Union)	12 Jun 61	Tech Assistance	10SUGG135	469777
Ghana	USSR (Soviet Union)	02 Jul 61	General Trade	0UNTS0	109380
Ghana	USSR (Soviet Union)	02 Jul 61	General Trade	16SUGG131	469996
Ghana	USSR (Soviet Union)	24 Jul 61	Finance	10SUGG139	469791
Ghana	USSR (Soviet Union)	04 Nov 61	General Trade	437UNTS213	106308
Ghana	USSR (Soviet Union)	04 Nov 61	Commodity Trade	10SUGG144	469803
Ghana	USSR (Soviet Union)	04 Nov 61	Finance	10SUGG144	469802
Ghana	USSR (Soviet Union)	04 Nov 61	Finance	0UNTS0	109381
Ghana	USSR (Soviet Union)	06 Apr 62	Air Transport	498UNTS41	107277
Ghana	USSR (Soviet Union)	27 Jul 62	Consul/Citizenship	16SUGG133	470009
Ghana	WHO (World Health)	21 Jan 58	Tech Assistance	307UNTS3	104437
Gibralter	Multilateral	24 Dec 68	Commodity Trade	0UNTS0	109369
Gilbert Islands	Multilateral	24 Dec 68	Commodity Trade	0UNTS0	109369
Greece	Argentina	21 Mar 50	Taxation	187UNTS213	102514
Greece	Australia	16 Jun 48	Claims and Debts	18UNTS211	100290
Greece	Australia	01 Jul 48	Direct Aid	22UNTS33	100329
Greece	Australia	23 May 52	Visas	223UNTS17	103042
Greece	Australia	24 May 54	Postal Service	191UNTS255	102586
Greece	Australia	24 May 54	Visas	193UNTS175	102614
Greece	Australia	15 Mar 56	Consul/Citizenship	241UNTS313	103438
Greece	Austria	11 May 50	General Trade	184UNTS217	102450
Greece	Austria	22 Mar 52	General Economic	187UNTS255	102517
Greece	Austria	20 Sep 52	General Trade	187UNTS191	102512
Greece	Austria	12 Aug 53	Visas	53ABGB158	403084
Greece	Austria	15 Jan 62	Air Transport	498UNTS3	107275
Greece	Austria	06 Dec 65	Admin Cooperation	71ABGB2	403085
Greece	Austria	04 Mar 70	Land Transport	71ABGB83	403086
Greece	Austria	22 Sep 70	Taxation	72ABGB39	403087
Greece	Belgium	27 Dec 48	General Trade	77UNTS265	101004
Greece	Belgium	27 Dec 48	Finance	77UNTS293	101005
Greece	Belgium	21 Jun 49	Air Transport	137UNTS215	101854
Greece	Belgium	24 Apr 52	Finance	166UNTS261	102191
Greece	Belgium	05 Aug 53	Visas	173UNTS53	102260
Greece	Belgium	23 Jun 54	Taxation	199UNTS43	102676
Greece	Belgium	09 Dec 54	Culture	257UNTS243	103660
Greece	Belgium	16 Dec 54	Claims and Debts	223UNTS73	103056
Greece	Belgium	01 Apr 58	Non-ILO Labor	388UNTS93	105574
Greece	Belgium	24 May 68	Taxation	0UNTS0	110552
Greece	Belgium	16 Jul 69	General Transport	0UNTS0	109869
Greece	Brazil	30 Jul 60	General Trade	607UNTS245	108808
Greece	Bulgaria	05 Dec 53	General Trade	225UNTS135	103095
Greece	Bulgaria	05 Dec 53	Finance	225UNTS145	103096
Greece	Bulgaria	19 Apr 56	Sanitation	594UNTS131	108600
Greece	Bulgaria	09 Jul 64	Land Transport	0UNTS0	110295
Greece	Bulgaria	09 Jul 64	Visas	0UNTS0	110296
Greece	Bulgaria	09 Jul 64	Air Transport	0UNTS0	110297
Greece	Bulgaria	09 Jul 64	Postal Service	0UNTS0	110294
Greece	Cameroon	29 Oct 62	General Trade	538UNTS185	107815
Greece	Canada	28 Jul 47	Customs	43UNTS111	100665
Greece	Canada	01 Jul 57	Visas	316UNTS201	104585
Greece	Canada	30 Sep 59	Visas	470UNTS87	106798
Greece	Canada	18 Jul 62	General Military	528UNTS265	107647
Greece	Cyprus	23 Nov 61	Air Transport	497UNTS311	107274
Greece	Cyprus	23 Aug 62	General Trade	609UNTS15	108825
Greece	Cyprus	30 Mar 68	Taxation	0UNTS0	109465
Greece	Czechoslovakia	30 Jul 47	Reparations	185UNTS149	102466
Greece	Czechoslovakia	30 Jul 47	General Trade	185UNTS133	102464
Greece	Czechoslovakia	30 Jul 47	Finance	185UNTS115	102463
Greece	Czechoslovakia	30 Jul 47	Claims and Debts	185UNTS143	102465
Greece	Czechoslovakia	01 Feb 54	General Trade	225UNTS77	103091
Greece	Czechoslovakia	01 Feb 54	Finance	225UNTS95	103092
Greece	Denmark	14 Nov 47	Air Transport	35UNTS295	100560
Greece	Denmark	25 Feb 49	General Trade	78UNTS325	101022
Greece	Denmark	25 Feb 49	Finance	78UNTS335	101023
Greece	Denmark	15 Sep 52	General Trade	187UNTS207	102513

PARTY ONE	PARTY TWO	DATE	TOPIC	CITATION	NUMBER
Greece	Denmark	19 Oct 53	General Trade	225UNTS9	103082
Greece	Denmark	29 Aug 55	General Trade	230UNTS25	103174
Greece	Denmark	04 Sep 56	General Trade	256UNTS319	103643
Greece	Denmark	04 Mar 61	Taxation	534UNTS157	107760
Greece	Denmark	26 Sep 63	General Trade	534UNTS43	107752
Greece	Ethiopia	20 Jan 54	Air Transport	222UNTS281	103035
Greece	Ethiopia	31 Jul 54	Culture	241UNTS319	103439
Greece	Ethiopia	22 Jun 59	General Economic	534UNTS147	107759
Greece	Ethiopia	07 Nov 62	Taxation	550UNTS189	108015
Greece	Ethiopia	07 Nov 62	Taxation	550UNTS179	108014
Greece	Finland	24 Mar 49	General Trade	78UNTS3	101008
Greece	Finland	24 Mar 49	Finance	78UNTS13	101009
Greece	France	24 Apr 46	Finance	91UNTS83	101243
Greece	France	05 May 47	Air Transport	76UNTS61	100980
Greece	France	06 Aug 49	General Trade	91UNTS95	101244
Greece	France	09 Dec 50	Taxation	166UNTS315	102196
Greece	France	03 Sep 51	Mostfavored Nation	187UNTS113	102505
Greece	France	31 Jul 52	General Trade	187UNTS169	102510
Greece	France	23 Dec 52	General Trade	187UNTS175	102511
Greece	France	08 Feb 54	Status of Forces	225UNTS107	103093
Greece	France	08 Feb 54	Status of Forces	225UNTS121	103094
Greece	France	13 May 54	Non-ILO Labor	222UNTS299	103036
Greece	France	30 Jun 54	Non-ILO Labor	257UNTS83	103651
Greece	France	22 Jul 54	General Trade	225UNTS199	103099
Greece	France	28 Jun 55	General Trade	225UNTS219	103100
Greece	France	25 Jun 56	General Trade	251UNTS167	103540
Greece	France	19 Apr 58	Non-ILO Labor	59FRRT14	415204
Greece	France	25 Jul 60	General Aid	533UNTS227	107745
Greece	France	21 Aug 63	Taxation	533UNTS235	107746
Greece	France	14 Dec 65	Loans and Credits	67FRJO1005	416205
Greece	France	09 Apr 69	Land Transport	69FRJO3007	416206
Greece	France	09 Apr 69	Land Transport	0UNTS0	110738
Greece	Germany, West	16 Mar 49	Finance	77UNTS327	101007
Greece	Germany, West	16 Mar 49	General Trade	77UNTS307	101006
Greece	Germany, West	12 Feb 51	General Trade	198UNTS193	102665
Greece	Germany, West	28 Jul 52	General Trade	182UNTS85	102424
Greece	Germany, West	11 Nov 53	General Economic	53WBGA228	424228
Greece	Germany, West	21 Sep 55	Admin Cooperation	55WBGA203	424229
Greece	Germany, West	17 May 56	Culture	57WGBB501	425230
Greece	Germany, West	27 Nov 58	General Economic	59WBGA3	424231
Greece	Germany, West	18 Feb 60	Non-ILO Labor	60WBGA173	424232
Greece	Germany, West	18 Mar 60	Specif Claim/Waive	61WGBB1596	425233
Greece	Germany, West	18 Mar 60	General Economic	62WGBB1505	425234
Greece	Germany, West	30 Mar 60	Non-ILO Labor	61WBGA25	424235
Greece	Germany, West	27 Mar 61	Claims and Debts	63WGBB216	425236
Greece	Germany, West	25 Apr 61	Non-ILO Labor	63WGBB678	425237
Greece	Germany, West	31 May 61	Non-ILO Labor	62WGBB1109	425238
Greece	Germany, West	04 Nov 61	Admin Cooperation	63WGBB109	425239
Greece	Germany, West	08 Mar 62	Land Transport	533UNTS269	107747
Greece	Germany, West	07 Jun 63	Air Transport	544UNTS193	107919
Greece	Germany, West	26 Sep 63	Other Military	550UNTS203	108017
Greece	Germany, West	16 Apr 64	Other Economic	609UNTS27	108826
Greece	Germany, West	18 Apr 66	Taxation	0UNTS0	109395
Greece	Germany, West	18 Apr 66	Taxation	67WGBB852	425240
Greece	Hungary	05 Jun 54	Finance	299UNTS295	104321
Greece	Hungary	05 Jun 54	General Trade	299UNTS285	104320
Greece	Hungary	27 Apr 63	Finance	550UNTS197	108016
Greece	Hungary	27 Apr 63	Air Transport	534UNTS3	107750
Greece	IBRD (World Bank)	18 Mar 68	IBRD Project	0UNTS0	109326
Greece	ILO (Labor Org)	25 Apr 51	Tech Assistance	100UNTS93	101390
Greece	India	18 Apr 51	Reparations	166UNTS305	102195
Greece	India	14 Feb 58	General Trade	609UNTS94	108827
Greece	India	11 Feb 65	Taxation	606UNTS9	108771
Greece	Iran	09 Jan 31	General Amity	166UNTS331	200497
Greece	Iran	09 Jan 31	General Amity	166UNTS323	200496

PARTY ONE	PARTY TWO	DATE	TOPIC	CITATION	NUMBER
Greece	Iran	20 Nov 56	Culture	0IRTB34	433043
Greece	Iran	06 Aug 69	Visas	0IRTB34	433044
Greece	Ireland	05 Jun 56	Visas	553UNTS93	108072
Greece	Israel	22 Jul 52	Taxation	215UNTS365	102924
Greece	Israel	22 Jul 52	General Economic	219UNTS231	102978
Greece	Israel	20 Jan 69	Visas	0UNTS0	110382
Greece	Israel	26 Feb 69	Visas	0UNTS0	110383
Greece	Italy	21 Sep 48	Culture	77UNTS259	101003
Greece	Italy	05 Nov 48	General Amity	50ITGU265	435195
Greece	Italy	05 Nov 48	Admin Cooperation	51ITGU205	435196
Greece	Italy	31 Aug 49	Reparations	78UNTS89	101014
Greece	Italy	05 Jul 52	Visas	187UNTS157	102508
Greece	Italy	04 Feb 53	Finance	189UNTS295	102552
Greece	Italy	04 Feb 53	General Trade	189UNTS269	102551
Greece	Italy	03 Dec 53	General Economic	53ITDI374	436197
Greece	Italy	11 Sep 54	Culture	284UNTS313	104145
Greece	Italy	10 Nov 54	General Trade	227UNTS9	103128
Greece	Italy	26 May 56	Air Transport	496UNTS301	107258
Greece	Italy	02 Aug 57	Air Transport	533UNTS217	107744
Greece	Italy	20 Jun 62	General Trade	62ITDI289	436198
Greece	Italy	26 Jun 65	Finance	66ITDI138	436199
Greece	Japan	12 Mar 55	General Trade	227UNTS33	103130
Greece	Japan	10 May 56	Visas	0JGJI1302	441091
Greece	Japan	09 Apr 65	General Trade	0JGJI1584	441136
Greece	Japan	09 Apr 65	General Trade	632UNTS61	109008
Greece	Japan	20 Sep 66	Claims and Debts	609UNTS103	108828
Greece	Japan	13 Feb 67	General Trade	67JJS201	442185
Greece	Japan	24 Jun 69	General Economic	69JJS183	442243
Greece	Lebanon	10 Sep 47	Dispute Settlement	187UNTS107	102504
Greece	Lebanon	06 Sep 48	Air Transport	178UNTS37	102335
Greece	Lebanon	06 Oct 48	Consul/Citizenship	87UNTS351	101179
Greece	Lebanon	10 Jun 49	Culture	178UNTS29	102334
Greece	Luxembourg	22 Oct 51	Air Transport	187UNTS119	102506
Greece	Malta	01 Oct 65	Visas	550UNTS329	108027
Greece	Mexico	12 Apr 60	General Trade	64MEXD3012	444025
Greece	Morocco	01 Nov 61	General Trade	483UNTS113	107009
Greece	Multilateral	27 Mar 41	Military Mission	67UNTS231	200222
Greece	Multilateral	19 Apr 44	Scientific Project	89UNTS279	200257
Greece	Multilateral	02 Aug 44	Scientific Project	67UNTS221	200221
Greece	Multilateral	07 Dec 44	Air Transport	171UNTS387	200502
Greece	Multilateral	07 Dec 44	Air Transport	171UNTS345	200501
Greece	Multilateral	07 Dec 44	IGO Establishment	15UNTS295	200102
Greece	Multilateral	07 Dec 44	Air Transport	84UNTS389	200252
Greece	Multilateral	15 Dec 44	Sanitation	17UNTS305	200110
Greece	Multilateral	15 Dec 44	Sanitation	16UNTS247	200106
Greece	Multilateral	08 Aug 45	General Military	82UNTS279	200251
Greece	Multilateral	27 Sep 45	IGO Establishment	5UNTS327	200035
Greece	Multilateral	16 Nov 45	IGO Establishment	4UNTS275	100052
Greece	Multilateral	27 Dec 45	IGO Establishment	2UNTS39	100020
Greece	Multilateral	04 Jan 46	IGO Establishment	6UNTS35	100066
Greece	Multilateral	14 Jan 46	Reparations	555UNTS69	108105
Greece	Multilateral	23 Apr 46	Sanitation	17UNTS3	100265
Greece	Multilateral	23 Apr 46	Sanitation	16UNTS179	100257
Greece	Multilateral	22 Jul 46	IGO Establishment	14UNTS185	100221
Greece	Multilateral	22 Jul 46	IGO Establishment	9UNTS3	100125
Greece	Multilateral	15 Oct 46	Refugees	11UNTS73	100150
Greece	Multilateral	30 Oct 46	IGO Establishment	11UNTS107	100151
Greece	Multilateral	11 Dec 46	Sanitation	12UNTS179	100186
Greece	Multilateral	08 Feb 47	Patents/Copyrights	14UNTS287	100222
Greece	Multilateral	10 Feb 47	Peace/Disarmament	41UNTS21	100643
Greece	Multilateral	10 Feb 47	Peace/Disarmament	49UNTS3	100747
Greece	Multilateral	02 Oct 47	Telecommunications	193UNTS188	102616
Greece	Multilateral	11 Oct 47	IGO Establishment	77UNTS143	100998
Greece	Multilateral	12 Nov 47	Admin Cooperation	53UNTS13	100770
Greece	Multilateral	12 Nov 47	Admin Cooperation	53UNTS39	100771

PARTY ONE	PARTY TWO	DATE	TOPIC	CITATION	NUMBER
Greece	Multilateral	12 Nov 47	Admin Cooperation	46UNTS201	100710
Greece	Multilateral	12 Nov 47	Admin Cooperation	53UNTS49	100772
Greece	Multilateral	12 Nov 47	Admin Cooperation	46UNTS169	100709
Greece	Multilateral	06 Mar 48	Water Transport	289UNTS3	104214
Greece	Multilateral	10 May 48	Culture	289UNTS111	104215
Greece	Multilateral	10 Jun 48	Humanitarian	164UNTS113	102163
Greece	Multilateral	10 Jun 48	Humanitarian	191UNTS3	102576
Greece	Multilateral	19 Jun 48	Air Transport	310UNTS151	104492
Greece	Multilateral	26 Jun 48	Culture	331UNTS217	104757
Greece	Multilateral	24 Jul 48	Sanitation	66UNTS25	100847
Greece	Multilateral	14 Sep 48	Milit Occupation	18UNTS267	100296
Greece	Multilateral	17 Sep 48	Telecommunications	97UNTS31	101345
Greece	Multilateral	19 Nov 48	Sanitation	44UNTS277	100688
Greece	Multilateral	09 Dec 48	Humanitarian	78UNTS277	101021
Greece	Multilateral	09 Dec 48	Scientific Project	73UNTS39	100942
Greece	Multilateral	09 Dec 48	Scientific Project	20UNTS229	100318
Greece	Multilateral	23 Mar 49	Commodity Trade	203UNTS179	102746
Greece	Multilateral	04 Apr 49	General Military	34UNTS243	100541
Greece	Multilateral	05 May 49	IGO Establishment	87UNTS103	101168
Greece	Multilateral	15 Jul 49	Health/Educ/Welfare	197UNTS3	102631
Greece	Multilateral	12 Aug 49	Humanitarian	75UNTS85	100971
Greece	Multilateral	12 Aug 49	General Military	75UNTS135	100972
Greece	Multilateral	12 Aug 49	Humanitarian	75UNTS287	100973
Greece	Multilateral	12 Aug 49	Humanitarian	75UNTS31	100970
Greece	Multilateral	02 Sep 49	IGO Status/Immunit	250UNTS12	103515
Greece	Multilateral	24 Sep 49	IGO Establishment	126UNTS237	101691
Greece	Multilateral	16 Dec 49	Admin Cooperation	72UNTS3	100924
Greece	Multilateral	06 Apr 50	Admin Cooperation	119UNTS99	101610
Greece	Multilateral	13 May 50	Land Transport	128UNTS171	101719
Greece	Multilateral	16 Sep 50	General Transport	92UNTS91	101264
Greece	Multilateral	18 Oct 50	Specific Resources	638UNTS185	109134
Greece	Multilateral	04 Nov 50	Humanitarian	213UNTS221	102889
Greece	Multilateral	22 Nov 50	Culture	131UNTS25	101734
Greece	Multilateral	07 Dec 50	Admin Cooperation	212UNTS17	102861
Greece	Multilateral	15 Dec 50	Customs	171UNTS305	102234
Greece	Multilateral	15 Dec 50	Customs	347UNTS127	104994
Greece	Multilateral	15 Dec 50	Customs	157UNTS129	102052
Greece	Multilateral	15 Dec 50	IGO Operations	160UNTS267	102111
Greece	Multilateral	25 May 51	Status of Forces	175UNTS215	102303
Greece	Multilateral	19 Jun 51	Status of Forces	199UNTS67	102678
Greece	Multilateral	02 Jul 51	Refugees	189UNTS137	102545
Greece	Multilateral	08 Sep 51	Peace/Disarmament	136UNTS45	101832
Greece	Multilateral	08 Sep 51	General Military	136UNTS165	101833
Greece	Multilateral	20 Sep 51	IGO Status/Immunit	200UNTS3	102691
Greece	Multilateral	09 Oct 51	IGO Establishment	220UNTS121	102997
Greece	Multilateral	06 Dec 51	IGO Establishment	425UNTS61	106119
Greece	Multilateral	06 Dec 51	Admin Cooperation	150UNTS67	101963
Greece	Multilateral	15 Feb 52	Scientific Project	132UNTS51	101751
Greece	Multilateral	10 May 52	Admin Cooperation	439UNTS193	106330
Greece	Multilateral	10 May 52	Admin Cooperation	439UNTS217	106331
Greece	Multilateral	10 May 52	Taxation	439UNTS233	106332
Greece	Multilateral	20 May 52	Sanitation	219UNTS55	102966
Greece	Multilateral	12 Jun 52	Dispute Settlement	138UNTS183	101869
Greece	Multilateral	11 Jul 52	Postal Service	170UNTS63	102222
Greece	Multilateral	11 Jul 52	Postal Service	171UNTS3	102224
Greece	Multilateral	11 Jul 52	Postal Service	171UNTS143	102226
Greece	Multilateral	11 Jul 52	IGO Establishment	169UNTS3	102220
Greece	Multilateral	11 Jul 52	Postal Service	171UNTS89	102225
Greece	Multilateral	11 Jul 52	Postal Service	170UNTS269	102223
Greece	Multilateral	11 Jul 52	Postal Service	170UNTS3	102221
Greece	Multilateral	07 Oct 52	Admin Cooperation	310UNTS181	104493
Greece	Multilateral	07 Nov 52	General Trade	221UNTS255	103010
Greece	Multilateral	27 Feb 53	Claims and Debts	333UNTS3	104764
Greece	Multilateral	28 Feb 53	General Amity	167UNTS21	102199
Greece	Multilateral	31 Mar 53	Privil/Immunities	193UNTS136	102613

PARTY ONE	PARTY TWO	DATE	TOPIC	CITATION	NUMBER
Greece	Multilateral	11 May 53	Sanitation	456UNTS3	106555
Greece	Multilateral	01 Jul 53	IGO Establishment	200UNTS149	102701
Greece	Multilateral	01 Oct 53	Commodity Trade	258UNTS153	103677
Greece	Multilateral	17 Oct 53	General Transport	184UNTS42	102438
Greece	Multilateral	19 Oct 53	IGO Establishment	207UNTS189	102807
Greece	Multilateral	07 Dec 53	Admin Cooperation	182UNTS51	102422
Greece	Multilateral	11 Dec 53	Patents/Copyrights	218UNTS27	102952
Greece	Multilateral	11 Dec 53	Non-ILO Labor	218UNTS211	102957
Greece	Multilateral	11 Dec 53	Sanitation	191UNTS285	102588
Greece	Multilateral	11 Dec 53	Non-ILO Labor	218UNTS153	102956
Greece	Multilateral	11 Dec 53	Non-ILO Labor	218UNTS255	102958
Greece	Multilateral	11 Dec 53	Education	218UNTS125	102954
Greece	Multilateral	12 May 54	Admin Cooperation	327UNTS3	104714
Greece	Multilateral	14 May 54	Culture	249UNTS215	103511
Greece	Multilateral	14 Jun 54	Air Transport	320UNTS217	104644
Greece	Multilateral	14 Jun 54	Air Transport	320UNTS209	104643
Greece	Multilateral	09 Aug 54	General Amity	211UNTS237	102855
Greece	Multilateral	19 Dec 54	Patents/Copyrights	218UNTS51	102953
Greece	Multilateral	19 Dec 54	Culture	218UNTS139	102955
Greece	Multilateral	02 Mar 55	IGO Establishment	225UNTS233	103101
Greece	Multilateral	01 May 55	Admin Cooperation	0UNTS0	110416
Greece	Multilateral	25 May 55	IGO Establishment	264UNTS117	103791
Greece	Multilateral	22 Jun 55	Atomic Energy	249UNTS3	103498
Greece	Multilateral	28 Sep 55	Air Transport	478UNTS371	106943
Greece	Multilateral	20 Oct 55	IGO Establishment	378UNTS159	105425
Greece	Multilateral	13 Dec 55	IGO Operations	529UNTS141	107660
Greece	Multilateral	13 Dec 55	Humanitarian	250UNTS3	103514
Greece	Multilateral	04 Jan 56	Scientific Project	256UNTS171	103627
Greece	Multilateral	10 Feb 56	Tech Assistance	228UNTS189	103151
Greece	Multilateral	25 Apr 56	Commodity Trade	270UNTS103	103896
Greece	Multilateral	18 May 56	Customs	338UNTS103	104834
Greece	Multilateral	18 May 56	Customs	327UNTS123	104721
Greece	Multilateral	20 Jun 56	Admin Cooperation	268UNTS3	103850
Greece	Multilateral	07 Sep 56	Humanitarian	266UNTS3	103822
Greece	Multilateral	24 Oct 56	Admin Cooperation	510UNTS161	107412
Greece	Multilateral	26 Oct 56	IGO Establishment	276UNTS3	103988
Greece	Multilateral	15 Dec 56	Education	278UNTS73	104023
Greece	Multilateral	29 Apr 57	Dispute Settlement	320UNTS243	104646
Greece	Multilateral	03 Oct 57	Postal Service	366UNTS3	105215
Greece	Multilateral	03 Oct 57	Postal Service	364UNTS331	105212
Greece	Multilateral	03 Oct 57	Postal Service	366UNTS87	105216
Greece	Multilateral	03 Oct 57	Postal Service	366UNTS141	105217
Greece	Multilateral	03 Oct 57	Postal Service	365UNTS3	105213
Greece	Multilateral	03 Oct 57	Postal Service	364UNTS3	105211
Greece	Multilateral	03 Oct 57	Postal Service	365UNTS207	105214
Greece	Multilateral	03 Oct 57	Postal Service	366UNTS255	105219
Greece	Multilateral	13 Dec 57	Extradition	359UNTS273	105146
Greece	Multilateral	13 Dec 57	Visas	315UNTS139	104565
Greece	Multilateral	03 Apr 58	Commodity Trade	336UNTS177	104806
Greece	Multilateral	15 Apr 58	Health/Educ/Welfare	539UNTS27	107822
Greece	Multilateral	10 Jun 58	Admin Cooperation	330UNTS3	104739
Greece	Multilateral	01 Dec 58	Commodity Trade	385UNTS137	105534
Greece	Multilateral	15 Dec 58	Sanitation	351UNTS159	105022
Greece	Multilateral	15 Dec 58	Mass Media	546UNTS235	107950
Greece	Multilateral	15 Jan 59	Customs	348UNTS13	104996
Greece	Multilateral	06 Apr 59	Commodity Trade	349UNTS167	105013
Greece	Multilateral	20 Apr 59	Admin Cooperation	472UNTS185	106841
Greece	Multilateral	20 Apr 59	Land Transport	0UNTS0	110345
Greece	Multilateral	14 Dec 59	Admin Cooperation	444UNTS193	106369
Greece	Multilateral	26 Jan 60	IGO Establishment	439UNTS249	106333
Greece	Multilateral	22 Apr 60	Air Transport	418UNTS211	106023
Greece	Multilateral	28 Apr 60	Health/Educ/Welfare	376UNTS111	105377
Greece	Multilateral	17 Jun 60	Humanitarian	536UNTS27	107794
Greece	Multilateral	22 Jun 60	Mass Media	546UNTS247	107951
Greece	Multilateral	16 Aug 60	Recognition	382UNTS3	105475

PARTY ONE	PARTY TWO	DATE	TOPIC	CITATION	NUMBER
Greece	Multilateral	16 Aug 60	General Amity	397UNTS287	105712
Greece	Multilateral	16 Aug 60	Recognition	382UNTS8	105476
Greece	Multilateral	21 Sep 60	Patents/Copyrights	394UNTS3	105664
Greece	Multilateral	30 Mar 61	Sanitation	520UNTS151	107515
Greece	Multilateral	18 Apr 61	Consul/Citizenship	500UNTS95	107310
Greece	Multilateral	08 Jun 61	Customs	473UNTS153	106862
Greece	Multilateral	08 Jun 61	Customs	473UNTS187	106863
Greece	Multilateral	05 Oct 61	Patents/Copyrights	527UNTS181	107625
Greece	Multilateral	05 Oct 61	Dispute Settlement	510UNTS175	107413
Greece	Multilateral	18 Oct 61	IGO Establishment	529UNTS89	107659
Greece	Multilateral	16 Dec 61	Visas	544UNTS19	107909
Greece	Multilateral	14 May 62	Scientific Project	544UNTS39	107910
Greece	Multilateral	14 May 62	Sanitation	544UNTS81	107911
Greece	Multilateral	10 Dec 62	Culture	521UNTS231	107525
Greece	Multilateral	17 Dec 62	Admin Cooperation	590UNTS81	108548
Greece	Multilateral	20 Apr 63	IGO Establishment	495UNTS3	107239
Greece	Multilateral	09 Jun 63	General Economic	538UNTS309	107818
Greece	Multilateral	05 Aug 63	Sanitation	480UNTS43	106964
Greece	Multilateral	09 Nov 63	Direct Aid	489UNTS209	107141
Greece	Multilateral	10 Feb 64	Visas	496UNTS151	107249
Greece	Multilateral	15 Jun 64	Atomic Energy	573UNTS85	108324
Greece	Multilateral	18 Jun 64	Atomic Energy	542UNTS145	107886
Greece	Multilateral	20 Jun 64	General Economic	539UNTS3	107819
Greece	Multilateral	10 Jul 64	Postal Service	612UNTS233	108848
Greece	Multilateral	10 Jul 64	Postal Service	613UNTS3	108850
Greece	Multilateral	10 Jul 64	Postal Service	613UNTS127	108853
Greece	Multilateral	10 Jul 64	Postal Service	612UNTS361	108849
Greece	Multilateral	10 Jul 64	Postal Service	611UNTS7	108844
Greece	Multilateral	10 Jul 64	Postal Service	613UNTS3	108851
Greece	Multilateral	10 Jul 64	Postal Service	613UNTS193	108852
Greece	Multilateral	10 Jul 64	Postal Service	612UNTS3	108847
Greece	Multilateral	10 Jul 64	Postal Service	611UNTS105	108845
Greece	Multilateral	10 Jul 64	Postal Service	611UNTS387	108846
Greece	Multilateral	22 Jan 65	Gen Communications	634UNTS239	109066
Greece	Multilateral	09 Mar 65	Water Transport	591UNTS265	108564
Greece	Multilateral	18 Mar 65	Dispute Settlement	575UNTS159	108359
Greece	Multilateral	08 Jul 65	General Trade	597UNTS3	108641
Greece	Multilateral	05 Apr 66	Water Transport	640UNTS133	109159
Greece	Multilateral	31 Jan 67	Refugees	606UNTS267	108791
Greece	Multilateral	24 Apr 67	Humanitarian	634UNTS255	109067
Greece	Netherlands	17 Apr 47	Air Transport	32UNTS115	100494
Greece	Netherlands	26 Jul 51	Taxation	109UNTS103	101495
Greece	Netherlands	14 Aug 51	Finance	51NET104	447030
Greece	Netherlands	05 Feb 53	General Trade	263UNTS361	103783
Greece	Netherlands	29 Apr 53	Culture	191UNTS235	102583
Greece	Netherlands	26 Sep 53	Visas	292UNTS23	104263
Greece	Netherlands	01 Nov 54	General Trade	223UNTS79	103057
Greece	Netherlands	14 Jul 55	General Trade	227UNTS27	103129
Greece	Netherlands	22 Nov 55	Visas	292UNTS31	104264
Greece	Netherlands	30 Apr 59	Finance	485UNTS135	107051
Greece	Netherlands	13 Sep 66	Non-ILO Labor	0UNTS0	110746
Greece	Netherlands	13 Sep 66	Non-ILO Labor	0UNTS0	109833
Greece	Netherlands	13 Sep 66	Non-ILO Labor	596UNTS245	108637
Greece	New Zealand	06 Dec 61	Visas	486UNTS3	107067
Greece	Norway	08 Dec 47	Loans and Credits	30UNTS171	100455
Greece	Norway	12 Mar 49	Finance	33UNTS13	100510
Greece	Norway	12 Mar 49	General Trade	30UNTS161	100454
Greece	Norway	28 May 51	Air Transport	187UNTS141	102507
Greece	Norway	25 May 55	Taxation	423UNTS77	106085
Greece	Norway	20 Jun 58	Visas	3NORT747	451066
Greece	Norway	25 Sep 64	General Economic	610UNTS0	108835
Greece	Pakistan	05 Mar 59	Visas	338UNTS97	104833
Greece	Pakistan	17 Jan 63	General Trade	538UNTS175	107814
Greece	Philippines	08 Oct 49	Air Transport	187UNTS221	102515
Greece	Philippines	28 Aug 50	General Amity	225UNTS155	103097

PARTY ONE	PARTY TWO	DATE	TOPIC	CITATION	NUMBER
Greece	Poland	08 Nov 60	General Trade	483UNTS127	107010
Greece	Poland	08 Nov 60	Finance	483UNTS141	107011
Greece	Poland	30 Sep 63	General Trade	534UNTS23	107751
Greece	Poland	21 Dec 63	Air Transport	538UNTS155	107813
Greece	Poland	21 Jan 64	Taxation	533UNTS309	107749
Greece	Portugal	31 Dec 49	Finance	92UNTS83	101263
Greece	Portugal	31 Dec 49	General Trade	92UNTS71	101262
Greece	Portugal	13 Jul 54	General Trade	230UNTS19	103173
Greece	Romania	19 May 54	Finance	225UNTS27	103084
Greece	Romania	19 May 54	General Trade	225UNTS17	103083
Greece	Romania	25 Aug 56	Reparations	299UNTS231	104315
Greece	Romania	02 May 60	Air Transport	485UNTS17	107043
Greece	Romania	20 Jul 63	Taxation	609UNTS109	108829
Greece	South Africa	28 Jul 47	Reparations	185UNTS161	102467
Greece	South Africa	27 Jan 53	Mostfavored Nation	533UNTS303	107748
Greece	South Africa	11 Nov 64	Taxation	631UNTS319	109001
Greece	Spain	03 Feb 53	Claims and Debts	225UNTS3	103081
Greece	Spain	15 May 54	General Trade	299UNTS261	104318
Greece	Spain	15 May 54	Finance	299UNTS277	104319
Greece	Spain	01 Jun 55	General Trade	56SPBO2701	460155
Greece	Spain	14 May 56	General Trade	56SPBO1406	460156
Greece	Spain	08 May 57	General Trade	57SPBO3005	460157
Greece	Sweden	08 Apr 47	Air Transport	94UNTS73	101307
Greece	Sweden	25 Jun 48	General Trade	267UNTS337	103849
Greece	Sweden	08 Dec 50	General Trade	50SOFM1045	461127
Greece	Sweden	08 Dec 50	Finance	50SOFM1056	461128
Greece	Sweden	17 Jul 51	General Trade	51SOFM343	461149
Greece	Sweden	19 Aug 52	General Trade	189UNTS117	102544
Greece	Sweden	08 Sep 52	Finance	52SOFM506	461173
Greece	Sweden	08 Sep 52	General Trade	52SOFM491	461172
Greece	Sweden	24 Jul 53	General Trade	189UNTS309	102553
Greece	Sweden	27 May 54	Taxation	219UNTS147	102971
Greece	Sweden	30 Jul 55	General Trade	225UNTS243	103102
Greece	Sweden	11 Dec 56	Dispute Settlement	299UNTS247	104316
Greece	Sweden	06 Oct 61	Taxation	481UNTS137	106981
Greece	Switzerland	01 Apr 47	Mostfavored Nation	180UNTS115	102378
Greece	Switzerland	26 May 48	Air Transport	94UNTS217	101312
Greece	Switzerland	04 Apr 52	Finance	166UNTS271	102192
Greece	Switzerland	12 Jun 62	Taxation	492UNTS47	107186
Greece	Syria	05 Jul 49	Air Transport	78UNTS71	101013
Greece	Syria	02 Jun 52	General Trade	183UNTS251	102434
Greece	Syria	17 Oct 68	Taxation	0UNTS0	110032
Greece	Taiwan	30 Nov 57	General Trade	0CTRC202	413007
Greece	Tunisia	02 Mar 60	General Trade	483UNTS89	107008
Greece	Tunisia	26 May 62	General Aid	534UNTS163	107761
Greece	Turkey	22 Jul 47	Air Transport	72UNTS131	100931
Greece	Turkey	02 Apr 49	Finance	78UNTS23	101010
Greece	Turkey	21 Jul 49	General Trade	78UNTS55	101011
Greece	Turkey	21 Jul 49	Claims and Debts	78UNTS65	101012
Greece	Turkey	20 Apr 51	Culture	178UNTS17	102333
Greece	Turkey	05 Aug 52	Visas	187UNTS163	102509
Greece	Turkey	07 Nov 53	General Trade	225UNTS163	103098
Greece	Turkey	10 Feb 55	Visas	55TURG1402	466015
Greece	UK Great Britain	11 Oct 45	Reparations	183UNTS329	200509
Greece	UK Great Britain	26 Nov 45	Air Transport	35UNTS161	100555
Greece	UK Great Britain	30 Nov 45	Reparations	183UNTS197	102428
Greece	UK Great Britain	24 Jan 46	Finance	6UNTS45	100067
Greece	UK Great Britain	21 Mar 46	Claims and Debts	91UNTS149	101247
Greece	UK Great Britain	21 Feb 47	Air Transport	70UNTS215	100905
Greece	UK Great Britain	07 Apr 47	Territory Boundary	11UNTS201	100158
Greece	UK Great Britain	05 Jun 47	Status of Forces	9UNTS197	100133
Greece	UK Great Britain	07 Sep 48	Status of Forces	180UNTS144	102380
Greece	UK Great Britain	29 Jun 49	Finance	86UNTS203	101160
Greece	UK Great Britain	17 Oct 49	Postal Service	93UNTS185	101300
Greece	UK Great Britain	16 Nov 50	Taxation	166UNTS281	102193

PARTY ONE	PARTY TWO	DATE	TOPIC	CITATION	NUMBER
Greece	UK Great Britain	21 Feb 51	General Economic	88UNTS205	101192
Greece	UK Great Britain	29 Sep 51	Culture	190UNTS260	102570
Greece	UK Great Britain	17 Apr 53	Consul/Citizenship	191UNTS151	102582
Greece	UK Great Britain	01 Jun 53	Visas	172UNTS265	102250
Greece	UK Great Britain	25 Jun 53	Taxation	190UNTS281	102571
Greece	UK Great Britain	05 Oct 53	Reparations	243UNTS73	103447
Greece	UK Great Britain	24 Feb 55	Specif Claim/Waive	209UNTS187	102827
Greece	UK Great Britain	07 Mar 55	General Military	211UNTS249	102856
Greece	UK Great Britain	14 May 59	Specif Claim/Waive	360UNTS69	105154
Greece	UK Great Britain	21 May 59	Claims and Debts	344UNTS3	104939
Greece	UK Great Britain	06 Apr 61	Visas	403UNTS267	105797
Greece	UK Great Britain	09 May 63	Specific Property	398UNTS179	105722
Greece	UK Great Britain	08 Jun 65	Visas	551UNTS205	108042
Greece	UK Great Britain	12 Oct 66	Other Military	578UNTS33	108385
Greece	UK Great Britain	15 Apr 68	Atomic Energy	0UNTS0	109782
Greece	UK Great Britain	02 Mar 70	Land Transport	0UNTS0	110756
Greece	UN Special Fund	13 Nov 59	Direct Aid	345UNTS171	104966
Greece	UNICEF (Children)	14 Oct 47	Humanitarian	102UNTS39	101409
Greece	United Arab Rep	30 Mar 46	Reparations	187UNTS263	102518
Greece	United Arab Rep	24 Apr 50	Air Transport	163UNTS229	102149
Greece	United Arab Rep	21 May 53	Finance	256UNTS25	103621
Greece	United Arab Rep	21 May 53	General Trade	256UNTS17	103620
Greece	United Arab Rep	04 Sep 56	Culture	299UNTS253	104317
Greece	United Nations	12 Feb 48	Humanitarian	47UNTS223	100732
Greece	United Nations	05 Mar 52	Tech Assistance	123UNTS3	101650
Greece	United Nations	18 May 62	Tech Assistance	429UNTS61	106190
Greece	United Nations	31 Mar 64	IGO Status/Immunit	492UNTS267	107195
Greece	United Nations	20 Jun 66	Claims and Debts	565UNTS3	108230
Greece	United Nations	14 Apr 67	IGO Operations	595UNTS83	108613
Greece	USA (United States)	10 Jul 42	Milit Assistance	103UNTS289	200319
Greece	USA (United States)	16 Mar 43	Milit Servic/Citiz	105UNTS227	200335
Greece	USA (United States)	11 Jan 46	General Trade	3UNTS203	100032
Greece	USA (United States)	27 Mar 46	Air Transport	15UNTS233	100239
Greece	USA (United States)	16 May 46	Direct Aid	184UNTS230	102451
Greece	USA (United States)	08 Oct 46	Claims and Debts	180UNTS119	102379
Greece	USA (United States)	20 Jun 47	Direct Aid	7UNTS267	100105
Greece	USA (United States)	08 Jul 47	Direct Aid	16UNTS157	100256
Greece	USA (United States)	03 Dec 47	Milit Assistance	89UNTS119	101213
Greece	USA (United States)	23 Apr 48	Education	74UNTS107	100958
Greece	USA (United States)	02 Jul 48	Mostfavored Nation	31UNTS131	100474
Greece	USA (United States)	02 Jul 48	Direct Aid	23UNTS43	100342
Greece	USA (United States)	25 Oct 48	General Trade	185UNTS103	102462
Greece	USA (United States)	01 Nov 48	Direct Aid	185UNTS169	102468
Greece	USA (United States)	29 Jan 49	Visas	88UNTS35	101183
Greece	USA (United States)	09 Feb 49	Direct Aid	79UNTS95	101034
Greece	USA (United States)	21 Feb 49	Status of Forces	88UNTS29	101182
Greece	USA (United States)	20 Feb 50	Taxation	196UNTS291	102630
Greece	USA (United States)	20 Feb 50	Taxation	196UNTS269	102629
Greece	USA (United States)	24 Oct 50	Admin Cooperation	133UNTS41	101778
Greece	USA (United States)	03 Aug 51	General Amity	224UNTS279	103080
Greece	USA (United States)	07 Jan 52	Milit Assistance	177UNTS249	102323
Greece	USA (United States)	07 Jan 52	Milit Assistance	180UNTS171	102382
Greece	USA (United States)	23 Apr 52	Direct Aid	177UNTS283	102327
Greece	USA (United States)	25 Jun 52	Air Transport	181UNTS53	102398
Greece	USA (United States)	24 Dec 52	Milit Assistance	185UNTS193	102470
Greece	USA (United States)	04 Feb 53	Milit Assistance	189UNTS3	102538
Greece	USA (United States)	12 Oct 53	Milit Installation	191UNTS319	102589
Greece	USA (United States)	30 Jul 54	Milit Assistance	234UNTS43	103272
Greece	USA (United States)	18 Aug 54	Telecommunications	234UNTS161	103282
Greece	USA (United States)	27 May 55	Milit Assistance	251UNTS349	103552
Greece	USA (United States)	16 Jun 55	Patents/Copyrights	262UNTS137	103742
Greece	USA (United States)	24 Jun 55	US Agri Commod Aid	270UNTS351	103905
Greece	USA (United States)	24 Jun 55	US Agri Commod Aid	270UNTS361	103906
Greece	USA (United States)	04 Aug 55	Atomic Energy	235UNTS257	103307
Greece	USA (United States)	08 Aug 56	US Agri Commod Aid	277UNTS203	104007

PARTY ONE	PARTY TWO	DATE	TOPIC	CITATION	NUMBER
Greece	USA (United States)	07 Sep 56	Status of Forces	278UNTS141	104030
Greece	USA (United States)	19 Jan 57	Milit Installation	280UNTS45	104049
Greece	USA (United States)	05 Aug 57	Milit Assistance	290UNTS167	104235
Greece	USA (United States)	18 Dec 57	US Agri Commod Aid	303UNTS159	104379
Greece	USA (United States)	15 Jan 59	Milit Assistance	357UNTS281	105120
Greece	USA (United States)	06 May 59	Milit Assistance	357UNTS163	105115
Greece	USA (United States)	07 Jan 60	US Agri Commod Aid	368UNTS221	105243
Greece	USA (United States)	15 Feb 60	Milit Assistance	377UNTS95	105397
Greece	USA (United States)	26 Apr 60	Patents/Copyrights	372UNTS299	105306
Greece	USA (United States)	07 Nov 60	US Agri Commod Aid	400UNTS57	105748
Greece	USA (United States)	18 Oct 61	US Agri Commod Aid	426UNTS209	106139
Greece	USA (United States)	24 Apr 62	Water Transport	459UNTS3	106609
Greece	USA (United States)	22 Oct 62	US Agri Commod Aid	462UNTS187	106678
Greece	USA (United States)	30 Oct 63	US Agri Commod Aid	493UNTS29	107205
Greece	USA (United States)	13 Dec 63	Education	494UNTS55	107226
Greece	USA (United States)	28 May 64	Claims and Debts	0UNTS0	109676
Greece	USA (United States)	17 Jul 64	Commodity Trade	530UNTS13	107669
Greece	USA (United States)	17 Nov 64	US Agri Commod Aid	532UNTS107	107714
Greece	USA (United States)	12 Jan 67	General Military	0UNTS0	109842
Greece	USA (United States)	08 Apr 69	Commodity Trade	0UNTS0	110157
Greece	USSR (Soviet Union)	28 Jul 53	General Economic	0SUST298	468170
Greece	USSR (Soviet Union)	02 Sep 54	General Trade	230UNTS33	103175
Greece	USSR (Soviet Union)	23 Aug 55	General Trade	233UNTS39	103249
Greece	USSR (Soviet Union)	06 Sep 56	Humanitarian	16SUGG73	469926
Greece	USSR (Soviet Union)	23 Jan 61	Postal Service	16SUGG130	469990
Greece	USSR (Soviet Union)	25 Apr 62	General Trade	11SUGG139	469835
Greece	Yugoslavia	15 Mar 51	Air Transport	187UNTS237	102516
Greece	Yugoslavia	02 Feb 52	Sanitation	188UNTS311	102535
Greece	Yugoslavia	28 Feb 53	General Economic	252UNTS27	103557
Greece	Yugoslavia	11 Sep 56	Health/Educ/Welfare	552UNTS311	108063
Greece	Yugoslavia	11 Sep 56	Admin Cooperation	391UNTS117	105620
Greece	Yugoslavia	22 Apr 57	Postal Service	391UNTS109	105619
Greece	Yugoslavia	18 Jun 59	Culture	368UNTS137	105238
Greece	Yugoslavia	18 Jun 59	Specific Resources	363UNTS133	105205
Greece	Yugoslavia	18 Jun 59	Visas	388UNTS3	105570
Greece	Yugoslavia	18 Jun 59	Admin Cooperation	368UNTS125	105237
Greece	Yugoslavia	18 Jun 59	IGO Establishment	368UNTS17	105233
Greece	Yugoslavia	18 Jun 59	Admin Cooperation	368UNTS69	105235
Greece	Yugoslavia	18 Jun 59	Land Transport	368UNTS27	105234
Greece	Yugoslavia	18 Jun 59	Admin Cooperation	368UNTS81	105236
Greece	Yugoslavia	18 Jun 59	Claims and Debts	368UNTS9	105232
Greece	Yugoslavia	18 Jun 59	Claims and Debts	368UNTS3	105231
Greece	Yugoslavia	05 Nov 64	Territory Boundary	539UNTS13	107820
Greece	Yugoslavia	05 Nov 64	Land Transport	539UNTS19	107821
Greece	Yugoslavia	15 Apr 67	Taxation	633UNTS373	109046
Grenada	Multilateral	01 Jul 68	Peace/Disarmament	0UNTS0	110485
Grenada	Multilateral	18 Oct 69	IGO Establishment	0UNTS0	110232
Guatemala	Argentina	30 Oct 64	Culture	601UNTS175	108695
Guatemala	Austria	18 Mar 60	General Trade	379UNTS89	105435
Guatemala	Costa Rica	20 Dec 55	General Economic	280UNTS121	104056
Guatemala	Denmark	04 Mar 48	General Economic	96UNTS223	101339
Guatemala	El Salvador	14 Dec 51	General Economic	131UNTS131	101740
Guatemala	France	26 Sep 50	Culture	60FRRT82	415207
Guatemala	Germany, West	24 Apr 66	Tech Assistance	67WBGA39	424241
Guatemala	Honduras	22 Aug 56	General Economic	263UNTS49	103767
Guatemala	IBRD (World Bank)	29 Jul 55	IBRD Project	229UNTS167	103165
Guatemala	IBRD (World Bank)	10 Mar 67	Loans and Credits	616UNTS139	108894
Guatemala	IBRD (World Bank)	28 Jun 68	IBRD Project	0UNTS0	109482
Guatemala	IBRD (World Bank)	16 Dec 68	IBRD Project	0UNTS0	110214
Guatemala	ICJ Option Clause	27 Jan 47	ICJ Option Clause	1UNTS49	100012
Guatemala	ILO (Labor Org)	13 Apr 51	Tech Assistance	126UNTS249	101692
Guatemala	Israel	27 Nov 61	Culture	448UNTS191	106431
Guatemala	Italy	10 Sep 49	General Amity	102UNTS53	101410
Guatemala	Mexico	12 Jun 63	Telecommunications	65MEXD2901	444023
Guatemala	Mexico	16 Dec 66	Culture	67MEXD402	444024

PARTY ONE	PARTY TWO	DATE	TOPIC	CITATION	NUMBER
Guatemala	Multilateral	30 Jul 40	Admin Cooperation	161UNTS253	200488
Guatemala	Multilateral	12 Oct 40	Specific Resources	161UNTS193	200485
Guatemala	Multilateral	28 Nov 40	Commodity Trade	139UNTS159	200452
Guatemala	Multilateral	15 Jan 44	IGO Establishment	161UNTS281	200489
Guatemala	Multilateral	02 Aug 44	Scientific Project	67UNTS221	200221
Guatemala	Multilateral	07 Dec 44	Air Transport	171UNTS345	200501
Guatemala	Multilateral	07 Dec 44	Air Transport	84UNTS389	200252
Guatemala	Multilateral	07 Dec 44	Air Transport	171UNTS387	200502
Guatemala	Multilateral	07 Dec 44	IGO Establishment	15UNTS295	200102
Guatemala	Multilateral	16 Nov 45	IGO Establishment	4UNTS275	100052
Guatemala	Multilateral	27 Dec 45	IGO Establishment	2UNTS39	100020
Guatemala	Multilateral	22 Jul 46	IGO Establishment	14UNTS185	100221
Guatemala	Multilateral	22 Jul 46	IGO Establishment	9UNTS3	100125
Guatemala	Multilateral	27 Jul 46	Patents/Copyrights	90UNTS229	101238
Guatemala	Multilateral	03 Sep 46	Commodity Trade	139UNTS3	101872
Guatemala	Multilateral	11 Dec 46	Sanitation	12UNTS179	100186
Guatemala	Multilateral	15 Dec 46	IGO Establishment	18UNTS3	100283
Guatemala	Multilateral	02 Sep 47	General Military	21UNTS77	100324
Guatemala	Multilateral	02 Oct 47	Telecommunications	193UNTS188	102616
Guatemala	Multilateral	11 Oct 47	IGO Establishment	77UNTS143	100998
Guatemala	Multilateral	12 Nov 47	Admin Cooperation	46UNTS169	100709
Guatemala	Multilateral	12 Nov 47	Admin Cooperation	46UNTS201	100710
Guatemala	Multilateral	30 Apr 48	IGO Establishment	119UNTS3	101609
Guatemala	Multilateral	30 Apr 48	Dispute Settlement	30UNTS55	100449
Guatemala	Multilateral	24 Jul 48	Sanitation	66UNTS25	100847
Guatemala	Multilateral	19 Nov 48	Sanitation	44UNTS277	100688
Guatemala	Multilateral	29 Nov 48	IGO Establishment	120UNTS13	101613
Guatemala	Multilateral	09 Dec 48	Humanitarian	78UNTS277	101021
Guatemala	Multilateral	23 Mar 49	Commodity Trade	203UNTS179	102746
Guatemala	Multilateral	09 Jul 49	Telecommunications	168UNTS143	102218
Guatemala	Multilateral	12 Aug 49	Humanitarian	75UNTS287	100973
Guatemala	Multilateral	12 Aug 49	General Military	75UNTS135	100972
Guatemala	Multilateral	12 Aug 49	Humanitarian	75UNTS31	100970
Guatemala	Multilateral	12 Aug 49	Humanitarian	75UNTS85	100971
Guatemala	Multilateral	06 Apr 50	Admin Cooperation	119UNTS99	101610
Guatemala	Multilateral	22 Nov 50	Culture	131UNTS25	101734
Guatemala	Multilateral	25 May 51	Status of Forces	175UNTS215	102303
Guatemala	Multilateral	01 Jun 51	Tech Assistance	118UNTS57	101596
Guatemala	Multilateral	08 Sep 51	Peace/Disarmament	136UNTS45	101832
Guatemala	Multilateral	14 Oct 51	IGO Establishment	122UNTS3	101631
Guatemala	Multilateral	06 Dec 51	Admin Cooperation	150UNTS67	101963
Guatemala	Multilateral	11 Jul 52	IGO Establishment	169UNTS3	102220
Guatemala	Multilateral	11 Jul 52	Postal Service	170UNTS63	102222
Guatemala	Multilateral	06 Sep 52	Patents/Copyrights	216UNTS132	102937
Guatemala	Multilateral	31 Mar 53	Mass Media	435UNTS191	106280
Guatemala	Multilateral	31 Mar 53	Privil/Immunities	193UNTS136	102613
Guatemala	Multilateral	11 May 53	Sanitation	456UNTS3	106555
Guatemala	Multilateral	04 Jun 54	Customs	276UNTS191	103992
Guatemala	Multilateral	04 Jun 54	Customs	282UNTS249	104101
Guatemala	Multilateral	14 Jun 54	Air Transport	320UNTS217	104644
Guatemala	Multilateral	14 Jun 54	Air Transport	320UNTS209	104643
Guatemala	Multilateral	28 Sep 54	Refugees	360UNTS117	105158
Guatemala	Multilateral	25 May 55	IGO Establishment	264UNTS117	103791
Guatemala	Multilateral	25 Apr 56	Commodity Trade	270UNTS103	103896
Guatemala	Multilateral	20 Jun 56	Admin Cooperation	268UNTS3	103850
Guatemala	Multilateral	07 Sep 56	Humanitarian	266UNTS3	103822
Guatemala	Multilateral	26 Oct 56	IGO Establishment	276UNTS3	103988
Guatemala	Multilateral	08 Nov 56	Commodity Trade	470UNTS171	106809
Guatemala	Multilateral	20 Feb 57	Consul/Citizenship	309UNTS65	104468
Guatemala	Multilateral	22 Feb 57	Tech Assistance	274UNTS93	103960
Guatemala	Multilateral	03 Oct 57	Postal Service	365UNTS3	105213
Guatemala	Multilateral	03 Oct 57	Postal Service	364UNTS3	105211
Guatemala	Multilateral	29 Apr 58	Territory Boundary	499UNTS311	107302
Guatemala	Multilateral	29 Apr 58	Water Transport	450UNTS11	106465
Guatemala	Multilateral	29 Apr 58	Territory Boundary	516UNTS205	107477

PARTY ONE	PARTY TWO	DATE	TOPIC	CITATION	NUMBER
Guatemala	Multilateral	10 Jun 58	Land Transport	454UNTS115	106540
Guatemala	Multilateral	10 Jun 58	General Economic	454UNTS47	106539
Guatemala	Multilateral	10 Jun 58	Land Transport	454UNTS211	106541
Guatemala	Multilateral	01 Dec 58	Commodity Trade	385UNTS137	105534
Guatemala	Multilateral	03 Dec 58	Admin Cooperation	416UNTS51	105995
Guatemala	Multilateral	03 Dec 58	Admin Cooperation	398UNTS9	105715
Guatemala	Multilateral	06 Apr 59	Commodity Trade	349UNTS167	105013
Guatemala	Multilateral	08 Apr 59	IGO Establishment	389UNTS69	105593
Guatemala	Multilateral	01 Sep 59	Customs	454UNTS289	106542
Guatemala	Multilateral	18 Nov 59	IGO Establishment	390UNTS227	105610
Guatemala	Multilateral	03 Dec 59	Tech Assistance	345UNTS251	104971
Guatemala	Multilateral	26 Jan 60	IGO Establishment	439UNTS249	106333
Guatemala	Multilateral	06 Feb 60	General Economic	383UNTS3	105494
Guatemala	Multilateral	26 Feb 60	Air Transport	418UNTS171	106022
Guatemala	Multilateral	28 Jul 60	IGO Establishment	485UNTS3	107042
Guatemala	Multilateral	13 Dec 60	General Economic	455UNTS3	106543
Guatemala	Multilateral	13 Dec 60	IGO Establishment	455UNTS204	106544
Guatemala	Multilateral	30 Mar 61	Sanitation	520UNTS151	107515
Guatemala	Multilateral	18 Apr 61	Consul/Citizenship	500UNTS95	107310
Guatemala	Multilateral	28 Jun 62	ILO Labor	494UNTS271	107238
Guatemala	Multilateral	28 Sep 62	IGO Establishment	469UNTS169	106791
Guatemala	Multilateral	05 Aug 63	Sanitation	480UNTS43	106964
Guatemala	Multilateral	21 Oct 63	Tech Assistance	480UNTS197	106969
Guatemala	Multilateral	14 Dec 63	IGO Establishment	507UNTS149	107399
Guatemala	Multilateral	28 Jan 64	Tech Assistance	502UNTS321	107336
Guatemala	Multilateral	10 Jul 64	Postal Service	612UNTS3	108847
Guatemala	Multilateral	10 Jul 64	Postal Service	611UNTS105	108845
Guatemala	Multilateral	10 Jul 64	Postal Service	611UNTS7	108844
Guatemala	Multilateral	14 Feb 67	General Military	634UNTS281	109068
Guatemala	Multilateral	18 Mar 68	Commodity Trade	0UNTS0	109262
Guatemala	Multilateral	01 Jun 68	General Trade	0UNTS0	110835
Guatemala	Multilateral	24 Dec 68	Commodity Trade	0UNTS0	109369
Guatemala	Norway	25 Oct 62	Visas	3NORT869	451067
Guatemala	Norway	27 Apr 65	Visas	3NORT869	451068
Guatemala	Norway	29 Aug 67	Visas	3NORT869	451069
Guatemala	Spain	31 Dec 55	General Trade	56SPBO2801	460158
Guatemala	Spain	28 Jul 61	Consul/Citizenship	62SPBO1003	460159
Guatemala	Spain	27 Apr 64	Culture	65SPBO2506	460160
Guatemala	Switzerland	01 Apr 55	General Trade	55SWRO407	462137
Guatemala	Taiwan	08 Nov 64	General Trade	543UNTS227	107903
Guatemala	UN Special Fund	17 Nov 60	Direct Aid	383UNTS67	105495
Guatemala	UNICEF (Children)	09 Feb 50	Tech Assistance	65UNTS84	100836
Guatemala	UNICEF (Children)	22 Nov 55	Direct Aid	221UNTS305	103012
Guatemala	United Nations	10 Mar 54	Tech Assistance	191UNTS271	102587
Guatemala	USA (United States)	21 Jul 42	Military Mission	103UNTS299	200320
Guatemala	USA (United States)	19 May 43	Land Transport	28UNTS377	200161
Guatemala	USA (United States)	17 Jul 43	Military Mission	28UNTS431	200166
Guatemala	USA (United States)	13 Apr 44	Admin Cooperation	106UNTS213	200342
Guatemala	USA (United States)	15 Jul 44	Scientific Project	106UNTS285	200347
Guatemala	USA (United States)	16 Sep 44	Education	135UNTS315	200444
Guatemala	USA (United States)	21 Feb 45	Military Mission	121UNTS133	200396
Guatemala	USA (United States)	21 May 45	Military Mission	121UNTS185	200399
Guatemala	USA (United States)	25 Oct 45	Postal Service	139UNTS45	101875
Guatemala	USA (United States)	29 Aug 47	Status of Forces	27UNTS11	100393
Guatemala	USA (United States)	05 Jan 48	Education	135UNTS104	101817
Guatemala	USA (United States)	18 May 48	Land Transport	67UNTS161	100875
Guatemala	USA (United States)	08 Oct 48	Military Mission	121UNTS31	101623
Guatemala	USA (United States)	08 Oct 48	Military Mission	121UNTS37	101624
Guatemala	USA (United States)	20 Dec 49	Status of Forces	70UNTS71	100897
Guatemala	USA (United States)	08 Jan 52	Tech Assistance	181UNTS31	102395
Guatemala	USA (United States)	30 Jul 54	Milit Assistance	234UNTS235	103286
Guatemala	USA (United States)	01 Sep 54	Tech Assistance	199UNTS51	102677
Guatemala	USA (United States)	01 Dec 54	Visas	237UNTS161	103342
Guatemala	USA (United States)	13 Dec 54	Direct Aid	237UNTS169	103343
Guatemala	USA (United States)	23 Mar 55	Claims and Debts	252UNTS143	103563

PARTY ONE	PARTY TWO	DATE	TOPIC	CITATION	NUMBER
Guatemala	USA (United States)	18 Jun 55	Milit Assistance	262UNTS105	103740
Guatemala	USA (United States)	28 Sep 55	General Trade	257UNTS307	103663
Guatemala	USA (United States)	30 May 56	Visas	275UNTS271	103986
Guatemala	USA (United States)	15 Aug 56	Atomic Energy	288UNTS181	104205
Guatemala	USA (United States)	23 Apr 60	Atomic Energy	373UNTS23	105312
Guatemala	USA (United States)	09 Aug 60	Finance	461UNTS15	106648
Guatemala	USA (United States)	21 May 62	General Trade	451UNTS205	106495
Guatemala	USA (United States)	02 Aug 62	Milit Assistance	461UNTS199	106664
Guatemala	USA (United States)	29 Dec 62	Tech Assistance	474UNTS31	106869
Guatemala	USA (United States)	03 Oct 63	Direct Aid	493UNTS45	107206
Guatemala	USA (United States)	04 May 65	Status of Forces	545UNTS163	107932
Guatemala	USA (United States)	11 Dec 67	Gen Communications	0UNTS0	110444
Guatemala	USSR (Soviet Union)	19 Apr 45	Consul/Citizenship	0SUST176	468171
Guatemala	WHO (World Health)	28 Nov 50	Sanitation	103UNTS51	101423
Guatemala	WHO (World Health)	17 Dec 51	Sanitation	120UNTS133	101619
Guatemala	WHO (World Health)	29 Dec 51	Sanitation	124UNTS89	101668
Guinea	Accept UN Charter	03 Dec 58	UN Charter	317UNTS77	104595
Guinea	Accept UN Charter	25 Oct 68	UN Charter	0UNTS0	109295
Guinea	China People's Rep	07 Oct 59	Culture	29CCJC595	410637
Guinea	China People's Rep	13 Sep 60	General Amity	60CCJC93	410717
Guinea	China People's Rep	13 Sep 60	Direct Aid	60CCJC94	410718
Guinea	China People's Rep	13 Sep 60	General Trade	60CCJC95	410719
Guinea	China People's Rep	07 Jan 64	General Trade	64CCJC4	411157
Guinea	China People's Rep	05 Aug 64	Mass Media	64CCJC107	411161
Guinea	China People's Rep	05 Jun 65	Culture	65CCJC74	411165
Guinea	China People's Rep	14 Sep 65	Postal Service	65CCJC114	411182
Guinea	China People's Rep	14 Sep 65	Telecommunications	65CCJC115	411183
Guinea	China People's Rep	02 Oct 65	Culture	65CCJC127	411167
Guinea	China People's Rep	01 Feb 66	General Trade	66CCJC2	411168
Guinea	China People's Rep	30 Apr 66	Culture	66CCJC24	411186
Guinea	China People's Rep	02 Jun 66	Scientific Project	66CCJC46	411169
Guinea	China People's Rep	16 Nov 66	Loans and Credits	66CCJC94	411190
Guinea	China People's Rep	16 Nov 66	General Trade	66CCJC95	411191
Guinea	China People's Rep	16 Nov 66	Direct Aid	66CCJC93	411189
Guinea	China People's Rep	16 Nov 66	General Economic	66CCJC92	411188
Guinea	Czechoslovakia	30 Nov 59	Culture	386UNTS63	105538
Guinea	Czechoslovakia	16 Dec 61	Air Transport	559UNTS49	108154
Guinea	France	29 Jul 61	Culture	62FRRT17	415208
Guinea	France	21 Mar 62	Air Transport	63FRRT59	415209
Guinea	France	22 May 63	General Trade	63FRRT62	415211
Guinea	France	22 May 63	Tech Assistance	63FRRT61	415210
Guinea	Germany, East	17 Nov 58	General Economic	6EGDA309	419115
Guinea	Germany, East	17 Nov 58	Culture	6EGDA309	419116
Guinea	Germany, East	17 Nov 58	Consul/Citizenship	6EGDA309	419114
Guinea	Germany, East	03 Mar 59	General Trade	7EGDA365	419117
Guinea	Germany, East	10 Jan 60	General Economic	8EGDA345	419118
Guinea	Germany, East	11 Feb 63	General Economic	11EGDA584	419119
Guinea	Germany, East	29 May 64	Education	12EGDA765	419121
Guinea	Germany, East	29 May 64	Non-ILO Labor	12EGDA759	419120
Guinea	Germany, East	09 Aug 65	General Economic	52EGDZ341	420122
Guinea	Germany, East	10 Dec 65	General Economic	51EGDZ349	420123
Guinea	Germany, West	18 Mar 59	Direct Aid	59WBGA77	424242
Guinea	Germany, West	09 Mar 61	Water Transport	61WBGA160	424243
Guinea	Germany, West	19 Apr 62	Claims and Debts	64WGBB145	425244
Guinea	Germany, West	19 Apr 62	General Economic	62WBGA134	424245
Guinea	Germany, West	19 Apr 62	Air Transport	62WBGA134	424247
Guinea	Germany, West	19 Apr 62	Loans and Credits	62WBGA134	424246
Guinea	Germany, West	10 Jul 64	Commodity Trade	64WBGA195	424248
Guinea	Germany, West	03 Jun 65	Loans and Credits	65WBGA136	424249
Guinea	Hungary	12 Jan 60	Culture	519UNTS131	107505
Guinea	IBRD (World Bank)	30 Mar 66	IBRD Project	568UNTS3	108262
Guinea	IBRD (World Bank)	18 Sep 68	IBRD Project	0UNTS0	110596
Guinea	Italy	30 Oct 62	Air Transport	65ITGU280	435200
Guinea	Italy	20 Feb 64	Claims and Debts	65ITDI130	436202
Guinea	Italy	20 Feb 64	Tech Assistance	65ITDI191	436201

PARTY ONE	PARTY TWO	DATE	TOPIC	CITATION	NUMBER
Guinea	Italy	29 Oct 64	Water Transport	65ITDI131	436203
Guinea	Ivory Coast	26 Jun 63	Air Transport	499UNTS71	107293
Guinea	Multilateral	07 Dec 44	IGO Establishment	15UNTS295	200102
Guinea	Multilateral	11 Dec 46	Sanitation	12UNTS179	100186
Guinea	Multilateral	27 May 47	Air Transport	418UNTS161	106021
Guinea	Multilateral	24 Jul 48	Sanitation	66UNTS25	100847
Guinea	Multilateral	21 Mar 50	Admin Cooperation	96UNTS271	101342
Guinea	Multilateral	07 Dec 50	Admin Cooperation	212UNTS17	102861
Guinea	Multilateral	02 Jul 51	Refugees	189UNTS137	102545
Guinea	Multilateral	07 Nov 52	General Trade	221UNTS255	103010
Guinea	Multilateral	07 Dec 53	Admin Cooperation	182UNTS51	102422
Guinea	Multilateral	18 Jan 54	IGO Establishment	330UNTS121	104743
Guinea	Multilateral	14 May 54	Culture	249UNTS215	103511
Guinea	Multilateral	14 Jun 54	Air Transport	320UNTS209	104643
Guinea	Multilateral	14 Jun 54	Air Transport	320UNTS217	104644
Guinea	Multilateral	29 Jul 54	Sanitation	249UNTS45	103500
Guinea	Multilateral	28 Sep 54	Refugees	360UNTS117	105158
Guinea	Multilateral	12 Oct 55	IGO Establishment	560UNTS3	108165
Guinea	Multilateral	03 Dec 59	Tech Assistance	348UNTS246	105003
Guinea	Multilateral	14 Dec 60	Education	429UNTS93	106193
Guinea	Multilateral	18 Apr 61	Consul/Citizenship	500UNTS95	107310
Guinea	Multilateral	18 Apr 61	Consul/Citizenship	500UNTS223	107311
Guinea	Multilateral	18 Apr 61	Dispute Settlement	500UNTS243	107312
Guinea	Multilateral	21 Jun 61	IGO Establishment	514UNTS209	107449
Guinea	Multilateral	25 May 62	IGO Establishment	486UNTS103	107075
Guinea	Multilateral	28 Jun 62	ILO Labor	494UNTS271	107238
Guinea	Multilateral	10 Dec 62	Culture	521UNTS231	107525
Guinea	Multilateral	25 May 63	IGO Establishment	479UNTS39	106947
Guinea	Multilateral	04 Aug 63	IGO Establishment	510UNTS3	107408
Guinea	Multilateral	26 Oct 63	Water Transport	587UNTS9	108506
Guinea	Multilateral	10 Jul 64	Postal Service	612UNTS3	108847
Guinea	Multilateral	10 Jul 64	Postal Service	612UNTS233	108848
Guinea	Multilateral	10 Jul 64	Postal Service	611UNTS7	108844
Guinea	Multilateral	10 Jul 64	Postal Service	612UNTS361	108849
Guinea	Multilateral	10 Jul 64	Postal Service	611UNTS105	108845
Guinea	Multilateral	10 Jul 64	Postal Service	611UNTS387	108846
Guinea	Multilateral	25 Nov 64	Water Transport	587UNTS19	108507
Guinea	Multilateral	28 May 65	IGO Establishment	559UNTS273	108163
Guinea	Multilateral	18 Mar 68	Commodity Trade	OUNTSO	109262
Guinea	Multilateral	24 Mar 68	IGO Establishment	OUNTSO	109577
Guinea	Multilateral	18 Jun 69	IGO Operations	OUNTSO	109741
Guinea	Multilateral	18 Jun 69	IGO Operations	OUNTSO	109740
Guinea	Netherlands	09 Mar 60	Air Transport	392UNTS243	105646
Guinea	Norway	21 Jun 62	Air Transport	466UNTS81	106738
Guinea	Poland	17 Jun 63	Tech Assistance	63PZUM61	458105
Guinea	Poland	10 Mar 66	Culture	67PDZU201	457130
Guinea	Romania	01 Dec 66	General Trade	642UNTS89	109167
Guinea	Sweden	17 Jun 61	Air Transport	465UNTS236	106729
Guinea	Switzerland	26 Apr 62	General Economic	63SWRO732	462138
Guinea	Switzerland	01 Feb 63	Air Transport	499UNTS35	107291
Guinea	UK Great Britain	22 Oct 59	General Trade	351UNTS341	105033
Guinea	UN Special Fund	02 Dec 59	Direct Aid	345UNTS215	104969
Guinea	UN Special Fund	18 Jun 69	General Aid	OUNTSO	109742
Guinea	UNICEF (Children)	08 Jun 59	Direct Aid	334UNTS277	104772
Guinea	UNICEF (Children)	22 Dec 66	IGO Operations	585UNTS137	108486
Guinea	United Nations	15 Oct 59	Tech Assistance	344UNTS47	104942
Guinea	USA (United States)	28 Oct 59	Culture	358UNTS169	105134
Guinea	USA (United States)	30 Sep 60	General Aid	394UNTS103	105671
Guinea	USA (United States)	02 Feb 62	US Agri Commod Aid	435UNTS35	106269
Guinea	USA (United States)	09 May 62	Claims and Debts	451UNTS197	106494
Guinea	USA (United States)	03 Nov 62	Mass Media	459UNTS259	106628
Guinea	USA (United States)	14 Dec 62	General Aid	462UNTS247	106684
Guinea	USA (United States)	22 May 63	US Agri Commod Aid	487UNTS251	107108
Guinea	USA (United States)	13 Jun 64	US Agri Commod Aid	531UNTS263	107708
Guinea	USA (United States)	29 Jun 65	Milit Installation	549UNTS139	107997

PARTY ONE	PARTY TWO	DATE	TOPIC	CITATION	NUMBER
Guinea	USA (United States)	04 Feb 66	US Agri Commod Aid	579UNTS213	108409
Guinea	USA (United States)	18 Oct 67	US Agri Commod Aid	OUNTSO	110050
Guinea	USA (United States)	03 Feb 69	Commodity Trade	OUNTSO	110266
Guinea	USSR (Soviet Union)	04 Oct 58	Consul/Citizenship	7SUGG121	469533
Guinea	USSR (Soviet Union)	13 Feb 59	General Economic	8SUGG137	469560
Guinea	USSR (Soviet Union)	24 Aug 59	General Aid	8SUGG152	469600
Guinea	USSR (Soviet Union)	24 Aug 59	Loans and Credits	8SUGG152	469601
Guinea	USSR (Soviet Union)	26 Nov 59	Culture	8SUGG159	469611
Guinea	USSR (Soviet Union)	01 Mar 60	Direct Aid	9SUGG128	469634
Guinea	USSR (Soviet Union)	01 Mar 60	Tech Assistance	9SUGG128	469635
Guinea	USSR (Soviet Union)	01 Mar 60	Tech Assistance	9SUGG127	469633
Guinea	USSR (Soviet Union)	17 Aug 60	Consul/Citizenship	16SUGG128	469980
Guinea	USSR (Soviet Union)	08 Sep 60	General Trade	9SUGG147	469691
Guinea	USSR (Soviet Union)	29 Apr 61	Non-IBRD Project	10SUGG130	469765
Guinea	USSR (Soviet Union)	29 May 61	General Aid	10SUGG132	469772
Guinea	USSR (Soviet Union)	16 Jan 62	Air Transport	11SUGG130	469817
Guinea	USSR (Soviet Union)	26 Feb 62	General Aid	11SUGG134	469824
Guinea	WHO (World Health)	11 Feb 61	Tech Assistance	394UNTS173	105677
Guyana	Accept UN Charter	04 Jun 66	UN Charter	572UNTS225	108316
Guyana	IBRD (World Bank)	27 Sep 68	IBRD Project	OUNTSO	109612
Guyana	IBRD (World Bank)	31 Jan 69	IBRD Project	OUNTSO	110096
Guyana	IDA (Devel Assoc)	31 Jan 69	Non-IBRD Project	OUNTSO	110097
Guyana	Multilateral	25 May 55	IGO Establishment	264UNTS117	103791
Guyana	Multilateral	01 Dec 58	Commodity Trade	385UNTS137	105534
Guyana	Multilateral	26 Jan 60	IGO Establishment	439UNTS249	106333
Guyana	Multilateral	10 Jul 64	Postal Service	611UNTS7	108844
Guyana	Multilateral	10 Jul 64	Postal Service	612UNTS3	108847
Guyana	Multilateral	10 Jul 64	Postal Service	611UNTS105	108845
Guyana	Multilateral	10 Jul 64	Postal Service	611UNTS387	108846
Guyana	Multilateral	22 Aug 66	Tech Assistance	571UNTS298	200624
Guyana	Multilateral	24 Dec 68	Commodity Trade	OUNTSO	109369
Guyana	Multilateral	27 Jan 69	Telecommunications	OUNTSO	109664
Guyana	Multilateral	18 Oct 69	IGO Establishment	OUNTSO	110232
Guyana	UK Great Britain	26 May 66	Status of Forces	595UNTS255	108621
Guyana	UK Great Britain	26 May 66	Admin Cooperation	588UNTS143	108521
Guyana	UK Great Britain	15 Jun 67	Military Mission	632UNTS15	109005
Guyana	UK Great Britain	20 Sep 68	Finance	OUNTSO	109803
Guyana	UN Special Fund	11 Jun 66	Non-IBRD Project	564UNTS201	200622
Guyana	UNICEF (Children)	02 Jul 69	IGO Operations	OUNTSO	109744
Guyana	United Nations	22 Aug 66	IGO Operations	571UNTS305	200625
Guyana	USA (United States)	07 Jun 67	Admin Cooperation	OUNTSO	109771
Guyana	USA (United States)	13 May 68	Gen Communications	OUNTSO	110017
Guyana	USA (United States)	17 Sep 68	US Agri Commod Aid	OUNTSO	110076
Guyana	WHO (World Health)	03 Jul 68	Direct Aid	642UNTS13	109161
Hague Private IL	Netherlands	01 Dec 59	IGO Status/Immunit	510UNTS191	107414
Haiti	France	08 Apr 52	Education	52FRJO2404	416212
Haiti	France	15 Jun 65	Air Transport	67FRJO1205	416213
Haiti	IBRD (World Bank)	07 May 56	IBRD Project	252UNTS279	103570
Haiti	IDA (Devel Assoc)	02 Nov 62	Non-IBRD Project	468UNTS205	106774
Haiti	Israel	28 Mar 67	General Amity	630UNTS293	108975
Haiti	Italy	14 Jun 54	General Economic	267UNTS97	103837
Haiti	Japan	17 Dec 58	General Economic	518UNTS91	107492
Haiti	Multilateral	30 Jul 40	Admin Cooperation	161UNTS253	200488
Haiti	Multilateral	12 Oct 40	Specific Resources	161UNTS193	200485
Haiti	Multilateral	28 Nov 40	Commodity Trade	139UNTS159	200452
Haiti	Multilateral	15 Jan 44	IGO Establishment	161UNTS281	200489
Haiti	Multilateral	19 Apr 44	Scientific Project	89UNTS279	200257
Haiti	Multilateral	02 Aug 44	Scientific Project	67UNTS221	200221
Haiti	Multilateral	07 Dec 44	Air Transport	171UNTS345	200501
Haiti	Multilateral	07 Dec 44	Air Transport	171UNTS387	200502
Haiti	Multilateral	07 Dec 44	Air Transport	84UNTS389	200252
Haiti	Multilateral	07 Dec 44	IGO Establishment	15UNTS295	200102
Haiti	Multilateral	15 Dec 44	Sanitation	16UNTS247	200106
Haiti	Multilateral	15 Dec 44	Sanitation	17UNTS305	200110
Haiti	Multilateral	08 Aug 45	General Military	82UNTS279	200251

PARTY ONE	PARTY TWO	DATE	TOPIC	CITATION	NUMBER
Haiti	Multilateral	16 Nov 45	IGO Establishment	4UNTS275	100052
Haiti	Multilateral	23 Apr 46	Sanitation	16UNTS179	100257
Haiti	Multilateral	23 Apr 46	Sanitation	17UNTS3	100265
Haiti	Multilateral	22 Jul 46	IGO Establishment	14UNTS185	100221
Haiti	Multilateral	22 Jul 46	IGO Establishment	9UNTS3	100125
Haiti	Multilateral	27 Jul 46	Patents/Copyrights	90UNTS229	101238
Haiti	Multilateral	03 Sep 46	Commodity Trade	139UNTS3	101872
Haiti	Multilateral	11 Dec 46	Sanitation	12UNTS179	100186
Haiti	Multilateral	02 Sep 47	General Military	21UNTS77	100324
Haiti	Multilateral	02 Oct 47	Telecommunications	193UNTS188	102616
Haiti	Multilateral	12 Nov 47	Admin Cooperation	46UNTS201	100710
Haiti	Multilateral	12 Nov 47	Admin Cooperation	46UNTS169	100709
Haiti	Multilateral	06 Mar 48	Water Transport	289UNTS3	104214
Haiti	Multilateral	30 Apr 48	IGO Establishment	119UNTS3	101609
Haiti	Multilateral	30 Apr 48	Dispute Settlement	30UNTS55	100449
Haiti	Multilateral	10 May 48	Culture	289UNTS111	104215
Haiti	Multilateral	10 Jun 48	Humanitarian	191UNTS3	102576
Haiti	Multilateral	10 Jun 48	Humanitarian	164UNTS113	102163
Haiti	Multilateral	19 Jun 48	Air Transport	310UNTS151	104492
Haiti	Multilateral	24 Jul 48	Sanitation	66UNTS25	100847
Haiti	Multilateral	09 Dec 48	Humanitarian	78UNTS277	101021
Haiti	Multilateral	23 Mar 49	Commodity Trade	203UNTS179	102746
Haiti	Multilateral	04 May 49	Admin Cooperation	47UNTS159	100728
Haiti	Multilateral	09 Jul 49	Telecommunications	168UNTS143	102218
Haiti	Multilateral	15 Jul 49	Health/Educ/Welfare	197UNTS3	102631
Haiti	Multilateral	16 Dec 49	Admin Cooperation	72UNTS3	100924
Haiti	Multilateral	21 Mar 50	Admin Cooperation	96UNTS271	101342
Haiti	Multilateral	22 Nov 50	Culture	131UNTS25	101734
Haiti	Multilateral	15 Dec 50	Customs	347UNTS127	104994
Haiti	Multilateral	15 Dec 50	Customs	157UNTS129	102052
Haiti	Multilateral	15 Dec 50	Customs	171UNTS305	102234
Haiti	Multilateral	25 May 51	Status of Forces	175UNTS215	102303
Haiti	Multilateral	28 Jun 51	Tech Assistance	118UNTS154	101604
Haiti	Multilateral	08 Sep 51	General Military	136UNTS165	101833
Haiti	Multilateral	08 Sep 51	Peace/Disarmament	136UNTS45	101832
Haiti	Multilateral	10 May 52	Taxation	439UNTS233	106332
Haiti	Multilateral	10 May 52	Admin Cooperation	439UNTS193	106330
Haiti	Multilateral	12 Jun 52	Dispute Settlement	138UNTS183	101869
Haiti	Multilateral	11 Jul 52	Postal Service	171UNTS143	102226
Haiti	Multilateral	11 Jul 52	Postal Service	170UNTS269	102223
Haiti	Multilateral	11 Jul 52	Postal Service	170UNTS63	102222
Haiti	Multilateral	11 Jul 52	Postal Service	170UNTS3	102221
Haiti	Multilateral	11 Jul 52	IGO Establishment	169UNTS3	102220
Haiti	Multilateral	11 Jul 52	Postal Service	171UNTS3	102224
Haiti	Multilateral	06 Sep 52	Patents/Copyrights	216UNTS132	102937
Haiti	Multilateral	07 Oct 52	Admin Cooperation	310UNTS181	104493
Haiti	Multilateral	07 Nov 52	General Trade	221UNTS255	103010
Haiti	Multilateral	31 Mar 53	Privil/Immunities	193UNTS136	102613
Haiti	Multilateral	01 Oct 53	Commodity Trade	258UNTS153	103677
Haiti	Multilateral	04 Jun 54	Customs	282UNTS249	104101
Haiti	Multilateral	04 Jun 54	Customs	276UNTS191	103992
Haiti	Multilateral	14 Jun 54	Air Transport	320UNTS209	104643
Haiti	Multilateral	25 May 55	IGO Establishment	264UNTS117	103791
Haiti	Multilateral	01 Mar 56	Customs	343UNTS129	104923
Haiti	Multilateral	25 Apr 56	Commodity Trade	270UNTS103	103896
Haiti	Multilateral	20 Jun 56	Admin Cooperation	268UNTS3	103850
Haiti	Multilateral	26 Jun 56	Tech Assistance	321UNTS2	104650
Haiti	Multilateral	07 Sep 56	Humanitarian	266UNTS3	103822
Haiti	Multilateral	26 Oct 56	IGO Establishment	276UNTS3	103988
Haiti	Multilateral	01 May 57	Admin Cooperation	284UNTS201	104138
Haiti	Multilateral	03 Oct 57	Postal Service	365UNTS207	105214
Haiti	Multilateral	03 Oct 57	Postal Service	365UNTS3	105213
Haiti	Multilateral	03 Oct 57	Postal Service	366UNTS255	105219
Haiti	Multilateral	03 Oct 57	Postal Service	366UNTS3	105215
Haiti	Multilateral	03 Oct 57	Postal Service	364UNTS3	105211

PARTY ONE	PARTY TWO	DATE	TOPIC	CITATION	NUMBER
Haiti	Multilateral	03 Oct 57	Postal Service	366UNTS141	105217
Haiti	Multilateral	03 Oct 57	Postal Service	364UNTS331	105212
Haiti	Multilateral	29 Apr 58	Specific Resources	559UNTS285	108164
Haiti	Multilateral	29 Apr 58	Territory Boundary	516UNTS205	107477
Haiti	Multilateral	29 Apr 58	Territory Boundary	499UNTS311	107302
Haiti	Multilateral	29 Apr 58	Dispute Settlement	450UNTS169	106466
Haiti	Multilateral	29 Apr 58	Water Transport	450UNTS11	106465
Haiti	Multilateral	01 Dec 58	Commodity Trade	385UNTS137	105534
Haiti	Multilateral	06 Apr 59	Commodity Trade	349UNTS167	105013
Haiti	Multilateral	08 Apr 59	IGO Establishment	389UNTS69	105593
Haiti	Multilateral	18 Nov 59	IGO Establishment	390UNTS227	105610
Haiti	Multilateral	26 Jan 60	IGO Establishment	439UNTS249	106333
Haiti	Multilateral	17 Jun 60	Humanitarian	536UNTS27	107794
Haiti	Multilateral	30 Mar 61	Sanitation	520UNTS151	107515
Haiti	Multilateral	26 Mar 62	IGO Establishment	539UNTS67	107825
Haiti	Multilateral	28 Sep 62	IGO Establishment	469UNTS169	106791
Haiti	Multilateral	05 Aug 63	Sanitation	480UNTS43	106964
Haiti	Multilateral	10 Jul 64	Postal Service	611UNTS105	108845
Haiti	Multilateral	10 Jul 64	Postal Service	611UNTS7	108844
Haiti	Multilateral	14 Feb 67	General Military	634UNTS281	109068
Haiti	Multilateral	18 Mar 68	Commodity Trade	0UNTS0	109262
Haiti	Norway	24 Oct 62	Visas	3NORT868	451070
Haiti	Taiwan	25 Feb 66	Admin Cooperation	0UNTS0	110433
Haiti	UN Special Fund	28 Jun 61	Direct Aid	399UNTS171	105741
Haiti	UNICEF (Children)	20 Dec 49	Tech Assistance	65UNTS68	100829
Haiti	United Nations	28 Jun 61	Tech Assistance	399UNTS159	105740
Haiti	USA (United States)	23 May 41	Military Mission	117UNTS191	200370
Haiti	USA (United States)	05 Jun 41	Admin Cooperation	101UNTS125	200289
Haiti	USA (United States)	13 Sep 41	Other Ad Hoc	103UNTS141	200311
Haiti	USA (United States)	19 Feb 42	Customs	105UNTS238	200336
Haiti	USA (United States)	07 Apr 42	Sanitation	106UNTS319	200349
Haiti	USA (United States)	21 Sep 42	Other Ad Hoc	120UNTS177	200391
Haiti	USA (United States)	30 Sep 42	Other Ad Hoc	24UNTS205	200144
Haiti	USA (United States)	19 Oct 42	Territory Boundary	120UNTS171	200390
Haiti	USA (United States)	08 Jan 45	Specific Resources	121UNTS153	200397
Haiti	USA (United States)	24 Aug 45	Visas	139UNTS311	200458
Haiti	USA (United States)	14 May 46	Finance	4UNTS179	100044
Haiti	USA (United States)	30 Sep 46	Other Ad Hoc	15UNTS257	100241
Haiti	USA (United States)	04 Jul 47	Other Ad Hoc	22UNTS165	100335
Haiti	USA (United States)	27 Sep 47	Sanitation	136UNTS258	101839
Haiti	USA (United States)	01 Oct 47	Other Ad Hoc	102UNTS67	101411
Haiti	USA (United States)	19 Dec 47	Direct Aid	135UNTS130	101818
Haiti	USA (United States)	11 Feb 48	Specific Resources	149UNTS11	101946
Haiti	USA (United States)	04 Jan 49	Military Mission	44UNTS69	100679
Haiti	USA (United States)	14 Apr 49	Military Mission	80UNTS37	101043
Haiti	USA (United States)	29 Dec 49	General Trade	133UNTS21	101775
Haiti	USA (United States)	28 Sep 50	Sanitation	162UNTS85	102132
Haiti	USA (United States)	02 May 51	Tech Assistance	151UNTS191	101994
Haiti	USA (United States)	29 Aug 52	Direct Aid	186UNTS35	102480
Haiti	USA (United States)	13 Mar 53	Direct Aid	212UNTS143	102866
Haiti	USA (United States)	28 May 54	Non-IBRD Project	233UNTS281	103267
Haiti	USA (United States)	28 Jan 55	Milit Assistance	270UNTS83	103894
Haiti	USA (United States)	01 Apr 55	Direct Aid	261UNTS361	103734
Haiti	USA (United States)	05 Apr 55	Milit Assistance	270UNTS97	103895
Haiti	USA (United States)	27 Apr 55	IGO Establishment	240UNTS17	103391
Haiti	USA (United States)	24 Jun 55	Non-IBRD Project	264UNTS291	103800
Haiti	USA (United States)	28 Dec 55	Non-IBRD Project	240UNTS95	103397
Haiti	USA (United States)	28 Dec 56	Direct Aid	279UNTS107	104035
Haiti	USA (United States)	09 Sep 58	Direct Aid	335UNTS257	104793
Haiti	USA (United States)	27 Oct 58	Military Mission	336UNTS235	104807
Haiti	USA (United States)	24 Dec 58	Military Mission	338UNTS265	104840
Haiti	USA (United States)	06 Jan 60	Gen Communications	367UNTS75	105226
Haiti	USA (United States)	08 Jul 60	Milit Assistance	380UNTS135	105454
Haiti	USA (United States)	01 Sep 60	Milit Assistance	388UNTS249	105582
Haiti	USA (United States)	06 Jun 62	General Trade	452UNTS59	106504

PARTY ONE	PARTY TWO	DATE	TOPIC	CITATION	NUMBER
Haiti	WHO (World Health)	21 Jun 50	Sanitation	103UNTS61	101424
Haiti	WHO (World Health)	27 Jun 50	Tech Assistance	110UNTS99	101504
Honduras	Argentina	26 Nov 64	Culture	0UNTS0	109557
Honduras	Canada	11 Jul 56	Mostfavored Nation	305UNTS39	104411
Honduras	France	15 Aug 55	Consul/Citizenship	60FRRT29	415219
Honduras	France	13 Jan 68	Health/Educ/Welfare	69FRJO1101	416220
Honduras	France	13 Jan 68	Culture	0UNTS0	109530
Honduras	Germany, West	18 Apr 64	Tech Assistance	66WBGA33	424250
Honduras	Guatemala	22 Aug 56	General Economic	263UNTS49	103767
Honduras	IBRD (World Bank)	22 Dec 55	IBRD Project	230UNTS262	103189
Honduras	IBRD (World Bank)	09 May 58	IBRD Project	323UNTS4	104662
Honduras	IBRD (World Bank)	20 May 59	IBRD Project	359UNTS119	105141
Honduras	IBRD (World Bank)	29 Jun 60	IBRD Project	400UNTS137	105751
Honduras	IBRD (World Bank)	02 Feb 65	IBRD Project	561UNTS255	108188
Honduras	IBRD (World Bank)	25 Aug 66	IBRD Project	582UNTS79	108460
Honduras	IBRD (World Bank)	26 May 67	IGO Operations	615UNTS145	108879
Honduras	IBRD (World Bank)	12 Jul 68	IBRD Project	0UNTS0	109408
Honduras	ICJ Option Clause	02 Feb 48	ICJ Option Clause	15UNTS217	100236
Honduras	IDA (Devel Assoc)	12 May 61	Loans and Credits	414UNTS180	105973
Honduras	IDA (Devel Assoc)	02 Feb 65	Non-IBRD Project	561UNTS279	108189
Honduras	IDA (Devel Assoc)	12 Jun 68	Non-IBRD Project	0UNTS0	109409
Honduras	Israel	10 Oct 62	Visas	484UNTS189	107028
Honduras	Italy	12 May 47	Peace/Disarmament	47ITGU140	435204
Honduras	Mexico	15 Jan 66	Culture	70MEXD703	444027
Honduras	Mexico	27 Oct 66	Tech Assistance	68MEXD1902	444026
Honduras	Multilateral	30 Jul 40	Admin Cooperation	161UNTS253	200488
Honduras	Multilateral	28 Nov 40	Commodity Trade	139UNTS159	200452
Honduras	Multilateral	15 Jan 44	IGO Establishment	161UNTS281	200489
Honduras	Multilateral	19 Apr 44	Scientific Project	89UNTS279	200257
Honduras	Multilateral	02 Aug 44	Scientific Project	67UNTS221	200221
Honduras	Multilateral	07 Dec 44	Air Transport	171UNTS387	200502
Honduras	Multilateral	07 Dec 44	Air Transport	171UNTS345	200501
Honduras	Multilateral	07 Dec 44	Air Transport	84UNTS389	200252
Honduras	Multilateral	07 Dec 44	IGO Establishment	15UNTS295	200102
Honduras	Multilateral	15 Dec 44	Sanitation	16UNTS247	200106
Honduras	Multilateral	15 Dec 44	Sanitation	17UNTS305	200110
Honduras	Multilateral	08 Aug 45	General Military	82UNTS279	200251
Honduras	Multilateral	27 Dec 45	IGO Establishment	2UNTS39	100020
Honduras	Multilateral	23 Apr 46	Sanitation	16UNTS179	100257
Honduras	Multilateral	23 Apr 46	Sanitation	17UNTS3	100265
Honduras	Multilateral	22 Jul 46	IGO Establishment	9UNTS3	100125
Honduras	Multilateral	22 Jul 46	IGO Establishment	14UNTS185	100221
Honduras	Multilateral	27 Jul 46	Patents/Copyrights	90UNTS229	101238
Honduras	Multilateral	03 Sep 46	Commodity Trade	139UNTS3	101872
Honduras	Multilateral	11 Dec 46	Sanitation	12UNTS179	100186
Honduras	Multilateral	15 Dec 46	IGO Establishment	18UNTS3	100283
Honduras	Multilateral	02 Sep 47	General Military	21UNTS77	100324
Honduras	Multilateral	02 Oct 47	Telecommunications	193UNTS188	102616
Honduras	Multilateral	06 Mar 48	Water Transport	289UNTS3	104214
Honduras	Multilateral	30 Apr 48	IGO Establishment	119UNTS3	101609
Honduras	Multilateral	30 Apr 48	Dispute Settlement	30UNTS55	100449
Honduras	Multilateral	24 Jul 48	Sanitation	66UNTS25	100847
Honduras	Multilateral	19 Nov 48	Sanitation	44UNTS277	100688
Honduras	Multilateral	09 Dec 48	Humanitarian	78UNTS277	101021
Honduras	Multilateral	23 Mar 49	Commodity Trade	203UNTS179	102746
Honduras	Multilateral	04 May 49	Admin Cooperation	30UNTS3	100445
Honduras	Multilateral	09 Jul 49	Telecommunications	168UNTS143	102218
Honduras	Multilateral	25 May 51	Status of Forces	175UNTS215	102303
Honduras	Multilateral	01 Jun 51	Tech Assistance	118UNTS57	101596
Honduras	Multilateral	08 Sep 51	Peace/Disarmament	136UNTS45	101832
Honduras	Multilateral	14 Oct 51	IGO Establishment	122UNTS3	101631
Honduras	Multilateral	11 Jul 52	IGO Establishment	169UNTS3	102220
Honduras	Multilateral	11 Jul 52	Postal Service	170UNTS63	102222
Honduras	Multilateral	11 Jul 52	Postal Service	170UNTS269	102223
Honduras	Multilateral	11 Jul 52	Postal Service	171UNTS3	102224
Honduras	Multilateral	11 Jul 52	Postal Service	170UNTS3	102221
Honduras	Multilateral	11 Jul 52	Postal Service	171UNTS143	102226
Honduras	Multilateral	06 Sep 52	Patents/Copyrights	216UNTS132	102937
Honduras	Multilateral	07 Oct 52	Admin Cooperation	310UNTS181	104493
Honduras	Multilateral	29 Dec 52	Tech Assistance	151UNTS317	102002
Honduras	Multilateral	04 Jun 54	Customs	276UNTS191	103992
Honduras	Multilateral	04 Jun 54	Customs	282UNTS249	104101
Honduras	Multilateral	14 Jun 54	Air Transport	320UNTS217	104644
Honduras	Multilateral	14 Jun 54	Air Transport	320UNTS209	104643
Honduras	Multilateral	28 Sep 54	Refugees	360UNTS117	105158
Honduras	Multilateral	25 May 55	IGO Establishment	264UNTS117	103791
Honduras	Multilateral	25 Apr 56	Commodity Trade	270UNTS103	103896
Honduras	Multilateral	26 Oct 56	IGO Establishment	276UNTS3	103988
Honduras	Multilateral	08 Nov 56	Commodity Trade	470UNTS171	106809
Honduras	Multilateral	22 Feb 57	Tech Assistance	274UNTS93	103960
Honduras	Multilateral	01 May 57	Admin Cooperation	284UNTS201	104138
Honduras	Multilateral	09 Jul 57	Tech Assistance	274UNTS300	103972
Honduras	Multilateral	03 Oct 57	Postal Service	364UNTS3	105211
Honduras	Multilateral	03 Oct 57	Postal Service	366UNTS255	105219
Honduras	Multilateral	03 Oct 57	Postal Service	366UNTS141	105217
Honduras	Multilateral	03 Oct 57	Postal Service	364UNTS331	105212
Honduras	Multilateral	03 Oct 57	Postal Service	365UNTS207	105214
Honduras	Multilateral	03 Oct 57	Postal Service	365UNTS3	105213
Honduras	Multilateral	03 Oct 57	Postal Service	366UNTS3	105215
Honduras	Multilateral	10 Jun 58	Land Transport	454UNTS211	106541
Honduras	Multilateral	10 Jun 58	General Economic	454UNTS47	106539
Honduras	Multilateral	10 Jun 58	Land Transport	454UNTS115	106540
Honduras	Multilateral	30 Jan 59	General Trade	0UNTS0	109234
Honduras	Multilateral	06 Apr 59	Commodity Trade	349UNTS167	105013
Honduras	Multilateral	08 Apr 59	IGO Establishment	389UNTS69	105593
Honduras	Multilateral	01 Sep 59	Customs	454UNTS289	106542
Honduras	Multilateral	18 Nov 59	IGO Establishment	390UNTS227	105610
Honduras	Multilateral	03 Dec 59	Tech Assistance	345UNTS251	104971
Honduras	Multilateral	26 Jan 60	IGO Establishment	439UNTS249	106333
Honduras	Multilateral	06 Feb 60	General Economic	383UNTS3	105494
Honduras	Multilateral	26 Feb 60	Air Transport	418UNTS171	106022
Honduras	Multilateral	17 Jun 60	Humanitarian	536UNTS27	107794
Honduras	Multilateral	28 Jul 60	IGO Establishment	485UNTS3	107042
Honduras	Multilateral	13 Dec 60	IGO Establishment	455UNTS204	106544
Honduras	Multilateral	13 Dec 60	General Economic	455UNTS3	106543
Honduras	Multilateral	21 Jun 61	IGO Establishment	514UNTS209	107449
Honduras	Multilateral	26 Mar 62	IGO Establishment	539UNTS67	107825
Honduras	Multilateral	28 Sep 62	IGO Establishment	469UNTS169	106791
Honduras	Multilateral	12 Dec 62	IGO Establishment	552UNTS15	108048
Honduras	Multilateral	05 Aug 63	Sanitation	480UNTS43	106964
Honduras	Multilateral	21 Oct 63	Tech Assistance	480UNTS197	106969
Honduras	Multilateral	08 Nov 63	Tech Assistance	482UNTS286	106999
Honduras	Multilateral	14 Dec 63	IGO Establishment	507UNTS149	107399
Honduras	Multilateral	10 Jul 64	Postal Service	612UNTS3	108847
Honduras	Multilateral	10 Jul 64	Postal Service	611UNTS7	108844
Honduras	Multilateral	10 Jul 64	Postal Service	611UNTS105	108845
Honduras	Multilateral	22 Jul 65	IBRD Project	561UNTS333	200618
Honduras	Multilateral	14 Feb 67	General Military	634UNTS281	109068
Honduras	Multilateral	21 Jun 67	Tech Assistance	598UNTS2	108653
Honduras	Multilateral	18 Mar 68	Commodity Trade	0UNTS0	109262
Honduras	Multilateral	01 Jun 68	General Trade	0UNTS0	110835
Honduras	Nicaragua	22 Jun 57	Specif Claim/Waive	277UNTS159	104005
Honduras	Norway	29 Nov 62	Visas	3NORT873	451071
Honduras	Spain	12 Jun 57	Culture	63SPBO1105	460161
Honduras	UK Great Britain	30 Apr 62	Visas	449UNTS159	106457
Honduras	UN Special Fund	20 Dec 60	Direct Aid	383UNTS103	105497
Honduras	UNICEF (Children)	17 Jan 50	Tech Assistance	65UNTS74	100831
Honduras	USA (United States)	28 Feb 41	Specific Resources	117UNTS205	200371
Honduras	USA (United States)	08 May 42	Sanitation	166UNTS351	200498
Honduras	USA (United States)	26 Oct 42	Land Transport	24UNTS209	200145

PARTY ONE	PARTY TWO	DATE	TOPIC	CITATION	NUMBER
Honduras	USA (United States)	12 Apr 44	Education	138UNTS271	200450
Honduras	USA (United States)	28 Dec 45	Military Mission	3UNTS185	100031
Honduras	USA (United States)	13 May 47	Sanitation	166UNTS159	102189
Honduras	USA (United States)	06 Mar 50	Military Mission	80UNTS51	101044
Honduras	USA (United States)	06 Mar 50	Military Mission	80UNTS71	101045
Honduras	USA (United States)	24 Mar 50	Admin Cooperation	93UNTS11	101283
Honduras	USA (United States)	26 Jan 51	Tech Assistance	99UNTS49	101370
Honduras	USA (United States)	30 Jan 51	Direct Aid	124UNTS63	101667
Honduras	USA (United States)	24 Apr 51	Education	140UNTS287	101894
Honduras	USA (United States)	07 Mar 52	Tech Assistance	233UNTS151	103260
Honduras	USA (United States)	23 Apr 52	Status of Forces	198UNTS251	102669
Honduras	USA (United States)	20 May 54	Milit Assistance	222UNTS87	103025
Honduras	USA (United States)	24 May 54	Milit Installation	433UNTS155	106238
Honduras	USA (United States)	21 Mar 55	Direct Aid	253UNTS3	103572
Honduras	USA (United States)	12 May 55	Direct Aid	270UNTS3	103886
Honduras	USA (United States)	10 Jun 55	Claims and Debts	258UNTS51	103669
Honduras	USA (United States)	25 Apr 56	Military Mission	269UNTS25	103869
Honduras	USA (United States)	25 Jun 56	Taxation	279UNTS113	104036
Honduras	USA (United States)	19 Feb 60	Gen Communications	371UNTS109	105273
Honduras	USA (United States)	18 Jan 61	General Trade	402UNTS169	105785
Honduras	USA (United States)	12 Apr 61	Direct Aid	413UNTS182	105952
Honduras	USA (United States)	20 Jul 62	General Aid	460UNTS125	106635
Honduras	USA (United States)	24 Oct 62	Milit Assistance	459UNTS211	106624
Honduras	USA (United States)	17 Apr 67	Gen Communications	0UNTS0	109760
Honduras	USA (United States)	27 Nov 69	Commodity Trade	0UNTS0	110454
Honduras	USA (United States)	30 Apr 70	General Trade	0UNTS0	110778
Honduras	WHO (World Health)	20 Apr 51	Tech Assistance	110UNTS111	101505
Hungary	Accept UN Charter	10 Mar 49	UN Charter	223UNTS55	103051
Hungary	Albania	12 Jan 60	Admin Cooperation	520UNTS3	107511
Hungary	Argentina	06 Nov 67	General Trade	0UNTS0	109561
Hungary	Australia	01 Jul 48	Direct Aid	22UNTS3	100325
Hungary	Australia	07 Jan 49	Admin Cooperation	189UNTS233	102548
Hungary	Australia	10 Feb 55	Postal Service	207UNTS173	102806
Hungary	Australia	05 Dec 67	General Trade	638UNTS209	109137
Hungary	Austria	18 May 55	Water Transport	55ABGB195	403088
Hungary	Austria	09 Apr 56	Specific Resources	438UNTS123	106315
Hungary	Austria	17 Jul 59	Air Transport	60ABGB76	403089
Hungary	Austria	17 Jul 59	Air Transport	0UNTS0	109237
Hungary	Austria	17 Jan 61	Customs	61ABGB42	403091
Hungary	Austria	09 Jul 63	Sanitation	482UNTS29	106989
Hungary	Austria	31 Oct 64	Claims and Debts	605UNTS77	108760
Hungary	Austria	31 Oct 64	Finance	605UNTS3	108758
Hungary	Austria	31 Oct 64	Claims and Debts	605UNTS63	108759
Hungary	Austria	31 Oct 64	Visas	545UNTS241	107937
Hungary	Austria	31 Oct 64	Visas	545UNTS223	107936
Hungary	Austria	11 Nov 64	Sanitation	576UNTS163	108368
Hungary	Austria	09 Apr 65	Admin Cooperation	638UNTS135	109133
Hungary	Austria	09 Apr 65	Visas	564UNTS179	108228
Hungary	Austria	09 Apr 65	Visas	638UNTS53	109131
Hungary	Austria	09 Apr 65	Recognition	638UNTS105	109132
Hungary	Austria	31 Oct 67	Claims and Debts	67ABGB293	403092
Hungary	Austria	08 Jun 68	Customs	68ABGB293	403093
Hungary	Austria	27 Nov 68	Customs	69ABGB261	403094
Hungary	Austria	29 Apr 69	Visas	69ABGB167	403095
Hungary	Austria	28 May 69	Health/Educ/Welfare	72ABGB111	403096
Hungary	Austria	28 Apr 71	Visas	71ABGB203	403097
Hungary	Austria	05 May 71	Air Transport	71ABGB403	403090
Hungary	Austria	17 May 71	Visas	71ABGB252	403098
Hungary	Austria	28 Oct 71	Finance	71ABGB421	403099
Hungary	Belgium	01 Jun 57	Air Transport	291UNTS17	104242
Hungary	Belgium	11 Feb 65	Culture	544UNTS3	107908
Hungary	Belgium	20 Mar 67	Land Transport	601UNTS37	108686
Hungary	Bulgaria	16 Jul 48	General Amity	477UNTS169	106921
Hungary	Bulgaria	13 Mar 58	Sanitation	438UNTS191	106317
Hungary	Bulgaria	13 Mar 58	Sanitation	438UNTS173	106316

PARTY ONE	PARTY TWO	DATE	TOPIC	CITATION	NUMBER
Hungary	Bulgaria	27 Jun 58	Culture	438UNTS235	106318
Hungary	Bulgaria	03 Apr 59	Sanitation	438UNTS269	106319
Hungary	Bulgaria	30 Jun 61	Admin Cooperation	438UNTS287	106320
Hungary	Bulgaria	19 Aug 65	Culture	577UNTS67	108373
Hungary	Bulgaria	16 May 66	Admin Cooperation	0UNTS0	110417
Hungary	Bulgaria	22 Jan 69	Visas	0UNTS0	110837
Hungary	Bulgaria	10 Jul 69	General Amity	0UNTS0	110111
Hungary	Canada	08 Mar 56	Commodity Trade	305UNTS27	104409
Hungary	Ceylon (Sri Lanka)	04 Jun 56	General Trade	315UNTS13	104555
Hungary	China People's Rep	22 Jan 51	General Economic	51CCJC3	410026
Hungary	China People's Rep	12 Jul 51	Culture	51CCJC21	410041
Hungary	China People's Rep	30 Mar 53	General Economic	53CCJC17	410098
Hungary	China People's Rep	16 Jul 53	Postal Service	53CCJC40	410112
Hungary	China People's Rep	16 Jul 53	Telecommunications	53CCJC41	410113
Hungary	China People's Rep	03 Oct 53	Scientific Project	53CCJC56	410119
Hungary	China People's Rep	15 Oct 53	Mass Media	53CCJC57	410120
Hungary	China People's Rep	28 Dec 54	Sanitation	54CCJC96	410200
Hungary	China People's Rep	26 Apr 55	General Economic	55CCJC32	410232
Hungary	China People's Rep	27 Jan 56	General Economic	56CCJC15	410303
Hungary	China People's Rep	08 Jun 57	General Economic	57CCJC65	410432
Hungary	China People's Rep	21 Mar 58	General Economic	58CCJC30	410504
Hungary	China People's Rep	17 May 58	Scientific Project	58CCJC62	410526
Hungary	China People's Rep	17 Mar 59	General Economic	59CCJC49	410602
Hungary	China People's Rep	06 Apr 59	Mass Media	59CCJC62	410611
Hungary	China People's Rep	06 May 59	General Amity	59CCJC75	410621
Hungary	China People's Rep	28 Feb 60	General Economic	60CCJC29	410677
Hungary	China People's Rep	15 Jul 61	Finance	61CCJC100	410812
Hungary	China People's Rep	15 Jul 61	General Economic	61CCJC102	410813
Hungary	China People's Rep	30 Mar 62	General Economic	62CCJC33	410880
Hungary	China People's Rep	10 Apr 63	General Economic	63CCJC42	410968
Hungary	China People's Rep	31 Jan 64	Mass Media	64CCJC20	411195
Hungary	China People's Rep	28 Mar 64	General Economic	64CCJC42	411197
Hungary	China People's Rep	26 Mar 65	General Economic	65CCJC46	411198
Hungary	China People's Rep	28 May 65	Scientific Project	65CCJC71	411199
Hungary	China People's Rep	05 Jun 65	Culture	65CCJC73	411193
Hungary	China People's Rep	20 Feb 66	General Economic	66CCJC5	411200
Hungary	China People's Rep	20 Jul 66	Culture	66CCJC69	411201
Hungary	China People's Rep	09 Aug 66	Scientific Project	66CCJC76	411194
Hungary	China People's Rep	22 Jun 67	General Economic	67CCJC25	411202
Hungary	COMECON (Econ Aid)	28 Feb 63	IGO Operations	506UNTS281	107390
Hungary	Cyprus	02 Jun 64	Air Transport	602UNTS3	108704
Hungary	Czechoslovakia	27 Feb 49	Admin Cooperation	26UNTS119	100383
Hungary	Czechoslovakia	16 Apr 49	General Amity	477UNTS183	106922
Hungary	Czechoslovakia	16 Apr 54	Specific Resources	504UNTS231	107360
Hungary	Czechoslovakia	28 Apr 55	Sanitation	477UNTS197	106923
Hungary	Czechoslovakia	13 Oct 56	Territory Boundary	300UNTS177	104337
Hungary	Czechoslovakia	13 Oct 56	Territory Boundary	300UNTS125	104336
Hungary	Czechoslovakia	12 Mar 58	Sanitation	408UNTS178	105870
Hungary	Czechoslovakia	08 May 58	Customs	407UNTS92	105862
Hungary	Czechoslovakia	27 Jun 58	Consul/Citizenship	477UNTS321	106927
Hungary	Czechoslovakia	30 Jan 59	Non-ILO Labor	351UNTS3	105016
Hungary	Czechoslovakia	27 Mar 59	Consul/Citizenship	351UNTS57	105017
Hungary	Czechoslovakia	04 Nov 60	Consul/Citizenship	397UNTS227	105708
Hungary	Czechoslovakia	24 Feb 61	Culture	422UNTS15	106066
Hungary	Czechoslovakia	02 Nov 61	Admin Cooperation	438UNTS3	106313
Hungary	Czechoslovakia	16 Oct 62	Visas	479UNTS301	106961
Hungary	Czechoslovakia	22 Oct 63	Land Transport	514UNTS95	107444
Hungary	Czechoslovakia	20 Dec 63	General Economic	538UNTS127	107812
Hungary	Czechoslovakia	17 Oct 64	Land Transport	545UNTS21	107924
Hungary	Czechoslovakia	27 Feb 68	IGO Establishment	640UNTS49	109154
Hungary	Czechoslovakia	14 Jun 68	General Amity	0UNTS0	109645
Hungary	Denmark	28 Feb 48	Finance	85UNTS35	101144
Hungary	Denmark	10 Feb 51	General Trade	85UNTS49	101145
Hungary	Denmark	17 Jul 58	Air Transport	344UNTS281	104954
Hungary	Denmark	20 Oct 69	Scientific Project	0UNTS0	110525

PARTY ONE	PARTY TWO	DATE	TOPIC	CITATION	NUMBER
Hungary	Ethiopia	25 May 65	Health/Educ/Welfare	577UNTS193	108377
Hungary	Finland	10 Jun 59	Culture	439UNTS3	106321
Hungary	Finland	13 Feb 62	Air Transport	463UNTS61	106693
Hungary	Finland	10 Nov 67	Land Transport	643UNTS95	109186
Hungary	Finland	01 Oct 69	General Economic	0UNTS0	110481
Hungary	Finland	01 Oct 69	Visas	0UNTS0	110358
Hungary	France	12 Jun 50	Claims and Debts	52FRJO2509	416221
Hungary	France	02 May 60	Air Transport	60FRRT63	415222
Hungary	France	14 May 65	Claims and Debts	65FRRT68	415223
Hungary	France	15 Feb 66	General Trade	66FRMD2602	417224
Hungary	France	28 Jul 66	Consul/Citizenship	67FRJO2210	416225
Hungary	France	28 Jul 66	Culture	67FRJO204	416227
Hungary	France	28 Jul 66	Scientific Project	67FRJO201	416226
Hungary	France	08 Oct 66	Land Transport	67FRJO3003	416228
Hungary	France	19 Mar 68	Admin Cooperation	0UNTS0	109532
Hungary	Germany, East	19 Oct 49	General Economic	1EGDA426	419431
Hungary	Germany, East	24 Jun 50	General Trade	1EGDA428	419434
Hungary	Germany, East	24 Jun 50	Scientific Project	4EGDA378	419432
Hungary	Germany, East	24 Jun 50	Finance	4EGDA380	419433
Hungary	Germany, East	24 Jun 50	Culture	4EGDA382	419435
Hungary	Germany, East	03 Mar 51	Mass Media	4EGDA384	419436
Hungary	Germany, East	01 Aug 51	Finance	1EGDA438	419437
Hungary	Germany, East	07 Mar 52	General Trade	1EGDA439	419438
Hungary	Germany, East	25 Mar 52	Postal Service	4EGDA390	419440
Hungary	Germany, East	25 Mar 52	Postal Service	4EGDA387	419439
Hungary	Germany, East	26 Mar 52	Telecommunications	4EGDA394	419441
Hungary	Germany, East	17 Oct 53	Consul/Citizenship	1EGDA446	419442
Hungary	Germany, East	23 Oct 54	General Economic	2EGDA448	419443
Hungary	Germany, East	10 Sep 55	Air Transport	407UNTS132	105863
Hungary	Germany, East	23 Sep 55	Mass Media	4EGDA405	419444
Hungary	Germany, East	10 Nov 55	Other Military	3EGDA527	419445
Hungary	Germany, East	01 Dec 55	Mass Media	4EGDA410	419446
Hungary	Germany, East	12 Dec 55	General Economic	3EGDA528	419447
Hungary	Germany, East	30 Jan 56	General Economic	3EGDA530	419448
Hungary	Germany, East	06 Jul 56	Health/Educ/Welfare	5EGDA582	419449
Hungary	Germany, East	05 Oct 56	Finance	5EGDA583	419450
Hungary	Germany, East	29 Jun 57	Patents/Copyrights	5EGDA792	419451
Hungary	Germany, East	03 Jul 57	Consul/Citizenship	407UNTS186	105865
Hungary	Germany, East	25 Oct 57	Sanitation	408UNTS156	105869
Hungary	Germany, East	30 Oct 57	Admin Cooperation	408UNTS4	105867
Hungary	Germany, East	13 Nov 57	Sanitation	407UNTS216	105866
Hungary	Germany, East	14 Jun 58	Sanitation	407UNTS78	105861
Hungary	Germany, East	14 Oct 58	General Trade	6EGDA422	419452
Hungary	Germany, East	14 Oct 58	General Economic	6EGDA422	419453
Hungary	Germany, East	19 Dec 59	Health/Educ/Welfare	7EGDA490	419454
Hungary	Germany, East	19 Dec 59	Health/Educ/Welfare	409UNTS4	105874
Hungary	Germany, East	12 Jan 60	Patents/Copyrights	409UNTS22	105875
Hungary	Germany, East	30 Jan 60	Health/Educ/Welfare	408UNTS230	105873
Hungary	Germany, East	08 Apr 60	General Trade	8EGDA478	419455
Hungary	Germany, East	27 Apr 60	Specif Goods/Equip	8EGDA479	419456
Hungary	Germany, East	09 Jul 60	Mass Media	8EGDA480	419457
Hungary	Germany, East	26 Apr 61	General Economic	9EGDA402	419458
Hungary	Germany, East	11 May 62	Education	10EGDA497	419459
Hungary	Germany, East	05 Sep 63	Non-ILO Labor	11EGDA648	419460
Hungary	Germany, East	18 Sep 63	Visas	11EGDA619	419461
Hungary	Germany, East	18 Jan 65	General Economic	51EGDZ328	420462
Hungary	Germany, East	15 Dec 65	General Trade	52EGDZ349	420463
Hungary	Germany, East	19 Feb 66	Scientific Project	51EGDZ354	420464
Hungary	Germany, East	11 Mar 66	Specific Property	51EGDZ355	420465
Hungary	Germany, East	01 Aug 66	Land Transport	49EGDZ365	420466
Hungary	Germany, East	03 Oct 66	Mass Media	45EGDZ369	420467
Hungary	Germany, East	18 May 67	General Amity	617UNTS3	108905
Hungary	Germany, East	30 May 67	Admin Cooperation	38EGDZ384	420468
Hungary	Germany, East	24 Jun 67	Admin Cooperation	42EGDZ386	420469
Hungary	Germany, East	07 Jul 67	Health/Educ/Welfare	48EGDZ387	420470

PARTY ONE	PARTY TWO	DATE	TOPIC	CITATION	NUMBER
Hungary	Germany, West	27 Jul 57	Commodity Trade	57WBGA164	424704
Hungary	Germany, West	10 Nov 63	General Economic	64WBGA14	424705
Hungary	Germany, West	27 Oct 70	General Economic	70WBGA218	424706
Hungary	Ghana	27 Apr 61	Culture	439UNTS17	106322
Hungary	Greece	05 Jun 54	Finance	299UNTS295	104321
Hungary	Greece	05 Jun 54	General Trade	299UNTS285	104320
Hungary	Greece	27 Apr 63	Finance	550UNTS197	108016
Hungary	Greece	27 Apr 63	Air Transport	534UNTS3	107750
Hungary	Guinea	12 Jan 60	Culture	519UNTS131	107505
Hungary	India	30 Mar 62	Culture	519UNTS119	107504
Hungary	Indonesia	23 Aug 61	General Amity	519UNTS163	107507
Hungary	Iran	10 May 65	General Economic	0IRTB37	433054
Hungary	Iran	10 Apr 68	General Economic	0IRTB37	433055
Hungary	Iran	24 May 68	Culture	0IRTB37	433051
Hungary	Iran	21 May 69	General Trade	0IRTB7	433052
Hungary	Iran	21 May 69	Finance	0IRTB7	433053
Hungary	Iraq	11 Apr 59	Culture	439UNTS25	106323
Hungary	Iraq	11 Oct 61	Gen Communications	577UNTS231	108380
Hungary	Italy	28 Mar 50	Customs	52ITGU68	435415
Hungary	Italy	17 Dec 57	Finance	58ITGU19	435416
Hungary	Italy	21 Sep 61	General Economic	66ITDI247	436417
Hungary	Korea, North	29 Mar 63	Sanitation	577UNTS219	108379
Hungary	Mongolia	10 Jul 63	Consul/Citizenship	519UNTS173	107508
Hungary	Mongolia	02 Oct 65	General Amity	587UNTS35	108508
Hungary	Mongolia	22 Nov 68	Admin Cooperation	0UNTS0	109646
Hungary	Multilateral	27 Mar 41	Military Mission	67UNTS231	200222
Hungary	Multilateral	02 Aug 44	Scientific Project	67UNTS221	200221
Hungary	Multilateral	20 Jan 45	Peace/Disarmament	140UNTS397	200471
Hungary	Multilateral	22 Jul 46	IGO Establishment	9UNTS3	100125
Hungary	Multilateral	22 Jul 46	IGO Establishment	14UNTS185	100221
Hungary	Multilateral	11 Dec 46	Sanitation	12UNTS179	100186
Hungary	Multilateral	08 Feb 47	Patents/Copyrights	14UNTS287	100222
Hungary	Multilateral	10 Feb 47	Peace/Disarmament	41UNTS135	100644
Hungary	Multilateral	02 Oct 47	Telecommunications	193UNTS188	102616
Hungary	Multilateral	11 Oct 47	IGO Establishment	77UNTS143	100998
Hungary	Multilateral	12 Nov 47	Admin Cooperation	53UNTS49	100772
Hungary	Multilateral	12 Nov 47	Admin Cooperation	46UNTS201	100710
Hungary	Multilateral	12 Nov 47	Admin Cooperation	53UNTS39	100771
Hungary	Multilateral	12 Nov 47	Admin Cooperation	46UNTS169	100709
Hungary	Multilateral	10 Jun 48	Humanitarian	164UNTS113	102163
Hungary	Multilateral	26 Jun 48	Culture	331UNTS217	104757
Hungary	Multilateral	24 Jul 48	Sanitation	66UNTS25	100847
Hungary	Multilateral	18 Aug 48	Water Transport	33UNTS181	100518
Hungary	Multilateral	09 Dec 48	Humanitarian	78UNTS277	101021
Hungary	Multilateral	12 Aug 49	Humanitarian	75UNTS31	100970
Hungary	Multilateral	12 Aug 49	Humanitarian	75UNTS287	100973
Hungary	Multilateral	12 Aug 49	Humanitarian	75UNTS85	100971
Hungary	Multilateral	12 Aug 49	General Military	75UNTS135	100972
Hungary	Multilateral	02 Sep 49	IGO Status/Immunit	250UNTS12	103515
Hungary	Multilateral	16 Sep 50	General Transport	92UNTS91	101264
Hungary	Multilateral	07 Dec 50	Admin Cooperation	212UNTS17	102861
Hungary	Multilateral	06 Dec 51	Admin Cooperation	150UNTS67	101963
Hungary	Multilateral	11 Jul 52	Postal Service	171UNTS143	102226
Hungary	Multilateral	11 Jul 52	Postal Service	171UNTS191	102227
Hungary	Multilateral	11 Jul 52	Postal Service	170UNTS269	102223
Hungary	Multilateral	11 Jul 52	IGO Establishment	169UNTS3	102220
Hungary	Multilateral	11 Jul 52	Postal Service	171UNTS89	102225
Hungary	Multilateral	11 Jul 52	Postal Service	170UNTS3	102221
Hungary	Multilateral	11 Jul 52	Postal Service	170UNTS63	102222
Hungary	Multilateral	07 Nov 52	General Trade	221UNTS255	103010
Hungary	Multilateral	31 Mar 53	Privil/Immunities	193UNTS136	102613
Hungary	Multilateral	01 Oct 53	Commodity Trade	258UNTS153	103677
Hungary	Multilateral	07 Dec 53	Admin Cooperation	182UNTS51	102422
Hungary	Multilateral	14 May 54	Culture	249UNTS215	103511
Hungary	Multilateral	14 May 55	General Amity	219UNTS3	102962

PARTY ONE	PARTY TWO	DATE	TOPIC	CITATION	NUMBER
Hungary	Multilateral	28 Sep 55	Air Transport	478UNTS371	106943
Hungary	Multilateral	12 Oct 55	IGO Establishment	560UNTS3	108165
Hungary	Multilateral	26 Mar 56	IGO Establishment	259UNTS125	103686
Hungary	Multilateral	18 May 56	Customs	338UNTS103	104834
Hungary	Multilateral	18 May 56	Customs	319UNTS21	104630
Hungary	Multilateral	18 May 56	Customs	327UNTS123	104721
Hungary	Multilateral	20 Jun 56	Admin Cooperation	268UNTS3	103850
Hungary	Multilateral	09 Jul 56	Non-ILO Labor	314UNTS3	104539
Hungary	Multilateral	07 Sep 56	Humanitarian	266UNTS3	103822
Hungary	Multilateral	26 Oct 56	IGO Establishment	276UNTS3	103988
Hungary	Multilateral	20 Feb 57	Consul/Citizenship	309UNTS65	104468
Hungary	Multilateral	15 Jun 57	Patents/Copyrights	583UNTS3	108470
Hungary	Multilateral	15 Jun 57	General Trade	550UNTS45	108008
Hungary	Multilateral	03 Oct 57	Postal Service	365UNTS3	105213
Hungary	Multilateral	03 Oct 57	Postal Service	364UNTS3	105211
Hungary	Multilateral	03 Oct 57	Postal Service	365UNTS207	105214
Hungary	Multilateral	03 Oct 57	Postal Service	366UNTS255	105219
Hungary	Multilateral	03 Oct 57	Postal Service	364UNTS331	105212
Hungary	Multilateral	03 Oct 57	Postal Service	366UNTS141	105217
Hungary	Multilateral	03 Oct 57	Postal Service	366UNTS87	105216
Hungary	Multilateral	13 Dec 57	Land Transport	372UNTS159	105296
Hungary	Multilateral	29 Jan 58	Specific Resources	339UNTS23	104845
Hungary	Multilateral	20 Mar 58	Admin Cooperation	335UNTS211	104789
Hungary	Multilateral	15 Apr 58	Health/Educ/Welfare	539UNTS27	107822
Hungary	Multilateral	29 Apr 58	Water Transport	450UNTS11	106465
Hungary	Multilateral	29 Apr 58	Territory Boundary	516UNTS205	107477
Hungary	Multilateral	01 Dec 58	Commodity Trade	385UNTS137	105534
Hungary	Multilateral	03 Dec 58	Admin Cooperation	398UNTS9	105715
Hungary	Multilateral	03 Dec 58	Admin Cooperation	416UNTS51	105995
Hungary	Multilateral	15 Jan 59	Customs	348UNTS13	104996
Hungary	Multilateral	14 Dec 59	Land Transport	422UNTS75	106069
Hungary	Multilateral	14 Dec 59	Sanitation	422UNTS57	106068
Hungary	Multilateral	14 Dec 59	Sanitation	422UNTS33	106067
Hungary	Multilateral	14 Dec 59	IGO Status/Immunit	368UNTS237	105244
Hungary	Multilateral	14 Dec 59	IGO Establishment	368UNTS253	105245
Hungary	Multilateral	17 Jun 60	Humanitarian	536UNTS27	107794
Hungary	Multilateral	09 Dec 60	Customs	429UNTS211	106200
Hungary	Multilateral	14 Dec 60	Education	429UNTS93	106193
Hungary	Multilateral	30 Mar 61	Sanitation	520UNTS151	107515
Hungary	Multilateral	18 Apr 61	Consul/Citizenship	500UNTS95	107310
Hungary	Multilateral	21 Apr 61	IGO Establishment	484UNTS349	107041
Hungary	Multilateral	08 Jun 61	Customs	473UNTS187	106863
Hungary	Multilateral	08 Jun 61	Customs	473UNTS153	106862
Hungary	Multilateral	06 Dec 61	Customs	473UNTS219	106864
Hungary	Multilateral	15 Dec 61	Admin Cooperation	424UNTS43	106098
Hungary	Multilateral	25 Jul 62	Specific Property	506UNTS177	107387
Hungary	Multilateral	08 Dec 62	Finance	510UNTS235	107418
Hungary	Multilateral	05 Aug 63	Sanitation	480UNTS43	106964
Hungary	Multilateral	23 Oct 63	IGO Establishment	506UNTS197	107388
Hungary	Multilateral	10 Jul 64	Postal Service	613UNTS3	108851
Hungary	Multilateral	10 Jul 64	Postal Service	613UNTS3	108850
Hungary	Multilateral	10 Jul 64	Postal Service	612UNTS233	108848
Hungary	Multilateral	10 Jul 64	Postal Service	612UNTS3	108847
Hungary	Multilateral	10 Jul 64	Postal Service	613UNTS193	108852
Hungary	Multilateral	10 Jul 64	Postal Service	611UNTS387	108846
Hungary	Multilateral	10 Jul 64	Postal Service	611UNTS105	108845
Hungary	Multilateral	10 Jul 64	Postal Service	611UNTS7	108844
Hungary	Multilateral	15 Jul 64	IGO Establishment	610UNTS143	108840
Hungary	Multilateral	09 Mar 65	Water Transport	591UNTS265	108564
Hungary	Multilateral	23 Jun 65	General IGO	614UNTS239	108873
Hungary	Multilateral	08 Jul 65	General Trade	597UNTS3	108641
Hungary	Multilateral	18 Nov 65	Customs	609UNTS115	108830
Hungary	Multilateral	09 Sep 66	IGO Status/Immunit	0UNTS0	109343
Hungary	Multilateral	26 Apr 67	General Trade	0UNTS0	109890
Hungary	Multilateral	01 Jul 68	Peace/Disarmament	0UNTS0	110485

PARTY ONE	PARTY TWO	DATE	TOPIC	CITATION	NUMBER
Hungary	Multilateral	24 Sep 68	Air Transport	0UNTS0	110612
Hungary	Multilateral	26 Nov 68	Humanitarian	0UNTS0	110823
Hungary	Netherlands	20 Dec 47	Finance	51NET95	447006
Hungary	Netherlands	01 Apr 55	General Trade	55NET62	447054
Hungary	Netherlands	28 May 57	Air Transport	334UNTS291	104773
Hungary	Netherlands	11 Jan 64	Taxation	522UNTS243	107550
Hungary	Netherlands	02 Jul 65	Finance	564UNTS49	108220
Hungary	Netherlands	14 Feb 68	Culture	0UNTS0	110419
Hungary	Norway	27 Aug 46	General Trade	31UNTS3	100465
Hungary	Norway	22 Feb 57	Claims and Debts	3NORT712	451072
Hungary	Norway	30 Apr 59	Air Transport	3NORT769	451073
Hungary	Norway	09 May 63	Finance	3NORT883	451074
Hungary	Norway	09 Dec 66	General Trade	3NORT981	451075
Hungary	Poland	28 Aug 47	Air Transport	15UNTS145	100231
Hungary	Poland	31 Jan 48	Culture	25UNTS283	100368
Hungary	Poland	13 May 48	General Economic	25UNTS301	100369
Hungary	Poland	18 Jun 48	Culture	25UNTS319	100370
Hungary	Poland	29 Oct 49	Sanitation	260UNTS113	103706
Hungary	Poland	29 Oct 49	Sanitation	260UNTS91	103705
Hungary	Poland	25 Apr 56	Telecommunications	56PZUM140	458044
Hungary	Poland	25 Apr 56	Postal Service	56PZUM128	458043
Hungary	Poland	25 Apr 56	Gen Communications	56PZUM156	458045
Hungary	Poland	18 Jun 56	Telecommunications	56PZUM185	458046
Hungary	Poland	08 May 58	Sanitation	408UNTS212	105872
Hungary	Poland	25 Oct 58	General Economic	58PZUM87	458061
Hungary	Poland	14 Feb 59	Non-ILO Labor	431UNTS157	106215
Hungary	Poland	06 Mar 59	Admin Cooperation	432UNTS3	106216
Hungary	Poland	20 May 59	Consul/Citizenship	432UNTS115	106217
Hungary	Poland	05 Jul 61	Consul/Citizenship	437UNTS3	106296
Hungary	Poland	18 Apr 64	Visas	64PZUM20	458111
Hungary	Poland	18 Jul 65	Land Transport	577UNTS161	108376
Hungary	Poland	16 Sep 67	Admin Cooperation	68PZUM32	458148
Hungary	Poland	16 May 68	General Amity	68PDZU257	457157
Hungary	Poland	16 May 68	General Amity	0UNTS0	109292
Hungary	Poland	31 Oct 68	Health/Educ/Welfare	70PDZU91	457161
Hungary	Romania	24 Jan 48	General Amity	477UNTS155	106920
Hungary	Romania	14 Dec 53	Sanitation	342UNTS151	104906
Hungary	Romania	03 Feb 56	Air Transport	362UNTS233	105190
Hungary	Romania	17 Dec 57	Sanitation	477UNTS303	106926
Hungary	Romania	07 Oct 58	Admin Cooperation	416UNTS199	106004
Hungary	Romania	18 Mar 59	Consul/Citizenship	417UNTS3	106005
Hungary	Romania	07 Sep 61	Non-ILO Labor	519UNTS141	107506
Hungary	Romania	13 Jun 63	Territory Boundary	576UNTS275	108369
Hungary	Romania	01 Feb 68	Customs	0UNTS0	109704
Hungary	South Africa	16 Nov 48	Admin Cooperation	225UNTS65	103089
Hungary	Sweden	26 Jul 46	Finance	46SOFM250	461030
Hungary	Sweden	26 Jul 46	General Trade	46SOFM247	461029
Hungary	Sweden	28 Nov 47	General Trade	47SOFM575	461058
Hungary	Sweden	19 Jan 49	General Trade	49SOFM155	461080
Hungary	Sweden	30 Nov 49	General Trade	49SOFM561	461093
Hungary	Sweden	31 Mar 51	Claims and Debts	51SOFM145	461139
Hungary	Sweden	17 Nov 53	General Economic	53SOFM1049	461190
Hungary	Sweden	02 Aug 57	Air Transport	334UNTS307	104774
Hungary	Switzerland	02 Feb 48	Taxation	49SWRO135	462053
Hungary	Switzerland	27 Jun 50	General Economic	50SWRO612	462139
Hungary	Switzerland	19 Jul 50	Claims and Debts	50SWRO736	462169
Hungary	Syria	18 Oct 62	Air Transport	491UNTS209	107178
Hungary	Turkey	12 May 49	General Economic	49TURG2812	466068
Hungary	UK Great Britain	12 Aug 46	Finance	89UNTS219	101220
Hungary	UK Great Britain	12 Mar 48	Admin Cooperation	104UNTS35	101434
Hungary	UK Great Britain	19 Aug 54	Finance	199UNTS149	102681
Hungary	UK Great Britain	27 Jun 56	Claims and Debts	249UNTS19	103499
Hungary	UK Great Britain	25 Oct 60	Air Transport	419UNTS309	106034
Hungary	UK Great Britain	09 Aug 67	Scientific Project	632UNTS39	109006
Hungary	UK Great Britain	12 Aug 69	Commodity Trade	0UNTS0	110239

PARTY ONE	PARTY TWO	DATE	TOPIC	CITATION	NUMBER
Hungary	UN Special Fund	28 Apr 67	General Aid	595UNTS171	108619
Hungary	UNICEF (Children)	28 Aug 47	IGO Operations	68UNTS226	200234
Hungary	United Nations	04 Mar 66	IGO Operations	559UNTS3	108151
Hungary	USA (United States)	09 Aug 46	Other Military	148UNTS313	101941
Hungary	USA (United States)	09 Mar 48	Admin Cooperation	183UNTS3	102426
Hungary	USA (United States)	19 Sep 69	Consul/Citizenship	0UNTS0	110447
Hungary	USSR (Soviet Union)	15 Jun 45	Reparations	0SUST180	468172
Hungary	USSR (Soviet Union)	25 Sep 45	Consul/Citizenship	0SUST98	468173
Hungary	USSR (Soviet Union)	29 Mar 46	Specific Property	0SUST208	468174
Hungary	USSR (Soviet Union)	29 Mar 46	Specific Property	0SUST208	468175
Hungary	USSR (Soviet Union)	08 Apr 46	Specific Property	0SUST209	468176
Hungary	USSR (Soviet Union)	08 Apr 46	Specific Property	0SUST209	468177
Hungary	USSR (Soviet Union)	10 Feb 47	Peace/Disarmament	0SUST227	468178
Hungary	USSR (Soviet Union)	15 Jul 47	General Economic	0SUST234	468179
Hungary	USSR (Soviet Union)	15 Jul 47	General Economic	216UNTS247	102940
Hungary	USSR (Soviet Union)	22 Sep 47	Gen Communications	0SUST236	468180
Hungary	USSR (Soviet Union)	01 Oct 47	Postal Service	0SUST237	468181
Hungary	USSR (Soviet Union)	09 Dec 47	General Economic	0SUST239	468182
Hungary	USSR (Soviet Union)	18 Feb 48	General Military	48UNTS163	100743
Hungary	USSR (Soviet Union)	01 Mar 48	Consul/Citizenship	0SUST438	468184
Hungary	USSR (Soviet Union)	07 Jun 48	Reparations	0SUST249	468185
Hungary	USSR (Soviet Union)	02 Oct 48	General Economic	0SUST253	468186
Hungary	USSR (Soviet Union)	26 Jul 49	Scientific Project	0SUST261	468187
Hungary	USSR (Soviet Union)	30 Jul 49	Territory Boundary	0SUST261	468188
Hungary	USSR (Soviet Union)	24 Feb 50	Admin Cooperation	0SUST271	468189
Hungary	USSR (Soviet Union)	24 Feb 50	Admin Cooperation	0SUST271	468190
Hungary	USSR (Soviet Union)	12 Apr 50	Mass Media	0SUST273	468191
Hungary	USSR (Soviet Union)	09 Jun 50	Specific Resources	0SUST274	468192
Hungary	USSR (Soviet Union)	13 Jul 50	Sanitation	221UNTS35	103001
Hungary	USSR (Soviet Union)	20 Jan 52	General Aid	0SUST284	468194
Hungary	USSR (Soviet Union)	23 Jan 52	General Trade	0SUST284	468193
Hungary	USSR (Soviet Union)	19 May 52	Education	0SUST284	468195
Hungary	USSR (Soviet Union)	30 Sep 52	Specific Property	0SUST291	468196
Hungary	USSR (Soviet Union)	06 Nov 54	Finance	0SUST319	468197
Hungary	USSR (Soviet Union)	27 May 55	Status of Forces	407UNTS156	105864
Hungary	USSR (Soviet Union)	13 Jun 55	Atomic Energy	0SUST330	468198
Hungary	USSR (Soviet Union)	14 Jun 56	Mass Media	0SUST385	468199
Hungary	USSR (Soviet Union)	28 Jun 56	Health/Educ/Welfare	259UNTS405	103700
Hungary	USSR (Soviet Union)	05 Oct 56	Loans and Credits	0SUST368	468200
Hungary	USSR (Soviet Union)	27 May 57	Status of Forces	0SUST383	468201
Hungary	USSR (Soviet Union)	15 Jun 57	Mass Media	16SUGG121	469942
Hungary	USSR (Soviet Union)	24 Aug 57	Consul/Citizenship	318UNTS35	104608
Hungary	USSR (Soviet Union)	24 Aug 57	Consul/Citizenship	318UNTS3	104607
Hungary	USSR (Soviet Union)	18 Dec 57	General Aid	0SUST394	468204
Hungary	USSR (Soviet Union)	13 Jan 58	General Trade	7SUGG101	469484
Hungary	USSR (Soviet Union)	24 Apr 58	Status of Forces	408UNTS118	105868
Hungary	USSR (Soviet Union)	11 May 58	Atomic Energy	7SUGG112	469509
Hungary	USSR (Soviet Union)	15 Jul 58	Admin Cooperation	322UNTS3	104656
Hungary	USSR (Soviet Union)	21 Jul 58	Customs	16SUGG125	469960
Hungary	USSR (Soviet Union)	21 Jul 58	Customs	408UNTS194	105871
Hungary	USSR (Soviet Union)	05 Nov 58	General Aid	7SUGG124	469538
Hungary	USSR (Soviet Union)	05 Nov 58	Tech Assistance	7SUGG125	469539
Hungary	USSR (Soviet Union)	28 Jan 59	Scientific Project	8SUGG135	469554
Hungary	USSR (Soviet Union)	17 Apr 59	Sanitation	16SUGG126	469964
Hungary	USSR (Soviet Union)	17 Apr 59	Sanitation	439UNTS41	106324
Hungary	USSR (Soviet Union)	07 Aug 59	General Trade	8SUGG151	469596
Hungary	USSR (Soviet Union)	07 Aug 59	Tech Assistance	8SUGG151	469597
Hungary	USSR (Soviet Union)	06 May 60	General Trade	9SUGG135	469655
Hungary	USSR (Soviet Union)	16 Jun 60	Mass Media	16SUGG128	469977
Hungary	USSR (Soviet Union)	04 Nov 60	Education	16SUGG129	469985
Hungary	USSR (Soviet Union)	20 Jun 61	General Aid	10SUGG136	469785
Hungary	USSR (Soviet Union)	01 Aug 61	General Trade	10SUGG140	469792
Hungary	USSR (Soviet Union)	03 Oct 61	Admin Cooperation	10SUGG142	469796
Hungary	USSR (Soviet Union)	15 Nov 62	General Trade	11SUGG157	469873
Hungary	USSR (Soviet Union)	17 Nov 62	General Trade	11SUGG157	469874

PARTY ONE	PARTY TWO	DATE	TOPIC	CITATION	NUMBER
Hungary	USSR (Soviet Union)	20 Dec 62	Non-ILO Labor	577UNTS245	108381
Hungary	USSR (Soviet Union)	20 Dec 62	Non-ILO Labor	11SUGG160	469878
Hungary	USSR (Soviet Union)	21 Jan 63	Consul/Citizenship	577UNTS201	108378
Hungary	USSR (Soviet Union)	07 Sep 67	General Amity	632UNTS89	109011
Hungary	USSR (Soviet Union)	16 Nov 68	Culture	0UNTS0	110283
Hungary	Yemen	30 May 64	General Amity	577UNTS39	108371
Hungary	Yugoslavia	13 Aug 44	Dispute Settlement	113UNTS233	101553
Hungary	Yugoslavia	11 May 46	Reparations	129UNTS3	101725
Hungary	Yugoslavia	23 Dec 46	Finance	113UNTS125	101549
Hungary	Yugoslavia	01 Jan 47	General Trade	113UNTS63	101548
Hungary	Yugoslavia	25 Jan 47	Reparations	130UNTS3	101726
Hungary	Yugoslavia	11 May 47	Direct Aid	130UNTS171	101730
Hungary	Yugoslavia	24 Jul 47	General Trade	114UNTS3	101554
Hungary	Yugoslavia	15 Oct 47	Culture	33UNTS73	100515
Hungary	Yugoslavia	18 Mar 48	Finance	113UNTS201	101551
Hungary	Yugoslavia	18 Mar 48	Finance	113UNTS219	101552
Hungary	Yugoslavia	18 Mar 48	General Trade	113UNTS141	101550
Hungary	Yugoslavia	17 Apr 48	Reparations	130UNTS121	101729
Hungary	Yugoslavia	17 Apr 48	Reparations	130UNTS101	101727
Hungary	Yugoslavia	17 Apr 48	Reparations	130UNTS111	101728
Hungary	Yugoslavia	25 May 57	Sanitation	477UNTS219	106924
Hungary	Yugoslavia	07 Oct 57	Non-ILO Labor	439UNTS61	106325
Hungary	Yugoslavia	20 Nov 57	Sanitation	477UNTS267	106925
Hungary	Yugoslavia	06 Dec 57	Sanitation	519UNTS215	107509
Hungary	Yugoslavia	07 May 60	Admin Cooperation	519UNTS237	107510
Hungary	Yugoslavia	09 Feb 62	Land Transport	577UNTS3	108370
Hungary	Yugoslavia	15 Oct 63	Health/Educ/Welfare	577UNTS49	108372
Hungary	Yugoslavia	08 Apr 65	Territory Boundary	587UNTS169	108511
Hungary	Yugoslavia	25 May 65	Customs	576UNTS145	108367
Hungary	Yugoslavia	09 Aug 65	Visas	577UNTS103	108375
Hungary	Yugoslavia	23 Nov 65	Visas	577UNTS89	108374
Hungary	Yugoslavia	26 Sep 66	Sanitation	601UNTS21	108685
IAEA (Atom Energy)	Afghanistan	24 Sep 65	Atomic Energy	556UNTS101	108121
IAEA (Atom Energy)	Argentina	02 Dec 64	Atomic Energy	525UNTS29	107582
IAEA (Atom Energy)	Argentina	03 Jun 69	Atomic Energy	0UNTS0	109947
IAEA (Atom Energy)	Austria	11 Dec 57	Atomic Energy	339UNTS110	104849
IAEA (Atom Energy)	Austria	21 Jun 63	Atomic Energy	490UNTS351	107164
IAEA (Atom Energy)	Burma	11 Oct 67	Atomic Energy	630UNTS49	108964
IAEA (Atom Energy)	Canada	24 Mar 59	Atomic Energy	339UNTS315	104851
IAEA (Atom Energy)	Chile	19 Dec 69	Atomic Energy	0UNTS0	110521
IAEA (Atom Energy)	Congo (Zaire)	27 Jun 62	Direct Aid	463UNTS31	106691
IAEA (Atom Energy)	FAO (Food Agri)	01 Oct 58	IGO Operations	361UNTS211	200571
IAEA (Atom Energy)	Finland	30 Dec 60	Atomic Energy	395UNTS257	105690
IAEA (Atom Energy)	Finland	02 Jul 63	Atomic Energy	490UNTS403	107167
IAEA (Atom Energy)	Finland	30 Jul 63	Atomic Energy	490UNTS413	107168
IAEA (Atom Energy)	Finland	27 Jan 64	Scientific Project	501UNTS213	107319
IAEA (Atom Energy)	ICAO (Civil Aviat)	01 Oct 59	IGO Operations	361UNTS193	200570
IAEA (Atom Energy)	ILO (Labor Org)	08 May 59	IGO Operations	328UNTS273	200555
IAEA (Atom Energy)	IMCO (Maritime Org)	13 Apr 61	IGO Operations	425UNTS281	200595
IAEA (Atom Energy)	India	09 Dec 66	Atomic Energy	603UNTS35	108722
IAEA (Atom Energy)	Indonesia	19 Dec 69	Atomic Energy	0UNTS0	110523
IAEA (Atom Energy)	Inter-Am Nuc Energ	22 Dec 60	IGO Operations	396UNTS285	200586
IAEA (Atom Energy)	Iran	10 May 67	Atomic Energy	0IRTB86	433141
IAEA (Atom Energy)	Iran	10 May 67	IGO Operations	614UNTS93	108865
IAEA (Atom Energy)	Iran	07 Jun 67	Atomic Energy	0IRTB87	433143
IAEA (Atom Energy)	Iran	04 Mar 69	Atomic Energy	0IRTB87	433142
IAEA (Atom Energy)	Iraq	21 Sep 67	Atomic Energy	630UNTS41	108963
IAEA (Atom Energy)	Israel	31 Aug 67	Atomic Energy	0UNTS0	109310
IAEA (Atom Energy)	Italy	11 Oct 63	IGO Establishment	639UNTS25	109142
IAEA (Atom Energy)	Japan	24 Mar 59	Atomic Energy	339UNTS327	104852
IAEA (Atom Energy)	Japan	26 Sep 67	Atomic Energy	637UNTS0	109113
IAEA (Atom Energy)	Mexico	18 Dec 63	Atomic Energy	490UNTS361	107165
IAEA (Atom Energy)	Mexico	20 Jun 66	Atomic Energy	573UNTS25	108321
IAEA (Atom Energy)	Mexico	18 Aug 67	IGO Operations	614UNTS123	108867
IAEA (Atom Energy)	Mexico	23 Aug 67	IGO Operations	614UNTS133	108868

PARTY ONE	PARTY TWO	DATE	TOPIC	CITATION	NUMBER
IAEA (Atom Energy)	Mexico	06 Sep 68	Atomic Energy	0UNTS0	109318
IAEA (Atom Energy)	Morocco	24 Sep 65	Atomic Energy	556UNTS109	108122
IAEA (Atom Energy)	Multilateral	27 Oct 54	Tech Assistance	201UNTS95	102712
IAEA (Atom Energy)	Multilateral	10 May 56	Tech Assistance	243UNTS103	103449
IAEA (Atom Energy)	Multilateral	15 Mar 58	Tech Assistance	292UNTS273	104276
IAEA (Atom Energy)	Multilateral	09 Oct 59	Tech Assistance	376UNTS382	105391
IAEA (Atom Energy)	Multilateral	03 Dec 59	Tech Assistance	348UNTS246	105003
IAEA (Atom Energy)	Multilateral	12 Apr 60	Tech Assistance	359UNTS323	105150
IAEA (Atom Energy)	Multilateral	04 Jun 60	Tech Assistance	360UNTS208	105159
IAEA (Atom Energy)	Multilateral	19 Jun 60	IGO Operations	537UNTS214	107803
IAEA (Atom Energy)	Multilateral	08 Jul 60	Tech Assistance	366UNTS310	105220
IAEA (Atom Energy)	Multilateral	30 Dec 60	Atomic Energy	395UNTS241	105689
IAEA (Atom Energy)	Multilateral	28 Jan 61	Tech Assistance	387UNTS202	105563
IAEA (Atom Energy)	Multilateral	08 Mar 61	Scientific Project	396UNTS255	200584
IAEA (Atom Energy)	Multilateral	10 Apr 61	Atomic Energy	402UNTS281	105791
IAEA (Atom Energy)	Multilateral	20 Sep 61	Tech Assistance	407UNTS52	105859
IAEA (Atom Energy)	Multilateral	04 Oct 61	Scientific Project	412UNTS210	105934
IAEA (Atom Energy)	Multilateral	16 Oct 61	Tech Assistance	410UNTS242	105908
IAEA (Atom Energy)	Multilateral	07 Nov 61	Tech Assistance	412UNTS258	105937
IAEA (Atom Energy)	Multilateral	27 Dec 61	Tech Assistance	425UNTS83	106120
IAEA (Atom Energy)	Multilateral	17 Jan 62	Tech Assistance	419UNTS294	106033
IAEA (Atom Energy)	Multilateral	20 Jan 62	Tech Assistance	429UNTS230	200596
IAEA (Atom Energy)	Multilateral	13 Feb 62	Tech Assistance	422UNTS288	200594
IAEA (Atom Energy)	Multilateral	21 Feb 62	Tech Assistance	423UNTS151	106091
IAEA (Atom Energy)	Multilateral	01 Mar 62	Tech Assistance	423UNTS122	106089
IAEA (Atom Energy)	Multilateral	05 Mar 62	Scientific Project	425UNTS3	106114
IAEA (Atom Energy)	Multilateral	10 Apr 62	Tech Assistance	429UNTS78	106192
IAEA (Atom Energy)	Multilateral	18 Apr 62	Tech Assistance	463UNTS44	106692
IAEA (Atom Energy)	Multilateral	17 May 62	Tech Assistance	429UNTS46	106189
IAEA (Atom Energy)	Multilateral	27 Jun 62	Atomic Energy	463UNTS11	106689
IAEA (Atom Energy)	Multilateral	27 Jun 62	Atomic Energy	463UNTS3	106688
IAEA (Atom Energy)	Multilateral	27 Jun 62	Atomic Energy	463UNTS17	106690
IAEA (Atom Energy)	Multilateral	12 Aug 62	Tech Assistance	443UNTS266	106365
IAEA (Atom Energy)	Multilateral	29 Aug 62	Tech Assistance	443UNTS280	106366
IAEA (Atom Energy)	Multilateral	11 Sep 62	Tech Assistance	455UNTS402	106553
IAEA (Atom Energy)	Multilateral	14 Sep 62	Visas	443UNTS73	106360
IAEA (Atom Energy)	Multilateral	14 Sep 62	IGO Status/Immunit	494UNTS219	107236
IAEA (Atom Energy)	Multilateral	15 Nov 62	Tech Assistance	448UNTS50	106424
IAEA (Atom Energy)	Multilateral	06 Dec 62	Tech Assistance	450UNTS240	106471
IAEA (Atom Energy)	Multilateral	12 Dec 62	Tech Assistance	457UNTS72	106578
IAEA (Atom Energy)	Multilateral	21 Jan 63	Tech Assistance	453UNTS20	106517
IAEA (Atom Energy)	Multilateral	05 Feb 63	Tech Assistance	453UNTS36	106518
IAEA (Atom Energy)	Multilateral	14 Feb 63	Tech Assistance	453UNTS168	106524
IAEA (Atom Energy)	Multilateral	06 Mar 63	Tech Assistance	455UNTS386	106552
IAEA (Atom Energy)	Multilateral	18 Apr 63	Tech Assistance	463UNTS121	106697
IAEA (Atom Energy)	Multilateral	06 May 63	Tech Assistance	463UNTS78	106694
IAEA (Atom Energy)	Multilateral	09 May 63	Tech Assistance	463UNTS159	106700
IAEA (Atom Energy)	Multilateral	22 May 63	Tech Assistance	483UNTS72	107007
IAEA (Atom Energy)	Multilateral	24 May 63	Tech Assistance	466UNTS346	106754
IAEA (Atom Energy)	Multilateral	23 Jul 63	Tech Assistance	471UNTS158	106831
IAEA (Atom Energy)	Multilateral	31 Jul 63	Tech Assistance	472UNTS220	106842
IAEA (Atom Energy)	Multilateral	27 Aug 63	Tech Assistance	511UNTS210	107435
IAEA (Atom Energy)	Multilateral	10 Sep 63	Tech Assistance	480UNTS100	106965
IAEA (Atom Energy)	Multilateral	23 Sep 63	Atomic Energy	488UNTS99	107122
IAEA (Atom Energy)	Multilateral	17 Oct 63	Atomic Energy	525UNTS75	107585
IAEA (Atom Energy)	Multilateral	30 Oct 63	Tech Assistance	480UNTS180	106968
IAEA (Atom Energy)	Multilateral	07 Nov 63	Tech Assistance	480UNTS232	106971
IAEA (Atom Energy)	Multilateral	08 Nov 63	Tech Assistance	482UNTS286	106999
IAEA (Atom Energy)	Multilateral	18 Dec 63	Atomic Energy	490UNTS383	107166
IAEA (Atom Energy)	Multilateral	28 Jan 64	Tech Assistance	502UNTS321	107336
IAEA (Atom Energy)	Multilateral	20 Feb 64	Tech Assistance	491UNTS30	107172
IAEA (Atom Energy)	Multilateral	28 Feb 64	Atomic Energy	501UNTS245	107321
IAEA (Atom Energy)	Multilateral	08 Apr 64	Loans and Credits	501UNTS221	107320
IAEA (Atom Energy)	Multilateral	11 Jun 64	Atomic Energy	525UNTS61	107584
IAEA (Atom Energy)	Multilateral	15 Jun 64	Atomic Energy	573UNTS85	108324

PARTY ONE	PARTY TWO	DATE	TOPIC	CITATION	NUMBER
IAEA (Atom Energy)	Multilateral	23 Jun 64	Tech Assistance	506UNTS108	107383
IAEA (Atom Energy)	Multilateral	28 Jun 64	Tech Assistance	519UNTS14	107499
IAEA (Atom Energy)	Multilateral	28 Jul 64	IGO Operations	555UNTS183	108113
IAEA (Atom Energy)	Multilateral	03 Aug 64	Tech Assistance	503UNTS239	107347
IAEA (Atom Energy)	Multilateral	18 Sep 64	IGO Operations	555UNTS205	108114
IAEA (Atom Energy)	Multilateral	18 Sep 64	IGO Operations	556UNTS25	108117
IAEA (Atom Energy)	Multilateral	21 Sep 64	IGO Operations	555UNTS227	108115
IAEA (Atom Energy)	Multilateral	30 Sep 64	IGO Operations	556UNTS3	108116
IAEA (Atom Energy)	Multilateral	24 Oct 64	Tech Assistance	514UNTS220	200608
IAEA (Atom Energy)	Multilateral	11 Nov 64	Tech Assistance	515UNTS94	107456
IAEA (Atom Energy)	Multilateral	02 Dec 64	Scientific Project	572UNTS229	108317
IAEA (Atom Energy)	Multilateral	02 Dec 64	Atomic Energy	525UNTS51	107583
IAEA (Atom Energy)	Multilateral	11 Dec 64	IGO Operations	547UNTS297	107964
IAEA (Atom Energy)	Multilateral	15 Dec 64	Tech Assistance	522UNTS20	107533
IAEA (Atom Energy)	Multilateral	27 Jan 65	Tech Assistance	523UNTS102	107556
IAEA (Atom Energy)	Multilateral	02 Feb 65	Tech Assistance	523UNTS256	107560
IAEA (Atom Energy)	Multilateral	12 Feb 65	Tech Assistance	525UNTS148	107587
IAEA (Atom Energy)	Multilateral	23 Feb 65	IGO Operations	527UNTS120	107622
IAEA (Atom Energy)	Multilateral	24 Feb 65	IGO Operations	556UNTS47	108118
IAEA (Atom Energy)	Multilateral	26 Feb 65	IGO Operations	556UNTS69	108119
IAEA (Atom Energy)	Multilateral	05 Mar 65	IGO Operations	527UNTS221	107627
IAEA (Atom Energy)	Multilateral	08 Apr 65	IGO Operations	533UNTS66	107733
IAEA (Atom Energy)	Multilateral	26 Apr 65	IGO Operations	533UNTS50	107732
IAEA (Atom Energy)	Multilateral	12 May 65	IGO Operations	534UNTS390	107769
IAEA (Atom Energy)	Multilateral	14 May 65	IGO Operations	550UNTS310	108026
IAEA (Atom Energy)	Multilateral	25 May 65	IGO Operations	535UNTS374	107791
IAEA (Atom Energy)	Multilateral	02 Jun 65	Tech Assistance	551UNTS2	108030
IAEA (Atom Energy)	Multilateral	02 Jun 65	Tech Assistance	537UNTS348	200611
IAEA (Atom Energy)	Multilateral	18 Jun 65	Atomic Energy	573UNTS3	108320
IAEA (Atom Energy)	Multilateral	23 Jun 65	Atomic Energy	548UNTS241	107981
IAEA (Atom Energy)	Multilateral	05 Jul 65	General Aid	563UNTS104	108207
IAEA (Atom Energy)	Multilateral	20 Jul 65	IGO Operations	541UNTS12	107857
IAEA (Atom Energy)	Multilateral	13 Sep 65	Tech Assistance	547UNTS264	107962
IAEA (Atom Energy)	Multilateral	13 Sep 65	IGO Operations	547UNTS248	107961
IAEA (Atom Energy)	Multilateral	21 Sep 65	IGO Operations	547UNTS280	107963
IAEA (Atom Energy)	Multilateral	24 Sep 65	Atomic Energy	556UNTS141	108124
IAEA (Atom Energy)	Multilateral	07 Oct 65	Atomic Energy	556UNTS175	108125
IAEA (Atom Energy)	Multilateral	21 Oct 65	Tech Assistance	547UNTS216	107959
IAEA (Atom Energy)	Multilateral	12 Nov 65	IGO Operations	550UNTS160	108013
IAEA (Atom Energy)	Multilateral	30 Dec 65	Atomic Energy	557UNTS3	108126
IAEA (Atom Energy)	Multilateral	31 Dec 65	Recognition	552UNTS292	108060
IAEA (Atom Energy)	Multilateral	12 May 66	General Aid	563UNTS54	108204
IAEA (Atom Energy)	Multilateral	20 Jun 66	Scientific Project	572UNTS263	108318
IAEA (Atom Energy)	Multilateral	20 Jun 66	Atomic Energy	573UNTS41	108322
IAEA (Atom Energy)	Multilateral	08 Jul 66	Atomic Energy	572UNTS283	108319
IAEA (Atom Energy)	Multilateral	06 Aug 66	Tech Assistance	570UNTS178	108294
IAEA (Atom Energy)	Multilateral	22 Aug 66	Tech Assistance	571UNTS298	200624
IAEA (Atom Energy)	Multilateral	23 Sep 66	IGO Operations	573UNTS132	108327
IAEA (Atom Energy)	Multilateral	23 Sep 66	General Aid	573UNTS148	108328
IAEA (Atom Energy)	Multilateral	28 Sep 66	Specif Goods/Equip	589UNTS41	108534
IAEA (Atom Energy)	Multilateral	30 Sep 66	IGO Operations	576UNTS8	108361
IAEA (Atom Energy)	Multilateral	17 Nov 66	IGO Operations	580UNTS22	108417
IAEA (Atom Energy)	Multilateral	25 Jan 67	IGO Operations	588UNTS212	108527
IAEA (Atom Energy)	Multilateral	27 Feb 67	IGO Operations	590UNTS156	108552
IAEA (Atom Energy)	Multilateral	03 Mar 67	Tech Assistance	594UNTS96	108597
IAEA (Atom Energy)	Multilateral	13 Apr 67	IGO Operations	595UNTS60	108612
IAEA (Atom Energy)	Multilateral	19 Apr 67	Tech Assistance	595UNTS120	108617
IAEA (Atom Energy)	Multilateral	10 Jun 67	Direct Aid	602UNTS212	108714
IAEA (Atom Energy)	Multilateral	14 Jun 67	Direct Aid	603UNTS2	108719
IAEA (Atom Energy)	Multilateral	20 Jun 67	Tech Assistance	0UNTS0	109290
IAEA (Atom Energy)	Multilateral	21 Jun 67	Tech Assistance	598UNTS2	108653
IAEA (Atom Energy)	Multilateral	23 Jun 67	IGO Operations	614UNTS185	108871
IAEA (Atom Energy)	Multilateral	26 Jul 67	IGO Operations	614UNTS217	108872
IAEA (Atom Energy)	Multilateral	23 Aug 67	IGO Operations	614UNTS145	108869
IAEA (Atom Energy)	Multilateral	26 Sep 67	Atomic Energy	633UNTS73	109035

PARTY ONE	PARTY TWO	DATE	TOPIC	CITATION	NUMBER
IAEA (Atom Energy)	Multilateral	12 Oct 67	Direct Aid	607UNTS20	108793
IAEA (Atom Energy)	Multilateral	12 Oct 67	Direct Aid	607UNTS2	108792
IAEA (Atom Energy)	Multilateral	19 Oct 67	Atomic Energy	630UNTS69	108966
IAEA (Atom Energy)	Multilateral	27 Oct 67	General Aid	608UNTS37	108811
IAEA (Atom Energy)	Multilateral	05 Nov 67	Atomic Energy	630UNTS77	108967
IAEA (Atom Energy)	Multilateral	14 Nov 67	Admin Cooperation	614UNTS2	108860
IAEA (Atom Energy)	Multilateral	18 Jun 69	IGO Operations	0UNTS0	109741
IAEA (Atom Energy)	Multilateral	18 Jun 69	IGO Operations	0UNTS0	109740
IAEA (Atom Energy)	Multilateral	24 Jun 69	IGO Operations	0UNTS0	109743
IAEA (Atom Energy)	Multilateral	17 Oct 69	Atomic Energy	0UNTS0	110518
IAEA (Atom Energy)	Multilateral	27 Nov 69	Atomic Energy	0UNTS0	110519
IAEA (Atom Energy)	Multilateral	19 Dec 69	Atomic Energy	0UNTS0	110522
IAEA (Atom Energy)	Multilateral	19 Dec 69	Atomic Energy	0UNTS0	110520
IAEA (Atom Energy)	Norway	10 Apr 61	Scientific Project	402UNTS255	105790
IAEA (Atom Energy)	OAU (Afri Unity)	26 Mar 69	Atomic Energy	0UNTS0	200646
IAEA (Atom Energy)	OECD (Econ Coop)	24 Nov 60	IGO Operations	396UNTS273	200585
IAEA (Atom Energy)	Other Party Combin	21 May 69	Scientific Project	0UNTS0	200650
IAEA (Atom Energy)	Pakistan	05 Mar 62	Scientific Project	425UNTS17	106115
IAEA (Atom Energy)	Pakistan	15 Mar 66	Claims and Debts	588UNTS261	108530
IAEA (Atom Energy)	Pakistan	17 Jun 68	Atomic Energy	0UNTS0	109314
IAEA (Atom Energy)	Philippines	28 Sep 66	Atomic Energy	589UNTS25	108533
IAEA (Atom Energy)	Romania	22 Apr 66	Atomic Energy	603UNTS23	108721
IAEA (Atom Energy)	Romania	27 Jun 68	Atomic Energy	0UNTS0	109315
IAEA (Atom Energy)	Spain	23 Jun 67	IGO Operations	614UNTS169	108870
IAEA (Atom Energy)	State/IGO Group	04 Dec 64	Atomic Energy	637UNTS0	109111
IAEA (Atom Energy)	State/IGO Group	10 Mar 67	Atomic Energy	0UNTS0	109526
IAEA (Atom Energy)	State/IGO Group	19 Jun 67	Atomic Energy	637UNTS0	109112
IAEA (Atom Energy)	State/IGO Group	05 Jan 68	Atomic Energy	637UNTS0	109114
IAEA (Atom Energy)	State/IGO Group	12 Feb 68	Atomic Energy	0UNTS0	109311
IAEA (Atom Energy)	State/IGO Group	28 Feb 68	Atomic Energy	637UNTS0	109115
IAEA (Atom Energy)	State/IGO Group	27 Mar 68	Atomic Energy	0UNTS0	109312
IAEA (Atom Energy)	State/IGO Group	17 Jun 68	Atomic Energy	0UNTS0	109313
IAEA (Atom Energy)	State/IGO Group	10 Jul 68	Atomic Energy	0UNTS0	109316
IAEA (Atom Energy)	State/IGO Group	15 Jul 68	Atomic Energy	0UNTS0	109317
IAEA (Atom Energy)	State/IGO Group	15 Oct 68	Atomic Energy	0UNTS0	109533
IAEA (Atom Energy)	State/IGO Group	13 Jun 69	Atomic Energy	0UNTS0	109948
IAEA (Atom Energy)	State/IGO Group	11 Jul 69	Atomic Energy	0UNTS0	109950
IAEA (Atom Energy)	Subsahara Tech Com	06 Feb 64	IGO Operations	501UNTS285	200606
IAEA (Atom Energy)	Sweden	19 Dec 69	Atomic Energy	0UNTS0	110524
IAEA (Atom Energy)	Taiwan	13 Oct 69	Atomic Energy	0UNTS0	110517
IAEA (Atom Energy)	Thailand	18 Mar 59	Tech Assistance	339UNTS307	104850
IAEA (Atom Energy)	Turkey	08 Feb 66	Atomic Energy	573UNTS75	108323
IAEA (Atom Energy)	Turkey	08 Dec 66	Atomic Energy	608UNTS69	108813
IAEA (Atom Energy)	UK Great Britain	11 May 59	Atomic Energy	339UNTS351	104854
IAEA (Atom Energy)	UK Great Britain	20 Jun 66	IGO Operations	588UNTS269	108531
IAEA (Atom Energy)	UN Special Fund	29 Nov 61	IGO Operations	415UNTS408	200593
IAEA (Atom Energy)	UNESCO (Educ/Cult)	01 Oct 58	IGO Operations	339UNTS373	200558
IAEA (Atom Energy)	UNESCO (Educ/Cult)	15 Jul 69	IGO Operations	0UNTS0	200654
IAEA (Atom Energy)	United Arab Rep	17 Sep 64	Atomic Energy	525UNTS19	107581
IAEA (Atom Energy)	United Arab Rep	14 Jan 65	Atomic Energy	603UNTS45	108723
IAEA (Atom Energy)	United Nations	23 Oct 57	IGO Operations	281UNTS369	200548
IAEA (Atom Energy)	United Nations	22 Sep 58	IGO Operations	313UNTS323	200552
IAEA (Atom Energy)	Uruguay	24 Sep 65	Atomic Energy	556UNTS117	108123
IAEA (Atom Energy)	USA (United States)	11 May 59	Atomic Energy	339UNTS359	104855
IAEA (Atom Energy)	USA (United States)	28 Jun 60	Direct Aid	374UNTS133	105333
IAEA (Atom Energy)	USA (United States)	30 Mar 62	Specific Property	442UNTS49	106338
IAEA (Atom Energy)	USA (United States)	20 Aug 62	Commodity Trade	456UNTS447	106570
IAEA (Atom Energy)	USA (United States)	15 Jun 64	Atomic Energy	525UNTS3	107580
IAEA (Atom Energy)	USA (United States)	26 Sep 66	Atomic Energy	589UNTS3	108532
IAEA (Atom Energy)	USA (United States)	09 Dec 66	Atomic Energy	589UNTS55	108535
IAEA (Atom Energy)	USA (United States)	07 Jun 67	IGO Operations	614UNTS109	108866
IAEA (Atom Energy)	USA (United States)	16 Oct 67	Atomic Energy	630UNTS57	108965
IAEA (Atom Energy)	USA (United States)	23 Aug 68	Atomic Energy	0UNTS0	110516
IAEA (Atom Energy)	USA (United States)	30 Sep 68	Atomic Energy	0UNTS0	109944
IAEA (Atom Energy)	USA (United States)	04 Mar 69	Atomic Energy	0UNTS0	109945

PARTY ONE	PARTY TWO	DATE	TOPIC	CITATION	NUMBER
IAEA (Atom Energy)	USSR (Soviet Union)	11 May 59	Atomic Energy	339UNTS341	104853
IAEA (Atom Energy)	Vietnam, South	16 Oct 67	Atomic Energy	630UNTS379	200636
IAEA (Atom Energy)	WHO (World Health)	28 May 59	IGO Operations	339UNTS387	200559
IAEA (Atom Energy)	WMO (Meteorology)	12 Aug 59	IGO Operations	341UNTS341	200561
IAEA (Atom Energy)	Yugoslavia	04 Oct 61	Scientific Project	412UNTS226	105935
IAEA (Atom Energy)	Yugoslavia	04 Mar 63	Atomic Energy	490UNTS333	107162
IAEA (Atom Energy)	Yugoslavia	04 Jun 63	Atomic Energy	490UNTS343	107163
IAEA (Atom Energy)	Yugoslavia	07 Dec 63	Scientific Project	501UNTS273	107322
IBRD (World Bank)	Afghanistan	22 Nov 66	IBRD Project	632UNTS171	109019
IBRD (World Bank)	Afghanistan	26 Jun 69	IBRD Project	0UNTS0	110649
IBRD (World Bank)	AID (Int Devel)	03 Jan 67	Direct Aid	619UNTS321	200635
IBRD (World Bank)	Algeria	14 May 64	IBRD Project	522UNTS265	107552
IBRD (World Bank)	Argentina	30 Jun 61	IBRD Project	445UNTS85	106379
IBRD (World Bank)	Argentina	19 Jan 62	IBRD Project	446UNTS305	106407
IBRD (World Bank)	Argentina	31 Jul 67	IBRD Project	633UNTS289	109042
IBRD (World Bank)	Argentina	25 Jan 68	IBRD Project	639UNTS187	109150
IBRD (World Bank)	Argentina	19 Dec 68	IBRD Project	0UNTS0	109631
IBRD (World Bank)	Argentina	24 Jun 69	IBRD Project	0UNTS0	110290
IBRD (World Bank)	Argentina	14 Nov 69	IBRD Project	0UNTS0	110675
IBRD (World Bank)	Australia	14 Nov 50	IBRD Project	156UNTS147	102041
IBRD (World Bank)	Australia	08 Jul 52	IBRD Project	159UNTS295	102092
IBRD (World Bank)	Australia	02 Mar 54	IBRD Project	191UNTS103	102579
IBRD (World Bank)	Australia	18 Mar 55	IBRD Project	220UNTS131	102998
IBRD (World Bank)	Australia	15 Nov 56	IBRD Project	288UNTS117	104201
IBRD (World Bank)	Australia	03 Dec 56	IBRD Project	288UNTS99	104200
IBRD (World Bank)	Australia	23 Jan 62	IBRD Project	430UNTS3	106201
IBRD (World Bank)	Australia	28 Jun 68	IBRD Project	0UNTS0	109483
IBRD (World Bank)	Austria	08 Nov 54	IBRD Project	216UNTS305	200528
IBRD (World Bank)	Austria	14 Jun 55	IBRD Project	221UNTS375	200531
IBRD (World Bank)	Austria	21 Sep 56	IBRD Project	259UNTS17	103681
IBRD (World Bank)	Austria	21 Sep 56	IBRD Project	259UNTS43	103682
IBRD (World Bank)	Austria	10 Oct 57	IBRD Project	301UNTS95	104343
IBRD (World Bank)	Austria	28 Apr 58	IBRD Project	359UNTS145	105142
IBRD (World Bank)	Austria	02 Dec 58	IBRD Project	340UNTS3	104856
IBRD (World Bank)	Austria	25 Sep 59	IBRD Project	355UNTS223	105079
IBRD (World Bank)	Austria	15 Jun 62	IBRD Project	447UNTS127	106414
IBRD (World Bank)	Belgium	01 Mar 49	IBRD Project	154UNTS133	102029
IBRD (World Bank)	Belgium	13 Sep 51	IBRD Project	158UNTS349	102071
IBRD (World Bank)	Belgium	13 Sep 51	IBRD Project	158UNTS323	102070
IBRD (World Bank)	Belgium	14 Dec 54	IBRD Project	210UNTS113	102837
IBRD (World Bank)	Belgium	26 Jun 57	IBRD Project	322UNTS301	104661
IBRD (World Bank)	Belgium	10 Sep 57	IBRD Project	286UNTS291	104174
IBRD (World Bank)	Belgium	27 Nov 57	IBRD Project	292UNTS175	104273
IBRD (World Bank)	Belgium	30 Mar 60	IBRD Project	379UNTS129	105438
IBRD (World Bank)	Belgium	30 Mar 60	IBRD Project	379UNTS161	105439
IBRD (World Bank)	Belgium	30 Mar 60	IBRD Project	379UNTS103	105437
IBRD (World Bank)	Brazil	27 Jan 49	IBRD Project	153UNTS264	102026
IBRD (World Bank)	Brazil	26 May 50	IBRD Project	301UNTS165	104345
IBRD (World Bank)	Brazil	27 Jun 52	IBRD Project	190UNTS115	102561
IBRD (World Bank)	Brazil	27 Jun 52	IBRD Project	190UNTS85	102560
IBRD (World Bank)	Brazil	30 Apr 53	IBRD Project	190UNTS133	102562
IBRD (World Bank)	Brazil	17 Jul 53	IBRD Project	190UNTS149	102563
IBRD (World Bank)	Brazil	18 Dec 53	IBRD Project	301UNTS229	104346
IBRD (World Bank)	Brazil	18 Dec 53	IBRD Project	190UNTS179	102564
IBRD (World Bank)	Brazil	24 Feb 54	IBRD Project	301UNTS249	104347
IBRD (World Bank)	Brazil	22 Jan 58	IBRD Project	323UNTS99	104666
IBRD (World Bank)	Brazil	03 Oct 58	IBRD Project	337UNTS177	104823
IBRD (World Bank)	Brazil	17 Jun 59	IBRD Project	377UNTS111	105398
IBRD (World Bank)	Brazil	26 Feb 65	IBRD Project	553UNTS3	108065
IBRD (World Bank)	Brazil	26 Feb 65	IBRD Project	567UNTS91	108253
IBRD (World Bank)	Brazil	15 Mar 66	IBRD Project	599UNTS52	108664
IBRD (World Bank)	Brazil	19 Dec 66	IBRD Project	599UNTS177	108667
IBRD (World Bank)	Brazil	19 Dec 66	IBRD Project	599UNTS107	108665
IBRD (World Bank)	Brazil	19 Dec 66	IBRD Project	599UNTS205	108668
IBRD (World Bank)	Brazil	19 Dec 66	IBRD Project	599UNTS149	108666

PARTY ONE	PARTY TWO	DATE	TOPIC	CITATION	NUMBER
IBRD (World Bank)	Brazil	23 Sep 67	IBRD Project	620UNTS77	108951
IBRD (World Bank)	Brazil	26 Jan 68	IBRD Project	0UNTS0	109613
IBRD (World Bank)	Brazil	23 Oct 68	IBRD Project	0UNTS0	110119
IBRD (World Bank)	Brazil	23 Oct 68	IBRD Project	0UNTS0	109629
IBRD (World Bank)	Brazil	23 Oct 68	IBRD Project	0UNTS0	109628
IBRD (World Bank)	Brazil	16 Feb 70	IBRD Project	0UNTS0	110826
IBRD (World Bank)	Burma	04 May 56	IBRD Project	253UNTS209	103585
IBRD (World Bank)	Burma	04 May 56	IBRD Project	253UNTS179	103584
IBRD (World Bank)	Burma	16 Jan 61	IBRD Project	400UNTS73	105749
IBRD (World Bank)	Cameroon	28 Mar 67	IBRD Project	618UNTS89	108925
IBRD (World Bank)	Cameroon	15 Apr 69	IBRD Project	0UNTS0	110171
IBRD (World Bank)	Cameroon	02 Jun 69	IBRD Project	0UNTS0	110122
IBRD (World Bank)	Cameroon	27 Mar 70	IBRD Project	0UNTS0	110681
IBRD (World Bank)	Ceylon (Sri Lanka)	09 Jul 54	IBRD Project	198UNTS313	200517
IBRD (World Bank)	Ceylon (Sri Lanka)	17 Sep 58	IBRD Project	323UNTS51	104664
IBRD (World Bank)	Ceylon (Sri Lanka)	06 Jun 61	IBRD Project	414UNTS349	105978
IBRD (World Bank)	Ceylon (Sri Lanka)	24 Aug 67	IBRD Project	632UNTS217	109025
IBRD (World Bank)	Ceylon (Sri Lanka)	22 Nov 67	IBRD Project	639UNTS221	109151
IBRD (World Bank)	Ceylon (Sri Lanka)	12 Nov 68	IBRD Project	0UNTS0	109623
IBRD (World Bank)	Ceylon (Sri Lanka)	18 Jul 69	IBRD Project	0UNTS0	110484
IBRD (World Bank)	Ceylon (Sri Lanka)	28 Jul 69	IBRD Project	0UNTS0	110483
IBRD (World Bank)	Chile	23 Mar 49	IBRD Project	153UNTS141	102019
IBRD (World Bank)	Chile	23 Mar 49	IBRD Project	153UNTS61	102018
IBRD (World Bank)	Chile	10 Oct 51	IBRD Project	158UNTS369	102072
IBRD (World Bank)	Chile	10 Sep 53	IBRD Project	188UNTS25	102520
IBRD (World Bank)	Chile	01 Nov 56	IBRD Project	261UNTS27	103724
IBRD (World Bank)	Chile	24 Jul 57	IBRD Project	282UNTS139	104098
IBRD (World Bank)	Chile	24 Jul 57	IBRD Project	282UNTS189	104099
IBRD (World Bank)	Chile	28 Apr 58	IBRD Project	359UNTS89	105140
IBRD (World Bank)	Chile	28 Jun 61	IBRD Project	426UNTS33	106129
IBRD (World Bank)	Chile	18 Dec 63	IBRD Project	504UNTS3	107351
IBRD (World Bank)	Chile	18 Dec 63	IBRD Project	504UNTS29	107352
IBRD (World Bank)	Chile	12 Feb 65	IBRD Project	537UNTS35	107796
IBRD (World Bank)	Chile	06 Oct 65	IBRD Project	567UNTS293	108261
IBRD (World Bank)	Chile	23 Dec 66	IBRD Project	595UNTS141	108618
IBRD (World Bank)	Chile	19 Sep 68	IBRD Project	0UNTS0	109590
IBRD (World Bank)	Chile	23 Apr 70	IBRD Project	0UNTS0	110827
IBRD (World Bank)	China	14 Jun 67	IGO Operations	615UNTS243	108882
IBRD (World Bank)	Colombia	19 Aug 49	IBRD Project	154UNTS329	102032
IBRD (World Bank)	Colombia	02 Nov 50	IBRD Project	158UNTS59	102062
IBRD (World Bank)	Colombia	28 Dec 50	IBRD Project	158UNTS87	102063
IBRD (World Bank)	Colombia	10 Apr 51	IBRD Project	158UNTS155	102066
IBRD (World Bank)	Colombia	13 Oct 51	IBRD Project	159UNTS75	102084
IBRD (World Bank)	Colombia	26 Aug 52	IBRD Project	159UNTS339	102094
IBRD (World Bank)	Colombia	10 Sep 53	IBRD Project	203UNTS3	102738
IBRD (World Bank)	Colombia	29 Dec 54	IBRD Project	211UNTS135	102851
IBRD (World Bank)	Colombia	24 Mar 55	IBRD Project	212UNTS217	102874
IBRD (World Bank)	Colombia	15 Jun 55	IBRD Project	248UNTS161	103494
IBRD (World Bank)	Colombia	06 Jun 56	IBRD Project	248UNTS139	103493
IBRD (World Bank)	Colombia	15 Dec 58	IBRD Project	354UNTS233	105065
IBRD (World Bank)	Colombia	30 Jan 59	IBRD Project	337UNTS327	104828
IBRD (World Bank)	Colombia	20 May 59	IBRD Project	344UNTS251	104953
IBRD (World Bank)	Colombia	20 Jan 60	IBRD Project	375UNTS49	105353
IBRD (World Bank)	Colombia	10 May 60	IBRD Project	379UNTS218	105441
IBRD (World Bank)	Colombia	20 Sep 60	IBRD Project	390UNTS173	105608
IBRD (World Bank)	Colombia	12 May 61	IBRD Project	415UNTS172	105985
IBRD (World Bank)	Colombia	28 Aug 61	IBRD Project	416UNTS23	105993
IBRD (World Bank)	Colombia	23 May 62	IBRD Project	447UNTS39	106411
IBRD (World Bank)	Colombia	03 Jun 63	IBRD Project	490UNTS199	107155
IBRD (World Bank)	Colombia	21 Jun 63	IBRD Project	482UNTS159	106994
IBRD (World Bank)	Colombia	28 Jun 63	IBRD Project	489UNTS113	107137
IBRD (World Bank)	Colombia	16 Jul 63	IBRD Project	482UNTS256	106998
IBRD (World Bank)	Colombia	07 Feb 64	IBRD Project	516UNTS99	107473
IBRD (World Bank)	Colombia	16 May 66	Loans and Credits	608UNTS249	108819
IBRD (World Bank)	Colombia	31 May 66	Loans and Credits	608UNTS279	108820

PARTY ONE	PARTY TWO	DATE	TOPIC	CITATION	NUMBER
IBRD (World Bank)	Colombia	15 Jun 67	Gen Communications	615UNTS47	108877
IBRD (World Bank)	Colombia	29 Jun 67	IBRD Project	619UNTS99	108941
IBRD (World Bank)	Colombia	22 May 68	IBRD Project	0UNTS0	109614
IBRD (World Bank)	Colombia	03 Jun 68	IBRD Project	0UNTS0	109333
IBRD (World Bank)	Colombia	03 Jun 68	IBRD Project	0UNTS0	109334
IBRD (World Bank)	Colombia	25 Jul 68	IBRD Project	0UNTS0	109484
IBRD (World Bank)	Colombia	27 Jul 68	IBRD Project	0UNTS0	109485
IBRD (World Bank)	Colombia	31 Jul 68	IBRD Project	0UNTS0	109512
IBRD (World Bank)	Colombia	02 Dec 68	IBRD Project	0UNTS0	109592
IBRD (World Bank)	Colombia	27 Jun 69	IBRD Project	0UNTS0	110500
IBRD (World Bank)	Colombia	27 Jun 69	IBRD Project	0UNTS0	110104
IBRD (World Bank)	Congo (Brazzaville)	30 Jun 59	IBRD Project	452UNTS123	106506
IBRD (World Bank)	Congo (Brazzaville)	09 Jan 67	IBRD Project	598UNTS161	108659
IBRD (World Bank)	Congo (Brazzaville)	10 May 67	IBRD Project	632UNTS185	109021
IBRD (World Bank)	Costa Rica	18 Sep 56	IBRD Project	260UNTS369	103721
IBRD (World Bank)	Costa Rica	11 Feb 59	IBRD Project	337UNTS245	104825
IBRD (World Bank)	Costa Rica	04 May 60	IBRD Project	390UNTS201	105609
IBRD (World Bank)	Costa Rica	03 Feb 61	IBRD Project	414UNTS314	105977
IBRD (World Bank)	Costa Rica	06 Sep 61	IBRD Project	446UNTS345	106408
IBRD (World Bank)	Costa Rica	13 Oct 61	IBRD Project	430UNTS27	106202
IBRD (World Bank)	Costa Rica	10 Jul 63	IBRD Project	482UNTS69	106991
IBRD (World Bank)	Costa Rica	05 Jun 68	IBRD Project	0UNTS0	109365
IBRD (World Bank)	Costa Rica	10 Jul 69	IBRD Project	0UNTS0	110488
IBRD (World Bank)	Costa Rica	10 Jul 69	IBRD Project	0UNTS0	110487
IBRD (World Bank)	Costa Rica	02 Apr 70	IBRD Project	0UNTS0	110683
IBRD (World Bank)	Cyprus	17 Apr 63	IBRD Project	476UNTS185	106909
IBRD (World Bank)	Cyprus	16 May 67	Loans and Credits	617UNTS21	108906
IBRD (World Bank)	Cyprus	30 Jun 69	IBRD Project	0UNTS0	110309
IBRD (World Bank)	Cyprus	24 Dec 69	IBRD Project	0UNTS0	110676
IBRD (World Bank)	Denmark	22 Aug 47	IBRD Project	152UNTS223	102016
IBRD (World Bank)	Denmark	04 Feb 59	IBRD Project	328UNTS143	104733
IBRD (World Bank)	Denmark	24 Jul 63	IBRD Project	481UNTS171	106982
IBRD (World Bank)	Dominican Republic	10 Dec 69	IBRD Project	0UNTS0	110689
IBRD (World Bank)	East Afri Service	29 Sep 65	IBRD Project	568UNTS327	200623
IBRD (World Bank)	East Afri Service	17 Feb 67	IBRD Project	599UNTS335	200629
IBRD (World Bank)	Ecuador	10 Feb 54	IBRD Project	209UNTS261	102830
IBRD (World Bank)	Ecuador	26 Mar 56	IBRD Project	292UNTS391	104277
IBRD (World Bank)	Ecuador	20 Sep 57	IBRD Project	293UNTS135	104291
IBRD (World Bank)	Ecuador	20 Sep 57	IBRD Project	289UNTS237	104221
IBRD (World Bank)	Ecuador	09 Oct 58	IBRD Project	337UNTS299	104827
IBRD (World Bank)	Ecuador	26 May 64	IBRD Project	534UNTS113	107758
IBRD (World Bank)	Ecuador	05 Sep 68	IBRD Project	0UNTS0	110112
IBRD (World Bank)	El Salvador	14 Dec 49	IBRD Project	155UNTS43	102035
IBRD (World Bank)	El Salvador	12 Oct 54	IBRD Project	203UNTS37	102739
IBRD (World Bank)	El Salvador	07 Jan 59	IBRD Project	346UNTS51	104977
IBRD (World Bank)	El Salvador	20 Feb 59	IBRD Project	362UNTS75	105183
IBRD (World Bank)	El Salvador	29 Jul 60	IBRD Project	390UNTS101	105605
IBRD (World Bank)	El Salvador	19 Jun 63	IBRD Project	481UNTS59	106978
IBRD (World Bank)	El Salvador	01 Oct 63	IBRD Project	517UNTS3	107481
IBRD (World Bank)	El Salvador	07 Dec 67	Loans and Credits	0UNTS0	109299
IBRD (World Bank)	El Salvador	11 Jun 69	IBRD Project	0UNTS0	110288
IBRD (World Bank)	Ethiopia	13 Sep 50	IBRD Project	157UNTS213	102055
IBRD (World Bank)	Ethiopia	13 Sep 50	IBRD Project	157UNTS233	102056
IBRD (World Bank)	Ethiopia	19 Feb 51	IBRD Project	186UNTS101	102486
IBRD (World Bank)	Ethiopia	28 Jan 57	IBRD Project	286UNTS307	104175
IBRD (World Bank)	Ethiopia	22 Nov 61	IBRD Project	426UNTS255	106142
IBRD (World Bank)	Ethiopia	31 May 62	IBRD Project	467UNTS237	106765
IBRD (World Bank)	Ethiopia	08 May 64	IBRD Project	505UNTS51	107364
IBRD (World Bank)	Ethiopia	28 Dec 65	IBRD Project	567UNTS229	108258
IBRD (World Bank)	Ethiopia	09 May 69	IBRD Project	0UNTS0	110219
IBRD (World Bank)	Fed of Malaya	22 Sep 58	IBRD Project	323UNTS71	104665
IBRD (World Bank)	Fed Rhod/Nyasaland	21 Jun 56	IBRD Project	285UNTS317	104156
IBRD (World Bank)	Finland	01 Aug 49	IBRD Project	156UNTS289	200480
IBRD (World Bank)	Finland	17 Oct 49	IBRD Project	156UNTS355	200481
IBRD (World Bank)	Finland	30 Apr 52	IBRD Project	159UNTS408	200483

PARTY ONE	PARTY TWO	DATE	TOPIC	CITATION	NUMBER
IBRD (World Bank)	Finland	24 Mar 55	IBRD Project	211UNTS305	200525
IBRD (World Bank)	Finland	22 May 56	IBRD Project	248UNTS57	103485
IBRD (World Bank)	Finland	16 Mar 59	IBRD Project	337UNTS269	104826
IBRD (World Bank)	Finland	09 Aug 61	IBRD Project	415UNTS204	105986
IBRD (World Bank)	Finland	15 Aug 62	IBRD Project	467UNTS177	106763
IBRD (World Bank)	Finland	18 Sep 63	IBRD Project	491UNTS345	107183
IBRD (World Bank)	Finland	10 Jul 64	IBRD Project	516UNTS125	107474
IBRD (World Bank)	Finland	30 Jun 65	IBRD Project	550UNTS63	108009
IBRD (World Bank)	Finland	27 Apr 66	IBRD Project	568UNTS107	108266
IBRD (World Bank)	Finland	24 Jan 69	IBRD Project	0UNTS0	109596
IBRD (World Bank)	France	09 May 47	IBRD Project	152UNTS111	102014
IBRD (World Bank)	France	10 Jun 54	IBRD Project	210UNTS89	102836
IBRD (World Bank)	France	26 Aug 55	IBRD Project	247UNTS305	103478
IBRD (World Bank)	France	30 Jun 59	IBRD Project	452UNTS67	106505
IBRD (World Bank)	France	10 Dec 59	IBRD Project	380UNTS319	105464
IBRD (World Bank)	France	17 Mar 60	IBRD Project	452UNTS147	106508
IBRD (World Bank)	Gabon	30 Jun 59	IBRD Project	452UNTS135	106507
IBRD (World Bank)	Gabon	10 Jul 64	IBRD Project	537UNTS63	107797
IBRD (World Bank)	Gabon	07 Jul 68	IBRD Project	0UNTS0	109361
IBRD (World Bank)	Gabon	10 Jan 69	IBRD Project	0UNTS0	109654
IBRD (World Bank)	Ghana	08 Feb 62	IBRD Project	449UNTS207	106462
IBRD (World Bank)	Ghana	23 Jun 69	IBRD Project	0UNTS0	110107
IBRD (World Bank)	Greece	18 Mar 68	IBRD Project	0UNTS0	109326
IBRD (World Bank)	Guatemala	29 Jul 55	IBRD Project	229UNTS167	103165
IBRD (World Bank)	Guatemala	10 Mar 67	Loans and Credits	616UNTS139	108894
IBRD (World Bank)	Guatemala	28 Jun 68	IBRD Project	0UNTS0	109482
IBRD (World Bank)	Guatemala	16 Dec 68	IBRD Project	0UNTS0	110214
IBRD (World Bank)	Guinea	30 Mar 66	IBRD Project	568UNTS3	108262
IBRD (World Bank)	Guinea	18 Sep 68	IBRD Project	0UNTS0	110596
IBRD (World Bank)	Guyana	27 Sep 68	IBRD Project	0UNTS0	109612
IBRD (World Bank)	Guyana	31 Jan 69	IBRD Project	0UNTS0	110096
IBRD (World Bank)	Haiti	07 May 56	IBRD Project	252UNTS279	103570
IBRD (World Bank)	Honduras	22 Dec 55	IBRD Project	230UNTS262	103189
IBRD (World Bank)	Honduras	09 May 58	IBRD Project	323UNTS4	104662
IBRD (World Bank)	Honduras	20 May 59	IBRD Project	359UNTS119	105141
IBRD (World Bank)	Honduras	29 Jun 60	IBRD Project	400UNTS137	105751
IBRD (World Bank)	Honduras	02 Feb 65	IBRD Project	561UNTS255	108188
IBRD (World Bank)	Honduras	25 Aug 66	IBRD Project	582UNTS79	108460
IBRD (World Bank)	Honduras	26 May 67	IGO Operations	615UNTS145	108879
IBRD (World Bank)	Honduras	12 Jul 68	IBRD Project	0UNTS0	109408
IBRD (World Bank)	Iceland	20 Jun 51	IBRD Project	158UNTS301	102069
IBRD (World Bank)	Iceland	01 Nov 51	IBRD Project	159UNTS55	102083
IBRD (World Bank)	Iceland	26 Aug 52	IBRD Project	159UNTS363	102095
IBRD (World Bank)	Iceland	04 Sep 53	IBRD Project	188UNTS3	102519
IBRD (World Bank)	Iceland	04 Sep 53	IBRD Project	178UNTS275	102344
IBRD (World Bank)	Iceland	14 Feb 62	IBRD Project	447UNTS95	106413
IBRD (World Bank)	Iceland	14 Sep 66	IBRD Project	598UNTS223	108660
IBRD (World Bank)	IFC (Finance Corp)	28 Oct 66	Loans and Credits	586UNTS225	200628
IBRD (World Bank)	IFC (Finance Corp)	23 Dec 69	IBRD Project	0UNTS0	200653
IBRD (World Bank)	India	18 Aug 49	IBRD Project	154UNTS269	102031
IBRD (World Bank)	India	29 Sep 49	IBRD Project	154UNTS393	102033
IBRD (World Bank)	India	18 Apr 50	IBRD Project	155UNTS117	102036
IBRD (World Bank)	India	18 Dec 52	IBRD Project	201UNTS241	102719
IBRD (World Bank)	India	23 Jan 53	IBRD Project	201UNTS145	102715
IBRD (World Bank)	India	19 Nov 54	IBRD Project	309UNTS159	104473
IBRD (World Bank)	India	14 Mar 55	IBRD Project	309UNTS129	104472
IBRD (World Bank)	India	26 Jun 56	IBRD Project	301UNTS3	104341
IBRD (World Bank)	India	19 Dec 56	IBRD Project	310UNTS75	104489
IBRD (World Bank)	India	05 Mar 57	IBRD Project	272UNTS201	103939
IBRD (World Bank)	India	29 May 57	IBRD Project	309UNTS201	104474
IBRD (World Bank)	India	12 Jul 57	IBRD Project	288UNTS135	104202
IBRD (World Bank)	India	20 Nov 57	IBRD Project	301UNTS47	104342
IBRD (World Bank)	India	25 Jun 58	IBRD Project	323UNTS131	104667
IBRD (World Bank)	India	25 Jun 58	IBRD Project	323UNTS157	104668
IBRD (World Bank)	India	23 Jul 58	IBRD Project	317UNTS3	104590

PARTY ONE	PARTY TWO	DATE	TOPIC	CITATION	NUMBER
IBRD (World Bank)	India	16 Sep 58	IBRD Project	323UNTS235	104671
IBRD (World Bank)	India	08 Apr 59	IBRD Project	348UNTS131	104998
IBRD (World Bank)	India	15 Jul 59	IBRD Project	355UNTS95	105075
IBRD (World Bank)	India	15 Jul 59	IBRD Project	346UNTS33	104976
IBRD (World Bank)	India	29 Jul 60	IBRD Project	377UNTS153	105399
IBRD (World Bank)	India	28 Oct 60	IBRD Project	406UNTS27	105838
IBRD (World Bank)	India	09 Aug 61	IBRD Project	417UNTS297	106011
IBRD (World Bank)	India	17 Aug 61	IBRD Project	417UNTS319	106012
IBRD (World Bank)	India	13 Oct 61	IBRD Project	418UNTS3	106013
IBRD (World Bank)	India	22 Dec 61	IBRD Project	481UNTS85	106979
IBRD (World Bank)	India	28 Feb 62	IBRD Project	447UNTS3	106410
IBRD (World Bank)	India	05 Jun 63	IBRD Project	481UNTS191	106983
IBRD (World Bank)	India	28 May 65	Loans and Credits	552UNTS39	108049
IBRD (World Bank)	India	11 Jun 65	IBRD Project	557UNTS101	108130
IBRD (World Bank)	India	11 Jun 65	IBRD Project	557UNTS59	108128
IBRD (World Bank)	India	07 Jul 66	IBRD Project	595UNTS3	108610
IBRD (World Bank)	India	19 Sep 67	IGO Operations	615UNTS165	108880
IBRD (World Bank)	India	18 Jun 69	IBRD Project	0UNTS0	109894
IBRD (World Bank)	India	18 Jun 69	IBRD Project	0UNTS0	110093
IBRD (World Bank)	India	03 Jun 70	IBRD Project	0UNTS0	110830
IBRD (World Bank)	Iran	22 Jan 57	IBRD Project	317UNTS129	104600
IBRD (World Bank)	Iran	29 May 59	IBRD Project	348UNTS103	104997
IBRD (World Bank)	Iran	23 Nov 59	IBRD Project	380UNTS245	105459
IBRD (World Bank)	Iran	20 Feb 60	IBRD Project	384UNTS213	105521
IBRD (World Bank)	Iran	10 Jun 64	IBRD Project	537UNTS111	107799
IBRD (World Bank)	Iran	28 Apr 65	IBRD Project	555UNTS45	108104
IBRD (World Bank)	Iran	28 Apr 65	IBRD Project	555UNTS21	108103
IBRD (World Bank)	Iran	12 Jul 65	IBRD Project	554UNTS3	108095
IBRD (World Bank)	Iran	26 Jul 66	IBRD Project	582UNTS107	108461
IBRD (World Bank)	Iran	17 Oct 67	IBRD Project	0UNTS0	109331
IBRD (World Bank)	Iran	05 Jun 68	IBRD Project	0UNTS0	109373
IBRD (World Bank)	Iran	18 Apr 69	IBRD Project	0UNTS0	110198
IBRD (World Bank)	Iran	28 May 69	IBRD Project	0UNTS0	110308
IBRD (World Bank)	Iraq	15 Jun 50	IBRD Project	155UNTS267	102038
IBRD (World Bank)	Iraq	22 Jul 66	IBRD Project	584UNTS233	108480
IBRD (World Bank)	Ireland	24 Mar 69	IBRD Project	0UNTS0	110222
IBRD (World Bank)	Israel	09 Sep 60	IBRD Project	406UNTS3	105837
IBRD (World Bank)	Israel	11 Jul 61	IBRD Project	429UNTS3	106188
IBRD (World Bank)	Israel	01 Feb 62	IBRD Project	435UNTS155	106277
IBRD (World Bank)	Israel	17 Oct 62	IBRD Project	467UNTS107	106760
IBRD (World Bank)	Israel	16 Sep 65	Claims and Debts	566UNTS212	108245
IBRD (World Bank)	Israel	15 Nov 67	IBRD Project	619UNTS129	108942
IBRD (World Bank)	Israel	15 Jun 70	IBRD Project	0UNTS0	110831
IBRD (World Bank)	Italy	10 Oct 51	IBRD Project	159UNTS383	200482
IBRD (World Bank)	Italy	06 Oct 53	IBRD Project	301UNTS135	104344
IBRD (World Bank)	Italy	01 Jun 55	IBRD Project	358UNTS203	105137
IBRD (World Bank)	Italy	11 Oct 56	IBRD Project	359UNTS3	105138
IBRD (World Bank)	Italy	28 Feb 58	IBRD Project	359UNTS47	105139
IBRD (World Bank)	Italy	21 Apr 59	IBRD Project	359UNTS191	105143
IBRD (World Bank)	Italy	16 Sep 59	IBRD Project	375UNTS159	105366
IBRD (World Bank)	Italy	28 Jun 65	IBRD Project	567UNTS127	108254
IBRD (World Bank)	Ivory Coast	21 Jun 68	IBRD Project	0UNTS0	109412
IBRD (World Bank)	Ivory Coast	13 Jun 69	IBRD Project	0UNTS0	110568
IBRD (World Bank)	Ivory Coast	13 Jun 69	IBRD Project	0UNTS0	110567
IBRD (World Bank)	Ivory Coast	13 Jun 69	IBRD Project	0UNTS0	110569
IBRD (World Bank)	Jamaica	08 Apr 65	IBRD Project	539UNTS303	107841
IBRD (World Bank)	Jamaica	20 Jun 66	IBRD Project	582UNTS145	108462
IBRD (World Bank)	Jamaica	30 Sep 66	IBRD Project	582UNTS179	108463
IBRD (World Bank)	Jamaica	23 Jan 67	IBRD Project	594UNTS311	108608
IBRD (World Bank)	Jamaica	14 May 69	IBRD Project	0UNTS0	109889
IBRD (World Bank)	Japan	12 Nov 52	IBRD Project	354UNTS313	105068
IBRD (World Bank)	Japan	15 Oct 53	IBRD Project	187UNTS321	200512
IBRD (World Bank)	Japan	15 Oct 53	IBRD Project	187UNTS367	200513
IBRD (World Bank)	Japan	15 Oct 53	IBRD Project	187UNTS271	200511
IBRD (World Bank)	Japan	25 Oct 55	IBRD Project	230UNTS379	200534

PARTY ONE	PARTY TWO	DATE	TOPIC	CITATION	NUMBER
IBRD (World Bank)	Japan	21 Feb 56	IBRD Project	248UNTS321	200543
IBRD (World Bank)	Japan	19 Dec 56	IBRD Project	264UNTS179	103793
IBRD (World Bank)	Japan	19 Dec 56	IBRD Project	268UNTS203	103859
IBRD (World Bank)	Japan	09 Aug 57	IBRD Project	293UNTS59	104286
IBRD (World Bank)	Japan	29 Jan 58	IBRD Project	310UNTS111	104490
IBRD (World Bank)	Japan	13 Jun 58	IBRD Project	312UNTS159	104518
IBRD (World Bank)	Japan	27 Jun 58	IBRD Project	312UNTS193	104519
IBRD (World Bank)	Japan	11 Jul 58	IBRD Project	318UNTS103	104611
IBRD (World Bank)	Japan	18 Aug 58	IBRD Project	323UNTS205	104670
IBRD (World Bank)	Japan	10 Sep 58	IBRD Project	318UNTS133	104612
IBRD (World Bank)	Japan	10 Sep 58	IBRD Project	323UNTS297	104673
IBRD (World Bank)	Japan	17 Feb 59	IBRD Project	337UNTS205	104824
IBRD (World Bank)	Japan	12 Nov 59	IBRD Project	354UNTS279	105067
IBRD (World Bank)	Japan	17 Mar 60	IBRD Project	362UNTS43	105182
IBRD (World Bank)	Japan	20 Dec 60	IBRD Project	400UNTS167	105752
IBRD (World Bank)	Japan	20 Dec 60	IBRD Project	400UNTS279	105754
IBRD (World Bank)	Japan	16 Mar 61	IBRD Project	400UNTS201	105753
IBRD (World Bank)	Japan	02 May 61	IBRD Project	415UNTS144	105984
IBRD (World Bank)	Japan	29 Nov 61	IBRD Project	426UNTS3	106128
IBRD (World Bank)	Japan	27 Sep 63	IBRD Project	485UNTS283	107061
IBRD (World Bank)	Japan	22 Apr 64	IBRD Project	505UNTS21	107363
IBRD (World Bank)	Japan	23 Dec 64	IBRD Project	538UNTS37	107809
IBRD (World Bank)	Japan	13 Jan 65	IBRD Project	537UNTS293	107806
IBRD (World Bank)	Japan	26 May 65	IBRD Project	550UNTS95	108010
IBRD (World Bank)	Japan	10 Sep 65	Claims and Debts	566UNTS249	108246
IBRD (World Bank)	Japan	29 Jul 66	IBRD Project	582UNTS209	108464
IBRD (World Bank)	Japan	09 Sep 69	IGO Establishment	70JHZ5	439032
IBRD (World Bank)	Kenya	29 Sep 65	IBRD Project	568UNTS289	108274
IBRD (World Bank)	Kenya	17 Feb 67	IBRD Project	599UNTS233	108669
IBRD (World Bank)	Kenya	10 Oct 69	IBRD Project	0UNTS0	110671
IBRD (World Bank)	Kenya	07 Nov 69	IBRD Project	0UNTS0	110673
IBRD (World Bank)	Korea, South	31 Jan 68	IBRD Project	639UNTS263	200638
IBRD (World Bank)	Korea, South	23 May 69	Loans and Credits	0UNTS0	200655
IBRD (World Bank)	Lebanon	25 Aug 55	IBRD Project	230UNTS233	103188
IBRD (World Bank)	Liberia	08 Jan 64	IBRD Project	504UNTS53	107353
IBRD (World Bank)	Liberia	05 Jun 67	Tech Assistance	633UNTS13	109031
IBRD (World Bank)	Liberia	20 Jun 69	IBRD Project	0UNTS0	109949
IBRD (World Bank)	Liberia	04 Jun 70	IBRD Project	0UNTS0	110685
IBRD (World Bank)	Luxembourg	28 Aug 47	IBRD Project	153UNTS3	102017
IBRD (World Bank)	Madagascar	23 Aug 67	IBRD Project	618UNTS215	108929
IBRD (World Bank)	Madagascar	12 Nov 68	IBRD Project	0UNTS0	109670
IBRD (World Bank)	Madagascar	14 Feb 69	IBRD Project	0UNTS0	110103
IBRD (World Bank)	Malaysia	15 Jul 63	IBRD Project	482UNTS123	106993
IBRD (World Bank)	Malaysia	07 Aug 63	IBRD Project	485UNTS253	107060
IBRD (World Bank)	Malaysia	26 Feb 65	IBRD Project	549UNTS239	108002
IBRD (World Bank)	Malaysia	17 Nov 65	IBRD Project	568UNTS23	108263
IBRD (World Bank)	Malaysia	26 Jul 66	IBRD Project	586UNTS195	108504
IBRD (World Bank)	Malaysia	15 Jun 67	IBRD Project	618UNTS235	108930
IBRD (World Bank)	Malaysia	17 Apr 68	IBRD Project	0UNTS0	109360
IBRD (World Bank)	Malaysia	27 Sep 68	IBRD Project	0UNTS0	109506
IBRD (World Bank)	Malaysia	27 Sep 68	IBRD Project	0UNTS0	109505
IBRD (World Bank)	Malaysia	09 Jan 69	IBRD Project	0UNTS0	109594
IBRD (World Bank)	Malaysia	23 May 69	IBRD Project	0UNTS0	110169
IBRD (World Bank)	Malaysia	20 May 70	IBRD Project	0UNTS0	110828
IBRD (World Bank)	Malaysia	20 May 70	IBRD Project	0UNTS0	110829
IBRD (World Bank)	Mauritania	17 Mar 60	IBRD Project	452UNTS211	106509
IBRD (World Bank)	Mexico	06 Jan 49	IBRD Project	154UNTS81	102028
IBRD (World Bank)	Mexico	06 Jan 49	IBRD Project	154UNTS3	102027
IBRD (World Bank)	Mexico	28 Apr 50	IBRD Project	155UNTS185	102037
IBRD (World Bank)	Mexico	18 Oct 50	IBRD Project	157UNTS259	102057
IBRD (World Bank)	Mexico	11 Jan 52	IBRD Project	159UNTS129	102086
IBRD (World Bank)	Mexico	24 Aug 54	IBRD Project	286UNTS211	104168
IBRD (World Bank)	Mexico	14 Jan 58	IBRD Project	293UNTS167	104292
IBRD (World Bank)	Mexico	05 May 58	IBRD Project	309UNTS3	104466
IBRD (World Bank)	Mexico	18 Oct 60	IBRD Project	422UNTS177	106075
IBRD (World Bank)	Mexico	16 Jan 61	IBRD Project	422UNTS203	106076
IBRD (World Bank)	Mexico	20 Jun 62	IBRD Project	468UNTS109	106771
IBRD (World Bank)	Mexico	20 Jun 62	IBRD Project	467UNTS205	106764
IBRD (World Bank)	Mexico	29 Apr 63	IBRD Project	489UNTS151	107138
IBRD (World Bank)	Mexico	20 Sep 63	IBRD Project	491UNTS317	107182
IBRD (World Bank)	Mexico	04 Feb 65	IBRD Project	549UNTS189	108000
IBRD (World Bank)	Mexico	01 Oct 65	IBRD Project	589UNTS339	108542
IBRD (World Bank)	Mexico	15 Dec 65	IBRD Project	568UNTS125	108267
IBRD (World Bank)	Mexico	25 May 66	IBRD Project	596UNTS3	108627
IBRD (World Bank)	Mexico	26 Jan 68	IBRD Project	0UNTS0	109511
IBRD (World Bank)	Mexico	26 Jan 68	IBRD Project	640UNTS3	109152
IBRD (World Bank)	Mexico	28 Jun 68	IBRD Project	0UNTS0	109335
IBRD (World Bank)	Mexico	12 Jun 69	IBRD Project	0UNTS0	110289
IBRD (World Bank)	Morocco	21 Dec 62	IBRD Project	478UNTS205	106937
IBRD (World Bank)	Morocco	26 Aug 64	IBRD Project	537UNTS193	107802
IBRD (World Bank)	Morocco	08 Nov 65	Claims and Debts	566UNTS279	108247
IBRD (World Bank)	Morocco	13 Jun 66	IGO Operations	615UNTS205	108881
IBRD (World Bank)	Morocco	26 Jan 67	IBRD Project	642UNTS3	109160
IBRD (World Bank)	Morocco	13 Nov 67	IBRD Project	0UNTS0	110544
IBRD (World Bank)	Morocco	14 Nov 68	IBRD Project	0UNTS0	110597
IBRD (World Bank)	Morocco	13 Nov 69	IBRD Project	0UNTS0	110674
IBRD (World Bank)	Morocco	06 Mar 70	IBRD Project	0UNTS0	110679
IBRD (World Bank)	Multilateral	02 Oct 54	IBRD Project	201UNTS171	102716
IBRD (World Bank)	Multilateral	02 Oct 54	IBRD Project	201UNTS179	102717
IBRD (World Bank)	Multilateral	25 May 55	IGO Establishment	264UNTS117	103791
IBRD (World Bank)	Multilateral	19 Sep 60	IBRD Project	444UNTS259	106371
IBRD (World Bank)	Multilateral	19 Sep 60	IBRD Project	419UNTS125	106032
IBRD (World Bank)	Multilateral	14 Jun 61	IBRD Project	415UNTS4	105979
IBRD (World Bank)	Multilateral	28 Aug 61	IBRD Project	416UNTS45	105994
IBRD (World Bank)	Multilateral	30 Dec 63	IBRD Project	568UNTS243	108272
IBRD (World Bank)	Multilateral	30 Dec 63	IBRD Project	568UNTS233	108271
IBRD (World Bank)	Multilateral	30 Dec 63	IBRD Project	568UNTS215	108270
IBRD (World Bank)	Multilateral	30 Dec 63	IBRD Project	551UNTS105	108036
IBRD (World Bank)	Multilateral	30 Dec 63	IBRD Project	551UNTS119	108037
IBRD (World Bank)	Multilateral	30 Dec 63	IBRD Project	551UNTS75	108035
IBRD (World Bank)	Multilateral	26 May 64	IBRD Project	541UNTS271	200613
IBRD (World Bank)	Multilateral	18 Mar 65	Dispute Settlement	575UNTS159	108359
IBRD (World Bank)	Multilateral	22 Jul 65	IBRD Project	561UNTS333	200618
IBRD (World Bank)	Multilateral	04 May 66	IBRD Project	575UNTS49	108354
IBRD (World Bank)	Multilateral	12 Jun 67	IGO Operations	615UNTS321	108885
IBRD (World Bank)	Netherlands	07 Aug 47	IBRD Project	152UNTS165	102015
IBRD (World Bank)	Netherlands	15 Jul 48	IBRD Project	153UNTS259	102023
IBRD (World Bank)	Netherlands	15 Jul 48	IBRD Project	153UNTS211	102020
IBRD (World Bank)	Netherlands	15 Jul 48	IBRD Project	153UNTS259	102024
IBRD (World Bank)	Netherlands	15 Jul 48	IBRD Project	153UNTS259	102025
IBRD (World Bank)	Netherlands	15 Jul 48	IBRD Project	153UNTS259	102021
IBRD (World Bank)	Netherlands	15 Jul 48	IBRD Project	153UNTS259	102022
IBRD (World Bank)	Netherlands	26 Jul 49	IBRD Project	154UNTS178	102030
IBRD (World Bank)	Netherlands	20 Mar 52	IBRD Project	159UNTS207	102089
IBRD (World Bank)	Netherlands	15 May 57	IBRD Project	274UNTS211	103967
IBRD (World Bank)	New Zealand	12 Nov 63	IBRD Project	485UNTS233	107059
IBRD (World Bank)	New Zealand	12 Mar 64	IBRD Project	505UNTS3	107362
IBRD (World Bank)	New Zealand	17 Dec 65	IBRD Project	567UNTS255	108259
IBRD (World Bank)	New Zealand	17 Dec 65	IBRD Project	567UNTS275	108260
IBRD (World Bank)	Nicaragua	07 Jun 51	IBRD Project	158UNTS277	102068
IBRD (World Bank)	Nicaragua	07 Jun 51	IBRD Project	158UNTS215	102067
IBRD (World Bank)	Nicaragua	29 Oct 51	IBRD Project	159UNTS35	102082
IBRD (World Bank)	Nicaragua	04 Sep 53	IBRD Project	186UNTS117	102487
IBRD (World Bank)	Nicaragua	04 Sep 53	IBRD Project	186UNTS137	102488
IBRD (World Bank)	Nicaragua	08 Jul 55	IBRD Project	229UNTS123	103163
IBRD (World Bank)	Nicaragua	08 Jul 55	IBRD Project	229UNTS97	103162
IBRD (World Bank)	Nicaragua	26 Aug 55	IBRD Project	229UNTS145	103164
IBRD (World Bank)	Nicaragua	22 May 56	IBRD Project	253UNTS233	103586
IBRD (World Bank)	Nicaragua	22 Jun 60	IBRD Project	384UNTS243	105522
IBRD (World Bank)	Nicaragua	01 Mar 63	IBRD Project	481UNTS15	106976

PARTY ONE	PARTY TWO	DATE	TOPIC	CITATION	NUMBER
IBRD (World Bank)	Nicaragua	05 Oct 66	IBRD Project	582UNTS231	108465
IBRD (World Bank)	Nicaragua	13 Mar 67	IBRD Project	632UNTS177	109020
IBRD (World Bank)	Nicaragua	10 Apr 68	Loans and Credits	0UNTS0	109300
IBRD (World Bank)	Nicaragua	21 Jun 68	IBRD Project	0UNTS0	109366
IBRD (World Bank)	Nigeria	10 Dec 62	IBRD Project	468UNTS255	106776
IBRD (World Bank)	Nigeria	12 Mar 64	IBRD Project	516UNTS325	107480
IBRD (World Bank)	Nigeria	07 Jul 64	IBRD Project	537UNTS3	107795
IBRD (World Bank)	Nigeria	26 Sep 65	IBRD Project	570UNTS233	108296
IBRD (World Bank)	Nigeria	26 Sep 65	IBRD Project	571UNTS39	108298
IBRD (World Bank)	Nigeria	27 Nov 68	IBRD Project	0UNTS0	109591
IBRD (World Bank)	Nigeria	05 Mar 69	IBRD Project	0UNTS0	109644
IBRD (World Bank)	Nigeria	06 Nov 69	IBRD Project	0UNTS0	110672
IBRD (World Bank)	Nigeria	26 Jun 70	IBRD Project	0UNTS0	110832
IBRD (World Bank)	Norway	08 Apr 54	IBRD Project	201UNTS131	102714
IBRD (World Bank)	Norway	19 Apr 55	IBRD Project	211UNTS159	102852
IBRD (World Bank)	Norway	03 May 56	IBRD Project	243UNTS281	103455
IBRD (World Bank)	Norway	08 Jul 59	IBRD Project	344UNTS229	104952
IBRD (World Bank)	Norway	02 Dec 60	IBRD Project	390UNTS131	105606
IBRD (World Bank)	Norway	15 Oct 63	IBRD Project	482UNTS103	106992
IBRD (World Bank)	Other Party Combin	12 Jun 68	IBRD Project	0UNTS0	200644
IBRD (World Bank)	Pakistan	27 Mar 52	IBRD Project	159UNTS251	102090
IBRD (World Bank)	Pakistan	13 Jun 52	IBRD Project	191UNTS85	102578
IBRD (World Bank)	Pakistan	02 Jun 54	IBRD Project	324UNTS59	104678
IBRD (World Bank)	Pakistan	20 Jun 55	IBRD Project	230UNTS41	103176
IBRD (World Bank)	Pakistan	04 Aug 55	IBRD Project	230UNTS79	103177
IBRD (World Bank)	Pakistan	06 Aug 55	IBRD Project	236UNTS195	103325
IBRD (World Bank)	Pakistan	18 Oct 57	IBRD Project	299UNTS303	104322
IBRD (World Bank)	Pakistan	17 Dec 57	IBRD Project	299UNTS321	104323
IBRD (World Bank)	Pakistan	23 Apr 58	IBRD Project	323UNTS253	104672
IBRD (World Bank)	Pakistan	13 Aug 59	IBRD Project	355UNTS129	105076
IBRD (World Bank)	Pakistan	25 Sep 59	IBRD Project	355UNTS169	105077
IBRD (World Bank)	Pakistan	30 Nov 59	IBRD Project	355UNTS203	105078
IBRD (World Bank)	Pakistan	19 Sep 60	IBRD Project	444UNTS207	106370
IBRD (World Bank)	Pakistan	27 Jun 61	IBRD Project	425UNTS241	106127
IBRD (World Bank)	Pakistan	14 Sep 62	IBRD Project	467UNTS152	106762
IBRD (World Bank)	Pakistan	14 Sep 62	IBRD Project	467UNTS125	106761
IBRD (World Bank)	Pakistan	13 Feb 63	IBRD Project	467UNTS3	106756
IBRD (World Bank)	Pakistan	14 May 64	IBRD Project	516UNTS145	107475
IBRD (World Bank)	Pakistan	30 Jun 64	IBRD Project	519UNTS57	107502
IBRD (World Bank)	Pakistan	26 Aug 64	IBRD Project	632UNTS201	109023
IBRD (World Bank)	Pakistan	09 Jul 65	IBRD Project	554UNTS39	108096
IBRD (World Bank)	Pakistan	15 Mar 67	IBRD Project	599UNTS245	108670
IBRD (World Bank)	Pakistan	26 May 67	Loans and Credits	616UNTS167	108895
IBRD (World Bank)	Pakistan	10 Aug 67	IBRD Project	618UNTS261	108931
IBRD (World Bank)	Pakistan	10 Jul 68	IBRD Project	0UNTS0	109302
IBRD (World Bank)	Pakistan	10 Jul 68	IBRD Project	0UNTS0	109588
IBRD (World Bank)	Pakistan	20 Dec 68	IBRD Project	0UNTS0	109593
IBRD (World Bank)	Pakistan	21 Mar 69	IBRD Project	0UNTS0	109672
IBRD (World Bank)	Pakistan	13 May 69	IBRD Project	0UNTS0	110098
IBRD (World Bank)	Pakistan	26 Jun 69	IBRD Project	0UNTS0	110357
IBRD (World Bank)	Pakistan	29 Jun 70	IBRD Project	0UNTS0	110833
IBRD (World Bank)	Panama	25 Sep 53	IBRD Project	188UNTS95	102522
IBRD (World Bank)	Panama	25 Sep 53	IBRD Project	188UNTS71	102521
IBRD (World Bank)	Panama	12 Jul 55	IBRD Project	219UNTS127	102970
IBRD (World Bank)	Panama	19 Aug 60	IBRD Project	390UNTS153	105607
IBRD (World Bank)	Panama	14 Sep 62	IBRD Project	476UNTS153	106908
IBRD (World Bank)	Panama	16 Mar 70	IBRD Project	0UNTS0	110680
IBRD (World Bank)	Paraguay	07 Dec 51	IBRD Project	159UNTS103	102085
IBRD (World Bank)	Paraguay	16 Dec 64	IBRD Project	549UNTS173	107999
IBRD (World Bank)	Paraguay	16 Dec 65	IBRD Project	568UNTS165	108268
IBRD (World Bank)	Paraguay	04 Apr 66	IBRD Project	570UNTS41	108287
IBRD (World Bank)	Paraguay	09 Jan 69	IBRD Project	0UNTS0	110825
IBRD (World Bank)	Paraguay	25 Jun 69	IBRD Project	0UNTS0	110225
IBRD (World Bank)	Peru	23 Jan 52	IBRD Project	159UNTS163	102087
IBRD (World Bank)	Peru	08 Jul 52	IBRD Project	159UNTS321	102093

PARTY ONE	PARTY TWO	DATE	TOPIC	CITATION	NUMBER
IBRD (World Bank)	Peru	12 Apr 54	IBRD Project	190UNTS231	102567
IBRD (World Bank)	Peru	12 Nov 54	IBRD Project	209UNTS287	102831
IBRD (World Bank)	Peru	05 Apr 55	IBRD Project	211UNTS115	102850
IBRD (World Bank)	Peru	19 Apr 55	IBRD Project	221UNTS153	103007
IBRD (World Bank)	Peru	05 Aug 55	IBRD Project	218UNTS3	102950
IBRD (World Bank)	Peru	13 Mar 57	IBRD Project	274UNTS59	103958
IBRD (World Bank)	Peru	17 Sep 58	IBRD Project	323UNTS27	104663
IBRD (World Bank)	Peru	01 Jun 60	IBRD Project	380UNTS15	105448
IBRD (World Bank)	Peru	29 Jun 60	IBRD Project	400UNTS99	105750
IBRD (World Bank)	Peru	19 Dec 60	IBRD Project	417UNTS275	106010
IBRD (World Bank)	Peru	03 Nov 61	IBRD Project	430UNTS47	106203
IBRD (World Bank)	Peru	13 Mar 63	IBRD Project	478UNTS245	106938
IBRD (World Bank)	Peru	22 Nov 63	IBRD Project	491UNTS101	107175
IBRD (World Bank)	Peru	22 Apr 64	IBRD Project	519UNTS95	107503
IBRD (World Bank)	Peru	15 Mar 65	IBRD Project	632UNTS209	109024
IBRD (World Bank)	Peru	03 Jun 65	IBRD Project	551UNTS227	108045
IBRD (World Bank)	Peru	18 Jun 65	IBRD Project	568UNTS191	108269
IBRD (World Bank)	Peru	17 Sep 65	Loans and Credits	566UNTS311	108248
IBRD (World Bank)	Peru	13 May 66	IBRD Project	570UNTS61	108288
IBRD (World Bank)	Peru	07 Sep 66	IBRD Project	585UNTS3	108481
IBRD (World Bank)	Peru	11 Sep 67	IBRD Project	619UNTS171	108943
IBRD (World Bank)	Philippines	22 Nov 57	IBRD Project	293UNTS83	104287
IBRD (World Bank)	Philippines	26 Jul 61	IBRD Project	414UNTS253	105976
IBRD (World Bank)	Philippines	13 Oct 61	IBRD Project	415UNTS269	105989
IBRD (World Bank)	Philippines	07 Nov 62	Loans and Credits	468UNTS281	106777
IBRD (World Bank)	Philippines	15 Feb 63	IBRD Project	478UNTS161	106936
IBRD (World Bank)	Philippines	22 Jul 64	IBRD Project	516UNTS171	107476
IBRD (World Bank)	Philippines	28 Oct 64	IBRD Project	537UNTS165	107801
IBRD (World Bank)	Philippines	02 Nov 65	IBRD Project	567UNTS3	108249
IBRD (World Bank)	Philippines	23 Sep 66	IBRD Project	596UNTS71	108629
IBRD (World Bank)	Philippines	05 Apr 67	IBRD Project	598UNTS261	108661
IBRD (World Bank)	Philippines	04 Jun 69	IBRD Project	0UNTS0	109893
IBRD (World Bank)	Philippines	10 Jul 69	IBRD Project	0UNTS0	110105
IBRD (World Bank)	Philippines	18 Aug 69	IBRD Project	0UNTS0	110490
IBRD (World Bank)	Portugal	06 Nov 63	IBRD Project	492UNTS89	107188
IBRD (World Bank)	Portugal	06 Nov 63	IBRD Project	491UNTS137	107176
IBRD (World Bank)	Portugal	29 Apr 65	IBRD Project	549UNTS69	107991
IBRD (World Bank)	Portugal	14 Jun 66	IBRD Project	581UNTS29	108431
IBRD (World Bank)	Portugal	14 Jun 66	IBRD Project	581UNTS3	108430
IBRD (World Bank)	Senegal	01 May 67	IGO Operations	615UNTS267	108883
IBRD (World Bank)	Senegal	10 Feb 69	IBRD Project	0UNTS0	110120
IBRD (World Bank)	Sierra Leone	18 Aug 64	IBRD Project	516UNTS295	107479
IBRD (World Bank)	Sierra Leone	05 Aug 68	IBRD Project	0UNTS0	109487
IBRD (World Bank)	Singapore	11 Aug 66	IBRD Project	585UNTS39	108482
IBRD (World Bank)	Singapore	04 Nov 66	IBRD Project	585UNTS155	108488
IBRD (World Bank)	Singapore	05 Jul 67	IBRD Project	618UNTS189	108928
IBRD (World Bank)	Singapore	15 Sep 67	IGO Operations	615UNTS295	108884
IBRD (World Bank)	Singapore	03 Jul 68	IBRD Project	0UNTS0	109364
IBRD (World Bank)	Singapore	25 Apr 69	IBRD Project	0UNTS0	109946
IBRD (World Bank)	Singapore	19 Dec 69	Loans and Credits	0UNTS0	110547
IBRD (World Bank)	Singapore	25 Feb 70	IBRD Project	0UNTS0	110678
IBRD (World Bank)	South Africa	23 Jan 51	IBRD Project	158UNTS135	102065
IBRD (World Bank)	South Africa	23 Jan 51	IBRD Project	158UNTS115	102064
IBRD (World Bank)	South Africa	28 Aug 53	IBRD Project	180UNTS73	102376
IBRD (World Bank)	South Africa	28 Aug 53	IBRD Project	180UNTS91	102377
IBRD (World Bank)	South Africa	28 Nov 55	IBRD Project	230UNTS101	103178
IBRD (World Bank)	South Africa	01 Oct 57	IBRD Project	280UNTS285	104065
IBRD (World Bank)	South Africa	02 Dec 58	IBRD Project	324UNTS3	104676
IBRD (World Bank)	South Africa	10 Jun 59	IBRD Project	340UNTS33	104857
IBRD (World Bank)	South Africa	01 Dec 61	IBRD Project	425UNTS215	106126
IBRD (World Bank)	South Africa	01 Dec 61	IBRD Project	425UNTS197	106125
IBRD (World Bank)	South Africa	08 Sep 66	IBRD Project	585UNTS71	108483
IBRD (World Bank)	Spain	25 Oct 63	IBRD Project	491UNTS297	107181
IBRD (World Bank)	Spain	31 Jul 64	IBRD Project	537UNTS81	107798
IBRD (World Bank)	Spain	29 Sep 65	IBRD Project	568UNTS49	108264

PARTY ONE	PARTY TWO	DATE	TOPIC	CITATION	NUMBER
IBRD (World Bank)	Spain	04 Aug 67	IBRD Project	619UNTS209	108944
IBRD (World Bank)	Spain	17 Jul 69	IBRD Project	0UNTS0	110489
IBRD (World Bank)	State/IGO Group	02 May 68	Direct Aid	637UNTS0	109110
IBRD (World Bank)	Sudan	21 Jul 58	IBRD Project	323UNTS183	104669
IBRD (World Bank)	Sudan	17 Jun 60	IBRD Project	379UNTS253	105442
IBRD (World Bank)	Sudan	14 Jun 61	IBRD Project	415UNTS26	105980
IBRD (World Bank)	Sudan	27 Dec 65	IBRD Project	567UNTS27	108250
IBRD (World Bank)	Sudan	15 Jul 68	IBRD Project	0UNTS0	109319
IBRD (World Bank)	Sudan	06 Sep 68	IBRD Project	0UNTS0	110595
IBRD (World Bank)	Switzerland	29 Jun 51	IGO Status/Immunit	216UNTS347	200529
IBRD (World Bank)	Switzerland	17 Sep 56	Loans and Credits	340UNTS311	200560
IBRD (World Bank)	Switzerland	11 Oct 61	IBRD Project	415UNTS396	200592
IBRD (World Bank)	Taiwan	27 Sep 63	IBRD Project	483UNTS151	107012
IBRD (World Bank)	Taiwan	17 Dec 64	IBRD Project	538UNTS3	107808
IBRD (World Bank)	Taiwan	28 Apr 65	IBRD Project	549UNTS145	107998
IBRD (World Bank)	Taiwan	02 Aug 67	IBRD Project	618UNTS301	108932
IBRD (World Bank)	Taiwan	07 Aug 67	IBRD Project	620UNTS113	108952
IBRD (World Bank)	Taiwan	02 Dec 68	IBRD Project	0UNTS0	109639
IBRD (World Bank)	Taiwan	29 May 69	IBRD Project	0UNTS0	109892
IBRD (World Bank)	Taiwan	16 May 70	IBRD Project	0UNTS0	110688
IBRD (World Bank)	Tanzania	29 Sep 65	IBRD Project	568UNTS309	108275
IBRD (World Bank)	Tanzania	17 Feb 67	IBRD Project	599UNTS287	108671
IBRD (World Bank)	Tanzania	13 Dec 67	IBRD Project	619UNTS239	108945
IBRD (World Bank)	Thailand	27 Oct 50	IBRD Project	158UNTS25	102060
IBRD (World Bank)	Thailand	27 Oct 50	IBRD Project	158UNTS3	102059
IBRD (World Bank)	Thailand	27 Oct 50	IBRD Project	158UNTS43	102061
IBRD (World Bank)	Thailand	09 Aug 55	IBRD Project	221UNTS283	103011
IBRD (World Bank)	Thailand	12 Oct 56	IBRD Project	261UNTS117	103728
IBRD (World Bank)	Thailand	12 Sep 57	IBRD Project	299UNTS349	104324
IBRD (World Bank)	Thailand	28 Apr 61	IBRD Project	415UNTS121	105983
IBRD (World Bank)	Thailand	21 Dec 62	IBRD Project	467UNTS43	106757
IBRD (World Bank)	Thailand	21 Dec 62	IBRD Project	467UNTS63	106758
IBRD (World Bank)	Thailand	07 Mar 63	IBRD Project	467UNTS83	106759
IBRD (World Bank)	Thailand	11 Jun 63	IBRD Project	481UNTS227	106984
IBRD (World Bank)	Thailand	11 Mar 64	IBRD Project	504UNTS73	107354
IBRD (World Bank)	Thailand	25 Nov 64	IBRD Project	537UNTS273	107805
IBRD (World Bank)	Thailand	22 Mar 65	IBRD Project	538UNTS63	107810
IBRD (World Bank)	Thailand	24 Jun 66	IBRD Project	582UNTS259	108466
IBRD (World Bank)	Thailand	19 Oct 66	IBRD Project	594UNTS347	108609
IBRD (World Bank)	Thailand	24 Mar 67	IBRD Project	599UNTS299	108672
IBRD (World Bank)	Thailand	19 Sep 67	IBRD Project	619UNTS275	108946
IBRD (World Bank)	Thailand	23 May 68	IBRD Project	0UNTS0	109332
IBRD (World Bank)	Thailand	27 Jun 69	IBRD Project	0UNTS0	110311
IBRD (World Bank)	Thailand	10 Feb 70	IBRD Project	0UNTS0	110677
IBRD (World Bank)	Trinidad/Tobago	10 Mar 67	IBRD Project	599UNTS3	108662
IBRD (World Bank)	Trinidad/Tobago	16 Oct 68	IBRD Project	0UNTS0	109651
IBRD (World Bank)	Trinidad/Tobago	28 May 69	IBRD Project	0UNTS0	110220
IBRD (World Bank)	Tunisia	03 Jul 63	IBRD Project	480UNTS209	106970
IBRD (World Bank)	Tunisia	05 Jun 64	IBRD Project	539UNTS129	107827
IBRD (World Bank)	Tunisia	16 May 66	IBRD Project	584UNTS155	108477
IBRD (World Bank)	Tunisia	21 Feb 67	IBRD Project	618UNTS39	108923
IBRD (World Bank)	Tunisia	14 Sep 67	IBRD Project	639UNTS147	109149
IBRD (World Bank)	Tunisia	29 Nov 68	IBRD Project	0UNTS0	110598
IBRD (World Bank)	Tunisia	04 Jun 69	IBRD Project	0UNTS0	110286
IBRD (World Bank)	Tunisia	04 Jun 69	IBRD Project	0UNTS0	110648
IBRD (World Bank)	Tunisia	24 Dec 69	Non-IBRD Project	0UNTS0	110548
IBRD (World Bank)	Turkey	07 Jul 50	IBRD Project	156UNTS3	102039
IBRD (World Bank)	Turkey	07 Jul 50	IBRD Project	156UNTS75	102040
IBRD (World Bank)	Turkey	19 Oct 50	IBRD Project	157UNTS333	102058
IBRD (World Bank)	Turkey	18 Jun 52	IBRD Project	159UNTS269	102091
IBRD (World Bank)	Turkey	10 Sep 53	IBRD Project	187UNTS71	102502
IBRD (World Bank)	Turkey	31 Oct 61	IBRD Project	0UNTS0	109630
IBRD (World Bank)	Turkey	10 Aug 66	IBRD Project	585UNTS199	108490
IBRD (World Bank)	Turkey	11 May 67	IBRD Project	632UNTS193	109022
IBRD (World Bank)	Turkey	28 Feb 69	IBRD Project	0UNTS0	110091

PARTY ONE	PARTY TWO	DATE	TOPIC	CITATION	NUMBER
IBRD (World Bank)	Turkey	12 Mar 69	IBRD Project	0UNTS0	110113
IBRD (World Bank)	Turkey	27 Jun 69	IBRD Project	0UNTS0	110559
IBRD (World Bank)	Uganda	29 Sep 65	IBRD Project	568UNTS317	108276
IBRD (World Bank)	Uganda	17 Feb 67	IBRD Project	599UNTS321	108673
IBRD (World Bank)	UK Great Britain	27 Feb 52	IBRD Project	159UNTS181	102088
IBRD (World Bank)	UK Great Britain	11 Mar 53	IBRD Project	172UNTS115	102243
IBRD (World Bank)	UK Great Britain	15 Mar 55	IBRD Project	265UNTS85	103808
IBRD (World Bank)	UK Great Britain	21 Jun 56	IBRD Project	285UNTS355	104157
IBRD (World Bank)	UK Great Britain	02 May 58	IBRD Project	324UNTS25	104677
IBRD (World Bank)	UK Great Britain	16 Jun 58	IBRD Project	309UNTS35	104467
IBRD (World Bank)	UK Great Britain	01 Apr 60	IBRD Project	379UNTS397	105446
IBRD (World Bank)	UK Great Britain	27 May 60	IBRD Project	375UNTS201	105367
IBRD (World Bank)	UK Great Britain	29 Mar 61	IBRD Project	415UNTS300	105990
IBRD (World Bank)	UK Great Britain	23 Jun 61	IBRD Project	415UNTS358	105991
IBRD (World Bank)	UK Great Britain	16 Aug 61	IBRD Project	426UNTS287	106143
IBRD (World Bank)	UK Great Britain	29 Nov 61	IBRD Project	426UNTS49	106130
IBRD (World Bank)	UK Great Britain	16 May 63	IBRD Project	477UNTS361	106929
IBRD (World Bank)	UK Great Britain	16 May 63	IBRD Project	476UNTS211	106910
IBRD (World Bank)	UK Great Britain	06 Sep 63	IBRD Project	483UNTS173	107013
IBRD (World Bank)	UK Great Britain	23 Sep 63	IBRD Project	503UNTS247	107348
IBRD (World Bank)	UK Great Britain	18 Apr 66	IGO Operations	573UNTS209	108334
IBRD (World Bank)	UK Great Britain	24 Apr 67	IBRD Project	600UNTS3	108674
IBRD (World Bank)	United Arab Rep	22 Dec 59	IBRD Project	354UNTS197	105063
IBRD (World Bank)	United Nations	15 Apr 48	IGO Operations	16UNTS341	200109
IBRD (World Bank)	United Nations	20 Feb 57	IGO Operations	265UNTS312	200546
IBRD (World Bank)	United Nations	05 Jan 61	IGO Operations	384UNTS303	200577
IBRD (World Bank)	Uruguay	25 Aug 50	IBRD Project	156UNTS203	102042
IBRD (World Bank)	Uruguay	29 Aug 55	IBRD Project	243UNTS123	103450
IBRD (World Bank)	Uruguay	25 Oct 56	IBRD Project	265UNTS59	103807
IBRD (World Bank)	Uruguay	30 Dec 59	IBRD Project	384UNTS275	105523
IBRD (World Bank)	Uruguay	26 Oct 62	IBRD Project	481UNTS39	106977
IBRD (World Bank)	Uruguay	30 Mar 65	IBRD Project	567UNTS45	108251
IBRD (World Bank)	Venezuela	13 Dec 61	IBRD Project	446UNTS371	106409
IBRD (World Bank)	Venezuela	20 Sep 63	IBRD Project	482UNTS227	106997
IBRD (World Bank)	Venezuela	28 Aug 64	IBRD Project	537UNTS135	107800
IBRD (World Bank)	Venezuela	28 Aug 64	IBRD Project	520UNTS97	107512
IBRD (World Bank)	Venezuela	13 Dec 65	IBRD Project	568UNTS77	108265
IBRD (World Bank)	Venezuela	21 Apr 66	IBRD Project	568UNTS257	108273
IBRD (World Bank)	Venezuela	26 Jan 67	IBRD Project	596UNTS35	108628
IBRD (World Bank)	Venezuela	18 Jun 69	IBRD Project	0UNTS0	110221
IBRD (World Bank)	Venezuela	30 Jun 69	IGO Operations	0UNTS0	110514
IBRD (World Bank)	Yugoslavia	17 Sep 49	IBRD Project	155UNTS3	102034
IBRD (World Bank)	Yugoslavia	11 Oct 51	IBRD Project	159UNTS3	102081
IBRD (World Bank)	Yugoslavia	11 Feb 53	IBRD Project	165UNTS231	102179
IBRD (World Bank)	Yugoslavia	23 Feb 61	IBRD Project	415UNTS92	105982
IBRD (World Bank)	Yugoslavia	11 Jul 62	IBRD Project	468UNTS143	106772
IBRD (World Bank)	Yugoslavia	21 Jun 63	IBRD Project	482UNTS43	106990
IBRD (World Bank)	Yugoslavia	28 Oct 63	IBRD Project	503UNTS289	107349
IBRD (World Bank)	Yugoslavia	11 Dec 64	IBRD Project	537UNTS321	107807
IBRD (World Bank)	Yugoslavia	24 Feb 67	IBRD Project	599UNTS27	108663
IBRD (World Bank)	Yugoslavia	18 Jul 67	IGO Operations	615UNTS343	108886
IBRD (World Bank)	Yugoslavia	22 Mar 68	Loans and Credits	0UNTS0	109301
IBRD (World Bank)	Yugoslavia	15 Aug 68	IBRD Project	0UNTS0	109595
IBRD (World Bank)	Yugoslavia	05 Jun 69	IBRD Project	0UNTS0	110480
IBRD (World Bank)	Yugoslavia	30 Jan 70	Non-IBRD Project	0UNTS0	110549
IBRD (World Bank)	Zambia	04 Oct 66	IBRD Project	585UNTS181	108489
IBRD (World Bank)	Zambia	05 Oct 68	IBRD Project	0UNTS0	109650
IBRD (World Bank)	Zambia	05 Oct 68	IBRD Project	0UNTS0	109608
IBRD (World Bank)	Zambia	11 Apr 69	IBRD Project	0UNTS0	109891
IBRD (World Bank)	Zambia	30 Jun 69	IBRD Project	0UNTS0	110310
IBRD (World Bank)	Zambia	20 Nov 69	Loans and Credits	0UNTS0	110546
ICAO (Civil Aviat)	Austria	01 Apr 71	IGO Operations	71ABGB152	403101
ICAO (Civil Aviat)	Canada	14 Apr 51	IGO Status/Immunit	96UNTS155	101335
ICAO (Civil Aviat)	Denmark	09 Sep 49	Air Transport	53UNTS341	100791
ICAO (Civil Aviat)	Ethiopia	02 Feb 51	Tech Assistance	96UNTS123	101333

PARTY ONE	PARTY TWO	DATE	TOPIC	CITATION	NUMBER
ICAO (Civil Aviat)	France	14 Mar 47	IGO Status/Immunit	94UNTS59	101306
ICAO (Civil Aviat)	IAEA (Atom Energy)	01 Oct 59	IGO Operations	361UNTS193	200570
ICAO (Civil Aviat)	Iceland	16 Sep 48	Air Transport	28UNTS267	100429
ICAO (Civil Aviat)	Iceland	07 Jun 51	Tech Assistance	96UNTS193	101337
ICAO (Civil Aviat)	India	29 Apr 52	Tech Assistance	151UNTS123	101987
ICAO (Civil Aviat)	Iraq	18 Sep 51	Tech Assistance	108UNTS219	101475
ICAO (Civil Aviat)	Israel	19 Feb 51	Tech Assistance	96UNTS141	101334
ICAO (Civil Aviat)	Lebanon	14 Feb 52	Tech Assistance	128UNTS83	101714
ICAO (Civil Aviat)	Mexico	28 Nov 52	Tech Assistance	164UNTS15	102156
ICAO (Civil Aviat)	Mexico	20 Dec 56	IGO Operations	497UNTS3	107259
ICAO (Civil Aviat)	Multilateral	02 Nov 50	Tech Assistance	81UNTS160	101071
ICAO (Civil Aviat)	Multilateral	24 Nov 50	Tech Assistance	81UNTS188	101072
ICAO (Civil Aviat)	Multilateral	15 Dec 50	Tech Assistance	76UNTS120	100985
ICAO (Civil Aviat)	Multilateral	18 Jan 51	Tech Assistance	81UNTS233	101073
ICAO (Civil Aviat)	Multilateral	15 Feb 51	Tech Assistance	81UNTS245	101074
ICAO (Civil Aviat)	Multilateral	05 Mar 51	Tech Assistance	81UNTS261	101075
ICAO (Civil Aviat)	Multilateral	20 Mar 51	IGO Operations	82UNTS172	101091
ICAO (Civil Aviat)	Multilateral	05 Apr 51	Tech Assistance	84UNTS299	101139
ICAO (Civil Aviat)	Multilateral	25 Jun 51	Tech Assistance	92UNTS27	101258
ICAO (Civil Aviat)	Multilateral	27 Jul 51	Tech Assistance	97UNTS291	200273
ICAO (Civil Aviat)	Multilateral	05 Sep 51	Tech Assistance	173UNTS15	102256
ICAO (Civil Aviat)	Multilateral	01 Oct 51	Tech Assistance	104UNTS249	101446
ICAO (Civil Aviat)	Multilateral	24 Dec 51	Tech Assistance	118UNTS290	200383
ICAO (Civil Aviat)	Multilateral	23 Jan 52	Tech Assistance	127UNTS269	101708
ICAO (Civil Aviat)	Multilateral	18 Feb 52	Tech Assistance	126UNTS319	200434
ICAO (Civil Aviat)	Multilateral	11 Apr 52	Tech Assistance	173UNTS2	102255
ICAO (Civil Aviat)	Multilateral	22 May 52	Tech Assistance	131UNTS115	101739
ICAO (Civil Aviat)	Multilateral	19 Jun 52	Tech Assistance	133UNTS165	101787
ICAO (Civil Aviat)	Multilateral	15 Oct 52	Tech Assistance	141UNTS96	101909
ICAO (Civil Aviat)	Multilateral	16 Dec 52	Tech Assistance	158UNTS407	102074
ICAO (Civil Aviat)	Multilateral	29 Dec 52	Tech Assistance	151UNTS317	102002
ICAO (Civil Aviat)	Multilateral	09 Oct 53	Tech Assistance	190UNTS49	102557
ICAO (Civil Aviat)	Multilateral	20 Apr 54	Tech Assistance	189UNTS11	102539
ICAO (Civil Aviat)	Multilateral	31 May 54	Tech Assistance	192UNTS20	102592
ICAO (Civil Aviat)	Multilateral	01 Jun 54	Tech Assistance	200UNTS235	200520
ICAO (Civil Aviat)	Multilateral	30 Jun 54	Tech Assistance	193UNTS67	102611
ICAO (Civil Aviat)	Multilateral	19 Aug 54	Tech Assistance	201UNTS51	102710
ICAO (Civil Aviat)	Multilateral	06 Oct 54	Tech Assistance	201UNTS75	102711
ICAO (Civil Aviat)	Multilateral	27 Oct 54	Tech Assistance	201UNTS95	102712
ICAO (Civil Aviat)	Multilateral	29 Oct 54	Tech Assistance	201UNTS115	102713
ICAO (Civil Aviat)	Multilateral	16 Dec 54	Tech Assistance	204UNTS323	200523
ICAO (Civil Aviat)	Multilateral	04 Apr 55	Tech Assistance	208UNTS239	102816
ICAO (Civil Aviat)	Multilateral	14 Jun 55	Tech Assistance	212UNTS263	200526
ICAO (Civil Aviat)	Multilateral	04 Jul 55	Tech Assistance	214UNTS10	102897
ICAO (Civil Aviat)	Multilateral	13 Dec 55	Tech Assistance	407UNTS8	105857
ICAO (Civil Aviat)	Multilateral	02 Feb 56	Tech Assistance	227UNTS153	103137
ICAO (Civil Aviat)	Multilateral	10 Feb 56	Tech Assistance	228UNTS189	103151
ICAO (Civil Aviat)	Multilateral	10 Feb 56	Tech Assistance	228UNTS167	103150
ICAO (Civil Aviat)	Multilateral	30 Mar 56	IGO Operations	604UNTS114	108748
ICAO (Civil Aviat)	Multilateral	10 May 56	Tech Assistance	243UNTS103	103449
ICAO (Civil Aviat)	Multilateral	31 May 56	Tech Assistance	251UNTS181	103541
ICAO (Civil Aviat)	Multilateral	08 Jun 56	Tech Assistance	247UNTS366	200541
ICAO (Civil Aviat)	Multilateral	12 Jun 56	Tech Assistance	243UNTS187	103453
ICAO (Civil Aviat)	Multilateral	14 Jun 56	Tech Assistance	265UNTS125	103809
ICAO (Civil Aviat)	Multilateral	26 Jun 56	Tech Assistance	321UNTS2	104650
ICAO (Civil Aviat)	Multilateral	26 Jun 56	Tech Assistance	253UNTS12	103573
ICAO (Civil Aviat)	Multilateral	02 Jul 56	Tech Assistance	248UNTS37	103484
ICAO (Civil Aviat)	Multilateral	02 Jul 56	Tech Assistance	540UNTS110	107846
ICAO (Civil Aviat)	Multilateral	31 Aug 56	Tech Assistance	249UNTS158	103506
ICAO (Civil Aviat)	Multilateral	05 Oct 56	Tech Assistance	251UNTS267	103545
ICAO (Civil Aviat)	Multilateral	05 Oct 56	Tech Assistance	251UNTS245	103544
ICAO (Civil Aviat)	Multilateral	21 Nov 56	Tech Assistance	253UNTS266	103588
ICAO (Civil Aviat)	Multilateral	15 Jan 57	Tech Assistance	376UNTS122	105378
ICAO (Civil Aviat)	Multilateral	23 Jan 57	Tech Assistance	259UNTS426	103701
ICAO (Civil Aviat)	Multilateral	17 Feb 57	Tech Assistance	271UNTS2	103907

PARTY ONE	PARTY TWO	DATE	TOPIC	CITATION	NUMBER
ICAO (Civil Aviat)	Multilateral	01 Mar 57	Tech Assistance	264UNTS94	103790
ICAO (Civil Aviat)	Multilateral	28 Mar 57	Tech Assistance	271UNTS30	103908
ICAO (Civil Aviat)	Multilateral	09 Apr 57	Tech Assistance	274UNTS172	103965
ICAO (Civil Aviat)	Multilateral	24 May 57	Tech Assistance	268UNTS270	103861
ICAO (Civil Aviat)	Multilateral	30 Jun 57	Tech Assistance	286UNTS171	104165
ICAO (Civil Aviat)	Multilateral	05 Nov 57	Tech Assistance	285UNTS301	104155
ICAO (Civil Aviat)	Multilateral	15 Mar 58	Tech Assistance	292UNTS273	104276
ICAO (Civil Aviat)	Multilateral	19 Jun 58	Tech Assistance	306UNTS236	200550
ICAO (Civil Aviat)	Multilateral	09 Oct 59	Tech Assistance	376UNTS382	105391
ICAO (Civil Aviat)	Multilateral	03 Dec 59	Tech Assistance	348UNTS246	105003
ICAO (Civil Aviat)	Multilateral	12 Apr 60	Tech Assistance	359UNTS323	105150
ICAO (Civil Aviat)	Multilateral	04 Jun 60	Tech Assistance	360UNTS208	105159
ICAO (Civil Aviat)	Multilateral	17 Jun 60	Humanitarian	536UNTS27	107794
ICAO (Civil Aviat)	Multilateral	19 Jun 60	IGO Operations	537UNTS214	107803
ICAO (Civil Aviat)	Multilateral	08 Jul 60	Tech Assistance	366UNTS310	105220
ICAO (Civil Aviat)	Multilateral	28 Jan 61	Tech Assistance	387UNTS202	105563
ICAO (Civil Aviat)	Multilateral	20 Sep 61	Tech Assistance	407UNTS52	105859
ICAO (Civil Aviat)	Multilateral	16 Oct 61	Tech Assistance	410UNTS242	105908
ICAO (Civil Aviat)	Multilateral	07 Nov 61	Tech Assistance	412UNTS258	105937
ICAO (Civil Aviat)	Multilateral	27 Dec 61	Tech Assistance	425UNTS83	106120
ICAO (Civil Aviat)	Multilateral	17 Jan 62	Tech Assistance	419UNTS294	106033
ICAO (Civil Aviat)	Multilateral	20 Jan 62	Tech Assistance	429UNTS230	200596
ICAO (Civil Aviat)	Multilateral	13 Feb 62	Tech Assistance	422UNTS288	200594
ICAO (Civil Aviat)	Multilateral	21 Feb 62	Tech Assistance	423UNTS151	106091
ICAO (Civil Aviat)	Multilateral	01 Mar 62	Tech Assistance	423UNTS122	106089
ICAO (Civil Aviat)	Multilateral	10 Apr 62	Tech Assistance	429UNTS78	106192
ICAO (Civil Aviat)	Multilateral	18 Apr 62	Tech Assistance	463UNTS44	106692
ICAO (Civil Aviat)	Multilateral	17 May 62	Tech Assistance	429UNTS46	106189
ICAO (Civil Aviat)	Multilateral	12 Aug 62	Tech Assistance	443UNTS266	106365
ICAO (Civil Aviat)	Multilateral	29 Aug 62	Tech Assistance	443UNTS280	106366
ICAO (Civil Aviat)	Multilateral	11 Sep 62	Tech Assistance	455UNTS402	106553
ICAO (Civil Aviat)	Multilateral	14 Sep 62	Visas	443UNTS73	106360
ICAO (Civil Aviat)	Multilateral	15 Nov 62	Tech Assistance	448UNTS50	106424
ICAO (Civil Aviat)	Multilateral	06 Dec 62	Tech Assistance	450UNTS240	106471
ICAO (Civil Aviat)	Multilateral	12 Dec 62	Tech Assistance	457UNTS72	106578
ICAO (Civil Aviat)	Multilateral	21 Jan 63	Tech Assistance	453UNTS20	106517
ICAO (Civil Aviat)	Multilateral	05 Feb 63	Tech Assistance	453UNTS36	106518
ICAO (Civil Aviat)	Multilateral	14 Feb 63	Tech Assistance	453UNTS168	106524
ICAO (Civil Aviat)	Multilateral	06 Mar 63	Tech Assistance	455UNTS386	106552
ICAO (Civil Aviat)	Multilateral	18 Apr 63	Tech Assistance	463UNTS121	106697
ICAO (Civil Aviat)	Multilateral	06 May 63	Tech Assistance	463UNTS78	106694
ICAO (Civil Aviat)	Multilateral	09 May 63	Tech Assistance	463UNTS159	106700
ICAO (Civil Aviat)	Multilateral	22 May 63	Tech Assistance	483UNTS72	107007
ICAO (Civil Aviat)	Multilateral	24 May 63	Tech Assistance	470UNTS208	106810
ICAO (Civil Aviat)	Multilateral	24 May 63	Tech Assistance	466UNTS346	106754
ICAO (Civil Aviat)	Multilateral	23 Jul 63	Tech Assistance	471UNTS158	106831
ICAO (Civil Aviat)	Multilateral	31 Jul 63	Tech Assistance	472UNTS220	106842
ICAO (Civil Aviat)	Multilateral	27 Aug 63	Tech Assistance	511UNTS210	107435
ICAO (Civil Aviat)	Multilateral	10 Sep 63	Tech Assistance	480UNTS100	106965
ICAO (Civil Aviat)	Multilateral	30 Oct 63	Tech Assistance	480UNTS180	106968
ICAO (Civil Aviat)	Multilateral	07 Nov 63	Tech Assistance	480UNTS232	106971
ICAO (Civil Aviat)	Multilateral	08 Nov 63	Tech Assistance	482UNTS286	106999
ICAO (Civil Aviat)	Multilateral	28 Jan 64	Tech Assistance	502UNTS321	107336
ICAO (Civil Aviat)	Multilateral	20 Feb 64	Tech Assistance	491UNTS30	107172
ICAO (Civil Aviat)	Multilateral	23 Jun 64	Tech Assistance	506UNTS108	107383
ICAO (Civil Aviat)	Multilateral	28 Jun 64	Tech Assistance	519UNTS14	107499
ICAO (Civil Aviat)	Multilateral	03 Aug 64	Tech Assistance	503UNTS239	107347
ICAO (Civil Aviat)	Multilateral	24 Oct 64	Tech Assistance	514UNTS220	200608
ICAO (Civil Aviat)	Multilateral	11 Nov 64	Tech Assistance	515UNTS94	107456
ICAO (Civil Aviat)	Multilateral	11 Dec 64	IGO Operations	547UNTS297	107964
ICAO (Civil Aviat)	Multilateral	15 Dec 64	Tech Assistance	522UNTS20	107533
ICAO (Civil Aviat)	Multilateral	27 Jan 65	Tech Assistance	523UNTS102	107556
ICAO (Civil Aviat)	Multilateral	02 Feb 65	Tech Assistance	523UNTS256	107560
ICAO (Civil Aviat)	Multilateral	12 Feb 65	Tech Assistance	525UNTS148	107587
ICAO (Civil Aviat)	Multilateral	23 Feb 65	IGO Operations	527UNTS120	107622

PARTY ONE	PARTY TWO	DATE	TOPIC	CITATION	NUMBER
ICAO (Civil Aviat)	Multilateral	05 Mar 65	IGO Operations	527UNTS221	107627
ICAO (Civil Aviat)	Multilateral	08 Apr 65	IGO Operations	533UNTS66	107733
ICAO (Civil Aviat)	Multilateral	26 Apr 65	IGO Operations	533UNTS50	107732
ICAO (Civil Aviat)	Multilateral	12 May 65	IGO Operations	534UNTS390	107769
ICAO (Civil Aviat)	Multilateral	14 May 65	IGO Operations	550UNTS310	108026
ICAO (Civil Aviat)	Multilateral	25 May 65	IGO Operations	535UNTS374	107791
ICAO (Civil Aviat)	Multilateral	02 Jun 65	Tech Assistance	551UNTS2	108030
ICAO (Civil Aviat)	Multilateral	02 Jun 65	Tech Assistance	537UNTS348	200611
ICAO (Civil Aviat)	Multilateral	05 Jul 65	General Aid	563UNTS104	108207
ICAO (Civil Aviat)	Multilateral	20 Jul 65	IGO Operations	541UNTS12	107857
ICAO (Civil Aviat)	Multilateral	13 Sep 65	IGO Operations	547UNTS248	107961
ICAO (Civil Aviat)	Multilateral	13 Sep 65	Tech Assistance	547UNTS264	107962
ICAO (Civil Aviat)	Multilateral	21 Sep 65	IGO Operations	547UNTS280	107963
ICAO (Civil Aviat)	Multilateral	21 Oct 65	Tech Assistance	547UNTS216	107959
ICAO (Civil Aviat)	Multilateral	12 Nov 65	IGO Operations	550UNTS160	108013
ICAO (Civil Aviat)	Multilateral	31 Dec 65	Recognition	552UNTS292	108060
ICAO (Civil Aviat)	Multilateral	12 May 66	General Aid	563UNTS54	108204
ICAO (Civil Aviat)	Multilateral	06 Aug 66	Tech Assistance	570UNTS178	108294
ICAO (Civil Aviat)	Multilateral	22 Aug 66	Tech Assistance	571UNTS298	200624
ICAO (Civil Aviat)	Multilateral	23 Sep 66	IGO Operations	573UNTS132	108327
ICAO (Civil Aviat)	Multilateral	23 Sep 66	General Aid	573UNTS148	108328
ICAO (Civil Aviat)	Multilateral	30 Sep 66	IGO Operations	576UNTS8	108361
ICAO (Civil Aviat)	Multilateral	17 Nov 66	IGO Operations	580UNTS22	108417
ICAO (Civil Aviat)	Multilateral	25 Jan 67	IGO Operations	588UNTS212	108527
ICAO (Civil Aviat)	Multilateral	27 Feb 67	IGO Operations	590UNTS156	108552
ICAO (Civil Aviat)	Multilateral	03 Mar 67	Tech Assistance	594UNTS96	108597
ICAO (Civil Aviat)	Multilateral	13 Apr 67	IGO Operations	595UNTS60	108612
ICAO (Civil Aviat)	Multilateral	19 Apr 67	Tech Assistance	595UNTS120	108617
ICAO (Civil Aviat)	Multilateral	10 Jun 67	Direct Aid	602UNTS212	108714
ICAO (Civil Aviat)	Multilateral	14 Jun 67	Direct Aid	603UNTS2	108719
ICAO (Civil Aviat)	Multilateral	20 Jun 67	Tech Assistance	0UNTS0	109290
ICAO (Civil Aviat)	Multilateral	21 Jun 67	Tech Assistance	598UNTS2	108653
ICAO (Civil Aviat)	Multilateral	10 Jul 67	Air Transport	0UNTS0	109971
ICAO (Civil Aviat)	Multilateral	12 Oct 67	Direct Aid	607UNTS2	108792
ICAO (Civil Aviat)	Multilateral	12 Oct 67	Direct Aid	607UNTS20	108793
ICAO (Civil Aviat)	Multilateral	27 Oct 67	General Aid	608UNTS37	108811
ICAO (Civil Aviat)	Multilateral	14 Nov 67	Admin Cooperation	614UNTS2	108860
ICAO (Civil Aviat)	Multilateral	18 Jun 69	IGO Operations	0UNTS0	109740
ICAO (Civil Aviat)	Multilateral	18 Jun 69	IGO Operations	0UNTS0	109741
ICAO (Civil Aviat)	Multilateral	24 Jun 69	IGO Operations	0UNTS0	109743
ICAO (Civil Aviat)	Peru	22 Oct 48	IGO Status/Immunit	95UNTS3	101315
ICAO (Civil Aviat)	Syria	28 May 53	Tech Assistance	173UNTS199	102267
ICAO (Civil Aviat)	Thailand	19 Apr 51	Tech Assistance	96UNTS181	101336
ICAO (Civil Aviat)	Thailand	18 Oct 65	Air Transport	0UNTS0	110162
ICAO (Civil Aviat)	UN Special Fund	21 Apr 60	IGO Operations	360UNTS367	200569
ICAO (Civil Aviat)	United Arab Rep	06 Mar 52	Tech Assistance	151UNTS111	101986
ICAO (Civil Aviat)	United Arab Rep	27 Aug 53	IGO Status/Immunit	215UNTS371	102925
ICAO (Civil Aviat)	United Nations	01 Oct 47	IGO Operations	8UNTS315	200045
ICAO (Civil Aviat)	United Nations	28 Feb 51	IGO Operations	139UNTS429	200469
ICAO (Civil Aviat)	Yugoslavia	06 Feb 52	Tech Assistance	128UNTS97	101715
Iceland	Accept UN Charter	19 Nov 46	UN Charter	1UNTS41	100008
Iceland	Australia	13 Nov 52	General Trade	161UNTS59	102122
Iceland	Australia	29 Apr 69	Visas	0UNTS0	110176
Iceland	Belgium	10 Dec 52	Patents/Copyrights	158UNTS445	102078
Iceland	Belgium	09 Jul 70	Taxation	0UNTS0	110607
Iceland	Bulgaria	10 Apr 68	Visas	0UNTS0	110304
Iceland	Canada	17 Oct 62	Visas	528UNTS281	107649
Iceland	Denmark	14 May 48	Non-ILO Labor	23UNTS163	100346
Iceland	Denmark	22 Mar 50	Air Transport	72UNTS273	100939
Iceland	Denmark	10 Oct 55	Taxation	230UNTS3	103171
Iceland	Denmark	01 Aug 61	Specific Resources	425UNTS191	106124
Iceland	Finland	10 Mar 60	Air Transport	497UNTS95	107264
Iceland	Germany, West	19 Dec 50	Patents/Copyrights	56WGBB899	425278
Iceland	Germany, West	19 Dec 50	General Amity	51WGBB153	425279
Iceland	Germany, West	20 May 54	General Trade	54WBGA124	424280

PARTY ONE	PARTY TWO	DATE	TOPIC	CITATION	NUMBER
Iceland	Germany, West	14 Sep 56	Visas	57WBGA192	424281
Iceland	Germany, West	12 Aug 59	Air Transport	411UNTS224	105921
Iceland	Germany, West	19 Jul 61	Specific Resources	409UNTS47	105877
Iceland	IBRD (World Bank)	20 Jun 51	IBRD Project	158UNTS301	102069
Iceland	IBRD (World Bank)	01 Nov 51	IBRD Project	159UNTS55	102083
Iceland	IBRD (World Bank)	26 Aug 52	IBRD Project	159UNTS363	102095
Iceland	IBRD (World Bank)	04 Sep 53	IBRD Project	178UNTS275	102344
Iceland	IBRD (World Bank)	04 Sep 53	IBRD Project	188UNTS3	102519
Iceland	IBRD (World Bank)	14 Feb 62	IBRD Project	447UNTS95	106413
Iceland	IBRD (World Bank)	14 Sep 66	IBRD Project	598UNTS223	108660
Iceland	ICAO (Civil Aviat)	16 Sep 48	Air Transport	28UNTS267	100429
Iceland	ICAO (Civil Aviat)	07 Jun 51	Tech Assistance	96UNTS193	101337
Iceland	Ireland	20 May 49	Visas	553UNTS99	108073
Iceland	Ireland	02 Dec 50	General Trade	558UNTS231	108143
Iceland	Israel	29 Dec 55	Visas	227UNTS147	103136
Iceland	Israel	15 Jun 60	Patents/Copyrights	377UNTS261	105405
Iceland	Israel	23 Feb 66	Visas	581UNTS211	108446
Iceland	Jamaica	02 Jul 69	Visas	0UNTS0	109943
Iceland	Japan	15 Nov 66	Visas	66JJS153	442183
Iceland	Luxembourg	23 Oct 52	Air Transport	193UNTS39	102609
Iceland	Multilateral	12 May 40	Scientific Project	101UNTS91	101405
Iceland	Multilateral	02 Aug 44	Scientific Project	67UNTS221	200221
Iceland	Multilateral	07 Dec 44	IGO Establishment	15UNTS295	200102
Iceland	Multilateral	07 Dec 44	Air Transport	171UNTS387	200502
Iceland	Multilateral	07 Dec 44	Air Transport	84UNTS389	200252
Iceland	Multilateral	07 Dec 44	Air Transport	171UNTS345	200501
Iceland	Multilateral	27 Dec 45	IGO Establishment	2UNTS39	100020
Iceland	Multilateral	05 Apr 46	Specific Resources	231UNTS199	103221
Iceland	Multilateral	02 Dec 46	Specific Resources	161UNTS72	102124
Iceland	Multilateral	15 Dec 46	IGO Establishment	18UNTS3	100283
Iceland	Multilateral	03 Mar 47	Humanitarian	11UNTS43	100148
Iceland	Multilateral	10 Jun 47	Water Transport	208UNTS3	102814
Iceland	Multilateral	02 Oct 47	Telecommunications	193UNTS188	102616
Iceland	Multilateral	11 Oct 47	IGO Establishment	77UNTS143	100998
Iceland	Multilateral	06 Mar 48	Water Transport	289UNTS3	104214
Iceland	Multilateral	10 Jun 48	Humanitarian	164UNTS113	102163
Iceland	Multilateral	10 Jun 48	Humanitarian	191UNTS3	102576
Iceland	Multilateral	19 Jun 48	Air Transport	310UNTS151	104492
Iceland	Multilateral	26 Jun 48	Culture	331UNTS217	104757
Iceland	Multilateral	24 Jul 48	Sanitation	66UNTS25	100847
Iceland	Multilateral	17 Sep 48	Telecommunications	97UNTS31	101345
Iceland	Multilateral	09 Dec 48	Humanitarian	78UNTS277	101021
Iceland	Multilateral	08 Feb 49	Specific Resources	157UNTS157	102053
Iceland	Multilateral	23 Mar 49	Commodity Trade	203UNTS179	102746
Iceland	Multilateral	04 Apr 49	General Military	34UNTS243	100541
Iceland	Multilateral	04 May 49	Admin Cooperation	30UNTS3	100445
Iceland	Multilateral	04 May 49	Admin Cooperation	47UNTS159	100728
Iceland	Multilateral	05 May 49	IGO Establishment	87UNTS103	101168
Iceland	Multilateral	18 Jun 49	ILO Labor	605UNTS295	108768
Iceland	Multilateral	27 Aug 49	Non-ILO Labor	47UNTS127	100727
Iceland	Multilateral	02 Sep 49	IGO Status/Immunit	250UNTS12	103515
Iceland	Multilateral	18 Oct 50	Specific Resources	638UNTS185	109134
Iceland	Multilateral	04 Nov 50	Humanitarian	213UNTS221	102889
Iceland	Multilateral	15 Dec 50	Customs	347UNTS127	104994
Iceland	Multilateral	15 Dec 50	Customs	157UNTS129	102052
Iceland	Multilateral	15 Dec 50	Customs	171UNTS305	102234
Iceland	Multilateral	15 Dec 50	IGO Operations	160UNTS267	102111
Iceland	Multilateral	09 Jan 51	Humanitarian	197UNTS341	102647
Iceland	Multilateral	25 May 51	Status of Forces	175UNTS215	102303
Iceland	Multilateral	19 Jun 51	Status of Forces	199UNTS67	102678
Iceland	Multilateral	28 Aug 51	Non-ILO Labor	198UNTS17	102654
Iceland	Multilateral	20 Sep 51	IGO Status/Immunit	200UNTS3	102691
Iceland	Multilateral	20 May 52	Sanitation	219UNTS55	102966
Iceland	Multilateral	11 Jul 52	Postal Service	170UNTS3	102221
Iceland	Multilateral	11 Jul 52	Postal Service	170UNTS63	102222

PARTY ONE	PARTY TWO	DATE	TOPIC	CITATION	NUMBER
Iceland	Multilateral	11 Jul 52	Postal Service	171UNTS89	102225
Iceland	Multilateral	11 Jul 52	Postal Service	170UNTS269	102223
Iceland	Multilateral	11 Jul 52	Postal Service	171UNTS143	102226
Iceland	Multilateral	11 Jul 52	IGO Establishment	169UNTS3	102220
Iceland	Multilateral	14 Jul 52	Consul/Citizenship	198UNTS47	102656
Iceland	Multilateral	23 Mar 53	Admin Cooperation	202UNTS241	102732
Iceland	Multilateral	31 Mar 53	Privil/Immunities	193UNTS136	102613
Iceland	Multilateral	01 Apr 53	Non-ILO Labor	227UNTS169	103138
Iceland	Multilateral	20 Jul 53	Non-ILO Labor	228UNTS41	103142
Iceland	Multilateral	20 Jul 53	Non-ILO Labor	227UNTS217	103140
Iceland	Multilateral	20 Jul 53	Non-ILO Labor	228UNTS3	103141
Iceland	Multilateral	11 Dec 53	Education	218UNTS125	102954
Iceland	Multilateral	11 Dec 53	Sanitation	191UNTS285	102588
Iceland	Multilateral	11 Dec 53	Non-ILO Labor	218UNTS255	102958
Iceland	Multilateral	11 Dec 53	Non-ILO Labor	218UNTS211	102957
Iceland	Multilateral	11 Dec 53	Non-ILO Labor	218UNTS153	102956
Iceland	Multilateral	11 Dec 53	Patents/Copyrights	218UNTS27	102952
Iceland	Multilateral	25 Feb 54	Air Transport	215UNTS249	102922
Iceland	Multilateral	12 May 54	Admin Cooperation	327UNTS3	104714
Iceland	Multilateral	22 May 54	Visas	199UNTS29	102675
Iceland	Multilateral	14 Jun 54	Air Transport	320UNTS209	104643
Iceland	Multilateral	14 Jun 54	Air Transport	320UNTS217	104644
Iceland	Multilateral	19 Dec 54	Culture	218UNTS139	102955
Iceland	Multilateral	25 May 55	IGO Establishment	264UNTS117	103791
Iceland	Multilateral	22 Jun 55	Atomic Energy	249UNTS3	103498
Iceland	Multilateral	15 Sep 55	Non-ILO Labor	254UNTS55	103593
Iceland	Multilateral	28 Sep 55	Air Transport	478UNTS371	106943
Iceland	Multilateral	13 Dec 55	IGO Operations	529UNTS141	107660
Iceland	Multilateral	25 Apr 56	Commodity Trade	270UNTS103	103896
Iceland	Multilateral	30 Apr 56	Air Transport	310UNTS229	104494
Iceland	Multilateral	25 Sep 56	Air Transport	334UNTS13	104766
Iceland	Multilateral	25 Sep 56	Air Transport	334UNTS89	104767
Iceland	Multilateral	26 Oct 56	IGO Establishment	276UNTS3	103988
Iceland	Multilateral	21 Nov 56	Tech Assistance	253UNTS266	103588
Iceland	Multilateral	15 Dec 56	Education	278UNTS73	104023
Iceland	Multilateral	19 Dec 56	Non-ILO Labor	427UNTS93	106148
Iceland	Multilateral	29 Apr 57	Dispute Settlement	320UNTS243	104646
Iceland	Multilateral	03 Oct 57	Postal Service	364UNTS3	105211
Iceland	Multilateral	03 Oct 57	Postal Service	366UNTS141	105217
Iceland	Multilateral	03 Oct 57	Postal Service	365UNTS207	105214
Iceland	Multilateral	03 Oct 57	Postal Service	366UNTS87	105216
Iceland	Multilateral	03 Oct 57	Postal Service	365UNTS3	105213
Iceland	Multilateral	03 Oct 57	Postal Service	364UNTS331	105212
Iceland	Multilateral	13 Dec 57	Extradition	359UNTS273	105146
Iceland	Multilateral	29 Apr 58	Specific Resources	559UNTS285	108164
Iceland	Multilateral	29 Apr 58	Territory Boundary	516UNTS205	107477
Iceland	Multilateral	29 Apr 58	Territory Boundary	499UNTS311	107302
Iceland	Multilateral	29 Apr 58	Water Transport	450UNTS11	106465
Iceland	Multilateral	24 Jan 59	IGO Establishment	486UNTS157	107078
Iceland	Multilateral	06 Apr 59	Commodity Trade	349UNTS167	105013
Iceland	Multilateral	20 Apr 59	Visas	376UNTS85	105375
Iceland	Multilateral	08 Sep 59	Non-ILO Labor	383UNTS203	105502
Iceland	Multilateral	14 Dec 59	Admin Cooperation	444UNTS193	106369
Iceland	Multilateral	17 Jun 60	Humanitarian	536UNTS27	107794
Iceland	Multilateral	26 Oct 61	Patents/Copyrights	496UNTS43	107247
Iceland	Multilateral	23 Mar 62	Admin Cooperation	470UNTS25	106793
Iceland	Multilateral	23 Mar 62	General Amity	434UNTS145	106262
Iceland	Multilateral	05 Aug 63	Sanitation	480UNTS43	106964
Iceland	Multilateral	18 Jun 64	Atomic Energy	542UNTS145	107886
Iceland	Multilateral	10 Jul 64	Postal Service	612UNTS3	108847
Iceland	Multilateral	10 Jul 64	Postal Service	611UNTS105	108845
Iceland	Multilateral	10 Jul 64	Postal Service	611UNTS387	108846
Iceland	Multilateral	10 Jul 64	Postal Service	611UNTS7	108844
Iceland	Multilateral	10 Jul 64	Postal Service	613UNTS3	108850
Iceland	Multilateral	10 Jul 64	Postal Service	612UNTS233	108848

PARTY ONE	PARTY TWO	DATE	TOPIC	CITATION	NUMBER
Iceland	Multilateral	12 Sep 64	Specific Resources	0UNTS0	109344
Iceland	Multilateral	09 Mar 65	Water Transport	591UNTS265	108564
Iceland	Multilateral	18 Mar 65	Dispute Settlement	575UNTS159	108359
Iceland	Multilateral	03 Dec 65	Admin Cooperation	572UNTS105	108309
Iceland	Multilateral	05 Apr 66	Water Transport	640UNTS133	109159
Iceland	Multilateral	03 Oct 66	Culture	610UNTS169	108841
Iceland	Multilateral	27 Jan 67	Scientific Project	610UNTS205	108843
Iceland	Multilateral	24 Feb 67	Health/Educ/Welfare	596UNTS133	108631
Iceland	Multilateral	17 Apr 67	Consul/Citizenship	0UNTS0	110377
Iceland	Multilateral	03 May 67	IGO Operations	0UNTS0	110764
Iceland	Multilateral	07 Jun 68	Admin Cooperation	0UNTS0	110346
Iceland	Multilateral	01 Jul 68	Peace/Disarmament	0UNTS0	110485
Iceland	Multilateral	05 Dec 68	Scientific Project	0UNTS0	109952
Iceland	Multilateral	12 Dec 69	General Economic	0UNTS0	110755
Iceland	Netherlands	22 Mar 50	Air Transport	95UNTS237	101323
Iceland	Netherlands	28 Dec 54	Finance	287UNTS159	104182
Iceland	Netherlands	30 Apr 59	Finance	487UNTS13	107091
Iceland	Norway	14 Jul 51	Air Transport	163UNTS265	102150
Iceland	Norway	17 Sep 55	Taxation	2NORT664	451076
Iceland	Norway	30 Mar 66	Taxation	566UNTS51	108240
Iceland	Norway	30 Mar 66	Taxation	3NORT959	451077
Iceland	Norway	09 Sep 68	Gen Communications	3NORT0	451078
Iceland	Spain	21 Dec 54	General Trade	55SPBO401	460165
Iceland	Spain	31 Dec 55	General Trade	56SPBO2701	460166
Iceland	Spain	13 Feb 57	General Trade	57SPBO103	460167
Iceland	Sweden	07 Apr 45	General Trade	45SOFM95	461006
Iceland	Sweden	20 Apr 45	Air Transport	45SOFM67	461002
Iceland	Sweden	18 May 46	General Trade	46SOFM197	461024
Iceland	Sweden	19 Oct 47	General Trade	47SOFM480	461047
Iceland	Sweden	15 Jul 49	General Trade	49SOFM497	461089
Iceland	Sweden	31 Mar 50	General Trade	50SOFM118	461106
Iceland	Sweden	12 Apr 51	General Trade	51SOFM211	461142
Iceland	Sweden	31 Mar 52	General Trade	52SOFM191	461162
Iceland	Sweden	03 Jun 52	Air Transport	215UNTS223	102921
Iceland	Sweden	03 Jul 53	General Trade	53SOFM733	461186
Iceland	Sweden	17 Sep 55	Taxation	262UNTS273	103755
Iceland	Sweden	23 Sep 55	Admin Cooperation	262UNTS241	103750
Iceland	Thailand	22 Jan 57	Air Transport	312UNTS63	104511
Iceland	UK Great Britain	04 Jul 46	Specific Property	6UNTS223	100077
Iceland	UK Great Britain	20 Jun 47	Visas	11UNTS223	100161
Iceland	UK Great Britain	26 May 50	Air Transport	95UNTS277	101326
Iceland	UK Great Britain	14 May 59	Finance	343UNTS301	104936
Iceland	UK Great Britain	09 Feb 61	Visas	398UNTS259	105728
Iceland	UK Great Britain	11 Mar 61	Dispute Settlement	397UNTS275	105710
Iceland	UK Great Britain	19 Sep 68	Finance	0UNTS0	109800
Iceland	UN Special Fund	10 Jul 64	IGO Operations	502UNTS343	107337
Iceland	United Nations	19 Apr 48	Humanitarian	47UNTS251	100733
Iceland	USA (United States)	01 Jul 41	Milit Assistance	12UNTS405	200071
Iceland	USA (United States)	21 Nov 41	Milit Assistance	124UNTS179	200418
Iceland	USA (United States)	17 Aug 42	Admin Cooperation	24UNTS163	200140
Iceland	USA (United States)	27 Sep 43	General Trade	29UNTS317	200170
Iceland	USA (United States)	27 Jan 45	Air Transport	122UNTS293	200411
Iceland	USA (United States)	11 Apr 45	Air Transport	16UNTS241	200105
Iceland	USA (United States)	07 Oct 46	Milit Installation	12UNTS163	100184
Iceland	USA (United States)	09 Dec 47	Visas	82UNTS31	101082
Iceland	USA (United States)	03 Jul 48	Direct Aid	20UNTS141	100316
Iceland	USA (United States)	03 Jul 48	Milit Occupation	27UNTS49	100398
Iceland	USA (United States)	05 May 51	Milit Assistance	205UNTS173	102776
Iceland	USA (United States)	08 Jan 52	Milit Assistance	180UNTS183	102383
Iceland	USA (United States)	18 Mar 52	Taxation	177UNTS263	102325
Iceland	USA (United States)	10 Dec 54	Milit Assistance	237UNTS191	103345
Iceland	USA (United States)	20 Jul 55	General Military	256UNTS245	103634
Iceland	USA (United States)	05 Oct 55	Claims and Debts	256UNTS285	103638
Iceland	USA (United States)	06 Mar 56	General Trade	270UNTS205	103898
Iceland	USA (United States)	04 Jun 56	Visas	275UNTS189	103982

PARTY ONE	PARTY TWO	DATE	TOPIC	CITATION	NUMBER
Iceland	USA (United States)	23 Nov 56	Specif Claim/Waive	281UNTS361	104088
Iceland	USA (United States)	06 Dec 56	General Military	265UNTS261	103818
Iceland	USA (United States)	23 Feb 57	Education	283UNTS73	104107
Iceland	USA (United States)	11 Apr 57	US Agri Commod Aid	283UNTS107	104110
Iceland	USA (United States)	03 May 58	US Agri Commod Aid	316UNTS137	104581
Iceland	USA (United States)	03 Mar 59	US Agri Commod Aid	341UNTS261	104889
Iceland	USA (United States)	23 Jun 59	Direct Aid	354UNTS3	105048
Iceland	USA (United States)	06 Apr 60	US Agri Commod Aid	372UNTS71	105289
Iceland	USA (United States)	30 Dec 60	Direct Aid	401UNTS43	105761
Iceland	USA (United States)	07 Apr 61	US Agri Commod Aid	406UNTS203	105850
Iceland	USA (United States)	06 Nov 61	US Agri Commod Aid	426UNTS225	106140
Iceland	USA (United States)	16 Mar 62	US Agri Commod Aid	445UNTS49	106376
Iceland	USA (United States)	27 Dec 62	Taxation	469UNTS91	106785
Iceland	USA (United States)	06 Feb 63	US Agri Commod Aid	473UNTS93	106858
Iceland	USA (United States)	15 Jul 63	General Trade	527UNTS45	107616
Iceland	USA (United States)	13 Feb 64	US Agri Commod Aid	510UNTS295	107420
Iceland	USA (United States)	13 Feb 64	US Agri Commod Aid	511UNTS3	107421
Iceland	USA (United States)	13 Feb 64	Education	524UNTS235	107576
Iceland	USA (United States)	30 Dec 64	US Agri Commod Aid	531UNTS287	107709
Iceland	USA (United States)	30 Dec 64	US Agri Commod Aid	542UNTS37	107878
Iceland	USA (United States)	05 Jun 67	US Agri Commod Aid	0UNTS0	109903
Iceland	USA (United States)	29 May 68	US Agri Commod Aid	0UNTS0	110066
Iceland	USA (United States)	23 May 69	Commodity Trade	0UNTS0	110276
Iceland	USA (United States)	24 Jun 70	Air Transport	0UNTS0	110783
Iceland	USSR (Soviet Union)	01 Aug 53	General Economic	0SUST298	468205
Iceland	USSR (Soviet Union)	05 Feb 54	General Economic	0SUST307	468206
Iceland	USSR (Soviet Union)	23 Sep 55	General Economic	0SUST338	468207
Iceland	USSR (Soviet Union)	03 Dec 55	Consul/Citizenship	0SUST343	468208
Iceland	USSR (Soviet Union)	13 Mar 58	Consul/Citizenship	16SUGG124	469956
Iceland	USSR (Soviet Union)	16 Jul 58	Specific Resources	7SUGG116	469519
Iceland	USSR (Soviet Union)	18 Aug 58	Loans and Credits	7SUGG118	469523
Iceland	USSR (Soviet Union)	14 Mar 60	Consul/Citizenship	16SUGG127	469973
Iceland	USSR (Soviet Union)	17 May 60	Finance	9SUGG136	469660
Iceland	USSR (Soviet Union)	25 Apr 61	Health/Educ/Welfare	10SUGG129	469764
Iceland	USSR (Soviet Union)	19 Dec 62	General Trade	11SUGG159	469877
Iceland	WHO (World Health)	06 Oct 50	Tech Assistance	110UNTS127	101506
ICJ (Int Court)	Netherlands	26 Jun 46	IGO Status/Immunit	8UNTS61	100114
IDA (Devel Assoc)	Afghanistan	23 Nov 64	Non-IBRD Project	567UNTS155	108255
IDA (Devel Assoc)	Australia	21 Jan 69	Non-IBRD Project	0UNTS0	110486
IDA (Devel Assoc)	Australia	30 Jan 70	Non-IBRD Project	0UNTS0	110654
IDA (Devel Assoc)	Bolivia	24 Jul 64	Non-IBRD Project	534UNTS171	107762
IDA (Devel Assoc)	Bolivia	24 Jul 64	Non-IBRD Project	534UNTS203	107763
IDA (Devel Assoc)	Bolivia	26 May 67	Non-IBRD Project	618UNTS159	108927
IDA (Devel Assoc)	Bolivia	28 Apr 69	Non-IBRD Project	0UNTS0	110235
IDA (Devel Assoc)	Bolivia	13 Jan 70	Non-IBRD Project	0UNTS0	110652
IDA (Devel Assoc)	Burundi	31 Mar 66	Loans and Credits	569UNTS3	108277
IDA (Devel Assoc)	Burundi	11 Apr 69	Non-IBRD Project	0UNTS0	110218
IDA (Devel Assoc)	Cameroon	28 Mar 67	Non-IBRD Project	618UNTS133	108926
IDA (Devel Assoc)	Cameroon	29 Jan 68	Non-IBRD Project	0UNTS0	109325
IDA (Devel Assoc)	Cameroon	23 Sep 69	Non-IBRD Project	0UNTS0	110580
IDA (Devel Assoc)	Cameroon	27 Mar 70	Non-IBRD Project	0UNTS0	110682
IDA (Devel Assoc)	Ceylon (Sri Lanka)	19 Jun 68	Non-IBRD Project	0UNTS0	109622
IDA (Devel Assoc)	Ceylon (Sri Lanka)	12 Nov 68	Non-IBRD Project	0UNTS0	109624
IDA (Devel Assoc)	Ceylon (Sri Lanka)	13 Nov 69	Non-IBRD Project	0UNTS0	110582
IDA (Devel Assoc)	Chad	14 Aug 68	Non-IBRD Project	0UNTS0	109641
IDA (Devel Assoc)	Chad	29 Aug 68	Non-IBRD Project	0UNTS0	109642
IDA (Devel Assoc)	Chile	28 Jun 61	Loans and Credits	426UNTS89	106131
IDA (Devel Assoc)	Colombia	28 Aug 61	Loans and Credits	416UNTS3	105992
IDA (Devel Assoc)	Congo (Zaire)	26 May 69	Loans and Credits	0UNTS0	110285
IDA (Devel Assoc)	Congo (Zaire)	09 Jun 69	Non-IBRD Project	0UNTS0	110588
IDA (Devel Assoc)	Congo (Zaire)	28 May 70	Non-IBRD Project	0UNTS0	110659
IDA (Devel Assoc)	Costa Rica	13 Oct 61	Non-IBRD Project	431UNTS3	106204
IDA (Devel Assoc)	Dahomey	05 Mar 69	Non-IBRD Project	0UNTS0	110216
IDA (Devel Assoc)	Ecuador	26 May 64	Non-IBRD Project	534UNTS93	107757
IDA (Devel Assoc)	Ecuador	27 Jun 68	Non-IBRD Project	0UNTS0	109321

PARTY ONE	PARTY TWO	DATE	TOPIC	CITATION	NUMBER
IDA (Devel Assoc)	Ecuador	20 Jan 70	Non-IBRD Project	0UNTS0	110653
IDA (Devel Assoc)	El Salvador	02 Nov 62	Non-IBRD Project	468UNTS331	106780
IDA (Devel Assoc)	Ethiopia	27 Feb 63	Non-IBRD Project	478UNTS289	106939
IDA (Devel Assoc)	Ethiopia	16 Feb 66	Loans and Credits	569UNTS43	108278
IDA (Devel Assoc)	Ethiopia	26 Nov 69	Non-IBRD Project	0UNTS0	110583
IDA (Devel Assoc)	France	05 Mar 69	Non-IBRD Project	0UNTS0	110217
IDA (Devel Assoc)	Ghana	14 Jun 68	Non-IBRD Project	0UNTS0	109303
IDA (Devel Assoc)	Ghana	29 Jul 69	Loans and Credits	0UNTS0	110291
IDA (Devel Assoc)	Ghana	28 Aug 69	Non-IBRD Project	0UNTS0	110573
IDA (Devel Assoc)	Ghana	25 Sep 69	Non-IBRD Project	0UNTS0	110591
IDA (Devel Assoc)	Guyana	31 Jan 69	Non-IBRD Project	0UNTS0	110097
IDA (Devel Assoc)	Haiti	02 Nov 62	Non-IBRD Project	468UNTS205	106774
IDA (Devel Assoc)	Honduras	12 May 61	Loans and Credits	414UNTS180	105973
IDA (Devel Assoc)	Honduras	02 Feb 65	Non-IBRD Project	561UNTS279	108189
IDA (Devel Assoc)	Honduras	12 Jun 68	Non-IBRD Project	0UNTS0	109409
IDA (Devel Assoc)	India	21 Jun 61	Loans and Credits	418UNTS61	106017
IDA (Devel Assoc)	India	06 Sep 61	Loans and Credits	418UNTS81	106018
IDA (Devel Assoc)	India	22 Nov 61	Loans and Credits	427UNTS29	106145
IDA (Devel Assoc)	India	22 Nov 61	Loans and Credits	427UNTS3	106144
IDA (Devel Assoc)	India	22 Nov 61	Loans and Credits	427UNTS55	106146
IDA (Devel Assoc)	India	14 Feb 62	Non-IBRD Project	468UNTS177	106773
IDA (Devel Assoc)	India	29 Jun 62	Non-IBRD Project	447UNTS221	106417
IDA (Devel Assoc)	India	18 Jul 62	Non-IBRD Project	447UNTS191	106416
IDA (Devel Assoc)	India	08 Aug 62	Non-IBRD Project	478UNTS335	106941
IDA (Devel Assoc)	India	14 Sep 62	Non-IBRD Project	448UNTS3	106422
IDA (Devel Assoc)	India	14 Sep 62	IBRD Project	467UNTS265	106766
IDA (Devel Assoc)	India	22 Mar 63	Non-IBRD Project	477UNTS3	106911
IDA (Devel Assoc)	India	24 May 63	Non-IBRD Project	483UNTS205	107014
IDA (Devel Assoc)	India	09 Jun 64	Non-IBRD Project	506UNTS31	107380
IDA (Devel Assoc)	India	06 Jul 64	Non-IBRD Project	534UNTS49	107753
IDA (Devel Assoc)	India	26 Oct 64	Non-IBRD Project	535UNTS245	107783
IDA (Devel Assoc)	India	11 Aug 65	Non-IBRD Project	562UNTS277	108199
IDA (Devel Assoc)	India	29 Jun 66	Non-IBRD Project	585UNTS101	108484
IDA (Devel Assoc)	India	29 Jun 66	Non-IBRD Project	582UNTS277	108467
IDA (Devel Assoc)	India	19 Aug 66	Non-IBRD Project	584UNTS193	108478
IDA (Devel Assoc)	India	23 Dec 66	Non-IBRD Project	594UNTS165	108603
IDA (Devel Assoc)	India	22 Jan 69	Non-IBRD Project	0UNTS0	109611
IDA (Devel Assoc)	India	18 Jun 69	Non-IBRD Project	0UNTS0	110094
IDA (Devel Assoc)	India	24 Sep 69	Non-IBRD Project	0UNTS0	110574
IDA (Devel Assoc)	India	24 Apr 70	Non-IBRD Project	0UNTS0	110657
IDA (Devel Assoc)	Indonesia	06 Sep 68	Non-IBRD Project	0UNTS0	109626
IDA (Devel Assoc)	Indonesia	27 Dec 68	Non-IBRD Project	0UNTS0	109653
IDA (Devel Assoc)	Indonesia	20 Jun 69	Non-IBRD Project	0UNTS0	110571
IDA (Devel Assoc)	Indonesia	20 Jun 69	Non-IBRD Project	0UNTS0	110570
IDA (Devel Assoc)	Indonesia	29 Oct 69	Non-IBRD Project	0UNTS0	110650
IDA (Devel Assoc)	Indonesia	15 Dec 69	Non-IBRD Project	0UNTS0	110651
IDA (Devel Assoc)	Jordan	22 Dec 61	Non-IBRD Project	448UNTS21	106423
IDA (Devel Assoc)	Jordan	12 Dec 63	Non-IBRD Project	506UNTS51	107381
IDA (Devel Assoc)	Jordan	12 Dec 63	Non-IBRD Project	492UNTS3	107184
IDA (Devel Assoc)	Jordan	09 May 67	Loans and Credits	617UNTS47	108907
IDA (Devel Assoc)	Kenya	17 Aug 64	Non-IBRD Project	535UNTS79	107776
IDA (Devel Assoc)	Kenya	29 Dec 64	Non-IBRD Project	535UNTS225	107782
IDA (Devel Assoc)	Kenya	30 Jun 65	Non-IBRD Project	554UNTS75	108097
IDA (Devel Assoc)	Kenya	19 Aug 66	Non-IBRD Project	585UNTS119	108485
IDA (Devel Assoc)	Kenya	11 May 67	General Aid	617UNTS111	108909
IDA (Devel Assoc)	Kenya	11 May 67	General Aid	617UNTS91	108908
IDA (Devel Assoc)	Kenya	17 Jun 68	Non-IBRD Project	0UNTS0	109320
IDA (Devel Assoc)	Kenya	17 Jun 68	Non-IBRD Project	0UNTS0	109304
IDA (Devel Assoc)	Kenya	20 May 70	Non-IBRD Project	0UNTS0	110684
IDA (Devel Assoc)	Korea, South	17 Aug 62	Non-IBRD Project	468UNTS387	200603
IDA (Devel Assoc)	Korea, South	18 Dec 67	Non-IBRD Project	639UNTS303	200639
IDA (Devel Assoc)	Korea, South	24 Jul 68	Non-IBRD Project	0UNTS0	200647
IDA (Devel Assoc)	Korea, South	04 Jun 69	Non-IBRD Project	0UNTS0	200657
IDA (Devel Assoc)	Madagascar	12 Nov 68	Non-IBRD Project	0UNTS0	109671
IDA (Devel Assoc)	Malawi	04 Oct 66	Non-IBRD Project	584UNTS215	108479

PARTY ONE	PARTY TWO	DATE	TOPIC	CITATION	NUMBER
IDA (Devel Assoc)	Malawi	04 May 67	Loans and Credits	617UNTS141	108910
IDA (Devel Assoc)	Malawi	05 Feb 68	Non-IBRD Project	0UNTS0	109308
IDA (Devel Assoc)	Malawi	05 Feb 68	Non-IBRD Project	0UNTS0	109307
IDA (Devel Assoc)	Malawi	05 Feb 68	Non-IBRD Project	0UNTS0	109309
IDA (Devel Assoc)	Malawi	11 Feb 70	Non-IBRD Project	0UNTS0	110655
IDA (Devel Assoc)	Mali	29 Sep 64	Non-IBRD Project	594UNTS187	108604
IDA (Devel Assoc)	Mauritania	28 Dec 64	Non-IBRD Project	540UNTS163	107849
IDA (Devel Assoc)	Mauritius	26 Jun 69	Non-IBRD Project	0UNTS0	110572
IDA (Devel Assoc)	Morocco	11 Oct 65	Non-IBRD Project	562UNTS299	108200
IDA (Devel Assoc)	Morocco	13 Nov 69	Non-IBRD Project	0UNTS0	110545
IDA (Devel Assoc)	Multilateral	14 Jun 61	IBRD Project	415UNTS4	105979
IDA (Devel Assoc)	Multilateral	28 Aug 61	IBRD Project	416UNTS45	105994
IDA (Devel Assoc)	Multilateral	26 May 64	IBRD Project	541UNTS271	200613
IDA (Devel Assoc)	Multilateral	29 Mar 65	Non-IBRD Project	540UNTS145	107848
IDA (Devel Assoc)	Multilateral	29 Apr 65	Non-IBRD Project	586UNTS123	108500
IDA (Devel Assoc)	Multilateral	22 Jul 65	IBRD Project	561UNTS333	200618
IDA (Devel Assoc)	Multilateral	10 Feb 66	Loans and Credits	575UNTS129	108356
IDA (Devel Assoc)	Multilateral	03 Mar 69	Commodity Trade	0UNTS0	110233
IDA (Devel Assoc)	Multilateral	18 Jun 69	IGO Operations	0UNTS0	109741
IDA (Devel Assoc)	Multilateral	18 Jun 69	IGO Operations	0UNTS0	109740
IDA (Devel Assoc)	Multilateral	24 Jun 69	IGO Operations	0UNTS0	109743
IDA (Devel Assoc)	Multilateral	26 Sep 70	IGO Operations	0UNTS0	110768
IDA (Devel Assoc)	Nepal	10 Nov 69	Non-IBRD Project	0UNTS0	110581
IDA (Devel Assoc)	Nicaragua	07 Sep 62	Non-IBRD Project	478UNTS313	106940
IDA (Devel Assoc)	Niger	24 Jun 64	Non-IBRD Project	554UNTS93	108098
IDA (Devel Assoc)	Niger	23 Sep 68	Non-IBRD Project	0UNTS0	109627
IDA (Devel Assoc)	Nigeria	01 Mar 65	Non-IBRD Project	563UNTS3	108201
IDA (Devel Assoc)	Nigeria	01 Mar 65	Non-IBRD Project	571UNTS3	108297
IDA (Devel Assoc)	Pakistan	19 Oct 61	Non-IBRD Project	447UNTS161	106415
IDA (Devel Assoc)	Pakistan	22 Nov 61	Non-IBRD Project	447UNTS295	106420
IDA (Devel Assoc)	Pakistan	29 Jun 62	Non-IBRD Project	447UNTS325	106421
IDA (Devel Assoc)	Pakistan	02 Nov 62	Non-IBRD Project	468UNTS351	106781
IDA (Devel Assoc)	Pakistan	26 Jun 63	Non-IBRD Project	492UNTS115	107189
IDA (Devel Assoc)	Pakistan	26 Jul 63	Non-IBRD Project	492UNTS143	107190
IDA (Devel Assoc)	Pakistan	16 Aug 63	Non-IBRD Project	492UNTS171	107191
IDA (Devel Assoc)	Pakistan	16 Aug 63	Non-IBRD Project	492UNTS205	107192
IDA (Devel Assoc)	Pakistan	25 Mar 64	Non-IBRD Project	534UNTS275	107765
IDA (Devel Assoc)	Pakistan	25 Mar 64	Non-IBRD Project	535UNTS43	107775
IDA (Devel Assoc)	Pakistan	11 Jun 64	Non-IBRD Project	506UNTS3	107379
IDA (Devel Assoc)	Pakistan	11 Jun 64	Non-IBRD Project	534UNTS309	107766
IDA (Devel Assoc)	Pakistan	24 Jun 64	Non-IBRD Project	533UNTS191	107743
IDA (Devel Assoc)	Pakistan	24 Jun 64	Non-IBRD Project	533UNTS165	107742
IDA (Devel Assoc)	Pakistan	21 Jul 64	Non-IBRD Project	534UNTS373	107768
IDA (Devel Assoc)	Pakistan	26 Aug 64	Non-IBRD Project	535UNTS263	107784
IDA (Devel Assoc)	Pakistan	22 Sep 64	Non-IBRD Project	594UNTS225	108605
IDA (Devel Assoc)	Pakistan	30 Jun 65	Non-IBRD Project	554UNTS111	108099
IDA (Devel Assoc)	Pakistan	13 Jan 66	Non-IBRD Project	567UNTS67	108252
IDA (Devel Assoc)	Pakistan	10 Feb 66	Non-IBRD Project	575UNTS89	108355
IDA (Devel Assoc)	Pakistan	17 Jun 66	Non-IBRD Project	582UNTS297	108468
IDA (Devel Assoc)	Pakistan	23 Dec 66	Non-IBRD Project	594UNTS255	108606
IDA (Devel Assoc)	Pakistan	13 Jan 69	Non-IBRD Project	0UNTS0	109610
IDA (Devel Assoc)	Pakistan	06 Mar 69	Non-IBRD Project	0UNTS0	109667
IDA (Devel Assoc)	Pakistan	26 Jun 69	Non-IBRD Project	0UNTS0	110227
IDA (Devel Assoc)	Pakistan	11 Feb 70	Non-IBRD Project	0UNTS0	110656
IDA (Devel Assoc)	Pakistan	22 May 70	Non-IBRD Project	0UNTS0	110658
IDA (Devel Assoc)	Pakistan	10 Jun 70	Non-IBRD Project	0UNTS0	110686
IDA (Devel Assoc)	Paraguay	26 Oct 61	Non-IBRD Project	447UNTS277	106419
IDA (Devel Assoc)	Paraguay	26 Dec 63	Non-IBRD Project	507UNTS3	107394
IDA (Devel Assoc)	Paraguay	04 Apr 66	Non-IBRD Project	582UNTS331	108469
IDA (Devel Assoc)	Paraguay	25 Jun 69	Non-IBRD Project	0UNTS0	110226
IDA (Devel Assoc)	Senegal	29 Sep 66	Non-IBRD Project	594UNTS277	108607
IDA (Devel Assoc)	Senegal	10 Feb 69	Non-IBRD Project	0UNTS0	110121
IDA (Devel Assoc)	Siam	02 Aug 66	Non-IBRD Project	585UNTS271	108492
IDA (Devel Assoc)	Somalia	29 Mar 65	Non-IBRD Project	586UNTS101	108499
IDA (Devel Assoc)	Somalia	26 Jun 68	Non-IBRD Project	0UNTS0	109634

PARTY ONE	PARTY TWO	DATE	TOPIC	CITATION	NUMBER
IDA (Devel Assoc)	Somalia	03 Apr 69	Loans and Credits	0UNTS0	110284
IDA (Devel Assoc)	Sudan	14 Jun 61	Loans and Credits	415UNTS50	105981
IDA (Devel Assoc)	Sudan	24 Jun 68	Non-IBRD Project	0UNTS0	109649
IDA (Devel Assoc)	Switzerland	26 Jun 67	Loans and Credits	0UNTS0	200648
IDA (Devel Assoc)	Syria	24 Dec 63	Non-IBRD Project	534UNTS253	107764
IDA (Devel Assoc)	Taiwan	30 Aug 61	Loans and Credits	417UNTS227	106008
IDA (Devel Assoc)	Taiwan	30 Aug 61	Loans and Credits	416UNTS175	106003
IDA (Devel Assoc)	Taiwan	06 Sep 61	Loans and Credits	417UNTS253	106009
IDA (Devel Assoc)	Taiwan	01 Dec 61	Loans and Credits	426UNTS105	106132
IDA (Devel Assoc)	Tanganyika	19 Dec 63	Non-IBRD Project	492UNTS241	107193
IDA (Devel Assoc)	Tanganyika	05 Feb 64	Non-IBRD Project	506UNTS91	107382
IDA (Devel Assoc)	Tanzania	13 Jan 66	Non-IBRD Project	567UNTS177	108256
IDA (Devel Assoc)	Tanzania	21 Mar 68	Non-IBRD Project	0UNTS0	109327
IDA (Devel Assoc)	Tanzania	31 Oct 68	Non-IBRD Project	0UNTS0	109652
IDA (Devel Assoc)	Tanzania	29 May 69	Non-IBRD Project	0UNTS0	110224
IDA (Devel Assoc)	Togo	10 Oct 68	Non-IBRD Project	0UNTS0	109643
IDA (Devel Assoc)	Tunisia	17 Sep 62	Non-IBRD Project	469UNTS33	106783
IDA (Devel Assoc)	Tunisia	16 Sep 66	Loans and Credits	616UNTS285	108903
IDA (Devel Assoc)	Tunisia	21 Feb 67	Non-IBRD Project	618UNTS69	108924
IDA (Devel Assoc)	Tunisia	04 Jun 69	IBRD Project	0UNTS0	110287
IDA (Devel Assoc)	Turkey	23 Nov 62	Non-IBRD Project	469UNTS3	106782
IDA (Devel Assoc)	Turkey	01 Feb 63	Non-IBRD Project	468UNTS223	106775
IDA (Devel Assoc)	Turkey	31 May 63	Non-IBRD Project	480UNTS127	106966
IDA (Devel Assoc)	Turkey	14 Jul 64	Non-IBRD Project	534UNTS339	107767
IDA (Devel Assoc)	Turkey	31 Aug 64	Non-IBRD Project	535UNTS111	107777
IDA (Devel Assoc)	Turkey	01 Apr 65	Non-IBRD Project	554UNTS137	108100
IDA (Devel Assoc)	Turkey	10 Aug 66	Non-IBRD Project	585UNTS237	108491
IDA (Devel Assoc)	Turkey	28 Feb 69	Non-IBRD Project	0UNTS0	110092
IDA (Devel Assoc)	Uganda	21 Apr 67	General Aid	617UNTS161	108911
IDA (Devel Assoc)	Uganda	28 Jul 67	General Aid	617UNTS177	108912
IDA (Devel Assoc)	Uganda	15 Sep 67	Non-IBRD Project	639UNTS115	109148
IDA (Devel Assoc)	Uganda	05 Oct 68	Non-IBRD Project	0UNTS0	109635
IDA (Devel Assoc)	Uganda	29 Sep 69	Non-IBRD Project	0UNTS0	110589
IDA (Devel Assoc)	UK Great Britain	13 Mar 62	Direct Aid	466UNTS331	106753
IDA (Devel Assoc)	UK Great Britain	31 Jul 64	Non-IBRD Project	535UNTS205	107781
IDA (Devel Assoc)	UK Great Britain	08 Feb 66	Non-IBRD Project	567UNTS207	108257
IDA (Devel Assoc)	United Nations	10 Apr 61	IGO Operations	394UNTS221	200582
IDA (Devel Assoc)	Upper Volta	18 Feb 69	Non-IBRD Project	0UNTS0	110215
IFC (Finance Corp)	IBRD (World Bank)	28 Oct 66	Loans and Credits	586UNTS225	200628
IFC (Finance Corp)	IBRD (World Bank)	23 Dec 69	IBRD Project	0UNTS0	200653
IFC (Finance Corp)	Multilateral	25 May 55	IGO Establishment	264UNTS117	103791
ILO (Labor Org)	Afromalagasy Org	30 May 63	IGO Operations	467UNTS482	200602
ILO (Labor Org)	Algeria	06 Apr 67	IGO Establishment	595UNTS99	108614
ILO (Labor Org)	Arab League	26 May 58	IGO Operations	302UNTS343	200549
ILO (Labor Org)	Argentina	06 Apr 70	IGO Operations	0UNTS0	110430
ILO (Labor Org)	Asian Productivity	27 Oct 64	IGO Operations	516UNTS367	200610
ILO (Labor Org)	Cameroon	07 May 67	IGO Operations	596UNTS209	108634
ILO (Labor Org)	Ceylon (Sri Lanka)	24 Jan 51	Tech Assistance	117UNTS355	200380
ILO (Labor Org)	Ceylon (Sri Lanka)	06 Apr 51	Tech Assistance	100UNTS235	200286
ILO (Labor Org)	Ceylon (Sri Lanka)	21 Nov 62	IGO Operations	449UNTS263	106463
ILO (Labor Org)	Chile	23 Jul 52	Tech Assistance	178UNTS323	102348
ILO (Labor Org)	Costa Rica	09 May 69	IGO Establishment	0UNTS0	110307
ILO (Labor Org)	Council of Europe	23 Nov 51	IGO Operations	126UNTS331	200435
ILO (Labor Org)	Council of Europe	08 Dec 60	IGO Operations	389UNTS291	200579
ILO (Labor Org)	Cuba	21 Apr 51	Tech Assistance	99UNTS205	101382
ILO (Labor Org)	Dominican Republic	18 Jun 51	Tech Assistance	100UNTS3	101383
ILO (Labor Org)	ECSC (Coal/Steel)	16 Jul 53	IGO Operations	412UNTS273	200591
ILO (Labor Org)	Ecuador	19 Apr 51	Tech Assistance	100UNTS77	101389
ILO (Labor Org)	EEC (Econ Commnty)	07 Jul 58	IGO Operations	312UNTS387	200551
ILO (Labor Org)	Ethiopia	10 Dec 64	IGO Establishment	521UNTS217	107524
ILO (Labor Org)	Euratom	26 Jan 61	IGO Operations	390UNTS323	200580
ILO (Labor Org)	FAO (Food Agri)	11 Sep 47	IGO Operations	18UNTS335	200111
ILO (Labor Org)	Greece	25 Apr 51	Tech Assistance	100UNTS93	101390
ILO (Labor Org)	Guatemala	13 Apr 51	Tech Assistance	126UNTS249	101692
ILO (Labor Org)	IAEA (Atom Energy)	08 May 59	IGO Operations	328UNTS273	200555

PARTY ONE	PARTY TWO	DATE	TOPIC	CITATION	NUMBER
ILO (Labor Org)	IMCO (Maritime Org)	16 Jan 59	IGO Operations	327UNTS309	200554
ILO (Labor Org)	India	26 Apr 51	Tech Assistance	100UNTS19	101384
ILO (Labor Org)	Indonesia	21 May 70	IGO Establishment	0UNTS0	110543
ILO (Labor Org)	Israel	19 Feb 51	Tech Assistance	100UNTS105	101391
ILO (Labor Org)	Italy	04 Sep 52	Tech Assistance	178UNTS371	200505
ILO (Labor Org)	Italy	24 Oct 64	IGO Establishment	541UNTS217	107871
ILO (Labor Org)	Jordan	29 Mar 51	Tech Assistance	100UNTS247	200287
ILO (Labor Org)	LAFTA (Free Trade)	02 Jul 65	IGO Operations	563UNTS327	200619
ILO (Labor Org)	League of Nations	04 May 46	IGO Operations	19UNTS187	200114
ILO (Labor Org)	Lebanon	14 May 66	IGO Establishment	600UNTS69	108676
ILO (Labor Org)	Liberia	02 Apr 51	Tech Assistance	100UNTS117	101392
ILO (Labor Org)	Mexico	06 Apr 51	Tech Assistance	100UNTS131	101393
ILO (Labor Org)	Mexico	05 Jan 55	IGO Status/Immunit	208UNTS225	102815
ILO (Labor Org)	Multilateral	02 Nov 50	Tech Assistance	81UNTS160	101071
ILO (Labor Org)	Multilateral	24 Nov 50	Tech Assistance	81UNTS188	101072
ILO (Labor Org)	Multilateral	15 Dec 50	Tech Assistance	76UNTS120	100985
ILO (Labor Org)	Multilateral	18 Jan 51	Tech Assistance	81UNTS233	101073
ILO (Labor Org)	Multilateral	15 Feb 51	Tech Assistance	81UNTS245	101074
ILO (Labor Org)	Multilateral	05 Mar 51	Tech Assistance	81UNTS261	101075
ILO (Labor Org)	Multilateral	20 Mar 51	IGO Operations	82UNTS172	101091
ILO (Labor Org)	Multilateral	28 Mar 51	Tech Assistance	181UNTS61	102399
ILO (Labor Org)	Multilateral	05 Apr 51	Tech Assistance	84UNTS299	101139
ILO (Labor Org)	Multilateral	25 Jun 51	Tech Assistance	92UNTS27	101258
ILO (Labor Org)	Multilateral	28 Jun 51	Tech Assistance	118UNTS154	101604
ILO (Labor Org)	Multilateral	27 Jul 51	Tech Assistance	97UNTS291	200273
ILO (Labor Org)	Multilateral	05 Sep 51	Tech Assistance	173UNTS15	102256
ILO (Labor Org)	Multilateral	01 Oct 51	Tech Assistance	104UNTS249	101446
ILO (Labor Org)	Multilateral	24 Dec 51	Tech Assistance	118UNTS290	200383
ILO (Labor Org)	Multilateral	23 Jan 52	Tech Assistance	127UNTS269	101708
ILO (Labor Org)	Multilateral	18 Feb 52	Tech Assistance	126UNTS319	200434
ILO (Labor Org)	Multilateral	11 Apr 52	Tech Assistance	173UNTS2	102255
ILO (Labor Org)	Multilateral	22 May 52	Tech Assistance	131UNTS115	101739
ILO (Labor Org)	Multilateral	15 Oct 52	Tech Assistance	141UNTS96	101909
ILO (Labor Org)	Multilateral	16 Dec 52	Tech Assistance	158UNTS407	102074
ILO (Labor Org)	Multilateral	29 Dec 52	Tech Assistance	151UNTS317	102002
ILO (Labor Org)	Multilateral	26 Feb 53	Tech Assistance	161UNTS31	102120
ILO (Labor Org)	Multilateral	09 Oct 53	Tech Assistance	190UNTS49	102557
ILO (Labor Org)	Multilateral	20 Apr 54	Tech Assistance	189UNTS11	102539
ILO (Labor Org)	Multilateral	31 May 54	Tech Assistance	192UNTS20	102592
ILO (Labor Org)	Multilateral	01 Jun 54	Tech Assistance	200UNTS235	200520
ILO (Labor Org)	Multilateral	30 Jun 54	Tech Assistance	193UNTS67	102611
ILO (Labor Org)	Multilateral	19 Aug 54	Tech Assistance	201UNTS51	102710
ILO (Labor Org)	Multilateral	06 Oct 54	Tech Assistance	201UNTS75	102711
ILO (Labor Org)	Multilateral	27 Oct 54	Tech Assistance	201UNTS95	102712
ILO (Labor Org)	Multilateral	29 Oct 54	Tech Assistance	201UNTS115	102713
ILO (Labor Org)	Multilateral	16 Dec 54	Tech Assistance	204UNTS323	200523
ILO (Labor Org)	Multilateral	04 Apr 55	Tech Assistance	208UNTS239	102816
ILO (Labor Org)	Multilateral	14 Jun 55	Tech Assistance	212UNTS263	200526
ILO (Labor Org)	Multilateral	04 Jul 55	Tech Assistance	214UNTS10	102897
ILO (Labor Org)	Multilateral	13 Dec 55	Tech Assistance	407UNTS8	105857
ILO (Labor Org)	Multilateral	02 Feb 56	Tech Assistance	227UNTS153	103137
ILO (Labor Org)	Multilateral	10 Feb 56	Tech Assistance	228UNTS189	103151
ILO (Labor Org)	Multilateral	10 Feb 56	Tech Assistance	228UNTS167	103150
ILO (Labor Org)	Multilateral	30 Mar 56	IGO Operations	604UNTS114	108748
ILO (Labor Org)	Multilateral	10 May 56	Tech Assistance	243UNTS103	103449
ILO (Labor Org)	Multilateral	31 May 56	Tech Assistance	251UNTS181	103541
ILO (Labor Org)	Multilateral	08 Jun 56	Tech Assistance	247UNTS366	200541
ILO (Labor Org)	Multilateral	12 Jun 56	Tech Assistance	243UNTS187	103453
ILO (Labor Org)	Multilateral	14 Jun 56	Tech Assistance	265UNTS125	103809
ILO (Labor Org)	Multilateral	26 Jun 56	Tech Assistance	321UNTS2	104650
ILO (Labor Org)	Multilateral	26 Jun 56	Tech Assistance	253UNTS12	103573
ILO (Labor Org)	Multilateral	02 Jul 56	Tech Assistance	540UNTS110	107846
ILO (Labor Org)	Multilateral	02 Jul 56	Tech Assistance	248UNTS37	103484
ILO (Labor Org)	Multilateral	31 Aug 56	Tech Assistance	249UNTS158	103506
ILO (Labor Org)	Multilateral	05 Oct 56	Tech Assistance	251UNTS245	103544

PARTY ONE	PARTY TWO	DATE	TOPIC	CITATION	NUMBER
ILO (Labor Org)	Multilateral	05 Oct 56	Tech Assistance	251UNTS267	103545
ILO (Labor Org)	Multilateral	21 Nov 56	Tech Assistance	253UNTS266	103588
ILO (Labor Org)	Multilateral	15 Jan 57	Tech Assistance	376UNTS122	105378
ILO (Labor Org)	Multilateral	23 Jan 57	Tech Assistance	259UNTS426	103701
ILO (Labor Org)	Multilateral	17 Feb 57	Tech Assistance	271UNTS2	103907
ILO (Labor Org)	Multilateral	01 Mar 57	Tech Assistance	264UNTS94	103790
ILO (Labor Org)	Multilateral	28 Mar 57	Tech Assistance	271UNTS30	103908
ILO (Labor Org)	Multilateral	09 Apr 57	Tech Assistance	274UNTS172	103965
ILO (Labor Org)	Multilateral	24 May 57	Tech Assistance	268UNTS270	103861
ILO (Labor Org)	Multilateral	30 Jun 57	Tech Assistance	286UNTS171	104165
ILO (Labor Org)	Multilateral	09 Jul 57	Tech Assistance	274UNTS300	103972
ILO (Labor Org)	Multilateral	05 Nov 57	Tech Assistance	285UNTS301	104155
ILO (Labor Org)	Multilateral	15 Mar 58	Tech Assistance	292UNTS273	104276
ILO (Labor Org)	Multilateral	19 Jun 58	Tech Assistance	306UNTS236	200550
ILO (Labor Org)	Multilateral	09 Oct 59	Tech Assistance	376UNTS382	105391
ILO (Labor Org)	Multilateral	03 Dec 59	Tech Assistance	348UNTS246	105003
ILO (Labor Org)	Multilateral	12 Apr 60	Tech Assistance	359UNTS323	105150
ILO (Labor Org)	Multilateral	04 Jun 60	Tech Assistance	360UNTS208	105159
ILO (Labor Org)	Multilateral	17 Jun 60	Humanitarian	536UNTS27	107794
ILO (Labor Org)	Multilateral	19 Jun 60	IGO Operations	537UNTS214	107803
ILO (Labor Org)	Multilateral	08 Jul 60	Tech Assistance	366UNTS310	105220
ILO (Labor Org)	Multilateral	28 Jan 61	Tech Assistance	387UNTS202	105563
ILO (Labor Org)	Multilateral	20 Sep 61	Tech Assistance	407UNTS52	105859
ILO (Labor Org)	Multilateral	16 Oct 61	Tech Assistance	410UNTS242	105908
ILO (Labor Org)	Multilateral	07 Nov 61	Tech Assistance	412UNTS258	105937
ILO (Labor Org)	Multilateral	27 Dec 61	Tech Assistance	425UNTS83	106120
ILO (Labor Org)	Multilateral	17 Jan 62	Tech Assistance	419UNTS294	106033
ILO (Labor Org)	Multilateral	20 Jan 62	Tech Assistance	429UNTS230	200596
ILO (Labor Org)	Multilateral	13 Feb 62	Tech Assistance	422UNTS288	200594
ILO (Labor Org)	Multilateral	21 Feb 62	Tech Assistance	423UNTS151	106091
ILO (Labor Org)	Multilateral	01 Mar 62	Tech Assistance	423UNTS122	106089
ILO (Labor Org)	Multilateral	10 Apr 62	Tech Assistance	429UNTS78	106192
ILO (Labor Org)	Multilateral	18 Apr 62	Tech Assistance	463UNTS44	106692
ILO (Labor Org)	Multilateral	17 May 62	Tech Assistance	429UNTS46	106189
ILO (Labor Org)	Multilateral	12 Aug 62	Tech Assistance	443UNTS266	106365
ILO (Labor Org)	Multilateral	29 Aug 62	Tech Assistance	443UNTS280	106366
ILO (Labor Org)	Multilateral	11 Sep 62	Tech Assistance	455UNTS402	106553
ILO (Labor Org)	Multilateral	14 Sep 62	Visas	443UNTS73	106360
ILO (Labor Org)	Multilateral	15 Nov 62	Tech Assistance	448UNTS50	106424
ILO (Labor Org)	Multilateral	06 Dec 62	Tech Assistance	450UNTS240	106471
ILO (Labor Org)	Multilateral	12 Dec 62	Tech Assistance	457UNTS72	106578
ILO (Labor Org)	Multilateral	21 Jan 63	Tech Assistance	453UNTS20	106517
ILO (Labor Org)	Multilateral	05 Feb 63	Tech Assistance	453UNTS36	106518
ILO (Labor Org)	Multilateral	14 Feb 63	Tech Assistance	453UNTS168	106524
ILO (Labor Org)	Multilateral	06 Mar 63	Tech Assistance	455UNTS386	106552
ILO (Labor Org)	Multilateral	18 Apr 63	Tech Assistance	463UNTS121	106697
ILO (Labor Org)	Multilateral	06 May 63	Tech Assistance	463UNTS78	106694
ILO (Labor Org)	Multilateral	09 May 63	Tech Assistance	463UNTS159	106700
ILO (Labor Org)	Multilateral	22 May 63	Tech Assistance	483UNTS72	107007
ILO (Labor Org)	Multilateral	24 May 63	Tech Assistance	466UNTS346	106754
ILO (Labor Org)	Multilateral	24 May 63	Tech Assistance	470UNTS208	106810
ILO (Labor Org)	Multilateral	23 Jul 63	Tech Assistance	471UNTS158	106831
ILO (Labor Org)	Multilateral	31 Jul 63	Tech Assistance	472UNTS220	106842
ILO (Labor Org)	Multilateral	27 Aug 63	Tech Assistance	511UNTS210	107435
ILO (Labor Org)	Multilateral	10 Sep 63	Tech Assistance	480UNTS100	106965
ILO (Labor Org)	Multilateral	30 Oct 63	Tech Assistance	480UNTS180	106968
ILO (Labor Org)	Multilateral	07 Nov 63	Tech Assistance	480UNTS232	106971
ILO (Labor Org)	Multilateral	08 Nov 63	Tech Assistance	482UNTS286	106999
ILO (Labor Org)	Multilateral	28 Jan 64	Tech Assistance	502UNTS321	107336
ILO (Labor Org)	Multilateral	20 Feb 64	Tech Assistance	491UNTS30	107172
ILO (Labor Org)	Multilateral	23 Jun 64	Tech Assistance	506UNTS108	107383
ILO (Labor Org)	Multilateral	28 Jun 64	Tech Assistance	519UNTS14	107499
ILO (Labor Org)	Multilateral	03 Aug 64	Tech Assistance	503UNTS239	107347
ILO (Labor Org)	Multilateral	24 Oct 64	Tech Assistance	514UNTS220	200608
ILO (Labor Org)	Multilateral	11 Nov 64	Tech Assistance	515UNTS94	107456

PARTY ONE	PARTY TWO	DATE	TOPIC	CITATION	NUMBER
ILO (Labor Org)	Multilateral	11 Dec 64	IGO Operations	547UNTS297	107964
ILO (Labor Org)	Multilateral	15 Dec 64	Tech Assistance	522UNTS20	107533
ILO (Labor Org)	Multilateral	27 Jan 65	Tech Assistance	523UNTS102	107556
ILO (Labor Org)	Multilateral	02 Feb 65	Tech Assistance	523UNTS256	107560
ILO (Labor Org)	Multilateral	12 Feb 65	Tech Assistance	525UNTS148	107587
ILO (Labor Org)	Multilateral	23 Feb 65	IGO Operations	527UNTS120	107622
ILO (Labor Org)	Multilateral	05 Mar 65	IGO Operations	527UNTS221	107627
ILO (Labor Org)	Multilateral	08 Apr 65	IGO Operations	533UNTS66	107733
ILO (Labor Org)	Multilateral	26 Apr 65	IGO Operations	533UNTS50	107732
ILO (Labor Org)	Multilateral	12 May 65	IGO Operations	534UNTS390	107769
ILO (Labor Org)	Multilateral	14 May 65	IGO Operations	550UNTS310	108026
ILO (Labor Org)	Multilateral	25 May 65	IGO Operations	535UNTS374	107791
ILO (Labor Org)	Multilateral	02 Jun 65	Tech Assistance	551UNTS2	108030
ILO (Labor Org)	Multilateral	02 Jun 65	Tech Assistance	537UNTS348	200611
ILO (Labor Org)	Multilateral	05 Jul 65	General Aid	563UNTS104	108207
ILO (Labor Org)	Multilateral	20 Jul 65	IGO Operations	541UNTS12	107857
ILO (Labor Org)	Multilateral	13 Sep 65	IGO Operations	547UNTS248	107961
ILO (Labor Org)	Multilateral	13 Sep 65	Tech Assistance	547UNTS264	107962
ILO (Labor Org)	Multilateral	21 Sep 65	IGO Operations	547UNTS280	107963
ILO (Labor Org)	Multilateral	21 Oct 65	Tech Assistance	547UNTS216	107959
ILO (Labor Org)	Multilateral	12 Nov 65	IGO Operations	550UNTS160	108013
ILO (Labor Org)	Multilateral	31 Dec 65	Recognition	552UNTS292	108060
ILO (Labor Org)	Multilateral	12 May 66	General Aid	563UNTS54	108204
ILO (Labor Org)	Multilateral	21 Jun 66	ILO Labor	0UNTS0	109728
ILO (Labor Org)	Multilateral	21 Jun 66	Non-ILO Labor	0UNTS0	109298
ILO (Labor Org)	Multilateral	06 Aug 66	Tech Assistance	570UNTS178	108294
ILO (Labor Org)	Multilateral	22 Aug 66	Tech Assistance	571UNTS298	200624
ILO (Labor Org)	Multilateral	23 Sep 66	General Aid	573UNTS148	108328
ILO (Labor Org)	Multilateral	23 Sep 66	IGO Operations	573UNTS132	108327
ILO (Labor Org)	Multilateral	30 Sep 66	IGO Operations	576UNTS8	108361
ILO (Labor Org)	Multilateral	17 Nov 66	IGO Operations	580UNTS22	108417
ILO (Labor Org)	Multilateral	25 Jan 67	IGO Operations	588UNTS212	108527
ILO (Labor Org)	Multilateral	27 Feb 67	IGO Operations	590UNTS156	108552
ILO (Labor Org)	Multilateral	03 Mar 67	Tech Assistance	594UNTS96	108597
ILO (Labor Org)	Multilateral	13 Apr 67	IGO Operations	595UNTS60	108612
ILO (Labor Org)	Multilateral	19 Apr 67	Tech Assistance	595UNTS120	108617
ILO (Labor Org)	Multilateral	10 Jun 67	Direct Aid	602UNTS212	108714
ILO (Labor Org)	Multilateral	14 Jun 67	Direct Aid	603UNTS2	108719
ILO (Labor Org)	Multilateral	20 Jun 67	Tech Assistance	0UNTS0	109290
ILO (Labor Org)	Multilateral	21 Jun 67	Tech Assistance	598UNTS2	108653
ILO (Labor Org)	Multilateral	28 Jun 67	ILO Labor	0UNTS0	110355
ILO (Labor Org)	Multilateral	29 Jun 67	Non-ILO Labor	0UNTS0	110030
ILO (Labor Org)	Multilateral	12 Oct 67	Direct Aid	607UNTS20	108793
ILO (Labor Org)	Multilateral	12 Oct 67	Direct Aid	607UNTS2	108792
ILO (Labor Org)	Multilateral	27 Oct 67	General Aid	608UNTS37	108811
ILO (Labor Org)	Multilateral	14 Nov 67	Admin Cooperation	614UNTS2	108860
ILO (Labor Org)	Multilateral	18 Jun 69	IGO Operations	0UNTS0	109741
ILO (Labor Org)	Multilateral	18 Jun 69	IGO Operations	0UNTS0	109740
ILO (Labor Org)	Multilateral	24 Jun 69	IGO Operations	0UNTS0	109743
ILO (Labor Org)	Multilateral	26 Sep 70	IGO Operations	0UNTS0	110768
ILO (Labor Org)	OAS (Am States)	07 Jun 50	IGO Operations	70UNTS223	200240
ILO (Labor Org)	OAU (Afri Unity)	25 Nov 65	General Amity	550UNTS389	200617
ILO (Labor Org)	Org Ctrl Am States	26 Jul 65	IGO Operations	563UNTS341	200620
ILO (Labor Org)	Pakistan	16 May 51	Tech Assistance	100UNTS147	101394
ILO (Labor Org)	Panama	10 Nov 51	Tech Assistance	126UNTS269	101693
ILO (Labor Org)	Paraguay	12 Jul 51	Tech Assistance	117UNTS155	101591
ILO (Labor Org)	Peru	13 Apr 51	Tech Assistance	100UNTS31	101385
ILO (Labor Org)	Peru	22 Jun 60	IGO Status/Immunit	423UNTS165	106092
ILO (Labor Org)	Philippines	23 Jan 70	IGO Establishment	0UNTS0	110348
ILO (Labor Org)	Senegal	09 Feb 67	IGO Establishment	600UNTS75	108677
ILO (Labor Org)	Subsahara Tech Com	25 Jul 59	IGO Operations	409UNTS290	200590
ILO (Labor Org)	Switzerland	11 Mar 46	IGO Status/Immunit	15UNTS377	200103
ILO (Labor Org)	Syria	03 Mar 51	Tech Assistance	110UNTS69	101502
ILO (Labor Org)	Taiwan	13 Feb 53	Tech Assistance	178UNTS337	102349
ILO (Labor Org)	Tanganyika	03 May 62	IGO Operations	429UNTS73	106191

PARTY ONE	PARTY TWO	DATE	TOPIC	CITATION	NUMBER
ILO (Labor Org)	Thailand	11 Jul 51	Tech Assistance	100UNTS159	101395
ILO (Labor Org)	Thailand	30 Aug 61	IGO Operations	422UNTS125	106072
ILO (Labor Org)	Trinidad/Tobago	14 Mar 69	IGO Operations	0UNTS0	109500
ILO (Labor Org)	Turkey	21 Mar 52	Tech Assistance	52TURG1306	466135
ILO (Labor Org)	UK Great Britain	14 Jan 59	IGO Operations	355UNTS283	105081
ILO (Labor Org)	UN Relief Palestin	31 Dec 52	Tech Assistance	182UNTS201	200506
ILO (Labor Org)	UN Special Fund	12 Oct 59	IGO Operations	343UNTS325	200563
ILO (Labor Org)	United Nations	19 Dec 46	IGO Operations	1UNTS183	200009
ILO (Labor Org)	United Nations	17 Feb 49	IGO Operations	26UNTS323	200154
ILO (Labor Org)	United Nations	07 Jun 50	Visas	68UNTS213	200231
ILO (Labor Org)	United Nations	12 Oct 50	IGO Operations	139UNTS395	200466
ILO (Labor Org)	Uruguay	20 Sep 52	Tech Assistance	187UNTS25	102499
ILO (Labor Org)	USA (United States)	22 Feb 63	IGO Operations	489UNTS347	107149
ILO (Labor Org)	Venezuela	22 Oct 51	Tech Assistance	117UNTS139	101590
ILO (Labor Org)	Vietnam, South	26 Jun 51	Tech Assistance	100UNTS223	200285
ILO (Labor Org)	WHO (World Health)	10 Jul 48	IGO Operations	19UNTS269	200121
ILO (Labor Org)	Zambia	20 Dec 67	IGO Operations	619UNTS293	108947
IMCO (Maritime Org)	FAO (Food Agri)	11 Jul 66	IGO Operations	575UNTS238	200627
IMCO (Maritime Org)	IAEA (Atom Energy)	13 Apr 61	IGO Operations	425UNTS281	200595
IMCO (Maritime Org)	ILO (Labor Org)	16 Jan 59	IGO Operations	327UNTS309	200554
IMCO (Maritime Org)	Multilateral	06 Mar 48	Water Transport	289UNTS3	104214
IMCO (Maritime Org)	Multilateral	27 Oct 54	Tech Assistance	201UNTS95	102712
IMCO (Maritime Org)	Multilateral	13 Dec 55	Tech Assistance	407UNTS8	105857
IMCO (Maritime Org)	Multilateral	10 May 56	Tech Assistance	243UNTS103	103449
IMCO (Maritime Org)	Multilateral	31 May 56	Tech Assistance	251UNTS181	103541
IMCO (Maritime Org)	Multilateral	02 Jul 56	Tech Assistance	248UNTS37	103484
IMCO (Maritime Org)	Multilateral	01 Mar 57	Tech Assistance	264UNTS94	103790
IMCO (Maritime Org)	Multilateral	24 May 57	Tech Assistance	268UNTS270	103861
IMCO (Maritime Org)	Multilateral	30 Jun 57	Tech Assistance	286UNTS171	104165
IMCO (Maritime Org)	Multilateral	15 Mar 58	Tech Assistance	292UNTS273	104276
IMCO (Maritime Org)	Multilateral	28 Jan 61	Tech Assistance	387UNTS202	105563
IMCO (Maritime Org)	Multilateral	27 Dec 61	Tech Assistance	425UNTS83	106120
IMCO (Maritime Org)	Multilateral	20 Jan 62	Tech Assistance	429UNTS230	200596
IMCO (Maritime Org)	Multilateral	13 Feb 62	Tech Assistance	422UNTS288	200594
IMCO (Maritime Org)	Multilateral	12 Aug 62	Tech Assistance	443UNTS266	106365
IMCO (Maritime Org)	Multilateral	21 Jan 63	Tech Assistance	453UNTS20	106517
IMCO (Maritime Org)	Multilateral	05 Feb 63	Tech Assistance	453UNTS36	106518
IMCO (Maritime Org)	Multilateral	09 May 63	Tech Assistance	463UNTS159	106700
IMCO (Maritime Org)	Multilateral	23 Jun 64	Tech Assistance	506UNTS108	107383
IMCO (Maritime Org)	Multilateral	28 Jun 64	Tech Assistance	519UNTS14	107499
IMCO (Maritime Org)	Multilateral	03 Aug 64	Tech Assistance	503UNTS239	107347
IMCO (Maritime Org)	Multilateral	11 Dec 64	IGO Operations	547UNTS297	107964
IMCO (Maritime Org)	Multilateral	15 Dec 64	Tech Assistance	522UNTS20	107533
IMCO (Maritime Org)	Multilateral	27 Jan 65	Tech Assistance	523UNTS102	107556
IMCO (Maritime Org)	Multilateral	23 Feb 65	IGO Operations	527UNTS120	107622
IMCO (Maritime Org)	Multilateral	12 May 65	IGO Operations	534UNTS390	107769
IMCO (Maritime Org)	Multilateral	02 Jun 65	Tech Assistance	537UNTS348	200611
IMCO (Maritime Org)	Multilateral	02 Jun 65	Tech Assistance	551UNTS2	108030
IMCO (Maritime Org)	Multilateral	05 Jul 65	General Aid	563UNTS104	108207
IMCO (Maritime Org)	Multilateral	20 Jul 65	IGO Operations	541UNTS12	107857
IMCO (Maritime Org)	Multilateral	13 Sep 65	Tech Assistance	547UNTS264	107962
IMCO (Maritime Org)	Multilateral	13 Sep 65	IGO Operations	547UNTS248	107961
IMCO (Maritime Org)	Multilateral	21 Sep 65	IGO Operations	547UNTS280	107963
IMCO (Maritime Org)	Multilateral	21 Oct 65	Tech Assistance	547UNTS216	107959
IMCO (Maritime Org)	Multilateral	12 Nov 65	IGO Operations	550UNTS160	108013
IMCO (Maritime Org)	Multilateral	12 May 66	General Aid	563UNTS54	108204
IMCO (Maritime Org)	Multilateral	06 Aug 66	Tech Assistance	570UNTS178	108294
IMCO (Maritime Org)	Multilateral	23 Sep 66	IGO Operations	573UNTS132	108327
IMCO (Maritime Org)	Multilateral	23 Sep 66	General Aid	573UNTS148	108328
IMCO (Maritime Org)	Multilateral	25 Jan 67	IGO Operations	588UNTS212	108527
IMCO (Maritime Org)	Multilateral	27 Feb 67	IGO Operations	590UNTS156	108552
IMCO (Maritime Org)	Multilateral	13 Apr 67	IGO Operations	595UNTS60	108612
IMCO (Maritime Org)	Multilateral	19 Apr 67	Tech Assistance	595UNTS120	108617
IMCO (Maritime Org)	Multilateral	10 Jun 67	Direct Aid	602UNTS212	108714
IMCO (Maritime Org)	Multilateral	14 Jun 67	Direct Aid	603UNTS2	108719

PARTY ONE	PARTY TWO	DATE	TOPIC	CITATION	NUMBER
IMCO (Maritime Org)	Multilateral	20 Jun 67	Tech Assistance	0UNTS0	109290
IMCO (Maritime Org)	Multilateral	21 Jun 67	Tech Assistance	598UNTS2	108653
IMCO (Maritime Org)	Multilateral	12 Oct 67	Direct Aid	607UNTS20	108793
IMCO (Maritime Org)	Multilateral	12 Oct 67	Direct Aid	607UNTS2	108792
IMCO (Maritime Org)	Multilateral	27 Oct 67	General Aid	608UNTS37	108811
IMCO (Maritime Org)	Multilateral	14 Nov 67	Admin Cooperation	614UNTS2	108860
IMCO (Maritime Org)	Multilateral	18 Jun 69	IGO Operations	0UNTS0	109740
IMCO (Maritime Org)	Multilateral	18 Jun 69	IGO Operations	0UNTS0	109741
IMCO (Maritime Org)	Multilateral	24 Jun 69	IGO Operations	0UNTS0	109743
IMCO (Maritime Org)	Multilateral	26 Sep 70	IGO Operations	0UNTS0	110768
IMCO (Maritime Org)	UK Great Britain	28 Nov 68	IGO Operations	0UNTS0	109632
IMCO (Maritime Org)	United Nations	13 Jan 59	IGO Operations	324UNTS273	200553
IMCO (Maritime Org)	United Nations	23 Jun 59	IGO Operations	336UNTS317	200556
IMCO (Maritime Org)	United Nations	11 Feb 64	IGO Operations	489UNTS357	200605
IMF (Fund)	United Nations	15 Apr 48	IGO Operations	16UNTS325	200108
IMF (Fund)	United Nations	22 Dec 60	IGO Operations	384UNTS315	200578
India	Afghanistan	14 Dec 49	Telecommunications	53UNTS95	100774
India	Afghanistan	04 Jan 50	General Amity	81UNTS75	101064
India	Afghanistan	04 Apr 50	General Trade	167UNTS105	102201
India	Argentina	26 Mar 66	General Trade	601UNTS201	108697
India	Argentina	04 Sep 68	Visas	0UNTS0	109571
India	Australia	11 Jul 49	Air Transport	35UNTS83	100552
India	Australia	23 Jan 63	Patents/Copyrights	456UNTS185	106556
India	Australia	03 Dec 63	Milit Assistance	486UNTS279	107082
India	Austria	24 Sep 63	Taxation	545UNTS199	107935
India	Austria	10 Jul 68	Other Military	68ABGB326	403100
India	Austria	10 Jul 68	Other Military	0UNTS0	109227
India	Belgium	04 Aug 47	Reparations	76UNTS23	100976
India	Belgium	16 Jul 62	Admin Cooperation	453UNTS259	106529
India	Belgium	26 Mar 70	Scientific Project	0UNTS0	110551
India	Bulgaria	20 Feb 63	Culture	0UNTS0	109955
India	Burma	07 Jul 51	General Amity	149UNTS35	101949
India	Burma	29 Sep 51	General Trade	132UNTS71	101752
India	Burma	12 Mar 57	Finance	312UNTS131	104515
India	Canada	26 Jan 51	Visas	248UNTS89	103486
India	Canada	10 Sep 51	General Aid	391UNTS237	105629
India	Canada	12 Jun 53	Admin Cooperation	248UNTS113	103490
India	Canada	30 Aug 56	Patents/Copyrights	305UNTS59	104413
India	Canada	20 Feb 58	Loans and Credits	391UNTS231	105628
India	Canada	22 Oct 58	Finance	392UNTS21	105635
India	Canada	14 May 63	Loans and Credits	529UNTS31	107653
India	Canada	16 Dec 63	Atomic Energy	529UNTS45	107655
India	Ceylon (Sri Lanka)	12 Aug 46	Postal Service	196UNTS209	102626
India	Ceylon (Sri Lanka)	21 Dec 48	Air Transport	28UNTS223	100427
India	Ceylon (Sri Lanka)	30 Apr 51	General Trade	196UNTS199	102625
India	Ceylon (Sri Lanka)	10 Sep 56	Taxation	315UNTS59	104560
India	Ceylon (Sri Lanka)	13 Jan 58	Commodity Trade	315UNTS107	104562
India	China People's Rep	29 Apr 54	Specif Claim/Waive	54CCJC23	410145
India	China People's Rep	29 Apr 54	General Economic	54CCJC22	410144
India	China People's Rep	29 Apr 54	General Trade	299UNTS57	104307
India	China People's Rep	14 Oct 54	General Trade	54CCJC72	410179
India	China People's Rep	14 Oct 54	General Trade	54CCJC74	410181
India	China People's Rep	14 Oct 54	Privil/Immunities	54CCJC73	410180
India	China People's Rep	01 Apr 55	Specific Property	55CCJC20	410223
India	Czechoslovakia	07 Jul 59	Culture	359UNTS259	105145
India	Czechoslovakia	19 Sep 60	Air Transport	465UNTS67	106722
India	Denmark	20 Dec 46	Reparations	7UNTS309	100107
India	Denmark	16 Sep 59	Taxation	405UNTS13	105820
India	Denmark	15 May 63	Direct Aid	616UNTS23	108889
India	Denmark	15 May 63	Tech Assistance	616UNTS49	108891
India	Denmark	15 May 63	Direct Aid	616UNTS39	108890
India	Denmark	12 Jul 63	Loans and Credits	616UNTS3	108888
India	Denmark	06 Feb 65	Water Transport	531UNTS23	107690
India	Denmark	01 Sep 67	Direct Aid	616UNTS69	108892
India	Denmark	25 Mar 68	Direct Aid	0UNTS0	109229

PARTY ONE	PARTY TWO	DATE	TOPIC	CITATION	NUMBER
India	Denmark	29 Apr 68	Direct Aid	0UNTS0	109230
India	Denmark	10 Jun 68	Sanitation	0UNTS0	109219
India	Denmark	08 May 69	General Aid	0UNTS0	109887
India	Denmark	30 Sep 69	Non-IBRD Project	0UNTS0	110541
India	Denmark	16 Feb 70	Tech Assistance	0UNTS0	110697
India	Ethiopia	07 Jun 49	Air Transport	35UNTS13	100548
India	Finland	14 Jun 57	Tech Assistance	277UNTS327	104016
India	Finland	23 Jun 61	Taxation	421UNTS49	106051
India	France	16 Jul 47	Air Transport	27UNTS325	100415
India	France	02 Feb 51	Territory Boundary	203UNTS155	102744
India	France	21 Oct 54	Specific Property	62FRRT33	415229
India	France	28 May 56	Specific Property	62FRRT33	415230
India	France	07 Jun 66	Health/Educ/Welfare	66FRRT32	415231
India	France	31 Jul 67	Air Transport	69FRJO709	416232
India	France	26 Mar 69	Taxation	70FRJO2803	416233
India	France	26 Mar 69	Taxation	0UNTS0	110735
India	Germany, East	16 Oct 54	Tech Assistance	2EGDA521	419126
India	Germany, East	16 Oct 54	General Economic	2EGDA521	419125
India	Germany, East	08 Oct 56	General Trade	5EGDA342	419127
India	Germany, East	18 Dec 59	General Economic	7EGDA367	419128
India	Germany, East	23 Nov 63	Water Transport	11EGDA388	419129
India	Germany, East	20 Feb 64	Culture	12EGDA1128	419130
India	Germany, East	12 Sep 64	General Economic	12EGDA771	419131
India	Germany, West	19 Mar 52	General Trade	52WBGA83	424251
India	Germany, West	31 Mar 55	General Trade	55WBGA174	424252
India	Germany, West	05 Mar 56	Other Military	68WBGA202	424253
India	Germany, West	07 Aug 58	Education	58WBGA178	424254
India	Germany, West	18 Mar 59	Taxation	60WGBB1828	425255
India	Germany, West	31 May 63	Air Transport	64WGBB677	425256
India	Germany, West	15 Oct 64	Claims and Debts	64WBGA235	424257
India	Germany, West	15 Jun 66	Water Transport	66WBGA190	424258
India	Germany, West	24 Jul 68	Customs	69WGBB1012	425259
India	Germany, West	20 Mar 69	Culture	69WGBB1713	425260
India	Greece	18 Apr 51	Reparations	166UNTS305	102195
India	Greece	14 Feb 58	General Trade	609UNTS94	108827
India	Greece	11 Feb 65	Taxation	606UNTS9	108771
India	Hungary	30 Mar 62	Culture	519UNTS119	107504
India	IAEA (Atom Energy)	09 Dec 66	Atomic Energy	603UNTS35	108722
India	IBRD (World Bank)	18 Aug 49	IBRD Project	154UNTS269	102031
India	IBRD (World Bank)	29 Sep 49	IBRD Project	154UNTS393	102033
India	IBRD (World Bank)	18 Apr 50	IBRD Project	155UNTS117	102036
India	IBRD (World Bank)	18 Dec 52	IBRD Project	201UNTS241	102719
India	IBRD (World Bank)	23 Jan 53	IBRD Project	201UNTS145	102715
India	IBRD (World Bank)	19 Nov 54	IBRD Project	309UNTS159	104473
India	IBRD (World Bank)	14 Mar 55	IBRD Project	309UNTS129	104472
India	IBRD (World Bank)	26 Jun 56	IBRD Project	301UNTS3	104341
India	IBRD (World Bank)	19 Dec 56	IBRD Project	310UNTS75	104489
India	IBRD (World Bank)	05 Mar 57	IBRD Project	272UNTS201	103939
India	IBRD (World Bank)	29 May 57	IBRD Project	309UNTS201	104474
India	IBRD (World Bank)	12 Jul 57	IBRD Project	288UNTS135	104202
India	IBRD (World Bank)	20 Nov 57	IBRD Project	301UNTS47	104342
India	IBRD (World Bank)	25 Jun 58	IBRD Project	323UNTS157	104668
India	IBRD (World Bank)	25 Jun 58	IBRD Project	323UNTS131	104667
India	IBRD (World Bank)	23 Jul 58	IBRD Project	317UNTS3	104590
India	IBRD (World Bank)	16 Sep 58	IBRD Project	323UNTS235	104671
India	IBRD (World Bank)	08 Apr 59	IBRD Project	348UNTS131	104998
India	IBRD (World Bank)	15 Jul 59	IBRD Project	346UNTS33	104976
India	IBRD (World Bank)	15 Jul 59	IBRD Project	355UNTS95	105075
India	IBRD (World Bank)	29 Jul 60	IBRD Project	377UNTS153	105399
India	IBRD (World Bank)	28 Oct 60	IBRD Project	406UNTS27	105838
India	IBRD (World Bank)	09 Aug 61	IBRD Project	417UNTS297	106011
India	IBRD (World Bank)	17 Aug 61	IBRD Project	417UNTS319	106012
India	IBRD (World Bank)	13 Oct 61	IBRD Project	418UNTS3	106013
India	IBRD (World Bank)	22 Dec 61	IBRD Project	481UNTS85	106979
India	IBRD (World Bank)	28 Feb 62	IBRD Project	447UNTS3	106410

PARTY ONE	PARTY TWO	DATE	TOPIC	CITATION	NUMBER
India	IBRD (World Bank)	05 Jun 63	IBRD Project	481UNTS191	106983
India	IBRD (World Bank)	28 May 65	Loans and Credits	552UNTS39	108049
India	IBRD (World Bank)	11 Jun 65	IBRD Project	557UNTS59	108128
India	IBRD (World Bank)	11 Jun 65	IBRD Project	557UNTS101	108130
India	IBRD (World Bank)	07 Jul 66	IBRD Project	595UNTS3	108610
India	IBRD (World Bank)	19 Sep 67	IGO Operations	615UNTS165	108880
India	IBRD (World Bank)	18 Jun 69	IBRD Project	OUNTSO	110093
India	IBRD (World Bank)	18 Jun 69	IBRD Project	OUNTSO	109894
India	IBRD (World Bank)	03 Jun 70	IBRD Project	OUNTSO	110830
India	ICAO (Civil Aviat)	29 Apr 52	Tech Assistance	151UNTS123	101987
India	ICJ Option Clause	07 Jan 56	ICJ Option Clause	226UNTS235	103116
India	ICJ Option Clause	14 Sep 59	ICJ Option Clause	340UNTS289	104871
India	IDA (Devel Assoc)	21 Jun 61	Loans and Credits	418UNTS61	106017
India	IDA (Devel Assoc)	06 Sep 61	Loans and Credits	418UNTS81	106018
India	IDA (Devel Assoc)	22 Nov 61	Loans and Credits	427UNTS55	106146
India	IDA (Devel Assoc)	22 Nov 61	Loans and Credits	427UNTS29	106145
India	IDA (Devel Assoc)	22 Nov 61	Loans and Credits	427UNTS3	106144
India	IDA (Devel Assoc)	14 Feb 62	Non-IBRD Project	468UNTS177	106773
India	IDA (Devel Assoc)	29 Jun 62	Non-IBRD Project	447UNTS221	106417
India	IDA (Devel Assoc)	18 Jul 62	Non-IBRD Project	447UNTS191	106416
India	IDA (Devel Assoc)	08 Aug 62	Non-IBRD Project	478UNTS335	106941
India	IDA (Devel Assoc)	14 Sep 62	Non-IBRD Project	448UNTS3	106422
India	IDA (Devel Assoc)	14 Sep 62	IBRD Project	467UNTS265	106766
India	IDA (Devel Assoc)	22 Mar 63	Non-IBRD Project	477UNTS3	106911
India	IDA (Devel Assoc)	24 May 63	Non-IBRD Project	483UNTS205	107014
India	IDA (Devel Assoc)	09 Jun 64	Non-IBRD Project	506UNTS31	107380
India	IDA (Devel Assoc)	06 Jul 64	Non-IBRD Project	534UNTS49	107753
India	IDA (Devel Assoc)	26 Oct 64	Non-IBRD Project	535UNTS245	107783
India	IDA (Devel Assoc)	11 Aug 65	Non-IBRD Project	562UNTS277	108199
India	IDA (Devel Assoc)	29 Jun 66	Non-IBRD Project	585UNTS101	108484
India	IDA (Devel Assoc)	29 Jun 66	Non-IBRD Project	582UNTS277	108467
India	IDA (Devel Assoc)	19 Aug 66	Non-IBRD Project	584UNTS193	108478
India	IDA (Devel Assoc)	23 Dec 66	Non-IBRD Project	594UNTS165	108603
India	IDA (Devel Assoc)	22 Jan 69	Non-IBRD Project	OUNTSO	109611
India	IDA (Devel Assoc)	18 Jun 69	Non-IBRD Project	OUNTSO	110094
India	IDA (Devel Assoc)	24 Sep 69	Non-IBRD Project	OUNTSO	110574
India	IDA (Devel Assoc)	24 Apr 70	Non-IBRD Project	OUNTSO	110657
India	ILO (Labor Org)	26 Apr 51	Tech Assistance	100UNTS19	101384
India	Indonesia	03 Mar 51	General Amity	167UNTS3	102197
India	Iran	15 Mar 50	General Amity	161UNTS15	102118
India	Iran	14 Jul 54	Sanitation	OIRTB38	433058
India	Iran	15 Dec 54	General Economic	327UNTS245	104724
India	Iran	01 Dec 56	Culture	OIRTB38	433056
India	Iran	11 Mar 64	General Trade	OIRTB38	433057
India	Iraq	10 Nov 52	General Amity	172UNTS103	102242
India	Italy	27 Aug 53	Other Military	275UNTS279	103987
India	Italy	16 Jul 59	Air Transport	464UNTS129	106714
India	Italy	06 Oct 59	General Trade	378UNTS267	105427
India	Italy	20 Aug 64	General Amity	66ITGU218	435206
India	Japan	09 Jun 52	Peace/Disarmament	OJGJI1000	441070
India	Japan	26 Nov 55	Air Transport	311UNTS243	104506
India	Japan	29 Oct 56	Culture	318UNTS289	104622
India	Japan	04 Feb 58	General Trade	324UNTS215	104687
India	Japan	05 Jan 60	Taxation	384UNTS3	105507
India	Japan	25 Jan 60	Tech Assistance	384UNTS31	105508
India	Japan	31 Mar 62	Education	451UNTS143	106490
India	Japan	23 Apr 62	Education	451UNTS155	106491
India	Japan	14 Dec 63	Claims and Debts	OJGJI1529	441118
India	Japan	17 Dec 64	Education	OJGJI1567	441127
India	Japan	26 Jan 65	Postal Service	OJGJI1606	441128
India	Japan	24 Feb 65	Postal Service	570UNTS3	108284
India	Japan	12 Aug 66	Direct Aid	66JJS57	442173
India	Japan	16 Dec 66	Loans and Credits	66JJS161	442184
India	Japan	14 Jul 67	Loans and Credits	67JJS207	442196
India	Japan	29 Aug 67	Claims and Debts	67JJS205	442200

PARTY ONE	PARTY TWO	DATE	TOPIC	CITATION	NUMBER
India	Japan	05 Sep 67	Loans and Credits	67JJS221	442201
India	Japan	05 Mar 68	Education	69JAIL171	440210
India	Japan	14 Feb 69	Loans and Credits	69JJS211	442232
India	Multilateral	19 Apr 44	Scientific Project	89UNTS279	200257
India	Multilateral	02 Aug 44	Scientific Project	67UNTS221	200221
India	Multilateral	07 Dec 44	IGO Establishment	15UNTS295	200102
India	Multilateral	07 Dec 44	Air Transport	171UNTS345	200501
India	Multilateral	07 Dec 44	Air Transport	84UNTS389	200252
India	Multilateral	15 Dec 44	Sanitation	17UNTS305	200110
India	Multilateral	15 Dec 44	Sanitation	16UNTS247	200106
India	Multilateral	08 Aug 45	General Military	82UNTS279	200251
India	Multilateral	16 Nov 45	IGO Establishment	4UNTS275	100052
India	Multilateral	04 Dec 45	Telecommunications	9UNTS101	100128
India	Multilateral	27 Dec 45	IGO Establishment	2UNTS39	100020
India	Multilateral	01 Jan 46	Peace/Disarmament	99UNTS131	101375
India	Multilateral	14 Jan 46	Reparations	555UNTS69	108105
India	Multilateral	23 Apr 46	Sanitation	16UNTS179	100257
India	Multilateral	23 Apr 46	Sanitation	17UNTS3	100265
India	Multilateral	22 Jul 46	IGO Establishment	9UNTS3	100125
India	Multilateral	22 Jul 46	IGO Establishment	14UNTS185	100221
India	Multilateral	27 Jul 46	Patents/Copyrights	90UNTS229	101238
India	Multilateral	15 Oct 46	Refugees	11UNTS73	100150
India	Multilateral	11 Dec 46	Sanitation	12UNTS179	100186
India	Multilateral	10 Feb 47	Peace/Disarmament	42UNTS3	100645
India	Multilateral	10 Feb 47	Peace/Disarmament	41UNTS21	100643
India	Multilateral	10 Feb 47	Peace/Disarmament	49UNTS3	100747
India	Multilateral	10 Feb 47	Peace/Disarmament	48UNTS203	100746
India	Multilateral	10 Feb 47	Peace/Disarmament	41UNTS135	100644
India	Multilateral	27 May 47	Air Transport	418UNTS161	106021
India	Multilateral	02 Oct 47	Telecommunications	193UNTS188	102616
India	Multilateral	11 Oct 47	IGO Establishment	77UNTS143	100998
India	Multilateral	12 Nov 47	Admin Cooperation	46UNTS201	100710
India	Multilateral	12 Nov 47	Admin Cooperation	53UNTS39	100771
India	Multilateral	12 Nov 47	Admin Cooperation	46UNTS169	100709
India	Multilateral	12 Nov 47	Admin Cooperation	53UNTS13	100770
India	Multilateral	06 Mar 48	Water Transport	289UNTS3	104214
India	Multilateral	11 May 48	Telecommunications	500UNTS267	107313
India	Multilateral	10 Jun 48	Humanitarian	164UNTS113	102163
India	Multilateral	10 Jun 48	Humanitarian	191UNTS3	102576
India	Multilateral	26 Jun 48	Culture	331UNTS217	104757
India	Multilateral	24 Jul 48	Sanitation	66UNTS25	100847
India	Multilateral	14 Sep 48	Milit Occupation	18UNTS267	100296
India	Multilateral	15 Nov 48	IGO Establishment	120UNTS59	101615
India	Multilateral	19 Nov 48	Sanitation	44UNTS277	100688
India	Multilateral	29 Nov 48	IGO Establishment	120UNTS13	101613
India	Multilateral	09 Dec 48	Humanitarian	78UNTS277	101021
India	Multilateral	09 Dec 48	Scientific Project	73UNTS39	100942
India	Multilateral	09 Dec 48	Scientific Project	20UNTS229	100318
India	Multilateral	23 Mar 49	Commodity Trade	203UNTS179	102746
India	Multilateral	04 May 49	Admin Cooperation	30UNTS23	100446
India	Multilateral	04 May 49	Admin Cooperation	47UNTS159	100728
India	Multilateral	04 May 49	Admin Cooperation	98UNTS101	101358
India	Multilateral	04 May 49	Admin Cooperation	30UNTS3	100445
India	Multilateral	04 May 49	Admin Cooperation	92UNTS19	101257
India	Multilateral	12 Aug 49	IGO Establishment	87UNTS131	101169
India	Multilateral	12 Aug 49	General Military	75UNTS135	100972
India	Multilateral	12 Aug 49	Humanitarian	75UNTS31	100970
India	Multilateral	12 Aug 49	Humanitarian	75UNTS85	100971
India	Multilateral	12 Aug 49	Humanitarian	75UNTS287	100973
India	Multilateral	19 Sep 49	Land Transport	125UNTS3	101671
India	Multilateral	16 Dec 49	Admin Cooperation	72UNTS3	100924
India	Multilateral	21 Mar 50	Admin Cooperation	96UNTS271	101342
India	Multilateral	06 Apr 50	Admin Cooperation	119UNTS99	101610
India	Multilateral	28 Jun 50	Loans and Credits	87UNTS153	101170
India	Multilateral	02 Nov 50	Tech Assistance	81UNTS160	101071

PARTY ONE	PARTY TWO	DATE	TOPIC	CITATION	NUMBER
India	Multilateral	07 Dec 50	Admin Cooperation	212UNTS17	102861
India	Multilateral	25 May 51	Status of Forces	175UNTS215	102303
India	Multilateral	10 Jul 51	Other Military	108UNTS287	101481
India	Multilateral	29 Jul 51	Other Military	117UNTS85	101585
India	Multilateral	04 Aug 51	Sanitation	104UNTS197	101441
India	Multilateral	31 Oct 51	Other Military	172UNTS193	102247
India	Multilateral	06 Dec 51	Admin Cooperation	150UNTS67	101963
India	Multilateral	08 Jun 52	Other Military	210UNTS317	102843
India	Multilateral	11 Jul 52	Postal Service	170UNTS63	102222
India	Multilateral	11 Jul 52	Postal Service	170UNTS3	102221
India	Multilateral	11 Jul 52	IGO Establishment	169UNTS3	102220
India	Multilateral	06 Sep 52	Patents/Copyrights	216UNTS132	102937
India	Multilateral	07 Oct 52	Admin Cooperation	310UNTS181	104493
India	Multilateral	17 Oct 52	Direct Aid	141UNTS121	101911
India	Multilateral	07 Nov 52	General Trade	221UNTS255	103010
India	Multilateral	31 Mar 53	Privil/Immunities	193UNTS136	102613
India	Multilateral	11 May 53	Sanitation	456UNTS3	106555
India	Multilateral	27 Aug 53	Other Military	213UNTS137	102884
India	Multilateral	07 Dec 53	Admin Cooperation	182UNTS51	102422
India	Multilateral	22 Feb 54	Other Military	188UNTS273	102531
India	Multilateral	01 Mar 54	Commodity Trade	256UNTS31	103622
India	Multilateral	14 May 54	Culture	249UNTS215	103511
India	Multilateral	04 Jun 54	Customs	276UNTS191	103992
India	Multilateral	04 Jun 54	Customs	282UNTS249	104101
India	Multilateral	14 Jun 54	Air Transport	320UNTS209	104643
India	Multilateral	14 Jun 54	Air Transport	320UNTS217	104644
India	Multilateral	24 Aug 54	Other Military	247UNTS213	103471
India	Multilateral	06 Apr 55	General Amity	261UNTS55	103725
India	Multilateral	25 May 55	IGO Establishment	264UNTS117	103791
India	Multilateral	21 Sep 55	Other Military	269UNTS241	103885
India	Multilateral	12 Oct 55	IGO Establishment	560UNTS3	108165
India	Multilateral	05 Mar 56	Other Military	326UNTS169	104711
India	Multilateral	05 Mar 56	Other Military	326UNTS181	104712
India	Multilateral	25 Apr 56	Commodity Trade	270UNTS103	103896
India	Multilateral	31 Aug 56	Tech Assistance	249UNTS158	103506
India	Multilateral	07 Sep 56	Humanitarian	266UNTS3	103822
India	Multilateral	26 Oct 56	IGO Establishment	276UNTS3	103988
India	Multilateral	20 Feb 57	Consul/Citizenship	309UNTS65	104468
India	Multilateral	01 Jul 57	Culture	0UNTS0	110418
India	Multilateral	03 Oct 57	Postal Service	364UNTS331	105212
India	Multilateral	03 Oct 57	Postal Service	364UNTS3	105211
India	Multilateral	03 Oct 57	Postal Service	365UNTS3	105213
India	Multilateral	06 Jan 58	General Transport	304UNTS227	104399
India	Multilateral	10 Jun 58	Admin Cooperation	330UNTS3	104739
India	Multilateral	01 Dec 58	Commodity Trade	385UNTS137	105534
India	Multilateral	06 Apr 59	Commodity Trade	349UNTS167	105013
India	Multilateral	19 Nov 59	IGO Operations	410UNTS156	105902
India	Multilateral	26 Jan 60	IGO Establishment	439UNTS249	106333
India	Multilateral	17 Jun 60	Humanitarian	536UNTS27	107794
India	Multilateral	01 Sep 60	Commodity Trade	403UNTS3	105792
India	Multilateral	19 Sep 60	IBRD Project	419UNTS125	106032
India	Multilateral	30 Mar 61	Sanitation	520UNTS151	107515
India	Multilateral	14 Apr 61	IGO Establishment	422UNTS101	106071
India	Multilateral	18 Apr 61	Dispute Settlement	500UNTS243	107312
India	Multilateral	18 Apr 61	Consul/Citizenship	500UNTS95	107310
India	Multilateral	18 Apr 61	Consul/Citizenship	500UNTS223	107311
India	Multilateral	21 Jun 61	IGO Establishment	514UNTS209	107449
India	Multilateral	26 Oct 61	Patents/Copyrights	496UNTS43	107247
India	Multilateral	15 May 62	Commodity Trade	444UNTS3	106367
India	Multilateral	28 Jun 62	ILO Labor	494UNTS271	107238
India	Multilateral	23 Jul 62	Recognition	456UNTS302	106564
India	Multilateral	10 Sep 62	Other Military	502UNTS3	107323
India	Multilateral	28 Sep 62	IGO Establishment	469UNTS169	106791
India	Multilateral	05 Aug 63	Sanitation	480UNTS43	106964
India	Multilateral	09 Nov 63	Direct Aid	489UNTS209	107141

PARTY ONE	PARTY TWO	DATE	TOPIC	CITATION	NUMBER
India	Multilateral	03 Dec 63	IGO Establishment	529UNTS217	107663
India	Multilateral	11 Jun 64	Atomic Energy	525UNTS61	107584
India	Multilateral	10 Jul 64	Postal Service	612UNTS3	108847
India	Multilateral	10 Jul 64	Postal Service	611UNTS105	108845
India	Multilateral	10 Jul 64	Postal Service	611UNTS387	108846
India	Multilateral	10 Jul 64	Postal Service	611UNTS7	108844
India	Multilateral	08 Jul 65	General Trade	597UNTS3	108641
India	Multilateral	04 Dec 65	IGO Establishment	571UNTS123	108303
India	Multilateral	17 Jan 66	IGO Establishment	592UNTS101	108573
India	Multilateral	05 Apr 66	Water Transport	640UNTS133	109159
India	Multilateral	27 Jan 67	Scientific Project	610UNTS205	108843
India	Multilateral	17 Mar 67	Non-IBRD Project	594UNTS105	108598
India	Multilateral	03 May 67	IGO Operations	0UNTS0	110764
India	Multilateral	06 Nov 67	Other Military	640UNTS87	109155
India	Multilateral	18 Mar 68	Commodity Trade	0UNTS0	109262
India	Multilateral	24 Sep 68	Air Transport	0UNTS0	110612
India	Multilateral	28 Sep 68	Tech Assistance	0UNTS0	109296
India	Multilateral	12 Dec 68	IGO Establishment	0UNTS0	109733
India	Multilateral	27 Jan 69	Telecommunications	0UNTS0	109664
India	Muscat and Oman	15 Mar 53	General Amity	190UNTS69	102559
India	Nepal	31 Jul 50	General Amity	94UNTS3	101302
India	Nepal	31 Jul 50	General Economic	104UNTS3	101430
India	Netherlands	31 May 47	Air Transport	17UNTS65	100268
India	Netherlands	24 May 51	Air Transport	108UNTS151	101471
India	Netherlands	04 Dec 54	Reparations	289UNTS221	104219
India	Netherlands	16 Jan 59	Tech Assistance	506UNTS153	107386
India	Netherlands	27 Apr 59	Tech Assistance	506UNTS141	107385
India	Netherlands	11 Dec 64	Scientific Project	570UNTS165	108292
India	Netherlands	27 Jul 65	Direct Aid	0UNTS0	110196
India	Netherlands	17 Feb 67	Direct Aid	0UNTS0	109389
India	Netherlands	21 Dec 67	Direct Aid	0UNTS0	109390
India	Netherlands	06 Feb 68	Scientific Project	0UNTS0	110754
India	Netherlands	30 Aug 68	Non-IBRD Project	0UNTS0	109475
India	New Zealand	22 Feb 63	Loans and Credits	486UNTS19	107069
India	Norway	29 Aug 50	General Trade	73UNTS179	100952
India	Norway	20 Jul 59	Taxation	356UNTS257	105099
India	Norway	19 Apr 61	Culture	404UNTS307	105818
India	Norway	17 Mar 67	Specific Resources	3NORT992	451079
India	Norway	16 Sep 68	Loans and Credits	3NORTO	451080
India	Norway	14 Nov 68	Visas	3NORTO	451081
India	Pakistan	10 Dec 47	Taxation	51UNTS173	100764
India	Pakistan	31 Mar 48	Finance	54UNTS33	100793
India	Pakistan	04 May 48	Dispute Settlement	54UNTS45	100794
India	Pakistan	23 Jun 48	Air Transport	28UNTS143	100423
India	Pakistan	30 Jun 48	Finance	29UNTS199	100441
India	Pakistan	23 Apr 49	Finance	54UNTS51	100795
India	Pakistan	27 Jul 49	Peace/Disarmament	81UNTS273	101076
India	Pakistan	08 Apr 50	Visas	131UNTS3	101733
India	Pakistan	21 Aug 52	Territory Boundary	207UNTS161	102805
India	Pakistan	20 Feb 53	Air Transport	164UNTS3	102155
India	Pakistan	08 May 54	Extradition	203UNTS167	102745
India	Pakistan	15 Apr 55	Land Transport	247UNTS25	103458
India	Pakistan	12 Jun 55	Finance	228UNTS211	103153
India	Pakistan	10 Sep 58	Territory Boundary	369UNTS81	105252
India	Pakistan	23 Oct 59	Territory Boundary	362UNTS3	105180
India	Pakistan	11 Jan 60	Territory Boundary	375UNTS119	105364
India	Pakistan	30 Jun 65	Territory Boundary	548UNTS277	107983
India	Pakistan	10 Jan 66	General Amity	560UNTS39	108166
India	Philippines	20 Oct 49	Air Transport	72UNTS191	100934
India	Philippines	11 Jul 52	General Amity	203UNTS73	102741
India	Philippines	14 Mar 69	Atomic Energy	0UNTS0	109796
India	Poland	29 Sep 56	Telecommunications	276UNTS305	103993
India	Poland	27 Mar 57	Culture	319UNTS263	104635
India	Poland	27 Jun 60	Water Transport	60PZUM63	458076
India	Romania	30 Apr 57	Culture	342UNTS251	104911

PARTY ONE	PARTY TWO	DATE	TOPIC	CITATION	NUMBER
India	Romania	25 Sep 68	Taxation	0UNTS0	109882
India	Sweden	21 May 48	Air Transport	34UNTS285	100543
India	Sweden	24 Feb 50	General Trade	50SOFM43	461099
India	Sweden	01 Jul 50	General Trade	50SOFM178	461110
India	Sweden	28 Feb 51	General Trade	51SOFM123	461137
India	Sweden	30 Jun 53	General Trade	53SOFM1067	461193
India	Sweden	30 Jul 58	Taxation	369UNTS211	105259
India	Switzerland	14 Aug 48	General Amity	33UNTS3	100509
India	Switzerland	24 Jun 49	Air Transport	95UNTS109	101319
India	Switzerland	28 Aug 58	Taxation	58SWRO795	462054
India	Switzerland	30 Jul 60	Finance	60SWRO1678	462140
India	Syria	25 Feb 52	General Amity	163UNTS55	102141
India	Thailand	12 Jun 56	Air Transport	255UNTS341	103617
India	Thailand	13 Dec 68	General Trade	0UNTS0	109386
India	Turkey	29 Jun 51	Culture	213UNTS183	102886
India	Turkey	14 Dec 51	General Amity	137UNTS15	101845
India	Turkey	04 Jun 53	General Trade	54TURG2203	466069
India	UK Great Britain	14 Aug 47	Finance	11UNTS371	100176
India	UK Great Britain	15 Feb 48	Finance	134UNTS70	101796
India	UK Great Britain	07 Dec 49	Postal Service	281UNTS245	104082
India	UK Great Britain	05 Jun 51	Postal Service	135UNTS3	101811
India	UK Great Britain	01 Dec 51	Air Transport	128UNTS39	101712
India	UK Great Britain	20 Jul 53	Finance	196UNTS251	102628
India	UK Great Britain	27 Nov 62	Milit Installation	466UNTS189	106744
India	UK Great Britain	31 Jul 64	Commodity Trade	522UNTS153	107542
India	UK Great Britain	20 Oct 64	Customs	534UNTS77	107755
India	UK Great Britain	20 Nov 64	Milit Assistance	534UNTS85	107756
India	UK Great Britain	21 Sep 68	Finance	0UNTS0	109809
India	UN Special Fund	20 Oct 59	Direct Aid	344UNTS143	104946
India	UNICEF (Children)	10 May 49	IGO Operations	68UNTS96	100887
India	United Arab Rep	14 Jun 52	Air Transport	173UNTS209	102268
India	United Arab Rep	20 Feb 69	Taxation	0UNTS0	110590
India	United Nations	14 Aug 51	Tech Assistance	98UNTS115	101359
India	United Nations	12 Jan 52	Tech Assistance	118UNTS175	101606
India	United Nations	02 Apr 52	Tech Assistance	126UNTS145	101687
India	United Nations	14 Aug 57	Milit Assistance	274UNTS233	103968
India	United Nations	19 Feb 62	Direct Aid	423UNTS3	106082
India	United Nations	27 Dec 62	Scientific Project	450UNTS3	106464
India	United Nations	25 Nov 64	Scientific Project	519UNTS47	107501
India	United Nations	04 Nov 67	IGO Operations	609UNTS3	108824
India	United Nations	22 Jul 68	IGO Operations	640UNTS121	109158
India	USA (United States)	30 Sep 42	Milit Servic/Citiz	13UNTS185	200078
India	USA (United States)	16 Oct 42	Status of Forces	109UNTS111	200353
India	USA (United States)	16 May 46	Milit Assistance	4UNTS183	100045
India	USA (United States)	14 Nov 46	Air Transport	22UNTS55	100331
India	USA (United States)	05 Jul 47	Status of Forces	185UNTS293	102476
India	USA (United States)	11 Aug 48	Visas	224UNTS115	103072
India	USA (United States)	04 Jul 49	Status of Forces	200UNTS181	102702
India	USA (United States)	02 Feb 50	Education	89UNTS127	101214
India	USA (United States)	28 Dec 50	Tech Assistance	99UNTS39	101369
India	USA (United States)	11 Jan 51	Admin Cooperation	148UNTS49	101934
India	USA (United States)	16 Mar 51	Milit Assistance	141UNTS47	101904
India	USA (United States)	09 Jul 51	Customs	147UNTS43	101927
India	USA (United States)	05 Jan 52	Tech Assistance	157UNTS39	102045
India	USA (United States)	29 Jul 54	Postal Service	239UNTS69	103373
India	USA (United States)	21 Oct 54	Patents/Copyrights	234UNTS119	103277
India	USA (United States)	04 Oct 55	Direct Aid	268UNTS115	103853
India	USA (United States)	03 Feb 56	Air Transport	272UNTS75	103932
India	USA (United States)	29 Aug 56	US Agri Commod Aid	278UNTS25	104019
India	USA (United States)	27 Sep 56	Direct Aid	281UNTS289	104085
India	USA (United States)	19 Sep 57	Claims and Debts	290UNTS175	104236
India	USA (United States)	23 Jun 58	US Agri Commod Aid	317UNTS181	104603
India	USA (United States)	26 Sep 58	US Agri Commod Aid	336UNTS59	104798
India	USA (United States)	17 Dec 58	Milit Assistance	358UNTS77	105125
India	USA (United States)	03 Mar 59	US Agri Commod Aid	341UNTS235	104886

PARTY ONE	PARTY TWO	DATE	TOPIC	CITATION	NUMBER
India	USA (United States)	13 Nov 59	US Agri Commod Aid	360UNTS287	105164
India	USA (United States)	04 May 60	US Agri Commod Aid	376UNTS279	105384
India	USA (United States)	13 Jun 60	Atomic Energy	377UNTS37	105394
India	USA (United States)	07 Feb 61	Scientific Project	462UNTS57	106671
India	USA (United States)	16 Apr 62	General Trade	445UNTS257	106393
India	USA (United States)	01 May 62	US Agri Commod Aid	451UNTS179	106493
India	USA (United States)	09 Oct 62	Scientific Project	471UNTS39	106820
India	USA (United States)	21 Nov 62	General Aid	462UNTS255	106685
India	USA (United States)	26 Nov 62	US Agri Commod Aid	460UNTS203	106641
India	USA (United States)	30 Nov 62	US Agri Commod Aid	459UNTS231	106626
India	USA (United States)	01 Feb 63	Scientific Project	473UNTS37	106852
India	USA (United States)	09 May 63	US Agri Commod Aid	476UNTS43	106902
India	USA (United States)	19 Jun 63	Education	479UNTS175	106952
India	USA (United States)	27 Jun 63	US Agri Commod Aid	479UNTS215	106955
India	USA (United States)	08 Aug 63	Scientific Project	488UNTS21	107117
India	USA (United States)	15 Apr 64	Commodity Trade	527UNTS19	107614
India	USA (United States)	30 Sep 64	US Agri Commod Aid	532UNTS321	107726
India	USA (United States)	13 Jan 65	Milit Assistance	541UNTS107	107864
India	USA (United States)	25 May 66	Gen Communications	593UNTS157	108582
India	USA (United States)	14 Feb 67	Scientific Project	0UNTS0	109752
India	USA (United States)	20 Feb 67	US Agri Commod Aid	0UNTS0	109850
India	USA (United States)	24 Jun 67	US Agri Commod Aid	0UNTS0	109906
India	USA (United States)	31 Aug 67	Commodity Trade	0UNTS0	109916
India	USA (United States)	12 Sep 67	US Agri Commod Aid	0UNTS0	109917
India	USA (United States)	30 Dec 67	US Agri Commod Aid	0UNTS0	109993
India	USA (United States)	05 Dec 68	Customs	0UNTS0	110253
India	USA (United States)	23 Dec 68	General Aid	0UNTS0	110259
India	USA (United States)	23 Dec 68	Commodity Trade	0UNTS0	110260
India	USA (United States)	13 Oct 69	US Agri Commod Aid	0UNTS0	110449
India	USSR (Soviet Union)	07 Apr 47	Consul/Citizenship	0SUST231	468209
India	USSR (Soviet Union)	02 Dec 53	General Trade	240UNTS143	103402
India	USSR (Soviet Union)	02 Dec 53	General Trade	0SUST304	468211
India	USSR (Soviet Union)	24 Jan 55	Non-IBRD Project	0SUST322	468212
India	USSR (Soviet Union)	22 Jun 55	General Amity	0SUST330	468213
India	USSR (Soviet Union)	23 Dec 55	Specif Goods/Equip	0SUST345	468214
India	USSR (Soviet Union)	06 Apr 56	Water Transport	0SUST352	468215
India	USSR (Soviet Union)	21 May 56	Specif Goods/Equip	0SUST356	468216
India	USSR (Soviet Union)	09 Nov 57	General Economic	0SUST391	468217
India	USSR (Soviet Union)	02 Jun 58	Air Transport	393UNTS3	105650
India	USSR (Soviet Union)	16 Nov 58	General Trade	16SUGG125	469962
India	USSR (Soviet Union)	16 Nov 58	General Trade	7SUGG126	469542
India	USSR (Soviet Union)	12 Dec 58	General Aid	7SUGG128	469544
India	USSR (Soviet Union)	29 May 59	General Aid	8SUGG146	469577
India	USSR (Soviet Union)	23 Jun 59	Non-IBRD Project	8SUGG147	469583
India	USSR (Soviet Union)	23 Jul 59	Tech Assistance	8SUGG150	469592
India	USSR (Soviet Union)	12 Sep 59	Loans and Credits	8SUGG153	469603
India	USSR (Soviet Union)	28 Sep 59	Non-IBRD Project	8SUGG154	469604
India	USSR (Soviet Union)	12 Feb 60	General Aid	9SUGG125	469630
India	USSR (Soviet Union)	12 Feb 60	Culture	392UNTS153	105642
India	USSR (Soviet Union)	14 Mar 60	General Trade	9SUGG130	469643
India	USSR (Soviet Union)	16 Jun 60	Tech Assistance	9SUGG138	469665
India	USSR (Soviet Union)	22 Aug 60	Education	9SUGG145	469685
India	USSR (Soviet Union)	21 Feb 61	General Aid	10SUGG122	469744
India	USSR (Soviet Union)	06 Oct 61	Atomic Energy	10SUGG143	469797
India	USSR (Soviet Union)	12 Feb 62	General Aid	11SUGG132	469820
India	USSR (Soviet Union)	10 Mar 62	Consul/Citizenship	16SUGG132	470003
India	USSR (Soviet Union)	20 Nov 62	Water Transport	11SUGG157	469875
India	USSR (Soviet Union)	10 Jun 63	General Trade	0UNTS0	109382
India	WHO (World Health)	09 Nov 49	IGO Status/Immunit	67UNTS43	100865
India	WHO (World Health)	11 Oct 51	Non-IBRD Project	118UNTS27	101594
India	WHO (World Health)	16 Oct 51	Tech Assistance	109UNTS49	101490
India	WHO (World Health)	23 Oct 51	Sanitation	109UNTS59	101491
India	WHO (World Health)	01 Nov 51	Scientific Project	118UNTS13	101593
India	WHO (World Health)	20 Dec 51	Tech Assistance	124UNTS109	101669
India	WHO (World Health)	02 Apr 52	Sanitation	131UNTS227	101743

PARTY ONE	PARTY TWO	DATE	TOPIC	CITATION	NUMBER
India	WHO (World Health)	14 Apr 52	Tech Assistance	131UNTS265	101746
India	WHO (World Health)	17 Apr 52	Tech Assistance	131UNTS241	101744
India	WHO (World Health)	19 Apr 52	Tech Assistance	131UNTS253	101745
India	WHO (World Health)	04 Jun 52	Sanitation	135UNTS279	101827
India	WHO (World Health)	19 Jun 52	Sanitation	134UNTS307	101809
India	WHO (World Health)	16 Jul 52	Tech Assistance	135UNTS291	101828
India	WHO (World Health)	11 Dec 52	Sanitation	158UNTS391	102073
India	WHO (World Health)	11 Feb 53	Tech Assistance	163UNTS43	102140
India	Yugoslavia	24 Jul 53	General Trade	394UNTS13	105665
Indo-Pac Fish Coun	Multilateral	15 Nov 48	IGO Establishment	120UNTS59	101615
Indonesia	Accept UN Charter	25 Sep 50	UN Charter	71UNTS153	100916
Indonesia	Australia	17 Dec 59	General Trade	354UNTS109	105058
Indonesia	Australia	14 Jun 68	Culture	0UNTS0	110173
Indonesia	Australia	07 Mar 69	Air Transport	0UNTS0	109735
Indonesia	China People's Rep	30 Nov 53	General Trade	53CCJC68	410128
Indonesia	China People's Rep	01 Sep 54	General Trade	54CCJC54	410168
Indonesia	China People's Rep	01 Sep 54	Finance	54CCJC55	410169
Indonesia	China People's Rep	22 Apr 55	Consul/Citizenship	55CCJC28	410230
Indonesia	China People's Rep	03 Nov 56	Direct Aid	56CCJC129	410379
Indonesia	China People's Rep	03 Nov 56	Finance	56CCJC128	410378
Indonesia	China People's Rep	03 Nov 56	General Trade	56CCJC126	410377
Indonesia	China People's Rep	01 Apr 61	General Amity	61CCJC43	410774
Indonesia	China People's Rep	01 Apr 61	Culture	61CCJC44	410775
Indonesia	China People's Rep	11 Oct 61	General Aid	61CCJC134	410837
Indonesia	China People's Rep	01 Nov 62	Scientific Project	62CCJC98	410924
Indonesia	China People's Rep	06 Nov 64	Air Transport	64CCJC161	411203
Indonesia	China People's Rep	12 Jan 65	Visas	65CCJC4	411209
Indonesia	China People's Rep	28 Jan 65	Direct Aid	65CCJC11	411210
Indonesia	China People's Rep	28 Jan 65	Loans and Credits	65CCJC12	411211
Indonesia	China People's Rep	16 Mar 65	Tech Assistance	65CCJC28	411212
Indonesia	China People's Rep	24 Jul 65	Water Transport	65CCJC100	411213
Indonesia	China People's Rep	14 Sep 65	Non-IBRD Project	65CCJC117	411214
Indonesia	China People's Rep	30 Sep 65	Direct Aid	65CCJC122	411215
Indonesia	China People's Rep	30 Sep 65	General Trade	65CCJC123	411216
Indonesia	China People's Rep	30 Sep 65	Finance	65CCJC124	411217
Indonesia	Czechoslovakia	29 May 61	General Amity	479UNTS337	106962
Indonesia	Denmark	30 Jan 68	General Economic	0UNTS0	110352
Indonesia	Denmark	22 Oct 69	Loans and Credits	0UNTS0	110393
Indonesia	France	24 Nov 67	Air Transport	68FRJO3103	416234
Indonesia	France	03 Apr 69	Atomic Energy	69FRJO2707	416235
Indonesia	France	03 Apr 69	Atomic Energy	0UNTS0	110736
Indonesia	France	20 Sep 69	Culture	0UNTS0	110737
Indonesia	Germany, East	12 Dec 56	General Trade	5EGDA344	419132
Indonesia	Germany, East	16 Feb 61	General Trade	9EGDA350	419133
Indonesia	Germany, East	16 Feb 61	Commodity Trade	9EGDA351	419135
Indonesia	Germany, East	16 Feb 61	Water Transport	9EGDA351	419136
Indonesia	Germany, East	16 Feb 61	Health/Educ/Welfare	9EGDA350	419134
Indonesia	Germany, West	22 Apr 53	General Trade	53WBGA163	424261
Indonesia	Germany, West	29 Aug 57	Direct Aid	57WBGA228	424262
Indonesia	Germany, West	17 May 68	Loans and Credits	68WBGA139	424263
Indonesia	Germany, West	08 Nov 68	Loans and Credits	70WGBB492	425264
Indonesia	Germany, West	08 May 69	Loans and Credits	69WBGA189	424265
Indonesia	Germany, West	23 Oct 69	Loans and Credits	70WBGA28	424266
Indonesia	Germany, West	04 Dec 69	Air Transport	71WGBB192	425267
Indonesia	Germany, West	27 Aug 70	Loans and Credits	70WBGA226	424268
Indonesia	Hungary	23 Aug 61	General Amity	519UNTS163	107507
Indonesia	IAEA (Atom Energy)	19 Dec 69	Atomic Energy	0UNTS0	110523
Indonesia	IDA (Devel Assoc)	06 Sep 68	Non-IBRD Project	0UNTS0	109626
Indonesia	IDA (Devel Assoc)	27 Dec 68	Non-IBRD Project	0UNTS0	109653
Indonesia	IDA (Devel Assoc)	20 Jun 69	Non-IBRD Project	0UNTS0	110571
Indonesia	IDA (Devel Assoc)	20 Jun 69	Non-IBRD Project	0UNTS0	110570
Indonesia	IDA (Devel Assoc)	29 Oct 69	Non-IBRD Project	0UNTS0	110650
Indonesia	IDA (Devel Assoc)	15 Dec 69	Non-IBRD Project	0UNTS0	110651
Indonesia	ILO (Labor Org)	21 May 70	IGO Establishment	0UNTS0	110543
Indonesia	India	03 Mar 51	General Amity	167UNTS3	102197

PARTY ONE	PARTY TWO	DATE	TOPIC	CITATION	NUMBER
Indonesia	Iran	29 Dec 58	General Amity	0IRTB39	433059
Indonesia	Iran	27 Apr 71	Culture	0IRTB39	433060
Indonesia	Italy	19 Apr 63	Admin Cooperation	64ITDI260	436207
Indonesia	Japan	16 Dec 53	Reparations	57JAIL78	440154
Indonesia	Japan	20 Jan 58	Loans and Credits	0JGJI1365	441104
Indonesia	Japan	20 Jan 58	Loans and Credits	325UNTS13	104691
Indonesia	Japan	20 Jan 58	Peace/Disarmament	324UNTS227	104688
Indonesia	Japan	20 Jan 58	Claims and Debts	325UNTS3	104690
Indonesia	Japan	20 Jan 58	Reparations	324UNTS247	104689
Indonesia	Japan	01 Jul 61	General Amity	517UNTS107	107484
Indonesia	Japan	23 Jan 62	Air Transport	559UNTS77	108155
Indonesia	Japan	09 Jun 67	Loans and Credits	67JJS229	442193
Indonesia	Japan	10 Nov 67	General Aid	67JJS243	442205
Indonesia	Japan	29 May 68	Tech Assistance	68JJS247	442213
Indonesia	Japan	02 Jul 68	Loans and Credits	68JJS263	442216
Indonesia	Japan	04 Jul 69	Direct Aid	69JJS211	442244
Indonesia	Japan	18 Jul 69	Tech Assistance	69JJS235	442245
Indonesia	Malaysia	17 Apr 59	General Amity	470UNTS273	106813
Indonesia	Mexico	10 Nov 61	General Trade	62MEXD1602	444028
Indonesia	Multilateral	11 Dec 46	Sanitation	12UNTS179	100186
Indonesia	Multilateral	27 May 47	Air Transport	418UNTS161	106021
Indonesia	Multilateral	11 Oct 47	IGO Establishment	77UNTS143	100998
Indonesia	Multilateral	06 Mar 48	Water Transport	289UNTS3	104214
Indonesia	Multilateral	24 Jul 48	Sanitation	66UNTS25	100847
Indonesia	Multilateral	15 Nov 48	IGO Establishment	120UNTS59	101615
Indonesia	Multilateral	29 Nov 48	IGO Establishment	120UNTS13	101613
Indonesia	Multilateral	23 Mar 49	Commodity Trade	203UNTS179	102746
Indonesia	Multilateral	31 May 50	General Trade	74UNTS95	100957
Indonesia	Multilateral	02 Nov 50	Tech Assistance	81UNTS160	101071
Indonesia	Multilateral	15 Dec 50	Customs	157UNTS129	102052
Indonesia	Multilateral	25 May 51	Status of Forces	175UNTS215	102303
Indonesia	Multilateral	08 Sep 51	General Military	136UNTS165	101833
Indonesia	Multilateral	08 Sep 51	Peace/Disarmament	136UNTS45	101832
Indonesia	Multilateral	06 Dec 51	Admin Cooperation	150UNTS67	101963
Indonesia	Multilateral	11 Feb 52	Direct Aid	165UNTS77	102169
Indonesia	Multilateral	11 Jul 52	Postal Service	170UNTS269	102223
Indonesia	Multilateral	11 Jul 52	Postal Service	170UNTS63	102222
Indonesia	Multilateral	11 Jul 52	Postal Service	171UNTS89	102225
Indonesia	Multilateral	11 Jul 52	Postal Service	171UNTS3	102224
Indonesia	Multilateral	11 Jul 52	Postal Service	170UNTS3	102221
Indonesia	Multilateral	11 Jul 52	IGO Establishment	169UNTS3	102220
Indonesia	Multilateral	11 Jul 52	Postal Service	171UNTS143	102226
Indonesia	Multilateral	07 Nov 52	General Trade	221UNTS255	103010
Indonesia	Multilateral	31 Mar 53	Privil/Immunities	193UNTS136	102613
Indonesia	Multilateral	11 May 53	Sanitation	456UNTS3	106555
Indonesia	Multilateral	01 Mar 54	Commodity Trade	256UNTS31	103622
Indonesia	Multilateral	14 May 54	Culture	249UNTS215	103511
Indonesia	Multilateral	14 Jun 54	Air Transport	320UNTS209	104643
Indonesia	Multilateral	14 Jun 54	Air Transport	320UNTS217	104644
Indonesia	Multilateral	29 Oct 54	Tech Assistance	201UNTS115	102713
Indonesia	Multilateral	25 May 55	IGO Establishment	264UNTS117	103791
Indonesia	Multilateral	12 Oct 55	IGO Establishment	560UNTS3	108165
Indonesia	Multilateral	25 Apr 56	Commodity Trade	270UNTS103	103896
Indonesia	Multilateral	26 Oct 56	IGO Establishment	276UNTS3	103988
Indonesia	Multilateral	03 Oct 57	Postal Service	364UNTS3	105211
Indonesia	Multilateral	03 Oct 57	Postal Service	365UNTS3	105213
Indonesia	Multilateral	03 Oct 57	Postal Service	365UNTS207	105214
Indonesia	Multilateral	03 Oct 57	Postal Service	366UNTS3	105215
Indonesia	Multilateral	03 Oct 57	Postal Service	366UNTS87	105216
Indonesia	Multilateral	03 Oct 57	Postal Service	366UNTS141	105217
Indonesia	Multilateral	29 Apr 58	Specific Resources	559UNTS285	108164
Indonesia	Multilateral	29 Apr 58	Dispute Settlement	450UNTS169	106466
Indonesia	Multilateral	29 Apr 58	Territory Boundary	499UNTS311	107302
Indonesia	Multilateral	29 Apr 58	Water Transport	450UNTS11	106465
Indonesia	Multilateral	01 Dec 58	Commodity Trade	385UNTS137	105534

PARTY ONE	PARTY TWO	DATE	TOPIC	CITATION	NUMBER
Indonesia	Multilateral	06 Apr 59	Commodity Trade	349UNTS167	105013
Indonesia	Multilateral	01 Sep 60	Commodity Trade	403UNTS3	105792
Indonesia	Multilateral	14 Sep 60	IGO Establishment	443UNTS247	106363
Indonesia	Multilateral	30 Mar 61	Sanitation	520UNTS151	107515
Indonesia	Multilateral	21 Jun 61	IGO Establishment	514UNTS209	107449
Indonesia	Multilateral	15 May 62	Commodity Trade	444UNTS3	106367
Indonesia	Multilateral	15 Aug 62	Territory Boundary	437UNTS292	106312
Indonesia	Multilateral	10 Sep 62	Other Military	502UNTS3	107323
Indonesia	Multilateral	28 Sep 62	IGO Establishment	469UNTS169	106791
Indonesia	Multilateral	31 Jul 63	General Amity	550UNTS343	108029
Indonesia	Multilateral	05 Aug 63	Sanitation	480UNTS43	106964
Indonesia	Multilateral	10 Jul 64	Postal Service	611UNTS387	108846
Indonesia	Multilateral	10 Jul 64	Postal Service	612UNTS233	108848
Indonesia	Multilateral	10 Jul 64	Postal Service	611UNTS7	108844
Indonesia	Multilateral	10 Jul 64	Postal Service	611UNTS105	108845
Indonesia	Multilateral	10 Jul 64	Postal Service	612UNTS361	108849
Indonesia	Multilateral	10 Jul 64	Postal Service	612UNTS3	108847
Indonesia	Multilateral	10 Jul 64	Postal Service	613UNTS3	108851
Indonesia	Multilateral	10 Jul 64	Postal Service	613UNTS3	108850
Indonesia	Multilateral	20 Aug 64	Telecommunications	514UNTS25	107441
Indonesia	Multilateral	18 Mar 65	Dispute Settlement	575UNTS159	108359
Indonesia	Multilateral	31 Dec 65	Specific Resources	616UNTS317	108904
Indonesia	Multilateral	25 Jan 67	IGO Operations	588UNTS212	108527
Indonesia	Multilateral	27 Jan 67	Scientific Project	610UNTS205	108843
Indonesia	Multilateral	03 May 67	IGO Operations	0UNTS0	110764
Indonesia	Multilateral	18 Mar 68	Commodity Trade	0UNTS0	109262
Indonesia	Multilateral	12 Dec 68	IGO Establishment	0UNTS0	109733
Indonesia	Multilateral	24 Dec 68	Commodity Trade	0UNTS0	109369
Indonesia	Multilateral	19 Dec 69	Atomic Energy	0UNTS0	110522
Indonesia	Netherlands	02 Nov 49	Recognition	69UNTS3	100894
Indonesia	Netherlands	14 Jul 50	Status of Forces	51NET4	447014
Indonesia	Netherlands	08 Jun 54	Taxation	54NET92	447047
Indonesia	Netherlands	10 Aug 54	General Amity	54NET113	447049
Indonesia	Netherlands	11 Aug 54	Claims and Debts	241UNTS129	103429
Indonesia	Netherlands	15 Aug 62	Territory Boundary	437UNTS273	106311
Indonesia	Netherlands	03 Apr 64	Tech Assistance	566UNTS45	108239
Indonesia	Netherlands	12 Jul 66	Air Transport	0UNTS0	110164
Indonesia	Netherlands	07 Sep 66	Finance	0UNTS0	109779
Indonesia	Netherlands	07 Jul 68	Culture	0UNTS0	110604
Indonesia	Norway	30 Apr 51	General Trade	2NORT552	451082
Indonesia	Norway	22 Jun 54	Finance	2NORT621	451083
Indonesia	Pakistan	03 Mar 51	General Amity	188UNTS333	102537
Indonesia	Philippines	21 Jun 51	General Amity	2PTS689	465027
Indonesia	Philippines	04 Jul 56	Admin Cooperation	401UNTS59	105763
Indonesia	Philippines	27 Jul 60	Admin Cooperation	4PTS349	465044
Indonesia	Philippines	30 Jan 61	General Military	4PTS425	465047
Indonesia	Philippines	27 May 63	General Trade	4PTS739	465050
Indonesia	Philippines	27 May 63	Tech Assistance	4PTS749	465052
Indonesia	Philippines	27 May 63	General Economic	4PTS753	465053
Indonesia	Philippines	27 May 63	Admin Cooperation	4PTS747	465051
Indonesia	Philippines	25 Jul 63	General Military	4PTS761	465054
Indonesia	Philippines	19 Mar 64	Gen Communications	4PTS859	465063
Indonesia	Philippines	19 Mar 64	IGO Establishment	4PTS855	465062
Indonesia	Philippines	21 Feb 67	Gen Communications	593UNTS109	108578
Indonesia	Poland	06 May 53	General Economic	53PZUM85	458009
Indonesia	Poland	10 Oct 61	Tech Assistance	61PZUM211	458089
Indonesia	Sweden	05 Apr 51	General Trade	51SOFM193	461140
Indonesia	Sweden	01 Jul 52	General Trade	52SOFM265	461167
Indonesia	Switzerland	30 Dec 54	General Trade	55SWRO64	462141
Indonesia	Thailand	03 Mar 54	General Amity	213UNTS297	102893
Indonesia	Turkey	14 Sep 59	General Trade	64TURG2909	466070
Indonesia	UK Great Britain	02 Jul 56	Commodity Trade	265UNTS285	103820
Indonesia	UK Great Britain	02 Jul 56	Commodity Trade	265UNTS271	103819
Indonesia	UK Great Britain	23 Nov 60	Air Transport	398UNTS71	105718
Indonesia	UK Great Britain	29 Jun 61	General Economic	443UNTS255	106364
Indonesia	UK Great Britain	01 Dec 66	Claims and Debts	606UNTS125	108782
Indonesia	UK Great Britain	01 Aug 67	Claims and Debts	638UNTS3	109128
Indonesia	UK Great Britain	31 Oct 67	Claims and Debts	0UNTS0	109497
Indonesia	UK Great Britain	02 Dec 67	Loans and Credits	0UNTS0	109339
Indonesia	UK Great Britain	06 May 68	Loans and Credits	0UNTS0	109340
Indonesia	UK Great Britain	11 Nov 68	Loans and Credits	0UNTS0	109659
Indonesia	UK Great Britain	16 Jan 69	Loans and Credits	0UNTS0	109660
Indonesia	UK Great Britain	13 Mar 69	Loans and Credits	0UNTS0	109879
Indonesia	UK Great Britain	13 Mar 69	Claims and Debts	0UNTS0	109790
Indonesia	UK Great Britain	29 Apr 69	Loans and Credits	0UNTS0	110036
Indonesia	UK Great Britain	25 Jun 69	Loans and Credits	0UNTS0	110116
Indonesia	UK Great Britain	22 Oct 69	Loans and Credits	0UNTS0	110440
Indonesia	UK Great Britain	13 Mar 70	Finance	0UNTS0	110757
Indonesia	UK Great Britain	13 Apr 70	Finance	0UNTS0	110786
Indonesia	UN Special Fund	07 Oct 60	Direct Aid	378UNTS141	105424
Indonesia	UNICEF (Children)	06 Apr 50	IGO Operations	68UNTS254	200238
Indonesia	UNICEF (Children)	04 Jul 55	Admin Cooperation	212UNTS13	102860
Indonesia	UNICEF (Children)	17 Nov 66	IGO Operations	578UNTS47	108386
Indonesia	United Nations	06 Feb 52	Tech Assistance	121UNTS3	101621
Indonesia	United Nations	17 Apr 56	Non-IBRD Project	233UNTS267	103266
Indonesia	USA (United States)	24 Mar 50	Direct Aid	92UNTS387	101281
Indonesia	USA (United States)	07 Jun 50	Admin Cooperation	98UNTS167	101362
Indonesia	USA (United States)	15 Aug 50	Milit Assistance	134UNTS255	101804
Indonesia	USA (United States)	16 Oct 50	Direct Aid	281UNTS105	104074
Indonesia	USA (United States)	05 Jan 52	Tech Assistance	215UNTS121	102916
Indonesia	USA (United States)	15 Sep 55	Mass Media	256UNTS293	103639
Indonesia	USA (United States)	02 Mar 56	US Agri Commod Aid	271UNTS345	103925
Indonesia	USA (United States)	13 Aug 58	Milit Assistance	335UNTS187	104785
Indonesia	USA (United States)	02 Mar 59	Air Transport	357UNTS145	105113
Indonesia	USA (United States)	29 May 59	US Agri Commod Aid	347UNTS85	104992
Indonesia	USA (United States)	08 Jun 60	Atomic Energy	388UNTS287	105585
Indonesia	USA (United States)	05 Nov 60	US Agri Commod Aid	400UNTS35	105746
Indonesia	USA (United States)	31 Mar 61	Visas	405UNTS119	105828
Indonesia	USA (United States)	26 Oct 61	US Agri Commod Aid	433UNTS249	106248
Indonesia	USA (United States)	19 Feb 62	US Agri Commod Aid	435UNTS137	106276
Indonesia	USA (United States)	14 Mar 63	General Aid	505UNTS79	107365
Indonesia	USA (United States)	18 Apr 66	US Agri Commod Aid	578UNTS106	108390
Indonesia	USA (United States)	28 Jun 66	US Agri Commod Aid	593UNTS201	108585
Indonesia	USA (United States)	30 Sep 66	US Agri Commod Aid	616UNTS199	108897
Indonesia	USA (United States)	07 Jan 67	Finance	0UNTS0	109896
Indonesia	USA (United States)	14 Apr 67	Milit Assistance	0UNTS0	109859
Indonesia	USA (United States)	15 Sep 67	US Agri Commod Aid	0UNTS0	109918
Indonesia	USA (United States)	01 Nov 67	US Agri Commod Aid	0UNTS0	110054
Indonesia	USA (United States)	22 Nov 67	US Agri Commod Aid	0UNTS0	109987
Indonesia	USA (United States)	30 Dec 67	Finance	0UNTS0	109994
Indonesia	USA (United States)	15 Feb 68	US Agri Commod Aid	0UNTS0	109988
Indonesia	USA (United States)	05 Aug 68	US Agri Commod Aid	0UNTS0	110070
Indonesia	USA (United States)	16 Aug 68	US Agri Commod Aid	0UNTS0	110071
Indonesia	USA (United States)	05 Sep 68	US Agri Commod Aid	0UNTS0	110072
Indonesia	USA (United States)	10 Dec 68	Gen Communications	0UNTS0	110151
Indonesia	USA (United States)	15 Dec 68	Air Transport	0UNTS0	109999
Indonesia	USA (United States)	17 Apr 69	General Military	0UNTS0	110330
Indonesia	USA (United States)	17 Nov 69	US Agri Commod Aid	0UNTS0	110453
Indonesia	USA (United States)	16 Jan 70	Scientific Project	0UNTS0	110616
Indonesia	USA (United States)	10 Apr 70	Commodity Trade	0UNTS0	110813
Indonesia	USSR (Soviet Union)	22 May 48	Consul/Citizenship	0SUST248	468218
Indonesia	USSR (Soviet Union)	03 Feb 50	Consul/Citizenship	0SUST268	468219
Indonesia	USSR (Soviet Union)	17 Dec 53	Consul/Citizenship	0SUST304	468220
Indonesia	USSR (Soviet Union)	12 Jun 56	Mostfavored Nation	0SUST367	468222
Indonesia	USSR (Soviet Union)	12 Aug 56	General Trade	16SUGG72	469924
Indonesia	USSR (Soviet Union)	18 Aug 56	General Economic	0SUST366	468221
Indonesia	USSR (Soviet Union)	15 Sep 56	General Aid	0SUST368	468223
Indonesia	USSR (Soviet Union)	03 Jan 59	General Aid	8SUGG132	469549
Indonesia	USSR (Soviet Union)	28 Jul 59	Loans and Credits	8SUGG150	469594
Indonesia	USSR (Soviet Union)	28 Jul 59	Loans and Credits	8SUGG150	469593

PARTY ONE	PARTY TWO	DATE	TOPIC	CITATION	NUMBER
Indonesia	USSR (Soviet Union)	14 Aug 59	Tech Assistance	8SUGG152	469598
Indonesia	USSR (Soviet Union)	28 Feb 60	General Aid	392UNTS173	105643
Indonesia	USSR (Soviet Union)	28 Feb 60	Culture	392UNTS191	105644
Indonesia	USSR (Soviet Union)	01 Jul 60	Atomic Energy	9SUGG141	469670
Indonesia	USSR (Soviet Union)	09 Jul 60	General Trade	9SUGG141	469672
Indonesia	USSR (Soviet Union)	09 Jul 60	Tech Assistance	9SUGG142	469673
Indonesia	USSR (Soviet Union)	14 Oct 60	Non-IBRD Project	9SUGG150	469706
Indonesia	USSR (Soviet Union)	06 Jan 61	Milit Assistance	10SUGG117	469734
Indonesia	USSR (Soviet Union)	24 Feb 61	General Aid	10SUGG123	469745
Indonesia	USSR (Soviet Union)	21 Dec 61	Gen Communications	10SUGG147	469812
Indonesia	USSR (Soviet Union)	17 Jan 62	Education	16SUGG132	469998
Indonesia	USSR (Soviet Union)	08 May 62	Direct Aid	11SUGG139	469837
Indonesia	USSR (Soviet Union)	19 May 62	Consul/Citizenship	16SUGG133	470007
Indonesia	USSR (Soviet Union)	10 Nov 62	Mass Media	16SUGG134	470012
Indonesia	USSR (Soviet Union)	05 Dec 62	Education	16SUGG134	470013
Indonesia	WHO (World Health)	28 Mar 51	Tech Assistance	103UNTS71	101425
Indonesia	WHO (World Health)	05 Feb 58	Tech Assistance	307UNTS15	104438
Indonesia	Yugoslavia	14 Dec 56	General Trade	378UNTS117	105422
Int Bureau Educ	Switzerland	15 Nov 46	IGO Status/Immunit	56SWRO1210	462187
Int Bureau Educ	UNESCO (Educ/Cult)	29 Nov 68	IGO Operations	0UNTS0	200642
Int Coffee Org	UK Great Britain	29 May 69	IGO Operations	0UNTS0	110037
Int Coun Expl Sea	Denmark	24 Jul 68	IGO Status/Immunit	0UNTS0	109413
Int Exhibit Bureau	France	11 Jan 65	IGO Status/Immunit	66FRRT36	415513
Int Org Metrology	France	01 Sep 64	IGO Status/Immunit	65FRRT76	415502
Int Rail Transport	Switzerland	28 Sep 56	IGO Status/Immunit	56SWRO1367	462188
Int Relief Union	UNESCO (Educ/Cult)	24 Dec 68	IGO Operations	0UNTS0	200643
Int Rice Commission	Multilateral	29 Nov 48	IGO Establishment	120UNTS13	101613
Int Sugar Council	UK Great Britain	29 May 69	IGO Operations	0UNTS0	110038
Int Whaling Com	Multilateral	02 Dec 46	Specific Resources	161UNTS72	102124
Int Wheat Coun	UK Great Britain	28 Nov 68	General IGO	0UNTS0	109498
Int Wine Office	France	20 Jan 65	IGO Status/Immunit	66FRRT35	415503
Inter-Am Devel Bnk	Multilateral	26 May 64	IBRD Project	541UNTS271	200613
Inter-Am Devel Bnk	Multilateral	22 Jul 65	IBRD Project	561UNTS333	200618
Inter-Am Devel Bnk	Multilateral	02 Aug 66	Tech Assistance	582UNTS59	108457
Inter-Am Devel Bnk	UN Special Fund	16 Jul 68	Non-IBRD Project	640UNTS305	200640
Inter-Am Devel Bnk	USA (United States)	19 Jun 61	Direct Aid	410UNTS34	105895
Inter-Am Nuc Energ	IAEA (Atom Energy)	22 Dec 60	IGO Operations	396UNTS285	200586
Intgov Eur Migrat	Switzerland	03 May 54	IGO Status/Immunit	56SWRO1213	462192
Iran	Afghanistan	30 Jun 48	Territory Boundary	0IRTB1	433001
Iran	Afghanistan	26 Jun 56	Admin Cooperation	0IRTB2	433002
Iran	Afghanistan	01 Feb 62	General Transport	0IRTB2	433005
Iran	Afghanistan	31 Oct 63	General Trade	0IRTB2	433003
Iran	Afghanistan	31 Oct 63	Finance	0IRTB2	433004
Iran	Afghanistan	02 Nov 63	Telecommunications	0IRTB2	433006
Iran	Afghanistan	31 Dec 63	Taxation	0IRTB3	433008
Iran	Afghanistan	11 Jan 69	Telecommunications	0IRTB3	433007
Iran	Algeria	08 Aug 68	Culture	0IRTB5	433010
Iran	Argentina	12 May 65	Culture	0IRTB11	433019
Iran	Austria	09 Sep 59	General Amity	66ABGB45	403103
Iran	Austria	05 Mar 70	General Amity	70ABGB111	403104
Iran	Belgium	14 Apr 58	Air Transport	381UNTS309	105473
Iran	Belgium	14 May 60	Culture	522UNTS249	107551
Iran	Belgium	19 Nov 64	Visas	0IRTB14	433022
Iran	Belgium	01 Sep 65	Taxation	0IRTB14	433021
Iran	Belgium	12 Mar 70	Health/Educ/Welfare	0IRTB14	433023
Iran	Brazil	22 Nov 57	Culture	0IRTB15	433024
Iran	Bulgaria	09 Feb 67	Finance	0IRTB16	433027
Iran	Bulgaria	09 Feb 67	General Economic	0IRTB16	433028
Iran	Bulgaria	09 Feb 67	General Trade	0IRTB16	433026
Iran	Bulgaria	26 Nov 67	Culture	0IRTB16	433025
Iran	Canada	10 Mar 61	Visas	470UNTS139	106805
Iran	Czechoslovakia	29 Jan 66	General Economic	0IRTB66	433106
Iran	Czechoslovakia	26 May 67	Culture	0IRTB66	433105
Iran	Czechoslovakia	12 Mar 69	Finance	0IRTB67	433109
Iran	Czechoslovakia	12 Mar 69	General Economic	0IRTB66	433107

PARTY ONE	PARTY TWO	DATE	TOPIC	CITATION	NUMBER
Iran	Czechoslovakia	12 Mar 69	General Trade	0IRTB66	433108
Iran	Denmark	18 Jun 51	Air Transport	255UNTS3	103602
Iran	Denmark	16 Sep 56	Taxation	0IRTB19	433030
Iran	Denmark	14 Jun 66	Tech Assistance	597UNTS283	108652
Iran	Denmark	23 Jun 67	Visas	0IRTB19	433031
Iran	Denmark	02 Nov 67	Loans and Credits	638UNTS217	109138
Iran	EEC (Econ Commnty)	14 Oct 63	General Trade	0IRTB85	433138
Iran	Ethiopia	06 Jun 68	General Amity	0IRTB28	433039
Iran	Finland	25 Apr 69	Visas	0IRTB29	433040
Iran	France	30 Aug 56	Taxation	0IRTB30	433041
Iran	France	12 May 59	General Trade	0IRTB31	433042
Iran	France	21 Apr 60	Air Transport	86FRRT5009	415238
Iran	France	24 Jun 64	Water Transport	69FRJO511	416240
Iran	France	24 Jun 64	Extradition	67FRJO3003	416239
Iran	France	24 Jun 64	Consul/Citizenship	0UNTS0	110722
Iran	France	03 Feb 66	Visas	66FRRT14	415241
Iran	France	27 Dec 67	Tech Assistance	69FRJO1304	416242
Iran	Germany, West	04 Nov 54	Direct Aid	56WGBB2091	425271
Iran	Germany, West	07 Apr 57	Taxation	0IRTB7	433011
Iran	Germany, West	22 Dec 59	Admin Cooperation	61WGBB105	425272
Iran	Germany, West	04 Feb 60	Non-IBRD Project	0IRTB8	433013
Iran	Germany, West	16 Apr 60	Non-IBRD Project	0IRTB9	433014
Iran	Germany, West	01 Jul 61	Air Transport	63WGBB1086	425273
Iran	Germany, West	01 Jul 61	Air Transport	0UNTS0	110465
Iran	Germany, West	11 Nov 65	Loans and Credits	67WGBB2549	425274
Iran	Germany, West	22 Apr 68	Loans and Credits	68WBGA112	424275
Iran	Germany, West	04 May 68	Taxation	0IRTB7	433012
Iran	Germany, West	08 Sep 68	Loans and Credits	69WBGA216	424276
Iran	Germany, West	07 Nov 68	Tech Assistance	0IRTB9	433015
Iran	Germany, West	20 Dec 68	Taxation	69WGBB2133	425277
Iran	Germany, West	27 Nov 69	Non-IBRD Project	0IRTB9	433016
Iran	Greece	09 Jan 31	General Amity	166UNTS331	200497
Iran	Greece	09 Jan 31	General Amity	166UNTS323	200496
Iran	Greece	20 Nov 56	Culture	0IRTB34	433043
Iran	Greece	06 Aug 69	Visas	0IRTB34	433044
Iran	Hungary	10 May 65	General Economic	0IRTB37	433054
Iran	Hungary	10 Apr 68	General Economic	0IRTB37	433055
Iran	Hungary	24 May 68	Culture	0IRTB37	433051
Iran	Hungary	21 May 69	Finance	0IRTB7	433053
Iran	Hungary	21 May 69	General Trade	0IRTB7	433052
Iran	IAEA (Atom Energy)	10 May 67	IGO Operations	614UNTS93	108865
Iran	IAEA (Atom Energy)	10 May 67	Atomic Energy	0IRTB86	433141
Iran	IAEA (Atom Energy)	07 Jun 67	Atomic Energy	0IRTB87	433143
Iran	IAEA (Atom Energy)	04 Mar 69	Atomic Energy	0IRTB87	433142
Iran	IBRD (World Bank)	22 Jan 57	IBRD Project	317UNTS129	104600
Iran	IBRD (World Bank)	29 May 59	IBRD Project	348UNTS103	104997
Iran	IBRD (World Bank)	23 Nov 59	IBRD Project	380UNTS245	105459
Iran	IBRD (World Bank)	20 Feb 60	IBRD Project	384UNTS213	105521
Iran	IBRD (World Bank)	10 Jun 64	IBRD Project	537UNTS111	107799
Iran	IBRD (World Bank)	28 Apr 65	IBRD Project	555UNTS21	108103
Iran	IBRD (World Bank)	28 Apr 65	IBRD Project	555UNTS45	108104
Iran	IBRD (World Bank)	12 Jul 65	IBRD Project	554UNTS3	108095
Iran	IBRD (World Bank)	26 Jul 66	IBRD Project	582UNTS107	108461
Iran	IBRD (World Bank)	17 Oct 67	IBRD Project	0UNTS0	109331
Iran	IBRD (World Bank)	05 Jun 68	IBRD Project	0UNTS0	109373
Iran	IBRD (World Bank)	18 Apr 69	IBRD Project	0UNTS0	110198
Iran	IBRD (World Bank)	28 May 69	IBRD Project	0UNTS0	110308
Iran	India	15 Mar 50	General Amity	161UNTS15	102118
Iran	India	14 Jul 54	Sanitation	0IRTB38	433058
Iran	India	15 Dec 54	General Economic	327UNTS245	104724
Iran	India	01 Dec 56	Culture	0IRTB38	433056
Iran	India	11 Mar 64	General Trade	0IRTB38	433057
Iran	Indonesia	29 Dec 58	General Amity	0IRTB39	433059
Iran	Indonesia	27 Apr 71	Culture	0IRTB39	433060
Iran	Iraq	01 Jun 65	Visas	0IRTB40	433061

PARTY ONE	PARTY TWO	DATE	TOPIC	CITATION	NUMBER
Iran	Italy	24 Sep 50	General Amity	281UNTS157	104077
Iran	Italy	26 Jan 55	General Trade	57ITGU149	435208
Iran	Italy	29 Jan 58	General Economic	58ITGU39	435210
Iran	Italy	29 Jan 58	Finance	302UNTS181	104358
Iran	Italy	07 May 58	General Trade	60ITDI329	436211
Iran	Italy	29 Nov 58	Culture	0IRTB43	433062
Iran	Italy	25 Jul 59	Visas	61ITDI281	436213
Iran	Italy	28 Jun 69	Visas	0IRTB43	433063
Iran	Italy	07 Oct 69	Taxation	0IRTB43	433064
Iran	Italy	27 Sep 70	Scientific Project	0IRTB44	433065
Iran	Japan	16 Apr 57	Culture	325UNTS113	104697
Iran	Japan	09 Dec 58	General Aid	325UNTS221	104701
Iran	Japan	12 Sep 60	Education	384UNTS43	105509
Iran	Japan	11 Oct 60	General Economic	0IRTB45	433066
Iran	Japan	23 Jul 63	Admin Cooperation	0IRTB46	433067
Iran	Japan	23 Jun 68	General Trade	68JJS283	442214
Iran	Japan	17 Mar 70	Taxation	0IRTB46	433068
Iran	Japan	16 Aug 70	Telecommunications	0IRTB46	433069
Iran	Jordan	16 Nov 49	General Amity	0IRTB47	433070
Iran	Jordan	26 Apr 60	Culture	0IRTB47	433071
Iran	Jordan	07 Jul 63	General Trade	0IRTB47	433072
Iran	Jordan	10 Jul 71	Taxation	0IRTB47	433073
Iran	Korea, South	05 May 69	General Amity	0IRTB17	433029
Iran	Kuwait	08 May 68	Taxation	0IRTB48	433075
Iran	Kuwait	06 Nov 68	General Trade	0IRTB48	433074
Iran	Lebanon	07 Oct 53	General Amity	0IRTB49	433076
Iran	Lebanon	17 Oct 56	Culture	0IRTB49	433077
Iran	Luxembourg	19 Nov 64	Visas	0IRTB50	433078
Iran	Multilateral	29 Jan 42	General Military	93UNTS279	200271
Iran	Multilateral	04 Dec 42	Direct Aid	24UNTS247	200150
Iran	Multilateral	02 Aug 44	Scientific Project	67UNTS221	200221
Iran	Multilateral	07 Dec 44	Air Transport	171UNTS345	200501
Iran	Multilateral	07 Dec 44	Air Transport	171UNTS387	200502
Iran	Multilateral	07 Dec 44	IGO Establishment	15UNTS295	200102
Iran	Multilateral	07 Dec 44	Air Transport	84UNTS389	200252
Iran	Multilateral	16 Nov 45	IGO Establishment	4UNTS275	100052
Iran	Multilateral	27 Dec 45	IGO Establishment	2UNTS39	100020
Iran	Multilateral	22 Jul 46	IGO Establishment	14UNTS185	100221
Iran	Multilateral	22 Jul 46	IGO Establishment	9UNTS3	100125
Iran	Multilateral	27 Jul 46	Patents/Copyrights	90UNTS229	101238
Iran	Multilateral	11 Dec 46	Sanitation	12UNTS179	100186
Iran	Multilateral	27 May 47	Air Transport	418UNTS161	106021
Iran	Multilateral	02 Oct 47	Telecommunications	193UNTS188	102616
Iran	Multilateral	06 Mar 48	Water Transport	289UNTS3	104214
Iran	Multilateral	19 Jun 48	Air Transport	310UNTS151	104492
Iran	Multilateral	24 Jul 48	Sanitation	66UNTS25	100847
Iran	Multilateral	29 Nov 48	IGO Establishment	120UNTS13	101613
Iran	Multilateral	09 Dec 48	Humanitarian	78UNTS277	101021
Iran	Multilateral	04 May 49	Admin Cooperation	98UNTS101	101358
Iran	Multilateral	04 May 49	Admin Cooperation	92UNTS19	101257
Iran	Multilateral	04 May 49	Admin Cooperation	47UNTS159	100728
Iran	Multilateral	04 May 49	Admin Cooperation	30UNTS3	100445
Iran	Multilateral	04 May 49	Admin Cooperation	30UNTS23	100446
Iran	Multilateral	15 Jul 49	Health/Educ/Welfare	197UNTS3	102631
Iran	Multilateral	12 Aug 49	Humanitarian	75UNTS85	100971
Iran	Multilateral	12 Aug 49	Humanitarian	75UNTS287	100973
Iran	Multilateral	12 Aug 49	Humanitarian	75UNTS31	100970
Iran	Multilateral	12 Aug 49	General Military	75UNTS135	100972
Iran	Multilateral	16 Dec 49	Admin Cooperation	72UNTS3	100924
Iran	Multilateral	06 Apr 50	Admin Cooperation	119UNTS99	101610
Iran	Multilateral	22 Nov 50	Culture	131UNTS25	101734
Iran	Multilateral	15 Dec 50	Customs	157UNTS129	102052
Iran	Multilateral	15 Dec 50	Customs	347UNTS127	104994
Iran	Multilateral	18 Jan 51	Tech Assistance	81UNTS233	101073
Iran	Multilateral	25 May 51	Status of Forces	175UNTS215	102303

PARTY ONE	PARTY TWO	DATE	TOPIC	CITATION	NUMBER
Iran	Multilateral	08 Sep 51	General Military	136UNTS165	101833
Iran	Multilateral	08 Sep 51	Peace/Disarmament	136UNTS45	101832
Iran	Multilateral	11 Jul 52	Postal Service	170UNTS3	102221
Iran	Multilateral	11 Jul 52	Postal Service	170UNTS269	102223
Iran	Multilateral	11 Jul 52	IGO Establishment	169UNTS3	102220
Iran	Multilateral	11 Jul 52	Postal Service	170UNTS63	102222
Iran	Multilateral	27 Feb 53	Claims and Debts	333UNTS3	104764
Iran	Multilateral	11 May 53	Sanitation	456UNTS3	106555
Iran	Multilateral	14 May 54	Culture	249UNTS215	103511
Iran	Multilateral	25 May 55	IGO Establishment	264UNTS117	103791
Iran	Multilateral	12 Oct 55	IGO Establishment	560UNTS3	108165
Iran	Multilateral	02 Feb 56	Tech Assistance	227UNTS153	103137
Iran	Multilateral	26 Oct 56	IGO Establishment	276UNTS3	103988
Iran	Multilateral	03 Oct 57	Postal Service	365UNTS3	105213
Iran	Multilateral	03 Oct 57	Postal Service	365UNTS207	105214
Iran	Multilateral	03 Oct 57	Postal Service	364UNTS331	105212
Iran	Multilateral	29 Apr 58	Specific Resources	559UNTS285	108164
Iran	Multilateral	29 Apr 58	Territory Boundary	516UNTS205	107477
Iran	Multilateral	29 Apr 58	Territory Boundary	499UNTS311	107302
Iran	Multilateral	29 Apr 58	Water Transport	450UNTS11	106465
Iran	Multilateral	28 Jul 58	General Military	335UNTS205	104788
Iran	Multilateral	19 Nov 59	IGO Operations	410UNTS156	105902
Iran	Multilateral	26 Jan 60	IGO Establishment	439UNTS249	106333
Iran	Multilateral	14 Sep 60	IGO Establishment	443UNTS247	106363
Iran	Multilateral	06 Oct 60	Customs	473UNTS131	106861
Iran	Multilateral	14 Dec 60	Education	429UNTS93	106193
Iran	Multilateral	30 Mar 61	Sanitation	520UNTS151	107515
Iran	Multilateral	18 Apr 61	Consul/Citizenship	500UNTS223	107311
Iran	Multilateral	18 Apr 61	Dispute Settlement	500UNTS243	107312
Iran	Multilateral	18 Apr 61	Consul/Citizenship	500UNTS95	107310
Iran	Multilateral	08 Jun 61	Customs	473UNTS153	106862
Iran	Multilateral	08 Jun 61	Customs	473UNTS187	106863
Iran	Multilateral	06 Dec 61	Customs	473UNTS219	106864
Iran	Multilateral	24 Apr 63	Consul/Citizenship	596UNTS261	108638
Iran	Multilateral	05 Aug 63	Sanitation	480UNTS43	106964
Iran	Multilateral	03 Dec 63	IGO Establishment	529UNTS217	107663
Iran	Multilateral	10 Jul 64	Postal Service	612UNTS3	108847
Iran	Multilateral	10 Jul 64	Postal Service	611UNTS387	108846
Iran	Multilateral	10 Jul 64	Postal Service	611UNTS7	108844
Iran	Multilateral	10 Jul 64	Postal Service	611UNTS105	108845
Iran	Multilateral	19 Nov 64	Visas	523UNTS3	107553
Iran	Multilateral	04 Dec 65	IGO Establishment	571UNTS123	108303
Iran	Multilateral	03 May 67	IGO Operations	0UNTS0	110764
Iran	Multilateral	01 Jul 68	Peace/Disarmament	0UNTS0	110485
Iran	Multilateral	04 May 70	Visas	0UNTS0	110579
Iran	Netherlands	31 Oct 49	Air Transport	0IRTB35	433046
Iran	Netherlands	31 Oct 49	Air Transport	254UNTS257	103596
Iran	Netherlands	27 Jul 56	Taxation	0IRTB35	433047
Iran	Netherlands	06 Feb 58	Consul/Citizenship	0IRTB36	433050
Iran	Netherlands	22 May 59	Culture	0IRTB35	433045
Iran	Netherlands	22 May 59	Culture	474UNTS195	106882
Iran	Netherlands	19 Nov 64	Visas	0IRTB36	433049
Iran	Netherlands	13 Jul 68	Taxation	0IRTB36	433048
Iran	Norway	31 May 50	Air Transport	2NORT535	451084
Iran	Norway	04 Nov 56	Taxation	3NORT699	451085
Iran	Norway	10 Mar 66	Tech Assistance	3NORT958	451086
Iran	Norway	25 Jan 68	Visas	3NORT0	451087
Iran	Pakistan	18 Feb 50	General Amity	161UNTS23	102119
Iran	Pakistan	09 Mar 56	Culture	449UNTS183	106460
Iran	Pakistan	20 Mar 56	Sanitation	0IRTB55	433084
Iran	Pakistan	18 May 57	Air Transport	0IRTB54	433081
Iran	Pakistan	06 Feb 58	Territory Boundary	0IRTB54	433079
Iran	Pakistan	16 Feb 59	Specific Property	0IRTB55	433087
Iran	Pakistan	20 Apr 59	Extradition	0IRTB54	433080
Iran	Pakistan	14 Dec 60	Sanitation	0IRTB55	433085

PARTY ONE	PARTY TWO	DATE	TOPIC	CITATION	NUMBER
Iran	Pakistan	20 May 62	General Trade	OIRTB55	433083
Iran	Pakistan	18 Oct 64	Visas	OIRTB55	433086
Iran	Pakistan	27 Jan 68	Admin Cooperation	OIRTB56	433088
Iran	Pakistan	01 Nov 71	Taxation	OIRTB54	433082
Iran	Poland	13 Feb 64	General Economic	OIRTB57	433092
Iran	Poland	13 May 68	Culture	69PDZU73	457156
Iran	Poland	13 Aug 68	Taxation	OIRTB58	433094
Iran	Poland	04 Oct 69	Taxation	OIRTB57	433093
Iran	Poland	16 Dec 69	General Trade	OIRTB57	433090
Iran	Poland	16 Dec 69	Finance	OIRTB57	433091
Iran	Qatar	20 Sep 69	Territory Boundary	OIRTB59	433095
Iran	Romania	25 Oct 65	General Economic	OIRTB60	433099
Iran	Romania	08 Aug 66	Specific Property	OIRTB60	433100
Iran	Romania	15 Aug 67	Culture	OIRTB60	433096
Iran	Romania	24 Jan 68	Finance	OIRTB60	433098
Iran	Romania	24 Jan 68	General Trade	OIRTB60	433097
Iran	Saudi Arabia	14 Nov 67	Culture	OIRTB10	433018
Iran	Saudi Arabia	24 Oct 68	Territory Boundary	OIRTB10	433017
Iran	Saudi Arabia	24 Oct 68	Territory Boundary	OUNTSO	109976
Iran	South Africa	11 Oct 71	Visas	OIRTB4	433009
Iran	Spain	12 Mar 56	Culture	OIRTB21	433033
Iran	Spain	12 Mar 56	General Amity	57SPBO1912	460162
Iran	Spain	20 Sep 67	Visas	OIRTB21	433034
Iran	Sweden	31 Oct 49	Air Transport	49SOFM767	461097
Iran	Sweden	16 Sep 56	Taxation	OIRTB63	433101
Iran	Sweden	30 Oct 68	Visas	OIRTB63	433102
Iran	Switzerland	27 May 54	Air Transport	496UNTS273	107257
Iran	Switzerland	07 Feb 57	Taxation	57SWRO213	462055
Iran	Switzerland	01 Feb 64	General Economic	64SWRO87	462142
Iran	Switzerland	20 Mar 66	Claims and Debts	OIRTB65	433103
Iran	Switzerland	31 Dec 68	Visas	OIRTB65	433104
Iran	Taiwan	11 Nov 57	Culture	563UNTS31	108202
Iran	Thailand	02 Feb 67	General Amity	614UNTS251	108874
Iran	Thailand	12 Nov 69	General Trade	OUNTSO	110563
Iran	Thailand	12 Nov 69	General Trade	OIRTB68	433110
Iran	Tunisia	20 Jul 68	General Trade	OIRTB69	433113
Iran	Tunisia	17 Apr 69	General Amity	OIRTB69	433111
Iran	Tunisia	17 Apr 69	Culture	OIRTB69	433112
Iran	Tunisia	17 Apr 69	Visas	OIRTB69	433114
Iran	Turkey	25 Dec 49	General Transport	51TURG1512	466136
Iran	Turkey	25 Dec 49	Customs	51TURG1512	466099
Iran	Turkey	25 Dec 49	Finance	51TURG1512	466071
Iran	Turkey	20 Mar 51	Air Transport	51TURG1512	466137
Iran	Turkey	08 Nov 55	Water Transport	OTURG217	466139
Iran	Turkey	13 Oct 56	General Economic	57TURG2506	466072
Iran	Turkey	02 Jan 59	Culture	64TURG601	466037
Iran	Turkey	08 Oct 64	Visas	64TURG2912	466017
Iran	UK Great Britain	25 Oct 54	Finance	204UNTS131	102754
Iran	UK Great Britain	06 May 59	Culture	398UNTS51	105717
Iran	UK Great Britain	09 Apr 60	Taxation	385UNTS63	105529
Iran	UK Great Britain	02 May 60	Air Transport	566UNTS129	108241
Iran	UN Special Fund	06 Oct 59	Direct Aid	OIRTB86	433139
Iran	UN Special Fund	06 Oct 59	Direct Aid	342UNTS89	104902
Iran	UNESCO (Educ/Cult)	16 Dec 68	Non-IBRD Project	OIRTB87	433144
Iran	UNICEF (Children)	02 Aug 51	Direct Aid	247UNTS11	103457
Iran	UNICEF (Children)	21 Nov 63	Direct Aid	OIRTB86	433140
Iran	UNICEF (Children)	21 Nov 63	IGO Operations	485UNTS35	107044
Iran	United Arab Rep	09 Sep 58	Culture	OIRTB20	433032
Iran	United Nations	05 Sep 62	Specific Resources	442UNTS249	106353
Iran	United Nations	16 Feb 65	Admin Cooperation	525UNTS211	107593
Iran	United Nations	15 Feb 68	Consul/Citizenship	631UNTS103	108990
Iran	USA (United States)	08 Apr 43	General Trade	106UNTS155	200340
Iran	USA (United States)	21 Aug 43	Admin Cooperation	101UNTS189	200293
Iran	USA (United States)	27 Nov 43	Military Mission	31UNTS451	200176
Iran	USA (United States)	08 Aug 46	Military Mission	31UNTS423	100484

PARTY ONE	PARTY TWO	DATE	TOPIC	CITATION	NUMBER
Iran	USA (United States)	06 Oct 47	Military Mission	11UNTS303	100171
Iran	USA (United States)	01 Sep 49	Direct Aid	79UNTS155	101039
Iran	USA (United States)	23 May 50	Milit Assistance	81UNTS3	101057
Iran	USA (United States)	19 Oct 50	Tech Assistance	92UNTS135	101266
Iran	USA (United States)	05 Jan 52	Direct Aid	OIRTB24	433038
Iran	USA (United States)	20 Jan 52	Tech Assistance	200UNTS191	102703
Iran	USA (United States)	24 Apr 52	Milit Assistance	OIRTB23	433035
Iran	USA (United States)	13 Oct 53	Customs	222UNTS67	103023
Iran	USA (United States)	15 Aug 55	General Amity	284UNTS93	104132
Iran	USA (United States)	20 Feb 56	US Agri Commod Aid	272UNTS135	103934
Iran	USA (United States)	16 Jan 57	Air Transport	308UNTS147	104460
Iran	USA (United States)	05 Mar 57	Atomic Energy	342UNTS29	104898
Iran	USA (United States)	21 Sep 57	Claims and Debts	293UNTS287	104296
Iran	USA (United States)	31 Oct 57	Milit Installation	OIRTB23	433036
Iran	USA (United States)	05 Mar 59	General Military	327UNTS277	104725
Iran	USA (United States)	12 Apr 60	General Trade	372UNTS63	105288
Iran	USA (United States)	26 Jul 60	US Agri Commod Aid	384UNTS141	105516
Iran	USA (United States)	21 Dec 61	Direct Aid	433UNTS269	106249
Iran	USA (United States)	29 Jan 62	US Agri Commod Aid	435UNTS53	106270
Iran	USA (United States)	16 Sep 62	Tech Assistance	OIRTB23	433037
Iran	USA (United States)	15 Oct 62	US Agri Commod Aid	473UNTS291	106866
Iran	USA (United States)	24 Oct 63	Culture	489UNTS303	107146
Iran	USA (United States)	17 Nov 63	US Agri Commod Aid	530UNTS41	107671
Iran	USA (United States)	29 Sep 64	US Agri Commod Aid	531UNTS163	107702
Iran	USA (United States)	16 Nov 64	US Agri Commod Aid	532UNTS213	107719
Iran	USA (United States)	19 Dec 66	US Agri Commod Aid	OUNTSO	109696
Iran	USA (United States)	20 Dec 66	US Agri Commod Aid	OUNTSO	109697
Iran	USA (United States)	19 Mar 68	Specific Resources	OUNTSO	110010
Iran	USA (United States)	27 May 68	Scientific Project	OUNTSO	109883
Iran	USSR (Soviet Union)	03 Oct 45	Sanitation	OSUST199	468224
Iran	USSR (Soviet Union)	30 Jun 48	Territory Boundary	OIRTB75	433118
Iran	USSR (Soviet Union)	09 Aug 50	Admin Cooperation	16SUGG66	469895
Iran	USSR (Soviet Union)	04 Nov 50	General Trade	OSUST278	468225
Iran	USSR (Soviet Union)	02 Dec 54	Admin Cooperation	OIRTB74	433115
Iran	USSR (Soviet Union)	02 Dec 54	Finance	OSUST320	468227
Iran	USSR (Soviet Union)	02 Dec 54	Territory Boundary	OSUST320	468228
Iran	USSR (Soviet Union)	02 Dec 54	Territory Boundary	451UNTS227	106497
Iran	USSR (Soviet Union)	15 Feb 55	Commodity Trade	OSUST323	468229
Iran	USSR (Soviet Union)	09 Jun 55	Specific Property	OSUST329	468230
Iran	USSR (Soviet Union)	15 Oct 56	Territory Boundary	OIRTB75	433117
Iran	USSR (Soviet Union)	11 Apr 57	Territory Boundary	OSUST381	468231
Iran	USSR (Soviet Union)	16 Apr 57	General Trade	OSUST381	468232
Iran	USSR (Soviet Union)	25 Apr 57	Land Transport	OUNTSO	109578
Iran	USSR (Soviet Union)	27 Apr 57	General Trade	OSUST382	468233
Iran	USSR (Soviet Union)	14 May 57	Dispute Settlement	457UNTS161	106586
Iran	USSR (Soviet Union)	14 May 57	Admin Cooperation	16SUGG120	469939
Iran	USSR (Soviet Union)	11 Aug 57	Specific Resources	OSUST387	468235
Iran	USSR (Soviet Union)	20 Jan 58	Land Transport	7SUGG103	469489
Iran	USSR (Soviet Union)	05 Mar 58	Specific Resources	7SUGG107	469499
Iran	USSR (Soviet Union)	15 Apr 58	General Trade	7SUGG110	469504
Iran	USSR (Soviet Union)	03 Jul 58	Territory Boundary	7SUGG115	469518
Iran	USSR (Soviet Union)	09 Aug 62	General Trade	11SUGG149	469855
Iran	USSR (Soviet Union)	27 Jul 63	Non-IBRD Project	OIRTB80	433128
Iran	USSR (Soviet Union)	20 Jun 64	Finance	OIRTB80	433127
Iran	USSR (Soviet Union)	17 Aug 64	Air Transport	OIRTB79	433123
Iran	USSR (Soviet Union)	13 Jan 66	Commodity Trade	OIRTB81	433130
Iran	USSR (Soviet Union)	13 Jan 66	Non-IBRD Project	OIRTB81	433129
Iran	USSR (Soviet Union)	13 Jan 66	Non-IBRD Project	633UNTS123	109037
Iran	USSR (Soviet Union)	14 Jan 66	Visas	OIRTB80	433125
Iran	USSR (Soviet Union)	17 Jan 66	Admin Cooperation	OIRTB79	433121
Iran	USSR (Soviet Union)	22 Aug 66	Culture	OIRTB79	433122
Iran	USSR (Soviet Union)	22 Aug 66	Culture	643UNTS203	109192
Iran	USSR (Soviet Union)	24 Dec 66	Sanitation	OIRTB78	433120
Iran	USSR (Soviet Union)	13 Mar 67	Sanitation	OIRTB78	433119
Iran	USSR (Soviet Union)	22 Jun 68	General Economic	OIRTB81	433131

PARTY ONE	PARTY TWO	DATE	TOPIC	CITATION	NUMBER
Iran	USSR (Soviet Union)	07 May 70	Territory Boundary	OIRTB74	433116
Iran	USSR (Soviet Union)	30 Jul 70	Specific Property	OIRTB82	433134
Iran	USSR (Soviet Union)	30 Jul 70	General Trade	OIRTB80	433126
Iran	USSR (Soviet Union)	30 Jul 70	General Trade	OIRTB81	433132
Iran	USSR (Soviet Union)	25 Feb 71	Scientific Project	OIRTB81	433133
Iran	USSR (Soviet Union)	18 Jul 71	Taxation	OIRTB79	433124
Iran	WHO (World Health)	04 Jul 55	Tech Assistance	227UNTS65	103131
Iran	WHO (World Health)	07 Sep 55	Tech Assistance	OIRTB87	433145
Iran	Yugoslavia	05 Dec 63	Health/Educ/Welfare	OIRTB83	433135
Iran	Yugoslavia	24 Apr 66	General Economic	OIRTB83	433136
Iran	Yugoslavia	16 Apr 70	Visas	OIRTB83	433137
Iraq	Austria	21 Nov 70	Air Transport	71ABGB270	403102
Iraq	Belgium	05 Jul 50	Claims and Debts	68UNTS165	100893
Iraq	Bulgaria	15 Nov 66	Air Transport	OUNTSO	109965
Iraq	China People's Rep	03 Jan 59	General Economic	59CCJC2	410566
Iraq	China People's Rep	03 Jan 59	General Trade	59CCJC3	410567
Iraq	China People's Rep	04 Apr 59	Culture	59CCJC61	410610
Iraq	China People's Rep	18 Oct 61	General Trade	61CCJC140	410840
Iraq	China People's Rep	23 Sep 64	General Trade	64CCJC123	411207
Iraq	China People's Rep	04 Jun 66	Culture	66CCJC48	411204
Iraq	China People's Rep	04 Jun 66	Mass Media	66CCJC49	411205
Iraq	Czechoslovakia	11 Mar 60	Air Transport	464UNTS267	106718
Iraq	Denmark	18 Nov 51	Air Transport	232UNTS25	103227
Iraq	France	19 May 66	Air Transport	67FRJO1901	416236
Iraq	France	25 Sep 67	General Trade	69FRJO1408	416237
Iraq	France	25 Sep 67	General Trade	OUNTSO	110822
Iraq	France	24 Apr 69	Culture	OUNTSO	110739
Iraq	France	19 Jun 69	Tech Assistance	OUNTSO	110740
Iraq	Germany, East	26 Oct 58	Consul/Citizenship	6EGDA314	419137
Iraq	Germany, East	26 Oct 58	General Trade	6EGDA314	419138
Iraq	Germany, East	01 Apr 59	Health/Educ/Welfare	7EGDA370	419139
Iraq	Germany, East	24 May 62	Consul/Citizenship	10EGDA384	419140
Iraq	Germany, East	22 Oct 66	Air Transport	36EGDZ370	420141
Iraq	Germany, West	07 Oct 51	General Trade	53WGBB543	425269
Iraq	Germany, West	07 Nov 58	Admin Cooperation	59WBGA93	424270
Iraq	Hungary	11 Apr 59	Culture	439UNTS25	106323
Iraq	Hungary	11 Oct 61	Gen Communications	577UNTS231	108380
Iraq	IAEA (Atom Energy)	21 Sep 67	Atomic Energy	630UNTS41	108963
Iraq	IBRD (World Bank)	15 Jun 50	IBRD Project	155UNTS267	102038
Iraq	IBRD (World Bank)	22 Jul 66	IBRD Project	584UNTS233	108480
Iraq	ICAO (Civil Aviat)	18 Sep 51	Tech Assistance	108UNTS219	101475
Iraq	India	10 Nov 52	General Amity	172UNTS103	102242
Iraq	Iran	01 Jun 65	Visas	OIRTB40	433061
Iraq	Italy	30 Sep 63	Tech Assistance	64ITDI264	436215
Iraq	Italy	30 Sep 63	General Trade	64ITDI261	436214
Iraq	Japan	17 Jun 64	General Trade	65JAIL235	440165
Iraq	Jordan	14 Apr 47	General Amity	23UNTS148	100345
Iraq	Kuwait	04 Oct 63	Visas	485UNTS321	107063
Iraq	Multilateral	02 Aug 44	Scientific Project	67UNTS221	200221
Iraq	Multilateral	07 Dec 44	Air Transport	84UNTS389	200252
Iraq	Multilateral	07 Dec 44	IGO Establishment	15UNTS295	200102
Iraq	Multilateral	07 Dec 44	Air Transport	171UNTS345	200501
Iraq	Multilateral	22 Mar 45	General Amity	70UNTS237	200241
Iraq	Multilateral	16 Nov 45	IGO Establishment	4UNTS275	100052
Iraq	Multilateral	27 Dec 45	IGO Establishment	2UNTS39	100020
Iraq	Multilateral	22 Jul 46	IGO Establishment	14UNTS185	100221
Iraq	Multilateral	22 Jul 46	IGO Establishment	9UNTS3	100125
Iraq	Multilateral	27 Jul 46	Patents/Copyrights	90UNTS229	101238
Iraq	Multilateral	11 Dec 46	Sanitation	12UNTS179	100186
Iraq	Multilateral	27 May 47	Air Transport	418UNTS161	106021
Iraq	Multilateral	02 Oct 47	Telecommunications	193UNTS188	102616
Iraq	Multilateral	11 Oct 47	IGO Establishment	77UNTS143	100998
Iraq	Multilateral	24 Jul 48	Sanitation	66UNTS25	100847
Iraq	Multilateral	19 Nov 48	Sanitation	44UNTS277	100688
Iraq	Multilateral	09 Dec 48	Humanitarian	78UNTS277	101021

PARTY ONE	PARTY TWO	DATE	TOPIC	CITATION	NUMBER
Iraq	Multilateral	04 May 49	Admin Cooperation	98UNTS101	101358
Iraq	Multilateral	04 May 49	Admin Cooperation	30UNTS3	100445
Iraq	Multilateral	04 May 49	Admin Cooperation	47UNTS159	100728
Iraq	Multilateral	04 May 49	Admin Cooperation	92UNTS19	101257
Iraq	Multilateral	15 Jul 49	Health/Educ/Welfare	197UNTS3	102631
Iraq	Multilateral	16 Dec 49	Admin Cooperation	72UNTS3	100924
Iraq	Multilateral	21 Mar 50	Admin Cooperation	96UNTS271	101342
Iraq	Multilateral	07 Dec 50	Admin Cooperation	212UNTS17	102861
Iraq	Multilateral	25 May 51	Status of Forces	175UNTS215	102303
Iraq	Multilateral	08 Sep 51	Peace/Disarmament	136UNTS45	101832
Iraq	Multilateral	08 Sep 51	General Military	136UNTS165	101833
Iraq	Multilateral	06 Dec 51	IGO Establishment	425UNTS61	106119
Iraq	Multilateral	06 Dec 51	Admin Cooperation	150UNTS67	101963
Iraq	Multilateral	12 Jun 52	Dispute Settlement	138UNTS183	101869
Iraq	Multilateral	11 Jul 52	IGO Establishment	169UNTS3	102220
Iraq	Multilateral	11 Jul 52	Postal Service	170UNTS3	102221
Iraq	Multilateral	11 Jul 52	Postal Service	170UNTS63	102222
Iraq	Multilateral	11 May 53	Sanitation	456UNTS3	106555
Iraq	Multilateral	07 Dec 53	Admin Cooperation	182UNTS51	102422
Iraq	Multilateral	14 May 54	Culture	249UNTS215	103511
Iraq	Multilateral	14 Jun 54	Air Transport	320UNTS209	104643
Iraq	Multilateral	14 Jun 54	Air Transport	320UNTS217	104644
Iraq	Multilateral	30 Jun 54	Tech Assistance	193UNTS67	102611
Iraq	Multilateral	25 May 55	IGO Establishment	264UNTS117	103791
Iraq	Multilateral	07 Sep 56	Humanitarian	266UNTS3	103822
Iraq	Multilateral	26 Oct 56	IGO Establishment	276UNTS3	103988
Iraq	Multilateral	03 Oct 57	Postal Service	366UNTS87	105216
Iraq	Multilateral	03 Oct 57	Postal Service	364UNTS3	105211
Iraq	Multilateral	03 Oct 57	Postal Service	365UNTS3	105213
Iraq	Multilateral	03 Oct 57	Postal Service	364UNTS331	105212
Iraq	Multilateral	26 Jan 60	IGO Establishment	439UNTS249	106333
Iraq	Multilateral	19 Jun 60	IGO Operations	537UNTS214	107803
Iraq	Multilateral	14 Sep 60	IGO Establishment	443UNTS247	106363
Iraq	Multilateral	30 Mar 61	Sanitation	520UNTS151	107515
Iraq	Multilateral	18 Apr 61	Consul/Citizenship	500UNTS95	107310
Iraq	Multilateral	18 Apr 61	Dispute Settlement	500UNTS243	107312
Iraq	Multilateral	18 Apr 61	Consul/Citizenship	500UNTS223	107311
Iraq	Multilateral	14 Sep 62	IGO Status/Immunit	494UNTS219	107236
Iraq	Multilateral	05 Aug 63	Sanitation	480UNTS43	106964
Iraq	Multilateral	10 Jul 64	Postal Service	612UNTS3	108847
Iraq	Multilateral	10 Jul 64	Postal Service	611UNTS105	108845
Iraq	Multilateral	10 Jul 64	Postal Service	613UNTS3	108850
Iraq	Multilateral	10 Jul 64	Postal Service	611UNTS7	108844
Iraq	Multilateral	10 Jul 64	Postal Service	611UNTS387	108846
Iraq	Multilateral	20 Aug 64	Telecommunications	514UNTS25	107441
Iraq	Multilateral	27 Jan 67	Scientific Project	610UNTS205	108843
Iraq	Multilateral	01 Jul 68	Peace/Disarmament	OUNTSO	110485
Iraq	Netherlands	16 Oct 54	Air Transport	55NET23	447051
Iraq	Norway	12 Jul 49	Air Transport	53UNTS137	100778
Iraq	Pakistan	02 Mar 49	Visas	141UNTS319	101921
Iraq	Pakistan	26 Feb 50	General Amity	214UNTS3	102896
Iraq	Pakistan	20 Jun 50	Air Transport	77UNTS215	101001
Iraq	Poland	03 Jan 59	General Economic	59PZUM9	458065
Iraq	Poland	02 Apr 59	Culture	432UNTS147	106218
Iraq	Poland	27 Jul 61	Air Transport	61PZUM183	458086
Iraq	Romania	24 Dec 58	General Trade	405UNTS243	105836
Iraq	Romania	04 Aug 59	Culture	502UNTS17	107324
Iraq	Spain	03 Sep 51	General Amity	55SPBO101	460163
Iraq	Spain	14 Feb 55	Culture	57SPBO1502	460164
Iraq	Sweden	28 Aug 51	Air Transport	52SOFM483	461171
Iraq	Switzerland	31 Mar 52	Air Transport	311UNTS43	104498
Iraq	Syria	03 Nov 61	General Trade	489UNTS45	107134
Iraq	Taiwan	16 Mar 42	General Amity	14UNTS335	200091
Iraq	Taiwan	14 Aug 57	Culture	OCTRC210	413008
Iraq	Turkey	29 Mar 46	Admin Cooperation	37UNTS333	100581

PARTY ONE	PARTY TWO	DATE	TOPIC	CITATION	NUMBER
Iraq	Turkey	29 Mar 46	General Amity	37UNTS226	100580
Iraq	Turkey	29 Mar 46	Extradition	37UNTS369	100582
Iraq	Turkey	30 Jun 47	Air Transport	72UNTS107	100930
Iraq	Turkey	24 Feb 55	General Military	233UNTS199	103264
Iraq	Turkey	25 Sep 68	Land Transport	0UNTS0	110585
Iraq	UK Great Britain	02 Aug 46	Consul/Citizenship	14UNTS93	100213
Iraq	UK Great Britain	13 Aug 47	Finance	9UNTS259	100136
Iraq	UK Great Britain	19 Apr 51	Air Transport	108UNTS121	101470
Iraq	UK Great Britain	22 May 52	Claims and Debts	175UNTS97	102298
Iraq	UK Great Britain	21 Jun 52	Admin Cooperation	149UNTS221	101954
Iraq	UK Great Britain	10 Jul 52	Finance	151UNTS227	101998
Iraq	UK Great Britain	04 Apr 55	General Military	233UNTS118	103265
Iraq	UK Great Britain	30 Apr 55	Claims and Debts	226UNTS319	103126
Iraq	UK Great Britain	14 Dec 59	Culture	374UNTS253	105339
Iraq	UK Great Britain	16 Aug 65	Commodity Trade	0UNTS0	109878
Iraq	UN Special Fund	19 Jun 60	Direct Aid	376UNTS357	105389
Iraq	UNICEF (Children)	10 Dec 51	Direct Aid	126UNTS57	101682
Iraq	UNICEF (Children)	03 Dec 63	IGO Operations	482UNTS319	107001
Iraq	United Arab Rep	23 Mar 55	Air Transport	311UNTS199	104504
Iraq	United Nations	05 Mar 61	Tech Assistance	409UNTS56	105878
Iraq	USA (United States)	16 Feb 44	Admin Cooperation	109UNTS223	200362
Iraq	USA (United States)	31 Jul 45	Milit Assistance	121UNTS239	200402
Iraq	USA (United States)	10 Apr 51	Tech Assistance	151UNTS179	101993
Iraq	USA (United States)	08 Aug 51	Visas	229UNTS185	103166
Iraq	USA (United States)	16 Aug 51	Education	147UNTS65	101929
Iraq	USA (United States)	21 Feb 52	Tech Assistance	198UNTS225	102666
Iraq	USA (United States)	18 Mar 52	Tech Assistance	223UNTS131	103061
Iraq	USA (United States)	21 May 52	Tech Assistance	205UNTS33	102768
Iraq	USA (United States)	21 May 52	Tech Assistance	212UNTS183	102870
Iraq	USA (United States)	21 May 52	Tech Assistance	205UNTS25	102767
Iraq	USA (United States)	21 May 52	Tech Assistance	206UNTS3	102782
Iraq	USA (United States)	09 Jun 52	Tech Assistance	212UNTS193	102871
Iraq	USA (United States)	18 Aug 52	Direct Aid	184UNTS131	102444
Iraq	USA (United States)	23 Oct 52	Tech Assistance	212UNTS201	102872
Iraq	USA (United States)	21 Apr 54	Milit Assistance	222UNTS251	103032
Iraq	USA (United States)	02 Mar 55	Non-IBRD Project	250UNTS229	103526
Iraq	USA (United States)	03 Dec 55	Milit Assistance	241UNTS19	103420
Iraq	USA (United States)	06 Jun 56	Visas	275UNTS265	103985
Iraq	USA (United States)	22 May 57	Direct Aid	284UNTS13	104125
Iraq	USA (United States)	16 Jun 57	Tech Assistance	284UNTS39	104127
Iraq	USA (United States)	07 Jul 59	Milit Assistance	357UNTS153	105114
Iraq	USA (United States)	23 Jan 63	Culture	488UNTS163	107126
Iraq	USA (United States)	27 Aug 63	US Agri Commod Aid	489UNTS271	107144
Iraq	USSR (Soviet Union)	08 Jul 58	Consul/Citizenship	7SUGG116	469520
Iraq	USSR (Soviet Union)	11 Oct 58	General Trade	328UNTS95	104730
Iraq	USSR (Soviet Union)	11 Oct 58	General Trade	328UNTS117	104731
Iraq	USSR (Soviet Union)	16 Mar 59	General Aid	346UNTS107	104979
Iraq	USSR (Soviet Union)	05 May 59	Culture	356UNTS179	105095
Iraq	USSR (Soviet Union)	17 Aug 59	Atomic Energy	8SUGG152	469599
Iraq	USSR (Soviet Union)	17 Aug 59	Atomic Energy	0UNTS0	110362
Iraq	USSR (Soviet Union)	16 Dec 59	Tech Assistance	8SUGG162	469616
Iraq	USSR (Soviet Union)	27 Dec 59	Tech Assistance	8SUGG164	469620
Iraq	USSR (Soviet Union)	20 Mar 60	Non-IBRD Project	9SUGG131	469644
Iraq	USSR (Soviet Union)	18 Aug 60	Loans and Credits	9SUGG144	469684
Iraq	USSR (Soviet Union)	22 Mar 61	Consul/Citizenship	16SUGG131	469992
Iraq	WHO (World Health)	01 Jul 51	Tech Assistance	110UNTS139	101507
Iraq	WHO (World Health)	13 Sep 61	Tech Assistance	419UNTS69	106030
Ireland	Accept UN Charter	06 Nov 56	UN Charter	254UNTS223	103594
Ireland	Argentina	25 Jun 65	Visas	0UNTS0	109523
Ireland	Australia	30 Dec 57	Air Transport	497UNTS29	107260
Ireland	Austria	06 Oct 50	General Trade	557UNTS173	108133
Ireland	Austria	24 May 66	Taxation	636UNTS149	109102
Ireland	Austria	10 Dec 70	Visas	70ABGB428	403105
Ireland	Belgium	25 Mar 47	Visas	18UNTS227	100292
Ireland	Belgium	16 Apr 48	Visas	26UNTS159	100386

PARTY ONE	PARTY TWO	DATE	TOPIC	CITATION	NUMBER
Ireland	Belgium	30 Jun 54	Air Transport	212UNTS255	102876
Ireland	Belgium	10 Sep 55	Air Transport	255UNTS235	103612
Ireland	Belgium	23 Sep 60	Commodity Trade	557UNTS180	108134
Ireland	Belgium	04 Dec 67	Taxation	0UNTS0	110594
Ireland	Canada	20 Aug 32	General Trade	0UNTS0	200645
Ireland	Canada	08 Aug 47	Air Transport	28UNTS47	100419
Ireland	Canada	28 Oct 54	Taxation	304UNTS317	104406
Ireland	Canada	28 Oct 54	Taxation	305UNTS3	104407
Ireland	Canada	21 Dec 67	General Trade	0UNTS0	109448
Ireland	Ceylon (Sri Lanka)	20 Nov 53	General Economic	345UNTS189	104967
Ireland	Czechoslovakia	29 Jan 47	Air Transport	27UNTS267	100411
Ireland	Denmark	13 May 47	Visas	553UNTS37	108066
Ireland	Denmark	18 Nov 47	Air Transport	35UNTS309	100561
Ireland	Denmark	18 Oct 54	Taxation	218UNTS295	102959
Ireland	Denmark	04 Feb 64	Taxation	525UNTS233	107596
Ireland	Finland	06 Jan 51	General Trade	558UNTS120	108140
Ireland	Finland	01 Feb 55	Visas	553UNTS45	108067
Ireland	Finland	15 Sep 65	Taxation	0UNTS0	109372
Ireland	Finland	15 Sep 65	Water Transport	604UNTS199	108750
Ireland	Finland	21 Apr 69	Taxation	0UNTS0	110818
Ireland	France	16 May 46	Air Transport	44UNTS105	100681
Ireland	France	22 Apr 47	Visas	553UNTS51	108068
Ireland	France	06 May 48	General Trade	558UNTS170	108141
Ireland	France	21 Nov 49	Non-ILO Labor	553UNTS59	108069
Ireland	France	07 Jun 55	General Trade	558UNTS217	108142
Ireland	France	04 Nov 67	Culture	68FRJO2402	416243
Ireland	France	04 Nov 67	Culture	0UNTS0	109291
Ireland	Germany, West	12 Jul 50	General Trade	557UNTS221	108136
Ireland	Germany, West	23 Jul 51	General Trade	558UNTS3	108137
Ireland	Germany, West	26 Sep 52	General Trade	558UNTS27	108138
Ireland	Germany, West	02 Dec 53	General Trade	558UNTS38	108139
Ireland	Germany, West	12 Jun 56	Air Transport	353UNTS121	105040
Ireland	Germany, West	11 May 60	Non-ILO Labor	553UNTS69	108070
Ireland	Germany, West	17 Oct 62	Taxation	604UNTS135	108749
Ireland	Germany, West	13 May 64	Other Military	553UNTS87	108071
Ireland	Greece	05 Jun 56	Visas	553UNTS93	108072
Ireland	IBRD (World Bank)	24 Mar 69	IBRD Project	0UNTS0	110222
Ireland	Iceland	20 May 49	Visas	553UNTS99	108073
Ireland	Iceland	02 Dec 50	General Trade	558UNTS231	108143
Ireland	Italy	21 Nov 47	Air Transport	353UNTS73	105038
Ireland	Italy	28 Nov 49	Visas	553UNTS105	108074
Ireland	Italy	27 Jul 53	General Trade	558UNTS237	108144
Ireland	Italy	15 Nov 57	Air Transport	59ITDI320	436216
Ireland	Italy	18 May 60	Visas	62ITDI327	436217
Ireland	Japan	01 Sep 66	Visas	66JJS171	442174
Ireland	Japan	01 Sep 66	Visas	608UNTS339	108822
Ireland	Luxembourg	01 Dec 48	Visas	553UNTS111	108075
Ireland	Luxembourg	27 Jul 54	Air Transport	232UNTS91	103231
Ireland	Mexico	15 Aug 68	Visas	0UNTS0	109937
Ireland	Monaco	06 Jul 54	Visas	553UNTS117	108076
Ireland	Multilateral	12 May 40	Scientific Project	101UNTS91	101405
Ireland	Multilateral	27 Mar 41	Military Mission	67UNTS231	200222
Ireland	Multilateral	02 Aug 44	Scientific Project	67UNTS221	200221
Ireland	Multilateral	07 Dec 44	Air Transport	171UNTS345	200501
Ireland	Multilateral	07 Dec 44	IGO Establishment	15UNTS295	200102
Ireland	Multilateral	05 Apr 46	Specific Resources	231UNTS199	103221
Ireland	Multilateral	22 Jul 46	IGO Establishment	9UNTS3	100125
Ireland	Multilateral	22 Jul 46	IGO Establishment	14UNTS185	100221
Ireland	Multilateral	11 Dec 46	Sanitation	12UNTS179	100186
Ireland	Multilateral	08 Feb 47	Patents/Copyrights	14UNTS287	100222
Ireland	Multilateral	02 Oct 47	Telecommunications	193UNTS188	102616
Ireland	Multilateral	11 Oct 47	IGO Establishment	77UNTS143	100998
Ireland	Multilateral	12 Nov 47	Admin Cooperation	53UNTS49	100772
Ireland	Multilateral	12 Nov 47	Admin Cooperation	53UNTS39	100771
Ireland	Multilateral	12 Nov 47	Admin Cooperation	46UNTS169	100709

PARTY ONE	PARTY TWO	DATE	TOPIC	CITATION	NUMBER
Ireland	Multilateral	12 Nov 47	Admin Cooperation	46UNTS201	100710
Ireland	Multilateral	12 Nov 47	Admin Cooperation	53UNTS13	100770
Ireland	Multilateral	06 Mar 48	Water Transport	289UNTS3	104214
Ireland	Multilateral	10 Jun 48	Humanitarian	191UNTS3	102576
Ireland	Multilateral	10 Jun 48	Humanitarian	164UNTS113	102163
Ireland	Multilateral	19 Jun 48	Air Transport	310UNTS151	104492
Ireland	Multilateral	26 Jun 48	Culture	331UNTS217	104757
Ireland	Multilateral	24 Jul 48	Sanitation	66UNTS25	100847
Ireland	Multilateral	17 Sep 48	Telecommunications	97UNTS31	101345
Ireland	Multilateral	09 Dec 48	Scientific Project	73UNTS39	100942
Ireland	Multilateral	09 Dec 48	Scientific Project	20UNTS229	100318
Ireland	Multilateral	23 Mar 49	Commodity Trade	203UNTS179	102746
Ireland	Multilateral	04 May 49	Admin Cooperation	92UNTS19	101257
Ireland	Multilateral	04 May 49	Admin Cooperation	98UNTS101	101358
Ireland	Multilateral	04 May 49	Admin Cooperation	30UNTS3	100445
Ireland	Multilateral	04 May 49	Admin Cooperation	47UNTS159	100728
Ireland	Multilateral	04 May 49	Admin Cooperation	30UNTS23	100446
Ireland	Multilateral	05 May 49	IGO Establishment	87UNTS103	101168
Ireland	Multilateral	12 Aug 49	Humanitarian	75UNTS287	100973
Ireland	Multilateral	12 Aug 49	Humanitarian	75UNTS31	100970
Ireland	Multilateral	12 Aug 49	Humanitarian	75UNTS85	100971
Ireland	Multilateral	12 Aug 49	General Military	75UNTS135	100972
Ireland	Multilateral	02 Sep 49	IGO Status/Immunit	250UNTS12	103515
Ireland	Multilateral	16 Sep 50	General Transport	92UNTS91	101264
Ireland	Multilateral	04 Nov 50	Humanitarian	213UNTS221	102889
Ireland	Multilateral	07 Dec 50	Admin Cooperation	212UNTS17	102861
Ireland	Multilateral	15 Dec 50	Customs	157UNTS129	102052
Ireland	Multilateral	15 Dec 50	Customs	347UNTS127	104994
Ireland	Multilateral	15 Dec 50	Customs	171UNTS305	102234
Ireland	Multilateral	15 Dec 50	IGO Operations	160UNTS267	102111
Ireland	Multilateral	25 May 51	Status of Forces	175UNTS215	102303
Ireland	Multilateral	02 Jul 51	Refugees	189UNTS137	102545
Ireland	Multilateral	09 Oct 51	IGO Establishment	220UNTS121	102997
Ireland	Multilateral	06 Dec 51	Admin Cooperation	150UNTS67	101963
Ireland	Multilateral	11 Jul 52	IGO Establishment	169UNTS3	102220
Ireland	Multilateral	11 Jul 52	Postal Service	170UNTS63	102222
Ireland	Multilateral	11 Jul 52	Postal Service	170UNTS3	102221
Ireland	Multilateral	06 Sep 52	Patents/Copyrights	216UNTS132	102937
Ireland	Multilateral	07 Nov 52	General Trade	221UNTS255	103010
Ireland	Multilateral	27 Feb 53	Claims and Debts	333UNTS3	104764
Ireland	Multilateral	31 Mar 53	Privil/Immunities	193UNTS136	102613
Ireland	Multilateral	07 Dec 53	Admin Cooperation	182UNTS51	102422
Ireland	Multilateral	11 Dec 53	Education	218UNTS125	102954
Ireland	Multilateral	11 Dec 53	Patents/Copyrights	218UNTS27	102952
Ireland	Multilateral	11 Dec 53	Non-ILO Labor	218UNTS211	102957
Ireland	Multilateral	11 Dec 53	Non-ILO Labor	218UNTS153	102956
Ireland	Multilateral	11 Dec 53	Non-ILO Labor	218UNTS255	102958
Ireland	Multilateral	11 Dec 53	Sanitation	191UNTS285	102588
Ireland	Multilateral	25 Feb 54	Air Transport	215UNTS249	102922
Ireland	Multilateral	12 May 54	Admin Cooperation	327UNTS3	104714
Ireland	Multilateral	14 May 54	Culture	249UNTS215	103511
Ireland	Multilateral	14 Jun 54	Air Transport	320UNTS217	104644
Ireland	Multilateral	14 Jun 54	Air Transport	320UNTS209	104643
Ireland	Multilateral	28 Sep 54	Refugees	360UNTS117	105158
Ireland	Multilateral	19 Dec 54	Patents/Copyrights	218UNTS51	102953
Ireland	Multilateral	19 Dec 54	Culture	218UNTS139	102955
Ireland	Multilateral	25 May 55	IGO Establishment	264UNTS117	103791
Ireland	Multilateral	28 Sep 55	Air Transport	478UNTS371	106943
Ireland	Multilateral	13 Dec 55	IGO Operations	529UNTS141	107660
Ireland	Multilateral	13 Dec 55	Humanitarian	250UNTS3	103514
Ireland	Multilateral	01 Mar 56	Customs	343UNTS129	104923
Ireland	Multilateral	25 Apr 56	Commodity Trade	270UNTS103	103896
Ireland	Multilateral	30 Apr 56	Air Transport	310UNTS229	104494
Ireland	Multilateral	18 May 56	Land Transport	339UNTS3	104844
Ireland	Multilateral	25 Sep 56	Air Transport	334UNTS89	104767

PARTY ONE	PARTY TWO	DATE	TOPIC	CITATION	NUMBER
Ireland	Multilateral	25 Sep 56	Air Transport	334UNTS13	104766
Ireland	Multilateral	14 Dec 56	Taxation	436UNTS131	106293
Ireland	Multilateral	14 Dec 56	Taxation	436UNTS115	106292
Ireland	Multilateral	15 Dec 56	Education	278UNTS73	104023
Ireland	Multilateral	20 Feb 57	Consul/Citizenship	309UNTS65	104468
Ireland	Multilateral	29 Apr 57	Dispute Settlement	320UNTS243	104646
Ireland	Multilateral	03 Oct 57	Postal Service	365UNTS207	105214
Ireland	Multilateral	03 Oct 57	Postal Service	365UNTS3	105213
Ireland	Multilateral	03 Oct 57	Postal Service	364UNTS3	105211
Ireland	Multilateral	03 Oct 57	Postal Service	364UNTS331	105212
Ireland	Multilateral	23 Nov 57	Refugees	506UNTS125	107384
Ireland	Multilateral	13 Dec 57	Extradition	359UNTS273	105146
Ireland	Multilateral	29 Apr 58	Territory Boundary	499UNTS311	107302
Ireland	Multilateral	29 Apr 58	Water Transport	450UNTS11	106465
Ireland	Multilateral	29 Apr 58	Specific Resources	559UNTS285	108164
Ireland	Multilateral	29 Apr 58	Territory Boundary	516UNTS205	107477
Ireland	Multilateral	01 Dec 58	Commodity Trade	385UNTS137	105534
Ireland	Multilateral	15 Dec 58	Sanitation	351UNTS159	105022
Ireland	Multilateral	15 Dec 58	Mass Media	546UNTS235	107950
Ireland	Multilateral	24 Jan 59	IGO Establishment	486UNTS157	107078
Ireland	Multilateral	06 Apr 59	Commodity Trade	349UNTS167	105013
Ireland	Multilateral	19 Nov 59	IGO Operations	410UNTS156	105902
Ireland	Multilateral	14 Dec 59	Admin Cooperation	444UNTS193	106369
Ireland	Multilateral	26 Jan 60	IGO Establishment	439UNTS249	106333
Ireland	Multilateral	22 Apr 60	Air Transport	418UNTS211	106023
Ireland	Multilateral	28 Apr 60	Health/Educ/Welfare	376UNTS111	105377
Ireland	Multilateral	17 Jun 60	Humanitarian	536UNTS27	107794
Ireland	Multilateral	22 Jun 60	Mass Media	546UNTS247	107951
Ireland	Multilateral	06 Oct 60	Customs	473UNTS131	106861
Ireland	Multilateral	18 Apr 61	Consul/Citizenship	500UNTS95	107310
Ireland	Multilateral	18 Apr 61	Dispute Settlement	500UNTS243	107312
Ireland	Multilateral	08 Jun 61	Customs	473UNTS187	106863
Ireland	Multilateral	08 Jun 61	Customs	473UNTS153	106862
Ireland	Multilateral	21 Jun 61	IGO Establishment	514UNTS209	107449
Ireland	Multilateral	18 Oct 61	IGO Establishment	529UNTS89	107659
Ireland	Multilateral	26 Oct 61	Patents/Copyrights	496UNTS43	107247
Ireland	Multilateral	06 Dec 61	Customs	473UNTS219	106864
Ireland	Multilateral	16 Dec 61	Visas	544UNTS19	107909
Ireland	Multilateral	14 May 62	Sanitation	544UNTS81	107911
Ireland	Multilateral	15 May 62	Commodity Trade	444UNTS3	106367
Ireland	Multilateral	28 Jun 62	ILO Labor	494UNTS271	107238
Ireland	Multilateral	17 Dec 62	Admin Cooperation	590UNTS81	108548
Ireland	Multilateral	17 Dec 62	Sanitation	486UNTS119	107076
Ireland	Multilateral	24 Apr 63	Consul/Citizenship	596UNTS261	108638
Ireland	Multilateral	24 Apr 63	Consul/Citizenship	596UNTS487	108640
Ireland	Multilateral	05 Aug 63	Sanitation	480UNTS43	106964
Ireland	Multilateral	09 Mar 64	Specific Resources	581UNTS57	108432
Ireland	Multilateral	09 Mar 64	Specific Resources	581UNTS89	108434
Ireland	Multilateral	09 Mar 64	Specific Resources	581UNTS83	108433
Ireland	Multilateral	10 Jul 64	Postal Service	612UNTS3	108847
Ireland	Multilateral	10 Jul 64	Postal Service	611UNTS387	108846
Ireland	Multilateral	10 Jul 64	Postal Service	611UNTS105	108845
Ireland	Multilateral	10 Jul 64	Postal Service	611UNTS7	108844
Ireland	Multilateral	13 Jul 64	ILO Labor	569UNTS65	108279
Ireland	Multilateral	20 Aug 64	Telecommunications	514UNTS25	107441
Ireland	Multilateral	12 Sep 64	Specific Resources	0UNTS0	109344
Ireland	Multilateral	22 Jan 65	Gen Communications	634UNTS239	109066
Ireland	Multilateral	18 Mar 65	Dispute Settlement	575UNTS159	108359
Ireland	Multilateral	05 Apr 66	Water Transport	640UNTS133	109159
Ireland	Multilateral	27 Jan 67	Scientific Project	610UNTS205	108843
Ireland	Multilateral	31 Jan 67	Refugees	606UNTS267	108791
Ireland	Multilateral	24 Apr 67	Humanitarian	634UNTS255	109067
Ireland	Multilateral	10 Jul 67	Air Transport	0UNTS0	109971
Ireland	Multilateral	22 Apr 68	Scientific Project	0UNTS0	109574
Ireland	Multilateral	01 Jul 68	Peace/Disarmament	0UNTS0	110485

PARTY ONE	PARTY TWO	DATE	TOPIC	CITATION	NUMBER
Ireland	Multilateral	24 Sep 68	Air Transport	0UNTS0	110612
Ireland	Netherlands	01 May 47	Visas	247UNTS193	103468
Ireland	Netherlands	10 May 48	Air Transport	28UNTS121	100422
Ireland	Netherlands	02 Sep 48	General Trade	558UNTS249	108145
Ireland	Netherlands	25 Nov 49	General Trade	558UNTS256	108146
Ireland	Netherlands	22 Dec 50	General Trade	51NET11	447017
Ireland	Netherlands	29 Oct 51	General Trade	52NET27	447031
Ireland	Netherlands	28 May 59	Non-ILO Labor	344UNTS95	104944
Ireland	Netherlands	11 Feb 69	Taxation	0UNTS0	110605
Ireland	Norway	17 Dec 47	Visas	90UNTS71	101228
Ireland	Norway	21 Jun 48	Air Transport	34UNTS317	100545
Ireland	Norway	02 Jul 51	General Trade	100UNTS53	101387
Ireland	Norway	18 Oct 54	Taxation	553UNTS123	108077
Ireland	Norway	02 Apr 64	Culture	553UNTS129	108078
Ireland	Portugal	06 Feb 52	General Trade	558UNTS289	108147
Ireland	Portugal	29 Jul 55	Visas	553UNTS135	108079
Ireland	Portugal	11 Nov 57	Mostfavored Nation	553UNTS141	108080
Ireland	Portugal	24 Jun 60	Air Transport	412UNTS30	105924
Ireland	South Africa	01 May 58	Taxation	398UNTS3	105714
Ireland	South Africa	13 Apr 60	Postal Service	390UNTS307	105612
Ireland	Spain	11 May 50	Scientific Project	553UNTS147	108081
Ireland	Spain	19 Dec 51	General Trade	0UNTS0	109228
Ireland	Spain	17 Apr 59	Visas	553UNTS157	108082
Ireland	Sweden	29 May 46	Air Transport	35UNTS231	100557
Ireland	Sweden	19 Mar 47	Visas	553UNTS163	108083
Ireland	Sweden	25 Jun 49	General Trade	558UNTS299	108148
Ireland	Sweden	18 Oct 54	Taxation	262UNTS259	103753
Ireland	Sweden	05 Dec 57	Non-ILO Labor	428UNTS221	106176
Ireland	Sweden	06 Nov 59	Taxation	428UNTS231	106177
Ireland	Switzerland	09 Jun 47	Visas	553UNTS169	108084
Ireland	Switzerland	06 May 48	Air Transport	334UNTS187	104768
Ireland	Switzerland	14 Mar 49	Non-ILO Labor	553UNTS175	108085
Ireland	Switzerland	26 Dec 51	General Trade	558UNTS305	108149
Ireland	Switzerland	18 Jun 58	Taxation	553UNTS183	108086
Ireland	Switzerland	08 Nov 66	Taxation	0UNTS0	109499
Ireland	Turkey	27 Sep 55	Visas	553UNTS193	108087
Ireland	UK Great Britain	05 Apr 46	Air Transport	72UNTS57	100928
Ireland	UK Great Britain	31 Jul 48	General Trade	86UNTS37	101151
Ireland	UK Great Britain	18 May 49	Taxation	553UNTS209	108089
Ireland	UK Great Britain	06 Apr 54	Sanitation	553UNTS197	108088
Ireland	UK Great Britain	29 Mar 60	Non-ILO Labor	371UNTS3	105267
Ireland	UK Great Britain	25 Jun 64	Commodity Trade	553UNTS221	108090
Ireland	UK Great Britain	30 Jun 64	Commodity Trade	522UNTS141	107541
Ireland	UK Great Britain	14 Dec 65	General Trade	565UNTS58	108235
Ireland	UK Great Britain	28 Feb 66	Health/Educ/Welfare	565UNTS33	108234
Ireland	UK Great Britain	23 Sep 68	Finance	0UNTS0	109374
Ireland	UN Special Fund	03 Jun 64	Direct Aid	496UNTS205	107253
Ireland	USA (United States)	03 Feb 45	Air Transport	122UNTS305	200412
Ireland	USA (United States)	03 Jun 47	Air Transport	16UNTS151	100255
Ireland	USA (United States)	28 Jun 48	Mostfavored Nation	32UNTS69	100489
Ireland	USA (United States)	28 Jun 48	Direct Aid	24UNTS3	100349
Ireland	USA (United States)	01 Aug 49	Visas	82UNTS37	101083
Ireland	USA (United States)	13 Sep 49	Taxation	127UNTS89	101701
Ireland	USA (United States)	13 Sep 49	Taxation	127UNTS119	101702
Ireland	USA (United States)	21 Jan 50	General Amity	206UNTS269	102792
Ireland	USA (United States)	01 May 50	Consul/Citizenship	222UNTS107	103026
Ireland	USA (United States)	17 Jun 54	Direct Aid	241UNTS173	103432
Ireland	USA (United States)	16 Mar 56	Atomic Energy	317UNTS195	104604
Ireland	USA (United States)	24 Mar 60	Atomic Energy	371UNTS237	105280
Ireland	USA (United States)	03 May 62	General Trade	442UNTS117	106343
Ireland	USA (United States)	25 Feb 64	Commodity Trade	511UNTS27	107423
Ireland	USA (United States)	18 Jun 64	Water Transport	530UNTS217	107684
Ireland	USA (United States)	10 Oct 68	Gen Communications	0UNTS0	110082
Ireland	USA (United States)	10 Oct 68	Gen Communications	0UNTS0	109938
Ireland	USA (United States)	30 Jan 70	General Trade	0UNTS0	110619

PARTY ONE	PARTY TWO	DATE	TOPIC	CITATION	NUMBER
Ireland	Vietnam, South	01 Dec 64	General Trade	553UNTS233	108091
IRO (Refugee Org)	Multilateral	06 Apr 50	Admin Cooperation	119UNTS99	101610
IRO (Refugee Org)	Netherlands	20 Jun 50	Refugees	76UNTS55	100979
IRO (Refugee Org)	Netherlands	13 Feb 51	IGO Operations	87UNTS239	101175
IRO (Refugee Org)	United Nations	07 Feb 49	IGO Operations	26UNTS299	200153
Israel	Accept UN Charter	29 Nov 48	UN Charter	30UNTS53	100448
Israel	Argentina	23 May 57	Culture	280UNTS199	104059
Israel	Australia	06 Sep 51	Mostfavored Nation	188UNTS303	102534
Israel	Australia	18 Jun 54	Postal Service	220UNTS29	102985
Israel	Australia	14 Apr 64	Visas	496UNTS233	107255
Israel	Austria	17 Nov 55	Air Transport	232UNTS153	103235
Israel	Austria	17 Jan 56	Air Transport	59ABGB162	403106
Israel	Austria	25 Nov 57	Visas	314UNTS81	104542
Israel	Austria	10 Oct 61	Extradition	448UNTS161	106430
Israel	Austria	22 Aug 63	Air Transport	63ABGB260	403107
Israel	Austria	06 Jun 66	Admin Cooperation	68ABGB349	403108
Israel	Austria	06 Jun 66	Admin Cooperation	68ABGB348	403109
Israel	Austria	06 Jun 66	Admin Cooperation	0UNTS0	109346
Israel	Austria	06 Jun 66	Admin Cooperation	0UNTS0	109347
Israel	Austria	03 Apr 67	Gen Communications	630UNTS301	108976
Israel	Austria	22 Nov 68	Visas	68ABGB438	403110
Israel	Austria	22 Nov 68	Visas	0UNTS0	109388
Israel	Austria	29 Jan 70	Taxation	71ABGB85	403111
Israel	Barbados	18 Jun 69	Visas	0UNTS0	110387
Israel	Belgium	30 Jun 52	Air Transport	183UNTS263	102435
Israel	Belgium	29 May 53	Admin Cooperation	219UNTS197	102975
Israel	Belgium	08 Feb 54	Extradition	188UNTS251	102528
Israel	Belgium	22 Jun 54	Visas	196UNTS245	102627
Israel	Belgium	14 Dec 54	Admin Cooperation	220UNTS49	102987
Israel	Belgium	15 Apr 55	Visas	211UNTS43	102845
Israel	Belgium	26 Mar 56	Extradition	260UNTS3	103702
Israel	Belgium	26 Apr 66	Admin Cooperation	566UNTS187	108243
Israel	Belgium	23 Mar 67	Culture	630UNTS275	108974
Israel	Belgium	25 Sep 68	Consul/Citizenship	0UNTS0	109359
Israel	Brazil	24 Jun 59	Culture	515UNTS151	107458
Israel	Brazil	27 Jan 67	Commodity Trade	0UNTS0	109845
Israel	Burma	05 Mar 56	Direct Aid	280UNTS209	104060
Israel	Cameroon	24 Oct 62	General Aid	449UNTS3	106446
Israel	Cameroon	24 Oct 62	Culture	449UNTS15	106447
Israel	Cameroon	09 Aug 63	Air Transport	499UNTS121	107295
Israel	Canada	02 Aug 55	Visas	226UNTS265	103121
Israel	Canada	12 Sep 66	Telecommunications	581UNTS167	108440
Israel	Canada	30 Nov 66	Taxation	630UNTS267	108973
Israel	Canada	10 Mar 67	Extradition	0UNTS0	110380
Israel	Canada	05 Apr 67	Gen Communications	0UNTS0	109350
Israel	Central Afri Rep	14 Feb 62	Visas	484UNTS143	107022
Israel	Central Afri Rep	13 Jun 62	Tech Assistance	448UNTS265	106439
Israel	Chad	07 Oct 64	Tech Assistance	630UNTS175	108969
Israel	Chile	29 Dec 65	Scientific Project	0UNTS0	110375
Israel	Colombia	21 Dec 62	Visas	484UNTS149	107023
Israel	Colombia	15 Jan 65	Tech Assistance	581UNTS173	108441
Israel	Colombia	12 Jul 66	Visas	581UNTS181	108442
Israel	Congo (Zaire)	14 Apr 64	Visas	552UNTS305	108062
Israel	Costa Rica	01 Sep 61	Visas	448UNTS247	106436
Israel	Costa Rica	31 Jul 62	Education	484UNTS155	107024
Israel	Costa Rica	06 Apr 68	Visas	0UNTS0	109355
Israel	Cyprus	17 Aug 61	Visas	484UNTS169	107025
Israel	Dahomey	28 Sep 61	Tech Assistance	448UNTS151	106429
Israel	Dahomey	18 Dec 61	Visas	448UNTS259	106438
Israel	Denmark	14 Nov 52	Finance	160UNTS289	102114
Israel	Denmark	14 Nov 52	General Economic	160UNTS275	102112
Israel	Denmark	14 Nov 52	General Trade	160UNTS279	102113
Israel	Denmark	04 Apr 55	Taxation	213UNTS283	102891
Israel	Denmark	29 Apr 55	Visas	220UNTS87	102992
Israel	Denmark	23 Feb 66	Visas	581UNTS187	108443

PARTY ONE	PARTY TWO	DATE	TOPIC	CITATION	NUMBER
Israel	Denmark	27 Jun 66	Taxation	581UNTS227	108448
Israel	Denmark	14 Feb 67	Admin Cooperation	620UNTS211	108957
Israel	Dominican Republic	25 Dec 63	Tech Assistance	550UNTS221	108018
Israel	Dominican Republic	02 May 68	Visas	0UNTS0	109357
Israel	Ecuador	20 Jun 66	Visas	581UNTS265	108449
Israel	Ecuador	09 Aug 67	Visas	630UNTS319	108979
Israel	El Salvador	14 Nov 58	Culture	345UNTS67	104959
Israel	El Salvador	05 Sep 60	Visas	413UNTS73	105941
Israel	El Salvador	04 Oct 61	Visas	448UNTS253	106437
Israel	Finland	16 Nov 55	Visas	257UNTS39	103647
Israel	Finland	21 Jan 65	Taxation	581UNTS275	108450
Israel	Finland	23 Feb 66	Visas	581UNTS219	108447
Israel	France	03 Jun 51	Extradition	219UNTS215	102977
Israel	France	24 Jan 52	Taxation	220UNTS55	102988
Israel	France	29 Apr 52	Air Transport	189UNTS55	102542
Israel	France	15 Sep 52	Customs	220UNTS65	102989
Israel	France	10 Jul 53	General Economic	53FRMD2307	417244
Israel	France	01 Mar 58	Visas	314UNTS87	104543
Israel	France	12 Nov 58	Admin Cooperation	345UNTS79	104960
Israel	France	19 May 59	Admin Cooperation	377UNTS231	105403
Israel	France	30 Jun 59	Milit Servic/Citiz	448UNTS107	106428
Israel	France	30 Nov 59	Culture	377UNTS237	105404
Israel	France	07 Jul 60	Visas	413UNTS79	105942
Israel	France	20 Aug 63	Taxation	515UNTS173	107460
Israel	France	20 Dec 63	Customs	515UNTS165	107459
Israel	France	17 Dec 65	Non-ILO Labor	581UNTS311	108451
Israel	France	17 Dec 65	Non-ILO Labor	582UNTS3	108452
Israel	France	28 Nov 69	Visas	0UNTS0	110388
Israel	Gabon	15 May 62	General Amity	484UNTS181	107027
Israel	Gabon	15 May 62	Tech Assistance	448UNTS211	106433
Israel	Gabon	10 Oct 62	Visas	484UNTS175	107026
Israel	Gambia	11 Jul 66	Visas	582UNTS11	108453
Israel	Germany, West	10 Sep 52	Reparations	162UNTS205	102137
Israel	Germany, West	10 Sep 52	Consul/Citizenship	345UNTS91	104961
Israel	Germany, West	01 Jun 62	Specific Property	448UNTS227	106435
Israel	Germany, West	09 Jul 62	Taxation	630UNTS87	108968
Israel	Germany, West	12 May 66	Direct Aid	66WBGA111	424282
Israel	Germany, West	12 Sep 66	Education	582UNTS17	108454
Israel	Germany, West	19 Sep 66	Admin Cooperation	67WGBB719	425283
Israel	Germany, West	25 Feb 68	Admin Cooperation	69WBGA94	424284
Israel	Germany, West	18 Jul 68	Direct Aid	68WBGA165	424285
Israel	Germany, West	31 Mar 69	Admin Cooperation	0UNTS0	110384
Israel	Ghana	25 May 62	Tech Assistance	515UNTS237	107461
Israel	Ghana	30 Nov 64	Tech Assistance	550UNTS231	108019
Israel	Greece	22 Jul 52	General Economic	219UNTS231	102978
Israel	Greece	22 Jul 52	Taxation	215UNTS365	102924
Israel	Greece	20 Jan 69	Visas	0UNTS0	110382
Israel	Greece	26 Feb 69	Visas	0UNTS0	110383
Israel	Guatemala	27 Nov 61	Culture	448UNTS191	106431
Israel	Haiti	28 Mar 67	General Amity	630UNTS293	108975
Israel	Honduras	10 Oct 62	Visas	484UNTS189	107028
Israel	IAEA (Atom Energy)	31 Aug 67	Atomic Energy	0UNTS0	109310
Israel	IBRD (World Bank)	09 Sep 60	IBRD Project	406UNTS3	105837
Israel	IBRD (World Bank)	11 Jul 61	IBRD Project	429UNTS3	106188
Israel	IBRD (World Bank)	01 Feb 62	IBRD Project	435UNTS155	106277
Israel	IBRD (World Bank)	17 Oct 62	IBRD Project	467UNTS107	106760
Israel	IBRD (World Bank)	16 Sep 65	Claims and Debts	566UNTS212	108245
Israel	IBRD (World Bank)	15 Nov 67	IBRD Project	619UNTS129	108942
Israel	IBRD (World Bank)	15 Jun 70	IBRD Project	0UNTS0	110831
Israel	ICAO (Civil Aviat)	19 Feb 51	Tech Assistance	96UNTS141	101334
Israel	Iceland	29 Dec 55	Visas	227UNTS147	103136
Israel	Iceland	15 Jun 60	Patents/Copyrights	377UNTS261	105405
Israel	Iceland	23 Feb 66	Visas	581UNTS211	108446
Israel	ICJ Option Clause	04 Sep 50	ICJ Option Clause	108UNTS239	101477
Israel	ICJ Option Clause	03 Oct 56	ICJ Option Clause	252UNTS301	103571

PARTY ONE	PARTY TWO	DATE	TOPIC	CITATION	NUMBER
Israel	ILO (Labor Org)	19 Feb 51	Tech Assistance	100UNTS105	101391
Israel	Italy	08 Nov 51	Mostfavored Nation	219UNTS293	102980
Israel	Italy	22 May 53	Mostfavored Nation	219UNTS297	102981
Israel	Italy	05 Mar 54	General Trade	55ITGU17	435218
Israel	Italy	28 Jun 54	Dispute Settlement	56ITGU292	435219
Israel	Italy	10 Jun 55	Taxation	280UNTS219	104061
Israel	Italy	24 Feb 56	Extradition	316UNTS97	104580
Israel	Italy	30 Aug 61	Visas	484UNTS197	107029
Israel	Ivory Coast	26 Oct 61	Visas	515UNTS251	107462
Israel	Jamaica	05 Dec 67	Visas	632UNTS83	109010
Israel	Jordan	03 Apr 49	Peace/Disarmament	42UNTS303	100656
Israel	Kenya	25 Feb 66	Tech Assistance	582UNTS23	108455
Israel	Lebanon	23 Mar 49	Peace/Disarmament	42UNTS287	100655
Israel	Lesotho	21 Jan 70	Visas	0UNTS0	110390
Israel	Liberia	09 Apr 59	General Amity	448UNTS95	106427
Israel	Liberia	03 Aug 61	Visas	484UNTS203	107030
Israel	Liberia	25 Jun 62	Tech Assistance	448UNTS287	106441
Israel	Liberia	25 Jun 62	Culture	448UNTS295	106442
Israel	Liberia	18 Sep 62	Postal Service	484UNTS209	107031
Israel	Luxembourg	27 Oct 54	Visas	226UNTS241	103117
Israel	Luxembourg	30 Mar 55	Visas	226UNTS247	103118
Israel	Luxembourg	26 Jul 56	Extradition	550UNTS239	108020
Israel	Malagasy	27 Aug 61	Direct Aid	413UNTS86	105943
Israel	Malagasy	27 Aug 61	General Amity	484UNTS217	107032
Israel	Malagasy	04 May 63	Visas	484UNTS225	107033
Israel	Malawi	03 Aug 66	Visas	582UNTS53	108456
Israel	Mali	24 Nov 60	Culture	413UNTS104	105945
Israel	Mali	24 Nov 60	Tech Assistance	413UNTS95	105944
Israel	Mauritius	15 May 69	Visas	0UNTS0	110385
Israel	Mexico	15 Jun 59	Culture	377UNTS267	105406
Israel	Mexico	11 Jul 66	Tech Assistance	68MEXD2510	444029
Israel	Mexico	11 Jul 66	Tech Assistance	0UNTS0	109348
Israel	Mexico	28 Jan 67	Scientific Project	0UNTS0	109846
Israel	Multilateral	07 Dec 44	IGO Establishment	15UNTS295	200102
Israel	Multilateral	07 Dec 44	Air Transport	84UNTS389	200252
Israel	Multilateral	11 Dec 46	Sanitation	12UNTS179	100186
Israel	Multilateral	11 Oct 47	IGO Establishment	77UNTS143	100998
Israel	Multilateral	06 Mar 48	Water Transport	289UNTS3	104214
Israel	Multilateral	10 May 48	Culture	289UNTS111	104215
Israel	Multilateral	10 Jun 48	Humanitarian	164UNTS113	102163
Israel	Multilateral	26 Jun 48	Culture	331UNTS217	104757
Israel	Multilateral	24 Jul 48	Sanitation	66UNTS25	100847
Israel	Multilateral	09 Dec 48	Scientific Project	73UNTS39	100942
Israel	Multilateral	09 Dec 48	Humanitarian	78UNTS277	101021
Israel	Multilateral	23 Mar 49	Commodity Trade	203UNTS179	102746
Israel	Multilateral	18 Jun 49	ILO Labor	605UNTS295	108768
Israel	Multilateral	12 Aug 49	Humanitarian	75UNTS287	100973
Israel	Multilateral	12 Aug 49	Humanitarian	75UNTS85	100971
Israel	Multilateral	12 Aug 49	General Military	75UNTS135	100972
Israel	Multilateral	12 Aug 49	Humanitarian	75UNTS31	100970
Israel	Multilateral	19 Sep 49	Land Transport	125UNTS3	101671
Israel	Multilateral	24 Sep 49	IGO Establishment	126UNTS237	101691
Israel	Multilateral	21 Mar 50	Admin Cooperation	96UNTS271	101342
Israel	Multilateral	06 Apr 50	Admin Cooperation	119UNTS99	101610
Israel	Multilateral	22 Nov 50	Culture	131UNTS25	101734
Israel	Multilateral	07 Dec 50	Admin Cooperation	212UNTS17	102861
Israel	Multilateral	15 Dec 50	Customs	157UNTS129	102052
Israel	Multilateral	25 May 51	Status of Forces	175UNTS215	102303
Israel	Multilateral	02 Jul 51	Refugees	189UNTS137	102545
Israel	Multilateral	06 Dec 51	IGO Establishment	425UNTS61	106119
Israel	Multilateral	06 Dec 51	Admin Cooperation	150UNTS67	101963
Israel	Multilateral	22 May 52	Tech Assistance	131UNTS115	101739
Israel	Multilateral	11 Jul 52	IGO Establishment	169UNTS3	102220
Israel	Multilateral	06 Sep 52	Patents/Copyrights	216UNTS132	102937
Israel	Multilateral	07 Oct 52	Admin Cooperation	310UNTS181	104493

PARTY ONE	PARTY TWO	DATE	TOPIC	CITATION	NUMBER
Israel	Multilateral	07 Nov 52	General Trade	221UNTS255	103010
Israel	Multilateral	27 Feb 53	Claims and Debts	333UNTS3	104764
Israel	Multilateral	31 Mar 53	Privil/Immunities	193UNTS136	102613
Israel	Multilateral	11 May 53	Sanitation	456UNTS3	106555
Israel	Multilateral	19 Oct 53	IGO Establishment	207UNTS189	102807
Israel	Multilateral	07 Dec 53	Admin Cooperation	182UNTS51	102422
Israel	Multilateral	11 Dec 53	Patents/Copyrights	218UNTS27	102952
Israel	Multilateral	25 Feb 54	Air Transport	215UNTS249	102922
Israel	Multilateral	01 Mar 54	Commodity Trade	256UNTS31	103622
Israel	Multilateral	12 May 54	Admin Cooperation	327UNTS3	104714
Israel	Multilateral	14 May 54	Culture	249UNTS215	103511
Israel	Multilateral	04 Jun 54	Customs	282UNTS249	104101
Israel	Multilateral	14 Jun 54	Air Transport	320UNTS217	104644
Israel	Multilateral	28 Sep 54	Refugees	360UNTS117	105158
Israel	Multilateral	25 May 55	IGO Establishment	264UNTS117	103791
Israel	Multilateral	06 Jun 55	IGO Establishment	219UNTS79	102968
Israel	Multilateral	28 Sep 55	Air Transport	478UNTS371	106943
Israel	Multilateral	25 Apr 56	Commodity Trade	270UNTS103	103896
Israel	Multilateral	18 May 56	Customs	338UNTS103	104834
Israel	Multilateral	20 Jun 56	Admin Cooperation	268UNTS3	103850
Israel	Multilateral	07 Sep 56	Humanitarian	266UNTS3	103822
Israel	Multilateral	25 Sep 56	Air Transport	334UNTS13	104766
Israel	Multilateral	25 Sep 56	Air Transport	334UNTS89	104767
Israel	Multilateral	26 Oct 56	IGO Establishment	276UNTS3	103988
Israel	Multilateral	20 Feb 57	Consul/Citizenship	309UNTS65	104468
Israel	Multilateral	15 Jun 57	General Trade	550UNTS45	108008
Israel	Multilateral	30 Jun 57	Tech Assistance	286UNTS171	104165
Israel	Multilateral	03 Oct 57	Postal Service	364UNTS3	105211
Israel	Multilateral	13 Dec 57	Extradition	359UNTS273	105146
Israel	Multilateral	03 Apr 58	Commodity Trade	336UNTS177	104806
Israel	Multilateral	29 Apr 58	Territory Boundary	499UNTS311	107302
Israel	Multilateral	29 Apr 58	Territory Boundary	516UNTS205	107477
Israel	Multilateral	29 Apr 58	Water Transport	450UNTS11	106465
Israel	Multilateral	29 Apr 58	Dispute Settlement	450UNTS169	106466
Israel	Multilateral	29 Apr 58	Specific Resources	559UNTS285	108164
Israel	Multilateral	10 Jun 58	Admin Cooperation	330UNTS3	104739
Israel	Multilateral	01 Dec 58	Commodity Trade	385UNTS137	105534
Israel	Multilateral	03 Dec 58	Admin Cooperation	416UNTS51	105995
Israel	Multilateral	03 Dec 58	Admin Cooperation	398UNTS9	105715
Israel	Multilateral	06 Apr 59	Commodity Trade	349UNTS167	105013
Israel	Multilateral	20 Apr 59	Admin Cooperation	472UNTS185	106841
Israel	Multilateral	26 Jan 60	IGO Establishment	439UNTS249	106333
Israel	Multilateral	17 Jun 60	Humanitarian	536UNTS27	107794
Israel	Multilateral	06 Oct 60	Customs	473UNTS131	106861
Israel	Multilateral	13 Dec 60	Air Transport	523UNTS117	107557
Israel	Multilateral	14 Dec 60	Education	429UNTS93	106193
Israel	Multilateral	30 Mar 61	Sanitation	520UNTS151	107515
Israel	Multilateral	18 Apr 61	Dispute Settlement	500UNTS243	107312
Israel	Multilateral	18 Apr 61	Consul/Citizenship	500UNTS95	107310
Israel	Multilateral	08 Jun 61	Customs	473UNTS153	106862
Israel	Multilateral	08 Jun 61	Customs	473UNTS187	106863
Israel	Multilateral	21 Jun 61	IGO Establishment	514UNTS209	107449
Israel	Multilateral	26 Oct 61	Patents/Copyrights	496UNTS43	107247
Israel	Multilateral	06 Dec 61	Customs	473UNTS219	106864
Israel	Multilateral	15 May 62	Commodity Trade	444UNTS3	106367
Israel	Multilateral	22 Jun 62	ILO Labor	494UNTS249	107237
Israel	Multilateral	28 Jun 62	ILO Labor	494UNTS271	107238
Israel	Multilateral	10 Dec 62	Culture	521UNTS231	107525
Israel	Multilateral	20 Apr 63	IGO Establishment	495UNTS3	107239
Israel	Multilateral	24 Apr 63	Consul/Citizenship	596UNTS261	108638
Israel	Multilateral	05 Aug 63	Sanitation	480UNTS43	106964
Israel	Multilateral	03 Mar 64	Consul/Citizenship	516UNTS53	107470
Israel	Multilateral	10 Jul 64	Postal Service	611UNTS7	108844
Israel	Multilateral	10 Jul 64	Postal Service	611UNTS105	108845
Israel	Multilateral	10 Jul 64	Postal Service	612UNTS3	108847

PARTY ONE	PARTY TWO	DATE	TOPIC	CITATION	NUMBER
Israel	Multilateral	20 Aug 64	Telecommunications	514UNTS25	107441
Israel	Multilateral	27 Nov 64	Visas	548UNTS47	107968
Israel	Multilateral	18 Jun 65	Atomic Energy	573UNTS3	108320
Israel	Multilateral	31 Dec 65	Specific Resources	616UNTS317	108904
Israel	Multilateral	05 Apr 66	Water Transport	640UNTS133	109159
Israel	Multilateral	02 Aug 66	Tech Assistance	582UNTS59	108457
Israel	Multilateral	27 Jan 67	Scientific Project	610UNTS205	108843
Israel	Multilateral	17 Apr 67	Consul/Citizenship	0UNTS0	110377
Israel	Multilateral	18 Mar 68	Commodity Trade	0UNTS0	109262
Israel	Netherlands	23 Oct 50	Air Transport	189UNTS89	102543
Israel	Netherlands	16 Jun 53	Visas	220UNTS93	102993
Israel	Netherlands	18 Jun 53	Visas	220UNTS99	102994
Israel	Netherlands	21 Aug 55	Visas	299UNTS51	104306
Israel	Netherlands	18 Dec 56	Extradition	276UNTS153	103991
Israel	Netherlands	28 May 62	Postal Service	448UNTS219	106434
Israel	Netherlands	25 Apr 63	Admin Cooperation	484UNTS231	107034
Israel	New Zealand	29 Apr 58	Visas	314UNTS93	104544
Israel	Niger	23 Jul 63	Visas	515UNTS257	107463
Israel	Norway	24 May 55	Taxation	220UNTS71	102990
Israel	Norway	26 Jul 55	Visas	226UNTS257	103120
Israel	Norway	26 Nov 57	Culture	345UNTS99	104962
Israel	Norway	15 Jun 61	General Economic	3NORT836	451088
Israel	Norway	23 Feb 66	Visas	581UNTS203	108445
Israel	Norway	02 Nov 66	Taxation	630UNTS225	108972
Israel	Norway	18 Apr 67	Admin Cooperation	630UNTS307	108977
Israel	OAS (Am States)	11 Oct 62	Tech Assistance	484UNTS241	107035
Israel	Paraguay	21 Nov 65	Visas	582UNTS65	108458
Israel	Peru	25 Jun 62	Culture	515UNTS263	107464
Israel	Peru	02 Apr 63	Tech Assistance	515UNTS279	107465
Israel	Peru	01 Apr 68	Visas	0UNTS0	109354
Israel	Philippines	07 Aug 51	Air Transport	192UNTS81	102596
Israel	Philippines	26 Feb 58	General Amity	507UNTS135	107398
Israel	Philippines	14 Dec 60	Visas	449UNTS23	106448
Israel	Philippines	10 Jan 63	Atomic Energy	588UNTS205	108526
Israel	Philippines	16 Mar 64	Tech Assistance	550UNTS269	108021
Israel	Philippines	20 Feb 67	Atomic Energy	597UNTS139	108642
Israel	Philippines	14 Jan 69	Atomic Energy	0UNTS0	109437
Israel	Philippines	10 Dec 69	Visas	0UNTS0	110389
Israel	Rwanda	23 Oct 62	Tech Assistance	515UNTS291	107466
Israel	Sierra Leone	30 Aug 62	Visas	448UNTS309	106444
Israel	Sierra Leone	22 Aug 65	Tech Assistance	550UNTS285	108023
Israel	Sierra Leone	22 Aug 65	Culture	550UNTS275	108022
Israel	Singapore	24 Apr 68	General Trade	642UNTS235	109176
Israel	South Africa	24 Dec 52	Taxation	207UNTS303	102813
Israel	South Africa	05 May 53	Air Transport	192UNTS183	102600
Israel	South Africa	31 Dec 54	Postal Service	220UNTS11	102984
Israel	South Africa	01 Sep 56	Visas	251UNTS161	103539
Israel	South Africa	18 Sep 59	Extradition	373UNTS47	105314
Israel	Sweden	02 Mar 55	Visas	220UNTS105	102995
Israel	Sweden	17 Jun 56	Taxation	257UNTS47	103648
Israel	Sweden	20 Mar 58	Admin Cooperation	314UNTS99	104545
Israel	Sweden	22 Dec 59	Taxation	377UNTS277	105407
Israel	Sweden	15 May 62	Taxation	484UNTS261	107036
Israel	Sweden	10 Sep 63	Extradition	516UNTS3	107467
Israel	Sweden	23 Feb 66	Visas	581UNTS195	108444
Israel	Switzerland	19 Nov 52	Air Transport	232UNTS3	103226
Israel	Switzerland	01 Jul 53	Postal Service	220UNTS41	102986
Israel	Switzerland	14 Sep 56	General Trade	56SWRO1281	462143
Israel	Switzerland	31 Dec 58	Extradition	377UNTS305	105408
Israel	Switzerland	29 Jun 62	Visas	448UNTS303	106443
Israel	Switzerland	01 May 67	Visas	630UNTS313	108978
Israel	Syria	20 Jul 49	Peace/Disarmament	42UNTS327	100657
Israel	Tanganyika	28 Jan 63	Tech Assistance	516UNTS39	107468
Israel	Tanganyika	17 Sep 63	Visas	516UNTS47	107469
Israel	Thailand	07 Jul 60	Visas	377UNTS325	105409

PARTY ONE	PARTY TWO	DATE	TOPIC	CITATION	NUMBER
Israel	Togo	09 Feb 65	Visas	550UNTS297	108024
Israel	Trinidad/Tobago	31 Dec 68	Visas	0UNTS0	110379
Israel	Turkey	04 Jul 50	Mostfavored Nation	220UNTS3	102982
Israel	Turkey	05 Feb 51	Air Transport	193UNTS3	102607
Israel	Turkey	13 Nov 64	Tech Assistance	550UNTS303	108025
Israel	Uganda	04 Feb 63	Tech Assistance	484UNTS273	107037
Israel	Uganda	11 Oct 68	Culture	0UNTS0	110378
Israel	UK Great Britain	10 Feb 50	Taxation	86UNTS211	101161
Israel	UK Great Britain	30 Mar 50	Claims and Debts	86UNTS231	101162
Israel	UK Great Britain	06 Dec 50	Air Transport	151UNTS33	101983
Israel	UK Great Britain	10 Dec 50	Patents/Copyrights	88UNTS211	101193
Israel	UK Great Britain	13 May 53	Finance	175UNTS179	102300
Israel	UK Great Britain	29 Apr 57	Non-ILO Labor	280UNTS227	104062
Israel	UK Great Britain	04 Apr 60	Extradition	377UNTS331	105410
Israel	UK Great Britain	31 Aug 60	Culture	385UNTS71	105530
Israel	UK Great Britain	26 Sep 62	Taxation	474UNTS233	106885
Israel	UK Great Britain	15 Sep 64	Taxation	539UNTS283	107839
Israel	UK Great Britain	15 Apr 65	Finance	551UNTS19	108031
Israel	UK Great Britain	05 Jul 66	Admin Cooperation	630UNTS189	108971
Israel	UK Great Britain	09 Feb 67	Visas	0UNTS0	109349
Israel	UK Great Britain	10 Jun 69	Culture	0UNTS0	110386
Israel	UN Relief Palestin	09 Nov 56	Direct Aid	280UNTS261	104063
Israel	UN Relief Palestin	14 Jun 67	Direct Aid	620UNTS183	108955
Israel	UN Special Fund	01 Dec 59	Direct Aid	345UNTS197	104968
Israel	UNICEF (Children)	20 Sep 48	Direct Aid	71UNTS17	100907
Israel	United Arab Rep	24 Feb 49	Peace/Disarmament	42UNTS251	100654
Israel	United Nations	25 Jun 51	Tech Assistance	97UNTS21	101344
Israel	United Nations	07 Jan 63	Tech Assistance	450UNTS229	106470
Israel	Upper Volta	11 Jun 61	Tech Assistance	413UNTS113	105946
Israel	Uruguay	30 Apr 53	Culture	280UNTS269	104064
Israel	Uruguay	03 Apr 66	Visas	582UNTS73	108459
Israel	Uruguay	03 Mar 69	Taxation	0UNTS0	110381
Israel	USA (United States)	19 Feb 50	Admin Cooperation	122UNTS117	101641
Israel	USA (United States)	04 May 50	Patents/Copyrights	132UNTS189	101760
Israel	USA (United States)	13 Jun 50	Air Transport	212UNTS93	102863
Israel	USA (United States)	26 Feb 51	Tech Assistance	137UNTS57	101848
Israel	USA (United States)	28 Feb 51	Taxation	220UNTS79	102991
Israel	USA (United States)	01 Jun 51	Visas	212UNTS129	102864
Israel	USA (United States)	23 Aug 51	General Amity	219UNTS237	102979
Israel	USA (United States)	07 Dec 51	Tech Assistance	157UNTS53	102046
Israel	USA (United States)	27 Feb 52	Direct Aid	177UNTS123	102314
Israel	USA (United States)	01 May 52	Direct Aid	177UNTS89	102311
Israel	USA (United States)	09 May 52	Tech Assistance	177UNTS63	102309
Israel	USA (United States)	09 May 52	Tech Assistance	177UNTS269	102326
Israel	USA (United States)	09 Jun 52	Mass Media	178UNTS297	102345
Israel	USA (United States)	23 Jul 52	Milit Assistance	179UNTS139	102363
Israel	USA (United States)	08 Aug 52	Direct Aid	181UNTS37	102396
Israel	USA (United States)	25 Nov 53	Direct Aid	219UNTS205	102976
Israel	USA (United States)	02 Mar 55	Visas	220UNTS113	102996
Israel	USA (United States)	29 Apr 55	US Agri Commod Aid	261UNTS331	103731
Israel	USA (United States)	12 Jul 55	Atomic Energy	219UNTS185	102974
Israel	USA (United States)	10 Nov 55	US Agri Commod Aid	240UNTS3	103390
Israel	USA (United States)	26 Jun 56	Education	257UNTS55	103649
Israel	USA (United States)	11 Sep 56	US Agri Commod Aid	277UNTS215	104008
Israel	USA (United States)	07 Nov 57	US Agri Commod Aid	302UNTS255	104365
Israel	USA (United States)	06 Nov 58	US Agri Commod Aid	336UNTS275	104810
Israel	USA (United States)	07 Jan 60	US Agri Commod Aid	368UNTS181	105241
Israel	USA (United States)	19 Dec 60	Direct Aid	401UNTS195	105772
Israel	USA (United States)	10 May 61	US Agri Commod Aid	409UNTS213	105887
Israel	USA (United States)	05 Mar 62	General Economic	446UNTS29	106400
Israel	USA (United States)	03 May 62	US Agri Commod Aid	442UNTS83	106340
Israel	USA (United States)	22 Jun 62	Education	448UNTS273	106440
Israel	USA (United States)	28 Aug 62	US Agri Commod Aid	448UNTS317	106445
Israel	USA (United States)	06 Dec 62	US Agri Commod Aid	460UNTS151	106638
Israel	USA (United States)	10 Dec 62	Extradition	484UNTS283	107038

PARTY ONE	PARTY TWO	DATE	TOPIC	CITATION	NUMBER
Israel	USA (United States)	21 Mar 63	Education	476UNTS131	106907
Israel	USA (United States)	21 May 63	Telecommunications	487UNTS319	107113
Israel	USA (United States)	22 Nov 63	Commodity Trade	494UNTS89	107228
Israel	USA (United States)	22 Dec 64	US Agri Commod Aid	532UNTS231	107720
Israel	USA (United States)	07 Jul 65	Gen Communications	549UNTS281	108004
Israel	USA (United States)	20 Jul 65	Milit Assistance	549UNTS55	107989
Israel	USA (United States)	26 Jul 65	Status of Forces	549UNTS49	107988
Israel	USA (United States)	06 Jun 66	US Agri Commod Aid	593UNTS165	108583
Israel	USA (United States)	06 Jun 66	US Agri Commod Aid	578UNTS143	108392
Israel	USA (United States)	15 Jun 66	Telecommunications	578UNTS159	108393
Israel	USA (United States)	13 Jul 67	General Trade	0UNTS0	109778
Israel	USA (United States)	04 Aug 67	US Agri Commod Aid	0UNTS0	109351
Israel	USA (United States)	29 Mar 68	US Agri Commod Aid	0UNTS0	109352
Israel	USA (United States)	22 May 68	Scientific Project	0UNTS0	109356
Israel	USA (United States)	23 Jul 68	Air Transport	0UNTS0	109358
Israel	USA (United States)	17 Jan 69	Commodity Trade	0UNTS0	110263
Israel	USA (United States)	07 May 70	US Agri Commod Aid	0UNTS0	110696
Israel	USSR (Soviet Union)	18 May 48	Recognition	0SUST248	468236
Israel	USSR (Soviet Union)	26 May 48	Consul/Citizenship	0SUST248	468237
Israel	USSR (Soviet Union)	15 Jul 53	Consul/Citizenship	0SUST297	468238
Israel	USSR (Soviet Union)	13 May 54	Consul/Citizenship	0SUST312	468239
Israel	USSR (Soviet Union)	15 Jul 55	Mostfavored Nation	226UNTS253	103119
Israel	USSR (Soviet Union)	07 Oct 64	Specific Property	516UNTS59	107471
Israel	Venezuela	19 Jun 66	Culture	0UNTS0	110376
Israel	Vietnam, South	11 Apr 62	Mostfavored Nation	448UNTS205	106432
Israel	WHO (World Health)	07 Aug 51	Tech Assistance	104UNTS213	101442
Israel	WHO (World Health)	11 Apr 58	Tech Assistance	307UNTS27	104439
Israel	Yugoslavia	29 Jul 51	Mostfavored Nation	220UNTS7	102983
Israel	Yugoslavia	11 Dec 58	General Trade	386UNTS271	105547
Israel	Yugoslavia	11 Dec 58	Finance	386UNTS283	105548
Israel	Yugoslavia	13 Jun 64	Visas	516UNTS91	107472
Italy	Accept UN Charter	22 Feb 56	UN Charter	231UNTS175	103217
Italy	Afghanistan	30 Jan 59	Air Transport	61ITDI347	436001
Italy	Afghanistan	10 Dec 60	Tech Assistance	63ITGU9	435002
Italy	Albania	22 Jun 57	Peace/Disarmament	57ITGU263	435003
Italy	Albania	22 Jun 57	Other Military	59ITDI216	436005
Italy	Albania	22 Jun 57	Admin Cooperation	59ITDI216	436004
Italy	Albania	26 May 58	Finance	362UNTS259	105191
Italy	Albania	11 Jun 58	Water Transport	58ITGU244	435006
Italy	Albania	21 Apr 62	Air Transport	63ITDI273	436007
Italy	Albania	19 Dec 64	General Trade	65ITDI115	436008
Italy	Algeria	12 Jan 55	Admin Cooperation	57ITGU87	435009
Italy	Algeria	03 Jun 65	Air Transport	67ITGU137	435010
Italy	Argentina	16 Apr 47	Sanitation	61ITMA451	437011
Italy	Argentina	26 Jan 48	Health/Educ/Welfare	1ITMA82	437012
Italy	Argentina	18 Feb 48	Air Transport	48ITGU179	435013
Italy	Argentina	12 Apr 49	Taxation	52ITGU22	435014
Italy	Argentina	25 Jun 52	Health/Educ/Welfare	52ITDI223	436015
Italy	Argentina	05 Dec 52	Mass Media	52ITDI225	436016
Italy	Argentina	23 May 56	Claims and Debts	267UNTS255	103846
Italy	Argentina	25 Nov 57	Health/Educ/Welfare	58ITGU120	435017
Italy	Argentina	25 Nov 57	General Economic	305UNTS275	104424
Italy	Argentina	19 Nov 59	Visas	61ITDI245	436018
Italy	Argentina	21 Jan 60	General Economic	62ITDI313	436019
Italy	Argentina	14 Jun 60	Atomic Energy	62ITDI314	436020
Italy	Argentina	01 Aug 60	Taxation	63ITGU9	435021
Italy	Argentina	12 Apr 61	Loans and Credits	62ITDI490	436024
Italy	Argentina	12 Apr 61	Culture	63ITGU86	435022
Italy	Argentina	12 Apr 61	Non-ILO Labor	63ITGU8	435023
Italy	Argentina	12 Apr 61	Non-ILO Labor	0UNTS0	109522
Italy	Argentina	21 Feb 68	Visas	0UNTS0	109562
Italy	Australia	08 Jul 48	Direct Aid	22UNTS11	100326
Italy	Australia	02 Aug 48	Air Transport	28UNTS165	100424
Italy	Australia	07 Jan 49	Admin Cooperation	189UNTS239	102549
Italy	Australia	29 Mar 51	Non-ILO Labor	131UNTS187	101741

PARTY ONE	PARTY TWO	DATE	TOPIC	CITATION	NUMBER
Italy	Australia	19 Jun 51	Visas	184UNTS185	102447
Italy	Australia	20 Dec 51	Peace/Disarmament	190UNTS223	102566
Italy	Australia	24 May 52	Reparations	161UNTS65	102123
Italy	Australia	27 Aug 53	Other Military	225UNTS47	103086
Italy	Australia	12 Feb 59	Commodity Trade	328UNTS133	104732
Italy	Australia	10 Nov 60	Air Transport	497UNTS247	107271
Italy	Australia	31 Jan 64	Non-ILO Labor	488UNTS197	107129
Italy	Austria	05 Sep 46	Peace/Disarmament	47ITGU295	435027
Italy	Austria	09 Nov 48	Land Transport	51ITGU71	435029
Italy	Austria	09 Nov 48	Land Transport	50ITGU44	435028
Italy	Austria	12 May 49	General Trade	51ITGU201	435030
Italy	Austria	19 May 49	General Trade	50ITGU137	435031
Italy	Austria	04 Oct 50	Finance	50ABGB220	403112
Italy	Austria	30 Dec 50	Non-ILO Labor	54ITGU278	435032
Italy	Austria	02 Aug 51	General Trade	53ITGU78	435033
Italy	Austria	02 Aug 51	Visas	51ABGB253	403113
Italy	Austria	01 Feb 52	Admin Cooperation	54ABGB235	403254
Italy	Austria	01 Feb 52	Patents/Copyrights	54ITGU143	435034
Italy	Austria	01 Feb 52	Patents/Copyrights	53ABGB130	403114
Italy	Austria	14 Mar 52	Admin Cooperation	56ABGB87	403116
Italy	Austria	14 Mar 52	Culture	54ABGB270	403115
Italy	Austria	14 Mar 53	Culture	54ITGU215	435035
Italy	Austria	10 Jul 54	Admin Cooperation	55ITGU75	435036
Italy	Austria	16 Jul 54	Admin Cooperation	67ITGU3	435037
Italy	Austria	05 Feb 55	Specific Resources	56ABGB42	403117
Italy	Austria	22 Oct 55	Specific Property	260UNTS327	103716
Italy	Austria	28 Dec 55	Visas	260UNTS345	103718
Italy	Austria	23 Jan 56	Air Transport	393UNTS97	105653
Italy	Austria	07 May 56	Finance	284UNTS351	104147
Italy	Austria	09 May 56	Education	267UNTS227	103845
Italy	Austria	12 Jul 56	Non-ILO Labor	378UNTS249	105426
Italy	Austria	19 Nov 56	Admin Cooperation	284UNTS293	104143
Italy	Austria	22 Apr 63	Visas	491UNTS53	107173
Italy	Austria	24 Oct 63	Mass Media	65ITGU152	435039
Italy	Austria	02 Aug 65	Air Transport	66ITDI118	436040
Italy	Austria	21 Apr 67	Admin Cooperation	72ABGB15	403118
Italy	Austria	24 Apr 68	Culture	68ABGB197	403119
Italy	Belgium	23 Jun 46	Non-ILO Labor	19UNTS65	100305
Italy	Belgium	09 Feb 48	Non-ILO Labor	71UNTS143	100915
Italy	Belgium	30 Apr 48	Non-ILO Labor	36UNTS305	100571
Italy	Belgium	29 Nov 48	Culture	41UNTS3	100641
Italy	Belgium	01 Jan 49	Visas	26UNTS151	100385
Italy	Belgium	30 Dec 49	Visas	51UNTS83	100754
Italy	Belgium	20 Oct 50	Non-ILO Labor	50ITGU296	435041
Italy	Belgium	24 Oct 50	Admin Cooperation	110UNTS39	101499
Italy	Belgium	19 Jan 51	Non-ILO Labor	51ITGU45	435042
Italy	Belgium	19 Jan 51	Non-ILO Labor	51ITGU46	435043
Italy	Belgium	24 Jan 52	Peace/Disarmament	53ITGU51	435046
Italy	Belgium	10 May 52	Non-ILO Labor	54ITGU244	435044
Italy	Belgium	25 Jun 52	Visas	137UNTS239	101855
Italy	Belgium	01 Aug 52	Non-ILO Labor	54ITGU185	435045
Italy	Belgium	22 Sep 52	Customs	157UNTS121	102051
Italy	Belgium	06 Aug 53	Non-ILO Labor	54ITGU123	435047
Italy	Belgium	12 Jul 54	Finance	288UNTS59	104198
Italy	Belgium	09 Dec 57	Non-ILO Labor	58ITGU9	435048
Italy	Belgium	10 Dec 57	Non-ILO Labor	58ITGU19	435049
Italy	Belgium	11 Dec 57	Health/Educ/Welfare	59ITDI245	436050
Italy	Belgium	28 Oct 61	Culture	429UNTS199	106199
Italy	Belgium	06 Apr 62	Admin Cooperation	490UNTS317	107161
Italy	Belgium	21 Feb 64	Health/Educ/Welfare	65ITDI119	436051
Italy	Belgium	23 Apr 65	Privil/Immunities	66ITGU165	435052
Italy	Bolivia	31 Jan 53	Culture	281UNTS181	104079
Italy	Bolivia	06 Dec 60	Visas	62ITDI317	436053
Italy	Brazil	08 Oct 49	Peace/Disarmament	50ITGU195	435054
Italy	Brazil	12 Oct 49	General Amity	1ITMA365	437055

PARTY ONE	PARTY TWO	DATE	TOPIC	CITATION	NUMBER
Italy	Brazil	05 Jul 50	General Economic	51ITGU36	435056
Italy	Brazil	05 Jul 50	General Economic	51ITGU38	435057
Italy	Brazil	25 Jan 51	Air Transport	52ITGU169	435058
Italy	Brazil	24 Nov 54	Dispute Settlement	284UNTS325	104146
Italy	Brazil	04 Oct 57	Taxation	62ITGU240	435059
Italy	Brazil	08 Jan 58	Reparations	362UNTS273	105192
Italy	Brazil	06 Sep 58	Atomic Energy	60ITGU96	435061
Italy	Brazil	06 Sep 58	Milit Servic/Citiz	60ITGU215	435060
Italy	Brazil	06 Sep 58	Culture	62ITGU153	435062
Italy	Brazil	21 Apr 60	Visas	62ITDI319	436063
Italy	Brazil	28 Nov 60	Consul/Citizenship	62ITDI468	436064
Italy	Brazil	09 Dec 60	Health/Educ/Welfare	63ITGU109	435065
Italy	Brazil	06 Sep 63	Patents/Copyrights	64ITDI240	436066
Italy	Brazil	18 Apr 64	Mass Media	65ITDI120	436067
Italy	Bulgaria	19 Dec 50	Customs	52ITGU224	435068
Italy	Bulgaria	25 Feb 58	General Trade	362UNTS291	105194
Italy	Bulgaria	25 Feb 58	Finance	362UNTS279	105193
Italy	Bulgaria	30 May 63	Tech Assistance	64ITDI344	436069
Italy	Bulgaria	10 Dec 65	Water Transport	66ITDI121	436071
Italy	Bulgaria	10 Dec 65	General Trade	66ITDI120	436070
Italy	Bulgaria	20 Sep 66	General Economic	0UNTS0	109964
Italy	Bulgaria	29 Jul 67	Mass Media	631UNTS33	108985
Italy	Bulgaria	11 Jan 68	Land Transport	0UNTS0	110303
Italy	Canada	28 Apr 48	General Economic	231UNTS69	103206
Italy	Canada	30 May 50	Culture	53ITDI80	436072
Italy	Canada	20 Sep 51	Reparations	236UNTS251	103328
Italy	Canada	10 Oct 52	Visas	233UNTS137	103258
Italy	Canada	12 Feb 54	Culture	55ITGU53	435074
Italy	Canada	02 Feb 60	Air Transport	62ITGU22	435075
Italy	Canada	18 Dec 61	Specific Resources	470UNTS153	106807
Italy	Canada	18 Sep 63	Specific Resources	64ITDI245	436076
Italy	Ceylon (Sri Lanka)	23 Apr 57	General Trade	337UNTS115	104820
Italy	Ceylon (Sri Lanka)	01 Jun 59	Air Transport	63ITDI14	436083
Italy	Chad	04 Jun 64	General Aid	65ITDI216	436084
Italy	Chile	24 Mar 49	General Amity	1ITMA525	437085
Italy	Chile	01 Dec 49	Health/Educ/Welfare	1ITMA526	437086
Italy	Chile	04 Jun 56	Milit Servic/Citiz	362UNTS309	105195
Italy	Chile	02 Aug 60	General Aid	62ITDI320	436087
Italy	Chile	30 Jun 65	Water Transport	66ITDI229	436089
Italy	Chile	30 Jun 65	Claims and Debts	66ITDI127	436088
Italy	Colombia	27 Aug 49	General Amity	1ITMA551	437091
Italy	Colombia	19 Jun 52	General Trade	53ITGU77	435092
Italy	Colombia	20 Dec 55	Specif Goods/Equip	260UNTS315	103714
Italy	Colombia	25 May 62	Visas	63ITDI279	436093
Italy	Congo (Zaire)	07 Dec 62	Air Transport	66ITGU211	435094
Italy	Costa Rica	20 Feb 53	General Trade	54ITGU198	435098
Italy	Cuba	30 Jun 47	Peace/Disarmament	47ITGU300	435099
Italy	Cuba	19 Sep 49	General Amity	1ITMA616	437100
Italy	Cuba	18 May 64	Loans and Credits	65ITDI219	436101
Italy	Czechoslovakia	02 Jul 47	Mostfavored Nation	48ITGU167	435077
Italy	Czechoslovakia	25 Feb 48	Admin Cooperation	26UNTS103	100380
Italy	Czechoslovakia	05 May 58	Finance	58ITGU129	435078
Italy	Czechoslovakia	22 Sep 60	Finance	62ITDI470	436079
Italy	Czechoslovakia	02 Oct 62	Admin Cooperation	63ITDI277	436080
Italy	Czechoslovakia	27 Mar 65	Tech Assistance	66ITDI123	436081
Italy	Czechoslovakia	15 Jul 65	General Trade	66ITDI124	436082
Italy	Dahomey	10 Mar 65	Tech Assistance	66ITDI175	436102
Italy	Denmark	01 Jul 50	Patents/Copyrights	133UNTS181	101788
Italy	Denmark	04 Oct 50	General Trade	78UNTS341	101024
Italy	Denmark	04 Oct 50	Finance	78UNTS353	101025
Italy	Denmark	24 Oct 51	General Trade	118UNTS91	101598
Italy	Denmark	28 Oct 52	General Trade	167UNTS125	102202
Italy	Denmark	10 Apr 54	General Trade	196UNTS175	102623
Italy	Denmark	15 Jul 54	Milit Servic/Citiz	250UNTS43	103516
Italy	Denmark	12 May 56	General Trade	260UNTS357	103720

PARTY ONE	PARTY TWO	DATE	TOPIC	CITATION	NUMBER
Italy	Denmark	26 Oct 56	Culture	267UNTS261	103847
Italy	Denmark	12 Jul 57	General Trade	291UNTS169	104251
Italy	Denmark	18 Jul 63	Privil/Immunities	64ITDI252	436103
Italy	Denmark	10 Mar 66	Taxation	0UNTS0	109217
Italy	Denmark	10 Mar 66	Taxation	643UNTS349	109201
Italy	Dominican Republic	27 Sep 49	Peace/Disarmament	51ITGU15	435104
Italy	Dominican Republic	18 Feb 54	General Trade	55ITGU124	435105
Italy	Ecuador	24 Aug 49	General Amity	72UNTS35	100926
Italy	Ecuador	07 Mar 52	Education	55ITGU80	435107
Italy	Ecuador	16 Apr 64	Visas	65ITDI127	436108
Italy	El Salvador	30 Mar 53	General Trade	53ITDI410	436106
Italy	Ethiopia	05 Mar 56	Reparations	267UNTS189	103844
Italy	Eur Space Research	23 May 64	IGO Operations	528UNTS75	107635
Italy	Finland	10 Apr 52	Consul/Citizenship	52ITDI295	436109
Italy	Finland	17 Dec 57	Finance	291UNTS133	104248
Italy	Finland	18 Feb 61	Non-ILO Labor	434UNTS199	106263
Italy	France	29 Nov 47	Peace/Disarmament	48ITGU38	435110
Italy	France	09 Feb 48	Education	50FRJO702	416245
Italy	France	31 Mar 48	Non-ILO Labor	49ITGU157	435111
Italy	France	29 May 48	Patents/Copyrights	49ITGU250	435113
Italy	France	29 May 48	Patents/Copyrights	49ITGU247	435112
Italy	France	03 Feb 49	Air Transport	53ITGU91	435114
Italy	France	30 May 49	Peace/Disarmament	50ITGU89	435115
Italy	France	26 Sep 49	Patents/Copyrights	52ITGU124	435116
Italy	France	04 Nov 49	Culture	52ITGU213	435117
Italy	France	07 Mar 50	Gen Communications	53ITGU296	435118
Italy	France	14 Mar 50	Patents/Copyrights	52ITGU127	435119
Italy	France	20 Jun 50	Other Military	52ITGU203	435121
Italy	France	04 Oct 50	Non-ILO Labor	50ITGU240	435122
Italy	France	29 Jan 51	Visas	52ITGU10	435124
Italy	France	29 Jan 51	Sanitation	52ITGU24	435125
Italy	France	29 Jan 51	Land Transport	52ITGU287	435123
Italy	France	02 Feb 51	General Trade	52ITGU68	435126
Italy	France	21 Mar 51	Non-ILO Labor	53ITGU22	435129
Italy	France	21 Mar 51	Non-ILO Labor	53ITGU22	435128
Italy	France	21 Mar 51	Health/Educ/Welfare	53ITGU22	435127
Italy	France	23 Aug 51	Consul/Citizenship	291UNTS143	104249
Italy	France	22 Mar 52	Consul/Citizenship	52ITDI336	436131
Italy	France	05 Apr 52	Patents/Copyrights	52ITGU127	435132
Italy	France	02 Dec 52	Claims and Debts	53ITGU51	435133
Italy	France	14 Mar 53	Land Transport	284UNTS221	104140
Italy	France	29 Jul 53	Peace/Disarmament	53ITDI289	436134
Italy	France	28 Dec 53	Milit Servic/Citiz	267UNTS89	103836
Italy	France	08 Jan 55	Patents/Copyrights	57ITGU68	435138
Italy	France	08 Jan 55	Patents/Copyrights	57ITGU137	435137
Italy	France	12 Jan 55	Consul/Citizenship	58ITGU99	435139
Italy	France	12 Jan 55	Specific Resources	56ITGU13	435141
Italy	France	12 Jan 55	Admin Cooperation	57ITGU87	435140
Italy	France	14 Feb 56	Culture	57ITGU139	435142
Italy	France	03 Mar 56	Non-ILO Labor	267UNTS181	103843
Italy	France	06 Apr 56	Admin Cooperation	60FRRT15	415246
Italy	France	28 Dec 56	Non-ILO Labor	291UNTS203	104255
Italy	France	11 Jan 57	Non-ILO Labor	59ITDI264	436144
Italy	France	27 Feb 57	Non-ILO Labor	59ITDI264	436145
Italy	France	28 Feb 57	Visas	291UNTS191	104253
Italy	France	29 Jul 57	Patents/Copyrights	291UNTS163	104250
Italy	France	01 Aug 57	Non-ILO Labor	302UNTS221	104360
Italy	France	19 Sep 57	Non-ILO Labor	302UNTS225	104361
Italy	France	08 Nov 57	Mass Media	305UNTS393	104427
Italy	France	25 Jan 58	Non-ILO Labor	58ITGU123	435146
Italy	France	27 Mar 58	Non-ILO Labor	305UNTS409	104428
Italy	France	27 Mar 58	Visas	305UNTS387	104426
Italy	France	29 Oct 58	Taxation	68FRJO1403	416247
Italy	France	30 Oct 58	Visas	363UNTS3	105196
Italy	France	21 Oct 59	General Economic	61ITDI264	436147

PARTY ONE	PARTY TWO	DATE	TOPIC	CITATION	NUMBER
Italy	France	06 Feb 60	Non-ILO Labor	62ITDI325	436151
Italy	France	01 Jun 60	General Military	62ITDI325	436152
Italy	France	14 Sep 60	General Ad Hoc	61ITDI213	436153
Italy	France	18 Dec 61	Culture	62ITDI506	436154
Italy	France	17 Jul 63	Non-ILO Labor	64ITDI254	436156
Italy	France	17 Jul 63	Non-ILO Labor	64ITDI253	436155
Italy	France	11 Oct 63	Land Transport	65ITGU181	435157
Italy	France	28 Apr 64	Territory Boundary	65ITDI128	436158
Italy	France	28 Apr 64	Patents/Copyrights	69FRJO2704	416248
Italy	France	02 Jun 64	Finance	634UNTS117	109056
Italy	France	25 Mar 65	Land Transport	65ITGU193	435159
Italy	France	16 Jul 65	Visas	65FRRT71	415249
Italy	France	29 Oct 65	Taxation	0UNTS0	109445
Italy	France	01 Mar 66	Admin Cooperation	67FRJO1108	416250
Italy	France	03 Jun 66	Visas	66FRRT30	415251
Italy	France	01 Aug 66	Culture	66FRRT40	415252
Italy	France	01 Aug 66	Mass Media	0UNTS0	110728
Italy	France	16 Feb 70	Mass Media	0UNTS0	110729
Italy	Gambia	09 Dec 65	Visas	66ITDI131	436161
Italy	Germany, West	26 Oct 51	Non-ILO Labor	53ITGU90	435162
Italy	Germany, West	30 Apr 52	Patents/Copyrights	52WGBB975	425286
Italy	Germany, West	05 May 53	Non-ILO Labor	53WBGA134	424288
Italy	Germany, West	05 May 53	Non-ILO Labor	267UNTS9	103835
Italy	Germany, West	05 May 53	Non-ILO Labor	54WGBB485	425287
Italy	Germany, West	12 Nov 53	Patents/Copyrights	56WGBB1883	425289
Italy	Germany, West	20 Apr 54	Admin Cooperation	55WGBB108	425290
Italy	Germany, West	28 Jun 54	Loans and Credits	288UNTS83	104199
Italy	Germany, West	18 Oct 55	Commodity Trade	56WBGA17	424291
Italy	Germany, West	22 Dec 55	Other Military	57WGBB1277	425292
Italy	Germany, West	08 Feb 56	Culture	58WGBB77	425293
Italy	Germany, West	19 Apr 56	General Trade	281UNTS195	104080
Italy	Germany, West	04 Jul 57	General Transport	64WBGA97	424294
Italy	Germany, West	12 Jul 57	Finance	291UNTS181	104252
Italy	Germany, West	21 Nov 57	General Amity	59WGBB949	425295
Italy	Germany, West	17 Apr 59	Status of Forces	60WGBB1961	425296
Italy	Germany, West	02 Jun 61	Specif Claim/Waive	63WGBB791	425297
Italy	Germany, West	02 Jun 61	Claims and Debts	63WGBB668	425298
Italy	Germany, West	12 Jul 61	Privil/Immunities	65WGBB843	425299
Italy	Germany, West	12 Jul 62	Non-ILO Labor	63WBGA75	424300
Italy	Germany, West	27 Jun 63	Non-ILO Labor	63WBGA231	424301
Italy	Germany, West	23 Jul 63	Patents/Copyrights	65WGBB156	425302
Italy	Germany, West	27 Feb 64	Non-ILO Labor	65ITDI129	436177
Italy	Germany, West	20 Dec 64	Dispute Settlement	66ITGU214	435178
Italy	Germany, West	23 Feb 65	Non-ILO Labor	65WBGA63	424303
Italy	Germany, West	27 Jul 66	Commodity Trade	67WBGA81	424304
Italy	Germany, West	19 Oct 67	Specif Claim/Waive	67WGBB1997	425305
Italy	Germany, West	17 Sep 68	Taxation	70WGBB723	425307
Italy	Germany, West	05 Nov 68	Non-ILO Labor	70WGBB797	425308
Italy	Germany, West	17 Jul 69	Admin Cooperation	69WBGA197	424309
Italy	Ghana	20 Jun 63	Air Transport	65ITGU193	435180
Italy	Greece	21 Sep 48	Culture	77UNTS259	101003
Italy	Greece	05 Nov 48	General Amity	50ITGU265	435195
Italy	Greece	05 Nov 48	Admin Cooperation	51ITGU205	435196
Italy	Greece	31 Aug 49	Reparations	78UNTS89	101014
Italy	Greece	05 Jul 52	Visas	187UNTS157	102508
Italy	Greece	04 Feb 53	General Trade	189UNTS269	102551
Italy	Greece	04 Feb 53	Finance	189UNTS295	102552
Italy	Greece	03 Dec 53	General Economic	53ITDI374	436197
Italy	Greece	11 Sep 54	Culture	284UNTS313	104145
Italy	Greece	10 Nov 54	General Trade	227UNTS9	103128
Italy	Greece	26 May 56	Air Transport	496UNTS301	107258
Italy	Greece	02 Aug 57	Air Transport	533UNTS217	107744
Italy	Greece	20 Jun 62	General Trade	62ITDI289	436198
Italy	Greece	26 Jun 65	Finance	66ITDI138	436199
Italy	Guatemala	10 Sep 49	General Amity	102UNTS53	101410

PARTY ONE	PARTY TWO	DATE	TOPIC	CITATION	NUMBER
Italy	Guinea	30 Oct 62	Air Transport	65ITGU280	435200
Italy	Guinea	20 Feb 64	Claims and Debts	65ITDI130	436202
Italy	Guinea	20 Feb 64	Tech Assistance	65ITDI191	436201
Italy	Guinea	29 Oct 64	Water Transport	65ITDI131	436203
Italy	Haiti	14 Jun 54	General Economic	267UNTS97	103837
Italy	Honduras	12 May 47	Peace/Disarmament	47ITGU140	435204
Italy	Hungary	28 Mar 50	Customs	52ITGU68	435415
Italy	Hungary	17 Dec 57	Finance	58ITGU19	435416
Italy	Hungary	21 Sep 61	General Economic	66ITDI247	436417
Italy	IAEA (Atom Energy)	11 Oct 63	IGO Establishment	639UNTS25	109142
Italy	IBRD (World Bank)	10 Oct 51	IBRD Project	159UNTS383	200482
Italy	IBRD (World Bank)	06 Oct 53	IBRD Project	301UNTS135	104344
Italy	IBRD (World Bank)	01 Jun 55	IBRD Project	358UNTS203	105137
Italy	IBRD (World Bank)	11 Oct 56	IBRD Project	359UNTS3	105138
Italy	IBRD (World Bank)	28 Feb 58	IBRD Project	359UNTS47	105139
Italy	IBRD (World Bank)	21 Apr 59	IBRD Project	359UNTS191	105143
Italy	IBRD (World Bank)	16 Sep 59	IBRD Project	375UNTS159	105366
Italy	IBRD (World Bank)	28 Jun 65	IBRD Project	567UNTS127	108254
Italy	ILO (Labor Org)	04 Sep 52	Tech Assistance	178UNTS371	200505
Italy	ILO (Labor Org)	24 Oct 64	IGO Establishment	541UNTS217	107871
Italy	India	27 Aug 53	Other Military	275UNTS279	103987
Italy	India	16 Jul 59	Air Transport	464UNTS129	106714
Italy	India	06 Oct 59	General Trade	378UNTS267	105427
Italy	India	20 Aug 64	General Amity	66ITGU218	435206
Italy	Indonesia	19 Apr 63	Admin Cooperation	64ITDI260	436207
Italy	Iran	24 Sep 50	General Amity	281UNTS157	104077
Italy	Iran	26 Jan 55	General Trade	57ITGU149	435208
Italy	Iran	29 Jan 58	Finance	302UNTS181	104358
Italy	Iran	29 Jan 58	General Economic	58ITGU39	435210
Italy	Iran	07 May 58	General Trade	60ITDI329	436211
Italy	Iran	29 Nov 58	Culture	0IRTB43	433062
Italy	Iran	25 Jul 59	Visas	61ITDI281	436213
Italy	Iran	28 Jun 69	Visas	0IRTB43	433063
Italy	Iran	07 Oct 69	Taxation	0IRTB43	433064
Italy	Iran	27 Sep 70	Scientific Project	0IRTB44	433065
Italy	Iraq	30 Sep 63	Tech Assistance	64ITDI264	436215
Italy	Iraq	30 Sep 63	General Trade	64ITDI261	436214
Italy	Ireland	21 Nov 47	Air Transport	353UNTS73	105038
Italy	Ireland	28 Nov 49	Visas	553UNTS105	108074
Italy	Ireland	27 Jul 53	General Trade	558UNTS237	108144
Italy	Ireland	15 Nov 57	Air Transport	59ITDI320	436216
Italy	Ireland	18 May 60	Visas	62ITDI327	436217
Italy	Israel	08 Nov 51	Mostfavored·Nation	219UNTS293	102980
Italy	Israel	22 May 53	Mostfavored Nation	219UNTS297	102981
Italy	Israel	05 Mar 54	General Trade	55ITGU17	435218
Italy	Israel	28 Jun 54	Dispute Settlement	56ITGU292	435219
Italy	Israel	10 Jun 55	Taxation	280UNTS219	104061
Italy	Israel	24 Feb 56	Extradition	316UNTS97	104580
Italy	Israel	30 Aug 61	Visas	484UNTS197	107029
Italy	Japan	05 Dec 53	General Military	53ITDI336	436181
Italy	Japan	31 Jul 54	Culture	55ITGU286	435182
Italy	Japan	11 Jan 56	Visas	267UNTS175	103842
Italy	Japan	31 Jan 62	Air Transport	498UNTS23	107276
Italy	Japan	15 Mar 63	Visas	64ITDI258	436183
Italy	Japan	22 Oct 69	Commodity Trade	69JJS259	442253
Italy	Jordan	24 Apr 52	General Amity	281UNTS167	104078
Italy	Jordan	25 Mar 63	Air Transport	64ITDI258	436184
Italy	Jordan	26 May 65	Air Transport	66ITDI265	436185
Italy	Korea, South	07 Mar 61	Patents/Copyrights	62ITDI497	436095
Italy	Korea, South	21 Nov 61	General Economic	62ITDI577	436096
Italy	Lebanon	24 Jan 49	Air Transport	231UNTS241	103223
Italy	Lebanon	15 Feb 49	General Amity	51ITGU106	435257
Italy	Lebanon	15 Feb 49	Admin Cooperation	50ITGU187	435256
Italy	Lebanon	04 Nov 55	General Trade	267UNTS113	103838
Italy	Lebanon	04 Nov 55	Tech Assistance	267UNTS147	103840

PARTY ONE	PARTY TWO	DATE	TOPIC	CITATION	NUMBER
Italy	Lebanon	13 Feb 60	Air Transport	62ITDI353	436258
Italy	Libya	02 Oct 56	Tech Assistance	57ITGU237	435259
Italy	Libya	25 Jan 63	General Trade	61ITDI272	436260
Italy	Luxembourg	06 Apr 48	Non-ILO Labor	49ITGU166	435261
Italy	Luxembourg	29 May 51	Non-ILO Labor	54ITGU194	435262
Italy	Luxembourg	05 Jun 54	Reparations	55ITGU162	435263
Italy	Luxembourg	03 May 56	Culture	58ITGU121	435265
Italy	Luxembourg	16 Jan 57	Non-ILO Labor	59ITDI347	436266
Italy	Malagasy	01 Jul 64	General Economic	65ITDI195	436267
Italy	Malagasy	01 Jul 64	Tech Assistance	65ITDI197	436268
Italy	Mali	03 Jun 64	Tech Assistance	65ITDI142	436269
Italy	Malta	23 Oct 65	Visas	550UNTS337	108028
Italy	Mexico	15 Sep 49	General Trade	52ITGU69	435273
Italy	Mexico	30 Mar 65	Commodity Trade	66ITDI142	436274
Italy	Mexico	07 Jun 65	Visas	66ITDI143	436275
Italy	Mexico	20 Jul 65	IGO Establishment	66ITDI144	436276
Italy	Mexico	08 Dec 65	Tech Assistance	66ITDI146	436277
Italy	Mexico	08 Dec 65	Loans and Credits	66ITDI147	436278
Italy	Mexico	23 Dec 65	Air Transport	66ITDI210	436279
Italy	Monaco	04 Dec 51	Reparations	52ITGU226	435280
Italy	Monaco	01 Jun 57	Visas	291UNTS197	104254
Italy	Monaco	06 Dec 57	Non-ILO Labor	363UNTS59	105199
Italy	Monaco	06 Dec 57	Non-ILO Labor	363UNTS45	105198
Italy	Monaco	08 Apr 58	Visas	60ITDI263	436281
Italy	Monaco	11 Oct 61	Non-ILO Labor	63ITGU122	435282
Italy	Monaco	02 Apr 64	Non-ILO Labor	65ITDI131	436283
Italy	Morocco	24 Jun 58	General Trade	363UNTS23	105197
Italy	Morocco	25 Nov 60	Visas	62ITDI356	436270
Italy	Morocco	28 Jan 61	General Trade	62ITDI511	436271
Italy	Morocco	10 Feb 61	Tech Assistance	62ITDI513	436272
Italy	Multilateral	27 Mar 41	Military Mission	67UNTS231	200222
Italy	Multilateral	19 Apr 44	Scientific Project	89UNTS279	200257
Italy	Multilateral	02 Aug 44	Scientific Project	67UNTS221	200221
Italy	Multilateral	07 Dec 44	IGO Establishment	15UNTS295	200102
Italy	Multilateral	15 Dec 44	Sanitation	17UNTS305	200110
Italy	Multilateral	15 Dec 44	Sanitation	16UNTS247	200106
Italy	Multilateral	14 Jan 46	Reparations	555UNTS69	108105
Italy	Multilateral	23 Apr 46	Sanitation	16UNTS179	100257
Italy	Multilateral	23 Apr 46	Sanitation	17UNTS3	100265
Italy	Multilateral	22 Jul 46	IGO Establishment	14UNTS185	100221
Italy	Multilateral	22 Jul 46	IGO Establishment	9UNTS3	100125
Italy	Multilateral	15 Oct 46	Refugees	11UNTS73	100150
Italy	Multilateral	11 Dec 46	Sanitation	12UNTS179	100186
Italy	Multilateral	15 Dec 46	IGO Establishment	18UNTS3	100283
Italy	Multilateral	08 Feb 47	Patents/Copyrights	14UNTS287	100222
Italy	Multilateral	10 Feb 47	Peace/Disarmament	49UNTS3	100747
Italy	Multilateral	27 May 47	Air Transport	418UNTS161	106021
Italy	Multilateral	14 Aug 47	Reparations	138UNTS111	101863
Italy	Multilateral	02 Oct 47	Telecommunications	193UNTS188	102616
Italy	Multilateral	10 Oct 47	Claims and Debts	54UNTS193	100804
Italy	Multilateral	11 Oct 47	IGO Establishment	77UNTS143	100998
Italy	Multilateral	12 Nov 47	Admin Cooperation	53UNTS39	100771
Italy	Multilateral	12 Nov 47	Admin Cooperation	46UNTS201	100710
Italy	Multilateral	12 Nov 47	Admin Cooperation	46UNTS169	100709
Italy	Multilateral	18 Nov 47	Finance	17UNTS89	100269
Italy	Multilateral	16 Dec 47	Reparations	82UNTS237	101096
Italy	Multilateral	06 Mar 48	Water Transport	289UNTS3	104214
Italy	Multilateral	17 Mar 48	General Military	19UNTS51	100304
Italy	Multilateral	10 May 48	Culture	289UNTS111	104215
Italy	Multilateral	10 Jun 48	Humanitarian	164UNTS113	102163
Italy	Multilateral	10 Jun 48	Humanitarian	191UNTS3	102576
Italy	Multilateral	19 Jun 48	Air Transport	310UNTS151	104492
Italy	Multilateral	26 Jun 48	Culture	331UNTS217	104757
Italy	Multilateral	24 Jul 48	Sanitation	66UNTS25	100847
Italy	Multilateral	17 Sep 48	Telecommunications	97UNTS31	101345

PARTY ONE	PARTY TWO	DATE	TOPIC	CITATION	NUMBER
Italy	Multilateral	19 Nov 48	Sanitation	44UNTS277	100688
Italy	Multilateral	29 Nov 48	IGO Establishment	120UNTS13	101613
Italy	Multilateral	09 Dec 48	Humanitarian	78UNTS277	101021
Italy	Multilateral	09 Dec 48	Scientific Project	73UNTS39	100942
Italy	Multilateral	08 Feb 49	Specific Resources	157UNTS157	102053
Italy	Multilateral	23 Mar 49	Commodity Trade	203UNTS179	102746
Italy	Multilateral	04 Apr 49	General Military	34UNTS243	100541
Italy	Multilateral	04 May 49	Admin Cooperation	92UNTS19	101257
Italy	Multilateral	04 May 49	Admin Cooperation	98UNTS101	101358
Italy	Multilateral	04 May 49	Admin Cooperation	47UNTS159	100728
Italy	Multilateral	04 May 49	Admin Cooperation	30UNTS3	100445
Italy	Multilateral	04 May 49	Admin Cooperation	30UNTS23	100446
Italy	Multilateral	05 May 49	IGO Establishment	87UNTS103	101168
Italy	Multilateral	16 Jun 49	Land Transport	45UNTS149	100696
Italy	Multilateral	12 Aug 49	Humanitarian	75UNTS31	100970
Italy	Multilateral	12 Aug 49	General Military	75UNTS135	100972
Italy	Multilateral	12 Aug 49	Humanitarian	75UNTS287	100973
Italy	Multilateral	12 Aug 49	Humanitarian	75UNTS85	100971
Italy	Multilateral	02 Sep 49	IGO Status/Immunit	250UNTS12	103515
Italy	Multilateral	19 Sep 49	Land Transport	125UNTS3	101671
Italy	Multilateral	24 Sep 49	IGO Establishment	126UNTS237	101691
Italy	Multilateral	16 Dec 49	Admin Cooperation	72UNTS3	100924
Italy	Multilateral	06 Apr 50	Admin Cooperation	119UNTS99	101610
Italy	Multilateral	17 Apr 50	Visas	131UNTS99	101738
Italy	Multilateral	17 Apr 50	Non-ILO Labor	126UNTS285	101694
Italy	Multilateral	13 May 50	Land Transport	128UNTS171	101719
Italy	Multilateral	04 Nov 50	Humanitarian	213UNTS221	102889
Italy	Multilateral	22 Nov 50	Culture	131UNTS25	101734
Italy	Multilateral	29 Nov 50	Patents/Copyrights	88UNTS221	101194
Italy	Multilateral	07 Dec 50	Admin Cooperation	212UNTS17	102861
Italy	Multilateral	15 Dec 50	IGO Operations	160UNTS267	102111
Italy	Multilateral	15 Dec 50	Customs	347UNTS127	104994
Italy	Multilateral	15 Dec 50	Customs	171UNTS305	102234
Italy	Multilateral	15 Dec 50	Customs	157UNTS129	102052
Italy	Multilateral	18 Apr 51	IGO Establishment	261UNTS140	103729
Italy	Multilateral	25 May 51	Status of Forces	175UNTS215	102303
Italy	Multilateral	19 Jun 51	Status of Forces	199UNTS67	102678
Italy	Multilateral	02 Jul 51	Refugees	189UNTS137	102545
Italy	Multilateral	27 Jul 51	Tech Assistance	97UNTS291	200273
Italy	Multilateral	20 Sep 51	IGO Status/Immunit	200UNTS3	102691
Italy	Multilateral	09 Oct 51	IGO Establishment	220UNTS121	102997
Italy	Multilateral	06 Dec 51	Admin Cooperation	150UNTS67	101963
Italy	Multilateral	06 Dec 51	IGO Establishment	425UNTS61	106119
Italy	Multilateral	10 Jan 52	Visas	163UNTS27	102139
Italy	Multilateral	10 Jan 52	Visas	163UNTS3	102138
Italy	Multilateral	15 Feb 52	Scientific Project	132UNTS51	101751
Italy	Multilateral	09 May 52	Milit Occupation	168UNTS65	102213
Italy	Multilateral	10 May 52	Admin Cooperation	439UNTS217	106331
Italy	Multilateral	10 May 52	Admin Cooperation	439UNTS193	106330
Italy	Multilateral	10 May 52	Taxation	439UNTS233	106332
Italy	Multilateral	20 May 52	Sanitation	219UNTS55	102966
Italy	Multilateral	11 Jul 52	IGO Establishment	169UNTS3	102220
Italy	Multilateral	11 Jul 52	Postal Service	171UNTS89	102225
Italy	Multilateral	11 Jul 52	Postal Service	171UNTS3	102224
Italy	Multilateral	11 Jul 52	Postal Service	170UNTS63	102222
Italy	Multilateral	11 Jul 52	Postal Service	170UNTS269	102223
Italy	Multilateral	11 Ju' 52	Postal Service	170UNTS3	102221
Italy	Multilateral	11 Jul 52	Postal Service	171UNTS143	102226
Italy	Multilateral	06 Sep 52	Patents/Copyrights	216UNTS132	102937
Italy	Multilateral	07 Oct 52	Admin Cooperation	310UNTS181	104493
Italy	Multilateral	07 Nov 52	General Trade	221UNTS255	103010
Italy	Multilateral	10 Nov 52	Admin Cooperation	214UNTS265	102904
Italy	Multilateral	30 Apr 53	Admin Cooperation	175UNTS89	102297
Italy	Multilateral	11 May 53	Sanitation	456UNTS3	106555
Italy	Multilateral	01 Jul 53	IGO Establishment	200UNTS149	102701

PARTY ONE	PARTY TWO	DATE	TOPIC	CITATION	NUMBER
Italy	Multilateral	27 Aug 53	Other Military	213UNTS137	102884
Italy	Multilateral	17 Oct 53	General Transport	184UNTS42	102438
Italy	Multilateral	19 Oct 53	IGO Establishment	207UNTS189	102807
Italy	Multilateral	26 Oct 53	Status of Forces	207UNTS237	102809
Italy	Multilateral	07 Dec 53	Admin Cooperation	182UNTS51	102422
Italy	Multilateral	11 Dec 53	Non-ILO Labor	218UNTS211	102957
Italy	Multilateral	11 Dec 53	Patents/Copyrights	218UNTS27	102952
Italy	Multilateral	11 Dec 53	Non-ILO Labor	218UNTS255	102958
Italy	Multilateral	11 Dec 53	Sanitation	191UNTS285	102588
Italy	Multilateral	11 Dec 53	Non-ILO Labor	218UNTS153	102956
Italy	Multilateral	11 Dec 53	Education	218UNTS125	102954
Italy	Multilateral	19 Feb 54	Status of Forces	214UNTS51	102899
Italy	Multilateral	25 Feb 54	Air Transport	215UNTS249	102922
Italy	Multilateral	01 Mar 54	Commodity Trade	256UNTS31	103622
Italy	Multilateral	01 Mar 54	Admin Cooperation	286UNTS265	104173
Italy	Multilateral	12 May 54	Admin Cooperation	327UNTS3	104714
Italy	Multilateral	14 May 54	Culture	249UNTS215	103511
Italy	Multilateral	04 Jun 54	Customs	282UNTS249	104101
Italy	Multilateral	04 Jun 54	Customs	276UNTS191	103992
Italy	Multilateral	14 Jun 54	Air Transport	320UNTS217	104644
Italy	Multilateral	14 Jun 54	Air Transport	320UNTS209	104643
Italy	Multilateral	28 Sep 54	Refugees	360UNTS117	105158
Italy	Multilateral	05 Oct 54	Territory Boundary	235UNTS99	103297
Italy	Multilateral	19 Dec 54	Culture	218UNTS139	102955
Italy	Multilateral	19 Dec 54	Patents/Copyrights	218UNTS51	102953
Italy	Multilateral	21 Dec 54	General Amity	258UNTS322	103678
Italy	Multilateral	06 Apr 55	General Amity	261UNTS55	103725
Italy	Multilateral	01 May 55	Admin Cooperation	0UNTS0	110416
Italy	Multilateral	25 May 55	IGO Establishment	264UNTS117	103791
Italy	Multilateral	06 Jun 55	IGO Establishment	219UNTS79	102968
Italy	Multilateral	22 Jun 55	Atomic Energy	249UNTS3	103498
Italy	Multilateral	28 Sep 55	Air Transport	478UNTS371	106943
Italy	Multilateral	12 Oct 55	IGO Establishment	560UNTS3	108165
Italy	Multilateral	20 Oct 55	IGO Establishment	378UNTS159	105425
Italy	Multilateral	13 Dec 55	Humanitarian	250UNTS3	103514
Italy	Multilateral	13 Dec 55	IGO Operations	529UNTS141	107660
Italy	Multilateral	04 Jan 56	Scientific Project	256UNTS171	103627
Italy	Multilateral	01 Mar 56	Customs	343UNTS129	104923
Italy	Multilateral	25 Apr 56	Commodity Trade	270UNTS103	103896
Italy	Multilateral	30 Apr 56	Air Transport	310UNTS229	104494
Italy	Multilateral	18 May 56	Customs	338UNTS103	104834
Italy	Multilateral	18 May 56	Customs	327UNTS123	104721
Italy	Multilateral	18 May 56	Customs	319UNTS21	104630
Italy	Multilateral	19 May 56	Land Transport	399UNTS189	105742
Italy	Multilateral	20 Jun 56	Admin Cooperation	268UNTS3	103850
Italy	Multilateral	05 Jul 56	Patents/Copyrights	258UNTS371	103679
Italy	Multilateral	09 Jul 56	Non-ILO Labor	314UNTS3	104539
Italy	Multilateral	07 Sep 56	Humanitarian	266UNTS3	103822
Italy	Multilateral	25 Sep 56	Air Transport	334UNTS13	104766
Italy	Multilateral	25 Sep 56	Air Transport	334UNTS89	104767
Italy	Multilateral	24 Oct 56	Admin Cooperation	510UNTS161	107412
Italy	Multilateral	26 Oct 56	IGO Establishment	276UNTS3	103988
Italy	Multilateral	29 Oct 56	Territory Boundary	263UNTS165	103772
Italy	Multilateral	15 Dec 56	Education	278UNTS73	104023
Italy	Multilateral	25 Mar 57	IGO Establishment	294UNTS259	104301
Italy	Multilateral	25 Mar 57	IGO Establishment	294UNTS2	104300
Italy	Multilateral	25 Mar 57	IGO Status/Immunit	294UNTS411	104302
Italy	Multilateral	29 Mar 57	Claims and Debts	283UNTS137	104113
Italy	Multilateral	12 Apr 57	Education	443UNTS128	106362
Italy	Multilateral	29 Apr 57	Dispute Settlement	320UNTS243	104646
Italy	Multilateral	15 Jun 57	Patents/Copyrights	583UNTS3	108470
Italy	Multilateral	15 Jun 57	General Trade	550UNTS45	108008
Italy	Multilateral	26 Jul 57	Land Transport	386UNTS3	105535
Italy	Multilateral	30 Sep 57	General Transport	619UNTS77	108940
Italy	Multilateral	03 Oct 57	Postal Service	366UNTS141	105217

PARTY ONE	PARTY TWO	DATE	TOPIC	CITATION	NUMBER
Italy	Multilateral	03 Oct 57	Postal Service	365UNTS3	105213
Italy	Multilateral	03 Oct 57	Postal Service	366UNTS255	105219
Italy	Multilateral	03 Oct 57	Postal Service	364UNTS331	105212
Italy	Multilateral	03 Oct 57	Postal Service	364UNTS3	105211
Italy	Multilateral	03 Oct 57	Postal Service	366UNTS193	105218
Italy	Multilateral	03 Oct 57	Postal Service	366UNTS87	105216
Italy	Multilateral	03 Oct 57	Postal Service	366UNTS3	105215
Italy	Multilateral	03 Oct 57	Postal Service	365UNTS207	105214
Italy	Multilateral	25 Nov 57	General Trade	403UNTS169	105795
Italy	Multilateral	13 Dec 57	Extradition	359UNTS273	105146
Italy	Multilateral	13 Dec 57	Visas	315UNTS139	104565
Italy	Multilateral	13 Dec 57	Land Transport	372UNTS159	105296
Italy	Multilateral	15 Jan 58	Customs	383UNTS229	105503
Italy	Multilateral	20 Mar 58	Admin Cooperation	335UNTS211	104789
Italy	Multilateral	31 Mar 58	Specific Property	320UNTS103	104639
Italy	Multilateral	03 Apr 58	Commodity Trade	336UNTS177	104806
Italy	Multilateral	03 Apr 58	Commodity Trade	302UNTS121	104355
Italy	Multilateral	15 Apr 58	Health/Educ/Welfare	539UNTS27	107822
Italy	Multilateral	29 Apr 58	Territory Boundary	516UNTS205	107477
Italy	Multilateral	01 Dec 58	Commodity Trade	385UNTS137	105534
Italy	Multilateral	03 Dec 58	Admin Cooperation	416UNTS51	105995
Italy	Multilateral	03 Dec 58	Admin Cooperation	398UNTS9	105715
Italy	Multilateral	15 Dec 58	Mass Media	546UNTS235	107950
Italy	Multilateral	15 Dec 58	Sanitation	351UNTS159	105022
Italy	Multilateral	15 Jan 59	Customs	348UNTS13	104996
Italy	Multilateral	06 Apr 59	Commodity Trade	349UNTS167	105013
Italy	Multilateral	20 Apr 59	Admin Cooperation	472UNTS185	106841
Italy	Multilateral	20 Apr 59	Visas	376UNTS85	105375
Italy	Multilateral	11 May 59	Claims and Debts	527UNTS145	107623
Italy	Multilateral	19 Nov 59	IGO Operations	410UNTS156	105902
Italy	Multilateral	14 Dec 59	Admin Cooperation	444UNTS193	106369
Italy	Multilateral	26 Jan 60	IGO Establishment	439UNTS249	106333
Italy	Multilateral	22 Apr 60	Air Transport	418UNTS211	106023
Italy	Multilateral	28 Apr 60	Health/Educ/Welfare	376UNTS111	105377
Italy	Multilateral	17 Jun 60	Humanitarian	536UNTS27	107794
Italy	Multilateral	22 Jun 60	Mass Media	546UNTS247	107951
Italy	Multilateral	01 Sep 60	Commodity Trade	403UNTS3	105792
Italy	Multilateral	21 Sep 60	Patents/Copyrights	394UNTS3	105664
Italy	Multilateral	06 Oct 60	Customs	473UNTS131	106861
Italy	Multilateral	01 Dec 60	Scientific Project	414UNTS110	105970
Italy	Multilateral	09 Dec 60	Customs	429UNTS211	106200
Italy	Multilateral	30 Mar 61	Sanitation	520UNTS151	107515
Italy	Multilateral	18 Apr 61	Consul/Citizenship	500UNTS95	107310
Italy	Multilateral	18 Apr 61	Consul/Citizenship	500UNTS223	107311
Italy	Multilateral	18 Apr 61	Dispute Settlement	500UNTS243	107312
Italy	Multilateral	21 Apr 61	IGO Establishment	484UNTS349	107041
Italy	Multilateral	08 Jun 61	Customs	473UNTS187	106863
Italy	Multilateral	08 Jun 61	Customs	473UNTS153	106862
Italy	Multilateral	21 Jun 61	IGO Establishment	514UNTS209	107449
Italy	Multilateral	05 Oct 61	Dispute Settlement	510UNTS175	107413
Italy	Multilateral	05 Oct 61	Patents/Copyrights	527UNTS181	107625
Italy	Multilateral	18 Oct 61	IGO Establishment	529UNTS89	107659
Italy	Multilateral	26 Oct 61	Patents/Copyrights	496UNTS43	107247
Italy	Multilateral	06 Dec 61	Customs	473UNTS219	106864
Italy	Multilateral	16 Dec 61	Visas	544UNTS19	107909
Italy	Multilateral	20 Feb 62	Water Transport	597UNTS159	108644
Italy	Multilateral	07 Mar 62	Commodity Trade	445UNTS199	106388
Italy	Multilateral	07 Mar 62	Commodity Trade	445UNTS205	106389
Italy	Multilateral	29 Mar 62	IGO Establishment	507UNTS177	107401
Italy	Multilateral	09 May 62	IGO Establishment	453UNTS299	106531
Italy	Multilateral	14 May 62	Sanitation	544UNTS81	107911
Italy	Multilateral	14 May 62	Scientific Project	544UNTS39	107910
Italy	Multilateral	15 May 62	Commodity Trade	444UNTS3	106367
Italy	Multilateral	14 Jun 62	IGO Establishment	528UNTS33	107634
Italy	Multilateral	28 Sep 62	IGO Establishment	469UNTS169	106791

PARTY ONE	PARTY TWO	DATE	TOPIC	CITATION	NUMBER
Italy	Multilateral	08 Dec 62	Finance	510UNTS235	107418
Italy	Multilateral	10 Dec 62	Culture	521UNTS231	107525
Italy	Multilateral	17 Dec 62	General Economic	523UNTS93	107555
Italy	Multilateral	17 Dec 62	Sanitation	486UNTS119	107076
Italy	Multilateral	20 Apr 63	IGO Establishment	495UNTS3	107239
Italy	Multilateral	24 Apr 63	Consul/Citizenship	596UNTS487	108640
Italy	Multilateral	24 Apr 63	Consul/Citizenship	596UNTS261	108638
Italy	Multilateral	06 May 63	Consul/Citizenship	634UNTS221	109065
Italy	Multilateral	05 Aug 63	Sanitation	480UNTS43	106964
Italy	Multilateral	14 Sep 63	Air Transport	0UNTS0	110106
Italy	Multilateral	09 Nov 63	Direct Aid	489UNTS209	107141
Italy	Multilateral	09 Mar 64	Specific Resources	581UNTS57	108432
Italy	Multilateral	18 Jun 64	Atomic Energy	542UNTS145	107886
Italy	Multilateral	10 Jul 64	Postal Service	613UNTS3	108850
Italy	Multilateral	10 Jul 64	Postal Service	613UNTS3	108851
Italy	Multilateral	10 Jul 64	Postal Service	613UNTS127	108853
Italy	Multilateral	10 Jul 64	Postal Service	612UNTS3	108847
Italy	Multilateral	10 Jul 64	Postal Service	612UNTS233	108848
Italy	Multilateral	10 Jul 64	Postal Service	613UNTS193	108852
Italy	Multilateral	10 Jul 64	Postal Service	611UNTS105	108845
Italy	Multilateral	10 Jul 64	Postal Service	611UNTS7	108844
Italy	Multilateral	10 Jul 64	Postal Service	611UNTS387	108846
Italy	Multilateral	10 Jul 64	Postal Service	612UNTS361	108849
Italy	Multilateral	20 Aug 64	Telecommunications	514UNTS25	107441
Italy	Multilateral	12 Sep 64	Specific Resources	0UNTS0	109344
Italy	Multilateral	15 Sep 64	General Trade	510UNTS147	107411
Italy	Multilateral	01 Dec 64	Water Transport	550UNTS133	108012
Italy	Multilateral	22 Jan 65	Gen Communications	634UNTS239	109066
Italy	Multilateral	18 Mar 65	Dispute Settlement	575UNTS159	108359
Italy	Multilateral	08 Jul 65	General Trade	597UNTS3	108641
Italy	Multilateral	08 Sep 65	Visas	578UNTS3	108382
Italy	Multilateral	04 Dec 65	IGO Establishment	571UNTS123	108303
Italy	Multilateral	31 Dec 65	Specific Resources	616UNTS317	108904
Italy	Multilateral	05 Apr 66	Water Transport	640UNTS133	109159
Italy	Multilateral	27 Jan 67	Scientific Project	610UNTS205	108843
Italy	Multilateral	24 Apr 67	Humanitarian	634UNTS255	109067
Italy	Multilateral	18 Mar 68	Commodity Trade	0UNTS0	109262
Italy	Multilateral	28 Sep 68	Tech Assistance	0UNTS0	109296
Italy	Multilateral	03 Mar 69	Commodity Trade	0UNTS0	110233
Italy	Multilateral	12 Jan 70	Commodity Trade	0UNTS0	110603
Italy	Multilateral	13 Apr 70	Education	0UNTS0	110793
Italy	Netherlands	04 Dec 48	Non-ILO Labor	46UNTS271	100716
Italy	Netherlands	16 Aug 49	Admin Cooperation	98UNTS21	101357
Italy	Netherlands	04 Mar 50	Air Transport	254UNTS305	103598
Italy	Netherlands	19 May 51	Finance	51NET97	447023
Italy	Netherlands	15 Jun 51	Reparations	150UNTS103	101964
Italy	Netherlands	05 Dec 51	Culture	52ITGU207	435286
Italy	Netherlands	05 Dec 51	Culture	0UNTS0	109323
Italy	Netherlands	22 Sep 52	Reparations	150UNTS113	101965
Italy	Netherlands	28 Oct 52	Non-ILO Labor	289UNTS144	104218
Italy	Netherlands	07 Aug 53	General Trade	53NET95	447041
Italy	Netherlands	21 Dec 53	Visas	189UNTS25	102540
Italy	Netherlands	04 Jun 54	Non-ILO Labor	289UNTS261	104222
Italy	Netherlands	24 Dec 54	Non-ILO Labor	55NET26	447052
Italy	Netherlands	29 Jun 56	Finance	287UNTS193	104185
Italy	Netherlands	24 Jan 57	Taxation	485UNTS67	107047
Italy	Netherlands	17 Apr 59	Admin Cooperation	474UNTS207	106883
Italy	Netherlands	29 Apr 59	Finance	486UNTS387	107089
Italy	Netherlands	22 Oct 59	Visas	61ITDI288	436288
Italy	Netherlands	01 Dec 59	Sanitation	455UNTS241	106545
Italy	Netherlands	08 Dec 59	Land Transport	484UNTS309	107039
Italy	Netherlands	06 Aug 60	Non-ILO Labor	455UNTS259	106546
Italy	Netherlands	24 Jan 61	Milit Servic/Citiz	450UNTS207	106468
Italy	Netherlands	29 May 64	Other Military	541UNTS147	107867
Italy	New Zealand	19 Apr 50	Claims and Debts	67UNTS81	100867

PARTY ONE	PARTY TWO	DATE	TOPIC	CITATION	NUMBER
Italy	New Zealand	20 Dec 51	Peace/Disarmament	150UNTS157	101970
Italy	New Zealand	25 Jan 61	Visas	435UNTS255	106282
Italy	Norway	20 Jul 46	General Trade	30UNTS177	100456
Italy	Norway	20 Jul 46	Finance	17UNTS273	100281
Italy	Norway	19 Nov 49	Finance	47UNTS89	100724
Italy	Norway	19 Nov 49	General Trade	47UNTS75	100723
Italy	Norway	24 Jul 50	Visas	90UNTS187	101236
Italy	Norway	22 Jan 51	Finance	88UNTS339	101202
Italy	Norway	20 Apr 53	General Trade	54ITGU107	435284
Italy	Norway	14 Jun 55	Culture	260UNTS307	103713
Italy	Norway	16 Dec 56	Patents/Copyrights	291UNTS207	104256
Italy	Norway	12 Jun 59	Non-ILO Labor	428UNTS363	106187
Italy	Norway	25 Aug 61	Taxation	475UNTS269	106896
Italy	Norway	29 Apr 66	Taxation	3NORT961	451090
Italy	Pakistan	05 Oct 57	Air Transport	353UNTS91	105039
Italy	Pakistan	10 Jan 61	General Trade	62ITDI516	436290
Italy	Panama	29 Mar 47	Peace/Disarmament	47ITGU127	435291
Italy	Panama	02 Sep 49	General Amity	2ITMA442	437292
Italy	Panama	06 Jan 64	Visas	65ITDI155	436293
Italy	Paraguay	08 Jul 59	Finance	63ITDI293	436295
Italy	Paraguay	08 Jul 59	General Trade	61ITGU76	435294
Italy	Peru	21 Aug 49	General Amity	2ITMA387	437296
Italy	Peru	18 Feb 60	Admin Cooperation	62ITDI362	436298
Italy	Peru	18 Feb 60	Visas	62ITDI361	436297
Italy	Peru	02 Sep 60	Visas	62ITDI363	436299
Italy	Peru	08 Apr 61	Culture	63ITGU36	435300
Italy	Philippines	09 Jul 47	General Amity	44UNTS3	100674
Italy	Philippines	14 Jul 59	Visas	490UNTS237	107157
Italy	Poland	15 Jun 49	General Trade	50ITGU130	435301
Italy	Poland	25 Feb 58	Admin Cooperation	58ITGU105	435303
Italy	Poland	25 Feb 58	Finance	58ITGU105	435302
Italy	Poland	03 Feb 59	Finance	61ITDI382	436304
Italy	Poland	27 Nov 60	Scientific Project	58PZUM132	458080
Italy	Poland	27 Nov 60	Tech Assistance	62ITDI437	436305
Italy	Poland	09 Dec 61	Culture	61PZUM266	458093
Italy	Poland	09 Dec 61	Culture	62ITDI517	436306
Italy	Poland	08 Jun 62	General Trade	63ITDI294	436307
Italy	Poland	29 Dec 62	Customs	63ITDI295	436308
Italy	Poland	25 Feb 65	General Trade	66ITDI150	436309
Italy	Poland	25 Mar 65	Culture	69PZUM213	458119
Italy	Poland	14 Jul 65	General Economic	65PZUM50	458124
Italy	Poland	14 Jul 65	General Economic	66ITDI154	436310
Italy	Poland	13 Jul 68	Land Transport	68PZUM94	458159
Italy	Portugal	05 Apr 50	Air Transport	254UNTS329	103599
Italy	Portugal	04 Jan 57	Visas	59ITDI369	436311
Italy	Romania	25 Nov 50	Customs	52ITGU39	435323
Italy	Romania	28 Jan 58	Finance	302UNTS231	104362
Italy	Romania	16 Jun 64	Scientific Project	558UNTS313	108150
Italy	Romania	14 Apr 65	Sanitation	66ITGU290	435324
Italy	Romania	06 Sep 65	General Economic	604UNTS49	108742
Italy	Romania	08 Aug 67	Culture	642UNTS191	109174
Italy	Romania	08 Aug 67	Culture	642UNTS213	109175
Italy	San Marino	20 Oct 53	Telecommunications	55ITGU45	435328
Italy	San Marino	20 Nov 58	Land Transport	62ITGU6	435329
Italy	San Marino	20 Dec 60	Reparations	62ITGU6	435332
Italy	San Marino	20 Dec 60	Finance	62ITGU6	435311
Italy	San Marino	26 Oct 63	Commodity Trade	66ITGU21	435333
Italy	Senegal	02 Oct 62	Tech Assistance	63ITDI347	436341
Italy	Somalia	01 Jul 60	General Economic	62ITGU148	435345
Italy	Somalia	01 Jul 60	Air Transport	62ITGU148	435347
Italy	Somalia	01 Jul 60	General Amity	62ITGU148	435343
Italy	Somalia	01 Jul 60	Consul/Citizenship	62ITGU148	435344
Italy	Somalia	01 Jul 60	Admin Cooperation	62ITDI366	436346
Italy	Somalia	26 Apr 61	Culture	63ITGU36	435348
Italy	South Africa	01 May 48	Admin Cooperation	225UNTS53	103087

PARTY ONE	PARTY TWO	DATE	TOPIC	CITATION	NUMBER
Italy	South Africa	26 Jun 53	Taxation	211UNTS255	102857
Italy	South Africa	27 Aug 53	Other Military	212UNTS211	102873
Italy	South Africa	20 Dec 53	Postal Service	277UNTS293	104014
Italy	South Africa	21 May 56	Air Transport	255UNTS323	103616
Italy	Spain	20 Jun 47	General Trade	47SPBO2008	460168
Italy	Spain	31 May 49	Air Transport	231UNTS251	103224
Italy	Spain	20 Apr 55	Mass Media	55SPBO505	460169
Italy	Spain	16 Jun 55	General Trade	55SPBO2908	460170
Italy	Spain	11 Aug 55	Culture	267UNTS125	103839
Italy	Spain	13 Apr 56	General Trade	56SPBO3004	460171
Italy	Spain	16 Apr 56	Mass Media	57SPBO102	460172
Italy	Spain	21 Jul 56	Non-ILO Labor	58SPBO1503	460173
Italy	Spain	05 Sep 56	Mass Media	302UNTS195	104359
Italy	Spain	12 Oct 57	Patents/Copyrights	291UNTS229	104258
Italy	Spain	25 Nov 57	Non-ILO Labor	59SPBO1601	460174
Italy	Spain	25 Nov 57	Non-ILO Labor	378UNTS289	105428
Italy	Spain	28 Mar 58	Non-ILO Labor	58SPBO2605	460175
Italy	Spain	08 May 58	General Trade	56SPBO406	460176
Italy	Spain	08 May 58	Finance	58ITGU237	435352
Italy	Spain	28 Aug 58	Customs	60ITDI282	436353
Italy	Spain	14 Mar 59	Non-ILO Labor	59SPBO904	460177
Italy	Spain	28 Jun 60	General Trade	62ITDI370	436354
Italy	Spain	28 Jun 61	Taxation	66ITGU159	435355
Italy	Sudan	22 Jul 65	Tech Assistance	66ITDI243	436360
Italy	Sweden	24 Nov 45	General Trade	45SOFM143	461017
Italy	Sweden	24 Nov 45	Finance	45SOFM146	461018
Italy	Sweden	23 Jun 46	General Trade	46SOFM199	461025
Italy	Sweden	19 Apr 47	Non-ILO Labor	48ITGU27	435361
Italy	Sweden	15 Nov 49	Finance	50SOFM840	461115
Italy	Sweden	15 Nov 49	General Trade	50SOFM817	461114
Italy	Sweden	18 Apr 50	General Trade	50SOFM69	461101
Italy	Sweden	02 Dec 50	General Trade	50SOFM1017	461125
Italy	Sweden	06 Dec 50	Finance	50SOFM1036	461126
Italy	Sweden	18 Jan 52	General Trade	52SOFM103	461158
Italy	Sweden	17 Jun 52	Finance	54ITGU144	435362
Italy	Sweden	27 Nov 53	General Trade	53SOFM1063	461192
Italy	Sweden	25 May 55	Non-ILO Labor	291UNTS235	104259
Italy	Sweden	20 Dec 56	Taxation	369UNTS357	105265
Italy	Sweden	20 Dec 56	Taxation	369UNTS305	105263
Italy	Sweden	14 Apr 58	Admin Cooperation	427UNTS167	106151
Italy	Sweden	29 Oct 64	Non-ILO Labor	65ITDI161	436363
Italy	Switzerland	09 Jul 47	Health/Educ/Welfare	14SWRS526	463145
Italy	Switzerland	22 Jun 48	Non-ILO Labor	48SWRO818	462019
Italy	Switzerland	18 Jun 49	Specific Property	55SWRO611	462037
Italy	Switzerland	24 Mar 50	Water Transport	52ITGU29	435367
Italy	Switzerland	21 Oct 50	General Trade	52ITGU57	435368
Italy	Switzerland	05 Apr 51	Territory Boundary	53SWRO409	462178
Italy	Switzerland	05 Apr 51	Territory Boundary	53SWRO403	462177
Italy	Switzerland	05 Apr 51	Territory Boundary	53ITGU91	435372
Italy	Switzerland	14 May 51	Admin Cooperation	51SWRO644	462031
Italy	Switzerland	17 Oct 51	Non-ILO Labor	54SWRO250	462097
Italy	Switzerland	04 Jul 52	Territory Boundary	55SWRO557	462180
Italy	Switzerland	25 Nov 52	Territory Boundary	55SWRO626	462176
Italy	Switzerland	02 Jul 53	Customs	257UNTS99	103653
Italy	Switzerland	23 Jul 55	Land Transport	284UNTS279	104142
Italy	Switzerland	17 Sep 55	Specific Resources	291UNTS213	104257
Italy	Switzerland	22 Dec 55	Finance	260UNTS339	103717
Italy	Switzerland	02 Feb 56	Sanitation	291UNTS113	104247
Italy	Switzerland	01 Jun 56	Telecommunications	57ITGU159	435376
Italy	Switzerland	04 Jun 56	Air Transport	378UNTS311	105429
Italy	Switzerland	29 Jun 56	Finance	284UNTS299	104144
Italy	Switzerland	31 Oct 56	Taxation	58ITGU50	435377
Italy	Switzerland	22 Dec 56	Taxation	57SWRO44	462020
Italy	Switzerland	01 Apr 57	Loans and Credits	59ITDI411	436378
Italy	Switzerland	27 May 57	Specific Resources	59SWRO432	462036

PARTY ONE	PARTY TWO	DATE	TOPIC	CITATION	NUMBER
Italy	Switzerland	19 Sep 57	Land Transport	363UNTS69	105200
Italy	Switzerland	23 May 58	Land Transport	363UNTS81	105201
Italy	Switzerland	31 Jul 58	Taxation	61SWRO413	462056
Italy	Switzerland	22 Nov 58	Commodity Trade	62ITGU312	435382
Italy	Switzerland	10 Dec 58	Admin Cooperation	60ITDI306	436383
Italy	Switzerland	10 Dec 59	Water Transport	61ITDI298	436384
Italy	Switzerland	04 Mar 60	Land Transport	62ITGU212	435385
Italy	Switzerland	11 Mar 61	Customs	63SWRO711	462075
Italy	Switzerland	25 Apr 61	Commodity Trade	62SWRO189	462144
Italy	Switzerland	16 May 61	Territory Boundary	63SWRO520	462179
Italy	Switzerland	15 Dec 61	Customs	63SWRO724	462064
Italy	Switzerland	16 Apr 62	Land Transport	63ITDI301	436390
Italy	Switzerland	14 Aug 62	Land Transport	63ITDI302	436391
Italy	Switzerland	14 Dec 62	Non-ILO Labor	64SWRO730	462098
Italy	Switzerland	16 Dec 62	General Ad Hoc	63ITDI303	436392
Italy	Switzerland	31 May 63	Customs	64ITDI283	436394
Italy	Switzerland	10 Aug 64	Non-ILO Labor	65ITGU54	435396
Italy	Syria	10 Nov 55	General Trade	267UNTS157	103841
Italy	Syria	28 May 58	Sanitation	60ITDI265	436342
Italy	Taiwan	30 Jul 47	Consul/Citizenship	12UNTS383	100195
Italy	Taiwan	30 Jul 47	Reparations	12UNTS377	100194
Italy	Taiwan	22 Apr 49	General Amity	0CTRC222	413009
Italy	Taiwan	25 Aug 49	General Trade	0CTRC227	413010
Italy	Taiwan	02 Feb 57	General Trade	0CTRC229	413011
Italy	Tanzania	04 Aug 65	Tech Assistance	66ITDI246	436397
Italy	Thailand	30 Dec 55	Visas	260UNTS351	103719
Italy	Tunisia	05 Apr 51	Telecommunications	52ITGU206	435398
Italy	Tunisia	08 Apr 58	General Trade	378UNTS327	105430
Italy	Tunisia	31 Oct 59	General Trade	378UNTS349	105431
Italy	Tunisia	23 Nov 61	Tech Assistance	62ITDI530	436400
Italy	Tunisia	26 Jul 62	Non-ILO Labor	63ITDI397	436403
Italy	Tunisia	26 Jul 62	Non-ILO Labor	63ITDI399	436402
Italy	Tunisia	26 Jul 62	Loans and Credits	63ITDI398	436401
Italy	Turkey	12 Apr 47	General Economic	47TURG109	466073
Italy	Turkey	10 Nov 48	General Economic	50TURG301	466074
Italy	Turkey	25 Nov 49	Air Transport	192UNTS39	102594
Italy	Turkey	24 Mar 50	General Amity	96UNTS207	101338
Italy	Turkey	17 Jul 51	Culture	52ITGU203	435404
Italy	Turkey	22 Oct 51	Visas	52ITDI481	436405
Italy	Turkey	24 Jan 52	General Trade	53ITGU27	435406
Italy	Turkey	29 Jan 55	General Aid	56TURG202	466109
Italy	Turkey	10 Apr 55	Commodity Trade	56TURG409	466076
Italy	Turkey	15 Apr 57	General Trade	58TURG407	466077
Italy	Turkey	29 Nov 58	Direct Aid	60ITDI306	436408
Italy	Turkey	10 Jun 59	Tech Assistance	61ITDI302	436409
Italy	Turkey	21 Jun 63	General Economic	63TURG609	466111
Italy	Turkey	23 Jan 65	Finance	66ITDI159	436411
Italy	Turkey	18 Sep 65	Loans and Credits	66ITDI162	436413
Italy	Turkey	18 Sep 65	Finance	66ITDI161	436412
Italy	Turkey	01 Dec 65	General Trade	66ITDI163	436419
Italy	Turkey	01 Dec 65	General Economic	66ITDI248	436418
Italy	UK Great Britain	16 Jan 47	Non-ILO Labor	48ITGU168	435186
Italy	UK Great Britain	17 Apr 47	Claims and Debts	54UNTS169	100802
Italy	UK Great Britain	17 Apr 47	Finance	54UNTS149	100801
Italy	UK Great Britain	30 May 47	Non-ILO Labor	54UNTS131	100800
Italy	UK Great Britain	06 Dec 47	Visas	82UNTS243	101097
Italy	UK Great Britain	21 Jan 48	Milit Installation	77UNTS23	100989
Italy	UK Great Britain	13 Mar 48	Admin Cooperation	104UNTS41	101435
Italy	UK Great Britain	25 Jun 48	Air Transport	94UNTS239	101313
Italy	UK Great Britain	28 Oct 48	Visas	77UNTS129	100996
Italy	UK Great Britain	14 Jun 49	Specific Property	135UNTS49	101813
Italy	UK Great Britain	20 Mar 50	Territory Boundary	128UNTS201	101721
Italy	UK Great Britain	21 Mar 50	Territory Boundary	128UNTS225	101722
Italy	UK Great Britain	28 Jul 50	Non-ILO Labor	101UNTS25	101399
Italy	UK Great Britain	21 Dec 50	Finance	175UNTS187	102301

PARTY ONE	PARTY TWO	DATE	TOPIC	CITATION	NUMBER
Italy	UK Great Britain	16 Jun 51	Patents/Copyrights	172UNTS293	102253
Italy	UK Great Britain	28 Jun 51	Claims and Debts	118UNTS115	101600
Italy	UK Great Britain	24 Oct 51	Air Transport	118UNTS143	101602
Italy	UK Great Britain	07 Nov 51	Claims and Debts	118UNTS133	101601
Italy	UK Great Britain	12 Nov 51	Specif Claim/Waive	135UNTS55	101814
Italy	UK Great Britain	28 Nov 51	Non-ILO Labor	172UNTS205	102248
Italy	UK Great Britain	28 Nov 51	Culture	172UNTS27	102238
Italy	UK Great Britain	21 Dec 51	Peace/Disarmament	121UNTS89	101628
Italy	UK Great Britain	12 Feb 52	Claims and Debts	126UNTS297	101695
Italy	UK Great Britain	06 Nov 52	Specif Claim/Waive	158UNTS431	102076
Italy	UK Great Britain	13 Apr 53	Reparations	172UNTS271	102251
Italy	UK Great Britain	01 Jun 54	Consul/Citizenship	403UNTS275	105798
Italy	UK Great Britain	01 Jun 54	Admin Cooperation	312UNTS353	104525
Italy	UK Great Britain	29 Jan 57	Non-ILO Labor	326UNTS119	104710
Italy	UK Great Britain	29 Mar 57	Reparations	310UNTS11	104481
Italy	UK Great Britain	12 Jun 57	Non-ILO Labor	310UNTS35	104484
Italy	UK Great Britain	28 Dec 57	Atomic Energy	305UNTS357	104425
Italy	UK Great Britain	09 Sep 58	Non-ILO Labor	60ITDI243	436190
Italy	UK Great Britain	14 Oct 58	Patents/Copyrights	60ITDI245	436191
Italy	UK Great Britain	14 Apr 59	Claims and Debts	343UNTS289	104934
Italy	UK Great Britain	04 Jul 60	Taxation	466UNTS195	106745
Italy	UK Great Britain	06 Mar 61	Visas	404UNTS3	105799
Italy	UK Great Britain	20 Apr 61	Other Military	63ITGU99	435192
Italy	UK Great Britain	23 Oct 61	Admin Cooperation	424UNTS225	106111
Italy	UK Great Britain	01 Sep 65	Taxation	0UNTS0	109284
Italy	UK Great Britain	01 Sep 65	Customs	0UNTS0	109283
Italy	UK Great Britain	15 Feb 66	Taxation	67ITGU230	435194
Italy	UK Great Britain	30 Sep 67	Culture	642UNTS271	109180
Italy	UK Great Britain	15 Feb 68	Taxation	0UNTS0	109263
Italy	UN Special Fund	01 Apr 60	Direct Aid	354UNTS261	105066
Italy	UNICEF (Children)	06 Nov 47	IGO Operations	68UNTS240	200236
Italy	UNICEF (Children)	28 May 56	Direct Aid	243UNTS43	103445
Italy	United Arab Rep	25 May 50	Air Transport	53ITGU67	435313
Italy	United Arab Rep	17 Oct 52	Other Military	52ITDI291	436314
Italy	United Arab Rep	06 Jul 57	Finance	302UNTS147	104357
Italy	United Arab Rep	08 Jan 59	Culture	61ITDI342	436315
Italy	United Arab Rep	08 Jan 59	Admin Cooperation	61ITDI289	436316
Italy	United Arab Rep	08 Jan 59	Claims and Debts	61ITDI289	436317
Italy	United Arab Rep	29 Apr 59	Tech Assistance	363UNTS91	105202
Italy	United Arab Rep	29 Apr 59	General Trade	61ITDI291	436318
Italy	United Arab Rep	19 Apr 61	Specific Resources	62ITDI518	436319
Italy	United Arab Rep	13 Apr 62	Claims and Debts	63ITDI380	436320
Italy	United Arab Rep	23 Mar 65	Claims and Debts	66ITDI231	436322
Italy	United Arab Rep	23 Mar 65	Claims and Debts	66ITGU215	435321
Italy	United Nations	23 Aug 61	IGO Operations	405UNTS3	105819
Italy	United Nations	26 Jul 63	IGO Operations	472UNTS173	106840
Italy	United Nations	18 Mar 64	Education	491UNTS21	107171
Italy	United Nations	23 May 66	IGO Operations	565UNTS11	108231
Italy	United Nations	18 Jan 67	Specif Claim/Waive	588UNTS197	108525
Italy	United Nations	15 Jan 68	Scientific Project	635UNTS11	109070
Italy	Uruguay	26 Feb 47	General Trade	48ITGU82	435426
Italy	USA (United States)	06 Dec 45	General Trade	3UNTS131	100027
Italy	USA (United States)	17 Apr 46	Extradition	206UNTS263	102791
Italy	USA (United States)	24 Sep 46	Other Military	148UNTS323	101942
Italy	USA (United States)	09 Jun 47	Air Transport	104UNTS157	101437
Italy	USA (United States)	04 Jul 47	Direct Aid	22UNTS173	100336
Italy	USA (United States)	14 Aug 47	Reparations	36UNTS53	100566
Italy	USA (United States)	14 Aug 47	Claims and Debts	36UNTS105	100567
Italy	USA (United States)	03 Sep 47	Status of Forces	67UNTS15	100863
Italy	USA (United States)	03 Jan 48	Direct Aid	31UNTS105	100471
Italy	USA (United States)	02 Feb 48	General Amity	79UNTS171	101040
Italy	USA (United States)	06 Feb 48	Air Transport	73UNTS113	100950
Italy	USA (United States)	14 Feb 48	Reparations	67UNTS115	100871
Italy	USA (United States)	28 Jun 48	Direct Aid	20UNTS43	100314
Italy	USA (United States)	28 Jun 48	Milit Occupation	25UNTS45	100356

PARTY ONE	PARTY TWO	DATE	TOPIC	CITATION	NUMBER
Italy	USA (United States)	29 Sep 48	Visas	84UNTS43	101117
Italy	USA (United States)	26 Nov 48	Direct Aid	79UNTS71	101032
Italy	USA (United States)	18 Dec 48	Education	79UNTS133	101037
Italy	USA (United States)	27 Jan 50	Milit Assistance	80UNTS145	101050
Italy	USA (United States)	13 Feb 51	IGO Establishment	148UNTS57	101935
Italy	USA (United States)	16 May 51	Reparations	206UNTS325	102795
Italy	USA (United States)	12 Dec 51	Patents/Copyrights	137UNTS175	101852
Italy	USA (United States)	21 Dec 51	Peace/Disarmament	167UNTS163	102206
Italy	USA (United States)	28 Dec 51	General Economic	157UNTS63	102047
Italy	USA (United States)	07 Jan 52	Milit Assistance	179UNTS165	102365
Italy	USA (United States)	05 Mar 52	Taxation	179UNTS3	102351
Italy	USA (United States)	31 Mar 54	Milit Assistance	235UNTS293	103311
Italy	USA (United States)	27 Apr 54	Milit Assistance	234UNTS103	103275
Italy	USA (United States)	16 Jun 54	Loans and Credits	236UNTS149	103322
Italy	USA (United States)	24 Jun 54	Tech Assistance	235UNTS3	103290
Italy	USA (United States)	28 Jun 54	Tech Assistance	237UNTS121	103340
Italy	USA (United States)	26 Jan 55	Air Transport	238UNTS179	103361
Italy	USA (United States)	11 Feb 55	Direct Aid	241UNTS91	103426
Italy	USA (United States)	11 Feb 55	Milit Assistance	240UNTS87	103396
Italy	USA (United States)	30 Mar 55	Taxation	257UNTS169	103654
Italy	USA (United States)	30 Mar 55	Taxation	257UNTS199	103655
Italy	USA (United States)	19 May 55	Direct Aid	269UNTS83	103876
Italy	USA (United States)	23 May 55	US Agri Commod Aid	251UNTS303	103547
Italy	USA (United States)	30 Jun 55	US Agri Commod Aid	258UNTS15	103667
Italy	USA (United States)	08 Jul 55	Milit Installation	270UNTS29	103889
Italy	USA (United States)	28 Jul 55	Atomic Energy	239UNTS235	103382
Italy	USA (United States)	27 Feb 56	Direct Aid	291UNTS287	104260
Italy	USA (United States)	27 Apr 56	Direct Aid	273UNTS149	103949
Italy	USA (United States)	30 Oct 56	US Agri Commod Aid	263UNTS221	103775
Italy	USA (United States)	29 Mar 57	Reparations	299UNTS157	104311
Italy	USA (United States)	22 Jun 57	Milit Assistance	284UNTS51	104128
Italy	USA (United States)	03 Jul 57	Atomic Energy	308UNTS195	104462
Italy	USA (United States)	07 Mar 58	US Agri Commod Aid	303UNTS205	104381
Italy	USA (United States)	08 May 58	Direct Aid	316UNTS177	104584
Italy	USA (United States)	30 Jul 59	Direct Aid	355UNTS393	105088
Italy	USA (United States)	18 Aug 59	Milit Assistance	361UNTS11	105169
Italy	USA (United States)	07 Jul 60	Milit Assistance	380UNTS143	105455
Italy	USA (United States)	19 Jul 60	Direct Aid	389UNTS237	105595
Italy	USA (United States)	04 Aug 60	Admin Cooperation	62ITDI376	436357
Italy	USA (United States)	03 Dec 60	Atomic Energy	410UNTS3	105893
Italy	USA (United States)	06 Jul 62	Commodity Trade	459UNTS123	106617
Italy	USA (United States)	28 Aug 62	Sanitation	461UNTS137	106657
Italy	USA (United States)	05 Sep 62	Scientific Project	461UNTS185	106663
Italy	USA (United States)	14 Nov 62	Telecommunications	459UNTS197	106622
Italy	USA (United States)	04 Aug 64	General Military	529UNTS205	107662
Italy	USA (United States)	18 Aug 64	Admin Cooperation	0UNTS0	109836
Italy	USA (United States)	18 Aug 64	Admin Cooperation	65ITGU279	435358
Italy	USA (United States)	23 Nov 64	Milit Assistance	532UNTS133	107716
Italy	USA (United States)	16 Dec 65	Specif Claim/Waive	574UNTS139	108346
Italy	USA (United States)	27 Dec 65	Specific Property	574UNTS145	108347
Italy	USA (United States)	12 Jan 66	Reparations	587UNTS309	108515
Italy	USA (United States)	19 Oct 66	Commodity Trade	0UNTS0	109686
Italy	USA (United States)	19 Jun 67	Scientific Project	0UNTS0	109773
Italy	USA (United States)	24 Jun 68	Scientific Project	0UNTS0	110328
Italy	USA (United States)	11 Sep 69	Scientific Project	0UNTS0	110506
Italy	USA (United States)	20 Jun 70	Scientific Project	0UNTS0	110814
Italy	USSR (Soviet Union)	11 Dec 48	General Trade	0SUST255	471028
Italy	USSR (Soviet Union)	11 Dec 48	Reparations	0SUST255	468240
Italy	USSR (Soviet Union)	11 Dec 48	General Trade	0UNTS0	109576
Italy	USSR (Soviet Union)	11 Dec 48	General Economic	217UNTS181	102948
Italy	USSR (Soviet Union)	11 Dec 48	Finance	0SUST255	468241
Italy	USSR (Soviet Union)	11 Dec 48	General Trade	50ITGU5	435420
Italy	USSR (Soviet Union)	28 Dec 57	Finance	58ITGU10	435421
Italy	USSR (Soviet Union)	28 Dec 57	Finance	0UNTS0	109579
Italy	USSR (Soviet Union)	18 Oct 59	Refugees	8SUGG155	469605

PARTY ONE	PARTY TWO	DATE	TOPIC	CITATION	NUMBER
Italy	USSR (Soviet Union)	20 Jan 60	Visas	16SUGG127	469969
Italy	USSR (Soviet Union)	20 Jan 60	Visas	62ITDI382	436422
Italy	USSR (Soviet Union)	09 Feb 60	Visas	9SUGG124	469627
Italy	USSR (Soviet Union)	09 Feb 60	Culture	399UNTS75	105735
Italy	USSR (Soviet Union)	25 Feb 60	Visas	16SUGG127	469972
Italy	USSR (Soviet Union)	30 Jun 60	Patents/Copyrights	62ITDI385	436423
Italy	USSR (Soviet Union)	07 Jun 61	General Trade	10SUGG134	469775
Italy	USSR (Soviet Union)	21 Sep 61	Specif Goods/Equip	10SUGG142	469794
Italy	USSR (Soviet Union)	05 Feb 64	General Trade	65ITDI165	436424
Italy	USSR (Soviet Union)	22 Feb 65	Air Transport	67ITGU231	435425
Italy	USSR (Soviet Union)	16 May 67	Admin Cooperation	608UNTS79	108814
Italy	Vatican/Holy See	16 Apr 45	Territory Boundary	47ITGU169	435335
Italy	Vatican/Holy See	21 Aug 46	Admin Cooperation	60ITMA422	437336
Italy	Vatican/Holy See	31 Apr 47	Territory Boundary	48ITGU190	435337
Italy	Vatican/Holy See	24 Apr 48	Territory Boundary	50ITGU99	435338
Italy	Vatican/Holy See	08 Oct 51	Telecommunications	52ITGU150	435339
Italy	Vatican/Holy See	16 Dec 55	Taxation	260UNTS319	103715
Italy	Vatican/Holy See	31 Jul 62	Finance	64ITGU281	435340
Italy	Venezuela	04 Jul 62	Air Transport	65ITGU194	435427
Italy	Vietnam, South	14 Nov 53	General Trade	0VKNG63	496015
Italy	Yemen	05 Oct 59	General Economic	61ITDI306	436429
Italy	Yemen	03 Oct 63	Admin Cooperation	64ITDI288	436430
Italy	Yugoslavia	03 Feb 49	Visas	33UNTS105	100517
Italy	Yugoslavia	13 Apr 49	Commodity Trade	171UNTS279	102232
Italy	Yugoslavia	23 May 49	Reparations	150UNTS179	101972
Italy	Yugoslavia	23 Dec 50	Admin Cooperation	150UNTS199	101974
Italy	Yugoslavia	23 Dec 50	Admin Cooperation	171UNTS291	102233
Italy	Yugoslavia	23 Dec 50	Reparations	150UNTS213	101975
Italy	Yugoslavia	23 Dec 50	Finance	150UNTS191	101973
Italy	Yugoslavia	23 Dec 50	Peace/Disarmament	55ITGU73	435220
Italy	Yugoslavia	23 Dec 50	Consul/Citizenship	58ITGU136	435223
Italy	Yugoslavia	23 Dec 50	Air Transport	52ITGU142	435222
Italy	Yugoslavia	23 Dec 50	Patents/Copyrights	55ITGU73	435221
Italy	Yugoslavia	18 Dec 54	Peace/Disarmament	284UNTS239	104141
Italy	Yugoslavia	26 Mar 55	Sanitation	379UNTS3	105432
Italy	Yugoslavia	31 Mar 55	General Trade	57ITGU32	435229
Italy	Yugoslavia	31 Mar 55	General Trade	386UNTS317	105551
Italy	Yugoslavia	31 Mar 55	General Trade	57ITGU32	435230
Italy	Yugoslavia	31 Mar 55	Visas	386UNTS307	105550
Italy	Yugoslavia	18 Jul 57	Specific Resources	58ITGU64	435231
Italy	Yugoslavia	03 Aug 57	Finance	59ITDI327	436234
Italy	Yugoslavia	14 Nov 57	Non-ILO Labor	60ITGU210	435232
Italy	Yugoslavia	12 Dec 57	Mass Media	386UNTS293	105549
Italy	Yugoslavia	20 Nov 58	Territory Boundary	379UNTS23	105433
Italy	Yugoslavia	13 Dec 58	Specific Resources	60ITDI345	436235
Italy	Yugoslavia	21 Apr 59	Visas	61ITDI284	436237
Italy	Yugoslavia	05 Oct 59	Land Transport	62ITGU255	435238
Italy	Yugoslavia	12 Feb 60	Other Military	379UNTS77	105434
Italy	Yugoslavia	27 Jul 60	Land Transport	6ITGU6	435024
Italy	Yugoslavia	03 Dec 60	Admin Cooperation	62ITGU237	435243
Italy	Yugoslavia	03 Dec 60	Culture	63ITGU30	435241
Italy	Yugoslavia	03 Dec 60	Consul/Citizenship	63ITGU15	435242
Italy	Yugoslavia	15 Sep 61	Culture	62ITGU80	435244
Italy	Yugoslavia	31 Oct 62	Visas	65ITGU192	435245
Italy	Yugoslavia	23 Dec 63	Visas	64ITDI321	436247
Italy	Yugoslavia	28 Nov 64	General Economic	65ITDI140	436250
Italy	Yugoslavia	28 Nov 64	General Economic	65ITDI194	436249
Italy	Yugoslavia	05 Nov 65	Specific Resources	67ITGU210	435252
Italy	Yugoslavia	10 Nov 65	Admin Cooperation	67ITGU169	435254
Italy	Yugoslavia	10 Nov 65	Admin Cooperation	66ITGU244	435253
ITU (Telecommun)	Multilateral	27 Oct 54	Tech Assistance	201UNTS95	102712
ITU (Telecommun)	Multilateral	04 Apr 55	Tech Assistance	208UNTS239	102816
ITU (Telecommun)	Multilateral	14 Jun 55	Tech Assistance	212UNTS263	200526
ITU (Telecommun)	Multilateral	04 Jul 55	Tech Assistance	214UNTS10	102897
ITU (Telecommun)	Multilateral	13 Dec 55	Tech Assistance	407UNTS8	105857

PARTY ONE	PARTY TWO	DATE	TOPIC	CITATION	NUMBER
ITU (Telecommun)	Multilateral	02 Feb 56	Tech Assistance	227UNTS153	103137
ITU (Telecommun)	Multilateral	10 Feb 56	Tech Assistance	228UNTS189	103151
ITU (Telecommun)	Multilateral	30 Mar 56	IGO Operations	604UNTS114	108748
ITU (Telecommun)	Multilateral	10 May 56	Tech Assistance	243UNTS103	103449
ITU (Telecommun)	Multilateral	31 May 56	Tech Assistance	251UNTS181	103541
ITU (Telecommun)	Multilateral	08 Jun 56	Tech Assistance	247UNTS366	200541
ITU (Telecommun)	Multilateral	12 Jun 56	Tech Assistance	243UNTS187	103453
ITU (Telecommun)	Multilateral	14 Jun 56	Tech Assistance	265UNTS125	103809
ITU (Telecommun)	Multilateral	26 Jun 56	Tech Assistance	253UNTS12	103573
ITU (Telecommun)	Multilateral	26 Jun 56	Tech Assistance	321UNTS2	104650
ITU (Telecommun)	Multilateral	02 Jul 56	Tech Assistance	540UNTS110	107846
ITU (Telecommun)	Multilateral	31 Aug 56	Tech Assistance	249UNTS158	103506
ITU (Telecommun)	Multilateral	05 Oct 56	Tech Assistance	251UNTS245	103544
ITU (Telecommun)	Multilateral	05 Oct 56	Tech Assistance	251UNTS267	103545
ITU (Telecommun)	Multilateral	21 Nov 56	Tech Assistance	253UNTS266	103588
ITU (Telecommun)	Multilateral	15 Jan 57	Tech Assistance	376UNTS122	105378
ITU (Telecommun)	Multilateral	23 Jan 57	Tech Assistance	259UNTS426	103701
ITU (Telecommun)	Multilateral	17 Feb 57	Tech Assistance	271UNTS2	103907
ITU (Telecommun)	Multilateral	01 Mar 57	Tech Assistance	264UNTS94	103790
ITU (Telecommun)	Multilateral	28 Mar 57	Tech Assistance	271UNTS30	103908
ITU (Telecommun)	Multilateral	09 Apr 57	Tech Assistance	274UNTS172	103965
ITU (Telecommun)	Multilateral	24 May 57	Tech Assistance	268UNTS270	103861
ITU (Telecommun)	Multilateral	09 Jul 57	Tech Assistance	274UNTS300	103972
ITU (Telecommun)	Multilateral	05 Nov 57	Tech Assistance	285UNTS301	104155
ITU (Telecommun)	Multilateral	15 Mar 58	Tech Assistance	292UNTS273	104276
ITU (Telecommun)	Multilateral	19 Jun 58	Tech Assistance	306UNTS236	200550
ITU (Telecommun)	Multilateral	09 Oct 59	Tech Assistance	376UNTS382	105391
ITU (Telecommun)	Multilateral	03 Dec 59	Tech Assistance	348UNTS246	105003
ITU (Telecommun)	Multilateral	12 Apr 60	Tech Assistance	359UNTS323	105150
ITU (Telecommun)	Multilateral	04 Jun 60	Tech Assistance	360UNTS208	105159
ITU (Telecommun)	Multilateral	19 Jun 60	IGO Operations	537UNTS214	107803
ITU (Telecommun)	Multilateral	08 Jul 60	Tech Assistance	366UNTS310	105220
ITU (Telecommun)	Multilateral	28 Jan 61	Tech Assistance	387UNTS202	105563
ITU (Telecommun)	Multilateral	20 Sep 61	Tech Assistance	407UNTS52	105859
ITU (Telecommun)	Multilateral	16 Oct 61	Tech Assistance	410UNTS242	105908
ITU (Telecommun)	Multilateral	07 Nov 61	Tech Assistance	412UNTS258	105937
ITU (Telecommun)	Multilateral	27 Dec 61	Tech Assistance	425UNTS83	106120
ITU (Telecommun)	Multilateral	17 Jan 62	Tech Assistance	419UNTS294	106033
ITU (Telecommun)	Multilateral	20 Jan 62	Tech Assistance	429UNTS230	200596
ITU (Telecommun)	Multilateral	13 Feb 62	Tech Assistance	422UNTS288	200594
ITU (Telecommun)	Multilateral	21 Feb 62	Tech Assistance	423UNTS151	106091
ITU (Telecommun)	Multilateral	01 Mar 62	Tech Assistance	423UNTS122	106089
ITU (Telecommun)	Multilateral	10 Apr 62	Tech Assistance	429UNTS78	106192
ITU (Telecommun)	Multilateral	18 Apr 62	Tech Assistance	463UNTS44	106692
ITU (Telecommun)	Multilateral	17 May 62	Tech Assistance	429UNTS46	106189
ITU (Telecommun)	Multilateral	12 Aug 62	Tech Assistance	443UNTS266	106365
ITU (Telecommun)	Multilateral	29 Aug 62	Tech Assistance	443UNTS280	106366
ITU (Telecommun)	Multilateral	14 Sep 62	Visas	443UNTS73	106360
ITU (Telecommun)	Multilateral	15 Nov 62	Tech Assistance	448UNTS50	106424
ITU (Telecommun)	Multilateral	06 Dec 62	Tech Assistance	450UNTS240	106471
ITU (Telecommun)	Multilateral	12 Dec 62	Tech Assistance	457UNTS72	106578
ITU (Telecommun)	Multilateral	21 Jan 63	Tech Assistance	453UNTS20	106517
ITU (Telecommun)	Multilateral	05 Feb 63	Tech Assistance	453UNTS36	106518
ITU (Telecommun)	Multilateral	14 Feb 63	Tech Assistance	453UNTS168	106524
ITU (Telecommun)	Multilateral	06 Mar 63	Tech Assistance	455UNTS386	106552
ITU (Telecommun)	Multilateral	18 Apr 63	Tech Assistance	463UNTS121	106697
ITU (Telecommun)	Multilateral	06 May 63	Tech Assistance	463UNTS78	106694
ITU (Telecommun)	Multilateral	09 May 63	Tech Assistance	463UNTS159	106700
ITU (Telecommun)	Multilateral	22 May 63	Tech Assistance	483UNTS72	107007
ITU (Telecommun)	Multilateral	24 May 63	Tech Assistance	466UNTS346	106754
ITU (Telecommun)	Multilateral	24 May 63	Tech Assistance	470UNTS208	106810
ITU (Telecommun)	Multilateral	23 Jul 63	Tech Assistance	471UNTS158	106831
ITU (Telecommun)	Multilateral	31 Jul 63	Tech Assistance	472UNTS220	106842
ITU (Telecommun)	Multilateral	27 Aug 63	Tech Assistance	511UNTS210	107435
ITU (Telecommun)	Multilateral	10 Sep 63	Tech Assistance	480UNTS100	106965

PARTY ONE	PARTY TWO	DATE	TOPIC	CITATION	NUMBER
ITU (Telecommun)	Multilateral	30 Oct 63	Tech Assistance	480UNTS180	106968
ITU (Telecommun)	Multilateral	07 Nov 63	Tech Assistance	480UNTS232	106971
ITU (Telecommun)	Multilateral	08 Nov 63	Tech Assistance	482UNTS286	106999
ITU (Telecommun)	Multilateral	28 Jan 64	Tech Assistance	502UNTS321	107336
ITU (Telecommun)	Multilateral	20 Feb 64	Tech Assistance	491UNTS30	107172
ITU (Telecommun)	Multilateral	23 Jun 64	Tech Assistance	506UNTS108	107383
ITU (Telecommun)	Multilateral	28 Jun 64	Tech Assistance	519UNTS14	107499
ITU (Telecommun)	Multilateral	03 Aug 64	Tech Assistance	503UNTS239	107347
ITU (Telecommun)	Multilateral	24 Oct 64	Tech Assistance	514UNTS220	200608
ITU (Telecommun)	Multilateral	11 Nov 64	Tech Assistance	515UNTS94	107456
ITU (Telecommun)	Multilateral	15 Dec 64	Tech Assistance	522UNTS20	107533
ITU (Telecommun)	Multilateral	27 Jan 65	Tech Assistance	523UNTS102	107556
ITU (Telecommun)	Multilateral	02 Feb 65	Tech Assistance	523UNTS256	107560
ITU (Telecommun)	Multilateral	12 Feb 65	Tech Assistance	525UNTS148	107587
ITU (Telecommun)	Multilateral	23 Feb 65	IGO Operations	527UNTS120	107622
ITU (Telecommun)	Multilateral	05 Mar 65	IGO Operations	527UNTS221	107627
ITU (Telecommun)	Multilateral	08 Apr 65	IGO Operations	533UNTS66	107733
ITU (Telecommun)	Multilateral	26 Apr 65	IGO Operations	533UNTS50	107732
ITU (Telecommun)	Multilateral	12 May 65	IGO Operations	534UNTS390	107769
ITU (Telecommun)	Multilateral	14 May 65	IGO Operations	550UNTS310	108026
ITU (Telecommun)	Multilateral	25 May 65	IGO Operations	535UNTS374	107791
ITU (Telecommun)	Multilateral	02 Jun 65	Tech Assistance	537UNTS348	200611
ITU (Telecommun)	Multilateral	02 Jun 65	Tech Assistance	551UNTS2	108030
ITU (Telecommun)	Multilateral	05 Jul 65	General Aid	563UNTS104	108207
ITU (Telecommun)	Multilateral	20 Jul 65	IGO Operations	541UNTS12	107857
ITU (Telecommun)	Multilateral	13 Sep 65	IGO Operations	547UNTS248	107961
ITU (Telecommun)	Multilateral	13 Sep 65	Tech Assistance	547UNTS264	107962
ITU (Telecommun)	Multilateral	21 Sep 65	IGO Operations	547UNTS280	107963
ITU (Telecommun)	Multilateral	21 Oct 65	Tech Assistance	547UNTS216	107959
ITU (Telecommun)	Multilateral	12 Nov 65	IGO Operations	550UNTS160	108013
ITU (Telecommun)	Multilateral	31 Dec 65	Recognition	552UNTS292	108060
ITU (Telecommun)	Multilateral	12 May 66	General Aid	563UNTS54	108204
ITU (Telecommun)	Multilateral	06 Aug 66	Tech Assistance	570UNTS178	108294
ITU (Telecommun)	Multilateral	22 Aug 66	Tech Assistance	571UNTS298	200624
ITU (Telecommun)	Multilateral	23 Sep 66	General Aid	573UNTS148	108328
ITU (Telecommun)	Multilateral	23 Sep 66	IGO Operations	573UNTS132	108327
ITU (Telecommun)	Multilateral	30 Sep 66	IGO Operations	576UNTS8	108361
ITU (Telecommun)	Multilateral	25 Jan 67	IGO Operations	588UNTS212	108527
ITU (Telecommun)	Multilateral	27 Feb 67	IGO Operations	590UNTS156	108552
ITU (Telecommun)	Multilateral	03 Mar 67	Tech Assistance	594UNTS96	108597
ITU (Telecommun)	Multilateral	13 Apr 67	IGO Operations	595UNTS60	108612
ITU (Telecommun)	Multilateral	19 Apr 67	Tech Assistance	595UNTS120	108617
ITU (Telecommun)	Multilateral	10 Jun 67	Direct Aid	602UNTS212	108714
ITU (Telecommun)	Multilateral	14 Jun 67	Direct Aid	603UNTS2	108719
ITU (Telecommun)	Multilateral	20 Jun 67	Tech Assistance	0UNTS0	109290
ITU (Telecommun)	Multilateral	21 Jun 67	Tech Assistance	598UNTS2	108653
ITU (Telecommun)	Multilateral	12 Oct 67	Direct Aid	607UNTS2	108792
ITU (Telecommun)	Multilateral	12 Oct 67	Direct Aid	607UNTS20	108793
ITU (Telecommun)	Multilateral	27 Oct 67	General Aid	608UNTS37	108811
ITU (Telecommun)	Multilateral	14 Nov 67	Admin Cooperation	614UNTS2	108860
ITU (Telecommun)	Multilateral	18 Jun 69	IGO Operations	0UNTS0	109741
ITU (Telecommun)	Multilateral	18 Jun 69	IGO Operations	0UNTS0	109740
ITU (Telecommun)	Multilateral	24 Jun 69	IGO Operations	0UNTS0	109743
ITU (Telecommun)	Multilateral	26 Sep 70	IGO Operations	0UNTS0	110768
ITU (Telecommun)	Switzerland	25 Feb 48	IGO Status/Immunit	56SWRO1196	462190
ITU (Telecommun)	UN Special Fund	13 Jul 60	IGO Operations	368UNTS329	200573
ITU (Telecommun)	United Nations	26 Apr 49	IGO Operations	30UNTS315	200175
ITU (Telecommun)	United Nations	14 Jan 60	IGO Operations	348UNTS331	200566
Ivory Coast	Accept UN Charter	07 Aug 60	UN Charter	375UNTS103	105360
Ivory Coast	Algeria	16 Feb 67	Air Transport	0UNTS0	109245
Ivory Coast	Belgium	12 Feb 62	Visas	429UNTS193	106198
Ivory Coast	Denmark	07 Jun 66	Air Transport	595UNTS313	108626
Ivory Coast	Denmark	23 Nov 66	General Trade	0UNTS0	110554
Ivory Coast	Denmark	23 Dec 68	Loans and Credits	0UNTS0	110178
Ivory Coast	France	11 Jul 60	Recognition	60FRRT52	415138

PARTY ONE	PARTY TWO	DATE	TOPIC	CITATION	NUMBER
Ivory Coast	France	24 Apr 61	Admin Cooperation	0UNTS0	110717
Ivory Coast	France	24 Apr 61	Culture	0UNTS0	110718
Ivory Coast	France	24 Apr 61	General Amity	62FRRT8	415139
Ivory Coast	France	26 Oct 61	Customs	62FRRT37	415140
Ivory Coast	France	19 Oct 62	Air Transport	498UNTS317	107286
Ivory Coast	France	06 Apr 66	Finance	69FRJO2201	416141
Ivory Coast	France	07 May 66	Claims and Debts	66FRJO2011	416142
Ivory Coast	France	21 Feb 70	Visas	0UNTS0	110536
Ivory Coast	Germany, West	18 Dec 61	General Economic	62WBGA58	424120
Ivory Coast	Germany, West	18 Dec 61	Direct Aid	62WBGA58	424121
Ivory Coast	Germany, West	18 Dec 61	Water Transport	62WBGA58	424122
Ivory Coast	Germany, West	03 Sep 63	Loans and Credits	63WBGA210	424123
Ivory Coast	Germany, West	27 Oct 66	Claims and Debts	68WBGA61	424124
Ivory Coast	Germany, West	11 Jun 68	Loans and Credits	68WGBB167	425125
Ivory Coast	Germany, West	17 Jun 68	Loans and Credits	68WBGA153	424126
Ivory Coast	Germany, West	05 May 70	Loans and Credits	70WBGA145	424127
Ivory Coast	Guinea	26 Jun 63	Air Transport	499UNTS71	107293
Ivory Coast	IBRD (World Bank)	21 Jun 68	IBRD Project	0UNTS0	109412
Ivory Coast	IBRD (World Bank)	13 Jun 69	IBRD Project	0UNTS0	110569
Ivory Coast	IBRD (World Bank)	13 Jun 69	IBRD Project	0UNTS0	110567
Ivory Coast	IBRD (World Bank)	13 Jun 69	IBRD Project	0UNTS0	110568
Ivory Coast	Israel	26 Oct 61	Visas	515UNTS251	107462
Ivory Coast	Mali	09 Jul 64	Air Transport	524UNTS121	107569
Ivory Coast	Multilateral	07 Dec 44	IGO Establishment	15UNTS295	200102
Ivory Coast	Multilateral	07 Dec 44	Air Transport	84UNTS389	200252
Ivory Coast	Multilateral	11 Dec 46	Sanitation	12UNTS179	100186
Ivory Coast	Multilateral	27 May 47	Air Transport	418UNTS161	106021
Ivory Coast	Multilateral	12 Nov 47	Admin Cooperation	53UNTS49	100772
Ivory Coast	Multilateral	12 Nov 47	Admin Cooperation	53UNTS13	100770
Ivory Coast	Multilateral	06 Mar 48	Water Transport	289UNTS3	104214
Ivory Coast	Multilateral	24 Jul 48	Sanitation	66UNTS25	100847
Ivory Coast	Multilateral	04 May 49	Admin Cooperation	98UNTS101	101358
Ivory Coast	Multilateral	04 May 49	Admin Cooperation	92UNTS19	101257
Ivory Coast	Multilateral	22 Nov 50	Culture	131UNTS25	101734
Ivory Coast	Multilateral	02 Jul 51	Refugees	189UNTS137	102545
Ivory Coast	Multilateral	18 Jan 54	IGO Establishment	330UNTS121	104743
Ivory Coast	Multilateral	14 Jun 54	Air Transport	320UNTS217	104644
Ivory Coast	Multilateral	14 Jun 54	Air Transport	320UNTS209	104643
Ivory Coast	Multilateral	29 Jul 54	Sanitation	249UNTS45	103500
Ivory Coast	Multilateral	25 May 55	IGO Establishment	264UNTS117	103791
Ivory Coast	Multilateral	28 Sep 55	Air Transport	478UNTS371	106943
Ivory Coast	Multilateral	26 Jan 60	IGO Establishment	439UNTS249	106333
Ivory Coast	Multilateral	17 Jun 60	Humanitarian	536UNTS27	107794
Ivory Coast	Multilateral	30 Mar 61	Sanitation	520UNTS151	107515
Ivory Coast	Multilateral	18 Apr 61	Consul/Citizenship	500UNTS95	107310
Ivory Coast	Multilateral	21 Jun 61	IGO Establishment	514UNTS209	107449
Ivory Coast	Multilateral	06 Dec 61	Customs	473UNTS219	106864
Ivory Coast	Multilateral	10 Apr 62	Tech Assistance	429UNTS78	106192
Ivory Coast	Multilateral	25 May 62	IGO Establishment	486UNTS103	107075
Ivory Coast	Multilateral	28 Sep 62	IGO Establishment	469UNTS169	106791
Ivory Coast	Multilateral	24 Apr 63	Consul/Citizenship	596UNTS487	108640
Ivory Coast	Multilateral	24 Apr 63	Consul/Citizenship	596UNTS261	108638
Ivory Coast	Multilateral	25 May 63	IGO Establishment	479UNTS39	106947
Ivory Coast	Multilateral	04 Aug 63	IGO Establishment	510UNTS3	107408
Ivory Coast	Multilateral	05 Aug 63	Sanitation	480UNTS43	106964
Ivory Coast	Multilateral	26 Oct 63	Water Transport	587UNTS9	108506
Ivory Coast	Multilateral	10 Jul 64	Postal Service	612UNTS233	108848
Ivory Coast	Multilateral	10 Jul 64	Postal Service	611UNTS387	108846
Ivory Coast	Multilateral	10 Jul 64	Postal Service	613UNTS3	108850
Ivory Coast	Multilateral	10 Jul 64	Postal Service	612UNTS3	108847
Ivory Coast	Multilateral	10 Jul 64	Postal Service	611UNTS7	108844
Ivory Coast	Multilateral	10 Jul 64	Postal Service	612UNTS361	108849
Ivory Coast	Multilateral	10 Jul 64	Postal Service	613UNTS3	108851
Ivory Coast	Multilateral	10 Jul 64	Postal Service	611UNTS105	108845
Ivory Coast	Multilateral	25 Nov 64	Water Transport	587UNTS19	108507

PARTY ONE	PARTY TWO	DATE	TOPIC	CITATION	NUMBER
Ivory Coast	Multilateral	01 Dec 64	Water Transport	550UNTS133	108012
Ivory Coast	Multilateral	09 Mar 65	Water Transport	591UNTS265	108564
Ivory Coast	Multilateral	18 Mar 65	Dispute Settlement	575UNTS159	108359
Ivory Coast	Multilateral	28 May 65	IGO Establishment	559UNTS273	108163
Ivory Coast	Multilateral	08 Jul 65	General Trade	597UNTS3	108641
Ivory Coast	Multilateral	05 Apr 66	Water Transport	640UNTS133	109159
Ivory Coast	Multilateral	27 May 66	IGO Establishment	637UNTS0	109121
Ivory Coast	Multilateral	04 May 67	IGO Establishment	595UNTS287	108623
Ivory Coast	Multilateral	27 Oct 67	General Aid	608UNTS37	108811
Ivory Coast	Multilateral	18 Mar 68	Commodity Trade	0UNTS0	109262
Ivory Coast	Multilateral	24 Sep 68	Air Transport	0UNTS0	110612
Ivory Coast	Netherlands	12 Feb 62	Visas	485UNTS219	107057
Ivory Coast	Netherlands	09 Oct 63	Air Transport	499UNTS141	107296
Ivory Coast	Netherlands	26 Apr 65	General Economic	634UNTS81	109053
Ivory Coast	Netherlands	03 Jun 65	Non-ILO Labor	634UNTS95	109054
Ivory Coast	Netherlands	01 Aug 66	Education	591UNTS245	108561
Ivory Coast	Norway	30 Apr 66	General Trade	3NORT963	451043
Ivory Coast	Norway	07 Jun 66	Visas	3NORT968	451045
Ivory Coast	Norway	07 Jun 66	Air Transport	3NORT967	451044
Ivory Coast	Norway	07 Jun 66	Air Transport	0UNTS0	109249
Ivory Coast	Norway	04 Dec 67	Privil/Immunities	3NORT1009	451046
Ivory Coast	Sweden	07 Jun 65	Air Transport	0UNTS0	109240
Ivory Coast	Switzerland	26 Jun 62	General Economic	63SWRO53	462127
Ivory Coast	Switzerland	17 Nov 62	Air Transport	499UNTS3	107289
Ivory Coast	UK Great Britain	29 Mar 65	Visas	551UNTS53	108032
Ivory Coast	UN Special Fund	29 Aug 61	Direct Aid	406UNTS129	105844
Ivory Coast	UNICEF (Children)	10 Jan 62	Direct Aid	422UNTS261	106080
Ivory Coast	United Nations	10 Dec 62	Tech Assistance	451UNTS269	106498
Ivory Coast	USA (United States)	17 May 61	General Aid	409UNTS241	105889
Ivory Coast	USA (United States)	01 Dec 61	Claims and Debts	462UNTS221	106681
Ivory Coast	USA (United States)	21 Apr 62	General Aid	526UNTS39	107598
Ivory Coast	USA (United States)	10 Mar 64	US Agri Commod Aid	526UNTS285	107611
Ivory Coast	USA (United States)	05 Apr 65	US Agri Commod Aid	546UNTS143	107941
Ivory Coast	WHO (World Health)	30 Jan 61	Tech Assistance	395UNTS205	105686
Jamaica	Accept UN Charter	06 Aug 62	UN Charter	437UNTS153	106304
Jamaica	Austria	25 Aug 70	Visas	70ABGB306	403120
Jamaica	Canada	16 Jul 65	Milit Assistance	548UNTS265	107982
Jamaica	Denmark	25 Mar 69	Visas	0UNTS0	109940
Jamaica	France	24 Sep 68	Visas	69FRJO2810	416253
Jamaica	France	24 Sep 68	Visas	0UNTS0	109336
Jamaica	Germany, West	07 Oct 64	Air Transport	514UNTS187	107447
Jamaica	Germany, West	16 Dec 64	Tech Assistance	531UNTS129	107699
Jamaica	Germany, West	03 Feb 65	Scientific Project	531UNTS143	107700
Jamaica	IBRD (World Bank)	08 Apr 65	IBRD Project	539UNTS303	107841
Jamaica	IBRD (World Bank)	20 Jun 66	IBRD Project	582UNTS145	108462
Jamaica	IBRD (World Bank)	30 Sep 66	IBRD Project	582UNTS179	108463
Jamaica	IBRD (World Bank)	23 Jan 67	IBRD Project	594UNTS311	108608
Jamaica	IBRD (World Bank)	14 May 69	IBRD Project	0UNTS0	109889
Jamaica	Iceland	02 Jul 69	Visas	0UNTS0	109943
Jamaica	Israel	05 Dec 67	Visas	632UNTS83	109010
Jamaica	Japan	17 Mar 64	Consul/Citizenship	65JAIL233	440163
Jamaica	Mexico	15 Mar 68	Visas	0UNTS0	109235
Jamaica	Multilateral	07 Dec 44	IGO Establishment	15UNTS295	200102
Jamaica	Multilateral	11 Dec 46	Sanitation	12UNTS179	100186
Jamaica	Multilateral	27 May 47	Air Transport	418UNTS161	106021
Jamaica	Multilateral	12 Nov 47	Admin Cooperation	53UNTS39	100771
Jamaica	Multilateral	12 Nov 47	Admin Cooperation	46UNTS201	100710
Jamaica	Multilateral	12 Nov 47	Admin Cooperation	53UNTS13	100770
Jamaica	Multilateral	09 Dec 48	Humanitarian	78UNTS277	101021
Jamaica	Multilateral	04 May 49	Admin Cooperation	92UNTS19	101257
Jamaica	Multilateral	04 May 49	Admin Cooperation	98UNTS101	101358
Jamaica	Multilateral	07 Dec 50	Admin Cooperation	212UNTS17	102861
Jamaica	Multilateral	02 Jul 51	Refugees	189UNTS137	102545
Jamaica	Multilateral	07 Nov 52	General Trade	221UNTS255	103010
Jamaica	Multilateral	14 Jun 54	Air Transport	320UNTS217	104644

PARTY ONE	PARTY TWO	DATE	TOPIC	CITATION	NUMBER
Jamaica	Multilateral	14 Jun 54	Air Transport	320UNTS209	104643
Jamaica	Multilateral	25 May 55	IGO Establishment	264UNTS117	103791
Jamaica	Multilateral	18 May 56	Customs	319UNTS21	104630
Jamaica	Multilateral	18 May 56	Customs	338UNTS103	104834
Jamaica	Multilateral	20 Feb 57	Consul/Citizenship	309UNTS65	104468
Jamaica	Multilateral	29 Apr 58	Specific Resources	559UNTS285	108164
Jamaica	Multilateral	29 Apr 58	Territory Boundary	499UNTS311	107302
Jamaica	Multilateral	29 Apr 58	Water Transport	450UNTS11	106465
Jamaica	Multilateral	29 Apr 58	Territory Boundary	516UNTS205	107477
Jamaica	Multilateral	01 Dec 58	Commodity Trade	385UNTS137	105534
Jamaica	Multilateral	30 Mar 61	Sanitation	520UNTS151	107515
Jamaica	Multilateral	18 Apr 61	Consul/Citizenship	500UNTS95	107310
Jamaica	Multilateral	21 Jun 61	IGO Establishment	514UNTS209	107449
Jamaica	Multilateral	22 Jun 62	ILO Labor	494UNTS249	107237
Jamaica	Multilateral	22 May 63	Tech Assistance	483UNTS72	107007
Jamaica	Multilateral	05 Aug 63	Sanitation	480UNTS43	106964
Jamaica	Multilateral	10 Jul 64	Postal Service	611UNTS7	108844
Jamaica	Multilateral	10 Jul 64	Postal Service	611UNTS105	108845
Jamaica	Multilateral	10 Jul 64	Postal Service	611UNTS387	108846
Jamaica	Multilateral	10 Jul 64	Postal Service	612UNTS3	108847
Jamaica	Multilateral	18 Mar 65	Dispute Settlement	575UNTS159	108359
Jamaica	Multilateral	08 Dec 65	IGO Establishment	600UNTS161	108680
Jamaica	Multilateral	27 Jan 67	Scientific Project	610UNTS205	108843
Jamaica	Multilateral	14 Feb 67	General Military	634UNTS281	109068
Jamaica	Multilateral	14 Nov 67	Admin Cooperation	614UNTS2	108860
Jamaica	Multilateral	08 Mar 68	Visas	634UNTS199	109062
Jamaica	Multilateral	18 Mar 68	Commodity Trade	0UNTS0	109262
Jamaica	Multilateral	01 Jul 68	Peace/Disarmament	0UNTS0	110485
Jamaica	Multilateral	24 Dec 68	Commodity Trade	0UNTS0	109369
Jamaica	Multilateral	27 Jan 69	Telecommunications	0UNTS0	109664
Jamaica	Multilateral	18 Oct 69	IGO Establishment	0UNTS0	110232
Jamaica	Norway	31 Mar 69	Visas	0UNTS0	109941
Jamaica	Sweden	01 Apr 69	Visas	0UNTS0	109942
Jamaica	UK Great Britain	01 Jun 61	Recognition	478UNTS9	106932
Jamaica	UK Great Britain	20 Feb 64	Military Mission	496UNTS239	107256
Jamaica	UK Great Britain	31 Mar 65	Military Mission	539UNTS59	107824
Jamaica	UK Great Britain	02 Apr 65	Taxation	552UNTS219	108056
Jamaica	UK Great Britain	20 Sep 68	Finance	0UNTS0	109804
Jamaica	UK Great Britain	25 Mar 70	Air Transport	0UNTS0	110759
Jamaica	UN Special Fund	22 May 63	Direct Aid	489UNTS191	107140
Jamaica	UNICEF (Children)	19 May 64	IGO Operations	500UNTS75	107308
Jamaica	United Nations	22 May 63	IGO Status/Immunit	479UNTS19	106945
Jamaica	United Nations	06 Dec 66	IGO Operations	580UNTS211	108424
Jamaica	USA (United States)	29 Nov 62	Air Transport	462UNTS229	106682
Jamaica	USA (United States)	04 Jan 63	Finance	471UNTS119	106826
Jamaica	USA (United States)	06 Jun 63	Milit Assistance	477UNTS29	106913
Jamaica	USA (United States)	01 Oct 63	Commodity Trade	488UNTS133	107124
Jamaica	USA (United States)	24 Oct 63	General Aid	489UNTS337	107148
Jamaica	USA (United States)	20 Dec 66	Admin Cooperation	0UNTS0	109698
Jamaica	USA (United States)	29 Sep 67	Commodity Trade	0UNTS0	109923
Jamaica	USA (United States)	02 Oct 69	Air Transport	0UNTS0	110448
Jamaica	USSR (Soviet Union)	05 Aug 62	Recognition	11SUGG149	469853
Jamaica	WHO (World Health)	25 Sep 63	Tech Assistance	481UNTS125	106980
Japan	Accept UN Charter	16 Jun 52	UN Charter	256UNTS167	103626
Japan	Afghanistan	15 Mar 61	Education	450UNTS373	106480
Japan	Afghanistan	27 Nov 68	Loans and Credits	69JJS3	442257
Japan	Afghanistan	04 Oct 69	Direct Aid	69JJS11	442249
Japan	Argentina	20 Dec 61	Health/Educ/Welfare	0JGJI1504	441112
Japan	Argentina	20 Dec 61	Sanitation	451UNTS77	106486
Japan	Argentina	20 Dec 61	General Amity	67JHZ9	439038
Japan	Argentina	20 Dec 61	Taxation	451UNTS91	106487
Japan	Argentina	20 Dec 61	Sanitation	0JGJI1462	441111
Japan	Argentina	20 Dec 61	Sanitation	0JGJI1460	441109
Japan	Argentina	20 Dec 61	General Amity	613UNTS323	108859
Japan	Argentina	20 Dec 61	Visas	451UNTS71	106485

PARTY ONE	PARTY TWO	DATE	TOPIC	CITATION	NUMBER
Japan	Argentina	20 Dec 61	Commodity Trade	0JGJI1461	441110
Japan	Argentina	15 Oct 65	Finance	0JGJI1613	441142
Japan	Asian Productivity	05 Apr 67	IGO Status/Immunit	67JHZ7	439008
Japan	Australia	27 Apr 53	Admin Cooperation	193UNTS78	102612
Japan	Australia	24 May 54	Specif Claim/Waive	191UNTS125	102580
Japan	Australia	19 Jan 56	Air Transport	311UNTS291	104507
Japan	Australia	06 Jul 57	General Trade	318UNTS381	104627
Japan	Australia	07 Feb 61	Postal Service	450UNTS343	106478
Japan	Australia	01 Mar 62	Postal Service	517UNTS81	107483
Japan	Australia	07 Aug 62	Atomic Energy	435UNTS261	106283
Japan	Australia	27 Nov 68	Specific Resources	69JHZ8	439025
Japan	Australia	27 Nov 68	Specific Resources	0UNTS0	110174
Japan	Australia	10 Jan 69	Visas	69JJS35	442229
Japan	Australia	20 Mar 69	Taxation	70JHZ7	439028
Japan	Austria	16 Nov 55	Recognition	0JGJI1280	441087
Japan	Austria	20 Mar 58	Visas	324UNTS205	104686
Japan	Austria	20 Dec 61	Taxation	517UNTS155	107485
Japan	Austria	30 Apr 65	General Trade	0JGJI1598	441137
Japan	Austria	04 Nov 66	General Trade	66JJS1	442182
Japan	Austria	24 Dec 68	General Trade	68JJS1	442225
Japan	Belgium	29 Aug 50	General Trade	82UNTS147	101089
Japan	Belgium	29 Aug 50	General Trade	76UNTS113	100984
Japan	Belgium	11 Jul 56	Visas	248UNTS129	103492
Japan	Belgium	18 Mar 58	Admin Cooperation	303UNTS149	104378
Japan	Belgium	30 Apr 58	Finance	303UNTS109	104373
Japan	Belgium	20 Jun 59	Air Transport	411UNTS3	105911
Japan	Belgium	28 Mar 68	Taxation	70JHZ4	439021
Japan	Belgium	28 Mar 68	Taxation	0UNTS0	110513
Japan	Benelux Econ Union	22 Jul 66	General Trade	66JJS31	442172
Japan	Benelux Econ Union	22 Oct 69	Commodity Trade	69JJS45	442250
Japan	Bolivia	02 Aug 56	Health/Educ/Welfare	0JGJI1299	441096
Japan	Brazil	14 Dec 56	Air Transport	0JGJI1485	441101
Japan	Brazil	14 Nov 60	Consul/Citizenship	518UNTS29	107491
Japan	Brazil	23 Jan 61	Culture	569UNTS81	108281
Japan	Brazil	28 Mar 62	Education	451UNTS125	106489
Japan	Brazil	19 Feb 65	Finance	0JGJI1585	441130
Japan	Brazil	26 Mar 65	Finance	0JGJI1587	441133
Japan	Brazil	07 Oct 66	Loans and Credits	68JJS39	442178
Japan	Brazil	24 Jan 67	Taxation	67JHZ12	439005
Japan	Brazil	24 Jan 67	Taxation	0UNTS0	109716
Japan	Brazil	23 Jun 67	Customs	67JJS93	442195
Japan	Bulgaria	28 Mar 67	General Trade	67JJS103	442190
Japan	Bulgaria	15 Mar 68	Visas	68JJS3	442211
Japan	Bulgaria	28 Feb 70	General Economic	70JHZ8	439035
Japan	Burma	05 Nov 54	Reparations	251UNTS215	103543
Japan	Burma	05 Nov 54	Peace/Disarmament	251UNTS201	103542
Japan	Burma	18 Oct 55	Admin Cooperation	0JGJI1254	441146
Japan	Burma	20 Jun 56	Admin Cooperation	306UNTS61	104431
Japan	Burma	29 Mar 63	General Aid	518UNTS3	107490
Japan	Burma	15 Feb 69	Loans and Credits	69JJS69	442233
Japan	Cambodia	09 Dec 55	General Amity	0JGJI1301	441089
Japan	Cambodia	02 Mar 59	General Economic	341UNTS163	104882
Japan	Cambodia	16 May 59	General Economic	0JGJI1401	441149
Japan	Cambodia	30 Sep 66	Tech Assistance	66JJS53	442177
Japan	Cambodia	02 Nov 68	Tech Assistance	68JJS49	442221
Japan	Cambodia	21 Mar 69	Direct Aid	69JJS75	442237
Japan	Cambodia	21 Mar 69	Non-IBRD Project	0UNTS0	110577
Japan	Cambodia	01 Aug 69	Non-IBRD Project	69JHZ8	439030
Japan	Canada	31 Mar 54	General Trade	236UNTS329	103334
Japan	Canada	12 Jan 55	Air Transport	311UNTS167	104503
Japan	Canada	13 Jun 55	Visas	247UNTS151	103464
Japan	Canada	20 Mar 56	Postal Service	517UNTS33	107482
Japan	Canada	02 Jul 59	Atomic Energy	383UNTS243	105504
Japan	Canada	05 Sep 61	Reparations	451UNTS47	106483
Japan	Canada	05 Sep 64	Visas	0JGJI1558	441122

PARTY ONE	PARTY TWO	DATE	TOPIC	CITATION	NUMBER
Japan	Canada	05 Sep 64	Taxation	569UNTS99	108282
Japan	Central Afri Rep	15 Oct 68	General Economic	68JJS57	442219
Japan	Ceylon (Sri Lanka)	06 Sep 52	General Economic	314UNTS279	104552
Japan	Ceylon (Sri Lanka)	20 Mar 61	Education	450UNTS385	106481
Japan	Ceylon (Sri Lanka)	09 Sep 66	Loans and Credits	66JJS89	442175
Japan	Ceylon (Sri Lanka)	22 Sep 67	Loans and Credits	67JJS119	442202
Japan	Ceylon (Sri Lanka)	12 Dec 67	Taxation	68JHZ9	439015
Japan	Ceylon (Sri Lanka)	12 Dec 67	Taxation	0UNTS0	109721
Japan	Ceylon (Sri Lanka)	03 Sep 68	Loans and Credits	68JJS113	442218
Japan	Ceylon (Sri Lanka)	27 Dec 68	Loans and Credits	68JJS121	442227
Japan	Ceylon (Sri Lanka)	24 Oct 69	Loans and Credits	69JJS117	442254
Japan	Ceylon (Sri Lanka)	02 Nov 69	Direct Aid	69JJS125	442256
Japan	Chad	24 Nov 64	General Trade	0JGJI1591	441126
Japan	Chile	31 Aug 65	Finance	0JGJI1610	441141
Japan	Chile	22 Oct 69	Visas	69JJS133	442252
Japan	China People's Rep	15 Apr 55	Specif Claim/Waive	55CCJC26	410228
Japan	China People's Rep	15 Apr 55	Territory Boundary	55CCJC25	410227
Japan	China People's Rep	15 Apr 55	Specific Resources	55CCJC24	410226
Japan	China People's Rep	04 May 55	General Trade	55CCJC36	410234
Japan	China People's Rep	27 Nov 55	Culture	55CCJC90	410275
Japan	China People's Rep	05 Mar 58	General Trade	58CCJC24	410499
Japan	China People's Rep	09 Nov 62	General Trade	62CCJC103	410928
Japan	China People's Rep	27 Dec 62	General Trade	62CCJC118	410939
Japan	China People's Rep	09 Nov 63	General Ad Hoc	63CCJC130	411029
Japan	China People's Rep	09 Nov 63	Specific Resources	63CCJC129	411028
Japan	China People's Rep	09 Nov 63	Dispute Settlement	63CCJC131	411030
Japan	China People's Rep	05 Aug 65	Specific Resources	65CCJC104	411218
Japan	China People's Rep	17 Dec 65	Specific Resources	65CCJC156	411219
Japan	Cuba	22 Apr 60	General Trade	442UNTS261	106354
Japan	Czechoslovakia	13 Feb 57	General Amity	300UNTS119	104335
Japan	Czechoslovakia	15 Dec 59	General Trade	383UNTS277	105505
Japan	Denmark	29 Feb 52	Consul/Citizenship	126UNTS139	101686
Japan	Denmark	28 Apr 52	Air Transport	166UNTS3	102182
Japan	Denmark	26 Feb 53	Air Transport	173UNTS329	102273
Japan	Denmark	21 Oct 53	Patents/Copyrights	0JGJI1171	441076
Japan	Denmark	31 May 54	Patents/Copyrights	0JGJI1173	441079
Japan	Denmark	20 Jul 56	Visas	0JGJI1296	441095
Japan	Denmark	10 Mar 59	Taxation	341UNTS55	104878
Japan	Denmark	25 May 59	Reparations	341UNTS157	104881
Japan	Denmark	03 Feb 68	Taxation	68JHZ7	439016
Japan	Denmark	03 Feb 68	Taxation	0UNTS0	109405
Japan	Dominican Republic	20 Mar 57	Visas	318UNTS245	104619
Japan	EEC (Econ Commnty)	30 Jun 67	General Trade	68JHZ5	439011
Japan	El Salvador	19 Jul 63	General Economic	518UNTS135	107494
Japan	El Salvador	26 Jul 68	Direct Aid	68JJS165	442217
Japan	Ethiopia	19 Dec 57	General Amity	325UNTS91	104695
Japan	Ethiopia	18 Aug 67	General Trade	68JJS175	442199
Japan	Export-Import Bank	06 Jul 55	Loans and Credits	0JGJI1234	441145
Japan	Export-Import Bank	10 Aug 56	Loans and Credits	0JGJI1300	441147
Japan	FAO (Food Agri)	22 Jan 69	Direct Aid	69JJS561	442231
Japan	Fed of Malaya	10 May 60	General Trade	383UNTS293	105506
Japan	Finland	22 Dec 58	Visas	341UNTS41	104876
Japan	France	11 Jun 52	Admin Cooperation	0JGJI1021	441144
Japan	France	25 Apr 53	Admin Cooperation	187UNTS41	102500
Japan	France	12 May 53	Culture	53FRJO610	416254
Japan	France	18 Nov 55	Visas	0JGJI1263	441088
Japan	France	17 Jan 56	Air Transport	255UNTS275	103614
Japan	France	27 Mar 57	Specif Claim/Waive	318UNTS233	104617
Japan	France	21 Dec 62	Taxation	0JGJI1502	441115
Japan	France	14 May 63	General Economic	518UNTS111	107493
Japan	France	27 Nov 64	Taxation	65FRRT75	415255
Japan	France	27 Nov 64	Taxation	569UNTS157	108283
Japan	France	23 Jul 65	Atomic Energy	0JGJI1604	441139
Japan	France	30 Mar 68	General Trade	68JJS187	442212
Japan	France	30 Sep 69	Commodity Trade	69JJS155	442248

PARTY ONE	PARTY TWO	DATE	TOPIC	CITATION	NUMBER
Japan	Germany, West	08 Aug 52	Admin Cooperation	0JGJI4507	441071
Japan	Germany, West	08 May 53	Patents/Copyrights	0JGJI1172	441073
Japan	Germany, West	24 May 54	Admin Cooperation	0JGJI4508	441080
Japan	Germany, West	18 Jun 55	Visas	0JGJI1262	441085
Japan	Germany, West	02 Nov 56	Non-ILO Labor	0JGJI1325	441099
Japan	Germany, West	14 Feb 57	Culture	318UNTS361	104626
Japan	Germany, West	27 Jun 57	Admin Cooperation	318UNTS335	104624
Japan	Germany, West	26 Jul 57	Visas	0JGJI1262	441102
Japan	Germany, West	01 Jul 60	General Trade	60WBGA156	424750
Japan	Germany, West	18 Jan 61	Air Transport	465UNTS173	106727
Japan	Germany, West	08 Apr 64	General Trade	65JAIL234	440164
Japan	Germany, West	05 Oct 64	Taxation	0JGJI1559	441123
Japan	Germany, West	22 Apr 66	Taxation	68JAIL201	440069
Japan	Germany, West	22 Apr 66	Taxation	0UNTS0	109715
Japan	Germany, West	27 Dec 67	General Trade	68JAIL169	440206
Japan	Germany, West	27 Dec 67	Water Transport	68WBGA43	424751
Japan	Germany, West	22 Oct 69	Commodity Trade	69JJS169	442251
Japan	Ghana	24 Sep 62	Direct Aid	0JGJI1501	441114
Japan	Ghana	23 May 63	Education	0JGJI1506	441116
Japan	Ghana	22 May 67	Education	67JJS193	442189
Japan	Greece	12 Mar 55	General Trade	227UNTS33	103130
Japan	Greece	10 May 56	Visas	0JGJI1302	441091
Japan	Greece	09 Apr 65	General Trade	0JGJI1584	441136
Japan	Greece	09 Apr 65	General Trade	632UNTS61	109008
Japan	Greece	20 Sep 66	Claims and Debts	609UNTS103	108828
Japan	Greece	13 Feb 67	General Trade	67JJS201	442185
Japan	Greece	24 Jun 69	General Economic	69JJS183	442243
Japan	Haiti	17 Dec 58	General Economic	518UNTS91	107492
Japan	IAEA (Atom Energy)	24 Mar 59	Atomic Energy	339UNTS327	104852
Japan	IAEA (Atom Energy)	26 Sep 67	Atomic Energy	637UNTS0	109113
Japan	IBRD (World Bank)	12 Nov 52	IBRD Project	354UNTS313	105068
Japan	IBRD (World Bank)	15 Oct 53	IBRD Project	187UNTS321	200512
Japan	IBRD (World Bank)	15 Oct 53	IBRD Project	187UNTS271	200511
Japan	IBRD (World Bank)	15 Oct 53	IBRD Project	187UNTS367	200513
Japan	IBRD (World Bank)	25 Oct 55	IBRD Project	230UNTS379	200534
Japan	IBRD (World Bank)	21 Feb 56	IBRD Project	248UNTS321	200543
Japan	IBRD (World Bank)	19 Dec 56	IBRD Project	268UNTS203	103859
Japan	IBRD (World Bank)	19 Dec 56	IBRD Project	264UNTS179	103793
Japan	IBRD (World Bank)	09 Aug 57	IBRD Project	293UNTS59	104286
Japan	IBRD (World Bank)	29 Jan 58	IBRD Project	310UNTS111	104490
Japan	IBRD (World Bank)	13 Jun 58	IBRD Project	312UNTS159	104518
Japan	IBRD (World Bank)	27 Jun 58	IBRD Project	312UNTS193	104519
Japan	IBRD (World Bank)	11 Jul 58	IBRD Project	318UNTS103	104611
Japan	IBRD (World Bank)	18 Aug 58	IBRD Project	323UNTS205	104670
Japan	IBRD (World Bank)	10 Sep 58	IBRD Project	323UNTS297	104673
Japan	IBRD (World Bank)	10 Sep 58	IBRD Project	318UNTS133	104612
Japan	IBRD (World Bank)	17 Feb 59	IBRD Project	337UNTS205	104824
Japan	IBRD (World Bank)	12 Nov 59	IBRD Project	354UNTS279	105067
Japan	IBRD (World Bank)	17 Mar 60	IBRD Project	362UNTS43	105182
Japan	IBRD (World Bank)	20 Dec 60	IBRD Project	400UNTS167	105752
Japan	IBRD (World Bank)	20 Dec 60	IBRD Project	400UNTS279	105754
Japan	IBRD (World Bank)	16 Mar 61	IBRD Project	400UNTS201	105753
Japan	IBRD (World Bank)	02 May 61	IBRD Project	415UNTS144	105984
Japan	IBRD (World Bank)	29 Nov 61	IBRD Project	426UNTS3	106128
Japan	IBRD (World Bank)	27 Sep 63	IBRD Project	485UNTS283	107061
Japan	IBRD (World Bank)	22 Apr 64	IBRD Project	505UNTS21	107363
Japan	IBRD (World Bank)	23 Dec 64	IBRD Project	538UNTS37	107809
Japan	IBRD (World Bank)	13 Jan 65	IBRD Project	537UNTS293	107806
Japan	IBRD (World Bank)	26 May 65	IBRD Project	550UNTS95	108010
Japan	IBRD (World Bank)	10 Sep 65	Claims and Debts	566UNTS249	108246
Japan	IBRD (World Bank)	29 Jul 66	IBRD Project	582UNTS209	108464
Japan	IBRD (World Bank)	09 Sep 69	IGO Establishment	70JHZ5	439032
Japan	Iceland	15 Nov 66	Visas	66JJS153	442183
Japan	ICJ Option Clause	24 Nov 51	ICJ Option Clause	137UNTS3	101842
Japan	ICJ Option Clause	25 Mar 54	ICJ Option Clause	188UNTS137	102524

PARTY ONE	PARTY TWO	DATE	TOPIC	CITATION	NUMBER
Japan	ICJ Option Clause	15 Sep 58	ICJ Option Clause	312UNTS155	104517
Japan	India	09 Jun 52	Peace/Disarmament	0JGJI1000	441070
Japan	India	26 Nov 55	Air Transport	311UNTS243	104506
Japan	India	29 Oct 56	Culture	318UNTS289	104622
Japan	India	04 Feb 58	General Trade	324UNTS215	104687
Japan	India	05 Jan 60	Taxation	384UNTS3	105507
Japan	India	25 Jan 60	Tech Assistance	384UNTS31	105508
Japan	India	31 Mar 62	Education	451UNTS143	106490
Japan	India	23 Apr 62	Education	451UNTS155	106491
Japan	India	14 Dec 63	Claims and Debts	0JGJI1529	441118
Japan	India	17 Dec 64	Education	0JGJI1567	441127
Japan	India	26 Jan 65	Postal Service	0JGJI1606	441128
Japan	India	24 Feb 65	Postal Service	570UNTS3	108284
Japan	India	12 Aug 66	Direct Aid	66JJS57	442173
Japan	India	16 Dec 66	Loans and Credits	66JJS161	442184
Japan	India	14 Jul 67	Loans and Credits	67JJS207	442196
Japan	India	29 Aug 67	Claims and Debts	67JJS205	442200
Japan	India	05 Sep 67	Loans and Credits	67JJS221	442201
Japan	India	05 Mar 68	Education	69JAIL171	440210
Japan	India	14 Feb 69	Loans and Credits	69JJS211	442232
Japan	Indonesia	16 Dec 53	Reparations	57JAIL78	440154
Japan	Indonesia	20 Jan 58	Claims and Debts	325UNTS3	104690
Japan	Indonesia	20 Jan 58	Reparations	324UNTS247	104689
Japan	Indonesia	20 Jan 58	Peace/Disarmament	324UNTS227	104688
Japan	Indonesia	20 Jan 58	Loans and Credits	325UNTS13	104691
Japan	Indonesia	20 Jan 58	Loans and Credits	0JGJI1365	441104
Japan	Indonesia	01 Jul 61	General Amity	517UNTS107	107484
Japan	Indonesia	23 Jan 62	Air Transport	559UNTS77	108155
Japan	Indonesia	09 Jun 67	Loans and Credits	67JJS229	442193
Japan	Indonesia	10 Nov 67	General Aid	67JJS243	442205
Japan	Indonesia	29 May 68	Tech Assistance	68JJS247	442213
Japan	Indonesia	02 Jul 68	Loans and Credits	68JJS263	442216
Japan	Indonesia	04 Jul 69	Direct Aid	69JJS211	442244
Japan	Indonesia	18 Jul 69	Tech Assistance	69JJS235	442245
Japan	Iran	16 Apr 57	Culture	325UNTS113	104697
Japan	Iran	09 Dec 58	General Aid	325UNTS221	104701
Japan	Iran	12 Sep 60	Education	384UNTS43	105509
Japan	Iran	11 Oct 60	General Economic	0IRTB45	433066
Japan	Iran	23 Jul 63	Admin Cooperation	0IRTB46	433067
Japan	Iran	23 Jun 68	General Trade	68JJS283	442214
Japan	Iran	17 Mar 70	Taxation	0IRTB46	433068
Japan	Iran	16 Aug 70	Telecommunications	0IRTB46	433069
Japan	Iraq	17 Jun 64	General Trade	65JAIL235	440165
Japan	Ireland	01 Sep 66	Visas	66JJS171	442174
Japan	Ireland	01 Sep 66	Visas	608UNTS339	108822
Japan	Italy	05 Dec 53	General Military	53ITDI336	436181
Japan	Italy	31 Jul 54	Culture	55ITGU286	435182
Japan	Italy	11 Jan 56	Visas	267UNTS175	103842
Japan	Italy	31 Jan 62	Air Transport	498UNTS23	107276
Japan	Italy	15 Mar 63	Visas	64ITDI258	436183
Japan	Italy	22 Oct 69	Commodity Trade	69JJS259	442253
Japan	Jamaica	17 Mar 64	Consul/Citizenship	65JAIL233	440163
Japan	Kenya	30 Jul 64	Education	0JGJI1550	441121
Japan	Kenya	31 Mar 66	Direct Aid	66JJS177	442171
Japan	Kenya	21 Jan 69	Direct Aid	69JJS275	442230
Japan	Korea, South	31 Dec 57	Admin Cooperation	0JGJI1369	441103
Japan	Korea, South	22 Jun 65	General Amity	583UNTS33	108471
Japan	Korea, South	22 Jun 65	Culture	584UNTS49	108475
Japan	Korea, South	22 Jun 65	Claims and Debts	583UNTS173	108473
Japan	Korea, South	22 Jun 65	Dispute Settlement	584UNTS147	108476
Japan	Korea, South	22 Jun 65	Specific Resources	583UNTS51	108472
Japan	Korea, South	22 Jun 65	Consul/Citizenship	584UNTS3	108474
Japan	Korea, South	24 Mar 66	General Trade	66JJS183	442170
Japan	Korea, South	18 Oct 66	Specific Resources	66JJS187	442180
Japan	Korea, South	28 Apr 67	Scientific Project	67JJS249	442186

PARTY ONE	PARTY TWO	DATE	TOPIC	CITATION	NUMBER
Japan	Korea, South	28 Apr 67	Scientific Project	67JJS251	442187
Japan	Korea, South	16 May 67	Air Transport	67JHZ8	439010
Japan	Korea, South	16 May 67	Air Transport	0UNTS0	109479
Japan	Korea, South	25 Oct 67	Education	67JJS291	442204
Japan	Korea, South	03 Dec 68	Patents/Copyrights	68JJS293	442224
Japan	Korea, South	01 Apr 69	Taxation	69JJS287	442239
Japan	Korea, South	03 Mar 70	Taxation	70JHZ10	439036
Japan	Kuwait	06 Oct 62	Air Transport	498UNTS235	107284
Japan	Laos	15 Oct 58	General Aid	341UNTS25	104875
Japan	Laos	07 Apr 65	Postal Service	0JGJI1589	441135
Japan	Laos	29 Jan 66	Postal Service	66JJS201	442167
Japan	Laos	05 Jun 67	Postal Service	67JJS299	442192
Japan	Laos	28 Feb 68	Loans and Credits	68JJS299	442209
Japan	Laos	24 Dec 68	General Aid	68JJS305	442226
Japan	Laos	05 Dec 69	Loans and Credits	69JJS303	442259
Japan	Laos	23 Dec 69	Direct Aid	69JJS309	442260
Japan	Lebanon	02 Jun 67	Air Transport	71JHZ3	439191
Japan	Lebanon	19 Jun 69	Taxation	69JJS317	442242
Japan	Luxembourg	18 Dec 56	Visas	318UNTS227	104616
Japan	Luxembourg	21 Jul 60	Visas	384UNTS55	105510
Japan	Malaysia	04 Jun 63	Taxation	517UNTS245	107488
Japan	Malaysia	11 Feb 65	Air Transport	0JGJI1614	441129
Japan	Malaysia	11 Feb 65	Air Transport	0UNTS0	109477
Japan	Malaysia	21 Sep 67	General Economic	68JHZ5	439014
Japan	Malaysia	21 Sep 67	General Economic	0UNTS0	109719
Japan	Malaysia	30 Jan 70	Taxation	70JHZ12	439034
Japan	Malta	13 Nov 68	General Trade	68JJS327	442222
Japan	Mexico	25 Oct 54	Culture	0JGJI1250	441082
Japan	Mexico	24 Jul 67	Tech Assistance	67JJS311	442198
Japan	Mexico	07 Mar 68	Specific Resources	68JHZ6	439019
Japan	Mexico	07 Mar 68	Water Transport	0UNTS0	109723
Japan	Mexico	30 Jan 69	General Trade	69JHZ12	439026
Japan	Morocco	05 Aug 61	Milit Installation	61JGJI38	441301
Japan	Morocco	13 Feb 62	Tech Assistance	62JGJI18	441302
Japan	Morocco	17 Feb 62	Non-IBRD Project	62JGJI19	441303
Japan	Morocco	30 Mar 62	Education	62JGJI20	441304
Japan	Morocco	10 May 63	Claims and Debts	63JGJI46	441305
Japan	Morocco	31 May 63	Mass Media	65JGJI49	441306
Japan	Morocco	01 Jun 63	Non-ILO Labor	63JGJI52	441308
Japan	Morocco	01 Jun 63	Non-ILO Labor	63JGJI52	441307
Japan	Morocco	11 Sep 67	Direct Aid	67JJS325	442203
Japan	Multilateral	07 Dec 44	Air Transport	84UNTS389	200252
Japan	Multilateral	07 Dec 44	IGO Establishment	15UNTS295	200102
Japan	Multilateral	02 Sep 45	Peace/Disarmament	139UNTS387	200465
Japan	Multilateral	22 Jul 46	IGO Establishment	9UNTS3	100125
Japan	Multilateral	02 Dec 46	Specific Resources	161UNTS72	102124
Japan	Multilateral	11 Dec 46	Sanitation	12UNTS179	100186
Japan	Multilateral	06 Mar 48	Water Transport	289UNTS3	104214
Japan	Multilateral	10 Jun 48	Humanitarian	164UNTS113	102163
Japan	Multilateral	24 Jul 48	Sanitation	66UNTS25	100847
Japan	Multilateral	15 Nov 48	IGO Establishment	120UNTS59	101615
Japan	Multilateral	29 Nov 48	IGO Establishment	120UNTS13	101613
Japan	Multilateral	09 Dec 48	Scientific Project	20UNTS229	100318
Japan	Multilateral	09 Dec 48	Scientific Project	73UNTS39	100942
Japan	Multilateral	23 Mar 49	Commodity Trade	203UNTS179	102746
Japan	Multilateral	16 Dec 49	Admin Cooperation	72UNTS3	100924
Japan	Multilateral	21 Mar 50	Admin Cooperation	96UNTS271	101342
Japan	Multilateral	25 May 51	Status of Forces	175UNTS215	102303
Japan	Multilateral	08 Sep 51	General Military	136UNTS165	101833
Japan	Multilateral	08 Sep 51	Peace/Disarmament	136UNTS45	101832
Japan	Multilateral	09 Oct 51	IGO Establishment	220UNTS121	102997
Japan	Multilateral	06 Dec 51	IGO Establishment	425UNTS61	106119
Japan	Multilateral	06 Dec 51	Admin Cooperation	150UNTS67	101963
Japan	Multilateral	04 Feb 52	General Economic	124UNTS3	101662
Japan	Multilateral	01 Mar 52	Specific Resources	168UNTS9	102210

PARTY ONE	PARTY TWO	DATE	TOPIC	CITATION	NUMBER
Japan	Multilateral	16 Apr 52	General Economic	139UNTS35	101874
Japan	Multilateral	09 May 52	Specific Resources	205UNTS65	102770
Japan	Multilateral	12 Jun 52	Dispute Settlement	138UNTS183	101869
Japan	Multilateral	11 Jul 52	Postal Service	171UNTS89	102225
Japan	Multilateral	11 Jul 52	IGO Establishment	169UNTS3	102220
Japan	Multilateral	11 Jul 52	Postal Service	170UNTS63	102222
Japan	Multilateral	11 Jul 52	Postal Service	170UNTS3	102221
Japan	Multilateral	11 Jul 52	Postal Service	170UNTS269	102223
Japan	Multilateral	11 Jul 52	Postal Service	171UNTS3	102224
Japan	Multilateral	06 Sep 52	Patents/Copyrights	216UNTS132	102937
Japan	Multilateral	07 Nov 52	General Trade	221UNTS255	103010
Japan	Multilateral	31 Mar 53	Privil/Immunities	193UNTS136	102613
Japan	Multilateral	11 May 53	Sanitation	456UNTS3	106555
Japan	Multilateral	01 Oct 53	Commodity Trade	258UNTS153	103677
Japan	Multilateral	26 Oct 53	Status of Forces	207UNTS237	102809
Japan	Multilateral	19 Feb 54	Status of Forces	214UNTS51	102899
Japan	Multilateral	25 Feb 54	Air Transport	215UNTS249	102922
Japan	Multilateral	01 Mar 54	Commodity Trade	256UNTS31	103622
Japan	Multilateral	12 May 54	Admin Cooperation	327UNTS3	104714
Japan	Multilateral	14 May 54	Culture	249UNTS215	103511
Japan	Multilateral	04 Jun 54	Customs	282UNTS249	104101
Japan	Multilateral	04 Jun 54	Customs	276UNTS191	103992
Japan	Multilateral	14 Jun 54	Air Transport	320UNTS217	104644
Japan	Multilateral	14 Jun 54	Air Transport	320UNTS209	104643
Japan	Multilateral	25 May 55	IGO Establishment	264UNTS117	103791
Japan	Multilateral	21 Sep 55	Other Military	269UNTS241	103885
Japan	Multilateral	28 Sep 55	Air Transport	478UNTS371	106943
Japan	Multilateral	12 Oct 55	IGO Establishment	560UNTS3	108165
Japan	Multilateral	04 Jan 56	Scientific Project	256UNTS171	103627
Japan	Multilateral	25 Apr 56	Commodity Trade	270UNTS103	103896
Japan	Multilateral	25 Sep 56	Air Transport	334UNTS13	104766
Japan	Multilateral	25 Sep 56	Air Transport	334UNTS89	104767
Japan	Multilateral	26 Oct 56	IGO Establishment	276UNTS3	103988
Japan	Multilateral	09 Feb 57	Specific Resources	314UNTS105	104546
Japan	Multilateral	01 Jul 57	Culture	0UNTS0	110418
Japan	Multilateral	03 Oct 57	Postal Service	364UNTS3	105211
Japan	Multilateral	03 Oct 57	Postal Service	364UNTS331	105212
Japan	Multilateral	03 Oct 57	Postal Service	366UNTS3	105215
Japan	Multilateral	03 Oct 57	Postal Service	366UNTS193	105218
Japan	Multilateral	03 Oct 57	Postal Service	365UNTS3	105213
Japan	Multilateral	03 Oct 57	Postal Service	365UNTS207	105214
Japan	Multilateral	03 Oct 57	Postal Service	366UNTS87	105216
Japan	Multilateral	29 Apr 58	Territory Boundary	516UNTS205	107477
Japan	Multilateral	01 Dec 58	Commodity Trade	385UNTS137	105534
Japan	Multilateral	06 Apr 59	Commodity Trade	349UNTS167	105013
Japan	Multilateral	19 Nov 59	IGO Operations	410UNTS156	105902
Japan	Multilateral	01 Dec 59	Territory Boundary	402UNTS71	105778
Japan	Multilateral	26 Jan 60	IGO Establishment	439UNTS249	106333
Japan	Multilateral	17 Jun 60	Humanitarian	536UNTS27	107794
Japan	Multilateral	01 Sep 60	Commodity Trade	403UNTS3	105792
Japan	Multilateral	08 Oct 60	General Trade	450UNTS309	106476
Japan	Multilateral	30 Mar 61	Sanitation	520UNTS151	107515
Japan	Multilateral	14 Apr 61	IGO Establishment	422UNTS101	106071
Japan	Multilateral	18 Apr 61	Consul/Citizenship	500UNTS95	107310
Japan	Multilateral	18 Apr 61	Dispute Settlement	500UNTS243	107312
Japan	Multilateral	21 Jun 61	IGO Establishment	514UNTS209	107449
Japan	Multilateral	05 Oct 61	Dispute Settlement	510UNTS175	107413
Japan	Multilateral	15 May 62	Commodity Trade	444UNTS3	106367
Japan	Multilateral	06 Jun 62	Privil/Immunities	486UNTS271	107081
Japan	Multilateral	06 Jun 62	Privil/Immunities	486UNTS263	107080
Japan	Multilateral	28 Sep 62	IGO Establishment	469UNTS169	106791
Japan	Multilateral	30 Apr 63	General Trade	570UNTS23	108285
Japan	Multilateral	05 Aug 63	Sanitation	480UNTS43	106964
Japan	Multilateral	23 Sep 63	Atomic Energy	488UNTS99	107122
Japan	Multilateral	09 Nov 63	Direct Aid	489UNTS209	107141

PARTY ONE	PARTY TWO	DATE	TOPIC	CITATION	NUMBER
Japan	Multilateral	10 Jul 64	Postal Service	613UNTS127	108853
Japan	Multilateral	10 Jul 64	Postal Service	613UNTS3	108850
Japan	Multilateral	10 Jul 64	Postal Service	612UNTS361	108849
Japan	Multilateral	10 Jul 64	Postal Service	611UNTS105	108845
Japan	Multilateral	10 Jul 64	Postal Service	611UNTS7	108844
Japan	Multilateral	10 Jul 64	Postal Service	611UNTS387	108846
Japan	Multilateral	10 Jul 64	Postal Service	612UNTS3	108847
Japan	Multilateral	10 Jul 64	Postal Service	612UNTS233	108848
Japan	Multilateral	20 Aug 64	Telecommunications	514UNTS25	107441
Japan	Multilateral	01 Dec 64	Water Transport	550UNTS133	108012
Japan	Multilateral	09 Mar 65	Water Transport	591UNTS265	108564
Japan	Multilateral	18 Mar 65	Dispute Settlement	575UNTS159	108359
Japan	Multilateral	08 Jul 65	General Trade	597UNTS3	108641
Japan	Multilateral	04 Dec 65	IGO Establishment	571UNTS123	108303
Japan	Multilateral	31 Dec 65	Specific Resources	616UNTS317	108904
Japan	Multilateral	05 Apr 66	Water Transport	640UNTS133	109159
Japan	Multilateral	04 May 66	IBRD Project	575UNTS49	108354
Japan	Multilateral	14 May 66	Specific Resources	0UNTS0	109587
Japan	Multilateral	20 Jun 66	Scientific Project	572UNTS263	108318
Japan	Multilateral	26 Sep 67	Atomic Energy	633UNTS73	109035
Japan	Multilateral	28 Dec 67	Scientific Project	0UNTS0	109322
Japan	Multilateral	18 Mar 68	Commodity Trade	0UNTS0	109262
Japan	Multilateral	01 Aug 68	Culture	0UNTS0	109368
Japan	Multilateral	28 Sep 68	Tech Assistance	0UNTS0	109296
Japan	Multilateral	24 Dec 68	Commodity Trade	0UNTS0	109369
Japan	Multilateral	11 Jun 69	Scientific Project	0UNTS0	110100
Japan	Multilateral	12 Jan 70	Commodity Trade	0UNTS0	110603
Japan	Netherlands	13 Apr 51	Finance	51NET51	447021
Japan	Netherlands	13 Apr 51	General Trade	51NET50	447020
Japan	Netherlands	17 Feb 53	Air Transport	192UNTS215	102602
Japan	Netherlands	13 Mar 56	Claims and Debts	252UNTS3	103554
Japan	Netherlands	16 May 56	Visas	305UNTS97	104417
Japan	Netherlands	20 Sep 57	Visas	305UNTS105	104418
Japan	Netherlands	03 Mar 70	Taxation	70JHZ10	439037
Japan	New Zealand	09 Sep 58	General Trade	325UNTS119	104698
Japan	New Zealand	09 Mar 62	General Trade	485UNTS351	107066
Japan	New Zealand	09 Mar 62	General Trade	485UNTS339	107065
Japan	New Zealand	30 Jan 63	Taxation	517UNTS183	107486
Japan	New Zealand	15 Mar 63	Postal Service	517UNTS229	107487
Japan	New Zealand	12 Jul 67	Specific Resources	0UNTS0	109718
Japan	New Zealand	12 Jul 67	Specific Resources	68JHZ7	439012
Japan	Norway	23 Feb 53	Air Transport	192UNTS191	102601
Japan	Norway	22 Aug 56	Visas	3NORT692	451091
Japan	Norway	28 Feb 57	General Economic	280UNTS87	104054
Japan	Norway	21 Feb 59	Taxation	356UNTS231	105098
Japan	Norway	11 May 67	Taxation	0UNTS0	109717
Japan	Norway	11 May 67	Taxation	3NORT997	451092
Japan	Norway	11 May 67	Taxation	68JHZ10	439009
Japan	Norway	10 Jan 69	General Trade	70JAIL190	440228
Japan	OECD (Econ Coop)	14 Mar 67	IGO Status/Immunit	67JHZ7	439007
Japan	Pakistan	24 Apr 53	Admin Cooperation	221UNTS325	103013
Japan	Pakistan	04 Apr 56	General Trade	57JAIL82	440161
Japan	Pakistan	27 May 57	Culture	325UNTS21	104692
Japan	Pakistan	17 Feb 59	Taxation	341UNTS127	104880
Japan	Pakistan	30 Jul 60	Education	384UNTS63	105511
Japan	Pakistan	01 Dec 60	Visas	450UNTS337	106477
Japan	Pakistan	18 Dec 60	General Amity	423UNTS197	106093
Japan	Pakistan	07 Mar 61	Postal Service	450UNTS359	106479
Japan	Pakistan	17 Oct 61	Air Transport	466UNTS17	106734
Japan	Pakistan	01 Aug 62	Visas	0JGJI1477	441113
Japan	Pakistan	16 Nov 63	Education	0JGJI1527	441117
Japan	Pakistan	25 Jul 69	Finance	69JJS341	442246
Japan	Paraguay	22 Jul 59	Loans and Credits	0JGJI9	441105
Japan	Paraguay	22 Jul 59	Visas	373UNTS85	105316
Japan	Peru	15 May 61	General Trade	451UNTS3	106482

PARTY ONE	PARTY TWO	DATE	TOPIC	CITATION	NUMBER
Japan	Philippines	24 Jan 53	Water Transport	3PTS63	465031
Japan	Philippines	12 Mar 53	Reparations	3PTS85	465032
Japan	Philippines	09 May 54	Reparations	57JAIL78	440155
Japan	Philippines	08 Dec 55	General Trade	3PTS529	465036
Japan	Philippines	09 May 56	Direct Aid	0JGJI1291	441090
Japan	Philippines	09 May 56	Reparations	285UNTS3	104148
Japan	Philippines	30 Nov 56	Reparations	0JGJI1313	441148
Japan	Philippines	07 Jan 58	General Trade	3PTS699	465037
Japan	Philippines	24 Jul 58	Visas	325UNTS103	104696
Japan	Philippines	02 Mar 59	Air Transport	341UNTS49	104877
Japan	Philippines	07 Sep 59	Loans and Credits	0JGJI9	441106
Japan	Philippines	09 Dec 60	General Amity	4PTS383	465046
Japan	Philippines	06 Dec 61	Visas	449UNTS29	106449
Japan	Philippines	19 Jan 63	Postal Service	517UNTS281	107489
Japan	Philippines	15 Feb 66	Direct Aid	66JJS217	442168
Japan	Philippines	29 Sep 66	Education	66JJS221	442176
Japan	Philippines	26 Jun 68	Postal Service	69JHZ8	439023
Japan	Philippines	08 Aug 68	Postal Service	69JJS349	442247
Japan	Philippines	08 Aug 68	Postal Service	0UNTS0	109834
Japan	Philippines	29 Nov 68	Tech Assistance	68JJS417	442223
Japan	Philippines	21 Feb 69	Loans and Credits	69JJS357	442234
Japan	Philippines	17 Jun 69	Tech Assistance	69JJS367	442241
Japan	Philippines	20 Jan 70	Air Transport	70JHZ5	439033
Japan	Poland	08 Feb 57	General Amity	318UNTS251	104620
Japan	Poland	26 Apr 58	General Economic	340UNTS221	104866
Japan	Romania	01 Sep 69	General Economic	70JHZ7	439031
Japan	San Marino	15 Jan 68	Visas	68JJS421	442208
Japan	Sierra Leone	07 Jan 66	Commodity Trade	66JJS229	442166
Japan	Singapore	15 Oct 66	Education	66JJS247	442179
Japan	Singapore	14 Feb 67	Air Transport	0UNTS0	109244
Japan	Singapore	14 Feb 67	Air Transport	67JHZ8	439006
Japan	Singapore	21 Sep 67	Reparations	68JHZ5	439013
Japan	Singapore	21 Sep 67	Reparations	0UNTS0	109720
Japan	South Africa	27 Mar 53	Admin Cooperation	173UNTS37	102258
Japan	South Africa	06 Apr 63	Postal Service	484UNTS319	107040
Japan	South Africa	21 Oct 68	Taxation	68JJS439	442220
Japan	Spain	24 Dec 55	General Trade	56SPB0801	460178
Japan	Spain	21 Dec 56	General Military	57JAIL88	440068
Japan	Spain	08 Jan 57	Claims and Debts	318UNTS221	104615
Japan	Spain	16 Mar 65	Visas	0JGJI1572	441132
Japan	Spain	22 Feb 66	General Trade	66JJS257	442169
Japan	Sweden	01 Apr 50	General Trade	50SOFM153	461107
Japan	Sweden	01 Apr 50	Finance	50SOFM165	461108
Japan	Sweden	13 Nov 51	Consul/Citizenship	51SOFM623	461156
Japan	Sweden	05 Mar 52	General Trade	52SOFM127	461159
Japan	Sweden	05 Mar 52	Finance	52SOFM142	461160
Japan	Sweden	28 Apr 52	Air Transport	52SOFM231	461165
Japan	Sweden	20 Feb 53	Air Transport	173UNTS307	102272
Japan	Sweden	06 May 53	General Trade	53SOFM1155	461195
Japan	Sweden	31 Mar 54	Claims and Debts	262UNTS187	103744
Japan	Sweden	08 Aug 56	Visas	0JGJI1303	441097
Japan	Sweden	12 Dec 56	Taxation	318UNTS309	104623
Japan	Sweden	20 Sep 57	Reparations	325UNTS29	104693
Japan	Switzerland	25 Jun 53	Claims and Debts	54SWR0530	462027
Japan	Switzerland	21 Jan 55	Claims and Debts	55SWR0357	462170
Japan	Switzerland	24 May 56	Air Transport	312UNTS3	104509
Japan	Switzerland	25 Mar 57	Visas	318UNTS239	104618
Japan	Syria	08 Jun 53	General Trade	184UNTS3	102436
Japan	Syria	30 Oct 69	Direct Aid	69JJS391	442255
Japan	Taiwan	24 Apr 52	General Trade	0CTCY447	414048
Japan	Taiwan	28 Apr 52	Peace/Disarmament	138UNTS3	101858
Japan	Taiwan	13 Jun 53	Finance	0CTCY447	414049
Japan	Taiwan	13 Jun 53	General Economic	0CTRC263	413012
Japan	Taiwan	15 Mar 55	Air Transport	0CTRC281	413013
Japan	Taiwan	18 May 60	Air Transport	0CTRC26	413022
Japan	Taiwan	05 Dec 69	Education	69JJS145	442258
Japan	Tanzania	20 Oct 66	Direct Aid	66JJS317	442181
Japan	Thailand	19 Jun 53	Air Transport	174UNTS29	102276
Japan	Thailand	06 Apr 55	Culture	230UNTS219	103187
Japan	Thailand	09 Jul 55	Finance	230UNTS13	103172
Japan	Thailand	06 Sep 55	Culture	55JHZ9	439002
Japan	Thailand	09 Apr 56	General Trade	57JAIL82	440162
Japan	Thailand	24 Aug 60	Education	384UNTS73	105512
Japan	Thailand	25 Nov 61	Sanitation	451UNTS55	106484
Japan	Thailand	01 Mar 63	Taxation	475UNTS233	106895
Japan	Thailand	16 Nov 64	Education	0JGJI1564	441125
Japan	Thailand	12 Jan 68	Loans and Credits	69JAIL169	440207
Japan	Tunisia	31 May 56	Visas	0JGJI1294	441094
Japan	Turkey	08 Feb 55	General Economic	56TURG301	466078
Japan	Turkey	05 Nov 57	Visas	318UNTS411	104628
Japan	Uganda	28 Jun 68	Education	68JJS445	442215
Japan	UK Great Britain	31 Aug 51	Finance	149UNTS227	101955
Japan	UK Great Britain	31 Aug 51	Finance	108UNTS273	101480
Japan	UK Great Britain	04 Nov 52	Specific Property	164UNTS101	102161
Japan	UK Great Britain	04 Nov 52	Specific Property	164UNTS107	102162
Japan	UK Great Britain	21 Nov 52	Reparations	172UNTS303	102254
Japan	UK Great Britain	29 Dec 52	Air Transport	175UNTS129	102299
Japan	UK Great Britain	27 Apr 53	Admin Cooperation	228UNTS227	103154
Japan	UK Great Britain	29 Jan 54	Finance	190UNTS319	102572
Japan	UK Great Britain	21 Sep 55	Other Military	0JGJI1287	441086
Japan	UK Great Britain	30 Aug 57	Visas	313UNTS63	104529
Japan	UK Great Britain	16 Jun 58	Atomic Energy	325UNTS185	104700
Japan	UK Great Britain	07 Oct 60	Reparations	384UNTS89	105513
Japan	UK Great Britain	03 Dec 60	Culture	414UNTS61	105966
Japan	UK Great Britain	11 Apr 61	Taxation	420UNTS75	106042
Japan	UK Great Britain	04 Sep 62	Taxation	475UNTS31	106888
Japan	UK Great Britain	02 Nov 62	Visas	466UNTS277	106749
Japan	UK Great Britain	14 Nov 62	General Trade	478UNTS29	106934
Japan	UK Great Britain	06 Jan 64	Specific Resources	502UNTS183	107329
Japan	UK Great Britain	04 May 64	Consul/Citizenship	561UNTS25	108179
Japan	UK Great Britain	22 Feb 65	Finance	560UNTS123	108171
Japan	UK Great Britain	14 Dec 65	Admin Cooperation	0JGJI1615	441143
Japan	UK Great Britain	06 Mar 68	Atomic Energy	68JHZ10	439018
Japan	UK Great Britain	06 Mar 68	Atomic Energy	0UNTS0	109494
Japan	UK Great Britain	10 Feb 69	Taxation	70JHZ12	439027
Japan	UN Special Fund	31 Oct 62	Tech Assistance	444UNTS171	106368
Japan	UN Special Fund	27 Mar 69	IGO Operations	70JAIL191	440238
Japan	UN Special Fund	09 Sep 69	Education	0UNTS0	109930
Japan	UNICEF (Children)	21 Nov 53	Direct Aid	183UNTS297	200507
Japan	United Arab Rep	20 Mar 57	Culture	318UNTS345	104625
Japan	United Arab Rep	10 May 62	Air Transport	498UNTS69	107278
Japan	United Arab Rep	27 Apr 64	Taxation	0JGJI1536	441119
Japan	United Arab Rep	03 Sep 68	Taxation	69JHZ8	439024
Japan	United Arab Rep	03 Sep 68	Taxation	0UNTS0	110576
Japan	United Nations	25 Jul 52	IGO Status/Immunit	135UNTS305	200443
Japan	United Nations	24 Jun 53	Tech Assistance	167UNTS249	200499
Japan	United Nations	26 Oct 53	IGO Operations	57JAIL86	440066
Japan	United Nations	19 Feb 54	Status of Forces	0JGJI7	441078
Japan	United Nations	19 Feb 54	Status of Forces	0JGJI1162	441077
Japan	United Nations	03 May 60	IGO Operations	0JGJI1413	441107
Japan	United Nations	15 Mar 61	IGO Operations	397UNTS199	105706
Japan	United Nations	04 Oct 61	Education	410UNTS133	105900
Japan	United Nations	11 Apr 62	IGO Operations	425UNTS45	106117
Japan	USA (United States)	14 Apr 49	Specif Claim/Waive	89UNTS141	101215
Japan	USA (United States)	04 Apr 51	Specific Resources	57JAIL85	440064
Japan	USA (United States)	28 Aug 51	Education	147UNTS81	101930
Japan	USA (United States)	08 Sep 51	Milit Assistance	136UNTS203	101834
Japan	USA (United States)	08 Sep 51	General Military	136UNTS211	101835
Japan	USA (United States)	28 Feb 52	Milit Assistance	208UNTS255	102817
Japan	USA (United States)	25 Jul 52	Milit Assistance	198UNTS281	102671

PARTY ONE	PARTY TWO	DATE	TOPIC	CITATION	NUMBER
Japan	USA (United States)	11 Aug 52	Air Transport	212UNTS27	102862
Japan	USA (United States)	18 Sep 52	Visas	227UNTS85	103133
Japan	USA (United States)	12 Nov 52	Milit Assistance	184UNTS111	102443
Japan	USA (United States)	22 Nov 52	Milit Installation	52JHZ12	439001
Japan	USA (United States)	18 Mar 53	Tech Assistance	212UNTS149	102867
Japan	USA (United States)	23 Mar 53	Direct Aid	185UNTS93	102461
Japan	USA (United States)	02 Apr 53	General Amity	206UNTS143	102788
Japan	USA (United States)	22 Apr 53	Admin Cooperation	178UNTS169	102341
Japan	USA (United States)	23 Oct 53	Visas	57JAIL86	440065
Japan	USA (United States)	29 Oct 53	Postal Service	57JAIL86	440067
Japan	USA (United States)	10 Nov 53	Patents/Copyrights	224UNTS161	103076
Japan	USA (United States)	24 Dec 53	Territory Boundary	222UNTS193	103028
Japan	USA (United States)	21 Jan 54	Tech Assistance	223UNTS145	103063
Japan	USA (United States)	08 Mar 54	Claims and Debts	232UNTS251	103240
Japan	USA (United States)	08 Mar 54	Direct Aid	232UNTS227	103238
Japan	USA (United States)	08 Mar 54	Direct Aid	232UNTS243	103239
Japan	USA (United States)	08 Mar 54	Milit Assistance	232UNTS215	103237
Japan	USA (United States)	08 Mar 54	Milit Assistance	232UNTS169	103236
Japan	USA (United States)	08 Mar 54	General Economic	232UNTS267	103241
Japan	USA (United States)	16 Apr 54	Taxation	238UNTS3	103353
Japan	USA (United States)	16 Apr 54	Taxation	238UNTS39	103354
Japan	USA (United States)	14 May 54	Milit Assistance	247UNTS273	103476
Japan	USA (United States)	19 Nov 54	Milit Installation	238UNTS207	103364
Japan	USA (United States)	04 Jan 55	Specif Claim/Waive	237UNTS197	103346
Japan	USA (United States)	07 Apr 55	Tech Assistance	263UNTS285	103778
Japan	USA (United States)	31 May 55	Direct Aid	241UNTS197	103434
Japan	USA (United States)	31 May 55	Direct Aid	241UNTS243	103435
Japan	USA (United States)	03 Jun 55	Milit Assistance	270UNTS51	103891
Japan	USA (United States)	24 Aug 55	Specif Claim/Waive	257UNTS297	103662
Japan	USA (United States)	14 Nov 55	Atomic Energy	240UNTS361	103413
Japan	USA (United States)	10 Feb 56	Direct Aid	275UNTS181	103981
Japan	USA (United States)	10 Feb 56	Direct Aid	275UNTS105	103979
Japan	USA (United States)	10 Feb 56	Direct Aid	275UNTS157	103980
Japan	USA (United States)	22 Mar 56	Patents/Copyrights	275UNTS195	103983
Japan	USA (United States)	13 Apr 56	Milit Assistance	273UNTS223	103953
Japan	USA (United States)	05 Sep 56	Admin Cooperation	277UNTS267	104011
Japan	USA (United States)	23 Nov 56	Atomic Energy	324UNTS177	104685
Japan	USA (United States)	10 Dec 56	Postal Service	0JGJI1146	441100
Japan	USA (United States)	22 Mar 57	Visas	288UNTS201	104206
Japan	USA (United States)	08 May 57	Atomic Energy	318UNTS257	104621
Japan	USA (United States)	14 Sep 57	Admin Cooperation	293UNTS247	104293
Japan	USA (United States)	11 Jan 58	Education	304UNTS35	104390
Japan	USA (United States)	25 Jan 58	Milit Assistance	304UNTS81	104392
Japan	USA (United States)	19 Jun 58	Atomic Energy	325UNTS143	104699
Japan	USA (United States)	03 Nov 58	Postal Service	341UNTS83	104879
Japan	USA (United States)	31 Jul 59	Milit Assistance	357UNTS107	105110
Japan	USA (United States)	12 Nov 59	Direct Aid	361UNTS27	105171
Japan	USA (United States)	19 Jan 60	Status of Forces	373UNTS207	105321
Japan	USA (United States)	19 Jan 60	General Military	373UNTS179	105320
Japan	USA (United States)	18 Feb 60	Direct Aid	372UNTS117	105292
Japan	USA (United States)	23 Mar 60	Tech Assistance	372UNTS289	105305
Japan	USA (United States)	15 Apr 60	Milit Assistance	372UNTS267	105303
Japan	USA (United States)	31 May 60	Direct Aid	376UNTS301	105385
Japan	USA (United States)	19 May 61	Atomic Energy	0JGJI1445	441108
Japan	USA (United States)	08 Jun 61	Reparations	410UNTS183	105903
Japan	USA (United States)	22 Jun 61	General Economic	410UNTS53	105896
Japan	USA (United States)	16 Oct 61	General Trade	433UNTS287	106250
Japan	USA (United States)	09 Jan 62	Direct Aid	451UNTS97	106488
Japan	USA (United States)	09 Feb 62	General Trade	13UST948	486001
Japan	USA (United States)	28 Aug 62	Loans and Credits	460UNTS267	106645
Japan	USA (United States)	24 Oct 62	Sanitation	462UNTS119	106673
Japan	USA (United States)	06 Nov 62	Telecommunications	459UNTS203	106623
Japan	USA (United States)	31 Dec 62	Mostfavored Nation	471UNTS83	106823
Japan	USA (United States)	01 Feb 63	Air Transport	473UNTS49	106854
Japan	USA (United States)	19 Feb 63	Direct Aid	473UNTS107	106859

PARTY ONE	PARTY TWO	DATE	TOPIC	CITATION	NUMBER
Japan	USA (United States)	22 Mar 63	Consul/Citizenship	518UNTS179	107495
Japan	USA (United States)	26 Apr 63	Milit Installation	477UNTS37	106914
Japan	USA (United States)	14 Jun 63	Finance	479UNTS165	106951
Japan	USA (United States)	27 Aug 63	Commodity Trade	487UNTS197	107105
Japan	USA (United States)	28 Aug 63	Commodity Trade	487UNTS237	107106
Japan	USA (United States)	25 Apr 64	General Economic	530UNTS61	107672
Japan	USA (United States)	30 Oct 64	Atomic Energy	0JGJI1563	441124
Japan	USA (United States)	25 Nov 64	Specific Property	533UNTS31	107730
Japan	USA (United States)	04 Dec 64	Milit Installation	532UNTS249	107721
Japan	USA (United States)	02 Apr 65	IGO Operations	16UST657	486002
Japan	USA (United States)	02 Apr 65	Admin Cooperation	0JGJI1588	441134
Japan	USA (United States)	30 Aug 65	Atomic Energy	0JGJI1609	441140
Japan	USA (United States)	23 Aug 66	Visas	606UNTS219	108787
Japan	USA (United States)	06 Sep 66	General Trade	616UNTS215	108898
Japan	USA (United States)	19 Sep 66	Scientific Project	0TIAS6170	487003
Japan	USA (United States)	19 Sep 66	Scientific Project	0UNTS0	109681
Japan	USA (United States)	09 May 67	Specific Resources	18UST1309	486004
Japan	USA (United States)	09 May 67	Specific Resources	0UNTS0	109766
Japan	USA (United States)	09 May 67	Specific Resources	0UNTS0	109765
Japan	USA (United States)	08 Aug 67	Milit Assistance	18UST1678	486005
Japan	USA (United States)	13 Oct 67	General Military	0UNTS0	110048
Japan	USA (United States)	13 Dec 67	Milit Assistance	18UST2804	486006
Japan	USA (United States)	12 Jan 68	General Trade	0UNTS0	109998
Japan	USA (United States)	12 Jan 68	Commodity Trade	19UST4419	486007
Japan	USA (United States)	19 Jan 68	Admin Cooperation	0UNTS0	110001
Japan	USA (United States)	19 Jan 68	Military Mission	0TIAS6442	487008
Japan	USA (United States)	26 Feb 68	Atomic Energy	0UNTS0	109722
Japan	USA (United States)	26 Feb 68	Atomic Energy	68JHZ7	439017
Japan	USA (United States)	05 Apr 68	Territory Boundary	0UNTS0	109724
Japan	USA (United States)	05 Apr 68	Territory Boundary	68JHZ6	439022
Japan	USA (United States)	02 Sep 68	Scientific Project	19UST6011	486009
Japan	USA (United States)	02 Sep 68	Scientific Project	0UNTS0	110073
Japan	USA (United States)	08 Nov 68	Culture	0UNTS0	110085
Japan	USA (United States)	23 Dec 68	Specific Resources	0TIAS6600	487010
Japan	USA (United States)	04 Apr 69	Milit Assistance	0UNTS0	110156
Japan	USA (United States)	04 Apr 69	Milit Installation	20UST545	486011
Japan	USA (United States)	18 Apr 69	Territory Boundary	0UNTS0	110331
Japan	USA (United States)	18 Apr 69	Territory Boundary	69JHZ7	439029
Japan	USA (United States)	31 Jul 69	Scientific Project	0UNTS0	110342
Japan	USA (United States)	31 Jul 69	Scientific Project	20UST2720	486012
Japan	USA (United States)	03 Mar 70	Recognition	0UNTS0	110625
Japan	USA (United States)	03 Mar 70	IGO Operations	21UST473	486013
Japan	USA (United States)	01 May 70	Admin Cooperation	0UNTS0	110695
Japan	USA (United States)	01 May 70	IGO Operations	21UST1167	486014
Japan	USA (United States)	11 Dec 70	Specific Resources	0TIAS7019	487015
Japan	USA (United States)	11 Dec 70	Specific Resources	0TIAS7020	487016
Japan	USA (United States)	11 Dec 70	Specific Resources	0TIAS7021	487017
Japan	USSR (Soviet Union)	19 Aug 46	Refugees	0SUST224	468242
Japan	USSR (Soviet Union)	14 May 56	Humanitarian	0JGJI1315	441093
Japan	USSR (Soviet Union)	14 May 56	Specific Resources	0JGJI1314	441092
Japan	USSR (Soviet Union)	19 Oct 56	General Economic	263UNTS119	103769
Japan	USSR (Soviet Union)	19 Oct 56	General Amity	263UNTS99	103768
Japan	USSR (Soviet Union)	06 Apr 57	Specific Resources	0SUST380	468243
Japan	USSR (Soviet Union)	06 Dec 57	General Economic	0SUST392	468245
Japan	USSR (Soviet Union)	06 Dec 57	Water Transport	16SUGG122	469949
Japan	USSR (Soviet Union)	06 Dec 57	General Economic	325UNTS35	104694
Japan	USSR (Soviet Union)	03 Jun 58	Water Transport	7SUGG113	469512
Japan	USSR (Soviet Union)	23 Jun 58	General Trade	16SUGG125	469959
Japan	USSR (Soviet Union)	13 May 59	Specific Resources	8SUGG145	469575
Japan	USSR (Soviet Union)	20 Nov 59	General Trade	8SUGG158	469610
Japan	USSR (Soviet Union)	02 Mar 60	General Trade	9SUGG128	469636
Japan	USSR (Soviet Union)	02 Mar 60	General Trade	9SUGG128	469637
Japan	USSR (Soviet Union)	18 May 60	Specific Resources	9SUGG136	469661
Japan	USSR (Soviet Union)	31 Mar 62	Admin Cooperation	16SUGG133	470006
Japan	USSR (Soviet Union)	26 Feb 65	Visas	0JGJI1622	441131

PARTY ONE	PARTY TWO	DATE	TOPIC	CITATION	NUMBER
Japan	USSR (Soviet Union)	21 Jan 66	General Trade	633UNTS165	109038
Japan	USSR (Soviet Union)	21 Jan 66	Air Transport	67JHZ3	439003
Japan	USSR (Soviet Union)	29 Jul 66	Consul/Citizenship	67JHZ8	439004
Japan	USSR (Soviet Union)	29 Jul 66	Consul/Citizenship	608UNTS93	108815
Japan	USSR (Soviet Union)	19 May 67	Consul/Citizenship	68JAIL163	440188
Japan	USSR (Soviet Union)	20 Jul 67	Scientific Project	67JJS455	442197
Japan	USSR (Soviet Union)	07 Mar 69	Air Transport	69JJS397	442235
Japan	USSR (Soviet Union)	14 Mar 69	General Trade	70JAIL191	440236
Japan	USSR (Soviet Union)	18 Apr 69	Specific Resources	69JJS423	442240
Japan	Vietnam, South	12 Jun 52	Dispute Settlement	OVKNG48	496009
Japan	Vietnam, South	13 May 59	Reparations	373UNTS101	105317
Japan	Vietnam, South	13 May 59	Loans and Credits	373UNTS149	105318
Japan	Vietnam, South	13 May 59	Loans and Credits	373UNTS173	105319
Japan	Vietnam, South	11 Jan 65	Specific Resources	OVKNG208	496060
Japan	Vietnam, South	10 Jun 67	Sanitation	67JJS537	442194
Japan	Vietnam, South	07 Mar 70	Tech Assistance	OVKNG316	496079
Japan	Vietnam, South	20 May 70	Refugees	OVKNG326	496082
Japan	Vietnam, South	09 Jun 70	Direct Aid	OVKNG339	496088
Japan	Vietnam, South	17 Oct 70	Direct Aid	OVKNG391	496090
Japan	Vietnam, South	16 Dec 70	Direct Aid	OVKNG366	496091
Japan	Vietnam, South	30 Mar 71	Privil/Immunities	OVKNG377	496094
Japan	Vietnam, South	18 Sep 71	Direct Aid	OVKNG389	496100
Japan	Vietnam, South	02 Oct 71	Direct Aid	OVKNG391	496101
Japan	Vietnam, South	27 Nov 71	Direct Aid	OVKNG394	496102
Japan	Vietnam, South	24 Dec 71	Direct Aid	OVKNG397	496103
Japan	WHO (World Health)	26 Nov 52	Tech Assistance	204UNTS301	200521
Japan	Yemen	27 May 55	General Amity	57JAIL80	440156
Japan	Yugoslavia	28 Feb 59	General Economic	341UNTS179	104883
Japan	Yugoslavia	25 Jun 64	Visas	OJGJI1548	441120
Japan	Yugoslavia	15 Mar 68	Culture	69JHZ5	439020
Japan	Yugoslavia	15 Mar 68	Culture	OUNTSO	110575
Japan	Zambia	21 May 65	General Trade	OJGJI1607	441138
Japan	Zambia	19 Feb 70	Taxation	71JHZ1	439261
Jordan	Accept UN Charter	11 Oct 55	UN Charter	223UNTS43	103048
Jordan	Belgium	19 Oct 60	Air Transport	479UNTS277	106959
Jordan	Denmark	07 Dec 61	Air Transport	631UNTS333	109003
Jordan	Denmark	28 Jun 66	Loans and Credits	574UNTS3	108338
Jordan	France	16 Jun 65	Health/Educ/Welfare	65FRRT86	415256
Jordan	France	30 Apr 66	Air Transport	66FRJO2606	416257
Jordan	Germany, West	14 Mar 67	Loans and Credits	67WBGA90	424314
Jordan	Germany, West	24 Oct 67	Loans and Credits	68WBGA42	424315
Jordan	Germany, West	25 Jul 68	Loans and Credits	68WBGA199	424316
Jordan	Germany, West	29 Jan 70	Air Transport	71WGBB1080	425318
Jordan	Germany, West	29 Jan 70	Loans and Credits	70WBGA54	424317
Jordan	IDA (Devel Assoc)	22 Dec 61	Non-IBRD Project	448UNTS21	106423
Jordan	IDA (Devel Assoc)	12 Dec 63	Non-IBRD Project	506UNTS51	107381
Jordan	IDA (Devel Assoc)	12 Dec 63	Non-IBRD Project	492UNTS3	107184
Jordan	IDA (Devel Assoc)	09 May 67	Loans and Credits	617UNTS47	108907
Jordan	ILO (Labor Org)	29 Mar 51	Tech Assistance	100UNTS247	200287
Jordan	Iran	16 Nov 49	General Amity	OIRTB47	433070
Jordan	Iran	26 Apr 60	Culture	OIRTB47	433071
Jordan	Iran	07 Jul 63	General Trade	OIRTB47	433072
Jordan	Iran	10 Jul 71	Taxation	OIRTB47	433073
Jordan	Iraq	14 Apr 47	General Amity	23UNTS148	100345
Jordan	Israel	03 Apr 49	Peace/Disarmament	42UNTS303	100656
Jordan	Italy	24 Apr 52	General Amity	281UNTS167	104078
Jordan	Italy	25 Mar 63	Air Transport	64ITDI258	436184
Jordan	Italy	26 May 65	Air Transport	66ITDI265	436185
Jordan	Multilateral	07 Dec 44	Air Transport	171UNTS345	200501
Jordan	Multilateral	07 Dec 44	Air Transport	84UNTS389	200252
Jordan	Multilateral	11 Dec 46	Sanitation	12UNTS179	100186
Jordan	Multilateral	12 Nov 47	Admin Cooperation	46UNTS201	100710
Jordan	Multilateral	09 Dec 48	Humanitarian	78UNTS277	101021
Jordan	Multilateral	04 May 49	Admin Cooperation	47UNTS159	100728
Jordan	Multilateral	22 Nov 50	Culture	131UNTS25	101734

PARTY ONE	PARTY TWO	DATE	TOPIC	CITATION	NUMBER
Jordan	Multilateral	07 Dec 50	Admin Cooperation	212UNTS17	102861
Jordan	Multilateral	25 May 51	Status of Forces	175UNTS215	102303
Jordan	Multilateral	11 Jul 52	Postal Service	170UNTS63	102222
Jordan	Multilateral	11 Jul 52	Postal Service	170UNTS269	102223
Jordan	Multilateral	11 Jul 52	IGO Establishment	169UNTS3	102220
Jordan	Multilateral	11 May 53	Sanitation	456UNTS3	106555
Jordan	Multilateral	12 May 54	Admin Cooperation	327UNTS3	104714
Jordan	Multilateral	14 May 54	Culture	249UNTS215	103511
Jordan	Multilateral	25 May 55	IGO Establishment	264UNTS117	103791
Jordan	Multilateral	14 Jun 55	Tech Assistance	212UNTS263	200526
Jordan	Multilateral	03 Oct 57	Postal Service	364UNTS331	105212
Jordan	Multilateral	03 Oct 57	Postal Service	364UNTS3	105211
Jordan	Multilateral	03 Oct 57	Postal Service	365UNTS3	105213
Jordan	Multilateral	10 Jun 58	Admin Cooperation	330UNTS3	104739
Jordan	Multilateral	26 Jan 60	IGO Establishment	439UNTS249	106333
Jordan	Multilateral	30 Mar 61	Sanitation	520UNTS151	107515
Jordan	Multilateral	21 Jun 61	IGO Establishment	514UNTS209	107449
Jordan	Multilateral	22 Jun 62	ILO Labor	494UNTS249	107237
Jordan	Multilateral	28 Jun 62	ILO Labor	494UNTS271	107238
Jordan	Multilateral	05 Aug 63	Sanitation	480UNTS43	106964
Jordan	Multilateral	10 Jul 64	Postal Service	612UNTS3	108847
Jordan	Multilateral	10 Jul 64	Postal Service	611UNTS387	108846
Jordan	Multilateral	10 Jul 64	Postal Service	611UNTS7	108844
Jordan	Multilateral	10 Jul 64	Postal Service	611UNTS105	108845
Jordan	Multilateral	13 Jul 64	ILO Labor	569UNTS65	108279
Jordan	Multilateral	03 Aug 64	Tech Assistance	503UNTS239	107347
Jordan	Multilateral	20 Aug 64	Telecommunications	514UNTS25	107441
Jordan	Multilateral	23 Jun 65	General IGO	614UNTS239	108873
Jordan	Multilateral	27 Jan 67	Scientific Project	610UNTS205	108843
Jordan	Multilateral	01 Jul 68	Peace/Disarmament	OUNTSO	110485
Jordan	Multilateral	24 Sep 68	Air Transport	OUNTSO	110612
Jordan	Netherlands	24 Aug 61	Air Transport	466UNTS3	106733
Jordan	Norway	21 Aug 61	Air Transport	465UNTS275	106731
Jordan	Spain	07 Oct 50	General Amity	51SPBO1710	460179
Jordan	State/IGO Group	03 Apr 68	Direct Aid	632UNTS66	109009
Jordan	Sweden	09 Jan 61	Air Transport	465UNTS155	106726
Jordan	Syria	04 Jun 53	Specific Resources	184UNTS15	102437
Jordan	Syria	23 Dec 53	Admin Cooperation	204UNTS207	102759
Jordan	Taiwan	19 Nov 57	General Amity	308UNTS227	104463
Jordan	Taiwan	17 Oct 61	Culture	435UNTS267	106284
Jordan	Turkey	11 Jan 47	General Amity	14UNTS49	100210
Jordan	Turkey	07 May 48	Air Transport	32UNTS313	100505
Jordan	Turkey	01 Apr 68	Land Transport	OUNTSO	110584
Jordan	UK Great Britain	19 Jul 41	Extradition	9UNTS389	200055
Jordan	UK Great Britain	19 Jul 41	Territory Boundary	9UNTS381	200054
Jordan	UK Great Britain	22 Mar 46	General Amity	6UNTS143	100074
Jordan	UK Great Britain	15 Mar 48	General Military	77UNTS77	100994
Jordan	UK Great Britain	01 May 51	Finance	117UNTS19	101582
Jordan	UK Great Britain	26 Mar 58	Loans and Credits	312UNTS373	104526
Jordan	UK Great Britain	07 May 58	Loans and Credits	312UNTS379	104527
Jordan	UK Great Britain	11 Jun 59	Loans and Credits	351UNTS283	105028
Jordan	UK Great Britain	04 May 60	Loans and Credits	385UNTS81	105531
Jordan	UK Great Britain	17 Jul 61	Loans and Credits	420UNTS53	106039
Jordan	UK Great Britain	28 Feb 62	Postal Service	466UNTS249	106748
Jordan	UK Great Britain	30 May 62	Loans and Credits	449UNTS167	106458
Jordan	UK Great Britain	27 Apr 63	Loans and Credits	475UNTS169	106892
Jordan	UK Great Britain	31 Aug 64	Loans and Credits	541UNTS3	107856
Jordan	UK Great Britain	08 Jun 65	Loans and Credits	552UNTS251	108057
Jordan	UK Great Britain	26 Jul 66	Loans and Credits	597UNTS219	108647
Jordan	UK Great Britain	02 May 67	Finance	610UNTSO	108837
Jordan	UK Great Britain	15 Aug 67	Loans and Credits	632UNTS269	109028
Jordan	UK Great Britain	30 Jul 68	Loans and Credits	OUNTSO	109784
Jordan	UK Great Britain	22 Sep 68	Finance	OUNTSO	109811
Jordan	UK Great Britain	14 Jan 69	Loans and Credits	OUNTSO	109785
Jordan	UK Great Britain	27 Mar 69	Loans and Credits	OUNTSO	110114

PARTY ONE	PARTY TWO	DATE	TOPIC	CITATION	NUMBER
Jordan	UK Great Britain	24 May 69	Loans and Credits	0UNTS0	110115
Jordan	UK Great Britain	09 Aug 69	Air Transport	0UNTS0	110424
Jordan	UK Great Britain	13 Oct 69	Loans and Credits	0UNTS0	110427
Jordan	UN Relief Palestin	20 Aug 51	Refugees	120UNTS277	200394
Jordan	UN Relief Palestin	30 Mar 53	Direct Aid	165UNTS317	200495
Jordan	UN Special Fund	15 Dec 59	Direct Aid	346UNTS3	104974
Jordan	UNICEF (Children)	08 Jul 52	Direct Aid	173UNTS353	200503
Jordan	UNICEF (Children)	09 Aug 58	Direct Aid	309UNTS297	104478
Jordan	UNICEF (Children)	24 Mar 69	IGO Operations	0UNTS0	109488
Jordan	United Arab Rep	21 Apr 47	General Trade	11UNTS3	100146
Jordan	United Arab Rep	02 Jan 52	Air Transport	192UNTS157	102599
Jordan	United Nations	29 Mar 51	Tech Assistance	137UNTS267	200448
Jordan	United Nations	18 Nov 58	IGO Operations	315UNTS125	104564
Jordan	United Nations	11 Sep 61	Tech Assistance	406UNTS255	105855
Jordan	USA (United States)	27 Feb 51	Tech Assistance	141UNTS55	101905
Jordan	USA (United States)	20 Dec 51	Tech Assistance	157UNTS69	102048
Jordan	USA (United States)	12 Feb 52	Tech Assistance	168UNTS25	102211
Jordan	USA (United States)	21 Oct 53	Direct Aid	222UNTS31	103020
Jordan	USA (United States)	13 May 54	Direct Aid	234UNTS225	103285
Jordan	USA (United States)	17 Jun 54	Direct Aid	266UNTS137	103828
Jordan	USA (United States)	29 Jun 54	Direct Aid	237UNTS111	103339
Jordan	USA (United States)	24 Sep 56	Milit Assistance	278UNTS51	104020
Jordan	USA (United States)	29 Apr 57	Direct Aid	290UNTS111	104230
Jordan	USA (United States)	27 Jun 57	General Aid	288UNTS269	104209
Jordan	USA (United States)	29 Jun 57	Direct Aid	288UNTS263	104208
Jordan	USA (United States)	11 Feb 64	US Agri Commod Aid	511UNTS85	107429
Jordan	USA (United States)	05 Apr 66	Direct Aid	593UNTS239	108587
Jordan	USA (United States)	25 Aug 66	US Agri Commod Aid	606UNTS237	108788
Jordan	USA (United States)	04 Apr 68	US Agri Commod Aid	0UNTS0	110011
Jordan	USA (United States)	21 Apr 69	US Agri Commod Aid	0UNTS0	110160
Jordan	USSR (Soviet Union)	04 Oct 67	Culture	0UNTS0	110278
Jordan	USSR (Soviet Union)	21 Jan 69	General Trade	0UNTS0	110364
Jordan	WHO (World Health)	03 Apr 51	Tech Assistance	110UNTS297	200367
Jordan	WHO (World Health)	16 Jun 52	Direct Aid	135UNTS323	200445
Jordan	WHO (World Health)	21 Aug 52	Direct Aid	141UNTS341	200472
Jordan	WHO (World Health)	03 Aug 60	Tech Assistance	381UNTS133	105469
Kenya	Accept UN Charter	12 Dec 63	UN Charter	483UNTS233	107015
Kenya	China People's Rep	10 May 64	Direct Aid	64CCJC64	411229
Kenya	Denmark	26 Jun 64	Education	573UNTS107	108325
Kenya	Denmark	26 Jun 68	Loans and Credits	0UNTS0	109210
Kenya	Denmark	28 Jun 68	Direct Aid	0UNTS0	109393
Kenya	France	28 Jul 64	Air Transport	65FRJO2511	416258
Kenya	Germany, West	04 Dec 64	General Economic	66WBGA165	424356
Kenya	Germany, West	04 Dec 64	Claims and Debts	66WGBB899	425355
Kenya	Germany, West	04 Dec 64	Tech Assistance	66WBGA165	424357
Kenya	Germany, West	04 Dec 64	Loans and Credits	66WBGA165	424358
Kenya	Germany, West	08 Dec 66	Loans and Credits	67WBGA52	424359
Kenya	Germany, West	30 Nov 67	Loans and Credits	68WBGA47	424360
Kenya	Germany, West	08 Aug 68	Visas	68WBGA184	424361
Kenya	Germany, West	11 Apr 69	Loans and Credits	69WBGA115	424362
Kenya	Germany, West	13 Mar 70	Loans and Credits	70WBGA98	424363
Kenya	Germany, West	20 Jun 70	Admin Cooperation	71WGBB924	425364
Kenya	Germany, West	01 Jul 70	Loans and Credits	70WBGA151	424365
Kenya	Germany, West	13 May 71	Loans and Credits	71WBGA114	424366
Kenya	IBRD (World Bank)	29 Sep 65	IBRD Project	568UNTS289	108274
Kenya	IBRD (World Bank)	17 Feb 67	IBRD Project	599UNTS233	108669
Kenya	IBRD (World Bank)	10 Oct 69	IBRD Project	0UNTS0	110671
Kenya	IBRD (World Bank)	07 Nov 69	IBRD Project	0UNTS0	110673
Kenya	ICJ Option Clause	12 Apr 65	ICJ Option Clause	531UNTS113	107697
Kenya	IDA (Devel Assoc)	17 Aug 64	Non-IBRD Project	535UNTS79	107776
Kenya	IDA (Devel Assoc)	29 Dec 64	Non-IBRD Project	535UNTS225	107782
Kenya	IDA (Devel Assoc)	30 Jun 65	Non-IBRD Project	554UNTS75	108097
Kenya	IDA (Devel Assoc)	19 Aug 66	Non-IBRD Project	585UNTS119	108485
Kenya	IDA (Devel Assoc)	11 May 67	General Aid	617UNTS111	108909
Kenya	IDA (Devel Assoc)	11 May 67	General Aid	617UNTS91	108908

PARTY ONE	PARTY TWO	DATE	TOPIC	CITATION	NUMBER
Kenya	IDA (Devel Assoc)	17 Jun 68	Non-IBRD Project	0UNTS0	109320
Kenya	IDA (Devel Assoc)	17 Jun 68	Non-IBRD Project	0UNTS0	109304
Kenya	IDA (Devel Assoc)	20 May 70	Non-IBRD Project	0UNTS0	110684
Kenya	Israel	25 Feb 66	Tech Assistance	582UNTS23	108455
Kenya	Japan	30 Jul 64	Education	0JGJI1550	441121
Kenya	Japan	31 Mar 66	Direct Aid	66JJS177	442171
Kenya	Japan	21 Jan 69	Direct Aid	69JJS275	442230
Kenya	Multilateral	27 May 47	Air Transport	418UNTS161	106021
Kenya	Multilateral	02 Jul 51	Refugees	189UNTS137	102545
Kenya	Multilateral	07 Nov 52	General Trade	221UNTS255	103010
Kenya	Multilateral	14 Jun 54	Air Transport	320UNTS209	104643
Kenya	Multilateral	14 Jun 54	Air Transport	320UNTS217	104644
Kenya	Multilateral	25 May 55	IGO Establishment	264UNTS117	103791
Kenya	Multilateral	30 Mar 61	Sanitation	520UNTS151	107515
Kenya	Multilateral	18 Apr 61	Dispute Settlement	500UNTS243	107312
Kenya	Multilateral	18 Apr 61	Consul/Citizenship	500UNTS95	107310
Kenya	Multilateral	18 Apr 61	Consul/Citizenship	500UNTS223	107311
Kenya	Multilateral	21 Jun 61	IGO Establishment	514UNTS209	107449
Kenya	Multilateral	25 May 62	IGO Establishment	486UNTS103	107075
Kenya	Multilateral	24 Apr 63	Consul/Citizenship	596UNTS261	108638
Kenya	Multilateral	24 Apr 63	Consul/Citizenship	596UNTS487	108640
Kenya	Multilateral	04 Aug 63	IGO Establishment	510UNTS3	107408
Kenya	Multilateral	10 Jul 64	Postal Service	611UNTS7	108844
Kenya	Multilateral	10 Jul 64	Postal Service	612UNTS3	108847
Kenya	Multilateral	10 Jul 64	Postal Service	611UNTS387	108846
Kenya	Multilateral	10 Jul 64	Postal Service	611UNTS105	108845
Kenya	Multilateral	11 Nov 64	Tech Assistance	515UNTS94	107456
Kenya	Multilateral	11 Dec 64	IGO Operations	547UNTS297	107964
Kenya	Multilateral	18 Mar 65	Dispute Settlement	575UNTS159	108359
Kenya	Multilateral	26 Apr 65	IGO Operations	533UNTS50	107732
Kenya	Multilateral	08 Jul 65	General Trade	597UNTS3	108641
Kenya	Multilateral	04 Mar 66	US Agri Commod Aid	578UNTS57	108387
Kenya	Multilateral	18 Mar 68	Commodity Trade	0UNTS0	109262
Kenya	Multilateral	24 Dec 68	Commodity Trade	0UNTS0	109369
Kenya	Multilateral	27 Jan 69	Telecommunications	0UNTS0	109664
Kenya	Netherlands	19 Nov 66	Admin Cooperation	643UNTS285	109198
Kenya	Netherlands	09 Feb 67	General Aid	0UNTS0	109780
Kenya	Netherlands	09 Feb 67	Non-ILO Labor	610UNTS0	108833
Kenya	Netherlands	10 Nov 67	Extradition	0UNTS0	109232
Kenya	Netherlands	23 Jul 69	Sanitation	0UNTS0	110750
Kenya	Netherlands	08 Jan 70	Sanitation	0UNTS0	110752
Kenya	Norway	03 Apr 65	Tech Assistance	3NORT937	451100
Kenya	Norway	09 Jul 65	Taxation	2NORT553	451101
Kenya	Norway	28 Aug 66	Tech Assistance	3NORT973	451102
Kenya	Poland	20 Apr 64	Tech Assistance	64PZUM23	458112
Kenya	UK Great Britain	16 Jan 64	Admin Cooperation	502UNTS213	107332
Kenya	UK Great Britain	25 Aug 64	Commodity Trade	522UNTS165	107543
Kenya	UK Great Britain	27 Nov 64	Milit Assistance	0UNTS0	110039
Kenya	UK Great Britain	14 Jul 67	Status of Forces	643UNTS231	109195
Kenya	UK Great Britain	14 Jul 67	Military Mission	643UNTS254	109196
Kenya	UK Great Britain	20 Sep 68	Finance	0UNTS0	109805
Kenya	UN Special Fund	01 Oct 64	IGO Operations	511UNTS181	107433
Kenya	UNICEF (Children)	24 Jun 70	IGO Operations	0UNTS0	110562
Kenya	United Nations	01 Oct 64	IGO Operations	511UNTS199	107434
Kenya	USA (United States)	20 Apr 64	Claims and Debts	524UNTS165	107571
Kenya	USA (United States)	26 Aug 64	General Aid	531UNTS51	107692
Kenya	USA (United States)	07 Dec 64	US Agri Commod Aid	532UNTS263	107722
Kenya	USA (United States)	19 Aug 65	Extradition	574UNTS153	108348
Korea, North	China People's Rep	25 Dec 49	Telecommunications	49CCJC3	410384
Korea, North	China People's Rep	25 Dec 49	Postal Service	49CCJC1	410383
Korea, North	China People's Rep	25 Dec 49	Telecommunications	49CCJC4	410385
Korea, North	China People's Rep	18 Aug 50	General Trade	50CCJC25	410020
Korea, North	China People's Rep	23 Nov 53	Health/Educ/Welfare	53CCJC66	410126
Korea, North	China People's Rep	30 Mar 54	Postal Service	54CCJC11	410137
Korea, North	China People's Rep	30 Jun 54	General Trade	54CCJC41	410159

PARTY ONE	PARTY TWO	DATE	TOPIC	CITATION	NUMBER
Korea, North	China People's Rep	14 Jan 56	Specific Resources	56CCJC10	410299
Korea, North	China People's Rep	30 May 56	Culture	56CCJC68	410339
Korea, North	China People's Rep	13 Aug 56	Mass Media	56CCJC92	410356
Korea, North	China People's Rep	02 Sep 56	Specific Resources	56CCJC97	410360
Korea, North	China People's Rep	10 Apr 57	Sanitation	57CCJC40	410418
Korea, North	China People's Rep	07 Jun 57	Postal Service	57CCJC59	410427
Korea, North	China People's Rep	07 Jun 57	Telecommunications	57CCJC60	410428
Korea, North	China People's Rep	31 Dec 57	Scientific Project	57CCJC130	410480
Korea, North	China People's Rep	31 Dec 57	Scientific Project	57CCJC129	410479
Korea, North	China People's Rep	21 Jan 58	General Trade	58CCJC10	410488
Korea, North	China People's Rep	27 Sep 58	Specif Goods/Equip	58CCJC88	410545
Korea, North	China People's Rep	19 Nov 58	General Trade	58CCJC99	410554
Korea, North	China People's Rep	18 Feb 59	Air Transport	59CCJC34	410589
Korea, North	China People's Rep	21 Feb 59	Culture	59CCJC38	410592
Korea, North	China People's Rep	29 Feb 60	General Trade	60CCJC31	410678
Korea, North	China People's Rep	23 May 60	Water Transport	60CCJC66	410702
Korea, North	China People's Rep	11 Jul 61	General Amity	61CCJC96	410809
Korea, North	China People's Rep	08 Jan 62	General Trade	62CCJC1	410854
Korea, North	China People's Rep	05 Nov 62	General Amity	62CCJC100	410925
Korea, North	China People's Rep	14 Oct 63	General Trade	63CCJC118	411019
Korea, North	China People's Rep	24 Sep 64	General Trade	64CCJC126	411232
Korea, North	China People's Rep	27 Dec 64	Mass Media	64CCJC188	411237
Korea, North	China People's Rep	18 Jun 65	Commodity Trade	65CCJC85	411238
Korea, North	China People's Rep	30 Jul 65	Culture	65CCJC102	411239
Korea, North	China People's Rep	01 Nov 65	Scientific Project	65CCJC135	411221
Korea, North	China People's Rep	09 Nov 65	Sanitation	65CCJC138	411222
Korea, North	China People's Rep	18 Nov 65	Land Transport	65CCJC144	411240
Korea, North	China People's Rep	02 Dec 65	Water Transport	65CCJC150	411223
Korea, North	China People's Rep	14 Dec 65	General Trade	65CCJC154	411241
Korea, North	China People's Rep	25 Feb 66	Culture	66CCJC6	411242
Korea, North	China People's Rep	01 Jun 66	Sanitation	66CCJC44	411224
Korea, North	China People's Rep	05 Jul 66	Tech Assistance	66CCJC66	411225
Korea, North	China People's Rep	30 Jul 66	Direct Aid	66CCJC74	411243
Korea, North	China People's Rep	03 Dec 66	General Trade	66CCJC103	411226
Korea, North	China People's Rep	30 Dec 66	Mass Media	66CCJC106	411244
Korea, North	Cuba	29 Aug 60	Culture	473UNTS117	106860
Korea, North	Cuba	29 Aug 60	Consul/Citizenship	469UNTS163	106790
Korea, North	Czechoslovakia	04 Jun 59	Sanitation	338UNTS291	104842
Korea, North	Germany, East	30 Dec 54	Finance	4EGDA505	419171
Korea, North	Germany, East	27 Jan 55	Tech Assistance	4EGDA507	419172
Korea, North	Germany, East	01 Dec 55	Postal Service	4EGDA508	419173
Korea, North	Germany, East	01 Dec 55	Telecommunications	4EGDA516	419174
Korea, North	Germany, East	12 Jun 56	Health/Educ/Welfare	4EGDA532	419175
Korea, North	Germany, East	12 Jun 56	Mass Media	1EGDA534	419176
Korea, North	Germany, East	22 Feb 57	General Trade	5EGDA355	419177
Korea, North	Germany, East	12 Mar 57	Tech Assistance	5EGDA355	419178
Korea, North	Germany, East	18 Apr 58	Health/Educ/Welfare	6EGDA323	419179
Korea, North	Germany, East	07 Dec 59	Education	7EGDA384	419180
Korea, North	Germany, East	03 Jun 60	Consul/Citizenship	8EGDA381	419181
Korea, North	Germany, East	29 Dec 61	General Economic	10EGDA399	419182
Korea, North	Germany, East	27 Jul 65	Sanitation	52EGDZ340	420183
Korea, North	Hungary	29 Mar 63	Sanitation	577UNTS219	108379
Korea, North	Multilateral	26 Mar 56	IGO Establishment	259UNTS125	103686
Korea, North	Multilateral	26 Oct 56	IGO Establishment	276UNTS3	103988
Korea, North	Multilateral	14 Dec 59	Sanitation	422UNTS33	106067
Korea, North	Multilateral	14 Dec 59	Sanitation	422UNTS57	106068
Korea, North	Poland	08 May 53	Tech Assistance	53PZUM109	458010
Korea, North	Poland	30 Dec 55	Telecommunications	55PZUM67	458030
Korea, North	Poland	30 Dec 55	Postal Service	55PZUM57	458031
Korea, North	Poland	11 May 56	Culture	432UNTS161	106219
Korea, North	Poland	17 Apr 57	Scientific Project	57PZUM67	458049
Korea, North	Romania	05 Dec 55	Telecommunications	362UNTS141	105186
Korea, North	Romania	05 Dec 55	Postal Service	362UNTS163	105187
Korea, North	Romania	12 May 56	Culture	342UNTS189	104908
Korea, North	USSR (Soviet Union)	18 Sep 48	Milit Occupation	OSUST253	468246
Korea, North	USSR (Soviet Union)	12 Oct 48	General Amity	OSUST253	468247
Korea, North	USSR (Soviet Union)	17 Mar 49	General Economic	OSUST257	468248
Korea, North	USSR (Soviet Union)	17 Mar 49	General Economic	221UNTS3	102999
Korea, North	USSR (Soviet Union)	06 May 52	Education	OSUST287	468249
Korea, North	USSR (Soviet Union)	19 Jun 53	Direct Aid	OSUST302	468250
Korea, North	USSR (Soviet Union)	28 Dec 54	Telecommunications	OSUST321	468252
Korea, North	USSR (Soviet Union)	28 Dec 54	Postal Service	OSUST321	468251
Korea, North	USSR (Soviet Union)	31 May 55	Finance	OSUST329	468253
Korea, North	USSR (Soviet Union)	31 Aug 55	Finance	OSUST335	468254
Korea, North	USSR (Soviet Union)	30 Nov 55	Sanitation	OSUST342	468255
Korea, North	USSR (Soviet Union)	09 Dec 55	Air Transport	OSUST343	468256
Korea, North	USSR (Soviet Union)	12 Jul 56	Direct Aid	OSUST363	468257
Korea, North	USSR (Soviet Union)	04 Aug 56	Direct Aid	16SUGG72	469923
Korea, North	USSR (Soviet Union)	05 Sep 56	Culture	259UNTS329	103695
Korea, North	USSR (Soviet Union)	20 Apr 57	Mass Media	16SUGG120	469937
Korea, North	USSR (Soviet Union)	25 Apr 57	Specific Property	OSUST382	468258
Korea, North	USSR (Soviet Union)	14 Aug 57	Non-IBRD Project	OSUST387	468260
Korea, North	USSR (Soviet Union)	14 Aug 57	Tech Assistance	OSUST387	468259
Korea, North	USSR (Soviet Union)	11 Oct 57	Education	OSUST390	468261
Korea, North	USSR (Soviet Union)	14 Oct 57	Admin Cooperation	OSUST390	468262
Korea, North	USSR (Soviet Union)	16 Dec 57	Consul/Citizenship	292UNTS107	104269
Korea, North	USSR (Soviet Union)	16 Dec 57	Admin Cooperation	301UNTS301	104349
Korea, North	USSR (Soviet Union)	16 Dec 57	Consul/Citizenship	292UNTS121	104270
Korea, North	USSR (Soviet Union)	11 May 58	General Economic	7SUGG112	469510
Korea, North	USSR (Soviet Union)	17 Mar 59	Tech Assistance	8SUGG140	469566
Korea, North	USSR (Soviet Union)	07 Sep 59	Atomic Energy	8SUGG153	469602
Korea, North	USSR (Soviet Union)	22 Jun 60	General Economic	399UNTS3	105732
Korea, North	USSR (Soviet Union)	11 Jul 60	Tech Assistance	9SUGG142	469674
Korea, North	USSR (Soviet Union)	31 Aug 60	Tech Assistance	9SUGG146	469690
Korea, North	USSR (Soviet Union)	30 Sep 60	Tech Assistance	9SUGG148	469700
Korea, North	USSR (Soviet Union)	13 Oct 60	Finance	9SUGG149	469705
Korea, North	USSR (Soviet Union)	24 Dec 60	Tech Assistance	9SUGG158	469728
Korea, North	USSR (Soviet Union)	24 Dec 60	General Trade	9SUGG158	469729
Korea, North	USSR (Soviet Union)	15 Feb 61	Education	16SUGG130	469991
Korea, North	USSR (Soviet Union)	06 Jul 61	General Aid	10SUGG137	469786
Korea, North	USSR (Soviet Union)	06 Jul 61	General Amity	420UNTS145	106045
Korea, North	USSR (Soviet Union)	06 Jul 61	General Aid	10SUGG137	469784
Korea, South	Argentina	08 Jul 68	Culture	OUNTSO	110186
Korea, South	Australia	21 Sep 65	General Trade	548UNTS163	107977
Korea, South	Austria	29 Jun 70	Visas	70ABGB242	403121
Korea, South	Austria	01 Sep 71	General Trade	71ABGB398	403122
Korea, South	Brazil	07 Feb 66	Culture	OUNTSO	109524
Korea, South	Denmark	04 Dec 69	Loans and Credits	OUNTSO	110396
Korea, South	France	01 Feb 61	Patents/Copyrights	61FRRT11	415130
Korea, South	France	26 Apr 63	Patents/Copyrights	64FRRT2	415131
Korea, South	France	28 Dec 65	Health/Educ/Welfare	68FRJO1909	416132
Korea, South	France	11 Feb 67	Visas	67FRJO1204	416133
Korea, South	Germany, West	22 Sep 61	Visas	62WBGA8	424389
Korea, South	Germany, West	16 Dec 63	Non-ILO Labor	64WGBB143	425390
Korea, South	Germany, West	04 Feb 64	Claims and Debts	66WGBB841	425391
Korea, South	Germany, West	07 Dec 64	Loans and Credits	65WBGA29	424393
Korea, South	Germany, West	08 Apr 65	General Trade	65WBGA29	424394
Korea, South	Germany, West	09 Apr 65	Water Transport	71WGBB1259	425395
Korea, South	Germany, West	18 Feb 70	Non-ILO Labor	70WBGA99	424396
Korea, South	Germany, West	21 May 71	Loans and Credits	71WBGA142	424397
Korea, South	Germany, West	02 Jun 71	Non-ILO Labor	71WGBB927	425398
Korea, South	IBRD (World Bank)	31 Jan 68	IBRD Project	639UNTS263	200638
Korea, South	IBRD (World Bank)	23 May 69	Loans and Credits	OUNTSO	200655
Korea, South	IDA (Devel Assoc)	17 Aug 62	Non-IBRD Project	468UNTS387	200603
Korea, South	IDA (Devel Assoc)	18 Dec 67	Non-IBRD Project	639UNTS303	200639
Korea, South	IDA (Devel Assoc)	24 Jul 68	Non-IBRD Project	OUNTSO	200647
Korea, South	IDA (Devel Assoc)	04 Jun 69	Non-IBRD Project	OUNTSO	200657
Korea, South	Iran	05 May 69	General Amity	OIRTB17	433029
Korea, South	Italy	07 Mar 61	Patents/Copyrights	62ITDI497	436095
Korea, South	Italy	21 Nov 61	General Economic	62ITDI577	436096

PARTY ONE	PARTY TWO	DATE	TOPIC	CITATION	NUMBER
Korea, South	Japan	31 Dec 57	Admin Cooperation	0JGJI1369	441103
Korea, South	Japan	22 Jun 65	General Amity	583UNTS33	108471
Korea, South	Japan	22 Jun 65	Claims and Debts	583UNTS173	108473
Korea, South	Japan	22 Jun 65	Specific Resources	583UNTS51	108472
Korea, South	Japan	22 Jun 65	Dispute Settlement	584UNTS147	108476
Korea, South	Japan	22 Jun 65	Consul/Citizenship	584UNTS3	108474
Korea, South	Japan	22 Jun 65	Culture	584UNTS49	108475
Korea, South	Japan	24 Mar 66	General Trade	66JJS183	442170
Korea, South	Japan	18 Oct 66	Specific Resources	66JJS187	442180
Korea, South	Japan	28 Apr 67	Scientific Project	67JJS249	442186
Korea, South	Japan	28 Apr 67	Scientific Project	67JJS251	442187
Korea, South	Japan	16 May 67	Air Transport	67JHZ8	439010
Korea, South	Japan	16 May 67	Air Transport	0UNTS0	109479
Korea, South	Japan	25 Oct 67	Education	67JJS291	442204
Korea, South	Japan	03 Dec 68	Patents/Copyrights	68JJS293	442224
Korea, South	Japan	01 Apr 69	Taxation	69JJS287	442239
Korea, South	Japan	03 Mar 70	Taxation	70JHZ10	439036
Korea, South	Mexico	29 Apr 66	Culture	70MEXD2904	444005
Korea, South	Mexico	12 Dec 66	General Trade	70MEXD2904	444006
Korea, South	Multilateral	07 Dec 44	IGO Establishment	15UNTS295	200102
Korea, South	Multilateral	07 Dec 44	Air Transport	84UNTS389	200252
Korea, South	Multilateral	06 Mar 48	Water Transport	289UNTS3	104214
Korea, South	Multilateral	10 Jun 48	Humanitarian	164UNTS113	102163
Korea, South	Multilateral	24 Jul 48	Sanitation	66UNTS25	100847
Korea, South	Multilateral	15 Nov 48	IGO Establishment	120UNTS59	101615
Korea, South	Multilateral	29 Nov 48	IGO Establishment	120UNTS13	101613
Korea, South	Multilateral	09 Dec 48	Humanitarian	78UNTS277	101021
Korea, South	Multilateral	21 Mar 50	Admin Cooperation	96UNTS271	101342
Korea, South	Multilateral	25 May 51	Status of Forces	175UNTS215	102303
Korea, South	Multilateral	06 Dec 51	Admin Cooperation	150UNTS67	101963
Korea, South	Multilateral	11 Jul 52	Postal Service	170UNTS63	102222
Korea, South	Multilateral	11 Jul 52	Postal Service	171UNTS3	102224
Korea, South	Multilateral	11 Jul 52	Postal Service	170UNTS3	102221
Korea, South	Multilateral	11 Jul 52	IGO Establishment	169UNTS3	102220
Korea, South	Multilateral	11 Jul 52	Postal Service	171UNTS191	102227
Korea, South	Multilateral	11 Jul 52	Postal Service	170UNTS269	102223
Korea, South	Multilateral	11 Jul 52	Postal Service	171UNTS89	102225
Korea, South	Multilateral	11 Jul 52	Postal Service	171UNTS143	102226
Korea, South	Multilateral	31 Mar 53	Privil/Immunities	193UNTS136	102613
Korea, South	Multilateral	11 May 53	Sanitation	456UNTS3	106555
Korea, South	Multilateral	14 Jun 54	Air Transport	320UNTS217	104644
Korea, South	Multilateral	14 Jun 54	Air Transport	320UNTS209	104643
Korea, South	Multilateral	28 Sep 54	Reparations	207UNTS293	102812
Korea, South	Multilateral	28 Sep 54	Refugees	360UNTS117	105158
Korea, South	Multilateral	25 May 55	IGO Establishment	264UNTS117	103791
Korea, South	Multilateral	13 Mar 56	Humanitarian	427UNTS245	106158
Korea, South	Multilateral	25 Apr 56	Commodity Trade	270UNTS103	103896
Korea, South	Multilateral	03 Oct 57	Postal Service	364UNTS3	105211
Korea, South	Multilateral	03 Oct 57	Postal Service	365UNTS3	105213
Korea, South	Multilateral	03 Oct 57	Postal Service	365UNTS207	105214
Korea, South	Multilateral	19 Jun 58	Tech Assistance	306UNTS236	200550
Korea, South	Multilateral	06 Apr 59	Commodity Trade	349UNTS167	105013
Korea, South	Multilateral	26 Jan 60	IGO Establishment	439UNTS249	106333
Korea, South	Multilateral	17 Jun 60	Humanitarian	536UNTS27	107794
Korea, South	Multilateral	01 Sep 60	Commodity Trade	403UNTS3	105792
Korea, South	Multilateral	23 Jan 61	Postal Service	530UNTS141	107679
Korea, South	Multilateral	30 Mar 61	Sanitation	520UNTS151	107515
Korea, South	Multilateral	14 Apr 61	IGO Establishment	422UNTS101	106071
Korea, South	Multilateral	18 Apr 61	Consul/Citizenship	500UNTS95	107310
Korea, South	Multilateral	18 Apr 61	Consul/Citizenship	500UNTS223	107311
Korea, South	Multilateral	18 Apr 61	Dispute Settlement	500UNTS243	107312
Korea, South	Multilateral	21 Jun 61	IGO Establishment	514UNTS209	107449
Korea, South	Multilateral	15 May 62	Commodity Trade	444UNTS3	106367
Korea, South	Multilateral	05 Aug 63	Sanitation	480UNTS43	106964
Korea, South	Multilateral	10 Jul 64	Postal Service	612UNTS3	108847

PARTY ONE	PARTY TWO	DATE	TOPIC	CITATION	NUMBER
Korea, South	Multilateral	10 Jul 64	Postal Service	611UNTS7	108844
Korea, South	Multilateral	10 Jul 64	Postal Service	611UNTS105	108845
Korea, South	Multilateral	10 Jul 64	Postal Service	612UNTS233	108848
Korea, South	Multilateral	09 Mar 65	Water Transport	591UNTS265	108564
Korea, South	Multilateral	18 Mar 65	Dispute Settlement	575UNTS159	108359
Korea, South	Multilateral	08 Jul 65	General Trade	597UNTS3	108641
Korea, South	Multilateral	04 Dec 65	IGO Establishment	571UNTS123	108303
Korea, South	Multilateral	16 Dec 65	Postal Service	570UNTS201	108295
Korea, South	Multilateral	31 Dec 65	Specific Resources	616UNTS317	108904
Korea, South	Multilateral	05 Apr 66	Water Transport	640UNTS133	109159
Korea, South	Multilateral	22 Apr 68	Scientific Project	0UNTS0	109574
Korea, South	Multilateral	01 Aug 68	Culture	0UNTS0	109368
Korea, South	Multilateral	11 Jun 69	Scientific Project	0UNTS0	110100
Korea, South	Multilateral	28 Apr 70	Visas	0UNTS0	110805
Korea, South	Netherlands	26 Oct 53	Air Transport	200UNTS103	102697
Korea, South	Netherlands	08 Dec 65	Patents/Copyrights	571UNTS83	108301
Korea, South	Netherlands	16 May 68	Non-IBRD Project	0UNTS0	109260
Korea, South	New Zealand	31 Jan 67	General Trade	598UNTS91	108656
Korea, South	Norway	24 May 65	Patents/Copyrights	3NORT942	451103
Korea, South	Philippines	11 Nov 60	Visas	490UNTS249	107159
Korea, South	Philippines	24 Feb 61	General Trade	423UNTS217	106094
Korea, South	Philippines	22 Jul 69	Air Transport	0UNTS0	110199
Korea, South	Taiwan	01 Mar 52	Air Transport	255UNTS35	103603
Korea, South	Taiwan	03 Mar 61	General Trade	0CTRC33	413014
Korea, South	Taiwan	27 Nov 64	General Amity	555UNTS3	108102
Korea, South	Thailand	15 Sep 61	General Trade	413UNTS137	105948
Korea, South	UK Great Britain	18 Nov 69	Visas	0UNTS0	110428
Korea, South	UN Special Fund	21 Apr 61	Direct Aid	394UNTS231	200583
Korea, South	UNICEF (Children)	25 Mar 50	IGO Operations	65UNTS171	200209
Korea, South	United Nations	21 Sep 51	IGO Status/Immunit	104UNTS323	200322
Korea, South	United Nations	06 Nov 59	Other Military	346UNTS289	200565
Korea, South	USA (United States)	24 Aug 48	General Military	79UNTS57	101031
Korea, South	USA (United States)	11 Sep 48	Milit Assistance	89UNTS155	101216
Korea, South	USA (United States)	10 Dec 48	Direct Aid	55UNTS157	100813
Korea, South	USA (United States)	17 Feb 49	Postal Service	74UNTS167	100963
Korea, South	USA (United States)	29 Jun 49	Air Transport	55UNTS79	100809
Korea, South	USA (United States)	26 Jan 50	Military Mission	178UNTS97	102337
Korea, South	USA (United States)	26 Jan 50	Milit Assistance	80UNTS205	101053
Korea, South	USA (United States)	28 Apr 50	Education	93UNTS21	101284
Korea, South	USA (United States)	12 Jul 50	Status of Forces	222UNTS229	103029
Korea, South	USA (United States)	28 Jul 50	Finance	140UNTS57	101883
Korea, South	USA (United States)	07 Jan 52	Milit Assistance	179UNTS105	102359
Korea, South	USA (United States)	24 May 52	Direct Aid	179UNTS23	102353
Korea, South	USA (United States)	01 Oct 53	General Military	238UNTS199	103363
Korea, South	USA (United States)	17 Nov 54	Milit Assistance	256UNTS251	103635
Korea, South	USA (United States)	29 Jan 55	Milit Assistance	239UNTS53	103371
Korea, South	USA (United States)	02 May 55	Direct Aid	258UNTS3	103666
Korea, South	USA (United States)	29 May 55	Milit Installation	256UNTS263	103636
Korea, South	USA (United States)	31 May 55	US Agri Commod Aid	251UNTS321	103548
Korea, South	USA (United States)	03 Feb 56	Atomic Energy	240UNTS129	103401
Korea, South	USA (United States)	13 Mar 56	US Agri Commod Aid	272UNTS3	103928
Korea, South	USA (United States)	02 Jul 56	Milit Assistance	281UNTS41	104067
Korea, South	USA (United States)	28 Nov 56	General Amity	302UNTS281	104367
Korea, South	USA (United States)	30 Jan 57	US Agri Commod Aid	278UNTS85	104024
Korea, South	USA (United States)	24 Apr 57	Air Transport	288UNTS219	104207
Korea, South	USA (United States)	05 Feb 58	US Agri Commod Aid	307UNTS121	104447
Korea, South	USA (United States)	18 Dec 58	Reparations	325UNTS233	104702
Korea, South	USA (United States)	30 Jun 59	US Agri Commod Aid	353UNTS297	105047
Korea, South	USA (United States)	25 Sep 59	Mass Media	358UNTS163	105133
Korea, South	USA (United States)	01 Oct 59	Direct Aid	358UNTS115	105129
Korea, South	USA (United States)	19 Feb 60	Claims and Debts	372UNTS109	105291
Korea, South	USA (United States)	17 Aug 60	Postal Service	400UNTS339	105757
Korea, South	USA (United States)	18 Nov 60	Atomic Energy	400UNTS49	105747
Korea, South	USA (United States)	28 Dec 60	US Agri Commod Aid	402UNTS3	105773
Korea, South	USA (United States)	08 Feb 61	General Aid	405UNTS37	105821

PARTY ONE	PARTY TWO	DATE	TOPIC	CITATION	NUMBER
Korea, South	USA (United States)	02 Mar 62	US Agri Commod Aid	442UNTS185	106349
Korea, South	USA (United States)	25 May 62	Visas	454UNTS25	106537
Korea, South	USA (United States)	07 Nov 62	US Agri Commod Aid	462UNTS129	106674
Korea, South	USA (United States)	08 Jan 63	Consul/Citizenship	493UNTS105	107211
Korea, South	USA (United States)	18 Jun 63	Education	487UNTS297	107112
Korea, South	USA (United States)	18 Mar 64	US Agri Commod Aid	524UNTS263	107578
Korea, South	USA (United States)	12 May 64	Commodity Trade	529UNTS299	107667
Korea, South	USA (United States)	31 Dec 64	US Agri Commod Aid	535UNTS315	107787
Korea, South	USA (United States)	26 Jan 65	Commodity Trade	541UNTS77	107862
Korea, South	USA (United States)	07 Mar 66	US Agri Commod Aid	579UNTS137	108404
Korea, South	USA (United States)	14 Sep 66	Direct Aid	606UNTS55	108774
Korea, South	USA (United States)	24 Sep 66	Admin Cooperation	607UNTS157	108803
Korea, South	USA (United States)	09 Feb 67	Milit Installation	0UNTS0	109605
Korea, South	USA (United States)	23 Feb 67	General Aid	0UNTS0	109852
Korea, South	USA (United States)	25 Mar 67	US Agri Commod Aid	0UNTS0	109756
Korea, South	USA (United States)	11 Dec 67	Commodity Trade	0UNTS0	110060
Korea, South	USA (United States)	28 Mar 68	Visas	0UNTS0	109926
Korea, South	USA (United States)	10 May 68	US Agri Commod Aid	0UNTS0	110139
Korea, South	USA (United States)	23 Oct 68	US Agri Commod Aid	0UNTS0	110140
Korea, South	USA (United States)	26 Feb 69	US Agri Commod Aid	0UNTS0	110141
Korea, South	USA (United States)	08 Apr 69	US Agri Commod Aid	0UNTS0	110142
Korea, South	USA (United States)	20 Mar 70	US Agri Commod Aid	0UNTS0	110631
Korea, South	Vietnam, South	19 Dec 62	General Trade	0VKNG187	496055
Korea, South	Vietnam, South	31 Oct 64	Milit Assistance	0VKNG323	496081
Korea, South	Vietnam, South	16 Jan 67	Air Transport	0VKNG241	496066
Korea, South	Vietnam, South	16 Jan 67	Claims and Debts	0VKNG240	496065
Korea, South	Vietnam, South	04 Oct 67	Finance	0VKNG255	496071
Korea, South	Vietnam, South	04 Jun 70	General Economic	0VKNG337	496087
Korea, South	Vietnam, South	04 Jun 70	General Economic	0VKNG384	496098
Korea, South	WHO (World Health)	19 Sep 51	Sanitation	109UNTS297	200366
Korea, South	WHO (World Health)	20 Jan 61	Tech Assistance	406UNTS269	200589
Kuwait	Accept UN Charter	20 Apr 63	UN Charter	463UNTS213	106705
Kuwait	France	18 Sep 69	Culture	0UNTS0	110742
Kuwait	Iran	08 May 68	Taxation	0IRTB48	433075
Kuwait	Iran	06 Nov 68	General Trade	0IRTB48	433074
Kuwait	Iraq	04 Oct 63	Visas	485UNTS321	107063
Kuwait	Japan	06 Oct 62	Air Transport	498UNTS235	107284
Kuwait	Multilateral	07 Dec 44	IGO Establishment	15UNTS295	200102
Kuwait	Multilateral	07 Dec 44	Air Transport	84UNTS389	200252
Kuwait	Multilateral	06 Mar 48	Water Transport	289UNTS3	104214
Kuwait	Multilateral	10 Jun 48	Humanitarian	164UNTS113	102163
Kuwait	Multilateral	24 Jul 48	Sanitation	66UNTS25	100847
Kuwait	Multilateral	07 Dec 50	Admin Cooperation	212UNTS17	102861
Kuwait	Multilateral	12 May 54	Admin Cooperation	327UNTS3	104714
Kuwait	Multilateral	25 May 55	IGO Establishment	264UNTS117	103791
Kuwait	Multilateral	26 Jan 60	IGO Establishment	439UNTS249	106333
Kuwait	Multilateral	17 Jun 60	Humanitarian	536UNTS27	107794
Kuwait	Multilateral	14 Sep 60	IGO Establishment	443UNTS247	106363
Kuwait	Multilateral	14 Dec 60	Education	429UNTS93	106193
Kuwait	Multilateral	30 Mar 61	Sanitation	520UNTS151	107515
Kuwait	Multilateral	21 Jun 61	IGO Establishment	514UNTS209	107449
Kuwait	Multilateral	13 Feb 62	Tech Assistance	422UNTS288	200594
Kuwait	Multilateral	22 Jun 62	ILO Labor	494UNTS249	107237
Kuwait	Multilateral	14 Sep 62	IGO Status/Immunit	494UNTS219	107236
Kuwait	Multilateral	24 Apr 63	Consul/Citizenship	596UNTS487	108640
Kuwait	Multilateral	24 Apr 63	Consul/Citizenship	596UNTS261	108638
Kuwait	Multilateral	05 Aug 63	Sanitation	480UNTS43	106964
Kuwait	Multilateral	10 Jul 64	Postal Service	611UNTS105	108845
Kuwait	Multilateral	10 Jul 64	Postal Service	611UNTS7	108844
Kuwait	Multilateral	10 Jul 64	Postal Service	612UNTS3	108847
Kuwait	Multilateral	10 Jul 64	Postal Service	611UNTS387	108846
Kuwait	Multilateral	20 Aug 64	Telecommunications	514UNTS25	107441
Kuwait	Multilateral	05 Apr 66	Water Transport	640UNTS133	109159
Kuwait	Multilateral	09 Jan 68	IGO Establishment	0UNTS0	109707
Kuwait	UK Great Britain	24 May 60	Air Transport	412UNTS4	105923

PARTY ONE	PARTY TWO	DATE	TOPIC	CITATION	NUMBER
Kuwait	UK Great Britain	19 Jun 61	General Amity	399UNTS239	105743
Kuwait	UK Great Britain	26 Nov 66	Culture	633UNTS58	109034
Kuwait	UK Great Britain	29 Dec 66	Postal Service	617UNTS203	108914
Kuwait	UN Special Fund	29 Jun 60	Tech Assistance	369UNTS419	200575
Kuwait	UNICEF (Children)	26 Jan 69	IGO Operations	0UNTS0	109792
Kuwait	United Nations	31 Oct 60	Tech Assistance	391UNTS295	200581
Kuwait	USA (United States)	27 Dec 60	Visas	401UNTS185	105771
Kuwait	USA (United States)	21 Oct 63	Postal Service	530UNTS281	107688
Kuwait	USA (United States)	24 Jul 66	Gen Communications	593UNTS289	108590
Kuwait	USSR (Soviet Union)	27 Mar 67	Culture	643UNTS135	109189
Kuwait	WHO (World Health)	16 Mar 61	Tech Assistance	397UNTS315	200588
LAFTA (Free Trade)	ILO (Labor Org)	02 Jul 65	IGO Operations	563UNTS327	200619
Laos	Accept UN Charter	30 Jun 52	UN Charter	223UNTS47	103049
Laos	Australia	24 Dec 63	Finance	503UNTS315	107350
Laos	France	22 Oct 53	Admin Cooperation	59FRRT7	415259
Laos	France	16 Nov 56	Admin Cooperation	60FRRT22	415260
Laos	ICJ Option Clause	24 Oct 52	UN Charter	149UNTS285	101957
Laos	Japan	15 Oct 58	General Aid	341UNTS25	104875
Laos	Japan	07 Apr 65	Postal Service	0JGJI1589	441135
Laos	Japan	29 Jan 66	Postal Service	66JJS201	442167
Laos	Japan	05 Jun 67	Postal Service	67JJS299	442192
Laos	Japan	28 Feb 68	Loans and Credits	68JJS299	442209
Laos	Japan	24 Dec 68	General Aid	68JJS305	442226
Laos	Japan	05 Dec 69	Loans and Credits	69JJS303	442259
Laos	Japan	23 Dec 69	Direct Aid	69JJS309	442260
Laos	Multilateral	07 Dec 44	IGO Establishment	15UNTS295	200102
Laos	Multilateral	11 Dec 46	Sanitation	12UNTS179	100186
Laos	Multilateral	19 Jun 48	Air Transport	310UNTS151	104492
Laos	Multilateral	24 Jul 48	Sanitation	66UNTS25	100847
Laos	Multilateral	29 Nov 48	IGO Establishment	120UNTS13	101613
Laos	Multilateral	09 Dec 48	Humanitarian	78UNTS277	101021
Laos	Multilateral	22 Nov 50	Culture	131UNTS25	101734
Laos	Multilateral	23 Dec 50	Tech Assistance	185UNTS3	102456
Laos	Multilateral	25 May 51	Status of Forces	175UNTS215	102303
Laos	Multilateral	08 Sep 51	Peace/Disarmament	136UNTS45	101832
Laos	Multilateral	08 Sep 51	General Military	136UNTS165	101833
Laos	Multilateral	06 Dec 51	Admin Cooperation	150UNTS67	101963
Laos	Multilateral	11 Jul 52	Postal Service	171UNTS3	102224
Laos	Multilateral	11 Jul 52	Postal Service	170UNTS269	102223
Laos	Multilateral	11 Jul 52	Postal Service	171UNTS89	102225
Laos	Multilateral	11 Jul 52	Postal Service	171UNTS191	102227
Laos	Multilateral	11 Jul 52	Postal Service	170UNTS63	102222
Laos	Multilateral	11 Jul 52	IGO Establishment	169UNTS3	102220
Laos	Multilateral	11 Jul 52	Postal Service	171UNTS143	102226
Laos	Multilateral	11 Jul 52	Postal Service	170UNTS3	102221
Laos	Multilateral	06 Sep 52	Patents/Copyrights	216UNTS132	102937
Laos	Multilateral	01 Jun 54	Tech Assistance	200UNTS235	200520
Laos	Multilateral	14 Jun 54	Air Transport	320UNTS217	104644
Laos	Multilateral	14 Jun 54	Air Transport	320UNTS209	104643
Laos	Multilateral	28 Sep 55	Air Transport	478UNTS371	106943
Laos	Multilateral	26 Oct 56	IGO Establishment	276UNTS3	103988
Laos	Multilateral	03 Oct 57	Postal Service	366UNTS3	105215
Laos	Multilateral	03 Oct 57	Postal Service	365UNTS3	105213
Laos	Multilateral	03 Oct 57	Postal Service	364UNTS331	105212
Laos	Multilateral	03 Oct 57	Postal Service	364UNTS3	105211
Laos	Multilateral	03 Oct 57	Postal Service	365UNTS207	105214
Laos	Multilateral	03 Oct 57	Postal Service	366UNTS87	105216
Laos	Multilateral	03 Oct 57	Postal Service	366UNTS255	105219
Laos	Multilateral	03 Oct 57	Postal Service	366UNTS141	105217
Laos	Multilateral	26 Jan 60	IGO Establishment	439UNTS249	106333
Laos	Multilateral	26 Nov 60	Taxation	500UNTS25	107304
Laos	Multilateral	18 Apr 61	Dispute Settlement	500UNTS243	107312
Laos	Multilateral	18 Apr 61	Consul/Citizenship	500UNTS223	107311
Laos	Multilateral	18 Apr 61	Consul/Citizenship	500UNTS95	107310
Laos	Multilateral	21 Jun 61	IGO Establishment	514UNTS209	107449

PARTY ONE	PARTY TWO	DATE	TOPIC	CITATION	NUMBER
Laos	Multilateral	23 Jul 62	Recognition	456UNTS302	106564
Laos	Multilateral	05 Aug 63	Sanitation	480UNTS43	106964
Laos	Multilateral	19 Oct 63	Direct Aid	523UNTS249	107559
Laos	Multilateral	10 Jul 64	Postal Service	612UNTS361	108849
Laos	Multilateral	10 Jul 64	Postal Service	613UNTS3	108851
Laos	Multilateral	10 Jul 64	Postal Service	613UNTS3	108850
Laos	Multilateral	10 Jul 64	Postal Service	611UNTS387	108846
Laos	Multilateral	10 Jul 64	Postal Service	612UNTS233	108848
Laos	Multilateral	10 Jul 64	Postal Service	611UNTS105	108845
Laos	Multilateral	10 Jul 64	Postal Service	612UNTS3	108847
Laos	Multilateral	10 Jul 64	Postal Service	611UNTS7	108844
Laos	Multilateral	10 Jul 64	Postal Service	613UNTS193	108852
Laos	Multilateral	08 Jul 65	General Trade	597UNTS3	108641
Laos	Multilateral	04 Dec 65	IGO Establishment	571UNTS123	108303
Laos	Multilateral	04 May 66	IBRD Project	575UNTS49	108354
Laos	Multilateral	27 Jan 67	Scientific Project	610UNTS205	108843
Laos	Multilateral	14 Jun 67	Direct Aid	603UNTS2	108719
Laos	Multilateral	01 Jul 68	Peace/Disarmament	0UNTS0	110485
Laos	Thailand	07 Jul 54	Air Transport	200UNTS115	102698
Laos	Thailand	12 Aug 65	Specific Property	547UNTS209	107958
Laos	UK Great Britain	17 May 63	Direct Aid	475UNTS155	106891
Laos	UK Great Britain	24 Dec 63	Finance	502UNTS189	107330
Laos	UK Great Britain	09 Aug 69	Finance	0UNTS0	110238
Laos	UK Great Britain	24 Mar 70	Loans and Credits	0UNTS0	110758
Laos	UN Special Fund	30 Apr 60	Tech Assistance	361UNTS171	105179
Laos	UNICEF (Children)	15 Aug 52	Direct Aid	161UNTS323	200491
Laos	UNICEF (Children)	11 Jan 58	Claims and Debts	287UNTS255	104191
Laos	United Nations	06 Jul 59	Tech Assistance	337UNTS41	104814
Laos	USA (United States)	09 Sep 51	Direct Aid	174UNTS141	102283
Laos	USA (United States)	31 Dec 51	Tech Assistance	198UNTS243	102668
Laos	USA (United States)	08 Jul 55	Direct Aid	278UNTS59	104021
Laos	USA (United States)	29 Dec 64	Claims and Debts	542UNTS23	107876
Laos	USSR (Soviet Union)	07 Oct 60	Consul/Citizenship	9SUGG149	469702
Laos	USSR (Soviet Union)	01 Dec 62	Direct Aid	11SUGG158	469876
Laos	USSR (Soviet Union)	01 Dec 62	Direct Aid	472UNTS3	106834
Laos	USSR (Soviet Union)	01 Dec 62	Finance	471UNTS181	106832
Laos	USSR (Soviet Union)	01 Dec 62	General Trade	458UNTS21	106590
Laos	Vietnam, South	29 Dec 54	Water Transport	0VKNG85	496026
Laos	Vietnam, South	12 Sep 58	Admin Cooperation	0VKNG131	496038
Laos	Vietnam, South	11 Jun 59	General Amity	0VKNG143	496041
Laos	WHO (World Health)	04 Aug 60	Tech Assistance	373UNTS313	105322
Lat Am Nuclear Arm	Mexico	12 Jan 70	IGO Establishment	0UNTS0	110564
League of Nations	ILO (Labor Org)	04 May 46	IGO Operations	19UNTS187	200114
League of Nations	Multilateral	19 Jul 46	IGO Operations	1UNTS97	200001
League of Nations	Multilateral	28 Aug 46	IGO Operations	1UNTS139	200006
League of Nations	Multilateral	10 Jul 47	Specific Property	5UNTS401	200038
League of Nations	United Nations	19 Jul 46	Specific Property	1UNTS109	200002
League of Nations	United Nations	31 Jul 46	Specific Property	1UNTS119	200003
League of Nations	United Nations	01 Aug 46	Specific Property	1UNTS131	200004
League of Nations	United Nations	01 Aug 46	Specific Property	1UNTS135	200005
League of Nations	United Nations	11 Apr 47	Specific Property	4UNTS443	200026
League of Nations	United Nations	14 Apr 47	Specific Property	4UNTS449	200027
League of Nations	United Nations	27 Jun 47	Specific Property	5UNTS395	200037
League of Nations	United Nations	27 Jun 47	Specific Property	5UNTS389	200036
Lebanon	Belgium	24 Dec 53	Air Transport	219UNTS153	102972
Lebanon	Belgium	24 Dec 53	Extradition	539UNTS321	107842
Lebanon	Bulgaria	17 Feb 67	Air Transport	0UNTS0	110538
Lebanon	China People's Rep	31 Dec 55	General Trade	55CCJC112	410293
Lebanon	China People's Rep	31 Dec 55	General Trade	55CCJC110	410291
Lebanon	China People's Rep	31 Dec 55	General Trade	55CCJC111	410292
Lebanon	Denmark	21 Oct 55	Air Transport	248UNTS17	103482
Lebanon	Denmark	29 Mar 67	Taxation	602UNTS251	108717
Lebanon	France	24 Jan 48	Finance	173UNTS99	102263
Lebanon	France	24 Jul 62	Taxation	64FRRT6	415261
Lebanon	Germany, East	20 May 63	General Economic	11EGDA603	419196

PARTY ONE	PARTY TWO	DATE	TOPIC	CITATION	NUMBER
Lebanon	Germany, West	16 Nov 51	Mostfavored Nation	53WGBB540	425403
Lebanon	Germany, West	08 Mar 55	Patents/Copyrights	55WGBB897	425404
Lebanon	Germany, West	12 Jun 56	Admin Cooperation	57WBGA173	424405
Lebanon	Germany, West	15 Mar 61	Air Transport	62WGBB184	425406
Lebanon	Germany, West	21 May 65	General Economic	67WGBB1673	425407
Lebanon	Greece	10 Sep 47	Dispute Settlement	187UNTS107	102504
Lebanon	Greece	06 Sep 48	Air Transport	178UNTS37	102335
Lebanon	Greece	06 Oct 48	Consul/Citizenship	87UNTS351	101179
Lebanon	Greece	10 Jun 49	Culture	178UNTS29	102334
Lebanon	IBRD (World Bank)	25 Aug 55	IBRD Project	230UNTS233	103188
Lebanon	ICAO (Civil Aviat)	14 Feb 52	Tech Assistance	128UNTS83	101714
Lebanon	ILO (Labor Org)	14 May 66	IGO Establishment	600UNTS69	108676
Lebanon	Iran	07 Oct 53	General Amity	0IRTB49	433076
Lebanon	Iran	17 Oct 56	Culture	0IRTB49	433077
Lebanon	Israel	23 Mar 49	Peace/Disarmament	42UNTS287	100655
Lebanon	Italy	24 Jan 49	Air Transport	231UNTS241	103223
Lebanon	Italy	15 Feb 49	General Amity	51ITGU106	435257
Lebanon	Italy	15 Feb 49	Admin Cooperation	50ITGU187	435256
Lebanon	Italy	04 Nov 55	General Trade	267UNTS113	103838
Lebanon	Italy	04 Nov 55	Tech Assistance	267UNTS147	103840
Lebanon	Italy	13 Feb 60	Air Transport	62ITDI353	436258
Lebanon	Japan	02 Jun 67	Air Transport	71JHZ3	439191
Lebanon	Japan	19 Jun 69	Taxation	69JJS317	442242
Lebanon	Mexico	26 Jul 50	Culture	52MEXD1502	444030
Lebanon	Multilateral	27 Mar 41	Military Mission	67UNTS231	200222
Lebanon	Multilateral	02 Aug 44	Scientific Project	67UNTS221	200221
Lebanon	Multilateral	07 Dec 44	Air Transport	171UNTS345	200501
Lebanon	Multilateral	07 Dec 44	Air Transport	171UNTS387	200502
Lebanon	Multilateral	07 Dec 44	IGO Establishment	15UNTS295	200102
Lebanon	Multilateral	07 Dec 44	Air Transport	84UNTS389	200252
Lebanon	Multilateral	22 Mar 45	General Amity	70UNTS237	200241
Lebanon	Multilateral	16 Nov 45	IGO Establishment	4UNTS275	100052
Lebanon	Multilateral	22 Jul 46	IGO Establishment	14UNTS185	100221
Lebanon	Multilateral	22 Jul 46	IGO Establishment	9UNTS3	100125
Lebanon	Multilateral	27 Jul 46	Patents/Copyrights	90UNTS229	101238
Lebanon	Multilateral	11 Dec 46	Sanitation	12UNTS179	100186
Lebanon	Multilateral	08 Feb 47	Patents/Copyrights	14UNTS287	100222
Lebanon	Multilateral	02 Oct 47	Telecommunications	193UNTS188	102616
Lebanon	Multilateral	11 Oct 47	IGO Establishment	77UNTS143	100998
Lebanon	Multilateral	12 Nov 47	Admin Cooperation	53UNTS13	100770
Lebanon	Multilateral	12 Nov 47	Admin Cooperation	53UNTS39	100771
Lebanon	Multilateral	06 Mar 48	Water Transport	289UNTS3	104214
Lebanon	Multilateral	10 May 48	Culture	289UNTS111	104215
Lebanon	Multilateral	26 Jun 48	Culture	331UNTS217	104757
Lebanon	Multilateral	24 Jul 48	Sanitation	66UNTS25	100847
Lebanon	Multilateral	19 Nov 48	Sanitation	44UNTS277	100688
Lebanon	Multilateral	09 Dec 48	Humanitarian	78UNTS277	101021
Lebanon	Multilateral	23 Mar 49	Commodity Trade	203UNTS179	102746
Lebanon	Multilateral	15 Jul 49	Health/Educ/Welfare	197UNTS3	102631
Lebanon	Multilateral	12 Aug 49	General Military	75UNTS135	100972
Lebanon	Multilateral	12 Aug 49	Humanitarian	75UNTS31	100970
Lebanon	Multilateral	12 Aug 49	Humanitarian	75UNTS287	100973
Lebanon	Multilateral	12 Aug 49	Humanitarian	75UNTS85	100971
Lebanon	Multilateral	19 Sep 49	Land Transport	125UNTS3	101671
Lebanon	Multilateral	24 Sep 49	IGO Establishment	126UNTS237	101691
Lebanon	Multilateral	16 Dec 49	Admin Cooperation	72UNTS3	100924
Lebanon	Multilateral	25 May 51	Status of Forces	175UNTS215	102303
Lebanon	Multilateral	08 Sep 51	Peace/Disarmament	136UNTS45	101832
Lebanon	Multilateral	08 Sep 51	General Military	136UNTS165	101833
Lebanon	Multilateral	10 May 52	Admin Cooperation	439UNTS217	106331
Lebanon	Multilateral	10 May 52	Admin Cooperation	439UNTS193	106330
Lebanon	Multilateral	10 May 52	Taxation	439UNTS233	106332
Lebanon	Multilateral	12 Jun 52	Dispute Settlement	138UNTS183	101869
Lebanon	Multilateral	11 Jul 52	Postal Service	170UNTS3	102221
Lebanon	Multilateral	11 Jul 52	Postal Service	170UNTS63	102222

PARTY ONE	PARTY TWO	DATE	TOPIC	CITATION	NUMBER
Lebanon	Multilateral	11 Jul 52	IGO Establishment	169UNTS3	102220
Lebanon	Multilateral	11 Jul 52	Postal Service	171UNTS89	102225
Lebanon	Multilateral	11 Jul 52	Postal Service	171UNTS143	102226
Lebanon	Multilateral	11 Jul 52	Postal Service	171UNTS3	102224
Lebanon	Multilateral	11 Jul 52	Postal Service	170UNTS269	102223
Lebanon	Multilateral	31 Mar 53	Privil/Immunities	193UNTS136	102613
Lebanon	Multilateral	11 May 53	Sanitation	456UNTS3	106555
Lebanon	Multilateral	01 Oct 53	Commodity Trade	258UNTS153	103677
Lebanon	Multilateral	09 Oct 53	Tech Assistance	190UNTS49	102557
Lebanon	Multilateral	01 Mar 54	Commodity Trade	256UNTS31	103622
Lebanon	Multilateral	14 May 54	Culture	249UNTS215	103511
Lebanon	Multilateral	04 Jun 54	Customs	276UNTS191	103992
Lebanon	Multilateral	25 May 55	IGO Establishment	264UNTS117	103791
Lebanon	Multilateral	12 Oct 55	IGO Establishment	560UNTS3	108165
Lebanon	Multilateral	25 Apr 56	Commodity Trade	270UNTS103	103896
Lebanon	Multilateral	26 Oct 56	IGO Establishment	276UNTS3	103988
Lebanon	Multilateral	15 Jun 57	General Trade	550UNTS45	108008
Lebanon	Multilateral	03 Oct 57	Postal Service	364UNTS3	105211
Lebanon	Multilateral	03 Oct 57	Postal Service	365UNTS207	105214
Lebanon	Multilateral	03 Oct 57	Postal Service	366UNTS3	105215
Lebanon	Multilateral	03 Oct 57	Postal Service	366UNTS87	105216
Lebanon	Multilateral	03 Oct 57	Postal Service	364UNTS331	105212
Lebanon	Multilateral	03 Oct 57	Postal Service	365UNTS3	105213
Lebanon	Multilateral	03 Oct 57	Postal Service	366UNTS141	105217
Lebanon	Multilateral	29 Apr 58	Specific Resources	559UNTS285	108164
Lebanon	Multilateral	29 Apr 58	Water Transport	450UNTS11	106465
Lebanon	Multilateral	29 Apr 58	Territory Boundary	499UNTS311	107302
Lebanon	Multilateral	01 Dec 58	Commodity Trade	385UNTS137	105534
Lebanon	Multilateral	19 Nov 59	IGO Operations	410UNTS156	105902
Lebanon	Multilateral	26 Jan 60	IGO Establishment	439UNTS249	106333
Lebanon	Multilateral	17 Jun 60	Humanitarian	536UNTS27	107794
Lebanon	Multilateral	14 Dec 60	Education	429UNTS93	106193
Lebanon	Multilateral	30 Mar 61	Sanitation	520UNTS151	107515
Lebanon	Multilateral	18 Apr 61	Consul/Citizenship	500UNTS223	107311
Lebanon	Multilateral	18 Apr 61	Dispute Settlement	500UNTS243	107312
Lebanon	Multilateral	18 Apr 61	Consul/Citizenship	500UNTS95	107310
Lebanon	Multilateral	21 Jun 61	IGO Establishment	514UNTS209	107449
Lebanon	Multilateral	26 Oct 61	Patents/Copyrights	496UNTS43	107247
Lebanon	Multilateral	11 Sep 62	Tech Assistance	455UNTS402	106553
Lebanon	Multilateral	14 Sep 62	IGO Status/Immunit	494UNTS219	107236
Lebanon	Multilateral	28 Sep 62	IGO Establishment	469UNTS169	106791
Lebanon	Multilateral	24 Apr 63	Consul/Citizenship	596UNTS487	108640
Lebanon	Multilateral	24 Apr 63	Consul/Citizenship	596UNTS261	108638
Lebanon	Multilateral	05 Aug 63	Sanitation	480UNTS43	106964
Lebanon	Multilateral	10 Jul 64	Postal Service	612UNTS233	108848
Lebanon	Multilateral	10 Jul 64	Postal Service	612UNTS361	108849
Lebanon	Multilateral	10 Jul 64	Postal Service	613UNTS3	108851
Lebanon	Multilateral	10 Jul 64	Postal Service	612UNTS3	108847
Lebanon	Multilateral	10 Jul 64	Postal Service	613UNTS3	108850
Lebanon	Multilateral	10 Jul 64	Postal Service	611UNTS7	108844
Lebanon	Multilateral	10 Jul 64	Postal Service	611UNTS105	108845
Lebanon	Multilateral	10 Jul 64	Postal Service	611UNTS387	108846
Lebanon	Multilateral	20 Aug 64	Telecommunications	514UNTS25	107441
Lebanon	Multilateral	01 Dec 64	Water Transport	550UNTS133	108012
Lebanon	Multilateral	09 Mar 65	Water Transport	591UNTS265	108564
Lebanon	Multilateral	27 Jan 67	Scientific Project	610UNTS205	108843
Lebanon	Multilateral	22 Apr 68	Scientific Project	0UNTS0	109574
Lebanon	Multilateral	24 Sep 68	Air Transport	0UNTS0	110612
Lebanon	Netherlands	20 Sep 49	Air Transport	108UNTS205	101474
Lebanon	Norway	02 Feb 56	Air Transport	3NORT674	451104
Lebanon	Norway	10 Dec 68	Taxation	3NORT0	451105
Lebanon	Pakistan	03 Oct 50	Visas	219UNTS41	102964
Lebanon	Pakistan	16 Jan 53	General Amity	284UNTS193	104137
Lebanon	Pakistan	04 Feb 64	Air Transport	614UNTS55	108863
Lebanon	Spain	07 Mar 49	Culture	49SPBO1812	460180

PARTY ONE	PARTY TWO	DATE	TOPIC	CITATION	NUMBER
Lebanon	Spain	06 May 50	General Amity	51SPBO607	460181
Lebanon	Sweden	23 Mar 53	Air Transport	255UNTS83	103605
Lebanon	Switzerland	03 Dec 45	Recognition	11SWRS673	463021
Lebanon	Switzerland	03 Mar 54	Air Transport	255UNTS127	103608
Lebanon	Switzerland	11 Sep 57	Taxation	57SWRO846	462057
Lebanon	Taiwan	06 Apr 57	General Trade	0CTRC305	413015
Lebanon	Turkey	07 Dec 46	Consul/Citizenship	48TURG702	466007
Lebanon	Turkey	24 Dec 46	Visas	4UNTS269	100051
Lebanon	Turkey	16 Sep 47	Air Transport	44UNTS123	100682
Lebanon	Turkey	28 Jan 57	Consul/Citizenship	57TURG1309	466008
Lebanon	UK Great Britain	20 Jun 49	Postal Service	90UNTS137	101232
Lebanon	UK Great Britain	15 Aug 51	Air Transport	160UNTS327	102116
Lebanon	UK Great Britain	19 May 58	Milit Assistance	327UNTS43	104716
Lebanon	UK Great Britain	24 Oct 63	Taxation	535UNTS3	107772
Lebanon	UN Relief Palestin	26 Nov 54	Direct Aid	202UNTS123	102728
Lebanon	UN Special Fund	07 May 60	Tech Assistance	360UNTS225	105160
Lebanon	UNICEF (Children)	03 Jul 56	Direct Aid	324UNTS145	104683
Lebanon	United Nations	01 May 57	IGO Establishment	266UNTS125	103827
Lebanon	United Nations	20 Jan 58	Postal Service	286UNTS199	104167
Lebanon	United Nations	20 Jan 58	Milit Installation	286UNTS189	104166
Lebanon	United Nations	13 Jun 58	IGO Status/Immunit	303UNTS271	104386
Lebanon	United Nations	26 Aug 61	Tech Assistance	406UNTS105	105842
Lebanon	USA (United States)	08 Sep 44	Recognition	124UNTS187	200419
Lebanon	USA (United States)	21 Jan 46	Postal Service	140UNTS73	101884
Lebanon	USA (United States)	11 Aug 46	Air Transport	66UNTS211	100856
Lebanon	USA (United States)	24 Feb 51	Tech Assistance	223UNTS121	103060
Lebanon	USA (United States)	29 May 51	Tech Assistance	160UNTS49	102101
Lebanon	USA (United States)	05 Jan 52	Tech Assistance	180UNTS199	102385
Lebanon	USA (United States)	26 Jun 52	Tech Assistance	181UNTS187	102409
Lebanon	USA (United States)	23 Mar 53	Milit Assistance	239UNTS45	103370
Lebanon	USA (United States)	18 Jun 54	Direct Aid	233UNTS177	103262
Lebanon	USA (United States)	18 Jul 55	Atomic Energy	239UNTS247	103383
Lebanon	USA (United States)	06 Jun 57	Tech Assistance	284UNTS155	104134
Lebanon	USA (United States)	06 Aug 58	Status of Forces	366UNTS361	105223
Lebanon	USA (United States)	03 Sep 58	Direct Aid	336UNTS91	104801
Lebanon	USA (United States)	16 Sep 59	Scientific Project	358UNTS175	105135
Lebanon	USSR (Soviet Union)	30 Apr 54	General Economic	226UNTS109	103111
Lebanon	WHO (World Health)	05 Jun 51	Scientific Project	104UNTS225	101443
Lebanon	WHO (World Health)	07 Jun 51	Tech Assistance	126UNTS221	101690
Lebanon	WHO (World Health)	08 Sep 60	Tech Assistance	387UNTS49	105557
Lebanon	Yugoslavia	17 Apr 54	Air Transport	602UNTS199	108713
Lesotho	Accept UN Charter	04 Oct 66	UN Charter	575UNTS155	108358
Lesotho	Israel	21 Jan 70	Visas	0UNTS0	110390
Lesotho	Multilateral	10 Jul 64	Postal Service	611UNTS7	108844
Lesotho	Multilateral	10 Jul 64	Postal Service	611UNTS105	108845
Lesotho	Multilateral	17 Nov 66	IGO Operations	580UNTS22	108417
Lesotho	Multilateral	01 Jul 68	Peace/Disarmament	0UNTS0	110485
Lesotho	South Africa	28 Sep 67	Air Transport	0UNTS0	110166
Lesotho	UK Great Britain	17 Feb 67	Admin Cooperation	632UNTS3	109004
Lesotho	UK Great Britain	03 Jul 68	Taxation	0UNTS0	109783
Lesotho	UK Great Britain	06 Jan 70	Finance	0UNTS0	110699
Lesotho	UN Special Fund	17 Nov 66	Recognition	580UNTS17	108416
Lesotho	United Nations	17 Nov 66	IGO Operations	580UNTS29	108418
Lesotho	USA (United States)	04 Oct 66	Admin Cooperation	0UNTS0	109684
Lesotho	USA (United States)	24 Feb 67	Finance	0UNTS0	109853
Lesotho	USA (United States)	22 Sep 67	Direct Aid	0UNTS0	109922
Lesotho	WHO (World Health)	07 Nov 67	Tech Assistance	632UNTS143	109016
Liberia	France	13 Jan 66	Air Transport	68FRJO1904	416262
Liberia	Germany, West	17 Nov 59	Direct Aid	60WBGA69	424408
Liberia	Germany, West	12 Dec 61	Direct Aid	62WBGA46	424411
Liberia	Germany, West	12 Dec 61	General Transport	62WBGA46	424410
Liberia	Germany, West	12 Dec 61	Claims and Debts	67WGBB1537	425409
Liberia	Germany, West	05 Dec 66	Loans and Credits	67WBGA40	424412
Liberia	Germany, West	27 May 70	Specific Property	71WGBB953	425413
Liberia	IBRD (World Bank)	08 Jan 64	IBRD Project	504UNTS53	107353

PARTY ONE	PARTY TWO	DATE	TOPIC	CITATION	NUMBER
Liberia	IBRD (World Bank)	05 Jun 67	Tech Assistance	633UNTS13	109031
Liberia	IBRD (World Bank)	20 Jun 69	IBRD Project	0UNTS0	109949
Liberia	IBRD (World Bank)	04 Jun 70	IBRD Project	0UNTS0	110685
Liberia	ICJ Option Clause	03 Mar 52	ICJ Option Clause	163UNTS117	102145
Liberia	ILO (Labor Org)	02 Apr 51	Tech Assistance	100UNTS117	101392
Liberia	Israel	09 Apr 59	General Amity	448UNTS95	106427
Liberia	Israel	03 Aug 61	Visas	484UNTS203	107030
Liberia	Israel	25 Jun 62	Tech Assistance	448UNTS287	106441
Liberia	Israel	25 Jun 62	Culture	448UNTS295	106442
Liberia	Israel	18 Sep 62	Postal Service	484UNTS209	107031
Liberia	Multilateral	02 Aug 44	Scientific Project	67UNTS221	200221
Liberia	Multilateral	07 Dec 44	Air Transport	171UNTS387	200502
Liberia	Multilateral	07 Dec 44	IGO Establishment	15UNTS295	200102
Liberia	Multilateral	07 Dec 44	Air Transport	171UNTS345	200501
Liberia	Multilateral	07 Dec 44	Air Transport	84UNTS389	200252
Liberia	Multilateral	16 Nov 45	IGO Establishment	4UNTS275	100052
Liberia	Multilateral	22 Jul 46	IGO Establishment	9UNTS3	100125
Liberia	Multilateral	22 Jul 46	IGO Establishment	14UNTS185	100221
Liberia	Multilateral	15 Oct 46	Refugees	11UNTS73	100150
Liberia	Multilateral	11 Dec 46	Sanitation	12UNTS179	100186
Liberia	Multilateral	15 Dec 46	IGO Establishment	18UNTS3	100283
Liberia	Multilateral	06 Mar 48	Water Transport	289UNTS3	104214
Liberia	Multilateral	10 Jun 48	Humanitarian	164UNTS113	102163
Liberia	Multilateral	24 Jul 48	Sanitation	66UNTS25	100847
Liberia	Multilateral	19 Nov 48	Sanitation	44UNTS277	100688
Liberia	Multilateral	09 Dec 48	Humanitarian	78UNTS277	101021
Liberia	Multilateral	23 Mar 49	Commodity Trade	203UNTS179	102746
Liberia	Multilateral	21 Mar 50	Admin Cooperation	96UNTS271	101342
Liberia	Multilateral	07 Dec 50	Admin Cooperation	212UNTS17	102861
Liberia	Multilateral	25 May 51	Status of Forces	175UNTS215	102303
Liberia	Multilateral	02 Jul 51	Refugees	189UNTS137	102545
Liberia	Multilateral	08 Sep 51	General Military	136UNTS165	101833
Liberia	Multilateral	08 Sep 51	Peace/Disarmament	136UNTS45	101832
Liberia	Multilateral	06 Dec 51	IGO Establishment	425UNTS61	106119
Liberia	Multilateral	12 Jun 52	Dispute Settlement	138UNTS183	101869
Liberia	Multilateral	11 Jul 52	Postal Service	170UNTS63	102222
Liberia	Multilateral	11 Jul 52	IGO Establishment	169UNTS3	102220
Liberia	Multilateral	11 Jul 52	Postal Service	170UNTS269	102223
Liberia	Multilateral	06 Sep 52	Patents/Copyrights	216UNTS132	102937
Liberia	Multilateral	07 Oct 52	Admin Cooperation	310UNTS181	104493
Liberia	Multilateral	31 Mar 53	Privil/Immunities	193UNTS136	102613
Liberia	Multilateral	07 Dec 53	Admin Cooperation	182UNTS51	102422
Liberia	Multilateral	18 Jan 54	IGO Establishment	330UNTS121	104743
Liberia	Multilateral	12 May 54	Admin Cooperation	327UNTS3	104714
Liberia	Multilateral	29 Jul 54	Sanitation	249UNTS45	103500
Liberia	Multilateral	28 Sep 54	Refugees	360UNTS117	105158
Liberia	Multilateral	25 May 55	IGO Establishment	264UNTS117	103791
Liberia	Multilateral	04 Jan 56	Scientific Project	256UNTS171	103627
Liberia	Multilateral	25 Apr 56	Commodity Trade	270UNTS103	103896
Liberia	Multilateral	07 Sep 56	Humanitarian	266UNTS3	103822
Liberia	Multilateral	26 Oct 56	IGO Establishment	276UNTS3	103988
Liberia	Multilateral	03 Oct 57	Postal Service	364UNTS3	105211
Liberia	Multilateral	03 Oct 57	Postal Service	365UNTS207	105214
Liberia	Multilateral	03 Oct 57	Postal Service	366UNTS255	105219
Liberia	Multilateral	03 Oct 57	Postal Service	365UNTS3	105213
Liberia	Multilateral	05 Nov 57	Tech Assistance	285UNTS301	104155
Liberia	Multilateral	29 Apr 58	Water Transport	450UNTS11	106465
Liberia	Multilateral	29 Apr 58	Territory Boundary	499UNTS311	107302
Liberia	Multilateral	29 Apr 58	Specific Resources	559UNTS285	108164
Liberia	Multilateral	29 Apr 58	Dispute Settlement	450UNTS169	106466
Liberia	Multilateral	29 Apr 58	Territory Boundary	516UNTS205	107477
Liberia	Multilateral	26 Jan 60	IGO Establishment	439UNTS249	106333
Liberia	Multilateral	17 Jun 60	Humanitarian	536UNTS27	107794
Liberia	Multilateral	14 Dec 60	Education	429UNTS93	106193
Liberia	Multilateral	30 Mar 61	Sanitation	520UNTS151	107515

PARTY ONE	PARTY TWO	DATE	TOPIC	CITATION	NUMBER
Liberia	Multilateral	18 Apr 61	Consul/Citizenship	500UNTS95	107310
Liberia	Multilateral	15 May 62	Commodity Trade	444UNTS3	106367
Liberia	Multilateral	24 Apr 63	Consul/Citizenship	596UNTS261	108638
Liberia	Multilateral	24 Apr 63	Consul/Citizenship	596UNTS487	108640
Liberia	Multilateral	25 May 63	IGO Establishment	479UNTS39	106947
Liberia	Multilateral	04 Aug 63	IGO Establishment	510UNTS3	107408
Liberia	Multilateral	05 Aug 63	Sanitation	480UNTS43	106964
Liberia	Multilateral	10 Jul 64	Postal Service	611UNTS105	108845
Liberia	Multilateral	10 Jul 64	Postal Service	611UNTS7	108844
Liberia	Multilateral	10 Jul 64	Postal Service	612UNTS3	108847
Liberia	Multilateral	12 Feb 65	Tech Assistance	525UNTS148	107587
Liberia	Multilateral	09 Mar 65	Water Transport	591UNTS265	108564
Liberia	Multilateral	18 Mar 65	Dispute Settlement	575UNTS159	108359
Liberia	Multilateral	28 May 65	IGO Establishment	559UNTS273	108163
Liberia	Multilateral	08 Jul 65	General Trade	597UNTS3	108641
Liberia	Multilateral	05 Apr 66	Water Transport	640UNTS133	109159
Liberia	Multilateral	04 May 67	IGO Establishment	595UNTS287	108623
Liberia	Multilateral	18 Mar 68	Commodity Trade	0UNTS0	109262
Liberia	Multilateral	01 Jul 68	Peace/Disarmament	0UNTS0	110485
Liberia	Netherlands	28 Nov 58	Air Transport	393UNTS55	105651
Liberia	Norway	29 Jun 62	Air Transport	466UNTS95	106739
Liberia	Spain	02 Apr 53	General Amity	53SPBO912	460182
Liberia	Spain	26 May 54	General Trade	56SPBO2603	460183
Liberia	Sweden	09 Dec 59	Air Transport	464UNTS219	106716
Liberia	Switzerland	31 Aug 61	Air Transport	559UNTS215	108160
Liberia	Taiwan	15 Jun 63	Culture	521UNTS361	107531
Liberia	UN Special Fund	11 Oct 60	Direct Aid	376UNTS341	105388
Liberia	UNICEF (Children)	17 Apr 52	Direct Aid	133UNTS3	101773
Liberia	UNICEF (Children)	08 Jun 66	General Amity	570UNTS31	108286
Liberia	United Nations	09 Mar 54	Tech Assistance	187UNTS61	102501
Liberia	USA (United States)	15 Jan 42	Admin Cooperation	117UNTS227	200372
Liberia	USA (United States)	31 Mar 42	General Military	23UNTS302	200137
Liberia	USA (United States)	08 Jun 43	Milit Assistance	117UNTS242	200373
Liberia	USA (United States)	31 Dec 43	Non-IBRD Project	106UNTS199	200341
Liberia	USA (United States)	28 Oct 47	Visas	82UNTS23	101081
Liberia	USA (United States)	26 Jul 48	Customs	182UNTS73	102423
Liberia	USA (United States)	22 Jul 49	Visas	232UNTS283	103242
Liberia	USA (United States)	22 Dec 50	Direct Aid	133UNTS69	101781
Liberia	USA (United States)	22 Dec 50	Tech Assistance	92UNTS145	101267
Liberia	USA (United States)	10 Jan 51	Gen Communications	132UNTS255	101765
Liberia	USA (United States)	11 Jan 51	Military Mission	122UNTS125	101642
Liberia	USA (United States)	19 Nov 51	Milit Assistance	167UNTS141	102204
Liberia	USA (United States)	15 Dec 52	Tech Assistance	185UNTS45	102457
Liberia	USA (United States)	23 Jun 53	Education	213UNTS57	102880
Liberia	USA (United States)	23 Jun 53	Tech Assistance	213UNTS37	102879
Liberia	USA (United States)	06 Oct 55	Tech Assistance	275UNTS93	103978
Liberia	USA (United States)	06 Oct 55	Direct Aid	275UNTS87	103977
Liberia	USA (United States)	22 Sep 56	Specific Property	278UNTS109	104027
Liberia	USA (United States)	16 Mar 57	Postal Service	290UNTS59	104228
Liberia	USA (United States)	08 Jul 59	Milit Assistance	357UNTS93	105108
Liberia	USA (United States)	13 Aug 59	Telecommunications	357UNTS181	105116
Liberia	USA (United States)	06 Sep 60	Admin Cooperation	389UNTS245	105596
Liberia	USA (United States)	17 Jun 61	Milit Assistance	410UNTS233	105907
Liberia	USA (United States)	08 Mar 62	Direct Aid	445UNTS41	106375
Liberia	USA (United States)	12 Apr 62	US Agri Commod Aid	445UNTS213	106390
Liberia	USA (United States)	14 Apr 64	Specific Property	526UNTS221	107606
Liberia	USA (United States)	08 May 64	Education	526UNTS239	107608
Liberia	USA (United States)	06 Jan 66	US Agri Commod Aid	592UNTS101	108570
Liberia	USA (United States)	23 Oct 67	US Agri Commod Aid	0UNTS0	110051
Liberia	WHO (World Health)	11 Jun 51	Tech Assistance	103UNTS83	101426
Libya	Accept UN Charter	24 Dec 51	UN Charter	223UNTS51	103050
Libya	France	10 Aug 55	General Amity	57FRJO704	416263
Libya	France	26 Dec 56	Territory Boundary	300UNTS263	104340
Libya	Germany, West	08 Jul 60	Direct Aid	61WBGA21	424414
Libya	Italy	02 Oct 56	Tech Assistance	57ITGU237	435259

PARTY ONE	PARTY TWO	DATE	TOPIC	CITATION	NUMBER
Libya	Italy	25 Jan 63	General Trade	61ITDI272	436260
Libya	Multilateral	07 Dec 44	IGO Establishment	15UNTS295	200102
Libya	Multilateral	12 Nov 47	Admin Cooperation	53UNTS39	100771
Libya	Multilateral	12 Nov 47	Admin Cooperation	53UNTS49	100772
Libya	Multilateral	24 Jul 48	Sanitation	66UNTS25	100847
Libya	Multilateral	24 Sep 49	IGO Establishment	126UNTS237	101691
Libya	Multilateral	21 Mar 50	Admin Cooperation	96UNTS271	101342
Libya	Multilateral	07 Dec 50	Admin Cooperation	212UNTS17	102861
Libya	Multilateral	25 May 51	Status of Forces	175UNTS215	102303
Libya	Multilateral	06 Dec 51	IGO Establishment	425UNTS61	106119
Libya	Multilateral	24 Dec 51	Tech Assistance	118UNTS290	200383
Libya	Multilateral	11 Jul 52	IGO Establishment	169UNTS3	102220
Libya	Multilateral	07 Oct 52	Admin Cooperation	310UNTS181	104493
Libya	Multilateral	14 May 54	Culture	249UNTS215	103511
Libya	Multilateral	14 Jun 54	Air Transport	320UNTS209	104643
Libya	Multilateral	14 Jun 54	Air Transport	320UNTS217	104644
Libya	Multilateral	25 May 55	IGO Establishment	264UNTS117	103791
Libya	Multilateral	26 Oct 56	IGO Establishment	276UNTS3	103988
Libya	Multilateral	03 Oct 57	Postal Service	364UNTS331	105212
Libya	Multilateral	03 Oct 57	Postal Service	365UNTS207	105214
Libya	Multilateral	03 Oct 57	Postal Service	364UNTS3	105211
Libya	Multilateral	03 Oct 57	Postal Service	366UNTS87	105216
Libya	Multilateral	03 Oct 57	Postal Service	365UNTS3	105213
Libya	Multilateral	03 Apr 58	Commodity Trade	336UNTS177	104806
Libya	Multilateral	26 Jan 60	IGO Establishment	439UNTS249	106333
Libya	Multilateral	14 Sep 60	IGO Establishment	443UNTS247	106363
Libya	Multilateral	21 Jun 61	IGO Establishment	514UNTS209	107449
Libya	Multilateral	14 Sep 62	IGO Status/Immunit	494UNTS219	107236
Libya	Multilateral	20 Apr 63	IGO Establishment	495UNTS3	107239
Libya	Multilateral	25 May 63	IGO Establishment	479UNTS39	106947
Libya	Multilateral	04 Aug 63	IGO Establishment	510UNTS3	107408
Libya	Multilateral	05 Aug 63	Sanitation	480UNTS43	106964
Libya	Multilateral	09 Nov 63	Direct Aid	489UNTS209	107141
Libya	Multilateral	28 Jun 64	Tech Assistance	519UNTS14	107499
Libya	Multilateral	10 Jul 64	Postal Service	613UNTS3	108850
Libya	Multilateral	10 Jul 64	Postal Service	612UNTS233	108848
Libya	Multilateral	10 Jul 64	Postal Service	611UNTS105	108845
Libya	Multilateral	10 Jul 64	Postal Service	612UNTS3	108847
Libya	Multilateral	10 Jul 64	Postal Service	611UNTS387	108846
Libya	Multilateral	10 Jul 64	Postal Service	611UNTS7	108844
Libya	Multilateral	20 Aug 64	Telecommunications	514UNTS25	107441
Libya	Multilateral	09 Mar 65	Water Transport	591UNTS265	108564
Libya	Multilateral	09 Jan 68	IGO Establishment	0UNTS0	109707
Libya	Multilateral	11 Jun 68	Scientific Project	0UNTS0	109884
Libya	Netherlands	07 Jan 54	Air Transport	54NET157	447044
Libya	Spain	05 May 59	Culture	62SPBO2307	460184
Libya	Turkey	09 Feb 58	Culture	59TURG206	466039
Libya	UK Great Britain	13 Dec 51	Direct Aid	123UNTS167	101658
Libya	UK Great Britain	31 Mar 52	Air Transport	151UNTS69	101984
Libya	UK Great Britain	21 Feb 53	Air Transport	311UNTS115	104501
Libya	UK Great Britain	21 Mar 53	General Military	172UNTS85	102240
Libya	UK Great Britain	25 Mar 53	Finance	172UNTS281	102252
Libya	UK Great Britain	29 Jul 53	Finance	186UNTS277	102493
Libya	UK Great Britain	29 Jul 53	General Amity	186UNTS185	102491
Libya	UK Great Britain	29 Jul 53	Status of Forces	186UNTS201	102492
Libya	UK Great Britain	19 Oct 53	Admin Cooperation	186UNTS285	102494
Libya	UK Great Britain	24 Sep 68	Finance	0UNTS0	109815
Libya	UN Special Fund	19 Apr 60	Direct Aid	356UNTS11	105090
Libya	UNICEF (Children)	05 Apr 52	Direct Aid	133UNTS287	200441
Libya	United Nations	27 Jun 59	Tech Assistance	336UNTS291	104811
Libya	USA (United States)	21 Jan 52	Tech Assistance	183UNTS177	102427
Libya	USA (United States)	20 May 52	Direct Aid	178UNTS307	102346
Libya	USA (United States)	20 May 52	Tech Assistance	178UNTS155	102339
Libya	USA (United States)	20 May 52	Tech Assistance	177UNTS81	102310
Libya	USA (United States)	11 Jan 54	Direct Aid	229UNTS15	103157

PARTY ONE	PARTY TWO	DATE	TOPIC	CITATION	NUMBER
Libya	USA (United States)	09 Sep 54	Direct Aid	238UNTS217	103365
Libya	USA (United States)	09 Sep 54	Milit Installation	224UNTS217	103078
Libya	USA (United States)	03 Nov 54	Direct Aid	238UNTS227	103366
Libya	USA (United States)	30 May 55	Direct Aid	270UNTS43	103890
Libya	USA (United States)	18 Jul 55	Direct Aid	241UNTS305	103437
Libya	USA (United States)	21 Jul 55	Tech Assistance	264UNTS247	103796
Libya	USA (United States)	28 Jul 55	Non-IBRD Project	270UNTS293	103902
Libya	USA (United States)	28 Jul 55	Non-IBRD Project	270UNTS245	103900
Libya	USA (United States)	28 Jul 55	Non-IBRD Project	270UNTS317	103903
Libya	USA (United States)	28 Jul 55	Non-IBRD Project	270UNTS269	103901
Libya	USA (United States)	22 Dec 55	Direct Aid	240UNTS111	103399
Libya	USA (United States)	27 Jun 56	Direct Aid	273UNTS89	103945
Libya	USA (United States)	04 Apr 57	Tech Assistance	283UNTS181	104116
Libya	USA (United States)	30 Jun 57	Milit Assistance	284UNTS177	104136
Libya	USA (United States)	21 May 59	Tech Assistance	361UNTS123	105176
Libya	USA (United States)	11 Dec 60	Health/Educ/Welfare	445UNTS125	106381
Libya	USSR (Soviet Union)	04 Sep 55	Consul/Citizenship	16SUGG69	469910
Libya	WHO (World Health)	05 Jul 55	Tech Assistance	219UNTS305	200530
Libya	WHO (World Health)	16 Jun 62	Tech Assistance	437UNTS127	106301
Liechtenstein	Austria	01 Apr 55	Admin Cooperation	56ABGB212	403124
Liechtenstein	Austria	01 Apr 55	Admin Cooperation	56ABGB213	403123
Liechtenstein	Austria	07 Dec 55	Taxation	56ABGB214	403126
Liechtenstein	Austria	17 Mar 60	Territory Boundary	60ABGB228	403128
Liechtenstein	Austria	02 Sep 63	Visas	65ABGB11	403129
Liechtenstein	Austria	01 Jun 66	Admin Cooperation	68ABGB99	403125
Liechtenstein	Austria	24 Oct 67	Visas	68ABGB21	403130
Liechtenstein	Austria	26 Sep 68	Non-ILO Labor	0UNTS0	109492
Liechtenstein	Austria	26 Sep 68	Non-ILO Labor	69ABGB72	403131
Liechtenstein	Austria	30 Oct 68	Non-ILO Labor	69ABGB73	403132
Liechtenstein	Austria	05 Nov 69	Taxation	71ABGB24	403133
Liechtenstein	Austria	06 Nov 69	Taxation	69ABGB479	403134
Liechtenstein	Austria	06 Nov 69	Taxation	0UNTS0	110323
Liechtenstein	Austria	12 Oct 71	Taxation	71ABGB493	403135
Liechtenstein	Germany, West	30 Jan 53	Claims and Debts	54WGBB522	425415
Liechtenstein	Germany, West	29 May 58	Admin Cooperation	59WBGA73	424416
Liechtenstein	ICJ Option Clause	10 Mar 50	ICJ Option Clause	51UNTS115	100758
Liechtenstein	ICJ Option Clause	10 Mar 50	ICJ Option Clause	51UNTS119	100759
Liechtenstein	Multilateral	27 Mar 41	Military Mission	67UNTS231	200222
Liechtenstein	Multilateral	11 Dec 46	Sanitation	12UNTS179	100186
Liechtenstein	Multilateral	08 Feb 47	Patents/Copyrights	14UNTS287	100222
Liechtenstein	Multilateral	13 Nov 47	Visas	251UNTS79	103534
Liechtenstein	Multilateral	26 Jun 48	Culture	331UNTS217	104757
Liechtenstein	Multilateral	19 Nov 48	Sanitation	44UNTS277	100688
Liechtenstein	Multilateral	16 Jun 49	Land Transport	45UNTS149	100696
Liechtenstein	Multilateral	12 Aug 49	Humanitarian	75UNTS85	100971
Liechtenstein	Multilateral	12 Aug 49	Humanitarian	75UNTS31	100970
Liechtenstein	Multilateral	12 Aug 49	Humanitarian	75UNTS287	100973
Liechtenstein	Multilateral	12 Aug 49	General Military	75UNTS135	100972
Liechtenstein	Multilateral	13 May 50	Land Transport	128UNTS171	101719
Liechtenstein	Multilateral	02 Jul 51	Refugees	189UNTS137	102545
Liechtenstein	Multilateral	27 Feb 53	Claims and Debts	333UNTS3	104764
Liechtenstein	Multilateral	11 May 53	Sanitation	456UNTS3	106555
Liechtenstein	Multilateral	14 May 54	Culture	249UNTS215	103511
Liechtenstein	Multilateral	28 Sep 54	Refugees	360UNTS117	105158
Liechtenstein	Multilateral	28 Sep 55	Air Transport	478UNTS371	106943
Liechtenstein	Multilateral	15 Jun 57	Patents/Copyrights	583UNTS3	108470
Liechtenstein	Multilateral	15 Jun 57	General Trade	550UNTS45	108008
Liechtenstein	Multilateral	15 Jan 58	Customs	383UNTS229	105503
Liechtenstein	Multilateral	30 Mar 61	Sanitation	520UNTS151	107515
Liechtenstein	Multilateral	18 Apr 61	Dispute Settlement	500UNTS243	107312
Liechtenstein	Multilateral	18 Apr 61	Consul/Citizenship	500UNTS95	107310
Liechtenstein	Multilateral	05 Oct 61	Patents/Copyrights	527UNTS181	107625
Liechtenstein	Multilateral	24 Apr 63	Consul/Citizenship	596UNTS261	108638
Liechtenstein	Multilateral	24 Apr 63	Consul/Citizenship	596UNTS487	108640
Liechtenstein	Multilateral	02 Sep 63	General Transport	548UNTS129	107974

PARTY ONE	PARTY TWO	DATE	TOPIC	CITATION	NUMBER
Liechtenstein	Multilateral	10 Jul 64	Postal Service	612UNTS361	108849
Liechtenstein	Multilateral	10 Jul 64	Postal Service	611UNTS105	108845
Liechtenstein	Multilateral	10 Jul 64	Postal Service	613UNTS3	108851
Liechtenstein	Multilateral	10 Jul 64	Postal Service	612UNTS3	108847
Liechtenstein	Multilateral	10 Jul 64	Postal Service	612UNTS233	108848
Liechtenstein	Multilateral	10 Jul 64	Postal Service	613UNTS3	108850
Liechtenstein	Multilateral	10 Jul 64	Postal Service	613UNTS193	108852
Liechtenstein	Multilateral	10 Jul 64	Postal Service	611UNTS7	108844
Liechtenstein	Multilateral	10 Jul 64	Postal Service	611UNTS387	108846
Liechtenstein	Multilateral	09 Mar 65	Water Transport	591UNTS265	108564
Liechtenstein	Multilateral	08 Mar 68	Visas	634UNTS199	109062
Liechtenstein	Norway	23 Dec 63	Visas	3NORT889	451106
Liechtenstein	Switzerland	10 Dec 54	Non-ILO Labor	55SWRO537	462186
Liechtenstein	Switzerland	07 May 55	Territory Boundary	56SWRO143	462181
Liechtenstein	Switzerland	06 Nov 63	Consul/Citizenship	64SWRO5	462184
Liechtenstein	Switzerland	06 Nov 63	Consul/Citizenship	64SWRO1	462183
Liechtenstein	Switzerland	24 Sep 64	Customs	64SWRO849	462185
Liechtenstein	Switzerland	24 Sep 64	Customs	64SWRO851	462182
Luxembourg	Australia	05 Sep 51	Visas	109UNTS31	101487
Luxembourg	Austria	13 Oct 52	Air Transport	192UNTS291	102606
Luxembourg	Austria	12 Sep 58	Non-ILO Labor	59ABGB27	403136
Luxembourg	Austria	18 Oct 62	Taxation	496UNTS97	107248
Luxembourg	Austria	10 Apr 64	Taxation	64ABGB143	403137
Luxembourg	Austria	16 Jul 71	Land Transport	71ABGB404	403138
Luxembourg	Belgium	28 Apr 45	Visas	41UNTS265	200181
Luxembourg	Belgium	14 May 45	Refugees	19UNTS243	200118
Luxembourg	Belgium	25 Mar 48	Taxation	18UNTS323	100300
Luxembourg	Belgium	27 Mar 48	Culture	178UNTS265	102343
Luxembourg	Belgium	24 Aug 48	Extradition	117UNTS131	101589
Luxembourg	Belgium	09 Oct 48	Taxation	123UNTS29	101652
Luxembourg	Belgium	14 Jan 49	Direct Aid	36UNTS339	100572
Luxembourg	Belgium	25 Feb 49	Admin Cooperation	47UNTS3	100719
Luxembourg	Belgium	07 Jun 49	Postal Service	34UNTS117	100531
Luxembourg	Belgium	15 Jul 49	Visas	41UNTS13	100642
Luxembourg	Belgium	03 Dec 49	Non-ILO Labor	91UNTS31	101241
Luxembourg	Belgium	06 Apr 50	Visas	65UNTS147	100843
Luxembourg	Belgium	12 Sep 50	Customs	110UNTS21	101497
Luxembourg	Belgium	07 Feb 52	Taxation	147UNTS3	101924
Luxembourg	Belgium	26 Sep 52	Reparations	141UNTS111	101910
Luxembourg	Belgium	04 Apr 55	Refugees	211UNTS57	102847
Luxembourg	Belgium	28 Mar 58	General Trade	303UNTS101	104372
Luxembourg	Belgium	29 Nov 61	Visas	486UNTS37	107071
Luxembourg	Belgium	30 Aug 62	Taxation	485UNTS313	107062
Luxembourg	Belgium	29 Jan 63	Direct Aid	0UNTS0	110432
Luxembourg	Belgium	29 Jan 63	IGO Establishment	547UNTS39	107955
Luxembourg	Belgium	14 Jan 65	Claims and Debts	620UNTS3	108949
Luxembourg	Belgium	11 Mar 65	Taxation	540UNTS297	107854
Luxembourg	Belgium	30 Sep 65	Consul/Citizenship	590UNTS35	108545
Luxembourg	Belgium	22 Feb 67	Culture	639UNTS3	109140
Luxembourg	Belgium	07 Feb 68	Finance	0UNTS0	110811
Luxembourg	Canada	26 Nov 49	Visas	231UNTS51	103203
Luxembourg	Denmark	21 May 46	Claims and Debts	4UNTS435	100060
Luxembourg	Denmark	10 Jun 58	Air Transport	356UNTS193	105096
Luxembourg	Finland	15 Aug 61	Air Transport	541UNTS45	107859
Luxembourg	France	30 Mar 49	Milit Servic/Citiz	50FRJO1003	416264
Luxembourg	France	27 Jun 49	Education	49FRJO2510	416265
Luxembourg	France	12 Nov 49	Non-ILO Labor	50FRJO110	416266
Luxembourg	France	29 Apr 52	Customs	55FRJO601	416267
Luxembourg	France	08 Feb 54	Culture	55FRJO1603	416268
Luxembourg	France	23 Jul 56	Admin Cooperation	60FRRT45	415269
Luxembourg	France	01 Apr 58	Taxation	60FRRT18	415270
Luxembourg	France	25 Jul 58	Postal Service	58FRJO2507	416271
Luxembourg	France	29 Mar 62	Air Transport	563UNTS227	108212
Luxembourg	France	10 Dec 62	Humanitarian	63FRRT9	415272
Luxembourg	France	16 Jul 63	Territory Boundary	68FRJO1101	416273

PARTY ONE	PARTY TWO	DATE	TOPIC	CITATION	NUMBER
Luxembourg	France	21 May 64	Territory Boundary	0UNTS0	110527
Luxembourg	France	03 Jun 64	Non-ILO Labor	67FRJO2412	416274
Luxembourg	France	16 Jul 64	Territory Boundary	0UNTS0	109225
Luxembourg	France	31 Aug 65	Health/Educ/Welfare	68FRJO1910	416275
Luxembourg	Germany, West	30 Apr 52	General Transport	61WBGA173	424417
Luxembourg	Germany, West	09 Dec 53	Extradition	63WBGA47	424418
Luxembourg	Germany, West	25 Jul 56	Visas	51WBGA114	424419
Luxembourg	Germany, West	13 May 57	Sanitation	60WBGA180	424420
Luxembourg	Germany, West	01 Dec 57	Non-ILO Labor	60WGBB2305	425421
Luxembourg	Germany, West	28 Aug 58	Taxation	59WGBB1269	425422
Luxembourg	Germany, West	11 Jul 59	Admin Cooperation	60WGBB2077	425423
Luxembourg	Germany, West	14 Feb 60	Non-ILO Labor	63WGBB385	425424
Luxembourg	Germany, West	14 Jul 60	Non-ILO Labor	63WGBB397	425425
Luxembourg	Germany, West	31 May 61	Admin Cooperation	62WBGA23	424427
Luxembourg	Germany, West	31 May 61	Consul/Citizenship	61WBGA141	424426
Luxembourg	Germany, West	05 Jul 61	Air Transport	62WGBB195	425428
Luxembourg	Germany, West	16 Feb 62	Visas	63WGBB141	425429
Luxembourg	Germany, West	12 Jul 62	Non-ILO Labor	63WBGA75	424430
Luxembourg	Germany, West	07 Dec 62	Admin Cooperation	64WGBB193	425431
Luxembourg	Germany, West	27 Jun 63	Non-ILO Labor	63WBGA231	424432
Luxembourg	Germany, West	06 Oct 64	Non-ILO Labor	65WBGA157	424433
Luxembourg	Germany, West	09 Dec 65	Visas	67WGBB909	425434
Luxembourg	Germany, West	17 May 66	Extradition	66WBGA131	424435
Luxembourg	Germany, West	28 Feb 67	Specif Claim/Waive	67WGBB1694	425436
Luxembourg	Germany, West	09 Dec 69	Non-ILO Labor	71WGBB40	425437
Luxembourg	Greece	22 Oct 51	Air Transport	187UNTS119	102506
Luxembourg	IBRD (World Bank)	28 Aug 47	IBRD Project	153UNTS3	102017
Luxembourg	Iceland	23 Oct 52	Air Transport	193UNTS39	102609
Luxembourg	Iran	19 Nov 64	Visas	0IRTB50	433078
Luxembourg	Ireland	01 Dec 48	Visas	553UNTS111	108075
Luxembourg	Ireland	27 Jul 54	Air Transport	232UNTS91	103231
Luxembourg	Israel	27 Oct 54	Visas	226UNTS241	103117
Luxembourg	Israel	30 Mar 55	Visas	226UNTS247	103118
Luxembourg	Israel	26 Jul 56	Extradition	550UNTS239	108020
Luxembourg	Italy	06 Apr 48	Non-ILO Labor	49ITGU166	435261
Luxembourg	Italy	29 May 51	Non-ILO Labor	54ITGU194	435262
Luxembourg	Italy	05 Jun 54	Reparations	55ITGU162	435263
Luxembourg	Italy	03 May 56	Culture	58ITGU121	435265
Luxembourg	Italy	16 Jan 57	Non-ILO Labor	59ITDI347	436266
Luxembourg	Japan	18 Dec 56	Visas	318UNTS227	104616
Luxembourg	Japan	21 Jul 60	Visas	384UNTS55	105510
Luxembourg	Multilateral	27 Mar 41	Military Mission	67UNTS231	200222
Luxembourg	Multilateral	21 Oct 43	Finance	2UNTS281	200021
Luxembourg	Multilateral	19 Apr 44	Scientific Project	89UNTS279	200257
Luxembourg	Multilateral	02 Aug 44	Scientific Project	67UNTS221	200221
Luxembourg	Multilateral	07 Dec 44	Air Transport	171UNTS345	200501
Luxembourg	Multilateral	07 Dec 44	IGO Establishment	15UNTS295	200102
Luxembourg	Multilateral	07 Dec 44	Air Transport	84UNTS389	200252
Luxembourg	Multilateral	15 Dec 44	Sanitation	17UNTS305	200110
Luxembourg	Multilateral	15 Dec 44	Sanitation	16UNTS247	200106
Luxembourg	Multilateral	20 Mar 45	General Economic	2UNTS299	200022
Luxembourg	Multilateral	08 Aug 45	General Military	82UNTS279	200251
Luxembourg	Multilateral	27 Sep 45	IGO Establishment	5UNTS327	200035
Luxembourg	Multilateral	16 Nov 45	IGO Establishment	4UNTS275	100052
Luxembourg	Multilateral	27 Dec 45	IGO Establishment	2UNTS39	100020
Luxembourg	Multilateral	04 Jan 46	IGO Establishment	6UNTS35	100066
Luxembourg	Multilateral	14 Jan 46	Reparations	555UNTS69	108105
Luxembourg	Multilateral	17 Apr 46	Land Transport	27UNTS103	100402
Luxembourg	Multilateral	23 Apr 46	Sanitation	17UNTS3	100265
Luxembourg	Multilateral	23 Apr 46	Sanitation	16UNTS179	100257
Luxembourg	Multilateral	22 Jul 46	IGO Establishment	14UNTS185	100221
Luxembourg	Multilateral	22 Jul 46	IGO Establishment	9UNTS3	100125
Luxembourg	Multilateral	27 Jul 46	Patents/Copyrights	90UNTS229	101238
Luxembourg	Multilateral	15 Oct 46	Refugees	11UNTS73	100150
Luxembourg	Multilateral	11 Dec 46	Sanitation	12UNTS179	100186

PARTY ONE	PARTY TWO	DATE	TOPIC	CITATION	NUMBER
Luxembourg	Multilateral	15 Dec 46	IGO Establishment	18UNTS3	100283
Luxembourg	Multilateral	08 Feb 47	Patents/Copyrights	14UNTS287	100222
Luxembourg	Multilateral	06 Jun 47	Patents/Copyrights	46UNTS249	100714
Luxembourg	Multilateral	02 Oct 47	Telecommunications	193UNTS188	102616
Luxembourg	Multilateral	12 Nov 47	Admin Cooperation	53UNTS49	100772
Luxembourg	Multilateral	12 Nov 47	Admin Cooperation	46UNTS169	100709
Luxembourg	Multilateral	12 Nov 47	Admin Cooperation	46UNTS201	100710
Luxembourg	Multilateral	12 Nov 47	Admin Cooperation	53UNTS39	100771
Luxembourg	Multilateral	12 Nov 47	Admin Cooperation	53UNTS13	100770
Luxembourg	Multilateral	18 Nov 47	Finance	17UNTS89	100269
Luxembourg	Multilateral	22 Dec 47	Customs	32UNTS143	100496
Luxembourg	Multilateral	17 Mar 48	General Military	19UNTS51	100304
Luxembourg	Multilateral	26 Jun 48	Culture	331UNTS217	104757
Luxembourg	Multilateral	24 Jul 48	Sanitation	66UNTS25	100847
Luxembourg	Multilateral	14 Sep 48	Milit Occupation	18UNTS267	100296
Luxembourg	Multilateral	08 Oct 48	Education	19UNTS113	100308
Luxembourg	Multilateral	19 Nov 48	Sanitation	44UNTS277	100688
Luxembourg	Multilateral	09 Dec 48	Scientific Project	73UNTS39	100942
Luxembourg	Multilateral	04 Apr 49	General Military	34UNTS243	100541
Luxembourg	Multilateral	28 Apr 49	IGO Establishment	83UNTS105	101105
Luxembourg	Multilateral	04 May 49	Admin Cooperation	92UNTS19	101257
Luxembourg	Multilateral	04 May 49	Admin Cooperation	98UNTS101	101358
Luxembourg	Multilateral	04 May 49	Admin Cooperation	30UNTS3	100445
Luxembourg	Multilateral	04 May 49	Admin Cooperation	30UNTS23	100446
Luxembourg	Multilateral	04 May 49	Admin Cooperation	47UNTS159	100728
Luxembourg	Multilateral	05 May 49	IGO Establishment	87UNTS103	101168
Luxembourg	Multilateral	12 Aug 49	Humanitarian	75UNTS85	100971
Luxembourg	Multilateral	12 Aug 49	Humanitarian	75UNTS287	100973
Luxembourg	Multilateral	12 Aug 49	Humanitarian	75UNTS31	100970
Luxembourg	Multilateral	12 Aug 49	General Military	75UNTS135	100972
Luxembourg	Multilateral	02 Sep 49	IGO Status/Immunit	250UNTS12	103515
Luxembourg	Multilateral	19 Sep 49	Land Transport	125UNTS3	101671
Luxembourg	Multilateral	07 Nov 49	Non-ILO Labor	132UNTS31	101749
Luxembourg	Multilateral	07 Nov 49	Sanitation	132UNTS3	101748
Luxembourg	Multilateral	16 Dec 49	Admin Cooperation	72UNTS3	100924
Luxembourg	Multilateral	18 Feb 50	Customs	123UNTS45	101654
Luxembourg	Multilateral	21 Mar 50	Admin Cooperation	96UNTS271	101342
Luxembourg	Multilateral	08 Apr 50	Specif Goods/Equip	68UNTS99	100889
Luxembourg	Multilateral	08 Apr 50	IGO Establishment	66UNTS285	100860
Luxembourg	Multilateral	17 Apr 50	Non-ILO Labor	126UNTS285	101694
Luxembourg	Multilateral	17 Apr 50	Visas	131UNTS99	101738
Luxembourg	Multilateral	13 May 50	Land Transport	128UNTS171	101719
Luxembourg	Multilateral	16 Sep 50	General Transport	92UNTS91	101264
Luxembourg	Multilateral	18 Oct 50	Specific Resources	638UNTS185	109134
Luxembourg	Multilateral	04 Nov 50	Humanitarian	213UNTS221	102889
Luxembourg	Multilateral	22 Nov 50	Culture	131UNTS25	101734
Luxembourg	Multilateral	15 Dec 50	Customs	347UNTS127	104994
Luxembourg	Multilateral	15 Dec 50	Customs	171UNTS305	102234
Luxembourg	Multilateral	15 Dec 50	Customs	157UNTS129	102052
Luxembourg	Multilateral	15 Dec 50	IGO Operations	160UNTS267	102111
Luxembourg	Multilateral	18 Apr 51	IGO Establishment	261UNTS140	103729
Luxembourg	Multilateral	25 May 51	Status of Forces	175UNTS215	102303
Luxembourg	Multilateral	19 Jun 51	Status of Forces	199UNTS67	102678
Luxembourg	Multilateral	02 Jul 51	Refugees	189UNTS137	102545
Luxembourg	Multilateral	08 Sep 51	Peace/Disarmament	136UNTS45	101832
Luxembourg	Multilateral	08 Sep 51	General Military	136UNTS165	101833
Luxembourg	Multilateral	20 Sep 51	IGO Status/Immunit	200UNTS3	102691
Luxembourg	Multilateral	09 Oct 51	IGO Establishment	220UNTS121	102997
Luxembourg	Multilateral	06 Dec 51	Admin Cooperation	150UNTS67	101963
Luxembourg	Multilateral	10 Jan 52	Visas	163UNTS3	102138
Luxembourg	Multilateral	10 Jan 52	Visas	163UNTS27	102139
Luxembourg	Multilateral	16 Apr 52	General Economic	139UNTS35	101874
Luxembourg	Multilateral	20 May 52	Sanitation	219UNTS55	102966
Luxembourg	Multilateral	11 Jul 52	Postal Service	170UNTS269	102223
Luxembourg	Multilateral	11 Jul 52	Postal Service	170UNTS3	102221

PARTY ONE	PARTY TWO	DATE	TOPIC	CITATION	NUMBER
Luxembourg	Multilateral	11 Jul 52	Postal Service	171UNTS89	102225
Luxembourg	Multilateral	11 Jul 52	Postal Service	170UNTS63	102222
Luxembourg	Multilateral	11 Jul 52	Postal Service	171UNTS3	102224
Luxembourg	Multilateral	11 Jul 52	IGO Establishment	169UNTS3	102220
Luxembourg	Multilateral	11 Jul 52	Postal Service	171UNTS143	102226
Luxembourg	Multilateral	05 Sep 52	Taxation	256UNTS3	103619
Luxembourg	Multilateral	05 Sep 52	Customs	247UNTS329	103479
Luxembourg	Multilateral	06 Sep 52	Patents/Copyrights	216UNTS132	102937
Luxembourg	Multilateral	07 Oct 52	Admin Cooperation	310UNTS181	104493
Luxembourg	Multilateral	07 Nov 52	General Trade	221UNTS255	103010
Luxembourg	Multilateral	27 Feb 53	Claims and Debts	333UNTS3	104764
Luxembourg	Multilateral	11 May 53	Sanitation	456UNTS3	106555
Luxembourg	Multilateral	24 Jul 53	General Amity	250UNTS108	103520
Luxembourg	Multilateral	17 Oct 53	General Transport	184UNTS42	102438
Luxembourg	Multilateral	09 Dec 53	General Economic	249UNTS197	103509
Luxembourg	Multilateral	11 Dec 53	Non-ILO Labor	218UNTS255	102958
Luxembourg	Multilateral	11 Dec 53	Patents/Copyrights	218UNTS27	102952
Luxembourg	Multilateral	11 Dec 53	Non-ILO Labor	218UNTS211	102957
Luxembourg	Multilateral	11 Dec 53	Sanitation	191UNTS285	102588
Luxembourg	Multilateral	11 Dec 53	Non-ILO Labor	218UNTS153	102956
Luxembourg	Multilateral	11 Dec 53	Education	218UNTS125	102954
Luxembourg	Multilateral	01 Mar 54	Admin Cooperation	286UNTS265	104173
Luxembourg	Multilateral	14 May 54	Culture	249UNTS215	103511
Luxembourg	Multilateral	04 Jun 54	Customs	276UNTS191	103992
Luxembourg	Multilateral	04 Jun 54	Customs	282UNTS249	104101
Luxembourg	Multilateral	14 Jun 54	Air Transport	320UNTS209	104643
Luxembourg	Multilateral	14 Jun 54	Air Transport	320UNTS217	104644
Luxembourg	Multilateral	08 Jul 54	Finance	287UNTS27	104178
Luxembourg	Multilateral	28 Sep 54	Refugees	360UNTS117	105158
Luxembourg	Multilateral	23 Oct 54	Status of Forces	334UNTS3	104765
Luxembourg	Multilateral	29 Nov 54	General Trade	287UNTS209	104187
Luxembourg	Multilateral	19 Dec 54	Culture	218UNTS139	102955
Luxembourg	Multilateral	21 Dec 54	General Amity	258UNTS322	103678
Luxembourg	Multilateral	06 Apr 55	General Amity	261UNTS55	103725
Luxembourg	Multilateral	25 May 55	IGO Establishment	264UNTS117	103791
Luxembourg	Multilateral	06 Jun 55	IGO Establishment	219UNTS79	102968
Luxembourg	Multilateral	22 Jun 55	Atomic Energy	249UNTS3	103498
Luxembourg	Multilateral	28 Sep 55	Air Transport	478UNTS371	106943
Luxembourg	Multilateral	20 Oct 55	IGO Establishment	378UNTS159	105425
Luxembourg	Multilateral	05 Nov 55	IGO Establishment	250UNTS201	103524
Luxembourg	Multilateral	13 Dec 55	IGO Operations	529UNTS141	107660
Luxembourg	Multilateral	13 Dec 55	Humanitarian	250UNTS3	103514
Luxembourg	Multilateral	21 Dec 55	General Trade	292UNTS63	104267
Luxembourg	Multilateral	01 Mar 56	Customs	343UNTS129	104923
Luxembourg	Multilateral	30 Apr 56	Air Transport	310UNTS229	104494
Luxembourg	Multilateral	18 May 56	Customs	327UNTS123	104721
Luxembourg	Multilateral	18 May 56	Customs	319UNTS21	104630
Luxembourg	Multilateral	18 May 56	Customs	338UNTS103	104834
Luxembourg	Multilateral	18 May 56	Land Transport	339UNTS3	104844
Luxembourg	Multilateral	19 May 56	Land Transport	399UNTS189	105742
Luxembourg	Multilateral	07 Jun 56	Non-ILO Labor	381UNTS145	105470
Luxembourg	Multilateral	06 Jul 56	Admin Cooperation	312UNTS109	104514
Luxembourg	Multilateral	09 Jul 56	Non-ILO Labor	314UNTS3	104539
Luxembourg	Multilateral	16 Aug 56	General Trade	287UNTS223	104188
Luxembourg	Multilateral	07 Sep 56	Humanitarian	266UNTS3	103822
Luxembourg	Multilateral	24 Oct 56	Admin Cooperation	510UNTS161	107412
Luxembourg	Multilateral	26 Oct 56	IGO Establishment	276UNTS3	103988
Luxembourg	Multilateral	14 Dec 56	Taxation	436UNTS131	106293
Luxembourg	Multilateral	14 Dec 56	Taxation	436UNTS115	106292
Luxembourg	Multilateral	15 Dec 56	Education	278UNTS73	104023
Luxembourg	Multilateral	25 Mar 57	IGO Status/Immunit	294UNTS411	104302
Luxembourg	Multilateral	25 Mar 57	IGO Establishment	294UNTS259	104301
Luxembourg	Multilateral	25 Mar 57	IGO Establishment	294UNTS2	104300
Luxembourg	Multilateral	12 Apr 57	Education	443UNTS128	106362
Luxembourg	Multilateral	29 Apr 57	Dispute Settlement	320UNTS243	104646

PARTY ONE	PARTY TWO	DATE	TOPIC	CITATION	NUMBER
Luxembourg	Multilateral	15 Jun 57	General Trade	550UNTS45	108008
Luxembourg	Multilateral	15 Jun 57	Patents/Copyrights	583UNTS3	108470
Luxembourg	Multilateral	26 Jul 57	Land Transport	386UNTS3	105535
Luxembourg	Multilateral	27 Sep 57	Admin Cooperation	299UNTS211	104314
Luxembourg	Multilateral	03 Oct 57	Postal Service	366UNTS87	105216
Luxembourg	Multilateral	03 Oct 57	Postal Service	366UNTS3	105215
Luxembourg	Multilateral	03 Oct 57	Postal Service	366UNTS255	105219
Luxembourg	Multilateral	03 Oct 57	Postal Service	364UNTS3	105211
Luxembourg	Multilateral	03 Oct 57	Postal Service	365UNTS207	105214
Luxembourg	Multilateral	03 Oct 57	Postal Service	365UNTS3	105213
Luxembourg	Multilateral	03 Oct 57	Postal Service	364UNTS331	105212
Luxembourg	Multilateral	03 Oct 57	Postal Service	366UNTS141	105217
Luxembourg	Multilateral	25 Nov 57	General Trade	403UNTS169	105795
Luxembourg	Multilateral	13 Dec 57	Land Transport	372UNTS159	105296
Luxembourg	Multilateral	13 Dec 57	Extradition	359UNTS273	105146
Luxembourg	Multilateral	13 Dec 57	Visas	315UNTS139	104565
Luxembourg	Multilateral	15 Jan 58	Customs	383UNTS229	105503
Luxembourg	Multilateral	03 Feb 58	IGO Establishment	381UNTS165	105471
Luxembourg	Multilateral	15 Apr 58	Health/Educ/Welfare	539UNTS27	107822
Luxembourg	Multilateral	29 Apr 58	Dispute Settlement	450UNTS169	106466
Luxembourg	Multilateral	10 Jun 58	Admin Cooperation	330UNTS3	104739
Luxembourg	Multilateral	25 Jul 58	Customs	352UNTS3	105035
Luxembourg	Multilateral	03 Dec 58	Admin Cooperation	416UNTS51	105995
Luxembourg	Multilateral	03 Dec 58	Admin Cooperation	398UNTS9	105715
Luxembourg	Multilateral	15 Dec 58	Mass Media	546UNTS235	107950
Luxembourg	Multilateral	15 Dec 58	Sanitation	351UNTS159	105022
Luxembourg	Multilateral	15 Jan 59	Customs	348UNTS13	104996
Luxembourg	Multilateral	30 Jan 59	General Trade	0UNTS0	109234
Luxembourg	Multilateral	06 Apr 59	Commodity Trade	349UNTS167	105013
Luxembourg	Multilateral	20 Apr 59	Admin Cooperation	472UNTS185	106841
Luxembourg	Multilateral	20 Apr 59	Visas	376UNTS85	105375
Luxembourg	Multilateral	11 May 59	Claims and Debts	527UNTS145	107623
Luxembourg	Multilateral	14 Dec 59	Admin Cooperation	444UNTS193	106369
Luxembourg	Multilateral	11 Apr 60	Visas	374UNTS3	105323
Luxembourg	Multilateral	15 Apr 60	Finance	470UNTS239	106811
Luxembourg	Multilateral	22 Apr 60	Air Transport	418UNTS211	106023
Luxembourg	Multilateral	28 Apr 60	Health/Educ/Welfare	376UNTS111	105377
Luxembourg	Multilateral	22 Jun 60	Mass Media	546UNTS247	107951
Luxembourg	Multilateral	21 Sep 60	Patents/Copyrights	394UNTS3	105664
Luxembourg	Multilateral	06 Oct 60	Customs	473UNTS131	106861
Luxembourg	Multilateral	09 Dec 60	Customs	429UNTS211	106200
Luxembourg	Multilateral	13 Dec 60	Air Transport	523UNTS117	107557
Luxembourg	Multilateral	13 Feb 61	ILO Labor	0UNTS0	110306
Luxembourg	Multilateral	16 Mar 61	General Trade	638UNTS235	109139
Luxembourg	Multilateral	30 Mar 61	Sanitation	520UNTS151	107515
Luxembourg	Multilateral	18 Apr 61	Consul/Citizenship	500UNTS95	107310
Luxembourg	Multilateral	18 Apr 61	Dispute Settlement	500UNTS243	107312
Luxembourg	Multilateral	08 Jun 61	Customs	473UNTS153	106862
Luxembourg	Multilateral	05 Oct 61	Admin Cooperation	0UNTS0	109431
Luxembourg	Multilateral	05 Oct 61	Patents/Copyrights	527UNTS181	107625
Luxembourg	Multilateral	18 Oct 61	IGO Establishment	529UNTS89	107659
Luxembourg	Multilateral	06 Dec 61	Customs	473UNTS219	106864
Luxembourg	Multilateral	16 Dec 61	Visas	544UNTS19	107909
Luxembourg	Multilateral	07 Mar 62	Commodity Trade	445UNTS199	106388
Luxembourg	Multilateral	07 Mar 62	Commodity Trade	445UNTS205	106389
Luxembourg	Multilateral	19 Mar 62	Patents/Copyrights	0UNTS0	110108
Luxembourg	Multilateral	14 May 62	Scientific Project	544UNTS39	107910
Luxembourg	Multilateral	14 May 62	Sanitation	544UNTS81	107911
Luxembourg	Multilateral	15 May 62	Commodity Trade	444UNTS3	106367
Luxembourg	Multilateral	27 Jun 62	Extradition	616UNTS79	108893
Luxembourg	Multilateral	28 Sep 62	IGO Establishment	469UNTS169	106791
Luxembourg	Multilateral	29 Nov 62	Visas	457UNTS63	106577
Luxembourg	Multilateral	17 Dec 62	Sanitation	486UNTS119	107076
Luxembourg	Multilateral	20 Apr 63	IGO Establishment	495UNTS3	107239
Luxembourg	Multilateral	24 Apr 63	Consul/Citizenship	596UNTS487	108640

PARTY ONE	PARTY TWO	DATE	TOPIC	CITATION	NUMBER
Luxembourg	Multilateral	24 Apr 63	Consul/Citizenship	596UNTS261	108638
Luxembourg	Multilateral	19 Jun 63	Visas	482UNTS19	106988
Luxembourg	Multilateral	05 Aug 63	Sanitation	480UNTS43	106964
Luxembourg	Multilateral	14 Nov 63	Finance	619UNTS299	108948
Luxembourg	Multilateral	10 Feb 64	Visas	496UNTS151	107249
Luxembourg	Multilateral	09 Mar 64	Specific Resources	581UNTS57	108432
Luxembourg	Multilateral	16 Apr 64	Visas	548UNTS27	107967
Luxembourg	Multilateral	14 May 64	Visas	528UNTS3	107631
Luxembourg	Multilateral	14 May 64	Refugees	528UNTS23	107633
Luxembourg	Multilateral	14 May 64	Refugees	528UNTS13	107632
Luxembourg	Multilateral	25 May 64	Taxation	620UNTS149	108953
Luxembourg	Multilateral	18 Jun 64	Atomic Energy	542UNTS145	107886
Luxembourg	Multilateral	10 Jul 64	Postal Service	611UNTS105	108845
Luxembourg	Multilateral	10 Jul 64	Postal Service	613UNTS193	108852
Luxembourg	Multilateral	10 Jul 64	Postal Service	613UNTS3	108851
Luxembourg	Multilateral	10 Jul 64	Postal Service	612UNTS361	108849
Luxembourg	Multilateral	10 Jul 64	Postal Service	612UNTS233	108848
Luxembourg	Multilateral	10 Jul 64	Postal Service	612UNTS3	108847
Luxembourg	Multilateral	10 Jul 64	Postal Service	611UNTS7	108844
Luxembourg	Multilateral	10 Jul 64	Postal Service	613UNTS3	108850
Luxembourg	Multilateral	10 Jul 64	Postal Service	611UNTS387	108846
Luxembourg	Multilateral	15 Sep 64	General Trade	510UNTS147	107411
Luxembourg	Multilateral	19 Nov 64	Visas	523UNTS3	107553
Luxembourg	Multilateral	27 Nov 64	Visas	548UNTS47	107968
Luxembourg	Multilateral	22 Jan 65	Gen Communications	634UNTS239	109066
Luxembourg	Multilateral	15 Feb 65	Visas	547UNTS3	107953
Luxembourg	Multilateral	15 Feb 65	Refugees	546UNTS277	107952
Luxembourg	Multilateral	09 Mar 65	Water Transport	591UNTS265	108564
Luxembourg	Multilateral	18 Mar 65	Dispute Settlement	575UNTS159	108359
Luxembourg	Multilateral	25 Apr 65	Finance	0UNTS0	110810
Luxembourg	Multilateral	08 Jul 65	General Trade	597UNTS3	108641
Luxembourg	Multilateral	16 Jul 65	General Trade	600UNTS49	108675
Luxembourg	Multilateral	08 Sep 65	Visas	578UNTS3	108382
Luxembourg	Multilateral	17 May 66	Visas	571UNTS89	108302
Luxembourg	Multilateral	12 Jul 66	Visas	578UNTS23	108384
Luxembourg	Multilateral	27 Jan 67	Scientific Project	610UNTS205	108843
Luxembourg	Multilateral	24 Apr 67	Humanitarian	634UNTS255	109067
Luxembourg	Multilateral	26 Apr 67	General Trade	0UNTS0	109890
Luxembourg	Multilateral	20 Jun 67	Visas	607UNTS97	108799
Luxembourg	Multilateral	22 Aug 67	General Trade	0UNTS0	110687
Luxembourg	Multilateral	15 Nov 67	General Trade	0UNTS0	109703
Luxembourg	Multilateral	27 Mar 68	Visas	0UNTS0	109293
Luxembourg	Multilateral	16 Aug 68	Non-ILO Labor	0UNTS0	109281
Luxembourg	Multilateral	10 Dec 68	Visas	0UNTS0	109387
Luxembourg	Multilateral	12 Jun 69	Visas	0UNTS0	110305
Luxembourg	Multilateral	17 Jul 69	Visas	0UNTS0	109729
Luxembourg	Multilateral	03 Dec 69	Visas	0UNTS0	110526
Luxembourg	Multilateral	13 Apr 70	Education	0UNTS0	110793
Luxembourg	Multilateral	28 Apr 70	Visas	0UNTS0	110805
Luxembourg	Multilateral	04 May 70	Visas	0UNTS0	110579
Luxembourg	Netherlands	23 Jun 48	Air Transport	32UNTS229	100500
Luxembourg	Netherlands	26 Apr 49	Culture	182UNTS187	102425
Luxembourg	Netherlands	08 Jul 50	Non-ILO Labor	135UNTS229	101824
Luxembourg	Netherlands	25 Aug 50	Non-ILO Labor	81UNTS13	101058
Luxembourg	Netherlands	06 Nov 53	Admin Cooperation	198UNTS187	102664
Luxembourg	Netherlands	04 May 55	Refugees	292UNTS17	104262
Luxembourg	Netherlands	06 Feb 56	Reparations	261UNTS17	103723
Luxembourg	Netherlands	22 Feb 56	Visas	286UNTS249	104171
Luxembourg	Netherlands	24 Mar 64	Consul/Citizenship	548UNTS137	107975
Luxembourg	Netherlands	08 May 68	Taxation	0UNTS0	110089
Luxembourg	New Zealand	29 Jun 51	Visas	101UNTS71	101403
Luxembourg	Norway	12 Jul 47	Visas	90UNTS59	101226
Luxembourg	Norway	17 Sep 51	Finance	2NORT568	451107
Luxembourg	Norway	17 Nov 52	Air Transport	311UNTS95	104500
Luxembourg	Norway	28 May 57	General Trade	3NORT717	451108

PARTY ONE	PARTY TWO	DATE	TOPIC	CITATION	NUMBER
Luxembourg	Philippines	17 Feb 60	Visas	359UNTS311	105148
Luxembourg	Portugal	21 Oct 50	Air Transport	108UNTS67	101468
Luxembourg	Portugal	12 Feb 65	Non-ILO Labor	571UNTS239	108305
Luxembourg	South Africa	30 May 61	Visas	412UNTS203	105933
Luxembourg	South Africa	31 Jan 62	Air Transport	563UNTS153	108209
Luxembourg	Spain	26 Mar 62	Air Transport	563UNTS205	108211
Luxembourg	Spain	22 Jun 63	Non-ILO Labor	65SPBO1509	460186
Luxembourg	Spain	22 Jun 63	Non-ILO Labor	65SPBO2408	460185
Luxembourg	Sweden	17 Nov 52	Air Transport	173UNTS277	102270
Luxembourg	Sweden	06 Apr 57	Admin Cooperation	427UNTS173	106152
Luxembourg	Sweden	12 Mar 58	Admin Cooperation	427UNTS179	106153
Luxembourg	Switzerland	09 Apr 51	Air Transport	254UNTS389	103601
Luxembourg	Switzerland	14 Nov 55	Non-ILO Labor	57SWRO282	462099
Luxembourg	Taiwan	19 Jul 63	Air Transport	564UNTS23	108218
Luxembourg	Thailand	29 Dec 60	Air Transport	465UNTS131	106725
Luxembourg	Tunisia	13 Jun 60	Air Transport	497UNTS143	107267
Luxembourg	UK Great Britain	29 May 39	Extradition	99UNTS301	200284
Luxembourg	UK Great Britain	11 Dec 46	Claims and Debts	11UNTS167	100155
Luxembourg	UK Great Britain	14 Feb 47	Visas	11UNTS267	100165
Luxembourg	UK Great Britain	27 May 48	Air Transport	53UNTS115	100776
Luxembourg	UK Great Britain	27 Jun 50	Culture	183UNTS217	102431
Luxembourg	UK Great Britain	13 Oct 53	Non-ILO Labor	209UNTS87	102825
Luxembourg	UK Great Britain	18 Jun 54	Reparations	192UNTS33	102593
Luxembourg	UK Great Britain	01 Apr 60	Visas	374UNTS267	105340
Luxembourg	UK Great Britain	21 Feb 61	Visas	398UNTS243	105726
Luxembourg	UK Great Britain	24 May 67	Taxation	0UNTS0	109341
Luxembourg	United Nations	28 Dec 66	Claims and Debts	585UNTS147	108487
Luxembourg	USA (United States)	03 Jul 46	Mostfavored Nation	32UNTS85	100491
Luxembourg	USA (United States)	29 Aug 46	Reparations	140UNTS101	101885
Luxembourg	USA (United States)	12 Sep 46	Reparations	149UNTS19	101947
Luxembourg	USA (United States)	03 Jul 48	Direct Aid	24UNTS35	100350
Luxembourg	USA (United States)	27 Jan 50	Milit Assistance	80UNTS187	101052
Luxembourg	USA (United States)	20 Mar 51	Other Military	180UNTS283	102392
Luxembourg	USA (United States)	08 Jan 52	Milit Assistance	180UNTS191	102384
Luxembourg	USA (United States)	13 Mar 52	Taxation	168UNTS57	102212
Luxembourg	USA (United States)	17 Aug 53	Mass Media	234UNTS219	103284
Luxembourg	USA (United States)	17 Apr 54	Milit Assistance	257UNTS255	103661
Luxembourg	USA (United States)	07 Jul 54	Milit Assistance	233UNTS23	103247
Luxembourg	USA (United States)	15 Jun 55	Reparations	264UNTS279	103798
Luxembourg	USA (United States)	07 Dec 56	General Military	265UNTS255	103817
Luxembourg	USA (United States)	23 Feb 62	General Amity	474UNTS3	106868
Luxembourg	USA (United States)	18 Dec 62	Taxation	532UNTS277	107723
Luxembourg	USA (United States)	29 Jul 65	Gen Communications	573UNTS197	108332
Luxembourg	USSR (Soviet Union)	01 Dec 60	Consul/Citizenship	10SUGG118	469736
Luxembourg	Yugoslavia	09 Apr 60	Air Transport	464UNTS293	106719
Madagascar	Denmark	10 Dec 65	General Trade	0UNTS0	110553
Madagascar	IBRD (World Bank)	23 Aug 67	IBRD Project	618UNTS215	108929
Madagascar	IBRD (World Bank)	12 Nov 68	IBRD Project	0UNTS0	109670
Madagascar	IBRD (World Bank)	14 Feb 69	IBRD Project	0UNTS0	110103
Madagascar	IDA (Devel Assoc)	12 Nov 68	Non-IBRD Project	0UNTS0	109671
Madagascar	Multilateral	07 Dec 44	Air Transport	84UNTS389	200252
Madagascar	Multilateral	07 Dec 44	IGO Establishment	15UNTS295	200102
Madagascar	Multilateral	27 May 47	Air Transport	418UNTS161	106021
Madagascar	Multilateral	12 Nov 47	Admin Cooperation	53UNTS39	100771
Madagascar	Multilateral	12 Nov 47	Admin Cooperation	46UNTS201	100710
Madagascar	Multilateral	06 Mar 48	Water Transport	289UNTS3	104214
Madagascar	Multilateral	24 Jul 48	Sanitation	66UNTS25	100847
Madagascar	Multilateral	04 May 49	Admin Cooperation	47UNTS159	100728
Madagascar	Multilateral	04 May 49	Admin Cooperation	92UNTS19	101257
Madagascar	Multilateral	15 Jul 49	Health/Educ/Welfare	197UNTS3	102631
Madagascar	Multilateral	22 Nov 50	Culture	131UNTS25	101734
Madagascar	Multilateral	25 Jun 51	Tech Assistance	92UNTS27	101258
Madagascar	Multilateral	02 Jul 51	Refugees	189UNTS137	102545
Madagascar	Multilateral	11 May 53	Sanitation	456UNTS3	106555
Madagascar	Multilateral	18 Jan 54	IGO Establishment	330UNTS121	104743

PARTY ONE	PARTY TWO	DATE	TOPIC	CITATION	NUMBER
Madagascar	Multilateral	12 May 54	Admin Cooperation	327UNTS3	104714
Madagascar	Multilateral	14 May 54	Culture	249UNTS215	103511
Madagascar	Multilateral	14 Jun 54	Air Transport	320UNTS217	104644
Madagascar	Multilateral	14 Jun 54	Air Transport	320UNTS209	104643
Madagascar	Multilateral	29 Jul 54	Sanitation	249UNTS45	103500
Madagascar	Multilateral	28 Sep 54	Refugees	360UNTS117	105158
Madagascar	Multilateral	25 May 55	IGO Establishment	264UNTS117	103791
Madagascar	Multilateral	28 Sep 55	Air Transport	478UNTS371	106943
Madagascar	Multilateral	01 Jul 57	Culture	0UNTS0	110418
Madagascar	Multilateral	29 Apr 58	Specific Resources	559UNTS285	108164
Madagascar	Multilateral	29 Apr 58	Territory Boundary	516UNTS205	107477
Madagascar	Multilateral	29 Apr 58	Territory Boundary	499UNTS311	107302
Madagascar	Multilateral	29 Apr 58	Water Transport	450UNTS11	106465
Madagascar	Multilateral	29 Apr 58	Dispute Settlement	450UNTS169	106466
Madagascar	Multilateral	10 Jun 58	Admin Cooperation	330UNTS3	104739
Madagascar	Multilateral	26 Jan 60	IGO Establishment	439UNTS249	106333
Madagascar	Multilateral	14 Dec 60	Education	429UNTS93	106193
Madagascar	Multilateral	30 Mar 61	Sanitation	520UNTS151	107515
Madagascar	Multilateral	18 Apr 61	Consul/Citizenship	500UNTS223	107311
Madagascar	Multilateral	18 Apr 61	Dispute Settlement	500UNTS243	107312
Madagascar	Multilateral	18 Apr 61	Consul/Citizenship	500UNTS95	107310
Madagascar	Multilateral	08 Jun 61	Customs	473UNTS153	106862
Madagascar	Multilateral	08 Jun 61	Customs	473UNTS187	106863
Madagascar	Multilateral	17 May 62	Tech Assistance	429UNTS46	106189
Madagascar	Multilateral	22 Jun 62	ILO Labor	494UNTS249	107237
Madagascar	Multilateral	28 Jun 62	ILO Labor	494UNTS271	107238
Madagascar	Multilateral	28 Sep 62	IGO Establishment	469UNTS169	106791
Madagascar	Multilateral	24 Apr 63	Consul/Citizenship	596UNTS487	108640
Madagascar	Multilateral	24 Apr 63	Consul/Citizenship	596UNTS261	108638
Madagascar	Multilateral	25 May 63	IGO Establishment	479UNTS39	106947
Madagascar	Multilateral	10 Jul 64	Postal Service	612UNTS233	108848
Madagascar	Multilateral	10 Jul 64	Postal Service	613UNTS3	108850
Madagascar	Multilateral	10 Jul 64	Postal Service	612UNTS361	108849
Madagascar	Multilateral	10 Jul 64	Postal Service	613UNTS3	108851
Madagascar	Multilateral	10 Jul 64	Postal Service	611UNTS105	108845
Madagascar	Multilateral	10 Jul 64	Postal Service	612UNTS3	108847
Madagascar	Multilateral	10 Jul 64	Postal Service	611UNTS387	108846
Madagascar	Multilateral	10 Jul 64	Postal Service	611UNTS7	108844
Madagascar	Multilateral	01 Dec 64	Water Transport	550UNTS133	108012
Madagascar	Multilateral	18 Mar 65	Dispute Settlement	575UNTS159	108359
Madagascar	Multilateral	23 Jun 65	General IGO	614UNTS239	108873
Madagascar	Multilateral	05 Apr 66	Water Transport	640UNTS133	109159
Madagascar	Multilateral	18 Mar 68	Commodity Trade	0UNTS0	109262
Madagascar	Multilateral	22 Apr 68	Scientific Project	0UNTS0	109574
Madagascar	Multilateral	24 Sep 68	Air Transport	0UNTS0	110612
Madagascar	Multilateral	24 Dec 68	Commodity Trade	0UNTS0	109369
Madagascar	USA (United States)	22 Jun 61	General Aid	413UNTS219	105956
Madagascar	USSR (Soviet Union)	23 Oct 64	General Trade	0UNTS0	109829
Malagasy	Accept UN Charter	26 Jun 60	UN Charter	375UNTS87	105356
Malagasy	China People's Rep	13 Aug 66	Tech Assistance	66CCJC77	411264
Malagasy	France	02 Apr 60	Recognition	60FRRT38	415278
Malagasy	France	27 Jun 60	General Amity	60FRRT46	415279
Malagasy	France	18 Oct 61	Specific Property	63FRRT21	415280
Malagasy	France	23 May 62	Customs	62FRRT40	415281
Malagasy	France	29 Sep 62	General Economic	65FRRT69	415282
Malagasy	France	25 Apr 63	Consul/Citizenship	65FRRT83	415283
Malagasy	France	06 Jul 63	Claims and Debts	63FRRT81	415284
Malagasy	France	19 Jun 64	Visas	64FRRT69	415285
Malagasy	France	08 May 67	Non-ILO Labor	68FRJO708	416286
Malagasy	France	22 May 68	Tech Assistance	68FRJO2211	416287
Malagasy	Germany, West	06 Jun 62	General Economic	62WBGA153	424438
Malagasy	Germany, West	06 Jun 62	Water Transport	62WBGA153	424440
Malagasy	Germany, West	06 Jun 62	Direct Aid	62WBGA153	424439
Malagasy	Germany, West	21 Sep 62	Claims and Debts	65WGBB369	425441
Malagasy	Germany, West	10 Mar 66	Loans and Credits	66WBGA151	424442

PARTY ONE	PARTY TWO	DATE	TOPIC	CITATION	NUMBER
Malagasy	Germany, West	18 Jul 68	Loans and Credits	68WBGA175	424443
Malagasy	Israel	27 Aug 61	General Amity	484UNTS217	107032
Malagasy	Israel	27 Aug 61	Direct Aid	413UNTS86	105943
Malagasy	Israel	04 May 63	Visas	484UNTS225	107033
Malagasy	Italy	01 Jul 64	General Economic	65ITDI195	436267
Malagasy	Italy	01 Jul 64	Tech Assistance	65ITDI197	436268
Malagasy	Multilateral	17 Jun 60	Humanitarian	536UNTS27	107794
Malagasy	Multilateral	21 Jun 61	IGO Establishment	514UNTS209	107449
Malagasy	Multilateral	17 May 62	Tech Assistance	429UNTS46	106189
Malagasy	Multilateral	05 Aug 63	Sanitation	480UNTS43	106964
Malagasy	Multilateral	10 Jul 64	Postal Service	612UNTS233	108848
Malagasy	Multilateral	10 Jul 64	Postal Service	611UNTS387	108846
Malagasy	Multilateral	10 Jul 64	Postal Service	611UNTS7	108844
Malagasy	Multilateral	10 Jul 64	Postal Service	611UNTS105	108845
Malagasy	Multilateral	10 Jul 64	Postal Service	612UNTS361	108849
Malagasy	Multilateral	10 Jul 64	Postal Service	612UNTS3	108847
Malagasy	Multilateral	10 Jul 64	Postal Service	613UNTS3	108850
Malagasy	Multilateral	10 Jul 64	Postal Service	613UNTS3	108851
Malagasy	Multilateral	09 Mar 65	Water Transport	591UNTS265	108564
Malagasy	Multilateral	05 Apr 66	Water Transport	640UNTS133	109159
Malagasy	Multilateral	27 May 66	IGO Establishment	637UNTS0	109121
Malagasy	Norway	13 May 66	General Amity	3NORT964	451109
Malagasy	Norway	13 May 66	General Economic	3NORT965	451110
Malagasy	Taiwan	04 Apr 62	General Amity	463UNTS195	106703
Malagasy	UN Special Fund	05 Jan 62	Direct Aid	419UNTS29	106028
Malagasy	UNICEF (Children)	16 Nov 61	Direct Aid	422UNTS251	106079
Malagasy	USA (United States)	26 Jul 63	Finance	487UNTS189	107104
Malagasy	USA (United States)	07 Oct 63	Scientific Project	494UNTS3	107221
Malagasy	WHO (World Health)	13 Oct 61	Tech Assistance	421UNTS273	106064
Malawi	Accept UN Charter	04 Aug 64	UN Charter	519UNTS3	107496
Malawi	Denmark	01 Sep 66	Loans and Credits	586UNTS3	108493
Malawi	Denmark	03 Sep 68	Education	0UNTS0	109414
Malawi	Denmark	16 Dec 68	Loans and Credits	0UNTS0	109461
Malawi	Germany, West	30 Jul 56	Consul/Citizenship	57WGBB284	425444
Malawi	Germany, West	25 Sep 64	Loans and Credits	65WBGA67	424445
Malawi	Germany, West	08 Aug 66	Loans and Credits	66WBGA188	424446
Malawi	Germany, West	22 Apr 68	Loans and Credits	68WBGA129	424447
Malawi	Germany, West	04 Sep 68	Loans and Credits	68WBGA215	424448
Malawi	Germany, West	07 Oct 70	Loans and Credits	70WBGA221	424449
Malawi	Ghana	04 May 65	Air Transport	541UNTS163	107869
Malawi	ICJ Option Clause	22 Nov 66	ICJ Option Clause	581UNTS135	108438
Malawi	IDA (Devel Assoc)	04 Oct 66	Non-IBRD Project	584UNTS215	108479
Malawi	IDA (Devel Assoc)	04 May 67	Loans and Credits	617UNTS141	108910
Malawi	IDA (Devel Assoc)	05 Feb 68	Non-IBRD Project	0UNTS0	109308
Malawi	IDA (Devel Assoc)	05 Feb 68	Non-IBRD Project	0UNTS0	109309
Malawi	IDA (Devel Assoc)	05 Feb 68	Non-IBRD Project	0UNTS0	109307
Malawi	IDA (Devel Assoc)	11 Feb 70	Non-IBRD Project	0UNTS0	110655
Malawi	Israel	03 Aug 66	Visas	582UNTS53	108456
Malawi	Multilateral	11 Dec 46	Sanitation	12UNTS179	100186
Malawi	Multilateral	06 Feb 47	IGO Establishment	97UNTS227	101352
Malawi	Multilateral	12 Nov 47	Admin Cooperation	46UNTS201	100710
Malawi	Multilateral	12 Nov 47	Admin Cooperation	53UNTS39	100771
Malawi	Multilateral	22 Feb 49	Sanitation	93UNTS129	101296
Malawi	Multilateral	04 May 49	Admin Cooperation	92UNTS19	101257
Malawi	Multilateral	04 May 49	Admin Cooperation	98UNTS101	101358
Malawi	Multilateral	04 May 49	Admin Cooperation	47UNTS159	100728
Malawi	Multilateral	22 Nov 50	Culture	131UNTS25	101734
Malawi	Multilateral	07 Dec 50	Admin Cooperation	212UNTS17	102861
Malawi	Multilateral	31 Mar 53	Privil/Immunities	193UNTS136	102613
Malawi	Multilateral	25 May 55	IGO Establishment	264UNTS117	103791
Malawi	Multilateral	20 Feb 57	Consul/Citizenship	309UNTS65	104468
Malawi	Multilateral	29 Apr 58	Water Transport	450UNTS11	106465
Malawi	Multilateral	29 Apr 58	Territory Boundary	516UNTS205	107477
Malawi	Multilateral	29 Apr 58	Specific Resources	559UNTS285	108164
Malawi	Multilateral	29 Apr 58	Territory Boundary	499UNTS311	107302

PARTY ONE	PARTY TWO	DATE	TOPIC	CITATION	NUMBER
Malawi	Multilateral	29 Apr 58	Dispute Settlement	450UNTS169	106466
Malawi	Multilateral	26 Jan 60	IGO Establishment	439UNTS249	106333
Malawi	Multilateral	18 Apr 61	Consul/Citizenship	500UNTS95	107310
Malawi	Multilateral	05 Oct 61	Patents/Copyrights	527UNTS181	107625
Malawi	Multilateral	10 Jul 64	Postal Service	611UNTS387	108846
Malawi	Multilateral	10 Jul 64	Postal Service	611UNTS105	108845
Malawi	Multilateral	10 Jul 64	Postal Service	612UNTS3	108847
Malawi	Multilateral	10 Jul 64	Postal Service	611UNTS7	108844
Malawi	Multilateral	24 Oct 64	Tech Assistance	514UNTS220	200608
Malawi	Multilateral	09 Mar 65	Water Transport	591UNTS265	108564
Malawi	Multilateral	18 Mar 65	Dispute Settlement	575UNTS159	108359
Malawi	Multilateral	08 Jul 65	General Trade	597UNTS3	108641
Malawi	Multilateral	20 Jul 65	IGO Operations	541UNTS12	107857
Malawi	Multilateral	24 Sep 68	Air Transport	0UNTS0	110612
Malawi	Multilateral	27 Jan 69	Telecommunications	0UNTS0	109664
Malawi	Multilateral	03 Dec 69	Visas	0UNTS0	110526
Malawi	Netherlands	28 Jun 68	Extradition	0UNTS0	109504
Malawi	Netherlands	18 Jun 69	Taxation	0UNTS0	110429
Malawi	Norway	12 Jul 65	Taxation	2NORT553	451111
Malawi	Norway	30 Apr 66	Visas	3NORT962	451112
Malawi	UK Great Britain	28 Aug 64	Consul/Citizenship	522UNTS223	107548
Malawi	UK Great Britain	01 Sep 64	Commodity Trade	522UNTS117	107539
Malawi	UK Great Britain	19 Jul 66	Admin Cooperation	637UNTS0	109125
Malawi	UK Great Britain	21 Nov 66	Admin Cooperation	637UNTS0	109126
Malawi	UK Great Britain	02 Apr 68	Taxation	0UNTS0	109450
Malawi	UK Great Britain	24 Sep 68	Finance	0UNTS0	109816
Malawi	UK Great Britain	27 Sep 68	Air Transport	0UNTS0	109713
Malawi	UN Special Fund	24 Oct 64	Direct Aid	514UNTS235	200609
Malawi	USA (United States)	20 Apr 65	General Aid	546UNTS175	107943
Malawi	USA (United States)	04 Apr 67	Recognition	0UNTS0	109899
Malawi	USA (United States)	21 Jul 67	Finance	0UNTS0	109910
Malawi	WHO (World Health)	06 Jan 65	Tech Assistance	525UNTS165	107588
Malawi	WHO (World Health)	08 Jan 65	Tech Assistance	524UNTS281	107579
Malaya	Multilateral	03 Oct 57	Postal Service	365UNTS3	105213
Malaya	Multilateral	09 Jul 63	Admin Cooperation	0UNTS0	110760
Malaysia	Australia	21 Jun 65	Humanitarian	542UNTS75	107880
Malaysia	Denmark	26 Mar 65	Air Transport	540UNTS205	107851
Malaysia	Denmark	14 Dec 67	Air Transport	614UNTS26	108862
Malaysia	Denmark	29 Feb 68	Loans and Credits	640UNTS29	109153
Malaysia	France	22 May 67	Air Transport	67FRJO508	416277
Malaysia	Germany, West	22 Dec 60	Claims and Debts	62WGBB1064	425450
Malaysia	Germany, West	09 Dec 63	Loans and Credits	64WBGA13	424451
Malaysia	Germany, West	08 Nov 65	Loans and Credits	65WBGA242	424452
Malaysia	Germany, West	23 Jul 68	Air Transport	70WGBB681	425453
Malaysia	Germany, West	18 Mar 69	Loans and Credits	69WBGA99	424454
Malaysia	Germany, West	11 Feb 71	Loans and Credits	71WBGA82	424455
Malaysia	IBRD (World Bank)	15 Jul 63	IBRD Project	482UNTS123	106993
Malaysia	IBRD (World Bank)	07 Aug 63	IBRD Project	485UNTS253	107060
Malaysia	IBRD (World Bank)	26 Feb 65	IBRD Project	549UNTS239	108002
Malaysia	IBRD (World Bank)	17 Nov 65	IBRD Project	568UNTS23	108263
Malaysia	IBRD (World Bank)	26 Jul 66	IBRD Project	586UNTS195	108504
Malaysia	IBRD (World Bank)	15 Jun 67	IBRD Project	618UNTS235	108930
Malaysia	IBRD (World Bank)	17 Apr 68	IBRD Project	0UNTS0	109360
Malaysia	IBRD (World Bank)	27 Sep 68	IBRD Project	0UNTS0	109506
Malaysia	IBRD (World Bank)	27 Sep 68	IBRD Project	0UNTS0	109505
Malaysia	IBRD (World Bank)	09 Jan 69	IBRD Project	0UNTS0	109594
Malaysia	IBRD (World Bank)	23 May 69	IBRD Project	0UNTS0	110169
Malaysia	IBRD (World Bank)	20 May 70	IBRD Project	0UNTS0	110828
Malaysia	IBRD (World Bank)	20 May 70	IBRD Project	0UNTS0	110829
Malaysia	Indonesia	17 Apr 59	General Amity	470UNTS273	106813
Malaysia	Japan	04 Jun 63	Taxation	517UNTS245	107488
Malaysia	Japan	11 Feb 65	Air Transport	0UNTS0	109477
Malaysia	Japan	11 Feb 65	Air Transport	0JGJI1614	441129
Malaysia	Japan	21 Sep 67	General Economic	68JHZ5	439014
Malaysia	Japan	21 Sep 67	General Economic	0UNTS0	109719

PARTY ONE	PARTY TWO	DATE	TOPIC	CITATION	NUMBER
Malaysia	Japan	30 Jan 70	Taxation	70JHZ12	439034
Malaysia	Multilateral	29 Apr 58	Specific Resources	559UNTS285	108164
Malaysia	Multilateral	29 Apr 58	Territory Boundary	499UNTS311	107302
Malaysia	Multilateral	29 Apr 58	Territory Boundary	516UNTS205	107477
Malaysia	Multilateral	17 Jun 60	Humanitarian	536UNTS27	107794
Malaysia	Multilateral	18 Apr 61	Consul/Citizenship	500UNTS223	107311
Malaysia	Multilateral	18 Apr 61	Dispute Settlement	500UNTS243	107312
Malaysia	Multilateral	18 Apr 61	Consul/Citizenship	500UNTS95	107310
Malaysia	Multilateral	09 Nov 63	Direct Aid	489UNTS209	107141
Malaysia	Multilateral	10 Jul 64	Postal Service	611UNTS105	108845
Malaysia	Multilateral	10 Jul 64	Postal Service	611UNTS7	108844
Malaysia	Multilateral	10 Jul 64	Postal Service	611UNTS387	108846
Malaysia	Multilateral	10 Jul 64	Postal Service	612UNTS3	108847
Malaysia	Multilateral	09 Mar 65	Water Transport	591UNTS265	108564
Malaysia	Multilateral	18 Mar 65	Dispute Settlement	575UNTS159	108359
Malaysia	Multilateral	04 Dec 65	IGO Establishment	571UNTS123	108303
Malaysia	Multilateral	31 Dec 65	Specific Resources	616UNTS317	108904
Malaysia	Multilateral	27 Jan 67	Scientific Project	610UNTS205	108843
Malaysia	Multilateral	28 Dec 67	Scientific Project	0UNTS0	109322
Malaysia	Multilateral	01 Jul 68	Peace/Disarmament	0UNTS0	110485
Malaysia	Multilateral	01 Aug 68	Culture	0UNTS0	109368
Malaysia	Multilateral	27 Jan 69	Telecommunications	0UNTS0	109664
Malaysia	Multilateral	11 Jun 69	Scientific Project	0UNTS0	110100
Malaysia	Netherlands	20 Jan 59	Visas	493UNTS147	107212
Malaysia	Netherlands	07 Apr 64	Air Transport	524UNTS81	107567
Malaysia	New Zealand	03 Feb 61	General Trade	447UNTS251	106418
Malaysia	Norway	19 Sep 60	Visas	3NORT812	451113
Malaysia	Norway	26 May 65	Air Transport	602UNTS157	108711
Malaysia	Norway	19 Oct 67	Air Transport	3NORT1005	451114
Malaysia	Philippines	31 Jul 62	Visas	452UNTS223	106510
Malaysia	Philippines	07 Feb 66	Admin Cooperation	608UNTS3	108809
Malaysia	Philippines	01 Sep 67	Commodity Trade	608UNTS13	108810
Malaysia	Singapore	07 Aug 65	Recognition	563UNTS89	108206
Malaysia	State/IGO Group	10 May 68	IGO Operations	636UNTS276	109105
Malaysia	UK Great Britain	09 Jul 64	Consul/Citizenship	522UNTS213	107547
Malaysia	UK Great Britain	09 Jul 64	Consul/Citizenship	522UNTS201	107546
Malaysia	UK Great Britain	09 Jul 64	Consul/Citizenship	522UNTS189	107545
Malaysia	UK Great Britain	07 May 65	Admin Cooperation	552UNTS259	108058
Malaysia	UK Great Britain	17 Jul 67	Taxation	637UNTS0	109127
Malaysia	UK Great Britain	01 Aug 67	Air Transport	633UNTS93	109036
Malaysia	UK Great Britain	05 Dec 67	Military Mission	642UNTS293	109181
Malaysia	UK Great Britain	24 Sep 68	Finance	0UNTS0	109817
Malaysia	UNICEF (Children)	01 Jul 64	IGO Operations	503UNTS229	107346
Malaysia	USA (United States)	28 Jan 63	Education	473UNTS15	106850
Malaysia	USA (United States)	02 Feb 70	Air Transport	0UNTS0	110620
Malaysia	USSR (Soviet Union)	03 Apr 67	General Trade	0UNTS0	109832
Malaysia	Vietnam, South	10 Dec 70	Air Transport	0VKNG368	496092
Maldive Islands	Accept UN Charter	26 Aug 65	UN Charter	545UNTS147	107929
Maldive Islands	Multilateral	17 Jun 60	Humanitarian	536UNTS27	107794
Maldive Islands	Multilateral	10 Jul 64	Postal Service	611UNTS7	108844
Maldive Islands	Multilateral	10 Jul 64	Postal Service	611UNTS105	108845
Maldive Islands	Multilateral	05 Apr 66	Water Transport	640UNTS133	109159
Maldive Islands	Multilateral	01 Jul 68	Peace/Disarmament	0UNTS0	110485
Maldive Islands	UK Great Britain	26 Jul 65	General Amity	548UNTS223	107980
Maldive Islands	UNICEF (Children)	06 Apr 70	IGO Operations	0UNTS0	110414
Maldive Islands	WHO (World Health)	23 May 66	Tech Assistance	566UNTS19	108237
Mali	Accept UN Charter	22 Oct 60	UN Charter	377UNTS361	105412
Mali	Algeria	22 Jul 63	Air Transport	564UNTS29	108219
Mali	Cameroon	17 Mar 64	Air Transport	524UNTS61	107566
Mali	China People's Rep	28 Feb 61	General Trade	61CCJC27	410761
Mali	China People's Rep	22 Sep 61	General Aid	61CCJC125	410830
Mali	China People's Rep	15 May 63	Culture	63CCJC58	410976
Mali	China People's Rep	31 Aug 63	Mass Media	63CCJC103	411007
Mali	China People's Rep	03 Nov 64	General Amity	64CCJC157	411246
Mali	China People's Rep	17 Mar 65	Direct Aid	65CCJC30	411257

PARTY ONE	PARTY TWO	DATE	TOPIC	CITATION	NUMBER
Mali	China People's Rep	17 Apr 65	Culture	65CCJC54	411259
Mali	China People's Rep	15 Jul 65	Specific Property	65CCJC95	411260
Mali	China People's Rep	13 May 66	Culture	66CCJC33	411262
Mali	China People's Rep	09 Jun 66	Loans and Credits	66CCJC51	411250
Mali	China People's Rep	14 Aug 67	Direct Aid	67CCJC30	411269
Mali	Czechoslovakia	27 Nov 61	Air Transport	466UNTS41	106736
Mali	France	22 Aug 61	Claims and Debts	63FRRT27	415288
Mali	France	09 Mar 62	General Amity	64FRRT49	415289
Mali	France	08 Mar 63	Visas	63FRRT42	415290
Mali	France	11 Mar 65	Non-ILO Labor	67FRJO3008	416291
Mali	France	15 Feb 67	Finance	67FRJO2706	416292
Mali	Germany, East	01 Apr 61	Consul/Citizenship	9EGDA462	419197
Mali	Germany, East	17 Apr 61	Finance	9EGDA372	419198
Mali	Germany, East	30 Sep 63	Tech Assistance	11EGDA424	419199
Mali	Germany, East	03 Jun 64	Education	12EGDA849	419201
Mali	Germany, East	03 Jun 64	Health/Educ/Welfare	12EGDA844	419200
Mali	Germany, East	17 May 65	Mass Media	50EGDZ336	420202
Mali	Germany, East	30 May 65	Tech Assistance	51EGDZ336	420203
Mali	Germany, East	12 Nov 65	Tech Assistance	44EGDZ347	420204
Mali	Germany, East	08 Jun 66	Air Transport	42EGDZ361	420205
Mali	Germany, East	17 Sep 66	Mass Media	34EGDZ368	420206
Mali	Germany, West	14 Feb 62	Loans and Credits	62WBGA75	424456
Mali	Germany, West	06 May 66	Loans and Credits	66WBGA124	424457
Mali	Germany, West	21 Nov 69	Loans and Credits	70WBGA15	424458
Mali	Germany, West	13 Mar 71	Loans and Credits	71WBGA86	424459
Mali	Ghana	09 Jan 63	Air Transport	466UNTS165	106742
Mali	IDA (Devel Assoc)	29 Sep 64	Non-IBRD Project	594UNTS187	108604
Mali	Israel	24 Nov 60	Tech Assistance	413UNTS95	105944
Mali	Israel	24 Nov 60	Culture	413UNTS104	105945
Mali	Italy	03 Jun 64	Tech Assistance	65ITDI142	436269
Mali	Ivory Coast	09 Jul 64	Air Transport	524UNTS121	107569
Mali	Multilateral	07 Dec 44	IGO Establishment	15UNTS295	200102
Mali	Multilateral	27 May 47	Air Transport	418UNTS161	106021
Mali	Multilateral	19 Jun 48	Air Transport	310UNTS151	104492
Mali	Multilateral	24 Jul 48	Sanitation	66UNTS25	100847
Mali	Multilateral	29 Nov 48	IGO Establishment	120UNTS13	101613
Mali	Multilateral	07 Oct 52	Admin Cooperation	310UNTS181	104493
Mali	Multilateral	18 Jan 54	IGO Establishment	330UNTS121	104743
Mali	Multilateral	14 May 54	Culture	249UNTS215	103511
Mali	Multilateral	14 Jun 54	Air Transport	320UNTS217	104644
Mali	Multilateral	14 Jun 54	Air Transport	320UNTS209	104643
Mali	Multilateral	29 Jul 54	Sanitation	249UNTS45	103500
Mali	Multilateral	28 Sep 55	Air Transport	478UNTS371	106943
Mali	Multilateral	26 Jan 60	IGO Establishment	439UNTS249	106333
Mali	Multilateral	30 Mar 61	Sanitation	520UNTS151	107515
Mali	Multilateral	21 Jun 61	IGO Establishment	514UNTS209	107449
Mali	Multilateral	25 May 62	IGO Establishment	486UNTS103	107075
Mali	Multilateral	10 Dec 62	Culture	521UNTS231	107525
Mali	Multilateral	09 May 63	Tech Assistance	463UNTS159	106700
Mali	Multilateral	25 May 63	IGO Establishment	479UNTS39	106947
Mali	Multilateral	04 Aug 63	IGO Establishment	510UNTS3	107408
Mali	Multilateral	05 Aug 63	Sanitation	480UNTS43	106964
Mali	Multilateral	26 Oct 63	Water Transport	587UNTS9	108506
Mali	Multilateral	09 Nov 63	Direct Aid	489UNTS209	107141
Mali	Multilateral	10 Jul 64	Postal Service	612UNTS233	108848
Mali	Multilateral	10 Jul 64	Postal Service	613UNTS127	108853
Mali	Multilateral	10 Jul 64	Postal Service	613UNTS193	108852
Mali	Multilateral	10 Jul 64	Postal Service	612UNTS361	108849
Mali	Multilateral	10 Jul 64	Postal Service	613UNTS3	108851
Mali	Multilateral	10 Jul 64	Postal Service	612UNTS3	108847
Mali	Multilateral	10 Jul 64	Postal Service	611UNTS105	108845
Mali	Multilateral	10 Jul 64	Postal Service	611UNTS7	108844
Mali	Multilateral	10 Jul 64	Postal Service	611UNTS387	108846
Mali	Multilateral	10 Jul 64	Postal Service	613UNTS3	108850
Mali	Multilateral	25 Nov 64	Water Transport	587UNTS19	108507

PARTY ONE	PARTY TWO	DATE	TOPIC	CITATION	NUMBER
Mali	Multilateral	09 Mar 65	Water Transport	591UNTS265	108564
Mali	Multilateral	08 Jul 65	General Trade	597UNTS3	108641
Mali	Multilateral	04 May 67	IGO Establishment	595UNTS287	108623
Mali	Multilateral	20 Jul 67	General Economic	0UNTS0	109259
Mali	Multilateral	22 Sep 67	Non-IBRD Project	0UNTS0	109258
Mali	Multilateral	24 Mar 68	IGO Establishment	0UNTS0	109577
Mali	Multilateral	01 Jul 68	Peace/Disarmament	0UNTS0	110485
Mali	Multilateral	24 Sep 68	Air Transport	0UNTS0	110612
Mali	Niger	15 Jan 64	Air Transport	499UNTS197	107299
Mali	Poland	02 Nov 61	Tech Assistance	61PZUM217	458091
Mali	Poland	02 Nov 61	Culture	64PDZU361	457090
Mali	Poland	02 Nov 62	Culture	572UNTS219	108315
Mali	Romania	26 Sep 63	Culture	528UNTS193	107642
Mali	Senegal	07 Feb 63	Air Transport	524UNTS41	107565
Mali	Tunisia	24 Jul 63	Air Transport	602UNTS91	108708
Mali	UN Special Fund	21 Jul 61	Direct Aid	401UNTS141	105768
Mali	UNICEF (Children)	17 Nov 60	Direct Aid	402UNTS23	105775
Mali	United Nations	09 May 63	Tech Assistance	463UNTS147	106699
Mali	USA (United States)	04 Jan 61	General Aid	405UNTS165	105832
Mali	USA (United States)	20 May 61	Milit Assistance	413UNTS205	105954
Mali	USA (United States)	09 Jun 64	Claims and Debts	530UNTS133	107678
Mali	USA (United States)	14 Jul 65	US Agri Commod Aid	564UNTS101	108223
Mali	USA (United States)	17 Jan 68	Scientific Project	0UNTS0	110000
Mali	USSR (Soviet Union)	14 Oct 60	Recognition	16SUGG129	469984
Mali	USSR (Soviet Union)	18 Mar 61	General Trade	0UNTS0	109826
Mali	USSR (Soviet Union)	18 Mar 61	Culture	10SUGG125	469754
Mali	USSR (Soviet Union)	18 Mar 61	General Trade	10SUGG125	469753
Mali	USSR (Soviet Union)	18 Mar 61	General Aid	10SUGG125	469752
Mali	USSR (Soviet Union)	17 May 61	Consul/Citizenship	16SUGG131	469993
Mali	USSR (Soviet Union)	20 Mar 62	Air Transport	16SUGG132	470004
Mali	USSR (Soviet Union)	10 Oct 62	Tech Assistance	493UNTS219	107216
Mali	WHO (World Health)	27 Apr 61	Tech Assistance	407UNTS66	105860
Malta	Accept UN Charter	29 Sep 64	UN Charter	519UNTS7	107497
Malta	Australia	28 Apr 65	Non-ILO Labor	548UNTS203	107979
Malta	Austria	21 Dec 66	Visas	595UNTS307	108625
Malta	Denmark	30 Dec 65	Visas	561UNTS199	108182
Malta	Denmark	06 May 69	Air Transport	0UNTS0	109931
Malta	Finland	08 Dec 65	Visas	561UNTS205	108183
Malta	France	14 Feb 68	Culture	68FRRT60	415293
Malta	France	24 Mar 69	Visas	0UNTS0	110734
Malta	France	27 Mar 69	Visas	69FRRT50	415294
Malta	Germany, West	29 Feb 64	General Trade	64WBGA87	424461
Malta	Germany, West	09 May 68	Water Transport	68WBGA119	424462
Malta	Greece	01 Oct 65	Visas	550UNTS329	108027
Malta	ICJ Option Clause	29 Nov 66	ICJ Option Clause	580UNTS205	108423
Malta	Italy	23 Oct 65	Visas	550UNTS337	108028
Malta	Japan	13 Nov 68	General Trade	68JJS327	442222
Malta	Multilateral	11 Dec 46	Sanitation	12UNTS179	100186
Malta	Multilateral	06 Mar 48	Water Transport	289UNTS3	104214
Malta	Multilateral	05 May 49	IGO Establishment	87UNTS103	101168
Malta	Multilateral	15 Jul 49	Health/Educ/Welfare	197UNTS3	102631
Malta	Multilateral	02 Sep 49	IGO Status/Immunit	250UNTS12	103515
Malta	Multilateral	24 Sep 49	IGO Establishment	126UNTS237	101691
Malta	Multilateral	07 Dec 50	Admin Cooperation	212UNTS17	102861
Malta	Multilateral	07 Nov 52	General Trade	221UNTS255	103010
Malta	Multilateral	31 Mar 53	Privil/Immunities	193UNTS136	102613
Malta	Multilateral	13 Dec 55	Humanitarian	250UNTS3	103514
Malta	Multilateral	18 May 56	Customs	319UNTS21	104630
Malta	Multilateral	29 Apr 58	Territory Boundary	516UNTS205	107477
Malta	Multilateral	29 Apr 58	Dispute Settlement	450UNTS169	106466
Malta	Multilateral	03 Dec 58	Admin Cooperation	398UNTS9	105715
Malta	Multilateral	28 Apr 60	Health/Educ/Welfare	376UNTS111	105377
Malta	Multilateral	14 Dec 60	Education	429UNTS93	106193
Malta	Multilateral	17 Dec 62	Admin Cooperation	590UNTS81	108548
Malta	Multilateral	10 Jul 64	Postal Service	611UNTS387	108846

PARTY ONE	PARTY TWO	DATE	TOPIC	CITATION	NUMBER
Malta	Multilateral	15 Dec 64	Tech Assistance	522UNTS20	107533
Malta	Multilateral	09 Mar 65	Water Transport	591UNTS265	108564
Malta	Multilateral	05 Apr 66	Water Transport	640UNTS133	109159
Malta	Multilateral	12 May 66	General Aid	563UNTS54	108204
Malta	Multilateral	24 Apr 67	Humanitarian	634UNTS255	109067
Malta	Multilateral	25 Oct 67	Scientific Project	0UNTS0	110322
Malta	Multilateral	07 Jun 68	Admin Cooperation	0UNTS0	110346
Malta	Multilateral	01 Jul 68	Peace/Disarmament	0UNTS0	110485
Malta	Norway	29 Dec 65	Visas	561UNTS211	108184
Malta	Portugal	01 Sep 66	Visas	579UNTS231	108410
Malta	Sweden	29 Dec 65	Visas	561UNTS217	108185
Malta	Switzerland	20 Jan 65	General Trade	548UNTS193	107978
Malta	Turkey	06 Jun 66	Visas	579UNTS237	108411
Malta	UK Great Britain	21 Sep 64	Military Mission	588UNTS55	108518
Malta	UK Great Britain	21 Sep 64	Direct Aid	588UNTS125	108519
Malta	UK Great Britain	31 Dec 64	Admin Cooperation	525UNTS221	107594
Malta	UK Great Britain	10 Jul 67	Air Transport	619UNTS11	108936
Malta	UK Great Britain	22 Sep 68	Finance	0UNTS0	109812
Malta	UNICEF (Children)	22 Apr 65	IGO Operations	533UNTS107	107737
Malta	USA (United States)	15 Jan 66	Specif Goods/Equip	579UNTS109	108402
Malta	USA (United States)	03 Aug 66	Milit Assistance	601UNTS125	108691
Malta	USA (United States)	16 Nov 66	Finance	0UNTS0	109837
Malta	USA (United States)	28 Dec 66	General Military	0UNTS0	109838
Malta	USA (United States)	14 Jun 67	Commodity Trade	604UNTS231	108753
Malta	USA (United States)	25 Jul 67	General Military	0UNTS0	109911
Malta	USA (United States)	16 Apr 68	Military Mission	0UNTS0	110012
Malta	USA (United States)	30 Sep 68	Military Mission	0UNTS0	110080
Malta	USA (United States)	18 Jun 69	Specific Property	0UNTS0	110332
Malta	USA (United States)	23 Apr 70	Military Mission	0UNTS0	110694
Malta	USA (United States)	24 Jun 70	Non-ILO Labor	0UNTS0	110816
Malta	WHO (World Health)	10 May 67	Tech Assistance	603UNTS99	108727
Malta	Yugoslavia	15 Jul 65	General Trade	561UNTS223	108186
Mauritania	Accept UN Charter	20 Mar 63	UN Charter	457UNTS59	106576
Mauritania	China People's Rep	16 Feb 67	Culture	67CCJC7	411268
Mauritania	China People's Rep	16 Feb 67	Direct Aid	67CCJC6	411267
Mauritania	China People's Rep	16 Feb 67	General Trade	67CCJC5	411266
Mauritania	France	19 Oct 60	Recognition	60FRRT75	415311
Mauritania	France	19 Jun 61	General Amity	62FRRT9	415312
Mauritania	France	10 May 63	Specific Property	63FRRT72	415313
Mauritania	France	29 May 63	Direct Aid	65FRRT99	415314
Mauritania	France	15 Jul 63	Visas	64FRRT8	415315
Mauritania	France	24 Oct 63	Air Transport	64FRRT10	415316
Mauritania	France	07 Feb 64	Consul/Citizenship	66FRJO1901	416317
Mauritania	France	16 Nov 64	Education	65FRRT91	415318
Mauritania	France	22 Jul 65	Non-ILO Labor	67FRJO1202	416319
Mauritania	France	22 Jul 65	Non-ILO Labor	0UNTS0	109329
Mauritania	France	15 Nov 67	Taxation	0UNTS0	110244
Mauritania	France	15 Nov 67	Finance	69FRJO2704	416320
Mauritania	France	17 Feb 68	Scientific Project	68FRJO706	416321
Mauritania	Germany, West	02 Oct 67	Loans and Credits	56WBGA91	424475
Mauritania	IBRD (World Bank)	17 Mar 60	IBRD Project	452UNTS211	106509
Mauritania	IDA (Devel Assoc)	28 Dec 64	Non-IBRD Project	540UNTS163	107849
Mauritania	Multilateral	07 Dec 44	IGO Establishment	15UNTS295	200102
Mauritania	Multilateral	27 May 47	Air Transport	418UNTS161	106021
Mauritania	Multilateral	19 Jun 48	Air Transport	310UNTS151	104492
Mauritania	Multilateral	24 Jul 48	Sanitation	66UNTS25	100847
Mauritania	Multilateral	24 Jul 48	Sanitation	66UNTS25	100847
Mauritania	Multilateral	18 Jun 49	ILO Labor	605UNTS295	108768
Mauritania	Multilateral	07 Oct 52	Admin Cooperation	310UNTS181	104493
Mauritania	Multilateral	14 Jun 54	Air Transport	320UNTS217	104644
Mauritania	Multilateral	14 Jun 54	Air Transport	320UNTS209	104643
Mauritania	Multilateral	26 Jan 60	IGO Establishment	439UNTS249	106333
Mauritania	Multilateral	17 Jun 60	Humanitarian	536UNTS27	107794
Mauritania	Multilateral	18 Apr 61	Consul/Citizenship	500UNTS95	107310
Mauritania	Multilateral	21 Jun 61	IGO Establishment	514UNTS209	107449

PARTY ONE	PARTY TWO	DATE	TOPIC	CITATION	NUMBER
Mauritania	Multilateral	07 Nov 61	Tech Assistance	412UNTS258	105937
Mauritania	Multilateral	28 Jun 62	ILO Labor	494UNTS271	107238
Mauritania	Multilateral	25 May 63	IGO Establishment	479UNTS39	106947
Mauritania	Multilateral	04 Aug 63	IGO Establishment	510UNTS3	107408
Mauritania	Multilateral	05 Aug 63	Sanitation	480UNTS43	106964
Mauritania	Multilateral	10 Jul 64	Postal Service	613UNTS3	108850
Mauritania	Multilateral	10 Jul 64	Postal Service	611UNTS105	108845
Mauritania	Multilateral	10 Jul 64	Postal Service	611UNTS7	108844
Mauritania	Multilateral	10 Jul 64	Postal Service	612UNTS361	108849
Mauritania	Multilateral	10 Jul 64	Postal Service	613UNTS3	108851
Mauritania	Multilateral	10 Jul 64	Postal Service	612UNTS233	108848
Mauritania	Multilateral	10 Jul 64	Postal Service	613UNTS193	108852
Mauritania	Multilateral	10 Jul 64	Postal Service	613UNTS193	108852
Mauritania	Multilateral	10 Jul 64	Postal Service	613UNTS3	108851
Mauritania	Multilateral	10 Jul 64	Postal Service	612UNTS3	108847
Mauritania	Multilateral	10 Jul 64	Postal Service	611UNTS387	108846
Mauritania	Multilateral	09 Mar 65	Water Transport	591UNTS265	108564
Mauritania	Multilateral	18 Mar 65	Dispute Settlement	575UNTS159	108359
Mauritania	Multilateral	29 Mar 65	Non-IBRD Project	540UNTS145	107848
Mauritania	Multilateral	05 Apr 66	Water Transport	640UNTS133	109159
Mauritania	Multilateral	04 May 67	IGO Establishment	595UNTS287	108623
Mauritania	Multilateral	04 May 67	IGO Establishment	595UNTS287	108623
Mauritania	Multilateral	24 Mar 68	IGO Establishment	0UNTS0	109577
Mauritania	Multilateral	01 Jul 68	Peace/Disarmament	0UNTS0	110485
Mauritania	Multilateral	24 Sep 68	Air Transport	0UNTS0	110612
Mauritania	Spain	11 May 65	Air Transport	602UNTS111	108709
Mauritania	UN Special Fund	07 Nov 61	Direct Aid	412UNTS240	105936
Mauritania	UNICEF (Children)	19 Jan 63	Direct Aid	452UNTS271	106514
Mauritania	USA (United States)	03 Jul 64	Finance	532UNTS307	107724
Mauritania	USA (United States)	17 Oct 66	Direct Aid	0UNTS0	109618
Mauritania	USSR (Soviet Union)	17 Oct 66	General Trade	633UNTS231	109040
Mauritania	WHO (World Health)	17 Apr 61	Tech Assistance	396UNTS301	200587
Mauritius	Accept UN Charter	12 Mar 68	UN Charter	634UNTS217	109064
Mauritius	France	19 May 69	General Trade	69FRMD3107	417310
Mauritius	Germany, West	20 Nov 69	Visas	70WBGA84	424476
Mauritius	ICJ Option Clause	23 Sep 68	ICJ Option Clause	0UNTS0	109251
Mauritius	IDA (Devel Assoc)	26 Jun 69	Non-IBRD Project	0UNTS0	110572
Mauritius	Israel	15 May 69	Visas	0UNTS0	110385
Mauritius	Multilateral	06 Mar 48	Water Transport	289UNTS3	104214
Mauritius	Multilateral	18 Jan 54	IGO Establishment	330UNTS121	104743
Mauritius	Multilateral	29 Jul 54	Sanitation	249UNTS45	103500
Mauritius	Multilateral	04 Aug 63	IGO Establishment	510UNTS3	107408
Mauritius	Multilateral	24 Mar 68	IGO Establishment	0UNTS0	109577
Mauritius	Multilateral	22 Apr 68	Scientific Project	0UNTS0	109574
Mauritius	Multilateral	24 Dec 68	Commodity Trade	0UNTS0	109369
Mauritius	UK Great Britain	12 Mar 68	Scientific Project	0UNTS0	109270
Mauritius	UK Great Britain	12 Mar 68	Admin Cooperation	0UNTS0	109269
Mauritius	UK Great Britain	12 Mar 68	Tech Assistance	0UNTS0	109268
Mauritius	UK Great Britain	12 Mar 68	Milit Assistance	0UNTS0	109267
Mauritius	UK Great Britain	16 Sep 68	Finance	0UNTS0	109797
Mauritius	United Nations	29 Aug 69	Tech Assistance	0UNTS0	110246
Mauritius	United Nations	29 Aug 69	General Aid	0UNTS0	110247
Mauritius	United Nations	29 Aug 69	Tech Assistance	0UNTS0	110245
Mauritius	USA (United States)	03 Sep 68	Milit Installation	0UNTS0	109737
Mauritius	USA (United States)	29 Dec 69	Scientific Project	0UNTS0	110615
Mauritius	USA (United States)	11 May 70	Finance	0UNTS0	110781
Medit Fish Council	Multilateral	24 Sep 49	IGO Establishment	126UNTS237	101691
Mexico	Argentina	26 Jan 60	Culture	635UNTS79	109073
Mexico	Australia	13 Jan 67	Visas	607UNTS77	108797
Mexico	Austria	06 Jun 58	Visas	59ABGB44	403139
Mexico	Belgium	16 Sep 50	General Trade	188UNTS119	102523
Mexico	Belgium	18 Mar 58	Visas	301UNTS291	104348
Mexico	Belgium	19 Nov 64	Culture	546UNTS217	107949
Mexico	Bolivia	12 Apr 62	Culture	66MEXD1708	444001
Mexico	Brazil	20 Jan 60	Culture	65MEXD2306	444002

PARTY ONE	PARTY TWO	DATE	TOPIC	CITATION	NUMBER
Mexico	Brazil	17 Oct 66	Air Transport	71MEXD903	444003
Mexico	Canada	08 Feb 46	General Trade	230UNTS183	103183
Mexico	Canada	27 Jul 53	Air Transport	192UNTS255	102604
Mexico	Canada	21 Dec 61	Air Transport	64MEXD607	444004
Mexico	Canada	30 Jul 62	Gen Communications	528UNTS257	107646
Mexico	Chile	28 Jan 60	Culture	63MEXD3010	444012
Mexico	Costa Rica	04 Feb 46	General Trade	50MEXD1810	444007
Mexico	Costa Rica	19 Jan 66	Tech Assistance	67MEXD2511	444008
Mexico	Costa Rica	19 Jan 66	Culture	67MEXD2511	444009
Mexico	Costa Rica	08 Sep 66	Air Transport	70MEXD304	444010
Mexico	Czechoslovakia	09 Aug 68	Culture	71MEXD903	444011
Mexico	Denmark	12 Jul 54	Patents/Copyrights	55MEXD2608	444013
Mexico	Denmark	04 Feb 70	Air Transport	71MEXD503	444014
Mexico	Ecuador	10 Aug 48	Culture	52MEXD2810	444015
Mexico	El Salvador	14 Dec 50	General Trade	52MEXD605	444016
Mexico	El Salvador	13 Jan 66	Culture	67MEXD1711	444017
Mexico	El Salvador	23 Jun 66	Tech Assistance	68MEXD1403	444018
Mexico	France	11 Dec 50	Patents/Copyrights	51FRJO1111	416322
Mexico	France	29 Nov 51	General Trade	53FRJO2905	416323
Mexico	France	17 Apr 52	Air Transport	163UNTS321	102153
Mexico	France	22 Apr 65	Tech Assistance	63FRRT13	415324
Mexico	Germany, West	04 Nov 54	Patents/Copyrights	55WGBB903	425477
Mexico	Germany, West	18 Dec 56	Admin Cooperation	57WGBB500	425478
Mexico	Germany, West	19 Nov 59	Visas	60WBGA101	424479
Mexico	Germany, West	08 Mar 67	Air Transport	69WGBB193	425480
Mexico	Greece	12 Apr 60	General Trade	64MEXD3012	444025
Mexico	Guatemala	12 Jun 63	Telecommunications	65MEXD2901	444023
Mexico	Guatemala	16 Dec 66	Culture	67MEXD402	444024
Mexico	Honduras	15 Jan 66	Culture	70MEXD703	444027
Mexico	Honduras	27 Oct 66	Tech Assistance	68MEXD1902	444026
Mexico	IAEA (Atom Energy)	18 Dec 63	Atomic Energy	490UNTS361	107165
Mexico	IAEA (Atom Energy)	20 Jun 66	Atomic Energy	573UNTS25	108321
Mexico	IAEA (Atom Energy)	18 Aug 67	IGO Operations	614UNTS123	108867
Mexico	IAEA (Atom Energy)	23 Aug 67	IGO Operations	614UNTS133	108868
Mexico	IAEA (Atom Energy)	06 Sep 68	Atomic Energy	0UNTS0	109318
Mexico	IBRD (World Bank)	06 Jan 49	IBRD Project	154UNTS3	102027
Mexico	IBRD (World Bank)	06 Jan 49	IBRD Project	154UNTS81	102028
Mexico	IBRD (World Bank)	28 Apr 50	IBRD Project	155UNTS185	102037
Mexico	IBRD (World Bank)	18 Oct 50	IBRD Project	157UNTS259	102057
Mexico	IBRD (World Bank)	11 Jan 52	IBRD Project	159UNTS129	102086
Mexico	IBRD (World Bank)	24 Aug 54	IBRD Project	286UNTS211	104168
Mexico	IBRD (World Bank)	14 Jan 58	IBRD Project	293UNTS167	104292
Mexico	IBRD (World Bank)	05 May 58	IBRD Project	309UNTS3	104466
Mexico	IBRD (World Bank)	18 Oct 60	IBRD Project	422UNTS177	106075
Mexico	IBRD (World Bank)	16 Jan 61	IBRD Project	422UNTS203	106076
Mexico	IBRD (World Bank)	20 Jun 62	IBRD Project	467UNTS205	106764
Mexico	IBRD (World Bank)	20 Jun 62	IBRD Project	468UNTS109	106771
Mexico	IBRD (World Bank)	29 Apr 63	IBRD Project	489UNTS151	107138
Mexico	IBRD (World Bank)	20 Sep 63	IBRD Project	491UNTS317	107182
Mexico	IBRD (World Bank)	04 Feb 65	IBRD Project	549UNTS189	108000
Mexico	IBRD (World Bank)	01 Oct 65	IBRD Project	589UNTS339	108542
Mexico	IBRD (World Bank)	15 Dec 65	IBRD Project	568UNTS125	108267
Mexico	IBRD (World Bank)	25 May 66	IBRD Project	596UNTS3	108627
Mexico	IBRD (World Bank)	26 Jan 68	IBRD Project	640UNTS3	109152
Mexico	IBRD (World Bank)	26 Jan 68	IBRD Project	0UNTS0	109511
Mexico	IBRD (World Bank)	28 Jun 68	IBRD Project	0UNTS0	109335
Mexico	IBRD (World Bank)	12 Jun 69	IBRD Project	0UNTS0	110289
Mexico	ICAO (Civil Aviat)	28 Nov 52	Tech Assistance	164UNTS15	102156
Mexico	ICAO (Civil Aviat)	20 Dec 56	IGO Operations	497UNTS3	107259
Mexico	ICJ Option Clause	23 Oct 47	ICJ Option Clause	9UNTS97	100127
Mexico	ILO (Labor Org)	06 Apr 51	Tech Assistance	100UNTS131	101393
Mexico	ILO (Labor Org)	05 Jan 55	IGO Status/Immunit	208UNTS225	102815
Mexico	Indonesia	10 Nov 61	General Trade	62MEXD1602	444028
Mexico	Ireland	15 Aug 68	Visas	0UNTS0	109937
Mexico	Israel	15 Jun 59	Culture	377UNTS267	105406

PARTY ONE	PARTY TWO	DATE	TOPIC	CITATION	NUMBER
Mexico	Israel	11 Jul 66	Tech Assistance	0UNTS0	109348
Mexico	Israel	11 Jul 66	Tech Assistance	68MEXD2510	444029
Mexico	Israel	28 Jan 67	Scientific Project	0UNTS0	109846
Mexico	Italy	15 Sep 49	General Trade	52ITGU69	435273
Mexico	Italy	30 Mar 65	Commodity Trade	66ITDI142	436274
Mexico	Italy	07 Jun 65	Visas	66ITDI143	436275
Mexico	Italy	20 Jul 65	IGO Establishment	66ITDI144	436276
Mexico	Italy	08 Dec 65	Tech Assistance	66ITDI146	436277
Mexico	Italy	08 Dec 65	Loans and Credits	66ITDI147	436278
Mexico	Italy	23 Dec 65	Air Transport	66ITDI210	436279
Mexico	Jamaica	15 Mar 68	Visas	0UNTS0	109235
Mexico	Japan	25 Oct 54	Culture	0JGJI1250	441082
Mexico	Japan	24 Jul 67	Tech Assistance	67JJS311	442198
Mexico	Japan	07 Mar 68	Specific Resources	68JHZ6	439019
Mexico	Japan	07 Mar 68	Water Transport	0UNTS0	109723
Mexico	Japan	30 Jan 69	General Trade	69JHZ12	439026
Mexico	Korea, South	29 Apr 66	Culture	70MEXD2904	444005
Mexico	Korea, South	12 Dec 66	General Trade	70MEXD2904	444006
Mexico	Lat Am Nuclear Arm	12 Jan 70	IGO Establishment	0UNTS0	110564
Mexico	Lebanon	26 Jul 50	Culture	52MEXD1502	444030
Mexico	Multilateral	30 Jul 40	Admin Cooperation	161UNTS253	200488
Mexico	Multilateral	12 Oct 40	Specific Resources	161UNTS193	200485
Mexico	Multilateral	28 Nov 40	Commodity Trade	139UNTS159	200452
Mexico	Multilateral	15 Jan 44	IGO Establishment	161UNTS281	200489
Mexico	Multilateral	19 Apr 44	Scientific Project	89UNTS279	200257
Mexico	Multilateral	02 Aug 44	Scientific Project	67UNTS221	200221
Mexico	Multilateral	07 Dec 44	Air Transport	171UNTS387	200502
Mexico	Multilateral	07 Dec 44	Air Transport	84UNTS389	200252
Mexico	Multilateral	07 Dec 44	IGO Establishment	15UNTS295	200102
Mexico	Multilateral	07 Dec 44	Air Transport	171UNTS345	200501
Mexico	Multilateral	16 Nov 45	IGO Establishment	4UNTS275	100052
Mexico	Multilateral	27 Dec 45	IGO Establishment	2UNTS39	100020
Mexico	Multilateral	22 Jul 46	IGO Establishment	9UNTS3	100125
Mexico	Multilateral	22 Jul 46	IGO Establishment	14UNTS185	100221
Mexico	Multilateral	03 Sep 46	Commodity Trade	139UNTS3	101872
Mexico	Multilateral	02 Dec 46	Specific Resources	161UNTS72	102124
Mexico	Multilateral	11 Dec 46	Sanitation	12UNTS179	100186
Mexico	Multilateral	10 Feb 47	Peace/Disarmament	49UNTS3	100747
Mexico	Multilateral	03 Mar 47	Humanitarian	11UNTS43	100148
Mexico	Multilateral	27 May 47	Air Transport	418UNTS161	106021
Mexico	Multilateral	02 Sep 47	General Military	21UNTS77	100324
Mexico	Multilateral	02 Oct 47	Telecommunications	193UNTS188	102616
Mexico	Multilateral	11 Oct 47	IGO Establishment	77UNTS143	100998
Mexico	Multilateral	12 Nov 47	Admin Cooperation	53UNTS49	100772
Mexico	Multilateral	12 Nov 47	Admin Cooperation	53UNTS39	100771
Mexico	Multilateral	12 Nov 47	Admin Cooperation	53UNTS13	100770
Mexico	Multilateral	12 Nov 47	Admin Cooperation	46UNTS169	100709
Mexico	Multilateral	12 Nov 47	Admin Cooperation	46UNTS201	100710
Mexico	Multilateral	06 Mar 48	Water Transport	289UNTS3	104214
Mexico	Multilateral	30 Apr 48	IGO Establishment	119UNTS3	101609
Mexico	Multilateral	30 Apr 48	Dispute Settlement	30UNTS55	100449
Mexico	Multilateral	10 Jun 48	Humanitarian	164UNTS113	102163
Mexico	Multilateral	19 Jun 48	Air Transport	310UNTS151	104492
Mexico	Multilateral	24 Jul 48	Sanitation	66UNTS25	100847
Mexico	Multilateral	19 Nov 48	Sanitation	44UNTS277	100688
Mexico	Multilateral	29 Nov 48	IGO Establishment	120UNTS13	101613
Mexico	Multilateral	09 Dec 48	Humanitarian	78UNTS277	101021
Mexico	Multilateral	23 Mar 49	Commodity Trade	203UNTS179	102746
Mexico	Multilateral	04 May 49	Admin Cooperation	92UNTS19	101257
Mexico	Multilateral	04 May 49	Admin Cooperation	98UNTS101	101358
Mexico	Multilateral	04 May 49	Admin Cooperation	30UNTS3	100445
Mexico	Multilateral	04 May 49	Admin Cooperation	47UNTS159	100728
Mexico	Multilateral	09 Jul 49	Telecommunications	168UNTS143	102218
Mexico	Multilateral	12 Aug 49	Humanitarian	75UNTS287	100973
Mexico	Multilateral	12 Aug 49	Humanitarian	75UNTS31	100970

PARTY ONE	PARTY TWO	DATE	TOPIC	CITATION	NUMBER
Mexico	Multilateral	12 Aug 49	General Military	75UNTS135	100972
Mexico	Multilateral	12 Aug 49	Humanitarian	75UNTS85	100971
Mexico	Multilateral	16 Dec 49	Admin Cooperation	72UNTS3	100924
Mexico	Multilateral	06 Apr 50	Admin Cooperation	119UNTS99	101610
Mexico	Multilateral	07 Dec 50	Admin Cooperation	212UNTS17	102861
Mexico	Multilateral	25 May 51	Status of Forces	175UNTS215	102303
Mexico	Multilateral	08 Sep 51	Peace/Disarmament	136UNTS45	101832
Mexico	Multilateral	06 Dec 51	IGO Establishment	425UNTS61	106119
Mexico	Multilateral	12 Jun 52	Dispute Settlement	138UNTS183	101869
Mexico	Multilateral	11 Jul 52	Postal Service	170UNTS63	102222
Mexico	Multilateral	11 Jul 52	Postal Service	170UNTS269	102223
Mexico	Multilateral	11 Jul 52	Postal Service	171UNTS89	102225
Mexico	Multilateral	11 Jul 52	IGO Establishment	169UNTS3	102220
Mexico	Multilateral	06 Sep 52	Patents/Copyrights	216UNTS132	102937
Mexico	Multilateral	07 Oct 52	Admin Cooperation	310UNTS181	104493
Mexico	Multilateral	31 Mar 53	Privil/Immunities	193UNTS136	102613
Mexico	Multilateral	11 May 53	Sanitation	456UNTS3	106555
Mexico	Multilateral	01 Oct 53	Commodity Trade	258UNTS153	103677
Mexico	Multilateral	07 Dec 53	Admin Cooperation	182UNTS51	102422
Mexico	Multilateral	12 May 54	Admin Cooperation	327UNTS3	104714
Mexico	Multilateral	14 May 54	Culture	249UNTS215	103511
Mexico	Multilateral	04 Jun 54	Customs	282UNTS249	104101
Mexico	Multilateral	04 Jun 54	Customs	276UNTS191	103992
Mexico	Multilateral	14 Jun 54	Air Transport	320UNTS217	104644
Mexico	Multilateral	14 Jun 54	Air Transport	320UNTS209	104643
Mexico	Multilateral	15 May 55	Recognition	217UNTS223	102949
Mexico	Multilateral	25 May 55	IGO Establishment	264UNTS117	103791
Mexico	Multilateral	28 Sep 55	Air Transport	478UNTS371	106943
Mexico	Multilateral	25 Apr 56	Commodity Trade	270UNTS103	103896
Mexico	Multilateral	20 Jun 56	Admin Cooperation	268UNTS3	103850
Mexico	Multilateral	07 Sep 56	Humanitarian	266UNTS3	103822
Mexico	Multilateral	26 Oct 56	IGO Establishment	276UNTS3	103988
Mexico	Multilateral	03 Oct 57	Postal Service	365UNTS207	105214
Mexico	Multilateral	03 Oct 57	Postal Service	364UNTS3	105211
Mexico	Multilateral	03 Oct 57	Postal Service	365UNTS3	105213
Mexico	Multilateral	03 Oct 57	Postal Service	366UNTS87	105216
Mexico	Multilateral	01 Dec 58	Commodity Trade	385UNTS137	105534
Mexico	Multilateral	06 Apr 59	Commodity Trade	349UNTS167	105013
Mexico	Multilateral	08 Apr 59	IGO Establishment	389UNTS69	105593
Mexico	Multilateral	26 Jan 60	IGO Establishment	439UNTS249	106333
Mexico	Multilateral	01 Sep 60	Commodity Trade	403UNTS3	105792
Mexico	Multilateral	30 Mar 61	Sanitation	520UNTS151	107515
Mexico	Multilateral	18 Apr 61	Consul/Citizenship	500UNTS95	107310
Mexico	Multilateral	21 Jun 61	IGO Establishment	514UNTS209	107449
Mexico	Multilateral	18 Sep 61	Air Transport	500UNTS31	107305
Mexico	Multilateral	26 Oct 61	Patents/Copyrights	496UNTS43	107247
Mexico	Multilateral	26 Mar 62	IGO Establishment	539UNTS67	107825
Mexico	Multilateral	15 May 62	Commodity Trade	444UNTS3	106367
Mexico	Multilateral	28 Sep 62	IGO Establishment	469UNTS169	106791
Mexico	Multilateral	24 Apr 63	Consul/Citizenship	596UNTS261	108638
Mexico	Multilateral	23 Jul 63	Tech Assistance	471UNTS158	106831
Mexico	Multilateral	05 Aug 63	Sanitation	480UNTS43	106964
Mexico	Multilateral	14 Sep 63	Air Transport	0UNTS0	110106
Mexico	Multilateral	18 Dec 63	Atomic Energy	490UNTS383	107166
Mexico	Multilateral	10 Jul 64	Postal Service	612UNTS233	108848
Mexico	Multilateral	10 Jul 64	Postal Service	611UNTS105	108845
Mexico	Multilateral	10 Jul 64	Postal Service	612UNTS3	108847
Mexico	Multilateral	10 Jul 64	Postal Service	611UNTS7	108844
Mexico	Multilateral	23 Jun 65	General IGO	614UNTS239	108873
Mexico	Multilateral	07 Oct 65	Atomic Energy	556UNTS175	108125
Mexico	Multilateral	31 Dec 65	Specific Resources	616UNTS317	108904
Mexico	Multilateral	17 Jan 66	IGO Establishment	592UNTS101	108573
Mexico	Multilateral	20 Jun 66	Atomic Energy	573UNTS41	108322
Mexico	Multilateral	27 Jan 67	Scientific Project	610UNTS205	108843
Mexico	Multilateral	14 Feb 67	General Military	634UNTS281	109068

PARTY ONE	PARTY TWO	DATE	TOPIC	CITATION	NUMBER
Mexico	Multilateral	23 Aug 67	IGO Operations	614UNTS145	108869
Mexico	Multilateral	18 Mar 68	Commodity Trade	0UNTS0	109262
Mexico	Multilateral	22 Apr 68	Scientific Project	0UNTS0	109574
Mexico	Multilateral	01 Jul 68	Peace/Disarmament	0UNTS0	110485
Mexico	Multilateral	24 Sep 68	Air Transport	0UNTS0	110612
Mexico	Multilateral	24 Dec 68	Commodity Trade	0UNTS0	109369
Mexico	Netherlands	07 Feb 46	Specif Claim/Waive	3UNTS13	100022
Mexico	Netherlands	27 Jan 50	General Trade	123UNTS197	101661
Mexico	Netherlands	13 Oct 52	Air Transport	163UNTS341	102154
Mexico	Netherlands	24 Aug 61	Air Transport	465UNTS291	106732
Mexico	Netherlands	08 Apr 64	Culture	575UNTS35	108353
Mexico	Nicaragua	19 Nov 46	Telecommunications	51MEXD1105	444031
Mexico	Nicaragua	17 Jan 66	Tech Assistance	68MEXD510	444032
Mexico	Nicaragua	17 Jan 66	Culture	68MEXD1005	444033
Mexico	Norway	10 Dec 59	Visas	3NORT792	451116
Mexico	Norway	04 Feb 70	Air Transport	71MEXD603	444034
Mexico	Panama	20 Jan 66	Culture	67MEXD807	444035
Mexico	Paraguay	13 Aug 58	Culture	60MEXD907	444036
Mexico	Peru	03 Feb 60	Culture	62MEXD3010	444037
Mexico	Poland	24 Jul 70	Health/Educ/Welfare	71PDZU321	457166
Mexico	Portugal	22 Oct 48	Air Transport	34UNTS329	100546
Mexico	Sweden	04 Feb 70	Air Transport	71MEXD803	444040
Mexico	Switzerland	02 Sep 50	General Trade	50SWRO915	462147
Mexico	Switzerland	02 Jun 66	Air Transport	68MEXD2702	444041
Mexico	Taiwan	01 Aug 44	General Amity	14UNTS441	200099
Mexico	Taiwan	25 Sep 64	General Trade	547UNTS233	107960
Mexico	UK Great Britain	07 Feb 46	Claims and Debts	6UNTS55	100068
Mexico	UK Great Britain	27 Sep 46	Consul/Citizenship	91UNTS161	101248
Mexico	UK Great Britain	12 Jun 52	Telecommunications	196UNTS149	102622
Mexico	UK Great Britain	20 Mar 54	Consul/Citizenship	331UNTS21	104750
Mexico	UK Great Britain	13 Nov 59	Visas	360UNTS3	105152
Mexico	UN Special Fund	23 Feb 61	Direct Aid	388UNTS151	105576
Mexico	UNICEF (Children)	20 May 54	Direct Aid	192UNTS3	102591
Mexico	United Arab Rep	08 Apr 60	Culture	64MEXD1408	444038
Mexico	United Arab Rep	25 Oct 63	General Trade	66MEXD1708	444039
Mexico	United Nations	20 May 51	IGO Operations	102UNTS103	101413
Mexico	United Nations	07 Apr 59	IGO Operations	381UNTS123	105468
Mexico	United Nations	18 Aug 61	Humanitarian	404UNTS297	105817
Mexico	United Nations	17 Jul 64	IGO Operations	533UNTS117	107738
Mexico	USA (United States)	11 Apr 41	Non-IBRD Project	117UNTS323	200379
Mexico	USA (United States)	19 Nov 41	Claims and Debts	148UNTS367	200474
Mexico	USA (United States)	19 Nov 41	Claims and Debts	125UNTS287	200430
Mexico	USA (United States)	04 Aug 42	Non-ILO Labor	148UNTS379	200475
Mexico	USA (United States)	12 Aug 42	Consul/Citizenship	125UNTS301	200431
Mexico	USA (United States)	24 Oct 42	Non-IBRD Project	21UNTS189	200123
Mexico	USA (United States)	10 Nov 42	Scientific Project	66UNTS307	200219
Mexico	USA (United States)	18 Nov 42	Claims and Debts	120UNTS183	200392
Mexico	USA (United States)	23 Dec 42	Finance	13UNTS231	200081
Mexico	USA (United States)	22 Jan 43	Milit Servic/Citiz	105UNTS259	200337
Mexico	USA (United States)	26 Apr 43	Non-ILO Labor	21UNTS245	200127
Mexico	USA (United States)	29 Apr 43	Non-ILO Labor	105UNTS119	200327
Mexico	USA (United States)	14 Jun 43	Scientific Project	66UNTS331	200220
Mexico	USA (United States)	01 Jul 43	Sanitation	28UNTS407	200164
Mexico	USA (United States)	29 Sep 43	Claims and Debts	106UNTS265	200345
Mexico	USA (United States)	27 Jan 44	IGO Establishment	106UNTS275	200346
Mexico	USA (United States)	03 Feb 44	Specific Resources	3UNTS313	200025
Mexico	USA (United States)	08 Nov 45	Specific Resources	46MEXD3003	444019
Mexico	USA (United States)	05 Mar 46	Claims and Debts	120UNTS3	101612
Mexico	USA (United States)	12 Apr 46	Scientific Project	66UNTS293	100861
Mexico	USA (United States)	22 Oct 46	Non-IBRD Project	21UNTS13	100321
Mexico	USA (United States)	15 Nov 46	Non-ILO Labor	105UNTS3	101450
Mexico	USA (United States)	17 Mar 47	Sanitation	167UNTS30	102200
Mexico	USA (United States)	02 Apr 47	Non-ILO Labor	148UNTS104	101939
Mexico	USA (United States)	25 Jan 49	IGO Establishment	99UNTS3	101367
Mexico	USA (United States)	14 Feb 49	Sanitation	160UNTS75	102103
Mexico	USA (United States)	21 Jun 49	Scientific Project	89UNTS3	101204
Mexico	USA (United States)	05 Jul 49	Military Mission	68UNTS55	100884
Mexico	USA (United States)	15 Aug 49	Scientific Project	66UNTS13	100846
Mexico	USA (United States)	30 Aug 49	IGO Establishment	98UNTS183	101364
Mexico	USA (United States)	03 May 50	Visas	98UNTS201	101366
Mexico	USA (United States)	27 Jun 51	Tech Assistance	141UNTS211	101916
Mexico	USA (United States)	10 Aug 51	Telecommunications	152UNTS27	102009
Mexico	USA (United States)	11 Aug 51	Non-ILO Labor	162UNTS103	102133
Mexico	USA (United States)	15 Jul 52	Air Transport	181UNTS263	102416
Mexico	USA (United States)	26 Aug 52	IGO Establishment	264UNTS269	103797
Mexico	USA (United States)	12 Nov 53	Visas	224UNTS187	103077
Mexico	USA (United States)	06 Apr 54	Non-IBRD Project	233UNTS163	103261
Mexico	USA (United States)	06 Apr 54	Tech Assistance	236UNTS69	103317
Mexico	USA (United States)	07 Jun 54	Tech Assistance	234UNTS11	103269
Mexico	USA (United States)	17 Jun 54	Non-IBRD Project	237UNTS275	103352
Mexico	USA (United States)	30 Jul 54	Sanitation	269UNTS39	103871
Mexico	USA (United States)	19 Nov 54	Non-ILO Labor	238UNTS237	103367
Mexico	USA (United States)	09 Mar 55	Tech Assistance	263UNTS247	103776
Mexico	USA (United States)	29 Jan 57	Telecommunications	418UNTS253	106025
Mexico	USA (United States)	07 Mar 57	Air Transport	279UNTS205	104042
Mexico	USA (United States)	23 Oct 57	US Agri Commod Aid	300UNTS35	104330
Mexico	USA (United States)	16 Jul 58	Telecommunications	335UNTS139	104782
Mexico	USA (United States)	31 Jul 59	Gen Communications	357UNTS187	105117
Mexico	USA (United States)	05 Aug 59	Customs	356UNTS3	105089
Mexico	USA (United States)	04 Feb 60	Scientific Project	586UNTS57	108496
Mexico	USA (United States)	12 Apr 60	Scientific Project	372UNTS47	105287
Mexico	USA (United States)	15 Aug 60	Air Transport	402UNTS177	105786
Mexico	USA (United States)	24 Oct 60	Specific Property	401UNTS137	105767
Mexico	USA (United States)	26 Jun 61	Direct Aid	413UNTS229	105957
Mexico	USA (United States)	19 Jul 61	Air Transport	433UNTS43	106230
Mexico	USA (United States)	15 Nov 61	Non-IBRD Project	460UNTS113	106634
Mexico	USA (United States)	08 Jan 62	Humanitarian	433UNTS163	106239
Mexico	USA (United States)	18 Apr 62	Telecommunications	452UNTS3	106501
Mexico	USA (United States)	29 Aug 63	Territory Boundary	505UNTS185	107374
Mexico	USA (United States)	14 Feb 64	Scientific Project	524UNTS197	107574
Mexico	USA (United States)	14 May 64	Commodity Trade	526UNTS228	107607
Mexico	USA (United States)	07 Aug 64	Taxation	530UNTS123	107677
Mexico	USA (United States)	27 Feb 65	Scientific Project	542UNTS181	107889
Mexico	USA (United States)	27 Feb 65	Scientific Project	546UNTS135	107940
Mexico	USA (United States)	24 Aug 66	Non-IBRD Project	606UNTS251	108789
Mexico	USA (United States)	26 Oct 66	Education	0UNTS0	109619
Mexico	USA (United States)	03 Dec 66	Admin Cooperation	0UNTS0	109692
Mexico	USA (United States)	02 Jun 67	General Trade	0UNTS0	109770
Mexico	USA (United States)	01 Aug 67	Claims and Debts	0UNTS0	109982
Mexico	USA (United States)	27 Oct 67	Specific Resources	0UNTS0	109925
Mexico	USA (United States)	03 May 68	Admin Cooperation	0UNTS0	110014
Mexico	USA (United States)	11 Dec 68	Telecommunications	71MEXD2001	444020
Mexico	USA (United States)	20 Dec 68	Scientific Project	0UNTS0	110258
Mexico	USA (United States)	20 Mar 70	Commodity Trade	0UNTS0	110629
Mexico	USA (United States)	23 Jun 70	Direct Aid	0UNTS0	110815
Mexico	USA (United States)	17 Jul 70	Admin Cooperation	71MEXD906	444021
Mexico	USA (United States)	23 Nov 70	Territory Boundary	72MEXD1501	444022
Mexico	USSR (Soviet Union)	28 May 68	Culture	0UNTS0	110282
Mexico	USSR (Soviet Union)	28 May 68	Health/Educ/Welfare	70MEXD808	444042
Mexico	Venezuela	25 Jul 46	Culture	48MEXD1011	444043
Mexico	WHO (World Health)	30 Apr 51	Tech Assistance	103UNTS95	101427
Mexico	WHO (World Health)	17 Dec 51	Tech Assistance	124UNTS121	101670
Mexico	WHO (World Health)	28 May 52	Sanitation	134UNTS319	101810
Mexico	Yugoslavia	17 Mar 50	General Trade	54MEXD2202	444044
Mexico	Yugoslavia	26 Mar 60	Culture	66MEXD1607	444045
Mexico	Yugoslavia	03 Jul 63	General Trade	67MEXD1711	444046
Monaco	Australia	07 Jul 59	Visas	354UNTS105	105057
Monaco	Austria	04 Jun 54	Visas	55ABGB215	403140
Monaco	Belgium	05 Jun 48	Admin Cooperation	18UNTS245	100294
Monaco	Belgium	06 Feb 50	Visas	51UNTS93	100755

PARTY ONE	PARTY TWO	DATE	TOPIC	CITATION	NUMBER
Monaco	Canada	20 Mar 52	Visas	233UNTS123	103256
Monaco	France	14 Apr 45	Finance	45FRJO106	416325
Monaco	France	14 Apr 45	Finance	45FRJO106	416326
Monaco	France	14 Apr 45	Admin Cooperation	45FRJO106	416327
Monaco	France	26 Oct 46	Reparations	60FRJO44	416328
Monaco	France	16 Jun 47	Consul/Citizenship	47FRJO2106	416329
Monaco	France	01 Apr 50	Taxation	53FRJO1006	416330
Monaco	France	13 Sep 50	Claims and Debts	54FRJO2706	416331
Monaco	France	13 Nov 52	Claims and Debts	54FRJO508	416332
Monaco	France	18 May 63	Finance	63FRRT66	415333
Monaco	France	18 May 63	Non-ILO Labor	0UNTS0	110719
Monaco	France	18 May 63	Taxation	0UNTS0	109438
Monaco	France	15 Oct 63	Admin Cooperation	63FRRT77	415334
Monaco	France	31 Aug 64	Visas	64FRRT66	415335
Monaco	France	09 Dec 66	Finance	0UNTS0	109439
Monaco	France	18 May 67	Culture	0UNTS0	110662
Monaco	France	26 Sep 68	Non-ILO Labor	0UNTS0	110720
Monaco	France	26 Sep 68	General Economic	70FRJO1601	416336
Monaco	France	23 Jan 70	Education	0UNTS0	110664
Monaco	France	23 Jan 70	Culture	0UNTS0	110663
Monaco	France	16 Apr 70	Admin Cooperation	0UNTS0	110721
Monaco	Germany, West	14 May 59	Visas	60WBGA85	424481
Monaco	Germany, West	21 May 62	Admin Cooperation	64WGBB1297	425483
Monaco	Germany, West	21 May 62	Extradition	64WGBB1297	425482
Monaco	Ireland	06 Jul 54	Visas	553UNTS117	108076
Monaco	Italy	04 Dec 51	Reparations	52ITGU226	435280
Monaco	Italy	01 Jun 57	Visas	291UNTS197	104254
Monaco	Italy	06 Dec 57	Non-ILO Labor	363UNTS45	105198
Monaco	Italy	06 Dec 57	Non-ILO Labor	363UNTS59	105199
Monaco	Italy	08 Apr 58	Visas	60ITDI263	436281
Monaco	Italy	11 Oct 61	Non-ILO Labor	63ITGU122	435282
Monaco	Italy	02 Apr 64	Non-ILO Labor	65ITDI131	436283
Monaco	Multilateral	11 Dec 46	Sanitation	12UNTS179	100186
Monaco	Multilateral	06 Jun 47	Patents/Copyrights	46UNTS249	100714
Monaco	Multilateral	02 Oct 47	Telecommunications	193UNTS188	102616
Monaco	Multilateral	10 Jun 48	Humanitarian	191UNTS3	102576
Monaco	Multilateral	10 Jun 48	Humanitarian	164UNTS113	102163
Monaco	Multilateral	26 Jun 48	Culture	331UNTS217	104757
Monaco	Multilateral	24 Jul 48	Sanitation	66UNTS25	100847
Monaco	Multilateral	17 Sep 48	Telecommunications	97UNTS31	101345
Monaco	Multilateral	19 Nov 48	Sanitation	44UNTS277	100688
Monaco	Multilateral	09 Dec 48	Humanitarian	78UNTS277	101021
Monaco	Multilateral	15 Jul 49	Health/Educ/Welfare	197UNTS3	102631
Monaco	Multilateral	12 Aug 49	Humanitarian	75UNTS31	100970
Monaco	Multilateral	12 Aug 49	Humanitarian	75UNTS85	100971
Monaco	Multilateral	12 Aug 49	Humanitarian	75UNTS287	100973
Monaco	Multilateral	19 Sep 49	Land Transport	125UNTS3	101671
Monaco	Multilateral	24 Sep 49	IGO Establishment	126UNTS237	101691
Monaco	Multilateral	18 Oct 50	Specific Resources	638UNTS185	109134
Monaco	Multilateral	22 Nov 50	Culture	131UNTS25	101734
Monaco	Multilateral	07 Dec 50	Admin Cooperation	212UNTS17	102861
Monaco	Multilateral	25 May 51	Status of Forces	175UNTS215	102303
Monaco	Multilateral	02 Jul 51	Refugees	189UNTS137	102545
Monaco	Multilateral	10 May 52	Admin Cooperation	439UNTS217	106331
Monaco	Multilateral	10 May 52	Admin Cooperation	439UNTS193	106330
Monaco	Multilateral	10 May 52	Taxation	439UNTS233	106332
Monaco	Multilateral	06 Sep 52	Patents/Copyrights	216UNTS132	102937
Monaco	Multilateral	11 May 53	Sanitation	456UNTS3	106555
Monaco	Multilateral	07 Dec 53	Admin Cooperation	182UNTS51	102422
Monaco	Multilateral	14 May 54	Culture	249UNTS215	103511
Monaco	Multilateral	04 Jun 54	Customs	282UNTS249	104101
Monaco	Multilateral	04 Jun 54	Customs	276UNTS191	103992
Monaco	Multilateral	12 Oct 55	IGO Establishment	560UNTS3	108165
Monaco	Multilateral	20 Jun 56	Admin Cooperation	268UNTS3	103850
Monaco	Multilateral	26 Oct 56	IGO Establishment	276UNTS3	103988

PARTY ONE	PARTY TWO	DATE	TOPIC	CITATION	NUMBER
Monaco	Multilateral	15 Jun 57	Patents/Copyrights	583UNTS3	108470
Monaco	Multilateral	15 Jun 57	General Trade	550UNTS45	108008
Monaco	Multilateral	03 Oct 57	Postal Service	366UNTS3	105215
Monaco	Multilateral	03 Oct 57	Postal Service	364UNTS3	105211
Monaco	Multilateral	03 Oct 57	Postal Service	366UNTS255	105219
Monaco	Multilateral	03 Oct 57	Postal Service	366UNTS141	105217
Monaco	Multilateral	03 Oct 57	Postal Service	366UNTS87	105216
Monaco	Multilateral	03 Oct 57	Postal Service	365UNTS3	105213
Monaco	Multilateral	03 Oct 57	Postal Service	364UNTS331	105212
Monaco	Multilateral	03 Oct 57	Postal Service	365UNTS207	105214
Monaco	Multilateral	23 Nov 57	Refugees	506UNTS125	107384
Monaco	Multilateral	10 Jun 58	Admin Cooperation	330UNTS3	104739
Monaco	Multilateral	08 Mar 61	Scientific Project	396UNTS255	200584
Monaco	Multilateral	26 Oct 61	Patents/Copyrights	496UNTS43	107247
Monaco	Multilateral	10 Jul 64	Postal Service	612UNTS3	108847
Monaco	Multilateral	10 Jul 64	Postal Service	611UNTS7	108844
Monaco	Multilateral	10 Jul 64	Postal Service	612UNTS233	108848
Monaco	Multilateral	10 Jul 64	Postal Service	612UNTS361	108849
Monaco	Multilateral	10 Jul 64	Postal Service	613UNTS3	108851
Monaco	Multilateral	10 Jul 64	Postal Service	613UNTS193	108852
Monaco	Multilateral	10 Jul 64	Postal Service	611UNTS387	108846
Monaco	Multilateral	10 Jul 64	Postal Service	611UNTS105	108845
Monaco	Multilateral	10 Jul 64	Postal Service	613UNTS127	108853
Monaco	Multilateral	10 Jul 64	Postal Service	613UNTS3	108850
Monaco	Multilateral	20 Aug 64	Telecommunications	514UNTS25	107441
Monaco	Multilateral	09 Mar 65	Water Transport	591UNTS265	108564
Monaco	Multilateral	03 May 67	IGO Operations	0UNTS0	110764
Monaco	Netherlands	25 Sep 46	Visas	247UNTS199	103469
Monaco	Netherlands	04 May 54	Admin Cooperation	291UNTS3	104240
Monaco	Netherlands	20 Oct 59	Visas	487UNTS29	107093
Monaco	New Zealand	13 Jun 52	Visas	171UNTS269	102230
Monaco	Norway	16 Jul 48	Visas	90UNTS77	101229
Monaco	UK Great Britain	10 Nov 48	Visas	81UNTS85	101065
Monaco	UK Great Britain	11 Apr 61	Visas	404UNTS11	105800
Monaco	United Nations	17 Dec 65	IGO Operations	550UNTS365	200615
Monaco	USA (United States)	31 Mar 52	Visas	177UNTS195	102318
Monaco	USA (United States)	24 Sep 52	Patents/Copyrights	186UNTS43	102481
Monaco	USA (United States)	16 Oct 68	Gen Communications	0UNTS0	110329
Mongolia	Accept UN Charter	04 Dec 61	UN Charter	434UNTS141	106261
Mongolia	Austria	15 Jul 63	General Trade	496UNTS171	107251
Mongolia	Bulgaria	18 Oct 66	Visas	0UNTS0	110301
Mongolia	Bulgaria	21 Jul 67	General Amity	610UNTS0	108839
Mongolia	Bulgaria	27 Nov 68	Admin Cooperation	0UNTS0	109885
Mongolia	Bulgaria	27 Nov 68	Admin Cooperation	0UNTS0	109633
Mongolia	China People's Rep	04 Oct 52	Health/Educ/Welfare	52CCJC54	410078
Mongolia	China People's Rep	16 Jan 53	Postal Service	53CCJC2	410087
Mongolia	China People's Rep	16 Jan 53	Telecommunications	53CCJC3	410088
Mongolia	China People's Rep	07 Apr 54	General Economic	54CCJC14	410139
Mongolia	China People's Rep	16 Dec 54	General Trade	54CCJC85	410190
Mongolia	China People's Rep	21 Dec 55	Mass Media	55CCJC98	410282
Mongolia	China People's Rep	07 Feb 56	General Trade	56CCJC20	410307
Mongolia	China People's Rep	25 Feb 56	Postal Service	56CCJC37	410321
Mongolia	China People's Rep	29 Aug 56	Direct Aid	56CCJC96	410359
Mongolia	China People's Rep	22 Dec 56	General Trade	56CCJC141	410390
Mongolia	China People's Rep	17 Jan 58	Air Transport	58CCJC6	410484
Mongolia	China People's Rep	24 Jan 58	Air Transport	58CCJC13	410490
Mongolia	China People's Rep	28 Jan 58	General Trade	58CCJC14	410491
Mongolia	China People's Rep	21 Feb 58	Culture	58CCJC19	410494
Mongolia	China People's Rep	30 Jan 59	General Trade	59CCJC21	410581
Mongolia	China People's Rep	23 Feb 60	General Trade	60CCJC23	410673
Mongolia	China People's Rep	06 May 60	Mass Media	60CCJC60	410699
Mongolia	China People's Rep	31 May 60	General Amity	60CCJC72	410705
Mongolia	China People's Rep	31 May 60	Tech Assistance	60CCJC74	410707
Mongolia	China People's Rep	26 Apr 61	General Trade	61CCJC70	410793
Mongolia	China People's Rep	26 Apr 61	General Amity	61CCJC69	410792

PARTY ONE	PARTY TWO	DATE	TOPIC	CITATION	NUMBER
Mongolia	China People's Rep	25 Feb 62	General Trade	62CCJC20	410869
Mongolia	China People's Rep	26 Dec 62	Territory Boundary	62CCJC117	410938
Mongolia	China People's Rep	18 Mar 63	General Trade	63CCJC34	410961
Mongolia	China People's Rep	20 Jan 64	General Trade	64CCJC13	411252
Mongolia	China People's Rep	30 Jun 64	Territory Boundary	64CCJC90	411255
Mongolia	China People's Rep	24 Mar 65	General Trade	65CCJC38	411258
Mongolia	China People's Rep	09 Jun 65	Culture	65CCJC80	411249
Mongolia	China People's Rep	28 Mar 66	General Trade	66CCJC11	411261
Mongolia	China People's Rep	30 May 66	Tech Assistance	66CCJC42	411263
Mongolia	China People's Rep	29 Sep 66	Culture	66CCJC82	411265
Mongolia	Czechoslovakia	08 Apr 57	General Amity	501UNTS171	107317
Mongolia	Czechoslovakia	08 Nov 63	Consul/Citizenship	503UNTS125	107341
Mongolia	Czechoslovakia	21 Oct 64	Sanitation	545UNTS91	107926
Mongolia	Czechoslovakia	09 Dec 66	Sanitation	637UNTS0	109124
Mongolia	Czechoslovakia	31 Mar 68	Sanitation	0UNTS0	109279
Mongolia	France	31 Jan 68	Culture	68FRJO1010	416337
Mongolia	Germany, East	16 Oct 53	Consul/Citizenship	1EGDA482	419211
Mongolia	Germany, East	18 Jul 55	Mass Media	4EGDA559	419212
Mongolia	Germany, East	17 Oct 55	Consul/Citizenship	3EGDA600	419213
Mongolia	Germany, East	22 Aug 57	Health/Educ/Welfare	5EGDA363	419214
Mongolia	Germany, East	22 Aug 57	General Amity	521UNTS351	107530
Mongolia	Germany, East	30 Oct 57	Finance	5EGDA366	419215
Mongolia	Germany, East	06 Nov 57	General Trade	5EGDA370	419216
Mongolia	Germany, East	01 Jul 58	Health/Educ/Welfare	6EGDA518	419217
Mongolia	Germany, East	11 Apr 59	Tech Assistance	7EGDA399	419218
Mongolia	Germany, East	12 Jun 59	Telecommunications	7EGDA399	419220
Mongolia	Germany, East	12 Jun 59	Postal Service	7EGDA392	419219
Mongolia	Germany, East	07 Jan 63	Consul/Citizenship	11EGDA430	419221
Mongolia	Germany, East	26 Aug 64	Tech Assistance	12EGDA1153	419222
Mongolia	Germany, East	28 May 65	Education	51EGDZ336	420223
Mongolia	Germany, East	11 Aug 65	Sanitation	52EGDZ341	420224
Mongolia	Germany, East	19 Mar 66	Tech Assistance	51EGDZ356	420225
Mongolia	Germany, East	12 Sep 68	General Amity	0UNTS0	109453
Mongolia	Germany, East	30 Apr 69	Admin Cooperation	0UNTS0	110320
Mongolia	Hungary	10 Jul 63	Consul/Citizenship	519UNTS173	107508
Mongolia	Hungary	02 Oct 65	General Amity	587UNTS35	108508
Mongolia	Hungary	22 Nov 68	Admin Cooperation	0UNTS0	109646
Mongolia	Multilateral	07 Dec 50	Admin Cooperation	212UNTS17	102861
Mongolia	Multilateral	31 Mar 53	Privil/Immunities	193UNTS136	102613
Mongolia	Multilateral	14 May 54	Culture	249UNTS215	103511
Mongolia	Multilateral	26 Mar 56	IGO Establishment	259UNTS125	103686
Mongolia	Multilateral	14 Dec 59	Sanitation	422UNTS57	106068
Mongolia	Multilateral	14 Dec 59	Sanitation	422UNTS33	106067
Mongolia	Multilateral	14 Dec 60	Education	429UNTS93	106193
Mongolia	Multilateral	24 May 63	Tech Assistance	470UNTS208	106810
Mongolia	Multilateral	05 Aug 63	Sanitation	480UNTS43	106964
Mongolia	Multilateral	23 Oct 63	IGO Establishment	506UNTS197	107388
Mongolia	Multilateral	10 Jul 64	Postal Service	611UNTS7	108844
Mongolia	Multilateral	10 Jul 64	Postal Service	612UNTS3	108847
Mongolia	Multilateral	10 Jul 64	Postal Service	611UNTS387	108846
Mongolia	Multilateral	10 Jul 64	Postal Service	611UNTS105	108845
Mongolia	Multilateral	08 Jul 65	General Trade	597UNTS3	108641
Mongolia	Multilateral	22 Apr 68	Scientific Project	0UNTS0	109574
Mongolia	Multilateral	01 Jul 68	Peace/Disarmament	0UNTS0	110485
Mongolia	Multilateral	26 Nov 68	Humanitarian	0UNTS0	110823
Mongolia	Poland	26 May 54	Mass Media	54PZUM14	458015
Mongolia	Poland	23 Dec 58	Culture	432UNTS177	106220
Mongolia	Poland	28 Feb 61	Tech Assistance	61PZUM88	458081
Mongolia	Poland	28 Oct 64	Consul/Citizenship	552UNTS115	108052
Mongolia	Poland	14 Sep 71	Admin Cooperation	72PDZU321	457175
Mongolia	Romania	08 May 56	Culture	342UNTS291	104913
Mongolia	Romania	29 Apr 67	Consul/Citizenship	0UNTS0	110204
Mongolia	Romania	23 Dec 67	Land Transport	CUNTS0	110205
Mongolia	State/IGO Group	15 Jan 70	Tech Assistance	0UNTS0	110202
Mongolia	UN Special Fund	26 Jan 66	Direct Aid	552UNTS201	108055

PARTY ONE	PARTY TWO	DATE	TOPIC	CITATION	NUMBER
Mongolia	UNICEF (Children)	23 Jun 65	IGO Operations	540UNTS83	107844
Mongolia	United Nations	06 Jan 65	IGO Operations	522UNTS45	107535
Mongolia	USSR (Soviet Union)	27 Feb 46	General Economic	216UNTS221	102938
Mongolia	USSR (Soviet Union)	27 Feb 46	General Military	48UNTS177	100744
Mongolia	USSR (Soviet Union)	24 Feb 49	Water Transport	16SUGG65	469889
Mongolia	USSR (Soviet Union)	24 Feb 49	Specific Resources	0SUST439	468266
Mongolia	USSR (Soviet Union)	12 Mar 49	Specific Property	0SUST439	468267
Mongolia	USSR (Soviet Union)	06 Jun 49	Specific Property	0SUST260	468268
Mongolia	USSR (Soviet Union)	06 Jun 49	Loans and Credits	0SUST439	468269
Mongolia	USSR (Soviet Union)	09 Dec 49	General Trade	0SUST265	468270
Mongolia	USSR (Soviet Union)	01 Nov 50	Specific Property	0SUST439	468271
Mongolia	USSR (Soviet Union)	16 Jun 51	Specific Property	16SUGG66	469896
Mongolia	USSR (Soviet Union)	21 Dec 51	Non-ILO Labor	0SUST440	468272
Mongolia	USSR (Soviet Union)	29 Dec 51	General Trade	0SUST440	468273
Mongolia	USSR (Soviet Union)	30 Apr 52	Education	0SUST286	468277
Mongolia	USSR (Soviet Union)	13 Jun 52	Tech Assistance	0SUST440	468274
Mongolia	USSR (Soviet Union)	20 Aug 52	Air Transport	16SUGG66	469898
Mongolia	USSR (Soviet Union)	15 Sep 52	Specific Property	16SUGG67	469899
Mongolia	USSR (Soviet Union)	08 Apr 53	Specific Property	0SUST441	468275
Mongolia	USSR (Soviet Union)	27 Aug 53	Education	16SUGG67	469901
Mongolia	USSR (Soviet Union)	11 Sep 53	Mass Media	0SUST301	468278
Mongolia	USSR (Soviet Union)	28 Nov 53	Loans and Credits	16SUGG67	469902
Mongolia	USSR (Soviet Union)	31 Dec 53	Specific Property	16SUGG68	469903
Mongolia	USSR (Soviet Union)	19 Nov 54	General Trade	0SUST319	468279
Mongolia	USSR (Soviet Union)	12 Aug 55	General Aid	0SUST443	468280
Mongolia	USSR (Soviet Union)	17 Oct 55	Land Transport	0SUST340	468281
Mongolia	USSR (Soviet Union)	23 Apr 56	Tech Assistance	16SUGG70	469914
Mongolia	USSR (Soviet Union)	23 Apr 56	Specific Property	16SUGG70	469913
Mongolia	USSR (Soviet Union)	24 Apr 56	Culture	259UNTS297	103693
Mongolia	USSR (Soviet Union)	19 Oct 56	Scientific Project	16SUGG74	469929
Mongolia	USSR (Soviet Union)	01 Dec 56	Air Transport	0SUST373	468282
Mongolia	USSR (Soviet Union)	16 Apr 57	Specific Property	0SUST381	468283
Mongolia	USSR (Soviet Union)	20 Apr 57	Air Transport	0SUST382	468285
Mongolia	USSR (Soviet Union)	22 Apr 57	Air Transport	0SUST381	468284
Mongolia	USSR (Soviet Union)	15 May 57	Specific Property	16SUGG120	469940
Mongolia	USSR (Soviet Union)	15 May 57	Direct Aid	16SUGG120	469941
Mongolia	USSR (Soviet Union)	16 Dec 57	Health/Educ/Welfare	0SUST393	468286
Mongolia	USSR (Soviet Union)	17 Dec 57	General Trade	0SUST394	468287
Mongolia	USSR (Soviet Union)	17 Dec 57	General Trade	0SUST394	468288
Mongolia	USSR (Soviet Union)	11 Apr 58	Education	16SUGG125	469958
Mongolia	USSR (Soviet Union)	11 Apr 58	Tech Assistance	16SUGG124	469957
Mongolia	USSR (Soviet Union)	25 Aug 58	Consul/Citizenship	322UNTS215	104659
Mongolia	USSR (Soviet Union)	25 Aug 58	Admin Cooperation	322UNTS105	104657
Mongolia	USSR (Soviet Union)	25 Aug 58	Consul/Citizenship	322UNTS201	104658
Mongolia	USSR (Soviet Union)	19 Nov 58	Loans and Credits	7SUGG126	469543
Mongolia	USSR (Soviet Union)	10 Feb 59	General Aid	8SUGG136	469559
Mongolia	USSR (Soviet Union)	28 Jul 59	Tech Assistance	16SUGG126	469965
Mongolia	USSR (Soviet Union)	09 Dec 59	General Aid	16SUGG126	469967
Mongolia	USSR (Soviet Union)	11 Feb 60	General Aid	9SUGG124	469629
Mongolia	USSR (Soviet Union)	11 Feb 60	General Aid	9SUGG124	469628
Mongolia	USSR (Soviet Union)	28 Mar 60	Direct Aid	9SUGG131	469646
Mongolia	USSR (Soviet Union)	09 Sep 60	General Aid	9SUGG147	469692
Mongolia	USSR (Soviet Union)	27 Sep 60	Tech Assistance	9SUGG148	469697
Mongolia	USSR (Soviet Union)	27 Sep 60	Tech Assistance	9SUGG148	469696
Mongolia	USSR (Soviet Union)	03 Oct 60	Education	16SUGG129	469983
Mongolia	USSR (Soviet Union)	08 Oct 60	Education	9SUGG149	469704
Mongolia	USSR (Soviet Union)	14 Nov 60	Tech Assistance	9SUGG151	469711
Mongolia	USSR (Soviet Union)	20 Dec 60	General Trade	9SUGG156	469725
Mongolia	USSR (Soviet Union)	25 Feb 61	Non-IBRD Project	10SUGG123	469746
Mongolia	USSR (Soviet Union)	13 Apr 61	Direct Aid	10SUGG128	469762
Mongolia	USSR (Soviet Union)	08 Jun 61	Tech Assistance	10SUGG134	469776
Mongolia	USSR (Soviet Union)	17 Jul 61	Tech Assistance	10SUGG138	469788
Mongolia	USSR (Soviet Union)	22 Jul 61	Tech Assistance	10SUGG139	469790
Mongolia	USSR (Soviet Union)	15 Jan 66	General Amity	562UNTS43	108194
Mongolia	USSR (Soviet Union)	17 Dec 67	General Trade	0UNTS0	109825

PARTY ONE	PARTY TWO	DATE	TOPIC	CITATION	NUMBER
Mongolia	WHO (World Health)	21 Jun 63	Tech Assistance	472UNTS373	106848
Montserrat	Multilateral	24 Dec 68	Commodity Trade	0UNTS0	109369
Montserrat	Multilateral	18 Oct 69	IGO Establishment	0UNTS0	110232
Morocco	Accept UN Charter	17 Jul 56	UN Charter	253UNTS77	103575
Morocco	Algeria	30 Apr 63	Air Transport	564UNTS3	108217
Morocco	Algeria	15 Jan 69	General Amity	0UNTS0	110095
Morocco	Argentina	10 Nov 64	Culture	0UNTS0	110179
Morocco	Bel-Lux Econ Union	28 Apr 65	General Economic	620UNTS171	108954
Morocco	Belgium	20 Jan 58	Air Transport	288UNTS3	104192
Morocco	Belgium	12 Apr 58	Visas	303UNTS141	104377
Morocco	Belgium	27 Feb 59	Extradition	390UNTS275	105611
Morocco	China People's Rep	27 Oct 61	Finance	61CCJC145	410844
Morocco	China People's Rep	30 Mar 63	General Trade	63CCJC39	410966
Morocco	Czechoslovakia	08 Jun 61	Air Transport	497UNTS275	107272
Morocco	Denmark	22 Apr 68	Tech Assistance	0UNTS0	109218
Morocco	Denmark	05 Nov 68	Loans and Credits	0UNTS0	109415
Morocco	France	06 Feb 57	Admin Cooperation	60FRRT11	415295
Morocco	France	06 Feb 57	Admin Cooperation	0UNTS0	109933
Morocco	France	05 Oct 57	Admin Cooperation	60FRRT4	415296
Morocco	France	05 Oct 57	Admin Cooperation	0UNTS0	110712
Morocco	France	05 Oct 57	Admin Cooperation	0UNTS0	110713
Morocco	France	25 Oct 57	Air Transport	559UNTS95	108156
Morocco	France	14 May 60	Non-IBRD Project	60FRRT40	415297
Morocco	France	20 Sep 60	Health/Educ/Welfare	60FRRT80	415298
Morocco	France	10 Mar 61	Air Transport	61FRRT52	415299
Morocco	France	21 Jun 61	Customs	61FRRT38	415300
Morocco	France	23 Jul 63	Non-ILO Labor	0UNTS0	109934
Morocco	France	17 Oct 64	Non-ILO Labor	0UNTS0	109935
Morocco	France	09 Jul 65	Non-ILO Labor	67FRJO605	416309
Morocco	France	09 Jul 65	Non-ILO Labor	0UNTS0	109936
Morocco	Germany, East	08 Aug 60	Finance	8EGDA401	419207
Morocco	Germany, East	31 Jul 64	Finance	12EGDA859	419209
Morocco	Germany, East	31 Jul 64	General Trade	12EGDA856	419208
Morocco	Germany, West	17 Jul 58	Admin Cooperation	59WGBB118	425463
Morocco	Germany, West	15 Apr 61	General Trade	61WBGA150	424464
Morocco	Germany, West	31 Aug 61	Claims and Debts	67WGBB1641	425465
Morocco	Germany, West	12 Oct 61	Air Transport	523UNTS289	107562
Morocco	Germany, West	21 May 63	Non-ILO Labor	71WGBB1365	425466
Morocco	Germany, West	13 Sep 66	Loans and Credits	66WBGA207	424467
Morocco	Germany, West	24 Nov 66	Water Transport	67WBGA49	424469
Morocco	Germany, West	24 Nov 66	General Economic	67WBGA49	424470
Morocco	Germany, West	24 Nov 66	Loans and Credits	67WBGA49	424468
Morocco	Germany, West	22 Jun 68	Loans and Credits	68WBGA154	424471
Morocco	Germany, West	19 Jun 69	Loans and Credits	69WBGA165	424472
Morocco	Germany, West	02 Jul 70	Loans and Credits	70WBGA165	424473
Morocco	Germany, West	10 Jun 71	Loans and Credits	71WBGA151	424474
Morocco	Greece	01 Nov 61	General Trade	483UNTS113	107009
Morocco	IAEA (Atom Energy)	24 Sep 65	Atomic Energy	556UNTS109	108122
Morocco	IBRD (World Bank)	21 Dec 62	IBRD Project	478UNTS205	106937
Morocco	IBRD (World Bank)	26 Aug 64	IBRD Project	537UNTS193	107802
Morocco	IBRD (World Bank)	08 Nov 65	Claims and Debts	566UNTS279	108247
Morocco	IBRD (World Bank)	13 Jun 66	IGO Operations	615UNTS205	108881
Morocco	IBRD (World Bank)	26 Jan 67	IBRD Project	642UNTS3	109160
Morocco	IBRD (World Bank)	13 Nov 67	IBRD Project	0UNTS0	110544
Morocco	IBRD (World Bank)	14 Nov 68	IBRD Project	0UNTS0	110597
Morocco	IBRD (World Bank)	13 Nov 69	IBRD Project	0UNTS0	110674
Morocco	IBRD (World Bank)	06 Mar 70	IBRD Project	0UNTS0	110679
Morocco	IDA (Devel Assoc)	11 Oct 65	Non-IBRD Project	562UNTS299	108200
Morocco	IDA (Devel Assoc)	13 Nov 69	Non-IBRD Project	0UNTS0	110545
Morocco	Italy	24 Jun 58	General Trade	363UNTS23	105197
Morocco	Italy	25 Nov 60	Visas	62ITDI356	436270
Morocco	Italy	28 Jan 61	General Trade	62ITDI511	436271
Morocco	Italy	10 Feb 61	Tech Assistance	62ITDI513	436272
Morocco	Japan	05 Aug 61	Milit Installation	61JGJI38	441301
Morocco	Japan	13 Feb 62	Tech Assistance	62JGJI18	441302

PARTY ONE	PARTY TWO	DATE	TOPIC	CITATION	NUMBER
Morocco	Japan	17 Feb 62	Non-IBRD Project	62JGJI19	441303
Morocco	Japan	30 Mar 62	Education	62JGJI20	441304
Morocco	Japan	10 May 63	Claims and Debts	63JGJI46	441305
Morocco	Japan	31 May 63	Mass Media	65JGJI49	441306
Morocco	Japan	01 Jun 63	Non-ILO Labor	63JGJI52	441307
Morocco	Japan	01 Jun 63	Non-ILO Labor	63JGJI52	441308
Morocco	Japan	11 Sep 67	Direct Aid	67JJS325	442203
Morocco	Multilateral	27 Mar 41	Military Mission	67UNTS231	200222
Morocco	Multilateral	07 Dec 44	IGO Establishment	15UNTS295	200102
Morocco	Multilateral	11 Dec 46	Sanitation	12UNTS179	100186
Morocco	Multilateral	08 Feb 47	Patents/Copyrights	14UNTS287	100222
Morocco	Multilateral	27 May 47	Air Transport	418UNTS161	106021
Morocco	Multilateral	06 Jun 47	Patents/Copyrights	46UNTS249	100714
Morocco	Multilateral	10 Jun 47	Water Transport	208UNTS3	102814
Morocco	Multilateral	02 Oct 47	Telecommunications	193UNTS188	102616
Morocco	Multilateral	06 Mar 48	Water Transport	289UNTS3	104214
Morocco	Multilateral	10 May 48	Culture	289UNTS111	104215
Morocco	Multilateral	26 Jun 48	Culture	331UNTS217	104757
Morocco	Multilateral	17 Sep 48	Telecommunications	97UNTS31	101345
Morocco	Multilateral	09 Dec 48	Humanitarian	78UNTS277	101021
Morocco	Multilateral	04 May 49	Admin Cooperation	92UNTS19	101257
Morocco	Multilateral	04 May 49	Admin Cooperation	98UNTS101	101358
Morocco	Multilateral	15 Jul 49	Health/Educ/Welfare	197UNTS3	102631
Morocco	Multilateral	24 Sep 49	IGO Establishment	126UNTS237	101691
Morocco	Multilateral	22 Nov 50	Culture	131UNTS25	101734
Morocco	Multilateral	07 Dec 50	Admin Cooperation	212UNTS17	102861
Morocco	Multilateral	02 Jul 51	Refugees	189UNTS137	102545
Morocco	Multilateral	11 Jul 52	Postal Service	170UNTS3	102221
Morocco	Multilateral	11 Jul 52	Postal Service	170UNTS269	102223
Morocco	Multilateral	11 Jul 52	Postal Service	171UNTS89	102225
Morocco	Multilateral	11 Jul 52	Postal Service	170UNTS63	102222
Morocco	Multilateral	11 Jul 52	Postal Service	171UNTS3	102224
Morocco	Multilateral	11 Jul 52	Postal Service	171UNTS143	102226
Morocco	Multilateral	11 Jul 52	IGO Establishment	169UNTS3	102220
Morocco	Multilateral	07 Oct 52	Admin Cooperation	310UNTS181	104493
Morocco	Multilateral	07 Dec 53	Admin Cooperation	182UNTS51	102422
Morocco	Multilateral	14 May 54	Culture	249UNTS215	103511
Morocco	Multilateral	04 Jun 54	Customs	282UNTS249	104101
Morocco	Multilateral	14 Jun 54	Air Transport	320UNTS209	104643
Morocco	Multilateral	14 Jun 54	Air Transport	320UNTS217	104644
Morocco	Multilateral	01 May 55	Admin Cooperation	0UNTS0	110416
Morocco	Multilateral	25 May 55	IGO Establishment	264UNTS117	103791
Morocco	Multilateral	28 Sep 55	Air Transport	478UNTS371	106943
Morocco	Multilateral	12 Oct 55	IGO Establishment	560UNTS3	108165
Morocco	Multilateral	20 Jun 56	Admin Cooperation	268UNTS3	103850
Morocco	Multilateral	26 Oct 56	IGO Establishment	276UNTS3	103988
Morocco	Multilateral	29 Oct 56	Territory Boundary	263UNTS165	103772
Morocco	Multilateral	14 Dec 56	Taxation	436UNTS115	106292
Morocco	Multilateral	28 Mar 57	Tech Assistance	271UNTS30	103908
Morocco	Multilateral	15 Jun 57	Patents/Copyrights	583UNTS3	108470
Morocco	Multilateral	15 Jun 57	General Trade	550UNTS45	108008
Morocco	Multilateral	03 Oct 57	Postal Service	364UNTS331	105212
Morocco	Multilateral	03 Oct 57	Postal Service	366UNTS87	105216
Morocco	Multilateral	03 Oct 57	Postal Service	366UNTS3	105215
Morocco	Multilateral	03 Oct 57	Postal Service	365UNTS3	105213
Morocco	Multilateral	03 Oct 57	Postal Service	366UNTS141	105217
Morocco	Multilateral	03 Oct 57	Postal Service	365UNTS207	105214
Morocco	Multilateral	03 Oct 57	Postal Service	366UNTS255	105219
Morocco	Multilateral	03 Oct 57	Postal Service	364UNTS3	105211
Morocco	Multilateral	23 Nov 57	Refugees	506UNTS125	107384
Morocco	Multilateral	31 Mar 58	Specific Property	320UNTS103	104639
Morocco	Multilateral	03 Apr 58	Commodity Trade	336UNTS177	104806
Morocco	Multilateral	10 Jun 58	Admin Cooperation	330UNTS3	104739
Morocco	Multilateral	01 Dec 58	Commodity Trade	385UNTS137	105534
Morocco	Multilateral	03 Dec 58	Admin Cooperation	398UNTS9	105715

PARTY ONE	PARTY TWO	DATE	TOPIC	CITATION	NUMBER
Morocco	Multilateral	03 Dec 58	Admin Cooperation	416UNTS51	105995
Morocco	Multilateral	19 Nov 59	IGO Operations	410UNTS156	105902
Morocco	Multilateral	26 Jan 60	IGO Establishment	439UNTS249	106333
Morocco	Multilateral	17 Jun 60	Humanitarian	536UNTS27	107794
Morocco	Multilateral	30 Mar 61	Sanitation	520UNTS151	107515
Morocco	Multilateral	18 Apr 61	Consul/Citizenship	500UNTS95	107310
Morocco	Multilateral	08 Jun 61	Customs	473UNTS187	106863
Morocco	Multilateral	20 Apr 63	IGO Establishment	495UNTS3	107239
Morocco	Multilateral	25 May 63	IGO Establishment	479UNTS39	106947
Morocco	Multilateral	04 Aug 63	IGO Establishment	510UNTS3	107408
Morocco	Multilateral	05 Aug 63	Sanitation	480UNTS43	106964
Morocco	Multilateral	10 Jul 64	Postal Service	613UNTS3	108851
Morocco	Multilateral	10 Jul 64	Postal Service	613UNTS193	108852
Morocco	Multilateral	10 Jul 64	Postal Service	612UNTS361	108849
Morocco	Multilateral	10 Jul 64	Postal Service	611UNTS105	108845
Morocco	Multilateral	10 Jul 64	Postal Service	612UNTS233	108848
Morocco	Multilateral	10 Jul 64	Postal Service	613UNTS3	108850
Morocco	Multilateral	10 Jul 64	Postal Service	611UNTS387	108846
Morocco	Multilateral	10 Jul 64	Postal Service	612UNTS3	108847
Morocco	Multilateral	10 Jul 64	Postal Service	611UNTS7	108844
Morocco	Multilateral	18 Mar 65	Dispute Settlement	575UNTS159	108359
Morocco	Multilateral	05 Apr 66	Water Transport	640UNTS133	109159
Morocco	Multilateral	27 Jan 67	Scientific Project	610UNTS205	108843
Morocco	Netherlands	14 May 69	Non-ILO Labor	0UNTS0	109781
Morocco	Norway	11 Feb 60	Visas	3NORT798	451115
Morocco	Poland	15 Oct 62	Tech Assistance	62PZUM100	458099
Morocco	Portugal	03 Apr 58	Air Transport	393UNTS203	105657
Morocco	Senegal	15 Sep 66	General Amity	634UNTS105	109055
Morocco	Spain	07 Apr 56	Recognition	57SPBO403	460188
Morocco	Spain	07 Apr 56	Recognition	57SPBO403	460187
Morocco	Spain	07 Apr 56	Recognition	57SPBO403	460189
Morocco	Spain	11 Feb 57	General Amity	57SPBO403	460190
Morocco	Spain	11 Feb 57	Admin Cooperation	57SPBO403	460191
Morocco	Spain	04 Jun 57	General Trade	57SPBO1706	460192
Morocco	Spain	07 Jul 57	Finance	57SPBO709	460194
Morocco	Spain	07 Jul 57	General Trade	57SPBO709	460195
Morocco	Spain	07 Jul 57	Finance	57SPBO709	460193
Morocco	Spain	07 Jul 57	Specific Resources	57SPBO709	460198
Morocco	Spain	07 Jul 57	Tech Assistance	58SPBO502	460200
Morocco	Spain	07 Jul 57	Commodity Trade	57SPBO709	460197
Morocco	Spain	07 Jul 57	Culture	58SPBO402	460199
Morocco	Spain	07 Jul 57	General Trade	57SPBO709	460196
Morocco	Sweden	30 Mar 61	Taxation	427UNTS185	106154
Morocco	Switzerland	29 Aug 57	Mostfavored Nation	58SWRO271	462146
Morocco	Switzerland	05 Jul 62	Air Transport	498UNTS171	107281
Morocco	Switzerland	05 Jul 62	Air Transport	498UNTS189	107282
Morocco	Taiwan	27 May 57	General Trade	0CTRC317	413016
Morocco	UK Great Britain	01 Mar 57	General Economic	310UNTS3	104480
Morocco	UK Great Britain	01 Oct 58	Visas	331UNTS119	104751
Morocco	UN Special Fund	04 Apr 59	Direct Aid	354UNTS347	105069
Morocco	UNESCO (Educ/Cult)	13 May 64	Tech Assistance	0UNTS0	109220
Morocco	UNESCO (Educ/Cult)	18 Dec 67	IGO Operations	0UNTS0	109221
Morocco	UNICEF (Children)	31 Jul 57	Direct Aid	282UNTS99	104095
Morocco	United Arab Rep	19 May 60	Air Transport	563UNTS121	108208
Morocco	United Nations	03 Mar 64	IGO Status/Immunit	490UNTS187	107154
Morocco	USA (United States)	02 Apr 57	General Aid	288UNTS157	104203
Morocco	USA (United States)	31 Mar 61	Admin Cooperation	406UNTS249	105854
Morocco	USA (United States)	30 Nov 61	Postal Service	451UNTS167	106492
Morocco	USA (United States)	09 Feb 62	Direct Aid	442UNTS135	106345
Morocco	USA (United States)	11 Sep 62	US Agri Commod Aid	462UNTS207	106680
Morocco	USA (United States)	29 Dec 64	Commodity Trade	593UNTS185	108584
Morocco	USA (United States)	23 Apr 65	US Agri Commod Aid	594UNTS3	108591
Morocco	USA (United States)	21 Apr 66	US Agri Commod Aid	0UNTS0	109679
Morocco	USA (United States)	12 Aug 66	US Agri Commod Aid	0UNTS0	109616
Morocco	USA (United States)	10 Feb 67	Culture	0UNTS0	109847

PARTY ONE	PARTY TWO	DATE	TOPIC	CITATION	NUMBER
Morocco	USA (United States)	20 Apr 67	US Agri Commod Aid	0UNTS0	109761
Morocco	USA (United States)	27 Oct 67	US Agri Commod Aid	0UNTS0	110053
Morocco	USA (United States)	02 May 68	US Agri Commod Aid	0UNTS0	110013
Morocco	USA (United States)	25 Feb 69	Commodity Trade	0UNTS0	110268
Morocco	USSR (Soviet Union)	18 Apr 57	General Trade	0SUST381	468289
Morocco	USSR (Soviet Union)	19 Apr 58	General Trade	7SUGG110	469505
Morocco	USSR (Soviet Union)	19 Apr 58	Finance	7SUGG110	469506
Morocco	USSR (Soviet Union)	04 Sep 58	Consul/Citizenship	7SUGG120	469525
Morocco	USSR (Soviet Union)	31 Jul 59	General Trade	8SUGG150	469595
Morocco	USSR (Soviet Union)	15 Nov 60	Milit Assistance	9SUGG151	469712
Morocco	USSR (Soviet Union)	28 Mar 62	Air Transport	11SUGG136	469831
Morocco	USSR (Soviet Union)	27 Oct 66	Scientific Project	608UNTS197	108816
Morocco	USSR (Soviet Union)	27 Oct 66	Mass Media	608UNTS207	108817
Morocco	WHO (World Health)	09 Aug 61	Tech Assistance	412UNTS192	105932
Muscat and Oman	India	15 Mar 53	General Amity	190UNTS69	102559
Muscat and Oman	Netherlands	25 Aug 68	Consul/Citizenship	0UNTS0	109835
Muscat and Oman	UK Great Britain	05 Apr 47	Air Transport	27UNTS287	100412
Muscat and Oman	UK Great Britain	20 Dec 51	General Amity	149UNTS247	101956
Muscat and Oman	UK Great Britain	25 Jul 58	General Military	312UNTS347	104524
Muscat and Oman	UK Great Britain	15 Nov 67	Territory Boundary	617UNTS319	108919
Muscat and Oman	USA (United States)	20 Dec 58	General Amity	380UNTS181	105457
NATO (North Atlan)	Germany, West	13 Mar 67	Military Mission	69WGBB1997	425744
NATO (North Atlan)	Multilateral	22 Jun 55	Atomic Energy	249UNTS3	103498
NATO (North Atlan)	Netherlands	25 May 64	Status of Forces	544UNTS237	107920
NATO (North Atlan)	USA (United States)	22 Oct 54	IGO Establishment	249UNTS175	103507
NE Atlantic Fish	Multilateral	05 Apr 46	Specific Resources	231UNTS199	103221
Nepal	Accept UN Charter	15 Dec 55	UN Charter	223UNTS65	103054
Nepal	China People's Rep	20 Sep 56	General Amity	56CCJC104	410365
Nepal	China People's Rep	20 Sep 56	Consul/Citizenship	56CCJC105	410366
Nepal	China People's Rep	20 Sep 56	Consul/Citizenship	56CCJC106	410367
Nepal	China People's Rep	07 Oct 56	Finance	56CCJC112	410369
Nepal	China People's Rep	07 Oct 56	Finance	56CCJC113	410370
Nepal	China People's Rep	07 Oct 56	Direct Aid	56CCJC111	410368
Nepal	China People's Rep	21 Mar 60	Direct Aid	60CCJC48	410691
Nepal	China People's Rep	21 Mar 60	Territory Boundary	60CCJC47	410690
Nepal	China People's Rep	28 Apr 60	General Amity	60CCJC58	410698
Nepal	China People's Rep	05 Oct 61	Territory Boundary	61CCJC128	410832
Nepal	China People's Rep	15 Oct 61	Non-IBRD Project	61CCJC138	410839
Nepal	China People's Rep	14 Aug 62	Consul/Citizenship	62CCJC79	410911
Nepal	China People's Rep	20 Jan 63	Territory Boundary	63CCJC10	410947
Nepal	China People's Rep	11 Oct 64	Culture	64CCJC147	411276
Nepal	China People's Rep	21 Jan 65	Postal Service	65CCJC8	411277
Nepal	China People's Rep	29 Aug 65	Non-IBRD Project	65CCJC109	411278
Nepal	China People's Rep	03 Sep 65	Culture	65CCJC111	411272
Nepal	China People's Rep	02 May 66	General Trade	66CCJC26	411273
Nepal	China People's Rep	18 Oct 66	Direct Aid	66CCJC85	411280
Nepal	China People's Rep	21 Dec 66	Direct Aid	66CCJC104	411281
Nepal	China People's Rep	14 Mar 67	Direct Aid	67CCJC10	411282
Nepal	China People's Rep	25 May 67	Non-IBRD Project	67CCJC20	411283
Nepal	China People's Rep	28 May 67	Non-IBRD Project	67CCJC21	411284
Nepal	Germany, West	06 Oct 67	Scientific Project	68WGBB81	425484
Nepal	IDA (Devel Assoc)	10 Nov 69	Non-IBRD Project	0UNTS0	110581
Nepal	India	31 Jul 50	General Economic	104UNTS3	101430
Nepal	India	31 Jul 50	General Amity	94UNTS3	101302
Nepal	Multilateral	07 Dec 44	IGO Establishment	15UNTS295	200102
Nepal	Multilateral	24 Jul 48	Sanitation	66UNTS25	100847
Nepal	Multilateral	07 Dec 50	Admin Cooperation	212UNTS17	102861
Nepal	Multilateral	06 Dec 51	Admin Cooperation	150UNTS67	101963
Nepal	Multilateral	31 Mar 53	Privil/Immunities	193UNTS136	102613
Nepal	Multilateral	25 May 55	IGO Establishment	264UNTS117	103791
Nepal	Multilateral	03 Oct 57	Postal Service	364UNTS3	105211
Nepal	Multilateral	06 Jan 58	General Transport	304UNTS227	104399
Nepal	Multilateral	29 Apr 58	Specific Resources	559UNTS285	108164
Nepal	Multilateral	29 Apr 58	Territory Boundary	516UNTS205	107477
Nepal	Multilateral	29 Apr 58	Water Transport	450UNTS11	106465

PARTY ONE	PARTY TWO	DATE	TOPIC	CITATION	NUMBER
Nepal	Multilateral	29 Apr 58	Territory Boundary	499UNTS311	107302
Nepal	Multilateral	29 Apr 58	Dispute Settlement	450UNTS169	106466
Nepal	Multilateral	26 Jan 60	IGO Establishment	439UNTS249	106333
Nepal	Multilateral	14 Apr 61	IGO Establishment	422UNTS101	106071
Nepal	Multilateral	18 Apr 61	Consul/Citizenship	500UNTS223	107311
Nepal	Multilateral	18 Apr 61	Consul/Citizenship	500UNTS95	107310
Nepal	Multilateral	18 Apr 61	Dispute Settlement	500UNTS243	107312
Nepal	Multilateral	14 Feb 63	Tech Assistance	453UNTS168	106524
Nepal	Multilateral	24 Apr 63	Consul/Citizenship	596UNTS261	108638
Nepal	Multilateral	24 Apr 63	Consul/Citizenship	596UNTS487	108640
Nepal	Multilateral	05 Aug 63	Sanitation	480UNTS43	106964
Nepal	Multilateral	10 Jul 64	Postal Service	611UNTS7	108844
Nepal	Multilateral	10 Jul 64	Postal Service	611UNTS105	108845
Nepal	Multilateral	18 Mar 65	Dispute Settlement	575UNTS159	108359
Nepal	Multilateral	25 May 65	IGO Operations	535UNTS374	107791
Nepal	Multilateral	08 Jul 65	General Trade	597UNTS3	108641
Nepal	Multilateral	04 Dec 65	IGO Establishment	571UNTS123	108303
Nepal	Multilateral	22 Apr 68	Scientific Project	0UNTS0	109574
Nepal	Multilateral	01 Jul 68	Peace/Disarmament	0UNTS0	110485
Nepal	UK Great Britain	30 Oct 50	General Amity	97UNTS121	101346
Nepal	UK Great Britain	31 Mar 69	Loans and Credits	0UNTS0	109881
Nepal	UK Great Britain	08 Aug 69	Direct Aid	0UNTS0	110237
Nepal	UN Special Fund	17 Nov 60	Direct Aid	380UNTS289	105461
Nepal	UNICEF (Children)	12 Dec 60	Direct Aid	382UNTS273	105488
Nepal	United Nations	02 Mar 53	Tech Assistance	161UNTS347	200493
Nepal	United Nations	18 Aug 58	Admin Cooperation	508UNTS3	107403
Nepal	USA (United States)	25 Apr 47	Consul/Citizenship	16UNTS97	100251
Nepal	USA (United States)	23 Jan 51	Tech Assistance	184UNTS65	102439
Nepal	USA (United States)	17 May 60	Claims and Debts	372UNTS313	105307
Nepal	USA (United States)	09 Jun 61	Education	421UNTS223	106061
Nepal	USA (United States)	24 Aug 62	General Aid	460UNTS143	106637
Nepal	USSR (Soviet Union)	09 Jul 56	Consul/Citizenship	16SUGG72	469921
Nepal	USSR (Soviet Union)	24 Apr 59	General Aid	8SUGG143	469573
Nepal	USSR (Soviet Union)	24 Apr 59	Non-IBRD Project	8SUGG143	469574
Nepal	USSR (Soviet Union)	12 Aug 60	Tech Assistance	9SUGG144	469683
Nepal	USSR (Soviet Union)	06 Feb 62	Direct Aid	11SUGG131	469819
Nepal	WHO (World Health)	13 May 54	Tech Assistance	204UNTS311	200522
Netherlands	Afghanistan	26 Jul 39	General Amity	32UNTS381	200177
Netherlands	Argentina	29 Oct 48	Air Transport	95UNTS21	101316
Netherlands	Argentina	15 Jan 49	Taxation	46UNTS241	100713
Netherlands	Argentina	06 May 54	General Economic	54NET175	447046
Netherlands	Australia	24 Jan 47	Finance	10UNTS77	100144
Netherlands	Australia	12 Aug 49	Reparations	34UNTS213	100539
Netherlands	Australia	26 Apr 50	Claims and Debts	54UNTS83	100796
Netherlands	Australia	20 Feb 51	Visas	97UNTS283	101354
Netherlands	Australia	22 Feb 51	Non-ILO Labor	128UNTS115	101717
Netherlands	Australia	25 Sep 51	Air Transport	128UNTS63	101713
Netherlands	Australia	22 Oct 53	Postal Service	184UNTS193	102448
Netherlands	Australia	01 Aug 56	Non-ILO Labor	280UNTS3	104047
Netherlands	Australia	29 Nov 56	Air Transport	302UNTS141	104356
Netherlands	Australia	09 Oct 57	Dispute Settlement	312UNTS225	104520
Netherlands	Australia	23 Jul 58	Postal Service	328UNTS227	104736
Netherlands	Australia	01 Jun 65	Consul/Citizenship	560UNTS85	108170
Netherlands	Austria	22 Jan 48	Air Transport	17UNTS99	100270
Netherlands	Austria	22 Mar 51	General Transport	51NET59	447018
Netherlands	Austria	22 Mar 51	Finance	51NET60	447019
Netherlands	Austria	24 May 51	Visas	51NET88	447024
Netherlands	Austria	24 May 51	Visas	52ABGB26	403142
Netherlands	Austria	17 Nov 54	Non-ILO Labor	292UNTS45	104266
Netherlands	Austria	18 Feb 55	Finance	55NET95	447053
Netherlands	Austria	03 May 58	Admin Cooperation	342UNTS3	104895
Netherlands	Austria	30 May 58	Visas	458UNTS147	106598
Netherlands	Austria	19 Mar 59	Admin Cooperation	485UNTS117	107048
Netherlands	Austria	29 Apr 59	Finance	486UNTS373	107087
Netherlands	Austria	06 May 59	Land Transport	485UNTS175	107055

PARTY ONE	PARTY TWO	DATE	TOPIC	CITATION	NUMBER
Netherlands	Austria	06 May 59	Land Transport	485UNTS153	107054
Netherlands	Austria	30 Sep 59	Specific Property	507UNTS111	107397
Netherlands	Austria	16 Oct 59	Admin Cooperation	458UNTS173	106600
Netherlands	Austria	06 Feb 63	Admin Cooperation	570UNTS101	108290
Netherlands	Austria	23 Jul 64	Admin Cooperation	544UNTS265	107921
Netherlands	Austria	02 Feb 70	Land Transport	70ABGB86	403143
Netherlands	Austria	01 Sep 70	Taxation	71ABGB191	403144
Netherlands	Belgium	02 Jan 45	Refugees	19UNTS259	200120
Netherlands	Belgium	16 May 46	Culture	17UNTS13	100266
Netherlands	Belgium	24 May 46	Finance	31UNTS169	100477
Netherlands	Belgium	12 Oct 46	Claims and Debts	23UNTS179	100347
Netherlands	Belgium	25 Mar 47	Postal Service	18UNTS309	100299
Netherlands	Belgium	28 Apr 47	Visas	37UNTS199	100577
Netherlands	Belgium	29 Aug 47	Non-ILO Labor	36UNTS349	100573
Netherlands	Belgium	13 Apr 48	Customs	32UNTS153	100497
Netherlands	Belgium	25 Sep 48	Taxation	123UNTS81	101655
Netherlands	Belgium	11 Oct 48	Finance	26UNTS95	100379
Netherlands	Belgium	13 May 49	Customs	65UNTS133	100841
Netherlands	Belgium	20 Aug 49	Visas	46UNTS133	100706
Netherlands	Belgium	07 Sep 49	Loans and Credits	117UNTS3	101581
Netherlands	Belgium	17 Feb 50	Water Transport	51UNTS101	100756
Netherlands	Belgium	29 Mar 50	Visas	68UNTS45	100883
Netherlands	Belgium	23 Oct 50	Territory Boundary	136UNTS31	101831
Netherlands	Belgium	25 Nov 50	Non-ILO Labor	51NET15	447016
Netherlands	Belgium	15 Mar 51	Reparations	93UNTS97	101294
Netherlands	Belgium	21 Apr 51	Non-ILO Labor	51NET64	447022
Netherlands	Belgium	14 Jun 51	Reparations	101UNTS3	101397
Netherlands	Belgium	15 Jun 51	Claims and Debts	51NET106	447026
Netherlands	Belgium	14 Nov 51	Admin Cooperation	123UNTS91	101656
Netherlands	Belgium	26 Mar 53	Visas	165UNTS297	102180
Netherlands	Belgium	29 Apr 53	Admin Cooperation	173UNTS61	102261
Netherlands	Belgium	27 Jan 54	Non-ILO Labor	54NET46	447045
Netherlands	Belgium	09 Jun 54	Milit Servic/Citiz	216UNTS121	102936
Netherlands	Belgium	28 Jun 54	Territory Boundary	272UNTS235	103942
Netherlands	Belgium	10 Sep 54	Customs	54NET153	447050
Netherlands	Belgium	13 Jan 55	Visas	210UNTS63	102834
Netherlands	Belgium	16 Feb 55	Refugees	211UNTS49	102846
Netherlands	Belgium	07 Mar 57	Dispute Settlement	282UNTS241	104100
Netherlands	Belgium	23 Oct 57	Water Transport	0UNTS0	109725
Netherlands	Belgium	24 Oct 57	Water Transport	292UNTS199	104274
Netherlands	Belgium	24 Oct 57	Water Transport	489UNTS11	107132
Netherlands	Belgium	24 Oct 57	Water Transport	489UNTS3	107131
Netherlands	Belgium	03 Feb 58	Territory Boundary	381UNTS305	105472
Netherlands	Belgium	04 Feb 58	Extradition	330UNTS83	104740
Netherlands	Belgium	28 Apr 59	Finance	485UNTS123	107049
Netherlands	Belgium	20 Jan 60	Admin Cooperation	373UNTS3	105310
Netherlands	Belgium	20 Jun 60	Specific Property	423UNTS19	106084
Netherlands	Belgium	24 Feb 61	Water Transport	474UNTS167	106881
Netherlands	Belgium	24 Feb 61	Admin Cooperation	474UNTS161	106880
Netherlands	Belgium	13 May 63	Territory Boundary	540UNTS3	107843
Netherlands	Belgium	06 Jan 64	Reparations	531UNTS119	107698
Netherlands	Belgium	27 Apr 65	Specific Resources	596UNTS235	108636
Netherlands	Belgium	21 Mar 68	Non-ILO Labor	0UNTS0	109363
Netherlands	Belgium	12 Dec 68	Water Transport	0UNTS0	109793
Netherlands	Belgium	04 Feb 69	Non-ILO Labor	0UNTS0	109714
Netherlands	Bolivia	30 Sep 61	Visas	487UNTS105	107097
Netherlands	Bolivia	31 Mar 69	Non-ILO Labor	0UNTS0	110749
Netherlands	Brazil	06 Nov 47	Air Transport	53UNTS59	100773
Netherlands	Brazil	15 Dec 50	Non-ILO Labor	123UNTS101	101657
Netherlands	Brazil	29 Nov 55	General Economic	56NET96	447059
Netherlands	Brazil	16 Mar 59	Admin Cooperation	499UNTS219	107300
Netherlands	Brazil	12 Oct 66	Culture	643UNTS271	109197
Netherlands	Bulgaria	07 Feb 58	Air Transport	335UNTS45	104777
Netherlands	Bulgaria	07 Jul 61	Finance	489UNTS21	107133
Netherlands	Burma	06 Sep 51	Air Transport	108UNTS187	101473

PARTY ONE	PARTY TWO	DATE	TOPIC	CITATION	NUMBER
Netherlands	Cambodia	04 Jul 69	Non-IBRD Project	0UNTS0	110391
Netherlands	Cameroon	18 Dec 63	General Aid	521UNTS303	107527
Netherlands	Cameroon	06 Jul 65	Tech Assistance	571UNTS75	108300
Netherlands	Cameroon	06 Jul 65	Tech Assistance	571UNTS63	108299
Netherlands	Canada	05 Feb 46	General Trade	230UNTS199	103184
Netherlands	Canada	05 Feb 46	Finance	43UNTS3	100658
Netherlands	Canada	30 Dec 46	Reparations	230UNTS205	103185
Netherlands	Canada	02 Jun 48	Air Transport	32UNTS215	100499
Netherlands	Canada	28 Oct 48	Reparations	231UNTS95	103210
Netherlands	Canada	09 May 49	Reparations	46UNTS263	100715
Netherlands	Canada	14 Dec 49	Visas	230UNTS337	103192
Netherlands	Canada	10 Apr 52	Reparations	233UNTS129	103257
Netherlands	Canada	02 Apr 57	Taxation	285UNTS193	104153
Netherlands	Canada	13 Apr 57	Milit Assistance	316UNTS223	104588
Netherlands	Ceylon (Sri Lanka)	14 Sep 53	Air Transport	193UNTS21	102608
Netherlands	Chile	18 Jun 54	Visas	292UNTS37	104265
Netherlands	Chile	07 Apr 61	Visas	453UNTS239	106527
Netherlands	Chile	28 May 62	Admin Cooperation	0UNTS0	110029
Netherlands	Chile	13 Jul 62	Air Transport	466UNTS109	106740
Netherlands	Colombia	03 Aug 62	Visas	485UNTS225	107058
Netherlands	Colombia	06 Jul 64	General Aid	543UNTS289	107906
Netherlands	Colombia	19 Jul 66	Tech Assistance	591UNTS201	108558
Netherlands	Congo (Zaire)	03 Feb 69	Air Transport	0UNTS0	110469
Netherlands	Cyprus	18 Apr 69	Air Transport	0UNTS0	110472
Netherlands	Czechoslovakia	15 Nov 46	Finance	51NET162	447003
Netherlands	Czechoslovakia	01 Sep 47	Air Transport	32UNTS129	100495
Netherlands	Czechoslovakia	24 Jun 48	General Trade	51NET49	447008
Netherlands	Czechoslovakia	07 Jul 49	General Trade	51NET163	447011
Netherlands	Czechoslovakia	11 Jun 64	Claims and Debts	556UNTS89	108120
Netherlands	Czechoslovakia	15 Nov 67	Land Transport	0UNTS0	109223
Netherlands	Denmark	31 Jan 46	Finance	3UNTS3	100021
Netherlands	Denmark	03 May 46	General Trade	52NET139	447001
Netherlands	Denmark	08 May 52	Reparations	131UNTS91	101737
Netherlands	Denmark	31 Jan 56	Finance	286UNTS255	104172
Netherlands	Denmark	20 Feb 57	Taxation	287UNTS41	104179
Netherlands	Denmark	13 Nov 57	Land Transport	306UNTS67	104432
Netherlands	Denmark	30 Apr 59	Finance	487UNTS23	107092
Netherlands	Denmark	06 Jun 63	Patents/Copyrights	484UNTS137	107021
Netherlands	Denmark	31 Mar 66	Territory Boundary	604UNTS209	108751
Netherlands	Denmark	20 Jun 67	Non-ILO Labor	619UNTS67	108939
Netherlands	Denmark	30 May 68	Specific Resources	0UNTS0	109233
Netherlands	Ecuador	14 Dec 54	Air Transport	232UNTS115	103233
Netherlands	Ecuador	21 Jan 63	Visas	514UNTS87	107443
Netherlands	Ecuador	14 Jan 65	Health/Educ/Welfare	551UNTS129	108038
Netherlands	Ethiopia	28 Oct 64	Tech Assistance	541UNTS235	107872
Netherlands	Euratom	25 Jul 61	Scientific Project	462UNTS263	106686
Netherlands	Euratom	25 Jul 61	IGO Status/Immunit	462UNTS313	106687
Netherlands	Fed Rhod/Nyasaland	02 Nov 55	Non-ILO Labor	263UNTS381	103784
Netherlands	Finland	25 Feb 49	Air Transport	53UNTS123	100777
Netherlands	Finland	30 May 51	General Trade	51NET83	447025
Netherlands	Finland	11 Jul 51	Non-ILO Labor	51NET113	447029
Netherlands	Finland	24 Jul 52	Visas	52NET106	447035
Netherlands	Finland	29 Mar 54	Taxation	252UNTS185	103567
Netherlands	Finland	29 Mar 54	Taxation	252UNTS239	103568
Netherlands	Finland	29 Jun 55	Finance	55NET91	447055
Netherlands	France	14 Jun 40	Finance	2UNTS263	200019
Netherlands	France	27 Mar 46	Visas	247UNTS3	103456
Netherlands	France	09 Apr 46	Finance	3UNTS57	100024
Netherlands	France	19 Nov 46	Culture	32UNTS101	100493
Netherlands	France	02 Dec 47	Finance	63FRRT76	415356
Netherlands	France	02 Jan 48	Visas	70UNTS105	100899
Netherlands	France	02 Jun 48	Education	50FRJO1002	416357
Netherlands	France	02 Jun 48	Non-ILO Labor	204UNTS275	102762
Netherlands	France	20 Jul 49	Mostfavored Nation	204UNTS287	102763
Netherlands	France	03 Aug 49	General Trade	51NET40	447012
Netherlands	France	30 Dec 49	Taxation	203UNTS133	102743
Netherlands	France	30 Dec 49	Taxation	203UNTS85	102742
Netherlands	France	07 Jan 50	Non-ILO Labor	120UNTS25	101614
Netherlands	France	03 Jul 51	Finance	63FRRT76	415358
Netherlands	France	07 Feb 52	General Trade	54NET90	447032
Netherlands	France	20 Jun 53	Land Transport	187UNTS97	102503
Netherlands	France	27 Nov 53	Reparations	302UNTS245	104363
Netherlands	France	30 Apr 54	Reparations	202UNTS115	102727
Netherlands	France	09 Jul 54	Finance	287UNTS169	104183
Netherlands	France	15 Dec 54	Reparations	288UNTS37	104195
Netherlands	France	15 Feb 57	Refugees	286UNTS243	104170
Netherlands	France	21 May 57	Visas	299UNTS43	104305
Netherlands	France	29 Apr 59	Finance	486UNTS379	107088
Netherlands	Germany, West	14 Dec 50	Water Transport	87UNTS257	101177
Netherlands	Germany, West	29 Mar 51	Non-ILO Labor	149UNTS71	101952
Netherlands	Germany, West	29 Jun 51	General Trade	51NET119	447028
Netherlands	Germany, West	18 Jan 52	Specific Property	179UNTS147	102364
Netherlands	Germany, West	31 Jan 52	Admin Cooperation	492UNTS295	107199
Netherlands	Germany, West	19 May 52	Reparations	134UNTS3	101794
Netherlands	Germany, West	20 Jun 52	Reparations	136UNTS221	101836
Netherlands	Germany, West	13 Mar 53	Visas	293UNTS123	104289
Netherlands	Germany, West	17 Mar 53	Visas	293UNTS129	104290
Netherlands	Germany, West	10 Oct 53	Visas	293UNTS115	104288
Netherlands	Germany, West	13 Aug 54	Admin Cooperation	492UNTS305	107200
Netherlands	Germany, West	11 Oct 54	Other Military	291UNTS9	104241
Netherlands	Germany, West	29 Oct 54	Non-ILO Labor	237UNTS3	103335
Netherlands	Germany, West	20 Sep 56	Specific Property	509UNTS269	107405
Netherlands	Germany, West	28 Sep 56	Air Transport	327UNTS185	104722
Netherlands	Germany, West	31 Oct 56	Admin Cooperation	287UNTS21	104177
Netherlands	Germany, West	01 Dec 56	Extradition	276UNTS127	103989
Netherlands	Germany, West	29 Jan 57	Status of Forces	314UNTS173	104548
Netherlands	Germany, West	10 Jul 57	Status of Forces	339UNTS97	104848
Netherlands	Germany, West	28 Jan 58	Specif Goods/Equip	453UNTS183	106525
Netherlands	Germany, West	30 Jan 58	Humanitarian	315UNTS117	104563
Netherlands	Germany, West	09 Apr 58	Visas	335UNTS237	104791
Netherlands	Germany, West	16 Apr 58	Sanitation	486UNTS331	107084
Netherlands	Germany, West	30 May 58	Visas	570UNTS127	108291
Netherlands	Germany, West	30 Jun 58	Non-ILO Labor	315UNTS179	104568
Netherlands	Germany, West	10 Oct 58	Visas	486UNTS345	107085
Netherlands	Germany, West	30 Apr 59	Finance	485UNTS141	107052
Netherlands	Germany, West	16 Jun 59	Taxation	593UNTS3	108576
Netherlands	Germany, West	08 Apr 60	Territory Boundary	508UNTS14	107404
Netherlands	Germany, West	03 Jun 60	Visas	487UNTS37	107094
Netherlands	Germany, West	09 Mar 61	Admin Cooperation	485UNTS185	107056
Netherlands	Germany, West	27 Apr 61	Culture	487UNTS77	107095
Netherlands	Germany, West	16 May 61	General Military	64WBGA168	424487
Netherlands	Germany, West	18 Jul 61	Sanitation	487UNTS95	107096
Netherlands	Germany, West	03 Aug 61	Admin Cooperation	492UNTS321	107201
Netherlands	Germany, West	12 Jul 62	Non-ILO Labor	63WBGA75	424488
Netherlands	Germany, West	30 Aug 62	Admin Cooperation	547UNTS173	107957
Netherlands	Germany, West	30 Aug 62	Admin Cooperation	500UNTS3	107303
Netherlands	Germany, West	27 Jun 63	Non-ILO Labor	63WBGA231	424489
Netherlands	Germany, West	27 May 64	Non-ILO Labor	64WBGA237	424490
Netherlands	Germany, West	06 Oct 64	Non-ILO Labor	65WBGA157	424491
Netherlands	Germany, West	01 Dec 64	Territory Boundary	550UNTS123	108011
Netherlands	Germany, West	14 Sep 65	Status of Forces	65WBGA203	424492
Netherlands	Germany, West	22 Sep 66	Land Transport	0UNTS0	109226
Netherlands	Germany, West	02 Feb 67	Dispute Settlement	606UNTS105	108779
Netherlands	Germany, West	14 Mar 68	Status of Forces	68WBGA81	424493
Netherlands	Germany, West	15 Mar 68	Admin Cooperation	68WBGA106	424494
Netherlands	Germany, West	28 Oct 68	Specific Property	69WGBB1121	425495
Netherlands	Germany, West	20 Dec 68	Admin Cooperation	69WGBB609	425496
Netherlands	Germany, West	21 Jan 69	Non-ILO Labor	0UNTS0	110751
Netherlands	Germany, West	21 Jan 69	Non-ILO Labor	70WGBB277	425497
Netherlands	Germany, West	03 Sep 69	Non-ILO Labor	71WGBB37	425498

PARTY ONE	PARTY TWO	DATE	TOPIC	CITATION	NUMBER
Netherlands	Germany, West	22 Sep 70	Land Transport	70WGBB1056	425499
Netherlands	Germany, West	22 Sep 70	Land Transport	70WGBB1056	425500
Netherlands	Germany, West	18 Dec 70	Specific Property	71WGBB122	425501
Netherlands	Ghana	30 Jul 60	Air Transport	412UNTS51	105925
Netherlands	Ghana	28 Dec 67	Education	0UNTS0	110747
Netherlands	Greece	17 Apr 47	Air Transport	32UNTS115	100494
Netherlands	Greece	26 Jul 51	Taxation	109UNTS103	101495
Netherlands	Greece	14 Aug 51	Finance	51NET104	447030
Netherlands	Greece	05 Feb 53	General Trade	263UNTS361	103783
Netherlands	Greece	29 Apr 53	Culture	191UNTS235	102583
Netherlands	Greece	26 Sep 53	Visas	292UNTS23	104263
Netherlands	Greece	01 Nov 54	General Trade	223UNTS79	103057
Netherlands	Greece	14 Jul 55	General Trade	227UNTS27	103129
Netherlands	Greece	22 Nov 55	Visas	292UNTS31	104264
Netherlands	Greece	30 Apr 59	Finance	485UNTS135	107051
Netherlands	Greece	13 Sep 66	Non-ILO Labor	596UNTS245	108637
Netherlands	Greece	13 Sep 66	Non-ILO Labor	0UNTS0	109833
Netherlands	Greece	13 Sep 66	Non-ILO Labor	0UNTS0	110746
Netherlands	Guinea	09 Mar 60	Air Transport	392UNTS243	105646
Netherlands	Hague Private IL	01 Dec 59	IGO Status/Immunit	510UNTS191	107414
Netherlands	Hungary	20 Dec 47	Finance	51NET95	447006
Netherlands	Hungary	01 Apr 55	General Trade	55NET62	447054
Netherlands	Hungary	28 May 57	Air Transport	334UNTS291	104773
Netherlands	Hungary	11 Jan 64	Taxation	522UNTS243	107550
Netherlands	Hungary	02 Jul 65	Finance	564UNTS49	108220
Netherlands	Hungary	14 Feb 68	Culture	0UNTS0	110419
Netherlands	IBRD (World Bank)	07 Aug 47	IBRD Project	152UNTS165	102015
Netherlands	IBRD (World Bank)	15 Jul 48	IBRD Project	153UNTS211	102020
Netherlands	IBRD (World Bank)	15 Jul 48	IBRD Project	153UNTS259	102024
Netherlands	IBRD (World Bank)	15 Jul 48	IBRD Project	153UNTS259	102022
Netherlands	IBRD (World Bank)	15 Jul 48	IBRD Project	153UNTS259	102021
Netherlands	IBRD (World Bank)	15 Jul 48	IBRD Project	153UNTS259	102023
Netherlands	IBRD (World Bank)	15 Jul 48	IBRD Project	153UNTS259	102025
Netherlands	IBRD (World Bank)	26 Jul 49	IBRD Project	154UNTS178	102030
Netherlands	IBRD (World Bank)	20 Mar 52	IBRD Project	159UNTS207	102089
Netherlands	IBRD (World Bank)	15 May 57	IBRD Project	274UNTS211	103967
Netherlands	Iceland	22 Mar 50	Air Transport	95UNTS237	101323
Netherlands	Iceland	28 Dec 54	Finance	287UNTS159	104182
Netherlands	Iceland	30 Apr 59	Finance	487UNTS13	107091
Netherlands	ICJ (Int Court)	26 Jun 46	IGO Status/Immunit	8UNTS61	100114
Netherlands	ICJ Option Clause	05 Aug 46	ICJ Option Clause	1UNTS7	100002
Netherlands	ICJ Option Clause	01 Aug 56	ICJ Option Clause	248UNTS33	103483
Netherlands	India	31 May 47	Air Transport	17UNTS65	100268
Netherlands	India	24·May 51	Air Transport	108UNTS151	101471
Netherlands	India	04 Dec 54	Reparations	289UNTS221	104219
Netherlands	India	16 Jan 59	Tech Assistance	506UNTS153	107386
Netherlands	India	27 Apr 59	Tech Assistance	506UNTS141	107385
Netherlands	India	11 Dec 64	Scientific Project	570UNTS165	108292
Netherlands	India	27 Jul 65	Direct Aid	0UNTS0	110196
Netherlands	India	17 Feb 67	Direct Aid	0UNTS0	109389
Netherlands	India	21 Dec 67	Direct Aid	0UNTS0	109390
Netherlands	India	06 Feb 68	Scientific Project	0UNTS0	110754
Netherlands	India	30 Aug 68	Non-IBRD Project	0UNTS0	109475
Netherlands	Indonesia	02 Nov 49	Recognition	69UNTS3	100894
Netherlands	Indonesia	14 Jul 50	Status of Forces	51NET4	447014
Netherlands	Indonesia	08 Jun 54	Taxation	54NET92	447047
Netherlands	Indonesia	10 Aug 54	General Amity	54NET113	447049
Netherlands	Indonesia	11 Aug 54	Claims and Debts	241UNTS129	103429
Netherlands	Indonesia	15 Aug 62	Territory Boundary	437UNTS273	106311
Netherlands	Indonesia	03 Apr 64	Tech Assistance	566UNTS45	108239
Netherlands	Indonesia	12 Jul 66	Air Transport	0UNTS0	110164
Netherlands	Indonesia	07 Sep 66	Finance	0UNTS0	109779
Netherlands	Indonesia	07 Jul 68	Culture	0UNTS0	110604
Netherlands	Iran	31 Oct 49	Air Transport	254UNTS257	103596
Netherlands	Iran	31 Oct 49	Air Transport	0IRTB35	433046

PARTY ONE	PARTY TWO	DATE	TOPIC	CITATION	NUMBER
Netherlands	Iran	27 Jul 56	Taxation	0IRTB35	433047
Netherlands	Iran	06 Feb 58	Consul/Citizenship	0IRTB36	433050
Netherlands	Iran	22 May 59	Culture	474UNTS195	106882
Netherlands	Iran	22 May 59	Culture	0IRTB35	433045
Netherlands	Iran	19 Nov 64	Visas	0IRTB36	433049
Netherlands	Iran	13 Jul 68	Taxation	0IRTB36	433048
Netherlands	Iraq	16 Oct 54	Air Transport	55NET23	447051
Netherlands	Ireland	01 May 47	Visas	247UNTS193	103468
Netherlands	Ireland	10 May 48	Air Transport	28UNTS121	100422
Netherlands	Ireland	02 Sep 48	General Trade	558UNTS249	108145
Netherlands	Ireland	25 Nov 49	General Trade	558UNTS256	108146
Netherlands	Ireland	22 Dec 50	General Trade	51NET11	447017
Netherlands	Ireland	29 Oct 51	General Trade	52NET27	447031
Netherlands	Ireland	28 May 59	Non-ILO Labor	344UNTS95	104944
Netherlands	Ireland	11 Feb 69	Taxation	0UNTS0	110605
Netherlands	IRO (Refugee Org)	20 Jun 50	Refugees	76UNTS55	100979
Netherlands	IRO (Refugee Org)	13 Feb 51	IGO Operations	87UNTS239	101175
Netherlands	Israel	23 Oct 50	Air Transport	189UNTS89	102543
Netherlands	Israel	16 Jun 53	Visas	220UNTS93	102993
Netherlands	Israel	18 Jun 53	Visas	220UNTS99	102994
Netherlands	Israel	21 Aug 55	Visas	299UNTS51	104306
Netherlands	Israel	18 Dec 56	Extradition	276UNTS153	103991
Netherlands	Israel	28 May 62	Postal Service	448UNTS219	106434
Netherlands	Israel	25 Apr 63	Admin Cooperation	484UNTS231	107034
Netherlands	Italy	04 Dec 48	Non-ILO Labor	46UNTS271	100716
Netherlands	Italy	16 Aug 49	Admin Cooperation	98UNTS21	101357
Netherlands	Italy	04 Mar 50	Air Transport	254UNTS305	103598
Netherlands	Italy	19 May 51	Finance	51NET97	447023
Netherlands	Italy	15 Jun 51	Reparations	150UNTS103	101964
Netherlands	Italy	05 Dec 51	Culture	0UNTS0	109323
Netherlands	Italy	05 Dec 51	Culture	52ITGU207	435286
Netherlands	Italy	22 Sep 52	Reparations	150UNTS113	101965
Netherlands	Italy	28 Oct 52	Non-ILO Labor	289UNTS144	104218
Netherlands	Italy	07 Aug 53	General Trade	53NET95	447041
Netherlands	Italy	21 Dec 53	Visas	189UNTS25	102540
Netherlands	Italy	04 Jun 54	Non-ILO Labor	289UNTS261	104222
Netherlands	Italy	24 Dec 54	Non-ILO Labor	55NET26	447052
Netherlands	Italy	29 Jun 56	Finance	287UNTS193	104185
Netherlands	Italy	24 Jan 57	Taxation	485UNTS67	107047
Netherlands	Italy	17 Apr 59	Admin Cooperation	474UNTS207	106883
Netherlands	Italy	29 Apr 59	Finance	486UNTS387	107089
Netherlands	Italy	22 Oct 59	Visas	61ITDI288	436288
Netherlands	Italy	01 Dec 59	Sanitation	455UNTS241	106545
Netherlands	Italy	08 Dec 59	Land Transport	484UNTS309	107039
Netherlands	Italy	06 Aug 60	Non-ILO Labor	455UNTS259	106546
Netherlands	Italy	24 Jan 61	Milit Servic/Citiz	450UNTS207	106468
Netherlands	Italy	29 May 64	Other Military	541UNTS147	107867
Netherlands	Ivory Coast	12 Feb 62	Visas	485UNTS219	107057
Netherlands	Ivory Coast	09 Oct 63	Air Transport	499UNTS141	107296
Netherlands	Ivory Coast	26 Apr 65	General Economic	634UNTS81	109053
Netherlands	Ivory Coast	03 Jun 65	Non-ILO Labor	634UNTS95	109054
Netherlands	Ivory Coast	01 Aug 66	Education	591UNTS245	108561
Netherlands	Japan	13 Apr 51	General Trade	51NET50	447020
Netherlands	Japan	13 Apr 51	Finance	51NET51	447021
Netherlands	Japan	17 Feb 53	Air Transport	192UNTS215	102602
Netherlands	Japan	13 Mar 56	Claims and Debts	252UNTS3	103554
Netherlands	Japan	16 May 56	Visas	305UNTS97	104417
Netherlands	Japan	20 Sep 57	Visas	305UNTS105	104418
Netherlands	Japan	03 Mar 70	Taxation	70JHZ10	439037
Netherlands	Jordan	24 Aug 61	Air Transport	466UNTS3	106733
Netherlands	Kenya	19 Nov 66	Admin Cooperation	643UNTS285	109198
Netherlands	Kenya	09 Feb 67	General Aid	0UNTS0	109780
Netherlands	Kenya	09 Feb 67	Non-ILO Labor	610UNTS0	108833
Netherlands	Kenya	10 Nov 67	Extradition	0UNTS0	109232
Netherlands	Kenya	23 Jul 69	Sanitation	0UNTS0	110750

PARTY ONE	PARTY TWO	DATE	TOPIC	CITATION	NUMBER
Netherlands	Kenya	08 Jan 70	Sanitation	0UNTS0	110752
Netherlands	Korea, South	26 Oct 53	Air Transport	200UNTS103	102697
Netherlands	Korea, South	08 Dec 65	Patents/Copyrights	571UNTS83	108301
Netherlands	Korea, South	16 May 68	Non-IBRD Project	0UNTS0	109260
Netherlands	Lebanon	20 Sep 49	Air Transport	108UNTS205	101474
Netherlands	Liberia	28 Nov 58	Air Transport	393UNTS55	105651
Netherlands	Libya	07 Jan 54	Air Transport	54NET157	447044
Netherlands	Luxembourg	23 Jun 48	Air Transport	32UNTS229	100500
Netherlands	Luxembourg	26 Apr 49	Culture	182UNTS187	102425
Netherlands	Luxembourg	08 Jul 50	Non-ILO Labor	135UNTS229	101824
Netherlands	Luxembourg	25 Aug 50	Non-ILO Labor	81UNTS13	101058
Netherlands	Luxembourg	06 Nov 53	Admin Cooperation	198UNTS187	102664
Netherlands	Luxembourg	04 May 55	Refugees	292UNTS17	104262
Netherlands	Luxembourg	06 Feb 56	Reparations	261UNTS17	103723
Netherlands	Luxembourg	22 Feb 56	Visas	286UNTS249	104171
Netherlands	Luxembourg	24 Mar 64	Consul/Citizenship	548UNTS137	107975
Netherlands	Luxembourg	08 May 68	Taxation	0UNTS0	110089
Netherlands	Malawi	28 Jun 68	Extradition	0UNTS0	109504
Netherlands	Malawi	18 Jun 69	Taxation	0UNTS0	110429
Netherlands	Malaysia	20 Jan 59	Visas	493UNTS147	107212
Netherlands	Malaysia	07 Apr 64	Air Transport	524UNTS81	107567
Netherlands	Mexico	07 Feb 46	Specif Claim/Waive	3UNTS13	100022
Netherlands	Mexico	27 Jan 50	General Trade	123UNTS197	101661
Netherlands	Mexico	13 Oct 52	Air Transport	163UNTS341	102154
Netherlands	Mexico	24 Aug 61	Air Transport	465UNTS291	106732
Netherlands	Mexico	08 Apr 64	Culture	575UNTS35	108353
Netherlands	Monaco	25 Sep 46	Visas	247UNTS199	103469
Netherlands	Monaco	04 May 54	Admin Cooperation	291UNTS3	104240
Netherlands	Monaco	20 Oct 59	Visas	487UNTS29	107093
Netherlands	Morocco	14 May 69	Non-ILO Labor	0UNTS0	109781
Netherlands	Multilateral	12 May 40	Scientific Project	101UNTS91	101405
Netherlands	Multilateral	27 Mar 41	Military Mission	67UNTS231	200222
Netherlands	Multilateral	21 Oct 43	Finance	2UNTS281	200021
Netherlands	Multilateral	02 Aug 44	Scientific Project	67UNTS221	200221
Netherlands	Multilateral	07 Dec 44	Air Transport	171UNTS345	200501
Netherlands	Multilateral	07 Dec 44	Air Transport	171UNTS387	200502
Netherlands	Multilateral	07 Dec 44	IGO Establishment	15UNTS295	200102
Netherlands	Multilateral	07 Dec 44	Air Transport	84UNTS389	200252
Netherlands	Multilateral	15 Dec 44	Sanitation	16UNTS247	200106
Netherlands	Multilateral	15 Dec 44	Sanitation	17UNTS305	200110
Netherlands	Multilateral	20 Mar 45	General Economic	2UNTS299	200022
Netherlands	Multilateral	08 Aug 45	General Military	82UNTS279	200251
Netherlands	Multilateral	02 Sep 45	Peace/Disarmament	139UNTS387	200465
Netherlands	Multilateral	27 Sep 45	IGO Establishment	5UNTS327	200035
Netherlands	Multilateral	16 Nov 45	IGO Establishment	4UNTS275	100052
Netherlands	Multilateral	27 Dec 45	IGO Establishment	2UNTS39	100020
Netherlands	Multilateral	04 Jan 46	IGO Establishment	6UNTS35	100066
Netherlands	Multilateral	14 Jan 46	Reparations	555UNTS69	108105
Netherlands	Multilateral	05 Apr 46	Specific Resources	231UNTS199	103221
Netherlands	Multilateral	23 Apr 46	Sanitation	17UNTS3	100265
Netherlands	Multilateral	23 Apr 46	Sanitation	16UNTS179	100257
Netherlands	Multilateral	22 Jul 46	IGO Establishment	9UNTS3	100125
Netherlands	Multilateral	22 Jul 46	IGO Establishment	14UNTS185	100221
Netherlands	Multilateral	27 Jul 46	Patents/Copyrights	90UNTS229	101238
Netherlands	Multilateral	15 Oct 46	Refugees	11UNTS73	100150
Netherlands	Multilateral	30 Oct 46	IGO Establishment	27UNTS77	100401
Netherlands	Multilateral	30 Oct 46	IGO Establishment	11UNTS107	100151
Netherlands	Multilateral	02 Dec 46	Specific Resources	161UNTS72	102124
Netherlands	Multilateral	11 Dec 46	Sanitation	12UNTS179	100186
Netherlands	Multilateral	15 Dec 46	IGO Establishment	18UNTS3	100283
Netherlands	Multilateral	20 Jan 47	Water Transport	87UNTS247	101176
Netherlands	Multilateral	06 Feb 47	IGO Establishment	97UNTS227	101352
Netherlands	Multilateral	08 Feb 47	Patents/Copyrights	14UNTS287	100222
Netherlands	Multilateral	10 Feb 47	Peace/Disarmament	49UNTS3	100747
Netherlands	Multilateral	03 Mar 47	Humanitarian	11UNTS43	100148

PARTY ONE	PARTY TWO	DATE	TOPIC	CITATION	NUMBER
Netherlands	Multilateral	27 May 47	Air Transport	418UNTS161	106021
Netherlands	Multilateral	06 Jun 47	Patents/Copyrights	46UNTS249	100714
Netherlands	Multilateral	10 Jun 47	Water Transport	208UNTS3	102814
Netherlands	Multilateral	02 Oct 47	Telecommunications	193UNTS188	102616
Netherlands	Multilateral	11 Oct 47	IGO Establishment	77UNTS143	100998
Netherlands	Multilateral	12 Nov 47	Admin Cooperation	46UNTS201	100710
Netherlands	Multilateral	12 Nov 47	Admin Cooperation	53UNTS39	100771
Netherlands	Multilateral	12 Nov 47	Admin Cooperation	53UNTS49	100772
Netherlands	Multilateral	12 Nov 47	Admin Cooperation	46UNTS169	100709
Netherlands	Multilateral	12 Nov 47	Admin Cooperation	53UNTS13	100770
Netherlands	Multilateral	18 Nov 47	Finance	17UNTS89	100269
Netherlands	Multilateral	22 Dec 47	Customs	32UNTS143	100496
Netherlands	Multilateral	06 Mar 48	Water Transport	289UNTS3	104214
Netherlands	Multilateral	17 Mar 48	General Military	19UNTS51	100304
Netherlands	Multilateral	10 May 48	Culture	289UNTS111	104215
Netherlands	Multilateral	10 Jun 48	Humanitarian	191UNTS3	102576
Netherlands	Multilateral	10 Jun 48	Humanitarian	164UNTS113	102163
Netherlands	Multilateral	19 Jun 48	Air Transport	310UNTS151	104492
Netherlands	Multilateral	26 Jun 48	Culture	331UNTS217	104757
Netherlands	Multilateral	24 Jul 48	Sanitation	66UNTS25	100847
Netherlands	Multilateral	14 Sep 48	Milit Occupation	18UNTS267	100296
Netherlands	Multilateral	17 Sep 48	Telecommunications	97UNTS31	101345
Netherlands	Multilateral	15 Nov 48	IGO Establishment	120UNTS59	101615
Netherlands	Multilateral	19 Nov 48	Sanitation	44UNTS277	100688
Netherlands	Multilateral	29 Nov 48	IGO Establishment	120UNTS13	101613
Netherlands	Multilateral	09 Dec 48	Scientific Project	73UNTS39	100942
Netherlands	Multilateral	09 Dec 48	Scientific Project	20UNTS229	100318
Netherlands	Multilateral	09 Dec 48	Humanitarian	78UNTS277	101021
Netherlands	Multilateral	12 Feb 49	Customs	189UNTS33	102541
Netherlands	Multilateral	23 Mar 49	Commodity Trade	203UNTS179	102746
Netherlands	Multilateral	04 Apr 49	General Military	34UNTS243	100541
Netherlands	Multilateral	28 Apr 49	IGO Establishment	83UNTS105	101105
Netherlands	Multilateral	04 May 49	Admin Cooperation	30UNTS23	100446
Netherlands	Multilateral	04 May 49	Admin Cooperation	30UNTS3	100445
Netherlands	Multilateral	04 May 49	Admin Cooperation	47UNTS159	100728
Netherlands	Multilateral	04 May 49	Admin Cooperation	92UNTS19	101257
Netherlands	Multilateral	04 May 49	Admin Cooperation	98UNTS101	101358
Netherlands	Multilateral	05 May 49	IGO Establishment	87UNTS103	101168
Netherlands	Multilateral	16 Jun 49	Land Transport	45UNTS149	100696
Netherlands	Multilateral	18 Jun 49	ILO Labor	605UNTS295	108768
Netherlands	Multilateral	15 Jul 49	Health/Educ/Welfare	197UNTS3	102631
Netherlands	Multilateral	12 Aug 49	Humanitarian	75UNTS31	100970
Netherlands	Multilateral	12 Aug 49	General Military	75UNTS135	100972
Netherlands	Multilateral	12 Aug 49	Humanitarian	75UNTS287	100973
Netherlands	Multilateral	12 Aug 49	Humanitarian	75UNTS85	100971
Netherlands	Multilateral	02 Sep 49	IGO Status/Immunit	250UNTS12	103515
Netherlands	Multilateral	19 Sep 49	Land Transport	125UNTS3	101671
Netherlands	Multilateral	07 Nov 49	Non-ILO Labor	132UNTS31	101749
Netherlands	Multilateral	07 Nov 49	Sanitation	132UNTS3	101748
Netherlands	Multilateral	16 Dec 49	Admin Cooperation	72UNTS3	100924
Netherlands	Multilateral	18 Feb 50	Customs	123UNTS45	101654
Netherlands	Multilateral	06 Apr 50	Admin Cooperation	119UNTS99	101610
Netherlands	Multilateral	17 Apr 50	Visas	131UNTS99	101738
Netherlands	Multilateral	17 Apr 50	Non-ILO Labor	126UNTS285	101694
Netherlands	Multilateral	13 May 50	Land Transport	128UNTS171	101719
Netherlands	Multilateral	31 May 50	General Trade	74UNTS95	100957
Netherlands	Multilateral	27 Jul 50	Non-ILO Labor	166UNTS73	102186
Netherlands	Multilateral	16 Sep 50	General Transport	92UNTS91	101264
Netherlands	Multilateral	18 Oct 50	Specific Resources	638UNTS185	109134
Netherlands	Multilateral	04 Nov 50	Humanitarian	213UNTS221	102889
Netherlands	Multilateral	22 Nov 50	Culture	131UNTS25	101734
Netherlands	Multilateral	07 Dec 50	Admin Cooperation	212UNTS17	102861
Netherlands	Multilateral	15 Dec 50	Customs	347UNTS127	104994
Netherlands	Multilateral	15 Dec 50	IGO Operations	160UNTS267	102111
Netherlands	Multilateral	15 Dec 50	Customs	157UNTS129	102052

PARTY ONE	PARTY TWO	DATE	TOPIC	CITATION	NUMBER
Netherlands	Multilateral	15 Dec 50	Customs	171UNTS305	102234
Netherlands	Multilateral	18 Apr 51	IGO Establishment	261UNTS140	103729
Netherlands	Multilateral	25 May 51	Status of Forces	175UNTS215	102303
Netherlands	Multilateral	19 Jun 51	Status of Forces	199UNTS67	102678
Netherlands	Multilateral	02 Jul 51	Refugees	189UNTS137	102545
Netherlands	Multilateral	10 Jul 51	Other Military	108UNTS287	101481
Netherlands	Multilateral	08 Sep 51	General Military	136UNTS165	101833
Netherlands	Multilateral	08 Sep 51	Peace/Disarmament	136UNTS45	101832
Netherlands	Multilateral	20 Sep 51	IGO Status/Immunit	200UNTS3	102691
Netherlands	Multilateral	09 Oct 51	IGO Establishment	220UNTS121	102997
Netherlands	Multilateral	06 Dec 51	Admin Cooperation	150UNTS67	101963
Netherlands	Multilateral	06 Dec 51	IGO Establishment	425UNTS61	106119
Netherlands	Multilateral	10 Jan 52	Visas	163UNTS27	102139
Netherlands	Multilateral	10 Jan 52	Visas	163UNTS3	102138
Netherlands	Multilateral	11 Feb 52	Direct Aid	165UNTS77	102169
Netherlands	Multilateral	15 Feb 52	Scientific Project	132UNTS51	101751
Netherlands	Multilateral	20 May 52	Sanitation	219UNTS55	102966
Netherlands	Multilateral	12 Jun 52	Dispute Settlement	138UNTS183	101869
Netherlands	Multilateral	11 Jul 52	Postal Service	171UNTS89	102225
Netherlands	Multilateral	11 Jul 52	Postal Service	170UNTS269	102223
Netherlands	Multilateral	11 Jul 52	Postal Service	170UNTS63	102222
Netherlands	Multilateral	11 Jul 52	Postal Service	170UNTS3	102221
Netherlands	Multilateral	11 Jul 52	Postal Service	171UNTS143	102226
Netherlands	Multilateral	11 Jul 52	Postal Service	171UNTS3	102224
Netherlands	Multilateral	11 Jul 52	Postal Service	171UNTS191	102227
Netherlands	Multilateral	11 Jul 52	IGO Establishment	169UNTS3	102220
Netherlands	Multilateral	05 Sep 52	Taxation	256UNTS3	103619
Netherlands	Multilateral	05 Sep 52	Customs	247UNTS329	103479
Netherlands	Multilateral	06 Sep 52	Patents/Copyrights	216UNTS132	102937
Netherlands	Multilateral	07 Oct 52	Admin Cooperation	310UNTS181	104493
Netherlands	Multilateral	07 Nov 52	General Trade	221UNTS255	103010
Netherlands	Multilateral	10 Nov 52	Admin Cooperation	214UNTS265	102904
Netherlands	Multilateral	27 Feb 53	Claims and Debts	333UNTS3	104764
Netherlands	Multilateral	11 May 53	Sanitation	456UNTS3	106555
Netherlands	Multilateral	01 Jul 53	IGO Establishment	200UNTS149	102701
Netherlands	Multilateral	24 Jul 53	General Amity	250UNTS108	103520
Netherlands	Multilateral	01 Oct 53	Commodity Trade	258UNTS153	103677
Netherlands	Multilateral	17 Oct 53	General Transport	184UNTS42	102438
Netherlands	Multilateral	19 Oct 53	IGO Establishment	207UNTS189	102807
Netherlands	Multilateral	26 Oct 53	Status of Forces	207UNTS237	102809
Netherlands	Multilateral	07 Dec 53	Admin Cooperation	182UNTS51	102422
Netherlands	Multilateral	09 Dec 53	General Economic	249UNTS197	103509
Netherlands	Multilateral	11 Dec 53	Non-ILO Labor	218UNTS255	102958
Netherlands	Multilateral	11 Dec 53	Non-ILO Labor	218UNTS153	102956
Netherlands	Multilateral	11 Dec 53	Education	218UNTS125	102954
Netherlands	Multilateral	11 Dec 53	Non-ILO Labor	218UNTS211	102957
Netherlands	Multilateral	11 Dec 53	Sanitation	191UNTS285	102588
Netherlands	Multilateral	11 Dec 53	Patents/Copyrights	218UNTS27	102952
Netherlands	Multilateral	25 Feb 54	Air Transport	215UNTS249	102922
Netherlands	Multilateral	01 Mar 54	Commodity Trade	256UNTS31	103622
Netherlands	Multilateral	01 Mar 54	Admin Cooperation	286UNTS265	104173
Netherlands	Multilateral	12 May 54	Admin Cooperation	327UNTS3	104714
Netherlands	Multilateral	14 May 54	Culture	249UNTS215	103511
Netherlands	Multilateral	21 May 54	Non-ILO Labor	345UNTS285	104973
Netherlands	Multilateral	04 Jun 54	Customs	282UNTS249	104101
Netherlands	Multilateral	04 Jun 54	Customs	276UNTS191	103992
Netherlands	Multilateral	14 Jun 54	Air Transport	320UNTS209	104643
Netherlands	Multilateral	14 Jun 54	Air Transport	320UNTS217	104644
Netherlands	Multilateral	08 Jul 54	Finance	287UNTS27	104178
Netherlands	Multilateral	28 Sep 54	Refugees	360UNTS117	105158
Netherlands	Multilateral	06 Oct 54	Tech Assistance	201UNTS75	102711
Netherlands	Multilateral	23 Oct 54	Status of Forces	334UNTS3	104765
Netherlands	Multilateral	29 Nov 54	General Trade	287UNTS209	104187
Netherlands	Multilateral	19 Dec 54	Patents/Copyrights	218UNTS51	102953
Netherlands	Multilateral	19 Dec 54	Culture	218UNTS139	102955
Netherlands	Multilateral	21 Dec 54	General Amity	258UNTS322	103678
Netherlands	Multilateral	06 Apr 55	General Amity	261UNTS55	103725
Netherlands	Multilateral	25 May 55	IGO Establishment	264UNTS117	103791
Netherlands	Multilateral	03 Jun 55	Specific Resources	310UNTS145	104491
Netherlands	Multilateral	06 Jun 55	IGO Establishment	219UNTS79	102968
Netherlands	Multilateral	22 Jun 55	Atomic Energy	249UNTS3	103498
Netherlands	Multilateral	28 Sep 55	Air Transport	478UNTS371	106943
Netherlands	Multilateral	12 Oct 55	IGO Establishment	560UNTS3	108165
Netherlands	Multilateral	20 Oct 55	IGO Establishment	378UNTS159	105425
Netherlands	Multilateral	05 Nov 55	IGO Establishment	250UNTS201	103524
Netherlands	Multilateral	13 Dec 55	IGO Operations	529UNTS141	107660
Netherlands	Multilateral	13 Dec 55	Humanitarian	250UNTS3	103514
Netherlands	Multilateral	21 Dec 55	General Trade	292UNTS63	104267
Netherlands	Multilateral	04 Jan 56	Scientific Project	256UNTS171	103627
Netherlands	Multilateral	01 Mar 56	Customs	343UNTS129	104923
Netherlands	Multilateral	25 Apr 56	Commodity Trade	270UNTS103	103896
Netherlands	Multilateral	30 Apr 56	Air Transport	310UNTS229	104494
Netherlands	Multilateral	18 May 56	Customs	338UNTS103	104834
Netherlands	Multilateral	18 May 56	Land Transport	339UNTS3	104844
Netherlands	Multilateral	18 May 56	Customs	327UNTS123	104721
Netherlands	Multilateral	18 May 56	Customs	319UNTS21	104630
Netherlands	Multilateral	19 May 56	Land Transport	399UNTS189	105742
Netherlands	Multilateral	07 Jun 56	Non-ILO Labor	381UNTS145	105470
Netherlands	Multilateral	20 Jun 56	Admin Cooperation	268UNTS3	103850
Netherlands	Multilateral	06 Jul 56	Admin Cooperation	312UNTS109	104514
Netherlands	Multilateral	09 Jul 56	Non-ILO Labor	314UNTS3	104539
Netherlands	Multilateral	16 Aug 56	General Trade	287UNTS223	104188
Netherlands	Multilateral	07 Sep 56	Humanitarian	266UNTS3	103822
Netherlands	Multilateral	25 Sep 56	Air Transport	334UNTS89	104767
Netherlands	Multilateral	25 Sep 56	Air Transport	334UNTS13	104766
Netherlands	Multilateral	24 Oct 56	Admin Cooperation	510UNTS161	107412
Netherlands	Multilateral	26 Oct 56	IGO Establishment	276UNTS3	103988
Netherlands	Multilateral	29 Oct 56	Territory Boundary	263UNTS165	103772
Netherlands	Multilateral	14 Dec 56	Taxation	436UNTS115	106292
Netherlands	Multilateral	14 Dec 56	Taxation	436UNTS131	106293
Netherlands	Multilateral	15 Dec 56	Education	278UNTS73	104023
Netherlands	Multilateral	25 Mar 57	IGO Status/Immunit	294UNTS411	104302
Netherlands	Multilateral	25 Mar 57	IGO Establishment	294UNTS2	104300
Netherlands	Multilateral	25 Mar 57	IGO Establishment	294UNTS259	104301
Netherlands	Multilateral	12 Apr 57	Education	443UNTS128	106362
Netherlands	Multilateral	29 Apr 57	Dispute Settlement	320UNTS243	104646
Netherlands	Multilateral	15 Jun 57	General Trade	550UNTS45	108008
Netherlands	Multilateral	15 Jun 57	Patents/Copyrights	583UNTS3	108470
Netherlands	Multilateral	27 Jun 57	General Economic	284UNTS139	104133
Netherlands	Multilateral	26 Jul 57	Land Transport	386UNTS3	105535
Netherlands	Multilateral	27 Sep 57	Admin Cooperation	299UNTS211	104314
Netherlands	Multilateral	30 Sep 57	General Transport	619UNTS77	108940
Netherlands	Multilateral	03 Oct 57	Postal Service	365UNTS3	105213
Netherlands	Multilateral	03 Oct 57	Postal Service	366UNTS141	105217
Netherlands	Multilateral	03 Oct 57	Postal Service	365UNTS207	105214
Netherlands	Multilateral	03 Oct 57	Postal Service	366UNTS3	105215
Netherlands	Multilateral	03 Oct 57	Postal Service	364UNTS331	105212
Netherlands	Multilateral	03 Oct 57	Postal Service	366UNTS193	105218
Netherlands	Multilateral	03 Oct 57	Postal Service	366UNTS255	105219
Netherlands	Multilateral	03 Oct 57	Postal Service	364UNTS3	105211
Netherlands	Multilateral	03 Oct 57	Postal Service	366UNTS87	105216
Netherlands	Multilateral	23 Nov 57	Refugees	506UNTS125	107384
Netherlands	Multilateral	25 Nov 57	General Trade	403UNTS169	105795
Netherlands	Multilateral	13 Dec 57	Land Transport	372UNTS159	105296
Netherlands	Multilateral	13 Dec 57	Extradition	359UNTS273	105146
Netherlands	Multilateral	15 Jan 58	Customs	383UNTS229	105503
Netherlands	Multilateral	03 Feb 58	IGO Establishment	381UNTS165	105471
Netherlands	Multilateral	20 Mar 58	Admin Cooperation	335UNTS211	104789
Netherlands	Multilateral	31 Mar 58	Specific Property	320UNTS103	104639
Netherlands	Multilateral	15 Apr 58	Health/Educ/Welfare	539UNTS27	107822

PARTY ONE	PARTY TWO	DATE	TOPIC	CITATION	NUMBER
Netherlands	Multilateral	29 Apr 58	Specific Resources	559UNTS285	108164
Netherlands	Multilateral	29 Apr 58	Territory Boundary	499UNTS311	107302
Netherlands	Multilateral	29 Apr 58	Territory Boundary	516UNTS205	107477
Netherlands	Multilateral	29 Apr 58	Dispute Settlement	450UNTS169	106466
Netherlands	Multilateral	29 Apr 58	Water Transport	450UNTS11	106465
Netherlands	Multilateral	10 Jun 58	Admin Cooperation	330UNTS3	104739
Netherlands	Multilateral	18 Jun 58	Finance	386UNTS355	105553
Netherlands	Multilateral	18 Jun 58	General Trade	386UNTS345	105552
Netherlands	Multilateral	25 Jul 58	Customs	352UNTS3	105035
Netherlands	Multilateral	01 Dec 58	Commodity Trade	385UNTS137	105534
Netherlands	Multilateral	15 Dec 58	Mass Media	546UNTS235	107950
Netherlands	Multilateral	15 Dec 58	Sanitation	351UNTS159	105022
Netherlands	Multilateral	15 Jan 59	Customs	348UNTS13	104996
Netherlands	Multilateral	24 Jan 59	IGO Establishment	486UNTS157	107078
Netherlands	Multilateral	30 Jan 59	General Trade	0UNTS0	109234
Netherlands	Multilateral	06 Apr 59	Commodity Trade	349UNTS167	105013
Netherlands	Multilateral	20 Apr 59	Visas	376UNTS85	105375
Netherlands	Multilateral	11 May 59	Claims and Debts	527UNTS145	107623
Netherlands	Multilateral	03 Aug 59	Status of Forces	481UNTS262	106986
Netherlands	Multilateral	18 Nov 59	IGO Establishment	390UNTS227	105610
Netherlands	Multilateral	19 Nov 59	IGO Operations	410UNTS156	105902
Netherlands	Multilateral	01 Dec 59	Territory Boundary	402UNTS71	105778
Netherlands	Multilateral	14 Dec 59	Admin Cooperation	444UNTS193	106369
Netherlands	Multilateral	26 Jan 60	IGO Establishment	439UNTS249	106333
Netherlands	Multilateral	15 Mar 60	Water Transport	572UNTS133	108310
Netherlands	Multilateral	11 Apr 60	Visas	374UNTS3	105323
Netherlands	Multilateral	22 Apr 60	Air Transport	418UNTS211	106023
Netherlands	Multilateral	28 Apr 60	Health/Educ/Welfare	376UNTS111	105377
Netherlands	Multilateral	17 Jun 60	Humanitarian	536UNTS27	107794
Netherlands	Multilateral	21 Jun 60	IGO Establishment	418UNTS109	106019
Netherlands	Multilateral	22 Jun 60	Mass Media	546UNTS247	107951
Netherlands	Multilateral	01 Sep 60	Commodity Trade	403UNTS3	105792
Netherlands	Multilateral	21 Sep 60	Patents/Copyrights	394UNTS3	105664
Netherlands	Multilateral	06 Oct 60	Customs	473UNTS131	106861
Netherlands	Multilateral	08 Oct 60	General Trade	450UNTS309	106476
Netherlands	Multilateral	01 Dec 60	Scientific Project	414UNTS110	105970
Netherlands	Multilateral	09 Dec 60	Customs	429UNTS211	106200
Netherlands	Multilateral	13 Dec 60	Air Transport	523UNTS117	107557
Netherlands	Multilateral	14 Dec 60	Education	429UNTS93	106193
Netherlands	Multilateral	13 Feb 61	ILO Labor	0UNTS0	110306
Netherlands	Multilateral	16 Mar 61	General Trade	638UNTS235	109139
Netherlands	Multilateral	30 Mar 61	Sanitation	520UNTS151	107515
Netherlands	Multilateral	08 Jun 61	Customs	473UNTS153	106862
Netherlands	Multilateral	08 Jun 61	Customs	473UNTS187	106863
Netherlands	Multilateral	21 Jun 61	IGO Establishment	514UNTS209	107449
Netherlands	Multilateral	18 Sep 61	Air Transport	500UNTS31	107305
Netherlands	Multilateral	05 Oct 61	Patents/Copyrights	527UNTS181	107625
Netherlands	Multilateral	18 Oct 61	IGO Establishment	529UNTS89	107659
Netherlands	Multilateral	06 Dec 61	Customs	473UNTS219	106864
Netherlands	Multilateral	16 Dec 61	Visas	544UNTS19	107909
Netherlands	Multilateral	20 Feb 62	Water Transport	597UNTS159	108644
Netherlands	Multilateral	07 Mar 62	Commodity Trade	445UNTS199	106388
Netherlands	Multilateral	07 Mar 62	Commodity Trade	445UNTS205	106389
Netherlands	Multilateral	19 Mar 62	Patents/Copyrights	0UNTS0	110108
Netherlands	Multilateral	29 Mar 62	IGO Establishment	507UNTS177	107401
Netherlands	Multilateral	09 May 62	IGO Establishment	453UNTS299	106531
Netherlands	Multilateral	14 May 62	Scientific Project	544UNTS39	107910
Netherlands	Multilateral	15 May 62	Commodity Trade	444UNTS3	106367
Netherlands	Multilateral	06 Jun 62	Privil/Immunities	486UNTS271	107081
Netherlands	Multilateral	06 Jun 62	Privil/Immunities	486UNTS263	107080
Netherlands	Multilateral	14 Jun 62	IGO Establishment	528UNTS33	107634
Netherlands	Multilateral	27 Jun 62	Extradition	616UNTS79	108893
Netherlands	Multilateral	28 Jun 62	ILO Labor	494UNTS271	107238
Netherlands	Multilateral	15 Aug 62	Territory Boundary	437UNTS292	106312
Netherlands	Multilateral	28 Sep 62	IGO Establishment	469UNTS169	106791

PARTY ONE	PARTY TWO	DATE	TOPIC	CITATION	NUMBER
Netherlands	Multilateral	05 Oct 62	IGO Establishment	502UNTS225	107333
Netherlands	Multilateral	29 Nov 62	Visas	457UNTS63	106577
Netherlands	Multilateral	10 Dec 62	Culture	521UNTS231	107525
Netherlands	Multilateral	17 Dec 62	Sanitation	486UNTS119	107076
Netherlands	Multilateral	30 Apr 63	General Trade	570UNTS23	108285
Netherlands	Multilateral	06 May 63	Consul/Citizenship	634UNTS221	109065
Netherlands	Multilateral	19 Jun 63	Visas	482UNTS19	106988
Netherlands	Multilateral	05 Aug 63	Sanitation	480UNTS43	106964
Netherlands	Multilateral	13 Aug 63	General Trade	592UNTS139	108572
Netherlands	Multilateral	19 Oct 63	Direct Aid	523UNTS249	107559
Netherlands	Multilateral	09 Nov 63	Direct Aid	489UNTS209	107141
Netherlands	Multilateral	10 Feb 64	Visas	496UNTS151	107249
Netherlands	Multilateral	09 Mar 64	Specific Resources	581UNTS57	108432
Netherlands	Multilateral	09 Mar 64	Specific Resources	581UNTS89	108434
Netherlands	Multilateral	09 Mar 64	Specific Resources	581UNTS83	108433
Netherlands	Multilateral	16 Apr 64	Visas	548UNTS27	107967
Netherlands	Multilateral	14 May 64	Refugees	528UNTS13	107632
Netherlands	Multilateral	14 May 64	Refugees	528UNTS23	107633
Netherlands	Multilateral	14 May 64	Visas	528UNTS3	107631
Netherlands	Multilateral	25 May 64	Taxation	620UNTS149	108953
Netherlands	Multilateral	18 Jun 64	Atomic Energy	542UNTS145	107886
Netherlands	Multilateral	10 Jul 64	Postal Service	613UNTS3	108850
Netherlands	Multilateral	10 Jul 64	Postal Service	612UNTS361	108849
Netherlands	Multilateral	10 Jul 64	Postal Service	612UNTS233	108848
Netherlands	Multilateral	10 Jul 64	Postal Service	611UNTS105	108845
Netherlands	Multilateral	10 Jul 64	Postal Service	613UNTS3	108851
Netherlands	Multilateral	10 Jul 64	Postal Service	611UNTS387	108846
Netherlands	Multilateral	10 Jul 64	Postal Service	612UNTS3	108847
Netherlands	Multilateral	10 Jul 64	Postal Service	613UNTS193	108852
Netherlands	Multilateral	10 Jul 64	Postal Service	611UNTS7	108844
Netherlands	Multilateral	20 Aug 64	Telecommunications	514UNTS25	107441
Netherlands	Multilateral	12 Sep 64	Specific Resources	0UNTS0	109344
Netherlands	Multilateral	15 Sep 64	General Trade	510UNTS147	107411
Netherlands	Multilateral	19 Nov 64	Visas	523UNTS3	107553
Netherlands	Multilateral	27 Nov 64	Visas	548UNTS47	107968
Netherlands	Multilateral	22 Jan 65	Gen Communications	634UNTS239	109066
Netherlands	Multilateral	15 Feb 65	Visas	547UNTS3	107953
Netherlands	Multilateral	15 Feb 65	Refugees	546UNTS277	107952
Netherlands	Multilateral	09 Mar 65	Water Transport	591UNTS265	108564
Netherlands	Multilateral	18 Mar 65	Dispute Settlement	575UNTS159	108359
Netherlands	Multilateral	08 Jul 65	General Trade	597UNTS3	108641
Netherlands	Multilateral	16 Jul 65	General Trade	600UNTS49	108675
Netherlands	Multilateral	08 Sep 65	Visas	578UNTS3	108382
Netherlands	Multilateral	04 Dec 65	IGO Establishment	571UNTS123	108303
Netherlands	Multilateral	31 Dec 65	Specific Resources	616UNTS317	108904
Netherlands	Multilateral	05 Apr 66	Water Transport	640UNTS133	109159
Netherlands	Multilateral	28 Apr 66	Non-ILO Labor	604UNTS219	108752
Netherlands	Multilateral	04 May 66	IBRD Project	575UNTS49	108354
Netherlands	Multilateral	17 May 66	Visas	571UNTS89	108302
Netherlands	Multilateral	12 Jul 66	Visas	578UNTS23	108384
Netherlands	Multilateral	31 Jan 67	Refugees	606UNTS267	108791
Netherlands	Multilateral	02 Feb 67	Dispute Settlement	606UNTS89	108777
Netherlands	Multilateral	19 Apr 67	Tech Assistance	595UNTS120	108617
Netherlands	Multilateral	26 Apr 67	General Trade	0UNTS0	109890
Netherlands	Multilateral	20 Jun 67	Visas	607UNTS97	108799
Netherlands	Multilateral	29 Jun 67	Non-ILO Labor	0UNTS0	110030
Netherlands	Multilateral	03 Jul 67	Air Transport	0UNTS0	109248
Netherlands	Multilateral	20 Jul 67	General Economic	0UNTS0	109259
Netherlands	Multilateral	22 Aug 67	General Trade	0UNTS0	110687
Netherlands	Multilateral	22 Sep 67	Non-IBRD Project	0UNTS0	109258
Netherlands	Multilateral	27 Oct 67	Telecommunications	0UNTS0	109861
Netherlands	Multilateral	15 Nov 67	General Trade	0UNTS0	109703
Netherlands	Multilateral	18 Mar 68	Commodity Trade	0UNTS0	109262
Netherlands	Multilateral	27 Mar 68	Visas	0UNTS0	109293
Netherlands	Multilateral	16 Aug 68	Non-ILO Labor	0UNTS0	109281

PARTY ONE	PARTY TWO	DATE	TOPIC	CITATION	NUMBER
Netherlands	Multilateral	24 Sep 68	Air Transport	0UNTS0	110612
Netherlands	Multilateral	28 Sep 68	Tech Assistance	0UNTS0	109296
Netherlands	Multilateral	10 Dec 68	Visas	0UNTS0	109387
Netherlands	Multilateral	07 Feb 69	Status of Forces	0UNTS0	110586
Netherlands	Multilateral	09 Jun 69	Specific Resources	0UNTS0	110099
Netherlands	Multilateral	12 Jun 69	Visas	0UNTS0	110305
Netherlands	Multilateral	24 Jun 69	IGO Operations	0UNTS0	109743
Netherlands	Multilateral	17 Jul 69	Visas	0UNTS0	109729
Netherlands	Multilateral	03 Dec 69	Visas	0UNTS0	110526
Netherlands	Multilateral	12 Jan 70	Commodity Trade	0UNTS0	110603
Netherlands	Multilateral	13 Apr 70	Education	0UNTS0	110793
Netherlands	Multilateral	28 Apr 70	Visas	0UNTS0	110805
Netherlands	Multilateral	04 May 70	Visas	0UNTS0	110579
Netherlands	Muscat and Oman	25 Aug 68	Consul/Citizenship	0UNTS0	109835
Netherlands	NATO (North Atlan)	25 May 64	Status of Forces	544UNTS237	107920
Netherlands	New Zealand	30 Oct 47	General Economic	76UNTS41	100977
Netherlands	New Zealand	03 Mar 49	Visas	34UNTS207	100538
Netherlands	New Zealand	16 Oct 50	Non-ILO Labor	83UNTS269	101111
Netherlands	Nigeria	04 Dec 64	Education	545UNTS155	107931
Netherlands	Nigeria	28 Oct 65	Scientific Project	578UNTS15	108383
Netherlands	Nigeria	18 Oct 66	Education	603UNTS53	108724
Netherlands	Norway	06 Nov 45	Finance	2UNTS5	100017
Netherlands	Norway	28 Jan 47	General Trade	31UNTS29	100467
Netherlands	Norway	03 Jun 47	Visas	2NORT456	451117
Netherlands	Norway	26 Feb 49	General Economic	29UNTS33	100432
Netherlands	Norway	29 Dec 50	Taxation	134UNTS19	101795
Netherlands	Norway	28 Jun 51	Non-ILO Labor	2NORT562	451118
Netherlands	Norway	28 Jun 51	Non-ILO Labor	51NET98	447027
Netherlands	Norway	09 Jun 54	Finance	287UNTS179	104184
Netherlands	Norway	09 Jul 54	Claims and Debts	54NET187	447048
Netherlands	Norway	18 May 55	Culture	252UNTS269	103569
Netherlands	Norway	28 May 57	General Trade	3NORT717	451119
Netherlands	Norway	30 Jun 58	Reparations	346UNTS217	104982
Netherlands	Norway	30 Jun 58	Reparations	348UNTS3	104995
Netherlands	Norway	30 Apr 59	Finance	487UNTS3	107090
Netherlands	Norway	18 Oct 62	Air Transport	466UNTS145	106741
Netherlands	Norway	17 Nov 64	Sanitation	579UNTS243	108412
Netherlands	Norway	22 Sep 66	Taxation	600UNTS227	108683
Netherlands	Pakistan	17 Jul 52	Air Transport	150UNTS277	101980
Netherlands	Pakistan	01 May 53	Visas	293UNTS11	104281
Netherlands	Pakistan	30 Oct 64	Tech Assistance	541UNTS243	107873
Netherlands	Pakistan	08 Nov 67	Scientific Project	0UNTS0	110753
Netherlands	Pakistan	13 Dec 68	Water Transport	0UNTS0	109739
Netherlands	Paraguay	05 Mar 52	Air Transport	52NET67	447033
Netherlands	Paraguay	13 Apr 57	Finance	593UNTS85	108577
Netherlands	Paraguay	21 Nov 60	Visas	450UNTS201	106467
Netherlands	Peru	22 Sep 52	Air Transport	255UNTS49	103604
Netherlands	Philippines	05 Feb 53	Air Transport	216UNTS99	102934
Netherlands	Philippines	17 Feb 60	Visas	359UNTS317	105149
Netherlands	Philippines	02 Mar 66	Tech Assistance	631UNTS325	109002
Netherlands	Philippines	13 Feb 68	Non-ILO Labor	0UNTS0	110748
Netherlands	Poland	20 May 49	General Trade	51NET67	447010
Netherlands	Poland	29 Oct 55	Finance	56NET19	447058
Netherlands	Poland	29 Oct 55	General Trade	56NET18	447057
Netherlands	Poland	21 Jul 60	Air Transport	497UNTS189	107269
Netherlands	Poland	20 Dec 63	Claims and Debts	514UNTS169	107446
Netherlands	Poland	22 Aug 67	Culture	0UNTS0	109275
Netherlands	Poland	22 Aug 67	Culture	68PDZU209	457147
Netherlands	Poland	22 Aug 67	General Economic	68PZUM26	458146
Netherlands	Poland	22 Aug 67	General Economic	0UNTS0	109276
Netherlands	Portugal	12 Apr 46	Air Transport	4UNTS317	100054
Netherlands	Portugal	14 Mar 52	Visas	309UNTS117	104470
Netherlands	Portugal	08 Jan 53	General Trade	53NET37	447036
Netherlands	Portugal	14 Dec 54	Visas	289UNTS121	104216
Netherlands	Portugal	26 Mar 57	Visas	288UNTS47	104196

PARTY ONE	PARTY TWO	DATE	TOPIC	CITATION	NUMBER
Netherlands	Portugal	30 Apr 59	Finance	485UNTS129	107050
Netherlands	Portugal	22 Nov 63	Non-ILO Labor	492UNTS31	107185
Netherlands	Portugal	12 Oct 66	Non-ILO Labor	0UNTS0	109273
Netherlands	Romania	27 Aug 57	Air Transport	342UNTS309	104914
Netherlands	Romania	30 Sep 60	General Economic	479UNTS91	106948
Netherlands	Romania	13 Feb 67	Culture	604UNTS287	108756
Netherlands	Romania	08 May 67	Finance	607UNTS105	108800
Netherlands	Romania	20 Jul 67	Sanitation	633UNTS21	109032
Netherlands	Romania	23 Apr 68	Land Transport	0UNTS0	109481
Netherlands	Senegal	12 Jun 65	General Economic	602UNTS231	108715
Netherlands	Sierra Leone	13 Jun 67	Air Transport	0UNTS0	109247
Netherlands	South Africa	22 Jul 47	Air Transport	12UNTS257	100188
Netherlands	South Africa	31 May 51	Culture	188UNTS289	102533
Netherlands	South Africa	21 Jun 52	Visas	309UNTS123	104471
Netherlands	South Africa	22 Apr 54	Taxation	211UNTS215	102853
Netherlands	Spain	13 Jul 46	Air Transport	4UNTS351	100055
Netherlands	Spain	21 Oct 46	General Trade	46SPBO3010	460207
Netherlands	Spain	21 Oct 46	Finance	46SPBO3010	460208
Netherlands	Spain	22 Oct 47	Air Transport	48SPBO1108	460209
Netherlands	Spain	08 Oct 48	Air Transport	28UNTS209	100426
Netherlands	Spain	20 Jun 50	Air Transport	95UNTS303	101327
Netherlands	Spain	08 Dec 53	General Trade	53NET134	447043
Netherlands	Spain	12 Jul 55	General Trade	55SPBO2908	460210
Netherlands	Spain	12 Jul 55	Finance	55SPBO2908	460211
Netherlands	Spain	27 May 59	Visas	458UNTS165	106599
Netherlands	Spain	08 Apr 61	Non-ILO Labor	482UNTS193	106996
Netherlands	Spain	17 Dec 62	Health/Educ/Welfare	499UNTS227	107301
Netherlands	Spain	16 Apr 64	Non-ILO Labor	64SPBO1306	460212
Netherlands	Spain	10 Feb 65	Visas	545UNTS3	107922
Netherlands	Sudan	12 Feb 56	Air Transport	311UNTS319	104508
Netherlands	Sweden	30 Nov 45	General Trade	45SOFM151	461019
Netherlands	Sweden	30 Nov 45	Finance	2UNTS27	100019
Netherlands	Sweden	29 Jun 46	General Trade	46SOFM204	461028
Netherlands	Sweden	23 Dec 46	General Trade	47SOFM1	461037
Netherlands	Sweden	20 Mar 47	Visas	247UNTS145	103463
Netherlands	Sweden	30 Dec 47	General Trade	47SOFM583	461059
Netherlands	Sweden	30 Dec 47	General Trade	51NET91	447007
Netherlands	Sweden	07 Apr 49	General Trade	49SOFM391	461086
Netherlands	Sweden	06 Jul 49	Non-ILO Labor	197UNTS189	102639
Netherlands	Sweden	19 Dec 49	General Trade	49SOFM625	461096
Netherlands	Sweden	18 Apr 50	General Trade	50SOFM781	461113
Netherlands	Sweden	29 May 51	General Trade	51SOFM253	461145
Netherlands	Sweden	31 Mar 52	General Trade	52SOFM167	461161
Netherlands	Sweden	25 Apr 52	Taxation	163UNTS131	102147
Netherlands	Sweden	25 Apr 52	Taxation	163UNTS195	102148
Netherlands	Sweden	10 Apr 53	General Trade	53SOFM81	461182
Netherlands	Sweden	23 Nov 55	Admin Cooperation	262UNTS247	103751
Netherlands	Sweden	21 May 57	Land Transport	286UNTS237	104169
Netherlands	Sweden	23 Oct 57	Land Transport	306UNTS75	104433
Netherlands	Sweden	30 Apr 59	Finance	485UNTS147	107053
Netherlands	Sweden	08 Jan 62	Air Transport	466UNTS65	106737
Netherlands	Switzerland	24 Oct 45	Finance	3UNTS73	100025
Netherlands	Switzerland	07 Mar 49	Air Transport	35UNTS69	100551
Netherlands	Switzerland	15 Sep 49	Visas	252UNTS13	103555
Netherlands	Switzerland	12 Nov 51	Taxation	126UNTS173	101689
Netherlands	Switzerland	12 Nov 51	Taxation	126UNTS157	101688
Netherlands	Switzerland	20 May 52	Land Transport	52SWRO603	462085
Netherlands	Switzerland	22 Jul 52	Land Transport	52NET97	447034
Netherlands	Switzerland	20 Nov 52	Non-ILO Labor	163UNTS121	102146
Netherlands	Switzerland	28 May 53	General Trade	54NET25	447040
Netherlands	Switzerland	26 Aug 53	Finance	53NET84	447042
Netherlands	Switzerland	03 Nov 53	Customs	293UNTS53	104285
Netherlands	Switzerland	23 Oct 56	Admin Cooperation	287UNTS203	104186
Netherlands	Switzerland	21 Jun 57	General Trade	57SWRO521	462149
Netherlands	Switzerland	28 Mar 58	Non-ILO Labor	318UNTS175	104614

PARTY ONE	PARTY TWO	DATE	TOPIC	CITATION	NUMBER
Netherlands	Switzerland	29 Mar 58	Visas	330UNTS101	104741
Netherlands	Switzerland	14 Apr 59	Finance	486UNTS367	107086
Netherlands	Syria	13 Feb 50	Air Transport	108UNTS53	101467
Netherlands	Taiwan	29 May 45	Privil/Immunities	2UNTS307	200023
Netherlands	Taiwan	06 Dec 47	Air Transport	43UNTS185	100669
Netherlands	Tanzania	27 Apr 65	Tech Assistance	594UNTS123	108599
Netherlands	Tanzania	09 May 68	Extradition	0UNTS0	109621
Netherlands	Thailand	30 Jan 47	General Amity	247UNTS353	103480
Netherlands	Thailand	18 Jul 47	Air Transport	28UNTS27	100417
Netherlands	Thailand	30 May 53	Reparations	293UNTS17	104282
Netherlands	Thailand	09 Dec 57	Visas	309UNTS291	104477
Netherlands	Tunisia	19 Mar 59	Air Transport	497UNTS61	107262
Netherlands	Tunisia	23 May 63	Finance	523UNTS237	107558
Netherlands	Tunisia	11 Feb 64	Culture	570UNTS173	108293
Netherlands	Tunisia	03 Mar 64	Tech Assistance	533UNTS133	107739
Netherlands	Tunisia	08 Jul 66	Tech Assistance	591UNTS235	108560
Netherlands	Turkey	19 Mar 47	Air Transport	14UNTS59	100211
Netherlands	Turkey	06 Sep 49	General Economic	50TURG1901	466079
Netherlands	Turkey	04 Nov 53	Visas	293UNTS3	104280
Netherlands	Turkey	26 Jul 55	General Economic	55NET140	447056
Netherlands	Turkey	29 Nov 58	Direct Aid	335UNTS229	104790
Netherlands	Turkey	12 Aug 59	Admin Cooperation	527UNTS181	107624
Netherlands	Turkey	12 May 60	Culture	463UNTS207	106704
Netherlands	Turkey	19 Aug 64	Non-ILO Labor	521UNTS197	107523
Netherlands	Turkey	05 Apr 66	Non-ILO Labor	0UNTS0	109204
Netherlands	Uganda	27 Jan 67	Extradition	608UNTS345	108823
Netherlands	UK Great Britain	13 Jun 39	Sanitation	5UNTS65	200028
Netherlands	UK Great Britain	14 Jun 40	Finance	2UNTS251	200018
Netherlands	UK Great Britain	25 Jul 40	Finance	2UNTS275	200020
Netherlands	UK Great Britain	02 Oct 44	Claims and Debts	231UNTS317	200535
Netherlands	UK Great Britain	07 Sep 45	Finance	2UNTS325	200024
Netherlands	UK Great Britain	20 Dec 45	Milit Assistance	4UNTS303	100053
Netherlands	UK Great Britain	13 Aug 46	Air Transport	4UNTS367	100056
Netherlands	UK Great Britain	16 Sep 46	Finance	4UNTS401	100057
Netherlands	UK Great Britain	04 Dec 46	Milit Installation	12UNTS241	100187
Netherlands	UK Great Britain	26 Feb 47	Finance	11UNTS279	100167
Netherlands	UK Great Britain	21 Mar 47	Visas	11UNTS297	100170
Netherlands	UK Great Britain	21 Mar 47	Visas	52NET64	447004
Netherlands	UK Great Britain	08 Oct 47	Reparations	252UNTS19	103556
Netherlands	UK Great Britain	11 Mar 48	Reparations	77UNTS69	100993
Netherlands	UK Great Britain	11 Jun 48	General Economic	66UNTS183	100853
Netherlands	UK Great Britain	07 Jul 48	Culture	82UNTS259	101099
Netherlands	UK Great Britain	06 Sep 48	Finance	32UNTS235	100501
Netherlands	UK Great Britain	15 Oct 48	Taxation	74UNTS3	100955
Netherlands	UK Great Britain	15 Oct 48	Taxation	73UNTS203	100954
Netherlands	UK Great Britain	17 Jan 49	Reparations	83UNTS67	101102
Netherlands	UK Great Britain	20 Sep 49	Reparations	51NET137	447013
Netherlands	UK Great Britain	30 Apr 51	Consul/Citizenship	91UNTS177	101250
Netherlands	UK Great Britain	17 May 51	Air Transport	118UNTS103	101599
Netherlands	UK Great Britain	30 Nov 51	Postal Service	123UNTS177	101659
Netherlands	UK Great Britain	19 Oct 53	Customs	306UNTS99	104435
Netherlands	UK Great Britain	09 Jul 54	Finance	199UNTS157	102682
Netherlands	UK Great Britain	11 Aug 54	Non-ILO Labor	248UNTS235	103497
Netherlands	UK Great Britain	11 Jun 56	Status of Forces	306UNTS107	104436
Netherlands	UK Great Britain	12 Jun 56	Non-ILO Labor	250UNTS81	103519
Netherlands	UK Great Britain	22 Oct 57	Air Transport	313UNTS309	104538
Netherlands	UK Great Britain	30 Apr 59	Claims and Debts	343UNTS307	104937
Netherlands	UK Great Britain	01 Apr 60	Visas	374UNTS277	105341
Netherlands	UK Great Britain	21 Feb 61	Visas	398UNTS235	105725
Netherlands	UK Great Britain	27 Aug 63	Other Military	490UNTS3	107150
Netherlands	UK Great Britain	30 Oct 63	Other Military	490UNTS11	107151
Netherlands	UK Great Britain	06 Oct 65	Territory Boundary	595UNTS105	108615
Netherlands	UK Great Britain	06 Oct 65	Territory Boundary	595UNTS113	108616
Netherlands	UK Great Britain	31 Oct 67	Taxation	0UNTS0	109222
Netherlands	UK Great Britain	17 Nov 67	Dispute Settlement	0UNTS0	110022

PARTY ONE	PARTY TWO	DATE	TOPIC	CITATION	NUMBER
Netherlands	UK Great Britain	17 Nov 67	Admin Cooperation	0UNTS0	110356
Netherlands	UK Great Britain	01 May 69	Taxation	0UNTS0	110438
Netherlands	UK Great Britain	19 Sep 69	Land Transport	0UNTS0	110807
Netherlands	UN Special Fund	12 Aug 60	Tech Assistance	372UNTS331	105309
Netherlands	UN Special Fund	24 May 63	Direct Aid	466UNTS289	106750
Netherlands	UNICEF (Children)	31 Dec 54	Direct Aid	202UNTS135	102729
Netherlands	United Arab Rep	08 Dec 49	Air Transport	95UNTS123	101320
Netherlands	United Arab Rep	21 Mar 53	Finance	53NET44	447039
Netherlands	United Arab Rep	21 Mar 53	General Trade	53NET43	447038
Netherlands	United Arab Rep	15 May 57	Taxation	288UNTS29	104194
Netherlands	United Arab Rep	08 Dec 60	Culture	455UNTS276	106547
Netherlands	United Arab Rep	05 Aug 65	Air Transport	0UNTS0	110161
Netherlands	United Nations	09 Apr 53	Direct Aid	163UNTS89	102143
Netherlands	United Nations	27 May 64	IGO Status/Immunit	548UNTS79	107971
Netherlands	Uruguay	12 May 47	Air Transport	51NET151	447005
Netherlands	USA (United States)	17 Jan 33	Status of Forces	474UNTS119	106877
Netherlands	USA (United States)	08 Jul 42	Milit Assistance	103UNTS277	200318
Netherlands	USA (United States)	30 Sep 42	Milit Servic/Citiz	13UNTS151	200076
Netherlands	USA (United States)	14 Jun 43	General Military	28UNTS397	200163
Netherlands	USA (United States)	16 May 44	Milit Occupation	132UNTS355	200440
Netherlands	USA (United States)	30 Apr 45	Milit Installation	139UNTS319	200459
Netherlands	USA (United States)	30 Apr 45	Milit Assistance	139UNTS341	200460
Netherlands	USA (United States)	09 Feb 46	Commodity Trade	3UNTS247	100035
Netherlands	USA (United States)	11 Feb 46	Claims and Debts	3UNTS37	100023
Netherlands	USA (United States)	13 Mar 46	Visas	84UNTS3	101113
Netherlands	USA (United States)	21 Nov 46	General Trade	12UNTS173	100185
Netherlands	USA (United States)	11 Apr 47	Other Military	148UNTS343	101943
Netherlands	USA (United States)	28 May 47	General Military	17UNTS29	100267
Netherlands	USA (United States)	20 Aug 47	Visas	84UNTS11	101114
Netherlands	USA (United States)	30 Oct 47	General Economic	76UNTS47	100978
Netherlands	USA (United States)	29 Apr 48	Taxation	32UNTS167	100498
Netherlands	USA (United States)	02 Jul 48	Direct Aid	20UNTS91	100315
Netherlands	USA (United States)	02 Jul 48	Mostfavored Nation	32UNTS77	100490
Netherlands	USA (United States)	17 Jan 49	Direct Aid	32UNTS241	100502
Netherlands	USA (United States)	26 Apr 49	Finance	70UNTS123	100901
Netherlands	USA (United States)	17 May 49	Milit Assistance	46UNTS291	100717
Netherlands	USA (United States)	27 Jan 50	Milit Assistance	80UNTS219	101054
Netherlands	USA (United States)	06 Oct 50	Finance	51NET1	447015
Netherlands	USA (United States)	07 Oct 50	Loans and Credits	79UNTS33	101029
Netherlands	USA (United States)	19 Jan 51	Reparations	141UNTS221	101917
Netherlands	USA (United States)	26 Sep 51	Milit Installation	158UNTS469	102080
Netherlands	USA (United States)	08 Jan 52	Milit Assistance	179UNTS175	102366
Netherlands	USA (United States)	07 Mar 52	Taxation	135UNTS199	101821
Netherlands	USA (United States)	15 May 52	Milit Assistance	177UNTS233	102321
Netherlands	USA (United States)	12 Mar 53	Claims and Debts	53NET135	447037
Netherlands	USA (United States)	19 Jun 53	Admin Cooperation	212UNTS249	102875
Netherlands	USA (United States)	27 Oct 53	Tech Assistance	221UNTS357	103017
Netherlands	USA (United States)	22 Jan 54	Tech Assistance	190UNTS207	102565
Netherlands	USA (United States)	07 May 54	Milit Assistance	213UNTS325	102895
Netherlands	USA (United States)	13 Aug 54	Milit Installation	251UNTS91	103535
Netherlands	USA (United States)	14 Dec 54	Milit Assistance	262UNTS35	103737
Netherlands	USA (United States)	21 Mar 55	Telecommunications	289UNTS129	104217
Netherlands	USA (United States)	29 Apr 55	Milit Assistance	251UNTS357	103553
Netherlands	USA (United States)	29 Apr 55	Milit Installation	219UNTS105	102969
Netherlands	USA (United States)	25 May 55	Claims and Debts	289UNTS227	104220
Netherlands	USA (United States)	18 Jul 55	Atomic Energy	240UNTS347	103412
Netherlands	USA (United States)	04 Nov 55	Air Transport	269UNTS3	103867
Netherlands	USA (United States)	22 Jan 56	Atomic Energy	287UNTS121	104181
Netherlands	USA (United States)	27 Mar 56	General Amity	285UNTS231	104154
Netherlands	USA (United States)	07 Aug 56	US Agri Commod Aid	281UNTS57	104069
Netherlands	USA (United States)	16 Aug 56	Specific Property	279UNTS3	104031
Netherlands	USA (United States)	15 Feb 57	Atomic Energy	287UNTS239	104190
Netherlands	USA (United States)	03 Apr 57	Air Transport	410UNTS193	105904
Netherlands	USA (United States)	06 May 59	Milit Installation	355UNTS327	105084
Netherlands	USA (United States)	24 Mar 60	Milit Assistance	406UNTS165	105847

PARTY ONE	PARTY TWO	DATE	TOPIC	CITATION	NUMBER
Netherlands	USA (United States)	24 Apr 62	Specific Property	436UNTS93	106289
Netherlands	USA (United States)	06 Feb 63	Status of Forces	487UNTS113	107098
Netherlands	USA (United States)	20 May 63	Specif Goods/Equip	487UNTS123	107099
Netherlands	USA (United States)	26 Nov 63	Milit Assistance	388UNTS303	105586
Netherlands	USA (United States)	22 Jun 66	Gen Communications	590UNTS109	108550
Netherlands	USSR (Soviet Union)	10 Jul 42	Consul/Citizenship	241UNTS475	200540
Netherlands	USSR (Soviet Union)	24 Oct 45	General Trade	16SUGG62	469883
Netherlands	USSR (Soviet Union)	02 Jul 48	General Economic	0NETO	447009
Netherlands	USSR (Soviet Union)	27 Jun 56	General Trade	0SUST359	468291
Netherlands	USSR (Soviet Union)	17 Jun 58	Air Transport	335UNTS77	104779
Netherlands	USSR (Soviet Union)	06 Nov 59	General Trade	8SUGG157	469609
Netherlands	USSR (Soviet Union)	14 Jul 67	Culture	0UNTS0	110497
Netherlands	USSR (Soviet Union)	20 Oct 67	Claims and Debts	0UNTS0	109391
Netherlands	Venezuela	26 Oct 54	Air Transport	232UNTS103	103232
Netherlands	Venezuela	11 Apr 57	Admin Cooperation	288UNTS23	104193
Netherlands	Vietnam, South	14 Nov 53	General Trade	0VKNG64	496016
Netherlands	Vietnam, South	05 Mar 55	Patents/Copyrights	288UNTS53	104197
Netherlands	Vietnam, South	24 Mar 67	Sanitation	610UNTS0	108834
Netherlands	Yemen	12 Apr 39	General Amity	79UNTS257	200249
Netherlands	Yugoslavia	03 Aug 46	Finance	52NET25	447002
Netherlands	Yugoslavia	01 Jun 56	Non-ILO Labor	276UNTS319	103994
Netherlands	Yugoslavia	13 Mar 57	Air Transport	327UNTS227	104723
Netherlands	Yugoslavia	22 Jul 58	Claims and Debts	386UNTS263	105546
Netherlands	Yugoslavia	09 Feb 61	Claims and Debts	453UNTS221	106526
Netherlands	Yugoslavia	28 May 64	Visas	521UNTS191	107522
Netherlands	Yugoslavia	11 Aug 66	Culture	602UNTS243	108716
Netherlands	Yugoslavia	08 Sep 66	Land Transport	597UNTS147	108643
Netherlands	Yugoslavia	13 Mar 68	General Economic	0UNTS0	109297
Netherlands	Yugoslavia	09 Mar 70	Non-ILO Labor	0UNTS0	110804
Netherlands	Zambia	17 Dec 65	Non-ILO Labor	631UNTS311	109000
Netherlands Antilles	Multilateral	03 Oct 57	Postal Service	365UNTS3	105213
Netherlands Antilles	Multilateral	10 Jul 64	Postal Service	612UNTS233	108848
Netherlands Antilles	Multilateral	10 Jul 64	Postal Service	612UNTS3	108847
Nevis	Multilateral	01 Jul 68	Peace/Disarmament	0UNTS0	110485
New Guinea	Multilateral	24 Dec 68	Commodity Trade	0UNTS0	109369
New Zealand	Australia	21 Jan 44	General Amity	18UNTS357	200113
New Zealand	Australia	15 Apr 49	Non-ILO Labor	34UNTS225	100540
New Zealand	Australia	26 Nov 49	Territory Boundary	198UNTS161	102662
New Zealand	Australia	30 Sep 58	Territory Boundary	340UNTS61	104859
New Zealand	Australia	12 May 60	Taxation	369UNTS119	105254
New Zealand	Australia	25 Jul 61	Air Transport	523UNTS271	107561
New Zealand	Australia	29 Apr 63	Customs	483UNTS241	107017
New Zealand	Australia	31 Aug 65	General Trade	554UNTS169	108101
New Zealand	Austria	10 Jun 52	Admin Cooperation	171UNTS263	102229
New Zealand	Austria	14 May 58	Visas	317UNTS117	104598
New Zealand	Belgium	01 Nov 51	Visas	118UNTS169	101605
New Zealand	Belgium	01 Sep 53	Air Transport	192UNTS283	102605
New Zealand	Bulgaria	03 Nov 67	General Trade	0UNTS0	109207
New Zealand	Canada	12 Mar 48	Taxation	231UNTS219	103222
New Zealand	Canada	16 Aug 50	Air Transport	77UNTS239	101002
New Zealand	Czechoslovakia	08 Aug 47	Claims and Debts	18UNTS161	100285
New Zealand	Czechoslovakia	22 Jan 48	Commodity Trade	16UNTS229	100264
New Zealand	Denmark	18 Sep 46	Claims and Debts	10UNTS39	100141
New Zealand	Denmark	13 Dec 48	Visas	92UNTS65	101261
New Zealand	Finland	12 Nov 62	Water Transport	485UNTS331	107064
New Zealand	France	02 Jul 47	Commodity Trade	16UNTS219	100263
New Zealand	France	22 Nov 47	Visas	15UNTS29	100228
New Zealand	France	15 Nov 49	Air Transport	53UNTS247	100785
New Zealand	France	13 Jan 50	Reparations	150UNTS151	101969
New Zealand	France	27 Feb 64	Air Transport	499UNTS191	107298
New Zealand	France	09 Nov 67	Air Transport	68FRJO103	416347
New Zealand	Germany, West	30 Mar 55	Admin Cooperation	271UNTS207	103916
New Zealand	Germany, West	10 Jun 55	Visas	380UNTS307	105462
New Zealand	Germany, West	05 Mar 56	Other Military	402UNTS103	105779
New Zealand	Germany, West	20 Apr 59	General Trade	402UNTS125	105782

PARTY ONE	PARTY TWO	DATE	TOPIC	CITATION	NUMBER
New Zealand	Greece	06 Dec 61	Visas	486UNTS3	107067
New Zealand	IBRD (World Bank)	12 Nov 63	IBRD Project	485UNTS233	107059
New Zealand	IBRD (World Bank)	12 Mar 64	IBRD Project	505UNTS3	107362
New Zealand	IBRD (World Bank)	17 Dec 65	IBRD Project	567UNTS275	108260
New Zealand	IBRD (World Bank)	17 Dec 65	IBRD Project	567UNTS255	108259
New Zealand	India	22 Feb 63	Loans and Credits	486UNTS19	107069
New Zealand	Israel	29 Apr 58	Visas	314UNTS93	104544
New Zealand	Italy	19 Apr 50	Claims and Debts	67UNTS81	100867
New Zealand	Italy	20 Dec 51	Peace/Disarmament	150UNTS157	101970
New Zealand	Italy	25 Jan 61	Visas	435UNTS255	106282
New Zealand	Japan	09 Sep 58	General Trade	325UNTS119	104698
New Zealand	Japan	09 Mar 62	General Trade	485UNTS339	107065
New Zealand	Japan	09 Mar 62	General Trade	485UNTS351	107066
New Zealand	Japan	30 Jan 63	Taxation	517UNTS183	107486
New Zealand	Japan	15 Mar 63	Postal Service	517UNTS229	107487
New Zealand	Japan	12 Jul 67	Specific Resources	0UNTS0	109718
New Zealand	Japan	12 Jul 67	Specific Resources	68JHZ7	439012
New Zealand	Korea, South	31 Jan 67	General Trade	598UNTS91	108656
New Zealand	Luxembourg	29 Jun 51	Visas	101UNTS71	101403
New Zealand	Malaysia	03 Feb 61	General Trade	447UNTS251	106418
New Zealand	Monaco	13 Jun 52	Visas	171UNTS269	102230
New Zealand	Multilateral	27 Mar 41	Military Mission	67UNTS231	200222
New Zealand	Multilateral	19 Apr 44	Scientific Project	89UNTS279	200257
New Zealand	Multilateral	02 Aug 44	Scientific Project	67UNTS221	200221
New Zealand	Multilateral	07 Dec 44	Air Transport	171UNTS345	200501
New Zealand	Multilateral	07 Dec 44	Air Transport	84UNTS389	200252
New Zealand	Multilateral	07 Dec 44	IGO Establishment	15UNTS295	200102
New Zealand	Multilateral	15 Dec 44	Sanitation	16UNTS247	200106
New Zealand	Multilateral	15 Dec 44	Sanitation	17UNTS305	200110
New Zealand	Multilateral	08 Aug 45	General Military	82UNTS279	200251
New Zealand	Multilateral	02 Sep 45	Peace/Disarmament	139UNTS387	200465
New Zealand	Multilateral	16 Nov 45	IGO Establishment	4UNTS275	100052
New Zealand	Multilateral	04 Dec 45	Telecommunications	9UNTS101	100128
New Zealand	Multilateral	14 Jan 46	Reparations	555UNTS69	108105
New Zealand	Multilateral	23 Apr 46	Sanitation	17UNTS3	100265
New Zealand	Multilateral	23 Apr 46	Sanitation	16UNTS179	100257
New Zealand	Multilateral	22 Jul 46	IGO Establishment	14UNTS185	100221
New Zealand	Multilateral	22 Jul 46	IGO Establishment	9UNTS3	100125
New Zealand	Multilateral	27 Jul 46	Patents/Copyrights	90UNTS229	101238
New Zealand	Multilateral	02 Dec 46	Specific Resources	161UNTS72	102124
New Zealand	Multilateral	11 Dec 46	Sanitation	12UNTS179	100186
New Zealand	Multilateral	15 Dec 46	IGO Establishment	18UNTS3	100283
New Zealand	Multilateral	06 Feb 47	IGO Establishment	97UNTS227	101352
New Zealand	Multilateral	08 Feb 47	Patents/Copyrights	14UNTS287	100222
New Zealand	Multilateral	10 Feb 47	Peace/Disarmament	41UNTS135	100644
New Zealand	Multilateral	10 Feb 47	Peace/Disarmament	49UNTS3	100747
New Zealand	Multilateral	10 Feb 47	Peace/Disarmament	41UNTS21	100643
New Zealand	Multilateral	10 Feb 47	Peace/Disarmament	48UNTS203	100746
New Zealand	Multilateral	10 Feb 47	Peace/Disarmament	42UNTS3	100645
New Zealand	Multilateral	03 Mar 47	Humanitarian	11UNTS43	100148
New Zealand	Multilateral	27 May 47	Air Transport	418UNTS161	106021
New Zealand	Multilateral	04 Aug 47	Air Transport	28UNTS41	100418
New Zealand	Multilateral	02 Oct 47	Telecommunications	193UNTS188	102616
New Zealand	Multilateral	11 Oct 47	IGO Establishment	77UNTS143	100998
New Zealand	Multilateral	12 Nov 47	Admin Cooperation	46UNTS169	100709
New Zealand	Multilateral	12 Nov 47	Admin Cooperation	46UNTS201	100710
New Zealand	Multilateral	10 May 48	Culture	289UNTS111	104215
New Zealand	Multilateral	11 May 48	Telecommunications	500UNTS267	107313
New Zealand	Multilateral	10 Jun 48	Humanitarian	191UNTS3	102576
New Zealand	Multilateral	10 Jun 48	Humanitarian	164UNTS113	102163
New Zealand	Multilateral	26 Jun 48	Culture	331UNTS217	104757
New Zealand	Multilateral	24 Jul 48	Sanitation	66UNTS25	100847
New Zealand	Multilateral	15 Nov 48	IGO Establishment	120UNTS59	101615
New Zealand	Multilateral	19 Nov 48	Sanitation	44UNTS277	100688
New Zealand	Multilateral	09 Dec 48	Humanitarian	78UNTS277	101021

PARTY ONE	PARTY TWO	DATE	TOPIC	CITATION	NUMBER
New Zealand	Multilateral	23 Mar 49	Commodity Trade	203UNTS179	102746
New Zealand	Multilateral	04 May 49	Admin Cooperation	30UNTS3	100445
New Zealand	Multilateral	04 May 49	Admin Cooperation	47UNTS159	100728
New Zealand	Multilateral	12 Aug 49	Humanitarian	75UNTS31	100970
New Zealand	Multilateral	12 Aug 49	Humanitarian	75UNTS85	100971
New Zealand	Multilateral	12 Aug 49	IGO Establishment	87UNTS131	101169
New Zealand	Multilateral	12 Aug 49	Humanitarian	75UNTS287	100973
New Zealand	Multilateral	12 Aug 49	General Military	75UNTS135	100972
New Zealand	Multilateral	15 Sep 49	Air Transport	53UNTS235	100783
New Zealand	Multilateral	27 Oct 49	Air Transport	53UNTS241	100784
New Zealand	Multilateral	22 Nov 50	Culture	131UNTS25	101734
New Zealand	Multilateral	07 Dec 50	Admin Cooperation	212UNTS17	102861
New Zealand	Multilateral	25 May 51	Status of Forces	175UNTS215	102303
New Zealand	Multilateral	02 Jul 51	Refugees	189UNTS137	102545
New Zealand	Multilateral	10 Jul 51	Other Military	108UNTS287	101481
New Zealand	Multilateral	29 Jul 51	Other Military	117UNTS85	101585
New Zealand	Multilateral	01 Sep 51	General Military	131UNTS83	101736
New Zealand	Multilateral	08 Sep 51	Peace/Disarmament	136UNTS45	101832
New Zealand	Multilateral	31 Oct 51	Other Military	172UNTS193	102247
New Zealand	Multilateral	06 Dec 51	Admin Cooperation	150UNTS67	101963
New Zealand	Multilateral	08 Jun 52	Other Military	210UNTS317	102843
New Zealand	Multilateral	12 Jun 52	Dispute Settlement	138UNTS183	101869
New Zealand	Multilateral	11 Jul 52	Postal Service	170UNTS3	102221
New Zealand	Multilateral	07 Nov 52	General Trade	221UNTS255	103010
New Zealand	Multilateral	27 Feb 53	Claims and Debts	333UNTS3	104764
New Zealand	Multilateral	11 May 53	Sanitation	456UNTS3	106555
New Zealand	Multilateral	27 Aug 53	Other Military	213UNTS137	102884
New Zealand	Multilateral	26 Oct 53	Status of Forces	207UNTS237	102809
New Zealand	Multilateral	07 Dec 53	Admin Cooperation	182UNTS51	102422
New Zealand	Multilateral	19 Feb 54	Status of Forces	214UNTS51	102899
New Zealand	Multilateral	22 Feb 54	Other Military	188UNTS273	102531
New Zealand	Multilateral	12 May 54	Admin Cooperation	327UNTS3	104714
New Zealand	Multilateral	14 May 54	Culture	249UNTS215	103511
New Zealand	Multilateral	14 Jun 54	Air Transport	320UNTS217	104644
New Zealand	Multilateral	14 Jun 54	Air Transport	320UNTS209	104643
New Zealand	Multilateral	08 Sep 54	Milit Assistance	209UNTS23	102819
New Zealand	Multilateral	28 Sep 54	Reparations	207UNTS293	102812
New Zealand	Multilateral	25 May 55	IGO Establishment	264UNTS117	103791
New Zealand	Multilateral	21 Sep 55	Other Military	269UNTS241	103885
New Zealand	Multilateral	28 Sep 55	Air Transport	478UNTS371	106943
New Zealand	Multilateral	12 Oct 55	IGO Establishment	560UNTS3	108165
New Zealand	Multilateral	05 Mar 56	Other Military	326UNTS181	104712
New Zealand	Multilateral	05 Mar 56	Other Military	326UNTS169	104711
New Zealand	Multilateral	25 Apr 56	Commodity Trade	270UNTS103	103896
New Zealand	Multilateral	26 Oct 56	IGO Establishment	276UNTS3	103988
New Zealand	Multilateral	20 Feb 57	Consul/Citizenship	309UNTS65	104468
New Zealand	Multilateral	03 Oct 57	Postal Service	364UNTS3	105211
New Zealand	Multilateral	03 Oct 57	Postal Service	364UNTS331	105212
New Zealand	Multilateral	29 Apr 58	Territory Boundary	499UNTS311	107302
New Zealand	Multilateral	29 Apr 58	Dispute Settlement	450UNTS169	106466
New Zealand	Multilateral	29 Apr 58	Water Transport	450UNTS11	106465
New Zealand	Multilateral	29 Apr 58	Specific Resources	559UNTS285	108164
New Zealand	Multilateral	29 Apr 58	Territory Boundary	516UNTS205	107477
New Zealand	Multilateral	01 Dec 58	Commodity Trade	385UNTS137	105534
New Zealand	Multilateral	03 Dec 58	Admin Cooperation	416UNTS51	105995
New Zealand	Multilateral	03 Dec 58	Admin Cooperation	398UNTS9	105715
New Zealand	Multilateral	06 Apr 59	Commodity Trade	349UNTS167	105013
New Zealand	Multilateral	01 Dec 59	Territory Boundary	402UNTS71	105778
New Zealand	Multilateral	17 Jun 60	Humanitarian	536UNTS27	107794
New Zealand	Multilateral	19 Sep 60	IBRD Project	444UNTS259	106371
New Zealand	Multilateral	14 Dec 60	Education	429UNTS93	106193
New Zealand	Multilateral	23 Jan 61	Postal Service	530UNTS141	107679
New Zealand	Multilateral	30 Mar 61	Sanitation	520UNTS151	107515
New Zealand	Multilateral	18 Apr 61	Dispute Settlement	500UNTS243	107312
New Zealand	Multilateral	18 Apr 61	Consul/Citizenship	500UNTS95	107310

PARTY ONE	PARTY TWO	DATE	TOPIC	CITATION	NUMBER
New Zealand	Multilateral	21 Jun 61	IGO Establishment	514UNTS209	107449
New Zealand	Multilateral	15 May 62	Commodity Trade	444UNTS3	106367
New Zealand	Multilateral	10 Sep 62	Other Military	502UNTS3	107323
New Zealand	Multilateral	28 Sep 62	IGO Establishment	469UNTS169	106791
New Zealand	Multilateral	10 Dec 62	Culture	521UNTS231	107525
New Zealand	Multilateral	05 Aug 63	Sanitation	480UNTS43	106964
New Zealand	Multilateral	10 Jul 64	Postal Service	611UNTS105	108845
New Zealand	Multilateral	10 Jul 64	Postal Service	611UNTS387	108846
New Zealand	Multilateral	10 Jul 64	Postal Service	612UNTS3	108847
New Zealand	Multilateral	10 Jul 64	Postal Service	611UNTS7	108844
New Zealand	Multilateral	13 Jul 64	ILO Labor	569UNTS65	108279
New Zealand	Multilateral	20 Aug 64	Telecommunications	514UNTS25	107441
New Zealand	Multilateral	07 Nov 64	Sanitation	548UNTS3	107965
New Zealand	Multilateral	01 Dec 64	Water Transport	550UNTS133	108012
New Zealand	Multilateral	26 Nov 65	Recognition	598UNTS81	108655
New Zealand	Multilateral	04 Dec 65	IGO Establishment	571UNTS123	108303
New Zealand	Multilateral	05 Apr 66	Water Transport	640UNTS133	109159
New Zealand	Multilateral	04 May 66	IBRD Project	575UNTS49	108354
New Zealand	Multilateral	27 Jan 67	Scientific Project	610UNTS205	108843
New Zealand	Multilateral	09 Mar 67	Other Military	603UNTS135	108730
New Zealand	Multilateral	03 May 67	IGO Operations	0UNTS0	110764
New Zealand	Multilateral	06 Nov 67	Other Military	640UNTS87	109155
New Zealand	Multilateral	18 Mar 68	Commodity Trade	0UNTS0	109262
New Zealand	Multilateral	01 Jul 68	Peace/Disarmament	0UNTS0	110485
New Zealand	Multilateral	01 Aug 68	Culture	0UNTS0	109368
New Zealand	Multilateral	24 Dec 68	Commodity Trade	0UNTS0	109369
New Zealand	Multilateral	27 Jan 69	Telecommunications	0UNTS0	109664
New Zealand	Multilateral	11 Jun 69	Scientific Project	0UNTS0	110100
New Zealand	Multilateral	12 Jan 70	Commodity Trade	0UNTS0	110603
New Zealand	Netherlands	30 Oct 47	General Economic	76UNTS41	100977
New Zealand	Netherlands	03 Mar 49	Visas	34UNTS207	100538
New Zealand	Netherlands	16 Oct 50	Non-ILO Labor	83UNTS269	101111
New Zealand	Norway	03 May 46	Claims and Debts	16UNTS211	100262
New Zealand	Norway	22 Nov 49	Visas	51UNTS123	100760
New Zealand	Pakistan	28 Jun 48	Postal Service	91UNTS235	101253
New Zealand	Pakistan	17 Sep 48	Postal Service	91UNTS275	101254
New Zealand	Philippines	09 May 60	Postal Service	486UNTS65	107073
New Zealand	Poland	07 Jul 65	General Trade	548UNTS19	107966
New Zealand	Singapore	04 Apr 68	Air Transport	0UNTS0	109480
New Zealand	Spain	02 Oct 61	Visas	453UNTS11	106516
New Zealand	State/IGO Group	17 Jul 70	Tech Assistance	0UNTS0	110593
New Zealand	State/IGO Group	17 Jul 70	IGO Operations	0UNTS0	110592
New Zealand	Sweden	04 Jun 48	Visas	18UNTS171	100286
New Zealand	Sweden	16 Apr 56	Taxation	274UNTS259	103971
New Zealand	Switzerland	30 Jul 48	Visas	18UNTS177	100287
New Zealand	Switzerland	09 Oct 52	General Trade	171UNTS275	102231
New Zealand	Switzerland	30 Dec 58	Taxation	380UNTS313	105463
New Zealand	Thailand	24 Dec 59	Customs	351UNTS197	105023
New Zealand	Turkey	05 Jun 58	Visas	317UNTS123	104599
New Zealand	UK Great Britain	27 May 47	Taxation	17UNTS211	100277
New Zealand	UK Great Britain	12 Nov 48	Milit Assistance	162UNTS197	102136
New Zealand	UK Great Britain	28 Nov 51	General Trade	127UNTS263	101707
New Zealand	UK Great Britain	20 Dec 55	Non-ILO Labor	268UNTS243	103860
New Zealand	UK Great Britain	04 Jul 57	Milit Assistance	402UNTS109	105780
New Zealand	UK Great Britain	20 Sep 57	Sanitation	287UNTS105	104180
New Zealand	UK Great Britain	12 Aug 59	General Trade	354UNTS161	105062
New Zealand	UK Great Britain	21 Sep 59	Milit Assistance	401UNTS51	105762
New Zealand	UK Great Britain	13 Jun 61	Air Transport	497UNTS293	107273
New Zealand	UK Great Britain	15 May 63	Commodity Trade	486UNTS11	107068
New Zealand	UK Great Britain	13 Jul 66	Taxation	598UNTS121	108658
New Zealand	UK Great Britain	02 Apr 68	General Military	0UNTS0	109206
New Zealand	UK Great Britain	24 Sep 68	Finance	0UNTS0	109818
New Zealand	UK Great Britain	19 Jun 69	Non-ILO Labor	0UNTS0	110439
New Zealand	UN Special Fund	28 Jun 63	Non-IBRD Project	470UNTS3	106792
New Zealand	UNICEF (Children)	26 Aug 54	Direct Aid	198UNTS173	102663

PARTY ONE	PARTY TWO	DATE	TOPIC	CITATION	NUMBER
New Zealand	United Nations	02 Feb 61	Humanitarian	391UNTS23	105614
New Zealand	United Nations	21 Feb 66	IGO Operations	555UNTS163	108110
New Zealand	USA (United States)	03 Sep 42	Milit Assistance	24UNTS185	200142
New Zealand	USA (United States)	30 Sep 42	Milit Servic/Citiz	13UNTS139	200075
New Zealand	USA (United States)	28 Jan 43	Admin Cooperation	121UNTS123	200395
New Zealand	USA (United States)	10 Jul 46	Milit Assistance	6UNTS341	100087
New Zealand	USA (United States)	03 Dec 46	Air Transport	7UNTS175	100099
New Zealand	USA (United States)	24 Apr 47	Patents/Copyrights	16UNTS79	100250
New Zealand	USA (United States)	16 Mar 48	Taxation	127UNTS133	101703
New Zealand	USA (United States)	14 Sep 48	General Military	18UNTS251	100295
New Zealand	USA (United States)	14 Mar 49	Visas	32UNTS369	100508
New Zealand	USA (United States)	19 Jun 52	Milit Assistance	178UNTS315	102347
New Zealand	USA (United States)	13 Jun 56	Atomic Energy	253UNTS155	103582
New Zealand	USA (United States)	05 May 58	Visas	317UNTS59	104594
New Zealand	USA (United States)	24 Dec 58	Scientific Project	324UNTS111	104680
New Zealand	USA (United States)	30 Oct 59	Tech Assistance	361UNTS21	105170
New Zealand	USA (United States)	23 Mar 60	Atomic Energy	371UNTS147	105276
New Zealand	USA (United States)	05 Mar 62	General Economic	446UNTS39	106401
New Zealand	USA (United States)	08 Jun 62	Loans and Credits	458UNTS209	106602
New Zealand	USA (United States)	15 May 63	Military Mission	477UNTS55	106915
New Zealand	USA (United States)	17 Feb 64	Commodity Trade	511UNTS37	107424
New Zealand	USA (United States)	24 Jun 64	Air Transport	524UNTS101	107568
New Zealand	USA (United States)	21 Jun 67	Gen Communications	0UNTS0	109205
New Zealand	USA (United States)	09 Jul 68	Scientific Project	0UNTS0	109208
New Zealand	USA (United States)	03 Sep 69	Milit Assistance	0UNTS0	110407
New Zealand	USA (United States)	29 Jan 70	General Trade	0UNTS0	110617
New Zealand	USA (United States)	03 Feb 70	Education	0UNTS0	110621
New Zealand	USA (United States)	20 Mar 70	Air Transport	0UNTS0	110630
New Zealand	USSR (Soviet Union)	27 Mar 62	Visas	16SUGG132	470005
New Zealand	USSR (Soviet Union)	01 Aug 63	General Trade	486UNTS27	107070
New Zealand	Western Samoa	01 Aug 62	General Amity	453UNTS3	106515
New Zealand	Western Samoa	30 Nov 62	Recognition	476UNTS3	106898
New Zealand	Western Samoa	24 Jan 63	Air Transport	499UNTS21	107290
New Zealand	Western Samoa	31 Dec 63	Scientific Project	521UNTS163	107519
New Zealand	Western Samoa	23 Jul 64	Non-IBRD Project	521UNTS173	107520
New Zealand	Western Samoa	29 Jul 66	Direct Aid	598UNTS115	108657
New Zealand	WHO (World Health)	29 Aug 67	Direct Aid	607UNTS57	108795
New Zealand	Yugoslavia	27 Feb 51	Reparations	150UNTS165	101971
New Zealand	Yugoslavia	09 Sep 60	General Trade	402UNTS119	105781
Newfoundland	Canada	29 Jul 46	Air Transport	17UNTS169	100275
Newfoundland	Multilateral	31 Mar 46	Milit Installation	17UNTS159	100274
Newfoundland	Multilateral	08 Feb 49	Specific Resources	157UNTS157	102053
Nicaragua	Argentina	25 Nov 64	Culture	0UNTS0	109556
Nicaragua	Canada	19 Dec 46	General Trade	236UNTS229	103326
Nicaragua	France	22 Dec 66	Health/Educ/Welfare	68FRJO1105	416338
Nicaragua	Germany, West	08 Apr 65	Tech Assistance	65WBGA169	424485
Nicaragua	Germany, West	09 Oct 68	Loans and Credits	69WBGA11	424486
Nicaragua	Honduras	22 Jun 57	Specif Claim/Waive	277UNTS159	104005
Nicaragua	IBRD (World Bank)	07 Jun 51	IBRD Project	158UNTS277	102068
Nicaragua	IBRD (World Bank)	07 Jun 51	IBRD Project	158UNTS215	102067
Nicaragua	IBRD (World Bank)	29 Oct 51	IBRD Project	159UNTS35	102082
Nicaragua	IBRD (World Bank)	04 Sep 53	IBRD Project	186UNTS117	102487
Nicaragua	IBRD (World Bank)	04 Sep 53	IBRD Project	186UNTS137	102488
Nicaragua	IBRD (World Bank)	08 Jul 55	IBRD Project	229UNTS97	103162
Nicaragua	IBRD (World Bank)	08 Jul 55	IBRD Project	229UNTS123	103163
Nicaragua	IBRD (World Bank)	26 Aug 55	IBRD Project	229UNTS145	103164
Nicaragua	IBRD (World Bank)	22 May 56	IBRD Project	253UNTS233	103586
Nicaragua	IBRD (World Bank)	22 Jun 60	IBRD Project	384UNTS243	105522
Nicaragua	IBRD (World Bank)	01 Mar 63	IBRD Project	481UNTS15	106976
Nicaragua	IBRD (World Bank)	05 Oct 66	IBRD Project	582UNTS231	108465
Nicaragua	IBRD (World Bank)	13 Mar 67	IBRD Project	632UNTS177	109020
Nicaragua	IBRD (World Bank)	10 Apr 68	Loans and Credits	0UNTS0	109300
Nicaragua	IBRD (World Bank)	21 Jun 68	IBRD Project	0UNTS0	109366
Nicaragua	IDA (Devel Assoc)	07 Sep 62	Non-IBRD Project	478UNTS313	106940
Nicaragua	Mexico	19 Nov 46	Telecommunications	51MEXD1105	444031

PARTY ONE	PARTY TWO	DATE	TOPIC	CITATION	NUMBER
Nicaragua	Mexico	17 Jan 66	Culture	68MEXD1005	444033
Nicaragua	Mexico	17 Jan 66	Tech Assistance	68MEXD510	444032
Nicaragua	Multilateral	25 Jun 36	Privil/Immunities	161UNTS217	200486
Nicaragua	Multilateral	17 Feb 40	Privil/Immunities	161UNTS229	200487
Nicaragua	Multilateral	30 Jul 40	Admin Cooperation	161UNTS253	200488
Nicaragua	Multilateral	12 Oct 40	Specific Resources	161UNTS193	200485
Nicaragua	Multilateral	28 Nov 40	Commodity Trade	139UNTS159	200452
Nicaragua	Multilateral	15 Jan 44	IGO Establishment	161UNTS281	200489
Nicaragua	Multilateral	19 Apr 44	Scientific Project	89UNTS279	200257
Nicaragua	Multilateral	02 Aug 44	Scientific Project	67UNTS221	200221
Nicaragua	Multilateral	07 Dec 44	Air Transport	171UNTS387	200502
Nicaragua	Multilateral	07 Dec 44	Air Transport	171UNTS345	200501
Nicaragua	Multilateral	07 Dec 44	Air Transport	84UNTS389	200252
Nicaragua	Multilateral	07 Dec 44	IGO Establishment	15UNTS295	200102
Nicaragua	Multilateral	15 Dec 44	Sanitation	16UNTS247	200106
Nicaragua	Multilateral	15 Dec 44	Sanitation	17UNTS305	200110
Nicaragua	Multilateral	16 Nov 45	IGO Establishment	4UNTS275	100052
Nicaragua	Multilateral	23 Apr 46	Sanitation	17UNTS3	100265
Nicaragua	Multilateral	23 Apr 46	Sanitation	16UNTS179	100257
Nicaragua	Multilateral	22 Jul 46	IGO Establishment	9UNTS3	100125
Nicaragua	Multilateral	22 Jul 46	IGO Establishment	14UNTS185	100221
Nicaragua	Multilateral	27 Jul 46	Patents/Copyrights	90UNTS229	101238
Nicaragua	Multilateral	03 Sep 46	Commodity Trade	139UNTS3	101872
Nicaragua	Multilateral	11 Dec 46	Sanitation	12UNTS179	100186
Nicaragua	Multilateral	27 May 47	Air Transport	418UNTS161	106021
Nicaragua	Multilateral	02 Sep 47	General Military	21UNTS77	100324
Nicaragua	Multilateral	02 Oct 47	Telecommunications	193UNTS188	102616
Nicaragua	Multilateral	12 Nov 47	Admin Cooperation	53UNTS49	100772
Nicaragua	Multilateral	12 Nov 47	Admin Cooperation	53UNTS39	100771
Nicaragua	Multilateral	12 Nov 47	Admin Cooperation	53UNTS13	100770
Nicaragua	Multilateral	30 Apr 48	IGO Establishment	119UNTS3	101609
Nicaragua	Multilateral	30 Apr 48	Dispute Settlement	30UNTS55	100449
Nicaragua	Multilateral	10 Jun 48	Humanitarian	164UNTS113	102163
Nicaragua	Multilateral	19 Nov 48	Sanitation	44UNTS277	100688
Nicaragua	Multilateral	29 Nov 48	IGO Establishment	120UNTS13	101613
Nicaragua	Multilateral	09 Dec 48	Humanitarian	78UNTS277	101021
Nicaragua	Multilateral	23 Mar 49	Commodity Trade	203UNTS179	102746
Nicaragua	Multilateral	04 May 49	Admin Cooperation	30UNTS3	100445
Nicaragua	Multilateral	09 Jul 49	Telecommunications	168UNTS143	102218
Nicaragua	Multilateral	12 Aug 49	Humanitarian	75UNTS287	100973
Nicaragua	Multilateral	12 Aug 49	Humanitarian	75UNTS85	100971
Nicaragua	Multilateral	12 Aug 49	Humanitarian	75UNTS31	100970
Nicaragua	Multilateral	12 Aug 49	General Military	75UNTS135	100972
Nicaragua	Multilateral	06 Apr 50	Admin Cooperation	119UNTS99	101610
Nicaragua	Multilateral	22 Nov 50	Culture	131UNTS25	101734
Nicaragua	Multilateral	25 May 51	Status of Forces	175UNTS215	102303
Nicaragua	Multilateral	08 Sep 51	Peace/Disarmament	136UNTS45	101832
Nicaragua	Multilateral	14 Oct 51	IGO Establishment	122UNTS3	101631
Nicaragua	Multilateral	06 Dec 51	Admin Cooperation	150UNTS67	101963
Nicaragua	Multilateral	10 May 52	Taxation	439UNTS233	106332
Nicaragua	Multilateral	10 May 52	Admin Cooperation	439UNTS193	106330
Nicaragua	Multilateral	10 May 52	Admin Cooperation	439UNTS217	106331
Nicaragua	Multilateral	11 Jul 52	Postal Service	170UNTS269	102223
Nicaragua	Multilateral	11 Jul 52	Postal Service	170UNTS63	102222
Nicaragua	Multilateral	11 Jul 52	Postal Service	170UNTS3	102221
Nicaragua	Multilateral	11 Jul 52	Postal Service	171UNTS3	102224
Nicaragua	Multilateral	11 Jul 52	IGO Establishment	169UNTS3	102220
Nicaragua	Multilateral	11 Jul 52	Postal Service	171UNTS143	102226
Nicaragua	Multilateral	11 Jul 52	Postal Service	171UNTS89	102225
Nicaragua	Multilateral	06 Sep 52	Patents/Copyrights	216UNTS132	102937
Nicaragua	Multilateral	16 Dec 52	Tech Assistance	158UNTS407	102074
Nicaragua	Multilateral	31 Mar 53	Privil/Immunities	193UNTS136	102613
Nicaragua	Multilateral	11 May 53	Sanitation	456UNTS3	106555
Nicaragua	Multilateral	14 May 54	Culture	249UNTS215	103511
Nicaragua	Multilateral	14 Jun 54	Air Transport	320UNTS217	104644

PARTY ONE	PARTY TWO	DATE	TOPIC	CITATION	NUMBER
Nicaragua	Multilateral	14 Jun 54	Air Transport	320UNTS209	104643
Nicaragua	Multilateral	25 May 55	IGO Establishment	264UNTS117	103791
Nicaragua	Multilateral	10 Feb 56	Tech Assistance	228UNTS189	103151
Nicaragua	Multilateral	25 Apr 56	Commodity Trade	270UNTS103	103896
Nicaragua	Multilateral	02 Jul 56	Tech Assistance	248UNTS37	103484
Nicaragua	Multilateral	26 Oct 56	IGO Establishment	276UNTS3	103988
Nicaragua	Multilateral	08 Nov 56	Commodity Trade	470UNTS171	106809
Nicaragua	Multilateral	22 Feb 57	Tech Assistance	274UNTS93	103960
Nicaragua	Multilateral	03 Oct 57	Postal Service	366UNTS87	105216
Nicaragua	Multilateral	03 Oct 57	Postal Service	366UNTS3	105215
Nicaragua	Multilateral	03 Oct 57	Postal Service	364UNTS331	105212
Nicaragua	Multilateral	03 Oct 57	Postal Service	365UNTS3	105213
Nicaragua	Multilateral	03 Oct 57	Postal Service	366UNTS141	105217
Nicaragua	Multilateral	03 Oct 57	Postal Service	364UNTS3	105211
Nicaragua	Multilateral	03 Oct 57	Postal Service	365UNTS207	105214
Nicaragua	Multilateral	03 Oct 57	Postal Service	366UNTS255	105219
Nicaragua	Multilateral	10 Jun 58	Land Transport	454UNTS115	106540
Nicaragua	Multilateral	10 Jun 58	General Economic	454UNTS47	106539
Nicaragua	Multilateral	10 Jun 58	Land Transport	454UNTS211	106541
Nicaragua	Multilateral	01 Dec 58	Commodity Trade	385UNTS137	105534
Nicaragua	Multilateral	08 Apr 59	IGO Establishment	389UNTS69	105593
Nicaragua	Multilateral	01 Sep 59	Customs	454UNTS289	106542
Nicaragua	Multilateral	18 Nov 59	IGO Establishment	390UNTS227	105610
Nicaragua	Multilateral	03 Dec 59	Tech Assistance	345UNTS251	104971
Nicaragua	Multilateral	26 Jan 60	IGO Establishment	439UNTS249	106333
Nicaragua	Multilateral	26 Feb 60	Air Transport	418UNTS171	106022
Nicaragua	Multilateral	17 Jun 60	Humanitarian	536UNTS27	107794
Nicaragua	Multilateral	28 Jul 60	IGO Establishment	485UNTS3	107042
Nicaragua	Multilateral	13 Dec 60	IGO Establishment	455UNTS204	106544
Nicaragua	Multilateral	13 Dec 60	General Economic	455UNTS3	106543
Nicaragua	Multilateral	30 Mar 61	Sanitation	520UNTS151	107515
Nicaragua	Multilateral	21 Jun 61	IGO Establishment	514UNTS209	107449
Nicaragua	Multilateral	26 Mar 62	IGO Establishment	539UNTS67	107825
Nicaragua	Multilateral	28 Sep 62	IGO Establishment	469UNTS169	106791
Nicaragua	Multilateral	12 Dec 62	IGO Establishment	552UNTS15	108048
Nicaragua	Multilateral	05 Aug 63	Sanitation	480UNTS43	106964
Nicaragua	Multilateral	21 Oct 63	Tech Assistance	480UNTS197	106969
Nicaragua	Multilateral	14 Dec 63	IGO Establishment	507UNTS149	107399
Nicaragua	Multilateral	10 Jul 64	Postal Service	611UNTS387	108846
Nicaragua	Multilateral	10 Jul 64	Postal Service	613UNTS3	108851
Nicaragua	Multilateral	10 Jul 64	Postal Service	612UNTS361	108849
Nicaragua	Multilateral	10 Jul 64	Postal Service	613UNTS3	108850
Nicaragua	Multilateral	10 Jul 64	Postal Service	612UNTS233	108848
Nicaragua	Multilateral	10 Jul 64	Postal Service	611UNTS7	108844
Nicaragua	Multilateral	10 Jul 64	Postal Service	612UNTS3	108847
Nicaragua	Multilateral	10 Jul 64	Postal Service	613UNTS193	108852
Nicaragua	Multilateral	10 Jul 64	Postal Service	611UNTS105	108845
Nicaragua	Multilateral	09 Mar 65	Water Transport	591UNTS265	108564
Nicaragua	Multilateral	14 Feb 67	General Military	634UNTS281	109068
Nicaragua	Multilateral	18 Mar 68	Commodity Trade	0UNTS0	109262
Nicaragua	Multilateral	01 Jun 68	General Trade	0UNTS0	110835
Nicaragua	Multilateral	24 Dec 68	Commodity Trade	0UNTS0	109369
Nicaragua	Norway	17 Oct 60	Visas	3NORT815	451120
Nicaragua	Norway	27 Mar 68	Visas	3NORT815	451121
Nicaragua	Peru	14 Oct 59	Air Transport	392UNTS303	105649
Nicaragua	Spain	25 Jul 61	Consul/Citizenship	62SPBO205	460201
Nicaragua	Taiwan	25 Apr 61	Culture	423UNTS139	106090
Nicaragua	UK Great Britain	25 May 51	Sanitation	101UNTS77	101404
Nicaragua	UK Great Britain	05 Feb 69	Visas	0UNTS0	109666
Nicaragua	UN Special Fund	20 Jan 61	Direct Aid	387UNTS15	105555
Nicaragua	UNICEF (Children)	17 Jan 50	Tech Assistance	65UNTS76	100832
Nicaragua	United Nations	03 Dec 63	IGO Status/Immunit	482UNTS329	107002
Nicaragua	USA (United States)	11 Jan 41	Specific Resources	117UNTS253	200374
Nicaragua	USA (United States)	08 Apr 42	Land Transport	24UNTS145	200138
Nicaragua	USA (United States)	08 Apr 42	Milit Installation	132UNTS343	200439

PARTY ONE	PARTY TWO	DATE	TOPIC	CITATION	NUMBER
Nicaragua	USA (United States)	22 May 42	Sanitation	105UNTS141	200328
Nicaragua	USA (United States)	27 Oct 42	Scientific Project	99UNTS287	200283
Nicaragua	USA (United States)	25 Oct 43	Military Mission	29UNTS383	200173
Nicaragua	USA (United States)	01 Feb 50	Tech Assistance	99UNTS25	101368
Nicaragua	USA (United States)	28 Feb 50	General Trade	132UNTS169	101758
Nicaragua	USA (United States)	23 Dec 50	Tech Assistance	92UNTS155	101268
Nicaragua	USA (United States)	31 Jan 51	Education	150UNTS3	101960
Nicaragua	USA (United States)	31 Jan 51	Sanitation	160UNTS121	102105
Nicaragua	USA (United States)	20 Apr 51	Land Transport	138UNTS57	101859
Nicaragua	USA (United States)	12 Dec 51	Status of Forces	167UNTS151	102205
Nicaragua	USA (United States)	09 Oct 52	Consul/Citizenship	184UNTS105	102442
Nicaragua	USA (United States)	19 Nov 52	Military Mission	186UNTS3	102478
Nicaragua	USA (United States)	30 Jun 53	Tech Assistance	215UNTS133	102917
Nicaragua	USA (United States)	02 Sep 53	Land Transport	215UNTS69	102911
Nicaragua	USA (United States)	19 Nov 53	Military Mission	206UNTS117	102787
Nicaragua	USA (United States)	23 Apr 54	Milit Assistance	229UNTS37	103159
Nicaragua	USA (United States)	22 Oct 55	Visas	358UNTS51	105123
Nicaragua	USA (United States)	21 Jan 56	General Amity	367UNTS3	105224
Nicaragua	USA (United States)	19 Mar 56	Postal Service	275UNTS231	103984
Nicaragua	USA (United States)	02 Aug 56	Land Transport	281UNTS99	104073
Nicaragua	USA (United States)	16 Oct 56	Gen Communications	282UNTS29	104090
Nicaragua	USA (United States)	09 Feb 57	Milit Assistance	279UNTS191	104040
Nicaragua	USA (United States)	11 Jun 57	Atomic Energy	304UNTS267	104402
Nicaragua	USA (United States)	05 Sep 58	Milit Installation	336UNTS33	104797
Nicaragua	USA (United States)	14 Apr 59	Admin Cooperation	343UNTS119	104922
Nicaragua	USA (United States)	30 Mar 62	Tech Assistance	456UNTS241	106559
Nicaragua	USA (United States)	09 May 66	Finance	0UNTS0	110043
Nicaragua	USA (United States)	20 Sep 66	Gen Communications	607UNTS167	108804
Nicaragua	USA (United States)	25 May 68	General Aid	0UNTS0	110143
Nicaragua	USA (United States)	25 Feb 70	General Trade	0UNTS0	110812
Nicaragua	WHO (World Health)	10 Nov 50	Tech Assistance	110UNTS155	101508
Nicaragua	WHO (World Health)	02 Jan 51	Sanitation	103UNTS107	101428
Niger	Accept UN Charter	07 Aug 60	UN Charter	375UNTS95	105358
Niger	France	11 Jul 60	Recognition	60FRRT52	415339
Niger	France	24 Apr 61	General Amity	62FRRT8	415340
Niger	France	28 May 62	Air Transport	63FRRT1	415341
Niger	France	29 Nov 62	Customs	63FRRT28	415342
Niger	France	01 Jun 65	Finance	66FRRT48	415343
Niger	France	23 Sep 65	Extradition	65FRRT90	415344
Niger	France	25 Feb 67	Mass Media	68FRJO204	416345
Niger	France	25 Feb 67	Mass Media	0UNTS0	109261
Niger	France	16 Feb 70	Visas	0UNTS0	110535
Niger	Germany, West	14 Jun 61	Direct Aid	61WBGA195	424503
Niger	Germany, West	14 Jun 61	General Economic	61WBGA195	424502
Niger	Germany, West	30 Jun 64	Loans and Credits	65WBGA14	424504
Niger	Germany, West	29 Oct 64	Claims and Debts	65WGBB1402	425505
Niger	Germany, West	18 Mar 68	Loans and Credits	68WBGA108	424506
Niger	Germany, West	19 Jul 69	Loans and Credits	69WBGA193	424507
Niger	IDA (Devel Assoc)	24 Jun 64	Non-IBRD Project	554UNTS93	108098
Niger	IDA (Devel Assoc)	23 Sep 68	Non-IBRD Project	0UNTS0	109627
Niger	Israel	23 Jul 63	Visas	515UNTS257	107463
Niger	Mali	15 Jan 64	Air Transport	499UNTS197	107299
Niger	Multilateral	07 Dec 44	Air Transport	84UNTS389	200252
Niger	Multilateral	07 Dec 44	IGO Establishment	15UNTS295	200102
Niger	Multilateral	11 Dec 46	Sanitation	12UNTS179	100186
Niger	Multilateral	12 Nov 47	Admin Cooperation	53UNTS49	100772
Niger	Multilateral	12 Nov 47	Admin Cooperation	53UNTS13	100770
Niger	Multilateral	19 Jun 48	Air Transport	310UNTS151	104492
Niger	Multilateral	24 Jul 48	Sanitation	66UNTS25	100847
Niger	Multilateral	04 May 49	Admin Cooperation	98UNTS101	101358
Niger	Multilateral	04 May 49	Admin Cooperation	92UNTS19	101257
Niger	Multilateral	07 Dec 50	Admin Cooperation	212UNTS17	102861
Niger	Multilateral	02 Jul 51	Refugees	189UNTS137	102545
Niger	Multilateral	07 Oct 52	Admin Cooperation	310UNTS181	104493
Niger	Multilateral	31 Mar 53	Privil/Immunities	193UNTS136	102613

PARTY ONE	PARTY TWO	DATE	TOPIC	CITATION	NUMBER
Niger	Multilateral	11 May 53	Sanitation	456UNTS3	106555
Niger	Multilateral	07 Dec 53	Admin Cooperation	182UNTS51	102422
Niger	Multilateral	29 Jul 54	Sanitation	249UNTS45	103500
Niger	Multilateral	28 Sep 55	Air Transport	478UNTS371	106943
Niger	Multilateral	20 Jun 56	Admin Cooperation	268UNTS3	103850
Niger	Multilateral	01 May 57	Admin Cooperation	284UNTS201	104138
Niger	Multilateral	29 Apr 58	Territory Boundary	516UNTS205	107477
Niger	Multilateral	10 Jun 58	Admin Cooperation	330UNTS3	104739
Niger	Multilateral	26 Jan 60	IGO Establishment	439UNTS249	106333
Niger	Multilateral	14 Dec 60	Education	429UNTS93	106193
Niger	Multilateral	30 Mar 61	Sanitation	520UNTS151	107515
Niger	Multilateral	18 Apr 61	Consul/Citizenship	500UNTS223	107311
Niger	Multilateral	18 Apr 61	Consul/Citizenship	500UNTS95	107310
Niger	Multilateral	18 Apr 61	Dispute Settlement	500UNTS243	107312
Niger	Multilateral	08 Jun 61	Customs	473UNTS153	106862
Niger	Multilateral	08 Jun 61	Customs	473UNTS187	106863
Niger	Multilateral	21 Jun 61	IGO Establishment	514UNTS209	107449
Niger	Multilateral	26 Oct 61	Patents/Copyrights	496UNTS43	107247
Niger	Multilateral	25 May 62	IGO Establishment	486UNTS103	107075
Niger	Multilateral	22 Jun 62	ILO Labor	494UNTS249	107237
Niger	Multilateral	12 Aug 62	Tech Assistance	443UNTS266	106365
Niger	Multilateral	10 Dec 62	Culture	521UNTS231	107525
Niger	Multilateral	24 Apr 63	Consul/Citizenship	596UNTS487	108640
Niger	Multilateral	24 Apr 63	Consul/Citizenship	596UNTS261	108638
Niger	Multilateral	25 May 63	IGO Establishment	479UNTS39	106947
Niger	Multilateral	04 Aug 63	IGO Establishment	510UNTS3	107408
Niger	Multilateral	05 Aug 63	Sanitation	480UNTS43	106964
Niger	Multilateral	14 Sep 63	Air Transport	0UNTS0	110106
Niger	Multilateral	26 Oct 63	Water Transport	587UNTS9	108506
Niger	Multilateral	10 Jul 64	Postal Service	613UNTS127	108853
Niger	Multilateral	10 Jul 64	Postal Service	612UNTS3	108847
Niger	Multilateral	10 Jul 64	Postal Service	611UNTS387	108846
Niger	Multilateral	10 Jul 64	Postal Service	613UNTS193	108852
Niger	Multilateral	10 Jul 64	Postal Service	613UNTS3	108851
Niger	Multilateral	10 Jul 64	Postal Service	612UNTS361	108849
Niger	Multilateral	10 Jul 64	Postal Service	611UNTS105	108845
Niger	Multilateral	10 Jul 64	Postal Service	613UNTS3	108850
Niger	Multilateral	10 Jul 64	Postal Service	612UNTS233	108848
Niger	Multilateral	10 Jul 64	Postal Service	611UNTS7	108844
Niger	Multilateral	25 Nov 64	Water Transport	587UNTS19	108507
Niger	Multilateral	01 Dec 64	Water Transport	550UNTS133	108012
Niger	Multilateral	18 Mar 65	Dispute Settlement	575UNTS159	108359
Niger	Multilateral	08 Jul 65	General Trade	597UNTS3	108641
Niger	Multilateral	27 May 66	IGO Establishment	637UNTS0	109121
Niger	Multilateral	12 Jul 66	Visas	578UNTS23	108384
Niger	Multilateral	27 Jan 67	Scientific Project	610UNTS205	108843
Niger	Multilateral	04 May 67	IGO Establishment	595UNTS287	108623
Niger	Multilateral	20 Jul 67	General Economic	0UNTS0	109259
Niger	Multilateral	22 Sep 67	Non-IBRD Project	0UNTS0	109258
Niger	Multilateral	22 Apr 68	Scientific Project	0UNTS0	109574
Niger	Multilateral	11 Jun 68	Scientific Project	0UNTS0	109884
Niger	Multilateral	24 Sep 68	Air Transport	0UNTS0	110612
Niger	Norway	15 Feb 66	Visas	3NORT956	451122
Niger	Poland	09 Nov 61	Health/Educ/Welfare	61PZUM229	458092
Niger	Switzerland	28 Mar 62	General Economic	63SWRO46	462148
Niger	Tunisia	18 Oct 66	Air Transport	0UNTS0	110468
Niger	UN Special Fund	26 Feb 62	Direct Aid	423UNTS83	106086
Niger	UNICEF (Children)	05 Dec 62	IGO Operations	503UNTS195	107344
Niger	United Nations	01 Oct 62	Tech Assistance	439UNTS181	106329
Niger	United Nations	20 Nov 63	IGO Establishment	536UNTS3	107793
Niger	United Nations	07 May 68	IGO Operations	639UNTS71	109145
Niger	USA (United States)	26 May 61	General Aid	410UNTS213	105905
Niger	USA (United States)	26 Apr 62	Claims and Debts	459UNTS129	106618
Niger	USA (United States)	14 Jun 62	Milit Assistance	458UNTS233	106605
Niger	USA (United States)	23 Jul 62	Tech Assistance	487UNTS325	107114
Niger	WHO (World Health)	28 Dec 60	Tech Assistance	394UNTS195	105679
Nigeria	Accept UN Charter	21 Mar 61	UN Charter	395UNTS237	105688
Nigeria	Canada	03 Jul 63	Milit Assistance	529UNTS57	107656
Nigeria	Denmark	08 Sep 66	Air Transport	591UNTS177	108557
Nigeria	Germany, West	25 Mar 63	Loans and Credits	64WBGA5	424509
Nigeria	Germany, West	25 Mar 63	Tech Assistance	64WBGA5	424510
Nigeria	Germany, West	25 Mar 63	General Transport	64WBGA5	424511
Nigeria	Germany, West	25 Mar 63	General Trade	64WBGA5	424508
Nigeria	Germany, West	31 Jul 69	Loans and Credits	69WBGA193	424512
Nigeria	Germany, West	12 Feb 71	Loans and Credits	71WBGA102	424513
Nigeria	Germany, West	13 May 71	Loans and Credits	71WBGA115	424514
Nigeria	IBRD (World Bank)	10 Dec 62	IBRD Project	468UNTS255	106776
Nigeria	IBRD (World Bank)	12 Mar 64	IBRD Project	516UNTS325	107480
Nigeria	IBRD (World Bank)	07 Jul 64	IBRD Project	537UNTS3	107795
Nigeria	IBRD (World Bank)	26 Sep 65	IBRD Project	571UNTS39	108298
Nigeria	IBRD (World Bank)	26 Sep 65	IBRD Project	570UNTS233	108296
Nigeria	IBRD (World Bank)	27 Nov 68	IBRD Project	0UNTS0	109591
Nigeria	IBRD (World Bank)	05 Mar 69	IBRD Project	0UNTS0	109644
Nigeria	IBRD (World Bank)	06 Nov 69	IBRD Project	0UNTS0	110672
Nigeria	IBRD (World Bank)	26 Jun 70	IBRD Project	0UNTS0	110832
Nigeria	ICJ Option Clause	14 Aug 65	ICJ Option Clause	544UNTS113	107913
Nigeria	IDA (Devel Assoc)	01 Mar 65	Non-IBRD Project	571UNTS3	108297
Nigeria	IDA (Devel Assoc)	01 Mar 65	Non-IBRD Project	563UNTS3	108201
Nigeria	Multilateral	07 Dec 44	Air Transport	84UNTS389	200252
Nigeria	Multilateral	07 Dec 44	IGO Establishment	15UNTS295	200102
Nigeria	Multilateral	11 Dec 46	Sanitation	12UNTS179	100186
Nigeria	Multilateral	12 Nov 47	Admin Cooperation	46UNTS201	100710
Nigeria	Multilateral	06 Mar 48	Water Transport	289UNTS3	104214
Nigeria	Multilateral	11 May 48	Telecommunications	500UNTS267	107313
Nigeria	Multilateral	10 Jun 48	Humanitarian	164UNTS113	102163
Nigeria	Multilateral	24 Jul 48	Sanitation	66UNTS25	100847
Nigeria	Multilateral	29 Nov 48	IGO Establishment	120UNTS13	101613
Nigeria	Multilateral	09 Dec 48	Scientific Project	73UNTS39	100942
Nigeria	Multilateral	04 May 49	Admin Cooperation	47UNTS159	100728
Nigeria	Multilateral	04 May 49	Admin Cooperation	92UNTS19	101257
Nigeria	Multilateral	22 Nov 50	Culture	131UNTS25	101734
Nigeria	Multilateral	07 Dec 50	Admin Cooperation	212UNTS17	102861
Nigeria	Multilateral	02 Jul 51	Refugees	189UNTS137	102545
Nigeria	Multilateral	10 May 52	Taxation	439UNTS233	106332
Nigeria	Multilateral	10 May 52	Admin Cooperation	439UNTS217	106331
Nigeria	Multilateral	07 Nov 52	General Trade	221UNTS255	103010
Nigeria	Multilateral	18 Jan 54	IGO Establishment	330UNTS121	104743
Nigeria	Multilateral	12 May 54	Admin Cooperation	327UNTS3	104714
Nigeria	Multilateral	14 May 54	Culture	249UNTS215	103511
Nigeria	Multilateral	29 Jul 54	Sanitation	249UNTS45	103500
Nigeria	Multilateral	25 May 55	IGO Establishment	264UNTS117	103791
Nigeria	Multilateral	29 Apr 58	Specific Resources	559UNTS285	108164
Nigeria	Multilateral	29 Apr 58	Water Transport	450UNTS11	106465
Nigeria	Multilateral	01 Dec 58	Commodity Trade	385UNTS137	105534
Nigeria	Multilateral	06 Apr 59	Commodity Trade	349UNTS167	105013
Nigeria	Multilateral	26 Jan 60	IGO Establishment	439UNTS249	106333
Nigeria	Multilateral	17 Jun 60	Humanitarian	536UNTS27	107794
Nigeria	Multilateral	01 Sep 60	Commodity Trade	403UNTS3	105792
Nigeria	Multilateral	30 Mar 61	Sanitation	520UNTS151	107515
Nigeria	Multilateral	18 Apr 61	Consul/Citizenship	500UNTS95	107310
Nigeria	Multilateral	21 Jun 61	IGO Establishment	514UNTS209	107449
Nigeria	Multilateral	15 May 62	Commodity Trade	444UNTS3	106367
Nigeria	Multilateral	28 Sep 62	IGO Establishment	469UNTS169	106791
Nigeria	Multilateral	24 Apr 63	Consul/Citizenship	596UNTS261	108638
Nigeria	Multilateral	25 May 63	IGO Establishment	479UNTS39	106947
Nigeria	Multilateral	04 Aug 63	IGO Establishment	510UNTS3	107408
Nigeria	Multilateral	05 Aug 63	Sanitation	480UNTS43	106964
Nigeria	Multilateral	26 Oct 63	Water Transport	587UNTS9	108506
Nigeria	Multilateral	09 Nov 63	Direct Aid	489UNTS209	107141
Nigeria	Multilateral	23 Jun 64	Tech Assistance	506UNTS108	107383

PARTY ONE	PARTY TWO	DATE	TOPIC	CITATION	NUMBER
Nigeria	Multilateral	10 Jul 64	Postal Service	611UNTS7	108844
Nigeria	Multilateral	10 Jul 64	Postal Service	611UNTS387	108846
Nigeria	Multilateral	10 Jul 64	Postal Service	612UNTS3	108847
Nigeria	Multilateral	10 Jul 64	Postal Service	611UNTS105	108845
Nigeria	Multilateral	25 Nov 64	Water Transport	587UNTS19	108507
Nigeria	Multilateral	09 Mar 65	Water Transport	591UNTS265	108564
Nigeria	Multilateral	18 Mar 65	Dispute Settlement	575UNTS159	108359
Nigeria	Multilateral	08 Jul 65	General Trade	597UNTS3	108641
Nigeria	Multilateral	31 Dec 65	Specific Resources	616UNTS317	108904
Nigeria	Multilateral	05 Apr 66	Water Transport	640UNTS133	109159
Nigeria	Multilateral	27 Jan 67	Scientific Project	610UNTS205	108843
Nigeria	Multilateral	04 May 67	IGO Establishment	595UNTS287	108623
Nigeria	Multilateral	20 Jul 67	General Economic	0UNTS0	109259
Nigeria	Multilateral	22 Sep 67	Non-IBRD Project	0UNTS0	109258
Nigeria	Multilateral	18 Mar 68	Commodity Trade	0UNTS0	109262
Nigeria	Multilateral	01 Jul 68	Peace/Disarmament	0UNTS0	110485
Nigeria	Multilateral	24 Sep 68	Air Transport	0UNTS0	110612
Nigeria	Multilateral	27 Jan 69	Telecommunications	0UNTS0	109664
Nigeria	Netherlands	04 Dec 64	Education	545UNTS155	107931
Nigeria	Netherlands	28 Oct 65	Scientific Project	578UNTS15	108383
Nigeria	Netherlands	18 Oct 66	Education	603UNTS53	108724
Nigeria	Norway	18 May 55	Taxation	2NORT553	451123
Nigeria	Norway	08 Sep 66	Air Transport	3NORT974	451124
Nigeria	State/IGO Group	20 Apr 68	IGO Operations	636UNTS294	109106
Nigeria	Switzerland	11 Oct 65	Air Transport	602UNTS137	108710
Nigeria	UK Great Britain	01 Oct 60	Recognition	384UNTS207	105520
Nigeria	UK Great Britain	29 May 61	Recognition	478UNTS3	106931
Nigeria	UK Great Britain	24 Sep 68	Finance	0UNTS0	109819
Nigeria	UN Special Fund	10 Feb 61	Direct Aid	390UNTS85	105604
Nigeria	United Nations	07 Aug 62	Tech Assistance	435UNTS167	106278
Nigeria	United Nations	07 Feb 67	IGO Operations	590UNTS25	108544
Nigeria	United Nations	02 Jul 68	General Economic	639UNTS81	109146
Nigeria	USA (United States)	19 Oct 60	Scientific Project	394UNTS113	105672
Nigeria	USA (United States)	24 Dec 62	Claims and Debts	462UNTS180	106677
Nigeria	USSR (Soviet Union)	12 Jan 61	Recognition	16SUGG130	469989
Nigeria	USSR (Soviet Union)	03 Apr 61	Consul/Citizenship	10SUGG127	469759
Nigeria	WHO (World Health)	27 Mar 62	Tech Assistance	429UNTS123	106194
North Borneo	Multilateral	09 Jul 63	Admin Cooperation	0UNTS0	110760
Northern Rhodesia	Multilateral	02 Oct 54	IBRD Project	201UNTS179	102717
Northern Rhodesia	Multilateral	30 Dec 63	IBRD Project	551UNTS119	108037
Northern Rhodesia	Multilateral	30 Dec 63	IBRD Project	568UNTS215	108270
Norway	Allied Milit Occup	17 Feb 49	Milit Occupation	30UNTS137	100451
Norway	Allied Milit Occup	16 Sep 49	General Trade	53UNTS3	100769
Norway	Argentina	18 Mar 48	Air Transport	2NORT475	451001
Norway	Argentina	09 Nov 48	Taxation	2NORT488	451002
Norway	Argentina	09 Sep 49	Finance	42UNTS125	100646
Norway	Argentina	10 Mar 61	Milit Servic/Citiz	3NORT826	451003
Norway	Argentina	06 Sep 61	Visas	3NORT842	451004
Norway	Australia	24 Mar 47	Claims and Debts	18UNTS185	100288
Norway	Australia	19 Oct 51	Visas	128UNTS109	101716
Norway	Australia	04 Jan 68	Water Transport	3NORT999	451005
Norway	Austria	14 Apr 47	Finance	15UNTS211	100235
Norway	Austria	14 Apr 47	General Trade	31UNTS21	100466
Norway	Austria	27 Nov 48	General Trade	2NORT490	451221
Norway	Austria	28 Jan 49	General Trade	30UNTS145	100452
Norway	Austria	02 Dec 49	Air Transport	72UNTS230	100936
Norway	Austria	23 Apr 54	Visas	2NORT626	451222
Norway	Austria	18 Mar 55	Finance	2NORT650	451223
Norway	Austria	12 Dec 56	Patents/Copyrights	3NORT701	451224
Norway	Austria	07 Jul 58	Admin Cooperation	3NORT750	451225
Norway	Austria	25 Feb 60	Taxation	376UNTS155	105380
Norway	Austria	25 Feb 60	Taxation	60ABGB205	403145
Norway	Austria	24 May 63	Visas	3NORT888	451226
Norway	Austria	16 Dec 70	Taxation	71ABGB414	403146
Norway	Belgium	23 Oct 45	Finance	16UNTS311	200107
Norway	Belgium	23 Oct 45	Claims and Debts	183UNTS337	200510
Norway	Belgium	21 Feb 46	General Trade	31UNTS435	100485
Norway	Belgium	21 Feb 46	Finance	31UNTS199	100479
Norway	Belgium	15 Jul 47	Visas	33UNTS25	100511
Norway	Belgium	20 Feb 48	Culture	32UNTS39	100487
Norway	Belgium	08 Mar 49	General Trade	29UNTS83	100435
Norway	Belgium	21 Jan 52	Claims and Debts	123UNTS39	101653
Norway	Belgium	24 Mar 54	Sanitation	219UNTS73	102967
Norway	Belgium	28 May 57	General Trade	3NORT0	451006
Norway	Belgium	30 Jun 67	Taxation	0UNTS0	110020
Norway	Belgium	30 Jun 67	Taxation	3NORT999	451007
Norway	Bolivia	19 Jul 61	Visas	3NORT838	451008
Norway	Brazil	14 Nov 47	Air Transport	44UNTS163	100684
Norway	Brazil	27 May 52	Consul/Citizenship	2NORT583	451009
Norway	Brazil	19 Dec 56	Patents/Copyrights	3NORT705	451010
Norway	Brazil	29 May 59	Visas	3NORT772	451011
Norway	Brazil	11 Aug 61	Finance	3NORT839	451012
Norway	Brazil	20 Oct 67	Taxation	3NORT1005	451013
Norway	Brazil	30 Oct 67	Taxation	0UNTS0	110602
Norway	Bulgaria	19 Jun 58	Air Transport	3NORT746	451014
Norway	Bulgaria	28 Oct 67	Visas	0UNTS0	110302
Norway	Bulgaria	28 Oct 67	Visas	3NORT1007	451015
Norway	Bulgaria	15 Nov 68	General Trade	3NORT0	451016
Norway	Burma	22 Jun 53	Air Transport	174UNTS49	102277
Norway	Canada	25 Jun 45	Finance	45UNTS297	200186
Norway	Canada	06 Jun 46	Finance	43UNTS67	100661
Norway	Canada	14 Feb 50	Air Transport	53UNTS329	100790
Norway	Canada	13 Mar 50	Visas	90UNTS181	101235
Norway	Canada	18 Mar 50	Reparations	230UNTS349	103194
Norway	Canada	06 Jul 54	Privil/Immunities	2NORT637	451017
Norway	Canada	20 Dec 55	Milit Assistance	305UNTS17	104408
Norway	Canada	17 Apr 57	Milit Assistance	316UNTS215	104587
Norway	Canada	25 Apr 60	Milit Installation	470UNTS109	106801
Norway	Canada	24 May 60	Milit Installation	470UNTS125	106803
Norway	Canada	23 Nov 66	Taxation	604UNTS295	108757
Norway	Canada	26 Apr 68	Specific Resources	3NORT0	451018
Norway	Canada	08 Oct 68	Gen Communications	3NORT0	451019
Norway	Ceylon (Sri Lanka)	29 May 59	Air Transport	411UNTS165	105919
Norway	Ceylon (Sri Lanka)	11 Jun 64	Taxation	559UNTS23	108153
Norway	Chile	27 Oct 52	Air Transport	2NORT592	451020
Norway	Chile	16 Mar 53	Visas	167UNTS13	102198
Norway	Chile	05 Feb 62	Claims and Debts	3NORT849	451021
Norway	China People's Rep	04 Jun 58	General Economic	3NORT742	451022
Norway	China People's Rep	04 Jun 58	General Economic	58CCJC65	410527
Norway	China People's Rep	04 Apr 61	Visas	3NORT829	451023
Norway	China People's Rep	04 Apr 61	Visas	61CCJC45	410776
Norway	China People's Rep	18 Jun 63	Culture	3NORT890	451024
Norway	China People's Rep	18 Jun 63	Culture	63CCJC76	410987
Norway	China People's Rep	30 Apr 66	Culture	66CCJC23	411279
Norway	China People's Rep	02 Dec 67	Consul/Citizenship	3NORT1008	451025
Norway	Colombia	01 Oct 59	Visas	3NORT785	451026
Norway	Costa Rica	15 Oct 52	General Trade	2NORT590	451027
Norway	Costa Rica	21 Oct 59	Visas	3NORT785	451028
Norway	Costa Rica	06 Jan 60	Visas	3NORT785	451029
Norway	Cuba	06 Mar 53	Visas	2NORT599	451030
Norway	Cyprus	18 May 55	Taxation	2NORT553	451031
Norway	Cyprus	25 May 62	Visas	3NORT857	451032
Norway	Cyprus	05 Mar 63	Air Transport	563UNTS305	108216
Norway	Czechoslovakia	13 Dec 45	Finance	17UNTS261	100280
Norway	Czechoslovakia	20 Mar 47	General Trade	30UNTS223	100460
Norway	Czechoslovakia	09 Jun 54	Claims and Debts	2NORT636	451033
Norway	Czechoslovakia	25 Oct 62	Taxation	498UNTS335	107287
Norway	Czechoslovakia	03 Dec 68	General Trade	3NORT0	451035
Norway	Czechoslovakia	03 Dec 68	Air Transport	3NORT0	451034
Norway	Denmark	07 Aug 45	Telecommunications	10UNTS203	200062

PARTY ONE	PARTY TWO	DATE	TOPIC	CITATION	NUMBER
Norway	Denmark	10 Oct 45	Visas	104UNTS335	200323
Norway	Denmark	30 Mar 46	General Trade	29UNTS163	100438
Norway	Denmark	08 Jul 46	Territory Boundary	7UNTS247	100103
Norway	Denmark	30 Dec 46	Taxation	8UNTS21	100111
Norway	Denmark	15 Apr 47	Finance	12UNTS323	100191
Norway	Denmark	09 Jul 47	Territory Boundary	7UNTS321	100108
Norway	Denmark	21 Jan 48	Non-ILO Labor	14UNTS307	100223
Norway	Denmark	21 Apr 48	Finance	18UNTS139	100284
Norway	Denmark	18 Jan 51	Non-ILO Labor	82UNTS153	101090
Norway	Denmark	14 Jan 52	Claims and Debts	120UNTS119	101618
Norway	Denmark	23 May 56	Taxation	271UNTS75	103910
Norway	Denmark	23 May 56	Taxation	271UNTS49	103909
Norway	Denmark	15 Sep 56	General Transport	259UNTS3	103680
Norway	Denmark	22 Feb 57	Taxation	286UNTS127	104164
Norway	Denmark	31 Oct 58	Privil/Immunities	3NORT752	451036
Norway	Denmark	05 Sep 62	Water Transport	3NORT863	451037
Norway	Denmark	11 May 63	General Trade	613UNTS271	108856
Norway	Denmark	12 Sep 63	General Trade	613UNTS289	108857
Norway	Denmark	08 Dec 65	Territory Boundary	634UNTS71	109052
Norway	Denmark	19 Dec 66	Specific Resources	606UNTS3	108770
Norway	Denmark	23 Dec 66	General Trade	613UNTS265	108855
Norway	Denmark	20 Apr 67	Specific Resources	604UNTS103	108747
Norway	Denmark	26 Apr 68	Specific Resources	3NORTO	451038
Norway	Denmark	26 Apr 68	Specific Resources	OUNTSO	109211
Norway	Denmark	28 Apr 69	Admin Cooperation	OUNTSO	110578
Norway	Dominican Republic	27 Oct 59	Visas	3NORT786	451039
Norway	Dominican Republic	28 Apr 60	Visas	3NORT786	451040
Norway	Ecuador	15 Jan 51	General Trade	2NORT548	451041
Norway	Ecuador	29 Jan 64	Visas	3NORT899	451042
Norway	El Salvador	21 Oct 59	Visas	3NORT786	451138
Norway	Eur Space Research	21 Sep 65	IGO Operations	579UNTS251	108413
Norway	Eur Space Research	31 Jan 66	Specific Property	580UNTS3	108414
Norway	Fed Rhod/Nyasaland	18 Jun 66	Taxation	580UNTS9	108415
Norway	Finland	27 Nov 45	Finance	17UNTS247	100279
Norway	Finland	15 Nov 47	General Trade	29UNTS179	100439
Norway	Finland	10 Sep 48	Specific Resources	32UNTS3	100486
Norway	Finland	13 Jun 49	Commodity Trade	34UNTS9	100523
Norway	Finland	24 Aug 49	Air Transport	53UNTS167	100780
Norway	Finland	30 Dec 49	Visas	90UNTS175	101234
Norway	Finland	25 Apr 51	Specific Resources	2NORT551	451048
Norway	Finland	16 Jan 52	General Ad Hoc	2NORT578	451049
Norway	Finland	18 Mar 52	Specific Resources	188UNTS187	102527
Norway	Finland	20 May 53	Specific Resources	173UNTS163	102265
Norway	Finland	22 Sep 53	Milit Servic/Citiz	183UNTS245	102433
Norway	Finland	29 Mar 54	Taxation	2NORT623	451051
Norway	Finland	29 Mar 54	Taxation	2NORT624	451052
Norway	Finland	29 Mar 54	Taxation	2NORT625	451053
Norway	Finland	15 Sep 56	Admin Cooperation	254UNTS17	103590
Norway	Finland	28 Jun 57	Non-IBRD Project	272UNTS191	103938
Norway	Finland	21 Jan 59	Non-ILO Labor	325UNTS295	104705
Norway	Finland	15 Nov 60	Specific Resources	383UNTS159	105501
Norway	Finland	29 Jun 61	Extradition	2NORT241	451055
Norway	Finland	09 Jun 64	Specific Resources	503UNTS205	107345
Norway	Finland	10 Dec 68	Territory Boundary	OUNTSO	109977
Norway	Finland	10 Dec 68	Customs	3NORTO	451056
Norway	France	06 Mar 46	Finance	15UNTS13	100227
Norway	France	26 Mar 46	General Trade	31UNTS69	100468
Norway	France	30 Jun 47	Visas	104UNTS313	101449
Norway	France	15 Jul 47	Specific Property	15UNTS5	100226
Norway	France	11 Jun 48	General Trade	31UNTS83	100469
Norway	France	05 Jul 48	General Trade	30UNTS281	100463
Norway	France	09 Feb 49	General Economic	29UNTS13	100431
Norway	France	06 Nov 51	Education	2NORT572	451057
Norway	France	22 Sep 53	Taxation	2NORT607	451058
Norway	France	04 Dec 53	Culture	2NORT611	451059

PARTY ONE	PARTY TWO	DATE	TOPIC	CITATION	NUMBER
Norway	France	30 Sep 54	Non-ILO Labor	2NORT641	451060
Norway	France	06 Dec 54	Milit Servic/Citiz	202UNTS313	102737
Norway	France	20 Nov 56	Patents/Copyrights	3NORT699	451061
Norway	France	02 Apr 60	General Trade	60FRMD904	417346
Norway	France	24 May 63	Visas	3NORT886	451062
Norway	France	16 Jul 64	Patents/Copyrights	510UNTS229	107417
Norway	Gambia	18 May 55	Taxation	2NORT553	451063
Norway	Gambia	28 Oct 65	Visas	3NORT948	451064
Norway	Germany, West	20 Dec 50	General Trade	2NORT545	451183
Norway	Germany, West	07 May 51	Claims and Debts	92UNTS51	101260
Norway	Germany, West	15 Feb 52	Land Transport	61WBGA58	424516
Norway	Germany, West	30 Dec 53	Customs	2NORT618	451184
Norway	Germany, West	25 May 54	Visas	2NORT633	451185
Norway	Germany, West	27 Jul 54	Privil/Immunities	2NORT639	451186
Norway	Germany, West	18 Mar 55	Extradition	209UNTS309	102832
Norway	Germany, West	29 May 56	Culture	3NORT688	451187
Norway	Germany, West	29 Jan 57	Air Transport	353UNTS39	105037
Norway	Germany, West	30 Oct 57	Milit Installation	3NORT728	451188
Norway	Germany, West	18 Nov 58	Taxation	357UNTS205	105119
Norway	Germany, West	07 Aug 59	Reparations	358UNTS185	105136
Norway	Germany, West	17 Dec 60	Milit Installation	3NORT822	451189
Norway	Germany, West	24 May 63	Visas	3NORT887	451190
Norway	Germany, West	30 Nov 63	Milit Installation	3NORT896	451191
Norway	Germany, West	04 Sep 64	Customs	3NORT923	451192
Norway	Germany, West	06 Sep 65	General Aid	3NORT946	451193
Norway	Germany, West	29 Oct 68	Gen Communications	3NORTO	451194
Norway	Germany, West	09 Sep 71	Admin Cooperation	71WGBB1266	425520
Norway	Ghana	29 Jun 68	Tech Assistance	3NORTO	451065
Norway	Greece	08 Dec 47	Loans and Credits	30UNTS171	100455
Norway	Greece	12 Mar 49	Finance	33UNTS13	100510
Norway	Greece	12 Mar 49	General Trade	30UNTS161	100454
Norway	Greece	28 May 51	Air Transport	187UNTS141	102507
Norway	Greece	25 May 55	Taxation	423UNTS77	106085
Norway	Greece	20 Jun 58	Visas	3NORT747	451066
Norway	Greece	25 Sep 64	General Economic	610UNTSO	108835
Norway	Guatemala	25 Oct 62	Visas	3NORT869	451067
Norway	Guatemala	27 Apr 65	Visas	3NORT869	451068
Norway	Guatemala	29 Aug 67	Visas	3NORT869	451069
Norway	Guinea	21 Jun 62	Air Transport	466UNTS81	106738
Norway	Haiti	24 Oct 62	Visas	3NORT868	451070
Norway	Honduras	29 Nov 62	Visas	3NORT873	451071
Norway	Hungary	27 Aug 46	General Trade	31UNTS3	100465
Norway	Hungary	22 Feb 57	Claims and Debts	3NORT712	451072
Norway	Hungary	30 Apr 59	Air Transport	3NORT769	451073
Norway	Hungary	09 May 63	Finance	3NORT883	451074
Norway	Hungary	09 Dec 66	General Trade	3NORT981	451075
Norway	IAEA (Atom Energy)	10 Apr 61	Scientific Project	402UNTS255	105790
Norway	IBRD (World Bank)	08 Apr 54	IBRD Project	201UNTS131	102714
Norway	IBRD (World Bank)	19 Apr 55	IBRD Project	211UNTS159	102852
Norway	IBRD (World Bank)	03 May 56	IBRD Project	243UNTS281	103455
Norway	IBRD (World Bank)	08 Jul 59	IBRD Project	344UNTS229	104952
Norway	IBRD (World Bank)	02 Dec 60	IBRD Project	390UNTS131	105606
Norway	IBRD (World Bank)	15 Oct 63	IBRD Project	482UNTS103	106992
Norway	Iceland	14 Jul 51	Air Transport	163UNTS265	102150
Norway	Iceland	17 Sep 55	Taxation	2NORT664	451076
Norway	Iceland	30 Mar 66	Taxation	566UNTS51	108240
Norway	Iceland	30 Mar 66	Taxation	3NORT959	451077
Norway	Iceland	09 Sep 68	Gen Communications	3NORTO	451078
Norway	ICJ Option Clause	16 Nov 46	ICJ Option Clause	1UNTS37	100006
Norway	ICJ Option Clause	17 Dec 56	ICJ Option Clause	256UNTS315	103642
Norway	India	29 Aug 50	General Trade	73UNTS179	100952
Norway	India	20 Jul 59	Taxation	356UNTS257	105099
Norway	India	19 Apr 61	Culture	404UNTS307	105818
Norway	India	17 Mar 67	Specific Resources	3NORT992	451079
Norway	India	16 Sep 68	Loans and Credits	3NORTO	451080

PARTY ONE	PARTY TWO	DATE	TOPIC	CITATION	NUMBER
Norway	India	14 Nov 68	Visas	3NORTO	451081
Norway	Indonesia	30 Apr 51	General Trade	2NORT552	451082
Norway	Indonesia	22 Jun 54	Finance	2NORT621	451083
Norway	Iran	31 May 50	Air Transport	2NORT535	451084
Norway	Iran	04 Nov 56	Taxation	3NORT699	451085
Norway	Iran	10 Mar 66	Tech Assistance	3NORT958	451086
Norway	Iran	25 Jan 68	Visas	3NORTO	451087
Norway	Iraq	12 Jul 49	Air Transport	53UNTS137	100778
Norway	Ireland	17 Dec 47	Visas	90UNTS71	101228
Norway	Ireland	21 Jun 48	Air Transport	34UNTS317	100545
Norway	Ireland	02 Jul 51	General Trade	100UNTS53	101387
Norway	Ireland	18 Oct 54	Taxation	553UNTS123	108077
Norway	Ireland	02 Apr 64	Culture	553UNTS129	108078
Norway	Israel	24 May 55	Taxation	220UNTS71	102990
Norway	Israel	26 Jul 55	Visas	226UNTS257	103120
Norway	Israel	26 Nov 57	Culture	345UNTS99	104962
Norway	Israel	15 Jun 61	General Economic	3NORT836	451088
Norway	Israel	23 Feb 66	Visas	581UNTS203	108445
Norway	Israel	02 Nov 66	Taxation	630UNTS225	108972
Norway	Israel	18 Apr 67	Admin Cooperation	630UNTS307	108977
Norway	Italy	20 Jul 46	General Trade	30UNTS177	100456
Norway	Italy	20 Jul 46	Finance	17UNTS273	100281
Norway	Italy	19 Nov 49	General Trade	47UNTS75	100723
Norway	Italy	19 Nov 49	Finance	47UNTS89	100724
Norway	Italy	24 Jul 50	Visas	90UNTS187	101236
Norway	Italy	22 Jan 51	Finance	88UNTS339	101202
Norway	Italy	20 Apr 53	General Trade	54ITGU107	435284
Norway	Italy	14 Jun 55	Culture	260UNTS307	103713
Norway	Italy	16 Dec 56	Patents/Copyrights	291UNTS207	104256
Norway	Italy	12 Jun 59	Non-ILO Labor	428UNTS363	106187
Norway	Italy	25 Aug 61	Taxation	475UNTS269	106896
Norway	Italy	29 Apr 66	Taxation	3NORT961	451090
Norway	Ivory Coast	30 Apr 66	General Trade	3NORT963	451043
Norway	Ivory Coast	07 Jun 66	Visas	3NORT968	451045
Norway	Ivory Coast	07 Jun 66	Air Transport	3NORT967	451044
Norway	Ivory Coast	07 Jun 66	Air Transport	0UNTS0	109249
Norway	Ivory Coast	04 Dec 67	Privil/Immunities	3NORT1009	451046
Norway	Jamaica	31 Mar 69	Visas	0UNTS0	109941
Norway	Japan	23 Feb 53	Air Transport	192UNTS191	102601
Norway	Japan	22 Aug 56	Visas	3NORT692	451091
Norway	Japan	28 Feb 57	General Economic	280UNTS87	104054
Norway	Japan	21 Feb 59	Taxation	356UNTS231	105098
Norway	Japan	11 May 67	Taxation	68JHZ10	439009
Norway	Japan	11 May 67	Taxation	3NORT997	451092
Norway	Japan	11 May 67	Taxation	0UNTS0	109717
Norway	Japan	10 Jan 69	General Trade	70JAIL190	440228
Norway	Jordan	21 Aug 61	Air Transport	465UNTS275	106731
Norway	Kenya	03 Apr 65	Tech Assistance	3NORT937	451100
Norway	Kenya	09 Jul 65	Taxation	2NORT553	451101
Norway	Kenya	28 Aug 66	Tech Assistance	3NORT973	451102
Norway	Korea, South	24 May 65	Patents/Copyrights	3NORT942	451103
Norway	Lebanon	02 Feb 56	Air Transport	3NORT674	451104
Norway	Lebanon	10 Dec 68	Taxation	3NORTO	451105
Norway	Liberia	29 Jun 62	Air Transport	466UNTS95	106739
Norway	Liechtenstein	23 Dec 63	Visas	3NORT889	451106
Norway	Luxembourg	12 Jul 47	Visas	90UNTS59	101226
Norway	Luxembourg	17 Sep 51	Finance	2NORT568	451107
Norway	Luxembourg	17 Nov 52	Air Transport	311UNTS95	104500
Norway	Luxembourg	28 May 57	General Trade	3NORT717	451108
Norway	Malagasy	13 May 66	General Economic	3NORT965	451110
Norway	Malagasy	13 May 66	General Amity	3NORT964	451109
Norway	Malawi	12 Jul 65	Taxation	2NORT553	451111
Norway	Malawi	30 Apr 66	Visas	3NORT962	451112
Norway	Malaysia	19 Sep 60	Visas	3NORT812	451113
Norway	Malaysia	26 May 65	Air Transport	602UNTS157	108711

PARTY ONE	PARTY TWO	DATE	TOPIC	CITATION	NUMBER
Norway	Malaysia	19 Oct 67	Air Transport	3NORT1005	451114
Norway	Malta	29 Dec 65	Visas	561UNTS211	108184
Norway	Mexico	10 Dec 59	Visas	3NORT792	451116
Norway	Mexico	04 Feb 70	Air Transport	71MEXD603	444034
Norway	Monaco	16 Jul 48	Visas	90UNTS77	101229
Norway	Morocco	11 Feb 60	Visas	3NORT798	451115
Norway	Multilateral	12 May 40	Scientific Project	101UNTS91	101405
Norway	Multilateral	27 Mar 41	Military Mission	67UNTS231	200222
Norway	Multilateral	02 Aug 44	Scientific Project	67UNTS221	200221
Norway	Multilateral	07 Dec 44	Air Transport	84UNTS389	200252
Norway	Multilateral	07 Dec 44	Air Transport	171UNTS345	200501
Norway	Multilateral	07 Dec 44	IGO Establishment	15UNTS295	200102
Norway	Multilateral	08 Aug 45	General Military	82UNTS279	200251
Norway	Multilateral	27 Sep 45	IGO Establishment	5UNTS327	200035
Norway	Multilateral	16 Nov 45	IGO Establishment	4UNTS275	100052
Norway	Multilateral	27 Dec 45	IGO Establishment	2UNTS39	100020
Norway	Multilateral	04 Jan 46	IGO Establishment	6UNTS35	100066
Norway	Multilateral	14 Jan 46	Reparations	555UNTS69	108105
Norway	Multilateral	05 Apr 46	Specific Resources	231UNTS199	103221
Norway	Multilateral	22 Jul 46	IGO Establishment	9UNTS3	100125
Norway	Multilateral	22 Jul 46	IGO Establishment	14UNTS185	100221
Norway	Multilateral	15 Oct 46	Refugees	11UNTS73	100150
Norway	Multilateral	30 Oct 46	IGO Establishment	11UNTS107	100151
Norway	Multilateral	02 Dec 46	Specific Resources	161UNTS72	102124
Norway	Multilateral	11 Dec 46	Sanitation	12UNTS179	100186
Norway	Multilateral	15 Dec 46	IGO Establishment	18UNTS3	100283
Norway	Multilateral	08 Feb 47	Patents/Copyrights	14UNTS287	100222
Norway	Multilateral	03 Mar 47	Humanitarian	11UNTS43	100148
Norway	Multilateral	27 May 47	Air Transport	418UNTS161	106021
Norway	Multilateral	10 Jun 47	Water Transport	208UNTS3	102814
Norway	Multilateral	19 Sep 47	Finance	30UNTS269	100462
Norway	Multilateral	19 Sep 47	General Trade	30UNTS249	100461
Norway	Multilateral	02 Oct 47	Telecommunications	193UNTS188	102616
Norway	Multilateral	11 Oct 47	IGO Establishment	77UNTS143	100998
Norway	Multilateral	12 Nov 47	Admin Cooperation	53UNTS39	100771
Norway	Multilateral	12 Nov 47	Admin Cooperation	46UNTS201	100710
Norway	Multilateral	12 Nov 47	Admin Cooperation	53UNTS49	100772
Norway	Multilateral	12 Nov 47	Admin Cooperation	53UNTS13	100770
Norway	Multilateral	12 Nov 47	Admin Cooperation	46UNTS169	100709
Norway	Multilateral	08 Mar 48	Admin Cooperation	27UNTS117	100403
Norway	Multilateral	10 May 48	Culture	289UNTS111	104215
Norway	Multilateral	10 Jun 48	Humanitarian	191UNTS3	102576
Norway	Multilateral	10 Jun 48	Humanitarian	164UNTS113	102163
Norway	Multilateral	19 Jun 48	Air Transport	310UNTS151	104492
Norway	Multilateral	26 Jun 48	Culture	331UNTS217	104757
Norway	Multilateral	24 Jul 48	Sanitation	66UNTS25	100847
Norway	Multilateral	14 Sep 48	Milit Occupation	18UNTS267	100296
Norway	Multilateral	17 Sep 48	Telecommunications	97UNTS31	101345
Norway	Multilateral	19 Nov 48	Sanitation	44UNTS277	100688
Norway	Multilateral	09 Dec 48	Humanitarian	78UNTS277	101021
Norway	Multilateral	09 Dec 48	Scientific Project	20UNTS229	100318
Norway	Multilateral	09 Dec 48	Scientific Project	73UNTS39	100942
Norway	Multilateral	08 Feb 49	Specific Resources	157UNTS157	102053
Norway	Multilateral	28 Feb 49	Scientific Project	29UNTS53	100434
Norway	Multilateral	16 Mar 49	Finance	29UNTS95	100436
Norway	Multilateral	23 Mar 49	Commodity Trade	203UNTS179	102746
Norway	Multilateral	04 Apr 49	General Military	34UNTS243	100541
Norway	Multilateral	04 May 49	Admin Cooperation	92UNTS19	101257
Norway	Multilateral	04 May 49	Admin Cooperation	98UNTS101	101358
Norway	Multilateral	04 May 49	Admin Cooperation	30UNTS3	100445
Norway	Multilateral	04 May 49	Admin Cooperation	30UNTS23	100446
Norway	Multilateral	04 May 49	Admin Cooperation	47UNTS159	100728
Norway	Multilateral	05 May 49	IGO Establishment	87UNTS103	101168
Norway	Multilateral	16 Jun 49	Land Transport	45UNTS149	100696
Norway	Multilateral	18 Jun 49	ILO Labor	605UNTS295	108768

PARTY ONE	PARTY TWO	DATE	TOPIC	CITATION	NUMBER
Norway	Multilateral	15 Jul 49	Health/Educ/Welfare	197UNTS3	102631
Norway	Multilateral	12 Aug 49	General Military	75UNTS135	100972
Norway	Multilateral	12 Aug 49	Humanitarian	75UNTS31	100970
Norway	Multilateral	12 Aug 49	Humanitarian	75UNTS287	100973
Norway	Multilateral	12 Aug 49	Humanitarian	75UNTS85	100971
Norway	Multilateral	27 Aug 49	Non-ILO Labor	47UNTS127	100727
Norway	Multilateral	02 Sep 49	IGO Status/Immunit	250UNTS12	103515
Norway	Multilateral	19 Sep 49	Land Transport	125UNTS3	101671
Norway	Multilateral	16 Dec 49	Admin Cooperation	72UNTS3	100924
Norway	Multilateral	21 Mar 50	Admin Cooperation	96UNTS271	101342
Norway	Multilateral	13 May 50	Land Transport	128UNTS171	101719
Norway	Multilateral	16 Sep 50	General Transport	92UNTS91	101264
Norway	Multilateral	04 Nov 50	Humanitarian	213UNTS221	102889
Norway	Multilateral	22 Nov 50	Culture	131UNTS25	101734
Norway	Multilateral	07 Dec 50	Admin Cooperation	212UNTS17	102861
Norway	Multilateral	15 Dec 50	Customs	171UNTS305	102234
Norway	Multilateral	15 Dec 50	Customs	347UNTS127	104994
Norway	Multilateral	15 Dec 50	IGO Operations	160UNTS267	102111
Norway	Multilateral	15 Dec 50	Customs	157UNTS129	102052
Norway	Multilateral	21 Dec 50	Admin Cooperation	90UNTS3	101222
Norway	Multilateral	09 Jan 51	Humanitarian	197UNTS341	102647
Norway	Multilateral	25 May 51	Status of Forces	175UNTS215	102303
Norway	Multilateral	19 Jun 51	Status of Forces	199UNTS67	102678
Norway	Multilateral	02 Jul 51	Refugees	189UNTS137	102545
Norway	Multilateral	28 Aug 51	Non-ILO Labor	198UNTS17	102654
Norway	Multilateral	08 Sep 51	Peace/Disarmament	136UNTS45	101832
Norway	Multilateral	20 Sep 51	IGO Status/Immunit	200UNTS3	102691
Norway	Multilateral	09 Oct 51	IGO Establishment	220UNTS121	102997
Norway	Multilateral	20 Dec 51	Air Transport	163UNTS293	102151
Norway	Multilateral	20 Dec 51	Air Transport	163UNTS309	102152
Norway	Multilateral	10 Jan 52	Visas	163UNTS27	102139
Norway	Multilateral	10 Jan 52	Visas	163UNTS3	102138
Norway	Multilateral	15 Feb 52	Scientific Project	132UNTS51	101751
Norway	Multilateral	07 Mar 52	Specific Resources	175UNTS205	102302
Norway	Multilateral	20 May 52	Sanitation	219UNTS55	102966
Norway	Multilateral	12 Jun 52	Dispute Settlement	138UNTS183	101869
Norway	Multilateral	11 Jul 52	Postal Service	171UNTS143	102226
Norway	Multilateral	11 Jul 52	Postal Service	171UNTS191	102227
Norway	Multilateral	11 Jul 52	Postal Service	171UNTS89	102225
Norway	Multilateral	11 Jul 52	Postal Service	170UNTS63	102222
Norway	Multilateral	11 Jul 52	Postal Service	170UNTS269	102223
Norway	Multilateral	11 Jul 52	Postal Service	170UNTS3	102221
Norway	Multilateral	11 Jul 52	Postal Service	171UNTS3	102224
Norway	Multilateral	11 Jul 52	IGO Establishment	169UNTS3	102220
Norway	Multilateral	14 Jul 52	Visas	198UNTS37	102655
Norway	Multilateral	14 Jul 52	Consul/Citizenship	198UNTS47	102656
Norway	Multilateral	06 Sep 52	Patents/Copyrights	216UNTS132	102937
Norway	Multilateral	07 Oct 52	Admin Cooperation	310UNTS181	104493
Norway	Multilateral	17 Oct 52	Direct Aid	141UNTS121	101911
Norway	Multilateral	07 Nov 52	General Trade	221UNTS255	103010
Norway	Multilateral	07 Feb 53	Territory Boundary	173UNTS143	102264
Norway	Multilateral	27 Feb 53	Claims and Debts	333UNTS3	104764
Norway	Multilateral	23 Mar 53	Admin Cooperation	202UNTS241	102732
Norway	Multilateral	31 Mar 53	Privil/Immunities	193UNTS136	102613
Norway	Multilateral	01 Apr 53	Non-ILO Labor	227UNTS169	103138
Norway	Multilateral	01 Jul 53	IGO Establishment	200UNTS149	102701
Norway	Multilateral	20 Jul 53	Non-ILO Labor	228UNTS3	103141
Norway	Multilateral	20 Jul 53	Non-ILO Labor	227UNTS217	103140
Norway	Multilateral	20 Jul 53	Non-ILO Labor	228UNTS41	103142
Norway	Multilateral	17 Oct 53	General Transport	184UNTS42	102438
Norway	Multilateral	19 Oct 53	IGO Establishment	207UNTS189	102807
Norway	Multilateral	07 Dec 53	Admin Cooperation	182UNTS51	102422
Norway	Multilateral	11 Dec 53	Education	218UNTS125	102954
Norway	Multilateral	11 Dec 53	Sanitation	191UNTS285	102588
Norway	Multilateral	11 Dec 53	Patents/Copyrights	218UNTS27	102952
Norway	Multilateral	11 Dec 53	Non-ILO Labor	218UNTS255	102958
Norway	Multilateral	11 Dec 53	Non-ILO Labor	218UNTS211	102957
Norway	Multilateral	11 Dec 53	Non-ILO Labor	218UNTS153	102956
Norway	Multilateral	25 Feb 54	Air Transport	215UNTS249	102922
Norway	Multilateral	01 Mar 54	Admin Cooperation	286UNTS265	104173
Norway	Multilateral	14 May 54	Culture	249UNTS215	103511
Norway	Multilateral	22 May 54	Non-ILO Labor	199UNTS3	102674
Norway	Multilateral	22 May 54	Visas	199UNTS29	102675
Norway	Multilateral	14 Jun 54	Air Transport	320UNTS209	104643
Norway	Multilateral	14 Jun 54	Air Transport	320UNTS217	104644
Norway	Multilateral	28 Sep 54	Refugees	360UNTS117	105158
Norway	Multilateral	19 Dec 54	Patents/Copyrights	218UNTS51	102953
Norway	Multilateral	19 Dec 54	Culture	218UNTS139	102955
Norway	Multilateral	12 Mar 55	Land Transport	211UNTS3	102844
Norway	Multilateral	19 Mar 55	Sanitation	228UNTS95	103144
Norway	Multilateral	25 May 55	IGO Establishment	264UNTS117	103791
Norway	Multilateral	22 Jun 55	Atomic Energy	249UNTS3	103498
Norway	Multilateral	15 Sep 55	Non-ILO Labor	254UNTS55	103593
Norway	Multilateral	28 Sep 55	Air Transport	478UNTS371	106943
Norway	Multilateral	29 Sep 55	Air Transport	222UNTS313	103037
Norway	Multilateral	12 Oct 55	IGO Establishment	560UNTS3	108165
Norway	Multilateral	20 Oct 55	IGO Establishment	378UNTS159	105425
Norway	Multilateral	13 Dec 55	IGO Operations	529UNTS141	107660
Norway	Multilateral	13 Dec 55	Humanitarian	250UNTS3	103514
Norway	Multilateral	04 Jan 56	Scientific Project	256UNTS171	103627
Norway	Multilateral	24 Feb 56	Specific Resources	243UNTS147	103451
Norway	Multilateral	01 Mar 56	Customs	343UNTS129	104923
Norway	Multilateral	03 Mar 56	Milit Servic/Citiz	243UNTS169	103452
Norway	Multilateral	13 Mar 56	Humanitarian	427UNTS245	106158
Norway	Multilateral	25 Apr 56	Commodity Trade	270UNTS103	103896
Norway	Multilateral	30 Apr 56	Air Transport	310UNTS229	104494
Norway	Multilateral	18 May 56	Customs	338UNTS103	104834
Norway	Multilateral	18 May 56	Customs	327UNTS123	104721
Norway	Multilateral	18 May 56	Land Transport	339UNTS3	104844
Norway	Multilateral	07 Sep 56	Humanitarian	266UNTS3	103822
Norway	Multilateral	15 Sep 56	Admin Cooperation	254UNTS45	103592
Norway	Multilateral	25 Sep 56	Air Transport	334UNTS89	104767
Norway	Multilateral	25 Sep 56	Air Transport	334UNTS13	104766
Norway	Multilateral	24 Oct 56	Admin Cooperation	510UNTS161	107412
Norway	Multilateral	26 Oct 56	IGO Establishment	276UNTS3	103988
Norway	Multilateral	14 Dec 56	Taxation	436UNTS115	106292
Norway	Multilateral	14 Dec 56	Taxation	436UNTS131	106293
Norway	Multilateral	15 Dec 56	Education	278UNTS73	104023
Norway	Multilateral	19 Dec 56	Non-ILO Labor	427UNTS93	106148
Norway	Multilateral	21 Dec 56	Humanitarian	427UNTS81	106147
Norway	Multilateral	20 Feb 57	Consul/Citizenship	309UNTS65	104468
Norway	Multilateral	29 Apr 57	Dispute Settlement	320UNTS243	104646
Norway	Multilateral	15 Jun 57	General Trade	550UNTS45	108008
Norway	Multilateral	12 Jul 57	Visas	322UNTS245	104660
Norway	Multilateral	03 Oct 57	Postal Service	365UNTS3	105213
Norway	Multilateral	03 Oct 57	Postal Service	366UNTS141	105217
Norway	Multilateral	03 Oct 57	Postal Service	364UNTS331	105212
Norway	Multilateral	03 Oct 57	Postal Service	366UNTS193	105218
Norway	Multilateral	03 Oct 57	Postal Service	366UNTS3	105215
Norway	Multilateral	03 Oct 57	Postal Service	366UNTS255	105219
Norway	Multilateral	03 Oct 57	Postal Service	366UNTS87	105216
Norway	Multilateral	03 Oct 57	Postal Service	365UNTS207	105214
Norway	Multilateral	03 Oct 57	Postal Service	364UNTS3	105211
Norway	Multilateral	23 Nov 57	Refugees	506UNTS125	107384
Norway	Multilateral	13 Dec 57	Extradition	359UNTS273	105146
Norway	Multilateral	15 Apr 58	Health/Educ/Welfare	539UNTS27	107822
Norway	Multilateral	26 Jun 58	Admin Cooperation	324UNTS97	104679
Norway	Multilateral	05 Nov 58	Land Transport	428UNTS73	106169
Norway	Multilateral	03 Dec 58	Admin Cooperation	416UNTS51	105995
Norway	Multilateral	03 Dec 58	Admin Cooperation	398UNTS9	105715

PARTY ONE	PARTY TWO	DATE	TOPIC	CITATION	NUMBER
Norway	Multilateral	15 Dec 58	Mass Media	546UNTS235	107950
Norway	Multilateral	15 Dec 58	Sanitation	351UNTS159	105022
Norway	Multilateral	15 Jan 59	Customs	348UNTS13	104996
Norway	Multilateral	24 Jan 59	IGO Establishment	486UNTS157	107078
Norway	Multilateral	06 Apr 59	Commodity Trade	349UNTS167	105013
Norway	Multilateral	20 Apr 59	Land Transport	0UNTS0	110345
Norway	Multilateral	20 Apr 59	Admin Cooperation	472UNTS185	106841
Norway	Multilateral	20 Apr 59	Visas	376UNTS85	105375
Norway	Multilateral	29 Apr 59	Specific Property	346UNTS167	104980
Norway	Multilateral	11 May 59	Claims and Debts	527UNTS145	107623
Norway	Multilateral	20 Aug 59	Air Transport	376UNTS99	105376
Norway	Multilateral	08 Sep 59	Non-ILO Labor	383UNTS203	105502
Norway	Multilateral	01 Dec 59	Territory Boundary	402UNTS71	105778
Norway	Multilateral	14 Dec 59	Admin Cooperation	444UNTS193	106369
Norway	Multilateral	04 Jan 60	IGO Establishment	370UNTS3	105266
Norway	Multilateral	26 Jan 60	IGO Establishment	439UNTS249	106333
Norway	Multilateral	22 Apr 60	Air Transport	418UNTS211	106023
Norway	Multilateral	28 Apr 60	Health/Educ/Welfare	376UNTS111	105377
Norway	Multilateral	17 Jun 60	Humanitarian	536UNTS27	107794
Norway	Multilateral	22 Jun 60	Mass Media	546UNTS247	107951
Norway	Multilateral	28 Jul 60	IGO Status/Immunit	394UNTS37	105667
Norway	Multilateral	21 Sep 60	Patents/Copyrights	394UNTS3	105664
Norway	Multilateral	06 Oct 60	Customs	473UNTS131	106861
Norway	Multilateral	01 Dec 60	Scientific Project	414UNTS110	105970
Norway	Multilateral	09 Dec 60	Customs	429UNTS211	106200
Norway	Multilateral	14 Dec 60	Education	429UNTS93	106193
Norway	Multilateral	27 Mar 61	IGO Establishment	420UNTS109	106043
Norway	Multilateral	30 Mar 61	Sanitation	520UNTS151	107515
Norway	Multilateral	10 Apr 61	Atomic Energy	402UNTS281	105791
Norway	Multilateral	18 Apr 61	Consul/Citizenship	500UNTS223	107311
Norway	Multilateral	18 Apr 61	Dispute Settlement	500UNTS243	107312
Norway	Multilateral	18 Apr 61	Consul/Citizenship	500UNTS95	107310
Norway	Multilateral	08 Jun 61	Customs	473UNTS187	106863
Norway	Multilateral	08 Jun 61	Customs	473UNTS153	106862
Norway	Multilateral	21 Jun 61	IGO Establishment	514UNTS209	107449
Norway	Multilateral	05 Oct 61	Dispute Settlement	510UNTS175	107413
Norway	Multilateral	18 Oct 61	IGO Establishment	529UNTS89	107659
Norway	Multilateral	06 Dec 61	Customs	473UNTS219	106864
Norway	Multilateral	16 Dec 61	Visas	544UNTS19	107909
Norway	Multilateral	20 Dec 61	Water Transport	419UNTS79	106031
Norway	Multilateral	20 Feb 62	Water Transport	597UNTS159	108644
Norway	Multilateral	23 Mar 62	Admin Cooperation	470UNTS25	106793
Norway	Multilateral	23 Mar 62	General Amity	434UNTS145	106262
Norway	Multilateral	14 May 62	Scientific Project	544UNTS39	107910
Norway	Multilateral	14 May 62	Sanitation	544UNTS81	107911
Norway	Multilateral	15 May 62	Commodity Trade	444UNTS3	106367
Norway	Multilateral	06 Jun 62	Privil/Immunities	486UNTS271	107081
Norway	Multilateral	06 Jun 62	Privil/Immunities	486UNTS263	107080
Norway	Multilateral	28 Jun 62	ILO Labor	494UNTS271	107238
Norway	Multilateral	18 Sep 62	Water Transport	442UNTS215	106351
Norway	Multilateral	28 Sep 62	IGO Establishment	469UNTS169	106791
Norway	Multilateral	10 Dec 62	Culture	521UNTS231	107525
Norway	Multilateral	15 Jan 63	Tech Assistance	456UNTS409	106567
Norway	Multilateral	24 Apr 63	Consul/Citizenship	596UNTS487	108640
Norway	Multilateral	24 Apr 63	Consul/Citizenship	596UNTS261	108638
Norway	Multilateral	06 May 63	Consul/Citizenship	634UNTS221	109065
Norway	Multilateral	05 Aug 63	Sanitation	480UNTS43	106964
Norway	Multilateral	14 Sep 63	Telecommunications	488UNTS121	107123
Norway	Multilateral	14 Sep 63	Air Transport	0UNTS0	110106
Norway	Multilateral	17 Oct 63	Atomic Energy	525UNTS75	107585
Norway	Multilateral	28 Feb 64	Atomic Energy	501UNTS245	107321
Norway	Multilateral	08 Apr 64	Loans and Credits	501UNTS221	107320
Norway	Multilateral	18 Jun 64	Atomic Energy	542UNTS145	107886
Norway	Multilateral	10 Jul 64	Postal Service	611UNTS105	108845
Norway	Multilateral	10 Jul 64	Postal Service	611UNTS7	108844

PARTY ONE	PARTY TWO	DATE	TOPIC	CITATION	NUMBER
Norway	Multilateral	10 Jul 64	Postal Service	611UNTS387	108846
Norway	Multilateral	10 Jul 64	Postal Service	613UNTS193	108852
Norway	Multilateral	10 Jul 64	Postal Service	613UNTS127	108853
Norway	Multilateral	10 Jul 64	Postal Service	612UNTS233	108848
Norway	Multilateral	10 Jul 64	Postal Service	612UNTS3	108847
Norway	Multilateral	10 Jul 64	Postal Service	613UNTS3	108851
Norway	Multilateral	10 Jul 64	Postal Service	612UNTS361	108849
Norway	Multilateral	10 Jul 64	Postal Service	613UNTS3	108850
Norway	Multilateral	13 Jul 64	ILO Labor	569UNTS65	108279
Norway	Multilateral	20 Aug 64	Telecommunications	514UNTS25	107441
Norway	Multilateral	12 Sep 64	Specific Resources	0UNTS0	109344
Norway	Multilateral	15 Sep 64	General Trade	510UNTS147	107411
Norway	Multilateral	01 Dec 64	Water Transport	550UNTS133	108012
Norway	Multilateral	22 Jan 65	Gen Communications	634UNTS239	109066
Norway	Multilateral	09 Mar 65	Water Transport	591UNTS265	108564
Norway	Multilateral	18 Mar 65	Dispute Settlement	575UNTS159	108359
Norway	Multilateral	08 Jul 65	General Trade	597UNTS3	108641
Norway	Multilateral	03 Dec 65	Admin Cooperation	572UNTS105	108309
Norway	Multilateral	04 Dec 65	IGO Establishment	571UNTS123	108303
Norway	Multilateral	05 Apr 66	Water Transport	640UNTS133	109159
Norway	Multilateral	21 Jun 66	Non-ILO Labor	0UNTS0	109298
Norway	Multilateral	03 Oct 66	Culture	610UNTS169	108841
Norway	Multilateral	19 Dec 66	Specific Resources	605UNTS313	108769
Norway	Multilateral	24 Feb 67	Health/Educ/Welfare	596UNTS133	108631
Norway	Multilateral	17 Mar 67	Non-IBRD Project	594UNTS105	108598
Norway	Multilateral	17 Apr 67	Consul/Citizenship	0UNTS0	110377
Norway	Multilateral	24 Apr 67	Humanitarian	634UNTS255	109067
Norway	Multilateral	29 Jun 67	Non-ILO Labor	0UNTS0	110030
Norway	Multilateral	08 Dec 67	Specific Resources	620UNTS225	108959
Norway	Multilateral	18 Mar 68	Commodity Trade	0UNTS0	109262
Norway	Multilateral	07 Jun 68	Admin Cooperation	0UNTS0	110346
Norway	Multilateral	01 Jul 68	Peace/Disarmament	0UNTS0	110485
Norway	Multilateral	16 Aug 68	Non-ILO Labor	0UNTS0	109281
Norway	Multilateral	05 Dec 68	Scientific Project	0UNTS0	109952
Norway	Multilateral	15 Jan 69	Consul/Citizenship	0UNTS0	109491
Norway	Multilateral	09 Jun 69	Specific Resources	0UNTS0	110099
Norway	Multilateral	12 Dec 69	General Economic	0UNTS0	110755
Norway	Netherlands	06 Nov 45	Finance	2UNTS5	100017
Norway	Netherlands	28 Jan 47	General Trade	31UNTS29	100467
Norway	Netherlands	03 Jun 47	Visas	2NORT456	451117
Norway	Netherlands	26 Feb 49	General Economic	29UNTS33	100432
Norway	Netherlands	29 Dec 50	Taxation	134UNTS19	101795
Norway	Netherlands	28 Jun 51	Non-ILO Labor	2NORT562	451118
Norway	Netherlands	28 Jun 51	Non-ILO Labor	51NET98	447027
Norway	Netherlands	09 Jun 54	Finance	287UNTS179	104184
Norway	Netherlands	09 Jul 54	Claims and Debts	54NET187	447048
Norway	Netherlands	18 May 55	Culture	252UNTS269	103569
Norway	Netherlands	28 May 57	General Trade	3NORT717	451119
Norway	Netherlands	30 Jun 58	Reparations	348UNTS3	104995
Norway	Netherlands	30 Jun 58	Reparations	346UNTS217	104982
Norway	Netherlands	30 Apr 59	Finance	487UNTS3	107090
Norway	Netherlands	18 Oct 62	Air Transport	466UNTS145	106741
Norway	Netherlands	17 Nov 64	Sanitation	579UNTS243	108412
Norway	Netherlands	22 Sep 66	Taxation	600UNTS227	108683
Norway	New Zealand	03 May 46	Claims and Debts	16UNTS211	100262
Norway	New Zealand	22 Nov 49	Visas	51UNTS123	100760
Norway	Nicaragua	17 Oct 60	Visas	3NORT815	451120
Norway	Nicaragua	27 Mar 68	Visas	3NORT815	451121
Norway	Niger	15 Feb 66	Visas	3NORT956	451122
Norway	Nigeria	18 May 55	Taxation	2NORT553	451123
Norway	Nigeria	08 Sep 66	Air Transport	3NORT974	451124
Norway	Pakistan	08 Jun 49	Visas	90UNTS131	101231
Norway	Pakistan	23 Jun 49	Air Transport	35UNTS49	100550
Norway	Pakistan	21 May 51	General Trade	318UNTS163	104613
Norway	Pakistan	22 May 51	General Trade	2NORT555	451125

PARTY ONE	PARTY TWO	DATE	TOPIC	CITATION	NUMBER
Norway	Pakistan	05 Mar 58	Air Transport	334UNTS199	104769
Norway	Panama	16 Jun 59	Visas	3NORT775	451126
Norway	Panama	30 Jan 62	Visas	3NORT848	451127
Norway	Paraguay	21 Mar 63	Visas	3NORT880	451128
Norway	Peru	27 Jul 59	Visas	3NORT778	451129
Norway	Peru	02 Nov 60	Air Transport	497UNTS207	107270
Norway	Philippines	20 Oct 54	Air Transport	216UNTS11	102928
Norway	Philippines	18 Feb 59	Visas	359UNTS305	105147
Norway	Philippines	14 Dec 66	Visas	591UNTS253	108562
Norway	Philippines	08 May 69	Air Transport	0UNTS0	109867
Norway	Poland	03 Dec 46	Finance	15UNTS203	100234
Norway	Poland	04 Feb 48	General Trade	30UNTS205	100458
Norway	Poland	31 Dec 48	General Trade	29UNTS3	100430
Norway	Poland	21 Dec 49	Finance	47UNTS107	100725
Norway	Poland	23 Dec 55	Claims and Debts	2NORT671	451130
Norway	Poland	17 Dec 58	Culture	432UNTS193	106221
Norway	Poland	17 Jan 61	Air Transport	412UNTS130	105928
Norway	Poland	30 Oct 64	Finance	3NORT928	451131
Norway	Poland	21 Sep 67	General Trade	3NORT1004	451132
Norway	Poland	18 Oct 68	General Trade	3NORT0	451133
Norway	Portugal	16 Aug 46	Commodity Trade	30UNTS215	100459
Norway	Portugal	11 Nov 47	Air Transport	34UNTS257	100542
Norway	Portugal	28 Nov 49	Finance	47UNTS117	100726
Norway	Portugal	24 Sep 58	Visas	3NORT751	451134
Norway	Romania	16 Jun 58	Air Transport	405UNTS223	105835
Norway	Romania	21 May 64	Claims and Debts	563UNTS45	108203
Norway	Romania	21 Oct 67	General Trade	3NORT1006	451135
Norway	Romania	26 Nov 68	Visas	3NORT0	451136
Norway	Romania	29 Nov 68	General Economic	0UNTS0	109705
Norway	Romania	29 Nov 68	General Economic	3NORT0	451137
Norway	Sierra Leone	02 May 51	Taxation	2NORT553	451139
Norway	Singapore	09 Sep 66	Taxation	3NORT975	451140
Norway	Singapore	20 Dec 66	Air Transport	3NORT985	451141
Norway	Singapore	20 Dec 66	Air Transport	0UNTS0	109242
Norway	Singapore	28 Nov 68	Visas	3NORT0	451142
Norway	South Africa	19 Jun 51	Taxation	2NORT560	451170
Norway	South Africa	21 Sep 53	Air Transport	192UNTS105	102597
Norway	South Africa	17 Feb 56	Visas	230UNTS213	103186
Norway	South Africa	28 Mar 58	Air Transport	300UNTS83	104332
Norway	South Africa	30 Oct 59	Specific Property	346UNTS21	104975
Norway	South Africa	22 Jun 67	Scientific Project	643UNTS121	109888
Norway	Spain	31 Dec 54	General Trade	55SPBO2101	460202
Norway	Spain	25 Jun 55	General Trade	55SPBO2607	460203
Norway	Spain	17 Jul 56	General Trade	56SPBO808	460204
Norway	Spain	21 Dec 56	Patents/Copyrights	56SPBO803	460205
Norway	Spain	21 Dec 56	Patents/Copyrights	3NORT705	451143
Norway	Spain	22 Jul 57	General Trade	57SPBO808	460206
Norway	Spain	22 May 59	Visas	3NORT771	451144
Norway	Spain	19 Aug 59	Culture	376UNTS145	105379
Norway	Spain	16 Mar 60	Claims and Debts	3NORT801	451145
Norway	Spain	17 May 60	General Trade	3NORT805	451146
Norway	Spain	25 Apr 63	Taxation	503UNTS41	107340
Norway	Spain	05 May 65	Air Transport	3NORT941	451147
Norway	Spain	03 Jun 65	Patents/Copyrights	3NORT943	451148
Norway	Sudan	05 Apr 59	Air Transport	3NORT765	451153
Norway	Sweden	22 Nov 46	Finance	15UNTS171	100233
Norway	Sweden	22 Nov 46	Specific Resources	46SOFM307	461034
Norway	Sweden	21 Jun 47	Taxation	94UNTS107	101309
Norway	Sweden	05 Aug 47	General Trade	47SOFM511	461052
Norway	Sweden	22 Dec 47	Non-ILO Labor	22UNTS203	100337
Norway	Sweden	22 Dec 47	Non-ILO Labor	47SOFM631	461060
Norway	Sweden	29 Apr 48	Commodity Trade	26UNTS41	100376
Norway	Sweden	29 Apr 48	Finance	26UNTS11	100374
Norway	Sweden	29 Apr 48	Commodity Trade	26UNTS33	100375
Norway	Sweden	18 Dec 48	Non-ILO Labor	30UNTS117	100450

PARTY ONE	PARTY TWO	DATE	TOPIC	CITATION	NUMBER
Norway	Sweden	28 Jan 49	Specific Resources	196UNTS3	102617
Norway	Sweden	14 Dec 49	Specific Resources	196UNTS19	102618
Norway	Sweden	17 Dec 49	Taxation	197UNTS197	102640
Norway	Sweden	17 Dec 49	Taxation	197UNTS215	102641
Norway	Sweden	28 Jan 50	Land Transport	202UNTS151	102730
Norway	Sweden	24 Feb 50	Claims and Debts	2NORT530	451160
Norway	Sweden	19 Dec 50	General Trade	50SOFM1065	461130
Norway	Sweden	20 Dec 50	Specific Resources	92UNTS3	101256
Norway	Sweden	19 Feb 51	Finance	51SOFM567	461155
Norway	Sweden	07 Dec 51	General Trade	51SOFM447	461152
Norway	Sweden	10 Nov 52	Scientific Project	52SOFM893	461179
Norway	Sweden	22 Nov 52	General Trade	52SOFM535	461175
Norway	Sweden	16 Nov 53	General Trade	53SOFM1047	461189
Norway	Sweden	12 May 54	Visas	198UNTS157	102661
Norway	Sweden	09 Jul 54	Claims and Debts	2NORT638	451161
Norway	Sweden	10 Jan 55	Patents/Copyrights	204UNTS293	102764
Norway	Sweden	28 May 55	Scientific Project	262UNTS151	103743
Norway	Sweden	07 Oct 55	Admin Cooperation	262UNTS253	103752
Norway	Sweden	26 Jan 56	General Ad Hoc	3NORT673	451162
Norway	Sweden	09 Mar 56	Land Transport	369UNTS285	105262
Norway	Sweden	29 Jun 56	Specific Resources	262UNTS335	103759
Norway	Sweden	15 Sep 56	Admin Cooperation	263UNTS17	103765
Norway	Sweden	27 Sep 56	Taxation	261UNTS71	103726
Norway	Sweden	16 Sep 57	Territory Boundary	428UNTS263	106178
Norway	Sweden	09 Jun 58	Water Transport	427UNTS221	106156
Norway	Sweden	28 Oct 59	Visas	427UNTS225	106157
Norway	Sweden	16 Mar 61	Customs	3NORT827	451163
Norway	Sweden	31 Oct 62	Claims and Debts	466UNTS361	106755
Norway	Sweden	28 Jun 63	Specific Resources	3NORT891	451164
Norway	Sweden	05 Apr 67	Specific Resources	3NORT994	451165
Norway	Sweden	05 Apr 67	Specific Resources	3NORT994	451166
Norway	Sweden	14 Dec 67	Admin Cooperation	3NORT1012	451167
Norway	Sweden	24 Jul 68	Territory Boundary	3NORT0	451168
Norway	Sweden	10 Dec 68	Taxation	0UNTS0	109615
Norway	Switzerland	15 Jul 47	Finance	12UNTS351	100192
Norway	Switzerland	01 Aug 47	Visas	90UNTS65	101227
Norway	Switzerland	26 Jun 48	General Trade	29UNTS193	100440
Norway	Switzerland	13 Jan 51	General Trade	2NORT547	451154
Norway	Switzerland	31 Mar 53	Milit Servic/Citiz	2NORT602	451155
Norway	Switzerland	30 Dec 54	Air Transport	311UNTS147	104502
Norway	Switzerland	07 Dec 56	Taxation	57SWRO715	462058
Norway	Switzerland	07 Dec 56	Taxation	57SWRO728	462059
Norway	Switzerland	07 Dec 56	Taxation	3NORT701	451157
Norway	Switzerland	07 Dec 56	Taxation	3NORT700	451156
Norway	Switzerland	03 Jul 57	Taxation	57SWRO733	462060
Norway	Switzerland	29 Jan 59	Visas	3NORT761	451158
Norway	Switzerland	25 May 63	Visas	3NORT889	451159
Norway	Syria	25 Feb 56	Air Transport	3NORT676	451169
Norway	Syria	25 Feb 56	Air Transport	463UNTS217	106706
Norway	Thailand	26 Nov 49	Air Transport	53UNTS269	100787
Norway	Thailand	11 Dec 62	Visas	3NORT875	451171
Norway	Thailand	09 Jan 64	Taxation	522UNTS65	107537
Norway	Trinidad/Tobago	27 Sep 68	Visas	3NORT0	451172
Norway	Tunisia	28 Mar 59	Air Transport	497UNTS77	107263
Norway	Tunisia	27 May 60	Visas	3NORT807	451173
Norway	Tunisia	09 Jun 60	General Trade	3NORT808	451174
Norway	Turkey	20 May 48	Air Transport	26UNTS137	100384
Norway	Turkey	24 Feb 49	General Trade	29UNTS47	100433
Norway	Turkey	24 Feb 49	Finance	30UNTS151	100453
Norway	Turkey	23 Aug 52	Visas	2NORT588	451175
Norway	Turkey	24 Apr 57	General Trade	2NORT715	451176
Norway	Turkey	10 Jan 58	Culture	351UNTS229	105025
Norway	Turkey	19 Dec 58	Loans and Credits	2NORT758	451177
Norway	Turkey	24 Apr 59	Visas	59TURG1006	466023
Norway	Turkey	14 Jul 59	Claims and Debts	2NORT770	451178

PARTY ONE	PARTY TWO	DATE	TOPIC	CITATION	NUMBER
Norway	Turkey	23 Dec 64	Loans and Credits	2NORT931	451179
Norway	Turkey	24 Dec 64	Loans and Credits	2NORT953	451180
Norway	Turkey	27 Dec 66	Loans and Credits	3NORT987	451181
Norway	Turkey	13 Jun 68	Loans and Credits	3NORTO	451182
Norway	Uganda	23 Mar 64	Tech Assistance	3NORT900	451196
Norway	Uganda	04 May 65	Visas	3NORT940	451195
Norway	UK Great Britain	11 Oct 45	Milit Installation	2NORT430	451149
Norway	UK Great Britain	08 Nov 45	Finance	5UNTS27	100063
Norway	UK Great Britain	31 Aug 46	Air Transport	6UNTS235	100078
Norway	UK Great Britain	27 Sep 46	Milit Installation	6UNTS259	100079
Norway	UK Great Britain	15 Jan 47	Consul/Citizenship	11UNTS187	100156
Norway	UK Great Britain	26 Feb 47	Visas	11UNTS273	100166
Norway	UK Great Britain	05 Jun 47	Milit Occupation	54UNTS181	100803
Norway	UK Great Britain	19 Feb 48	Culture	34UNTS33	100526
Norway	UK Great Britain	06 Nov 50	Finance	88UNTS257	101197
Norway	UK Great Britain	15 Dec 50	General Trade	106UNTS87	101459
Norway	UK Great Britain	22 Feb 51	Consul/Citizenship	326UNTS209	104713
Norway	UK Great Britain	02 May 51	Taxation	106UNTS101	101460
Norway	UK Great Britain	23 Jun 52	Air Transport	151UNTS81	101985
Norway	UK Great Britain	12 May 54	General Trade	2NORT627	451150
Norway	UK Great Britain	12 Jul 57	Atomic Energy	310UNTS41	104485
Norway	UK Great Britain	25 Jul 57	Non-ILO Labor	313UNTS3	104528
Norway	UK Great Britain	23 Apr 59	Finance	343UNTS283	104933
Norway	UK Great Britain	17 Nov 60	Specific Resources	398UNTS189	105723
Norway	UK Great Britain	10 May 61	Visas	414UNTS9	105960
Norway	UK Great Britain	12 Jun 61	Admin Cooperation	424UNTS173	106107
Norway	UK Great Britain	28 Sep 64	Specific Property	548UNTS63	107970
Norway	UK Great Britain	10 Mar 65	Territory Boundary	551UNTS213	108043
Norway	UK Great Britain	06 Mar 67	Non-ILO Labor	3NORT991	451151
Norway	UK Great Britain	06 Nov 68	Commodity Trade	3NORTO	451152
Norway	UK Great Britain	22 Jan 69	Taxation	OUNTSO	110436
Norway	United Arab Rep	11 Mar 50	Air Transport	95UNTS157	101321
Norway	United Arab Rep	20 Oct 64	Taxation	543UNTS3	107895
Norway	United Nations	09 Jul 57	Status of Forces	271UNTS223	103917
Norway	Uruguay	20 Mar 52	Air Transport	310UNTS279	104496
Norway	Uruguay	20 Oct 55	Consul/Citizenship	2NORT666	451197
Norway	Uruguay	24 Jan 61	Visas	3NORT824	451198
Norway	USA (United States)	28 Mar 40	Specif Claim/Waive	88UNTS365	200253
Norway	USA (United States)	28 Aug 42	Other Military	139UNTS361	200461
Norway	USA (United States)	16 Jan 43	Milit Servic/Citiz	13UNTS335	200082
Norway	USA (United States)	16 May 44	Privil/Immunities	67UNTS253	200223
Norway	USA (United States)	29 May 45	Water Transport	34UNTS371	200180
Norway	USA (United States)	06 Oct 45	Air Transport	122UNTS319	200413
Norway	USA (United States)	08 Jul 46	Mostfavored Nation	13UNTS35	100199
Norway	USA (United States)	12 Nov 46	Air Transport	42UNTS227	100651
Norway	USA (United States)	29 Jul 47	Visas	87UNTS343	101178
Norway	USA (United States)	24 Feb 48	Milit Assistance	34UNTS155	100535
Norway	USA (United States)	15 Mar 48	Admin Cooperation	73UNTS81	100946
Norway	USA (United States)	03 Jul 48	Direct Aid	20UNTS185	100317
Norway	USA (United States)	03 Jul 48	Milit Occupation	27UNTS59	100399
Norway	USA (United States)	25 May 49	Education	32UNTS345	100507
Norway	USA (United States)	13 Jun 49	Taxation	127UNTS163	101704
Norway	USA (United States)	13 Jun 49	Taxation	127UNTS189	101705
Norway	USA (United States)	31 Oct 49	Direct Aid	68UNTS3	100879
Norway	USA (United States)	27 Jan 50	Milit Assistance	80UNTS241	101055
Norway	USA (United States)	28 Dec 50	Milit Assistance	240UNTS391	103414
Norway	USA (United States)	17 Sep 51	Milit Assistance	140UNTS313	101895
Norway	USA (United States)	08 Jan 52	Milit Assistance	179UNTS185	102367
Norway	USA (United States)	01 Apr 52	Direct Aid	177UNTS291	102328
Norway	USA (United States)	21 Jun 52	Reparations	236UNTS9	103313
Norway	USA (United States)	27 Jun 52	Tech Assistance	184UNTS271	102452
Norway	USA (United States)	13 Apr 54	Status of Forces	229UNTS223	103169
Norway	USA (United States)	07 May 54	Milit Assistance	231UNTS157	103215
Norway	USA (United States)	06 Aug 54	Air Transport	222UNTS269	103034
Norway	USA (United States)	06 Aug 54	Air Transport	222UNTS261	103033

PARTY ONE	PARTY TWO	DATE	TOPIC	CITATION	NUMBER
Norway	USA (United States)	06 Apr 55	General Military	269UNTS65	103874
Norway	USA (United States)	05 Feb 57	Air Transport	279UNTS169	104038
Norway	USA (United States)	25 Feb 57	Atomic Energy	284UNTS19	104126
Norway	USA (United States)	08 May 58	Milit Installation	2NORT528	451199
Norway	USA (United States)	13 Feb 60	Milit Assistance	388UNTS255	105583
Norway	USA (United States)	06 Jul 60	Milit Assistance	378UNTS25	105415
Norway	USA (United States)	29 Nov 60	Milit Assistance	404UNTS251	105815
Norway	USA (United States)	05 Mar 62	General Economic	446UNTS47	106402
Norway	USA (United States)	01 Mar 63	Water Transport	524UNTS185	107573
Norway	USA (United States)	13 Jul 66	Claims and Debts	3NORT972	451200
Norway	USA (United States)	04 May 67	Atomic Energy	3NORT997	451201
Norway	USA (United States)	04 May 67	Atomic Energy	OUNTSO	109763
Norway	USA (United States)	01 Jun 67	Gen Communications	631UNTS119	108991
Norway	USA (United States)	15 Jun 68	Scientific Project	3NORTO	451202
Norway	USA (United States)	15 Jun 68	Scientific Project	OUNTSO	110145
Norway	USA (United States)	26 Jun 68	Non-ILO Labor	3NORTO	451203
Norway	USA (United States)	26 Feb 70	Admin Cooperation	OUNTSO	110624
Norway	USSR (Soviet Union)	27 Dec 46	Finance	17UNTS283	100282
Norway	USSR (Soviet Union)	11 Feb 47	Telecommunications	OSUST228	468292
Norway	USSR (Soviet Union)	11 Feb 47	Postal Service	OSUST229	468293
Norway	USSR (Soviet Union)	19 Feb 47	General Trade	30UNTS293	100464
Norway	USSR (Soviet Union)	18 Dec 47	Territory Boundary	52UNTS3	100768
Norway	USSR (Soviet Union)	21 May 48	Claims and Debts	2NORT478	451205
Norway	USSR (Soviet Union)	23 May 49	Territory Boundary	2NORT500	451206
Norway	USSR (Soviet Union)	30 Nov 49	Finance	16SUGG65	469893
Norway	USSR (Soviet Union)	29 Dec 49	Territory Boundary	83UNTS291	101112
Norway	USSR (Soviet Union)	02 Jul 53	Other Military	OSUST441	468294
Norway	USSR (Soviet Union)	15 Nov 55	General Trade	OSUST341	468295
Norway	USSR (Soviet Union)	31 Mar 56	Air Transport	259UNTS205	103690
Norway	USSR (Soviet Union)	12 Oct 56	Culture	308UNTS95	104457
Norway	USSR (Soviet Union)	19 Oct 56	Humanitarian	257UNTS3	103644
Norway	USSR (Soviet Union)	15 Feb 57	Territory Boundary	312UNTS289	104523
Norway	USSR (Soviet Union)	07 Jun 57	Specific Resources	OSUST384	468298
Norway	USSR (Soviet Union)	01 Aug 57	Territory Boundary	OSUST386	468299
Norway	USSR (Soviet Union)	22 Nov 57	Specific Resources	309UNTS269	104476
Norway	USSR (Soviet Union)	29 Nov 57	Territory Boundary	OSUST392	468301
Norway	USSR (Soviet Union)	18 Dec 57	Specific Resources	312UNTS257	104522
Norway	USSR (Soviet Union)	20 Oct 58	Culture	7SUGG122	469536
Norway	USSR (Soviet Union)	30 Sep 59	Claims and Debts	3NORT784	451209
Norway	USSR (Soviet Union)	09 Dec 59	Specif Claim/Waive	361UNTS93	105173
Norway	USSR (Soviet Union)	12 May 61	Consul/Citizenship	3NORT833	451210
Norway	USSR (Soviet Union)	22 Feb 62	Specific Resources	11SUGG133	469823
Norway	USSR (Soviet Union)	16 Apr 62	Specific Resources	437UNTS175	106307
Norway	USSR (Soviet Union)	24 Dec 63	Territory Boundary	3NORT897	451211
Norway	USSR (Soviet Union)	08 Aug 64	Territory Boundary	3NORT921	451212
Norway	USSR (Soviet Union)	29 Jan 65	Finance	3NORT932	451213
Norway	USSR (Soviet Union)	06 Mar 65	Consul/Citizenship	3NORT934	451214
Norway	USSR (Soviet Union)	18 Dec 67	Territory Boundary	3NORT1013	451215
Norway	USSR (Soviet Union)	09 Jul 68	Admin Cooperation	3NORTO	451216
Norway	Venezuela	30 Jul 57	General Trade	3NORT725	451217
Norway	Venezuela	01 Dec 59	Visas	3NORT790	451218
Norway	WHO (World Health)	09 May 52	Tech Assistance	131UNTS281	101747
Norway	Yugoslavia	30 Aug 46	General Trade	30UNTS187	100457
Norway	Yugoslavia	30 Aug 46	Finance	15UNTS163	100232
Norway	Yugoslavia	31 May 51	Claims and Debts	2NORT558	451093
Norway	Yugoslavia	24 Jun 55	Culture	2NORT660	451094
Norway	Yugoslavia	30 May 56	General Trade	3NORT689	451095
Norway	Yugoslavia	18 Nov 59	Finance	383UNTS131	105499
Norway	Yugoslavia	21 Dec 59	General Trade	3NORT794	451096
Norway	Yugoslavia	15 Apr 64	Air Transport	602UNTS177	108712
Norway	Yugoslavia	06 May 64	Visas	3NORT909	451097
Norway	Yugoslavia	18 May 66	Taxation	3NORT970	451098
Norway	Yugoslavia	21 Aug 68	General Economic	3NORTO	451099
Norway	Zambia	21 Dec 63	Taxation	2NORT553	451219
Norway	Zambia	31 Mar 67	Tech Assistance	3NORT993	451220

PARTY ONE	PARTY TWO	DATE	TOPIC	CITATION	NUMBER
NW Atlantic Fish	Multilateral	08 Feb 49	Specific Resources	157UNTS157	102053
Nyasaland	Multilateral	04 Aug 63	IGO Establishment	510UNTS3	107408
OAS (Am States)	ILO (Labor Org)	07 Jun 50	IGO Operations	70UNTS223	200240
OAS (Am States)	Israel	11 Oct 62	Tech Assistance	484UNTS241	107035
OAS (Am States)	Multilateral	02 Aug 66	Tech Assistance	582UNTS59	108457
OAS (Am States)	USA (United States)	03 Mar 52	Tech Assistance	165UNTS67	102168
OAS (Am States)	USA (United States)	22 Jun 52	IGO Status/Immunit	181UNTS147	102405
OAS (Am States)	USA (United States)	29 Nov 61	Direct Aid	424UNTS119	106104
OAU (Afri Unity)	IAEA (Atom Energy)	26 Mar 69	Atomic Energy	0UNTS0	200646
OAU (Afri Unity)	ILO (Labor Org)	25 Nov 65	General Amity	550UNTS389	200617
OAU (Afri Unity)	United Nations	15 Nov 65	IGO Operations	548UNTS315	200614
OAU (Afri Unity)	WHO (World Health)	24 Sep 69	IGO Operations	0UNTS0	200651
OECD (Econ Coop)	France	05 Mar 59	Non-ILO Labor	59FRRT40	415499
OECD (Econ Coop)	France	26 Jan 66	Non-ILO Labor	66FRRT12	415506
OECD (Econ Coop)	IAEA (Atom Energy)	24 Nov 60	IGO Operations	396UNTS273	200585
OECD (Econ Coop)	Japan	14 Mar 67	IGO Status/Immunit	67JHZ7	439007
OECD (Econ Coop)	Spain	10 Jan 58	IGO Operations	58SPBO1207	460274
Org Ctrl Am States	ILO (Labor Org)	26 Jul 65	IGO Operations	563UNTS341	200620
Org Rail Collabor	Poland	12 Dec 57	IGO Operations	57PZUM125	458057
Pakistan	Accept UN Charter	30 Sep 47	UN Charter	8UNTS57	100112
Pakistan	Afghanistan	13 Jun 57	Air Transport	327UNTS51	104717
Pakistan	Australia	03 Jun 49	Air Transport	35UNTS23	100549
Pakistan	Australia	16 Jan 52	Postal Service	151UNTS281	102001
Pakistan	Austria	24 Dec 56	General Trade	316UNTS83	104579
Pakistan	Austria	16 Aug 57	Visas	306UNTS3	104429
Pakistan	Austria	10 Jan 68	Other Military	636UNTS133	109100
Pakistan	Austria	06 Jul 70	Taxation	71ABGB297	403147
Pakistan	Austria	28 May 71	Air Transport	71ABGB296	403148
Pakistan	Belgium	20 Feb 52	Extradition	133UNTS199	101790
Pakistan	Belgium	15 Mar 52	General Trade	316UNTS65	104578
Pakistan	Belgium	19 Oct 56	Visas	257UNTS221	103657
Pakistan	Belgium	04 Jul 58	Air Transport	387UNTS305	105569
Pakistan	Belgium	14 Nov 63	Culture	535UNTS393	107792
Pakistan	Burma	18 Nov 47	Air Transport	35UNTS321	100562
Pakistan	Burma	22 Jun 48	Postal Service	91UNTS197	101252
Pakistan	Burma	25 Jun 52	General Amity	173UNTS41	102259
Pakistan	Canada	10 Sep 51	Direct Aid	122UNTS21	101632
Pakistan	Canada	23 Oct 51	Visas	248UNTS95	103487
Pakistan	Canada	15 Jan 58	Patents/Copyrights	392UNTS35	105637
Pakistan	Canada	14 May 59	Atomic Energy	426UNTS129	106133
Pakistan	Canada	21 Dec 60	Air Transport	465UNTS115	106724
Pakistan	Ceylon (Sri Lanka)	15 Dec 48	Postal Service	91UNTS303	101255
Pakistan	Ceylon (Sri Lanka)	03 Jan 49	Air Transport	28UNTS247	100428
Pakistan	Ceylon (Sri Lanka)	23 May 55	General Trade	286UNTS15	104159
Pakistan	China People's Rep	14 Mar 53	Commodity Trade	53CCJC11	410094
Pakistan	China People's Rep	19 Mar 56	Direct Aid	56CCJC41	410325
Pakistan	China People's Rep	03 Jun 58	Commodity Trade	58CCJC64	410431
Pakistan	China People's Rep	04 Oct 58	Mostfavored Nation	58CCJC89	410546
Pakistan	China People's Rep	02 Mar 63	Territory Boundary	63CCJC28	410957
Pakistan	China People's Rep	29 Aug 63	Air Transport	63CCJC101	411005
Pakistan	China People's Rep	18 Feb 65	Direct Aid	65CCJC19	411295
Pakistan	China People's Rep	26 Mar 65	Culture	65CCJC45	411298
Pakistan	China People's Rep	26 Mar 65	Territory Boundary	65CCJC44	411297
Pakistan	China People's Rep	01 Nov 65	Direct Aid	65CCJC134	411288
Pakistan	China People's Rep	01 Jun 66	Culture	66CCJC45	411289
Pakistan	China People's Rep	23 Jun 66	Direct Aid	66CCJC56	411303
Pakistan	China People's Rep	04 Jul 66	General Trade	66CCJC64	411290
Pakistan	China People's Rep	21 Oct 66	Water Transport	66CCJC87	411305
Pakistan	China People's Rep	17 Jan 67	Direct Aid	67CCJC1	411306
Pakistan	China People's Rep	14 Sep 67	Culture	67CCJC34	411308
Pakistan	Denmark	09 Nov 49	Air Transport	44UNTS255	100687
Pakistan	Denmark	30 Aug 54	Visas	203UNTS59	102740
Pakistan	Denmark	10 Apr 57	Air Transport	302UNTS53	104353
Pakistan	Denmark	05 Sep 59	Admin Cooperation	354UNTS377	105071
Pakistan	Denmark	04 Sep 61	Taxation	455UNTS305	106549

PARTY ONE	PARTY TWO	DATE	TOPIC	CITATION	NUMBER
Pakistan	Denmark	12 Dec 64	Tech Assistance	636UNTS313	109107
Pakistan	Denmark	01 Jun 67	Water Transport	620UNTS217	108958
Pakistan	Denmark	21 Oct 67	Tech Assistance	632UNTS105	109012
Pakistan	Denmark	05 Sep 68	Tech Assistance	0UNTS0	109396
Pakistan	Ethiopia	01 Jan 48	Air Transport	35UNTS3	100547
Pakistan	Ethiopia	29 Aug 52	Air Transport	150UNTS257	101979
Pakistan	Finland	11 Dec 67	Water Transport	631UNTS99	108989
Pakistan	France	31 Jul 50	Air Transport	96UNTS23	101329
Pakistan	France	17 Feb 58	General Trade	58FRMD2202	417349
Pakistan	France	27 Aug 64	Visas	64FRMD67	417350
Pakistan	France	22 Jul 66	Taxation	69FRMD25	417351
Pakistan	France	22 Jul 66	Taxation	0UNTS0	109648
Pakistan	France	22 Oct 69	Water Transport	0UNTS0	110633
Pakistan	Germany, West	04 Mar 50	General Trade	50WGBB717	425562
Pakistan	Germany, West	05 Mar 56	Other Military	68WBGA203	424563
Pakistan	Germany, West	09 Mar 57	General Trade	52WBGA132	424564
Pakistan	Germany, West	07 Aug 58	Taxation	60WGBB1799	425565
Pakistan	Germany, West	25 Nov 59	General Economic	457UNTS22	106575
Pakistan	Germany, West	20 Jul 60	Air Transport	465UNTS41	106721
Pakistan	Germany, West	09 Nov 61	Culture	63WGBB43	425566
Pakistan	Greece	05 Mar 59	Visas	338UNTS97	104833
Pakistan	Greece	17 Jan 63	General Trade	538UNTS175	107814
Pakistan	IAEA (Atom Energy)	05 Mar 62	Scientific Project	425UNTS17	106115
Pakistan	IAEA (Atom Energy)	15 Mar 66	Claims and Debts	588UNTS261	108530
Pakistan	IAEA (Atom Energy)	17 Jun 68	Atomic Energy	0UNTS0	109314
Pakistan	IBRD (World Bank)	27 Mar 52	IBRD Project	159UNTS251	102090
Pakistan	IBRD (World Bank)	13 Jun 52	IBRD Project	191UNTS85	102578
Pakistan	IBRD (World Bank)	02 Jun 54	IBRD Project	324UNTS59	104678
Pakistan	IBRD (World Bank)	20 Jun 55	IBRD Project	230UNTS41	103176
Pakistan	IBRD (World Bank)	04 Aug 55	IBRD Project	230UNTS79	103177
Pakistan	IBRD (World Bank)	06 Aug 55	IBRD Project	236UNTS195	103325
Pakistan	IBRD (World Bank)	18 Oct 57	IBRD Project	299UNTS303	104322
Pakistan	IBRD (World Bank)	17 Dec 57	IBRD Project	299UNTS321	104323
Pakistan	IBRD (World Bank)	23 Apr 58	IBRD Project	323UNTS253	104672
Pakistan	IBRD (World Bank)	13 Aug 59	IBRD Project	355UNTS129	105076
Pakistan	IBRD (World Bank)	25 Sep 59	IBRD Project	355UNTS169	105077
Pakistan	IBRD (World Bank)	30 Nov 59	IBRD Project	355UNTS203	105078
Pakistan	IBRD (World Bank)	19 Sep 60	IBRD Project	444UNTS207	106370
Pakistan	IBRD (World Bank)	27 Jun 61	IBRD Project	425UNTS241	106127
Pakistan	IBRD (World Bank)	14 Sep 62	IBRD Project	467UNTS125	106761
Pakistan	IBRD (World Bank)	14 Sep 62	IBRD Project	467UNTS152	106762
Pakistan	IBRD (World Bank)	13 Feb 63	IBRD Project	467UNTS3	106756
Pakistan	IBRD (World Bank)	14 May 64	IBRD Project	516UNTS145	107475
Pakistan	IBRD (World Bank)	30 Jun 64	IBRD Project	519UNTS57	107502
Pakistan	IBRD (World Bank)	26 Aug 64	IBRD Project	632UNTS201	109023
Pakistan	IBRD (World Bank)	09 Jul 65	IBRD Project	554UNTS39	108096
Pakistan	IBRD (World Bank)	15 Mar 67	IBRD Project	599UNTS245	108670
Pakistan	IBRD (World Bank)	26 May 67	Loans and Credits	616UNTS167	108895
Pakistan	IBRD (World Bank)	10 Aug 67	IBRD Project	618UNTS261	108931
Pakistan	IBRD (World Bank)	10 Jul 68	IBRD Project	0UNTS0	109588
Pakistan	IBRD (World Bank)	10 Jul 68	IBRD Project	0UNTS0	109302
Pakistan	IBRD (World Bank)	20 Dec 68	IBRD Project	0UNTS0	109593
Pakistan	IBRD (World Bank)	21 Mar 69	IBRD Project	0UNTS0	109672
Pakistan	IBRD (World Bank)	13 May 69	IBRD Project	0UNTS0	110098
Pakistan	IBRD (World Bank)	26 Jun 69	IBRD Project	0UNTS0	110357
Pakistan	IBRD (World Bank)	29 Jun 70	IBRD Project	0UNTS0	110833
Pakistan	ICJ Option Clause	22 Jun 48	ICJ Option Clause	16UNTS197	100259
Pakistan	ICJ Option Clause	23 May 57	ICJ Option Clause	269UNTS77	103875
Pakistan	ICJ Option Clause	12 Sep 60	ICJ Option Clause	374UNTS127	105332
Pakistan	IDA (Devel Assoc)	19 Oct 61	Non-IBRD Project	447UNTS161	106415
Pakistan	IDA (Devel Assoc)	22 Nov 61	Non-IBRD Project	447UNTS295	106420
Pakistan	IDA (Devel Assoc)	29 Jun 62	Non-IBRD Project	447UNTS325	106421
Pakistan	IDA (Devel Assoc)	02 Nov 62	Non-IBRD Project	468UNTS351	106781
Pakistan	IDA (Devel Assoc)	26 Jun 63	Non-IBRD Project	492UNTS115	107189
Pakistan	IDA (Devel Assoc)	26 Jul 63	Non-IBRD Project	492UNTS143	107190

PARTY ONE	PARTY TWO	DATE	TOPIC	CITATION	NUMBER
Pakistan	IDA (Devel Assoc)	16 Aug 63	Non-IBRD Project	492UNTS205	107192
Pakistan	IDA (Devel Assoc)	16 Aug 63	Non-IBRD Project	492UNTS171	107191
Pakistan	IDA (Devel Assoc)	25 Mar 64	Non-IBRD Project	535UNTS43	107775
Pakistan	IDA (Devel Assoc)	25 Mar 64	Non-IBRD Project	534UNTS275	107765
Pakistan	IDA (Devel Assoc)	11 Jun 64	Non-IBRD Project	506UNTS3	107379
Pakistan	IDA (Devel Assoc)	11 Jun 64	Non-IBRD Project	534UNTS309	107766
Pakistan	IDA (Devel Assoc)	24 Jun 64	Non-IBRD Project	533UNTS165	107742
Pakistan	IDA (Devel Assoc)	24 Jun 64	Non-IBRD Project	533UNTS191	107743
Pakistan	IDA (Devel Assoc)	21 Jul 64	Non-IBRD Project	534UNTS373	107768
Pakistan	IDA (Devel Assoc)	26 Aug 64	Non-IBRD Project	535UNTS263	107784
Pakistan	IDA (Devel Assoc)	22 Sep 64	Non-IBRD Project	594UNTS225	108605
Pakistan	IDA (Devel Assoc)	30 Jun 65	Non-IBRD Project	554UNTS111	108099
Pakistan	IDA (Devel Assoc)	13 Jan 66	Non-IBRD Project	567UNTS67	108252
Pakistan	IDA (Devel Assoc)	10 Feb 66	Non-IBRD Project	575UNTS89	108355
Pakistan	IDA (Devel Assoc)	17 Jun 66	Non-IBRD Project	582UNTS297	108468
Pakistan	IDA (Devel Assoc)	23 Dec 66	Non-IBRD Project	594UNTS255	108606
Pakistan	IDA (Devel Assoc)	13 Jan 69	Non-IBRD Project	0UNTS0	109610
Pakistan	IDA (Devel Assoc)	06 Mar 69	Non-IBRD Project	0UNTS0	109667
Pakistan	IDA (Devel Assoc)	26 Jun 69	Non-IBRD Project	0UNTS0	110227
Pakistan	IDA (Devel Assoc)	11 Feb 70	Non-IBRD Project	0UNTS0	110656
Pakistan	IDA (Devel Assoc)	22 May 70	Non-IBRD Project	0UNTS0	110658
Pakistan	IDA (Devel Assoc)	10 Jun 70	Non-IBRD Project	0UNTS0	110686
Pakistan	ILO (Labor Org)	16 May 51	Tech Assistance	100UNTS147	101394
Pakistan	India	10 Dec 47	Taxation	51UNTS173	100764
Pakistan	India	31 Mar 48	Finance	54UNTS33	100793
Pakistan	India	04 May.48	Dispute Settlement	54UNTS45	100794
Pakistan	India	23 Jun 48	Air Transport	28UNTS143	100423
Pakistan	India	30 Jun 48	Finance	29UNTS199	100441
Pakistan	India	23 Apr 49	Finance	54UNTS51	100795
Pakistan	India	27 Jul 49	Peace/Disarmament	81UNTS273	101076
Pakistan	India	08 Apr 50	Visas	131UNTS3	101733
Pakistan	India	21 Aug 52	Territory Boundary	207UNTS161	102805
Pakistan	India	20 Feb 53	Air Transport	164UNTS3	102155
Pakistan	India	08 May 54	Extradition	203UNTS167	102745
Pakistan	India	15 Apr 55	Land Transport	247UNTS25	103458
Pakistan	India	12 Jun 55	Finance	228UNTS211	103153
Pakistan	India	10 Sep 58	Territory Boundary	369UNTS81	105252
Pakistan	India	23 Oct 59	Territory Boundary	362UNTS3	105180
Pakistan	India	11 Jan 60	Territory Boundary	375UNTS119	105364
Pakistan	India	30 Jun 65	Territory Boundary	548UNTS277	107983
Pakistan	India	10 Jan 66	General Amity	560UNTS39	108166
Pakistan	Indonesia	03 Mar 51	General Amity	188UNTS333	102537
Pakistan	Iran	18 Feb 50	General Amity	161UNTS23	102119
Pakistan	Iran	09 Mar 56	Culture	449UNTS183	106460
Pakistan	Iran	20 Mar 56	Sanitation	0IRTB55	433084
Pakistan	Iran	20 Mar 56	Sanitation	0IRTB55	433084
Pakistan	Iran	18 May 57	Air Transport	0IRTB54	433081
Pakistan	Iran	06 Feb 58	Territory Boundary	0IRTB54	433079
Pakistan	Iran	16 Feb 59	Specific Property	0IRTB55	433087
Pakistan	Iran	20 Apr 59	Extradition	0IRTB54	433080
Pakistan	Iran	14 Dec 60	Sanitation	0IRTB55	433085
Pakistan	Iran	20 May 62	General Trade	0IRTB55	433083
Pakistan	Iran	18 Oct 64	Visas	0IRTB55	433086
Pakistan	Iran	27 Jan 68	Admin Cooperation	0IRTB56	433088
Pakistan	Iran	01 Nov 71	Taxation	0IRTB54	433082
Pakistan	Iraq	02 Mar 49	Visas	141UNTS319	101921
Pakistan	Iraq	26 Feb 50	General Amity	214UNTS3	102896
Pakistan	Iraq	20 Jun 50	Air Transport	77UNTS215	101001
Pakistan	Italy	05 Oct 57	Air Transport	353UNTS91	105039
Pakistan	Italy	10 Jan 61	General Trade	62ITDI516	436290
Pakistan	Japan	24 Apr 53	Admin Cooperation	221UNTS325	103013
Pakistan	Japan	04 Apr 56	General Trade	57JAIL82	440161
Pakistan	Japan	27 May 57	Culture	325UNTS21	104692
Pakistan	Japan	17 Feb 59	Taxation	341UNTS127	104880
Pakistan	Japan	30 Jul 60	Education	384UNTS63	105511
Pakistan	Japan	01 Dec 60	Visas	450UNTS337	106477

PARTY ONE	PARTY TWO	DATE	TOPIC	CITATION	NUMBER
Pakistan	Japan	18 Dec 60	General Amity	423UNTS197	106093
Pakistan	Japan	07 Mar 61	Postal Service	450UNTS359	106479
Pakistan	Japan	17 Oct 61	Air Transport	466UNTS17	106734
Pakistan	Japan	01 Aug 62	Visas	0JGJI1477	441113
Pakistan	Japan	16 Nov 63	Education	0JGJI1527	441117
Pakistan	Japan	25 Jul 69	Finance	69JJS341	442246
Pakistan	Lebanon	03 Oct 50	Visas	219UNTS41	102964
Pakistan	Lebanon	16 Jan 53	General Amity	284UNTS193	104137
Pakistan	Lebanon	04 Feb 64	Air Transport	614UNTS55	108863
Pakistan	Multilateral	07 Dec 44	IGO Establishment	15UNTS295	200102
Pakistan	Multilateral	07 Dec 44	Air Transport	84UNTS389	200252
Pakistan	Multilateral	11 Dec 46	Sanitation	12UNTS179	100186
Pakistan	Multilateral	10 Feb 47	Peace/Disarmament	49UNTS3	100747
Pakistan	Multilateral	27 May 47	Air Transport	418UNTS161	106021
Pakistan	Multilateral	02 Oct 47	Telecommunications	193UNTS188	102616
Pakistan	Multilateral	11 Oct 47	IGO Establishment	77UNTS143	100998
Pakistan	Multilateral	12 Nov 47	Admin Cooperation	46UNTS201	100710
Pakistan	Multilateral	12 Nov 47	Admin Cooperation	46UNTS169	100709
Pakistan	Multilateral	12 Nov 47	Admin Cooperation	53UNTS39	100771
Pakistan	Multilateral	12 Nov 47	Admin Cooperation	53UNTS13	100770
Pakistan	Multilateral	06 Mar 48	Water Transport	289UNTS3	104214
Pakistan	Multilateral	10 Jun 48	Humanitarian	191UNTS3	102576
Pakistan	Multilateral	10 Jun 48	Humanitarian	164UNTS113	102163
Pakistan	Multilateral	19 Jun 48	Air Transport	310UNTS151	104492
Pakistan	Multilateral	26 Jun 48	Culture	331UNTS217	104757
Pakistan	Multilateral	14 Sep 48	Milit Occupation	18UNTS267	100296
Pakistan	Multilateral	15 Nov 48	IGO Establishment	120UNTS59	101615
Pakistan	Multilateral	19 Nov 48	Sanitation	44UNTS277	100688
Pakistan	Multilateral	29 Nov 48	IGO Establishment	120UNTS13	101613
Pakistan	Multilateral	09 Dec 48	Scientific Project	73UNTS39	100942
Pakistan	Multilateral	09 Dec 48	Humanitarian	78UNTS277	101021
Pakistan	Multilateral	09 Dec 48	Scientific Project	20UNTS229	100318
Pakistan	Multilateral	04 May 49	Admin Cooperation	30UNTS23	100446
Pakistan	Multilateral	04 May 49	Admin Cooperation	47UNTS159	100728
Pakistan	Multilateral	04 May 49	Admin Cooperation	30UNTS3	100445
Pakistan	Multilateral	04 May 49	Admin Cooperation	98UNTS101	101358
Pakistan	Multilateral	04 May 49	Admin Cooperation	92UNTS19	101257
Pakistan	Multilateral	15 Jul 49	Health/Educ/Welfare	197UNTS3	102631
Pakistan	Multilateral	12 Aug 49	IGO Establishment	87UNTS131	101169
Pakistan	Multilateral	12 Aug 49	General Military	75UNTS135	100972
Pakistan	Multilateral	12 Aug 49	Humanitarian	75UNTS287	100973
Pakistan	Multilateral	12 Aug 49	Humanitarian	75UNTS31	100970
Pakistan	Multilateral	12 Aug 49	Humanitarian	75UNTS85	100971
Pakistan	Multilateral	16 Dec 49	Admin Cooperation	72UNTS3	100924
Pakistan	Multilateral	21 Mar 50	Admin Cooperation	96U24	
Pakistan	Multilateral	21 Mar 50	Admin Cooperation	96UNTS271	101342
Pakistan	Multilateral	06 Apr 50	Admin Cooperation	119UNTS99	101610
Pakistan	Multilateral	28 Jun 50	Loans and Credits	87UNTS153	101170
Pakistan	Multilateral	22 Nov 50	Culture	131UNTS25	101734
Pakistan	Multilateral	07 Dec 50	Admin Cooperation	212UNTS17	102861
Pakistan	Multilateral	15 Dec 50	Customs	171UNTS305	102234
Pakistan	Multilateral	15 Dec 50	Customs	157UNTS129	102052
Pakistan	Multilateral	25 May 51	Status of Forces	175UNTS215	102303
Pakistan	Multilateral	10 Jul 51	Other Military	108UNTS287	101481
Pakistan	Multilateral	29 Jul 51	Other Military	117UNTS85	101585
Pakistan	Multilateral	08 Sep 51	Peace/Disarmament	136UNTS45	101832
Pakistan	Multilateral	08 Sep 51	General Military	136UNTS165	101833
Pakistan	Multilateral	31 Oct 51	Other Military	172UNTS193	102247
Pakistan	Multilateral	06 Dec 51	Admin Cooperation	150UNTS67	101963
Pakistan	Multilateral	08 Jun 52	Other Military	210UNTS317	102843
Pakistan	Multilateral	12 Jun 52	Dispute Settlement	138UNTS183	101869
Pakistan	Multilateral	11 Jul 52	IGO Establishment	169UNTS3	102220
Pakistan	Multilateral	11 Jul 52	Postal Service	170UNTS3	102221
Pakistan	Multilateral	11 Jul 52	Postal Service	170UNTS63	102222
Pakistan	Multilateral	06 Sep 52	Patents/Copyrights	216UNTS132	102937
Pakistan	Multilateral	07 Oct 52	Admin Cooperation	310UNTS181	104493

PARTY ONE	PARTY TWO	DATE	TOPIC	CITATION	NUMBER
Pakistan	Multilateral	07 Nov 52	General Trade	221UNTS255	103010
Pakistan	Multilateral	27 Feb 53	Claims and Debts	333UNTS3	104764
Pakistan	Multilateral	31 Mar 53	Privil/Immunities	193UNTS136	102613
Pakistan	Multilateral	11 May 53	Sanitation	456UNTS3	106555
Pakistan	Multilateral	27 Aug 53	Other Military	213UNTS137	102884
Pakistan	Multilateral	22 Feb 54	Other Military	188UNTS273	102531
Pakistan	Multilateral	25 Feb 54	Air Transport	215UNTS249	102922
Pakistan	Multilateral	14 May 54	Culture	249UNTS215	103511
Pakistan	Multilateral	14 Jun 54	Air Transport	320UNTS209	104643
Pakistan	Multilateral	14 Jun 54	Air Transport	320UNTS217	104644
Pakistan	Multilateral	08 Sep 54	Milit Assistance	209UNTS23	102819
Pakistan	Multilateral	25 May 55	IGO Establishment	264UNTS117	103791
Pakistan	Multilateral	21 Sep 55	Other Military	269UNTS241	103885
Pakistan	Multilateral	28 Sep 55	Air Transport	478UNTS371	106943
Pakistan	Multilateral	12 Oct 55	IGO Establishment	560UNTS3	108165
Pakistan	Multilateral	05 Mar 56	Other Military	326UNTS169	104711
Pakistan	Multilateral	05 Mar 56	Other Military	326UNTS181	104712
Pakistan	Multilateral	20 Jun 56	Admin Cooperation	268UNTS3	103850
Pakistan	Multilateral	02 Jul 56	Tech Assistance	540UNTS110	107846
Pakistan	Multilateral	07 Sep 56	Humanitarian	266UNTS3	103822
Pakistan	Multilateral	25 Sep 56	Air Transport	334UNTS89	104767
Pakistan	Multilateral	25 Sep 56	Air Transport	334UNTS13	104766
Pakistan	Multilateral	26 Oct 56	IGO Establishment	276UNTS3	103988
Pakistan	Multilateral	20 Feb 57	Consul/Citizenship	309UNTS65	104468
Pakistan	Multilateral	03 Oct 57	Postal Service	365UNTS3	105213
Pakistan	Multilateral	03 Oct 57	Postal Service	364UNTS331	105212
Pakistan	Multilateral	03 Oct 57	Postal Service	364UNTS3	105211
Pakistan	Multilateral	29 Apr 58	Specific Resources	559UNTS285	108164
Pakistan	Multilateral	29 Apr 58	Territory Boundary	516UNTS205	107477
Pakistan	Multilateral	29 Apr 58	Dispute Settlement	450UNTS169	106466
Pakistan	Multilateral	29 Apr 58	Water Transport	450UNTS11	106465
Pakistan	Multilateral	29 Apr 58	Territory Boundary	499UNTS311	107302
Pakistan	Multilateral	10 Jun 58	Admin Cooperation	330UNTS3	104739
Pakistan	Multilateral	28 Jul 58	General Military	335UNTS205	104788
Pakistan	Multilateral	19 Nov 59	IGO Operations	410UNTS156	105902
Pakistan	Multilateral	26 Jan 60	IGO Establishment	439UNTS249	106333
Pakistan	Multilateral	17 Jun 60	Humanitarian	536UNTS27	107794
Pakistan	Multilateral	19 Sep 60	IBRD Project	444UNTS259	106371
Pakistan	Multilateral	19 Sep 60	IBRD Project	419UNTS125	106032
Pakistan	Multilateral	30 Mar 61	Sanitation	520UNTS151	107515
Pakistan	Multilateral	14 Apr 61	IGO Establishment	422UNTS101	106071
Pakistan	Multilateral	18 Apr 61	Consul/Citizenship	500UNTS95	107310
Pakistan	Multilateral	21 Jun 61	IGO Establishment	514UNTS209	107449
Pakistan	Multilateral	20 Feb 62	Water Transport	597UNTS159	108644
Pakistan	Multilateral	05 Mar 62	Scientific Project	425UNTS3	106114
Pakistan	Multilateral	10 Sep 62	Other Military	502UNTS3	107323
Pakistan	Multilateral	24 Apr 63	Consul/Citizenship	596UNTS261	108638
Pakistan	Multilateral	05 Aug 63	Sanitation	480UNTS43	106964
Pakistan	Multilateral	03 Dec 63	IGO Establishment	529UNTS217	107663
Pakistan	Multilateral	10 Jul 64	Postal Service	611UNTS105	108845
Pakistan	Multilateral	10 Jul 64	Postal Service	611UNTS7	108844
Pakistan	Multilateral	10 Jul 64	Postal Service	611UNTS387	108846
Pakistan	Multilateral	10 Jul 64	Postal Service	612UNTS3	108847
Pakistan	Multilateral	18 Mar 65	Dispute Settlement	575UNTS159	108359
Pakistan	Multilateral	08 Jul 65	General Trade	597UNTS3	108641
Pakistan	Multilateral	04 Dec 65	IGO Establishment	571UNTS123	108303
Pakistan	Multilateral	10 Feb 66	Loans and Credits	575UNTS129	108356
Pakistan	Multilateral	05 Apr 66	Water Transport	640UNTS133	109159
Pakistan	Multilateral	27 Jan 67	Scientific Project	610UNTS205	108843
Pakistan	Multilateral	03 May 67	IGO Operations	0UNTS0	110764
Pakistan	Multilateral	20 Jun 67	Visas	607UNTS97	108799
Pakistan	Multilateral	19 Oct 67	Atomic Energy	630UNTS69	108966
Pakistan	Multilateral	06 Nov 67	Other Military	640UNTS87	109155
Pakistan	Multilateral	28 Sep 68	Tech Assistance	0UNTS0	109296
Pakistan	Multilateral	17 Oct 69	Atomic Energy	0UNTS0	110518

PARTY ONE	PARTY TWO	DATE	TOPIC	CITATION	NUMBER
Pakistan	Netherlands	17 Jul 52	Air Transport	150UNTS277	101980
Pakistan	Netherlands	01 May 53	Visas	293UNTS11	104281
Pakistan	Netherlands	30 Oct 64	Tech Assistance	541UNTS243	107873
Pakistan	Netherlands	08 Nov 67	Scientific Project	0UNTS0	110753
Pakistan	Netherlands	13 Dec 68	Water Transport	0UNTS0	109739
Pakistan	New Zealand	28 Jun 48	Postal Service	91UNTS235	101253
Pakistan	New Zealand	17 Sep 48	Postal Service	91UNTS275	101254
Pakistan	Norway	08 Jun 49	Visas	90UNTS131	101231
Pakistan	Norway	23 Jun 49	Air Transport	35UNTS49	100550
Pakistan	Norway	21 May 51	General Trade	318UNTS163	104613
Pakistan	Norway	22 May 51	General Trade	2NORT555	451125
Pakistan	Norway	05 Mar 58	Air Transport	334UNTS199	104769
Pakistan	Philippines	16 Jul 49	Air Transport	35UNTS111	100553
Pakistan	Philippines	03 Jan 51	General Amity	2PTS605	465023
Pakistan	Philippines	15 Aug 61	Culture	522UNTS35	107534
Pakistan	Philippines	29 Sep 61	General Trade	422UNTS3	106065
Pakistan	Poland	21 Mar 67	Admin Cooperation	67PZUM69	458140
Pakistan	Portugal	07 Jun 58	Air Transport	320UNTS225	104645
Pakistan	Saudi Arabia	25 Nov 51	General Amity	177UNTS3	102304
Pakistan	Spain	08 Jul 57	General Amity	59SPBO1706	460213
Pakistan	Sweden	06 May 48	Air Transport	36UNTS3	100564
Pakistan	Sweden	04 Jun 55	Tech Assistance	228UNTS121	103146
Pakistan	Sweden	06 Mar 58	Air Transport	393UNTS181	105656
Pakistan	Sweden	25 Aug 58	Taxation	369UNTS183	105258
Pakistan	Switzerland	17 Mar 52	Air Transport	192UNTS237	102603
Pakistan	Switzerland	30 Dec 59	Taxation	60SWRO1058	462061
Pakistan	Syria	29 Aug 50	General Amity	109UNTS95	101494
Pakistan	Syria	18 Dec 55	General Trade	320UNTS269	104647
Pakistan	Thailand	28 Aug 58	General Amity	394UNTS53	105668
Pakistan	Turkey	27 May 49	Visas	141UNTS325	101922
Pakistan	Turkey	26 Jul 51	General Amity	188UNTS323	102536
Pakistan	Turkey	22 Oct 51	Visas	219UNTS47	102965
Pakistan	Turkey	29 Jun 53	Culture	211UNTS225	102854
Pakistan	Turkey	04 Feb 54	General Amity	211UNTS263	102858
Pakistan	Turkey	02 Nov 55	Air Transport	311UNTS217	104505
Pakistan	Turkey	12 Dec 55	Visas	55TURG1912	466024
Pakistan	UK Great Britain	21 Feb 48	Finance	134UNTS128	101797
Pakistan	UK Great Britain	27 Jul 49	Air Transport	44UNTS199	100685
Pakistan	UK Great Britain	02 Apr 51	General Trade	168UNTS281	102219
Pakistan	UK Great Britain	26 Sep 51	Postal Service	118UNTS221	101608
Pakistan	UK Great Britain	29 Sep 51	Finance	134UNTS183	101798
Pakistan	UK Great Britain	22 Jul 52	Postal Service	157UNTS185	102054
Pakistan	UK Great Britain	10 Jun 55	Taxation	243UNTS15	103444
Pakistan	UK Great Britain	13 Mar 63	Atomic Energy	482UNTS347	107003
Pakistan	UK Great Britain	13 Oct 64	Atomic Energy	534UNTS71	107754
Pakistan	UK Great Britain	25 Sep 68	Finance	0UNTS0	109820
Pakistan	UN Special Fund	25 Feb 60	Direct Aid	351UNTS141	105021
Pakistan	UNICEF (Children)	20 Jun 49	Tech Assistance	65UNTS60	100826
Pakistan	United Arab Rep	28 Aug 51	General Amity	214UNTS247	102902
Pakistan	United Arab Rep	08 Sep 51	Postal Service	133UNTS257	101793
Pakistan	United Arab Rep	14 Nov 53	Culture	485UNTS55	107046
Pakistan	United Arab Rep	13 Dec 54	Air Transport	255UNTS167	103610
Pakistan	United Nations	27 Aug 48	Humanitarian	47UNTS269	100734
Pakistan	United Nations	28 Apr 52	Tech Assistance	128UNTS191	101720
Pakistan	United Nations	25 Jan 54	Tech Assistance	185UNTS213	102472
Pakistan	United Nations	17 Nov 60	Tech Assistance	380UNTS277	105460
Pakistan	United Nations	18 Apr 63	IGO Operations	503UNTS25	107339
Pakistan	USA (United States)	16 Jun 48	Air Transport	235UNTS29	103293
Pakistan	USA (United States)	18 Oct 49	Visas	141UNTS333	101923
Pakistan	USA (United States)	23 Sep 50	Education	82UNTS131	101088
Pakistan	USA (United States)	15 Dec 50	Milit Assistance	122UNTS89	101639
Pakistan	USA (United States)	09 Feb 51	Tech Assistance	100UNTS67	101388
Pakistan	USA (United States)	23 May 51	Admin Cooperation	134UNTS265	101805
Pakistan	USA (United States)	17 Sep 52	Loans and Credits	227UNTS77	103132
Pakistan	USA (United States)	25 Jun 53	Direct Aid	205UNTS139	102773

PARTY ONE	PARTY TWO	DATE	TOPIC	CITATION	NUMBER
Pakistan	USA (United States)	01 May 54	Mass Media	237UNTS231	103349
Pakistan	USA (United States)	19 May 54	Milit Assistance	202UNTS301	102736
Pakistan	USA (United States)	23 Aug 54	Direct Aid	234UNTS243	103287
Pakistan	USA (United States)	02 Oct 54	Direct Aid	236UNTS187	103324
Pakistan	USA (United States)	11 Jan 55	Milit Assistance	251UNTS111	103537
Pakistan	USA (United States)	18 Jan 55	US Agri Commod Aid	239UNTS61	103372
Pakistan	USA (United States)	18 Jan 55	Direct Aid	241UNTS53	103423
Pakistan	USA (United States)	26 May 55	General Economic	257UNTS93	103652
Pakistan	USA (United States)	20 Jul 55	Postal Service	241UNTS255	103436
Pakistan	USA (United States)	11 Aug 55	Atomic Energy	239UNTS259	103384
Pakistan	USA (United States)	02 Mar 56	US Agri Commod Aid	271UNTS371	103927
Pakistan	USA (United States)	28 May 56	Milit Assistance	269UNTS15	103868
Pakistan	USA (United States)	07 Aug 56	US Agri Commod Aid	281UNTS75	104071
Pakistan	USA (United States)	10 Sep 56	Milit Assistance	277UNTS259	104010
Pakistan	USA (United States)	01 Jul 57	Taxation	344UNTS203	104951
Pakistan	USA (United States)	15 Nov 57	US Agri Commod Aid	303UNTS173	104380
Pakistan	USA (United States)	26 Nov 58	US Agri Commod Aid	337UNTS3	104812
Pakistan	USA (United States)	05 Mar 59	General Military	327UNTS285	104726
Pakistan	USA (United States)	18 Jul 59	Gen Communications	355UNTS367	105087
Pakistan	USA (United States)	28 Jul 59	Visas	360UNTS327	105166
Pakistan	USA (United States)	12 Nov 59	General Amity	404UNTS259	105816
Pakistan	USA (United States)	11 Apr 60	US Agri Commod Aid	372UNTS251	105302
Pakistan	USA (United States)	14 Oct 61	US Agri Commod Aid	426UNTS237	106141
Pakistan	USA (United States)	05 Mar 62	General Trade	446UNTS57	106403
Pakistan	USA (United States)	31 May 62	General Aid	460UNTS75	106631
Pakistan	USA (United States)	25 Jul 62	Direct Aid	459UNTS87	106614
Pakistan	USA (United States)	16 Jan 63	Milit Assistance	471UNTS133	106828
Pakistan	USA (United States)	29 Jun 63	Milit Assistance	487UNTS243	107107
Pakistan	USA (United States)	26 Feb 65	Commodity Trade	542UNTS103	107883
Pakistan	USA (United States)	26 May 66	US Agri Commod Aid	594UNTS27	108592
Pakistan	USA (United States)	21 Nov 66	Commodity Trade	0UNTS0	109689
Pakistan	USA (United States)	11 May 67	US Agri Commod Aid	0UNTS0	109767
Pakistan	USA (United States)	03 Jul 67	General Trade	0UNTS0	109777
Pakistan	USA (United States)	03 Aug 67	US Agri Commod Aid	0UNTS0	109912
Pakistan	USA (United States)	26 Dec 67	US Agri Commod Aid	0UNTS0	109990
Pakistan	USA (United States)	16 May 68	US Agri Commod Aid	0UNTS0	109996
Pakistan	USA (United States)	03 Jul 69	US Agri Commod Aid	0UNTS0	110446
Pakistan	USA (United States)	03 Oct 69	US Agri Commod Aid	0UNTS0	110508
Pakistan	USA (United States)	10 Jan 70	US Agri Commod Aid	0UNTS0	110509
Pakistan	USA (United States)	06 May 70	Commodity Trade	0UNTS0	110780
Pakistan	USSR (Soviet Union)	01 May 48	Consul/Citizenship	0SUST248	468303
Pakistan	USSR (Soviet Union)	27 Jun 56	Finance	16SUGG71	469920
Pakistan	USSR (Soviet Union)	27 Jun 56	General Trade	16SUGG71	469919
Pakistan	USSR (Soviet Union)	27 Jun 56	General Trade	0SUST359	468304
Pakistan	USSR (Soviet Union)	27 Jun 57	General Trade	0UNTS0	109823
Pakistan	USSR (Soviet Union)	04 Mar 61	General Aid	10SUGG124	469749
Pakistan	USSR (Soviet Union)	07 Oct 63	Air Transport	499UNTS161	107297
Pakistan	USSR (Soviet Union)	05 Jun 65	Culture	593UNTS115	108579
Pakistan	WHO (World Health)	07 Oct 51	Tech Assistance	126UNTS101	101684
Pakistan	WHO (World Health)	21 Feb 52	IGO Operations	131UNTS221	101742
Pakistan	WHO (World Health)	20 Jan 60	Tech Assistance	351UNTS355	105034
Pakistan	Yugoslavia	15 May 54	General Trade	286UNTS3	104158
Pan Am Health Org	WHO (World Health)	24 May 49	Sanitation	32UNTS387	200178
Panama	Argentina	21 Nov 64	Culture	635UNTS205	109083
Panama	France	10 Jul 53	Consul/Citizenship	58FRRT19	415352
Panama	Germany, West	09 Feb 60	Admin Cooperation	60WBGA169	424567
Panama	Germany, West	30 Sep 64	Tech Assistance	65WBGA7	424568
Panama	Germany, West	31 Jul 67	Visas	67WBGA171	424569
Panama	Germany, West	05 Jul 68	Air Transport	69WGBB1560	425570
Panama	IBRD (World Bank)	25 Sep 53	IBRD Project	188UNTS71	102521
Panama	IBRD (World Bank)	25 Sep 53	IBRD Project	188UNTS95	102522
Panama	IBRD (World Bank)	12 Jul 55	IBRD Project	219UNTS127	102970
Panama	IBRD (World Bank)	19 Aug 60	IBRD Project	390UNTS153	105607
Panama	IBRD (World Bank)	14 Sep 62	IBRD Project	476UNTS153	106908
Panama	IBRD (World Bank)	16 Mar 70	IBRD Project	0UNTS0	110680

PARTY ONE	PARTY TWO	DATE	TOPIC	CITATION	NUMBER
Panama	ILO (Labor Org)	10 Nov 51	Tech Assistance	126UNTS269	101693
Panama	Italy	29 Mar 47	Peace/Disarmament	47ITGU127	435291
Panama	Italy	02 Sep 49	General Amity	2ITMA442	437292
Panama	Italy	06 Jan 64	Visas	65ITDI155	436293
Panama	Mexico	20 Jan 66	Culture	67MEXD807	444035
Panama	Multilateral	17 Feb 40	Privil/Immunities	161UNTS229	200487
Panama	Multilateral	30 Jul 40	Admin Cooperation	161UNTS253	200488
Panama	Multilateral	15 Jan 44	IGO Establishment	161UNTS281	200489
Panama	Multilateral	02 Aug 44	Scientific Project	67UNTS221	200221
Panama	Multilateral	07 Dec 44	Air Transport	171UNTS345	200501
Panama	Multilateral	07 Dec 44	IGO Establishment	15UNTS295	200102
Panama	Multilateral	08 Aug 45	General Military	82UNTS279	200251
Panama	Multilateral	16 Nov 45	IGO Establishment	4UNTS275	100052
Panama	Multilateral	22 Jul 46	IGO Establishment	9UNTS3	100125
Panama	Multilateral	22 Jul 46	IGO Establishment	14UNTS185	100221
Panama	Multilateral	27 Jul 46	Patents/Copyrights	90UNTS229	101238
Panama	Multilateral	02 Dec 46	Specific Resources	161UNTS72	102124
Panama	Multilateral	11 Dec 46	Sanitation	12UNTS179	100186
Panama	Multilateral	15 Dec 46	IGO Establishment	18UNTS3	100283
Panama	Multilateral	27 May 47	Air Transport	418UNTS161	106021
Panama	Multilateral	02 Sep 47	General Military	21UNTS77	100324
Panama	Multilateral	02 Oct 47	Telecommunications	193UNTS188	102616
Panama	Multilateral	12 Nov 47	Admin Cooperation	46UNTS169	100709
Panama	Multilateral	06 Mar 48	Water Transport	289UNTS3	104214
Panama	Multilateral	30 Apr 48	IGO Establishment	119UNTS3	101609
Panama	Multilateral	30 Apr 48	Dispute Settlement	30UNTS55	100449
Panama	Multilateral	10 Jun 48	Humanitarian	191UNTS3	102576
Panama	Multilateral	10 Jun 48	Humanitarian	164UNTS113	102163
Panama	Multilateral	24 Jul 48	Sanitation	66UNTS25	100847
Panama	Multilateral	19 Nov 48	Sanitation	44UNTS277	100688
Panama	Multilateral	09 Dec 48	Humanitarian	78UNTS277	101021
Panama	Multilateral	23 Mar 49	Commodity Trade	203UNTS179	102746
Panama	Multilateral	09 Jul 49	Telecommunications	168UNTS143	102218
Panama	Multilateral	25 May 51	Status of Forces	175UNTS215	102303
Panama	Multilateral	01 Jun 51	Tech Assistance	118UNTS57	101596
Panama	Multilateral	08 Sep 51	Peace/Disarmament	136UNTS45	101832
Panama	Multilateral	11 Jul 52	Postal Service	170UNTS63	102222
Panama	Multilateral	11 Jul 52	Postal Service	170UNTS269	102223
Panama	Multilateral	11 Jul 52	IGO Establishment	169UNTS3	102220
Panama	Multilateral	11 May 53	Sanitation	456UNTS3	106555
Panama	Multilateral	12 May 54	Admin Cooperation	327UNTS3	104714
Panama	Multilateral	14 May 54	Culture	249UNTS215	103511
Panama	Multilateral	04 Jun 54	Customs	282UNTS249	104101
Panama	Multilateral	04 Jun 54	Customs	276UNTS191	103992
Panama	Multilateral	14 Jun 54	Air Transport	320UNTS209	104643
Panama	Multilateral	14 Jun 54	Air Transport	320UNTS217	104644
Panama	Multilateral	25 May 55	IGO Establishment	264UNTS117	103791
Panama	Multilateral	04 Jan 56	Scientific Project	256UNTS171	103627
Panama	Multilateral	25 Apr 56	Commodity Trade	270UNTS103	103896
Panama	Multilateral	26 Oct 56	IGO Establishment	276UNTS3	103988
Panama	Multilateral	09 Apr 57	Tech Assistance	274UNTS172	103965
Panama	Multilateral	03 Oct 57	Postal Service	365UNTS3	105213
Panama	Multilateral	03 Oct 57	Postal Service	364UNTS3	105211
Panama	Multilateral	03 Oct 57	Postal Service	365UNTS207	105214
Panama	Multilateral	29 Apr 58	Territory Boundary	516UNTS205	107477
Panama	Multilateral	29 Apr 58	Territory Boundary	499UNTS311	107302
Panama	Multilateral	29 Apr 58	Water Transport	450UNTS11	106465
Panama	Multilateral	29 Apr 58	Specific Resources	559UNTS285	108164
Panama	Multilateral	29 Apr 58	Dispute Settlement	450UNTS169	106466
Panama	Multilateral	01 Dec 58	Commodity Trade	385UNTS137	105534
Panama	Multilateral	03 Dec 58	Admin Cooperation	416UNTS51	105995
Panama	Multilateral	03 Dec 58	Admin Cooperation	398UNTS9	105715
Panama	Multilateral	06 Apr 59	Commodity Trade	349UNTS167	105013
Panama	Multilateral	08 Apr 59	IGO Establishment	389UNTS69	105593
Panama	Multilateral	18 Nov 59	IGO Establishment	390UNTS227	105610

PARTY ONE	PARTY TWO	DATE	TOPIC	CITATION	NUMBER
Panama	Multilateral	26 Jan 60	IGO Establishment	439UNTS249	106333
Panama	Multilateral	17 Jun 60	Humanitarian	536UNTS27	107794
Panama	Multilateral	28 Jul 60	IGO Establishment	485UNTS3	107042
Panama	Multilateral	30 Mar 61	Sanitation	520UNTS151	107515
Panama	Multilateral	18 Apr 61	Consul/Citizenship	500UNTS95	107310
Panama	Multilateral	18 Apr 61	Dispute Settlement	500UNTS243	107312
Panama	Multilateral	18 Apr 61	Consul/Citizenship	500UNTS223	107311
Panama	Multilateral	21 Jun 61	IGO Establishment	514UNTS209	107449
Panama	Multilateral	26 Mar 62	IGO Establishment	539UNTS67	107825
Panama	Multilateral	28 Sep 62	IGO Establishment	469UNTS169	106791
Panama	Multilateral	24 Apr 63	Consul/Citizenship	596UNTS487	108640
Panama	Multilateral	24 Apr 63	Consul/Citizenship	596UNTS261	108638
Panama	Multilateral	05 Aug 63	Sanitation	480UNTS43	106964
Panama	Multilateral	21 Oct 63	Tech Assistance	480UNTS197	106969
Panama	Multilateral	14 Dec 63	IGO Establishment	507UNTS149	107399
Panama	Multilateral	10 Jul 64	Postal Service	611UNTS105	108845
Panama	Multilateral	10 Jul 64	Postal Service	611UNTS7	108844
Panama	Multilateral	05 Apr 66	Water Transport	640UNTS133	109159
Panama	Multilateral	27 Jan 67	Scientific Project	610UNTS205	108843
Panama	Multilateral	14 Feb 67	General Military	634UNTS281	109068
Panama	Multilateral	24 Sep 68	Air Transport	0UNTS0	110612
Panama	Norway	16 Jun 59	Visas	3NORT775	451126
Panama	Norway	30 Jan 62	Visas	3NORT848	451127
Panama	Spain	18 Mar 53	General Amity	54SPB0607	460214
Panama	Taiwan	26 Feb 60	Culture	435UNTS281	106285
Panama	UK Great Britain	15 Sep 51	Air Transport	560UNTS143	108172
Panama	UK Great Britain	07 Jan 66	Visas	565UNTS25	108233
Panama	UN Special Fund	09 Mar 61	Direct Aid	396UNTS3	105691
Panama	UNICEF (Children)	14 Jun 51	IGO Operations	97UNTS3	101343
Panama	United Nations	20 Aug 52	Tech Assistance	136UNTS3	101829
Panama	United Nations	24 Jun 59	IGO Operations	507UNTS245	107402
Panama	USA (United States)	31 Jan 35	Consul/Citizenship	234UNTS277	200536
Panama	USA (United States)	23 Mar 40	Land Transport	124UNTS195	200420
Panama	USA (United States)	06 Sep 40	Land Transport	124UNTS209	200421
Panama	USA (United States)	28 Mar 41	Taxation	103UNTS163	200312
Panama	USA (United States)	07 Mar 42	Admin Cooperation	101UNTS157	200291
Panama	USA (United States)	18 May 42	General Amity	124UNTS221	200422
Panama	USA (United States)	07 Jul 42	Military Mission	9UNTS289	200048
Panama	USA (United States)	02 Mar 43	Sanitation	107UNTS55	200351
Panama	USA (United States)	07 Jun 43	Specific Property	21UNTS269	200128
Panama	USA (United States)	14 Nov 44	Education	139UNTS367	200462
Panama	USA (United States)	13 May 45	Visas	89UNTS273	200256
Panama	USA (United States)	26 May 47	Territory Boundary	138UNTS137	101866
Panama	USA (United States)	24 Sep 48	Education	150UNTS25	101961
Panama	USA (United States)	05 Nov 48	Visas	89UNTS27	101206
Panama	USA (United States)	31 Mar 49	Air Transport	55UNTS87	100810
Panama	USA (United States)	31 Mar 49	Telecommunications	55UNTS125	100811
Panama	USA (United States)	31 Mar 49	Air Transport	55UNTS141	100812
Panama	USA (United States)	14 Jun 49	Visas	89UNTS37	101207
Panama	USA (United States)	26 Jan 50	Claims and Debts	132UNTS233	101763
Panama	USA (United States)	24 May 50	Territory Boundary	241UNTS139	103430
Panama	USA (United States)	14 Sep 50	Land Transport	241UNTS159	103431
Panama	USA (United States)	14 Sep 50	Land Transport	124UNTS25	101664
Panama	USA (United States)	20 Dec 50	Tech Assistance	92UNTS167	101269
Panama	USA (United States)	26 Jan 51	Land Transport	137UNTS69	101849
Panama	USA (United States)	26 Feb 51	Sanitation	160UNTS153	102106
Panama	USA (United States)	30 Jul 51	Direct Aid	140UNTS321	101896
Panama	USA (United States)	23 Oct 51	Direct Aid	140UNTS3	101880
Panama	USA (United States)	30 Jun 52	Tech Assistance	181UNTS121	102404
Panama	USA (United States)	21 Jul 52	Tech Assistance	181UNTS285	102417
Panama	USA (United States)	08 Aug 52	Air Transport	181UNTS257	102415
Panama	USA (United States)	26 Jun 53	Tech Assistance	215UNTS77	102912
Panama	USA (United States)	25 Mar 54	Specific Property	232UNTS289	103243
Panama	USA (United States)	11 May 54	Direct Aid	236UNTS107	103319
Panama	USA (United States)	25 Jan 55	General Ad Hoc	243UNTS211	103454

PARTY ONE	PARTY TWO	DATE	TOPIC	CITATION	NUMBER
Panama	USA (United States)	25 May 56	Visas	268UNTS333	103866
Panama	USA (United States)	01 Aug 56	Telecommunications	281UNTS49	104068
Panama	USA (United States)	05 Aug 57	Visas	299UNTS113	104309
Panama	USA (United States)	20 May 59	Milit Assistance	346UNTS235	104983
Panama	USA (United States)	24 Jun 59	Scientific Project	479UNTS145	106950
Panama	USA (United States)	31 Oct 60	Admin Cooperation	405UNTS63	105823
Panama	USA (United States)	23 Jan 61	Admin Cooperation	445UNTS135	106382
Panama	USA (United States)	11 Dec 61	General Aid	445UNTS161	106384
Panama	USA (United States)	23 May 62	Milit Assistance	458UNTS225	106604
Panama	USA (United States)	30 Aug 63	Taxation	488UNTS11	107116
Panama	USA (United States)	30 Oct 63	General Aid	530UNTS3	107668
Panama	USA (United States)	15 Feb 66	Scientific Project	586UNTS27	108494
Panama	USA (United States)	16 Nov 66	Gen Communications	0UNTS0	109688
Panama	USA (United States)	22 Feb 68	Air Transport	0UNTS0	110006
Panama	USA (United States)	20 Mar 69	Scientific Project	0UNTS0	110155
Panama	USA (United States)	04 Mar 70	Commodity Trade	0UNTS0	110626
Panama	WHO (World Health)	09 Nov 51	Sanitation	118UNTS43	101595
Papua	Multilateral	24 Dec 68	Commodity Trade	0UNTS0	109369
Paraguay	Argentina	23 Jan 58	Scientific Project	0UNTS0	109294
Paraguay	Argentina	07 Feb 64	Air Transport	634UNTS127	109057
Paraguay	Argentina	21 Oct 64	Specific Property	635UNTS177	109081
Paraguay	Argentina	21 Oct 64	Specific Property	635UNTS189	109082
Paraguay	Argentina	23 Jan 67	Water Transport	634UNTS181	109060
Paraguay	Argentina	23 Jan 67	General Trade	634UNTS193	109061
Paraguay	Argentina	14 Jul 67	Culture	0UNTS0	110181
Paraguay	Argentina	20 Jul 67	Atomic Energy	0UNTS0	110182
Paraguay	Argentina	20 Jul 67	Tech Assistance	0UNTS0	110183
Paraguay	Argentina	15 Jul 69	Territory Boundary	0UNTS0	110193
Paraguay	Austria	17 Jan 69	Visas	69ABGB92	403149
Paraguay	Belgium	21 Nov 60	Visas	387UNTS237	105565
Paraguay	Brazil	14 Apr 41	Commodity Trade	54UNTS269	200199
Paraguay	Brazil	14 Jun 41	Finance	54UNTS313	200203
Paraguay	Brazil	14 Jun 41	Culture	54UNTS235	200196
Paraguay	Brazil	14 Jun 41	Culture	54UNTS249	200197
Paraguay	Brazil	14 Jun 41	Specific Property	54UNTS259	200198
Paraguay	Brazil	14 Jun 41	Land Transport	54UNTS289	200201
Paraguay	Brazil	14 Jun 41	Admin Cooperation	54UNTS279	200200
Paraguay	Brazil	14 Jun 41	IGO Establishment	54UNTS303	200202
Paraguay	Brazil	14 Jun 41	Visas	88UNTS401	200255
Paraguay	Brazil	14 Jun 41	IGO Establishment	54UNTS323	200204
Paraguay	Brazil	08 Oct 42	Telecommunications	65UNTS191	200211
Paraguay	Brazil	11 Aug 44	Land Transport	67UNTS303	200227
Paraguay	Denmark	18 May 57	Finance	286UNTS117	104163
Paraguay	Denmark	03 May 67	General Trade	608UNTS55	108812
Paraguay	France	11 Sep 56	General Trade	58FRRT18	415353
Paraguay	France	05 Apr 63	Visas	63FRRT50	415354
Paraguay	France	10 Dec 63	Health/Educ/Welfare	65FRRT15	415355
Paraguay	Germany, West	25 Jul 55	General Trade	55WBGA187	424571
Paraguay	Germany, West	25 Jul 55	Finance	55WBGA187	424572
Paraguay	Germany, West	30 Jul 55	Mostfavored Nation	57WGBB1273	425573
Paraguay	Germany, West	11 Nov 69	Loans and Credits	70WBGA41	424574
Paraguay	Germany, West	29 Apr 71	Loans and Credits	71WBGA114	424575
Paraguay	IBRD (World Bank)	07 Dec 51	IBRD Project	159UNTS103	102085
Paraguay	IBRD (World Bank)	16 Dec 64	IBRD Project	549UNTS173	107999
Paraguay	IBRD (World Bank)	16 Dec 65	IBRD Project	568UNTS165	108268
Paraguay	IBRD (World Bank)	04 Apr 66	IBRD Project	570UNTS41	108287
Paraguay	IBRD (World Bank)	09 Jan 69	IBRD Project	0UNTS0	110825
Paraguay	IBRD (World Bank)	25 Jun 69	IBRD Project	0UNTS0	110225
Paraguay	IDA (Devel Assoc)	26 Oct 61	Non-IBRD Project	447UNTS277	106419
Paraguay	IDA (Devel Assoc)	26 Dec 63	Non-IBRD Project	507UNTS3	107394
Paraguay	IDA (Devel Assoc)	04 Apr 66	Non-IBRD Project	582UNTS331	108469
Paraguay	IDA (Devel Assoc)	25 Jun 69	Non-IBRD Project	0UNTS0	110226
Paraguay	ILO (Labor Org)	12 Jul 51	Tech Assistance	117UNTS155	101591
Paraguay	Israel	21 Nov 65	Visas	582UNTS65	108458
Paraguay	Italy	08 Jul 59	Finance	63ITDI293	436295

PARTY ONE	PARTY TWO	DATE	TOPIC	CITATION	NUMBER
Paraguay	Italy	08 Jul 59	General Trade	61ITGU76	435294
Paraguay	Japan	22 Jul 59	Loans and Credits	0JGJI9	441105
Paraguay	Japan	22 Jul 59	Visas	373UNTS85	105316
Paraguay	Mexico	13 Aug 58	Culture	60MEXD907	444036
Paraguay	Multilateral	30 Jul 40	Admin Cooperation	161UNTS253	200488
Paraguay	Multilateral	02 Aug 44	Scientific Project	67UNTS221	200221
Paraguay	Multilateral	07 Dec 44	Air Transport	84UNTS389	200252
Paraguay	Multilateral	07 Dec 44	IGO Establishment	15UNTS295	200102
Paraguay	Multilateral	07 Dec 44	Air Transport	171UNTS345	200501
Paraguay	Multilateral	07 Dec 44	Air Transport	171UNTS387	200502
Paraguay	Multilateral	08 Aug 45	General Military	82UNTS279	200251
Paraguay	Multilateral	27 Dec 45	IGO Establishment	2UNTS39	100020
Paraguay	Multilateral	22 Jul 46	IGO Establishment	9UNTS3	100125
Paraguay	Multilateral	22 Jul 46	IGO Establishment	14UNTS185	100221
Paraguay	Multilateral	11 Dec 46	Sanitation	12UNTS179	100186
Paraguay	Multilateral	02 Sep 47	General Military	21UNTS77	100324
Paraguay	Multilateral	11 Oct 47	IGO Establishment	77UNTS143	100998
Paraguay	Multilateral	30 Apr 48	IGO Establishment	119UNTS3	101609
Paraguay	Multilateral	30 Apr 48	Dispute Settlement	30UNTS55	100449
Paraguay	Multilateral	24 Jul 48	Sanitation	66UNTS25	100847
Paraguay	Multilateral	19 Nov 48	Sanitation	44UNTS277	100688
Paraguay	Multilateral	29 Nov 48	IGO Establishment	120UNTS13	101613
Paraguay	Multilateral	09 Dec 48	Humanitarian	78UNTS277	101021
Paraguay	Multilateral	09 Jul 49	Telecommunications	168UNTS143	102218
Paraguay	Multilateral	12 Aug 49	General Military	75UNTS135	100972
Paraguay	Multilateral	12 Aug 49	Humanitarian	75UNTS85	100971
Paraguay	Multilateral	12 Aug 49	Humanitarian	75UNTS287	100973
Paraguay	Multilateral	12 Aug 49	Humanitarian	75UNTS31	100970
Paraguay	Multilateral	25 May 51	Status of Forces	175UNTS215	102303
Paraguay	Multilateral	08 Sep 51	Peace/Disarmament	136UNTS45	101832
Paraguay	Multilateral	11 Jul 52	Postal Service	170UNTS3	102221
Paraguay	Multilateral	11 Jul 52	Postal Service	170UNTS63	102222
Paraguay	Multilateral	11 Jul 52	IGO Establishment	169UNTS3	102220
Paraguay	Multilateral	11 Jul 52	Postal Service	171UNTS89	102225
Paraguay	Multilateral	11 Jul 52	Postal Service	170UNTS269	102223
Paraguay	Multilateral	11 Jul 52	Postal Service	171UNTS143	102226
Paraguay	Multilateral	31 Mar 53	Mass Media	435UNTS191	106280
Paraguay	Multilateral	31 Mar 53	Privil/Immunities	193UNTS136	102613
Paraguay	Multilateral	19 Oct 53	IGO Establishment	207UNTS189	102807
Paraguay	Multilateral	25 May 55	IGO Establishment	264UNTS117	103791
Paraguay	Multilateral	04 Jul 55	Tech Assistance	214UNTS10	102897
Paraguay	Multilateral	26 Oct 56	IGO Establishment	276UNTS3	103988
Paraguay	Multilateral	03 Oct 57	Postal Service	366UNTS141	105217
Paraguay	Multilateral	03 Oct 57	Postal Service	364UNTS3	105211
Paraguay	Multilateral	03 Oct 57	Postal Service	364UNTS331	105212
Paraguay	Multilateral	03 Oct 57	Postal Service	366UNTS193	105218
Paraguay	Multilateral	03 Oct 57	Postal Service	365UNTS3	105213
Paraguay	Multilateral	03 Oct 57	Postal Service	366UNTS87	105216
Paraguay	Multilateral	03 Oct 57	Postal Service	366UNTS255	105219
Paraguay	Multilateral	03 Oct 57	Postal Service	366UNTS3	105215
Paraguay	Multilateral	03 Oct 57	Postal Service	365UNTS207	105214
Paraguay	Multilateral	01 Dec 58	Commodity Trade	385UNTS137	105534
Paraguay	Multilateral	08 Apr 59	IGO Establishment	389UNTS69	105593
Paraguay	Multilateral	26 Jan 60	IGO Establishment	439UNTS249	106333
Paraguay	Multilateral	17 Jun 60	Humanitarian	536UNTS27	107794
Paraguay	Multilateral	28 Jul 60	IGO Establishment	485UNTS3	107042
Paraguay	Multilateral	30 Mar 61	Sanitation	520UNTS151	107515
Paraguay	Multilateral	26 Oct 61	Patents/Copyrights	496UNTS43	107247
Paraguay	Multilateral	26 Mar 62	IGO Establishment	539UNTS67	107825
Paraguay	Multilateral	22 Jun 62	ILO Labor	494UNTS249	107237
Paraguay	Multilateral	05 Aug 63	Sanitation	480UNTS43	106964
Paraguay	Multilateral	13 Aug 63	General Trade	592UNTS139	108572
Paraguay	Multilateral	10 Jul 64	Postal Service	613UNTS3	108850
Paraguay	Multilateral	10 Jul 64	Postal Service	611UNTS7	108844
Paraguay	Multilateral	10 Jul 64	Postal Service	611UNTS387	108846

PARTY ONE	PARTY TWO	DATE	TOPIC	CITATION	NUMBER
Paraguay	Multilateral	10 Jul 64	Postal Service	612UNTS233	108848
Paraguay	Multilateral	10 Jul 64	Postal Service	613UNTS3	108851
Paraguay	Multilateral	10 Jul 64	Postal Service	613UNTS193	108852
Paraguay	Multilateral	10 Jul 64	Postal Service	611UNTS105	108845
Paraguay	Multilateral	10 Jul 64	Postal Service	612UNTS3	108847
Paraguay	Multilateral	10 Jul 64	Postal Service	613UNTS127	108853
Paraguay	Multilateral	10 Jul 64	Postal Service	612UNTS361	108849
Paraguay	Multilateral	13 Jul 64	ILO Labor	569UNTS65	108279
Paraguay	Multilateral	23 Jun 65	General IGO	614UNTS239	108873
Paraguay	Multilateral	08 Jul 65	General Trade	597UNTS3	108641
Paraguay	Multilateral	14 Feb 67	General Military	634UNTS281	109068
Paraguay	Multilateral	18 Mar 68	Commodity Trade	0UNTS0	109262
Paraguay	Multilateral	01 Jul 68	Peace/Disarmament	0UNTS0	110485
Paraguay	Netherlands	05 Mar 52	Air Transport	52NET67	447033
Paraguay	Netherlands	13 Apr 57	Finance	593UNTS85	108577
Paraguay	Netherlands	21 Nov 60	Visas	450UNTS201	106467
Paraguay	Norway	21 Mar 63	Visas	3NORT880	451128
Paraguay	Spain	12 Oct 49	General Amity	51SPBO908	460215
Paraguay	Spain	25 Aug 50	General Economic	52SPBO1211	460216
Paraguay	Spain	26 Mar 57	Culture	58SPBO2904	460217
Paraguay	Spain	11 Aug 58	Commodity Trade	59SPBO1007	460218
Paraguay	Spain	25 Jun 59	General Trade	60SPBO1804	460220
Paraguay	Spain	25 Jun 59	General Trade	60SPBO1804	460221
Paraguay	Spain	25 Jun 59	Water Transport	60SPBO1904	460223
Paraguay	Spain	25 Jun 59	Non-ILO Labor	60SPBO1804	460219
Paraguay	Spain	25 Jun 59	Consul/Citizenship	60SPBO1904	460222
Paraguay	Spain	21 May 63	Specif Goods/Equip	65SPBO2207	460224
Paraguay	Spain	13 Nov 64	Specif Goods/Equip	65SPBO1108	460225
Paraguay	Taiwan	18 Aug 61	Culture	438UNTS109	106314
Paraguay	Taiwan	11 Jul 62	General Trade	458UNTS41	106591
Paraguay	Taiwan	07 Jun 68	General Amity	0UNTS0	110435
Paraguay	UK Great Britain	03 Apr 50	General Economic	99UNTS81	101372
Paraguay	UK Great Britain	21 Nov 55	General Economic	252UNTS107	103560
Paraguay	UK Great Britain	27 Oct 66	Visas	597UNTS229	108648
Paraguay	UN Special Fund	22 Jun 61	Direct Aid	399UNTS117	105738
Paraguay	UNICEF (Children)	25 Jan 51	IGO Operations	79UNTS9	101027
Paraguay	United Nations	27 Sep 51	Tech Assistance	120UNTS105	101617
Paraguay	United Nations	01 Aug 59	Tech Assistance	341UNTS319	104894
Paraguay	USA (United States)	22 May 42	Sanitation	124UNTS243	200423
Paraguay	USA (United States)	28 Nov 42	Admin Cooperation	101UNTS173	200292
Paraguay	USA (United States)	27 Oct 43	Military Mission	29UNTS391	200174
Paraguay	USA (United States)	10 Dec 43	Military Mission	21UNTS305	200131
Paraguay	USA (United States)	12 Sep 46	General Trade	125UNTS179	101677
Paraguay	USA (United States)	28 Feb 47	Air Transport	44UNTS25	100676
Paraguay	USA (United States)	03 Mar 47	Tech Assistance	135UNTS156	101819
Paraguay	USA (United States)	01 Jan 48	Scientific Project	89UNTS191	101217
Paraguay	USA (United States)	12 Mar 48	Education	162UNTS30	102131
Paraguay	USA (United States)	30 Jun 48	Sanitation	124UNTS34	101665
Paraguay	USA (United States)	27 Nov 50	Direct Aid	122UNTS147	101644
Paraguay	USA (United States)	29 Dec 50	Tech Assistance	122UNTS157	101645
Paraguay	USA (United States)	30 Jul 51	Military Mission	178UNTS163	102340
Paraguay	USA (United States)	22 Jul 55	Military Mission	265UNTS3	103802
Paraguay	USA (United States)	22 Jul 55	Military Mission	265UNTS15	103803
Paraguay	USA (United States)	28 Oct 55	Claims and Debts	273UNTS97	103946
Paraguay	USA (United States)	02 May 56	US Agri Commod Aid	268UNTS299	103863
Paraguay	USA (United States)	11 May 56	Visas	269UNTS33	103870
Paraguay	USA (United States)	04 Apr 57	Taxation	283UNTS193	104117
Paraguay	USA (United States)	04 Apr 57	Education	284UNTS161	104135
Paraguay	USA (United States)	06 Oct 60	Gen Communications	393UNTS281	105662
Paraguay	USA (United States)	07 Jul 61	US Agri Commod Aid	433UNTS53	106231
Paraguay	USA (United States)	26 Sep 61	General Aid	461UNTS91	106653
Paraguay	USA (United States)	16 Jan 62	Scientific Project	433UNTS169	106240
Paraguay	USA (United States)	25 Aug 62	Milit Assistance	461UNTS207	106665
Paraguay	USA (United States)	24 Nov 62	US Agri Commod Aid	471UNTS49	106821
Paraguay	USA (United States)	20 Aug 63	Education	531UNTS197	107704

PARTY ONE	PARTY TWO	DATE	TOPIC	CITATION	NUMBER
Paraguay	USA (United States)	16 Sep 63	US Agri Commod Aid	494UNTS101	107229
Paraguay	USA (United States)	14 Nov 63	US Agri Commod Aid	505UNTS87	107366
Paraguay	USA (United States)	10 Feb 64	Milit Assistance	511UNTS53	107426
Paraguay	USA (United States)	05 Sep 64	US Agri Commod Aid	530UNTS225	107685
Paraguay	USA (United States)	11 Apr 66	Milit Assistance	578UNTS99	108389
Paraguay	USA (United States)	18 Apr 66	Gen Communications	586UNTS189	108503
Paraguay	USA (United States)	27 Apr 66	US Agri Commod Aid	578UNTS121	108391
Paraguay	USA (United States)	04 Nov 66	Direct Aid	0UNTS0	109620
Paraguay	USA (United States)	07 Jun 69	US Agri Commod Aid	0UNTS0	110333
Paraguay	WHO (World Health)	15 Feb 51	Tech Assistance	110UNTS171	101509
Peru	Argentina	25 May 68	Atomic Energy	0UNTS0	110184
Peru	Austria	25 Jul 59	Visas	59ABGB242	403150
Peru	Belgium	03 May 57	Visas	274UNTS251	103970
Peru	Belgium	22 Jan 65	Tech Assistance	0UNTS0	110565
Peru	Canada	18 Feb 54	Air Transport	411UNTS64	105915
Peru	Denmark	10 Jun 57	General Economic	406UNTS63	105839
Peru	Denmark	22 Jun 60	Air Transport	439UNTS113	106326
Peru	Denmark	30 Dec 64	Tech Assistance	595UNTS47	108611
Peru	Denmark	20 Jun 67	Loans and Credits	0UNTS0	109446
Peru	France	23 Apr 59	Air Transport	61FRRT19	415359
Peru	Germany, West	20 Jul 51	General Trade	52WGBB333	425576
Peru	Germany, West	20 Dec 56	Admin Cooperation	61WBGA200	424577
Peru	Germany, West	30 Apr 62	Air Transport	0UNTS0	110466
Peru	Germany, West	30 Apr 62	Air Transport	63WGBB373	425578
Peru	Germany, West	20 Nov 64	Culture	66WGBB76	425579
Peru	Germany, West	21 Jul 65	Tech Assistance	69WBGA126	424580
Peru	IBRD (World Bank)	23 Jan 52	IBRD Project	159UNTS163	102087
Peru	IBRD (World Bank)	08 Jul 52	IBRD Project	159UNTS321	102093
Peru	IBRD (World Bank)	12 Apr 54	IBRD Project	190UNTS231	102567
Peru	IBRD (World Bank)	12 Nov 54	IBRD Project	209UNTS287	102831
Peru	IBRD (World Bank)	05 Apr 55	IBRD Project	211UNTS115	102850
Peru	IBRD (World Bank)	19 Apr 55	IBRD Project	221UNTS153	103007
Peru	IBRD (World Bank)	05 Aug 55	IBRD Project	218UNTS3	102950
Peru	IBRD (World Bank)	13 Mar 57	IBRD Project	274UNTS59	103958
Peru	IBRD (World Bank)	17 Sep 58	IBRD Project	323UNTS27	104663
Peru	IBRD (World Bank)	01 Jun 60	IBRD Project	380UNTS15	105448
Peru	IBRD (World Bank)	29 Jun 60	IBRD Project	400UNTS99	105750
Peru	IBRD (World Bank)	19 Dec 60	IBRD Project	417UNTS275	106010
Peru	IBRD (World Bank)	03 Nov 61	IBRD Project	430UNTS47	106203
Peru	IBRD (World Bank)	13 Mar 63	IBRD Project	478UNTS245	106938
Peru	IBRD (World Bank)	22 Nov 63	IBRD Project	491UNTS101	107175
Peru	IBRD (World Bank)	22 Apr 64	IBRD Project	519UNTS95	107503
Peru	IBRD (World Bank)	15 Mar 65	IBRD Project	632UNTS209	109024
Peru	IBRD (World Bank)	03 Jun 65	IBRD Project	551UNTS227	108045
Peru	IBRD (World Bank)	18 Jun 65	IBRD Project	568UNTS191	108269
Peru	IBRD (World Bank)	17 Sep 65	Loans and Credits	566UNTS311	108248
Peru	IBRD (World Bank)	13 May 66	IBRD Project	570UNTS61	108288
Peru	IBRD (World Bank)	07 Sep 66	IBRD Project	585UNTS3	108481
Peru	IBRD (World Bank)	11 Sep 67	IBRD Project	619UNTS171	108943
Peru	ICAO (Civil Aviat)	22 Oct 48	IGO Status/Immunit	95UNTS3	101315
Peru	ILO (Labor Org)	13 Apr 51	Tech Assistance	100UNTS31	101385
Peru	ILO (Labor Org)	22 Jun 60	IGO Status/Immunit	423UNTS165	106092
Peru	Israel	25 Jun 62	Culture	515UNTS263	107464
Peru	Israel	02 Apr 63	Tech Assistance	515UNTS279	107465
Peru	Israel	01 Apr 68	Visas	0UNTS0	109354
Peru	Italy	21 Aug 49	General Amity	2ITMA387	437296
Peru	Italy	18 Feb 60	Admin Cooperation	62ITDI362	436298
Peru	Italy	18 Feb 60	Visas	62ITDI361	436297
Peru	Italy	02 Sep 60	Visas	62ITDI363	436299
Peru	Italy	08 Apr 61	Culture	63ITGU36	435300
Peru	Japan	15 May 61	General Trade	451UNTS3	106482
Peru	Mexico	03 Feb 60	Culture	62MEXD3010	444037
Peru	Multilateral	25 Jun 36	Privil/Immunities	161UNTS217	200486
Peru	Multilateral	30 Jul 40	Admin Cooperation	161UNTS253	200488
Peru	Multilateral	12 Oct 40	Specific Resources	161UNTS193	200485
Peru	Multilateral	28 Nov 40	Commodity Trade	139UNTS159	200452
Peru	Multilateral	02 Aug 44	Scientific Project	67UNTS221	200221
Peru	Multilateral	07 Dec 44	Air Transport	171UNTS387	200502
Peru	Multilateral	07 Dec 44	Air Transport	171UNTS345	200501
Peru	Multilateral	07 Dec 44	IGO Establishment	15UNTS295	200102
Peru	Multilateral	15 Dec 44	Sanitation	17UNTS305	200110
Peru	Multilateral	15 Dec 44	Sanitation	16UNTS247	200106
Peru	Multilateral	16 Nov 45	IGO Establishment	4UNTS275	100052
Peru	Multilateral	27 Dec 45	IGO Establishment	2UNTS39	100020
Peru	Multilateral	22 Jul 46	IGO Establishment	14UNTS185	100221
Peru	Multilateral	22 Jul 46	IGO Establishment	9UNTS3	100125
Peru	Multilateral	03 Sep 46	Commodity Trade	139UNTS3	101872
Peru	Multilateral	02 Dec 46	Specific Resources	161UNTS72	102124
Peru	Multilateral	11 Dec 46	Sanitation	12UNTS179	100186
Peru	Multilateral	15 Dec 46	IGO Establishment	18UNTS3	100283
Peru	Multilateral	02 Sep 47	General Military	21UNTS77	100324
Peru	Multilateral	02 Oct 47	Telecommunications	193UNTS188	102616
Peru	Multilateral	11 Oct 47	IGO Establishment	77UNTS143	100998
Peru	Multilateral	30 Apr 48	IGO Establishment	119UNTS3	101609
Peru	Multilateral	30 Apr 48	Dispute Settlement	30UNTS55	100449
Peru	Multilateral	19 Jun 48	Air Transport	310UNTS151	104492
Peru	Multilateral	24 Jul 48	Sanitation	66UNTS25	100847
Peru	Multilateral	19 Nov 48	Sanitation	44UNTS277	100688
Peru	Multilateral	09 Dec 48	Humanitarian	78UNTS277	101021
Peru	Multilateral	23 Mar 49	Commodity Trade	203UNTS179	102746
Peru	Multilateral	12 Aug 49	Humanitarian	75UNTS31	100970
Peru	Multilateral	12 Aug 49	Humanitarian	75UNTS287	100973
Peru	Multilateral	12 Aug 49	Humanitarian	75UNTS85	100971
Peru	Multilateral	12 Aug 49	General Military	75UNTS135	100972
Peru	Multilateral	16 Dec 49	Admin Cooperation	72UNTS3	100924
Peru	Multilateral	06 Apr 50	Admin Cooperation	119UNTS99	101610
Peru	Multilateral	25 May 51	Status of Forces	175UNTS215	102303
Peru	Multilateral	02 Jul 51	Refugees	189UNTS137	102545
Peru	Multilateral	08 Sep 51	Peace/Disarmament	136UNTS45	101832
Peru	Multilateral	11 Jul 52	IGO Establishment	169UNTS3	102220
Peru	Multilateral	11 Jul 52	Postal Service	170UNTS269	102223
Peru	Multilateral	11 Jul 52	Postal Service	170UNTS63	102222
Peru	Multilateral	06 Sep 52	Patents/Copyrights	216UNTS132	102937
Peru	Multilateral	27 Feb 53	Claims and Debts	333UNTS3	104764
Peru	Multilateral	31 Mar 53	Mass Media	435UNTS191	106280
Peru	Multilateral	14 Jun 54	Air Transport	320UNTS217	104644
Peru	Multilateral	14 Jun 54	Air Transport	320UNTS209	104643
Peru	Multilateral	25 May 55	IGO Establishment	264UNTS117	103791
Peru	Multilateral	30 Mar 56	IGO Operations	604UNTS114	108748
Peru	Multilateral	25 Apr 56	Commodity Trade	270UNTS103	103896
Peru	Multilateral	07 Sep 56	Humanitarian	266UNTS3	103822
Peru	Multilateral	26 Oct 56	IGO Establishment	276UNTS3	103988
Peru	Multilateral	01 May 57	Admin Cooperation	284UNTS201	104138
Peru	Multilateral	03 Oct 57	Postal Service	365UNTS207	105214
Peru	Multilateral	03 Oct 57	Postal Service	364UNTS3	105211
Peru	Multilateral	03 Oct 57	Postal Service	365UNTS3	105213
Peru	Multilateral	29 Apr 58	Territory Boundary	499UNTS311	107302
Peru	Multilateral	01 Dec 58	Commodity Trade	385UNTS137	105534
Peru	Multilateral	06 Apr 59	Commodity Trade	349UNTS167	105013
Peru	Multilateral	08 Apr 59	IGO Establishment	389UNTS69	105593
Peru	Multilateral	18 Nov 59	IGO Establishment	390UNTS227	105610
Peru	Multilateral	26 Jan 60	IGO Establishment	439UNTS249	106333
Peru	Multilateral	17 Jun 60	Humanitarian	536UNTS27	107794
Peru	Multilateral	28 Jul 60	IGO Establishment	485UNTS3	107042
Peru	Multilateral	30 Mar 61	Sanitation	520UNTS151	107515
Peru	Multilateral	21 Jun 61	IGO Establishment	514UNTS209	107449
Peru	Multilateral	26 Mar 62	IGO Establishment	539UNTS67	107825
Peru	Multilateral	28 Sep 62	IGO Establishment	469UNTS169	106791
Peru	Multilateral	24 Apr 63	Consul/Citizenship	596UNTS261	108638
Peru	Multilateral	24 Apr 63	Consul/Citizenship	596UNTS487	108640

PARTY ONE	PARTY TWO	DATE	TOPIC	CITATION	NUMBER
Peru	Multilateral	05 Aug 63	Sanitation	480UNTS43	106964
Peru	Multilateral	10 Jul 64	Postal Service	611UNTS105	108845
Peru	Multilateral	10 Jul 64	Postal Service	611UNTS7	108844
Peru	Multilateral	13 Jul 64	ILO Labor	569UNTS65	108279
Peru	Multilateral	05 Apr 66	Water Transport	640UNTS133	109159
Peru	Multilateral	27 Jan 67	Scientific Project	610UNTS205	108843
Peru	Multilateral	14 Feb 67	General Military	634UNTS281	109068
Peru	Multilateral	18 Mar 68	Commodity Trade	0UNTS0	109262
Peru	Multilateral	01 Jul 68	Peace/Disarmament	0UNTS0	110485
Peru	Multilateral	24 Dec 68	Commodity Trade	0UNTS0	109369
Peru	Multilateral	29 Jul 70	Tech Assistance	0UNTS0	110608
Peru	Netherlands	22 Sep 52	Air Transport	255UNTS49	103604
Peru	Nicaragua	14 Oct 59	Air Transport	392UNTS303	105649
Peru	Norway	27 Jul 59	Visas	3NORT778	451129
Peru	Norway	02 Nov 60	Air Transport	497UNTS207	107270
Peru	Spain	23 May 53	General Trade	54SPBO1810	460226
Peru	Spain	31 Mar 54	Air Transport	232UNTS65	103230
Peru	Spain	16 May 59	Consul/Citizenship	60SPBO1904	460227
Peru	Switzerland	20 Jul 53	General Trade	55SWRO287	462150
Peru	Switzerland	23 Nov 56	Air Transport	411UNTS97	105916
Peru	Taiwan	08 Jun 64	General Trade	548UNTS151	107976
Peru	UK Great Britain	22 Dec 47	Air Transport	72UNTS143	100932
Peru	UK Great Britain	20 Jul 48	Finance	66UNTS197	100855
Peru	UK Great Britain	03 Dec 66	Loans and Credits	617UNTS231	108915
Peru	UK Great Britain	19 Dec 67	Loans and Credits	0UNTS0	109447
Peru	UN Special Fund	19 Jan 60	Direct Aid	349UNTS83	105010
Peru	UNICEF (Children)	31 Jan 50	Tech Assistance	65UNTS80	100834
Peru	USA (United States)	11 Mar 42	Military Mission	117UNTS266	200375
Peru	USA (United States)	21 Apr 42	Scientific Project	89UNTS317	200260
Peru	USA (United States)	07 May 42	General Trade	103UNTS219	200316
Peru	USA (United States)	11 May 42	Sanitation	136UNTS353	200447
Peru	USA (United States)	24 Aug 42	Education	24UNTS153	200139
Peru	USA (United States)	20 May 43	Non-IBRD Project	100UNTS259	200288
Peru	USA (United States)	20 Dec 43	Military Mission	117UNTS285	200376
Peru	USA (United States)	31 Mar 44	Military Mission	109UNTS165	200357
Peru	USA (United States)	04 Apr 44	Scientific Project	89UNTS291	200258
Peru	USA (United States)	15 Apr 44	Education	150UNTS317	200479
Peru	USA (United States)	02 May 44	Military Mission	109UNTS211	200361
Peru	USA (United States)	10 Jul 44	Military Mission	117UNTS291	200377
Peru	USA (United States)	12 Jun 45	Milit Servic/Citiz	121UNTS283	200406
Peru	USA (United States)	19 Aug 46	Military Mission	109UNTS15	101485
Peru	USA (United States)	07 Oct 46	Military Mission	7UNTS71	100092
Peru	USA (United States)	22 Nov 46	Non-IBRD Project	100UNTS170	101396
Peru	USA (United States)	27 Dec 46	Air Transport	152UNTS93	102013
Peru	USA (United States)	27 Dec 46	Air Transport	26UNTS227	100390
Peru	USA (United States)	19 Apr 47	Sanitation	136UNTS284	101840
Peru	USA (United States)	02 Mar 48	Military Mission	109UNTS9	101484
Peru	USA (United States)	30 Jun 48	Education	150UNTS45	101962
Peru	USA (United States)	25 Mar 49	Scientific Project	89UNTS15	101205
Peru	USA (United States)	20 Jun 49	Military Mission	92UNTS249	101276
Peru	USA (United States)	28 Sep 51	General Trade	160UNTS35	102099
Peru	USA (United States)	04 Feb 52	Education	121UNTS255	200403
Peru	USA (United States)	22 Feb 52	Milit Assistance	165UNTS31	102166
Peru	USA (United States)	09 Apr 52	Tech Assistance	184UNTS295	102454
Peru	USA (United States)	13 Apr 54	Tech Assistance	236UNTS87	103318
Peru	USA (United States)	25 Oct 54	Direct Aid	238UNTS247	103368
Peru	USA (United States)	31 Dec 54	Non-ILO Labor	251UNTS51	103533
Peru	USA (United States)	07 Jan 55	Milit Assistance	261UNTS321	103730
Peru	USA (United States)	07 Feb 55	Direct Aid	241UNTS63	103424
Peru	USA (United States)	16 Mar 55	Claims and Debts	252UNTS151	103564
Peru	USA (United States)	30 Apr 55	General Aid	263UNTS309	103780
Peru	USA (United States)	28 Oct 55	Military Mission	239UNTS181	103378
Peru	USA (United States)	25 Jan 56	Atomic Energy	240UNTS425	103417
Peru	USA (United States)	03 May 56	Direct Aid	272UNTS59	103931
Peru	USA (United States)	07 May 56	US Agri Commod Aid	268UNTS285	103862

PARTY ONE	PARTY TWO	DATE	TOPIC	CITATION	NUMBER
Peru	USA (United States)	08 May 56	Direct Aid	278UNTS117	104028
Peru	USA (United States)	06 Sep 56	Military Mission	277UNTS231	104009
Peru	USA (United States)	09 Oct 56	Visas	288UNTS165	104204
Peru	USA (United States)	17 Apr 57	Scientific Project	283UNTS3	104102
Peru	USA (United States)	02 May 57	US Agri Commod Aid	283UNTS55	104106
Peru	USA (United States)	19 Jul 57	Direct Aid	289UNTS271	104223
Peru	USA (United States)	09 Apr 58	US Agri Commod Aid	316UNTS37	104576
Peru	USA (United States)	15 Jun 59	Milit Assistance	346UNTS279	104987
Peru	USA (United States)	22 Aug 59	Atomic Energy	357UNTS99	105109
Peru	USA (United States)	12 Feb 60	US Agri Commod Aid	372UNTS83	105290
Peru	USA (United States)	26 Feb 60	Milit Assistance	394UNTS141	105674
Peru	USA (United States)	15 Jul 60	Military Mission	384UNTS159	105517
Peru	USA (United States)	13 Feb 61	Visas	406UNTS177	105848
Peru	USA (United States)	25 Jan 62	Tech Assistance	473UNTS57	106855
Peru	USA (United States)	05 Mar 62	General Economic	446UNTS65	106404
Peru	USA (United States)	20 Mar 62	US Agri Commod Aid	445UNTS61	106377
Peru	USA (United States)	20 Dec 62	Milit Installation	471UNTS75	106822
Peru	USA (United States)	23 Sep 63	US Agri Commod Aid	488UNTS91	107121
Peru	USA (United States)	13 Feb 64	US Agri Commod Aid	511UNTS119	107431
Peru	USA (United States)	07 Jul 64	Scientific Project	530UNTS113	107676
Peru	USA (United States)	28 Jan 65	Education	587UNTS273	108513
Peru	USA (United States)	11 Aug 65	Gen Communications	564UNTS135	108225
Peru	USA (United States)	23 Apr 70	Visas	0UNTS0	110776
Peru	WHO (World Health)	26 Sep 50	Sanitation	104UNTS233	101444
Peru	WHO (World Health)	10 Nov 50	Tech Assistance	110UNTS187	101510
Petrol Export Org	Austria	24 Jun 65	IGO Operations	589UNTS135	108540
Philippines	Argentina	12 Feb 60	General Amity	535UNTS293	107785
Philippines	Asian Devel Bank	22 Dec 66	IGO Establishment	615UNTS375	108887
Philippines	Australia	01 Sep 49	Postal Service	46UNTS215	100711
Philippines	Australia	14 Apr 50	Air Transport	127UNTS281	101709
Philippines	Australia	23 Feb 60	Visas	358UNTS139	105131
Philippines	Australia	16 Jun 65	General Trade	541UNTS31	107858
Philippines	Belgium	05 Feb 57	Patents/Copyrights	269UNTS49	103872
Philippines	Belgium	17 Feb 60	Visas	356UNTS303	105101
Philippines	Bolivia	22 Feb 63	Visas	490UNTS231	107156
Philippines	Burma	15 Aug 52	Air Transport	200UNTS97	102696
Philippines	Cuba	03 Sep 52	General Amity	3PTS3	465030
Philippines	Denmark	20 Oct 54	Air Transport	216UNTS3	102927
Philippines	Denmark	21 Apr 59	Visas	3PTS827	465040
Philippines	Denmark	20 Dec 66	Visas	591UNTS259	108563
Philippines	Denmark	08 May 69	Air Transport	0UNTS0	109866
Philippines	Dominican Republic	02 Nov 52	General Amity	543UNTS175	107901
Philippines	Ecuador	24 Mar 48	General Amity	1PTS695	465014
Philippines	FAO (Food Agri)	03 Apr 52	Tech Assistance	2PTS785	465073
Philippines	FAO (Food Agri)	30 Oct 52	Tech Assistance	3PTS36	465075
Philippines	FAO (Food Agri)	14 Nov 52	Tech Assistance	3PTS49	465078
Philippines	FAO (Food Agri)	25 Jun 53	Tech Assistance	3PTS165	465081
Philippines	France	26 Jun 47	General Amity	1PTS427	465008
Philippines	France	08 Mar 63	Visas	569UNTS77	108280
Philippines	France	29 Oct 68	Air Transport	0UNTS0	109972
Philippines	France	21 May 70	Visas	0UNTS0	110744
Philippines	Germany, West	25 Apr 55	General Trade	3PTS417	465035
Philippines	Germany, West	09 Mar 62	Visas	449UNTS35	106450
Philippines	Germany, West	05 Feb 63	Tech Assistance	4PTS639	465049
Philippines	Germany, West	28 Feb 64	General Trade	4PTS831	465057
Philippines	Germany, West	29 Feb 64	Direct Aid	4PTS835	465058
Philippines	Germany, West	03 Mar 64	General Economic	4PTS843	465061
Philippines	Germany, West	03 Mar 64	Water Transport	4PTS841	465060
Philippines	Germany, West	03 Mar 64	Admin Cooperation	64WBGA89	424581
Philippines	Germany, West	03 Mar 64	General Amity	64WBGA89	424781
Philippines	Germany, West	03 Mar 64	Visas	4PTS839	465059
Philippines	Germany, West	30 Apr 68	Visas	68WBGA135	424782
Philippines	Germany, West	30 Apr 68	Visas	68WBGA135	424582
Philippines	Germany, West	27 May 71	Loans and Credits	71WBGA158	424583
Philippines	Germany, West	27 May 71	Loans and Credits	71WBGA158	424783

PARTY ONE	PARTY TWO	DATE	TOPIC	CITATION	NUMBER
Philippines	Greece	08 Oct 49	Air Transport	187UNTS221	102515
Philippines	Greece	28 Aug 50	General Amity	225UNTS155	103097
Philippines	IAEA (Atom Energy)	28 Sep 66	Atomic Energy	589UNTS25	108533
Philippines	IBRD (World Bank)	22 Nov 57	IBRD Project	293UNTS83	104287
Philippines	IBRD (World Bank)	26 Jul 61	IBRD Project	414UNTS253	105976
Philippines	IBRD (World Bank)	13 Oct 61	IBRD Project	415UNTS269	105989
Philippines	IBRD (World Bank)	07 Nov 62	Loans and Credits	468UNTS281	106777
Philippines	IBRD (World Bank)	15 Feb 63	IBRD Project	478UNTS161	106936
Philippines	IBRD (World Bank)	22 Jul 64	IBRD Project	516UNTS171	107476
Philippines	IBRD (World Bank)	28 Oct 64	IBRD Project	537UNTS165	107801
Philippines	IBRD (World Bank)	02 Nov 65	IBRD Project	567UNTS3	108249
Philippines	IBRD (World Bank)	23 Sep 66	IBRD Project	596UNTS71	108629
Philippines	IBRD (World Bank)	05 Apr 67	IBRD Project	598UNTS261	108661
Philippines	IBRD (World Bank)	04 Jun 69	IBRD Project	0UNTS0	109893
Philippines	IBRD (World Bank)	10 Jul 69	IBRD Project	0UNTS0	110105
Philippines	IBRD (World Bank)	18 Aug 69	IBRD Project	0UNTS0	110490
Philippines	ICJ Option Clause	12 Jul 47	ICJ Option Clause	7UNTS229	100101
Philippines	ILO (Labor Org)	23 Jan 70	IGO Establishment	0UNTS0	110348
Philippines	India	20 Oct 49	Air Transport	72UNTS191	100934
Philippines	India	11 Jul 52	General Amity	203UNTS73	102741
Philippines	India	14 Mar 69	Atomic Energy	0UNTS0	109796
Philippines	Indonesia	21 Jun 51	General Amity	2PTS689	465027
Philippines	Indonesia	04 Jul 56	Admin Cooperation	401UNTS59	105763
Philippines	Indonesia	27 Jul 60	Admin Cooperation	4PTS349	465044
Philippines	Indonesia	30 Jan 61	General Military	4PTS425	465047
Philippines	Indonesia	27 May 63	General Trade	4PTS739	465050
Philippines	Indonesia	27 May 63	General Economic	4PTS753	465053
Philippines	Indonesia	27 May 63	Admin Cooperation	4PTS747	465051
Philippines	Indonesia	27 May 63	Tech Assistance	4PTS749	465052
Philippines	Indonesia	25 Jul 63	General Military	4PTS761	465054
Philippines	Indonesia	19 Mar 64	Gen Communications	4PTS859	465063
Philippines	Indonesia	19 Mar 64	IGO Establishment	4PTS855	465062
Philippines	Indonesia	21 Feb 67	Gen Communications	593UNTS109	108578
Philippines	Israel	07 Aug 51	Air Transport	192UNTS81	102596
Philippines	Israel	26 Feb 58	General Amity	507UNTS135	107398
Philippines	Israel	14 Dec 60	Visas	449UNTS23	106448
Philippines	Israel	10 Jan 63	Atomic Energy	588UNTS205	108526
Philippines	Israel	16 Mar 64	Tech Assistance	550UNTS269	108021
Philippines	Israel	20 Feb 67	Atomic Energy	597UNTS139	108642
Philippines	Israel	14 Jan 69	Atomic Energy	0UNTS0	109437
Philippines	Israel	10 Dec 69	Visas	0UNTS0	110389
Philippines	Italy	09 Jul 47	General Amity	44UNTS3	100674
Philippines	Italy	14 Jul 59	Visas	490UNTS237	107157
Philippines	Japan	24 Jan 53	Water Transport	3PTS63	465031
Philippines	Japan	12 Mar 53	Reparations	3PTS85	465032
Philippines	Japan	09 May 54	Reparations	57JAIL78	440155
Philippines	Japan	08 Dec 55	General Trade	3PTS529	465036
Philippines	Japan	09 May 56	Direct Aid	0JGJI1291	441090
Philippines	Japan	09 May 56	Reparations	285UNTS3	104148
Philippines	Japan	30 Nov 56	Reparations	0JGJI1313	441148
Philippines	Japan	07 Jan 58	General Trade	3PTS699	465037
Philippines	Japan	24 Jul 58	Visas	325UNTS103	104696
Philippines	Japan	02 Mar 59	Air Transport	341UNTS49	104877
Philippines	Japan	07 Sep 59	Loans and Credits	0JGJI9	441106
Philippines	Japan	09 Dec 60	General Amity	4PTS383	465046
Philippines	Japan	06 Dec 61	Visas	449UNTS29	106449
Philippines	Japan	19 Jan 63	Postal Service	517UNTS281	107489
Philippines	Japan	15 Feb 66	Direct Aid	66JJS217	442168
Philippines	Japan	29 Sep 66	Education	66JJS221	442176
Philippines	Japan	26 Jun 68	Postal Service	69JHZ8	439023
Philippines	Japan	08 Aug 68	Postal Service	69JJS349	442247
Philippines	Japan	08 Aug 68	Postal Service	0UNTS0	109834
Philippines	Japan	29 Nov 68	Tech Assistance	68JJS417	442223
Philippines	Japan	21 Feb 69	Loans and Credits	69JJS357	442234
Philippines	Japan	17 Jun 69	Tech Assistance	69JJS367	442241

PARTY ONE	PARTY TWO	DATE	TOPIC	CITATION	NUMBER
Philippines	Japan	20 Jan 70	Air Transport	70JHZ5	439033
Philippines	Korea, South	11 Nov 60	Visas	490UNTS249	107159
Philippines	Korea, South	24 Feb 61	General Trade	423UNTS217	106094
Philippines	Korea, South	22 Jul 69	Air Transport	0UNTS0	110199
Philippines	Luxembourg	17 Feb 60	Visas	359UNTS311	105148
Philippines	Malaysia	31 Jul 62	Visas	452UNTS223	106510
Philippines	Malaysia	07 Feb 66	Admin Cooperation	608UNTS3	108809
Philippines	Malaysia	01 Sep 67	Commodity Trade	608UNTS13	108810
Philippines	Multilateral	19 Apr 44	Scientific Project	89UNTS279	200257
Philippines	Multilateral	02 Aug 44	Scientific Project	67UNTS221	200221
Philippines	Multilateral	07 Dec 44	Air Transport	171UNTS345	200501
Philippines	Multilateral	07 Dec 44	Air Transport	84UNTS389	200252
Philippines	Multilateral	16 Nov 45	IGO Establishment	4UNTS275	100052
Philippines	Multilateral	27 Dec 45	IGO Establishment	2UNTS39	100020
Philippines	Multilateral	23 Apr 46	Sanitation	16UNTS179	100257
Philippines	Multilateral	23 Apr 46	Sanitation	17UNTS3	100265
Philippines	Multilateral	22 Jul 46	IGO Establishment	9UNTS3	100125
Philippines	Multilateral	22 Jul 46	IGO Establishment	14UNTS185	100221
Philippines	Multilateral	11 Dec 46	Sanitation	12UNTS179	100186
Philippines	Multilateral	15 Dec 46	IGO Establishment	18UNTS3	100283
Philippines	Multilateral	27 May 47	Air Transport	418UNTS161	106021
Philippines	Multilateral	02 Oct 47	Telecommunications	193UNTS188	102616
Philippines	Multilateral	11 Oct 47	IGO Establishment	77UNTS143	100998
Philippines	Multilateral	12 Nov 47	Admin Cooperation	53UNTS39	100771
Philippines	Multilateral	12 Nov 47	Admin Cooperation	53UNTS49	100772
Philippines	Multilateral	06 Mar 48	Water Transport	289UNTS3	104214
Philippines	Multilateral	10 Jun 48	Humanitarian	164UNTS113	102163
Philippines	Multilateral	10 Jun 48	Humanitarian	191UNTS3	102576
Philippines	Multilateral	26 Jun 48	Culture	331UNTS217	104757
Philippines	Multilateral	24 Jul 48	Sanitation	66UNTS25	100847
Philippines	Multilateral	15 Nov 48	IGO Establishment	120UNTS59	101615
Philippines	Multilateral	19 Nov 48	Sanitation	44UNTS277	100688
Philippines	Multilateral	29 Nov 48	IGO Establishment	120UNTS13	101613
Philippines	Multilateral	09 Dec 48	Humanitarian	78UNTS277	101021
Philippines	Multilateral	23 Mar 49	Commodity Trade	203UNTS179	102746
Philippines	Multilateral	15 Jul 49	Health/Educ/Welfare	197UNTS3	102631
Philippines	Multilateral	12 Aug 49	General Military	75UNTS135	100972
Philippines	Multilateral	12 Aug 49	Humanitarian	75UNTS31	100970
Philippines	Multilateral	12 Aug 49	Humanitarian	75UNTS85	100971
Philippines	Multilateral	12 Aug 49	Humanitarian	75UNTS287	100973
Philippines	Multilateral	19 Sep 49	Land Transport	125UNTS3	101671
Philippines	Multilateral	16 Dec 49	Admin Cooperation	72UNTS3	100924
Philippines	Multilateral	21 Mar 50	Admin Cooperation	96UNTS271	101342
Philippines	Multilateral	06 Apr 50	Admin Cooperation	119UNTS99	101610
Philippines	Multilateral	22 Nov 50	Culture	131UNTS25	101734
Philippines	Multilateral	07 Dec 50	Admin Cooperation	212UNTS17	102861
Philippines	Multilateral	05 Apr 51	Tech Assistance	84UNTS299	101139
Philippines	Multilateral	25 May 51	Status of Forces	175UNTS215	102303
Philippines	Multilateral	08 Sep 51	Peace/Disarmament	136UNTS45	101832
Philippines	Multilateral	06 Dec 51	Admin Cooperation	150UNTS67	101963
Philippines	Multilateral	11 Jul 52	IGO Establishment	169UNTS3	102220
Philippines	Multilateral	06 Sep 52	Patents/Copyrights	216UNTS132	102937
Philippines	Multilateral	07 Oct 52	Admin Cooperation	310UNTS181	104493
Philippines	Multilateral	31 Mar 53	Privil/Immunities	193UNTS136	102613
Philippines	Multilateral	11 May 53	Sanitation	456UNTS3	106555
Philippines	Multilateral	01 Oct 53	Commodity Trade	258UNTS153	103677
Philippines	Multilateral	26 Oct 53	Status of Forces	207UNTS237	102809
Philippines	Multilateral	19 Feb 54	Status of Forces	214UNTS51	102899
Philippines	Multilateral	12 May 54	Admin Cooperation	327UNTS3	104714
Philippines	Multilateral	14 May 54	Culture	249UNTS215	103511
Philippines	Multilateral	04 Jun 54	Customs	282UNTS249	104101
Philippines	Multilateral	04 Jun 54	Customs	276UNTS191	103992
Philippines	Multilateral	14 Jun 54	Air Transport	320UNTS209	104643
Philippines	Multilateral	14 Jun 54	Air Transport	320UNTS217	104644
Philippines	Multilateral	08 Sep 54	Milit Assistance	209UNTS23	102819

PARTY ONE	PARTY TWO	DATE	TOPIC	CITATION	NUMBER
Philippines	Multilateral	28 Sep 54	Refugees	360UNTS117	105158
Philippines	Multilateral	27 Oct 54	Tech Assistance	201UNTS95	102712
Philippines	Multilateral	25 May 55	IGO Establishment	264UNTS117	103791
Philippines	Multilateral	28 Sep 55	Air Transport	478UNTS371	106943
Philippines	Multilateral	25 Apr 56	Commodity Trade	270UNTS103	103896
Philippines	Multilateral	20 Jun 56	Admin Cooperation	268UNTS3	103850
Philippines	Multilateral	26 Oct 56	IGO Establishment	276UNTS3	103988
Philippines	Multilateral	03 Oct 57	Postal Service	364UNTS3	105211
Philippines	Multilateral	10 Jun 58	Admin Cooperation	330UNTS3	104739
Philippines	Multilateral	01 Dec 58	Commodity Trade	385UNTS137	105534
Philippines	Multilateral	06 Apr 59	Commodity Trade	349UNTS167	105013
Philippines	Multilateral	26 Jan 60	IGO Establishment	439UNTS249	106333
Philippines	Multilateral	17 Jun 60	Humanitarian	536UNTS27	107794
Philippines	Multilateral	14 Dec 60	Education	429UNTS93	106193
Philippines	Multilateral	23 Jan 61	Postal Service	530UNTS141	107679
Philippines	Multilateral	30 Mar 61	Sanitation	520UNTS151	107515
Philippines	Multilateral	14 Apr 61	IGO Establishment	422UNTS101	106071
Philippines	Multilateral	18 Apr 61	Consul/Citizenship	500UNTS95	107310
Philippines	Multilateral	18 Apr 61	Dispute Settlement	500UNTS243	107312
Philippines	Multilateral	18 Apr 61	Consul/Citizenship	500UNTS223	107311
Philippines	Multilateral	21 Jun 61	IGO Establishment	514UNTS209	107449
Philippines	Multilateral	15 May 62	Commodity Trade	444UNTS3	106367
Philippines	Multilateral	10 Dec 62	Culture	521UNTS231	107525
Philippines	Multilateral	24 Apr 63	Consul/Citizenship	596UNTS487	108640
Philippines	Multilateral	24 Apr 63	Consul/Citizenship	596UNTS261	108638
Philippines	Multilateral	31 Jul 63	General Amity	550UNTS343	108029
Philippines	Multilateral	05 Aug 63	Sanitation	480UNTS43	106964
Philippines	Multilateral	14 Sep 63	Air Transport	0UNTS0	110106
Philippines	Multilateral	09 Nov 63	Direct Aid	489UNTS209	107141
Philippines	Multilateral	11 Jun 64	Atomic Energy	525UNTS61	107584
Philippines	Multilateral	10 Jul 64	Postal Service	611UNTS7	108844
Philippines	Multilateral	10 Jul 64	Postal Service	611UNTS105	108845
Philippines	Multilateral	18 Sep 64	IGO Operations	555UNTS205	108114
Philippines	Multilateral	09 Mar 65	Water Transport	591UNTS265	108564
Philippines	Multilateral	04 Dec 65	IGO Establishment	571UNTS123	108303
Philippines	Multilateral	16 Dec 65	Postal Service	570UNTS201	108295
Philippines	Multilateral	05 Apr 66	Water Transport	640UNTS133	109159
Philippines	Multilateral	28 Sep 66	Specif Goods/Equip	589UNTS41	108534
Philippines	Multilateral	27 Jan 67	Scientific Project	610UNTS205	108843
Philippines	Multilateral	28 Dec 67	Scientific Project	0UNTS0	109322
Philippines	Multilateral	01 Aug 68	Culture	0UNTS0	109368
Philippines	Multilateral	28 Sep 68	Tech Assistance	0UNTS0	109296
Philippines	Multilateral	11 Jun 69	Scientific Project	0UNTS0	110100
Philippines	Netherlands	05 Feb 53	Air Transport	216UNTS99	102934
Philippines	Netherlands	17 Feb 60	Visas	359UNTS317	105149
Philippines	Netherlands	02 Mar 66	Tech Assistance	631UNTS325	109002
Philippines	Netherlands	13 Feb 68	Non-ILO Labor	0UNTS0	110748
Philippines	New Zealand	09 May 60	Postal Service	486UNTS65	107073
Philippines	Norway	20 Oct 54	Air Transport	216UNTS11	102928
Philippines	Norway	18 Feb 59	Visas	359UNTS305	105147
Philippines	Norway	14 Dec 66	Visas	591UNTS253	108562
Philippines	Norway	08 May 69	Air Transport	0UNTS0	109867
Philippines	Pakistan	16 Jul 49	Air Transport	35UNTS111	100553
Philippines	Pakistan	03 Jan 51	General Amity	2PTS605	465023
Philippines	Pakistan	15 Aug 61	Culture	522UNTS35	107534
Philippines	Pakistan	29 Sep 61	General Trade	422UNTS3	106065
Philippines	SCAP Japan	18 May 50	General Economic	2PTS555	465022
Philippines	SCAP Japan	03 Mar 51	General Trade	2PTS613	465025
Philippines	SCAP Japan	12 Mar 51	General Trade	2PTS615	465026
Philippines	SCAP Japan	19 Mar 52	Finance	2PTS783	465029
Philippines	Spain	27 Sep 47	General Amity	70UNTS133	100902
Philippines	Spain	20 May 48	Consul/Citizenship	70UNTS143	100903
Philippines	Spain	22 Dec 48	Dispute Settlement	2PTS93	465016
Philippines	Spain	04 Mar 49	Culture	49SPBO1306	460096
Philippines	Spain	04 Mar 49	Culture	49SPBO1812	460097

PARTY ONE	PARTY TWO	DATE	TOPIC	CITATION	NUMBER
Philippines	Spain	06 Oct 51	Postal Service	54SPBO2101	460098
Philippines	Spain	06 Oct 51	Air Transport	215UNTS193	102920
Philippines	Spain	04 Jul 62	Visas	490UNTS243	107158
Philippines	Sweden	20 Aug 54	Air Transport	200UNTS121	102699
Philippines	Sweden	12 Apr 66	Taxation	0UNTS0	110197
Philippines	Sweden	11 Nov 66	Visas	587UNTS3	108505
Philippines	Sweden	08 May 69	Air Transport	0UNTS0	109868
Philippines	Switzerland	26 Oct 46	General Trade	1PTS319	465005
Philippines	Switzerland	08 Mar 52	Air Transport	231UNTS301	103225
Philippines	Switzerland	30 Aug 56	General Amity	293UNTS43	104284
Philippines	Taiwan	18 Apr 47	General Amity	11UNTS361	100175
Philippines	Taiwan	23 Oct 50	Air Transport	215UNTS159	102918
Philippines	Taiwan	18 Oct 56	General Trade	541UNTS57	107860
Philippines	Taiwan	05 Aug 58	Postal Service	3PTS761	465039
Philippines	Taiwan	18 Dec 59	Consul/Citizenship	4PTS25	465043
Philippines	Taiwan	25 Aug 64	Tech Assistance	511UNTS233	107436
Philippines	Thailand	14 Jun 49	General Amity	81UNTS53	101062
Philippines	Thailand	27 Apr 53	Air Transport	174UNTS3	102274
Philippines	Thailand	31 Jul 62	Visas	452UNTS235	106511
Philippines	Turkey	13 Jun 49	General Amity	2PTS155	465020
Philippines	UK Great Britain	07 Jan 48	Air Transport	28UNTS63	100420
Philippines	UK Great Britain	20 Apr 48	Territory Boundary	1PTS705	465015
Philippines	UK Great Britain	24 May 49	Consul/Citizenship	2PTS145	465019
Philippines	UK Great Britain	23 Jan 51	Admin Cooperation	2PTS609	465024
Philippines	UK Great Britain	31 Jan 55	Air Transport	216UNTS51	102932
Philippines	UK Great Britain	29 Aug 55	Non-ILO Labor	221UNTS241	103009
Philippines	UK Great Britain	14 Apr 58	Air Transport	3PTS715	465038
Philippines	UN Special Fund	28 Jun 61	Direct Aid	399UNTS141	105739
Philippines	UNICEF (Children)	20 Nov 48	Tech Assistance	65UNTS48	100819
Philippines	United Arab Rep	18 Jan 55	General Amity	3PTS399	465034
Philippines	United Arab Rep	03 May 62	Culture	4PTS551	465048
Philippines	United Nations	15 Sep 64	IGO Operations	510UNTS137	107410
Philippines	United Nations	05 Apr 66	Health/Educ/Welfare	560UNTS191	108174
Philippines	UNTAB (Tech Assis)	01 Mar 52	Tech Assistance	2PTS775	465072
Philippines	UNTAB (Tech Assis)	24 Apr 52	Tech Assistance	2PTS789	465074
Philippines	UNTAB (Tech Assis)	05 Nov 52	Tech Assistance	3PTS45	465077
Philippines	UNTAB (Tech Assis)	05 Nov 52	Tech Assistance	3PTS41	465076
Philippines	UNTAB (Tech Assis)	19 Jun 53	Tech Assistance	3PTS137	465079
Philippines	UNTAB (Tech Assis)	25 Jun 53	Tech Assistance	3PTS161	465080
Philippines	UNTAB (Tech Assis)	06 Aug 53	Tech Assistance	3PTS191	465084
Philippines	UNTAB (Tech Assis)	06 Aug 53	Tech Assistance	3PTS187	465083
Philippines	UNTAB (Tech Assis)	04 May 57	Tech Assistance	3PTS661	465085
Philippines	UNTAB (Tech Assis)	23 Jul 58	Tech Assistance	3PTS749	465086
Philippines	USA (United States)	01 Apr 46	Specific Property	1PTS393	465007
Philippines	USA (United States)	04 Jul 46	General Trade	43UNTS135	100668
Philippines	USA (United States)	04 Jul 46	General Amity	6UNTS335	100086
Philippines	USA (United States)	04 Jul 46	General Amity	7UNTS3	100088
Philippines	USA (United States)	04 Aug 46	General Trade	1PTS243	465001
Philippines	USA (United States)	08 Aug 46	General Trade	1PTS251	465002
Philippines	USA (United States)	22 Aug 46	Reparations	1PTS255	465003
Philippines	USA (United States)	11 Sep 46	Milit Assistance	43UNTS231	100670
Philippines	USA (United States)	17 Sep 46	IGO Establishment	15UNTS249	100240
Philippines	USA (United States)	04 Oct 46	Specif Goods/Equip	1PTS271	465004
Philippines	USA (United States)	19 Oct 46	Telecommunications	43UNTS263	100672
Philippines	USA (United States)	16 Nov 46	Dispute Settlement	1PTS321	465006
Philippines	USA (United States)	16 Nov 46	Air Transport	7UNTS151	100097
Philippines	USA (United States)	14 Feb 47	Non-IBRD Project	16UNTS3	100245
Philippines	USA (United States)	14 Mar 47	Milit Installation	43UNTS271	100673
Philippines	USA (United States)	14 Mar 47	Non-IBRD Project	16UNTS31	100247
Philippines	USA (United States)	14 Mar 47	Consul/Citizenship	45UNTS23	100690
Philippines	USA (United States)	21 Mar 47	Milit Assistance	45UNTS47	100691
Philippines	USA (United States)	12 May 47	Scientific Project	16UNTS137	100254
Philippines	USA (United States)	12 May 47	Scientific Project	16UNTS123	100253
Philippines	USA (United States)	12 May 47	Scientific Project	16UNTS109	100252
Philippines	USA (United States)	16 May 47	Non-ILO Labor	280UNTS177	104057

PARTY ONE	PARTY TWO	DATE	TOPIC	CITATION	NUMBER
Philippines	USA (United States)	04 Sep 47	Gen Communications	1PTS435	465009
Philippines	USA (United States)	17 Sep 47	Postal Service	206UNTS249	102790
Philippines	USA (United States)	30 Sep 47	Postal Service	1PTS445	465010
Philippines	USA (United States)	12 Oct 47	Territory Boundary	1PTS519	465011
Philippines	USA (United States)	19 Dec 47	Territory Boundary	1PTS639	465012
Philippines	USA (United States)	24 Dec 47	Territory Boundary	1PTS645	465013
Philippines	USA (United States)	23 Mar 48	Education	43UNTS247	100671
Philippines	USA (United States)	07 Jun 48	Admin Cooperation	73UNTS89	100947
Philippines	USA (United States)	23 Aug 48	Patents/Copyrights	82UNTS11	101080
Philippines	USA (United States)	27 Aug 48	Reparations	44UNTS13	100675
Philippines	USA (United States)	21 Oct 48	Patents/Copyrights	77UNTS197	101000
Philippines	USA (United States)	16 May 49	Milit Installation	67UNTS199	100878
Philippines	USA (United States)	07 Jun 49	Direct Aid	45UNTS63	100692
Philippines	USA (United States)	08 Aug 49	Milit Installation	163UNTS103	102144
Philippines	USA (United States)	20 Dec 49	Finance	2PTS517	465021
Philippines	USA (United States)	16 Mar 50	Air Transport	89UNTS199	101218
Philippines	USA (United States)	20 Apr 50	Specif Goods/Equip	2PTS553	465071
Philippines	USA (United States)	06 Nov 50	Finance	122UNTS63	101637
Philippines	USA (United States)	27 Apr 51	Direct Aid	174UNTS251	102290
Philippines	USA (United States)	30 Aug 51	Milit Assistance	177UNTS133	102315
Philippines	USA (United States)	07 Jan 52	Milit Assistance	179UNTS193	102368
Philippines	USA (United States)	19 Feb 52	Direct Aid	177UNTS307	102330
Philippines	USA (United States)	24 Nov 52	Visas	181UNTS155	102406
Philippines	USA (United States)	09 Mar 53	Milit Servic/Citiz	227UNTS101	103134
Philippines	USA (United States)	26 Jun 53	Milit Assistance	213UNTS77	102881
Philippines	USA (United States)	27 Apr 55	Direct Aid	261UNTS351	103733
Philippines	USA (United States)	27 Jul 55	Atomic Energy	239UNTS271	103385
Philippines	USA (United States)	06 Sep 55	Visas	238UNTS109	103356
Philippines	USA (United States)	28 Oct 55	Milit Installation	239UNTS165	103376
Philippines	USA (United States)	18 Oct 56	Taxation	280UNTS55	104050
Philippines	USA (United States)	06 Feb 57	Status of Forces	303UNTS237	104383
Philippines	USA (United States)	08 Apr 57	Specific Resources	303UNTS227	104382
Philippines	USA (United States)	18 Jun 57	Milit Installation	289UNTS289	104225
Philippines	USA (United States)	25 Jun 57	US Agri Commod Aid	289UNTS279	104224
Philippines	USA (United States)	01 Nov 57	Status of Forces	307UNTS39	104440
Philippines	USA (United States)	20 Feb 58	Status of Forces	303UNTS261	104385
Philippines	USA (United States)	15 May 58	Milit Assistance	316UNTS163	104583
Philippines	USA (United States)	03 Jun 58	US Agri Commod Aid	316UNTS3	104573
Philippines	USA (United States)	30 Jun 58	Direct Aid	321UNTS51	104653
Philippines	USA (United States)	17 Jul 58	Specific Property	335UNTS199	104787
Philippines	USA (United States)	21 Jan 59	Specif Claim/Waive	341UNTS255	104888
Philippines	USA (United States)	12 Oct 59	General Military	4PTS11	465042
Philippines	USA (United States)	07 Dec 59	Milit Installation	359UNTS227	105144
Philippines	USA (United States)	06 Dec 60	Other Economic	4PTS371	465045
Philippines	USA (United States)	12 Mar 61	Postal Service	288UNTS285	104210
Philippines	USA (United States)	04 Oct 61	Specif Goods/Equip	433UNTS83	106232
Philippines	USA (United States)	31 Oct 61	Direct Aid	424UNTS129	106105
Philippines	USA (United States)	24 Nov 61	US Agri Commod Aid	433UNTS315	106251
Philippines	USA (United States)	21 Aug 62	Milit Assistance	461UNTS163	106660
Philippines	USA (United States)	11 Jan 63	Specific Resources	473UNTS43	106853
Philippines	USA (United States)	23 Mar 63	Education	474UNTS80	106873
Philippines	USA (United States)	06 May 63	Telecommunications	477UNTS67	106916
Philippines	USA (United States)	15 Aug 63	Tech Assistance	4PTS791	465055
Philippines	USA (United States)	30 Aug 63	Non-ILO Labor	489UNTS323	107147
Philippines	USA (United States)	08 Oct 63	Non-ILO Labor	4PTS811	465056
Philippines	USA (United States)	24 Feb 64	Commodity Trade	505UNTS283	107378
Philippines	USA (United States)	14 May 64	US Agri Commod Aid	526UNTS113	107604
Philippines	USA (United States)	05 Oct 64	Taxation	4PTS879	465064
Philippines	USA (United States)	12 Nov 64	Postal Service	574UNTS159	108349
Philippines	USA (United States)	10 Mar 65	Non-ILO Labor	4PTS925	465066
Philippines	USA (United States)	10 Mar 65	Non-IBRD Project	0UNTS0	110124
Philippines	USA (United States)	16 Mar 65	Status of Forces	542UNTS199	107890
Philippines	USA (United States)	23 Apr 65	US Agri Commod Aid	546UNTS157	107942
Philippines	USA (United States)	28 May 65	Visas	0UNTS0	110248
Philippines	USA (United States)	15 Jul 65	Non-IBRD Project	0UNTS0	110125

PARTY ONE	PARTY TWO	DATE	TOPIC	CITATION	NUMBER
Philippines	USA (United States)	12 Aug 65	Milit Installation	579UNTS47	108397
Philippines	USA (United States)	10 Sep 65	Gen Communications	4PTS919	465065
Philippines	USA (United States)	05 Oct 65	General Trade	4PTS973	465067
Philippines	USA (United States)	15 Nov 65	Milit Assistance	574UNTS205	108350
Philippines	USA (United States)	16 Dec 65	General Military	4PTS1037	465068
Philippines	USA (United States)	20 Dec 65	Admin Cooperation	4PTS1041	465069
Philippines	USA (United States)	29 Dec 65	Taxation	4PTS1051	465070
Philippines	USA (United States)	26 Aug 66	Milit Installation	606UNTS259	108790
Philippines	USA (United States)	22 Dec 66	Other Military	579UNTS203	108408
Philippines	USA (United States)	22 Dec 66	US Agri Commod Aid	591UNTS219	108559
Philippines	USA (United States)	04 Jan 67	Customs	590UNTS51	108546
Philippines	USA (United States)	28 Mar 67	Water Transport	0UNTS0	109757
Philippines	USA (United States)	25 Apr 67	Tech Assistance	0UNTS0	109860
Philippines	USA (United States)	18 May 67	Non-IBRD Project	0UNTS0	110126
Philippines	USA (United States)	26 Jun 67	Non-IBRD Project	0UNTS0	110127
Philippines	USA (United States)	29 Jun 67	Claims and Debts	0UNTS0	109776
Philippines	USA (United States)	11 Aug 67	Non-IBRD Project	0UNTS0	110128
Philippines	USA (United States)	24 Aug 67	General Military	0UNTS0	109915
Philippines	USA (United States)	21 Sep 67	Commodity Trade	0UNTS0	109921
Philippines	USA (United States)	16 Oct 67	General Military	632UNTS113	109013
Philippines	USA (United States)	22 Dec 67	US Agri Commod Aid	0UNTS0	110133
Philippines	USA (United States)	23 Jan 68	Finance	0UNTS0	110003
Philippines	USA (United States)	30 Apr 68	Milit Installation	0UNTS0	110129
Philippines	USA (United States)	27 May 68	Non-ILO Labor	0UNTS0	109435
Philippines	USA (United States)	11 Jun 68	Non-IBRD Project	0UNTS0	110130
Philippines	USA (United States)	13 Jun 68	Atomic Energy	0UNTS0	110131
Philippines	USA (United States)	28 Dec 68	Milit Installation	0UNTS0	109436
Philippines	USA (United States)	24 Apr 69	Customs	0UNTS0	110403
Philippines	USA (United States)	24 Apr 69	Non-IBRD Project	0UNTS0	110132
Philippines	USA (United States)	05 Sep 69	Education	0UNTS0	110408
Philippines	USA (United States)	24 Mar 70	US Agri Commod Aid	0UNTS0	110692
Philippines	Vatican/Holy See	18 Jun 52	Status of Forces	543UNTS165	107900
Philippines	Vietnam, South	26 Apr 59	General Amity	3PTS829	465041
Philippines	WHO (World Health)	28 Dec 50	Tech Assistance	110UNTS203	101511
Philippines	WHO (World Health)	22 Jul 51	IGO Status/Immunit	149UNTS197	101953
Philippines	WHO (World Health)	16 Jul 53	Tech Assistance	3PTS175	465033
Philippines	WHO (World Health)	16 Jul 53	Tech Assistance	3PTS175	465082
Poland	Afghanistan	19 Sep 60	Tech Assistance	60PZUM116	458079
Poland	Afghanistan	27 Jun 62	Air Transport	62PZUM57	458096
Poland	Afghanistan	25 Jun 66	Culture	72PDZU373	457137
Poland	Albania	02 Dec 50	Culture	260UNTS131	103707
Poland	Albania	25 Jan 51	Scientific Project	260UNTS217	103710
Poland	Albania	08 Jul 57	Air Transport	57PZUM74	458051
Poland	Algeria	26 Jan 63	Tech Assistance	63PZUM11	458100
Poland	Algeria	22 Jul 64	Culture	64PDZU71	457114
Poland	Algeria	06 Feb 65	Air Transport	64PZUM9	458117
Poland	Argentina	29 Oct 52	General Economic	53PZUM67	458007
Poland	Australia	03 Jun 48	Direct Aid	16UNTS189	100258
Poland	Australia	25 Nov 54	Postal Service	521UNTS281	107526
Poland	Australia	30 Dec 58	Privil/Immunities	58PZUM122	458063
Poland	Australia	20 Jun 66	General Trade	638UNTS201	109136
Poland	Austria	08 Feb 56	Air Transport	334UNTS221	104770
Poland	Austria	21 Jun 63	Air Transport	63ABGB294	403151
Poland	Austria	25 Oct 63	Land Transport	63PZUM67	458106
Poland	Austria	11 Dec 63	Admin Cooperation	63PZUM76	458108
Poland	Austria	05 Feb 68	Taxation	68ABGB123	403152
Poland	Austria	05 Feb 68	Taxation	0UNTS0	109213
Poland	Austria	09 Jun 70	General Amity	70ABGB278	403153
Poland	Austria	09 Sep 71	General Economic	71ABGB495	403154
Poland	Belgium	24 Mar 47	Non-ILO Labor	18UNTS279	100297
Poland	Belgium	17 Oct 56	Air Transport	356UNTS279	105100
Poland	Belgium	14 Nov 63	Claims and Debts	66PZUM85	458107
Poland	Belgium	09 Dec 63	Culture	514UNTS195	107448
Poland	Belgium	26 Nov 65	Non-ILO Labor	620UNTS13	108950
Poland	Belgium	07 Dec 65	Atomic Energy	65PZUM77	458127

PARTY ONE	PARTY TWO	DATE	TOPIC	CITATION	NUMBER
Poland	Belgium	30 Oct 68	Land Transport	0UNTS0	109597
Poland	Benelux Econ Union	17 Feb 65	General Economic	547UNTS165	107956
Poland	Brazil	24 Oct 52	General Economic	53PZUM59	458006
Poland	Brazil	19 Oct 61	Culture	552UNTS75	108050
Poland	Brazil	25 May 68	Water Transport	68PZUM88	458158
Poland	Bulgaria	28 Jun 47	Culture	15UNTS123	100230
Poland	Bulgaria	29 May 48	General Military	26UNTS213	100389
Poland	Bulgaria	30 May 48	General Trade	37UNTS3	100574
Poland	Bulgaria	16 May 49	Air Transport	84UNTS313	101140
Poland	Bulgaria	26 Sep 49	Sanitation	260UNTS249	103712
Poland	Bulgaria	26 Sep 49	Sanitation	260UNTS227	103711
Poland	Bulgaria	19 Oct 53	Gen Communications	53PZUM117	458013
Poland	Bulgaria	30 Dec 58	General Economic	58PZUM124	458064
Poland	Bulgaria	20 Jun 59	Customs	59PZUM78	458068
Poland	Bulgaria	12 Jul 61	Admin Cooperation	436UNTS147	106294
Poland	Bulgaria	19 Sep 61	Consul/Citizenship	483UNTS249	107018
Poland	Bulgaria	04 Dec 61	Admin Cooperation	484UNTS3	107019
Poland	Bulgaria	03 Oct 64	Land Transport	64PZUM48	458115
Poland	Bulgaria	08 Jun 65	Visas	65PZUM44	458122
Poland	Bulgaria	08 Jun 65	Visas	0UNTS0	110300
Poland	Bulgaria	07 Apr 66	Culture	66PZUM14	458131
Poland	Bulgaria	03 Oct 66	Culture	618UNTS3	108921
Poland	Bulgaria	06 Apr 67	General Amity	617UNTS327	108920
Poland	Bulgaria	06 Dec 68	Sanitation	70PDZU13	457162
Poland	Bulgaria	07 Feb 72	Consul/Citizenship	72PDZU401	457178
Poland	Cambodia	17 Dec 57	Tech Assistance	57PZUM130	458058
Poland	Cameroon	26 Apr 63	Culture	63PZUM31	458102
Poland	Cameroon	26 Apr 63	Tech Assistance	63PZUM27	458101
Poland	Canada	05 Nov 63	Commodity Trade	529UNTS81	107658
Poland	China People's Rep	29 Jan 51	Telecommunications	51CCJC5	410028
Poland	China People's Rep	29 Jan 51	General Economic	51CCJC4	410027
Poland	China People's Rep	29 Jan 51	Water Transport	51CCJC7	410030
Poland	China People's Rep	29 Jan 51	Postal Service	51CCJC6	410029
Poland	China People's Rep	03 Apr 51	Culture	51CCJC12	410033
Poland	China People's Rep	03 Apr 51	Culture	304UNTS187	104396
Poland	China People's Rep	25 May 53	General Economic	53CCJC27	410103
Poland	China People's Rep	15 Oct 53	Mass Media	53PZUM115	458012
Poland	China People's Rep	15 Oct 53	Mass Media	53CCJC58	410121
Poland	China People's Rep	19 Feb 54	General Economic	54CCJC5	410133
Poland	China People's Rep	20 Jul 54	Scientific Project	54PZUM50	458019
Poland	China People's Rep	20 Jul 54	Scientific Project	54CCJC47	410164
Poland	China People's Rep	21 Mar 55	General Economic	55CCJC16	410221
Poland	China People's Rep	21 Dec 55	General Trade	55CCJC99	410283
Poland	China People's Rep	24 Feb 56	Gen Communications	56CCJC35	410319
Poland	China People's Rep	25 Feb 56	Postal Service	56PZUM109	458040
Poland	China People's Rep	25 Feb 56	Gen Communications	56CCJC36	410320
Poland	China People's Rep	23 Apr 56	Scientific Project	56CCJC53	410332
Poland	China People's Rep	14 Jul 56	Education	56CCJC86	410351
Poland	China People's Rep	01 Apr 57	General Trade	57CCJC34	410414
Poland	China People's Rep	29 Oct 57	Sanitation	57CCJC102	410457
Poland	China People's Rep	07 Apr 58	General Trade	58CCJC47	410514
Poland	China People's Rep	14 Feb 59	General Trade	59CCJC26	410585
Poland	China People's Rep	06 Mar 59	General Trade	59CCJC43	410597
Poland	China People's Rep	15 Apr 59	Mass Media	59CCJC66	410615
Poland	China People's Rep	15 May 61	Finance	61CCJC75	410796
Poland	China People's Rep	10 Jul 61	General Trade	61CCJC95	410808
Poland	China People's Rep	16 Mar 65	General Economic	65CCJC29	411296
Poland	China People's Rep	26 Apr 65	Scientific Project	65CCJC56	411299
Poland	China People's Rep	05 May 65	Culture	65CCJC62	411287
Poland	China People's Rep	15 Dec 65	Scientific Project	65CCJC155	411300
Poland	China People's Rep	22 Mar 66	General Economic	66CCJC9	411301
Poland	China People's Rep	20 Jun 66	Scientific Project	66CCJC54	411302
Poland	China People's Rep	24 Jun 66	Culture	66CCJC57	411304
Poland	China People's Rep	30 Jun 67	General Economic	67CCJC26	411307
Poland	COMECON (Econ Aid)	22 Feb 63	IGO Operations	506UNTS303	107391

PARTY ONE	PARTY TWO	DATE	TOPIC	CITATION	NUMBER
Poland	Cuba	01 Jul 60	Tech Assistance	60PZUM71	458077
Poland	Cuba	06 Mar 61	Culture	484UNTS123	107020
Poland	Cuba	12 Oct 62	Mass Media	62PZUM93	458098
Poland	Czechoslovakia	24 Jan 46	Air Transport	25UNTS181	100363
Poland	Czechoslovakia	12 Feb 46	Reparations	25UNTS207	100364
Poland	Czechoslovakia	10 Mar 47	General Military	25UNTS231	100365
Poland	Czechoslovakia	04 Apr 47	General Economic	85UNTS62	101146
Poland	Czechoslovakia	04 Jul 47	General Economic	50PDZU93	457002
Poland	Czechoslovakia	04 Jul 47	Culture	25UNTS249	100366
Poland	Czechoslovakia	05 Apr 48	Non-ILO Labor	31UNTS355	100482
Poland	Czechoslovakia	05 Apr 48	Admin Cooperation	31UNTS325	100481
Poland	Czechoslovakia	12 Nov 48	Land Transport	84UNTS347	101141
Poland	Czechoslovakia	21 Jan 49	Admin Cooperation	31UNTS205	100480
Poland	Czechoslovakia	22 Jan 49	Sanitation	85UNTS3	101142
Poland	Czechoslovakia	02 Jul 49	Land Transport	260UNTS149	103708
Poland	Czechoslovakia	02 Jul 49	Land Transport	260UNTS179	103709
Poland	Czechoslovakia	17 Nov 50	Sanitation	530UNTS195	107682
Poland	Czechoslovakia	20 Dec 52	General Economic	53PZUM77	458008
Poland	Czechoslovakia	00 Feb 54	Mass Media	54PZUM11	458014
Poland	Czechoslovakia	29 May 54	Postal Service	54PZUM34	458018
Poland	Czechoslovakia	06 Sep 55	Visas	55PZUM23	458024
Poland	Czechoslovakia	23 Sep 55	Territory Boundary	55PZUM27	458025
Poland	Czechoslovakia	30 Sep 55	Non-ILO Labor	55PZUM33	458026
Poland	Czechoslovakia	13 Jan 56	Water Transport	56PZUM25	458033
Poland	Czechoslovakia	13 Jan 56	Land Transport	56PZUM30	458034
Poland	Czechoslovakia	13 Jan 56	Gen Communications	265UNTS157	103811
Poland	Czechoslovakia	07 May 57	General Economic	57PZUM69	458050
Poland	Czechoslovakia	31 Jan 58	Land Transport	431UNTS99	106214
Poland	Czechoslovakia	21 Mar 58	Specific Resources	538UNTS89	107811
Poland	Czechoslovakia	27 Mar 58	Culture	58PZUM61	458060
Poland	Czechoslovakia	29 Mar 58	Reparations	340UNTS199	104865
Poland	Czechoslovakia	13 Jun 58	Territory Boundary	354UNTS221	105064
Poland	Czechoslovakia	25 Nov 58	Customs	372UNTS205	105299
Poland	Czechoslovakia	08 Apr 59	Sanitation	59PZUM60	458066
Poland	Czechoslovakia	04 Jul 59	Visas	363UNTS333	105210
Poland	Czechoslovakia	16 Dec 59	Admin Cooperation	372UNTS223	105300
Poland	Czechoslovakia	02 Apr 60	General Economic	60PZUM16	458073
Poland	Czechoslovakia	17 May 60	Consul/Citizenship	424UNTS3	106096
Poland	Czechoslovakia	10 Sep 60	General Economic	60PZUM110	458078
Poland	Czechoslovakia	14 Nov 60	Sanitation	413UNTS4	105938
Poland	Czechoslovakia	04 Jul 61	Admin Cooperation	436UNTS189	106295
Poland	Czechoslovakia	29 Sep 62	Specific Property	62PZUM81	458097
Poland	Czechoslovakia	16 Nov 62	Land Transport	526UNTS3	107597
Poland	Czechoslovakia	27 Apr 63	Mass Media	63PZUM39	458104
Poland	Czechoslovakia	27 Apr 63	Mass Media	63PZUM34	458103
Poland	Czechoslovakia	17 May 65	Consul/Citizenship	66PDZU135	457121
Poland	Czechoslovakia	17 May 65	Consul/Citizenship	572UNTS181	108312
Poland	Czechoslovakia	29 Jul 65	Dispute Settlement	572UNTS203	108313
Poland	Czechoslovakia	23 Sep 65	Admin Cooperation	72PDZU237	457138
Poland	Czechoslovakia	22 Jan 66	Culture	588UNTS175	108524
Poland	Czechoslovakia	01 Mar 67	General Amity	632UNTS255	109027
Poland	Czechoslovakia	08 Apr 67	Land Transport	72PDZU240	457143
Poland	Czechoslovakia	26 Apr 67	Education	610UNTS0	108832
Poland	Czechoslovakia	02 Dec 67	Admin Cooperation	71PDZU117	457150
Poland	Dahomey	05 Mar 65	Culture	66PDZU395	457118
Poland	Denmark	14 Dec 48	Finance	81UNTS33	101060
Poland	Denmark	12 May 49	Claims and Debts	87UNTS179	101172
Poland	Denmark	07 Dec 49	Commodity Trade	81UNTS21	101059
Poland	Denmark	01 Oct 50	General Economic	81UNTS43	101061
Poland	Denmark	09 Jun 52	General Trade	135UNTS209	101822
Poland	Denmark	09 Jun 52	Finance	135UNTS221	101823
Poland	Denmark	26 Feb 53	Claims and Debts	186UNTS301	102496
Poland	Denmark	08 Jun 60	Culture	424UNTS37	106097
Poland	Denmark	17 Jan 61	Air Transport	412UNTS111	105927
Poland	Denmark	15 Nov 67	General Economic	643UNTS383	109203

PARTY ONE	PARTY TWO	DATE	TOPIC	CITATION	NUMBER
Poland	Denmark	26 Feb 68	Water Transport	643UNTS371	109202
Poland	Denmark	01 Jun 71	Specific Property	72PDZU33	457172
Poland	Ethiopia	01 Dec 65	Tech Assistance	65PZUM71	458126
Poland	Finland	10 Jun 63	Air Transport	503UNTS179	107343
Poland	Finland	18 Dec 63	Non-ILO Labor	486UNTS57	107072
Poland	Finland	18 Oct 69	Land Transport	0UNTS0	110463
Poland	France	11 Feb 47	Reparations	12UNTS287	100189
Poland	France	19 Feb 47	Scientific Project	47PDZU1044	457001
Poland	France	19 May 47	Education	12UNTS95	100181
Poland	France	19 Mar 48	Claims and Debts	51FRJO1111	416360
Poland	France	09 Jun 48	Non-ILO Labor	32UNTS251	100503
Poland	France	17 Aug 48	Non-ILO Labor	0UNTS0	110700
Poland	France	07 Sep 51	Claims and Debts	57FRJO708	416361
Poland	France	12 Nov 59	Taxation	59PZUM106	458071
Poland	France	25 Jun 60	Air Transport	61FRRT20	415362
Poland	France	25 Jun 60	Air Transport	60PZUM53	458075
Poland	France	25 May 61	Non-ILO Labor	61PZUM118	458083
Poland	France	25 May 61	Non-ILO Labor	0UNTS0	110701
Poland	France	15 Jun 61	Consul/Citizenship	61PZUM127	458085
Poland	France	22 Oct 65	General Trade	65FRMD611	417363
Poland	France	28 Apr 66	Non-ILO Labor	0UNTS0	110702
Poland	France	28 Apr 66	Non-ILO Labor	66PZUM76	458133
Poland	France	20 May 66	Scientific Project	66PZUM79	458135
Poland	France	20 May 66	Culture	67FRJO204	416365
Poland	France	20 May 66	Tech Assistance	67FRJO404	416364
Poland	France	22 May 66	Culture	66PZUM70	458136
Poland	France	05 Apr 67	Admin Cooperation	69PDZU29	457142
Poland	France	05 Apr 67	Consul/Citizenship	69FRJO2202	416366
Poland	France	05 Apr 67	Admin Cooperation	0UNTS0	109636
Poland	France	05 Apr 67	Admin Cooperation	0UNTS0	109510
Poland	France	03 Mar 68	Land Transport	68PZUM65	458153
Poland	France	03 Mar 68	General Transport	68FRJO308	416367
Poland	Germany, East	06 Jun 50	General Economic	4EGDA114	419229
Poland	Germany, East	06 Jun 50	Finance	4EGDA115	419228
Poland	Germany, East	06 Jun 50	Territory Boundary	4EGDA113	419227
Poland	Germany, East	06 Jun 50	Culture	4EGDA118	419230
Poland	Germany, East	23 Jun 50	Sanitation	304UNTS91	104393
Poland	Germany, East	06 Jul 50	Telecommunications	4EGDA128	419232
Poland	Germany, East	06 Jul 50	Territory Boundary	319UNTS93	104631
Poland	Germany, East	19 Jan 51	Territory Boundary	4EGDA130	419233
Poland	Germany, East	03 Feb 51	Postal Service	4EGDA137	419234
Poland	Germany, East	03 Feb 51	Telecommunications	4EGDA144	419235
Poland	Germany, East	08 Jan 52	Culture	304UNTS113	104394
Poland	Germany, East	18 Jan 52	Finance	4EGDA153	419236
Poland	Germany, East	06 Feb 52	Water Transport	304UNTS131	104395
Poland	Germany, East	06 Oct 53	Consul/Citizenship	1EGDA370	419237
Poland	Germany, East	06 Oct 53	Consul/Citizenship	53PZUM113	458011
Poland	Germany, East	19 Dec 53	Culture	4EGDA171	419238
Poland	Germany, East	27 May 54	Water Transport	54PZUM16	458016
Poland	Germany, East	27 May 54	Water Transport	54PZUM22	458017
Poland	Germany, East	27 May 54	Water Transport	4EGDA175	419239
Poland	Germany, East	27 May 54	Water Transport	4EGDA193	419240
Poland	Germany, East	02 Aug 54	Specific Resources	2EGDA426	419241
Poland	Germany, East	02 Aug 54	Specific Resources	54PZUM53	458020
Poland	Germany, East	05 Nov 54	Land Transport	4EGDA204	419242
Poland	Germany, East	21 Feb 55	General Economic	2EGDA431	419244
Poland	Germany, East	28 May 55	Postal Service	3EGDA458	419245
Poland	Germany, East	20 Jun 55	Air Transport	55PZUM13	458022
Poland	Germany, East	20 Jun 55	Air Transport	4EGDA224	419246
Poland	Germany, East	09 Jul 55	Sanitation	55PZUM19	458023
Poland	Germany, East	09 Jul 55	Sanitation	4EGDA230	419247
Poland	Germany, East	07 Oct 55	Sanitation	55PZUM41	458027
Poland	Germany, East	07 Oct 55	Sanitation	4EGDA234	419248
Poland	Germany, East	12 Jan 56	Water Transport	56PZUM11	458032
Poland	Germany, East	12 Jan 56	Water Transport	4EGDA237	419249

PARTY ONE	PARTY TWO	DATE	TOPIC	CITATION	NUMBER
Poland	Germany, East	27 Jan 56	Scientific Project	3EGDA504	419250
Poland	Germany, East	31 Jan 56	Water Transport	3EGDA504	419251
Poland	Germany, East	01 Feb 57	Admin Cooperation	319UNTS115	104632
Poland	Germany, East	17 Apr 57	Specific Resources	5EGDA407	419252
Poland	Germany, East	13 Jul 57	Health/Educ/Welfare	319UNTS229	104634
Poland	Germany, East	05 Sep 57	Customs	57PZUM94	458053
Poland	Germany, East	05 Sep 57	Customs	5EGDA433	419253
Poland	Germany, East	17 Sep 57	Atomic Energy	5EGDA438	419254
Poland	Germany, East	17 Sep 57	Atomic Energy	57PZUM99	458054
Poland	Germany, East	16 Nov 57	General Economic	5EGDA440	419255
Poland	Germany, East	25 Nov 57	Consul/Citizenship	340UNTS99	104862
Poland	Germany, East	03 Dec 57	General Economic	5EGDA794	419256
Poland	Germany, East	14 Mar 58	Health/Educ/Welfare	6EGDA332	419257
Poland	Germany, East	24 Oct 58	General Economic	6EGDA332	419259
Poland	Germany, East	24 Oct 58	Commodity Trade	6EGDA332	419258
Poland	Germany, East	06 May 59	Culture	7EGDA409	419260
Poland	Germany, East	08 May 59	Culture	59PZUM64	458067
Poland	Germany, East	27 May 59	Commodity Trade	7EGDA568	419261
Poland	Germany, East	23 Sep 59	Land Transport	59PZUM90	458069
Poland	Germany, East	23 Sep 59	Visas	7EGDA416	419262
Poland	Germany, East	10 Nov 59	Specific Resources	59PZUM100	458070
Poland	Germany, East	10 Nov 59	Specific Resources	7EGDA426	419263
Poland	Germany, East	09 Jan 60	Water Transport	8EGDA414	419264
Poland	Germany, East	09 Jan 60	Water Transport	8EGDA419	419265
Poland	Germany, East	22 Apr 60	General Economic	60PZUM20	458074
Poland	Germany, East	22 Apr 60	General Economic	8EGDA423	419266
Poland	Germany, East	18 Jan 61	Specific Property	9EGDA379	419267
Poland	Germany, East	13 May 61	Admin Cooperation	9EGDA469	419268
Poland	Germany, East	09 May 62	Visas	10EGDA575	419269
Poland	Germany, East	17 Mar 63	Non-ILO Labor	11EGDA589	419270
Poland	Germany, East	30 Dec 63	Air Transport	11EGDA416	419271
Poland	Germany, East	14 Mar 64	Visas	64PZUM16	458110
Poland	Germany, East	07 Jun 64	Visas	12EGDA1144	419272
Poland	Germany, East	06 Oct 64	Culture	552UNTS89	108051
Poland	Germany, East	11 Mar 65	Specific Resources	52EGDZ331	420273
Poland	Germany, East	12 May 65	Specific Property	44EGDZ335	420274
Poland	Germany, East	04 Nov 65	Education	65PZUM65	458125
Poland	Germany, East	30 Dec 65	General Economic	60EGDZ350	420275
Poland	Germany, East	05 Mar 66	Commodity Trade	51EGDZ355	420276
Poland	Germany, East	15 Mar 67	General Amity	618UNTS21	108922
Poland	Germany, East	05 May 67	Scientific Project	48EGDZ383	420277
Poland	Germany, East	29 Oct 67	Territory Boundary	69PDZU217	457160
Poland	Germany, East	15 May 69	Water Transport	70PDZU96	457163
Poland	Germany, East	28 Oct 69	Admin Cooperation	70PDZU221	457165
Poland	Germany, East	16 Jul 71	Gen Communications	72PDZU41	457174
Poland	Germany, East	25 Nov 71	Visas	71PDZU357	457177
Poland	Germany, East	25 Nov 71	Admin Cooperation	72PDZU48	457176
Poland	Germany, West	16 Nov 56	General Economic	57WBGA1	424584
Poland	Germany, West	07 Mar 63	General Economic	63WBGA64	424585
Poland	Germany, West	11 Sep 69	Land Transport	69WBGA191	424586
Poland	Germany, West	15 Oct 70	General Economic	70WBGA211	424587
Poland	Germany, West	07 Dec 70	Territory Boundary	72PDZU229	457169
Poland	Ghana	17 Jan 61	Culture	572UNTS209	108314
Poland	Ghana	19 Apr 61	Tech Assistance	61PZUM94	458082
Poland	Ghana	17 Jan 64	Culture	65PDZU393	457109
Poland	Greece	08 Nov 60	Finance	483UNTS141	107011
Poland	Greece	08 Nov 60	General Trade	483UNTS127	107010
Poland	Greece	30 Sep 63	General Trade	534UNTS23	107751
Poland	Greece	21 Dec 63	Air Transport	538UNTS155	107813
Poland	Greece	21 Jan 64	Taxation	533UNTS309	107749
Poland	Guinea	17 Jun 63	Tech Assistance	63PZUM61	458105
Poland	Guinea	10 Mar 66	Culture	67PDZU201	457130
Poland	Hungary	28 Aug 47	Air Transport	15UNTS145	100231
Poland	Hungary	31 Jan 48	Culture	25UNTS283	100368
Poland	Hungary	13 May 48	General Economic	25UNTS301	100369

PARTY ONE	PARTY TWO	DATE	TOPIC	CITATION	NUMBER
Poland	Hungary	18 Jun 48	Culture	25UNTS319	100370
Poland	Hungary	29 Oct 49	Sanitation	260UNTS113	103706
Poland	Hungary	29 Oct 49	Sanitation	260UNTS91	103705
Poland	Hungary	25 Apr 56	Gen Communications	56PZUM156	458045
Poland	Hungary	25 Apr 56	Telecommunications	56PZUM140	458044
Poland	Hungary	25 Apr 56	Postal Service	56PZUM128	458043
Poland	Hungary	18 Jun 56	Telecommunications	56PZUM185	458046
Poland	Hungary	08 May 58	Sanitation	408UNTS212	105872
Poland	Hungary	25 Oct 58	General Economic	58PZUM87	458061
Poland	Hungary	14 Feb 59	Non-ILO Labor	431UNTS157	106215
Poland	Hungary	06 Mar 59	Admin Cooperation	432UNTS3	106216
Poland	Hungary	20 May 59	Consul/Citizenship	432UNTS115	106217
Poland	Hungary	05 Jul 61	Consul/Citizenship	437UNTS3	106296
Poland	Hungary	18 Apr 64	Visas	64PZUM20	458111
Poland	Hungary	18 Jul 65	Land Transport	577UNTS161	108376
Poland	Hungary	16 Sep 67	Admin Cooperation	68PZUM32	458148
Poland	Hungary	16 May 68	General Amity	68PDZU257	457157
Poland	Hungary	16 May 68	General Amity	OUNTSO	109292
Poland	Hungary	31 Oct 68	Health/Educ/Welfare	70PDZU91	457161
Poland	India	29 Sep 56	Telecommunications	276UNTS305	103993
Poland	India	27 Mar 57	Culture	319UNTS263	104635
Poland	India	27 Jun 60	Water Transport	60PZUM63	458076
Poland	Indonesia	06 May 53	General Economic	53PZUM85	458009
Poland	Indonesia	10 Oct 61	Tech Assistance	61PZUM211	458089
Poland	Iran	13 Feb 64	General Economic	OIRTB57	433092
Poland	Iran	13 May 68	Culture	69PDZU73	457156
Poland	Iran	13 Aug 68	Taxation	OIRTB58	433094
Poland	Iran	04 Oct 69	Taxation	OIRTB57	433093
Poland	Iran	16 Dec 69	General Trade	OIRTB57	433090
Poland	Iran	16 Dec 69	Finance	OIRTB57	433091
Poland	Iraq	03 Jan 59	General Economic	59PZUM9	458065
Poland	Iraq	02 Apr 59	Culture	432UNTS147	106218
Poland	Iraq	27 Jul 61	Air Transport	61PZUM183	458086
Poland	Italy	15 Jun 49	General Trade	50ITGU130	435301
Poland	Italy	25 Feb 58	Finance	58ITGU105	435302
Poland	Italy	25 Feb 58	Admin Cooperation	58ITGU105	435303
Poland	Italy	03 Feb 59	Finance	61ITDI382	436304
Poland	Italy	27 Nov 60	Tech Assistance	62ITDI437	436305
Poland	Italy	27 Nov 60	Scientific Project	58PZUM132	458080
Poland	Italy	09 Dec 61	Culture	62ITDI517	436306
Poland	Italy	09 Dec 61	Culture	61PZUM266	458093
Poland	Italy	08 Jun 62	General Trade	63ITDI294	436307
Poland	Italy	29 Dec 62	Customs	63ITDI295	436308
Poland	Italy	25 Feb 65	General Trade	66ITDI150	436309
Poland	Italy	25 Mar 65	Culture	69PZUM213	458119
Poland	Italy	14 Jul 65	General Economic	66ITDI154	436310
Poland	Italy	14 Jul 65	General Economic	65PZUM50	458124
Poland	Italy	13 Jul 68	Land Transport	68PZUM94	458159
Poland	Japan	08 Feb 57	General Amity	318UNTS251	104620
Poland	Japan	26 Apr 58	General Economic	340UNTS221	104866
Poland	Kenya	20 Apr 64	Tech Assistance	64PZUM23	458112
Poland	Korea, North	08 May 53	Tech Assistance	53PZUM109	458010
Poland	Korea, North	30 Dec 55	Postal Service	55PZUM57	458031
Poland	Korea, North	30 Dec 55	Telecommunications	55PZUM67	458030
Poland	Korea, North	11 May 56	Culture	432UNTS161	106219
Poland	Korea, North	17 Apr 57	Scientific Project	57PZUM67	458049
Poland	Mali	02 Nov 61	Tech Assistance	61PZUM217	458091
Poland	Mali	02 Nov 61	Culture	64PDZU361	457090
Poland	Mali	02 Nov 62	Culture	572UNTS219	108315
Poland	Mexico	24 Jul 70	Health/Educ/Welfare	71PDZU321	457166
Poland	Mongolia	26 May 54	Mass Media	54PZUM14	458015
Poland	Mongolia	23 Dec 58	Culture	432UNTS177	106220
Poland	Mongolia	28 Feb 61	Tech Assistance	61PZUM88	458081
Poland	Mongolia	28 Oct 64	Consul/Citizenship	552UNTS115	108052
Poland	Mongolia	14 Sep 71	Admin Cooperation	72PDZU321	457175

PARTY ONE	PARTY TWO	DATE	TOPIC	CITATION	NUMBER
Poland	Morocco	15 Oct 62	Tech Assistance	62PZUM100	458099
Poland	Multilateral	27 Mar 41	Military Mission	67UNTS231	200222
Poland	Multilateral	19 Apr 44	Scientific Project	89UNTS279	200257
Poland	Multilateral	02 Aug 44	Scientific Project	67UNTS221	200221
Poland	Multilateral	07 Dec 44	Air Transport	171UNTS345	200501
Poland	Multilateral	07 Dec 44	Air Transport	84UNTS389	200252
Poland	Multilateral	07 Dec 44	IGO Establishment	15UNTS295	200102
Poland	Multilateral	15 Dec 44	Sanitation	16UNTS247	200106
Poland	Multilateral	15 Dec 44	Sanitation	17UNTS305	200110
Poland	Multilateral	08 Aug 45	General Military	82UNTS279	200251
Poland	Multilateral	27 Sep 45	IGO Establishment	5UNTS327	200035
Poland	Multilateral	16 Nov 45	IGO Establishment	4UNTS275	100052
Poland	Multilateral	27 Dec 45	IGO Establishment	2UNTS39	100020
Poland	Multilateral	04 Jan 46	IGO Establishment	6UNTS35	100066
Poland	Multilateral	05 Apr 46	Specific Resources	231UNTS199	103221
Poland	Multilateral	23 Apr 46	Sanitation	17UNTS3	100265
Poland	Multilateral	23 Apr 46	Sanitation	16UNTS179	100257
Poland	Multilateral	22 Jul 46	IGO Establishment	14UNTS185	100221
Poland	Multilateral	22 Jul 46	IGO Establishment	9UNTS3	100125
Poland	Multilateral	27 Jul 46	Patents/Copyrights	90UNTS229	101238
Poland	Multilateral	30 Oct 46	IGO Establishment	11UNTS107	100151
Poland	Multilateral	11 Dec 46	Sanitation	12UNTS179	100186
Poland	Multilateral	08 Feb 47	Patents/Copyrights	14UNTS287	100222
Poland	Multilateral	10 Feb 47	Peace/Disarmament	49UNTS3	100747
Poland	Multilateral	10 Jun 47	Water Transport	208UNTS3	102814
Poland	Multilateral	02 Oct 47	Telecommunications	193UNTS188	102616
Poland	Multilateral	11 Oct 47	IGO Establishment	77UNTS143	100998
Poland	Multilateral	12 Nov 47	Admin Cooperation	53UNTS39	100771
Poland	Multilateral	12 Nov 47	Admin Cooperation	46UNTS169	100709
Poland	Multilateral	12 Nov 47	Admin Cooperation	53UNTS13	100770
Poland	Multilateral	12 Nov 47	Admin Cooperation	46UNTS201	100710
Poland	Multilateral	12 Nov 47	Admin Cooperation	53UNTS49	100772
Poland	Multilateral	06 Mar 48	Water Transport	289UNTS3	104214
Poland	Multilateral	10 Jun 48	Humanitarian	191UNTS3	102576
Poland	Multilateral	10 Jun 48	Humanitarian	164UNTS113	102163
Poland	Multilateral	24 Jul 48	Sanitation	66UNTS25	100847
Poland	Multilateral	19 Nov 48	Sanitation	44UNTS277	100688
Poland	Multilateral	09 Dec 48	Humanitarian	78UNTS277	101021
Poland	Multilateral	08 Feb 49	Specific Resources	157UNTS157	102053
Poland	Multilateral	16 Jun 49	Land Transport	45UNTS149	100696
Poland	Multilateral	18 Jun 49	ILO Labor	605UNTS295	108768
Poland	Multilateral	12 Aug 49	Humanitarian	75UNTS85	100971
Poland	Multilateral	12 Aug 49	General Military	75UNTS135	100972
Poland	Multilateral	12 Aug 49	Humanitarian	75UNTS287	100973
Poland	Multilateral	12 Aug 49	Humanitarian	75UNTS31	100970
Poland	Multilateral	21 Mar 50	Admin Cooperation	96UNTS271	101342
Poland	Multilateral	16 Sep 50	General Transport	92UNTS91	101264
Poland	Multilateral	11 Jul 52	Postal Service	171UNTS191	102227
Poland	Multilateral	11 Jul 52	Postal Service	171UNTS89	102225
Poland	Multilateral	11 Jul 52	Postal Service	170UNTS63	102222
Poland	Multilateral	11 Jul 52	Postal Service	170UNTS269	102223
Poland	Multilateral	11 Jul 52	Postal Service	170UNTS3	102221
Poland	Multilateral	11 Jul 52	IGO Establishment	169UNTS3	102220
Poland	Multilateral	07 Nov 52	General Trade	221UNTS255	103010
Poland	Multilateral	31 Mar 53	Privil/Immunities	193UNTS136	102613
Poland	Multilateral	01 Oct 53	Commodity Trade	258UNTS153	103677
Poland	Multilateral	12 May 54	Admin Cooperation	327UNTS3	104714
Poland	Multilateral	14 May 54	Culture	249UNTS215	103511
Poland	Multilateral	14 Jun 54	Air Transport	320UNTS217	104644
Poland	Multilateral	14 Jun 54	Air Transport	320UNTS209	104643
Poland	Multilateral	14 May 55	General Amity	219UNTS3	102962
Poland	Multilateral	15 May 55	Recognition	217UNTS223	102949
Poland	Multilateral	28 Sep 55	Air Transport	478UNTS371	106943
Poland	Multilateral	12 Oct 55	IGO Establishment	560UNTS3	108165
Poland	Multilateral	26 Mar 56	IGO Establishment	259UNTS125	103686

PARTY ONE	PARTY TWO	DATE	TOPIC	CITATION	NUMBER
Poland	Multilateral	18 May 56	Land Transport	339UNTS3	104844
Poland	Multilateral	18 May 56	Customs	338UNTS103	104834
Poland	Multilateral	18 May 56	Customs	327UNTS123	104721
Poland	Multilateral	19 May 56	Land Transport	399UNTS189	105742
Poland	Multilateral	20 Jun 56	Admin Cooperation	268UNTS3	103850
Poland	Multilateral	09 Jul 56	Non-ILO Labor	314UNTS3	104539
Poland	Multilateral	07 Sep 56	Humanitarian	266UNTS3	103822
Poland	Multilateral	26 Oct 56	IGO Establishment	276UNTS3	103988
Poland	Multilateral	14 Dec 56	Taxation	436UNTS131	106293
Poland	Multilateral	14 Dec 56	Taxation	436UNTS115	106292
Poland	Multilateral	20 Feb 57	Consul/Citizenship	309UNTS65	104468
Poland	Multilateral	15 Jun 57	General Trade	550UNTS45	108008
Poland	Multilateral	03 Oct 57	Postal Service	365UNTS207	105214
Poland	Multilateral	03 Oct 57	Postal Service	366UNTS255	105219
Poland	Multilateral	03 Oct 57	Postal Service	364UNTS3	105211
Poland	Multilateral	03 Oct 57	Postal Service	364UNTS331	105212
Poland	Multilateral	03 Oct 57	Postal Service	365UNTS3	105213
Poland	Multilateral	03 Oct 57	Postal Service	366UNTS87	105216
Poland	Multilateral	29 Apr 58	Territory Boundary	499UNTS311	107302
Poland	Multilateral	29 Apr 58	Water Transport	450UNTS11	106465
Poland	Multilateral	10 Jun 58	Admin Cooperation	330UNTS3	104739
Poland	Multilateral	01 Dec 58	Commodity Trade	385UNTS137	105534
Poland	Multilateral	15 Jan 59	Customs	348UNTS13	104996
Poland	Multilateral	24 Jan 59	IGO Establishment	486UNTS157	107078
Poland	Multilateral	01 Dec 59	Territory Boundary	402UNTS71	105778
Poland	Multilateral	14 Dec 59	Land Transport	422UNTS75	106069
Poland	Multilateral	14 Dec 59	Sanitation	422UNTS33	106067
Poland	Multilateral	14 Dec 59	IGO Status/Immunit	368UNTS237	105244
Poland	Multilateral	14 Dec 59	IGO Establishment	368UNTS253	105245
Poland	Multilateral	14 Dec 59	Sanitation	422UNTS57	106068
Poland	Multilateral	17 Jun 60	Humanitarian	536UNTS27	107794
Poland	Multilateral	06 Oct 60	Customs	473UNTS131	106861
Poland	Multilateral	14 Dec 60	Education	429UNTS93	106193
Poland	Multilateral	30 Mar 61	Sanitation	520UNTS151	107515
Poland	Multilateral	18 Apr 61	Consul/Citizenship	500UNTS95	107310
Poland	Multilateral	21 Apr 61	IGO Establishment	484UNTS349	107041
Poland	Multilateral	21 Jun 61	IGO Establishment	514UNTS209	107449
Poland	Multilateral	15 Dec 61	Admin Cooperation	424UNTS43	106098
Poland	Multilateral	23 Jul 62	Recognition	456UNTS302	106564
Poland	Multilateral	25 Jul 62	Specific Property	506UNTS177	107387
Poland	Multilateral	28 Jul 62	Specific Resources	460UNTS219	106642
Poland	Multilateral	10 Dec 62	Culture	521UNTS231	107525
Poland	Multilateral	24 Apr 63	Consul/Citizenship	596UNTS261	108638
Poland	Multilateral	07 Jun 63	Water Transport	472UNTS95	106837
Poland	Multilateral	05 Aug 63	Sanitation	480UNTS43	106964
Poland	Multilateral	23 Oct 63	IGO Establishment	506UNTS197	107388
Poland	Multilateral	14 Nov 63	Finance	619UNTS299	108948
Poland	Multilateral	28 Feb 64	Atomic Energy	501UNTS245	107321
Poland	Multilateral	10 Jul 64	Postal Service	611UNTS387	108846
Poland	Multilateral	10 Jul 64	Postal Service	613UNTS3	108850
Poland	Multilateral	10 Jul 64	Postal Service	611UNTS7	108844
Poland	Multilateral	10 Jul 64	Postal Service	613UNTS193	108852
Poland	Multilateral	10 Jul 64	Postal Service	611UNTS105	108845
Poland	Multilateral	10 Jul 64	Postal Service	612UNTS233	108848
Poland	Multilateral	10 Jul 64	Postal Service	612UNTS3	108847
Poland	Multilateral	15 Jul 64	IGO Establishment	610UNTS143	108840
Poland	Multilateral	12 Sep 64	Specific Resources	0UNTS0	109344
Poland	Multilateral	01 Dec 64	Water Transport	550UNTS133	108012
Poland	Multilateral	02 Feb 65	Tech Assistance	523UNTS256	107560
Poland	Multilateral	09 Mar 65	Water Transport	591UNTS265	108564
Poland	Multilateral	23 Jun 65	General IGO	614UNTS239	108873
Poland	Multilateral	08 Jul 65	General Trade	597UNTS3	108641
Poland	Multilateral	18 Nov 65	Customs	609UNTS115	108830
Poland	Multilateral	31 Dec 65	Specific Resources	616UNTS317	108904
Poland	Multilateral	05 Apr 66	Water Transport	640UNTS133	109159

PARTY ONE	PARTY TWO	DATE	TOPIC	CITATION	NUMBER
Poland	Multilateral	28 Apr 66	Non-ILO Labor	604UNTS219	108752
Poland	Multilateral	09 Sep 66	IGO Status/Immunit	0UNTS0	109343
Poland	Multilateral	27 Jan 67	Scientific Project	610UNTS205	108843
Poland	Multilateral	22 Aug 67	General Trade	0UNTS0	110687
Poland	Multilateral	22 Apr 68	Scientific Project	0UNTS0	109574
Poland	Multilateral	01 Jul 68	Peace/Disarmament	0UNTS0	110485
Poland	Multilateral	26 Nov 68	Humanitarian	0UNTS0	110823
Poland	Multilateral	24 Dec 68	Commodity Trade	0UNTS0	109369
Poland	Netherlands	20 May 49	General Trade	51NET67	447010
Poland	Netherlands	29 Oct 55	Finance	56NET19	447058
Poland	Netherlands	29 Oct 55	General Trade	56NET18	447057
Poland	Netherlands	21 Jul 60	Air Transport	497UNTS189	107269
Poland	Netherlands	20 Dec 63	Claims and Debts	514UNTS169	107446
Poland	Netherlands	22 Aug 67	General Economic	68PZUM26	458146
Poland	Netherlands	22 Aug 67	Culture	68PDZU209	457147
Poland	Netherlands	22 Aug 67	Culture	0UNTS0	109275
Poland	Netherlands	22 Aug 67	General Economic	0UNTS0	109276
Poland	New Zealand	07 Jul 65	General Trade	548UNTS19	107966
Poland	Niger	09 Nov 61	Health/Educ/Welfare	61PZUM229	458092
Poland	Norway	03 Dec 46	Finance	15UNTS203	100234
Poland	Norway	04 Feb 48	General Trade	30UNTS205	100458
Poland	Norway	31 Dec 48	General Trade	29UNTS3	100430
Poland	Norway	21 Dec 49	Finance	47UNTS107	100725
Poland	Norway	23 Dec 55	Claims and Debts	2NORT671	451130
Poland	Norway	17 Dec 58	Culture	432UNTS193	106221
Poland	Norway	17 Jan 61	Air Transport	412UNTS130	105928
Poland	Norway	30 Oct 64	Finance	3NORT928	451131
Poland	Norway	21 Sep 67	General Trade	3NORT1004	451132
Poland	Norway	18 Oct 68	General Trade	3NORT0	451133
Poland	Org Rail Collabor	12 Dec 57	IGO Operations	57PZUM125	458057
Poland	Pakistan	21 Mar 67	Admin Cooperation	67PZUM69	458140
Poland	Romania	09 Aug 47	Air Transport	12UNTS363	100193
Poland	Romania	27 Feb 48	Culture	46UNTS143	100707
Poland	Romania	26 Jan 49	General Military	85UNTS21	101143
Poland	Romania	09 Dec 58	General Economic	58PZUM111	458062
Poland	Romania	25 Jan 62	Admin Cooperation	468UNTS3	106770
Poland	Romania	05 Oct 62	Consul/Citizenship	521UNTS3	107516
Poland	Romania	26 Nov 64	Health/Educ/Welfare	552UNTS157	108053
Poland	Romania	29 Jan 68	Land Transport	68PZUM52	458152
Poland	Romania	29 Jan 68	Land Transport	0UNTS0	109538
Poland	Romania	29 Jan 68	Land Transport	68PZUM42	458151
Poland	Romania	10 Feb 69	Specific Resources	0UNTS0	110213
Poland	Romania	12 Nov 70	General Amity	71PDZU53	457168
Poland	Romania	28 Jun 71	Visas	72PDZU1	457173
Poland	Senegal	18 Jun 62	Culture	62PZUM48	458094
Poland	Senegal	18 Jun 62	General Economic	62PZUM51	458095
Poland	Singapore	07 Jun 66	General Trade	631UNTS189	108994
Poland	Sweden	09 Jul 45	General Trade	45SOFM115	461011
Poland	Sweden	20 Aug 45	General Economic	45SOFM125	461014
Poland	Sweden	24 Aug 45	Air Transport	45SOFM70	461004
Poland	Sweden	16 Feb 46	General Economic	46SOFM183	461021
Poland	Sweden	26 Oct 46	General Economic	46SOFM311	461035
Poland	Sweden	18 Mar 47	Finance	47SOFM137	461039
Poland	Sweden	18 Mar 47	General Economic	12UNTS295	100190
Poland	Sweden	22 Apr 48	Claims and Debts	49PDZU27	457004
Poland	Sweden	18 Oct 49	Finance	49SOFM529	461091
Poland	Sweden	03 Nov 49	General Economic	49SOFM549	461092
Poland	Sweden	16 Nov 49	Claims and Debts	50SOFM921	461119
Poland	Sweden	03 Dec 51	Finance	51SOFM461	461153
Poland	Sweden	18 Oct 52	General Trade	52SOFM529	461174
Poland	Sweden	08 Jun 56	Air Transport	334UNTS257	104771
Poland	Sweden	21 Aug 57	Admin Cooperation	427UNTS277	106159
Poland	Sweden	19 Jan 66	Finance	66PZUM25	458129
Poland	Sweden	04 Apr 68	Land Transport	68PZUM71	458154
Poland	Sweden	05 Oct 70	Specific Property	71PDZU37	457167

PARTY ONE	PARTY TWO	DATE	TOPIC	CITATION	NUMBER
Poland	Switzerland	25 Jun 49	General Economic	49SWRO832	462151
Poland	Switzerland	25 Jun 49	Claims and Debts	49SWRO839	462171
Poland	Switzerland	18 May 61	Air Transport	559UNTS233	108161
Poland	Switzerland	13 Jun 61	Taxation	61PZUM121	458084
Poland	Switzerland	13 Jun 61	Taxation	61SWRO570	462062
Poland	Syria	10 Nov 62	Air Transport	491UNTS228	107179
Poland	Syria	18 Jun 65	Tech Assistance	66PZUM33	458123
Poland	Tanzania	15 May 65	Tech Assistance	65PZUM38	458120
Poland	Tunisia	16 Sep 61	Tech Assistance	61PZUM192	458087
Poland	Tunisia	27 Apr 66	Culture	67PDZU249	457132
Poland	Turkey	18 Jul 48	General Economic	49TURG1802	466081
Poland	Turkey	18 Jul 49	General Economic	49TURG1802	466082
Poland	Turkey	04 Dec 53	Commodity Trade	55TURG204	466083
Poland	UK Great Britain	24 Jun 46	Claims and Debts	11UNTS59	100149
Poland	UK Great Britain	24 Jan 48	Claims and Debts	87UNTS3	101163
Poland	UK Great Britain	02 Mar 48	Finance	77UNTS47	100991
Poland	UK Great Britain	14 Jan 49	General Economic	83UNTS3	101100
Poland	UK Great Britain	14 Jan 49	Reparations	83UNTS51	101101
Poland	UK Great Britain	22 Aug 49	Admin Cooperation	404UNTS17	105801
Poland	UK Great Britain	11 Nov 54	Finance	204UNTS137	102755
Poland	UK Great Britain	03 Apr 59	Air Transport	351UNTS295	105030
Poland	UK Great Britain	02 Jul 60	Air Transport	385UNTS87	105532
Poland	UK Great Britain	26 Sep 64	Specific Property	539UNTS153	107828
Poland	UK Great Britain	23 Feb 67	Consul/Citizenship	71PDZU186	457139
Poland	UK Great Britain	21 Jul 67	Sanitation	0UNTS0	110421
Poland	UK Great Britain	21 Jul 67	Sanitation	70PDZU1	457145
Poland	UK Great Britain	10 Oct 67	Scientific Project	0UNTS0	109496
Poland	UK Great Britain	10 Oct 67	Scientific Project	68PZUM35	458149
Poland	UN Special Fund	15 Oct 59	Direct Aid	344UNTS29	104941
Poland	UNICEF (Children)	23 Aug 47	Tech Assistance	65UNTS22	100815
Poland	UNICEF (Children)	24 Aug 61	Direct Aid	406UNTS95	105841
Poland	United Arab Rep	14 Feb 56	Air Transport	56PZUM82	458039
Poland	United Arab Rep	02 Feb 57	Culture	319UNTS221	104633
Poland	United Arab Rep	26 Oct 64	Tech Assistance	64PZUM63	458116
Poland	United Nations	16 Jul 63	IGO Operations	471UNTS3	106817
Poland	United Nations	20 Feb 67	IGO Operations	590UNTS71	108547
Poland	USA (United States)	01 Jul 42	Milit Assistance	103UNTS267	200317
Poland	USA (United States)	25 Feb 43	Milit Servic/Citiz	13UNTS395	200086
Poland	USA (United States)	22 Apr 46	Loans and Credits	406UNTS215	105851
Poland	USA (United States)	24 Apr 46	General Economic	4UNTS155	100042
Poland	USA (United States)	29 Aug 46	Status of Forces	160UNTS11	102097
Poland	USA (United States)	30 Oct 48	Consul/Citizenship	15UNTS225	100238
Poland	USA (United States)	28 Jun 56	Claims and Debts	273UNTS79	103944
Poland	USA (United States)	07 Jun 57	Direct Aid	291UNTS41	104243
Poland	USA (United States)	12 Feb 58	Mass Media	304UNTS287	104403
Poland	USA (United States)	15 Feb 58	US Agri Commod Aid	307UNTS217	104452
Poland	USA (United States)	30 May 58	Mass Media	315UNTS231	104572
Poland	USA (United States)	10 Jun 59	US Agri Commod Aid	347UNTS41	104989
Poland	USA (United States)	16 Jul 60	Specif Claim/Waive	384UNTS169	105518
Poland	USA (United States)	21 Jul 60	US Agri Commod Aid	380UNTS157	105456
Poland	USA (United States)	15 Dec 61	US Agri Commod Aid	434UNTS3	106252
Poland	USA (United States)	21 Jan 63	Visas	471UNTS151	106830
Poland	USA (United States)	01 Feb 63	US Agri Commod Aid	487UNTS143	107100
Poland	USA (United States)	03 Feb 64	US Agri Commod Aid	505UNTS215	107375
Poland	USA (United States)	03 Feb 64	US Agri Commod Aid	505UNTS245	107376
Poland	USA (United States)	24 Jun 65	Commodity Trade	593UNTS147	108581
Poland	USA (United States)	27 Sep 65	Air Transport	564UNTS169	108227
Poland	USA (United States)	15 Mar 67	Commodity Trade	0UNTS0	109856
Poland	USA (United States)	12 Jun 69	Specific Resources	0UNTS0	110335
Poland	USSR (Soviet Union)	05 Jan 45	Consul/Citizenship	0SUST169	468305
Poland	USSR (Soviet Union)	21 Apr 45	General Military	12UNTS391	200070
Poland	USSR (Soviet Union)	06 Jul 45	Consul/Citizenship	0SUST182	468306
Poland	USSR (Soviet Union)	07 Jul 45	General Trade	0SUST182	468307
Poland	USSR (Soviet Union)	11 Jul 45	Admin Cooperation	0SUST183	468308
Poland	USSR (Soviet Union)	16 Aug 45	Territory Boundary	10UNTS193	200061

PARTY ONE	PARTY TWO	DATE	TOPIC	CITATION	NUMBER
Poland	USSR (Soviet Union)	16 Aug 45	Reparations	0SUST193	468309
Poland	USSR (Soviet Union)	23 Nov 45	Land Transport	0SUST201	468310
Poland	USSR (Soviet Union)	08 Feb 46	Loans and Credits	0SUST206	468311
Poland	USSR (Soviet Union)	20 Mar 46	Gen Communications	0SUST207	468312
Poland	USSR (Soviet Union)	12 Apr 46	General Trade	0SUST210	468313
Poland	USSR (Soviet Union)	05 Mar 47	Loans and Credits	0SUST230	468314
Poland	USSR (Soviet Union)	05 Mar 47	Finance	0SUST230	468315
Poland	USSR (Soviet Union)	05 Mar 47	Milit Assistance	0SUST230	468319
Poland	USSR (Soviet Union)	05 Mar 47	Tech Assistance	0SUST230	468318
Poland	USSR (Soviet Union)	05 Mar 47	Commodity Trade	0SUST230	468316
Poland	USSR (Soviet Union)	05 Mar 47	Specif Goods/Equip	0SUST230	468317
Poland	USSR (Soviet Union)	30 Apr 47	Territory Boundary	0SUST232	468321
Poland	USSR (Soviet Union)	06 May 47	Refugees	0SUST232	468320
Poland	USSR (Soviet Union)	04 Aug 47	General Trade	0SUST235	468322
Poland	USSR (Soviet Union)	01 Oct 47	Postal Service	0SUST237	468323
Poland	USSR (Soviet Union)	26 Jan 48	Loans and Credits	0SUST244	468325
Poland	USSR (Soviet Union)	26 Jan 48	General Trade	0SUST243	468324
Poland	USSR (Soviet Union)	08 Apr 48	Sanitation	26UNTS191	100388
Poland	USSR (Soviet Union)	08 Jul 48	Territory Boundary	37UNTS25	100575
Poland	USSR (Soviet Union)	08 Jul 48	Dispute Settlement	37UNTS107	100576
Poland	USSR (Soviet Union)	22 Oct 49	Mass Media	0SUST263	468327
Poland	USSR (Soviet Union)	29 Jun 50	Loans and Credits	0SUST275	468329
Poland	USSR (Soviet Union)	29 Jun 50	General Trade	0SUST275	468328
Poland	USSR (Soviet Union)	15 Feb 51	Territory Boundary	432UNTS199	106222
Poland	USSR (Soviet Union)	29 Feb 52	General Trade	0SUST285	468332
Poland	USSR (Soviet Union)	05 Apr 52	Culture	0SUST285	468333
Poland	USSR (Soviet Union)	19 May 52	Education	0SUST287	468334
Poland	USSR (Soviet Union)	05 Sep 53	Mass Media	0SUST301	468335
Poland	USSR (Soviet Union)	18 Feb 55	Air Transport	0SUST323	468336
Poland	USSR (Soviet Union)	18 Feb 55	Air Transport	55PZUM9	458021
Poland	USSR (Soviet Union)	23 Apr 55	Atomic Energy	0SUST326	468337
Poland	USSR (Soviet Union)	21 Jul 55	Direct Aid	16SUGG68	469907
Poland	USSR (Soviet Union)	01 Feb 56	Specific Property	56PZUM70	458038
Poland	USSR (Soviet Union)	07 Feb 56	Mass Media	0SUST349	468338
Poland	USSR (Soviet Union)	30 Jun 56	Culture	259UNTS311	103694
Poland	USSR (Soviet Union)	18 Sep 56	Loans and Credits	0SUST368	468339
Poland	USSR (Soviet Union)	02 Oct 56	Specific Property	56PZUM205	458047
Poland	USSR (Soviet Union)	17 Dec 56	Status of Forces	266UNTS179	103830
Poland	USSR (Soviet Union)	05 Mar 57	Territory Boundary	274UNTS133	103963
Poland	USSR (Soviet Union)	25 Mar 57	Extradition	281UNTS121	104075
Poland	USSR (Soviet Union)	27 Mar 57	Education	0SUST379	468340
Poland	USSR (Soviet Union)	23 May 57	Education	0SUST388	468341
Poland	USSR (Soviet Union)	22 Jun 57	Mass Media	16SUGG121	469943
Poland	USSR (Soviet Union)	23 Aug 57	Education	56PZUM90	458052
Poland	USSR (Soviet Union)	26 Oct 57	Status of Forces	432UNTS221	106223
Poland	USSR (Soviet Union)	28 Dec 57	Admin Cooperation	320UNTS3	104638
Poland	USSR (Soviet Union)	21 Jan 58	Consul/Citizenship	319UNTS277	104636
Poland	USSR (Soviet Union)	21 Jan 58	Consul/Citizenship	319UNTS291	104637
Poland	USSR (Soviet Union)	22 Jan 58	Atomic Energy	7SUGG103	469492
Poland	USSR (Soviet Union)	04 Feb 58	General Trade	7SUGG104	469494
Poland	USSR (Soviet Union)	05 Feb 58	Scientific Project	7SUGG105	469495
Poland	USSR (Soviet Union)	18 Mar 58	Territory Boundary	340UNTS89	104861
Poland	USSR (Soviet Union)	22 May 58	Culture	7SUGG112	469511
Poland	USSR (Soviet Union)	14 Jun 58	Water Transport	7SUGG114	469513
Poland	USSR (Soviet Union)	18 Jun 58	Status of Forces	7SUGG114	469514
Poland	USSR (Soviet Union)	10 Sep 58	Territory Boundary	7SUGG120	469528
Poland	USSR (Soviet Union)	02 Oct 58	General Trade	7SUGG121	469532
Poland	USSR (Soviet Union)	03 Mar 59	Tech Assistance	8SUGG138	469561
Poland	USSR (Soviet Union)	03 Apr 59	Non-IBRD Project	8SUGG141	469571
Poland	USSR (Soviet Union)	05 Jun 59	Non-IBRD Project	8SUGG147	469580
Poland	USSR (Soviet Union)	19 Feb 60	Customs	16SUGG127	469971
Poland	USSR (Soviet Union)	19 Feb 60	Customs	60PZUM11	458072
Poland	USSR (Soviet Union)	10 Mar 60	General Trade	9SUGG129	469641
Poland	USSR (Soviet Union)	10 Mar 60	Tech Assistance	9SUGG130	469642
Poland	USSR (Soviet Union)	01 Apr 60	Finance	9SUGG132	469648

PARTY ONE	PARTY TWO	DATE	TOPIC	CITATION	NUMBER
Poland	USSR (Soviet Union)	13 Sep 60	Tech Assistance	9SUGG148	469694
Poland	USSR (Soviet Union)	13 Sep 60	Tech Assistance	9SUGG148	469693
Poland	USSR (Soviet Union)	29 Sep 60	Commodity Trade	9SUGG148	469698
Poland	USSR (Soviet Union)	04 Jan 61	Health/Educ/Welfare	10SUGG117	469733
Poland	USSR (Soviet Union)	07 Jan 61	Direct Aid	10SUGG117	469735
Poland	USSR (Soviet Union)	05 Feb 61	Territory Boundary	420UNTS161	106046
Poland	USSR (Soviet Union)	15 Feb 61	Admin Cooperation	10SUGG121	469741
Poland	USSR (Soviet Union)	21 Apr 61	Non-IBRD Project	10SUGG128	469763
Poland	USSR (Soviet Union)	19 May 61	Tech Assistance	10SUGG130	469767
Poland	USSR (Soviet Union)	19 May 61	Direct Aid	10SUGG130	469766
Poland	USSR (Soviet Union)	22 Jun 61	Non-IBRD Project	10SUGG136	469780
Poland	USSR (Soviet Union)	30 Jun 61	Specif Goods/Equip	10SUGG137	469783
Poland	USSR (Soviet Union)	07 Jul 61	Atomic Energy	10SUGG137	469787
Poland	USSR (Soviet Union)	20 Jul 61	Non-IBRD Project	10SUGG138	469789
Poland	USSR (Soviet Union)	04 Oct 61	Specific Property	61PZUM209	458088
Poland	USSR (Soviet Union)	03 Dec 61	Atomic Energy	10SUGG145	469808
Poland	USSR (Soviet Union)	13 Dec 61	General Aid	10SUGG146	469809
Poland	USSR (Soviet Union)	22 Apr 63	Land Transport	493UNTS229	107217
Poland	USSR (Soviet Union)	17 Jul 64	Specific Resources	552UNTS175	108054
Poland	USSR (Soviet Union)	31 Mar 65	Consul/Citizenship	571UNTS217	108304
Poland	USSR (Soviet Union)	08 Apr 65	General Amity	540UNTS97	107845
Poland	USSR (Soviet Union)	07 May 66	Land Transport	66PZUM60	458134
Poland	USSR (Soviet Union)	24 Apr 68	Air Transport	68PZUM77	458155
Poland	USSR (Soviet Union)	29 Aug 69	Territory Boundary	70PDZU165	457164
Poland	USSR (Soviet Union)	14 Oct 70	Health/Educ/Welfare	71PDZU213	457170
Poland	USSR (Soviet Union)	27 May 71	Consul/Citizenship	72PDZU125	457171
Poland	Vietnam, North	24 Jan 56	Gen Communications	56PZUM66	458037
Poland	Vietnam, North	24 Jan 56	Telecommunications	56PZUM50	458036
Poland	Vietnam, North	24 Jan 56	Postal Service	56PZUM32	458035
Poland	Vietnam, North	06 Apr 57	Culture	432UNTS255	106224
Poland	WHO (World Health)	26 Aug 65	Tech Assistance	552UNTS3	108047
Poland	Yugoslavia	23 Nov 45	General Economic	115UNTS3	101555
Poland	Yugoslavia	02 Jan 46	Visas	115UNTS21	101556
Poland	Yugoslavia	18 Jan 46	General Trade	115UNTS83	101559
Poland	Yugoslavia	16 Mar 46	Culture	10UNTS11	100139
Poland	Yugoslavia	18 Mar 46	General Military	1UNTS53	100013
Poland	Yugoslavia	24 May 47	General Trade	115UNTS37	101557
Poland	Yugoslavia	24 May 47	Finance	115UNTS69	101558
Poland	Yugoslavia	24 May 47	General Trade	115UNTS89	101560
Poland	Yugoslavia	22 Aug 47	Air Transport	47PDZU293	457003
Poland	Yugoslavia	07 Nov 47	General Economic	115UNTS137	101561
Poland	Yugoslavia	21 Jan 48	Non-IBRD Project	115UNTS155	101562
Poland	Yugoslavia	12 Apr 48	General Trade	115UNTS167	101563
Poland	Yugoslavia	16 Jan 49	General Trade	115UNTS241	101564
Poland	Yugoslavia	14 Nov 55	Air Transport	55PZUM49	458029
Poland	Yugoslavia	14 Nov 55	Scientific Project	55PZUM45	458028
Poland	Yugoslavia	07 Mar 56	Telecommunications	56PZUM115	458041
Poland	Yugoslavia	07 Mar 56	Postal Service	56PZUM121	458042
Poland	Yugoslavia	06 Jul 56	Culture	281UNTS143	104076
Poland	Yugoslavia	12 Nov 56	General Economic	57PZUM114	458056
Poland	Yugoslavia	04 Apr 57	Atomic Energy	57PZUM62	458048
Poland	Yugoslavia	20 Oct 57	Sanitation	57PZUM102	458055
Poland	Yugoslavia	16 Jan 58	Non-ILO Labor	340UNTS137	104863
Poland	Yugoslavia	16 Jan 58	Non-ILO Labor	340UNTS181	104864
Poland	Yugoslavia	20 Feb 58	General Economic	58PZUM48	458059
Poland	Yugoslavia	17 Nov 58	Consul/Citizenship	432UNTS267	106225
Poland	Yugoslavia	06 Feb 60	Admin Cooperation	521UNTS37	107517
Poland	Yugoslavia	05 May 60	Sanitation	423UNTS229	106095
Poland	Yugoslavia	30 Jun 64	General Economic	64PZUM29	458113
Poland	Yugoslavia	10 Dec 65	Sanitation	66PDZU279	457128
Poland	Yugoslavia	09 May 67	Customs	67PZUM88	458144
Portugal	Accept UN Charter	04 Feb 56	UN Charter	229UNTS3	103155
Portugal	Argentina	20 May 66	Non-ILO Labor	635UNTS301	109090
Portugal	Australia	29 Mar 63	Visas	468UNTS313	106778
Portugal	Austria	14 Dec 54	Visas	55ABGB175	403155

PARTY ONE	PARTY TWO	DATE	TOPIC	CITATION	NUMBER
Portugal	Austria	29 Dec 70	Taxation	72ABGB85	403156
Portugal	Belgium	07 Jan 46	Finance	19UNTS159	100310
Portugal	Belgium	22 Oct 46	Air Transport	34UNTS49	100527
Portugal	Belgium	01 Mar 49	Finance	32UNTS49	100488
Portugal	Belgium	03 Jul 51	Visas	101UNTS17	101398
Portugal	Belgium	30 Jul 55	Culture	250UNTS213	103525
Portugal	Benelux Econ Union	24 May 67	Visas	601UNTS153	108693
Portugal	Brazil	30 Apr 42	Postal Service	65UNTS183	200210
Portugal	Brazil	10 Dec 46	Air Transport	200UNTS67	102695
Portugal	Canada	25 Apr 47	Air Transport	94UNTS87	101308
Portugal	Canada	28 May 54	General Trade	391UNTS253	105631
Portugal	Canada	24 Jan 58	Visas	392UNTS15	105634
Portugal	Colombia	09 Mar 51	Air Transport	108UNTS87	101469
Portugal	Cuba	26 Jun 51	Air Transport	192UNTS115	102598
Portugal	Denmark	15 Dec 47	Air Transport	35UNTS329	100563
Portugal	Denmark	08 Apr 49	General Trade	74UNTS209	100964
Portugal	Denmark	08 Apr 49	Finance	74UNTS221	100965
Portugal	Denmark	02 Jun 50	General Trade	74UNTS229	100966
Portugal	Denmark	05 Jun 51	General Trade	101UNTS61	101402
Portugal	Denmark	29 Aug 52	General Trade	149UNTS49	101950
Portugal	Denmark	20 Feb 65	Commodity Trade	639UNTS43	109143
Portugal	Fed Rhod/Nyasaland	29 Nov 58	General Trade	354UNTS137	105060
Portugal	France	30 Apr 46	Air Transport	35UNTS197	100556
Portugal	France	16 Nov 57	Non-ILO Labor	59FRRT16	415368
Portugal	France	30 Oct 58	Non-ILO Labor	59FRRT16	415369
Portugal	France	31 Dec 63	Non-ILO Labor	64FRRT12	415370
Portugal	France	16 Oct 64	Education	64FRRT68	415371
Portugal	France	26 Jan 65	Admin Cooperation	65FRRT25	415372
Portugal	France	11 Sep 67	Non-ILO Labor	67FRJO2910	416373
Portugal	Germany, West	24 Aug 50	General Economic	50WBGA164	424588
Portugal	Germany, West	26 Sep 51	Customs	52WGBB505	425589
Portugal	Germany, West	21 Mar 58	Air Transport	464UNTS71	106712
Portugal	Germany, West	03 Apr 58	Patents/Copyrights	59WGBB264	425591
Portugal	Germany, West	03 Apr 58	Finance	59WGBB264	425592
Portugal	Germany, West	03 Jun 58	Claims and Debts	59WGBB264	425590
Portugal	Germany, West	30 May 59	General Economic	59WBGA131	424593
Portugal	Germany, West	13 May 61	Admin Cooperation	61WBGA125	424594
Portugal	Germany, West	17 Mar 64	Non-ILO Labor	64WBGA104	424595
Portugal	Germany, West	15 Jun 64	Extradition	67WGBB2345	425596
Portugal	Germany, West	06 Nov 64	Non-ILO Labor	68WGBB473	425597
Portugal	Germany, West	22 Oct 65	Culture	67WGBB721	425598
Portugal	Greece	31 Dec 49	Finance	92UNTS83	101263
Portugal	Greece	31 Dec 49	General Trade	92UNTS71	101262
Portugal	Greece	13 Jul 54	General Trade	230UNTS19	103173
Portugal	IBRD (World Bank)	06 Nov 63	IBRD Project	492UNTS89	107188
Portugal	IBRD (World Bank)	06 Nov 63	IBRD Project	491UNTS137	107176
Portugal	IBRD (World Bank)	29 Apr 65	IBRD Project	549UNTS69	107991
Portugal	IBRD (World Bank)	14 Jun 66	IBRD Project	581UNTS29	108431
Portugal	IBRD (World Bank)	14 Jun 66	IBRD Project	581UNTS3	108430
Portugal	ICJ Option Clause	19 Dec 55	ICJ Option Clause	224UNTS275	103079
Portugal	Ireland	06 Feb 52	General Trade	558UNTS289	108147
Portugal	Ireland	29 Jul 55	Visas	553UNTS135	108079
Portugal	Ireland	11 Nov 57	Mostfavored Nation	553UNTS141	108080
Portugal	Ireland	24 Jun 60	Air Transport	412UNTS30	105924
Portugal	Italy	05 Apr 50	Air Transport	254UNTS329	103599
Portugal	Italy	04 Jan 57	Visas	59ITDI369	436311
Portugal	Luxembourg	21 Oct 50	Air Transport	108UNTS67	101468
Portugal	Luxembourg	12 Feb 65	Non-ILO Labor	571UNTS239	108305
Portugal	Malta	01 Sep 66	Visas	579UNTS231	108410
Portugal	Mexico	22 Oct 48	Air Transport	34UNTS329	100546
Portugal	Morocco	03 Apr 58	Air Transport	393UNTS203	105657
Portugal	Multilateral	12 May 40	Scientific Project	101UNTS91	101405
Portugal	Multilateral	27 Mar 41	Military Mission	67UNTS231	200222
Portugal	Multilateral	02 Aug 44	Scientific Project	67UNTS221	200221
Portugal	Multilateral	07 Dec 44	Air Transport	171UNTS345	200501

PARTY ONE	PARTY TWO	DATE	TOPIC	CITATION	NUMBER
Portugal	Multilateral	07 Dec 44	IGO Establishment	15UNTS295	200102
Portugal	Multilateral	07 Dec 44	Air Transport	84UNTS389	200252
Portugal	Multilateral	05 Apr 46	Specific Resources	231UNTS199	103221
Portugal	Multilateral	22 Jul 46	IGO Establishment	9UNTS3	100125
Portugal	Multilateral	22 Jul 46	IGO Establishment	14UNTS185	100221
Portugal	Multilateral	08 Feb 47	Patents/Copyrights	14UNTS287	100222
Portugal	Multilateral	02 Oct 47	Telecommunications	193UNTS188	102616
Portugal	Multilateral	11 Oct 47	IGO Establishment	77UNTS143	100998
Portugal	Multilateral	06 Mar 48	Water Transport	289UNTS3	104214
Portugal	Multilateral	10 May 48	Culture	289UNTS111	104215
Portugal	Multilateral	10 Jun 48	Humanitarian	191UNTS3	102576
Portugal	Multilateral	10 Jun 48	Humanitarian	164UNTS113	102163
Portugal	Multilateral	19 Jun 48	Air Transport	310UNTS151	104492
Portugal	Multilateral	26 Jun 48	Culture	331UNTS217	104757
Portugal	Multilateral	24 Jul 48	Sanitation	66UNTS25	100847
Portugal	Multilateral	17 Sep 48	Telecommunications	97UNTS31	101345
Portugal	Multilateral	29 Nov 48	IGO Establishment	120UNTS13	101613
Portugal	Multilateral	08 Feb 49	Specific Resources	157UNTS157	102053
Portugal	Multilateral	22 Feb 49	Sanitation	93UNTS129	101296
Portugal	Multilateral	23 Mar 49	Commodity Trade	203UNTS179	102746
Portugal	Multilateral	04 Apr 49	General Military	34UNTS243	100541
Portugal	Multilateral	18 Jun 49	ILO Labor	605UNTS295	108768
Portugal	Multilateral	12 Aug 49	Humanitarian	75UNTS85	100971
Portugal	Multilateral	12 Aug 49	Humanitarian	75UNTS287	100973
Portugal	Multilateral	12 Aug 49	General Military	75UNTS135	100972
Portugal	Multilateral	12 Aug 49	Humanitarian	75UNTS31	100970
Portugal	Multilateral	13 May 50	Land Transport	128UNTS171	101719
Portugal	Multilateral	18 Oct 50	Specific Resources	638UNTS185	109134
Portugal	Multilateral	15 Dec 50	Customs	347UNTS127	104994
Portugal	Multilateral	15 Dec 50	Customs	171UNTS305	102234
Portugal	Multilateral	15 Dec 50	IGO Operations	160UNTS267	102111
Portugal	Multilateral	15 Dec 50	Customs	157UNTS129	102052
Portugal	Multilateral	25 May 51	Status of Forces	175UNTS215	102303
Portugal	Multilateral	19 Jun 51	Status of Forces	199UNTS67	102678
Portugal	Multilateral	02 Jul 51	Refugees	189UNTS137	102545
Portugal	Multilateral	20 Sep 51	IGO Status/Immunit	200UNTS3	102691
Portugal	Multilateral	09 Oct 51	IGO Establishment	220UNTS121	102997
Portugal	Multilateral	06 Dec 51	Admin Cooperation	150UNTS67	101963
Portugal	Multilateral	10 Jan 52	Visas	163UNTS3	102138
Portugal	Multilateral	10 Jan 52	Visas	163UNTS27	102139
Portugal	Multilateral	10 May 52	Taxation	439UNTS233	106332
Portugal	Multilateral	10 May 52	Admin Cooperation	439UNTS193	106330
Portugal	Multilateral	10 May 52	Admin Cooperation	439UNTS217	106331
Portugal	Multilateral	11 Jul 52	Postal Service	170UNTS3	102221
Portugal	Multilateral	11 Jul 52	Postal Service	171UNTS3	102224
Portugal	Multilateral	11 Jul 52	IGO Establishment	169UNTS3	102220
Portugal	Multilateral	11 Jul 52	Postal Service	170UNTS63	102222
Portugal	Multilateral	11 Jul 52	Postal Service	171UNTS143	102226
Portugal	Multilateral	11 Jul 52	Postal Service	171UNTS89	102225
Portugal	Multilateral	11 Jul 52	Postal Service	170UNTS269	102223
Portugal	Multilateral	06 Sep 52	Patents/Copyrights	216UNTS132	102937
Portugal	Multilateral	07 Oct 52	Admin Cooperation	310UNTS181	104493
Portugal	Multilateral	07 Nov 52	General Trade	221UNTS255	103010
Portugal	Multilateral	10 Nov 52	Admin Cooperation	214UNTS265	102904
Portugal	Multilateral	01 Oct 53	Commodity Trade	258UNTS153	103677
Portugal	Multilateral	17 Oct 53	General Transport	184UNTS42	102438
Portugal	Multilateral	11 Dec 53	Sanitation	191UNTS285	102588
Portugal	Multilateral	18 Jan 54	IGO Establishment	330UNTS121	104743
Portugal	Multilateral	01 Mar 54	Admin Cooperation	286UNTS265	104173
Portugal	Multilateral	14 May 54	Culture	249UNTS215	103511
Portugal	Multilateral	04 Jun 54	Customs	282UNTS249	104101
Portugal	Multilateral	04 Jun 54	Customs	276UNTS191	103992
Portugal	Multilateral	14 Jun 54	Air Transport	320UNTS209	104643
Portugal	Multilateral	14 Jun 54	Air Transport	320UNTS217	104644
Portugal	Multilateral	29 Jul 54	Sanitation	249UNTS45	103500
Portugal	Multilateral	01 May 55	Admin Cooperation	0UNTS0	110416
Portugal	Multilateral	25 May 55	IGO Establishment	264UNTS117	103791
Portugal	Multilateral	22 Jun 55	Atomic Energy	249UNTS3	103498
Portugal	Multilateral	28 Sep 55	Air Transport	478UNTS371	106943
Portugal	Multilateral	20 Oct 55	IGO Establishment	378UNTS159	105425
Portugal	Multilateral	01 Mar 56	Customs	343UNTS129	104923
Portugal	Multilateral	25 Apr 56	Commodity Trade	270UNTS103	103896
Portugal	Multilateral	30 Apr 56	Air Transport	310UNTS229	104494
Portugal	Multilateral	18 May 56	Customs	338UNTS103	104834
Portugal	Multilateral	18 May 56	Customs	319UNTS21	104630
Portugal	Multilateral	20 Jun 56	Admin Cooperation	268UNTS3	103850
Portugal	Multilateral	07 Sep 56	Humanitarian	266UNTS3	103822
Portugal	Multilateral	24 Oct 56	Admin Cooperation	510UNTS161	107412
Portugal	Multilateral	26 Oct 56	IGO Establishment	276UNTS3	103988
Portugal	Multilateral	29 Oct 56	Territory Boundary	263UNTS165	103772
Portugal	Multilateral	20 Feb 57	Consul/Citizenship	309UNTS65	104468
Portugal	Multilateral	15 Jun 57	Patents/Copyrights	583UNTS3	108470
Portugal	Multilateral	15 Jun 57	General Trade	550UNTS45	108008
Portugal	Multilateral	30 Sep 57	General Transport	619UNTS77	108940
Portugal	Multilateral	03 Oct 57	Postal Service	366UNTS3	105215
Portugal	Multilateral	03 Oct 57	Postal Service	365UNTS207	105214
Portugal	Multilateral	03 Oct 57	Postal Service	365UNTS3	105213
Portugal	Multilateral	03 Oct 57	Postal Service	364UNTS3	105211
Portugal	Multilateral	03 Oct 57	Postal Service	366UNTS141	105217
Portugal	Multilateral	03 Oct 57	Postal Service	364UNTS331	105212
Portugal	Multilateral	03 Oct 57	Postal Service	366UNTS87	105216
Portugal	Multilateral	03 Oct 57	Postal Service	366UNTS255	105219
Portugal	Multilateral	13 Dec 57	Land Transport	372UNTS159	105296
Portugal	Multilateral	31 Mar 58	Specific Property	320UNTS103	104639
Portugal	Multilateral	03 Apr 58	Commodity Trade	336UNTS177	104806
Portugal	Multilateral	03 Apr 58	Commodity Trade	302UNTS121	104355
Portugal	Multilateral	29 Apr 58	Specific Resources	559UNTS285	108164
Portugal	Multilateral	29 Apr 58	Territory Boundary	516UNTS205	107477
Portugal	Multilateral	29 Apr 58	Territory Boundary	499UNTS311	107302
Portugal	Multilateral	29 Apr 58	Dispute Settlement	450UNTS169	106466
Portugal	Multilateral	29 Apr 58	Water Transport	450UNTS11	106465
Portugal	Multilateral	27 Oct 58	Reparations	351UNTS303	105031
Portugal	Multilateral	01 Dec 58	Commodity Trade	385UNTS137	105534
Portugal	Multilateral	06 Apr 59	Commodity Trade	349UNTS167	105013
Portugal	Multilateral	11 May 59	Claims and Debts	527UNTS145	107623
Portugal	Multilateral	19 Nov 59	IGO Operations	410UNTS156	105902
Portugal	Multilateral	04 Jan 60	IGO Establishment	370UNTS3	105266
Portugal	Multilateral	22 Apr 60	Air Transport	418UNTS211	106023
Portugal	Multilateral	17 Jun 60	Humanitarian	536UNTS27	107794
Portugal	Multilateral	28 Jul 60	IGO Status/Immunit	394UNTS37	105667
Portugal	Multilateral	21 Sep 60	Patents/Copyrights	394UNTS3	105664
Portugal	Multilateral	09 Dec 60	Customs	429UNTS211	106200
Portugal	Multilateral	27 Mar 61	IGO Establishment	420UNTS109	106043
Portugal	Multilateral	30 Mar 61	Sanitation	520UNTS151	107515
Portugal	Multilateral	08 Jun 61	Customs	473UNTS153	106862
Portugal	Multilateral	08 Jun 61	Customs	473UNTS187	106863
Portugal	Multilateral	21 Jun 61	IGO Establishment	514UNTS209	107449
Portugal	Multilateral	05 Oct 61	Admin Cooperation	0UNTS0	109431
Portugal	Multilateral	06 Dec 61	Customs	473UNTS219	106864
Portugal	Multilateral	15 May 62	Commodity Trade	444UNTS3	106367
Portugal	Multilateral	28 Sep 62	IGO Establishment	469UNTS169	106791
Portugal	Multilateral	20 Apr 63	IGO Establishment	495UNTS3	107239
Portugal	Multilateral	05 Aug 63	Sanitation	480UNTS43	106964
Portugal	Multilateral	14 Sep 63	Air Transport	0UNTS0	110106
Portugal	Multilateral	09 Mar 64	Specific Resources	581UNTS57	108432
Portugal	Multilateral	18 Jun 64	Atomic Energy	542UNTS145	107886
Portugal	Multilateral	10 Jul 64	Postal Service	613UNTS193	108852
Portugal	Multilateral	10 Jul 64	Postal Service	611UNTS105	108845
Portugal	Multilateral	10 Jul 64	Postal Service	613UNTS3	108850
Portugal	Multilateral	10 Jul 64	Postal Service	613UNTS3	108851

PARTY ONE	PARTY TWO	DATE	TOPIC	CITATION	NUMBER
Portugal	Multilateral	10 Jul 64	Postal Service	612UNTS233	108848
Portugal	Multilateral	10 Jul 64	Postal Service	611UNTS387	108846
Portugal	Multilateral	10 Jul 64	Postal Service	612UNTS3	108847
Portugal	Multilateral	10 Jul 64	Postal Service	611UNTS7	108844
Portugal	Multilateral	20 Aug 64	Telecommunications	514UNTS25	107441
Portugal	Multilateral	12 Sep 64	Specific Resources	0UNTS0	109344
Portugal	Multilateral	24 Feb 65	IGO Operations	556UNTS47	108118
Portugal	Multilateral	08 Jul 65	General Trade	597UNTS3	108641
Portugal	Multilateral	03 May 67	IGO Operations	0UNTS0	110764
Portugal	Multilateral	10 Jul 67	Air Transport	0UNTS0	109971
Portugal	Multilateral	18 Mar 68	Commodity Trade	0UNTS0	109262
Portugal	Multilateral	24 Dec 68	Commodity Trade	0UNTS0	109369
Portugal	Netherlands	12 Apr 46	Air Transport	4UNTS317	100054
Portugal	Netherlands	14 Mar 52	Visas	309UNTS117	104470
Portugal	Netherlands	08 Jan 53	General Trade	53NET37	447036
Portugal	Netherlands	14 Dec 54	Visas	289UNTS121	104216
Portugal	Netherlands	26 Mar 57	Visas	288UNTS47	104196
Portugal	Netherlands	30 Apr 59	Finance	485UNTS129	107050
Portugal	Netherlands	22 Nov 63	Non-ILO Labor	492UNTS31	107185
Portugal	Netherlands	12 Oct 66	Non-ILO Labor	0UNTS0	109273
Portugal	Norway	16 Aug 46	Commodity Trade	30UNTS215	100459
Portugal	Norway	11 Nov 47	Air Transport	34UNTS257	100542
Portugal	Norway	28 Nov 49	Finance	47UNTS117	100726
Portugal	Norway	24 Sep 58	Visas	3NORT751	451134
Portugal	Pakistan	07 Jun 58	Air Transport	320UNTS225	104645
Portugal	South Africa	07 May 63	Air Transport	499UNTS49	107292
Portugal	Spain	31 Mar 47	Air Transport	47SPBO1107	460228
Portugal	Spain	21 Feb 55	General Economic	55SPBO2803	460229
Portugal	Spain	28 Feb 56	Sanitation	57SPBO802	460230
Portugal	Spain	21 Jan 57	Customs	57SPBO209	460231
Portugal	Spain	20 Oct 59	Sanitation	61SPBO1107	460232
Portugal	Spain	17 Feb 60	Customs	60SPBO312	460233
Portugal	Spain	20 Jan 62	Non-ILO Labor	62SPBO1809	460234
Portugal	Spain	27 Feb 63	Non-ILO Labor	63SPBO3010	460235
Portugal	Spain	27 Aug 63	Non-ILO Labor	63SPBO3010	460236
Portugal	Sweden	06 Mar 47	Air Transport	35UNTS243	100558
Portugal	Sweden	18 May 50	General Trade	50SOFM931	461120
Portugal	Sweden	18 May 50	Finance	50SOFM933	461121
Portugal	Sweden	13 Dec 51	General Trade	52SOFM193	461163
Portugal	Switzerland	09 Dec 46	Air Transport	310UNTS251	104495
Portugal	Switzerland	10 May 58	Water Transport	58SWRO781	462078
Portugal	Switzerland	22 Feb 62	Commodity Trade	62SWRO257	462152
Portugal	Taiwan	01 Apr 47	Privil/Immunities	14UNTS177	100220
Portugal	Taiwan	04 Mar 48	Finance	0CTRC415	413023
Portugal	Taiwan	20 May 48	Customs	0CTRC419	413024
Portugal	Turkey	18 Dec 58	Direct Aid	64TURG909	466113
Portugal	UK Great Britain	01 Jul 45	Postal Service	5UNTS263	200034
Portugal	UK Great Britain	06 Dec 45	Air Transport	6UNTS3	100065
Portugal	UK Great Britain	06 Dec 45	Air Transport	5UNTS37	100064
Portugal	UK Great Britain	16 Apr 46	Finance	6UNTS119	100071
Portugal	UK Great Britain	16 Oct 47	Sanitation	82UNTS203	101093
Portugal	UK Great Britain	25 May 48	Milit Installation	34UNTS311	100544
Portugal	UK Great Britain	20 Jul 51	Finance	105UNTS61	101453
Portugal	UK Great Britain	21 Nov 52	Milit Assistance	404UNTS27	105802
Portugal	UK Great Britain	21 Jan 53	Non-IBRD Project	175UNTS13	102293
Portugal	UK Great Britain	10 Jul 54	Finance	199UNTS169	102683
Portugal	UK Great Britain	18 Nov 54	Territory Boundary	325UNTS307	104706
Portugal	UK Great Britain	18 Nov 54	Territory Boundary	210UNTS265	102841
Portugal	UK Great Britain	19 Nov 54	Culture	226UNTS305	103125
Portugal	UK Great Britain	23 Nov 54	Visas	204UNTS183	102757
Portugal	UK Great Britain	24 Nov 54	Visas	313UNTS125	104533
Portugal	UK Great Britain	18 Jul 58	Atomic Energy	313UNTS109	104532
Portugal	UK Great Britain	27 Feb 61	Visas	404UNTS33	105803
Portugal	UK Great Britain	31 Jul 61	Taxation	449UNTS119	106454
Portugal	UK Great Britain	07 Apr 64	Land Transport	539UNTS167	107830

PARTY ONE	PARTY TWO	DATE	TOPIC	CITATION	NUMBER
Portugal	UK Great Britain	17 Apr 66	Air Transport	573UNTS223	108335
Portugal	UK Great Britain	27 Mar 68	Taxation	0UNTS0	109656
Portugal	USA (United States)	28 Nov 44	Milit Assistance	183UNTS311	200508
Portugal	USA (United States)	06 Dec 45	Air Transport	3UNTS139	100028
Portugal	USA (United States)	17 May 46	Commodity Trade	126UNTS3	101678
Portugal	USA (United States)	30 May 46	Air Transport	174UNTS187	102285
Portugal	USA (United States)	26 Aug 46	Mostfavored Nation	13UNTS67	100203
Portugal	USA (United States)	28 Sep 48	Mostfavored Nation	31UNTS139	100475
Portugal	USA (United States)	28 Sep 48	Direct Aid	29UNTS213	100442
Portugal	USA (United States)	04 Aug 49	Reparations	181UNTS15	102394
Portugal	USA (United States)	24 Feb 50	Visas	92UNTS219	101274
Portugal	USA (United States)	05 Jan 51	Milit Assistance	133UNTS75	101782
Portugal	USA (United States)	06 Sep 51	Milit Assistance	237UNTS217	103348
Portugal	USA (United States)	08 Jan 52	General Military	207UNTS51	102799
Portugal	USA (United States)	09 Jul 52	Milit Assistance	180UNTS251	102389
Portugal	USA (United States)	01 Apr 53	Taxation	205UNTS41	102769
Portugal	USA (United States)	21 Jul 55	Atomic Energy	239UNTS283	103386
Portugal	USA (United States)	24 May 56	US Agri Commod Aid	268UNTS323	103865
Portugal	USA (United States)	07 Nov 56	Milit Assistance	277UNTS133	104003
Portugal	USA (United States)	12 Jan 59	Postal Service	343UNTS49	104921
Portugal	USA (United States)	19 Mar 60	Education	371UNTS131	105275
Portugal	USA (United States)	26 Sep 60	Milit Assistance	393UNTS257	105660
Portugal	USA (United States)	31 Oct 60	Patents/Copyrights	394UNTS127	105673
Portugal	USA (United States)	28 Nov 61	US Agri Commod Aid	434UNTS31	106253
Portugal	USA (United States)	05 Mar 62	General Trade	436UNTS101	106290
Portugal	USA (United States)	12 Mar 64	Commodity Trade	542UNTS3	107875
Portugal	USA (United States)	12 Nov 64	Specific Property	541UNTS251	107874
Portugal	USA (United States)	26 May 65	Gen Communications	546UNTS189	107945
Portugal	USA (United States)	23 Mar 67	Commodity Trade	0UNTS0	109857
Portugal	USA (United States)	03 Jul 69	Atomic Energy	0UNTS0	110337
Portugal	Venezuela	16 May 56	Air Transport	463UNTS239	106707
Qatar	Iran	20 Sep 69	Territory Boundary	0IRTB59	433095
Qatar	Multilateral	14 Sep 60	IGO Establishment	443UNTS247	106363
Qatar	Multilateral	10 Jul 64	Postal Service	612UNTS3	108847
Qatar	Multilateral	10 Jul 64	Postal Service	611UNTS387	108846
Refrigeration Inst	France	05 Jul 66	IGO Status/Immunit	67FRJO1203	416508
Rhone Railroad	Multilateral	30 Dec 63	IBRD Project	568UNTS215	108270
Rhone Railroad	Multilateral	30 Dec 63	IBRD Project	568UNTS233	108271
Romania	Accept UN Charter	14 Dec 55	UN Charter	223UNTS59	103052
Romania	Accept UN Charter	15 Dec 55	UN Charter	223UNTS69	103055
Romania	Albania	14 Feb 53	Culture	342UNTS107	104903
Romania	Albania	03 May 61	Non-ILO Labor	592UNTS21	108567
Romania	Argentina	05 Nov 68	Culture	0UNTS0	109573
Romania	Argentina	03 Apr 69	General Trade	0UNTS0	110189
Romania	Australia	07 Jan 49	Admin Cooperation	189UNTS263	102550
Romania	Australia	18 May 67	General Trade	642UNTS25	109162
Romania	Austria	11 May 55	Water Transport	342UNTS119	104904
Romania	Austria	10 Jul 58	Air Transport	353UNTS155	105041
Romania	Austria	21 Jul 61	General Trade	421UNTS161	106057
Romania	Austria	03 Jul 63	Claims and Debts	588UNTS3	108516
Romania	Austria	27 May 64	Land Transport	588UNTS29	108517
Romania	Austria	18 Dec 64	Sanitation	65ABGB34	403157
Romania	Austria	17 Nov 65	Admin Cooperation	0UNTS0	109625
Romania	Austria	17 Nov 65	Visas	564UNTS185	108229
Romania	Austria	28 Apr 68	Customs	0UNTS0	109377
Romania	Austria	17 Dec 68	Visas	69ABGB39	403158
Romania	Austria	17 Dec 68	Visas	0UNTS0	109468
Romania	Austria	24 Sep 70	General Trade	70ABGB328	403159
Romania	Austria	02 Oct 70	Customs	70ABGB338	403160
Romania	Bel-Lux Econ Union	16 Sep 68	Tech Assistance	0UNTS0	110212
Romania	Bel-Lux Econ Union	16 Sep 68	General Economic	0UNTS0	110042
Romania	Belgium	04 Dec 56	Air Transport	317UNTS161	104602
Romania	Belgium	12 Oct 62	Sanitation	502UNTS31	107325
Romania	Belgium	13 Nov 63	Culture	520UNTS119	107513
Romania	Belgium	22 Sep 67	Land Transport	637UNTS0	109109

PARTY ONE	PARTY TWO	DATE	TOPIC	CITATION	NUMBER
Romania	Belgium	25 Oct 69	Visas	0UNTS0	110557
Romania	Bulgaria	29 Sep 50	Scientific Project	342UNTS141	104905
Romania	Bulgaria	22 Jul 54	Sanitation	362UNTS101	105184
Romania	Bulgaria	03 Dec 58	Admin Cooperation	417UNTS133	106007
Romania	Bulgaria	23 Apr 59	Consul/Citizenship	387UNTS81	105559
Romania	Bulgaria	21 Sep 59	Consul/Citizenship	387UNTS61	105558
Romania	Bulgaria	14 Mar 60	Admin Cooperation	472UNTS279	106844
Romania	Bulgaria	15 Jun 67	Visas	634UNTS57	109051
Romania	Bulgaria	22 Aug 67	Visas	631UNTS49	108986
Romania	Central Afri Rep	13 Sep 68	General Trade	0UNTS0	110208
Romania	Central Afri Rep	13 Sep 68	Tech Assistance	0UNTS0	110209
Romania	Ceylon (Sri Lanka)	16 Mar 56	General Trade	315UNTS41	104558
Romania	Ceylon (Sri Lanka)	16 Mar 56	Finance	315UNTS51	104559
Romania	China People's Rep	12 Dec 51	Culture	51CCJC27	410047
Romania	China People's Rep	30 Jul 52	General Economic	52CCJC42	410072
Romania	China People's Rep	09 Jan 53	Scientific Project	53CCJC1	410086
Romania	China People's Rep	19 Jan 53	General Trade	53CCJC4	410089
Romania	China People's Rep	15 Oct 53	Mass Media	53CCJC59	410122
Romania	China People's Rep	19 Apr 54	General Economic	54CCJC16	410140
Romania	China People's Rep	20 Jan 55	General Economic	55CCJC3	410210
Romania	China People's Rep	30 Jul 55	Gen Communications	55CCJC53	410246
Romania	China People's Rep	03 Jan 56	General Economic	56CCJC2	410295
Romania	China People's Rep	19 Apr 57	General Economic	57CCJC46	410422
Romania	China People's Rep	30 Mar 58	General Economic	58CCJC36	410508
Romania	China People's Rep	22 Mar 59	General Economic	59CCJC55	410607
Romania	China People's Rep	13 Apr 59	Scientific Project	59CCJC64	410613
Romania	China People's Rep	15 Mar 60	General Economic	60CCJC39	410685
Romania	China People's Rep	07 Jul 61	General Economic	61CCJC93	410807
Romania	China People's Rep	29 May 62	General Economic	62CCJC52	410893
Romania	China People's Rep	08 Apr 63	General Economic	63CCJC40	410967
Romania	China People's Rep	08 Jun 63	Scientific Project	63CCJC71	410985
Romania	China People's Rep	06 Jul 63	Scientific Project	63CCJC86	410994
Romania	China People's Rep	27 Dec 63	General Economic	63CCJC151	411041
Romania	China People's Rep	03 Oct 64	Mass Media	64CCJC140	411310
Romania	China People's Rep	15 May 65	Scientific Project	65CCJC66	411314
Romania	China People's Rep	27 May 65	Culture	592UNTS3	108566
Romania	China People's Rep	27 May 65	Culture	65CCJC70	411315
Romania	China People's Rep	01 Dec 65	Scientific Project	65CCJC149	411312
Romania	China People's Rep	21 Dec 65	General Trade	65CCJC159	411316
Romania	China People's Rep	11 Feb 66	Culture	66CCJC4	411317
Romania	China People's Rep	31 Jul 66	Scientific Project	66CCJC75	411318
Romania	China People's Rep	14 Feb 67	General Economic	67CCJC4	411319
Romania	Cuba	28 Oct 60	Culture	457UNTS9	106574
Romania	Czechoslovakia	05 Sep 47	Education	46UNTS37	100699
Romania	Czechoslovakia	01 Mar 48	Admin Cooperation	26UNTS109	100381
Romania	Czechoslovakia	31 Jul 52	Sanitation	362UNTS123	105185
Romania	Czechoslovakia	02 May 57	Health/Educ/Welfare	387UNTS167	105562
Romania	Czechoslovakia	25 Mar 58	Sanitation	339UNTS77	104846
Romania	Czechoslovakia	25 Oct 58	Admin Cooperation	417UNTS37	106006
Romania	Czechoslovakia	25 Oct 58	Culture	338UNTS301	104843
Romania	Czechoslovakia	21 May 60	Consul/Citizenship	397UNTS245	105709
Romania	Czechoslovakia	16 Dec 63	General Trade	527UNTS285	107630
Romania	Czechoslovakia	17 Nov 67	Sanitation	0UNTS0	109280
Romania	Czechoslovakia	06 Dec 67	Land Transport	0UNTS0	109537
Romania	Czechoslovakia	16 Aug 68	General Amity	0UNTS0	110392
Romania	Czechoslovakia	23 Nov 68	Culture	0UNTS0	110211
Romania	Denmark	25 Jun 58	Air Transport	345UNTS231	104970
Romania	Denmark	29 Aug 67	General Economic	0UNTS0	109404
Romania	Denmark	29 Aug 67	Culture	642UNTS357	109183
Romania	Denmark	29 Aug 67	Land Transport	0UNTS0	109231
Romania	Ecuador	10 Oct 67	General Trade	642UNTS33	109163
Romania	Finland	01 Apr 68	Land Transport	0UNTS0	109392
Romania	Finland	25 Sep 69	General Economic	0UNTS0	110398
Romania	France	09 Feb 59	Finance	59FRJO1903	416374
Romania	France	18 May 62	Air Transport	498UNTS115	107279

PARTY ONE	PARTY TWO	DATE	TOPIC	CITATION	NUMBER
Romania	France	31 Jul 64	Education	0UNTS0	110723
Romania	France	31 Jul 64	Tech Assistance	64FRRT64	415375
Romania	France	11 Jan 65	Culture	65FRRT46	415376
Romania	France	11 Jan 65	Culture	0UNTS0	110528
Romania	France	08 Feb 65	General Economic	65FRMD1302	417377
Romania	France	14 Mar 66	Land Transport	604UNTS33	108741
Romania	France	22 Apr 66	Culture	66FRRT38	415378
Romania	France	13 Feb 67	Sanitation	67FRJO508	416379
Romania	France	26 Jun 67	Culture	642UNTS181	109173
Romania	France	18 May 68	Consul/Citizenship	0UNTS0	110724
Romania	France	17 Jan 69	Admin Cooperation	0UNTS0	110725
Romania	France	12 Mar 69	Sanitation	69FRJO609	416380
Romania	France	12 Mar 69	Sanitation	0UNTS0	110531
Romania	France	25 Jun 69	Culture	0UNTS0	110533
Romania	Germany, East	22 Sep 50	Finance	4EGDA420	419280
Romania	Germany, East	22 Sep 50	Scientific Project	4EGDA419	419279
Romania	Germany, East	22 Sep 50	Culture	4EGDA422	419281
Romania	Germany, East	06 Nov 50	General Trade	1EGDA453	419282
Romania	Germany, East	23 Jan 52	General Trade	1EGDA454	419283
Romania	Germany, East	12 Sep 52	General Economic	1EGDA455	419284
Romania	Germany, East	31 Oct 52	Telecommunications	4EGDA431	419286
Romania	Germany, East	31 Oct 52	Postal Service	4EGDA425	419285
Romania	Germany, East	17 Oct 53	Consul/Citizenship	1EGDA457	419287
Romania	Germany, East	21 Dec 53	Mass Media	4EGDA437	419288
Romania	Germany, East	03 Jun 55	Scientific Project	3EGDA577	419290
Romania	Germany, East	28 Jul 55	Air Transport	342UNTS207	104909
Romania	Germany, East	05 Aug 55	Sanitation	342UNTS229	104910
Romania	Germany, East	21 Dec 55	Finance	4EGDA451	419291
Romania	Germany, East	08 Dec 56	Sanitation	362UNTS189	105188
Romania	Germany, East	28 Apr 57	Health/Educ/Welfare	5EGDA468	419292
Romania	Germany, East	28 Apr 57	Sanitation	5EGDA479	419293
Romania	Germany, East	15 Jul 58	Consul/Citizenship	387UNTS133	105561
Romania	Germany, East	15 Jul 58	Admin Cooperation	395UNTS3	105681
Romania	Germany, East	15 Jul 58	Health/Educ/Welfare	387UNTS115	105560
Romania	Germany, East	16 Mar 59	General Economic	7EGDA432	419294
Romania	Germany, East	18 Mar 59	Mass Media	7EGDA438	419295
Romania	Germany, East	12 Nov 59	Atomic Energy	7EGDA443	419296
Romania	Germany, East	17 Feb 61	General Trade	9EGDA388	419297
Romania	Germany, East	02 Mar 61	Scientific Project	9EGDA389	419298
Romania	Germany, East	18 Dec 62	IGO Establishment	51EGDZ278	420299
Romania	Germany, East	12 Jun 63	Non-ILO Labor	11EGDA605	419300
Romania	Germany, East	20 Nov 63	Air Transport	11EGDA478	419301
Romania	Germany, East	19 Dec 63	Education	11EGDA638	419302
Romania	Germany, East	15 Jun 65	Visas	44EGDZ337	420303
Romania	Germany, East	22 Jan 66	General Trade	40EGDZ352	420304
Romania	Germany, East	07 Jul 66	Mass Media	48EGDZ363	420305
Romania	Germany, West	24 Dec 63	General Trade	64WBGA57	424604
Romania	Germany, West	03 Aug 67	General Economic	642UNTS47	109164
Romania	Germany, West	16 Jul 68	Land Transport	0UNTS0	110207
Romania	Germany, West	10 Jun 69	Tech Assistance	69WBGA72	424605
Romania	Germany, West	12 Oct 70	Land Transport	70WGBB1217	425606
Romania	Ghana	30 Sep 61	Air Transport	467UNTS443	106769
Romania	Ghana	30 Sep 61	Culture	457UNTS3	106573
Romania	Ghana	23 Nov 66	Loans and Credits	642UNTS79	109166
Romania	Ghana	23 Nov 66	General Trade	642UNTS63	109165
Romania	Greece	19 May 54	General Trade	225UNTS17	103083
Romania	Greece	19 May 54	Finance	225UNTS27	103084
Romania	Greece	25 Aug 56	Reparations	299UNTS231	104315
Romania	Greece	02 May 60	Air Transport	485UNTS17	107043
Romania	Greece	20 Jul 63	Taxation	609UNTS109	108829
Romania	Guinea	01 Dec 66	General Trade	642UNTS89	109167
Romania	Hungary	24 Jan 48	General Amity	477UNTS155	106920
Romania	Hungary	14 Dec 53	Sanitation	342UNTS151	104906
Romania	Hungary	03 Feb 56	Air Transport	362UNTS233	105190
Romania	Hungary	17 Dec 57	Sanitation	477UNTS303	106926

PARTY ONE	PARTY TWO	DATE	TOPIC	CITATION	NUMBER
Romania	Hungary	07 Oct 58	Admin Cooperation	416UNTS199	106004
Romania	Hungary	18 Mar 59	Consul/Citizenship	417UNTS3	106005
Romania	Hungary	07 Sep 61	Non-ILO Labor	519UNTS141	107506
Romania	Hungary	13 Jun 63	Territory Boundary	576UNTS275	108369
Romania	Hungary	01 Feb 68	Customs	0UNTS0	109704
Romania	IAEA (Atom Energy)	22 Apr 66	Atomic Energy	603UNTS23	108721
Romania	IAEA (Atom Energy)	27 Jun 68	Atomic Energy	0UNTS0	109315
Romania	India	30 Apr 57	Culture	342UNTS251	104911
Romania	India	25 Sep 68	Taxation	0UNTS0	109882
Romania	Iran	25 Oct 65	General Economic	0IRTB60	433099
Romania	Iran	08 Aug 66	Specific Property	0IRTB60	433100
Romania	Iran	15 Aug 67	Culture	0IRTB60	433096
Romania	Iran	24 Jan 68	Finance	0IRTB60	433098
Romania	Iran	24 Jan 68	General Trade	0IRTB60	433097
Romania	Iraq	24 Dec 58	General Trade	405UNTS243	105836
Romania	Iraq	04 Aug 59	Culture	502UNTS17	107324
Romania	Italy	25 Nov 50	Customs	52ITGU39	435323
Romania	Italy	28 Jan 58	Finance	302UNTS231	104362
Romania	Italy	16 Jun 64	Scientific Project	558UNTS313	108150
Romania	Italy	14 Apr 65	Sanitation	66ITGU290	435324
Romania	Italy	06 Sep 65	General Economic	604UNTS49	108742
Romania	Italy	08 Aug 67	Culture	642UNTS213	109175
Romania	Italy	08 Aug 67	Culture	642UNTS191	109174
Romania	Japan	01 Sep 69	General Economic	70JHZ7	439031
Romania	Korea, North	05 Dec 55	Postal Service	362UNTS163	105187
Romania	Korea, North	05 Dec 55	Telecommunications	362UNTS141	105186
Romania	Korea, North	12 May 56	Culture	342UNTS189	104908
Romania	Mali	26 Sep 63	Culture	528UNTS193	107642
Romania	Mongolia	08 May 56	Culture	342UNTS291	104913
Romania	Mongolia	29 Apr 67	Consul/Citizenship	0UNTS0	110204
Romania	Mongolia	23 Dec 67	Land Transport	0UNTS0	110205
Romania	Multilateral	27 Mar 41	Military Mission	67UNTS231	200222
Romania	Multilateral	02 Aug 44	Scientific Project	67UNTS221	200221
Romania	Multilateral	11 Dec 46	Sanitation	12UNTS179	100186
Romania	Multilateral	08 Feb 47	Patents/Copyrights	14UNTS287	100222
Romania	Multilateral	10 Feb 47	Peace/Disarmament	42UNTS3	100645
Romania	Multilateral	02 Oct 47	Telecommunications	193UNTS188	102616
Romania	Multilateral	11 Oct 47	IGO Establishment	77UNTS143	100998
Romania	Multilateral	12 Nov 47	Admin Cooperation	53UNTS49	100772
Romania	Multilateral	12 Nov 47	Admin Cooperation	53UNTS39	100771
Romania	Multilateral	12 Nov 47	Admin Cooperation	53UNTS13	100770
Romania	Multilateral	12 Nov 47	Admin Cooperation	46UNTS169	100709
Romania	Multilateral	12 Nov 47	Admin Cooperation	46UNTS201	100710
Romania	Multilateral	06 Mar 48	Water Transport	289UNTS3	104214
Romania	Multilateral	10 Jun 48	Humanitarian	164UNTS113	102163
Romania	Multilateral	24 Jul 48	Sanitation	66UNTS25	100847
Romania	Multilateral	18 Aug 48	Water Transport	33UNTS181	100518
Romania	Multilateral	19 Nov 48	Sanitation	44UNTS277	100688
Romania	Multilateral	09 Dec 48	Humanitarian	78UNTS277	101021
Romania	Multilateral	04 May 49	Admin Cooperation	47UNTS159	100728
Romania	Multilateral	04 May 49	Admin Cooperation	30UNTS3	100445
Romania	Multilateral	12 Aug 49	Humanitarian	75UNTS85	100971
Romania	Multilateral	12 Aug 49	Humanitarian	75UNTS287	100973
Romania	Multilateral	12 Aug 49	General Military	75UNTS135	100972
Romania	Multilateral	12 Aug 49	Humanitarian	75UNTS31	100970
Romania	Multilateral	16 Sep 50	General Transport	92UNTS91	101264
Romania	Multilateral	07 Dec 50	Admin Cooperation	212UNTS17	102861
Romania	Multilateral	11 Jul 52	Postal Service	170UNTS269	102223
Romania	Multilateral	11 Jul 52	Postal Service	170UNTS3	102221
Romania	Multilateral	11 Jul 52	IGO Establishment	169UNTS3	102220
Romania	Multilateral	11 Jul 52	Postal Service	171UNTS3	102224
Romania	Multilateral	11 Jul 52	Postal Service	171UNTS89	102225
Romania	Multilateral	11 Jul 52	Postal Service	171UNTS191	102227
Romania	Multilateral	11 Jul 52	Postal Service	170UNTS63	102222
Romania	Multilateral	11 Jul 52	Postal Service	171UNTS143	102226

PARTY ONE	PARTY TWO	DATE	TOPIC	CITATION	NUMBER
Romania	Multilateral	07 Nov 52	General Trade	221UNTS255	103010
Romania	Multilateral	31 Mar 53	Privil/Immunities	193UNTS136	102613
Romania	Multilateral	07 Dec 53	Admin Cooperation	182UNTS51	102422
Romania	Multilateral	14 May 54	Culture	249UNTS215	103511
Romania	Multilateral	14 May 55	General Amity	219UNTS3	102962
Romania	Multilateral	28 Sep 55	Air Transport	478UNTS371	106943
Romania	Multilateral	12 Oct 55	IGO Establishment	560UNTS3	108165
Romania	Multilateral	26 Mar 56	IGO Establishment	259UNTS125	103686
Romania	Multilateral	18 May 56	Customs	327UNTS123	104721
Romania	Multilateral	18 May 56	Customs	338UNTS103	104834
Romania	Multilateral	07 Sep 56	Humanitarian	266UNTS3	103822
Romania	Multilateral	11 Sep 56	Humanitarian	266UNTS221	103832
Romania	Multilateral	26 Oct 56	IGO Establishment	276UNTS3	103988
Romania	Multilateral	20 Feb 57	Consul/Citizenship	309UNTS65	104468
Romania	Multilateral	15 Jun 57	Patents/Copyrights	583UNTS3	108470
Romania	Multilateral	15 Jun 57	General Trade	550UNTS45	108008
Romania	Multilateral	01 Jul 57	Culture	0UNTS0	110418
Romania	Multilateral	03 Oct 57	Postal Service	364UNTS3	105211
Romania	Multilateral	03 Oct 57	Postal Service	366UNTS3	105215
Romania	Multilateral	03 Oct 57	Postal Service	366UNTS255	105219
Romania	Multilateral	03 Oct 57	Postal Service	366UNTS87	105216
Romania	Multilateral	03 Oct 57	Postal Service	366UNTS141	105217
Romania	Multilateral	03 Oct 57	Postal Service	364UNTS331	105212
Romania	Multilateral	03 Oct 57	Postal Service	365UNTS207	105214
Romania	Multilateral	13 Dec 57	Land Transport	372UNTS159	105296
Romania	Multilateral	29 Jan 58	Specific Resources	339UNTS23	104845
Romania	Multilateral	29 Apr 58	Territory Boundary	516UNTS205	107477
Romania	Multilateral	29 Apr 58	Territory Boundary	499UNTS311	107302
Romania	Multilateral	29 Apr 58	Water Transport	450UNTS11	106465
Romania	Multilateral	10 Jun 58	Admin Cooperation	330UNTS3	104739
Romania	Multilateral	03 Dec 58	Admin Cooperation	416UNTS51	105995
Romania	Multilateral	03 Dec 58	Admin Cooperation	398UNTS9	105715
Romania	Multilateral	15 Jan 59	Customs	348UNTS13	104996
Romania	Multilateral	07 Jul 59	Specific Resources	377UNTS203	105402
Romania	Multilateral	19 Nov 59	IGO Operations	410UNTS156	105902
Romania	Multilateral	14 Dec 59	Sanitation	422UNTS57	106068
Romania	Multilateral	14 Dec 59	Land Transport	422UNTS75	106069
Romania	Multilateral	14 Dec 59	IGO Establishment	368UNTS253	105245
Romania	Multilateral	14 Dec 59	Sanitation	422UNTS33	106067
Romania	Multilateral	14 Dec 59	IGO Status/Immunit	368UNTS237	105244
Romania	Multilateral	29 Jul 60	Water Transport	392UNTS69	105640
Romania	Multilateral	09 Dec 60	Customs	429UNTS211	106200
Romania	Multilateral	18 Apr 61	Consul/Citizenship	500UNTS95	107310
Romania	Multilateral	21 Apr 61	IGO Establishment	484UNTS349	107041
Romania	Multilateral	08 Jun 61	Customs	473UNTS187	106863
Romania	Multilateral	08 Jun 61	Customs	473UNTS153	106862
Romania	Multilateral	15 Dec 61	Admin Cooperation	424UNTS43	106098
Romania	Multilateral	25 Jul 62	Specific Property	506UNTS177	107387
Romania	Multilateral	28 Jul 62	Specific Resources	460UNTS219	106642
Romania	Multilateral	10 Dec 62	Culture	521UNTS231	107525
Romania	Multilateral	05 Aug 63	Sanitation	480UNTS43	106964
Romania	Multilateral	23 Oct 63	IGO Establishment	506UNTS197	107388
Romania	Multilateral	10 Jul 64	Postal Service	611UNTS387	108846
Romania	Multilateral	10 Jul 64	Postal Service	612UNTS233	108848
Romania	Multilateral	10 Jul 64	Postal Service	612UNTS361	108849
Romania	Multilateral	10 Jul 64	Postal Service	611UNTS105	108845
Romania	Multilateral	10 Jul 64	Postal Service	613UNTS193	108852
Romania	Multilateral	10 Jul 64	Postal Service	613UNTS3	108850
Romania	Multilateral	10 Jul 64	Postal Service	612UNTS3	108847
Romania	Multilateral	10 Jul 64	Postal Service	611UNTS7	108844
Romania	Multilateral	01 Dec 64	Water Transport	550UNTS133	108012
Romania	Multilateral	27 Jan 65	Tech Assistance	523UNTS102	107556
Romania	Multilateral	08 Jul 65	General Trade	597UNTS3	108641
Romania	Multilateral	27 Jan 67	Scientific Project	610UNTS205	108843
Romania	Multilateral	20 Jul 67	General Economic	0UNTS0	109259

PARTY ONE	PARTY TWO	DATE	TOPIC	CITATION	NUMBER
Romania	Multilateral	22 Sep 67	Non-IBRD Project	0UNTS0	109258
Romania	Multilateral	01 Jul 68	Peace/Disarmament	0UNTS0	110485
Romania	Multilateral	24 Sep 68	Air Transport	0UNTS0	110612
Romania	Multilateral	26 Nov 68	Humanitarian	0UNTS0	110823
Romania	Netherlands	27 Aug 57	Air Transport	342UNTS309	104914
Romania	Netherlands	30 Sep 60	General Economic	479UNTS91	106948
Romania	Netherlands	13 Feb 67	Culture	604UNTS287	108756
Romania	Netherlands	08 May 67	Finance	607UNTS105	108800
Romania	Netherlands	20 Jul 67	Sanitation	633UNTS21	109032
Romania	Netherlands	23 Apr 68	Land Transport	0UNTS0	109481
Romania	Norway	16 Jun 58	Air Transport	405UNTS223	105835
Romania	Norway	21 May 64	Claims and Debts	563UNTS45	108203
Romania	Norway	21 Oct 67	General Trade	3NORT1006	451135
Romania	Norway	26 Nov 68	Visas	3NORT0	451136
Romania	Norway	29 Nov 68	General Economic	3NORT0	451137
Romania	Norway	29 Nov 68	General Economic	0UNTS0	109705
Romania	Poland	09 Aug 47	Air Transport	12UNTS363	100193
Romania	Poland	27 Feb 48	Culture	46UNTS143	100707
Romania	Poland	26 Jan 49	General Military	85UNTS21	101143
Romania	Poland	09 Dec 58	General Economic	58PZUM111	458062
Romania	Poland	25 Jan 62	Admin Cooperation	468UNTS3	106770
Romania	Poland	05 Oct 62	Consul/Citizenship	521UNTS3	107516
Romania	Poland	26 Nov 64	Health/Educ/Welfare	552UNTS157	108053
Romania	Poland	29 Jan 68	Land Transport	0UNTS0	109538
Romania	Poland	29 Jan 68	Land Transport	68PZUM52	458152
Romania	Poland	29 Jan 68	Land Transport	68PZUM42	458151
Romania	Poland	10 Feb 69	Specific Resources	0UNTS0	110213
Romania	Poland	12 Nov 70	General Amity	71PDZU53	457168
Romania	Poland	28 Jun 71	Visas	72PDZU1	457173
Romania	Somalia	20 Apr 67	Scientific Project	642UNTS155	109171
Romania	South Africa	16 Nov 48	Admin Cooperation	225UNTS71	103090
Romania	Southern Yemen	17 Jun 68	General Trade	0UNTS0	110206
Romania	Spain	05 Jan 67	Consul/Citizenship	642UNTS103	109168
Romania	Sweden	15 Apr 57	Air Transport	342UNTS325	104915
Romania	Sweden	01 Mar 67	General Transport	642UNTS163	109172
Romania	Switzerland	03 Aug 51	General Economic	51SWR0827	462153
Romania	Thailand	20 Mar 70	General Trade	0UNTS0	110458
Romania	Tunisia	21 Apr 66	Culture	604UNTS57	108743
Romania	Tunisia	21 Apr 66	Scientific Project	604UNTS65	108744
Romania	Turkey	05 Apr 54	General Economic	55TURG1602	466084
Romania	Turkey	19 May 67	Sanitation	0UNTS0	109536
Romania	UK Great Britain	13 Mar 48	Admin Cooperation	104UNTS117	101436
Romania	UK Great Britain	10 Nov 60	Finance	385UNTS113	105533
Romania	UK Great Britain	22 Mar 66	Commodity Trade	571UNTS281	108307
Romania	UK Great Britain	09 Mar 67	Scientific Project	605UNTS195	108764
Romania	UK Great Britain	17 Mar 67	Air Transport	0UNTS0	109706
Romania	UK Great Britain	16 Jul 68	Atomic Energy	0UNTS0	109710
Romania	UK Great Britain	18 Oct 68	General Trade	0UNTS0	110210
Romania	UN Special Fund	24 Oct 64	IGO Operations	519UNTS29	107500
Romania	UNICEF (Children)	28 Aug 47	IGO Operations	68UNTS228	200235
Romania	United Arab Rep	15 Apr 57	Culture	389UNTS21	105589
Romania	United Arab Rep	14 Aug 58	Air Transport	405UNTS189	105834
Romania	United Arab Rep	03 Sep 66	Direct Aid	604UNTS73	108745
Romania	United Arab Rep	14 Nov 66	Finance	642UNTS141	109170
Romania	United Arab Rep	14 Nov 66	General Trade	642UNTS129	109169
Romania	United Nations	29 May 61	IGO Operations	406UNTS147	105845
Romania	United Nations	08 Apr 67	Privil/Immunities	594UNTS159	108602
Romania	USA (United States)	28 Jun 46	Other Military	148UNTS355	101944
Romania	USA (United States)	26 Feb 48	Admin Cooperation	48UNTS9	100738
Romania	USA (United States)	30 Mar 60	Claims and Debts	371UNTS163	105278
Romania	USA (United States)	09 Dec 60	Culture	401UNTS19	105759
Romania	USA (United States)	26 May 62	Visas	456UNTS265	106561
Romania	USA (United States)	02 Apr 63	Culture	474UNTS95	106874
Romania	USA (United States)	23 Dec 64	Health/Educ/Welfare	535UNTS359	107790
Romania	USA (United States)	18 Feb 67	Tech Assistance	0UNTS0	109849

PARTY ONE	PARTY TWO	DATE	TOPIC	CITATION	NUMBER
Romania	USA (United States)	26 Nov 68	Education	0UNTS0	110402
Romania	USA (United States)	25 Apr 69	Visas	0UNTS0	110272
Romania	USA (United States)	03 Aug 69	Education	0UNTS0	110343
Romania	USSR (Soviet Union)	16 Jan 45	Reparations	0SUST169	468344
Romania	USSR (Soviet Union)	09 Mar 45	Admin Cooperation	0SUST174	468345
Romania	USSR (Soviet Union)	08 May 45	Finance	0SUST178	468347
Romania	USSR (Soviet Union)	08 May 45	General Trade	0SUST178	468346
Romania	USSR (Soviet Union)	17 Jul 45	Specific Property	0SUST183	468348
Romania	USSR (Soviet Union)	19 Jul 45	Specific Property	0SUST183	468349
Romania	USSR (Soviet Union)	06 Aug 45	Consul/Citizenship	0SUST188	468350
Romania	USSR (Soviet Union)	08 Aug 45	Specific Property	0SUST189	468351
Romania	USSR (Soviet Union)	15 Aug 45	Specific Property	0SUST193	468352
Romania	USSR (Soviet Union)	20 Aug 45	Consul/Citizenship	0SUST194	468353
Romania	USSR (Soviet Union)	13 Sep 45	Reparations	0SUST197	468356
Romania	USSR (Soviet Union)	13 Sep 45	Refugees	0SUST197	468359
Romania	USSR (Soviet Union)	13 Sep 45	Land Transport	0SUST197	468358
Romania	USSR (Soviet Union)	13 Sep 45	Reparations	0SUST197	468357
Romania	USSR (Soviet Union)	13 Sep 45	Reparations	0SUST197	468355
Romania	USSR (Soviet Union)	13 Sep 45	Health/Educ/Welfare	0SUST198	468360
Romania	USSR (Soviet Union)	13 Sep 45	Commodity Trade	0SUST197	468354
Romania	USSR (Soviet Union)	15 Feb 46	Finance	0SUST206	468361
Romania	USSR (Soviet Union)	15 Feb 46	Mostfavored Nation	0SUST206	468362
Romania	USSR (Soviet Union)	20 Mar 46	Specific Property	0SUST208	468363
Romania	USSR (Soviet Union)	15 Apr 46	Reparations	0SUST210	468364
Romania	USSR (Soviet Union)	20 Feb 47	General Economic	0SUST229	468365
Romania	USSR (Soviet Union)	20 Feb 47	General Economic	226UNTS79	103110
Romania	USSR (Soviet Union)	12 Jun 47	Land Transport	0SUST232	468366
Romania	USSR (Soviet Union)	04 Feb 48	Territory Boundary	0SUST244	468367
Romania	USSR (Soviet Union)	04 Feb 48	General Military	48UNTS189	100745
Romania	USSR (Soviet Union)	18 Feb 48	General Economic	0SUST245	468368
Romania	USSR (Soviet Union)	07 Jun 48	Reparations	0SUST249	468369
Romania	USSR (Soviet Union)	20 Aug 48	Gen Communications	0SUST252	468370
Romania	USSR (Soviet Union)	20 Aug 48	Postal Service	0SUST252	468371
Romania	USSR (Soviet Union)	01 Nov 48	Specific Property	16SUGG64	469887
Romania	USSR (Soviet Union)	24 Jan 49	General Economic	0SUST257	468373
Romania	USSR (Soviet Union)	24 Jan 49	Tech Assistance	0SUST257	468372
Romania	USSR (Soviet Union)	20 Feb 49	Specific Property	16SUGG64	469888
Romania	USSR (Soviet Union)	27 Apr 49	Mass Media	0SUST258	468374
Romania	USSR (Soviet Union)	27 Apr 49	Territory Boundary	0SUST263	468375
Romania	USSR (Soviet Union)	04 Jul 49	Specific Property	16SUGG65	469890
Romania	USSR (Soviet Union)	04 Aug 49	Specific Property	16SUGG65	469891
Romania	USSR (Soviet Union)	25 Nov 49	Dispute Settlement	0SUST264	468377
Romania	USSR (Soviet Union)	25 Nov 49	Admin Cooperation	0SUST264	468376
Romania	USSR (Soviet Union)	17 Feb 50	General Economic	0SUST270	468379
Romania	USSR (Soviet Union)	17 Feb 50	Scientific Project	0SUST270	468378
Romania	USSR (Soviet Union)	27 May 50	Sanitation	221UNTS13	103000
Romania	USSR (Soviet Union)	15 Mar 51	General Economic	0SUST280	468380
Romania	USSR (Soviet Union)	24 Aug 51	General Aid	0SUST282	468381
Romania	USSR (Soviet Union)	20 Mar 52	Education	0SUST285	468382
Romania	USSR (Soviet Union)	15 Aug 52	Specific Property	16SUGG66	469897
Romania	USSR (Soviet Union)	25 Dec 52	Specific Resources	0SUST292	468383
Romania	USSR (Soviet Union)	17 Aug 53	Mass Media	0SUST299	468384
Romania	USSR (Soviet Union)	05 Dec 53	Specific Property	0SUST304	468385
Romania	USSR (Soviet Union)	05 Dec 53	Admin Cooperation	0SUST304	468386
Romania	USSR (Soviet Union)	31 Mar 54	Finance	0SUST309	468387
Romania	USSR (Soviet Union)	31 Mar 54	Loans and Credits	0SUST310	468388
Romania	USSR (Soviet Union)	25 Jan 55	Air Transport	0SUST323	468389
Romania	USSR (Soviet Union)	22 Apr 55	Atomic Energy	0SUST326	468390
Romania	USSR (Soviet Union)	13 Dec 55	Finance	0SUST344	468391
Romania	USSR (Soviet Union)	03 Jan 56	Air Transport	0SUST346	468392
Romania	USSR (Soviet Union)	07 Apr 56	Culture	259UNTS377	103698
Romania	USSR (Soviet Union)	14 Apr 56	Gen Communications	0SUST353	468393
Romania	USSR (Soviet Union)	21 Jul 56	Commodity Trade	0SUST364	468394
Romania	USSR (Soviet Union)	24 Sep 56	Specific Resources	16SUGG73	469928
Romania	USSR (Soviet Union)	22 Oct 56	Finance	0SUST370	468395

PARTY ONE	PARTY TWO	DATE	TOPIC	CITATION	NUMBER
Romania	USSR (Soviet Union)	03 Dec 56	Loans and Credits	OSUST373	468396
Romania	USSR (Soviet Union)	04 Mar 57	General Trade	OSUST379	468397
Romania	USSR (Soviet Union)	14 Mar 57	Mass Media	16SUGG119	469934
Romania	USSR (Soviet Union)	15 Apr 57	Status of Forces	274UNTS143	103964
Romania	USSR (Soviet Union)	06 May 57	Commodity Trade	16SUGG120	469938
Romania	USSR (Soviet Union)	18 Jun 57	Specific Property	OSUST385	468398
Romania	USSR (Soviet Union)	18 Jul 57	Admin Cooperation	OSUST386	468399
Romania	USSR (Soviet Union)	31 Jul 57	Specific Resources	16SUGG121	469944
Romania	USSR (Soviet Union)	01 Aug 57	Admin Cooperation	OSUST386	468400
Romania	USSR (Soviet Union)	04 Sep 57	Consul/Citizenship	318UNTS55	104609
Romania	USSR (Soviet Union)	04 Sep 57	Consul/Citizenship	318UNTS89	104610
Romania	USSR (Soviet Union)	19 Dec 57	Tech Assistance	16SUGG123	469950
Romania	USSR (Soviet Union)	19 Dec 57	Education	16SUGG123	469951
Romania	USSR (Soviet Union)	07 Mar 58	Claims and Debts	7SUGG107	469500
Romania	USSR (Soviet Union)	03 Apr 58	Admin Cooperation	313UNTS167	104535
Romania	USSR (Soviet Union)	02 Feb 59	General Trade	8SUGG136	469555
Romania	USSR (Soviet Union)	20 Mar 59	Tech Assistance	8SUGG141	469567
Romania	USSR (Soviet Union)	15 Oct 59	Specific Resources	16SUGG126	469966
Romania	USSR (Soviet Union)	01 Dec 59	Tech Assistance	8SUGG159	469612
Romania	USSR (Soviet Union)	02 Dec 59	Tech Assistance	8SUGG160	469614
Romania	USSR (Soviet Union)	11 Nov 60	General Trade	9SUGG151	469707
Romania	USSR (Soviet Union)	11 Nov 60	Tech Assistance	9SUGG151	469710
Romania	USSR (Soviet Union)	08 Dec 60	Education	16SUGG129	469986
Romania	USSR (Soviet Union)	22 Dec 60	Customs	16SUGG130	469987
Romania	USSR (Soviet Union)	24 Dec 60	Admin Cooperation	472UNTS245	106843
Romania	USSR (Soviet Union)	27 Feb 61	Admin Cooperation	10SUGG123	469747
Romania	USSR (Soviet Union)	28 Mar 61	Tech Assistance	10SUGG126	469755
Romania	USSR (Soviet Union)	01 Dec 61	Tech Assistance	10SUGG145	469807
Romania	USSR (Soviet Union)	23 Dec 61	Non-IBRD Project	10SUGG148	469814
Romania	USSR (Soviet Union)	19 Apr 62	Atomic Energy	11SUGG138	469834
Romania	USSR (Soviet Union)	04 Mar 66	Visas	591UNTS327	108565
Romania	USSR (Soviet Union)	21 Jun 66	Land Transport	604UNTS81	108746
Romania	Vietnam, North	12 Oct 56	Culture	342UNTS173	104907
Romania	Vietnam, North	30 Jun 58	Scientific Project	389UNTS43	105591
Romania	Yugoslavia	15 Dec 45	General Economic	116UNTS3	101565
Romania	Yugoslavia	26 Jun 46	Finance	116UNTS21	101566
Romania	Yugoslavia	23 Dec 46	Loans and Credits	116UNTS33	101567
Romania	Yugoslavia	26 Jun 47	Culture	116UNTS39	101568
Romania	Yugoslavia	30 Jun 47	Air Transport	116UNTS57	101569
Romania	Yugoslavia	30 Sep 47	Finance	116UNTS71	101570
Romania	Yugoslavia	19 Dec 47	General Amity	116UNTS89	101571
Romania	Yugoslavia	31 Dec 48	Visas	116UNTS103	101572
Romania	Yugoslavia	13 Jan 56	Postal Service	342UNTS265	104912
Romania	Yugoslavia	01 Feb 56	Air Transport	362UNTS203	105189
Romania	Yugoslavia	04 Aug 56	Sanitation	395UNTS99	105682
Romania	Yugoslavia	25 Sep 56	Sanitation	395UNTS147	105683
Romania	Yugoslavia	27 Oct 56	Culture	389UNTS33	105590
Romania	Yugoslavia	27 Oct 56	Scientific Project	389UNTS55	105592
Romania	Yugoslavia	08 Nov 62	Consul/Citizenship	472UNTS305	106845
Romania	Yugoslavia	30 Nov 63	Specific Property	512UNTS2	107438
Romania	Yugoslavia	20 Dec 63	Visas	527UNTS245	107629
Romania	Yugoslavia	25 Dec 63	Land Transport	576UNTS95	108366
Ruanda-Urundi	Multilateral	02 Oct 47	Telecommunications	193UNTS188	102616
Ruanda-Urundi	Multilateral	04 Jun 54	Customs	282UNTS249	104101
Rwanda	Accept UN Charter	01 Jul 62	UN Charter	437UNTS145	106302
Rwanda	Belgium	13 Oct 62	Tech Assistance	456UNTS425	106568
Rwanda	Belgium	13 Oct 62	Tech Assistance	456UNTS431	106569
Rwanda	Belgium	07 Aug 70	Admin Cooperation	OUNTSO	110834
Rwanda	France	04 Dec 62	General Amity	65FRRT20	415381
Rwanda	Germany, West	25 Apr 64	Loans and Credits	64WBGA243	424600
Rwanda	Germany, West	16 Feb 65	Tech Assistance	65WBGA90	424601
Rwanda	Germany, West	18 May 67	Claims and Debts	68WGBB1260	425602
Rwanda	Germany, West	08 Apr 71	Loans and Credits	71WBGA112	424603
Rwanda	Israel	23 Oct 62	Tech Assistance	515UNTS291	107466
Rwanda	Multilateral	11 Dec 46	Sanitation	12UNTS179	100186

PARTY ONE	PARTY TWO	DATE	TOPIC	CITATION	NUMBER
Rwanda	Multilateral	22 Nov 50	Culture	131UNTS25	101734
Rwanda	Multilateral	07 Nov 52	General Trade	221UNTS255	103010
Rwanda	Multilateral	11 May 53	Sanitation	456UNTS3	106555
Rwanda	Multilateral	26 Jan 60	IGO Establishment	439UNTS249	106333
Rwanda	Multilateral	18 Apr 61	Consul/Citizenship	500UNTS95	107310
Rwanda	Multilateral	28 Sep 62	IGO Establishment	469UNTS169	106791
Rwanda	Multilateral	21 Jan 63	Tech Assistance	453UNTS20	106517
Rwanda	Multilateral	25 May 63	IGO Establishment	479UNTS39	106947
Rwanda	Multilateral	04 Aug 63	IGO Establishment	510UNTS3	107408
Rwanda	Multilateral	05 Aug 63	Sanitation	480UNTS43	106964
Rwanda	Multilateral	10 Jul 64	Postal Service	611UNTS7	108844
Rwanda	Multilateral	10 Jul 64	Postal Service	611UNTS105	108845
Rwanda	Multilateral	10 Jul 64	Postal Service	612UNTS3	108847
Rwanda	Multilateral	10 Jul 64	Postal Service	611UNTS387	108846
Rwanda	Multilateral	08 Jul 65	General Trade	597UNTS3	108641
Rwanda	Multilateral	31 Dec 65	Specific Resources	616UNTS317	108904
Rwanda	Multilateral	27 Jan 67	Scientific Project	610UNTS205	108843
Rwanda	Multilateral	27 Oct 67	Telecommunications	OUNTSO	109861
Rwanda	Multilateral	18 Mar 68	Commodity Trade	OUNTSO	109262
Rwanda	UN Special Fund	18 Mar 64	Direct Aid	491UNTS3	107170
Rwanda	UNICEF (Children)	11 Sep 64	IGO Operations	510UNTS127	107409
Rwanda	United Nations	28 Nov 62	Tech Assistance	450UNTS267	106473
Rwanda	USA (United States)	09 Aug 65	Finance	OUNTSO	109895
Rwanda	USSR (Soviet Union)	30 Jun 62	Recognition	11SUGG145	469849
Rwanda	USSR (Soviet Union)	06 May 66	Culture	633UNTS217	109039
Rwanda	WHO (World Health)	22 Jun 64	Tech Assistance	514UNTS11	107440
Rwanda	WHO (World Health)	23 Jun 64	Tech Assistance	514UNTS157	107445
Saar	Multilateral	05 May 49	IGO Establishment	87UNTS103	101168
Saar	Multilateral	02 Sep 49	IGO Status/Immunit	250UNTS12	103515
Saar	Multilateral	04 Nov 50	Humanitarian	213UNTS221	102889
Saar	Multilateral	11 Dec 53	Non-ILO Labor	218UNTS255	102958
Saar	Multilateral	11 Dec 53	Non-ILO Labor	218UNTS153	102956
Saar	Multilateral	11 Dec 53	Non-ILO Labor	218UNTS211	102957
Saar	Multilateral	11 Dec 53	Patents/Copyrights	218UNTS27	102952
Saar	Multilateral	11 Dec 53	Education	218UNTS125	102954
Saar	Multilateral	19 Dec 54	Patents/Copyrights	218UNTS51	102953
Saar	Multilateral	19 Dec 54	Culture	218UNTS139	102955
Saar	Multilateral	13 Dec 55	Humanitarian	250UNTS3	103514
Saar	Multilateral	13 Dec 55	IGO Operations	529UNTS141	107660
Saar	Multilateral	15 Dec 56	Education	278UNTS73	104023
San Marino	Austria	30 May 72	Visas	72ABGB259	403163
San Marino	Belgium	14 Dec 49	Visas	51UNTS107	100757
San Marino	Belgium	22 Apr 55	Non-ILO Labor	253UNTS41	103574
San Marino	Canada	16 Oct 62	Visas	529UNTS3	107650
San Marino	France	12 Jul 49	Non-ILO Labor	51FRJO203	416382
San Marino	France	15 Jan 54	Consul/Citizenship	56FRJO106	416383
San Marino	France	21 May 65	Non-ILO Labor	65FRRT58	415384
San Marino	France	25 May 67	Admin Cooperation	69FRJO1503	416385
San Marino	France	25 May 67	Admin Cooperation	OUNTSO	109527
San Marino	Germany, West	08 Oct 68	Visas	69WGBB203	425612
San Marino	ICJ Option Clause	11 Jan 54	ICJ Option Clause	186UNTS295	102495
San Marino	Italy	20 Oct 53	Telecommunications	55ITGU45	435328
San Marino	Italy	20 Nov 58	Land Transport	62ITGU6	435329
San Marino	Italy	20 Dec 60	Reparations	62ITGU6	435332
San Marino	Italy	20 Dec 60	Finance	62ITGU6	435311
San Marino	Italy	26 Oct 63	Commodity Trade	66ITGU21	435333
San Marino	Japan	15 Jan 68	Visas	68JJS421	442208
San Marino	Multilateral	19 Nov 48	Sanitation	44UNTS277	100688
San Marino	Multilateral	11 Jul 52	Postal Service	171UNTS89	102225
San Marino	Multilateral	11 Jul 52	Postal Service	170UNTS269	102223
San Marino	Multilateral	11 Jul 52	Postal Service	170UNTS3	102221
San Marino	Multilateral	11 Jul 52	Postal Service	171UNTS3	102224
San Marino	Multilateral	11 Jul 52	IGO Establishment	169UNTS3	102220
San Marino	Multilateral	11 Jul 52	Postal Service	171UNTS143	102226
San Marino	Multilateral	11 Jul 52	Postal Service	170UNTS63	102222

PARTY ONE	PARTY TWO	DATE	TOPIC	CITATION	NUMBER
San Marino	Multilateral	06 Sep 52	Patents/Copyrights	216UNTS132	102937
San Marino	Multilateral	14 May 54	Culture	249UNTS215	103511
San Marino	Multilateral	07 Sep 56	Humanitarian	266UNTS3	103822
San Marino	Multilateral	03 Oct 57	Postal Service	366UNTS3	105215
San Marino	Multilateral	03 Oct 57	Postal Service	366UNTS87	105216
San Marino	Multilateral	03 Oct 57	Postal Service	365UNTS3	105213
San Marino	Multilateral	03 Oct 57	Postal Service	365UNTS207	105214
San Marino	Multilateral	03 Oct 57	Postal Service	364UNTS3	105211
San Marino	Multilateral	03 Oct 57	Postal Service	366UNTS141	105217
San Marino	Multilateral	03 Oct 57	Postal Service	366UNTS255	105219
San Marino	Multilateral	03 Oct 57	Postal Service	364UNTS331	105212
San Marino	Multilateral	18 Apr 61	Consul/Citizenship	500UNTS95	107310
San Marino	Multilateral	05 Aug 63	Sanitation	480UNTS43	106964
San Marino	Multilateral	10 Jul 64	Postal Service	613UNTS3	108850
San Marino	Multilateral	10 Jul 64	Postal Service	613UNTS127	108853
San Marino	Multilateral	10 Jul 64	Postal Service	613UNTS3	108851
San Marino	Multilateral	10 Jul 64	Postal Service	611UNTS387	108846
San Marino	Multilateral	10 Jul 64	Postal Service	612UNTS233	108848
San Marino	Multilateral	10 Jul 64	Postal Service	611UNTS7	108844
San Marino	Multilateral	10 Jul 64	Postal Service	612UNTS361	108849
San Marino	Multilateral	10 Jul 64	Postal Service	611UNTS105	108845
San Marino	Multilateral	10 Jul 64	Postal Service	612UNTS3	108847
San Marino	Multilateral	08 Jul 65	General Trade	597UNTS3	108641
San Marino	Multilateral	27 Jan 67	Scientific Project	610UNTS205	108843
San Marino	Multilateral	12 Jun 69	Visas	0UNTS0	110305
San Marino	UK Great Britain	12 Sep 49	Visas	87UNTS37	101164
San Marino	UK Great Britain	08 Mar 61	Visas	414UNTS46	105964
San Marino	UK Great Britain	22 Jul 61	Reparations	420UNTS3	106035
San Marino	United Nations	07 Oct 48	Humanitarian	47UNTS337	200190
San Marino	USSR (Soviet Union)	29 Feb 56	Consul/Citizenship	16SUGG70	469912
Sarawak	Multilateral	09 Jul 63	Admin Cooperation	0UNTS0	110760
Saudi Arabia	France	07 Jul 63	Health/Educ/Welfare	65FRRT21	415051
Saudi Arabia	Iran	14 Nov 67	Culture	0IRTB10	433018
Saudi Arabia	Iran	24 Oct 68	Territory Boundary	0IRTB10	433017
Saudi Arabia	Iran	24 Oct 68	Territory Boundary	0UNTS0	109976
Saudi Arabia	Multilateral	02 Aug 44	Scientific Project	67UNTS221	200221
Saudi Arabia	Multilateral	07 Dec 44	IGO Establishment	15UNTS295	200102
Saudi Arabia	Multilateral	22 Mar 45	General Amity	70UNTS237	200241
Saudi Arabia	Multilateral	16 Nov 45	IGO Establishment	4UNTS275	100052
Saudi Arabia	Multilateral	22 Jul 46	IGO Establishment	14UNTS185	100221
Saudi Arabia	Multilateral	22 Jul 46	IGO Establishment	9UNTS3	100125
Saudi Arabia	Multilateral	27 Jul 46	Patents/Copyrights	90UNTS229	101238
Saudi Arabia	Multilateral	11 Dec 46	Sanitation	12UNTS179	100186
Saudi Arabia	Multilateral	02 Oct 47	Telecommunications	193UNTS188	102616
Saudi Arabia	Multilateral	06 Mar 48	Water Transport	289UNTS3	104214
Saudi Arabia	Multilateral	24 Jul 48	Sanitation	66UNTS25	100847
Saudi Arabia	Multilateral	19 Nov 48	Sanitation	44UNTS277	100688
Saudi Arabia	Multilateral	09 Dec 48	Humanitarian	78UNTS277	101021
Saudi Arabia	Multilateral	23 Mar 49	Commodity Trade	203UNTS179	102746
Saudi Arabia	Multilateral	25 May 51	Status of Forces	175UNTS215	102303
Saudi Arabia	Multilateral	08 Sep 51	General Military	136UNTS165	101833
Saudi Arabia	Multilateral	08 Sep 51	Peace/Disarmament	136UNTS45	101832
Saudi Arabia	Multilateral	11 Jul 52	IGO Establishment	169UNTS3	102220
Saudi Arabia	Multilateral	25 May 55	IGO Establishment	264UNTS117	103791
Saudi Arabia	Multilateral	25 Apr 56	Commodity Trade	270UNTS103	103896
Saudi Arabia	Multilateral	17 Feb 57	Tech Assistance	271UNTS2	103907
Saudi Arabia	Multilateral	03 Oct 57	Postal Service	364UNTS3	105211
Saudi Arabia	Multilateral	03 Oct 57	Postal Service	365UNTS207	105214
Saudi Arabia	Multilateral	03 Oct 57	Postal Service	364UNTS331	105212
Saudi Arabia	Multilateral	03 Oct 57	Postal Service	365UNTS3	105213
Saudi Arabia	Multilateral	06 Apr 59	Commodity Trade	349UNTS167	105013
Saudi Arabia	Multilateral	26 Jan 60	IGO Establishment	439UNTS249	106333
Saudi Arabia	Multilateral	17 Jun 60	Humanitarian	536UNTS27	107794
Saudi Arabia	Multilateral	14 Sep 60	IGO Establishment	443UNTS247	106363
Saudi Arabia	Multilateral	15 May 62	Commodity Trade	444UNTS3	106367

PARTY ONE	PARTY TWO	DATE	TOPIC	CITATION	NUMBER
Saudi Arabia	Multilateral	24 Apr 63	Consul/Citizenship	596UNTS261	108638
Saudi Arabia	Multilateral	10 Jul 64	Postal Service	611UNTS387	108846
Saudi Arabia	Multilateral	10 Jul 64	Postal Service	611UNTS105	108845
Saudi Arabia	Multilateral	10 Jul 64	Postal Service	612UNTS3	108847
Saudi Arabia	Multilateral	10 Jul 64	Postal Service	612UNTS233	108848
Saudi Arabia	Multilateral	10 Jul 64	Postal Service	611UNTS7	108844
Saudi Arabia	Multilateral	20 Aug 64	Telecommunications	514UNTS25	107441
Saudi Arabia	Multilateral	09 Jan 68	IGO Establishment	0UNTS0	109707
Saudi Arabia	Multilateral	24 Sep 68	Air Transport	0UNTS0	110612
Saudi Arabia	Pakistan	25 Nov 51	General Amity	177UNTS3	102304
Saudi Arabia	Spain	09 Jan 61	General Amity	62SPBO606	460038
Saudi Arabia	Syria	16 Nov 61	General Economic	491UNTS163	107177
Saudi Arabia	Taiwan	15 Nov 46	General Amity	18UNTS197	100289
Saudi Arabia	UK Great Britain	20 Apr 42	Extradition	10UNTS99	200056
Saudi Arabia	UK Great Britain	20 Apr 42	General Trade	10UNTS151	200058
Saudi Arabia	UK Great Britain	20 Apr 42	General Amity	10UNTS117	200057
Saudi Arabia	UK Great Britain	31 Oct 43	General Amity	10UNTS165	200059
Saudi Arabia	UK Great Britain	30 Jul 54	Dispute Settlement	201UNTS317	102722
Saudi Arabia	UN Special Fund	19 Jan 61	Direct Aid	396UNTS27	105692
Saudi Arabia	UNICEF (Children)	04 Jul 61	Direct Aid	413UNTS122	105947
Saudi Arabia	United Nations	16 Mar 62	Tech Assistance	456UNTS379	106566
Saudi Arabia	United Nations	23 Aug 63	IGO Status/Immunit	474UNTS155	106879
Saudi Arabia	USA (United States)	17 Jan 51	Direct Aid	140UNTS335	101897
Saudi Arabia	USA (United States)	18 Jun 51	Specific Property	102UNTS73	101412
Saudi Arabia	USA (United States)	18 Jun 51	Milit Assistance	141UNTS67	101906
Saudi Arabia	USA (United States)	10 Nov 51	Scientific Project	180UNTS263	102390
Saudi Arabia	USA (United States)	10 Nov 52	Direct Aid	181UNTS307	102419
Saudi Arabia	USA (United States)	10 Nov 52	Tech Assistance	181UNTS235	102413
Saudi Arabia	USA (United States)	10 Nov 52	Tech Assistance	181UNTS225	102412
Saudi Arabia	USA (United States)	10 Nov 52	Direct Aid	181UNTS295	102418
Saudi Arabia	USA (United States)	15 Dec 52	Direct Aid	185UNTS55	102458
Saudi Arabia	USA (United States)	15 Dec 52	Tech Assistance	185UNTS67	102459
Saudi Arabia	USA (United States)	25 Jan 53	Education	201UNTS3	102706
Saudi Arabia	USA (United States)	29 Jun 53	Sanitation	206UNTS23	102784
Saudi Arabia	USA (United States)	02 Apr 57	Milit Installation	283UNTS97	104109
Saudi Arabia	USA (United States)	01 May 58	Direct Aid	315UNTS221	104571
Saudi Arabia	USA (United States)	13 Nov 62	Loans and Credits	488UNTS175	107127
Saudi Arabia	USA (United States)	06 Jan 64	Telecommunications	531UNTS3	107689
Saudi Arabia	USA (United States)	05 Jun 65	Milit Installation	548UNTS285	107984
Saudi Arabia	USA (United States)	11 Nov 65	Milit Installation	606UNTS65	108775
Saudi Arabia	USA (United States)	19 Nov 65	Non-IBRD Project	580UNTS35	108419
Saudi Arabia	USA (United States)	25 Jul 68	Culture	0UNTS0	110401
Saudi Arabia	WHO (World Health)	29 Aug 51	Tech Assistance	110UNTS277	101516
Saudi Arabia	WHO (World Health)	06 Sep 60	Tech Assistance	395UNTS169	105684
SCAP Japan	Multilateral	04 Feb 52	General Economic	124UNTS3	101662
SCAP Japan	Philippines	18 May 50	General Economic	2PTS555	465022
SCAP Japan	Philippines	03 Mar 51	General Trade	2PTS613	465025
SCAP Japan	Philippines	12 Mar 51	General Trade	2PTS615	465026
SCAP Japan	Philippines	19 Mar 52	Finance	2PTS783	465029
SEATO (SE Asia)	UK Great Britain	12 Mar 65	IGO Status/Immunit	561UNTS313	108191
SEATO (SE Asia)	USA (United States)	29 May 59	Sanitation	347UNTS77	104991
Senegal	Accept UN Charter	20 Sep 60	UN Charter	376UNTS79	105374
Senegal	Czechoslovakia	20 Jun 62	Air Transport	498UNTS145	107280
Senegal	Denmark	11 Apr 62	General Trade	0UNTS0	110769
Senegal	Denmark	03 Aug 68	Loans and Credits	0UNTS0	109282
Senegal	France	22 Jun 60	General Amity	60FRRT47	415388
Senegal	France	19 Sep 60	Admin Cooperation	61FRRT22	415389
Senegal	France	14 Jun 62	Admin Cooperation	65FRRT28	415390
Senegal	France	15 Jun 62	Air Transport	524UNTS3	107563
Senegal	France	18 Sep 62	Specific Property	63FRRT22	415391
Senegal	France	13 Oct 62	Customs	63FRRT55	415392
Senegal	France	16 Feb 63	Consul/Citizenship	65FRRT51	415393
Senegal	France	24 Apr 63	Claims and Debts	65FRRT7	415394
Senegal	France	21 Jan 64	Visas	64FRRT32	415395
Senegal	France	21 Jan 64	Education	64FRRT25	415396

PARTY ONE	PARTY TWO	DATE	TOPIC	CITATION	NUMBER
Senegal	France	15 May 64	Education	66FRJO1601	416397
Senegal	France	05 Mar 65	Non-ILO Labor	67FRJO3110	416398
Senegal	France	03 May 65	General Economic	0UNTS0	109489
Senegal	Gambia	19 Apr 67	General Amity	640UNTS101	109156
Senegal	Germany, West	27 Jun 61	Water Transport	61WBGA171	424620
Senegal	Germany, West	27 Jun 61	Direct Aid	61WBGA194	424619
Senegal	Germany, West	24 Jan 64	Claims and Debts	65WGBB1391	425621
Senegal	Germany, West	29 Oct 64	Air Transport	66WGBB118	425622
Senegal	Germany, West	29 Oct 64	Air Transport	0UNTS0	110467
Senegal	Germany, West	13 Feb 68	Loans and Credits	68WBGA78	424623
Senegal	Germany, West	23 Sep 68	Culture	70WGBB1224	425624
Senegal	Germany, West	20 Nov 68	Loans and Credits	69WBGA28	424625
Senegal	Germany, West	17 Apr 69	Admin Cooperation	71WGBB1309	425626
Senegal	Germany, West	28 Sep 70	Loans and Credits	70WBGA214	424627
Senegal	IBRD (World Bank)	01 May 67	IGO Operations	615UNTS267	108883
Senegal	IBRD (World Bank)	10 Feb 69	IBRD Project	0UNTS0	110120
Senegal	IDA (Devel Assoc)	29 Sep 66	Non-IBRD Project	594UNTS277	108607
Senegal	IDA (Devel Assoc)	10 Feb 69	Non-IBRD Project	0UNTS0	110121
Senegal	ILO (Labor Org)	09 Feb 67	IGO Establishment	600UNTS75	108677
Senegal	Italy	02 Oct 62	Tech Assistance	63ITDI347	436341
Senegal	Mali	07 Feb 63	Air Transport	524UNTS41	107565
Senegal	Morocco	15 Sep 66	General Amity	634UNTS105	109055
Senegal	Multilateral	07 Dec 44	Air Transport	84UNTS389	200252
Senegal	Multilateral	07 Dec 44	IGO Establishment	15UNTS295	200102
Senegal	Multilateral	11 Dec 46	Sanitation	12UNTS179	100186
Senegal	Multilateral	27 May 47	Air Transport	418UNTS161	106021
Senegal	Multilateral	06 Mar 48	Water Transport	289UNTS3	104214
Senegal	Multilateral	24 Jul 48	Sanitation	66UNTS25	100847
Senegal	Multilateral	04 May 49	Admin Cooperation	98UNTS101	101358
Senegal	Multilateral	04 May 49	Admin Cooperation	92UNTS19	101257
Senegal	Multilateral	02 Jul 51	Refugees	189UNTS137	102545
Senegal	Multilateral	31 Mar 53	Privil/Immunities	193UNTS136	102613
Senegal	Multilateral	11 May 53	Sanitation	456UNTS3	106555
Senegal	Multilateral	18 Jan 54	IGO Establishment	330UNTS121	104743
Senegal	Multilateral	14 Jun 54	Air Transport	320UNTS209	104643
Senegal	Multilateral	14 Jun 54	Air Transport	320UNTS217	104644
Senegal	Multilateral	29 Jul 54	Sanitation	249UNTS45	103500
Senegal	Multilateral	25 May 55	IGO Establishment	264UNTS117	103791
Senegal	Multilateral	29 Apr 58	Specific Resources	559UNTS285	108164
Senegal	Multilateral	29 Apr 58	Territory Boundary	499UNTS311	107302
Senegal	Multilateral	29 Apr 58	Territory Boundary	516UNTS205	107477
Senegal	Multilateral	29 Apr 58	Water Transport	450UNTS11	106465
Senegal	Multilateral	26 Jan 60	IGO Establishment	439UNTS249	106333
Senegal	Multilateral	14 Dec 60	Education	429UNTS93	106193
Senegal	Multilateral	30 Mar 61	Sanitation	520UNTS151	107515
Senegal	Multilateral	18 Apr 61	Consul/Citizenship	500UNTS95	107310
Senegal	Multilateral	18 Apr 61	Consul/Citizenship	500UNTS223	107311
Senegal	Multilateral	21 Jun 61	IGO Establishment	514UNTS209	107449
Senegal	Multilateral	27 Dec 61	Tech Assistance	425UNTS83	106120
Senegal	Multilateral	25 May 62	IGO Establishment	486UNTS103	107075
Senegal	Multilateral	22 Jun 62	ILO Labor	494UNTS249	107237
Senegal	Multilateral	24 Apr 63	Consul/Citizenship	596UNTS487	108640
Senegal	Multilateral	25 May 63	IGO Establishment	479UNTS39	106947
Senegal	Multilateral	04 Aug 63	IGO Establishment	510UNTS3	107408
Senegal	Multilateral	05 Aug 63	Sanitation	480UNTS43	106964
Senegal	Multilateral	10 Jul 64	Postal Service	612UNTS361	108849
Senegal	Multilateral	10 Jul 64	Postal Service	613UNTS3	108851
Senegal	Multilateral	10 Jul 64	Postal Service	611UNTS105	108845
Senegal	Multilateral	10 Jul 64	Postal Service	611UNTS7	108844
Senegal	Multilateral	10 Jul 64	Postal Service	612UNTS233	108848
Senegal	Multilateral	10 Jul 64	Postal Service	611UNTS387	108846
Senegal	Multilateral	10 Jul 64	Postal Service	612UNTS3	108847
Senegal	Multilateral	10 Jul 64	Postal Service	613UNTS3	108850
Senegal	Multilateral	13 Jul 64	ILO Labor	569UNTS65	108279
Senegal	Multilateral	09 Mar 65	Water Transport	591UNTS265	108564

PARTY ONE	PARTY TWO	DATE	TOPIC	CITATION	NUMBER
Senegal	Multilateral	18 Mar 65	Dispute Settlement	575UNTS159	108359
Senegal	Multilateral	08 Jul 65	General Trade	597UNTS3	108641
Senegal	Multilateral	27 May 66	IGO Establishment	637UNTS0	109121
Senegal	Multilateral	21 Jun 66	ILO Labor	0UNTS0	109728
Senegal	Multilateral	31 Jan 67	Refugees	606UNTS267	108791
Senegal	Multilateral	04 May 67	IGO Establishment	595UNTS287	108623
Senegal	Multilateral	24 Mar 68	IGO Establishment	0UNTS0	109577
Senegal	Netherlands	12 Jun 65	General Economic	602UNTS231	108715
Senegal	Poland	18 Jun 62	General Economic	62PZUM51	458095
Senegal	Poland	18 Jun 62	Culture	62PZUM48	458094
Senegal	Switzerland	16 Aug 62	General Economic	64SWRO718	462155
Senegal	Switzerland	23 Jan 63	Air Transport	524UNTS23	107564
Senegal	UN Special Fund	16 Dec 61	Direct Aid	425UNTS97	106121
Senegal	UNICEF (Children)	22 Jan 64	IGO Operations	486UNTS91	107074
Senegal	United Nations	12 Jan 66	Health/Educ/Welfare	551UNTS147	108039
Senegal	United Nations	08 Nov 67	Admin Cooperation	613UNTS255	108854
Senegal	USA (United States)	13 May 61	General Aid	409UNTS232	105888
Senegal	USA (United States)	20 Jul 62	Milit Assistance	458UNTS137	106596
Senegal	USA (United States)	17 Jan 63	General Aid	493UNTS97	107210
Senegal	USA (United States)	12 Jun 63	Finance	0UNTS0	109979
Senegal	USA (United States)	03 Jul 63	US Agri Commod Aid	527UNTS95	107620
Senegal	USSR (Soviet Union)	14 Jun 62	General Aid	11SUGG143	469843
Senegal	USSR (Soviet Union)	14 Jun 62	Culture	437UNTS233	106309
Senegal	USSR (Soviet Union)	14 Jun 62	Consul/Citizenship	16SUGG133	470008
Senegal	USSR (Soviet Union)	14 Jun 62	General Trade	11SUGG143	469842
Senegal	WHO (World Health)	06 Aug 62	Tech Assistance	435UNTS179	106279
Seychelles	Multilateral	24 Dec 68	Commodity Trade	0UNTS0	109369
Siam	IDA (Devel Assoc)	02 Aug 66	Non-IBRD Project	585UNTS271	108492
Siam	Multilateral	02 Aug 44	Scientific Project	67UNTS221	200221
Siam	Multilateral	01 Jan 46	Peace/Disarmament	99UNTS131	101375
Siam	Multilateral	06 May 46	Commodity Trade	99UNTS181	101379
Siam	Multilateral	06 May 46	Commodity Trade	157UNTS85	102049
Siam	Multilateral	22 Jul 46	IGO Establishment	9UNTS3	100125
Siam	Multilateral	22 Jul 46	IGO Establishment	14UNTS185	100221
Siam	Multilateral	07 Dec 46	Commodity Trade	157UNTS103	102050
Siam	Multilateral	11 Dec 46	Sanitation	12UNTS179	100186
Siam	Multilateral	02 Oct 47	Telecommunications	193UNTS188	102616
Siam	Multilateral	11 Oct 47	IGO Establishment	77UNTS143	100998
Siam	Multilateral	24 Jul 48	Sanitation	66UNTS25	100847
Sierra Leone	Accept UN Charter	27 Apr 61	UN Charter	409UNTS44	105876
Sierra Leone	France	19 Oct 64	Health/Educ/Welfare	65FRRT30	415399
Sierra Leone	France	18 Jul 67	Air Transport	67FRJO1410	416400
Sierra Leone	Germany, West	13 Sep 63	Loans and Credits	63WBGA222	424630
Sierra Leone	Germany, West	13 Sep 63	Tech Assistance	63WBGA222	424629
Sierra Leone	Germany, West	13 Sep 63	General Economic	63WBGA222	424628
Sierra Leone	Germany, West	13 Sep 63	Water Transport	63WBGA222	424631
Sierra Leone	Germany, West	08 Apr 65	Claims and Debts	66WGBB861	425632
Sierra Leone	Germany, West	05 Sep 67	Loans and Credits	67WBGA214	424633
Sierra Leone	Germany, West	15 Dec 70	Loans and Credits	71WBGA64	424634
Sierra Leone	IBRD (World Bank)	18 Aug 64	IBRD Project	516UNTS295	107479
Sierra Leone	IBRD (World Bank)	05 Aug 68	IBRD Project	0UNTS0	109487
Sierra Leone	Israel	30 Aug 62	Visas	448UNTS309	106444
Sierra Leone	Israel	22 Aug 65	Culture	550UNTS275	108022
Sierra Leone	Israel	22 Aug 65	Tech Assistance	550UNTS285	108023
Sierra Leone	Japan	07 Jan 66	Commodity Trade	66JJS229	442166
Sierra Leone	Multilateral	07 Dec 44	IGO Establishment	15UNTS295	200102
Sierra Leone	Multilateral	11 Dec 46	Sanitation	12UNTS179	100186
Sierra Leone	Multilateral	12 Nov 47	Admin Cooperation	53UNTS13	100770
Sierra Leone	Multilateral	12 Nov 47	Admin Cooperation	46UNTS201	100710
Sierra Leone	Multilateral	12 Nov 47	Admin Cooperation	53UNTS39	100771
Sierra Leone	Multilateral	24 Jul 48	Sanitation	66UNTS25	100847
Sierra Leone	Multilateral	29 Nov 48	IGO Establishment	120UNTS13	101613
Sierra Leone	Multilateral	04 May 49	Admin Cooperation	47UNTS159	100728
Sierra Leone	Multilateral	04 May 49	Admin Cooperation	98UNTS101	101358
Sierra Leone	Multilateral	04 May 49	Admin Cooperation	92UNTS19	101257

PARTY ONE	PARTY TWO	DATE	TOPIC	CITATION	NUMBER
Sierra Leone	Multilateral	22 Nov 50	Culture	131UNTS25	101734
Sierra Leone	Multilateral	07 Nov 52	General Trade	221UNTS255	103010
Sierra Leone	Multilateral	31 Mar 53	Mass Media	435UNTS191	106280
Sierra Leone	Multilateral	31 Mar 53	Privil/Immunities	193UNTS136	102613
Sierra Leone	Multilateral	18 Jan 54	IGO Establishment	330UNTS121	104743
Sierra Leone	Multilateral	29 Jul 54	Sanitation	249UNTS45	103500
Sierra Leone	Multilateral	25 May 55	IGO Establishment	264UNTS117	103791
Sierra Leone	Multilateral	18 May 56	Customs	319UNTS21	104630
Sierra Leone	Multilateral	18 May 56	Customs	327UNTS123	104721
Sierra Leone	Multilateral	18 May 56	Customs	338UNTS103	104834
Sierra Leone	Multilateral	20 Feb 57	Consul/Citizenship	309UNTS65	104468
Sierra Leone	Multilateral	29 Apr 58	Territory Boundary	516UNTS205	107477
Sierra Leone	Multilateral	29 Apr 58	Specific Resources	559UNTS285	108164
Sierra Leone	Multilateral	29 Apr 58	Dispute Settlement	450UNTS169	106466
Sierra Leone	Multilateral	29 Apr 58	Water Transport	450UNTS11	106465
Sierra Leone	Multilateral	06 Apr 59	Commodity Trade	349UNTS167	105013
Sierra Leone	Multilateral	26 Jan 60	IGO Establishment	439UNTS249	106333
Sierra Leone	Multilateral	18 Apr 61	Consul/Citizenship	500UNTS95	107310
Sierra Leone	Multilateral	21 Jun 61	IGO Establishment	514UNTS209	107449
Sierra Leone	Multilateral	16 Oct 61	Tech Assistance	410UNTS242	105908
Sierra Leone	Multilateral	28 Sep 62	IGO Establishment	469UNTS169	106791
Sierra Leone	Multilateral	25 May 63	IGO Establishment	479UNTS39	106947
Sierra Leone	Multilateral	04 Aug 63	IGO Establishment	510UNTS3	107408
Sierra Leone	Multilateral	05 Aug 63	Sanitation	480UNTS43	106964
Sierra Leone	Multilateral	10 Jul 64	Postal Service	611UNTS7	108844
Sierra Leone	Multilateral	10 Jul 64	Postal Service	611UNTS387	108846
Sierra Leone	Multilateral	10 Jul 64	Postal Service	611UNTS105	108845
Sierra Leone	Multilateral	10 Jul 64	Postal Service	612UNTS3	108847
Sierra Leone	Multilateral	01 Dec 64	Water Transport	550UNTS133	108012
Sierra Leone	Multilateral	18 Mar 65	Dispute Settlement	575UNTS159	108359
Sierra Leone	Multilateral	28 May 65	IGO Establishment	559UNTS273	108163
Sierra Leone	Multilateral	21 Jun 66	Non-ILO Labor	0UNTS0	109298
Sierra Leone	Multilateral	21 Jun 66	ILO Labor	0UNTS0	109728
Sierra Leone	Multilateral	04 May 67	IGO Establishment	595UNTS287	108623
Sierra Leone	Multilateral	18 Mar 68	Commodity Trade	0UNTS0	109262
Sierra Leone	Multilateral	27 Jan 69	Telecommunications	0UNTS0	109664
Sierra Leone	Netherlands	13 Jun 67	Air Transport	0UNTS0	109247
Sierra Leone	Norway	02 May 51	Taxation	2NORT553	451139
Sierra Leone	State/IGO Group	29 May 68	Direct Aid	637UNTS0	109120
Sierra Leone	UK Great Britain	05 May 61	Consul/Citizenship	420UNTS17	106037
Sierra Leone	UK Great Britain	05 May 61	Recognition	420UNTS11	106036
Sierra Leone	UK Great Britain	05 Apr 62	Air Transport	434UNTS227	106265
Sierra Leone	UK Great Britain	18 Mar 68	Taxation	0UNTS0	109655
Sierra Leone	UK Great Britain	20 Sep 68	Finance	0UNTS0	109806
Sierra Leone	UN Special Fund	02 Oct 61	Direct Aid	422UNTS131	106073
Sierra Leone	UNICEF (Children)	11 Apr 62	Direct Aid	431UNTS55	106209
Sierra Leone	United Nations	19 Feb 64	IGO Status/Immunit	489UNTS91	107136
Sierra Leone	USA (United States)	05 May 61	General Aid	409UNTS194	105885
Sierra Leone	USA (United States)	19 May 61	Admin Cooperation	409UNTS251	105890
Sierra Leone	USA (United States)	29 Dec 61	Direct Aid	434UNTS43	106254
Sierra Leone	USA (United States)	29 Jan 65	US Agri Commod Aid	542UNTS87	107882
Sierra Leone	USA (United States)	16 Aug 65	Telecommunications	579UNTS55	108398
Sierra Leone	USA (United States)	06 May 66	Admin Cooperation	594UNTS47	108593
Sierra Leone	USA (United States)	23 Jan 68	US Agri Commod Aid	0UNTS0	110004
Sierra Leone	USA (United States)	08 Apr 69	US Agri Commod Aid	0UNTS0	110158
Sierra Leone	USSR (Soviet Union)	18 Jan 62	Recognition	16SUGG132	469999
Sierra Leone	USSR (Soviet Union)	26 Apr 65	General Trade	0UNTS0	109831
Sierra Leone	WHO (World Health)	19 Jun 62	Tech Assistance	439UNTS151	106327
Sierra Leone	WHO (World Health)	22 Nov 63	IGO Operations	493UNTS255	107219
Singapore	Accept UN Charter	04 Sep 65	UN Charter	545UNTS151	107930
Singapore	Australia	03 Nov 67	Air Transport	0UNTS0	110167
Singapore	Australia	27 Jun 68	Health/Educ/Welfare	0UNTS0	109669
Singapore	Australia	11 Feb 69	Taxation	0UNTS0	110175
Singapore	Austria	13 Jan 69	Admin Cooperation	69ABGB435	403164
Singapore	Austria	13 Jan 69	Admin Cooperation	0UNTS0	110409

PARTY ONE	PARTY TWO	DATE	TOPIC	CITATION	NUMBER
Singapore	Bulgaria	05 May 66	General Trade	631UNTS165	108993
Singapore	Cambodia	25 Nov 69	General Economic	0UNTS0	110561
Singapore	Denmark	20 Dec 66	Air Transport	593UNTS125	108580
Singapore	Denmark	07 Mar 69	Taxation	0UNTS0	110771
Singapore	France	29 Jun 67	Air Transport	67FRJO1110	416401
Singapore	Germany, West	15 Feb 69	Air Transport	71WGBB184	425643
Singapore	IBRD (World Bank)	11 Aug 66	IBRD Project	585UNTS39	108482
Singapore	IBRD (World Bank)	04 Nov 66	IBRD Project	585UNTS155	108488
Singapore	IBRD (World Bank)	05 Jul 67	IBRD Project	618UNTS189	108928
Singapore	IBRD (World Bank)	15 Sep 67	IGO Operations	615UNTS295	108884
Singapore	IBRD (World Bank)	03 Jul 68	IBRD Project	0UNTS0	109364
Singapore	IBRD (World Bank)	25 Apr 69	IBRD Project	0UNTS0	109946
Singapore	IBRD (World Bank)	19 Dec 69	Loans and Credits	0UNTS0	110547
Singapore	IBRD (World Bank)	25 Feb 70	IBRD Project	0UNTS0	110678
Singapore	Israel	24 Apr 68	General Trade	642UNTS235	109176
Singapore	Japan	15 Oct 66	Education	66JJS247	442179
Singapore	Japan	14 Feb 67	Air Transport	0UNTS0	109244
Singapore	Japan	14 Feb 67	Air Transport	67JHZ8	439006
Singapore	Japan	21 Sep 67	Reparations	0UNTS0	109720
Singapore	Japan	21 Sep 67	Reparations	68JHZ5	439013
Singapore	Malaysia	07 Aug 65	Recognition	563UNTS89	108206
Singapore	Multilateral	06 Mar 48	Water Transport	289UNTS3	104214
Singapore	Multilateral	20 Feb 57	Consul/Citizenship	309UNTS65	104468
Singapore	Multilateral	17 Jun 60	Humanitarian	536UNTS27	107794
Singapore	Multilateral	09 Jul 63	Admin Cooperation	0UNTS0	110760
Singapore	Multilateral	10 Jul 64	Postal Service	611UNTS7	108844
Singapore	Multilateral	10 Jul 64	Postal Service	611UNTS105	108845
Singapore	Multilateral	10 Jul 64	Postal Service	612UNTS3	108847
Singapore	Multilateral	10 Jul 64	Postal Service	611UNTS387	108846
Singapore	Multilateral	04 Dec 65	IGO Establishment	571UNTS123	108303
Singapore	Multilateral	31 Dec 65	Recognition	552UNTS292	108060
Singapore	Multilateral	23 Sep 66	IGO Operations	573UNTS132	108327
Singapore	Multilateral	23 Sep 66	General Aid	573UNTS148	108328
Singapore	Multilateral	28 Dec 67	Scientific Project	0UNTS0	109322
Singapore	Multilateral	11 Jun 68	Scientific Project	0UNTS0	109884
Singapore	Multilateral	27 Jan 69	Telecommunications	0UNTS0	109664
Singapore	New Zealand	04 Apr 68	Air Transport	0UNTS0	109480
Singapore	Norway	09 Sep 66	Taxation	3NORT975	451140
Singapore	Norway	20 Dec 66	Air Transport	0UNTS0	109242
Singapore	Norway	20 Dec 66	Air Transport	3NORT985	451141
Singapore	Norway	28 Nov 68	Visas	3NORT0	451142
Singapore	Poland	07 Jun 66	General Trade	631UNTS189	108994
Singapore	Sweden	20 Dec 66	Air Transport	0UNTS0	109243
Singapore	UK Great Britain	01 Dec 66	Taxation	605UNTS153	108763
Singapore	UK Great Britain	01 Aug 67	Air Transport	619UNTS29	108937
Singapore	UK Great Britain	19 Sep 68	Finance	0UNTS0	109801
Singapore	UN Special Fund	31 Dec 65	Admin Cooperation	552UNTS299	108061
Singapore	UN Special Fund	23 Sep 66	General Aid	573UNTS115	108326
Singapore	UNICEF (Children)	31 Jul 69	IGO Operations	0UNTS0	109736
Singapore	United Arab Rep	30 May 68	General Trade	0UNTS0	110420
Singapore	USA (United States)	25 Mar 66	Finance	580UNTS221	108425
Singapore	USA (United States)	30 Aug 66	General Trade	616UNTS242	108899
Singapore	USA (United States)	10 Jun 69	Extradition	0UNTS0	110404
Singapore	USSR (Soviet Union)	02 Apr 66	General Trade	631UNTS125	108992
Singapore	WHO (World Health)	28 Mar 66	Tech Assistance	562UNTS59	108195
Solomon Islands	Multilateral	24 Dec 68	Commodity Trade	0UNTS0	109369
Somalia	Accept UN Charter	11 Feb 61	UN Charter	388UNTS179	105577
Somalia	China People's Rep	10 Jan 63	Culture	63CCJC6	410943
Somalia	China People's Rep	15 May 63	General Economic	63CCJC61	410979
Somalia	China People's Rep	17 Aug 65	Culture	65CCJC107	411324
Somalia	China People's Rep	11 Jun 66	Culture	66CCJC53	411326
Somalia	China People's Rep	23 Oct 66	Non-ILO Labor	66CCJC88	411328
Somalia	China People's Rep	19 Aug 67	Culture	67CCJC32	411330
Somalia	Czechoslovakia	04 Jun 61	Culture	479UNTS291	106960
Somalia	Czechoslovakia	04 Jun 61	Tech Assistance	480UNTS261	106973

PARTY ONE	PARTY TWO	DATE	TOPIC	CITATION	NUMBER
Somalia	Germany, West	19 Jan 62	General Trade	62WBGA113	424635
Somalia	Germany, West	19 Jan 62	General Transport	62WBGA113	424637
Somalia	Germany, West	19 Jan 62	Loans and Credits	62WBGA113	424638
Somalia	Germany, West	19 Jan 62	Direct Aid	62WBGA113	424636
Somalia	Germany, West	30 Nov 67	Loans and Credits	68WBGA77	424639
Somalia	Germany, West	06 Jun 68	Loans and Credits	68WBGA149	424640
Somalia	Germany, West	28 Nov 68	Loans and Credits	69WBGA157	424641
Somalia	Germany, West	20 Jan 70	Loans and Credits	70WBGA48	424642
Somalia	ICJ Option Clause	25 Mar 63	ICJ Option Clause	458UNTS143	106597
Somalia	IDA (Devel Assoc)	29 Mar 65	Non-IBRD Project	586UNTS101	108499
Somalia	IDA (Devel Assoc)	26 Jun 68	Non-IBRD Project	0UNTS0	109634
Somalia	IDA (Devel Assoc)	03 Apr 69	Loans and Credits	0UNTS0	110284
Somalia	Italy	01 Jul 60	Admin Cooperation	62ITDI366	436346
Somalia	Italy	01 Jul 60	General Economic	62ITGU148	435345
Somalia	Italy	01 Jul 60	Consul/Citizenship	62ITGU148	435344
Somalia	Italy	01 Jul 60	Air Transport	62ITGU148	435347
Somalia	Italy	01 Jul 60	General Amity	62ITGU148	435343
Somalia	Italy	26 Apr 61	Culture	63ITGU36	435348
Somalia	Multilateral	27 May 47	Air Transport	418UNTS161	106021
Somalia	Multilateral	24 Jul 48	Sanitation	66UNTS25	100847
Somalia	Multilateral	18 Jan 54	IGO Establishment	330UNTS121	104743
Somalia	Multilateral	14 Jun 54	Air Transport	320UNTS217	104644
Somalia	Multilateral	14 Jun 54	Air Transport	320UNTS209	104643
Somalia	Multilateral	25 May 55	IGO Establishment	264UNTS117	103791
Somalia	Multilateral	03 Oct 57	Postal Service	366UNTS87	105216
Somalia	Multilateral	03 Oct 57	Postal Service	364UNTS3	105211
Somalia	Multilateral	03 Oct 57	Postal Service	366UNTS3	105215
Somalia	Multilateral	03 Oct 57	Postal Service	364UNTS331	105212
Somalia	Multilateral	03 Oct 57	Postal Service	366UNTS141	105217
Somalia	Multilateral	03 Oct 57	Postal Service	365UNTS207	105214
Somalia	Multilateral	03 Oct 57	Postal Service	366UNTS255	105219
Somalia	Multilateral	26 Jan 60	IGO Establishment	439UNTS249	106333
Somalia	Multilateral	28 Jan 61	Tech Assistance	387UNTS202	105563
Somalia	Multilateral	21 Jun 61	IGO Establishment	514UNTS209	107449
Somalia	Multilateral	25 May 63	IGO Establishment	479UNTS39	106947
Somalia	Multilateral	04 Aug 63	IGO Establishment	510UNTS3	107408
Somalia	Multilateral	05 Aug 63	Sanitation	480UNTS43	106964
Somalia	Multilateral	10 Jul 64	Postal Service	612UNTS3	108847
Somalia	Multilateral	10 Jul 64	Postal Service	613UNTS3	108850
Somalia	Multilateral	10 Jul 64	Postal Service	613UNTS193	108852
Somalia	Multilateral	10 Jul 64	Postal Service	611UNTS387	108846
Somalia	Multilateral	10 Jul 64	Postal Service	613UNTS3	108851
Somalia	Multilateral	10 Jul 64	Postal Service	611UNTS7	108844
Somalia	Multilateral	10 Jul 64	Postal Service	611UNTS105	108845
Somalia	Multilateral	10 Jul 64	Postal Service	612UNTS361	108849
Somalia	Multilateral	10 Jul 64	Postal Service	612UNTS233	108848
Somalia	Multilateral	18 Mar 65	Dispute Settlement	575UNTS159	108359
Somalia	Multilateral	29 Apr 65	Non-IBRD Project	586UNTS123	108500
Somalia	Multilateral	21 Sep 65	IGO Operations	547UNTS280	107963
Somalia	Multilateral	05 Apr 66	Water Transport	640UNTS133	109159
Somalia	Multilateral	27 Jan 67	Scientific Project	610UNTS205	108843
Somalia	Multilateral	01 Jul 68	Peace/Disarmament	0UNTS0	110485
Somalia	Romania	20 Apr 67	Scientific Project	642UNTS155	109171
Somalia	UK Great Britain	26 Jun 60	Recognition	374UNTS357	105349
Somalia	UK Great Britain	26 Jun 60	Non-ILO Labor	374UNTS339	105347
Somalia	UK Great Britain	26 Jun 60	Finance	374UNTS363	105350
Somalia	UK Great Britain	26 Jun 60	Non-ILO Labor	374UNTS347	105348
Somalia	UK Great Britain	26 Jun 60	Direct Aid	374UNTS331	105346
Somalia	UN Special Fund	28 Jan 61	Direct Aid	388UNTS75	105573
Somalia	UNICEF (Children)	01 Apr 62	Direct Aid	431UNTS75	106211
Somalia	United Nations	20 Jan 62	Tech Assistance	420UNTS133	106044
Somalia	USA (United States)	04 Feb 61	Tech Assistance	433UNTS179	106241
Somalia	USA (United States)	17 Apr 62	Direct Aid	436UNTS107	106291
Somalia	USA (United States)	08 Jan 64	Claims and Debts	505UNTS165	107372
Somalia	USA (United States)	15 Mar 68	US Agri Commod Aid	0UNTS0	110008

PARTY ONE	PARTY TWO	DATE	TOPIC	CITATION	NUMBER
Somalia	USSR (Soviet Union)	11 Sep 60	Consul/Citizenship	9SUGG149	469701
Somalia	USSR (Soviet Union)	02 Jun 61	Culture	528UNTS147	107638
Somalia	USSR (Soviet Union)	02 Jun 61	Tech Assistance	457UNTS263	106587
Somalia	USSR (Soviet Union)	02 Jun 61	General Trade	493UNTS173	107214
Somalia	USSR (Soviet Union)	27 Mar 62	General Aid	11SUGG136	469829
Somalia	USSR (Soviet Union)	27 Mar 62	Direct Aid	11SUGG136	469830
Somalia	WHO (World Health)	17 Aug 61	Tech Assistance	423UNTS111	106088
Somalia	WHO (World Health)	08 Nov 63	IGO Operations	493UNTS243	107218
South Africa	Australia	04 Nov 55	Air Transport	232UNTS143	103234
South Africa	Australia	26 Sep 58	Air Transport	335UNTS121	104780
South Africa	Austria	11 Jun 57	Visas	272UNTS229	103941
South Africa	Austria	26 Sep 57	Postal Service	287UNTS3	104176
South Africa	Austria	31 Aug 62	Visas	443UNTS65	106359
South Africa	Austria	08 Nov 67	Other Military	636UNTS125	109099
South Africa	Austria	26 Mar 69	Air Transport	0UNTS0	110471
South Africa	Belgium	04 Jul 47	Claims and Debts	47UNTS9	100720
South Africa	Belgium	01 Jun 54	Culture	201UNTS25	102708
South Africa	Belgium	13 Sep 54	Air Transport	201UNTS15	102707
South Africa	Belgium	11 Jun 57	Taxation	292UNTS165	104272
South Africa	Belgium	28 Apr 58	Visas	303UNTS131	104375
South Africa	Belgium	11 Jun 58	Air Transport	335UNTS63	104778
South Africa	Belgium	25 May 65	Non-ILO Labor	0UNTS0	110762
South Africa	Belgium	13 Nov 67	Air Transport	0UNTS0	110168
South Africa	Canada	26 Nov 51	Taxation	248UNTS107	103489
South Africa	Canada	04 Aug 54	Postal Service	261UNTS3	103722
South Africa	Canada	21 Mar 55	Commodity Trade	213UNTS291	102892
South Africa	Canada	28 Sep 56	Taxation	299UNTS3	104303
South Africa	Canada	28 Sep 56	Taxation	299UNTS17	104304
South Africa	Denmark	14 Oct 46	Claims and Debts	10UNTS29	100140
South Africa	Denmark	30 Nov 50	Taxation	84UNTS51	101118
South Africa	Denmark	30 Apr 53	Air Transport	174UNTS19	102275
South Africa	Denmark	28 Mar 58	Air Transport	300UNTS107	104334
South Africa	Fed Rhod/Nyasaland	28 Jun 53	General Trade	267UNTS270	103848
South Africa	Fed Rhod/Nyasaland	22 May 56	Taxation	254UNTS227	103595
South Africa	Fed Rhod/Nyasaland	30 May 56	Air Transport	255UNTS317	103615
South Africa	Fed Rhod/Nyasaland	11 Oct 58	Non-ILO Labor	373UNTS75	105315
South Africa	Fed Rhod/Nyasaland	16 May 60	General Trade	376UNTS217	105381
South Africa	Fed Rhod/Nyasaland	19 Nov 62	Extradition	458UNTS59	106592
South Africa	Finland	15 Nov 48	Admin Cooperation	225UNTS59	103088
South Africa	Finland	24 Mar 54	Admin Cooperation	230UNTS121	103179
South Africa	Finland	05 Dec 56	Visas	258UNTS59	103670
South Africa	Finland	12 Jun 64	Water Transport	505UNTS107	107367
South Africa	France	18 Apr 47	Reparations	225UNTS35	103085
South Africa	France	05 May 54	Air Transport	215UNTS401	102926
South Africa	France	17 Sep 54	Air Transport	216UNTS29	102930
South Africa	France	22 Nov 54	Taxation	219UNTS35	102963
South Africa	France	06 Jan 64	Scientific Project	601UNTS229	108699
South Africa	France	27 Mar 68	Scientific Project	643UNTS343	109200
South Africa	Germany, West	28 Aug 51	General Economic	51WBGA216	424645
South Africa	Germany, West	05 Mar 56	Other Military	68WBGA205	424646
South Africa	Germany, West	28 Sep 56	Taxation	327UNTS83	104718
South Africa	Germany, West	11 Jun 62	Culture	64WGBB13	425647
South Africa	Greece	28 Jul 47	Reparations	185UNTS161	102467
South Africa	Greece	27 Jan 53	Mostfavored Nation	533UNTS303	107748
South Africa	Greece	11 Nov 64	Taxation	631UNTS319	109001
South Africa	Hungary	16 Nov 48	Admin Cooperation	225UNTS65	103089
South Africa	IBRD (World Bank)	23 Jan 51	IBRD Project	158UNTS135	102065
South Africa	IBRD (World Bank)	23 Jan 51	IBRD Project	158UNTS115	102064
South Africa	IBRD (World Bank)	28 Aug 53	IBRD Project	180UNTS91	102377
South Africa	IBRD (World Bank)	28 Aug 53	IBRD Project	180UNTS73	102376
South Africa	IBRD (World Bank)	28 Nov 55	IBRD Project	230UNTS101	103178
South Africa	IBRD (World Bank)	01 Oct 57	IBRD Project	280UNTS285	104065
South Africa	IBRD (World Bank)	02 Dec 58	IBRD Project	324UNTS3	104676
South Africa	IBRD (World Bank)	10 Jun 59	IBRD Project	340UNTS33	104857
South Africa	IBRD (World Bank)	01 Dec 61	IBRD Project	425UNTS197	106125

PARTY ONE	PARTY TWO	DATE	TOPIC	CITATION	NUMBER
South Africa	IBRD (World Bank)	01 Dec 61	IBRD Project	425UNTS215	106126
South Africa	IBRD (World Bank)	08 Sep 66	IBRD Project	585UNTS71	108483
South Africa	ICJ Option Clause	12 Sep 55	ICJ Option Clause	216UNTS115	102935
South Africa	Iran	11 Oct 71	Visas	0IRTB4	433009
South Africa	Ireland	01 May 58	Taxation	398UNTS3	105714
South Africa	Ireland	13 Apr 60	Postal Service	390UNTS307	105612
South Africa	Israel	24 Dec 52	Taxation	207UNTS303	102813
South Africa	Israel	05 May 53	Air Transport	192UNTS183	102600
South Africa	Israel	31 Dec 54	Postal Service	220UNTS11	102984
South Africa	Israel	01 Sep 56	Visas	251UNTS161	103539
South Africa	Israel	18 Sep 59	Extradition	373UNTS47	105314
South Africa	Italy	01 May 48	Admin Cooperation	225UNTS53	103087
South Africa	Italy	26 Jun 53	Taxation	211UNTS255	102857
South Africa	Italy	27 Aug 53	Other Military	212UNTS211	102873
South Africa	Italy	20 Dec 53	Postal Service	277UNTS293	104014
South Africa	Italy	21 May 56	Air Transport	255UNTS323	103616
South Africa	Japan	27 Mar 53	Admin Cooperation	173UNTS37	102258
South Africa	Japan	06 Apr 63	Postal Service	484UNTS319	107040
South Africa	Japan	21 Oct 68	Taxation	68JJS439	442220
South Africa	Lesotho	28 Sep 67	Air Transport	0UNTS0	110166
South Africa	Luxembourg	30 May 61	Visas	412UNTS203	105933
South Africa	Luxembourg	31 Jan 62	Air Transport	563UNTS153	108209
South Africa	Multilateral	27 Mar 41	Military Mission	67UNTS231	200222
South Africa	Multilateral	19 Apr 44	Scientific Project	89UNTS279	200257
South Africa	Multilateral	02 Aug 44	Scientific Project	67UNTS221	200221
South Africa	Multilateral	07 Dec 44	IGO Establishment	15UNTS295	200102
South Africa	Multilateral	07 Dec 44	Air Transport	84UNTS389	200252
South Africa	Multilateral	07 Dec 44	Air Transport	171UNTS345	200501
South Africa	Multilateral	15 Dec 44	Sanitation	17UNTS305	200110
South Africa	Multilateral	15 Dec 44	Sanitation	16UNTS247	200106
South Africa	Multilateral	16 Nov 45	IGO Establishment	4UNTS275	100052
South Africa	Multilateral	04 Dec 45	Telecommunications	9UNTS101	100128
South Africa	Multilateral	27 Dec 45	IGO Establishment	2UNTS39	100020
South Africa	Multilateral	14 Jan 46	Reparations	555UNTS69	108105
South Africa	Multilateral	23 Apr 46	Sanitation	17UNTS3	100265
South Africa	Multilateral	23 Apr 46	Sanitation	16UNTS179	100257
South Africa	Multilateral	22 Jul 46	IGO Establishment	9UNTS3	100125
South Africa	Multilateral	22 Jul 46	IGO Establishment	14UNTS185	100221
South Africa	Multilateral	27 Jul 46	Patents/Copyrights	90UNTS229	101238
South Africa	Multilateral	15 Oct 46	Refugees	11UNTS73	100150
South Africa	Multilateral	02 Dec 46	Specific Resources	161UNTS72	102124
South Africa	Multilateral	11 Dec 46	Sanitation	12UNTS179	100186
South Africa	Multilateral	08 Feb 47	Patents/Copyrights	14UNTS287	100222
South Africa	Multilateral	10 Feb 47	Peace/Disarmament	41UNTS135	100644
South Africa	Multilateral	10 Feb 47	Peace/Disarmament	49UNTS3	100747
South Africa	Multilateral	10 Feb 47	Peace/Disarmament	42UNTS3	100645
South Africa	Multilateral	10 Feb 47	Peace/Disarmament	48UNTS203	100746
South Africa	Multilateral	10 Feb 47	Peace/Disarmament	41UNTS21	100643
South Africa	Multilateral	03 Mar 47	Humanitarian	11UNTS43	100148
South Africa	Multilateral	02 Oct 47	Telecommunications	193UNTS188	102616
South Africa	Multilateral	11 Oct 47	IGO Establishment	77UNTS143	100998
South Africa	Multilateral	12 Nov 47	Admin Cooperation	53UNTS39	100771
South Africa	Multilateral	12 Nov 47	Admin Cooperation	53UNTS49	100772
South Africa	Multilateral	12 Nov 47	Admin Cooperation	46UNTS201	100710
South Africa	Multilateral	12 Nov 47	Admin Cooperation	53UNTS13	100770
South Africa	Multilateral	12 Nov 47	Admin Cooperation	46UNTS169	100709
South Africa	Multilateral	10 Jun 48	Humanitarian	164UNTS113	102163
South Africa	Multilateral	10 Jun 48	Humanitarian	191UNTS3	102576
South Africa	Multilateral	26 Jun 48	Culture	331UNTS217	104757
South Africa	Multilateral	24 Jul 48	Sanitation	66UNTS25	100847
South Africa	Multilateral	14 Sep 48	Milit Occupation	18UNTS267	100296
South Africa	Multilateral	19 Nov 48	Sanitation	44UNTS277	100688
South Africa	Multilateral	09 Dec 48	Scientific Project	20UNTS229	100318
South Africa	Multilateral	09 Dec 48	Scientific Project	73UNTS39	100942
South Africa	Multilateral	22 Feb 49	Sanitation	93UNTS129	101296

PARTY ONE	PARTY TWO	DATE	TOPIC	CITATION	NUMBER
South Africa	Multilateral	23 Mar 49	Commodity Trade	203UNTS179	102746
South Africa	Multilateral	04 May 49	Admin Cooperation	30UNTS23	100446
South Africa	Multilateral	04 May 49	Admin Cooperation	98UNTS101	101358
South Africa	Multilateral	04 May 49	Admin Cooperation	47UNTS159	100728
South Africa	Multilateral	04 May 49	Admin Cooperation	92UNTS19	101257
South Africa	Multilateral	04 May 49	Admin Cooperation	30UNTS3	100445
South Africa	Multilateral	12 Aug 49	IGO Establishment	87UNTS131	101169
South Africa	Multilateral	19 Sep 49	Land Transport	125UNTS3	101671
South Africa	Multilateral	16 Dec 49	Admin Cooperation	72UNTS3	100924
South Africa	Multilateral	21 Mar 50	Admin Cooperation	96UNTS271	101342
South Africa	Multilateral	07 Dec 50	Admin Cooperation	212UNTS17	102861
South Africa	Multilateral	25 May 51	Status of Forces	175UNTS215	102303
South Africa	Multilateral	10 Jul 51	Other Military	108UNTS287	101481
South Africa	Multilateral	29 Jul 51	Other Military	117UNTS85	101585
South Africa	Multilateral	08 Sep 51	Peace/Disarmament	136UNTS45	101832
South Africa	Multilateral	31 Oct 51	Other Military	172UNTS193	102247
South Africa	Multilateral	06 Dec 51	Admin Cooperation	150UNTS67	101963
South Africa	Multilateral	10 May 52	Taxation	439UNTS233	106332
South Africa	Multilateral	08 Jun 52	Other Military	210UNTS317	102843
South Africa	Multilateral	12 Jun 52	Dispute Settlement	138UNTS183	101869
South Africa	Multilateral	11 Jul 52	IGO Establishment	169UNTS3	102220
South Africa	Multilateral	11 Jul 52	Postal Service	170UNTS3	102221
South Africa	Multilateral	27 Feb 53	Claims and Debts	333UNTS3	104764
South Africa	Multilateral	11 May 53	Sanitation	456UNTS3	106555
South Africa	Multilateral	27 Aug 53	Other Military	213UNTS137	102884
South Africa	Multilateral	01 Oct 53	Commodity Trade	258UNTS153	103677
South Africa	Multilateral	26 Oct 53	Status of Forces	207UNTS237	102809
South Africa	Multilateral	07 Dec 53	Admin Cooperation	182UNTS51	102422
South Africa	Multilateral	11 Dec 53	Patents/Copyrights	218UNTS27	102952
South Africa	Multilateral	18 Jan 54	IGO Establishment	330UNTS121	104743
South Africa	Multilateral	19 Feb 54	Status of Forces	214UNTS51	102899
South Africa	Multilateral	22 Feb 54	Other Military	188UNTS273	102531
South Africa	Multilateral	14 Jun 54	Air Transport	320UNTS217	104644
South Africa	Multilateral	14 Jun 54	Air Transport	320UNTS209	104643
South Africa	Multilateral	29 Jul 54	Sanitation	249UNTS45	103500
South Africa	Multilateral	01 May 55	Admin Cooperation	0UNTS0	110416
South Africa	Multilateral	25 May 55	IGO Establishment	264UNTS117	103791
South Africa	Multilateral	21 Sep 55	Other Military	269UNTS241	103885
South Africa	Multilateral	05 Mar 56	Other Military	326UNTS169	104711
South Africa	Multilateral	05 Mar 56	Other Military	326UNTS181	104712
South Africa	Multilateral	25 Apr 56	Commodity Trade	270UNTS103	103896
South Africa	Multilateral	26 Oct 56	IGO Establishment	276UNTS3	103988
South Africa	Multilateral	03 Oct 57	Postal Service	364UNTS3	105211
South Africa	Multilateral	29 Apr 58	Specific Resources	559UNTS285	108164
South Africa	Multilateral	29 Apr 58	Territory Boundary	516UNTS205	107477
South Africa	Multilateral	29 Apr 58	Territory Boundary	499UNTS311	107302
South Africa	Multilateral	01 Dec 58	Commodity Trade	385UNTS137	105534
South Africa	Multilateral	06 Apr 59	Commodity Trade	349UNTS167	105013
South Africa	Multilateral	01 Dec 59	Territory Boundary	402UNTS71	105778
South Africa	Multilateral	26 Jan 60	IGO Establishment	439UNTS249	106333
South Africa	Multilateral	18 Apr 61	Consul/Citizenship	500UNTS95	107310
South Africa	Multilateral	21 Jun 61	IGO Establishment	514UNTS209	107449
South Africa	Multilateral	15 May 62	Commodity Trade	444UNTS3	106367
South Africa	Multilateral	14 Sep 62	Visas	443UNTS73	106360
South Africa	Multilateral	05 Aug 63	Sanitation	480UNTS43	106964
South Africa	Multilateral	30 Oct 63	Tech Assistance	480UNTS180	106968
South Africa	Multilateral	10 Jul 64	Postal Service	612UNTS3	108847
South Africa	Multilateral	10 Jul 64	Postal Service	611UNTS7	108844
South Africa	Multilateral	10 Jul 64	Postal Service	611UNTS105	108845
South Africa	Multilateral	20 Aug 64	Telecommunications	514UNTS25	107441
South Africa	Multilateral	01 Dec 64	Water Transport	550UNTS133	108012
South Africa	Multilateral	26 Feb 65	IGO Operations	556UNTS69	108119
South Africa	Multilateral	08 Jul 65	General Trade	597UNTS3	108641
South Africa	Multilateral	05 Apr 66	Water Transport	640UNTS133	109159
South Africa	Multilateral	14 May 66	Specific Resources	0UNTS0	109587

PARTY ONE	PARTY TWO	DATE	TOPIC	CITATION	NUMBER
South Africa	Multilateral	27 Jan 67	Scientific Project	610UNTS205	108843
South Africa	Multilateral	03 May 67	IGO Operations	0UNTS0	110764
South Africa	Multilateral	26 Jul 67	IGO Operations	614UNTS217	108872
South Africa	Multilateral	24 Dec 68	Commodity Trade	0UNTS0	109369
South Africa	Multilateral	12 Jan 70	Commodity Trade	0UNTS0	110603
South Africa	Netherlands	22 Jul 47	Air Transport	12UNTS257	100188
South Africa	Netherlands	31 May 51	Culture	188UNTS289	102533
South Africa	Netherlands	21 Jun 52	Visas	309UNTS123	104471
South Africa	Netherlands	22 Apr 54	Taxation	211UNTS215	102853
South Africa	Norway	19 Jun 51	Taxation	2NORT560	451170
South Africa	Norway	21 Sep 53	Air Transport	192UNTS105	102597
South Africa	Norway	17 Feb 56	Visas	230UNTS213	103186
South Africa	Norway	28 Mar 58	Air Transport	300UNTS83	104332
South Africa	Norway	30 Oct 59	Specific Property	346UNTS21	104975
South Africa	Norway	22 Jun 67	Scientific Project	643UNTS121	109888
South Africa	Portugal	07 May 63	Air Transport	499UNTS49	107292
South Africa	Romania	16 Nov 48	Admin Cooperation	225UNTS71	103090
South Africa	Spain	08 Feb 63	Mostfavored Nation	458UNTS79	106593
South Africa	Sweden	25 May 51	Taxation	197UNTS425	102649
South Africa	Sweden	26 Nov 52	Air Transport	52SOFM541	461176
South Africa	Sweden	09 Jan 53	Air Transport	173UNTS299	102271
South Africa	Sweden	28 Jul 55	Taxation	230UNTS287	103191
South Africa	Sweden	28 Mar 58	Air Transport	300UNTS95	104333
South Africa	Sweden	29 May 61	Taxation	442UNTS15	106335
South Africa	Switzerland	26 Aug 54	Air Transport	216UNTS19	102929
South Africa	Switzerland	07 Nov 55	Taxation	230UNTS279	103190
South Africa	Switzerland	07 Nov 55	Taxation	56SWR0655	462041
South Africa	Switzerland	19 Oct 59	Air Transport	559UNTS257	108162
South Africa	Switzerland	19 Oct 59	Air Transport	61SWR0907	462090
South Africa	Switzerland	03 Jul 67	Taxation	643UNTS3	109184
South Africa	UK Great Britain	26 Oct 45	Air Transport	72UNTS41	100927
South Africa	UK Great Britain	24 Aug 46	Telecommunications	51UNTS187	100765
South Africa	UK Great Britain	14 Oct 46	Taxation	86UNTS77	101153
South Africa	UK Great Britain	14 Oct 46	Taxation	86UNTS51	101152
South Africa	UK Great Britain	09 Oct 47	Finance	17UNTS239	100278
South Africa	UK Great Britain	06 Dec 48	Customs	118UNTS183	101607
South Africa	UK Great Britain	22 Feb 49	Territory Boundary	93UNTS75	101291
South Africa	UK Great Britain	12 Jun 50	Customs	93UNTS67	101290
South Africa	UK Great Britain	30 Jun 55	General Military	248UNTS191	103495
South Africa	UK Great Britain	18 Jun 59	Taxation	380UNTS103	105452
South Africa	UK Great Britain	18 Jun 59	Taxation	380UNTS81	105451
South Africa	UK Great Britain	18 Jun 59	Taxation	380UNTS59	105450
South Africa	UK Great Britain	28 May 62	Taxation	443UNTS79	106361
South Africa	UK Great Britain	22 Jun 64	Commodity Trade	515UNTS71	107454
South Africa	UK Great Britain	15 Nov 67	Consul/Citizenship	616UNTS277	108902
South Africa	UK Great Britain	21 Nov 68	Taxation	0UNTS0	110023
South Africa	USA (United States)	31 Oct 42	Milit Servic/Citiz	105UNTS269	200338
South Africa	USA (United States)	17 Apr 45	Direct Aid	90UNTS267	200264
South Africa	USA (United States)	17 Apr 45	Reparations	90UNTS275	200265
South Africa	USA (United States)	13 Dec 46	Taxation	167UNTS171	102207
South Africa	USA (United States)	21 Mar 47	Milit Assistance	16UNTS47	100248
South Africa	USA (United States)	10 Apr 47	Taxation	167UNTS211	102208
South Africa	USA (United States)	23 May 47	Air Transport	66UNTS233	100857
South Africa	USA (United States)	18 Dec 47	Extradition	148UNTS85	101938
South Africa	USA (United States)	16 Nov 49	Admin Cooperation	73UNTS97	100948
South Africa	USA (United States)	09 Nov 51	Milit Assistance	160UNTS41	102100
South Africa	USA (United States)	26 Mar 52	Education	165UNTS187	102176
South Africa	USA (United States)	24 Jun 52	Milit Assistance	177UNTS241	102322
South Africa	USA (United States)	22 Feb 55	Air Transport	247UNTS247	103473
South Africa	USA (United States)	03 Apr 56	Visas	249UNTS395	103513
South Africa	USA (United States)	08 Jul 57	Atomic Energy	290UNTS147	104234
South Africa	USA (United States)	13 Sep 60	Specific Property	388UNTS65	105572
South Pacific Com	United Nations	24 Jan 63	Tech Assistance	470UNTS361	200604
South Pacific Com	United Nations	20 Feb 63	Tech Assistance	453UNTS333	200600
Southern Rhodesia	Multilateral	04 Dec 45	Telecommunications	9UNTS101	100128

PARTY ONE	PARTY TWO	DATE	TOPIC	CITATION	NUMBER
Southern Rhodesia	Multilateral	02 Oct 47	Telecommunications	193UNTS188	102616
Southern Rhodesia	Multilateral	09 Dec 48	Scientific Project	73UNTS39	100942
Southern Rhodesia	Multilateral	22 Feb 49	Sanitation	93UNTS129	101296
Southern Rhodesia	Multilateral	12 Aug 49	IGO Establishment	87UNTS131	101169
Southern Rhodesia	Multilateral	02 Oct 54	IBRD Project	201UNTS171	102716
Southern Rhodesia	Multilateral	02 Oct 54	IBRD Project	201UNTS179	102717
Southern Rhodesia	Multilateral	30 Dec 63	IBRD Project	568UNTS243	108272
Southern Rhodesia	Multilateral	30 Dec 63	IBRD Project	568UNTS233	108271
Southern Rhodesia	Multilateral	30 Dec 63	IBRD Project	551UNTS105	108036
Southern Yemen	Accept UN Charter	30 Nov 67	UN Charter	614UNTS21	108861
Southern Yemen	Multilateral	10 Jul 64	Postal Service	611UNTS387	108846
Southern Yemen	Romania	17 Jun 68	General Trade	0UNTS0	110206
Southern Yemen	State/IGO Group	04 Apr 69	Direct Aid	0UNTS0	109455
Southern Yemen	State/IGO Group	04 Apr 69	Direct Aid	0UNTS0	109454
Southern Yemen	UN Special Fund	04 Apr 69	Direct Aid	0UNTS0	109456
Southern Yemen	UNICEF (Children)	26 Jul 69	IGO Operations	0UNTS0	109730
Spain	Accept UN Charter	23 Sep 55	UN Charter	223UNTS63	103053
Spain	Afghanistan	28 Oct 57	General Amity	58SPBO2507	460001
Spain	Argentina	01 Mar 47	Air Transport	47SPBO2004	460031
Spain	Argentina	18 Oct 48	Culture	48SPBO3110	460035
Spain	Argentina	18 Oct 48	Health/Educ/Welfare	48SPBO3110	460034
Spain	Argentina	18 Oct 48	Milit Servic/Citiz	48SPBO3110	460032
Spain	Argentina	18 Oct 48	Culture	48SPBO3110	460033
Spain	Argentina	22 Apr 60	Mass Media	61SPBO2109	460037
Spain	Argentina	08 Jul 60	Health/Educ/Welfare	60SPBO508	460036
Spain	Argentina	12 Oct 65	Visas	635UNTS221	109085
Spain	Argentina	10 Nov 65	Culture	0UNTS0	109559
Spain	Argentina	28 May 66	Non-ILO Labor	0UNTS0	109525
Spain	Argentina	28 Aug 69	Culture	0UNTS0	110194
Spain	Australia	27 Sep 61	Visas	426UNTS159	106135
Spain	Austria	21 Mar 56	Finance	56SPBO2404	460040
Spain	Austria	21 Mar 56	General Trade	56SPBO2404	460039
Spain	Austria	09 Nov 56	Visas	56ABGB241	403165
Spain	Austria	28 Mar 57	General Trade	57SPBO2004	460041
Spain	Austria	10 Jun 59	Visas	59ABGB223	403166
Spain	Austria	04 Aug 59	Culture	61ABGB256	403167
Spain	Austria	17 Jun 60	General Trade	390UNTS17	105600
Spain	Austria	19 Feb 62	Air Transport	62SPBO2910	460042
Spain	Austria	19 Feb 62	Air Transport	0UNTS0	109238
Spain	Austria	02 May 62	Non-ILO Labor	62SPBO606	460043
Spain	Austria	15 Jul 64	Non-ILO Labor	589UNTS169	108541
Spain	Austria	14 Oct 64	Non-ILO Labor	66ABGB9	403168
Spain	Austria	24 Mar 66	Land Transport	590UNTS203	108555
Spain	Austria	20 Dec 66	Taxation	636UNTS197	109103
Spain	Austria	23 Oct 69	Non-ILO Labor	70ABGB358	403169
Spain	Austria	09 Feb 70	Culture	70ABGB87	403170
Spain	Austria	14 May 70	Non-ILO Labor	70ABGB358	403171
Spain	Austria	14 Mar 72	Admin Cooperation	72ABGB249	403172
Spain	Belgium	24 Jan 47	Admin Cooperation	19UNTS3	100301
Spain	Belgium	04 Jan 52	Visas	121UNTS25	101622
Spain	Belgium	10 Mar 52	Air Transport	178UNTS243	102342
Spain	Belgium	27 Jan 55	General Economic	55SPBO2302	460044
Spain	Belgium	22 Jun 55	Finance	55SPBO908	460045
Spain	Belgium	30 Jan 56	General Economic	56SPBO803	460046
Spain	Belgium	25 Apr 56	Finance	56SPBO2405	460047
Spain	Belgium	30 Jul 56	Finance	56SPBO610	460048
Spain	Belgium	07 Aug 56	General Trade	56SPBO3108	460049
Spain	Belgium	28 Nov 56	Non-ILO Labor	58SPBO2605	460050
Spain	Belgium	28 Nov 56	Non-ILO Labor	308UNTS285	104465
Spain	Belgium	28 Nov 56	Non-ILO Labor	308UNTS239	104464
Spain	Belgium	28 Nov 56	Non-ILO Labor	58SPBO2705	460052
Spain	Belgium	28 Nov 56	Non-ILO Labor	58SPBO2705	460051
Spain	Belgium	26 Jul 57	Finance	57SPBO2208	460053
Spain	Belgium	10 Sep 57	Non-ILO Labor	58SPBO3005	460054
Spain	Belgium	27 Oct 58	Culture	327UNTS107	104720

PARTY ONE	PARTY TWO	DATE	TOPIC	CITATION	NUMBER
Spain	Belgium	27 May 59	Visas	340UNTS81	104860
Spain	Belgium	11 Sep 59	Visas	345UNTS29	104956
Spain	Belgium	19 Jul 66	Land Transport	575UNTS3	108352
Spain	Bolivia	12 Oct 61	Consul/Citizenship	64SPBO1406	460055
Spain	Brazil	28 Nov 49	Air Transport	215UNTS303	102923
Spain	Brazil	30 Dec 54	General Economic	55SPBO2201	460056
Spain	Brazil	30 Sep 57	General Economic	57SPBO1810	460057
Spain	Brazil	25 Jun 60	Culture	OUNTSO	109427
Spain	Brazil	25 Jun 60	Culture	65SPBO907	460058
Spain	Brazil	13 Oct 60	Visas	OUNTSO	109416
Spain	Brazil	27 Dec 60	Health/Educ/Welfare	64SPBO508	460060
Spain	Brazil	27 Dec 60	Health/Educ/Welfare	64SPBO508	460061
Spain	Brazil	27 Dec 60	Health/Educ/Welfare	64SPBO508	460059
Spain	Brazil	27 Dec 60	Visas	OUNTSO	109428
Spain	Brazil	11 Aug 64	Health/Educ/Welfare	OUNTSO	109417
Spain	Brazil	12 Aug 65	Visas	OUNTSO	109486
Spain	Canada	29 Jan 52	Claims and Debts	233UNTS117	103255
Spain	Canada	26 May 54	General Trade	391UNTS273	105632
Spain	Canada	18 Dec 59	Visas	470UNTS117	106802
Spain	Canada	08 Sep 64	Atomic Energy	65SPBO2505	460062
Spain	Ceylon (Sri Lanka)	22 Jul 55	General Trade	56SPBO2310	460063
Spain	Chile	09 Aug 50	General Economic	54SPBO1308	460073
Spain	Chile	24 May 58	Health/Educ/Welfare	58SPBO1411	460074
Spain	Chile	23 Jun 58	Health/Educ/Welfare	58SPBO1411	460075
Spain	Chile	07 Jun 61	Health/Educ/Welfare	65SPBO1911	460076
Spain	Colombia	11 Dec 51	Air Transport	216UNTS73	102933
Spain	Colombia	01 Apr 53	Culture	65SPBO1201	460064
Spain	Colombia	10 Nov 55	Telecommunications	56SPBO1704	460065
Spain	Costa Rica	09 Jan 53	General Amity	54SPBO303	460066
Spain	Costa Rica	08 Jun 64	Consul/Citizenship	65SPBO2506	460067
Spain	Cuba	19 Jun 51	Air Transport	53SPBO2504	460068
Spain	Cuba	18 Aug 53	General Economic	54SPBO408	460069
Spain	Cuba	06 Jul 54	General Economic	56SPBO1702	460070
Spain	Cuba	21 Jul 55	General Economic	55SPBO1508	460071
Spain	Cuba	14 Aug 56	General Economic	56SPBO609	460072
Spain	Denmark	12 Jul 50	Finance	71UNTS129	100913
Spain	Denmark	12 Jul 50	General Trade	71UNTS135	100914
Spain	Denmark	03 Jul 51	General Trade	101UNTS51	101401
Spain	Denmark	28 Jul 52	Commodity Trade	135UNTS255	101825
Spain	Denmark	01 Jul 57	General Trade	57SPBO1009	460078
Spain	Denmark	15 Jul 57	General Trade	57SPBO1009	460079
Spain	Denmark	05 May 65	Air Transport	543UNTS255	107905
Spain	Dominican Republic	10 Nov 52	General Amity	53SPBO309	460080
Spain	Dominican Republic	27 Jan 53	Culture	53SPBO112	460081
Spain	Dominican Republic	14 Jan 54	General Trade	54SPBO1808	460082
Spain	Dominican Republic	01 Feb 56	Health/Educ/Welfare	57SPBO2901	460083
Spain	Dominican Republic	01 May 67	Admin Cooperation	OUNTSO	110410
Spain	Dominican Republic	15 Mar 68	Consul/Citizenship	OUNTSO	110411
Spain	Ecuador	05 May 53	Culture	54SPBO3001	460084
Spain	Ecuador	12 Jul 54	General Trade	55SPBO1909	460085
Spain	Ecuador	12 Jul 54	Finance	55SPBO1909	460086
Spain	Ecuador	06 Dec 54	Culture	56SPBO706	460088
Spain	Ecuador	09 Jun 55	General Economic	55SPBO3009	460087
Spain	Ecuador	01 Apr 60	Non-ILO Labor	62SPBO2310	460089
Spain	Ecuador	04 Mar 64	Consul/Citizenship	65SPBO1301	460090
Spain	El Salvador	19 Feb 52	General Amity	52SPBO1611	460091
Spain	El Salvador	02 Dec 52	Finance	53SPBO511	460093
Spain	El Salvador	02 Dec 52	General Trade	53SPBO511	460092
Spain	El Salvador	06 Nov 53	Consul/Citizenship	54SPBO508	460094
Spain	Finland	21 May 56	Finance	56SPBO906	460100
Spain	Finland	21 May 56	General Trade	56SPBO906	460099
Spain	Finland	25 May 57	General Trade	57SPBO2007	460279
Spain	Finland	10 May 58	General Trade	58SPBO2405	460278
Spain	Finland	15 Nov 67	Taxation	OUNTSO	109375
Spain	France	29 Apr 48	Air Transport	48SPBO1605	460101

PARTY ONE	PARTY TWO	DATE	TOPIC	CITATION	NUMBER
Spain	France	23 Aug 48	Air Transport	28UNTS173	100425
Spain	France	24 Sep 52	Territory Boundary	54SPBO1230	460102
Spain	France	15 May 53	Admin Cooperation	55SPBO1508	460103
Spain	France	19 Nov 54	General Trade	55SPBO1301	460104
Spain	France	17 Dec 54	Mass Media	55SPBO2101	460105
Spain	France	17 Feb 55	Specific Resources	55SPBO1503	460106
Spain	France	15 Mar 55	General Trade	55SPBO304	460107
Spain	France	31 Mar 55	Mass Media	55SPBO105	460109
Spain	France	31 Mar 55	General Trade	55SPBO105	460108
Spain	France	13 May 55	Customs	55FRJO2408	416161
Spain	France	25 Nov 55	General Trade	56SPBO202	460110
Spain	France	28 Mar 56	General Trade	56SPBO2704	460111
Spain	France	02 Jun 56	Mass Media	56SPBO2406	460112
Spain	France	01 Dec 56	General Trade	57SPBO301	460113
Spain	France	17 May 57	General Trade	57SPBO606	460114
Spain	France	21 Jun 57	Patents/Copyrights	51FRJO1108	416162
Spain	France	25 Jun 57	Patents/Copyrights	58SPBO2203	460115
Spain	France	27 Jun 57	Non-ILO Labor	59SPBO3003	460276
Spain	France	27 Jun 57	Non-ILO Labor	57SPBO1409	460118
Spain	France	27 Jun 57	Non-ILO Labor	OUNTSO	110704
Spain	France	27 Jun 57	Non-ILO Labor	59SPBO3003	460116
Spain	France	27 Jun 57	Non-ILO Labor	59SPBO1104	460277
Spain	France	27 Jun 57	Non-ILO Labor	57SPBO1409	460117
Spain	France	19 Nov 57	General Economic	58SPBO301	460119
Spain	France	29 Nov 57	Non-ILO Labor	57SPBO3112	460120
Spain	France	04 Dec 57	General Trade	58SPBO301	460121
Spain	France	28 Mar 58	Non-ILO Labor	58SPBO1504	460122
Spain	France	28 Mar 58	Non-ILO Labor	58SPBO2204	460123
Spain	France	19 Apr 58	General Trade	58SPBO805	460124
Spain	France	14 Jul 59	Visas	60SPBO404	460128
Spain	France	14 Jul 59	Health/Educ/Welfare	60SPBO404	460127
Spain	France	14 Jul 59	Specific Resources	65SPBO202	460125
Spain	France	14 Jul 59	Sanitation	60SPBO305	460126
Spain	France	20 Oct 59	Non-ILO Labor	60SPBO2603	460129
Spain	France	11 Apr 60	Non-ILO Labor	60SPBO2007	460130
Spain	France	25 Jan 61	Non-ILO Labor	61SPBO2802	460131
Spain	France	25 Jan 61	Non-ILO Labor	62SPBO2103	460132
Spain	France	17 Apr 61	Admin Cooperation	61SPBO2505	460133
Spain	France	30 May 61	Customs	63SPBO1009	460134
Spain	France	15 Jun 61	Admin Cooperation	61FRRT42	415163
Spain	France	04 Oct 61	Non-ILO Labor	62SPBO401	460135
Spain	France	14 Dec 61	Non-ILO Labor	62SPBO1902	460136
Spain	France	14 Dec 61	Non-ILO Labor	62SPBO2002	460137
Spain	France	30 Mar 62	Admin Cooperation	62SPBO1711	460140
Spain	France	30 Mar 62	General Transport	62SPBO1911	460138
Spain	France	30 Mar 62	General Transport	62SPBO2311	460139
Spain	France	12 Apr 62	Non-ILO Labor	62SPBO3107	460141
Spain	France	30 May 62	Customs	63FRRT68	415164
Spain	France	17 Jul 62	Culture	66FRRT17	415165
Spain	France	02 Nov 62	Non-ILO Labor	63SPBO403	460142
Spain	France	23 Nov 62	Non-ILO Labor	63SPBO202	460143
Spain	France	08 Jan 63	Taxation	64SPBO701	460144
Spain	France	08 Jul 63	Non-ILO Labor	OUNTSO	110705
Spain	France	08 Jul 63	Non-ILO Labor	63SPBO1312	460145
Spain	France	29 Jul 63	Specific Resources	64SPBO108	460146
Spain	France	11 Oct 63	Non-ILO Labor	63SPBO1612	460147
Spain	France	15 Nov 63	Loans and Credits	64SPBO1403	460148
Spain	France	23 May 64	General Trade	64FRRT48	415166
Spain	France	04 Jun 64	Scientific Project	65SPBO1805	460149
Spain	France	03 Jul 64	Non-ILO Labor	64SPBO1509	460151
Spain	France	11 Jul 64	General Ad Hoc	67FRJO2502	416167
Spain	France	11 Jul 64	Specific Property	OUNTSO	110374
Spain	France	29 Aug 64	Non-ILO Labor	OUNTSO	110706
Spain	France	29 Aug 64	Non-ILO Labor	65SPBO1602	460152
Spain	France	29 Aug 64	Non-ILO Labor	64SPBO112	460153

PARTY ONE	PARTY TWO	DATE	TOPIC	CITATION	NUMBER
Spain	France	29 Aug 64	Non-ILO Labor	65SPBO302	460150
Spain	France	01 Jun 65	Non-ILO Labor	65SPBO2906	460154
Spain	France	07 Jul 65	Admin Cooperation	66FRRT16	415168
Spain	France	22 Jul 66	Admin Cooperation	67FRJO408	416169
Spain	France	20 Mar 67	Specific Resources	67FRJO408	416170
Spain	France	20 Mar 67	Specific Resources	0UNTS0	110234
Spain	France	03 May 67	Admin Cooperation	67FRJO1108	416171
Spain	France	15 Jun 67	Visas	67FRJO608	416172
Spain	France	20 Jun 67	Visas	67FRJO608	416173
Spain	France	15 Mar 68	Admin Cooperation	70FRJO2503	416174
Spain	France	02 Aug 68	Non-ILO Labor	69FRJO1809	416175
Spain	France	07 Feb 69	Culture	0UNTS0	110707
Spain	France	11 Mar 69	Specific Resources	69FRJO909	416176
Spain	France	09 Apr 69	Milit Servic/Citiz	0UNTS0	110709
Spain	France	09 Apr 69	Admin Cooperation	0UNTS0	110708
Spain	France	28 May 69	Admin Cooperation	0UNTS0	110710
Spain	France	30 May 69	Specific Resources	76FRJO9070	416177
Spain	France	17 Jun 69	General Ad Hoc	64FRJO1010	416178
Spain	France	28 Jul 69	Non-ILO Labor	0UNTS0	110711
Spain	Germany, West	25 Jan 52	Non-ILO Labor	53SPBO1616	460002
Spain	Germany, West	10 Dec 54	Culture	56SPBO2503	460003
Spain	Germany, West	16 May 55	General Trade	55SPBO2106	460006
Spain	Germany, West	16 May 55	Finance	55SPBO2106	460007
Spain	Germany, West	03 May 56	Mass Media	56SPBO706	460004
Spain	Germany, West	03 May 56	Mass Media	56SPBO706	460005
Spain	Germany, West	18 May 56	Finance	56SPBO307	460009
Spain	Germany, West	18 May 56	General Trade	56SPBO307	460008
Spain	Germany, West	27 May 57	General Trade	57SPBO1007	460010
Spain	Germany, West	08 Apr 58	Finance	59SPBO2606	460018
Spain	Germany, West	08 Apr 58	Claims and Debts	59SPBO2606	460011
Spain	Germany, West	08 Apr 58	Patents/Copyrights	59SPBO2606	460020
Spain	Germany, West	08 Apr 58	Finance	59SPBO2606	460013
Spain	Germany, West	08 Apr 58	Finance	59SPBO2606	460017
Spain	Germany, West	08 Apr 58	Finance	59SPBO2606	460012
Spain	Germany, West	08 Apr 58	Finance	59SPBO2606	460019
Spain	Germany, West	08 Apr 58	Finance	59SPBO2606	460015
Spain	Germany, West	08 Apr 58	Patents/Copyrights	59SPBO2606	460016
Spain	Germany, West	08 Apr 58	Specif Goods/Equip	59SPBO2606	460014
Spain	Germany, West	29 Oct 59	Non-ILO Labor	61SPBO1110	460022
Spain	Germany, West	29 Oct 59	Non-ILO Labor	61SPBO1110	460021
Spain	Germany, West	29 Oct 59	Non-ILO Labor	61SPBO1110	460023
Spain	Germany, West	29 Oct 59	Non-ILO Labor	61SPBO2312	460024
Spain	Germany, West	29 Mar 60	Non-ILO Labor	60SPBO505	460025
Spain	Germany, West	28 Apr 60	Air Transport	465UNTS3	106720
Spain	Germany, West	24 Oct 60	Non-ILO Labor	61SPBO710	460026
Spain	Germany, West	09 May 61	General Economic	61SPBO2905	460027
Spain	Germany, West	29 May 62	Humanitarian	65SPBO706	460028
Spain	Germany, West	27 Apr 63	Scientific Project	63SPBO2205	460029
Spain	Germany, West	15 May 64	Non-ILO Labor	65SPBO1907	460030
Spain	Greece	03 Feb 53	Claims and Debts	225UNTS3	103081
Spain	Greece	15 May 54	General Trade	299UNTS261	104318
Spain	Greece	15 May 54	Finance	299UNTS277	104319
Spain	Greece	01 Jun 55	General Trade	56SPBO2701	460155
Spain	Greece	14 May 56	General Trade	56SPBO1406	460156
Spain	Greece	08 May 57	General Trade	57SPBO3005	460157
Spain	Guatemala	31 Dec 55	General Trade	56SPBO2801	460158
Spain	Guatemala	28 Jul 61	Consul/Citizenship	62SPBO1003	460159
Spain	Guatemala	27 Apr 64	Culture	65SPBO2506	460160
Spain	Honduras	12 Jun 57	Culture	63SPBO1105	460161
Spain	IAEA (Atom Energy)	23 Jun 67	IGO Operations	614UNTS169	108870
Spain	IBRD (World Bank)	25 Oct 63	IBRD Project	491UNTS297	107181
Spain	IBRD (World Bank)	31 Jul 64	IBRD Project	537UNTS81	107798
Spain	IBRD (World Bank)	29 Sep 65	IBRD Project	568UNTS49	108264
Spain	IBRD (World Bank)	04 Aug 67	IBRD Project	619UNTS209	108944
Spain	IBRD (World Bank)	17 Jul 69	IBRD Project	0UNTS0	110489

PARTY ONE	PARTY TWO	DATE	TOPIC	CITATION	NUMBER
Spain	Iceland	21 Dec 54	General Trade	55SPBO401	460165
Spain	Iceland	31 Dec 55	General Trade	56SPBO2701	460166
Spain	Iceland	13 Feb 57	General Trade	57SPBO103	460167
Spain	Iran	12 Mar 56	General Amity	57SPBO1912	460162
Spain	Iran	12 Mar 56	Culture	0IRTB21	433033
Spain	Iran	20 Sep 67	Visas	0IRTB21	433034
Spain	Iraq	03 Sep 51	General Amity	55SPBO101	460163
Spain	Iraq	14 Feb 55	Culture	57SPBO1502	460164
Spain	Ireland	11 May 50	Scientific Project	553UNTS147	108081
Spain	Ireland	19 Dec 51	General Trade	0UNTS0	109228
Spain	Ireland	17 Apr 59	Visas	553UNTS157	108082
Spain	Italy	20 Jun 47	General Trade	47SPBO2008	460168
Spain	Italy	31 May 49	Air Transport	231UNTS251	103224
Spain	Italy	20 Apr 55	Mass Media	55SPBO505	460169
Spain	Italy	16 Jun 55	General Trade	55SPBO2908	460170
Spain	Italy	11 Aug 55	Culture	267UNTS125	103839
Spain	Italy	13 Apr 56	General Trade	56SPBO3004	460171
Spain	Italy	16 Apr 56	Mass Media	57SPBO102	460172
Spain	Italy	21 Jul 56	Non-ILO Labor	58SPBO1503	460173
Spain	Italy	05 Sep 56	Mass Media	302UNTS195	104359
Spain	Italy	12 Oct 57	Patents/Copyrights	291UNTS229	104258
Spain	Italy	25 Nov 57	Non-ILO Labor	378UNTS289	105428
Spain	Italy	25 Nov 57	Non-ILO Labor	59SPBO1601	460174
Spain	Italy	28 Mar 58	Non-ILO Labor	58SPBO2605	460175
Spain	Italy	08 May 58	General Trade	56SPBO406	460176
Spain	Italy	08 May 58	Finance	58ITGU237	435352
Spain	Italy	28 Aug 58	Customs	60ITDI282	436353
Spain	Italy	14 Mar 59	Non-ILO Labor	59SPBO904	460177
Spain	Italy	28 Jun 60	General Trade	62ITDI370	436354
Spain	Italy	28 Jun 61	Taxation	66ITGU159	435355
Spain	Japan	24 Dec 55	General Trade	56SPBO801	460178
Spain	Japan	21 Dec 56	General Military	57JAIL88	440068
Spain	Japan	08 Jan 57	Claims and Debts	318UNTS221	104615
Spain	Japan	16 Mar 65	Visas	0JGJI1572	441132
Spain	Japan	22 Feb 66	General Trade	66JJS257	442169
Spain	Jordan	07 Oct 50	General Amity	51SPBO1710	460179
Spain	Lebanon	07 Mar 49	Culture	49SPBO1812	460180
Spain	Lebanon	06 May 50	General Amity	51SPBO607	460181
Spain	Liberia	02 Apr 53	General Amity	53SPBO912	460182
Spain	Liberia	26 May 54	General Trade	56SPBO2603	460183
Spain	Libya	05 May 59	Culture	62SPBO2307	460184
Spain	Luxembourg	26 Mar 62	Air Transport	563UNTS205	108211
Spain	Luxembourg	22 Jun 63	Non-ILO Labor	65SPBO1509	460186
Spain	Luxembourg	22 Jun 63	Non-ILO Labor	65SPBO2408	460185
Spain	Mauritania	11 May 65	Air Transport	602UNTS111	108709
Spain	Morocco	07 Apr 56	Recognition	57SPBO403	460189
Spain	Morocco	07 Apr 56	Recognition	57SPBO403	460188
Spain	Morocco	07 Apr 56	Recognition	57SPBO403	460187
Spain	Morocco	11 Feb 57	Admin Cooperation	57SPBO403	460191
Spain	Morocco	11 Feb 57	General Amity	57SPBO403	460190
Spain	Morocco	04 Jun 57	General Trade	57SPBO1706	460192
Spain	Morocco	07 Jul 57	Finance	57SPBO709	460194
Spain	Morocco	07 Jul 57	Commodity Trade	57SPBO709	460197
Spain	Morocco	07 Jul 57	General Trade	57SPBO709	460195
Spain	Morocco	07 Jul 57	Tech Assistance	58SPBO502	460200
Spain	Morocco	07 Jul 57	General Trade	57SPBO709	460196
Spain	Morocco	07 Jul 57	Specific Resources	57SPBO709	460198
Spain	Morocco	07 Jul 57	Finance	57SPBO709	460193
Spain	Morocco	07 Jul 57	Culture	58SPBO402	460199
Spain	Multilateral	27 Mar 41	Military Mission	67UNTS231	200222
Spain	Multilateral	07 Dec 44	Air Transport	171UNTS345	200501
Spain	Multilateral	07 Dec 44	IGO Establishment	15UNTS295	200102
Spain	Multilateral	07 Dec 44	Air Transport	84UNTS389	200252
Spain	Multilateral	05 Apr 46	Specific Resources	231UNTS199	103221
Spain	Multilateral	11 Dec 46	Sanitation	12UNTS179	100186

PARTY ONE	PARTY TWO	DATE	TOPIC	CITATION	NUMBER
Spain	Multilateral	08 Feb 47	Patents/Copyrights	14UNTS287	100222
Spain	Multilateral	06 Mar 48	Water Transport	289UNTS3	104214
Spain	Multilateral	10 May 48	Reparations	140UNTS129	101887
Spain	Multilateral	10 Jun 48	Humanitarian	164UNTS113	102163
Spain	Multilateral	26 Jun 48	Culture	331UNTS217	104757
Spain	Multilateral	24 Jul 48	Sanitation	66UNTS25	100847
Spain	Multilateral	08 Feb 49	Specific Resources	157UNTS157	102053
Spain	Multilateral	23 Mar 49	Commodity Trade	203UNTS179	102746
Spain	Multilateral	12 Aug 49	Humanitarian	75UNTS287	100973
Spain	Multilateral	12 Aug 49	General Military	75UNTS135	100972
Spain	Multilateral	12 Aug 49	Humanitarian	75UNTS85	100971
Spain	Multilateral	12 Aug 49	Humanitarian	75UNTS31	100970
Spain	Multilateral	24 Sep 49	IGO Establishment	126UNTS237	101691
Spain	Multilateral	16 Dec 49	Admin Cooperation	72UNTS3	100924
Spain	Multilateral	21 Mar 50	Admin Cooperation	96UNTS271	101342
Spain	Multilateral	13 May 50	Land Transport	128UNTS171	101719
Spain	Multilateral	16 Sep 50	General Transport	92UNTS91	101264
Spain	Multilateral	18 Oct 50	Specific Resources	638UNTS185	109134
Spain	Multilateral	22 Nov 50	Culture	131UNTS25	101734
Spain	Multilateral	15 Dec 50	Customs	157UNTS129	102052
Spain	Multilateral	25 May 51	Status of Forces	175UNTS215	102303
Spain	Multilateral	09 Oct 51	IGO Establishment	220UNTS121	102997
Spain	Multilateral	06 Dec 51	Admin Cooperation	150UNTS67	101963
Spain	Multilateral	10 Jan 52	Visas	163UNTS27	102139
Spain	Multilateral	10 May 52	Admin Cooperation	439UNTS217	106331
Spain	Multilateral	10 May 52	Taxation	439UNTS233	106332
Spain	Multilateral	10 May 52	Admin Cooperation	439UNTS193	106330
Spain	Multilateral	20 May 52	Sanitation	219UNTS55	102966
Spain	Multilateral	11 Jul 52	Postal Service	171UNTS3	102224
Spain	Multilateral	11 Jul 52	Postal Service	170UNTS63	102222
Spain	Multilateral	11 Jul 52	Postal Service	171UNTS191	102227
Spain	Multilateral	11 Jul 52	Postal Service	171UNTS89	102225
Spain	Multilateral	11 Jul 52	Postal Service	171UNTS143	102226
Spain	Multilateral	11 Jul 52	IGO Establishment	169UNTS3	102220
Spain	Multilateral	11 Jul 52	Postal Service	170UNTS269	102223
Spain	Multilateral	11 Jul 52	Postal Service	170UNTS3	102221
Spain	Multilateral	06 Sep 52	Patents/Copyrights	216UNTS132	102937
Spain	Multilateral	07 Oct 52	Admin Cooperation	310UNTS181	104493
Spain	Multilateral	07 Nov 52	General Trade	221UNTS255	103010
Spain	Multilateral	10 Nov 52	Admin Cooperation	214UNTS265	102904
Spain	Multilateral	27 Feb 53	Claims and Debts	333UNTS3	104764
Spain	Multilateral	11 May 53	Sanitation	456UNTS3	106555
Spain	Multilateral	01 Jul 53	IGO Establishment	200UNTS149	102701
Spain	Multilateral	17 Oct 53	General Transport	184UNTS42	102438
Spain	Multilateral	11 Dec 53	Patents/Copyrights	218UNTS27	102952
Spain	Multilateral	11 Dec 53	Education	218UNTS125	102954
Spain	Multilateral	01 Mar 54	Commodity Trade	256UNTS31	103622
Spain	Multilateral	01 Mar 54	Admin Cooperation	286UNTS265	104173
Spain	Multilateral	12 May 54	Admin Cooperation	327UNTS3	104714
Spain	Multilateral	14 May 54	Culture	249UNTS215	103511
Spain	Multilateral	04 Jun 54	Customs	276UNTS191	103992
Spain	Multilateral	04 Jun 54	Customs	282UNTS249	104101
Spain	Multilateral	14 Jun 54	Air Transport	320UNTS209	104643
Spain	Multilateral	14 Jun 54	Air Transport	320UNTS217	104644
Spain	Multilateral	19 Dec 54	Culture	218UNTS139	102955
Spain	Multilateral	01 May 55	Admin Cooperation	0UNTS0	110416
Spain	Multilateral	25 May 55	IGO Establishment	264UNTS117	103791
Spain	Multilateral	12 Oct 55	IGO Establishment	560UNTS3	108165
Spain	Multilateral	20 Oct 55	IGO Establishment	378UNTS159	105425
Spain	Multilateral	04 Jan 56	Scientific Project	256UNTS171	103627
Spain	Multilateral	01 Mar 56	Customs	343UNTS129	104923
Spain	Multilateral	25 Apr 56	Commodity Trade	270UNTS103	103896
Spain	Multilateral	30 Apr 56	Air Transport	310UNTS229	104494
Spain	Multilateral	18 May 56	Customs	338UNTS103	104834
Spain	Multilateral	18 May 56	Customs	327UNTS123	104721

PARTY ONE	PARTY TWO	DATE	TOPIC	CITATION	NUMBER
Spain	Multilateral	18 May 56	Customs	319UNTS21	104630
Spain	Multilateral	09 Jul 56	Non-ILO Labor	314UNTS3	104539
Spain	Multilateral	24 Oct 56	Admin Cooperation	510UNTS161	107412
Spain	Multilateral	26 Oct 56	IGO Establishment	276UNTS3	103988
Spain	Multilateral	29 Oct 56	Territory Boundary	263UNTS165	103772
Spain	Multilateral	15 Jun 57	Patents/Copyrights	583UNTS3	108470
Spain	Multilateral	15 Jun 57	General Trade	550UNTS45	108008
Spain	Multilateral	01 Jul 57	Culture	0UNTS0	110418
Spain	Multilateral	03 Oct 57	Postal Service	366UNTS193	105218
Spain	Multilateral	03 Oct 57	Postal Service	366UNTS141	105217
Spain	Multilateral	03 Oct 57	Postal Service	366UNTS87	105216
Spain	Multilateral	03 Oct 57	Postal Service	364UNTS3	105211
Spain	Multilateral	03 Oct 57	Postal Service	366UNTS255	105219
Spain	Multilateral	03 Oct 57	Postal Service	364UNTS331	105212
Spain	Multilateral	03 Oct 57	Postal Service	365UNTS207	105214
Spain	Multilateral	03 Oct 57	Postal Service	366UNTS3	105215
Spain	Multilateral	03 Oct 57	Postal Service	365UNTS3	105213
Spain	Multilateral	13 Dec 57	Land Transport	372UNTS159	105296
Spain	Multilateral	20 Mar 58	Admin Cooperation	335UNTS211	104789
Spain	Multilateral	31 Mar 58	Specific Property	320UNTS103	104639
Spain	Multilateral	03 Apr 58	Commodity Trade	336UNTS177	104806
Spain	Multilateral	03 Apr 58	Commodity Trade	302UNTS121	104355
Spain	Multilateral	03 Dec 58	Admin Cooperation	398UNTS9	105715
Spain	Multilateral	03 Dec 58	Admin Cooperation	416UNTS51	105995
Spain	Multilateral	15 Jan 59	Customs	348UNTS13	104996
Spain	Multilateral	24 Jan 59	IGO Establishment	486UNTS157	107078
Spain	Multilateral	06 Apr 59	Commodity Trade	349UNTS167	105013
Spain	Multilateral	19 Nov 59	IGO Operations	410UNTS156	105902
Spain	Multilateral	26 Jan 60	IGO Establishment	439UNTS249	106333
Spain	Multilateral	22 Apr 60	Air Transport	418UNTS211	106023
Spain	Multilateral	17 Jun 60	Humanitarian	536UNTS27	107794
Spain	Multilateral	28 Jul 60	IGO Establishment	485UNTS3	107042
Spain	Multilateral	01 Sep 60	Commodity Trade	403UNTS3	105792
Spain	Multilateral	06 Oct 60	Customs	473UNTS131	106861
Spain	Multilateral	01 Dec 60	Scientific Project	414UNTS110	105970
Spain	Multilateral	30 Mar 61	Sanitation	520UNTS151	107515
Spain	Multilateral	21 Apr 61	IGO Establishment	484UNTS349	107041
Spain	Multilateral	08 Jun 61	Customs	473UNTS187	106863
Spain	Multilateral	08 Jun 61	Customs	473UNTS153	106862
Spain	Multilateral	21 Jun 61	IGO Establishment	514UNTS209	107449
Spain	Multilateral	26 Oct 61	Patents/Copyrights	496UNTS43	107247
Spain	Multilateral	06 Dec 61	Customs	473UNTS219	106864
Spain	Multilateral	15 May 62	Commodity Trade	444UNTS3	106367
Spain	Multilateral	14 Jun 62	IGO Establishment	528UNTS33	107634
Spain	Multilateral	28 Sep 62	IGO Establishment	469UNTS169	106791
Spain	Multilateral	10 Dec 62	Culture	521UNTS231	107525
Spain	Multilateral	20 Apr 63	IGO Establishment	495UNTS3	107239
Spain	Multilateral	19 Jun 63	Visas	482UNTS19	106988
Spain	Multilateral	05 Aug 63	Sanitation	480UNTS43	106964
Spain	Multilateral	09 Nov 63	Direct Aid	489UNTS209	107141
Spain	Multilateral	09 Mar 64	Specific Resources	581UNTS57	108432
Spain	Multilateral	09 Mar 64	Specific Resources	581UNTS89	108434
Spain	Multilateral	10 Jul 64	Postal Service	613UNTS193	108852
Spain	Multilateral	10 Jul 64	Postal Service	611UNTS105	108845
Spain	Multilateral	10 Jul 64	Postal Service	612UNTS361	108849
Spain	Multilateral	10 Jul 64	Postal Service	612UNTS233	108848
Spain	Multilateral	10 Jul 64	Postal Service	611UNTS7	108844
Spain	Multilateral	10 Jul 64	Postal Service	613UNTS127	108853
Spain	Multilateral	10 Jul 64	Postal Service	613UNTS3	108851
Spain	Multilateral	10 Jul 64	Postal Service	612UNTS3	108847
Spain	Multilateral	10 Jul 64	Postal Service	611UNTS387	108846
Spain	Multilateral	10 Jul 64	Postal Service	613UNTS3	108850
Spain	Multilateral	20 Aug 64	Telecommunications	514UNTS25	107441
Spain	Multilateral	12 Sep 64	Specific Resources	0UNTS0	109344
Spain	Multilateral	15 Sep 64	General Trade	510UNTS147	107411

PARTY ONE	PARTY TWO	DATE	TOPIC	CITATION	NUMBER
Spain	Multilateral	01 Dec 64	Water Transport	550UNTS133	108012
Spain	Multilateral	08 Jul 65	General Trade	597UNTS3	108641
Spain	Multilateral	31 Dec 65	Specific Resources	616UNTS317	108904
Spain	Multilateral	17 Jan 66	IGO Establishment	592UNTS101	108573
Spain	Multilateral	05 Apr 66	Water Transport	640UNTS133	109159
Spain	Multilateral	14 May 66	Specific Resources	0UNTS0	109587
Spain	Multilateral	21 Jun 66	Non-ILO Labor	0UNTS0	109298
Spain	Multilateral	23 Jun 67	IGO Operations	614UNTS185	108871
Spain	Multilateral	28 Jun 67	ILO Labor	0UNTS0	110355
Spain	Multilateral	10 Jul 67	Air Transport	0UNTS0	109971
Spain	Multilateral	18 Mar 68	Commodity Trade	0UNTS0	109262
Spain	Netherlands	13 Jul 46	Air Transport	4UNTS351	100055
Spain	Netherlands	21 Oct 46	General Trade	46SPBO3010	460207
Spain	Netherlands	21 Oct 46	Finance	46SPBO3010	460208
Spain	Netherlands	22 Oct 47	Air Transport	48SPBO1108	460209
Spain	Netherlands	08 Oct 48	Air Transport	28UNTS209	100426
Spain	Netherlands	20 Jun 50	Air Transport	95UNTS303	101327
Spain	Netherlands	08 Dec 53	General Trade	53NET134	447043
Spain	Netherlands	12 Jul 55	Finance	55SPBO2908	460211
Spain	Netherlands	12 Jul 55	General Trade	55SPBO2908	460210
Spain	Netherlands	27 May 59	Visas	458UNTS165	106599
Spain	Netherlands	08 Apr 61	Non-ILO Labor	482UNTS193	106996
Spain	Netherlands	17 Dec 62	Health/Educ/Welfare	499UNTS227	107301
Spain	Netherlands	16 Apr 64	Non-ILO Labor	64SPBO1306	460212
Spain	Netherlands	10 Feb 65	Visas	545UNTS3	107922
Spain	New Zealand	02 Oct 61	Visas	453UNTS11	106516
Spain	Nicaragua	25 Jul 61	Consul/Citizenship	62SPBO205	460201
Spain	Norway	31 Dec 54	General Trade	55SPBO2101	460202
Spain	Norway	25 Jun 55	General Trade	55SPBO2607	460203
Spain	Norway	17 Jul 56	General Trade	56SPBO808	460204
Spain	Norway	21 Dec 56	Patents/Copyrights	56SPBO803	460205
Spain	Norway	21 Dec 56	Patents/Copyrights	3NORT705	451143
Spain	Norway	22 Jul 57	General Trade	57SPBO808	460206
Spain	Norway	22 May 59	Visas	3NORT771	451144
Spain	Norway	19 Aug 59	Culture	376UNTS145	105379
Spain	Norway	16 Mar 60	Claims and Debts	3NORT801	451145
Spain	Norway	17 May 60	General Trade	3NORT805	451146
Spain	Norway	25 Apr 63	Taxation	503UNTS41	107340
Spain	Norway	05 May 65	Air Transport	3NORT941	451147
Spain	Norway	03 Jun 65	Patents/Copyrights	3NORT943	451148
Spain	OECD (Econ Coop)	10 Jan 58	IGO Operations	58SPBO1207	460274
Spain	Pakistan	08 Jul 57	General Amity	59SPBO1706	460213
Spain	Panama	18 Mar 53	General Amity	54SPBO607	460214
Spain	Paraguay	12 Oct 49	General Amity	51SPBO908	460215
Spain	Paraguay	25 Aug 50	General Economic	52SPBO1211	460216
Spain	Paraguay	26 Mar 57	Culture	58SPBO2904	460217
Spain	Paraguay	11 Aug 58	Commodity Trade	59SPBO1007	460218
Spain	Paraguay	25 Jun 59	Non-ILO Labor	60SPBO1804	460219
Spain	Paraguay	25 Jun 59	Consul/Citizenship	60SPBO1904	460222
Spain	Paraguay	25 Jun 59	Water Transport	60SPBO1904	460223
Spain	Paraguay	25 Jun 59	General Trade	60SPBO1804	460220
Spain	Paraguay	25 Jun 59	General Trade	60SPBO1804	460221
Spain	Paraguay	21 May 63	Specif Goods/Equip	65SPBO2207	460224
Spain	Paraguay	13 Nov 64	Specif Goods/Equip	65SPBO1108	460225
Spain	Peru	23 May 53	General Trade	54SPBO1810	460226
Spain	Peru	31 Mar 54	Air Transport	232UNTS65	103230
Spain	Peru	16 May 59	Consul/Citizenship	60SPBO1904	460227
Spain	Philippines	27 Sep 47	General Amity	70UNTS133	100902
Spain	Philippines	20 May 48	Consul/Citizenship	70UNTS143	100903
Spain	Philippines	22 Dec 48	Dispute Settlement	2PTS93	465016
Spain	Philippines	04 Mar 49	Culture	49SPBO1812	460097
Spain	Philippines	04 Mar 49	Culture	49SPBO1306	460096
Spain	Philippines	06 Oct 51	Air Transport	215UNTS193	102920
Spain	Philippines	06 Oct 51	Postal Service	54SPBO2101	460098
Spain	Philippines	04 Jul 62	Visas	490UNTS243	107158

PARTY ONE	PARTY TWO	DATE	TOPIC	CITATION	NUMBER
Spain	Portugal	31 Mar 47	Air Transport	47SPBO1107	460228
Spain	Portugal	21 Feb 55	General Economic	55SPBO2803	460229
Spain	Portugal	28 Feb 56	Sanitation	57SPBO802	460230
Spain	Portugal	21 Jan 57	Customs	57SPBO209	460231
Spain	Portugal	20 Oct 59	Sanitation	61SPBO1107	460232
Spain	Portugal	17 Feb 60	Customs	60SPBO312	460233
Spain	Portugal	20 Jan 62	Non-ILO Labor	62SPBO1809	460234
Spain	Portugal	27 Feb 63	Non-ILO Labor	63SPBO3010	460235
Spain	Portugal	27 Aug 63	Non-ILO Labor	63SPBO3010	460236
Spain	Romania	05 Jan 67	Consul/Citizenship	642UNTS103	109168
Spain	Saudi Arabia	09 Jan 61	General Amity	62SPBO606	460038
Spain	South Africa	08 Feb 63	Mostfavored Nation	458UNTS79	106593
Spain	State/IGO Group	03 May 69	Tech Assistance	0UNTS0	109534
Spain	Sweden	26 Jan 46	General Economic	46SOFM169	461020
Spain	Sweden	03 Oct 46	General Trade	46SOFM257	461033
Spain	Sweden	17 Jul 47	General Economic	47SOFM667	461070
Spain	Sweden	17 Jul 47	General Trade	47SPBO1008	460244
Spain	Sweden	18 Feb 50	Air Transport	166UNTS15	102184
Spain	Sweden	12 Oct 50	Scientific Project	197UNTS305	102644
Spain	Sweden	24 Jan 51	General Economic	51SOFM18	461133
Spain	Sweden	10 Jul 51	General Trade	51SOFM307	461148
Spain	Sweden	14 Jul 52	General Economic	52SOFM303	461169
Spain	Sweden	11 Jun 55	General Economic	55SPBO1108	460245
Spain	Sweden	11 Apr 56	General Economic	56SPBO705	460246
Spain	Sweden	05 Nov 58	General Economic	58SPBO1612	460247
Spain	Sweden	25 Apr 63	Taxation	64SPBO1801	460249
Spain	Sweden	25 Apr 63	Taxation	64SPBO1601	460248
Spain	Sweden	05 May 65	Air Transport	0UNTS0	109239
Spain	Switzerland	17 Jul 46	Air Transport	47SPBO2004	460250
Spain	Switzerland	03 Aug 50	Air Transport	254UNTS365	103600
Spain	Switzerland	27 Nov 54	General Economic	55SPBO1001	460251
Spain	Switzerland	21 Sep 59	Non-ILO Labor	60SPBO1406	460252
Spain	Switzerland	21 Nov 59	General Trade	59SWRO2095	462131
Spain	Switzerland	25 Jan 60	Non-ILO Labor	60SPBO2707	460253
Spain	Switzerland	02 Apr 60	General Trade	60SWRO457	462132
Spain	Switzerland	02 Mar 61	Non-ILO Labor	61SPBO912	460254
Spain	Switzerland	23 Jan 63	Land Transport	63SPBO1109	460255
Spain	Switzerland	27 Nov 63	Taxation	64SWRO953	462047
Spain	Switzerland	27 Nov 63	Taxation	65SPBO1201	460256
Spain	Syria	18 Apr 52	Culture	53SPBO2401	460243
Spain	Syria	18 Apr 52	General Amity	53SPBO2401	460242
Spain	Taiwan	19 Feb 53	General Amity	181UNTS81	102400
Spain	Taiwan	03 Dec 56	General Trade	56SPBO1512	460077
Spain	Taiwan	07 Feb 57	Culture	314UNTS161	104547
Spain	Taiwan	07 Feb 57	Culture	0CTRC439	413025
Spain	Turkey	08 Sep 47	Finance	48TURG902	466085
Spain	Turkey	19 Jun 51	General Economic	52TURG2805	466086
Spain	Turkey	23 Jan 54	Commodity Trade	55TURG204	466087
Spain	Turkey	28 Mar 56	Culture	58SPBO908	460257
Spain	Turkey	16 Apr 59	General Amity	61SPBO803	460258
Spain	UK Great Britain	30 Oct 44	Air Transport	47SPBO2004	460237
Spain	UK Great Britain	28 Mar 47	Finance	66UNTS91	100849
Spain	UK Great Britain	23 Jun 48	General Economic	66UNTS193	100854
Spain	UK Great Britain	15 Dec 48	Finance	87UNTS49	101165
Spain	UK Great Britain	20 Jul 50	Air Transport	398UNTS101	105719
Spain	UK Great Britain	20 Dec 51	Finance	123UNTS187	101660
Spain	UK Great Britain	21 Dec 54	General Trade	55SPBO301	460238
Spain	UK Great Britain	01 Jul 55	General Economic	55SPBO608	460239
Spain	UK Great Britain	21 Dec 56	General Trade	57SPBO1601	460240
Spain	UK Great Britain	19 Feb 58	General Trade	58SPBO803	460241
Spain	UK Great Britain	19 Jan 60	Atomic Energy	404UNTS41	105804
Spain	UK Great Britain	13 May 60	Visas	374UNTS287	105342
Spain	UK Great Britain	12 Jul 60	Culture	414UNTS123	105971
Spain	UK Great Britain	15 Feb 61	Visas	404UNTS75	105805
Spain	UK Great Britain	30 May 61	Consul/Citizenship	562UNTS169	108198

PARTY ONE	PARTY TWO	DATE	TOPIC	CITATION	NUMBER
Spain	UK Great Britain	21 Dec 68	Taxation	0UNTS0	109663
Spain	UN Special Fund	30 Jun 65	Direct Aid	544UNTS159	107918
Spain	UNICEF (Children)	07 May 54	Direct Aid	190UNTS357	200515
Spain	United Arab Rep	26 Apr 52	Culture	53SPB02006	460095
Spain	Uruguay	24 Feb 54	Finance	57SPB02502	460259
Spain	Uruguay	24 Feb 54	General Trade	57SPB02502	460261
Spain	Uruguay	24 Feb 54	General Trade	57SPB02502	460260
Spain	Uruguay	24 Jan 55	Customs	55SPB01902	460262
Spain	Uruguay	25 Jun 55	General Trade	55SPB01508	460263
Spain	Uruguay	21 Jan 56	General Trade	56SPB01003	460264
Spain	Uruguay	09 Aug 56	General Trade	56SPB02310	460265
Spain	USA (United States)	02 Dec 44	Air Transport	89UNTS345	200262
Spain	USA (United States)	15 Jan 46	Air Transport	89UNTS241	101221
Spain	USA (United States)	11 Jul 46	Mostfavored Nation	13UNTS51	100201
Spain	USA (United States)	03 May 48	Finance	132UNTS155	101756
Spain	USA (United States)	08 May 50	Admin Cooperation	98UNTS175	101363
Spain	USA (United States)	21 Jan 52	Visas	160UNTS63	102102
Spain	USA (United States)	26 Sep 53	Milit Assistance	207UNTS83	102801
Spain	USA (United States)	26 Sep 53	Direct Aid	207UNTS93	102802
Spain	USA (United States)	26 Sep 53	Milit Assistance	207UNTS61	102800
Spain	USA (United States)	19 May 54	Tech Assistance	235UNTS87	103296
Spain	USA (United States)	30 Jul 54	Milit Assistance	235UNTS45	103295
Spain	USA (United States)	20 Apr 55	US Agri Commod Aid	239UNTS117	103374
Spain	USA (United States)	16 Jul 55	Postal Service	270UNTS211	103899
Spain	USA (United States)	19 Jul 55	Atomic Energy	239UNTS299	103387
Spain	USA (United States)	05 Mar 56	US Agri Commod Aid	271UNTS329	103924
Spain	USA (United States)	23 Oct 56	US Agri Commod Aid	277UNTS105	104001
Spain	USA (United States)	09 Mar 57	Milit Assistance	283UNTS89	104108
Spain	USA (United States)	16 Aug 57	Atomic Energy	307UNTS169	104449
Spain	USA (United States)	23 Sep 57	Air Transport	290UNTS261	104238
Spain	USA (United States)	27 Jan 58	US Agri Commod Aid	303UNTS247	104384
Spain	USA (United States)	16 Oct 58	Education	336UNTS153	104804
Spain	USA (United States)	13 Jan 59	US Agri Commod Aid	341UNTS241	104887
Spain	USA (United States)	23 Jun 59	Milit Assistance	354UNTS11	105049
Spain	USA (United States)	13 Feb 60	Milit Installation	371UNTS185	105279
Spain	USA (United States)	18 Mar 60	Scientific Project	372UNTS13	105284
Spain	USA (United States)	22 Jun 60	US Agri Commod Aid	378UNTS3	105414
Spain	USA (United States)	21 Jul 60	Milit Assistance	393UNTS289	105663
Spain	USA (United States)	22 May 61	US Agri Commod Aid	409UNTS260	105891
Spain	USA (United States)	31 Dec 62	Commodity Trade	471UNTS99	106825
Spain	USA (United States)	16 Jul 63	Commodity Trade	488UNTS77	107120
Spain	USA (United States)	29 Jan 64	Specific Property	511UNTS61	107427
Spain	USA (United States)	18 Mar 64	Culture	535UNTS343	107789
Spain	USA (United States)	16 Jul 64	Water Transport	529UNTS187	107661
Spain	USA (United States)	26 Jan 65	Scientific Project	542UNTS81	107881
Spain	USA (United States)	01 Oct 65	Scientific Project	65SPB0611	460280
Spain	USA (United States)	14 Apr 66	Scientific Project	586UNTS79	108497
Spain	USA (United States)	14 Apr 66	Specific Property	579UNTS173	108406
Spain	USA (United States)	21 Apr 66	Milit Assistance	580UNTS231	108426
Spain	USA (United States)	13 Oct 67	Commodity Trade	0UNTS0	110049
Spain	USA (United States)	25 Jun 68	Non-IBRD Project	0UNTS0	110147
Spain	USA (United States)	15 Jul 68	General Economic	0UNTS0	110252
Spain	Vatican/Holy See	07 Jun 41	Admin Cooperation	53SPB01911	460267
Spain	Vatican/Holy See	16 Jul 46	Non-ILO Labor	53SPB01911	460268
Spain	Vatican/Holy See	05 Aug 50	Admin Cooperation	50SPB01811	460270
Spain	Vatican/Holy See	27 Aug 53	General Amity	53SPB01910	460271
Spain	Vatican/Holy See	06 Jul 57	Admin Cooperation	57SPB01207	460272
Spain	Vatican/Holy See	05 Apr 62	Education	62SPB02007	460273
Spain	WHO (World Health)	30 Jan 52	Tech Assistance	124UNTS259	200425
Spain	Yemen	19 May 52	General Amity	55SPB01505	460266
Spanish Colonies	Multilateral	08 Feb 47	Patents/Copyrights	14UNTS287	100222
Spanish Colonies	Multilateral	11 Jul 52	Postal Service	171UNTS3	102224
Spanish Colonies	Multilateral	11 Jul 52	Postal Service	171UNTS143	102226
Spanish Colonies	Multilateral	11 Jul 52	Postal Service	171UNTS89	102225
Spanish Colonies	Multilateral	11 Jul 52	Postal Service	170UNTS3	102221

PARTY ONE	PARTY TWO	DATE	TOPIC	CITATION	NUMBER
Spanish Colonies	Multilateral	11 Jul 52	Postal Service	170UNTS63	102222
Spanish Colonies	Multilateral	11 Jul 52	Postal Service	170UNTS269	102223
Spanish Colonies	Multilateral	03 Oct 57	Postal Service	365UNTS207	105214
Spanish Colonies	Multilateral	03 Oct 57	Postal Service	365UNTS3	105213
Spanish Colonies	Multilateral	10 Jul 64	Postal Service	612UNTS3	108847
Spanish Morroco	Multilateral	08 Feb 47	Patents/Copyrights	14UNTS287	100222
Spanish Morroco	Multilateral	11 Jul 52	Postal Service	171UNTS143	102226
Spanish Morroco	Multilateral	11 Jul 52	Postal Service	171UNTS3	102224
Spanish Morroco	Multilateral	11 Jul 52	Postal Service	171UNTS89	102225
Spanish Morroco	Multilateral	11 Jul 52	Postal Service	170UNTS3	102221
Spanish Morroco	Multilateral	11 Jul 52	Postal Service	170UNTS63	102222
St. Christopher	Multilateral	18 Oct 69	IGO Establishment	0UNTS0	110232
St. Helena	Multilateral	24 Dec 68	Commodity Trade	0UNTS0	109369
St. Kitts	Multilateral	01 Jul 68	Peace/Disarmament	0UNTS0	110485
St. Lucia	Multilateral	01 Jul 68	Peace/Disarmament	0UNTS0	110485
St. Lucia	Multilateral	18 Oct 69	IGO Establishment	0UNTS0	110232
St. Vincent	Multilateral	18 Oct 69	IGO Establishment	0UNTS0	110232
Subsahara Tech Com	IAEA (Atom Energy)	06 Feb 64	IGO Operations	501UNTS285	200606
Subsahara Tech Com	ILO (Labor Org)	25 Jul 59	IGO Operations	409UNTS290	200590
Sudan	Accept UN Charter	12 Jan 56	UN Charter	253UNTS81	103576
Sudan	Bulgaria	06 Mar 67	Scientific Project	0UNTS0	109966
Sudan	China People's Rep	12 Apr 56	General Trade	56CCJC50	410330
Sudan	China People's Rep	23 May 62	General Trade	62CCJC49	410891
Sudan	China People's Rep	27 Jul 66	General Trade	66CCJC72	411327
Sudan	Denmark	11 May 59	Air Transport	445UNTS105	106380
Sudan	France	22 Dec 69	Culture	0UNTS0	110743
Sudan	Germany, East	10 Jun 55	Finance	3EGDA660	419308
Sudan	Germany, East	03 Mar 60	Scientific Project	46EGDZ364	420309
Sudan	Germany, West	07 Feb 63	Tech Assistance	64WBGA6	424649
Sudan	Germany, West	07 Feb 63	Claims and Debts	66WGBB889	425648
Sudan	IBRD (World Bank)	21 Jul 58	IBRD Project	323UNTS183	104669
Sudan	IBRD (World Bank)	17 Jun 60	IBRD Project	379UNTS253	105442
Sudan	IBRD (World Bank)	14 Jun 61	IBRD Project	415UNTS26	105980
Sudan	IBRD (World Bank)	27 Dec 65	IBRD Project	567UNTS27	108250
Sudan	IBRD (World Bank)	15 Jul 68	IBRD Project	0UNTS0	109319
Sudan	IBRD (World Bank)	06 Sep 68	IBRD Project	0UNTS0	110595
Sudan	ICJ Option Clause	30 Dec 57	ICJ Option Clause	284UNTS215	104139
Sudan	IDA (Devel Assoc)	14 Jun 61	Loans and Credits	415UNTS50	105981
Sudan	IDA (Devel Assoc)	24 Jun 68	Non-IBRD Project	0UNTS0	109649
Sudan	Italy	22 Jul 65	Tech Assistance	66ITDI243	436360
Sudan	Multilateral	07 Dec 44	IGO Establishment	15UNTS295	200102
Sudan	Multilateral	27 May 47	Air Transport	418UNTS161	106021
Sudan	Multilateral	07 Dec 50	Admin Cooperation	212UNTS17	102861
Sudan	Multilateral	14 Jun 54	Air Transport	320UNTS217	104644
Sudan	Multilateral	14 Jun 54	Air Transport	320UNTS209	104643
Sudan	Multilateral	04 Apr 55	Tech Assistance	208UNTS239	102816
Sudan	Multilateral	25 May 55	IGO Establishment	264UNTS117	103791
Sudan	Multilateral	07 Sep 56	Humanitarian	266UNTS3	103822
Sudan	Multilateral	26 Oct 56	IGO Establishment	276UNTS3	103988
Sudan	Multilateral	03 Oct 57	Postal Service	365UNTS3	105213
Sudan	Multilateral	03 Oct 57	Postal Service	365UNTS207	105214
Sudan	Multilateral	03 Oct 57	Postal Service	364UNTS3	105211
Sudan	Multilateral	26 Jan 60	IGO Establishment	439UNTS249	106333
Sudan	Multilateral	14 Jun 61	IBRD Project	415UNTS4	105979
Sudan	Multilateral	21 Jun 61	IGO Establishment	514UNTS209	107449
Sudan	Multilateral	25 May 63	IGO Establishment	479UNTS39	106947
Sudan	Multilateral	04 Aug 63	IGO Establishment	510UNTS3	107408
Sudan	Multilateral	05 Aug 63	Sanitation	480UNTS43	106964
Sudan	Multilateral	10 Jul 64	Postal Service	612UNTS3	108847
Sudan	Multilateral	10 Jul 64	Postal Service	611UNTS7	108844
Sudan	Multilateral	10 Jul 64	Postal Service	612UNTS233	108848
Sudan	Multilateral	10 Jul 64	Postal Service	611UNTS387	108846
Sudan	Multilateral	10 Jul 64	Postal Service	611UNTS105	108845
Sudan	Multilateral	20 Aug 64	Telecommunications	514UNTS25	107441
Sudan	Multilateral	08 Jul 65	General Trade	597UNTS3	108641

PARTY ONE	PARTY TWO	DATE	TOPIC	CITATION	NUMBER
Sudan	Multilateral	13 Sep 65	IGO Operations	547UNTS248	107961
Sudan	Multilateral	13 Sep 65	Tech Assistance	547UNTS264	107962
Sudan	Multilateral	17 Jan 66	IGO Establishment	592UNTS101	108573
Sudan	Netherlands	12 Feb 56	Air Transport	311UNTS319	104508
Sudan	Norway	05 Apr 59	Air Transport	3NORT765	451153
Sudan	Sweden	17 Feb 58	Air Transport	393UNTS161	105655
Sudan	Switzerland	18 Feb 63	Air Transport	563UNTS281	108215
Sudan	UK Great Britain	16 Jan 61	Air Transport	424UNTS233	106112
Sudan	UK Great Britain	11 Dec 68	Loans and Credits	0UNTS0	109786
Sudan	UK Great Britain	23 Aug 69	Loans and Credits	0UNTS0	110425
Sudan	UN Special Fund	21 Apr 60	Direct Aid	356UNTS213	105097
Sudan	UNICEF (Children)	07 Aug 56	Direct Aid	248UNTS307	200542
Sudan	United Arab Rep	08 Nov 59	Specific Resources	453UNTS51	106519
Sudan	United Nations	28 Mar 59	Tech Assistance	327UNTS95	104719
Sudan	United Nations	08 Nov 66	Scientific Project	576UNTS85	108365
Sudan	USA (United States)	31 Mar 58	General Aid	308UNTS105	104458
Sudan	USA (United States)	17 Mar 59	Admin Cooperation	342UNTS13	104896
Sudan	USA (United States)	14 Nov 61	US Agri Commod Aid	434UNTS51	106255
Sudan	USA (United States)	31 Jan 63	US Agri Commod Aid	494UNTS119	107230
Sudan	USA (United States)	02 Mar 64	US Agri Commod Aid	524UNTS217	107575
Sudan	USA (United States)	13 Apr 66	US Agri Commod Aid	586UNTS39	108495
Sudan	USSR (Soviet Union)	07 Jan 56	Consul/Citizenship	0SUST351	468415
Sudan	USSR (Soviet Union)	16 Mar 59	General Trade	8SUGG140	469565
Sudan	USSR (Soviet Union)	01 Nov 61	General Trade	10SUGG143	469801
Sudan	USSR (Soviet Union)	01 Nov 61	General Trade	0UNTS0	109827
Sudan	USSR (Soviet Union)	21 Nov 61	Direct Aid	10SUGG145	469805
Sudan	USSR (Soviet Union)	20 Oct 62	Air Transport	11SUGG156	469870
Sudan	WHO (World Health)	21 Jun 58	Tech Assistance	307UNTS235	104453
Sudan	WHO (World Health)	11 Mar 62	Tech Assistance	432UNTS325	106226
Surinam	Multilateral	10 Jul 64	Postal Service	612UNTS233	108848
Surinam	Multilateral	10 Jul 64	Postal Service	612UNTS3	108847
Swaziland	ICJ Option Clause	06 Sep 68	UN Charter	0UNTS0	109252
Swaziland	ICJ Option Clause	09 May 69	ICJ Option Clause	0UNTS0	109589
Swaziland	Multilateral	01 Jul 68	Peace/Disarmament	0UNTS0	110485
Swaziland	Multilateral	24 Dec 68	Commodity Trade	0UNTS0	109369
Swaziland	State/IGO Group	18 Aug 69	Tech Assistance	0UNTS0	109927
Swaziland	State/IGO Group	18 Aug 69	IGO Operations	0UNTS0	109928
Swaziland	UK Great Britain	08 Sep 68	Admin Cooperation	0UNTS0	109474
Swaziland	UN Special Fund	18 Aug 69	Direct Aid	0UNTS0	109929
Swaziland	USA (United States)	29 Sep 67	Finance	0UNTS0	109924
Sweden	Accept UN Charter	19 Nov 46	UN Charter	1UNTS43	100009
Sweden	Afghanistan	22 Oct 40	General Amity	191UNTS349	200516
Sweden	Argentina	31 Jul 45	General Trade	45SOFM119	461012
Sweden	Argentina	20 Nov 48	Taxation	197UNTS47	102633
Sweden	Argentina	23 Nov 48	General Economic	49SOFM571	461094
Sweden	Argentina	16 Jan 59	Milit Servic/Citiz	427UNTS327	106163
Sweden	Argentina	12 Jun 59	Culture	427UNTS337	106164
Sweden	Australia	16 Sep 46	General Trade	10UNTS63	100143
Sweden	Australia	22 Sep 50	General Trade	50SOFM1075	461131
Sweden	Australia	26 Sep 51	Visas	109UNTS39	101488
Sweden	Australia	25 May 53	General Trade	53SOFM1099	461194
Sweden	Austria	02 Dec 49	Air Transport	108UNTS3	101465
Sweden	Austria	02 Mar 50	General Trade	50SOFM59	461100
Sweden	Austria	31 Oct 50	Non-ILO Labor	197UNTS311	102645
Sweden	Austria	23 May 51	Finance	51SOFM251	461144
Sweden	Austria	23 May 51	General Trade	51SOFM243	461143
Sweden	Austria	29 May 51	General Amity	197UNTS431	102650
Sweden	Austria	19 Jul 51	Taxation	198UNTS9	102652
Sweden	Austria	01 Aug 51	Taxation	198UNTS13	102653
Sweden	Austria	29 Apr 52	General Trade	52SOFM235	461166
Sweden	Austria	01 Jun 53	General Trade	53SOFM699	461184
Sweden	Austria	09 Apr 54	Visas	55ABGB193	403173
Sweden	Austria	17 Oct 55	Taxation	262UNTS283	103756
Sweden	Austria	03 Nov 55	Non-ILO Labor	262UNTS289	103757
Sweden	Austria	14 Aug 56	Taxation	262UNTS355	103760

PARTY ONE	PARTY TWO	DATE	TOPIC	CITATION	NUMBER
Sweden	Austria	10 Apr 57	Admin Cooperation	427UNTS343	106165
Sweden	Austria	18 Feb 58	Land Transport	427UNTS349	106166
Sweden	Austria	19 Feb 58	Land Transport	427UNTS211	106155
Sweden	Austria	18 Jun 58	Visas	59ABGB30	403174
Sweden	Austria	14 May 59	Taxation	428UNTS3	106167
Sweden	Austria	22 Feb 60	Taxation	60ABGB143	403175
Sweden	Austria	21 Nov 62	Taxation	63ABGB212	403176
Sweden	Austria	06 Apr 70	Taxation	70ABGB341	403177
Sweden	Austria	14 Mar 72	Taxation	72ABGB298	403178
Sweden	Belgium	30 May 45	General Trade	45SOFM99	461007
Sweden	Belgium	30 May 45	Finance	45SOFM100	461008
Sweden	Belgium	30 Dec 46	General Trade	47SOFM23	461038
Sweden	Belgium	30 Dec 46	Claims and Debts	23UNTS197	100348
Sweden	Belgium	20 Mar 47	Visas	34UNTS3	100522
Sweden	Belgium	16 Dec 48	Visas	26UNTS3	100372
Sweden	Belgium	14 Feb 49	Finance	49SOFM87	461076
Sweden	Belgium	21 Feb 49	Air Transport	95UNTS73	101317
Sweden	Belgium	29 Dec 50	Finance	50SOFM900	461118
Sweden	Belgium	18 Sep 51	Non-ILO Labor	133UNTS187	101789
Sweden	Belgium	21 Apr 52	Air Transport	166UNTS9	102183
Sweden	Belgium	01 Apr 53	Taxation	185UNTS225	102473
Sweden	Belgium	20 Nov 53	General Trade	53SOFM1057	461191
Sweden	Belgium	18 Jan 56	Taxation	293UNTS23	104283
Sweden	Belgium	20 Nov 56	Taxation	281UNTS239	104081
Sweden	Belgium	08 May 58	Land Transport	312UNTS145	104516
Sweden	Belgium	18 May 59	Admin Cooperation	341UNTS277	104890
Sweden	Belgium	11 Jan 65	Education	533UNTS157	107741
Sweden	Belgium	02 Jul 65	Taxation	0UNTS0	109367
Sweden	Belgium	20 Mar 67	Land Transport	0UNTS0	109795
Sweden	Brazil	14 Nov 47	Air Transport	94UNTS139	101310
Sweden	Brazil	29 Apr 55	Patents/Copyrights	228UNTS115	103145
Sweden	Bulgaria	22 Sep 47	Finance	47SOFM508	461051
Sweden	Bulgaria	22 Sep 47	General Trade	47SOFM499	461050
Sweden	Bulgaria	11 Oct 49	General Trade	49SOFM519	461090
Sweden	Bulgaria	17 Apr 57	Air Transport	464UNTS3	106709
Sweden	Bulgaria	19 Oct 67	Education	0UNTS0	109968
Sweden	Burma	14 Sep 50	Air Transport	96UNTS45	101330
Sweden	Burma	06 Mar 56	General Trade	369UNTS275	105261
Sweden	Canada	12 Apr 45	Air Transport	45SOFM65	461001
Sweden	Canada	27 Jun 47	Air Transport	27UNTS313	100414
Sweden	Canada	30 Jun 49	Visas	231UNTS37	103201
Sweden	Canada	06 Apr 51	Taxation	197UNTS393	102648
Sweden	Canada	11 Sep 62	Atomic Energy	529UNTS9	107651
Sweden	Ceylon (Sri Lanka)	18 May 57	Taxation	315UNTS85	104561
Sweden	Ceylon (Sri Lanka)	22 May 58	Tech Assistance	428UNTS65	106168
Sweden	Ceylon (Sri Lanka)	29 May 59	Air Transport	464UNTS109	106713
Sweden	Chile	27 Oct 52	Air Transport	311UNTS63	104499
Sweden	China People's Rep	24 Jun 55	Consul/Citizenship	55CCJC45	410239
Sweden	China People's Rep	24 Jun 55	Consul/Citizenship	228UNTS153	103148
Sweden	China People's Rep	08 Apr 57	Patents/Copyrights	428UNTS267	106179
Sweden	China People's Rep	08 Apr 57	Patents/Copyrights	57CCJC38	410416
Sweden	China People's Rep	08 Nov 57	General Trade	57CCJC108	410462
Sweden	Colombia	27 Jan 53	General Trade	53SOFM1	461180
Sweden	Czechoslovakia	23 Oct 45	Admin Cooperation	46SOFM313	461036
Sweden	Czechoslovakia	15 Nov 45	Air Transport	45SOFM71	461005
Sweden	Czechoslovakia	17 Nov 45	General Trade	45SOFM137	461015
Sweden	Czechoslovakia	17 Nov 45	Finance	45SOFM138	461016
Sweden	Czechoslovakia	29 Jul 46	General Trade	46SOFM253	461031
Sweden	Czechoslovakia	29 Jul 46	Finance	46SOFM255	461032
Sweden	Czechoslovakia	22 Oct 46	Admin Cooperation	200UNTS31	102692
Sweden	Czechoslovakia	10 Mar 47	General Trade	47SOFM571	461055
Sweden	Czechoslovakia	15 Mar 47	Claims and Debts	47SOFM572	461056
Sweden	Czechoslovakia	15 Oct 47	Air Transport	44UNTS149	100683
Sweden	Czechoslovakia	30 Oct 47	General Trade	47SOFM485	461048
Sweden	Czechoslovakia	30 Oct 47	Finance	47SOFM494	461049

PARTY ONE	PARTY TWO	DATE	TOPIC	CITATION	NUMBER
Sweden	Czechoslovakia	01 Feb 49	General Trade	49SOFM63	461073
Sweden	Czechoslovakia	01 Feb 49	Finance	49SOFM76	461074
Sweden	Czechoslovakia	30 Mar 50	Finance	50SOFM116	461105
Sweden	Czechoslovakia	30 Mar 50	General Trade	50SOFM95	461104
Sweden	Czechoslovakia	16 Mar 51	General Trade	51SOFM125	461138
Sweden	Czechoslovakia	14 Mar 52	General Trade	52SOFM83	461157
Sweden	Czechoslovakia	25 Oct 62	Air Transport	498UNTS343	107288
Sweden	Denmark	18 Nov 46	Non-ILO Labor	7UNTS251	100104
Sweden	Denmark	12 Dec 46	General Trade	47SOFM573	461057
Sweden	Denmark	14 Nov 47	General Trade	47SOFM513	461054
Sweden	Denmark	23 Dec 47	Non-ILO Labor	47SOFM635	461061
Sweden	Denmark	23 Dec 47	Non-ILO Labor	14UNTS3	100207
Sweden	Denmark	08 Feb 49	General Trade	49SOFM1	461071
Sweden	Denmark	08 Feb 49	Finance	33UNTS227	100519
Sweden	Denmark	17 Jun 49	Commodity Trade	49SOFM307	461084
Sweden	Denmark	08 Mar 50	General Trade	50SOFM89	461102
Sweden	Denmark	08 Mar 50	Finance	50SOFM93	461103
Sweden	Denmark	16 Aug 50	Commodity Trade	50SOFM943	461122
Sweden	Denmark	10 Feb 51	Finance	51SOFM104	461135
Sweden	Denmark	10 Feb 51	General Trade	51SOFM94	461134
Sweden	Denmark	11 Feb 53	General Trade	53SOFM5	461181
Sweden	Denmark	27 Oct 53	Taxation	198UNTS129	102660
Sweden	Denmark	27 Oct 53	Taxation	198UNTS111	102659
Sweden	Denmark	27 Oct 53	Taxation	198UNTS71	102658
Sweden	Denmark	30 Sep 54	Patents/Copyrights	262UNTS199	103745
Sweden	Denmark	28 Oct 54	Sanitation	262UNTS211	103747
Sweden	Denmark	07 Dec 55	Admin Cooperation	262UNTS235	103749
Sweden	Denmark	15 Sep 56	General Transport	263UNTS3	103764
Sweden	Denmark	21 Jul 58	Taxation	320UNTS163	104642
Sweden	Denmark	04 Jan 60	General Trade	376UNTS375	105390
Sweden	Denmark	05 Dec 67	Specific Resources	631UNTS257	108998
Sweden	Denmark	11 Sep 70	General Military	0UNTS0	110840
Sweden	Ethiopia	13 Oct 54	Tech Assistance	202UNTS273	102734
Sweden	Ethiopia	16 Mar 57	Tech Assistance	304UNTS214	104398
Sweden	Eur Space Research	29 Jul 64	IGO Operations	528UNTS81	107636
Sweden	Finland	10 Mar 43	Taxation	198UNTS333	200518
Sweden	Finland	17 Aug 45	General Trade	45SOFM124	461013
Sweden	Finland	17 Feb 49	Specific Resources	197UNTS123	102636
Sweden	Finland	18 Mar 49	General Trade	49SOFM137	461078
Sweden	Finland	26 Apr 49	Air Transport	95UNTS83	101318
Sweden	Finland	17 Nov 49	Claims and Debts	50SOFM849	461116
Sweden	Finland	21 Dec 49	Taxation	197UNTS243	102642
Sweden	Finland	31 Mar 50	Taxation	197UNTS285	102643
Sweden	Finland	01 Apr 50	General Economic	50SOFM169	461109
Sweden	Finland	29 Dec 50	Taxation	197UNTS333	102646
Sweden	Finland	16 Mar 51	General Economic	51SOFM109	461136
Sweden	Finland	15 Jun 51	Visas	198UNTS3	102651
Sweden	Finland	09 Apr 52	General Trade	52SOFM203	461164
Sweden	Finland	09 Apr 53	Dispute Settlement	198UNTS61	102657
Sweden	Finland	07 Jul 56	General Transport	258UNTS83	103672
Sweden	Finland	15 Sep 56	Admin Cooperation	254UNTS31	103591
Sweden	Finland	22 Sep 58	Water Transport	428UNTS119	106170
Sweden	Finland	16 Oct 58	Culture	428UNTS125	106171
Sweden	Finland	13 Apr 60	Culture	428UNTS131	106172
Sweden	Finland	21 Nov 60	Territory Boundary	383UNTS125	105498
Sweden	Finland	18 Feb 61	Visas	428UNTS145	106173
Sweden	Finland	05 Nov 62	Customs	455UNTS289	106548
Sweden	Finland	29 Jun 63	Land Transport	477UNTS21	106912
Sweden	Finland	07 Oct 68	General Ad Hoc	0UNTS0	109376
Sweden	Finland	15 Oct 68	Atomic Energy	0UNTS0	110798
Sweden	France	21 Jun 45	Finance	45SOFM107	461010
Sweden	France	21 Jun 45	General Trade	45SOFM105	461009
Sweden	France	16 Aug 45	Air Transport	45SOFM69	461003
Sweden	France	28 Jun 46	Finance	46SOFM203	461027
Sweden	France	28 Jun 46	General Trade	46SOFM201	461026

PARTY ONE	PARTY TWO	DATE	TOPIC	CITATION	NUMBER
Sweden	France	02 Aug 46	Air Transport	27UNTS251	100410
Sweden	France	31 Oct 47	General Trade	47SOFM455	461045
Sweden	France	31 Oct 47	Finance	47SOFM480	461046
Sweden	France	03 Mar 49	General Trade	49SOFM97	461077
Sweden	France	08 Apr 49	Taxation	197UNTS177	102637
Sweden	France	08 Apr 49	Taxation	197UNTS183	102638
Sweden	France	30 Jun 49	General Trade	49SOFM484	461088
Sweden	France	17 Dec 49	General Trade	49SOFM584	461095
Sweden	France	31 Oct 50	General Trade	50SOFM981	461124
Sweden	France	02 Dec 50	Non-ILO Labor	50SOFM1061	461129
Sweden	France	11 Apr 51	General Trade	51SOFM203	461141
Sweden	France	16 Nov 51	General Trade	51SOFM411	461151
Sweden	France	29 Nov 52	General Trade	52SOFM545	461177
Sweden	France	24 Apr 53	General Trade	53SOFM577	461183
Sweden	France	07 Nov 53	General Trade	53SOFM1023	461188
Sweden	France	16 Feb 54	General Transport	228UNTS137	103147
Sweden	France	05 Nov 54	Taxation	262UNTS229	103748
Sweden	France	05 Mar 55	Consul/Citizenship	427UNTS133	106150
Sweden	France	07 Mar 56	Admin Cooperation	369UNTS155	105256
Sweden	France	07 Mar 56	Admin Cooperation	369UNTS171	105257
Sweden	France	10 May 57	Admin Cooperation	427UNTS127	106149
Sweden	France	13 Oct 65	Culture	65FRRT103	415402
Sweden	France	16 Dec 68	General Transport	69FRJO2702	416403
Sweden	France	16 Dec 68	Land Transport	0UNTS0	109865
Sweden	Germany, East	24 Jan 49	General Trade	49SOFM13	461072
Sweden	Germany, East	19 Jul 49	General Economic	49SOFM251	461082
Sweden	Germany, West	05 Oct 47	Finance	47SOFM651	461062
Sweden	Germany, West	14 Jan 49	Finance	49SOFM84	461075
Sweden	Germany, West	25 May 49	Finance	49SOFM457	461087
Sweden	Germany, West	04 Sep 50	Finance	50SOFM196	461112
Sweden	Germany, West	04 Sep 50	General Trade	50SOFM181	461111
Sweden	Germany, West	26 Jan 51	General Trade	51WBGA23	424613
Sweden	Germany, West	02 Feb 51	Patents/Copyrights	51WGBB105	425614
Sweden	Germany, West	15 May 53	Non-ILO Labor	227UNTS195	103139
Sweden	Germany, West	31 May 54	Extradition	200UNTS39	102693
Sweden	Germany, West	05 Aug 55	Land Transport	262UNTS265	103754
Sweden	Germany, West	17 Jan 56	Reparations	262UNTS301	103758
Sweden	Germany, West	22 Mar 56	Claims and Debts	262UNTS361	103761
Sweden	Germany, West	22 Mar 56	Reparations	262UNTS401	103762
Sweden	Germany, West	22 Mar 56	Patents/Copyrights	262UNTS423	103763
Sweden	Germany, West	29 Jan 57	Air Transport	393UNTS113	105654
Sweden	Germany, West	13 Feb 57	Admin Cooperation	428UNTS149	106174
Sweden	Germany, West	29 Aug 58	Admin Cooperation	59WGBB401	425615
Sweden	Germany, West	17 Apr 59	Taxation	428UNTS155	106175
Sweden	Germany, West	07 Jun 60	Admin Cooperation	60WGBB2299	425616
Sweden	Germany, West	03 Aug 64	Specif Claim/Waive	64WGBB1402	425617
Sweden	Germany, West	21 Sep 66	Other Military	66WBGA213	424618
Sweden	Greece	08 Apr 47	Air Transport	94UNTS73	101307
Sweden	Greece	25 Jun 48	General Trade	267UNTS337	103849
Sweden	Greece	08 Dec 50	Finance	50SOFM1056	461128
Sweden	Greece	08 Dec 50	General Trade	50SOFM1045	461127
Sweden	Greece	17 Jul 51	General Trade	51SOFM343	461149
Sweden	Greece	19 Aug 52	General Trade	189UNTS117	102544
Sweden	Greece	08 Sep 52	Finance	52SOFM506	461173
Sweden	Greece	08 Sep 52	General Trade	52SOFM491	461172
Sweden	Greece	24 Jul 53	General Trade	189UNTS309	102553
Sweden	Greece	27 May 54	Taxation	219UNTS147	102971
Sweden	Greece	30 Jul 55	General Trade	225UNTS243	103102
Sweden	Greece	11 Dec 56	Dispute Settlement	299UNTS247	104316
Sweden	Greece	06 Oct 61	Taxation	481UNTS137	106981
Sweden	Guinea	17 Jun 61	Air Transport	465UNTS236	106729
Sweden	Hungary	26 Jul 46	General Trade	46SOFM247	461029
Sweden	Hungary	26 Jul 46	Finance	46SOFM250	461030
Sweden	Hungary	28 Nov 47	General Trade	47SOFM575	461058
Sweden	Hungary	19 Jan 49	General Trade	49SOFM155	461080

PARTY ONE	PARTY TWO	DATE	TOPIC	CITATION	NUMBER
Sweden	Hungary	30 Nov 49	General Trade	49SOFM561	461093
Sweden	Hungary	31 Mar 51	Claims and Debts	51SOFM145	461139
Sweden	Hungary	17 Nov 53	General Economic	53SOFM1049	461190
Sweden	Hungary	02 Aug 57	Air Transport	334UNTS307	104774
Sweden	IAEA (Atom Energy)	19 Dec 69	Atomic Energy	0UNTS0	110524
Sweden	Iceland	07 Apr 45	General Trade	45SOFM95	461006
Sweden	Iceland	20 Apr 45	Air Transport	45SOFM67	461002
Sweden	Iceland	18 May 46	General Trade	46SOFM197	461024
Sweden	Iceland	19 Oct 47	General Trade	47SOFM480	461047
Sweden	Iceland	15 Jul 49	General Trade	49SOFM497	461089
Sweden	Iceland	31 Mar 50	General Trade	50SOFM118	461106
Sweden	Iceland	12 Apr 51	General Trade	51SOFM211	461142
Sweden	Iceland	31 Mar 52	General Trade	52SOFM191	461162
Sweden	Iceland	03 Jun 52	Air Transport	215UNTS223	102921
Sweden	Iceland	03 Jul 53	General Trade	53SOFM733	461186
Sweden	Iceland	17 Sep 55	Taxation	262UNTS273	103755
Sweden	Iceland	23 Sep 55	Admin Cooperation	262UNTS241	103750
Sweden	ICJ Option Clause	05 Apr 47	ICJ Option Clause	2UNTS3	100016
Sweden	ICJ Option Clause	06 Apr 57	ICJ Option Clause	264UNTS221	103794
Sweden	India	21 May 48	Air Transport	34UNTS285	100543
Sweden	India	24 Feb 50	General Trade	50SOFM43	461099
Sweden	India	01 Jul 50	General Trade	50SOFM178	461110
Sweden	India	28 Feb 51	General Trade	51SOFM123	461137
Sweden	India	30 Jun 53	General Trade	53SOFM1067	461193
Sweden	India	30 Jul 58	Taxation	369UNTS211	105259
Sweden	Indonesia	05 Apr 51	General Trade	51SOFM193	461140
Sweden	Indonesia	01 Jul 52	General Trade	52SOFM265	461167
Sweden	Iran	31 Oct 49	Air Transport	49SOFM767	461097
Sweden	Iran	16 Sep 56	Taxation	0IRTB63	433101
Sweden	Iran	30 Oct 68	Visas	0IRTB63	433102
Sweden	Iraq	28 Aug 51	Air Transport	52SOFM483	461171
Sweden	Ireland	29 May 46	Air Transport	35UNTS231	100557
Sweden	Ireland	19 Mar 47	Visas	553UNTS163	108083
Sweden	Ireland	25 Jun 49	General Trade	558UNTS299	108148
Sweden	Ireland	18 Oct 54	Taxation	262UNTS259	103753
Sweden	Ireland	05 Dec 57	Non-ILO Labor	428UNTS221	106176
Sweden	Ireland	06 Nov 59	Taxation	428UNTS231	106177
Sweden	Israel	02 Mar 55	Visas	220UNTS105	102995
Sweden	Israel	17 Jun 56	Taxation	257UNTS47	103648
Sweden	Israel	20 Mar 58	Admin Cooperation	314UNTS99	104545
Sweden	Israel	22 Dec 59	Taxation	377UNTS277	105407
Sweden	Israel	15 May 62	Taxation	484UNTS261	107036
Sweden	Israel	10 Sep 63	Extradition	516UNTS3	107467
Sweden	Israel	23 Feb 66	Visas	581UNTS195	108444
Sweden	Italy	24 Nov 45	General Trade	45SOFM143	461017
Sweden	Italy	24 Nov 45	Finance	45SOFM146	461018
Sweden	Italy	23 Jun 46	General Trade	46SOFM199	461025
Sweden	Italy	19 Apr 47	Non-ILO Labor	48ITGU27	435361
Sweden	Italy	15 Nov 49	Finance	50SOFM840	461115
Sweden	Italy	15 Nov 49	General Trade	50SOFM817	461114
Sweden	Italy	18 Apr 50	General Trade	50SOFM69	461101
Sweden	Italy	02 Dec 50	General Trade	50SOFM1017	461125
Sweden	Italy	06 Dec 50	Finance	50SOFM1036	461126
Sweden	Italy	18 Jan 52	General Trade	52SOFM103	461158
Sweden	Italy	17 Jun 52	Finance	54ITGU144	435362
Sweden	Italy	27 Nov 53	General Trade	53SOFM1063	461192
Sweden	Italy	25 May 55	Non-ILO Labor	291UNTS235	104259
Sweden	Italy	20 Dec 56	Taxation	369UNTS357	105265
Sweden	Italy	20 Dec 56	Taxation	369UNTS305	105263
Sweden	Italy	14 Apr 58	Admin Cooperation	427UNTS167	106151
Sweden	Italy	29 Oct 64	Non-ILO Labor	65ITDI161	436363
Sweden	Ivory Coast	07 Jun 65	Air Transport	0UNTS0	109240
Sweden	Jamaica	01 Apr 69	Visas	0UNTS0	109942
Sweden	Japan	01 Apr 50	General Trade	50SOFM153	461107
Sweden	Japan	01 Apr 50	Finance	50SOFM165	461108

PARTY ONE	PARTY TWO	DATE	TOPIC	CITATION	NUMBER
Sweden	Japan	13 Nov 51	Consul/Citizenship	51SOFM623	461156
Sweden	Japan	05 Mar 52	General Trade	52SOFM127	461159
Sweden	Japan	05 Mar 52	Finance	52SOFM142	461160
Sweden	Japan	28 Apr 52	Air Transport	52SOFM231	461165
Sweden	Japan	20 Feb 53	Air Transport	173UNTS307	102272
Sweden	Japan	06 May 53	General Trade	53SOFM1155	461195
Sweden	Japan	31 Mar 54	Claims and Debts	262UNTS187	103744
Sweden	Japan	08 Aug 56	Visas	0JGJI1303	441097
Sweden	Japan	12 Dec 56	Taxation	318UNTS309	104623
Sweden	Japan	20 Sep 57	Reparations	325UNTS29	104693
Sweden	Jordan	09 Jan 61	Air Transport	465UNTS155	106726
Sweden	Lebanon	23 Mar 53	Air Transport	255UNTS83	103605
Sweden	Liberia	09 Dec 59	Air Transport	464UNTS219	106716
Sweden	Luxembourg	17 Nov 52	Air Transport	173UNTS277	102270
Sweden	Luxembourg	06 Apr 57	Admin Cooperation	427UNTS173	106152
Sweden	Luxembourg	12 Mar 58	Admin Cooperation	427UNTS179	106153
Sweden	Malta	29 Dec 65	Visas	561UNTS217	108185
Sweden	Mexico	04 Feb 70	Air Transport	71MEXD803	444040
Sweden	Morocco	30 Mar 61	Taxation	427UNTS185	106154
Sweden	Multilateral	12 May 40	Scientific Project	101UNTS91	101405
Sweden	Multilateral	27 Mar 41	Military Mission	67UNTS231	200222
Sweden	Multilateral	02 Aug 44	Scientific Project	67UNTS221	200221
Sweden	Multilateral	07 Dec 44	Air Transport	171UNTS345	200501
Sweden	Multilateral	07 Dec 44	Air Transport	171UNTS387	200502
Sweden	Multilateral	07 Dec 44	IGO Establishment	15UNTS295	200102
Sweden	Multilateral	07 Dec 44	Air Transport	84UNTS389	200252
Sweden	Multilateral	05 Apr 46	Specific Resources	231UNTS199	103221
Sweden	Multilateral	18 Jul 46	Reparations	125UNTS119	101674
Sweden	Multilateral	22 Jul 46	IGO Establishment	9UNTS3	100125
Sweden	Multilateral	22 Jul 46	IGO Establishment	14UNTS185	100221
Sweden	Multilateral	15 Oct 46	Refugees	11UNTS73	100150
Sweden	Multilateral	02 Dec 46	Specific Resources	161UNTS72	102124
Sweden	Multilateral	11 Dec 46	Sanitation	12UNTS179	100186
Sweden	Multilateral	08 Feb 47	Patents/Copyrights	14UNTS287	100222
Sweden	Multilateral	10 Jun 47	Water Transport	208UNTS3	102814
Sweden	Multilateral	02 Oct 47	Telecommunications	193UNTS188	102616
Sweden	Multilateral	11 Oct 47	IGO Establishment	77UNTS143	100998
Sweden	Multilateral	12 Nov 47	Admin Cooperation	53UNTS49	100772
Sweden	Multilateral	12 Nov 47	Admin Cooperation	53UNTS13	100770
Sweden	Multilateral	12 Nov 47	Admin Cooperation	53UNTS39	100771
Sweden	Multilateral	06 Mar 48	Water Transport	289UNTS3	104214
Sweden	Multilateral	08 Mar 48	Admin Cooperation	27UNTS117	100403
Sweden	Multilateral	10 May 48	Culture	289UNTS111	104215
Sweden	Multilateral	10 Jun 48	Humanitarian	191UNTS3	102576
Sweden	Multilateral	10 Jun 48	Humanitarian	164UNTS113	102163
Sweden	Multilateral	19 Jun 48	Air Transport	310UNTS151	104492
Sweden	Multilateral	26 Jun 48	Culture	331UNTS217	104757
Sweden	Multilateral	24 Jul 48	Sanitation	66UNTS25	100847
Sweden	Multilateral	17 Sep 48	Telecommunications	97UNTS31	101345
Sweden	Multilateral	19 Nov 48	Sanitation	44UNTS277	100688
Sweden	Multilateral	09 Dec 48	Scientific Project	20UNTS229	100318
Sweden	Multilateral	09 Dec 48	Humanitarian	78UNTS277	101021
Sweden	Multilateral	09 Dec 48	Scientific Project	73UNTS39	100942
Sweden	Multilateral	28 Feb 49	Scientific Project	29UNTS53	100434
Sweden	Multilateral	23 Mar 49	Commodity Trade	203UNTS179	102746
Sweden	Multilateral	04 May 49	Admin Cooperation	98UNTS101	101358
Sweden	Multilateral	04 May 49	Admin Cooperation	92UNTS19	101257
Sweden	Multilateral	04 May 49	Admin Cooperation	30UNTS23	100446
Sweden	Multilateral	05 May 49	IGO Establishment	87UNTS103	101168
Sweden	Multilateral	16 Jun 49	Land Transport	45UNTS149	100696
Sweden	Multilateral	12 Aug 49	General Military	75UNTS135	100972
Sweden	Multilateral	12 Aug 49	Humanitarian	75UNTS287	100973
Sweden	Multilateral	12 Aug 49	Humanitarian	75UNTS85	100971
Sweden	Multilateral	12 Aug 49	Humanitarian	75UNTS31	100970
Sweden	Multilateral	27 Aug 49	Non-ILO Labor	47UNTS127	100727

PARTY ONE	PARTY TWO	DATE	TOPIC	CITATION	NUMBER
Sweden	Multilateral	02 Sep 49	IGO Status/Immunit	250UNTS12	103515
Sweden	Multilateral	19 Sep 49	Land Transport	125UNTS3	101671
Sweden	Multilateral	16 Dec 49	Admin Cooperation	72UNTS3	100924
Sweden	Multilateral	06 Apr 50	Admin Cooperation	119UNTS99	101610
Sweden	Multilateral	13 May 50	Land Transport	128UNTS171	101719
Sweden	Multilateral	16 Sep 50	General Transport	92UNTS91	101264
Sweden	Multilateral	18 Oct 50	Specific Resources	638UNTS185	109134
Sweden	Multilateral	04 Nov 50	Humanitarian	213UNTS221	102889
Sweden	Multilateral	22 Nov 50	Culture	131UNTS25	101734
Sweden	Multilateral	07 Dec 50	Admin Cooperation	212UNTS17	102861
Sweden	Multilateral	15 Dec 50	Customs	157UNTS129	102052
Sweden	Multilateral	15 Dec 50	IGO Operations	160UNTS267	102111
Sweden	Multilateral	15 Dec 50	Customs	171UNTS305	102234
Sweden	Multilateral	15 Dec 50	Customs	347UNTS127	104994
Sweden	Multilateral	21 Dec 50	Admin Cooperation	90UNTS3	101222
Sweden	Multilateral	09 Jan 51	Humanitarian	197UNTS341	102647
Sweden	Multilateral	25 May 51	Status of Forces	175UNTS215	102303
Sweden	Multilateral	02 Jul 51	Refugees	189UNTS137	102545
Sweden	Multilateral	28 Aug 51	Non-ILO Labor	198UNTS17	102654
Sweden	Multilateral	09 Oct 51	IGO Establishment	220UNTS121	102997
Sweden	Multilateral	06 Dec 51	Admin Cooperation	150UNTS67	101963
Sweden	Multilateral	20 Dec 51	Air Transport	163UNTS293	102151
Sweden	Multilateral	20 Dec 51	Air Transport	163UNTS309	102152
Sweden	Multilateral	10 Jan 52	Visas	163UNTS27	102139
Sweden	Multilateral	10 Jan 52	Visas	163UNTS3	102138
Sweden	Multilateral	15 Feb 52	Scientific Project	132UNTS51	101751
Sweden	Multilateral	07 Mar 52	Specific Resources	175UNTS205	102302
Sweden	Multilateral	20 May 52	Sanitation	219UNTS55	102966
Sweden	Multilateral	11 Jul 52	Postal Service	170UNTS63	102222
Sweden	Multilateral	11 Jul 52	Postal Service	171UNTS143	102226
Sweden	Multilateral	11 Jul 52	IGO Establishment	169UNTS3	102220
Sweden	Multilateral	11 Jul 52	Postal Service	171UNTS3	102224
Sweden	Multilateral	11 Jul 52	Postal Service	171UNTS89	102225
Sweden	Multilateral	11 Jul 52	Postal Service	170UNTS3	102221
Sweden	Multilateral	11 Jul 52	Postal Service	170UNTS269	102223
Sweden	Multilateral	14 Jul 52	Consul/Citizenship	198UNTS47	102656
Sweden	Multilateral	14 Jul 52	Visas	198UNTS37	102655
Sweden	Multilateral	06 Sep 52	Patents/Copyrights	216UNTS132	102937
Sweden	Multilateral	07 Oct 52	Admin Cooperation	310UNTS181	104493
Sweden	Multilateral	07 Nov 52	General Trade	221UNTS255	103010
Sweden	Multilateral	10 Nov 52	Admin Cooperation	214UNTS265	102904
Sweden	Multilateral	27 Feb 53	Claims and Debts	333UNTS3	104764
Sweden	Multilateral	23 Mar 53	Admin Cooperation	202UNTS241	102732
Sweden	Multilateral	31 Mar 53	Privil/Immunities	193UNTS136	102613
Sweden	Multilateral	01 Apr 53	Non-ILO Labor	227UNTS169	103138
Sweden	Multilateral	11 May 53	Sanitation	456UNTS3	106555
Sweden	Multilateral	01 Jul 53	IGO Establishment	200UNTS149	102701
Sweden	Multilateral	20 Jul 53	Non-ILO Labor	227UNTS217	103140
Sweden	Multilateral	20 Jul 53	Non-ILO Labor	228UNTS3	103141
Sweden	Multilateral	20 Jul 53	Non-ILO Labor	228UNTS41	103142
Sweden	Multilateral	17 Oct 53	General Transport	184UNTS42	102438
Sweden	Multilateral	19 Oct 53	IGO Establishment	207UNTS189	102807
Sweden	Multilateral	07 Dec 53	Admin Cooperation	182UNTS51	102422
Sweden	Multilateral	11 Dec 53	Non-ILO Labor	218UNTS211	102957
Sweden	Multilateral	11 Dec 53	Non-ILO Labor	218UNTS153	102956
Sweden	Multilateral	11 Dec 53	Patents/Copyrights	218UNTS27	102952
Sweden	Multilateral	11 Dec 53	Non-ILO Labor	218UNTS255	102958
Sweden	Multilateral	11 Dec 53	Education	218UNTS125	102954
Sweden	Multilateral	11 Dec 53	Sanitation	191UNTS285	102588
Sweden	Multilateral	25 Feb 54	Air Transport	215UNTS249	102922
Sweden	Multilateral	01 Mar 54	Admin Cooperation	286UNTS265	104173
Sweden	Multilateral	12 May 54	Admin Cooperation	327UNTS3	104714
Sweden	Multilateral	22 May 54	Non-ILO Labor	199UNTS3	102674
Sweden	Multilateral	22 May 54	Visas	199UNTS29	102675
Sweden	Multilateral	04 Jun 54	Customs	282UNTS249	104101

PARTY ONE	PARTY TWO	DATE	TOPIC	CITATION	NUMBER
Sweden	Multilateral	04 Jun 54	Customs	276UNTS191	103992
Sweden	Multilateral	14 Jun 54	Air Transport	320UNTS209	104643
Sweden	Multilateral	14 Jun 54	Air Transport	320UNTS217	104644
Sweden	Multilateral	28 Sep 54	Refugees	360UNTS117	105158
Sweden	Multilateral	19 Dec 54	Patents/Copyrights	218UNTS51	102953
Sweden	Multilateral	19 Dec 54	Culture	218UNTS139	102955
Sweden	Multilateral	12 Mar 55	Land Transport	211UNTS3	102844
Sweden	Multilateral	19 Mar 55	Sanitation	228UNTS95	103144
Sweden	Multilateral	25 May 55	IGO Establishment	264UNTS117	103791
Sweden	Multilateral	15 Sep 55	Non-ILO Labor	254UNTS55	103593
Sweden	Multilateral	28 Sep 55	Air Transport	478UNTS371	106943
Sweden	Multilateral	29 Sep 55	Air Transport	222UNTS313	103037
Sweden	Multilateral	12 Oct 55	IGO Establishment	560UNTS3	108165
Sweden	Multilateral	20 Oct 55	IGO Establishment	378UNTS159	105425
Sweden	Multilateral	13 Dec 55	IGO Operations	529UNTS141	107660
Sweden	Multilateral	13 Dec 55	Humanitarian	250UNTS3	103514
Sweden	Multilateral	04 Jan 56	Scientific Project	256UNTS171	103627
Sweden	Multilateral	01 Mar 56	Customs	343UNTS129	104923
Sweden	Multilateral	03 Mar 56	Milit Servic/Citiz	243UNTS169	103452
Sweden	Multilateral	13 Mar 56	Humanitarian	427UNTS245	106158
Sweden	Multilateral	25 Apr 56	Commodity Trade	270UNTS103	103896
Sweden	Multilateral	30 Apr 56	Air Transport	310UNTS229	104494
Sweden	Multilateral	18 May 56	Customs	338UNTS103	104834
Sweden	Multilateral	18 May 56	Customs	327UNTS123	104721
Sweden	Multilateral	18 May 56	Land Transport	339UNTS3	104844
Sweden	Multilateral	18 May 56	Customs	319UNTS21	104630
Sweden	Multilateral	19 May 56	Land Transport	399UNTS189	105742
Sweden	Multilateral	20 Jun 56	Admin Cooperation	268UNTS3	103850
Sweden	Multilateral	15 Sep 56	Admin Cooperation	254UNTS45	103592
Sweden	Multilateral	25 Sep 56	Air Transport	334UNTS89	104767
Sweden	Multilateral	25 Sep 56	Air Transport	334UNTS13	104766
Sweden	Multilateral	26 Oct 56	IGO Establishment	276UNTS3	103988
Sweden	Multilateral	14 Dec 56	Taxation	436UNTS131	106293
Sweden	Multilateral	14 Dec 56	Taxation	436UNTS115	106292
Sweden	Multilateral	15 Dec 56	Education	278UNTS73	104023
Sweden	Multilateral	19 Dec 56	Non-ILO Labor	427UNTS93	106148
Sweden	Multilateral	21 Dec 56	Humanitarian	427UNTS81	106147
Sweden	Multilateral	20 Feb 57	Consul/Citizenship	309UNTS65	104468
Sweden	Multilateral	29 Apr 57	Dispute Settlement	320UNTS243	104646
Sweden	Multilateral	15 Jun 57	General Trade	550UNTS45	108008
Sweden	Multilateral	12 Jul 57	Visas	322UNTS245	104660
Sweden	Multilateral	03 Oct 57	Postal Service	366UNTS87	105216
Sweden	Multilateral	03 Oct 57	Postal Service	365UNTS207	105214
Sweden	Multilateral	03 Oct 57	Postal Service	364UNTS3	105211
Sweden	Multilateral	03 Oct 57	Postal Service	366UNTS255	105219
Sweden	Multilateral	03 Oct 57	Postal Service	365UNTS3	105213
Sweden	Multilateral	03 Oct 57	Postal Service	366UNTS193	105218
Sweden	Multilateral	03 Oct 57	Postal Service	366UNTS141	105217
Sweden	Multilateral	03 Oct 57	Postal Service	364UNTS331	105212
Sweden	Multilateral	03 Oct 57	Postal Service	366UNTS3	105215
Sweden	Multilateral	23 Nov 57	Refugees	506UNTS125	107384
Sweden	Multilateral	13 Dec 57	Extradition	359UNTS273	105146
Sweden	Multilateral	20 Mar 58	Admin Cooperation	335UNTS211	104789
Sweden	Multilateral	31 Mar 58	Specific Property	320UNTS103	104639
Sweden	Multilateral	15 Apr 58	Health/Educ/Welfare	539UNTS27	107822
Sweden	Multilateral	29 Apr 58	Dispute Settlement	450UNTS169	106466
Sweden	Multilateral	29 Apr 58	Territory Boundary	499UNTS311	107302
Sweden	Multilateral	26 Jun 58	Admin Cooperation	324UNTS97	104679
Sweden	Multilateral	05 Nov 58	Land Transport	428UNTS73	106169
Sweden	Multilateral	15 Dec 58	Mass Media	546UNTS235	107950
Sweden	Multilateral	15 Dec 58	Sanitation	351UNTS159	105022
Sweden	Multilateral	15 Jan 59	Customs	348UNTS13	104996
Sweden	Multilateral	24 Jan 59	IGO Establishment	486UNTS157	107078
Sweden	Multilateral	06 Apr 59	Commodity Trade	349UNTS167	105013
Sweden	Multilateral	20 Apr 59	Visas	376UNTS85	105375

PARTY ONE	PARTY TWO	DATE	TOPIC	CITATION	NUMBER
Sweden	Multilateral	20 Apr 59	Land Transport	0UNTS0	110345
Sweden	Multilateral	20 Apr 59	Admin Cooperation	472UNTS185	106841
Sweden	Multilateral	11 May 59	Claims and Debts	527UNTS145	107623
Sweden	Multilateral	20 Aug 59	Air Transport	376UNTS99	105376
Sweden	Multilateral	08 Sep 59	Non-ILO Labor	383UNTS203	105502
Sweden	Multilateral	14 Dec 59	Admin Cooperation	444UNTS193	106369
Sweden	Multilateral	04 Jan 60	IGO Establishment	370UNTS3	105266
Sweden	Multilateral	26 Jan 60	IGO Establishment	439UNTS249	106333
Sweden	Multilateral	22 Apr 60	Air Transport	418UNTS211	106023
Sweden	Multilateral	28 Apr 60	Health/Educ/Welfare	376UNTS111	105377
Sweden	Multilateral	17 Jun 60	Humanitarian	536UNTS27	107794
Sweden	Multilateral	22 Jun 60	Mass Media	546UNTS247	107951
Sweden	Multilateral	28 Jul 60	IGO Status/Immunit	394UNTS37	105667
Sweden	Multilateral	06 Oct 60	Customs	473UNTS131	106861
Sweden	Multilateral	01 Dec 60	Scientific Project	414UNTS110	105970
Sweden	Multilateral	09 Dec 60	Customs	429UNTS211	106200
Sweden	Multilateral	27 Mar 61	IGO Establishment	420UNTS109	106043
Sweden	Multilateral	30 Mar 61	Sanitation	520UNTS151	107515
Sweden	Multilateral	18 Apr 61	Consul/Citizenship	500UNTS223	107311
Sweden	Multilateral	18 Apr 61	Consul/Citizenship	500UNTS95	107310
Sweden	Multilateral	18 Apr 61	Dispute Settlement	500UNTS243	107312
Sweden	Multilateral	08 Jun 61	Customs	473UNTS187	106863
Sweden	Multilateral	08 Jun 61	Customs	473UNTS153	106862
Sweden	Multilateral	21 Jun 61	IGO Establishment	514UNTS209	107449
Sweden	Multilateral	05 Oct 61	Dispute Settlement	510UNTS175	107413
Sweden	Multilateral	18 Oct 61	IGO Establishment	529UNTS89	107659
Sweden	Multilateral	26 Oct 61	Patents/Copyrights	496UNTS43	107247
Sweden	Multilateral	06 Dec 61	Customs	473UNTS219	106864
Sweden	Multilateral	16 Dec 61	Visas	544UNTS19	107909
Sweden	Multilateral	20 Dec 61	Water Transport	419UNTS79	106031
Sweden	Multilateral	20 Feb 62	Water Transport	597UNTS159	108644
Sweden	Multilateral	23 Mar 62	Admin Cooperation	470UNTS25	106793
Sweden	Multilateral	23 Mar 62	General Amity	434UNTS145	106262
Sweden	Multilateral	14 May 62	Scientific Project	544UNTS39	107910
Sweden	Multilateral	14 May 62	Sanitation	544UNTS81	107911
Sweden	Multilateral	15 May 62	Commodity Trade	444UNTS3	106367
Sweden	Multilateral	14 Jun 62	IGO Establishment	528UNTS33	107634
Sweden	Multilateral	28 Jun 62	ILO Labor	494UNTS271	107238
Sweden	Multilateral	18 Sep 62	Water Transport	442UNTS215	106351
Sweden	Multilateral	28 Sep 62	IGO Establishment	469UNTS169	106791
Sweden	Multilateral	05 Oct 62	IGO Establishment	502UNTS225	107333
Sweden	Multilateral	10 Dec 62	Culture	521UNTS231	107525
Sweden	Multilateral	15 Jan 63	Tech Assistance	456UNTS409	106567
Sweden	Multilateral	24 Apr 63	Consul/Citizenship	596UNTS487	108640
Sweden	Multilateral	24 Apr 63	Consul/Citizenship	596UNTS261	108638
Sweden	Multilateral	05 Aug 63	Sanitation	480UNTS43	106964
Sweden	Multilateral	14 Sep 63	Air Transport	0UNTS0	110106
Sweden	Multilateral	14 Sep 63	Telecommunications	488UNTS121	107123
Sweden	Multilateral	17 Oct 63	Atomic Energy	525UNTS75	107585
Sweden	Multilateral	09 Nov 63	Direct Aid	489UNTS209	107141
Sweden	Multilateral	09 Mar 64	Specific Resources	581UNTS57	108432
Sweden	Multilateral	10 Jul 64	Postal Service	611UNTS387	108846
Sweden	Multilateral	10 Jul 64	Postal Service	611UNTS105	108845
Sweden	Multilateral	10 Jul 64	Postal Service	613UNTS127	108853
Sweden	Multilateral	10 Jul 64	Postal Service	613UNTS3	108850
Sweden	Multilateral	10 Jul 64	Postal Service	612UNTS3	108847
Sweden	Multilateral	10 Jul 64	Postal Service	613UNTS193	108852
Sweden	Multilateral	10 Jul 64	Postal Service	612UNTS361	108849
Sweden	Multilateral	10 Jul 64	Postal Service	612UNTS233	108848
Sweden	Multilateral	10 Jul 64	Postal Service	611UNTS7	108844
Sweden	Multilateral	13 Jul 64	ILO Labor	569UNTS65	108279
Sweden	Multilateral	20 Aug 64	Telecommunications	514UNTS25	107441
Sweden	Multilateral	12 Sep 64	Specific Resources	0UNTS0	109344
Sweden	Multilateral	15 Sep 64	General Trade	510UNTS147	107411
Sweden	Multilateral	01 Dec 64	Water Transport	550UNTS133	108012

PARTY ONE	PARTY TWO	DATE	TOPIC	CITATION	NUMBER
Sweden	Multilateral	22 Jan 65	Gen Communications	634UNTS239	109066
Sweden	Multilateral	18 Mar 65	Dispute Settlement	575UNTS159	108359
Sweden	Multilateral	03 Dec 65	Admin Cooperation	572UNTS105	108309
Sweden	Multilateral	04 Dec 65	IGO Establishment	571UNTS123	108303
Sweden	Multilateral	10 Feb 66	Loans and Credits	575UNTS129	108356
Sweden	Multilateral	05 Apr 66	Water Transport	640UNTS133	109159
Sweden	Multilateral	03 Oct 66	Culture	610UNTS169	108841
Sweden	Multilateral	19 Dec 66	Specific Resources	605UNTS313	108769
Sweden	Multilateral	27 Jan 67	Scientific Project	610UNTS205	108843
Sweden	Multilateral	31 Jan 67	Refugees	606UNTS267	108791
Sweden	Multilateral	24 Feb 67	Health/Educ/Welfare	596UNTS133	108631
Sweden	Multilateral	17 Apr 67	Consul/Citizenship	0UNTS0	110377
Sweden	Multilateral	24 Apr 67	Humanitarian	634UNTS255	109067
Sweden	Multilateral	29 Jun 67	Non-ILO Labor	0UNTS0	110030
Sweden	Multilateral	08 Dec 67	Specific Resources	620UNTS225	108959
Sweden	Multilateral	18 Mar 68	Commodity Trade	0UNTS0	109262
Sweden	Multilateral	07 Jun 68	Admin Cooperation	0UNTS0	110346
Sweden	Multilateral	01 Jul 68	Peace/Disarmament	0UNTS0	110485
Sweden	Multilateral	16 Aug 68	Non-ILO Labor	0UNTS0	109281
Sweden	Multilateral	05 Dec 68	Scientific Project	0UNTS0	109952
Sweden	Multilateral	15 Jan 69	Consul/Citizenship	0UNTS0	109491
Sweden	Multilateral	09 Jun 69	Specific Resources	0UNTS0	110099
Sweden	Multilateral	12 Dec 69	General Economic	0UNTS0	110755
Sweden	Multilateral	29 Jul 70	Tech Assistance	0UNTS0	110608
Sweden	Netherlands	30 Nov 45	General Trade	45SOFM151	461019
Sweden	Netherlands	30 Nov 45	Finance	2UNTS27	100019
Sweden	Netherlands	29 Jun 46	General Trade	46SOFM204	461028
Sweden	Netherlands	23 Dec 46	General Trade	47SOFM1	461037
Sweden	Netherlands	20 Mar 47	Visas	247UNTS145	103463
Sweden	Netherlands	30 Dec 47	General Trade	51NET91	447007
Sweden	Netherlands	30 Dec 47	General Trade	47SOFM583	461059
Sweden	Netherlands	07 Apr 49	General Trade	49SOFM391	461086
Sweden	Netherlands	06 Jul 49	Non-ILO Labor	197UNTS189	102639
Sweden	Netherlands	19 Dec 49	General Trade	49SOFM625	461096
Sweden	Netherlands	18 Apr 50	General Trade	50SOFM781	461113
Sweden	Netherlands	29 May 51	General Trade	51SOFM253	461145
Sweden	Netherlands	31 Mar 52	General Trade	52SOFM167	461161
Sweden	Netherlands	25 Apr 52	Taxation	163UNTS195	102148
Sweden	Netherlands	25 Apr 52	Taxation	163UNTS131	102147
Sweden	Netherlands	10 Apr 53	General Trade	53SOFM81	461182
Sweden	Netherlands	23 Nov 55	Admin Cooperation	262UNTS247	103751
Sweden	Netherlands	21 May 57	Land Transport	286UNTS237	104169
Sweden	Netherlands	23 Oct 57	Land Transport	306UNTS75	104433
Sweden	Netherlands	30 Apr 59	Finance	485UNTS147	107053
Sweden	Netherlands	08 Jan 62	Air Transport	466UNTS65	106737
Sweden	New Zealand	04 Jun 48	Visas	18UNTS171	100286
Sweden	New Zealand	16 Apr 56	Taxation	274UNTS259	103971
Sweden	Norway	22 Nov 46	Specific Resources	46SOFM307	461034
Sweden	Norway	22 Nov 46	Finance	15UNTS171	100233
Sweden	Norway	21 Jun 47	Taxation	94UNTS107	101309
Sweden	Norway	05 Aug 47	General Trade	47SOFM511	461052
Sweden	Norway	22 Dec 47	Non-ILO Labor	47SOFM631	461060
Sweden	Norway	22 Dec 47	Non-ILO Labor	22UNTS203	100337
Sweden	Norway	29 Apr 48	Commodity Trade	26UNTS41	100376
Sweden	Norway	29 Apr 48	Finance	26UNTS11	100374
Sweden	Norway	29 Apr 48	Commodity Trade	26UNTS33	100375
Sweden	Norway	18 Dec 48	Non-ILO Labor	30UNTS117	100450
Sweden	Norway	28 Jan 49	Specific Resources	196UNTS3	102617
Sweden	Norway	14 Dec 49	Specific Resources	196UNTS19	102618
Sweden	Norway	17 Dec 49	Taxation	197UNTS197	102640
Sweden	Norway	17 Dec 49	Taxation	197UNTS215	102641
Sweden	Norway	28 Jan 50	Land Transport	202UNTS151	102730
Sweden	Norway	24 Feb 50	Claims and Debts	2NORT530	451160
Sweden	Norway	19 Dec 50	General Trade	50SOFM1065	461130
Sweden	Norway	20 Dec 50	Specific Resources	92UNTS3	101256

PARTY ONE	PARTY TWO	DATE	TOPIC	CITATION	NUMBER
Sweden	Norway	19 Feb 51	Finance	51SOFM567	461155
Sweden	Norway	07 Dec 51	General Trade	51SOFM447	461152
Sweden	Norway	10 Nov 52	Scientific Project	52SOFM893	461179
Sweden	Norway	22 Nov 52	General Trade	52SOFM535	461175
Sweden	Norway	16 Nov 53	General Trade	53SOFM1047	461189
Sweden	Norway	12 May 54	Visas	198UNTS157	102661
Sweden	Norway	09 Jul 54	Claims and Debts	2NORT638	451161
Sweden	Norway	10 Jan 55	Patents/Copyrights	204UNTS293	102764
Sweden	Norway	28 May 55	Scientific Project	262UNTS151	103743
Sweden	Norway	07 Oct 55	Admin Cooperation	262UNTS253	103752
Sweden	Norway	26 Jan 56	General Ad Hoc	3NORT673	451162
Sweden	Norway	09 Mar 56	Land Transport	369UNTS285	105262
Sweden	Norway	29 Jun 56	Specific Resources	262UNTS335	103759
Sweden	Norway	15 Sep 56	Admin Cooperation	263UNTS17	103765
Sweden	Norway	27 Sep 56	Taxation	261UNTS71	103726
Sweden	Norway	16 Sep 57	Territory Boundary	428UNTS263	106178
Sweden	Norway	09 Jun 58	Water Transport	427UNTS221	106156
Sweden	Norway	28 Oct 59	Visas	427UNTS225	106157
Sweden	Norway	16 Mar 61	Customs	3NORT827	451163
Sweden	Norway	31 Oct 62	Claims and Debts	466UNTS361	106755
Sweden	Norway	28 Jun 63	Specific Resources	3NORT891	451164
Sweden	Norway	05 Apr 67	Specific Resources	3NORT994	451165
Sweden	Norway	05 Apr 67	Specific Resources	3NORT994	451166
Sweden	Norway	14 Dec 67	Admin Cooperation	3NORT1012	451167
Sweden	Norway	24 Jul 68	Territory Boundary	3NORTO	451168
Sweden	Norway	10 Dec 68	Taxation	0UNTSO	109615
Sweden	Pakistan	06 May 48	Air Transport	36UNTS3	100564
Sweden	Pakistan	04 Jun 55	Tech Assistance	228UNTS121	103146
Sweden	Pakistan	06 Mar 58	Air Transport	393UNTS181	105656
Sweden	Pakistan	25 Aug 58	Taxation	369UNTS183	105258
Sweden	Philippines	20 Aug 54	Air Transport	200UNTS121	102699
Sweden	Philippines	12 Apr 66	Taxation	0UNTSO	110197
Sweden	Philippines	11 Nov 66	Visas	587UNTS3	108505
Sweden	Philippines	08 May 69	Air Transport	0UNTSO	109868
Sweden	Poland	09 Jul 45	General Trade	45SOFM115	461011
Sweden	Poland	20 Aug 45	General Economic	45SOFM125	461014
Sweden	Poland	24 Aug 45	Air Transport	45SOFM70	461004
Sweden	Poland	16 Feb 46	General Economic	46SOFM183	461021
Sweden	Poland	26 Oct 46	General Economic	46SOFM311	461035
Sweden	Poland	18 Mar 47	Finance	47SOFM137	461039
Sweden	Poland	18 Mar 47	General Economic	12UNTS295	100190
Sweden	Poland	22 Apr 48	Claims and Debts	49PDZU27	457004
Sweden	Poland	18 Oct 49	Finance	49SOFM529	461091
Sweden	Poland	03 Nov 49	General Economic	49SOFM549	461092
Sweden	Poland	16 Nov 49	Claims and Debts	50SOFM921	461119
Sweden	Poland	03 Dec 51	Finance	51SOFM461	461153
Sweden	Poland	18 Oct 52	General Trade	52SOFM529	461174
Sweden	Poland	08 Jun 56	Air Transport	334UNTS257	104771
Sweden	Poland	21 Aug 57	Admin Cooperation	427UNTS277	106159
Sweden	Poland	19 Jan 66	Finance	66PZUM25	458129
Sweden	Poland	04 Apr 68	Land Transport	68PZUM71	458154
Sweden	Poland	05 Oct 70	Specific Property	71PDZU37	457167
Sweden	Portugal	06 Mar 47	Air Transport	35UNTS243	100558
Sweden	Portugal	18 May 50	General Trade	50SOFM931	461120
Sweden	Portugal	18 May 50	Finance	50SOFM933	461121
Sweden	Portugal	13 Dec 51	General Trade	52SOFM193	461163
Sweden	Romania	15 Apr 57	Air Transport	342UNTS325	104915
Sweden	Romania	01 Mar 67	General Transport	642UNTS163	109172
Sweden	Singapore	20 Dec 66	Air Transport	0UNTSO	109243
Sweden	South Africa	25 May 51	Taxation	197UNTS425	102649
Sweden	South Africa	26 Nov 52	Air Transport	52SOFM541	461176
Sweden	South Africa	09 Jan 53	Air Transport	173UNTS299	102271
Sweden	South Africa	28 Jul 55	Taxation	230UNTS287	103191
Sweden	South Africa	28 Mar 58	Air Transport	300UNTS95	104333
Sweden	South Africa	29 May 61	Taxation	442UNTS15	106335

PARTY ONE	PARTY TWO	DATE	TOPIC	CITATION	NUMBER
Sweden	Spain	26 Jan 46	General Economic	46SOFM169	461020
Sweden	Spain	03 Oct 46	General Trade	46SOFM257	461033
Sweden	Spain	17 Jul 47	General Trade	47SPBO1008	460244
Sweden	Spain	17 Jul 47	General Economic	47SOFM667	461070
Sweden	Spain	18 Feb 50	Air Transport	166UNTS15	102184
Sweden	Spain	12 Oct 50	Scientific Project	197UNTS305	102644
Sweden	Spain	24 Jan 51	General Economic	51SOFM18	461133
Sweden	Spain	10 Jul 51	General Trade	51SOFM307	461148
Sweden	Spain	14 Jul 52	General Economic	52SOFM303	461169
Sweden	Spain	11 Jun 55	General Economic	55SPBO1108	460245
Sweden	Spain	11 Apr 56	General Economic	56SPBO705	460246
Sweden	Spain	05 Nov 58	General Economic	58SPBO1612	460247
Sweden	Spain	25 Apr 63	Taxation	64SPBO1601	460248
Sweden	Spain	25 Apr 63	Taxation	64SPBO1801	460249
Sweden	Spain	05 May 65	Air Transport	0UNTSO	109239
Sweden	Sudan	17 Feb 58	Air Transport	393UNTS161	105655
Sweden	Switzerland	16 Mar 48	Non-ILO Labor	197UNTS39	102632
Sweden	Switzerland	16 Oct 48	Taxation	197UNTS55	102634
Sweden	Switzerland	16 Oct 48	Taxation	197UNTS101	102635
Sweden	Switzerland	03 Jun 50	General Trade	50SOFM853	461117
Sweden	Switzerland	18 Oct 50	Air Transport	166UNTS49	102185
Sweden	Switzerland	11 Jan 51	General Economic	51SOFM1	461132
Sweden	Switzerland	20 Jun 51	General Trade	51SOFM277	461146
Sweden	Switzerland	20 Jun 51	General Trade	51SWRO619	462156
Sweden	Switzerland	20 Jun 51	Finance	51SOFM296	461147
Sweden	Switzerland	18 Oct 51	Air Transport	51SOFM477	461154
Sweden	Switzerland	02 Jul 52	General Trade	52SOFM289	461168
Sweden	Switzerland	05 Jun 53	General Trade	53SOFM708	461185
Sweden	Switzerland	12 Aug 53	Customs	232UNTS59	103229
Sweden	Switzerland	25 Sep 54	Patents/Copyrights	262UNTS205	103746
Sweden	Switzerland	17 Dec 54	Non-ILO Labor	369UNTS233	105260
Sweden	Switzerland	30 Apr 58	Land Transport	427UNTS295	106161
Sweden	Taiwan	05 Apr 45	Privil/Immunities	0CTRC448	413026
Sweden	Thailand	23 Nov 49	Air Transport	72UNTS217	100935
Sweden	Thailand	20 Oct 61	Taxation	428UNTS275	106180
Sweden	Tunisia	19 Mar 59	Air Transport	497UNTS43	107261
Sweden	Tunisia	06 Sep 60	Taxation	427UNTS301	106162
Sweden	Turkey	24 Apr 46	Finance	46SOFM192	461023
Sweden	Turkey	24 Apr 46	General Economic	46TURG2312	466088
Sweden	Turkey	24 Apr 46	General Trade	45SOFM191	461022
Sweden	Turkey	26 Jun 46	Air Transport	14UNTS21	100208
Sweden	Turkey	07 Jun 48	General Economic	49TURG1902	466089
Sweden	Turkey	17 Dec 58	Direct Aid	64TURG909	466114
Sweden	Turkey	01 Jun 60	Visas	60TURG2106	466027
Sweden	UK Great Britain	06 Mar 45	Finance	5UNTS241	200032
Sweden	UK Great Britain	06 Mar 45	Finance	82UNTS219	101095
Sweden	UK Great Britain	27 Nov 46	Air Transport	11UNTS229	100162
Sweden	UK Great Britain	20 Mar 47	Visas	11UNTS291	100169
Sweden	UK Great Britain	30 Mar 49	Taxation	209UNTS129	102826
Sweden	UK Great Britain	30 Dec 49	Finance	87UNTS59	101166
Sweden	UK Great Britain	05 Apr 50	Air Transport	99UNTS107	101374
Sweden	UK Great Britain	10 Nov 50	Finance	88UNTS265	101198
Sweden	UK Great Britain	17 Jan 51	Postal Service	93UNTS225	101301
Sweden	UK Great Britain	14 Mar 52	Consul/Citizenship	202UNTS157	102731
Sweden	UK Great Britain	23 Jun 52	Air Transport	52SOFM468	461170
Sweden	UK Great Britain	28 Jul 54	Finance	199UNTS181	102684
Sweden	UK Great Britain	29 Oct 54	Visas	209UNTS75	102823
Sweden	UK Great Britain	22 Dec 55	Claims and Debts	231UNTS179	103218
Sweden	UK Great Britain	18 Jan 56	Admin Cooperation	428UNTS301	106181
Sweden	UK Great Britain	09 Jun 56	Non-ILO Labor	309UNTS301	104479
Sweden	UK Great Britain	08 Dec 56	Claims and Debts	264UNTS61	103788
Sweden	UK Great Britain	20 Sep 57	Atomic Energy	310UNTS49	104486
Sweden	UK Great Britain	18 Apr 59	Claims and Debts	360UNTS89	105156
Sweden	UK Great Britain	28 Jul 60	Taxation	404UNTS85	105806
Sweden	UK Great Britain	28 Jul 60	Taxation	404UNTS113	105808

PARTY ONE	PARTY TWO	DATE	TOPIC	CITATION	NUMBER
Sweden	UK Great Britain	05 May 61	Visas	404UNTS105	105807
Sweden	UK Great Britain	26 Apr 63	Extradition	590UNTS117	108551
Sweden	UK Great Britain	30 Jun 64	Commodity Trade	515UNTS83	107455
Sweden	UK Great Britain	14 Oct 64	Taxation	543UNTS135	107898
Sweden	UK Great Britain	26 Oct 67	Milit Assistance	632UNTS277	109029
Sweden	UK Great Britain	21 Nov 67	Land Transport	0UNTS0	109338
Sweden	UK Great Britain	12 Feb 68	Taxation	0UNTS0	109449
Sweden	UN Hi Com Refugees	08 Oct 56	Refugees	428UNTS307	106182
Sweden	United Arab Rep	12 Dec 49	Air Transport	108UNTS15	101466
Sweden	United Arab Rep	21 Jul 58	Mostfavored Nation	427UNTS285	106160
Sweden	United Arab Rep	29 Jul 58	Taxation	369UNTS323	105264
Sweden	United Nations	11 Feb 53	Tech Assistance	160UNTS3	102096
Sweden	United Nations	01 Jul 57	Status of Forces	271UNTS187	103914
Sweden	United Nations	01 Jun 62	Admin Cooperation	429UNTS135	106195
Sweden	United Nations	16 Jun 65	Admin Cooperation	539UNTS45	107823
Sweden	United Nations	21 Feb 66	IGO Operations	555UNTS169	108111
Sweden	Uruguay	13 Jun 49	Finance	49SOFM301	461083
Sweden	Uruguay	20 Mar 52	Air Transport	311UNTS3	104497
Sweden	USA (United States)	16 Dec 44	Air Transport	6UNTS397	200041
Sweden	USA (United States)	04 Dec 45	Air Transport	6UNTS273	100080
Sweden	USA (United States)	30 Sep 46	Air Transport	42UNTS213	100649
Sweden	USA (United States)	30 Apr 47	Visas	84UNTS33	101116
Sweden	USA (United States)	24 Jun 47	General Economic	36UNTS25	100565
Sweden	USA (United States)	16 Dec 47	Admin Cooperation	73UNTS65	100944
Sweden	USA (United States)	03 Jul 48	Direct Aid	23UNTS101	100343
Sweden	USA (United States)	03 Jul 48	Milit Occupation	27UNTS69	100400
Sweden	USA (United States)	27 Jun 49	General Trade	49SOFM311	461085
Sweden	USA (United States)	25 May 50	General Trade	88UNTS43	101184
Sweden	USA (United States)	27 Jun 51	Milit Assistance	148UNTS77	101937
Sweden	USA (United States)	01 Jul 52	Milit Assistance	187UNTS3	102497
Sweden	USA (United States)	20 Nov 52	Education	177UNTS203	102319
Sweden	USA (United States)	06 Aug 54	Air Transport	221UNTS331	103014
Sweden	USA (United States)	22 Dec 54	Air Transport	228UNTS85	103143
Sweden	USA (United States)	18 Jan 56	Atomic Energy	240UNTS413	103416
Sweden	USA (United States)	05 Sep 61	General Economic	421UNTS241	106062
Sweden	USA (United States)	24 Oct 61	Extradition	494UNTS141	107231
Sweden	USA (United States)	05 Mar 62	Commodity Trade	459UNTS17	106610
Sweden	USA (United States)	04 Oct 62	Milit Assistance	462UNTS31	106669
Sweden	USA (United States)	22 Oct 63	Taxation	530UNTS247	107686
Sweden	USA (United States)	06 Jul 64	Water Transport	529UNTS287	107666
Sweden	USA (United States)	28 Jul 66	Atomic Energy	603UNTS61	108725
Sweden	USA (United States)	02 Jun 69	Telecommunications	0UNTS0	110277
Sweden	USSR (Soviet Union)	07 Oct 46	General Trade	0SUST219	468406
Sweden	USSR (Soviet Union)	07 Oct 46	Claims and Debts	0SUST219	468407
Sweden	USSR (Soviet Union)	07 Oct 46	General Trade	0SUST218	468404
Sweden	USSR (Soviet Union)	07 Oct 46	Loans and Credits	0SUST218	468405
Sweden	USSR (Soviet Union)	25 Oct 46	Air Transport	0SUST220	468409
Sweden	USSR (Soviet Union)	25 Oct 46	Air Transport	0SUST220	468408
Sweden	USSR (Soviet Union)	05 Nov 46	Postal Service	0SUST221	468410
Sweden	USSR (Soviet Union)	30 Jan 47	General Trade	0SUST225	468411
Sweden	USSR (Soviet Union)	31 Dec 47	General Trade	47SOFM511	461053
Sweden	USSR (Soviet Union)	02 Apr 49	General Trade	49SOFM145	461079
Sweden	USSR (Soviet Union)	23 Jan 54	Air Transport	0SUST306	468412
Sweden	USSR (Soviet Union)	29 Sep 54	Humanitarian	202UNTS259	102733
Sweden	USSR (Soviet Union)	31 Mar 56	Air Transport	259UNTS239	103691
Sweden	USSR (Soviet Union)	28 Jan 57	Finance	428UNTS315	106183
Sweden	USSR (Soviet Union)	27 Mar 58	Specific Property	7SUGG108	469501
Sweden	USSR (Soviet Union)	28 Mar 58	Privil/Immunities	428UNTS321	106184
Sweden	USSR (Soviet Union)	02 Feb 62	General Trade	11SUGG131	469818
Sweden	USSR (Soviet Union)	30 Nov 67	Consul/Citizenship	0UNTS0	109385
Sweden	Venezuela	13 Mar 57	Admin Cooperation	428UNTS351	106185
Sweden	Yugoslavia	12 Apr 47	General Trade	47SOFM161	461040
Sweden	Yugoslavia	12 Apr 47	Finance	47SOFM181	461041
Sweden	Yugoslavia	06 Oct 47	Air Transport	53UNTS107	100775
Sweden	Yugoslavia	21 May 49	General Trade	49SOFM157	461081

PARTY ONE	PARTY TWO	DATE	TOPIC	CITATION	NUMBER
Sweden	Yugoslavia	02 Jan 50	General Trade	50SOFM1	461098
Sweden	Yugoslavia	19 Aug 50	General Economic	50SOFM945	461123
Sweden	Yugoslavia	29 Oct 51	General Trade	51SOFM401	461150
Sweden	Yugoslavia	20 Dec 52	General Trade	52SOFM569	461178
Sweden	Yugoslavia	16 Oct 53	General Trade	53SOFM1013	461197
Sweden	Yugoslavia	18 Apr 58	Air Transport	393UNTS225	105658
Sweden	Yugoslavia	31 May 58	Admin Cooperation	428UNTS357	106186
Switzerland	Afghanistan	27 Sep 61	Air Transport	63SWRO874	462089
Switzerland	Argentina	13 Jan 50	Taxation	50SWRO584	462042
Switzerland	Argentina	25 Jan 56	Air Transport	559UNTS121	108157
Switzerland	Argentina	25 Nov 57	General Economic	58SWRO38	462120
Switzerland	Argentina	05 Sep 68	Loans and Credits	0UNTS0	109572
Switzerland	Australia	21 May 59	Taxation	341UNTS283	104891
Switzerland	Austria	30 Apr 47	Sanitation	48SWRO192	462104
Switzerland	Austria	30 Apr 47	Customs	48SWRO197	462073
Switzerland	Austria	30 Apr 47	Land Transport	48SWRO183	462068
Switzerland	Austria	30 Apr 47	Customs	48SWRO204	462011
Switzerland	Austria	19 Dec 49	Air Transport	254UNTS287	103597
Switzerland	Austria	30 May 50	Land Transport	50SWRO781	462069
Switzerland	Austria	15 Jul 50	Non-ILO Labor	51SWRO787	462093
Switzerland	Austria	15 Jul 50	Non-ILO Labor	51ABGB232	403179
Switzerland	Austria	14 Sep 50	Visas	51SWRO642	462013
Switzerland	Austria	14 Sep 50	Admin Cooperation	51SWRO639	462010
Switzerland	Austria	17 May 52	Admin Cooperation	52SWRO529	462030
Switzerland	Austria	12 Nov 53	Taxation	54SWRO1109	462043
Switzerland	Austria	09 Dec 53	Admin Cooperation	54ABGB164	403181
Switzerland	Austria	08 Apr 54	Taxation	54SWRO1125	462044
Switzerland	Austria	10 Apr 54	Specific Resources	55SWRO741	462035
Switzerland	Austria	13 Jul 54	Finance	55ABGB42	403184
Switzerland	Austria	15 Sep 54	General Economic	54SWRO1005	462122
Switzerland	Austria	05 Jan 55	Extradition	55SWRO61	462009
Switzerland	Austria	19 Mar 56	Non-ILO Labor	56SWRO663	462012
Switzerland	Austria	01 Jun 57	Visas	57ABGB159	403185
Switzerland	Austria	22 Jul 57	Land Transport	57ABGB268	403186
Switzerland	Austria	22 Jul 57	Land Transport	57SWRO906	462076
Switzerland	Austria	16 Dec 57	Claims and Debts	58SWRO239	462121
Switzerland	Austria	22 Oct 58	Land Transport	59SWRO329	462080
Switzerland	Austria	22 Dec 58	Land Transport	59ABGB123	403187
Switzerland	Austria	06 Apr 59	Taxation	59ABGB196	403182
Switzerland	Austria	16 Dec 60	Admin Cooperation	62SWRO270	462029
Switzerland	Austria	06 Apr 62	Admin Cooperation	62SWRO1659	462024
Switzerland	Austria	26 Apr 62	Admin Cooperation	62ABGB320	403189
Switzerland	Austria	02 Sep 63	Visas	548UNTS91	107973
Switzerland	Austria	20 Feb 65	Non-ILO Labor	66ABGB41	403190
Switzerland	Austria	20 Feb 65	Non-ILO Labor	66ABGB41	403180
Switzerland	Austria	29 Dec 66	Taxation	67ABGB355	403183
Switzerland	Austria	23 Aug 67	Tech Assistance	67ABGB333	403191
Switzerland	Austria	24 Oct 67	Visas	68ABGB21	403192
Switzerland	Austria	15 Nov 67	Non-ILO Labor	69ABGB4	403193
Switzerland	Austria	15 Nov 67	Non-ILO Labor	0UNTS0	109434
Switzerland	Austria	29 Dec 67	Admin Cooperation	68ABGB84	403188
Switzerland	Austria	26 Aug 68	Admin Cooperation	0UNTS0	110354
Switzerland	Austria	01 Oct 68	Non-ILO Labor	69ABGB5	403194
Switzerland	Belgium	03 Jul 47	Visas	29UNTS277	100444
Switzerland	Belgium	01 Sep 48	Visas	23UNTS139	100344
Switzerland	Belgium	21 Mar 49	Admin Cooperation	34UNTS17	100524
Switzerland	Belgium	28 Jul 50	Visas	71UNTS91	100911
Switzerland	Belgium	17 Jun 52	Non-ILO Labor	180UNTS23	102373
Switzerland	Belgium	05 Jan 56	Reparations	228UNTS159	103149
Switzerland	Belgium	21 Jun 57	General Trade	57SWRO521	462162
Switzerland	Belgium	05 Dec 57	Taxation	293UNTS317	104299
Switzerland	Belgium	29 Apr 59	Admin Cooperation	443UNTS35	106356
Switzerland	Belgium	24 Mar 60	Air Transport	416UNTS81	105996
Switzerland	Brazil	10 Aug 48	Air Transport	94UNTS269	101314
Switzerland	Brazil	22 Jun 56	Taxation	56SWRO1087	462045

PARTY ONE	PARTY TWO	DATE	TOPIC	CITATION	NUMBER
Switzerland	Bulgaria	26 Nov 54	General Economic	54SWRO1171	462123
Switzerland	Burma	31 Oct 60	Air Transport	465UNTS97	106723
Switzerland	Cameroon	28 Jan 63	General Economic	64SWRO400	462124
Switzerland	Canada	14 Jul 47	Admin Cooperation	43UNTS103	100664
Switzerland	Canada	10 Jan 58	Air Transport	464UNTS21	106710
Switzerland	Canada	06 Mar 58	Atomic Energy	58SWRO724	462040
Switzerland	Canada	23 Jun 58	Admin Cooperation	391UNTS213	105625
Switzerland	Canada	22 Sep 59	Taxation	470UNTS101	106800
Switzerland	CERN (Nuc Resrch)	11 Jun 55	IGO Status/Immunit	249UNTS405	200544
Switzerland	Chile	17 Jun 55	General Trade	55SWRO705	462125
Switzerland	Chile	24 Nov 61	Loans and Credits	62SWRO77	462107
Switzerland	China People's Rep	14 Apr 57	Patents/Copyrights	57CCJC23	410405
Switzerland	Colombia	15 Jan 59	Milit Servic/Citiz	63SWRO143	462005
Switzerland	Congo (Brazzaville)	18 Oct 62	General Economic	64SWRO635	462126
Switzerland	Congo (Zaire)	29 Jun 59	Taxation	59SWRO639	462046
Switzerland	Cuba	30 Mar 54	General Trade	54SWRO537	462128
Switzerland	Czechoslovakia	10 Sep 47	Air Transport	35UNTS275	100559
Switzerland	Czechoslovakia	22 Dec 49	General Economic	50SWRO15	462158
Switzerland	Czechoslovakia	24 Nov 53	General Trade	54SWRO745	462157
Switzerland	Czechoslovakia	04 Jun 59	Non-ILO Labor	349UNTS121	105012
Switzerland	Czechoslovakia	26 Apr 60	Taxation	60SWRO538	462063
Switzerland	Denmark	21 Feb 48	Non-ILO Labor	14UNTS321	100224
Switzerland	Denmark	06 Apr 50	General Trade	87UNTS197	101173
Switzerland	Denmark	22 Jun 50	Air Transport	96UNTS3	101328
Switzerland	Denmark	20 Jan 51	Finance	87UNTS223	101174
Switzerland	Denmark	15 Sep 51	General Trade	110UNTS55	101501
Switzerland	Denmark	21 May 54	Non-ILO Labor	55SWRO290	462094
Switzerland	Denmark	14 Jan 57	Taxation	286UNTS27	104160
Switzerland	Denmark	14 Jan 57	Taxation	286UNTS85	104161
Switzerland	Denmark	21 Dec 59	Commodity Trade	633UNTS351	109045
Switzerland	Denmark	14 Aug 63	Land Transport	63SWRO797	462081
Switzerland	Ecuador	08 Oct 57	General Trade	59SWRO194	462130
Switzerland	EFTA (Free Trade)	10 Aug 61	IGO Status/Immunit	61SWRO763	462193
Switzerland	El Salvador	11 Feb 54	General Trade	54SWRO687	462154
Switzerland	Finland	15 Oct 55	Finance	55SWRO1014	462134
Switzerland	Finland	15 Oct 55	General Trade	55SWRO1017	462135
Switzerland	Finland	27 Dec 56	Taxation	277UNTS59	103997
Switzerland	Finland	27 Dec 56	Taxation	277UNTS7	103996
Switzerland	Finland	17 Jun 57	Taxation	57SWRO756	462048
Switzerland	Finland	07 Jan 59	Air Transport	353UNTS173	105042
Switzerland	France	29 Jun 46	Refugees	47FRJO2905	416404
Switzerland	France	01 Aug 46	Customs	12SWRS656	463071
Switzerland	France	01 Aug 46	Non-ILO Labor	11SWRS615	463015
Switzerland	France	01 Aug 46	Non-ILO Labor	11SWRS623	463018
Switzerland	France	01 Aug 46	Non-ILO Labor	11SWRS621	463016
Switzerland	France	27 Apr 48	Non-ILO Labor	51SWRO1019	462017
Switzerland	France	15 Jun 48	Specific Resources	66FRRT33	415405
Switzerland	France	04 Jul 49	Specific Property	50SWRO1334	462088
Switzerland	France	09 Jul 49	Non-ILO Labor	50SWRO1164	462096
Switzerland	France	21 Nov 49	Claims and Debts	49SWRO1953	462168
Switzerland	France	20 Nov 51	Land Transport	52SWRO623	462083
Switzerland	France	25 Feb 53	Territory Boundary	60SWRO1546	462174
Switzerland	France	25 Feb 53	Territory Boundary	57SWRO884	462002
Switzerland	France	31 Dec 53	Taxation	55SWRO115	462049
Switzerland	France	31 Dec 53	Taxation	55SWRO138	462050
Switzerland	France	31 Dec 53	Taxation	55SWRO132	462051
Switzerland	France	11 May 54	Land Transport	54SWRO1148	462077
Switzerland	France	29 Oct 55	General Trade	55SWRO1092	462136
Switzerland	France	25 Apr 56	Specific Property	58SWRO135	462087
Switzerland	France	25 Apr 56	Specific Property	58SWRO135	462004
Switzerland	France	14 Oct 57	Visas	58FRRT4	415406
Switzerland	France	04 Dec 57	Specific Resources	58SWRO49	462106
Switzerland	France	01 Aug 58	Milit Servic/Citiz	59SWRO223	462006
Switzerland	France	24 Sep 58	Non-ILO Labor	62SWRO1016	462102
Switzerland ·	France	16 Oct 58	Land Transport	58SWRO1087	462084

PARTY ONE	PARTY TWO	DATE	TOPIC	CITATION	NUMBER
Switzerland	France	16 Apr 59	Non-ILO Labor	61SWRO24	462101
Switzerland	France	03 Dec 59	Territory Boundary	60SWRO1555	462175
Switzerland	France	03 Dec 59	Specific Resources	60SWRO1548	462033
Switzerland	France	03 Dec 59	Territory Boundary	60SWRO1554	462173
Switzerland	France	03 Dec 59	Specific Resources	60SWRO1552	462034
Switzerland	France	03 Dec 59	Territory Boundary	60SWRO1550	462003
Switzerland	France	12 Apr 60	Refugees	60FRRT41	415407
Switzerland	France	28 Sep 60	Customs	61SWRO574	462074
Switzerland	France	28 Sep 60	General Transport	OUNTSO	110716
Switzerland	France	17 Sep 62	Customs	62SWRO1657	462070
Switzerland	France	16 Nov 62	Specific Resources	63SWRO961	462039
Switzerland	France	28 Feb 63	Visas	63FRRT34	415408
Switzerland	France	28 Feb 63	Visas	63FRRT37	415409
Switzerland	France	04 Apr 63	Claims and Debts	63FRRT45	415410
Switzerland	France	23 Aug 63	Specific Property	64SWRO1255	462032
Switzerland	France	23 Aug 63	Territory Boundary	64SWRO1272	462001
Switzerland	France	19 Sep 63	Finance	63FRRT83	415411
Switzerland	France	27 May 64	Non-ILO Labor	64FRRT42	415412
Switzerland	France	28 Sep 64	Admin Cooperation	64FRRT63	415413
Switzerland	France	10 Mar 65	Admin Cooperation	67FRJO604	416414
Switzerland	France	30 Jun 65	Admin Cooperation	65FRRT78	415415
Switzerland	France	24 Jul 65	Land Transport	65FRRT80	415417
Switzerland	France	24 Jul 65	General Transport	65FRRT80	415416
Switzerland	France	13 Sep 65	IGO Status/Immunit	69FRJO1004	416418
Switzerland	France	13 Sep 65	Atomic Energy	OUNTSO	109863
Switzerland	France	12 May 66	Visas	66FRJO2406	416419
Switzerland	France	09 Sep 66	Taxation	67FRJO1010	416420
Switzerland	France	16 Jun 67	Admin Cooperation	67FRJO1108	416421
Switzerland	France	19 Jul 67	Admin Cooperation	67FRJO1108	416422
Switzerland	Germany, West	24 Oct 50	Non-ILO Labor	51SWRO937	462092
Switzerland	Germany, West	02 Nov 50	Patents/Copyrights	51WGBB63	425752
Switzerland	Germany, West	20 Dec 51	Customs	52SWRO367	462114
Switzerland	Germany, West	25 Jan 52	Land Transport	53SWRO4	462067
Switzerland	Germany, West	14 Jul 52	Non-ILO Labor	53SWRO423	462103
Switzerland	Germany, West	19 Jul 52	Claims and Debts	53SWRO413	462026
Switzerland	Germany, West	26 Aug 52	Claims and Debts	53SWRO119	462115
Switzerland	Germany, West	26 Aug 52	Finance	53SWRO134	462116
Switzerland	Germany, West	26 Aug 52	Claims and Debts	53WGBB703	425753
Switzerland	Germany, West	08 Oct 52	Admin Cooperation	53WGBB519	425754
Switzerland	Germany, West	27 Feb 53	Claims and Debts	54SWRO3	462118
Switzerland	Germany, West	11 Jul 53	Claims and Debts	53SWRO936	462117
Switzerland	Germany, West	17 Dec 53	Land Transport	54SWRO449	462079
Switzerland	Germany, West	25 Oct 54	Extradition	55SWRO25	462007
Switzerland	Germany, West	02 Dec 54	General Trade	54SWRO1291	462112
Switzerland	Germany, West	28 Dec 54	Extradition	55WBGA19	424755
Switzerland	Germany, West	02 Feb 55	Non-ILO Labor	55SWRO315	462008
Switzerland	Germany, West	02 Feb 55	Non-ILO Labor	55WBGA48	424756
Switzerland	Germany, West	06 Dec 55	Admin Cooperation	57SWRO821	462025
Switzerland	Germany, West	02 May 56	Air Transport	559UNTS157	108158
Switzerland	Germany, West	06 Jun 56	Admin Cooperation	60SWRO617	462023
Switzerland	Germany, West	16 Jul 56	Finance	57SWRO399	462113
Switzerland	Germany, West	21 Jul 56	Visas	57WBGA107	424757
Switzerland	Germany, West	01 Nov 57	Specific Resources	59SWRO369	462105
Switzerland	Germany, West	05 Feb 58	Land Transport	60SWRO1639	462065
Switzerland	Germany, West	05 Feb 58	Land Transport	60SWRO1671	462066
Switzerland	Germany, West	21 Nov 58	Customs	60WGBB941	425758
Switzerland	Germany, West	01 Jun 61	Customs	64SWRO387	462072
Switzerland	Germany, West	29 Jun 61	Claims and Debts	62SWRO1311	462167
Switzerland	Germany, West	25 Feb 64	Non-ILO Labor	65WGBB1293	425759
Switzerland	Germany, West	23 Nov 64	Territory Boundary	67WGBB2040	425760
Switzerland	Germany, West	23 Nov 64	Territory Boundary	67WGBB2029	425761
Switzerland	Germany, West	29 Apr 65	Humanitarian	67WGBB773	425762
Switzerland	Germany, West	25 May 66	Territory Boundary	67WBGA165	424763
Switzerland	Germany, West	07 Mar 67	Patents/Copyrights	69WGBB138	425764
Switzerland	Germany, West	26 Mar 69	Admin Cooperation	69WBGA142	424765

PARTY ONE	PARTY TWO	DATE	TOPIC	CITATION	NUMBER
Switzerland	Germany, West	26 May 69	Admin Cooperation	71WGBB90	425766
Switzerland	Germany, West	21 May 70	Visas	70WGBB745	425767
Switzerland	Ghana	17 May 61	Air Transport	559UNTS193	108159
Switzerland	Ghana	06 Dec 63	Taxation	64SWRO426	462052
Switzerland	Greece	01 Apr 47	Mostfavored Nation	180UNTS115	102378
Switzerland	Greece	26 May 48	Air Transport	94UNTS217	101312
Switzerland	Greece	04 Apr 52	Finance	166UNTS271	102192
Switzerland	Greece	12 Jun 62	Taxation	492UNTS47	107186
Switzerland	Guatemala	01 Apr 55	General Trade	55SWRO407	462137
Switzerland	Guinea	26 Apr 62	General Economic	63SWRO732	462138
Switzerland	Guinea	01 Feb 63	Air Transport	499UNTS35	107291
Switzerland	Hungary	02 Feb 48	Taxation	49SWRO135	462053
Switzerland	Hungary	27 Jun 50	General Economic	50SWRO612	462139
Switzerland	Hungary	19 Jul 50	Claims and Debts	50SWRO736	462169
Switzerland	IBRD (World Bank)	29 Jun 51	IGO Status/Immunit	216UNTS347	200529
Switzerland	IBRD (World Bank)	17 Sep 56	Loans and Credits	340UNTS311	200560
Switzerland	IBRD (World Bank)	11 Oct 61	IBRD Project	415UNTS396	200592
Switzerland	ICJ Option Clause	06 Jul 48	ICJ Option Clause	17UNTS115	100272
Switzerland	ICJ Option Clause	06 Jul 48	ICJ Option Clause	17UNTS111	100271
Switzerland	IDA (Devel Assoc)	26 Jun 67	Loans and Credits	0UNTS0	200648
Switzerland	ILO (Labor Org)	11 Mar 46	IGO Status/Immunit	15UNTS377	200103
Switzerland	India	14 Aug 48	General Amity	33UNTS3	100509
Switzerland	India	24 Jun 49	Air Transport	95UNTS109	101319
Switzerland	India	28 Aug 58	Taxation	58SWRO795	462054
Switzerland	India	30 Jul 60	Finance	60SWRO1678	462140
Switzerland	Indonesia	30 Dec 54	General Trade	55SWRO64	462141
Switzerland	Int Bureau Educ	15 Nov 46	IGO Status/Immunit	56SWRO1210	462187
Switzerland	Int Rail Transport	28 Sep 56	IGO Status/Immunit	56SWRO1367	462188
Switzerland	Intgov Eur Migrat	03 May 54	IGO Status/Immunit	56SWRO1213	462192
Switzerland	Iran	27 May 54	Air Transport	496UNTS273	107257
Switzerland	Iran	07 Feb 57	Taxation	57SWRO213	462055
Switzerland	Iran	01 Feb 64	General Economic	64SWRO87	462142
Switzerland	Iran	20 Mar 66	Claims and Debts	0IRTB65	433103
Switzerland	Iran	31 Dec 68	Visas	0IRTB65	433104
Switzerland	Iraq	31 Mar 52	Air Transport	311UNTS43	104498
Switzerland	Ireland	09 Jun 47	Visas	553UNTS169	108084
Switzerland	Ireland	06 May 48	Air Transport	334UNTS187	104768
Switzerland	Ireland	14 Mar 49	Non-ILO Labor	553UNTS175	108085
Switzerland	Ireland	26 Dec 51	General Trade	558UNTS305	108149
Switzerland	Ireland	18 Jun 58	Taxation	553UNTS183	108086
Switzerland	Ireland	08 Nov 66	Taxation	0UNTS0	109499
Switzerland	Israel	19 Nov 52	Air Transport	232UNTS3	103226
Switzerland	Israel	01 Jul 53	Postal Service	220UNTS41	102986
Switzerland	Israel	14 Sep 56	General Trade	56SWRO1281	462143
Switzerland	Israel	31 Dec 58	Extradition	377UNTS305	105408
Switzerland	Israel	29 Jun 62	Visas	448UNTS303	106443
Switzerland	Israel	01 May 67	Visas	630UNTS313	108978
Switzerland	Italy	09 Jul 47	Health/Educ/Welfare	14SWRS526	463145
Switzerland	Italy	22 Jun 48	Non-ILO Labor	48SWRO818	462019
Switzerland	Italy	18 Jun 49	Specific Property	55SWRO611	462037
Switzerland	Italy	24 Mar 50	Water Transport	52ITGU29	435367
Switzerland	Italy	21 Oct 50	General Trade	52ITGU57	435368
Switzerland	Italy	05 Apr 51	Territory Boundary	53ITGU91	435372
Switzerland	Italy	05 Apr 51	Territory Boundary	53SWRO409	462178
Switzerland	Italy	05 Apr 51	Territory Boundary	53SWRO403	462177
Switzerland	Italy	14 May 51	Admin Cooperation	51SWRO644	462031
Switzerland	Italy	17 Oct 51	Non-ILO Labor	54SWRO250	462097
Switzerland	Italy	04 Jul 52	Territory Boundary	55SWRO557	462180
Switzerland	Italy	25 Nov 52	Territory Boundary	55SWRO626	462176
Switzerland	Italy	02 Jul 53	Customs	257UNTS99	103653
Switzerland	Italy	23 Jul 55	Land Transport	284UNTS279	104142
Switzerland	Italy	17 Sep 55	Specific Resources	291UNTS213	104257
Switzerland	Italy	22 Dec 55	Finance	260UNTS339	103717
Switzerland	Italy	02 Feb 56	Sanitation	291UNTS113	104247
Switzerland	Italy	01 Jun 56	Telecommunications	57ITGU159	435376

PARTY ONE	PARTY TWO	DATE	TOPIC	CITATION	NUMBER
Switzerland	Italy	04 Jun 56	Air Transport	378UNTS311	105429
Switzerland	Italy	29 Jun 56	Finance	284UNTS299	104144
Switzerland	Italy	31 Oct 56	Taxation	58ITGU50	435377
Switzerland	Italy	22 Dec 56	Taxation	57SWRO44	462020
Switzerland	Italy	01 Apr 57	Loans and Credits	59ITDI411	436378
Switzerland	Italy	27 May 57	Specific Resources	59SWRO432	462036
Switzerland	Italy	19 Sep 57	Land Transport	363UNTS69	105200
Switzerland	Italy	23 May 58	Land Transport	363UNTS81	105201
Switzerland	Italy	31 Jul 58	Taxation	61SWRO413	462056
Switzerland	Italy	22 Nov 58	Commodity Trade	62ITGU312	435382
Switzerland	Italy	10 Dec 58	Admin Cooperation	60ITDI306	436383
Switzerland	Italy	10 Dec 59	Water Transport	61ITDI298	436384
Switzerland	Italy	04 Mar 60	Land Transport	62ITGU212	435385
Switzerland	Italy	11 Mar 61	Customs	63SWRO711	462075
Switzerland	Italy	25 Apr 61	Commodity Trade	62SWRO189	462144
Switzerland	Italy	16 May 61	Territory Boundary	63SWRO520	462179
Switzerland	Italy	15 Dec 61	Customs	63SWRO724	462064
Switzerland	Italy	16 Apr 62	Land Transport	63ITDI301	436390
Switzerland	Italy	14 Aug 62	Land Transport	63ITDI302	436391
Switzerland	Italy	14 Dec 62	Non-ILO Labor	64SWRO730	462098
Switzerland	Italy	16 Dec 62	General Ad Hoc	63ITDI303	436392
Switzerland	Italy	31 May 63	Customs	64ITDI283	436394
Switzerland	Italy	10 Aug 64	Non-ILO Labor	65ITGU54	435396
Switzerland	ITU (Telecommun)	25 Feb 48	IGO Status/Immunit	56SWRO1196	462190
Switzerland	Ivory Coast	26 Jun 62	General Economic	63SWRO53	462127
Switzerland	Ivory Coast	17 Nov 62	Air Transport	499UNTS3	107289
Switzerland	Japan	25 Jun 53	Claims and Debts	54SWRO530	462027
Switzerland	Japan	21 Jan 55	Claims and Debts	55SWRO357	462170
Switzerland	Japan	24 May 56	Air Transport	312UNTS3	104509
Switzerland	Japan	25 Mar 57	Visas	318UNTS239	104618
Switzerland	Lebanon	03 Dec 45	Recognition	11SWRS673	463021
Switzerland	Lebanon	03 Mar 54	Air Transport	255UNTS127	103608
Switzerland	Lebanon	11 Sep 57	Taxation	57SWRO846	462057
Switzerland	Liberia	31 Aug 61	Air Transport	559UNTS215	108160
Switzerland	Liechtenstein	10 Dec 54	Non-ILO Labor	55SWRO537	462186
Switzerland	Liechtenstein	07 May 55	Territory Boundary	56SWRO143	462181
Switzerland	Liechtenstein	06 Nov 63	Consul/Citizenship	64SWRO1	462183
Switzerland	Liechtenstein	06 Nov 63	Consul/Citizenship	64SWRO5	462184
Switzerland	Liechtenstein	24 Sep 64	Customs	64SWRO851	462182
Switzerland	Liechtenstein	24 Sep 64	Customs	64SWRO849	462185
Switzerland	Luxembourg	09 Apr 51	Air Transport	254UNTS389	103601
Switzerland	Luxembourg	14 Nov 55	Non-ILO Labor	57SWRO282	462099
Switzerland	Malta	20 Jan 65	General Trade	548UNTS193	107978
Switzerland	Mexico	02 Sep 50	General Trade	50SWRO915	462147
Switzerland	Mexico	02 Jun 66	Air Transport	68MEXD2702	444041
Switzerland	Morocco	29 Aug 57	Mostfavored Nation	58SWRO271	462146
Switzerland	Morocco	05 Jul 62	Air Transport	498UNTS189	107282
Switzerland	Morocco	05 Jul 62	Air Transport	498UNTS171	107281
Switzerland	Multilateral	27 Mar 41	Military Mission	67UNTS231	200222
Switzerland	Multilateral	02 Aug 44	Scientific Project	67UNTS221	200221
Switzerland	Multilateral	07 Dec 44	Air Transport	84UNTS389	200252
Switzerland	Multilateral	07 Dec 44	Air Transport	171UNTS345	200501
Switzerland	Multilateral	07 Dec 44	IGO Establishment	15UNTS295	200102
Switzerland	Multilateral	22 Jul 46	IGO Establishment	9UNTS3	100125
Switzerland	Multilateral	22 Jul 46	IGO Establishment	14UNTS185	100221
Switzerland	Multilateral	15 Oct 46	Refugees	11UNTS73	100150
Switzerland	Multilateral	11 Dec 46	Sanitation	12UNTS179	100186
Switzerland	Multilateral	08 Feb 47	Patents/Copyrights	14UNTS287	100222
Switzerland	Multilateral	06 Jun 47	Patents/Copyrights	46UNTS249	100714
Switzerland	Multilateral	02 Oct 47	Telecommunications	193UNTS188	102616
Switzerland	Multilateral	11 Oct 47	IGO Establishment	77UNTS143	100998
Switzerland	Multilateral	13 Nov 47	Visas	251UNTS79	103534
Switzerland	Multilateral	06 Mar 48	Water Transport	289UNTS3	104214
Switzerland	Multilateral	10 May 48	Culture	289UNTS111	104215
Switzerland	Multilateral	10 Jun 48	Humanitarian	164UNTS113	102163

PARTY ONE	PARTY TWO	DATE	TOPIC	CITATION	NUMBER
Switzerland	Multilateral	10 Jun 48	Humanitarian	191UNTS3	102576
Switzerland	Multilateral	19 Jun 48	Air Transport	310UNTS151	104492
Switzerland	Multilateral	26 Jun 48	Culture	331UNTS217	104757
Switzerland	Multilateral	24 Jul 48	Sanitation	66UNTS25	100847
Switzerland	Multilateral	19 Nov 48	Sanitation	44UNTS277	100688
Switzerland	Multilateral	09 Dec 48	Scientific Project	20UNTS229	100318
Switzerland	Multilateral	12 Feb 49	Customs	189UNTS33	102541
Switzerland	Multilateral	23 Mar 49	Commodity Trade	203UNTS179	102746
Switzerland	Multilateral	04 May 49	Admin Cooperation	30UNTS23	100446
Switzerland	Multilateral	04 May 49	Admin Cooperation	98UNTS101	101358
Switzerland	Multilateral	04 May 49	Admin Cooperation	92UNTS19	101257
Switzerland	Multilateral	04 May 49	Admin Cooperation	30UNTS3	100445
Switzerland	Multilateral	04 May 49	Admin Cooperation	47UNTS159	100728
Switzerland	Multilateral	05 May 49	IGO Establishment	87UNTS103	101168
Switzerland	Multilateral	16 Jun 49	Land Transport	45UNTS149	100696
Switzerland	Multilateral	12 Aug 49	Humanitarian	75UNTS287	100973
Switzerland	Multilateral	12 Aug 49	Humanitarian	75UNTS31	100970
Switzerland	Multilateral	12 Aug 49	Humanitarian	75UNTS85	100971
Switzerland	Multilateral	12 Aug 49	General Military	75UNTS135	100972
Switzerland	Multilateral	02 Sep 49	IGO Status/Immunit	250UNTS12	103515
Switzerland	Multilateral	19 Sep 49	Land Transport	125UNTS3	101671
Switzerland	Multilateral	16 Dec 49	Admin Cooperation	72UNTS3	100924
Switzerland	Multilateral	13 May 50	Land Transport	128UNTS171	101719
Switzerland	Multilateral	27 Jul 50	Non-ILO Labor	166UNTS73	102186
Switzerland	Multilateral	18 Oct 50	Specific Resources	638UNTS185	109134
Switzerland	Multilateral	22 Nov 50	Culture	131UNTS25	101734
Switzerland	Multilateral	07 Dec 50	Admin Cooperation	212UNTS17	102861
Switzerland	Multilateral	15 Dec 50	IGO Operations	160UNTS267	102111
Switzerland	Multilateral	15 Dec 50	Customs	347UNTS127	104994
Switzerland	Multilateral	15 Dec 50	Customs	157UNTS129	102052
Switzerland	Multilateral	25 May 51	Status of Forces	175UNTS215	102303
Switzerland	Multilateral	02 Jul 51	Refugees	189UNTS137	102545
Switzerland	Multilateral	09 Oct 51	IGO Establishment	220UNTS121	102997
Switzerland	Multilateral	06 Dec 51	Admin Cooperation	150UNTS67	101963
Switzerland	Multilateral	10 Jan 52	Visas	163UNTS27	102139
Switzerland	Multilateral	10 Jan 52	Visas	163UNTS3	102138
Switzerland	Multilateral	15 Feb 52	Scientific Project	132UNTS51	101751
Switzerland	Multilateral	10 May 52	Admin Cooperation	439UNTS217	106331
Switzerland	Multilateral	10 May 52	Admin Cooperation	439UNTS193	106330
Switzerland	Multilateral	10 May 52	Taxation	439UNTS233	106332
Switzerland	Multilateral	11 Jul 52	Postal Service	171UNTS3	102224
Switzerland	Multilateral	11 Jul 52	Postal Service	170UNTS3	102221
Switzerland	Multilateral	11 Jul 52	Postal Service	171UNTS89	102225
Switzerland	Multilateral	11 Jul 52	Postal Service	170UNTS269	102223
Switzerland	Multilateral	11 Jul 52	Postal Service	171UNTS143	102226
Switzerland	Multilateral	11 Jul 52	IGO Establishment	169UNTS3	102220
Switzerland	Multilateral	11 Jul 52	Postal Service	170UNTS63	102222
Switzerland	Multilateral	28 Aug 52	Claims and Debts	175UNTS69	102296
Switzerland	Multilateral	06 Sep 52	Patents/Copyrights	216UNTS132	102937
Switzerland	Multilateral	07 Oct 52	Admin Cooperation	310UNTS181	104493
Switzerland	Multilateral	07 Nov 52	General Trade	221UNTS255	103010
Switzerland	Multilateral	27 Feb 53	Claims and Debts	333UNTS3	104764
Switzerland	Multilateral	11 May 53	Sanitation	456UNTS3	106555
Switzerland	Multilateral	01 Jul 53	IGO Establishment	200UNTS149	102701
Switzerland	Multilateral	17 Oct 53	General Transport	184UNTS42	102438
Switzerland	Multilateral	19 Oct 53	IGO Establishment	207UNTS189	102807
Switzerland	Multilateral	07 Dec 53	Admin Cooperation	182UNTS51	102422
Switzerland	Multilateral	11 Dec 53	Patents/Copyrights	218UNTS27	102952
Switzerland	Multilateral	11 Dec 53	Sanitation	191UNTS285	102588
Switzerland	Multilateral	25 Feb 54	Air Transport	215UNTS249	102922
Switzerland	Multilateral	01 Mar 54	Admin Cooperation	286UNTS265	104173
Switzerland	Multilateral	12 May 54	Admin Cooperation	327UNTS3	104714
Switzerland	Multilateral	21 May 54	Non-ILO Labor	345UNTS285	104973
Switzerland	Multilateral	04 Jun 54	Customs	276UNTS191	103992
Switzerland	Multilateral	04 Jun 54	Customs	282UNTS249	104101

PARTY ONE	PARTY TWO	DATE	TOPIC	CITATION	NUMBER
Switzerland	Multilateral	14 Jun 54	Air Transport	320UNTS209	104643
Switzerland	Multilateral	14 Jun 54	Air Transport	320UNTS217	104644
Switzerland	Multilateral	28 Sep 54	Refugees	360UNTS117	105158
Switzerland	Multilateral	19 Dec 54	Culture	218UNTS139	102955
Switzerland	Multilateral	28 Sep 55	Air Transport	478UNTS371	106943
Switzerland	Multilateral	12 Oct 55	IGO Establishment	560UNTS3	108165
Switzerland	Multilateral	20 Oct 55	IGO Establishment	378UNTS159	105425
Switzerland	Multilateral	01 Mar 56	Customs	343UNTS129	104923
Switzerland	Multilateral	25 Apr 56	Commodity Trade	270UNTS103	103896
Switzerland	Multilateral	30 Apr 56	Air Transport	310UNTS229	104494
Switzerland	Multilateral	18 May 56	Customs	327UNTS123	104721
Switzerland	Multilateral	18 May 56	Customs	338UNTS103	104834
Switzerland	Multilateral	18 May 56	Customs	319UNTS21	104630
Switzerland	Multilateral	19 May 56	Land Transport	399UNTS189	105742
Switzerland	Multilateral	09 Jul 56	Non-ILO Labor	314UNTS3	104539
Switzerland	Multilateral	25 Sep 56	Air Transport	334UNTS89	104767
Switzerland	Multilateral	25 Sep 56	Air Transport	334UNTS13	104766
Switzerland	Multilateral	24 Oct 56	Admin Cooperation	510UNTS161	107412
Switzerland	Multilateral	26 Oct 56	IGO Establishment	276UNTS3	103988
Switzerland	Multilateral	15 Jun 57	General Trade	550UNTS45	108008
Switzerland	Multilateral	15 Jun 57	Patents/Copyrights	583UNTS3	108470
Switzerland	Multilateral	27 Sep 57	Admin Cooperation	299UNTS211	104314
Switzerland	Multilateral	30 Sep 57	General Transport	619UNTS77	108940
Switzerland	Multilateral	03 Oct 57	Postal Service	364UNTS3	105211
Switzerland	Multilateral	03 Oct 57	Postal Service	365UNTS3	105213
Switzerland	Multilateral	03 Oct 57	Postal Service	366UNTS3	105215
Switzerland	Multilateral	03 Oct 57	Postal Service	366UNTS141	105217
Switzerland	Multilateral	03 Oct 57	Postal Service	365UNTS207	105214
Switzerland	Multilateral	03 Oct 57	Postal Service	366UNTS87	105216
Switzerland	Multilateral	03 Oct 57	Postal Service	366UNTS255	105219
Switzerland	Multilateral	03 Oct 57	Postal Service	364UNTS331	105212
Switzerland	Multilateral	23 Nov 57	Refugees	506UNTS125	107384
Switzerland	Multilateral	13 Dec 57	Land Transport	372UNTS159	105296
Switzerland	Multilateral	15 Jan 58	Customs	383UNTS229	105503
Switzerland	Multilateral	15 Apr 58	Health/Educ/Welfare	539UNTS27	107822
Switzerland	Multilateral	29 Apr 58	Specific Resources	559UNTS285	108164
Switzerland	Multilateral	29 Apr 58	Dispute Settlement	450UNTS169	106466
Switzerland	Multilateral	29 Apr 58	Territory Boundary	516UNTS205	107477
Switzerland	Multilateral	29 Apr 58	Territory Boundary	499UNTS311	107302
Switzerland	Multilateral	29 Apr 58	Water Transport	450UNTS11	106465
Switzerland	Multilateral	15 Dec 58	Sanitation	351UNTS159	105022
Switzerland	Multilateral	15 Jan 59	Customs	348UNTS13	104996
Switzerland	Multilateral	06 Apr 59	Commodity Trade	349UNTS167	105013
Switzerland	Multilateral	11 May 59	Claims and Debts	527UNTS145	107623
Switzerland	Multilateral	19 Nov 59	IGO Operations	410UNTS156	105902
Switzerland	Multilateral	04 Jan 60	IGO Establishment	370UNTS3	105266
Switzerland	Multilateral	22 Apr 60	Air Transport	418UNTS211	106023
Switzerland	Multilateral	28 Apr 60	Health/Educ/Welfare	376UNTS111	105377
Switzerland	Multilateral	17 Jun 60	Humanitarian	536UNTS27	107794
Switzerland	Multilateral	28 Jul 60	IGO Status/Immunit	394UNTS37	105667
Switzerland	Multilateral	06 Oct 60	Customs	473UNTS131	106861
Switzerland	Multilateral	01 Dec 60	Scientific Project	414UNTS110	105970
Switzerland	Multilateral	09 Dec 60	Customs	429UNTS211	106200
Switzerland	Multilateral	13 Feb 61	ILO Labor	0UNTS0	110306
Switzerland	Multilateral	27 Mar 61	IGO Establishment	420UNTS109	106043
Switzerland	Multilateral	30 Mar 61	Sanitation	520UNTS151	107515
Switzerland	Multilateral	18 Apr 61	Dispute Settlement	500UNTS243	107312
Switzerland	Multilateral	18 Apr 61	Consul/Citizenship	500UNTS95	107310
Switzerland	Multilateral	08 Jun 61	Customs	473UNTS187	106863
Switzerland	Multilateral	08 Jun 61	Customs	473UNTS153	106862
Switzerland	Multilateral	21 Jun 61	IGO Establishment	514UNTS209	107449
Switzerland	Multilateral	18 Sep 61	Air Transport	500UNTS31	107305
Switzerland	Multilateral	05 Oct 61	Admin Cooperation	0UNTS0	109431
Switzerland	Multilateral	05 Oct 61	Patents/Copyrights	527UNTS181	107625
Switzerland	Multilateral	06 Dec 61	Customs	473UNTS219	106864

PARTY ONE	PARTY TWO	DATE	TOPIC	CITATION	NUMBER
Switzerland	Multilateral	14 May 62	Scientific Project	544UNTS39	107910
Switzerland	Multilateral	15 May 62	Commodity Trade	444UNTS3	106367
Switzerland	Multilateral	14 Jun 62	IGO Establishment	528UNTS33	107634
Switzerland	Multilateral	28 Sep 62	IGO Establishment	469UNTS169	106791
Switzerland	Multilateral	24 Apr 63	Consul/Citizenship	596UNTS487	108640
Switzerland	Multilateral	24 Apr 63	Consul/Citizenship	596UNTS261	108638
Switzerland	Multilateral	05 Aug 63	Sanitation	480UNTS43	106964
Switzerland	Multilateral	02 Sep 63	General Transport	548UNTS129	107974
Switzerland	Multilateral	14 May 64	Refugees	528UNTS23	107633
Switzerland	Multilateral	14 May 64	Refugees	528UNTS13	107632
Switzerland	Multilateral	14 May 64	Visas	528UNTS3	107631
Switzerland	Multilateral	10 Jul 64	Postal Service	613UNTS3	108850
Switzerland	Multilateral	10 Jul 64	Postal Service	613UNTS193	108852
Switzerland	Multilateral	10 Jul 64	Postal Service	612UNTS3	108847
Switzerland	Multilateral	10 Jul 64	Postal Service	612UNTS361	108849
Switzerland	Multilateral	10 Jul 64	Postal Service	613UNTS3	108851
Switzerland	Multilateral	10 Jul 64	Postal Service	611UNTS387	108846
Switzerland	Multilateral	10 Jul 64	Postal Service	611UNTS105	108845
Switzerland	Multilateral	10 Jul 64	Postal Service	612UNTS233	108848
Switzerland	Multilateral	10 Jul 64	Postal Service	611UNTS7	108844
Switzerland	Multilateral	20 Aug 64	Telecommunications	514UNTS25	107441
Switzerland	Multilateral	01 Dec 64	Water Transport	550UNTS133	108012
Switzerland	Multilateral	09 Mar 65	Water Transport	591UNTS265	108564
Switzerland	Multilateral	08 Jul 65	General Trade	597UNTS3	108641
Switzerland	Multilateral	05 Apr 66	Water Transport	640UNTS133	109159
Switzerland	Multilateral	30 Apr 66	Specific Resources	620UNTS191	108956
Switzerland	Multilateral	27 Jan 67	Scientific Project	610UNTS205	108843
Switzerland	Multilateral	08 Mar 68	Visas	634UNTS199	109062
Switzerland	Multilateral	18 Mar 68	Commodity Trade	0UNTS0	109262
Switzerland	Multilateral	24 Sep 68	Air Transport	0UNTS0	110612
Switzerland	Netherlands	24 Oct 45	Finance	3UNTS73	100025
Switzerland	Netherlands	07 Mar 49	Air Transport	35UNTS69	100551
Switzerland	Netherlands	15 Sep 49	Visas	252UNTS13	103555
Switzerland	Netherlands	12 Nov 51	Taxation	126UNTS157	101688
Switzerland	Netherlands	12 Nov 51	Taxation	126UNTS173	101689
Switzerland	Netherlands	20 May 52	Land Transport	52SWRO603	462085
Switzerland	Netherlands	22 Jul 52	Land Transport	52NET97	447034
Switzerland	Netherlands	20 Nov 52	Non-ILO Labor	163UNTS121	102146
Switzerland	Netherlands	28 May 53	General Trade	54NET25	447040
Switzerland	Netherlands	26 Aug 53	Finance	53NET84	447042
Switzerland	Netherlands	03 Nov 53	Customs	293UNTS53	104285
Switzerland	Netherlands	23 Oct 56	Admin Cooperation	287UNTS203	104186
Switzerland	Netherlands	21 Jun 57	General Trade	57SWRO521	462149
Switzerland	Netherlands	28 Mar 58	Non-ILO Labor	318UNTS175	104614
Switzerland	Netherlands	29 Mar 58	Visas	330UNTS101	104741
Switzerland	Netherlands	14 Apr 59	Finance	486UNTS367	107086
Switzerland	New Zealand	30 Jul 48	Visas	18UNTS177	100287
Switzerland	New Zealand	09 Oct 52	General Trade	171UNTS275	102231
Switzerland	New Zealand	30 Dec 58	Taxation	380UNTS313	105463
Switzerland	Niger	28 Mar 62	General Economic	63SWRO46	462148
Switzerland	Nigeria	11 Oct 65	Air Transport	602UNTS137	108710
Switzerland	Norway	15 Jul 47	Finance	12UNTS351	100192
Switzerland	Norway	01 Aug 47	Visas	90UNTS65	101227
Switzerland	Norway	26 Jun 48	General Trade	29UNTS193	100440
Switzerland	Norway	13 Jan 51	General Trade	2NORT547	451154
Switzerland	Norway	31 Mar 53	Milit Servic/Citiz	2NORT602	451155
Switzerland	Norway	30 Dec 54	Air Transport	311UNTS147	104502
Switzerland	Norway	07 Dec 56	Taxation	3NORT700	451156
Switzerland	Norway	07 Dec 56	Taxation	57SWRO728	462059
Switzerland	Norway	07 Dec 56	Taxation	57SWRO715	462058
Switzerland	Norway	07 Dec 56	Taxation	3NORT701	451157
Switzerland	Norway	03 Jul 57	Taxation	57SWRO733	462060
Switzerland	Norway	29 Jan 59	Visas	3NORT761	451158
Switzerland	Norway	25 May 63	Visas	3NORT889	451159
Switzerland	Pakistan	17 Mar 52	Air Transport	192UNTS237	102603

PARTY ONE	PARTY TWO	DATE	TOPIC	CITATION	NUMBER
Switzerland	Pakistan	30 Dec 59	Taxation	60SWRO1058	462061
Switzerland	Peru	20 Jul 53	General Trade	55SWRO287	462150
Switzerland	Peru	23 Nov 56	Air Transport	411UNTS97	105916
Switzerland	Philippines	26 Oct 46	General Trade	1PTS319	465005
Switzerland	Philippines	08 Mar 52	Air Transport	231UNTS301	103225
Switzerland	Philippines	30 Aug 56	General Amity	293UNTS43	104284
Switzerland	Poland	25 Jun 49	General Economic	49SWRO832	462151
Switzerland	Poland	25 Jun 49	Claims and Debts	49SWRO839	462171
Switzerland	Poland	18 May 61	Air Transport	559UNTS233	108161
Switzerland	Poland	13 Jun 61	Taxation	61SWRO570	462062
Switzerland	Poland	13 Jun 61	Taxation	61PZUM121	458084
Switzerland	Portugal	09 Dec 46	Air Transport	310UNTS251	104495
Switzerland	Portugal	10 May 58	Water Transport	58SWRO781	462078
Switzerland	Portugal	22 Feb 62	Commodity Trade	62SWRO257	462152
Switzerland	Romania	03 Aug 51	General Economic	51SWRO827	462153
Switzerland	Senegal	16 Aug 62	General Economic	64SWRO718	462155
Switzerland	Senegal	23 Jan 63	Air Transport	524UNTS23	107564
Switzerland	South Africa	26 Aug 54	Air Transport	216UNTS19	102929
Switzerland	South Africa	07 Nov 55	Taxation	56SWRO655	462041
Switzerland	South Africa	07 Nov 55	Taxation	230UNTS279	103190
Switzerland	South Africa	19 Oct 59	Air Transport	61SWRO907	462090
Switzerland	South Africa	19 Oct 59	Air Transport	559UNTS257	108162
Switzerland	South Africa	03 Jul 67	Taxation	643UNTS3	109184
Switzerland	Spain	17 Jul 46	Air Transport	47SPBO2004	460250
Switzerland	Spain	03 Aug 50	Air Transport	254UNTS365	103600
Switzerland	Spain	27 Nov 54	General Economic	55SPBO1001	460251
Switzerland	Spain	21 Sep 59	Non-ILO Labor	60SPBO1406	460252
Switzerland	Spain	21 Nov 59	General Trade	59SWRO2095	462131
Switzerland	Spain	25 Jan 60	Non-ILO Labor	60SPBO2707	460253
Switzerland	Spain	02 Apr 60	General Trade	60SWRO457	462132
Switzerland	Spain	02 Mar 61	Non-ILO Labor	61SPBO912	460254
Switzerland	Spain	23 Jan 63	Land Transport	63SPBO1109	460255
Switzerland	Spain	27 Nov 63	Taxation	64SWRO953	462047
Switzerland	Spain	27 Nov 63	Taxation	65SPBO1201	460256
Switzerland	Sudan	18 Feb 63	Air Transport	563UNTS281	108215
Switzerland	Sweden	16 Mar 48	Non-ILO Labor	197UNTS39	102632
Switzerland	Sweden	16 Oct 48	Taxation	197UNTS55	102634
Switzerland	Sweden	16 Oct 48	Taxation	197UNTS101	102635
Switzerland	Sweden	03 Jun 50	General Trade	50SOFM853	461117
Switzerland	Sweden	18 Oct 50	Air Transport	166UNTS49	102185
Switzerland	Sweden	11 Jan 51	General Economic	51SOFM1	461132
Switzerland	Sweden	20 Jun 51	General Trade	51SWRO619	462156
Switzerland	Sweden	20 Jun 51	Finance	51SOFM296	461147
Switzerland	Sweden	20 Jun 51	General Trade	51SOFM277	461146
Switzerland	Sweden	18 Oct 51	Air Transport	51SOFM477	461154
Switzerland	Sweden	02 Jul 52	General Trade	52SOFM289	461168
Switzerland	Sweden	05 Jun 53	General Trade	53SOFM708	461185
Switzerland	Sweden	12 Aug 53	Customs	232UNTS59	103229
Switzerland	Sweden	25 Sep 54	Patents/Copyrights	262UNTS205	103746
Switzerland	Sweden	17 Dec 54	Non-ILO Labor	369UNTS233	105260
Switzerland	Sweden	30 Apr 58	Land Transport	427UNTS295	106161
Switzerland	Syria	03 Dec 45	Recognition	11SWRS708	463022
Switzerland	Syria	26 May 54	Air Transport	255UNTS145	103609
Switzerland	Taiwan	13 Mar 46	Consul/Citizenship	14UNTS159	100218
Switzerland	Tanganyika	30 Jan 64	Admin Cooperation	64SWRO276	462028
Switzerland	Thailand	13 Oct 56	Air Transport	312UNTS43	104510
Switzerland	Thailand	07 Oct 70	General Economic	0UNTS0	110824
Switzerland	Tunisia	26 Oct 57	Mostfavored Nation	58SWRO260	462159
Switzerland	Tunisia	21 May 60	Air Transport	497UNTS109	107265
Switzerland	Tunisia	02 Dec 61	General Trade	62SWRO1517	462160
Switzerland	Tunisia	02 Dec 61	Tech Assistance	64SWRO70	462109
Switzerland	Tunisia	02 Dec 61	Finance	64SWRO67	462108
Switzerland	Tunisia	15 Nov 63	Claims and Debts	63SWRO1073	462161
Switzerland	Turkey	12 Sep 45	General Economic	46TURG2301	466090
Switzerland	Turkey	16 Feb 49	Air Transport	72UNTS175	100933

PARTY ONE	PARTY TWO	DATE	TOPIC	CITATION	NUMBER
Switzerland	Turkey	22 Dec 58	Direct Aid	64TURG909	466115
Switzerland	UK Great Britain	12 Mar 46	Finance	6UNTS107	100070
Switzerland	UK Great Britain	10 Jun 47	Visas	11UNTS217	100160
Switzerland	UK Great Britain	05 Apr 50	Air Transport	51SWRO573	462091
Switzerland	UK Great Britain	08 Dec 50	Claims and Debts	175UNTS55	102295
Switzerland	UK Great Britain	13 May 52	Air Transport	164UNTS91	102160
Switzerland	UK Great Britain	16 Jan 53	Non-ILO Labor	196UNTS119	102621
Switzerland	UK Great Britain	16 Jul 54	Claims and Debts	199UNTS197	102685
Switzerland	UK Great Britain	30 Sep 54	Taxation	209UNTS197	102828
Switzerland	UK Great Britain	12 Jun 56	Taxation	269UNTS133	103879
Switzerland	UK Great Britain	06 May 59	Claims and Debts	343UNTS315	104938
Switzerland	UK Great Britain	27 Feb 61	Visas	404UNTS167	105809
Switzerland	UK Great Britain	20 Oct 61	Loans and Credits	431UNTS29	106206
Switzerland	UK Great Britain	27 Aug 63	General Transport	486UNTS183	107079
Switzerland	UK Great Britain	11 Aug 64	Atomic Energy	552UNTS271	108059
Switzerland	UK Great Britain	07 Jul 65	Dispute Settlement	605UNTS205	108765
Switzerland	UK Great Britain	29 Jun 67	Gen Communications	617UNTS261	108916
Switzerland	UK Great Britain	21 Feb 68	Non-ILO Labor	0UNTS0	110034
Switzerland	UK Great Britain	26 Nov 68	Taxation	0UNTS0	109662
Switzerland	UK Great Britain	12 Dec 68	Atomic Energy	0UNTS0	109787
Switzerland	United Arab Rep	06 Apr 50	Finance	50SWRO329	462129
Switzerland	United Arab Rep	15 May 50	Air Transport	95UNTS255	101325
Switzerland	United Arab Rep	05 Jan 55	Taxation	216UNTS41	102931
Switzerland	United Arab Rep	14 Jul 60	Air Transport	497UNTS161	107268
Switzerland	United Nations	01 Jul 46	Specific Property	1UNTS153	200007
Switzerland	United Nations	01 Jul 46	IGO Status/Immunit	1UNTS163	200008
Switzerland	United Nations	14 Sep 49	IGO Operations	43UNTS327	200183
Switzerland	United Nations	09 Jul 56	Telecommunications	56SWRO1273	462191
Switzerland	United Nations	03 Jun 66	Claims and Debts	564UNTS193	200621
Switzerland	United Nations	13 May 68	IGO Operations	636UNTS353	200637
Switzerland	United Nations	11 Dec 68	Postal Service	0UNTS0	200649
Switzerland	UPU (Postal Union)	22 Apr 48	IGO Status/Immunit	56SWRO1194	462189
Switzerland	USA (United States)	03 Aug 45	Air Transport	51UNTS233	200191
Switzerland	USA (United States)	22 Nov 46	Claims and Debts	14SWRS351	463111
Switzerland	USA (United States)	30 Apr 47	Specif Goods/Equip	42UNTS235	100652
Switzerland	USA (United States)	13 May 49	Air Transport	51UNTS129	100761
Switzerland	USA (United States)	21 Oct 49	Reparations	132UNTS163	101757
Switzerland	USA (United States)	24 Feb 50	Admin Cooperation	93UNTS3	101282
Switzerland	USA (United States)	13 Oct 50	General Trade	133UNTS33	101777
Switzerland	USA (United States)	24 May 51	Taxation	127UNTS227	101706
Switzerland	USA (United States)	09 Jul 51	Taxation	165UNTS51	102167
Switzerland	USA (United States)	08 Jun 55	General Trade	55SWRO579	462133
Switzerland	USA (United States)	18 Jul 55	Atomic Energy	239UNTS311	103388
Switzerland	USA (United States)	21 Jun 56	Atomic Energy	279UNTS41	104033
Switzerland	USA (United States)	29 Mar 60	General Trade	371UNTS155	105277
Switzerland	USA (United States)	13 Oct 61	Air Transport	459UNTS219	106625
Switzerland	USA (United States)	11 Jul 63	General Trade	487UNTS177	107102
Switzerland	USA (United States)	30 Jan 65	Atomic Energy	594UNTS55	108594
Switzerland	USA (United States)	16 May 67	Gen Communications	0UNTS0	109768
Switzerland	USA (United States)	28 Oct 68	General Economic	0UNTS0	110084
Switzerland	USSR (Soviet Union)	18 Mar 46	Consul/Citizenship	0SUST207	468413
Switzerland	USSR (Soviet Union)	17 Mar 48	General Trade	0SUST246	468414
Switzerland	USSR (Soviet Union)	17 Mar 48	General Trade	217UNTS73	102944
Switzerland	USSR (Soviet Union)	17 Mar 48	General Trade	217UNTS87	102945
Switzerland	Venezuela	11 Jul 55	General Trade	55SWRO729	462163
Switzerland	WHO (World Health)	12 Jan 49	IGO Status/Immunit	26UNTS331	200155
Switzerland	WMO (Meteorology)	10 Mar 55	IGO Status/Immunit	211UNTS277	200524
Switzerland	Yugoslavia	27 Sep 48	Claims and Debts	48SWRO995	462172
Switzerland	Yugoslavia	27 Sep 48	General Economic	48SWRO990	462165
Switzerland	Yugoslavia	27 Sep 48	General Trade	48SWRO986	462164
Switzerland	Yugoslavia	28 May 53	Air Transport	232UNTS45	103228
Switzerland	Yugoslavia	23 Oct 59	Claims and Debts	60SWRO475	462166
Switzerland	Yugoslavia	24 Apr 61	Loans and Credits	62SWRO99	462110
Switzerland	Yugoslavia	29 Mar 62	Land Transport	62SWRO1359	462086
Switzerland	Yugoslavia	08 Jun 62	Non-ILO Labor	64SWRO157	462100

PARTY ONE	PARTY TWO	DATE	TOPIC	CITATION	NUMBER
Syria	Bulgaria	28 Jun 62	Culture	0UNTS0	109954
Syria	Bulgaria	13 Dec 64	Air Transport	0UNTS0	109956
Syria	Bulgaria	08 Nov 65	Scientific Project	0UNTS0	109959
Syria	Bulgaria	12 Jun 66	Visas	0UNTS0	109961
Syria	China People's Rep	30 Nov 55	General Trade	55CCJC92	410277
Syria	China People's Rep	30 Nov 55	Finance	55CCJC93	410278
Syria	China People's Rep	12 Jun 56	Culture	56CCJC71	410341
Syria	China People's Rep	12 Jun 56	Culture	56CCJC72	410342
Syria	China People's Rep	03 Jul 57	General Trade	57CCJC69	410434
Syria	China People's Rep	21 Feb 63	Finance	63CCJC16	410950
Syria	China People's Rep	21 Feb 63	General Trade	63CCJC15	410949
Syria	China People's Rep	21 Feb 63	Direct Aid	63CCJC17	410951
Syria	China People's Rep	18 Mar 65	Culture	65CCJC31	411323
Syria	China People's Rep	06 Oct 65	Mass Media	65CCJC130	411322
Syria	China People's Rep	20 Apr 66	Culture	66CCJC19	411325
Syria	China People's Rep	13 Apr 67	Tech Assistance	67CCJC12	411329
Syria	Cyprus	22 Dec 64	Air Transport	602UNTS25	108705
Syria	Czechoslovakia	18 Jun 57	Culture	303UNTS119	104374
Syria	Denmark	20 Oct 55	Air Transport	250UNTS61	103518
Syria	Denmark	28 Dec 65	Tech Assistance	588UNTS163	108523
Syria	France	07 Feb 49	Finance	50FRJO1003	416423
Syria	France	07 Jan 66	Air Transport	67FRJO404	416424
Syria	Germany, East	07 Nov 55	Consul/Citizenship	3EGDA668	419310
Syria	Germany, East	27 Nov 55	General Economic	3EGDA668	419311
Syria	Germany, East	08 Jul 56	Culture	5EGDA485	419312
Syria	Germany, East	03 Sep 57	General Trade	5EGDA485	419313
Syria	Germany, East	27 Jan 58	Mass Media	6EGDA515	419314
Syria	Germany, East	06 Jun 65	Air Transport	43EGDZ337	420315
Syria	Germany, East	02 Aug 65	Finance	51EGDZ341	420318
Syria	Germany, East	02 Aug 65	Water Transport	51EGDZ341	420319
Syria	Germany, East	02 Aug 65	Tech Assistance	51EGDZ341	420317
Syria	Germany, East	02 Aug 65	General Trade	51EGDZ341	420316
Syria	Germany, East	17 Oct 65	General Economic	52EGDZ356	420320
Syria	Germany, East	23 Apr 66	Mass Media	47EGDZ358	420321
Syria	Germany, East	30 Aug 66	General Economic	42EGDZ366	420322
Syria	Germany, East	14 Sep 66	Culture	37EGDZ367	420323
Syria	Germany, East	30 Oct 66	Tech Assistance	37EGDZ370	420324
Syria	Germany, West	25 Jun 62	Tech Assistance	489UNTS71	107135
Syria	Germany, West	22 Aug 63	Direct Aid	64WBGA79	424650
Syria	Greece	05 Jul 49	Air Transport	78UNTS71	101013
Syria	Greece	02 Jun 52	General Trade	183UNTS251	102434
Syria	Greece	17 Oct 68	Taxation	0UNTS0	110032
Syria	Hungary	18 Oct 62	Air Transport	491UNTS209	107178
Syria	ICAO (Civil Aviat)	28 May 53	Tech Assistance	173UNTS199	102267
Syria	IDA (Devel Assoc)	24 Dec 63	Non-IBRD Project	534UNTS253	107764
Syria	ILO (Labor Org)	03 Mar 51	Tech Assistance	110UNTS69	101502
Syria	India	25 Feb 52	General Amity	163UNTS55	102141
Syria	Iraq	03 Nov 61	General Trade	489UNTS45	107134
Syria	Israel	20 Jul 49	Peace/Disarmament	42UNTS327	100657
Syria	Italy	10 Nov 55	General Trade	267UNTS157	103841
Syria	Italy	28 May 58	Sanitation	60ITDI265	436342
Syria	Japan	08 Jun 53	General Trade	184UNTS3	102436
Syria	Japan	30 Oct 69	Direct Aid	69JJS391	442255
Syria	Jordan	04 Jun 53	Specific Resources	184UNTS15	102437
Syria	Jordan	23 Dec 53	Admin Cooperation	204UNTS207	102759
Syria	Multilateral	27 Mar 41	Military Mission	67UNTS231	200222
Syria	Multilateral	19 Apr 44	Scientific Project	89UNTS279	200257
Syria	Multilateral	02 Aug 44	Scientific Project	67UNTS221	200221
Syria	Multilateral	07 Dec 44	IGO Establishment	15UNTS295	200102
Syria	Multilateral	07 Dec 44	Air Transport	171UNTS387	200502
Syria	Multilateral	07 Dec 44	Air Transport	171UNTS345	200501
Syria	Multilateral	07 Dec 44	Air Transport	84UNTS389	200252
Syria	Multilateral	15 Dec 44	Sanitation	16UNTS247	200106
Syria	Multilateral	22 Mar 45	General Amity	70UNTS237	200241
Syria	Multilateral	16 Nov 45	IGO Establishment	4UNTS275	100052

PARTY ONE	PARTY TWO	DATE	TOPIC	CITATION	NUMBER
Syria	Multilateral	23 Apr 46	Sanitation	16UNTS179	100257
Syria	Multilateral	23 Apr 46	Sanitation	17UNTS3	100265
Syria	Multilateral	22 Jul 46	IGO Establishment	9UNTS3	100125
Syria	Multilateral	22 Jul 46	IGO Establishment	14UNTS185	100221
Syria	Multilateral	27 Jul 46	Patents/Copyrights	90UNTS229	101238
Syria	Multilateral	11 Dec 46	Sanitation	12UNTS179	100186
Syria	Multilateral	08 Feb 47	Patents/Copyrights	14UNTS287	100222
Syria	Multilateral	27 May 47	Air Transport	418UNTS161	106021
Syria	Multilateral	02 Oct 47	Telecommunications	193UNTS188	102616
Syria	Multilateral	12 Nov 47	Admin Cooperation	53UNTS39	100771
Syria	Multilateral	12 Nov 47	Admin Cooperation	53UNTS13	100770
Syria	Multilateral	06 Mar 48	Water Transport	289UNTS3	104214
Syria	Multilateral	26 Jun 48	Culture	331UNTS217	104757
Syria	Multilateral	24 Jul 48	Sanitation	66UNTS25	100847
Syria	Multilateral	14 Sep 48	Milit Occupation	18UNTS267	100296
Syria	Multilateral	09 Dec 48	Humanitarian	78UNTS277	101021
Syria	Multilateral	15 Jul 49	Health/Educ/Welfare	197UNTS3	102631
Syria	Multilateral	12 Aug 49	Humanitarian	75UNTS287	100973
Syria	Multilateral	12 Aug 49	Humanitarian	75UNTS85	100971
Syria	Multilateral	12 Aug 49	Humanitarian	75UNTS31	100970
Syria	Multilateral	12 Aug 49	General Military	75UNTS135	100972
Syria	Multilateral	16 Dec 49	Admin Cooperation	72UNTS3	100924
Syria	Multilateral	06 Apr 50	Admin Cooperation	119UNTS99	101610
Syria	Multilateral	07 Dec 50	Admin Cooperation	212UNTS17	102861
Syria	Multilateral	15 Dec 50	Customs	157UNTS129	102052
Syria	Multilateral	25 May 51	Status of Forces	175UNTS215	102303
Syria	Multilateral	08 Sep 51	General Military	136UNTS165	101833
Syria	Multilateral	08 Sep 51	Peace/Disarmament	136UNTS45	101832
Syria	Multilateral	11 Jul 52	Postal Service	170UNTS3	102221
Syria	Multilateral	11 Jul 52	Postal Service	170UNTS63	102222
Syria	Multilateral	11 Jul 52	Postal Service	171UNTS89	102225
Syria	Multilateral	11 Jul 52	Postal Service	170UNTS269	102223
Syria	Multilateral	11 Jul 52	IGO Establishment	169UNTS3	102220
Syria	Multilateral	07 Dec 53	Admin Cooperation	182UNTS51	102422
Syria	Multilateral	14 May 54	Culture	249UNTS215	103511
Syria	Multilateral	14 Jun 54	Air Transport	320UNTS217	104644
Syria	Multilateral	14 Jun 54	Air Transport	320UNTS209	104643
Syria	Multilateral	25 May 55	IGO Establishment	264UNTS117	103791
Syria	Multilateral	14 Jun 56	Tech Assistance	265UNTS125	103809
Syria	Multilateral	26 Oct 56	IGO Establishment	276UNTS3	103988
Syria	Multilateral	03 Oct 57	Postal Service	364UNTS331	105212
Syria	Multilateral	03 Oct 57	Postal Service	366UNTS87	105216
Syria	Multilateral	03 Oct 57	Postal Service	365UNTS207	105214
Syria	Multilateral	03 Oct 57	Postal Service	364UNTS3	105211
Syria	Multilateral	03 Oct 57	Postal Service	365UNTS3	105213
Syria	Multilateral	19 Nov 59	IGO Operations	410UNTS156	105902
Syria	Multilateral	26 Jan 60	IGO Establishment	439UNTS249	106333
Syria	Multilateral	30 Mar 61	Sanitation	520UNTS151	107515
Syria	Multilateral	21 Jun 61	IGO Establishment	514UNTS209	107449
Syria	Multilateral	22 Jun 62	ILO Labor	494UNTS249	107237
Syria	Multilateral	28 Jun 62	ILO Labor	494UNTS271	107238
Syria	Multilateral	12 Dec 62	Tech Assistance	457UNTS72	106578
Syria	Multilateral	20 Apr 63	IGO Establishment	495UNTS3	107239
Syria	Multilateral	05 Aug 63	Sanitation	480UNTS43	106964
Syria	Multilateral	10 Jul 64	Postal Service	612UNTS3	108847
Syria	Multilateral	10 Jul 64	Postal Service	611UNTS387	108846
Syria	Multilateral	10 Jul 64	Postal Service	612UNTS233	108848
Syria	Multilateral	10 Jul 64	Postal Service	611UNTS7	108844
Syria	Multilateral	10 Jul 64	Postal Service	613UNTS3	108850
Syria	Multilateral	10 Jul 64	Postal Service	611UNTS105	108845
Syria	Multilateral	20 Aug 64	Telecommunications	514UNTS25	107441
Syria	Multilateral	21 Jun 66	ILO Labor	0UNTS0	109728
Syria	Multilateral	01 Jul 68	Peace/Disarmament	0UNTS0	110485
Syria	Netherlands	13 Feb 50	Air Transport	108UNTS53	101467
Syria	Norway	25 Feb 56	Air Transport	3NORT676	451169
Syria	Norway	25 Feb 56	Air Transport	463UNTS217	106706
Syria	Pakistan	29 Aug 50	General Amity	109UNTS95	101494
Syria	Pakistan	18 Dec 55	General Trade	320UNTS269	104647
Syria	Poland	10 Nov 62	Air Transport	491UNTS228	107179
Syria	Poland	18 Jun 65	Tech Assistance	66PZUM33	458123
Syria	Saudi Arabia	16 Nov 61	General Economic	491UNTS163	107177
Syria	Spain	18 Apr 52	Culture	53SPBO2401	460243
Syria	Spain	18 Apr 52	General Amity	53SPBO2401	460242
Syria	Switzerland	03 Dec 45	Recognition	11SWRS708	463022
Syria	Switzerland	26 May 54	Air Transport	255UNTS145	103609
Syria	Turkey	12 Feb 46	Air Transport	49TURG1712	466138
Syria	Turkey	23 Jul 49	Commodity Trade	50TURG403	466091
Syria	Turkey	28 Apr 53	Telecommunications	204UNTS255	102760
Syria	Turkey	03 Mar 56	General Trade	57TURG701	466092
Syria	UK Great Britain	02 Nov 46	Dispute Settlement	11UNTS153	100153
Syria	UK Great Britain	30 Jan 54	Air Transport	449UNTS47	106452
Syria	UK Great Britain	05 Feb 54	Telecommunications	204UNTS267	102761
Syria	UK Great Britain	31 Aug 64	Commodity Trade	539UNTS259	107837
Syria	UN Special Fund	07 Jul 62	Direct Aid	443UNTS3	106355
Syria	UN Special Fund	22 Apr 68	IGO Operations	634UNTS207	109063
Syria	UNICEF (Children)	10 Jul 52	Direct Aid	136UNTS17	101830
Syria	United Arab Rep	03 Jul 55	Air Transport	393UNTS67	105652
Syria	United Arab Rep	20 Oct 55	General Military	247UNTS117	103461
Syria	United Arab Rep	27 Dec 62	Air Transport	491UNTS245	107180
Syria	United Nations	17 Nov 62	IGO Status/Immunit	456UNTS359	106565
Syria	USA (United States)	08 Sep 44	Recognition	124UNTS251	200424
Syria	USA (United States)	28 Apr 47	Air Transport	262UNTS121	103741
Syria	USA (United States)	09 Nov 61	US Agri Commod Aid	435UNTS75	106271
Syria	USA (United States)	18 Nov 63	US Agri Commod Aid	494UNTS169	107232
Syria	USSR (Soviet Union)	16 Nov 55	General Economic	259UNTS71	103683
Syria	USSR (Soviet Union)	19 Nov 55	Consul/Citizenship	0SUST444	468416
Syria	USSR (Soviet Union)	20 Aug 56	Culture	274UNTS105	103961
Syria	USSR (Soviet Union)	29 Jun 57	Telecommunications	0SUST385	468417
Syria	USSR (Soviet Union)	28 Oct 57	General Aid	0SUST391	468418
Syria	USSR (Soviet Union)	19 Dec 57	General Trade	0SUST394	468419
Syria	USSR (Soviet Union)	07 Oct 61	Consul/Citizenship	10SUGG143	469798
Syria	USSR (Soviet Union)	28 Feb 62	Consul/Citizenship	16SUGG132	470002
Syria	USSR (Soviet Union)	19 Aug 62	Culture	457UNTS285	106588
Syria	USSR (Soviet Union)	18 Dec 66	Non-IBRD Project	633UNTS247	109041
Syria	WHO (World Health)	20 Jun 52	Tech Assistance	165UNTS219	102178
Syria	WHO (World Health)	18 Nov 62	Tech Assistance	480UNTS249	106972
Syria	Yugoslavia	17 Jul 66	Air Transport	0UNTS0	110165
Taiwan	Argentina	10 Feb 47	General Amity	486UNTS143	107077
Taiwan	Argentina	19 Mar 66	Culture	635UNTS281	109089
Taiwan	Australia	22 Mar 55	Postal Service	209UNTS3	102818
Taiwan	Australia	29 Jul 55	Patents/Copyrights	213UNTS193	102887
Taiwan	Australia	22 Apr 68	General Trade	0UNTS0	109734
Taiwan	Belgium	20 Oct 43	Privil/Immunities	14UNTS376	200095
Taiwan	Belgium	13 Jan 54	Milit Assistance	223UNTS111	103059
Taiwan	Bolivia	29 Jul 66	Admin Cooperation	0UNTS0	110434
Taiwan	Brazil	20 Aug 43	General Amity	14UNTS365	200094
Taiwan	Brazil	27 Mar 46	Culture	0CTRC43	413001
Taiwan	Brazil	28 Dec 62	General Trade	500UNTS61	107307
Taiwan	Canada	22 Mar 44	Milit Assistance	14UNTS397	200096
Taiwan	Canada	14 Apr 44	Privil/Immunities	14UNTS408	200097
Taiwan	Canada	07 Feb 46	Finance	43UNTS23	100659
Taiwan	Canada	26 Sep 46	General Trade	14UNTS167	100219
Taiwan	Canada	28 May 47	Direct Aid	0CTRC63	413017
Taiwan	Costa Rica	05 May 44	General Amity	14UNTS427	200098
Taiwan	Costa Rica	10 Apr 58	Culture	315UNTS165	104567
Taiwan	Cuba	12 Nov 42	General Amity	10UNTS243	200065
Taiwan	Denmark	20 May 46	Privil/Immunities	12UNTS59	100180
Taiwan	Dominican Republic	11 May 40	General Amity	10UNTS285	200067
Taiwan	Ecuador	06 Jan 46	General Amity	7UNTS233	100102
Taiwan	Ecuador	12 Jun 59	Culture	387UNTS3	105554

PARTY ONE	PARTY TWO	DATE	TOPIC	CITATION	NUMBER
Taiwan	Ecuador	17 Jun 64	General Trade	533UNTS141	107740
Taiwan	Ecuador	23 Oct 64	General Trade	543UNTS241	107904
Taiwan	El Salvador	09 Dec 54	General Amity	214UNTS217	102900
Taiwan	El Salvador	27 Nov 61	Culture	437UNTS161	106306
Taiwan	France	18 Aug 45	Territory Boundary	14UNTS477	200101
Taiwan	France	28 Feb 46	Milit Occupation	14UNTS151	100217
Taiwan	France	28 Feb 46	General Amity	14UNTS137	100216
Taiwan	France	28 Feb 46	Privil/Immunities	14UNTS113	100215
Taiwan	France	14 Dec 46	Air Transport	0CTRC160	413002
Taiwan	France	28 Jun 47	Air Transport	0CTRC165	413018
Taiwan	France	10 May 48	Air Transport	0CTRC169	413019
Taiwan	France	30 Apr 49	Air Transport	0CTRC172	413020
Taiwan	France	12 May 54	Finance	0CTRC178	413004
Taiwan	France	12 May 54	General Trade	0CTRC174	413003
Taiwan	France	15 Apr 55	General Economic	0CTRC183	413021
Taiwan	France	21 Oct 55	Telecommunications	0CTRC186	413005
Taiwan	France	24 May 58	Patents/Copyrights	0CTRC10	413006
Taiwan	Greece	30 Nov 57	General Trade	0CTRC202	413007
Taiwan	Guatemala	08 Nov 64	General Trade	543UNTS227	107903
Taiwan	Haiti	25 Feb 66	Admin Cooperation	0UNTS0	110433
Taiwan	IAEA (Atom Energy)	13 Oct 69	Atomic Energy	0UNTS0	110517
Taiwan	IBRD (World Bank)	27 Sep 63	IBRD Project	483UNTS151	107012
Taiwan	IBRD (World Bank)	17 Dec 64	IBRD Project	538UNTS3	107808
Taiwan	IBRD (World Bank)	28 Apr 65	IBRD Project	549UNTS145	107998
Taiwan	IBRD (World Bank)	02 Aug 67	IBRD Project	618UNTS301	108932
Taiwan	IBRD (World Bank)	07 Aug 67	IBRD Project	620UNTS113	108952
Taiwan	IBRD (World Bank)	02 Dec 68	IBRD Project	0UNTS0	109639
Taiwan	IBRD (World Bank)	29 May 69	IBRD Project	0UNTS0	109892
Taiwan	IBRD (World Bank)	16 May 70	IBRD Project	0UNTS0	110688
Taiwan	ICJ Option Clause	26 Oct 46	ICJ Option Clause	1UNTS35	100005
Taiwan	IDA (Devel Assoc)	30 Aug 61	Loans and Credits	416UNTS175	106003
Taiwan	IDA (Devel Assoc)	30 Aug 61	Loans and Credits	417UNTS227	106008
Taiwan	IDA (Devel Assoc)	06 Sep 61	Loans and Credits	417UNTS253	106009
Taiwan	IDA (Devel Assoc)	01 Dec 61	Loans and Credits	426UNTS105	106132
Taiwan	ILO (Labor Org)	13 Feb 53	Tech Assistance	178UNTS337	102349
Taiwan	Iran	11 Nov 57	Culture	563UNTS31	108202
Taiwan	Iraq	16 Mar 42	General Amity	14UNTS335	200091
Taiwan	Iraq	14 Aug 57	Culture	0CTRC210	413008
Taiwan	Italy	30 Jul 47	Reparations	12UNTS377	100194
Taiwan	Italy	30 Jul 47	Consul/Citizenship	12UNTS383	100195
Taiwan	Italy	22 Apr 49	General Amity	0CTRC222	413009
Taiwan	Italy	25 Aug 49	General Trade	0CTRC227	413010
Taiwan	Italy	02 Feb 57	General Trade	0CTRC229	413011
Taiwan	Japan	24 Apr 52	General Trade	0CTCY447	414048
Taiwan	Japan	28 Apr 52	Peace/Disarmament	138UNTS3	101858
Taiwan	Japan	13 Jun 53	General Economic	0CTRC263	413012
Taiwan	Japan	13 Jun 53	Finance	0CTCY447	414049
Taiwan	Japan	15 Mar 55	Air Transport	0CTRC281	413013
Taiwan	Japan	18 May 60	Air Transport	0CTRC26	413022
Taiwan	Japan	05 Dec 69	Education	69JJS145	442258
Taiwan	Jordan	19 Nov 57	General Amity	308UNTS227	104463
Taiwan	Jordan	17 Oct 61	Culture	435UNTS267	106284
Taiwan	Korea, South	01 Mar 52	Air Transport	255UNTS35	103603
Taiwan	Korea, South	03 Mar 61	General Trade	0CTRC33	413014
Taiwan	Korea, South	27 Nov 64	General Amity	555UNTS3	108102
Taiwan	Lebanon	06 Apr 57	General Trade	0CTRC305	413015
Taiwan	Liberia	15 Jun 63	Culture	521UNTS361	107531
Taiwan	Luxembourg	19 Jul 63	Air Transport	564UNTS23	108218
Taiwan	Malagasy	04 Apr 62	General Amity	463UNTS195	106703
Taiwan	Mexico	01 Aug 44	General Amity	14UNTS441	200099
Taiwan	Mexico	25 Sep 64	General Trade	547UNTS233	107960
Taiwan	Morocco	27 May 57	General Trade	0CTRC317	413016
Taiwan	Multilateral	19 Apr 44	Scientific Project	89UNTS279	200257
Taiwan	Multilateral	02 Aug 44	Scientific Project	67UNTS221	200221
Taiwan	Multilateral	07 Dec 44	Air Transport	171UNTS387	200502

PARTY ONE	PARTY TWO	DATE	TOPIC	CITATION	NUMBER
Taiwan	Multilateral	07 Dec 44	IGO Establishment	15UNTS295	200102
Taiwan	Multilateral	07 Dec 44	Air Transport	171UNTS345	200501
Taiwan	Multilateral	15 Dec 44	Sanitation	16UNTS247	200106
Taiwan	Multilateral	15 Dec 44	Sanitation	17UNTS305	200110
Taiwan	Multilateral	16 Nov 45	IGO Establishment	4UNTS275	100052
Taiwan	Multilateral	23 Apr 46	Sanitation	16UNTS179	100257
Taiwan	Multilateral	23 Apr 46	Sanitation	17UNTS3	100265
Taiwan	Multilateral	22 Jul 46	IGO Establishment	14UNTS185	100221
Taiwan	Multilateral	22 Jul 46	IGO Establishment	9UNTS3	100125
Taiwan	Multilateral	15 Oct 46	Refugees	11UNTS73	100150
Taiwan	Multilateral	11 Dec 46	Sanitation	12UNTS179	100186
Taiwan	Multilateral	15 Dec 46	IGO Establishment	18UNTS3	100283
Taiwan	Multilateral	10 Feb 47	Peace/Disarmament	49UNTS3	100747
Taiwan	Multilateral	02 Oct 47	Telecommunications	193UNTS188	102616
Taiwan	Multilateral	12 Nov 47	Admin Cooperation	53UNTS39	100771
Taiwan	Multilateral	12 Nov 47	Admin Cooperation	53UNTS13	100770
Taiwan	Multilateral	12 Nov 47	Admin Cooperation	46UNTS169	100709
Taiwan	Multilateral	10 Jun 48	Humanitarian	164UNTS113	102163
Taiwan	Multilateral	10 Jun 48	Humanitarian	191UNTS3	102576
Taiwan	Multilateral	19 Jun 48	Air Transport	310UNTS151	104492
Taiwan	Multilateral	14 Sep 48	Milit Occupation	18UNTS267	100296
Taiwan	Multilateral	15 Nov 48	IGO Establishment	120UNTS59	101615
Taiwan	Multilateral	19 Nov 48	Sanitation	44UNTS277	100688
Taiwan	Multilateral	29 Nov 48	IGO Establishment	120UNTS13	101613
Taiwan	Multilateral	09 Dec 48	Humanitarian	78UNTS277	101021
Taiwan	Multilateral	23 Mar 49	Commodity Trade	203UNTS179	102746
Taiwan	Multilateral	04 May 49	Admin Cooperation	92UNTS19	101257
Taiwan	Multilateral	04 May 49	Admin Cooperation	98UNTS101	101358
Taiwan	Multilateral	04 May 49	Admin Cooperation	30UNTS3	100445
Taiwan	Multilateral	04 May 49	Admin Cooperation	30UNTS23	100446
Taiwan	Multilateral	04 May 49	Admin Cooperation	47UNTS159	100728
Taiwan	Multilateral	18 Jun 49	ILO Labor	605UNTS295	108768
Taiwan	Multilateral	12 Aug 49	General Military	75UNTS135	100972
Taiwan	Multilateral	12 Aug 49	Humanitarian	75UNTS287	100973
Taiwan	Multilateral	12 Aug 49	Humanitarian	75UNTS85	100971
Taiwan	Multilateral	12 Aug 49	Humanitarian	75UNTS31	100970
Taiwan	Multilateral	06 Apr 50	Admin Cooperation	119UNTS99	101610
Taiwan	Multilateral	22 Nov 50	Culture	131UNTS25	101734
Taiwan	Multilateral	07 Dec 50	Admin Cooperation	212UNTS17	102861
Taiwan	Multilateral	25 May 51	Status of Forces	175UNTS215	102303
Taiwan	Multilateral	11 Jul 52	Postal Service	170UNTS63	102222
Taiwan	Multilateral	11 Jul 52	Postal Service	170UNTS269	102223
Taiwan	Multilateral	11 Jul 52	Postal Service	171UNTS89	102225
Taiwan	Multilateral	11 Jul 52	IGO Establishment	169UNTS3	102220
Taiwan	Multilateral	11 Jul 52	Postal Service	170UNTS3	102221
Taiwan	Multilateral	31 Mar 53	Privil/Immunities	193UNTS136	102613
Taiwan	Multilateral	11 May 53	Sanitation	456UNTS3	106555
Taiwan	Multilateral	01 Oct 53	Commodity Trade	258UNTS153	103677
Taiwan	Multilateral	07 Dec 53	Admin Cooperation	182UNTS51	102422
Taiwan	Multilateral	14 May 54	Culture	249UNTS215	103511
Taiwan	Multilateral	14 Jun 54	Air Transport	320UNTS217	104644
Taiwan	Multilateral	20 Jun 56	Admin Cooperation	268UNTS3	103850
Taiwan	Multilateral	26 Oct 56	IGO Establishment	276UNTS3	103988
Taiwan	Multilateral	20 Feb 57	Consul/Citizenship	309UNTS65	104468
Taiwan	Multilateral	03 Oct 57	Postal Service	366UNTS87	105216
Taiwan	Multilateral	29 Apr 58	Territory Boundary	516UNTS205	107477
Taiwan	Multilateral	29 Apr 58	Specific Resources	559UNTS285	108164
Taiwan	Multilateral	29 Apr 58	Territory Boundary	499UNTS311	107302
Taiwan	Multilateral	29 Apr 58	Water Transport	450UNTS11	106465
Taiwan	Multilateral	29 Apr 58	Dispute Settlement	450UNTS169	106466
Taiwan	Multilateral	01 Dec 58	Commodity Trade	385UNTS137	105534
Taiwan	Multilateral	03 Dec 58	Admin Cooperation	416UNTS51	105995
Taiwan	Multilateral	03 Dec 58	Admin Cooperation	398UNTS9	105715
Taiwan	Multilateral	26 Jan 60	IGO Establishment	439UNTS249	106333
Taiwan	Multilateral	17 Jun 60	Humanitarian	536UNTS27	107794

PARTY ONE	PARTY TWO	DATE	TOPIC	CITATION	NUMBER
Taiwan	Multilateral	14 Dec 60	Education	429UNTS93	106193
Taiwan	Multilateral	23 Jan 61	Postal Service	530UNTS141	107679
Taiwan	Multilateral	30 Mar 61	Sanitation	520UNTS151	107515
Taiwan	Multilateral	14 Apr 61	IGO Establishment	422UNTS101	106071
Taiwan	Multilateral	18 Apr 61	Consul/Citizenship	500UNTS95	107310
Taiwan	Multilateral	18 Apr 61	Consul/Citizenship	500UNTS223	107311
Taiwan	Multilateral	18 Apr 61	Dispute Settlement	500UNTS243	107312
Taiwan	Multilateral	21 Jun 61	IGO Establishment	514UNTS209	107449
Taiwan	Multilateral	22 Jun 62	ILO Labor	494UNTS249	107237
Taiwan	Multilateral	28 Jun 62	ILO Labor	494UNTS271	107238
Taiwan	Multilateral	23 Jul 62	Recognition	456UNTS302	106564
Taiwan	Multilateral	10 Dec 62	Culture	521UNTS231	107525
Taiwan	Multilateral	24 Apr 63	Consul/Citizenship	596UNTS487	108640
Taiwan	Multilateral	05 Aug 63	Sanitation	480UNTS43	106964
Taiwan	Multilateral	14 Sep 63	Air Transport	0UNTS0	110106
Taiwan	Multilateral	10 Jul 64	Postal Service	611UNTS105	108845
Taiwan	Multilateral	10 Jul 64	Postal Service	611UNTS7	108844
Taiwan	Multilateral	10 Jul 64	Postal Service	611UNTS387	108846
Taiwan	Multilateral	10 Jul 64	Postal Service	612UNTS233	108848
Taiwan	Multilateral	10 Jul 64	Postal Service	612UNTS3	108847
Taiwan	Multilateral	20 Aug 64	Telecommunications	514UNTS25	107441
Taiwan	Multilateral	21 Sep 64	IGO Operations	555UNTS227	108115
Taiwan	Multilateral	09 Mar 65	Water Transport	591UNTS265	108564
Taiwan	Multilateral	18 Mar 65	Dispute Settlement	575UNTS159	108359
Taiwan	Multilateral	04 Dec 65	IGO Establishment	571UNTS123	108303
Taiwan	Multilateral	16 Dec 65	Postal Service	570UNTS201	108295
Taiwan	Multilateral	05 Apr 66	Water Transport	640UNTS133	109159
Taiwan	Multilateral	03 May 67	IGO Operations	0UNTS0	110764
Taiwan	Multilateral	28 Jun 67	ILO Labor	0UNTS0	110355
Taiwan	Multilateral	01 Jul 68	Peace/Disarmament	0UNTS0	110485
Taiwan	Multilateral	01 Aug 68	Culture	0UNTS0	109368
Taiwan	Multilateral	11 Jun 69	Scientific Project	0UNTS0	110100
Taiwan	Netherlands	29 May 45	Privil/Immunities	2UNTS307	200023
Taiwan	Netherlands	06 Dec 47	Air Transport	43UNTS185	100669
Taiwan	Nicaragua	25 Apr 61	Culture	423UNTS139	106090
Taiwan	Panama	26 Feb 60	Culture	435UNTS281	106285
Taiwan	Paraguay	18 Aug 61	Culture	438UNTS109	106314
Taiwan	Paraguay	11 Jul 62	General Trade	458UNTS41	106591
Taiwan	Paraguay	07 Jun 68	General Amity	0UNTS0	110435
Taiwan	Peru	08 Jun 64	General Trade	548UNTS151	107976
Taiwan	Philippines	18 Apr 47	General Amity	11UNTS361	100175
Taiwan	Philippines	23 Oct 50	Air Transport	215UNTS159	102918
Taiwan	Philippines	18 Oct 56	General Trade	541UNTS57	107860
Taiwan	Philippines	05 Aug 58	Postal Service	3PTS761	465039
Taiwan	Philippines	18 Dec 59	Consul/Citizenship	4PTS25	465043
Taiwan	Philippines	25 Aug 64	Tech Assistance	511UNTS233	107436
Taiwan	Portugal	01 Apr 47	Privil/Immunities	14UNTS177	100220
Taiwan	Portugal	04 Mar 48	Finance	0CTRC415	413023
Taiwan	Portugal	20 May 48	Customs	0CTRC419	413024
Taiwan	Saudi Arabia	15 Nov 46	General Amity	18UNTS197	100289
Taiwan	Spain	19 Feb 53	General Amity	181UNTS81	102400
Taiwan	Spain	03 Dec 56	General Trade	56SPBO1512	460077
Taiwan	Spain	07 Feb 57	Culture	0CTRC439	413025
Taiwan	Spain	07 Feb 57	Culture	314UNTS161	104547
Taiwan	Sweden	05 Apr 45	Privil/Immunities	0CTRC448	413026
Taiwan	Switzerland	13 Mar 46	Consul/Citizenship	14UNTS159	100218
Taiwan	Thailand	23 Jan 46	General Amity	161UNTS127	102126
Taiwan	Thailand	29 Sep 51	Air Transport	215UNTS166	102919
Taiwan	Thailand	09 Mar 60	Air Transport	0CTRC46	413027
Taiwan	Thailand	23 Nov 66	General Trade	581UNTS125	108436
Taiwan	Turkey	12 Feb 57	Culture	282UNTS125	104097
Taiwan	UK Great Britain	18 Jun 41	Territory Boundary	10UNTS227	200064
Taiwan	UK Great Britain	07 Jul 45	Status of Forces	14UNTS455	200100
Taiwan	UK Great Britain	23 Jul 47	Air Transport	9UNTS207	100135
Taiwan	UK Great Britain	12 Jan 48	Customs	14UNTS74	100212

PARTY ONE	PARTY TWO	DATE	TOPIC	CITATION	NUMBER
Taiwan	UK Great Britain	18 May 48	Milit Assistance	66UNTS113	100850
Taiwan	UK Great Britain	18 Oct 48	Customs	0CTRC645	413028
Taiwan	UN Special Fund	20 Sep 60	Tech Assistance	375UNTS29	105352
Taiwan	UNICEF (Children)	21 May 48	Tech Assistance	65UNTS38	100818
Taiwan	UNICEF (Children)	19 Jul 50	IGO Operations	94UNTS21	101304
Taiwan	UNICEF (Children)	08 Apr 64	IGO Operations	500UNTS49	107306
Taiwan	United Nations	05 Feb 54	Tech Assistance	186UNTS85	102485
Taiwan	Uruguay	03 May 61	Culture	596UNTS121	108630
Taiwan	USA (United States)	02 Jun 42	Milit Assistance	14UNTS343	200092
Taiwan	USA (United States)	11 Jan 43	Privil/Immunities	10UNTS261	200066
Taiwan	USA (United States)	21 May 43	Status of Forces	14UNTS353	200093
Taiwan	USA (United States)	13 Jun 44	Status of Forces	107UNTS43	200350
Taiwan	USA (United States)	14 Jun 46	Milit Assistance	4UNTS253	100049
Taiwan	USA (United States)	28 Jun 46	Milit Assistance	34UNTS121	100532
Taiwan	USA (United States)	30 Aug 46	Direct Aid	12UNTS39	100179
Taiwan	USA (United States)	04 Nov 46	General Amity	25UNTS69	100359
Taiwan	USA (United States)	20 Dec 46	Air Transport	22UNTS87	100332
Taiwan	USA (United States)	29 Apr 47	Milit Assistance	0CTRC719	413029
Taiwan	USA (United States)	03 Sep 47	Status of Forces	9UNTS91	100126
Taiwan	USA (United States)	27 Oct 47	Direct Aid	12UNTS11	100178
Taiwan	USA (United States)	10 Nov 47	Education	0CTRC747	413030
Taiwan	USA (United States)	08 Dec 47	Milit Installation	70UNTS3	100895
Taiwan	USA (United States)	17 Mar 48	Reparations	76UNTS157	100987
Taiwan	USA (United States)	30 Apr 48	Direct Aid	0CTRC753	413031
Taiwan	USA (United States)	03 Jul 48	Mostfavored Nation	0CTRC767	413032
Taiwan	USA (United States)	03 Jul 48	Direct Aid	17UNTS119	100273
Taiwan	USA (United States)	05 Aug 48	IGO Establishment	82UNTS109	101087
Taiwan	USA (United States)	18 Nov 48	Direct Aid	198UNTS287	102672
Taiwan	USA (United States)	27 Jan 49	Direct Aid	0CTRC790	413036
Taiwan	USA (United States)	27 Mar 49	Direct Aid	0CTRC770	413033
Taiwan	USA (United States)	27 Jun 49	Tech Assistance	0CTRC783	413035
Taiwan	USA (United States)	26 Jan 50	Direct Aid	0CTRC772	413034
Taiwan	USA (United States)	19 Dec 50	Air Transport	0CTRC792	413037
Taiwan	USA (United States)	09 Feb 51	Milit Assistance	132UNTS273	101767
Taiwan	USA (United States)	02 Jan 52	Milit Assistance	181UNTS161	102407
Taiwan	USA (United States)	25 Jun 52	Direct Aid	136UNTS229	101837
Taiwan	USA (United States)	01 Nov 52	Admin Cooperation	0CTRC809	413039
Taiwan	USA (United States)	12 Dec 52	Direct Aid	0CTRC807	413038
Taiwan	USA (United States)	04 Feb 53	Patents/Copyrights	0CTRC815	413040
Taiwan	USA (United States)	14 May 54	Milit Installation	231UNTS165	103216
Taiwan	USA (United States)	26 Oct 54	Direct Aid	0CTRC823	413041
Taiwan	USA (United States)	10 Dec 54	General Military	248UNTS213	103496
Taiwan	USA (United States)	15 Apr 55	Air Transport	0CTRC827	413042
Taiwan	USA (United States)	18 Jul 55	Atomic Energy	235UNTS221	103304
Taiwan	USA (United States)	14 Oct 55	Milit Installation	268UNTS165	103857
Taiwan	USA (United States)	20 Feb 56	Visas	275UNTS73	103976
Taiwan	USA (United States)	03 Apr 56	Milit Assistance	268UNTS315	103864
Taiwan	USA (United States)	14 Aug 56	US Agri Commod Aid	281UNTS257	104083
Taiwan	USA (United States)	14 Sep 56	Loans and Credits	0CTRC868	413043
Taiwan	USA (United States)	21 Nov 56	Milit Installation	265UNTS241	103816
Taiwan	USA (United States)	27 Dec 56	Admin Cooperation	0CTRC874	413044
Taiwan	USA (United States)	03 May 57	Claims and Debts	0CTRC877	413045
Taiwan	USA (United States)	28 Jun 57	Loans and Credits	0CTRC880	413046
Taiwan	USA (United States)	30 Jul 57	Postal Service	300UNTS61	104331
Taiwan	USA (United States)	08 Oct 57	Postal Service	304UNTS241	104400
Taiwan	USA (United States)	30 Nov 57	Culture	0CTRC885	413047
Taiwan	USA (United States)	18 Apr 58	US Agri Commod Aid	308UNTS179	104461
Taiwan	USA (United States)	06 Aug 58	Milit Installation	462UNTS3	106666
Taiwan	USA (United States)	24 Dec 58	Loans and Credits	340UNTS251	104868
Taiwan	USA (United States)	07 Feb 59	Milit Assistance	341UNTS225	104885
Taiwan	USA (United States)	09 Jun 59	US Agri Commod Aid	353UNTS257	105046
Taiwan	USA (United States)	08 Jul 59	Milit Assistance	354UNTS47	105052
Taiwan	USA (United States)	22 Jul 59	Milit Assistance	357UNTS293	105121
Taiwan	USA (United States)	02 Dec 59	Atomic Energy	361UNTS115	105175
Taiwan	USA (United States)	15 Apr 60	Milit Installation	462UNTS19	106667

PARTY ONE	PARTY TWO	DATE	TOPIC	CITATION	NUMBER
Taiwan	USA (United States)	30 Aug 60	US Agri Commod Aid	388UNTS191	105579
Taiwan	USA (United States)	21 Jul 61	US Agri Commod Aid	416UNTS101	105998
Taiwan	USA (United States)	28 Feb 62	Milit Installation	462UNTS25	106668
Taiwan	USA (United States)	16 Apr 62	General Trade	445UNTS249	106392
Taiwan	USA (United States)	27 Apr 62	US Agri Commod Aid	436UNTS25	106287
Taiwan	USA (United States)	15 Aug 62	Loans and Credits	460UNTS237	106643
Taiwan	USA (United States)	31 Aug 62	US Agri Commod Aid	460UNTS247	106644
Taiwan	USA (United States)	19 Nov 62	US Agri Commod Aid	459UNTS263	106629
Taiwan	USA (United States)	19 Oct 63	Commodity Trade	494UNTS27	107224
Taiwan	USA (United States)	19 Dec 63	Status of Forces	527UNTS69	107617
Taiwan	USA (United States)	23 Apr 64	Health/Educ/Welfare	524UNTS141	107570
Taiwan	USA (United States)	03 Jun 64	US Agri Commod Aid	526UNTS257	107610
Taiwan	USA (United States)	19 Dec 64	Status of Forces	532UNTS313	107725
Taiwan	USA (United States)	31 Dec 64	US Agri Commod Aid	532UNTS59	107712
Taiwan	USA (United States)	31 Dec 64	US Agri Commod Aid	532UNTS29	107711
Taiwan	USA (United States)	09 Apr 65	General Economic	546UNTS81	107939
Taiwan	USA (United States)	06 Mar 67	Water Transport	0UNTS0	109753
Taiwan	USA (United States)	01 Apr 67	Water Transport	0UNTS0	109758
Taiwan	USA (United States)	08 Jun 67	Water Transport	0UNTS0	109904
Taiwan	USA (United States)	12 Oct 67	Commodity Trade	0UNTS0	110047
Taiwan	USA (United States)	12 Dec 67	US Agri Commod Aid	0UNTS0	110062
Taiwan	USA (United States)	12 Dec 67	US Agri Commod Aid	0UNTS0	110061
Taiwan	USA (United States)	15 Dec 67	Loans and Credits	0UNTS0	109989
Taiwan	USA (United States)	18 Jun 68	Milit Assistance	0UNTS0	110146
Taiwan	USA (United States)	16 Dec 68	Milit Assistance	0UNTS0	110256
Taiwan	USA (United States)	23 Jan 69	Scientific Project	0UNTS0	110264
Taiwan	USA (United States)	18 Jun 69	Milit Installation	0UNTS0	110334
Taiwan	USA (United States)	22 Aug 69	Education	0UNTS0	110405
Taiwan	USSR (Soviet Union)	14 Aug 45	General Amity	10UNTS300	200068
Taiwan	Vietnam, South	19 Aug 66	Air Transport	0VKNG238	496064
Taiwan	Vietnam, South	19 Aug 66	Air Transport	0UNTS0	109241
Taiwan	WHO (World Health)	25 Oct 51	Sanitation	126UNTS77	101683
Taiwan	WHO (World Health)	07 Mar 52	Sanitation	128UNTS233	101723
Taiwan	WHO (World Health)	21 Apr 55	Tech Assistance	210UNTS71	102835
Tanganyika	Accept UN Charter	09 Dec 61	UN Charter	416UNTS147	106000
Tanganyika	China People's Rep	13 Dec 62	Culture	62CCJC114	410935
Tanganyika	Denmark	04 Aug 64	Dispute Settlement	544UNTS123	107915
Tanganyika	Denmark	04 Aug 64	Taxation	544UNTS117	107914
Tanganyika	IDA (Devel Assoc)	19 Dec 63	Non-IBRD Project	492UNTS241	107193
Tanganyika	IDA (Devel Assoc)	05 Feb 64	Non-IBRD Project	506UNTS91	107382
Tanganyika	ILO (Labor Org)	03 May 62	IGO Operations	429UNTS73	106191
Tanganyika	Israel	28 Jan 63	Tech Assistance	516UNTS39	107468
Tanganyika	Israel	17 Sep 63	Visas	516UNTS47	107469
Tanganyika	Multilateral	07 Dec 44	IGO Establishment	15UNTS295	200102
Tanganyika	Multilateral	27 May 47	Air Transport	418UNTS161	106021
Tanganyika	Multilateral	12 Nov 47	Admin Cooperation	46UNTS201	100710
Tanganyika	Multilateral	22 Feb 49	Sanitation	93UNTS129	101296
Tanganyika	Multilateral	04 May 49	Admin Cooperation	98UNTS101	101358
Tanganyika	Multilateral	04 May 49	Admin Cooperation	92UNTS19	101257
Tanganyika	Multilateral	22 Nov 50	Culture	131UNTS25	101734
Tanganyika	Multilateral	07 Dec 50	Admin Cooperation	212UNTS17	102861
Tanganyika	Multilateral	07 Nov 52	General Trade	221UNTS255	103010
Tanganyika	Multilateral	18 Jan 54	IGO Establishment	330UNTS121	104743
Tanganyika	Multilateral	14 Jun 54	Air Transport	320UNTS209	104643
Tanganyika	Multilateral	14 Jun 54	Air Transport	320UNTS217	104644
Tanganyika	Multilateral	29 Jul 54	Sanitation	249UNTS45	103500
Tanganyika	Multilateral	25 May 55	IGO Establishment	264UNTS117	103791
Tanganyika	Multilateral	20 Feb 57	Consul/Citizenship	309UNTS65	104468
Tanganyika	Multilateral	26 Jan 60	IGO Establishment	439UNTS249	106333
Tanganyika	Multilateral	18 Apr 61	Consul/Citizenship	500UNTS223	107311
Tanganyika	Multilateral	18 Apr 61	Dispute Settlement	500UNTS243	107312
Tanganyika	Multilateral	18 Apr 61	Consul/Citizenship	500UNTS95	107310
Tanganyika	Multilateral	21 Jun 61	IGO Establishment	514UNTS209	107449
Tanganyika	Multilateral	28 Sep 62	IGO Establishment	469UNTS169	106791
Tanganyika	Multilateral	06 Mar 63	Tech Assistance	455UNTS386	106552

PARTY ONE	PARTY TWO	DATE	TOPIC	CITATION	NUMBER
Tanganyika	Multilateral	25 May 63	IGO Establishment	479UNTS39	106947
Tanganyika	Multilateral	04 Aug 63	IGO Establishment	510UNTS3	107408
Tanganyika	Multilateral	05 Aug 63	Sanitation	480UNTS43	106964
Tanganyika	Multilateral	14 May 65	IGO Operations	550UNTS310	108026
Tanganyika	Switzerland	30 Jan 64	Admin Cooperation	64SWRO276	462028
Tanganyika	UK Great Britain	09 Dec 61	IGO Establishment	437UNTS47	106299
Tanganyika	UK Great Britain	14 Mar 62	Admin Cooperation	449UNTS147	106456
Tanganyika	UK Great Britain	03 Apr 63	Admin Cooperation	478UNTS23	106933
Tanganyika	UK Great Britain	02 Sep 64	Commodity Trade	522UNTS177	107544
Tanganyika	UN Special Fund	17 Jul 62	Direct Aid	435UNTS237	106281
Tanganyika	UNICEF (Children)	25 Jan 63	Direct Aid	453UNTS249	106528
Tanganyika	United Nations	01 Jun 62	Tech Assistance	479UNTS3	106944
Tanganyika	USA (United States)	21 Jul 61	Direct Aid	445UNTS33	106374
Tanganyika	USA (United States)	14 Nov 63	Claims and Debts	493UNTS75	107208
Tanganyika	USA (United States)	09 Dec 63	Tech Assistance	526UNTS301	107612
Tanganyika	USSR (Soviet Union)	10 Dec 61	Recognition	16SUGG132	469997
Tanganyika	USSR (Soviet Union)	14 Aug 63	General Trade	493UNTS195	107215
Tanganyika	USSR (Soviet Union)	06 Nov 63	Culture	528UNTS157	107639
Tanganyika	WHO (World Health)	05 Nov 63	Tech Assistance	496UNTS193	107252
Tanzania	Bulgaria	15 Jul 66	Scientific Project	0UNTS0	109962
Tanzania	China People's Rep	16 Jun 64	Direct Aid	64CCJC85	411335
Tanzania	China People's Rep	05 Jan 65	Tech Assistance	65CCJC3	411332
Tanzania	China People's Rep	05 Jan 65	Direct Aid	65CCJC2	411331
Tanzania	China People's Rep	10 Feb 65	General Trade	65CCJC16	411337
Tanzania	China People's Rep	10 Feb 65	General Trade	65CCJC15	411336
Tanzania	China People's Rep	20 Feb 65	General Amity	65CCJC21	411338
Tanzania	China People's Rep	22 Apr 66	Water Transport	66CCJC21	411339
Tanzania	China People's Rep	07 May 66	Culture	66CCJC29	411333
Tanzania	China People's Rep	08 Jun 66	General Economic	66CCJC50	411334
Tanzania	China People's Rep	10 Oct 66	Direct Aid	66CCJC83	411340
Tanzania	Denmark	05 Apr 67	Scientific Project	604UNTS19	108740
Tanzania	Denmark	05 Apr 67	Tech Assistance	603UNTS111	108728
Tanzania	Denmark	01 Nov 67	Loans and Credits	619UNTS47	108938
Tanzania	Denmark	27 May 69	Education	0UNTS0	110763
Tanzania	Finland	01 Jun 68	Non-ILO Labor	0UNTS0	109791
Tanzania	France	28 Apr 64	Air Transport	65FRRT97	415425
Tanzania	Germany, East	17 May 64	General Amity	12EGDA1139	419485
Tanzania	Germany, West	06 Sep 62	Tech Assistance	62WBGA225	424652
Tanzania	Germany, West	06 Sep 62	General Economic	62WBGA225	424651
Tanzania	Germany, West	11 Sep 62	Water Transport	62WBGA225	424654
Tanzania	Germany, West	11 Sep 62	Loans and Credits	62WBGA225	424653
Tanzania	Germany, West	30 Jan 65	Claims and Debts	66WGBB873	425655
Tanzania	Germany, West	06 Feb 71	Loans and Credits	71WBGA114	424656
Tanzania	IBRD (World Bank)	29 Sep 65	IBRD Project	568UNTS309	108275
Tanzania	IBRD (World Bank)	17 Feb 67	IBRD Project	599UNTS287	108671
Tanzania	IBRD (World Bank)	13 Dec 67	IBRD Project	619UNTS239	108945
Tanzania	IDA (Devel Assoc)	13 Jan 66	Non-IBRD Project	567UNTS177	108256
Tanzania	IDA (Devel Assoc)	21 Mar 68	Non-IBRD Project	0UNTS0	109327
Tanzania	IDA (Devel Assoc)	31 Oct 68	Non-IBRD Project	0UNTS0	109652
Tanzania	IDA (Devel Assoc)	29 May 69	Non-IBRD Project	0UNTS0	110224
Tanzania	Italy	04 Aug 65	Tech Assistance	66ITDI246	436397
Tanzania	Japan	20 Oct 66	Direct Aid	66JJS317	442181
Tanzania	Multilateral	11 Dec 46	Sanitation	12UNTS179	100186
Tanzania	Multilateral	02 Jul 51	Refugees	189UNTS137	102545
Tanzania	Multilateral	10 Jun 58	Admin Cooperation	330UNTS3	104739
Tanzania	Multilateral	10 Jul 64	Postal Service	612UNTS3	108847
Tanzania	Multilateral	10 Jul 64	Postal Service	611UNTS387	108846
Tanzania	Multilateral	10 Jul 64	Postal Service	611UNTS105	108845
Tanzania	Multilateral	10 Jul 64	Postal Service	611UNTS7	108844
Tanzania	Multilateral	14 May 65	IGO Operations	550UNTS310	108026
Tanzania	Multilateral	08 Jul 65	General Trade	597UNTS3	108641
Tanzania	Multilateral	17 Jan 66	IGO Establishment	592UNTS101	108573
Tanzania	Multilateral	04 Mar 66	US Agri Commod Aid	578UNTS57	108387
Tanzania	Multilateral	31 Jan 67	Refugees	606UNTS267	108791
Tanzania	Multilateral	18 Mar 68	Commodity Trade	0UNTS0	109262

PARTY ONE	PARTY TWO	DATE	TOPIC	CITATION	NUMBER
Tanzania	Multilateral	24 Sep 68	Air Transport	0UNTS0	110612
Tanzania	Multilateral	27 Jan 69	Telecommunications	0UNTS0	109664
Tanzania	Netherlands	27 Apr 65	Tech Assistance	594UNTS123	108599
Tanzania	Netherlands	09 May 68	Extradition	0UNTS0	109621
Tanzania	Poland	15 May 65	Tech Assistance	65FZUM38	458120
Tanzania	UK Great Britain	23 Sep 68	Finance	0UNTS0	109813
Tanzania	USA (United States)	06 Dec 65	Consul/Citizenship	592UNTS51	108568
Tanzania	USA (United States)	08 Feb 68	General Economic	0UNTS0	110005
Thailand	Accept UN Charter	16 Dec 46	UN Charter	1UNTS47	100011
Thailand	Argentina	10 Dec 61	General Trade	422UNTS87	106070
Thailand	Australia	26 Oct 53	Air Transport	255UNTS117	103607
Thailand	Australia	20 Dec 56	Admin Cooperation	265UNTS149	103810
Thailand	Australia	28 Jul 59	Customs	339UNTS91	104847
Thailand	Australia	26 Feb 60	Air Transport	392UNTS255	105647
Thailand	Austria	30 Sep 64	General Trade	527UNTS239	107628
Thailand	Austria	25 Apr 66	Admin Cooperation	66ABGB135	403195
Thailand	Belgium	02 Dec 59	Visas	351UNTS89	105018
Thailand	Burma	15 Oct 56	General Amity	277UNTS87	104000
Thailand	Burma	08 Jun 60	Visas	372UNTS321	105308
Thailand	Burma	17 May 63	Visas	468UNTS319	106779
Thailand	Burma	15 Aug 69	Air Transport	0UNTS0	109978
Thailand	Cambodia	15 Dec 60	Extradition	382UNTS315	105492
Thailand	Cambodia	15 Dec 60	Extradition	382UNTS321	105493
Thailand	Cambodia	15 Dec 60	Admin Cooperation	382UNTS307	105491
Thailand	Cambodia	15 Dec 60	Mass Media	382UNTS301	105490
Thailand	Canada	27 Apr 69	General Economic	0UNTS0	109675
Thailand	Ceylon (Sri Lanka)	24 Feb 50	Air Transport	72UNTS261	100938
Thailand	Denmark	23 Nov 49	Air Transport	53UNTS255	100786
Thailand	Denmark	25 Jan 65	Tech Assistance	530UNTS173	107680
Thailand	Denmark	01 Jun 65	Taxation	551UNTS157	108040
Thailand	Denmark	16 Oct 68	Scientific Project	0UNTS0	109463
Thailand	Denmark	16 Jun 69	Scientific Project	0UNTS0	109794
Thailand	Denmark	18 Nov 69	Admin Cooperation	0UNTS0	110765
Thailand	Denmark	18 Nov 69	Culture	0UNTS0	110766
Thailand	France	17 Nov 46	Admin Cooperation	47FRJO1503	416448
Thailand	France	17 Nov 46	Reparations	344UNTS59	104943
Thailand	France	26 Feb 60	Air Transport	392UNTS279	105648
Thailand	Germany, West	09 Oct 56	Direct Aid	258UNTS143	103676
Thailand	Germany, West	13 Dec 61	Claims and Debts	541UNTS181	107870
Thailand	Germany, West	05 Mar 62	Air Transport	563UNTS165	108210
Thailand	Germany, West	02 Apr 64	Tech Assistance	503UNTS3	107338
Thailand	Germany, West	28 Oct 64	Loans and Credits	521UNTS333	107529
Thailand	Germany, West	28 Oct 64	Non-IBRD Project	521UNTS311	107528
Thailand	Germany, West	23 Dec 64	Scientific Project	525UNTS177	107589
Thailand	Germany, West	23 Dec 64	Tech Assistance	525UNTS185	107590
Thailand	Germany, West	23 Dec 64	Sanitation	525UNTS201	107592
Thailand	Germany, West	23 Dec 64	Non-IBRD Project	525UNTS193	107591
Thailand	Germany, West	10 Jul 67	Taxation	68WGBB589	425657
Thailand	Germany, West	29 Mar 68	Direct Aid	637UNTS0	109122
Thailand	Germany, West	08 Oct 68	Loans and Credits	0UNTS0	109637
Thailand	Germany, West	08 Oct 68	Loans and Credits	68WBGA234	424658
Thailand	Germany, West	04 Dec 68	Loans and Credits	0UNTS0	109638
Thailand	IAEA (Atom Energy)	18 Mar 59	Tech Assistance	339UNTS307	104850
Thailand	IBRD (World Bank)	27 Oct 50	IBRD Project	158UNTS3	102059
Thailand	IBRD (World Bank)	27 Oct 50	IBRD Project	158UNTS43	102061
Thailand	IBRD (World Bank)	27 Oct 50	IBRD Project	158UNTS25	102060
Thailand	IBRD (World Bank)	09 Aug 55	IBRD Project	221UNTS283	103011
Thailand	IBRD (World Bank)	12 Oct 56	IBRD Project	261UNTS117	103728
Thailand	IBRD (World Bank)	12 Sep 57	IBRD Project	299UNTS349	104324
Thailand	IBRD (World Bank)	28 Apr 61	IBRD Project	415UNTS121	105983
Thailand	IBRD (World Bank)	21 Dec 62	IBRD Project	467UNTS63	106758
Thailand	IBRD (World Bank)	21 Dec 62	IBRD Project	467UNTS43	106757
Thailand	IBRD (World Bank)	07 Mar 63	IBRD Project	467UNTS83	106759
Thailand	IBRD (World Bank)	11 Jun 63	IBRD Project	481UNTS227	106984
Thailand	IBRD (World Bank)	11 Mar 64	IBRD Project	504UNTS73	107354

PARTY ONE	PARTY TWO	DATE	TOPIC	CITATION	NUMBER
Thailand	IBRD (World Bank)	25 Nov 64	IBRD Project	537UNTS273	107805
Thailand	IBRD (World Bank)	22 Mar 65	IBRD Project	538UNTS63	107810
Thailand	IBRD (World Bank)	24 Jun 66	IBRD Project	582UNTS259	108466
Thailand	IBRD (World Bank)	19 Oct 66	IBRD Project	594UNTS347	108609
Thailand	IBRD (World Bank)	24 Mar 67	IBRD Project	599UNTS299	108672
Thailand	IBRD (World Bank)	19 Sep 67	IBRD Project	619UNTS275	108946
Thailand	IBRD (World Bank)	23 May 68	IBRD Project	0UNTS0	109332
Thailand	IBRD (World Bank)	27 Jun 69	IBRD Project	0UNTS0	110311
Thailand	IBRD (World Bank)	10 Feb 70	IBRD Project	0UNTS0	110677
Thailand	ICAO (Civil Aviat)	19 Apr 51	Tech Assistance	96UNTS181	101336
Thailand	ICAO (Civil Aviat)	18 Oct 65	Air Transport	0UNTS0	110162
Thailand	Iceland	22 Jan 57	Air Transport	312UNTS63	104511
Thailand	ICJ Option Clause	20 May 50	ICJ Option Clause	65UNTS157	100844
Thailand	ILO (Labor Org)	11 Jul 51	Tech Assistance	100UNTS159	101395
Thailand	ILO (Labor Org)	30 Aug 61	IGO Operations	422UNTS125	106072
Thailand	India	12 Jun 56	Air Transport	255UNTS341	103617
Thailand	India	13 Dec 68	General Trade	0UNTS0	109386
Thailand	Indonesia	03 Mar 54	General Amity	213UNTS297	102893
Thailand	Iran	02 Feb 67	General Amity	614UNTS251	108874
Thailand	Iran	12 Nov 69	General Trade	0IRTB68	433110
Thailand	Iran	12 Nov 69	General Trade	0UNTS0	110563
Thailand	Israel	07 Jul 60	Visas	377UNTS325	105409
Thailand	Italy	30 Dec 55	Visas	260UNTS351	103719
Thailand	Japan	19 Jun 53	Air Transport	174UNTS29	102276
Thailand	Japan	06 Apr 55	Culture	230UNTS219	103187
Thailand	Japan	09 Jul 55	Finance	230UNTS13	103172
Thailand	Japan	06 Sep 55	Culture	55JHZ9	439002
Thailand	Japan	09 Apr 56	General Trade	57JAIL82	440162
Thailand	Japan	24 Aug 60	Education	384UNTS73	105512
Thailand	Japan	25 Nov 61	Sanitation	451UNTS55	106484
Thailand	Japan	01 Mar 63	Taxation	475UNTS233	106895
Thailand	Japan	16 Nov 64	Education	0JGJI1564	441125
Thailand	Japan	12 Jan 68	Loans and Credits	69JAIL169	440207
Thailand	Korea, South	15 Sep 61	General Trade	413UNTS137	105948
Thailand	Laos	07 Jul 54	Air Transport	200UNTS115	102698
Thailand	Laos	12 Aug 65	Specific Property	547UNTS209	107958
Thailand	Luxembourg	29 Dec 60	Air Transport	465UNTS131	106725
Thailand	Multilateral	07 Dec 44	IGO Establishment	15UNTS295	200102
Thailand	Multilateral	07 Dec 44	Air Transport	84UNTS389	200252
Thailand	Multilateral	07 Dec 44	Air Transport	171UNTS345	200501
Thailand	Multilateral	07 Dec 44	Air Transport	171UNTS387	200502
Thailand	Multilateral	01 Jan 46	Peace/Disarmament	99UNTS131	101375
Thailand	Multilateral	27 May 47	Air Transport	418UNTS161	106021
Thailand	Multilateral	15 Nov 48	IGO Establishment	120UNTS59	101615
Thailand	Multilateral	29 Nov 48	IGO Establishment	120UNTS13	101613
Thailand	Multilateral	06 Apr 50	Admin Cooperation	119UNTS99	101610
Thailand	Multilateral	22 Nov 50	Culture	131UNTS25	101734
Thailand	Multilateral	25 May 51	Status of Forces	175UNTS215	102303
Thailand	Multilateral	06 Dec 51	Admin Cooperation	150UNTS67	101963
Thailand	Multilateral	11 Jul 52	Postal Service	170UNTS269	102223
Thailand	Multilateral	11 Jul 52	IGO Establishment	169UNTS3	102220
Thailand	Multilateral	11 Jul 52	Postal Service	171UNTS89	102225
Thailand	Multilateral	11 Jul 52	Postal Service	171UNTS143	102226
Thailand	Multilateral	11 Jul 52	Postal Service	170UNTS3	102221
Thailand	Multilateral	11 Jul 52	Postal Service	170UNTS63	102222
Thailand	Multilateral	07 Oct 52	Admin Cooperation	310UNTS181	104493
Thailand	Multilateral	27 Feb 53	Claims and Debts	333UNTS3	104764
Thailand	Multilateral	31 Mar 53	Privil/Immunities	193UNTS136	102613
Thailand	Multilateral	30 Jul 53	Reparations	215UNTS97	102913
Thailand	Multilateral	19 Feb 54	Status of Forces	214UNTS51	102899
Thailand	Multilateral	01 Mar 54	Commodity Trade	256UNTS31	103622
Thailand	Multilateral	14 May 54	Culture	249UNTS215	103511
Thailand	Multilateral	14 Jun 54	Air Transport	320UNTS209	104643
Thailand	Multilateral	14 Jun 54	Air Transport	320UNTS217	104644
Thailand	Multilateral	24 Aug 54	Other Military	247UNTS213	103471

PARTY ONE	PARTY TWO	DATE	TOPIC	CITATION	NUMBER
Thailand	Multilateral	08 Sep 54	Milit Assistance	209UNTS23	102819
Thailand	Multilateral	25 May 55	IGO Establishment	264UNTS117	103791
Thailand	Multilateral	26 Oct 56	IGO Establishment	276UNTS3	103988
Thailand	Multilateral	31 Jan 57	Claims and Debts	278UNTS105	104026
Thailand	Multilateral	03 Oct 57	Postal Service	365UNTS207	105214
Thailand	Multilateral	03 Oct 57	Postal Service	366UNTS141	105217
Thailand	Multilateral	03 Oct 57	Postal Service	364UNTS3	105211
Thailand	Multilateral	03 Oct 57	Postal Service	365UNTS3	105213
Thailand	Multilateral	03 Oct 57	Postal Service	366UNTS87	105216
Thailand	Multilateral	03 Oct 57	Postal Service	366UNTS255	105219
Thailand	Multilateral	03 Oct 57	Postal Service	364UNTS331	105212
Thailand	Multilateral	29 Apr 58	Territory Boundary	499UNTS311	107302
Thailand	Multilateral	29 Apr 58	Water Transport	450UNTS11	106465
Thailand	Multilateral	29 Apr 58	Specific Resources	559UNTS285	108164
Thailand	Multilateral	29 Apr 58	Territory Boundary	516UNTS205	107477
Thailand	Multilateral	26 Jan 60	IGO Establishment	439UNTS249	106333
Thailand	Multilateral	04 Jun 60	Tech Assistance	360UNTS208	105159
Thailand	Multilateral	01 Sep 60	Commodity Trade	403UNTS3	105792
Thailand	Multilateral	26 Nov 60	Taxation	500UNTS25	107304
Thailand	Multilateral	23 Jan 61	Postal Service	530UNTS141	107679
Thailand	Multilateral	30 Mar 61	Sanitation	520UNTS151	107515
Thailand	Multilateral	14 Apr 61	IGO Establishment	422UNTS101	106071
Thailand	Multilateral	18 Apr 61	Consul/Citizenship	500UNTS95	107310
Thailand	Multilateral	18 Apr 61	Consul/Citizenship	500UNTS223	107311
Thailand	Multilateral	21 Jun 61	IGO Establishment	514UNTS209	107449
Thailand	Multilateral	23 Jul 62	Recognition	456UNTS302	106564
Thailand	Multilateral	05 Aug 63	Sanitation	480UNTS43	106964
Thailand	Multilateral	19 Oct 63	Direct Aid	523UNTS249	107559
Thailand	Multilateral	10 Jul 64	Postal Service	611UNTS105	108845
Thailand	Multilateral	10 Jul 64	Postal Service	611UNTS387	108846
Thailand	Multilateral	10 Jul 64	Postal Service	613UNTS3	108851
Thailand	Multilateral	10 Jul 64	Postal Service	613UNTS193	108852
Thailand	Multilateral	10 Jul 64	Postal Service	612UNTS3	108847
Thailand	Multilateral	10 Jul 64	Postal Service	613UNTS3	108850
Thailand	Multilateral	10 Jul 64	Postal Service	611UNTS7	108844
Thailand	Multilateral	10 Jul 64	Postal Service	612UNTS233	108848
Thailand	Multilateral	13 Jul 64	ILO Labor	569UNTS65	108279
Thailand	Multilateral	30 Sep 64	IGO Operations	556UNTS3	108116
Thailand	Multilateral	08 Jul 65	General Trade	597UNTS3	108641
Thailand	Multilateral	04 Dec 65	IGO Establishment	571UNTS123	108303
Thailand	Multilateral	16 Dec 65	Postal Service	570UNTS201	108295
Thailand	Multilateral	31 Dec 65	Specific Resources	616UNTS317	108904
Thailand	Multilateral	04 May 66	IBRD Project	575UNTS49	108354
Thailand	Multilateral	27 Jan 67	Scientific Project	610UNTS205	108843
Thailand	Multilateral	28 Jun 67	ILO Labor	0UNTS0	110355
Thailand	Multilateral	28 Dec 67	Scientific Project	0UNTS0	109322
Thailand	Multilateral	01 Aug 68	Culture	0UNTS0	109368
Thailand	Multilateral	11 Jun 69	Scientific Project	0UNTS0	110100
Thailand	Netherlands	30 Jan 47	General Amity	247UNTS353	103480
Thailand	Netherlands	18 Jul 47	Air Transport	28UNTS27	100417
Thailand	Netherlands	30 May 53	Reparations	293UNTS17	104282
Thailand	Netherlands	09 Dec 57	Visas	309UNTS291	104477
Thailand	New Zealand	24 Dec 59	Customs	351UNTS197	105023
Thailand	Norway	26 Nov 49	Air Transport	53UNTS269	100787
Thailand	Norway	11 Dec 62	Visas	3NORT875	451171
Thailand	Norway	09 Jan 64	Taxation	522UNTS65	107537
Thailand	Pakistan	28 Aug 58	General Amity	394UNTS53	105668
Thailand	Philippines	14 Jun 49	General Amity	81UNTS53	101062
Thailand	Philippines	27 Apr 53	Air Transport	174UNTS3	102274
Thailand	Philippines	31 Jul 62	Visas	452UNTS235	106511
Thailand	Romania	20 Mar 70	General Trade	0UNTS0	110458
Thailand	Sweden	23 Nov 49	Air Transport	72UNTS217	100935
Thailand	Sweden	20 Oct 61	Taxation	428UNTS275	106180
Thailand	Switzerland	13 Oct 56	Air Transport	312UNTS43	104510
Thailand	Switzerland	07 Oct 70	General Economic	0UNTS0	110824

PARTY ONE	PARTY TWO	DATE	TOPIC	CITATION	NUMBER
Thailand	Taiwan	23 Jan 46	General Amity	161UNTS127	102126
Thailand	Taiwan	29 Sep 51	Air Transport	215UNTS166	102919
Thailand	Taiwan	09 Mar 60	Air Transport	0CTRC46	413027
Thailand	Taiwan	23 Nov 66	General Trade	581UNTS125	108436
Thailand	UK Great Britain	22 Mar 40	General Economic	2UNTS215	200013
Thailand	UK Great Britain	01 May 46	Commodity Trade	99UNTS175	101378
Thailand	UK Great Britain	01 May 46	Commodity Trade	99UNTS169	101377
Thailand	UK Great Britain	06 May 46	Commodity Trade	99UNTS193	101380
Thailand	UK Great Britain	06 Jan 47	Reparations	99UNTS149	101376
Thailand	UK Great Britain	08 May 47	Claims and Debts	100UNTS47	101386
Thailand	UK Great Britain	10 Nov 50	Air Transport	96UNTS77	101332
Thailand	UK Great Britain	29 Sep 52	General Economic	173UNTS31	102257
Thailand	UK Great Britain	25 Jul 57	Customs	277UNTS81	103999
Thailand	UK Great Britain	20 Nov 62	Tech Assistance	466UNTS243	106747
Thailand	UK Great Britain	09 Jan 63	Admin Cooperation	470UNTS59	106795
Thailand	UN Special Fund	04 Jun 60	Tech Assistance	360UNTS97	105157
Thailand	UNESCO (Educ/Cult)	25 Aug 61	IGO Operations	410UNTS125	105899
Thailand	UNICEF (Children)	01 Dec 48	IGO Operations	68UNTS94	100886
Thailand	United Nations	05 Oct 48	Humanitarian	47UNTS287	100735
Thailand	United Nations	11 Jun 51	Tech Assistance	90UNTS45	101225
Thailand	United Nations	26 May 54	IGO Status/Immunit	260UNTS35	103703
Thailand	USA (United States)	26 Feb 47	Air Transport	16UNTS17	100246
Thailand	USA (United States)	08 May 47	Air Transport	42UNTS241	100653
Thailand	USA (United States)	05 Sep 47	Admin Cooperation	73UNTS57	100943
Thailand	USA (United States)	01 Jul 50	Education	81UNTS61	101063
Thailand	USA (United States)	19 Sep 50	Tech Assistance	132UNTS199	101761
Thailand	USA (United States)	17 Oct 50	Milit Assistance	79UNTS41	101030
Thailand	USA (United States)	29 Dec 51	Milit Assistance	179UNTS113	102360
Thailand	USA (United States)	03 Dec 53	Tech Assistance	213UNTS91	102882
Thailand	USA (United States)	11 Aug 54	Commodity Trade	234UNTS155	103281
Thailand	USA (United States)	01 Sep 54	Claims and Debts	237UNTS209	103347
Thailand	USA (United States)	21 Jun 55	US Agri Commod Aid	262UNTS87	103738
Thailand	USA (United States)	09 Sep 55	Commodity Trade	264UNTS285	103799
Thailand	USA (United States)	14 Nov 55	Commodity Trade	239UNTS201	103380
Thailand	USA (United States)	13 Mar 56	Atomic Energy	253UNTS105	103579
Thailand	USA (United States)	04 Mar 57	US Agri Commod Aid	279UNTS235	104043
Thailand	USA (United States)	19 May 59	Milit Assistance	346UNTS271	104986
Thailand	USA (United States)	23 Dec 60	IGO Establishment	405UNTS135	105830
Thailand	USA (United States)	28 Nov 61	Direct Aid	434UNTS77	106256
Thailand	USA (United States)	12 Jan 62	Postal Service	459UNTS95	106615
Thailand	USA (United States)	31 May 62	Postal Service	459UNTS135	106619
Thailand	USA (United States)	25 Apr 63	Sanitation	476UNTS115	106906
Thailand	USA (United States)	24 May 63	Education	477UNTS123	106918
Thailand	USA (United States)	29 May 66	General Amity	0UNTS0	109345
Thailand	USSR (Soviet Union)	31 Dec 46	Consul/Citizenship	0SUST225	468420
Thailand	USSR (Soviet Union)	17 May 56	Consul/Citizenship	16SUGG71	469916
Thailand	USSR (Soviet Union)	20 May 56	Consul/Citizenship	0SUST355	468421
Thailand	Vietnam, South	18 Sep 67	Refugees	0VKNG252	496070
Thailand	Vietnam, South	13 Jan 70	Air Transport	0VKNG312	496076
Thailand	WHO (World Health)	12 Aug 49	Sanitation	178UNTS347	102350
Thailand	WHO (World Health)	04 Oct 51	Scientific Project	109UNTS85	101493
Thailand	WHO (World Health)	04 Oct 51	Sanitation	109UNTS77	101492
Tobago	Multilateral	12 Jun 67	IGO Operations	615UNTS321	108885
Togo	Accept UN Charter	21 May 60	UN Charter	375UNTS83	105355
Togo	France	09 Apr 62	Direct Aid	62FRRT41	415449
Togo	France	10 Jul 63	General Amity	64FRRT39	415450
Togo	France	10 Jul 63	Finance	0UNTS0	110372
Togo	France	10 Jul 63	General Economic	0UNTS0	110371
Togo	France	10 Jul 63	Consul/Citizenship	0UNTS0	110366
Togo	France	10 Jul 63	General Military	0UNTS0	110365
Togo	France	10 Jul 63	Tech Assistance	0UNTS0	110369
Togo	France	10 Jul 63	Admin Cooperation	0UNTS0	110367
Togo	France	10 Jul 63	Culture	0UNTS0	110368
Togo	France	10 Jul 63	Admin Cooperation	0UNTS0	110370
Togo	France	30 Apr 68	Claims and Debts	69FRJO2006	416451

PARTY ONE	PARTY TWO	DATE	TOPIC	CITATION	NUMBER
Togo	France	30 Apr 68	Territory Boundary	0UNTS0	110373
Togo	France	03 Feb 69	Scientific Project	0UNTS0	110670
Togo	France	25 Feb 70	Visas	0UNTS0	110537
Togo	Germany, West	20 Jul 60	Water Transport	60WBGA237	424659
Togo	Germany, West	20 Jul 60	Direct Aid	60WBGA243	424660
Togo	Germany, West	16 May 61	Claims and Debts	64WGBB154	425661
Togo	Germany, West	09 Jul 63	Loans and Credits	63WBGA199	424662
Togo	Germany, West	25 Mar 66	Non-IBRD Project	66WBGA111	424663
Togo	Germany, West	03 Feb 67	Loans and Credits	67WBGA136	424664
Togo	Germany, West	31 Jul 67	Loans and Credits	67WBGA218	424665
Togo	Germany, West	28 Aug 68	Tech Assistance	68WBGA219	424666
Togo	Germany, West	18 Jun 70	Loans and Credits	70WBGA196	424667
Togo	Germany, West	20 Mar 71	Loans and Credits	71WBGA115	424668
Togo	Germany, West	27 May 71	Loans and Credits	71WBGA114	424669
Togo	IDA (Devel Assoc)	10 Oct 68	Non-IBRD Project	0UNTS0	109643
Togo	Israel	09 Feb 65	Visas	550UNTS297	108024
Togo	Multilateral	11 Dec 46	Sanitation	12UNTS179	100186
Togo	Multilateral	24 Jul 48	Sanitation	66UNTS25	100847
Togo	Multilateral	02 Jul 51	Refugees	189UNTS137	102545
Togo	Multilateral	25 May 55	IGO Establishment	264UNTS117	103791
Togo	Multilateral	26 Jan 60	IGO Establishment	439UNTS249	106333
Togo	Multilateral	30 Mar 61	Sanitation	520UNTS151	107515
Togo	Multilateral	20 Sep 61	Tech Assistance	407UNTS52	105859
Togo	Multilateral	04 Aug 63	IGO Establishment	510UNTS3	107408
Togo	Multilateral	05 Aug 63	Sanitation	480UNTS43	106964
Togo	Multilateral	10 Jul 64	Postal Service	613UNTS3	108850
Togo	Multilateral	10 Jul 64	Postal Service	611UNTS7	108844
Togo	Multilateral	10 Jul 64	Postal Service	613UNTS193	108852
Togo	Multilateral	10 Jul 64	Postal Service	612UNTS233	108848
Togo	Multilateral	10 Jul 64	Postal Service	613UNTS3	108851
Togo	Multilateral	10 Jul 64	Postal Service	611UNTS105	108845
Togo	Multilateral	10 Jul 64	Postal Service	611UNTS387	108846
Togo	Multilateral	10 Jul 64	Postal Service	612UNTS361	108849
Togo	Multilateral	10 Jul 64	Postal Service	613UNTS127	108853
Togo	Multilateral	10 Jul 64	Postal Service	612UNTS3	108847
Togo	Multilateral	09 Mar 65	Water Transport	591UNTS265	108564
Togo	Multilateral	18 Mar 65	Dispute Settlement	575UNTS159	108359
Togo	Multilateral	27 May 66	IGO Establishment	637UNTS0	109121
Togo	Multilateral	27 Jan 67	Scientific Project	610UNTS205	108843
Togo	Multilateral	04 May 67	IGO Establishment	595UNTS287	108623
Togo	Multilateral	18 Mar 68	Commodity Trade	0UNTS0	109262
Togo	Multilateral	01 Jul 68	Peace/Disarmament	0UNTS0	110485
Togo	Multilateral	24 Sep 68	Air Transport	0UNTS0	110612
Togo	UN Special Fund	08 Jun 60	Tech Assistance	369UNTS401	200574
Togo	UNICEF (Children)	27 Jun 63	IGO Operations	540UNTS135	107847
Togo	United Nations	06 May 60	Tech Assistance	388UNTS53	105571
Togo	United Nations	03 Jul 64	Education	502UNTS287	107334
Togo	USA (United States)	22 Dec 60	Direct Aid	401UNTS33	105760
Togo	USA (United States)	20 Mar 62	Admin Cooperation	445UNTS79	106378
Togo	USA (United States)	05 Sep 62	General Aid	461UNTS47	106650
Togo	USA (United States)	08 Feb 66	General Amity	0UNTS0	109677
Togo	USSR (Soviet Union)	01 May 60	Consul/Citizenship	9SUGG134	469652
Togo	USSR (Soviet Union)	12 Jun 61	General Trade	0UNTS0	110495
Togo	USSR (Soviet Union)	12 Jun 61	General Trade	0SUST135	471030
Togo	USSR (Soviet Union)	14 Jun 61	General Trade	0UNTS0	110496
Togo	WHO (World Health)	03 Feb 61	Tech Assistance	394UNTS207	105680
Tonga	Multilateral	07 Nov 64	Sanitation	548UNTS3	107965
Transjordan	Multilateral	02 Aug 44	Scientific Project	67UNTS221	200221
Transjordan	Multilateral	07 Dec 44	IGO Establishment	15UNTS295	200102
Transjordan	Multilateral	22 Mar 45	General Amity	70UNTS237	200241
Transjordan	Multilateral	22 Jul 46	IGO Establishment	14UNTS185	100221
Transjordan	Multilateral	22 Jul 46	IGO Establishment	9UNTS3	100125
Transjordan	Multilateral	24 Jul 48	Sanitation	66UNTS25	100847
Trieste	Multilateral	17 Oct 53	General Transport	184UNTS42	102438
Trieste	United Nations	30 Sep 52	Tech Assistance	140UNTS11	101881

PARTY ONE	PARTY TWO	DATE	TOPIC	CITATION	NUMBER
Trieste	USA (United States)	15 Oct 48	Direct Aid	29UNTS249	100443
Trieste	USA (United States)	11 Feb 49	Direct Aid	79UNTS123	101036
Trinidad	Multilateral	15 Oct 46	Refugees	11UNTS73	100150
Trinidad	Multilateral	12 Jun 67	IGO Operations	615UNTS321	108885
Trinidad/Tobago	Accept UN Charter	06 Sep 62	UN Charter	437UNTS157	106305
Trinidad/Tobago	Denmark	02 Nov 69	Air Transport	0UNTS0	110395
Trinidad/Tobago	France	12 Oct 64	Air Transport	535UNTS25	107774
Trinidad/Tobago	IBRD (World Bank)	10 Mar 67	IBRD Project	599UNTS3	108662
Trinidad/Tobago	IBRD (World Bank)	16 Oct 68	IBRD Project	0UNTS0	109651
Trinidad/Tobago	IBRD (World Bank)	28 May 69	IBRD Project	0UNTS0	110220
Trinidad/Tobago	ILO (Labor Org)	14 Mar 69	IGO Operations	0UNTS0	109500
Trinidad/Tobago	Israel	31 Dec 68	Visas	0UNTS0	110379
Trinidad/Tobago	Multilateral	07 Dec 44	IGO Establishment	15UNTS295	200102
Trinidad/Tobago	Multilateral	07 Dec 44	Air Transport	84UNTS389	200252
Trinidad/Tobago	Multilateral	11 Dec 46	Sanitation	12UNTS179	100186
Trinidad/Tobago	Multilateral	12 Nov 47	Admin Cooperation	46UNTS201	100710
Trinidad/Tobago	Multilateral	06 Mar 48	Water Transport	289UNTS3	104214
Trinidad/Tobago	Multilateral	04 May 49	Admin Cooperation	98UNTS101	101358
Trinidad/Tobago	Multilateral	04 May 49	Admin Cooperation	92UNTS19	101257
Trinidad/Tobago	Multilateral	15 Jul 49	Health/Educ/Welfare	197UNTS3	102631
Trinidad/Tobago	Multilateral	22 Nov 50	Culture	131UNTS25	101734
Trinidad/Tobago	Multilateral	07 Dec 50	Admin Cooperation	212UNTS17	102861
Trinidad/Tobago	Multilateral	07 Nov 52	General Trade	221UNTS255	103010
Trinidad/Tobago	Multilateral	31 Mar 53	Privil/Immunities	193UNTS136	102613
Trinidad/Tobago	Multilateral	28 Sep 54	Refugees	360UNTS117	105158
Trinidad/Tobago	Multilateral	18 May 56	Customs	319UNTS21	104630
Trinidad/Tobago	Multilateral	18 May 56	Customs	338UNTS103	104834
Trinidad/Tobago	Multilateral	20 Feb 57	Consul/Citizenship	309UNTS65	104468
Trinidad/Tobago	Multilateral	29 Apr 58	Territory Boundary	516UNTS205	107477
Trinidad/Tobago	Multilateral	29 Apr 58	Territory Boundary	499UNTS311	107302
Trinidad/Tobago	Multilateral	29 Apr 58	Water Transport	450UNTS11	106465
Trinidad/Tobago	Multilateral	29 Apr 58	Specific Resources	559UNTS285	108164
Trinidad/Tobago	Multilateral	10 Jun 58	Admin Cooperation	330UNTS3	104739
Trinidad/Tobago	Multilateral	01 Dec 58	Commodity Trade	385UNTS137	105534
Trinidad/Tobago	Multilateral	17 Jun 60	Humanitarian	536UNTS27	107794
Trinidad/Tobago	Multilateral	30 Mar 61	Sanitation	520UNTS151	107515
Trinidad/Tobago	Multilateral	18 Apr 61	Consul/Citizenship	500UNTS95	107310
Trinidad/Tobago	Multilateral	28 Sep 62	IGO Establishment	469UNTS169	106791
Trinidad/Tobago	Multilateral	24 Apr 63	Consul/Citizenship	596UNTS261	108638
Trinidad/Tobago	Multilateral	06 May 63	Tech Assistance	463UNTS78	106694
Trinidad/Tobago	Multilateral	05 Aug 63	Sanitation	480UNTS43	106964
Trinidad/Tobago	Multilateral	10 Jul 64	Postal Service	611UNTS105	108845
Trinidad/Tobago	Multilateral	10 Jul 64	Postal Service	612UNTS3	108847
Trinidad/Tobago	Multilateral	10 Jul 64	Postal Service	611UNTS7	108844
Trinidad/Tobago	Multilateral	10 Jul 64	Postal Service	611UNTS387	108846
Trinidad/Tobago	Multilateral	18 Mar 65	Dispute Settlement	575UNTS159	108359
Trinidad/Tobago	Multilateral	08 Dec 65	IGO Establishment	600UNTS161	108680
Trinidad/Tobago	Multilateral	05 Apr 66	Water Transport	640UNTS133	109159
Trinidad/Tobago	Multilateral	22 Dec 66	Taxation	0UNTS0	109980
Trinidad/Tobago	Multilateral	27 Jan 67	Scientific Project	610UNTS205	108843
Trinidad/Tobago	Multilateral	14 Feb 67	General Military	634UNTS281	109068
Trinidad/Tobago	Multilateral	16 Mar 67	Gen Communications	0UNTS0	109755
Trinidad/Tobago	Multilateral	12 Jun 67	IGO Operations	615UNTS321	108885
Trinidad/Tobago	Multilateral	03 Jul 67	Air Transport	0UNTS0	109248
Trinidad/Tobago	Multilateral	18 Mar 68	Commodity Trade	0UNTS0	109262
Trinidad/Tobago	Multilateral	18 Mar 68	Postal Service	0UNTS0	110009
Trinidad/Tobago	Multilateral	09 Oct 68	Finance	0UNTS0	109822
Trinidad/Tobago	Multilateral	24 Dec 68	Commodity Trade	0UNTS0	109369
Trinidad/Tobago	Multilateral	27 Jan 69	Telecommunications	0UNTS0	109664
Trinidad/Tobago	Multilateral	18 Oct 69	IGO Establishment	0UNTS0	110232
Trinidad/Tobago	Norway	27 Sep 68	Visas	3NORT0	451172
Trinidad/Tobago	UK Great Britain	09 May 64	Admin Cooperation	633UNTS327	109043
Trinidad/Tobago	UK Great Britain	29 Dec 66	Taxation	605UNTS237	108766
Trinidad/Tobago	UK Great Britain	23 Jan 67	Telecommunications	605UNTS277	108767
Trinidad/Tobago	UK Great Britain	01 Mar 67	Air Transport	606UNTS149	108784

PARTY ONE	PARTY TWO	DATE	TOPIC	CITATION	NUMBER
Trinidad/Tobago	UN Special Fund	06 May 63	Direct Aid	463UNTS93	106695
Trinidad/Tobago	UNICEF (Children)	08 Aug 63	IGO Operations	473UNTS281	106865
Trinidad/Tobago	United Nations	06 May 63	IGO Status/Immunit	463UNTS109	106696
Trinidad/Tobago	USA (United States)	08 Oct 62	Air Transport	462UNTS145	106675
Trinidad/Tobago	USA (United States)	15 Jan 63	Finance	471UNTS141	106829
Trinidad/Tobago	USA (United States)	05 Dec 64	Milit Installation	535UNTS331	107788
Trinidad/Tobago	USA (United States)	21 Jul 69	Non-ILO Labor	0UNTS0	110339
Trinidad/Tobago	USSR (Soviet Union)	30 Aug 62	Recognition	11SUGG150	469859
Trinidad/Tobago	WHO (World Health)	23 Jun 64	Tech Assistance	503UNTS167	107342
Tunis	Multilateral	01 Jul 68	Peace/Disarmament	0UNTS0	110485
Tunisia	Accept UN Charter	14 Jul 56	UN Charter	253UNTS85	103577
Tunisia	Algeria	01 Sep 63	Air Transport	601UNTS275	108701
Tunisia	Austria	28 Jun 65	Admin Cooperation	65ABGB255	403196
Tunisia	Austria	28 Jun 65	Visas	65ABGB254	403197
Tunisia	Austria	30 Dec 65	Tech Assistance	589UNTS119	108539
Tunisia	Austria	17 Oct 66	Air Transport	67ABGB251	403198
Tunisia	Belgium	13 Oct 60	Visas	421UNTS71	106052
Tunisia	Belgium	21 Dec 62	Culture	482UNTS3	106987
Tunisia	Belgium	15 Jul 64	Tech Assistance	560UNTS57	108168
Tunisia	Belgium	15 Jul 64	Tech Assistance	560UNTS65	108169
Tunisia	Belgium	15 Jul 64	General Economic	561UNTS297	108190
Tunisia	Belgium	07 Aug 69	Education	0UNTS0	109974
Tunisia	Belgium	07 Aug 69	Non-ILO Labor	0UNTS0	109973
Tunisia	Bulgaria	29 Apr 69	Water Transport	0UNTS0	110839
Tunisia	China People's Rep	25 Sep 58	General Trade	58CCJC84	410541
Tunisia	Czechoslovakia	06 Apr 63	Culture	555UNTS111	108106
Tunisia	Denmark	14 Apr 59	Air Transport	340UNTS273	104870
Tunisia	Denmark	07 Jun 68	Loans and Credits	0UNTS0	109407
Tunisia	Denmark	10 Jun 69	Loans and Credits	0UNTS0	110772
Tunisia	France	16 Apr 53	Health/Educ/Welfare	53FRJO2407	416452
Tunisia	France	03 Jun 55	General Amity	55FRJO609	416453
Tunisia	France	09 Mar 57	General Amity	58FRRT8	415454
Tunisia	France	27 Oct 58	Water Transport	60FRRT17	415455
Tunisia	France	15 Apr 59	Health/Educ/Welfare	59FRRT47	415456
Tunisia	France	20 May 61	Air Transport	65FRRT53	415457
Tunisia	France	08 Jan 63	Health/Educ/Welfare	63FRRT10	415458
Tunisia	France	31 Jan 63	Customs	63FRRT32	415459
Tunisia	France	09 Aug 63	Claims and Debts	65FRRT77	415461
Tunisia	France	09 Aug 63	Education	63FRRT70	415460
Tunisia	France	29 Jan 64	Visas	64FRRT26	415463
Tunisia	France	29 Jan 64	Visas	64FRRT30	415462
Tunisia	France	17 Dec 65	Non-ILO Labor	66FRRT37	415464
Tunisia	France	17 Dec 65	Non-ILO Labor	0UNTS0	110665
Tunisia	France	20 Mar 68	Non-ILO Labor	0UNTS0	110730
Tunisia	France	14 Feb 69	Culture	0UNTS0	110316
Tunisia	France	17 Feb 69	Culture	69FRJO110	416465
Tunisia	France	05 Jun 69	Tech Assistance	69FRJO2109	416466
Tunisia	France	05 Jun 69	Tech Assistance	0UNTS0	110317
Tunisia	France	20 Mar 70	Finance	0UNTS0	110666
Tunisia	Germany, East	26 May 61	Mass Media	9EGDA400	419372
Tunisia	Germany, East	28 Feb 62	Finance	10EGDA566	419373
Tunisia	Germany, East	27 Nov 64	General Trade	12EGDA1171	419374
Tunisia	Germany, East	27 Nov 64	Finance	12EGDA903	419375
Tunisia	Germany, West	29 Jan 60	General Trade	60WBGA107	424678
Tunisia	Germany, West	20 Dec 63	Loans and Credits	64WBGA73	424680
Tunisia	Germany, West	20 Dec 63	Claims and Debts	65WGBB1377	425679
Tunisia	Germany, West	20 Apr 65	Tech Assistance	65WBGA123	424681
Tunisia	Germany, West	14 Jul 65	Loans and Credits	65WBGA182	424682
Tunisia	Germany, West	18 Oct 65	Non-ILO Labor	66WBGA57	424683
Tunisia	Germany, West	28 Mar 66	Other Military	66WBGA90	424684
Tunisia	Germany, West	03 Jun 66	Loans and Credits	66WBGA148	424685
Tunisia	Germany, West	19 Jul 66	Admin Cooperation	69WGBB889	425688
Tunisia	Germany, West	19 Jul 66	Extradition	69WGBB1157	425689
Tunisia	Germany, West	19 Jul 66	Water Transport	67WBGA66	424686
Tunisia	Germany, West	19 Jul 66	Culture	67WGBB1210	425687

PARTY ONE	PARTY TWO	DATE	TOPIC	CITATION	NUMBER
Tunisia	Germany, West	02 Jun 67	Loans and Credits	67WBGA128	424690
Tunisia	Germany, West	28 May 68	Loans and Credits	68WBGA156	424691
Tunisia	Germany, West	24 Apr 69	Loans and Credits	69WBGA144	424692
Tunisia	Germany, West	26 May 69	Air Transport	71WGBB177	425693
Tunisia	Germany, West	23 Apr 70	Tech Assistance	70WBGA196	424695
Tunisia	Germany, West	23 Apr 70	Finance	70WBGA126	424694
Tunisia	Germany, West	07 May 71	Finance	71WBGA116	424696
Tunisia	Ghana	11 Dec 62	Air Transport	563UNTS243	108213
Tunisia	Greece	02 Mar 60	General Trade	483UNTS89	107008
Tunisia	Greece	26 May 62	General Aid	534UNTS163	107761
Tunisia	IBRD (World Bank)	03 Jul 63	IBRD Project	480UNTS209	106970
Tunisia	IBRD (World Bank)	05 Jun 64	IBRD Project	539UNTS129	107827
Tunisia	IBRD (World Bank)	16 May 66	IBRD Project	584UNTS155	108477
Tunisia	IBRD (World Bank)	21 Feb 67	IBRD Project	618UNTS39	108923
Tunisia	IBRD (World Bank)	14 Sep 67	IBRD Project	639UNTS147	109149
Tunisia	IBRD (World Bank)	29 Nov 68	IBRD Project	0UNTS0	110598
Tunisia	IBRD (World Bank)	04 Jun 69	IBRD Project	0UNTS0	110286
Tunisia	IBRD (World Bank)	04 Jun 69	IBRD Project	0UNTS0	110648
Tunisia	IBRD (World Bank)	24 Dec 69	Non-IBRD Project	0UNTS0	110548
Tunisia	IDA (Devel Assoc)	17 Sep 62	Non-IBRD Project	469UNTS33	106783
Tunisia	IDA (Devel Assoc)	16 Sep 66	Loans and Credits	616UNTS285	108903
Tunisia	IDA (Devel Assoc)	21 Feb 67	Non-IBRD Project	618UNTS69	108924
Tunisia	IDA (Devel Assoc)	04 Jun 69	IBRD Project	0UNTS0	110287
Tunisia	Iran	20 Jul 68	General Trade	0IRTB69	433113
Tunisia	Iran	17 Apr 69	General Amity	0IRTB69	433111
Tunisia	Iran	17 Apr 69	Visas	0IRTB69	433114
Tunisia	Iran	17 Apr 69	Culture	0IRTB69	433112
Tunisia	Italy	05 Apr 51	Telecommunications	52ITGU206	435398
Tunisia	Italy	08 Apr 58	General Trade	378UNTS327	105430
Tunisia	Italy	31 Oct 59	General Trade	378UNTS349	105431
Tunisia	Italy	23 Nov 61	Tech Assistance	62ITDI530	436400
Tunisia	Italy	26 Jul 62	Non-ILO Labor	63ITDI399	436402
Tunisia	Italy	26 Jul 62	Non-ILO Labor	63ITDI397	436403
Tunisia	Italy	26 Jul 62	Loans and Credits	63ITDI398	436401
Tunisia	Japan	31 May 56	Visas	0JGJI1294	441094
Tunisia	Luxembourg	13 Jun 60	Air Transport	497UNTS143	107267
Tunisia	Mali	24 Jul 63	Air Transport	602UNTS91	108708
Tunisia	Multilateral	27 Mar 41	Military Mission	67UNTS231	200222
Tunisia	Multilateral	07 Dec 44	Air Transport	84UNTS389	200252
Tunisia	Multilateral	07 Dec 44	IGO Establishment	15UNTS295	200102
Tunisia	Multilateral	08 Feb 47	Patents/Copyrights	14UNTS287	100222
Tunisia	Multilateral	27 May 47	Air Transport	418UNTS161	106021
Tunisia	Multilateral	06 Jun 47	Patents/Copyrights	46UNTS249	100714
Tunisia	Multilateral	02 Oct 47	Telecommunications	193UNTS188	102616
Tunisia	Multilateral	06 Mar 48	Water Transport	289UNTS3	104214
Tunisia	Multilateral	10 May 48	Culture	289UNTS111	104215
Tunisia	Multilateral	10 Jun 48	Humanitarian	164UNTS113	102163
Tunisia	Multilateral	26 Jun 48	Culture	331UNTS217	104757
Tunisia	Multilateral	17 Sep 48	Telecommunications	97UNTS31	101345
Tunisia	Multilateral	09 Dec 48	Humanitarian	78UNTS277	101021
Tunisia	Multilateral	07 Dec 50	Admin Cooperation	212UNTS17	102861
Tunisia	Multilateral	02 Jul 51	Refugees	189UNTS137	102545
Tunisia	Multilateral	11 Jul 52	Postal Service	171UNTS89	102225
Tunisia	Multilateral	11 Jul 52	Postal Service	170UNTS269	102223
Tunisia	Multilateral	11 Jul 52	Postal Service	171UNTS143	102226
Tunisia	Multilateral	11 Jul 52	Postal Service	170UNTS63	102222
Tunisia	Multilateral	11 Jul 52	IGO Establishment	169UNTS3	102220
Tunisia	Multilateral	11 Jul 52	Postal Service	170UNTS3	102221
Tunisia	Multilateral	11 Jul 52	Postal Service	171UNTS3	102224
Tunisia	Multilateral	07 Oct 52	Admin Cooperation	310UNTS181	104493
Tunisia	Multilateral	31 Mar 53	Privil/Immunities	193UNTS136	102613
Tunisia	Multilateral	14 Jun 54	Air Transport	320UNTS217	104644
Tunisia	Multilateral	14 Jun 54	Air Transport	320UNTS209	104643
Tunisia	Multilateral	25 May 55	IGO Establishment	264UNTS117	103791
Tunisia	Multilateral	20 Jun 56	Admin Cooperation	268UNTS3	103850

PARTY ONE	PARTY TWO	DATE	TOPIC	CITATION	NUMBER
Tunisia	Multilateral	26 Oct 56	IGO Establishment	276UNTS3	103988
Tunisia	Multilateral	20 Feb 57	Consul/Citizenship	309UNTS65	104468
Tunisia	Multilateral	15 Jun 57	General Trade	550UNTS45	108008
Tunisia	Multilateral	01 Jul 57	Culture	0UNTS0	110418
Tunisia	Multilateral	03 Oct 57	Postal Service	365UNTS3	105213
Tunisia	Multilateral	03 Oct 57	Postal Service	365UNTS207	105214
Tunisia	Multilateral	03 Oct 57	Postal Service	366UNTS3	105215
Tunisia	Multilateral	03 Oct 57	Postal Service	364UNTS331	105212
Tunisia	Multilateral	03 Oct 57	Postal Service	366UNTS141	105217
Tunisia	Multilateral	03 Oct 57	Postal Service	366UNTS255	105219
Tunisia	Multilateral	03 Oct 57	Postal Service	364UNTS3	105211
Tunisia	Multilateral	03 Oct 57	Postal Service	366UNTS87	105216
Tunisia	Multilateral	03 Apr 58	Commodity Trade	336UNTS177	104806
Tunisia	Multilateral	03 Apr 58	Commodity Trade	302UNTS121	104355
Tunisia	Multilateral	29 Apr 58	Water Transport	450UNTS11	106465
Tunisia	Multilateral	29 Apr 58	Specific Resources	559UNTS285	108164
Tunisia	Multilateral	29 Apr 58	Territory Boundary	499UNTS311	107302
Tunisia	Multilateral	29 Apr 58	Territory Boundary	516UNTS205	107477
Tunisia	Multilateral	19 Nov 59	IGO Operations	410UNTS156	105902
Tunisia	Multilateral	26 Jan 60	IGO Establishment	439UNTS249	106333
Tunisia	Multilateral	12 Apr 60	Tech Assistance	359UNTS323	105150
Tunisia	Multilateral	17 Jun 60	Humanitarian	536UNTS27	107794
Tunisia	Multilateral	30 Mar 61	Sanitation	520UNTS151	107515
Tunisia	Multilateral	18 Apr 61	Consul/Citizenship	500UNTS95	107310
Tunisia	Multilateral	18 Apr 61	Consul/Citizenship	500UNTS223	107311
Tunisia	Multilateral	21 Jun 61	IGO Establishment	514UNTS209	107449
Tunisia	Multilateral	06 Dec 61	Customs	473UNTS219	106864
Tunisia	Multilateral	28 Jun 62	ILO Labor	494UNTS271	107238
Tunisia	Multilateral	14 Sep 62	IGO Status/Immunit	494UNTS219	107236
Tunisia	Multilateral	10 Dec 62	Culture	521UNTS231	107525
Tunisia	Multilateral	20 Apr 63	IGO Establishment	495UNTS3	107239
Tunisia	Multilateral	24 Apr 63	Consul/Citizenship	596UNTS261	108638
Tunisia	Multilateral	25 May 63	IGO Establishment	479UNTS39	106947
Tunisia	Multilateral	04 Aug 63	IGO Establishment	510UNTS3	107408
Tunisia	Multilateral	05 Aug 63	Sanitation	480UNTS43	106964
Tunisia	Multilateral	10 Jul 64	Postal Service	612UNTS233	108848
Tunisia	Multilateral	10 Jul 64	Postal Service	613UNTS3	108851
Tunisia	Multilateral	10 Jul 64	Postal Service	611UNTS105	108845
Tunisia	Multilateral	10 Jul 64	Postal Service	611UNTS7	108844
Tunisia	Multilateral	10 Jul 64	Postal Service	612UNTS3	108847
Tunisia	Multilateral	10 Jul 64	Postal Service	611UNTS387	108846
Tunisia	Multilateral	10 Jul 64	Postal Service	613UNTS193	108852
Tunisia	Multilateral	10 Jul 64	Postal Service	613UNTS3	108850
Tunisia	Multilateral	10 Jul 64	Postal Service	612UNTS361	108849
Tunisia	Multilateral	13 Jul 64	ILO Labor	569UNTS65	108279
Tunisia	Multilateral	20 Aug 64	Telecommunications	514UNTS25	107441
Tunisia	Multilateral	01 Dec 64	Water Transport	550UNTS133	108012
Tunisia	Multilateral	18 Mar 65	Dispute Settlement	575UNTS159	108359
Tunisia	Multilateral	08 Apr 65	IGO Operations	533UNTS66	107733
Tunisia	Multilateral	23 Jun 65	General IGO	614UNTS239	108873
Tunisia	Multilateral	05 Apr 66	Water Transport	640UNTS133	109159
Tunisia	Multilateral	27 Jan 67	Scientific Project	610UNTS205	108843
Tunisia	Multilateral	31 Jan 67	Refugees	606UNTS267	108791
Tunisia	Netherlands	19 Mar 59	Air Transport	497UNTS61	107262
Tunisia	Netherlands	23 May 63	Finance	523UNTS237	107558
Tunisia	Netherlands	11 Feb 64	Culture	570UNTS173	108293
Tunisia	Netherlands	03 Mar 64	Tech Assistance	533UNTS133	107739
Tunisia	Netherlands	08 Jul 66	Tech Assistance	591UNTS235	108560
Tunisia	Niger	18 Oct 66	Air Transport	0UNTS0	110468
Tunisia	Norway	28 Mar 59	Air Transport	497UNTS77	107263
Tunisia	Norway	27 May 60	Visas	3NORT807	451173
Tunisia	Norway	09 Jun 60	General Trade	3NORT808	451174
Tunisia	Poland	16 Sep 61	Tech Assistance	61PZUM192	458087
Tunisia	Poland	27 Apr 66	Culture	67PDZU249	457132
Tunisia	Romania	21 Apr 66	Culture	604UNTS57	108743

PARTY ONE	PARTY TWO	DATE	TOPIC	CITATION	NUMBER
Tunisia	Romania	21 Apr 66	Scientific Project	604UNTS65	108744
Tunisia	Sweden	19 Mar 59	Air Transport	497UNTS43	107261
Tunisia	Sweden	06 Sep 60	Taxation	427UNTS301	106162
Tunisia	Switzerland	26 Oct 57	Mostfavored Nation	58SWRO260	462159
Tunisia	Switzerland	21 May 60	Air Transport	497UNTS109	107265
Tunisia	Switzerland	02 Dec 61	Finance	64SWRO67	462108
Tunisia	Switzerland	02 Dec 61	Tech Assistance	64SWRO70	462109
Tunisia	Switzerland	02 Dec 61	General Trade	62SWRO1517	462160
Tunisia	Switzerland	15 Nov 63	Claims and Debts	63SWRO1073	462161
Tunisia	Turkey	17 Apr 58	Mostfavored Nation	59TURG606	466093
Tunisia	UK Great Britain	16 Nov 59	General Trade	354UNTS367	105070
Tunisia	UK Great Britain	17 Jan 61	General Trade	566UNTS2	108236
Tunisia	UK Great Britain	14 Jul 62	Visas	466UNTS235	106746
Tunisia	UN Special Fund	12 Apr 60	Direct Aid	355UNTS289	105082
Tunisia	UNESCO (Educ/Cult)	03 Jan 57	Direct Aid	257UNTS21	103645
Tunisia	United Nations	23 Dec 58	Tech Assistance	321UNTS23	104651
Tunisia	United Nations	04 Aug 66	IGO Operations	576UNTS23	108363
Tunisia	United Nations	18 Mar 68	IGO Operations	633UNTS3	109030
Tunisia	USA (United States)	26 Mar 57	General Aid	283UNTS117	104111
Tunisia	USA (United States)	28 Jun 57	Direct Aid	289UNTS301	104226
Tunisia	USA (United States)	18 Mar 59	Admin Cooperation	344UNTS179	104948
Tunisia	USA (United States)	30 Jun 61	US Agri Commod Aid	434UNTS85	106257
Tunisia	USA (United States)	13 Feb 62	Direct Aid	442UNTS155	106346
Tunisia	USA (United States)	16 Feb 62	US Agri Commod Aid	442UNTS161	106347
Tunisia	USA (United States)	14 Sep 62	US Agri Commod Aid	461UNTS31	106649
Tunisia	USA (United States)	29 Oct 62	Direct Aid	462UNTS201	106679
Tunisia	USA (United States)	18 Nov 63	Education	494UNTS193	107233
Tunisia	USA (United States)	07 Apr 64	US Agri Commod Aid	527UNTS3	107613
Tunisia	USA (United States)	17 Feb 65	US Agri Commod Aid	542UNTS125	107885
Tunisia	USA (United States)	30 Jul 66	US Agri Commod Aid	601UNTS133	108692
Tunisia	USA (United States)	26 Sep 66	Scientific Project	616UNTS259	108900
Tunisia	USA (United States)	17 Mar 67	US Agri Commod Aid	0UNTS0	109898
Tunisia	USA (United States)	06 Nov 67	US Agri Commod Aid	0UNTS0	110056
Tunisia	USA (United States)	17 May 68	US Agri Commod Aid	0UNTS0	110019
Tunisia	USA (United States)	17 Jul 68	Scientific Project	0UNTS0	110149
Tunisia	USA (United States)	24 Dec 68	Commodity Trade	0UNTS0	110261
Tunisia	USA (United States)	11 Jul 69	US Agri Commod Aid	0UNTS0	110338
Tunisia	USA (United States)	18 Dec 69	US Agri Commod Aid	0UNTS0	110510
Tunisia	USSR (Soviet Union)	11 Jul 56	Recognition	16SUGG72	469922
Tunisia	USSR (Soviet Union)	16 Jan 60	General Trade	9SUGG121	469622
Tunisia	USSR (Soviet Union)	04 May 60	Consul/Citizenship	9SUGG134	469654
Tunisia	USSR (Soviet Union)	10 Jan 61	Consul/Citizenship	16SUGG130	469988
Tunisia	USSR (Soviet Union)	30 Aug 61	General Aid	437UNTS243	106310
Tunisia	USSR (Soviet Union)	14 Mar 62	Finance	11SUGG135	469827
Tunisia	USSR (Soviet Union)	14 Mar 62	Mostfavored Nation	11SUGG135	469826
Tunisia	USSR (Soviet Union)	14 Mar 62	General Trade	11SUGG135	469825
Tunisia	Vietnam, South	10 May 66	General Trade	0VKNG235	496062
Tunisia	WHO (World Health)	04 Aug 60	Tech Assistance	381UNTS335	105474
Tunisia	WHO (World Health)	27 Jan 65	IGO Operations	528UNTS209	107644
Turk-Caicose Is	Multilateral	18 Oct 69	IGO Establishment	0UNTS0	110232
Turkey	Afghanistan	08 Feb 58	Air Transport	464UNTS39	106711
Turkey	Afghanistan	07 Nov 59	Culture	64TURG601	466034
Turkey	Argentina	19 Aug 65	Culture	0UNTS0	109558
Turkey	Australia	10 Apr 56	Visas	247UNTS139	103462
Turkey	Australia	05 Oct 67	Visas	0UNTS0	109457
Turkey	Austria	08 Aug 49	Mostfavored Nation	49ABGB234	403199
Turkey	Austria	07 Apr 54	Visas	55ABGB194	403200
Turkey	Austria	09 Oct 54	General Aid	56TURG404	466100
Turkey	Austria	19 Oct 56	Visas	56TURG2710	466010
Turkey	Austria	06 Apr 57	Admin Cooperation	58TURG2602	466032
Turkey	Austria	30 Dec 63	Direct Aid	64TURG903	466101
Turkey	Austria	15 May 64	Non-ILO Labor	515UNTS109	107457
Turkey	Austria	12 Oct 66	Non-ILO Labor	69ABGB338	403201
Turkey	Austria	08 Feb 68	Customs	68ABGB280	403202
Turkey	Austria	07 Nov 69	Land Transport	70ABGB274	403203

PARTY ONE	PARTY TWO	DATE	TOPIC	CITATION	NUMBER
Turkey	Belgium	12 Mar 47	Finance	33UNTS43	100513
Turkey	Belgium	12 Mar 47	General Trade	37UNTS215	100578
Turkey	Belgium	12 Mar 47	Mostfavored Nation	37UNTS221	100579
Turkey	Belgium	25 Feb 48	Visas	18UNTS237	100293
Turkey	Belgium	25 Mar 48	General Economic	48TURG2906	466044
Turkey	Belgium	02 Dec 48	General Economic	50TURG3001	466045
Turkey	Belgium	16 Oct 52	Visas	149UNTS289	101958
Turkey	Belgium	15 Apr 55	General Economic	58TURG2903	466046
Turkey	Belgium	02 Jan 56	Visas	228UNTS203	103152
Turkey	Belgium	25 Oct 56	Air Transport	380UNTS3	105447
Turkey	Belgium	28 Nov 58	Loans and Credits	64TURG909	466102
Turkey	Belgium	29 Dec 58	Culture	357UNTS195	105118
Turkey	Belgium	23 Sep 63	Direct Aid	566UNTS195	108244
Turkey	Belgium	04 Jul 66	Non-ILO Labor	0UNTS0	109397
Turkey	Brazil	21 Sep 50	Air Transport	150UNTS299	101981
Turkey	Bulgaria	07 Jun 46	General Trade	46TURG2112	466048
Turkey	Bulgaria	05 Dec 46	General Economic	47TURG2802	466049
Turkey	Bulgaria	07 Sep 49	General Economic	50TURG1001	466050
Turkey	Bulgaria	23 Feb 55	General Economic	56TURG202	466047
Turkey	Bulgaria	18 Apr 66	Air Transport	631UNTS263	108999
Turkey	Bulgaria	30 May 67	Sanitation	631UNTS19	108984
Turkey	Bulgaria	30 May 67	Sanitation	0UNTS0	109967
Turkey	Bulgaria	15 Dec 67	Land Transport	0UNTS0	110836
Turkey	Canada	15 Mar 48	General Economic	231UNTS63	103205
Turkey	Canada	28 Feb 49	Visas	231UNTS57	103204
Turkey	Canada	09 Feb 51	Visas	233UNTS95	103252
Turkey	Canada	21 Aug 56	Visas	305UNTS89	104416
Turkey	Czechoslovakia	05 Mar 47	Air Transport	14UNTS101	100214
Turkey	Denmark	30 Jun 47	Air Transport	32UNTS301	100504
Turkey	Denmark	15 Dec 48	General Trade	76UNTS17	100975
Turkey	Denmark	15 Dec 48	Finance	76UNTS3	100974
Turkey	Denmark	17 Dec 58	Direct Aid	64TURG909	466103
Turkey	Denmark	06 Mar 70	Finance	0UNTS0	110542
Turkey	Dominican Republic	28 Nov 51	General Amity	52TURG605	466001
Turkey	EEC (Econ Commnty)	12 Sep 63	Other Economic	64TURG1202	466005
Turkey	FAO (Food Agri)	14 Apr 51	Tech Assistance	51TURG407	466134
Turkey	Finland	15 May 46	General Economic	46TURG2312	466052
Turkey	Finland	12 Jun 48	General Trade	49TURG1902	466054
Turkey	Finland	12 Jun 48	Finance	49TURG1902	466053
Turkey	Finland	27 Oct 53	General Trade	55TURG702	466055
Turkey	Finland	29 Sep 54	Visas	59TURG1006	466012
Turkey	Finland	13 May 60	Finance	60TURG1908	466057
Turkey	Finland	13 May 60	General Trade	60TURG1908	466056
Turkey	France	31 Aug 46	General Economic	47FRJO310	416467
Turkey	France	12 Oct 46	Air Transport	14UNTS33	100209
Turkey	France	21 Oct 46	General Trade	48TURG2302	466060
Turkey	France	22 Dec 50	Non-ILO Labor	98UNTS11	101356
Turkey	France	17 Jun 52	Culture	60FRRT2	415515
Turkey	France	18 Jan 54	Claims and Debts	54TURG1003	466104
Turkey	France	19 Jan 54	Commodity Trade	55TURG3105	466062
Turkey	France	06 Apr 57	General Economic	58TURG407	466063
Turkey	France	08 Apr 61	Commodity Trade	61TURG1109	466064
Turkey	France	08 Jan 65	Non-ILO Labor	65FRRT57	415468
Turkey	Germany, West	19 Apr 48	General Trade	49TURG1902	466065
Turkey	Germany, West	18 Dec 48	General Economic	50TURG1001	466140
Turkey	Germany, West	15 Jan 49	General Economic	49TURG2812	466066
Turkey	Germany, West	14 Nov 49	Mostfavored Nation	50TURG1002	466029
Turkey	Germany, West	16 Feb 52	General Economic	52TURG305	466067
Turkey	Germany, West	16 Feb 52	Extradition	52TURG305	466006
Turkey	Germany, West	16 Feb 52	General Trade	53TURG202	466028
Turkey	Germany, West	16 Feb 52	Admin Cooperation	52TURG1602	466033
Turkey	Germany, West	16 Feb 52	Finance	52WBGA50	424769
Turkey	Germany, West	16 Feb 52	Customs	52WGBB616	425768
Turkey	Germany, West	06 Aug 53	Commodity Trade	54TURG2203	466043
Turkey	Germany, West	08 May 57	Culture	58WBGA336	424770

PARTY ONE	PARTY TWO	DATE	TOPIC	CITATION	NUMBER
Turkey	Germany, West	05 Jul 57	Air Transport	62WGBB2376	425771
Turkey	Germany, West	05 Jul 57	Air Transport	0UNTS0	110464
Turkey	Germany, West	07 May 58	Culture	58TURG1505	466036
Turkey	Germany, West	27 Nov 58	Direct Aid	64TURG909	466106
Turkey	Germany, West	26 Jun 59	Claims and Debts	60WGBB2365	425772
Turkey	Germany, West	19 Apr 60	Direct Aid	60TURG2208	466107
Turkey	Germany, West	06 Jun 61	Loans and Credits	61TURG1907	466108
Turkey	Germany, West	20 Jun 62	Loans and Credits	65WGBB1193	425774
Turkey	Germany, West	11 Sep 62	Visas	62WBGA217	424775
Turkey	Germany, West	30 Apr 64	Health/Educ/Welfare	65WGBB1169	425776
Turkey	Germany, West	30 Sep 64	Non-ILO Labor	68WBGA22	424773
Turkey	Germany, West	08 Dec 65	Admin Cooperation	67WGBB1692	425777
Turkey	Germany, West	03 Jun 69	Loans and Credits	69WBGA133	424778
Turkey	Germany, West	16 Jun 70	Loans and Credits	70WBGA135	424779
Turkey	Germany, West	03 Dec 71	Loans and Credits	71WBGA242	424780
Turkey	Greece	22 Jul 47	Air Transport	72UNTS131	100931
Turkey	Greece	02 Apr 49	Finance	78UNTS23	101010
Turkey	Greece	21 Jul 49	General Trade	78UNTS55	101011
Turkey	Greece	21 Jul 49	Claims and Debts	78UNTS65	101012
Turkey	Greece	20 Apr 51	Culture	178UNTS17	102333
Turkey	Greece	05 Aug 52	Visas	187UNTS163	102509
Turkey	Greece	07 Nov 53	General Trade	225UNTS163	103098
Turkey	Greece	10 Feb 55	Visas	55TURG1402	466015
Turkey	Hungary	12 May 49	General Economic	49TURG2812	466068
Turkey	IAEA (Atom Energy)	08 Feb 66	Atomic Energy	573UNTS75	108323
Turkey	IAEA (Atom Energy)	08 Dec 66	Atomic Energy	608UNTS69	108813
Turkey	IBRD (World Bank)	07 Jul 50	IBRD Project	156UNTS3	102039
Turkey	IBRD (World Bank)	07 Jul 50	IBRD Project	156UNTS75	102040
Turkey	IBRD (World Bank)	19 Oct 50	IBRD Project	157UNTS333	102058
Turkey	IBRD (World Bank)	18 Jun 52	IBRD Project	159UNTS269	102091
Turkey	IBRD (World Bank)	10 Sep 53	IBRD Project	187UNTS71	102502
Turkey	IBRD (World Bank)	31 Oct 61	IBRD Project	0UNTS0	109630
Turkey	IBRD (World Bank)	10 Aug 66	IBRD Project	585UNTS199	108490
Turkey	IBRD (World Bank)	11 May 67	IBRD Project	632UNTS193	109022
Turkey	IBRD (World Bank)	28 Feb 69	IBRD Project	0UNTS0	110091
Turkey	IBRD (World Bank)	12 Mar 69	IBRD Project	0UNTS0	110113
Turkey	IBRD (World Bank)	27 Jun 69	IBRD Project	0UNTS0	110559
Turkey	ICJ Option Clause	22 May 47	ICJ Option Clause	4UNTS265	100050
Turkey	IDA (Devel Assoc)	23 Nov 62	Non-IBRD Project	469UNTS3	106782
Turkey	IDA (Devel Assoc)	01 Feb 63	Non-IBRD Project	468UNTS223	106775
Turkey	IDA (Devel Assoc)	31 May 63	Non-IBRD Project	480UNTS127	106966
Turkey	IDA (Devel Assoc)	14 Jul 64	Non-IBRD Project	534UNTS339	107767
Turkey	IDA (Devel Assoc)	31 Aug 64	Non-IBRD Project	535UNTS111	107777
Turkey	IDA (Devel Assoc)	01 Apr 65	Non-IBRD Project	554UNTS137	108100
Turkey	IDA (Devel Assoc)	10 Aug 66	Non-IBRD Project	585UNTS237	108491
Turkey	IDA (Devel Assoc)	28 Feb 69	Non-IBRD Project	0UNTS0	110092
Turkey	ILO (Labor Org)	21 Mar 52	Tech Assistance	52TURG1306	466135
Turkey	India	29 Jun 51	Culture	213UNTS183	102886
Turkey	India	14 Dec 51	General Amity	137UNTS15	101845
Turkey	India	04 Jun 53	General Trade	54TURG2203	466069
Turkey	Indonesia	14 Sep 59	General Trade	64TURG2909	466070
Turkey	Iran	25 Dec 49	General Transport	51TURG1512	466136
Turkey	Iran	25 Dec 49	Customs	51TURG1512	466099
Turkey	Iran	25 Dec 49	Finance	51TURG1512	466071
Turkey	Iran	20 Mar 51	Air Transport	51TURG1512	466137
Turkey	Iran	08 Nov 55	Water Transport	0TURG217	466139
Turkey	Iran	13 Oct 56	General Economic	57TURG2506	466072
Turkey	Iran	02 Jan 59	Culture	64TURG601	466037
Turkey	Iran	08 Oct 64	Visas	64TURG2912	466017
Turkey	Iraq	29 Mar 46	Extradition	37UNTS369	100582
Turkey	Iraq	29 Mar 46	Admin Cooperation	37UNTS333	100581
Turkey	Iraq	29 Mar 46	General Amity	37UNTS226	100580
Turkey	Iraq	30 Jun 47	Air Transport	72UNTS107	100930
Turkey	Iraq	24 Feb 55	General Military	233UNTS199	103264
Turkey	Iraq	25 Sep 68	Land Transport	0UNTS0	110585

PARTY ONE	PARTY TWO	DATE	TOPIC	CITATION	NUMBER
Turkey	Ireland	27 Sep 55	Visas	553UNTS193	108087
Turkey	Israel	04 Jul 50	Mostfavored Nation	220UNTS3	102982
Turkey	Israel	05 Feb 51	Air Transport	193UNTS3	102607
Turkey	Israel	13 Nov 64	Tech Assistance	550UNTS303	108025
Turkey	Italy	12 Apr 47	General Economic	47TURG109	466073
Turkey	Italy	10 Nov 48	General Economic	50TURG301	466074
Turkey	Italy	25 Nov 49	Air Transport	192UNTS39	102594
Turkey	Italy	24 Mar 50	General Amity	96UNTS207	101338
Turkey	Italy	17 Jul 51	Culture	52ITGU203	435404
Turkey	Italy	22 Oct 51	Visas	52ITDI481	436405
Turkey	Italy	24 Jan 52	General Trade	53ITGU27	435406
Turkey	Italy	29 Jan 55	General Aid	56TURG202	466109
Turkey	Italy	10 Apr 55	Commodity Trade	56TURG409	466076
Turkey	Italy	15 Apr 57	General Trade	58TURG407	466077
Turkey	Italy	29 Nov 58	Direct Aid	60ITDI306	436408
Turkey	Italy	10 Jun 59	Tech Assistance	61ITDI302	436409
Turkey	Italy	21 Jun 63	General Economic	63TURG609	466111
Turkey	Italy	23 Jan 65	Finance	66ITDI159	436411
Turkey	Italy	18 Sep 65	Finance	66ITDI161	436412
Turkey	Italy	18 Sep 65	Loans and Credits	66ITDI162	436413
Turkey	Italy	01 Dec 65	General Trade	66ITDI163	436419
Turkey	Italy	01 Dec 65	General Economic	66ITDI248	436418
Turkey	Japan	08 Feb 55	General Economic	56TURG301	466078
Turkey	Japan	05 Nov 57	Visas	318UNTS411	104628
Turkey	Jordan	11 Jan 47	General Amity	14UNTS49	100210
Turkey	Jordan	07 May 48	Air Transport	32UNTS313	100505
Turkey	Jordan	01 Apr 68	Land Transport	0UNTS0	110584
Turkey	Lebanon	07 Dec 46	Consul/Citizenship	48TURG702	466007
Turkey	Lebanon	24 Dec 46	Visas	4UNTS269	100051
Turkey	Lebanon	16 Sep 47	Air Transport	44UNTS123	100682
Turkey	Lebanon	28 Jan 57	Consul/Citizenship	57TURG1309	466008
Turkey	Libya	09 Feb 58	Culture	59TURG206	466039
Turkey	Malta	06 Jun 66	Visas	579UNTS237	108411
Turkey	Multilateral	27 Mar 41	Military Mission	67UNTS231	200222
Turkey	Multilateral	02 Aug 44	Scientific Project	67UNTS221	200221
Turkey	Multilateral	07 Dec 44	Air Transport	84UNTS389	200252
Turkey	Multilateral	07 Dec 44	IGO Establishment	15UNTS295	200102
Turkey	Multilateral	07 Dec 44	Air Transport	171UNTS387	200502
Turkey	Multilateral	07 Dec 44	Air Transport	171UNTS345	200501
Turkey	Multilateral	16 Nov 45	IGO Establishment	4UNTS275	100052
Turkey	Multilateral	04 Jan 46	IGO Establishment	6UNTS35	100066
Turkey	Multilateral	22 Jul 46	IGO Establishment	9UNTS3	100125
Turkey	Multilateral	22 Jul 46	IGO Establishment	14UNTS185	100221
Turkey	Multilateral	27 Jul 46	Patents/Copyrights	90UNTS229	101238
Turkey	Multilateral	11 Dec 46	Sanitation	12UNTS179	100186
Turkey	Multilateral	08 Feb 47	Patents/Copyrights	14UNTS287	100222
Turkey	Multilateral	06 Jun 47	Patents/Copyrights	46UNTS249	100714
Turkey	Multilateral	02 Oct 47	Telecommunications	193UNTS188	102616
Turkey	Multilateral	11 Oct 47	IGO Establishment	77UNTS143	100998
Turkey	Multilateral	12 Nov 47	Admin Cooperation	53UNTS49	100772
Turkey	Multilateral	12 Nov 47	Admin Cooperation	53UNTS39	100771
Turkey	Multilateral	12 Nov 47	Admin Cooperation	53UNTS13	100770
Turkey	Multilateral	12 Nov 47	Admin Cooperation	46UNTS169	100709
Turkey	Multilateral	12 Nov 47	Admin Cooperation	46UNTS201	100710
Turkey	Multilateral	06 Mar 48	Water Transport	289UNTS3	104214
Turkey	Multilateral	10 Jun 48	Humanitarian	164UNTS113	102163
Turkey	Multilateral	26 Jun 48	Culture	331UNTS217	104757
Turkey	Multilateral	24 Jul 48	Sanitation	66UNTS25	100847
Turkey	Multilateral	17 Sep 48	Telecommunications	97UNTS31	101345
Turkey	Multilateral	19 Nov 48	Sanitation	44UNTS277	100688
Turkey	Multilateral	09 Dec 48	Humanitarian	78UNTS277	101021
Turkey	Multilateral	04 Apr 49	General Military	34UNTS243	100541
Turkey	Multilateral	04 May 49	Admin Cooperation	30UNTS23	100446
Turkey	Multilateral	04 May 49	Admin Cooperation	30UNTS3	100445
Turkey	Multilateral	04 May 49	Admin Cooperation	98UNTS101	101358

PARTY ONE	PARTY TWO	DATE	TOPIC	CITATION	NUMBER
Turkey	Multilateral	04 May 49	Admin Cooperation	47UNTS159	100728
Turkey	Multilateral	04 May 49	Admin Cooperation	92UNTS19	101257
Turkey	Multilateral	05 May 49	IGO Establishment	87UNTS103	101168
Turkey	Multilateral	16 Jun 49	Land Transport	45UNTS149	100696
Turkey	Multilateral	12 Aug 49	Humanitarian	75UNTS85	100971
Turkey	Multilateral	12 Aug 49	General Military	75UNTS135	100972
Turkey	Multilateral	12 Aug 49	Humanitarian	75UNTS31	100970
Turkey	Multilateral	12 Aug 49	Humanitarian	75UNTS287	100973
Turkey	Multilateral	02 Sep 49	IGO Status/Immunit	250UNTS12	103515
Turkey	Multilateral	24 Sep 49	IGO Establishment	126UNTS237	101691
Turkey	Multilateral	06 Apr 50	Admin Cooperation	119UNTS99	101610
Turkey	Multilateral	13 May 50	Land Transport	128UNTS171	101719
Turkey	Multilateral	16 Sep 50	General Transport	92UNTS91	101264
Turkey	Multilateral	18 Oct 50	Specific Resources	638UNTS185	109134
Turkey	Multilateral	04 Nov 50	Humanitarian	213UNTS221	102889
Turkey	Multilateral	07 Dec 50	Admin Cooperation	212UNTS17	102861
Turkey	Multilateral	15 Dec 50	Customs	347UNTS127	104994
Turkey	Multilateral	15 Dec 50	Customs	157UNTS129	102052
Turkey	Multilateral	15 Dec 50	Customs	171UNTS305	102234
Turkey	Multilateral	15 Dec 50	IGO Operations	160UNTS267	102111
Turkey	Multilateral	25 May 51	Status of Forces	175UNTS215	102303
Turkey	Multilateral	19 Jun 51	Status of Forces	199UNTS67	102678
Turkey	Multilateral	02 Jul 51	Refugees	189UNTS137	102545
Turkey	Multilateral	05 Sep 51	Tech Assistance	173UNTS15	102256
Turkey	Multilateral	08 Sep 51	Peace/Disarmament	136UNTS45	101832
Turkey	Multilateral	08 Sep 51	General Military	136UNTS165	101833
Turkey	Multilateral	20 Sep 51	IGO Status/Immunit	200UNTS3	102691
Turkey	Multilateral	09 Oct 51	IGO Establishment	220UNTS121	102997
Turkey	Multilateral	06 Dec 51	IGO Establishment	425UNTS61	106119
Turkey	Multilateral	12 Jun 52	Dispute Settlement	138UNTS183	101869
Turkey	Multilateral	11 Jul 52	Postal Service	170UNTS269	102223
Turkey	Multilateral	11 Jul 52	Postal Service	170UNTS3	102221
Turkey	Multilateral	11 Jul 52	Postal Service	171UNTS3	102224
Turkey	Multilateral	11 Jul 52	Postal Service	171UNTS143	102226
Turkey	Multilateral	11 Jul 52	Postal Service	170UNTS63	102222
Turkey	Multilateral	11 Jul 52	Postal Service	171UNTS89	102225
Turkey	Multilateral	11 Jul 52	IGO Establishment	169UNTS3	102220
Turkey	Multilateral	07 Nov 52	General Trade	221UNTS255	103010
Turkey	Multilateral	28 Feb 53	General Amity	167UNTS21	102199
Turkey	Multilateral	31 Mar 53	Privil/Immunities	193UNTS136	102613
Turkey	Multilateral	11 May 53	Sanitation	456UNTS3	106555
Turkey	Multilateral	17 Oct 53	General Transport	184UNTS42	102438
Turkey	Multilateral	07 Dec 53	Admin Cooperation	182UNTS51	102422
Turkey	Multilateral	11 Dec 53	Patents/Copyrights	218UNTS27	102952
Turkey	Multilateral	11 Dec 53	Non-ILO Labor	218UNTS255	102958
Turkey	Multilateral	11 Dec 53	Non-ILO Labor	218UNTS153	102956
Turkey	Multilateral	11 Dec 53	Non-ILO Labor	218UNTS211	102957
Turkey	Multilateral	11 Dec 53	Sanitation	191UNTS285	102588
Turkey	Multilateral	11 Dec 53	Education	218UNTS125	102954
Turkey	Multilateral	01 Mar 54	Commodity Trade	256UNTS31	103622
Turkey	Multilateral	14 May 54	Culture	249UNTS215	103511
Turkey	Multilateral	14 Jun 54	Air Transport	320UNTS209	104643
Turkey	Multilateral	14 Jun 54	Air Transport	320UNTS217	104644
Turkey	Multilateral	09 Aug 54	General Amity	211UNTS237	102855
Turkey	Multilateral	19 Dec 54	Culture	218UNTS139	102955
Turkey	Multilateral	19 Dec 54	Patents/Copyrights	218UNTS51	102953
Turkey	Multilateral	02 Mar 55	IGO Establishment	225UNTS233	103101
Turkey	Multilateral	01 May 55	Admin Cooperation	0UNTS0	110416
Turkey	Multilateral	25 May 55	IGO Establishment	264UNTS117	103791
Turkey	Multilateral	22 Jun 55	Atomic Energy	249UNTS3	103498
Turkey	Multilateral	12 Oct 55	IGO Establishment	560UNTS3	108165
Turkey	Multilateral	20 Oct 55	IGO Establishment	378UNTS159	105425
Turkey	Multilateral	13 Dec 55	Humanitarian	250UNTS3	103514
Turkey	Multilateral	13 Dec 55	IGO Operations	529UNTS141	107660
Turkey	Multilateral	01 Mar 56	Customs	343UNTS129	104923

PARTY ONE	PARTY TWO	DATE	TOPIC	CITATION	NUMBER
Turkey	Multilateral	30 Apr 56	Air Transport	310UNTS229	104494
Turkey	Multilateral	09 Jul 56	Non-ILO Labor	314UNTS3	104539
Turkey	Multilateral	26 Oct 56	IGO Establishment	276UNTS3	103988
Turkey	Multilateral	15 Dec 56	Education	278UNTS73	104023
Turkey	Multilateral	23 Jan 57	Tech Assistance	259UNTS426	103701
Turkey	Multilateral	29 Apr 57	Dispute Settlement	320UNTS243	104646
Turkey	Multilateral	15 Jun 57	General Trade	550UNTS45	108008
Turkey	Multilateral	27 Sep 57	Admin Cooperation	299UNTS211	104314
Turkey	Multilateral	03 Oct 57	Postal Service	366UNTS193	105218
Turkey	Multilateral	03 Oct 57	Postal Service	365UNTS207	105214
Turkey	Multilateral	03 Oct 57	Postal Service	366UNTS255	105219
Turkey	Multilateral	03 Oct 57	Postal Service	366UNTS3	105215
Turkey	Multilateral	03 Oct 57	Postal Service	366UNTS87	105216
Turkey	Multilateral	03 Oct 57	Postal Service	366UNTS141	105217
Turkey	Multilateral	03 Oct 57	Postal Service	365UNTS3	105213
Turkey	Multilateral	03 Oct 57	Postal Service	364UNTS3	105211
Turkey	Multilateral	03 Oct 57	Postal Service	364UNTS331	105212
Turkey	Multilateral	13 Dec 57	Land Transport	372UNTS159	105296
Turkey	Multilateral	13 Dec 57	Extradition	359UNTS273	105146
Turkey	Multilateral	28 Jul 58	General Military	335UNTS205	104788
Turkey	Multilateral	15 Dec 58	Mass Media	546UNTS235	107950
Turkey	Multilateral	15 Dec 58	Sanitation	351UNTS159	105022
Turkey	Multilateral	15 Jan 59	Customs	348UNTS13	104996
Turkey	Multilateral	20 Apr 59	Admin Cooperation	472UNTS185	106841
Turkey	Multilateral	11 May 59	Claims and Debts	527UNTS145	107623
Turkey	Multilateral	19 Nov 59	IGO Operations	410UNTS156	105902
Turkey	Multilateral	14 Dec 59	Admin Cooperation	444UNTS193	106369
Turkey	Multilateral	26 Jan 60	IGO Establishment	439UNTS249	106333
Turkey	Multilateral	28 Apr 60	Health/Educ/Welfare	376UNTS111	105377
Turkey	Multilateral	22 Jun 60	Mass Media	546UNTS247	107951
Turkey	Multilateral	16 Aug 60	Recognition	382UNTS3	105475
Turkey	Multilateral	16 Aug 60	General Amity	397UNTS287	105712
Turkey	Multilateral	16 Aug 60	Recognition	382UNTS8	105476
Turkey	Multilateral	01 Sep 60	Commodity Trade	403UNTS3	105792
Turkey	Multilateral	21 Sep 60	Patents/Copyrights	394UNTS3	105664
Turkey	Multilateral	06 Oct 60	Customs	473UNTS131	106861
Turkey	Multilateral	08 Jun 61	Customs	473UNTS187	106863
Turkey	Multilateral	08 Jun 61	Customs	473UNTS153	106862
Turkey	Multilateral	05 Oct 61	Patents/Copyrights	527UNTS181	107625
Turkey	Multilateral	18 Oct 61	IGO Establishment	529UNTS89	107659
Turkey	Multilateral	16 Dec 61	Visas	544UNTS19	107909
Turkey	Multilateral	14 May 62	Scientific Project	544UNTS39	107910
Turkey	Multilateral	14 May 62	Sanitation	544UNTS81	107911
Turkey	Multilateral	17 Dec.62	Admin Cooperation	590UNTS81	108548
Turkey	Multilateral	20 Apr 63	IGO Establishment	495UNTS3	107239
Turkey	Multilateral	09 Jun 63	General Economic	538UNTS309	107818
Turkey	Multilateral	05 Aug 63	Sanitation	480UNTS43	106964
Turkey	Multilateral	18 Jun 64	Atomic Energy	542UNTS145	107886
Turkey	Multilateral	20 Jun 64	General Economic	539UNTS3	107819
Turkey	Multilateral	10 Jul 64	Postal Service	613UNTS193	108852
Turkey	Multilateral	10 Jul 64	Postal Service	613UNTS3	108851
Turkey	Multilateral	10 Jul 64	Postal Service	611UNTS105	108845
Turkey	Multilateral	10 Jul 64	Postal Service	611UNTS387	108846
Turkey	Multilateral	10 Jul 64	Postal Service	612UNTS3	108847
Turkey	Multilateral	10 Jul 64	Postal Service	611UNTS7	108844
Turkey	Multilateral	10 Jul 64	Postal Service	613UNTS127	108853
Turkey	Multilateral	10 Jul 64	Postal Service	613UNTS3	108850
Turkey	Multilateral	10 Jul 64	Postal Service	612UNTS233	108848
Turkey	Multilateral	10 Jul 64	Postal Service	612UNTS361	108849
Turkey	Multilateral	08 Jul 65	General Trade	597UNTS3	108641
Turkey	Multilateral	21 Oct 65	Tech Assistance	547UNTS216	107959
Turkey	Multilateral	31 Dec 65	Specific Resources	616UNTS317	108904
Turkey	Multilateral	05 Apr 66	Water Transport	640UNTS133	109159
Turkey	Multilateral	27 Jan 67	Scientific Project	610UNTS205	108843
Turkey	Multilateral	31 Jan 67	Refugees	606UNTS267	108791

PARTY ONE	PARTY TWO	DATE	TOPIC	CITATION	NUMBER
Turkey	Multilateral	24 Sep 68	Air Transport	0UNTS0	110612
Turkey	Netherlands	19 Mar 47	Air Transport	14UNTS59	100211
Turkey	Netherlands	06 Sep 49	General Economic	50TURG1901	466079
Turkey	Netherlands	04 Nov 53	Visas	293UNTS3	104280
Turkey	Netherlands	26 Jul 55	General Economic	55NET140	447056
Turkey	Netherlands	29 Nov 58	Direct Aid	335UNTS229	104790
Turkey	Netherlands	12 Aug 59	Admin Cooperation	527UNTS181	107624
Turkey	Netherlands	12 May 60	Culture	463UNTS207	106704
Turkey	Netherlands	19 Aug 64	Non-ILO Labor	521UNTS197	107523
Turkey	Netherlands	05 Apr 66	Non-ILO Labor	0UNTS0	109204
Turkey	New Zealand	05 Jun 58	Visas	317UNTS123	104599
Turkey	Norway	20 May 48	Air Transport	26UNTS137	100384
Turkey	Norway	24 Feb 49	General Trade	29UNTS47	100433
Turkey	Norway	24 Feb 49	Finance	30UNTS151	100453
Turkey	Norway	23 Aug 52	Visas	2NORT588	451175
Turkey	Norway	24 Apr 57	General Trade	2NORT715	451176
Turkey	Norway	10 Jan 58	Culture	351UNTS229	105025
Turkey	Norway	19 Dec 58	Loans and Credits	2NORT758	451177
Turkey	Norway	24 Apr 59	Visas	59TURG1006	466023
Turkey	Norway	14 Jul 59	Claims and Debts	2NORT770	451178
Turkey	Norway	23 Dec 64	Loans and Credits	2NORT931	451179
Turkey	Norway	24 Dec 64	Loans and Credits	2NORT953	451180
Turkey	Norway	27 Dec 66	Loans and Credits	3NORT987	451181
Turkey	Norway	13 Jun 68	Loans and Credits	3NORTO	451182
Turkey	Pakistan	27 May 49	Visas	141UNTS325	101922
Turkey	Pakistan	26 Jul 51	General Amity	188UNTS323	102536
Turkey	Pakistan	22 Oct 51	Visas	219UNTS47	102965
Turkey	Pakistan	29 Jun 53	Culture	211UNTS225	102854
Turkey	Pakistan	04 Feb 54	General Amity	211UNTS263	102858
Turkey	Pakistan	02 Nov 55	Air Transport	311UNTS217	104505
Turkey	Pakistan	12 Dec 55	Visas	55TURG1912	466024
Turkey	Philippines	13 Jun 49	General Amity	2PTS155	465020
Turkey	Poland	18 Jul 48	General Economic	49TURG1802	466081
Turkey	Poland	18 Jul 49	General Economic	49TURG1802	466082
Turkey	Poland	04 Dec 53	Commodity Trade	55TURG204	466083
Turkey	Portugal	18 Dec 58	Direct Aid	64TURG909	466113
Turkey	Romania	05 Apr 54	General Economic	55TURG1602	466084
Turkey	Romania	19 May 67	Sanitation	0UNTS0	109536
Turkey	Spain	08 Sep 47	Finance	48TURG902	466085
Turkey	Spain	19 Jun 51	General Economic	52TURG2805	466086
Turkey	Spain	23 Jan 54	Commodity Trade	55TURG204	466087
Turkey	Spain	28 Mar 56	Culture	58SPBO908	460257
Turkey	Spain	16 Apr 59	General Amity	61SPBO803	460258
Turkey	Sweden	24 Apr 46	General Trade	45SOFM191	461022
Turkey	Sweden	24 Apr 46	Finance	46SOFM192	461023
Turkey	Sweden	24 Apr 46	General Economic	46TURG2312	466088
Turkey	Sweden	26 Jun 46	Air Transport	14UNTS21	100208
Turkey	Sweden	07 Jun 48	General Economic	49TURG1902	466089
Turkey	Sweden	17 Dec 58	Direct Aid	64TURG909	466114
Turkey	Sweden	01 Jun 60	Visas	60TURG2106	466027
Turkey	Switzerland	12 Sep 45	General Economic	46TURG2301	466090
Turkey	Switzerland	16 Feb 49	Air Transport	72UNTS175	100933
Turkey	Switzerland	22 Dec 58	Direct Aid	64TURG909	466115
Turkey	Syria	12 Feb 46	Air Transport	49TURG1712	466138
Turkey	Syria	23 Jul 49	Commodity Trade	50TURG403	466091
Turkey	Syria	28 Apr 53	Telecommunications	204UNTS255	102760
Turkey	Syria	03 Mar 56	General Trade	57TURG701	466092
Turkey	Taiwan	12 Feb 57	Culture	282UNTS125	104097
Turkey	Tunisia	17 Apr 58	Mostfavored Nation	59TURG606	466093
Turkey	UK Great Britain	23 Mar 44	Specif Claim/Waive	2UNTS227	200015
Turkey	UK Great Britain	04 May 45	General Economic	46TURG2301	466095
Turkey	UK Great Britain	12 Feb 46	Air Transport	6UNTS79	100069
Turkey	UK Great Britain	16 Oct 48	Finance	83UNTS85	101103
Turkey	UK Great Britain	09 Oct 52	Visas	151UNTS233	101999
Turkey	UK Great Britain	11 Feb 54	Milit Assistance	190UNTS343	102575

PARTY ONE	PARTY TWO	DATE	TOPIC	CITATION	NUMBER
Turkey	UK Great Britain	17 Jan 55	Finance	204UNTS195	102758
Turkey	UK Great Britain	12 Mar 56	Culture	313UNTS73	104530
Turkey	UK Great Britain	28 Feb 57	Customs	310UNTS29	104483
Turkey	UK Great Britain	28 Feb 57	General Economic	310UNTS69	104488
Turkey	UK Great Britain	16 Aug 57	Milit Assistance	310UNTS21	104482
Turkey	UK Great Britain	25 Nov 58	Loans and Credits	327UNTS35	104715
Turkey	UK Great Britain	13 Jun 59	Claims and Debts	551UNTS59	108033
Turkey	UK Great Britain	09 Sep 59	Non-ILO Labor	424UNTS267	106113
Turkey	UK Great Britain	01 Mar 60	Visas	374UNTS295	105343
Turkey	UK Great Britain	28 Jun 61	Visas	414UNTS93	105968
Turkey	UK Great Britain	01 May 63	Loans and Credits	63TURG2109	466116
Turkey	UK Great Britain	21 Oct 65	Loans and Credits	561UNTS185	108180
Turkey	UK Great Britain	29 Jul 66	Loans and Credits	597UNTS241	108649
Turkey	UK Great Britain	21 Apr 67	Loans and Credits	610UNTS0	108838
Turkey	UK Great Britain	04 Mar 68	Loans and Credits	0UNTS0	109265
Turkey	UK Great Britain	04 Mar 68	Loans and Credits	0UNTS0	109266
Turkey	UK Great Britain	29 Mar 68	Loans and Credits	0UNTS0	109286
Turkey	UK Great Britain	02 Apr 68	Taxation	0UNTS0	109452
Turkey	UK Great Britain	22 May 68	Loans and Credits	0UNTS0	109287
Turkey	UK Great Britain	06 Aug 68	Loans and Credits	0UNTS0	109451
Turkey	UK Great Britain	12 Aug 68	Loans and Credits	0UNTS0	109495
Turkey	UK Great Britain	23 Jun 69	Loans and Credits	0UNTS0	110027
Turkey	UK Great Britain	15 Sep 69	Loans and Credits	0UNTS0	110242
Turkey	UK Great Britain	14 Nov 69	Loans and Credits	0UNTS0	110441
Turkey	UN Special Fund	20 Nov 59	Direct Aid	345UNTS105	104963
Turkey	UNICEF (Children)	05 Sep 51	Direct Aid	193UNTS55	102610
Turkey	United Arab Rep	12 Apr 50	Air Transport	128UNTS3	101711
Turkey	United Arab Rep	15 Aug 53	General Economic	55TURG204	466094
Turkey	United Nations	31 Mar 64	IGO Status/Immunit	492UNTS273	107196
Turkey	USA (United States)	22 Apr 44	Customs	109UNTS279	200364
Turkey	USA (United States)	23 Feb 45	Direct Aid	121UNTS165	200398
Turkey	USA (United States)	12 Feb 46	Air Transport	13UNTS3	100196
Turkey	USA (United States)	27 Feb 46	Loans and Credits	46TURG1005	466117
Turkey	USA (United States)	07 May 46	Milit Assistance	6UNTS293	100083
Turkey	USA (United States)	12 Jul 47	Direct Aid	7UNTS299	100106
Turkey	USA (United States)	04 Jul 48	Mostfavored Nation	34UNTS185	100536
Turkey	USA (United States)	04 Jul 48	Direct Aid	24UNTS67	100351
Turkey	USA (United States)	27 Dec 49	Direct Aid	98UNTS141	101361
Turkey	USA (United States)	21 Jan 50	Direct Aid	50TURG3003	466118
Turkey	USA (United States)	15 Nov 51	Direct Aid	177UNTS315	102331
Turkey	USA (United States)	07 Jan 52	Milit Assistance	179UNTS121	102361
Turkey	USA (United States)	23 Jun 54	Status of Forces	233UNTS189	103263
Turkey	USA (United States)	23 Jun 54	Taxation	222UNTS161	103027
Turkey	USA (United States)	01 Jul 54	Milit Assistance	234UNTS147	103280
Turkey	USA (United States)	15 Nov 54	Commodity Trade	238UNTS135	103358
Turkey	USA (United States)	25 Apr 55	Milit Assistance	263UNTS299	103779
Turkey	USA (United States)	26 May 55	Milit Assistance	262UNTS97	103739
Turkey	USA (United States)	10 Jun 55	Atomic Energy	238UNTS149	103359
Turkey	USA (United States)	29 Jun 55	Milit Assistance	269UNTS97	103878
Turkey	USA (United States)	11 Oct 55	Visas	272UNTS145	103935
Turkey	USA (United States)	12 Mar 56	US Agri Commod Aid	272UNTS21	103929
Turkey	USA (United States)	18 May 56	Patents/Copyrights	283UNTS167	104115
Turkey	USA (United States)	12 Nov 56	US Agri Commod Aid	282UNTS77	104093
Turkey	USA (United States)	23 Nov 56	Direct Aid	290UNTS273	104239
Turkey	USA (United States)	15 Jan 57	Claims and Debts	280UNTS79	104053
Turkey	USA (United States)	12 Sep 57	Direct Aid	58TURG1004	466119
Turkey	USA (United States)	20 Jan 58	US Agri Commod Aid	304UNTS15	104389
Turkey	USA (United States)	06 Sep 58	Loans and Credits	336UNTS85	104800
Turkey	USA (United States)	14 Oct 58	Milit Assistance	336UNTS145	104803
Turkey	USA (United States)	13 Feb 59	US Agri Commod Aid	340UNTS235	104867
Turkey	USA (United States)	05 Mar 59	General Military	327UNTS293	104727
Turkey	USA (United States)	05 May 59	Milit Assistance	355UNTS341	105085
Turkey	USA (United States)	26 May 59	Direct Aid	354UNTS57	105053
Turkey	USA (United States)	20 Aug 59	Claims and Debts	61TURG2207	466120
Turkey	USA (United States)	29 Aug 59	Claims and Debts	61TURG2207	466121

PARTY ONE	PARTY TWO	DATE	TOPIC	CITATION	NUMBER
Turkey	USA (United States)	28 Oct 59	Milit Assistance	360UNTS265	105162
Turkey	USA (United States)	13 Nov 59	Milit Assistance	361UNTS3	105168
Turkey	USA (United States)	30 Nov 59	Tech Assistance	361UNTS107	105174
Turkey	USA (United States)	22 Dec 59	US Agri Commod Aid	367UNTS57	105225
Turkey	USA (United States)	02 Mar 60	Milit Assistance	372UNTS37	105286
Turkey	USA (United States)	31 Dec 60	Loans and Credits	61TURG2407	466122
Turkey	USA (United States)	09 Jan 61	General Economic	61TURG1707	466123
Turkey	USA (United States)	11 Jan 61	US Agri Commod Aid	405UNTS173	105833
Turkey	USA (United States)	21 Jan 61	Loans and Credits	61TURG2407	466124
Turkey	USA (United States)	07 Feb 61	Atomic Energy	61TURG509	466040
Turkey	USA (United States)	29 Jul 61	US Agri Commod Aid	416UNTS151	106001
Turkey	USA (United States)	08 Feb 62	Loans and Credits	63TURG106	466125
Turkey	USA (United States)	29 Mar 62	Loans and Credits	63TURG106	466126
Turkey	USA (United States)	23 Jul 62	Loans and Credits	63TURG106	466127
Turkey	USA (United States)	27 Aug 62	General Aid	461UNTS55	106651
Turkey	USA (United States)	23 Nov 62	Loans and Credits	63TURG404	466128
Turkey	USA (United States)	07 Dec 62	Loans and Credits	63TURG504	466129
Turkey	USA (United States)	21 Feb 63	US Agri Commod Aid	473UNTS311	106867
Turkey	USA (United States)	13 May 63	Loans and Credits	65TURG1506	466130
Turkey	USA (United States)	15 Jul 63	Loans and Credits	63TURG2809	466131
Turkey	USA (United States)	11 Sep 63	Loans and Credits	63TURG2509	466132
Turkey	USA (United States)	15 Oct 63	Loans and Credits	64TURG904	466133
Turkey	USA (United States)	17 Jul 64	Commodity Trade	530UNTS25	107670
Turkey	USA (United States)	02 Apr 66	US Agri Commod Aid	0UNTS0	109678
Turkey	USA (United States)	24 Sep 68	Status of Forces	0UNTS0	110079
Turkey	USA (United States)	12 Nov 68	Milit Installation	0UNTS0	110087
Turkey	USA (United States)	06 Feb 69	Commodity Trade	0UNTS0	110267
Turkey	USA (United States)	03 Nov 69	US Agri Commod Aid	0UNTS0	110452
Turkey	USA (United States)	16 Mar 70	US Agri Commod Aid	0UNTS0	110628
Turkey	USSR (Soviet Union)	18 Jul 53	Dispute Settlement	0SUST298	468422
Turkey	USSR (Soviet Union)	15 Sep 53	Specific Resources	0SUST301	468423
Turkey	USSR (Soviet Union)	27 Apr 61	Land Transport	420UNTS307	106047
Turkey	USSR (Soviet Union)	09 Jun 62	Telecommunications	493UNTS155	107213
Turkey	USSR (Soviet Union)	24 Feb 67	Scientific Project	643UNTS153	109190
Turkey	WHO (World Health)	19 Oct 50	Tech Assistance	110UNTS215	101512
Turkey	Yemen	09 Oct 52	General Amity	53TURG2107	466004
Turkey	Yugoslavia	18 Sep 47	General Economic	48TURG2302	466096
Turkey	Yugoslavia	05 Jan 50	General Economic	50TURG1803	466030
Turkey	Yugoslavia	05 Jan 50	General Economic	50TURG2503	466097
Turkey	Yugoslavia	26 Feb 53	General Trade	247UNTS54	103460
Turkey	Yugoslavia	16 Apr 53	Air Transport	255UNTS99	103606
Turkey	Yugoslavia	10 Apr 54	General Trade	55TURG1602	466098
Turkey	Yugoslavia	13 Jul 56	Claims and Debts	57TURG1309	466031
Turkey	Yugoslavia	22 Sep 60	Sanitation	61TURG504	466041
Uganda	Accept UN Charter	09 Oct 62	UN Charter	443UNTS47	106357
Uganda	China People's Rep	21 Apr 65	Direct Aid	65CCJC55	411353
Uganda	Denmark	01 Apr 68	Loans and Credits	0UNTS0	109209
Uganda	Denmark	03 Jul 68	Direct Aid	0UNTS0	109305
Uganda	Denmark	03 Jul 68	Tech Assistance	0UNTS0	109466
Uganda	Denmark	03 Jul 68	Non-IBRD Project	0UNTS0	109467
Uganda	Denmark	20 Jun 69	Education	0UNTS0	109932
Uganda	France	28 Apr 64	Air Transport	65FRRT95	415348
Uganda	Germany, West	17 Mar 64	Water Transport	66WBGA167	424697
Uganda	Germany, West	17 Mar 64	General Trade	67WBGA89	424698
Uganda	Germany, West	20 Mar 64	Loans and Credits	66WBGA167	424699
Uganda	Germany, West	20 Mar 64	Tech Assistance	66WBGA167	424700
Uganda	Germany, West	29 Nov 66	Claims and Debts	68WGBB449	425701
Uganda	Germany, West	19 Oct 67	Loans and Credits	68WBGA224	424702
Uganda	Germany, West	15 Jan 69	Loans and Credits	69WBGA123	424703
Uganda	IBRD (World Bank)	29 Sep 65	IBRD Project	568UNTS317	108276
Uganda	IBRD (World Bank)	17 Feb 67	IBRD Project	599UNTS321	108673
Uganda	ICJ Option Clause	03 Oct 63	ICJ Option Clause	479UNTS35	106946
Uganda	IDA (Devel Assoc)	21 Apr 67	General Aid	617UNTS161	108911
Uganda	IDA (Devel Assoc)	28 Jul 67	General Aid	617UNTS177	108912
Uganda	IDA (Devel Assoc)	15 Sep 67	Non-IBRD Project	639UNTS115	109148

PARTY ONE	PARTY TWO	DATE	TOPIC	CITATION	NUMBER
Uganda	IDA (Devel Assoc)	05 Oct 68	Non-IBRD Project	0UNTSO	109635
Uganda	IDA (Devel Assoc)	29 Sep 69	Non-IBRD Project	0UNTSO	110589
Uganda	Israel	04 Feb 63	Tech Assistance	484UNTS273	107037
Uganda	Israel	11 Oct 68	Culture	0UNTSO	110378
Uganda	Japan	28 Jun 68	Education	68JJS445	442215
Uganda	Multilateral	11 Dec 46	Sanitation	12UNTS179	100186
Uganda	Multilateral	22 Nov 50	Culture	131UNTS25	101734
Uganda	Multilateral	07 Dec 50	Admin Cooperation	212UNTS17	102861
Uganda	Multilateral	07 Nov 52	General Trade	221UNTS255	103010
Uganda	Multilateral	28 Sep 54	Refugees	360UNTS117	105158
Uganda	Multilateral	25 May 55	IGO Establishment	264UNTS117	103791
Uganda	Multilateral	20 Feb 57	Consul/Citizenship	309UNTS65	104468
Uganda	Multilateral	29 Apr 58	Territory Boundary	516UNTS205	107477
Uganda	Multilateral	29 Apr 58	Water Transport	450UNTS11	106465
Uganda	Multilateral	29 Apr 58	Specific Resources	559UNTS285	108164
Uganda	Multilateral	29 Apr 58	Territory Boundary	499UNTS311	107302
Uganda	Multilateral	29 Apr 58	Dispute Settlement	450UNTS169	106466
Uganda	Multilateral	26 Jan 60	IGO Establishment	439UNTS249	106333
Uganda	Multilateral	18 Apr 61	Consul/Citizenship	500UNTS95	107310
Uganda	Multilateral	28 Sep 62	IGO Establishment	469UNTS169	106791
Uganda	Multilateral	24 May 63	Tech Assistance	466UNTS346	106754
Uganda	Multilateral	25 May 63	IGO Establishment	479UNTS39	106947
Uganda	Multilateral	04 Aug 63	IGO Establishment	510UNTS3	107408
Uganda	Multilateral	05 Aug 63	Sanitation	480UNTS43	106964
Uganda	Multilateral	10 Jul 64	Postal Service	612UNTS3	108847
Uganda	Multilateral	10 Jul 64	Postal Service	611UNTS7	108844
Uganda	Multilateral	10 Jul 64	Postal Service	611UNTS105	108845
Uganda	Multilateral	10 Jul 64	Postal Service	611UNTS387	108846
Uganda	Multilateral	13 Jul 64	ILO Labor	569UNTS65	108279
Uganda	Multilateral	18 Mar 65	Dispute Settlement	575UNTS159	108359
Uganda	Multilateral	23 Jun 65	General IGO	614UNTS239	108873
Uganda	Multilateral	08 Jul 65	General Trade	597UNTS3	108641
Uganda	Multilateral	17 Jan 66	IGO Establishment	592UNTS101	108573
Uganda	Multilateral	04 Mar 66	US Agri Commod Aid	578UNTS57	108387
Uganda	Multilateral	27 Feb 67	IGO Operations	590UNTS156	108552
Uganda	Multilateral	27 Oct 67	Telecommunications	0UNTSO	109861
Uganda	Multilateral	18 Mar 68	Commodity Trade	0UNTSO	109262
Uganda	Multilateral	27 Jan 69	Telecommunications	0UNTSO	109664
Uganda	Netherlands	27 Jan 67	Extradition	608UNTS345	108823
Uganda	Norway	23 Mar 64	Tech Assistance	3NORT900	451196
Uganda	Norway	04 May 65	Visas	3NORT940	451195
Uganda	UK Great Britain	10 Oct 62	Admin Cooperation	475UNTS177	106893
Uganda	UK Great Britain	21 Sep 68	Finance	0UNTSO	109810
Uganda	UN Special Fund	19 Dec 62	Admin Cooperation	449UNTS41	106451
Uganda	UN Special Fund	22 Mar 63	Direct Aid	456UNTS466	106572
Uganda	United Nations	29 May 63	IGO Status/Immunit	466UNTS311	106751
Uganda	USA (United States)	16 Nov 64	General Aid	586UNTS143	108501
Uganda	USA (United States)	29 May 65	Claims and Debts	546UNTS209	107948
Uganda	USSR (Soviet Union)	08 Oct 62	Recognition	11SUGG155	469868
Uganda	USSR (Soviet Union)	13 Oct 62	Consul/Citizenship	11SUGG156	469869
Uganda	USSR (Soviet Union)	24 Jul 65	Culture	596UNTS199	108633
UK Great Britain	Afghanistan	19 Apr 65	Culture	633UNTS45	109033
UK Great Britain	Argentina	17 Apr 46	Air Transport	164UNTS53	102159
UK Great Britain	Argentina	17 Sep 46	General Economic	88UNTS47	101185
UK Great Britain	Argentina	19 Mar 47	General Trade	11UNTS195	100157
UK Great Britain	Argentina	14 Mar 49	Taxation	83UNTS193	101108
UK Great Britain	Argentina	27 Jun 49	General Economic	83UNTS217	101110
UK Great Britain	Argentina	31 Mar 55	General Economic	210UNTS223	102840
UK Great Britain	Argentina	30 Jun 56	General Economic	269UNTS235	103884
UK Great Britain	Argentina	31 Oct 56	Finance	269UNTS229	103883
UK Great Britain	Argentina	25 Nov 57	Claims and Debts	313UNTS95	104531
UK Great Britain	Argentina	19 Jun 61	Culture	470UNTS71	106797
UK Great Britain	Argentina	05 Jun 63	Loans and Credits	482UNTS353	107004
UK Great Britain	Argentina	12 Sep 63	Milit Servic/Citiz	601UNTS213	108698
UK Great Britain	Argentina	15 Apr 64	Commodity Trade	515UNTS3	107450

PARTY ONE	PARTY TWO	DATE	TOPIC	CITATION	NUMBER
UK Great Britain	Argentina	12 Jan 65	Air Transport	597UNTS177	108645
UK Great Britain	Argentina	15 Sep 66	Loans and Credits	603UNTS151	108732
UK Great Britain	Argentina	17 Feb 67	Visas	617UNTS193	108913
UK Great Britain	Australia	29 Oct 46	Taxation	17UNTS181	100276
UK Great Britain	Australia	28 Apr 50	Air Transport	95UNTS249	101324
UK Great Britain	Australia	19 Dec 50	Territory Boundary	93UNTS81	101292
UK Great Britain	Australia	08 Jun 53	Non-ILO Labor	201UNTS187	102718
UK Great Britain	Australia	26 Feb 57	General Trade	265UNTS197	103813
UK Great Britain	Australia	01 Apr 57	Non-ILO Labor	271UNTS235	103918
UK Great Britain	Australia	29 Jan 58	Non-ILO Labor	292UNTS233	104275
UK Great Britain	Australia	07 Feb 58	Air Transport	335UNTS23	104776
UK Great Britain	Australia	14 Nov 61	Air Transport	466UNTS35	106735
UK Great Britain	Australia	28 May 62	Admin Cooperation	434UNTS219	106264
UK Great Britain	Australia	16 Aug 62	Non-ILO Labor	439UNTS163	106328
UK Great Britain	Australia	06 Dec 62	Postal Service	457UNTS145	106584
UK Great Britain	Australia	06 Jun 63	Sanitation	472UNTS157	106838
UK Great Britain	Australia	23 Sep 63	Postal Service	483UNTS39	107006
UK Great Britain	Australia	15 Apr 64	Commodity Trade	515UNTS23	107451
UK Great Britain	Australia	07 Dec 67	Taxation	0UNTSO	109458
UK Great Britain	Australia	03 Oct 68	Finance	0UNTSO	109821
UK Great Britain	Australia	16 Oct 68	Scientific Project	0UNTSO	109459
UK Great Britain	Austria	23 Dec 46	General Aid	88UNTS93	101186
UK Great Britain	Austria	28 Apr 47	Reparations	93UNTS53	101287
UK Great Britain	Austria	26 Jan 50	Finance	97UNTS183	101350
UK Great Britain	Austria	31 Jan 51	Finance	88UNTS107	101187
UK Great Britain	Austria	28 Jun 51	Admin Cooperation	117UNTS99	101586
UK Great Britain	Austria	30 Jun 52	Reparations	138UNTS153	101867
UK Great Britain	Austria	12 Dec 52	Culture	172UNTS9	102237
UK Great Britain	Austria	31 May 54	Claims and Debts	54ABGB259	403213
UK Great Britain	Austria	09 Jul 54	Finance	201UNTS277	102720
UK Great Britain	Austria	14 Oct 54	Claims and Debts	204UNTS87	102751
UK Great Britain	Austria	15 May 55	Claims and Debts	344UNTS9	104940
UK Great Britain	Austria	09 Jul 56	Non-ILO Labor	310UNTS61	104487
UK Great Britain	Austria	20 Jul 56	Taxation	269UNTS147	103880
UK Great Britain	Austria	27 Oct 56	Air Transport	264UNTS67	103789
UK Great Britain	Austria	14 Mar 59	Claims and Debts	343UNTS263	104930
UK Great Britain	Austria	24 Jun 60	Consul/Citizenship	502UNTS79	107327
UK Great Britain	Austria	14 Jul 61	Admin Cooperation	453UNTS267	106530
UK Great Britain	Austria	09 Jan 63	Extradition	0UNTSO	110806
UK Great Britain	Austria	01 Mar 67	Air Transport	67ABGB119	403214
UK Great Britain	Austria	09 Mar 67	Other Military	67ABGB192	403216
UK Great Britain	Austria	03 Apr 68	Visas	0UNTSO	109214
UK Great Britain	Austria	15 Jan 69	Extradition	70ABGB169	403215
UK Great Britain	Austria	30 Apr 69	Taxation	70ABGB390	403250
UK Great Britain	Austria	29 May 69	Land Transport	70ABGB39	403218
UK Great Britain	Austria	09 Jun 69	Visas	69ABGB260	403217
UK Great Britain	Austria	27 May 70	Visas	70ABGB167	403219
UK Great Britain	Austria	12 Jul 71	Visas	71ABGB278	403220
UK Great Britain	Barbados	25 Sep 68	Finance	0UNTSO	109802
UK Great Britain	Belgium	16 May 44	Admin Cooperation	90UNTS283	200266
UK Great Britain	Belgium	22 Aug 44	Direct Aid	90UNTS295	200267
UK Great Britain	Belgium	05 Oct 44	Finance	5UNTS227	200031
UK Great Britain	Belgium	25 Jun 45	Reparations	90UNTS307	200268
UK Great Britain	Belgium	11 Mar 46	Status of Forces	26UNTS167	100387
UK Great Britain	Belgium	17 Apr 46	Health/Educ/Welfare	6UNTS177	100075
UK Great Britain	Belgium	16 Jan 47	Milit Installation	54UNTS97	100797
UK Great Britain	Belgium	05 Feb 47	Visas	11UNTS261	100164
UK Great Britain	Belgium	14 Nov 47	Finance	25UNTS269	100367
UK Great Britain	Belgium	07 Jun 48	Reparations	20UNTS33	100313
UK Great Britain	Belgium	29 Dec 48	Visas	27UNTS135	100404
UK Great Britain	Belgium	14 Apr 49	Visas	65UNTS117	100840
UK Great Britain	Belgium	07 Sep 49	Loans and Credits	106UNTS61	101457
UK Great Britain	Belgium	23 Dec 49	Status of Forces	99UNTS61	101371
UK Great Britain	Belgium	15 Mar 50	Patents/Copyrights	76UNTS85	100981
UK Great Britain	Belgium	06 Apr 51	Specific Property	110UNTS3	101496

PARTY ONE	PARTY TWO	DATE	TOPIC	CITATION	NUMBER
UK Great Britain	Belgium	08 May 51	Air Transport	158UNTS451	102079
UK Great Britain	Belgium	30 Jun 52	Milit Assistance	199UNTS113	102679
UK Great Britain	Belgium	12 Nov 52	Status of Forces	180UNTS15	102372
UK Great Britain	Belgium	27 Mar 53	Taxation	188UNTS153	102526
UK Great Britain	Belgium	10 Sep 53	Admin Cooperation	183UNTS203	102429
UK Great Britain	Belgium	04 Jan 54	Sanitation	247UNTS47	103459
UK Great Britain	Belgium	09 Jul 54	Finance	201UNTS299	102721
UK Great Britain	Belgium	05 Nov 54	Visas	209UNTS69	102822
UK Great Britain	Belgium	10 Nov 55	Status of Forces	331UNTS209	104756
UK Great Britain	Belgium	18 Nov 55	Atomic Energy	222UNTS327	103038
UK Great Britain	Belgium	20 May 57	Non-ILO Labor	303UNTS53	104371
UK Great Britain	Belgium	03 Oct 57	Reparations	394UNTS69	105669
UK Great Britain	Belgium	23 Apr 59	Finance	343UNTS271	104931
UK Great Britain	Belgium	01 Apr 60	Visas	361UNTS135	105177
UK Great Britain	Belgium	21 Feb 61	Visas	398UNTS229	105724
UK Great Britain	Belgium	08 Mar 61	Consul/Citizenship	523UNTS17	107554
UK Great Britain	Belgium	29 Aug 67	Taxation	0UNTS0	110540
UK Great Britain	Belgium	11 Dec 68	Land Transport	0UNTS0	109586
UK Great Britain	Bolivia	18 Mar 60	Visas	374UNTS199	105335
UK Great Britain	Botswana	30 Sep 66	Consul/Citizenship	633UNTS339	109044
UK Great Britain	Botswana	30 Sep 66	Status of Forces	597UNTS211	108646
UK Great Britain	Botswana	09 Oct 68	Military Mission	0UNTS0	109711
UK Great Britain	Botswana	01 Sep 69	Finance	0UNTS0	110240
UK Great Britain	Botswana	06 Apr 70	Taxation	0UNTS0	110808
UK Great Britain	Brazil	15 Mar 40	Territory Boundary	5UNTS71	200029
UK Great Britain	Brazil	27 May 44	Milit Servic/Citiz	2UNTS235	200016
UK Great Britain	Brazil	31 Oct 46	Air Transport	11UNTS115	100152
UK Great Britain	Brazil	21 May 48	Finance	66UNTS121	100851
UK Great Britain	Brazil	03 Aug 49	General Trade	86UNTS113	101154
UK Great Britain	Brazil	18 Sep 50	General Trade	88UNTS115	101188
UK Great Britain	Brazil	01 Oct 53	Claims and Debts	183UNTS207	102430
UK Great Britain	Brazil	05 Apr 55	Milit Servic/Citiz	403UNTS139	105793
UK Great Britain	Brazil	21 Jul 61	Loans and Credits	414UNTS26	105962
UK Great Britain	Brazil	14 Oct 64	Loans and Credits	539UNTS289	107840
UK Great Britain	Brazil	29 Dec 67	Taxation	643UNTS217	109193
UK Great Britain	Brazil	18 Jan 68	Tech Assistance	0UNTS0	109472
UK Great Britain	Bulgaria	13 Mar 48	Postal Service	104UNTS25	101432
UK Great Britain	Bulgaria	22 Sep 55	Finance	222UNTS349	103039
UK Great Britain	Bulgaria	13 Mar 68	Sanitation	0UNTS0	109585
UK Great Britain	Bulgaria	13 Mar 68	Consul/Citizenship	0UNTS0	109708
UK Great Britain	Bulgaria	28 Feb 69	Scientific Project	0UNTS0	109789
UK Great Britain	Bulgaria	27 Apr 70	General Trade	0UNTS0	110787
UK Great Britain	Bulgaria	28 May 70	Air Transport	0UNTS0	110788
UK Great Britain	Burma	17 Oct 47	Recognition	70UNTS183	100904
UK Great Britain	Burma	12 Oct 48	Finance	71UNTS255	100923
UK Great Britain	Burma	13 Mar 50	Taxation	131UNTS53	101735
UK Great Britain	Burma	25 Oct 52	Air Transport	150UNTS237	101978
UK Great Britain	Burma	18 Jun 56	Commodity Trade	256UNTS125	103623
UK Great Britain	Burma	20 Jan 59	Commodity Trade	343UNTS201	104926
UK Great Britain	Burma	06 Feb 59	Commodity Trade	343UNTS223	104927
UK Great Britain	Burma	02 Apr 63	Commodity Trade	475UNTS139	106890
UK Great Britain	Cambodia	09 Jul 69	Loans and Credits	0UNTS0	110117
UK Great Britain	Cameroon	29 Jul 63	General Economic	478UNTS148	106935
UK Great Britain	Cameroon	20 Aug 63	Culture	539UNTS233	107834
UK Great Britain	Cameroon	16 Jun 67	Loans and Credits	618UNTS329	108933
UK Great Britain	Canada	21 Dec 45	Air Transport	27UNTS155	100405
UK Great Britain	Canada	06 Mar 46	Finance	20UNTS13	100312
UK Great Britain	Canada	06 Mar 46	Reparations	20UNTS3	100311
UK Great Britain	Canada	05 Jun 46	Taxation	86UNTS3	101147
UK Great Britain	Canada	05 Jun 46	Taxation	27UNTS207	100408
UK Great Britain	Canada	17 Jul 47	Air Transport	28UNTS3	100416
UK Great Britain	Canada	19 Aug 49	Air Transport	44UNTS223	100686
UK Great Britain	Canada	19 Oct 54	Milit Assistance	214UNTS309	102906
UK Great Britain	Canada	09 Jan 56	Status of Forces	331UNTS192	104755
UK Great Britain	Canada	21 Jun 56	Postal Service	381UNTS111	105467

PARTY ONE	PARTY TWO	DATE	TOPIC	CITATION	NUMBER
UK Great Britain	Canada	20 Oct 56	Postal Service	381UNTS99	105466
UK Great Britain	Canada	16 Nov 56	Postal Service	412UNTS166	105930
UK Great Britain	Canada	18 Oct 58	General Aid	392UNTS61	105639
UK Great Britain	Canada	10 Dec 59	Non-ILO Labor	379UNTS201	105440
UK Great Britain	Canada	05 Aug 60	Milit Installation	470UNTS133	106804
UK Great Britain	Canada	15 Apr 64	Commodity Trade	515UNTS39	107452
UK Great Britain	Canada	11 Sep 64	Status of Forces	522UNTS99	107538
UK Great Britain	Canada	06 Dec 65	Taxation	572UNTS161	108311
UK Great Britain	Canada	13 Dec 66	Non-ILO Labor	0UNTS0	109274
UK Great Britain	Ceylon (Sri Lanka)	11 Nov 47	Admin Cooperation	86UNTS31	101150
UK Great Britain	Ceylon (Sri Lanka)	11 Nov 47	Consul/Citizenship	86UNTS25	101149
UK Great Britain	Ceylon (Sri Lanka)	11 Nov 47	Milit Assistance	86UNTS19	101148
UK Great Britain	Ceylon (Sri Lanka)	30 Apr 48	Finance	182UNTS2	102421
UK Great Britain	Ceylon (Sri Lanka)	28 Feb 49	Gen Communications	314UNTS269	104551
UK Great Britain	Ceylon (Sri Lanka)	05 Aug 49	Air Transport	35UNTS137	100554
UK Great Britain	Ceylon (Sri Lanka)	26 Jul 50	Taxation	337UNTS77	104818
UK Great Britain	Ceylon (Sri Lanka)	07 Jun 57	Milit Installation	280UNTS107	104055
UK Great Britain	Ceylon (Sri Lanka)	18 Sep 68	Finance	0UNTS0	109798
UK Great Britain	Chile	01 Jul 44	General Trade	2UNTS243	200017
UK Great Britain	Chile	25 Jun 46	General Trade	91UNTS137	101246
UK Great Britain	Chile	16 Sep 47	Air Transport	133UNTS143	101786
UK Great Britain	Chile	27 Oct 47	Milit Servic/Citiz	82UNTS209	101094
UK Great Britain	Chile	24 Jun 48	Finance	77UNTS113	100995
UK Great Britain	Chile	31 Jul 54	Milit Servic/Citiz	618UNTS353	108934
UK Great Britain	Chile	21 Oct 60	Loans and Credits	385UNTS15	105525
UK Great Britain	Chile	09 May 61	Visas	414UNTS37	105963
UK Great Britain	Chile	23 Nov 65	Loans and Credits	560UNTS215	108176
UK Great Britain	Chile	07 Oct 66	Tech Assistance	603UNTS167	108733
UK Great Britain	Chile	18 Nov 68	Atomic Energy	0UNTS0	110236
UK Great Britain	China People's Rep	06 Jul 53	General Trade	53CCJC39	410111
UK Great Britain	China People's Rep	20 Sep 53	Reparations	53CCJC54	410118
UK Great Britain	China People's Rep	01 Jun 56	Patents/Copyrights	56CCJC69	410340
UK Great Britain	Colombia	16 Oct 47	Air Transport	160UNTS297	102115
UK Great Britain	Colombia	13 Dec 49	Finance	88UNTS133	101189
UK Great Britain	Colombia	26 May 61	Visas	414UNTS85	105967
UK Great Britain	Congo (Zaire)	03 Jan 64	Loans and Credits	534UNTS417	107770
UK Great Britain	Costa Rica	19 Nov 68	Visas	0UNTS0	109661
UK Great Britain	Cuba	02 Dec 46	Admin Cooperation	11UNTS161	100154
UK Great Britain	Cuba	19 Mar 48	Air Transport	175UNTS23	102294
UK Great Britain	Cuba	02 Mar 51	Visas	88UNTS191	101190
UK Great Britain	Cuba	10 Aug 51	General Trade	108UNTS243	101478
UK Great Britain	Cuba	18 Dec 53	General Trade	186UNTS157	102490
UK Great Britain	Cyprus	16 Aug 60	Specific Property	382UNTS201	105480
UK Great Britain	Cyprus	16 Aug 60	Specific Property	382UNTS189	105479
UK Great Britain	Cyprus	16 Aug 60	Specific Property	382UNTS207	105481
UK Great Britain	Cyprus	16 Aug 60	Dispute Settlement	382UNTS183	105478
UK Great Britain	Cyprus	16 Aug 60	Specific Property	382UNTS177	105477
UK Great Britain	Cyprus	16 Aug 60	Customs	382UNTS215	105482
UK Great Britain	Cyprus	16 Aug 60	Consul/Citizenship	382UNTS247	105486
UK Great Britain	Cyprus	16 Aug 60	Privil/Immunities	382UNTS225	105483
UK Great Britain	Cyprus	16 Aug 60	Direct Aid	382UNTS231	105484
UK Great Britain	Cyprus	16 Aug 60	Claims and Debts	382UNTS239	105485
UK Great Britain	Cyprus	02 Jul 64	Commodity Trade	522UNTS129	107540
UK Great Britain	Cyprus	07 Mar 68	Taxation	0UNTS0	109342
UK Great Britain	Cyprus	11 Mar 68	Military Mission	0UNTS0	109285
UK Great Britain	Cyprus	21 Sep 68	Finance	0UNTS0	109808
UK Great Britain	Cyprus	06 Oct 69	Non-ILO Labor	0UNTS0	110426
UK Great Britain	Czechoslovakia	01 Nov 45	Finance	5UNTS15	100062
UK Great Britain	Czechoslovakia	19 Feb 47	Milit Installation	9UNTS173	100131
UK Great Britain	Czechoslovakia	16 Jun 47	Education	46UNTS61	100700
UK Great Britain	Czechoslovakia	03 Mar 49	Other Military	83UNTS95	101104
UK Great Britain	Czechoslovakia	18 Aug 49	Finance	86UNTS129	101155
UK Great Britain	Czechoslovakia	28 Sep 49	General Economic	86UNTS141	101156
UK Great Britain	Czechoslovakia	28 Sep 49	Claims and Debts	86UNTS175	101158
UK Great Britain	Czechoslovakia	28 Sep 49	Reparations	86UNTS161	101157

PARTY ONE	PARTY TWO	DATE	TOPIC	CITATION	NUMBER
UK Great Britain	Czechoslovakia	15 Jan 60	Air Transport	374UNTS207	105336
UK Great Britain	Czechoslovakia	26 Mar 68	Scientific Project	0UNTS0	109278
UK Great Britain	Denmark	16 Aug 45	Finance	5UNTS251	200033
UK Great Britain	Denmark	24 Oct 45	Milit Assistance	93UNTS143	101297
UK Great Britain	Denmark	06 Dec 45	Finance	5UNTS3	100061
UK Great Britain	Denmark	16 Aug 46	Milit Installation	9UNTS163	100130
UK Great Britain	Denmark	20 Jan 47	Telecommunications	118UNTS73	101597
UK Great Britain	Denmark	20 Mar 47	Visas	11UNTS285	100168
UK Great Britain	Denmark	22 Apr 47	Milit Occupation	8UNTS3	100110
UK Great Britain	Denmark	19 Aug 47	Reparations	9UNTS277	100137
UK Great Britain	Denmark	01 Dec 47	Reparations	93UNTS151	101298
UK Great Britain	Denmark	04 Mar 48	Milit Assistance	77UNTS57	100992
UK Great Britain	Denmark	11 Nov 48	Finance	25UNTS333	100371
UK Great Britain	Denmark	13 Aug 49	General Trade	68UNTS105	100890
UK Great Britain	Denmark	27 Mar 50	Taxation	68UNTS117	100891
UK Great Britain	Denmark	19 Oct 50	Finance	79UNTS25	101028
UK Great Britain	Denmark	23 Jun 52	Air Transport	151UNTS3	101982
UK Great Britain	Denmark	15 Dec 53	Non-ILO Labor	196UNTS105	102620
UK Great Britain	Denmark	23 Jul 54	Specific Resources	213UNTS313	102894
UK Great Britain	Denmark	20 Jan 55	Milit Servic/Citiz	210UNTS303	102842
UK Great Britain	Denmark	27 Feb 56	Commodity Trade	252UNTS83	103558
UK Great Britain	Denmark	09 Jul 56	Non-ILO Labor	264UNTS45	103787
UK Great Britain	Denmark	08 Oct 56	Consul/Citizenship	331UNTS181	104754
UK Great Britain	Denmark	18 Nov 57	General Trade	403UNTS153	105794
UK Great Britain	Denmark	28 Apr 59	Finance	343UNTS257	104929
UK Great Britain	Denmark	27 Aug 59	Non-ILO Labor	360UNTS11	105153
UK Great Britain	Denmark	08 Apr 60	Customs	374UNTS233	105337
UK Great Britain	Denmark	20 May 60	Atomic Energy	374UNTS245	105338
UK Great Britain	Denmark	10 May 61	Visas	414UNTS17	105961
UK Great Britain	Denmark	15 Nov 61	Dispute Settlement	420UNTS67	106041
UK Great Britain	Denmark	27 Jun 62	Consul/Citizenship	562UNTS75	108197
UK Great Britain	Denmark	30 Jun 64	Water Transport	539UNTS203	107833
UK Great Britain	Denmark	16 Sep 64	Commodity Trade	534UNTS427	107771
UK Great Britain	Denmark	03 Mar 66	Territory Boundary	592UNTS207	108574
UK Great Britain	Dominican Republic	26 Nov 51	Milit Installation	133UNTS205	101791
UK Great Britain	Dominican Republic	09 Aug 56	Consul/Citizenship	252UNTS127	103561
UK Great Britain	Dominican Republic	20 Jun 67	Visas	619UNTS3	108935
UK Great Britain	Ecuador	13 Sep 63	Visas	490UNTS19	107152
UK Great Britain	Ecuador	15 Nov 69	Loans and Credits	0UNTS0	110600
UK Great Britain	El Salvador	16 Dec 43	General Trade	2UNTS221	200014
UK Great Britain	El Salvador	16 Dec 46	General Trade	6UNTS131	100072
UK Great Britain	El Salvador	20 Aug 62	Visas	453UNTS309	106532
UK Great Britain	El Salvador	20 Jun 67	Tech Assistance	0UNTS0	109471
UK Great Britain	Ethiopia	19 Dec 44	General Amity	93UNTS303	200272
UK Great Britain	Ethiopia	29 Sep 47	Territory Boundary	82UNTS191	101092
UK Great Britain	Ethiopia	03 Jul 52	Status of Forces	151UNTS207	101996
UK Great Britain	Ethiopia	29 Aug 52	Trusteeship	190UNTS329	102573
UK Great Britain	Ethiopia	06 Sep 52	Finance	149UNTS57	101951
UK Great Britain	Ethiopia	29 Nov 54	Status of Forces	207UNTS283	102811
UK Great Britain	Ethiopia	12 Aug 55	Territory Boundary	227UNTS3	103127
UK Great Britain	Ethiopia	07 Jul 58	Air Transport	331UNTS3	104749
UK Great Britain	Ethiopia	13 Feb 69	Admin Cooperation	0UNTS0	109788
UK Great Britain	Eur Space Research	24 Nov 67	Gen Communications	638UNTS17	109129
UK Great Britain	Eur Space Research	30 Jan 69	Scientific Project	0UNTS0	109665
UK Great Britain	Eur Space Research	19 Dec 69	Scientific Project	0UNTS0	110442
UK Great Britain	Euratom	04 Feb 59	Atomic Energy	331UNTS125	104752
UK Great Britain	Euratom	11 Jul 66	Taxation	639UNTS99	109147
UK Great Britain	FAO (Food Agri)	24 Apr 58	IGO Operations	642UNTS245	109177
UK Great Britain	FAO (Food Agri)	20 Feb 61	IGO Operations	642UNTS253	109178
UK Great Britain	FAO (Food Agri)	13 Jul 67	IGO Operations	642UNTS263	109179
UK Great Britain	Fed of Malaya	12 Sep 57	Recognition	279UNTS287	104046
UK Great Britain	Fed of Malaya	12 Oct 57	Milit Assistance	285UNTS59	104149
UK Great Britain	Fed of Malaya	18 Oct 57	Air Transport	335UNTS3	104775
UK Great Britain	Fed of Malaya	04 Mar 58	Admin Cooperation	314UNTS253	104550
UK Great Britain	Fed of Malaya	08 Nov 58	Recognition	327UNTS301	104728

PARTY ONE	PARTY TWO	DATE	TOPIC	CITATION	NUMBER
UK Great Britain	Fed of Malaya	01 May 59	Loans and Credits	345UNTS57	104958
UK Great Britain	Fed of Malaya	27 Jul 59	Non-ILO Labor	374UNTS21	105324
UK Great Britain	Fed of Malaya	07 Jun 60	Scientific Project	375UNTS141	105365
UK Great Britain	Fed of Malaya	11 Sep 63	Admin Cooperation	0UNTS0	110761
UK Great Britain	Finland	12 Mar 48	Admin Cooperation	104UNTS29	101433
UK Great Britain	Finland	28 Dec 49	Peace/Disarmament	86UNTS191	101159
UK Great Britain	Finland	07 Jul 50	Finance	138UNTS171	101868
UK Great Britain	Finland	12 Dec 51	Taxation	172UNTS45	102239
UK Great Britain	Finland	16 Nov 54	Visas	204UNTS177	102756
UK Great Britain	Finland	28 Jul 59	Non-ILO Labor	355UNTS31	105073
UK Great Britain	Finland	05 May 61	Visas	414UNTS101	105969
UK Great Britain	Finland	09 Jun 61	Visas	414UNTS53	105965
UK Great Britain	Finland	05 Dec 61	Admin Cooperation	424UNTS217	106110
UK Great Britain	Finland	12 Sep 64	Commodity Trade	535UNTS13	107773
UK Great Britain	Finland	25 Mar 65	Air Transport	539UNTS103	107826
UK Great Britain	Finland	24 May 68	Atomic Energy	0UNTS0	109575
UK Great Britain	Finland	17 Jul 69	Taxation	0UNTS0	110321
UK Great Britain	France	27 Mar 45	Finance	98UNTS227	200274
UK Great Britain	France	29 Aug 45	Patents/Copyrights	11UNTS397	200069
UK Great Britain	France	31 Aug 45	IGO Establishment	98UNTS249	200275
UK Great Britain	France	04 Dec 45	Milit Installation	9UNTS121	100129
UK Great Britain	France	26 Jan 46	Reparations	91UNTS183	101251
UK Great Britain	France	28 Feb 46	Air Transport	27UNTS173	100407
UK Great Britain	France	29 Apr 46	Finance	98UNTS123	101360
UK Great Britain	France	03 Dec 46	Finance	54UNTS117	100798
UK Great Britain	France	03 Dec 46	Reparations	54UNTS127	100799
UK Great Britain	France	14 Dec 46	Taxation	105UNTS27	101452
UK Great Britain	France	27 Dec 46	Visas	11UNTS255	100163
UK Great Britain	France	04 Mar 47	General Amity	9UNTS187	100132
UK Great Britain	France	18 Jun 47	Air Transport	9UNTS203	100134
UK Great Britain	France	13 Aug 47	Non-ILO Labor	91UNTS169	101249
UK Great Britain	France	02 Mar 48	Culture	77UNTS33	100990
UK Great Britain	France	19 Apr 48	Status of Forces	83UNTS201	101109
UK Great Britain	France	11 Jun 48	Non-ILO Labor	66UNTS151	100852
UK Great Britain	France	12 Jul 48	Postal Service	90UNTS83	101230
UK Great Britain	France	15 Jul 48	Claims and Debts	71UNTS215	100920
UK Great Britain	France	21 Dec 49	Milit Servic/Citiz	264UNTS37	103786
UK Great Britain	France	23 Jan 50	Reparations	97UNTS149	101348
UK Great Britain	France	28 Jan 50	Non-ILO Labor	97UNTS155	101349
UK Great Britain	France	06 Oct 50	Air Transport	96UNTS63	101331
UK Great Britain	France	14 Dec 50	Taxation	51FRJO2108	416198
UK Great Britain	France	29 Dec 50	Dispute Settlement	118UNTS149	101603
UK Great Britain	France	24 Jan 51	Postal Service	90UNTS193	101237
UK Great Britain	France	30 Jan 51	Specific Resources	51FRJO2010	416199
UK Great Britain	France	30 Jan 51	Privil/Immunities	121UNTS97	101629
UK Great Britain	France	17 Feb 51	Finance	88UNTS199	101191
UK Great Britain	France	11 Apr 51	Claims and Debts	106UNTS3	101456
UK Great Britain	France	20 Apr 51	Air Transport	106UNTS81	101458
UK Great Britain	France	20 Aug 51	Finance	108UNTS263	101479
UK Great Britain	France	31 Dec 51	Consul/Citizenship	330UNTS145	104744
UK Great Britain	France	10 Nov 52	Admin Cooperation	214UNTS255	102903
UK Great Britain	France	13 Apr 53	Admin Cooperation	172UNTS173	102245
UK Great Britain	France	14 Oct 53	Admin Cooperation	186UNTS151	102489
UK Great Britain	France	10 Jul 56	Non-ILO Labor	326UNTS23	104708
UK Great Britain	France	28 Nov 58	Taxation	351UNTS263	105027
UK Great Britain	France	26 Jan 59	Admin Cooperation	330UNTS207	104745
UK Great Britain	France	26 Jan 59	Admin Cooperation	330UNTS213	104746
UK Great Britain	France	05 Mar 59	Finance	343UNTS277	104932
UK Great Britain	France	14 Feb 61	Visas	398UNTS267	105729
UK Great Britain	France	29 Nov 62	Scientific Project	453UNTS325	106534
UK Great Britain	France	17 Apr 63	Admin Cooperation	474UNTS295	106886
UK Great Britain	France	21 Jun 63	Taxation	540UNTS311	107855
UK Great Britain	France	05 Nov 63	Taxation	539UNTS277	107838
UK Great Britain	France	10 Apr 64	Specific Resources	0UNTS0	109272
UK Great Britain	France	03 Jun 64	General Ad Hoc	65FRRT92	415200

PARTY ONE	PARTY TWO	DATE	TOPIC	CITATION	NUMBER
UK Great Britain	France	03 Jun 64	Scientific Project	539UNTS253	107836
UK Great Britain	France	25 Feb 65	Non-ILO Labor	543UNTS157	107899
UK Great Britain	France	21 Sep 65	Culture	561UNTS3	108177
UK Great Britain	France	19 Nov 65	Non-ILO Labor	65FRRT105	415201
UK Great Britain	France	19 Nov 65	Non-ILO Labor	561UNTS19	108178
UK Great Britain	France	14 Feb 67	Non-ILO Labor	0UNTS0	109493
UK Great Britain	France	15 Feb 67	Admin Cooperation	606UNTS119	108781
UK Great Britain	France	22 Nov 67	Gen Communications	643UNTS225	109194
UK Great Britain	France	22 May 68	Finance	69FRJO2511	416202
UK Great Britain	France	22 May 68	Taxation	0UNTS0	110422
UK Great Britain	France	13 Sep 68	Culture	69FRJO1001	416203
UK Great Britain	France	28 Mar 69	Land Transport	0UNTS0	110599
UK Great Britain	France	28 May 69	Taxation	0UNTS0	110423
UK Great Britain	France	19 May 70	Consul/Citizenship	0UNTS0	110809
UK Great Britain	Gambia	05 Jun 65	Admin Cooperation	551UNTS193	108041
UK Great Britain	Gambia	20 Jun 66	Recognition	573UNTS203	108333
UK Great Britain	Gambia	01 Apr 68	Taxation	0UNTS0	109709
UK Great Britain	Gambia	19 Sep 68	Finance	0UNTS0	109799
UK Great Britain	Germany, West	09 Dec 50	Finance	88UNTS247	101196
UK Great Britain	Germany, West	09 Sep 52	Milit Installation	151UNTS215	101997
UK Great Britain	Germany, West	27 Feb 53	Claims and Debts	330UNTS217	104747
UK Great Britain	Germany, West	22 May 53	Finance	172UNTS179	102246
UK Great Britain	Germany, West	10 Jul 54	Finance	199UNTS135	102680
UK Great Britain	Germany, West	18 Oct 54	Taxation	218UNTS301	102960
UK Great Britain	Germany, West	22 Jul 55	Air Transport	269UNTS189	103881
UK Great Britain	Germany, West	22 Jul 55	Air Transport	269UNTS223	103882
UK Great Britain	Germany, West	30 Jul 56	Consul/Citizenship	330UNTS233	104748
UK Great Britain	Germany, West	31 Jul 56	Atomic Energy	252UNTS93	103559
UK Great Britain	Germany, West	11 Apr 57	Status of Forces	331UNTS173	104753
UK Great Britain	Germany, West	07 Jun 57	Milit Assistance	398UNTS275	105730
UK Great Britain	Germany, West	18 Apr 58	Culture	343UNTS241	104928
UK Great Britain	Germany, West	03 Oct 58	Milit Assistance	398UNTS293	105731
UK Great Britain	Germany, West	10 Apr 59	Claims and Debts	343UNTS295	104935
UK Great Britain	Germany, West	03 Aug 59	Dispute Settlement	502UNTS197	107331
UK Great Britain	Germany, West	16 Oct 59	Other Military	385UNTS21	105526
UK Great Britain	Germany, West	28 Jan 60	Reparations	420UNTS29	106038
UK Great Britain	Germany, West	23 Feb 60	Extradition	385UNTS39	105527
UK Great Britain	Germany, West	09 Mar 60	Admin Cooperation	403UNTS253	105796
UK Great Britain	Germany, West	20 Apr 60	Non-ILO Labor	413UNTS236	105958
UK Great Britain	Germany, West	20 Apr 60	Non-ILO Labor	449UNTS77	106453
UK Great Britain	Germany, West	20 Jun 60	Visas	385UNTS55	105528
UK Great Britain	Germany, West	14 Jul 60	Admin Cooperation	414UNTS144	105972
UK Great Britain	Germany, West	20 Feb 61	Visas	398UNTS249	105727
UK Great Britain	Germany, West	02 May 61	Admin Cooperation	414UNTS3	105959
UK Great Britain	Germany, West	12 Jul 61	Status of Forces	424UNTS211	106109
UK Great Britain	Germany, West	26 Sep 61	Milit Assistance	424UNTS201	106108
UK Great Britain	Germany, West	06 Jun 62	Status of Forces	437UNTS39	106298
UK Great Britain	Germany, West	20 Sep 62	Admin Cooperation	453UNTS317	106533
UK Great Britain	Germany, West	09 Jun 64	Reparations	539UNTS187	107831
UK Great Britain	Germany, West	27 Jul 64	Status of Forces	539UNTS243	107835
UK Great Britain	Germany, West	26 Nov 64	Taxation	603UNTS183	108734
UK Great Britain	Germany, West	11 Jan 67	Commodity Trade	67WBGA22	424716
UK Great Britain	Germany, West	31 Mar 67	Commodity Trade	67WBGA83	424717
UK Great Britain	Germany, West	05 May 67	Finance	613UNTS313	108858
UK Great Britain	Germany, West	02 Jun 67	Land Transport	67WBGA135	424718
UK Great Britain	Germany, West	20 Jul 67	General Trade	67WBGA176	424719
UK Great Britain	Germany, West	11 Apr 68	Finance	0UNTS0	109288
UK Great Britain	Germany, West	19 May 69	Finance	0UNTS0	110025
UK Great Britain	Germany, West	01 Sep 69	Finance	0UNTS0	110241
UK Great Britain	Ghana	25 Nov 57	Recognition	287UNTS233	104189
UK Great Britain	Ghana	24 Sep 58	Air Transport	411UNTS146	105918
UK Great Britain	Ghana	17 Apr 59	Status of Forces	337UNTS353	104829
UK Great Britain	Ghana	04 Jun 60	Admin Cooperation	377UNTS197	105401
UK Great Britain	Ghana	05 Jul 60	Admin Cooperation	402UNTS17	105774
UK Great Britain	Ghana	27 Feb 67	Claims and Debts	606UNTS133	108783

PARTY ONE	PARTY TWO	DATE	TOPIC	CITATION	NUMBER
UK Great Britain	Ghana	21 Sep 68	Finance	0UNTS0	109807
UK Great Britain	Ghana	17 Dec 68	Claims and Debts	0UNTS0	109712
UK Great Britain	Greece	11 Oct 45	Reparations	183UNTS329	200509
UK Great Britain	Greece	26 Nov 45	Air Transport	35UNTS161	100555
UK Great Britain	Greece	30 Nov 45	Reparations	183UNTS197	102428
UK Great Britain	Greece	24 Jan 46	Finance	6UNTS45	100067
UK Great Britain	Greece	21 Mar 46	Claims and Debts	91UNTS149	101247
UK Great Britain	Greece	21 Feb 47	Air Transport	70UNTS215	100905
UK Great Britain	Greece	07 Apr 47	Territory Boundary	11UNTS201	100158
UK Great Britain	Greece	05 Jun 47	Status of Forces	9UNTS197	100133
UK Great Britain	Greece	07 Sep 48	Status of Forces	180UNTS144	102380
UK Great Britain	Greece	29 Jun 49	Finance	86UNTS203	101160
UK Great Britain	Greece	17 Oct 49	Postal Service	93UNTS185	101300
UK Great Britain	Greece	16 Nov 50	Taxation	166UNTS281	102193
UK Great Britain	Greece	21 Feb 51	General Economic	88UNTS205	101192
UK Great Britain	Greece	29 Sep 51	Culture	190UNTS260	102570
UK Great Britain	Greece	17 Apr 53	Consul/Citizenship	191UNTS151	102582
UK Great Britain	Greece	01 Jun 53	Visas	172UNTS265	102250
UK Great Britain	Greece	25 Jun 53	Taxation	190UNTS281	102571
UK Great Britain	Greece	05 Oct 53	Reparations	243UNTS73	103447
UK Great Britain	Greece	24 Feb 55	Specif Claim/Waive	209UNTS187	102827
UK Great Britain	Greece	07 Mar 55	General Military	211UNTS249	102856
UK Great Britain	Greece	14 May 59	Specif Claim/Waive	360UNTS69	105154
UK Great Britain	Greece	21 May 59	Claims and Debts	344UNTS3	104939
UK Great Britain	Greece	06 Apr 61	Visas	403UNTS267	105797
UK Great Britain	Greece	09 May 63	Specific Property	398UNTS179	105722
UK Great Britain	Greece	08 Jun 65	Visas	551UNTS205	108042
UK Great Britain	Greece	12 Oct 66	Other Military	578UNTS33	108385
UK Great Britain	Greece	15 Apr 68	Atomic Energy	0UNTS0	109782
UK Great Britain	Greece	02 Mar 70	Land Transport	0UNTS0	110756
UK Great Britain	Guinea	22 Oct 59	General Trade	351UNTS341	105033
UK Great Britain	Guyana	26 May 66	Status of Forces	595UNTS255	108621
UK Great Britain	Guyana	26 May 66	Admin Cooperation	588UNTS143	108521
UK Great Britain	Guyana	15 Jun 67	Military Mission	632UNTS15	109005
UK Great Britain	Guyana	20 Sep 68	Finance	0UNTS0	109803
UK Great Britain	Honduras	30 Apr 62	Visas	449UNTS159	106457
UK Great Britain	Hungary	12 Aug 46	Finance	89UNTS219	101220
UK Great Britain	Hungary	12 Mar 48	Admin Cooperation	104UNTS35	101434
UK Great Britain	Hungary	19 Aug 54	Finance	199UNTS149	102681
UK Great Britain	Hungary	27 Jun 56	Claims and Debts	249UNTS19	103499
UK Great Britain	Hungary	25 Oct 60	Air Transport	419UNTS309	106034
UK Great Britain	Hungary	09 Aug 67	Scientific Project	632UNTS39	109006
UK Great Britain	Hungary	12 Aug 69	Commodity Trade	0UNTS0	110239
UK Great Britain	IAEA (Atom Energy)	11 May 59	Atomic Energy	339UNTS351	104854
UK Great Britain	IAEA (Atom Energy)	20 Jun 66	IGO Operations	588UNTS269	108531
UK Great Britain	IBRD (World Bank)	27 Feb 52	IBRD Project	159UNTS181	102088
UK Great Britain	IBRD (World Bank)	11 Mar 53	IBRD Project	172UNTS115	102243
UK Great Britain	IBRD (World Bank)	15 Mar 55	IBRD Project	265UNTS85	103808
UK Great Britain	IBRD (World Bank)	21 Jun 56	IBRD Project	285UNTS355	104157
UK Great Britain	IBRD (World Bank)	02 May 58	IBRD Project	324UNTS25	104677
UK Great Britain	IBRD (World Bank)	16 Jun 58	IBRD Project	309UNTS35	104467
UK Great Britain	IBRD (World Bank)	01 Apr 60	IBRD Project	379UNTS397	105446
UK Great Britain	IBRD (World Bank)	27 May 60	IBRD Project	375UNTS201	105367
UK Great Britain	IBRD (World Bank)	29 Mar 61	IBRD Project	415UNTS300	105990
UK Great Britain	IBRD (World Bank)	23 Jun 61	IBRD Project	415UNTS358	105991
UK Great Britain	IBRD (World Bank)	16 Aug 61	IBRD Project	426UNTS287	106143
UK Great Britain	IBRD (World Bank)	29 Nov 61	IBRD Project	426UNTS49	106130
UK Great Britain	IBRD (World Bank)	16 May 63	IBRD Project	476UNTS211	106910
UK Great Britain	IBRD (World Bank)	16 May 63	IBRD Project	477UNTS361	106929
UK Great Britain	IBRD (World Bank)	06 Sep 63	IBRD Project	483UNTS173	107013
UK Great Britain	IBRD (World Bank)	23 Sep 63	IBRD Project	503UNTS247	107348
UK Great Britain	IBRD (World Bank)	18 Apr 66	IGO Operations	573UNTS209	108334
UK Great Britain	IBRD (World Bank)	24 Apr 67	IBRD Project	600UNTS3	108674
UK Great Britain	Iceland	04 Jul 46	Specific Property	6UNTS223	100077
UK Great Britain	Iceland	20 Jun 47	Visas	11UNTS223	100161

PARTY ONE	PARTY TWO	DATE	TOPIC	CITATION	NUMBER
UK Great Britain	Iceland	26 May 50	Air Transport	95UNTS277	101326
UK Great Britain	Iceland	14 May 59	Finance	343UNTS301	104936
UK Great Britain	Iceland	09 Feb 61	Visas	398UNTS259	105728
UK Great Britain	Iceland	11 Mar 61	Dispute Settlement	397UNTS275	105710
UK Great Britain	Iceland	19 Sep 68	Finance	0UNTS0	109800
UK Great Britain	ICJ Option Clause	13 Feb 46	ICJ Option Clause	1UNTS3	100001
UK Great Britain	ICJ Option Clause	02 Jun 55	ICJ Option Clause	211UNTS109	102849
UK Great Britain	ICJ Option Clause	31 Oct 55	ICJ Option Clause	219UNTS179	102973
UK Great Britain	ICJ Option Clause	18 Apr 57	ICJ Option Clause	265UNTS221	103814
UK Great Britain	ICJ Option Clause	26 Nov 58	ICJ Option Clause	316UNTS59	104577
UK Great Britain	ICJ Option Clause	27 Nov 63	ICJ Option Clause	482UNTS187	106995
UK Great Britain	ICJ Option Clause	01 Jan 69	ICJ Option Clause	0UNTS0	109370
UK Great Britain	IDA (Devel Assoc)	13 Mar 62	Direct Aid	466UNTS331	106753
UK Great Britain	IDA (Devel Assoc)	31 Jul 64	Non-IBRD Project	535UNTS205	107781
UK Great Britain	IDA (Devel Assoc)	08 Feb 66	Non-IBRD Project	567UNTS207	108257
UK Great Britain	ILO (Labor Org)	14 Jan 59	IGO Operations	355UNTS283	105081
UK Great Britain	IMCO (Maritime Org)	28 Nov 68	IGO Operations	0UNTS0	109632
UK Great Britain	India	14 Aug 47	Finance	11UNTS371	100176
UK Great Britain	India	15 Feb 48	Finance	134UNTS70	101796
UK Great Britain	India	07 Dec 49	Postal Service	281UNTS245	104082
UK Great Britain	India	05 Jun 51	Postal Service	135UNTS3	101811
UK Great Britain	India	01 Dec 51	Air Transport	128UNTS39	101712
UK Great Britain	India	20 Jul 53	Finance	196UNTS251	102628
UK Great Britain	India	27 Nov 62	Milit Installation	466UNTS189	106744
UK Great Britain	India	31 Jul 64	Commodity Trade	522UNTS153	107542
UK Great Britain	India	20 Oct 64	Customs	534UNTS77	107755
UK Great Britain	India	20 Nov 64	Milit Assistance	534UNTS85	107756
UK Great Britain	India	21 Sep 68	Finance	0UNTS0	109809
UK Great Britain	Indonesia	02 Jul 56	Commodity Trade	265UNTS271	103819
UK Great Britain	Indonesia	02 Jul 56	Commodity Trade	265UNTS285	103820
UK Great Britain	Indonesia	23 Nov 60	Air Transport	398UNTS71	105718
UK Great Britain	Indonesia	29 Jun 61	General Economic	443UNTS255	106364
UK Great Britain	Indonesia	01 Dec 66	Claims and Debts	606UNTS125	108782
UK Great Britain	Indonesia	01 Aug 67	Claims and Debts	638UNTS3	109128
UK Great Britain	Indonesia	31 Oct 67	Claims and Debts	0UNTS0	109497
UK Great Britain	Indonesia	02 Dec 67	Loans and Credits	0UNTS0	109339
UK Great Britain	Indonesia	06 May 68	Loans and Credits	0UNTS0	109340
UK Great Britain	Indonesia	11 Nov 68	Loans and Credits	0UNTS0	109659
UK Great Britain	Indonesia	16 Jan 69	Loans and Credits	0UNTS0	109660
UK Great Britain	Indonesia	13 Mar 69	Loans and Credits	0UNTS0	109879
UK Great Britain	Indonesia	13 Mar 69	Claims and Debts	0UNTS0	109790
UK Great Britain	Indonesia	29 Apr 69	Loans and Credits	0UNTS0	110036
UK Great Britain	Indonesia	25 Jun 69	Loans and Credits	0UNTS0	110116
UK Great Britain	Indonesia	22 Oct 69	Loans and Credits	0UNTS0	110440
UK Great Britain	Indonesia	13 Mar 70	Finance	0UNTS0	110757
UK Great Britain	Indonesia	13 Apr 70	Finance	0UNTS0	110786
UK Great Britain	Int Coffee Org	29 May 69	IGO Operations	0UNTS0	110037
UK Great Britain	Int Sugar Council	29 May 69	IGO Operations	0UNTS0	110038
UK Great Britain	Int Wheat Coun	28 Nov 68	General IGO	0UNTS0	109498
UK Great Britain	Iran	25 Oct 54	Finance	204UNTS131	102754
UK Great Britain	Iran	06 May 59	Culture	398UNTS51	105717
UK Great Britain	Iran	09 Apr 60	Taxation	385UNTS63	105529
UK Great Britain	Iran	02 May 60	Air Transport	566UNTS129	108241
UK Great Britain	Iraq	02 Aug 46	Consul/Citizenship	14UNTS93	100213
UK Great Britain	Iraq	13 Aug 47	Finance	9UNTS259	100136
UK Great Britain	Iraq	19 Apr 51	Air Transport	108UNTS121	101470
UK Great Britain	Iraq	22 May 52	Claims and Debts	175UNTS97	102298
UK Great Britain	Iraq	21 Jun 52	Admin Cooperation	149UNTS221	101954
UK Great Britain	Iraq	10 Jul 52	Finance	151UNTS227	101998
UK Great Britain	Iraq	04 Apr 55	General Military	233UNTS118	103265
UK Great Britain	Iraq	30 Apr 55	Claims and Debts	226UNTS319	103126
UK Great Britain	Iraq	14 Dec 59	Culture	374UNTS253	105339
UK Great Britain	Iraq	16 Aug 65	Commodity Trade	0UNTS0	109878
UK Great Britain	Ireland	05 Apr 46	Air Transport	72UNTS57	100928
UK Great Britain	Ireland	31 Jul 48	General Trade	86UNTS37	101151

PARTY ONE	PARTY TWO	DATE	TOPIC	CITATION	NUMBER
UK Great Britain	Ireland	18 May 49	Taxation	553UNTS209	108089
UK Great Britain	Ireland	06 Apr 54	Sanitation	553UNTS197	108088
UK Great Britain	Ireland	29 Mar 60	Non-ILO Labor	371UNTS3	105267
UK Great Britain	Ireland	25 Jun 64	Commodity Trade	553UNTS221	108090
UK Great Britain	Ireland	30 Jun 64	Commodity Trade	522UNTS141	107541
UK Great Britain	Ireland	14 Dec 65	General Trade	565UNTS58	108235
UK Great Britain	Ireland	28 Feb 66	Health/Educ/Welfare	565UNTS33	108234
UK Great Britain	Ireland	23 Sep 68	Finance	0UNTS0	109374
UK Great Britain	Israel	10 Feb 50	Taxation	86UNTS211	101161
UK Great Britain	Israel	30 Mar 50	Claims and Debts	86UNTS231	101162
UK Great Britain	Israel	06 Dec 50	Air Transport	151UNTS33	101983
UK Great Britain	Israel	10 Dec 50	Patents/Copyrights	88UNTS211	101193
UK Great Britain	Israel	13 May 53	Finance	175UNTS179	102300
UK Great Britain	Israel	29 Apr 57	Non-ILO Labor	280UNTS227	104062
UK Great Britain	Israel	04 Apr 60	Extradition	377UNTS331	105410
UK Great Britain	Israel	31 Aug 60	Culture	385UNTS71	105530
UK Great Britain	Israel	26 Sep 62	Taxation	474UNTS233	106885
UK Great Britain	Israel	15 Sep 64	Taxation	539UNTS283	107839
UK Great Britain	Israel	15 Apr 65	Finance	551UNTS19	108031
UK Great Britain	Israel	05 Jul 66	Admin Cooperation	630UNTS189	108971
UK Great Britain	Israel	09 Feb 67	Visas	0UNTS0	109349
UK Great Britain	Israel	10 Jun 69	Culture	0UNTS0	110386
UK Great Britain	Italy	16 Jan 47	Non-ILO Labor	48ITGU168	435186
UK Great Britain	Italy	17 Apr 47	Claims and Debts	54UNTS169	100802
UK Great Britain	Italy	17 Apr 47	Finance	54UNTS149	100801
UK Great Britain	Italy	30 May 47	Non-ILO Labor	54UNTS131	100800
UK Great Britain	Italy	06 Dec 47	Visas	82UNTS243	101097
UK Great Britain	Italy	21 Jan 48	Milit Installation	77UNTS23	100989
UK Great Britain	Italy	13 Mar 48	Admin Cooperation	104UNTS41	101435
UK Great Britain	Italy	25 Jun 48	Air Transport	94UNTS239	101313
UK Great Britain	Italy	28 Oct 48	Visas	77UNTS129	100996
UK Great Britain	Italy	14 Jun 49	Specific Property	135UNTS49	101813
UK Great Britain	Italy	20 Mar 50	Territory Boundary	128UNTS201	101721
UK Great Britain	Italy	21 Mar 50	Territory Boundary	128UNTS225	101722
UK Great Britain	Italy	28 Jul 50	Non-ILO Labor	101UNTS25	101399
UK Great Britain	Italy	21 Dec 50	Finance	175UNTS187	102301
UK Great Britain	Italy	16 Jun 51	Patents/Copyrights	172UNTS293	102253
UK Great Britain	Italy	28 Jun 51	Claims and Debts	118UNTS115	101600
UK Great Britain	Italy	24 Oct 51	Air Transport	118UNTS143	101602
UK Great Britain	Italy	07 Nov 51	Claims and Debts	118UNTS133	101601
UK Great Britain	Italy	12 Nov 51	Specif Claim/Waive	135UNTS55	101814
UK Great Britain	Italy	28 Nov 51	Culture	172UNTS27	102238
UK Great Britain	Italy	28 Nov 51	Non-ILO Labor	172UNTS205	102248
UK Great Britain	Italy	21 Dec 51	Peace/Disarmament	121UNTS89	101628
UK Great Britain	Italy	12 Feb 52	Claims and Debts	126UNTS297	101695
UK Great Britain	Italy	06 Nov 52	Specif Claim/Waive	158UNTS431	102076
UK Great Britain	Italy	13 Apr 53	Reparations	172UNTS271	102251
UK Great Britain	Italy	01 Jun 54	Admin Cooperation	312UNTS353	104525
UK Great Britain	Italy	01 Jun 54	Consul/Citizenship	403UNTS275	105798
UK Great Britain	Italy	29 Jan 57	Non-ILO Labor	326UNTS119	104710
UK Great Britain	Italy	29 Mar 57	Reparations	310UNTS11	104481
UK Great Britain	Italy	12 Jun 57	Non-ILO Labor	310UNTS35	104484
UK Great Britain	Italy	28 Dec 57	Atomic Energy	305UNTS357	104425
UK Great Britain	Italy	09 Sep 58	Non-ILO Labor	60ITDI243	436190
UK Great Britain	Italy	14 Oct 58	Patents/Copyrights	60ITDI245	436191
UK Great Britain	Italy	14 Apr 59	Claims and Debts	343UNTS289	104934
UK Great Britain	Italy	04 Jul 60	Taxation	466UNTS195	106745
UK Great Britain	Italy	06 Mar 61	Visas	404UNTS3	105799
UK Great Britain	Italy	20 Apr 61	Other Military	63ITGU99	435192
UK Great Britain	Italy	23 Oct 61	Admin Cooperation	424UNTS225	106111
UK Great Britain	Italy	01 Sep 65	Taxation	0UNTS0	109284
UK Great Britain	Italy	01 Sep 65	Customs	0UNTS0	109283
UK Great Britain	Italy	15 Feb 66	Taxation	67ITGU230	435194
UK Great Britain	Italy	30 Sep 67	Culture	642UNTS271	109180
UK Great Britain	Italy	15 Feb 68	Taxation	0UNTS0	109263

PARTY ONE	PARTY TWO	DATE	TOPIC	CITATION	NUMBER
UK Great Britain	Ivory Coast	29 Mar 65	Visas	551UNTS53	108032
UK Great Britain	Jamaica	01 Jun 61	Recognition	478UNTS9	106932
UK Great Britain	Jamaica	20 Feb 64	Military Mission	496UNTS239	107256
UK Great Britain	Jamaica	31 Mar 65	Military Mission	539UNTS59	107824
UK Great Britain	Jamaica	02 Apr 65	Taxation	552UNTS219	108056
UK Great Britain	Jamaica	20 Sep 68	Finance	0UNTS0	109804
UK Great Britain	Jamaica	25 Mar 70	Air Transport	0UNTS0	110759
UK Great Britain	Japan	31 Aug 51	Finance	149UNTS227	101955
UK Great Britain	Japan	31 Aug 51	Finance	108UNTS273	101480
UK Great Britain	Japan	04 Nov 52	Specific Property	164UNTS101	102161
UK Great Britain	Japan	04 Nov 52	Specific Property	164UNTS107	102162
UK Great Britain	Japan	21 Nov 52	Reparations	172UNTS303	102254
UK Great Britain	Japan	29 Dec 52	Air Transport	175UNTS129	102299
UK Great Britain	Japan	27 Apr 53	Admin Cooperation	228UNTS227	103154
UK Great Britain	Japan	29 Jan 54	Finance	190UNTS319	102572
UK Great Britain	Japan	21 Sep 55	Other Military	0JGJI1287	441086
UK Great Britain	Japan	30 Aug 57	Visas	313UNTS63	104529
UK Great Britain	Japan	16 Jun 58	Atomic Energy	325UNTS185	104700
UK Great Britain	Japan	07 Oct 60	Reparations	384UNTS89	105513
UK Great Britain	Japan	03 Dec 60	Culture	414UNTS61	105966
UK Great Britain	Japan	11 Apr 61	Taxation	420UNTS75	106042
UK Great Britain	Japan	04 Sep 62	Taxation	475UNTS31	106888
UK Great Britain	Japan	02 Nov 62	Visas	466UNTS277	106749
UK Great Britain	Japan	14 Nov 62	General Trade	478UNTS29	106934
UK Great Britain	Japan	06 Jan 64	Specific Resources	502UNTS183	107329
UK Great Britain	Japan	04 May 64	Consul/Citizenship	561UNTS25	108179
UK Great Britain	Japan	22 Feb 65	Finance	560UNTS123	108171
UK Great Britain	Japan	14 Dec 65	Admin Cooperation	0JGJI1615	441143
UK Great Britain	Japan	06 Mar 68	Atomic Energy	68JHZ10	439018
UK Great Britain	Japan	06 Mar 68	Atomic Energy	0UNTS0	109494
UK Great Britain	Japan	10 Feb 69	Taxation	70JHZ12	439027
UK Great Britain	Jordan	19 Jul 41	Territory Boundary	9UNTS381	200054
UK Great Britain	Jordan	19 Jul 41	Extradition	9UNTS389	200055
UK Great Britain	Jordan	22 Mar 46	General Amity	6UNTS143	100074
UK Great Britain	Jordan	15 Mar 48	General Military	77UNTS77	100994
UK Great Britain	Jordan	01 May 51	Finance	117UNTS19	101582
UK Great Britain	Jordan	26 Mar 58	Loans and Credits	312UNTS373	104526
UK Great Britain	Jordan	07 May 58	Loans and Credits	312UNTS379	104527
UK Great Britain	Jordan	11 Jun 59	Loans and Credits	351UNTS283	105028
UK Great Britain	Jordan	04 May 60	Loans and Credits	385UNTS81	105531
UK Great Britain	Jordan	17 Jul 61	Loans and Credits	420UNTS53	106039
UK Great Britain	Jordan	28 Feb 62	Postal Service	466UNTS249	106748
UK Great Britain	Jordan	30 May 62	Loans and Credits	449UNTS167	106458
UK Great Britain	Jordan	27 Apr 63	Loans and Credits	475UNTS169	106892
UK Great Britain	Jordan	31 Aug 64	Loans and Credits	541UNTS3	107856
UK Great Britain	Jordan	08 Jun 65	Loans and Credits	552UNTS251	108057
UK Great Britain	Jordan	26 Jul 66	Loans and Credits	597UNTS219	108647
UK Great Britain	Jordan	02 May 67	Finance	610UNTS0	108837
UK Great Britain	Jordan	15 Aug 67	Loans and Credits	632UNTS269	109028
UK Great Britain	Jordan	30 Jul 68	Loans and Credits	0UNTS0	109784
UK Great Britain	Jordan	22 Sep 68	Finance	0UNTS0	109811
UK Great Britain	Jordan	14 Jan 69	Loans and Credits	0UNTS0	109785
UK Great Britain	Jordan	27 Mar 69	Loans and Credits	0UNTS0	110114
UK Great Britain	Jordan	24 May 69	Loans and Credits	0UNTS0	110115
UK Great Britain	Jordan	09 Aug 69	Air Transport	0UNTS0	110424
UK Great Britain	Jordan	13 Oct 69	Loans and Credits	0UNTS0	110427
UK Great Britain	Kenya	16 Jan 64	Admin Cooperation	502UNTS213	107332
UK Great Britain	Kenya	25 Aug 64	Commodity Trade	522UNTS165	107543
UK Great Britain	Kenya	27 Nov 64	Milit Assistance	0UNTS0	110039
UK Great Britain	Kenya	14 Jul 67	Military Mission	643UNTS254	109196
UK Great Britain	Kenya	14 Jul 67	Status of Forces	643UNTS231	109195
UK Great Britain	Kenya	20 Sep 68	Finance	0UNTS0	109805
UK Great Britain	Korea, South	18 Nov 69	Visas	0UNTS0	110428
UK Great Britain	Kuwait	24 May 60	Air Transport	412UNTS4	105923
UK Great Britain	Kuwait	19 Jun 61	General Amity	399UNTS239	105743

PARTY ONE	PARTY TWO	DATE	TOPIC	CITATION	NUMBER
UK Great Britain	Kuwait	26 Nov 66	Culture	633UNTS58	109034
UK Great Britain	Kuwait	29 Dec 66	Postal Service	617UNTS203	108914
UK Great Britain	Laos	17 May 63	Direct Aid	475UNTS155	106891
UK Great Britain	Laos	24 Dec 63	Finance	502UNTS189	107330
UK Great Britain	Laos	09 Aug 69	Finance	0UNTS0	110238
UK Great Britain	Laos	24 Mar 70	Loans and Credits	0UNTS0	110758
UK Great Britain	Lebanon	20 Jun 49	Postal Service	90UNTS137	101232
UK Great Britain	Lebanon	15 Aug 51	Air Transport	160UNTS327	102116
UK Great Britain	Lebanon	19 May 58	Milit Assistance	327UNTS43	104716
UK Great Britain	Lebanon	24 Oct 63	Taxation	535UNTS3	107772
UK Great Britain	Lesotho	17 Feb 67	Admin Cooperation	632UNTS3	109004
UK Great Britain	Lesotho	03 Jul 68	Taxation	0UNTS0	109783
UK Great Britain	Lesotho	06 Jan 70	Finance	0UNTS0	110699
UK Great Britain	Libya	13 Dec 51	Direct Aid	123UNTS167	101658
UK Great Britain	Libya	31 Mar 52	Air Transport	151UNTS69	101984
UK Great Britain	Libya	21 Feb 53	Air Transport	311UNTS115	104501
UK Great Britain	Libya	21 Mar 53	General Military	172UNTS85	102240
UK Great Britain	Libya	25 Mar 53	Finance	172UNTS281	102252
UK Great Britain	Libya	29 Jul 53	General Amity	186UNTS185	102491
UK Great Britain	Libya	29 Jul 53	Status of Forces	186UNTS201	102492
UK Great Britain	Libya	29 Jul 53	Finance	186UNTS277	102493
UK Great Britain	Libya	19 Oct 53	Admin Cooperation	186UNTS285	102494
UK Great Britain	Libya	24 Sep 68	Finance	0UNTS0	109815
UK Great Britain	Luxembourg	29 May 39	Extradition	99UNTS301	200284
UK Great Britain	Luxembourg	11 Dec 46	Claims and Debts	11UNTS167	100155
UK Great Britain	Luxembourg	14 Feb 47	Visas	11UNTS267	100165
UK Great Britain	Luxembourg	27 May 48	Air Transport	53UNTS115	100776
UK Great Britain	Luxembourg	27 Jun 50	Culture	183UNTS217	102431
UK Great Britain	Luxembourg	13 Oct 53	Non-ILO Labor	209UNTS87	102825
UK Great Britain	Luxembourg	18 Jun 54	Reparations	192UNTS33	102593
UK Great Britain	Luxembourg	01 Apr 60	Visas	374UNTS267	105340
UK Great Britain	Luxembourg	21 Feb 61	Visas	398UNTS243	105726
UK Great Britain	Luxembourg	24 May 67	Taxation	0UNTS0	109341
UK Great Britain	Malawi	28 Aug 64	Consul/Citizenship	522UNTS223	107548
UK Great Britain	Malawi	01 Sep 64	Commodity Trade	522UNTS117	107539
UK Great Britain	Malawi	19 Jul 66	Admin Cooperation	637UNTS0	109125
UK Great Britain	Malawi	21 Nov 66	Admin Cooperation	637UNTS0	109126
UK Great Britain	Malawi	02 Apr 68	Taxation	0UNTS0	109450
UK Great Britain	Malawi	24 Sep 68	Finance	0UNTS0	109816
UK Great Britain	Malawi	27 Sep 68	Air Transport	0UNTS0	109713
UK Great Britain	Malaysia	09 Jul 64	Consul/Citizenship	522UNTS189	107545
UK Great Britain	Malaysia	09 Jul 64	Consul/Citizenship	522UNTS213	107547
UK Great Britain	Malaysia	09 Jul 64	Consul/Citizenship	522UNTS201	107546
UK Great Britain	Malaysia	07 May 65	Admin Cooperation	552UNTS259	108058
UK Great Britain	Malaysia	17 Jul 67	Taxation	637UNTS0	109127
UK Great Britain	Malaysia	01 Aug 67	Air Transport	633UNTS93	109036
UK Great Britain	Malaysia	05 Dec 67	Military Mission	642UNTS293	109181
UK Great Britain	Malaysia	24 Sep 68	Finance	0UNTS0	109817
UK Great Britain	Maldive Islands	26 Jul 65	General Amity	548UNTS223	107980
UK Great Britain	Malta	21 Sep 64	Direct Aid	588UNTS125	108519
UK Great Britain	Malta	21 Sep 64	Military Mission	588UNTS55	108518
UK Great Britain	Malta	31 Dec 64	Admin Cooperation	525UNTS221	107594
UK Great Britain	Malta	10 Jul 67	Air Transport	619UNTS11	108936
UK Great Britain	Malta	22 Sep 68	Finance	0UNTS0	109812
UK Great Britain	Mauritius	12 Mar 68	Admin Cooperation	0UNTS0	109269
UK Great Britain	Mauritius	12 Mar 68	Milit Assistance	0UNTS0	109267
UK Great Britain	Mauritius	12 Mar 68	Scientific Project	0UNTS0	109270
UK Great Britain	Mauritius	12 Mar 68	Tech Assistance	0UNTS0	109268
UK Great Britain	Mauritius	16 Sep 68	Finance	0UNTS0	109797
UK Great Britain	Mexico	07 Feb 46	Claims and Debts	6UNTS55	100068
UK Great Britain	Mexico	27 Sep 46	Consul/Citizenship	91UNTS161	101248
UK Great Britain	Mexico	12 Jun 52	Telecommunications	196UNTS149	102622
UK Great Britain	Mexico	20 Mar 54	Consul/Citizenship	331UNTS21	104750
UK Great Britain	Mexico	13 Nov 59	Visas	360UNTS3	105152
UK Great Britain	Monaco	10 Nov 48	Visas	81UNTS85	101065

PARTY ONE	PARTY TWO	DATE	TOPIC	CITATION	NUMBER
UK Great Britain	Monaco	11 Apr 61	Visas	404UNTS11	105800
UK Great Britain	Morocco	01 Mar 57	General Economic	310UNTS3	104480
UK Great Britain	Morocco	01 Oct 58	Visas	331UNTS119	104751
UK Great Britain	Multilateral	12 May 40	Scientific Project	101UNTS91	101405
UK Great Britain	Multilateral	27 Mar 41	Military Mission	67UNTS231	200222
UK Great Britain	Multilateral	29 Jan 42	General Military	93UNTS279	200271
UK Great Britain	Multilateral	22 Apr 42	Commodity Trade	8UNTS237	200044
UK Great Britain	Multilateral	04 Dec 42	Direct Aid	24UNTS247	200150
UK Great Britain	Multilateral	26 Mar 43	Specif Goods/Equip	13UNTS427	200089
UK Great Britain	Multilateral	21 Dec 43	Commodity Trade	65UNTS231	200214
UK Great Britain	Multilateral	19 Apr 44	Scientific Project	89UNTS279	200257
UK Great Britain	Multilateral	02 Aug 44	Scientific Project	67UNTS221	200221
UK Great Britain	Multilateral	12 Sep 44	Milit Occupation	227UNTS279	200532
UK Great Britain	Multilateral	08 Oct 44	Reparations	45UNTS311	200187
UK Great Britain	Multilateral	28 Oct 44	Peace/Disarmament	123UNTS223	200414
UK Great Britain	Multilateral	14 Nov 44	Milit Occupation	236UNTS359	200539
UK Great Britain	Multilateral	07 Dec 44	Air Transport	171UNTS345	200501
UK Great Britain	Multilateral	07 Dec 44	Air Transport	84UNTS389	200252
UK Great Britain	Multilateral	07 Dec 44	IGO Establishment	15UNTS295	200102
UK Great Britain	Multilateral	15 Dec 44	Sanitation	16UNTS247	200106
UK Great Britain	Multilateral	15 Dec 44	Sanitation	17UNTS305	200110
UK Great Britain	Multilateral	20 Jan 45	Peace/Disarmament	140UNTS397	200471
UK Great Britain	Multilateral	05 Jun 45	Milit Occupation	68UNTS189	200230
UK Great Britain	Multilateral	09 Jun 45	Milit Occupation	139UNTS381	200464
UK Great Britain	Multilateral	09 Jul 45	Milit Occupation	16CUNTS359	200484
UK Great Britain	Multilateral	26 Jul 45	Milit Occupation	227UNTS297	200533
UK Great Britain	Multilateral	08 Aug 45	General Military	82UNTS279	200251
UK Great Britain	Multilateral	02 Sep 45	Peace/Disarmament	139UNTS387	200465
UK Great Britain	Multilateral	27 Sep 45	IGO Establishment	5UNTS327	200035
UK Great Britain	Multilateral	15 Nov 45	Atomic Energy	3UNTS123	100026
UK Great Britain	Multilateral	16 Nov 45	IGO Establishment	4UNTS275	100052
UK Great Britain	Multilateral	04 Dec 45	Telecommunications	9UNTS101	100128
UK Great Britain	Multilateral	26 Dec 45	Peace/Disarmament	20UNTS259	100319
UK Great Britain	Multilateral	27 Dec 45	IGO Establishment	2UNTS39	100020
UK Great Britain	Multilateral	01 Jan 46	Peace/Disarmament	99UNTS131	101375
UK Great Britain	Multilateral	04 Jan 46	IGO Establishment	6UNTS35	100066
UK Great Britain	Multilateral	14 Jan 46	Reparations	555UNTS69	108105
UK Great Britain	Multilateral	31 Mar 46	Milit Installation	17UNTS159	100274
UK Great Britain	Multilateral	05 Apr 46	Specific Resources	231UNTS199	103221
UK Great Britain	Multilateral	23 Apr 46	Sanitation	16UNTS179	100257
UK Great Britain	Multilateral	23 Apr 46	Sanitation	17UNTS3	100265
UK Great Britain	Multilateral	06 May 46	Commodity Trade	157UNTS85	102049
UK Great Britain	Multilateral	06 May 46	Commodity Trade	99UNTS181	101379
UK Great Britain	Multilateral	03 Jun 46	Commodity Trade	7UNTS331	100109
UK Great Britain	Multilateral	28 Jun 46	Milit Occupation	138UNTS85	101862
UK Great Britain	Multilateral	18 Jul 46	Reparations	125UNTS119	101674
UK Great Britain	Multilateral	22 Jul 46	IGO Establishment	9UNTS3	100125
UK Great Britain	Multilateral	22 Jul 46	IGO Establishment	14UNTS185	100221
UK Great Britain	Multilateral	27 Jul 46	Patents/Copyrights	90UNTS229	101238
UK Great Britain	Multilateral	15 Oct 46	Refugees	11UNTS73	100150
UK Great Britain	Multilateral	30 Oct 46	IGO Establishment	27UNTS77	100401
UK Great Britain	Multilateral	30 Oct 46	IGO Establishment	11UNTS107	100151
UK Great Britain	Multilateral	02 Dec 46	Specific Resources	161UNTS72	102124
UK Great Britain	Multilateral	07 Dec 46	Commodity Trade	157UNTS103	102050
UK Great Britain	Multilateral	11 Dec 46	Sanitation	12UNTS179	100186
UK Great Britain	Multilateral	15 Dec 46	IGO Establishment	18UNTS3	100283
UK Great Britain	Multilateral	23 Dec 46	Commodity Trade	126UNTS47	101681
UK Great Britain	Multilateral	06 Feb 47	IGO Establishment	97UNTS227	101352
UK Great Britain	Multilateral	08 Feb 47	Patents/Copyrights	14UNTS287	100222
UK Great Britain	Multilateral	10 Feb 47	Peace/Disarmament	42UNTS3	100645
UK Great Britain	Multilateral	10 Feb 47	Peace/Disarmament	41UNTS21	100643
UK Great Britain	Multilateral	10 Feb 47	Reparations	140UNTS111	101886
UK Great Britain	Multilateral	10 Feb 47	Peace/Disarmament	49UNTS3	100747
UK Great Britain	Multilateral	10 Feb 47	Peace/Disarmament	48UNTS203	100746
UK Great Britain	Multilateral	10 Feb 47	Peace/Disarmament	41UNTS135	100644

PARTY ONE	PARTY TWO	DATE	TOPIC	CITATION	NUMBER
UK Great Britain	Multilateral	03 Mar 47	Humanitarian	11UNTS43	100148
UK Great Britain	Multilateral	27 May 47	Air Transport	418UNTS161	106021
UK Great Britain	Multilateral	06 Jun 47	Patents/Copyrights	46UNTS249	100714
UK Great Britain	Multilateral	04 Aug 47	Air Transport	28UNTS41	100418
UK Great Britain	Multilateral	14 Aug 47	Reparations	138UNTS111	101863
UK Great Britain	Multilateral	29 Sep 47	Peace/Disarmament	45UNTS125	100694
UK Great Britain	Multilateral	02 Oct 47	Telecommunications	193UNTS188	102616
UK Great Britain	Multilateral	10 Oct 47	Claims and Debts	54UNTS193	100804
UK Great Britain	Multilateral	11 Oct 47	IGO Establishment	77UNTS143	100998
UK Great Britain	Multilateral	04 Nov 47	Reparations	93UNTS61	101288
UK Great Britain	Multilateral	12 Nov 47	Admin Cooperation	46UNTS169	100709
UK Great Britain	Multilateral	12 Nov 47	Admin Cooperation	46UNTS201	100710
UK Great Britain	Multilateral	16 Dec 47	Reparations	82UNTS237	101096
UK Great Britain	Multilateral	06 Mar 48	Water Transport	289UNTS3	104214
UK Great Britain	Multilateral	17 Mar 48	General Military	19UNTS51	100304
UK Great Britain	Multilateral	10 May 48	Reparations	140UNTS129	101887
UK Great Britain	Multilateral	10 May 48	Culture	289UNTS111	104215
UK Great Britain	Multilateral	11 May 48	Telecommunications	500UNTS267	107313
UK Great Britain	Multilateral	13 May 48	Reparations	140UNTS187	101888
UK Great Britain	Multilateral	10 Jun 48	Humanitarian	164UNTS113	102163
UK Great Britain	Multilateral	10 Jun 48	Humanitarian	191UNTS3	102576
UK Great Britain	Multilateral	19 Jun 48	Air Transport	310UNTS151	104492
UK Great Britain	Multilateral	26 Jun 48	Culture	331UNTS217	104757
UK Great Britain	Multilateral	24 Jul 48	Sanitation	66UNTS25	100847
UK Great Britain	Multilateral	14 Sep 48	Milit Occupation	18UNTS267	100296
UK Great Britain	Multilateral	17 Sep 48	Telecommunications	97UNTS31	101345
UK Great Britain	Multilateral	15 Nov 48	IGO Establishment	120UNTS59	101615
UK Great Britain	Multilateral	19 Nov 48	Sanitation	44UNTS277	100688
UK Great Britain	Multilateral	29 Nov 48	IGO Establishment	120UNTS13	101613
UK Great Britain	Multilateral	09 Dec 48	Scientific Project	73UNTS39	100942
UK Great Britain	Multilateral	09 Dec 48	Scientific Project	20UNTS229	100318
UK Great Britain	Multilateral	16 Dec 48	Direct Aid	79UNTS85	101033
UK Great Britain	Multilateral	08 Feb 49	Specific Resources	157UNTS157	102053
UK Great Britain	Multilateral	22 Feb 49	Sanitation	93UNTS129	101296
UK Great Britain	Multilateral	28 Feb 49	Scientific Project	29UNTS53	100434
UK Great Britain	Multilateral	23 Mar 49	Commodity Trade	203UNTS179	102746
UK Great Britain	Multilateral	31 Mar 49	Reparations	122UNTS57	101636
UK Great Britain	Multilateral	04 Apr 49	General Military	34UNTS243	100541
UK Great Britain	Multilateral	08 Apr 49	Milit Occupation	140UNTS196	101889
UK Great Britain	Multilateral	28 Apr 49	IGO Establishment	83UNTS105	101105
UK Great Britain	Multilateral	04 May 49	Milit Occupation	138UNTS123	101864
UK Great Britain	Multilateral	04 May 49	Admin Cooperation	92UNTS19	101257
UK Great Britain	Multilateral	04 May 49	Admin Cooperation	30UNTS3	100445
UK Great Britain	Multilateral	04 May 49	Admin Cooperation	30UNTS23	100446
UK Great Britain	Multilateral	04 May 49	Admin Cooperation	47UNTS159	100728
UK Great Britain	Multilateral	04 May 49	Admin Cooperation	98UNTS101	101358
UK Great Britain	Multilateral	05 May 49	IGO Establishment	87UNTS103	101168
UK Great Britain	Multilateral	16 Jun 49	Land Transport	45UNTS149	100696
UK Great Britain	Multilateral	20 Jun 49	IGO Establishment	128UNTS141	101718
UK Great Britain	Multilateral	22 Jul 49	General Trade	557UNTS211	108135
UK Great Britain	Multilateral	05 Aug 49	Finance	88UNTS229	101195
UK Great Britain	Multilateral	12 Aug 49	General Military	75UNTS135	100972
UK Great Britain	Multilateral	12 Aug 49	IGO Establishment	87UNTS131	101169
UK Great Britain	Multilateral	12 Aug 49	Humanitarian	75UNTS287	100973
UK Great Britain	Multilateral	12 Aug 49	Humanitarian	75UNTS85	100971
UK Great Britain	Multilateral	12 Aug 49	Humanitarian	75UNTS31	100970
UK Great Britain	Multilateral	02 Sep 49	IGO Status/Immunit	250UNTS12	103515
UK Great Britain	Multilateral	15 Sep 49	Air Transport	53UNTS235	100783
UK Great Britain	Multilateral	19 Sep 49	Land Transport	125UNTS3	101671
UK Great Britain	Multilateral	24 Sep 49	IGO Establishment	126UNTS237	101691
UK Great Britain	Multilateral	27 Oct 49	Air Transport	53UNTS241	100784
UK Great Britain	Multilateral	07 Nov 49	Sanitation	132UNTS3	101748
UK Great Britain	Multilateral	07 Nov 49	Non-ILO Labor	132UNTS31	101749
UK Great Britain	Multilateral	22 Nov 49	Recognition	185UNTS307	102477
UK Great Britain	Multilateral	16 Dec 49	Admin Cooperation	72UNTS3	100924

PARTY ONE	PARTY TWO	DATE	TOPIC	CITATION	NUMBER
UK Great Britain	Multilateral	06 Apr 50	Admin Cooperation	119UNTS99	101610
UK Great Britain	Multilateral	17 Apr 50	Visas	131UNTS99	101738
UK Great Britain	Multilateral	17 Apr 50	Non-ILO Labor	126UNTS285	101694
UK Great Britain	Multilateral	28 Jun 50	Loans and Credits	87UNTS153	101170
UK Great Britain	Multilateral	16 Sep 50	General Transport	92UNTS91	101264
UK Great Britain	Multilateral	04 Nov 50	Humanitarian	213UNTS221	102889
UK Great Britain	Multilateral	22 Nov 50	Culture	131UNTS25	101734
UK Great Britain	Multilateral	29 Nov 50	Patents/Copyrights	88UNTS221	101194
UK Great Britain	Multilateral	07 Dec 50	Admin Cooperation	212UNTS17	102861
UK Great Britain	Multilateral	15 Dec 50	Customs	171UNTS305	102234
UK Great Britain	Multilateral	15 Dec 50	Customs	347UNTS127	104994
UK Great Britain	Multilateral	15 Dec 50	IGO Operations	160UNTS267	102111
UK Great Britain	Multilateral	15 Dec 50	Tech Assistance	76UNTS120	100985
UK Great Britain	Multilateral	15 Dec 50	Customs	157UNTS129	102052
UK Great Britain	Multilateral	06 Mar 51	Claims and Debts	106UNTS141	101461
UK Great Britain	Multilateral	06 Mar 51	Milit Assistance	138UNTS67	101860
UK Great Britain	Multilateral	03 Apr 51	Milit Occupation	141UNTS303	101920
UK Great Britain	Multilateral	25 Apr 51	Reparations	91UNTS21	101240
UK Great Britain	Multilateral	25 May 51	Status of Forces	175UNTS215	102303
UK Great Britain	Multilateral	15 Jun 51	Tech Assistance	148UNTS67	101936
UK Great Britain	Multilateral	19 Jun 51	Status of Forces	199UNTS67	102678
UK Great Britain	Multilateral	25 Jun 51	Tech Assistance	92UNTS27	101258
UK Great Britain	Multilateral	02 Jul 51	Refugees	189UNTS137	102545
UK Great Britain	Multilateral	10 Jul 51	Other Military	108UNTS287	101481
UK Great Britain	Multilateral	29 Jul 51	Other Military	117UNTS85	101585
UK Great Britain	Multilateral	08 Sep 51	Peace/Disarmament	136UNTS45	101832
UK Great Britain	Multilateral	08 Sep 51	General Military	136UNTS165	101833
UK Great Britain	Multilateral	20 Sep 51	IGO Status/Immunit	200UNTS3	102691
UK Great Britain	Multilateral	09 Oct 51	IGO Establishment	220UNTS121	102997
UK Great Britain	Multilateral	31 Oct 51	Other Military	172UNTS193	102247
UK Great Britain	Multilateral	06 Dec 51	Admin Cooperation	150UNTS67	101963
UK Great Britain	Multilateral	09 May 52	Milit Occupation	168UNTS65	102213
UK Great Britain	Multilateral	10 May 52	Admin Cooperation	439UNTS217	106331
UK Great Britain	Multilateral	10 May 52	Admin Cooperation	439UNTS193	106330
UK Great Britain	Multilateral	10 May 52	Taxation	439UNTS233	106332
UK Great Britain	Multilateral	15 May 52	Sanitation	0UNTS0	110476
UK Great Britain	Multilateral	20 May 52	Sanitation	219UNTS55	102966
UK Great Britain	Multilateral	08 Jun 52	Other Military	210UNTS317	102843
UK Great Britain	Multilateral	12 Jun 52	Dispute Settlement	138UNTS183	101869
UK Great Britain	Multilateral	11 Jul 52	Postal Service	170UNTS3	102221
UK Great Britain	Multilateral	11 Jul 52	IGO Establishment	169UNTS3	102220
UK Great Britain	Multilateral	28 Aug 52	Claims and Debts	175UNTS69	102296
UK Great Britain	Multilateral	06 Sep 52	Patents/Copyrights	216UNTS132	102937
UK Great Britain	Multilateral	07 Oct 52	Admin Cooperation	310UNTS181	104493
UK Great Britain	Multilateral	07 Nov 52	General Trade	221UNTS255	103010
UK Great Britain	Multilateral	10 Nov 52	Admin Cooperation	214UNTS265	102904
UK Great Britain	Multilateral	27 Feb 53	Claims and Debts	333UNTS3	104764
UK Great Britain	Multilateral	30 Apr 53	Admin Cooperation	175UNTS89	102297
UK Great Britain	Multilateral	11 May 53	Sanitation	456UNTS3	106555
UK Great Britain	Multilateral	01 Jul 53	IGO Establishment	200UNTS149	102701
UK Great Britain	Multilateral	30 Jul 53	Reparations	215UNTS97	102913
UK Great Britain	Multilateral	27 Aug 53	Other Military	213UNTS137	102884
UK Great Britain	Multilateral	01 Oct 53	Commodity Trade	258UNTS153	103677
UK Great Britain	Multilateral	17 Oct 53	General Transport	184UNTS42	102438
UK Great Britain	Multilateral	26 Oct 53	Status of Forces	207UNTS237	102809
UK Great Britain	Multilateral	07 Dec 53	Admin Cooperation	182UNTS51	102422
UK Great Britain	Multilateral	11 Dec 53	Non-ILO Labor	218UNTS153	102956
UK Great Britain	Multilateral	11 Dec 53	Non-ILO Labor	218UNTS255	102958
UK Great Britain	Multilateral	11 Dec 53	Sanitation	191UNTS285	102588
UK Great Britain	Multilateral	11 Dec 53	Patents/Copyrights	218UNTS27	102952
UK Great Britain	Multilateral	11 Dec 53	Non-ILO Labor	218UNTS211	102957
UK Great Britain	Multilateral	11 Dec 53	Education	218UNTS125	102954
UK Great Britain	Multilateral	18 Jan 54	IGO Establishment	330UNTS121	104743
UK Great Britain	Multilateral	19 Feb 54	Status of Forces	214UNTS51	102899
UK Great Britain	Multilateral	22 Feb 54	Other Military	188UNTS273	102531

PARTY ONE	PARTY TWO	DATE	TOPIC	CITATION	NUMBER
UK Great Britain	Multilateral	25 Feb 54	Air Transport	215UNTS249	102922
UK Great Britain	Multilateral	01 Mar 54	Commodity Trade	256UNTS31	103622
UK Great Britain	Multilateral	12 May 54	Admin Cooperation	327UNTS3	104714
UK Great Britain	Multilateral	14 May 54	Culture	249UNTS215	103511
UK Great Britain	Multilateral	04 Jun 54	Customs	276UNTS191	103992
UK Great Britain	Multilateral	04 Jun 54	Customs	282UNTS249	104101
UK Great Britain	Multilateral	14 Jun 54	Air Transport	320UNTS217	104644
UK Great Britain	Multilateral	14 Jun 54	Air Transport	320UNTS209	104643
UK Great Britain	Multilateral	30 Jun 54	Admin Cooperation	204UNTS99	102752
UK Great Britain	Multilateral	29 Jul 54	Sanitation	249UNTS45	103500
UK Great Britain	Multilateral	24 Aug 54	Other Military	247UNTS213	103471
UK Great Britain	Multilateral	08 Sep 54	Milit Assistance	209UNTS23	102819
UK Great Britain	Multilateral	28 Sep 54	Refugees	360UNTS117	105158
UK Great Britain	Multilateral	28 Sep 54	Reparations	207UNTS293	102812
UK Great Britain	Multilateral	02 Oct 54	IBRD Project	201UNTS171	102716
UK Great Britain	Multilateral	02 Oct 54	IBRD Project	201UNTS179	102717
UK Great Britain	Multilateral	05 Oct 54	Territory Boundary	235UNTS99	103297
UK Great Britain	Multilateral	23 Oct 54	Reparations	332UNTS219	104762
UK Great Britain	Multilateral	23 Oct 54	Status of Forces	334UNTS3	104765
UK Great Britain	Multilateral	23 Oct 54	Status of Forces	332UNTS387	104763
UK Great Britain	Multilateral	23 Oct 54	Status of Forces	332UNTS3	104760
UK Great Britain	Multilateral	23 Oct 54	Milit Occupation	331UNTS327	104759
UK Great Britain	Multilateral	23 Oct 54	Milit Occupation	331UNTS253	104758
UK Great Britain	Multilateral	23 Oct 54	Milit Occupation	332UNTS157	104761
UK Great Britain	Multilateral	01 Dec 54	Admin Cooperation	210UNTS197	102839
UK Great Britain	Multilateral	19 Dec 54	Culture	218UNTS139	102955
UK Great Britain	Multilateral	19 Dec 54	Patents/Copyrights	218UNTS51	102953
UK Great Britain	Multilateral	21 Dec 54	General Amity	258UNTS322	103678
UK Great Britain	Multilateral	04 Apr 55	Tech Assistance	208UNTS239	102816
UK Great Britain	Multilateral	10 May 55	Claims and Debts	273UNTS121	103948
UK Great Britain	Multilateral	15 May 55	Recognition	217UNTS223	102949
UK Great Britain	Multilateral	25 May 55	IGO Establishment	264UNTS117	103791
UK Great Britain	Multilateral	03 Jun 55	Specific Resources	310UNTS145	104491
UK Great Britain	Multilateral	06 Jun 55	IGO Establishment	219UNTS79	102968
UK Great Britain	Multilateral	22 Jun 55	Atomic Energy	249UNTS3	103498
UK Great Britain	Multilateral	21 Sep 55	Other Military	269UNTS241	103885
UK Great Britain	Multilateral	28 Sep 55	Air Transport	478UNTS371	106943
UK Great Britain	Multilateral	12 Oct 55	IGO Establishment	560UNTS3	108165
UK Great Britain	Multilateral	13 Dec 55	Humanitarian	250UNTS3	103514
UK Great Britain	Multilateral	13 Dec 55	IGO Operations	529UNTS141	107660
UK Great Britain	Multilateral	04 Jan 56	Scientific Project	256UNTS171	103627
UK Great Britain	Multilateral	01 Mar 56	Customs	343UNTS129	104923
UK Great Britain	Multilateral	05 Mar 56	Other Military	326UNTS169	104711
UK Great Britain	Multilateral	05 Mar 56	Other Military	326UNTS181	104712
UK Great Britain	Multilateral	30 Apr 56	Air Transport	310UNTS229	104494
UK Great Britain	Multilateral	18 May 56	Customs	338UNTS103	104834
UK Great Britain	Multilateral	18 May 56	Customs	327UNTS123	104721
UK Great Britain	Multilateral	18 May 56	Customs	319UNTS21	104630
UK Great Britain	Multilateral	18 May 56	Land Transport	339UNTS3	104844
UK Great Britain	Multilateral	19 May 56	Land Transport	399UNTS189	105742
UK Great Britain	Multilateral	05 Jul 56	Patents/Copyrights	258UNTS371	103679
UK Great Britain	Multilateral	13 Jul 56	Dispute Settlement	281UNTS3	104066
UK Great Britain	Multilateral	07 Sep 56	Humanitarian	266UNTS3	103822
UK Great Britain	Multilateral	24 Sep 56	Patents/Copyrights	253UNTS171	103583
UK Great Britain	Multilateral	25 Sep 56	Air Transport	334UNTS13	104766
UK Great Britain	Multilateral	25 Sep 56	Air Transport	334UNTS89	104767
UK Great Britain	Multilateral	26 Oct 56	IGO Establishment	276UNTS3	103988
UK Great Britain	Multilateral	29 Oct 56	Territory Boundary	263UNTS165	103772
UK Great Britain	Multilateral	14 Dec 56	Taxation	436UNTS131	106293
UK Great Britain	Multilateral	15 Dec 56	Education	278UNTS73	104023
UK Great Britain	Multilateral	31 Jan 57	Claims and Debts	278UNTS105	104026
UK Great Britain	Multilateral	20 Feb 57	Consul/Citizenship	309UNTS65	104468
UK Great Britain	Multilateral	29 Mar 57	Claims and Debts	283UNTS137	104113
UK Great Britain	Multilateral	29 Apr 57	Dispute Settlement	320UNTS243	104646
UK Great Britain	Multilateral	15 Jun 57	General Trade	550UNTS45	108008

PARTY ONE	PARTY TWO	DATE	TOPIC	CITATION	NUMBER
UK Great Britain	Multilateral	30 Sep 57	General Transport	619UNTS77	108940
UK Great Britain	Multilateral	03 Oct 57	Postal Service	364UNTS331	105212
UK Great Britain	Multilateral	03 Oct 57	Postal Service	365UNTS3	105213
UK Great Britain	Multilateral	03 Oct 57	Postal Service	364UNTS3	105211
UK Great Britain	Multilateral	23 Nov 57	Refugees	506UNTS125	107384
UK Great Britain	Multilateral	25 Nov 57	General Trade	403UNTS169	105795
UK Great Britain	Multilateral	13 Dec 57	Land Transport	372UNTS159	105296
UK Great Britain	Multilateral	13 Dec 57	Extradition	359UNTS273	105146
UK Great Britain	Multilateral	20 Mar 58	Admin Cooperation	335UNTS211	104789
UK Great Britain	Multilateral	31 Mar 58	Specific Property	320UNTS103	104639
UK Great Britain	Multilateral	03 Apr 58	Commodity Trade	336UNTS177	104806
UK Great Britain	Multilateral	29 Apr 58	Dispute Settlement	450UNTS169	106466
UK Great Britain	Multilateral	29 Apr 58	Territory Boundary	516UNTS205	107477
UK Great Britain	Multilateral	29 Apr 58	Water Transport	450UNTS11	106465
UK Great Britain	Multilateral	29 Apr 58	Territory Boundary	499UNTS311	107302
UK Great Britain	Multilateral	29 Apr 58	Specific Resources	559UNTS285	108164
UK Great Britain	Multilateral	28 Jul 58	General Military	335UNTS205	104788
UK Great Britain	Multilateral	27 Oct 58	Reparations	351UNTS303	105031
UK Great Britain	Multilateral	01 Dec 58	Commodity Trade	385UNTS137	105534
UK Great Britain	Multilateral	03 Dec 58	Admin Cooperation	398UNTS9	105715
UK Great Britain	Multilateral	03 Dec 58	Admin Cooperation	416UNTS51	105995
UK Great Britain	Multilateral	15 Dec 58	Mass Media	546UNTS235	107950
UK Great Britain	Multilateral	15 Dec 58	Sanitation	351UNTS159	105022
UK Great Britain	Multilateral	15 Jan 59	Customs	348UNTS13	104996
UK Great Britain	Multilateral	24 Jan 59	IGO Establishment	486UNTS157	107078
UK Great Britain	Multilateral	06 Apr 59	Commodity Trade	349UNTS167	105013
UK Great Britain	Multilateral	11 May 59	Claims and Debts	527UNTS145	107623
UK Great Britain	Multilateral	03 Aug 59	Status of Forces	481UNTS262	106986
UK Great Britain	Multilateral	18 Nov 59	IGO Establishment	390UNTS227	105610
UK Great Britain	Multilateral	19 Nov 59	IGO Operations	410UNTS156	105902
UK Great Britain	Multilateral	01 Dec 59	Territory Boundary	402UNTS71	105778
UK Great Britain	Multilateral	14 Dec 59	Admin Cooperation	444UNTS193	106369
UK Great Britain	Multilateral	04 Jan 60	IGO Establishment	370UNTS3	105266
UK Great Britain	Multilateral	26 Jan 60	IGO Establishment	439UNTS249	106333
UK Great Britain	Multilateral	22 Apr 60	Air Transport	418UNTS211	106023
UK Great Britain	Multilateral	28 Apr 60	Health/Educ/Welfare	376UNTS111	105377
UK Great Britain	Multilateral	17 Jun 60	Humanitarian	536UNTS27	107794
UK Great Britain	Multilateral	21 Jun 60	IGO Establishment	418UNTS109	106019
UK Great Britain	Multilateral	22 Jun 60	Mass Media	546UNTS247	107951
UK Great Britain	Multilateral	08 Jul 60	Tech Assistance	366UNTS310	105220
UK Great Britain	Multilateral	28 Jul 60	IGO Status/Immunit	394UNTS37	105667
UK Great Britain	Multilateral	16 Aug 60	Recognition	382UNTS3	105475
UK Great Britain	Multilateral	16 Aug 60	Recognition	382UNTS8	105476
UK Great Britain	Multilateral	01 Sep 60	Commodity Trade	403UNTS3	105792
UK Great Britain	Multilateral	19 Sep 60	IBRD Project	444UNTS259	106371
UK Great Britain	Multilateral	21 Sep 60	Patents/Copyrights	394UNTS3	105664
UK Great Britain	Multilateral	01 Dec 60	Scientific Project	414UNTS110	105970
UK Great Britain	Multilateral	09 Dec 60	Customs	429UNTS211	106200
UK Great Britain	Multilateral	13 Dec 60	Air Transport	523UNTS117	107557
UK Great Britain	Multilateral	14 Dec 60	Education	429UNTS93	106193
UK Great Britain	Multilateral	27 Mar 61	IGO Establishment	420UNTS109	106043
UK Great Britain	Multilateral	30 Mar 61	Sanitation	520UNTS151	107515
UK Great Britain	Multilateral	18 Apr 61	Consul/Citizenship	500UNTS95	107310
UK Great Britain	Multilateral	18 Apr 61	Dispute Settlement	500UNTS243	107312
UK Great Britain	Multilateral	08 Jun 61	Customs	473UNTS153	106862
UK Great Britain	Multilateral	08 Jun 61	Customs	473UNTS187	106863
UK Great Britain	Multilateral	21 Jun 61	IGO Establishment	514UNTS209	107449
UK Great Britain	Multilateral	18 Sep 61	Air Transport	500UNTS31	107305
UK Great Britain	Multilateral	05 Oct 61	Patents/Copyrights	527UNTS181	107625
UK Great Britain	Multilateral	05 Oct 61	Dispute Settlement	510UNTS175	107413
UK Great Britain	Multilateral	18 Oct 61	IGO Establishment	529UNTS89	107659
UK Great Britain	Multilateral	26 Oct 61	Patents/Copyrights	496UNTS43	107247
UK Great Britain	Multilateral	06 Dec 61	Customs	473UNTS219	106864
UK Great Britain	Multilateral	16 Dec 61	Visas	544UNTS19	107909
UK Great Britain	Multilateral	20 Feb 62	Water Transport	597UNTS159	108644

PARTY ONE	PARTY TWO	DATE	TOPIC	CITATION	NUMBER
UK Great Britain	Multilateral	29 Mar 62	IGO Establishment	507UNTS177	107401
UK Great Britain	Multilateral	09 May 62	IGO Establishment	453UNTS299	106531
UK Great Britain	Multilateral	14 May 62	Scientific Project	544UNTS39	107910
UK Great Britain	Multilateral	14 May 62	Sanitation	544UNTS81	107911
UK Great Britain	Multilateral	15 May 62	Commodity Trade	444UNTS3	106367
UK Great Britain	Multilateral	06 Jun 62	Privil/Immunities	486UNTS271	107081
UK Great Britain	Multilateral	06 Jun 62	Privil/Immunities	486UNTS263	107080
UK Great Britain	Multilateral	14 Jun 62	IGO Establishment	528UNTS33	107634
UK Great Britain	Multilateral	23 Jul 62	Recognition	456UNTS302	106564
UK Great Britain	Multilateral	10 Sep 62	Other Military	502UNTS3	107323
UK Great Britain	Multilateral	28 Sep 62	IGO Establishment	469UNTS169	106791
UK Great Britain	Multilateral	16 Oct 62	Postal Service	470UNTS336	106816
UK Great Britain	Multilateral	16 Oct 62	Postal Service	470UNTS321	106815
UK Great Britain	Multilateral	16 Oct 62	Postal Service	470UNTS291	106814
UK Great Britain	Multilateral	17 Dec 62	Sanitation	486UNTS119	107076
UK Great Britain	Multilateral	17 Dec 62	Admin Cooperation	590UNTS81	108548
UK Great Britain	Multilateral	02 Apr 63	Commodity Trade	475UNTS121	106889
UK Great Britain	Multilateral	20 Apr 63	IGO Establishment	495UNTS3	107239
UK Great Britain	Multilateral	24 Apr 63	Consul/Citizenship	596UNTS261	108638
UK Great Britain	Multilateral	24 Apr 63	Consul/Citizenship	596UNTS487	108640
UK Great Britain	Multilateral	06 May 63	Consul/Citizenship	634UNTS221	109065
UK Great Britain	Multilateral	09 Jul 63	Admin Cooperation	0UNTS0	110760
UK Great Britain	Multilateral	05 Aug 63	Sanitation	480UNTS43	106964
UK Great Britain	Multilateral	14 Sep 63	Air Transport	0UNTS0	110106
UK Great Britain	Multilateral	09 Nov 63	Direct Aid	489UNTS209	107141
UK Great Britain	Multilateral	30 Dec 63	IBRD Project	568UNTS233	108271
UK Great Britain	Multilateral	30 Dec 63	IBRD Project	568UNTS215	108270
UK Great Britain	Multilateral	30 Dec 63	IBRD Project	568UNTS243	108272
UK Great Britain	Multilateral	30 Dec 63	IBRD Project	551UNTS119	108037
UK Great Britain	Multilateral	30 Dec 63	IBRD Project	551UNTS105	108036
UK Great Britain	Multilateral	30 Dec 63	IBRD Project	551UNTS75	108035
UK Great Britain	Multilateral	09 Mar 64	Specific Resources	581UNTS57	108432
UK Great Britain	Multilateral	09 Mar 64	Specific Resources	581UNTS89	108434
UK Great Britain	Multilateral	09 Mar 64	Specific Resources	581UNTS83	108433
UK Great Britain	Multilateral	06 May 64	IGO Operations	514UNTS71	107442
UK Great Britain	Multilateral	18 Jun 64	Atomic Energy	542UNTS145	107886
UK Great Britain	Multilateral	10 Jul 64	Postal Service	612UNTS3	108847
UK Great Britain	Multilateral	10 Jul 64	Postal Service	611UNTS7	108844
UK Great Britain	Multilateral	10 Jul 64	Postal Service	611UNTS387	108846
UK Great Britain	Multilateral	10 Jul 64	Postal Service	611UNTS105	108845
UK Great Britain	Multilateral	13 Jul 64	ILO Labor	569UNTS65	108279
UK Great Britain	Multilateral	20 Aug 64	Telecommunications	514UNTS25	107441
UK Great Britain	Multilateral	12 Sep 64	Specific Resources	0UNTS0	109344
UK Great Britain	Multilateral	01 Dec 64	Water Transport	550UNTS133	108012
UK Great Britain	Multilateral	22 Jan 65	Gen Communications	634UNTS239	109066
UK Great Britain	Multilateral	09 Mar 65	Water Transport	591UNTS265	108564
UK Great Britain	Multilateral	18 Mar 65	Dispute Settlement	575UNTS159	108359
UK Great Britain	Multilateral	23 Jun 65	General IGO	614UNTS239	108873
UK Great Britain	Multilateral	23 Jun 65	Atomic Energy	548UNTS241	107981
UK Great Britain	Multilateral	08 Jul 65	General Trade	597UNTS3	108641
UK Great Britain	Multilateral	15 Nov 65	Admin Cooperation	0UNTS0	109432
UK Great Britain	Multilateral	26 Nov 65	Recognition	598UNTS81	108655
UK Great Britain	Multilateral	04 Dec 65	IGO Establishment	571UNTS123	108303
UK Great Britain	Multilateral	08 Dec 65	IGO Establishment	600UNTS161	108680
UK Great Britain	Multilateral	31 Dec 65	Specific Resources	616UNTS317	108904
UK Great Britain	Multilateral	30 Mar 66	Scientific Project	593UNTS261	108588
UK Great Britain	Multilateral	05 Apr 66	Water Transport	640UNTS133	109159
UK Great Britain	Multilateral	27 Jan 67	Scientific Project	610UNTS205	108843
UK Great Britain	Multilateral	31 Jan 67	Refugees	606UNTS267	108791
UK Great Britain	Multilateral	09 Mar 67	Other Military	603UNTS135	108730
UK Great Britain	Multilateral	24 Apr 67	Humanitarian	634UNTS255	109067
UK Great Britain	Multilateral	03 May 67	IGO Operations	0UNTS0	110764
UK Great Britain	Multilateral	30 Jun 67	Commodity Trade	0UNTS0	109864
UK Great Britain	Multilateral	10 Jul 67	Air Transport	0UNTS0	109971
UK Great Britain	Multilateral	20 Jul 67	General Economic	0UNTS0	109259

PARTY ONE	PARTY TWO	DATE	TOPIC	CITATION	NUMBER
UK Great Britain	Multilateral	26 Sep 67	Atomic Energy	633UNTS73	109035
UK Great Britain	Multilateral	25 Oct 67	Scientific Project	0UNTS0	110322
UK Great Britain	Multilateral	06 Nov 67	Other Military	640UNTS87	109155
UK Great Britain	Multilateral	18 Mar 68	Commodity Trade	0UNTS0	109262
UK Great Britain	Multilateral	22 Apr 68	Scientific Project	0UNTS0	109574
UK Great Britain	Multilateral	07 Jun 68	Admin Cooperation	0UNTS0	110346
UK Great Britain	Multilateral	11 Jun 68	Scientific Project	0UNTS0	109884
UK Great Britain	Multilateral	01 Jul 68	Peace/Disarmament	0UNTS0	110485
UK Great Britain	Multilateral	16 Aug 68	Non-ILO Labor	0UNTS0	109281
UK Great Britain	Multilateral	24 Sep 68	Air Transport	0UNTS0	110612
UK Great Britain	Multilateral	28 Sep 68	Tech Assistance	0UNTS0	109296
UK Great Britain	Multilateral	09 Oct 68	Finance	0UNTS0	109822
UK Great Britain	Multilateral	24 Dec 68	Commodity Trade	0UNTS0	109369
UK Great Britain	Multilateral	27 Jan 69	Telecommunications	0UNTS0	109664
UK Great Britain	Multilateral	07 Feb 69	Status of Forces	0UNTS0	110587
UK Great Britain	Multilateral	07 Feb 69	Status of Forces	0UNTS0	110586
UK Great Britain	Multilateral	09 Jun 69	Specific Resources	0UNTS0	110099
UK Great Britain	Multilateral	18 Oct 69	IGO Establishment	0UNTS0	110232
UK Great Britain	Multilateral	12 Jan 70	Commodity Trade	0UNTS0	110603
UK Great Britain	Muscat and Oman	05 Apr 47	Air Transport	27UNTS287	100412
UK Great Britain	Muscat and Oman	20 Dec 51	General Amity	149UNTS247	101956
UK Great Britain	Muscat and Oman	25 Jul 58	General Military	312UNTS347	104524
UK Great Britain	Muscat and Oman	15 Nov 67	Territory Boundary	617UNTS319	108919
UK Great Britain	Nepal	30 Oct 50	General Amity	97UNTS121	101346
UK Great Britain	Nepal	31 Mar 69	Loans and Credits	0UNTS0	109881
UK Great Britain	Nepal	08 Aug 69	Direct Aid	0UNTS0	110237
UK Great Britain	Netherlands	13 Jun 39	Sanitation	5UNTS65	200028
UK Great Britain	Netherlands	14 Jun 40	Finance	2UNTS251	200018
UK Great Britain	Netherlands	25 Jul 40	Finance	2UNTS275	200020
UK Great Britain	Netherlands	02 Oct 44	Claims and Debts	231UNTS317	200535
UK Great Britain	Netherlands	07 Sep 45	Finance	2UNTS325	200024
UK Great Britain	Netherlands	20 Dec 45	Milit Assistance	4UNTS303	100053
UK Great Britain	Netherlands	13 Aug 46	Air Transport	4UNTS367	100056
UK Great Britain	Netherlands	16 Sep 46	Finance	4UNTS401	100057
UK Great Britain	Netherlands	04 Dec 46	Milit Installation	12UNTS241	100187
UK Great Britain	Netherlands	26 Feb 47	Finance	11UNTS279	100167
UK Great Britain	Netherlands	21 Mar 47	Visas	52NET64	447004
UK Great Britain	Netherlands	21 Mar 47	Visas	11UNTS297	100170
UK Great Britain	Netherlands	08 Oct 47	Reparations	252UNTS19	103556
UK Great Britain	Netherlands	11 Mar 48	Reparations	77UNTS69	100993
UK Great Britain	Netherlands	11 Jun 48	General Economic	66UNTS183	100853
UK Great Britain	Netherlands	07 Jul 48	Culture	82UNTS259	101099
UK Great Britain	Netherlands	06 Sep 48	Finance	32UNTS235	100501
UK Great Britain	Netherlands	15 Oct 48	Taxation	73UNTS203	100954
UK Great Britain	Netherlands	15 Oct 48	Taxation	74UNTS3	100955
UK Great Britain	Netherlands	17 Jan 49	Reparations	83UNTS67	101102
UK Great Britain	Netherlands	20 Sep 49	Reparations	51NET137	447013
UK Great Britain	Netherlands	30 Apr 51	Consul/Citizenship	91UNTS177	101250
UK Great Britain	Netherlands	17 May 51	Air Transport	118UNTS103	101599
UK Great Britain	Netherlands	30 Nov 51	Postal Service	123UNTS177	101659
UK Great Britain	Netherlands	19 Oct 53	Customs	306UNTS99	104435
UK Great Britain	Netherlands	09 Jul 54	Finance	199UNTS157	102682
UK Great Britain	Netherlands	11 Aug 54	Non-ILO Labor	248UNTS235	103497
UK Great Britain	Netherlands	11 Jun 56	Status of Forces	306UNTS107	104436
UK Great Britain	Netherlands	12 Jun 56	Non-ILO Labor	250UNTS81	103519
UK Great Britain	Netherlands	22 Oct 57	Air Transport	313UNTS309	104538
UK Great Britain	Netherlands	30 Apr 59	Claims and Debts	343UNTS307	104937
UK Great Britain	Netherlands	01 Apr 60	Visas	374UNTS277	105341
UK Great Britain	Netherlands	21 Feb 61	Visas	398UNTS235	105725
UK Great Britain	Netherlands	27 Aug 63	Other Military	490UNTS3	107150
UK Great Britain	Netherlands	30 Oct 63	Other Military	490UNTS11	107151
UK Great Britain	Netherlands	06 Oct 65	Territory Boundary	595UNTS105	108615
UK Great Britain	Netherlands	06 Oct 65	Territory Boundary	595UNTS113	108616
UK Great Britain	Netherlands	31 Oct 67	Taxation	0UNTS0	109222
UK Great Britain	Netherlands	17 Nov 67	Dispute Settlement	0UNTS0	110022
UK Great Britain	Netherlands	17 Nov 67	Admin Cooperation	0UNTS0	110356
UK Great Britain	Netherlands	01 May 69	Taxation	0UNTS0	110438
UK Great Britain	Netherlands	19 Sep 69	Land Transport	0UNTS0	110807
UK Great Britain	New Zealand	27 May 47	Taxation	17UNTS211	100277
UK Great Britain	New Zealand	12 Nov 48	Milit Assistance	162UNTS197	102136
UK Great Britain	New Zealand	28 Nov 51	General Trade	127UNTS263	101707
UK Great Britain	New Zealand	20 Dec 55	Non-ILO Labor	268UNTS243	103860
UK Great Britain	New Zealand	04 Jul 57	Milit Assistance	402UNTS109	105780
UK Great Britain	New Zealand	20 Sep 57	Sanitation	287UNTS105	104180
UK Great Britain	New Zealand	12 Aug 59	General Trade	354UNTS161	105062
UK Great Britain	New Zealand	21 Sep 59	Milit Assistance	401UNTS51	105762
UK Great Britain	New Zealand	13 Jun 61	Air Transport	497UNTS293	107273
UK Great Britain	New Zealand	15 May 63	Commodity Trade	486UNTS11	107068
UK Great Britain	New Zealand	13 Jul 66	Taxation	598UNTS121	108658
UK Great Britain	New Zealand	02 Apr 68	General Military	0UNTS0	109206
UK Great Britain	New Zealand	24 Sep 68	Finance	0UNTS0	109818
UK Great Britain	New Zealand	19 Jun 69	Non-ILO Labor	0UNTS0	110439
UK Great Britain	Nicaragua	25 May 51	Sanitation	101UNTS77	101404
UK Great Britain	Nicaragua	05 Feb 69	Visas	0UNTS0	109666
UK Great Britain	Nigeria	01 Oct 60	Recognition	384UNTS207	105520
UK Great Britain	Nigeria	29 May 61	Recognition	478UNTS3	106931
UK Great Britain	Nigeria	24 Sep 68	Finance	0UNTS0	109819
UK Great Britain	Norway	11 Oct 45	Milit Installation	2NORT430	451149
UK Great Britain	Norway	08 Nov 45	Finance	5UNTS27	100063
UK Great Britain	Norway	31 Aug 46	Air Transport	6UNTS235	100078
UK Great Britain	Norway	27 Sep 46	Milit Installation	6UNTS259	100079
UK Great Britain	Norway	15 Jan 47	Consul/Citizenship	11UNTS187	100156
UK Great Britain	Norway	26 Feb 47	Visas	11UNTS273	100166
UK Great Britain	Norway	05 Jun 47	Milit Occupation	54UNTS181	100803
UK Great Britain	Norway	19 Feb 48	Culture	34UNTS33	100526
UK Great Britain	Norway	06 Nov 50	Finance	88UNTS257	101197
UK Great Britain	Norway	15 Dec 50	General Trade	106UNTS87	101459
UK Great Britain	Norway	22 Feb 51	Consul/Citizenship	326UNTS209	104713
UK Great Britain	Norway	02 May 51	Taxation	106UNTS101	101460
UK Great Britain	Norway	23 Jun 52	Air Transport	151UNTS81	101985
UK Great Britain	Norway	12 May 54	General Trade	2NORT627	451150
UK Great Britain	Norway	12 Jul 57	Atomic Energy	310UNTS41	104485
UK Great Britain	Norway	25 Jul 57	Non-ILO Labor	313UNTS3	104528
UK Great Britain	Norway	23 Apr 59	Finance	343UNTS283	104933
UK Great Britain	Norway	17 Nov 60	Specific Resources	398UNTS189	105723
UK Great Britain	Norway	10 May 61	Visas	414UNTS9	105960
UK Great Britain	Norway	12 Jun 61	Admin Cooperation	424UNTS173	106107
UK Great Britain	Norway	28 Sep 64	Specific Property	548UNTS63	107970
UK Great Britain	Norway	10 Mar 65	Territory Boundary	551UNTS213	108043
UK Great Britain	Norway	06 Mar 67	Non-ILO Labor	3NORT991	451151
UK Great Britain	Norway	06 Nov 68	Commodity Trade	3NORT0	451152
UK Great Britain	Norway	22 Jan 69	Taxation	0UNTS0	110436
UK Great Britain	Pakistan	21 Feb 48	Finance	134UNTS128	101797
UK Great Britain	Pakistan	27 Jul 49	Air Transport	44UNTS199	100685
UK Great Britain	Pakistan	02 Apr 51	General Trade	168UNTS281	102219
UK Great Britain	Pakistan	26 Sep 51	Postal Service	118UNTS221	101608
UK Great Britain	Pakistan	29 Sep 51	Finance	134UNTS183	101798
UK Great Britain	Pakistan	22 Jul 52	Postal Service	157UNTS185	102054
UK Great Britain	Pakistan	10 Jun 55	Taxation	243UNTS15	103444
UK Great Britain	Pakistan	13 Mar 63	Atomic Energy	482UNTS347	107003
UK Great Britain	Pakistan	13 Oct 64	Atomic Energy	534UNTS71	107754
UK Great Britain	Pakistan	25 Sep 68	Finance	0UNTS0	109820
UK Great Britain	Panama	15 Sep 51	Air Transport	560UNTS143	108172
UK Great Britain	Panama	07 Jan 66	Visas	565UNTS25	108233
UK Great Britain	Paraguay	03 Apr 50	General Economic	99UNTS81	101372
UK Great Britain	Paraguay	21 Nov 55	General Economic	252UNTS107	103560
UK Great Britain	Paraguay	27 Oct 66	Visas	597UNTS229	108648
UK Great Britain	Peru	22 Dec 47	Air Transport	72UNTS143	100932
UK Great Britain	Peru	20 Jul 48	Finance	66UNTS197	100855
UK Great Britain	Peru	03 Dec 66	Loans and Credits	617UNTS231	108915

PARTY ONE	PARTY TWO	DATE	TOPIC	CITATION	NUMBER
UK Great Britain	Peru	19 Dec 67	Loans and Credits	0UNTS0	109447
UK Great Britain	Philippines	07 Jan 48	Air Transport	28UNTS63	100420
UK Great Britain	Philippines	20 Apr 48	Territory Boundary	1PTS705	465015
UK Great Britain	Philippines	24 May 49	Consul/Citizenship	2PTS145	465019
UK Great Britain	Philippines	23 Jan 51	Admin Cooperation	2PTS609	465024
UK Great Britain	Philippines	31 Jan 55	Air Transport	216UNTS51	102932
UK Great Britain	Philippines	29 Aug 55	Non-ILO Labor	221UNTS241	103009
UK Great Britain	Philippines	14 Apr 58	Air Transport	3PTS715	465038
UK Great Britain	Poland	24 Jun 46	Claims and Debts	11UNTS59	100149
UK Great Britain	Poland	24 Jan 48	Claims and Debts	87UNTS3	101163
UK Great Britain	Poland	02 Mar 48	Finance	77UNTS47	100991
UK Great Britain	Poland	14 Jan 49	Reparations	83UNTS51	101101
UK Great Britain	Poland	14 Jan 49	General Economic	83UNTS3	101100
UK Great Britain	Poland	22 Aug 49	Admin Cooperation	404UNTS17	105801
UK Great Britain	Poland	11 Nov 54	Finance	204UNTS137	102755
UK Great Britain	Poland	03 Apr 59	Air Transport	351UNTS295	105030
UK Great Britain	Poland	02 Jul 60	Air Transport	385UNTS87	105532
UK Great Britain	Poland	26 Sep 64	Specific Property	539UNTS153	107828
UK Great Britain	Poland	23 Feb 67	Consul/Citizenship	71PDZU186	457139
UK Great Britain	Poland	21 Jul 67	Sanitation	0UNTS0	110421
UK Great Britain	Poland	21 Jul 67	Sanitation	70PDZU1	457145
UK Great Britain	Poland	10 Oct 67	Scientific Project	0UNTS0	109496
UK Great Britain	Poland	10 Oct 67	Scientific Project	68PZUM35	458149
UK Great Britain	Portugal	01 Jul 45	Postal Service	5UNTS263	200034
UK Great Britain	Portugal	06 Dec 45	Air Transport	5UNTS37	100064
UK Great Britain	Portugal	06 Dec 45	Air Transport	6UNTS3	100065
UK Great Britain	Portugal	16 Apr 46	Finance	6UNTS119	100071
UK Great Britain	Portugal	16 Oct 47	Sanitation	82UNTS203	101093
UK Great Britain	Portugal	25 May 48	Milit Installation	34UNTS311	100544
UK Great Britain	Portugal	20 Jul 51	Finance	105UNTS61	101453
UK Great Britain	Portugal	21 Nov 52	Milit Assistance	404UNTS27	105802
UK Great Britain	Portugal	21 Jan 53	Non-IBRD Project	175UNTS13	102293
UK Great Britain	Portugal	10 Jul 54	Finance	199UNTS169	102683
UK Great Britain	Portugal	18 Nov 54	Territory Boundary	325UNTS307	104706
UK Great Britain	Portugal	18 Nov 54	Territory Boundary	210UNTS265	102841
UK Great Britain	Portugal	19 Nov 54	Culture	226UNTS305	103125
UK Great Britain	Portugal	23 Nov 54	Visas	204UNTS183	102757
UK Great Britain	Portugal	24 Nov 54	Visas	313UNTS125	104533
UK Great Britain	Portugal	18 Jul 58	Atomic Energy	313UNTS109	104532
UK Great Britain	Portugal	27 Feb 61	Visas	404UNTS33	105803
UK Great Britain	Portugal	31 Jul 61	Taxation	449UNTS119	106454
UK Great Britain	Portugal	07 Apr 64	Land Transport	539UNTS167	107830
UK Great Britain	Portugal	17 Apr 66	Air Transport	573UNTS223	108335
UK Great Britain	Portugal	27 Mar 68	Taxation	0UNTS0	109656
UK Great Britain	Romania	13 Mar 48	Admin Cooperation	104UNTS117	101436
UK Great Britain	Romania	10 Nov 60	Finance	385UNTS113	105533
UK Great Britain	Romania	22 Mar 66	Commodity Trade	571UNTS281	108307
UK Great Britain	Romania	09 Mar 67	Scientific Project	605UNTS195	108764
UK Great Britain	Romania	17 Mar 67	Air Transport	0UNTS0	109706
UK Great Britain	Romania	16 Jul 68	Atomic Energy	0UNTS0	109710
UK Great Britain	Romania	18 Oct 68	General Trade	0UNTS0	110210
UK Great Britain	San Marino	12 Sep 49	Visas	87UNTS37	101164
UK Great Britain	San Marino	08 Mar 61	Visas	414UNTS46	105964
UK Great Britain	San Marino	22 Jul 61	Reparations	420UNTS3	106035
UK Great Britain	Saudi Arabia	20 Apr 42	Extradition	10UNTS99	200056
UK Great Britain	Saudi Arabia	20 Apr 42	General Amity	10UNTS117	200057
UK Great Britain	Saudi Arabia	20 Apr 42	General Trade	10UNTS151	200058
UK Great Britain	Saudi Arabia	31 Oct 43	General Amity	10UNTS165	200059
UK Great Britain	Saudi Arabia	30 Jul 54	Dispute Settlement	201UNTS317	102722
UK Great Britain	SEATO (SE Asia)	12 Mar 65	IGO Status/Immunit	561UNTS313	108191
UK Great Britain	Sierra Leone	05 May 61	Recognition	420UNTS11	106036
UK Great Britain	Sierra Leone	05 May 61	Consul/Citizenship	420UNTS17	106037
UK Great Britain	Sierra Leone	05 Apr 62	Air Transport	434UNTS227	106265
UK Great Britain	Sierra Leone	18 Mar 68	Taxation	0UNTS0	109655
UK Great Britain	Sierra Leone	20 Sep 68	Finance	0UNTS0	109806

PARTY ONE	PARTY TWO	DATE	TOPIC	CITATION	NUMBER
UK Great Britain	Singapore	01 Dec 66	Taxation	605UNTS153	108763
UK Great Britain	Singapore	01 Aug 67	Air Transport	619UNTS29	108937
UK Great Britain	Singapore	19 Sep 68	Finance	0UNTS0	109801
UK Great Britain	Somalia	26 Jun 60	Non-ILO Labor	374UNTS347	105348
UK Great Britain	Somalia	26 Jun 60	Direct Aid	374UNTS331	105346
UK Great Britain	Somalia	26 Jun 60	Recognition	374UNTS357	105349
UK Great Britain	Somalia	26 Jun 60	Finance	374UNTS363	105350
UK Great Britain	Somalia	26 Jun 60	Non-ILO Labor	374UNTS339	105347
UK Great Britain	South Africa	26 Oct 45	Air Transport	72UNTS41	100927
UK Great Britain	South Africa	24 Aug 46	Telecommunications	51UNTS187	100765
UK Great Britain	South Africa	14 Oct 46	Taxation	86UNTS51	101152
UK Great Britain	South Africa	14 Oct 46	Taxation	86UNTS77	101153
UK Great Britain	South Africa	09 Oct 47	Finance	17UNTS239	100278
UK Great Britain	South Africa	06 Dec 48	Customs	118UNTS183	101607
UK Great Britain	South Africa	22 Feb 49	Territory Boundary	93UNTS75	101291
UK Great Britain	South Africa	12 Jun 50	Customs	93UNTS67	101290
UK Great Britain	South Africa	30 Jun 55	General Military	248UNTS191	103495
UK Great Britain	South Africa	18 Jun 59	Taxation	380UNTS59	105450
UK Great Britain	South Africa	18 Jun 59	Taxation	380UNTS81	105451
UK Great Britain	South Africa	18 Jun 59	Taxation	380UNTS103	105452
UK Great Britain	South Africa	28 May 62	Taxation	443UNTS79	106361
UK Great Britain	South Africa	22 Jun 64	Commodity Trade	515UNTS71	107454
UK Great Britain	South Africa	15 Nov 67	Consul/Citizenship	616UNTS277	108902
UK Great Britain	South Africa	21 Nov 68	Taxation	0UNTS0	110023
UK Great Britain	Spain	30 Oct 44	Air Transport	47SPBO2004	460237
UK Great Britain	Spain	28 Mar 47	Finance	66UNTS91	100849
UK Great Britain	Spain	23 Jun 48	General Economic	66UNTS193	100854
UK Great Britain	Spain	15 Dec 48	Finance	87UNTS49	101165
UK Great Britain	Spain	20 Jul 50	Air Transport	398UNTS101	105719
UK Great Britain	Spain	20 Dec 51	Finance	123UNTS187	101660
UK Great Britain	Spain	21 Dec 54	General Trade	55SPBO301	460238
UK Great Britain	Spain	01 Jul 55	General Economic	55SPBO608	460239
UK Great Britain	Spain	21 Dec 56	General Trade	57SPBO1601	460240
UK Great Britain	Spain	19 Feb 58	General Trade	58SPBO803	460241
UK Great Britain	Spain	19 Jan 60	Atomic Energy	404UNTS41	105804
UK Great Britain	Spain	13 May 60	Visas	374UNTS287	105342
UK Great Britain	Spain	12 Jul 60	Culture	414UNTS123	105971
UK Great Britain	Spain	15 Feb 61	Visas	404UNTS75	105805
UK Great Britain	Spain	30 May 61	Consul/Citizenship	562UNTS169	108198
UK Great Britain	Spain	21 Dec 68	Taxation	0UNTS0	109663
UK Great Britain	Sudan	16 Jan 61	Air Transport	424UNTS233	106112
UK Great Britain	Sudan	11 Dec 68	Loans and Credits	0UNTS0	109786
UK Great Britain	Sudan	23 Aug 69	Loans and Credits	0UNTS0	110425
UK Great Britain	Swaziland	08 Sep 68	Admin Cooperation	0UNTS0	109474
UK Great Britain	Sweden	06 Mar 45	Finance	5UNTS241	200032
UK Great Britain	Sweden	06 Mar 45	Finance	82UNTS219	101095
UK Great Britain	Sweden	27 Nov 46	Air Transport	11UNTS229	100162
UK Great Britain	Sweden	20 Mar 47	Visas	11UNTS291	100169
UK Great Britain	Sweden	30 Mar 49	Taxation	209UNTS129	102826
UK Great Britain	Sweden	30 Dec 49	Finance	87UNTS59	101166
UK Great Britain	Sweden	05 Apr 50	Air Transport	99UNTS107	101374
UK Great Britain	Sweden	10 Nov 50	Finance	88UNTS265	101198
UK Great Britain	Sweden	17 Jan 51	Postal Service	93UNTS225	101301
UK Great Britain	Sweden	14 Mar 52	Consul/Citizenship	202UNTS157	102731
UK Great Britain	Sweden	23 Jun 52	Air Transport	52SOFM468	461170
UK Great Britain	Sweden	28 Jul 54	Finance	199UNTS181	102684
UK Great Britain	Sweden	29 Oct 54	Visas	209UNTS75	102823
UK Great Britain	Sweden	22 Dec 55	Claims and Debts	231UNTS179	103218
UK Great Britain	Sweden	18 Jan 56	Admin Cooperation	428UNTS301	106181
UK Great Britain	Sweden	09 Jun 56	Non-ILO Labor	309UNTS301	104479
UK Great Britain	Sweden	08 Dec 56	Claims and Debts	264UNTS61	103788
UK Great Britain	Sweden	20 Sep 57	Atomic Energy	310UNTS49	104486
UK Great Britain	Sweden	18 Apr 59	Claims and Debts	360UNTS89	105156
UK Great Britain	Sweden	28 Jul 60	Taxation	404UNTS85	105806
UK Great Britain	Sweden	28 Jul 60	Taxation	404UNTS113	105808

PARTY ONE	PARTY TWO	DATE	TOPIC	CITATION	NUMBER
UK Great Britain	Sweden	05 May 61	Visas	404UNTS105	105807
UK Great Britain	Sweden	26 Apr 63	Extradition	590UNTS117	108551
UK Great Britain	Sweden	30 Jun 64	Commodity Trade	515UNTS83	107455
UK Great Britain	Sweden	14 Oct 64	Taxation	543UNTS135	107898
UK Great Britain	Sweden	26 Oct 67	Milit Assistance	632UNTS277	109029
UK Great Britain	Sweden	21 Nov 67	Land Transport	0UNTS0	109338
UK Great Britain	Sweden	12 Feb 68	Taxation	0UNTS0	109449
UK Great Britain	Switzerland	12 Mar 46	Finance	6UNTS107	100070
UK Great Britain	Switzerland	10 Jun 47	Visas	11UNTS217	100160
UK Great Britain	Switzerland	05 Apr 50	Air Transport	51SWRO573	462091
UK Great Britain	Switzerland	08 Dec 50	Claims and Debts	175UNTS55	102295
UK Great Britain	Switzerland	13 May 52	Air Transport	164UNTS91	102160
UK Great Britain	Switzerland	16 Jan 53	Non-ILO Labor	196UNTS119	102621
UK Great Britain	Switzerland	16 Jul 54	Claims and Debts	199UNTS197	102685
UK Great Britain	Switzerland	30 Sep 54	Taxation	209UNTS197	102828
UK Great Britain	Switzerland	12 Jun 56	Taxation	269UNTS133	103879
UK Great Britain	Switzerland	06 May 59	Claims and Debts	343UNTS315	104938
UK Great Britain	Switzerland	27 Feb 61	Visas	404UNTS167	105809
UK Great Britain	Switzerland	20 Oct 61	Loans and Credits	431UNTS29	106206
UK Great Britain	Switzerland	27 Aug 63	General Transport	486UNTS183	107079
UK Great Britain	Switzerland	11 Aug 64	Atomic Energy	552UNTS271	108059
UK Great Britain	Switzerland	07 Jul 65	Dispute Settlement	605UNTS205	108765
UK Great Britain	Switzerland	29 Jun 67	Gen Communications	617UNTS261	108916
UK Great Britain	Switzerland	21 Feb 68	Non-ILO Labor	0UNTS0	110034
UK Great Britain	Switzerland	26 Nov 68	Taxation	0UNTS0	109662
UK Great Britain	Switzerland	12 Dec 68	Atomic Energy	0UNTS0	109787
UK Great Britain	Syria	02 Nov 46	Dispute Settlement	11UNTS153	100153
UK Great Britain	Syria	30 Jan 54	Air Transport	449UNTS47	106452
UK Great Britain	Syria	05 Feb 54	Telecommunications	204UNTS267	102761
UK Great Britain	Syria	31 Aug 64	Commodity Trade	539UNTS259	107837
UK Great Britain	Taiwan	18 Jun 41	Territory Boundary	10UNTS227	200064
UK Great Britain	Taiwan	07 Jul 45	Status of Forces	14UNTS455	200100
UK Great Britain	Taiwan	23 Jul 47	Air Transport	9UNTS207	100135
UK Great Britain	Taiwan	12 Jan 48	Customs	14UNTS74	100212
UK Great Britain	Taiwan	18 May 48	Milit Assistance	66UNTS113	100850
UK Great Britain	Taiwan	18 Oct 48	Customs	0CTRC645	413028
UK Great Britain	Tanganyika	09 Dec 61	IGO Establishment	437UNTS47	106299
UK Great Britain	Tanganyika	14 Mar 62	Admin Cooperation	449UNTS147	106456
UK Great Britain	Tanganyika	03 Apr 63	Admin Cooperation	478UNTS23	106933
UK Great Britain	Tanganyika	02 Sep 64	Commodity Trade	522UNTS177	107544
UK Great Britain	Tanzania	23 Sep 68	Finance	0UNTS0	109813
UK Great Britain	Thailand	22 Mar 40	General Economic	2UNTS215	200013
UK Great Britain	Thailand	01 May 46	Commodity Trade	99UNTS175	101378
UK Great Britain	Thailand	01 May 46	Commodity Trade	99UNTS169	101377
UK Great Britain	Thailand	06 May 46	Commodity Trade	99UNTS193	101380
UK Great Britain	Thailand	06 Jan 47	Reparations	99UNTS149	101376
UK Great Britain	Thailand	08 May 47	Claims and Debts	100UNTS47	101386
UK Great Britain	Thailand	10 Nov 50	Air Transport	96UNTS77	101332
UK Great Britain	Thailand	29 Sep 52	General Economic	173UNTS31	102257
UK Great Britain	Thailand	25 Jul 57	Customs	277UNTS81	103999
UK Great Britain	Thailand	20 Nov 62	Tech Assistance	466UNTS243	106747
UK Great Britain	Thailand	09 Jan 63	Admin Cooperation	470UNTS59	106795
UK Great Britain	Trinidad/Tobago	09 May 64	Admin Cooperation	633UNTS327	109043
UK Great Britain	Trinidad/Tobago	29 Dec 66	Taxation	605UNTS237	108766
UK Great Britain	Trinidad/Tobago	23 Jan 67	Telecommunications	605UNTS277	108767
UK Great Britain	Trinidad/Tobago	01 Mar 67	Air Transport	606UNTS149	108784
UK Great Britain	Tunisia	16 Nov 59	General Trade	354UNTS367	105070
UK Great Britain	Tunisia	17 Jan 61	General Trade	566UNTS2	108236
UK Great Britain	Tunisia	14 Jul 62	Visas	466UNTS235	106746
UK Great Britain	Turkey	23 Mar 44	Specif Claim/Waive	2UNTS227	200015
UK Great Britain	Turkey	04 May 45	General Economic	46TURG2301	466095
UK Great Britain	Turkey	12 Feb 46	Air Transport	6UNTS79	100069
UK Great Britain	Turkey	16 Oct 48	Finance	83UNTS85	101103
UK Great Britain	Turkey	09 Oct 52	Visas	151UNTS233	101999
UK Great Britain	Turkey	11 Feb 54	Milit Assistance	190UNTS343	102575
UK Great Britain	Turkey	17 Jan 55	Finance	204UNTS195	102758
UK Great Britain	Turkey	12 Mar 56	Culture	313UNTS73	104530
UK Great Britain	Turkey	28 Feb 57	Customs	310UNTS29	104483
UK Great Britain	Turkey	28 Feb 57	General Economic	310UNTS69	104488
UK Great Britain	Turkey	16 Aug 57	Milit Assistance	310UNTS21	104482
UK Great Britain	Turkey	25 Nov 58	Loans and Credits	327UNTS35	104715
UK Great Britain	Turkey	13 Jun 59	Claims and Debts	551UNTS59	108033
UK Great Britain	Turkey	09 Sep 59	Non-ILO Labor	424UNTS267	106113
UK Great Britain	Turkey	01 Mar 60	Visas	374UNTS295	105343
UK Great Britain	Turkey	28 Jun 61	Visas	414UNTS93	105968
UK Great Britain	Turkey	01 May 63	Loans and Credits	63TURG2109	466116
UK Great Britain	Turkey	21 Oct 65	Loans and Credits	561UNTS185	108180
UK Great Britain	Turkey	29 Jul 66	Loans and Credits	597UNTS241	108649
UK Great Britain	Turkey	21 Apr 67	Loans and Credits	610UNTS0	108838
UK Great Britain	Turkey	04 Mar 68	Loans and Credits	0UNTS0	109265
UK Great Britain	Turkey	04 Mar 68	Loans and Credits	0UNTS0	109266
UK Great Britain	Turkey	29 Mar 68	Loans and Credits	0UNTS0	109286
UK Great Britain	Turkey	02 Apr 68	Taxation	0UNTS0	109452
UK Great Britain	Turkey	22 May 68	Loans and Credits	0UNTS0	109287
UK Great Britain	Turkey	06 Aug 68	Loans and Credits	0UNTS0	109451
UK Great Britain	Turkey	12 Aug 68	Loans and Credits	0UNTS0	109495
UK Great Britain	Turkey	23 Jun 69	Loans and Credits	0UNTS0	110027
UK Great Britain	Turkey	15 Sep 69	Loans and Credits	0UNTS0	110242
UK Great Britain	Turkey	14 Nov 69	Loans and Credits	0UNTS0	110441
UK Great Britain	Uganda	10 Oct 62	Admin Cooperation	475UNTS177	106893
UK Great Britain	Uganda	21 Sep 68	Finance	0UNTS0	109810
UK Great Britain	UN Special Fund	07 Jan 60	Direct Aid	348UNTS177	105000
UK Great Britain	UNESCO (Educ/Cult)	09 Aug 56	Direct Aid	256UNTS139	103624
UK Great Britain	UNICEF (Children)	13 Jun 49	Tech Assistance	65UNTS58	100825
UK Great Britain	UNICEF (Children)	17 Jun 49	Tech Assistance	65UNTS56	100824
UK Great Britain	UNICEF (Children)	17 Jun 49	Tech Assistance	65UNTS54	100822
UK Great Britain	UNICEF (Children)	17 Jun 49	Tech Assistance	65UNTS50	100820
UK Great Britain	UNICEF (Children)	17 Jun 49	Tech Assistance	65UNTS56	100823
UK Great Britain	UNICEF (Children)	17 Jun 49	Tech Assistance	65UNTS54	100821
UK Great Britain	UNICEF (Children)	19 Dec 49	Tech Assistance	65UNTS64	100828
UK Great Britain	UNICEF (Children)	10 Feb 50	Direct Aid	65UNTS86	100837
UK Great Britain	UNICEF (Children)	02 Oct 51	Direct Aid	104UNTS301	101448
UK Great Britain	UNICEF (Children)	04 Feb 52	Direct Aid	120UNTS147	101620
UK Great Britain	UNICEF (Children)	15 Feb 52	Direct Aid	121UNTS63	101626
UK Great Britain	UNICEF (Children)	25 Jul 52	Direct Aid	135UNTS37	101812
UK Great Britain	UNICEF (Children)	16 Dec 52	Direct Aid	151UNTS359	102005
UK Great Britain	UNICEF (Children)	07 Oct 53	Tech Assistance	180UNTS59	102375
UK Great Britain	United Arab Rep	10 Dec 46	Specif Claim/Waive	105UNTS15	101451
UK Great Britain	United Arab Rep	30 Jun 47	Finance	93UNTS165	101299
UK Great Britain	United Arab Rep	05 Jan 48	Finance	77UNTS3	100988
UK Great Britain	United Arab Rep	31 Mar 49	Finance	83UNTS139	101106
UK Great Britain	United Arab Rep	17 Apr 49	Reparations	83UNTS183	101107
UK Great Britain	United Arab Rep	31 May 49	Specific Resources	226UNTS273	103122
UK Great Britain	United Arab Rep	20 Mar 50	Tech Assistance	226UNTS287	103123
UK Great Britain	United Arab Rep	01 Jul 51	Finance	249UNTS125	103503
UK Great Britain	United Arab Rep	01 Jul 51	Finance	249UNTS143	103504
UK Great Britain	United Arab Rep	19 Oct 52	General Trade	158UNTS423	102075
UK Great Britain	United Arab Rep	30 Oct 52	Finance	172UNTS3	102236
UK Great Britain	United Arab Rep	05 Jan 53	Specific Property	207UNTS277	102810
UK Great Britain	United Arab Rep	12 Feb 53	Recognition	161UNTS157	102127
UK Great Britain	United Arab Rep	19 Oct 54	General Amity	210UNTS3	102833
UK Great Britain	United Arab Rep	19 Oct 54	Milit Installation	221UNTS227	103008
UK Great Britain	United Arab Rep	28 Feb 59	Finance	343UNTS159	104925
UK Great Britain	United Arab Rep	14 Nov 61	Education	449UNTS129	106455
UK Great Britain	United Arab Rep	29 Sep 65	Culture	0UNTS0	109444
UK Great Britain	United Nations	18 Mar 49	Humanitarian	47UNTS305	100736
UK Great Britain	United Nations	27 Jun 63	Trusteeship	469UNTS145	106789
UK Great Britain	United Nations	02 Apr 64	IGO Status/Immunit	492UNTS279	107197
UK Great Britain	United Nations	21 Feb 66	General Economic	555UNTS177	108112
UK Great Britain	United Nations	12 Mar 68	IGO Operations	632UNTS121	109014

PARTY ONE	PARTY TWO	DATE	TOPIC	CITATION	NUMBER
UK Great Britain	Uruguay	15 Jul 47	Finance	71UNTS179	100918
UK Great Britain	Uruguay	12 Jul 48	Finance	71UNTS199	100919
UK Great Britain	USA (United States)	27 Jul 42	Status of Forces	117UNTS311	200378
UK Great Britain	USA (United States)	30 Sep 42	Milit Servic/Citiz	13UNTS169	200077
UK Great Britain	USA (United States)	03 Nov 42	Admin Cooperation	109UNTS127	200354
UK Great Britain	USA (United States)	30 Apr 43	Specific Resources	28UNTS341	200159
UK Great Britain	USA (United States)	10 May 43	Postal Service	147UNTS109	200473
UK Great Britain	USA (United States)	19 Aug 43	Atomic Energy	214UNTS341	200527
UK Great Britain	USA (United States)	24 Sep 43	Admin Cooperation	139UNTS373	200463
UK Great Britain	USA (United States)	01 Dec 43	Scientific Project	3UNTS209	100033
UK Great Britain	USA (United States)	10 Mar 44	Patents/Copyrights	5UNTS205	200030
UK Great Britain	USA (United States)	28 Mar 44	Status of Forces	15UNTS413	200104
UK Great Britain	USA (United States)	16 Apr 45	Taxation	6UNTS359	200039
UK Great Britain	USA (United States)	16 Apr 45	Taxation	6UNTS189	100076
UK Great Britain	USA (United States)	15 Jun 45	Reparations	89UNTS327	200261
UK Great Britain	USA (United States)	05 Nov 45	IGO Establishment	138UNTS75	101861
UK Great Britain	USA (United States)	06 Dec 45	Finance	126UNTS13	101679
UK Great Britain	USA (United States)	10 Dec 45	Refugees	3UNTS177	100030
UK Great Britain	USA (United States)	11 Feb 46	Air Transport	3UNTS253	100036
UK Great Britain	USA (United States)	21 Feb 46	General Trade	6UNTS137	100073
UK Great Britain	USA (United States)	01 Mar 46	Commodity Trade	3UNTS293	100037
UK Great Britain	USA (United States)	27 Mar 46	Patents/Copyrights	4UNTS101	100040
UK Great Britain	USA (United States)	27 Mar 46	Milit Assistance	4UNTS2	100039
UK Great Britain	USA (United States)	06 May 46	Admin Cooperation	99UNTS199	101381
UK Great Britain	USA (United States)	07 May 46	Water Transport	6UNTS285	100082
UK Great Britain	USA (United States)	31 Jul 46	Air Transport	42UNTS199	100648
UK Great Britain	USA (United States)	02 Dec 46	Milit Occupation	7UNTS163	100098
UK Great Britain	USA (United States)	23 Jan 47	Status of Forces	15UNTS281	100244
UK Great Britain	USA (United States)	23 May 47	Specific Property	11UNTS211	100159
UK Great Britain	USA (United States)	09 Oct 47	Milit Assistance	34UNTS129	100533
UK Great Britain	USA (United States)	13 Oct 47	Air Transport	66UNTS269	100858
UK Great Britain	USA (United States)	23 Oct 47	Territory Boundary	66UNTS277	100859
UK Great Britain	USA (United States)	30 Oct 47	General Economic	126UNTS39	101680
UK Great Britain	USA (United States)	24 Feb 48	Milit Installation	73UNTS143	100951
UK Great Britain	USA (United States)	06 Jul 48	Milit Occupation	25UNTS61	100358
UK Great Britain	USA (United States)	06 Jul 48	Direct Aid	22UNTS263	100339
UK Great Britain	USA (United States)	22 Sep 48	Milit Assistance	71UNTS64	100910
UK Great Britain	USA (United States)	30 Sep 48	Specific Resources	71UNTS241	100922
UK Great Britain	USA (United States)	12 Nov 48	Visas	84UNTS275	101136
UK Great Britain	USA (United States)	01 Dec 48	Direct Aid	81UNTS93	101066
UK Great Britain	USA (United States)	19 Sep 49	Milit Installation	68UNTS31	100882
UK Great Britain	USA (United States)	12 Dec 49	Visas	92UNTS191	101271
UK Great Britain	USA (United States)	27 Jan 50	Milit Assistance	80UNTS261	101056
UK Great Britain	USA (United States)	21 Jul 50	Milit Installation	97UNTS193	101351
UK Great Britain	USA (United States)	01 Aug 50	Milit Installation	88UNTS273	101199
UK Great Britain	USA (United States)	13 Sep 50	Visas	122UNTS51	101635
UK Great Britain	USA (United States)	06 Mar 51	Status of Forces	97UNTS137	101347
UK Great Britain	USA (United States)	25 Apr 51	Specific Property	99UNTS97	101373
UK Great Britain	USA (United States)	03 Jun 51	Postal Service	137UNTS81	101850
UK Great Britain	USA (United States)	06 Jun 51	Consul/Citizenship	165UNTS121	102174
UK Great Britain	USA (United States)	15 Jun 51	Tech Assistance	141UNTS79	101907
UK Great Britain	USA (United States)	13 Jul 51	Tech Assistance	105UNTS71	101454
UK Great Britain	USA (United States)	18 Jul 51	Land Transport	117UNTS49	101583
UK Great Britain	USA (United States)	30 Jul 51	Admin Cooperation	105UNTS81	101455
UK Great Britain	USA (United States)	08 Jan 52	Milit Assistance	179UNTS201	102369
UK Great Britain	USA (United States)	08 Jan 52	Direct Aid	126UNTS307	101696
UK Great Britain	USA (United States)	15 Jan 52	Milit Installation	127UNTS3	101697
UK Great Britain	USA (United States)	18 Jan 52	Commodity Trade	184UNTS79	102440
UK Great Britain	USA (United States)	18 Mar 52	Milit Assistance	177UNTS33	102307
UK Great Britain	USA (United States)	29 Jul 52	Status of Forces	179UNTS129	102362
UK Great Britain	USA (United States)	19 Jan 53	General Military	161UNTS3	102117
UK Great Britain	USA (United States)	25 Feb 53	Direct Aid	212UNTS157	102868
UK Great Britain	USA (United States)	02 Mar 53	Milit Installation	172UNTS257	102249
UK Great Britain	USA (United States)	24 Jun 53	Tech Assistance	224UNTS141	103074
UK Great Britain	USA (United States)	26 Jun 53	Loans and Credits	183UNTS225	102432

PARTY ONE	PARTY TWO	DATE	TOPIC	CITATION	NUMBER
UK Great Britain	USA (United States)	20 Jan 54	Tech Assistance	196UNTS95	102619
UK Great Britain	USA (United States)	15 Jun 54	Milit Assistance	236UNTS133	103320
UK Great Britain	USA (United States)	21 Jun 54	Other Military	209UNTS61	102821
UK Great Britain	USA (United States)	12 Jul 54	Tech Assistance	204UNTS123	102753
UK Great Britain	USA (United States)	19 Jul 54	Territory Boundary	250UNTS193	103523
UK Great Britain	USA (United States)	21 Jul 54	Status of Forces	222UNTS243	103031
UK Great Britain	USA (United States)	24 Sep 54	Milit Installation	300UNTS3	104326
UK Great Britain	USA (United States)	07 Jun 55	General Military	265UNTS27	103804
UK Great Britain	USA (United States)	15 Jun 55	Atomic Energy	214UNTS301	102905
UK Great Britain	USA (United States)	15 Jun 55	Atomic Energy	229UNTS73	103161
UK Great Britain	USA (United States)	15 Nov 55	Scientific Project	231UNTS185	103219
UK Great Britain	USA (United States)	05 Jun 56	Milit Installation	247UNTS205	103470
UK Great Britain	USA (United States)	25 Jun 56	Milit Installation	249UNTS59	103501
UK Great Britain	USA (United States)	25 Jun 56	Milit Installation	249UNTS91	103502
UK Great Britain	USA (United States)	01 Nov 56	Scientific Project	264UNTS3	103785
UK Great Britain	USA (United States)	27 Nov 56	Scientific Project	282UNTS43	104092
UK Great Britain	USA (United States)	27 Jun 57	Direct Aid	290UNTS133	104232
UK Great Britain	USA (United States)	27 Jun 57	General Economic	284UNTS75	104130
UK Great Britain	USA (United States)	01 Nov 57	Scientific Project	299UNTS167	104312
UK Great Britain	USA (United States)	20 Jan 58	Specific Property	304UNTS3	104387
UK Great Britain	USA (United States)	03 Feb 58	US Agri Commod Aid	307UNTS199	104450
UK Great Britain	USA (United States)	22 Feb 58	Milit Assistance	307UNTS207	104451
UK Great Britain	USA (United States)	03 Jul 58	Atomic Energy	326UNTS3	104707
UK Great Britain	USA (United States)	30 Dec 58	Specific Property	338UNTS281	104841
UK Great Britain	USA (United States)	16 Apr 59	IGO Status/Immunit	343UNTS11	104917
UK Great Britain	USA (United States)	15 Feb 60	Milit Assistance	371UNTS45	105269
UK Great Britain	USA (United States)	24 Jun 60	Gen Communications	377UNTS63	105396
UK Great Britain	USA (United States)	14 Oct 60	Scientific Project	398UNTS165	105721
UK Great Britain	USA (United States)	20 Jan 61	Scientific Project	402UNTS153	105783
UK Great Britain	USA (United States)	10 Feb 61	Milit Installation	409UNTS129	105880
UK Great Britain	USA (United States)	10 Feb 61	Milit Installation	409UNTS68	105879
UK Great Britain	USA (United States)	15 Mar 61	Scientific Project	404UNTS207	105811
UK Great Britain	USA (United States)	29 Mar 61	Scientific Project	405UNTS107	105826
UK Great Britain	USA (United States)	06 Apr 61	Scientific Project	404UNTS215	105812
UK Great Britain	USA (United States)	18 Jul 61	Milit Assistance	404UNTS227	105813
UK Great Britain	USA (United States)	28 Aug 61	Finance	434UNTS103	106258
UK Great Britain	USA (United States)	08 Sep 61	Scientific Project	418UNTS53	106016
UK Great Britain	USA (United States)	26 Sep 61	Scientific Project	421UNTS99	106055
UK Great Britain	USA (United States)	22 Feb 62	Direct Aid	435UNTS127	106275
UK Great Britain	USA (United States)	07 Mar 62	General Economic	446UNTS231	106406
UK Great Britain	USA (United States)	26 Apr 62	General Trade	445UNTS273	106395
UK Great Britain	USA (United States)	15 Aug 62	General Aid	580UNTS189	108421
UK Great Britain	USA (United States)	29 Aug 62	Milit Installation	449UNTS177	106459
UK Great Britain	USA (United States)	10 Dec 62	Mostfavored Nation	471UNTS91	106824
UK Great Britain	USA (United States)	15 Jan 63	Scientific Project	466UNTS181	106743
UK Great Britain	USA (United States)	06 Apr 63	Milit Installation	474UNTS49	106871
UK Great Britain	USA (United States)	11 Oct 63	Scientific Project	483UNTS3	107005
UK Great Britain	USA (United States)	15 Apr 64	Commodity Trade	515UNTS55	107453
UK Great Britain	USA (United States)	19 Jun 64	Water Transport	530UNTS99	107675
UK Great Britain	USA (United States)	20 Aug 64	Specific Property	531UNTS85	107694
UK Great Britain	USA (United States)	16 Nov 64	General Trade	0UNTS0	109749
UK Great Britain	USA (United States)	22 Apr 65	Postal Service	0UNTS0	109750
UK Great Britain	USA (United States)	10 May 65	Education	545UNTS181	107934
UK Great Britain	USA (United States)	07 Jul 65	Specific Property	551UNTS221	108044
UK Great Britain	USA (United States)	09 Aug 65	General Aid	580UNTS181	108420
UK Great Britain	USA (United States)	10 Nov 65	General Aid	580UNTS197	108422
UK Great Britain	USA (United States)	26 Nov 65	Gen Communications	561UNTS193	108181
UK Great Britain	USA (United States)	08 Feb 66	Finance	0UNTS0	109751
UK Great Britain	USA (United States)	05 Apr 66	General Trade	592UNTS61	108569
UK Great Britain	USA (United States)	02 Jun 66	Atomic Energy	573UNTS229	108336
UK Great Britain	USA (United States)	06 Jul 66	Extradition	588UNTS137	108520
UK Great Britain	USA (United States)	26 Aug 66	General Trade	0UNTS0	109769
UK Great Britain	USA (United States)	27 Oct 66	Claims and Debts	597UNTS265	108650
UK Great Britain	USA (United States)	12 Dec 66	Scientific Project	603UNTS235	108735
UK Great Britain	USA (United States)	28 Dec 66	Direct Aid	0UNTS0	109700

PARTY ONE	PARTY TWO	DATE	TOPIC	CITATION	NUMBER
UK Great Britain	USA (United States)	30 Dec 66	General Military	603UNTS273	108737
UK Great Britain	USA (United States)	30 Dec 66	Scientific Project	603UNTS245	108736
UK Great Britain	USA (United States)	01 Jan 67	Scientific Project	604UNTS3	108738
UK Great Britain	USA (United States)	10 Jan 67	General Aid	0UNTS0	109840
UK Great Britain	USA (United States)	11 Jan 67	General Aid	0UNTS0	109841
UK Great Britain	USA (United States)	18 Jan 67	General Aid	0UNTS0	109843
UK Great Britain	USA (United States)	12 Jun 67	Land Transport	0UNTS0	110785
UK Great Britain	USA (United States)	16 Dec 67	Direct Aid	0UNTS0	110063
UK Great Britain	USA (United States)	16 May 68	Admin Cooperation	0UNTS0	110018
UK Great Britain	USA (United States)	27 May 68	General Aid	0UNTS0	110144
UK Great Britain	USA (United States)	25 Jun 68	Direct Aid	0UNTS0	109271
UK Great Britain	USA (United States)	27 Jun 68	Finance	0UNTS0	110498
UK Great Britain	USA (United States)	09 Aug 68	Finance	0UNTS0	110499
UK Great Britain	USA (United States)	09 Oct 68	Finance	0UNTS0	110081
UK Great Britain	USA (United States)	11 Oct 68	Finance	0UNTS0	110083
UK Great Britain	USA (United States)	21 Nov 68	Finance	0UNTS0	110088
UK Great Britain	USA (United States)	25 Sep 69	Finance	0UNTS0	110243
UK Great Britain	USSR (Soviet Union)	16 Aug 41	Finance	91UNTS341	200269
UK Great Britain	USSR (Soviet Union)	22 Jun 42	Finance	91UNTS355	200270
UK Great Britain	USSR (Soviet Union)	23 Sep 44	Telecommunications	10UNTS171	200060
UK Great Britain	USSR (Soviet Union)	11 Feb 45	Refugees	0SUST173	468426
UK Great Britain	USSR (Soviet Union)	11 Feb 45	Refugees	0SUST173	468425
UK Great Britain	USSR (Soviet Union)	11 Feb 45	Refugees	0SUST173	468424
UK Great Britain	USSR (Soviet Union)	11 Feb 45	Refugees	0SUST174	468427
UK Great Britain	USSR (Soviet Union)	02 Oct 45	Milit Occupation	0SUST199	468428
UK Great Britain	USSR (Soviet Union)	09 Jul 46	Telecommunications	0SUST214	468429
UK Great Britain	USSR (Soviet Union)	27 Dec 47	General Economic	91UNTS113	101245
UK Great Britain	USSR (Soviet Union)	27 Dec 47	Finance	82UNTS251	101098
UK Great Britain	USSR (Soviet Union)	19 Mar 53	Refugees	0SUST293	468430
UK Great Britain	USSR (Soviet Union)	25 May 56	Specific Resources	266UNTS209	103831
UK Great Britain	USSR (Soviet Union)	19 Dec 57	Air Transport	351UNTS235	105026
UK Great Britain	USSR (Soviet Union)	03 Mar 59	Culture	8SUGG138	469562
UK Great Britain	USSR (Soviet Union)	28 Mar 59	Health/Educ/Welfare	8SUGG141	469569
UK Great Britain	USSR (Soviet Union)	24 May 59	General Trade	374UNTS305	105344
UK Great Britain	USSR (Soviet Union)	01 Dec 59	Health/Educ/Welfare	351UNTS313	105032
UK Great Britain	USSR (Soviet Union)	22 Dec 59	General Trade	8SUGG163	469618
UK Great Britain	USSR (Soviet Union)	09 Jan 61	Health/Educ/Welfare	404UNTS175	105810
UK Great Britain	USSR (Soviet Union)	12 Jan 61	Culture	398UNTS157	105720
UK Great Britain	USSR (Soviet Union)	19 May 61	Atomic Energy	10SUGG131	469768
UK Great Britain	USSR (Soviet Union)	21 Jan 63	Health/Educ/Welfare	475UNTS3	106887
UK Great Britain	USSR (Soviet Union)	13 Apr 64	Visas	539UNTS197	107832
UK Great Britain	USSR (Soviet Union)	30 Sep 64	Specific Property	539UNTS159	107829
UK Great Britain	USSR (Soviet Union)	06 Jan 65	Scientific Project	543UNTS77	107897
UK Great Britain	USSR (Soviet Union)	13 Feb 65	Health/Educ/Welfare	543UNTS43	107896
UK Great Britain	USSR (Soviet Union)	02 Dec 65	Consul/Citizenship	0UNTS0	109384
UK Great Britain	USSR (Soviet Union)	24 Feb 67	Scientific Project	606UNTS171	108785
UK Great Britain	USSR (Soviet Union)	25 Aug 67	Gen Communications	632UNTS49	109007
UK Great Britain	USSR (Soviet Union)	05 Jan 68	Claims and Debts	638UNTS41	109130
UK Great Britain	USSR (Soviet Union)	19 Jan 68	Scientific Project	0UNTS0	109277
UK Great Britain	USSR (Soviet Union)	15 Aug 68	Visas	0UNTS0	109473
UK Great Britain	USSR (Soviet Union)	28 Mar 69	Scientific Project	0UNTS0	109880
UK Great Britain	USSR (Soviet Union)	03 Jun 69	General Trade	0UNTS0	110026
UK Great Britain	Venezuela	20 Jul 56	Admin Cooperation	351UNTS289	105029
UK Great Britain	Venezuela	17 Feb 66	Territory Boundary	561UNTS321	108192
UK Great Britain	Vietnam, South	14 Oct 55	Patents/Copyrights	231UNTS193	103220
UK Great Britain	Vietnam, South	30 Nov 62	Admin Cooperation	470UNTS51	106794
UK Great Britain	Vietnam, South	27 Nov 68	Air Transport	0VKNG278	496072
UK Great Britain	Vietnam, South	20 Jul 70	Air Transport	0VKNG351	496089
UK Great Britain	Western Samoa	23 Jul 69	Finance	0UNTS0	110118
UK Great Britain	WHO (World Health)	07 Feb 52	Tech Assistance	121UNTS75	101627
UK Great Britain	WMO (Meteorology)	16 Dec 64	Tech Assistance	548UNTS57	107969
UK Great Britain	Yemen	20 Jan 51	General Amity	101UNTS39	101400
UK Great Britain	Yugoslavia	23 Dec 48	Reparations	81UNTS121	101068
UK Great Britain	Yugoslavia	23 Dec 48	General Trade	81UNTS133	101069
UK Great Britain	Yugoslavia	23 Dec 48	Reparations	81UNTS103	101067

PARTY ONE	PARTY TWO	DATE	TOPIC	CITATION	NUMBER
UK Great Britain	Yugoslavia	26 Dec 49	General Trade	87UNTS71	101167
UK Great Britain	Yugoslavia	09 Feb 50	Finance	88UNTS287	101200
UK Great Britain	Yugoslavia	28 Dec 50	Loans and Credits	88UNTS329	101201
UK Great Britain	Yugoslavia	10 May 51	Loans and Credits	102UNTS29	101408
UK Great Britain	Yugoslavia	28 Sep 51	Finance	117UNTS107	101587
UK Great Britain	Yugoslavia	20 Aug 52	Finance	158UNTS439	102077
UK Great Britain	Yugoslavia	31 Dec 53	Education	190UNTS335	102574
UK Great Britain	Yugoslavia	22 Dec 54	Claims and Debts	207UNTS227	102808
UK Great Britain	Yugoslavia	31 Dec 54	Education	209UNTS81	102824
UK Great Britain	Yugoslavia	24 May 58	Non-ILO Labor	326UNTS69	104709
UK Great Britain	Yugoslavia	03 Feb 59	Loans and Credits	343UNTS153	104924
UK Great Britain	Yugoslavia	03 Feb 59	Air Transport	359UNTS339	105151
UK Great Britain	Yugoslavia	22 Jul 59	Admin Cooperation	374UNTS319	105345
UK Great Britain	Yugoslavia	12 Apr 60	Culture	360UNTS79	105155
UK Great Britain	Yugoslavia	08 Jun 61	Mass Media	437UNTS111	106300
UK Great Britain	Yugoslavia	21 Jul 61	Loans and Credits	420UNTS61	106040
UK Great Britain	Yugoslavia	13 Feb 62	Culture	431UNTS35	106207
UK Great Britain	Yugoslavia	28 Nov 62	Commodity Trade	470UNTS65	106796
UK Great Britain	Yugoslavia	16 Feb 63	Air Transport	507UNTS171	107400
UK Great Britain	Yugoslavia	18 Dec 63	Commodity Trade	502UNTS177	107328
UK Great Britain	Yugoslavia	01 Mar 65	General Trade	548UNTS85	107972
UK Great Britain	Yugoslavia	20 Apr 65	Visas	551UNTS69	108034
UK Great Britain	Yugoslavia	21 Apr 65	Consul/Citizenship	595UNTS189	108620
UK Great Britain	Yugoslavia	27 Jan 66	Culture	573UNTS243	108337
UK Great Britain	Yugoslavia	02 Feb 66	Commodity Trade	571UNTS275	108306
UK Great Britain	Yugoslavia	05 Jan 67	Mass Media	604UNTS13	108739
UK Great Britain	Yugoslavia	30 Jun 67	Postal Service	642UNTS325	109182
UK Great Britain	Yugoslavia	19 Apr 68	Scientific Project	0UNTS0	109657
UK Great Britain	Yugoslavia	03 Feb 69	Land Transport	0UNTS0	110437
UK Great Britain	Yugoslavia	29 Apr 69	Visas	0UNTS0	110024
UK Great Britain	Zambia	30 Jan 62	Non-ILO Labor	590UNTS173	108553
UK Great Britain	Zambia	28 Jul 66	Non-ILO Labor	590UNTS191	108554
UK Great Britain	Zambia	21 Feb 68	Military Mission	0UNTS0	109264
UK Great Britain	Zambia	06 Apr 68	Taxation	0UNTS0	110698
UK Great Britain	Zambia	23 Sep 68	Finance	0UNTS0	109814
Ukrainian SSR	Multilateral	02 Aug 44	Scientific Project	67UNTS221	200221
Ukrainian SSR	Multilateral	22 Jul 46	IGO Establishment	9UNTS3	100125
Ukrainian SSR	Multilateral	22 Jul 46	IGO Establishment	14UNTS185	100221
Ukrainian SSR	Multilateral	11 Dec 46	Sanitation	12UNTS179	100186
Ukrainian SSR	Multilateral	10 Feb 47	Peace/Disarmament	41UNTS135	100644
Ukrainian SSR	Multilateral	10 Feb 47	Peace/Disarmament	49UNTS3	100747
Ukrainian SSR	Multilateral	10 Feb 47	Peace/Disarmament	48UNTS203	100746
Ukrainian SSR	Multilateral	10 Feb 47	Peace/Disarmament	42UNTS3	100645
Ukrainian SSR	Multilateral	10 Feb 47	Peace/Disarmament	41UNTS21	100643
Ukrainian SSR	Multilateral	02 Oct 47	Telecommunications	193UNTS188	102616
Ukrainian SSR	Multilateral	11 Oct 47	IGO Establishment	77UNTS143	100998
Ukrainian SSR	Multilateral	24 Jul 48	Sanitation	66UNTS25	100847
Ukrainian SSR	Multilateral	18 Aug 48	Water Transport	33UNTS181	100518
Ukrainian SSR	Multilateral	19 Nov 48	Sanitation	44UNTS277	100688
Ukrainian SSR	Multilateral	09 Dec 48	Humanitarian	78UNTS277	101021
Ukrainian SSR	Multilateral	12 Aug 49	Humanitarian	75UNTS287	100973
Ukrainian SSR	Multilateral	12 Aug 49	Humanitarian	75UNTS85	100971
Ukrainian SSR	Multilateral	12 Aug 49	Humanitarian	75UNTS31	100970
Ukrainian SSR	Multilateral	12 Aug 49	General Military	75UNTS135	100972
Ukrainian SSR	Multilateral	21 Mar 50	Admin Cooperation	96UNTS271	101342
Ukrainian SSR	Multilateral	07 Dec 50	Admin Cooperation	212UNTS17	102861
Ukrainian SSR	Multilateral	11 Jul 52	Postal Service	170UNTS3	102221
Ukrainian SSR	Multilateral	11 Jul 52	IGO Establishment	169UNTS3	102220
Ukrainian SSR	Multilateral	31 Mar 53	Privil/Immunities	193UNTS136	102613
Ukrainian SSR	Multilateral	14 May 54	Culture	249UNTS215	103511
Ukrainian SSR	Multilateral	28 Sep 55	Air Transport	478UNTS371	106943
Ukrainian SSR	Multilateral	07 Sep 56	Humanitarian	266UNTS3	103822
Ukrainian SSR	Multilateral	26 Oct 56	IGO Establishment	276UNTS3	103988
Ukrainian SSR	Multilateral	20 Feb 57	Consul/Citizenship	309UNTS65	104468
Ukrainian SSR	Multilateral	03 Oct 57	Postal Service	364UNTS331	105212

PARTY ONE	PARTY TWO	DATE	TOPIC	CITATION	NUMBER
Ukrainian SSR	Multilateral	03 Oct 57	Postal Service	364UNTS3	105211
Ukrainian SSR	Multilateral	03 Oct 57	Postal Service	365UNTS3	105213
Ukrainian SSR	Multilateral	29 Apr 58	Water Transport	450UNTS11	106465
Ukrainian SSR	Multilateral	29 Apr 58	Territory Boundary	516UNTS205	107477
Ukrainian SSR	Multilateral	29 Apr 58	Territory Boundary	499UNTS311	107302
Ukrainian SSR	Multilateral	03 Dec 58	Admin Cooperation	398UNTS9	105715
Ukrainian SSR	Multilateral	03 Dec 58	Admin Cooperation	416UNTS51	105995
Ukrainian SSR	Multilateral	14 Dec 60	Education	429UNTS93	106193
Ukrainian SSR	Multilateral	30 Mar 61	Sanitation	520UNTS151	107515
Ukrainian SSR	Multilateral	18 Apr 61	Consul/Citizenship	500UNTS95	107310
Ukrainian SSR	Multilateral	21 Apr 61	IGO Establishment	484UNTS349	107041
Ukrainian SSR	Multilateral	05 Aug 63	Sanitation	480UNTS43	106964
Ukrainian SSR	Multilateral	10 Jul 64	Postal Service	611UNTS387	108846
Ukrainian SSR	Multilateral	10 Jul 64	Postal Service	611UNTS7	108844
Ukrainian SSR	Multilateral	10 Jul 64	Postal Service	612UNTS3	108847
Ukrainian SSR	Multilateral	10 Jul 64	Postal Service	611UNTS105	108845
Ukrainian SSR	Multilateral	13 Jul 64	ILO Labor	569UNTS65	108279
Ukrainian SSR	Multilateral	09 Mar 65	Water Transport	591UNTS265	108564
Ukrainian SSR	Multilateral	08 Jul 65	General Trade	597UNTS3	108641
Ukrainian SSR	Multilateral	22 Apr 68	Scientific Project	0UNTS0	109574
Ukrainian SSR	Multilateral	26 Nov 68	Humanitarian	0UNTS0	110823
UN Emergency Fund	Multilateral	13 Mar 56	Humanitarian	427UNTS245	106158
UN Hi Com Refugees	Sweden	08 Oct 56	Refugees	428UNTS307	106182
UN Mission Congo	Multilateral	15 Feb 64	Milit Installation	533UNTS98	107736
UN Relief Palestin	ILO (Labor Org)	31 Dec 52	Tech Assistance	182UNTS201	200506
UN Relief Palestin	Israel	09 Nov 56	Direct Aid	280UNTS261	104063
UN Relief Palestin	Israel	14 Jun 67	Direct Aid	620UNTS183	108955
UN Relief Palestin	Jordan	20 Aug 51	Refugees	120UNTS277	200394
UN Relief Palestin	Jordan	30 Mar 53	Direct Aid	165UNTS317	200495
UN Relief Palestin	Lebanon	26 Nov 54	Direct Aid	202UNTS123	102728
UN Relief Palestin	United Arab Rep	12 Sep 50	Refugees	121UNTS107	101630
UN Relief Palestin	United Arab Rep	30 Jun 53	Tech Assistance	190UNTS3	102554
UN Relief Palestin	United Arab Rep	14 Oct 53	Tech Assistance	190UNTS13	102555
UN Relief Palestin	WHO (World Health)	23 Sep 50	Sanitation	103UNTS129	200310
UN Special Fund	Afghanistan	21 Feb 60	Direct Aid	351UNTS93	105019
UN Special Fund	African Devel Bank	09 Oct 68	Non-IBRD Project	0UNTS0	200641
UN Special Fund	Algeria	15 Nov 62	Tech Assistance	452UNTS243	106512
UN Special Fund	Argentina	04 Dec 59	Direct Aid	345UNTS263	104972
UN Special Fund	Australia	30 Sep 64	Scientific Project	510UNTS277	107419
UN Special Fund	Australia	06 Feb 67	IGO Operations	590UNTS3	108543
UN Special Fund	Barbados	03 Mar 67	Tech Assistance	594UNTS91	108596
UN Special Fund	Bolivia	09 Feb 60	Direct Aid	351UNTS203	105024
UN Special Fund	Botswana	30 Sep 66	IGO Operations	576UNTS3	108360
UN Special Fund	Botswana	12 Oct 67	Direct Aid	607UNTS37	108794
UN Special Fund	Brazil	16 Sep 60	Tech Assistance	375UNTS3	105351
UN Special Fund	Bulgaria	26 May 66	General Aid	563UNTS71	108205
UN Special Fund	Burma	03 Jan 61	Direct Aid	387UNTS219	105564
UN Special Fund	Burundi	22 Aug 63	Direct Aid	476UNTS49	106903
UN Special Fund	Cambodia	24 Nov 60	Direct Aid	382UNTS255	105487
UN Special Fund	Cameroon	13 Jun 61	Direct Aid	397UNTS297	105713
UN Special Fund	Central Afri Rep	30 Oct 63	Direct Aid	481UNTS247	106985
UN Special Fund	Ceylon (Sri Lanka)	03 May 61	Direct Aid	395UNTS217	105687
UN Special Fund	Chad	23 Jan 61	Direct Aid	390UNTS69	105603
UN Special Fund	Chile	22 Jan 60	Direct Aid	351UNTS115	105020
UN Special Fund	Colombia	04 Feb 60	Direct Aid	355UNTS257	105080
UN Special Fund	Congo (Brazzaville)	09 Nov 61	Direct Aid	413UNTS58	105940
UN Special Fund	Congo (Zaire)	26 Jul 63	Direct Aid	474UNTS137	106878
UN Special Fund	Costa Rica	10 Jan 61	Direct Aid	389UNTS253	105597
UN Special Fund	Cuba	10 Mar 61	Direct Aid	390UNTS35	105601
UN Special Fund	Cyprus	24 Feb 61	Direct Aid	389UNTS3	105588
UN Special Fund	Czechoslovakia	13 Jul 67	Non-IBRD Project	606UNTS71	108776
UN Special Fund	Dahomey	28 Mar 62	Tech Assistance	424UNTS55	106099
UN Special Fund	Dominican Republic	06 Jun 62	Direct Aid	429UNTS169	106197
UN Special Fund	Ecuador	10 Nov 59	Direct Aid	345UNTS3	104955
UN Special Fund	El Salvador	24 Oct 60	Direct Aid	377UNTS171	105400

PARTY ONE	PARTY TWO	DATE	TOPIC	CITATION	NUMBER
UN Special Fund	Ethiopia	13 Jul 60	Tech Assistance	368UNTS159	105240
UN Special Fund	FAO (Food Agri)	28 Sep 59	IGO Operations	341UNTS353	200562
UN Special Fund	Fed of Malaya	25 Jul 61	Direct Aid	401UNTS159	105769
UN Special Fund	Fiji Islands	13 Oct 70	IGO Operations	0UNTS0	110792
UN Special Fund	France	17 Mar 60	Direct Aid	354UNTS119	105059
UN Special Fund	Gabon	02 Feb 61	Direct Aid	387UNTS289	105568
UN Special Fund	Gambia	09 Jun 65	IGO Operations	538UNTS321	200612
UN Special Fund	Gambia	25 Mar 70	Tech Assistance	0UNTS0	110397
UN Special Fund	Ghana	12 Aug 59	Direct Aid	338UNTS203	104836
UN Special Fund	Greece	13 Nov 59	Direct Aid	345UNTS171	104966
UN Special Fund	Guatemala	17 Nov 60	Direct Aid	383UNTS67	105495
UN Special Fund	Guinea	02 Dec 59	Direct Aid	345UNTS215	104969
UN Special Fund	Guinea	18 Jun 69	General Aid	0UNTS0	109742
UN Special Fund	Guyana	11 Jun 66	Non-IBRD Project	564UNTS201	200622
UN Special Fund	Haiti	28 Jun 61	Direct Aid	399UNTS171	105741
UN Special Fund	Honduras	20 Dec 60	Direct Aid	383UNTS103	105497
UN Special Fund	Hungary	28 Apr 67	General Aid	595UNTS171	108619
UN Special Fund	IAEA (Atom Energy)	29 Nov 61	IGO Operations	415UNTS408	200593
UN Special Fund	ICAO (Civil Aviat)	21 Apr 60	IGO Operations	360UNTS367	200569
UN Special Fund	Iceland	10 Jul 64	IGO Operations	502UNTS343	107337
UN Special Fund	ILO (Labor Org)	12 Oct 59	IGO Operations	343UNTS325	200563
UN Special Fund	India	20 Oct 59	Direct Aid	344UNTS143	104946
UN Special Fund	Indonesia	07 Oct 60	Direct Aid	378UNTS141	105424
UN Special Fund	Inter-Am Devel Bnk	16 Jul 68	Non-IBRD Project	640UNTS305	200640
UN Special Fund	Iran	06 Oct 59	Direct Aid	0IRTB86	433139
UN Special Fund	Iran	06 Oct 59	Direct Aid	342UNTS89	104902
UN Special Fund	Iraq	19 Jun 60	Direct Aid	376UNTS357	105389
UN Special Fund	Ireland	03 Jun 64	Direct Aid	496UNTS205	107253
UN Special Fund	Israel	01 Dec 59	Direct Aid	345UNTS197	104968
UN Special Fund	Italy	01 Apr 60	Direct Aid	354UNTS261	105066
UN Special Fund	ITU (Telecommun)	13 Jul 60	IGO Operations	368UNTS329	200573
UN Special Fund	Ivory Coast	29 Aug 61	Direct Aid	406UNTS129	105844
UN Special Fund	Jamaica	22 May 63	Direct Aid	489UNTS191	107140
UN Special Fund	Japan	31 Oct 62	Tech Assistance	444UNTS171	106368
UN Special Fund	Japan	27 Mar 69	IGO Operations	70JAIL191	440238
UN Special Fund	Japan	09 Sep 69	Education	0UNTS0	109930
UN Special Fund	Jordan	15 Dec 59	Direct Aid	346UNTS3	104974
UN Special Fund	Kenya	01 Oct 64	IGO Operations	511UNTS181	107433
UN Special Fund	Korea, South	21 Apr 61	Direct Aid	394UNTS231	200583
UN Special Fund	Kuwait	29 Jun 60	Tech Assistance	369UNTS419	200575
UN Special Fund	Laos	30 Apr 60	Tech Assistance	361UNTS171	105179
UN Special Fund	Lebanon	07 May 60	Tech Assistance	360UNTS225	105160
UN Special Fund	Lesotho	17 Nov 66	Recognition	580UNTS17	108416
UN Special Fund	Liberia	11 Oct 60	Direct Aid	376UNTS341	105388
UN Special Fund	Libya	19 Apr 60	Direct Aid	356UNTS11	105090
UN Special Fund	Malagasy	05 Jan 62	Direct Aid	419UNTS29	106028
UN Special Fund	Malawi	24 Oct 64	Direct Aid	514UNTS235	200609
UN Special Fund	Mali	21 Jul 61	Direct Aid	401UNTS141	105768
UN Special Fund	Mauritania	07 Nov 61	Direct Aid	412UNTS240	105936
UN Special Fund	Mexico	23 Feb 61	Direct Aid	388UNTS151	105576
UN Special Fund	Mongolia	26 Jan 66	Direct Aid	552UNTS201	108055
UN Special Fund	Morocco	04 Apr 59	Direct Aid	354UNTS347	105069
UN Special Fund	Multilateral	25 Jan 67	IGO Operations	588UNTS212	108527
UN Special Fund	Nepal	17 Nov 60	Direct Aid	380UNTS289	105461
UN Special Fund	Netherlands	12 Aug 60	Tech Assistance	372UNTS331	105309
UN Special Fund	Netherlands	24 May 63	Direct Aid	466UNTS289	106750
UN Special Fund	New Zealand	28 Jun 63	Non-IBRD Project	470UNTS3	106792
UN Special Fund	Nicaragua	20 Jan 61	Direct Aid	387UNTS15	105555
UN Special Fund	Niger	26 Feb 62	Direct Aid	423UNTS83	106086
UN Special Fund	Nigeria	10 Feb 61	Direct Aid	390UNTS85	105604
UN Special Fund	Pakistan	25 Feb 60	Direct Aid	351UNTS141	105021
UN Special Fund	Panama	09 Mar 61	Direct Aid	396UNTS3	105691
UN Special Fund	Paraguay	22 Jun 61	Direct Aid	399UNTS117	105738
UN Special Fund	Peru	19 Jan 60	Direct Aid	349UNTS83	105010
UN Special Fund	Philippines	28 Jun 61	Direct Aid	399UNTS141	105739

PARTY ONE	PARTY TWO	DATE	TOPIC	CITATION	NUMBER
UN Special Fund	Poland	15 Oct 59	Direct Aid	344UNTS29	104941
UN Special Fund	Romania	24 Oct 64	IGO Operations	519UNTS29	107500
UN Special Fund	Rwanda	18 Mar 64	Direct Aid	491UNTS3	107170
UN Special Fund	Saudi Arabia	19 Jan 61	Direct Aid	396UNTS27	105692
UN Special Fund	Senegal	16 Dec 61	Direct Aid	425UNTS97	106121
UN Special Fund	Sierra Leone	02 Oct 61	Direct Aid	422UNTS131	106073
UN Special Fund	Singapore	31 Dec 65	Admin Cooperation	552UNTS299	108061
UN Special Fund	Singapore	23 Sep 66	General Aid	573UNTS115	108326
UN Special Fund	Somalia	28 Jan 61	Direct Aid	388UNTS75	105573
UN Special Fund	Southern Yemen	04 Apr 69	Direct Aid	0UNTS0	109456
UN Special Fund	Spain	30 Jun 65	Direct Aid	544UNTS159	107918
UN Special Fund	Sudan	21 Apr 60	Direct Aid	356UNTS213	105097
UN Special Fund	Swaziland	18 Aug 69	Direct Aid	0UNTS0	109929
UN Special Fund	Syria	07 Jul 62	Direct Aid	443UNTS3	106355
UN Special Fund	Syria	22 Apr 68	IGO Operations	634UNTS207	109063
UN Special Fund	Taiwan	20 Sep 60	Tech Assistance	375UNTS29	105352
UN Special Fund	Tanganyika	17 Jul 62	Direct Aid	435UNTS237	106281
UN Special Fund	Thailand	04 Jun 60	Tech Assistance	360UNTS97	105157
UN Special Fund	Togo	08 Jun 60	Tech Assistance	369UNTS401	200574
UN Special Fund	Trinidad/Tobago	06 May 63	Direct Aid	463UNTS93	106695
UN Special Fund	Tunisia	12 Apr 60	Direct Aid	355UNTS289	105082
UN Special Fund	Turkey	20 Nov 59	Direct Aid	345UNTS105	104963
UN Special Fund	Uganda	19 Dec 62	Admin Cooperation	449UNTS41	106451
UN Special Fund	Uganda	22 Mar 63	Direct Aid	456UNTS466	106572
UN Special Fund	UK Great Britain	07 Jan 60	Direct Aid	348UNTS177	105000
UN Special Fund	UNESCO (Educ/Cult)	29 Sep 54	IGO Operations	363UNTS367	200572
UN Special Fund	United Arab Rep	25 Nov 59	Direct Aid	345UNTS125	104964
UN Special Fund	Upper Volta	26 Jun 61	Direct Aid	400UNTS3	105744
UN Special Fund	UPU (Postal Union)	21 Sep 66	Non-IBRD Project	573UNTS259	200626
UN Special Fund	Uruguay	04 May 62	Direct Aid	429UNTS143	106196
UN Special Fund	Venezuela	11 Dec 61	Direct Aid	422UNTS149	106074
UN Special Fund	Vietnam, South	29 Apr 60	Direct Aid	357UNTS311	200567
UN Special Fund	Vietnam, South	29 Apr 60	Direct Aid	0VKNG154	496046
UN Special Fund	Western Samoa	05 Jun 63	Direct Aid	467UNTS463	200601
UN Special Fund	WHO (World Health)	25 May 60	IGO Operations	359UNTS375	200568
UN Special Fund	WMO (Meteorology)	17 Nov 59	IGO Operations	345UNTS311	200564
UN Special Fund	Yemen	02 Aug 61	Direct Aid	402UNTS43	105777
UN Special Fund	Yugoslavia	27 Oct 59	Direct Aid	344UNTS159	104947
UN Special Fund	Zambia	15 Dec 64	Direct Aid	522UNTS3	107532
UN Special Fund	Zambia	04 Feb 65	Admin Cooperation	527UNTS115	107621
UNESCO (Educ/Cult)	Afghanistan	08 Dec 48	Education	46UNTS3	100697
UNESCO (Educ/Cult)	Austria	04 Nov 63	IGO Establishment	63ABGB337	403204
UNESCO (Educ/Cult)	FAO (Food Agri)	23 Aug 48	IGO Operations	18UNTS345	200112
UNESCO (Educ/Cult)	FAO (Food Agri)	09 Feb 49	IGO Operations	43UNTS315	200182
UNESCO (Educ/Cult)	France	25 Jun 54	Specific Property	55FRJO1208	416497
UNESCO (Educ/Cult)	France	02 Jul 54	IGO Status/Immunit	357UNTS3	105103
UNESCO (Educ/Cult)	Germany, West	06 May 69	IGO Operations	69WBGA207	424745
UNESCO (Educ/Cult)	IAEA (Atom Energy)	01 Oct 58	IGO Operations	339UNTS373	200558
UNESCO (Educ/Cult)	IAEA (Atom Energy)	15 Jul 69	IGO Operations	0UNTS0	200654
UNESCO (Educ/Cult)	Int Bureau Educ	29 Nov 68	IGO Operations	0UNTS0	200642
UNESCO (Educ/Cult)	Int Relief Union	24 Dec 68	IGO Operations	0UNTS0	200643
UNESCO (Educ/Cult)	Iran	16 Dec 68	Non-IBRD Project	0IRTB87	433144
UNESCO (Educ/Cult)	Morocco	13 May 64	Tech Assistance	0UNTS0	109220
UNESCO (Educ/Cult)	Morocco	18 Dec 67	IGO Operations	0UNTS0	109221
UNESCO (Educ/Cult)	Multilateral	02 Nov 50	Tech Assistance	81UNTS160	101071
UNESCO (Educ/Cult)	Multilateral	24 Nov 50	Tech Assistance	81UNTS188	101072
UNESCO (Educ/Cult)	Multilateral	15 Dec 50	Tech Assistance	76UNTS120	100985
UNESCO (Educ/Cult)	Multilateral	18 Jan 51	Tech Assistance	81UNTS233	101073
UNESCO (Educ/Cult)	Multilateral	15 Feb 51	Tech Assistance	81UNTS245	101074
UNESCO (Educ/Cult)	Multilateral	05 Mar 51	Tech Assistance	81UNTS261	101075
UNESCO (Educ/Cult)	Multilateral	20 Mar 51	IGO Operations	82UNTS172	101091
UNESCO (Educ/Cult)	Multilateral	28 Mar 51	Tech Assistance	181UNTS61	102399
UNESCO (Educ/Cult)	Multilateral	05 Apr 51	Tech Assistance	84UNTS299	101139
UNESCO (Educ/Cult)	Multilateral	25 Jun 51	Tech Assistance	92UNTS27	101258
UNESCO (Educ/Cult)	Multilateral	28 Jun 51	Tech Assistance	118UNTS154	101604

PARTY ONE	PARTY TWO	DATE	TOPIC	CITATION	NUMBER
UNESCO (Educ/Cult)	Multilateral	27 Jul 51	Tech Assistance	97UNTS291	200273
UNESCO (Educ/Cult)	Multilateral	24 Dec 51	Tech Assistance	118UNTS290	200383
UNESCO (Educ/Cult)	Multilateral	18 Feb 52	Tech Assistance	126UNTS319	200434
UNESCO (Educ/Cult)	Multilateral	11 Apr 52	Tech Assistance	173UNTS2	102255
UNESCO (Educ/Cult)	Multilateral	22 May 52	Tech Assistance	131UNTS115	101739
UNESCO (Educ/Cult)	Multilateral	19 Jun 52	Tech Assistance	133UNTS165	101787
UNESCO (Educ/Cult)	Multilateral	15 Oct 52	Tech Assistance	141UNTS96	101909
UNESCO (Educ/Cult)	Multilateral	16 Dec 52	Tech Assistance	158UNTS407	102074
UNESCO (Educ/Cult)	Multilateral	29 Dec 52	Tech Assistance	151UNTS317	102002
UNESCO (Educ/Cult)	Multilateral	09 Oct 53	Tech Assistance	190UNTS49	102557
UNESCO (Educ/Cult)	Multilateral	20 Apr 54	Tech Assistance	189UNTS11	102539
UNESCO (Educ/Cult)	Multilateral	31 May 54	Tech Assistance	192UNTS20	102592
UNESCO (Educ/Cult)	Multilateral	01 Jun 54	Tech Assistance	200UNTS235	200520
UNESCO (Educ/Cult)	Multilateral	30 Jun 54	Tech Assistance	193UNTS67	102611
UNESCO (Educ/Cult)	Multilateral	19 Aug 54	Tech Assistance	201UNTS51	102710
UNESCO (Educ/Cult)	Multilateral	06 Oct 54	Tech Assistance	201UNTS75	102711
UNESCO (Educ/Cult)	Multilateral	27 Oct 54	Tech Assistance	201UNTS95	102712
UNESCO (Educ/Cult)	Multilateral	29 Oct 54	Tech Assistance	201UNTS115	102713
UNESCO (Educ/Cult)	Multilateral	16 Dec 54	Tech Assistance	204UNTS323	200523
UNESCO (Educ/Cult)	Multilateral	04 Apr 55	Tech Assistance	208UNTS239	102816
UNESCO (Educ/Cult)	Multilateral	14 Jun 55	Tech Assistance	212UNTS263	200526
UNESCO (Educ/Cult)	Multilateral	04 Jul 55	Tech Assistance	214UNTS10	102897
UNESCO (Educ/Cult)	Multilateral	13 Dec 55	Tech Assistance	407UNTS8	105857
UNESCO (Educ/Cult)	Multilateral	02 Feb 56	Tech Assistance	227UNTS153	103137
UNESCO (Educ/Cult)	Multilateral	10 Feb 56	Tech Assistance	228UNTS167	103150
UNESCO (Educ/Cult)	Multilateral	10 Feb 56	Tech Assistance	228UNTS189	103151
UNESCO (Educ/Cult)	Multilateral	30 Mar 56	IGO Operations	604UNTS114	108748
UNESCO (Educ/Cult)	Multilateral	10 May 56	Tech Assistance	243UNTS103	103449
UNESCO (Educ/Cult)	Multilateral	31 May 56	Tech Assistance	251UNTS181	103541
UNESCO (Educ/Cult)	Multilateral	08 Jun 56	Tech Assistance	247UNTS366	200541
UNESCO (Educ/Cult)	Multilateral	12 Jun 56	Tech Assistance	243UNTS187	103453
UNESCO (Educ/Cult)	Multilateral	14 Jun 56	Tech Assistance	265UNTS125	103809
UNESCO (Educ/Cult)	Multilateral	26 Jun 56	Tech Assistance	321UNTS2	104650
UNESCO (Educ/Cult)	Multilateral	26 Jun 56	Tech Assistance	253UNTS12	103573
UNESCO (Educ/Cult)	Multilateral	02 Jul 56	Tech Assistance	540UNTS110	107846
UNESCO (Educ/Cult)	Multilateral	02 Jul 56	Tech Assistance	248UNTS37	103484
UNESCO (Educ/Cult)	Multilateral	31 Aug 56	Tech Assistance	249UNTS158	103506
UNESCO (Educ/Cult)	Multilateral	05 Oct 56	Tech Assistance	251UNTS245	103544
UNESCO (Educ/Cult)	Multilateral	05 Oct 56	Tech Assistance	251UNTS267	103545
UNESCO (Educ/Cult)	Multilateral	21 Nov 56	Tech Assistance	253UNTS266	103588
UNESCO (Educ/Cult)	Multilateral	15 Jan 57	Tech Assistance	376UNTS122	105378
UNESCO (Educ/Cult)	Multilateral	23 Jan 57	Tech Assistance	259UNTS426	103701
UNESCO (Educ/Cult)	Multilateral	17 Feb 57	Tech Assistance	271UNTS2	103907
UNESCO (Educ/Cult)	Multilateral	01 Mar 57	Tech Assistance	264UNTS94	103790
UNESCO (Educ/Cult)	Multilateral	28 Mar 57	Tech Assistance	271UNTS30	103908
UNESCO (Educ/Cult)	Multilateral	09 Apr 57	Tech Assistance	274UNTS172	103965
UNESCO (Educ/Cult)	Multilateral	24 May 57	Tech Assistance	268UNTS270	103861
UNESCO (Educ/Cult)	Multilateral	30 Jun 57	Tech Assistance	286UNTS171	104165
UNESCO (Educ/Cult)	Multilateral	09 Jul 57	Tech Assistance	274UNTS300	103972
UNESCO (Educ/Cult)	Multilateral	05 Nov 57	Tech Assistance	285UNTS301	104155
UNESCO (Educ/Cult)	Multilateral	15 Mar 58	Tech Assistance	292UNTS273	104276
UNESCO (Educ/Cult)	Multilateral	19 Jun 58	Tech Assistance	306UNTS236	200550
UNESCO (Educ/Cult)	Multilateral	09 Oct 59	Tech Assistance	376UNTS382	105391
UNESCO (Educ/Cult)	Multilateral	03 Dec 59	Tech Assistance	348UNTS246	105003
UNESCO (Educ/Cult)	Multilateral	12 Apr 60	Tech Assistance	359UNTS323	105150
UNESCO (Educ/Cult)	Multilateral	04 Jun 60	Tech Assistance	360UNTS208	105159
UNESCO (Educ/Cult)	Multilateral	19 Jun 60	IGO Operations	537UNTS214	107803
UNESCO (Educ/Cult)	Multilateral	08 Jul 60	Tech Assistance	366UNTS310	105220
UNESCO (Educ/Cult)	Multilateral	28 Jan 61	Tech Assistance	387UNTS202	105563
UNESCO (Educ/Cult)	Multilateral	20 Sep 61	Tech Assistance	407UNTS52	105859
UNESCO (Educ/Cult)	Multilateral	16 Oct 61	Tech Assistance	410UNTS242	105908
UNESCO (Educ/Cult)	Multilateral	07 Nov 61	Tech Assistance	412UNTS258	105937
UNESCO (Educ/Cult)	Multilateral	27 Dec 61	Tech Assistance	425UNTS83	106120
UNESCO (Educ/Cult)	Multilateral	17 Jan 62	Tech Assistance	419UNTS294	106033
UNESCO (Educ/Cult)	Multilateral	20 Jan 62	Tech Assistance	429UNTS230	200596

PARTY ONE	PARTY TWO	DATE	TOPIC	CITATION	NUMBER
UNESCO (Educ/Cult)	Multilateral	13 Feb 62	Tech Assistance	422UNTS288	200594
UNESCO (Educ/Cult)	Multilateral	21 Feb 62	Tech Assistance	423UNTS151	106091
UNESCO (Educ/Cult)	Multilateral	01 Mar 62	Tech Assistance	423UNTS122	106089
UNESCO (Educ/Cult)	Multilateral	10 Apr 62	Tech Assistance	429UNTS78	106192
UNESCO (Educ/Cult)	Multilateral	18 Apr 62	Tech Assistance	463UNTS44	106692
UNESCO (Educ/Cult)	Multilateral	17 May 62	Tech Assistance	429UNTS46	106189
UNESCO (Educ/Cult)	Multilateral	12 Aug 62	Tech Assistance	443UNTS266	106365
UNESCO (Educ/Cult)	Multilateral	29 Aug 62	Tech Assistance	443UNTS280	106366
UNESCO (Educ/Cult)	Multilateral	11 Sep 62	Tech Assistance	455UNTS402	106553
UNESCO (Educ/Cult)	Multilateral	14 Sep 62	Visas	443UNTS73	106360
UNESCO (Educ/Cult)	Multilateral	15 Nov 62	Tech Assistance	448UNTS50	106424
UNESCO (Educ/Cult)	Multilateral	06 Dec 62	Tech Assistance	450UNTS240	106471
UNESCO (Educ/Cult)	Multilateral	12 Dec 62	Tech Assistance	457UNTS72	106578
UNESCO (Educ/Cult)	Multilateral	21 Jan 63	Tech Assistance	453UNTS20	106517
UNESCO (Educ/Cult)	Multilateral	05 Feb 63	Tech Assistance	453UNTS36	106518
UNESCO (Educ/Cult)	Multilateral	14 Feb 63	Tech Assistance	453UNTS168	106524
UNESCO (Educ/Cult)	Multilateral	06 Mar 63	Tech Assistance	455UNTS386	106552
UNESCO (Educ/Cult)	Multilateral	18 Apr 63	Tech Assistance	463UNTS121	106697
UNESCO (Educ/Cult)	Multilateral	06 May 63	Tech Assistance	463UNTS78	106694
UNESCO (Educ/Cult)	Multilateral	09 May 63	Tech Assistance	463UNTS159	106700
UNESCO (Educ/Cult)	Multilateral	22 May 63	Tech Assistance	483UNTS72	107007
UNESCO (Educ/Cult)	Multilateral	24 May 63	Tech Assistance	470UNTS208	106810
UNESCO (Educ/Cult)	Multilateral	24 May 63	Tech Assistance	466UNTS346	106754
UNESCO (Educ/Cult)	Multilateral	23 Jul 63	Tech Assistance	471UNTS158	106831
UNESCO (Educ/Cult)	Multilateral	31 Jul 63	Tech Assistance	472UNTS220	106842
UNESCO (Educ/Cult)	Multilateral	27 Aug 63	Tech Assistance	511UNTS210	107435
UNESCO (Educ/Cult)	Multilateral	10 Sep 63	Tech Assistance	480UNTS100	106965
UNESCO (Educ/Cult)	Multilateral	30 Oct 63	Tech Assistance	480UNTS180	106968
UNESCO (Educ/Cult)	Multilateral	07 Nov 63	Tech Assistance	480UNTS232	106971
UNESCO (Educ/Cult)	Multilateral	08 Nov 63	Tech Assistance	482UNTS286	106999
UNESCO (Educ/Cult)	Multilateral	09 Nov 63	Direct Aid	489UNTS209	107141
UNESCO (Educ/Cult)	Multilateral	28 Jan 64	Tech Assistance	502UNTS321	107336
UNESCO (Educ/Cult)	Multilateral	20 Feb 64	Tech Assistance	491UNTS30	107172
UNESCO (Educ/Cult)	Multilateral	23 Jun 64	Tech Assistance	506UNTS108	107383
UNESCO (Educ/Cult)	Multilateral	28 Jun 64	Tech Assistance	519UNTS14	107499
UNESCO (Educ/Cult)	Multilateral	03 Aug 64	Tech Assistance	503UNTS239	107347
UNESCO (Educ/Cult)	Multilateral	24 Oct 64	Tech Assistance	514UNTS220	200608
UNESCO (Educ/Cult)	Multilateral	11 Nov 64	Tech Assistance	515UNTS94	107456
UNESCO (Educ/Cult)	Multilateral	11 Dec 64	IGO Operations	547UNTS297	107964
UNESCO (Educ/Cult)	Multilateral	15 Dec 64	Tech Assistance	522UNTS20	107533
UNESCO (Educ/Cult)	Multilateral	27 Jan 65	Tech Assistance	523UNTS102	107556
UNESCO (Educ/Cult)	Multilateral	02 Feb 65	Tech Assistance	523UNTS256	107560
UNESCO (Educ/Cult)	Multilateral	12 Feb 65	Tech Assistance	525UNTS148	107587
UNESCO (Educ/Cult)	Multilateral	23 Feb 65	IGO Operations	527UNTS120	107622
UNESCO (Educ/Cult)	Multilateral	05 Mar 65	IGO Operations	527UNTS221	107627
UNESCO (Educ/Cult)	Multilateral	08 Apr 65	IGO Operations	533UNTS66	107733
UNESCO (Educ/Cult)	Multilateral	26 Apr 65	IGO Operations	533UNTS50	107732
UNESCO (Educ/Cult)	Multilateral	12 May 65	IGO Operations	534UNTS390	107769
UNESCO (Educ/Cult)	Multilateral	14 May 65	IGO Operations	550UNTS310	108026
UNESCO (Educ/Cult)	Multilateral	25 May 65	IGO Operations	535UNTS374	107791
UNESCO (Educ/Cult)	Multilateral	02 Jun 65	Tech Assistance	537UNTS348	200611
UNESCO (Educ/Cult)	Multilateral	02 Jun 65	Tech Assistance	551UNTS2	108030
UNESCO (Educ/Cult)	Multilateral	05 Jul 65	General Aid	563UNTS104	108207
UNESCO (Educ/Cult)	Multilateral	20 Jul 65	IGO Operations	541UNTS12	107857
UNESCO (Educ/Cult)	Multilateral	13 Sep 65	Tech Assistance	547UNTS264	107962
UNESCO (Educ/Cult)	Multilateral	13 Sep 65	IGO Operations	547UNTS248	107961
UNESCO (Educ/Cult)	Multilateral	21 Sep 65	IGO Operations	547UNTS280	107963
UNESCO (Educ/Cult)	Multilateral	21 Oct 65	Tech Assistance	547UNTS216	107959
UNESCO (Educ/Cult)	Multilateral	12 Nov 65	IGO Operations	550UNTS160	108013
UNESCO (Educ/Cult)	Multilateral	31 Dec 65	Recognition	552UNTS292	108060
UNESCO (Educ/Cult)	Multilateral	12 May 66	General Aid	563UNTS54	108204
UNESCO (Educ/Cult)	Multilateral	06 Aug 66	Tech Assistance	570UNTS178	108294
UNESCO (Educ/Cult)	Multilateral	22 Aug 66	Tech Assistance	571UNTS298	200624
UNESCO (Educ/Cult)	Multilateral	23 Sep 66	IGO Operations	573UNTS132	108327
UNESCO (Educ/Cult)	Multilateral	23 Sep 66	General Aid	573UNTS148	108328

PARTY ONE	PARTY TWO	DATE	TOPIC	CITATION	NUMBER
UNESCO (Educ/Cult)	Multilateral	30 Sep 66	IGO Operations	576UNTS8	108361
UNESCO (Educ/Cult)	Multilateral	17 Nov 66	IGO Operations	580UNTS22	108417
UNESCO (Educ/Cult)	Multilateral	25 Jan 67	IGO Operations	588UNTS212	108527
UNESCO (Educ/Cult)	Multilateral	27 Feb 67	IGO Operations	590UNTS156	108552
UNESCO (Educ/Cult)	Multilateral	03 Mar 67	Tech Assistance	594UNTS96	108597
UNESCO (Educ/Cult)	Multilateral	13 Apr 67	IGO Operations	595UNTS60	108612
UNESCO (Educ/Cult)	Multilateral	19 Apr 67	Tech Assistance	595UNTS120	108617
UNESCO (Educ/Cult)	Multilateral	10 Jun 67	Direct Aid	602UNTS212	108714
UNESCO (Educ/Cult)	Multilateral	14 Jun 67	Direct Aid	603UNTS2	108719
UNESCO (Educ/Cult)	Multilateral	20 Jun 67	Tech Assistance	0UNTS0	109290
UNESCO (Educ/Cult)	Multilateral	21 Jun 67	Tech Assistance	598UNTS2	108653
UNESCO (Educ/Cult)	Multilateral	12 Oct 67	Direct Aid	607UNTS2	108792
UNESCO (Educ/Cult)	Multilateral	12 Oct 67	Direct Aid	607UNTS20	108793
UNESCO (Educ/Cult)	Multilateral	27 Oct 67	General Aid	608UNTS37	108811
UNESCO (Educ/Cult)	Multilateral	14 Nov 67	Admin Cooperation	614UNTS2	108860
UNESCO (Educ/Cult)	Multilateral	18 Jun 69	IGO Operations	0UNTS0	109740
UNESCO (Educ/Cult)	Multilateral	18 Jun 69	IGO Operations	0UNTS0	109741
UNESCO (Educ/Cult)	Multilateral	24 Jun 69	IGO Operations	0UNTS0	109743
UNESCO (Educ/Cult)	Multilateral	26 Sep 70	IGO Operations	0UNTS0	110768
UNESCO (Educ/Cult)	Thailand	25 Aug 61	IGO Operations	410UNTS125	105899
UNESCO (Educ/Cult)	Tunisia	03 Jan 57	Direct Aid	257UNTS21	103645
UNESCO (Educ/Cult)	UK Great Britain	09 Aug 56	Direct Aid	256UNTS139	103624
UNESCO (Educ/Cult)	UN Special Fund	29 Sep 54	IGO Operations	363UNTS367	200572
UNESCO (Educ/Cult)	United Arab Rep	09 Nov 63	Culture	489UNTS233	107142
UNESCO (Educ/Cult)	United Nations	03 Feb 47	IGO Operations	1UNTS233	200011
UNESCO (Educ/Cult)	United Nations	07 Mar 51	IGO Operations	139UNTS417	200468
UNESCO (Educ/Cult)	USA (United States)	19 Jan 62	Culture	435UNTS99	106272
UNESCO (Educ/Cult)	USA (United States)	16 Oct 64	Specific Property	550UNTS23	108006
UNESCO (Educ/Cult)	WHO (World Health)	15 Jul 48	IGO Operations	44UNTS323	200184
UNESCO (Educ/Cult)	Yugoslavia	27 Feb 64	IGO Operations	489UNTS257	107143
UNICEF (Children)	Afghanistan	04 Jul 50	IGO Operations	71UNTS3	100906
UNICEF (Children)	Afghanistan	22 Oct 70	IGO Operations	0UNTS0	110797
UNICEF (Children)	Albania	20 Nov 47	IGO Operations	65UNTS163	200208
UNICEF (Children)	Algeria	20 Nov 62	Direct Aid	453UNTS151	106522
UNICEF (Children)	Argentina	19 Nov 57	Direct Aid	300UNTS229	104338
UNICEF (Children)	Australia	21 Dec 67	IGO Operations	614UNTS83	108864
UNICEF (Children)	Austria	07 Nov 47	IGO Operations	68UNTS252	200237
UNICEF (Children)	Barbados	30 Mar 68	IGO Operations	637UNTS0	109123
UNICEF (Children)	Belgium	17 Jun 52	Direct Aid	171UNTS249	102228
UNICEF (Children)	Bolivia	03 Feb 50	Tech Assistance	65UNTS82	100835
UNICEF (Children)	Botswana	25 Jun 68	IGO Operations	639UNTS61	109144
UNICEF (Children)	Brazil	09 Jun 50	IGO Operations	66UNTS75	100848
UNICEF (Children)	Brazil	28 Mar 66	IGO Operations	607UNTS235	108807
UNICEF (Children)	Bulgaria	23 Aug 47	IGO Operations	68UNTS223	200232
UNICEF (Children)	Bulgaria	10 Mar 66	IGO Operations	559UNTS13	108152
UNICEF (Children)	Burma	22 Apr 50	IGO Operations	68UNTS96	100888
UNICEF (Children)	Burundi	08 Jan 64	IGO Operations	485UNTS45	107045
UNICEF (Children)	Cambodia	28 Apr 56	Direct Aid	136UNTS341	200446
UNICEF (Children)	Cambodia	25 Jun 56	Direct Aid	249UNTS153	103505
UNICEF (Children)	Cameroon	12 Aug 61	Direct Aid	402UNTS235	105788
UNICEF (Children)	Central Afri Rep	21 Aug 61	Direct Aid	413UNTS48	105939
UNICEF (Children)	Ceylon (Sri Lanka)	07 Jun 50	IGO Operations	68UNTS256	200239
UNICEF (Children)	Ceylon (Sri Lanka)	27 Jan 69	IGO Operations	0UNTS0	109394
UNICEF (Children)	Chad	26 Aug 61	Direct Aid	422UNTS231	106077
UNICEF (Children)	Chile	03 Mar 50	Direct Aid	126UNTS119	101685
UNICEF (Children)	Chile	30 Nov 65	IGO Operations	596UNTS215	108635
UNICEF (Children)	Colombia	15 Mar 50	Tech Assistance	65UNTS104	100838
UNICEF (Children)	Congo (Brazzaville)	09 Apr 62	Direct Aid	431UNTS65	106210
UNICEF (Children)	Costa Rica	14 Jan 50	Tech Assistance	65UNTS70	100830
UNICEF (Children)	Cuba	11 Feb 60	Direct Aid	349UNTS277	105014
UNICEF (Children)	Cyprus	19 Apr 61	Direct Aid	394UNTS185	105678
UNICEF (Children)	Czechoslovakia	03 Oct 47	Tech Assistance	65UNTS26	100816
UNICEF (Children)	Dahomey	28 Aug 63	IGO Operations	507UNTS101	107396
UNICEF (Children)	Dominican Republic	15 Feb 52	Humanitarian	121UNTS43	101625
UNICEF (Children)	Ecuador	12 Oct 49	Tech Assistance	65UNTS62	100827

PARTY ONE	PARTY TWO	DATE	TOPIC	CITATION	NUMBER
UNICEF (Children)	El Salvador	18 Jan 50	Tech Assistance	65UNTS78	100833
UNICEF (Children)	Ethiopia	27 Apr 53	Direct Aid	213UNTS169	102885
UNICEF (Children)	Ethiopia	01 Apr 63	IGO Operations	457UNTS103	106579
UNICEF (Children)	Finland	23 Aug 47	IGO Operations	68UNTS224	200233
UNICEF (Children)	France	19 Feb 48	IGO Operations	68UNTS75	100885
UNICEF (Children)	Gabon	02 Nov 61	Direct Aid	422UNTS241	106078
UNICEF (Children)	Gambia	29 May 65	IGO Operations	547UNTS29	107954
UNICEF (Children)	Ghana	12 Aug 58	Direct Aid	309UNTS103	104469
UNICEF (Children)	Greece	14 Oct 47	Humanitarian	102UNTS39	101409
UNICEF (Children)	Guatemala	09 Feb 50	Tech Assistance	65UNTS84	100836
UNICEF (Children)	Guatemala	22 Nov 55	Direct Aid	221UNTS305	103012
UNICEF (Children)	Guinea	08 Jun 59	Direct Aid	334UNTS277	104772
UNICEF (Children)	Guinea	22 Dec 66	IGO Operations	585UNTS137	108486
UNICEF (Children)	Guyana	02 Jul 69	IGO Operations	0UNTS0	109744
UNICEF (Children)	Haiti	20 Dec 49	Tech Assistance	65UNTS68	100829
UNICEF (Children)	Honduras	17 Jan 50	Tech Assistance	65UNTS74	100831
UNICEF (Children)	Hungary	28 Aug 47	IGO Operations	68UNTS226	200234
UNICEF (Children)	India	10 May 49	IGO Operations	68UNTS96	100887
UNICEF (Children)	Indonesia	06 Apr 50	IGO Operations	68UNTS254	200238
UNICEF (Children)	Indonesia	04 Jul 55	Admin Cooperation	212UNTS13	102860
UNICEF (Children)	Indonesia	17 Nov 66	IGO Operations	578UNTS47	108386
UNICEF (Children)	Iran	02 Aug 51	Direct Aid	247UNTS11	103457
UNICEF (Children)	Iran	21 Nov 63	IGO Operations	485UNTS35	107044
UNICEF (Children)	Iran	21 Nov 63	Direct Aid	0IRTB86	433140
UNICEF (Children)	Iraq	10 Dec 51	Direct Aid	126UNTS57	101682
UNICEF (Children)	Iraq	03 Dec 63	IGO Operations	482UNTS319	107001
UNICEF (Children)	Israel	20 Sep 48	Direct Aid	71UNTS17	100907
UNICEF (Children)	Italy	06 Nov 47	IGO Operations	68UNTS240	200236
UNICEF (Children)	Italy	28 May 56	Direct Aid	243UNTS43	103445
UNICEF (Children)	Ivory Coast	10 Jan 62	Direct Aid	422UNTS261	106080
UNICEF (Children)	Jamaica	19 May 64	IGO Operations	500UNTS75	107308
UNICEF (Children)	Japan	21 Nov 53	Direct Aid	183UNTS297	200507
UNICEF (Children)	Jordan	08 Jul 52	Direct Aid	173UNTS353	200503
UNICEF (Children)	Jordan	09 Aug 58	Direct Aid	309UNTS297	104478
UNICEF (Children)	Jordan	24 Mar 69	IGO Operations	0UNTS0	109488
UNICEF (Children)	Kenya	24 Jun 70	IGO Operations	0UNTS0	110562
UNICEF (Children)	Korea, South	25 Mar 50	IGO Operations	65UNTS171	200209
UNICEF (Children)	Kuwait	26 Jan 69	IGO Operations	0UNTS0	109792
UNICEF (Children)	Laos	15 Aug 52	Direct Aid	161UNTS323	200491
UNICEF (Children)	Laos	11 Jan 58	Claims and Debts	287UNTS255	104191
UNICEF (Children)	Lebanon	03 Jul 56	Direct Aid	324UNTS145	104683
UNICEF (Children)	Liberia	17 Apr 52	Direct Aid	133UNTS3	101773
UNICEF (Children)	Liberia	08 Jun 66	General Amity	570UNTS31	108286
UNICEF (Children)	Libya	05 Apr 52	Direct Aid	133UNTS287	200441
UNICEF (Children)	Malagasy	16 Nov 61	Direct Aid	422UNTS251	106079
UNICEF (Children)	Malaysia	01 Jul 64	IGO Operations	503UNTS229	107346
UNICEF (Children)	Maldive Islands	06 Apr 70	IGO Operations	0UNTS0	110414
UNICEF (Children)	Mali	17 Nov 60	Direct Aid	402UNTS23	105775
UNICEF (Children)	Malta	22 Apr 65	IGO Operations	533UNTS107	107737
UNICEF (Children)	Mauritania	19 Jan 63	Direct Aid	452UNTS271	106514
UNICEF (Children)	Mexico	20 May 54	Direct Aid	192UNTS3	102591
UNICEF (Children)	Mongolia	23 Jun 65	IGO Operations	540UNTS83	107844
UNICEF (Children)	Morocco	31 Jul 57	Direct Aid	282UNTS99	104095
UNICEF (Children)	Multilateral	01 Aug 51	Sanitation	107UNTS19	101464
UNICEF (Children)	Nepal	12 Dec 60	Direct Aid	382UNTS273	105488
UNICEF (Children)	Netherlands	31 Dec 54	Direct Aid	202UNTS135	102729
UNICEF (Children)	New Zealand	26 Aug 54	Direct Aid	198UNTS173	102663
UNICEF (Children)	Nicaragua	17 Jan 50	Tech Assistance	65UNTS76	100832
UNICEF (Children)	Niger	05 Dec 62	IGO Operations	503UNTS195	107344
UNICEF (Children)	Pakistan	20 Jun 49	Tech Assistance	65UNTS60	100826
UNICEF (Children)	Panama	14 Jun 51	IGO Operations	97UNTS3	101343
UNICEF (Children)	Paraguay	25 Jan 51	IGO Operations	79UNTS9	101027
UNICEF (Children)	Peru	31 Jan 50	Tech Assistance	65UNTS80	100834
UNICEF (Children)	Philippines	20 Nov 48	Tech Assistance	65UNTS48	100819
UNICEF (Children)	Poland	23 Aug 47	Tech Assistance	65UNTS22	100815

PARTY ONE	PARTY TWO	DATE	TOPIC	CITATION	NUMBER
UNICEF (Children)	Poland	24 Aug 61	Direct Aid	406UNTS95	105841
UNICEF (Children)	Romania	28 Aug 47	IGO Operations	68UNTS228	200235
UNICEF (Children)	Rwanda	11 Sep 64	IGO Operations	510UNTS127	107409
UNICEF (Children)	Saudi Arabia	04 Jul 61	Direct Aid	413UNTS122	105947
UNICEF (Children)	Senegal	22 Jan 64	IGO Operations	486UNTS91	107074
UNICEF (Children)	Sierra Leone	11 Apr 62	Direct Aid	431UNTS55	106209
UNICEF (Children)	Singapore	31 Jul 69	IGO Operations	0UNTS0	109736
UNICEF (Children)	Somalia	01 Apr 62	Direct Aid	431UNTS75	106211
UNICEF (Children)	Southern Yemen	26 Jul 69	IGO Operations	0UNTS0	109730
UNICEF (Children)	Spain	07 May 54	Direct Aid	190UNTS357	200515
UNICEF (Children)	Sudan	07 Aug 56	Direct Aid	248UNTS307	200542
UNICEF (Children)	Syria	10 Jul 52	Direct Aid	136UNTS17	101830
UNICEF (Children)	Taiwan	21 May 48	Tech Assistance	65UNTS38	100818
UNICEF (Children)	Taiwan	19 Jul 50	IGO Operations	94UNTS21	101304
UNICEF (Children)	Taiwan	08 Apr 64	IGO Operations	500UNTS49	107306
UNICEF (Children)	Tanganyika	25 Jan 63	Direct Aid	453UNTS249	106528
UNICEF (Children)	Thailand	01 Dec 48	IGO Operations	68UNTS94	100886
UNICEF (Children)	Togo	27 Jun 63	IGO Operations	540UNTS135	107847
UNICEF (Children)	Trinidad/Tobago	08 Aug 63	IGO Operations	473UNTS281	106865
UNICEF (Children)	Turkey	05 Sep 51	Direct Aid	193UNTS55	102610
UNICEF (Children)	UK Great Britain	13 Jun 49	Tech Assistance	65UNTS58	100825
UNICEF (Children)	UK Great Britain	17 Jun 49	Tech Assistance	65UNTS54	100821
UNICEF (Children)	UK Great Britain	17 Jun 49	Tech Assistance	65UNTS56	100823
UNICEF (Children)	UK Great Britain	17 Jun 49	Tech Assistance	65UNTS50	100820
UNICEF (Children)	UK Great Britain	17 Jun 49	Tech Assistance	65UNTS54	100822
UNICEF (Children)	UK Great Britain	17 Jun 49	Tech Assistance	65UNTS56	100824
UNICEF (Children)	UK Great Britain	19 Dec 49	Tech Assistance	65UNTS64	100828
UNICEF (Children)	UK Great Britain	10 Feb 50	Direct Aid	65UNTS86	100837
UNICEF (Children)	UK Great Britain	02 Oct 51	Direct Aid	104UNTS301	101448
UNICEF (Children)	UK Great Britain	04 Feb 52	Direct Aid	120UNTS147	101620
UNICEF (Children)	UK Great Britain	15 Feb 52	Direct Aid	121UNTS63	101626
UNICEF (Children)	UK Great Britain	25 Jul 52	Direct Aid	135UNTS37	101812
UNICEF (Children)	UK Great Britain	16 Dec 52	Direct Aid	151UNTS359	102005
UNICEF (Children)	UK Great Britain	07 Oct 53	Tech Assistance	180UNTS59	102375
UNICEF (Children)	United Arab Rep	18 May 52	Direct Aid	324UNTS161	104684
UNICEF (Children)	Upper Volta	15 Nov 60	Direct Aid	402UNTS33	105776
UNICEF (Children)	Uruguay	18 Dec 56	IGO Operations	0UNTS0	109398
UNICEF (Children)	Venezuela	25 Oct 67	IGO Operations	0UNTS0	109337
UNICEF (Children)	Vietnam, South	29 Aug 52	Direct Aid	161UNTS335	200492
UNICEF (Children)	Yemen	31 Jan 62	Direct Aid	422UNTS271	106081
UNICEF (Children)	Yugoslavia	20 Nov 47	Tech Assistance	65UNTS28	100817
UNICEF (Children)	Zambia	02 Feb 67	IGO Operations	589UNTS89	108536
UNIDO (Industrial)	Multilateral	27 Oct 54	Tech Assistance	201UNTS95	102712
UNIDO (Industrial)	Multilateral	13 Dec 55	Tech Assistance	407UNTS8	105857
UNIDO (Industrial)	Multilateral	30 Mar 56	IGO Operations	604UNTS114	108748
UNIDO (Industrial)	Multilateral	10 May 56	Tech Assistance	243UNTS103	103449
UNIDO (Industrial)	Multilateral	31 May 56	Tech Assistance	251UNTS181	103541
UNIDO (Industrial)	Multilateral	26 Jun 56	Tech Assistance	253UNTS12	103573
UNIDO (Industrial)	Multilateral	02 Jul 56	Tech Assistance	248UNTS37	103484
UNIDO (Industrial)	Multilateral	01 Mar 57	Tech Assistance	264UNTS94	103790
UNIDO (Industrial)	Multilateral	24 May 57	Tech Assistance	268UNTS270	103861
UNIDO (Industrial)	Multilateral	30 Jun 57	Tech Assistance	286UNTS171	104165
UNIDO (Industrial)	Multilateral	15 Mar 58	Tech Assistance	292UNTS273	104276
UNIDO (Industrial)	Multilateral	28 Jan 61	Tech Assistance	387UNTS202	105563
UNIDO (Industrial)	Multilateral	27 Dec 61	Tech Assistance	425UNTS83	106120
UNIDO (Industrial)	Multilateral	20 Jan 62	Tech Assistance	429UNTS230	200596
UNIDO (Industrial)	Multilateral	13 Feb 62	Tech Assistance	422UNTS288	200594
UNIDO (Industrial)	Multilateral	10 Apr 62	Tech Assistance	429UNTS78	106192
UNIDO (Industrial)	Multilateral	12 Aug 62	Tech Assistance	443UNTS266	106365
UNIDO (Industrial)	Multilateral	21 Jan 63	Tech Assistance	453UNTS20	106517
UNIDO (Industrial)	Multilateral	09 May 63	Tech Assistance	463UNTS159	106700
UNIDO (Industrial)	Multilateral	28 Jun 64	Tech Assistance	519UNTS14	107499
UNIDO (Industrial)	Multilateral	03 Aug 64	Tech Assistance	503UNTS239	107347
UNIDO (Industrial)	Multilateral	15 Dec 64	Tech Assistance	522UNTS20	107533
UNIDO (Industrial)	Multilateral	27 Jan 65	Tech Assistance	523UNTS102	107556

PARTY ONE	PARTY TWO	DATE	TOPIC	CITATION	NUMBER
UNIDO (Industrial)	Multilateral	23 Feb 65	IGO Operations	527UNTS120	107622
UNIDO (Industrial)	Multilateral	12 May 65	IGO Operations	534UNTS390	107769
UNIDO (Industrial)	Multilateral	13 Sep 65	IGO Operations	547UNTS248	107961
UNIDO (Industrial)	Multilateral	13 Sep 65	Tech Assistance	547UNTS264	107962
UNIDO (Industrial)	Multilateral	21 Sep 65	IGO Operations	547UNTS280	107963
UNIDO (Industrial)	Multilateral	12 Nov 65	IGO Operations	550UNTS160	108013
UNIDO (Industrial)	Multilateral	12 May 66	General Aid	563UNTS54	108204
UNIDO (Industrial)	Multilateral	06 Aug 66	Tech Assistance	570UNTS178	108294
UNIDO (Industrial)	Multilateral	14 Jun 67	Direct Aid	603UNTS2	108719
UNIDO (Industrial)	Multilateral	27 Oct 67	General Aid	608UNTS37	108811
United Arab Rep	Accept UN Charter	30 Nov 66	UN Charter	581UNTS131	108437
United Arab Rep	Argentina	21 Jun 65	General Economic	634UNTS161	109058
United Arab Rep	Argentina	21 Jun 65	Commodity Trade	634UNTS177	109059
United Arab Rep	Australia	14 Jun 52	Air Transport	173UNTS241	102269
United Arab Rep	Austria	16 Oct 62	Taxation	491UNTS63	107174
United Arab Rep	Belgium	01 Jul 47	Claims and Debts	34UNTS93	100529
United Arab Rep	Belgium	19 Sep 49	Air Transport	137UNTS189	101853
United Arab Rep	Belgium	28 Nov 49	Culture	76UNTS91	100982
United Arab Rep	Belgium	31 Oct 56	Taxation	257UNTS235	103659
United Arab Rep	Belgium	30 Mar 66	Claims and Debts	632UNTS237	109026
United Arab Rep	Belgium	17 May 67	Culture	0UNTS0	109501
United Arab Rep	Bulgaria	09 Jul 59	Air Transport	411UNTS187	105920
United Arab Rep	Bulgaria	17 Nov 65	Visas	0UNTS0	109960
United Arab Rep	Bulgaria	29 Aug 66	Sanitation	0UNTS0	109963
United Arab Rep	Bulgaria	29 Aug 66	Sanitation	630UNTS325	108980
United Arab Rep	Bulgaria	12 Feb 67	Gen Communications	630UNTS353	108981
United Arab Rep	Bulgaria	12 Feb 67	Telecommunications	630UNTS363	108982
United Arab Rep	Bulgaria	24 May 69	Water Transport	0UNTS0	110566
United Arab Rep	Canada	03 Dec 52	Mostfavored Nation	233UNTS145	103259
United Arab Rep	Ceylon (Sri Lanka)	26 Sep 50	Air Transport	192UNTS53	102595
United Arab Rep	Ceylon (Sri Lanka)	17 Nov 54	General Trade	315UNTS3	104554
United Arab Rep	China People's Rep	22 Aug 55	General Trade	55CCJC58	410251
United Arab Rep	China People's Rep	22 Aug 55	General Trade	55CCJC59	410252
United Arab Rep	China People's Rep	15 Apr 56	Culture	56CCJC51	410331
United Arab Rep	China People's Rep	20 May 56	Culture	56CCJC66	410337
United Arab Rep	China People's Rep	22 Oct 56	General Trade	56CCJC117	410371
United Arab Rep	China People's Rep	22 Oct 56	Finance	56CCJC118	410372
United Arab Rep	China People's Rep	21 Dec 57	General Trade	57CCJC122	410474
United Arab Rep	China People's Rep	25 Aug 58	Postal Service	58CCJC81	410538
United Arab Rep	China People's Rep	15 Dec 58	General Trade	58CCJC106	410559
United Arab Rep	China People's Rep	15 Dec 58	Finance	58CCJC105	410558
United Arab Rep	China People's Rep	15 Dec 58	General Trade	58CCJC104	410557
United Arab Rep	China People's Rep	05 Feb 61	General Trade	61CCJC23	410758
United Arab Rep	China People's Rep	17 Mar 62	General Trade	62CCJC26	410875
United Arab Rep	China People's Rep	17 Mar 62	General Trade	62CCJC24	410873
United Arab Rep	China People's Rep	17 Mar 62	Finance	62CCJC25	410874
United Arab Rep	China People's Rep	05 Jan 63	Telecommunications	63CCJC2	410942
United Arab Rep	China People's Rep	14 Jul 63	General Trade	63CCJC88	410995
United Arab Rep	China People's Rep	22 Dec 64	General Trade	64CCJC186	411351
United Arab Rep	China People's Rep	22 Dec 64	Direct Aid	64CCJC184	411350
United Arab Rep	China People's Rep	13 Jan 65	Tech Assistance	65CCJC5	411352
United Arab Rep	China People's Rep	02 May 65	Air Transport	65CCJC58	411341
United Arab Rep	China People's Rep	04 May 66	General Trade	66CCJC28	411343
United Arab Rep	China People's Rep	07 May 66	Culture	66CCJC30	411344
United Arab Rep	China People's Rep	25 May 67	General Trade	67CCJC19	411360
United Arab Rep	Czechoslovakia	06 May 57	Tech Assistance	292UNTS317	104278
United Arab Rep	Czechoslovakia	30 Jun 57	Air Transport	411UNTS126	105917
United Arab Rep	Czechoslovakia	19 Oct 57	Culture	530UNTS181	107681
United Arab Rep	Czechoslovakia	07 Feb 59	General Economic	372UNTS243	105301
United Arab Rep	Czechoslovakia	26 Nov 64	Sanitation	545UNTS11	107923
United Arab Rep	Denmark	14 Mar 50	Air Transport	95UNTS197	101322
United Arab Rep	Denmark	01 Dec 58	Taxation	337UNTS69	104817
United Arab Rep	Denmark	12 Jan 65	Sanitation	0UNTS0	109732
United Arab Rep	Denmark	12 Apr 69	Loans and Credits	0UNTS0	109953
United Arab Rep	Denmark	24 Nov 69	Direct Aid	0UNTS0	110456

PARTY ONE	PARTY TWO	DATE	TOPIC	CITATION	NUMBER
United Arab Rep	Finland	01 Apr 65	Taxation	562UNTS3	108193
United Arab Rep	France	08 Aug 50	Air Transport	127UNTS293	101710
United Arab Rep	France	22 Aug 58	General Amity	0UNTS0	110511
United Arab Rep	France	05 Nov 64	Claims and Debts	64FRRT73	415048
United Arab Rep	France	28 Jul 66	Visas	0UNTS0	110512
United Arab Rep	France	28 Jul 66	Admin Cooperation	67FRJO810	416049
United Arab Rep	France	19 Mar 68	Education	0UNTS0	110102
United Arab Rep	France	19 Mar 68	Health/Educ/Welfare	69FRJO3005	416050
United Arab Rep	France	19 Mar 68	Culture	0UNTS0	110101
United Arab Rep	France	05 Sep 68	Taxation	0UNTS0	110801
United Arab Rep	Germany, East	10 Nov 55	General Trade	3EGDA621	419001
United Arab Rep	Germany, East	12 Nov 55	Consul/Citizenship	3EGDA624	419002
United Arab Rep	Germany, East	06 Aug 56	Mass Media	5EGDA278	419003
United Arab Rep	Germany, East	07 Sep 57	General Economic	5EGDA280	419005
United Arab Rep	Germany, East	07 Sep 57	Consul/Citizenship	5EGDA281	419004
United Arab Rep	Germany, East	27 Mar 58	Water Transport	6EGDA474	419471
United Arab Rep	Germany, East	29 Aug 58	Tech Assistance	6EGDA484	419473
United Arab Rep	Germany, East	29 Aug 58	General Aid	6EGDA484	419472
United Arab Rep	Germany, East	27 Nov 58	Specific Property	6EGDA521	419474
United Arab Rep	Germany, East	13 Dec 58	General Trade	8EGDA559	419476
United Arab Rep	Germany, East	13 Dec 58	Finance	6EGDA485	419475
United Arab Rep	Germany, East	02 Aug 62	Mass Media	10EGDA547	419477
United Arab Rep	Germany, East	16 Dec 62	General Trade	10EGDA620	419478
United Arab Rep	Germany, East	06 May 65	Tech Assistance	43EGDZ335	420479
United Arab Rep	Germany, East	20 May 65	Air Transport	52EGDZ329	420480
United Arab Rep	Germany, East	11 Feb 66	Water Transport	52EGDZ353	420481
United Arab Rep	Germany, East	03 May 66	General Economic	33EGDZ359	420482
United Arab Rep	Germany, East	03 May 66	General Economic	33EGDZ359	420483
United Arab Rep	Germany, East	02 Aug 66	Sanitation	49EGDZ365	420484
United Arab Rep	Germany, West	21 Apr 51	General Trade	52WGBB525	425710
United Arab Rep	Germany, West	31 Jul 54	Customs	55WGBB857	425711
United Arab Rep	Germany, West	18 Feb 56	General Trade	56WBGA110	424712
United Arab Rep	Germany, West	22 Feb 56	Other Military	57WBGA48	424713
United Arab Rep	Germany, West	11 Nov 59	Culture	60WGBB2351	425714
United Arab Rep	Germany, West	17 Nov 59	Taxation	61WGBB420	425715
United Arab Rep	Germany, West	16 Feb 60	Air Transport	464UNTS233	106717
United Arab Rep	Ghana	29 Aug 60	Air Transport	412UNTS71	105926
United Arab Rep	Greece	30 Mar 46	Reparations	187UNTS263	102518
United Arab Rep	Greece	24 Apr 50	Air Transport	163UNTS229	102149
United Arab Rep	Greece	21 May 53	General Trade	256UNTS17	103620
United Arab Rep	Greece	21 May 53	Finance	256UNTS25	103621
United Arab Rep	Greece	04 Sep 56	Culture	299UNTS253	104317
United Arab Rep	IAEA (Atom Energy)	17 Sep 64	Atomic Energy	525UNTS19	107581
United Arab Rep	IAEA (Atom Energy)	14 Jan 65	Atomic Energy	603UNTS45	108723
United Arab Rep	IBRD (World Bank)	22 Dec 59	IBRD Project	354UNTS197	105063
United Arab Rep	ICAO (Civil Aviat)	06 Mar 52	Tech Assistance	151UNTS111	101986
United Arab Rep	ICAO (Civil Aviat)	27 Aug 53	IGO Status/Immunit	215UNTS371	102925
United Arab Rep	India	14 Jun 52	Air Transport	173UNTS209	102268
United Arab Rep	India	20 Feb 69	Taxation	0UNTS0	110590
United Arab Rep	Iran	09 Sep 58	Culture	0IRTB20	433032
United Arab Rep	Iraq	23 Mar 55	Air Transport	311UNTS199	104504
United Arab Rep	Israel	24 Feb 49	Peace/Disarmament	42UNTS251	100654
United Arab Rep	Italy	25 May 50	Air Transport	53ITGU67	435313
United Arab Rep	Italy	17 Oct 52	Other Military	52ITDI291	436314
United Arab Rep	Italy	06 Jul 57	Finance	302UNTS147	104357
United Arab Rep	Italy	08 Jan 59	Culture	61ITDI342	436315
United Arab Rep	Italy	08 Jan 59	Admin Cooperation	61ITDI289	436316
United Arab Rep	Italy	08 Jan 59	Claims and Debts	61ITDI289	436317
United Arab Rep	Italy	29 Apr 59	Tech Assistance	363UNTS91	105202
United Arab Rep	Italy	29 Apr 59	General Trade	61ITDI291	436318
United Arab Rep	Italy	19 Apr 61	Specific Resources	62ITDI518	436319
United Arab Rep	Italy	13 Apr 62	Claims and Debts	63ITDI380	436320
United Arab Rep	Italy	23 Mar 65	Claims and Debts	66ITDI231	436322
United Arab Rep	Italy	23 Mar 65	Claims and Debts	66ITGU215	435321
United Arab Rep	Japan	20 Mar 57	Culture	318UNTS345	104625

PARTY ONE	PARTY TWO	DATE	TOPIC	CITATION	NUMBER
United Arab Rep	Japan	10 May 62	Air Transport	498UNTS69	107278
United Arab Rep	Japan	27 Apr 64	Taxation	0JGJI1536	441119
United Arab Rep	Japan	03 Sep 68	Taxation	69JHZ8	439024
United Arab Rep	Japan	03 Sep 68	Taxation	0UNTS0	110576
United Arab Rep	Jordan	21 Apr 47	General Trade	11UNTS3	100146
United Arab Rep	Jordan	02 Jan 52	Air Transport	192UNTS157	102599
United Arab Rep	Mexico	08 Apr 60	Culture	64MEXD1408	444038
United Arab Rep	Mexico	25 Oct 63	General Trade	66MEXD1708	444039
United Arab Rep	Morocco	19 May 60	Air Transport	563UNTS121	108208
United Arab Rep	Multilateral	02 Aug 44	Scientific Project	67UNTS221	200221
United Arab Rep	Multilateral	07 Dec 44	Air Transport	171UNTS345	200501
United Arab Rep	Multilateral	07 Dec 44	Air Transport	84UNTS389	200252
United Arab Rep	Multilateral	07 Dec 44	IGO Establishment	15UNTS295	200102
United Arab Rep	Multilateral	15 Dec 44	Sanitation	17UNTS305	200110
United Arab Rep	Multilateral	15 Dec 44	Sanitation	16UNTS247	200106
United Arab Rep	Multilateral	22 Mar 45	General Amity	70UNTS237	200241
United Arab Rep	Multilateral	16 Nov 45	IGO Establishment	4UNTS275	100052
United Arab Rep	Multilateral	27 Dec 45	IGO Establishment	2UNTS39	100020
United Arab Rep	Multilateral	14 Jan 46	Reparations	555UNTS69	108105
United Arab Rep	Multilateral	22 Jul 46	IGO Establishment	14UNTS185	100221
United Arab Rep	Multilateral	22 Jul 46	IGO Establishment	9UNTS3	100125
United Arab Rep	Multilateral	27 Jul 46	Patents/Copyrights	90UNTS229	101238
United Arab Rep	Multilateral	11 Dec 46	Sanitation	12UNTS179	100186
United Arab Rep	Multilateral	27 May 47	Air Transport	418UNTS161	106021
United Arab Rep	Multilateral	02 Oct 47	Telecommunications	193UNTS188	102616
United Arab Rep	Multilateral	11 Oct 47	IGO Establishment	77UNTS143	100998
United Arab Rep	Multilateral	12 Nov 47	Admin Cooperation	53UNTS13	100770
United Arab Rep	Multilateral	12 Nov 47	Admin Cooperation	46UNTS169	100709
United Arab Rep	Multilateral	12 Nov 47	Admin Cooperation	53UNTS39	100771
United Arab Rep	Multilateral	12 Nov 47	Admin Cooperation	46UNTS201	100710
United Arab Rep	Multilateral	06 Mar 48	Water Transport	289UNTS3	104214
United Arab Rep	Multilateral	06 Mar 48	Water Transport	289UNTS3	104214
United Arab Rep	Multilateral	10 Jun 48	Humanitarian	164UNTS113	102163
United Arab Rep	Multilateral	10 Jun 48	Humanitarian	164UNTS113	102163
United Arab Rep	Multilateral	10 Jun 48	Humanitarian	191UNTS3	102576
United Arab Rep	Multilateral	24 Jul 48	Sanitation	66UNTS25	100847
United Arab Rep	Multilateral	19 Nov 48	Sanitation	44UNTS277	100688
United Arab Rep	Multilateral	29 Nov 48	IGO Establishment	120UNTS13	101613
United Arab Rep	Multilateral	09 Dec 48	Scientific Project	73UNTS39	100942
United Arab Rep	Multilateral	09 Dec 48	Humanitarian	78UNTS277	101021
United Arab Rep	Multilateral	09 Dec 48	Scientific Project	20UNTS229	100318
United Arab Rep	Multilateral	23 Mar 49	Commodity Trade	203UNTS179	102746
United Arab Rep	Multilateral	04 May 49	Admin Cooperation	92UNTS19	101257
United Arab Rep	Multilateral	04 May 49	Admin Cooperation	47UNTS159	100728
United Arab Rep	Multilateral	04 May 49	Admin Cooperation	30UNTS23	100446
United Arab Rep	Multilateral	04 May 49	Admin Cooperation	30UNTS3	100445
United Arab Rep	Multilateral	04 May 49	Admin Cooperation	98UNTS101	101358
United Arab Rep	Multilateral	12 Aug 49	Humanitarian	75UNTS85	100971
United Arab Rep	Multilateral	12 Aug 49	Humanitarian	75UNTS287	100973
United Arab Rep	Multilateral	12 Aug 49	General Military	75UNTS135	100972
United Arab Rep	Multilateral	12 Aug 49	Humanitarian	75UNTS31	100970
United Arab Rep	Multilateral	19 Sep 49	Land Transport	125UNTS3	101671
United Arab Rep	Multilateral	24 Sep 49	IGO Establishment	126UNTS237	101691
United Arab Rep	Multilateral	16 Dec 49	Admin Cooperation	72UNTS3	100924
United Arab Rep	Multilateral	21 Mar 50	Admin Cooperation	96UNTS271	101342
United Arab Rep	Multilateral	06 Apr 50	Admin Cooperation	119UNTS99	101610
United Arab Rep	Multilateral	22 Nov 50	Culture	131UNTS25	101734
United Arab Rep	Multilateral	07 Dec 50	Admin Cooperation	212UNTS17	102861
United Arab Rep	Multilateral	15 Dec 50	Customs	157UNTS129	102052
United Arab Rep	Multilateral	01 Aug 51	Sanitation	107UNTS19	101464
United Arab Rep	Multilateral	08 Sep 51	Peace/Disarmament	136UNTS45	101832
United Arab Rep	Multilateral	08 Sep 51	General Military	136UNTS165	101833
United Arab Rep	Multilateral	09 Oct 51	IGO Establishment	220UNTS121	102997
United Arab Rep	Multilateral	06 Dec 51	IGO Establishment	425UNTS61	106119
United Arab Rep	Multilateral	06 Dec 51	IGO Establishment	425UNTS61	106119

PARTY ONE	PARTY TWO	DATE	TOPIC	CITATION	NUMBER
United Arab Rep	Multilateral	06 Dec 51	Admin Cooperation	150UNTS67	101963
United Arab Rep	Multilateral	10 May 52	Admin Cooperation	439UNTS193	106330
United Arab Rep	Multilateral	10 May 52	Admin Cooperation	439UNTS217	106331
United Arab Rep	Multilateral	10 May 52	Taxation	439UNTS233	106332
United Arab Rep	Multilateral	20 May 52	Sanitation	219UNTS55	102966
United Arab Rep	Multilateral	08 Jun 52	Other Military	210UNTS317	102843
United Arab Rep	Multilateral	11 Jul 52	Postal Service	171UNTS191	102227
United Arab Rep	Multilateral	11 Jul 52	IGO Establishment	169UNTS3	102220
United Arab Rep	Multilateral	11 Jul 52	Postal Service	171UNTS143	102226
United Arab Rep	Multilateral	11 Jul 52	Postal Service	171UNTS89	102225
United Arab Rep	Multilateral	11 Jul 52	Postal Service	170UNTS3	102221
United Arab Rep	Multilateral	11 Jul 52	Postal Service	170UNTS63	102222
United Arab Rep	Multilateral	11 Jul 52	Postal Service	170UNTS269	102223
United Arab Rep	Multilateral	07 Oct 52	Admin Cooperation	310UNTS181	104493
United Arab Rep	Multilateral	15 Oct 52	Tech Assistance	141UNTS96	101909
United Arab Rep	Multilateral	15 Oct 52	Tech Assistance	141UNTS96	101909
United Arab Rep	Multilateral	07 Nov 52	General Trade	221UNTS255	103010
United Arab Rep	Multilateral	26 Feb 53	Tech Assistance	161UNTS31	102120
United Arab Rep	Multilateral	26 Feb 53	Tech Assistance	161UNTS31	102120
United Arab Rep	Multilateral	27 Feb 53	Claims and Debts	333UNTS3	104764
United Arab Rep	Multilateral	27 Feb 53	Claims and Debts	333UNTS3	104764
United Arab Rep	Multilateral	31 Mar 53	Mass Media	435UNTS191	106280
United Arab Rep	Multilateral	11 May 53	Sanitation	456UNTS3	106555
United Arab Rep	Multilateral	07 Dec 53	Admin Cooperation	182UNTS51	102422
United Arab Rep	Multilateral	12 May 54	Admin Cooperation	327UNTS3	104714
United Arab Rep	Multilateral	14 May 54	Culture	249UNTS215	103511
United Arab Rep	Multilateral	04 Jun 54	Customs	276UNTS191	103992
United Arab Rep	Multilateral	04 Jun 54	Customs	282UNTS249	104101
United Arab Rep	Multilateral	14 Jun 54	Air Transport	320UNTS209	104643
United Arab Rep	Multilateral	14 Jun 54	Air Transport	320UNTS217	104644
United Arab Rep	Multilateral	04 Apr 55	Tech Assistance	208UNTS239	102816
United Arab Rep	Multilateral	06 Apr 55	General Amity	261UNTS55	103725
United Arab Rep	Multilateral	25 May 55	IGO Establishment	264UNTS117	103791
United Arab Rep	Multilateral	25 May 55	IGO Establishment	264UNTS117	103791
United Arab Rep	Multilateral	28 Sep 55	Air Transport	478UNTS371	106943
United Arab Rep	Multilateral	12 Oct 55	IGO Establishment	560UNTS3	108165
United Arab Rep	Multilateral	25 Apr 56	Commodity Trade	270UNTS103	103896
United Arab Rep	Multilateral	26 Oct 56	IGO Establishment	276UNTS3	103988
United Arab Rep	Multilateral	15 Jun 57	Patents/Copyrights	583UNTS3	108470
United Arab Rep	Multilateral	03 Oct 57	Postal Service	366UNTS255	105219
United Arab Rep	Multilateral	03 Oct 57	Postal Service	365UNTS207	105214
United Arab Rep	Multilateral	03 Oct 57	Postal Service	366UNTS141	105217
United Arab Rep	Multilateral	03 Oct 57	Postal Service	366UNTS87	105216
United Arab Rep	Multilateral	03 Oct 57	Postal Service	366UNTS3	105215
United Arab Rep	Multilateral	03 Oct 57	Postal Service	364UNTS3	105211
United Arab Rep	Multilateral	03 Oct 57	Postal Service	364UNTS331	105212
United Arab Rep	Multilateral	03 Oct 57	Postal Service	365UNTS3	105213
United Arab Rep	Multilateral	03 Oct 57	Postal Service	366UNTS193	105218
United Arab Rep	Multilateral	10 Jun 58	Admin Cooperation	330UNTS3	104739
United Arab Rep	Multilateral	03 Dec 58	Admin Cooperation	416UNTS51	105995
United Arab Rep	Multilateral	06 Apr 59	Commodity Trade	349UNTS167	105013
United Arab Rep	Multilateral	19 Nov 59	IGO Operations	410UNTS156	105902
United Arab Rep	Multilateral	26 Jan 60	IGO Establishment	439UNTS249	106333
United Arab Rep	Multilateral	17 Jun 60	Humanitarian	536UNTS27	107794
United Arab Rep	Multilateral	06 Oct 60	Customs	473UNTS131	106861
United Arab Rep	Multilateral	14 Dec 60	Education	429UNTS93	106193
United Arab Rep	Multilateral	30 Mar 61	Sanitation	520UNTS151	107515
United Arab Rep	Multilateral	18 Apr 61	Consul/Citizenship	500UNTS95	107310
United Arab Rep	Multilateral	18 Apr 61	Consul/Citizenship	500UNTS223	107311
United Arab Rep	Multilateral	08 Jun 61	Customs	473UNTS153	106862
United Arab Rep	Multilateral	08 Jun 61	Customs	473UNTS187	106863
United Arab Rep	Multilateral	21 Jun 61	IGO Establishment	514UNTS209	107449
United Arab Rep	Multilateral	06 Dec 61	Customs	473UNTS219	106864
United Arab Rep	Multilateral	20 Feb 62	Water Transport	597UNTS159	108644
United Arab Rep	Multilateral	15 May 62	Commodity Trade	444UNTS3	106367

PARTY ONE	PARTY TWO	DATE	TOPIC	CITATION	NUMBER
United Arab Rep	Multilateral	14 Sep 62	IGO Status/Immunit	494UNTS219	107236
United Arab Rep	Multilateral	20 Apr 63	IGO Establishment	495UNTS3	107239
United Arab Rep	Multilateral	24 Apr 63	Consul/Citizenship	596UNTS261	108638
United Arab Rep	Multilateral	25 May 63	IGO Establishment	479UNTS39	106947
United Arab Rep	Multilateral	04 Aug 63	IGO Establishment	510UNTS3	107408
United Arab Rep	Multilateral	05 Aug 63	Sanitation	480UNTS43	106964
United Arab Rep	Multilateral	10 Sep 63	Tech Assistance	480UNTS100	106965
United Arab Rep	Multilateral	10 Jul 64	Postal Service	612UNTS233	108848
United Arab Rep	Multilateral	10 Jul 64	Postal Service	613UNTS193	108852
United Arab Rep	Multilateral	10 Jul 64	Postal Service	612UNTS361	108849
United Arab Rep	Multilateral	10 Jul 64	Postal Service	613UNTS3	108851
United Arab Rep	Multilateral	10 Jul 64	Postal Service	611UNTS7	108844
United Arab Rep	Multilateral	10 Jul 64	Postal Service	611UNTS387	108846
United Arab Rep	Multilateral	10 Jul 64	Postal Service	612UNTS3	108847
United Arab Rep	Multilateral	10 Jul 64	Postal Service	613UNTS127	108853
United Arab Rep	Multilateral	10 Jul 64	Postal Service	611UNTS105	108845
United Arab Rep	Multilateral	10 Jul 64	Postal Service	613UNTS3	108850
United Arab Rep	Multilateral	20 Aug 64	Telecommunications	514UNTS25	107441
United Arab Rep	Multilateral	15 Nov 65	Admin Cooperation	0UNTS0	109432
United Arab Rep	Multilateral	17 Jan 66	IGO Establishment	592UNTS101	108573
United Arab Rep	Multilateral	05 Apr 66	Water Transport	640UNTS133	109159
United Arab Rep	Multilateral	27 Jan 67	Scientific Project	610UNTS205	108843
United Arab Rep	Multilateral	03 May 67	IGO Operations	0UNTS0	110764
United Arab Rep	Multilateral	22 Apr 68	Scientific Project	0UNTS0	109574
United Arab Rep	Multilateral	24 Sep 68	Air Transport	0UNTS0	110612
United Arab Rep	Netherlands	08 Dec 49	Air Transport	95UNTS123	101320
United Arab Rep	Netherlands	21 Mar 53	Finance	53NET44	447039
United Arab Rep	Netherlands	21 Mar 53	General Trade	53NET43	447038
United Arab Rep	Netherlands	15 May 57	Taxation	288UNTS29	104194
United Arab Rep	Netherlands	08 Dec 60	Culture	455UNTS276	106547
United Arab Rep	Netherlands	05 Aug 65	Air Transport	0UNTS0	110161
United Arab Rep	Norway	11 Mar 50	Air Transport	95UNTS157	101321
United Arab Rep	Norway	20 Oct 64	Taxation	543UNTS3	107895
United Arab Rep	Other Unilat Decla	24 Apr 57	General Ad Hoc	265UNTS299	103821
United Arab Rep	Pakistan	28 Aug 51	General Amity	214UNTS247	102902
United Arab Rep	Pakistan	08 Sep 51	Postal Service	133UNTS257	101793
United Arab Rep	Pakistan	14 Nov 53	Culture	485UNTS55	107046
United Arab Rep	Pakistan	13 Dec 54	Air Transport	255UNTS167	103610
United Arab Rep	Philippines	18 Jan 55	General Amity	3PTS399	465034
United Arab Rep	Philippines	03 May 62	Culture	4PTS551	465048
United Arab Rep	Poland	14 Feb 56	Air Transport	56PZUM82	458039
United Arab Rep	Poland	02 Feb 57	Culture	319UNTS221	104633
United Arab Rep	Poland	26 Oct 64	Tech Assistance	64PZUM63	458116
United Arab Rep	Romania	15 Apr 57	Culture	389UNTS21	105589
United Arab Rep	Romania	14 Aug 58	Air Transport	405UNTS189	105834
United Arab Rep	Romania	03 Sep 66	Direct Aid	604UNTS73	108745
United Arab Rep	Romania	14 Nov 66	Finance	642UNTS141	109170
United Arab Rep	Romania	14 Nov 66	General Trade	642UNTS129	109169
United Arab Rep	Singapore	30 May 68	General Trade	0UNTS0	110420
United Arab Rep	Spain	26 Apr 52	Culture	53SPBO2006	460095
United Arab Rep	Special Decla ICJ	18 Jun 57	ICJ Option Clause	272UNTS225	103940
United Arab Rep	Sudan	08 Nov 59	Specific Resources	453UNTS51	106519
United Arab Rep	Sweden	12 Dec 49	Air Transport	108UNTS15	101466
United Arab Rep	Sweden	21 Jul 58	Mostfavored Nation	427UNTS285	106160
United Arab Rep	Sweden	29 Jul 58	Taxation	369UNTS323	105264
United Arab Rep	Switzerland	06 Apr 50	Finance	50SWRO329	462129
United Arab Rep	Switzerland	15 May 50	Air Transport	95UNTS255	101325
United Arab Rep	Switzerland	05 Jan 55	Taxation	216UNTS41	102931
United Arab Rep	Switzerland	14 Jul 60	Air Transport	497UNTS161	107268
United Arab Rep	Syria	03 Jul 55	Air Transport	393UNTS67	105652
United Arab Rep	Syria	20 Oct 55	General Military	247UNTS117	103461
United Arab Rep	Syria	27 Dec 62	Air Transport	491UNTS245	107180
United Arab Rep	Turkey	12 Apr 50	Air Transport	128UNTS3	101711
United Arab Rep	Turkey	15 Aug 53	General Economic	55TURG204	466094
United Arab Rep	UK Great Britain	10 Dec 46	Specif Claim/Waive	105UNTS15	101451

PARTY ONE	PARTY TWO	DATE	TOPIC	CITATION	NUMBER
United Arab Rep	UK Great Britain	30 Jun 47	Finance	93UNTS165	101299
United Arab Rep	UK Great Britain	05 Jan 48	Finance	77UNTS3	100988
United Arab Rep	UK Great Britain	31 Mar 49	Finance	83UNTS139	101106
United Arab Rep	UK Great Britain	17 Apr 49	Reparations	83UNTS183	101107
United Arab Rep	UK Great Britain	31 May 49	Specific Resources	226UNTS273	103122
United Arab Rep	UK Great Britain	20 Mar 50	Tech Assistance	226UNTS287	103123
United Arab Rep	UK Great Britain	01 Jul 51	Finance	249UNTS125	103503
United Arab Rep	UK Great Britain	01 Jul 51	Finance	249UNTS143	103504
United Arab Rep	UK Great Britain	19 Oct 52	General Trade	158UNTS423	102075
United Arab Rep	UK Great Britain	30 Oct 52	Finance	172UNTS3	102236
United Arab Rep	UK Great Britain	05 Jan 53	Specific Property	207UNTS277	102810
United Arab Rep	UK Great Britain	12 Feb 53	Recognition	161UNTS157	102127
United Arab Rep	UK Great Britain	19 Oct 54	Milit Installation	221UNTS227	103008
United Arab Rep	UK Great Britain	19 Oct 54	General Amity	210UNTS3	102833
United Arab Rep	UK Great Britain	28 Feb 59	Finance	343UNTS159	104925
United Arab Rep	UK Great Britain	14 Nov 61	Education	449UNTS129	106455
United Arab Rep	UK Great Britain	29 Sep 65	Culture	0UNTS0	109444
United Arab Rep	UN Relief Palestin	12 Sep 50	Refugees	121UNTS107	101630
United Arab Rep	UN Relief Palestin	30 Jun 53	Tech Assistance	190UNTS3	102554
United Arab Rep	UN Relief Palestin	14 Oct 53	Tech Assistance	190UNTS13	102555
United Arab Rep	UN Special Fund	25 Nov 59	Direct Aid	345UNTS125	104964
United Arab Rep	UNESCO (Educ/Cult)	09 Nov 63	Culture	489UNTS233	107142
United Arab Rep	UNICEF (Children)	18 May 52	Direct Aid	324UNTS161	104684
United Arab Rep	United Nations	08 Jan 57	Specific Property	257UNTS75	103650
United Arab Rep	United Nations	08 Feb 57	Status of Forces	260UNTS61	103704
United Arab Rep	United Nations	17 Oct 60	Specif Claim/Waive	388UNTS143	105575
United Arab Rep	United Nations	08 Feb 63	Direct Aid	453UNTS79	106520
United Arab Rep	United Nations	27 Aug 63	Tech Assistance	474UNTS221	106884
United Arab Rep	United Nations	26 Nov 65	IGO Operations	551UNTS253	108046
United Arab Rep	United Nations	14 Nov 68	IGO Operations	0UNTS0	109371
United Arab Rep	USA (United States)	05 Jan 46	Status of Forces	160UNTS27	102098
United Arab Rep	USA (United States)	15 Jun 46	Air Transport	151UNTS135	101988
United Arab Rep	USA (United States)	15 Jun 46	Air Transport	71UNTS157	100917
United Arab Rep	USA (United States)	15 Aug 46	Mostfavored Nation	13UNTS59	100202
United Arab Rep	USA (United States)	03 Nov 49	Education	71UNTS31	100908
United Arab Rep	USA (United States)	05 May 51	Tech Assistance	198UNTS265	102670
United Arab Rep	USA (United States)	29 Apr 52	Milit Assistance	241UNTS3	103418
United Arab Rep	USA (United States)	12 Mar 53	Tech Assistance	204UNTS3	102747
United Arab Rep	USA (United States)	19 Mar 53	Tech Assistance	215UNTS17	102909
United Arab Rep	USA (United States)	21 May 53	Tech Assistance	204UNTS29	102748
United Arab Rep	USA (United States)	18 Jun 53	Education	204UNTS55	102749
United Arab Rep	USA (United States)	18 Jun 53	Sanitation	215UNTS45	102910
United Arab Rep	USA (United States)	24 Feb 54	Tech Assistance	236UNTS61	103316
United Arab Rep	USA (United States)	30 Oct 54	Direct Aid	234UNTS139	103279
United Arab Rep	USA (United States)	06 Nov 54	Tech Assistance	237UNTS183	103344
United Arab Rep	USA (United States)	07 Mar 55	Mass Media	252UNTS159	103565
United Arab Rep	USA (United States)	14 Dec 55	US Agri Commod Aid	240UNTS37	103392
United Arab Rep	USA (United States)	31 Oct 58	Postal Service	355UNTS355	105086
United Arab Rep	USA (United States)	24 Dec 58	US Agri Commod Aid	338UNTS221	104837
United Arab Rep	USA (United States)	13 Jan 59	Postal Service	358UNTS3	105122
United Arab Rep	USA (United States)	29 Jul 59	US Agri Commod Aid	357UNTS121	105111
United Arab Rep	USA (United States)	28 Sep 59	Education	358UNTS97	105128
United Arab Rep	USA (United States)	14 Nov 59	US Agri Commod Aid	360UNTS311	105165
United Arab Rep	USA (United States)	01 Aug 60	US Agri Commod Aid	384UNTS189	105519
United Arab Rep	USA (United States)	09 Aug 60	US Agri Commod Aid	388UNTS271	105584
United Arab Rep	USA (United States)	02 Sep 61	US Agri Commod Aid	421UNTS251	106063
United Arab Rep	USA (United States)	19 Jan 62	US Agri Commod Aid	435UNTS107	106273
United Arab Rep	USA (United States)	21 May 62	Culture	458UNTS197	106601
United Arab Rep	USA (United States)	08 Oct 62	US Agri Commod Aid	462UNTS39	106670
United Arab Rep	USA (United States)	29 Jun 63	Finance	479UNTS207	106954
United Arab Rep	USA (United States)	01 Aug 63	Visas	488UNTS189	107128
United Arab Rep	USA (United States)	04 Dec 63	Commodity Trade	505UNTS117	107368
United Arab Rep	USA (United States)	05 May 64	Air Transport	531UNTS229	107706
United Arab Rep	USA (United States)	03 Jan 66	US Agri Commod Aid	579UNTS63	108399
United Arab Rep	USA (United States)	03 Jan 66	US Agri Commod Aid	579UNTS83	108400

PARTY ONE	PARTY TWO	DATE	TOPIC	CITATION	NUMBER
United Arab Rep	USA (United States)	21 Feb 67	Culture	0UNTS0	109851
United Arab Rep	USSR (Soviet Union)	03 Mar 48	Mostfavored Nation	0SUST246	468123
United Arab Rep	USSR (Soviet Union)	18 Aug 53	General Trade	16SUGG67	469900
United Arab Rep	USSR (Soviet Union)	18 Aug 53	Finance	0SUST299	468124
United Arab Rep	USSR (Soviet Union)	23 Mar 54	Consul/Citizenship	0SUST308	468125
United Arab Rep	USSR (Soviet Union)	27 Mar 54	General Trade	0SUST309	468126
United Arab Rep	USSR (Soviet Union)	27 Mar 54	General Trade	0SUST309	468127
United Arab Rep	USSR (Soviet Union)	27 Mar 54	Non-ILO Labor	0SUST309	468128
United Arab Rep	USSR (Soviet Union)	12 Jul 56	Atomic Energy	0SUST363	468129
United Arab Rep	USSR (Soviet Union)	15 Jul 56	General Trade	0UNTS0	109824
United Arab Rep	USSR (Soviet Union)	19 Oct 57	Culture	292UNTS151	104271
United Arab Rep	USSR (Soviet Union)	19 Oct 57	Culture	0SUST391	468130
United Arab Rep	USSR (Soviet Union)	29 Jan 58	General Aid	7SUGG103	469493
United Arab Rep	USSR (Soviet Union)	10 Apr 58	Culture	7SUGG109	469503
United Arab Rep	USSR (Soviet Union)	10 Aug 58	General Trade	7SUGG118	469524
United Arab Rep	USSR (Soviet Union)	11 Sep 58	Air Transport	7SUGG121	469530
United Arab Rep	USSR (Soviet Union)	18 Sep 58	Water Transport	338UNTS29	104831
United Arab Rep	USSR (Soviet Union)	18 Jan 59	Non-IBRD Project	8SUGG134	469553
United Arab Rep	USSR (Soviet Union)	17 Jan 60	Non-IBRD Project	9SUGG121	469621
United Arab Rep	USSR (Soviet Union)	21 Mar 60	Visas	16SUGG127	469974
United Arab Rep	USSR (Soviet Union)	08 Jul 60	Loans and Credits	9SUGG154	469720
United Arab Rep	USSR (Soviet Union)	11 Aug 60	Tech Assistance	9SUGG144	469681
United Arab Rep	USSR (Soviet Union)	27 Aug 60	Tech Assistance	399UNTS37	105733
United Arab Rep	USSR (Soviet Union)	01 Feb 62	Consul/Citizenship	16SUGG132	470001
United Arab Rep	USSR (Soviet Union)	23 Jun 62	General Trade	11SUGG145	469847
United Arab Rep	USSR (Soviet Union)	23 Jun 62	Finance	472UNTS19	106835
United Arab Rep	USSR (Soviet Union)	23 Jun 62	Finance	11SUGG144	469846
United Arab Rep	USSR (Soviet Union)	23 Jun 62	General Trade	472UNTS43	106836
United Arab Rep	WHO (World Health)	25 Aug 50	IGO Operations	92UNTS39	101259
United Arab Rep	WHO (World Health)	25 Mar 51	IGO Status/Immunit	223UNTS87	103058
United Arab Rep	WHO (World Health)	03 Aug 60	Tech Assistance	385UNTS3	105524
United Arab Rep	Yemen	27 Sep 45	General Amity	9UNTS373	200053
United Arab Rep	Yugoslavia	20 Feb 55	Air Transport	255UNTS199	103611
United Arab Rep	Zambia	16 Feb 66	General Trade	0UNTS0	109535
United Nations	Afghanistan	24 Nov 59	Tech Assistance	397UNTS187	105705
United Nations	Afghanistan	28 Apr 64	Education	494UNTS77	107227
United Nations	Algeria	23 Sep 64	IGO Operations	510UNTS217	107416
United Nations	Australia	13 May 63	Education	463UNTS187	106702
United Nations	Australia	25 Feb 66	IGO Operations	557UNTS85	108129
United Nations	Austria	27 Feb 61	IGO Status/Immunit	394UNTS27	105666
United Nations	Austria	29 Jan 63	Consul/Citizenship	452UNTS261	106513
United Nations	Austria	11 Jun 64	IGO Status/Immunit	500UNTS85	107309
United Nations	Austria	24 Feb 66	IGO Operations	557UNTS129	108131
United Nations	Austria	13 Apr 67	IGO Establishment	600UNTS93	108679
United Nations	Austria	12 Mar 68	IGO Operations	632UNTS131	109015
United Nations	Austria	25 May 68	IGO Operations	637UNTS0	109117
United Nations	Austria	25 May 68	IGO Operations	637UNTS0	109118
United Nations	Austria	24 Sep 68	IGO Operations	0UNTS0	109253
United Nations	Austria	24 Sep 68	IGO Operations	68ABGB377	403249
United Nations	Austria	22 Sep 70	IGO Operations	70ABGB318	403252
United Nations	Austria	15 Dec 70	Non-ILO Labor	71ABGB424	403253
United Nations	Belgium	20 Mar 64	Milit Installation	533UNTS83	107734
United Nations	Belgium	20 Feb 65	Claims and Debts	535UNTS197	107780
United Nations	Belgium	20 Feb 65	Finance	535UNTS191	107779
United Nations	Bolivia	01 Oct 51	Tech Assistance	104UNTS263	101447
United Nations	Bolivia	14 Dec 60	Tech Assistance	382UNTS283	105489
United Nations	Botswana	30 Sep 66	Tech Assistance	576UNTS17	108362
United Nations	Brazil	04 Aug 52	Tech Assistance	135UNTS185	101820
United Nations	Brazil	13 Aug 57	Milit Assistance	274UNTS199	103966
United Nations	Brazil	24 Mar 66	IGO Establishment	560UNTS47	108167
United Nations	Burma	15 Dec 58	Tech Assistance	319UNTS3	104629
United Nations	Burundi	29 Dec 62	Tech Assistance	450UNTS279	106474
United Nations	Cambodia	24 Jun 53	Tech Assistance	168UNTS309	200500
United Nations	Cambodia	30 Nov 60	Tech Assistance	383UNTS147	105500
United Nations	Cameroon	29 Aug 62	Tech Assistance	442UNTS3	106334

PARTY ONE	PARTY TWO	DATE	TOPIC	CITATION	NUMBER
United Nations	Canada	27 Aug 48	Humanitarian	47UNTS167	100729
United Nations	Canada	29 Jul 57	Milit Assistance	274UNTS47	103957
United Nations	Canada	21 Feb 66	IGO Operations	555UNTS119	108107
United Nations	Ceylon (Sri Lanka)	21 Jan 52	Tech Assistance	118UNTS281	200382
United Nations	Ceylon (Sri Lanka)	04 Dec 61	Tech Assistance	415UNTS236	105987
United Nations	Chile	16 Feb 53	IGO Operations	314UNTS49	104541
United Nations	Colombia	17 Jul 52	Tech Assistance	135UNTS61	101815
United Nations	Colombia	27 Aug 63	Education	481UNTS3	106975
United Nations	Congo (Brazzaville)	13 Mar 68	IGO Operations	632UNTS161	109018
United Nations	Congo (Zaire)	23 Aug 60	Direct Aid	373UNTS327	200576
United Nations	Congo (Zaire)	12 Jun 61	General Aid	494UNTS205	107234
United Nations	Congo (Zaire)	27 Nov 61	IGO Status/Immunit	414UNTS229	105975
United Nations	Congo (Zaire)	02 Mar 64	Milit Installation	533UNTS93	107735
United Nations	Costa Rica	27 Feb 53	Tech Assistance	161UNTS45	102121
United Nations	Cyprus	15 Jun 61	Tech Assistance	398UNTS39	105716
United Nations	Cyprus	30 Mar 64	IGO Status/Immunit	492UNTS261	107194
United Nations	Cyprus	31 Mar 64	IGO Status/Immunit	492UNTS57	107187
United Nations	Czechoslovakia	07 Oct 48	Humanitarian	47UNTS185	100730
United Nations	Dahomey	15 Apr 69	IGO Operations	0UNTS0	110170
United Nations	Denmark	16 Jul 57	Milit Assistance	274UNTS81	103959
United Nations	Denmark	21 Feb 66	IGO Operations	555UNTS151	108108
United Nations	Dominican Republic	19 Nov 53	Tech Assistance	180UNTS45	102374
United Nations	Dominican Republic	05 Aug 63	IGO Status/Immunit	472UNTS353	106847
United Nations	East Afri Service	27 Nov 65	Health/Educ/Welfare	550UNTS375	200616
United Nations	Ecuador	16 Jun 53	Tech Assistance	166UNTS289	102194
United Nations	Ecuador	26 Nov 62	Tech Assistance	445UNTS3	106372
United Nations	Ethiopia	22 Jun 53	Tech Assistance	172UNTS93	102241
United Nations	Ethiopia	18 Jun 58	IGO Operations	317UNTS101	104597
United Nations	Ethiopia	13 Jul 60	Tech Assistance	368UNTS143	105239
United Nations	Ethiopia	14 Jun 61	Direct Aid	406UNTS81	105840
United Nations	FAO (Food Agri)	03 Feb 47	IGO Operations	1UNTS207	200010
United Nations	FAO (Food Agri)	02 Aug 50	IGO Operations	139UNTS407	200467
United Nations	Fed of Malaya	29 May 58	Tech Assistance	330UNTS109	104742
United Nations	Finland	20 May 48	Humanitarian	47UNTS319	200189
United Nations	Finland	27 Jun 57	Status of Forces	271UNTS135	103913
United Nations	Finland	21 Feb 66	IGO Operations	555UNTS157	108109
United Nations	Finland	16 Jan 67	Education	588UNTS153	108522
United Nations	France	10 Mar 48	Humanitarian	47UNTS203	100731
United Nations	France	17 Aug 51	IGO Operations	122UNTS191	101647
United Nations	Gabon	11 Jan 63	IGO Operations	450UNTS257	106472
United Nations	Germany, West	28 Jun 62	IGO Operations	434UNTS249	200597
United Nations	Ghana	27 Feb 59	Tech Assistance	324UNTS133	104682
United Nations	Ghana	29 Aug 61	Tech Assistance	406UNTS117	105843
United Nations	Ghana	08 Apr 67	IGO Operations	594UNTS149	108601
United Nations	Ghana	19 Sep 68	IGO Operations	0UNTS0	109250
United Nations	Greece	12 Feb 48	Humanitarian	47UNTS223	100732
United Nations	Greece	05 Mar 52	Tech Assistance	123UNTS3	101650
United Nations	Greece	18 May 62	Tech Assistance	429UNTS61	106190
United Nations	Greece	31 Mar 64	IGO Status/Immunit	492UNTS267	107195
United Nations	Greece	20 Jun 66	Claims and Debts	565UNTS3	108230
United Nations	Greece	14 Apr 67	IGO Operations	595UNTS83	108613
United Nations	Guatemala	10 Mar 54	Tech Assistance	191UNTS271	102587
United Nations	Guinea	15 Oct 59	Tech Assistance	344UNTS47	104942
United Nations	Guyana	22 Aug 66	IGO Operations	571UNTS305	200625
United Nations	Haiti	28 Jun 61	Tech Assistance	399UNTS159	105740
United Nations	Hungary	04 Mar 66	IGO Operations	559UNTS3	108151
United Nations	IAEA (Atom Energy)	23 Oct 57	IGO Operations	281UNTS369	200548
United Nations	IAEA (Atom Energy)	22 Sep 58	IGO Operations	313UNTS323	200552
United Nations	IBRD (World Bank)	15 Apr 48	IGO Operations	16UNTS341	200109
United Nations	IBRD (World Bank)	20 Feb 57	IGO Operations	265UNTS312	200546
United Nations	IBRD (World Bank)	05 Jan 61	IGO Operations	384UNTS303	200577
United Nations	ICAO (Civil Aviat)	01 Oct 47	IGO Operations	8UNTS315	200045
United Nations	ICAO (Civil Aviat)	28 Feb 51	IGO Operations	139UNTS429	200469
United Nations	Iceland	19 Apr 48	Humanitarian	47UNTS251	100733
United Nations	IDA (Devel Assoc)	10 Apr 61	IGO Operations	394UNTS221	200582

PARTY ONE	PARTY TWO	DATE	TOPIC	CITATION	NUMBER
United Nations	ILO (Labor Org)	19 Dec 46	IGO Operations	1UNTS183	200009
United Nations	ILO (Labor Org)	17 Feb 49	IGO Operations	26UNTS323	200154
United Nations	ILO (Labor Org)	07 Jun 50	Visas	68UNTS213	200231
United Nations	ILO (Labor Org)	12 Oct 50	IGO Operations	139UNTS395	200466
United Nations	IMCO (Maritime Org)	13 Jan 59	IGO Operations	324UNTS273	200553
United Nations	IMCO (Maritime Org)	23 Jun 59	IGO Operations	336UNTS317	200556
United Nations	IMCO (Maritime Org)	11 Feb 64	IGO Operations	489UNTS357	200605
United Nations	IMF (Fund)	15 Apr 48	IGO Operations	16UNTS325	200108
United Nations	IMF (Fund)	22 Dec 60	IGO Operations	384UNTS315	200578
United Nations	India	14 Aug 51	Tech Assistance	98UNTS115	101359
United Nations	India	12 Jan 52	Tech Assistance	118UNTS175	101606
United Nations	India	02 Apr 52	Tech Assistance	126UNTS145	101687
United Nations	India	14 Aug 57	Milit Assistance	274UNTS233	103968
United Nations	India	19 Feb 62	Direct Aid	423UNTS3	106082
United Nations	India	27 Dec 62	Scientific Project	450UNTS3	106464
United Nations	India	25 Nov 64	Scientific Project	519UNTS47	107501
United Nations	India	04 Nov 67	IGO Operations	609UNTS3	108824
United Nations	India	22 Jul 68	IGO Operations	640UNTS121	109158
United Nations	Indonesia	06 Feb 52	Tech Assistance	121UNTS3	101621
United Nations	Indonesia	17 Apr 56	Non-IBRD Project	233UNTS267	103266
United Nations	Iran	05 Sep 62	Specific Resources	442UNTS249	106353
United Nations	Iran	16 Feb 65	Admin Cooperation	525UNTS211	107593
United Nations	Iran	15 Feb 68	Consul/Citizenship	631UNTS103	108990
United Nations	Iraq	05 Mar 61	Tech Assistance	409UNTS56	105878
United Nations	IRO (Refugee Org)	07 Feb 49	IGO Operations	26UNTS299	200153
United Nations	Israel	25 Jun 51	Tech Assistance	97UNTS21	101344
United Nations	Israel	07 Jan 63	Tech Assistance	450UNTS229	106470
United Nations	Italy	23 Aug 61	IGO Operations	405UNTS3	105819
United Nations	Italy	26 Jul 63	IGO Operations	472UNTS173	106840
United Nations	Italy	18 Mar 64	Education	491UNTS21	107171
United Nations	Italy	23 May 66	IGO Operations	565UNTS11	108231
United Nations	Italy	18 Jan 67	Specif Claim/Waive	588UNTS197	108525
United Nations	Italy	15 Jan 68	Scientific Project	635UNTS11	109070
United Nations	ITU (Telecommun)	26 Apr 49	IGO Operations	30UNTS315	200175
United Nations	ITU (Telecommun)	14 Jan 60	IGO Operations	348UNTS331	200566
United Nations	Ivory Coast	10 Dec 62	Tech Assistance	451UNTS269	106498
United Nations	Jamaica	22 May 63	IGO Status/Immunit	479UNTS19	106945
United Nations	Jamaica	06 Dec 66	IGO Operations	580UNTS211	108424
United Nations	Japan	25 Jul 52	IGO Status/Immunit	135UNTS305	200443
United Nations	Japan	24 Jun 53	Tech Assistance	167UNTS249	200499
United Nations	Japan	26 Oct 53	IGO Operations	57JAIL86	440066
United Nations	Japan	19 Feb 54	Status of Forces	0JGJI1162	441077
United Nations	Japan	19 Feb 54	Status of Forces	0JGJI7	441078
United Nations	Japan	03 May 60	IGO Operations	0JGJI1413	441107
United Nations	Japan	15 Mar 61	IGO Operations	397UNTS199	105706
United Nations	Japan	04 Oct 61	Education	410UNTS133	105900
United Nations	Japan	11 Apr 62	IGO Operations	425UNTS45	106117
United Nations	Jordan	29 Mar 51	Tech Assistance	137UNTS267	200448
United Nations	Jordan	18 Nov 58	IGO Operations	315UNTS125	104564
United Nations	Jordan	11 Sep 61	Tech Assistance	406UNTS255	105855
United Nations	Kenya	01 Oct 64	IGO Operations	511UNTS199	107434
United Nations	Korea, South	21 Sep 51	IGO Status/Immunit	104UNTS323	200322
United Nations	Korea, South	06 Nov 59	Other Military	346UNTS289	200565
United Nations	Kuwait	31 Oct 60	Tech Assistance	391UNTS295	200581
United Nations	Laos	06 Jul 59	Tech Assistance	337UNTS41	104814
United Nations	League of Nations	19 Jul 46	Specific Property	1UNTS109	200002
United Nations	League of Nations	31 Jul 46	Specific Property	1UNTS119	200003
United Nations	League of Nations	01 Aug 46	Specific Property	1UNTS135	200005
United Nations	League of Nations	01 Aug 46	Specific Property	1UNTS131	200004
United Nations	League of Nations	11 Apr 47	Specific Property	4UNTS443	200026
United Nations	League of Nations	14 Apr 47	Specific Property	4UNTS449	200027
United Nations	League of Nations	27 Jun 47	Specific Property	5UNTS389	200036
United Nations	League of Nations	27 Jun 47	Specific Property	5UNTS395	200037
United Nations	Lebanon	01 May 57	IGO Establishment	266UNTS125	103827
United Nations	Lebanon	20 Jan 58	Milit Installation	286UNTS189	104166

PARTY ONE	PARTY TWO	DATE	TOPIC	CITATION	NUMBER
United Nations	Lebanon	20 Jan 58	Postal Service	286UNTS199	104167
United Nations	Lebanon	13 Jun 58	IGO Status/Immunit	303UNTS271	104386
United Nations	Lebanon	26 Aug 61	Tech Assistance	406UNTS105	105842
United Nations	Lesotho	17 Nov 66	IGO Operations	580UNTS29	108418
United Nations	Liberia	09 Mar 54	Tech Assistance	187UNTS61	102501
United Nations	Libya	27 Jun 59	Tech Assistance	336UNTS291	104811
United Nations	Luxembourg	28 Dec 66	Claims and Debts	585UNTS147	108487
United Nations	Mali	09 May 63	Tech Assistance	463UNTS147	106699
United Nations	Mauritius	29 Aug 69	General Aid	0UNTS0	110247
United Nations	Mauritius	29 Aug 69	Tech Assistance	0UNTS0	110245
United Nations	Mauritius	29 Aug 69	Tech Assistance	0UNTS0	110246
United Nations	Mexico	20 May 51	IGO Operations	102UNTS103	101413
United Nations	Mexico	07 Apr 59	IGO Operations	381UNTS123	105468
United Nations	Mexico	18 Aug 61	Humanitarian	404UNTS297	105817
United Nations	Mexico	17 Jul 64	IGO Operations	533UNTS117	107738
United Nations	Monaco	17 Dec 65	IGO Operations	550UNTS365	200615
United Nations	Mongolia	06 Jan 65	IGO Operations	522UNTS45	107535
United Nations	Morocco	03 Mar 64	IGO Status/Immunit	490UNTS187	107154
United Nations	Multilateral	19 Jul 46	IGO Operations	1UNTS97	200001
United Nations	Multilateral	28 Aug 46	IGO Operations	1UNTS139	200006
United Nations	Multilateral	10 Jul 47	Specific Property	5UNTS401	200038
United Nations	Multilateral	09 Dec 48	Humanitarian	78UNTS277	101021
United Nations	Multilateral	06 Apr 50	Admin Cooperation	119UNTS99	101610
United Nations	Multilateral	02 Nov 50	Tech Assistance	81UNTS160	101071
United Nations	Multilateral	24 Nov 50	Tech Assistance	81UNTS188	101072
United Nations	Multilateral	02 Dec 50	Trusteeship	118UNTS255	200381
United Nations	Multilateral	15 Dec 50	Tech Assistance	76UNTS120	100985
United Nations	Multilateral	18 Jan 51	Tech Assistance	81UNTS233	101073
United Nations	Multilateral	15 Feb 51	Tech Assistance	81UNTS245	101074
United Nations	Multilateral	05 Mar 51	Tech Assistance	81UNTS261	101075
United Nations	Multilateral	20 Mar 51	IGO Operations	82UNTS172	101091
United Nations	Multilateral	05 Apr 51	Tech Assistance	84UNTS299	101139
United Nations	Multilateral	25 Jun 51	Tech Assistance	92UNTS27	101258
United Nations	Multilateral	28 Jun 51	Tech Assistance	118UNTS154	101604
United Nations	Multilateral	18 Jul 51	Direct Aid	102UNTS291	200308
United Nations	Multilateral	27 Jul 51	Tech Assistance	97UNTS291	200273
United Nations	Multilateral	05 Sep 51	Tech Assistance	173UNTS15	102256
United Nations	Multilateral	01 Oct 51	Tech Assistance	104UNTS249	101446
United Nations	Multilateral	24 Dec 51	Tech Assistance	118UNTS290	200383
United Nations	Multilateral	23 Jan 52	Tech Assistance	127UNTS269	101708
United Nations	Multilateral	18 Feb 52	Tech Assistance	126UNTS319	200434
United Nations	Multilateral	11 Apr 52	Tech Assistance	173UNTS2	102255
United Nations	Multilateral	22 May 52	Tech Assistance	131UNTS115	101739
United Nations	Multilateral	19 Jun 52	Tech Assistance	133UNTS165	101787
United Nations	Multilateral	21 Aug 52	Tech Assistance	141UNTS129	101912
United Nations	Multilateral	15 Oct 52	Tech Assistance	141UNTS96	101909
United Nations	Multilateral	17 Oct 52	Direct Aid	141UNTS121	101911
United Nations	Multilateral	16 Dec 52	Tech Assistance	158UNTS407	102074
United Nations	Multilateral	29 Dec 52	Tech Assistance	151UNTS317	102002
United Nations	Multilateral	26 Feb 53	Tech Assistance	161UNTS31	102120
United Nations	Multilateral	09 Oct 53	Tech Assistance	190UNTS49	102557
United Nations	Multilateral	20 Apr 54	Tech Assistance	189UNTS11	102539
United Nations	Multilateral	31 May 54	Tech Assistance	192UNTS20	102592
United Nations	Multilateral	01 Jun 54	Tech Assistance	200UNTS235	200520
United Nations	Multilateral	30 Jun 54	Tech Assistance	193UNTS67	102611
United Nations	Multilateral	19 Aug 54	Tech Assistance	201UNTS51	102710
United Nations	Multilateral	06 Oct 54	Tech Assistance	201UNTS75	102711
United Nations	Multilateral	27 Oct 54	Tech Assistance	201UNTS95	102712
United Nations	Multilateral	29 Oct 54	Tech Assistance	201UNTS115	102713
United Nations	Multilateral	16 Dec 54	Tech Assistance	204UNTS323	200523
United Nations	Multilateral	04 Apr 55	Tech Assistance	208UNTS239	102816
United Nations	Multilateral	14 Jun 55	Tech Assistance	212UNTS263	200526
United Nations	Multilateral	04 Jul 55	Tech Assistance	214UNTS10	102897
United Nations	Multilateral	13 Dec 55	Tech Assistance	407UNTS8	105857
United Nations	Multilateral	02 Feb 56	Tech Assistance	227UNTS153	103137

PARTY ONE	PARTY TWO	DATE	TOPIC	CITATION	NUMBER
United Nations	Multilateral	10 Feb 56	Tech Assistance	228UNTS189	103151
United Nations	Multilateral	10 Feb 56	Tech Assistance	228UNTS167	103150
United Nations	Multilateral	30 Mar 56	IGO Operations	604UNTS114	108748
United Nations	Multilateral	10 May 56	Tech Assistance	243UNTS103	103449
United Nations	Multilateral	31 May 56	Tech Assistance	251UNTS181	103541
United Nations	Multilateral	08 Jun 56	Tech Assistance	247UNTS366	200541
United Nations	Multilateral	12 Jun 56	Tech Assistance	243UNTS187	103453
United Nations	Multilateral	14 Jun 56	Tech Assistance	265UNTS125	103809
United Nations	Multilateral	26 Jun 56	Tech Assistance	321UNTS2	104650
United Nations	Multilateral	26 Jun 56	Tech Assistance	253UNTS12	103573
United Nations	Multilateral	02 Jul 56	Tech Assistance	540UNTS110	107846
United Nations	Multilateral	02 Jul 56	Tech Assistance	248UNTS37	103484
United Nations	Multilateral	31 Aug 56	Tech Assistance	249UNTS158	103506
United Nations	Multilateral	05 Oct 56	Tech Assistance	251UNTS267	103545
United Nations	Multilateral	05 Oct 56	Tech Assistance	251UNTS245	103544
United Nations	Multilateral	21 Nov 56	Tech Assistance	253UNTS266	103588
United Nations	Multilateral	15 Jan 57	Tech Assistance	376UNTS122	105378
United Nations	Multilateral	23 Jan 57	Tech Assistance	259UNTS426	103701
United Nations	Multilateral	17 Feb 57	Tech Assistance	271UNTS2	103907
United Nations	Multilateral	22 Feb 57	Tech Assistance	274UNTS93	103960
United Nations	Multilateral	01 Mar 57	Tech Assistance	264UNTS94	103790
United Nations	Multilateral	28 Mar 57	Tech Assistance	271UNTS30	103908
United Nations	Multilateral	09 Apr 57	Tech Assistance	274UNTS172	103965
United Nations	Multilateral	24 May 57	Tech Assistance	268UNTS270	103861
United Nations	Multilateral	30 Jun 57	Tech Assistance	286UNTS171	104165
United Nations	Multilateral	09 Jul 57	Tech Assistance	274UNTS300	103972
United Nations	Multilateral	05 Nov 57	Tech Assistance	285UNTS301	104155
United Nations	Multilateral	15 Mar 58	Tech Assistance	292UNTS273	104276
United Nations	Multilateral	20 Mar 58	Admin Cooperation	335UNTS211	104789
United Nations	Multilateral	19 Jun 58	Tech Assistance	306UNTS236	200550
United Nations	Multilateral	09 Oct 59	Tech Assistance	376UNTS382	105391
United Nations	Multilateral	03 Dec 59	Tech Assistance	348UNTS246	105003
United Nations	Multilateral	03 Dec 59	Tech Assistance	345UNTS251	104971
United Nations	Multilateral	12 Apr 60	Tech Assistance	359UNTS323	105150
United Nations	Multilateral	04 Jun 60	Tech Assistance	360UNTS208	105159
United Nations	Multilateral	19 Jun 60	IGO Operations	537UNTS214	107803
United Nations	Multilateral	08 Jul 60	Tech Assistance	366UNTS310	105220
United Nations	Multilateral	28 Jan 61	Tech Assistance	387UNTS202	105563
United Nations	Multilateral	20 Sep 61	Tech Assistance	407UNTS52	105859
United Nations	Multilateral	16 Oct 61	Tech Assistance	410UNTS242	105908
United Nations	Multilateral	07 Nov 61	Tech Assistance	412UNTS258	105937
United Nations	Multilateral	27 Dec 61	Tech Assistance	425UNTS83	106120
United Nations	Multilateral	17 Jan 62	Tech Assistance	419UNTS294	106033
United Nations	Multilateral	20 Jan 62	Tech Assistance	429UNTS230	200596
United Nations	Multilateral	13 Feb 62	Tech Assistance	422UNTS288	200594
United Nations	Multilateral	21 Feb 62	Tech Assistance	423UNTS151	106091
United Nations	Multilateral	01 Mar 62	Tech Assistance	423UNTS122	106089
United Nations	Multilateral	10 Apr 62	Tech Assistance	429UNTS78	106192
United Nations	Multilateral	18 Apr 62	Tech Assistance	463UNTS44	106692
United Nations	Multilateral	17 May 62	Tech Assistance	429UNTS46	106189
United Nations	Multilateral	12 Aug 62	Tech Assistance	443UNTS266	106365
United Nations	Multilateral	15 Aug 62	Territory Boundary	437UNTS292	106312
United Nations	Multilateral	29 Aug 62	Tech Assistance	443UNTS280	106366
United Nations	Multilateral	11 Sep 62	Tech Assistance	455UNTS402	106553
United Nations	Multilateral	14 Sep 62	Visas	443UNTS73	106360
United Nations	Multilateral	15 Nov 62	Tech Assistance	448UNTS50	106424
United Nations	Multilateral	06 Dec 62	Tech Assistance	450UNTS240	106471
United Nations	Multilateral	12 Dec 62	Tech Assistance	457UNTS72	106578
United Nations	Multilateral	21 Jan 63	Tech Assistance	453UNTS20	106517
United Nations	Multilateral	05 Feb 63	Tech Assistance	453UNTS36	106518
United Nations	Multilateral	14 Feb 63	Tech Assistance	453UNTS168	106524
United Nations	Multilateral	06 Mar 63	Tech Assistance	455UNTS386	106552
United Nations	Multilateral	18 Apr 63	Tech Assistance	463UNTS121	106697
United Nations	Multilateral	06 May 63	Tech Assistance	463UNTS78	106694
United Nations	Multilateral	09 May 63	Tech Assistance	463UNTS159	106700

PARTY ONE	PARTY TWO	DATE	TOPIC	CITATION	NUMBER
United Nations	Multilateral	22 May 63	Tech Assistance	483UNTS72	107007
United Nations	Multilateral	24 May 63	Tech Assistance	470UNTS208	106810
United Nations	Multilateral	24 May 63	Tech Assistance	466UNTS346	106754
United Nations	Multilateral	23 Jul 63	Tech Assistance	471UNTS158	106831
United Nations	Multilateral	31 Jul 63	Tech Assistance	472UNTS220	106842
United Nations	Multilateral	27 Aug 63	Tech Assistance	511UNTS210	107435
United Nations	Multilateral	10 Sep 63	Tech Assistance	480UNTS100	106965
United Nations	Multilateral	21 Oct 63	Tech Assistance	480UNTS197	106969
United Nations	Multilateral	30 Oct 63	Tech Assistance	480UNTS180	106968
United Nations	Multilateral	07 Nov 63	Tech Assistance	480UNTS232	106971
United Nations	Multilateral	08 Nov 63	Tech Assistance	482UNTS286	106999
United Nations	Multilateral	28 Jan 64	Tech Assistance	502UNTS321	107336
United Nations	Multilateral	20 Feb 64	Tech Assistance	491UNTS30	107172
United Nations	Multilateral	23 Jun 64	Tech Assistance	506UNTS108	107383
United Nations	Multilateral	28 Jun 64	Tech Assistance	519UNTS14	107499
United Nations	Multilateral	03 Aug 64	Tech Assistance	503UNTS239	107347
United Nations	Multilateral	24 Oct 64	Tech Assistance	514UNTS220	200608
United Nations	Multilateral	11 Nov 64	Tech Assistance	515UNTS94	107456
United Nations	Multilateral	11 Dec 64	IGO Operations	547UNTS297	107964
United Nations	Multilateral	15 Dec 64	Tech Assistance	522UNTS20	107533
United Nations	Multilateral	27 Jan 65	Tech Assistance	523UNTS102	107556
United Nations	Multilateral	02 Feb 65	Tech Assistance	523UNTS256	107560
United Nations	Multilateral	12 Feb 65	Tech Assistance	525UNTS148	107587
United Nations	Multilateral	23 Feb 65	IGO Operations	527UNTS120	107622
United Nations	Multilateral	05 Mar 65	IGO Operations	527UNTS221	107627
United Nations	Multilateral	08 Apr 65	IGO Operations	533UNTS66	107733
United Nations	Multilateral	26 Apr 65	IGO Operations	533UNTS50	107732
United Nations	Multilateral	12 May 65	IGO Operations	534UNTS390	107769
United Nations	Multilateral	14 May 65	IGO Operations	550UNTS310	108026
United Nations	Multilateral	25 May 65	IGO Operations	535UNTS374	107791
United Nations	Multilateral	02 Jun 65	Tech Assistance	537UNTS348	200611
United Nations	Multilateral	02 Jun 65	Tech Assistance	551UNTS2	108030
United Nations	Multilateral	05 Jul 65	General Aid	563UNTS104	108207
United Nations	Multilateral	20 Jul 65	IGO Operations	541UNTS12	107857
United Nations	Multilateral	13 Sep 65	IGO Operations	547UNTS248	107961
United Nations	Multilateral	13 Sep 65	Tech Assistance	547UNTS264	107962
United Nations	Multilateral	21 Sep 65	IGO Operations	547UNTS280	107963
United Nations	Multilateral	21 Oct 65	Tech Assistance	547UNTS216	107959
United Nations	Multilateral	12 Nov 65	IGO Operations	550UNTS160	108013
United Nations	Multilateral	31 Dec 65	Recognition	552UNTS292	108060
United Nations	Multilateral	12 May 66	General Aid	563UNTS54	108204
United Nations	Multilateral	06 Aug 66	Tech Assistance	570UNTS178	108294
United Nations	Multilateral	22 Aug 66	Tech Assistance	571UNTS298	200624
United Nations	Multilateral	23 Sep 66	IGO Operations	573UNTS132	108327
United Nations	Multilateral	23 Sep 66	General Aid	573UNTS148	108328
United Nations	Multilateral	30 Sep 66	IGO Operations	576UNTS8	108361
United Nations	Multilateral	17 Nov 66	IGO Operations	580UNTS22	108417
United Nations	Multilateral	25 Jan 67	IGO Operations	588UNTS212	108527
United Nations	Multilateral	27 Feb 67	IGO Operations	590UNTS156	108552
United Nations	Multilateral	03 Mar 67	Tech Assistance	594UNTS96	108597
United Nations	Multilateral	17 Mar 67	Non-IBRD Project	594UNTS105	108598
United Nations	Multilateral	13 Apr 67	IGO Operations	595UNTS60	108612
United Nations	Multilateral	19 Apr 67	Tech Assistance	595UNTS120	108617
United Nations	Multilateral	10 Jun 67	Direct Aid	602UNTS212	108714
United Nations	Multilateral	14 Jun 67	Direct Aid	603UNTS2	108719
United Nations	Multilateral	21 Jun 67	Tech Assistance	598UNTS2	108653
United Nations	Multilateral	12 Oct 67	Direct Aid	607UNTS2	108792
United Nations	Multilateral	12 Oct 67	Direct Aid	607UNTS20	108793
United Nations	Multilateral	14 Nov 67	Admin Cooperation	614UNTS2	108860
United Nations	Multilateral	18 Jun 69	IGO Operations	0UNTS0	109741
United Nations	Multilateral	18 Jun 69	IGO Operations	0UNTS0	109740
United Nations	Multilateral	24 Jun 69	IGO Operations	0UNTS0	109743
United Nations	Multilateral	29 Jul 70	Tech Assistance	0UNTS0	110608
United Nations	Multilateral	26 Sep 70	IGO Operations	0UNTS0	110768
United Nations	Nepal	02 Mar 53	Tech Assistance	161UNTS347	200493

PARTY ONE	PARTY TWO	DATE	TOPIC	CITATION	NUMBER
United Nations	Nepal	18 Aug 58	Admin Cooperation	508UNTS3	107403
United Nations	Netherlands	09 Apr 53	Direct Aid	163UNTS89	102143
United Nations	Netherlands	27 May 64	IGO Status/Immunit	548UNTS79	107971
United Nations	New Zealand	02 Feb 61	Humanitarian	391UNTS23	105614
United Nations	New Zealand	21 Feb 66	IGO Operations	555UNTS163	108110
United Nations	Nicaragua	03 Dec 63	IGO Status/Immunit	482UNTS329	107002
United Nations	Niger	01 Oct 62	Tech Assistance	439UNTS181	106329
United Nations	Niger	20 Nov 63	IGO Establishment	536UNTS3	107793
United Nations	Niger	07 May 68	IGO Operations	639UNTS71	109145
United Nations	Nigeria	07 Aug 62	Tech Assistance	435UNTS167	106278
United Nations	Nigeria	07 Feb 67	IGO Operations	590UNTS25	108544
United Nations	Nigeria	02 Jul 68	General Economic	639UNTS81	109146
United Nations	Norway	09 Jul 57	Status of Forces	271UNTS223	103917
United Nations	OAU (Afri Unity)	15 Nov 65	IGO Operations	548UNTS315	200614
United Nations	Other Party Combin	05 Nov 58	Admin Cooperation	613UNTS385	200630
United Nations	Other Party Combin	22 Apr 59	Admin Cooperation	613UNTS391	200631
United Nations	Other Unilat Decla	31 Aug 65	IGO Establishment	557UNTS143	108132
United Nations	Pakistan	27 Aug 48	Humanitarian	47UNTS269	100734
United Nations	Pakistan	28 Apr 52	Tech Assistance	128UNTS191	101720
United Nations	Pakistan	25 Jan 54	Tech Assistance	185UNTS213	102472
United Nations	Pakistan	17 Nov 60	Tech Assistance	380UNTS277	105460
United Nations	Pakistan	18 Apr 63	IGO Operations	503UNTS25	107339
United Nations	Panama	20 Aug 52	Tech Assistance	136UNTS3	101829
United Nations	Panama	24 Jun 59	IGO Operations	507UNTS245	107402
United Nations	Paraguay	27 Sep 51	Tech Assistance	120UNTS105	101617
United Nations	Paraguay	01 Aug 59	Tech Assistance	341UNTS319	104894
United Nations	Philippines	15 Sep 64	IGO Operations	510UNTS137	107410
United Nations	Philippines	05 Apr 66	Health/Educ/Welfare	560UNTS191	108174
United Nations	Poland	16 Jul 63	IGO Operations	471UNTS3	106817
United Nations	Poland	20 Feb 67	IGO Operations	590UNTS71	108547
United Nations	Romania	29 May 61	IGO Operations	406UNTS147	105845
United Nations	Romania	08 Apr 67	Privil/Immunities	594UNTS159	108602
United Nations	Rwanda	28 Nov 62	Tech Assistance	450UNTS267	106473
United Nations	San Marino	07 Oct 48	Humanitarian	47UNTS337	200190
United Nations	Saudi Arabia	16 Mar 62	Tech Assistance	456UNTS379	106566
United Nations	Saudi Arabia	23 Aug 63	IGO Status/Immunit	474UNTS155	106879
United Nations	Senegal	12 Jan 66	Health/Educ/Welfare	551UNTS147	108039
United Nations	Senegal	08 Nov 67	Admin Cooperation	613UNTS255	108854
United Nations	Sierra Leone	19 Feb 64	IGO Status/Immunit	489UNTS91	107136
United Nations	Somalia	20 Jan 62	Tech Assistance	420UNTS133	106044
United Nations	South Pacific Com	24 Jan 63	Tech Assistance	470UNTS361	200604
United Nations	South Pacific Com	20 Feb 63	Tech Assistance	453UNTS333	200600
United Nations	Sudan	28 Mar 59	Tech Assistance	327UNTS95	104719
United Nations	Sudan	08 Nov 66	Scientific Project	576UNTS85	108365
United Nations	Sweden	11 Feb 53	Tech Assistance	160UNTS3	102096
United Nations	Sweden	01 Jul 57	Status of Forces	271UNTS187	103914
United Nations	Sweden	01 Jun 62	Admin Cooperation	429UNTS135	106195
United Nations	Sweden	16 Jun 65	Admin Cooperation	539UNTS45	107823
United Nations	Sweden	21 Feb 66	IGO Operations	555UNTS169	108111
United Nations	Switzerland	01 Jul 46	IGO Status/Immunit	1UNTS163	200008
United Nations	Switzerland	01 Jul 46	Specific Property	1UNTS153	200007
United Nations	Switzerland	14 Sep 49	IGO Operations	43UNTS327	200183
United Nations	Switzerland	09 Jul 56	Telecommunications	56SWRO1273	462191
United Nations	Switzerland	03 Jun 66	Claims and Debts	564UNTS193	200621
United Nations	Switzerland	13 May 68	IGO Operations	636UNTS353	200637
United Nations	Switzerland	11 Dec 68	Postal Service	0UNTS0	200649
United Nations	Syria	17 Nov 62	IGO Status/Immunit	456UNTS359	106565
United Nations	Taiwan	05 Feb 54	Tech Assistance	186UNTS85	102485
United Nations	Tanganyika	01 Jun 62	Tech Assistance	479UNTS3	106944
United Nations	Thailand	05 Oct 48	Humanitarian	47UNTS287	100735
United Nations	Thailand	11 Jun 51	Tech Assistance	90UNTS45	101225
United Nations	Thailand	26 May 54	IGO Status/Immunit	260UNTS35	103703
United Nations	Togo	06 May 60	Tech Assistance	388UNTS53	105571
United Nations	Togo	03 Jul 64	Education	502UNTS287	107334
United Nations	Trieste	30 Sep 52	Tech Assistance	140UNTS11	101881

PARTY ONE	PARTY TWO	DATE	TOPIC	CITATION	NUMBER
United Nations	Trinidad/Tobago	06 May 63	IGO Status/Immunit	463UNTS109	106696
United Nations	Tunisia	23 Dec 58	Tech Assistance	321UNTS23	104651
United Nations	Tunisia	04 Aug 66	IGO Operations	576UNTS23	108363
United Nations	Tunisia	18 Mar 68	IGO Operations	633UNTS3	109030
United Nations	Turkey	31 Mar 64	IGO Status/Immunit	492UNTS273	107196
United Nations	Uganda	29 May 63	IGO Status/Immunit	466UNTS311	106751
United Nations	UK Great Britain	18 Mar 49	Humanitarian	47UNTS305	100736
United Nations	UK Great Britain	27 Jun 63	Trusteeship	469UNTS145	106789
United Nations	UK Great Britain	02 Apr 64	IGO Status/Immunit	492UNTS279	107197
United Nations	UK Great Britain	21 Feb 66	General Economic	555UNTS177	108112
United Nations	UK Great Britain	12 Mar 68	IGO Operations	632UNTS121	109014
United Nations	UNESCO (Educ/Cult)	03 Feb 47	IGO Operations	1UNTS233	200011
United Nations	UNESCO (Educ/Cult)	07 Mar 51	IGO Operations	139UNTS417	200468
United Nations	United Arab Rep	08 Jan 57	Specific Property	257UNTS75	103650
United Nations	United Arab Rep	08 Feb 57	Status of Forces	260UNTS61	103704
United Nations	United Arab Rep	17 Oct 60	Specif Claim/Waive	388UNTS143	105575
United Nations	United Arab Rep	08 Feb 63	Direct Aid	453UNTS79	106520
United Nations	United Arab Rep	27 Aug 63	Tech Assistance	474UNTS221	106884
United Nations	United Arab Rep	26 Nov 65	IGO Operations	551UNTS253	108046
United Nations	United Arab Rep	14 Nov 68	IGO Operations	0UNTS0	109371
United Nations	UNRRA (Relief)	27 Sep 48	IGO Operations	27UNTS349	200158
United Nations	Upper Volta	26 Feb 64	IGO Status/Immunit	489UNTS179	107139
United Nations	UPU (Postal Union)	15 Nov 47	IGO Operations	19UNTS219	200116
United Nations	Uruguay	17 Oct 51	Tech Assistance	122UNTS29	101633
United Nations	USA (United States)	26 Jun 47	IGO Establishment	11UNTS11	100147
United Nations	USA (United States)	18 Dec 47	IGO Status/Immunit	11UNTS347	100174
United Nations	USA (United States)	23 Mar 48	Loans and Credits	19UNTS43	100303
United Nations	USA (United States)	28 Mar 51	Postal Service	108UNTS231	101476
United Nations	USA (United States)	18 Nov 61	US Agri Commod Aid	494UNTS213	107235
United Nations	USSR (Soviet Union)	04 May 70	Education	0UNTS0	110459
United Nations	Venezuela	05 Mar 54	Tech Assistance	187UNTS9	102498
United Nations	Venezuela	18 Nov 56	IGO Operations	588UNTS243	108529
United Nations	Vietnam, South	24 Mar 54	Tech Assistance	188UNTS345	200514
United Nations	Vietnam, South	03 Jun 59	IGO Status/Immunit	337UNTS361	200557
United Nations	Western Samoa	05 Nov 62	Tech Assistance	443UNTS297	200599
United Nations	WHO (World Health)	15 Nov 47	IGO Operations	19UNTS193	200115
United Nations	WHO (World Health)	10 Feb 50	IGO Operations	46UNTS327	200188
United Nations	WHO (World Health)	20 Apr 50	IGO Operations	139UNTS445	200470
United Nations	WMO (Meteorology)	10 Apr 51	IGO Status/Immunit	103UNTS245	200415
United Nations	WMO (Meteorology)	27 Mar 53	IGO Operations	178UNTS361	200504
United Nations	Yemen	07 Apr 53	Tech Assistance	163UNTS73	102142
United Nations	Yugoslavia	06 Jan 51	Direct Aid	78UNTS165	101015
United Nations	Yugoslavia	10 Apr 52	Tech Assistance	141UNTS89	101908
United Nations	Yugoslavia	01 Oct 57	Milit Assistance	277UNTS191	104006
United Nations	Yugoslavia	07 Jan 65	IGO Operations	522UNTS55	107536
United Nations	Yugoslavia	16 Mar 70	Humanitarian	0UNTS0	110360
United Nations	Zambia	23 Oct 65	IGO Operations	549UNTS101	107993
United Nations	Zambia	06 Jul 67	IGO Operations	600UNTS81	108678
United Nations	Zambia	30 Mar 70	Humanitarian	0UNTS0	110399
UNKRA (Korean Rec)	Multilateral	13 Mar 56	Humanitarian	427UNTS245	106158
UNRRA (Relief)	Austria	05 Apr 46	Direct Aid	46ABGB116	403205
UNRRA (Relief)	Brazil	12 Oct 44	IGO Establishment	67UNTS321	200228
UNRRA (Relief)	Multilateral	19 Jul 46	IGO Operations	1UNTS97	200001
UNRRA (Relief)	Multilateral	28 Aug 46	IGO Operations	1UNTS139	200006
UNRRA (Relief)	Multilateral	10 Jul 47	Specific Property	5UNTS401	200038
UNRRA (Relief)	United Nations	27 Sep 48	IGO Operations	27UNTS349	200158
UNTAB (Tech Assis)	Multilateral	07 Dec 44	IGO Establishment	15UNTS295	200102
UNTAB (Tech Assis)	Multilateral	02 Nov 50	Tech Assistance	81UNTS160	101071
UNTAB (Tech Assis)	Multilateral	18 Jan 51	Tech Assistance	81UNTS233	101073
UNTAB (Tech Assis)	Multilateral	05 Mar 51	Tech Assistance	81UNTS261	101075
UNTAB (Tech Assis)	Multilateral	05 Sep 51	Tech Assistance	173UNTS15	102256
UNTAB (Tech Assis)	Multilateral	01 Oct 51	Tech Assistance	104UNTS249	101446
UNTAB (Tech Assis)	Multilateral	23 Jan 52	Tech Assistance	127UNTS269	101708
UNTAB (Tech Assis)	Multilateral	11 Apr 52	Tech Assistance	173UNTS2	102255
UNTAB (Tech Assis)	Multilateral	15 Oct 52	Tech Assistance	141UNTS96	101909

PARTY ONE	PARTY TWO	DATE	TOPIC	CITATION	NUMBER
UNTAB (Tech Assis)	Multilateral	16 Dec 52	Tech Assistance	158UNTS407	102074
UNTAB (Tech Assis)	Multilateral	29 Dec 52	Tech Assistance	151UNTS317	102002
UNTAB (Tech Assis)	Multilateral	09 Oct 53	Tech Assistance	190UNTS49	102557
UNTAB (Tech Assis)	Multilateral	01 Jun 54	Tech Assistance	200UNTS235	200520
UNTAB (Tech Assis)	Multilateral	06 Oct 54	Tech Assistance	201UNTS75	102711
UNTAB (Tech Assis)	Multilateral	29 Oct 54	Tech Assistance	201UNTS115	102713
UNTAB (Tech Assis)	Multilateral	04 Jul 55	Tech Assistance	214UNTS10	102897
UNTAB (Tech Assis)	Multilateral	10 Feb 56	Tech Assistance	228UNTS189	103151
UNTAB (Tech Assis)	Multilateral	10 Feb 56	Tech Assistance	228UNTS167	103150
UNTAB (Tech Assis)	Multilateral	31 May 56	Tech Assistance	251UNTS181	103541
UNTAB (Tech Assis)	Multilateral	08 Jun 56	Tech Assistance	247UNTS366	200541
UNTAB (Tech Assis)	Multilateral	12 Jun 56	Tech Assistance	243UNTS187	103453
UNTAB (Tech Assis)	Multilateral	14 Jun 56	Tech Assistance	265UNTS125	103809
UNTAB (Tech Assis)	Multilateral	26 Jun 56	Tech Assistance	253UNTS12	103573
UNTAB (Tech Assis)	Multilateral	02 Jul 56	Tech Assistance	248UNTS37	103484
UNTAB (Tech Assis)	Multilateral	31 Aug 56	Tech Assistance	249UNTS158	103506
UNTAB (Tech Assis)	Multilateral	05 Oct 56	Tech Assistance	251UNTS245	103544
UNTAB (Tech Assis)	Multilateral	23 Jan 57	Tech Assistance	259UNTS426	103701
UNTAB (Tech Assis)	Multilateral	01 Mar 57	Tech Assistance	264UNTS94	103790
UNTAB (Tech Assis)	Multilateral	09 Apr 57	Tech Assistance	274UNTS172	103965
UNTAB (Tech Assis)	Multilateral	24 May 57	Tech Assistance	268UNTS270	103861
UNTAB (Tech Assis)	Multilateral	30 Jun 57	Tech Assistance	286UNTS171	104165
UNTAB (Tech Assis)	Multilateral	09 Jul 57	Tech Assistance	274UNTS300	103972
UNTAB (Tech Assis)	Multilateral	19 Jun 58	Tech Assistance	306UNTS236	200550
UNTAB (Tech Assis)	Multilateral	03 Dec 59	Tech Assistance	348UNTS246	105003
UNTAB (Tech Assis)	Multilateral	04 Jun 60	Tech Assistance	360UNTS208	105159
UNTAB (Tech Assis)	Multilateral	08 Jul 60	Tech Assistance	366UNTS310	105220
UNTAB (Tech Assis)	Multilateral	28 Jan 61	Tech Assistance	387UNTS202	105563
UNTAB (Tech Assis)	Multilateral	01 Mar 62	Tech Assistance	423UNTS122	106089
UNTAB (Tech Assis)	Multilateral	14 Feb 63	Tech Assistance	453UNTS168	106524
UNTAB (Tech Assis)	Multilateral	06 Mar 63	Tech Assistance	455UNTS386	106552
UNTAB (Tech Assis)	Multilateral	23 Jul 63	Tech Assistance	471UNTS158	106831
UNTAB (Tech Assis)	Multilateral	04 Aug 63	IGO Establishment	510UNTS3	107408
UNTAB (Tech Assis)	Multilateral	02 Feb 65	Tech Assistance	523UNTS256	107560
UNTAB (Tech Assis)	Multilateral	23 Feb 65	IGO Operations	527UNTS120	107622
UNTAB (Tech Assis)	Multilateral	18 Mar 65	Dispute Settlement	575UNTS159	108359
UNTAB (Tech Assis)	Multilateral	25 May 65	IGO Operations	535UNTS374	107791
UNTAB (Tech Assis)	Multilateral	23 Jun 65	General IGO	614UNTS239	108873
UNTAB (Tech Assis)	Multilateral	23 Sep 66	General Aid	573UNTS148	108328
UNTAB (Tech Assis)	Multilateral	30 Sep 66	IGO Operations	576UNTS8	108361
UNTAB (Tech Assis)	Philippines	01 Mar 52	Tech Assistance	2PTS775	465072
UNTAB (Tech Assis)	Philippines	24 Apr 52	Tech Assistance	2PTS789	465074
UNTAB (Tech Assis)	Philippines	05 Nov 52	Tech Assistance	3PTS41	465076
UNTAB (Tech Assis)	Philippines	05 Nov 52	Tech Assistance	3PTS45	465077
UNTAB (Tech Assis)	Philippines	19 Jun 53	Tech Assistance	3PTS137	465079
UNTAB (Tech Assis)	Philippines	25 Jun 53	Tech Assistance	3PTS161	465080
UNTAB (Tech Assis)	Philippines	06 Aug 53	Tech Assistance	3PTS191	465084
UNTAB (Tech Assis)	Philippines	06 Aug 53	Tech Assistance	3PTS187	465083
UNTAB (Tech Assis)	Philippines	04 May 57	Tech Assistance	3PTS661	465085
UNTAB (Tech Assis)	Philippines	23 Jul 58	Tech Assistance	3PTS749	465086
Upper Volta	Accept UN Charter	07 Aug 60	UN Charter	375UNTS99	105359
Upper Volta	France	11 Jul 60	Recognition	60FRRT52	415214
Upper Volta	France	24 Apr 61	General Amity	62FRRT8	415215
Upper Volta	France	31 Mar 62	Customs	62FRRT42	415216
Upper Volta	France	29 May 62	Air Transport	63FRRT2	415217
Upper Volta	France	11 Aug 65	Finance	67FRJO106	416218
Upper Volta	France	30 May 70	Visas	0UNTS0	110745
Upper Volta	Germany, West	08 Jun 61	Direct Aid	61WBGA193	424522
Upper Volta	Germany, West	08 Jun 61	General Economic	61WBGA193	424521
Upper Volta	IDA (Devel Assoc)	18 Feb 69	Non-IBRD Project	0UNTS0	110215
Upper Volta	Israel	11 Jun 61	Tech Assistance	413UNTS113	105946
Upper Volta	Multilateral	07 Dec 44	IGO Establishment	15UNTS295	200102
Upper Volta	Multilateral	11 Dec 46	Sanitation	12UNTS179	100186
Upper Volta	Multilateral	24 Jul 48	Sanitation	66UNTS25	100847
Upper Volta	Multilateral	09 Dec 48	Humanitarian	78UNTS277	101021

PARTY ONE	PARTY TWO	DATE	TOPIC	CITATION	NUMBER
Upper Volta	Multilateral	21 Mar 50	Admin Cooperation	96UNTS271	101342
Upper Volta	Multilateral	22 Nov 50	Culture	131UNTS25	101734
Upper Volta	Multilateral	18 Jan 54	IGO Establishment	330UNTS121	104743
Upper Volta	Multilateral	20 Jun 56	Admin Cooperation	268UNTS3	103850
Upper Volta	Multilateral	29 Apr 58	Specific Resources	559UNTS285	108164
Upper Volta	Multilateral	29 Apr 58	Water Transport	450UNTS11	106465
Upper Volta	Multilateral	26 Jan 60	IGO Establishment	439UNTS249	106333
Upper Volta	Multilateral	21 Apr 61	IGO Establishment	484UNTS349	107041
Upper Volta	Multilateral	25 May 62	IGO Establishment	486UNTS103	107075
Upper Volta	Multilateral	10 Dec 62	Culture	521UNTS231	107525
Upper Volta	Multilateral	18 Apr 63	Tech Assistance	463UNTS121	106697
Upper Volta	Multilateral	24 Apr 63	Consul/Citizenship	596UNTS487	108640
Upper Volta	Multilateral	24 Apr 63	Consul/Citizenship	596UNTS261	108638
Upper Volta	Multilateral	25 May 63	IGO Establishment	479UNTS39	106947
Upper Volta	Multilateral	04 Aug 63	IGO Establishment	510UNTS3	107408
Upper Volta	Multilateral	05 Aug 63	Sanitation	480UNTS43	106964
Upper Volta	Multilateral	14 Sep 63	Air Transport	0UNTS0	110106
Upper Volta	Multilateral	26 Oct 63	Water Transport	587UNTS9	108506
Upper Volta	Multilateral	10 Jul 64	Postal Service	613UNTS193	108852
Upper Volta	Multilateral	10 Jul 64	Postal Service	611UNTS105	108845
Upper Volta	Multilateral	10 Jul 64	Postal Service	611UNTS7	108844
Upper Volta	Multilateral	10 Jul 64	Postal Service	612UNTS233	108848
Upper Volta	Multilateral	10 Jul 64	Postal Service	611UNTS387	108846
Upper Volta	Multilateral	10 Jul 64	Postal Service	612UNTS3	108847
Upper Volta	Multilateral	10 Jul 64	Postal Service	613UNTS3	108850
Upper Volta	Multilateral	10 Jul 64	Postal Service	613UNTS3	108851
Upper Volta	Multilateral	10 Jul 64	Postal Service	612UNTS361	108849
Upper Volta	Multilateral	25 Nov 64	Water Transport	587UNTS19	108507
Upper Volta	Multilateral	18 Mar 65	Dispute Settlement	575UNTS159	108359
Upper Volta	Multilateral	08 Jul 65	General Trade	597UNTS3	108641
Upper Volta	Multilateral	27 May 66	IGO Establishment	637UNTS0	109121
Upper Volta	Multilateral	27 Jan 67	Scientific Project	610UNTS205	108843
Upper Volta	Multilateral	04 May 67	IGO Establishment	595UNTS287	108623
Upper Volta	Multilateral	01 Jul 68	Peace/Disarmament	0UNTS0	110485
Upper Volta	Multilateral	24 Sep 68	Air Transport	0UNTS0	110612
Upper Volta	Multilateral	10 Dec 68	Visas	0UNTS0	109387
Upper Volta	UN Special Fund	26 Jun 61	Direct Aid	400UNTS3	105744
Upper Volta	UNICEF (Children)	15 Nov 60	Direct Aid	402UNTS33	105776
Upper Volta	United Nations	26 Feb 64	IGO Status/Immunit	489UNTS179	107139
Upper Volta	USA (United States)	01 Jun 61	General Aid	410UNTS223	105906
Upper Volta	USA (United States)	18 Jun 65	Finance	549UNTS133	107996
Upper Volta	USA (United States)	21 Aug 67	Scientific Project	0UNTS0	110045
Upper Volta	USSR (Soviet Union)	08 Mar 68	General Trade	0UNTS0	110280
Upper Volta	WHO (World Health)	15 Nov 60	Tech Assistance	383UNTS91	105496
UPU (Postal Union)	Multilateral	27 Oct 54	Tech Assistance	201UNTS95	102712
UPU (Postal Union)	Multilateral	10 May 56	Tech Assistance	243UNTS103	103449
UPU (Postal Union)	Multilateral	31 May 56	Tech Assistance	251UNTS181	103541
UPU (Postal Union)	Multilateral	02 Jul 56	Tech Assistance	248UNTS37	103484
UPU (Postal Union)	Multilateral	27 Dec 61	Tech Assistance	425UNTS83	106120
UPU (Postal Union)	Multilateral	20 Jan 62	Tech Assistance	429UNTS230	200596
UPU (Postal Union)	Multilateral	13 Feb 62	Tech Assistance	422UNTS288	200594
UPU (Postal Union)	Multilateral	18 Apr 62	Tech Assistance	463UNTS44	106692
UPU (Postal Union)	Multilateral	12 Aug 62	Tech Assistance	443UNTS266	106365
UPU (Postal Union)	Multilateral	29 Aug 62	Tech Assistance	443UNTS280	106366
UPU (Postal Union)	Multilateral	14 Sep 62	Visas	443UNTS73	106360
UPU (Postal Union)	Multilateral	15 Nov 62	Tech Assistance	448UNTS50	106424
UPU (Postal Union)	Multilateral	06 Dec 62	Tech Assistance	450UNTS240	106471
UPU (Postal Union)	Multilateral	12 Dec 62	Tech Assistance	457UNTS72	106578
UPU (Postal Union)	Multilateral	21 Jan 63	Tech Assistance	453UNTS20	106517
UPU (Postal Union)	Multilateral	05 Feb 63	Tech Assistance	453UNTS36	106518
UPU (Postal Union)	Multilateral	14 Feb 63	Tech Assistance	453UNTS168	106524
UPU (Postal Union)	Multilateral	06 Mar 63	Tech Assistance	455UNTS386	106552
UPU (Postal Union)	Multilateral	18 Apr 63	Tech Assistance	463UNTS121	106697
UPU (Postal Union)	Multilateral	06 May 63	Tech Assistance	463UNTS78	106694
UPU (Postal Union)	Multilateral	09 May 63	Tech Assistance	463UNTS159	106700

PARTY ONE	PARTY TWO	DATE	TOPIC	CITATION	NUMBER
UPU (Postal Union)	Multilateral	22 May 63	Tech Assistance	483UNTS72	107007
UPU (Postal Union)	Multilateral	24 May 63	Tech Assistance	466UNTS346	106754
UPU (Postal Union)	Multilateral	24 May 63	Tech Assistance	470UNTS208	106810
UPU (Postal Union)	Multilateral	23 Jul 63	Tech Assistance	471UNTS158	106831
UPU (Postal Union)	Multilateral	31 Jul 63	Tech Assistance	472UNTS220	106842
UPU (Postal Union)	Multilateral	27 Aug 63	Tech Assistance	511UNTS210	107435
UPU (Postal Union)	Multilateral	10 Sep 63	Tech Assistance	480UNTS100	106965
UPU (Postal Union)	Multilateral	30 Oct 63	Tech Assistance	480UNTS180	106968
UPU (Postal Union)	Multilateral	07 Nov 63	Tech Assistance	480UNTS232	106971
UPU (Postal Union)	Multilateral	08 Nov 63	Tech Assistance	482UNTS286	106999
UPU (Postal Union)	Multilateral	28 Jan 64	Tech Assistance	502UNTS321	107336
UPU (Postal Union)	Multilateral	20 Feb 64	Tech Assistance	491UNTS30	107172
UPU (Postal Union)	Multilateral	23 Jun 64	Tech Assistance	506UNTS108	107383
UPU (Postal Union)	Multilateral	28 Jun 64	Tech Assistance	519UNTS14	107499
UPU (Postal Union)	Multilateral	03 Aug 64	Tech Assistance	503UNTS239	107347
UPU (Postal Union)	Multilateral	24 Oct 64	Tech Assistance	514UNTS220	200608
UPU (Postal Union)	Multilateral	11 Nov 64	Tech Assistance	515UNTS94	107456
UPU (Postal Union)	Multilateral	11 Dec 64	IGO Operations	547UNTS297	107964
UPU (Postal Union)	Multilateral	15 Dec 64	Tech Assistance	522UNTS20	107533
UPU (Postal Union)	Multilateral	27 Jan 65	Tech Assistance	523UNTS102	107556
UPU (Postal Union)	Multilateral	02 Feb 65	Tech Assistance	523UNTS256	107560
UPU (Postal Union)	Multilateral	12 Feb 65	Tech Assistance	525UNTS148	107587
UPU (Postal Union)	Multilateral	23 Feb 65	IGO Operations	527UNTS120	107622
UPU (Postal Union)	Multilateral	05 Mar 65	IGO Operations	527UNTS221	107627
UPU (Postal Union)	Multilateral	08 Apr 65	IGO Operations	533UNTS66	107733
UPU (Postal Union)	Multilateral	26 Apr 65	IGO Operations	533UNTS50	107732
UPU (Postal Union)	Multilateral	12 May 65	IGO Operations	534UNTS390	107769
UPU (Postal Union)	Multilateral	14 May 65	IGO Operations	550UNTS310	108026
UPU (Postal Union)	Multilateral	25 May 65	IGO Operations	535UNTS374	107791
UPU (Postal Union)	Multilateral	02 Jun 65	Tech Assistance	537UNTS348	200611
UPU (Postal Union)	Multilateral	02 Jun 65	Tech Assistance	551UNTS2	108030
UPU (Postal Union)	Multilateral	05 Jul 65	General Aid	563UNTS104	108207
UPU (Postal Union)	Multilateral	20 Jul 65	IGO Operations	541UNTS12	107857
UPU (Postal Union)	Multilateral	13 Sep 65	Tech Assistance	547UNTS264	107962
UPU (Postal Union)	Multilateral	13 Sep 65	IGO Operations	547UNTS248	107961
UPU (Postal Union)	Multilateral	21 Sep 65	IGO Operations	547UNTS280	107963
UPU (Postal Union)	Multilateral	21 Oct 65	Tech Assistance	547UNTS216	107959
UPU (Postal Union)	Multilateral	12 Nov 65	IGO Operations	550UNTS160	108013
UPU (Postal Union)	Multilateral	31 Dec 65	Recognition	552UNTS292	108060
UPU (Postal Union)	Multilateral	12 May 66	General Aid	563UNTS54	108204
UPU (Postal Union)	Multilateral	06 Aug 66	Tech Assistance	570UNTS178	108294
UPU (Postal Union)	Multilateral	22 Aug 66	Tech Assistance	571UNTS298	200624
UPU (Postal Union)	Multilateral	23 Sep 66	IGO Operations	573UNTS132	108327
UPU (Postal Union)	Multilateral	23 Sep 66	General Aid	573UNTS148	108328
UPU (Postal Union)	Multilateral	30 Sep 66	IGO Operations	576UNTS8	108361
UPU (Postal Union)	Multilateral	17 Nov 66	IGO Operations	580UNTS22	108417
UPU (Postal Union)	Multilateral	25 Jan 67	IGO Operations	588UNTS212	108527
UPU (Postal Union)	Multilateral	27 Feb 67	IGO Operations	590UNTS156	108552
UPU (Postal Union)	Multilateral	03 Mar 67	Tech Assistance	594UNTS96	108597
UPU (Postal Union)	Multilateral	19 Apr 67	Tech Assistance	595UNTS120	108617
UPU (Postal Union)	Multilateral	10 Jun 67	Direct Aid	602UNTS212	108714
UPU (Postal Union)	Multilateral	14 Jun 67	Direct Aid	603UNTS2	108719
UPU (Postal Union)	Multilateral	20 Jun 67	Tech Assistance	0UNTS0	109290
UPU (Postal Union)	Multilateral	21 Jun 67	Tech Assistance	598UNTS2	108653
UPU (Postal Union)	Multilateral	12 Oct 67	Direct Aid	607UNTS20	108793
UPU (Postal Union)	Multilateral	12 Oct 67	Direct Aid	607UNTS2	108792
UPU (Postal Union)	Multilateral	27 Oct 67	General Aid	608UNTS37	108811
UPU (Postal Union)	Multilateral	14 Nov 67	Admin Cooperation	614UNTS2	108860
UPU (Postal Union)	Multilateral	18 Jun 69	IGO Operations	0UNTS0	109740
UPU (Postal Union)	Multilateral	18 Jun 69	IGO Operations	0UNTS0	109741
UPU (Postal Union)	Multilateral	24 Jun 69	IGO Operations	0UNTS0	109743
UPU (Postal Union)	Switzerland	22 Apr 48	IGO Status/Immunit	56SWRO1194	462189
UPU (Postal Union)	UN Special Fund	21 Sep 66	Non-IBRD Project	573UNTS259	200626
UPU (Postal Union)	United Nations	15 Nov 47	IGO Operations	19UNTS219	200116
Uruguay	Argentina	30 Dec 46	Specific Resources	0UNTS0	109540

PARTY ONE	PARTY TWO	DATE	TOPIC	CITATION	NUMBER
Uruguay	Argentina	27 Apr 57	Non-ILO Labor	635UNTS69	109072
Uruguay	Argentina	23 Nov 60	Non-IBRD Project	0UNTS0	109519
Uruguay	Argentina	07 Apr 61	Territory Boundary	635UNTS91	109074
Uruguay	Argentina	04 Sep 63	General Economic	0UNTS0	109541
Uruguay	Argentina	12 Feb 66	Non-IBRD Project	0UNTS0	109520
Uruguay	Argentina	07 Mar 66	General Trade	635UNTS275	109088
Uruguay	Argentina	12 Feb 67	Water Transport	635UNTS125	109076
Uruguay	Argentina	30 May 67	Non-IBRD Project	0UNTS0	109521
Uruguay	Argentina	08 Jul 68	Visas	0UNTS0	109544
Uruguay	Argentina	08 Jul 68	Territory Boundary	0UNTS0	110185
Uruguay	Argentina	08 Jul 68	Non-IBRD Project	0UNTS0	109542
Uruguay	Argentina	16 Oct 68	Territory Boundary	0UNTS0	109543
Uruguay	Argentina	27 Jun 69	Commodity Trade	0UNTS0	110191
Uruguay	Argentina	18 Sep 69	Commodity Trade	0UNTS0	110192
Uruguay	Austria	06 Jul 61	Visas	63ABGB223	403206
Uruguay	Brazil	08 Jan 42	Admin Cooperation	54UNTS359	200206
Uruguay	Brazil	18 May 42	Telecommunications	54UNTS369	200207
Uruguay	Brazil	22 Nov 44	Specif Goods/Equip	65UNTS289	200217
Uruguay	Brazil	16 Dec 44	Admin Cooperation	65UNTS305	200218
Uruguay	Denmark	04 Mar 53	General Economic	250UNTS51	103517
Uruguay	Denmark	09 Sep 53	Finance	256UNTS149	103625
Uruguay	Denmark	04 Jun 57	Finance	286UNTS107	104162
Uruguay	France	09 May 60	Finance	60FRRT43	415478
Uruguay	Germany, West	18 Apr 53	General Trade	53WBGA94	424708
Uruguay	Germany, West	18 Apr 53	General Trade	54WGBB51	425707
Uruguay	Germany, West	31 Aug 57	Air Transport	59WGBB80	425709
Uruguay	IAEA (Atom Energy)	24 Sep 65	Atomic Energy	556UNTS117	108123
Uruguay	IBRD (World Bank)	25 Aug 50	IBRD Project	156UNTS203	102042
Uruguay	IBRD (World Bank)	29 Aug 55	IBRD Project	243UNTS123	103450
Uruguay	IBRD (World Bank)	25 Oct 56	IBRD Project	265UNTS59	103807
Uruguay	IBRD (World Bank)	30 Dec 59	IBRD Project	384UNTS275	105523
Uruguay	IBRD (World Bank)	26 Oct 62	IBRD Project	481UNTS39	106977
Uruguay	IBRD (World Bank)	30 Mar 65	IBRD Project	567UNTS45	108251
Uruguay	ILO (Labor Org)	20 Sep 52	Tech Assistance	187UNTS25	102499
Uruguay	Israel	30 Apr 53	Culture	280UNTS269	104064
Uruguay	Israel	03 Apr 66	Visas	582UNTS73	108459
Uruguay	Israel	03 Mar 69	Taxation	0UNTS0	110381
Uruguay	Italy	26 Feb 47	General Trade	48ITGU82	435426
Uruguay	Multilateral	30 Jul 40	Admin Cooperation	161UNTS253	200488
Uruguay	Multilateral	12 Oct 40	Specific Resources	161UNTS193	200485
Uruguay	Multilateral	15 Jan 44	IGO Establishment	161UNTS281	200489
Uruguay	Multilateral	02 Aug 44	Scientific Project	67UNTS221	200221
Uruguay	Multilateral	07 Dec 44	Air Transport	171UNTS387	200502
Uruguay	Multilateral	07 Dec 44	Air Transport	171UNTS345	200501
Uruguay	Multilateral	07 Dec 44	Air Transport	84UNTS389	200252
Uruguay	Multilateral	07 Dec 44	IGO Establishment	15UNTS295	200102
Uruguay	Multilateral	08 Aug 45	General Military	82UNTS279	200251
Uruguay	Multilateral	16 Nov 45	IGO Establishment	4UNTS275	100052
Uruguay	Multilateral	27 Dec 45	IGO Establishment	2UNTS39	100020
Uruguay	Multilateral	22 Jul 46	IGO Establishment	14UNTS185	100221
Uruguay	Multilateral	22 Jul 46	IGO Establishment	9UNTS3	100125
Uruguay	Multilateral	11 Dec 46	Sanitation	12UNTS179	100186
Uruguay	Multilateral	02 Sep 47	General Military	21UNTS77	100324
Uruguay	Multilateral	02 Oct 47	Telecommunications	193UNTS188	102616
Uruguay	Multilateral	11 Oct 47	IGO Establishment	77UNTS143	100998
Uruguay	Multilateral	06 Mar 48	Water Transport	289UNTS3	104214
Uruguay	Multilateral	30 Apr 48	IGO Establishment	119UNTS3	101609
Uruguay	Multilateral	30 Apr 48	Dispute Settlement	30UNTS55	100449
Uruguay	Multilateral	10 Jun 48	Humanitarian	191UNTS3	102576
Uruguay	Multilateral	10 Jun 48	Humanitarian	164UNTS113	102163
Uruguay	Multilateral	24 Jul 48	Sanitation	66UNTS25	100847
Uruguay	Multilateral	19 Nov 48	Sanitation	44UNTS277	100688
Uruguay	Multilateral	29 Nov 48	IGO Establishment	120UNTS13	101613
Uruguay	Multilateral	09 Dec 48	Humanitarian	78UNTS277	101021
Uruguay	Multilateral	23 Mar 49	Commodity Trade	203UNTS179	102746

PARTY ONE	PARTY TWO	DATE	TOPIC	CITATION	NUMBER
Uruguay	Multilateral	09 Jul 49	Telecommunications	168UNTS143	102218
Uruguay	Multilateral	15 Jul 49	Health/Educ/Welfare	197UNTS3	102631
Uruguay	Multilateral	12 Aug 49	Humanitarian	75UNTS31	100970
Uruguay	Multilateral	12 Aug 49	General Military	75UNTS135	100972
Uruguay	Multilateral	12 Aug 49	Humanitarian	75UNTS287	100973
Uruguay	Multilateral	12 Aug 49	Humanitarian	75UNTS85	100971
Uruguay	Multilateral	06 Apr 50	Admin Cooperation	119UNTS99	101610
Uruguay	Multilateral	08 Sep 51	Peace/Disarmament	136UNTS45	101832
Uruguay	Multilateral	08 Sep 51	General Military	136UNTS165	101833
Uruguay	Multilateral	06 Dec 51	Admin Cooperation	150UNTS67	101963
Uruguay	Multilateral	11 Jul 52	Postal Service	170UNTS269	102223
Uruguay	Multilateral	11 Jul 52	Postal Service	171UNTS3	102224
Uruguay	Multilateral	11 Jul 52	Postal Service	170UNTS63	102222
Uruguay	Multilateral	11 Jul 52	IGO Establishment	169UNTS3	102220
Uruguay	Multilateral	11 Jul 52	Postal Service	170UNTS3	102221
Uruguay	Multilateral	11 Jul 52	Postal Service	171UNTS143	102226
Uruguay	Multilateral	11 Jul 52	Postal Service	171UNTS89	102225
Uruguay	Multilateral	06 Sep 52	Patents/Copyrights	216UNTS132	102937
Uruguay	Multilateral	31 Mar 53	Privil/Immunities	193UNTS136	102613
Uruguay	Multilateral	14 May 54	Culture	249UNTS215	103511
Uruguay	Multilateral	04 Jun 54	Customs	282UNTS249	104101
Uruguay	Multilateral	04 Jun 54	Customs	276UNTS191	103992
Uruguay	Multilateral	25 May 55	IGO Establishment	264UNTS117	103791
Uruguay	Multilateral	13 Dec 55	Tech Assistance	407UNTS8	105857
Uruguay	Multilateral	20 Jun 56	Admin Cooperation	268UNTS3	103850
Uruguay	Multilateral	26 Oct 56	IGO Establishment	276UNTS3	103988
Uruguay	Multilateral	20 Feb 57	Consul/Citizenship	309UNTS65	104468
Uruguay	Multilateral	03 Oct 57	Postal Service	366UNTS87	105216
Uruguay	Multilateral	03 Oct 57	Postal Service	364UNTS3	105211
Uruguay	Multilateral	03 Oct 57	Postal Service	366UNTS141	105217
Uruguay	Multilateral	03 Oct 57	Postal Service	364UNTS331	105212
Uruguay	Multilateral	03 Oct 57	Postal Service	365UNTS207	105214
Uruguay	Multilateral	03 Oct 57	Postal Service	365UNTS3	105213
Uruguay	Multilateral	03 Oct 57	Postal Service	366UNTS255	105219
Uruguay	Multilateral	03 Oct 57	Postal Service	366UNTS3	105215
Uruguay	Multilateral	29 Apr 58	Territory Boundary	499UNTS311	107302
Uruguay	Multilateral	29 Apr 58	Specific Resources	559UNTS285	108164
Uruguay	Multilateral	29 Apr 58	Water Transport	450UNTS11	106465
Uruguay	Multilateral	29 Apr 58	Territory Boundary	516UNTS205	107477
Uruguay	Multilateral	29 Apr 58	Dispute Settlement	450UNTS169	106466
Uruguay	Multilateral	08 Apr 59	IGO Establishment	389UNTS69	105593
Uruguay	Multilateral	17 Jun 60	Humanitarian	536UNTS27	107794
Uruguay	Multilateral	28 Jul 60	IGO Establishment	485UNTS3	107042
Uruguay	Multilateral	18 Apr 61	Consul/Citizenship	500UNTS95	107310
Uruguay	Multilateral	26 Mar 62	IGO Establishment	539UNTS67	107825
Uruguay	Multilateral	24 Apr 63	Consul/Citizenship	596UNTS261	108638
Uruguay	Multilateral	24 Apr 63	Consul/Citizenship	596UNTS487	108640
Uruguay	Multilateral	05 Aug 63	Sanitation	480UNTS43	106964
Uruguay	Multilateral	10 Jul 64	Postal Service	612UNTS3	108847
Uruguay	Multilateral	10 Jul 64	Postal Service	611UNTS105	108845
Uruguay	Multilateral	10 Jul 64	Postal Service	612UNTS233	108848
Uruguay	Multilateral	10 Jul 64	Postal Service	611UNTS387	108846
Uruguay	Multilateral	10 Jul 64	Postal Service	611UNTS7	108844
Uruguay	Multilateral	10 Jul 64	Postal Service	613UNTS3	108851
Uruguay	Multilateral	10 Jul 64	Postal Service	613UNTS193	108852
Uruguay	Multilateral	10 Jul 64	Postal Service	613UNTS3	108850
Uruguay	Multilateral	10 Jul 64	Postal Service	612UNTS361	108849
Uruguay	Multilateral	24 Sep 65	Atomic Energy	556UNTS141	108124
Uruguay	Multilateral	27 Jan 67	Scientific Project	610UNTS205	108843
Uruguay	Multilateral	14 Feb 67	General Military	634UNTS281	109068
Uruguay	Multilateral	22 Apr 68	Scientific Project	0UNTS0	109574
Uruguay	Netherlands	12 May 47	Air Transport	51NET151	447005
Uruguay	Norway	20 Mar 52	Air Transport	310UNTS279	104496
Uruguay	Norway	20 Oct 55	Consul/Citizenship	2NORT666	451197
Uruguay	Norway	24 Jan 61	Visas	3NORT824	451198

PARTY ONE	PARTY TWO	DATE	TOPIC	CITATION	NUMBER
Uruguay	Spain	24 Feb 54	General Trade	57SPBO2502	460261
Uruguay	Spain	24 Feb 54	General Trade	57SPBO2502	460260
Uruguay	Spain	24 Feb 54	Finance	57SPBO2502	460259
Uruguay	Spain	24 Jan 55	Customs	55SPBO1902	460262
Uruguay	Spain	25 Jun 55	General Trade	55SPBO1508	460263
Uruguay	Spain	21 Jan 56	General Trade	56SPBO1003	460264
Uruguay	Spain	09 Aug 56	General Trade	56SPBO2310	460265
Uruguay	Sweden	13 Jun 49	Finance	49SOFM301	461083
Uruguay	Sweden	20 Mar 52	Air Transport	311UNTS3	104497
Uruguay	Taiwan	03 May 61	Culture	596UNTS121	108630
Uruguay	UK Great Britain	15 Jul 47	Finance	71UNTS179	100918
Uruguay	UK Great Britain	12 Jul 48	Finance	71UNTS199	100919
Uruguay	UN Special Fund	04 May 62	Direct Aid	429UNTS143	106196
Uruguay	UNICEF (Children)	18 Dec 56	IGO Operations	0UNTS0	109398
Uruguay	United Nations	17 Oct 51	Tech Assistance	122UNTS29	101633
Uruguay	USA (United States)	21 Jul 42	General Trade	120UNTS211	200393
Uruguay	USA (United States)	01 Nov 43	Sanitation	106UNTS311	200348
Uruguay	USA (United States)	23 Apr 46	Sanitation	160UNTS103	102104
Uruguay	USA (United States)	14 Dec 46	Air Transport	532UNTS87	107713
Uruguay	USA (United States)	27 Jul 49	Sanitation	151UNTS199	101995
Uruguay	USA (United States)	08 Nov 49	Visas	82UNTS45	101084
Uruguay	USA (United States)	07 Mar 51	Sanitation	165UNTS113	102173
Uruguay	USA (United States)	04 Dec 51	Military Mission	152UNTS41	102010
Uruguay	USA (United States)	30 Jun 52	Milit Assistance	207UNTS139	102804
Uruguay	USA (United States)	12 Nov 52	Visas	231UNTS145	103213
Uruguay	USA (United States)	30 Nov 53	General Trade	229UNTS25	103158
Uruguay	USA (United States)	13 Jan 56	Atomic Energy	240UNTS401	103415
Uruguay	USA (United States)	23 Mar 56	Tech Assistance	376UNTS311	105386
Uruguay	USA (United States)	20 Feb 59	US Agri Commod Aid	341UNTS201	104884
Uruguay	USA (United States)	22 Jul 60	Education	388UNTS315	105587
Uruguay	USA (United States)	12 Sep 61	Gen Communications	607UNTS175	108805
Uruguay	USA (United States)	27 Apr 62	US Agri Commod Aid	452UNTS25	106502
Uruguay	USA (United States)	31 Jul 63	Tech Assistance	488UNTS3	107115
Uruguay	USA (United States)	17 May 65	Education	564UNTS69	108221
Uruguay	USA (United States)	19 Jan 68	US Agri Commod Aid	0UNTS0	110002
Uruguay	USA (United States)	07 May 68	US Agri Commod Aid	0UNTS0	110015
Uruguay	USA (United States)	17 Apr 70	General Trade	0UNTS0	110775
Uruguay	USSR (Soviet Union)	28 Jul 54	Finance	0SUST315	468442
Uruguay	USSR (Soviet Union)	11 Aug 56	General Trade	0SUST366	468443
Uruguay	USSR (Soviet Union)	11 Aug 56	General Economic	0SUST366	468444
Uruguay	WHO (World Health)	11 Jun 51	Tech Assistance	128UNTS251	101724
US Occup Germ	Multilateral	20 Jan 47	Water Transport	87UNTS247	101176
US Occup Germ	Multilateral	19 Sep 47	General Trade	30UNTS249	100461
US Occup Germ	Multilateral	19 Sep 47	Finance	30UNTS269	100462
US Occup Germ	Multilateral	05 Oct 47	Finance	34UNTS23	100525
US Occup Germ	Multilateral	14 Jul 48	Direct Aid	23UNTS3	100340
US Occup Germ	Multilateral	14 Jul 48	Mostfavored Nation	31UNTS123	100473
US Occup Germ	Multilateral	16 Dec 48	Direct Aid	79UNTS85	101033
US Occup Germ	Multilateral	16 Mar 49	Finance	29UNTS95	100436
US Occup Germ	Multilateral	08 Apr 49	Milit Occupation	140UNTS196	101889
US Occup Germ	Multilateral	14 Apr 49	Milit Occupation	141UNTS281	101919
US Occup Germ	Multilateral	05 Aug 49	Finance	88UNTS229	101195
US Occup Germ	Multilateral	10 Aug 49	Finance	45UNTS3	100689
USA (United States)	Afghanistan	29 Feb 44	Admin Cooperation	106UNTS247	200344
USA (United States)	Afghanistan	07 Feb 51	Tech Assistance	132UNTS265	101766
USA (United States)	Afghanistan	30 Jun 53	Tech Assistance	215UNTS3	102908
USA (United States)	Afghanistan	20 Mar 54	Direct Aid	229UNTS7	103156
USA (United States)	Afghanistan	29 May 54	Direct Aid	234UNTS3	103268
USA (United States)	Afghanistan	23 Jun 56	Direct Aid	271UNTS295	103921
USA (United States)	Afghanistan	09 Jun 57	Admin Cooperation	307UNTS97	104445
USA (United States)	Afghanistan	26 Jun 58	Culture	321UNTS67	104654
USA (United States)	Afghanistan	15 Feb 61	Mass Media	406UNTS235	105852
USA (United States)	Afghanistan	11 Sep 62	General Aid	461UNTS169	106661
USA (United States)	Afghanistan	20 Aug 63	Education	488UNTS41	107118
USA (United States)	Afghanistan	22 May 65	US Agri Commod Aid	579UNTS29	108396

PARTY ONE	PARTY TWO	DATE	TOPIC	CITATION	NUMBER
USA (United States)	Afghanistan	20 Dec 66	US Agri Commod Aid	0UNTS0	109699
USA (United States)	Afghanistan	19 Jul 67	US Agri Commod Aid	0UNTS0	109909
USA (United States)	Afghanistan	02 Jul 68	US Agri Commod Aid	0UNTS0	110148
USA (United States)	Algeria	23 Feb 66	Direct Aid	592UNTS117	108571
USA (United States)	Argentina	15 Apr 41	Visas	103UNTS307	200321
USA (United States)	Argentina	14 Oct 41	General Trade	119UNTS193	200384
USA (United States)	Argentina	02 Sep 43	Military Mission	9UNTS363	200052
USA (United States)	Argentina	09 May 45	Commodity Trade	139UNTS227	200453
USA (United States)	Argentina	19 Sep 46	Commodity Trade	7UNTS131	100095
USA (United States)	Argentina	06 Oct 48	Military Mission	80UNTS91	101046
USA (United States)	Argentina	20 Jul 50	Taxation	89UNTS63	101209
USA (United States)	Argentina	08 Jan 51	Milit Assistance	165UNTS89	102170
USA (United States)	Argentina	25 Apr 55	US Agri Commod Aid	251UNTS283	103546
USA (United States)	Argentina	29 Jul 55	Atomic Energy	235UNTS121	103298
USA (United States)	Argentina	21 Dec 55	Commodity Trade	240UNTS329	103411
USA (United States)	Argentina	03 Oct 56	Military Mission	279UNTS13	104032
USA (United States)	Argentina	05 Nov 56	Education	277UNTS143	104004
USA (United States)	Argentina	03 Jun 57	Tech Assistance	291UNTS61	104244
USA (United States)	Argentina	28 Apr 58	Status of Forces	315UNTS211	104570
USA (United States)	Argentina	12 Jun 59	US Agri Commod Aid	347UNTS59	104990
USA (United States)	Argentina	22 Dec 59	Admin Cooperation	411UNTS42	105912
USA (United States)	Argentina	01 Apr 60	Milit Assistance	371UNTS245	105281
USA (United States)	Argentina	23 May 60	Atomic Energy	377UNTS3	105392
USA (United States)	Argentina	02 Aug 60	Military Mission	384UNTS105	105514
USA (United States)	Argentina	16 Mar 62	Scientific Project	454UNTS3	106535
USA (United States)	Argentina	22 Jun 62	Atomic Energy	458UNTS97	106594
USA (United States)	Argentina	24 Jul 63	General Trade	487UNTS183	107103
USA (United States)	Argentina	21 Aug 63	Education	488UNTS61	107119
USA (United States)	Argentina	30 Nov 63	Scientific Project	505UNTS131	107369
USA (United States)	Argentina	10 May 64	Milit Assistance	527UNTS77	107618
USA (United States)	Argentina	08 Aug 66	Admin Cooperation	606UNTS209	108786
USA (United States)	Argentina	31 Mar 67	Gen Communications	636UNTS95	109095
USA (United States)	Argentina	31 Mar 67	Gen Communications	636UNTS103	109096
USA (United States)	Argentina	25 Jun 69	Atomic Energy	0UNTS0	110336
USA (United States)	Argentina	05 May 70	General Military	0UNTS0	110779
USA (United States)	Ascension Island	22 Jun 67	Air Transport	0UNTS0	110021
USA (United States)	Australia	03 Sep 42	Milit Assistance	24UNTS195	200143
USA (United States)	Australia	30 Sep 42	Milit Servic/Citiz	13UNTS125	200074
USA (United States)	Australia	10 May 44	Reparations	106UNTS237	200343
USA (United States)	Australia	08 Mar 45	Claims and Debts	121UNTS205	200400
USA (United States)	Australia	07 Jun 46	Milit Assistance	4UNTS237	100048
USA (United States)	Australia	03 Dec 46	Air Transport	7UNTS201	100100
USA (United States)	Australia	10 Mar 47	Air Transport	10UNTS89	100145
USA (United States)	Australia	26 Nov 49	Reparations	45UNTS133	100695
USA (United States)	Australia	29 Dec 49	Patents/Copyrights	71UNTS45	100909
USA (United States)	Australia	10 Feb 50	Visas	51UNTS167	100763
USA (United States)	Australia	20 Feb 51	Milit Assistance	132UNTS297	101769
USA (United States)	Australia	16 Nov 51	Tech Assistance	168UNTS75	102214
USA (United States)	Australia	27 May 52	Postal Service	178UNTS113	102338
USA (United States)	Australia	14 May 53	Taxation	205UNTS237	102778
USA (United States)	Australia	14 May 53	Taxation	205UNTS277	102780
USA (United States)	Australia	14 May 53	Taxation	205UNTS253	102779
USA (United States)	Australia	20 Aug 55	Visas	268UNTS133	103855
USA (United States)	Australia	22 Jun 56	Atomic Energy	283UNTS275	104123
USA (United States)	Australia	31 Dec 56	Milit Assistance	266UNTS89	103823
USA (United States)	Australia	12 Jul 57	Milit Assistance	290UNTS139	104233
USA (United States)	Australia	24 Jan 58	Patents/Copyrights	307UNTS105	104446
USA (United States)	Australia	25 Feb 58	Tech Assistance	317UNTS153	104601
USA (United States)	Australia	20 Jun 58	Postal Service	336UNTS97	104802
USA (United States)	Australia	19 Aug 59	Visas	388UNTS183	105578
USA (United States)	Australia	20 Nov 59	Air Transport	349UNTS293	105015
USA (United States)	Australia	26 Feb 60	Specific Property	354UNTS95	105056
USA (United States)	Australia	23 Aug 60	General Military	388UNTS237	105581
USA (United States)	Australia	09 May 61	Scientific Project	409UNTS203	105886
USA (United States)	Australia	22 May 61	Scientific Project	419UNTS3	106026

PARTY ONE	PARTY TWO	DATE	TOPIC	CITATION	NUMBER
USA (United States)	Australia	05 Jun 61	Scientific Project	409UNTS279	105892
USA (United States)	Australia	09 May 63	Status of Forces	469UNTS55	106784
USA (United States)	Australia	09 May 63	Milit Installation	475UNTS331	106897
USA (United States)	Australia	03 Jan 64	Gen Communications	505UNTS159	107371
USA (United States)	Australia	05 Feb 64	Status of Forces	511UNTS103	107430
USA (United States)	Australia	17 Feb 64	Commodity Trade	511UNTS17	107422
USA (United States)	Australia	17 Aug 64	Scientific Project	530UNTS209	107683
USA (United States)	Australia	28 Aug 64	Education	510UNTS201	107415
USA (United States)	Australia	25 Jun 65	Gen Communications	541UNTS155	107868
USA (United States)	Australia	09 Dec 66	Scientific Project	607UNTS83	108798
USA (United States)	Australia	13 Jan 69	Scientific Project	0UNTS0	110262
USA (United States)	Australia	13 Jan 69	Scientific Project	0UNTS0	109460
USA (United States)	Australia	10 Nov 69	General Military	0UNTS0	110479
USA (United States)	Australia	30 Jan 70	General Trade	0UNTS0	110618
USA (United States)	Australia	25 Mar 70	Gen Communications	0UNTS0	110693
USA (United States)	Australia	22 May 70	General Military	0UNTS0	110661
USA (United States)	Austria	21 Jun 47	Milit Occupation	67UNTS99	100869
USA (United States)	Austria	21 Jun 47	Reparations	67UNTS89	100868
USA (United States)	Austria	25 Jun 47	Direct Aid	22UNTS141	100334
USA (United States)	Austria	08 Oct 47	Air Transport	25UNTS3	100354
USA (United States)	Austria	02 Jan 48	Direct Aid	34UNTS141	100534
USA (United States)	Austria	02 Jul 48	Direct Aid	21UNTS29	100323
USA (United States)	Austria	02 Jul 48	Milit Occupation	25UNTS53	100357
USA (United States)	Austria	11 Feb 49	Direct Aid	79UNTS113	101035
USA (United States)	Austria	23 Mar 49	Admin Cooperation	43UNTS127	100667
USA (United States)	Austria	12 Jul 49	Visas	84UNTS291	101138
USA (United States)	Austria	06 Jun 50	Education	92UNTS201	101273
USA (United States)	Austria	15 May 51	Direct Aid	139UNTS79	101876
USA (United States)	Austria	05 Jan 52	Milit Assistance	179UNTS73	102355
USA (United States)	Austria	16 Feb 52	Direct Aid	177UNTS299	102329
USA (United States)	Austria	14 Jun 55	US Agri Commod Aid	258UNTS37	103668
USA (United States)	Austria	26 Sep 55	Specific Property	272UNTS31	103930
USA (United States)	Austria	07 Feb 56	US Agri Commod Aid	272UNTS117	103933
USA (United States)	Austria	08 Jun 56	Atomic Energy	253UNTS139	103581
USA (United States)	Austria	25 Oct 56	Taxation	299UNTS123	104310
USA (United States)	Austria	21 Nov 56	Claims and Debts	290UNTS181	104237
USA (United States)	Austria	10 May 57	US Agri Commod Aid	283UNTS15	104103
USA (United States)	Austria	10 May 57	Direct Aid	283UNTS33	104104
USA (United States)	Austria	09 Aug 57	Milit Assistance	288UNTS299	104211
USA (United States)	Austria	30 Jan 59	Claims and Debts	511UNTS145	107432
USA (United States)	Austria	30 Apr 59	Air Transport	343UNTS41	104920
USA (United States)	Austria	22 May 59	Reparations	347UNTS3	104988
USA (United States)	Austria	22 Jul 59	Atomic Energy	368UNTS199	105242
USA (United States)	Austria	15 Jun 60	Patents/Copyrights	376UNTS267	105383
USA (United States)	Austria	29 Mar 61	Direct Aid	459UNTS45	106612
USA (United States)	Austria	03 Oct 61	Direct Aid	426UNTS187	106137
USA (United States)	Austria	25 Jun 63	Education	479UNTS223	106956
USA (United States)	Austria	23 Jun 66	Air Transport	601UNTS51	108687
USA (United States)	Austria	04 Jul 67	Taxation	0UNTS0	109981
USA (United States)	Austria	21 Nov 67	Gen Communications	634UNTS43	109049
USA (United States)	Austria	11 Jul 69	Atomic Energy	0UNTS0	110431
USA (United States)	Barbados	11 Mar 68	Finance	0UNTS0	110007
USA (United States)	Barbados	09 Jul 68	Scientific Project	0UNTS0	110068
USA (United States)	Barbados	12 Sep 68	Gen Communications	0UNTS0	110075
USA (United States)	Belgium	16 Jun 42	Milit Assistance	105UNTS159	200329
USA (United States)	Belgium	16 Oct 42	Milit Servic/Citiz	13UNTS211	200080
USA (United States)	Belgium	30 Jan 43	Milit Assistance	13UNTS371	200084
USA (United States)	Belgium	04 Aug 43	Status of Forces	109UNTS149	200356
USA (United States)	Belgium	17 Apr 45	Milit Assistance	139UNTS253	200454
USA (United States)	Belgium	19 Apr 45	Milit Installation	139UNTS179	200455
USA (United States)	Belgium	05 Apr 46	Air Transport	4UNTS125	100041
USA (United States)	Belgium	11 Jul 46	Mostfavored Nation	13UNTS43	100200
USA (United States)	Belgium	24 Sep 46	Claims and Debts	132UNTS80	101753
USA (United States)	Belgium	23 Jan 47	Visas	47UNTS23	100721
USA (United States)	Belgium	03 Feb 47	Visas	84UNTS255	101134

PARTY ONE	PARTY TWO	DATE	TOPIC	CITATION	NUMBER
USA (United States)	Belgium	23 Jul 47	Other Military	33UNTS33	100512
USA (United States)	Belgium	30 Oct 47	General Economic	125UNTS103	101672
USA (United States)	Belgium	02 Jul 48	Mostfavored Nation	27UNTS43	100397
USA (United States)	Belgium	02 Jul 48	Direct Aid	19UNTS127	100309
USA (United States)	Belgium	26 Oct 48	Visas	84UNTS265	101135
USA (United States)	Belgium	28 Oct 48	Taxation	173UNTS67	102262
USA (United States)	Belgium	27 Jan 50	Milit Assistance	51UNTS213	100767
USA (United States)	Belgium	16 Mar 51	Reparations	93UNTS109	101295
USA (United States)	Belgium	07 Jan 52	Milit Assistance	179UNTS81	102356
USA (United States)	Belgium	07 Apr 52	Taxation	205UNTS3	102765
USA (United States)	Belgium	12 May 52	Finance	179UNTS15	102352
USA (United States)	Belgium	18 Jun 53	Milit Assistance	222UNTS3	103019
USA (United States)	Belgium	18 Jul 53	Taxation	180UNTS9	102371
USA (United States)	Belgium	02 Sep 53	Milit Assistance	200UNTS127	102700
USA (United States)	Belgium	17 Nov 53	Milit Assistance	251UNTS105	103536
USA (United States)	Belgium	12 Oct 54	Patents/Copyrights	202UNTS289	102735
USA (United States)	Belgium	23 Nov 54	Tech Assistance	235UNTS19	103292
USA (United States)	Belgium	15 Jun 55	Atomic Energy	235UNTS133	103299
USA (United States)	Belgium	15 Jul 55	Milit Assistance	223UNTS3	103040
USA (United States)	Belgium	31 Aug 55	Milit Assistance	223UNTS111	103041
USA (United States)	Belgium	03 Dec 57	Air Transport	303UNTS45	104370
USA (United States)	Belgium	27 Nov 59	Other Military	366UNTS331	105221
USA (United States)	Belgium	22 Apr 60	Milit Assistance	372UNTS277	105304
USA (United States)	Belgium	18 May 60	Patents/Copyrights	373UNTS31	105313
USA (United States)	Belgium	21 Feb 61	General Amity	480UNTS149	106967
USA (United States)	Belgium	17 May 62	Milit Assistance	461UNTS3	106647
USA (United States)	Belgium	23 May 62	Visas	434UNTS133	106260
USA (United States)	Belgium	19 Apr 63	Water Transport	493UNTS83	107209
USA (United States)	Belgium	19 Apr 63	Gen Communications	476UNTS29	106900
USA (United States)	Belgium	14 Nov 63	Extradition	522UNTS237	107549
USA (United States)	Belgium	18 Jun 65	Gen Communications	549UNTS95	107992
USA (United States)	Bolivia	04 Sep 41	Military Mission	8UNTS345	200046
USA (United States)	Bolivia	31 Jan 42	Admin Cooperation	101UNTS137	200290
USA (United States)	Bolivia	16 Jul 42	Sanitation	13UNTS101	200072
USA (United States)	Bolivia	11 Aug 42	Military Mission	9UNTS309	200049
USA (United States)	Bolivia	07 Sep 44	Education	162UNTS315	200494
USA (United States)	Bolivia	10 Jun 46	Mostfavored Nation	13UNTS19	100197
USA (United States)	Bolivia	16 May 47	Tech Assistance	168UNTS89	102215
USA (United States)	Bolivia	03 Nov 47	Air Transport	51UNTS33	100750
USA (United States)	Bolivia	14 Jul 48	Sanitation	136UNTS238	101838
USA (United States)	Bolivia	29 Sep 48	Air Transport	505UNTS139	107370
USA (United States)	Bolivia	16 May 49	Education	162UNTS3	102129
USA (United States)	Bolivia	30 Mar 50	Military Mission	241UNTS77	103425
USA (United States)	Bolivia	22 Nov 50	Education	152UNTS17	102008
USA (United States)	Bolivia	14 Mar 51	Tech Assistance	132UNTS319	101771
USA (United States)	Bolivia	18 Jun 52	Tech Assistance	199UNTS211	102686
USA (United States)	Bolivia	06 Nov 53	Direct Aid	222UNTS41	103021
USA (United States)	Bolivia	15 Jan 54	Tech Assistance	229UNTS213	103168
USA (United States)	Bolivia	16 Jun 54	Direct Aid	234UNTS35	103271
USA (United States)	Bolivia	03 Aug 55	Non-IBRD Project	264UNTS225	103795
USA (United States)	Bolivia	09 Sep 55	Military Mission	256UNTS239	103633
USA (United States)	Bolivia	23 Sep 55	Claims and Debts	256UNTS275	103637
USA (United States)	Bolivia	10 Mar 56	Mass Media	270UNTS199	103897
USA (United States)	Bolivia	30 Jun 56	Military Mission	271UNTS243	103919
USA (United States)	Bolivia	30 Jun 56	Military Mission	271UNTS269	103920
USA (United States)	Bolivia	07 Jun 57	US Agri Commod Aid	291UNTS77	104245
USA (United States)	Bolivia	22 Apr 58	Milit Assistance	317UNTS209	104605
USA (United States)	Bolivia	09 Feb 61	Milit Assistance	405UNTS113	105827
USA (United States)	Bolivia	07 Apr 61	US Agri Commod Aid	433UNTS3	106227
USA (United States)	Bolivia	23 Oct 61	Telecommunications	424UNTS93	106101
USA (United States)	Bolivia	15 Nov 61	US Agri Commod Aid	456UNTS192	106557
USA (United States)	Bolivia	12 Feb 62	US Agri Commod Aid	451UNTS281	106499
USA (United States)	Bolivia	26 Apr 62	Milit Assistance	461UNTS105	106654
USA (United States)	Bolivia	19 Jun 62	General Aid	458UNTS239	106606
USA (United States)	Bolivia	17 Dec 62	US Agri Commod Aid	469UNTS121	106788

PARTY ONE	PARTY TWO	DATE	TOPIC	CITATION	NUMBER
USA (United States)	Bolivia	04 Feb 63	US Agri Commod Aid	473UNTS65	106856
USA (United States)	Bolivia	25 Mar 64	US Agri Commod Aid	532UNTS3	107710
USA (United States)	Bolivia	16 Mar 65	Gen Communications	542UNTS209	107891
USA (United States)	Bolivia	12 May 65	US Agri Commod Aid	564UNTS143	108226
USA (United States)	Bolivia	17 Aug 65	US Agri Commod Aid	587UNTS289	108514
USA (United States)	Bolivia	22 Apr 66	US Agri Commod Aid	578UNTS73	108388
USA (United States)	Bolivia	16 Jan 68	US Agri Commod Aid	0UNTS0	110064
USA (United States)	Bolivia	16 Jan 68	US Agri Commod Aid	0UNTS0	110065
USA (United States)	Bolivia	07 Mar 69	US Agri Commod Aid	0UNTS0	110153
USA (United States)	Bolivia	07 Mar 69	US Agri Commod Aid	0UNTS0	110154
USA (United States)	Botswana	30 Sep 66	Admin Cooperation	0UNTS0	109682
USA (United States)	Botswana	12 Jan 68	Finance	0UNTS0	109997
USA (United States)	Brazil	03 Mar 42	Tech Assistance	105UNTS91	200324
USA (United States)	Brazil	03 Mar 42	Tech Assistance	105UNTS99	200325
USA (United States)	Brazil	14 Mar 42	Sanitation	102UNTS195	200302
USA (United States)	Brazil	07 May 42	Military Mission	6UNTS377	200040
USA (United States)	Brazil	17 Jul 42	Sanitation	102UNTS203	200303
USA (United States)	Brazil	03 Sep 42	Non-IBRD Project	13UNTS109	200073
USA (United States)	Brazil	10 Feb 43	Sanitation	102UNTS217	200304
USA (United States)	Brazil	24 May 43	Status of Forces	28UNTS385	200162
USA (United States)	Brazil	25 Nov 43	Sanitation	102UNTS227	200305
USA (United States)	Brazil	29 Sep 44	Military Mission	65UNTS271	200216
USA (United States)	Brazil	15 Feb 46	Education	162UNTS21	102130
USA (United States)	Brazil	05 Apr 46	Education	12UNTS131	100183
USA (United States)	Brazil	28 Jun 46	Milit Assistance	6UNTS327	100085
USA (United States)	Brazil	06 Sep 46	Air Transport	54UNTS197	100805
USA (United States)	Brazil	17 Sep 46	Military Mission	7UNTS49	100091
USA (United States)	Brazil	02 Feb 48	Status of Forces	67UNTS109	100870
USA (United States)	Brazil	30 Jun 48	General Trade	125UNTS111	101673
USA (United States)	Brazil	29 Jul 48	Military Mission	80UNTS111	101047
USA (United States)	Brazil	26 Nov 48	Scientific Project	88UNTS3	101180
USA (United States)	Brazil	30 Dec 48	Sanitation	102UNTS3	101406
USA (United States)	Brazil	31 Aug 49	Sanitation	102UNTS13	101407
USA (United States)	Brazil	23 May 50	Admin Cooperation	151UNTS141	101989
USA (United States)	Brazil	16 Aug 50	Tech Assistance	140UNTS223	101890
USA (United States)	Brazil	19 Dec 50	Direct Aid	140UNTS365	101899
USA (United States)	Brazil	19 Dec 50	Tech Assistance	141UNTS3	101900
USA (United States)	Brazil	27 Dec 50	Sanitation	147UNTS33	101926
USA (United States)	Brazil	04 Jan 51	Milit Assistance	165UNTS97	102171
USA (United States)	Brazil	29 Jun 51	Tech Assistance	184UNTS303	102455
USA (United States)	Brazil	24 Jul 51	Direct Aid	134UNTS195	101799
USA (United States)	Brazil	15 Mar 52	Milit Assistance	199UNTS221	102687
USA (United States)	Brazil	02 Jun 52	Scientific Project	181UNTS109	102403
USA (United States)	Brazil	30 Jun 52	Tech Assistance	185UNTS79	102460
USA (United States)	Brazil	30 May 53	Tech Assistance	460UNTS89	106633
USA (United States)	Brazil	26 Jun 53	Direct Aid	336UNTS241	104808
USA (United States)	Brazil	30 Jun 54	Non-IBRD Project	237UNTS137	103341
USA (United States)	Brazil	20 Aug 54	Commodity Trade	410UNTS79	105898
USA (United States)	Brazil	03 Aug 55	Scientific Project	270UNTS71	103893
USA (United States)	Brazil	03 Aug 55	Atomic Energy	235UNTS159	103300
USA (United States)	Brazil	20 Sep 55	Military Mission	257UNTS349	103665
USA (United States)	Brazil	16 Nov 55	Commodity Trade	239UNTS207	103381
USA (United States)	Brazil	31 Dec 56	US Agri Commod Aid	266UNTS151	103829
USA (United States)	Brazil	16 Jan 57	Milit Assistance	266UNTS99	103824
USA (United States)	Brazil	21 Jan 57	Milit Installation	278UNTS97	104025
USA (United States)	Brazil	02 Apr 57	Patents/Copyrights	290UNTS119	104231
USA (United States)	Brazil	05 Nov 57	Education	303UNTS3	104368
USA (United States)	Brazil	19 Oct 59	Milit Assistance	372UNTS131	105293
USA (United States)	Brazil	27 Feb 60	Direct Aid	384UNTS131	105515
USA (United States)	Brazil	13 Jan 61	Extradition	532UNTS177	107718
USA (United States)	Brazil	17 Mar 61	Atomic Energy	406UNTS241	105853
USA (United States)	Brazil	04 May 61	US Agri Commod Aid	433UNTS91	106233
USA (United States)	Brazil	27 Oct 61	Telecommunications	433UNTS113	106234
USA (United States)	Brazil	11 Nov 61	Direct Aid	433UNTS199	106243
USA (United States)	Brazil	15 Mar 62	US Agri Commod Aid	456UNTS209	106558

PARTY ONE	PARTY TWO	DATE	TOPIC	CITATION	NUMBER
USA (United States)	Brazil	13 Apr 62	Non-IBRD Project	445UNTS227	106391
USA (United States)	Brazil	19 Apr 62	General Trade	456UNTS255	106560
USA (United States)	Brazil	29 Mar 63	Scientific Project	476UNTS67	106904
USA (United States)	Brazil	11 Sep 63	US Agri Commod Aid	493UNTS267	107220
USA (United States)	Brazil	30 Jan 64	Milit Assistance	511UNTS77	107428
USA (United States)	Brazil	06 Feb 65	Direct Aid	0UNTS0	110324
USA (United States)	Brazil	26 May 65	Visas	549UNTS125	107995
USA (United States)	Brazil	01 Jun 65	Gen Communications	546UNTS195	107946
USA (United States)	Brazil	08 Jul 65	Atomic Energy	0UNTS0	109603
USA (United States)	Brazil	23 Apr 66	US Agri Commod Aid	607UNTS117	108801
USA (United States)	Brazil	19 Oct 66	Education	0UNTS0	109685
USA (United States)	Brazil	27 Jan 67	Milit Installation	0UNTS0	109844
USA (United States)	Brazil	28 Jun 67	Water Transport	0UNTS0	109775
USA (United States)	Brazil	28 Jun 67	Water Transport	0UNTS0	109774
USA (United States)	Brazil	12 Mar 68	Scientific Project	0UNTS0	110138
USA (United States)	Brazil	10 Sep 68	Scientific Project	0UNTS0	110074
USA (United States)	Brazil	20 Sep 68	Gen Communications	0UNTS0	110078
USA (United States)	British Guiana	29 May 65	Loans and Credits	605UNTS87	108761
USA (United States)	Bulgaria	08 Mar 48	Admin Cooperation	29UNTS101	100437
USA (United States)	Bulgaria	02 Jul 63	Claims and Debts	479UNTS245	106957
USA (United States)	Burma	28 Feb 47	Direct Aid	25UNTS27	100355
USA (United States)	Burma	05 Apr 48	Admin Cooperation	73UNTS73	100945
USA (United States)	Burma	28 Sep 49	Air Transport	55UNTS3	100806
USA (United States)	Burma	13 Sep 50	Direct Aid	92UNTS361	101280
USA (United States)	Burma	06 Nov 50	Milit Assistance	122UNTS81	101638
USA (United States)	Burma	09 Feb 52	Milit Assistance	179UNTS91	102357
USA (United States)	Burma	24 Oct 52	Tech Assistance	222UNTS55	103022
USA (United States)	Burma	30 Jun 56	Tech Assistance	281UNTS65	104070
USA (United States)	Burma	23 Oct 56	Mass Media	282UNTS37	104091
USA (United States)	Burma	04 Dec 56	US Agri Commod Aid	268UNTS189	103858
USA (United States)	Burma	21 Mar 57	Direct Aid	300UNTS11	104327
USA (United States)	Burma	27 May 58	US Agri Commod Aid	315UNTS197	104569
USA (United States)	Burma	24 Jun 58	Milit Assistance	335UNTS193	104786
USA (United States)	Burma	25 Aug 58	Commodity Trade	336UNTS3	104795
USA (United States)	Burma	24 Jun 59	Direct Aid	358UNTS91	105127
USA (United States)	Burma	09 Nov 62	US Agri Commod Aid	461UNTS113	106655
USA (United States)	Burma	01 Jun 66	Loans and Credits	580UNTS253	108428
USA (United States)	Burundi	06 May 69	Finance	0UNTS0	110799
USA (United States)	Cambodia	08 Sep 51	Direct Aid	174UNTS115	102282
USA (United States)	Cambodia	28 Dec 51	Milit Assistance	179UNTS97	102358
USA (United States)	Cambodia	16 May 55	Milit Assistance	263UNTS273	103777
USA (United States)	Cambodia	17 Oct 57	Scientific Project	299UNTS203	104313
USA (United States)	Cambodia	15 Jul 60	Admin Cooperation	380UNTS129	105453
USA (United States)	Cameroon	26 May 61	General Aid	413UNTS195	105953
USA (United States)	Cameroon	10 Sep 62	Tech Assistance	461UNTS177	106662
USA (United States)	Cameroon	07 Mar 67	Finance	0UNTS0	109855
USA (United States)	Canada	10 Jun 39	Milit Assistance	149UNTS332	200476
USA (United States)	Canada	29 May 40	Status of Forces	119UNTS285	200385
USA (United States)	Canada	13 Dec 40	General Trade	117UNTS173	200368
USA (United States)	Canada	27 Jun 41	IGO Establishment	103UNTS205	200315
USA (United States)	Canada	10 Nov 41	Specific Resources	23UNTS275	200134
USA (United States)	Canada	27 Nov 41	Specific Resources	103UNTS193	200314
USA (United States)	Canada	04 Mar 42	Taxation	124UNTS271	200426
USA (United States)	Canada	12 Mar 42	Non-ILO Labor	119UNTS295	200386
USA (United States)	Canada	18 Mar 42	Land Transport	101UNTS205	200294
USA (United States)	Canada	20 Mar 42	Milit Servic/Citiz	105UNTS169	200330
USA (United States)	Canada	08 Apr 42	Milit Servic/Citiz	105UNTS179	200331
USA (United States)	Canada	09 May 42	Land Transport	101UNTS215	200295
USA (United States)	Canada	27 Jun 42	Other Military	99UNTS223	200276
USA (United States)	Canada	15 Aug 42	Other Military	99UNTS233	200277
USA (United States)	Canada	10 Sep 42	Land Transport	101UNTS221	200296
USA (United States)	Canada	04 Nov 42	Non-ILO Labor	24UNTS217	200146
USA (United States)	Canada	09 Nov 42	General Trade	101UNTS233	200298
USA (United States)	Canada	30 Nov 42	Reparations	119UNTS305	200387
USA (United States)	Canada	07 Dec 42	Land Transport	101UNTS227	200297

PARTY ONE	PARTY TWO	DATE	TOPIC	CITATION	NUMBER
USA (United States)	Canada	19 Dec 42	Commodity Trade	26UNTS363	200156
USA (United States)	Canada	28 Dec 42	Other Military	99UNTS241	200278
USA (United States)	Canada	27 Jan 43	Milit Installation	101UNTS257	200300
USA (United States)	Canada	23 Feb 43	Land Transport	101UNTS243	200299
USA (United States)	Canada	04 Mar 43	Air Transport	13UNTS411	200087
USA (United States)	Canada	13 Mar 43	Other Military	99UNTS249	200279
USA (United States)	Canada	10 Apr 43	Territory Boundary	21UNTS237	200126
USA (United States)	Canada	26 May 43	Privil/Immunities	7UNTS345	200043
USA (United States)	Canada	19 Jul 43	Land Transport	29UNTS289	200167
USA (United States)	Canada	09 Aug 43	Milit Installation	29UNTS295	200168
USA (United States)	Canada	13 Aug 43	Admin Cooperation	109UNTS135	200355
USA (United States)	Canada	17 Jan 44	Mass Media	109UNTS199	200360
USA (United States)	Canada	03 Mar 44	Specific Resources	109UNTS191	200359
USA (United States)	Canada	23 Mar 44	Claims and Debts	125UNTS345	200432
USA (United States)	Canada	07 Jun 44	Specific Property	99UNTS259	200280
USA (United States)	Canada	08 Jun 44	Taxation	124UNTS297	200427
USA (United States)	Canada	27 Jun 44	Milit Installation	101UNTS273	200301
USA (United States)	Canada	05 Aug 44	Specific Resources	121UNTS299	200408
USA (United States)	Canada	13 Feb 45	Status of Forces	200UNTS219	200519
USA (United States)	Canada	17 Feb 45	Air Transport	122UNTS261	200409
USA (United States)	Canada	26 Feb 45	Other Military	99UNTS273	200281
USA (United States)	Canada	15 May 45	Peace/Disarmament	125UNTS353	200433
USA (United States)	Canada	06 Sep 45	Other Military	99UNTS281	200282
USA (United States)	Canada	03 Mar 46	Specific Property	6UNTS279	100081
USA (United States)	Canada	30 Mar 46	Milit Installation	7UNTS15	100089
USA (United States)	Canada	27 Sep 46	Patents/Copyrights	21UNTS3	100320
USA (United States)	Canada	15 Nov 46	Specif Claim/Waive	7UNTS141	100096
USA (United States)	Canada	06 Dec 46	Milit Assistance	149UNTS3	101945
USA (United States)	Canada	09 Jan 47	Specific Property	11UNTS341	100173
USA (United States)	Canada	06 Mar 47	Specific Resources	11UNTS325	100172
USA (United States)	Canada	18 Mar 47	Commodity Trade	117UNTS79	101584
USA (United States)	Canada	12 Apr 47	Air Transport	122UNTS229	101648
USA (United States)	Canada	19 May 47	Non-ILO Labor	43UNTS97	100663
USA (United States)	Canada	20 Aug 47	Telecommunications	27UNTS3	100392
USA (United States)	Canada	15 Oct 47	Telecommunications	82UNTS53	101085
USA (United States)	Canada	30 Oct 47	General Economic	27UNTS19	100394
USA (United States)	Canada	26 Dec 47	Commodity Trade	27UNTS29	100395
USA (United States)	Canada	31 Mar 48	Specific Property	81UNTS285	101077
USA (United States)	Canada	01 Apr 48	Telecommunications	82UNTS99	101086
USA (United States)	Canada	30 Apr 48	Sanitation	77UNTS191	100999
USA (United States)	Canada	23 Nov 48	Commodity Trade	81UNTS295	101078
USA (United States)	Canada	31 Jan 49	Humanitarian	43UNTS119	100666
USA (United States)	Canada	14 Mar 49	Reparations	82UNTS3	101079
USA (United States)	Canada	12 Apr 49	Milit Assistance	206UNTS241	102789
USA (United States)	Canada	04 Jun 49	Air Transport	200UNTS201	102704
USA (United States)	Canada	04 Jun 49	Air Transport	122UNTS237	101649
USA (United States)	Canada	24 Jan 50	Specif Claim/Waive	151UNTS171	101992
USA (United States)	Canada	27 Feb 50	Specific Resources	132UNTS223	101762
USA (United States)	Canada	24 Mar 50	Customs	200UNTS211	102705
USA (United States)	Canada	12 Jun 50	Taxation	127UNTS67	101700
USA (United States)	Canada	12 Jun 50	Taxation	127UNTS57	101699
USA (United States)	Canada	22 Jun 50	Scientific Project	70UNTS115	100900
USA (United States)	Canada	26 Oct 50	Direct Aid	132UNTS247	101764
USA (United States)	Canada	08 Feb 51	Telecommunications	207UNTS17	102797
USA (United States)	Canada	27 Mar 51	Milit Assistance	132UNTS333	101772
USA (United States)	Canada	18 Apr 51	Milit Assistance	134UNTS205	101800
USA (United States)	Canada	01 Aug 51	Milit Installation	233UNTS109	103254
USA (United States)	Canada	11 Sep 51	Non-ILO Labor	206UNTS311	102793
USA (United States)	Canada	26 Oct 51	Extradition	206UNTS319	102794
USA (United States)	Canada	21 Feb 52	Humanitarian	205UNTS293	102781
USA (United States)	Canada	19 Mar 52	Status of Forces	174UNTS267	102291
USA (United States)	Canada	30 Apr 52	Milit Installation	235UNTS269	103308
USA (United States)	Canada	23 Jun 52	Telecommunications	207UNTS25	102798
USA (United States)	Canada	30 Jun 52	Water Transport	234UNTS199	103283
USA (United States)	Canada	08 Nov 52	Gen Communications	207UNTS3	102796

PARTY ONE	PARTY TWO	DATE	TOPIC	CITATION	NUMBER
USA (United States)	Canada	05 Dec 52	Milit Installation	206UNTS11	102783
USA (United States)	Canada	02 Mar 53	Specific Resources	222UNTS77	103024
USA (United States)	Canada	17 Mar 53	Telecommunications	236UNTS259	103329
USA (United States)	Canada	30 Jun 53	General Military	215UNTS103	102914
USA (United States)	Canada	30 Jun 53	Specific Property	206UNTS93	102786
USA (United States)	Canada	12 Nov 53	IGO Establishment	234UNTS97	103274
USA (United States)	Canada	12 Nov 53	General Economic	223UNTS139	103062
USA (United States)	Canada	03 May 54	Milit Assistance	221UNTS339	103015
USA (United States)	Canada	10 Sep 54	Specific Resources	238UNTS97	103355
USA (United States)	Canada	05 May 55	Milit Installation	241UNTS179	103433
USA (United States)	Canada	08 Jun 55	Customs	247UNTS163	103466
USA (United States)	Canada	13 Jun 55	Specif Goods/Equip	268UNTS87	103851
USA (United States)	Canada	15 Jun 55	Atomic Energy	235UNTS176	103301
USA (United States)	Canada	15 Jun 55	Milit Assistance	235UNTS201	103302
USA (United States)	Canada	15 Jun 55	Specif Goods/Equip	268UNTS101	103852
USA (United States)	Canada	21 Jul 55	Milit Assistance	269UNTS53	103873
USA (United States)	Canada	22 Sep 55	Specif Goods/Equip	256UNTS227	103632
USA (United States)	Canada	26 Jan 56	Status of Forces	241UNTS115	103428
USA (United States)	Canada	19 Apr 56	Milit Installation	274UNTS3	103955
USA (United States)	Canada	23 Apr 56	Non-ILO Labor	300UNTS29	104329
USA (United States)	Canada	24 Oct 56	Specif Goods/Equip	281UNTS281	104084
USA (United States)	Canada	28 Dec 56	Specific Resources	290UNTS103	104229
USA (United States)	Canada	17 Jan 57	Specif Goods/Equip	266UNTS109	103825
USA (United States)	Canada	26 Feb 57	Water Transport	279UNTS179	104039
USA (United States)	Canada	09 Apr 57	Water Transport	283UNTS217	104119
USA (United States)	Canada	12 May 58	General Military	316UNTS151	104582
USA (United States)	Canada	20 Jun 58	Milit Assistance	317UNTS37	104592
USA (United States)	Canada	02 Sep 58	General Military	335UNTS249	104792
USA (United States)	Canada	31 Oct 58	Non-ILO Labor	391UNTS219	105626
USA (United States)	Canada	07 Jan 59	Specific Property	391UNTS207	105624
USA (United States)	Canada	27 Feb 59	Specific Resources	341UNTS3	104873
USA (United States)	Canada	09 Mar 59	Territory Boundary	340UNTS295	104872
USA (United States)	Canada	13 Apr 59	Specific Property	342UNTS43	104899
USA (United States)	Canada	01 May 59	Specific Property	343UNTS27	104919
USA (United States)	Canada	22 May 59	Milit Assistance	354UNTS63	105054
USA (United States)	Canada	13 Jul 59	Milit Assistance	353UNTS237	105045
USA (United States)	Canada	31 Mar 60	Specif Goods/Equip	400UNTS315	105755
USA (United States)	Canada	14 Jun 60	Scientific Project	377UNTS365	105413
USA (United States)	Canada	24 Aug 60	Scientific Project	388UNTS225	105580
USA (United States)	Canada	31 Aug 60	Milit Assistance	393UNTS247	105659
USA (United States)	Canada	13 Jan 61	Postal Service	410UNTS62	105897
USA (United States)	Canada	17 Jan 61	Specific Resources	542UNTS224	107894
USA (United States)	Canada	17 Feb 61	Taxation	445UNTS143	106383
USA (United States)	Canada	05 May 61	Admin Cooperation	419UNTS9	106027
USA (United States)	Canada	12 Jun 61	Milit Assistance	410UNTS21	105894
USA (United States)	Canada	01 Sep 61	Claims and Debts	421UNTS199	106058
USA (United States)	Canada	23 Sep 61	Milit Installation	421UNTS79	106053
USA (United States)	Canada	27 Sep 61	Milit Assistance	421UNTS85	106054
USA (United States)	Canada	17 Oct 61	Specific Property	426UNTS201	106138
USA (United States)	Canada	17 Oct 61	Water Transport	424UNTS101	106102
USA (United States)	Canada	07 Mar 62	General Trade	436UNTS3	106286
USA (United States)	Canada	19 Apr 62	Specific Property	445UNTS265	106394
USA (United States)	Canada	13 Jul 62	Water Transport	460UNTS83	106632
USA (United States)	Canada	24 Oct 62	Telecommunications	462UNTS67	106672
USA (United States)	Canada	28 Dec 62	Scientific Project	471UNTS13	106818
USA (United States)	Canada	23 Aug 63	Telecommunications	494UNTS13	107222
USA (United States)	Canada	15 Nov 63	Other Military	493UNTS67	107207
USA (United States)	Canada	27 Dec 63	Air Transport	494UNTS21	107223
USA (United States)	Canada	22 Jan 64	Specific Property	530UNTS89	107674
USA (United States)	Canada	06 Mar 64	Specific Property	524UNTS255	107577
USA (United States)	Canada	06 May 64	Scientific Project	524UNTS173	107572
USA (United States)	Canada	25 May 64	Milit Installation	526UNTS251	107609
USA (United States)	Canada	16 Sep 64	Gen Communications	530UNTS267	107687
USA (United States)	Canada	16 Jan 65	Commodity Trade	606UNTS31	108772
USA (United States)	Canada	25 Mar 65	Dispute Settlement	607UNTS141	108802

PARTY ONE	PARTY TWO	DATE	TOPIC	CITATION	NUMBER
USA (United States)	Canada	12 May 65	Milit Installation	545UNTS169	107933
USA (United States)	Canada	08 Jun 65	Gen Communications	546UNTS201	107947
USA (United States)	Canada	11 Jun 65	Scientific Project	564UNTS83	108222
USA (United States)	Canada	29 Jun 65	Scientific Project	549UNTS273	108003
USA (United States)	Canada	01 Dec 65	Milit Installation	574UNTS37	108340
USA (United States)	Canada	17 Dec 65	General Trade	574UNTS49	108341
USA (United States)	Canada	17 Jan 66	Air Transport	586UNTS151	108502
USA (United States)	Canada	09 Jun 66	Non-IBRD Project	580UNTS263	108429
USA (United States)	Canada	10 Jun 66	Water Transport	639UNTS13	109141
USA (United States)	Canada	15 Jun 66	Milit Installation	594UNTS83	108595
USA (United States)	Canada	30 Sep 66	Milit Installation	616UNTS193	108896
USA (United States)	Canada	06 Oct 66	Scientific Project	0UNTS0	109607
USA (United States)	Canada	13 Apr 67	Water Transport	0UNTS0	109759
USA (United States)	Canada	05 May 67	Non-ILO Labor	0UNTS0	109764
USA (United States)	Canada	12 Jun 67	Gen Communications	0UNTS0	109772
USA (United States)	Canada	08 Aug 67	Scientific Project	0UNTS0	109913
USA (United States)	Canada	11 Aug 67	Scientific Project	0UNTS0	109914
USA (United States)	Canada	25 Sep 67	Commodity Trade	0UNTS0	110503
USA (United States)	Canada	25 Oct 67	Scientific Project	0UNTS0	110052
USA (United States)	Canada	30 Jan 69	Sanitation	0UNTS0	110265
USA (United States)	Canada	21 Mar 69	Other Ad Hoc	0UNTS0	110271
USA (United States)	Canada	21 Mar 69	Other Ad Hoc	0UNTS0	110270
USA (United States)	Canada	31 Jul 69	Water Transport	0UNTS0	110341
USA (United States)	Canada	29 Jan 70	Specific Resources	0UNTS0	110800
USA (United States)	Canada	25 Jun 70	Scientific Project	0UNTS0	110817
USA (United States)	Central Afri Rep	10 Feb 63	Direct Aid	473UNTS83	106857
USA (United States)	Central Afri Rep	31 Dec 64	Claims and Debts	542UNTS29	107877
USA (United States)	Central Afri Rep	24 Nov 66	Direct Aid	0UNTS0	109690
USA (United States)	Ceylon (Sri Lanka)	31 Jan 49	Admin Cooperation	88UNTS21	101181
USA (United States)	Ceylon (Sri Lanka)	07 Nov 50	Tech Assistance	92UNTS125	101265
USA (United States)	Ceylon (Sri Lanka)	14 May 51	Gen Communications	141UNTS159	101913
USA (United States)	Ceylon (Sri Lanka)	17 Nov 52	Education	180UNTS207	102386
USA (United States)	Ceylon (Sri Lanka)	23 Aug 54	Mass Media	314UNTS297	104553
USA (United States)	Ceylon (Sri Lanka)	18 Jul 55	Postal Service	281UNTS295	104086
USA (United States)	Ceylon (Sri Lanka)	28 Apr 56	Direct Aid	274UNTS35	103956
USA (United States)	Ceylon (Sri Lanka)	07 Sep 56	Visas	280UNTS35	104048
USA (United States)	Ceylon (Sri Lanka)	02 Nov 56	Milit Assistance	282UNTS93	104094
USA (United States)	Ceylon (Sri Lanka)	18 Jun 58	US Agri Commod Aid	316UNTS15	104574
USA (United States)	Ceylon (Sri Lanka)	13 Mar 59	US Agri Commod Aid	342UNTS51	104900
USA (United States)	Ceylon (Sri Lanka)	30 Sep 60	US Agri Commod Aid	389UNTS221	105594
USA (United States)	Ceylon (Sri Lanka)	19 Jul 62	US Agri Commod Aid	454UNTS31	106538
USA (United States)	Ceylon (Sri Lanka)	21 Nov 62	General Aid	462UNTS237	106683
USA (United States)	Ceylon (Sri Lanka)	29 Aug 64	Education	531UNTS93	107695
USA (United States)	Ceylon (Sri Lanka)	23 Feb 66	Finance	586UNTS91	108498
USA (United States)	Ceylon (Sri Lanka)	12 Mar 66	US Agri Commod Aid	579UNTS117	108403
USA (United States)	Ceylon (Sri Lanka)	24 Oct 67	US Agri Commod Aid	0UNTS0	109984
USA (United States)	Ceylon (Sri Lanka)	21 Jun 68	US Agri Commod Aid	0UNTS0	110327
USA (United States)	Ceylon (Sri Lanka)	19 Feb 69	US Agri Commod Aid	0UNTS0	110152
USA (United States)	Chad	12 May 65	Finance	546UNTS183	107944
USA (United States)	Chad	31 Aug 66	Direct Aid	606UNTS47	108773
USA (United States)	Chile	14 Apr 43	Military Mission	9UNTS331	200050
USA (United States)	Chile	11 May 43	Sanitation	139UNTS295	200456
USA (United States)	Chile	24 May 45	Military Mission	121UNTS219	200401
USA (United States)	Chile	11 Jun 45	Milit Servic/Citiz	121UNTS291	200407
USA (United States)	Chile	30 Jul 45	General Trade	6UNTS409	200042
USA (United States)	Chile	30 Jul 46	General Trade	7UNTS41	100090
USA (United States)	Chile	10 May 47	Air Transport	55UNTS21	100807
USA (United States)	Chile	21 Jan 49	Sanitation	160UNTS185	102107
USA (United States)	Chile	09 Apr 49	Customs	122UNTS169	101646
USA (United States)	Chile	12 May 50	Consul/Citizenship	177UNTS103	102312
USA (United States)	Chile	29 Aug 50	Visas	122UNTS43	101634
USA (United States)	Chile	04 Jan 51	Milit Assistance	165UNTS105	102172
USA (United States)	Chile	16 Jan 51	Direct Aid	157UNTS3	102043
USA (United States)	Chile	16 Jan 51	Education	147UNTS11	101925
USA (United States)	Chile	16 Jan 51	Tech Assistance	151UNTS147	101990

PARTY ONE	PARTY TWO	DATE	TOPIC	CITATION	NUMBER
USA (United States)	Chile	15 Feb 51	Military Mission	133UNTS117	101784
USA (United States)	Chile	15 Feb 51	Military Mission	133UNTS95	101783
USA (United States)	Chile	09 Apr 52	Milit Assistance	186UNTS53	102482
USA (United States)	Chile	30 Jun 52	Tech Assistance	199UNTS241	102688
USA (United States)	Chile	27 Jun 53	Tech Assistance	229UNTS53	103160
USA (United States)	Chile	27 Jun 53	Tech Assistance	229UNTS193	103167
USA (United States)	Chile	30 Dec 53	Tech Assistance	236UNTS41	103315
USA (United States)	Chile	10 May 54	Customs	247UNTS299	103477
USA (United States)	Chile	28 Jun 54	Tech Assistance	233UNTS3	103246
USA (United States)	Chile	14 Jan 55	Mass Media	238UNTS191	103362
USA (United States)	Chile	27 Jan 55	US Agri Commod Aid	262UNTS3	103735
USA (United States)	Chile	31 Mar 55	Education	262UNTS19	103736
USA (United States)	Chile	05 Apr 55	Direct Aid	250UNTS253	103527
USA (United States)	Chile	08 Aug 55	Atomic Energy	235UNTS209	103303
USA (United States)	Chile	13 Mar 56	US Agri Commod Aid	275UNTS49	103975
USA (United States)	Chile	20 Apr 56	Atomic Energy	293UNTS277	104295
USA (United States)	Chile	15 Nov 56	Military Mission	282UNTS3	104089
USA (United States)	Chile	01 Mar 57	Non-ILO Labor	283UNTS127	104112
USA (United States)	Chile	19 Feb 59	Specific Property	343UNTS17	104918
USA (United States)	Chile	19 Feb 60	Atomic Energy	371UNTS255	105282
USA (United States)	Chile	28 Mar 60	Scientific Project	401UNTS105	105765
USA (United States)	Chile	02 Jun 60	US Agri Commod Aid	377UNTS11	105393
USA (United States)	Chile	29 Jun 60	Direct Aid	377UNTS355	105411
USA (United States)	Chile	16 Jul 60	Milit Assistance	393UNTS271	105661
USA (United States)	Chile	29 Jul 60	Admin Cooperation	405UNTS127	105829
USA (United States)	Chile	28 Oct 60	Direct Aid	401UNTS177	105770
USA (United States)	Chile	08 Nov 60	US Agri Commod Aid	405UNTS85	105825
USA (United States)	Chile	03 Aug 61	Direct Aid	433UNTS21	106228
USA (United States)	Chile	12 Aug 61	Scientific Project	421UNTS209	106059
USA (United States)	Chile	07 Aug 62	US Agri Commod Aid	461UNTS61	106652
USA (United States)	Chile	04 Oct 62	Tech Assistance	461UNTS129	106656
USA (United States)	Chile	27 Oct 64	Military Mission	532UNTS347	107727
USA (United States)	Chile	27 Jul 65	US Agri Commod Aid	574UNTS83	108342
USA (United States)	Chile	30 Nov 67	Gen Communications	0UNTS0	110058
USA (United States)	Chile	29 Dec 67	US Agri Commod Aid	0UNTS0	109992
USA (United States)	Chile	29 Apr 69	Commodity Trade	0UNTS0	110273
USA (United States)	China	31 Aug 65	Status of Forces	572UNTS3	108308
USA (United States)	China People's Rep	10 Sep 55	Extradition	55CCJC63	410255
USA (United States)	Colombia	09 Sep 40	Extradition	125UNTS239	200428
USA (United States)	Colombia	19 Feb 42	Military Mission	117UNTS185	200369
USA (United States)	Colombia	29 May 42	Military Mission	8UNTS365	200047
USA (United States)	Colombia	23 Oct 42	Sanitation	105UNTS109	200326
USA (United States)	Colombia	05 Nov 42	Military Mission	24UNTS227	200147
USA (United States)	Colombia	29 Mar 43	Milit Installation	124UNTS139	200416
USA (United States)	Colombia	12 Feb 44	Milit Servic/Citiz	109UNTS287	200365
USA (United States)	Colombia	17 Apr 45	Customs	139UNTS303	200457
USA (United States)	Colombia	03 Dec 45	Military Mission	107UNTS3	101462
USA (United States)	Colombia	19 Feb 46	Sanitation	166UNTS104	102187
USA (United States)	Colombia	14 Oct 46	Military Mission	7UNTS97	100093
USA (United States)	Colombia	22 Dec 47	Air Transport	51UNTS45	100751
USA (United States)	Colombia	21 Feb 49	Military Mission	92UNTS227	101275
USA (United States)	Colombia	21 Feb 49	Military Mission	44UNTS83	100680
USA (United States)	Colombia	26 Jul 49	Admin Cooperation	73UNTS106	100949
USA (United States)	Colombia	12 Oct 49	General Trade	133UNTS15	101774
USA (United States)	Colombia	24 Nov 50	Scientific Project	133UNTS49	101779
USA (United States)	Colombia	09 Mar 51	Tech Assistance	141UNTS15	101901
USA (United States)	Colombia	12 Jan 52	Education	168UNTS109	102216
USA (United States)	Colombia	17 Apr 52	Milit Assistance	174UNTS215	102287
USA (United States)	Colombia	09 Jun 53	Tech Assistance	213UNTS3	102877
USA (United States)	Colombia	22 May 54	Visas	354UNTS21	105050
USA (United States)	Colombia	30 Jun 54	Non-IBRD Project	237UNTS263	103351
USA (United States)	Colombia	14 Jun 55	Non-IBRD Project	256UNTS211	103630
USA (United States)	Colombia	23 Jun 55	US Agri Commod Aid	263UNTS337	103781
USA (United States)	Colombia	19 Jul 55	Atomic Energy	235UNTS233	103305
USA (United States)	Colombia	16 Sep 55	Military Mission	256UNTS221	103631

PARTY ONE	PARTY TWO	DATE	TOPIC	CITATION	NUMBER
USA (United States)	Colombia	18 Nov 55	Claims and Debts	239UNTS173	103377
USA (United States)	Colombia	28 Nov 55	Non-IBRD Project	241UNTS39	103422
USA (United States)	Colombia	20 Dec 55	US Agri Commod Aid	241UNTS25	103421
USA (United States)	Colombia	14 Mar 56	Scientific Project	271UNTS303	103922
USA (United States)	Colombia	27 Mar 56	Air Transport	273UNTS235	103954
USA (United States)	Colombia	24 Oct 56	Air Transport	476UNTS77	106905
USA (United States)	Colombia	09 Jan 57	Education	462UNTS151	106676
USA (United States)	Colombia	16 Apr 57	US Agri Commod Aid	283UNTS245	104121
USA (United States)	Colombia	14 Mar 58	US Agri Commod Aid	308UNTS115	104459
USA (United States)	Colombia	08 May 59	Direct Aid	344UNTS193	104950
USA (United States)	Colombia	06 Oct 59	US Agri Commod Aid	358UNTS145	105132
USA (United States)	Colombia	11 Jan 60	Tech Assistance	371UNTS37	105268
USA (United States)	Colombia	07 Apr 60	Milit Assistance	372UNTS27	105285
USA (United States)	Colombia	03 Apr 61	Milit Assistance	407UNTS3	105856
USA (United States)	Colombia	04 Apr 61	Direct Aid	405UNTS55	105822
USA (United States)	Colombia	01 Aug 61	Taxation	433UNTS123	106235
USA (United States)	Colombia	09 Apr 62	Scientific Project	476UNTS9	106899
USA (United States)	Colombia	15 May 62	General Trade	445UNTS279	106396
USA (United States)	Colombia	23 Jul 62	General Aid	458UNTS123	106595
USA (United States)	Colombia	05 Oct 62	Finance	459UNTS191	106621
USA (United States)	Colombia	27 Mar 63	US Agri Commod Aid	489UNTS289	107145
USA (United States)	Colombia	29 Nov 63	Gen Communications	494UNTS49	107225
USA (United States)	Colombia	13 May 64	Scientific Project	530UNTS77	107673
USA (United States)	Colombia	08 Oct 64	US Agri Commod Aid	579UNTS3	108395
USA (United States)	Colombia	09 Jun 65	Commodity Trade	549UNTS3	107985
USA (United States)	Colombia	28 Oct 65	Telecommunications	574UNTS109	108343
USA (United States)	Colombia	10 Mar 66	US Agri Commod Aid	0UNTS0	109604
USA (United States)	Colombia	25 Oct 66	Tech Assistance	0UNTS0	109687
USA (United States)	Colombia	10 May 68	Customs	0UNTS0	110016
USA (United States)	Colombia	31 May 68	US Agri Commod Aid	0UNTS0	110067
USA (United States)	Colombia	18 Sep 68	Commodity Trade	0UNTS0	110077
USA (United States)	Colombia	19 Dec 68	Scientific Project	0UNTS0	110257
USA (United States)	Congo (Brazzaville)	05 Aug 61	Admin Cooperation	603UNTS19	108720
USA (United States)	Congo (Brazzaville)	01 Sep 62	Claims and Debts	459UNTS117	106616
USA (United States)	Congo (Brazzaville)	14 May 69	Commodity Trade	0UNTS0	110274
USA (United States)	Congo (Zaire)	18 Nov 61	US Agri Commod Aid	433UNTS207	106244
USA (United States)	Congo (Zaire)	17 Nov 62	Finance	474UNTS41	106870
USA (United States)	Congo (Zaire)	23 Feb 63	US Agri Commod Aid	493UNTS17	107204
USA (United States)	Congo (Zaire)	23 Feb 63	US Agri Commod Aid	493UNTS3	107203
USA (United States)	Congo (Zaire)	19 Jul 63	Milit Installation	511UNTS47	107425
USA (United States)	Congo (Zaire)	28 Apr 64	US Agri Commod Aid	526UNTS55	107600
USA (United States)	Congo (Zaire)	09 Dec 64	US Agri Commod Aid	531UNTS249	107707
USA (United States)	Congo (Zaire)	19 Jul 65	Direct Aid	593UNTS215	108586
USA (United States)	Congo (Zaire)	03 Oct 66	US Agri Commod Aid	0UNTS0	109683
USA (United States)	Congo (Zaire)	15 Mar 67	US Agri Commod Aid	0UNTS0	109897
USA (United States)	Congo (Zaire)	11 Dec 67	US Agri Commod Aid	0UNTS0	110059
USA (United States)	Congo (Zaire)	12 Aug 68	US Agri Commod Aid	0UNTS0	110150
USA (United States)	Congo (Zaire)	21 Oct 69	US Agri Commod Aid	0UNTS0	110450
USA (United States)	Costa Rica	18 Jun 41	Specific Resources	103UNTS173	200313
USA (United States)	Costa Rica	16 Jan 42	Land Transport	23UNTS285	200135
USA (United States)	Costa Rica	03 Apr 43	Specif Goods/Equip	13UNTS463	200090
USA (United States)	Costa Rica	29 May 44	Non-ILO Labor	124UNTS155	200417
USA (United States)	Costa Rica	10 Dec 45	Military Mission	3UNTS157	100029
USA (United States)	Costa Rica	12 Jan 48	Consul/Citizenship	70UNTS27	100896
USA (United States)	Costa Rica	27 Feb 48	Direct Aid	135UNTS74	101816
USA (United States)	Costa Rica	31 May 49	IGO Establishment	80UNTS3	101041
USA (United States)	Costa Rica	04 Apr 50	General Trade	132UNTS177	101759
USA (United States)	Costa Rica	02 Dec 50	Admin Cooperation	133UNTS61	101780
USA (United States)	Costa Rica	11 Jan 51	Tech Assistance	92UNTS179	101270
USA (United States)	Costa Rica	17 Jan 51	Land Transport	134UNTS215	101801
USA (United States)	Costa Rica	13 Feb 51	Sanitation	141UNTS169	101914
USA (United States)	Costa Rica	11 Sep 51	Air Transport	234UNTS255	103288
USA (United States)	Costa Rica	25 Feb 52	Status of Forces	174UNTS233	102288
USA (United States)	Costa Rica	30 Jun 54	Tech Assistance	235UNTS35	103294
USA (United States)	Costa Rica	26 Feb 55	Claims and Debts	252UNTS129	103562

PARTY ONE	PARTY TWO	DATE	TOPIC	CITATION	NUMBER
USA (United States)	Costa Rica	18 May 56	Atomic Energy	404UNTS237	105814
USA (United States)	Costa Rica	19 Oct 56	Gen Communications	278UNTS65	104022
USA (United States)	Costa Rica	22 Dec 61	General Aid	460UNTS277	106646
USA (United States)	Costa Rica	18 Jun 62	Milit Assistance	461UNTS155	106659
USA (United States)	Costa Rica	23 Nov 62	General Aid	541UNTS67	107861
USA (United States)	Costa Rica	24 Aug 64	Gen Communications	531UNTS107	107696
USA (United States)	Costa Rica	22 Nov 68	Finance	0UNTS0	110445
USA (United States)	Costa Rica	01 Oct 69	Commodity Trade	0UNTS0	110507
USA (United States)	Costa Rica	06 Mar 70	Commodity Trade	0UNTS0	110627
USA (United States)	Cuba	16 May 32	Consul/Citizenship	234UNTS283	200537
USA (United States)	Cuba	23 Dec 41	General Trade	119UNTS313	200388
USA (United States)	Cuba	01 Feb 43	Milit Servic/Citiz	13UNTS379	200085
USA (United States)	Cuba	30 Oct 47	General Economic	119UNTS163	101611
USA (United States)	Cuba	27 Jan 48	Scientific Project	67UNTS3	100862
USA (United States)	Cuba	21 Feb 49	Status of Forces	231UNTS108	103212
USA (United States)	Cuba	22 Dec 50	Military Mission	122UNTS97	101640
USA (United States)	Cuba	20 Jun 51	Tech Assistance	148UNTS3	101931
USA (United States)	Cuba	28 Aug 51	Military Mission	134UNTS225	101802
USA (United States)	Cuba	28 Aug 51	Military Mission	140UNTS239	101891
USA (United States)	Cuba	17 Dec 51	Visas	152UNTS87	102012
USA (United States)	Cuba	18 Dec 51	General Military	165UNTS3	102164
USA (United States)	Cuba	27 Feb 52	Gen Communications	168UNTS3	102209
USA (United States)	Cuba	07 Mar 52	Milit Assistance	165UNTS11	102165
USA (United States)	Cuba	26 May 53	Air Transport	224UNTS75	103070
USA (United States)	Cuba	26 Nov 53	Air Transport	205UNTS213	102777
USA (United States)	Cuba	03 Aug 55	Military Mission	265UNTS41	103805
USA (United States)	Cuba	10 Jan 56	Milit Assistance	240UNTS101	103398
USA (United States)	Cuba	26 Jun 56	Atomic Energy	293UNTS257	104294
USA (United States)	Cuba	04 Feb 57	Admin Cooperation	302UNTS273	104366
USA (United States)	Cuba	15 Aug 58	Specific Resources	358UNTS63	105124
USA (United States)	Cuba	06 Nov 65	Refugees	601UNTS81	108688
USA (United States)	Cyprus	08 Dec 60	Direct Aid	405UNTS145	105831
USA (United States)	Cyprus	29 Jun 61	General Aid	411UNTS56	105914
USA (United States)	Cyprus	15 Jan 62	Commodity Trade	435UNTS15	106267
USA (United States)	Cyprus	18 Jan 62	Education	435UNTS3	106266
USA (United States)	Cyprus	02 Mar 62	Direct Aid	445UNTS189	106386
USA (United States)	Cyprus	23 Aug 62	General Aid	461UNTS147	106658
USA (United States)	Cyprus	11 Jan 63	Visas	471UNTS127	106827
USA (United States)	Cyprus	23 Apr 63	Telecommunications	487UNTS291	107111
USA (United States)	Cyprus	29 May 63	Finance	487UNTS283	107110
USA (United States)	Cyprus	18 Jun 63	US Agri Commod Aid	479UNTS191	106953
USA (United States)	Czechoslovakia	11 Jul 42	Milit Assistance	90UNTS257	200263
USA (United States)	Czechoslovakia	21 Oct 43	Milit Servic/Citiz	29UNTS369	200172
USA (United States)	Czechoslovakia	03 Jan 46	Air Transport	6UNTS309	100084
USA (United States)	Czechoslovakia	14 Nov 46	General Trade	7UNTS119	100094
USA (United States)	Czechoslovakia	25 Jul 47	Reparations	90UNTS19	101223
USA (United States)	Czechoslovakia	16 Sep 48	Milit Assistance	90UNTS35	101224
USA (United States)	Czechoslovakia	29 Sep 50	Postal Service	290UNTS3	104227
USA (United States)	Czechoslovakia	21 Dec 62	Visas	469UNTS115	106787
USA (United States)	Czechoslovakia	28 Aug 67	Consul/Citizenship	0UNTS0	110443
USA (United States)	Czechoslovakia	28 Feb 69	Air Transport	0UNTS0	110269
USA (United States)	Czechoslovakia	29 Aug 69	General Trade	0UNTS0	110406
USA (United States)	Dahomey	27 May 61	General Aid	445UNTS23	106373
USA (United States)	Dahomey	13 Jun 62	Milit Assistance	458UNTS219	106603
USA (United States)	Dahomey	31 Dec 64	US Agri Commod Aid	541UNTS117	107865
USA (United States)	Dahomey	13 Mar 65	Claims and Debts	549UNTS43	107987
USA (United States)	Dahomey	03 Jul 67	Direct Aid	0UNTS0	109907
USA (United States)	Denmark	16 Dec 44	Air Transport	10UNTS213	200063
USA (United States)	Denmark	21 Mar 46	Air Transport	3UNTS301	100038
USA (United States)	Denmark	10 Sep 46	Mostfavored Nation	13UNTS75	100204
USA (United States)	Denmark	01 Oct 46	Air Transport	42UNTS219	100650
USA (United States)	Denmark	09 Jun 47	Visas	132UNTS145	101755
USA (United States)	Denmark	06 May 48	Taxation	26UNTS55	100377
USA (United States)	Denmark	29 Jun 48	Mostfavored Nation	27UNTS35	100396
USA (United States)	Denmark	29 Jun 48	Direct Aid	22UNTS217	100338

PARTY ONE	PARTY TWO	DATE	TOPIC	CITATION	NUMBER
USA (United States)	Denmark	01 Aug 49	Admin Cooperation	79UNTS147	101038
USA (United States)	Denmark	27 Jan 50	Milit Assistance	48UNTS115	100740
USA (United States)	Denmark	27 Apr 51	General Military	94UNTS35	101305
USA (United States)	Denmark	23 Aug 51	Education	147UNTS49	101928
USA (United States)	Denmark	01 Oct 51	General Amity	421UNTS105	106056
USA (United States)	Denmark	16 Nov 51	Milit Assistance	180UNTS275	102391
USA (United States)	Denmark	08 Jan 52	Milit Assistance	179UNTS65	102354
USA (United States)	Denmark	04 Feb 52	Patents/Copyrights	157UNTS25	102044
USA (United States)	Denmark	04 Apr 52	Telecommunications	177UNTS13	102305
USA (United States)	Denmark	07 Apr 52	Milit Assistance	177UNTS257	102324
USA (United States)	Denmark	08 Aug 52	Direct Aid	181UNTS249	102414
USA (United States)	Denmark	15 Oct 53	Patents/Copyrights	215UNTS111	102915
USA (United States)	Denmark	08 Jun 54	Milit Assistance	307UNTS133	104448
USA (United States)	Denmark	06 Aug 54	Air Transport	222UNTS235	103030
USA (United States)	Denmark	15 Dec 54	Air Transport	213UNTS273	102890
USA (United States)	Denmark	25 Jul 55	Atomic Energy	235UNTS245	103306
USA (United States)	Denmark	12 Dec 56	Status of Forces	304UNTS311	104405
USA (United States)	Denmark	28 Aug 58	Reparations	335UNTS133	104781
USA (United States)	Denmark	08 May 59	Milit Assistance	344UNTS185	104949
USA (United States)	Denmark	19 Feb 60	Patents/Copyrights	354UNTS151	105061
USA (United States)	Denmark	12 Apr 60	Milit Assistance	373UNTS9	105311
USA (United States)	Denmark	07 Jul 60	Air Transport	380UNTS39	105449
USA (United States)	Denmark	02 Dec 60	Milit Installation	402UNTS245	105789
USA (United States)	Denmark	05 Mar 62	General Economic	446UNTS9	106398
USA (United States)	Denmark	28 May 62	Education	450UNTS215	106469
USA (United States)	Denmark	02 Jul 64	Water Transport	529UNTS277	107665
USA (United States)	Dominican Republic	14 Nov 42	Customs	24UNTS233	200148
USA (United States)	Dominican Republic	10 Dec 42	Admin Cooperation	24UNTS257	200151
USA (United States)	Dominican Republic	25 Jan 43	Military Mission	13UNTS399	200083
USA (United States)	Dominican Republic	10 Jun 43	Specific Resources	21UNTS277	200129
USA (United States)	Dominican Republic	07 Jul 43	Sanitation	28UNTS419	200165
USA (United States)	Dominican Republic	19 Oct 43	Non-ILO Labor	21UNTS295	200130
USA (United States)	Dominican Republic	11 Feb 44	Milit Assistance	109UNTS251	200363
USA (United States)	Dominican Republic	13 Oct 45	Education	149UNTS361	200477
USA (United States)	Dominican Republic	07 Oct 46	Mostfavored Nation	13UNTS91	100206
USA (United States)	Dominican Republic	19 Jul 49	Air Transport	51UNTS145	100762
USA (United States)	Dominican Republic	23 Jan 50	Consul/Citizenship	236UNTS3	103312
USA (United States)	Dominican Republic	11 Aug 50	Status of Forces	92UNTS329	101278
USA (United States)	Dominican Republic	20 Feb 51	Tech Assistance	132UNTS305	101770
USA (United States)	Dominican Republic	16 Mar 51	Education	148UNTS15	101932
USA (United States)	Dominican Republic	26 Nov 51	Milit Installation	150UNTS227	101976
USA (United States)	Dominican Republic	07 Jan 52	Direct Aid	174UNTS243	102289
USA (United States)	Dominican Republic	06 Mar 53	Milit Assistance	199UNTS267	102689
USA (United States)	Dominican Republic	22 Apr 55	Milit Assistance	239UNTS325	103389
USA (United States)	Dominican Republic	30 Jun 55	Non-IBRD Project	257UNTS313	103664
USA (United States)	Dominican Republic	16 Dec 55	Visas	241UNTS101	103427
USA (United States)	Dominican Republic	15 Jun 56	Atomic Energy	265UNTS227	103815
USA (United States)	Dominican Republic	11 Aug 56	Scientific Project	263UNTS181	103773
USA (United States)	Dominican Republic	07 Dec 56	Military Mission	263UNTS193	103774
USA (United States)	Dominican Republic	09 Mar 57	Gen Communications	279UNTS249	104044
USA (United States)	Dominican Republic	11 Jan 62	General Aid	433UNTS133	106236
USA (United States)	Dominican Republic	08 Mar 62	Milit Assistance	527UNTS29	107615
USA (United States)	Dominican Republic	02 May 62	Direct Aid	442UNTS107	106342
USA (United States)	Dominican Republic	02 May 62	Claims and Debts	442UNTS99	106341
USA (United States)	Dominican Republic	25 Oct 62	Scientific Project	459UNTS247	106627
USA (United States)	Dominican Republic	30 Nov 62	US Agri Commod Aid	471UNTS25	106819
USA (United States)	Dominican Republic	22 Apr 63	Telecommunications	487UNTS169	107101
USA (United States)	Dominican Republic	13 Aug 63	US Agri Commod Aid	492UNTS327	107202
USA (United States)	Dominican Republic	28 Aug 64	Scientific Project	531UNTS35	107691
USA (United States)	Dominican Republic	02 Feb 65	Gen Communications	542UNTS117	107884
USA (United States)	Dominican Republic	18 Mar 65	US Agri Commod Aid	542UNTS215	107892
USA (United States)	Dominican Republic	21 Jul 66	Scientific Project	0UNTS0	109680
USA (United States)	Dominican Republic	01 Apr 68	General Aid	0UNTS0	110249
USA (United States)	Dominican Republic	10 May 68	US Agri Commod Aid	0UNTS0	110326
USA (United States)	Dominican Republic	11 Jun 68	General Aid	0UNTS0	110250

PARTY ONE	PARTY TWO	DATE	TOPIC	CITATION	NUMBER
USA (United States)	Dominican Republic	28 Mar 69	General Aid	0UNTS0	110251
USA (United States)	Dominican Republic	11 Apr 69	Scientific Project	0UNTS0	110159
USA (United States)	Dominican Republic	09 Mar 70	Commodity Trade	0UNTS0	110691
USA (United States)	Dominican Republic	31 Mar 70	US Agri Commod Aid	0UNTS0	110632
USA (United States)	ECSC (Coal/Steel)	23 Apr 54	Loans and Credits	229UNTS229	103170
USA (United States)	Ecuador	24 Feb 42	Sanitation	26UNTS379	200157
USA (United States)	Ecuador	02 Mar 42	General Trade	105UNTS195	200332
USA (United States)	Ecuador	29 Oct 42	Scientific Project	89UNTS301	200259
USA (United States)	Ecuador	13 Sep 43	Military Mission	29UNTS349	200171
USA (United States)	Ecuador	29 Jun 44	Military Mission	80UNTS283	200250
USA (United States)	Ecuador	22 Jan 45	Education	24UNTS273	200152
USA (United States)	Ecuador	05 Apr 45	Milit Servic/Citiz	121UNTS265	200404
USA (United States)	Ecuador	11 Jun 46	Status of Forces	167UNTS135	102203
USA (United States)	Ecuador	08 Jan 47	Air Transport	22UNTS119	100333
USA (United States)	Ecuador	21 Jun 47	Sanitation	26UNTS275	100391
USA (United States)	Ecuador	27 Oct 47	Air Transport	44UNTS45	100677
USA (United States)	Ecuador	29 Oct 47	Admin Cooperation	21UNTS21	100322
USA (United States)	Ecuador	14 Nov 47	Education	149UNTS297	101959
USA (United States)	Ecuador	14 May 48	Scientific Project	89UNTS71	101210
USA (United States)	Ecuador	21 Sep 48	Military Mission	80UNTS127	101048
USA (United States)	Ecuador	04 Feb 49	Military Mission	80UNTS137	101049
USA (United States)	Ecuador	17 May 49	Military Mission	66UNTS3	100845
USA (United States)	Ecuador	03 May 51	Tech Assistance	141UNTS27	101902
USA (United States)	Ecuador	20 Feb 52	Milit Assistance	177UNTS43	102308
USA (United States)	Ecuador	17 Mar 52	Telecommunications	177UNTS115	102313
USA (United States)	Ecuador	29 May 52	Tech Assistance	185UNTS203	102471
USA (United States)	Ecuador	30 Jun 54	Tech Assistance	236UNTS163	103323
USA (United States)	Ecuador	29 Mar 55	Claims and Debts	261UNTS343	103732
USA (United States)	Ecuador	08 Jul 55	Milit Assistance	265UNTS49	103806
USA (United States)	Ecuador	24 Aug 55	Military Mission	256UNTS299	103640
USA (United States)	Ecuador	06 Sep 55	Direct Aid	256UNTS187	103628
USA (United States)	Ecuador	07 Oct 55	US Agri Commod Aid	256UNTS197	103629
USA (United States)	Ecuador	19 Jul 56	Milit Assistance	372UNTS149	105295
USA (United States)	Ecuador	31 Oct 56	Education	283UNTS151	104114
USA (United States)	Ecuador	15 Feb 57	US Agri Commod Aid	279UNTS155	104037
USA (United States)	Ecuador	24 Apr 57	Scientific Project	284UNTS3	104124
USA (United States)	Ecuador	31 May 57	Atomic Energy	304UNTS61	104391
USA (United States)	Ecuador	06 Nov 57	Consul/Citizenship	307UNTS49	104441
USA (United States)	Ecuador	27 Jun 58	Direct Aid	317UNTS51	104593
USA (United States)	Ecuador	30 Jun 58	US Agri Commod Aid	336UNTS11	104796
USA (United States)	Ecuador	11 Feb 60	Milit Assistance	372UNTS141	105294
USA (United States)	Ecuador	24 Feb 60	Tech Assistance	371UNTS55	105270
USA (United States)	Ecuador	27 Sep 60	US Agri Commod Aid	401UNTS115	105766
USA (United States)	Ecuador	03 Apr 61	US Agri Commod Aid	409UNTS140	105882
USA (United States)	Ecuador	17 Jun 61	Direct Aid	411UNTS49	105913
USA (United States)	Ecuador	17 Apr 62	General Aid	442UNTS69	106339
USA (United States)	Ecuador	03 Aug 62	General Aid	460UNTS133	106636
USA (United States)	Ecuador	07 Jan 63	Visas	477UNTS101	106917
USA (United States)	Ecuador	05 Apr 63	US Agri Commod Aid	477UNTS135	106919
USA (United States)	Ecuador	20 Sep 63	Education	488UNTS147	107125
USA (United States)	Ecuador	26 Mar 65	Gen Communications	542UNTS237	107893
USA (United States)	Ecuador	25 Jun 65	US Agri Commod Aid	549UNTS23	107986
USA (United States)	Ecuador	20 Aug 68	Scientific Project	0UNTS0	110504
USA (United States)	Ecuador	30 Jun 69	US Agri Commod Aid	0UNTS0	110690
USA (United States)	EEC (Econ Commnty)	07 Mar 62	General Trade	445UNTS195	106387
USA (United States)	EEC (Econ Commnty)	07 Mar 62	General Trade	436UNTS49	106288
USA (United States)	EEC (Econ Commnty)	07 Mar 62	General Economic	446UNTS81	106405
USA (United States)	El Salvador	27 Nov 41	Admin Cooperation	120UNTS161	200389
USA (United States)	El Salvador	13 Feb 42	Land Transport	23UNTS293	200136
USA (United States)	El Salvador	05 May 42	Sanitation	21UNTS215	200124
USA (United States)	El Salvador	24 Nov 42	Military Mission	24UNTS241	200149
USA (United States)	El Salvador	02 Dec 42	Scientific Project	122UNTS277	200410
USA (United States)	El Salvador	25 Mar 43	Military Mission	13UNTS419	200088
USA (United States)	El Salvador	21 May 43	Military Mission	9UNTS341	200051
USA (United States)	El Salvador	31 May 43	Milit Servic/Citiz	105UNTS205	200333

PARTY ONE	PARTY TWO	DATE	TOPIC	CITATION	NUMBER
USA (United States)	El Salvador	09 Jun 45	Education	149UNTS379	200478
USA (United States)	El Salvador	19 Aug 47	Military Mission	51UNTS57	100752
USA (United States)	El Salvador	23 Sep 48	Sanitation	181UNTS101	102402
USA (United States)	El Salvador	27 Jul 49	Sanitation	180UNTS219	102387
USA (United States)	El Salvador	13 Dec 50	Sanitation	166UNTS149	102188
USA (United States)	El Salvador	19 Mar 51	Land Transport	134UNTS245	101803
USA (United States)	El Salvador	18 Apr 51	Tech Assistance	141UNTS37	101903
USA (United States)	El Salvador	11 May 51	Direct Aid	141UNTS191	101915
USA (United States)	El Salvador	19 Jul 51	Tech Assistance	140UNTS259	101892
USA (United States)	El Salvador	23 Jul 51	Direct Aid	138UNTS127	101865
USA (United States)	El Salvador	23 Oct 51	Direct Aid	137UNTS43	101847
USA (United States)	El Salvador	12 Dec 51	Education	132UNTS287	101768
USA (United States)	El Salvador	07 Jan 52	Tech Assistance	198UNTS231	102667
USA (United States)	El Salvador	04 Apr 52	Tech Assistance	177UNTS219	102320
USA (United States)	El Salvador	14 May 53	Direct Aid	234UNTS71	103273
USA (United States)	El Salvador	21 May 53	Military Mission	213UNTS15	102878
USA (United States)	El Salvador	15 Dec 53	Visas	236UNTS25	103314
USA (United States)	El Salvador	16 Jul 54	Non-IBRD Project	237UNTS237	103350
USA (United States)	El Salvador	31 Aug 54	Non-IBRD Project	237UNTS49	103336
USA (United States)	El Salvador	23 Sep 54	Military Mission	237UNTS91	103338
USA (United States)	El Salvador	21 Mar 55	Non-IBRD Project	250UNTS261	103528
USA (United States)	El Salvador	08 Aug 55	Non-IBRD Project	264UNTS301	103801
USA (United States)	El Salvador	21 Nov 57	Military Mission	303UNTS19	104369
USA (United States)	El Salvador	09 May 58	Visas	316UNTS29	104575
USA (United States)	El Salvador	29 Jan 60	Claims and Debts	372UNTS3	105283
USA (United States)	El Salvador	21 Aug 61	US Agri Commod Aid	418UNTS35	106015
USA (United States)	El Salvador	20 Nov 61	Direct Aid	433UNTS221	106245
USA (United States)	El Salvador	19 Dec 61	General Aid	445UNTS175	106385
USA (United States)	El Salvador	05 Apr 62	Telecommunications	442UNTS41	106337
USA (United States)	El Salvador	13 Apr 62	Milit Assistance	451UNTS307	106500
USA (United States)	El Salvador	15 May 62	General Trade	452UNTS49	106503
USA (United States)	El Salvador	07 May 63	US Agri Commod Aid	476UNTS35	106901
USA (United States)	El Salvador	05 Jun 67	Gen Communications	0UNTS0	109902
USA (United States)	Ethiopia	09 Aug 43	Milit Installation	29UNTS303	200169
USA (United States)	Ethiopia	04 Jul 46	Mostfavored Nation	13UNTS27	100198
USA (United States)	Ethiopia	20 May 49	Milit Assistance	89UNTS99	101211
USA (United States)	Ethiopia	02 May 51	Direct Aid	139UNTS85	101877
USA (United States)	Ethiopia	16 Jun 51	Tech Assistance	148UNTS39	101933
USA (United States)	Ethiopia	07 Sep 51	General Amity	206UNTS41	102785
USA (United States)	Ethiopia	15 May 52	Education	180UNTS227	102388
USA (United States)	Ethiopia	13 Jun 52	Milit Assistance	205UNTS17	102766
USA (United States)	Ethiopia	18 Jun 52	Tech Assistance	181UNTS207	102410
USA (United States)	Ethiopia	24 Jun 52	Tech Assistance	181UNTS215	102411
USA (United States)	Ethiopia	05 Nov 52	Sanitation	184UNTS139	102445
USA (United States)	Ethiopia	07 Nov 52	Tech Assistance	184UNTS285	102453
USA (United States)	Ethiopia	29 Apr 53	Sanitation	224UNTS121	103073
USA (United States)	Ethiopia	22 May 53	Milit Assistance	207UNTS127	102803
USA (United States)	Ethiopia	22 May 53	Milit Installation	191UNTS59	102577
USA (United States)	Ethiopia	25 Jun 53	Tech Assistance	212UNTS175	102869
USA (United States)	Ethiopia	30 Jun 53	Direct Aid	212UNTS135	102865
USA (United States)	Ethiopia	21 Apr 54	Tech Assistance	232UNTS299	103244
USA (United States)	Ethiopia	01 Jun 54	Direct Aid	232UNTS311	103245
USA (United States)	Ethiopia	12 Jun 54	Tech Assistance	234UNTS25	103270
USA (United States)	Ethiopia	25 Apr 57	Direct Aid	283UNTS205	104118
USA (United States)	Ethiopia	26 Dec 57	Milit Assistance	307UNTS71	104443
USA (United States)	Ethiopia	06 Dec 61	Education	433UNTS231	106246
USA (United States)	Ethiopia	23 May 62	General Aid	456UNTS293	106563
USA (United States)	Ethiopia	03 Aug 62	Claims and Debts	459UNTS79	106613
USA (United States)	Ethiopia	13 Aug 62	US Agri Commod Aid	459UNTS31	106611
USA (United States)	Ethiopia	25 Jan 63	Scientific Project	473UNTS27	106851
USA (United States)	Ethiopia	11 Jun 63	US Agri Commod Aid	487UNTS269	107109
USA (United States)	Ethiopia	25 Nov 64	Mass Media	532UNTS125	107715
USA (United States)	Ethiopia	17 Aug 65	US Agri Commod Aid	564UNTS119	108224
USA (United States)	Ethiopia	14 Dec 65	US Agri Commod Aid	574UNTS115	108344
USA (United States)	Ethiopia	30 Dec 65	Milit Installation	574UNTS129	108345

PARTY ONE	PARTY TWO	DATE	TOPIC	CITATION	NUMBER
USA (United States)	Ethiopia	15 Jun 67	Postal Service	0UNTS0	109905
USA (United States)	Eur Space Research	28 Nov 66	Scientific Project	0UNTS0	109691
USA (United States)	Euratom	29 May 58	Atomic Energy	335UNTS161	104783
USA (United States)	Euratom	08 Nov 58	Atomic Energy	338UNTS135	104835
USA (United States)	FAO (Food Agri)	29 Mar 62	IGO Operations	454UNTS13	106536
USA (United States)	FAO (Food Agri)	26 May 67	Direct Aid	0UNTS0	109901
USA (United States)	Fed of Malaya	09 Jul 58	Milit Assistance	336UNTS79	104799
USA (United States)	Fed of Malaya	21 Apr 59	Admin Cooperation	343UNTS3	104916
USA (United States)	Fed of Malaya	22 May 59	Tech Assistance	346UNTS263	104985
USA (United States)	Fed of Malaya	04 Sep 61	Direct Aid	421UNTS215	106060
USA (United States)	Finland	07 Jan 47	Taxation	15UNTS273	100243
USA (United States)	Finland	29 Mar 49	Air Transport	55UNTS59	100808
USA (United States)	Finland	01 Nov 49	Claims and Debts	68UNTS11	100880
USA (United States)	Finland	18 Jan 50	General Economic	92UNTS197	101272
USA (United States)	Finland	16 Nov 51	Patents/Copyrights	140UNTS273	101893
USA (United States)	Finland	03 Mar 52	Taxation	177UNTS141	102316
USA (United States)	Finland	03 Mar 52	Taxation	177UNTS163	102317
USA (United States)	Finland	02 Jul 52	Education	165UNTS203	102177
USA (United States)	Finland	04 Dec 52	General Amity	205UNTS149	102774
USA (United States)	Finland	06 May 55	US Agri Commod Aid	251UNTS3	103529
USA (United States)	Finland	14 Dec 55	Visas	335UNTS263	104794
USA (United States)	Finland	10 May 57	US Agri Commod Aid	283UNTS43	104105
USA (United States)	Finland	21 Feb 58	US Agri Commod Aid	304UNTS253	104401
USA (United States)	Finland	15 Aug 58	Visas	314UNTS43	104540
USA (United States)	Finland	30 Dec 58	US Agri Commod Aid	340UNTS259	104869
USA (United States)	Finland	22 Jul 59	Admin Cooperation	354UNTS39	105051
USA (United States)	Finland	23 Mar 60	US Agri Commod Aid	371UNTS117	105274
USA (United States)	Finland	16 Jun 61	Claims and Debts	413UNTS211	105955
USA (United States)	Finland	04 Aug 61	US Agri Commod Aid	418UNTS19	106014
USA (United States)	Finland	05 Mar 62	General Economic	446UNTS19	106399
USA (United States)	Finland	03 Nov 65	Air Transport	573UNTS175	108330
USA (United States)	Finland	27 Dec 67	Gen Communications	0UNTS0	109991
USA (United States)	Finland	08 Apr 70	Atomic Energy	0UNTS0	110767
USA (United States)	France	25 Jul 39	Taxation	125UNTS259	200429
USA (United States)	France	03 Sep 42	Milit Assistance	24UNTS177	200141
USA (United States)	France	25 Sep 43	Direct Aid	76UNTS183	200245
USA (United States)	France	25 Aug 44	Milit Occupation	138UNTS247	200449
USA (United States)	France	20 Feb 45	Direct Aid	76UNTS193	200246
USA (United States)	France	20 Feb 45	IGO Status/Immunit	76UNTS223	200248
USA (United States)	France	28 Feb 45	IGO Status/Immunit	76UNTS213	200247
USA (United States)	France	14 Aug 45	Admin Cooperation	73UNTS237	200243
USA (United States)	France	08 Nov 45	General Trade	76UNTS151	100986
USA (United States)	France	29 Dec 45	Air Transport	139UNTS105	101878
USA (United States)	France	07 Feb 46	Commodity Trade	3UNTS239	100034
USA (United States)	France	27 Mar 46	Air Transport	139UNTS114	101879
USA (United States)	France	28 May 46	General Trade	84UNTS151	101125
USA (United States)	France	28 May 46	Reparations	84UNTS93	101121
USA (United States)	France	28 May 46	General Economic	84UNTS167	101127
USA (United States)	France	28 May 46	Mass Media	84UNTS161	101126
USA (United States)	France	28 May 46	Reparations	84UNTS113	101122
USA (United States)	France	28 May 46	Status of Forces	84UNTS141	101124
USA (United States)	France	28 May 46	Milit Assistance	84UNTS79	101120
USA (United States)	France	28 May 46	Status of Forces	84UNTS121	101123
USA (United States)	France	28 May 46	Milit Assistance	84UNTS59	101119
USA (United States)	France	18 Jun 46	Air Transport	42UNTS183	100647
USA (United States)	France	18 Jul 46	Reparations	125UNTS165	101675
USA (United States)	France	18 Oct 46	Taxation	140UNTS23	101882
USA (United States)	France	10 Dec 46	Visas	15UNTS265	100242
USA (United States)	France	11 Mar 47	Humanitarian	151UNTS159	101991
USA (United States)	France	27 Mar 47	Patents/Copyrights	16UNTS65	100249
USA (United States)	France	04 Apr 47	Patents/Copyrights	24UNTS133	100353
USA (United States)	France	19 Apr 47	General Trade	132UNTS135	101754
USA (United States)	France	16 Sep 47	Visas	84UNTS19	101115
USA (United States)	France	01 Oct 47	Other Military	148UNTS303	101940
USA (United States)	France	25 Oct 47	Non-ILO Labor	89UNTS111	101212

PARTY ONE	PARTY TWO	DATE	TOPIC	CITATION	NUMBER
USA (United States)	France	30 Oct 47	General Economic	125UNTS171	101676
USA (United States)	France	02 Jan 48	Direct Aid	31UNTS97	100470
USA (United States)	France	25 Feb 48	Milit Servic/Citiz	67UNTS33	100864
USA (United States)	France	27 Feb 48	Reparations	84UNTS207	101131
USA (United States)	France	28 Jun 48	Mostfavored Nation	31UNTS115	100472
USA (United States)	France	28 Jun 48	Direct Aid	19UNTS9	100302
USA (United States)	France	09 Jul 48	Mostfavored Nation	32UNTS93	100492
USA (United States)	France	09 Jul 48	Direct Aid	24UNTS103	100352
USA (United States)	France	16 Sep 48	Culture	84UNTS185	101129
USA (United States)	France	19 Oct 48	Air Transport	98UNTS3	101355
USA (United States)	France	22 Oct 48	Education	84UNTS173	101128
USA (United States)	France	27 Nov 48	Scientific Project	168UNTS119	102217
USA (United States)	France	23 Dec 48	Direct Aid	67UNTS171	100876
USA (United States)	France	07 Feb 49	Direct Aid	67UNTS189	100877
USA (United States)	France	14 Mar 49	Claims and Debts	84UNTS225	101132
USA (United States)	France	14 Mar 49	Claims and Debts	84UNTS237	101133
USA (United States)	France	31 Mar 49	Visas	84UNTS283	101137
USA (United States)	France	27 Jan 50	Milit Assistance	80UNTS171	101051
USA (United States)	France	27 Feb 51	Milit Installation	0UNTS0	109598
USA (United States)	France	05 Jan 52	Milit Assistance	181UNTS177	102408
USA (United States)	France	02 Feb 52	Reparations	247UNTS223	103472
USA (United States)	France	13 Mar 52	Milit Assistance	177UNTS21	102306
USA (United States)	France	13 Jun 52	Taxation	181UNTS3	102393
USA (United States)	France	22 Jul 52	Direct Aid	181UNTS319	102420
USA (United States)	France	04 Oct 52	Milit Installation	0UNTS0	109599
USA (United States)	France	17 Jun 53	Milit Installation	0UNTS0	109600
USA (United States)	France	30 Jun 53	Milit Installation	0UNTS0	109601
USA (United States)	France	02 Sep 53	Milit Assistance	224UNTS153	103075
USA (United States)	France	31 May 54	Milit Assistance	236UNTS141	103321
USA (United States)	France	01 Jul 55	Other Military	270UNTS19	103888
USA (United States)	France	11 Aug 55	US Agri Commod Aid	251UNTS15	103530
USA (United States)	France	23 Sep 55	Milit Assistance	270UNTS341	103904
USA (United States)	France	19 Mar 56	Other Military	275UNTS37	103974
USA (United States)	France	23 Mar 56	Specific Property	278UNTS131	104029
USA (United States)	France	19 Jun 56	Atomic Energy	281UNTS341	104087
USA (United States)	France	22 Jun 56	Taxation	291UNTS101	104246
USA (United States)	France	06 Sep 56	Milit Installation	335UNTS173	104784
USA (United States)	France	08 Nov 56	Direct Aid	280UNTS189	104058
USA (United States)	France	14 Dec 56	Air Transport	266UNTS117	103826
USA (United States)	France	12 Mar 57	Patents/Copyrights	279UNTS275	104045
USA (United States)	France	23 Sep 57	Tech Assistance	293UNTS297	104297
USA (United States)	France	27 Dec 57	US Agri Commod Aid	307UNTS79	104444
USA (United States)	France	30 Jan 58	Specif Claim/Waive	304UNTS9	104388
USA (United States)	France	28 Feb 58	US Agri Commod Aid	366UNTS343	105222
USA (United States)	France	08 Dec 58	Milit Installation	0UNTS0	109602
USA (United States)	France	21 Mar 59	US Agri Commod Aid	342UNTS71	104901
USA (United States)	France	07 May 59	Milit Assistance	354UNTS83	105055
USA (United States)	France	10 Jul 59	Patents/Copyrights	62FRRT12	415179
USA (United States)	France	25 Nov 59	Admin Cooperation	401UNTS75	105764
USA (United States)	France	19 Sep 60	Milit Assistance	400UNTS21	105745
USA (United States)	France	04 Nov 60	US Agri Commod Aid	400UNTS323	105756
USA (United States)	France	31 Mar 61	Scientific Project	409UNTS136	105881
USA (United States)	France	27 Jul 61	Milit Assistance	433UNTS29	106229
USA (United States)	France	21 Sep 61	Visas	433UNTS243	106247
USA (United States)	France	22 Jan 63	Dispute Settlement	473UNTS3	106849
USA (United States)	France	01 Aug 63	Taxation	527UNTS89	107619
USA (United States)	France	07 May 65	Education	573UNTS183	108331
USA (United States)	France	05 May 66	Admin Cooperation	593UNTS279	108589
USA (United States)	France	17 Jun 66	Scientific Project	601UNTS113	108690
USA (United States)	France	18 Jul 66	Consul/Citizenship	68FRRT7	415180
USA (United States)	France	18 Jul 66	Consul/Citizenship	0UNTS0	110044
USA (United States)	France	24 Mar 67	Specific Property	0UNTS0	109858
USA (United States)	France	28 Jul 67	Taxation	68FRJO1210	416181
USA (United States)	France	28 Jul 67	Taxation	0UNTS0	110325
USA (United States)	France	24 May 68	Non-ILO Labor	69FRJO607	416182

PARTY ONE	PARTY TWO	DATE	TOPIC	CITATION	NUMBER
USA (United States)	Gabon	04 Oct 62	General Aid	459UNTS185	106620
USA (United States)	Gabon	10 Apr 63	Finance	474UNTS113	106876
USA (United States)	Gambia	05 Dec 66	Direct Aid	0UNTS0	109693
USA (United States)	Gambia	04 Nov 67	Finance	0UNTS0	110055
USA (United States)	Germany, West	30 Mar 42	Humanitarian	105UNTS219	200334
USA (United States)	Germany, West	15 Dec 49	Direct Aid	92UNTS269	101277
USA (United States)	Germany, West	07 Jun 51	Direct Aid	238UNTS161	103360
USA (United States)	Germany, West	19 Sep 51	General Trade	180UNTS161	102381
USA (United States)	Germany, West	28 Dec 51	Milit Assistance	181UNTS45	102397
USA (United States)	Germany, West	11 Jun 52	Mass Media	273UNTS105	103947
USA (United States)	Germany, West	18 Jul 52	Education	165UNTS167	102175
USA (United States)	Germany, West	09 Jan 53	Visas	212UNTS3	102859
USA (United States)	Germany, West	27 Feb 53	Claims and Debts	224UNTS31	103068
USA (United States)	Germany, West	27 Feb 53	Claims and Debts	223UNTS167	103065
USA (United States)	Germany, West	27 Feb 53	Claims and Debts	205UNTS103	102771
USA (United States)	Germany, West	27 Feb 53	Claims and Debts	224UNTS13	103067
USA (United States)	Germany, West	30 Mar 53	Reparations	235UNTS285	103310
USA (United States)	Germany, West	01 Apr 53	Claims and Debts	224UNTS3	103066
USA (United States)	Germany, West	09 Apr 53	Culture	204UNTS79	102750
USA (United States)	Germany, West	02 Jun 53	General Amity	231UNTS151	103214
USA (United States)	Germany, West	03 Jun 53	General Amity	253UNTS89	103578
USA (United States)	Germany, West	20 Aug 53	Milit Assistance	224UNTS49	103069
USA (United States)	Germany, West	23 Nov 53	Milit Installation	224UNTS107	103071
USA (United States)	Germany, West	12 Feb 54	Milit Assistance	223UNTS153	103064
USA (United States)	Germany, West	22 Jul 54	Taxation	221UNTS351	103016
USA (United States)	Germany, West	22 Jul 54	Taxation	239UNTS3	103369
USA (United States)	Germany, West	17 Aug 54	Direct Aid	233UNTS31	103248
USA (United States)	Germany, West	28 Aug 54	Milit Installation	299UNTS377	104325
USA (United States)	Germany, West	15 Oct 54	Milit Assistance	239UNTS135	103375
USA (United States)	Germany, West	27 Oct 54	Admin Cooperation	234UNTS131	103278
USA (United States)	Germany, West	29 Oct 54	General Amity	273UNTS3	103943
USA (United States)	Germany, West	18 Feb 55	Milit Assistance	247UNTS257	103474
USA (United States)	Germany, West	04 Apr 55	Milit Assistance	279UNTS73	104034
USA (United States)	Germany, West	14 Apr 55	General Military	263UNTS351	103782
USA (United States)	Germany, West	06 Jun 55	Humanitarian	315UNTS155	104566
USA (United States)	Germany, West	30 Jun 55	Milit Assistance	240UNTS69	103394
USA (United States)	Germany, West	30 Jun 55	Milit Assistance	240UNTS47	103393
USA (United States)	Germany, West	07 Jul 55	Air Transport	275UNTS3	103973
USA (United States)	Germany, West	02 Aug 55	Specif Goods/Equip	268UNTS121	103854
USA (United States)	Germany, West	23 Dec 55	US Agri Commod Aid	240UNTS79	103395
USA (United States)	Germany, West	04 Jan 56	General Military	268UNTS143	103856
USA (United States)	Germany, West	13 Feb 56	Atomic Energy	253UNTS119	103580
USA (United States)	Germany, West	02 Mar 56	Claims and Debts	273UNTS209	103952
USA (United States)	Germany, West	07 Mar 56	Sanitation	271UNTS361	103926
USA (United States)	Germany, West	18 Apr 56	Admin Cooperation	271UNTS319	103923
USA (United States)	Germany, West	26 Apr 56	Culture	283UNTS267	104122
USA (United States)	Germany, West	27 Jul 56	Admin Cooperation	278UNTS3	104017
USA (United States)	Germany, West	08 Oct 56	Milit Assistance	278UNTS9	104018
USA (United States)	Germany, West	12 Dec 56	Milit Assistance	280UNTS71	104052
USA (United States)	Germany, West	12 Dec 56	Milit Assistance	280UNTS63	104051
USA (United States)	Germany, West	11 Apr 57	Admin Cooperation	283UNTS233	104120
USA (United States)	Germany, West	01 May 57	Milit Assistance	284UNTS85	104131
USA (United States)	Germany, West	07 Jun 57	Milit Assistance	346UNTS241	104984
USA (United States)	Germany, West	28 Jun 57	Atomic Energy	288UNTS339	104213
USA (United States)	Germany, West	03 Jul 57	Atomic Energy	288UNTS305	104212
USA (United States)	Germany, West	10 Dec 57	Milit Assistance	307UNTS59	104442
USA (United States)	Germany, West	11 Dec 58	Air Transport	337UNTS31	104813
USA (United States)	Germany, West	20 Mar 59	Claims and Debts	341UNTS15	104874
USA (United States)	Germany, West	05 May 59	Atomic Energy	355UNTS307	105083
USA (United States)	Germany, West	03 Aug 59	Status of Forces	490UNTS28	107153
USA (United States)	Germany, West	01 Oct 59	Air Transport	358UNTS129	105130
USA (United States)	Germany, West	16 Mar 60	Specific Property	371UNTS101	105272
USA (United States)	Germany, West	27 May 60	Milit Assistance	377UNTS45	105395
USA (United States)	Germany, West	16 Aug 60	Claims and Debts	418UNTS235	106024
USA (United States)	Germany, West	03 Jan 61	Admin Cooperation	416UNTS93	105997
USA (United States)	Germany, West	29 Sep 61	Scientific Project	424UNTS113	106103
USA (United States)	Germany, West	25 May 62	Milit Assistance	458UNTS259	106608
USA (United States)	Germany, West	20 Nov 62	Education	505UNTS263	107377
USA (United States)	Germany, West	29 Nov 62	Water Transport	460UNTS169	106639
USA (United States)	Germany, West	14 Mar 63	Status of Forces	474UNTS71	106872
USA (United States)	Germany, West	17 Mar 64	Education	64WBGA113	424720
USA (United States)	Germany, West	18 Dec 65	Status of Forces	579UNTS193	108407
USA (United States)	Germany, West	25 Mar 66	Commodity Trade	66WBGA144	424721
USA (United States)	Germany, West	30 Jun 66	Gen Communications	601UNTS107	108689
USA (United States)	Germany, West	16 Dec 66	Culture	0UNTS0	109694
USA (United States)	Germany, West	23 Dec 66	Education	68WBGA21	424722
USA (United States)	Germany, West	29 Dec 66	General Aid	0UNTS0	109839
USA (United States)	Germany, West	16 Mar 67	Commodity Trade	67WBGA150	424723
USA (United States)	Germany, West	12 Jul 67	Patents/Copyrights	0UNTS0	109908
USA (United States)	Germany, West	24 Oct 67	Status of Forces	67WBGA213	424724
USA (United States)	Germany, West	27 Feb 68	Admin Cooperation	0UNTS0	110134
USA (United States)	Germany, West	24 Jun 69	Specific Property	69WBGA156	424725
USA (United States)	Germany, West	11 Sep 70	Non-ILO Labor	70WGBB2778	425726
USA (United States)	Germany, West	03 Dec 70	Milit Installation	71WGBB407	425727
USA (United States)	Ghana	03 Jun 57	Tech Assistance	284UNTS63	104129
USA (United States)	Ghana	12 Feb 58	Admin Cooperation	442UNTS175	106348
USA (United States)	Ghana	30 Sep 58	Admin Cooperation	336UNTS169	104805
USA (United States)	Ghana	09 Apr 59	Customs	342UNTS21	104897
USA (United States)	Ghana	19 Jul 61	Direct Aid	416UNTS167	106002
USA (United States)	Ghana	03 Jan 62	Scientific Project	433UNTS147	106237
USA (United States)	Ghana	24 Jan 62	Education	435UNTS23	106268
USA (United States)	Ghana	01 Apr 66	US Agri Commod Aid	579UNTS157	108405
USA (United States)	Ghana	03 Mar 67	US Agri Commod Aid	0UNTS0	109854
USA (United States)	Ghana	24 Oct 67	US Agri Commod Aid	0UNTS0	109985
USA (United States)	Ghana	03 Jan 68	US Agri Commod Aid	0UNTS0	109986
USA (United States)	Ghana	10 Dec 68	General Aid	0UNTS0	110254
USA (United States)	Ghana	09 Jun 69	General Aid	0UNTS0	110255
USA (United States)	Ghana	22 Jun 70	Commodity Trade	0UNTS0	110782
USA (United States)	Greece	10 Jul 42	Milit Assistance	103UNTS289	200319
USA (United States)	Greece	16 Mar 43	Milit Servic/Citiz	105UNTS227	200335
USA (United States)	Greece	11 Jan 46	General Trade	3UNTS203	100032
USA (United States)	Greece	27 Mar 46	Air Transport	15UNTS233	100239
USA (United States)	Greece	16 May 46	Direct Aid	184UNTS230	102451
USA (United States)	Greece	08 Oct 46	Claims and Debts	180UNTS119	102379
USA (United States)	Greece	20 Jun 47	Direct Aid	7UNTS267	100105
USA (United States)	Greece	08 Jul 47	Direct Aid	16UNTS157	100256
USA (United States)	Greece	03 Dec 47	Milit Assistance	89UNTS119	101213
USA (United States)	Greece	23 Apr 48	Education	74UNTS107	100958
USA (United States)	Greece	02 Jul 48	Direct Aid	23UNTS43	100342
USA (United States)	Greece	02 Jul 48	Mostfavored Nation	31UNTS131	100474
USA (United States)	Greece	25 Oct 48	General Trade	185UNTS103	102462
USA (United States)	Greece	01 Nov 48	Direct Aid	185UNTS169	102468
USA (United States)	Greece	29 Jan 49	Visas	88UNTS35	101183
USA (United States)	Greece	09 Feb 49	Direct Aid	79UNTS95	101034
USA (United States)	Greece	21 Feb 49	Status of Forces	88UNTS29	101182
USA (United States)	Greece	20 Feb 50	Taxation	196UNTS269	102629
USA (United States)	Greece	20 Feb 50	Taxation	196UNTS291	102630
USA (United States)	Greece	24 Oct 50	Admin Cooperation	133UNTS41	101778
USA (United States)	Greece	03 Aug 51	General Amity	224UNTS279	103080
USA (United States)	Greece	07 Jan 52	Milit Assistance	180UNTS171	102382
USA (United States)	Greece	07 Jan 52	Milit Assistance	177UNTS249	102323
USA (United States)	Greece	23 Apr 52	Direct Aid	177UNTS283	102327
USA (United States)	Greece	25 Jun 52	Air Transport	181UNTS53	102398
USA (United States)	Greece	24 Dec 52	Milit Assistance	185UNTS193	102470
USA (United States)	Greece	04 Feb 53	Milit Assistance	189UNTS3	102538
USA (United States)	Greece	12 Oct 53	Milit Installation	191UNTS319	102589
USA (United States)	Greece	30 Jul 54	Milit Assistance	234UNTS43	103272
USA (United States)	Greece	18 Aug 54	Telecommunications	234UNTS161	103282
USA (United States)	Greece	27 May 55	Milit Assistance	251UNTS349	103552
USA (United States)	Greece	16 Jun 55	Patents/Copyrights	262UNTS137	103742

PARTY ONE	PARTY TWO	DATE	TOPIC	CITATION	NUMBER
USA (United States)	Greece	24 Jun 55	US Agri Commod Aid	270UNTS351	103905
USA (United States)	Greece	24 Jun 55	US Agri Commod Aid	270UNTS361	103906
USA (United States)	Greece	04 Aug 55	Atomic Energy	235UNTS257	103307
USA (United States)	Greece	08 Aug 56	US Agri Commod Aid	277UNTS203	104007
USA (United States)	Greece	07 Sep 56	Status of Forces	278UNTS141	104030
USA (United States)	Greece	19 Jan 57	Milit Installation	280UNTS45	104049
USA (United States)	Greece	05 Aug 57	Milit Assistance	290UNTS167	104235
USA (United States)	Greece	18 Dec 57	US Agri Commod Aid	303UNTS159	104379
USA (United States)	Greece	15 Jan 59	Milit Assistance	357UNTS281	105120
USA (United States)	Greece	06 May 59	Milit Assistance	357UNTS163	105115
USA (United States)	Greece	07 Jan 60	US Agri Commod Aid	368UNTS221	105243
USA (United States)	Greece	15 Feb 60	Milit Assistance	377UNTS95	105397
USA (United States)	Greece	26 Apr 60	Patents/Copyrights	372UNTS299	105306
USA (United States)	Greece	07 Nov 60	US Agri Commod Aid	400UNTS57	105748
USA (United States)	Greece	18 Oct 61	US Agri Commod Aid	426UNTS209	106139
USA (United States)	Greece	24 Apr 62	Water Transport	459UNTS3	106609
USA (United States)	Greece	22 Oct 62	US Agri Commod Aid	462UNTS187	106678
USA (United States)	Greece	30 Oct 63	US Agri Commod Aid	493UNTS29	107205
USA (United States)	Greece	13 Dec 63	Education	494UNTS55	107226
USA (United States)	Greece	28 May 64	Claims and Debts	0UNTS0	109676
USA (United States)	Greece	17 Jul 64	Commodity Trade	530UNTS13	107669
USA (United States)	Greece	17 Nov 64	US Agri Commod Aid	532UNTS107	107714
USA (United States)	Greece	12 Jan 67	General Military	0UNTS0	109842
USA (United States)	Greece	08 Apr 69	Commodity Trade	0UNTS0	110157
USA (United States)	Guatemala	21 Jul 42	Military Mission	103UNTS299	200320
USA (United States)	Guatemala	19 May 43	Land Transport	28UNTS377	200161
USA (United States)	Guatemala	17 Jul 43	Military Mission	28UNTS431	200166
USA (United States)	Guatemala	13 Apr 44	Admin Cooperation	106UNTS213	200342
USA (United States)	Guatemala	15 Jul 44	Scientific Project	106UNTS285	200347
USA (United States)	Guatemala	16 Sep 44	Education	135UNTS315	200444
USA (United States)	Guatemala	21 Feb 45	Military Mission	121UNTS133	200396
USA (United States)	Guatemala	21 May 45	Military Mission	121UNTS185	200399
USA (United States)	Guatemala	25 Oct 45	Postal Service	139UNTS45	101875
USA (United States)	Guatemala	29 Aug 47	Status of Forces	27UNTS11	100393
USA (United States)	Guatemala	05 Jan 48	Education	135UNTS104	101817
USA (United States)	Guatemala	18 May 48	Land Transport	67UNTS161	100875
USA (United States)	Guatemala	08 Oct 48	Military Mission	121UNTS37	101624
USA (United States)	Guatemala	08 Oct 48	Military Mission	121UNTS31	101623
USA (United States)	Guatemala	20 Dec 49	Status of Forces	70UNTS71	100897
USA (United States)	Guatemala	08 Jan 52	Tech Assistance	181UNTS31	102395
USA (United States)	Guatemala	30 Jul 54	Milit Assistance	234UNTS235	103286
USA (United States)	Guatemala	01 Sep 54	Tech Assistance	199UNTS51	102677
USA (United States)	Guatemala	01 Dec 54	Visas	237UNTS161	103342
USA (United States)	Guatemala	13 Dec 54	Direct Aid	237UNTS169	103343
USA (United States)	Guatemala	23 Mar 55	Claims and Debts	252UNTS143	103563
USA (United States)	Guatemala	18 Jun 55	Milit Assistance	262UNTS105	103740
USA (United States)	Guatemala	28 Sep 55	General Trade	257UNTS307	103663
USA (United States)	Guatemala	30 May 56	Visas	275UNTS271	103986
USA (United States)	Guatemala	15 Aug 56	Atomic Energy	288UNTS181	104205
USA (United States)	Guatemala	23 Apr 60	Atomic Energy	373UNTS23	105312
USA (United States)	Guatemala	09 Aug 60	Finance	461UNTS15	106648
USA (United States)	Guatemala	21 May 62	General Trade	451UNTS205	106495
USA (United States)	Guatemala	02 Aug 62	Milit Assistance	461UNTS199	106664
USA (United States)	Guatemala	29 Dec 62	Tech Assistance	474UNTS31	106869
USA (United States)	Guatemala	03 Oct 63	Direct Aid	493UNTS45	107206
USA (United States)	Guatemala	04 May 65	Status of Forces	545UNTS163	107932
USA (United States)	Guatemala	11 Dec 67	Gen Communications	0UNTS0	110444
USA (United States)	Guinea	28 Oct 59	Culture	358UNTS169	105134
USA (United States)	Guinea	30 Sep 60	General Aid	394UNTS103	105671
USA (United States)	Guinea	02 Feb 62	US Agri Commod Aid	435UNTS35	106269
USA (United States)	Guinea	09 May 62	Claims and Debts	451UNTS197	106494
USA (United States)	Guinea	03 Nov 62	Mass Media	459UNTS259	106628
USA (United States)	Guinea	14 Dec 62	General Aid	462UNTS247	106684
USA (United States)	Guinea	22 May 63	US Agri Commod Aid	487UNTS251	107108
USA (United States)	Guinea	13 Jun 64	US Agri Commod Aid	531UNTS263	107708

PARTY ONE	PARTY TWO	DATE	TOPIC	CITATION	NUMBER
USA (United States)	Guinea	29 Jun 65	Milit Installation	549UNTS139	107997
USA (United States)	Guinea	04 Feb 66	US Agri Commod Aid	579UNTS213	108409
USA (United States)	Guinea	18 Oct 67	US Agri Commod Aid	0UNTS0	110050
USA (United States)	Guinea	03 Feb 69	Commodity Trade	0UNTS0	110266
USA (United States)	Guyana	07 Jun 67	Admin Cooperation	0UNTS0	109771
USA (United States)	Guyana	13 May 68	Gen Communications	0UNTS0	110017
USA (United States)	Guyana	17 Sep 68	US Agri Commod Aid	0UNTS0	110076
USA (United States)	Haiti	23 May 41	Military Mission	117UNTS191	200370
USA (United States)	Haiti	05 Jun 41	Admin Cooperation	101UNTS125	200289
USA (United States)	Haiti	13 Sep 41	Other Ad Hoc	103UNTS141	200311
USA (United States)	Haiti	19 Feb 42	Customs	105UNTS238	200336
USA (United States)	Haiti	07 Apr 42	Sanitation	106UNTS319	200349
USA (United States)	Haiti	21 Sep 42	Other Ad Hoc	120UNTS177	200391
USA (United States)	Haiti	30 Sep 42	Other Ad Hoc	24UNTS205	200144
USA (United States)	Haiti	19 Oct 42	Territory Boundary	120UNTS171	200390
USA (United States)	Haiti	08 Jan 45	Specific Resources	121UNTS153	200397
USA (United States)	Haiti	24 Aug 45	Visas	139UNTS311	200458
USA (United States)	Haiti	14 May 46	Finance	4UNTS179	100044
USA (United States)	Haiti	30 Sep 46	Other Ad Hoc	15UNTS257	100241
USA (United States)	Haiti	04 Jul 47	Other Ad Hoc	22UNTS165	100335
USA (United States)	Haiti	27 Sep 47	Sanitation	136UNTS258	101839
USA (United States)	Haiti	01 Oct 47	Other Ad Hoc	102UNTS67	101411
USA (United States)	Haiti	19 Dec 47	Direct Aid	135UNTS130	101818
USA (United States)	Haiti	11 Feb 48	Specific Resources	149UNTS11	101946
USA (United States)	Haiti	04 Jan 49	Military Mission	44UNTS69	100679
USA (United States)	Haiti	14 Apr 49	Military Mission	80UNTS37	101043
USA (United States)	Haiti	29 Dec 49	General Trade	133UNTS21	101775
USA (United States)	Haiti	28 Sep 50	Sanitation	162UNTS85	102132
USA (United States)	Haiti	02 May 51	Tech Assistance	151UNTS191	101994
USA (United States)	Haiti	29 Aug 52	Direct Aid	186UNTS35	102480
USA (United States)	Haiti	13 Mar 53	Direct Aid	212UNTS143	102866
USA (United States)	Haiti	28 May 54	Non-IBRD Project	233UNTS281	103267
USA (United States)	Haiti	28 Jan 55	Milit Assistance	270UNTS83	103894
USA (United States)	Haiti	01 Apr 55	Direct Aid	261UNTS361	103734
USA (United States)	Haiti	05 Apr 55	Milit Assistance	270UNTS97	103895
USA (United States)	Haiti	27 Apr 55	IGO Establishment	240UNTS17	103391
USA (United States)	Haiti	24 Jun 55	Non-IBRD Project	264UNTS291	103800
USA (United States)	Haiti	28 Dec 55	Non-IBRD Project	240UNTS95	103397
USA (United States)	Haiti	28 Dec 56	Direct Aid	279UNTS107	104035
USA (United States)	Haiti	09 Sep 58	Direct Aid	335UNTS257	104793
USA (United States)	Haiti	27 Oct 58	Military Mission	336UNTS235	104807
USA (United States)	Haiti	24 Dec 58	Military Mission	338UNTS265	104840
USA (United States)	Haiti	06 Jan 60	Gen Communications	367UNTS75	105226
USA (United States)	Haiti	08 Jul 60	Milit Assistance	380UNTS135	105454
USA (United States)	Haiti	01 Sep 60	Milit Assistance	388UNTS249	105582
USA (United States)	Haiti	06 Jun 62	General Trade	452UNTS59	106504
USA (United States)	Honduras	28 Feb 41	Specific Resources	117UNTS205	200371
USA (United States)	Honduras	08 May 42	Sanitation	166UNTS351	200498
USA (United States)	Honduras	26 Oct 42	Land Transport	24UNTS209	200145
USA (United States)	Honduras	12 Apr 44	Education	138UNTS271	200450
USA (United States)	Honduras	28 Dec 45	Military Mission	3UNTS185	100031
USA (United States)	Honduras	13 May 47	Sanitation	166UNTS159	102189
USA (United States)	Honduras	06 Mar 50	Military Mission	80UNTS51	101044
USA (United States)	Honduras	06 Mar 50	Military Mission	80UNTS71	101045
USA (United States)	Honduras	24 Mar 50	Admin Cooperation	93UNTS11	101283
USA (United States)	Honduras	26 Jan 51	Tech Assistance	99UNTS49	101370
USA (United States)	Honduras	30 Jan 51	Direct Aid	124UNTS63	101667
USA (United States)	Honduras	24 Apr 51	Education	140UNTS287	101894
USA (United States)	Honduras	07 Mar 52	Tech Assistance	233UNTS151	103260
USA (United States)	Honduras	23 Apr 52	Status of Forces	198UNTS251	102669
USA (United States)	Honduras	20 May 54	Milit Assistance	222UNTS87	103025
USA (United States)	Honduras	24 May 54	Milit Installation	433UNTS155	106238
USA (United States)	Honduras	21 Mar 55	Direct Aid	253UNTS3	103572
USA (United States)	Honduras	12 May 55	Direct Aid	270UNTS3	103886
USA (United States)	Honduras	10 Jun 55	Claims and Debts	258UNTS51	103669

PARTY ONE	PARTY TWO	DATE	TOPIC	CITATION	NUMBER
USA (United States)	Honduras	25 Apr 56	Military Mission	269UNTS25	103869
USA (United States)	Honduras	25 Jun 56	Taxation	279UNTS113	104036
USA (United States)	Honduras	19 Feb 60	Gen Communications	371UNTS109	105273
USA (United States)	Honduras	18 Jan 61	General Trade	402UNTS169	105785
USA (United States)	Honduras	12 Apr 61	Direct Aid	413UNTS182	105952
USA (United States)	Honduras	20 Jul 62	General Aid	460UNTS125	106635
USA (United States)	Honduras	24 Oct 62	Milit Assistance	459UNTS211	106624
USA (United States)	Honduras	17 Apr 67	Gen Communications	0UNTS0	109760
USA (United States)	Honduras	27 Nov 69	Commodity Trade	0UNTS0	110454
USA (United States)	Honduras	30 Apr 70	General Trade	0UNTS0	110778
USA (United States)	Hungary	09 Aug 46	Other Military	148UNTS313	101941
USA (United States)	Hungary	09 Mar 48	Admin Cooperation	183UNTS3	102426
USA (United States)	Hungary	19 Sep 69	Consul/Citizenship	0UNTS0	110447
USA (United States)	IAEA (Atom Energy)	11 May 59	Atomic Energy	339UNTS359	104855
USA (United States)	IAEA (Atom Energy)	28 Jun 60	Direct Aid	374UNTS133	105333
USA (United States)	IAEA (Atom Energy)	30 Mar 62	Specific Property	442UNTS49	106338
USA (United States)	IAEA (Atom Energy)	20 Aug 62	Commodity Trade	456UNTS447	106570
USA (United States)	IAEA (Atom Energy)	15 Jun 64	Atomic Energy	525UNTS3	107580
USA (United States)	IAEA (Atom Energy)	26 Sep 66	Atomic Energy	589UNTS3	108532
USA (United States)	IAEA (Atom Energy)	09 Dec 66	Atomic Energy	589UNTS55	108535
USA (United States)	IAEA (Atom Energy)	07 Jun 67	IGO Operations	614UNTS109	108866
USA (United States)	IAEA (Atom Energy)	16 Oct 67	Atomic Energy	630UNTS57	108965
USA (United States)	IAEA (Atom Energy)	23 Aug 68	Atomic Energy	0UNTS0	110516
USA (United States)	IAEA (Atom Energy)	30 Sep 68	Atomic Energy	0UNTS0	109944
USA (United States)	IAEA (Atom Energy)	04 Mar 69	Atomic Energy	0UNTS0	109945
USA (United States)	Iceland	01 Jul 41	Milit Assistance	12UNTS405	200071
USA (United States)	Iceland	21 Nov 41	Milit Assistance	124UNTS179	200418
USA (United States)	Iceland	17 Aug 42	Admin Cooperation	24UNTS163	200140
USA (United States)	Iceland	27 Sep 43	General Trade	29UNTS317	200170
USA (United States)	Iceland	27 Jan 45	Air Transport	122UNTS293	200411
USA (United States)	Iceland	11 Apr 45	Air Transport	16UNTS241	200105
USA (United States)	Iceland	07 Oct 46	Milit Installation	12UNTS163	100184
USA (United States)	Iceland	09 Dec 47	Visas	82UNTS31	101082
USA (United States)	Iceland	03 Jul 48	Milit Occupation	27UNTS49	100398
USA (United States)	Iceland	03 Jul 48	Direct Aid	20UNTS141	100316
USA (United States)	Iceland	05 May 51	Milit Assistance	205UNTS173	102776
USA (United States)	Iceland	08 Jan 52	Milit Assistance	180UNTS183	102383
USA (United States)	Iceland	18 Mar 52	Taxation	177UNTS263	102325
USA (United States)	Iceland	10 Dec 54	Milit Assistance	237UNTS191	103345
USA (United States)	Iceland	20 Jul 55	General Military	256UNTS245	103634
USA (United States)	Iceland	05 Oct 55	Claims and Debts	256UNTS285	103638
USA (United States)	Iceland	06 Mar 56	General Trade	270UNTS205	103898
USA (United States)	Iceland	04 Jun 56	Visas	275UNTS189	103982
USA (United States)	Iceland	23 Nov 56	Specif Claim/Waive	281UNTS361	104088
USA (United States)	Iceland	06 Dec 56	General Military	265UNTS261	103818
USA (United States)	Iceland	23 Feb 57	Education	283UNTS73	104107
USA (United States)	Iceland	11 Apr 57	US Agri Commod Aid	283UNTS107	104110
USA (United States)	Iceland	03 May 58	US Agri Commod Aid	316UNTS137	104581
USA (United States)	Iceland	03 Mar 59	US Agri Commod Aid	341UNTS261	104889
USA (United States)	Iceland	23 Jun 59	Direct Aid	354UNTS3	105048
USA (United States)	Iceland	06 Apr 60	US Agri Commod Aid	372UNTS71	105289
USA (United States)	Iceland	30 Dec 60	Direct Aid	401UNTS43	105761
USA (United States)	Iceland	07 Apr 61	US Agri Commod Aid	406UNTS203	105850
USA (United States)	Iceland	06 Nov 61	US Agri Commod Aid	426UNTS225	106140
USA (United States)	Iceland	16 Mar 62	US Agri Commod Aid	445UNTS49	106376
USA (United States)	Iceland	27 Dec 62	Taxation	469UNTS91	106785
USA (United States)	Iceland	06 Feb 63	US Agri Commod Aid	473UNTS93	106858
USA (United States)	Iceland	15 Jul 63	General Trade	527UNTS45	107616
USA (United States)	Iceland	13 Feb 64	Education	524UNTS235	107576
USA (United States)	Iceland	13 Feb 64	US Agri Commod Aid	510UNTS295	107420
USA (United States)	Iceland	13 Feb 64	US Agri Commod Aid	511UNTS3	107421
USA (United States)	Iceland	30 Dec 64	US Agri Commod Aid	542UNTS37	107878
USA (United States)	Iceland	30 Dec 64	US Agri Commod Aid	531UNTS287	107709
USA (United States)	Iceland	05 Jun 67	US Agri Commod Aid	0UNTS0	109903
USA (United States)	Iceland	29 May 68	US Agri Commod Aid	0UNTS0	110066

PARTY ONE	PARTY TWO	DATE	TOPIC	CITATION	NUMBER
USA (United States)	Iceland	23 May 69	Commodity Trade	0UNTS0	110276
USA (United States)	Iceland	24 Jun 70	Air Transport	0UNTS0	110783
USA (United States)	ICJ Option Clause	14 Aug 46	ICJ Option Clause	1UNTS9	100003
USA (United States)	ILO (Labor Org)	22 Feb 63	IGO Operations	489UNTS347	107149
USA (United States)	India	30 Sep 42	Milit Servic/Citiz	13UNTS185	200078
USA (United States)	India	16 Oct 42	Status of Forces	109UNTS111	200353
USA (United States)	India	16 May 46	Milit Assistance	4UNTS183	100045
USA (United States)	India	14 Nov 46	Air Transport	22UNTS55	100331
USA (United States)	India	05 Jul 47	Status of Forces	185UNTS293	102476
USA (United States)	India	11 Aug 48	Visas	224UNTS115	103072
USA (United States)	India	04 Jul 49	Status of Forces	200UNTS181	102702
USA (United States)	India	02 Feb 50	Education	89UNTS127	101214
USA (United States)	India	28 Dec 50	Tech Assistance	99UNTS39	101369
USA (United States)	India	11 Jan 51	Admin Cooperation	148UNTS49	101934
USA (United States)	India	16 Mar 51	Milit Assistance	141UNTS47	101904
USA (United States)	India	09 Jul 51	Customs	147UNTS43	101927
USA (United States)	India	05 Jan 52	Tech Assistance	157UNTS39	102045
USA (United States)	India	29 Jul 54	Postal Service	239UNTS69	103373
USA (United States)	India	21 Oct 54	Patents/Copyrights	234UNTS119	103277
USA (United States)	India	04 Oct 55	Direct Aid	268UNTS115	103853
USA (United States)	India	03 Feb 56	Air Transport	272UNTS75	103932
USA (United States)	India	29 Aug 56	US Agri Commod Aid	278UNTS25	104019
USA (United States)	India	27 Sep 56	Direct Aid	281UNTS289	104085
USA (United States)	India	19 Sep 57	Claims and Debts	290UNTS175	104236
USA (United States)	India	23 Jun 58	US Agri Commod Aid	317UNTS181	104603
USA (United States)	India	26 Sep 58	US Agri Commod Aid	336UNTS59	104798
USA (United States)	India	17 Dec 58	Milit Assistance	358UNTS77	105125
USA (United States)	India	03 Mar 59	US Agri Commod Aid	341UNTS235	104886
USA (United States)	India	13 Nov 59	US Agri Commod Aid	360UNTS287	105164
USA (United States)	India	04 May 60	US Agri Commod Aid	376UNTS279	105384
USA (United States)	India	13 Jun 60	Atomic Energy	377UNTS37	105394
USA (United States)	India	07 Feb 61	Scientific Project	462UNTS57	106671
USA (United States)	India	16 Apr 62	General Trade	445UNTS257	106393
USA (United States)	India	01 May 62	US Agri Commod Aid	451UNTS179	106493
USA (United States)	India	09 Oct 62	Scientific Project	471UNTS39	106820
USA (United States)	India	21 Nov 62	General Aid	462UNTS255	106685
USA (United States)	India	26 Nov 62	US Agri Commod Aid	460UNTS203	106641
USA (United States)	India	30 Nov 62	US Agri Commod Aid	459UNTS231	106626
USA (United States)	India	01 Feb 63	Scientific Project	473UNTS37	106852
USA (United States)	India	09 May 63	US Agri Commod Aid	476UNTS43	106902
USA (United States)	India	19 Jun 63	Education	479UNTS175	106952
USA (United States)	India	27 Jun 63	US Agri Commod Aid	479UNTS215	106955
USA (United States)	India	08 Aug 63	Scientific Project	488UNTS21	107117
USA (United States)	India	15 Apr 64	Commodity Trade	527UNTS19	107614
USA (United States)	India	30 Sep 64	US Agri Commod Aid	532UNTS321	107726
USA (United States)	India	13 Jan 65	Milit Assistance	541UNTS107	107864
USA (United States)	India	25 May 66	Gen Communications	593UNTS157	108582
USA (United States)	India	14 Feb 67	Scientific Project	0UNTS0	109752
USA (United States)	India	20 Feb 67	US Agri Commod Aid	0UNTS0	109850
USA (United States)	India	24 Jun 67	US Agri Commod Aid	0UNTS0	109906
USA (United States)	India	31 Aug 67	Commodity Trade	0UNTS0	109916
USA (United States)	India	12 Sep 67	US Agri Commod Aid	0UNTS0	109917
USA (United States)	India	30 Dec 67	US Agri Commod Aid	0UNTS0	109993
USA (United States)	India	05 Dec 68	Customs	0UNTS0	110253
USA (United States)	India	23 Dec 68	Commodity Trade	0UNTS0	110260
USA (United States)	India	23 Dec 68	General Aid	0UNTS0	110259
USA (United States)	India	13 Oct 69	US Agri Commod Aid	0UNTS0	110449
USA (United States)	Indonesia	24 Mar 50	Direct Aid	92UNTS387	101281
USA (United States)	Indonesia	07 Jun 50	Admin Cooperation	98UNTS167	101362
USA (United States)	Indonesia	15 Aug 50	Milit Assistance	134UNTS255	101804
USA (United States)	Indonesia	16 Oct 50	Direct Aid	281UNTS105	104074
USA (United States)	Indonesia	05 Jan 52	Tech Assistance	215UNTS121	102916
USA (United States)	Indonesia	15 Sep 55	Mass Media	256UNTS293	103639
USA (United States)	Indonesia	02 Mar 56	US Agri Commod Aid	271UNTS345	103925
USA (United States)	Indonesia	13 Aug 58	Milit Assistance	335UNTS187	104785

PARTY ONE	PARTY TWO	DATE	TOPIC	CITATION	NUMBER
USA (United States)	Indonesia	02 Mar 59	Air Transport	357UNTS145	105113
USA (United States)	Indonesia	29 May 59	US Agri Commod Aid	347UNTS85	104992
USA (United States)	Indonesia	08 Jun 60	Atomic Energy	388UNTS287	105585
USA (United States)	Indonesia	05 Nov 60	US Agri Commod Aid	400UNTS35	105746
USA (United States)	Indonesia	31 Mar 61	Visas	405UNTS119	105828
USA (United States)	Indonesia	26 Oct 61	US Agri Commod Aid	433UNTS249	106248
USA (United States)	Indonesia	19 Feb 62	US Agri Commod Aid	435UNTS137	106276
USA (United States)	Indonesia	14 Mar 63	General Aid	505UNTS79	107365
USA (United States)	Indonesia	18 Apr 66	US Agri Commod Aid	578UNTS106	108390
USA (United States)	Indonesia	28 Jun 66	US Agri Commod Aid	593UNTS201	108585
USA (United States)	Indonesia	30 Sep 66	US Agri Commod Aid	616UNTS199	108897
USA (United States)	Indonesia	07 Jan 67	Finance	0UNTS0	109896
USA (United States)	Indonesia	14 Apr 67	Milit Assistance	0UNTS0	109859
USA (United States)	Indonesia	15 Sep 67	US Agri Commod Aid	0UNTS0	109918
USA (United States)	Indonesia	01 Nov 67	US Agri Commod Aid	0UNTS0	110054
USA (United States)	Indonesia	22 Nov 67	US Agri Commod Aid	0UNTS0	109987
USA (United States)	Indonesia	30 Dec 67	Finance	0UNTS0	109994
USA (United States)	Indonesia	15 Feb 68	US Agri Commod Aid	0UNTS0	109988
USA (United States)	Indonesia	05 Aug 68	US Agri Commod Aid	0UNTS0	110070
USA (United States)	Indonesia	16 Aug 68	US Agri Commod Aid	0UNTS0	110071
USA (United States)	Indonesia	05 Sep 68	US Agri Commod Aid	0UNTS0	110072
USA (United States)	Indonesia	10 Dec 68	Gen Communications	0UNTS0	110151
USA (United States)	Indonesia	15 Dec 68	Air Transport	0UNTS0	109999
USA (United States)	Indonesia	17 Apr 69	General Military	0UNTS0	110330
USA (United States)	Indonesia	17 Nov 69	US Agri Commod Aid	0UNTS0	110453
USA (United States)	Indonesia	16 Jan 70	Scientific Project	0UNTS0	110616
USA (United States)	Indonesia	10 Apr 70	Commodity Trade	0UNTS0	110813
USA (United States)	Inter-Am Devel Bnk	19 Jun 61	Direct Aid	410UNTS34	105895
USA (United States)	Iran	08 Apr 43	General Trade	106UNTS155	200340
USA (United States)	Iran	21 Aug 43	Admin Cooperation	101UNTS189	200293
USA (United States)	Iran	27 Nov 43	Military Mission	31UNTS451	200176
USA (United States)	Iran	08 Aug 46	Military Mission	31UNTS423	100484
USA (United States)	Iran	06 Oct 47	Military Mission	11UNTS303	100171
USA (United States)	Iran	01 Sep 49	Direct Aid	79UNTS155	101039
USA (United States)	Iran	23 May 50	Milit Assistance	81UNTS3	101057
USA (United States)	Iran	19 Oct 50	Tech Assistance	92UNTS135	101266
USA (United States)	Iran	05 Jan 52	Direct Aid	0IRTB24	433038
USA (United States)	Iran	20 Jan 52	Tech Assistance	200UNTS191	102703
USA (United States)	Iran	24 Apr 52	Milit Assistance	0IRTB23	433035
USA (United States)	Iran	13 Oct 53	Customs	222UNTS67	103023
USA (United States)	Iran	15 Aug 55	General Amity	284UNTS93	104132
USA (United States)	Iran	20 Feb 56	US Agri Commod Aid	272UNTS135	103934
USA (United States)	Iran	16 Jan 57	Air Transport	308UNTS147	104460
USA (United States)	Iran	05 Mar 57	Atomic Energy	342UNTS29	104898
USA (United States)	Iran	21 Sep 57	Claims and Debts	293UNTS287	104296
USA (United States)	Iran	31 Oct 57	Milit Installation	0IRTB23	433036
USA (United States)	Iran	05 Mar 59	General Military	327UNTS277	104725
USA (United States)	Iran	12 Apr 60	General Trade	372UNTS63	105288
USA (United States)	Iran	26 Jul 60	US Agri Commod Aid	384UNTS141	105516
USA (United States)	Iran	21 Dec 61	Direct Aid	433UNTS269	106249
USA (United States)	Iran	29 Jan 62	US Agri Commod Aid	435UNTS53	106270
USA (United States)	Iran	16 Sep 62	Tech Assistance	0IRTB23	433037
USA (United States)	Iran	15 Oct 62	US Agri Commod Aid	473UNTS291	106866
USA (United States)	Iran	24 Oct 63	Culture	489UNTS303	107146
USA (United States)	Iran	17 Nov 63	US Agri Commod Aid	530UNTS41	107671
USA (United States)	Iran	29 Sep 64	US Agri Commod Aid	531UNTS163	107702
USA (United States)	Iran	16 Nov 64	US Agri Commod Aid	532UNTS213	107719
USA (United States)	Iran	19 Dec 66	US Agri Commod Aid	0UNTS0	109696
USA (United States)	Iran	20 Dec 66	US Agri Commod Aid	0UNTS0	109697
USA (United States)	Iran	19 Mar 68	Specific Resources	0UNTS0	110010
USA (United States)	Iran	27 May 68	Scientific Project	0UNTS0	109883
USA (United States)	Iraq	16 Feb 44	Admin Cooperation	109UNTS223	200362
USA (United States)	Iraq	31 Jul 45	Milit Assistance	121UNTS239	200402
USA (United States)	Iraq	10 Apr 51	Tech Assistance	151UNTS179	101993
USA (United States)	Iraq	08 Aug 51	Visas	229UNTS185	103166

PARTY ONE	PARTY TWO	DATE	TOPIC	CITATION	NUMBER
USA (United States)	Iraq	16 Aug 51	Education	147UNTS65	101929
USA (United States)	Iraq	21 Feb 52	Tech Assistance	198UNTS225	102666
USA (United States)	Iraq	18 Mar 52	Tech Assistance	223UNTS131	103061
USA (United States)	Iraq	21 May 52	Tech Assistance	212UNTS183	102870
USA (United States)	Iraq	21 May 52	Tech Assistance	205UNTS25	102767
USA (United States)	Iraq	21 May 52	Tech Assistance	205UNTS33	102768
USA (United States)	Iraq	21 May 52	Tech Assistance	206UNTS3	102782
USA (United States)	Iraq	09 Jun 52	Tech Assistance	212UNTS193	102871
USA (United States)	Iraq	18 Aug 52	Direct Aid	184UNTS131	102444
USA (United States)	Iraq	23 Oct 52	Tech Assistance	212UNTS201	102872
USA (United States)	Iraq	21 Apr 54	Milit Assistance	222UNTS251	103032
USA (United States)	Iraq	02 Mar 55	Non-IBRD Project	250UNTS229	103526
USA (United States)	Iraq	03 Dec 55	Milit Assistance	241UNTS19	103420
USA (United States)	Iraq	06 Jun 56	Visas	275UNTS265	103985
USA (United States)	Iraq	22 May 57	Direct Aid	284UNTS13	104125
USA (United States)	Iraq	16 Jun 57	Tech Assistance	284UNTS39	104127
USA (United States)	Iraq	07 Jul 59	Milit Assistance	357UNTS153	105114
USA (United States)	Iraq	23 Jan 63	Culture	488UNTS163	107126
USA (United States)	Iraq	27 Aug 63	US Agri Commod Aid	489UNTS271	107144
USA (United States)	Ireland	03 Feb 45	Air Transport	122UNTS305	200412
USA (United States)	Ireland	03 Jun 47	Air Transport	16UNTS151	100255
USA (United States)	Ireland	28 Jun 48	Mostfavored Nation	32UNTS69	100489
USA (United States)	Ireland	28 Jun 48	Direct Aid	24UNTS3	100349
USA (United States)	Ireland	01 Aug 49	Visas	82UNTS37	101083
USA (United States)	Ireland	13 Sep 49	Taxation	127UNTS119	101702
USA (United States)	Ireland	13 Sep 49	Taxation	127UNTS89	101701
USA (United States)	Ireland	21 Jan 50	General Amity	206UNTS269	102792
USA (United States)	Ireland	01 May 50	Consul/Citizenship	222UNTS107	103026
USA (United States)	Ireland	17 Jun 54	Direct Aid	241UNTS173	103432
USA (United States)	Ireland	16 Mar 56	Atomic Energy	317UNTS195	104604
USA (United States)	Ireland	24 Mar 60	Atomic Energy	371UNTS237	105280
USA (United States)	Ireland	03 May 62	General Trade	442UNTS117	106343
USA (United States)	Ireland	25 Feb 64	Commodity Trade	511UNTS27	107423
USA (United States)	Ireland	18 Jun 64	Water Transport	530UNTS217	107684
USA (United States)	Ireland	10 Oct 68	Gen Communications	0UNTS0	110082
USA (United States)	Ireland	10 Oct 68	Gen Communications	0UNTS0	109938
USA (United States)	Ireland	30 Jan 70	General Trade	0UNTS0	110619
USA (United States)	Israel	19 Feb 50	Admin Cooperation	122UNTS117	101641
USA (United States)	Israel	04 May 50	Patents/Copyrights	132UNTS189	101760
USA (United States)	Israel	13 Jun 50	Air Transport	212UNTS93	102863
USA (United States)	Israel	26 Feb 51	Tech Assistance	137UNTS57	101848
USA (United States)	Israel	28 Feb 51	Taxation	220UNTS79	102991
USA (United States)	Israel	01 Jun 51	Visas	212UNTS129	102864
USA (United States)	Israel	23 Aug 51	General Amity	219UNTS237	102979
USA (United States)	Israel	07 Dec 51	Tech Assistance	157UNTS53	102046
USA (United States)	Israel	27 Feb 52	Direct Aid	177UNTS123	102314
USA (United States)	Israel	01 May 52	Direct Aid	177UNTS89	102311
USA (United States)	Israel	09 May 52	Tech Assistance	177UNTS63	102309
USA (United States)	Israel	09 May 52	Tech Assistance	177UNTS269	102326
USA (United States)	Israel	09 Jun 52	Mass Media	178UNTS297	102345
USA (United States)	Israel	23 Jul 52	Milit Assistance	179UNTS139	102363
USA (United States)	Israel	08 Aug 52	Direct Aid	181UNTS37	102396
USA (United States)	Israel	25 Nov 53	Direct Aid	219UNTS205	102976
USA (United States)	Israel	02 Mar 55	Visas	220UNTS113	102996
USA (United States)	Israel	29 Apr 55	US Agri Commod Aid	261UNTS331	103731
USA (United States)	Israel	12 Jul 55	Atomic Energy	219UNTS185	102974
USA (United States)	Israel	10 Nov 55	US Agri Commod Aid	240UNTS3	103390
USA (United States)	Israel	26 Jun 56	Education	257UNTS55	103649
USA (United States)	Israel	11 Sep 56	US Agri Commod Aid	277UNTS215	104008
USA (United States)	Israel	07 Nov 57	US Agri Commod Aid	302UNTS255	104365
USA (United States)	Israel	06 Nov 58	US Agri Commod Aid	336UNTS275	104810
USA (United States)	Israel	07 Jan 60	US Agri Commod Aid	368UNTS181	105241
USA (United States)	Israel	19 Dec 60	Direct Aid	401UNTS195	105772
USA (United States)	Israel	10 May 61	US Agri Commod Aid	409UNTS213	105887
USA (United States)	Israel	05 Mar 62	General Economic	446UNTS29	106400

PARTY ONE	PARTY TWO	DATE	TOPIC	CITATION	NUMBER
USA (United States)	Israel	03 May 62	US Agri Commod Aid	442UNTS83	106340
USA (United States)	Israel	22 Jun 62	Education	448UNTS273	106440
USA (United States)	Israel	28 Aug 62	US Agri Commod Aid	448UNTS317	106445
USA (United States)	Israel	06 Dec 62	US Agri Commod Aid	460UNTS151	106638
USA (United States)	Israel	10 Dec 62	Extradition	484UNTS283	107038
USA (United States)	Israel	21 Mar 63	Education	476UNTS131	106907
USA (United States)	Israel	21 May 63	Telecommunications	487UNTS319	107113
USA (United States)	Israel	22 Nov 63	Commodity Trade	494UNTS89	107228
USA (United States)	Israel	22 Dec 64	US Agri Commod Aid	532UNTS231	107720
USA (United States)	Israel	07 Jul 65	Gen Communications	549UNTS281	108004
USA (United States)	Israel	20 Jul 65	Milit Assistance	549UNTS55	107989
USA (United States)	Israel	26 Jul 65	Status of Forces	549UNTS49	107988
USA (United States)	Israel	06 Jun 66	US Agri Commod Aid	593UNTS165	108583
USA (United States)	Israel	06 Jun 66	US Agri Commod Aid	578UNTS143	108392
USA (United States)	Israel	15 Jun 66	Telecommunications	578UNTS159	108393
USA (United States)	Israel	13 Jul 67	General Trade	0UNTS0	109778
USA (United States)	Israel	04 Aug 67	US Agri Commod Aid	0UNTS0	109351
USA (United States)	Israel	29 Mar 68	US Agri Commod Aid	0UNTS0	109352
USA (United States)	Israel	22 May 68	Scientific Project	0UNTS0	109356
USA (United States)	Israel	23 Jul 68	Air Transport	0UNTS0	109358
USA (United States)	Israel	17 Jan 69	Commodity Trade	0UNTS0	110263
USA (United States)	Israel	07 May 70	US Agri Commod Aid	0UNTS0	110696
USA (United States)	Italy	06 Dec 45	General Trade	3UNTS131	100027
USA (United States)	Italy	17 Apr 46	Extradition	206UNTS263	102791
USA (United States)	Italy	24 Sep 46	Other Military	148UNTS323	101942
USA (United States)	Italy	09 Jun 47	Air Transport	104UNTS157	101437
USA (United States)	Italy	04 Jul 47	Direct Aid	22UNTS173	100336
USA (United States)	Italy	14 Aug 47	Reparations	36UNTS53	100566
USA (United States)	Italy	14 Aug 47	Claims and Debts	36UNTS105	100567
USA (United States)	Italy	03 Sep 47	Status of Forces	67UNTS15	100863
USA (United States)	Italy	03 Jan 48	Direct Aid	31UNTS105	100471
USA (United States)	Italy	02 Feb 48	General Amity	79UNTS171	101040
USA (United States)	Italy	06 Feb 48	Air Transport	73UNTS113	100950
USA (United States)	Italy	14 Feb 48	Reparations	67UNTS115	100871
USA (United States)	Italy	28 Jun 48	Direct Aid	20UNTS43	100314
USA (United States)	Italy	28 Jun 48	Milit Occupation	25UNTS45	100356
USA (United States)	Italy	29 Sep 48	Visas	84UNTS43	101117
USA (United States)	Italy	26 Nov 48	Direct Aid	79UNTS71	101032
USA (United States)	Italy	18 Dec 48	Education	79UNTS133	101037
USA (United States)	Italy	27 Jan 50	Milit Assistance	80UNTS145	101050
USA (United States)	Italy	13 Feb 51	IGO Establishment	148UNTS57	101935
USA (United States)	Italy	16 May 51	Reparations	206UNTS325	102795
USA (United States)	Italy	12 Dec 51	Patents/Copyrights	137UNTS175	101852
USA (United States)	Italy	21 Dec 51	Peace/Disarmament	167UNTS163	102206
USA (United States)	Italy	28 Dec 51	General Economic	157UNTS63	102047
USA (United States)	Italy	07 Jan 52	Milit Assistance	179UNTS165	102365
USA (United States)	Italy	05 Mar 52	Taxation	179UNTS3	102351
USA (United States)	Italy	31 Mar 54	Milit Assistance	235UNTS293	103311
USA (United States)	Italy	27 Apr 54	Milit Assistance	234UNTS103	103275
USA (United States)	Italy	16 Jun 54	Loans and Credits	236UNTS149	103322
USA (United States)	Italy	24 Jun 54	Tech Assistance	235UNTS3	103290
USA (United States)	Italy	28 Jun 54	Tech Assistance	237UNTS121	103340
USA (United States)	Italy	26 Jan 55	Air Transport	238UNTS179	103361
USA (United States)	Italy	11 Feb 55	Direct Aid	241UNTS91	103426
USA (United States)	Italy	11 Feb 55	Milit Assistance	240UNTS87	103396
USA (United States)	Italy	30 Mar 55	Taxation	257UNTS199	103655
USA (United States)	Italy	30 Mar 55	Taxation	257UNTS169	103654
USA (United States)	Italy	19 May 55	Direct Aid	269UNTS83	103876
USA (United States)	Italy	23 May 55	US Agri Commod Aid	251UNTS303	103547
USA (United States)	Italy	30 Jun 55	US Agri Commod Aid	258UNTS15	103667
USA (United States)	Italy	08 Jul 55	Milit Installation	270UNTS29	103889
USA (United States)	Italy	28 Jul 55	Atomic Energy	239UNTS235	103382
USA (United States)	Italy	27 Feb 56	Direct Aid	291UNTS287	104260
USA (United States)	Italy	27 Apr 56	Direct Aid	273UNTS149	103949
USA (United States)	Italy	30 Oct 56	US Agri Commod Aid	263UNTS221	103775

PARTY ONE	PARTY TWO	DATE	TOPIC	CITATION	NUMBER
USA (United States)	Italy	29 Mar 57	Reparations	299UNTS157	104311
USA (United States)	Italy	22 Jun 57	Milit Assistance	284UNTS51	104128
USA (United States)	Italy	03 Jul 57	Atomic Energy	308UNTS195	104462
USA (United States)	Italy	07 Mar 58	US Agri Commod Aid	303UNTS205	104381
USA (United States)	Italy	08 May 58	Direct Aid	316UNTS177	104584
USA (United States)	Italy	30 Jul 59	Direct Aid	355UNTS393	105088
USA (United States)	Italy	18 Aug 59	Milit Assistance	361UNTS11	105169
USA (United States)	Italy	07 Jul 60	Milit Assistance	380UNTS143	105455
USA (United States)	Italy	19 Jul 60	Direct Aid	389UNTS237	105595
USA (United States)	Italy	04 Aug 60	Admin Cooperation	62ITDI376	436357
USA (United States)	Italy	03 Dec 60	Atomic Energy	410UNTS3	105893
USA (United States)	Italy	06 Jul 62	Commodity Trade	459UNTS123	106617
USA (United States)	Italy	28 Aug 62	Sanitation	461UNTS137	106657
USA (United States)	Italy	05 Sep 62	Scientific Project	461UNTS185	106663
USA (United States)	Italy	14 Nov 62	Telecommunications	459UNTS197	106622
USA (United States)	Italy	04 Aug 64	General Military	529UNTS205	107662
USA (United States)	Italy	18 Aug 64	Admin Cooperation	65ITGU279	435358
USA (United States)	Italy	18 Aug 64	Admin Cooperation	0UNTS0	109836
USA (United States)	Italy	23 Nov 64	Milit Assistance	532UNTS133	107716
USA (United States)	Italy	16 Dec 65	Specif Claim/Waive	574UNTS139	108346
USA (United States)	Italy	27 Dec 65	Specific Property	574UNTS145	108347
USA (United States)	Italy	12 Jan 66	Reparations	587UNTS309	108515
USA (United States)	Italy	19 Oct 66	Commodity Trade	0UNTS0	109686
USA (United States)	Italy	19 Jun 67	Scientific Project	0UNTS0	109773
USA (United States)	Italy	24 Jun 68	Scientific Project	0UNTS0	110328
USA (United States)	Italy	11 Sep 69	Scientific Project	0UNTS0	110506
USA (United States)	Italy	20 Jun 70	Scientific Project	0UNTS0	110814
USA (United States)	Ivory Coast	17 May 61	General Aid	409UNTS241	105889
USA (United States)	Ivory Coast	01 Dec 61	Claims and Debts	462UNTS221	106681
USA (United States)	Ivory Coast	21 Apr 62	General Aid	526UNTS39	107598
USA (United States)	Ivory Coast	10 Mar 64	US Agri Commod Aid	526UNTS285	107611
USA (United States)	Ivory Coast	05 Apr 65	US Agri Commod Aid	546UNTS143	107941
USA (United States)	Jamaica	29 Nov 62	Air Transport	462UNTS229	106682
USA (United States)	Jamaica	04 Jan 63	Finance	471UNTS119	106826
USA (United States)	Jamaica	06 Jun 63	Milit Assistance	477UNTS29	106913
USA (United States)	Jamaica	01 Oct 63	Commodity Trade	488UNTS133	107124
USA (United States)	Jamaica	24 Oct 63	General Aid	489UNTS337	107148
USA (United States)	Jamaica	20 Dec 66	Admin Cooperation	0UNTS0	109698
USA (United States)	Jamaica	29 Sep 67	Commodity Trade	0UNTS0	109923
USA (United States)	Jamaica	02 Oct 69	Air Transport	0UNTS0	110448
USA (United States)	Japan	14 Apr 49	Specif Claim/Waive	89UNTS141	101215
USA (United States)	Japan	04 Apr 51	Specific Resources	57JAIL85	440064
USA (United States)	Japan	28 Aug 51	Education	147UNTS81	101930
USA (United States)	Japan	08 Sep 51	General Military	136UNTS211	101835
USA (United States)	Japan	08 Sep 51	Milit Assistance	136UNTS203	101834
USA (United States)	Japan	28 Feb 52	Milit Assistance	208UNTS255	102817
USA (United States)	Japan	25 Jul 52	Milit Assistance	198UNTS281	102671
USA (United States)	Japan	11 Aug 52	Air Transport	212UNTS27	102862
USA (United States)	Japan	18 Sep 52	Visas	227UNTS85	103133
USA (United States)	Japan	12 Nov 52	Milit Assistance	184UNTS111	102443
USA (United States)	Japan	22 Nov 52	Milit Installation	52JHZ12	439001
USA (United States)	Japan	18 Mar 53	Tech Assistance	212UNTS149	102867
USA (United States)	Japan	23 Mar 53	Direct Aid	185UNTS93	102461
USA (United States)	Japan	02 Apr 53	General Amity	206UNTS143	102788
USA (United States)	Japan	22 Apr 53	Admin Cooperation	178UNTS169	102341
USA (United States)	Japan	23 Oct 53	Visas	57JAIL86	440065
USA (United States)	Japan	29 Oct 53	Postal Service	57JAIL86	440067
USA (United States)	Japan	10 Nov 53	Patents/Copyrights	224UNTS161	103076
USA (United States)	Japan	24 Dec 53	Territory Boundary	222UNTS193	103028
USA (United States)	Japan	21 Jan 54	Tech Assistance	223UNTS145	103063
USA (United States)	Japan	08 Mar 54	General Economic	232UNTS267	103241
USA (United States)	Japan	08 Mar 54	Milit Assistance	232UNTS169	103236
USA (United States)	Japan	08 Mar 54	Milit Assistance	232UNTS215	103237
USA (United States)	Japan	08 Mar 54	Claims and Debts	232UNTS251	103240
USA (United States)	Japan	08 Mar 54	Direct Aid	232UNTS243	103239

PARTY ONE	PARTY TWO	DATE	TOPIC	CITATION	NUMBER
USA (United States)	Japan	08 Mar 54	Direct Aid	232UNTS227	103238
USA (United States)	Japan	16 Apr 54	Taxation	238UNTS3	103353
USA (United States)	Japan	16 Apr 54	Taxation	238UNTS39	103354
USA (United States)	Japan	14 May 54	Milit Assistance	247UNTS273	103476
USA (United States)	Japan	19 Nov 54	Milit Installation	238UNTS207	103364
USA (United States)	Japan	04 Jan 55	Specif Claim/Waive	237UNTS197	103346
USA (United States)	Japan	07 Apr 55	Tech Assistance	263UNTS285	103778
USA (United States)	Japan	31 May 55	Direct Aid	241UNTS243	103435
USA (United States)	Japan	31 May 55	Direct Aid	241UNTS197	103434
USA (United States)	Japan	03 Jun 55	Milit Assistance	270UNTS51	103891
USA (United States)	Japan	24 Aug 55	Specif Claim/Waive	257UNTS297	103662
USA (United States)	Japan	14 Nov 55	Atomic Energy	240UNTS361	103413
USA (United States)	Japan	10 Feb 56	Direct Aid	275UNTS157	103980
USA (United States)	Japan	10 Feb 56	Direct Aid	275UNTS181	103981
USA (United States)	Japan	10 Feb 56	Direct Aid	275UNTS105	103979
USA (United States)	Japan	22 Mar 56	Patents/Copyrights	275UNTS195	103983
USA (United States)	Japan	13 Apr 56	Milit Assistance	273UNTS223	103953
USA (United States)	Japan	05 Sep 56	Admin Cooperation	277UNTS267	104011
USA (United States)	Japan	23 Nov 56	Atomic Energy	324UNTS177	104685
USA (United States)	Japan	10 Dec 56	Postal Service	0JGJI1146	441100
USA (United States)	Japan	22 Mar 57	Visas	288UNTS201	104206
USA (United States)	Japan	08 May 57	Atomic Energy	318UNTS257	104621
USA (United States)	Japan	14 Sep 57	Admin Cooperation	293UNTS247	104293
USA (United States)	Japan	11 Jan 58	Education	304UNTS35	104390
USA (United States)	Japan	25 Jan 58	Milit Assistance	304UNTS81	104392
USA (United States)	Japan	19 Jun 58	Atomic Energy	325UNTS143	104699
USA (United States)	Japan	03 Nov 58	Postal Service	341UNTS83	104879
USA (United States)	Japan	31 Jul 59	Milit Assistance	357UNTS107	105110
USA (United States)	Japan	12 Nov 59	Direct Aid	361UNTS27	105171
USA (United States)	Japan	19 Jan 60	General Military	373UNTS179	105320
USA (United States)	Japan	19 Jan 60	Status of Forces	373UNTS207	105321
USA (United States)	Japan	18 Feb 60	Direct Aid	372UNTS117	105292
USA (United States)	Japan	23 Mar 60	Tech Assistance	372UNTS289	105305
USA (United States)	Japan	15 Apr 60	Milit Assistance	372UNTS267	105303
USA (United States)	Japan	31 May 60	Direct Aid	376UNTS301	105385
USA (United States)	Japan	19 May 61	Atomic Energy	0JGJI1445	441108
USA (United States)	Japan	08 Jun 61	Reparations	410UNTS183	105903
USA (United States)	Japan	22 Jun 61	General Economic	410UNTS53	105896
USA (United States)	Japan	16 Oct 61	General Trade	433UNTS287	106250
USA (United States)	Japan	09 Jan 62	Direct Aid	451UNTS97	106488
USA (United States)	Japan	09 Feb 62	General Trade	13UST948	486001
USA (United States)	Japan	28 Aug 62	Loans and Credits	460UNTS267	106645
USA (United States)	Japan	24 Oct 62	Sanitation	462UNTS119	106673
USA (United States)	Japan	06 Nov 62	Telecommunications	459UNTS203	106623
USA (United States)	Japan	31 Dec 62	Mostfavored Nation	471UNTS83	106823
USA (United States)	Japan	01 Feb 63	Air Transport	473UNTS49	106854
USA (United States)	Japan	19 Feb 63	Direct Aid	473UNTS107	106859
USA (United States)	Japan	22 Mar 63	Consul/Citizenship	518UNTS179	107495
USA (United States)	Japan	26 Apr 63	Milit Installation	477UNTS37	106914
USA (United States)	Japan	14 Jun 63	Finance	479UNTS165	106951
USA (United States)	Japan	27 Aug 63	Commodity Trade	487UNTS197	107105
USA (United States)	Japan	28 Aug 63	Commodity Trade	487UNTS237	107106
USA (United States)	Japan	25 Apr 64	General Economic	530UNTS61	107672
USA (United States)	Japan	30 Oct 64	Atomic Energy	0JGJI1563	441124
USA (United States)	Japan	25 Nov 64	Specific Property	533UNTS31	107730
USA (United States)	Japan	04 Dec 64	Milit Installation	532UNTS249	107721
USA (United States)	Japan	02 Apr 65	IGO Operations	16UST657	486002
USA (United States)	Japan	02 Apr 65	Admin Cooperation	0JGJI1588	441134
USA (United States)	Japan	30 Aug 65	Atomic Energy	0JGJI1609	441140
USA (United States)	Japan	23 Aug 66	Visas	606UNTS219	108787
USA (United States)	Japan	06 Sep 66	General Trade	616UNTS215	108898
USA (United States)	Japan	19 Sep 66	Scientific Project	0UNTS0	109681
USA (United States)	Japan	19 Sep 66	Scientific Project	0TIAS6170	487003
USA (United States)	Japan	09 May 67	Specific Resources	18UST1309	486004
USA (United States)	Japan	09 May 67	Specific Resources	0UNTS0	109766

PARTY ONE	PARTY TWO	DATE	TOPIC	CITATION	NUMBER
USA (United States)	Japan	09 May 67	Specific Resources	0UNTS0	109765
USA (United States)	Japan	08 Aug 67	Milit Assistance	18UST1678	486005
USA (United States)	Japan	13 Oct 67	General Military	0UNTS0	110048
USA (United States)	Japan	13 Dec 67	Milit Assistance	18UST2804	486006
USA (United States)	Japan	12 Jan 68	General Trade	0UNTS0	109998
USA (United States)	Japan	12 Jan 68	Commodity Trade	19UST4419	486007
USA (United States)	Japan	19 Jan 68	Military Mission	0TIAS6442	487008
USA (United States)	Japan	19 Jan 68	Admin Cooperation	0UNTS0	110001
USA (United States)	Japan	26 Feb 68	Atomic Energy	0UNTS0	109722
USA (United States)	Japan	26 Feb 68	Atomic Energy	68JHZ7	439017
USA (United States)	Japan	05 Apr 68	Territory Boundary	68JHZ6	439022
USA (United States)	Japan	05 Apr 68	Territory Boundary	0UNTS0	109724
USA (United States)	Japan	02 Sep 68	Scientific Project	0UNTS0	110073
USA (United States)	Japan	02 Sep 68	Scientific Project	19UST6011	486009
USA (United States)	Japan	08 Nov 68	Culture	0UNTS0	110085
USA (United States)	Japan	23 Dec 68	Specific Resources	0TIAS6600	487010
USA (United States)	Japan	04 Apr 69	Milit Installation	20UST545	486011
USA (United States)	Japan	04 Apr 69	Milit Assistance	0UNTS0	110156
USA (United States)	Japan	18 Apr 69	Territory Boundary	69JHZ7	439029
USA (United States)	Japan	18 Apr 69	Territory Boundary	0UNTS0	110331
USA (United States)	Japan	31 Jul 69	Scientific Project	20UST2720	486012
USA (United States)	Japan	31 Jul 69	Scientific Project	0UNTS0	110342
USA (United States)	Japan	03 Mar 70	IGO Operations	21UST473	486013
USA (United States)	Japan	03 Mar 70	Recognition	0UNTS0	110625
USA (United States)	Japan	01 May 70	IGO Operations	21UST1167	486014
USA (United States)	Japan	01 May 70	Admin Cooperation	0UNTS0	110695
USA (United States)	Japan	11 Dec 70	Specific Resources	0TIAS7019	487015
USA (United States)	Japan	11 Dec 70	Specific Resources	0TIAS7021	487017
USA (United States)	Japan	11 Dec 70	Specific Resources	0TIAS7020	487016
USA (United States)	Jordan	27 Feb 51	Tech Assistance	141UNTS55	101905
USA (United States)	Jordan	20 Dec 51	Tech Assistance	157UNTS69	102048
USA (United States)	Jordan	12 Feb 52	Tech Assistance	168UNTS25	102211
USA (United States)	Jordan	21 Oct 53	Direct Aid	222UNTS31	103020
USA (United States)	Jordan	13 May 54	Direct Aid	234UNTS225	103285
USA (United States)	Jordan	17 Jun 54	Direct Aid	266UNTS137	103828
USA (United States)	Jordan	29 Jun 54	Direct Aid	237UNTS111	103339
USA (United States)	Jordan	24 Sep 56	Milit Assistance	278UNTS51	104020
USA (United States)	Jordan	29 Apr 57	Direct Aid	290UNTS111	104230
USA (United States)	Jordan	27 Jun 57	General Aid	288UNTS269	104209
USA (United States)	Jordan	29 Jun 57	Direct Aid	288UNTS263	104208
USA (United States)	Jordan	11 Feb 64	US Agri Commod Aid	511UNTS85	107429
USA (United States)	Jordan	05 Apr 66	Direct Aid	593UNTS239	108587
USA (United States)	Jordan	25 Aug 66	US Agri Commod Aid	606UNTS237	108788
USA (United States)	Jordan	04 Apr 68	US Agri Commod Aid	0UNTS0	110011
USA (United States)	Jordan	21 Apr 69	US Agri Commod Aid	0UNTS0	110160
USA (United States)	Kenya	20 Apr 64	Claims and Debts	524UNTS165	107571
USA (United States)	Kenya	26 Aug 64	General Aid	531UNTS51	107692
USA (United States)	Kenya	07 Dec 64	US Agri Commod Aid	532UNTS263	107722
USA (United States)	Kenya	19 Aug 65	Extradition	574UNTS153	108348
USA (United States)	Korea, South	24 Aug 48	General Military	79UNTS57	101031
USA (United States)	Korea, South	11 Sep 48	Milit Assistance	89UNTS155	101216
USA (United States)	Korea, South	10 Dec 48	Direct Aid	55UNTS157	100813
USA (United States)	Korea, South	17 Feb 49	Postal Service	74UNTS167	100963
USA (United States)	Korea, South	29 Jun 49	Air Transport	55UNTS79	100809
USA (United States)	Korea, South	26 Jan 50	Military Mission	178UNTS97	102337
USA (United States)	Korea, South	26 Jan 50	Milit Assistance	80UNTS205	101053
USA (United States)	Korea, South	28 Apr 50	Education	93UNTS21	101284
USA (United States)	Korea, South	12 Jul 50	Status of Forces	222UNTS229	103029
USA (United States)	Korea, South	28 Jul 50	Finance	140UNTS57	101883
USA (United States)	Korea, South	07 Jan 52	Milit Assistance	179UNTS105	102359
USA (United States)	Korea, South	24 May 52	Direct Aid	179UNTS23	102353
USA (United States)	Korea, South	01 Oct 53	General Military	238UNTS199	103363
USA (United States)	Korea, South	17 Nov 54	Milit Assistance	256UNTS251	103635
USA (United States)	Korea, South	29 Jan 55	Milit Assistance	239UNTS53	103371
USA (United States)	Korea, South	02 May 55	Direct Aid	258UNTS3	103666

PARTY ONE	PARTY TWO	DATE	TOPIC	CITATION	NUMBER
USA (United States)	Korea, South	29 May 55	Milit Installation	256UNTS263	103636
USA (United States)	Korea, South	31 May 55	US Agri Commod Aid	251UNTS321	103548
USA (United States)	Korea, South	03 Feb 56	Atomic Energy	240UNTS129	103401
USA (United States)	Korea, South	13 Mar 56	US Agri Commod Aid	272UNTS3	103928
USA (United States)	Korea, South	02 Jul 56	Milit Assistance	281UNTS41	104067
USA (United States)	Korea, South	28 Nov 56	General Amity	302UNTS281	104367
USA (United States)	Korea, South	30 Jan 57	US Agri Commod Aid	278UNTS85	104024
USA (United States)	Korea, South	24 Apr 57	Air Transport	288UNTS219	104207
USA (United States)	Korea, South	05 Feb 58	US Agri Commod Aid	307UNTS121	104447
USA (United States)	Korea, South	18 Dec 58	Reparations	325UNTS233	104702
USA (United States)	Korea, South	30 Jun 59	US Agri Commod Aid	353UNTS297	105047
USA (United States)	Korea, South	25 Sep 59	Mass Media	358UNTS163	105133
USA (United States)	Korea, South	01 Oct 59	Direct Aid	358UNTS115	105129
USA (United States)	Korea, South	19 Feb 60	Claims and Debts	372UNTS109	105291
USA (United States)	Korea, South	17 Aug 60	Postal Service	400UNTS339	105757
USA (United States)	Korea, South	18 Nov 60	Atomic Energy	400UNTS49	105747
USA (United States)	Korea, South	28 Dec 60	US Agri Commod Aid	402UNTS3	105773
USA (United States)	Korea, South	08 Feb 61	General Aid	405UNTS37	105821
USA (United States)	Korea, South	02 Mar 62	US Agri Commod Aid	442UNTS185	106349
USA (United States)	Korea, South	25 May 62	Visas	454UNTS25	106537
USA (United States)	Korea, South	07 Nov 62	US Agri Commod Aid	462UNTS129	106674
USA (United States)	Korea, South	08 Jan 63	Consul/Citizenship	493UNTS105	107211
USA (United States)	Korea, South	18 Jun 63	Education	487UNTS297	107112
USA (United States)	Korea, South	18 Mar 64	US Agri Commod Aid	524UNTS263	107578
USA (United States)	Korea, South	12 May 64	Commodity Trade	529UNTS299	107667
USA (United States)	Korea, South	31 Dec 64	US Agri Commod Aid	535UNTS315	107787
USA (United States)	Korea, South	26 Jan 65	Commodity Trade	541UNTS77	107862
USA (United States)	Korea, South	07 Mar 66	US Agri Commod Aid	579UNTS137	108404
USA (United States)	Korea, South	14 Sep 66	Direct Aid	606UNTS55	108774
USA (United States)	Korea, South	24 Sep 66	Admin Cooperation	607UNTS157	108803
USA (United States)	Korea, South	09 Feb 67	Milit Installation	0UNTS0	109605
USA (United States)	Korea, South	23 Feb 67	General Aid	0UNTS0	109852
USA (United States)	Korea, South	25 Mar 67	US Agri Commod Aid	0UNTS0	109756
USA (United States)	Korea, South	11 Dec 67	Commodity Trade	0UNTS0	110060
USA (United States)	Korea, South	28 Mar 68	Visas	0UNTS0	109926
USA (United States)	Korea, South	10 May 68	US Agri Commod Aid	0UNTS0	110139
USA (United States)	Korea, South	23 Oct 68	US Agri Commod Aid	0UNTS0	110140
USA (United States)	Korea, South	26 Feb 69	US Agri Commod Aid	0UNTS0	110141
USA (United States)	Korea, South	08 Apr 69	US Agri Commod Aid	0UNTS0	110142
USA (United States)	Korea, South	20 Mar 70	US Agri Commod Aid	0UNTS0	110631
USA (United States)	Kuwait	27 Dec 60	Visas	401UNTS185	105771
USA (United States)	Kuwait	21 Oct 63	Postal Service	530UNTS281	107688
USA (United States)	Kuwait	24 Jul 66	Gen Communications	593UNTS289	108590
USA (United States)	Laos	09 Sep 51	Direct Aid	174UNTS141	102283
USA (United States)	Laos	31 Dec 51	Tech Assistance	198UNTS243	102668
USA (United States)	Laos	08 Jul 55	Direct Aid	278UNTS59	104021
USA (United States)	Laos	29 Dec 64	Claims and Debts	542UNTS23	107876
USA (United States)	Lebanon	08 Sep 44	Recognition	124UNTS187	200419
USA (United States)	Lebanon	21 Jan 46	Postal Service	140UNTS73	101884
USA (United States)	Lebanon	11 Aug 46	Air Transport	66UNTS211	100856
USA (United States)	Lebanon	24 Feb 51	Tech Assistance	223UNTS121	103060
USA (United States)	Lebanon	29 May 51	Tech Assistance	160UNTS49	102101
USA (United States)	Lebanon	05 Jan 52	Tech Assistance	180UNTS199	102385
USA (United States)	Lebanon	26 Jun 52	Tech Assistance	181UNTS187	102409
USA (United States)	Lebanon	23 Mar 53	Milit Assistance	239UNTS45	103370
USA (United States)	Lebanon	18 Jun 54	Direct Aid	233UNTS177	103262
USA (United States)	Lebanon	18 Jul 55	Atomic Energy	239UNTS247	103383
USA (United States)	Lebanon	06 Jun 57	Tech Assistance	284UNTS155	104134
USA (United States)	Lebanon	06 Aug 58	Status of Forces	366UNTS361	105223
USA (United States)	Lebanon	03 Sep 58	Direct Aid	336UNTS91	104801
USA (United States)	Lebanon	16 Sep 59	Scientific Project	358UNTS175	105135
USA (United States)	Lesotho	04 Oct 66	Admin Cooperation	0UNTS0	109684
USA (United States)	Lesotho	24 Feb 67	Finance	0UNTS0	109853
USA (United States)	Lesotho	22 Sep 67	Direct Aid	0UNTS0	109922
USA (United States)	Liberia	15 Jan 42	Admin Cooperation	117UNTS227	200372

PARTY ONE	PARTY TWO	DATE	TOPIC	CITATION	NUMBER
USA (United States)	Liberia	31 Mar 42	General Military	23UNTS302	200137
USA (United States)	Liberia	08 Jun 43	Milit Assistance	117UNTS242	200373
USA (United States)	Liberia	31 Dec 43	Non-IBRD Project	106UNTS199	200341
USA (United States)	Liberia	28 Oct 47	Visas	82UNTS23	101081
USA (United States)	Liberia	26 Jul 48	Customs	182UNTS73	102423
USA (United States)	Liberia	22 Jul 49	Visas	232UNTS283	103242
USA (United States)	Liberia	22 Dec 50	Direct Aid	133UNTS69	101781
USA (United States)	Liberia	22 Dec 50	Tech Assistance	92UNTS145	101267
USA (United States)	Liberia	10 Jan 51	Gen Communications	132UNTS255	101765
USA (United States)	Liberia	11 Jan 51	Military Mission	122UNTS125	101642
USA (United States)	Liberia	19 Nov 51	Milit Assistance	167UNTS141	102204
USA (United States)	Liberia	15 Dec 52	Tech Assistance	185UNTS45	102457
USA (United States)	Liberia	23 Jun 53	Education	213UNTS57	102880
USA (United States)	Liberia	23 Jun 53	Tech Assistance	213UNTS37	102879
USA (United States)	Liberia	06 Oct 55	Tech Assistance	275UNTS93	103978
USA (United States)	Liberia	06 Oct 55	Direct Aid	275UNTS87	103977
USA (United States)	Liberia	22 Sep 56	Specific Property	278UNTS109	104027
USA (United States)	Liberia	16 Mar 57	Postal Service	290UNTS59	104228
USA (United States)	Liberia	08 Jul 59	Milit Assistance	357UNTS93	105108
USA (United States)	Liberia	13 Aug 59	Telecommunications	357UNTS181	105116
USA (United States)	Liberia	06 Sep 60	Admin Cooperation	389UNTS245	105596
USA (United States)	Liberia	17 Jun 61	Milit Assistance	410UNTS233	105907
USA (United States)	Liberia	08 Mar 62	Direct Aid	445UNTS41	106375
USA (United States)	Liberia	12 Apr 62	US Agri Commod Aid	445UNTS213	106390
USA (United States)	Liberia	14 Apr 64	Specific Property	526UNTS221	107606
USA (United States)	Liberia	08 May 64	Education	526UNTS239	107608
USA (United States)	Liberia	06 Jan 66	US Agri Commod Aid	592UNTS101	108570
USA (United States)	Liberia	23 Oct 67	US Agri Commod Aid	0UNTS0	110051
USA (United States)	Libya	21 Jan 52	Tech Assistance	183UNTS177	102427
USA (United States)	Libya	20 May 52	Direct Aid	178UNTS307	102346
USA (United States)	Libya	20 May 52	Tech Assistance	178UNTS155	102339
USA (United States)	Libya	20 May 52	Tech Assistance	177UNTS81	102310
USA (United States)	Libya	11 Jan 54	Direct Aid	229UNTS15	103157
USA (United States)	Libya	09 Sep 54	Milit Installation	224UNTS217	103078
USA (United States)	Libya	09 Sep 54	Direct Aid	238UNTS217	103365
USA (United States)	Libya	03 Nov 54	Direct Aid	238UNTS227	103366
USA (United States)	Libya	30 May 55	Direct Aid	270UNTS43	103890
USA (United States)	Libya	18 Jul 55	Direct Aid	241UNTS305	103437
USA (United States)	Libya	21 Jul 55	Tech Assistance	264UNTS247	103796
USA (United States)	Libya	28 Jul 55	Non-IBRD Project	270UNTS245	103900
USA (United States)	Libya	28 Jul 55	Non-IBRD Project	270UNTS293	103902
USA (United States)	Libya	28 Jul 55	Non-IBRD Project	270UNTS269	103901
USA (United States)	Libya	28 Jul 55	Non-IBRD Project	270UNTS317	103903
USA (United States)	Libya	22 Dec 55	Direct Aid	240UNTS111	103399
USA (United States)	Libya	27 Jun 56	Direct Aid	273UNTS89	103945
USA (United States)	Libya	04 Apr 57	Tech Assistance	283UNTS181	104116
USA (United States)	Libya	30 Jun 57	Milit Assistance	284UNTS177	104136
USA (United States)	Libya	21 May 59	Tech Assistance	361UNTS123	105176
USA (United States)	Libya	11 Dec 60	Health/Educ/Welfare	445UNTS125	106381
USA (United States)	Luxembourg	03 Jul 46	Mostfavored Nation	32UNTS85	100491
USA (United States)	Luxembourg	29 Aug 46	Reparations	140UNTS101	101885
USA (United States)	Luxembourg	12 Sep 46	Reparations	149UNTS19	101947
USA (United States)	Luxembourg	03 Jul 48	Direct Aid	24UNTS35	100350
USA (United States)	Luxembourg	27 Jan 50	Milit Assistance	80UNTS187	101052
USA (United States)	Luxembourg	20 Mar 51	Other Military	180UNTS283	102392
USA (United States)	Luxembourg	08 Jan 52	Milit Assistance	180UNTS191	102384
USA (United States)	Luxembourg	13 Mar 52	Taxation	168UNTS57	102212
USA (United States)	Luxembourg	17 Aug 53	Mass Media	234UNTS219	103284
USA (United States)	Luxembourg	17 Apr 54	Milit Assistance	257UNTS255	103661
USA (United States)	Luxembourg	07 Jul 54	Milit Assistance	233UNTS23	103247
USA (United States)	Luxembourg	15 Jun 55	Reparations	264UNTS279	103798
USA (United States)	Luxembourg	07 Dec 56	General Military	265UNTS255	103817
USA (United States)	Luxembourg	23 Feb 62	General Amity	474UNTS3	106868
USA (United States)	Luxembourg	18 Dec 62	Taxation	532UNTS277	107723
USA (United States)	Luxembourg	29 Jul 65	Gen Communications	573UNTS197	108332

PARTY ONE	PARTY TWO	DATE	TOPIC	CITATION	NUMBER
USA (United States)	Madagascar	22 Jun 61	General Aid	413UNTS219	105956
USA (United States)	Malagasy	26 Jul 63	Finance	487UNTS189	107104
USA (United States)	Malagasy	07 Oct 63	Scientific Project	494UNTS3	107221
USA (United States)	Malawi	20 Apr 65	General Aid	546UNTS175	107943
USA (United States)	Malawi	04 Apr 67	Recognition	0UNTS0	109899
USA (United States)	Malawi	21 Jul 67	Finance	0UNTS0	109910
USA (United States)	Malaysia	28 Jan 63	Education	473UNTS15	106850
USA (United States)	Malaysia	02 Feb 70	Air Transport	0UNTS0	110620
USA (United States)	Mali	04 Jan 61	General Aid	405UNTS165	105832
USA (United States)	Mali	20 May 61	Milit Assistance	413UNTS205	105954
USA (United States)	Mali	09 Jun 64	Claims and Debts	530UNTS133	107678
USA (United States)	Mali	14 Jul 65	US Agri Commod Aid	564UNTS101	108223
USA (United States)	Mali	17 Jan 68	Scientific Project	0UNTS0	110000
USA (United States)	Malta	15 Jan 66	Specif Goods/Equip	579UNTS109	108402
USA (United States)	Malta	03 Aug 66	Milit Assistance	601UNTS125	108691
USA (United States)	Malta	16 Nov 66	Finance	0UNTS0	109837
USA (United States)	Malta	28 Dec 66	General Military	0UNTS0	109838
USA (United States)	Malta	14 Jun 67	Commodity Trade	604UNTS231	108753
USA (United States)	Malta	25 Jul 67	General Military	0UNTS0	109911
USA (United States)	Malta	16 Apr 68	Military Mission	0UNTS0	110012
USA (United States)	Malta	30 Sep 68	Military Mission	0UNTS0	110080
USA (United States)	Malta	18 Jun 69	Specific Property	0UNTS0	110332
USA (United States)	Malta	23 Apr 70	Military Mission	0UNTS0	110694
USA (United States)	Malta	24 Jun 70	Non-ILO Labor	0UNTS0	110816
USA (United States)	Mauritania	03 Jul 64	Finance	532UNTS307	107724
USA (United States)	Mauritania	17 Oct 66	Direct Aid	0UNTS0	109618
USA (United States)	Mauritius	03 Sep 68	Milit Installation	0UNTS0	109737
USA (United States)	Mauritius	29 Dec 69	Scientific Project	0UNTS0	110615
USA (United States)	Mauritius	11 May 70	Finance	0UNTS0	110781
USA (United States)	Mexico	11 Apr 41	Non-IBRD Project	117UNTS323	200379
USA (United States)	Mexico	19 Nov 41	Claims and Debts	148UNTS367	200474
USA (United States)	Mexico	19 Nov 41	Claims and Debts	125UNTS287	200430
USA (United States)	Mexico	04 Aug 42	Non-ILO Labor	148UNTS379	200475
USA (United States)	Mexico	12 Aug 42	Consul/Citizenship	125UNTS301	200431
USA (United States)	Mexico	24 Oct 42	Non-IBRD Project	21UNTS189	200123
USA (United States)	Mexico	10 Nov 42	Scientific Project	66UNTS307	200219
USA (United States)	Mexico	18 Nov 42	Claims and Debts	120UNTS183	200392
USA (United States)	Mexico	23 Dec 42	Finance	13UNTS231	200081
USA (United States)	Mexico	22 Jan 43	Milit Servic/Citiz	105UNTS259	200337
USA (United States)	Mexico	26 Apr 43	Non-ILO Labor	21UNTS245	200127
USA (United States)	Mexico	29 Apr 43	Non-ILO Labor	105UNTS119	200327
USA (United States)	Mexico	14 Jun 43	Scientific Project	66UNTS331	200220
USA (United States)	Mexico	01 Jul 43	Sanitation	28UNTS407	200164
USA (United States)	Mexico	29 Sep 43	Claims and Debts	106UNTS265	200345
USA (United States)	Mexico	27 Jan 44	IGO Establishment	106UNTS275	200346
USA (United States)	Mexico	03 Feb 44	Specific Resources	3UNTS313	200025
USA (United States)	Mexico	08 Nov 45	Specific Resources	46MEXD3003	444019
USA (United States)	Mexico	05 Mar 46	Claims and Debts	120UNTS3	101612
USA (United States)	Mexico	12 Apr 46	Scientific Project	66UNTS293	100861
USA (United States)	Mexico	22 Oct 46	Non-IBRD Project	21UNTS13	100321
USA (United States)	Mexico	15 Nov 46	Non-ILO Labor	105UNTS3	101450
USA (United States)	Mexico	17 Mar 47	Sanitation	167UNTS30	102200
USA (United States)	Mexico	02 Apr 47	Non-ILO Labor	148UNTS104	101939
USA (United States)	Mexico	25 Jan 49	IGO Establishment	99UNTS3	101367
USA (United States)	Mexico	14 Feb 49	Sanitation	160UNTS75	102103
USA (United States)	Mexico	21 Jun 49	Scientific Project	89UNTS3	101204
USA (United States)	Mexico	05 Jul 49	Military Mission	68UNTS55	100884
USA (United States)	Mexico	15 Aug 49	Scientific Project	66UNTS13	100846
USA (United States)	Mexico	30 Aug 49	IGO Establishment	98UNTS183	101364
USA (United States)	Mexico	03 May 50	Visas	98UNTS201	101366
USA (United States)	Mexico	27 Jun 51	Tech Assistance	141UNTS211	101916
USA (United States)	Mexico	10 Aug 51	Telecommunications	152UNTS27	102009
USA (United States)	Mexico	11 Aug 51	Non-ILO Labor	162UNTS103	102133
USA (United States)	Mexico	15 Jul 52	Air Transport	181UNTS263	102416
USA (United States)	Mexico	26 Aug 52	IGO Establishment	264UNTS269	103797

PARTY ONE	PARTY TWO	DATE	TOPIC	CITATION	NUMBER
USA (United States)	Mexico	12 Nov 53	Visas	224UNTS187	103077
USA (United States)	Mexico	06 Apr 54	Non-IBRD Project	233UNTS163	103261
USA (United States)	Mexico	06 Apr 54	Tech Assistance	236UNTS69	103317
USA (United States)	Mexico	07 Jun 54	Tech Assistance	234UNTS11	103269
USA (United States)	Mexico	17 Jun 54	Non-IBRD Project	237UNTS275	103352
USA (United States)	Mexico	30 Jul 54	Sanitation	269UNTS39	103871
USA (United States)	Mexico	19 Nov 54	Non-ILO Labor	238UNTS237	103367
USA (United States)	Mexico	09 Mar 55	Tech Assistance	263UNTS247	103776
USA (United States)	Mexico	29 Jan 57	Telecommunications	418UNTS253	106025
USA (United States)	Mexico	07 Mar 57	Air Transport	279UNTS205	104042
USA (United States)	Mexico	23 Oct 57	US Agri Commod Aid	300UNTS35	104330
USA (United States)	Mexico	16 Jul 58	Telecommunications	335UNTS139	104782
USA (United States)	Mexico	31 Jul 59	Gen Communications	357UNTS187	105117
USA (United States)	Mexico	05 Aug 59	Customs	356UNTS3	105089
USA (United States)	Mexico	04 Feb 60	Scientific Project	586UNTS57	108496
USA (United States)	Mexico	12 Apr 60	Scientific Project	372UNTS47	105287
USA (United States)	Mexico	15 Aug 60	Air Transport	402UNTS177	105786
USA (United States)	Mexico	24 Oct 60	Specific Property	401UNTS137	105767
USA (United States)	Mexico	26 Jun 61	Direct Aid	413UNTS229	105957
USA (United States)	Mexico	19 Jul 61	Air Transport	433UNTS43	106230
USA (United States)	Mexico	15 Nov 61	Non-IBRD Project	460UNTS113	106634
USA (United States)	Mexico	08 Jan 62	Humanitarian	433UNTS163	106239
USA (United States)	Mexico	18 Apr 62	Telecommunications	452UNTS3	106501
USA (United States)	Mexico	29 Aug 63	Territory Boundary	505UNTS185	107374
USA (United States)	Mexico	14 Feb 64	Scientific Project	524UNTS197	107574
USA (United States)	Mexico	14 May 64	Commodity Trade	526UNTS228	107607
USA (United States)	Mexico	07 Aug 64	Taxation	530UNTS123	107677
USA (United States)	Mexico	27 Feb 65	Scientific Project	546UNTS135	107940
USA (United States)	Mexico	27 Feb 65	Scientific Project	542UNTS181	107889
USA (United States)	Mexico	24 Aug 66	Non-IBRD Project	606UNTS251	108789
USA (United States)	Mexico	26 Oct 66	Education	0UNTS0	109619
USA (United States)	Mexico	03 Dec 66	Admin Cooperation	0UNTS0	109692
USA (United States)	Mexico	02 Jun 67	General Trade	0UNTS0	109770
USA (United States)	Mexico	01 Aug 67	Claims and Debts	0UNTS0	109982
USA (United States)	Mexico	27 Oct 67	Specific Resources	0UNTS0	109925
USA (United States)	Mexico	03 May 68	Admin Cooperation	0UNTS0	110014
USA (United States)	Mexico	11 Dec 68	Telecommunications	71MEXD2001	444020
USA (United States)	Mexico	20 Dec 68	Scientific Project	0UNTS0	110258
USA (United States)	Mexico	20 Mar 70	Commodity Trade	0UNTS0	110629
USA (United States)	Mexico	23 Jun 70	Direct Aid	0UNTS0	110815
USA (United States)	Mexico	17 Jul 70	Admin Cooperation	71MEXD906	444021
USA (United States)	Mexico	23 Nov 70	Territory Boundary	72MEXD1501	444022
USA (United States)	Monaco	31 Mar 52	Visas	177UNTS195	102318
USA (United States)	Monaco	24 Sep 52	Patents/Copyrights	186UNTS43	102481
USA (United States)	Monaco	16 Oct 68	Gen Communications	0UNTS0	110329
USA (United States)	Morocco	02 Apr 57	General Aid	288UNTS157	104203
USA (United States)	Morocco	31 Mar 61	Admin Cooperation	406UNTS249	105854
USA (United States)	Morocco	30 Nov 61	Postal Service	451UNTS167	106492
USA (United States)	Morocco	09 Feb 62	Direct Aid	442UNTS135	106345
USA (United States)	Morocco	11 Sep 62	US Agri Commod Aid	462UNTS207	106680
USA (United States)	Morocco	29 Dec 64	Commodity Trade	593UNTS185	108584
USA (United States)	Morocco	23 Apr 65	US Agri Commod Aid	594UNTS3	108591
USA (United States)	Morocco	21 Apr 66	US Agri Commod Aid	0UNTS0	109679
USA (United States)	Morocco	12 Aug 66	US Agri Commod Aid	0UNTS0	109616
USA (United States)	Morocco	10 Feb 67	Culture	0UNTS0	109847
USA (United States)	Morocco	20 Apr 67	US Agri Commod Aid	0UNTS0	109761
USA (United States)	Morocco	27 Oct 67	US Agri Commod Aid	0UNTS0	110053
USA (United States)	Morocco	02 May 68	US Agri Commod Aid	0UNTS0	110013
USA (United States)	Morocco	25 Feb 69	Commodity Trade	0UNTS0	110268
USA (United States)	Multilateral	25 Jun 36	Privil/Immunities	161UNTS217	200486
USA (United States)	Multilateral	17 Feb 40	Privil/Immunities	161UNTS229	200487
USA (United States)	Multilateral	12 May 40	Scientific Project	101UNTS91	101405
USA (United States)	Multilateral	30 Jul 40	Admin Cooperation	161UNTS253	200488
USA (United States)	Multilateral	12 Oct 40	Specific Resources	161UNTS193	200485
USA (United States)	Multilateral	28 Nov 40	Commodity Trade	139UNTS159	200452

PARTY ONE	PARTY TWO	DATE	TOPIC	CITATION	NUMBER
USA (United States)	Multilateral	27 Mar 41	Military Mission	67UNTS231	200222
USA (United States)	Multilateral	22 Apr 42	Commodity Trade	8UNTS237	200044
USA (United States)	Multilateral	04 Dec 42	Direct Aid	24UNTS247	200150
USA (United States)	Multilateral	26 Mar 43	Specif Goods/Equip	13UNTS427	200089
USA (United States)	Multilateral	21 Dec 43	Commodity Trade	65UNTS231	200214
USA (United States)	Multilateral	15 Jan 44	IGO Establishment	161UNTS281	200489
USA (United States)	Multilateral	19 Apr 44	Scientific Project	89UNTS279	200257
USA (United States)	Multilateral	02 Aug 44	Scientific Project	67UNTS221	200221
USA (United States)	Multilateral	12 Sep 44	Milit Occupation	227UNTS279	200532
USA (United States)	Multilateral	28 Oct 44	Peace/Disarmament	123UNTS223	200414
USA (United States)	Multilateral	14 Nov 44	Milit Occupation	236UNTS359	200539
USA (United States)	Multilateral	07 Dec 44	Air Transport	171UNTS387	200502
USA (United States)	Multilateral	07 Dec 44	IGO Establishment	15UNTS295	200102
USA (United States)	Multilateral	07 Dec 44	Air Transport	84UNTS389	200252
USA (United States)	Multilateral	07 Dec 44	Air Transport	171UNTS345	200501
USA (United States)	Multilateral	15 Dec 44	Sanitation	17UNTS305	200110
USA (United States)	Multilateral	15 Dec 44	Sanitation	16UNTS247	200106
USA (United States)	Multilateral	20 Jan 45	Peace/Disarmament	140UNTS397	200471
USA (United States)	Multilateral	05 Jun 45	Milit Occupation	68UNTS189	200230
USA (United States)	Multilateral	09 Jun 45	Milit Occupation	139UNTS381	200464
USA (United States)	Multilateral	09 Jul 45	Milit Occupation	160UNTS359	200484
USA (United States)	Multilateral	26 Jul 45	Milit Occupation	227UNTS297	200533
USA (United States)	Multilateral	08 Aug 45	General Military	82UNTS279	200251
USA (United States)	Multilateral	02 Sep 45	Peace/Disarmament	139UNTS387	200465
USA (United States)	Multilateral	27 Sep 45	IGO Establishment	5UNTS327	200035
USA (United States)	Multilateral	15 Nov 45	Atomic Energy	3UNTS123	100026
USA (United States)	Multilateral	16 Nov 45	IGO Establishment	4UNTS275	100052
USA (United States)	Multilateral	04 Dec 45	Telecommunications	9UNTS101	100128
USA (United States)	Multilateral	26 Dec 45	Peace/Disarmament	20UNTS259	100319
USA (United States)	Multilateral	27 Dec 45	IGO Establishment	2UNTS39	100020
USA (United States)	Multilateral	04 Jan 46	IGO Establishment	6UNTS35	100066
USA (United States)	Multilateral	14 Jan 46	Reparations	555UNTS69	108105
USA (United States)	Multilateral	23 Apr 46	Sanitation	16UNTS179	100257
USA (United States)	Multilateral	23 Apr 46	Sanitation	17UNTS3	100265
USA (United States)	Multilateral	06 May 46	Commodity Trade	157UNTS85	102049
USA (United States)	Multilateral	06 May 46	Commodity Trade	99UNTS181	101379
USA (United States)	Multilateral	03 Jun 46	Commodity Trade	7UNTS331	100109
USA (United States)	Multilateral	28 Jun 46	Milit Occupation	138UNTS85	101862
USA (United States)	Multilateral	18 Jul 46	Reparations	125UNTS119	101674
USA (United States)	Multilateral	22 Jul 46	IGO Establishment	9UNTS3	100125
USA (United States)	Multilateral	22 Jul 46	IGO Establishment	14UNTS185	100221
USA (United States)	Multilateral	27 Jul 46	Patents/Copyrights	90UNTS229	101238
USA (United States)	Multilateral	03 Sep 46	Commodity Trade	139UNTS3	101872
USA (United States)	Multilateral	30 Oct 46	IGO Establishment	27UNTS77	100401
USA (United States)	Multilateral	30 Oct 46	IGO Establishment	11UNTS107	100151
USA (United States)	Multilateral	02 Dec 46	Specific Resources	161UNTS72	102124
USA (United States)	Multilateral	11 Dec 46	Sanitation	12UNTS179	100186
USA (United States)	Multilateral	15 Dec 46	IGO Establishment	18UNTS3	100283
USA (United States)	Multilateral	23 Dec 46	Commodity Trade	126UNTS47	101681
USA (United States)	Multilateral	06 Feb 47	IGO Establishment	97UNTS227	101352
USA (United States)	Multilateral	10 Feb 47	Reparations	140UNTS111	101886
USA (United States)	Multilateral	10 Feb 47	Peace/Disarmament	41UNTS135	100644
USA (United States)	Multilateral	10 Feb 47	Peace/Disarmament	42UNTS3	100645
USA (United States)	Multilateral	10 Feb 47	Peace/Disarmament	49UNTS3	100747
USA (United States)	Multilateral	10 Feb 47	Peace/Disarmament	41UNTS21	100643
USA (United States)	Multilateral	03 Mar 47	Humanitarian	11UNTS43	100148
USA (United States)	Multilateral	14 Aug 47	Reparations	138UNTS111	101863
USA (United States)	Multilateral	02 Sep 47	General Military	21UNTS77	100324
USA (United States)	Multilateral	02 Oct 47	Telecommunications	193UNTS188	102616
USA (United States)	Multilateral	10 Oct 47	Claims and Debts	54UNTS193	100804
USA (United States)	Multilateral	11 Oct 47	IGO Establishment	77UNTS143	100998
USA (United States)	Multilateral	04 Nov 47	Reparations	93UNTS61	101288
USA (United States)	Multilateral	13 Nov 47	Visas	251UNTS79	103534
USA (United States)	Multilateral	16 Dec 47	Reparations	82UNTS237	101096
USA (United States)	Multilateral	06 Mar 48	Water Transport	289UNTS3	104214

PARTY ONE	PARTY TWO	DATE	TOPIC	CITATION	NUMBER
USA (United States)	Multilateral	30 Apr 48	IGO Establishment	119UNTS3	101609
USA (United States)	Multilateral	30 Apr 48	Dispute Settlement	30UNTS55	100449
USA (United States)	Multilateral	10 May 48	Reparations	140UNTS129	101887
USA (United States)	Multilateral	13 May 48	Reparations	140UNTS187	101888
USA (United States)	Multilateral	10 Jun 48	Humanitarian	191UNTS3	102576
USA (United States)	Multilateral	10 Jun 48	Humanitarian	164UNTS113	102163
USA (United States)	Multilateral	19 Jun 48	Air Transport	310UNTS151	104492
USA (United States)	Multilateral	14 Jul 48	Mostfavored Nation	31UNTS123	100473
USA (United States)	Multilateral	14 Jul 48	Direct Aid	23UNTS3	100340
USA (United States)	Multilateral	24 Jul 48	Sanitation	66UNTS25	100847
USA (United States)	Multilateral	14 Sep 48	Milit Occupation	18UNTS267	100296
USA (United States)	Multilateral	08 Oct 48	Education	19UNTS113	100308
USA (United States)	Multilateral	19 Oct 48	Specif Claim/Waive	84UNTS201	101130
USA (United States)	Multilateral	15 Nov 48	IGO Establishment	120UNTS59	101615
USA (United States)	Multilateral	19 Nov 48	Sanitation	44UNTS277	100688
USA (United States)	Multilateral	29 Nov 48	IGO Establishment	120UNTS13	101613
USA (United States)	Multilateral	09 Dec 48	Humanitarian	78UNTS277	101021
USA (United States)	Multilateral	16 Dec 48	Direct Aid	79UNTS85	101033
USA (United States)	Multilateral	08 Feb 49	Specific Resources	157UNTS157	102053
USA (United States)	Multilateral	23 Mar 49	Commodity Trade	203UNTS179	102746
USA (United States)	Multilateral	31 Mar 49	Reparations	122UNTS57	101636
USA (United States)	Multilateral	04 Apr 49	General Military	34UNTS243	100541
USA (United States)	Multilateral	08 Apr 49	Milit Occupation	140UNTS196	101889
USA (United States)	Multilateral	28 Apr 49	IGO Establishment	83UNTS105	101105
USA (United States)	Multilateral	04 May 49	Milit Occupation	138UNTS123	101864
USA (United States)	Multilateral	04 May 49	Admin Cooperation	92UNTS19	101257
USA (United States)	Multilateral	04 May 49	Admin Cooperation	47UNTS159	100728
USA (United States)	Multilateral	04 May 49	Admin Cooperation	30UNTS23	100446
USA (United States)	Multilateral	04 May 49	Admin Cooperation	30UNTS3	100445
USA (United States)	Multilateral	20 Jun 49	IGO Establishment	128UNTS141	101718
USA (United States)	Multilateral	09 Jul 49	Telecommunications	168UNTS143	102218
USA (United States)	Multilateral	15 Jul 49	Health/Educ/Welfare	197UNTS3	102631
USA (United States)	Multilateral	22 Jul 49	General Trade	557UNTS211	108135
USA (United States)	Multilateral	12 Aug 49	IGO Establishment	87UNTS131	101169
USA (United States)	Multilateral	12 Aug 49	Humanitarian	75UNTS31	100970
USA (United States)	Multilateral	12 Aug 49	General Military	75UNTS135	100972
USA (United States)	Multilateral	12 Aug 49	Humanitarian	75UNTS85	100971
USA (United States)	Multilateral	12 Aug 49	Humanitarian	75UNTS287	100973
USA (United States)	Multilateral	19 Sep 49	Land Transport	125UNTS3	101671
USA (United States)	Multilateral	22 Nov 49	Recognition	185UNTS307	102477
USA (United States)	Multilateral	06 Apr 50	Admin Cooperation	119UNTS99	101610
USA (United States)	Multilateral	29 Nov 50	Patents/Copyrights	88UNTS221	101194
USA (United States)	Multilateral	07 Dec 50	Admin Cooperation	212UNTS17	102861
USA (United States)	Multilateral	23 Dec 50	Tech Assistance	185UNTS3	102456
USA (United States)	Multilateral	06 Mar 51	Milit Assistance	138UNTS67	101860
USA (United States)	Multilateral	06 Mar 51	Claims and Debts	106UNTS141	101461
USA (United States)	Multilateral	03 Apr 51	Milit Occupation	141UNTS303	101920
USA (United States)	Multilateral	25 Apr 51	Reparations	91UNTS21	101240
USA (United States)	Multilateral	25 May 51	Status of Forces	175UNTS215	102303
USA (United States)	Multilateral	15 Jun 51	Tech Assistance	148UNTS67	101936
USA (United States)	Multilateral	19 Jun 51	Status of Forces	199UNTS67	102678
USA (United States)	Multilateral	01 Sep 51	General Military	131UNTS83	101736
USA (United States)	Multilateral	08 Sep 51	Peace/Disarmament	136UNTS45	101832
USA (United States)	Multilateral	20 Sep 51	IGO Status/Immunit	200UNTS3	102691
USA (United States)	Multilateral	06 Dec 51	Admin Cooperation	150UNTS67	101963
USA (United States)	Multilateral	11 Feb 52	Direct Aid	165UNTS77	102169
USA (United States)	Multilateral	01 Mar 52	Specific Resources	168UNTS9	102210
USA (United States)	Multilateral	09 May 52	Specific Resources	205UNTS65	102770
USA (United States)	Multilateral	09 May 52	Milit Occupation	168UNTS65	102213
USA (United States)	Multilateral	20 May 52	Sanitation	219UNTS55	102966
USA (United States)	Multilateral	12 Jun 52	Dispute Settlement	138UNTS183	101869
USA (United States)	Multilateral	11 Jul 52	IGO Establishment	169UNTS3	102220
USA (United States)	Multilateral	28 Aug 52	Claims and Debts	175UNTS69	102296
USA (United States)	Multilateral	06 Sep 52	Patents/Copyrights	216UNTS132	102937
USA (United States)	Multilateral	07 Nov 52	General Trade	221UNTS255	103010

PARTY ONE	PARTY TWO	DATE	TOPIC	CITATION	NUMBER
USA (United States)	Multilateral	10 Nov 52	Admin Cooperation	214UNTS265	102904
USA (United States)	Multilateral	27 Feb 53	Claims and Debts	333UNTS3	104764
USA (United States)	Multilateral	30 Apr 53	Admin Cooperation	175UNTS89	102297
USA (United States)	Multilateral	11 May 53	Sanitation	456UNTS3	106555
USA (United States)	Multilateral	30 Jul 53	Reparations	215UNTS97	102913
USA (United States)	Multilateral	01 Oct 53	Commodity Trade	258UNTS153	103677
USA (United States)	Multilateral	19 Oct 53	IGO Establishment	207UNTS189	102807
USA (United States)	Multilateral	26 Oct 53	Status of Forces	207UNTS237	102809
USA (United States)	Multilateral	07 Dec 53	Admin Cooperation	182UNTS51	102422
USA (United States)	Multilateral	19 Feb 54	Status of Forces	214UNTS51	102899
USA (United States)	Multilateral	25 Feb 54	Air Transport	215UNTS249	102922
USA (United States)	Multilateral	12 May 54	Admin Cooperation	327UNTS3	104714
USA (United States)	Multilateral	14 May 54	Culture	249UNTS215	103511
USA (United States)	Multilateral	04 Jun 54	Customs	276UNTS191	103992
USA (United States)	Multilateral	04 Jun 54	Customs	282UNTS249	104101
USA (United States)	Multilateral	14 Jun 54	Air Transport	320UNTS217	104644
USA (United States)	Multilateral	30 Jun 54	Admin Cooperation	204UNTS99	102752
USA (United States)	Multilateral	08 Sep 54	Milit Assistance	209UNTS23	102819
USA (United States)	Multilateral	05 Oct 54	Territory Boundary	235UNTS99	103297
USA (United States)	Multilateral	23 Oct 54	Milit Occupation	331UNTS327	104759
USA (United States)	Multilateral	23 Oct 54	Reparations	332UNTS219	104762
USA (United States)	Multilateral	23 Oct 54	Milit Occupation	331UNTS253	104758
USA (United States)	Multilateral	23 Oct 54	Status of Forces	334UNTS3	104765
USA (United States)	Multilateral	23 Oct 54	Status of Forces	332UNTS387	104763
USA (United States)	Multilateral	23 Oct 54	Status of Forces	332UNTS3	104760
USA (United States)	Multilateral	23 Oct 54	Milit Occupation	332UNTS157	104761
USA (United States)	Multilateral	01 Dec 54	Admin Cooperation	210UNTS197	102839
USA (United States)	Multilateral	10 May 55	Claims and Debts	273UNTS121	103948
USA (United States)	Multilateral	15 May 55	Recognition	217UNTS223	102949
USA (United States)	Multilateral	25 May 55	IGO Establishment	264UNTS117	103791
USA (United States)	Multilateral	06 Jun 55	IGO Establishment	219UNTS79	102968
USA (United States)	Multilateral	22 Jun 55	Atomic Energy	249UNTS3	103498
USA (United States)	Multilateral	28 Sep 55	Air Transport	478UNTS371	106943
USA (United States)	Multilateral	04 Jan 56	Scientific Project	256UNTS171	103627
USA (United States)	Multilateral	10 Feb 56	Tech Assistance	228UNTS189	103151
USA (United States)	Multilateral	25 Apr 56	Commodity Trade	270UNTS103	103896
USA (United States)	Multilateral	18 May 56	Customs	338UNTS103	104834
USA (United States)	Multilateral	05 Jul 56	Patents/Copyrights	258UNTS371	103679
USA (United States)	Multilateral	13 Jul 56	Dispute Settlement	281UNTS3	104066
USA (United States)	Multilateral	24 Sep 56	Patents/Copyrights	253UNTS171	103583
USA (United States)	Multilateral	25 Sep 56	Air Transport	334UNTS89	104767
USA (United States)	Multilateral	25 Sep 56	Air Transport	334UNTS13	104766
USA (United States)	Multilateral	26 Oct 56	IGO Establishment	276UNTS3	103988
USA (United States)	Multilateral	29 Oct 56	Territory Boundary	263UNTS165	103772
USA (United States)	Multilateral	31 Jan 57	Claims and Debts	278UNTS105	104026
USA (United States)	Multilateral	09 Feb 57	Specific Resources	314UNTS105	104546
USA (United States)	Multilateral	29 Mar 57	Claims and Debts	283UNTS137	104113
USA (United States)	Multilateral	01 May 57	Admin Cooperation	284UNTS201	104138
USA (United States)	Multilateral	27 Jun 57	General Economic	284UNTS139	104133
USA (United States)	Multilateral	03 Oct 57	Postal Service	364UNTS3	105211
USA (United States)	Multilateral	06 Jan 58	General Transport	304UNTS227	104399
USA (United States)	Multilateral	31 Mar 58	Specific Property	320UNTS103	104639
USA (United States)	Multilateral	29 Apr 58	Territory Boundary	516UNTS205	107477
USA (United States)	Multilateral	29 Apr 58	Territory Boundary	499UNTS311	107302
USA (United States)	Multilateral	29 Apr 58	Specific Resources	559UNTS285	108164
USA (United States)	Multilateral	29 Apr 58	Water Transport	450UNTS11	106465
USA (United States)	Multilateral	29 Apr 58	Dispute Settlement	450UNTS169	106466
USA (United States)	Multilateral	28 Jul 58	General Military	335UNTS205	104788
USA (United States)	Multilateral	27 Oct 58	Reparations	351UNTS303	105031
USA (United States)	Multilateral	01 Dec 58	Commodity Trade	385UNTS137	105534
USA (United States)	Multilateral	15 Jan 59	Customs	348UNTS13	104996
USA (United States)	Multilateral	06 Apr 59	Commodity Trade	349UNTS167	105013
USA (United States)	Multilateral	08 Apr 59	IGO Establishment	389UNTS69	105593
USA (United States)	Multilateral	03 Aug 59	Status of Forces	481UNTS262	106986
USA (United States)	Multilateral	01 Dec 59	Territory Boundary	402UNTS71	105778

PARTY ONE	PARTY TWO	DATE	TOPIC	CITATION	NUMBER
USA (United States)	Multilateral	26 Jan 60	IGO Establishment	439UNTS249	106333
USA (United States)	Multilateral	17 Jun 60	Humanitarian	536UNTS27	107794
USA (United States)	Multilateral	21 Jun 60	IGO Establishment	418UNTS109	106019
USA (United States)	Multilateral	19 Sep 60	IBRD Project	444UNTS259	106371
USA (United States)	Multilateral	21 Sep 60	Patents/Copyrights	394UNTS3	105664
USA (United States)	Multilateral	30 Dec 60	Atomic Energy	395UNTS241	105689
USA (United States)	Multilateral	10 Apr 61	Atomic Energy	402UNTS281	105791
USA (United States)	Multilateral	18 Apr 61	Dispute Settlement	500UNTS243	107312
USA (United States)	Multilateral	18 Apr 61	Consul/Citizenship	500UNTS95	107310
USA (United States)	Multilateral	14 Jun 61	IBRD Project	415UNTS4	105979
USA (United States)	Multilateral	21 Jun 61	IGO Establishment	514UNTS209	107449
USA (United States)	Multilateral	04 Oct 61	Scientific Project	412UNTS210	105934
USA (United States)	Multilateral	20 Feb 62	Water Transport	597UNTS159	108644
USA (United States)	Multilateral	05 Mar 62	Scientific Project	425UNTS3	106114
USA (United States)	Multilateral	07 Mar 62	Commodity Trade	445UNTS199	106388
USA (United States)	Multilateral	07 Mar 62	Commodity Trade	445UNTS205	106389
USA (United States)	Multilateral	15 May 62	Commodity Trade	444UNTS3	106367
USA (United States)	Multilateral	27 Jun 62	Atomic Energy	463UNTS11	106689
USA (United States)	Multilateral	27 Jun 62	Atomic Energy	463UNTS17	106690
USA (United States)	Multilateral	23 Jul 62	Recognition	456UNTS302	106564
USA (United States)	Multilateral	28 Sep 62	IGO Establishment	469UNTS169	106791
USA (United States)	Multilateral	10 Dec 62	Culture	521UNTS231	107525
USA (United States)	Multilateral	06 Mar 63	Tech Assistance	455UNTS386	106552
USA (United States)	Multilateral	02 Apr 63	Commodity Trade	475UNTS121	106889
USA (United States)	Multilateral	24 Apr 63	Consul/Citizenship	596UNTS487	108640
USA (United States)	Multilateral	24 Apr 63	Consul/Citizenship	596UNTS261	108638
USA (United States)	Multilateral	05 Aug 63	Sanitation	480UNTS43	106964
USA (United States)	Multilateral	14 Sep 63	Air Transport	0UNTS0	110106
USA (United States)	Multilateral	14 Sep 63	Telecommunications	488UNTS121	107123
USA (United States)	Multilateral	23 Sep 63	Atomic Energy	488UNTS99	107122
USA (United States)	Multilateral	18 Dec 63	Atomic Energy	490UNTS383	107166
USA (United States)	Multilateral	08 Apr 64	Loans and Credits	501UNTS221	107320
USA (United States)	Multilateral	15 Jun 64	Atomic Energy	573UNTS85	108324
USA (United States)	Multilateral	18 Jun 64	Atomic Energy	542UNTS145	107886
USA (United States)	Multilateral	10 Jul 64	Postal Service	611UNTS7	108844
USA (United States)	Multilateral	10 Jul 64	Postal Service	611UNTS105	108845
USA (United States)	Multilateral	28 Jul 64	IGO Operations	555UNTS183	108113
USA (United States)	Multilateral	20 Aug 64	Telecommunications	514UNTS25	107441
USA (United States)	Multilateral	18 Sep 64	IGO Operations	555UNTS205	108114
USA (United States)	Multilateral	18 Sep 64	IGO Operations	556UNTS25	108117
USA (United States)	Multilateral	21 Sep 64	IGO Operations	555UNTS227	108115
USA (United States)	Multilateral	30 Sep 64	IGO Operations	556UNTS3	108116
USA (United States)	Multilateral	02 Dec 64	Scientific Project	572UNTS229	108317
USA (United States)	Multilateral	02 Dec 64	Atomic Energy	525UNTS51	107583
USA (United States)	Multilateral	24 Feb 65	IGO Operations	556UNTS47	108118
USA (United States)	Multilateral	26 Feb 65	IGO Operations	556UNTS69	108119
USA (United States)	Multilateral	18 Mar 65	Dispute Settlement	575UNTS159	108359
USA (United States)	Multilateral	18 Jun 65	Atomic Energy	573UNTS3	108320
USA (United States)	Multilateral	08 Jul 65	General Trade	597UNTS3	108641
USA (United States)	Multilateral	24 Sep 65	Atomic Energy	556UNTS141	108124
USA (United States)	Multilateral	07 Oct 65	Atomic Energy	556UNTS175	108125
USA (United States)	Multilateral	15 Nov 65	Admin Cooperation	0UNTS0	109432
USA (United States)	Multilateral	04 Dec 65	IGO Establishment	571UNTS123	108303
USA (United States)	Multilateral	30 Dec 65	Atomic Energy	557UNTS3	108126
USA (United States)	Multilateral	17 Jan 66	IGO Establishment	592UNTS101	108573
USA (United States)	Multilateral	04 Mar 66	US Agri Commod Aid	578UNTS57	108387
USA (United States)	Multilateral	30 Mar 66	Scientific Project	593UNTS261	108588
USA (United States)	Multilateral	05 Apr 66	Water Transport	640UNTS133	109159
USA (United States)	Multilateral	04 May 66	IBRD Project	575UNTS49	108354
USA (United States)	Multilateral	14 May 66	Specific Resources	0UNTS0	109587
USA (United States)	Multilateral	20 Jun 66	Atomic Energy	573UNTS41	108322
USA (United States)	Multilateral	08 Jul 66	Atomic Energy	572UNTS283	108319
USA (United States)	Multilateral	28 Sep 66	Specif Goods/Equip	589UNTS41	108534
USA (United States)	Multilateral	22 Dec 66	Taxation	0UNTS0	109980
USA (United States)	Multilateral	27 Jan 67	Scientific Project	610UNTS205	108843

PARTY ONE	PARTY TWO	DATE	TOPIC	CITATION	NUMBER
USA (United States)	Multilateral	31 Jan 67	Refugees	606UNTS267	108791
USA (United States)	Multilateral	16 Mar 67	Gen Communications	0UNTS0	109755
USA (United States)	Multilateral	03 May 67	IGO Operations	0UNTS0	110764
USA (United States)	Multilateral	23 Jun 67	IGO Operations	614UNTS185	108871
USA (United States)	Multilateral	30 Jun 67	Commodity Trade	0UNTS0	109864
USA (United States)	Multilateral	20 Jul 67	General Economic	0UNTS0	109259
USA (United States)	Multilateral	26 Jul 67	IGO Operations	614UNTS217	108872
USA (United States)	Multilateral	23 Aug 67	IGO Operations	614UNTS145	108869
USA (United States)	Multilateral	19 Oct 67	Atomic Energy	630UNTS69	108966
USA (United States)	Multilateral	05 Nov 67	Atomic Energy	630UNTS77	108967
USA (United States)	Multilateral	18 Mar 68	Postal Service	0UNTS0	110009
USA (United States)	Multilateral	18 Mar 68	Commodity Trade	0UNTS0	109262
USA (United States)	Multilateral	22 Apr 68	Scientific Project	0UNTS0	109574
USA (United States)	Multilateral	07 Feb 69	Status of Forces	0UNTS0	110586
USA (United States)	Multilateral	07 Feb 69	Status of Forces	0UNTS0	110587
USA (United States)	Multilateral	27 Nov 69	Atomic Energy	0UNTS0	110519
USA (United States)	Multilateral	19 Dec 69	Atomic Energy	0UNTS0	110520
USA (United States)	Multilateral	19 Dec 69	Atomic Energy	0UNTS0	110522
USA (United States)	Multilateral	24 Feb 70	Non-IBRD Project	0UNTS0	110623
USA (United States)	Muscat and Oman	20 Dec 58	General Amity	380UNTS181	105457
USA (United States)	NATO (North Atlan)	22 Oct 54	IGO Establishment	249UNTS175	103507
USA (United States)	Nepal	25 Apr 47	Consul/Citizenship	16UNTS97	100251
USA (United States)	Nepal	23 Jan 51	Tech Assistance	184UNTS65	102439
USA (United States)	Nepal	17 May 60	Claims and Debts	372UNTS313	105307
USA (United States)	Nepal	09 Jun 61	Education	421UNTS223	106061
USA (United States)	Nepal	24 Aug 62	General Aid	460UNTS143	106637
USA (United States)	Netherlands	17 Jan 33	Status of Forces	474UNTS119	106877
USA (United States)	Netherlands	08 Jul 42	Milit Assistance	103UNTS277	200318
USA (United States)	Netherlands	30 Sep 42	Milit Servic/Citiz	13UNTS151	200076
USA (United States)	Netherlands	14 Jun 43	General Military	28UNTS397	200163
USA (United States)	Netherlands	16 May 44	Milit Occupation	132UNTS355	200440
USA (United States)	Netherlands	30 Apr 45	Milit Assistance	139UNTS341	200460
USA (United States)	Netherlands	30 Apr 45	Milit Installation	139UNTS319	200459
USA (United States)	Netherlands	09 Feb 46	Commodity Trade	3UNTS247	100035
USA (United States)	Netherlands	11 Feb 46	Claims and Debts	3UNTS37	100023
USA (United States)	Netherlands	13 Mar 46	Visas	84UNTS3	101113
USA (United States)	Netherlands	21 Nov 46	General Trade	12UNTS173	100185
USA (United States)	Netherlands	11 Apr 47	Other Military	148UNTS343	101943
USA (United States)	Netherlands	28 May 47	General Military	17UNTS29	100267
USA (United States)	Netherlands	20 Aug 47	Visas	84UNTS11	101114
USA (United States)	Netherlands	30 Oct 47	General Economic	76UNTS47	100978
USA (United States)	Netherlands	29 Apr 48	Taxation	32UNTS167	100498
USA (United States)	Netherlands	02 Jul 48	Mostfavored Nation	32UNTS77	100490
USA (United States)	Netherlands	02 Jul 48	Direct Aid	20UNTS91	100315
USA (United States)	Netherlands	17 Jan 49	Direct Aid	32UNTS241	100502
USA (United States)	Netherlands	26 Apr 49	Finance	70UNTS123	100901
USA (United States)	Netherlands	17 May 49	Milit Assistance	46UNTS291	100717
USA (United States)	Netherlands	27 Jan 50	Milit Assistance	80UNTS219	101054
USA (United States)	Netherlands	06 Oct 50	Finance	51NET1	447015
USA (United States)	Netherlands	07 Oct 50	Loans and Credits	79UNTS33	101029
USA (United States)	Netherlands	19 Jan 51	Reparations	141UNTS221	101917
USA (United States)	Netherlands	26 Sep 51	Milit Installation	158UNTS469	102080
USA (United States)	Netherlands	08 Jan 52	Milit Assistance	179UNTS175	102366
USA (United States)	Netherlands	07 Mar 52	Taxation	135UNTS199	101821
USA (United States)	Netherlands	15 May 52	Milit Assistance	177UNTS233	102321
USA (United States)	Netherlands	12 Mar 53	Claims and Debts	53NET135	447037
USA (United States)	Netherlands	19 Jun 53	Admin Cooperation	212UNTS249	102875
USA (United States)	Netherlands	27 Oct 53	Tech Assistance	221UNTS357	103017
USA (United States)	Netherlands	22 Jan 54	Tech Assistance	190UNTS207	102565
USA (United States)	Netherlands	07 May 54	Milit Assistance	213UNTS325	102895
USA (United States)	Netherlands	13 Aug 54	Milit Installation	251UNTS91	103535
USA (United States)	Netherlands	14 Dec 54	Milit Assistance	262UNTS35	103737
USA (United States)	Netherlands	21 Mar 55	Telecommunications	289UNTS129	104217
USA (United States)	Netherlands	29 Apr 55	Milit Installation	219UNTS105	102969
USA (United States)	Netherlands	29 Apr 55	Milit Assistance	251UNTS357	103553

PARTY ONE	PARTY TWO	DATE	TOPIC	CITATION	NUMBER
USA (United States)	Netherlands	25 May 55	Claims and Debts	289UNTS227	104220
USA (United States)	Netherlands	18 Jul 55	Atomic Energy	240UNTS347	103412
USA (United States)	Netherlands	04 Nov 55	Air Transport	269UNTS3	103867
USA (United States)	Netherlands	22 Jan 56	Atomic Energy	287UNTS121	104181
USA (United States)	Netherlands	27 Mar 56	General Amity	285UNTS231	104154
USA (United States)	Netherlands	07 Aug 56	US Agri Commod Aid	281UNTS57	104069
USA (United States)	Netherlands	16 Aug 56	Specific Property	279UNTS3	104031
USA (United States)	Netherlands	15 Feb 57	Atomic Energy	287UNTS239	104190
USA (United States)	Netherlands	03 Apr 57	Air Transport	410UNTS193	105904
USA (United States)	Netherlands	06 May 59	Milit Installation	355UNTS327	105084
USA (United States)	Netherlands	24 Mar 60	Milit Assistance	406UNTS165	105847
USA (United States)	Netherlands	24 Apr 62	Specific Property	436UNTS93	106289
USA (United States)	Netherlands	06 Feb 63	Status of Forces	487UNTS113	107098
USA (United States)	Netherlands	20 May 63	Specif Goods/Equip	487UNTS123	107099
USA (United States)	Netherlands	26 Nov 63	Milit Assistance	388UNTS303	105586
USA (United States)	Netherlands	22 Jun 66	Gen Communications	590UNTS109	108550
USA (United States)	New Zealand	03 Sep 42	Milit Assistance	24UNTS185	200142
USA (United States)	New Zealand	30 Sep 42	Milit Servic/Citiz	13UNTS139	200075
USA (United States)	New Zealand	28 Jan 43	Admin Cooperation	121UNTS123	200395
USA (United States)	New Zealand	10 Jul 46	Milit Assistance	6UNTS341	100087
USA (United States)	New Zealand	03 Dec 46	Air Transport	7UNTS175	100099
USA (United States)	New Zealand	24 Apr 47	Patents/Copyrights	16UNTS79	100250
USA (United States)	New Zealand	16 Mar 48	Taxation	127UNTS133	101703
USA (United States)	New Zealand	14 Sep 48	General Military	18UNTS251	100295
USA (United States)	New Zealand	14 Mar 49	Visas	32UNTS369	100508
USA (United States)	New Zealand	19 Jun 52	Milit Assistance	178UNTS315	102347
USA (United States)	New Zealand	13 Jun 56	Atomic Energy	253UNTS155	103582
USA (United States)	New Zealand	05 May 58	Visas	317UNTS59	104594
USA (United States)	New Zealand	24 Dec 58	Scientific Project	324UNTS111	104680
USA (United States)	New Zealand	30 Oct 59	Tech Assistance	361UNTS21	105170
USA (United States)	New Zealand	23 Mar 60	Atomic Energy	371UNTS147	105276
USA (United States)	New Zealand	05 Mar 62	General Economic	446UNTS39	106401
USA (United States)	New Zealand	08 Jun 62	Loans and Credits	458UNTS209	106602
USA (United States)	New Zealand	15 May 63	Military Mission	477UNTS55	106915
USA (United States)	New Zealand	17 Feb 64	Commodity Trade	511UNTS37	107424
USA (United States)	New Zealand	24 Jun 64	Air Transport	524UNTS101	107568
USA (United States)	New Zealand	21 Jun 67	Gen Communications	0UNTS0	109205
USA (United States)	New Zealand	09 Jul 68	Scientific Project	0UNTS0	109208
USA (United States)	New Zealand	03 Sep 69	Milit Assistance	0UNTS0	110407
USA (United States)	New Zealand	29 Jan 70	General Trade	0UNTS0	110617
USA (United States)	New Zealand	03 Feb 70	Education	0UNTS0	110621
USA (United States)	New Zealand	20 Mar 70	Air Transport	0UNTS0	110630
USA (United States)	Nicaragua	11 Jan 41	Specific Resources	117UNTS253	200374
USA (United States)	Nicaragua	08 Apr 42	Milit Installation	132UNTS343	200439
USA (United States)	Nicaragua	08 Apr 42	Land Transport	24UNTS145	200138
USA (United States)	Nicaragua	22 May 42	Sanitation	105UNTS141	200328
USA (United States)	Nicaragua	27 Oct 42	Scientific Project	99UNTS287	200283
USA (United States)	Nicaragua	25 Oct 43	Military Mission	29UNTS383	200173
USA (United States)	Nicaragua	01 Feb 50	Tech Assistance	99UNTS25	101368
USA (United States)	Nicaragua	28 Feb 50	General Trade	132UNTS169	101758
USA (United States)	Nicaragua	23 Dec 50	Tech Assistance	92UNTS155	101268
USA (United States)	Nicaragua	31 Jan 51	Education	150UNTS3	101960
USA (United States)	Nicaragua	31 Jan 51	Sanitation	160UNTS121	102105
USA (United States)	Nicaragua	20 Apr 51	Land Transport	138UNTS57	101859
USA (United States)	Nicaragua	12 Dec 51	Status of Forces	167UNTS151	102205
USA (United States)	Nicaragua	09 Oct 52	Consul/Citizenship	184UNTS105	102442
USA (United States)	Nicaragua	19 Nov 52	Military Mission	186UNTS3	102478
USA (United States)	Nicaragua	30 Jun 53	Tech Assistance	215UNTS133	102917
USA (United States)	Nicaragua	02 Sep 53	Land Transport	215UNTS69	102911
USA (United States)	Nicaragua	19 Nov 53	Military Mission	206UNTS117	102787
USA (United States)	Nicaragua	23 Apr 54	Milit Assistance	229UNTS37	103159
USA (United States)	Nicaragua	22 Oct 55	Visas	358UNTS51	105123
USA (United States)	Nicaragua	21 Jan 56	General Amity	367UNTS3	105224
USA (United States)	Nicaragua	19 Mar 56	Postal Service	275UNTS231	103984
USA (United States)	Nicaragua	02 Aug 56	Land Transport	281UNTS99	104073

PARTY ONE	PARTY TWO	DATE	TOPIC	CITATION	NUMBER
USA (United States)	Nicaragua	16 Oct 56	Gen Communications	282UNTS29	104090
USA (United States)	Nicaragua	09 Feb 57	Milit Assistance	279UNTS191	104040
USA (United States)	Nicaragua	11 Jun 57	Atomic Energy	304UNTS267	104402
USA (United States)	Nicaragua	05 Sep 58	Milit Installation	336UNTS33	104797
USA (United States)	Nicaragua	14 Apr 59	Admin Cooperation	343UNTS119	104922
USA (United States)	Nicaragua	30 Mar 62	Tech Assistance	456UNTS241	106559
USA (United States)	Nicaragua	09 May 66	Finance	0UNTS0	110043
USA (United States)	Nicaragua	20 Sep 66	Gen Communications	607UNTS167	108804
USA (United States)	Nicaragua	25 May 68	General Aid	0UNTS0	110143
USA (United States)	Nicaragua	25 Feb 70	General Trade	0UNTS0	110812
USA (United States)	Niger	26 May 61	General Aid	410UNTS213	105905
USA (United States)	Niger	26 Apr 62	Claims and Debts	459UNTS129	106618
USA (United States)	Niger	14 Jun 62	Milit Assistance	458UNTS233	106605
USA (United States)	Niger	23 Jul 62	Tech Assistance	487UNTS325	107114
USA (United States)	Nigeria	19 Oct 60	Scientific Project	394UNTS113	105672
USA (United States)	Nigeria	24 Dec 62	Claims and Debts	462UNTS180	106677
USA (United States)	Norway	28 Mar 40	Specif Claim/Waive	88UNTS365	200253
USA (United States)	Norway	28 Aug 42	Other Military	139UNTS361	200461
USA (United States)	Norway	16 Jan 43	Milit Servic/Citiz	13UNTS335	200082
USA (United States)	Norway	16 May 44	Privil/Immunities	67UNTS253	200223
USA (United States)	Norway	29 May 45	Water Transport	34UNTS371	200180
USA (United States)	Norway	06 Oct 45	Air Transport	122UNTS319	200413
USA (United States)	Norway	08 Jul 46	Mostfavored Nation	13UNTS35	100199
USA (United States)	Norway	12 Nov 46	Air Transport	42UNTS227	100651
USA (United States)	Norway	29 Jul 47	Visas	87UNTS343	101178
USA (United States)	Norway	24 Feb 48	Milit Assistance	34UNTS155	100535
USA (United States)	Norway	15 Mar 48	Admin Cooperation	73UNTS81	100946
USA (United States)	Norway	03 Jul 48	Milit Occupation	27UNTS59	100399
USA (United States)	Norway	03 Jul 48	Direct Aid	20UNTS185	100317
USA (United States)	Norway	25 May 49	Education	32UNTS345	100507
USA (United States)	Norway	13 Jun 49	Taxation	127UNTS189	101705
USA (United States)	Norway	13 Jun 49	Taxation	127UNTS163	101704
USA (United States)	Norway	31 Oct 49	Direct Aid	68UNTS3	100879
USA (United States)	Norway	27 Jan 50	Milit Assistance	80UNTS241	101055
USA (United States)	Norway	28 Dec 50	Milit Assistance	240UNTS391	103414
USA (United States)	Norway	17 Sep 51	Milit Assistance	140UNTS313	101895
USA (United States)	Norway	08 Jan 52	Milit Assistance	179UNTS185	102367
USA (United States)	Norway	01 Apr 52	Direct Aid	177UNTS291	102328
USA (United States)	Norway	21 Jun 52	Reparations	236UNTS9	103313
USA (United States)	Norway	27 Jun 52	Tech Assistance	184UNTS271	102452
USA (United States)	Norway	13 Apr 54	Status of Forces	229UNTS223	103169
USA (United States)	Norway	07 May 54	Milit Assistance	231UNTS157	103215
USA (United States)	Norway	06 Aug 54	Air Transport	222UNTS269	103034
USA (United States)	Norway	06 Aug 54	Air Transport	222UNTS261	103033
USA (United States)	Norway	06 Apr 55	General Military	269UNTS65	103874
USA (United States)	Norway	05 Feb 57	Air Transport	279UNTS169	104038
USA (United States)	Norway	25 Feb 57	Atomic Energy	284UNTS19	104126
USA (United States)	Norway	08 May 58	Milit Installation	2NORT528	451199
USA (United States)	Norway	13 Feb 60	Milit Assistance	388UNTS255	105583
USA (United States)	Norway	06 Jul 60	Milit Assistance	378UNTS25	105415
USA (United States)	Norway	29 Nov 60	Milit Assistance	404UNTS251	105815
USA (United States)	Norway	05 Mar 62	General Economic	446UNTS47	106402
USA (United States)	Norway	01 Mar 63	Water Transport	524UNTS185	107573
USA (United States)	Norway	13 Jul 66	Claims and Debts	3NORT972	451200
USA (United States)	Norway	04 May 67	Atomic Energy	0UNTS0	109763
USA (United States)	Norway	04 May 67	Atomic Energy	3NORT997	451201
USA (United States)	Norway	01 Jun 67	Gen Communications	631UNTS119	108991
USA (United States)	Norway	15 Jun 68	Scientific Project	3NORT0	451202
USA (United States)	Norway	15 Jun 68	Scientific Project	0UNTS0	110145
USA (United States)	Norway	26 Jun 68	Non-ILO Labor	3NORT0	451203
USA (United States)	Norway	26 Feb 70	Admin Cooperation	0UNTS0	110624
USA (United States)	OAS (Am States)	03 Mar 52	Tech Assistance	165UNTS67	102168
USA (United States)	OAS (Am States)	22 Jun 52	IGO Status/Immunit	181UNTS147	102405
USA (United States)	OAS (Am States)	29 Nov 61	Direct Aid	424UNTS119	106104
USA (United States)	Pakistan	16 Jun 48	Air Transport	235UNTS29	103293

PARTY ONE	PARTY TWO	DATE	TOPIC	CITATION	NUMBER
USA (United States)	Pakistan	18 Oct 49	Visas	141UNTS333	101923
USA (United States)	Pakistan	23 Sep 50	Education	82UNTS131	101088
USA (United States)	Pakistan	15 Dec 50	Milit Assistance	122UNTS89	101639
USA (United States)	Pakistan	09 Feb 51	Tech Assistance	100UNTS67	101388
USA (United States)	Pakistan	23 May 51	Admin Cooperation	134UNTS265	101805
USA (United States)	Pakistan	17 Sep 52	Loans and Credits	227UNTS77	103132
USA (United States)	Pakistan	25 Jun 53	Direct Aid	205UNTS139	102773
USA (United States)	Pakistan	01 May 54	Mass Media	237UNTS231	103349
USA (United States)	Pakistan	19 May 54	Milit Assistance	202UNTS301	102736
USA (United States)	Pakistan	23 Aug 54	Direct Aid	234UNTS243	103287
USA (United States)	Pakistan	02 Oct 54	Direct Aid	236UNTS187	103324
USA (United States)	Pakistan	11 Jan 55	Milit Assistance	251UNTS111	103537
USA (United States)	Pakistan	18 Jan 55	Direct Aid	241UNTS53	103423
USA (United States)	Pakistan	18 Jan 55	US Agri Commod Aid	239UNTS61	103372
USA (United States)	Pakistan	26 May 55	General Economic	257UNTS93	103652
USA (United States)	Pakistan	20 Jul 55	Postal Service	241UNTS255	103436
USA (United States)	Pakistan	11 Aug 55	Atomic Energy	239UNTS259	103384
USA (United States)	Pakistan	02 Mar 56	US Agri Commod Aid	271UNTS371	103927
USA (United States)	Pakistan	28 May 56	Milit Assistance	269UNTS15	103868
USA (United States)	Pakistan	07 Aug 56	US Agri Commod Aid	281UNTS75	104071
USA (United States)	Pakistan	10 Sep 56	Milit Assistance	277UNTS259	104010
USA (United States)	Pakistan	01 Jul 57	Taxation	344UNTS203	104951
USA (United States)	Pakistan	15 Nov 57	US Agri Commod Aid	303UNTS173	104380
USA (United States)	Pakistan	26 Nov 58	US Agri Commod Aid	337UNTS3	104812
USA (United States)	Pakistan	05 Mar 59	General Military	327UNTS285	104726
USA (United States)	Pakistan	18 Jul 59	Gen Communications	355UNTS367	105087
USA (United States)	Pakistan	28 Jul 59	Visas	360UNTS327	105166
USA (United States)	Pakistan	12 Nov 59	General Amity	404UNTS259	105816
USA (United States)	Pakistan	11 Apr 60	US Agri Commod Aid	372UNTS251	105302
USA (United States)	Pakistan	14 Oct 61	US Agri Commod Aid	426UNTS237	106141
USA (United States)	Pakistan	05 Mar 62	General Trade	446UNTS57	106403
USA (United States)	Pakistan	31 May 62	General Aid	460UNTS75	106631
USA (United States)	Pakistan	25 Jul 62	Direct Aid	459UNTS87	106614
USA (United States)	Pakistan	16 Jan 63	Milit Assistance	471UNTS133	106828
USA (United States)	Pakistan	29 Jun 63	Milit Assistance	487UNTS243	107107
USA (United States)	Pakistan	26 Feb 65	Commodity Trade	542UNTS103	107883
USA (United States)	Pakistan	26 May 66	US Agri Commod Aid	594UNTS27	108592
USA (United States)	Pakistan	21 Nov 66	Commodity Trade	0UNTS0	109689
USA (United States)	Pakistan	11 May 67	US Agri Commod Aid	0UNTS0	109767
USA (United States)	Pakistan	03 Jul 67	General Trade	0UNTS0	109777
USA (United States)	Pakistan	03 Aug 67	US Agri Commod Aid	0UNTS0	109912
USA (United States)	Pakistan	26 Dec 67	US Agri Commod Aid	0UNTS0	109990
USA (United States)	Pakistan	16 May 68	US Agri Commod Aid	0UNTS0	109996
USA (United States)	Pakistan	03 Jul 69	US Agri Commod Aid	0UNTS0	110446
USA (United States)	Pakistan	03 Oct 69	US Agri Commod Aid	0UNTS0	110508
USA (United States)	Pakistan	10 Jan 70	US Agri Commod Aid	0UNTS0	110509
USA (United States)	Pakistan	06 May 70	Commodity Trade	0UNTS0	110780
USA (United States)	Panama	31 Jan 35	Consul/Citizenship	234UNTS277	200536
USA (United States)	Panama	23 Mar 40	Land Transport	124UNTS195	200420
USA (United States)	Panama	06 Sep 40	Land Transport	124UNTS209	200421
USA (United States)	Panama	28 Mar 41	Taxation	103UNTS163	200312
USA (United States)	Panama	07 Mar 42	Admin Cooperation	101UNTS157	200291
USA (United States)	Panama	18 May 42	General Amity	124UNTS221	200422
USA (United States)	Panama	07 Jul 42	Military Mission	9UNTS289	200048
USA (United States)	Panama	02 Mar 43	Sanitation	107UNTS55	200351
USA (United States)	Panama	07 Jun 43	Specific Property	21UNTS269	200128
USA (United States)	Panama	14 Nov 44	Education	139UNTS367	200462
USA (United States)	Panama	13 May 45	Visas	89UNTS273	200256
USA (United States)	Panama	26 May 47	Territory Boundary	138UNTS137	101866
USA (United States)	Panama	24 Sep 48	Education	150UNTS25	101961
USA (United States)	Panama	05 Nov 48	Visas	89UNTS27	101206
USA (United States)	Panama	31 Mar 49	Telecommunications	55UNTS125	100811
USA (United States)	Panama	31 Mar 49	Air Transport	55UNTS87	100810
USA (United States)	Panama	31 Mar 49	Air Transport	55UNTS141	100812
USA (United States)	Panama	14 Jun 49	Visas	89UNTS37	101207

PARTY ONE	PARTY TWO	DATE	TOPIC	CITATION	NUMBER
USA (United States)	Panama	26 Jan 50	Claims and Debts	132UNTS233	101763
USA (United States)	Panama	24 May 50	Territory Boundary	241UNTS139	103430
USA (United States)	Panama	14 Sep 50	Land Transport	241UNTS159	103431
USA (United States)	Panama	14 Sep 50	Land Transport	124UNTS25	101664
USA (United States)	Panama	20 Dec 50	Tech Assistance	92UNTS167	101269
USA (United States)	Panama	26 Jan 51	Land Transport	137UNTS69	101849
USA (United States)	Panama	26 Feb 51	Sanitation	160UNTS153	102106
USA (United States)	Panama	30 Jul 51	Direct Aid	140UNTS321	101896
USA (United States)	Panama	23 Oct 51	Direct Aid	140UNTS3	101880
USA (United States)	Panama	30 Jun 52	Tech Assistance	181UNTS121	102404
USA (United States)	Panama	21 Jul 52	Tech Assistance	181UNTS285	102417
USA (United States)	Panama	08 Aug 52	Air Transport	181UNTS257	102415
USA (United States)	Panama	26 Jun 53	Tech Assistance	215UNTS77	102912
USA (United States)	Panama	25 Mar 54	Specific Property	232UNTS289	103243
USA (United States)	Panama	11 May 54	Direct Aid	236UNTS107	103319
USA (United States)	Panama	25 Jan 55	General Ad Hoc	243UNTS211	103454
USA (United States)	Panama	25 May 56	Visas	268UNTS333	103866
USA (United States)	Panama	01 Aug 56	Telecommunications	281UNTS49	104068
USA (United States)	Panama	05 Aug 57	Visas	299UNTS113	104309
USA (United States)	Panama	20 May 59	Milit Assistance	346UNTS235	104983
USA (United States)	Panama	24 Jun 59	Scientific Project	479UNTS145	106950
USA (United States)	Panama	31 Oct 60	Admin Cooperation	405UNTS63	105823
USA (United States)	Panama	23 Jan 61	Admin Cooperation	445UNTS135	106382
USA (United States)	Panama	11 Dec 61	General Aid	445UNTS161	106384
USA (United States)	Panama	23 May 62	Milit Assistance	458UNTS225	106604
USA (United States)	Panama	30 Aug 63	Taxation	488UNTS11	107116
USA (United States)	Panama	30 Oct 63	General Aid	530UNTS3	107668
USA (United States)	Panama	15 Feb 66	Scientific Project	586UNTS27	108494
USA (United States)	Panama	16 Nov 66	Gen Communications	OUNTSO	109688
USA (United States)	Panama	22 Feb 68	Air Transport	OUNTSO	110006
USA (United States)	Panama	20 Mar 69	Scientific Project	OUNTSO	110155
USA (United States)	Panama	04 Mar 70	Commodity Trade	OUNTSO	110626
USA (United States)	Paraguay	22 May 42	Sanitation	124UNTS243	200423
USA (United States)	Paraguay	28 Nov 42	Admin Cooperation	101UNTS173	200292
USA (United States)	Paraguay	27 Oct 43	Military Mission	29UNTS391	200174
USA (United States)	Paraguay	10 Dec 43	Military Mission	21UNTS305	200131
USA (United States)	Paraguay	12 Sep 46	General Trade	125UNTS179	101677
USA (United States)	Paraguay	28 Feb 47	Air Transport	44UNTS25	100676
USA (United States)	Paraguay	03 Mar 47	Tech Assistance	135UNTS156	101819
USA (United States)	Paraguay	01 Jan 48	Scientific Project	89UNTS191	101217
USA (United States)	Paraguay	12 Mar 48	Education	162UNTS30	102131
USA (United States)	Paraguay	30 Jun 48	Sanitation	124UNTS34	101665
USA (United States)	Paraguay	27 Nov 50	Direct Aid	122UNTS147	101644
USA (United States)	Paraguay	29 Dec 50	Tech Assistance	122UNTS157	101645
USA (United States)	Paraguay	30 Jul 51	Military Mission	178UNTS163	102340
USA (United States)	Paraguay	22 Jul 55	Military Mission	265UNTS3	103802
USA (United States)	Paraguay	22 Jul 55	Military Mission	265UNTS15	103803
USA (United States)	Paraguay	28 Oct 55	Claims and Debts	273UNTS97	103946
USA (United States)	Paraguay	02 May 56	US Agri Commod Aid	268UNTS299	103863
USA (United States)	Paraguay	11 May 56	Visas	269UNTS33	103870
USA (United States)	Paraguay	04 Apr 57	Taxation	283UNTS193	104117
USA (United States)	Paraguay	04 Apr 57	Education	284UNTS161	104135
USA (United States)	Paraguay	06 Oct 60	Gen Communications	393UNTS281	105662
USA (United States)	Paraguay	07 Jul 61	US Agri Commod Aid	433UNTS53	106231
USA (United States)	Paraguay	26 Sep 61	General Aid	461UNTS91	106653
USA (United States)	Paraguay	16 Jan 62	Scientific Project	433UNTS169	106240
USA (United States)	Paraguay	25 Aug 62	Milit Assistance	461UNTS207	106665
USA (United States)	Paraguay	24 Nov 62	US Agri Commod Aid	471UNTS49	106821
USA (United States)	Paraguay	20 Aug 63	Education	531UNTS197	107704
USA (United States)	Paraguay	16 Sep 63	US Agri Commod Aid	494UNTS101	107229
USA (United States)	Paraguay	14 Nov 63	US Agri Commod Aid	505UNTS87	107366
USA (United States)	Paraguay	10 Feb 64	Milit Assistance	511UNTS53	107426
USA (United States)	Paraguay	05 Sep 64	US Agri Commod Aid	530UNTS225	107685
USA (United States)	Paraguay	11 Apr 66	Milit Assistance	578UNTS99	108389
USA (United States)	Paraguay	18 Apr 66	Gen Communications	586UNTS189	108503

PARTY ONE	PARTY TWO	DATE	TOPIC	CITATION	NUMBER
USA (United States)	Paraguay	27 Apr 66	US Agri Commod Aid	578UNTS121	108391
USA (United States)	Paraguay	04 Nov 66	Direct Aid	OUNTSO	109620
USA (United States)	Paraguay	07 Jun 69	US Agri Commod Aid	OUNTSO	110333
USA (United States)	Peru	11 Mar 42	Military Mission	117UNTS266	200375
USA (United States)	Peru	21 Apr 42	Scientific Project	89UNTS317	200260
USA (United States)	Peru	07 May 42	General Trade	103UNTS219	200316
USA (United States)	Peru	11 May 42	Sanitation	136UNTS353	200447
USA (United States)	Peru	24 Aug 42	Education	24UNTS153	200139
USA (United States)	Peru	20 May 43	Non-IBRD Project	100UNTS259	200288
USA (United States)	Peru	20 Dec 43	Military Mission	117UNTS285	200376
USA (United States)	Peru	31 Mar 44	Military Mission	109UNTS165	200357
USA (United States)	Peru	04 Apr 44	Scientific Project	89UNTS291	200258
USA (United States)	Peru	15 Apr 44	Education	150UNTS317	200479
USA (United States)	Peru	02 May 44	Military Mission	109UNTS211	200361
USA (United States)	Peru	10 Jul 44	Military Mission	117UNTS291	200377
USA (United States)	Peru	12 Jun 45	Milit Servic/Citiz	121UNTS283	200406
USA (United States)	Peru	19 Aug 46	Military Mission	109UNTS15	101485
USA (United States)	Peru	07 Oct 46	Military Mission	7UNTS71	100092
USA (United States)	Peru	22 Nov 46	Non-IBRD Project	100UNTS170	101396
USA (United States)	Peru	27 Dec 46	Air Transport	152UNTS93	102013
USA (United States)	Peru	27 Dec 46	Air Transport	26UNTS227	100390
USA (United States)	Peru	19 Apr 47	Sanitation	136UNTS284	101840
USA (United States)	Peru	02 Mar 48	Military Mission	109UNTS9	101484
USA (United States)	Peru	30 Jun 48	Education	150UNTS45	101962
USA (United States)	Peru	25 Mar 49	Scientific Project	89UNTS15	101205
USA (United States)	Peru	20 Jun 49	Military Mission	92UNTS249	101276
USA (United States)	Peru	28 Sep 51	General Trade	160UNTS35	102099
USA (United States)	Peru	04 Feb 52	Education	121UNTS255	200403
USA (United States)	Peru	22 Feb 52	Milit Assistance	165UNTS31	102166
USA (United States)	Peru	09 Apr 52	Tech Assistance	184UNTS295	102454
USA (United States)	Peru	13 Apr 54	Tech Assistance	236UNTS87	103318
USA (United States)	Peru	25 Oct 54	Direct Aid	238UNTS247	103368
USA (United States)	Peru	31 Dec 54	Non-ILO Labor	251UNTS51	103533
USA (United States)	Peru	07 Jan 55	Milit Assistance	261UNTS321	103730
USA (United States)	Peru	07 Feb 55	Direct Aid	241UNTS63	103424
USA (United States)	Peru	16 Mar 55	Claims and Debts	252UNTS151	103564
USA (United States)	Peru	30 Apr 55	General Aid	263UNTS309	103780
USA (United States)	Peru	28 Oct 55	Military Mission	239UNTS181	103378
USA (United States)	Peru	25 Jan 56	Atomic Energy	240UNTS425	103417
USA (United States)	Peru	03 May 56	Direct Aid	272UNTS59	103931
USA (United States)	Peru	07 May 56	US Agri Commod Aid	268UNTS285	103862
USA (United States)	Peru	08 May 56	Direct Aid	278UNTS117	104028
USA (United States)	Peru	06 Sep 56	Military Mission	277UNTS231	104009
USA (United States)	Peru	09 Oct 56	Visas	288UNTS165	104204
USA (United States)	Peru	17 Apr 57	Scientific Project	283UNTS3	104102
USA (United States)	Peru	02 May 57	US Agri Commod Aid	283UNTS55	104106
USA (United States)	Peru	19 Jul 57	Direct Aid	289UNTS271	104223
USA (United States)	Peru	09 Apr 58	US Agri Commod Aid	316UNTS37	104576
USA (United States)	Peru	15 Jun 59	Milit Assistance	346UNTS279	104987
USA (United States)	Peru	22 Aug 59	Atomic Energy	357UNTS99	105109
USA (United States)	Peru	12 Feb 60	US Agri Commod Aid	372UNTS83	105290
USA (United States)	Peru	26 Feb 60	Milit Assistance	394UNTS141	105674
USA (United States)	Peru	15 Jul 60	Military Mission	384UNTS159	105517
USA (United States)	Peru	13 Feb 61	Visas	406UNTS177	105848
USA (United States)	Peru	25 Jan 62	Tech Assistance	473UNTS57	106855
USA (United States)	Peru	05 Mar 62	General Economic	446UNTS65	106404
USA (United States)	Peru	20 Mar 62	US Agri Commod Aid	445UNTS61	106377
USA (United States)	Peru	20 Dec 62	Milit Installation	471UNTS75	106822
USA (United States)	Peru	23 Sep 63	US Agri Commod Aid	488UNTS91	107121
USA (United States)	Peru	13 Feb 64	US Agri Commod Aid	511UNTS119	107431
USA (United States)	Peru	07 Jul 64	Scientific Project	530UNTS113	107676
USA (United States)	Peru	28 Jan 65	Education	587UNTS273	108513
USA (United States)	Peru	11 Aug 65	Gen Communications	564UNTS135	108225
USA (United States)	Peru	23 Apr 70	Visas	OUNTSO	110776
USA (United States)	Philippines	01 Apr 46	Specific Property	1PTS393	465007

PARTY ONE	PARTY TWO	DATE	TOPIC	CITATION	NUMBER
USA (United States)	Philippines	04 Jul 46	General Amity	7UNTS3	100088
USA (United States)	Philippines	04 Jul 46	General Amity	6UNTS335	100086
USA (United States)	Philippines	04 Jul 46	General Trade	43UNTS135	100668
USA (United States)	Philippines	04 Aug 46	General Trade	1PTS243	465001
USA (United States)	Philippines	08 Aug 46	General Trade	1PTS251	465002
USA (United States)	Philippines	22 Aug 46	Reparations	1PTS255	465003
USA (United States)	Philippines	11 Sep 46	Milit Assistance	43UNTS231	100670
USA (United States)	Philippines	17 Sep 46	IGO Establishment	15UNTS249	100240
USA (United States)	Philippines	04 Oct 46	Specif Goods/Equip	1PTS271	465004
USA (United States)	Philippines	19 Oct 46	Telecommunications	43UNTS263	100672
USA (United States)	Philippines	16 Nov 46	Dispute Settlement	1PTS321	465006
USA (United States)	Philippines	16 Nov 46	Air Transport	7UNTS151	100097
USA (United States)	Philippines	14 Feb 47	Non-IBRD Project	16UNTS3	100245
USA (United States)	Philippines	14 Mar 47	Milit Installation	43UNTS271	100673
USA (United States)	Philippines	14 Mar 47	Non-IBRD Project	16UNTS31	100247
USA (United States)	Philippines	14 Mar 47	Consul/Citizenship	45UNTS23	100690
USA (United States)	Philippines	21 Mar 47	Milit Assistance	45UNTS47	100691
USA (United States)	Philippines	12 May 47	Scientific Project	16UNTS137	100254
USA (United States)	Philippines	12 May 47	Scientific Project	16UNTS123	100253
USA (United States)	Philippines	12 May 47	Scientific Project	16UNTS109	100252
USA (United States)	Philippines	16 May 47	Non-ILO Labor	280UNTS177	104057
USA (United States)	Philippines	04 Sep 47	Gen Communications	1PTS435	465009
USA (United States)	Philippines	17 Sep 47	Postal Service	206UNTS249	102790
USA (United States)	Philippines	30 Sep 47	Postal Service	1PTS445	465010
USA (United States)	Philippines	12 Oct 47	Territory Boundary	1PTS519	465011
USA (United States)	Philippines	19 Dec 47	Territory Boundary	1PTS639	465012
USA (United States)	Philippines	24 Dec 47	Territory Boundary	1PTS645	465013
USA (United States)	Philippines	23 Mar 48	Education	43UNTS247	100671
USA (United States)	Philippines	07 Jun 48	Admin Cooperation	73UNTS89	100947
USA (United States)	Philippines	23 Aug 48	Patents/Copyrights	82UNTS11	101080
USA (United States)	Philippines	27 Aug 48	Reparations	44UNTS13	100675
USA (United States)	Philippines	21 Oct 48	Patents/Copyrights	77UNTS197	101000
USA (United States)	Philippines	16 May 49	Milit Installation	67UNTS199	100878
USA (United States)	Philippines	07 Jun 49	Direct Aid	45UNTS63	100692
USA (United States)	Philippines	08 Aug 49	Milit Installation	163UNTS103	102144
USA (United States)	Philippines	20 Dec 49	Finance	2PTS517	465021
USA (United States)	Philippines	16 Mar 50	Air Transport	89UNTS199	101218
USA (United States)	Philippines	20 Apr 50	Specif Goods/Equip	2PTS553	465071
USA (United States)	Philippines	06 Nov 50	Finance	122UNTS63	101637
USA (United States)	Philippines	27 Apr 51	Direct Aid	174UNTS251	102290
USA (United States)	Philippines	30 Aug 51	Milit Assistance	177UNTS133	102315
USA (United States)	Philippines	07 Jan 52	Milit Assistance	179UNTS193	102368
USA (United States)	Philippines	19 Feb 52	Direct Aid	177UNTS307	102330
USA (United States)	Philippines	24 Nov 52	Visas	181UNTS155	102406
USA (United States)	Philippines	09 Mar 53	Milit Servic/Citiz	227UNTS101	103134
USA (United States)	Philippines	26 Jun 53	Milit Assistance	213UNTS77	102881
USA (United States)	Philippines	27 Apr 55	Direct Aid	261UNTS351	103733
USA (United States)	Philippines	27 Jul 55	Atomic Energy	239UNTS271	103385
USA (United States)	Philippines	06 Sep 55	Visas	238UNTS109	103356
USA (United States)	Philippines	28 Oct 55	Milit Installation	239UNTS165	103376
USA (United States)	Philippines	18 Oct 56	Taxation	280UNTS55	104050
USA (United States)	Philippines	06 Feb 57	Status of Forces	303UNTS237	104383
USA (United States)	Philippines	08 Apr 57	Specific Resources	303UNTS227	104382
USA (United States)	Philippines	18 Jun 57	Milit Installation	289UNTS289	104225
USA (United States)	Philippines	25 Jun 57	US Agri Commod Aid	289UNTS279	104224
USA (United States)	Philippines	01 Nov 57	Status of Forces	307UNTS39	104440
USA (United States)	Philippines	20 Feb 58	Status of Forces	303UNTS261	104385
USA (United States)	Philippines	15 May 58	Milit Assistance	316UNTS163	104583
USA (United States)	Philippines	03 Jun 58	US Agri Commod Aid	316UNTS3	104573
USA (United States)	Philippines	30 Jun 58	Direct Aid	321UNTS51	104653
USA (United States)	Philippines	17 Jul 58	Specific Property	335UNTS199	104787
USA (United States)	Philippines	21 Jan 59	Specif Claim/Waive	341UNTS255	104888
USA (United States)	Philippines	12 Oct 59	General Military	4PTS11	465042
USA (United States)	Philippines	07 Dec 59	Milit Installation	359UNTS227	105144
USA (United States)	Philippines	06 Dec 60	Other Economic	4PTS371	465045

PARTY ONE	PARTY TWO	DATE	TOPIC	CITATION	NUMBER
USA (United States)	Philippines	12 Mar 61	Postal Service	288UNTS285	104210
USA (United States)	Philippines	04 Oct 61	Specif Goods/Equip	433UNTS83	106232
USA (United States)	Philippines	31 Oct 61	Direct Aid	424UNTS129	106105
USA (United States)	Philippines	24 Nov 61	US Agri Commod Aid	433UNTS315	106251
USA (United States)	Philippines	21 Aug 62	Milit Assistance	461UNTS163	106660
USA (United States)	Philippines	11 Jan 63	Specific Resources	473UNTS43	106853
USA (United States)	Philippines	23 Mar 63	Education	474UNTS80	106873
USA (United States)	Philippines	06 May 63	Telecommunications	477UNTS67	106916
USA (United States)	Philippines	15 Aug 63	Tech Assistance	4PTS791	465055
USA (United States)	Philippines	30 Aug 63	Non-ILO Labor	489UNTS323	107147
USA (United States)	Philippines	08 Oct 63	Non-ILO Labor	4PTS811	465056
USA (United States)	Philippines	24 Feb 64	Commodity Trade	505UNTS283	107378
USA (United States)	Philippines	14 May 64	US Agri Commod Aid	526UNTS113	107604
USA (United States)	Philippines	05 Oct 64	Taxation	4PTS879	465064
USA (United States)	Philippines	12 Nov 64	Postal Service	574UNTS159	108349
USA (United States)	Philippines	10 Mar 65	Non-IBRD Project	0UNTS0	110124
USA (United States)	Philippines	10 Mar 65	Non-ILO Labor	4PTS925	465066
USA (United States)	Philippines	16 Mar 65	Status of Forces	542UNTS199	107890
USA (United States)	Philippines	23 Apr 65	US Agri Commod Aid	546UNTS157	107942
USA (United States)	Philippines	28 May 65	Visas	0UNTS0	110248
USA (United States)	Philippines	15 Jul 65	Non-IBRD Project	0UNTS0	110125
USA (United States)	Philippines	12 Aug 65	Milit Installation	579UNTS47	108397
USA (United States)	Philippines	10 Sep 65	Gen Communications	4PTS919	465065
USA (United States)	Philippines	05 Oct 65	General Trade	4PTS973	465067
USA (United States)	Philippines	15 Nov 65	Milit Assistance	574UNTS205	108350
USA (United States)	Philippines	16 Dec 65	General Military	4PTS1037	465068
USA (United States)	Philippines	20 Dec 65	Admin Cooperation	4PTS1041	465069
USA (United States)	Philippines	29 Dec 65	Taxation	4PTS1051	465070
USA (United States)	Philippines	26 Aug 66	Milit Installation	606UNTS259	108790
USA (United States)	Philippines	22 Dec 66	US Agri Commod Aid	591UNTS219	108559
USA (United States)	Philippines	22 Dec 66	Other Military	579UNTS203	108408
USA (United States)	Philippines	04 Jan 67	Customs	590UNTS51	108546
USA (United States)	Philippines	28 Mar 67	Water Transport	0UNTS0	109757
USA (United States)	Philippines	25 Apr 67	Tech Assistance	0UNTS0	109860
USA (United States)	Philippines	18 May 67	Non-IBRD Project	0UNTS0	110126
USA (United States)	Philippines	26 Jun 67	Non-IBRD Project	0UNTS0	110127
USA (United States)	Philippines	29 Jun 67	Claims and Debts	0UNTS0	109776
USA (United States)	Philippines	11 Aug 67	Non-IBRD Project	0UNTS0	110128
USA (United States)	Philippines	24 Aug 67	General Military	0UNTS0	109915
USA (United States)	Philippines	21 Sep 67	Commodity Trade	0UNTS0	109921
USA (United States)	Philippines	16 Oct 67	General Military	632UNTS113	109013
USA (United States)	Philippines	22 Dec 67	US Agri Commod Aid	0UNTS0	110133
USA (United States)	Philippines	23 Jan 68	Finance	0UNTS0	110003
USA (United States)	Philippines	30 Apr 68	Milit Installation	0UNTS0	110129
USA (United States)	Philippines	27 May 68	Non-ILO Labor	0UNTS0	109435
USA (United States)	Philippines	11 Jun 68	Non-IBRD Project	0UNTS0	110130
USA (United States)	Philippines	13 Jun 68	Atomic Energy	0UNTS0	110131
USA (United States)	Philippines	28 Dec 68	Milit Installation	0UNTS0	109436
USA (United States)	Philippines	24 Apr 69	Customs	0UNTS0	110403
USA (United States)	Philippines	24 Apr 69	Non-IBRD Project	0UNTS0	110132
USA (United States)	Philippines	05 Sep 69	Education	0UNTS0	110408
USA (United States)	Philippines	24 Mar 70	US Agri Commod Aid	0UNTS0	110692
USA (United States)	Poland	01 Jul 42	Milit Assistance	103UNTS267	200317
USA (United States)	Poland	25 Feb 43	Milit Servic/Citiz	13UNTS395	200086
USA (United States)	Poland	22 Apr 46	Loans and Credits	406UNTS215	105851
USA (United States)	Poland	24 Apr 46	General Economic	4UNTS155	100042
USA (United States)	Poland	29 Aug 46	Status of Forces	160UNTS11	102097
USA (United States)	Poland	30 Oct 48	Consul/Citizenship	15UNTS225	100238
USA (United States)	Poland	28 Jun 56	Claims and Debts	273UNTS79	103944
USA (United States)	Poland	07 Jun 57	Direct Aid	291UNTS41	104243
USA (United States)	Poland	12 Feb 58	Mass Media	304UNTS287	104403
USA (United States)	Poland	15 Feb 58	US Agri Commod Aid	307UNTS217	104452
USA (United States)	Poland	30 May 58	Mass Media	315UNTS231	104572
USA (United States)	Poland	10 Jun 59	US Agri Commod Aid	347UNTS41	104989
USA (United States)	Poland	16 Jul 60	Specif Claim/Waive	384UNTS169	105518

PARTY ONE	PARTY TWO	DATE	TOPIC	CITATION	NUMBER
USA (United States)	Poland	21 Jul 60	US Agri Commod Aid	380UNTS157	105456
USA (United States)	Poland	15 Dec 61	US Agri Commod Aid	434UNTS3	106252
USA (United States)	Poland	21 Jan 63	Visas	471UNTS151	106830
USA (United States)	Poland	01 Feb 63	US Agri Commod Aid	487UNTS143	107100
USA (United States)	Poland	03 Feb 64	US Agri Commod Aid	505UNTS245	107376
USA (United States)	Poland	03 Feb 64	US Agri Commod Aid	505UNTS215	107375
USA (United States)	Poland	24 Jun 65	Commodity Trade	593UNTS147	108581
USA (United States)	Poland	27 Sep 65	Air Transport	564UNTS169	108227
USA (United States)	Poland	15 Mar 67	Commodity Trade	0UNTS0	109856
USA (United States)	Poland	12 Jun 69	Specific Resources	0UNTS0	110335
USA (United States)	Portugal	28 Nov 44	Milit Assistance	183UNTS311	200508
USA (United States)	Portugal	06 Dec 45	Air Transport	3UNTS139	100028
USA (United States)	Portugal	17 May 46	Commodity Trade	126UNTS3	101678
USA (United States)	Portugal	30 May 46	Air Transport	174UNTS187	102285
USA (United States)	Portugal	26 Aug 46	Mostfavored Nation	13UNTS67	100203
USA (United States)	Portugal	28 Sep 48	Direct Aid	29UNTS213	100442
USA (United States)	Portugal	28 Sep 48	Mostfavored Nation	31UNTS139	100475
USA (United States)	Portugal	04 Aug 49	Reparations	181UNTS15	102394
USA (United States)	Portugal	24 Feb 50	Visas	92UNTS219	101274
USA (United States)	Portugal	05 Jan 51	Milit Assistance	133UNTS75	101782
USA (United States)	Portugal	06 Sep 51	Milit Assistance	237UNTS217	103348
USA (United States)	Portugal	08 Jan 52	General Military	207UNTS51	102799
USA (United States)	Portugal	09 Jul 52	Milit Assistance	180UNTS251	102389
USA (United States)	Portugal	01 Apr 53	Taxation	205UNTS41	102769
USA (United States)	Portugal	21 Jul 55	Atomic Energy	239UNTS283	103386
USA (United States)	Portugal	24 May 56	US Agri Commod Aid	268UNTS323	103865
USA (United States)	Portugal	07 Nov 56	Milit Assistance	277UNTS133	104003
USA (United States)	Portugal	12 Jan 59	Postal Service	343UNTS49	104921
USA (United States)	Portugal	19 Mar 60	Education	371UNTS131	105275
USA (United States)	Portugal	26 Sep 60	Milit Assistance	393UNTS257	105660
USA (United States)	Portugal	31 Oct 60	Patents/Copyrights	394UNTS127	105673
USA (United States)	Portugal	28 Nov 61	US Agri Commod Aid	434UNTS31	106253
USA (United States)	Portugal	05 Mar 62	General Trade	436UNTS101	106290
USA (United States)	Portugal	12 Mar 64	Commodity Trade	542UNTS3	107875
USA (United States)	Portugal	12 Nov 64	Specific Property	541UNTS251	107874
USA (United States)	Portugal	26 May 65	Gen Communications	546UNTS189	107945
USA (United States)	Portugal	23 Mar 67	Commodity Trade	0UNTS0	109857
USA (United States)	Portugal	03 Jul 69	Atomic Energy	0UNTS0	110337
USA (United States)	Romania	28 Jun 46	Other Military	148UNTS355	101944
USA (United States)	Romania	26 Feb 48	Admin Cooperation	48UNTS9	100738
USA (United States)	Romania	30 Mar 60	Claims and Debts	371UNTS163	105278
USA (United States)	Romania	09 Dec 60	Culture	401UNTS19	105759
USA (United States)	Romania	26 May 62	Visas	456UNTS265	106561
USA (United States)	Romania	02 Apr 63	Culture	474UNTS95	106874
USA (United States)	Romania	23 Dec 64	Health/Educ/Welfare	535UNTS359	107790
USA (United States)	Romania	18 Feb 67	Tech Assistance	0UNTS0	109849
USA (United States)	Romania	26 Nov 68	Education	0UNTS0	110402
USA (United States)	Romania	25 Apr 69	Visas	0UNTS0	110272
USA (United States)	Romania	03 Aug 69	Education	0UNTS0	110343
USA (United States)	Rwanda	09 Aug 65	Finance	0UNTS0	109895
USA (United States)	Saudi Arabia	17 Jan 51	Direct Aid	140UNTS335	101897
USA (United States)	Saudi Arabia	18 Jun 51	Milit Assistance	141UNTS67	101906
USA (United States)	Saudi Arabia	18 Jun 51	Specific Property	102UNTS73	101412
USA (United States)	Saudi Arabia	10 Nov 51	Scientific Project	180UNTS263	102390
USA (United States)	Saudi Arabia	10 Nov 52	Tech Assistance	181UNTS225	102412
USA (United States)	Saudi Arabia	10 Nov 52	Tech Assistance	181UNTS235	102413
USA (United States)	Saudi Arabia	10 Nov 52	Direct Aid	181UNTS307	102419
USA (United States)	Saudi Arabia	10 Nov 52	Direct Aid	181UNTS295	102418
USA (United States)	Saudi Arabia	15 Dec 52	Direct Aid	185UNTS55	102458
USA (United States)	Saudi Arabia	15 Dec 52	Tech Assistance	185UNTS67	102459
USA (United States)	Saudi Arabia	25 Jan 53	Education	201UNTS3	102706
USA (United States)	Saudi Arabia	29 Jun 53	Sanitation	206UNTS23	102784
USA (United States)	Saudi Arabia	02 Apr 57	Milit Installation	283UNTS97	104109
USA (United States)	Saudi Arabia	01 May 58	Direct Aid	315UNTS221	104571
USA (United States)	Saudi Arabia	13 Nov 62	Loans and Credits	488UNTS175	107127

PARTY ONE	PARTY TWO	DATE	TOPIC	CITATION	NUMBER
USA (United States)	Saudi Arabia	06 Jan 64	Telecommunications	531UNTS3	107689
USA (United States)	Saudi Arabia	05 Jun 65	Milit Installation	548UNTS285	107984
USA (United States)	Saudi Arabia	11 Nov 65	Milit Installation	606UNTS65	108775
USA (United States)	Saudi Arabia	19 Nov 65	Non-IBRD Project	580UNTS35	108419
USA (United States)	Saudi Arabia	25 Jul 68	Culture	0UNTS0	110401
USA (United States)	SEATO (SE Asia)	29 May 59	Sanitation	347UNTS77	104991
USA (United States)	Senegal	13 May 61	General Aid	409UNTS232	105888
USA (United States)	Senegal	20 Jul 62	Milit Assistance	458UNTS137	106596
USA (United States)	Senegal	17 Jan 63	General Aid	493UNTS97	107210
USA (United States)	Senegal	12 Jun 63	Finance	0UNTS0	109979
USA (United States)	Senegal	03 Jul 63	US Agri Commod Aid	527UNTS95	107620
USA (United States)	Sierra Leone	05 May 61	General Aid	409UNTS194	105885
USA (United States)	Sierra Leone	19 May 61	Admin Cooperation	409UNTS251	105890
USA (United States)	Sierra Leone	29 Dec 61	Direct Aid	434UNTS43	106254
USA (United States)	Sierra Leone	29 Jan 65	US Agri Commod Aid	542UNTS87	107882
USA (United States)	Sierra Leone	16 Aug 65	Telecommunications	579UNTS55	108398
USA (United States)	Sierra Leone	06 May 66	Admin Cooperation	594UNTS47	108593
USA (United States)	Sierra Leone	23 Jan 68	US Agri Commod Aid	0UNTS0	110004
USA (United States)	Sierra Leone	08 Apr 69	US Agri Commod Aid	0UNTS0	110158
USA (United States)	Singapore	25 Mar 66	Finance	580UNTS221	108425
USA (United States)	Singapore	30 Aug 66	General Trade	616UNTS242	108899
USA (United States)	Singapore	10 Jun 69	Extradition	0UNTS0	110404
USA (United States)	Somalia	04 Feb 61	Tech Assistance	433UNTS179	106241
USA (United States)	Somalia	17 Apr 62	Direct Aid	436UNTS107	106291
USA (United States)	Somalia	08 Jan 64	Claims and Debts	505UNTS165	107372
USA (United States)	Somalia	15 Mar 68	US Agri Commod Aid	0UNTS0	110008
USA (United States)	South Africa	31 Oct 42	Milit Servic/Citiz	105UNTS269	200338
USA (United States)	South Africa	17 Apr 45	Direct Aid	90UNTS267	200264
USA (United States)	South Africa	17 Apr 45	Reparations	90UNTS275	200265
USA (United States)	South Africa	13 Dec 46	Taxation	167UNTS171	102207
USA (United States)	South Africa	21 Mar 47	Milit Assistance	16UNTS47	100248
USA (United States)	South Africa	10 Apr 47	Taxation	167UNTS211	102208
USA (United States)	South Africa	23 May 47	Air Transport	66UNTS233	100857
USA (United States)	South Africa	18 Dec 47	Extradition	148UNTS85	101938
USA (United States)	South Africa	16 Nov 49	Admin Cooperation	73UNTS97	100948
USA (United States)	South Africa	09 Nov 51	Milit Assistance	160UNTS41	102100
USA (United States)	South Africa	26 Mar 52	Education	165UNTS187	102176
USA (United States)	South Africa	24 Jun 52	Milit Assistance	177UNTS241	102322
USA (United States)	South Africa	22 Feb 55	Air Transport	247UNTS247	103473
USA (United States)	South Africa	03 Apr 56	Visas	249UNTS395	103513
USA (United States)	South Africa	08 Jul 57	Atomic Energy	290UNTS147	104234
USA (United States)	South Africa	13 Sep 60	Specific Property	388UNTS65	105572
USA (United States)	Spain	02 Dec 44	Air Transport	89UNTS345	200262
USA (United States)	Spain	15 Jan 46	Air Transport	89UNTS241	101221
USA (United States)	Spain	11 Jul 46	Mostfavored Nation	13UNTS51	100201
USA (United States)	Spain	03 May 48	Finance	132UNTS155	101756
USA (United States)	Spain	08 May 50	Admin Cooperation	98UNTS175	101363
USA (United States)	Spain	21 Jan 52	Visas	160UNTS63	102102
USA (United States)	Spain	26 Sep 53	Direct Aid	207UNTS93	102802
USA (United States)	Spain	26 Sep 53	Milit Assistance	207UNTS61	102800
USA (United States)	Spain	26 Sep 53	Milit Assistance	207UNTS83	102801
USA (United States)	Spain	19 May 54	Tech Assistance	235UNTS87	103296
USA (United States)	Spain	30 Jul 54	Milit Assistance	235UNTS45	103295
USA (United States)	Spain	20 Apr 55	US Agri Commod Aid	239UNTS117	103374
USA (United States)	Spain	16 Jul 55	Postal Service	270UNTS211	103899
USA (United States)	Spain	19 Jul 55	Atomic Energy	239UNTS299	103387
USA (United States)	Spain	05 Mar 56	US Agri Commod Aid	271UNTS329	103924
USA (United States)	Spain	23 Oct 56	US Agri Commod Aid	277UNTS105	104001
USA (United States)	Spain	09 Mar 57	Milit Assistance	283UNTS89	104108
USA (United States)	Spain	16 Aug 57	Atomic Energy	307UNTS169	104449
USA (United States)	Spain	23 Sep 57	Air Transport	290UNTS261	104238
USA (United States)	Spain	27 Jan 58	US Agri Commod Aid	303UNTS247	104384
USA (United States)	Spain	16 Oct 58	Education	336UNTS153	104804
USA (United States)	Spain	13 Jan 59	US Agri Commod Aid	341UNTS241	104887
USA (United States)	Spain	23 Jun 59	Milit Assistance	354UNTS11	105049

PARTY ONE	PARTY TWO	DATE	TOPIC	CITATION	NUMBER
USA (United States)	Spain	13 Feb 60	Milit Installation	371UNTS185	105279
USA (United States)	Spain	18 Mar 60	Scientific Project	372UNTS13	105284
USA (United States)	Spain	22 Jun 60	US Agri Commod Aid	378UNTS3	105414
USA (United States)	Spain	21 Jul 60	Milit Assistance	393UNTS289	105663
USA (United States)	Spain	22 May 61	US Agri Commod Aid	409UNTS260	105891
USA (United States)	Spain	31 Dec 62	Commodity Trade	471UNTS99	106825
USA (United States)	Spain	16 Jul 63	Commodity Trade	488UNTS77	107120
USA (United States)	Spain	29 Jan 64	Specific Property	511UNTS61	107427
USA (United States)	Spain	18 Mar 64	Culture	535UNTS343	107789
USA (United States)	Spain	16 Jul 64	Water Transport	529UNTS187	107661
USA (United States)	Spain	26 Jan 65	Scientific Project	542UNTS81	107881
USA (United States)	Spain	01 Oct 65	Scientific Project	65SPBO611	460280
USA (United States)	Spain	14 Apr 66	Scientific Project	586UNTS79	108497
USA (United States)	Spain	14 Apr 66	Specific Property	579UNTS173	108406
USA (United States)	Spain	21 Apr 66	Milit Assistance	580UNTS231	108426
USA (United States)	Spain	13 Oct 67	Commodity Trade	0UNTS0	110049
USA (United States)	Spain	25 Jun 68	Non-IBRD Project	0UNTS0	110147
USA (United States)	Spain	15 Jul 68	General Economic	0UNTS0	110252
USA (United States)	Sudan	31 Mar 58	General Aid	308UNTS105	104458
USA (United States)	Sudan	17 Mar 59	Admin Cooperation	342UNTS13	104896
USA (United States)	Sudan	14 Nov 61	US Agri Commod Aid	434UNTS51	106255
USA (United States)	Sudan	31 Jan 63	US Agri Commod Aid	494UNTS119	107230
USA (United States)	Sudan	02 Mar 64	US Agri Commod Aid	524UNTS217	107575
USA (United States)	Sudan	13 Apr 66	US Agri Commod Aid	586UNTS39	108495
USA (United States)	Swaziland	29 Sep 67	Finance	0UNTS0	109924
USA (United States)	Sweden	16 Dec 44	Air Transport	6UNTS397	200041
USA (United States)	Sweden	04 Dec 45	Air Transport	6UNTS273	100080
USA (United States)	Sweden	30 Sep 46	Air Transport	42UNTS213	100649
USA (United States)	Sweden	30 Apr 47	Visas	84UNTS33	101116
USA (United States)	Sweden	24 Jun 47	General Economic	36UNTS25	100565
USA (United States)	Sweden	16 Dec 47	Admin Cooperation	73UNTS65	100944
USA (United States)	Sweden	03 Jul 48	Milit Occupation	27UNTS69	100400
USA (United States)	Sweden	03 Jul 48	Direct Aid	23UNTS101	100343
USA (United States)	Sweden	27 Jun 49	General Trade	49SOFM311	461085
USA (United States)	Sweden	25 May 50	General Trade	88UNTS43	101184
USA (United States)	Sweden	27 Jun 51	Milit Assistance	148UNTS77	101937
USA (United States)	Sweden	01 Jul 52	Milit Assistance	187UNTS3	102497
USA (United States)	Sweden	20 Nov 52	Education	177UNTS203	102319
USA (United States)	Sweden	06 Aug 54	Air Transport	221UNTS331	103014
USA (United States)	Sweden	22 Dec 54	Air Transport	228UNTS85	103143
USA (United States)	Sweden	18 Jan 56	Atomic Energy	240UNTS413	103416
USA (United States)	Sweden	05 Sep 61	General Economic	421UNTS241	106062
USA (United States)	Sweden	24 Oct 61	Extradition	494UNTS141	107231
USA (United States)	Sweden	05 Mar 62	Commodity Trade	459UNTS17	106610
USA (United States)	Sweden	04 Oct 62	Milit Assistance	462UNTS31	106669
USA (United States)	Sweden	22 Oct 63	Taxation	530UNTS247	107686
USA (United States)	Sweden	06 Jul 64	Water Transport	529UNTS287	107666
USA (United States)	Sweden	28 Jul 66	Atomic Energy	603UNTS61	108725
USA (United States)	Sweden	02 Jun 69	Telecommunications	0UNTS0	110277
USA (United States)	Switzerland	03 Aug 45	Air Transport	51UNTS233	200191
USA (United States)	Switzerland	22 Nov 46	Claims and Debts	14SWRS351	463111
USA (United States)	Switzerland	30 Apr 47	Specif Goods/Equip	42UNTS235	100652
USA (United States)	Switzerland	13 May 49	Air Transport	51UNTS129	100761
USA (United States)	Switzerland	21 Oct 49	Reparations	132UNTS163	101757
USA (United States)	Switzerland	24 Feb 50	Admin Cooperation	93UNTS3	101282
USA (United States)	Switzerland	13 Oct 50	General Trade	133UNTS33	101777
USA (United States)	Switzerland	24 May 51	Taxation	127UNTS227	101706
USA (United States)	Switzerland	09 Jul 51	Taxation	165UNTS51	102167
USA (United States)	Switzerland	08 Jun 55	General Trade	55SWRO579	462133
USA (United States)	Switzerland	18 Jul 55	Atomic Energy	239UNTS311	103388
USA (United States)	Switzerland	21 Jun 56	Atomic Energy	279UNTS41	104033
USA (United States)	Switzerland	29 Mar 60	General Trade	371UNTS155	105277
USA (United States)	Switzerland	13 Oct 61	Air Transport	459UNTS219	106625
USA (United States)	Switzerland	11 Jul 63	General Trade	487UNTS177	107102
USA (United States)	Switzerland	30 Jan 65	Atomic Energy	594UNTS55	108594

PARTY ONE	PARTY TWO	DATE	TOPIC	CITATION	NUMBER
USA (United States)	Switzerland	16 May 67	Gen Communications	0UNTS0	109768
USA (United States)	Switzerland	28 Oct 68	General Economic	0UNTS0	110084
USA (United States)	Syria	08 Sep 44	Recognition	124UNTS251	200424
USA (United States)	Syria	28 Apr 47	Air Transport	262UNTS121	103741
USA (United States)	Syria	09 Nov 61	US Agri Commod Aid	435UNTS75	106271
USA (United States)	Syria	18 Nov 63	US Agri Commod Aid	494UNTS169	107232
USA (United States)	Taiwan	02 Jun 42	Milit Assistance	14UNTS343	200092
USA (United States)	Taiwan	11 Jan 43	Privil/Immunities	10UNTS261	200066
USA (United States)	Taiwan	21 May 43	Status of Forces	14UNTS353	200093
USA (United States)	Taiwan	13 Jun 44	Status of Forces	107UNTS43	200350
USA (United States)	Taiwan	14 Jun 46	Milit Assistance	4UNTS253	100049
USA (United States)	Taiwan	28 Jun 46	Milit Assistance	34UNTS121	100532
USA (United States)	Taiwan	30 Aug 46	Direct Aid	12UNTS39	100179
USA (United States)	Taiwan	04 Nov 46	General Amity	25UNTS69	100359
USA (United States)	Taiwan	20 Dec 46	Air Transport	22UNTS87	100332
USA (United States)	Taiwan	29 Apr 47	Milit Assistance	0CTRC719	413029
USA (United States)	Taiwan	03 Sep 47	Status of Forces	9UNTS91	100126
USA (United States)	Taiwan	27 Oct 47	Direct Aid	12UNTS11	100178
USA (United States)	Taiwan	10 Nov 47	Education	0CTRC747	413030
USA (United States)	Taiwan	08 Dec 47	Milit Installation	70UNTS3	100895
USA (United States)	Taiwan	17 Mar 48	Reparations	76UNTS157	100987
USA (United States)	Taiwan	30 Apr 48	Direct Aid	0CTRC753	413031
USA (United States)	Taiwan	03 Jul 48	Mostfavored Nation	0CTRC767	413032
USA (United States)	Taiwan	03 Jul 48	Direct Aid	17UNTS119	100273
USA (United States)	Taiwan	05 Aug 48	IGO Establishment	82UNTS109	101087
USA (United States)	Taiwan	18 Nov 48	Direct Aid	198UNTS287	102672
USA (United States)	Taiwan	27 Jan 49	Direct Aid	0CTRC790	413036
USA (United States)	Taiwan	27 Mar 49	Direct Aid	0CTRC770	413033
USA (United States)	Taiwan	27 Jun 49	Tech Assistance	0CTRC783	413035
USA (United States)	Taiwan	26 Jan 50	Direct Aid	0CTRC772	413034
USA (United States)	Taiwan	19 Dec 50	Air Transport	0CTRC792	413037
USA (United States)	Taiwan	09 Feb 51	Milit Assistance	132UNTS273	101767
USA (United States)	Taiwan	02 Jan 52	Milit Assistance	181UNTS161	102407
USA (United States)	Taiwan	25 Jun 52	Direct Aid	136UNTS229	101837
USA (United States)	Taiwan	01 Nov 52	Admin Cooperation	0CTRC809	413039
USA (United States)	Taiwan	12 Dec 52	Direct Aid	0CTRC807	413038
USA (United States)	Taiwan	04 Feb 53	Patents/Copyrights	0CTRC815	413040
USA (United States)	Taiwan	14 May 54	Milit Installation	231UNTS165	103216
USA (United States)	Taiwan	26 Oct 54	Direct Aid	0CTRC823	413041
USA (United States)	Taiwan	10 Dec 54	General Military	248UNTS213	103496
USA (United States)	Taiwan	15 Apr 55	Air Transport	0CTRC827	413042
USA (United States)	Taiwan	18 Jul 55	Atomic Energy	235UNTS221	103304
USA (United States)	Taiwan	14 Oct 55	Milit Installation	268UNTS165	103857
USA (United States)	Taiwan	20 Feb 56	Visas	275UNTS73	103976
USA (United States)	Taiwan	03 Apr 56	Milit Assistance	268UNTS315	103864
USA (United States)	Taiwan	14 Aug 56	US Agri Commod Aid	281UNTS257	104083
USA (United States)	Taiwan	14 Sep 56	Loans and Credits	0CTRC868	413043
USA (United States)	Taiwan	21 Nov 56	Milit Installation	265UNTS241	103816
USA (United States)	Taiwan	27 Dec 56	Admin Cooperation	0CTRC874	413044
USA (United States)	Taiwan	03 May 57	Claims and Debts	0CTRC877	413045
USA (United States)	Taiwan	28 Jun 57	Loans and Credits	0CTRC880	413046
USA (United States)	Taiwan	30 Jul 57	Postal Service	300UNTS61	104331
USA (United States)	Taiwan	08 Oct 57	Postal Service	304UNTS241	104400
USA (United States)	Taiwan	30 Nov 57	Culture	0CTRC885	413047
USA (United States)	Taiwan	18 Apr 58	US Agri Commod Aid	308UNTS179	104461
USA (United States)	Taiwan	06 Aug 58	Milit Installation	462UNTS3	106666
USA (United States)	Taiwan	24 Dec 58	Loans and Credits	340UNTS251	104868
USA (United States)	Taiwan	07 Feb 59	Milit Assistance	341UNTS225	104885
USA (United States)	Taiwan	09 Jun 59	US Agri Commod Aid	353UNTS257	105046
USA (United States)	Taiwan	08 Jul 59	Milit Assistance	354UNTS47	105052
USA (United States)	Taiwan	22 Jul 59	Milit Assistance	357UNTS293	105121
USA (United States)	Taiwan	02 Dec 59	Atomic Energy	361UNTS115	105175
USA (United States)	Taiwan	15 Apr 60	Milit Installation	462UNTS19	106667
USA (United States)	Taiwan	30 Aug 60	US Agri Commod Aid	388UNTS191	105579
USA (United States)	Taiwan	21 Jul 61	US Agri Commod Aid	416UNTS101	105998

PARTY ONE	PARTY TWO	DATE	TOPIC	CITATION	NUMBER
USA (United States)	Taiwan	28 Feb 62	Milit Installation	462UNTS25	106668
USA (United States)	Taiwan	16 Apr 62	General Trade	445UNTS249	106392
USA (United States)	Taiwan	27 Apr 62	US Agri Commod Aid	436UNTS25	106287
USA (United States)	Taiwan	15 Aug 62	Loans and Credits	460UNTS237	106643
USA (United States)	Taiwan	31 Aug 62	US Agri Commod Aid	460UNTS247	106644
USA (United States)	Taiwan	19 Nov 62	US Agri Commod Aid	459UNTS263	106629
USA (United States)	Taiwan	19 Oct 63	Commodity Trade	494UNTS27	107224
USA (United States)	Taiwan	19 Dec 63	Status of Forces	527UNTS69	107617
USA (United States)	Taiwan	23 Apr 64	Health/Educ/Welfare	524UNTS141	107570
USA (United States)	Taiwan	03 Jun 64	US Agri Commod Aid	526UNTS257	107610
USA (United States)	Taiwan	19 Dec 64	Status of Forces	532UNTS313	107725
USA (United States)	Taiwan	31 Dec 64	US Agri Commod Aid	532UNTS59	107712
USA (United States)	Taiwan	31 Dec 64	US Agri Commod Aid	532UNTS29	107711
USA (United States)	Taiwan	09 Apr 65	General Economic	546UNTS81	107939
USA (United States)	Taiwan	06 Mar 67	Water Transport	0UNTS0	109753
USA (United States)	Taiwan	01 Apr 67	Water Transport	0UNTS0	109758
USA (United States)	Taiwan	08 Jun 67	Water Transport	0UNTS0	109904
USA (United States)	Taiwan	12 Oct 67	Commodity Trade	0UNTS0	110047
USA (United States)	Taiwan	12 Dec 67	US Agri Commod Aid	0UNTS0	110062
USA (United States)	Taiwan	12 Dec 67	US Agri Commod Aid	0UNTS0	110061
USA (United States)	Taiwan	15 Dec 67	Loans and Credits	0UNTS0	109989
USA (United States)	Taiwan	18 Jun 68	Milit Assistance	0UNTS0	110146
USA (United States)	Taiwan	16 Dec 68	Milit Assistance	0UNTS0	110256
USA (United States)	Taiwan	23 Jan 69	Scientific Project	0UNTS0	110264
USA (United States)	Taiwan	18 Jun 69	Milit Installation	0UNTS0	110334
USA (United States)	Taiwan	22 Aug 69	Education	0UNTS0	110405
USA (United States)	Tanganyika	21 Jul 61	Direct Aid	445UNTS33	106374
USA (United States)	Tanganyika	14 Nov 63	Claims and Debts	493UNTS75	107208
USA (United States)	Tanganyika	09 Dec 63	Tech Assistance	526UNTS301	107612
USA (United States)	Tanzania	06 Dec 65	Consul/Citizenship	592UNTS51	108568
USA (United States)	Tanzania	08 Feb 68	General Economic	0UNTS0	110005
USA (United States)	Thailand	26 Feb 47	Air Transport	16UNTS17	100246
USA (United States)	Thailand	08 May 47	Air Transport	42UNTS241	100653
USA (United States)	Thailand	05 Sep 47	Admin Cooperation	73UNTS57	100943
USA (United States)	Thailand	01 Jul 50	Education	81UNTS61	101063
USA (United States)	Thailand	19 Sep 50	Tech Assistance	132UNTS199	101761
USA (United States)	Thailand	17 Oct 50	Milit Assistance	79UNTS41	101030
USA (United States)	Thailand	29 Dec 51	Milit Assistance	179UNTS113	102360
USA (United States)	Thailand	03 Dec 53	Tech Assistance	213UNTS91	102882
USA (United States)	Thailand	11 Aug 54	Commodity Trade	234UNTS155	103281
USA (United States)	Thailand	01 Sep 54	Claims and Debts	237UNTS209	103347
USA (United States)	Thailand	21 Jun 55	US Agri Commod Aid	262UNTS87	103738
USA (United States)	Thailand	09 Sep 55	Commodity Trade	264UNTS285	103799
USA (United States)	Thailand	14 Nov 55	Commodity Trade	239UNTS201	103380
USA (United States)	Thailand	13 Mar 56	Atomic Energy	253UNTS105	103579
USA (United States)	Thailand	04 Mar 57	US Agri Commod Aid	279UNTS235	104043
USA (United States)	Thailand	19 May 59	Milit Assistance	346UNTS271	104986
USA (United States)	Thailand	23 Dec 60	IGO Establishment	405UNTS135	105830
USA (United States)	Thailand	28 Nov 61	Direct Aid	434UNTS77	106256
USA (United States)	Thailand	12 Jan 62	Postal Service	459UNTS95	106615
USA (United States)	Thailand	31 May 62	Postal Service	459UNTS135	106619
USA (United States)	Thailand	25 Apr 63	Sanitation	476UNTS115	106906
USA (United States)	Thailand	24 May 63	Education	477UNTS123	106918
USA (United States)	Thailand	29 May 66	General Amity	0UNTS0	109345
USA (United States)	Togo	22 Dec 60	Direct Aid	401UNTS33	105760
USA (United States)	Togo	20 Mar 62	Admin Cooperation	445UNTS79	106378
USA (United States)	Togo	05 Sep 62	General Aid	461UNTS47	106650
USA (United States)	Togo	08 Feb 66	General Amity	0UNTS0	109677
USA (United States)	Trieste	15 Oct 48	Direct Aid	29UNTS249	100443
USA (United States)	Trieste	11 Feb 49	Direct Aid	79UNTS123	101036
USA (United States)	Trinidad/Tobago	08 Oct 62	Air Transport	462UNTS145	106675
USA (United States)	Trinidad/Tobago	15 Jan 63	Finance	471UNTS141	106829
USA (United States)	Trinidad/Tobago	05 Dec 64	Milit Installation	535UNTS331	107788
USA (United States)	Trinidad/Tobago	21 Jul 69	Non-ILO Labor	0UNTS0	110339
USA (United States)	Tunisia	26 Mar 57	General Aid	283UNTS117	104111

PARTY ONE	PARTY TWO	DATE	TOPIC	CITATION	NUMBER
USA (United States)	Tunisia	28 Jun 57	Direct Aid	289UNTS301	104226
USA (United States)	Tunisia	18 Mar 59	Admin Cooperation	344UNTS179	104948
USA (United States)	Tunisia	30 Jun 61	US Agri Commod Aid	434UNTS85	106257
USA (United States)	Tunisia	13 Feb 62	Direct Aid	442UNTS155	106346
USA (United States)	Tunisia	16 Feb 62	US Agri Commod Aid	442UNTS161	106347
USA (United States)	Tunisia	14 Sep 62	US Agri Commod Aid	461UNTS31	106649
USA (United States)	Tunisia	29 Oct 62	Direct Aid	462UNTS201	106679
USA (United States)	Tunisia	18 Nov 63	Education	494UNTS193	107233
USA (United States)	Tunisia	07 Apr 64	US Agri Commod Aid	527UNTS3	107613
USA (United States)	Tunisia	17 Feb 65	US Agri Commod Aid	542UNTS125	107885
USA (United States)	Tunisia	30 Jul 66	US Agri Commod Aid	601UNTS133	108692
USA (United States)	Tunisia	26 Sep 66	Scientific Project	616UNTS259	108900
USA (United States)	Tunisia	17 Mar 67	US Agri Commod Aid	0UNTS0	109898
USA (United States)	Tunisia	06 Nov 67	US Agri Commod Aid	0UNTS0	110056
USA (United States)	Tunisia	17 May 68	US Agri Commod Aid	0UNTS0	110019
USA (United States)	Tunisia	17 Jul 68	Scientific Project	0UNTS0	110149
USA (United States)	Tunisia	24 Dec 68	Commodity Trade	0UNTS0	110261
USA (United States)	Tunisia	11 Jul 69	US Agri Commod Aid	0UNTS0	110338
USA (United States)	Tunisia	18 Dec 69	US Agri Commod Aid	0UNTS0	110510
USA (United States)	Turkey	22 Apr 44	Customs	109UNTS279	200364
USA (United States)	Turkey	23 Feb 45	Direct Aid	121UNTS165	200398
USA (United States)	Turkey	12 Feb 46	Air Transport	13UNTS3	100196
USA (United States)	Turkey	27 Feb 46	Loans and Credits	46TURG1005	466117
USA (United States)	Turkey	07 May 46	Milit Assistance	6UNTS293	100083
USA (United States)	Turkey	12 Jul 47	Direct Aid	7UNTS299	100106
USA (United States)	Turkey	04 Jul 48	Direct Aid	24UNTS67	100351
USA (United States)	Turkey	04 Jul 48	Mostfavored Nation	34UNTS185	100536
USA (United States)	Turkey	27 Dec 49	Direct Aid	98UNTS141	101361
USA (United States)	Turkey	21 Jan 50	Direct Aid	50TURG3003	466118
USA (United States)	Turkey	15 Nov 51	Direct Aid	177UNTS315	102331
USA (United States)	Turkey	07 Jan 52	Milit Assistance	179UNTS121	102361
USA (United States)	Turkey	23 Jun 54	Status of Forces	233UNTS189	103263
USA (United States)	Turkey	23 Jun 54	Taxation	222UNTS161	103027
USA (United States)	Turkey	01 Jul 54	Milit Assistance	234UNTS147	103280
USA (United States)	Turkey	15 Nov 54	Commodity Trade	238UNTS135	103358
USA (United States)	Turkey	25 Apr 55	Milit Assistance	263UNTS299	103779
USA (United States)	Turkey	26 May 55	Milit Assistance	262UNTS97	103739
USA (United States)	Turkey	10 Jun 55	Atomic Energy	238UNTS149	103359
USA (United States)	Turkey	29 Jun 55	Milit Assistance	269UNTS97	103878
USA (United States)	Turkey	11 Oct 55	Visas	272UNTS145	103935
USA (United States)	Turkey	12 Mar 56	US Agri Commod Aid	272UNTS21	103929
USA (United States)	Turkey	18 May 56	Patents/Copyrights	283UNTS167	104115
USA (United States)	Turkey	12 Nov 56	US Agri Commod Aid	282UNTS77	104093
USA (United States)	Turkey	23 Nov 56	Direct Aid	290UNTS273	104239
USA (United States)	Turkey	15 Jan 57	Claims and Debts	280UNTS79	104053
USA (United States)	Turkey	12 Sep 57	Direct Aid	58TURG1004	466119
USA (United States)	Turkey	20 Jan 58	US Agri Commod Aid	304UNTS15	104389
USA (United States)	Turkey	06 Sep 58	Loans and Credits	336UNTS85	104800
USA (United States)	Turkey	14 Oct 58	Milit Assistance	336UNTS145	104803
USA (United States)	Turkey	13 Feb 59	US Agri Commod Aid	340UNTS235	104867
USA (United States)	Turkey	05 Mar 59	General Military	327UNTS293	104727
USA (United States)	Turkey	05 May 59	Milit Assistance	355UNTS341	105085
USA (United States)	Turkey	26 May 59	Direct Aid	354UNTS57	105053
USA (United States)	Turkey	20 Aug 59	Claims and Debts	61TURG2207	466120
USA (United States)	Turkey	29 Aug 59	Claims and Debts	61TURG2207	466121
USA (United States)	Turkey	28 Oct 59	Milit Assistance	360UNTS265	105162
USA (United States)	Turkey	13 Nov 59	Milit Assistance	361UNTS3	105168
USA (United States)	Turkey	30 Nov 59	Tech Assistance	361UNTS107	105174
USA (United States)	Turkey	22 Dec 59	US Agri Commod Aid	367UNTS57	105225
USA (United States)	Turkey	02 Mar 60	Milit Assistance	372UNTS37	105286
USA (United States)	Turkey	31 Dec 60	Loans and Credits	61TURG2407	466122
USA (United States)	Turkey	09 Jan 61	General Economic	61TURG1707	466123
USA (United States)	Turkey	11 Jan 61	US Agri Commod Aid	405UNTS173	105833
USA (United States)	Turkey	21 Jan 61	Loans and Credits	61TURG2407	466124
USA (United States)	Turkey	07 Feb 61	Atomic Energy	61TURG509	466040

PARTY ONE	PARTY TWO	DATE	TOPIC	CITATION	NUMBER
USA (United States)	Turkey	29 Jul 61	US Agri Commod Aid	416UNTS151	106001
USA (United States)	Turkey	08 Feb 62	Loans and Credits	63TURG106	466125
USA (United States)	Turkey	29 Mar 62	Loans and Credits	63TURG106	466126
USA (United States)	Turkey	23 Jul 62	Loans and Credits	63TURG106	466127
USA (United States)	Turkey	27 Aug 62	General Aid	461UNTS55	106651
USA (United States)	Turkey	23 Nov 62	Loans and Credits	63TURG404	466128
USA (United States)	Turkey	07 Dec 62	Loans and Credits	63TURG504	466129
USA (United States)	Turkey	21 Feb 63	US Agri Commod Aid	473UNTS311	106867
USA (United States)	Turkey	13 May 63	Loans and Credits	65TURG1506	466130
USA (United States)	Turkey	15 Jul 63	Loans and Credits	63TURG2809	466131
USA (United States)	Turkey	11 Sep 63	Loans and Credits	63TURG2509	466132
USA (United States)	Turkey	15 Oct 63	Loans and Credits	64TURG904	466133
USA (United States)	Turkey	17 Jul 64	Commodity Trade	530UNTS25	107670
USA (United States)	Turkey	02 Apr 66	US Agri Commod Aid	0UNTS0	109678
USA (United States)	Turkey	24 Sep 68	Status of Forces	0UNTS0	110079
USA (United States)	Turkey	12 Nov 68	Milit Installation	0UNTS0	110087
USA (United States)	Turkey	06 Feb 69	Commodity Trade	0UNTS0	110267
USA (United States)	Turkey	03 Nov 69	US Agri Commod Aid	0UNTS0	110452
USA (United States)	Turkey	16 Mar 70	US Agri Commod Aid	0UNTS0	110628
USA (United States)	Uganda	16 Nov 64	General Aid	586UNTS143	108501
USA (United States)	Uganda	29 May 65	Claims and Debts	546UNTS209	107948
USA (United States)	UK Great Britain	27 Jul 42	Status of Forces	117UNTS311	200378
USA (United States)	UK Great Britain	30 Sep 42	Milit Servic/Citiz	13UNTS169	200077
USA (United States)	UK Great Britain	03 Nov 42	Admin Cooperation	109UNTS127	200354
USA (United States)	UK Great Britain	30 Apr 43	Specific Resources	28UNTS341	200159
USA (United States)	UK Great Britain	10 May 43	Postal Service	147UNTS109	200473
USA (United States)	UK Great Britain	19 Aug 43	Atomic Energy	214UNTS341	200527
USA (United States)	UK Great Britain	24 Sep 43	Admin Cooperation	139UNTS373	200463
USA (United States)	UK Great Britain	01 Dec 43	Scientific Project	3UNTS209	100033
USA (United States)	UK Great Britain	10 Mar 44	Patents/Copyrights	5UNTS205	200030
USA (United States)	UK Great Britain	28 Mar 44	Status of Forces	15UNTS413	200104
USA (United States)	UK Great Britain	16 Apr 45	Taxation	6UNTS359	200039
USA (United States)	UK Great Britain	16 Apr 45	Taxation	6UNTS189	100076
USA (United States)	UK Great Britain	15 Jun 45	Reparations	89UNTS327	200261
USA (United States)	UK Great Britain	05 Nov 45	IGO Establishment	138UNTS75	101861
USA (United States)	UK Great Britain	06 Dec 45	Finance	126UNTS13	101679
USA (United States)	UK Great Britain	10 Dec 45	Refugees	3UNTS177	100030
USA (United States)	UK Great Britain	11 Feb 46	Air Transport	3UNTS253	100036
USA (United States)	UK Great Britain	21 Feb 46	General Trade	6UNTS137	100073
USA (United States)	UK Great Britain	01 Mar 46	Commodity Trade	3UNTS293	100037
USA (United States)	UK Great Britain	27 Mar 46	Milit Assistance	4UNTS2	100039
USA (United States)	UK Great Britain	27 Mar 46	Patents/Copyrights	4UNTS101	100040
USA (United States)	UK Great Britain	06 May 46	Admin Cooperation	99UNTS199	101381
USA (United States)	UK Great Britain	07 May 46	Water Transport	6UNTS285	100082
USA (United States)	UK Great Britain	31 Jul 46	Air Transport	42UNTS199	100648
USA (United States)	UK Great Britain	02 Dec 46	Milit Occupation	7UNTS163	100098
USA (United States)	UK Great Britain	23 Jan 47	Status of Forces	15UNTS281	100244
USA (United States)	UK Great Britain	23 May 47	Specific Property	11UNTS211	100159
USA (United States)	UK Great Britain	09 Oct 47	Milit Assistance	34UNTS129	100533
USA (United States)	UK Great Britain	13 Oct 47	Air Transport	66UNTS269	100858
USA (United States)	UK Great Britain	23 Oct 47	Territory Boundary	66UNTS277	100859
USA (United States)	UK Great Britain	30 Oct 47	General Economic	126UNTS39	101680
USA (United States)	UK Great Britain	24 Feb 48	Milit Installation	73UNTS143	100951
USA (United States)	UK Great Britain	06 Jul 48	Direct Aid	22UNTS263	100339
USA (United States)	UK Great Britain	06 Jul 48	Milit Occupation	25UNTS61	100358
USA (United States)	UK Great Britain	22 Sep 48	Milit Assistance	71UNTS64	100910
USA (United States)	UK Great Britain	30 Sep 48	Specific Resources	71UNTS241	100922
USA (United States)	UK Great Britain	12 Nov 48	Visas	84UNTS275	101136
USA (United States)	UK Great Britain	01 Dec 48	Direct Aid	81UNTS93	101066
USA (United States)	UK Great Britain	19 Sep 49	Milit Installation	68UNTS31	100882
USA (United States)	UK Great Britain	12 Dec 49	Visas	92UNTS191	101271
USA (United States)	UK Great Britain	27 Jan 50	Milit Assistance	80UNTS261	101056
USA (United States)	UK Great Britain	21 Jul 50	Milit Installation	97UNTS193	101351
USA (United States)	UK Great Britain	01 Aug 50	Milit Installation	88UNTS273	101199
USA (United States)	UK Great Britain	13 Sep 50	Visas	122UNTS51	101635

PARTY ONE	PARTY TWO	DATE	TOPIC	CITATION	NUMBER
USA (United States)	UK Great Britain	06 Mar 51	Status of Forces	97UNTS137	101347
USA (United States)	UK Great Britain	25 Apr 51	Specific Property	99UNTS97	101373
USA (United States)	UK Great Britain	03 Jun 51	Postal Service	137UNTS81	101850
USA (United States)	UK Great Britain	06 Jun 51	Consul/Citizenship	165UNTS121	102174
USA (United States)	UK Great Britain	15 Jun 51	Tech Assistance	141UNTS79	101907
USA (United States)	UK Great Britain	13 Jul 51	Tech Assistance	105UNTS71	101454
USA (United States)	UK Great Britain	18 Jul 51	Land Transport	117UNTS49	101583
USA (United States)	UK Great Britain	30 Jul 51	Admin Cooperation	105UNTS81	101455
USA (United States)	UK Great Britain	08 Jan 52	Milit Assistance	179UNTS201	102369
USA (United States)	UK Great Britain	08 Jan 52	Direct Aid	126UNTS307	101696
USA (United States)	UK Great Britain	15 Jan 52	Milit Installation	127UNTS3	101697
USA (United States)	UK Great Britain	18 Jan 52	Commodity Trade	184UNTS79	102440
USA (United States)	UK Great Britain	18 Mar 52	Milit Assistance	177UNTS33	102307
USA (United States)	UK Great Britain	29 Jul 52	Status of Forces	179UNTS129	102362
USA (United States)	UK Great Britain	19 Jan 53	General Military	161UNTS3	102117
USA (United States)	UK Great Britain	25 Feb 53	Direct Aid	212UNTS157	102868
USA (United States)	UK Great Britain	02 Mar 53	Milit Installation	172UNTS257	102249
USA (United States)	UK Great Britain	24 Jun 53	Tech Assistance	224UNTS141	103074
USA (United States)	UK Great Britain	26 Jun 53	Loans and Credits	183UNTS225	102432
USA (United States)	UK Great Britain	20 Jan 54	Tech Assistance	196UNTS95	102619
USA (United States)	UK Great Britain	15 Jun 54	Milit Assistance	236UNTS133	103320
USA (United States)	UK Great Britain	21 Jun 54	Other Military	209UNTS61	102821
USA (United States)	UK Great Britain	12 Jul 54	Tech Assistance	204UNTS123	102753
USA (United States)	UK Great Britain	19 Jul 54	Territory Boundary	250UNTS193	103523
USA (United States)	UK Great Britain	21 Jul 54	Status of Forces	222UNTS243	103031
USA (United States)	UK Great Britain	24 Sep 54	Milit Installation	300UNTS3	104326
USA (United States)	UK Great Britain	07 Jun 55	General Military	265UNTS27	103804
USA (United States)	UK Great Britain	15 Jun 55	Atomic Energy	229UNTS73	103161
USA (United States)	UK Great Britain	15 Jun 55	Atomic Energy	214UNTS301	102905
USA (United States)	UK Great Britain	15 Nov 55	Scientific Project	231UNTS185	103219
USA (United States)	UK Great Britain	05 Jun 56	Milit Installation	247UNTS205	103470
USA (United States)	UK Great Britain	25 Jun 56	Milit Installation	249UNTS91	103502
USA (United States)	UK Great Britain	25 Jun 56	Milit Installation	249UNTS59	103501
USA (United States)	UK Great Britain	01 Nov 56	Scientific Project	264UNTS3	103785
USA (United States)	UK Great Britain	27 Nov 56	Scientific Project	282UNTS43	104092
USA (United States)	UK Great Britain	27 Jun 57	Direct Aid	290UNTS133	104232
USA (United States)	UK Great Britain	27 Jun 57	General Economic	284UNTS75	104130
USA (United States)	UK Great Britain	01 Nov 57	Scientific Project	299UNTS167	104312
USA (United States)	UK Great Britain	20 Jan 58	Specific Property	304UNTS3	104387
USA (United States)	UK Great Britain	03 Feb 58	US Agri Commod Aid	307UNTS199	104450
USA (United States)	UK Great Britain	22 Feb 58	Milit Assistance	307UNTS207	104451
USA (United States)	UK Great Britain	03 Jul 58	Atomic Energy	326UNTS3	104707
USA (United States)	UK Great Britain	30 Dec 58	Specific Property	338UNTS281	104841
USA (United States)	UK Great Britain	16 Apr 59	IGO Status/Immunit	343UNTS11	104917
USA (United States)	UK Great Britain	15 Feb 60	Milit Assistance	371UNTS45	105269
USA (United States)	UK Great Britain	24 Jun 60	Gen Communications	377UNTS63	105396
USA (United States)	UK Great Britain	14 Oct 60	Scientific Project	398UNTS165	105721
USA (United States)	UK Great Britain	20 Jan 61	Scientific Project	402UNTS153	105783
USA (United States)	UK Great Britain	10 Feb 61	Milit Installation	409UNTS129	105880
USA (United States)	UK Great Britain	10 Feb 61	Milit Installation	409UNTS68	105879
USA (United States)	UK Great Britain	15 Mar 61	Scientific Project	404UNTS207	105811
USA (United States)	UK Great Britain	29 Mar 61	Scientific Project	405UNTS107	105826
USA (United States)	UK Great Britain	06 Apr 61	Scientific Project	404UNTS215	105812
USA (United States)	UK Great Britain	18 Jul 61	Milit Assistance	404UNTS227	105813
USA (United States)	UK Great Britain	28 Aug 61	Finance	434UNTS103	106258
USA (United States)	UK Great Britain	08 Sep 61	Scientific Project	418UNTS53	106016
USA (United States)	UK Great Britain	26 Sep 61	Scientific Project	421UNTS99	106055
USA (United States)	UK Great Britain	22 Feb 62	Direct Aid	435UNTS127	106275
USA (United States)	UK Great Britain	07 Mar 62	General Economic	446UNTS231	106406
USA (United States)	UK Great Britain	26 Apr 62	General Trade	445UNTS273	106395
USA (United States)	UK Great Britain	15 Aug 62	General Aid	580UNTS189	108421
USA (United States)	UK Great Britain	29 Aug 62	Milit Installation	449UNTS177	106459
USA (United States)	UK Great Britain	10 Dec 62	Mostfavored Nation	471UNTS91	106824
USA (United States)	UK Great Britain	15 Jan 63	Scientific Project	466UNTS181	106743
USA (United States)	UK Great Britain	06 Apr 63	Milit Installation	474UNTS49	106871

PARTY ONE	PARTY TWO	DATE	TOPIC	CITATION	NUMBER
USA (United States)	UK Great Britain	11 Oct 63	Scientific Project	483UNTS3	107005
USA (United States)	UK Great Britain	15 Apr 64	Commodity Trade	515UNTS55	107453
USA (United States)	UK Great Britain	19 Jun 64	Water Transport	530UNTS99	107675
USA (United States)	UK Great Britain	20 Aug 64	Specific Property	531UNTS85	107694
USA (United States)	UK Great Britain	16 Nov 64	General Trade	0UNTS0	109749
USA (United States)	UK Great Britain	22 Apr 65	Postal Service	0UNTS0	109750
USA (United States)	UK Great Britain	10 May 65	Education	545UNTS181	107934
USA (United States)	UK Great Britain	07 Jul 65	Specific Property	551UNTS221	108044
USA (United States)	UK Great Britain	09 Aug 65	General Aid	580UNTS181	108420
USA (United States)	UK Great Britain	10 Nov 65	General Aid	580UNTS197	108422
USA (United States)	UK Great Britain	26 Nov 65	Gen Communications	561UNTS193	108181
USA (United States)	UK Great Britain	08 Feb 66	Finance	0UNTS0	109751
USA (United States)	UK Great Britain	05 Apr 66	General Trade	592UNTS61	108569
USA (United States)	UK Great Britain	02 Jun 66	Atomic Energy	573UNTS229	108336
USA (United States)	UK Great Britain	06 Jul 66	Extradition	588UNTS137	108520
USA (United States)	UK Great Britain	26 Aug 66	General Trade	0UNTS0	109769
USA (United States)	UK Great Britain	27 Oct 66	Claims and Debts	597UNTS265	108650
USA (United States)	UK Great Britain	12 Dec 66	Scientific Project	603UNTS235	108735
USA (United States)	UK Great Britain	28 Dec 66	Direct Aid	0UNTS0	109700
USA (United States)	UK Great Britain	30 Dec 66	Scientific Project	603UNTS245	108736
USA (United States)	UK Great Britain	30 Dec 66	General Military	603UNTS273	108737
USA (United States)	UK Great Britain	01 Jan 67	Scientific Project	604UNTS3	108738
USA (United States)	UK Great Britain	10 Jan 67	General Aid	0UNTS0	109840
USA (United States)	UK Great Britain	11 Jan 67	General Aid	0UNTS0	109841
USA (United States)	UK Great Britain	18 Jan 67	General Aid	0UNTS0	109843
USA (United States)	UK Great Britain	12 Jun 67	Land Transport	0UNTS0	110785
USA (United States)	UK Great Britain	16 Dec 67	Direct Aid	0UNTS0	110063
USA (United States)	UK Great Britain	16 May 68	Admin Cooperation	0UNTS0	110018
USA (United States)	UK Great Britain	27 May 68	General Aid	0UNTS0	110144
USA (United States)	UK Great Britain	25 Jun 68	Direct Aid	0UNTS0	109271
USA (United States)	UK Great Britain	27 Jun 68	Finance	0UNTS0	110498
USA (United States)	UK Great Britain	09 Aug 68	Finance	0UNTS0	110499
USA (United States)	UK Great Britain	09 Oct 68	Finance	0UNTS0	110081
USA (United States)	UK Great Britain	11 Oct 68	Finance	0UNTS0	110083
USA (United States)	UK Great Britain	21 Nov 68	Finance	0UNTS0	110088
USA (United States)	UK Great Britain	25 Sep 69	Finance	0UNTS0	110243
USA (United States)	UNESCO (Educ/Cult)	19 Jan 62	Culture	435UNTS99	106272
USA (United States)	UNESCO (Educ/Cult)	16 Oct 64	Specific Property	550UNTS23	108006
USA (United States)	United Arab Rep	05 Jan 46	Status of Forces	160UNTS27	102098
USA (United States)	United Arab Rep	15 Jun 46	Air Transport	151UNTS135	101988
USA (United States)	United Arab Rep	15 Jun 46	Air Transport	71UNTS157	100917
USA (United States)	United Arab Rep	15 Aug 46	Mostfavored Nation	13UNTS59	100202
USA (United States)	United Arab Rep	03 Nov 49	Education	71UNTS31	100908
USA (United States)	United Arab Rep	05 May 51	Tech Assistance	198UNTS265	102670
USA (United States)	United Arab Rep	29 Apr 52	Milit Assistance	241UNTS3	103418
USA (United States)	United Arab Rep	12 Mar 53	Tech Assistance	204UNTS3	102747
USA (United States)	United Arab Rep	19 Mar 53	Tech Assistance	215UNTS17	102909
USA (United States)	United Arab Rep	21 May 53	Tech Assistance	204UNTS29	102748
USA (United States)	United Arab Rep	18 Jun 53	Education	204UNTS55	102749
USA (United States)	United Arab Rep	18 Jun 53	Sanitation	215UNTS45	102910
USA (United States)	United Arab Rep	24 Feb 54	Tech Assistance	236UNTS61	103316
USA (United States)	United Arab Rep	30 Oct 54	Direct Aid	234UNTS139	103279
USA (United States)	United Arab Rep	06 Nov 54	Tech Assistance	237UNTS183	103344
USA (United States)	United Arab Rep	07 Mar 55	Mass Media	252UNTS159	103565
USA (United States)	United Arab Rep	14 Dec 55	US Agri Commod Aid	240UNTS37	103392
USA (United States)	United Arab Rep	31 Oct 58	Postal Service	355UNTS355	105086
USA (United States)	United Arab Rep	24 Dec 58	US Agri Commod Aid	338UNTS221	104837
USA (United States)	United Arab Rep	13 Jan 59	Postal Service	358UNTS3	105122
USA (United States)	United Arab Rep	29 Jul 59	US Agri Commod Aid	357UNTS121	105111
USA (United States)	United Arab Rep	28 Sep 59	Education	358UNTS97	105128
USA (United States)	United Arab Rep	14 Nov 59	US Agri Commod Aid	360UNTS311	105165
USA (United States)	United Arab Rep	01 Aug 60	US Agri Commod Aid	384UNTS189	105519
USA (United States)	United Arab Rep	09 Aug 60	US Agri Commod Aid	388UNTS271	105584
USA (United States)	United Arab Rep	02 Sep 61	US Agri Commod Aid	421UNTS251	106063
USA (United States)	United Arab Rep	19 Jan 62	US Agri Commod Aid	435UNTS107	106273

PARTY ONE	PARTY TWO	DATE	TOPIC	CITATION	NUMBER
USA (United States)	United Arab Rep	21 May 62	Culture	458UNTS197	106601
USA (United States)	United Arab Rep	08 Oct 62	US Agri Commod Aid	462UNTS39	106670
USA (United States)	United Arab Rep	29 Jun 63	Finance	479UNTS207	106954
USA (United States)	United Arab Rep	01 Aug 63	Visas	488UNTS189	107128
USA (United States)	United Arab Rep	04 Dec 63	Commodity Trade	505UNTS117	107368
USA (United States)	United Arab Rep	05 May 64	Air Transport	531UNTS229	107706
USA (United States)	United Arab Rep	03 Jan 66	US Agri Commod Aid	579UNTS63	108399
USA (United States)	United Arab Rep	03 Jan 66	US Agri Commod Aid	579UNTS83	108400
USA (United States)	United Arab Rep	21 Feb 67	Culture	0UNTS0	109851
USA (United States)	United Nations	26 Jun 47	IGO Establishment	11UNTS11	100147
USA (United States)	United Nations	18 Dec 47	IGO Status/Immunit	11UNTS347	100174
USA (United States)	United Nations	23 Mar 48	Loans and Credits	19UNTS43	100303
USA (United States)	United Nations	28 Mar 51	Postal Service	108UNTS231	101476
USA (United States)	United Nations	18 Nov 61	US Agri Commod Aid	494UNTS213	107235
USA (United States)	Upper Volta	01 Jun 61	General Aid	410UNTS223	105906
USA (United States)	Upper Volta	18 Jun 65	Finance	549UNTS133	107996
USA (United States)	Upper Volta	21 Aug 67	Scientific Project	0UNTS0	110045
USA (United States)	Uruguay	21 Jul 42	General Trade	120UNTS211	200393
USA (United States)	Uruguay	01 Nov 43	Sanitation	106UNTS311	200348
USA (United States)	Uruguay	23 Apr 46	Sanitation	160UNTS103	102104
USA (United States)	Uruguay	14 Dec 46	Air Transport	532UNTS87	107713
USA (United States)	Uruguay	27 Jul 49	Sanitation	151UNTS199	101995
USA (United States)	Uruguay	08 Nov 49	Visas	82UNTS45	101084
USA (United States)	Uruguay	07 Mar 51	Sanitation	165UNTS113	102173
USA (United States)	Uruguay	04 Dec 51	Military Mission	152UNTS41	102010
USA (United States)	Uruguay	30 Jun 52	Milit Assistance	207UNTS139	102804
USA (United States)	Uruguay	12 Nov 52	Visas	231UNTS145	103213
USA (United States)	Uruguay	30 Nov 53	General Trade	229UNTS25	103158
USA (United States)	Uruguay	13 Jan 56	Atomic Energy	240UNTS401	103415
USA (United States)	Uruguay	23 Mar 56	Tech Assistance	376UNTS311	105386
USA (United States)	Uruguay	20 Feb 59	US Agri Commod Aid	341UNTS201	104884
USA (United States)	Uruguay	22 Jul 60	Education	388UNTS315	105587
USA (United States)	Uruguay	12 Sep 61	Gen Communications	607UNTS175	108805
USA (United States)	Uruguay	27 Apr 62	US Agri Commod Aid	452UNTS25	106502
USA (United States)	Uruguay	31 Jul 63	Tech Assistance	488UNTS3	107115
USA (United States)	Uruguay	17 May 65	Education	564UNTS69	108221
USA (United States)	Uruguay	19 Jan 68	US Agri Commod Aid	0UNTS0	110002
USA (United States)	Uruguay	07 May 68	US Agri Commod Aid	0UNTS0	110015
USA (United States)	Uruguay	17 Apr 70	General Trade	0UNTS0	110775
USA (United States)	USSR (Soviet Union)	02 Aug 41	General Trade	102UNTS269	200306
USA (United States)	USSR (Soviet Union)	18 Apr 42	Milit Assistance	105UNTS285	200339
USA (United States)	USSR (Soviet Union)	11 Feb 45	Other Military	68UNTS175	200229
USA (United States)	USSR (Soviet Union)	17 Sep 45	Milit Occupation	235UNTS346	200538
USA (United States)	USSR (Soviet Union)	15 Oct 45	Milit Assistance	278UNTS151	200547
USA (United States)	USSR (Soviet Union)	05 Feb 46	General Ad Hoc	0SUST206	468432
USA (United States)	USSR (Soviet Union)	18 Apr 46	General Ad Hoc	0SUST210	468433
USA (United States)	USSR (Soviet Union)	23 Apr 46	Culture	0SUST210	468434
USA (United States)	USSR (Soviet Union)	24 May 46	Telecommunications	4UNTS201	100046
USA (United States)	USSR (Soviet Union)	19 Aug 46	Admin Cooperation	0SUST218	468435
USA (United States)	USSR (Soviet Union)	15 Apr 47	General Aid	0SUST438	468436
USA (United States)	USSR (Soviet Union)	16 Jun 47	Consul/Citizenship	0SUST232	468437
USA (United States)	USSR (Soviet Union)	27 Sep 49	Milit Assistance	149UNTS23	101948
USA (United States)	USSR (Soviet Union)	26 Dec 53	Specif Goods/Equip	0SUST305	468438
USA (United States)	USSR (Soviet Union)	26 Mar 54	Milit Assistance	247UNTS263	103475
USA (United States)	USSR (Soviet Union)	22 Dec 54	Milit Assistance	251UNTS41	103532
USA (United States)	USSR (Soviet Union)	26 May 55	Milit Assistance	270UNTS61	103892
USA (United States)	USSR (Soviet Union)	25 Jun 55	Territory Boundary	270UNTS15	103887
USA (United States)	USSR (Soviet Union)	05 Sep 55	Sanitation	256UNTS307	103641
USA (United States)	USSR (Soviet Union)	16 Dec 55	Culture	0SUST344	468439
USA (United States)	USSR (Soviet Union)	09 Jul 56	Specif Goods/Equip	0SUST363	468440
USA (United States)	USSR (Soviet Union)	29 Dec 56	Privil/Immunities	0SUST371	468441
USA (United States)	USSR (Soviet Union)	27 Jan 58	Health/Educ/Welfare	301UNTS405	104350
USA (United States)	USSR (Soviet Union)	20 Aug 58	Visas	336UNTS269	104809
USA (United States)	USSR (Soviet Union)	10 Sep 58	Culture	7SUGG121	469529
USA (United States)	USSR (Soviet Union)	09 Oct 58	Mass Media	7SUGG122	469534

PARTY ONE	PARTY TWO	DATE	TOPIC	CITATION	NUMBER
USA (United States)	USSR (Soviet Union)	29 Dec 58	Culture	7SUGG131	469548
USA (United States)	USSR (Soviet Union)	16 Apr 59	Culture	8SUGG142	469572
USA (United States)	USSR (Soviet Union)	21 Nov 59	Culture	361UNTS35	105172
USA (United States)	USSR (Soviet Union)	22 Dec 59	Claims and Debts	8SUGG163	469619
USA (United States)	USSR (Soviet Union)	08 Mar 62	Health/Educ/Welfare	460UNTS3	106630
USA (United States)	USSR (Soviet Union)	30 Oct 62	Scientific Project	11SUGG156	469871
USA (United States)	USSR (Soviet Union)	20 Jun 63	Specif Goods/Equip	472UNTS163	106839
USA (United States)	USSR (Soviet Union)	22 Feb 64	Health/Educ/Welfare	526UNTS131	107605
USA (United States)	USSR (Soviet Union)	01 Jun 64	Consul/Citizenship	0UNTS0	109383
USA (United States)	USSR (Soviet Union)	18 Nov 64	Atomic Energy	535UNTS307	107786
USA (United States)	USSR (Soviet Union)	14 Dec 64	Specific Property	531UNTS213	107705
USA (United States)	USSR (Soviet Union)	05 Feb 65	Specific Resources	541UNTS97	107863
USA (United States)	USSR (Soviet Union)	19 Mar 66	Scientific Project	0UNTS0	109617
USA (United States)	USSR (Soviet Union)	04 Nov 66	Air Transport	0UNTS0	109606
USA (United States)	USSR (Soviet Union)	13 Feb 67	Specific Resources	0UNTS0	109848
USA (United States)	USSR (Soviet Union)	25 Nov 67	Specific Resources	0UNTS0	110057
USA (United States)	USSR (Soviet Union)	15 Jul 68	Scientific Project	0UNTS0	110069
USA (United States)	USSR (Soviet Union)	16 May 69	Consul/Citizenship	0UNTS0	110275
USA (United States)	USSR (Soviet Union)	10 Feb 70	Scientific Project	0UNTS0	110774
USA (United States)	Venezuela	13 Oct 42	Commodity Trade	138UNTS282	200451
USA (United States)	Venezuela	18 Feb 43	Sanitation	21UNTS225	200125
USA (United States)	Venezuela	14 May 43	Non-IBRD Project	28UNTS359	200160
USA (United States)	Venezuela	13 Jan 44	Military Mission	109UNTS171	200358
USA (United States)	Venezuela	11 May 45	Milit Servic/Citiz	121UNTS273	200405
USA (United States)	Venezuela	29 Mar 46	Specific Resources	124UNTS57	101666
USA (United States)	Venezuela	03 Jun 46	Military Mission	4UNTS215	100047
USA (United States)	Venezuela	30 Jun 47	Sanitation	166UNTS198	102190
USA (United States)	Venezuela	30 Jan 48	Military Mission	109UNTS25	101486
USA (United States)	Venezuela	24 Mar 48	Air Transport	44UNTS57	100678
USA (United States)	Venezuela	23 Aug 50	Military Mission	92UNTS341	101279
USA (United States)	Venezuela	07 Jun 51	Tech Assistance	141UNTS273	101918
USA (United States)	Venezuela	10 Aug 51	Military Mission	140UNTS345	101898
USA (United States)	Venezuela	28 Aug 52	General Trade	178UNTS51	102336
USA (United States)	Venezuela	29 Sep 52	Tech Assistance	186UNTS23	102479
USA (United States)	Venezuela	16 Jan 53	Military Mission	199UNTS287	102690
USA (United States)	Venezuela	14 Aug 53	Air Transport	213UNTS99	102883
USA (United States)	Venezuela	21 Jul 55	Atomic Energy	238UNTS121	103357
USA (United States)	Venezuela	21 Feb 57	Water Transport	279UNTS199	104041
USA (United States)	Venezuela	24 Sep 57	Tech Assistance	293UNTS307	104298
USA (United States)	Venezuela	08 Oct 58	Atomic Energy	371UNTS69	105271
USA (United States)	Venezuela	17 Apr 59	Visas	358UNTS83	105126
USA (United States)	Venezuela	12 Nov 59	Gen Communications	367UNTS81	105227
USA (United States)	Venezuela	17 May 62	US Agri Commod Aid	456UNTS275	106562
USA (United States)	Venezuela	28 May 62	Tech Assistance	458UNTS249	106607
USA (United States)	Venezuela	29 Nov 62	Finance	474UNTS107	106875
USA (United States)	Venezuela	18 Sep 67	Gen Communications	0UNTS0	109919
USA (United States)	Vietnam, South	07 Sep 51	Direct Aid	174UNTS165	102284
USA (United States)	Vietnam, South	19 Jan 52	Milit Assistance	205UNTS127	102772
USA (United States)	Vietnam, South	20 Aug 54	Humanitarian	0VKNG74	496021
USA (United States)	Vietnam, South	26 Aug 54	Direct Aid	234UNTS111	103276
USA (United States)	Vietnam, South	22 Nov 54	Patents/Copyrights	235UNTS11	103291
USA (United States)	Vietnam, South	07 Mar 55	Direct Aid	277UNTS285	104013
USA (United States)	Vietnam, South	23 Apr 55	Milit Assistance	277UNTS279	104012
USA (United States)	Vietnam, South	10 May 55	Milit Assistance	273UNTS157	103950
USA (United States)	Vietnam, South	03 Nov 55	Mass Media	239UNTS195	103379
USA (United States)	Vietnam, South	15 Aug 57	Admin Cooperation	0VKNG122	496036
USA (United States)	Vietnam, South	05 Nov 57	Finance	300UNTS23	104328
USA (United States)	Vietnam, South	17 Jun 58	Atomic Energy	321UNTS35	104652
USA (United States)	Vietnam, South	22 Apr 59	Atomic Energy	347UNTS113	104993
USA (United States)	Vietnam, South	16 Oct 59	US Agri Commod Aid	360UNTS271	105163
USA (United States)	Vietnam, South	28 Oct 60	US Agri Commod Aid	401UNTS3	105758
USA (United States)	Vietnam, South	25 Mar 61	US Agri Commod Aid	406UNTS187	105849
USA (United States)	Vietnam, South	03 Apr 61	General Amity	424UNTS137	106106
USA (United States)	Vietnam, South	04 Apr 61	Admin Cooperation	405UNTS77	105824
USA (United States)	Vietnam, South	14 Jul 61	US Agri Commod Aid	416UNTS133	105999
USA (United States)	Vietnam, South	27 Dec 61	US Agri Commod Aid	433UNTS185	106242
USA (United States)	Vietnam, South	28 May 62	US Agri Commod Aid	0VKNG168	496049
USA (United States)	Vietnam, South	21 Nov 62	US Agri Commod Aid	469UNTS101	106786
USA (United States)	Vietnam, South	19 Aug 63	Atomic Energy	0VKNG178	496053
USA (United States)	Vietnam, South	09 Jan 64	US Agri Commod Aid	505UNTS173	107373
USA (United States)	Vietnam, South	29 Sep 64	US Agri Commod Aid	531UNTS183	107703
USA (United States)	Vietnam, South	09 Feb 65	Claims and Debts	542UNTS175	107888
USA (United States)	Vietnam, South	24 Apr 65	Specific Resources	0VKNG216	496061
USA (United States)	Vietnam, South	26 May 65	US Agri Commod Aid	550UNTS3	108005
USA (United States)	Vietnam, South	03 Jan 66	Mass Media	579UNTS99	108401
USA (United States)	Vietnam, South	21 Mar 66	US Agri Commod Aid	578UNTS165	108394
USA (United States)	Vietnam, South	15 Dec 66	US Agri Commod Aid	0VKNG319	496080
USA (United States)	Vietnam, South	15 Dec 66	US Agri Commod Aid	0UNTS0	109695
USA (United States)	Vietnam, South	13 Mar 67	US Agri Commod Aid	0VKNG244	496067
USA (United States)	Vietnam, South	13 Mar 67	US Agri Commod Aid	0UNTS0	109754
USA (United States)	Vietnam, South	03 May 67	Taxation	0VKNG246	496068
USA (United States)	Vietnam, South	03 May 67	Taxation	0UNTS0	109762
USA (United States)	Vietnam, South	29 Jun 67	Direct Aid	0VKNG251	496069
USA (United States)	Vietnam, South	21 Sep 67	US Agri Commod Aid	0UNTS0	109920
USA (United States)	Vietnam, South	24 Oct 67	US Agri Commod Aid	0UNTS0	109983
USA (United States)	Vietnam, South	06 Jan 68	US Agri Commod Aid	0UNTS0	109995
USA (United States)	Vietnam, South	11 Mar 68	US Agri Commod Aid	0UNTS0	110135
USA (United States)	Vietnam, South	09 Nov 68	Status of Forces	0VKNG281	496073
USA (United States)	Vietnam, South	09 Nov 68	Milit Servic/Citiz	0UNTS0	110086
USA (United States)	Vietnam, South	14 Jan 69	US Agri Commod Aid	0UNTS0	110136
USA (United States)	Vietnam, South	05 Feb 69	US Agri Commod Aid	0UNTS0	110137
USA (United States)	Vietnam, South	17 Oct 69	US Agri Commod Aid	0SUGG304	469074
USA (United States)	Vietnam, South	29 Oct 69	US Agri Commod Aid	0UNTS0	110451
USA (United States)	Vietnam, South	23 Dec 69	Commodity Trade	0UNTS0	110613
USA (United States)	Vietnam, South	20 Jan 70	Commodity Trade	0VKNG311	496075
USA (United States)	Vietnam, South	12 Feb 70	Claims and Debts	0VKNG314	496077
USA (United States)	Vietnam, South	17 Feb 70	US Agri Commod Aid	0VKNG315	496078
USA (United States)	Vietnam, South	25 Mar 70	Commodity Trade	0UNTS0	110614
USA (United States)	Vietnam, South	15 May 70	US Agri Commod Aid	0VKNG327	496083
USA (United States)	Western Samoa	03 Nov 64	Scientific Project	521UNTS181	107521
USA (United States)	Western Samoa	22 Jul 69	Loans and Credits	0UNTS0	110340
USA (United States)	Yemen	04 May 46	General Economic	4UNTS165	100043
USA (United States)	Yemen	30 Jun 59	Direct Aid	357UNTS137	105112
USA (United States)	Yugoslavia	30 Mar 42	Milit Servic/Citiz	13UNTS199	200079
USA (United States)	Yugoslavia	24 Jul 42	Milit Assistance	34UNTS361	200179
USA (United States)	Yugoslavia	03 Oct 46	Mostfavored Nation	13UNTS83	100205
USA (United States)	Yugoslavia	19 Jul 48	Claims and Debts	89UNTS43	101208
USA (United States)	Yugoslavia	19 Jul 48	Milit Assistance	34UNTS195	100537
USA (United States)	Yugoslavia	24 Dec 49	Air Transport	89UNTS209	101219
USA (United States)	Yugoslavia	25 Mar 50	Visas	98UNTS195	101365
USA (United States)	Yugoslavia	14 Aug 50	Postal Service	137UNTS131	101851
USA (United States)	Yugoslavia	09 Oct 50	Admin Cooperation	133UNTS25	101776
USA (United States)	Yugoslavia	21 Nov 50	Direct Aid	93UNTS39	101285
USA (United States)	Yugoslavia	21 Nov 50	Milit Assistance	93UNTS45	101286
USA (United States)	Yugoslavia	06 Jan 51	Direct Aid	122UNTS137	101643
USA (United States)	Yugoslavia	17 Apr 51	Milit Assistance	162UNTS173	102134
USA (United States)	Yugoslavia	14 Nov 51	Milit Assistance	174UNTS201	102286
USA (United States)	Yugoslavia	08 Jan 52	Direct Aid	152UNTS61	102011
USA (United States)	Yugoslavia	15 Aug 52	Direct Aid	184UNTS97	102441
USA (United States)	Yugoslavia	11 Oct 52	Direct Aid	235UNTS277	103309
USA (United States)	Yugoslavia	03 Dec 52	Direct Aid	185UNTS183	102469
USA (United States)	Yugoslavia	23 Jul 53	Taxation	221UNTS365	103018
USA (United States)	Yugoslavia	05 Jan 54	Direct Aid	234UNTS267	103289
USA (United States)	Yugoslavia	16 Apr 54	Direct Aid	237UNTS77	103337
USA (United States)	Yugoslavia	18 Oct 54	Milit Assistance	273UNTS163	103951
USA (United States)	Yugoslavia	05 Jan 55	US Agri Commod Aid	251UNTS29	103531
USA (United States)	Yugoslavia	09 Feb 55	Direct Aid	241UNTS13	103419
USA (United States)	Yugoslavia	12 May 55	Direct Aid	251UNTS337	103550
USA (United States)	Yugoslavia	12 May 55	Direct Aid	251UNTS343	103551
USA (United States)	Yugoslavia	12 May 55	Direct Aid	251UNTS331	103549

PARTY ONE	PARTY TWO	DATE	TOPIC	CITATION	NUMBER
USA (United States)	Yugoslavia	30 Sep 55	General Military	269UNTS89	103877
USA (United States)	Yugoslavia	19 Jan 56	Direct Aid	240UNTS121	103400
USA (United States)	Yugoslavia	21 May 56	Visas	281UNTS93	104072
USA (United States)	Yugoslavia	03 Nov 56	US Agri Commod Aid	277UNTS119	104002
USA (United States)	Yugoslavia	03 Feb 58	US Agri Commod Aid	304UNTS293	104404
USA (United States)	Yugoslavia	05 Apr 58	Tech Assistance	338UNTS233	104838
USA (United States)	Yugoslavia	16 Jun 58	Admin Cooperation	317UNTS31	104591
USA (United States)	Yugoslavia	22 Dec 58	US Agri Commod Aid	338UNTS243	104839
USA (United States)	Yugoslavia	25 Aug 59	Milit Assistance	357UNTS87	105107
USA (United States)	Yugoslavia	25 Aug 59	Milit Assistance	357UNTS77	105106
USA (United States)	Yugoslavia	22 Oct 59	Tech Assistance	360UNTS259	105161
USA (United States)	Yugoslavia	03 Jun 60	US Agri Commod Aid	376UNTS243	105382
USA (United States)	Yugoslavia	19 Jan 61	General Aid	402UNTS163	105784
USA (United States)	Yugoslavia	19 Apr 61	Direct Aid	409UNTS163	105883
USA (United States)	Yugoslavia	28 Apr 61	US Agri Commod Aid	409UNTS172	105884
USA (United States)	Yugoslavia	14 Jun 61	Admin Cooperation	0UNTS0	110400
USA (United States)	Yugoslavia	28 Dec 61	US Agri Commod Aid	434UNTS111	106259
USA (United States)	Yugoslavia	21 Apr 62	US Agri Commod Aid	442UNTS123	106344
USA (United States)	Yugoslavia	28 Nov 62	US Agri Commod Aid	460UNTS185	106640
USA (United States)	Yugoslavia	04 Apr 64	Visas	526UNTS47	107599
USA (United States)	Yugoslavia	27 Apr 64	US Agri Commod Aid	526UNTS73	107601
USA (United States)	Yugoslavia	27 Apr 64	US Agri Commod Aid	526UNTS89	107602
USA (United States)	Yugoslavia	28 Apr 64	US Agri Commod Aid	526UNTS103	107603
USA (United States)	Yugoslavia	05 Oct 64	Commodity Trade	531UNTS63	107693
USA (United States)	Yugoslavia	28 Oct 64	US Agri Commod Aid	533UNTS3	107728
USA (United States)	Yugoslavia	29 Oct 64	US Agri Commod Aid	533UNTS17	107729
USA (United States)	Yugoslavia	05 Nov 64	Claims and Debts	550UNTS31	108007
USA (United States)	Yugoslavia	09 Nov 64	Education	533UNTS39	107731
USA (United States)	Yugoslavia	16 Mar 65	US Agri Commod Aid	542UNTS161	107887
USA (United States)	Yugoslavia	16 Jul 65	US Agri Commod Aid	549UNTS111	107994
USA (United States)	Yugoslavia	22 Nov 65	US Agri Commod Aid	574UNTS211	108351
USA (United States)	Yugoslavia	11 Apr 66	US Agri Commod Aid	580UNTS239	108427
USA (United States)	Yugoslavia	24 Apr 67	Finance	0UNTS0	109900
USA (United States)	Yugoslavia	26 Sep 67	Commodity Trade	0UNTS0	110046
USA (United States)	Zambia	11 Aug 66	Finance	616UNTS267	108901
USSR (Soviet Union)	Afghanistan	13 Jun 46	Territory Boundary	31UNTS147	100476
USSR (Soviet Union)	Afghanistan	13 Apr 47	Telecommunications	0SUST231	468001
USSR (Soviet Union)	Afghanistan	17 Jul 50	General Economic	0SUST276	468002
USSR (Soviet Union)	Afghanistan	27 Jan 54	Loans and Credits	0SUST306	468003
USSR (Soviet Union)	Afghanistan	28 Jun 55	General Transport	240UNTS253	103407
USSR (Soviet Union)	Afghanistan	18 Dec 55	Admin Cooperation	259UNTS101	103684
USSR (Soviet Union)	Afghanistan	28 Jan 56	Loans and Credits	0SUST347	468005
USSR (Soviet Union)	Afghanistan	24 Mar 56	Air Transport	0SUST351	468006
USSR (Soviet Union)	Afghanistan	18 Jan 58	Admin Cooperation	7SUGG102	469486
USSR (Soviet Union)	Afghanistan	18 Jan 58	Visas	321UNTS77	104655
USSR (Soviet Union)	Afghanistan	25 Jun 58	Specific Resources	7SUGG114	469515
USSR (Soviet Union)	Afghanistan	04 Feb 59	Telecommunications	8SUGG136	469556
USSR (Soviet Union)	Afghanistan	28 May 59	General Aid	8SUGG145	469576
USSR (Soviet Union)	Afghanistan	18 Jul 59	Non-IBRD Project	8SUGG149	469591
USSR (Soviet Union)	Afghanistan	19 Jan 60	General Aid	9SUGG121	469623
USSR (Soviet Union)	Afghanistan	18 Feb 60	Education	9SUGG126	469631
USSR (Soviet Union)	Afghanistan	04 Mar 60	Culture	9SUGG129	469638
USSR (Soviet Union)	Afghanistan	25 May 60	Non-IBRD Project	9SUGG136	469662
USSR (Soviet Union)	Afghanistan	12 Aug 60	General Trade	9SUGG144	469682
USSR (Soviet Union)	Afghanistan	13 Nov 60	Tech Assistance	9SUGG151	469708
USSR (Soviet Union)	Afghanistan	16 Oct 61	General Aid	10SUGG143	469800
USSR (Soviet Union)	Afghanistan	13 Jan 62	General Trade	11SUGG130	469816
USSR (Soviet Union)	Afghanistan	11 Apr 62	Tech Assistance	11SUGG137	469832
USSR (Soviet Union)	Afghanistan	17 May 62	General Aid	11SUGG140	469839
USSR (Soviet Union)	Afghanistan	06 Feb 68	Tech Assistance	0UNTS0	110279
USSR (Soviet Union)	Albania	10 Nov 45	Consul/Citizenship	0SUST201	471019
USSR (Soviet Union)	Albania	26 Jul 47	General Economic	0SUST235	468007
USSR (Soviet Union)	Albania	03 Sep 48	Loans and Credits	0SUST252	471027
USSR (Soviet Union)	Albania	03 Sep 48	General Trade	0SUST252	471026
USSR (Soviet Union)	Albania	10 Apr 49	General Economic	0SUST258	468008

PARTY ONE	PARTY TWO	DATE	TOPIC	CITATION	NUMBER
USSR (Soviet Union)	Albania	27 Jun 50	Mass Media	0SUST275	468009
USSR (Soviet Union)	Albania	17 Feb 51	Loans and Credits	0SUST280	468010
USSR (Soviet Union)	Albania	19 Apr 52	Tech Assistance	0SUST286	468011
USSR (Soviet Union)	Albania	05 Jul 52	Education	0SUST288	468012
USSR (Soviet Union)	Albania	27 Aug 55	Sanitation	0SUST334	468013
USSR (Soviet Union)	Albania	03 May 56	Culture	259UNTS391	103699
USSR (Soviet Union)	Albania	17 Apr 57	General Amity	0SUST381	468014
USSR (Soviet Union)	Albania	18 Sep 57	Consul/Citizenship	307UNTS265	104455
USSR (Soviet Union)	Albania	18 Sep 57	Consul/Citizenship	307UNTS251	104454
USSR (Soviet Union)	Albania	26 Oct 57	Mass Media	16SUGG122	469948
USSR (Soviet Union)	Albania	22 Nov 57	General Aid	0SUST392	468017
USSR (Soviet Union)	Albania	15 Feb 58	General Trade	7SUGG105	469497
USSR (Soviet Union)	Albania	15 Feb 58	General Economic	313UNTS261	104536
USSR (Soviet Union)	Albania	30 Jun 58	Admin Cooperation	328UNTS3	104729
USSR (Soviet Union)	Albania	06 Feb 59	General Trade	8SUGG136	469557
USSR (Soviet Union)	Albania	03 Apr 59	General Economic	8SUGG141	469570
USSR (Soviet Union)	Albania	03 Jul 59	Non-IBRD Project	8SUGG148	469587
USSR (Soviet Union)	Albania	03 Jul 59	Tech Assistance	8SUGG148	469585
USSR (Soviet Union)	Albania	03 Jul 59	Non-IBRD Project	8SUGG148	469586
USSR (Soviet Union)	Albania	03 Jul 59	Culture	8SUGG148	469584
USSR (Soviet Union)	Albania	25 Jan 60	General Trade	9SUGG122	469626
USSR (Soviet Union)	Albania	19 Jul 60	Tech Assistance	9SUGG142	469676
USSR (Soviet Union)	Albania	31 Aug 60	Tech Assistance	9SUGG146	469689
USSR (Soviet Union)	Albania	04 Jan 61	General Economic	10SUGG117	469732
USSR (Soviet Union)	Algeria	23 Mar 62	Recognition	11SUGG136	469828
USSR (Soviet Union)	Argentina	05 Jun 46	General Amity	0SUST212	468018
USSR (Soviet Union)	Argentina	05 Aug 53	General Economic	221UNTS99	103004
USSR (Soviet Union)	Argentina	03 Jun 54	Culture	0SUST316	468019
USSR (Soviet Union)	Argentina	19 May 55	General Trade	0SUST328	468020
USSR (Soviet Union)	Argentina	27 Oct 58	Loans and Credits	7SUGG122	469537
USSR (Soviet Union)	Argentina	27 May 60	Loans and Credits	9SUGG137	469663
USSR (Soviet Union)	Australia	15 Jul 47	Consul/Citizenship	0SUST234	468021
USSR (Soviet Union)	Australia	13 Mar 59	Consul/Citizenship	8SUGG139	469564
USSR (Soviet Union)	Australia	29 Jun 60	Postal Service	392UNTS131	105641
USSR (Soviet Union)	Australia	15 Oct 65	General Trade	553UNTS239	108092
USSR (Soviet Union)	Austria	29 Apr 45	Recognition	0SUST176	471015
USSR (Soviet Union)	Austria	24 Oct 45	Consul/Citizenship	0SUST200	468050
USSR (Soviet Union)	Austria	16 Jul 46	Claims and Debts	0SUST215	468049
USSR (Soviet Union)	Austria	17 Jul 53	Specif Goods/Equip	0SUST297	468051
USSR (Soviet Union)	Austria	30 Jul 53	Milit Occupation	0SUST298	468052
USSR (Soviet Union)	Austria	15 Apr 55	General Ad Hoc	0SUST325	468053
USSR (Soviet Union)	Austria	15 May 55	Recognition	0SUST328	468054
USSR (Soviet Union)	Austria	31 Aug 55	Specific Property	0SUST335	468055
USSR (Soviet Union)	Austria	17 Oct 55	Finance	56ABGB86	403221
USSR (Soviet Union)	Austria	17 Oct 55	Non-IBRD Project	0UNTS0	109254
USSR (Soviet Union)	Austria	17 Oct 55	Finance	0UNTS0	109255
USSR (Soviet Union)	Austria	17 Oct 55	General Economic	240UNTS289	103409
USSR (Soviet Union)	Austria	09 Nov 55	Air Transport	255UNTS247	103613
USSR (Soviet Union)	Austria	06 Dec 55	General Amity	0SUST444	468058
USSR (Soviet Union)	Austria	28 Dec 55	Postal Service	0SUST345	468059
USSR (Soviet Union)	Austria	27 Apr 57	General Amity	0SUST382	468060
USSR (Soviet Union)	Austria	14 Jun 57	Water Transport	285UNTS169	104152
USSR (Soviet Union)	Austria	28 Feb 59	Consul/Citizenship	356UNTS39	105091
USSR (Soviet Union)	Austria	06 Jun 59	Air Transport	8SUGG147	469581
USSR (Soviet Union)	Austria	13 Dec 60	General Trade	9SUGG154	469722
USSR (Soviet Union)	Austria	22 Mar 68	Culture	0UNTS0	110281
USSR (Soviet Union)	Austria	02 Jul 68	Air Transport	68ABGB295	403222
USSR (Soviet Union)	Austria	15 Jan 70	Air Transport	70ABGB109	403223
USSR (Soviet Union)	Austria	11 Mar 70	Admin Cooperation	72ABGB112	403224
USSR (Soviet Union)	Austria	05 Aug 70	General Economic	70ABGB317	403225
USSR (Soviet Union)	Belgium	13 Mar 45	Refugees	19UNTS235	200117
USSR (Soviet Union)	Belgium	27 Nov 45	Admin Cooperation	0SUST212	468022
USSR (Soviet Union)	Belgium	10 Nov 47	Finance	18UNTS299	100298
USSR (Soviet Union)	Belgium	18 Feb 48	General Trade	0SUST244	468024
USSR (Soviet Union)	Belgium	18 Feb 48	Finance	0SUST245	468025

PARTY ONE	PARTY TWO	DATE	TOPIC	CITATION	NUMBER
USSR (Soviet Union)	Belgium	30 Jun 48	Finance	16SUGG64	469885
USSR (Soviet Union)	Belgium	02 Dec 49	Finance	16SUGG66	469894
USSR (Soviet Union)	Belgium	14 Nov 50	General Trade	0SUST278	468026
USSR (Soviet Union)	Belgium	02 Nov 56	General Amity	0SUST371	468023
USSR (Soviet Union)	Belgium	05 Jun 58	Air Transport	345UNTS145	104965
USSR (Soviet Union)	Bolivia	18 Apr 45	Consul/Citizenship	0SUST176	471014
USSR (Soviet Union)	Brazil	02 Apr 45	Consul/Citizenship	0SUST437	468027
USSR (Soviet Union)	Brazil	09 Dec 59	General Economic	8SUGG160	469615
USSR (Soviet Union)	Brazil	27 May 61	General Trade	10SUGG131	469771
USSR (Soviet Union)	Brazil	27 May 61	Loans and Credits	10SUGG131	469769
USSR (Soviet Union)	Brazil	27 May 61	General Trade	10SUGG131	469770
USSR (Soviet Union)	Brazil	23 Nov 61	Consul/Citizenship	10SUGG145	469806
USSR (Soviet Union)	Brazil	20 Apr 63	General Trade	0UNTS0	109256
USSR (Soviet Union)	Brazil	20 Apr 63	General Trade	0UNTS0	109257
USSR (Soviet Union)	Bulgaria	14 Mar 45	General Trade	0SUST175	468028
USSR (Soviet Union)	Bulgaria	16 Aug 45	Consul/Citizenship	0SUST193	471018
USSR (Soviet Union)	Bulgaria	10 Feb 47	Peace/Disarmament	0SUST226	468029
USSR (Soviet Union)	Bulgaria	05 Jul 47	General Economic	0SUST233	468030
USSR (Soviet Union)	Bulgaria	23 Aug 47	Loans and Credits	0SUST236	471022
USSR (Soviet Union)	Bulgaria	17 Dec 47	Gen Communications	0SUST241	468031
USSR (Soviet Union)	Bulgaria	17 Dec 47	Postal Service	0SUST241	468032
USSR (Soviet Union)	Bulgaria	18 Mar 48	General Military	48UNTS135	100741
USSR (Soviet Union)	Bulgaria	01 Apr 48	General Economic	217UNTS97	102946
USSR (Soviet Union)	Bulgaria	01 Apr 48	General Trade	0SUST247	471025
USSR (Soviet Union)	Bulgaria	09 Aug 48	Loans and Credits	0SUST251	468035
USSR (Soviet Union)	Bulgaria	18 Feb 50	Tech Assistance	0SUST271	468036
USSR (Soviet Union)	Bulgaria	24 May 50	Admin Cooperation	0SUST274	468037
USSR (Soviet Union)	Bulgaria	25 Aug 50	Sanitation	221UNTS57	103002
USSR (Soviet Union)	Bulgaria	07 Mar 51	Education	0SUST285	468040
USSR (Soviet Union)	Bulgaria	10 Apr 51	Scientific Project	0SUST281	468039
USSR (Soviet Union)	Bulgaria	09 Oct 54	Specific Property	0SUST317	468041
USSR (Soviet Union)	Bulgaria	26 Nov 55	Specific Property	0SUST342	468042
USSR (Soviet Union)	Bulgaria	03 Feb 56	General Aid	0SUST348	468043
USSR (Soviet Union)	Bulgaria	28 Apr 56	Culture	259UNTS363	103697
USSR (Soviet Union)	Bulgaria	22 Nov 56	Mass Media	16SUGG74	469930
USSR (Soviet Union)	Bulgaria	20 Feb 57	General Economic	0SUST378	468045
USSR (Soviet Union)	Bulgaria	19 Nov 57	General Trade	0SUST391	468046
USSR (Soviet Union)	Bulgaria	12 Dec 57	Admin Cooperation	317UNTS217	104606
USSR (Soviet Union)	Bulgaria	12 Dec 57	Consul/Citizenship	302UNTS3	104351
USSR (Soviet Union)	Bulgaria	12 Dec 57	Consul/Citizenship	302UNTS21	104352
USSR (Soviet Union)	Bulgaria	18 Jan 58	Claims and Debts	7SUGG102	469487
USSR (Soviet Union)	Bulgaria	26 Apr 58	General Trade	7SUGG111	469508
USSR (Soviet Union)	Bulgaria	26 Apr 58	Commodity Trade	7SUGG111	469507
USSR (Soviet Union)	Bulgaria	19 Jul 58	Tech Assistance	7SUGG116	469521
USSR (Soviet Union)	Bulgaria	26 Dec 58	Non-IBRD Project	7SUGG130	469547
USSR (Soviet Union)	Bulgaria	26 Dec 58	Non-IBRD Project	7SUGG130	469546
USSR (Soviet Union)	Bulgaria	04 Nov 59	General Trade	8SUGG156	469607
USSR (Soviet Union)	Bulgaria	04 Nov 59	Tech Assistance	8SUGG156	469608
USSR (Soviet Union)	Bulgaria	11 Dec 59	Non-ILO Labor	368UNTS287	105246
USSR (Soviet Union)	Bulgaria	20 Jan 60	Tech Assistance	9SUGG22	469624
USSR (Soviet Union)	Bulgaria	28 Jun 60	Tech Assistance	9SUGG140	469669
USSR (Soviet Union)	Bulgaria	22 Jul 60	Tech Assistance	9SUGG143	469678
USSR (Soviet Union)	Bulgaria	22 Sep 60	Education	16SUGG129	469982
USSR (Soviet Union)	Bulgaria	08 Oct 60	Tech Assistance	9SUGG149	469703
USSR (Soviet Union)	Bulgaria	29 Nov 60	Tech Assistance	9SUGG152	469716
USSR (Soviet Union)	Bulgaria	30 Nov 60	Tech Assistance	9SUGG153	469718
USSR (Soviet Union)	Bulgaria	30 Nov 60	General Aid	9SUGG153	469717
USSR (Soviet Union)	Bulgaria	31 Dec 60	Loans and Credits	9SUGG158	469730
USSR (Soviet Union)	Bulgaria	18 Jan 61	General Trade	10SUGG118	469737
USSR (Soviet Union)	Bulgaria	18 Feb 61	Tech Assistance	10SUGG122	469742
USSR (Soviet Union)	Bulgaria	29 Sep 61	Tech Assistance	10SUGG142	469795
USSR (Soviet Union)	Bulgaria	20 Jun 62	Commodity Trade	11SUGG144	469845
USSR (Soviet Union)	Bulgaria	20 Jun 62	General Trade	11SUGG144	469844
USSR (Soviet Union)	Bulgaria	25 Dec 62	Mass Media	11SUGG160	469879
USSR (Soviet Union)	Bulgaria	06 Jul 66	Consul/Citizenship	596UNTS177	108632

PARTY ONE	PARTY TWO	DATE	TOPIC	CITATION	NUMBER
USSR (Soviet Union)	Bulgaria	27 Apr 67	Atomic Energy	631UNTS3	108983
USSR (Soviet Union)	Bulgaria	12 May 67	General Amity	631UNTS239	108997
USSR (Soviet Union)	Burma	18 Feb 48	Consul/Citizenship	0SUST245	468061
USSR (Soviet Union)	Burma	01 Jul 55	General Trade	0SUST331	468062
USSR (Soviet Union)	Burma	01 Apr 56	Commodity Trade	0SUST352	468063
USSR (Soviet Union)	Burma	30 Sep 57	Specif Goods/Equip	16SUGG121	469946
USSR (Soviet Union)	Burma	04 May 60	Direct Aid	9SUGG134	469653
USSR (Soviet Union)	Burma	19 Feb 62	Direct Aid	11SUGG133	469821
USSR (Soviet Union)	Burma	30 Aug 62	Non-IBRD Project	11SUGG150	469857
USSR (Soviet Union)	Burundi	30 Jun 62	Recognition	11SUGG145	469848
USSR (Soviet Union)	Burundi	01 Oct 62	Consul/Citizenship	11SUGG154	469866
USSR (Soviet Union)	Cambodia	13 May 56	Consul/Citizenship	16SUGG70	469915
USSR (Soviet Union)	Cambodia	07 Jul 56	Direct Aid	0SUST363	468064
USSR (Soviet Union)	Cambodia	31 May 57	Finance	0SUST384	468067
USSR (Soviet Union)	Cambodia	31 May 57	Health/Educ/Welfare	0SUST384	468066
USSR (Soviet Union)	Cambodia	31 May 57	General Trade	0SUST384	468065
USSR (Soviet Union)	Cambodia	12 Sep 58	Non-IBRD Project	7SUGG121	469531
USSR (Soviet Union)	Cambodia	10 May 60	Direct Aid	9SUGG135	469657
USSR (Soviet Union)	Cambodia	10 May 60	Direct Aid	9SUGG165	469658
USSR (Soviet Union)	Cambodia	24 Jun 61	Non-IBRD Project	10SUGG136	469781
USSR (Soviet Union)	Cameroon	24 Sep 62	General Trade	11SUGG153	469862
USSR (Soviet Union)	Cameroon	24 Sep 62	General Trade	11SUGG153	469863
USSR (Soviet Union)	Cameroon	24 Sep 62	General Trade	0UNTS0	109580
USSR (Soviet Union)	Canada	29 Sep 50	Claims and Debts	230UNTS371	103197
USSR (Soviet Union)	Canada	24 Jun 55	Postal Service	16SUGG68	469906
USSR (Soviet Union)	Canada	29 Feb 56	General Trade	252UNTS165	103566
USSR (Soviet Union)	Canada	15 Jan 59	Consul/Citizenship	8SUGG133	469551
USSR (Soviet Union)	Canada	23 Dec 59	Visas	16SUGG127	469968
USSR (Soviet Union)	Central Afri Rep	07 Dec 60	Consul/Citizenship	9SUGG154	469721
USSR (Soviet Union)	Ceylon (Sri Lanka)	06 Dec 56	Consul/Citizenship	16SUGG74	469931
USSR (Soviet Union)	Ceylon (Sri Lanka)	15 Jan 58	Culture	305UNTS235	104421
USSR (Soviet Union)	Ceylon (Sri Lanka)	08 Feb 58	General Trade	16SUGG124	469955
USSR (Soviet Union)	Ceylon (Sri Lanka)	08 Feb 58	General Trade	7SUGG105	469496
USSR (Soviet Union)	Ceylon (Sri Lanka)	08 Feb 58	Finance	0UNTS0	110491
USSR (Soviet Union)	Ceylon (Sri Lanka)	08 Feb 58	General Trade	348UNTS159	104999
USSR (Soviet Union)	Ceylon (Sri Lanka)	22 Feb 62	General Trade	11SUGG133	469822
USSR (Soviet Union)	Ceylon (Sri Lanka)	12 Jun 62	General Aid	11SUGG143	469841
USSR (Soviet Union)	Ceylon (Sri Lanka)	09 Aug 62	General Aid	11SUGG149	469854
USSR (Soviet Union)	Ceylon (Sri Lanka)	22 Sep 62	Non-IBRD Project	11SUGG153	469861
USSR (Soviet Union)	Ceylon (Sri Lanka)	14 Nov 62	Water Transport	11SUGG156	469872
USSR (Soviet Union)	Ceylon (Sri Lanka)	25 Feb 70	General Economic	0UNTS0	110361
USSR (Soviet Union)	Chad	22 Jun 67	Mostfavored Nation	643UNTS121	109188
USSR (Soviet Union)	China People's Rep	02 Oct 49	Consul/Citizenship	0SUST263	468068
USSR (Soviet Union)	China People's Rep	07 Feb 50	Gen Communications	50CCJC2	410002
USSR (Soviet Union)	China People's Rep	07 Feb 50	Gen Communications	50CCJC1	410386
USSR (Soviet Union)	China People's Rep	07 Feb 50	Postal Service	0SUST268	468069
USSR (Soviet Union)	China People's Rep	07 Feb 50	Telecommunications	0SUST268	468070
USSR (Soviet Union)	China People's Rep	14 Feb 50	Milit Installation	0SUST270	468072
USSR (Soviet Union)	China People's Rep	14 Feb 50	Specific Property	0SUST270	468071
USSR (Soviet Union)	China People's Rep	14 Feb 50	General Amity	226UNTS3	103103
USSR (Soviet Union)	China People's Rep	14 Feb 50	Privil/Immunities	226UNTS31	103105
USSR (Soviet Union)	China People's Rep	14 Feb 50	General Amity	50CCJC4	410003
USSR (Soviet Union)	China People's Rep	14 Feb 50	Loans and Credits	226UNTS21	103104
USSR (Soviet Union)	China People's Rep	14 Feb 50	Consul/Citizenship	50CCJC5	410004
USSR (Soviet Union)	China People's Rep	14 Feb 50	Loans and Credits	50CCJC6	410005
USSR (Soviet Union)	China People's Rep	27 Mar 50	Specific Property	0SUST272	468073
USSR (Soviet Union)	China People's Rep	27 Mar 50	Specif Goods/Equip	50CCJC15	410011
USSR (Soviet Union)	China People's Rep	27 Mar 50	Specific Property	0SUST272	468075
USSR (Soviet Union)	China People's Rep	27 Mar 50	Specif Goods/Equip	50CCJC14	410010
USSR (Soviet Union)	China People's Rep	27 Mar 50	Specif Goods/Equip	50CCJC13	410009
USSR (Soviet Union)	China People's Rep	27 Mar 50	Non-ILO Labor	50CCJC16	410012
USSR (Soviet Union)	China People's Rep	27 Mar 50	Privil/Immunities	0SUST272	468076
USSR (Soviet Union)	China People's Rep	27 Mar 50	Specific Property	0SUST272	468074
USSR (Soviet Union)	China People's Rep	19 Apr 50	General Trade	0SUST273	468077
USSR (Soviet Union)	China People's Rep	19 Apr 50	General Trade	50CCJC18	410014

PARTY ONE	PARTY TWO	DATE	TOPIC	CITATION	NUMBER
USSR (Soviet Union)	China People's Rep	19 Apr 50	General Trade	50CCJC17	410013
USSR (Soviet Union)	China People's Rep	19 Apr 50	General Aid	50CCJC20	410015
USSR (Soviet Union)	China People's Rep	28 Aug 50	Specific Property	50CCJC26	410021
USSR (Soviet Union)	China People's Rep	25 Oct 50	Privil/Immunities	0SUST278	468078
USSR (Soviet Union)	China People's Rep	02 Jan 51	Water Transport	0SUST279	468079
USSR (Soviet Union)	China People's Rep	02 Jan 51	Water Transport	51CCJC1	410024
USSR (Soviet Union)	China People's Rep	14 Mar 51	Land Transport	0SUST280	468080
USSR (Soviet Union)	China People's Rep	15 Jun 51	General Trade	51CCJC17	410038
USSR (Soviet Union)	China People's Rep	28 Jul 51	Specific Property	0SUST282	468081
USSR (Soviet Union)	China People's Rep	06 Dec 51	Education	0SUST283	468082
USSR (Soviet Union)	China People's Rep	06 Dec 51	Tech Assistance	51CCJC26	410046
USSR (Soviet Union)	China People's Rep	12 Apr 52	General Trade	52CCJC5	410050
USSR (Soviet Union)	China People's Rep	09 Aug 52	Education	0SUST289	468083
USSR (Soviet Union)	China People's Rep	09 Aug 52	Education	52CCJC45	410073
USSR (Soviet Union)	China People's Rep	15 Sep 52	Specific Property	0SUST290	468084
USSR (Soviet Union)	China People's Rep	15 Sep 52	Milit Installation	226UNTS45	103106
USSR (Soviet Union)	China People's Rep	15 Sep 52	Milit Installation	52CCJC49	410076
USSR (Soviet Union)	China People's Rep	19 Sep 57	Direct Aid	53CCJC29	410104
USSR (Soviet Union)	China People's Rep	21 Mar 53	Direct Aid	0SUST294	468085
USSR (Soviet Union)	China People's Rep	21 Mar 53	General Trade	53CCJC13	410095
USSR (Soviet Union)	China People's Rep	21 Aug 54	Mass Media	0SUST315	468086
USSR (Soviet Union)	China People's Rep	21 Aug 54	Mass Media	54CCJC51	410166
USSR (Soviet Union)	China People's Rep	12 Oct 54	Loans and Credits	0SUST318	468090
USSR (Soviet Union)	China People's Rep	12 Oct 54	Specific Property	0SUST317	468087
USSR (Soviet Union)	China People's Rep	12 Oct 54	Scientific Project	54CCJC65	410174
USSR (Soviet Union)	China People's Rep	12 Oct 54	General Amity	226UNTS57	103108
USSR (Soviet Union)	China People's Rep	12 Oct 54	General Ad Hoc	0SUST318	468089
USSR (Soviet Union)	China People's Rep	12 Oct 54	General Amity	226UNTS69	103109
USSR (Soviet Union)	China People's Rep	12 Oct 54	Health/Educ/Welfare	0SUST318	468088
USSR (Soviet Union)	China People's Rep	12 Oct 54	Milit Installation	226UNTS51	103107
USSR (Soviet Union)	China People's Rep	12 Oct 54	Tech Assistance	0SUST318	468091
USSR (Soviet Union)	China People's Rep	30 Dec 54	Air Transport	54CCJC99	410202
USSR (Soviet Union)	China People's Rep	30 Dec 54	Air Transport	0SUST321	468092
USSR (Soviet Union)	China People's Rep	12 Feb 55	General Trade	16SUGG68	469904
USSR (Soviet Union)	China People's Rep	12 Feb 55	General Trade	55CCJC10	410215
USSR (Soviet Union)	China People's Rep	16 Aug 55	Sanitation	0SUST334	468093
USSR (Soviet Union)	China People's Rep	16 Aug 55	Sanitation	55CCJC56	410249
USSR (Soviet Union)	China People's Rep	27 Dec 55	General Trade	16SUGG70	469911
USSR (Soviet Union)	China People's Rep	27 Dec 55	General Trade	55CCJC105	410287
USSR (Soviet Union)	China People's Rep	07 Apr 56	Direct Aid	0SUST353	468094
USSR (Soviet Union)	China People's Rep	07 Apr 56	Direct Aid	0SUST353	468095
USSR (Soviet Union)	China People's Rep	14 Jun 56	Commodity Trade	16SUGG71	469918
USSR (Soviet Union)	China People's Rep	14 Jun 56	General Trade	56CCJC73	410343
USSR (Soviet Union)	China People's Rep	05 Jul 56	Culture	56CCJC84	410349
USSR (Soviet Union)	China People's Rep	05 Jul 56	Culture	263UNTS129	103770
USSR (Soviet Union)	China People's Rep	18 Aug 56	Scientific Project	0SUST366	468096
USSR (Soviet Union)	China People's Rep	18 Sep 56	Specif Goods/Equip	16SUGG73	469927
USSR (Soviet Union)	China People's Rep	24 Dec 56	Scientific Project	56CCJC143	410391
USSR (Soviet Union)	China People's Rep	15 Feb 57	Gen Communications	57CCJC17	410399
USSR (Soviet Union)	China People's Rep	27 Mar 57	Specific Property	16SUGG119	469935
USSR (Soviet Union)	China People's Rep	10 Apr 57	General Trade	57CCJC39	410417
USSR (Soviet Union)	China People's Rep	15 Oct 57	Atomic Energy	16SUGG122	469947
USSR (Soviet Union)	China People's Rep	11 Dec 57	Scientific Project	57CCJC114	410468
USSR (Soviet Union)	China People's Rep	21 Dec 57	Visas	305UNTS213	104420
USSR (Soviet Union)	China People's Rep	21 Dec 57	Water Transport	57CCJC120	410473
USSR (Soviet Union)	China People's Rep	28 Dec 57	Education	16SUGG124	469954
USSR (Soviet Union)	China People's Rep	28 Dec 57	Tech Assistance	16SUGG124	469953
USSR (Soviet Union)	China People's Rep	18 Jan 58	Scientific Project	7SUGG102	469488
USSR (Soviet Union)	China People's Rep	23 Apr 58	General Trade	58CCJC57	410521
USSR (Soviet Union)	China People's Rep	23 Apr 58	General Economic	313UNTS135	104534
USSR (Soviet Union)	China People's Rep	23 Apr 58	General Trade	58CCJC56	410520
USSR (Soviet Union)	China People's Rep	08 Aug 58	Tech Assistance	7SUGG118	469522
USSR (Soviet Union)	China People's Rep	17 Jan 59	General Trade	16SUGG126	469963
USSR (Soviet Union)	China People's Rep	07 Feb 59	Tech Assistance	8SUGG136	469558
USSR (Soviet Union)	China People's Rep	07 Feb 59	Direct Aid	59CCJC24	410583

PARTY ONE	PARTY TWO	DATE	TOPIC	CITATION	NUMBER
USSR (Soviet Union)	China People's Rep	01 Jun 59	Scientific Project	59CCJC81	410625
USSR (Soviet Union)	China People's Rep	23 Jun 59	Consul/Citizenship	356UNTS83	105092
USSR (Soviet Union)	China People's Rep	23 Jun 59	Consul/Citizenship	59CCJC86	410629
USSR (Soviet Union)	China People's Rep	29 Jan 60	Specific Resources	60CCJC9	410660
USSR (Soviet Union)	China People's Rep	29 Jan 60	Specific Resources	16SUGG127	469970
USSR (Soviet Union)	China People's Rep	28 May 60	Visas	16SUGG128	469976
USSR (Soviet Union)	China People's Rep	20 Mar 61	Finance	61CCJC38	410770
USSR (Soviet Union)	China People's Rep	07 Apr 61	Direct Aid	10SUGG127	469761
USSR (Soviet Union)	China People's Rep	07 Apr 61	Finance	10SUGG127	469760
USSR (Soviet Union)	China People's Rep	25 May 61	Mass Media	61CCJC79	410799
USSR (Soviet Union)	China People's Rep	19 Jun 61	Tech Assistance	16SUGG131	469994
USSR (Soviet Union)	China People's Rep	19 Jun 61	General Economic	10SUGG136	469778
USSR (Soviet Union)	China People's Rep	19 Jun 61	Scientific Project	61CCJC87	410803
USSR (Soviet Union)	China People's Rep	19 Jun 61	Scientific Project	10SUGG136	469779
USSR (Soviet Union)	China People's Rep	19 Jun 61	General Aid	16SUGG131	469995
USSR (Soviet Union)	China People's Rep	21 Jun 61	Scientific Project	61CCJC88	410804
USSR (Soviet Union)	China People's Rep	29 Apr 65	General Trade	65CCJC57	411354
USSR (Soviet Union)	China People's Rep	25 May 65	Culture	65CCJC69	411355
USSR (Soviet Union)	China People's Rep	12 Jun 65	Scientific Project	65CCJC82	411356
USSR (Soviet Union)	China People's Rep	18 Nov 65	Scientific Project	65CCJC143	411357
USSR (Soviet Union)	China People's Rep	04 Apr 66	Air Transport	66CCJC14	411342
USSR (Soviet Union)	China People's Rep	19 Apr 66	General Trade	66CCJC18	411358
USSR (Soviet Union)	China People's Rep	27 Jun 66	Culture	66CCJC59	411359
USSR (Soviet Union)	China People's Rep	06 Nov 66	Scientific Project	66CCJC91	411345
USSR (Soviet Union)	China People's Rep	27 Jul 67	General Trade	67CCJC27	411361
USSR (Soviet Union)	COMECON (Econ Aid)	07 Dec 61	IGO Operations	506UNTS325	107392
USSR (Soviet Union)	Congo (Zaire)	07 Jul 60	Recognition	16SUGG128	469978
USSR (Soviet Union)	Congo (Zaire)	07 Jul 60	Consul/Citizenship	9SUGG141	469671
USSR (Soviet Union)	Congo (Zaire)	26 May 64	General Trade	0UNTS0	109582
USSR (Soviet Union)	Cuba	13 Feb 60	General Economic	369UNTS17	105248
USSR (Soviet Union)	Cuba	13 Feb 60	Claims and Debts	369UNTS3	105247
USSR (Soviet Union)	Cuba	20 Feb 60	General Trade	9SUGG126	469632
USSR (Soviet Union)	Cuba	08 May 60	Consul/Citizenship	9SUGG135	469656
USSR (Soviet Union)	Cuba	18 Jun 60	General Trade	9SUGG139	469666
USSR (Soviet Union)	Cuba	18 Jun 60	Finance	9SUGG139	469667
USSR (Soviet Union)	Cuba	16 Nov 60	Education	9SUGG152	469714
USSR (Soviet Union)	Cuba	16 Nov 60	Tech Assistance	9SUGG152	469713
USSR (Soviet Union)	Cuba	12 Dec 60	Culture	421UNTS3	106048
USSR (Soviet Union)	Cuba	19 Dec 60	General Aid	9SUGG155	469723
USSR (Soviet Union)	Cuba	19 Dec 60	Education	9SUGG155	469724
USSR (Soviet Union)	Cuba	01 Jun 61	Tech Assistance	10SUGG132	469773
USSR (Soviet Union)	Cuba	11 Oct 61	Tech Assistance	10SUGG143	469799
USSR (Soviet Union)	Cuba	08 May 62	Direct Aid	11SUGG139	469836
USSR (Soviet Union)	Cuba	14 May 62	General Trade	11SUGG140	469838
USSR (Soviet Union)	Cuba	17 Jul 62	Air Transport	11SUGG147	469850
USSR (Soviet Union)	Cuba	17 Jul 62	Air Transport	0UNTS0	110123
USSR (Soviet Union)	Cuba	03 Aug 62	Tech Assistance	16SUGG134	470010
USSR (Soviet Union)	Cuba	04 Aug 62	Education	11SUGG149	469852
USSR (Soviet Union)	Cuba	30 Aug 62	Non-IBRD Project	11SUGG150	469858
USSR (Soviet Union)	Cuba	25 Sep 62	Non-IBRD Project	11SUGG153	469865
USSR (Soviet Union)	Cuba	25 Sep 62	Specific Resources	11SUGG153	469864
USSR (Soviet Union)	Cuba	26 Sep 62	Specific Resources	16SUGG134	470011
USSR (Soviet Union)	Cuba	17 Feb 65	Finance	0UNTS0	109830
USSR (Soviet Union)	Cuba	17 Feb 65	General Trade	0UNTS0	109583
USSR (Soviet Union)	Cyprus	18 Aug 60	Recognition	16SUGG128	469981
USSR (Soviet Union)	Cyprus	13 Nov 60	Consul/Citizenship	9SUGG151	469709
USSR (Soviet Union)	Cyprus	22 Dec 61	General Economic	10SUGG147	469813
USSR (Soviet Union)	Cyprus	22 Dec 61	General Trade	0UNTS0	109828
USSR (Soviet Union)	Cyprus	29 Feb 64	Air Transport	602UNTS45	108706
USSR (Soviet Union)	Cyprus	22 Feb 65	General Trade	0UNTS0	109584
USSR (Soviet Union)	Czechoslovakia	31 Mar 45	Claims and Debts	16SUGG61	469880
USSR (Soviet Union)	Czechoslovakia	31 Mar 45	General Military	16SUGG62	469881
USSR (Soviet Union)	Czechoslovakia	14 Apr 45	Milit Installation	16SUGG62	469882
USSR (Soviet Union)	Czechoslovakia	29 Jun 45	Territory Boundary	504UNTS299	200607
USSR (Soviet Union)	Czechoslovakia	22 Oct 45	Postal Service	0SUST200	468099

PARTY ONE	PARTY TWO	DATE	TOPIC	CITATION	NUMBER
USSR (Soviet Union)	Czechoslovakia	12 Apr 46	General Trade	0SUST210	468100
USSR (Soviet Union)	Czechoslovakia	12 Apr 46	Claims and Debts	0SUST210	468101
USSR (Soviet Union)	Czechoslovakia	10 Jul 46	Consul/Citizenship	0SUST214	468102
USSR (Soviet Union)	Czechoslovakia	25 Jul 46	Air Transport	27UNTS231	100409
USSR (Soviet Union)	Czechoslovakia	12 Jul 47	General Trade	0SUST234	468103
USSR (Soviet Union)	Czechoslovakia	28 Nov 47	Sanitation	216UNTS285	102941
USSR (Soviet Union)	Czechoslovakia	11 Dec 47	General Economic	217UNTS35	102943
USSR (Soviet Union)	Czechoslovakia	11 Dec 47	General Economic	0SUST240	471024
USSR (Soviet Union)	Czechoslovakia	11 Dec 47	Scientific Project	0SUST240	468104
USSR (Soviet Union)	Czechoslovakia	11 Dec 47	Loans and Credits	0SUST240	471023
USSR (Soviet Union)	Czechoslovakia	09 Feb 48	General Trade	0SUST244	468105
USSR (Soviet Union)	Czechoslovakia	15 Dec 48	General Economic	0SUST255	468106
USSR (Soviet Union)	Czechoslovakia	03 Nov 49	Mass Media	16SUGG65	469892
USSR (Soviet Union)	Czechoslovakia	03 Nov 50	General Economic	0SUST278	468107
USSR (Soviet Union)	Czechoslovakia	08 Aug 51	Postal Service	0SUST282	468108
USSR (Soviet Union)	Czechoslovakia	11 Apr 52	Education	0SUST286	468109
USSR (Soviet Union)	Czechoslovakia	23 Apr 55	Atomic Energy	0SUST326	468110
USSR (Soviet Union)	Czechoslovakia	28 Apr 55	Specific Resources	16SUGG68	469905
USSR (Soviet Union)	Czechoslovakia	01 Jun 56	Culture	259UNTS341	103696
USSR (Soviet Union)	Czechoslovakia	30 Nov 56	Territory Boundary	266UNTS243	103833
USSR (Soviet Union)	Czechoslovakia	14 Jan 57	General Trade	0SUST376	468111
USSR (Soviet Union)	Czechoslovakia	25 Jan 57	Mass Media	16SUGG118	469932
USSR (Soviet Union)	Czechoslovakia	01 Mar 57	Specif Goods/Equip	16SUGG119	469933
USSR (Soviet Union)	Czechoslovakia	06 Jul 57	Claims and Debts	0SUST385	468112
USSR (Soviet Union)	Czechoslovakia	31 Aug 57	Admin Cooperation	308UNTS3	104456
USSR (Soviet Union)	Czechoslovakia	05 Oct 57	Consul/Citizenship	320UNTS129	104641
USSR (Soviet Union)	Czechoslovakia	05 Oct 57	Consul/Citizenship	320UNTS111	104640
USSR (Soviet Union)	Czechoslovakia	04 Dec 57	Sanitation	313UNTS291	104537
USSR (Soviet Union)	Czechoslovakia	01 Apr 58	Customs	7SUGG108	469502
USSR (Soviet Union)	Czechoslovakia	30 Jun 58	Claims and Debts	7SUGG115	469517
USSR (Soviet Union)	Czechoslovakia	05 Sep 58	Scientific Project	7SUGG120	469526
USSR (Soviet Union)	Czechoslovakia	05 Sep 58	Scientific Project	7SUGG120	469527
USSR (Soviet Union)	Czechoslovakia	14 Oct 58	Commodity Trade	7SUGG122	469535
USSR (Soviet Union)	Czechoslovakia	07 Jan 59	Non-IBRD Project	8SUGG133	469550
USSR (Soviet Union)	Czechoslovakia	17 Jan 59	General Trade	8SUGG134	469552
USSR (Soviet Union)	Czechoslovakia	02 Dec 59	Non-ILO Labor	374UNTS63	105330
USSR (Soviet Union)	Czechoslovakia	20 Jan 60	General Trade	9SUGG122	469625
USSR (Soviet Union)	Czechoslovakia	07 Mar 60	Tech Assistance	9SUGG129	469639
USSR (Soviet Union)	Czechoslovakia	31 Mar 60	Non-IBRD Project	9SUGG132	469647
USSR (Soviet Union)	Czechoslovakia	28 Apr 60	General Trade	9SUGG134	469651
USSR (Soviet Union)	Czechoslovakia	12 May 60	Tech Assistance	9SUGG135	469659
USSR (Soviet Union)	Czechoslovakia	21 Feb 61	Scientific Project	10SUGG122	469743
USSR (Soviet Union)	Czechoslovakia	28 Jun 61	Non-IBRD Project	10SUGG136	469782
USSR (Soviet Union)	Czechoslovakia	21 Aug 61	Non-IBRD Project	10SUGG140	469793
USSR (Soviet Union)	Czechoslovakia	21 Dec 61	Non-IBRD Project	10SUGG147	469811
USSR (Soviet Union)	Czechoslovakia	17 Apr 62	Atomic Energy	11SUGG138	469833
USSR (Soviet Union)	Czechoslovakia	27 Nov 63	General Amity	496UNTS161	107250
USSR (Soviet Union)	Czechoslovakia	17 Sep 65	Visas	549UNTS221	108001
USSR (Soviet Union)	Czechoslovakia	23 Apr 66	Culture	566UNTS159	108242
USSR (Soviet Union)	Czechoslovakia	03 Feb 67	Land Transport	617UNTS267	108917
USSR (Soviet Union)	Czechoslovakia	23 Nov 67	Gen Communications	0UNTS0	109224
USSR (Soviet Union)	Czechoslovakia	06 May 70	General Amity	0UNTS0	110560
USSR (Soviet Union)	Dahomey	04 Jun 62	Consul/Citizenship	11SUGG141	469840
USSR (Soviet Union)	Dahomey	20 Mar 63	Culture	528UNTS181	107641
USSR (Soviet Union)	Dahomey	10 Jul 63	General Trade	528UNTS167	107640
USSR (Soviet Union)	Denmark	16 May 45	Consul/Citizenship	0SUST178	468115
USSR (Soviet Union)	Denmark	08 Jul 46	General Trade	0SUST214	468116
USSR (Soviet Union)	Denmark	08 Aug 46	Telecommunications	0SUST217	468117
USSR (Soviet Union)	Denmark	17 Aug 46	Finance	16SUGG63	469884
USSR (Soviet Union)	Denmark	17 Aug 46	Dispute Settlement	0SUST217	468118
USSR (Soviet Union)	Denmark	17 Aug 46	General Economic	8UNTS201	100124
USSR (Soviet Union)	Denmark	17 Jul 53	General Trade	175UNTS3	102292
USSR (Soviet Union)	Denmark	18 Aug 55	Consul/Citizenship	16SUGG69	469908
USSR (Soviet Union)	Denmark	17 Sep 55	Consul/Citizenship	0SUST336	468119
USSR (Soviet Union)	Denmark	06 Mar 56	Health/Educ/Welfare	0SUST350	468120

PARTY ONE	PARTY TWO	DATE	TOPIC	CITATION	NUMBER
USSR (Soviet Union)	Denmark	31 Mar 56	Air Transport	259UNTS169	103689
USSR (Soviet Union)	Denmark	14 May 56	General Trade	271UNTS125	103912
USSR (Soviet Union)	Denmark	30 May 59	Finance	8SUGG146	469578
USSR (Soviet Union)	Denmark	10 May 60	Taxation	16SUGG127	469975
USSR (Soviet Union)	Denmark	20 Jul 60	Consul/Citizenship	16SUGG128	469979
USSR (Soviet Union)	Denmark	11 Sep 62	Culture	458UNTS3	106589
USSR (Soviet Union)	Denmark	27 Feb 64	Specif Claim/Waive	509UNTS285	107407
USSR (Soviet Union)	Denmark	17 Jul 70	Scientific Project	0UNTS0	110784
USSR (Soviet Union)	Dominican Republic	08 Mar 45	Consul/Citizenship	0SUST174	468121
USSR (Soviet Union)	Ecuador	16 Jun 45	Consul/Citizenship	0SUST180	468122
USSR (Soviet Union)	Ethiopia	18 May 56	Consul/Citizenship	16SUGG71	469917
USSR (Soviet Union)	Ethiopia	02 Jun 56	Consul/Citizenship	0SUST357	468131
USSR (Soviet Union)	Ethiopia	11 Jul 59	General Trade	8SUGG149	469588
USSR (Soviet Union)	Ethiopia	11 Jul 59	General Trade	0UNTS0	110494
USSR (Soviet Union)	Ethiopia	12 Jul 59	General Aid	8SUGG149	469589
USSR (Soviet Union)	Ethiopia	12 Jul 59	Culture	8SUGG149	469590
USSR (Soviet Union)	Ethiopia	08 Mar 60	Non-IBRD Project	9SUGG129	469640
USSR (Soviet Union)	Ethiopia	25 Mar 60	Tech Assistance	9SUGG131	469645
USSR (Soviet Union)	Ethiopia	13 Jan 61	Culture	421UNTS13	106049
USSR (Soviet Union)	Ethiopia	29 Aug 62	Non-IBRD Project	11SUGG150	469856
USSR (Soviet Union)	Finland	28 Oct 22	Specific Resources	67UNTS157	100874
USSR (Soviet Union)	Finland	28 Oct 22	Specific Resources	67UNTS153	100873
USSR (Soviet Union)	Finland	11 Oct 40	Territory Boundary	67UNTS139	100872
USSR (Soviet Union)	Finland	31 Jan 45	General Trade	0SUST170	468132
USSR (Soviet Union)	Finland	08 May 45	General Trade	0SUST177	471016
USSR (Soviet Union)	Finland	06 Aug 45	Consul/Citizenship	0SUST188	471017
USSR (Soviet Union)	Finland	26 Oct 45	Territory Boundary	0SUST200	468133
USSR (Soviet Union)	Finland	31 Dec 45	Reparations	0SUST205	471020
USSR (Soviet Union)	Finland	30 Apr 46	Specific Property	0SUST211	468134
USSR (Soviet Union)	Finland	19 Aug 46	Telecommunications	0SUST217	468135
USSR (Soviet Union)	Finland	19 Aug 46	Postal Service	0SUST217	468137
USSR (Soviet Union)	Finland	05 Dec 46	General Economic	0SUST222	468136
USSR (Soviet Union)	Finland	03 Feb 47	Finance	0SUST225	468138
USSR (Soviet Union)	Finland	03 Feb 47	Territory Boundary	216UNTS231	102939
USSR (Soviet Union)	Finland	03 Feb 47	Specific Property	0SUST225	468139
USSR (Soviet Union)	Finland	03 Feb 47	Specific Property	0SUST226	468140
USSR (Soviet Union)	Finland	24 Apr 47	Specific Resources	0SUST231	468141
USSR (Soviet Union)	Finland	24 May 47	Specific Property	0SUST232	468142
USSR (Soviet Union)	Finland	01 Dec 47	General Trade	217UNTS3	102942
USSR (Soviet Union)	Finland	07 Dec 47	Territory Boundary	0SUST239	468143
USSR (Soviet Union)	Finland	19 Dec 47	Land Transport	0SUST242	468144
USSR (Soviet Union)	Finland	16 Mar 48	Admin Cooperation	0SUST246	468145
USSR (Soviet Union)	Finland	06 Apr 48	General Military	48UNTS149	100742
USSR (Soviet Union)	Finland	19 Jun 48	Dispute Settlement	0SUST249	468146
USSR (Soviet Union)	Finland	28 Jul 48	Reparations	16SUGG64	469886
USSR (Soviet Union)	Finland	09 Dec 48	Territory Boundary	217UNTS135	102947
USSR (Soviet Union)	Finland	17 Dec 48	General Trade	0SUST256	471029
USSR (Soviet Union)	Finland	13 Jun 50	General Trade	0SUST275	468147
USSR (Soviet Union)	Finland	06 Feb 54	Loans and Credits	221UNTS143	103006
USSR (Soviet Union)	Finland	29 Apr 54	Specific Resources	0SUST311	468148
USSR (Soviet Union)	Finland	17 Jul 54	General Trade	240UNTS173	103403
USSR (Soviet Union)	Finland	24 Jan 55	Loans and Credits	240UNTS243	103406
USSR (Soviet Union)	Finland	19 Sep 55	Milit Installation	226UNTS187	103113
USSR (Soviet Union)	Finland	19 Oct 55	Air Transport	353UNTS185	105043
USSR (Soviet Union)	Finland	14 Sep 56	Land Transport	255UNTS365	103618
USSR (Soviet Union)	Finland	07 Dec 56	Humanitarian	258UNTS89	103673
USSR (Soviet Union)	Finland	26 Jun 58	Commodity Trade	7SUGG114	469516
USSR (Soviet Union)	Finland	21 Feb 59	Specific Resources	338UNTS3	104830
USSR (Soviet Union)	Finland	29 Apr 59	Specif Claim/Waive	346UNTS209	104981
USSR (Soviet Union)	Finland	22 Oct 59	General Trade	8SUGG155	469606
USSR (Soviet Union)	Finland	22 Dec 59	Loans and Credits	8SUGG163	469617
USSR (Soviet Union)	Finland	27 May 60	Culture	379UNTS381	105444
USSR (Soviet Union)	Finland	23 Jun 60	Territory Boundary	379UNTS277	105443
USSR (Soviet Union)	Finland	24 Nov 60	Customs	9SUGG152	469715
USSR (Soviet Union)	Finland	03 Feb 61	Specific Property	10SUGG120	469740

PARTY ONE	PARTY TWO	DATE	TOPIC	CITATION	NUMBER
USSR (Soviet Union)	Finland	01 Apr 61	Customs	10SUGG127	469757
USSR (Soviet Union)	Finland	06 Apr 61	Tech Assistance	10SUGG127	469758
USSR (Soviet Union)	Finland	27 Sep 62	Territory Boundary	479UNTS99	106949
USSR (Soviet Union)	Finland	24 Apr 64	Territory Boundary	537UNTS231	107804
USSR (Soviet Union)	Finland	20 May 65	Territory Boundary	566UNTS31	108238
USSR (Soviet Union)	Finland	04 Jun 65	Specific Resources	560UNTS169	108173
USSR (Soviet Union)	Finland	24 Jan 66	Consul/Citizenship	576UNTS35	108364
USSR (Soviet Union)	Finland	05 May 67	Specific Resources	640UNTS111	109157
USSR (Soviet Union)	Finland	07 Mar 68	General Transport	643UNTS107	109187
USSR (Soviet Union)	Finland	18 Oct 68	Land Transport	0UNTS0	109609
USSR (Soviet Union)	Finland	14 May 69	Atomic Energy	0UNTS0	110040
USSR (Soviet Union)	Finland	30 May 69	Education	0UNTS0	110041
USSR (Soviet Union)	Finland	13 Jun 69	Specific Resources	0UNTS0	110606
USSR (Soviet Union)	France	29 Jun 45	Refugees	0SUST181	468150
USSR (Soviet Union)	France	29 Dec 45	General Trade	0SUST205	468151
USSR (Soviet Union)	France	06 Apr 46	Commodity Trade	0SUST209	471021
USSR (Soviet Union)	France	03 Sep 51	General Trade	221UNTS79	103003
USSR (Soviet Union)	France	15 Jul 53	General Trade	0UNTS0	110492
USSR (Soviet Union)	France	29 Jun 54	Air Transport	0SUST313	468155
USSR (Soviet Union)	France	31 Mar 56	General Trade	0SUST351	468156
USSR (Soviet Union)	France	31 Mar 56	Culture	0SUST355	468157
USSR (Soviet Union)	France	23 Jul 56	Culture	65FRRT52	415469
USSR (Soviet Union)	France	11 Feb 57	General Trade	0SUST377	468158
USSR (Soviet Union)	France	14 Nov 58	General Trade	7SUGG125	469541
USSR (Soviet Union)	France	14 Nov 58	General Trade	7SUGG125	469540
USSR (Soviet Union)	France	02 Apr 60	Finance	0UNTS0	110493
USSR (Soviet Union)	France	02 Apr 60	Finance	9SUGG132	469649
USSR (Soviet Union)	France	12 Jul 60	Culture	9SUGG142	469675
USSR (Soviet Union)	France	24 Jan 63	Finance	63FRMD1302	417470
USSR (Soviet Union)	France	30 Oct 64	General Trade	64FRMD411	417471
USSR (Soviet Union)	France	22 Mar 65	Mass Media	65FRRT60	415472
USSR (Soviet Union)	France	30 Jun 66	Scientific Project	589UNTS99	108537
USSR (Soviet Union)	France	30 Jun 66	Culture	589UNTS109	108538
USSR (Soviet Union)	France	08 Dec 66	Consul/Citizenship	69FRJO1610	416473
USSR (Soviet Union)	France	08 Dec 66	Consul/Citizenship	0UNTS0	110031
USSR (Soviet Union)	France	08 Dec 66	Consul/Citizenship	0UNTS0	110363
USSR (Soviet Union)	France	14 Mar 67	Patents/Copyrights	68FRJO2103	416474
USSR (Soviet Union)	France	14 Mar 67	Taxation	0UNTS0	109330
USSR (Soviet Union)	France	20 Apr 67	Water Transport	67FRJO2709	416475
USSR (Soviet Union)	France	08 Jul 67	Culture	68FRJO1603	416476
USSR (Soviet Union)	France	08 Jul 67	Mass Media	0UNTS0	109378
USSR (Soviet Union)	France	09 Jan 69	Health/Educ/Welfare	69FRJO3007	416477
USSR (Soviet Union)	France	09 Jan 69	Health/Educ/Welfare	0UNTS0	110733
USSR (Soviet Union)	France	13 Oct 69	Other Military	0UNTS0	110319
USSR (Soviet Union)	France	24 Oct 69	Scientific Project	0UNTS0	110460
USSR (Soviet Union)	Germany, East	19 Nov 49	Consul/Citizenship	1EGDA329	419376
USSR (Soviet Union)	Germany, East	12 Apr 50	General Economic	1EGDA245	419377
USSR (Soviet Union)	Germany, East	15 May 50	Reparations	0SUST274	468160
USSR (Soviet Union)	Germany, East	19 May 50	Claims and Debts	0SUST274	468161
USSR (Soviet Union)	Germany, East	01 Jul 50	Postal Service	4EGDA16	419379
USSR (Soviet Union)	Germany, East	01 Jul 50	Postal Service	4EGDA11	419378
USSR (Soviet Union)	Germany, East	01 Jul 50	Telecommunications	4EGDA27	419380
USSR (Soviet Union)	Germany, East	27 Sep 51	General Trade	1EGDA256	419381
USSR (Soviet Union)	Germany, East	27 Sep 51	Scientific Project	4EGDA33	419382
USSR (Soviet Union)	Germany, East	12 May 52	Education	4EGDA428	419383
USSR (Soviet Union)	Germany, East	13 Jan 53	Mass Media	4EGDA34	419384
USSR (Soviet Union)	Germany, East	20 Jul 53	Direct Aid	1EGDA273	419385
USSR (Soviet Union)	Germany, East	22 Aug 53	Consul/Citizenship	1EGDA286	419386
USSR (Soviet Union)	Germany, East	22 Aug 53	Reparations	221UNTS129	103005
USSR (Soviet Union)	Germany, East	22 Aug 53	Other Military	1EGDA286	419387
USSR (Soviet Union)	Germany, East	31 Dec 53	Specif Goods/Equip	1EGDA299	419388
USSR (Soviet Union)	Germany, East	30 Apr 54	Specif Goods/Equip	4EGDA41	419389
USSR (Soviet Union)	Germany, East	30 Sep 54	Consul/Citizenship	2EGDA275	419390
USSR (Soviet Union)	Germany, East	30 Sep 54	Finance	4EGDA42	419391
USSR (Soviet Union)	Germany, East	27 Apr 55	Specific Property	2EGDA337	419392

PARTY ONE	PARTY TWO	DATE	TOPIC	CITATION	NUMBER
USSR (Soviet Union)	Germany, East	28 Apr 55	Atomic Energy	0SUST327	468162
USSR (Soviet Union)	Germany, East	30 Jun 55	Specif Goods/Equip	3EGDA205	419393
USSR (Soviet Union)	Germany, East	01 Jul 55	Culture	2EGDA206	419394
USSR (Soviet Union)	Germany, East	25 Aug 55	Claims and Debts	0SUST334	468163
USSR (Soviet Union)	Germany, East	03 Sep 55	Scientific Project	3EGDA242	419395
USSR (Soviet Union)	Germany, East	20 Sep 55	Admin Cooperation	0SUST338	468164
USSR (Soviet Union)	Germany, East	20 Sep 55	General Amity	226UNTS201	103114
USSR (Soviet Union)	Germany, East	18 Oct 55	Air Transport	3EGDA327	419397
USSR (Soviet Union)	Germany, East	27 Nov 55	Specif Goods/Equip	4EGDA51	419398
USSR (Soviet Union)	Germany, East	23 Dec 55	Commodity Trade	3EGDA353	419399
USSR (Soviet Union)	Germany, East	26 Apr 56	Health/Educ/Welfare	259UNTS279	103692
USSR (Soviet Union)	Germany, East	30 May 56	Sanitation	263UNTS143	103771
USSR (Soviet Union)	Germany, East	18 Jun 56	Air Transport	4EGDA61	419400
USSR (Soviet Union)	Germany, East	17 Jul 56	Milit Occupation	5EGDA645	419401
USSR (Soviet Union)	Germany, East	12 Oct 56	Mass Media	0SUST369	468166
USSR (Soviet Union)	Germany, East	12 Oct 56	Mass Media	0SUST369	468165
USSR (Soviet Union)	Germany, East	26 Feb 57	Specific Property	5EGDA686	419402
USSR (Soviet Union)	Germany, East	12 Mar 57	Status of Forces	285UNTS105	104150
USSR (Soviet Union)	Germany, East	04 Apr 57	Specif Goods/Equip	16SUGG119	469936
USSR (Soviet Union)	Germany, East	10 May 57	Consul/Citizenship	285UNTS135	104151
USSR (Soviet Union)	Germany, East	25 May 57	General Economic	5EGDA697	419403
USSR (Soviet Union)	Germany, East	02 Aug 57	Status of Forces	5EGDA699	419404
USSR (Soviet Union)	Germany, East	27 Sep 57	General Economic	5EGDA730	419405
USSR (Soviet Union)	Germany, East	27 Sep 57	General Economic	292UNTS75	104268
USSR (Soviet Union)	Germany, East	28 Nov 57	Admin Cooperation	305UNTS113	104419
USSR (Soviet Union)	Germany, East	27 Dec 57	Admin Cooperation	0SUST395	468169
USSR (Soviet Union)	Germany, East	21 Feb 58	Specific Property	6EGDA429	419406
USSR (Soviet Union)	Germany, East	21 Feb 58	Education	6EGDA425	419407
USSR (Soviet Union)	Germany, East	25 Feb 58	General Economic	6EGDA431	419408
USSR (Soviet Union)	Germany, East	24 Jun 58	Milit Occupation	6EGDA447	419409
USSR (Soviet Union)	Germany, East	08 Sep 58	Specif Goods/Equip	6EGDA452	419410
USSR (Soviet Union)	Germany, East	21 Oct 58	Sanitation	16SUGG125	469961
USSR (Soviet Union)	Germany, East	21 Oct 58	Sanitation	6EGDA457	419411
USSR (Soviet Union)	Germany, East	22 Oct 58	Tech Assistance	6EGDA521	419412
USSR (Soviet Union)	Germany, East	22 Dec 58	Scientific Project	7SUGG129	469545
USSR (Soviet Union)	Germany, East	21 Nov 59	General Trade	7EGDA531	419414
USSR (Soviet Union)	Germany, East	01 Mar 60	Tech Assistance	8EGDA538	419415
USSR (Soviet Union)	Germany, East	24 May 60	Non-ILO Labor	392UNTS205	105645
USSR (Soviet Union)	Germany, East	29 Jul 60	Specif Goods/Equip	8EGDA577	419416
USSR (Soviet Union)	Germany, East	30 Aug 60	Education	9SUGG146	469688
USSR (Soviet Union)	Germany, East	27 Sep 60	Tech Assistance	9SUGG148	469695
USSR (Soviet Union)	Germany, East	31 Dec 60	General Economic	9SUGG159	469731
USSR (Soviet Union)	Germany, East	30 May 61	General Economic	9EGDA418	419417
USSR (Soviet Union)	Germany, East	10 Nov 61	Tech Assistance	10SUGG145	469804
USSR (Soviet Union)	Germany, East	28 Dec 61	Atomic Energy	9EGDA442	419418
USSR (Soviet Union)	Germany, East	05 Mar 62	Loans and Credits	10EGDA504	419419
USSR (Soviet Union)	Germany, East	03 May 62	Tech Assistance	10EGDA574	419420
USSR (Soviet Union)	Germany, East	08 Aug 62	Scientific Project	10EGDA521	419421
USSR (Soviet Union)	Germany, East	11 Mar 63	Commodity Trade	11EGDA588	419422
USSR (Soviet Union)	Germany, East	18 Jul 63	Tech Assistance	11EGDA611	419423
USSR (Soviet Union)	Germany, East	05 May 64	Tech Assistance	12EGDA1137	419424
USSR (Soviet Union)	Germany, East	12 Jun 64	General Amity	553UNTS249	108093
USSR (Soviet Union)	Germany, East	01 Oct 64	Health/Educ/Welfare	12EGDA1077	419425
USSR (Soviet Union)	Germany, East	14 Jul 65	Atomic Energy	48EGDZ339	420426
USSR (Soviet Union)	Germany, East	03 Dec 65	General Trade	61EGDZ349	420427
USSR (Soviet Union)	Germany, East	16 Mar 66	IGO Establishment	51EGDZ356	420428
USSR (Soviet Union)	Germany, East	01 Jun 66	Land Transport	41EGDZ361	420429
USSR (Soviet Union)	Germany, East	01 Sep 66	Air Transport	34EGDZ367	420430
USSR (Soviet Union)	Germany, West	13 Sep 55	Consul/Citizenship	0SUST334	468159
USSR (Soviet Union)	Germany, West	05 Aug 57	Admin Cooperation	16SUGG121	469945
USSR (Soviet Union)	Germany, West	25 Apr 58	General Economic	346UNTS71	104978
USSR (Soviet Union)	Germany, West	25 Apr 58	Consul/Citizenship	338UNTS49	104832
USSR (Soviet Union)	Germany, West	25 Mar 59	Scientific Project	8SUGG141	469568
USSR (Soviet Union)	Germany, West	30 May 59	Health/Educ/Welfare	8SUGG146	469579
USSR (Soviet Union)	Germany, West	31 Dec 60	General Economic	61WBGA12	424644

PARTY ONE	PARTY TWO	DATE	TOPIC	CITATION	NUMBER
USSR (Soviet Union)	Ghana	14 Jan 58	Consul/Citizenship	7SUGG102	469485
USSR (Soviet Union)	Ghana	10 Jun 59	General Trade	8SUGG147	469582
USSR (Soviet Union)	Ghana	04 Aug 60	General Aid	399UNTS61	105734
USSR (Soviet Union)	Ghana	04 Aug 60	General Trade	421UNTS27	106050
USSR (Soviet Union)	Ghana	25 Aug 60	Culture	9SUGG145	469686
USSR (Soviet Union)	Ghana	01 Feb 61	Specif Goods/Equip	10SUGG120	469739
USSR (Soviet Union)	Ghana	28 Feb 61	Atomic Energy	10SUGG124	469748
USSR (Soviet Union)	Ghana	12 Jun 61	Tech Assistance	10SUGG135	469777
USSR (Soviet Union)	Ghana	02 Jul 61	General Trade	0UNTS0	109380
USSR (Soviet Union)	Ghana	02 Jul 61	General Trade	16SUGG131	469996
USSR (Soviet Union)	Ghana	24 Jul 61	Finance	10SUGG139	469791
USSR (Soviet Union)	Ghana	04 Nov 61	Finance	10SUGG144	469802
USSR (Soviet Union)	Ghana	04 Nov 61	Commodity Trade	10SUGG144	469803
USSR (Soviet Union)	Ghana	04 Nov 61	General Trade	437UNTS213	106308
USSR (Soviet Union)	Ghana	04 Nov 61	Finance	0UNTS0	109381
USSR (Soviet Union)	Ghana	06 Apr 62	Air Transport	498UNTS41	107277
USSR (Soviet Union)	Ghana	27 Jul 62	Consul/Citizenship	16SUGG133	470009
USSR (Soviet Union)	Greece	28 Jul 53	General Economic	0SUST298	468170
USSR (Soviet Union)	Greece	02 Sep 54	General Trade	230UNTS33	103175
USSR (Soviet Union)	Greece	23 Aug 55	General Trade	233UNTS39	103249
USSR (Soviet Union)	Greece	06 Sep 56	Humanitarian	16SUGG73	469926
USSR (Soviet Union)	Greece	23 Jan 61	Postal Service	16SUGG130	469990
USSR (Soviet Union)	Greece	25 Apr 62	General Trade	11SUGG139	469835
USSR (Soviet Union)	Guatemala	19 Apr 45	Consul/Citizenship	0SUST176	468171
USSR (Soviet Union)	Guinea	04 Oct 58	Consul/Citizenship	7SUGG121	469533
USSR (Soviet Union)	Guinea	13 Feb 59	General Economic	8SUGG137	469560
USSR (Soviet Union)	Guinea	24 Aug 59	General Aid	8SUGG152	469600
USSR (Soviet Union)	Guinea	24 Aug 59	Loans and Credits	8SUGG152	469601
USSR (Soviet Union)	Guinea	26 Nov 59	Culture	8SUGG159	469611
USSR (Soviet Union)	Guinea	01 Mar 60	Direct Aid	9SUGG128	469634
USSR (Soviet Union)	Guinea	01 Mar 60	Tech Assistance	9SUGG128	469635
USSR (Soviet Union)	Guinea	01 Mar 60	Tech Assistance	9SUGG127	469633
USSR (Soviet Union)	Guinea	17 Aug 60	Consul/Citizenship	16SUGG128	469980
USSR (Soviet Union)	Guinea	08 Sep 60	General Trade	9SUGG147	469691
USSR (Soviet Union)	Guinea	29 Apr 61	Non-IBRD Project	10SUGG130	469765
USSR (Soviet Union)	Guinea	29 May 61	General Aid	10SUGG132	469772
USSR (Soviet Union)	Guinea	16 Jan 62	Air Transport	11SUGG130	469817
USSR (Soviet Union)	Guinea	26 Feb 62	General Aid	11SUGG134	469824
USSR (Soviet Union)	Hungary	15 Jun 45	Reparations	0SUST180	468172
USSR (Soviet Union)	Hungary	25 Sep 45	Consul/Citizenship	0SUST98	468173
USSR (Soviet Union)	Hungary	29 Mar 46	Specific Property	0SUST208	468174
USSR (Soviet Union)	Hungary	29 Mar 46	Specific Property	0SUST208	468175
USSR (Soviet Union)	Hungary	08 Apr 46	Specific Property	0SUST209	468176
USSR (Soviet Union)	Hungary	08 Apr 46	Specific Property	0SUST209	468177
USSR (Soviet Union)	Hungary	10 Feb 47	Peace/Disarmament	0SUST227	468178
USSR (Soviet Union)	Hungary	15 Jul 47	General Economic	0SUST234	468179
USSR (Soviet Union)	Hungary	15 Jul 47	General Economic	216UNTS247	102940
USSR (Soviet Union)	Hungary	22 Sep 47	Gen Communications	0SUST236	468180
USSR (Soviet Union)	Hungary	01 Oct 47	Postal Service	0SUST237	468181
USSR (Soviet Union)	Hungary	09 Dec 47	General Economic	0SUST239	468182
USSR (Soviet Union)	Hungary	18 Feb 48	General Military	48UNTS163	100743
USSR (Soviet Union)	Hungary	01 Mar 48	Consul/Citizenship	0SUST438	468184
USSR (Soviet Union)	Hungary	07 Jun 48	Reparations	0SUST249	468185
USSR (Soviet Union)	Hungary	02 Oct 48	General Economic	0SUST253	468186
USSR (Soviet Union)	Hungary	26 Jul 49	Scientific Project	0SUST261	468187
USSR (Soviet Union)	Hungary	30 Jul 49	Territory Boundary	0SUST261	468188
USSR (Soviet Union)	Hungary	24 Feb 50	Admin Cooperation	0SUST271	468189
USSR (Soviet Union)	Hungary	24 Feb 50	Admin Cooperation	0SUST271	468190
USSR (Soviet Union)	Hungary	12 Apr 50	Mass Media	0SUST273	468191
USSR (Soviet Union)	Hungary	09 Jun 50	Specific Resources	0SUST274	468192
USSR (Soviet Union)	Hungary	13 Jul 50	Sanitation	221UNTS35	103001
USSR (Soviet Union)	Hungary	20 Jan 52	General Aid	0SUST284	468194
USSR (Soviet Union)	Hungary	23 Jan 52	General Trade	0SUST284	468193
USSR (Soviet Union)	Hungary	19 May 52	Education	0SUST284	468195
USSR (Soviet Union)	Hungary	30 Sep 52	Specific Property	0SUST291	468196

PARTY ONE	PARTY TWO	DATE	TOPIC	CITATION	NUMBER
USSR (Soviet Union)	Hungary	06 Nov 54	Finance	0SUST319	468197
USSR (Soviet Union)	Hungary	27 May 55	Status of Forces	407UNTS156	105864
USSR (Soviet Union)	Hungary	13 Jun 55	Atomic Energy	0SUST330	468198
USSR (Soviet Union)	Hungary	14 Jun 56	Mass Media	0SUST385	468199
USSR (Soviet Union)	Hungary	28 Jun 56	Health/Educ/Welfare	259UNTS405	103700
USSR (Soviet Union)	Hungary	05 Oct 56	Loans and Credits	0SUST368	468200
USSR (Soviet Union)	Hungary	27 May 57	Status of Forces	0SUST383	468201
USSR (Soviet Union)	Hungary	15 Jun 57	Mass Media	16SUGG121	469942
USSR (Soviet Union)	Hungary	24 Aug 57	Consul/Citizenship	318UNTS3	104607
USSR (Soviet Union)	Hungary	24 Aug 57	Consul/Citizenship	318UNTS35	104608
USSR (Soviet Union)	Hungary	18 Dec 57	General Aid	0SUST394	468204
USSR (Soviet Union)	Hungary	13 Jan 58	General Trade	7SUGG101	469484
USSR (Soviet Union)	Hungary	24 Apr 58	Status of Forces	408UNTS118	105868
USSR (Soviet Union)	Hungary	11 May 58	Atomic Energy	7SUGG112	469509
USSR (Soviet Union)	Hungary	15 Jul 58	Admin Cooperation	322UNTS3	104656
USSR (Soviet Union)	Hungary	21 Jul 58	Customs	16SUGG125	469960
USSR (Soviet Union)	Hungary	21 Jul 58	Customs	408UNTS194	105871
USSR (Soviet Union)	Hungary	05 Nov 58	Tech Assistance	7SUGG125	469539
USSR (Soviet Union)	Hungary	05 Nov 58	General Aid	7SUGG124	469538
USSR (Soviet Union)	Hungary	28 Jan 59	Scientific Project	8SUGG135	469554
USSR (Soviet Union)	Hungary	17 Apr 59	Sanitation	16SUGG126	469964
USSR (Soviet Union)	Hungary	17 Apr 59	Sanitation	439UNTS41	106324
USSR (Soviet Union)	Hungary	07 Aug 59	General Trade	8SUGG151	469596
USSR (Soviet Union)	Hungary	07 Aug 59	Tech Assistance	8SUGG151	469597
USSR (Soviet Union)	Hungary	06 May 60	General Trade	9SUGG135	469655
USSR (Soviet Union)	Hungary	16 Jun 60	Mass Media	16SUGG128	469977
USSR (Soviet Union)	Hungary	04 Nov 60	Education	16SUGG129	469985
USSR (Soviet Union)	Hungary	20 Jun 61	General Aid	10SUGG136	469785
USSR (Soviet Union)	Hungary	01 Aug 61	General Trade	10SUGG140	469792
USSR (Soviet Union)	Hungary	03 Oct 61	Admin Cooperation	10SUGG142	469796
USSR (Soviet Union)	Hungary	15 Nov 62	General Trade	11SUGG157	469873
USSR (Soviet Union)	Hungary	17 Nov 62	General Trade	11SUGG157	469874
USSR (Soviet Union)	Hungary	20 Dec 62	Non-ILO Labor	11SUGG160	469878
USSR (Soviet Union)	Hungary	20 Dec 62	Non-ILO Labor	577UNTS245	108381
USSR (Soviet Union)	Hungary	21 Jan 63	Consul/Citizenship	577UNTS201	108378
USSR (Soviet Union)	Hungary	07 Sep 67	General Amity	632UNTS89	109011
USSR (Soviet Union)	Hungary	16 Nov 68	Culture	0UNTS0	110283
USSR (Soviet Union)	IAEA (Atom Energy)	11 May 59	Atomic Energy	339UNTS341	104853
USSR (Soviet Union)	Iceland	01 Aug 53	General Economic	0SUST298	468205
USSR (Soviet Union)	Iceland	05 Feb 54	General Economic	0SUST307	468206
USSR (Soviet Union)	Iceland	23 Sep 55	General Economic	0SUST338	468207
USSR (Soviet Union)	Iceland	03 Dec 55	Consul/Citizenship	0SUST343	468208
USSR (Soviet Union)	Iceland	13 Mar 58	Consul/Citizenship	16SUGG124	469956
USSR (Soviet Union)	Iceland	16 Jul 58	Specific Resources	7SUGG116	469519
USSR (Soviet Union)	Iceland	18 Aug 58	Loans and Credits	7SUGG118	469523
USSR (Soviet Union)	Iceland	14 Mar 60	Consul/Citizenship	16SUGG127	469973
USSR (Soviet Union)	Iceland	17 May 60	Finance	9SUGG136	469660
USSR (Soviet Union)	Iceland	25 Apr 61	Health/Educ/Welfare	10SUGG129	469764
USSR (Soviet Union)	Iceland	19 Dec 62	General Trade	11SUGG159	469877
USSR (Soviet Union)	India	07 Apr 47	Consul/Citizenship	0SUST231	468209
USSR (Soviet Union)	India	02 Dec 53	General Trade	0SUST304	468211
USSR (Soviet Union)	India	02 Dec 53	General Trade	240UNTS143	103402
USSR (Soviet Union)	India	24 Jan 55	Non-IBRD Project	0SUST322	468212
USSR (Soviet Union)	India	22 Jun 55	General Amity	0SUST330	468213
USSR (Soviet Union)	India	23 Dec 55	Specif Goods/Equip	0SUST345	468214
USSR (Soviet Union)	India	06 Apr 56	Water Transport	0SUST352	468215
USSR (Soviet Union)	India	21 May 56	Specif Goods/Equip	0SUST356	468216
USSR (Soviet Union)	India	09 Nov 57	General Economic	0SUST391	468217
USSR (Soviet Union)	India	02 Jun 58	Air Transport	393UNTS3	105650
USSR (Soviet Union)	India	16 Nov 58	General Trade	7SUGG126	469542
USSR (Soviet Union)	India	16 Nov 58	General Trade	16SUGG125	469962
USSR (Soviet Union)	India	12 Dec 58	General Aid	7SUGG128	469544
USSR (Soviet Union)	India	29 May 59	General Aid	8SUGG146	469577
USSR (Soviet Union)	India	23 Jun 59	Non-IBRD Project	8SUGG147	469583
USSR (Soviet Union)	India	23 Jul 59	Tech Assistance	8SUGG150	469592

PARTY ONE	PARTY TWO	DATE	TOPIC	CITATION	NUMBER
USSR (Soviet Union)	India	12 Sep 59	Loans and Credits	8SUGG153	469603
USSR (Soviet Union)	India	28 Sep 59	Non-IBRD Project	8SUGG154	469604
USSR (Soviet Union)	India	12 Feb 60	General Aid	9SUGG125	469630
USSR (Soviet Union)	India	12 Feb 60	Culture	392UNTS153	105642
USSR (Soviet Union)	India	14 Mar 60	General Trade	9SUGG130	469643
USSR (Soviet Union)	India	16 Jun 60	Tech Assistance	9SUGG138	469665
USSR (Soviet Union)	India	22 Aug 60	Education	9SUGG145	469685
USSR (Soviet Union)	India	21 Feb 61	General Aid	10SUGG122	469744
USSR (Soviet Union)	India	06 Oct 61	Atomic Energy	10SUGG143	469797
USSR (Soviet Union)	India	12 Feb 62	General Aid	11SUGG132	469820
USSR (Soviet Union)	India	10 Mar 62	Consul/Citizenship	16SUGG132	470003
USSR (Soviet Union)	India	20 Nov 62	Water Transport	11SUGG157	469875
USSR (Soviet Union)	India	10 Jun 63	General Trade	0UNTS0	109382
USSR (Soviet Union)	Indonesia	22 May 48	Consul/Citizenship	0SUST248	468218
USSR (Soviet Union)	Indonesia	03 Feb 50	Consul/Citizenship	0SUST268	468219
USSR (Soviet Union)	Indonesia	17 Dec 53	Consul/Citizenship	0SUST304	468220
USSR (Soviet Union)	Indonesia	12 Jun 56	Mostfavored Nation	0SUST367	468222
USSR (Soviet Union)	Indonesia	12 Aug 56	General Trade	16SUGG72	469924
USSR (Soviet Union)	Indonesia	18 Aug 56	General Economic	0SUST366	468221
USSR (Soviet Union)	Indonesia	15 Sep 56	General Aid	0SUST368	468223
USSR (Soviet Union)	Indonesia	03 Jan 59	General Aid	8SUGG132	469549
USSR (Soviet Union)	Indonesia	28 Jul 59	Loans and Credits	8SUGG150	469594
USSR (Soviet Union)	Indonesia	28 Jul 59	Loans and Credits	8SUGG150	469593
USSR (Soviet Union)	Indonesia	14 Aug 59	Tech Assistance	8SUGG152	469598
USSR (Soviet Union)	Indonesia	28 Feb 60	Culture	392UNTS191	105644
USSR (Soviet Union)	Indonesia	28 Feb 60	General Aid	392UNTS173	105643
USSR (Soviet Union)	Indonesia	01 Jul 60	Atomic Energy	9SUGG141	469670
USSR (Soviet Union)	Indonesia	09 Jul 60	General Trade	9SUGG141	469672
USSR (Soviet Union)	Indonesia	09 Jul 60	Tech Assistance	9SUGG142	469673
USSR (Soviet Union)	Indonesia	14 Oct 60	Non-IBRD Project	9SUGG150	469706
USSR (Soviet Union)	Indonesia	06 Jan 61	Milit Assistance	10SUGG117	469734
USSR (Soviet Union)	Indonesia	24 Feb 61	General Aid	10SUGG123	469745
USSR (Soviet Union)	Indonesia	21 Dec 61	Gen Communications	10SUGG147	469812
USSR (Soviet Union)	Indonesia	17 Jan 62	Education	16SUGG132	469998
USSR (Soviet Union)	Indonesia	08 May 62	Direct Aid	11SUGG139	469837
USSR (Soviet Union)	Indonesia	19 May 62	Consul/Citizenship	16SUGG133	470007
USSR (Soviet Union)	Indonesia	10 Nov 62	Mass Media	16SUGG134	470012
USSR (Soviet Union)	Indonesia	05 Dec 62	Education	16SUGG134	470013
USSR (Soviet Union)	Iran	03 Oct 45	Sanitation	0SUST199	468224
USSR (Soviet Union)	Iran	30 Jun 48	Territory Boundary	0IRTB75	433118
USSR (Soviet Union)	Iran	09 Aug 50	Admin Cooperation	16SUGG66	469895
USSR (Soviet Union)	Iran	04 Nov 50	General Trade	0SUST278	468225
USSR (Soviet Union)	Iran	02 Dec 54	Territory Boundary	0SUST320	468228
USSR (Soviet Union)	Iran	02 Dec 54	Finance	0SUST320	468227
USSR (Soviet Union)	Iran	02 Dec 54	Admin Cooperation	0IRTB74	433115
USSR (Soviet Union)	Iran	02 Dec 54	Territory Boundary	451UNTS227	106497
USSR (Soviet Union)	Iran	15 Feb 55	Commodity Trade	0SUST323	468229
USSR (Soviet Union)	Iran	09 Jun 55	Specific Property	0SUST329	468230
USSR (Soviet Union)	Iran	15 Oct 56	Territory Boundary	0IRTB75	433117
USSR (Soviet Union)	Iran	11 Apr 57	Territory Boundary	0SUST381	468231
USSR (Soviet Union)	Iran	16 Apr 57	General Trade	0SUST381	468232
USSR (Soviet Union)	Iran	25 Apr 57	Land Transport	0UNTS0	109578
USSR (Soviet Union)	Iran	27 Apr 57	General Trade	0SUST382	468233
USSR (Soviet Union)	Iran	14 May 57	Admin Cooperation	16SUGG120	469939
USSR (Soviet Union)	Iran	14 May 57	Dispute Settlement	457UNTS161	106586
USSR (Soviet Union)	Iran	11 Aug 57	Specific Resources	0SUST387	468235
USSR (Soviet Union)	Iran	20 Jan 58	Land Transport	7SUGG103	469489
USSR (Soviet Union)	Iran	05 Mar 58	Specific Resources	7SUGG107	469499
USSR (Soviet Union)	Iran	15 Apr 58	General Trade	7SUGG110	469504
USSR (Soviet Union)	Iran	03 Jul 58	Territory Boundary	7SUGG115	469518
USSR (Soviet Union)	Iran	09 Aug 62	General Trade	11SUGG149	469855
USSR (Soviet Union)	Iran	27 Jul 63	Non-IBRD Project	0IRTB80	433128
USSR (Soviet Union)	Iran	20 Jun 64	Finance	0IRTB80	433127
USSR (Soviet Union)	Iran	17 Aug 64	Air Transport	0IRTB79	433123
USSR (Soviet Union)	Iran	13 Jan 66	Non-IBRD Project	633UNTS123	109037

PARTY ONE	PARTY TWO	DATE	TOPIC	CITATION	NUMBER
USSR (Soviet Union)	Iran	13 Jan 66	Non-IBRD Project	0IRTB81	433129
USSR (Soviet Union)	Iran	13 Jan 66	Commodity Trade	0IRTB81	433130
USSR (Soviet Union)	Iran	14 Jan 66	Visas	0IRTB80	433125
USSR (Soviet Union)	Iran	17 Jan 66	Admin Cooperation	0IRTB79	433121
USSR (Soviet Union)	Iran	22 Aug 66	Culture	0IRTB79	433122
USSR (Soviet Union)	Iran	22 Aug 66	Culture	643UNTS203	109192
USSR (Soviet Union)	Iran	24 Dec 66	Sanitation	0IRTB78	433120
USSR (Soviet Union)	Iran	13 Mar 67	Sanitation	0IRTB78	433119
USSR (Soviet Union)	Iran	22 Jun 68	General Economic	0IRTB81	433131
USSR (Soviet Union)	Iran	07 May 70	Territory Boundary	0IRTB74	433116
USSR (Soviet Union)	Iran	30 Jul 70	General Trade	0IRTB81	433132
USSR (Soviet Union)	Iran	30 Jul 70	Specific Property	0IRTB82	433134
USSR (Soviet Union)	Iran	30 Jul 70	General Trade	0IRTB80	433126
USSR (Soviet Union)	Iran	25 Feb 71	Scientific Project	0IRTB81	433133
USSR (Soviet Union)	Iran	18 Jul 71	Taxation	0IRTB79	433124
USSR (Soviet Union)	Iraq	08 Jul 58	Consul/Citizenship	7SUGG116	469520
USSR (Soviet Union)	Iraq	11 Oct 58	General Trade	328UNTS95	104730
USSR (Soviet Union)	Iraq	11 Oct 58	General Trade	328UNTS117	104731
USSR (Soviet Union)	Iraq	16 Mar 59	General Aid	346UNTS107	104979
USSR (Soviet Union)	Iraq	05 May 59	Culture	356UNTS179	105095
USSR (Soviet Union)	Iraq	17 Aug 59	Atomic Energy	8SUGG152	469599
USSR (Soviet Union)	Iraq	17 Aug 59	Atomic Energy	0UNTS0	110362
USSR (Soviet Union)	Iraq	16 Dec 59	Tech Assistance	8SUGG162	469616
USSR (Soviet Union)	Iraq	27 Dec 59	Tech Assistance	8SUGG164	469620
USSR (Soviet Union)	Iraq	20 Mar 60	Non-IBRD Project	9SUGG131	469644
USSR (Soviet Union)	Iraq	18 Aug 60	Loans and Credits	9SUGG144	469684
USSR (Soviet Union)	Iraq	22 Mar 61	Consul/Citizenship	16SUGG131	469992
USSR (Soviet Union)	Israel	18 May 48	Recognition	0SUST248	468236
USSR (Soviet Union)	Israel	26 May 48	Consul/Citizenship	0SUST248	468237
USSR (Soviet Union)	Israel	15 Jul 53	Consul/Citizenship	0SUST297	468238
USSR (Soviet Union)	Israel	13 May 54	Consul/Citizenship	0SUST312	468239
USSR (Soviet Union)	Israel	15 Jul 55	Mostfavored Nation	226UNTS253	103119
USSR (Soviet Union)	Israel	07 Oct 64	Specific Property	516UNTS59	107471
USSR (Soviet Union)	Italy	11 Dec 48	General Trade	0UNTS0	109576
USSR (Soviet Union)	Italy	11 Dec 48	General Economic	217UNTS181	102948
USSR (Soviet Union)	Italy	11 Dec 48	General Trade	0SUST255	471028
USSR (Soviet Union)	Italy	11 Dec 48	General Trade	50ITGU5	435420
USSR (Soviet Union)	Italy	11 Dec 48	Finance	0SUST255	468241
USSR (Soviet Union)	Italy	11 Dec 48	Reparations	0SUST255	468240
USSR (Soviet Union)	Italy	28 Dec 57	Finance	58ITGU10	435421
USSR (Soviet Union)	Italy	28 Dec 57	Finance	0UNTS0	109579
USSR (Soviet Union)	Italy	18 Oct 59	Refugees	8SUGG155	469605
USSR (Soviet Union)	Italy	20 Jan 60	Visas	16SUGG127	469969
USSR (Soviet Union)	Italy	20 Jan 60	Visas	62ITDI382	436422
USSR (Soviet Union)	Italy	09 Feb 60	Visas	9SUGG124	469627
USSR (Soviet Union)	Italy	09 Feb 60	Culture	399UNTS75	105735
USSR (Soviet Union)	Italy	25 Feb 60	Visas	16SUGG127	469972
USSR (Soviet Union)	Italy	30 Jun 60	Patents/Copyrights	62ITDI385	436423
USSR (Soviet Union)	Italy	07 Jun 61	General Trade	10SUGG134	469775
USSR (Soviet Union)	Italy	21 Sep 61	Specif Goods/Equip	10SUGG142	469794
USSR (Soviet Union)	Italy	05 Feb 64	General Trade	65ITDI165	436424
USSR (Soviet Union)	Italy	22 Feb 65	Air Transport	67ITGU231	435425
USSR (Soviet Union)	Italy	16 May 67	Admin Cooperation	608UNTS79	108814
USSR (Soviet Union)	Jamaica	05 Aug 62	Recognition	11SUGG149	469853
USSR (Soviet Union)	Japan	19 Aug 46	Refugees	0SUST224	468242
USSR (Soviet Union)	Japan	14 May 56	Specific Resources	0JGJI1314	441092
USSR (Soviet Union)	Japan	14 May 56	Humanitarian	0JGJI1315	441093
USSR (Soviet Union)	Japan	19 Oct 56	General Amity	263UNTS99	103768
USSR (Soviet Union)	Japan	19 Oct 56	General Economic	263UNTS119	103769
USSR (Soviet Union)	Japan	06 Apr 57	Specific Resources	0SUST380	468243
USSR (Soviet Union)	Japan	06 Dec 57	Water Transport	16SUGG122	469949
USSR (Soviet Union)	Japan	06 Dec 57	General Economic	325UNTS35	104694
USSR (Soviet Union)	Japan	06 Dec 57	General Economic	0SUST392	468245
USSR (Soviet Union)	Japan	03 Jun 58	Water Transport	7SUGG113	469512
USSR (Soviet Union)	Japan	23 Jun 58	General Trade	16SUGG125	469959

PARTY ONE	PARTY TWO	DATE	TOPIC	CITATION	NUMBER
USSR (Soviet Union)	Japan	13 May 59	Specific Resources	8SUGG145	469575
USSR (Soviet Union)	Japan	20 Nov 59	General Trade	8SUGG158	469610
USSR (Soviet Union)	Japan	02 Mar 60	General Trade	9SUGG128	469636
USSR (Soviet Union)	Japan	02 Mar 60	General Trade	9SUGG128	469637
USSR (Soviet Union)	Japan	18 May 60	Specific Resources	9SUGG136	469661
USSR (Soviet Union)	Japan	31 Mar 62	Admin Cooperation	16SUGG133	470006
USSR (Soviet Union)	Japan	26 Feb 65	Visas	0JGJI1622	441131
USSR (Soviet Union)	Japan	21 Jan 66	General Trade	633UNTS165	109038
USSR (Soviet Union)	Japan	21 Jan 66	Air Transport	67JHZ3	439003
USSR (Soviet Union)	Japan	29 Jul 66	Consul/Citizenship	67JHZ8	439004
USSR (Soviet Union)	Japan	29 Jul 66	Consul/Citizenship	608UNTS93	108815
USSR (Soviet Union)	Japan	19 May 67	Consul/Citizenship	68JAIL163	440188
USSR (Soviet Union)	Japan	20 Jul 67	Scientific Project	67JJS455	442197
USSR (Soviet Union)	Japan	07 Mar 69	Air Transport	69JJS397	442235
USSR (Soviet Union)	Japan	14 Mar 69	General Trade	70JAIL191	440236
USSR (Soviet Union)	Japan	18 Apr 69	Specific Resources	69JJS423	442240
USSR (Soviet Union)	Jordan	04 Oct 67	Culture	0UNTS0	110278
USSR (Soviet Union)	Jordan	21 Jan 69	General Trade	0UNTS0	110364
USSR (Soviet Union)	Korea, North	18 Sep 48	Milit Occupation	0SUST253	468246
USSR (Soviet Union)	Korea, North	12 Oct 48	General Amity	0SUST253	468247
USSR (Soviet Union)	Korea, North	17 Mar 49	General Economic	221UNTS3	102999
USSR (Soviet Union)	Korea, North	17 Mar 49	General Economic	0SUST257	468248
USSR (Soviet Union)	Korea, North	06 May 52	Education	0SUST287	468249
USSR (Soviet Union)	Korea, North	19 Jun 53	Direct Aid	0SUST302	468250
USSR (Soviet Union)	Korea, North	28 Dec 54	Telecommunications	0SUST321	468252
USSR (Soviet Union)	Korea, North	28 Dec 54	Postal Service	0SUST321	468251
USSR (Soviet Union)	Korea, North	31 May 55	Finance	0SUST329	468253
USSR (Soviet Union)	Korea, North	31 Aug 55	Finance	0SUST335	468254
USSR (Soviet Union)	Korea, North	30 Nov 55	Sanitation	0SUST342	468255
USSR (Soviet Union)	Korea, North	09 Dec 55	Air Transport	0SUST343	468256
USSR (Soviet Union)	Korea, North	12 Jul 56	Direct Aid	0SUST363	468257
USSR (Soviet Union)	Korea, North	04 Aug 56	Direct Aid	16SUGG72	469923
USSR (Soviet Union)	Korea, North	05 Sep 56	Culture	259UNTS329	103695
USSR (Soviet Union)	Korea, North	20 Apr 57	Mass Media	16SUGG120	469937
USSR (Soviet Union)	Korea, North	25 Apr 57	Specific Property	0SUST382	468258
USSR (Soviet Union)	Korea, North	14 Aug 57	Non-IBRD Project	0SUST387	468260
USSR (Soviet Union)	Korea, North	14 Aug 57	Tech Assistance	0SUST387	468259
USSR (Soviet Union)	Korea, North	11 Oct 57	Education	0SUST390	468261
USSR (Soviet Union)	Korea, North	14 Oct 57	Admin Cooperation	0SUST390	468262
USSR (Soviet Union)	Korea, North	16 Dec 57	Admin Cooperation	301UNTS301	104349
USSR (Soviet Union)	Korea, North	16 Dec 57	Consul/Citizenship	292UNTS121	104270
USSR (Soviet Union)	Korea, North	16 Dec 57	Consul/Citizenship	292UNTS107	104269
USSR (Soviet Union)	Korea, North	11 May 58	General Economic	7SUGG112	469510
USSR (Soviet Union)	Korea, North	17 Mar 59	Tech Assistance	8SUGG140	469566
USSR (Soviet Union)	Korea, North	07 Sep 59	Atomic Energy	8SUGG153	469602
USSR (Soviet Union)	Korea, North	22 Jun 60	General Economic	399UNTS3	105732
USSR (Soviet Union)	Korea, North	11 Jul 60	Tech Assistance	9SUGG142	469674
USSR (Soviet Union)	Korea, North	31 Aug 60	Tech Assistance	9SUGG146	469690
USSR (Soviet Union)	Korea, North	30 Sep 60	Tech Assistance	9SUGG148	469700
USSR (Soviet Union)	Korea, North	13 Oct 60	Finance	9SUGG149	469705
USSR (Soviet Union)	Korea, North	24 Dec 60	Tech Assistance	9SUGG158	469728
USSR (Soviet Union)	Korea, North	24 Dec 60	General Trade	9SUGG158	469729
USSR (Soviet Union)	Korea, North	15 Feb 61	Education	16SUGG130	469991
USSR (Soviet Union)	Korea, North	06 Jul 61	General Aid	10SUGG137	469784
USSR (Soviet Union)	Korea, North	06 Jul 61	General Aid	10SUGG137	469786
USSR (Soviet Union)	Korea, North	06 Jul 61	General Amity	420UNTS145	106045
USSR (Soviet Union)	Kuwait	27 Mar 67	Culture	643UNTS135	109189
USSR (Soviet Union)	Laos	07 Oct 60	Consul/Citizenship	9SUGG149	469702
USSR (Soviet Union)	Laos	01 Dec 62	General Trade	458UNTS21	106590
USSR (Soviet Union)	Laos	01 Dec 62	Direct Aid	11SUGG158	469876
USSR (Soviet Union)	Laos	01 Dec 62	Direct Aid	472UNTS3	106834
USSR (Soviet Union)	Laos	01 Dec 62	Finance	471UNTS181	106832
USSR (Soviet Union)	Lebanon	30 Apr 54	General Economic	226UNTS109	103111
USSR (Soviet Union)	Libya	04 Sep 55	Consul/Citizenship	16SUGG69	469910
USSR (Soviet Union)	Luxembourg	01 Dec 60	Consul/Citizenship	10SUGG118	469736

PARTY ONE	PARTY TWO	DATE	TOPIC	CITATION	NUMBER
USSR (Soviet Union)	Madagascar	23 Oct 64	General Trade	0UNTS0	109829
USSR (Soviet Union)	Malaysia	03 Apr 67	General Trade	0UNTS0	109832
USSR (Soviet Union)	Mali	14 Oct 60	Recognition	16SUGG129	469984
USSR (Soviet Union)	Mali	18 Mar 61	Culture	10SUGG125	469754
USSR (Soviet Union)	Mali	18 Mar 61	General Trade	10SUGG125	469753
USSR (Soviet Union)	Mali	18 Mar 61	General Trade	0UNTS0	109826
USSR (Soviet Union)	Mali	18 Mar 61	General Aid	10SUGG125	469752
USSR (Soviet Union)	Mali	17 May 61	Consul/Citizenship	16SUGG131	469993
USSR (Soviet Union)	Mali	20 Mar 62	Air Transport	16SUGG132	470004
USSR (Soviet Union)	Mali	10 Oct 62	Tech Assistance	493UNTS219	107216
USSR (Soviet Union)	Mauritania	17 Oct 66	General Trade	633UNTS231	109040
USSR (Soviet Union)	Mexico	28 May 68	Health/Educ/Welfare	70MEXD808	444042
USSR (Soviet Union)	Mexico	28 May 68	Culture	0UNTS0	110282
USSR (Soviet Union)	Mongolia	27 Feb 46	General Economic	216UNTS221	102938
USSR (Soviet Union)	Mongolia	27 Feb 46	General Military	48UNTS177	100744
USSR (Soviet Union)	Mongolia	24 Feb 49	Water Transport	16SUGG65	469889
USSR (Soviet Union)	Mongolia	24 Feb 49	Specific Resources	0SUST439	468266
USSR (Soviet Union)	Mongolia	12 Mar 49	Specific Property	0SUST439	468267
USSR (Soviet Union)	Mongolia	06 Jun 49	Loans and Credits	0SUST439	468269
USSR (Soviet Union)	Mongolia	06 Jun 49	Specific Property	0SUST260	468268
USSR (Soviet Union)	Mongolia	09 Dec 49	General Trade	0SUST265	468270
USSR (Soviet Union)	Mongolia	01 Nov 50	Specific Property	0SUST439	468271
USSR (Soviet Union)	Mongolia	16 Jun 51	Specific Property	16SUGG66	469896
USSR (Soviet Union)	Mongolia	21 Dec 51	Non-ILO Labor	0SUST440	468272
USSR (Soviet Union)	Mongolia	29 Dec 51	General Trade	0SUST440	468273
USSR (Soviet Union)	Mongolia	30 Apr 52	Education	0SUST286	468277
USSR (Soviet Union)	Mongolia	13 Jun 52	Tech Assistance	0SUST440	468274
USSR (Soviet Union)	Mongolia	20 Aug 52	Air Transport	16SUGG66	469898
USSR (Soviet Union)	Mongolia	15 Sep 52	Specific Property	16SUGG67	469899
USSR (Soviet Union)	Mongolia	08 Apr 53	Specific Property	0SUST441	468275
USSR (Soviet Union)	Mongolia	27 Aug 53	Education	16SUGG67	469901
USSR (Soviet Union)	Mongolia	11 Sep 53	Mass Media	0SUST301	468278
USSR (Soviet Union)	Mongolia	28 Nov 53	Loans and Credits	16SUGG67	469902
USSR (Soviet Union)	Mongolia	31 Dec 53	Specific Property	16SUGG68	469903
USSR (Soviet Union)	Mongolia	19 Nov 54	General Trade	0SUST319	468279
USSR (Soviet Union)	Mongolia	12 Aug 55	General Aid	0SUST443	468280
USSR (Soviet Union)	Mongolia	17 Oct 55	Land Transport	0SUST340	468281
USSR (Soviet Union)	Mongolia	23 Apr 56	Specific Property	16SUGG70	469913
USSR (Soviet Union)	Mongolia	23 Apr 56	Tech Assistance	16SUGG70	469914
USSR (Soviet Union)	Mongolia	24 Apr 56	Culture	259UNTS297	103693
USSR (Soviet Union)	Mongolia	19 Oct 56	Scientific Project	16SUGG74	469929
USSR (Soviet Union)	Mongolia	01 Dec 56	Air Transport	0SUST373	468282
USSR (Soviet Union)	Mongolia	16 Apr 57	Specific Property	0SUST381	468283
USSR (Soviet Union)	Mongolia	20 Apr 57	Air Transport	0SUST382	468285
USSR (Soviet Union)	Mongolia	22 Apr 57	Air Transport	0SUST381	468284
USSR (Soviet Union)	Mongolia	15 May 57	Direct Aid	16SUGG120	469941
USSR (Soviet Union)	Mongolia	15 May 57	Specific Property	16SUGG120	469940
USSR (Soviet Union)	Mongolia	16 Dec 57	Health/Educ/Welfare	0SUST393	468286
USSR (Soviet Union)	Mongolia	17 Dec 57	General Trade	0SUST394	468288
USSR (Soviet Union)	Mongolia	17 Dec 57	General Trade	0SUST394	468287
USSR (Soviet Union)	Mongolia	11 Apr 58	Education	16SUGG125	469958
USSR (Soviet Union)	Mongolia	11 Apr 58	Tech Assistance	16SUGG124	469957
USSR (Soviet Union)	Mongolia	25 Aug 58	Admin Cooperation	322UNTS105	104657
USSR (Soviet Union)	Mongolia	25 Aug 58	Consul/Citizenship	322UNTS215	104659
USSR (Soviet Union)	Mongolia	25 Aug 58	Consul/Citizenship	322UNTS201	104658
USSR (Soviet Union)	Mongolia	19 Nov 58	Loans and Credits	7SUGG126	469543
USSR (Soviet Union)	Mongolia	10 Feb 59	General Aid	8SUGG136	469559
USSR (Soviet Union)	Mongolia	28 Jul 59	Tech Assistance	16SUGG126	469965
USSR (Soviet Union)	Mongolia	09 Dec 59	General Aid	16SUGG126	469967
USSR (Soviet Union)	Mongolia	11 Feb 60	General Aid	9SUGG124	469628
USSR (Soviet Union)	Mongolia	11 Feb 60	General Aid	9SUGG124	469629
USSR (Soviet Union)	Mongolia	28 Mar 60	Direct Aid	9SUGG131	469646
USSR (Soviet Union)	Mongolia	09 Sep 60	General Aid	9SUGG147	469692
USSR (Soviet Union)	Mongolia	27 Sep 60	Tech Assistance	9SUGG148	469697
USSR (Soviet Union)	Mongolia	27 Sep 60	Tech Assistance	9SUGG148	469696

PARTY ONE	PARTY TWO	DATE	TOPIC	CITATION	NUMBER
USSR (Soviet Union)	Mongolia	03 Oct 60	Education	16SUGG129	469983
USSR (Soviet Union)	Mongolia	08 Oct 60	Education	9SUGG149	469704
USSR (Soviet Union)	Mongolia	14 Nov 60	Tech Assistance	9SUGG151	469711
USSR (Soviet Union)	Mongolia	20 Dec 60	General Trade	9SUGG156	469725
USSR (Soviet Union)	Mongolia	25 Feb 61	Non-IBRD Project	10SUGG123	469746
USSR (Soviet Union)	Mongolia	13 Apr 61	Direct Aid	10SUGG128	469762
USSR (Soviet Union)	Mongolia	08 Jun 61	Tech Assistance	10SUGG134	469776
USSR (Soviet Union)	Mongolia	17 Jul 61	Tech Assistance	10SUGG138	469788
USSR (Soviet Union)	Mongolia	22 Jul 61	Tech Assistance	10SUGG139	469790
USSR (Soviet Union)	Mongolia	15 Jan 66	General Amity	562UNTS43	108194
USSR (Soviet Union)	Mongolia	17 Dec 67	General Trade	0UNTS0	109825
USSR (Soviet Union)	Morocco	18 Apr 57	General Trade	0SUST381	468289
USSR (Soviet Union)	Morocco	19 Apr 58	Finance	7SUGG110	469506
USSR (Soviet Union)	Morocco	19 Apr 58	General Trade	7SUGG110	469505
USSR (Soviet Union)	Morocco	04 Sep 58	Consul/Citizenship	7SUGG120	469525
USSR (Soviet Union)	Morocco	31 Jul 59	General Trade	8SUGG150	469595
USSR (Soviet Union)	Morocco	15 Nov 60	Milit Assistance	9SUGG151	469712
USSR (Soviet Union)	Morocco	28 Mar 62	Air Transport	11SUGG136	469831
USSR (Soviet Union)	Morocco	27 Oct 66	Mass Media	608UNTS207	108817
USSR (Soviet Union)	Morocco	27 Oct 66	Scientific Project	608UNTS197	108816
USSR (Soviet Union)	Multilateral	29 Jan 42	General Military	93UNTS279	200271
USSR (Soviet Union)	Multilateral	02 Aug 44	Scientific Project	67UNTS221	200221
USSR (Soviet Union)	Multilateral	12 Sep 44	Milit Occupation	227UNTS279	200532
USSR (Soviet Union)	Multilateral	08 Oct 44	Reparations	45UNTS311	200187
USSR (Soviet Union)	Multilateral	28 Oct 44	Peace/Disarmament	123UNTS223	200414
USSR (Soviet Union)	Multilateral	14 Nov 44	Milit Occupation	236UNTS359	200539
USSR (Soviet Union)	Multilateral	20 Jan 45	Peace/Disarmament	140UNTS397	200471
USSR (Soviet Union)	Multilateral	05 Jun 45	Milit Occupation	68UNTS189	200230
USSR (Soviet Union)	Multilateral	09 Jul 45	Milit Occupation	160UNTS359	200484
USSR (Soviet Union)	Multilateral	26 Jul 45	Milit Occupation	227UNTS297	200533
USSR (Soviet Union)	Multilateral	08 Aug 45	General Military	82UNTS279	200251
USSR (Soviet Union)	Multilateral	02 Sep 45	Peace/Disarmament	139UNTS387	200465
USSR (Soviet Union)	Multilateral	27 Sep 45	IGO Establishment	5UNTS327	200035
USSR (Soviet Union)	Multilateral	26 Dec 45	Peace/Disarmament	20UNTS259	100319
USSR (Soviet Union)	Multilateral	05 Apr 46	Specific Resources	231UNTS199	103221
USSR (Soviet Union)	Multilateral	28 Jun 46	Milit Occupation	138UNTS85	101862
USSR (Soviet Union)	Multilateral	22 Jul 46	IGO Establishment	14UNTS185	100221
USSR (Soviet Union)	Multilateral	22 Jul 46	IGO Establishment	9UNTS3	100125
USSR (Soviet Union)	Multilateral	02 Dec 46	Specific Resources	161UNTS72	102124
USSR (Soviet Union)	Multilateral	11 Dec 46	Sanitation	12UNTS179	100186
USSR (Soviet Union)	Multilateral	10 Feb 47	Reparations	140UNTS111	101886
USSR (Soviet Union)	Multilateral	10 Feb 47	Peace/Disarmament	48UNTS203	100746
USSR (Soviet Union)	Multilateral	10 Feb 47	Peace/Disarmament	49UNTS3	100747
USSR (Soviet Union)	Multilateral	10 Feb 47	Peace/Disarmament	41UNTS135	100644
USSR (Soviet Union)	Multilateral	10 Feb 47	Peace/Disarmament	41UNTS21	100643
USSR (Soviet Union)	Multilateral	10 Feb 47	Peace/Disarmament	42UNTS3	100645
USSR (Soviet Union)	Multilateral	03 Mar 47	Humanitarian	11UNTS43	100148
USSR (Soviet Union)	Multilateral	29 Sep 47	Peace/Disarmament	45UNTS125	100694
USSR (Soviet Union)	Multilateral	02 Oct 47	Telecommunications	193UNTS188	102616
USSR (Soviet Union)	Multilateral	11 Oct 47	IGO Establishment	77UNTS143	100998
USSR (Soviet Union)	Multilateral	12 Nov 47	Admin Cooperation	53UNTS13	100770
USSR (Soviet Union)	Multilateral	12 Nov 47	Admin Cooperation	53UNTS39	100771
USSR (Soviet Union)	Multilateral	12 Nov 47	Admin Cooperation	53UNTS49	100772
USSR (Soviet Union)	Multilateral	12 Nov 47	Admin Cooperation	46UNTS169	100709
USSR (Soviet Union)	Multilateral	12 Nov 47	Admin Cooperation	46UNTS201	100710
USSR (Soviet Union)	Multilateral	06 Mar 48	Water Transport	289UNTS3	104214
USSR (Soviet Union)	Multilateral	10 Jun 48	Humanitarian	164UNTS113	102163
USSR (Soviet Union)	Multilateral	24 Jul 48	Sanitation	66UNTS25	100847
USSR (Soviet Union)	Multilateral	18 Aug 48	Water Transport	33UNTS181	100518
USSR (Soviet Union)	Multilateral	19 Nov 48	Sanitation	44UNTS277	100688
USSR (Soviet Union)	Multilateral	09 Dec 48	Humanitarian	78UNTS277	101021
USSR (Soviet Union)	Multilateral	08 Feb 49	Specific Resources	157UNTS157	102053
USSR (Soviet Union)	Multilateral	04 May 49	Admin Cooperation	47UNTS159	100728
USSR (Soviet Union)	Multilateral	12 Aug 49	Humanitarian	75UNTS287	100973
USSR (Soviet Union)	Multilateral	12 Aug 49	Humanitarian	75UNTS31	100970

PARTY ONE	PARTY TWO	DATE	TOPIC	CITATION	NUMBER
USSR (Soviet Union)	Multilateral	12 Aug 49	General Military	75UNTS135	100972
USSR (Soviet Union)	Multilateral	12 Aug 49	Humanitarian	75UNTS85	100971
USSR (Soviet Union)	Multilateral	21 Mar 50	Admin Cooperation	96UNTS271	101342
USSR (Soviet Union)	Multilateral	07 Dec 50	Admin Cooperation	212UNTS17	102861
USSR (Soviet Union)	Multilateral	11 Jul 52	IGO Establishment	169UNTS3	102220
USSR (Soviet Union)	Multilateral	11 Jul 52	Postal Service	170UNTS3	102221
USSR (Soviet Union)	Multilateral	07 Feb 53	Territory Boundary	173UNTS143	102264
USSR (Soviet Union)	Multilateral	31 Mar 53	Privil/Immunities	193UNTS136	102613
USSR (Soviet Union)	Multilateral	01 Oct 53	Commodity Trade	258UNTS153	103677
USSR (Soviet Union)	Multilateral	12 May 54	Admin Cooperation	327UNTS3	104714
USSR (Soviet Union)	Multilateral	14 May 54	Culture	249UNTS215	103511
USSR (Soviet Union)	Multilateral	14 May 55	General Amity	219UNTS3	102962
USSR (Soviet Union)	Multilateral	15 May 55	Recognition	217UNTS223	102949
USSR (Soviet Union)	Multilateral	28 Sep 55	Air Transport	478UNTS371	106943
USSR (Soviet Union)	Multilateral	12 Oct 55	IGO Establishment	560UNTS3	108165
USSR (Soviet Union)	Multilateral	24 Feb 56	Specific Resources	243UNTS147	103451
USSR (Soviet Union)	Multilateral	26 Mar 56	IGO Establishment	259UNTS125	103686
USSR (Soviet Union)	Multilateral	07 Sep 56	Humanitarian	266UNTS3	103822
USSR (Soviet Union)	Multilateral	11 Sep 56	Humanitarian	266UNTS221	103832
USSR (Soviet Union)	Multilateral	26 Oct 56	IGO Establishment	276UNTS3	103988
USSR (Soviet Union)	Multilateral	09 Feb 57	Specific Resources	314UNTS105	104546
USSR (Soviet Union)	Multilateral	20 Feb 57	Consul/Citizenship	309UNTS65	104468
USSR (Soviet Union)	Multilateral	03 Oct 57	Postal Service	364UNTS331	105212
USSR (Soviet Union)	Multilateral	03 Oct 57	Postal Service	365UNTS3	105213
USSR (Soviet Union)	Multilateral	03 Oct 57	Postal Service	364UNTS3	105211
USSR (Soviet Union)	Multilateral	29 Jan 58	Specific Resources	339UNTS23	104845
USSR (Soviet Union)	Multilateral	29 Apr 58	Water Transport	450UNTS11	106465
USSR (Soviet Union)	Multilateral	29 Apr 58	Territory Boundary	499UNTS311	107302
USSR (Soviet Union)	Multilateral	29 Apr 58	Territory Boundary	516UNTS205	107477
USSR (Soviet Union)	Multilateral	01 Dec 58	Commodity Trade	385UNTS137	105534
USSR (Soviet Union)	Multilateral	03 Dec 58	Admin Cooperation	416UNTS51	105995
USSR (Soviet Union)	Multilateral	24 Jan 59	IGO Establishment	486UNTS157	107078
USSR (Soviet Union)	Multilateral	29 Apr 59	Specific Property	346UNTS167	104980
USSR (Soviet Union)	Multilateral	07 Jul 59	Specific Resources	377UNTS203	105402
USSR (Soviet Union)	Multilateral	01 Dec 59	Territory Boundary	402UNTS71	105778
USSR (Soviet Union)	Multilateral	14 Dec 59	Land Transport	422UNTS75	106069
USSR (Soviet Union)	Multilateral	14 Dec 59	IGO Status/Immunit	368UNTS237	105244
USSR (Soviet Union)	Multilateral	14 Dec 59	IGO Establishment	368UNTS253	105245
USSR (Soviet Union)	Multilateral	14 Dec 59	Sanitation	422UNTS33	106067
USSR (Soviet Union)	Multilateral	14 Dec 59	Sanitation	422UNTS57	106068
USSR (Soviet Union)	Multilateral	15 Mar 60	Water Transport	572UNTS133	108310
USSR (Soviet Union)	Multilateral	17 Jun 60	Humanitarian	536UNTS27	107794
USSR (Soviet Union)	Multilateral	29 Jul 60	Water Transport	392UNTS69	105640
USSR (Soviet Union)	Multilateral	14 Dec 60	Education	429UNTS93	106193
USSR (Soviet Union)	Multilateral	30 Mar 61	Sanitation	520UNTS151	107515
USSR (Soviet Union)	Multilateral	18 Apr 61	Consul/Citizenship	500UNTS95	107310
USSR (Soviet Union)	Multilateral	21 Apr 61	IGO Establishment	484UNTS349	107041
USSR (Soviet Union)	Multilateral	15 Dec 61	Admin Cooperation	424UNTS43	106098
USSR (Soviet Union)	Multilateral	20 Feb 62	Water Transport	597UNTS159	108644
USSR (Soviet Union)	Multilateral	15 May 62	Commodity Trade	444UNTS3	106367
USSR (Soviet Union)	Multilateral	06 Jun 62	Privil/Immunities	486UNTS263	107080
USSR (Soviet Union)	Multilateral	23 Jul 62	Recognition	456UNTS302	106564
USSR (Soviet Union)	Multilateral	25 Jul 62	Specific Property	506UNTS177	107387
USSR (Soviet Union)	Multilateral	28 Jul 62	Specific Resources	460UNTS219	106642
USSR (Soviet Union)	Multilateral	28 Sep 62	IGO Establishment	469UNTS169	106791
USSR (Soviet Union)	Multilateral	07 Jun 63	Water Transport	472UNTS95	106837
USSR (Soviet Union)	Multilateral	05 Aug 63	Sanitation	480UNTS43	106964
USSR (Soviet Union)	Multilateral	23 Oct 63	IGO Establishment	506UNTS197	107388
USSR (Soviet Union)	Multilateral	03 Mar 64	Consul/Citizenship	516UNTS53	107470
USSR (Soviet Union)	Multilateral	10 Jul 64	Postal Service	612UNTS3	108847
USSR (Soviet Union)	Multilateral	10 Jul 64	Postal Service	611UNTS7	108844
USSR (Soviet Union)	Multilateral	10 Jul 64	Postal Service	611UNTS387	108846
USSR (Soviet Union)	Multilateral	10 Jul 64	Postal Service	611UNTS105	108845
USSR (Soviet Union)	Multilateral	13 Jul 64	ILO Labor	569UNTS65	108279
USSR (Soviet Union)	Multilateral	12 Sep 64	Specific Resources	0UNTS0	109344

PARTY ONE	PARTY TWO	DATE	TOPIC	CITATION	NUMBER
USSR (Soviet Union)	Multilateral	09 Mar 65	Water Transport	591UNTS265	108564
USSR (Soviet Union)	Multilateral	08 Jul 65	General Trade	597UNTS3	108641
USSR (Soviet Union)	Multilateral	18 Nov 65	Customs	609UNTS115	108830
USSR (Soviet Union)	Multilateral	05 Apr 66	Water Transport	640UNTS133	109159
USSR (Soviet Union)	Multilateral	09 Sep 66	IGO Status/Immunit	0UNTS0	109343
USSR (Soviet Union)	Multilateral	27 Jan 67	Scientific Project	610UNTS205	108843
USSR (Soviet Union)	Multilateral	22 Apr 68	Scientific Project	0UNTS0	109574
USSR (Soviet Union)	Multilateral	01 Jul 68	Peace/Disarmament	0UNTS0	110485
USSR (Soviet Union)	Multilateral	26 Nov 68	Humanitarian	0UNTS0	110823
USSR (Soviet Union)	Multilateral	24 Dec 68	Commodity Trade	0UNTS0	109369
USSR (Soviet Union)	Nepal	09 Jul 56	Consul/Citizenship	16SUGG72	469921
USSR (Soviet Union)	Nepal	24 Apr 59	General Aid	8SUGG143	469573
USSR (Soviet Union)	Nepal	24 Apr 59	Non-IBRD Project	8SUGG143	469574
USSR (Soviet Union)	Nepal	12 Aug 60	Tech Assistance	9SUGG144	469683
USSR (Soviet Union)	Nepal	06 Feb 62	Direct Aid	11SUGG131	469819
USSR (Soviet Union)	Netherlands	10 Jul 42	Consul/Citizenship	241UNTS475	200540
USSR (Soviet Union)	Netherlands	24 Oct 45	General Trade	16SUGG62	469883
USSR (Soviet Union)	Netherlands	02 Jul 48	General Economic	0NETO	447009
USSR (Soviet Union)	Netherlands	27 Jun 56	General Trade	0SUST359	468291
USSR (Soviet Union)	Netherlands	17 Jun 58	Air Transport	335UNTS77	104779
USSR (Soviet Union)	Netherlands	06 Nov 59	General Trade	8SUGG157	469609
USSR (Soviet Union)	Netherlands	14 Jul 67	Culture	0UNTS0	110497
USSR (Soviet Union)	Netherlands	20 Oct 67	Claims and Debts	0UNTS0	109391
USSR (Soviet Union)	New Zealand	27 Mar 62	Visas	16SUGG132	470005
USSR (Soviet Union)	New Zealand	01 Aug 63	General Trade	486UNTS27	107070
USSR (Soviet Union)	Nigeria	12 Jan 61	Recognition	16SUGG130	469989
USSR (Soviet Union)	Nigeria	03 Apr 61	Consul/Citizenship	10SUGG127	469759
USSR (Soviet Union)	Norway	27 Dec 46	Finance	17UNTS283	100282
USSR (Soviet Union)	Norway	11 Feb 47	Telecommunications	0SUST228	468292
USSR (Soviet Union)	Norway	11 Feb 47	Postal Service	0SUST229	468293
USSR (Soviet Union)	Norway	19 Feb 47	General Trade	30UNTS293	100464
USSR (Soviet Union)	Norway	18 Dec 47	Territory Boundary	52UNTS3	100768
USSR (Soviet Union)	Norway	21 May 48	Claims and Debts	2NORT478	451205
USSR (Soviet Union)	Norway	23 May 49	Territory Boundary	2NORT500	451206
USSR (Soviet Union)	Norway	30 Nov 49	Finance	16SUGG65	469893
USSR (Soviet Union)	Norway	29 Dec 49	Territory Boundary	83UNTS291	101112
USSR (Soviet Union)	Norway	02 Jul 53	Other Military	0SUST441	468294
USSR (Soviet Union)	Norway	15 Nov 55	General Trade	0SUST341	468295
USSR (Soviet Union)	Norway	31 Mar 56	Air Transport	259UNTS205	103690
USSR (Soviet Union)	Norway	12 Oct 56	Culture	308UNTS95	104457
USSR (Soviet Union)	Norway	19 Oct 56	Humanitarian	257UNTS3	103644
USSR (Soviet Union)	Norway	15 Feb 57	Territory Boundary	312UNTS289	104523
USSR (Soviet Union)	Norway	07 Jun 57	Specific Resources	0SUST384	468298
USSR (Soviet Union)	Norway	01 Aug 57	Territory Boundary	0SUST386	468299
USSR (Soviet Union)	Norway	22 Nov 57	Specific Resources	309UNTS269	104476
USSR (Soviet Union)	Norway	29 Nov 57	Territory Boundary	0SUST392	468301
USSR (Soviet Union)	Norway	18 Dec 57	Specific Resources	312UNTS257	104522
USSR (Soviet Union)	Norway	20 Oct 58	Culture	7SUGG122	469536
USSR (Soviet Union)	Norway	30 Sep 59	Claims and Debts	3NORT784	451209
USSR (Soviet Union)	Norway	09 Dec 59	Specif Claim/Waive	361UNTS93	105173
USSR (Soviet Union)	Norway	12 May 61	Consul/Citizenship	3NORT833	451210
USSR (Soviet Union)	Norway	22 Feb 62	Specific Resources	11SUGG133	469823
USSR (Soviet Union)	Norway	16 Apr 62	Specific Resources	437UNTS175	106307
USSR (Soviet Union)	Norway	24 Dec 63	Territory Boundary	3NORT897	451211
USSR (Soviet Union)	Norway	08 Aug 64	Territory Boundary	3NORT921	451212
USSR (Soviet Union)	Norway	29 Jan 65	Finance	3NORT932	451213
USSR (Soviet Union)	Norway	06 Mar 65	Consul/Citizenship	3NORT934	451214
USSR (Soviet Union)	Norway	18 Dec 67	Territory Boundary	3NORT1013	451215
USSR (Soviet Union)	Norway	09 Jul 68	Admin Cooperation	3NORT0	451216
USSR (Soviet Union)	Pakistan	01 May 48	Consul/Citizenship	0SUST248	468303
USSR (Soviet Union)	Pakistan	27 Jun 56	General Trade	0SUST359	468304
USSR (Soviet Union)	Pakistan	27 Jun 56	Finance	16SUGG71	469920
USSR (Soviet Union)	Pakistan	27 Jun 56	General Trade	16SUGG71	469919
USSR (Soviet Union)	Pakistan	27 Jun 57	General Trade	0UNTS0	109823
USSR (Soviet Union)	Pakistan	04 Mar 61	General Aid	10SUGG124	469749

PARTY ONE	PARTY TWO	DATE	TOPIC	CITATION	NUMBER
USSR (Soviet Union)	Pakistan	07 Oct 63	Air Transport	499UNTS161	107297
USSR (Soviet Union)	Pakistan	05 Jun 65	Culture	593UNTS115	108579
USSR (Soviet Union)	Poland	05 Jan 45	Consul/Citizenship	0SUST169	468305
USSR (Soviet Union)	Poland	21 Apr 45	General Military	12UNTS391	200070
USSR (Soviet Union)	Poland	06 Jul 45	Consul/Citizenship	0SUST182	468306
USSR (Soviet Union)	Poland	07 Jul 45	General Trade	0SUST182	468307
USSR (Soviet Union)	Poland	11 Jul 45	Admin Cooperation	0SUST183	468308
USSR (Soviet Union)	Poland	16 Aug 45	Reparations	0SUST193	468309
USSR (Soviet Union)	Poland	16 Aug 45	Territory Boundary	10UNTS193	200061
USSR (Soviet Union)	Poland	23 Nov 45	Land Transport	0SUST201	468310
USSR (Soviet Union)	Poland	08 Feb 46	Loans and Credits	0SUST206	468311
USSR (Soviet Union)	Poland	20 Mar 46	Gen Communications	0SUST207	468312
USSR (Soviet Union)	Poland	12 Apr 46	General Trade	0SUST210	468313
USSR (Soviet Union)	Poland	05 Mar 47	Commodity Trade	0SUST230	468316
USSR (Soviet Union)	Poland	05 Mar 47	Tech Assistance	0SUST230	468318
USSR (Soviet Union)	Poland	05 Mar 47	Milit Assistance	0SUST230	468319
USSR (Soviet Union)	Poland	05 Mar 47	Loans and Credits	0SUST230	468314
USSR (Soviet Union)	Poland	05 Mar 47	Finance	0SUST230	468315
USSR (Soviet Union)	Poland	05 Mar 47	Specif Goods/Equip	0SUST230	468317
USSR (Soviet Union)	Poland	30 Apr 47	Territory Boundary	0SUST232	468321
USSR (Soviet Union)	Poland	06 May 47	Refugees	0SUST232	468320
USSR (Soviet Union)	Poland	04 Aug 47	General Trade	0SUST235	468322
USSR (Soviet Union)	Poland	01 Oct 47	Postal Service	0SUST237	468323
USSR (Soviet Union)	Poland	26 Jan 48	Loans and Credits	0SUST244	468325
USSR (Soviet Union)	Poland	26 Jan 48	General Trade	0SUST243	468324
USSR (Soviet Union)	Poland	08 Apr 48	Sanitation	26UNTS191	100388
USSR (Soviet Union)	Poland	08 Jul 48	Territory Boundary	37UNTS25	100575
USSR (Soviet Union)	Poland	08 Jul 48	Dispute Settlement	37UNTS107	100576
USSR (Soviet Union)	Poland	22 Oct 49	Mass Media	0SUST263	468327
USSR (Soviet Union)	Poland	29 Jun 50	Loans and Credits	0SUST275	468329
USSR (Soviet Union)	Poland	29 Jun 50	General Trade	0SUST275	468328
USSR (Soviet Union)	Poland	15 Feb 51	Territory Boundary	432UNTS199	106222
USSR (Soviet Union)	Poland	29 Feb 52	General Trade	0SUST285	468332
USSR (Soviet Union)	Poland	05 Apr 52	Culture	0SUST285	468333
USSR (Soviet Union)	Poland	19 May 52	Education	0SUST287	468334
USSR (Soviet Union)	Poland	05 Sep 53	Mass Media	0SUST301	468335
USSR (Soviet Union)	Poland	18 Feb 55	Air Transport	0SUST323	468336
USSR (Soviet Union)	Poland	18 Feb 55	Air Transport	55PZUM9	458021
USSR (Soviet Union)	Poland	23 Apr 55	Atomic Energy	0SUST326	468337
USSR (Soviet Union)	Poland	21 Jul 55	Direct Aid	16SUGG68	469907
USSR (Soviet Union)	Poland	01 Feb 56	Specific Property	56PZUM70	458038
USSR (Soviet Union)	Poland	07 Feb 56	Mass Media	0SUST349	468338
USSR (Soviet Union)	Poland	30 Jun 56	Culture	259UNTS311	103694
USSR (Soviet Union)	Poland	18 Sep 56	Loans and Credits	0SUST368	468339
USSR (Soviet Union)	Poland	02 Oct 56	Specific Property	56PZUM205	458047
USSR (Soviet Union)	Poland	17 Dec 56	Status of Forces	266UNTS179	103830
USSR (Soviet Union)	Poland	05 Mar 57	Territory Boundary	274UNTS133	103963
USSR (Soviet Union)	Poland	25 Mar 57	Extradition	281UNTS121	104075
USSR (Soviet Union)	Poland	27 Mar 57	Education	0SUST379	468340
USSR (Soviet Union)	Poland	23 May 57	Education	0SUST388	468341
USSR (Soviet Union)	Poland	22 Jun 57	Mass Media	16SUGG121	469943
USSR (Soviet Union)	Poland	23 Aug 57	Education	56PZUM90	458052
USSR (Soviet Union)	Poland	26 Oct 57	Status of Forces	432UNTS221	106223
USSR (Soviet Union)	Poland	28 Dec 57	Admin Cooperation	320UNTS3	104638
USSR (Soviet Union)	Poland	21 Jan 58	Consul/Citizenship	319UNTS291	104637
USSR (Soviet Union)	Poland	21 Jan 58	Consul/Citizenship	319UNTS277	104636
USSR (Soviet Union)	Poland	22 Jan 58	Atomic Energy	7SUGG103	469492
USSR (Soviet Union)	Poland	04 Feb 58	General Trade	7SUGG104	469494
USSR (Soviet Union)	Poland	05 Feb 58	Scientific Project	7SUGG105	469495
USSR (Soviet Union)	Poland	18 Mar 58	Territory Boundary	340UNTS89	104861
USSR (Soviet Union)	Poland	22 May 58	Culture	7SUGG112	469511
USSR (Soviet Union)	Poland	14 Jun 58	Water Transport	7SUGG114	469513
USSR (Soviet Union)	Poland	18 Jun 58	Status of Forces	7SUGG114	469514
USSR (Soviet Union)	Poland	10 Sep 58	Territory Boundary	7SUGG120	469528
USSR (Soviet Union)	Poland	02 Oct 58	General Trade	7SUGG121	469532

PARTY ONE	PARTY TWO	DATE	TOPIC	CITATION	NUMBER
USSR (Soviet Union)	Poland	03 Mar 59	Tech Assistance	8SUGG138	469561
USSR (Soviet Union)	Poland	03 Apr 59	Non-IBRD Project	8SUGG141	469571
USSR (Soviet Union)	Poland	05 Jun 59	Non-IBRD Project	8SUGG147	469580
USSR (Soviet Union)	Poland	19 Feb 60	Customs	16SUGG127	469971
USSR (Soviet Union)	Poland	19 Feb 60	Customs	60PZUM11	458072
USSR (Soviet Union)	Poland	10 Mar 60	Tech Assistance	9SUGG130	469642
USSR (Soviet Union)	Poland	10 Mar 60	General Trade	9SUGG129	469641
USSR (Soviet Union)	Poland	01 Apr 60	Finance	9SUGG132	469648
USSR (Soviet Union)	Poland	13 Sep 60	Tech Assistance	9SUGG148	469693
USSR (Soviet Union)	Poland	13 Sep 60	Tech Assistance	9SUGG148	469694
USSR (Soviet Union)	Poland	29 Sep 60	Commodity Trade	9SUGG148	469698
USSR (Soviet Union)	Poland	04 Jan 61	Health/Educ/Welfare	10SUGG117	469733
USSR (Soviet Union)	Poland	07 Jan 61	Direct Aid	10SUGG117	469735
USSR (Soviet Union)	Poland	05 Feb 61	Territory Boundary	420UNTS161	106046
USSR (Soviet Union)	Poland	15 Feb 61	Admin Cooperation	10SUGG121	469741
USSR (Soviet Union)	Poland	21 Apr 61	Non-IBRD Project	10SUGG128	469763
USSR (Soviet Union)	Poland	19 May 61	Tech Assistance	10SUGG130	469767
USSR (Soviet Union)	Poland	19 May 61	Direct Aid	10SUGG130	469766
USSR (Soviet Union)	Poland	22 Jun 61	Non-IBRD Project	10SUGG136	469780
USSR (Soviet Union)	Poland	30 Jun 61	Specif Goods/Equip	10SUGG137	469783
USSR (Soviet Union)	Poland	07 Jul 61	Atomic Energy	10SUGG137	469787
USSR (Soviet Union)	Poland	20 Jul 61	Non-IBRD Project	10SUGG138	469789
USSR (Soviet Union)	Poland	04 Oct 61	Specific Property	61PZUM209	458088
USSR (Soviet Union)	Poland	03 Dec 61	Atomic Energy	10SUGG145	469808
USSR (Soviet Union)	Poland	13 Dec 61	General Aid	10SUGG146	469809
USSR (Soviet Union)	Poland	22 Apr 63	Land Transport	493UNTS229	107217
USSR (Soviet Union)	Poland	17 Jul 64	Specific Resources	552UNTS175	108054
USSR (Soviet Union)	Poland	31 Mar 65	Consul/Citizenship	571UNTS217	108304
USSR (Soviet Union)	Poland	08 Apr 65	General Amity	540UNTS97	107845
USSR (Soviet Union)	Poland	07 May 66	Land Transport	66PZUM60	458134
USSR (Soviet Union)	Poland	24 Apr 68	Air Transport	68PZUM77	458155
USSR (Soviet Union)	Poland	29 Aug 69	Territory Boundary	70PDZU165	457164
USSR (Soviet Union)	Poland	14 Oct 70	Health/Educ/Welfare	71PDZU213	457170
USSR (Soviet Union)	Poland	27 May 71	Consul/Citizenship	72PDZU125	457171
USSR (Soviet Union)	Romania	16 Jan 45	Reparations	0SUST169	468344
USSR (Soviet Union)	Romania	09 Mar 45	Admin Cooperation	0SUST174	468345
USSR (Soviet Union)	Romania	08 May 45	General Trade	0SUST178	468346
USSR (Soviet Union)	Romania	08 May 45	Finance	0SUST178	468347
USSR (Soviet Union)	Romania	17 Jul 45	Specific Property	0SUST183	468348
USSR (Soviet Union)	Romania	19 Jul 45	Specific Property	0SUST183	468349
USSR (Soviet Union)	Romania	06 Aug 45	Consul/Citizenship	0SUST188	468350
USSR (Soviet Union)	Romania	08 Aug 45	Specific Property	0SUST189	468351
USSR (Soviet Union)	Romania	15 Aug 45	Specific Property	0SUST193	468352
USSR (Soviet Union)	Romania	20 Aug 45	Consul/Citizenship	0SUST194	468353
USSR (Soviet Union)	Romania	13 Sep 45	Health/Educ/Welfare	0SUST198	468360
USSR (Soviet Union)	Romania	13 Sep 45	Reparations	0SUST197	468355
USSR (Soviet Union)	Romania	13 Sep 45	Reparations	0SUST197	468357
USSR (Soviet Union)	Romania	13 Sep 45	Commodity Trade	0SUST197	468354
USSR (Soviet Union)	Romania	13 Sep 45	Land Transport	0SUST197	468358
USSR (Soviet Union)	Romania	13 Sep 45	Reparations	0SUST197	468356
USSR (Soviet Union)	Romania	13 Sep 45	Refugees	0SUST197	468359
USSR (Soviet Union)	Romania	15 Feb 46	Mostfavored Nation	0SUST206	468362
USSR (Soviet Union)	Romania	15 Feb 46	Finance	0SUST206	468361
USSR (Soviet Union)	Romania	20 Mar 46	Specific Property	0SUST208	468363
USSR (Soviet Union)	Romania	15 Apr 46	Reparations	0SUST210	468364
USSR (Soviet Union)	Romania	20 Feb 47	General Economic	0SUST229	468365
USSR (Soviet Union)	Romania	20 Feb 47	General Economic	226UNTS79	103110
USSR (Soviet Union)	Romania	12 Jun 47	Land Transport	0SUST232	468366
USSR (Soviet Union)	Romania	04 Feb 48	Territory Boundary	0SUST244	468367
USSR (Soviet Union)	Romania	04 Feb 48	General Military	48UNTS189	100745
USSR (Soviet Union)	Romania	18 Feb 48	General Economic	0SUST245	468368
USSR (Soviet Union)	Romania	07 Jun 48	Reparations	0SUST249	468369
USSR (Soviet Union)	Romania	20 Aug 48	Gen Communications	0SUST252	468370
USSR (Soviet Union)	Romania	20 Aug 48	Postal Service	0SUST252	468371
USSR (Soviet Union)	Romania	01 Nov 48	Specific Property	16SUGG64	469887

PARTY ONE	PARTY TWO	DATE	TOPIC	CITATION	NUMBER
USSR (Soviet Union)	Romania	24 Jan 49	General Economic	0SUST257	468373
USSR (Soviet Union)	Romania	24 Jan 49	Tech Assistance	0SUST257	468372
USSR (Soviet Union)	Romania	20 Feb 49	Specific Property	16SUGG64	469888
USSR (Soviet Union)	Romania	27 Apr 49	Territory Boundary	0SUST263	468375
USSR (Soviet Union)	Romania	27 Apr 49	Mass Media	0SUST258	468374
USSR (Soviet Union)	Romania	04 Jul 49	Specific Property	16SUGG65	469890
USSR (Soviet Union)	Romania	04 Aug 49	Specific Property	16SUGG65	469891
USSR (Soviet Union)	Romania	25 Nov 49	Admin Cooperation	0SUST264	468376
USSR (Soviet Union)	Romania	25 Nov 49	Dispute Settlement	0SUST264	468377
USSR (Soviet Union)	Romania	17 Feb 50	Scientific Project	0SUST270	468378
USSR (Soviet Union)	Romania	17 Feb 50	General Economic	0SUST270	468379
USSR (Soviet Union)	Romania	27 May 50	Sanitation	221UNTS13	103000
USSR (Soviet Union)	Romania	15 Mar 51	General Economic	0SUST280	468380
USSR (Soviet Union)	Romania	24 Aug 51	General Aid	0SUST282	468381
USSR (Soviet Union)	Romania	20 Mar 52	Education	0SUST285	468382
USSR (Soviet Union)	Romania	15 Aug 52	Specific Property	16SUGG66	469897
USSR (Soviet Union)	Romania	25 Dec 52	Specific Resources	0SUST292	468383
USSR (Soviet Union)	Romania	17 Aug 53	Mass Media	0SUST299	468384
USSR (Soviet Union)	Romania	05 Dec 53	Specific Property	0SUST304	468385
USSR (Soviet Union)	Romania	05 Dec 53	Admin Cooperation	0SUST304	468386
USSR (Soviet Union)	Romania	31 Mar 54	Loans and Credits	0SUST310	468388
USSR (Soviet Union)	Romania	31 Mar 54	Finance	0SUST309	468387
USSR (Soviet Union)	Romania	25 Jan 55	Air Transport	0SUST323	468389
USSR (Soviet Union)	Romania	22 Apr 55	Atomic Energy	0SUST326	468390
USSR (Soviet Union)	Romania	13 Dec 55	Finance	0SUST344	468391
USSR (Soviet Union)	Romania	03 Jan 56	Air Transport	0SUST346	468392
USSR (Soviet Union)	Romania	07 Apr 56	Culture	259UNTS377	103698
USSR (Soviet Union)	Romania	14 Apr 56	Gen Communications	0SUST353	468393
USSR (Soviet Union)	Romania	21 Jul 56	Commodity Trade	0SUST364	468394
USSR (Soviet Union)	Romania	24 Sep 56	Specific Resources	16SUGG73	469928
USSR (Soviet Union)	Romania	22 Oct 56	Finance	0SUST370	468395
USSR (Soviet Union)	Romania	03 Dec 56	Loans and Credits	0SUST373	468396
USSR (Soviet Union)	Romania	04 Mar 57	General Trade	0SUST379	468397
USSR (Soviet Union)	Romania	14 Mar 57	Mass Media	16SUGG119	469934
USSR (Soviet Union)	Romania	15 Apr 57	Status of Forces	274UNTS143	103964
USSR (Soviet Union)	Romania	06 May 57	Commodity Trade	16SUGG120	469938
USSR (Soviet Union)	Romania	18 Jun 57	Specific Property	0SUST385	468398
USSR (Soviet Union)	Romania	18 Jul 57	Admin Cooperation	0SUST386	468399
USSR (Soviet Union)	Romania	31 Jul 57	Specific Resources	16SUGG121	469944
USSR (Soviet Union)	Romania	01 Aug 57	Admin Cooperation	0SUST386	468400
USSR (Soviet Union)	Romania	04 Sep 57	Consul/Citizenship	318UNTS89	104610
USSR (Soviet Union)	Romania	04 Sep 57	Consul/Citizenship	318UNTS55	104609
USSR (Soviet Union)	Romania	19 Dec 57	Tech Assistance	16SUGG123	469950
USSR (Soviet Union)	Romania	19 Dec 57	Education	16SUGG123	469951
USSR (Soviet Union)	Romania	07 Mar 58	Claims and Debts	7SUGG107	469500
USSR (Soviet Union)	Romania	03 Apr 58	Admin Cooperation	313UNTS167	104535
USSR (Soviet Union)	Romania	02 Feb 59	General Trade	8SUGG136	469555
USSR (Soviet Union)	Romania	20 Mar 59	Tech Assistance	8SUGG141	469567
USSR (Soviet Union)	Romania	15 Oct 59	Specific Resources	16SUGG126	469966
USSR (Soviet Union)	Romania	01 Dec 59	Tech Assistance	8SUGG159	469612
USSR (Soviet Union)	Romania	02 Dec 59	Tech Assistance	8SUGG160	469614
USSR (Soviet Union)	Romania	11 Nov 60	General Trade	9SUGG151	469707
USSR (Soviet Union)	Romania	11 Nov 60	Tech Assistance	9SUGG151	469710
USSR (Soviet Union)	Romania	08 Dec 60	Education	16SUGG129	469986
USSR (Soviet Union)	Romania	22 Dec 60	Customs	16SUGG130	469987
USSR (Soviet Union)	Romania	24 Dec 60	Admin Cooperation	472UNTS245	106843
USSR (Soviet Union)	Romania	27 Feb 61	Admin Cooperation	10SUGG123	469747
USSR (Soviet Union)	Romania	28 Mar 61	Tech Assistance	10SUGG126	469755
USSR (Soviet Union)	Romania	01 Dec 61	Tech Assistance	10SUGG145	469807
USSR (Soviet Union)	Romania	23 Dec 61	Non-IBRD Project	10SUGG148	469814
USSR (Soviet Union)	Romania	19 Apr 62	Atomic Energy	11SUGG138	469834
USSR (Soviet Union)	Romania	04 Mar 66	Visas	591UNTS327	108565
USSR (Soviet Union)	Romania	21 Jun 66	Land Transport	604UNTS81	108746
USSR (Soviet Union)	Rwanda	30 Jun 62	Recognition	11SUGG145	469849
USSR (Soviet Union)	Rwanda	06 May 66	Culture	633UNTS217	109039

PARTY ONE	PARTY TWO	DATE	TOPIC	CITATION	NUMBER
USSR (Soviet Union)	San Marino	29 Feb 56	Consul/Citizenship	16SUGG70	469912
USSR (Soviet Union)	Senegal	14 Jun 62	General Trade	11SUGG143	469842
USSR (Soviet Union)	Senegal	14 Jun 62	Consul/Citizenship	16SUGG133	470008
USSR (Soviet Union)	Senegal	14 Jun 62	General Aid	11SUGG143	469843
USSR (Soviet Union)	Senegal	14 Jun 62	Culture	437UNTS233	106309
USSR (Soviet Union)	Sierra Leone	18 Jan 62	Recognition	16SUGG132	469999
USSR (Soviet Union)	Sierra Leone	26 Apr 65	General Trade	0UNTS0	109831
USSR (Soviet Union)	Singapore	02 Apr 66	General Trade	631UNTS125	108992
USSR (Soviet Union)	Somalia	11 Sep 60	Consul/Citizenship	9SUGG149	469701
USSR (Soviet Union)	Somalia	02 Jun 61	Culture	528UNTS147	107638
USSR (Soviet Union)	Somalia	02 Jun 61	General Trade	493UNTS173	107214
USSR (Soviet Union)	Somalia	02 Jun 61	Tech Assistance	457UNTS263	106587
USSR (Soviet Union)	Somalia	27 Mar 62	General Aid	11SUGG136	469829
USSR (Soviet Union)	Somalia	27 Mar 62	Direct Aid	11SUGG136	469830
USSR (Soviet Union)	Sudan	07 Jan 56	Consul/Citizenship	0SUST351	468415
USSR (Soviet Union)	Sudan	16 Mar 59	General Trade	8SUGG140	469565
USSR (Soviet Union)	Sudan	01 Nov 61	General Trade	10SUGG143	469801
USSR (Soviet Union)	Sudan	01 Nov 61	General Trade	0UNTS0	109827
USSR (Soviet Union)	Sudan	21 Nov 61	Direct Aid	10SUGG145	469805
USSR (Soviet Union)	Sudan	20 Oct 62	Air Transport	11SUGG156	469870
USSR (Soviet Union)	Sweden	07 Oct 46	Claims and Debts	0SUST219	468407
USSR (Soviet Union)	Sweden	07 Oct 46	General Trade	0SUST218	468404
USSR (Soviet Union)	Sweden	07 Oct 46	General Trade	0SUST219	468406
USSR (Soviet Union)	Sweden	07 Oct 46	Loans and Credits	0SUST218	468405
USSR (Soviet Union)	Sweden	25 Oct 46	Air Transport	0SUST220	468408
USSR (Soviet Union)	Sweden	25 Oct 46	Air Transport	0SUST220	468409
USSR (Soviet Union)	Sweden	05 Nov 46	Postal Service	0SUST221	468410
USSR (Soviet Union)	Sweden	30 Jan 47	General Trade	0SUST225	468411
USSR (Soviet Union)	Sweden	31 Dec 47	General Trade	47SOFM511	461053
USSR (Soviet Union)	Sweden	02 Apr 49	General Trade	49SOFM145	461079
USSR (Soviet Union)	Sweden	23 Jan 54	Air Transport	0SUST306	468412
USSR (Soviet Union)	Sweden	29 Sep 54	Humanitarian	202UNTS259	102733
USSR (Soviet Union)	Sweden	31 Mar 56	Air Transport	259UNTS239	103691
USSR (Soviet Union)	Sweden	28 Jan 57	Finance	428UNTS315	106183
USSR (Soviet Union)	Sweden	27 Mar 58	Specific Property	7SUGG108	469501
USSR (Soviet Union)	Sweden	28 Mar 58	Privil/Immunities	428UNTS321	106184
USSR (Soviet Union)	Sweden	02 Feb 62	General Trade	11SUGG131	469818
USSR (Soviet Union)	Sweden	30 Nov 67	Consul/Citizenship	0UNTS0	109385
USSR (Soviet Union)	Switzerland	18 Mar 46	Consul/Citizenship	0SUST207	468413
USSR (Soviet Union)	Switzerland	17 Mar 48	General Trade	0SUST246	468414
USSR (Soviet Union)	Switzerland	17 Mar 48	General Trade	217UNTS87	102945
USSR (Soviet Union)	Switzerland	17 Mar 48	General Trade	217UNTS73	102944
USSR (Soviet Union)	Syria	16 Nov 55	General Economic	259UNTS71	103683
USSR (Soviet Union)	Syria	19 Nov 55	Consul/Citizenship	0SUST444	468416
USSR (Soviet Union)	Syria	20 Aug 56	Culture	274UNTS105	103961
USSR (Soviet Union)	Syria	29 Jun 57	Telecommunications	0SUST385	468417
USSR (Soviet Union)	Syria	28 Oct 57	General Aid	0SUST391	468418
USSR (Soviet Union)	Syria	19 Dec 57	General Trade	0SUST394	468419
USSR (Soviet Union)	Syria	07 Oct 61	Consul/Citizenship	10SUGG143	469798
USSR (Soviet Union)	Syria	28 Feb 62	Consul/Citizenship	16SUGG132	470002
USSR (Soviet Union)	Syria	19 Aug 62	Culture	457UNTS285	106588
USSR (Soviet Union)	Syria	18 Dec 66	Non-IBRD Project	633UNTS247	109041
USSR (Soviet Union)	Taiwan	14 Aug 45	General Amity	10UNTS300	200068
USSR (Soviet Union)	Tanganyika	10 Dec 61	Recognition	16SUGG132	469997
USSR (Soviet Union)	Tanganyika	14 Aug 63	General Trade	493UNTS195	107215
USSR (Soviet Union)	Tanganyika	06 Nov 63	Culture	528UNTS157	107639
USSR (Soviet Union)	Thailand	31 Dec 46	Consul/Citizenship	0SUST225	468420
USSR (Soviet Union)	Thailand	17 May 56	Consul/Citizenship	16SUGG71	469916
USSR (Soviet Union)	Thailand	20 May 56	Consul/Citizenship	0SUST355	468421
USSR (Soviet Union)	Togo	01 May 60	Consul/Citizenship	9SUGG134	469652
USSR (Soviet Union)	Togo	12 Jun 61	General Trade	0SUST135	471030
USSR (Soviet Union)	Togo	12 Jun 61	General Trade	0UNTS0	110495
USSR (Soviet Union)	Togo	14 Jun 61	General Trade	0UNTS0	110496
USSR (Soviet Union)	Trinidad/Tobago	30 Aug 62	Recognition	11SUGG150	469859
USSR (Soviet Union)	Tunisia	11 Jul 56	Recognition	16SUGG72	469922
USSR (Soviet Union)	Tunisia	16 Jan 60	General Trade	9SUGG121	469622
USSR (Soviet Union)	Tunisia	04 May 60	Consul/Citizenship	9SUGG134	469654
USSR (Soviet Union)	Tunisia	10 Jan 61	Consul/Citizenship	16SUGG130	469988
USSR (Soviet Union)	Tunisia	30 Aug 61	General Aid	437UNTS243	106310
USSR (Soviet Union)	Tunisia	14 Mar 62	Finance	11SUGG135	469827
USSR (Soviet Union)	Tunisia	14 Mar 62	General Trade	11SUGG135	469825
USSR (Soviet Union)	Tunisia	14 Mar 62	Mostfavored Nation	11SUGG135	469826
USSR (Soviet Union)	Turkey	18 Jul 53	Dispute Settlement	0SUST298	468422
USSR (Soviet Union)	Turkey	15 Sep 53	Specific Resources	0SUST301	468423
USSR (Soviet Union)	Turkey	27 Apr 61	Land Transport	420UNTS307	106047
USSR (Soviet Union)	Turkey	09 Jun 62	Telecommunications	493UNTS155	107213
USSR (Soviet Union)	Turkey	24 Feb 67	Scientific Project	643UNTS153	109190
USSR (Soviet Union)	Uganda	08 Oct 62	Recognition	11SUGG155	469868
USSR (Soviet Union)	Uganda	13 Oct 62	Consul/Citizenship	11SUGG156	469869
USSR (Soviet Union)	Uganda	24 Jul 65	Culture	596UNTS199	108633
USSR (Soviet Union)	UK Great Britain	16 Aug 41	Finance	91UNTS341	200269
USSR (Soviet Union)	UK Great Britain	22 Jun 42	Finance	91UNTS355	200270
USSR (Soviet Union)	UK Great Britain	23 Sep 44	Telecommunications	10UNTS171	200060
USSR (Soviet Union)	UK Great Britain	11 Feb 45	Refugees	0SUST173	468424
USSR (Soviet Union)	UK Great Britain	11 Feb 45	Refugees	0SUST174	468427
USSR (Soviet Union)	UK Great Britain	11 Feb 45	Refugees	0SUST173	468425
USSR (Soviet Union)	UK Great Britain	11 Feb 45	Refugees	0SUST173	468426
USSR (Soviet Union)	UK Great Britain	02 Oct 45	Milit Occupation	0SUST199	468428
USSR (Soviet Union)	UK Great Britain	09 Jul 46	Telecommunications	0SUST214	468429
USSR (Soviet Union)	UK Great Britain	27 Dec 47	General Economic	91UNTS113	101245
USSR (Soviet Union)	UK Great Britain	27 Dec 47	Finance	82UNTS251	101098
USSR (Soviet Union)	UK Great Britain	19 Mar 53	Refugees	0SUST293	468430
USSR (Soviet Union)	UK Great Britain	25 May 56	Specific Resources	266UNTS209	103831
USSR (Soviet Union)	UK Great Britain	19 Dec 57	Air Transport	351UNTS235	105026
USSR (Soviet Union)	UK Great Britain	03 Mar 59	Culture	8SUGG138	469562
USSR (Soviet Union)	UK Great Britain	28 Mar 59	Health/Educ/Welfare	8SUGG141	469569
USSR (Soviet Union)	UK Great Britain	24 May 59	General Trade	374UNTS305	105344
USSR (Soviet Union)	UK Great Britain	01 Dec 59	Health/Educ/Welfare	351UNTS313	105032
USSR (Soviet Union)	UK Great Britain	22 Dec 59	General Trade	8SUGG163	469618
USSR (Soviet Union)	UK Great Britain	09 Jan 61	Health/Educ/Welfare	404UNTS175	105810
USSR (Soviet Union)	UK Great Britain	12 Jan 61	Culture	398UNTS157	105720
USSR (Soviet Union)	UK Great Britain	19 May 61	Atomic Energy	10SUGG131	469768
USSR (Soviet Union)	UK Great Britain	21 Jan 63	Health/Educ/Welfare	475UNTS3	106887
USSR (Soviet Union)	UK Great Britain	13 Apr 64	Visas	539UNTS197	107832
USSR (Soviet Union)	UK Great Britain	30 Sep 64	Specific Property	539UNTS159	107829
USSR (Soviet Union)	UK Great Britain	06 Jan 65	Scientific Project	543UNTS77	107897
USSR (Soviet Union)	UK Great Britain	13 Feb 65	Health/Educ/Welfare	543UNTS43	107896
USSR (Soviet Union)	UK Great Britain	02 Dec 65	Consul/Citizenship	0UNTS0	109384
USSR (Soviet Union)	UK Great Britain	24 Feb 67	Scientific Project	606UNTS171	108785
USSR (Soviet Union)	UK Great Britain	25 Aug 67	Gen Communications	632UNTS49	109007
USSR (Soviet Union)	UK Great Britain	05 Jan 68	Claims and Debts	638UNTS41	109130
USSR (Soviet Union)	UK Great Britain	19 Jan 68	Scientific Project	0UNTS0	109277
USSR (Soviet Union)	UK Great Britain	15 Aug 68	Visas	0UNTS0	109473
USSR (Soviet Union)	UK Great Britain	28 Mar 69	Scientific Project	0UNTS0	109880
USSR (Soviet Union)	UK Great Britain	03 Jun 69	General Trade	0UNTS0	110026
USSR (Soviet Union)	United Arab Rep	03 Mar 48	Mostfavored Nation	0SUST246	468123
USSR (Soviet Union)	United Arab Rep	18 Aug 53	Finance	0SUST299	468124
USSR (Soviet Union)	United Arab Rep	18 Aug 53	General Trade	16SUGG67	469900
USSR (Soviet Union)	United Arab Rep	23 Mar 54	Consul/Citizenship	0SUST308	468125
USSR (Soviet Union)	United Arab Rep	27 Mar 54	General Trade	0SUST309	468126
USSR (Soviet Union)	United Arab Rep	27 Mar 54	Non-ILO Labor	0SUST309	468128
USSR (Soviet Union)	United Arab Rep	27 Mar 54	General Trade	0SUST309	468127
USSR (Soviet Union)	United Arab Rep	12 Jul 56	Atomic Energy	0SUST363	468129
USSR (Soviet Union)	United Arab Rep	15 Jul 56	General Trade	0UNTS0	109824
USSR (Soviet Union)	United Arab Rep	19 Oct 57	Culture	0SUST391	468130
USSR (Soviet Union)	United Arab Rep	19 Oct 57	Culture	292UNTS151	104271
USSR (Soviet Union)	United Arab Rep	29 Jan 58	General Aid	7SUGG103	469493
USSR (Soviet Union)	United Arab Rep	10 Apr 58	Culture	7SUGG109	469503
USSR (Soviet Union)	United Arab Rep	10 Aug 58	General Trade	7SUGG118	469524
USSR (Soviet Union)	United Arab Rep	11 Sep 58	Air Transport	7SUGG121	469530

PARTY ONE	PARTY TWO	DATE	TOPIC	CITATION	NUMBER
USSR (Soviet Union)	United Arab Rep	18 Sep 58	Water Transport	338UNTS29	104831
USSR (Soviet Union)	United Arab Rep	18 Jan 59	Non-IBRD Project	8SUGG134	469553
USSR (Soviet Union)	United Arab Rep	17 Jan 60	Non-IBRD Project	9SUGG121	469621
USSR (Soviet Union)	United Arab Rep	21 Mar 60	Visas	16SUGG127	469974
USSR (Soviet Union)	United Arab Rep	08 Jul 60	Loans and Credits	9SUGG154	469720
USSR (Soviet Union)	United Arab Rep	11 Aug 60	Tech Assistance	9SUGG144	469681
USSR (Soviet Union)	United Arab Rep	27 Aug 60	Tech Assistance	399UNTS37	105733
USSR (Soviet Union)	United Arab Rep	01 Feb 62	Consul/Citizenship	16SUGG132	470001
USSR (Soviet Union)	United Arab Rep	23 Jun 62	General Trade	11SUGG145	469847
USSR (Soviet Union)	United Arab Rep	23 Jun 62	Finance	11SUGG144	469846
USSR (Soviet Union)	United Arab Rep	23 Jun 62	General Trade	472UNTS43	106836
USSR (Soviet Union)	United Arab Rep	23 Jun 62	Finance	472UNTS19	106835
USSR (Soviet Union)	United Nations	04 May 70	Education	0UNTS0	110459
USSR (Soviet Union)	Upper Volta	08 Mar 68	General Trade	0UNTS0	110280
USSR (Soviet Union)	Uruguay	28 Jul 54	Finance	0SUST315	468442
USSR (Soviet Union)	Uruguay	11 Aug 56	General Economic	0SUST366	468444
USSR (Soviet Union)	Uruguay	11 Aug 56	General Trade	0SUST366	468443
USSR (Soviet Union)	USA (United States)	02 Aug 41	General Trade	102UNTS269	200306
USSR (Soviet Union)	USA (United States)	18 Apr 42	Milit Assistance	105UNTS285	200339
USSR (Soviet Union)	USA (United States)	11 Feb 45	Other Military	68UNTS175	200229
USSR (Soviet Union)	USA (United States)	17 Sep 45	Milit Occupation	235UNTS346	200538
USSR (Soviet Union)	USA (United States)	15 Oct 45	Milit Assistance	278UNTS151	200547
USSR (Soviet Union)	USA (United States)	05 Feb 46	General Ad Hoc	0SUST206	468432
USSR (Soviet Union)	USA (United States)	18 Apr 46	General Ad Hoc	0SUST210	468433
USSR (Soviet Union)	USA (United States)	23 Apr 46	Culture	0SUST210	468434
USSR (Soviet Union)	USA (United States)	24 May 46	Telecommunications	4UNTS201	100046
USSR (Soviet Union)	USA (United States)	19 Aug 46	Admin Cooperation	0SUST218	468435
USSR (Soviet Union)	USA (United States)	15 Apr 47	General Aid	0SUST438	468436
USSR (Soviet Union)	USA (United States)	16 Jun 47	Consul/Citizenship	0SUST232	468437
USSR (Soviet Union)	USA (United States)	27 Sep 49	Milit Assistance	149UNTS23	101948
USSR (Soviet Union)	USA (United States)	26 Dec 53	Specif Goods/Equip	0SUST305	468438
USSR (Soviet Union)	USA (United States)	26 Mar 54	Milit Assistance	247UNTS263	103475
USSR (Soviet Union)	USA (United States)	22 Dec 54	Milit Assistance	251UNTS41	103532
USSR (Soviet Union)	USA (United States)	26 May 55	Milit Assistance	270UNTS61	103892
USSR (Soviet Union)	USA (United States)	25 Jun 55	Territory Boundary	270UNTS15	103887
USSR (Soviet Union)	USA (United States)	05 Sep 55	Sanitation	256UNTS307	103641
USSR (Soviet Union)	USA (United States)	16 Dec 55	Culture	0SUST344	468439
USSR (Soviet Union)	USA (United States)	09 Jul 56	Specif Goods/Equip	0SUST363	468440
USSR (Soviet Union)	USA (United States)	29 Dec 56	Privil/Immunities	0SUST371	468441
USSR (Soviet Union)	USA (United States)	27 Jan 58	Health/Educ/Welfare	301UNTS405	104350
USSR (Soviet Union)	USA (United States)	20 Aug 58	Visas	336UNTS269	104809
USSR (Soviet Union)	USA (United States)	10 Sep 58	Culture	7SUGG121	469529
USSR (Soviet Union)	USA (United States)	09 Oct 58	Mass Media	7SUGG122	469534
USSR (Soviet Union)	USA (United States)	29 Dec 58	Culture	7SUGG131	469548
USSR (Soviet Union)	USA (United States)	16 Apr 59	Culture	8SUGG142	469572
USSR (Soviet Union)	USA (United States)	21 Nov 59	Culture	361UNTS35	105172
USSR (Soviet Union)	USA (United States)	22 Dec 59	Claims and Debts	8SUGG163	469619
USSR (Soviet Union)	USA (United States)	08 Mar 62	Health/Educ/Welfare	460UNTS3	106630
USSR (Soviet Union)	USA (United States)	30 Oct 62	Scientific Project	11SUGG156	469871
USSR (Soviet Union)	USA (United States)	20 Jun 63	Specif Goods/Equip	472UNTS163	106839
USSR (Soviet Union)	USA (United States)	22 Feb 64	Health/Educ/Welfare	526UNTS131	107605
USSR (Soviet Union)	USA (United States)	01 Jun 64	Consul/Citizenship	0UNTS0	109383
USSR (Soviet Union)	USA (United States)	18 Nov 64	Atomic Energy	535UNTS307	107786
USSR (Soviet Union)	USA (United States)	14 Dec 64	Specific Property	531UNTS213	107705
USSR (Soviet Union)	USA (United States)	05 Feb 65	Specific Resources	541UNTS97	107863
USSR (Soviet Union)	USA (United States)	19 Mar 66	Scientific Project	0UNTS0	109617
USSR (Soviet Union)	USA (United States)	04 Nov 66	Air Transport	0UNTS0	109606
USSR (Soviet Union)	USA (United States)	13 Feb 67	Specific Resources	0UNTS0	109848
USSR (Soviet Union)	USA (United States)	25 Nov 67	Specific Resources	0UNTS0	110057
USSR (Soviet Union)	USA (United States)	15 Jul 68	Scientific Project	0UNTS0	110069
USSR (Soviet Union)	USA (United States)	16 May 69	Consul/Citizenship	0UNTS0	110275
USSR (Soviet Union)	USA (United States)	10 Feb 70	Scientific Project	0UNTS0	110774
USSR (Soviet Union)	Venezuela	14 Mar 45	Consul/Citizenship	0SUST175	468445
USSR (Soviet Union)	Vietnam, North	30 Jan 50	Consul/Citizenship	0SUST268	468446
USSR (Soviet Union)	Vietnam, North	08 Jul 55	General Trade	0SUST331	468448

PARTY ONE	PARTY TWO	DATE	TOPIC	CITATION	NUMBER
USSR (Soviet Union)	Vietnam, North	08 Jul 55	General Trade	0SUST331	468447
USSR (Soviet Union)	Vietnam, North	18 Jul 55	General Trade	0SUST333	468450
USSR (Soviet Union)	Vietnam, North	18 Jul 55	Direct Aid	0SUST333	468449
USSR (Soviet Union)	Vietnam, North	27 Aug 55	Education	16SUGG69	469909
USSR (Soviet Union)	Vietnam, North	01 Dec 56	Loans and Credits	0SUST445	468451
USSR (Soviet Union)	Vietnam, North	15 Feb 57	Culture	274UNTS115	103962
USSR (Soviet Union)	Vietnam, North	11 Mar 57	Finance	0SUST379	468452
USSR (Soviet Union)	Vietnam, North	08 Apr 57	General Trade	0SUST380	468453
USSR (Soviet Union)	Vietnam, North	25 Dec 57	Culture	0SUST395	468454
USSR (Soviet Union)	Vietnam, North	26 Dec 57	Postal Service	0SUST395	468456
USSR (Soviet Union)	Vietnam, North	26 Dec 57	Telecommunications	0SUST395	468455
USSR (Soviet Union)	Vietnam, North	12 Mar 58	General Economic	356UNTS149	105094
USSR (Soviet Union)	Vietnam, North	07 Mar 59	Tech Assistance	8SUGG139	469563
USSR (Soviet Union)	Vietnam, North	05 Jun 59	Consul/Citizenship	356UNTS111	105093
USSR (Soviet Union)	Vietnam, North	14 Jun 60	Loans and Credits	9SUGG138	469664
USSR (Soviet Union)	Vietnam, North	02 Aug 60	Tech Assistance	9SUGG143	469680
USSR (Soviet Union)	Vietnam, North	26 Aug 60	General Aid	9SUGG145	469687
USSR (Soviet Union)	Vietnam, North	30 Sep 60	Tech Assistance	9SUGG148	469699
USSR (Soviet Union)	Vietnam, North	23 Dec 60	General Aid	9SUGG157	469726
USSR (Soviet Union)	Vietnam, North	23 Dec 60	General Trade	9SUGG157	469727
USSR (Soviet Union)	Vietnam, North	27 Jan 61	Direct Aid	10SUGG119	469738
USSR (Soviet Union)	Vietnam, North	06 Mar 61	Tech Assistance	10SUGG124	469750
USSR (Soviet Union)	Vietnam, North	09 Mar 61	Tech Assistance	10SUGG124	469751
USSR (Soviet Union)	Vietnam, North	15 Sep 62	General Aid	11SUGG152	469860
USSR (Soviet Union)	Western Samoa	01 Jan 62	Recognition	11SUGG130	469815
USSR (Soviet Union)	Yemen	31 Oct 55	General Amity	240UNTS317	103410
USSR (Soviet Union)	Yemen	08 Mar 56	General Trade	0SUST350	468457
USSR (Soviet Union)	Yemen	11 Jul 56	General Economic	0SUST363	468458
USSR (Soviet Union)	Yemen	01 Dec 59	Tech Assistance	8SUGG160	469613
USSR (Soviet Union)	Yemen	04 Apr 60	Non-IBRD Project	9SUGG133	469650
USSR (Soviet Union)	Yemen	25 Jun 60	Tech Assistance	9SUGG140	469668
USSR (Soviet Union)	Yemen	04 Jun 61	Non-IBRD Project	10SUGG134	469774
USSR (Soviet Union)	Yemen	04 Oct 62	Recognition	11SUGG155	469867
USSR (Soviet Union)	Yemen	19 Mar 63	General Trade	0UNTS0	109581
USSR (Soviet Union)	Yemen	21 Mar 64	General Amity	553UNTS267	108094
USSR (Soviet Union)	Yugoslavia	11 Apr 45	General Amity	0SUST175	468459
USSR (Soviet Union)	Yugoslavia	13 Apr 45	General Trade	0SUST175	468460
USSR (Soviet Union)	Yugoslavia	13 Nov 45	Scientific Project	116UNTS139	101573
USSR (Soviet Union)	Yugoslavia	30 Nov 45	General Trade	116UNTS153	101574
USSR (Soviet Union)	Yugoslavia	26 Apr 46	General Trade	116UNTS163	101575
USSR (Soviet Union)	Yugoslavia	08 Jun 46	General Trade	0SUST213	468461
USSR (Soviet Union)	Yugoslavia	04 Feb 47	Air Transport	130UNTS235	101731
USSR (Soviet Union)	Yugoslavia	04 Feb 47	Admin Cooperation	116UNTS171	101576
USSR (Soviet Union)	Yugoslavia	05 Jul 47	General Economic	0SUST234	468462
USSR (Soviet Union)	Yugoslavia	05 Jul 47	Finance	0SUST234	468463
USSR (Soviet Union)	Yugoslavia	25 Jul 47	Tech Assistance	130UNTS315	101732
USSR (Soviet Union)	Yugoslavia	23 Aug 47	Reparations	116UNTS281	101577
USSR (Soviet Union)	Yugoslavia	15 Dec 47	Education	116UNTS313	101578
USSR (Soviet Union)	Yugoslavia	27 Dec 48	General Trade	116UNTS327	101579
USSR (Soviet Union)	Yugoslavia	31 Aug 49	Admin Cooperation	116UNTS345	101580
USSR (Soviet Union)	Yugoslavia	14 Jun 53	Consul/Citizenship	0SUST296	468464
USSR (Soviet Union)	Yugoslavia	01 Oct 54	General Trade	0SUST316	468465
USSR (Soviet Union)	Yugoslavia	05 Jan 55	General Trade	0SUST322	468466
USSR (Soviet Union)	Yugoslavia	05 Jan 55	Finance	240UNTS225	103405
USSR (Soviet Union)	Yugoslavia	05 Jan 55	General Trade	240UNTS207	103404
USSR (Soviet Union)	Yugoslavia	10 Jan 55	Air Transport	0SUST322	468467
USSR (Soviet Union)	Yugoslavia	10 Jan 55	Air Transport	0SUST322	468468
USSR (Soviet Union)	Yugoslavia	30 Jul 55	General Trade	0SUST334	468469
USSR (Soviet Union)	Yugoslavia	03 Sep 55	Air Transport	240UNTS267	103408
USSR (Soviet Union)	Yugoslavia	27 Sep 55	Postal Service	0SUST339	468471
USSR (Soviet Union)	Yugoslavia	27 Sep 55	Gen Communications	0SUST338	468470
USSR (Soviet Union)	Yugoslavia	12 Nov 55	Culture	0SUST340	468472
USSR (Soviet Union)	Yugoslavia	19 Dec 55	Scientific Project	378UNTS127	105423
USSR (Soviet Union)	Yugoslavia	12 Jan 56	Direct Aid	0SUST347	468474
USSR (Soviet Union)	Yugoslavia	28 Jan 56	Atomic Energy	0SUST348	468475

PARTY ONE	PARTY TWO	DATE	TOPIC	CITATION	NUMBER
USSR (Soviet Union)	Yugoslavia	02 Feb 56	Loans and Credits	259UNTS111	103685
USSR (Soviet Union)	Yugoslavia	03 Mar 56	Water Transport	0SUST350	468477
USSR (Soviet Union)	Yugoslavia	09 Mar 56	Claims and Debts	0SUST351	468478
USSR (Soviet Union)	Yugoslavia	17 May 56	Culture	259UNTS145	103687
USSR (Soviet Union)	Yugoslavia	22 May 56	Consul/Citizenship	259UNTS155	103688
USSR (Soviet Union)	Yugoslavia	20 Jun 56	Admin Cooperation	0SUST358	468479
USSR (Soviet Union)	Yugoslavia	27 Aug 56	Specif Goods/Equip	16SUGG73	469925
USSR (Soviet Union)	Yugoslavia	09 Feb 57	Scientific Project	0SUST377	468480
USSR (Soviet Union)	Yugoslavia	10 Apr 57	General Trade	0SUST381	468481
USSR (Soviet Union)	Yugoslavia	10 Jul 57	Mass Media	0SUST386	468482
USSR (Soviet Union)	Yugoslavia	29 Jul 57	Direct Aid	0SUST386	468483
USSR (Soviet Union)	Yugoslavia	21 Jul 60	Consul/Citizenship	9SUGG142	469677
USSR (Soviet Union)	Yugoslavia	30 Mar 61	General Trade	10SUGG126	469756
USSR (Soviet Union)	Yugoslavia	24 Feb 62	Admin Cooperation	471UNTS195	106833
USSR (Soviet Union)	Yugoslavia	29 Sep 66	General Aid	608UNTS219	108818
USSR (Soviet Union)	Zambia	26 May 67	General Economic	643UNTS179	109191
Vatican/Holy See	Argentina	10 Oct 66	Consul/Citizenship	601UNTS187	108696
Vatican/Holy See	Austria	23 Jun 60	Claims and Debts	60ABGB195	403207
Vatican/Holy See	Austria	23 Jun 60	Admin Cooperation	60ABGB196	403209
Vatican/Holy See	Austria	09 Jul 62	Education	62ABGB273	403210
Vatican/Holy See	Austria	07 Jul 64	Admin Cooperation	64ABGB227	403211
Vatican/Holy See	Austria	07 Oct 68	Admin Cooperation	68ABGB417	403212
Vatican/Holy See	Austria	29 Sep 69	Claims and Debts	70ABGB107	403208
Vatican/Holy See	Italy	16 Apr 45	Territory Boundary	47ITGU169	435335
Vatican/Holy See	Italy	21 Aug 46	Admin Cooperation	60ITMA422	437336
Vatican/Holy See	Italy	31 Apr 47	Territory Boundary	48ITGU190	435337
Vatican/Holy See	Italy	24 Apr 48	Territory Boundary	50ITGU99	435338
Vatican/Holy See	Italy	08 Oct 51	Telecommunications	52ITGU150	435339
Vatican/Holy See	Italy	16 Dec 55	Taxation	260UNTS319	103715
Vatican/Holy See	Italy	31 Jul 62	Finance	64ITGU281	435340
Vatican/Holy See	Multilateral	02 Oct 47	Telecommunications	193UNTS188	102616
Vatican/Holy See	Multilateral	26 Jun 48	Culture	331UNTS217	104757
Vatican/Holy See	Multilateral	12 Aug 49	Humanitarian	75UNTS85	100971
Vatican/Holy See	Multilateral	12 Aug 49	Humanitarian	75UNTS31	100970
Vatican/Holy See	Multilateral	12 Aug 49	General Military	75UNTS135	100972
Vatican/Holy See	Multilateral	12 Aug 49	Humanitarian	75UNTS287	100973
Vatican/Holy See	Multilateral	25 May 51	Status of Forces	175UNTS215	102303
Vatican/Holy See	Multilateral	02 Jul 51	Refugees	189UNTS137	102545
Vatican/Holy See	Multilateral	10 May 52	Taxation	439UNTS233	106332
Vatican/Holy See	Multilateral	10 May 52	Admin Cooperation	439UNTS217	106331
Vatican/Holy See	Multilateral	10 May 52	Admin Cooperation	439UNTS193	106330
Vatican/Holy See	Multilateral	11 Jul 52	Postal Service	171UNTS143	102226
Vatican/Holy See	Multilateral	11 Jul 52	Postal Service	171UNTS89	102225
Vatican/Holy See	Multilateral	11 Jul 52	Postal Service	170UNTS269	102223
Vatican/Holy See	Multilateral	11 Jul 52	Postal Service	170UNTS63	102222
Vatican/Holy See	Multilateral	11 Jul 52	Postal Service	171UNTS3	102224
Vatican/Holy See	Multilateral	11 Jul 52	Postal Service	170UNTS3	102221
Vatican/Holy See	Multilateral	11 Jul 52	IGO Establishment	169UNTS3	102220
Vatican/Holy See	Multilateral	06 Sep 52	Patents/Copyrights	216UNTS132	102937
Vatican/Holy See	Multilateral	04 Jun 54	Customs	276UNTS191	103992
Vatican/Holy See	Multilateral	04 Jun 54	Customs	282UNTS249	104101
Vatican/Holy See	Multilateral	28 Sep 54	Refugees	360UNTS117	105158
Vatican/Holy See	Multilateral	19 Dec 54	Culture	218UNTS139	102955
Vatican/Holy See	Multilateral	25 Apr 56	Commodity Trade	270UNTS103	103896
Vatican/Holy See	Multilateral	20 Jun 56	Admin Cooperation	268UNTS3	103850
Vatican/Holy See	Multilateral	26 Oct 56	IGO Establishment	276UNTS3	103988
Vatican/Holy See	Multilateral	03 Oct 57	Postal Service	366UNTS255	105219
Vatican/Holy See	Multilateral	03 Oct 57	Postal Service	366UNTS141	105217
Vatican/Holy See	Multilateral	03 Oct 57	Postal Service	364UNTS3	105211
Vatican/Holy See	Multilateral	03 Oct 57	Postal Service	366UNTS3	105215
Vatican/Holy See	Multilateral	03 Oct 57	Postal Service	365UNTS3	105213
Vatican/Holy See	Multilateral	03 Oct 57	Postal Service	365UNTS207	105214
Vatican/Holy See	Multilateral	03 Oct 57	Postal Service	366UNTS87	105216
Vatican/Holy See	Multilateral	03 Oct 57	Postal Service	364UNTS331	105212
Vatican/Holy See	Multilateral	29 Apr 58	Territory Boundary	516UNTS205	107477

PARTY ONE	PARTY TWO	DATE	TOPIC	CITATION	NUMBER
Vatican/Holy See	Multilateral	29 Apr 58	Water Transport	450UNTS11	106465
Vatican/Holy See	Multilateral	29 Apr 58	Dispute Settlement	450UNTS169	106466
Vatican/Holy See	Multilateral	06 Apr 59	Commodity Trade	349UNTS167	105013
Vatican/Holy See	Multilateral	30 Mar 61	Sanitation	520UNTS151	107515
Vatican/Holy See	Multilateral	18 Apr 61	Consul/Citizenship	500UNTS95	107310
Vatican/Holy See	Multilateral	26 Oct 61	Patents/Copyrights	496UNTS43	107247
Vatican/Holy See	Multilateral	15 May 62	Commodity Trade	444UNTS3	106367
Vatican/Holy See	Multilateral	24 Apr 63	Consul/Citizenship	596UNTS261	108638
Vatican/Holy See	Multilateral	10 Jul 64	Postal Service	612UNTS361	108849
Vatican/Holy See	Multilateral	10 Jul 64	Postal Service	613UNTS3	108851
Vatican/Holy See	Multilateral	10 Jul 64	Postal Service	612UNTS3	108847
Vatican/Holy See	Multilateral	10 Jul 64	Postal Service	611UNTS105	108845
Vatican/Holy See	Multilateral	10 Jul 64	Postal Service	611UNTS387	108846
Vatican/Holy See	Multilateral	10 Jul 64	Postal Service	612UNTS233	108848
Vatican/Holy See	Multilateral	10 Jul 64	Postal Service	613UNTS193	108852
Vatican/Holy See	Multilateral	10 Jul 64	Postal Service	611UNTS7	108844
Vatican/Holy See	Multilateral	10 Jul 64	Postal Service	613UNTS3	108850
Vatican/Holy See	Multilateral	10 Jul 64	Postal Service	613UNTS127	108853
Vatican/Holy See	Multilateral	20 Aug 64	Telecommunications	514UNTS25	107441
Vatican/Holy See	Multilateral	08 Jul 65	General Trade	597UNTS3	108641
Vatican/Holy See	Multilateral	31 Jan 67	Refugees	606UNTS267	108791
Vatican/Holy See	Philippines	18 Jun 52	Status of Forces	543UNTS165	107900
Vatican/Holy See	Spain	07 Jun 41	Admin Cooperation	53SPBO1911	460267
Vatican/Holy See	Spain	16 Jul 46	Non-ILO Labor	53SPBO1911	460268
Vatican/Holy See	Spain	05 Aug 50	Admin Cooperation	50SPBO1811	460270
Vatican/Holy See	Spain	27 Aug 53	General Amity	53SPBO1910	460271
Vatican/Holy See	Spain	06 Jul 57	Admin Cooperation	57SPBO1207	460272
Vatican/Holy See	Spain	05 Apr 62	Education	62SPBO2007	460273
Venezuela	Belgium	15 May 63	Culture	470UNTS259	106812
Venezuela	Brazil	30 Mar 40	Dispute Settlement	51UNTS291	200195
Venezuela	Brazil	22 Oct 42	Culture	65UNTS203	200212
Venezuela	Brazil	30 Jan 46	Consul/Citizenship	65UNTS107	100839
Venezuela	Canada	11 Oct 50	General Economic	231UNTS3	103198
Venezuela	Canada	08 Oct 59	Visas	470UNTS93	106799
Venezuela	Canada	22 Nov 61	Telecommunications	470UNTS148	106806
Venezuela	France	26 Jul 50	General Economic	50FRMD2408	417479
Venezuela	IBRD (World Bank)	13 Dec 61	IBRD Project	446UNTS371	106409
Venezuela	IBRD (World Bank)	20 Sep 63	IBRD Project	482UNTS227	106997
Venezuela	IBRD (World Bank)	28 Aug 64	IBRD Project	537UNTS135	107800
Venezuela	IBRD (World Bank)	28 Aug 64	IBRD Project	520UNTS97	107512
Venezuela	IBRD (World Bank)	13 Dec 65	IBRD Project	568UNTS77	108265
Venezuela	IBRD (World Bank)	21 Apr 66	IBRD Project	568UNTS257	108273
Venezuela	IBRD (World Bank)	26 Jan 67	IBRD Project	596UNTS35	108628
Venezuela	IBRD (World Bank)	18 Jun 69	IBRD Project	0UNTS0	110221
Venezuela	IBRD (World Bank)	30 Jun 69	IGO Operations	0UNTS0	110514
Venezuela	ILO (Labor Org)	22 Oct 51	Tech Assistance	117UNTS139	101590
Venezuela	Israel	19 Jun 66	Culture	0UNTS0	110376
Venezuela	Italy	04 Jul 62	Air Transport	65ITGU194	435427
Venezuela	Mexico	25 Jul 46	Culture	48MEXD1011	444043
Venezuela	Multilateral	25 Jun 36	Privil/Immunities	161UNTS217	200486
Venezuela	Multilateral	17 Feb 40	Privil/Immunities	161UNTS229	200487
Venezuela	Multilateral	30 Jul 40	Admin Cooperation	161UNTS253	200488
Venezuela	Multilateral	12 Oct 40	Specific Resources	161UNTS193	200485
Venezuela	Multilateral	28 Nov 40	Commodity Trade	139UNTS159	200452
Venezuela	Multilateral	15 Jan 44	IGO Establishment	161UNTS281	200489
Venezuela	Multilateral	02 Aug 44	Scientific Project	67UNTS221	200221
Venezuela	Multilateral	07 Dec 44	Air Transport	84UNTS389	200252
Venezuela	Multilateral	07 Dec 44	Air Transport	171UNTS387	200502
Venezuela	Multilateral	07 Dec 44	Air Transport	171UNTS345	200501
Venezuela	Multilateral	07 Dec 44	IGO Establishment	15UNTS295	200102
Venezuela	Multilateral	08 Aug 45	General Military	82UNTS279	200251
Venezuela	Multilateral	16 Nov 45	IGO Establishment	4UNTS275	100052
Venezuela	Multilateral	22 Jul 46	IGO Establishment	9UNTS3	100125
Venezuela	Multilateral	22 Jul 46	IGO Establishment	14UNTS185	100221
Venezuela	Multilateral	27 Jul 46	Patents/Copyrights	90UNTS229	101238

PARTY ONE	PARTY TWO	DATE	TOPIC	CITATION	NUMBER
Venezuela	Multilateral	03 Sep 46	Commodity Trade	139UNTS3	101872
Venezuela	Multilateral	15 Oct 46	Refugees	11UNTS73	100150
Venezuela	Multilateral	11 Dec 46	Sanitation	12UNTS179	100186
Venezuela	Multilateral	15 Dec 46	IGO Establishment	18UNTS3	100283
Venezuela	Multilateral	02 Sep 47	General Military	21UNTS77	100324
Venezuela	Multilateral	02 Oct 47	Telecommunications	193UNTS188	102616
Venezuela	Multilateral	11 Oct 47	IGO Establishment	77UNTS143	100998
Venezuela	Multilateral	30 Apr 48	IGO Establishment	119UNTS3	101609
Venezuela	Multilateral	30 Apr 48	Dispute Settlement	30UNTS55	100449
Venezuela	Multilateral	10 Jun 48	Humanitarian	164UNTS113	102163
Venezuela	Multilateral	19 Jun 48	Air Transport	310UNTS151	104492
Venezuela	Multilateral	24 Jul 48	Sanitation	66UNTS25	100847
Venezuela	Multilateral	19 Nov 48	Sanitation	44UNTS277	100688
Venezuela	Multilateral	29 Nov 48	IGO Establishment	120UNTS13	101613
Venezuela	Multilateral	09 Dec 48	Humanitarian	78UNTS277	101021
Venezuela	Multilateral	23 Mar 49	Commodity Trade	203UNTS179	102746
Venezuela	Multilateral	09 Jul 49	Telecommunications	168UNTS143	102218
Venezuela	Multilateral	12 Aug 49	Humanitarian	75UNTS31	100970
Venezuela	Multilateral	12 Aug 49	General Military	75UNTS135	100972
Venezuela	Multilateral	12 Aug 49	Humanitarian	75UNTS85	100971
Venezuela	Multilateral	12 Aug 49	Humanitarian	75UNTS287	100973
Venezuela	Multilateral	16 Dec 49	Admin Cooperation	72UNTS3	100924
Venezuela	Multilateral	21 Mar 50	Admin Cooperation	96UNTS271	101342
Venezuela	Multilateral	06 Apr 50	Admin Cooperation	119UNTS99	101610
Venezuela	Multilateral	25 May 51	Status of Forces	175UNTS215	102303
Venezuela	Multilateral	08 Sep 51	Peace/Disarmament	136UNTS45	101832
Venezuela	Multilateral	12 Jun 52	Dispute Settlement	138UNTS183	101869
Venezuela	Multilateral	11 Jul 52	Postal Service	170UNTS269	102223
Venezuela	Multilateral	11 Jul 52	Postal Service	171UNTS143	102226
Venezuela	Multilateral	11 Jul 52	Postal Service	170UNTS63	102222
Venezuela	Multilateral	11 Jul 52	Postal Service	171UNTS3	102224
Venezuela	Multilateral	11 Jul 52	IGO Establishment	169UNTS3	102220
Venezuela	Multilateral	11 Jul 52	Postal Service	170UNTS3	102221
Venezuela	Multilateral	11 Jul 52	Postal Service	171UNTS89	102225
Venezuela	Multilateral	11 May 53	Sanitation	456UNTS3	106555
Venezuela	Multilateral	12 May 54	Admin Cooperation	327UNTS3	104714
Venezuela	Multilateral	14 Jun 54	Air Transport	320UNTS217	104644
Venezuela	Multilateral	19 Aug 54	Tech Assistance	201UNTS51	102710
Venezuela	Multilateral	25 May 55	IGO Establishment	264UNTS117	103791
Venezuela	Multilateral	28 Sep 55	Air Transport	478UNTS371	106943
Venezuela	Multilateral	12 Oct 55	IGO Establishment	560UNTS3	108165
Venezuela	Multilateral	25 Apr 56	Commodity Trade	270UNTS103	103896
Venezuela	Multilateral	26 Oct 56	IGO Establishment	276UNTS3	103988
Venezuela	Multilateral	03 Oct 57	Postal Service	365UNTS207	105214
Venezuela	Multilateral	03 Oct 57	Postal Service	366UNTS255	105219
Venezuela	Multilateral	03 Oct 57	Postal Service	366UNTS87	105216
Venezuela	Multilateral	03 Oct 57	Postal Service	366UNTS3	105215
Venezuela	Multilateral	03 Oct 57	Postal Service	365UNTS3	105213
Venezuela	Multilateral	03 Oct 57	Postal Service	364UNTS3	105211
Venezuela	Multilateral	03 Oct 57	Postal Service	364UNTS331	105212
Venezuela	Multilateral	03 Oct 57	Postal Service	366UNTS141	105217
Venezuela	Multilateral	29 Apr 58	Water Transport	450UNTS11	106465
Venezuela	Multilateral	29 Apr 58	Specific Resources	559UNTS285	108164
Venezuela	Multilateral	29 Apr 58	Territory Boundary	499UNTS311	107302
Venezuela	Multilateral	29 Apr 58	Territory Boundary	516UNTS205	107477
Venezuela	Multilateral	06 Apr 59	Commodity Trade	349UNTS167	105013
Venezuela	Multilateral	08 Apr 59	IGO Establishment	389UNTS69	105593
Venezuela	Multilateral	09 Oct 59	Tech Assistance	376UNTS382	105391
Venezuela	Multilateral	18 Nov 59	IGO Establishment	390UNTS227	105610
Venezuela	Multilateral	17 Jun 60	Humanitarian	536UNTS27	107794
Venezuela	Multilateral	28 Jul 60	IGO Establishment	485UNTS3	107042
Venezuela	Multilateral	14 Sep 60	IGO Establishment	443UNTS247	106363
Venezuela	Multilateral	30 Mar 61	Sanitation	520UNTS151	107515
Venezuela	Multilateral	18 Apr 61	Consul/Citizenship	500UNTS95	107310
Venezuela	Multilateral	21 Jun 61	IGO Establishment	514UNTS209	107449

PARTY ONE	PARTY TWO	DATE	TOPIC	CITATION	NUMBER
Venezuela	Multilateral	26 Mar 62	IGO Establishment	539UNTS67	107825
Venezuela	Multilateral	15 May 62	Commodity Trade	444UNTS3	106367
Venezuela	Multilateral	28 Sep 62	IGO Establishment	469UNTS169	106791
Venezuela	Multilateral	24 Apr 63	Consul/Citizenship	596UNTS261	108638
Venezuela	Multilateral	05 Aug 63	Sanitation	480UNTS43	106964
Venezuela	Multilateral	10 Jul 64	Postal Service	613UNTS3	108851
Venezuela	Multilateral	10 Jul 64	Postal Service	612UNTS3	108847
Venezuela	Multilateral	10 Jul 64	Postal Service	612UNTS361	108849
Venezuela	Multilateral	10 Jul 64	Postal Service	613UNTS3	108850
Venezuela	Multilateral	10 Jul 64	Postal Service	611UNTS387	108846
Venezuela	Multilateral	10 Jul 64	Postal Service	611UNTS105	108845
Venezuela	Multilateral	10 Jul 64	Postal Service	613UNTS193	108852
Venezuela	Multilateral	10 Jul 64	Postal Service	611UNTS7	108844
Venezuela	Multilateral	10 Jul 64	Postal Service	612UNTS233	108848
Venezuela	Multilateral	05 Apr 66	Water Transport	640UNTS133	109159
Venezuela	Multilateral	27 Jan 67	Scientific Project	610UNTS205	108843
Venezuela	Multilateral	14 Feb 67	General Military	634UNTS281	109068
Venezuela	Multilateral	18 Mar 68	Commodity Trade	0UNTS0	109262
Venezuela	Netherlands	26 Oct 54	Air Transport	232UNTS103	103232
Venezuela	Netherlands	11 Apr 57	Admin Cooperation	288UNTS23	104193
Venezuela	Norway	30 Jul 57	General Trade	3NORT725	451217
Venezuela	Norway	01 Dec 59	Visas	3NORT790	451218
Venezuela	Portugal	16 May 56	Air Transport	463UNTS239	106707
Venezuela	Sweden	13 Mar 57	Admin Cooperation	428UNTS351	106185
Venezuela	Switzerland	11 Jul 55	General Trade	55SWRO729	462163
Venezuela	UK Great Britain	20 Jul 56	Admin Cooperation	351UNTS289	105029
Venezuela	UK Great Britain	17 Feb 66	Territory Boundary	561UNTS321	108192
Venezuela	UN Special Fund	11 Dec 61	Direct Aid	422UNTS149	106074
Venezuela	UNICEF (Children)	25 Oct 67	IGO Operations	0UNTS0	109337
Venezuela	United Nations	05 Mar 54	Tech Assistance	187UNTS9	102498
Venezuela	United Nations	18 Nov 56	IGO Operations	588UNTS243	108529
Venezuela	USA (United States)	13 Oct 42	Commodity Trade	138UNTS282	200451
Venezuela	USA (United States)	18 Feb 43	Sanitation	21UNTS225	200125
Venezuela	USA (United States)	14 May 43	Non-IBRD Project	28UNTS359	200160
Venezuela	USA (United States)	13 Jan 44	Military Mission	109UNTS171	200358
Venezuela	USA (United States)	11 May 45	Milit Servic/Citiz	121UNTS273	200405
Venezuela	USA (United States)	29 Mar 46	Specific Resources	124UNTS57	101666
Venezuela	USA (United States)	03 Jun 46	Military Mission	4UNTS215	100047
Venezuela	USA (United States)	30 Jun 47	Sanitation	166UNTS198	102190
Venezuela	USA (United States)	30 Jan 48	Military Mission	109UNTS25	101486
Venezuela	USA (United States)	24 Mar 48	Air Transport	44UNTS57	100678
Venezuela	USA (United States)	23 Aug 50	Military Mission	92UNTS341	101279
Venezuela	USA (United States)	07 Jun 51	Tech Assistance	141UNTS273	101918
Venezuela	USA (United States)	10 Aug 51	Military Mission	140UNTS345	101898
Venezuela	USA (United States)	28 Aug 52	General Trade	178UNTS51	102336
Venezuela	USA (United States)	29 Sep 52	Tech Assistance	186UNTS23	102479
Venezuela	USA (United States)	16 Jan 53	Military Mission	199UNTS287	102690
Venezuela	USA (United States)	14 Aug 53	Air Transport	213UNTS99	102883
Venezuela	USA (United States)	21 Jul 55	Atomic Energy	238UNTS121	103357
Venezuela	USA (United States)	21 Feb 57	Water Transport	279UNTS199	104041
Venezuela	USA (United States)	24 Sep 57	Tech Assistance	293UNTS307	104298
Venezuela	USA (United States)	08 Oct 58	Atomic Energy	371UNTS69	105271
Venezuela	USA (United States)	17 Apr 59	Visas	358UNTS83	105126
Venezuela	USA (United States)	12 Nov 59	Gen Communications	367UNTS81	105227
Venezuela	USA (United States)	17 May 62	US Agri Commod Aid	456UNTS275	106562
Venezuela	USA (United States)	28 May 62	Tech Assistance	458UNTS249	106607
Venezuela	USA (United States)	29 Nov 62	Finance	474UNTS107	106875
Venezuela	USA (United States)	18 Sep 67	Gen Communications	0UNTS0	109919
Venezuela	USSR (Soviet Union)	14 Mar 45	Consul/Citizenship	0SUST175	468445
Venezuela	WHO (World Health)	11 Sep 50	Tech Assistance	110UNTS237	101513
Vietnam	Multilateral	07 Dec 44	IGO Establishment	15UNTS295	200102
Vietnam	Multilateral	11 Dec 46	Sanitation	12UNTS179	100186
Vietnam	Multilateral	27 May 47	Air Transport	418UNTS161	106021
Vietnam	Multilateral	10 Jun 48	Humanitarian	164UNTS113	102163
Vietnam	Multilateral	24 Jul 48	Sanitation	66UNTS25	100847

PARTY ONE	PARTY TWO	DATE	TOPIC	CITATION	NUMBER
Vietnam	Multilateral	15 Nov 48	IGO Establishment	120UNTS59	101615
Vietnam	Multilateral	29 Nov 48	IGO Establishment	120UNTS13	101613
Vietnam	Multilateral	22 Nov 50	Culture	131UNTS25	101734
Vietnam	Multilateral	07 Dec 50	Admin Cooperation	212UNTS17	102861
Vietnam	Multilateral	23 Dec 50	Tech Assistance	185UNTS3	102456
Vietnam	Multilateral	08 Sep 51	Peace/Disarmament	136UNTS45	101832
Vietnam	Multilateral	08 Sep 51	General Military	136UNTS165	101833
Vietnam	Multilateral	11 Jul 52	Postal Service	170UNTS269	102223
Vietnam	Multilateral	11 Jul 52	Postal Service	170UNTS63	102222
Vietnam	Multilateral	11 Jul 52	Postal Service	170UNTS3	102221
Vietnam	Multilateral	11 Jul 52	IGO Establishment	169UNTS3	102220
Vietnam	Multilateral	11 May 53	Sanitation	456UNTS3	106555
Vietnam	Multilateral	04 Jun 54	Customs	282UNTS249	104101
Vietnam	Multilateral	04 Jun 54	Customs	276UNTS191	103992
Vietnam	Multilateral	08 Jun 56	Tech Assistance	247UNTS366	200541
Vietnam	Multilateral	07 Sep 56	Humanitarian	266UNTS3	103822
Vietnam	Multilateral	26 Oct 56	IGO Establishment	276UNTS3	103988
Vietnam	Multilateral	03 Oct 57	Postal Service	365UNTS207	105214
Vietnam	Multilateral	03 Oct 57	Postal Service	366UNTS141	105217
Vietnam	Multilateral	03 Oct 57	Postal Service	366UNTS255	105219
Vietnam	Multilateral	03 Oct 57	Postal Service	366UNTS87	105216
Vietnam	Multilateral	03 Oct 57	Postal Service	365UNTS3	105213
Vietnam	Multilateral	03 Oct 57	Postal Service	366UNTS193	105218
Vietnam	Multilateral	03 Oct 57	Postal Service	366UNTS3	105215
Vietnam	Multilateral	05 Aug 63	Sanitation	480UNTS43	106964
Vietnam	Multilateral	10 Jul 64	Postal Service	613UNTS3	108850
Vietnam	Multilateral	10 Jul 64	Postal Service	613UNTS193	108852
Vietnam	Multilateral	10 Jul 64	Postal Service	613UNTS127	108853
Vietnam	Multilateral	10 Jul 64	Postal Service	613UNTS3	108851
Vietnam, North	China People's Rep	25 Aug 53	General Trade	53CCJC51	410116
Vietnam, North	China People's Rep	07 Jul 54	General Trade	54CCJC44	410161
Vietnam, North	China People's Rep	24 Dec 54	Direct Aid	54CCJC90	410194
Vietnam, North	China People's Rep	24 Dec 54	Postal Service	54CCJC86	410191
Vietnam, North	China People's Rep	24 Dec 54	Telecommunications	54CCJC88	410192
Vietnam, North	China People's Rep	25 May 55	Land Transport	55CCJC38	410235
Vietnam, North	China People's Rep	07 Jul 55	General Trade	55CCJC48	410241
Vietnam, North	China People's Rep	07 Jul 55	Culture	55CCJC47	410240
Vietnam, North	China People's Rep	07 Jul 55	General Trade	55CCJC49	410242
Vietnam, North	China People's Rep	05 Apr 56	Air Transport	56CCJC45	410327
Vietnam, North	China People's Rep	18 Jun 56	General Trade	56CCJC74	410344
Vietnam, North	China People's Rep	20 Dec 56	Water Transport	56CCJC139	410388
Vietnam, North	China People's Rep	31 Jul 57	General Trade	57CCJC75	410440
Vietnam, North	China People's Rep	31 Jul 57	General Economic	57CCJC73	410438
Vietnam, North	China People's Rep	15 Mar 58	Mass Media	58CCJC28	410502
Vietnam, North	China People's Rep	31 Mar 58	General Economic	58CCJC38	410509
Vietnam, North	China People's Rep	08 Dec 58	Land Transport	58CCJC102	410556
Vietnam, North	China People's Rep	16 Jan 59	Culture	59CCJC11	410573
Vietnam, North	China People's Rep	18 Feb 59	General Economic	59CCJC28	410587
Vietnam, North	China People's Rep	20 Jun 59	Finance	59CCJC85	410628
Vietnam, North	China People's Rep	27 Jun 59	Scientific Project	59CCJC87	410630
Vietnam, North	China People's Rep	07 Mar 60	General Economic	60CCJC36	410682
Vietnam, North	China People's Rep	28 Nov 60	Scientific Project	60CCJC118	410735
Vietnam, North	China People's Rep	31 Jan 61	Land Transport	61CCJC12	410753
Vietnam, North	China People's Rep	05 Dec 62	General Amity	62CCJC108	410931
Vietnam, North	China People's Rep	05 Dec 62	General Economic	62CCJC109	410932
Vietnam, North	China People's Rep	09 Mar 64	Land Transport	64CCJC36	411363
Vietnam, North	China People's Rep	29 Jul 64	Postal Service	64CCJC102	411370
Vietnam, North	China People's Rep	29 Jul 64	Telecommunications	64CCJC103	411371
Vietnam, North	China People's Rep	31 Jul 64	Sanitation	64CCJC105	411372
Vietnam, North	China People's Rep	12 Sep 64	Air Transport	64CCJC116	411374
Vietnam, North	China People's Rep	19 Jun 65	Culture	65CCJC86	411376
Vietnam, North	China People's Rep	13 Jul 65	Direct Aid	65CCJC90	411377
Vietnam, North	China People's Rep	16 Sep 65	Sanitation	65CCJC118	411378
Vietnam, North	China People's Rep	13 Nov 65	Scientific Project	65CCJC142	411379
Vietnam, North	China People's Rep	03 Dec 65	Tech Assistance	65CCJC151	411364

PARTY ONE	PARTY TWO	DATE	TOPIC	CITATION	NUMBER
Vietnam, North	China People's Rep	05 Dec 65	Loans and Credits	65CCJC152	411365
Vietnam, North	China People's Rep	05 Dec 65	General Trade	65CCJC153	411366
Vietnam, North	China People's Rep	21 Mar 66	Land Transport	66CCJC8	411380
Vietnam, North	China People's Rep	22 Apr 66	Tech Assistance	66CCJC20	411381
Vietnam, North	China People's Rep	28 May 66	Culture	66CCJC41	411382
Vietnam, North	China People's Rep	02 Jul 66	Direct Aid	66CCJC63	411367
Vietnam, North	China People's Rep	21 Aug 66	Scientific Project	66CCJC78	411383
Vietnam, North	China People's Rep	29 Aug 66	Direct Aid	66CCJC81	411384
Vietnam, North	China People's Rep	12 Oct 66	Sanitation	66CCJC84	411385
Vietnam, North	China People's Rep	23 Nov 66	General Economic	66CCJC99	411386
Vietnam, North	China People's Rep	25 Apr 67	Culture	67CCJC15	411387
Vietnam, North	China People's Rep	03 Aug 67	Direct Aid	67CCJC28	411368
Vietnam, North	China People's Rep	05 Aug 67	Direct Aid	67CCJC29	411369
Vietnam, North	Czechoslovakia	14 Jan 63	Consul/Citizenship	501UNTS181	107318
Vietnam, North	Germany, East	14 Mar 56	Tech Assistance	4EGDA567	419486
Vietnam, North	Germany, East	15 Jun 56	Finance	3EGDA612	419487
Vietnam, North	Germany, East	31 Jul 57	Culture	5EGDA780	419488
Vietnam, North	Germany, East	14 May 58	Telecommunications	6EGDA505	419490
Vietnam, North	Germany, East	14 May 58	Postal Service	6EGDA494	419489
Vietnam, North	Germany, East	01 Dec 58	General Economic	7EGDA559	419491
Vietnam, North	Germany, East	07 Mar 59	General Economic	7EGDA541	419492
Vietnam, North	Germany, East	09 Oct 59	Consul/Citizenship	7EGDA547	419493
Vietnam, North	Germany, East	09 Feb 61	General Economic	9EGDA448	419494
Vietnam, North	Germany, East	04 Nov 65	Education	43EGDZ347	420495
Vietnam, North	Germany, East	10 Oct 66	Loans and Credits	46EGDZ369	420496
Vietnam, North	Germany, East	10 Oct 66	Education	46EGDZ369	420497
Vietnam, North	Multilateral	10 May 52	Taxation	439UNTS233	106332
Vietnam, North	Multilateral	26 Mar 56	IGO Establishment	259UNTS125	103686
Vietnam, North	Multilateral	23 Jul 62	Recognition	456UNTS302	106564
Vietnam, North	Poland	24 Jan 56	Postal Service	56PZUM32	458035
Vietnam, North	Poland	24 Jan 56	Telecommunications	56PZUM50	458036
Vietnam, North	Poland	24 Jan 56	Gen Communications	56PZUM66	458037
Vietnam, North	Poland	06 Apr 57	Culture	432UNTS255	106224
Vietnam, North	Romania	12 Oct 56	Culture	342UNTS173	104907
Vietnam, North	Romania	30 Jun 58	Scientific Project	389UNTS43	105591
Vietnam, North	USSR (Soviet Union)	30 Jan 50	Consul/Citizenship	0SUST268	468446
Vietnam, North	USSR (Soviet Union)	08 Jul 55	General Trade	0SUST331	468447
Vietnam, North	USSR (Soviet Union)	08 Jul 55	General Trade	0SUST331	468448
Vietnam, North	USSR (Soviet Union)	18 Jul 55	Direct Aid	0SUST333	468449
Vietnam, North	USSR (Soviet Union)	18 Jul 55	General Trade	0SUST333	468450
Vietnam, North	USSR (Soviet Union)	27 Aug 55	Education	16SUGG69	469909
Vietnam, North	USSR (Soviet Union)	01 Dec 56	Loans and Credits	0SUST445	468451
Vietnam, North	USSR (Soviet Union)	15 Feb 57	Culture	274UNTS115	103962
Vietnam, North	USSR (Soviet Union)	11 Mar 57	Finance	0SUST379	468452
Vietnam, North	USSR (Soviet Union)	08 Apr 57	General Trade	0SUST380	468453
Vietnam, North	USSR (Soviet Union)	25 Dec 57	Culture	0SUST395	468454
Vietnam, North	USSR (Soviet Union)	26 Dec 57	Telecommunications	0SUST395	468455
Vietnam, North	USSR (Soviet Union)	26 Dec 57	Postal Service	0SUST395	468456
Vietnam, North	USSR (Soviet Union)	12 Mar 58	General Economic	356UNTS149	105094
Vietnam, North	USSR (Soviet Union)	07 Mar 59	Tech Assistance	8SUGG139	469563
Vietnam, North	USSR (Soviet Union)	05 Jun 59	Consul/Citizenship	356UNTS111	105093
Vietnam, North	USSR (Soviet Union)	14 Jun 60	Loans and Credits	9SUGG138	469664
Vietnam, North	USSR (Soviet Union)	02 Aug 60	Tech Assistance	9SUGG143	469680
Vietnam, North	USSR (Soviet Union)	26 Aug 60	General Aid	9SUGG145	469687
Vietnam, North	USSR (Soviet Union)	30 Sep 60	Tech Assistance	9SUGG148	469699
Vietnam, North	USSR (Soviet Union)	23 Dec 60	General Aid	9SUGG157	469726
Vietnam, North	USSR (Soviet Union)	23 Dec 60	General Trade	9SUGG157	469727
Vietnam, North	USSR (Soviet Union)	27 Jan 61	Direct Aid	10SUGG119	469738
Vietnam, North	USSR (Soviet Union)	06 Mar 61	Tech Assistance	10SUGG124	469750
Vietnam, North	USSR (Soviet Union)	09 Mar 61	Tech Assistance	10SUGG124	469751
Vietnam, North	USSR (Soviet Union)	15 Sep 62	General Aid	11SUGG152	469860
Vietnam, South	Asian Devel Bank	16 Dec 70	Loans and Credits	0VKNG381	496095
Vietnam, South	Australia	04 Oct 54	Admin Cooperation	0VKNG81	496022
Vietnam, South	Australia	04 Oct 54	Admin Cooperation	201UNTS349	102723
Vietnam, South	Belgium	29 May 53	General Trade	0VKNG56	496012

PARTY ONE	PARTY TWO	DATE	TOPIC	CITATION	NUMBER
Vietnam, South	Cambodia	29 Dec 54	Water Transport	0VKNG85	496023
Vietnam, South	Cambodia	22 Aug 55	Finance	0VKNG100	496032
Vietnam, South	Cambodia	27 May 70	Consul/Citizenship	0VKNG332	496084
Vietnam, South	Cambodia	27 May 70	Consul/Citizenship	0VKNG334	496086
Vietnam, South	Cambodia	27 May 70	General Economic	0VKNG333	496085
Vietnam, South	Cambodia	22 Jan 71	General Amity	0VKNG370	496093
Vietnam, South	Cambodia	04 Jun 71	Visas	0VKNG383	496097
Vietnam, South	Cambodia	04 Jun 71	Customs	0VKNG382	496096
Vietnam, South	Canada	18 Sep 59	Direct Aid	0VKNG146	496042
Vietnam, South	Canada	25 Sep 61	Direct Aid	0VKNG172	496052
Vietnam, South	Chad	02 Jul 71	Consul/Citizenship	0VKNG387	496099
Vietnam, South	FAO (Food Agri)	28 Jan 53	Tech Assistance	0VKNG52	496010
Vietnam, South	France	30 May 50	Education	0VKNG9	496001
Vietnam, South	France	15 Jun 50	Education	0VKNG10	496002
Vietnam, South	France	16 Jun 50	Water Transport	0VKNG11	496003
Vietnam, South	France	17 Jun 50	IGO Establishment	0VKNG13	496004
Vietnam, South	France	12 Mar 51	Specific Property	0VKNG25	496005
Vietnam, South	France	08 Feb 52	Education	0VKNG41	496006
Vietnam, South	France	26 May 52	Land Transport	0VKNG45	496007
Vietnam, South	France	07 Jun 52	Education	0VKNG47	496008
Vietnam, South	France	09 May 53	General Military	0VKNG53	496011
Vietnam, South	France	09 Jul 53	Education	0VKNG59	496013
Vietnam, South	France	19 Oct 53	Admin Cooperation	0VKNG62	496014
Vietnam, South	France	05 Apr 54	Admin Cooperation	0VKNG67	496018
Vietnam, South	France	04 Jun 54	General Amity	0VKNG68	496019
Vietnam, South	France	20 Jul 54	Peace/Disarmament	0VKNG72	496020
Vietnam, South	France	16 Sep 54	Recognition	59FRRT7	415480
Vietnam, South	France	30 Dec 54	General Economic	0VKNG85	496024
Vietnam, South	France	30 Dec 54	Status of Forces	0VKNG85	496025
Vietnam, South	France	11 May 55	Education	0VKNG91	496027
Vietnam, South	France	15 May 55	Status of Forces	0VKNG92	496028
Vietnam, South	France	13 Jun 55	Milit Installation	0VKNG94	496029
Vietnam, South	France	20 Jun 55	Air Transport	0VKNG95	496030
Vietnam, South	France	16 Aug 55	Consul/Citizenship	59FRRT7	415481
Vietnam, South	France	17 Aug 55	Finance	0VKNG98	496031
Vietnam, South	France	05 Apr 56	Mass Media	0VKNG104	496033
Vietnam, South	France	14 Jul 56	Consul/Citizenship	0VKNG109	496034
Vietnam, South	France	28 Jul 56	Air Transport	0VKNG110	496035
Vietnam, South	France	10 Sep 58	Finance	0VKNG130	496037
Vietnam, South	France	29 Sep 59	Scientific Project	0VKNG151	496043
Vietnam, South	France	14 Nov 59	General Economic	0VKNG153	496044
Vietnam, South	France	24 Mar 60	General Economic	0VKNG153	496045
Vietnam, South	France	24 Mar 60	Specific Property	70FRJO2203	416482
Vietnam, South	France	24 Mar 60	Claims and Debts	0UNTS0	110473
Vietnam, South	France	28 Jan 61	Atomic Energy	0VKNG159	496047
Vietnam, South	France	11 Feb 61	Culture	0VKNG160	496048
Vietnam, South	France	10 Aug 61	Tech Assistance	0VKNG170	496050
Vietnam, South	France	22 Nov 62	Education	0VKNG184	496054
Vietnam, South	France	15 May 63	Admin Cooperation	0VKNG190	496056
Vietnam, South	France	22 May 63	Specific Property	0VKNG191	496057
Vietnam, South	Germany, West	10 Dec 53	General Trade	0VKNG66	496017
Vietnam, South	Germany, West	27 May 59	Education	0VKNG141	496040
Vietnam, South	Germany, West	10 Aug 61	Tech Assistance	0VKNG171	496051
Vietnam, South	Germany, West	19 Jul 63	Direct Aid	0VKNG192	496058
Vietnam, South	Germany, West	04 Dec 63	Loans and Credits	0VKNG194	496059
Vietnam, South	Germany, West	28 Mar 66	Specif Goods/Equip	66WGBB322	425728
Vietnam, South	Germany, West	28 Jun 66	Direct Aid	0VKNG237	496063
Vietnam, South	Germany, West	30 Mar 67	Humanitarian	67WGBB2105	425729
Vietnam, South	IAEA (Atom Energy)	16 Oct 67	Atomic Energy	630UNTS379	200636
Vietnam, South	ICJ Option Clause	05 Nov 52	ICJ Option Clause	150UNTS147	101968
Vietnam, South	ILO (Labor Org)	26 Jun 51	Tech Assistance	100UNTS223	200285
Vietnam, South	Ireland	01 Dec 64	General Trade	553UNTS233	108091
Vietnam, South	Israel	11 Apr 62	Mostfavored Nation	448UNTS205	106432
Vietnam, South	Italy	14 Nov 53	General Trade	0VKNG63	496015
Vietnam, South	Japan	12 Jun 52	Dispute Settlement	0VKNG48	496009

PARTY ONE	PARTY TWO	DATE	TOPIC	CITATION	NUMBER
Vietnam, South	Japan	13 May 59	Reparations	373UNTS101	105317
Vietnam, South	Japan	13 May 59	Loans and Credits	373UNTS149	105318
Vietnam, South	Japan	13 May 59	Loans and Credits	373UNTS173	105319
Vietnam, South	Japan	11 Jan 65	Specific Resources	0VKNG208	496060
Vietnam, South	Japan	10 Jun 67	Sanitation	67JJS537	442194
Vietnam, South	Japan	07 Mar 70	Tech Assistance	0VKNG316	496079
Vietnam, South	Japan	20 May 70	Refugees	0VKNG326	496082
Vietnam, South	Japan	09 Jun 70	Direct Aid	0VKNG339	496088
Vietnam, South	Japan	17 Oct 70	Direct Aid	0VKNG391	496090
Vietnam, South	Japan	16 Dec 70	Direct Aid	0VKNG366	496091
Vietnam, South	Japan	30 Mar 71	Privil/Immunities	0VKNG377	496094
Vietnam, South	Japan	18 Sep 71	Direct Aid	0VKNG389	496100
Vietnam, South	Japan	02 Oct 71	Direct Aid	0VKNG391	496101
Vietnam, South	Japan	27 Nov 71	Direct Aid	0VKNG394	496102
Vietnam, South	Japan	24 Dec 71	Direct Aid	0VKNG397	496103
Vietnam, South	Korea, South	19 Dec 62	General Trade	0VKNG187	496055
Vietnam, South	Korea, South	31 Oct 64	Milit Assistance	0VKNG323	496081
Vietnam, South	Korea, South	16 Jan 67	Air Transport	0VKNG241	496066
Vietnam, South	Korea, South	16 Jan 67	Claims and Debts	0VKNG240	496065
Vietnam, South	Korea, South	04 Oct 67	Finance	0VKNG255	496071
Vietnam, South	Korea, South	04 Jun 70	General Economic	0VKNG337	496087
Vietnam, South	Korea, South	04 Jun 70	General Economic	0VKNG384	496098
Vietnam, South	Laos	29 Dec 54	Water Transport	0VKNG85	496026
Vietnam, South	Laos	12 Sep 58	Admin Cooperation	0VKNG131	496038
Vietnam, South	Laos	11 Jun 59	General Amity	0VKNG143	496041
Vietnam, South	Malaysia	10 Dec 70	Air Transport	0VKNG368	496092
Vietnam, South	Multilateral	10 Jun 48	Humanitarian	164UNTS113	102163
Vietnam, South	Multilateral	09 Dec 48	Humanitarian	78UNTS277	101021
Vietnam, South	Multilateral	06 Dec 51	Admin Cooperation	150UNTS67	101963
Vietnam, South	Multilateral	14 Jun 54	Air Transport	320UNTS209	104643
Vietnam, South	Multilateral	14 Jun 54	Air Transport	320UNTS217	104644
Vietnam, South	Multilateral	25 May 55	IGO Establishment	264UNTS117	103791
Vietnam, South	Multilateral	08 Jun 56	Tech Assistance	247UNTS366	200541
Vietnam, South	Multilateral	03 Oct 57	Postal Service	364UNTS3	105211
Vietnam, South	Multilateral	03 Oct 57	Postal Service	364UNTS331	105212
Vietnam, South	Multilateral	26 Jan 60	IGO Establishment	439UNTS249	106333
Vietnam, South	Multilateral	17 Jun 60	Humanitarian	536UNTS27	107794
Vietnam, South	Multilateral	26 Nov 60	Taxation	500UNTS25	107304
Vietnam, South	Multilateral	14 Dec 60	Education	429UNTS93	106193
Vietnam, South	Multilateral	14 Jun 61	IBRD Project	415UNTS4	105979
Vietnam, South	Multilateral	21 Jun 61	IGO Establishment	514UNTS209	107449
Vietnam, South	Multilateral	23 Jul 62	Recognition	456UNTS302	106564
Vietnam, South	Multilateral	19 Oct 63	Direct Aid	523UNTS249	107559
Vietnam, South	Multilateral	10 Jul 64	Postal Service	611UNTS7	108844
Vietnam, South	Multilateral	10 Jul 64	Postal Service	612UNTS233	108848
Vietnam, South	Multilateral	10 Jul 64	Postal Service	611UNTS105	108845
Vietnam, South	Multilateral	10 Jul 64	Postal Service	612UNTS3	108847
Vietnam, South	Multilateral	10 Jul 64	Postal Service	611UNTS387	108846
Vietnam, South	Multilateral	18 Sep 64	IGO Operations	556UNTS25	108117
Vietnam, South	Multilateral	08 Jul 65	General Trade	597UNTS3	108641
Vietnam, South	Multilateral	04 Dec 65	IGO Establishment	571UNTS123	108303
Vietnam, South	Multilateral	05 Apr 66	Water Transport	640UNTS133	109159
Vietnam, South	Multilateral	28 Dec 67	Scientific Project	0UNTS0	109322
Vietnam, South	Multilateral	01 Aug 68	Culture	0UNTS0	109368
Vietnam, South	Multilateral	11 Jun 69	Scientific Project	0UNTS0	110100
Vietnam, South	Netherlands	14 Nov 53	General Trade	0VKNG64	496016
Vietnam, South	Netherlands	05 Mar 55	Patents/Copyrights	288UNTS53	104197
Vietnam, South	Netherlands	24 Mar 67	Sanitation	610UNTS0	108834
Vietnam, South	Philippines	26 Apr 59	General Amity	3PTS829	465041
Vietnam, South	Taiwan	19 Aug 66	Air Transport	0VKNG238	496064
Vietnam, South	Taiwan	19 Aug 66	Air Transport	0UNTS0	109241
Vietnam, South	Thailand	18 Sep 67	Refugees	0VKNG252	496070
Vietnam, South	Thailand	13 Jan 70	Air Transport	0VKNG312	496076
Vietnam, South	Tunisia	10 May 66	General Trade	0VKNG235	496062
Vietnam, South	UK Great Britain	14 Oct 55	Patents/Copyrights	231UNTS193	103220

PARTY ONE	PARTY TWO	DATE	TOPIC	CITATION	NUMBER
Vietnam, South	UK Great Britain	30 Nov 62	Admin Cooperation	470UNTS51	106794
Vietnam, South	UK Great Britain	27 Nov 68	Air Transport	0VKNG278	496072
Vietnam, South	UK Great Britain	20 Jul 70	Air Transport	0VKNG351	496089
Vietnam, South	UN Special Fund	29 Apr 60	Direct Aid	0VKNG154	496046
Vietnam, South	UN Special Fund	29 Apr 60	Direct Aid	357UNTS311	200567
Vietnam, South	UNICEF (Children)	29 Aug 52	Direct Aid	161UNTS335	200492
Vietnam, South	United Nations	24 Mar 54	Tech Assistance	188UNTS345	200514
Vietnam, South	United Nations	03 Jun 59	IGO Status/Immunit	337UNTS361	200557
Vietnam, South	USA (United States)	07 Sep 51	Direct Aid	174UNTS165	102284
Vietnam, South	USA (United States)	19 Jan 52	Milit Assistance	205UNTS127	102772
Vietnam, South	USA (United States)	20 Aug 54	Humanitarian	0VKNG74	496021
Vietnam, South	USA (United States)	26 Aug 54	Direct Aid	234UNTS111	103276
Vietnam, South	USA (United States)	22 Nov 54	Patents/Copyrights	235UNTS11	103291
Vietnam, South	USA (United States)	07 Mar 55	Direct Aid	277UNTS285	104013
Vietnam, South	USA (United States)	23 Apr 55	Milit Assistance	277UNTS279	104012
Vietnam, South	USA (United States)	10 May 55	Milit Assistance	273UNTS157	103950
Vietnam, South	USA (United States)	03 Nov 55	Mass Media	239UNTS195	103379
Vietnam, South	USA (United States)	15 Aug 57	Admin Cooperation	0VKNG122`	496036
Vietnam, South	USA (United States)	05 Nov 57	Finance	300UNTS23	104328
Vietnam, South	USA (United States)	17 Jun 58	Atomic Energy	321UNTS35	104652
Vietnam, South	USA (United States)	22 Apr 59	Atomic Energy	347UNTS113	104993
Vietnam, South	USA (United States)	16 Oct 59	US Agri Commod Aid	360UNTS271	105163
Vietnam, South	USA (United States)	28 Oct 60	US Agri Commod Aid	401UNTS3	105758
Vietnam, South	USA (United States)	25 Mar 61	US Agri Commod Aid	406UNTS187	105849
Vietnam, South	USA (United States)	03 Apr 61	General Amity	424UNTS137	106106
Vietnam, South	USA (United States)	04 Apr 61	Admin Cooperation	405UNTS77	105824
Vietnam, South	USA (United States)	14 Jul 61	US Agri Commod Aid	416UNTS133	105999
Vietnam, South	USA (United States)	27 Dec 61	US Agri Commod Aid	433UNTS185	106242
Vietnam, South	USA (United States)	28 May 62	US Agri Commod Aid	0VKNG168	496049
Vietnam, South	USA (United States)	21 Nov 62	US Agri Commod Aid	469UNTS101	106786
Vietnam, South	USA (United States)	19 Aug 63	Atomic Energy	0VKNG178	496053
Vietnam, South	USA (United States)	09 Jan 64	US Agri Commod Aid	505UNTS173	107373
Vietnam, South	USA (United States)	29 Sep 64	US Agri Commod Aid	531UNTS183	107703
Vietnam, South	USA (United States)	09 Feb 65	Claims and Debts	542UNTS175	107888
Vietnam, South	USA (United States)	24 Apr 65	Specific Resources	0VKNG216	496061
Vietnam, South	USA (United States)	26 May 65	US Agri Commod Aid	550UNTS3	108005
Vietnam, South	USA (United States)	03 Jan 66	Mass Media	579UNTS99	108401
Vietnam, South	USA (United States)	21 Mar 66	US Agri Commod Aid	578UNTS165	108394
Vietnam, South	USA (United States)	15 Dec 66	US Agri Commod Aid	0VKNG319	496080
Vietnam, South	USA (United States)	15 Dec 66	US Agri Commod Aid	0UNTS0	109695
Vietnam, South	USA (United States)	13 Mar 67	US Agri Commod Aid	0VKNG244	496067
Vietnam, South	USA (United States)	13 Mar 67	US Agri Commod Aid	0UNTS0	109754
Vietnam, South	USA (United States)	03 May 67	Taxation	0VKNG246	496068
Vietnam, South	USA (United States)	03 May 67	Taxation	0UNTS0	109762
Vietnam, South	USA (United States)	29 Jun 67	Direct Aid	0VKNG251	496069
Vietnam, South	USA (United States)	21 Sep 67	US Agri Commod Aid	0UNTS0	109920
Vietnam, South	USA (United States)	24 Oct 67	US Agri Commod Aid	0UNTS0	109983
Vietnam, South	USA (United States)	06 Jan 68	US Agri Commod Aid	0UNTS0	109995
Vietnam, South	USA (United States)	11 Mar 68	US Agri Commod Aid	0UNTS0	110135
Vietnam, South	USA (United States)	09 Nov 68	Milit Servic/Citiz	0UNTS0	110086
Vietnam, South	USA (United States)	09 Nov 68	Status of Forces	0VKNG281	496073
Vietnam, South	USA (United States)	14 Jan 69	US Agri Commod Aid	0UNTS0	110136
Vietnam, South	USA (United States)	05 Feb 69	US Agri Commod Aid	0UNTS0	110137
Vietnam, South	USA (United States)	17 Oct 69	US Agri Commod Aid	0SUGG304	469074
Vietnam, South	USA (United States)	29 Oct 69	US Agri Commod Aid	0UNTS0	110451
Vietnam, South	USA (United States)	23 Dec 69	Commodity Trade	0UNTS0	110613
Vietnam, South	USA (United States)	20 Jan 70	Commodity Trade	0VKNG311	496075
Vietnam, South	USA (United States)	12 Feb 70	Claims and Debts	0VKNG314	496077
Vietnam, South	USA (United States)	17 Feb 70	US Agri Commod Aid	0VKNG315	496078
Vietnam, South	USA (United States)	25 Mar 70	Commodity Trade	0UNTS0	110614
Vietnam, South	USA (United States)	15 May 70	US Agri Commod Aid	0VKNG327	496083
Vietnam, South	WHO (World Health)	21 Sep 51	Tech Assistance	107UNTS63	200352
Vietnam, South	WHO (World Health)	09 Mar 59	Sanitation	0VKNG135	496039
Virgin Islands	Multilateral	24 Dec 68	Commodity Trade	0UNTS0	109369
Virgin Islands	Multilateral	18 Oct 69	IGO Establishment	0UNTS0	110232

PARTY ONE	PARTY TWO	DATE	TOPIC	CITATION	NUMBER
W Pacif Hi Command	Multilateral	07 Nov 64	Sanitation	548UNTS3	107965
West Africa	Multilateral	03 Oct 57	Postal Service	364UNTS3	105211
Western Samoa	Multilateral	20 Jan 62	Tech Assistance	429UNTS230	200596
Western Samoa	Multilateral	10 Dec 62	Culture	521UNTS231	107525
Western Samoa	Multilateral	05 Aug 63	Sanitation	480UNTS43	106964
Western Samoa	Multilateral	07 Nov 64	Sanitation	548UNTS3	107965
Western Samoa	Multilateral	04 Dec 65	IGO Establishment	571UNTS123	108303
Western Samoa	New Zealand	01 Aug 62	General Amity	453UNTS3	106515
Western Samoa	New Zealand	30 Nov 62	Recognition	476UNTS3	106898
Western Samoa	New Zealand	24 Jan 63	Air Transport	499UNTS21	107290
Western Samoa	New Zealand	31 Dec 63	Scientific Project	521UNTS163	107519
Western Samoa	New Zealand	23 Jul 64	Non-IBRD Project	521UNTS173	107520
Western Samoa	New Zealand	29 Jul 66	Direct Aid	598UNTS115	108657
Western Samoa	State/IGO Group	30 Jul 70	IGO Operations	0UNTS0	200656
Western Samoa	UK Great Britain	23 Jul 69	Finance	0UNTS0	110118
Western Samoa	UN Special Fund	05 Jun 63	Direct Aid	467UNTS463	200601
Western Samoa	United Nations	05 Nov 62	Tech Assistance	443UNTS297	200599
Western Samoa	USA (United States)	03 Nov 64	Scientific Project	521UNTS181	107521
Western Samoa	USA (United States)	22 Jul 69	Loans and Credits	0UNTS0	110340
Western Samoa	USSR (Soviet Union)	01 Jan 62	Recognition	11SUGG130	469815
Western Samoa	WHO (World Health)	14 Aug 62	Tech Assistance	437UNTS317	200598
WEU (West Europe)	France	09 Jun 58	Non-ILO Labor	58FRRT32	415498
WEU (West Europe)	France	30 Nov 67	Non-ILO Labor	68FRJO506	416511
WHO (World Health)	Afghanistan	04 Dec 49	Direct Aid	102UNTS117	101414
WHO (World Health)	Afghanistan	18 Dec 58	Tech Assistance	324UNTS121	104681
WHO (World Health)	Algeria	20 Dec 62	Tech Assistance	463UNTS135	106698
WHO (World Health)	Austria	10 Jan 52	Tech Assistance	131UNTS295	200438
WHO (World Health)	Barbados	18 Jul 67	Tech Assistance	603UNTS87	108726
WHO (World Health)	Bolivia	07 Feb 51	Sanitation	104UNTS167	101438
WHO (World Health)	Brazil	12 Jun 52	Scientific Project	151UNTS333	102003
WHO (World Health)	Brazil	04 Feb 54	Tech Assistance	233UNTS49	103250
WHO (World Health)	Burma	13 Jun 51	Sanitation	117UNTS115	101588
WHO (World Health)	Burma	09 Jul 51	Sanitation	104UNTS187	101440
WHO (World Health)	Burma	09 Jul 51	Sanitation	102UNTS131	101416
WHO (World Health)	Burma	09 Jul 51	Sanitation	107UNTS9	101463
WHO (World Health)	Burma	09 Jul 51	Sanitation	104UNTS175	101439
WHO (World Health)	Burma	17 Jul 51	Tech Assistance	102UNTS127	101415
WHO (World Health)	Burma	18 Feb 52	Scientific Project	127UNTS43	101698
WHO (World Health)	Burma	09 Jun 52	Sanitation	134UNTS273	101806
WHO (World Health)	Burma	20 Sep 57	Tech Assistance	282UNTS113	104096
WHO (World Health)	Burundi	08 Aug 63	Tech Assistance	477UNTS346	106928
WHO (World Health)	Burundi	30 Aug 63	IGO Operations	490UNTS423	107169
WHO (World Health)	Cambodia	31 May 51	Tech Assistance	102UNTS279	200307
WHO (World Health)	Cambodia	19 May 60	Tech Assistance	372UNTS193	105298
WHO (World Health)	Cameroon	08 Dec 62	Tech Assistance	451UNTS215	106496
WHO (World Health)	Central Afri Rep	13 Feb 61	Tech Assistance	394UNTS149	105675
WHO (World Health)	Ceylon (Sri Lanka)	17 Feb 50	Direct Aid	102UNTS309	200309
WHO (World Health)	Ceylon (Sri Lanka)	04 Mar 52	Direct Aid	128UNTS281	200437
WHO (World Health)	Ceylon (Sri Lanka)	26 Mar 52	Sanitation	134UNTS341	200442
WHO (World Health)	Ceylon (Sri Lanka)	21 Nov 52	Sanitation	161UNTS315	200490
WHO (World Health)	Ceylon (Sri Lanka)	21 Dec 59	Tech Assistance	349UNTS109	105011
WHO (World Health)	Chad	03 Feb 61	Tech Assistance	394UNTS161	105676
WHO (World Health)	Chile	31 May 52	Sanitation	136UNTS323	101841
WHO (World Health)	Chile	11 Jul 52	Tech Assistance	137UNTS27	101846
WHO (World Health)	Chile	24 Oct 52	Sanitation	151UNTS339	102004
WHO (World Health)	Chile	04 Nov 52	Sanitation	150UNTS119	101966
WHO (World Health)	Colombia	05 Jan 51	Sanitation	102UNTS139	101417
WHO (World Health)	Colombia	04 May 51	Tech Assistance	110UNTS83	101503
WHO (World Health)	Colombia	18 Sep 51	Tech Assistance	109UNTS45	101489
WHO (World Health)	Congo (Brazzaville)	12 Dec 60	Tech Assistance	399UNTS105	105737
WHO (World Health)	Costa Rica	13 Apr 51	Sanitation	103UNTS3	101419
WHO (World Health)	Costa Rica	14 Jun 51	Sanitation	102UNTS151	101418
WHO (World Health)	Costa Rica	23 Jan 52	Sanitation	135UNTS265	101826
WHO (World Health)	Cyprus	07 Oct 67	Direct Aid	608UNTS327	108821
WHO (World Health)	Dahomey	07 Dec 60	Tech Assistance	387UNTS277	105567

PARTY ONE	PARTY TWO	DATE	TOPIC	CITATION	NUMBER
WHO (World Health)	Denmark	14 Feb 51	Sanitation	104UNTS243	101445
WHO (World Health)	Denmark	05 Nov 51	Sanitation	110UNTS253	101514
WHO (World Health)	Denmark	30 Nov 51	Scientific Project	118UNTS3	101592
WHO (World Health)	Denmark	26 Mar 52	Scientific Project	134UNTS285	101807
WHO (World Health)	Denmark	29 Jun 55	IGO Status/Immunit	247UNTS168	103467
WHO (World Health)	Denmark	03 Sep 56	Sanitation	258UNTS103	103674
WHO (World Health)	Dominican Republic	15 Feb 52	Sanitation	134UNTS291	101808
WHO (World Health)	Dominican Republic	10 Oct 52	Sanitation	150UNTS133	101967
WHO (World Health)	Ecuador	16 Oct 51	Tech Assistance	110UNTS263	101515
WHO (World Health)	El Salvador	21 Apr 50	Sanitation	103UNTS13	101420
WHO (World Health)	El Salvador	02 Jan 51	Sanitation	103UNTS29	101421
WHO (World Health)	Ethiopia	02 Jul 51	Tech Assistance	103UNTS39	101422
WHO (World Health)	Ethiopia	17 Feb 56	Tech Assistance	243UNTS91	103448
WHO (World Health)	Ethiopia	11 Jan 62	Tech Assistance	423UNTS99	106087
WHO (World Health)	Ethiopia	27 Jan 65	IGO Operations	541UNTS135	107866
WHO (World Health)	FAO (Food Agri)	17 Jul 48	IGO Operations	76UNTS171	200244
WHO (World Health)	Fed of Malaya	25 Nov 60	Tech Assistance	387UNTS37	105556
WHO (World Health)	Finland	07 Mar 52	Tech Assistance	128UNTS269	200436
WHO (World Health)	France	23 Jul 52	IGO Status/Immunit	209UNTS231	102829
WHO (World Health)	France	02 Apr 53	Tech Assistance	174UNTS83	102279
WHO (World Health)	France	30 Apr 53	Tech Assistance	174UNTS71	102278
WHO (World Health)	France	14 Mar 67	IGO Operations	0UNTS0	110667
WHO (World Health)	Gabon	27 Apr 61	Tech Assistance	397UNTS215	105707
WHO (World Health)	Ghana	21 Jan 58	Tech Assistance	307UNTS3	104437
WHO (World Health)	Guatemala	28 Nov 50	Sanitation	103UNTS51	101423
WHO (World Health)	Guatemala	17 Dec 51	Sanitation	120UNTS133	101619
WHO (World Health)	Guatemala	29 Dec 51	Sanitation	124UNTS89	101668
WHO (World Health)	Guinea	11 Feb 61	Tech Assistance	394UNTS173	105677
WHO (World Health)	Guyana	03 Jul 68	Direct Aid	642UNTS13	109161
WHO (World Health)	Haiti	21 Jun 50	Sanitation	103UNTS61	101424
WHO (World Health)	Haiti	27 Jun 50	Tech Assistance	110UNTS99	101504
WHO (World Health)	Honduras	20 Apr 51	Tech Assistance	110UNTS111	101505
WHO (World Health)	IAEA (Atom Energy)	28 May 59	IGO Operations	339UNTS387	200559
WHO (World Health)	Iceland	06 Oct 50	Tech Assistance	110UNTS127	101506
WHO (World Health)	ILO (Labor Org)	10 Jul 48	IGO Operations	19UNTS269	200121
WHO (World Health)	India	09 Nov 49	IGO Status/Immunit	67UNTS43	100865
WHO (World Health)	India	11 Oct 51	Non-IBRD Project	118UNTS27	101594
WHO (World Health)	India	16 Oct 51	Tech Assistance	109UNTS49	101490
WHO (World Health)	India	23 Oct 51	Sanitation	109UNTS59	101491
WHO (World Health)	India	01 Nov 51	Scientific Project	118UNTS13	101593
WHO (World Health)	India	20 Dec 51	Tech Assistance	124UNTS109	101669
WHO (World Health)	India	02 Apr 52	Sanitation	131UNTS227	101743
WHO (World Health)	India	14 Apr 52	Tech Assistance	131UNTS265	101746
WHO (World Health)	India	17 Apr 52	Tech Assistance	131UNTS241	101744
WHO (World Health)	India	19 Apr 52	Tech Assistance	131UNTS253	101745
WHO (World Health)	India	04 Jun 52	Sanitation	135UNTS279	101827
WHO (World Health)	India	19 Jun 52	Sanitation	134UNTS307	101809
WHO (World Health)	India	16 Jul 52	Tech Assistance	135UNTS291	101828
WHO (World Health)	India	11 Dec 52	Sanitation	158UNTS391	102073
WHO (World Health)	India	11 Feb 53	Tech Assistance	163UNTS43	102140
WHO (World Health)	Indonesia	28 Mar 51	Tech Assistance	103UNTS71	101425
WHO (World Health)	Indonesia	05 Feb 58	Tech Assistance	307UNTS15	104438
WHO (World Health)	Iran	04 Jul 55	Tech Assistance	227UNTS65	103131
WHO (World Health)	Iran	07 Sep 55	Tech Assistance	0IRTB87	433145
WHO (World Health)	Iraq	01 Jul 51	Tech Assistance	110UNTS139	101507
WHO (World Health)	Iraq	13 Sep 61	Tech Assistance	419UNTS69	106030
WHO (World Health)	Israel	07 Aug 51	Tech Assistance	104UNTS213	101442
WHO (World Health)	Israel	11 Apr 58	Tech Assistance	307UNTS27	104439
WHO (World Health)	Ivory Coast	30 Jan 61	Tech Assistance	395UNTS205	105686
WHO (World Health)	Jamaica	25 Sep 63	Tech Assistance	481UNTS125	106980
WHO (World Health)	Japan	26 Nov 52	Tech Assistance	204UNTS301	200521
WHO (World Health)	Jordan	03 Apr 51	Tech Assistance	110UNTS297	200367
WHO (World Health)	Jordan	16 Jun 52	Direct Aid	135UNTS323	200445
WHO (World Health)	Jordan	21 Aug 52	Direct Aid	141UNTS341	200472
WHO (World Health)	Jordan	03 Aug 60	Tech Assistance	381UNTS133	105469

PARTY ONE	PARTY TWO	DATE	TOPIC	CITATION	NUMBER
WHO (World Health)	Korea, South	19 Sep 51	Sanitation	109UNTS297	200366
WHO (World Health)	Korea, South	20 Jan 61	Tech Assistance	406UNTS269	200589
WHO (World Health)	Kuwait	16 Mar 61	Tech Assistance	397UNTS315	200588
WHO (World Health)	Laos	04 Aug 60	Tech Assistance	373UNTS313	105322
WHO (World Health)	Lebanon	05 Jun 51	Scientific Project	104UNTS225	101443
WHO (World Health)	Lebanon	07 Jun 51	Tech Assistance	126UNTS221	101690
WHO (World Health)	Lebanon	08 Sep 60	Tech Assistance	387UNTS49	105557
WHO (World Health)	Lesotho	07 Nov 67	Tech Assistance	632UNTS143	109016
WHO (World Health)	Liberia	11 Jun 51	Tech Assistance	103UNTS83	101426
WHO (World Health)	Libya	05 Jul 55	Tech Assistance	219UNTS305	200530
WHO (World Health)	Libya	16 Jun 62	Tech Assistance	437UNTS127	106301
WHO (World Health)	Malagasy	13 Oct 61	Tech Assistance	421UNTS273	106064
WHO (World Health)	Malawi	06 Jan 65	Tech Assistance	525UNTS165	107588
WHO (World Health)	Malawi	08 Jan 65	Tech Assistance	524UNTS281	107579
WHO (World Health)	Maldive Islands	23 May 66	Tech Assistance	566UNTS19	108237
WHO (World Health)	Mali	27 Apr 61	Tech Assistance	407UNTS66	105860
WHO (World Health)	Malta	10 May 67	Tech Assistance	603UNTS99	108727
WHO (World Health)	Mauritania	17 Apr 61	Tech Assistance	396UNTS301	200587
WHO (World Health)	Mexico	30 Apr 51	Tech Assistance	103UNTS95	101427
WHO (World Health)	Mexico	17 Dec 51	Tech Assistance	124UNTS121	101670
WHO (World Health)	Mexico	28 May 52	Sanitation	134UNTS319	101810
WHO (World Health)	Mongolia	21 Jun 63	Tech Assistance	472UNTS373	106848
WHO (World Health)	Morocco	09 Aug 61	Tech Assistance	412UNTS192	105932
WHO (World Health)	Multilateral	02 Nov 50	Tech Assistance	81UNTS160	101071
WHO (World Health)	Multilateral	24 Nov 50	Tech Assistance	81UNTS188	101072
WHO (World Health)	Multilateral	15 Dec 50	Tech Assistance	76UNTS120	100985
WHO (World Health)	Multilateral	18 Jan 51	Tech Assistance	81UNTS233	101073
WHO (World Health)	Multilateral	15 Feb 51	Tech Assistance	81UNTS245	101074
WHO (World Health)	Multilateral	05 Mar 51	Tech Assistance	81UNTS261	101075
WHO (World Health)	Multilateral	05 Apr 51	Tech Assistance	84UNTS299	101139
WHO (World Health)	Multilateral	01 Jun 51	Tech Assistance	118UNTS57	101596
WHO (World Health)	Multilateral	25 Jun 51	Tech Assistance	92UNTS27	101258
WHO (World Health)	Multilateral	28 Jun 51	Tech Assistance	118UNTS154	101604
WHO (World Health)	Multilateral	18 Jul 51	Direct Aid	102UNTS291	200308
WHO (World Health)	Multilateral	27 Jul 51	Tech Assistance	97UNTS291	200273
WHO (World Health)	Multilateral	01 Aug 51	Sanitation	107UNTS19	101464
WHO (World Health)	Multilateral	04 Aug 51	Sanitation	104UNTS197	101441
WHO (World Health)	Multilateral	05 Sep 51	Tech Assistance	173UNTS15	102256
WHO (World Health)	Multilateral	24 Dec 51	Tech Assistance	118UNTS290	200383
WHO (World Health)	Multilateral	18 Feb 52	Tech Assistance	126UNTS319	200434
WHO (World Health)	Multilateral	22 May 52	Tech Assistance	131UNTS115	101739
WHO (World Health)	Multilateral	19 Jun 52	Tech Assistance	133UNTS165	101787
WHO (World Health)	Multilateral	21 Aug 52	Tech Assistance	141UNTS129	101912
WHO (World Health)	Multilateral	15 Oct 52	Tech Assistance	141UNTS96	101909
WHO (World Health)	Multilateral	16 Dec 52	Tech Assistance	158UNTS407	102074
WHO (World Health)	Multilateral	29 Dec 52	Tech Assistance	151UNTS317	102002
WHO (World Health)	Multilateral	09 Oct 53	Tech Assistance	190UNTS49	102557
WHO (World Health)	Multilateral	20 Apr 54	Tech Assistance	189UNTS11	102539
WHO (World Health)	Multilateral	31 May 54	Tech Assistance	192UNTS20	102592
WHO (World Health)	Multilateral	01 Jun 54	Tech Assistance	200UNTS235	200520
WHO (World Health)	Multilateral	19 Aug 54	Tech Assistance	201UNTS51	102710
WHO (World Health)	Multilateral	06 Oct 54	Tech Assistance	201UNTS75	102711
WHO (World Health)	Multilateral	27 Oct 54	Tech Assistance	201UNTS95	102712
WHO (World Health)	Multilateral	29 Oct 54	Tech Assistance	201UNTS115	102713
WHO (World Health)	Multilateral	16 Dec 54	Tech Assistance	204UNTS323	200523
WHO (World Health)	Multilateral	04 Apr 55	Tech Assistance	208UNTS239	102816
WHO (World Health)	Multilateral	14 Jun 55	Tech Assistance	212UNTS263	200526
WHO (World Health)	Multilateral	04 Jul 55	Tech Assistance	214UNTS10	102897
WHO (World Health)	Multilateral	13 Dec 55	Tech Assistance	407UNTS8	105857
WHO (World Health)	Multilateral	02 Feb 56	Tech Assistance	227UNTS153	103137
WHO (World Health)	Multilateral	10 Feb 56	Tech Assistance	228UNTS167	103150
WHO (World Health)	Multilateral	10 Feb 56	Tech Assistance	228UNTS189	103151
WHO (World Health)	Multilateral	30 Mar 56	IGO Operations	604UNTS114	108748
WHO (World Health)	Multilateral	10 May 56	Tech Assistance	243UNTS103	103449
WHO (World Health)	Multilateral	31 May 56	Tech Assistance	251UNTS181	103541

PARTY ONE	PARTY TWO	DATE	TOPIC	CITATION	NUMBER
WHO (World Health)	Multilateral	08 Jun 56	Tech Assistance	247UNTS366	200541
WHO (World Health)	Multilateral	12 Jun 56	Tech Assistance	243UNTS187	103453
WHO (World Health)	Multilateral	14 Jun 56	Tech Assistance	265UNTS125	103809
WHO (World Health)	Multilateral	26 Jun 56	Tech Assistance	321UNTS2	104650
WHO (World Health)	Multilateral	26 Jun 56	Tech Assistance	253UNTS12	103573
WHO (World Health)	Multilateral	02 Jul 56	Tech Assistance	248UNTS37	103484
WHO (World Health)	Multilateral	02 Jul 56	Tech Assistance	540UNTS110	107846
WHO (World Health)	Multilateral	05 Oct 56	Tech Assistance	251UNTS267	103545
WHO (World Health)	Multilateral	05 Oct 56	Tech Assistance	251UNTS245	103544
WHO (World Health)	Multilateral	21 Nov 56	Tech Assistance	253UNTS266	103588
WHO (World Health)	Multilateral	15 Jan 57	Tech Assistance	376UNTS122	105378
WHO (World Health)	Multilateral	23 Jan 57	Tech Assistance	259UNTS426	103701
WHO (World Health)	Multilateral	17 Feb 57	Tech Assistance	271UNTS2	103907
WHO (World Health)	Multilateral	01 Mar 57	Tech Assistance	264UNTS94	103790
WHO (World Health)	Multilateral	28 Mar 57	Tech Assistance	271UNTS30	103908
WHO (World Health)	Multilateral	09 Apr 57	Tech Assistance	274UNTS172	103965
WHO (World Health)	Multilateral	24 May 57	Tech Assistance	268UNTS270	103861
WHO (World Health)	Multilateral	30 Jun 57	Tech Assistance	286UNTS171	104165
WHO (World Health)	Multilateral	09 Jul 57	Tech Assistance	274UNTS300	103972
WHO (World Health)	Multilateral	05 Nov 57	Tech Assistance	285UNTS301	104155
WHO (World Health)	Multilateral	15 Mar 58	Tech Assistance	292UNTS273	104276
WHO (World Health)	Multilateral	19 Jun 58	Tech Assistance	306UNTS236	200550
WHO (World Health)	Multilateral	09 Oct 59	Tech Assistance	376UNTS382	105391
WHO (World Health)	Multilateral	03 Dec 59	Tech Assistance	348UNTS246	105003
WHO (World Health)	Multilateral	12 Apr 60	Tech Assistance	359UNTS323	105150
WHO (World Health)	Multilateral	04 Jun 60	Tech Assistance	360UNTS208	105159
WHO (World Health)	Multilateral	19 Jun 60	IGO Operations	537UNTS214	107803
WHO (World Health)	Multilateral	08 Jul 60	Tech Assistance	366UNTS310	105220
WHO (World Health)	Multilateral	28 Jan 61	Tech Assistance	387UNTS202	105563
WHO (World Health)	Multilateral	20 Sep 61	Tech Assistance	407UNTS52	105859
WHO (World Health)	Multilateral	16 Oct 61	Tech Assistance	410UNTS242	105908
WHO (World Health)	Multilateral	07 Nov 61	Tech Assistance	412UNTS258	105937
WHO (World Health)	Multilateral	27 Dec 61	Tech Assistance	425UNTS83	106120
WHO (World Health)	Multilateral	17 Jan 62	Tech Assistance	419UNTS294	106033
WHO (World Health)	Multilateral	20 Jan 62	Tech Assistance	429UNTS230	200596
WHO (World Health)	Multilateral	13 Feb 62	Tech Assistance	422UNTS288	200594
WHO (World Health)	Multilateral	21 Feb 62	Tech Assistance	423UNTS151	106091
WHO (World Health)	Multilateral	01 Mar 62	Tech Assistance	423UNTS122	106089
WHO (World Health)	Multilateral	10 Apr 62	Tech Assistance	429UNTS78	106192
WHO (World Health)	Multilateral	18 Apr 62	Tech Assistance	463UNTS44	106692
WHO (World Health)	Multilateral	17 May 62	Tech Assistance	429UNTS46	106189
WHO (World Health)	Multilateral	12 Aug 62	Tech Assistance	443UNTS266	106365
WHO (World Health)	Multilateral	29 Aug 62	Tech Assistance	443UNTS280	106366
WHO (World Health)	Multilateral	11 Sep 62	Tech Assistance	455UNTS402	106553
WHO (World Health)	Multilateral	14 Sep 62	Visas	443UNTS73	106360
WHO (World Health)	Multilateral	15 Nov 62	Tech Assistance	448UNTS50	106424
WHO (World Health)	Multilateral	06 Dec 62	Tech Assistance	450UNTS240	106471
WHO (World Health)	Multilateral	12 Dec 62	Tech Assistance	457UNTS72	106578
WHO (World Health)	Multilateral	21 Jan 63	Tech Assistance	453UNTS20	106517
WHO (World Health)	Multilateral	05 Feb 63	Tech Assistance	453UNTS36	106518
WHO (World Health)	Multilateral	14 Feb 63	Tech Assistance	453UNTS168	106524
WHO (World Health)	Multilateral	06 Mar 63	Tech Assistance	455UNTS386	106552
WHO (World Health)	Multilateral	18 Apr 63	Tech Assistance	463UNTS121	106697
WHO (World Health)	Multilateral	06 May 63	Tech Assistance	463UNTS78	106694
WHO (World Health)	Multilateral	09 May 63	Tech Assistance	463UNTS159	106700
WHO (World Health)	Multilateral	22 May 63	Tech Assistance	483UNTS72	107007
WHO (World Health)	Multilateral	24 May 63	Tech Assistance	470UNTS208	106810
WHO (World Health)	Multilateral	24 May 63	Tech Assistance	466UNTS346	106754
WHO (World Health)	Multilateral	23 Jul 63	Tech Assistance	471UNTS158	106831
WHO (World Health)	Multilateral	31 Jul 63	Tech Assistance	472UNTS220	106842
WHO (World Health)	Multilateral	27 Aug 63	Tech Assistance	511UNTS210	107435
WHO (World Health)	Multilateral	10 Sep 63	Tech Assistance	480UNTS100	106965
WHO (World Health)	Multilateral	30 Oct 63	Tech Assistance	480UNTS180	106968
WHO (World Health)	Multilateral	07 Nov 63	Tech Assistance	480UNTS232	106971
WHO (World Health)	Multilateral	08 Nov 63	Tech Assistance	482UNTS286	106999

PARTY ONE	PARTY TWO	DATE	TOPIC	CITATION	NUMBER
WHO (World Health)	Multilateral	28 Jan 64	Tech Assistance	502UNTS321	107336
WHO (World Health)	Multilateral	20 Feb 64	Tech Assistance	491UNTS30	107172
WHO (World Health)	Multilateral	23 Jun 64	Tech Assistance	506UNTS108	107383
WHO (World Health)	Multilateral	28 Jun 64	Tech Assistance	519UNTS14	107499
WHO (World Health)	Multilateral	03 Aug 64	Tech Assistance	503UNTS239	107347
WHO (World Health)	Multilateral	24 Oct 64	Tech Assistance	514UNTS220	200608
WHO (World Health)	Multilateral	11 Nov 64	Tech Assistance	515UNTS94	107456
WHO (World Health)	Multilateral	11 Dec 64	IGO Operations	547UNTS297	107964
WHO (World Health)	Multilateral	15 Dec 64	Tech Assistance	522UNTS20	107533
WHO (World Health)	Multilateral	27 Jan 65	Tech Assistance	523UNTS102	107556
WHO (World Health)	Multilateral	02 Feb 65	Tech Assistance	523UNTS256	107560
WHO (World Health)	Multilateral	12 Feb 65	Tech Assistance	525UNTS148	107587
WHO (World Health)	Multilateral	23 Feb 65	IGO Operations	527UNTS120	107622
WHO (World Health)	Multilateral	05 Mar 65	IGO Operations	527UNTS221	107627
WHO (World Health)	Multilateral	08 Apr 65	IGO Operations	533UNTS66	107733
WHO (World Health)	Multilateral	26 Apr 65	IGO Operations	533UNTS50	107732
WHO (World Health)	Multilateral	12 May 65	IGO Operations	534UNTS390	107769
WHO (World Health)	Multilateral	14 May 65	IGO Operations	550UNTS310	108026
WHO (World Health)	Multilateral	25 May 65	IGO Operations	535UNTS374	107791
WHO (World Health)	Multilateral	02 Jun 65	Tech Assistance	537UNTS348	200611
WHO (World Health)	Multilateral	02 Jun 65	Tech Assistance	551UNTS2	108030
WHO (World Health)	Multilateral	05 Jul 65	General Aid	563UNTS104	108207
WHO (World Health)	Multilateral	20 Jul 65	IGO Operations	541UNTS12	107857
WHO (World Health)	Multilateral	13 Sep 65	Tech Assistance	547UNTS264	107962
WHO (World Health)	Multilateral	13 Sep 65	IGO Operations	547UNTS248	107961
WHO (World Health)	Multilateral	21 Sep 65	IGO Operations	547UNTS280	107963
WHO (World Health)	Multilateral	21 Oct 65	Tech Assistance	547UNTS216	107959
WHO (World Health)	Multilateral	12 Nov 65	IGO Operations	550UNTS160	108013
WHO (World Health)	Multilateral	31 Dec 65	Recognition	552UNTS292	108060
WHO (World Health)	Multilateral	12 May 66	General Aid	563UNTS54	108204
WHO (World Health)	Multilateral	06 Aug 66	Tech Assistance	570UNTS178	108294
WHO (World Health)	Multilateral	22 Aug 66	Tech Assistance	571UNTS298	200624
WHO (World Health)	Multilateral	23 Sep 66	General Aid	573UNTS148	108328
WHO (World Health)	Multilateral	23 Sep 66	IGO Operations	573UNTS132	108327
WHO (World Health)	Multilateral	30 Sep 66	IGO Operations	576UNTS8	108361
WHO (World Health)	Multilateral	17 Nov 66	IGO Operations	580UNTS22	108417
WHO (World Health)	Multilateral	25 Jan 67	IGO Operations	588UNTS212	108527
WHO (World Health)	Multilateral	27 Feb 67	IGO Operations	590UNTS156	108552
WHO (World Health)	Multilateral	03 Mar 67	Tech Assistance	594UNTS96	108597
WHO (World Health)	Multilateral	13 Apr 67	IGO Operations	595UNTS60	108612
WHO (World Health)	Multilateral	19 Apr 67	Tech Assistance	595UNTS120	108617
WHO (World Health)	Multilateral	10 Jun 67	Direct Aid	602UNTS212	108714
WHO (World Health)	Multilateral	14 Jun 67	Direct Aid	603UNTS2	108719
WHO (World Health)	Multilateral	20 Jun 67	Tech Assistance	0UNTS0	109290
WHO (World Health)	Multilateral	21 Jun 67	Tech Assistance	598UNTS2	108653
WHO (World Health)	Multilateral	12 Oct 67	Direct Aid	607UNTS20	108793
WHO (World Health)	Multilateral	12 Oct 67	Direct Aid	607UNTS2	108792
WHO (World Health)	Multilateral	27 Oct 67	General Aid	608UNTS37	108811
WHO (World Health)	Multilateral	14 Nov 67	Admin Cooperation	614UNTS2	108860
WHO (World Health)	Multilateral	18 Jun 69	IGO Operations	0UNTS0	109741
WHO (World Health)	Multilateral	18 Jun 69	IGO Operations	0UNTS0	109740
WHO (World Health)	Multilateral	24 Jun 69	IGO Operations	0UNTS0	109743
WHO (World Health)	Multilateral	26 Sep 70	IGO Operations	0UNTS0	110768
WHO (World Health)	Nepal	13 May 54	Tech Assistance	204UNTS311	200522
WHO (World Health)	New Zealand	29 Aug 67	Direct Aid	607UNTS57	108795
WHO (World Health)	Nicaragua	10 Nov 50	Tech Assistance	110UNTS155	101508
WHO (World Health)	Nicaragua	02 Jan 51	Sanitation	103UNTS107	101428
WHO (World Health)	Niger	28 Dec 60	Tech Assistance	394UNTS195	105679
WHO (World Health)	Nigeria	27 Mar 62	Tech Assistance	429UNTS123	106194
WHO (World Health)	Norway	09 May 52	Tech Assistance	131UNTS281	101747
WHO (World Health)	OAU (Afri Unity)	24 Sep 69	IGO Operations	0UNTS0	200651
WHO (World Health)	Pakistan	07 Oct 51	Tech Assistance	126UNTS101	101684
WHO (World Health)	Pakistan	21 Feb 52	IGO Operations	131UNTS221	101742
WHO (World Health)	Pakistan	20 Jan 60	Tech Assistance	351UNTS355	105034
WHO (World Health)	Pan Am Health Org	24 May 49	Sanitation	32UNTS387	200178

PARTY ONE	PARTY TWO	DATE	TOPIC	CITATION	NUMBER
WHO (World Health)	Panama	09 Nov 51	Sanitation	118UNTS43	101595
WHO (World Health)	Paraguay	15 Feb 51	Tech Assistance	110UNTS171	101509
WHO (World Health)	Peru	26 Sep 50	Sanitation	104UNTS233	101444
WHO (World Health)	Peru	10 Nov 50	Tech Assistance	110UNTS187	101510
WHO (World Health)	Philippines	28 Dec 50	Tech Assistance	110UNTS203	101511
WHO (World Health)	Philippines	22 Jul 51	IGO Status/Immunit	149UNTS197	101953
WHO (World Health)	Philippines	16 Jul 53	Tech Assistance	3PTS175	465082
WHO (World Health)	Philippines	16 Jul 53	Tech Assistance	3PTS175	465033
WHO (World Health)	Poland	26 Aug 65	Tech Assistance	552UNTS3	108047
WHO (World Health)	Rwanda	22 Jun 64	Tech Assistance	514UNTS11	107440
WHO (World Health)	Rwanda	23 Jun 64	Tech Assistance	514UNTS157	107445
WHO (World Health)	Saudi Arabia	29 Aug 51	Tech Assistance	110UNTS277	101516
WHO (World Health)	Saudi Arabia	06 Sep 60	Tech Assistance	395UNTS169	105684
WHO (World Health)	Senegal	06 Aug 62	Tech Assistance	435UNTS179	106279
WHO (World Health)	Sierra Leone	19 Jun 62	Tech Assistance	439UNTS151	106327
WHO (World Health)	Sierra Leone	22 Nov 63	IGO Operations	493UNTS255	107219
WHO (World Health)	Singapore	28 Mar 66	Tech Assistance	562UNTS59	108195
WHO (World Health)	Somalia	17 Aug 61	Tech Assistance	423UNTS111	106088
WHO (World Health)	Somalia	08 Nov 63	IGO Operations	493UNTS243	107218
WHO (World Health)	Spain	30 Jan 52	Tech Assistance	124UNTS259	200425
WHO (World Health)	Sudan	21 Jun 58	Tech Assistance	307UNTS235	104453
WHO (World Health)	Sudan	11 Mar 62	Tech Assistance	432UNTS325	106226
WHO (World Health)	Switzerland	12 Jan 49	IGO Status/Immunit	26UNTS331	200155
WHO (World Health)	Syria	20 Jun 52	Tech Assistance	165UNTS219	102178
WHO (World Health)	Syria	18 Nov 62	Tech Assistance	480UNTS249	106972
WHO (World Health)	Taiwan	25 Oct 51	Sanitation	126UNTS77	101683
WHO (World Health)	Taiwan	07 Mar 52	Sanitation	128UNTS233	101723
WHO (World Health)	Taiwan	21 Apr 55	Tech Assistance	210UNTS71	102835
WHO (World Health)	Tanganyika	05 Nov 63	Tech Assistance	496UNTS193	107252
WHO (World Health)	Thailand	12 Aug 49	Sanitation	178UNTS347	102350
WHO (World Health)	Thailand	04 Oct 51	Sanitation	109UNTS77	101492
WHO (World Health)	Thailand	04 Oct 51	Scientific Project	109UNTS85	101493
WHO (World Health)	Togo	03 Feb 61	Tech Assistance	394UNTS207	105680
WHO (World Health)	Trinidad/Tobago	23 Jun 64	Tech Assistance	503UNTS167	107342
WHO (World Health)	Tunisia	04 Aug 60	Tech Assistance	381UNTS335	105474
WHO (World Health)	Tunisia	27 Jan 65	IGO Operations	528UNTS209	107644
WHO (World Health)	Turkey	19 Oct 50	Tech Assistance	110UNTS215	101512
WHO (World Health)	UK Great Britain	07 Feb 52	Tech Assistance	121UNTS75	101627
WHO (World Health)	UN Relief Palestin	23 Sep 50	Sanitation	103UNTS129	200310
WHO (World Health)	UN Special Fund	25 May 60	IGO Operations	359UNTS375	200568
WHO (World Health)	UNESCO (Educ/Cult)	15 Jul 48	IGO Operations	44UNTS323	200184
WHO (World Health)	United Arab Rep	25 Aug 50	IGO Operations	92UNTS39	101259
WHO (World Health)	United Arab Rep	25 Mar 51	IGO Status/Immunit	223UNTS87	103058
WHO (World Health)	United Arab Rep	03 Aug 60	Tech Assistance	385UNTS3	105524
WHO (World Health)	United Nations	15 Nov 47	IGO Operations	19UNTS193	200115
WHO (World Health)	United Nations	10 Feb 50	IGO Operations	46UNTS327	200188
WHO (World Health)	United Nations	20 Apr 50	IGO Operations	139UNTS445	200470
WHO (World Health)	Upper Volta	15 Nov 60	Tech Assistance	383UNTS91	105496
WHO (World Health)	Uruguay	11 Jun 51	Tech Assistance	128UNTS251	101724
WHO (World Health)	Venezuela	11 Sep 50	Tech Assistance	110UNTS237	101513
WHO (World Health)	Vietnam, South	21 Sep 51	Tech Assistance	107UNTS63	200352
WHO (World Health)	Vietnam, South	09 Mar 59	Sanitation	0VKNG135	496039
WHO (World Health)	Western Samoa	14 Aug 62	Tech Assistance	437UNTS317	200598
WHO (World Health)	Yemen	03 Dec 60	Tech Assistance	395UNTS187	105685
WHO (World Health)	Yugoslavia	02 May 51	Tech Assistance	103UNTS117	101429
WMO (Meteorology)	IAEA (Atom Energy)	12 Aug 59	IGO Operations	341UNTS341	200561
WMO (Meteorology)	Multilateral	04 Apr 55	Tech Assistance	208UNTS239	102816
WMO (Meteorology)	Multilateral	14 Jun 55	Tech Assistance	212UNTS263	200526
WMO (Meteorology)	Multilateral	04 Jul 55	Tech Assistance	214UNTS10	102897
WMO (Meteorology)	Multilateral	13 Dec 55	Tech Assistance	407UNTS8	105857
WMO (Meteorology)	Multilateral	02 Feb 56	Tech Assistance	227UNTS153	103137
WMO (Meteorology)	Multilateral	10 Feb 56	Tech Assistance	228UNTS189	103151
WMO (Meteorology)	Multilateral	30 Mar 56	IGO Operations	604UNTS114	108748
WMO (Meteorology)	Multilateral	10 May 56	Tech Assistance	243UNTS103	103449
WMO (Meteorology)	Multilateral	31 May 56	Tech Assistance	251UNTS181	103541

PARTY ONE	PARTY TWO	DATE	TOPIC	CITATION	NUMBER
WMO (Meteorology)	Multilateral	08 Jun 56	Tech Assistance	247UNTS366	200541
WMO (Meteorology)	Multilateral	12 Jun 56	Tech Assistance	243UNTS187	103453
WMO (Meteorology)	Multilateral	14 Jun 56	Tech Assistance	265UNTS125	103809
WMO (Meteorology)	Multilateral	26 Jun 56	Tech Assistance	321UNTS2	104650
WMO (Meteorology)	Multilateral	26 Jun 56	Tech Assistance	253UNTS12	103573
WMO (Meteorology)	Multilateral	02 Jul 56	Tech Assistance	540UNTS110	107846
WMO (Meteorology)	Multilateral	31 Aug 56	Tech Assistance	249UNTS158	103506
WMO (Meteorology)	Multilateral	05 Oct 56	Tech Assistance	251UNTS267	103545
WMO (Meteorology)	Multilateral	05 Oct 56	Tech Assistance	251UNTS245	103544
WMO (Meteorology)	Multilateral	21 Nov 56	Tech Assistance	253UNTS266	103588
WMO (Meteorology)	Multilateral	15 Jan 57	Tech Assistance	376UNTS122	105378
WMO (Meteorology)	Multilateral	23 Jan 57	Tech Assistance	259UNTS426	103701
WMO (Meteorology)	Multilateral	17 Feb 57	Tech Assistance	271UNTS2	103907
WMO (Meteorology)	Multilateral	01 Mar 57	Tech Assistance	264UNTS94	103790
WMO (Meteorology)	Multilateral	28 Mar 57	Tech Assistance	271UNTS30	103908
WMO (Meteorology)	Multilateral	09 Apr 57	Tech Assistance	274UNTS172	103965
WMO (Meteorology)	Multilateral	24 May 57	Tech Assistance	268UNTS270	103861
WMO (Meteorology)	Multilateral	09 Jul 57	Tech Assistance	274UNTS300	103972
WMO (Meteorology)	Multilateral	05 Nov 57	Tech Assistance	285UNTS301	104155
WMO (Meteorology)	Multilateral	15 Mar 58	Tech Assistance	292UNTS273	104276
WMO (Meteorology)	Multilateral	19 Jun 58	Tech Assistance	306UNTS236	200550
WMO (Meteorology)	Multilateral	09 Oct 59	Tech Assistance	376UNTS382	105391
WMO (Meteorology)	Multilateral	03 Dec 59	Tech Assistance	348UNTS246	105003
WMO (Meteorology)	Multilateral	12 Apr 60	Tech Assistance	359UNTS323	105150
WMO (Meteorology)	Multilateral	04 Jun 60	Tech Assistance	360UNTS208	105159
WMO (Meteorology)	Multilateral	19 Jun 60	IGO Operations	537UNTS214	107803
WMO (Meteorology)	Multilateral	08 Jul 60	Tech Assistance	366UNTS310	105220
WMO (Meteorology)	Multilateral	28 Jan 61	Tech Assistance	387UNTS202	105563
WMO (Meteorology)	Multilateral	20 Sep 61	Tech Assistance	407UNTS52	105859
WMO (Meteorology)	Multilateral	16 Oct 61	Tech Assistance	410UNTS242	105908
WMO (Meteorology)	Multilateral	07 Nov 61	Tech Assistance	412UNTS258	105937
WMO (Meteorology)	Multilateral	27 Dec 61	Tech Assistance	425UNTS83	106120
WMO (Meteorology)	Multilateral	17 Jan 62	Tech Assistance	419UNTS294	106033
WMO (Meteorology)	Multilateral	20 Jan 62	Tech Assistance	429UNTS230	200596
WMO (Meteorology)	Multilateral	13 Feb 62	Tech Assistance	422UNTS288	200594
WMO (Meteorology)	Multilateral	21 Feb 62	Tech Assistance	423UNTS151	106091
WMO (Meteorology)	Multilateral	01 Mar 62	Tech Assistance	423UNTS122	106089
WMO (Meteorology)	Multilateral	10 Apr 62	Tech Assistance	429UNTS78	106192
WMO (Meteorology)	Multilateral	18 Apr 62	Tech Assistance	463UNTS44	106692
WMO (Meteorology)	Multilateral	17 May 62	Tech Assistance	429UNTS46	106189
WMO (Meteorology)	Multilateral	12 Aug 62	Tech Assistance	443UNTS266	106365
WMO (Meteorology)	Multilateral	29 Aug 62	Tech Assistance	443UNTS280	106366
WMO (Meteorology)	Multilateral	11 Sep 62	Tech Assistance	455UNTS402	106553
WMO (Meteorology)	Multilateral	14 Sep 62	Visas	443UNTS73	106360
WMO (Meteorology)	Multilateral	15 Nov 62	Tech Assistance	448UNTS50	106424
WMO (Meteorology)	Multilateral	06 Dec 62	Tech Assistance	450UNTS240	106471
WMO (Meteorology)	Multilateral	12 Dec 62	Tech Assistance	457UNTS72	106578
WMO (Meteorology)	Multilateral	21 Jan 63	Tech Assistance	453UNTS20	106517
WMO (Meteorology)	Multilateral	05 Feb 63	Tech Assistance	453UNTS36	106518
WMO (Meteorology)	Multilateral	14 Feb 63	Tech Assistance	453UNTS168	106524
WMO (Meteorology)	Multilateral	18 Apr 63	Tech Assistance	463UNTS121	106697
WMO (Meteorology)	Multilateral	06 May 63	Tech Assistance	463UNTS78	106694
WMO (Meteorology)	Multilateral	09 May 63	Tech Assistance	463UNTS159	106700
WMO (Meteorology)	Multilateral	22 May 63	Tech Assistance	483UNTS72	107007
WMO (Meteorology)	Multilateral	24 May 63	Tech Assistance	470UNTS208	106810
WMO (Meteorology)	Multilateral	24 May 63	Tech Assistance	466UNTS346	106754
WMO (Meteorology)	Multilateral	23 Jul 63	Tech Assistance	471UNTS158	106831
WMO (Meteorology)	Multilateral	31 Jul 63	Tech Assistance	472UNTS220	106842
WMO (Meteorology)	Multilateral	27 Aug 63	Tech Assistance	511UNTS210	107435
WMO (Meteorology)	Multilateral	10 Sep 63	Tech Assistance	480UNTS100	106965
WMO (Meteorology)	Multilateral	30 Oct 63	Tech Assistance	480UNTS180	106968
WMO (Meteorology)	Multilateral	07 Nov 63	Tech Assistance	480UNTS232	106971
WMO (Meteorology)	Multilateral	08 Nov 63	Tech Assistance	482UNTS286	106999
WMO (Meteorology)	Multilateral	28 Jan 64	Tech Assistance	502UNTS321	107336
WMO (Meteorology)	Multilateral	20 Feb 64	Tech Assistance	491UNTS30	107172

PARTY ONE	PARTY TWO	DATE	TOPIC	CITATION	NUMBER
WMO (Meteorology)	Multilateral	23 Jun 64	Tech Assistance	506UNTS108	107383
WMO (Meteorology)	Multilateral	28 Jun 64	Tech Assistance	519UNTS14	107499
WMO (Meteorology)	Multilateral	03 Aug 64	Tech Assistance	503UNTS239	107347
WMO (Meteorology)	Multilateral	24 Oct 64	Tech Assistance	514UNTS220	200608
WMO (Meteorology)	Multilateral	11 Nov 64	Tech Assistance	515UNTS94	107456
WMO (Meteorology)	Multilateral	11 Dec 64	IGO Operations	547UNTS297	107964
WMO (Meteorology)	Multilateral	15 Dec 64	Tech Assistance	522UNTS20	107533
WMO (Meteorology)	Multilateral	27 Jan 65	Tech Assistance	523UNTS102	107556
WMO (Meteorology)	Multilateral	02 Feb 65	Tech Assistance	523UNTS256	107560
WMO (Meteorology)	Multilateral	12 Feb 65	Tech Assistance	525UNTS148	107587
WMO (Meteorology)	Multilateral	23 Feb 65	IGO Operations	527UNTS120	107622
WMO (Meteorology)	Multilateral	05 Mar 65	IGO Operations	527UNTS221	107627
WMO (Meteorology)	Multilateral	08 Apr 65	IGO Operations	533UNTS66	107733
WMO (Meteorology)	Multilateral	26 Apr 65	IGO Operations	533UNTS50	107732
WMO (Meteorology)	Multilateral	12 May 65	IGO Operations	534UNTS390	107769
WMO (Meteorology)	Multilateral	14 May 65	IGO Operations	550UNTS310	108026
WMO (Meteorology)	Multilateral	25 May 65	IGO Operations	535UNTS374	107791
WMO (Meteorology)	Multilateral	02 Jun 65	Tech Assistance	551UNTS2	108030
WMO (Meteorology)	Multilateral	02 Jun 65	Tech Assistance	537UNTS348	200611
WMO (Meteorology)	Multilateral	05 Jul 65	General Aid	563UNTS104	108207
WMO (Meteorology)	Multilateral	20 Jul 65	IGO Operations	541UNTS12	107857
WMO (Meteorology)	Multilateral	13 Sep 65	Tech Assistance	547UNTS264	107962
WMO (Meteorology)	Multilateral	13 Sep 65	IGO Operations	547UNTS248	107961
WMO (Meteorology)	Multilateral	21 Sep 65	IGO Operations	547UNTS280	107963
WMO (Meteorology)	Multilateral	21 Oct 65	Tech Assistance	547UNTS216	107959
WMO (Meteorology)	Multilateral	12 Nov 65	IGO Operations	550UNTS160	108013
WMO (Meteorology)	Multilateral	31 Dec 65	Recognition	552UNTS292	108060
WMO (Meteorology)	Multilateral	12 May 66	General Aid	563UNTS54	108204
WMO (Meteorology)	Multilateral	06 Aug 66	Tech Assistance	570UNTS178	108294
WMO (Meteorology)	Multilateral	22 Aug 66	Tech Assistance	571UNTS298	200624
WMO (Meteorology)	Multilateral	23 Sep 66	General Aid	573UNTS148	108328
WMO (Meteorology)	Multilateral	23 Sep 66	IGO Operations	573UNTS132	108327
WMO (Meteorology)	Multilateral	30 Sep 66	IGO Operations	576UNTS8	108361
WMO (Meteorology)	Multilateral	17 Nov 66	IGO Operations	580UNTS22	108417
WMO (Meteorology)	Multilateral	25 Jan 67	IGO Operations	588UNTS212	108527
WMO (Meteorology)	Multilateral	27 Feb 67	IGO Operations	590UNTS156	108552
WMO (Meteorology)	Multilateral	03 Mar 67	Tech Assistance	594UNTS96	108597
WMO (Meteorology)	Multilateral	13 Apr 67	IGO Operations	595UNTS60	108612
WMO (Meteorology)	Multilateral	19 Apr 67	Tech Assistance	595UNTS120	108617
WMO (Meteorology)	Multilateral	10 Jun 67	Direct Aid	602UNTS212	108714
WMO (Meteorology)	Multilateral	14 Jun 67	Direct Aid	603UNTS2	108719
WMO (Meteorology)	Multilateral	20 Jun 67	Tech Assistance	0UNTS0	109290
WMO (Meteorology)	Multilateral	21 Jun 67	Tech Assistance	598UNTS2	108653
WMO (Meteorology)	Multilateral	12 Oct 67	Direct Aid	607UNTS2	108792
WMO (Meteorology)	Multilateral	12 Oct 67	Direct Aid	607UNTS20	108793
WMO (Meteorology)	Multilateral	27 Oct 67	General Aid	608UNTS37	108811
WMO (Meteorology)	Multilateral	14 Nov 67	Admin Cooperation	614UNTS2	108860
WMO (Meteorology)	Multilateral	18 Jun 69	IGO Operations	0UNTS0	109741
WMO (Meteorology)	Multilateral	18 Jun 69	IGO Operations	0UNTS0	109740
WMO (Meteorology)	Multilateral	24 Jun 69	IGO Operations	0UNTS0	109743
WMO (Meteorology)	Multilateral	26 Sep 70	IGO Operations	0UNTS0	110768
WMO (Meteorology)	Switzerland	10 Mar 55	IGO Status/Immunit	211UNTS277	200524
WMO (Meteorology)	UK Great Britain	16 Dec 64	Tech Assistance	548UNTS57	107969
WMO (Meteorology)	UN Special Fund	17 Nov 59	IGO Operations	345UNTS311	200564
WMO (Meteorology)	United Nations	10 Apr 51	IGO Status/Immunit	103UNTS245	200415
WMO (Meteorology)	United Nations	27 Mar 53	IGO Operations	178UNTS361	200504
Yemen	Accept UN Charter	30 Sep 47	UN Charter	8UNTS59	100113
Yemen	Bulgaria	08 Apr 64	Culture	0UNTS0	110293
Yemen	Bulgaria	08 Apr 64	General Amity	0UNTS0	110292
Yemen	China People's Rep	12 Jan 58	General Amity	58CCJC3	410481
Yemen	China People's Rep	12 Jan 58	General Trade	58CCJC4	410482
Yemen	China People's Rep	12 Jan 58	Health/Educ/Welfare	58CCJC5	410483
Yemen	China People's Rep	09 Jun 64	General Amity	64CCJC78	411388
Yemen	China People's Rep	09 Jun 64	Culture	64CCJC80	411390
Yemen	China People's Rep	23 Mar 65	Direct Aid	65CCJC37	411393

PARTY ONE	PARTY TWO	DATE	TOPIC	CITATION	NUMBER
Yemen	China People's Rep	03 May 65	Culture	65CCJC60	411391
Yemen	China People's Rep	23 May 66	Culture	66CCJC36	411395
Yemen	Czechoslovakia	02 Apr 68	General Amity	0UNTS0	110172
Yemen	Germany, East	28 Oct 63	Consul/Citizenship	11EGDA627	419143
Yemen	Germany, West	21 Apr 53	General Amity	54WGBB573	425310
Yemen	Germany, West	28 Nov 69	Loans and Credits	70WBGA37	424311
Yemen	Germany, West	28 Sep 70	Loans and Credits	70WBGA226	424312
Yemen	Germany, West	03 Jun 71	Loans and Credits	71WBGA146	424313
Yemen	Hungary	30 May 64	General Amity	577UNTS39	108371
Yemen	Italy	05 Oct 59	General Economic	61ITDI306	436429
Yemen	Italy	03 Oct 63	Admin Cooperation	64ITDI288	436430
Yemen	Japan	27 May 55	General Amity	57JAIL80	440156
Yemen	Multilateral	02 Aug 44	Scientific Project	67UNTS221	200221
Yemen	Multilateral	22 Mar 45	General Amity	70UNTS237	200241
Yemen	Multilateral	24 Jul 48	Sanitation	66UNTS25	100847
Yemen	Multilateral	11 Jul 52	Postal Service	170UNTS63	102222
Yemen	Multilateral	11 Jul 52	IGO Establishment	169UNTS3	102220
Yemen	Multilateral	11 Jul 52	Postal Service	170UNTS269	102223
Yemen	Multilateral	31 May 56	Tech Assistance	251UNTS181	103541
Yemen	Multilateral	03 Oct 57	Postal Service	366UNTS141	105217
Yemen	Multilateral	03 Oct 57	Postal Service	365UNTS3	105213
Yemen	Multilateral	03 Oct 57	Postal Service	366UNTS3	105215
Yemen	Multilateral	03 Oct 57	Postal Service	366UNTS255	105219
Yemen	Multilateral	03 Oct 57	Postal Service	364UNTS331	105212
Yemen	Multilateral	03 Oct 57	Postal Service	366UNTS87	105216
Yemen	Multilateral	03 Oct 57	Postal Service	364UNTS3	105211
Yemen	Multilateral	03 Oct 57	Postal Service	365UNTS207	105214
Yemen	Multilateral	14 Sep 62	IGO Status/Immunit	494UNTS219	107236
Yemen	Multilateral	05 Aug 63	Sanitation	480UNTS43	106964
Yemen	Multilateral	10 Jul 64	Postal Service	612UNTS3	108847
Yemen	Multilateral	10 Jul 64	Postal Service	611UNTS7	108844
Yemen	Multilateral	10 Jul 64	Postal Service	611UNTS105	108845
Yemen	Multilateral	10 Jul 64	Postal Service	612UNTS233	108848
Yemen	Multilateral	10 Jul 64	Postal Service	613UNTS193	108852
Yemen	Multilateral	10 Jul 64	Postal Service	613UNTS3	108850
Yemen	Multilateral	10 Jul 64	Postal Service	611UNTS387	108846
Yemen	Multilateral	10 Jul 64	Postal Service	612UNTS361	108849
Yemen	Multilateral	24 Sep 68	Air Transport	0UNTS0	110612
Yemen	Netherlands	12 Apr 39	General Amity	79UNTS257	200249
Yemen	Spain	19 May 52	General Amity	55SPBO1505	460266
Yemen	State/IGO Group	23 Apr 69	Direct Aid	0UNTS0	109514
Yemen	Turkey	09 Oct 52	General Amity	53TURG2107	466004
Yemen	UK Great Britain	20 Jan 51	General Amity	101UNTS39	101400
Yemen	UN Special Fund	02 Aug 61	Direct Aid	402UNTS43	105777
Yemen	UNICEF (Children)	31 Jan 62	Direct Aid	422UNTS271	106081
Yemen	United Arab Rep	27 Sep 45	General Amity	9UNTS373	200053
Yemen	United Nations	07 Apr 53	Tech Assistance	163UNTS73	102142
Yemen	USA (United States)	04 May 46	General Economic	4UNTS165	100043
Yemen	USA (United States)	30 Jun 59	Direct Aid	357UNTS137	105112
Yemen	USSR (Soviet Union)	31 Oct 55	General Amity	240UNTS317	103410
Yemen	USSR (Soviet Union)	08 Mar 56	General Trade	0SUST350	468457
Yemen	USSR (Soviet Union)	11 Jul 56	General Economic	0SUST363	468458
Yemen	USSR (Soviet Union)	01 Dec 59	Tech Assistance	8SUGG160	469613
Yemen	USSR (Soviet Union)	04 Apr 60	Non-IBRD Project	9SUGG133	469650
Yemen	USSR (Soviet Union)	25 Jun 60	Tech Assistance	9SUGG140	469668
Yemen	USSR (Soviet Union)	04 Jun 61	Non-IBRD Project	10SUGG134	469774
Yemen	USSR (Soviet Union)	04 Oct 62	Recognition	11SUGG155	469867
Yemen	USSR (Soviet Union)	19 Mar 63	General Trade	0UNTS0	109581
Yemen	USSR (Soviet Union)	21 Mar 64	General Amity	553UNTS267	108094
Yemen	WHO (World Health)	03 Dec 60	Tech Assistance	395UNTS187	105685
Yugoslavia	Albania	23 Mar 44	General Military	1UNTS81	100015
Yugoslavia	Albania	01 Jul 46	General Economic	111UNTS3	101517
Yugoslavia	Albania	01 Jul 46	Loans and Credits	111UNTS81	101518
Yugoslavia	Albania	11 Jul 46	Air Transport	4UNTS407	100058
Yugoslavia	Albania	03 Oct 46	General Trade	111UNTS227	101537

PARTY ONE	PARTY TWO	DATE	TOPIC	CITATION	NUMBER
Yugoslavia	Albania	03 Oct 46	Loans and Credits	111UNTS87	101519
Yugoslavia	Albania	28 Nov 46	Non-IBRD Project	111UNTS127	101525
Yugoslavia	Albania	28 Nov 46	Non-ILO Labor	111UNTS163	101529
Yugoslavia	Albania	28 Nov 46	Non-IBRD Project	111UNTS109	101522
Yugoslavia	Albania	28 Nov 46	Finance	111UNTS171	101530
Yugoslavia	Albania	28 Nov 46	Land Transport	111UNTS139	101526
Yugoslavia	Albania	28 Nov 46	Non-IBRD Project	111UNTS93	101520
Yugoslavia	Albania	28 Nov 46	Non-IBRD Project	111UNTS123	101524
Yugoslavia	Albania	28 Nov 46	Non-IBRD Project	111UNTS105	101521
Yugoslavia	Albania	28 Nov 46	Non-IBRD Project	111UNTS151	101528
Yugoslavia	Albania	28 Nov 46	Non-IBRD Project	111UNTS113	101523
Yugoslavia	Albania	28 Nov 46	Finance	111UNTS143	101527
Yugoslavia	Albania	12 Jun 47	IGO Establishment	111UNTS201	101535
Yugoslavia	Albania	12 Jun 47	Dispute Settlement	111UNTS183	101532
Yugoslavia	Albania	12 Jun 47	Loans and Credits	111UNTS189	101533
Yugoslavia	Albania	12 Jun 47	Direct Aid	111UNTS177	101531
Yugoslavia	Albania	12 Jun 47	Finance	111UNTS195	101534
Yugoslavia	Albania	22 Jun 47	General Trade	111UNTS207	101536
Yugoslavia	Albania	09 Jul 47	Culture	33UNTS91	100516
Yugoslavia	Albania	23 Nov 56	Air Transport	386UNTS73	105539
Yugoslavia	Albania	23 Nov 56	Air Transport	363UNTS123	105204
Yugoslavia	Albania	20 May 57	Sanitation	363UNTS99	105203
Yugoslavia	Albania	29 Aug 57	Postal Service	391UNTS127	105621
Yugoslavia	Albania	29 Aug 57	Postal Service	391UNTS167	105622
Yugoslavia	Albania	28 Apr 58	Consul/Citizenship	386UNTS103	105540
Yugoslavia	Albania	29 Dec 59	General Trade	396UNTS63	105693
Yugoslavia	Argentina	21 Mar 64	Claims and Debts	635UNTS153	109078
Yugoslavia	Argentina	09 Jun 65	General Trade	601UNTS3	108684
Yugoslavia	Australia	09 Jul 48	Direct Aid	22UNTS17	100327
Yugoslavia	Australia	22 Feb 50	Claims and Debts	51UNTS201	100766
Yugoslavia	Australia	19 Nov 53	Admin Cooperation	191UNTS241	102584
Yugoslavia	Australia	28 Feb 56	Postal Service	243UNTS53	103446
Yugoslavia	Australia	12 Feb 70	Non-ILO Labor	0UNTS0	110660
Yugoslavia	Austria	19 Mar 53	Visas	467UNTS293	106767
Yugoslavia	Austria	19 Mar 53	Visas	467UNTS323	106768
Yugoslavia	Austria	11 Nov 53	Air Transport	363UNTS149	105206
Yugoslavia	Austria	25 May 54	Specific Resources	227UNTS111	103135
Yugoslavia	Austria	02 Nov 54	Patents/Copyrights	55ABGB199	403229
Yugoslavia	Austria	10 Nov 54	Water Transport	56ABGB118	403230
Yugoslavia	Austria	27 Nov 54	Specific Resources	396UNTS75	105694
Yugoslavia	Austria	16 Dec 54	Territory Boundary	56ABGB119	403231
Yugoslavia	Austria	16 Dec 54	Admin Cooperation	55ABGB224	403232
Yugoslavia	Austria	18 Jan 55	Mass Media	378UNTS31	105416
Yugoslavia	Austria	15 Jun 56	Sanitation	396UNTS117	105695
Yugoslavia	Austria	19 Mar 58	Territory Boundary	58ABGB144	403233
Yugoslavia	Austria	14 Mar 59	Admin Cooperation	59ABGB163	403234
Yugoslavia	Austria	18 Mar 60	Consul/Citizenship	68ABGB378	403251
Yugoslavia	Austria	18 Mar 60	Admin Cooperation	60ABGB265	403255
Yugoslavia	Austria	18 Mar 60	Admin Cooperation	61ABGB115	403235
Yugoslavia	Austria	18 Mar 60	Visas	60ABGB232	403226
Yugoslavia	Austria	23 Mar 61	Land Transport	61ABGB223	403236
Yugoslavia	Austria	30 Jun 61	Admin Cooperation	443UNTS51	106358
Yugoslavia	Austria	10 Oct 61	Admin Cooperation	62ABGB310	403237
Yugoslavia	Austria	11 Dec 62	Land Transport	546UNTS3	107938
Yugoslavia	Austria	18 Jul 63	Visas	63ABGB244	403227
Yugoslavia	Austria	08 Apr 64	Territory Boundary	66ABGB229	403238
Yugoslavia	Austria	20 May 64	Extradition	514UNTS3	107439
Yugoslavia	Austria	27 Nov 64	Visas	64ABGB325	403228
Yugoslavia	Austria	28 Jun 65	Visas	66ABGB23	403240
Yugoslavia	Austria	28 Sep 65	Customs	66ABGB239	403239
Yugoslavia	Austria	19 Nov 65	Non-ILO Labor	591UNTS3	108556
Yugoslavia	Austria	19 Nov 65	Non-ILO Labor	587UNTS239	108512
Yugoslavia	Austria	17 Dec 65	Non-ILO Labor	66ABGB290	403241
Yugoslavia	Austria	20 Dec 65	Visas	573UNTS165	108329
Yugoslavia	Austria	10 Oct 66	Visas	595UNTS273	108622

PARTY ONE	PARTY TWO	DATE	TOPIC	CITATION	NUMBER
Yugoslavia	Austria	08 Apr 67	Visas	0UNTS0	109216
Yugoslavia	Austria	26 Apr 67	Admin Cooperation	603UNTS143	108731
Yugoslavia	Austria	26 Apr 67	Visas	67ABGB177	403243
Yugoslavia	Austria	28 Apr 67	Visas	68ABGB173	403244
Yugoslavia	Austria	28 Jul 67	Visas	68ABGB379	403245
Yugoslavia	Austria	22 Apr 68	Customs	68ABGB400	403246
Yugoslavia	Austria	12 Jul 68	Visas	68ABGB345	403247
Yugoslavia	Austria	05 Mar 69	Visas	70ABGB82	403242
Yugoslavia	Austria	03 Apr 70	Visas	70ABGB141	403248
Yugoslavia	Belgium	01 Nov 54	Non-ILO Labor	251UNTS123	103538
Yugoslavia	Belgium	05 Feb 57	Culture	276UNTS143	103990
Yugoslavia	Belgium	31 Oct 61	Sanitation	426UNTS165	106136
Yugoslavia	Bulgaria	22 Aug 47	Finance	111UNTS241	101538
Yugoslavia	Bulgaria	20 Feb 54	Territory Boundary	397UNTS13	105700
Yugoslavia	Bulgaria	22 Apr 54	Dispute Settlement	397UNTS43	105701
Yugoslavia	Bulgaria	02 Nov 54	Patents/Copyrights	375UNTS333	105371
Yugoslavia	Bulgaria	16 Mar 55	General Economic	397UNTS83	105702
Yugoslavia	Bulgaria	17 Jun 55	Sanitation	375UNTS287	105370
Yugoslavia	Bulgaria	01 Oct 55	Air Transport	396UNTS223	105698
Yugoslavia	Bulgaria	15 Nov 55	Consul/Citizenship	396UNTS179	105696
Yugoslavia	Bulgaria	15 Nov 55	General Transport	396UNTS191	105697
Yugoslavia	Bulgaria	11 Dec 55	Sanitation	378UNTS49	105417
Yugoslavia	Bulgaria	10 Feb 56	Scientific Project	349UNTS21	105007
Yugoslavia	Bulgaria	23 Mar 56	Admin Cooperation	367UNTS213	105230
Yugoslavia	Bulgaria	04 Apr 56	Air Transport	391UNTS47	105616
Yugoslavia	Bulgaria	22 May 56	Visas	367UNTS119	105229
Yugoslavia	Bulgaria	16 Jun 56	Territory Boundary	391UNTS3	105613
Yugoslavia	Bulgaria	16 Jun 56	Territory Boundary	375UNTS235	105368
Yugoslavia	Bulgaria	24 Dec 56	Culture	397UNTS3	105699
Yugoslavia	Bulgaria	19 Apr 57	Water Transport	349UNTS3	105006
Yugoslavia	Bulgaria	04 Jun 57	Sanitation	349UNTS35	105008
Yugoslavia	Bulgaria	17 Jun 57	Territory Boundary	375UNTS249	105369
Yugoslavia	Bulgaria	18 Dec 57	Non-ILO Labor	376UNTS3	105372
Yugoslavia	Bulgaria	21 Mar 58	Customs	376UNTS53	105373
Yugoslavia	Bulgaria	21 Mar 58	Land Transport	386UNTS119	105541
Yugoslavia	Bulgaria	21 Mar 58	Land Transport	349UNTS61	105009
Yugoslavia	Bulgaria	04 Apr 58	Water Transport	367UNTS89	105228
Yugoslavia	Burma	29 Jun 53	General Trade	378UNTS83	105418
Yugoslavia	Burma	14 Jun 55	Direct Aid	378UNTS93	105419
Yugoslavia	Burma	07 Mar 56	Direct Aid	378UNTS99	105420
Yugoslavia	Burma	07 Mar 56	Tech Assistance	386UNTS235	105543
Yugoslavia	Burma	07 Mar 56	Commodity Trade	386UNTS207	105542
Yugoslavia	Canada	29 Mar 50	Reparations	230UNTS357	103195
Yugoslavia	Ceylon (Sri Lanka)	30 Jul 53	General Trade	337UNTS103	104819
Yugoslavia	Ceylon (Sri Lanka)	05 May 59	Scientific Project	391UNTS101	105618
Yugoslavia	China People's Rep	14 Feb 56	Telecommunications	56CCJC24	410310
Yugoslavia	China People's Rep	14 Feb 56	Postal Service	56CCJC23	410309
Yugoslavia	China People's Rep	17 Feb 56	Dispute Settlement	56CCJC28	410314
Yugoslavia	China People's Rep	17 Feb 56	Dispute Settlement	56CCJC26	410312
Yugoslavia	China People's Rep	17 Feb 56	General Trade	56CCJC25	410311
Yugoslavia	China People's Rep	17 Feb 56	Dispute Settlement	56CCJC30	410316
Yugoslavia	China People's Rep	17 Feb 56	Finance	56CCJC27	410313
Yugoslavia	China People's Rep	17 Feb 56	Scientific Project	56CCJC29	410315
Yugoslavia	China People's Rep	04 Jan 57	General Transport	57CCJC2	410394
Yugoslavia	China People's Rep	04 Jan 57	General Trade	57CCJC1	410393
Yugoslavia	China People's Rep	07 Jun 57	Culture	57CCJC62	410429
Yugoslavia	China People's Rep	01 Nov 57	Scientific Project	57CCJC103	410458
Yugoslavia	China People's Rep	27 Dec 57	Scientific Project	57CCJC125	410475
Yugoslavia	China People's Rep	29 Mar 58	Culture	58CCJC35	410507
Yugoslavia	China People's Rep	18 Mar 59	General Trade	59CCJC53	410605
Yugoslavia	China People's Rep	25 Mar 60	General Trade	60CCJC52	410694
Yugoslavia	China People's Rep	15 Jul 61	General Trade	61CCJC103	410814
Yugoslavia	China People's Rep	28 Jun 62	General Trade	62CCJC60	410898
Yugoslavia	China People's Rep	05 Nov 63	General Trade	63CCJC128	411027
Yugoslavia	China People's Rep	11 Jun 64	General Trade	64CCJC82	411392

PARTY ONE	PARTY TWO	DATE	TOPIC	CITATION	NUMBER
Yugoslavia	China People's Rep	11 May 65	General Trade	65CCJC63	411394
Yugoslavia	China People's Rep	10 Jun 66	General Trade	66CCJC52	411396
Yugoslavia	Czechoslovakia	09 May 46	General Military	1UNTS67	100014
Yugoslavia	Czechoslovakia	25 Feb 47	General Trade	112UNTS3	101539
Yugoslavia	Czechoslovakia	27 Apr 47	Culture	33UNTS49	100514
Yugoslavia	Czechoslovakia	04 Sep 47	Claims and Debts	112UNTS91	101540
Yugoslavia	Czechoslovakia	14 Mar 48	Air Transport	28UNTS81	100421
Yugoslavia	Czechoslovakia	10 Apr 48	General Economic	112UNTS101	101541
Yugoslavia	Czechoslovakia	24 May 48	Finance	112UNTS225	101545
Yugoslavia	Czechoslovakia	24 May 48	Specif Goods/Equip	112UNTS215	101544
Yugoslavia	Czechoslovakia	24 May 48	General Trade	112UNTS111	101542
Yugoslavia	Czechoslovakia	24 May 48	Finance	112UNTS183	101543
Yugoslavia	Czechoslovakia	01 Mar 49	General Trade	113UNTS3	101547
Yugoslavia	Czechoslovakia	01 Mar 49	Finance	112UNTS241	101546
Yugoslavia	Czechoslovakia	11 Feb 56	Admin Cooperation	397UNTS135	105703
Yugoslavia	Czechoslovakia	16 Jun 56	Health/Educ/Welfare	552UNTS325	108064
Yugoslavia	Czechoslovakia	03 Jul 56	General Economic	397UNTS165	105704
Yugoslavia	Czechoslovakia	29 Jan 57	Culture	300UNTS249	104339
Yugoslavia	Czechoslovakia	22 May 57	Non-ILO Labor	391UNTS57	105617
Yugoslavia	Czechoslovakia	22 May 57	Non-ILO Labor	391UNTS33	105615
Yugoslavia	Czechoslovakia	11 Jun 57	Sanitation	504UNTS107	107355
Yugoslavia	Czechoslovakia	22 Oct 62	Land Transport	480UNTS267	106974
Yugoslavia	Czechoslovakia	24 Jun 63	Consul/Citizenship	496UNTS3	107246
Yugoslavia	Czechoslovakia	05 Oct 63	Sanitation	504UNTS151	107356
Yugoslavia	Czechoslovakia	20 Jan 64	Admin Cooperation	538UNTS197	107816
Yugoslavia	Czechoslovakia	14 Mar 64	Visas	544UNTS147	107917
Yugoslavia	Czechoslovakia	08 Oct 64	Visas	544UNTS129	107916
Yugoslavia	Czechoslovakia	17 May 67	Customs	617UNTS305	108918
Yugoslavia	Denmark	28 Jun 47	General Economic	78UNTS242	101020
Yugoslavia	Denmark	27 Jan 54	Admin Cooperation	193UNTS181	102615
Yugoslavia	Denmark	13 Jul 59	Specif Claim/Waive	386UNTS251	105545
Yugoslavia	Denmark	11 Feb 64	Air Transport	511UNTS241	107437
Yugoslavia	Denmark	11 Apr 68	Taxation	0UNTS0	109406
Yugoslavia	Denmark	13 May 68	Land Transport	0UNTS0	109727
Yugoslavia	Ethiopia	21 Aug 53	General Economic	378UNTS105	105421
Yugoslavia	Ethiopia	06 Jun 59	Loans and Credits	386UNTS243	105544
Yugoslavia	France	05 Jan 50	Non-ILO Labor	51FRJO2404	416483
Yugoslavia	France	05 Jan 50	Non-ILO Labor	0UNTS0	109502
Yugoslavia	France	14 Apr 51	Claims and Debts	53FRJO3107	416484
Yugoslavia	France	02 Aug 58	Claims and Debts	59FRRT11	415485
Yugoslavia	France	12 Jul 63	Claims and Debts	64FRRT31	415486
Yugoslavia	France	25 Jan 64	General Trade	64FRMD102	417487
Yugoslavia	France	19 Jun 64	Culture	65FRRT31	415488
Yugoslavia	France	17 Oct 64	General Transport	65FRRT88	415489
Yugoslavia	France	25 Jan 65	Non-ILO Labor	65FRRT82	415490
Yugoslavia	France	08 Feb 66	Sanitation	0UNTS0	109503
Yugoslavia	France	08 Feb 66	Sanitation	67FRJO102	416491
Yugoslavia	France	08 Feb 66	Health/Educ/Welfare	67FRJO1802	416492
Yugoslavia	France	27 Jun 66	Tech Assistance	67FRJO504	416493
Yugoslavia	France	23 Mar 67	Air Transport	67FRJO410	416494
Yugoslavia	France	15 Jan 69	General Economic	69FRJO2811	416495
Yugoslavia	France	15 Jan 69	Visas	69FRJO2205	416496
Yugoslavia	France	15 Jan 69	Scientific Project	0UNTS0	110530
Yugoslavia	France	05 Mar 70	Non-ILO Labor	0UNTS0	110803
Yugoslavia	Germany, East	10 Oct 57	Consul/Citizenship	5EGDA348	419144
Yugoslavia	Germany, East	19 Oct 57	Finance	5EGDA352	419146
Yugoslavia	Germany, East	19 Oct 57	General Trade	5EGDA352	419145
Yugoslavia	Germany, East	06 Feb 60	Air Transport	8EGDA354	419147
Yugoslavia	Germany, East	02 Dec 60	General Economic	8EGDA364	419148
Yugoslavia	Germany, East	27 Jul 61	General Economic	9EGDA484	419149
Yugoslavia	Germany, East	22 May 63	General Ad Hoc	11EGDA603	419150
Yugoslavia	Germany, East	20 Jul 63	General Trade	51EGDZ292	420151
Yugoslavia	Germany, East	28 Sep 63	Humanitarian	11EGDA620	419153
Yugoslavia	Germany, East	28 Sep 63	General Economic	11EGDA620	419152
Yugoslavia	Germany, East	19 Dec 63	Sanitation	11EGDA395	419154
Yugoslavia	Germany, East	12 Feb 64	Consul/Citizenship	12EGDA792	419155
Yugoslavia	Germany, East	15 May 64	IGO Establishment	12EGDA806	419156
Yugoslavia	Germany, East	10 Jul 64	Health/Educ/Welfare	12EGDA815	419157
Yugoslavia	Germany, East	22 Mar 65	Sanitation	50EGDZ332	420158
Yugoslavia	Germany, East	31 Aug 65	Sanitation	44EGDZ342	420159
Yugoslavia	Germany, East	22 Apr 66	Gen Communications	47EGDZ358	420160
Yugoslavia	Germany, East	20 May 66	Admin Cooperation	45EGDZ360	420161
Yugoslavia	Germany, East	18 Sep 66	Land Transport	34EGDZ368	420162
Yugoslavia	Germany, East	01 Oct 66	Consul/Citizenship	46EGDZ369	420163
Yugoslavia	Germany, East	03 Jun 67	Scientific Project	42EGDZ385	420164
Yugoslavia	Germany, West	12 Oct 36	Non-ILO Labor	56WGBB9437	425333
Yugoslavia	Germany, West	12 Oct 36	Non-ILO Labor	69WGBB1473	425336
Yugoslavia	Germany, West	11 Jun 52	General Trade	52WBGA169	424319
Yugoslavia	Germany, West	18 Dec 53	Admin Cooperation	55WBGA36	424320
Yugoslavia	Germany, West	26 Jun 54	Water Transport	59WGBB735	425321
Yugoslavia	Germany, West	21 Jul 54	Patents/Copyrights	55WGBB89	425322
Yugoslavia	Germany, West	14 May 55	Extradition	57WBGA146	424323
Yugoslavia	Germany, West	10 Mar 56	General Economic	56WGBB967	425325
Yugoslavia	Germany, West	10 Mar 56	Specif Claim/Waive	57WBGA9	424328
Yugoslavia	Germany, West	10 Mar 56	Claims and Debts	57WBGA9	424327
Yugoslavia	Germany, West	10 Mar 56	General Economic	57WBGA9	424326
Yugoslavia	Germany, West	10 Mar 56	Non-ILO Labor	58WGBB168	425324
Yugoslavia	Germany, West	17 Jul 56	Customs	59WGBB735	425329
Yugoslavia	Germany, West	17 Jul 56	Finance	56WBGA160	424330
Yugoslavia	Germany, West	10 Apr 57	Air Transport	463UNTS269	106708
Yugoslavia	Germany, West	19 Jul 57	Commodity Trade	57WBGA183	424331
Yugoslavia	Germany, West	16 Jul 64	Direct Aid	65WBGA17	424333
Yugoslavia	Germany, West	16 Jul 64	Visas	64WBGA192	424332
Yugoslavia	Germany, West	12 Oct 68	Non-ILO Labor	69WGBB1107	425337
Yugoslavia	Germany, West	23 Oct 68	Visas	69WBGA59	424338
Yugoslavia	Germany, West	10 Feb 69	General Economic	69WBGA145	424339
Yugoslavia	Germany, West	28 Jul 69	Health/Educ/Welfare	70WGBB1375	425341
Yugoslavia	Germany, West	28 Jul 69	Consul/Citizenship	70WGBB1191	425340
Yugoslavia	Greece	15 Mar 51	Air Transport	187UNTS237	102516
Yugoslavia	Greece	02 Feb 52	Sanitation	188UNTS311	102535
Yugoslavia	Greece	28 Feb 53	General Economic	252UNTS27	103557
Yugoslavia	Greece	11 Sep 56	Admin Cooperation	391UNTS117	105620
Yugoslavia	Greece	11 Sep 56	Health/Educ/Welfare	552UNTS311	108063
Yugoslavia	Greece	22 Apr 57	Postal Service	391UNTS109	105619
Yugoslavia	Greece	18 Jun 59	Admin Cooperation	368UNTS125	105237
Yugoslavia	Greece	18 Jun 59	Claims and Debts	368UNTS3	105231
Yugoslavia	Greece	18 Jun 59	Land Transport	368UNTS27	105234
Yugoslavia	Greece	18 Jun 59	Culture	368UNTS137	105238
Yugoslavia	Greece	18 Jun 59	Admin Cooperation	368UNTS69	105235
Yugoslavia	Greece	18 Jun 59	Visas	388UNTS3	105570
Yugoslavia	Greece	18 Jun 59	Claims and Debts	368UNTS9	105232
Yugoslavia	Greece	18 Jun 59	Admin Cooperation	368UNTS81	105236
Yugoslavia	Greece	18 Jun 59	IGO Establishment	368UNTS17	105233
Yugoslavia	Greece	18 Jun 59	Specific Resources	363UNTS133	105205
Yugoslavia	Greece	05 Nov 64	Territory Boundary	539UNTS13	107820
Yugoslavia	Greece	05 Nov 64	Land Transport	539UNTS19	107821
Yugoslavia	Greece	15 Apr 67	Taxation	633UNTS373	109046
Yugoslavia	Hungary	13 Aug 44	Dispute Settlement	113UNTS233	101553
Yugoslavia	Hungary	11 May 46	Reparations	129UNTS3	101725
Yugoslavia	Hungary	23 Dec 46	Finance	113UNTS125	101549
Yugoslavia	Hungary	01 Jan 47	General Trade	113UNTS63	101548
Yugoslavia	Hungary	25 Jan 47	Reparations	130UNTS3	101726
Yugoslavia	Hungary	11 May 47	Direct Aid	130UNTS171	101730
Yugoslavia	Hungary	24 Jul 47	General Trade	114UNTS3	101554
Yugoslavia	Hungary	15 Oct 47	Culture	33UNTS73	100515
Yugoslavia	Hungary	18 Mar 48	General Trade	113UNTS141	101550
Yugoslavia	Hungary	18 Mar 48	Finance	113UNTS201	101551
Yugoslavia	Hungary	18 Mar 48	Finance	113UNTS219	101552
Yugoslavia	Hungary	17 Apr 48	Reparations	130UNTS121	101729
Yugoslavia	Hungary	17 Apr 48	Reparations	130UNTS111	101728

PARTY ONE	PARTY TWO	DATE	TOPIC	CITATION	NUMBER
Yugoslavia	Hungary	17 Apr 48	Reparations	130UNTS101	101727
Yugoslavia	Hungary	25 May 57	Sanitation	477UNTS219	106924
Yugoslavia	Hungary	07 Oct 57	Non-ILO Labor	439UNTS61	106325
Yugoslavia	Hungary	20 Nov 57	Sanitation	477UNTS267	106925
Yugoslavia	Hungary	06 Dec 57	Sanitation	519UNTS215	107509
Yugoslavia	Hungary	07 May 60	Admin Cooperation	519UNTS237	107510
Yugoslavia	Hungary	09 Feb 62	Land Transport	577UNTS3	108370
Yugoslavia	Hungary	15 Oct 63	Health/Educ/Welfare	577UNTS49	108372
Yugoslavia	Hungary	08 Apr 65	Territory Boundary	587UNTS169	108511
Yugoslavia	Hungary	25 May 65	Customs	576UNTS145	108367
Yugoslavia	Hungary	09 Aug 65	Visas	577UNTS103	108375
Yugoslavia	Hungary	23 Nov 65	Visas	577UNTS89	108374
Yugoslavia	Hungary	26 Sep 66	Sanitation	601UNTS21	108685
Yugoslavia	IAEA (Atom Energy)	04 Oct 61	Scientific Project	412UNTS226	105935
Yugoslavia	IAEA (Atom Energy)	04 Mar 63	Atomic Energy	490UNTS333	107162
Yugoslavia	IAEA (Atom Energy)	04 Jun 63	Atomic Energy	490UNTS343	107163
Yugoslavia	IAEA (Atom Energy)	07 Dec 63	Scientific Project	501UNTS273	107322
Yugoslavia	IBRD (World Bank)	17 Sep 49	IBRD Project	155UNTS3	102034
Yugoslavia	IBRD (World Bank)	11 Oct 51	IBRD Project	159UNTS3	102081
Yugoslavia	IBRD (World Bank)	11 Feb 53	IBRD Project	165UNTS231	102179
Yugoslavia	IBRD (World Bank)	23 Feb 61	IBRD Project	415UNTS92	105982
Yugoslavia	IBRD (World Bank)	11 Jul 62	IBRD Project	468UNTS143	106772
Yugoslavia	IBRD (World Bank)	21 Jun 63	IBRD Project	482UNTS43	106990
Yugoslavia	IBRD (World Bank)	28 Oct 63	IBRD Project	503UNTS289	107349
Yugoslavia	IBRD (World Bank)	11 Dec 64	IBRD Project	537UNTS321	107807
Yugoslavia	IBRD (World Bank)	24 Feb 67	IBRD Project	599UNTS27	108663
Yugoslavia	IBRD (World Bank)	18 Jul 67	IGO Operations	615UNTS343	108886
Yugoslavia	IBRD (World Bank)	22 Mar 68	Loans and Credits	0UNTS0	109301
Yugoslavia	IBRD (World Bank)	15 Aug 68	IBRD Project	0UNTS0	109595
Yugoslavia	IBRD (World Bank)	05 Jun 69	IBRD Project	0UNTS0	110480
Yugoslavia	IBRD (World Bank)	30 Jan 70	Non-IBRD Project	0UNTS0	110549
Yugoslavia	ICAO (Civil Aviat)	06 Feb 52	Tech Assistance	128UNTS97	101715
Yugoslavia	India	24 Jul 53	General Trade	394UNTS13	105665
Yugoslavia	Indonesia	14 Dec 56	General Trade	378UNTS117	105422
Yugoslavia	Iran	05 Dec 63	Health/Educ/Welfare	0IRTB83	433135
Yugoslavia	Iran	24 Apr 66	General Economic	0IRTB83	433136
Yugoslavia	Iran	16 Apr 70	Visas	0IRTB83	433137
Yugoslavia	Israel	29 Jul 51	Mostfavored Nation	220UNTS7	102983
Yugoslavia	Israel	11 Dec 58	Finance	386UNTS283	105548
Yugoslavia	Israel	11 Dec 58	General Trade	386UNTS271	105547
Yugoslavia	Israel	13 Jun 64	Visas	516UNTS91	107472
Yugoslavia	Italy	03 Feb 49	Visas	33UNTS105	100517
Yugoslavia	Italy	13 Apr 49	Commodity Trade	171UNTS279	102232
Yugoslavia	Italy	23 May 49	Reparations	150UNTS179	101972
Yugoslavia	Italy	23 Dec 50	Peace/Disarmament	55ITGU73	435220
Yugoslavia	Italy	23 Dec 50	Patents/Copyrights	55ITGU73	435221
Yugoslavia	Italy	23 Dec 50	Consul/Citizenship	58ITGU136	435223
Yugoslavia	Italy	23 Dec 50	Air Transport	52ITGU142	435222
Yugoslavia	Italy	23 Dec 50	Admin Cooperation	171UNTS291	102233
Yugoslavia	Italy	23 Dec 50	Reparations	150UNTS213	101975
Yugoslavia	Italy	23 Dec 50	Admin Cooperation	150UNTS199	101974
Yugoslavia	Italy	23 Dec 50	Finance	150UNTS191	101973
Yugoslavia	Italy	18 Dec 54	Peace/Disarmament	284UNTS239	104141
Yugoslavia	Italy	26 Mar 55	Sanitation	379UNTS3	105432
Yugoslavia	Italy	31 Mar 55	General Trade	57ITGU32	435229
Yugoslavia	Italy	31 Mar 55	General Trade	386UNTS317	105551
Yugoslavia	Italy	31 Mar 55	Visas	386UNTS307	105550
Yugoslavia	Italy	31 Mar 55	General Trade	57ITGU32	435230
Yugoslavia	Italy	18 Jul 57	Specific Resources	58ITGU64	435231
Yugoslavia	Italy	03 Aug 57	Finance	59ITDI327	436234
Yugoslavia	Italy	14 Nov 57	Non-ILO Labor	60ITGU210	435232
Yugoslavia	Italy	12 Dec 57	Mass Media	386UNTS293	105549
Yugoslavia	Italy	20 Nov 58	Territory Boundary	379UNTS23	105433
Yugoslavia	Italy	13 Dec 58	Specific Resources	60ITDI345	436235
Yugoslavia	Italy	21 Apr 59	Visas	61ITDI284	436237
Yugoslavia	Italy	05 Oct 59	Land Transport	62ITGU255	435238
Yugoslavia	Italy	12 Feb 60	Other Military	379UNTS77	105434
Yugoslavia	Italy	27 Jul 60	Land Transport	6ITGU6	435024
Yugoslavia	Italy	03 Dec 60	Admin Cooperation	62ITGU237	435243
Yugoslavia	Italy	03 Dec 60	Culture	63ITGU30	435241
Yugoslavia	Italy	03 Dec 60	Consul/Citizenship	63ITGU15	435242
Yugoslavia	Italy	15 Sep 61	Culture	62ITGU80	435244
Yugoslavia	Italy	31 Oct 62	Visas	65ITGU192	435245
Yugoslavia	Italy	23 Dec 63	Visas	64ITDI321	436247
Yugoslavia	Italy	28 Nov 64	General Economic	65ITDI140	436250
Yugoslavia	Italy	28 Nov 64	General Economic	65ITDI194	436249
Yugoslavia	Italy	05 Nov 65	Specific Resources	67ITGU210	435252
Yugoslavia	Italy	10 Nov 65	Admin Cooperation	67ITGU169	435254
Yugoslavia	Italy	10 Nov 65	Admin Cooperation	66ITGU244	435253
Yugoslavia	Japan	28 Feb 59	General Economic	341UNTS179	104883
Yugoslavia	Japan	25 Jun 64	Visas	0JGJI1548	441120
Yugoslavia	Japan	15 Mar 68	Culture	69JHZ5	439020
Yugoslavia	Japan	15 Mar 68	Culture	0UNTS0	110575
Yugoslavia	Lebanon	17 Apr 54	Air Transport	602UNTS199	108713
Yugoslavia	Luxembourg	09 Apr 60	Air Transport	464UNTS293	106719
Yugoslavia	Malta	15 Jul 65	General Trade	561UNTS223	108186
Yugoslavia	Mexico	17 Mar 50	General Trade	54MEXD2202	444044
Yugoslavia	Mexico	26 Mar 60	Culture	66MEXD1607	444045
Yugoslavia	Mexico	03 Jul 63	General Trade	67MEXD1711	444046
Yugoslavia	Multilateral	02 Aug 44	Scientific Project	67UNTS221	200221
Yugoslavia	Multilateral	09 Jun 45	Milit Occupation	139UNTS381	200464
Yugoslavia	Multilateral	08 Aug 45	General Military	82UNTS279	200251
Yugoslavia	Multilateral	27 Sep 45	IGO Establishment	5UNTS327	200035
Yugoslavia	Multilateral	16 Nov 45	IGO Establishment	4UNTS275	100052
Yugoslavia	Multilateral	27 Dec 45	IGO Establishment	2UNTS39	100020
Yugoslavia	Multilateral	14 Jan 46	Reparations	555UNTS69	108105
Yugoslavia	Multilateral	22 Jul 46	IGO Establishment	14UNTS185	100221
Yugoslavia	Multilateral	22 Jul 46	IGO Establishment	9UNTS3	100125
Yugoslavia	Multilateral	27 Jul 46	Patents/Copyrights	90UNTS229	101238
Yugoslavia	Multilateral	11 Dec 46	Sanitation	12UNTS179	100186
Yugoslavia	Multilateral	10 Feb 47	Peace/Disarmament	41UNTS21	100643
Yugoslavia	Multilateral	10 Feb 47	Peace/Disarmament	49UNTS3	100747
Yugoslavia	Multilateral	10 Feb 47	Peace/Disarmament	41UNTS135	100644
Yugoslavia	Multilateral	27 May 47	Air Transport	418UNTS161	106021
Yugoslavia	Multilateral	02 Oct 47	Telecommunications	193UNTS188	102616
Yugoslavia	Multilateral	11 Oct 47	IGO Establishment	77UNTS143	100998
Yugoslavia	Multilateral	12 Nov 47	Admin Cooperation	53UNTS13	100770
Yugoslavia	Multilateral	12 Nov 47	Admin Cooperation	53UNTS39	100771
Yugoslavia	Multilateral	12 Nov 47	Admin Cooperation	46UNTS201	100710
Yugoslavia	Multilateral	12 Nov 47	Admin Cooperation	46UNTS169	100709
Yugoslavia	Multilateral	06 Mar 48	Water Transport	289UNTS3	104214
Yugoslavia	Multilateral	10 Jun 48	Humanitarian	164UNTS113	102163
Yugoslavia	Multilateral	26 Jun 48	Culture	331UNTS217	104757
Yugoslavia	Multilateral	24 Jul 48	Sanitation	66UNTS25	100847
Yugoslavia	Multilateral	18 Aug 48	Water Transport	33UNTS181	100518
Yugoslavia	Multilateral	19 Nov 48	Sanitation	44UNTS277	100688
Yugoslavia	Multilateral	09 Dec 48	Humanitarian	78UNTS277	101021
Yugoslavia	Multilateral	04 May 49	Admin Cooperation	47UNTS159	100728
Yugoslavia	Multilateral	04 May 49	Admin Cooperation	30UNTS3	100445
Yugoslavia	Multilateral	04 May 49	Admin Cooperation	30UNTS23	100446
Yugoslavia	Multilateral	04 May 49	Admin Cooperation	98UNTS101	101358
Yugoslavia	Multilateral	04 May 49	Admin Cooperation	92UNTS19	101257
Yugoslavia	Multilateral	16 Jun 49	Land Transport	45UNTS149	100696
Yugoslavia	Multilateral	18 Jun 49	ILO Labor	605UNTS295	108768
Yugoslavia	Multilateral	15 Jul 49	Health/Educ/Welfare	197UNTS3	102631
Yugoslavia	Multilateral	12 Aug 49	Humanitarian	75UNTS287	100973
Yugoslavia	Multilateral	12 Aug 49	Humanitarian	75UNTS85	100971
Yugoslavia	Multilateral	12 Aug 49	General Military	75UNTS135	100972
Yugoslavia	Multilateral	12 Aug 49	Humanitarian	75UNTS31	100970
Yugoslavia	Multilateral	19 Sep 49	Land Transport	125UNTS3	101671

PARTY ONE	PARTY TWO	DATE	TOPIC	CITATION	NUMBER
Yugoslavia	Multilateral	24 Sep 49	IGO Establishment	126UNTS237	101691
Yugoslavia	Multilateral	16 Dec 49	Admin Cooperation	72UNTS3	100924
Yugoslavia	Multilateral	21 Mar 50	Admin Cooperation	96UNTS271	101342
Yugoslavia	Multilateral	06 Apr 50	Admin Cooperation	119UNTS99	101610
Yugoslavia	Multilateral	13 May 50	Land Transport	128UNTS171	101719
Yugoslavia	Multilateral	22 Nov 50	Culture	131UNTS25	101734
Yugoslavia	Multilateral	07 Dec 50	Admin Cooperation	212UNTS17	102861
Yugoslavia	Multilateral	25 May 51	Status of Forces	175UNTS215	102303
Yugoslavia	Multilateral	02 Jul 51	Refugees	189UNTS137	102545
Yugoslavia	Multilateral	09 Oct 51	IGO Establishment	220UNTS121	102997
Yugoslavia	Multilateral	06 Dec 51	Admin Cooperation	150UNTS67	101963
Yugoslavia	Multilateral	15 Feb 52	Scientific Project	132UNTS51	101751
Yugoslavia	Multilateral	11 Apr 52	Tech Assistance	173UNTS2	102255
Yugoslavia	Multilateral	10 May 52	Admin Cooperation	439UNTS217	106331
Yugoslavia	Multilateral	10 May 52	Admin Cooperation	439UNTS193	106330
Yugoslavia	Multilateral	10 May 52	Taxation	439UNTS233	106332
Yugoslavia	Multilateral	20 May 52	Sanitation	219UNTS55	102966
Yugoslavia	Multilateral	11 Jul 52	Postal Service	171UNTS89	102225
Yugoslavia	Multilateral	11 Jul 52	Postal Service	170UNTS3	102221
Yugoslavia	Multilateral	11 Jul 52	IGO Establishment	169UNTS3	102220
Yugoslavia	Multilateral	11 Jul 52	Postal Service	171UNTS3	102224
Yugoslavia	Multilateral	11 Jul 52	Postal Service	171UNTS143	102226
Yugoslavia	Multilateral	11 Jul 52	Postal Service	170UNTS269	102223
Yugoslavia	Multilateral	11 Jul 52	Postal Service	170UNTS63	102222
Yugoslavia	Multilateral	06 Sep 52	Patents/Copyrights	216UNTS132	102937
Yugoslavia	Multilateral	27 Feb 53	Claims and Debts	333UNTS3	104764
Yugoslavia	Multilateral	28 Feb 53	General Amity	167UNTS21	102199
Yugoslavia	Multilateral	31 Mar 53	Mass Media	435UNTS191	106280
Yugoslavia	Multilateral	31 Mar 53	Privil/Immunities	193UNTS136	102613
Yugoslavia	Multilateral	11 May 53	Sanitation	456UNTS3	106555
Yugoslavia	Multilateral	01 Jul 53	IGO Establishment	200UNTS149	102701
Yugoslavia	Multilateral	01 Oct 53	Commodity Trade	258UNTS153	103677
Yugoslavia	Multilateral	17 Oct 53	General Transport	184UNTS42	102438
Yugoslavia	Multilateral	07 Dec 53	Admin Cooperation	182UNTS51	102422
Yugoslavia	Multilateral	11 Dec 53	Sanitation	191UNTS285	102588
Yugoslavia	Multilateral	01 Mar 54	Admin Cooperation	286UNTS265	104173
Yugoslavia	Multilateral	12 May 54	Admin Cooperation	327UNTS3	104714
Yugoslavia	Multilateral	14 May 54	Culture	249UNTS215	103511
Yugoslavia	Multilateral	04 Jun 54	Customs	276UNTS191	103992
Yugoslavia	Multilateral	14 Jun 54	Air Transport	320UNTS217	104644
Yugoslavia	Multilateral	14 Jun 54	Air Transport	320UNTS209	104643
Yugoslavia	Multilateral	09 Aug 54	General Amity	211UNTS237	102855
Yugoslavia	Multilateral	05 Oct 54	Territory Boundary	235UNTS99	103297
Yugoslavia	Multilateral	02 Mar 55	IGO Establishment	225UNTS233	103101
Yugoslavia	Multilateral	01 May 55	Admin Cooperation	0UNTS0	110416
Yugoslavia	Multilateral	28 Sep 55	Air Transport	478UNTS371	106943
Yugoslavia	Multilateral	12 Oct 55	IGO Establishment	560UNTS3	108165
Yugoslavia	Multilateral	20 Oct 55	IGO Establishment	378UNTS159	105425
Yugoslavia	Multilateral	04 Jan 56	Scientific Project	256UNTS171	103627
Yugoslavia	Multilateral	25 Apr 56	Commodity Trade	270UNTS103	103896
Yugoslavia	Multilateral	18 May 56	Customs	338UNTS103	104834
Yugoslavia	Multilateral	18 May 56	Land Transport	339UNTS3	104844
Yugoslavia	Multilateral	18 May 56	Customs	319UNTS21	104630
Yugoslavia	Multilateral	18 May 56	Customs	327UNTS123	104721
Yugoslavia	Multilateral	19 May 56	Land Transport	399UNTS189	105742
Yugoslavia	Multilateral	20 Jun 56	Admin Cooperation	268UNTS3	103850
Yugoslavia	Multilateral	26 Jun 56	Tech Assistance	253UNTS12	103573
Yugoslavia	Multilateral	09 Jul 56	Non-ILO Labor	314UNTS3	104539
Yugoslavia	Multilateral	07 Sep 56	Humanitarian	266UNTS3	103822
Yugoslavia	Multilateral	26 Oct 56	IGO Establishment	276UNTS3	103988
Yugoslavia	Multilateral	14 Dec 56	Taxation	436UNTS131	106293
Yugoslavia	Multilateral	14 Dec 56	Taxation	436UNTS115	106292
Yugoslavia	Multilateral	20 Feb 57	Consul/Citizenship	309UNTS65	104468
Yugoslavia	Multilateral	15 Jun 57	Patents/Copyrights	583UNTS3	108470
Yugoslavia	Multilateral	15 Jun 57	General Trade	550UNTS45	108008

PARTY ONE	PARTY TWO	DATE	TOPIC	CITATION	NUMBER
Yugoslavia	Multilateral	01 Jul 57	Culture	0UNTS0	110418
Yugoslavia	Multilateral	03 Oct 57	Postal Service	366UNTS141	105217
Yugoslavia	Multilateral	03 Oct 57	Postal Service	364UNTS3	105211
Yugoslavia	Multilateral	03 Oct 57	Postal Service	364UNTS331	105212
Yugoslavia	Multilateral	03 Oct 57	Postal Service	365UNTS207	105214
Yugoslavia	Multilateral	03 Oct 57	Postal Service	366UNTS255	105219
Yugoslavia	Multilateral	03 Oct 57	Postal Service	366UNTS87	105216
Yugoslavia	Multilateral	03 Oct 57	Postal Service	366UNTS3	105215
Yugoslavia	Multilateral	03 Oct 57	Postal Service	365UNTS3	105213
Yugoslavia	Multilateral	23 Nov 57	Refugees	506UNTS125	107384
Yugoslavia	Multilateral	13 Dec 57	Land Transport	372UNTS159	105296
Yugoslavia	Multilateral	29 Jan 58	Specific Resources	339UNTS23	104845
Yugoslavia	Multilateral	20 Mar 58	Admin Cooperation	335UNTS211	104789
Yugoslavia	Multilateral	29 Apr 58	Water Transport	450UNTS11	106465
Yugoslavia	Multilateral	29 Apr 58	Specific Resources	559UNTS285	108164
Yugoslavia	Multilateral	29 Apr 58	Dispute Settlement	450UNTS169	106466
Yugoslavia	Multilateral	29 Apr 58	Territory Boundary	516UNTS205	107477
Yugoslavia	Multilateral	29 Apr 58	Territory Boundary	499UNTS311	107302
Yugoslavia	Multilateral	18 Jun 58	General Trade	386UNTS345	105552
Yugoslavia	Multilateral	18 Jun 58	Finance	386UNTS355	105553
Yugoslavia	Multilateral	15 Jan 59	Customs	348UNTS13	104996
Yugoslavia	Multilateral	19 Nov 59	IGO Operations	410UNTS156	105902
Yugoslavia	Multilateral	26 Jan 60	IGO Establishment	439UNTS249	106333
Yugoslavia	Multilateral	15 Mar 60	Water Transport	572UNTS133	108310
Yugoslavia	Multilateral	15 Apr 60	Finance	470UNTS239	106811
Yugoslavia	Multilateral	17 Jun 60	Humanitarian	536UNTS27	107794
Yugoslavia	Multilateral	06 Oct 60	Customs	473UNTS131	106861
Yugoslavia	Multilateral	09 Dec 60	Customs	429UNTS211	106200
Yugoslavia	Multilateral	14 Dec 60	Education	429UNTS93	106193
Yugoslavia	Multilateral	30 Mar 61	Sanitation	520UNTS151	107515
Yugoslavia	Multilateral	18 Apr 61	Consul/Citizenship	500UNTS223	107311
Yugoslavia	Multilateral	18 Apr 61	Dispute Settlement	500UNTS243	107312
Yugoslavia	Multilateral	18 Apr 61	Consul/Citizenship	500UNTS95	107310
Yugoslavia	Multilateral	21 Apr 61	IGO Establishment	484UNTS349	107041
Yugoslavia	Multilateral	08 Jun 61	Customs	473UNTS187	106863
Yugoslavia	Multilateral	08 Jun 61	Customs	473UNTS153	106862
Yugoslavia	Multilateral	21 Jun 61	IGO Establishment	514UNTS209	107449
Yugoslavia	Multilateral	04 Oct 61	Scientific Project	412UNTS210	105934
Yugoslavia	Multilateral	05 Oct 61	Patents/Copyrights	527UNTS181	107625
Yugoslavia	Multilateral	05 Oct 61	Dispute Settlement	510UNTS175	107413
Yugoslavia	Multilateral	26 Oct 61	Patents/Copyrights	496UNTS43	107247
Yugoslavia	Multilateral	06 Dec 61	Customs	473UNTS219	106864
Yugoslavia	Multilateral	08 Dec 62	Finance	510UNTS235	107418
Yugoslavia	Multilateral	10 Dec 62	Culture	521UNTS231	107525
Yugoslavia	Multilateral	24 Apr 63	Consul/Citizenship	596UNTS487	108640
Yugoslavia	Multilateral	24 Apr 63	Consul/Citizenship	596UNTS261	108638
Yugoslavia	Multilateral	05 Aug 63	Sanitation	480UNTS43	106964
Yugoslavia	Multilateral	09 Nov 63	Direct Aid	489UNTS209	107141
Yugoslavia	Multilateral	28 Feb 64	Atomic Energy	501UNTS245	107321
Yugoslavia	Multilateral	10 Jul 64	Postal Service	613UNTS127	108853
Yugoslavia	Multilateral	10 Jul 64	Postal Service	612UNTS361	108849
Yugoslavia	Multilateral	10 Jul 64	Postal Service	613UNTS193	108852
Yugoslavia	Multilateral	10 Jul 64	Postal Service	612UNTS3	108847
Yugoslavia	Multilateral	10 Jul 64	Postal Service	611UNTS7	108844
Yugoslavia	Multilateral	10 Jul 64	Postal Service	613UNTS3	108851
Yugoslavia	Multilateral	10 Jul 64	Postal Service	611UNTS387	108846
Yugoslavia	Multilateral	10 Jul 64	Postal Service	611UNTS105	108845
Yugoslavia	Multilateral	10 Jul 64	Postal Service	613UNTS3	108850
Yugoslavia	Multilateral	10 Jul 64	Postal Service	612UNTS233	108848
Yugoslavia	Multilateral	01 Dec 64	Water Transport	550UNTS133	108012
Yugoslavia	Multilateral	09 Mar 65	Water Transport	591UNTS265	108564
Yugoslavia	Multilateral	08 Jul 65	General Trade	597UNTS3	108641
Yugoslavia	Multilateral	05 Apr 66	Water Transport	640UNTS133	109159
Yugoslavia	Multilateral	27 Jan 67	Scientific Project	610UNTS205	108843
Yugoslavia	Multilateral	31 Jan 67	Refugees	606UNTS267	108791

PARTY ONE	PARTY TWO	DATE	TOPIC	CITATION	NUMBER
Yugoslavia	Multilateral	03 May 67	IGO Operations	0UNTS0	110764
Yugoslavia	Multilateral	01 Jul 68	Peace/Disarmament	0UNTS0	110485
Yugoslavia	Multilateral	26 Nov 68	Humanitarian	0UNTS0	110823
Yugoslavia	Multilateral	17 Jul 69	Visas	0UNTS0	109729
Yugoslavia	Netherlands	03 Aug 46	Finance	52NET25	447002
Yugoslavia	Netherlands	01 Jun 56	Non-ILO Labor	276UNTS319	103994
Yugoslavia	Netherlands	13 Mar 57	Air Transport	327UNTS227	104723
Yugoslavia	Netherlands	22 Jul 58	Claims and Debts	386UNTS263	105546
Yugoslavia	Netherlands	09 Feb 61	Claims and Debts	453UNTS221	106526
Yugoslavia	Netherlands	28 May 64	Visas	521UNTS191	107522
Yugoslavia	Netherlands	11 Aug 66	Culture	602UNTS243	108716
Yugoslavia	Netherlands	08 Sep 66	Land Transport	597UNTS147	108643
Yugoslavia	Netherlands	13 Mar 68	General Economic	0UNTS0	109297
Yugoslavia	Netherlands	09 Mar 70	Non-ILO Labor	0UNTS0	110804
Yugoslavia	New Zealand	27 Feb 51	Reparations	150UNTS165	101971
Yugoslavia	New Zealand	09 Sep 60	General Trade	402UNTS119	105781
Yugoslavia	Norway	30 Aug 46	General Trade	30UNTS187	100457
Yugoslavia	Norway	30 Aug 46	Finance	15UNTS163	100232
Yugoslavia	Norway	31 May 51	Claims and Debts	2NORT558	451093
Yugoslavia	Norway	24 Jun 55	Culture	2NORT660	451094
Yugoslavia	Norway	30 May 56	General Trade	3NORT689	451095
Yugoslavia	Norway	18 Nov 59	Finance	383UNTS131	105499
Yugoslavia	Norway	21 Dec 59	General Trade	3NORT794	451096
Yugoslavia	Norway	15 Apr 64	Air Transport	602UNTS177	108712
Yugoslavia	Norway	06 May 64	Visas	3NORT909	451097
Yugoslavia	Norway	18 May 66	Taxation	3NORT970	451098
Yugoslavia	Norway	21 Aug 68	General Economic	3NORT0	451099
Yugoslavia	Pakistan	15 May 54	General Trade	286UNTS3	104158
Yugoslavia	Poland	23 Nov 45	General Economic	115UNTS3	101555
Yugoslavia	Poland	02 Jan 46	Visas	115UNTS21	101556
Yugoslavia	Poland	18 Jan 46	General Trade	115UNTS83	101559
Yugoslavia	Poland	16 Mar 46	Culture	10UNTS11	100139
Yugoslavia	Poland	18 Mar 46	General Military	1UNTS53	100013
Yugoslavia	Poland	24 May 47	General Trade	115UNTS89	101560
Yugoslavia	Poland	24 May 47	General Trade	115UNTS37	101557
Yugoslavia	Poland	24 May 47	Finance	115UNTS69	101558
Yugoslavia	Poland	22 Aug 47	Air Transport	47PDZU293	457003
Yugoslavia	Poland	07 Nov 47	General Economic	115UNTS137	101561
Yugoslavia	Poland	21 Jan 48	Non-IBRD Project	115UNTS155	101562
Yugoslavia	Poland	12 Apr 48	General Trade	115UNTS167	101563
Yugoslavia	Poland	16 Jan 49	General Trade	115UNTS241	101564
Yugoslavia	Poland	14 Nov 55	Air Transport	55PZUM49	458029
Yugoslavia	Poland	14 Nov 55	Scientific Project	55PZUM45	458028
Yugoslavia	Poland	07 Mar 56	Telecommunications	56PZUM115	458041
Yugoslavia	Poland	07 Mar 56	Postal Service	56PZUM121	458042
Yugoslavia	Poland	06 Jul 56	Culture	281UNTS143	104076
Yugoslavia	Poland	12 Nov 56	General Economic	57PZUM114	458056
Yugoslavia	Poland	04 Apr 57	Atomic Energy	57PZUM62	458048
Yugoslavia	Poland	20 Oct 57	Sanitation	57PZUM102	458055
Yugoslavia	Poland	16 Jan 58	Non-ILO Labor	340UNTS181	104864
Yugoslavia	Poland	16 Jan 58	Non-ILO Labor	340UNTS137	104863
Yugoslavia	Poland	20 Feb 58	General Economic	58PZUM48	458059
Yugoslavia	Poland	17 Nov 58	Consul/Citizenship	432UNTS267	106225
Yugoslavia	Poland	06 Feb 60	Admin Cooperation	521UNTS37	107517
Yugoslavia	Poland	05 May 60	Sanitation	423UNTS229	106095
Yugoslavia	Poland	30 Jun 64	General Economic	64PZUM29	458113
Yugoslavia	Poland	10 Dec 65	Sanitation	66PDZU279	457128
Yugoslavia	Poland	09 May 67	Customs	67PZUM88	458144
Yugoslavia	Romania	15 Dec 45	General Economic	116UNTS3	101565
Yugoslavia	Romania	26 Jun 46	Finance	116UNTS21	101566
Yugoslavia	Romania	23 Dec 46	Loans and Credits	116UNTS33	101567
Yugoslavia	Romania	26 Jun 47	Culture	116UNTS39	101568
Yugoslavia	Romania	30 Jun 47	Air Transport	116UNTS57	101569
Yugoslavia	Romania	30 Sep 47	Finance	116UNTS71	101570
Yugoslavia	Romania	19 Dec 47	General Amity	116UNTS89	101571

PARTY ONE	PARTY TWO	DATE	TOPIC	CITATION	NUMBER
Yugoslavia	Romania	31 Dec 48	Visas	116UNTS103	101572
Yugoslavia	Romania	13 Jan 56	Postal Service	342UNTS265	104912
Yugoslavia	Romania	01 Feb 56	Air Transport	362UNTS203	105189
Yugoslavia	Romania	04 Aug 56	Sanitation	395UNTS99	105682
Yugoslavia	Romania	25 Sep 56	Sanitation	395UNTS147	105683
Yugoslavia	Romania	27 Oct 56	Culture	389UNTS33	105590
Yugoslavia	Romania	27 Oct 56	Scientific Project	389UNTS55	105592
Yugoslavia	Romania	08 Nov 62	Consul/Citizenship	472UNTS305	106845
Yugoslavia	Romania	30 Nov 63	Specific Property	512UNTS2	107438
Yugoslavia	Romania	20 Dec 63	Visas	527UNTS245	107629
Yugoslavia	Romania	25 Dec 63	Land Transport	576UNTS95	108366
Yugoslavia	Sweden	12 Apr 47	General Trade	47SOFM161	461040
Yugoslavia	Sweden	12 Apr 47	Finance	47SOFM181	461041
Yugoslavia	Sweden	06 Oct 47	Air Transport	53UNTS107	100775
Yugoslavia	Sweden	21 May 49	General Trade	49SOFM157	461081
Yugoslavia	Sweden	02 Jan 50	General Trade	50SOFM1	461098
Yugoslavia	Sweden	19 Aug 50	General Economic	50SOFM945	461123
Yugoslavia	Sweden	29 Oct 51	General Trade	51SOFM401	461150
Yugoslavia	Sweden	20 Dec 52	General Trade	52SOFM569	461178
Yugoslavia	Sweden	16 Oct 53	General Trade	53SOFM1013	461197
Yugoslavia	Sweden	18 Apr 58	Air Transport	393UNTS225	105658
Yugoslavia	Sweden	31 May 58	Admin Cooperation	428UNTS357	106186
Yugoslavia	Switzerland	27 Sep 48	General Trade	48SWRO986	462164
Yugoslavia	Switzerland	27 Sep 48	General Economic	48SWRO990	462165
Yugoslavia	Switzerland	27 Sep 48	Claims and Debts	48SWRO995	462172
Yugoslavia	Switzerland	28 May 53	Air Transport	232UNTS45	103228
Yugoslavia	Switzerland	23 Oct 59	Claims and Debts	60SWRO475	462166
Yugoslavia	Switzerland	24 Apr 61	Loans and Credits	62SWRO99	462110
Yugoslavia	Switzerland	29 Mar 62	Land Transport	62SWRO1359	462086
Yugoslavia	Switzerland	08 Jun 62	Non-ILO Labor	64SWRO157	462100
Yugoslavia	Syria	17 Jul 66	Air Transport	0UNTS0	110165
Yugoslavia	Turkey	18 Sep 47	General Economic	48TURG2302	466096
Yugoslavia	Turkey	05 Jan 50	General Economic	50TURG1803	466030
Yugoslavia	Turkey	05 Jan 50	General Economic	50TURG2503	466097
Yugoslavia	Turkey	26 Feb 53	General Trade	247UNTS54	103460
Yugoslavia	Turkey	16 Apr 53	Air Transport	255UNTS99	103606
Yugoslavia	Turkey	10 Apr 54	General Trade	55TURG1602	466098
Yugoslavia	Turkey	13 Jul 56	Claims and Debts	57TURG1309	466031
Yugoslavia	Turkey	22 Sep 60	Sanitation	61TURG504	466041
Yugoslavia	UK Great Britain	23 Dec 48	Reparations	81UNTS103	101067
Yugoslavia	UK Great Britain	23 Dec 48	Reparations	81UNTS121	101068
Yugoslavia	UK Great Britain	23 Dec 48	General Trade	81UNTS133	101069
Yugoslavia	UK Great Britain	26 Dec 49	General Trade	87UNTS71	101167
Yugoslavia	UK Great Britain	09 Feb 50	Finance	88UNTS287	101200
Yugoslavia	UK Great Britain	28 Dec 50	Loans and Credits	88UNTS329	101201
Yugoslavia	UK Great Britain	10 May 51	Loans and Credits	102UNTS29	101408
Yugoslavia	UK Great Britain	28 Sep 51	Finance	117UNTS107	101587
Yugoslavia	UK Great Britain	20 Aug 52	Finance	158UNTS439	102077
Yugoslavia	UK Great Britain	31 Dec 53	Education	190UNTS335	102574
Yugoslavia	UK Great Britain	22 Dec 54	Claims and Debts	207UNTS227	102808
Yugoslavia	UK Great Britain	31 Dec 54	Education	209UNTS81	102824
Yugoslavia	UK Great Britain	24 May 58	Non-ILO Labor	326UNTS69	104709
Yugoslavia	UK Great Britain	03 Feb 59	Air Transport	359UNTS339	105151
Yugoslavia	UK Great Britain	03 Feb 59	Loans and Credits	343UNTS153	104924
Yugoslavia	UK Great Britain	22 Jul 59	Admin Cooperation	374UNTS319	105345
Yugoslavia	UK Great Britain	12 Apr 60	Culture	360UNTS79	105155
Yugoslavia	UK Great Britain	08 Jun 61	Mass Media	437UNTS111	106300
Yugoslavia	UK Great Britain	21 Jul 61	Loans and Credits	420UNTS61	106040
Yugoslavia	UK Great Britain	13 Feb 62	Culture	431UNTS35	106207
Yugoslavia	UK Great Britain	28 Nov 62	Commodity Trade	470UNTS65	106796
Yugoslavia	UK Great Britain	16 Feb 63	Air Transport	507UNTS171	107400
Yugoslavia	UK Great Britain	18 Dec 63	Commodity Trade	502UNTS177	107328
Yugoslavia	UK Great Britain	01 Mar 65	General Trade	548UNTS85	107972
Yugoslavia	UK Great Britain	20 Apr 65	Visas	551UNTS69	108034
Yugoslavia	UK Great Britain	21 Apr 65	Consul/Citizenship	595UNTS189	108620

PARTY ONE	PARTY TWO	DATE	TOPIC	CITATION	NUMBER
Yugoslavia	UK Great Britain	27 Jan 66	Culture	573UNTS243	108337
Yugoslavia	UK Great Britain	02 Feb 66	Commodity Trade	571UNTS275	108306
Yugoslavia	UK Great Britain	05 Jan 67	Mass Media	604UNTS13	108739
Yugoslavia	UK Great Britain	30 Jun 67	Postal Service	642UNTS325	109182
Yugoslavia	UK Great Britain	19 Apr 68	Scientific Project	0UNTS0	109657
Yugoslavia	UK Great Britain	03 Feb 69	Land Transport	0UNTS0	110437
Yugoslavia	UK Great Britain	29 Apr 69	Visas	0UNTS0	110024
Yugoslavia	UN Special Fund	27 Oct 59	Direct Aid	344UNTS159	104947
Yugoslavia	UNESCO (Educ/Cult)	27 Feb 64	IGO Operations	489UNTS257	107143
Yugoslavia	UNICEF (Children)	20 Nov 47	Tech Assistance	65UNTS28	100817
Yugoslavia	United Arab Rep	20 Feb 55	Air Transport	255UNTS199	103611
Yugoslavia	United Nations	06 Jan 51	Direct Aid	78UNTS165	101015
Yugoslavia	United Nations	10 Apr 52	Tech Assistance	141UNTS89	101908
Yugoslavia	United Nations	01 Oct 57	Milit Assistance	277UNTS191	104006
Yugoslavia	United Nations	07 Jan 65	IGO Operations	522UNTS55	107536
Yugoslavia	United Nations	16 Mar 70	Humanitarian	0UNTS0	110360
Yugoslavia	USA (United States)	30 Mar 42	Milit Servic/Citiz	13UNTS199	200079
Yugoslavia	USA (United States)	24 Jul 42	Milit Assistance	34UNTS361	200179
Yugoslavia	USA (United States)	03 Oct 46	Mostfavored Nation	13UNTS83	100205
Yugoslavia	USA (United States)	19 Jul 48	Milit Assistance	34UNTS195	100537
Yugoslavia	USA (United States)	19 Jul 48	Claims and Debts	89UNTS43	101208
Yugoslavia	USA (United States)	24 Dec 49	Air Transport	89UNTS209	101219
Yugoslavia	USA (United States)	25 Mar 50	Visas	98UNTS195	101365
Yugoslavia	USA (United States)	14 Aug 50	Postal Service	137UNTS131	101851
Yugoslavia	USA (United States)	09 Oct 50	Admin Cooperation	133UNTS25	101776
Yugoslavia	USA (United States)	21 Nov 50	Direct Aid	93UNTS39	101285
Yugoslavia	USA (United States)	21 Nov 50	Milit Assistance	93UNTS45	101286
Yugoslavia	USA (United States)	06 Jan 51	Direct Aid	122UNTS137	101643
Yugoslavia	USA (United States)	17 Apr 51	Milit Assistance	162UNTS173	102134
Yugoslavia	USA (United States)	14 Nov 51	Milit Assistance	174UNTS201	102286
Yugoslavia	USA (United States)	08 Jan 52	Direct Aid	152UNTS61	102011
Yugoslavia	USA (United States)	15 Aug 52	Direct Aid	184UNTS97	102441
Yugoslavia	USA (United States)	11 Oct 52	Direct Aid	235UNTS277	103309
Yugoslavia	USA (United States)	03 Dec 52	Direct Aid	185UNTS183	102469
Yugoslavia	USA (United States)	23 Jul 53	Taxation	221UNTS365	103018
Yugoslavia	USA (United States)	05 Jan 54	Direct Aid	234UNTS267	103289
Yugoslavia	USA (United States)	16 Apr 54	Direct Aid	237UNTS77	103337
Yugoslavia	USA (United States)	18 Oct 54	Milit Assistance	273UNTS163	103951
Yugoslavia	USA (United States)	05 Jan 55	US Agri Commod Aid	251UNTS29	103531
Yugoslavia	USA (United States)	09 Feb 55	Direct Aid	241UNTS13	103419
Yugoslavia	USA (United States)	12 May 55	Direct Aid	251UNTS337	103550
Yugoslavia	USA (United States)	12 May 55	Direct Aid	251UNTS343	103551
Yugoslavia	USA (United States)	12 May 55	Direct Aid	251UNTS331	103549
Yugoslavia	USA (United States)	30 Sep 55	General Military	269UNTS89	103877
Yugoslavia	USA (United States)	19 Jan 56	Direct Aid	240UNTS121	103400
Yugoslavia	USA (United States)	21 May 56	Visas	281UNTS93	104072
Yugoslavia	USA (United States)	03 Nov 56	US Agri Commod Aid	277UNTS119	104002
Yugoslavia	USA (United States)	03 Feb 58	US Agri Commod Aid	304UNTS293	104404
Yugoslavia	USA (United States)	05 Apr 58	Tech Assistance	338UNTS233	104838
Yugoslavia	USA (United States)	16 Jun 58	Admin Cooperation	317UNTS31	104591
Yugoslavia	USA (United States)	22 Dec 58	US Agri Commod Aid	338UNTS243	104839
Yugoslavia	USA (United States)	25 Aug 59	Milit Assistance	357UNTS87	105107
Yugoslavia	USA (United States)	25 Aug 59	Milit Assistance	357UNTS77	105106
Yugoslavia	USA (United States)	22 Oct 59	Tech Assistance	360UNTS259	105161
Yugoslavia	USA (United States)	03 Jun 60	US Agri Commod Aid	376UNTS243	105382
Yugoslavia	USA (United States)	19 Jan 61	General Aid	402UNTS163	105784
Yugoslavia	USA (United States)	19 Apr 61	Direct Aid	409UNTS163	105883
Yugoslavia	USA (United States)	28 Apr 61	US Agri Commod Aid	409UNTS172	105884
Yugoslavia	USA (United States)	14 Jun 61	Admin Cooperation	0UNTS0	110400
Yugoslavia	USA (United States)	28 Dec 61	US Agri Commod Aid	434UNTS111	106259
Yugoslavia	USA (United States)	21 Apr 62	US Agri Commod Aid	442UNTS123	106344
Yugoslavia	USA (United States)	28 Nov 62	US Agri Commod Aid	460UNTS185	106640
Yugoslavia	USA (United States)	04 Apr 64	Visas	526UNTS47	107599
Yugoslavia	USA (United States)	27 Apr 64	US Agri Commod Aid	526UNTS89	107602
Yugoslavia	USA (United States)	27 Apr 64	US Agri Commod Aid	526UNTS73	107601

PARTY ONE	PARTY TWO	DATE	TOPIC	CITATION	NUMBER
Yugoslavia	USA (United States)	28 Apr 64	US Agri Commod Aid	526UNTS103	107603
Yugoslavia	USA (United States)	05 Oct 64	Commodity Trade	531UNTS63	107693
Yugoslavia	USA (United States)	28 Oct 64	US Agri Commod Aid	533UNTS3	107728
Yugoslavia	USA (United States)	29 Oct 64	US Agri Commod Aid	533UNTS17	107729
Yugoslavia	USA (United States)	05 Nov 64	Claims and Debts	550UNTS31	108007
Yugoslavia	USA (United States)	09 Nov 64	Education	533UNTS39	107731
Yugoslavia	USA (United States)	16 Mar 65	US Agri Commod Aid	542UNTS161	107887
Yugoslavia	USA (United States)	16 Jul 65	US Agri Commod Aid	549UNTS111	107994
Yugoslavia	USA (United States)	22 Nov 65	US Agri Commod Aid	574UNTS211	108351
Yugoslavia	USA (United States)	11 Apr 66	US Agri Commod Aid	580UNTS239	108427
Yugoslavia	USA (United States)	24 Apr 67	Finance	0UNTS0	109900
Yugoslavia	USA (United States)	26 Sep 67	Commodity Trade	0UNTS0	110046
Yugoslavia	USSR (Soviet Union)	11 Apr 45	General Amity	0SUST175	468459
Yugoslavia	USSR (Soviet Union)	13 Apr 45	General Trade	0SUST175	468460
Yugoslavia	USSR (Soviet Union)	13 Nov 45	Scientific Project	116UNTS139	101573
Yugoslavia	USSR (Soviet Union)	30 Nov 45	General Trade	116UNTS153	101574
Yugoslavia	USSR (Soviet Union)	26 Apr 46	General Trade	116UNTS163	101575
Yugoslavia	USSR (Soviet Union)	08 Jun 46	General Trade	0SUST213	468461
Yugoslavia	USSR (Soviet Union)	04 Feb 47	Air Transport	130UNTS235	101731
Yugoslavia	USSR (Soviet Union)	04 Feb 47	Admin Cooperation	116UNTS171	101576
Yugoslavia	USSR (Soviet Union)	05 Jul 47	General Economic	0SUST234	468462
Yugoslavia	USSR (Soviet Union)	05 Jul 47	Finance	0SUST234	468463
Yugoslavia	USSR (Soviet Union)	25 Jul 47	Tech Assistance	130UNTS315	101732
Yugoslavia	USSR (Soviet Union)	23 Aug 47	Reparations	116UNTS281	101577
Yugoslavia	USSR (Soviet Union)	15 Dec 47	Education	116UNTS313	101578
Yugoslavia	USSR (Soviet Union)	27 Dec 48	General Trade	116UNTS327	101579
Yugoslavia	USSR (Soviet Union)	31 Aug 49	Admin Cooperation	116UNTS345	101580
Yugoslavia	USSR (Soviet Union)	14 Jun 53	Consul/Citizenship	0SUST296	468464
Yugoslavia	USSR (Soviet Union)	01 Oct 54	General Trade	0SUST316	468465
Yugoslavia	USSR (Soviet Union)	05 Jan 55	General Trade	0SUST322	468466
Yugoslavia	USSR (Soviet Union)	05 Jan 55	General Trade	240UNTS207	103404
Yugoslavia	USSR (Soviet Union)	05 Jan 55	Finance	240UNTS225	103405
Yugoslavia	USSR (Soviet Union)	10 Jan 55	Air Transport	0SUST322	468468
Yugoslavia	USSR (Soviet Union)	10 Jan 55	Air Transport	0SUST322	468467
Yugoslavia	USSR (Soviet Union)	30 Jul 55	General Trade	0SUST334	468469
Yugoslavia	USSR (Soviet Union)	03 Sep 55	Air Transport	240UNTS267	103408
Yugoslavia	USSR (Soviet Union)	27 Sep 55	Postal Service	0SUST339	468471
Yugoslavia	USSR (Soviet Union)	27 Sep 55	Gen Communications	0SUST338	468470
Yugoslavia	USSR (Soviet Union)	12 Nov 55	Culture	0SUST340	468472
Yugoslavia	USSR (Soviet Union)	19 Dec 55	Scientific Project	378UNTS127	105423
Yugoslavia	USSR (Soviet Union)	12 Jan 56	Direct Aid	0SUST347	468474
Yugoslavia	USSR (Soviet Union)	28 Jan 56	Atomic Energy	0SUST348	468475
Yugoslavia	USSR (Soviet Union)	02 Feb 56	Loans and Credits	259UNTS111	103685
Yugoslavia	USSR (Soviet Union)	03 Mar 56	Water Transport	0SUST350	468477
Yugoslavia	USSR (Soviet Union)	09 Mar 56	Claims and Debts	0SUST351	468478
Yugoslavia	USSR (Soviet Union)	17 May 56	Culture	259UNTS145	103687
Yugoslavia	USSR (Soviet Union)	22 May 56	Consul/Citizenship	259UNTS155	103688
Yugoslavia	USSR (Soviet Union)	20 Jun 56	Admin Cooperation	0SUST358	468479
Yugoslavia	USSR (Soviet Union)	27 Aug 56	Specif Goods/Equip	16SUGG73	469925
Yugoslavia	USSR (Soviet Union)	09 Feb 57	Scientific Project	0SUST377	468480
Yugoslavia	USSR (Soviet Union)	10 Apr 57	General Trade	0SUST381	468481
Yugoslavia	USSR (Soviet Union)	10 Jul 57	Mass Media	0SUST386	468482
Yugoslavia	USSR (Soviet Union)	29 Jul 57	Direct Aid	0SUST386	468483
Yugoslavia	USSR (Soviet Union)	21 Jul 60	Consul/Citizenship	9SUGG142	469677
Yugoslavia	USSR (Soviet Union)	30 Mar 61	General Trade	10SUGG126	469756
Yugoslavia	USSR (Soviet Union)	24 Feb 62	Admin Cooperation	471UNTS195	106833
Yugoslavia	USSR (Soviet Union)	29 Sep 66	General Aid	608UNTS219	108818
Yugoslavia	WHO (World Health)	02 May 51	Tech Assistance	103UNTS117	101429
Zambia	Accept UN Charter	26 Oct 64	UN Charter	519UNTS11	107498
Zambia	China People's Rep	22 Aug 66	Culture	66CCJC80	411397
Zambia	China People's Rep	28 Apr 67	General Trade	67CCJC18	411398
Zambia	Denmark	12 Dec 65	Tech Assistance	574UNTS21	108339
Zambia	Denmark	17 Oct 67	Tech Assistance	620UNTS239	108960
Zambia	Denmark	18 Oct 67	Loans and Credits	637UNTS0	109116
Zambia	Denmark	11 Jul 68	Tech Assistance	0UNTS0	110794

PARTY ONE	PARTY TWO	DATE	TOPIC	CITATION	NUMBER
Zambia	Denmark	11 Jul 68	Direct Aid	0UNTS0	109306
Zambia	Finland	29 Aug 70	Tech Assistance	0UNTS0	110841
Zambia	Germany, West	10 Dec 66	Claims and Debts	68WGBB33	425610
Zambia	Germany, West	10 Dec 66	General Economic	67WBGA51	424607
Zambia	Germany, West	10 Dec 66	Loans and Credits	67WBGA51	424608
Zambia	Germany, West	10 Dec 66	Tech Assistance	67WBGA51	424609
Zambia	Germany, West	11 Apr 68	Tech Assistance	68WBGA147	424611
Zambia	IBRD (World Bank)	04 Oct 66	IBRD Project	585UNTS181	108489
Zambia	IBRD (World Bank)	05 Oct 68	IBRD Project	0UNTS0	109650
Zambia	IBRD (World Bank)	05 Oct 68	IBRD Project	0UNTS0	109608
Zambia	IBRD (World Bank)	11 Apr 69	IBRD Project	0UNTS0	109891
Zambia	IBRD (World Bank)	30 Jun 69	IBRD Project	0UNTS0	110310
Zambia	IBRD (World Bank)	20 Nov 69	Loans and Credits	0UNTS0	110546
Zambia	ILO (Labor Org)	20 Dec 67	IGO Operations	619UNTS293	108947
Zambia	Japan	21 May 65	General Trade	0JGJI1607	441138
Zambia	Japan	19 Feb 70	Taxation	71JHZ1	439261
Zambia	Multilateral	25 May 55	IGO Establishment	264UNTS117	103791
Zambia	Multilateral	26 Jan 60	IGO Establishment	439UNTS249	106333
Zambia	Multilateral	22 Jun 62	ILO Labor	494UNTS249	107237
Zambia	Multilateral	04 Aug 63	IGO Establishment	510UNTS3	107408
Zambia	Multilateral	10 Jul 64	Postal Service	611UNTS105	108845
Zambia	Multilateral	10 Jul 64	Postal Service	611UNTS7	108844
Zambia	Multilateral	10 Jul 64	Postal Service	612UNTS3	108847
Zambia	Multilateral	09 Mar 65	Water Transport	591UNTS265	108564
Zambia	Multilateral	23 Jun 65	General IGO	614UNTS239	108873

PARTY ONE	PARTY TWO	DATE	TOPIC	CITATION	NUMBER
Zambia	Multilateral	08 Jul 65	General Trade	597UNTS3	108641
Zambia	Netherlands	17 Dec 65	Non-ILO Labor	631UNTS311	109000
Zambia	Norway	21 Dec 63	Taxation	2NORT553	451219
Zambia	Norway	31 Mar 67	Tech Assistance	3NORT993	451220
Zambia	State/IGO Group	29 May 70	Tech Assistance	0UNTS0	110502
Zambia	State/IGO Group	29 May 70	Tech Assistance	0UNTS0	110501
Zambia	UK Great Britain	30 Jan 62	Non-ILO Labor	590UNTS173	108553
Zambia	UK Great Britain	28 Jul 66	Non-ILO Labor	590UNTS191	108554
Zambia	UK Great Britain	21 Feb 68	Military Mission	0UNTS0	109264
Zambia	UK Great Britain	06 Apr 68	Taxation	0UNTS0	110698
Zambia	UK Great Britain	23 Sep 68	Finance	0UNTS0	109814
Zambia	UN Special Fund	15 Dec 64	Direct Aid	522UNTS3	107532
Zambia	UN Special Fund	04 Feb 65	Admin Cooperation	527UNTS115	107621
Zambia	UNICEF (Children)	02 Feb 67	IGO Operations	589UNTS89	108536
Zambia	United Arab Rep	16 Feb 66	General Trade	0UNTS0	109535
Zambia	United Nations	23 Oct 65	IGO Operations	549UNTS101	107993
Zambia	United Nations	06 Jul 67	IGO Operations	600UNTS81	108678
Zambia	United Nations	30 Mar 70	Humanitarian	0UNTS0	110399
Zambia	USA (United States)	11 Aug 66	Finance	616UNTS267	108901
Zambia	USSR (Soviet Union)	26 May 67	General Economic	643UNTS179	109191
Zanzibar	Accept UN Charter	10 Dec 63	UN Charter	483UNTS237	107016
Zanzibar	Germany, East	17 May 64	General Aid	12EGDA1139	419306
Zanzibar	Germany, East	27 Jun 64	Tech Assistance	12EGDA1146	419307
Zanzibar	Multilateral	04 Aug 63	IGO Establishment	510UNTS3	107408

INTERNATIONAL ORGANIZATION SECTION

User's Guide

This is one of the five specialized sections of the INDEX. Each specialized section lists treaties in a different order: (1) by date of signature, (2) by party, (3) by international organizations mentioned in the treaty text, (4) by the topical categories of the UNTS Index and (5) by the topical categories of this INDEX.

Within each section there is a standard set of information per treaty: (1) parties, (2) date of signature, (3) topic, (4) citation and (5) treaty number.

In many cases a user will satisfy a query within one of the five specialized sections and will not need to go to the Main Entry Section (Volumes 1–3). It is for limited use of this kind that the present USER'S GUIDE has been designed. However, if the user is unfamiliar with the general format and search techniques of this INDEX, or if the search involves more than one specialized section, it is advisable to consult the Introduction in Volume 1.

Sample of International Organization Section

PARTY ONE	PARTY TWO	DATE	TOPIC	CITATION	NUMBER
Caribbean Commission					
Multilateral		30 Oct 46	IGO Establishment	27UNTS77	100401
Netherlands	USA (United States)	22 Jan 54	Tech Assistance	190UNTS207	102565
States Multilateral		21 Jun 60	IGO Establishment	418UNTS109	106019
International Commission on Civil Status					
Multilateral		27 Sep 57	Admin Cooperation	299UNTS211	104314
Permanent Court of Arbitration					
League of Nations	United Nations	19 Jul 46	Specific Property	1UNTS109	200002
Taiwan	Spain	19 Feb 53	General Amity	181UNTS81	102400
Brazil	Italy	24 Nov 54	Dispute Settlement	284UNTS325	104146
United Arab Rep	Yugoslavia	20 Feb 55	Air Transport	255UNTS199	103611
Fed of Malaya	United Nations	29 May 58	Tech Assistance	330UNTS109	104742
Nepal	United Nations	18 Aug 58	Admin Cooperation	508UNTS3	107403

Key Item. This section is ordered alphabetically by international organizations (IGO's) referred to in the treaty text. In the above sample there are three treaties under Caribbean Commission, one under International Commission on Civil Status and six under Permanent Court of Arbitration. Each of these treaties contains at least one textual reference to the IGO under which it is listed. Treaties are listed in order of date of signature with any one IGO block.

Party One. In case of a bilateral treaty this column identifies one of the two parties. In case of a multilateral treaty it shows the word "Multilateral."

Party Two. In case of a bilateral treaty this column identifies the other of the two parties. In a multilateral treaty it remains blank.

Date. This column identifies the date of signature. Other dates (ratification, force, registration, accession, etc.) can be found in the Main Entry Section. Multiple dates of signature are represented only by the most recent date.

Topic. This column identifies the single dominant theme of each treaty. For a full list of INDEX topics see Volume 1, Introduction, Thesaurus, Topic List. The same information is reproduced also in the beginning of Volume 5.

Citation. This column identifies the printed source where the full text of the treaty can be found. For details on abbreviations see Volume 1, Introduction, Thesaurus, Sources and Citations.

Treaty Number. This column identifies the serial number of each treaty under which it is listed in the Main Entry Section. See that location for all further information on any treaty.

League of Nations Treaty Series

PARTY ONE	PARTY TWO	DATE	TOPIC	CITATION	NUMBER
Arbitration Commission					
Germany	UK Great Britain	05 Apr 23	Reparations	17LTS173	300435
Multilateral		28 Apr 23	Patents/Copyrights	33LTS47	300832
Multilateral		14 Dec 23	General Trade	29LTS37	300732
Netherlands	USA (United States)	23 Jan 25	Territory Boundary	33LTS445	300864
Germany	New Zealand	17 Jan 30	Reparations	109LTS485	302551
France	Spain	10 Jul 39	Dispute Settlement	148LTS369	303423
Bank for International Settlements					
Multilateral		20 Jan 30	Reparations	104LTS243	302394
Multilateral		10 Jun 30	Loans and Credits	112LTS237	302618
Belgium-Luxembourg Economic Union					
Bel-Lux Econ Union		07 Jul 25	General Economic	54LTS267	301290
Conciliation Commission					
Poland	Switzerland	07 Mar 25	Dispute Settlement	50LTS261	301209
Chile	Norway	27 Jan 36	Dispute Settlement	179LTS433	304169
Danube Commission					
Multilateral		23 Jul 21	Water Transport	26LTS173	300647
Multilateral		29 Mar 23	Land Transport	23LTS378	300594
International Labour Organization					
Multilateral		12 May 26	Refugees	89LTS47	302004
League of Nations					
Danzig	Poland	09 Nov 20	Territory Boundary	6LTS189	300153
Lithuania	Poland	29 Nov 20	Peace/Disarmament	9LTS63	300243
France	UK Great Britain	23 Dec 20	Territory Boundary	22LTS353	300564
Germany	UK Great Britain	18 Jun 21	Sanitation	16LTS139	300404
Czechoslovakia	UK Great Britain	04 Aug 21	Sanitation	16LTS157	300406
Multilateral		20 Oct 21	Peace/Disarmament	9LTS211	300255
Multilateral		31 Mar 22	Humanitarian	9LTS415	300269
Bulgaria	UK Great Britain	05 Apr 22	Sanitation	16LTS191	300410
Latvia	Poland	07 Jul 22	Sanitation	37LTS317	300958
Multilateral		04 Oct 22	Territory Boundary	12LTS391	300335
UK Great Britain	Uruguay	19 Oct 22	Sanitation	16LTS201	300411
France	USA (United States)	13 Feb 23	Territory Boundary	26LTS69	300641
France	USA (United States)	13 Feb 23	Territory Boundary	26LTS53	300640
Sweden	Uruguay	24 Feb 23	Dispute Settlement	63LTS239	301494
Turkey		24 Jul 23	Sanitation	36LTS157	300915
Multilateral		24 Jul 23	Territory Boundary	28LTS139	300703
Poland	Romania	24 Jul 23	Sanitation	18LTS103	300458
Other Unilat Decla	Ethiopia	27 Sep 23	UN Charter	25LTS180	300606
Multilateral		09 Dec 23	General Economic	58LTS315	301380
Multilateral		09 Dec 23	Non-IBRD Project	36LTS76	300905
Belgium	USA (United States)	21 Jan 24	Territory Boundary	31LTS137	300791
Multilateral		25 Jan 24	Sanitation	57LTS135	301360
Czechoslovakia	Hungary	09 Feb 24	Postal Service	30LTS325	300772
Multilateral		31 Mar 24	Sanitation	27LTS211	300685
League of Nations (Cont.)					
Multilateral		11 Feb 25	Sanitation	51LTS337	301239
Multilateral		19 Feb 25	Admin Cooperation	81LTS317	301845
Estonia	Sweden	29 May 25	Dispute Settlement	46LTS289	301123
Lithuania	Sweden	11 Jun 25	Dispute Settlement	57LTS191	301364
Czechoslovakia	Poland	05 Sep 25	Sanitation	58LTS143	301370
Multilateral		16 Oct 25	Peace/Disarmament	54LTS289	301292
France	Germany	16 Oct 25	General Military	54LTS315	301294
Belgium	Germany	16 Oct 25	General Military	54LTS303	301293
Czechoslovakia	Germany	16 Oct 25	General Military	54LTS341	301296
Germany	Poland	16 Oct 25	General Military	54LTS327	301295
Czechoslovakia	France	16 Oct 25	Peace/Disarmament	54LTS359	301298
France	Poland	16 Oct 25	Peace/Disarmament	54LTS353	301297
Poland	Romania	26 Mar 26	Peace/Disarmament	60LTS161	301411
Multilateral		12 May 26	Refugees	89LTS47	302004
France	Romania	10 Jun 26	Dispute Settlement	58LTS233	301374
France	Romania	10 Jun 26	General Amity	58LTS225	301373
Romania	Serb/Croat/Slovene	13 Jun 26	General Military	54LTS257	301289
Denmark	France	05 Jul 26	Dispute Settlement	71LTS455	301684
Bulgaria		09 Sep 26	Refugees	58LTS245	301375
Poland	Serb/Croat/Slovene	18 Sep 26	General Amity	78LTS413	301799
Multilateral		25 Sep 26	ILO Labor	60LTS253	301414
Czechoslovakia	Denmark	30 Nov 26	Dispute Settlement	67LTS105	301541
Other Unilat Decla	Estonia	10 Dec 26	Finance	62LTS277	301467
Denmark	Lithuania	11 Dec 26	Dispute Settlement	67LTS333	301555
Denmark	Estonia	18 Dec 26	Dispute Settlement	63LTS363	301500
Germany	Italy	29 Dec 26	Dispute Settlement	78LTS383	301797
Belgium	Switzerland	05 Feb 27	Dispute Settlement	68LTS45	301567
Denmark	Germany	23 Feb 27	Dispute Settlement	61LTS325	301444
Chile	France	24 Feb 27	Dispute Settlement	69LTS277	301610
Greece		15 Sep 27	Loans and Credits	70LTS9	301622
Italy	Lithuania	17 Sep 27	Dispute Settlement	72LTS439	301700
Multilateral		26 Sep 27	Dispute Settlement	92LTS301	302096
Belgium	Luxembourg	17 Oct 27	Dispute Settlement	124LTS203	302834
France	Serb/Croat/Slovene	11 Nov 27	General Amity	68LTS373	301592
Germany	Poland	07 Dec 27	Specific Property	92LTS203	302088
France	USA (United States)	06 Feb 28	Dispute Settlement	91LTS323	302072
France	Netherlands	10 Mar 28	Dispute Settlement	102LTS109	302356
Greece	Romania	21 Mar 28	General Military	108LTS187	302508
Italy	USA (United States)	19 Apr 28	Dispute Settlement	113LTS183	302645
Germany	USA (United States)	05 May 28	Dispute Settlement	90LTS177	302035
Multilateral		30 Jun 28	Refugees	89LTS63	302006
Czechoslovakia	USA (United States)	16 Aug 28	Dispute Settlement	89LTS225	302018
Austria	USA (United States)	16 Aug 28	Dispute Settlement	88LTS95	301988
Bulgaria		08 Sep 28	Loans and Credits	74LTS167	301738
Multilateral		26 Sep 28	Dispute Settlement	93LTS343	302123
Albania	USA (United States)	22 Oct 28	Dispute Settlement	92LTS217	302089

PARTY ONE	PARTY TWO	DATE	TOPIC	CITATION	NUMBER
League of Nations (Cont.)					
Sweden	USA (United States)	27 Oct 28	Dispute Settlement	91LTS225	302063
Luxembourg	Poland	29 Oct 28	Dispute Settlement	111LTS71	302581
Bulgaria	USA (United States)	21 Jan 29	Dispute Settlement	93LTS337	302122
Hungary	USA (United States)	26 Jan 29	Dispute Settlement	96LTS173	302200
Norway	USA (United States)	20 Feb 29	Dispute Settlement	91LTS413	302079
Belgium	USA (United States)	20 Mar 29	Dispute Settlement	109LTS267	302543
Multilateral		20 Apr 29	Admin Cooperation	112LTS371	302623
Multilateral		20 Apr 29	Admin Cooperation	112LTS395	302624
Belgium	Czechoslovakia	29 Apr 29	Dispute Settlement	110LTS113	302556
Multilateral		21 May 29	Dispute Settlement	96LTS311	302210
Italy	Norway	10 Jun 29	Dispute Settlement	105LTS161	302410
Multilateral		14 Jun 29	Visas	94LTS275	302148
Belgium	Greece	25 Jun 29	Dispute Settlement	113LTS117	302640
Czechoslovakia	Estonia	09 Jul 29	Dispute Settlement	101LTS423	302341
Multilateral		27 Jul 29	Other Military	118LTS343	302734
Estonia	USA (United States)	27 Aug 29	Dispute Settlement	102LTS233	302366
Multilateral		30 Aug 29	General Amity	104LTS487	302400
Germany	Luxembourg	11 Sep 29	Dispute Settlement	118LTS97	302715
Luxembourg	Switzerland	16 Sep 29	Dispute Settlement	107LTS23	302465
Luxembourg	Netherlands	17 Sep 29	Dispute Settlement	107LTS35	302466
Czechoslovakia	Luxembourg	18 Sep 29	Dispute Settlement	107LTS49	302467
Czechoslovakia	Switzerland	20 Sep 29	Dispute Settlement	102LTS123	302357
Czechoslovakia	Finland	02 Oct 29	Dispute Settlement	115LTS155	302684
Other Unilat Decla	Greece	14 Jan 30	Refugees	108LTS349	302518
Luxembourg	Romania	22 Jan 30	Dispute Settlement	110LTS151	302559
Denmark	Latvia	28 Feb 30	Dispute Settlement	113LTS27	302632
Czechoslovakia	Lithuania	08 Mar 30	Dispute Settlement	115LTS61	302677
Belgium	Yugoslavia	25 Mar 30	Dispute Settlement	106LTS343	302455
Multilateral		12 Apr 30	Milit Servic/Citiz	178LTS227	304117
Netherlands	Poland	12 Apr 30	Dispute Settlement	113LTS65	302636
Multilateral		07 Jun 30	Finance	143LTS257	303313
Multilateral		07 Jun 30	Finance	143LTS337	303315
Multilateral		07 Jun 30	Finance	143LTS317	303314
Austria	Greece	26 Jun 30	Dispute Settlement	119LTS353	302755
Iraq	UK Great Britain	30 Jun 30	General Military	132LTS363	303048
Hungary	Latvia	13 Aug 30	Dispute Settlement	117LTS395	302705
Austria	Norway	01 Oct 30	Extradition	119LTS15	302737
Czechoslovakia	Persia	29 Oct 30	General Amity	121LTS53	302783
Iceland	USA (United States)	15 May 30	Dispute Settlement	108LTS109	302503
Poland	Romania	15 Jan 31	Admin Cooperation	115LTS171	302685
Iraq	UK Great Britain	04 Mar 31	Privil/Immunities	123LTS77	302807
Multilateral		13 Jul 31	Other HEW	139LTS301	303219
Multilateral		15 Jul 32	Direct Aid	135LTS285	303118
Romania		28 Jan 33	Tech Assistance	138LTS271	303193
Czechoslovakia	Poland	10 Feb 34	General Trade	183LTS213	304238
Multilateral		20 Feb 35	Sanitation	193LTS37	304486
Multilateral		20 Feb 35	Sanitation	193LTS59	304487
Multilateral		20 Feb 35	Sanitation	186LTS173	304310
France	USSR (Soviet Union)	02 May 35	General Amity	167LTS395	303881
United Arab Rep	UK Great Britain	26 Aug 36	General Military	173LTS401	304031
Multilateral		23 Sep 36	Gen Communications	196LTS301	304319
France	UK Great Britain	24 Apr 37	Other Military	178LTS186	304112
Multilateral		08 Jul 37	General Amity	190LTS21	304402
USA (United States)	USSR (Soviet Union)	04 Aug 37	General Trade	182LTS113	304204
Multilateral		14 Sep 37	General Military	181LTS137	304184
Portugal	UK Great Britain	28 Dec 37	Territory Boundary	185LTS205	304284
Multilateral		09 Apr 38	Admin Cooperation	191LTS119	304441
Multilateral		09 Apr 38	Admin Cooperation	191LTS165	304442
Permanent Court of Arbitration					
Brazil	Spain	08 Apr 09	Dispute Settlement	88LTS86	301987
Chile	Colombia	16 Nov 14	Dispute Settlement	114LTS111	302659
Colombia	Peru	24 Mar 22	Territory Boundary	74LTS9	301726
Sweden	USA (United States)	24 Jun 24	Dispute Settlement	33LTS273	300851
Netherlands	USA (United States)	21 Aug 24	Sanitation	33LTS433	300863

PARTY ONE	PARTY TWO	DATE	TOPIC	CITATION	NUMBER
Permanent Court of Arbitration (Cont.)					
Germany	Sweden	29 Aug 24	Dispute Settlement	42LTS111	301036
Finland	Germany	14 Mar 25	Dispute Settlement	43LTS347	301070
Belgium	USA (United States)	09 Dec 25	Other Ad Hoc	72LTS171	301690
Cuba	USA (United States)	04 Mar 26	Admin Cooperation	61LTS369	301447
France	USA (United States)	06 Feb 28	Dispute Settlement	91LTS323	302072
Germany	USA (United States)	05 May 28	Dispute Settlement	90LTS177	302035
Finland	USA (United States)	07 Jun 28	Dispute Settlement	87LTS9	301958
Denmark	USA (United States)	14 Jun 28	Dispute Settlement	88LTS173	301995
Poland	USA (United States)	16 Aug 28	Dispute Settlement	99LTS409	302286
Czechoslovakia	USA (United States)	16 Aug 28	Dispute Settlement	89LTS225	302018
Austria	USA (United States)	16 Aug 28	Dispute Settlement	88LTS95	301988
Albania	USA (United States)	22 Oct 28	Dispute Settlement	92LTS217	302089
Sweden	USA (United States)	27 Oct 28	Dispute Settlement	91LTS225	302063
Lithuania	USA (United States)	14 Nov 28	Dispute Settlement	100LTS111	302297
Bulgaria	USA (United States)	21 Jan 29	Dispute Settlement	93LTS337	302122
Serb/Croat/Slovene	USA (United States)	21 Jan 29	Dispute Settlement	93LTS307	302118
Hungary	USA (United States)	26 Jan 29	Dispute Settlement	96LTS173	302200
Norway	USA (United States)	20 Feb 29	Dispute Settlement	91LTS413	302079
Portugal	USA (United States)	01 Mar 29	Dispute Settlement	99LTS375	302282
Latvia	USA (United States)	14 Jan 30	Dispute Settlement	105LTS301	302422
Germany	Romania	03 Oct 37	Air Transport	190LTS369	304429
Estonia	Germany	23 Dec 37	Air Transport	189LTS333	304393
Permanent Court of International Justice					
Multilateral		10 Aug 20	Consul/Citizenship	28LTS223	300711
Multilateral		05 Oct 21	IGO Establishment	51LTS361	301241
Other Unilat Decla	Lithuania	12 May 22	Admin Cooperation	22LTS393	300569
Sweden	Uruguay	24 Feb 23	Dispute Settlement	63LTS239	301494
Iraq	UK Great Britain	30 Apr 23	General Amity	35LTS13	300890
Turkey		24 Jul 23	Admin Cooperation	36LTS161	300916
Multilateral		18 Dec 23	Territory Boundary	28LTS541	300729
Finland	Norway	28 Apr 24	Territory Boundary	30LTS49	300758
Multilateral		08 May 24	Territory Boundary	29LTS85	300736
Sweden	Switzerland	02 Jun 24	Admin Cooperation	33LTS199	300844
Denmark	Switzerland	06 Jun 24	Dispute Settlement	34LTS175	300873
Brazil	Switzerland	23 Jun 24	Dispute Settlement	33LTS415	300861
Denmark	Norway	27 Jun 24	Dispute Settlement	33LTS173	300842
Denmark	Sweden	27 Jun 24	Dispute Settlement	33LTS149	300840
Denmark	Finland	27 Jun 24	Dispute Settlement	33LTS131	300839
Denmark	Norway	09 Jul 24	Territory Boundary	27LTS203	300684
Italy	Switzerland	20 Sep 24	Admin Cooperation	33LTS91	300834
Austria	Switzerland	11 Oct 24	Dispute Settlement	33LTS423	300862
Multilateral		17 Jan 25	Dispute Settlement	38LTS357	300991
Finland	Norway	14 Feb 25	Specific Resources	49LTS391	301194
Finland	Norway	14 Feb 25	Specific Resources	49LTS379	301193
France	Switzerland	06 Apr 25	Dispute Settlement	147LTS89	303393
Czechoslovakia	Poland	23 Apr 25	Dispute Settlement	48LTS383	301171
France	Germany	14 Aug 25	Territory Boundary	75LTS103	301756
Norway	Switzerland	21 Aug 25	Dispute Settlement	51LTS89	301224
Greece	Switzerland	21 Sep 25	Dispute Settlement	87LTS187	301969
Czechoslovakia	Germany	16 Oct 25	General Military	54LTS341	301296
Belgium	Germany	16 Oct 25	General Military	54LTS303	301293
Germany	Poland	16 Oct 25	General Military	54LTS327	301295
France	Germany	16 Oct 25	General Military	54LTS315	301294
Poland	Sweden	03 Nov 25	Dispute Settlement	62LTS263	301466
Siam	UK Great Britain	25 Nov 25	Dispute Settlement	63LTS161	301487
Norway	Sweden	25 Nov 25	Dispute Settlement	60LTS295	301417
Netherlands	Switzerland	12 Dec 25	Dispute Settlement	63LTS289	301496
Czechoslovakia	Sweden	02 Jan 26	Dispute Settlement	48LTS173	301159
Denmark	Sweden	14 Jan 26	Dispute Settlement	51LTS251	301235
Denmark	Norway	15 Jan 26	Dispute Settlement	60LTS311	301418
Finland	Sweden	29 Jan 26	Dispute Settlement	49LTS367	301192
France	Great Britain	02 Feb 26	General Amity	56LTS79	301324
Finland	Norway	03 Feb 26	Dispute Settlement	60LTS353	301420
Romania	Switzerland	03 Feb 26	Dispute Settlement	55LTS91	301306

PARTY ONE	PARTY TWO	DATE	TOPIC	CITATION	NUMBER
Permanent Court of International Justice (Cont.)					
Liberia	USA (United States)	10 Feb 26	Dispute Settlement	56LTS279	301336
Austria	Czechoslovakia	05 Mar 26	General Amity	51LTS349	301240
Austria	Poland	16 Apr 26	Dispute Settlement	62LTS329	301471
Spain	Switzerland	20 Apr 26	Dispute Settlement	60LTS23	301403
Belgium	Sweden	30 Apr 26	Dispute Settlement	67LTS91	301540
Germany	Netherlands	20 May 26	Dispute Settlement	66LTS103	301527
Austria	Sweden	28 May 26	Dispute Settlement	61LTS193	301434
France	Romania	10 Jun 26	Dispute Settlement	58LTS233	301374
Denmark	France	05 Jul 26	Dispute Settlement	71LTS455	301684
Italy	Spain	07 Aug 26	General Amity	67LTS365	301558
France	Switzerland	27 Aug 26	Admin Cooperation	71LTS63	301654
Poland	Serb/Croat/Slovene	18 Sep 26	Dispute Settlement	78LTS419	301800
Czechoslovakia	Denmark	30 Nov 26	Dispute Settlement	67LTS105	301541
Denmark	Lithuania	11 Dec 26	Dispute Settlement	67LTS333	301555
Denmark	Estonia	18 Dec 26	Dispute Settlement	63LTS363	301500
Germany	Italy	29 Dec 26	Dispute Settlement	78LTS383	301797
Belgium	Switzerland	05 Feb 27	Dispute Settlement	68LTS45	301567
Denmark	Germany	23 Feb 27	Dispute Settlement	61LTS325	301444
Chile	France	24 Feb 27	Dispute Settlement	69LTS277	301610
Belgium	Finland	04 Mar 27	Dispute Settlement	69LTS361	301618
Belgium	Denmark	13 Mar 27	Dispute Settlement	67LTS117	301542
Belgium	Netherlands	24 Mar 27	Sanitation	84LTS34	301902
Netherlands	Sweden	21 May 27	Dispute Settlement	79LTS147	301807
Belgium	Portugal	09 Jul 27	Dispute Settlement	74LTS39	301730
Multilateral		12 Jul 27	Direct Aid	135LTS247	303115
Belgium	Spain	19 Jul 27	Dispute Settlement	80LTS17	301820
Colombia	Switzerland	20 Aug 27	Dispute Settlement	111LTS229	302589
Brazil	France	27 Aug 27	Dispute Settlement	75LTS91	301754
Italy	Lithuania	17 Sep 27	Dispute Settlement	72LTS439	301700
Belgium	Luxembourg	17 Oct 27	Dispute Settlement	124LTS203	302834
France	Luxembourg	20 Oct 27	Dispute Settlement	106LTS457	302462
France	Serb/Croat/Slovene	11 Nov 27	Dispute Settlement	68LTS381	301593
Finland	Switzerland	16 Nov 27	Dispute Settlement	77LTS93	301765
Portugal	Spain	18 Jan 28	Dispute Settlement	77LTS105	301766
Germany	Lithuania	29 Jan 28	Dispute Settlement	90LTS233	302042
France	Sweden	03 Mar 28	Dispute Settlement	95LTS89	302168
France	Netherlands	10 Mar 28	Dispute Settlement	102LTS109	302356
Denmark	Spain	14 Mar 28	Dispute Settlement	74LTS93	301735
Greece	Romania	21 Mar 28	General Military	108LTS187	302508
Denmark	Haiti	05 Apr 28	Dispute Settlement	99LTS19	302264
Italy	USA (United States)	19 Apr 28	Dispute Settlement	113LTS183	302645
Spain	Sweden	26 Apr 28	Dispute Settlement	77LTS77	301764
Finland	Spain	31 May 28	Dispute Settlement	82LTS229	301874
Finland	Netherlands	09 Jun 28	Dispute Settlement	87LTS321	301978
Austria	Spain	11 Jun 28	Dispute Settlement	87LTS393	301984
Luxembourg	Spain	21 Jun 28	Dispute Settlement	109LTS137	302533
France	Portugal	06 Jul 28	Dispute Settlement	126LTS27	302869
Greece	Italy	23 Sep 28	Dispute Settlement	108LTS219	302510
Multilateral		26 Sep 28	Dispute Settlement	93LTS343	302123
Portugal	Switzerland	17 Oct 28	Dispute Settlement	96LTS287	302207
Netherlands	Siam	27 Oct 28	Dispute Settlement	93LTS131	302105
Luxembourg	Poland	29 Oct 28	Dispute Settlement	111LTS71	302581
Multilateral		30 Oct 28	Dispute Settlement	87LTS103	301963
Czechoslovakia	Serb/Croat/Slovene	07 Nov 28	Claims and Debts	95LTS101	302169
Germany	Romania	10 Nov 28	Dispute Settlement	91LTS101	302058
Czechoslovakia	Spain	16 Nov 28	Dispute Settlement	100LTS313	302303
Hungary	Poland	30 Nov 28	Dispute Settlement	100LTS67	302294
Poland	Spain	03 Dec 28	Dispute Settlement	101LTS501	302348
Switzerland	Turkey	09 Dec 28	Dispute Settlement	159LTS219	303664
Norway	Spain	27 Dec 28	Dispute Settlement	97LTS339	302231
Bulgaria	Turkey	06 Mar 29	Dispute Settlement	114LTS399	302668
Belgium	USA (United States)	20 Mar 29	Dispute Settlement	109LTS267	302543
Romania	USA (United States)	21 Mar 29	Dispute Settlement	105LTS79	302402
Greece	Serb/Croat/Slovene	27 Mar 29	Dispute Settlement	108LTS201	302509
Luxembourg	USA (United States)	06 Apr 29	Dispute Settlement	106LTS475	302464

PARTY ONE	PARTY TWO	DATE	TOPIC	CITATION	NUMBER
Permanent Court of International Justice (Cont.)					
Multilateral		20 Apr 29	Admin Cooperation	112LTS371	302623
Belgium	Czechoslovakia	29 Apr 29	Dispute Settlement	110LTS113	302556
France	Persia	10 May 29	General Amity	150LTS329	303465
Germany	Turkey	16 May 29	Dispute Settlement	109LTS451	302549
Multilateral		21 May 29	Dispute Settlement	96LTS311	302210
Belgium	Persia	23 May 29	General Amity	110LTS369	302568
Persia	Sweden	27 May 29	General Amity	105LTS279	302420
Czechoslovakia	Greece	08 Jun 29	General Amity	108LTS255	302512
Italy	Norway	10 Jun 29	Dispute Settlement	105LTS161	302410
Hungary	Spain	10 Jun 29	Dispute Settlement	101LTS251	302327
Belgium	Greece	25 Jun 29	Dispute Settlement	113LTS117	302640
Czechoslovakia	Estonia	09 Jul 29	Dispute Settlement	101LTS423	302341
Bulgaria	Hungary	22 Jul 29	Dispute Settlement	101LTS41	302317
Luxembourg	Portugal	15 Aug 29	Dispute Settlement	115LTS77	302678
Iceland	Spain	26 Aug 29	Dispute Settlement	104LTS183	302388
Estonia	USA (United States)	27 Aug 29	Dispute Settlement	102LTS233	302366
Czechoslovakia	Norway	09 Sep 29	Dispute Settlement	101LTS355	302336
Germany	Luxembourg	11 Sep 29	Dispute Settlement	118LTS97	302715
Czechoslovakia	Netherlands	14 Sep 29	Dispute Settlement	107LTS201	302477
Luxembourg	Switzerland	16 Sep 29	Dispute Settlement	107LTS23	302465
Luxembourg	Netherlands	17 Sep 29	Dispute Settlement	107LTS35	302466
Czechoslovakia	Luxembourg	18 Sep 29	Dispute Settlement	107LTS49	302467
Czechoslovakia	Switzerland	20 Sep 29	Dispute Settlement	102LTS123	302357
Czechoslovakia	Finland	02 Oct 29	Dispute Settlement	115LTS155	302684
Estonia	Hungary	27 Nov 29	Dispute Settlement	106LTS331	302454
Norway	Poland	09 Dec 29	Dispute Settlement	101LTS325	302334
Bulgaria	Poland	31 Dec 29	Dispute Settlement	113LTS89	302638
Lithuania	Persia	13 Jan 30	General Amity	131LTS221	303013
Netherlands	Romania	22 Jan 30	Dispute Settlement	112LTS121	302611
Luxembourg	Romania	22 Jan 30	Dispute Settlement	110LTS151	302559
Greece	Spain	23 Jan 30	Dispute Settlement	139LTS93	303205
Austria	Italy	06 Feb 30	Dispute Settlement	105LTS97	302405
Denmark	Latvia	28 Feb 30	Dispute Settlement	113LTS27	302632
Czechoslovakia	Lithuania	08 Mar 30	Dispute Settlement	115LTS61	302677
Belgium	Yugoslavia	25 Mar 30	Dispute Settlement	106LTS343	302455
Multilateral		12 Apr 30	Admin Cooperation	179LTS115	304138
Netherlands	Poland	12 Apr 30	Dispute Settlement	113LTS65	302636
Multilateral		12 Apr 30	Admin Cooperation	179LTS89	304137
Finland	France	28 Apr 30	Dispute Settlement	139LTS381	303222
Greece	Hungary	05 May 30	Dispute Settlement	118LTS293	302732
Germany	Irish Free State	12 May 30	General Economic	131LTS153	303008
Greece	USA (United States)	19 Jun 30	Dispute Settlement	136LTS393	303137
Austria	Greece	26 Jun 30	Dispute Settlement	119LTS353	302755
Denmark	Iceland	27 Jun 30	Dispute Settlement	118LTS121	302717
China	USA (United States)	27 Jun 30	Dispute Settlement	140LTS184	303236
Finland	Iceland	27 Jun 30	Dispute Settlement	167LTS271	303873
Iceland	Sweden	27 Jun 30	Dispute Settlement	127LTS67	302907
Iceland	Norway	27 Jun 30	Dispute Settlement	126LTS417	302900
Belgium	Romania	08 Jul 30	Dispute Settlement	128LTS403	302944
Norway	Portugal	26 Jul 30	Dispute Settlement	134LTS123	303087
Hungary	Latvia	13 Aug 30	Dispute Settlement	117LTS395	302705
Belgium	Lithuania	24 Sep 30	Dispute Settlement	129LTS399	302974
Austria	Norway	01 Oct 30	Extradition	119LTS15	302737
Greece	Turkey	30 Oct 30	Dispute Settlement	125LTS9	302841
Latvia	Lithuania	24 Nov 30	Dispute Settlement	112LTS405	302626
Iceland	USA (United States)	15 May 30	Dispute Settlement	108LTS109	302503
Austria	Hungary	26 Jan 31	General Amity	123LTS171	302814
Switzerland	USA (United States)	16 Feb 31	Dispute Settlement	129LTS465	302978
Netherlands	Yugoslavia	11 Mar 31	Dispute Settlement	129LTS89	302952
Czechoslovakia	Turkey	17 Mar 31	Dispute Settlement	133LTS151	303065
Netherlands	Spain	30 Mar 31	Dispute Settlement	137LTS161	303153
Italy	Latvia	28 Apr 31	Dispute Settlement	126LTS399	302898
Belgium	Bulgaria	23 Jun 31	Dispute Settlement	137LTS191	303156
Bulgaria	Spain	26 Jun 31	Dispute Settlement	166LTS341	303850
Multilateral		13 Jul 31	Other HEW	139LTS301	303219

PARTY ONE	PARTY TWO	DATE	TOPIC	CITATION	NUMBER
Permanent Court of International Justice (Cont.)					
Multilateral		21 Aug 31	Other Ad Hoc	185LTS45	304273
Bulgaria	Norway	26 Nov 31	Dispute Settlement	134LTS27	303081
Greece	Poland	04 Jan 32	Dispute Settlement	131LTS229	303014
Luxembourg	Norway	12 Feb 32	Dispute Settlement	142LTS29	303277
Denmark	Turkey	08 Mar 32	Dispute Settlement	143LTS223	303310
Italy	Luxembourg	15 Apr 32	Dispute Settlement	142LTS119	303284
Netherlands	Turkey	16 Apr 32	Dispute Settlement	143LTS237	303311
Brazil	UK Great Britain	01 Nov 32	Territory Boundary	177LTS127	304087
Portugal	Sweden	06 Dec 32	Dispute Settlement	145LTS91	303347
Norway	Turkey	16 Jan 33	Dispute Settlement	161LTS173	303710
Netherlands	Norway	23 Mar 33	Dispute Settlement	146LTS291	303380
Netherlands	Venezuela	05 Apr 33	Dispute Settlement	144LTS353	303338
Denmark	Greece	13 Apr 33	Dispute Settlement	150LTS465	303478
Japan	Netherlands	19 Apr 33	Dispute Settlement	163LTS351	303778
Multilateral		11 Oct 33	Consul/Citizenship	150LTS431	303476
Czechoslovakia	Latvia	11 Oct 33	Dispute Settlement	155LTS195	303577
Romania	Turkey	17 Oct 33	Dispute Settlement	165LTS273	303814
Turkey	Yugoslavia	27 Nov 33	Dispute Settlement	161LTS229	303715
Denmark	Venezuela	19 Dec 33	Dispute Settlement	158LTS249	303635
Denmark	Persia	20 Feb 34	General Amity	158LTS299	303640
Belgium	UK Great Britain	13 Apr 34	Dispute Settlement	154LTS361	303561
Persia	Switzerland	25 Apr 34	General Amity	159LTS235	303666
Multilateral		20 Feb 35	Sanitation	193LTS37	304486
Multilateral		20 Feb 35	Sanitation	193LTS59	304487
Norway	Venezuela	13 May 35	Dispute Settlement	167LTS407	303882
Hungary	Switzerland	18 Jun 35	Air Transport	174LTS7	304033
France	Hungary	23 Jul 35	Air Transport	173LTS243	304016

PARTY ONE	PARTY TWO	DATE	TOPIC	CITATION	NUMBER
Permanent Court of International Justice (Cont.)					
Bulgaria	Denmark	07 Dec 35	Dispute Settlement	182LTS183	304211
Denmark	Yugoslavia	14 Dec 35	Dispute Settlement	184LTS99	304245
Czechoslovakia	Finland	21 Mar 36	Admin Cooperation	179LTS295	304156
Multilateral		23 Sep 36	Gen Communications	186LTS301	304319
Hungary	UK Great Britain	22 Mar 37	Air Transport	190LTS59	304405
Iran	Iraq	24 Jul 37	Dispute Settlement	190LTS269	304425
France	UK Great Britain	29 Jul 37	Privil/Immunities	184LTS351	304257
Siam	Switzerland	04 Nov 37	General Amity	190LTS137	304412
Belgium	Siam	05 Nov 37	Privil/Immunities	190LTS163	304414
Bel-Lux Econ Union	Siam	05 Nov 37	General Amity	190LTS151	304413
Denmark	Siam	05 Nov 37	General Amity	188LTS187	304358
Siam	Sweden	08 Nov 37	General Amity	185LTS337	304298
Norway	Siam	15 Nov 37	General Amity	186LTS9	304301
Netherlands	Siam	01 Feb 38	General Amity	193LTS13	304485
Greece	UK Great Britain	30 May 39	Air Transport	202LTS7	304732
France	Spain	10 Jul 39	Dispute Settlement	148LTS369	303423
Special Commission					
Multilateral		03 May 23	Customs	33LTS11	300830
Italy	UK Great Britain	15 Jul 24	Territory Boundary	36LTS379	300936
Universal Postal Union					
Multilateral		15 Sep 21	Postal Service	30LTS141	300767
Belgium	Luxembourg	18 May 28	Postal Service	89LTS213	302016
Germany	UK Great Britain	17 Jul 29	Postal Service	100LTS439	302313
Bulgaria	Czechoslovakia	29 Aug 33	General Economic	148LTS15	303402
Lithuania	Sweden	17 May 38	Postal Service	192LTS237	304474

United Nations Treaty Series

PARTY ONE	PARTY TWO	DATE	TOPIC	CITATION	NUMBER
Administrative Centre of Social Security for Rhine Boatmen					
Multilateral		27 Jul 50	Non-ILO Labor	166UNTS73	102186
African Development Bank					
Multilateral		04 Aug 63	IGO Establishment	510UNTS3	107408
Allied Military Occupation					
Multilateral		12 Sep 44	Milit Occupation	227UNTS279	200532
Multilateral		28 Oct 44	Peace/Disarmament	123UNTS223	200414
Multilateral		14 Nov 44	Milit Occupation	236UNTS359	200539
Multilateral		20 Jan 45	Peace/Disarmament	140UNTS397	200471
Multilateral		09 Jun 45	Milit Occupation	139UNTS381	200464
Multilateral		09 Jul 45	Milit Occupation	160UNTS359	200484
Multilateral		26 Jul 45	Milit Occupation	227UNTS297	200533
Multilateral		08 Aug 45	General Military	82UNTS279	200251
Multilateral		02 Sep 45	Peace/Disarmament	139UNTS387	200465
Belgium	UK Great Britain	11 Mar 46	Status of Forces	26UNTS167	100387
Multilateral		28 Jun 46	Milit Occupation	138UNTS85	101862
Hungary	USA (United States)	09 Aug 46	Other Military	148UNTS313	101941
UK Great Britain	USA (United States)	02 Dec 46	Milit Occupation	7UNTS163	100098
Multilateral		10 Feb 47	Reparations	140UNTS111	101886
Multilateral		04 Nov 47	Reparations	93UNTS61	101288
Multilateral		16 Dec 47	Reparations	82UNTS237	101096
France	UK Great Britain	15 Jul 48	Claims and Debts	71UNTS215	100920
Multilateral		08 Apr 49	Milit Occupation	140UNTS196	101889
Multilateral		14 Apr 49	Milit Occupation	141UNTS281	101919
Canada	Netherlands	09 May 49	Reparations	46UNTS263	100715
Multilateral		20 Jun 49	IGO Establishment	128UNTS141	101718
Belgium	UK Great Britain	23 Dec 49	Status of Forces	99UNTS61	101371
Germany, West	Netherlands	14 Dec 50	Water Transport	87UNTS257	101177
Multilateral		03 Apr 51	Milit Occupation	141UNTS303	101920
South Africa	USA (United States)	26 Mar 52	Education	165UNTS187	102176
Multilateral		16 Apr 52	General Economic	139UNTS35	101874
Germany, West	Netherlands	19 May 52	Reparations	134UNTS3	101794
Finland	USA (United States)	02 Jul 52	Education	165UNTS203	102177
Germany, West	USA (United States)	18 Jul 52	Education	165UNTS167	102175
Multilateral		27 Feb 53	Claims and Debts	333UNTS3	104764
Germany, West	USA (United States)	27 Feb 53	Claims and Debts	224UNTS31	103068
Germany, West	USA (United States)	20 Aug 53	Milit Assistance	224UNTS49	103069
Multilateral		23 Oct 54	Milit Occupation	331UNTS253	104758
Multilateral		23 Oct 54	Reparations	332UNTS219	104762
Multilateral		23 Oct 54	Milit Occupation	331UNTS327	104759
Germany, West	USA (United States)	18 Apr 56	Admin Cooperation	271UNTS319	103923
Australia	Netherlands	09 Oct 57	Dispute Settlement	312UNTS225	104520
Arab League					
Multilateral		22 Mar 45	General Amity	70UNTS237	200241
Greece	Lebanon	06 Oct 48	Consul/Citizenship	87UNTS351	101179
United Arab Rep	UK Great Britain	19 Oct 54	General Amity	210UNTS3	102833

PARTY ONE	PARTY TWO	DATE	TOPIC	CITATION	NUMBER
Arbitration Commission					
Greece	Iran	09 Jan 31	General Amity	166UNTS323	200496
Brazil	France	27 Jan 40	Air Transport	72UNTS77	100929
Brazil	Venezuela	30 Mar 40	Dispute Settlement	51UNTS291	200195
Turkey	UK Great Britain	23 Mar 44	Specif Claim/Waive	2UNTS227	200015
South Africa	UK Great Britain	26 Oct 45	Air Transport	72UNTS41	100927
Greece	UK Great Britain	26 Nov 45	Air Transport	35UNTS161	100555
Portugal	UK Great Britain	06 Dec 45	Air Transport	6UNTS3	100065
Portugal	UK Great Britain	06 Dec 45	Air Transport	5UNTS37	100064
Canada	UK Great Britain	21 Dec 45	Air Transport	27UNTS155	100405
Czechoslovakia	Poland	24 Jan 46	Air Transport	25UNTS181	100363
Czechoslovakia	Poland	12 Feb 46	Reparations	25UNTS207	100364
Turkey	UK Great Britain	12 Feb 46	Air Transport	6UNTS79	100069
France	UK Great Britain	28 Feb 46	Air Transport	27UNTS173	100407
Ireland	UK Great Britain	05 Apr 46	Air Transport	72UNTS57	100928
Netherlands	Portugal	12 Apr 46	Air Transport	4UNTS317	100054
France	Portugal	30 Apr 46	Air Transport	35UNTS197	100556
France	Ireland	16 May 46	Air Transport	44UNTS105	100681
Ireland	Sweden	29 May 46	Air Transport	35UNTS231	100557
Australia	Canada	11 Jun 46	Air Transport	10UNTS47	100142
United Nations	Switzerland	01 Jul 46	Specific Property	1UNTS153	200007
France	Sweden	02 Aug 46	Air Transport	27UNTS251	100410
Netherlands	UK Great Britain	13 Aug 46	Air Transport	4UNTS367	100056
Norway	UK Great Britain	31 Aug 46	Air Transport	6UNTS235	100078
Brazil	UK Great Britain	31 Oct 46	Air Transport	11UNTS115	100152
Peru	USA (United States)	27 Dec 46	Air Transport	26UNTS227	100390
Czechoslovakia	Ireland	29 Jan 47	Air Transport	27UNTS267	100411
Paraguay	USA (United States)	28 Feb 47	Air Transport	44UNTS25	100676
Greece	Sweden	08 Apr 47	Air Transport	94UNTS73	101307
Canada	Portugal	25 Apr 47	Air Transport	94UNTS87	101308
Chile	USA (United States)	10 May 47	Air Transport	55UNTS21	100807
Hungary	Yugoslavia	11 May 47	Direct Aid	130UNTS171	101730
Albania	Yugoslavia	12 Jun 47	Dispute Settlement	111UNTS183	101532
Canada	Sweden	27 Jun 47	Air Transport	27UNTS313	100414
Iraq	Turkey	30 Jun 47	Air Transport	72UNTS107	100930
Hungary	USSR (Soviet Union)	15 Jul 47	General Economic	216UNTS247	102940
France	India	16 Jul 47	Air Transport	27UNTS325	100415
Canada	UK Great Britain	17 Jul 47	Air Transport	28UNTS3	100416
Netherlands	Thailand	18 Jul 47	Air Transport	28UNTS27	100417
Greece	Turkey	22 Jul 47	Air Transport	72UNTS131	100931
Taiwan	UK Great Britain	23 Jul 47	Air Transport	9UNTS207	100135
Hungary	Yugoslavia	24 Jul 47	General Trade	114UNTS3	101554
Netherlands	IBRD (World Bank)	07 Aug 47	IBRD Project	152UNTS165	102015
Canada	Ireland	08 Aug 47	Air Transport	28UNTS47	100419
Denmark	IBRD (World Bank)	22 Aug 47	IBRD Project	152UNTS223	102016
Luxembourg	IBRD (World Bank)	28 Aug 47	IBRD Project	153UNTS3	102017
Czechoslovakia	Switzerland	10 Sep 47	Air Transport	35UNTS275	100559

PARTY ONE	PARTY TWO	DATE	TOPIC	CITATION	NUMBER
Arbitration Commission (Cont.)					
Philippines	Spain	27 Sep 47	General Amity	70UNTS133	100902
Austria	USA (United States)	08 Oct 47	Air Transport	25UNTS3	100354
Colombia	UK Great Britain	16 Oct 47	Air Transport	160UNTS297	102115
Brazil	Netherlands	06 Nov 47	Air Transport	53UNTS59	100773
Norway	Portugal	11 Nov 47	Air Transport	34UNTS257	100542
Multilateral		12 Nov 47	Admin Cooperation	53UNTS49	100772
Brazil	Sweden	14 Nov 47	Air Transport	94UNTS139	101310
Brazil	Norway	14 Nov 47	Air Transport	44UNTS163	100684
Denmark	Greece	14 Nov 47	Air Transport	35UNTS295	100560
Brazil	Denmark	14 Nov 47	Air Transport	47UNTS39	100722
Denmark	Ireland	18 Nov 47	Air Transport	35UNTS309	100561
Ireland	Italy	21 Nov 47	Air Transport	353UNTS73	105038
Taiwan	Netherlands	06 Dec 47	Air Transport	43UNTS185	100669
Denmark	Portugal	15 Dec 47	Air Transport	35UNTS329	100563
Peru	UK Great Britain	22 Dec 47	Air Transport	72UNTS143	100932
Philippines	UK Great Britain	07 Jan 48	Air Transport	28UNTS63	100420
Italy	USA (United States)	06 Feb 48	Air Transport	73UNTS113	100950
Pakistan	Sweden	06 May 48	Air Transport	36UNTS3	100564
Ireland	Netherlands	10 May 48	Air Transport	28UNTS121	100422
Norway	Turkey	20 May 48	Air Transport	26UNTS137	100384
India	Sweden	21 May 48	Air Transport	34UNTS285	100543
Greece	Switzerland	26 May 48	Air Transport	94UNTS217	101312
Ireland	Norway	21 Jun 48	Air Transport	34UNTS317	100545
India	Pakistan	23 Jun 48	Air Transport	28UNTS143	100423
Italy	UK Great Britain	25 Jun 48	Air Transport	94UNTS239	101313
Brazil	Switzerland	10 Aug 48	Air Transport	94UNTS269	101314
France	Spain	23 Aug 48	Air Transport	28UNTS173	100425
Finland	Norway	10 Sep 48	Specific Resources	32UNTS3	100486
Bolivia	USA (United States)	29 Sep 48	Air Transport	505UNTS139	107370
Netherlands	Spain	08 Oct 48	Air Transport	28UNTS209	100426
Mexico	Portugal	22 Oct 48	Air Transport	34UNTS329	100546
Ceylon (Sri Lanka)	India	21 Dec 48	Air Transport	28UNTS223	100427
Ceylon (Sri Lanka)	Pakistan	03 Jan 49	Air Transport	28UNTS247	100428
Mexico	IBRD (World Bank)	06 Jan 49	IBRD Project	154UNTS81	102028
Mexico	IBRD (World Bank)	06 Jan 49	IBRD Project	154UNTS3	102027
WHO (World Health)	Switzerland	12 Jan 49	IGO Status/Immunit	26UNTS331	200155
Brazil	IBRD (World Bank)	27 Jan 49	IBRD Project	153UNTS264	102026
Switzerland	Turkey	16 Feb 49	Air Transport	72UNTS175	100933
Belgium	France	18 Feb 49	Claims and Debts	31UNTS173	100478
Finland	Netherlands	25 Feb 49	Air Transport	53UNTS123	100777
Belgium	IBRD (World Bank)	01 Mar 49	IBRD Project	154UNTS133	102029
Netherlands	Switzerland	07 Mar 49	Air Transport	35UNTS69	100551
Finland	USA (United States)	29 Mar 49	Air Transport	55UNTS59	100808
Panama	USA (United States)	31 Mar 49	Air Transport	55UNTS87	100810
Switzerland	USA (United States)	13 May 49	Air Transport	51UNTS129	100761
Italy	Yugoslavia	23 May 49	Reparations	150UNTS179	101972
Australia	Pakistan	03 Jun 49	Air Transport	35UNTS23	100549
Belgium	Greece	21 Jun 49	Air Transport	137UNTS215	101854
Norway	Pakistan	23 Jun 49	Air Transport	35UNTS49	100550
Australia	India	11 Jul 49	Air Transport	35UNTS83	100552
Iraq	Norway	12 Jul 49	Air Transport	53UNTS137	100778
Czechoslovakia	Finland	13 Jul 49	Air Transport	53UNTS153	100779
Multilateral		15 Jul 49	Health/Educ/Welfare	197UNTS3	102631
Pakistan	Philippines	16 Jul 49	Air Transport	35UNTS111	100553
Dominican Republic	USA (United States)	19 Jul 49	Air Transport	51UNTS145	100762
Netherlands	IBRD (World Bank)	26 Jul 49	IBRD Project	154UNTS178	102030
Pakistan	UK Great Britain	27 Jul 49	Air Transport	44UNTS199	100685
Finland	IBRD (World Bank)	01 Aug 49	IBRD Project	156UNTS289	200480
Ceylon (Sri Lanka)	UK Great Britain	05 Aug 49	Air Transport	35UNTS137	100554
India	IBRD (World Bank)	18 Aug 49	IBRD Project	154UNTS269	102031
Colombia	IBRD (World Bank)	19 Aug 49	IBRD Project	154UNTS329	102032
Canada	UK Great Britain	19 Aug 49	Air Transport	44UNTS223	100686
Finland	Norway	24 Aug 49	Air Transport	53UNTS167	100780
Denmark	Finland	26 Aug 49	Air Transport	53UNTS191	100781
IBRD (World Bank)	Yugoslavia	17 Sep 49	IBRD Project	155UNTS3	102034

PARTY ONE	PARTY TWO	DATE	TOPIC	CITATION	NUMBER
Arbitration Commission (Cont.)					
Belgium	United Arab Rep	19 Sep 49	Air Transport	137UNTS189	101853
Lebanon	Netherlands	20 Sep 49	Air Transport	108UNTS205	101474
Burma	USA (United States)	28 Sep 49	Air Transport	55UNTS3	100806
India	IBRD (World Bank)	29 Sep 49	IBRD Project	154UNTS393	102033
Finland	IBRD (World Bank)	17 Oct 49	IBRD Project	156UNTS355	200481
India	Philippines	20 Oct 49	Air Transport	72UNTS191	100934
Denmark	Pakistan	09 Nov 49	Air Transport	44UNTS255	100687
Sweden	Thailand	23 Nov 49	Air Transport	72UNTS217	100935
Denmark	Thailand	23 Nov 49	Air Transport	53UNTS255	100786
Norway	Thailand	26 Nov 49	Air Transport	53UNTS269	100787
Brazil	Spain	28 Nov 49	Air Transport	215UNTS303	102923
Austria	Denmark	02 Dec 49	Air Transport	53UNTS281	100788
Austria	Sweden	02 Dec 49	Air Transport	108UNTS3	101465
Austria	Norway	02 Dec 49	Air Transport	72UNTS230	100936
Sweden	United Arab Rep	12 Dec 49	Air Transport	108UNTS15	101466
Canada	Denmark	13 Dec 49	Air Transport	72UNTS247	100937
El Salvador	IBRD (World Bank)	14 Dec 49	IBRD Project	155UNTS43	102035
Australia	Ceylon (Sri Lanka)	12 Jan 50	Air Transport	53UNTS295	100789
United Nations	WHO (World Health)	10 Feb 50	IGO Operations	46UNTS327	200188
Ceylon (Sri Lanka)	Thailand	24 Feb 50	Air Transport	72UNTS261	100938
India	Iran	15 Mar 50	General Amity	161UNTS15	102118
Denmark	Iceland	22 Mar 50	Air Transport	72UNTS273	100939
Multilateral		17 Apr 50	Non-ILO Labor	126UNTS285	101694
India	IBRD (World Bank)	18 Apr 50	IBRD Project	155UNTS117	102036
Greece	United Arab Rep	24 Apr 50	Air Transport	163UNTS229	102149
Mexico	IBRD (World Bank)	28 Apr 50	IBRD Project	155UNTS185	102037
Israel	USA (United States)	13 Jun 50	Air Transport	212UNTS93	102863
Iraq	IBRD (World Bank)	15 Jun 50	IBRD Project	155UNTS267	102038
Burma	Ceylon (Sri Lanka)	29 Jun 50	Air Transport	73UNTS3	100940
IBRD (World Bank)	Turkey	07 Jul 50	IBRD Project	156UNTS75	102040
IBRD (World Bank)	Turkey	07 Jul 50	IBRD Project	156UNTS3	102039
Spain	UK Great Britain	20 Jul 50	Air Transport	398UNTS101	105719
Canada	France	01 Aug 50	Air Transport	73UNTS21	100941
Spain	Switzerland	03 Aug 50	Air Transport	254UNTS365	103600
IBRD (World Bank)	Uruguay	25 Aug 50	IBRD Project	156UNTS203	102042
WHO (World Health)	United Arab Rep	25 Aug 50	IGO Operations	92UNTS39	101259
Brazil	Turkey	21 Sep 50	Air Transport	150UNTS299	101981
Luxembourg	Portugal	21 Oct 50	Air Transport	108UNTS67	101468
Israel	UK Great Britain	06 Dec 50	Air Transport	151UNTS33	101983
Multilateral		07 Dec 50	Admin Cooperation	212UNTS17	102861
Israel	Turkey	05 Feb 51	Air Transport	193UNTS3	102607
Colombia	Portugal	09 Mar 51	Air Transport	108UNTS87	101469
WHO (World Health)	United Arab Rep	25 Mar 51	IGO Status/Immunit	223UNTS87	103058
WHO (World Health)	United Arab Rep	25 Mar 51	IGO Status/Immunit	223UNTS87	103058
Germany, West	Netherlands	29 Mar 51	Non-ILO Labor	149UNTS71	101952
Guatemala	ILO (Labor Org)	13 Apr 51	Tech Assistance	126UNTS249	101692
Iraq	UK Great Britain	19 Apr 51	Air Transport	108UNTS121	101470
Belgium	UK Great Britain	08 May 51	Air Transport	158UNTS451	102079
India	Netherlands	24 May 51	Air Transport	108UNTS151	101471
Lebanon	WHO (World Health)	07 Jun 51	Tech Assistance	126UNTS221	101690
WHO (World Health)	Uruguay	11 Jun 51	Tech Assistance	128UNTS251	101724
Denmark	Iran	18 Jun 51	Air Transport	255UNTS3	103602
IBRD (World Bank)	Switzerland	29 Jun 51	IGO Status/Immunit	216UNTS347	200529
Burma	WHO (World Health)	09 Jul 51	Sanitation	104UNTS187	101440
Burma	WHO (World Health)	09 Jul 51	Sanitation	104UNTS175	101439
Iceland	Norway	14 Jul 51	Air Transport	163UNTS265	102150
Burma	Denmark	30 Jul 51	Air Transport	108UNTS167	101472
Lebanon	UK Great Britain	15 Aug 51	Air Transport	160UNTS327	102116
Burma	Netherlands	06 Sep 51	Air Transport	108UNTS187	101473
Philippines	Spain	06 Oct 51	Air Transport	215UNTS193	102920
India	WHO (World Health)	16 Oct 51	Tech Assistance	109UNTS49	101490
Panama	ILO (Labor Org)	10 Nov 51	Tech Assistance	126UNTS269	101693
Colombia	Spain	11 Dec 51	Air Transport	216UNTS73	102933
El Salvador	Guatemala	14 Dec 51	General Economic	131UNTS131	101740
Multilateral		20 Dec 51	Air Transport	163UNTS293	102151

PARTY ONE	PARTY TWO	DATE	TOPIC	CITATION	NUMBER
Arbitration Commission (Cont.)					
Jordan	United Arab Rep	02 Jan 52	Air Transport	192UNTS157	102599
Multilateral		10 Jan 52	Visas	163UNTS27	102139
Multilateral		10 Jan 52	Visas	163UNTS3	102138
Costa Rica	WHO (World Health)	23 Jan 52	Sanitation	135UNTS265	101826
Indonesia	United Nations	06 Feb 52	Tech Assistance	121UNTS3	101621
Finland	Norway	18 Mar 52	Specific Resources	188UNTS187	102527
India	WHO (World Health)	17 Apr 52	Tech Assistance	131UNTS241	101744
India	WHO (World Health)	19 Apr 52	Tech Assistance	131UNTS253	101745
Norway	WHO (World Health)	09 May 52	Tech Assistance	131UNTS281	101747
Australia	Italy	24 May 52	Reparations	161UNTS65	102123
Iceland	Sweden	03 Jun 52	Air Transport	215UNTS223	102921
India	WHO (World Health)	04 Jun 52	Sanitation	135UNTS279	101827
Norway	UK Great Britain	23 Jun 52	Air Transport	151UNTS81	101985
Denmark	UK Great Britain	23 Jun 52	Air Transport	151UNTS3	101982
Taiwan	USA (United States)	25 Jun 52	Direct Aid	136UNTS229	101837
Multilateral		11 Jul 52	Postal Service	171UNTS3	102224
Multilateral		11 Jul 52	Postal Service	171UNTS191	102227
Netherlands	Pakistan	17 Jul 52	Air Transport	150UNTS277	101980
Japan	USA (United States)	11 Aug 52	Air Transport	212UNTS27	102862
Ethiopia	Pakistan	29 Aug 52	Air Transport	150UNTS257	101979
Germany, West	Israel	10 Sep 52	Reparations	162UNTS205	102137
Netherlands	Peru	22 Sep 52	Air Transport	255UNTS49	103604
Dominican Republic	WHO (World Health)	10 Oct 52	Sanitation	150UNTS133	101967
Mexico	Netherlands	13 Oct 52	Air Transport	163UNTS341	102154
Iceland	Luxembourg	23 Oct 52	Air Transport	193UNTS39	102609
Multilateral		25 Oct 52	Land Transport	241UNTS336	103442
Burma	UK Great Britain	25 Oct 52	Air Transport	150UNTS237	101978
Multilateral		07 Nov 52	General Trade	221UNTS255	103010
Israel	Switzerland	19 Nov 52	Air Transport	232UNTS3	103226
Switzerland	UK Great Britain	16 Jan 53	Non-ILO Labor	196UNTS119	102621
Taiwan	Spain	19 Feb 53	General Amity	181UNTS81	102400
Libya	UK Great Britain	21 Feb 53	Air Transport	311UNTS115	104501
Multilateral		27 Feb 53	Claims and Debts	333UNTS3	104764
Germany, West	USA (United States)	27 Feb 53	Claims and Debts	223UNTS167	103065
Lebanon	Sweden	23 Mar 53	Air Transport	255UNTS83	103605
Turkey	Yugoslavia	16 Apr 53	Air Transport	255UNTS99	103606
Cuba	USA (United States)	26 May 53	Air Transport	224UNTS75	103070
Switzerland	Yugoslavia	28 May 53	Air Transport	232UNTS45	103228
Libya	UK Great Britain	29 Jul 53	Status of Forces	186UNTS201	102492
USA (United States)	Venezuela	14 Aug 53	Air Transport	213UNTS99	102883
ICAO (Civil Aviat)	United Arab Rep	27 Aug 53	IGO Status/Immunit	215UNTS371	102925
Ceylon (Sri Lanka)	Netherlands	14 Sep 53	Air Transport	193UNTS21	102608
Greece	UK Great Britain	05 Oct 53	Reparations	243UNTS73	103447
France	Netherlands	27 Nov 53	Reparations	302UNTS245	104363
Belgium	Lebanon	24 Dec 53	Air Transport	219UNTS153	102972
Ethiopia	Greece	20 Jan 54	Air Transport	222UNTS281	103035
Syria	UK Great Britain	30 Jan 54	Air Transport	449UNTS47	106452
Canada	Peru	18 Feb 54	Air Transport	411UNTS64	105915
Lebanon	Switzerland	03 Mar 54	Air Transport	255UNTS127	103608
Peru	Spain	31 Mar 54	Air Transport	232UNTS65	103230
Switzerland	Syria	26 May 54	Air Transport	255UNTS145	103609
Saudi Arabia	UK Great Britain	30 Jul 54	Dispute Settlement	201UNTS317	102722
Norway	USA (United States)	06 Aug 54	Air Transport	222UNTS269	103034
Multilateral		23 Oct 54	Milit Occupation	331UNTS327	104759
Multilateral		23 Oct 54	Status of Forces	332UNTS3	104760
Multilateral		23 Oct 54	Status of Forces	332UNTS387	104763
Multilateral		23 Oct 54	Reparations	332UNTS219	104762
Multilateral		01 Dec 54	Admin Cooperation	210UNTS197	102839
Pakistan	United Arab Rep	13 Dec 54	Air Transport	255UNTS167	103610
Sweden	Switzerland	17 Dec 54	Non-ILO Labor	369UNTS233	105260
Austria	Belgium	07 Jan 55	Air Transport	380UNTS219	105458
Canada	Japan	12 Jan 55	Air Transport	311UNTS167	104503
Philippines	UK Great Britain	31 Jan 55	Air Transport	216UNTS51	102932
United Arab Rep	Yugoslavia	20 Feb 55	Air Transport	255UNTS199	103611
Greece	UK Great Britain	24 Feb 55	Specif Claim/Waive	209UNTS187	102827

PARTY ONE	PARTY TWO	DATE	TOPIC	CITATION	NUMBER
Arbitration Commission (Cont.)					
WMO (Meteorology)	Switzerland	10 Mar 55	IGO Status/Immunit	211UNTS277	200524
Syria	United Arab Rep	03 Jul 55	Air Transport	393UNTS67	105652
Germany, West	UK Great Britain	22 Jul 55	Air Transport	269UNTS189	103881
Belgium	Ireland	10 Sep 55	Air Transport	255UNTS235	103612
France	Germany, West	04 Oct 55	Air Transport	353UNTS203	105044
Denmark	Lebanon	21 Oct 55	Air Transport	248UNTS17	103482
Austria	Israel	17 Nov 55	Air Transport	232UNTS153	103235
India	Japan	26 Nov 55	Air Transport	311UNTS243	104506
Costa Rica	Guatemala	20 Dec 55	General Economic	280UNTS121	104056
France	Japan	17 Jan 56	Air Transport	255UNTS275	103614
Australia	Japan	19 Jan 56	Air Transport	311UNTS291	104507
Austria	Italy	23 Jan 56	Air Transport	393UNTS97	105653
Italy	Switzerland	02 Feb 56	Sanitation	291UNTS113	104247
India	USA (United States)	03 Feb 56	Air Transport	272UNTS75	103932
Netherlands	Sudan	12 Feb 56	Air Transport	311UNTS319	104508
Norway	Syria	25 Feb 56	Air Transport	463UNTS217	106706
Belgium	Germany, West	14 Apr 56	Air Transport	344UNTS103	104945
Indonesia	United Nations	17 Apr 56	Non-IBRD Project	233UNTS267	103266
Multilateral		30 Apr 56	Air Transport	310UNTS229	104494
Germany, West	Switzerland	02 May 56	Air Transport	559UNTS157	108158
Brazil	France	04 May 56	Finance	323UNTS339	104675
Japan	Philippines	09 May 56	Reparations	285UNTS3	104148
Multilateral		18 May 56	Customs	319UNTS21	104630
Japan	Switzerland	24 May 56	Air Transport	312UNTS3	104509
Greece	Italy	26 May 56	Air Transport	496UNTS301	107258
Netherlands	Yugoslavia	01 Jun 56	Non-ILO Labor	276UNTS319	103994
Italy	Switzerland	04 Jun 56	Air Transport	378UNTS311	105429
Germany, West	Ireland	12 Jun 56	Air Transport	353UNTS121	105040
India	Thailand	12 Jun 56	Air Transport	255UNTS341	103617
Norway	Sweden	29 Jun 56	Specific Resources	262UNTS335	103759
Multilateral		06 Jul 56	Admin Cooperation	312UNTS109	104514
Multilateral		13 Jul 56	Dispute Settlement	281UNTS3	104066
Germany, West	USA (United States)	27 Jul 56	Admin Cooperation	278UNTS3	104017
IBRD (World Bank)	Switzerland	17 Sep 56	Loans and Credits	340UNTS311	200560
UN Hi Com Refugees	Sweden	08 Oct 56	Refugees	428UNTS307	106182
Switzerland	Thailand	13 Oct 56	Air Transport	312UNTS43	104510
Colombia	USA (United States)	24 Oct 56	Air Transport	476UNTS77	106905
Austria	USA (United States)	21 Nov 56	Claims and Debts	290UNTS181	104237
Peru	Switzerland	23 Nov 56	Air Transport	411UNTS97	105916
Multilateral		14 Dec 56	Taxation	436UNTS115	106292
Multilateral		14 Dec 56	Taxation	436UNTS131	106293
Iceland	Thailand	22 Jan 57	Air Transport	312UNTS63	104511
Germany, West	Norway	29 Jan 57	Air Transport	353UNTS39	105037
Germany, West	Sweden	29 Jan 57	Air Transport	393UNTS113	105654
Denmark	Germany, West	29 Jan 57	Air Transport	302UNTS75	104354
United Nations	United Arab Rep	08 Feb 57	Status of Forces	260UNTS61	103704
Mexico	USA (United States)	07 Mar 57	Air Transport	279UNTS205	104042
Germany, West	Yugoslavia	10 Apr 57	Air Transport	463UNTS269	106708
Denmark	Pakistan	10 Apr 57	Air Transport	302UNTS53	104353
Korea, South	USA (United States)	24 Apr 57	Air Transport	288UNTS219	104207
Multilateral		29 Apr 57	Dispute Settlement	320UNTS243	104646
Australia	Germany, West	22 May 57	Air Transport	357UNTS45	105105
Finland	United Nations	27 Jun 57	Status of Forces	271UNTS135	103913
Czechoslovakia	United Arab Rep	30 Jun 57	Air Transport	411UNTS126	105917
Norway	United Nations	09 Jul 57	Status of Forces	271UNTS223	103917
Denmark	United Nations	16 Jul 57	Milit Assistance	274UNTS81	103959
Norway	UK Great Britain	25 Jul 57	Non-ILO Labor	313UNTS3	104528
Canada	United Nations	29 Jul 57	Milit Assistance	274UNTS47	103957
United Nations	Yugoslavia	01 Oct 57	Milit Assistance	277UNTS191	104006
Austria	IAEA (Atom Energy)	11 Dec 57	Atomic Energy	339UNTS110	104849
Australia	Ireland	30 Dec 57	Air Transport	497UNTS29	107260
Canada	Switzerland	10 Jan 58	Air Transport	464UNTS21	106710
Indonesia	Japan	20 Jan 58	Reparations	324UNTS247	104689
Afghanistan	Turkey	08 Feb 58	Air Transport	464UNTS39	106711
Sudan	Sweden	17 Feb 58	Air Transport	393UNTS161	105655

Arbitration Commission (Cont.)

PARTY ONE	PARTY TWO	DATE	TOPIC	CITATION	NUMBER
Pakistan	Sweden	06 Mar 58	Air Transport	393UNTS181	105656
USSR (Soviet Union)	Vietnam, North	12 Mar 58	General Economic	356UNTS149	105094
Germany, West	Portugal	21 Mar 58	Air Transport	464UNTS71	106712
Netherlands	Switzerland	28 Mar 58	Non-ILO Labor	318UNTS175	104614
Morocco	Portugal	03 Apr 58	Air Transport	393UNTS203	105657
Belgium	Iran	14 Apr 58	Air Transport	381UNTS309	105473
Sweden	Yugoslavia	18 Apr 58	Air Transport	393UNTS225	105658
Multilateral		29 Apr 58	Dispute Settlement	450UNTS169	106466
Pakistan	Portugal	07 Jun 58	Air Transport	320UNTS225	104645
Multilateral		10 Jun 58	General Economic	454UNTS47	106539
Nepal	United Nations	18 Aug 58	Admin Cooperation	508UNTS3	107403
Ghana	UK Great Britain	24 Sep 58	Air Transport	411UNTS146	105918
Liberia	Netherlands	28 Nov 58	Air Transport	393UNTS55	105651
Burma	United Nations	15 Dec 58	Tech Assistance	319UNTS3	104629
United Nations	Tunisia	23 Dec 58	Tech Assistance	321UNTS23	104651
Multilateral		15 Jan 59	Customs	348UNTS13	104996
UK Great Britain	Yugoslavia	03 Feb 59	Air Transport	359UNTS339	105151
Ghana	United Nations	27 Feb 59	Tech Assistance	324UNTS133	104682
Japan	Yugoslavia	28 Feb 59	General Economic	341UNTS179	104883
Sudan	USA (United States)	17 Mar 59	Admin Cooperation	342UNTS13	104896
Tunisia	USA (United States)	18 Mar 59	Admin Cooperation	344UNTS179	104948
Sweden	Tunisia	19 Mar 59	Air Transport	497UNTS43	107261
Japan	IAEA (Atom Energy)	24 Mar 59	Atomic Energy	339UNTS327	104852
Canada	IAEA (Atom Energy)	24 Mar 59	Atomic Energy	339UNTS315	104851
Norway	Tunisia	28 Mar 59	Air Transport	497UNTS77	107263
Nicaragua	USA (United States)	14 Apr 59	Admin Cooperation	343UNTS119	104922
Fed of Malaya	USA (United States)	21 Apr 59	Admin Cooperation	343UNTS3	104916
Denmark	Sudan	11 May 59	Air Transport	445UNTS105	106380
Ceylon (Sri Lanka)	Denmark	29 May 59	Air Transport	348UNTS225	105002
Ceylon (Sri Lanka)	Sweden	29 May 59	Air Transport	464UNTS109	106713
Ceylon (Sri Lanka)	Norway	29 May 59	Air Transport	411UNTS165	105919
United Nations	Vietnam, South	03 Jun 59	IGO Status/Immunit	337UNTS361	200557
Czechoslovakia	Switzerland	04 Jun 59	Non-ILO Labor	349UNTS121	105012
Italy	Norway	12 Jun 59	Non-ILO Labor	428UNTS363	106187
Greece	Yugoslavia	18 Jun 59	Admin Cooperation	368UNTS69	105235
Greece	Yugoslavia	18 Jun 59	Specific Resources	363UNTS133	105205
Panama	United Nations	24 Jun 59	IGO Operations	507UNTS245	107402
India	Italy	16 Jul 59	Air Transport	464UNTS129	106714
Afghanistan	Germany, West	22 Jul 59	Air Transport	464UNTS177	106715
Paraguay	United Nations	01 Aug 59	Tech Assistance	341UNTS319	104894
Multilateral		03 Aug 59	Status of Forces	481UNTS262	106986
Germany, West	UK Great Britain	03 Aug 59	Dispute Settlement	502UNTS197	107331
Germany, West	Iceland	12 Aug 59	Air Transport	411UNTS224	105921
Ghana	UN Special Fund	12 Aug 59	Direct Aid	338UNTS203	104836
Canada	Germany, West	04 Sep 59	Air Transport	411UNTS260	105922
Turkey	UK Great Britain	09 Sep 59	Non-ILO Labor	424UNTS267	106113
Iran	UN Special Fund	06 Oct 59	Direct Aid	342UNTS89	104902
Poland	UN Special Fund	15 Oct 59	Direct Aid	344UNTS29	104941
Guinea	United Nations	15 Oct 59	Tech Assistance	344UNTS47	104942
India	UN Special Fund	20 Oct 59	Direct Aid	344UNTS143	104946
UN Special Fund	Yugoslavia	27 Oct 59	Direct Aid	344UNTS159	104947
Korea, South	United Nations	06 Nov 59	Other Military	346UNTS289	200565
Ecuador	UN Special Fund	10 Nov 59	Direct Aid	345UNTS3	104955
Ethiopia	France	12 Nov 59	Specific Property	381UNTS3	105465
Greece	UN Special Fund	13 Nov 59	Direct Aid	345UNTS171	104966
UN Special Fund	Turkey	20 Nov 59	Direct Aid	345UNTS105	104963
UN Special Fund	United Arab Rep	25 Nov 59	Direct Aid	345UNTS125	104964
Israel	UN Special Fund	01 Dec 59	Direct Aid	345UNTS197	104968
Guinea	UN Special Fund	02 Dec 59	Direct Aid	345UNTS215	104969
Argentina	UN Special Fund	04 Dec 59	Direct Aid	345UNTS263	104972
Liberia	Sweden	09 Dec 59	Air Transport	464UNTS219	106716
Jordan	UN Special Fund	15 Dec 59	Direct Aid	346UNTS3	104974
UN Special Fund	UK Great Britain	07 Jan 60	Direct Aid	348UNTS177	105000
Czechoslovakia	UK Great Britain	15 Jan 60	Air Transport	374UNTS207	105336
Peru	UN Special Fund	19 Jan 60	Direct Aid	349UNTS83	105010

Arbitration Commission (Cont.)

PARTY ONE	PARTY TWO	DATE	TOPIC	CITATION	NUMBER
Multilateral		06 Feb 60	General Economic	383UNTS3	105494
Germany, West	United Arab Rep	16 Feb 60	Air Transport	464UNTS233	106717
Finland	Iceland	10 Mar 60	Air Transport	497UNTS95	107264
Luxembourg	Yugoslavia	09 Apr 60	Air Transport	464UNTS293	106719
Germany, West	UK Great Britain	20 Apr 60	Non-ILO Labor	449UNTS77	106453
Germany, West	Spain	28 Apr 60	Air Transport	465UNTS3	106720
Morocco	United Arab Rep	19 May 60	Air Transport	563UNTS121	108208
Switzerland	Tunisia	21 May 60	Air Transport	497UNTS109	107265
Kuwait	UK Great Britain	24 May 60	Air Transport	412UNTS4	105923
Iraq	UN Special Fund	19 Jun 60	Direct Aid	376UNTS357	105389
Denmark	Peru	22 Jun 60	Air Transport	439UNTS113	106326
Korea, North	USSR (Soviet Union)	22 Jun 60	General Economic	399UNTS3	105732
Ireland	Portugal	24 Jun 60	Air Transport	412UNTS30	105924
IAEA (Atom Energy)	USA (United States)	28 Jun 60	Direct Aid	374UNTS133	105333
Switzerland	United Arab Rep	14 Jul 60	Air Transport	497UNTS161	107268
Germany, West	Pakistan	20 Jul 60	Air Transport	465UNTS41	106721
Ghana	Netherlands	30 Jul 60	Air Transport	412UNTS51	105925
Guatemala	USA (United States)	09 Aug 60	Finance	461UNTS15	106648
Ghana	United Arab Rep	29 Aug 60	Air Transport	412UNTS71	105926
Brazil	UN Special Fund	16 Sep 60	Tech Assistance	375UNTS3	105351
Taiwan	UN Special Fund	20 Sep 60	Tech Assistance	375UNTS29	105352
Indonesia	UN Special Fund	07 Oct 60	Direct Aid	378UNTS141	105424
Belgium	Jordan	19 Oct 60	Air Transport	479UNTS277	106959
El Salvador	UN Special Fund	24 Oct 60	Direct Aid	377UNTS171	105400
Norway	Peru	02 Nov 60	Air Transport	497UNTS207	107270
Australia	Italy	10 Nov 60	Air Transport	497UNTS247	107271
Indonesia	UK Great Britain	23 Nov 60	Air Transport	398UNTS71	105718
Multilateral		09 Dec 60	Customs	429UNTS211	106200
Multilateral		13 Dec 60	Air Transport	523UNTS117	107557
Canada	Pakistan	21 Dec 60	Air Transport	465UNTS115	106724
Luxembourg	Thailand	29 Dec 60	Air Transport	465UNTS131	106725
Multilateral		30 Dec 60	Atomic Energy	395UNTS241	105689
Jordan	Sweden	09 Jan 61	Air Transport	465UNTS155	106726
Sudan	UK Great Britain	16 Jan 61	Air Transport	424UNTS233	106112
Germany, West	Japan	18 Jan 61	Air Transport	465UNTS173	106727
UN Special Fund	Saudi Arabia	19 Jan 61	Direct Aid	396UNTS27	105692
Panama	UN Special Fund	09 Mar 61	Direct Aid	396UNTS3	105691
Multilateral		18 Apr 61	Dispute Settlement	500UNTS243	107312
Korea, South	UN Special Fund	21 Apr 61	Direct Aid	394UNTS231	200583
Multilateral		21 Apr 61	IGO Establishment	484UNTS349	107041
Ceylon (Sri Lanka)	UN Special Fund	03 May 61	Direct Aid	395UNTS217	105687
Honduras	IDA (Devel Assoc)	12 May 61	Loans and Credits	414UNTS180	105973
Czechoslovakia	Morocco	08 Jun 61	Air Transport	497UNTS275	107272
New Zealand	UK Great Britain	13 Jun 61	Air Transport	497UNTS293	107273
Cameroon	UN Special Fund	13 Jun 61	Direct Aid	397UNTS297	105713
Cyprus	United Nations	15 Jun 61	Tech Assistance	398UNTS39	105716
Guinea	Sweden	17 Jun 61	Air Transport	465UNTS236	106729
Paraguay	UN Special Fund	22 Jun 61	Direct Aid	399UNTS117	105738
Philippines	UN Special Fund	28 Jun 61	Direct Aid	399UNTS141	105739
Haiti	United Nations	28 Jun 61	Tech Assistance	399UNTS159	105740
Haiti	UN Special Fund	28 Jun 61	Direct Aid	399UNTS171	105741
Australia	New Zealand	25 Jul 61	Air Transport	523UNTS271	107561
Czechoslovakia	Ghana	02 Aug 61	Air Transport	465UNTS249	106730
Jordan	Norway	21 Aug 61	Air Transport	465UNTS275	106731
Mexico	Netherlands	24 Aug 61	Air Transport	465UNTS291	106732
Jordan	Netherlands	24 Aug 61	Air Transport	466UNTS3	106733
Liberia	Switzerland	31 Aug 61	Air Transport	559UNTS215	108160
UN Special Fund	Sierra Leone	02 Oct 61	Direct Aid	422UNTS131	106073
Germany, West	Morocco	12 Oct 61	Air Transport	523UNTS289	107562
Japan	Pakistan	17 Oct 61	Air Transport	466UNTS17	106734
Cyprus	Greece	23 Nov 61	Air Transport	497UNTS311	107274
UN Special Fund	Senegal	16 Dec 61	Direct Aid	425UNTS97	106121
Netherlands	Sweden	08 Jan 62	Air Transport	466UNTS65	106737
Austria	Greece	15 Jan 62	Air Transport	498UNTS3	107275
Italy	Japan	31 Jan 62	Air Transport	498UNTS23	107276

PARTY ONE	PARTY TWO	DATE	TOPIC	CITATION	NUMBER
Arbitration Commission (Cont.)					
Germany, West	Thailand	05 Mar 62	Air Transport	563UNTS165	108210
Multilateral		05 Mar 62	Scientific Project	425UNTS3	106114
Pakistan	IAEA (Atom Energy)	05 Mar 62	Scientific Project	425UNTS17	106115
Luxembourg	Spain	26 Mar 62	Air Transport	563UNTS205	108211
Dahomey	UN Special Fund	28 Mar 62	Tech Assistance	424UNTS55	106099
France	Luxembourg	29 Mar 62	Air Transport	563UNTS227	108212
Multilateral		29 Mar 62	IGO Establishment	507UNTS177	107401
IAEA (Atom Energy)	USA (United States)	30 Mar 62	Specific Property	442UNTS49	106338
UN Special Fund	Uruguay	04 May 62	Direct Aid	429UNTS143	106196
Japan	United Arab Rep	10 May 62	Air Transport	498UNTS69	107278
Greece	United Nations	18 May 62	Tech Assistance	429UNTS61	106190
United Nations	Tanganyika	01 Jun 62	Tech Assistance	479UNTS3	106944
Dominican Republic	UN Special Fund	06 Jun 62	Direct Aid	429UNTS169	106197
France	Senegal	15 Jun 62	Air Transport	524UNTS3	107563
Czechoslovakia	Senegal	20 Jun 62	Air Transport	498UNTS145	107280
Guinea	Norway	21 Jun 62	Air Transport	466UNTS81	106738
Liberia	Norway	29 Jun 62	Air Transport	466UNTS95	106739
Morocco	Switzerland	05 Jul 62	Air Transport	498UNTS189	107282
Morocco	Switzerland	05 Jul 62	Air Transport	498UNTS171	107281
UN Special Fund	Syria	07 Jul 62	Direct Aid	443UNTS3	106355
Chile	Netherlands	13 Jul 62	Air Transport	466UNTS109	106740
UN Special Fund	Tanganyika	17 Jul 62	Direct Aid	435UNTS237	106281
Nigeria	United Nations	07 Aug 62	Tech Assistance	435UNTS167	106278
Cameroon	United Nations	29 Aug 62	Tech Assistance	442UNTS3	106334
Ecuador	Germany, West	20 Sep 62	Air Transport	498UNTS199	107283
Belgium	Germany, West	21 Sep 62	Reparations	502UNTS63	107326
Austria	Czechoslovakia	22 Sep 62	Land Transport	495UNTS157	107244
Finland	USSR (Soviet Union)	27 Sep 62	Territory Boundary	479UNTS99	106949
Niger	United Nations	01 Oct 62	Tech Assistance	439UNTS181	106329
Japan	Kuwait	06 Oct 62	Air Transport	498UNTS235	107284
Finland	France	12 Oct 62	Air Transport	498UNTS299	107285
Netherlands	Norway	18 Oct 62	Air Transport	466UNTS145	106741
France	Ivory Coast	19 Oct 62	Air Transport	498UNTS317	107286
Japan	UN Special Fund	31 Oct 62	Tech Assistance	444UNTS171	106368
United Nations	Western Samoa	05 Nov 62	Tech Assistance	443UNTS297	200599
Algeria	UN Special Fund	15 Nov 62	Tech Assistance	452UNTS243	106512
Ivory Coast	Switzerland	17 Nov 62	Air Transport	499UNTS3	107289
Ecuador	United Nations	26 Nov 62	Tech Assistance	445UNTS3	106372
Rwanda	United Nations	28 Nov 62	Tech Assistance	450UNTS267	106473
Ivory Coast	United Nations	10 Dec 62	Tech Assistance	451UNTS269	106498
Ghana	Tunisia	11 Dec 62	Air Transport	563UNTS243	108213
Netherlands	Spain	17 Dec 62	Health/Educ/Welfare	499UNTS227	107301
Nigeria	USA (United States)	24 Dec 62	Claims and Debts	462UNTS180	106677
Burundi	United Nations	29 Dec 62	Tech Assistance	450UNTS279	106474
Israel	United Nations	07 Jan 63	Tech Assistance	450UNTS229	106470
Ghana	Mali	09 Jan 63	Air Transport	466UNTS165	106742
France	USA (United States)	22 Jan 63	Dispute Settlement	473UNTS3	106849
Senegal	Switzerland	23 Jan 63	Air Transport	524UNTS23	107564
Guinea	Switzerland	01 Feb 63	Air Transport	499UNTS35	107291
Mali	Senegal	07 Feb 63	Air Transport	524UNTS41	107565
Algeria	France	18 Feb 63	Air Transport	563UNTS263	108214
Sudan	Switzerland	18 Feb 63	Air Transport	563UNTS281	108215
Cyprus	Norway	05 Mar 63	Air Transport	563UNTS305	108216
Austria	Czechoslovakia	08 Mar 63	General Economic	495UNTS219	107245
Burma	Japan	29 Mar 63	General Aid	518UNTS3	107490
Cyprus	Denmark	27 Apr 63	Air Transport	529UNTS255	107664
Algeria	Morocco	30 Apr 63	Air Transport	564UNTS3	108217
UN Special Fund	Trinidad/Tobago	06 May 63	Direct Aid	463UNTS93	106695
Jamaica	UN Special Fund	22 May 63	Direct Aid	489UNTS191	107140
Jamaica	United Nations	22 May 63	IGO Status/Immunit	479UNTS19	106945
Netherlands	Tunisia	23 May 63	Finance	523UNTS237	107558
Netherlands	UN Special Fund	24 May 63	Direct Aid	466UNTS289	106750
Multilateral		25 May 63	IGO Establishment	479UNTS39	106947
UN Special Fund	Western Samoa	05 Jun 63	Direct Aid	467UNTS463	200601
Multilateral		09 Jun 63	General Economic	538UNTS309	107818

PARTY ONE	PARTY TWO	DATE	TOPIC	CITATION	NUMBER
Arbitration Commission (Cont.)					
Guinea	Ivory Coast	26 Jun 63	Air Transport	499UNTS71	107293
New Zealand	UN Special Fund	28 Jun 63	Non-IBRD Project	470UNTS3	106792
Finland	IAEA (Atom Energy)	02 Jul 63	Atomic Energy	490UNTS403	107167
IBRD (World Bank)	Tunisia	03 Jul 63	IBRD Project	480UNTS209	106970
Austria	France	12 Jul 63	Air Transport	499UNTS91	107294
Algeria	Mali	22 Jul 63	Air Transport	564UNTS29	108219
Congo (Zaire)	UN Special Fund	26 Jul 63	Direct Aid	474UNTS137	106878
Cameroon	UK Great Britain	29 Jul 63	General Economic	478UNTS148	106935
Dominican Republic	United Nations	05 Aug 63	IGO Status/Immunit	472UNTS353	106847
Cameroon	Israel	09 Aug 63	Air Transport	499UNTS121	107295
Burundi	UN Special Fund	22 Aug 63	Direct Aid	476UNTS49	106903
United Nations	United Arab Rep	27 Aug 63	Tech Assistance	474UNTS221	106884
Burundi	WHO (World Health)	30 Aug 63	IGO Operations	490UNTS423	107169
Multilateral		23 Sep 63	Atomic Energy	488UNTS99	107122
Ivory Coast	Netherlands	09 Oct 63	Air Transport	499UNTS141	107296
Central Afri Rep	UN Special Fund	30 Oct 63	Direct Aid	481UNTS247	106985
WHO (World Health)	Somalia	08 Nov 63	IGO Operations	493UNTS243	107218
WHO (World Health)	Sierra Leone	22 Nov 63	IGO Operations	493UNTS255	107219
Romania	Yugoslavia	30 Nov 63	Specific Property	512UNTS2	107438
Nicaragua	United Nations	03 Dec 63	IGO Status/Immunit	482UNTS329	107002
IAEA (Atom Energy)	Yugoslavia	07 Dec 63	Scientific Project	501UNTS273	107322
Multilateral		18 Dec 63	Atomic Energy	490UNTS383	107166
Romania	Yugoslavia	25 Dec 63	Land Transport	576UNTS95	108366
Somalia	USA (United States)	08 Jan 64	Claims and Debts	505UNTS165	107372
Mali	Niger	15 Jan 64	Air Transport	499UNTS197	107299
Denmark	Yugoslavia	11 Feb 64	Air Transport	511UNTS241	107437
United Nations	Upper Volta	26 Feb 64	IGO Status/Immunit	489UNTS179	107139
Multilateral		28 Feb 64	Atomic Energy	501UNTS245	107321
Morocco	United Nations	03 Mar 64	IGO Status/Immunit	490UNTS187	107154
Cameroon	Mali	17 Mar 64	Air Transport	524UNTS61	107566
Rwanda	UN Special Fund	18 Mar 64	Direct Aid	491UNTS3	107170
Cyprus	United Nations	31 Mar 64	IGO Status/Immunit	492UNTS57	107187
Portugal	UK Great Britain	07 Apr 64	Land Transport	539UNTS167	107830
Malaysia	Netherlands	07 Apr 64	Air Transport	524UNTS81	107567
Multilateral		08 Apr 64	Loans and Credits	501UNTS221	107320
United Arab Rep	USA (United States)	05 May 64	Air Transport	531UNTS229	107706
Multilateral		06 May 64	IGO Operations	514UNTS71	107442
Mali	USA (United States)	09 Jun 64	Claims and Debts	530UNTS133	107678
Multilateral		15 Jun 64	Atomic Energy	573UNTS85	108324
New Zealand	USA (United States)	24 Jun 64	Air Transport	524UNTS101	107568
Mauritania	USA (United States)	03 Jul 64	Finance	532UNTS307	107724
Ivory Coast	Mali	09 Jul 64	Air Transport	524UNTS121	107569
Iceland	UN Special Fund	10 Jul 64	IGO Operations	502UNTS343	107337
Austria	Spain	15 Jul 64	Non-ILO Labor	589UNTS169	108541
Belgium	Tunisia	15 Jul 64	General Economic	561UNTS297	108190
Eur Space Research	Sweden	29 Jul 64	IGO Operations	528UNTS81	107636
France	Eur Space Research	10 Aug 64	IGO Operations	528UNTS135	107637
Multilateral		20 Aug 64	Telecommunications	514UNTS25	107441
Multilateral		18 Sep 64	IGO Operations	556UNTS25	108117
Algeria	United Nations	23 Sep 64	IGO Operations	510UNTS217	107416
Australia	UN Special Fund	30 Sep 64	Scientific Project	510UNTS277	107419
Kenya	United Nations	01 Oct 64	IGO Operations	511UNTS199	107434
Kenya	UN Special Fund	01 Oct 64	IGO Operations	511UNTS181	107433
France	Trinidad/Tobago	12 Oct 64	Air Transport	535UNTS25	107774
Malawi	UN Special Fund	24 Oct 64	Direct Aid	514UNTS235	200609
Romania	UN Special Fund	24 Oct 64	IGO Operations	519UNTS29	107500
Austria	Hungary	11 Nov 64	Sanitation	576UNTS163	108368
Ethiopia	ILO (Labor Org)	10 Dec 64	IGO Establishment	521UNTS217	107524
UN Special Fund	Zambia	15 Dec 64	Direct Aid	522UNTS3	107532
Multilateral		23 Feb 65	IGO Operations	527UNTS120	107622
Multilateral		24 Feb 65	IGO Operations	556UNTS47	108118
Multilateral		05 Mar 65	IGO Operations	527UNTS221	107627
Finland	UK Great Britain	25 Mar 65	Air Transport	539UNTS103	107826
Hungary	Yugoslavia	08 Apr 65	Territory Boundary	587UNTS169	108511
Multilateral		08 Apr 65	IGO Operations	533UNTS66	107733

PARTY ONE	PARTY TWO	DATE	TOPIC	CITATION	NUMBER
Arbitration Commission (Cont.)					
Multilateral		26 Apr 65	IGO Operations	533UNTS50	107732
Multilateral		12 May 65	IGO Operations	534UNTS390	107769
Multilateral		25 May 65	IGO Operations	535UNTS374	107791
Multilateral		18 Jun 65	Atomic Energy	573UNTS3	108320
Japan	Korea, South	22 Jun 65	Claims and Debts	583UNTS173	108473
Japan	Korea, South	22 Jun 65	Dispute Settlement	584UNTS147	108476
Japan	Korea, South	22 Jun 65	Specific Resources	583UNTS51	108472
Austria	Petrol Export Org	24 Jun 65	IGO Operations	589UNTS135	108540
Hungary	Yugoslavia	09 Aug 65	Visas	577UNTS103	108375
Multilateral		24 Sep 65	Atomic Energy	556UNTS141	108124
Austria	Yugoslavia	19 Nov 65	Non-ILO Labor	587UNTS239	108512
Multilateral		17 Jan 66	IGO Establishment	592UNTS101	108573
IAEA (Atom Energy)	Turkey	08 Feb 66	Atomic Energy	573UNTS75	108323
Canada	United Nations	21 Feb 66	IGO Operations	555UNTS119	108107
Pakistan	IAEA (Atom Energy)	15 Mar 66	Claims and Debts	588UNTS261	108530
Bulgaria	UN Special Fund	26 May 66	General Aid	563UNTS71	108205
Multilateral		20 Jun 66	Atomic Energy	573UNTS41	108322
IAEA (Atom Energy)	UK Great Britain	20 Jun 66	IGO Operations	588UNTS269	108531
Brazil	Denmark	08 Jul 66	Loans and Credits	581UNTS95	108435
UN Special Fund	Singapore	23 Sep 66	General Aid	573UNTS115	108326
IAEA (Atom Energy)	USA (United States)	26 Sep 66	Atomic Energy	589UNTS3	108532
Multilateral		28 Sep 66	Specif Goods/Equip	589UNTS41	108534
IAEA (Atom Energy)	USA (United States)	09 Dec 66	Atomic Energy	589UNTS55	108535
Australia	UN Special Fund	06 Feb 67	IGO Operations	590UNTS3	108543
Asia Economic Development Organization					
India	United Nations	25 Nov 64	Scientific Project	519UNTS47	107501
Asia Oceania Postal Union					
Multilateral		23 Jan 61	Postal Service	530UNTS141	107679
Asian Crime Prevention Organization					
Japan	United Nations	15 Mar 61	IGO Operations	397UNTS199	105706
Asian Productivity Organization					
Multilateral		14 Apr 61	IGO Establishment	422UNTS101	106071
Balkan Alliance					
Multilateral		02 Mar 55	IGO Establishment	225UNTS233	103101
Bank for International Settlements					
Belgium	UK Great Britain	07 Sep 49	Loans and Credits	106UNTS61	101457
Belgium	Netherlands	07 Sep 49	Loans and Credits	117UNTS3	101581
Belgium	France	07 Sep 49	Loans and Credits	123UNTS13	101651
Multilateral		08 Sep 51	Peace/Disarmament	136UNTS45	101832
Other Unilat Decla	United Arab Rep	24 Apr 57	General Ad Hoc	265UNTS299	103821
Benelux Customs Union					
Multilateral		24 Jul 53	General Amity	250UNTS108	103520
Benelux Economic Union					
Multilateral		22 Dec 47	Customs	32UNTS143	100496
Multilateral		24 Jul 53	General Amity	250UNTS108	103520
Multilateral		29 Nov 54	General Trade	287UNTS209	104187
Multilateral		21 Dec 55	General Trade	292UNTS63	104267
Multilateral		06 Jul 56	Admin Cooperation	312UNTS109	104514
Multilateral		03 Feb 58	IGO Establishment	381UNTS165	105471
Belgium	Netherlands	03 Feb 58	Territory Boundary	381UNTS305	105472
Multilateral		25 Jul 58	Customs	352UNTS3	105035
Multilateral		11 Apr 60	Visas	374UNTS3	105323
Belgium	Luxembourg	29 Jan 63	IGO Establishment	547UNTS39	107955
Multilateral		13 Aug 63	General Trade	592UNTS139	108572
Benelux Econ Union	Poland	17 Feb 65	General Economic	547UNTS165	107956
Belgium	Luxembourg	30 Sep 65	Consul/Citizenship	590UNTS35	108545
Benelux Parliament					
Multilateral		05 Nov 55	IGO Establishment	250UNTS201	103524
Multilateral		11 Apr 60	Visas	374UNTS3	105323

PARTY ONE	PARTY TWO	DATE	TOPIC	CITATION	NUMBER
Canadian American Defense Organization					
Canada	USA (United States)	02 Sep 58	General Military	335UNTS249	104792
Caribbean Commission					
Multilateral		30 Oct 46	IGO Establishment	27UNTS77	100401
Netherlands	USA (United States)	22 Jan 54	Tech Assistance	190UNTS207	102565
Multilateral		21 Jun 60	IGO Establishment	418UNTS109	106019
Central American Bank					
Multilateral		13 Dec 60	IGO Establishment	455UNTS204	106544
Central American Economic Association					
Multilateral		06 Feb 60	General Economic	383UNTS3	105494
Central American Economic Council					
Multilateral		13 Dec 60	General Economic	455UNTS3	106543
Central American Trade Council					
Multilateral		10 Jun 58	General Economic	454UNTS47	106539
Multilateral		01 Sep 59	Customs	454UNTS289	106542
Central Commission for the Navigation of the Rhine					
UK Great Britain	USA (United States)	05 Nov 45	IGO Establishment	138UNTS75	101861
Multilateral		10 May 52	Admin Cooperation	439UNTS193	106330
Multilateral		10 May 52	Admin Cooperation	439UNTS217	106331
Multilateral		21 May 54	Non-ILO Labor	345UNTS285	104973
Central Control Office for Electric Power Systems					
Multilateral		25 Jul 62	Specific Property	506UNTS177	107387
Central Office for International Rail Transport					
Multilateral		25 Oct 52	Land Transport	241UNTS336	103442
Finland	Sweden	07 Jul 56	General Transport	258UNTS83	103672
Central Treaty Organization					
Iraq	Turkey	24 Feb 55	General Military	233UNTS199	103264
Multilateral		28 Jul 58	General Military	335UNTS205	104788
Claims Commission					
Mexico	USA (United States)	19 Nov 41	Claims and Debts	148UNTS367	200474
Mexico	USA (United States)	19 Nov 41	Claims and Debts	125UNTS287	200430
Czechoslovakia	Poland	12 Feb 46	Reparations	25UNTS207	100364
Thailand	UK Great Britain	06 Jan 47	Reparations	99UNTS149	101376
Czechoslovakia	Yugoslavia	25 Feb 47	General Trade	112UNTS3	101539
Germany, West	Norway	07 May 51	Claims and Debts	92UNTS51	101260
Germany, West	USA (United States)	27 Feb 53	Claims and Debts	224UNTS31	103068
Hungary	USSR (Soviet Union)	27 May 55	Status of Forces	407UNTS156	105864
Greece	Romania	25 Aug 56	Reparations	299UNTS231	104315
Poland	USSR (Soviet Union)	17 Dec 56	Status of Forces	266UNTS179	103830
United Nations	United Arab Rep	08 Feb 57	Status of Forces	260UNTS61	103704
Bulgaria	Yugoslavia	04 Apr 58	Water Transport	367UNTS89	105228
Norway	USSR (Soviet Union)	09 Dec 59	Specif Claim/Waive	361UNTS93	105173
Congo (Zaire)	United Nations	27 Nov 61	IGO Status/Immunit	414UNTS229	105975
Colombo Plan					
Canada	Pakistan	10 Sep 51	Direct Aid	122UNTS21	101632
Canada	India	10 Sep 51	General Aid	391UNTS237	105629
Canada	Ceylon (Sri Lanka)	11 Jul 52	General Aid	391UNTS245	105630
Canada	India	20 Feb 58	Loans and Credits	391UNTS231	105628
Canada	Ceylon (Sri Lanka)	05 Nov 58	Loans and Credits	391UNTS225	105627
Australia	Thailand	28 Jul 59	Customs	339UNTS91	104847
Commission for Technical Co-operation in Africa South of the Sahara					
Multilateral		18 Jan 54	IGO Establishment	330UNTS121	104743
Multilateral		29 Jul 54	Sanitation	249UNTS45	103500
Committee of Control of the International Zone of Tangier					
France	UK Great Britain	31 Aug 45	IGO Establishment	98UNTS249	200275
Multilateral		10 Nov 52	Admin Cooperation	214UNTS265	102904
France	UK Great Britain	10 Nov 52	Admin Cooperation	214UNTS255	102903
Commonwealth Telecommunications Board					
Multilateral		11 May 48	Telecommunications	500UNTS267	107313

PARTY ONE	PARTY TWO	DATE	TOPIC	CITATION	NUMBER
Conciliation Commission					
Brazil	Venezuela	30 Mar 40	Dispute Settlement	51UNTS291	200195
France	Thailand	17 Nov 46	Reparations	344UNTS59	104943
Multilateral		10 Feb 47	Peace/Disarmament	48UNTS203	100746
Philippines	Spain	27 Sep 47	General Amity	70UNTS133	100902
Italy	USA (United States)	13 Feb 51	IGO Establishment	148UNTS57	101935
Italy	Netherlands	15 Jun 51	Reparations	150UNTS103	101964
Multilateral		22 Feb 54	Other Military	188UNTS273	102531
Brazil	Italy	24 Nov 54	Dispute Settlement	284UNTS325	104146
Multilateral		15 May 55	Recognition	217UNTS223	102949
Italy	USA (United States)	29 Mar 57	Reparations	299UNTS157	104311
Italy	UK Great Britain	29 Mar 57	Reparations	310UNTS11	104481
Multilateral		29 Apr 57	Dispute Settlement	320UNTS243	104646
Multilateral		29 Apr 58	Dispute Settlement	450UNTS169	106466
Ethiopia	France	12 Nov 59	Specific Property	381UNTS3	105465
Council for Mutual Economic Assistance					
Multilateral		14 Dec 59	IGO Establishment	368UNTS253	105245
Multilateral		14 Dec 59	IGO Status/Immunit	368UNTS237	105244
Multilateral		25 Jul 62	Specific Property	506UNTS177	107387
Multilateral		23 Oct 63	IGO Establishment	506UNTS197	107388
Germany, East	USSR (Soviet Union)	12 Jun 64	General Amity	553UNTS249	108093
Poland	USSR (Soviet Union)	08 Apr 65	General Amity	540UNTS97	107845
New Zealand	Poland	07 Jul 65	General Trade	548UNTS19	107966
Mongolia	USSR (Soviet Union)	15 Jan 66	General Amity	562UNTS43	108194
Council for Mutual Economic Assistance					
Germany, East	Poland	15 Mar 67	General Amity	618UNTS21	108922
Council of Europe					
Multilateral		05 May 49	IGO Establishment	87UNTS103	101168
Multilateral		02 Sep 49	IGO Status/Immunit	250UNTS12	103515
Multilateral		22 Nov 49	Recognition	185UNTS307	102477
Multilateral		04 Nov 50	Humanitarian	213UNTS221	102889
Multilateral		18 Apr 51	IGO Establishment	261UNTS140	103729
Greece	Italy	05 Jul 52	Visas	187UNTS157	102508
Greece	Turkey	05 Aug 52	Visas	187UNTS163	102509
Belgium	Germany, West	06 Dec 52	Visas	152UNTS11	102007
Belgium	Greece	05 Aug 53	Visas	173UNTS53	102260
Greece	Netherlands	26 Sep 53	Visas	292UNTS23	104263
Germany, West	Netherlands	10 Oct 53	Visas	293UNTS115	104288
Multilateral		11 Dec 53	Non-ILO Labor	218UNTS153	102956
Multilateral		11 Dec 53	Patents/Copyrights	218UNTS27	102952
Multilateral		11 Dec 53	Education	218UNTS125	102954
Multilateral		11 Dec 53	Non-ILO Labor	218UNTS211	102957
Multilateral		11 Dec 53	Non-ILO Labor	218UNTS255	102958
Multilateral		19 Dec 54	Culture	218UNTS139	102955
Multilateral		19 Dec 54	Patents/Copyrights	218UNTS51	102953
Multilateral		13 Dec 55	IGO Operations	529UNTS141	107660
Multilateral		13 Dec 55	Humanitarian	250UNTS3	103514
Belgium	Germany, West	26 Jul 56	Visas	249UNTS187	103508
Multilateral		15 Dec 56	Education	278UNTS73	104023
Multilateral		25 Mar 57	IGO Establishment	294UNTS2	104300
Multilateral		25 Mar 57	IGO Establishment	294UNTS259	104301
Multilateral		29 Apr 57	Dispute Settlement	320UNTS243	104646
Multilateral		30 Sep 57	General Transport	619UNTS77	108940
Multilateral		13 Dec 57	Extradition	359UNTS273	105146
Multilateral		13 Dec 57	Visas	315UNTS139	104565
Multilateral		15 Dec 58	Mass Media	546UNTS235	107950
Multilateral		15 Dec 58	Sanitation	351UNTS159	105022
Multilateral		20 Apr 59	Admin Cooperation	472UNTS185	106841
Multilateral		20 Apr 59	Visas	376UNTS85	105375
Multilateral		14 Dec 59	Admin Cooperation	444UNTS193	106369
Multilateral		28 Apr 60	Health/Educ/Welfare	376UNTS111	105377
Germany, West	UK Great Britain	20 Jun 60	Visas	385UNTS55	105528
Multilateral		22 Jun 60	Mass Media	546UNTS247	107951
Spain	UK Great Britain	15 Feb 61	Visas	404UNTS75	105805

PARTY ONE	PARTY TWO	DATE	TOPIC	CITATION	NUMBER
Council of Europe (Cont.)					
Switzerland	UK Great Britain	27 Feb 61	Visas	404UNTS167	105809
Portugal	UK Great Britain	27 Feb 61	Visas	404UNTS33	105803
Sweden	UK Great Britain	05 May 61	Visas	404UNTS105	105807
Norway	UK Great Britain	10 May 61	Visas	414UNTS9	105960
Denmark	UK Great Britain	10 May 61	Visas	414UNTS17	105961
Turkey	UK Great Britain	28 Jun 61	Visas	414UNTS93	105968
Multilateral		18 Oct 61	IGO Establishment	529UNTS89	107659
Multilateral		16 Dec 61	Visas	544UNTS19	107909
Multilateral		14 May 62	Scientific Project	544UNTS39	107910
Multilateral		14 May 62	Sanitation	544UNTS81	107911
Multilateral		17 Dec 62	Admin Cooperation	590UNTS81	108548
Multilateral		17 Dec 62	General Economic	523UNTS93	107555
Multilateral		17 Dec 62	Sanitation	486UNTS119	107076
Court of Justice of the European Community					
Netherlands	Euratom	25 Jul 61	Scientific Project	462UNTS263	106686
Netherlands	Euratom	25 Jul 61	IGO Status/Immunit	462UNTS313	106687
Multilateral		29 Mar 62	IGO Establishment	507UNTS177	107401
Customs Co-operation Council					
Multilateral		15 Dec 50	Customs	347UNTS127	104994
Multilateral		15 Dec 50	Customs	157UNTS129	102052
Multilateral		15 Dec 50	IGO Operations	160UNTS267	102111
Multilateral		01 Mar 56	Customs	343UNTS129	104923
Multilateral		06 Oct 60	Customs	473UNTS131	106861
Multilateral		08 Jun 61	Customs	473UNTS187	106863
Multilateral		08 Jun 61	Customs	473UNTS153	106862
Multilateral		06 Dec 61	Customs	473UNTS219	106864
Danube Commission					
Multilateral		18 Aug 48	Water Transport	33UNTS181	100518
Czechoslovakia	Romania	16 Dec 63	General Trade	527UNTS285	107630
Czechoslovakia	Hungary	27 Feb 68	IGO Establishment	640UNTS49	109154
Demographic Centre					
India	United Nations	25 Nov 64	Scientific Project	519UNTS47	107501
Diplomatic Conference of International Maritime Law					
Multilateral		10 May 52	Taxation	439UNTS233	106332
Multilateral		10 May 52	Admin Cooperation	439UNTS193	106330
Multilateral		10 May 52	Admin Cooperation	439UNTS217	106331
East African Common Services Organization					
Tanganyika	UK Great Britain	09 Dec 61	IGO Establishment	437UNTS47	106299
Economic Commission for Asia and the Far East					
Iran	United Nations	05 Sep 62	Specific Resources	442UNTS249	106353
European Atomic Energy Commission					
Multilateral		25 Mar 57	IGO Status/Immunit	294UNTS411	104302
Italy	USA (United States)	03 Jul 57	Atomic Energy	308UNTS195	104462
Germany, West	USA (United States)	03 Jul 57	Atomic Energy	288UNTS305	104212
Italy	UK Great Britain	28 Dec 57	Atomic Energy	305UNTS357	104425
Netherlands	Euratom	25 Jul 61	IGO Status/Immunit	462UNTS313	106687
Belgium	Netherlands	13 May 63	Territory Boundary	540UNTS3	107843
European Civil Aviation Conference					
Multilateral		30 Apr 56	Air Transport	310UNTS229	104494
European Coal and Steel Community					
Multilateral		04 Jan 46	IGO Establishment	6UNTS35	100066
France	USA (United States)	19 Apr 47	General Trade	132UNTS135	101754
Multilateral		23 Oct 54	Reparations	332UNTS219	104762
Multilateral		25 Mar 57	IGO Establishment	294UNTS2	104300
Multilateral		12 Apr 57	Education	443UNTS128	106362
EEC (Econ Commnty)	USA (United States)	07 Mar 62	General Trade	436UNTS49	106288

PARTY ONE	PARTY TWO	DATE	TOPIC	CITATION	NUMBER
European Commission for the Control of Foot and Mouth Disease					
Multilateral		11 Dec 53	Sanitation	191UNTS285	102588
European Company for the Financing of Railway Rolling Stock					
Multilateral		20 Oct 55	IGO Establishment	378UNTS159	105425
European Conference of Ministers of Transportation					
Multilateral		17 Oct 53	General Transport	184UNTS42	102438
European Court of Human Rights					
Multilateral		04 Nov 50	Humanitarian	213UNTS221	102889
European Defense Community					
Luxembourg	USA (United States)	17 Apr 54	Milit Assistance	257UNTS255	103661
Netherlands	USA (United States)	07 May 54	Milit Assistance	213UNTS325	102895
Multilateral		02 Dec 54	General Amity	226UNTS153	103112
European Economic Community					
Multilateral		10 Jan 52	Visas	163UNTS3	102138
Multilateral		10 Jan 52	Visas	163UNTS27	102139
Multilateral		18 May 56	Customs	338UNTS103	104834
Multilateral		18 May 56	Land Transport	339UNTS3	104844
Multilateral		25 Mar 57	IGO Establishment	294UNTS2	104300
Multilateral		25 Mar 57	IGO Status/Immunit	294UNTS411	104302
Multilateral		03 Feb 58	IGO Establishment	381UNTS165	105471
Multilateral		15 Jan 59	Customs	348UNTS13	104996
Germany, West	New Zealand	20 Apr 59	General Trade	402UNTS125	105782
Multilateral		04 Jan 60	IGO Establishment	370UNTS3	105266
Germany, West	UK Great Britain	20 Apr 60	Non-ILO Labor	449UNTS77	106453
Germany, West	UK Great Britain	20 Apr 60	Non-ILO Labor	413UNTS236	105958
Italy	Netherlands	06 Aug 60	Non-ILO Labor	455UNTS259	106546
Greece	UK Great Britain	06 Apr 61	Visas	403UNTS267	105797
Multilateral		14 May 62	Sanitation	544UNTS81	107911
France	Japan	14 May 63	General Economic	518UNTS111	107493
Multilateral		13 Aug 63	General Trade	592UNTS139	108572
Mauritania	IDA (Devel Assoc)	28 Dec 64	Non-IBRD Project	540UNTS163	107849
Denmark	Portugal	20 Feb 65	Commodity Trade	639UNTS43	109143
European Free Trade Association					
Austria	Denmark	14 Nov 59	Commodity Trade	630UNTS29	108962
Denmark	Switzerland	21 Dec 59	Commodity Trade	633UNTS351	109045
Denmark	Sweden	04 Jan 60	General Trade	376UNTS375	105390
Multilateral		28 Jul 60	IGO Status/Immunit	394UNTS37	105667
Denmark	Finland	27 Mar 61	Commodity Trade	630UNTS3	108961
Multilateral		27 Mar 61	IGO Establishment	420UNTS109	106043
Denmark	Norway	11 May 63	General Trade	613UNTS271	108856
Denmark	Norway	12 Sep 63	General Trade	613UNTS289	108857
Denmark	Portugal	20 Feb 65	Commodity Trade	639UNTS43	109143
Denmark	Norway	23 Dec 66	General Trade	613UNTS265	108855
European Inland Transportation Organization					
UK Great Britain	USA (United States)	05 Nov 45	IGO Establishment	138UNTS75	101861
European Nuclear Energy Agency					
Portugal	UK Great Britain	18 Jul 58	Atomic Energy	313UNTS109	104532
Euratom	UK Great Britain	04 Feb 59	Atomic Energy	331UNTS125	104752
Denmark	UK Great Britain	20 May 60	Atomic Energy	374UNTS245	105338
European Organization for Astronomical Research					
Multilateral		05 Oct 62	IGO Establishment	502UNTS225	107333
European Organization for Nuclear Research					
Multilateral		15 Feb 52	Scientific Project	132UNTS51	101751
Multilateral		01 Jul 53	IGO Establishment	200UNTS149	102701
European Payments Union					
Netherlands	USA (United States)	07 Oct 50	Loans and Credits	79UNTS33	101029
Denmark	UK Great Britain	19 Oct 50	Finance	79UNTS25	101028
Norway	UK Great Britain	06 Nov 50	Finance	88UNTS257	101197
Sweden	UK Great Britain	10 Nov 50	Finance	88UNTS265	101198
Germany, West	UK Great Britain	09 Dec 50	Finance	88UNTS247	101196
Denmark	Switzerland	20 Jan 51	Finance	87UNTS223	101174

PARTY ONE	PARTY TWO	DATE	TOPIC	CITATION	NUMBER
European Payments Union (Cont.)					
Italy	Norway	22 Jan 51	Finance	88UNTS339	101202
Austria	UK Great Britain	31 Jan 51	Finance	88UNTS107	101187
Austria	USA (United States)	15 May 51	Direct Aid	139UNTS79	101876
Portugal	UK Great Britain	20 Jul 51	Finance	105UNTS61	101453
France	UK Great Britain	20 Aug 51	Finance	108UNTS263	101479
Belgium	Greece	24 Apr 52	Finance	166UNTS261	102191
Belgium	UK Great Britain	30 Jun 52	Milit Assistance	199UNTS113	102679
Germany, West	Greece	28 Jul 52	General Trade	182UNTS85	102424
Greece	Sweden	19 Aug 52	General Trade	189UNTS117	102544
Denmark	Greece	15 Sep 52	General Trade	187UNTS207	102513
Austria	Greece	20 Sep 52	General Trade	187UNTS191	102512
France	Greece	23 Dec 52	General Trade	187UNTS175	102511
Greece	Italy	04 Feb 53	General Trade	189UNTS269	102551
Greece	Italy	04 Feb 53	Finance	189UNTS295	102552
Denmark	Germany, West	26 Feb 53	Claims and Debts	178UNTS3	102332
Greece	Yugoslavia	28 Feb 53	General Economic	252UNTS27	103557
Multilateral		09 Dec 53	General Economic	249UNTS197	103509
Netherlands	Norway	09 Jun 54	Finance	287UNTS179	104184
Germany, West	Italy	28 Jun 54	Loans and Credits	288UNTS83	104199
France	Netherlands	09 Jul 54	Finance	287UNTS169	104183
Belgium	UK Great Britain	09 Jul 54	Finance	201UNTS299	102721
Austria	UK Great Britain	09 Jul 54	Finance	201UNTS277	102720
Netherlands	UK Great Britain	09 Jul 54	Finance	199UNTS157	102682
Germany, West	UK Great Britain	10 Jul 54	Finance	199UNTS135	102680
Portugal	UK Great Britain	10 Jul 54	Finance	199UNTS169	102683
Belgium	Italy	12 Jul 54	Finance	288UNTS59	104198
Switzerland	UK Great Britain	16 Jul 54	Claims and Debts	199UNTS197	102685
France	Greece	22 Jul 54	General Trade	225UNTS199	103099
Sweden	UK Great Britain	28 Jul 54	Finance	199UNTS181	102684
Greece	Italy	10 Nov 54	General Trade	227UNTS9	103128
Iceland	Netherlands	28 Dec 54	Finance	287UNTS159	104182
France	Greece	28 Jun 55	General Trade	225UNTS219	103100
Sweden	UK Great Britain	22 Dec 55	Claims and Debts	231UNTS179	103218
Denmark	Netherlands	31 Jan 56	Finance	286UNTS255	104172
Austria	Italy	07 May 56	Finance	284UNTS351	104147
Italy	Switzerland	29 Jun 56	Finance	284UNTS299	104144
Italy	Netherlands	29 Jun 56	Finance	287UNTS193	104185
Sweden	UK Great Britain	08 Dec 56	Claims and Debts	264UNTS61	103788
Ceylon (Sri Lanka)	Italy	23 Apr 57	General Trade	337UNTS115	104820
Germany, West	Italy	12 Jul 57	Finance	291UNTS181	104252
Italy	Tunisia	08 Apr 58	General Trade	378UNTS327	105430
Netherlands	Turkey	29 Nov 58	Direct Aid	335UNTS229	104790
France	UK Great Britain	05 Mar 59	Finance	343UNTS277	104932
Austria	UK Great Britain	14 Mar 59	Claims and Debts	343UNTS263	104930
Germany, West	UK Great Britain	10 Apr 59	Claims and Debts	343UNTS295	104935
Netherlands	Switzerland	14 Apr 59	Finance	486UNTS367	107086
Italy	UK Great Britain	14 Apr 59	Claims and Debts	343UNTS289	104934
Norway	UK Great Britain	23 Apr 59	Finance	343UNTS283	104933
Belgium	UK Great Britain	23 Apr 59	Finance	343UNTS271	104931
Belgium	Netherlands	28 Apr 59	Finance	485UNTS123	107049
Denmark	UK Great Britain	28 Apr 59	Finance	343UNTS257	104929
Italy	Netherlands	29 Apr 59	Finance	486UNTS387	107089
Austria	Netherlands	29 Apr 59	Finance	486UNTS373	107087
France	Netherlands	29 Apr 59	Finance	486UNTS379	107088
Netherlands	Norway	30 Apr 59	Finance	487UNTS3	107090
Netherlands	UK Great Britain	30 Apr 59	Claims and Debts	343UNTS307	104937
Netherlands	Portugal	30 Apr 59	Finance	485UNTS129	107050
Iceland	Netherlands	30 Apr 59	Finance	487UNTS13	107091
Germany, West	Netherlands	30 Apr 59	Finance	485UNTS141	107052
Denmark	Netherlands	30 Apr 59	Finance	487UNTS23	107092
Netherlands	Sweden	30 Apr 59	Finance	485UNTS147	107053
Greece	Netherlands	30 Apr 59	Finance	485UNTS135	107051
Switzerland	UK Great Britain	06 May 59	Claims and Debts	343UNTS315	104938
Iceland	UK Great Britain	14 May 59	Finance	343UNTS301	104936
Greece	UK Great Britain	21 May 59	Claims and Debts	344UNTS3	104939

PARTY ONE	PARTY TWO	DATE	TOPIC	CITATION	NUMBER
European Schools Committee					
Multilateral		12 Apr 57	Education	443UNTS128	106362
European Space Launcher Development Organization					
Multilateral		29 Mar 62	IGO Establishment	507UNTS177	107401
European Space Research Organization					
Multilateral		14 Jun 62	IGO Establishment	528UNTS33	107634
Food and Agricultural Organization of the United Nations					
Multilateral		15 Nov 48	IGO Establishment	120UNTS59	101615
Multilateral		29 Nov 48	IGO Establishment	120UNTS13	101613
Multilateral		08 Feb 49	Specific Resources	157UNTS157	102053
Multilateral		24 Sep 49	IGO Establishment	126UNTS237	101691
Multilateral		06 Dec 51	Admin Cooperation	150UNTS67	101963
Multilateral		01 Mar 57	Tech Assistance	264UNTS94	103790
Multilateral		24 May 57	Tech Assistance	268UNTS270	103861
Multilateral		26 Jun 57	ILO Labor	328UNTS247	104738
Multilateral		03 Apr 58	Commodity Trade	336UNTS177	104806
Multilateral		29 Apr 58	Specific Resources	559UNTS285	108164
Multilateral		29 Apr 58	Water Transport	450UNTS11	106465
FAO (Food Agri)	IAEA (Atom Energy)	01 Oct 58	IGO Operations	361UNTS211	200571
India	Netherlands	16 Jan 59	Tech Assistance	506UNTS153	107386
Multilateral		06 Apr 59	Commodity Trade	349UNTS167	105013
Multilateral		18 Nov 59	IGO Establishment	390UNTS227	105610
Multilateral		19 Nov 59	IGO Operations	410UNTS156	105902
Italy	United Nations	23 Aug 61	IGO Operations	405UNTS3	105819
Multilateral		15 May 62	Commodity Trade	444UNTS3	106367
Multilateral		25 May 62	IGO Establishment	486UNTS103	107075
Multilateral		20 Apr 63	IGO Establishment	495UNTS3	107239
Multilateral		09 Jun 63	General Economic	538UNTS309	107818
Italy	United Nations	18 Mar 64	Education	491UNTS21	107171
Jordan	UK Great Britain	31 Aug 64	Loans and Credits	541UNTS3	107856
Multilateral		02 Jul 65	Sanitation	592UNTS215	108575
Multilateral		17 Jan 66	IGO Establishment	592UNTS101	108573
Multilateral		24 Dec 68	Commodity Trade	0UNTS0	109369
General Agreement on Tariffs and Trade					
Cuba	USA (United States)	30 Oct 47	General Economic	119UNTS163	101611
Multilateral		30 Oct 47	General Economic	55UNTS188	100814
Italy	USA (United States)	28 Jun 48	Milit Occupation	25UNTS45	100356
Denmark	USA (United States)	29 Jun 48	Mostfavored Nation	27UNTS35	100396
Belgium	USA (United States)	02 Jul 48	Mostfavored Nation	27UNTS43	100397
Austria	USA (United States)	02 Jul 48	Milit Occupation	25UNTS53	100357
Sweden	USA (United States)	03 Jul 48	Milit Occupation	27UNTS69	100400
Norway	USA (United States)	03 Jul 48	Milit Occupation	27UNTS59	100399
Iceland	USA (United States)	03 Jul 48	Milit Occupation	27UNTS49	100398
UK Great Britain	USA (United States)	06 Jul 48	Milit Occupation	25UNTS61	100358
Multilateral		23 Mar 49	Commodity Trade	203UNTS179	102746
Denmark	UK Great Britain	13 Aug 49	General Trade	68UNTS105	100890
Finland	USA (United States)	18 Jan 50	General Economic	92UNTS197	101272
Ireland	USA (United States)	21 Jan 50	General Amity	206UNTS269	102792
Nicaragua	USA (United States)	28 Feb 50	General Trade	132UNTS169	101758
Sweden	USA (United States)	25 May 50	General Trade	88UNTS43	101184
South Africa	UK Great Britain	12 Jun 50	Customs	93UNTS67	101290
Multilateral		22 Nov 50	Culture	131UNTS25	101734
Multilateral		18 Apr 51	IGO Establishment	261UNTS140	103729
Peru	USA (United States)	28 Sep 51	General Trade	160UNTS35	102099
Australia	Iceland	13 Nov 52	General Trade	161UNTS59	102122
Chile	USA (United States)	10 May 54	Customs	247UNTS299	103477
Denmark	UK Great Britain	27 Feb 56	Commodity Trade	252UNTS83	103558
Korea, South	USA (United States)	28 Nov 56	General Amity	302UNTS281	104367
Multilateral		25 Mar 57	IGO Establishment	294UNTS259	104301
Muscat and Oman	USA (United States)	20 Dec 58	General Amity	380UNTS181	105457
New Zealand	UK Great Britain	12 Aug 59	General Trade	354UNTS161	105062
Pakistan	USA (United States)	12 Nov 59	General Amity	404UNTS259	105816
Czechoslovakia	Japan	15 Dec 59	General Trade	383UNTS277	105505
General Agreement on Tariffs and Trade (Cont.)					
Australia	Indonesia	17 Dec 59	General Trade	354UNTS109	105058
Multilateral		04 Jan 60	IGO Establishment	370UNTS3	105266
Switzerland	USA (United States)	29 Mar 60	General Trade	371UNTS155	105277
Cuba	Japan	22 Apr 60	General Trade	442UNTS261	106354
Fed of Malaya	Japan	10 May 60	General Trade	383UNTS293	105506
Multilateral		06 Oct 60	Customs	473UNTS131	106861
Multilateral		08 Oct 60	General Trade	450UNTS309	106476
Japan	Pakistan	18 Dec 60	General Amity	423UNTS197	106093
Belgium	USA (United States)	21 Feb 61	General Amity	480UNTS149	106967
Japan	Peru	15 May 61	General Trade	451UNTS3	106482
Multilateral		08 Jun 61	Customs	473UNTS153	106862
Indonesia	Japan	01 Jul 61	General Amity	517UNTS107	107484
Multilateral		06 Dec 61	Customs	473UNTS219	106864
Argentina	Japan	20 Dec 61	General Amity	613UNTS323	108859
Denmark	USA (United States)	05 Mar 62	General Economic	446UNTS9	106398
Norway	USA (United States)	05 Mar 62	General Economic	446UNTS47	106402
Pakistan	USA (United States)	05 Mar 62	General Trade	446UNTS57	106403
New Zealand	USA (United States)	05 Mar 62	General Economic	446UNTS39	106401
Israel	USA (United States)	05 Mar 62	General Economic	446UNTS29	106400
Peru	USA (United States)	05 Mar 62	General Economic	446UNTS65	106404
Finland	USA (United States)	05 Mar 62	General Economic	446UNTS19	106399
Portugal	USA (United States)	05 Mar 62	General Trade	436UNTS101	106290
EEC (Econ Commnty)	USA (United States)	07 Mar 62	General Trade	445UNTS195	106387
EEC (Econ Commnty)	USA (United States)	07 Mar 62	General Economic	446UNTS81	106405
Multilateral		07 Mar 62	Commodity Trade	445UNTS199	106388
UK Great Britain	USA (United States)	07 Mar 62	General Economic	446UNTS231	106406
Canada	USA (United States)	07 Mar 62	General Trade	436UNTS3	106286
EEC (Econ Commnty)	USA (United States)	07 Mar 62	General Trade	436UNTS49	106288
Multilateral		07 Mar 62	Commodity Trade	445UNTS205	106389
Japan	New Zealand	09 Mar 62	General Trade	485UNTS339	107065
Haiti	USA (United States)	06 Jun 62	General Trade	452UNTS59	106504
UK Great Britain	USA (United States)	10 Dec 62	Mostfavored Nation	471UNTS91	106824
Spain	USA (United States)	31 Dec 62	Commodity Trade	471UNTS99	106825
Japan	USA (United States)	31 Dec 62	Mostfavored Nation	471UNTS83	106823
Greece	Pakistan	17 Jan 63	General Trade	538UNTS175	107814
France	Japan	14 May 63	General Economic	518UNTS111	107493
Australia	USA (United States)	17 Feb 64	Commodity Trade	511UNTS17	107422
New Zealand	USA (United States)	17 Feb 64	Commodity Trade	511UNTS37	107424
Australia	UK Great Britain	15 Apr 64	Commodity Trade	515UNTS23	107451
Canada	UK Great Britain	15 Apr 64	Commodity Trade	515UNTS39	107452
UK Great Britain	USA (United States)	15 Apr 64	Commodity Trade	515UNTS55	107453
India	USA (United States)	15 Apr 64	Commodity Trade	527UNTS19	107614
Argentina	UK Great Britain	15 Apr 64	Commodity Trade	515UNTS3	107450
South Africa	UK Great Britain	22 Jun 64	Commodity Trade	515UNTS71	107454
Ireland	UK Great Britain	30 Jun 64	Commodity Trade	522UNTS141	107541
Sweden	UK Great Britain	30 Jun 64	Commodity Trade	515UNTS83	107455
Cyprus	UK Great Britain	02 Jul 64	Commodity Trade	522UNTS129	107540
India	UK Great Britain	31 Jul 64	Commodity Trade	522UNTS153	107542
Kenya	UK Great Britain	25 Aug 64	Commodity Trade	522UNTS165	107543
Syria	UK Great Britain	31 Aug 64	Commodity Trade	539UNTS259	107837
Malawi	UK Great Britain	01 Sep 64	Commodity Trade	522UNTS117	107539
Tanganyika	UK Great Britain	02 Sep 64	Commodity Trade	522UNTS177	107544
Finland	UK Great Britain	12 Sep 64	Commodity Trade	535UNTS13	107773
Denmark	UK Great Britain	16 Sep 64	Commodity Trade	534UNTS427	107771
Australia	Philippines	16 Jun 65	General Trade	541UNTS31	107858
Australia	Korea, South	21 Sep 65	General Trade	548UNTS163	107977
UK Great Britain	USA (United States)	05 Apr 66	General Trade	592UNTS61	108569
Indo-Pacific Fisheries Council					
Multilateral		15 Nov 48	IGO Establishment	120UNTS59	101615
Institute of Nutrition of Central America and Panama					
Multilateral		01 Jun 51	Tech Assistance	118UNTS57	101596
Inter-Allied Reparations Agency					
Multilateral		14 Jan 46	Reparations	555UNTS69	108105
Multilateral		20 Jan 47	Water Transport	87UNTS247	101176

PARTY ONE	PARTY TWO	DATE	TOPIC	CITATION	NUMBER
Inter-Allied Reparations Agency (Cont.)					
Netherlands	Norway	30 Jun 58	Reparations	348UNTS3	104995
Inter-American Bank					
Multilateral		08 Apr 59	IGO Establishment	389UNTS69	105593
Ecuador	IBRD (World Bank)	26 May 64	IBRD Project	534UNTS113	107758
Bolivia	IDA (Devel Assoc)	24 Jul 64	Non-IBRD Project	534UNTS203	107763
Honduras	IBRD (World Bank)	02 Feb 65	IBRD Project	561UNTS255	108188
Inter-American Coffee Board					
Multilateral		28 Nov 40	Commodity Trade	139UNTS159	200452
Multilateral		03 Sep 46	Commodity Trade	139UNTS3	101872
Multilateral		28 Sep 62	IGO Establishment	469UNTS169	106791
Inter-American Institute of Agricultural Sciences					
Multilateral		15 Jan 44	IGO Establishment	161UNTS281	200489
Inter-American Territory Committee					
Multilateral		30 Jul 40	Admin Cooperation	161UNTS253	200488
Inter-Governmental Maritime Consultative Organization					
Multilateral		30 Oct 46	IGO Establishment	11UNTS107	100151
Multilateral		06 Mar 48	Water Transport	289UNTS3	104214
Multilateral		10 Jun 48	Humanitarian	191UNTS3	102576
Multilateral		10 Jun 48	Humanitarian	164UNTS113	102163
Italy	Yugoslavia	13 Apr 49	Commodity Trade	171UNTS279	102232
Denmark	Iraq	18 Nov 51	Air Transport	232UNTS25	103227
Israel	Switzerland	19 Nov 52	Air Transport	232UNTS3	103226
Cuba	USA (United States)	26 May 53	Air Transport	224UNTS75	103070
Switzerland	Yugoslavia	28 May 53	Air Transport	232UNTS45	103228
Peru	Spain	31 Mar 54	Air Transport	232UNTS65	103230
Ireland	Luxembourg	27 Jul 54	Air Transport	232UNTS91	103231
Ecuador	Netherlands	14 Dec 54	Air Transport	232UNTS115	103233
Austria	Israel	17 Nov 55	Air Transport	232UNTS153	103235
Multilateral		04 Jan 56	Scientific Project	256UNTS171	103627
Multilateral		17 Jun 60	Humanitarian	536UNTS27	107794
Mexico	USA (United States)	08 Jan 62	Humanitarian	433UNTS163	106239
Japan	UK Great Britain	14 Nov 62	General Trade	478UNTS29	106934
Multilateral		09 Mar 65	Water Transport	591UNTS265	108564
Finland	UK Great Britain	25 Mar 65	Air Transport	539UNTS103	107826
Intergovernmental Committee for European Migration					
Multilateral		19 Oct 53	IGO Establishment	207UNTS189	102807
Multilateral		20 Jun 56	Admin Cooperation	268UNTS3	103850
Intergovernmental Committee on Refugees					
Multilateral		18 Jul 46	Reparations	125UNTS119	101674
Belgium	USA (United States)	23 Jan 47	Visas	47UNTS23	100721
Intergovernmental Copyright Committee					
Multilateral		06 Sep 52	Patents/Copyrights	216UNTS132	102937
International Air Transport Association					
Malaysia	UK Great Britain	01 Aug 67	Air Transport	633UNTS93	109036
International Atomic Energy Agency					
Multilateral		26 Oct 56	IGO Establishment	276UNTS3	103988
Norway	UK Great Britain	12 Jul 57	Atomic Energy	310UNTS41	104485
Sweden	UK Great Britain	20 Sep 57	Atomic Energy	310UNTS49	104486
Portugal	UK Great Britain	18 Jul 58	Atomic Energy	313UNTS109	104532
USA (United States)	Venezuela	08 Oct 58	Atomic Energy	371UNTS69	105271
Euratom	USA (United States)	08 Nov 58	Atomic Energy	338UNTS135	104835
Euratom	UK Great Britain	04 Feb 59	Atomic Energy	331UNTS125	104752
Morocco	UN Special Fund	04 Apr 59	Direct Aid	354UNTS347	105069
USA (United States)	Vietnam, South	22 Apr 59	Atomic Energy	347UNTS113	104993
Canada	Pakistan	14 May 59	Atomic Energy	426UNTS129	106133
Multilateral		01 Jul 59	IGO Status/Immunit	374UNTS147	105334
Canada	Japan	02 Jul 59	Atomic Energy	383UNTS243	105504
Austria	USA (United States)	22 Jul 59	Atomic Energy	368UNTS199	105242
Australia	Canada	04 Aug 59	Atomic Energy	391UNTS191	105623
Ghana	UN Special Fund	12 Aug 59	Direct Aid	338UNTS203	104836
Iran	UN Special Fund	06 Oct 59	Direct Aid	342UNTS89	104902

PARTY ONE	PARTY TWO	DATE	TOPIC	CITATION	NUMBER
International Atomic Energy Agency (Cont.)					
Poland	UN Special Fund	15 Oct 59	Direct Aid	344UNTS29	104941
India	UN Special Fund	20 Oct 59	Direct Aid	344UNTS143	104946
UN Special Fund	Yugoslavia	27 Oct 59	Direct Aid	344UNTS159	104947
Ecuador	UN Special Fund	10 Nov 59	Direct Aid	345UNTS3	104955
Greece	UN Special Fund	13 Nov 59	Direct Aid	345UNTS171	104966
UN Special Fund	WMO (Meteorology)	17 Nov 59	IGO Operations	345UNTS311	200564
UN Special Fund	Turkey	20 Nov 59	Direct Aid	345UNTS105	104963
UN Special Fund	United Arab Rep	25 Nov 59	Direct Aid	345UNTS125	104964
Israel	UN Special Fund	01 Dec 59	Direct Aid	345UNTS197	104968
Guinea	UN Special Fund	02 Dec 59	Direct Aid	345UNTS215	104969
Argentina	UN Special Fund	04 Dec 59	Direct Aid	345UNTS263	104972
Jordan	UN Special Fund	15 Dec 59	Direct Aid	346UNTS3	104974
UN Special Fund	UK Great Britain	07 Jan 60	Direct Aid	348UNTS177	105000
Peru	UN Special Fund	19 Jan 60	Direct Aid	349UNTS83	105010
Chile	UN Special Fund	22 Jan 60	Direct Aid	351UNTS115	105020
Colombia	UN Special Fund	04 Feb 60	Direct Aid	355UNTS257	105080
Bolivia	UN Special Fund	09 Feb 60	Direct Aid	351UNTS203	105024
Afghanistan	UN Special Fund	21 Feb 60	Direct Aid	351UNTS93	105019
Pakistan	UN Special Fund	25 Feb 60	Direct Aid	351UNTS141	105021
France	UN Special Fund	17 Mar 60	Direct Aid	354UNTS119	105059
Italy	UN Special Fund	01 Apr 60	Direct Aid	354UNTS261	105066
UN Special Fund	Tunisia	12 Apr 60	Direct Aid	355UNTS289	105082
Libya	UN Special Fund	19 Apr 60	Direct Aid	356UNTS11	105090
ICAO (Civil Aviat)	UN Special Fund	21 Apr 60	IGO Operations	360UNTS367	200569
UN Special Fund	Sudan	21 Apr 60	Direct Aid	356UNTS213	105097
UN Special Fund	Vietnam, South	29 Apr 60	Direct Aid	357UNTS311	200567
Laos	UN Special Fund	30 Apr 60	Tech Assistance	361UNTS171	105179
Lebanon	UN Special Fund	07 May 60	Tech Assistance	360UNTS225	105160
UN Special Fund	Thailand	04 Jun 60	Tech Assistance	360UNTS97	105157
UN Special Fund	Togo	08 Jun 60	Tech Assistance	369UNTS401	200574
Indonesia	USA (United States)	08 Jun 60	Atomic Energy	388UNTS287	105585
Kuwait	UN Special Fund	29 Jun 60	Tech Assistance	369UNTS419	200575
ITU (Telecommun)	UN Special Fund	13 Jul 60	IGO Operations	368UNTS329	200573
Netherlands	UN Special Fund	12 Aug 60	Tech Assistance	372UNTS331	105309
Brazil	UN Special Fund	16 Sep 60	Tech Assistance	375UNTS3	105351
Taiwan	UN Special Fund	20 Sep 60	Tech Assistance	375UNTS29	105352
Liberia	UN Special Fund	11 Oct 60	Direct Aid	376UNTS341	105388
El Salvador	UN Special Fund	24 Oct 60	Direct Aid	377UNTS171	105400
Guatemala	UN Special Fund	17 Nov 60	Direct Aid	383UNTS67	105495
IAEA (Atom Energy)	OECD (Econ Coop)	24 Nov 60	IGO Operations	396UNTS273	200585
Cambodia	UN Special Fund	24 Nov 60	Direct Aid	382UNTS255	105487
Burma	UN Special Fund	03 Jan 61	Direct Aid	387UNTS219	105564
Gabon	UN Special Fund	02 Feb 61	Direct Aid	387UNTS289	105568
Ceylon (Sri Lanka)	UN Special Fund	03 May 61	Direct Aid	395UNTS217	105687
Paraguay	UN Special Fund	22 Jun 61	Direct Aid	399UNTS117	105738
Haiti	UN Special Fund	28 Jun 61	Direct Aid	399UNTS171	105741
Philippines	UN Special Fund	28 Jun 61	Direct Aid	399UNTS141	105739
UN Special Fund	Sierra Leone	02 Oct 61	Direct Aid	422UNTS131	106073
Mauritania	UN Special Fund	07 Nov 61	Direct Aid	412UNTS240	105936
Congo (Brazzaville)	UN Special Fund	09 Nov 61	Direct Aid	413UNTS58	105940
USA (United States)	USSR (Soviet Union)	08 Mar 62	Health/Educ/Welfare	460UNTS3	106630
Dahomey	UN Special Fund	28 Mar 62	Tech Assistance	424UNTS55	106099
Colombia	USA (United States)	09 Apr 62	Scientific Project	476UNTS9	106899
UN Special Fund	Uruguay	04 May 62	Direct Aid	429UNTS143	106196
Dominican Republic	UN Special Fund	06 Jun 62	Direct Aid	429UNTS169	106197
Argentina	USA (United States)	22 Jun 62	Atomic Energy	458UNTS97	106594
UN Special Fund	Syria	07 Jul 62	Direct Aid	443UNTS3	106355
UN Special Fund	Tanganyika	17 Jul 62	Direct Aid	435UNTS237	106281
Australia	Japan	07 Aug 62	Atomic Energy	435UNTS261	106283
Canada	Sweden	11 Sep 62	Atomic Energy	529UNTS9	107651
Algeria	UN Special Fund	15 Nov 62	Tech Assistance	452UNTS243	106512
Austria	United Nations	29 Jan 63	Consul/Citizenship	452UNTS261	106513
UN Special Fund	Trinidad/Tobago	06 May 63	Direct Aid	463UNTS93	106695
Jamaica	UN Special Fund	22 May 63	Direct Aid	489UNTS191	107140
Netherlands	UN Special Fund	24 May 63	Direct Aid	466UNTS289	106750

PARTY ONE	PARTY TWO	DATE	TOPIC	CITATION	NUMBER
International Atomic Energy Agency (Cont.)					
UN Special Fund	Western Samoa	05 Jun 63	Direct Aid	467UNTS463	200601
New Zealand	UN Special Fund	28 Jun 63	Non-IBRD Project	470UNTS3	106792
Congo (Zaire)	UN Special Fund	26 Jul 63	Direct Aid	474UNTS137	106878
India	USA (United States)	08 Aug 63	Scientific Project	488UNTS21	107117
Burundi	UN Special Fund	22 Aug 63	Direct Aid	476UNTS49	106903
Central Afri Rep	UN Special Fund	30 Oct 63	Direct Aid	481UNTS247	106985
Canada	India	16 Dec 63	Atomic Energy	529UNTS45	107655
Rwanda	UN Special Fund	18 Mar 64	Direct Aid	491UNTS3	107170
Ireland	UN Special Fund	03 Jun 64	Direct Aid	496UNTS205	107253
Austria	United Nations	11 Jun 64	IGO Status/Immunit	500UNTS85	107309
Iceland	UN Special Fund	10 Jul 64	IGO Operations	502UNTS343	107337
Switzerland	UK Great Britain	11 Aug 64	Atomic Energy	552UNTS271	108059
Malawi	UN Special Fund	24 Oct 64	Direct Aid	514UNTS235	200609
Romania	UN Special Fund	24 Oct 64	IGO Operations	519UNTS29	107500
USA (United States)	USSR (Soviet Union)	18 Nov 64	Atomic Energy	535UNTS307	107786
Multilateral		09 Mar 65	Water Transport	591UNTS265	108564
Brazil	USA (United States)	08 Jul 65	Atomic Energy	0UNTS0	109603
United Nations	United Arab Rep	26 Nov 65	IGO Operations	551UNTS253	108046
Mongolia	UN Special Fund	26 Jan 66	Direct Aid	552UNTS201	108055
Bulgaria	UN Special Fund	26 May 66	General Aid	563UNTS71	108205
UN Special Fund	Singapore	23 Sep 66	General Aid	573UNTS115	108326
Australia	UN Special Fund	06 Feb 67	IGO Operations	590UNTS3	108543
Multilateral		14 Feb 67	General Military	634UNTS281	109068
Hungary	UN Special Fund	28 Apr 67	General Aid	595UNTS171	108619
International Authority for the Ruhr					
Multilateral		28 Apr 49	IGO Establishment	83UNTS105	101105
International Bank for Economic Cooperation					
Multilateral		23 Oct 63	IGO Establishment	506UNTS197	107388
International Bank for Reconstruction and Development					
Multilateral		27 Dec 45	IGO Establishment	2UNTS39	100020
Turkey	USA (United States)	07 May 46	Milit Assistance	6UNTS293	100083
France	USA (United States)	28 May 46	General Economic	84UNTS167	101127
Ceylon (Sri Lanka)	UK Great Britain	30 Apr 48	Finance	182UNTS2	102421
Ireland	USA (United States)	28 Jun 48	Direct Aid	24UNTS3	100349
Greece	USA (United States)	02 Jul 48	Direct Aid	23UNTS43	100342
Luxembourg	USA (United States)	03 Jul 48	Direct Aid	24UNTS35	100350
UK Great Britain	USA (United States)	06 Jul 48	Direct Aid	22UNTS263	100339
Germany, West	USA (United States)	15 Dec 49	Direct Aid	92UNTS269	101277
Ethiopia	USA (United States)	02 May 51	Direct Aid	139UNTS85	101877
Bolivia	United Nations	01 Oct 51	Tech Assistance	104UNTS263	101447
USA (United States)	Yugoslavia	11 Oct 52	Direct Aid	235UNTS277	103309
Netherlands	USA (United States)	29 Apr 55	Milit Installation	219UNTS105	102969
Multilateral		25 May 55	IGO Establishment	264UNTS117	103791
Israel	USA (United States)	06 Nov 58	US Agri Commod Aid	336UNTS275	104810
Multilateral		26 Jan 60	IGO Establishment	439UNTS249	106333
IDA (Devel Assoc)	United Nations	10 Apr 61	IGO Operations	394UNTS221	200582
Honduras	IDA (Devel Assoc)	12 May 61	Loans and Credits	414UNTS180	105973
IDA (Devel Assoc)	Sudan	14 Jun 61	Loans and Credits	415UNTS50	105981
Colombia	IDA (Devel Assoc)	28 Aug 61	Loans and Credits	416UNTS3	105992
Costa Rica	IDA (Devel Assoc)	13 Oct 61	Non-IBRD Project	431UNTS3	106204
Pakistan	USA (United States)	14 Oct 61	US Agri Commod Aid	426UNTS237	106141
India	IDA (Devel Assoc)	08 Aug 62	Non-IBRD Project	478UNTS335	106941
Ethiopia	IDA (Devel Assoc)	27 Feb 63	Non-IBRD Project	478UNTS289	106939
India	IDA (Devel Assoc)	22 Mar 63	Non-IBRD Project	477UNTS3	106911
Ecuador	IDA (Devel Assoc)	26 May 64	Non-IBRD Project	534UNTS93	107757
Pakistan	IDA (Devel Assoc)	21 Jul 64	Non-IBRD Project	534UNTS373	107768
Honduras	IDA (Devel Assoc)	02 Feb 65	Non-IBRD Project	561UNTS279	108189
Belgium	Congo (Zaire)	06 Feb 65	Claims and Debts	540UNTS227	107852
International Civil Aviation Organization					
Brazil	France	27 Jan 40	Air Transport	72UNTS77	100929
Multilateral		12 May 40	Scientific Project	101UNTS91	101405
Multilateral		07 Dec 44	IGO Establishment	15UNTS295	200102
Multilateral		07 Dec 44	Air Transport	171UNTS345	200501

PARTY ONE	PARTY TWO	DATE	TOPIC	CITATION	NUMBER
International Civil Aviation Organization (Cont.)					
Multilateral		07 Dec 44	Air Transport	84UNTS389	200252
Denmark	USA (United States)	16 Dec 44	Air Transport	10UNTS213	200063
Sweden	USA (United States)	16 Dec 44	Air Transport	6UNTS397	200041
Iceland	USA (United States)	27 Jan 45	Air Transport	122UNTS293	200411
Ireland	USA (United States)	03 Feb 45	Air Transport	122UNTS305	200412
Canada	USA (United States)	17 Feb 45	Air Transport	122UNTS261	200409
Norway	USA (United States)	06 Oct 45	Air Transport	122UNTS319	200413
South Africa	UK Great Britain	26 Oct 45	Air Transport	72UNTS41	100927
Greece	UK Great Britain	26 Nov 45	Air Transport	35UNTS161	100555
Portugal	UK Great Britain	06 Dec 45	Air Transport	6UNTS3	100065
Portugal	UK Great Britain	06 Dec 45	Air Transport	5UNTS37	100064
Portugal	USA (United States)	06 Dec 45	Air Transport	3UNTS139	100028
Canada	UK Great Britain	21 Dec 45	Air Transport	27UNTS155	100405
Czechoslovakia	USA (United States)	03 Jan 46	Air Transport	6UNTS309	100084
Czechoslovakia	Poland	24 Jan 46	Air Transport	25UNTS181	100363
UK Great Britain	USA (United States)	11 Feb 46	Air Transport	3UNTS253	100036
Turkey	UK Great Britain	12 Feb 46	Air Transport	6UNTS79	100069
France	UK Great Britain	28 Feb 46	Air Transport	27UNTS173	100407
France	USA (United States)	27 Mar 46	Air Transport	139UNTS114	101879
Greece	USA (United States)	27 Mar 46	Air Transport	15UNTS233	100239
Ireland	UK Great Britain	05 Apr 46	Air Transport	72UNTS57	100928
Belgium	USA (United States)	05 Apr 46	Air Transport	4UNTS125	100041
Netherlands	Portugal	12 Apr 46	Air Transport	4UNTS317	100054
France	Portugal	30 Apr 46	Air Transport	35UNTS197	100556
France	Ireland	16 May 46	Air Transport	44UNTS105	100681
Ireland	Sweden	29 May 46	Air Transport	35UNTS231	100557
Australia	Canada	11 Jun 46	Air Transport	10UNTS47	100142
United Arab Rep	USA (United States)	15 Jun 46	Air Transport	151UNTS135	101988
United Arab Rep	USA (United States)	15 Jun 46	Air Transport	71UNTS157	100917
France	USA (United States)	18 Jun 46	Air Transport	42UNTS183	100647
Sweden	Turkey	26 Jun 46	Air Transport	14UNTS21	100208
Iceland	UK Great Britain	04 Jul 46	Specific Property	6UNTS223	100077
Netherlands	Spain	13 Jul 46	Air Transport	4UNTS351	100055
Canada	Newfoundland	29 Jul 46	Air Transport	17UNTS169	100275
UK Great Britain	USA (United States)	31 Jul 46	Air Transport	42UNTS199	100648
France	Sweden	02 Aug 46	Air Transport	27UNTS251	100410
Lebanon	USA (United States)	11 Aug 46	Air Transport	66UNTS211	100856
Netherlands	UK Great Britain	13 Aug 46	Air Transport	4UNTS367	100056
Norway	UK Great Britain	31 Aug 46	Air Transport	6UNTS235	100078
Brazil	USA (United States)	06 Sep 46	Air Transport	54UNTS197	100805
Sweden	USA (United States)	30 Sep 46	Air Transport	42UNTS213	100649
Denmark	USA (United States)	01 Oct 46	Air Transport	42UNTS219	100650
France	Turkey	12 Oct 46	Air Transport	14UNTS33	100209
Belgium	Portugal	22 Oct 46	Air Transport	34UNTS49	100527
Brazil	UK Great Britain	31 Oct 46	Air Transport	11UNTS115	100152
Norway	USA (United States)	12 Nov 46	Air Transport	42UNTS227	100651
India	USA (United States)	14 Nov 46	Air Transport	22UNTS55	100331
Philippines	USA (United States)	16 Nov 46	Air Transport	7UNTS151	100097
Sweden	UK Great Britain	27 Nov 46	Air Transport	11UNTS229	100162
Australia	USA (United States)	03 Dec 46	Air Transport	7UNTS201	100100
New Zealand	USA (United States)	03 Dec 46	Air Transport	7UNTS175	100099
Portugal	Switzerland	09 Dec 46	Air Transport	310UNTS251	104495
Brazil	Portugal	10 Dec 46	Air Transport	200UNTS67	102695
USA (United States)	Uruguay	14 Dec 46	Air Transport	532UNTS87	107713
Taiwan	USA (United States)	20 Dec 46	Air Transport	22UNTS87	100332
Peru	USA (United States)	27 Dec 46	Air Transport	26UNTS227	100390
Ecuador	USA (United States)	08 Jan 47	Air Transport	22UNTS119	100333
Czechoslovakia	Ireland	29 Jan 47	Air Transport	27UNTS267	100411
Multilateral		10 Feb 47	Peace/Disarmament	41UNTS21	100643
Multilateral		10 Feb 47	Peace/Disarmament	42UNTS3	100645
Multilateral		10 Feb 47	Peace/Disarmament	41UNTS135	100644
Thailand	USA (United States)	26 Feb 47	Air Transport	16UNTS17	100246
Paraguay	USA (United States)	28 Feb 47	Air Transport	44UNTS25	100676
Czechoslovakia	Turkey	05 Mar 47	Air Transport	14UNTS101	100214
Portugal	Sweden	06 Mar 47	Air Transport	35UNTS243	100558

International Civil Aviation Organization (Cont.)

PARTY ONE	PARTY TWO	DATE	TOPIC	CITATION	NUMBER
Australia	USA (United States)	10 Mar 47	Air Transport	10UNTS89	100145
Netherlands	Turkey	19 Mar 47	Air Transport	14UNTS59	100211
Greece	Sweden	08 Apr 47	Air Transport	94UNTS73	101307
Greece	Netherlands	17 Apr 47	Air Transport	32UNTS115	100494
Canada	Portugal	25 Apr 47	Air Transport	94UNTS87	101308
Syria	USA (United States)	28 Apr 47	Air Transport	262UNTS121	103741
Switzerland	USA (United States)	30 Apr 47	Specif Goods/Equip	42UNTS235	100652
France	Greece	05 May 47	Air Transport	76UNTS61	100980
Thailand	USA (United States)	08 May 47	Air Transport	42UNTS241	100653
Chile	USA (United States)	10 May 47	Air Transport	55UNTS21	100807
Czechoslovakia	Denmark	14 May 47	Air Transport	27UNTS297	100413
South Africa	USA (United States)	23 May 47	Air Transport	66UNTS233	100857
Multilateral		27 May 47	Air Transport	418UNTS161	106021
India	Netherlands	31 May 47	Air Transport	17UNTS65	100268
Italy	USA (United States)	09 Jun 47	Air Transport	104UNTS157	101437
Canada	Sweden	27 Jun 47	Air Transport	27UNTS313	100414
Iraq	Turkey	30 Jun 47	Air Transport	72UNTS107	100930
Denmark	Turkey	30 Jun 47	Air Transport	32UNTS301	100504
France	India	16 Jul 47	Air Transport	27UNTS325	100415
Canada	UK Great Britain	17 Jul 47	Air Transport	28UNTS3	100416
Netherlands	Thailand	18 Jul 47	Air Transport	28UNTS27	100417
Greece	Turkey	22 Jul 47	Air Transport	72UNTS131	100931
Taiwan	UK Great Britain	23 Jul 47	Air Transport	9UNTS207	100135
Canada	Ireland	08 Aug 47	Air Transport	28UNTS47	100419
Czechoslovakia	Netherlands	01 Sep 47	Air Transport	32UNTS129	100495
Czechoslovakia	Switzerland	10 Sep 47	Air Transport	35UNTS275	100559
Chile	UK Great Britain	16 Sep 47	Air Transport	133UNTS143	101786
Lebanon	Turkey	16 Sep 47	Air Transport	44UNTS123	100682
Austria	USA (United States)	08 Oct 47	Air Transport	25UNTS3	100354
UK Great Britain	USA (United States)	13 Oct 47	Air Transport	66UNTS269	100858
Czechoslovakia	Sweden	15 Oct 47	Air Transport	44UNTS149	100683
Colombia	UK Great Britain	16 Oct 47	Air Transport	160UNTS297	102115
Brazil	Netherlands	06 Nov 47	Air Transport	53UNTS59	100773
Norway	Portugal	11 Nov 47	Air Transport	34UNTS257	100542
Brazil	Sweden	14 Nov 47	Air Transport	94UNTS139	101310
Brazil	Norway	14 Nov 47	Air Transport	44UNTS163	100684
Brazil	Denmark	14 Nov 47	Air Transport	47UNTS39	100722
Denmark	Greece	14 Nov 47	Air Transport	35UNTS295	100560
Denmark	Ireland	18 Nov 47	Air Transport	35UNTS309	100561
Ireland	Italy	21 Nov 47	Air Transport	353UNTS73	105038
Taiwan	Netherlands	06 Dec 47	Air Transport	43UNTS185	100669
Denmark	Portugal	15 Dec 47	Air Transport	35UNTS329	100563
Peru	UK Great Britain	22 Dec 47	Air Transport	72UNTS143	100932
Ethiopia	Pakistan	01 Jan 48	Air Transport	35UNTS3	100547
Philippines	UK Great Britain	07 Jan 48	Air Transport	28UNTS63	100420
Italy	USA (United States)	06 Feb 48	Air Transport	73UNTS113	100950
UK Great Britain	USA (United States)	24 Feb 48	Milit Installation	73UNTS143	100951
Argentina	Denmark	18 Mar 48	Air Transport	94UNTS175	101311
Cuba	UK Great Britain	19 Mar 48	Air Transport	175UNTS23	102294
Ireland	Switzerland	06 May 48	Air Transport	334UNTS187	104768
Pakistan	Sweden	06 May 48	Air Transport	36UNTS3	100564
Jordan	Turkey	07 May 48	Air Transport	32UNTS313	100505
Ireland	Netherlands	10 May 48	Air Transport	28UNTS121	100422
Norway	Turkey	20 May 48	Air Transport	26UNTS137	100384
India	Sweden	21 May 48	Air Transport	34UNTS285	100543
Greece	Switzerland	26 May 48	Air Transport	94UNTS217	101312
Canada	Netherlands	02 Jun 48	Air Transport	32UNTS215	100499
Ireland	Norway	21 Jun 48	Air Transport	34UNTS317	100545
India	Pakistan	23 Jun 48	Air Transport	28UNTS143	100423
Italy	UK Great Britain	25 Jun 48	Air Transport	94UNTS239	101313
Brazil	Switzerland	10 Aug 48	Air Transport	94UNTS269	101314
Greece	Lebanon	06 Sep 48	Air Transport	178UNTS37	102335
Bolivia	USA (United States)	29 Sep 48	Air Transport	505UNTS139	107370
France	USA (United States)	19 Oct 48	Air Transport	98UNTS3	101355
Mexico	Portugal	22 Oct 48	Air Transport	34UNTS329	100546

International Civil Aviation Organization (Cont.)

PARTY ONE	PARTY TWO	DATE	TOPIC	CITATION	NUMBER
Argentina	Netherlands	29 Oct 48	Air Transport	95UNTS21	101316
Argentina	Chile	14 Dec 48	Air Transport	635UNTS21	109071
Ceylon (Sri Lanka)	India	21 Dec 48	Air Transport	28UNTS223	100427
Ceylon (Sri Lanka)	Pakistan	03 Jan 49	Air Transport	28UNTS247	100428
Italy	Lebanon	24 Jan 49	Air Transport	231UNTS241	103223
Switzerland	Turkey	16 Feb 49	Air Transport	72UNTS175	100933
Finland	Netherlands	25 Feb 49	Air Transport	53UNTS123	100777
Netherlands	Switzerland	07 Mar 49	Air Transport	35UNTS69	100551
Finland	USA (United States)	29 Mar 49	Air Transport	55UNTS59	100808
Panama	USA (United States)	31 Mar 49	Air Transport	55UNTS87	100810
Finland	Sweden	26 Apr 49	Air Transport	95UNTS83	101318
Switzerland	USA (United States)	13 May 49	Air Transport	51UNTS129	100761
Australia	Pakistan	03 Jun 49	Air Transport	35UNTS23	100549
Canada	USA (United States)	04 Jun 49	Air Transport	122UNTS237	101649
Ethiopia	India	07 Jun 49	Air Transport	35UNTS13	100548
Belgium	Greece	21 Jun 49	Air Transport	137UNTS215	101854
Norway	Pakistan	23 Jun 49	Air Transport	35UNTS49	100550
India	Switzerland	24 Jun 49	Air Transport	95UNTS109	101319
Greece	Syria	05 Jul 49	Air Transport	78UNTS71	101013
Australia	India	11 Jul 49	Air Transport	35UNTS83	100552
Iraq	Norway	12 Jul 49	Air Transport	53UNTS137	100778
Czechoslovakia	Finland	13 Jul 49	Air Transport	53UNTS153	100779
Pakistan	Philippines	16 Jul 49	Air Transport	35UNTS111	100553
Dominican Republic	USA (United States)	19 Jul 49	Air Transport	51UNTS145	100762
Pakistan	UK Great Britain	27 Jul 49	Air Transport	44UNTS199	100685
Ceylon (Sri Lanka)	UK Great Britain	05 Aug 49	Air Transport	35UNTS137	100554
Canada	UK Great Britain	19 Aug 49	Air Transport	44UNTS223	100686
Finland	Norway	24 Aug 49	Air Transport	53UNTS167	100780
Denmark	Finland	26 Aug 49	Air Transport	53UNTS191	100781
Belgium	Canada	30 Aug 49	Air Transport	53UNTS221	100782
Belgium	United Arab Rep	19 Sep 49	Air Transport	137UNTS189	101853
Lebanon	Netherlands	20 Sep 49	Air Transport	108UNTS205	101474
Burma	USA (United States)	28 Sep 49	Air Transport	55UNTS3	100806
Greece	Philippines	08 Oct 49	Air Transport	187UNTS221	102515
India	Philippines	20 Oct 49	Air Transport	72UNTS191	100934
Iran	Netherlands	31 Oct 49	Air Transport	254UNTS257	103596
Denmark	Pakistan	09 Nov 49	Air Transport	44UNTS255	100687
France	New Zealand	15 Nov 49	Air Transport	53UNTS247	100785
Denmark	Thailand	23 Nov 49	Air Transport	53UNTS255	100786
Sweden	Thailand	23 Nov 49	Air Transport	72UNTS217	100935
Italy	Turkey	25 Nov 49	Air Transport	192UNTS39	102594
Norway	Thailand	26 Nov 49	Air Transport	53UNTS269	100787
Austria	Sweden	02 Dec 49	Air Transport	108UNTS3	101465
Austria	Norway	02 Dec 49	Air Transport	72UNTS230	100936
Austria	Denmark	02 Dec 49	Air Transport	53UNTS281	100788
Netherlands	United Arab Rep	08 Dec 49	Air Transport	95UNTS123	101320
Sweden	United Arab Rep	12 Dec 49	Air Transport	108UNTS15	101466
Canada	Denmark	13 Dec 49	Air Transport	72UNTS247	100937
Austria	Switzerland	19 Dec 49	Air Transport	254UNTS287	103597
USA (United States)	Yugoslavia	24 Dec 49	Air Transport	89UNTS209	101219
Australia	Ceylon (Sri Lanka)	12 Jan 50	Air Transport	53UNTS295	100789
Netherlands	Syria	13 Feb 50	Air Transport	108UNTS53	101467
Canada	Norway	14 Feb 50	Air Transport	53UNTS329	100790
Ceylon (Sri Lanka)	Thailand	24 Feb 50	Air Transport	72UNTS261	100938
Italy	Netherlands	04 Mar 50	Air Transport	254UNTS305	103598
Norway	United Arab Rep	11 Mar 50	Air Transport	95UNTS157	101321
Denmark	United Arab Rep	14 Mar 50	Air Transport	95UNTS197	101322
Philippines	USA (United States)	16 Mar 50	Air Transport	89UNTS199	101218
Iceland	Netherlands	22 Mar 50	Air Transport	95UNTS237	101323
Denmark	Iceland	22 Mar 50	Air Transport	72UNTS273	100939
Italy	Portugal	05 Apr 50	Air Transport	254UNTS329	103599
Sweden	UK Great Britain	05 Apr 50	Air Transport	99UNTS107	101374
Turkey	United Arab Rep	12 Apr 50	Air Transport	128UNTS3	101711
Greece	United Arab Rep	24 Apr 50	Air Transport	163UNTS229	102149
Switzerland	United Arab Rep	15 May 50	Air Transport	95UNTS255	101325

International Civil Aviation Organization (Cont.)

PARTY ONE	PARTY TWO	DATE	TOPIC	CITATION	NUMBER
Iceland	UK Great Britain	26 May 50	Air Transport	95UNTS277	101326
Israel	USA (United States)	13 Jun 50	Air Transport	212UNTS93	102863
Iraq	Pakistan	20 Jun 50	Air Transport	77UNTS215	101001
Denmark	Switzerland	22 Jun 50	Air Transport	96UNTS3	101328
Canada	USA (United States)	22 Jun 50	Scientific Project	70UNTS115	100900
Burma	Ceylon (Sri Lanka)	29 Jun 50	Air Transport	73UNTS3	100940
Spain	UK Great Britain	20 Jul 50	Air Transport	398UNTS101	105719
France	Pakistan	31 Jul 50	Air Transport	96UNTS23	101329
Canada	France	01 Aug 50	Air Transport	73UNTS21	100941
France	United Arab Rep	08 Aug 50	Air Transport	127UNTS293	101710
Canada	New Zealand	16 Aug 50	Air Transport	77UNTS239	101002
Burma	Sweden	14 Sep 50	Air Transport	96UNTS45	101330
Brazil	Turkey	21 Sep 50	Air Transport	150UNTS299	101981
Ceylon (Sri Lanka)	United Arab Rep	26 Sep 50	Air Transport	192UNTS53	102595
France	UK Great Britain	06 Oct 50	Air Transport	96UNTS63	101331
Sweden	Switzerland	18 Oct 50	Air Transport	166UNTS49	102185
Luxembourg	Portugal	21 Oct 50	Air Transport	108UNTS67	101468
Israel	Netherlands	23 Oct 50	Air Transport	189UNTS89	102543
Thailand	UK Great Britain	10 Nov 50	Air Transport	96UNTS77	101332
Israel	UK Great Britain	06 Dec 50	Air Transport	151UNTS33	101983
Israel	Turkey	05 Feb 51	Air Transport	193UNTS3	102607
Colombia	Portugal	09 Mar 51	Air Transport	108UNTS87	101469
Greece	Yugoslavia	15 Mar 51	Air Transport	187UNTS237	102516
Jordan	United Nations	29 Mar 51	Tech Assistance	137UNTS267	200448
Luxembourg	Switzerland	09 Apr 51	Air Transport	254UNTS389	103601
Iraq	UK Great Britain	19 Apr 51	Air Transport	108UNTS121	101470
Belgium	UK Great Britain	08 May 51	Air Transport	158UNTS451	102079
India	Netherlands	24 May 51	Air Transport	108UNTS151	101471
Greece	Norway	28 May 51	Air Transport	187UNTS141	102507
Denmark	Iran	18 Jun 51	Air Transport	255UNTS3	103602
Cuba	Portugal	26 Jun 51	Air Transport	192UNTS115	102598
Iceland	Norway	14 Jul 51	Air Transport	163UNTS265	102150
Burma	Denmark	30 Jul 51	Air Transport	108UNTS167	101472
Israel	Philippines	07 Aug 51	Air Transport	192UNTS81	102596
Lebanon	UK Great Britain	15 Aug 51	Air Transport	160UNTS327	102116
Burma	Netherlands	06 Sep 51	Air Transport	108UNTS187	101473
Multilateral		08 Sep 51	Peace/Disarmament	136UNTS45	101832
Panama	UK Great Britain	15 Sep 51	Air Transport	560UNTS143	108172
Australia	Netherlands	25 Sep 51	Air Transport	128UNTS63	101713
Taiwan	Thailand	29 Sep 51	Air Transport	215UNTS166	102919
Philippines	Spain	06 Oct 51	Air Transport	215UNTS193	102920
Greece	Luxembourg	22 Oct 51	Air Transport	187UNTS119	102506
India	UK Great Britain	01 Dec 51	Air Transport	128UNTS39	101712
Colombia	Spain	11 Dec 51	Air Transport	216UNTS73	102933
Jordan	United Arab Rep	02 Jan 52	Air Transport	192UNTS157	102599
WHO (World Health)	Spain	30 Jan 52	Tech Assistance	124UNTS259	200425
Costa Rica	USA (United States)	25 Feb 52	Status of Forces	174UNTS233	102288
Japan	USA (United States)	28 Feb 52	Milit Assistance	208UNTS255	102817
Taiwan	Korea, South	01 Mar 52	Air Transport	255UNTS35	103603
Philippines	Switzerland	08 Mar 52	Air Transport	231UNTS301	103225
Belgium	Spain	10 Mar 52	Air Transport	178UNTS243	102342
Pakistan	Switzerland	17 Mar 52	Air Transport	192UNTS237	102603
Norway	Uruguay	20 Mar 52	Air Transport	310UNTS279	104496
Sweden	Uruguay	20 Mar 52	Air Transport	311UNTS3	104497
Iraq	Switzerland	31 Mar 52	Air Transport	311UNTS43	104498
France	Mexico	17 Apr 52	Air Transport	163UNTS321	102153
Honduras	USA (United States)	23 Apr 52	Status of Forces	198UNTS251	102669
France	Israel	29 Apr 52	Air Transport	189UNTS55	102542
Iceland	Sweden	03 Jun 52	Air Transport	215UNTS223	102921
India	United Arab Rep	14 Jun 52	Air Transport	173UNTS209	102268
Australia	United Arab Rep	14 Jun 52	Air Transport	173UNTS241	102269
Norway	UK Great Britain	23 Jun 52	Air Transport	151UNTS81	101985
Denmark	UK Great Britain	23 Jun 52	Air Transport	151UNTS3	101982
Greece	USA (United States)	25 Jun 52	Air Transport	181UNTS53	102398
Belgium	Israel	30 Jun 52	Air Transport	183UNTS263	102435

International Civil Aviation Organization (Cont.)

PARTY ONE	PARTY TWO	DATE	TOPIC	CITATION	NUMBER
Netherlands	Pakistan	17 Jul 52	Air Transport	150UNTS277	101980
Japan	USA (United States)	11 Aug 52	Air Transport	212UNTS27	102862
Ethiopia	Pakistan	29 Aug 52	Air Transport	150UNTS257	101979
Netherlands	Peru	22 Sep 52	Air Transport	255UNTS49	103604
Multilateral		07 Oct 52	Admin Cooperation	310UNTS181	104493
Austria	Luxembourg	13 Oct 52	Air Transport	192UNTS291	102606
Mexico	Netherlands	13 Oct 52	Air Transport	163UNTS341	102154
Iceland	Luxembourg	23 Oct 52	Air Transport	193UNTS39	102609
Burma	UK Great Britain	25 Oct 52	Air Transport	150UNTS237	101978
Chile	Sweden	27 Oct 52	Air Transport	311UNTS63	104499
Chile	Denmark	27 Oct 52	Air Transport	271UNTS93	103911
Luxembourg	Norway	17 Nov 52	Air Transport	311UNTS95	104500
Luxembourg	Sweden	17 Nov 52	Air Transport	173UNTS277	102270
Japan	UK Great Britain	29 Dec 52	Air Transport	175UNTS129	102299
South Africa	Sweden	09 Jan 53	Air Transport	173UNTS299	102271
Japan	Netherlands	17 Feb 53	Air Transport	192UNTS215	102602
Japan	Sweden	20 Feb 53	Air Transport	173UNTS307	102272
India	Pakistan	20 Feb 53	Air Transport	164UNTS3	102155
Libya	UK Great Britain	21 Feb 53	Air Transport	311UNTS115	104501
Japan	Norway	23 Feb 53	Air Transport	192UNTS191	102601
Denmark	Japan	26 Feb 53	Air Transport	173UNTS329	102273
Lebanon	Sweden	23 Mar 53	Air Transport	255UNTS83	103605
Turkey	Yugoslavia	16 Apr 53	Air Transport	255UNTS99	103606
Philippines	Thailand	27 Apr 53	Air Transport	174UNTS3	102274
Denmark	South Africa	30 Apr 53	Air Transport	174UNTS19	102275
Israel	South Africa	05 May 53	Air Transport	192UNTS183	102600
Japan	Thailand	19 Jun 53	Air Transport	174UNTS29	102276
Burma	Norway	22 Jun 53	Air Transport	174UNTS49	102277
Canada	Mexico	27 Jul 53	Air Transport	192UNTS255	102604
USA (United States)	Venezuela	14 Aug 53	Air Transport	213UNTS99	102883
Ceylon (Sri Lanka)	Netherlands	14 Sep 53	Air Transport	193UNTS21	102608
Austria	Yugoslavia	11 Nov 53	Air Transport	363UNTS149	105206
Mexico	USA (United States)	12 Nov 53	Visas	224UNTS187	103077
Belgium	Lebanon	24 Dec 53	Air Transport	219UNTS153	102972
Ethiopia	Greece	20 Jan 54	Air Transport	222UNTS281	103035
Syria	UK Great Britain	30 Jan 54	Air Transport	449UNTS47	106452
Canada	Peru	18 Feb 54	Air Transport	411UNTS64	105915
Multilateral		25 Feb 54	Air Transport	215UNTS249	102922
Multilateral		01 Mar 54	Commodity Trade	256UNTS31	103622
Lebanon	Switzerland	03 Mar 54	Air Transport	255UNTS127	103608
Switzerland	Syria	26 May 54	Air Transport	255UNTS145	103609
Iran	Switzerland	27 May 54	Air Transport	496UNTS273	107257
Multilateral		14 Jun 54	Air Transport	320UNTS209	104643
Multilateral		14 Jun 54	Air Transport	320UNTS217	104644
Belgium	Ireland	30 Jun 54	Air Transport	212UNTS255	102876
Pakistan	United Arab Rep	13 Dec 54	Air Transport	255UNTS167	103610
Norway	Switzerland	30 Dec 54	Air Transport	311UNTS147	104502
Austria	Belgium	07 Jan 55	Air Transport	380UNTS219	105458
Canada	Japan	12 Jan 55	Air Transport	311UNTS167	104503
Philippines	UK Great Britain	31 Jan 55	Air Transport	216UNTS51	102932
Iraq	United Arab Rep	23 Mar 55	Air Transport	311UNTS199	104504
Norway	Sweden	28 May 55	Scientific Project	262UNTS151	103743
Syria	United Arab Rep	03 Jul 55	Air Transport	393UNTS67	105652
Germany, West	USA (United States)	07 Jul 55	Air Transport	275UNTS3	103973
Germany, West	UK Great Britain	22 Jul 55	Air Transport	269UNTS189	103881
Germany, West	UK Great Britain	22 Jul 55	Air Transport	269UNTS223	103882
Germany, West	USA (United States)	02 Aug 55	Specif Goods/Equip	268UNTS121	103854
Belgium	Ireland	10 Sep 55	Air Transport	255UNTS235	103612
Bulgaria	Yugoslavia	01 Oct 55	Air Transport	396UNTS223	105698
France	Germany, West	04 Oct 55	Air Transport	353UNTS203	105044
Denmark	Syria	20 Oct 55	Air Transport	250UNTS61	103518
Denmark	Lebanon	21 Oct 55	Air Transport	248UNTS17	103482
Pakistan	Turkey	02 Nov 55	Air Transport	311UNTS217	104505
India	Japan	26 Nov 55	Air Transport	311UNTS243	104506
France	Japan	17 Jan 56	Air Transport	255UNTS275	103614

International Civil Aviation Organization (Cont.)

PARTY ONE	PARTY TWO	DATE	TOPIC	CITATION	NUMBER
Australia	Japan	19 Jan 56	Air Transport	311UNTS291	104507
Austria	Italy	23 Jan 56	Air Transport	393UNTS97	105653
Argentina	Switzerland	25 Jan 56	Air Transport	559UNTS121	108157
India	USA (United States)	03 Feb 56	Air Transport	272UNTS75	103932
Norway	Syria	25 Feb 56	Air Transport	463UNTS217	106706
Belgium	Germany, West	14 Apr 56	Air Transport	344UNTS103	104945
Multilateral		30 Apr 56	Air Transport	310UNTS229	104494
Germany, West	Switzerland	02 May 56	Air Transport	559UNTS157	108158
Portugal	Venezuela	16 May 56	Air Transport	463UNTS239	106707
Japan	Switzerland	24 May 56	Air Transport	312UNTS3	104509
Greece	Italy	26 May 56	Air Transport	496UNTS301	107258
Italy	Switzerland	04 Jun 56	Air Transport	378UNTS311	105429
Germany, West	Ireland	12 Jun 56	Air Transport	353UNTS121	105040
India	Thailand	12 Jun 56	Air Transport	255UNTS341	103617
Multilateral		25 Sep 56	Air Transport	334UNTS89	104767
Multilateral		25 Sep 56	Air Transport	334UNTS13	104766
Germany, West	Netherlands	28 Sep 56	Air Transport	327UNTS185	104722
Switzerland	Thailand	13 Oct 56	Air Transport	312UNTS43	104510
Colombia	USA (United States)	24 Oct 56	Air Transport	476UNTS77	106905
Belgium	Turkey	25 Oct 56	Air Transport	380UNTS3	105447
Austria	UK Great Britain	27 Oct 56	Air Transport	264UNTS67	103789
Peru	Switzerland	23 Nov 56	Air Transport	411UNTS97	105916
Iran	USA (United States)	16 Jan 57	Air Transport	308UNTS147	104460
Iceland	Thailand	22 Jan 57	Air Transport	312UNTS63	104511
Germany, West	Sweden	29 Jan 57	Air Transport	393UNTS113	105654
Germany, West	Norway	29 Jan 57	Air Transport	353UNTS39	105037
Denmark	Germany, West	29 Jan 57	Air Transport	302UNTS75	104354
Mexico	USA (United States)	07 Mar 57	Air Transport	279UNTS205	104042
Netherlands	Yugoslavia	13 Mar 57	Air Transport	327UNTS227	104723
Netherlands	USA (United States)	03 Apr 57	Air Transport	410UNTS193	105904
Germany, West	Yugoslavia	10 Apr 57	Air Transport	463UNTS269	106708
Denmark	Pakistan	10 Apr 57	Air Transport	302UNTS53	104353
Korea, South	USA (United States)	24 Apr 57	Air Transport	288UNTS219	104207
Australia	Germany, West	22 May 57	Air Transport	357UNTS45	105105
Afghanistan	Pakistan	13 Jun 57	Air Transport	327UNTS51	104717
Czechoslovakia	United Arab Rep	30 Jun 57	Air Transport	411UNTS126	105917
Greece	Italy	02 Aug 57	Air Transport	533UNTS217	107744
Italy	Pakistan	05 Oct 57	Air Transport	353UNTS91	105039
Fed of Malaya	UK Great Britain	18 Oct 57	Air Transport	335UNTS3	104775
France	Morocco	25 Oct 57	Air Transport	559UNTS95	108156
Australia	Ireland	30 Dec 57	Air Transport	497UNTS29	107260
Canada	Switzerland	10 Jan 58	Air Transport	464UNTS21	106710
Belgium	Morocco	20 Jan 58	Air Transport	288UNTS3	104192
Australia	UK Great Britain	07 Feb 58	Air Transport	335UNTS23	104776
Afghanistan	Turkey	08 Feb 58	Air Transport	464UNTS39	106711
Sudan	Sweden	17 Feb 58	Air Transport	393UNTS161	105655
Norway	Pakistan	05 Mar 58	Air Transport	334UNTS199	104769
Pakistan	Sweden	06 Mar 58	Air Transport	393UNTS181	105656
Germany, West	Portugal	21 Mar 58	Air Transport	464UNTS71	106712
South Africa	Sweden	28 Mar 58	Air Transport	300UNTS95	104333
Norway	South Africa	28 Mar 58	Air Transport	300UNTS83	104332
Denmark	South Africa	28 Mar 58	Air Transport	300UNTS107	104334
Morocco	Portugal	03 Apr 58	Air Transport	393UNTS203	105657
Belgium	Iran	14 Apr 58	Air Transport	381UNTS309	105473
Sweden	Yugoslavia	18 Apr 58	Air Transport	393UNTS225	105658
Pakistan	Portugal	07 Jun 58	Air Transport	320UNTS225	104645
Denmark	Luxembourg	10 Jun 58	Air Transport	356UNTS193	105096
Netherlands	USSR (Soviet Union)	17 Jun 58	Air Transport	335UNTS77	104779
Belgium	Pakistan	04 Jul 58	Air Transport	387UNTS305	105569
Ethiopia	UK Great Britain	07 Jul 58	Air Transport	331UNTS3	104749
Ghana	UK Great Britain	24 Sep 58	Air Transport	411UNTS146	105918
Liberia	Netherlands	28 Nov 58	Air Transport	393UNTS55	105651
Finland	Switzerland	07 Jan 59	Air Transport	353UNTS173	105042
Sweden	Tunisia	19 Mar 59	Air Transport	497UNTS43	107261
Netherlands	Tunisia	19 Mar 59	Air Transport	497UNTS61	107262

International Civil Aviation Organization (Cont.)

PARTY ONE	PARTY TWO	DATE	TOPIC	CITATION	NUMBER
Norway	Tunisia	28 Mar 59	Air Transport	497UNTS77	107263
Denmark	Tunisia	14 Apr 59	Air Transport	340UNTS273	104870
Denmark	Sudan	11 May 59	Air Transport	445UNTS105	106380
Ceylon (Sri Lanka)	Sweden	29 May 59	Air Transport	464UNTS109	106713
Ceylon (Sri Lanka)	Norway	29 May 59	Air Transport	411UNTS165	105919
Ceylon (Sri Lanka)	Denmark	29 May 59	Air Transport	348UNTS225	105002
Belgium	Japan	20 Jun 59	Air Transport	411UNTS3	105911
Bulgaria	United Arab Rep	09 Jul 59	Air Transport	411UNTS187	105920
India	Italy	16 Jul 59	Air Transport	464UNTS129	106714
Afghanistan	Germany, West	22 Jul 59	Air Transport	464UNTS177	106715
Multilateral		03 Aug 59	Status of Forces	481UNTS262	106986
Germany, West	Iceland	12 Aug 59	Air Transport	411UNTS224	105921
Canada	Germany, West	04 Sep 59	Air Transport	411UNTS260	105922
Australia	Fed of Malaya	29 Sep 59	Air Transport	357UNTS29	105104
Nicaragua	Peru	14 Oct 59	Air Transport	392UNTS303	105649
South Africa	Switzerland	19 Oct 59	Air Transport	559UNTS257	108162
Czechoslovakia	UK Great Britain	15 Jan 60	Air Transport	374UNTS207	105336
Germany, West	United Arab Rep	16 Feb 60	Air Transport	464UNTS233	106717
Multilateral		26 Feb 60	Air Transport	418UNTS171	106022
Australia	Thailand	26 Feb 60	Air Transport	392UNTS255	105647
Guinea	Netherlands	09 Mar 60	Air Transport	392UNTS243	105646
Finland	Iceland	10 Mar 60	Air Transport	497UNTS95	107264
Belgium	Switzerland	24 Mar 60	Air Transport	416UNTS81	105996
Luxembourg	Yugoslavia	09 Apr 60	Air Transport	464UNTS293	106719
Multilateral		22 Apr 60	Air Transport	418UNTS211	106023
Germany, West	Spain	28 Apr 60	Air Transport	465UNTS3	106720
Morocco	United Arab Rep	19 May 60	Air Transport	563UNTS121	108208
Switzerland	Tunisia	21 May 60	Air Transport	497UNTS109	107265
Kuwait	UK Great Britain	24 May 60	Air Transport	412UNTS4	105923
Luxembourg	Tunisia	13 Jun 60	Air Transport	497UNTS143	107267
Denmark	Peru	22 Jun 60	Air Transport	439UNTS113	106326
Ireland	Portugal	24 Jun 60	Air Transport	412UNTS30	105924
Denmark	USA (United States)	07 Jul 60	Air Transport	380UNTS39	105449
Switzerland	United Arab Rep	14 Jul 60	Air Transport	497UNTS161	107268
Germany, West	Pakistan	20 Jul 60	Air Transport	465UNTS41	106721
Ghana	Netherlands	30 Jul 60	Air Transport	412UNTS51	105925
Mexico	USA (United States)	15 Aug 60	Air Transport	402UNTS177	105786
Belgium	Burma	17 Aug 60	Air Transport	540UNTS185	107850
Ghana	United Arab Rep	29 Aug 60	Air Transport	412UNTS71	105926
Czechoslovakia	India	19 Sep 60	Air Transport	465UNTS67	106722
Belgium	Jordan	19 Oct 60	Air Transport	479UNTS277	106959
Burma	Switzerland	31 Oct 60	Air Transport	465UNTS97	106723
Norway	Peru	02 Nov 60	Air Transport	497UNTS207	107270
Australia	Italy	10 Nov 60	Air Transport	497UNTS247	107271
Indonesia	UK Great Britain	23 Nov 60	Air Transport	398UNTS71	105718
Multilateral		13 Dec 60	Air Transport	523UNTS117	107557
Canada	Pakistan	21 Dec 60	Air Transport	465UNTS115	106724
Luxembourg	Thailand	29 Dec 60	Air Transport	465UNTS131	106725
Jordan	Sweden	09 Jan 61	Air Transport	465UNTS155	106726
Sudan	UK Great Britain	16 Jan 61	Air Transport	424UNTS233	106112
Germany, West	Japan	18 Jan 61	Air Transport	465UNTS173	106727
Ghana	Switzerland	17 May 61	Air Transport	559UNTS193	108159
Czechoslovakia	Morocco	08 Jun 61	Air Transport	497UNTS275	107272
New Zealand	UK Great Britain	13 Jun 61	Air Transport	497UNTS293	107273
Cameroon	France	16 Jun 61	Air Transport	412UNTS148	105929
Guinea	Sweden	17 Jun 61	Air Transport	465UNTS236	106729
Multilateral		21 Jun 61	IGO Establishment	514UNTS209	107449
Australia	New Zealand	25 Jul 61	Air Transport	523UNTS271	107561
Czechoslovakia	Ghana	02 Aug 61	Air Transport	465UNTS249	106730
Finland	Luxembourg	15 Aug 61	Air Transport	541UNTS45	107859
Jordan	Norway	21 Aug 61	Air Transport	465UNTS275	106731
Mexico	Netherlands	24 Aug 61	Air Transport	465UNTS291	106732
Jordan	Netherlands	24 Aug 61	Air Transport	466UNTS3	106733
Liberia	Switzerland	31 Aug 61	Air Transport	559UNTS215	108160
Multilateral		18 Sep 61	Air Transport	500UNTS31	107305

PARTY ONE	PARTY TWO	DATE	TOPIC	CITATION	NUMBER
International Civil Aviation Organization (Cont.)					
Germany, West	Morocco	12 Oct 61	Air Transport	523UNTS289	107562
Japan	Pakistan	17 Oct 61	Air Transport	466UNTS17	106734
Cyprus	Greece	23 Nov 61	Air Transport	497UNTS311	107274
Denmark	Jordan	07 Dec 61	Air Transport	631UNTS333	109003
Czechoslovakia	Guinea	16 Dec 61	Air Transport	559UNTS49	108154
Netherlands	Sweden	08 Jan 62	Air Transport	466UNTS65	106737
Austria	Greece	15 Jan 62	Air Transport	498UNTS3	107275
Indonesia	Japan	23 Jan 62	Air Transport	559UNTS77	108155
Italy	Japan	31 Jan 62	Air Transport	498UNTS23	107276
Germany, West	Thailand	05 Mar 62	Air Transport	563UNTS165	108210
Luxembourg	Spain	26 Mar 62	Air Transport	563UNTS205	108211
France	Luxembourg	29 Mar 62	Air Transport	563UNTS227	108212
Sierra Leone	UK Great Britain	05 Apr 62	Air Transport	434UNTS227	106265
Netherlands	USA (United States)	24 Apr 62	Specific Property	436UNTS93	106289
Japan	United Arab Rep	10 May 62	Air Transport	498UNTS69	107278
France	Senegal	15 Jun 62	Air Transport	524UNTS3	107563
Czechoslovakia	Senegal	20 Jun 62	Air Transport	498UNTS145	107280
Guinea	Norway	21 Jun 62	Air Transport	466UNTS81	106738
Morocco	Switzerland	05 Jul 62	Air Transport	498UNTS171	107281
Morocco	Switzerland	05 Jul 62	Air Transport	498UNTS189	107282
Chile	Netherlands	13 Jul 62	Air Transport	466UNTS109	106740
Ecuador	Germany, West	20 Sep 62	Air Transport	498UNTS199	107283
Japan	Kuwait	06 Oct 62	Air Transport	498UNTS235	107284
Finland	France	12 Oct 62	Air Transport	498UNTS299	107285
Netherlands	Norway	18 Oct 62	Air Transport	466UNTS145	106741
France	Ivory Coast	19 Oct 62	Air Transport	498UNTS317	107286
Ivory Coast	Switzerland	17 Nov 62	Air Transport	499UNTS3	107289
Ghana	Tunisia	11 Dec 62	Air Transport	563UNTS243	108213
Ghana	Mali	09 Jan 63	Air Transport	466UNTS165	106742
France	USA (United States)	22 Jan 63	Dispute Settlement	473UNTS3	106849
Senegal	Switzerland	23 Jan 63	Air Transport	524UNTS23	107564
Guinea	Switzerland	01 Feb 63	Air Transport	499UNTS35	107291
Mali	Senegal	07 Feb 63	Air Transport	524UNTS41	107565
Algeria	France	18 Feb 63	Air Transport	563UNTS263	108214
Sudan	Switzerland	18 Feb 63	Air Transport	563UNTS281	108215
Cyprus	Norway	05 Mar 63	Air Transport	563UNTS305	108216
Cyprus	Denmark	27 Apr 63	Air Transport	529UNTS255	107664
Algeria	Morocco	30 Apr 63	Air Transport	564UNTS3	108217
Portugal	South Africa	07 May 63	Air Transport	499UNTS49	107292
Germany, West	Greece	07 Jun 63	Air Transport	544UNTS193	107919
Belgium	Cyprus	08 Jun 63	Air Transport	601UNTS311	108703
Guinea	Ivory Coast	26 Jun 63	Air Transport	499UNTS71	107293
Austria	France	12 Jul 63	Air Transport	499UNTS91	107294
Algeria	Mali	22 Jul 63	Air Transport	564UNTS29	108219
Mali	Tunisia	24 Jul 63	Air Transport	602UNTS91	108708
Cameroon	Israel	09 Aug 63	Air Transport	499UNTS121	107295
Algeria	Tunisia	01 Sep 63	Air Transport	601UNTS275	108701
Ivory Coast	Netherlands	09 Oct 63	Air Transport	499UNTS141	107296
Canada	Denmark	28 Nov 63	Air Transport	496UNTS223	107254
Greece	Poland	21 Dec 63	Air Transport	538UNTS155	107813
Mali	Niger	15 Jan 64	Air Transport	499UNTS197	107299
Lebanon	Pakistan	04 Feb 64	Air Transport	614UNTS55	108863
Argentina	Paraguay	07 Feb 64	Air Transport	634UNTS127	109057
Denmark	Yugoslavia	11 Feb 64	Air Transport	511UNTS241	107437
Cameroon	Mali	17 Mar 64	Air Transport	524UNTS61	107566
Malaysia	Netherlands	07 Apr 64	Air Transport	524UNTS81	107567
Norway	Yugoslavia	15 Apr 64	Air Transport	602UNTS177	108712
United Arab Rep	USA (United States)	05 May 64	Air Transport	531UNTS229	107706
Jamaica	UNICEF (Children)	19 May 64	IGO Operations	500UNTS75	107308
Cyprus	Hungary	02 Jun 64	Air Transport	602UNTS3	108704
New Zealand	USA (United States)	24 Jun 64	Air Transport	524UNTS101	107568
Ivory Coast	Mali	09 Jul 64	Air Transport	524UNTS121	107569
France	Trinidad/Tobago	12 Oct 64	Air Transport	535UNTS25	107774
Cyprus	Syria	22 Dec 64	Air Transport	602UNTS25	108705
Argentina	UK Great Britain	12 Jan 65	Air Transport	597UNTS177	108645
Denmark	Malaysia	26 Mar 65	Air Transport	540UNTS205	107851
Australia	France	13 Apr 65	Air Transport	601UNTS293	108702
Ghana	Malawi	04 May 65	Air Transport	541UNTS163	107869
Denmark	Spain	05 May 65	Air Transport	543UNTS255	107905
Mauritania	Spain	11 May 65	Air Transport	602UNTS111	108709
Malaysia	Norway	26 May 65	Air Transport	602UNTS157	108711
Ivory Coast	Sweden	07 Jun 65	Air Transport	0UNTS0	109240
Nigeria	Switzerland	11 Oct 65	Air Transport	602UNTS137	108710
Burma	Czechoslovakia	15 Dec 65	Air Transport	602UNTS71	108707
Canada	USA (United States)	17 Jan 66	Air Transport	586UNTS151	108502
Denmark	Ivory Coast	07 Jun 66	Air Transport	595UNTS313	108626
Denmark	Nigeria	08 Sep 66	Air Transport	591UNTS177	108557
Denmark	Singapore	20 Dec 66	Air Transport	593UNTS125	108580
Trinidad/Tobago	UK Great Britain	01 Mar 67	Air Transport	606UNTS149	108784
Malta	UK Great Britain	10 Jul 67	Air Transport	619UNTS11	108936
Malaysia	UK Great Britain	01 Aug 67	Air Transport	633UNTS93	109036
Singapore	UK Great Britain	01 Aug 67	Air Transport	619UNTS29	108937
Denmark	Malaysia	14 Dec 67	Air Transport	614UNTS26	108862
International Commission on Civil Status					
Multilateral		27 Sep 57	Admin Cooperation	299UNTS211	104314
International Committee of the Red Cross					
Multilateral		12 Aug 49	Humanitarian	75UNTS85	100971
Multilateral		12 Aug 49	Humanitarian	75UNTS287	100973
Multilateral		12 Aug 49	General Military	75UNTS135	100972
Multilateral		12 Aug 49	Humanitarian	75UNTS31	100970
International Computation Centre					
Multilateral		06 Dec 51	IGO Establishment	425UNTS61	106119
International Cotton Institute					
Multilateral		17 Jan 66	IGO Establishment	592UNTS101	108573
International Court of Justice					
Greece	Iran	09 Jan 31	General Amity	166UNTS323	200496
Multilateral		16 Nov 45	IGO Establishment	4UNTS275	100052
ICJ Option Clause	UK Great Britain	13 Feb 46	ICJ Option Clause	1UNTS3	100001
Jordan	UK Great Britain	22 Mar 46	General Amity	6UNTS143	100074
Multilateral		17 Apr 46	Land Transport	27UNTS103	100402
United Nations	Switzerland	01 Jul 46	IGO Status/Immunit	1UNTS163	200008
United Nations	Switzerland	01 Jul 46	Specific Property	1UNTS153	200007
Multilateral		19 Jul 46	IGO Operations	1UNTS97	200001
ICJ Option Clause	Netherlands	05 Aug 46	ICJ Option Clause	1UNTS7	100002
ICJ Option Clause	USA (United States)	14 Aug 46	ICJ Option Clause	1UNTS9	100003
ICJ Option Clause	Taiwan	26 Oct 46	ICJ Option Clause	1UNTS35	100005
Taiwan	USA (United States)	04 Nov 46	General Amity	25UNTS69	100359
ICJ Option Clause	Norway	16 Nov 46	ICJ Option Clause	1UNTS37	100006
ICJ Option Clause	Denmark	10 Dec 46	ICJ Option Clause	1UNTS45	100010
Multilateral		13 Dec 46	Trusteeship	8UNTS165	100121
Multilateral		13 Dec 46	Trusteeship	8UNTS151	100120
Multilateral		13 Dec 46	Trusteeship	8UNTS71	100115
Multilateral		13 Dec 46	Trusteeship	8UNTS105	100117
Multilateral		13 Dec 46	Trusteeship	8UNTS91	100116
Multilateral		13 Dec 46	Trusteeship	8UNTS135	100119
Multilateral		13 Dec 46	Trusteeship	8UNTS119	100118
Multilateral		15 Dec 46	IGO Establishment	18UNTS3	100283
ICJ Option Clause	Guatemala	27 Jan 47	ICJ Option Clause	1UNTS49	100012
UNESCO (Educ/Cult)	United Nations	03 Feb 47	IGO Operations	1UNTS233	200011
FAO (Food Agri)	United Nations	03 Feb 47	IGO Operations	1UNTS207	200010
ICJ Option Clause	France	18 Feb 47	ICJ Option Clause	26UNTS91	100378
ICJ Option Clause	Sweden	05 Apr 47	ICJ Option Clause	2UNTS3	100016
ICJ Option Clause	Turkey	22 May 47	ICJ Option Clause	4UNTS265	100050
Italy	Philippines	09 Jul 47	General Amity	44UNTS3	100674
ICJ Option Clause	Philippines	12 Jul 47	ICJ Option Clause	7UNTS229	100101
Burma	UK Great Britain	17 Oct 47	Recognition	70UNTS183	100904
ICJ Option Clause	Mexico	23 Oct 47	ICJ Option Clause	9UNTS97	100127
Multilateral		12 Nov 47	Admin Cooperation	46UNTS201	100710

PARTY ONE	PARTY TWO	DATE	TOPIC	CITATION	NUMBER
International Court of Justice (Cont.)					
Multilateral		12 Nov 47	Admin Cooperation	53UNTS49	100772
Italy	USA (United States)	02 Feb 48	General Amity	79UNTS171	101040
ICJ Option Clause	Honduras	02 Feb 48	ICJ Option Clause	15UNTS217	100236
ICJ Option Clause	Brazil	12 Feb 48	ICJ Option Clause	15UNTS221	100237
Multilateral		06 Mar 48	Water Transport	289UNTS3	104214
Jordan	UK Great Britain	15 Mar 48	General Military	77UNTS77	100994
Multilateral		17 Mar 48	General Military	19UNTS51	100304
IMF (Fund)	United Nations	15 Apr 48	IGO Operations	16UNTS325	200108
Multilateral		30 Apr 48	Dispute Settlement	30UNTS55	100449
Pakistan	Sweden	06 May 48	Air Transport	36UNTS3	100564
India	Sweden	21 May 48	Air Transport	34UNTS285	100543
ICJ Option Clause	Belgium	10 Jun 48	ICJ Option Clause	16UNTS203	100260
ICJ Option Clause	Pakistan	22 Jun 48	ICJ Option Clause	16UNTS197	100259
Multilateral		26 Jun 48	Culture	331UNTS217	104757
Ireland	USA (United States)	28 Jun 48	Direct Aid	24UNTS3	100349
Italy	USA (United States)	28 Jun 48	Direct Aid	20UNTS43	100314
France	USA (United States)	28 Jun 48	Direct Aid	19UNTS9	100302
Denmark	USA (United States)	29 Jun 48	Direct Aid	22UNTS217	100338
Greece	USA (United States)	02 Jul 48	Direct Aid	23UNTS43	100342
Belgium	USA (United States)	02 Jul 48	Direct Aid	19UNTS127	100309
Austria	USA (United States)	02 Jul 48	Direct Aid	21UNTS29	100323
Netherlands	USA (United States)	02 Jul 48	Direct Aid	20UNTS91	100315
Luxembourg	USA (United States)	03 Jul 48	Direct Aid	24UNTS35	100350
Iceland	USA (United States)	03 Jul 48	Direct Aid	20UNTS141	100316
Taiwan	USA (United States)	03 Jul 48	Direct Aid	17UNTS119	100273
Sweden	USA (United States)	03 Jul 48	Direct Aid	23UNTS101	100343
Norway	USA (United States)	03 Jul 48	Direct Aid	20UNTS185	100317
Turkey	USA (United States)	04 Jul 48	Direct Aid	24UNTS67	100351
ICJ Option Clause	Bolivia	05 Jul 48	ICJ Option Clause	16UNTS207	100261
UK Great Britain	USA (United States)	06 Jul 48	Direct Aid	22UNTS263	100339
ICJ Option Clause	Switzerland	06 Jul 48	ICJ Option Clause	17UNTS115	100272
ICJ Option Clause	Switzerland	06 Jul 48	ICJ Option Clause	17UNTS111	100271
Portugal	USA (United States)	28 Sep 48	Direct Aid	29UNTS213	100442
Greece	Lebanon	06 Oct 48	Consul/Citizenship	87UNTS351	101179
Peru	ICAO (Civil Aviat)	22 Oct 48	IGO Status/Immunit	95UNTS3	101315
Multilateral		09 Dec 48	Humanitarian	78UNTS277	101021
WHO (World Health)	Switzerland	12 Jan 49	IGO Status/Immunit	26UNTS331	200155
Italy	Lebanon	24 Jan 49	Air Transport	231UNTS241	103223
IRO (Refugee Org)	United Nations	07 Feb 49	IGO Operations	26UNTS299	200153
Belgium	France	18 Feb 49	Claims and Debts	31UNTS173	100478
Multilateral		28 Apr 49	Dispute Settlement	71UNTS101	100912
Australia	Pakistan	03 Jun 49	Air Transport	35UNTS23	100549
Philippines	Thailand	14 Jun 49	General Amity	81UNTS53	101062
Norway	Pakistan	23 Jun 49	Air Transport	35UNTS49	100550
Australia	India	11 Jul 49	Air Transport	35UNTS83	100552
Multilateral		15 Jul 49	Health/Educ/Welfare	197UNTS3	102631
Pakistan	Philippines	16 Jul 49	Air Transport	35UNTS111	100553
Belgium	Canada	30 Aug 49	Air Transport	53UNTS221	100782
Guatemala	Italy	10 Sep 49	General Amity	102UNTS53	101410
Multilateral		19 Sep 49	Land Transport	125UNTS3	101671
Lebanon	Netherlands	20 Sep 49	Air Transport	108UNTS205	101474
Iran	Netherlands	31 Oct 49	Air Transport	254UNTS257	103596
Indonesia	Netherlands	02 Nov 49	Recognition	69UNTS3	100894
India	WHO (World Health)	09 Nov 49	IGO Status/Immunit	67UNTS43	100865
Australia	Ceylon (Sri Lanka)	12 Jan 50	Air Transport	53UNTS295	100789
Ireland	USA (United States)	21 Jan 50	General Amity	206UNTS269	102792
Mexico	Netherlands	27 Jan 50	General Trade	123UNTS197	101661
United Nations	WHO (World Health)	10 Feb 50	IGO Operations	46UNTS327	200188
Iran	Pakistan	18 Feb 50	General Amity	161UNTS23	102119
ICJ Option Clause	Liechtenstein	10 Mar 50	ICJ Option Clause	51UNTS115	100758
ICJ Option Clause	Liechtenstein	10 Mar 50	ICJ Option Clause	51UNTS119	100759
Multilateral		21 Mar 50	Admin Cooperation	96UNTS271	101342
Italy	Turkey	24 Mar 50	General Amity	96UNTS207	101338
Multilateral		06 Apr 50	Admin Cooperation	119UNTS99	101610
ICJ Option Clause	Thailand	20 May 50	ICJ Option Clause	65UNTS157	100844

PARTY ONE	PARTY TWO	DATE	TOPIC	CITATION	NUMBER
International Court of Justice (Cont.)					
Haiti	WHO (World Health)	27 Jun 50	Tech Assistance	110UNTS99	101504
France	United Arab Rep	08 Aug 50	Air Transport	127UNTS293	101710
Canada	New Zealand	16 Aug 50	Air Transport	77UNTS239	101002
Greece	Philippines	28 Aug 50	General Amity	225UNTS155	103097
ICJ Option Clause	Israel	04 Sep 50	ICJ Option Clause	108UNTS239	101477
WHO (World Health)	Venezuela	11 Sep 50	Tech Assistance	110UNTS237	101513
Belgium	Mexico	16 Sep 50	General Trade	188UNTS119	102523
Iceland	WHO (World Health)	06 Oct 50	Tech Assistance	110UNTS127	101506
WHO (World Health)	Turkey	19 Oct 50	Tech Assistance	110UNTS215	101512
Nicaragua	WHO (World Health)	10 Nov 50	Tech Assistance	110UNTS155	101508
Peru	WHO (World Health)	10 Nov 50	Tech Assistance	110UNTS187	101510
Multilateral		02 Dec 50	Trusteeship	118UNTS255	200381
Multilateral		07 Dec 50	Admin Cooperation	212UNTS17	102861
Norway	UK Great Britain	15 Dec 50	General Trade	106UNTS87	101459
Philippines	WHO (World Health)	28 Dec 50	Tech Assistance	110UNTS203	101511
France	UK Great Britain	29 Dec 50	Dispute Settlement	118UNTS149	101603
France	India	02 Feb 51	Territory Boundary	203UNTS155	102744
Paraguay	WHO (World Health)	15 Feb 51	Tech Assistance	110UNTS171	101509
WHO (World Health)	United Arab Rep	25 Mar 51	IGO Status/Immunit	223UNTS87	103058
Indonesia	WHO (World Health)	28 Mar 51	Tech Assistance	103UNTS71	101425
Jordan	WHO (World Health)	03 Apr 51	Tech Assistance	110UNTS297	200367
United Nations	WMO (Meteorology)	10 Apr 51	IGO Status/Immunit	103UNTS245	200415
France	UK Great Britain	11 Apr 51	Claims and Debts	106UNTS3	101456
Canada	ICAO (Civil Aviat)	14 Apr 51	IGO Status/Immunit	96UNTS155	101335
Honduras	WHO (World Health)	20 Apr 51	Tech Assistance	110UNTS111	101505
Multilateral		25 Apr 51	Reparations	91UNTS21	101240
Colombia	WHO (World Health)	04 May 51	Tech Assistance	110UNTS83	101503
Belgium	UK Great Britain	08 May 51	Air Transport	158UNTS451	102079
India	Netherlands	24 May 51	Air Transport	108UNTS151	101471
Cambodia	WHO (World Health)	31 May 51	Tech Assistance	102UNTS279	200307
Liberia	WHO (World Health)	11 Jun 51	Tech Assistance	103UNTS83	101426
WHO (World Health)	Uruguay	11 Jun 51	Tech Assistance	128UNTS251	101724
Burma	WHO (World Health)	13 Jun 51	Sanitation	117UNTS115	101588
Denmark	Iran	18 Jun 51	Air Transport	255UNTS3	103602
IBRD (World Bank)	Switzerland	29 Jun 51	IGO Status/Immunit	216UNTS347	200529
Iraq	WHO (World Health)	01 Jul 51	Tech Assistance	110UNTS139	101507
Multilateral		02 Jul 51	Refugees	189UNTS137	102545
Burma	WHO (World Health)	09 Jul 51	Sanitation	104UNTS175	101439
Burma	WHO (World Health)	09 Jul 51	Sanitation	104UNTS187	101440
Philippines	WHO (World Health)	22 Jul 51	IGO Status/Immunit	149UNTS197	101953
Greece	USA (United States)	03 Aug 51	General Amity	224UNTS279	103080
Israel	Philippines	07 Aug 51	Air Transport	192UNTS81	102596
France	Italy	23 Aug 51	Consul/Citizenship	291UNTS143	104249
Israel	USA (United States)	23 Aug 51	General Amity	219UNTS237	102979
Multilateral		08 Sep 51	Peace/Disarmament	136UNTS45	101832
WHO (World Health)	Vietnam, South	21 Sep 51	Tech Assistance	107UNTS63	200352
Denmark	USA (United States)	01 Oct 51	General Amity	421UNTS105	106056
Bolivia	United Nations	01 Oct 51	Tech Assistance	104UNTS263	101447
ICJ Option Clause	Japan	24 Nov 51	ICJ Option Clause	137UNTS3	101842
India	WHO (World Health)	20 Dec 51	Tech Assistance	124UNTS109	101669
Jordan	USA (United States)	20 Dec 51	Tech Assistance	157UNTS69	102048
Italy	USA (United States)	28 Dec 51	General Economic	157UNTS63	102047
France	UK Great Britain	31 Dec 51	Consul/Citizenship	330UNTS145	104744
Indonesia	United Nations	06 Feb 52	Tech Assistance	121UNTS3	101621
ICJ Option Clause	Liberia	03 Mar 52	ICJ Option Clause	163UNTS117	102145
Sweden	UK Great Britain	14 Mar 52	Consul/Citizenship	202UNTS157	102731
India	WHO (World Health)	17 Apr 52	Tech Assistance	131UNTS241	101744
India	WHO (World Health)	19 Apr 52	Tech Assistance	131UNTS253	101745
ICJ Option Clause	Ceylon (Sri Lanka)	23 Apr 52	UN Charter	137UNTS7	101843
France	Israel	29 Apr 52	Air Transport	189UNTS55	102542
Norway	WHO (World Health)	09 May 52	Tech Assistance	131UNTS281	101747
Multilateral		10 May 52	Taxation	439UNTS233	106332
Multilateral		10 May 52	Admin Cooperation	439UNTS193	106330
Multilateral		10 May 52	Admin Cooperation	439UNTS217	106331
India	WHO (World Health)	04 Jun 52	Sanitation	135UNTS279	101827

International Court of Justice (Cont.)

PARTY ONE	PARTY TWO	DATE	TOPIC	CITATION	NUMBER
Multilateral		12 Jun 52	Dispute Settlement	138UNTS183	101869
Taiwan	USA (United States)	25 Jun 52	Direct Aid	136UNTS229	101837
Belgium	Israel	30 Jun 52	Air Transport	183UNTS263	102435
India	Philippines	11 Jul 52	General Amity	203UNTS73	102741
Netherlands	Pakistan	17 Jul 52	Air Transport	150UNTS277	101980
ICJ Option Clause	Cambodia	17 Jul 52	UN Charter	137UNTS11	101844
Japan	United Nations	25 Jul 52	IGO Status/Immunit	135UNTS305	200443
Ethiopia	Pakistan	29 Aug 52	Air Transport	150UNTS257	101979
Multilateral		06 Sep 52	Patents/Copyrights	216UNTS132	102937
Germany, West	Israel	10 Sep 52	Reparations	162UNTS205	102137
ICJ Option Clause	Laos	24 Oct 52	UN Charter	149UNTS285	101957
ICJ Option Clause	Vietnam, South	05 Nov 52	ICJ Option Clause	150UNTS147	101968
Multilateral		07 Nov 52	General Trade	221UNTS255	103010
Israel	Switzerland	19 Nov 52	Air Transport	232UNTS3	103226
Switzerland	UK Great Britain	16 Jan 53	Non-ILO Labor	196UNTS119	102621
Japan	Netherlands	17 Feb 53	Air Transport	192UNTS215	102602
Japan	Norway	23 Feb 53	Air Transport	192UNTS191	102601
France	Italy	14 Mar 53	Land Transport	284UNTS221	104140
Multilateral		31 Mar 53	Mass Media	435UNTS191	106280
Multilateral		31 Mar 53	Privil/Immunities	193UNTS136	102613
Finland	Sweden	09 Apr 53	Dispute Settlement	198UNTS61	102657
Greece	UK Great Britain	17 Apr 53	Consul/Citizenship	191UNTS151	102582
Multilateral		01 Jul 53	IGO Establishment	200UNTS149	102701
Multilateral		24 Jul 53	General Amity	250UNTS108	103520
Libya	UK Great Britain	29 Jul 53	General Amity	186UNTS185	102491
Libya	UK Great Britain	29 Jul 53	Status of Forces	186UNTS201	102492
USA (United States)	Venezuela	14 Aug 53	Air Transport	213UNTS99	102883
ICAO (Civil Aviat)	United Arab Rep	27 Aug 53	IGO Status/Immunit	215UNTS371	102925
Ceylon (Sri Lanka)	Netherlands	14 Sep 53	Air Transport	193UNTS21	102608
Denmark	Finland	24 Sep 53	Dispute Settlement	188UNTS283	102532
Spain	USA (United States)	26 Sep 53	Direct Aid	207UNTS93	102802
Multilateral		19 Oct 53	IGO Establishment	207UNTS189	102807
Multilateral		11 Dec 53	Non-ILO Labor	218UNTS255	102958
Multilateral		11 Dec 53	Non-ILO Labor	218UNTS153	102956
Belgium	Lebanon	24 Dec 53	Air Transport	219UNTS153	102972
ICJ Option Clause	San Marino	11 Jan 54	ICJ Option Clause	186UNTS295	102495
Multilateral		18 Jan 54	IGO Establishment	330UNTS121	104743
ICJ Option Clause	Australia	06 Feb 54	ICJ Option Clause	186UNTS77	102484
France	Sweden	16 Feb 54	General Transport	228UNTS137	103147
ICJ Option Clause	Finland	26 Feb 54	Dispute Settlement	189UNTS223	102546
Indonesia	Thailand	03 Mar 54	General Amity	213UNTS297	102893
Japan	USA (United States)	08 Mar 54	Claims and Debts	232UNTS251	103240
Mexico	UK Great Britain	20 Mar 54	Consul/Citizenship	331UNTS21	104750
ICJ Option Clause	Japan	25 Mar 54	ICJ Option Clause	188UNTS137	102524
Australia	Japan	24 May 54	Specif Claim/Waive	191UNTS125	102580
Multilateral		04 Jun 54	Customs	282UNTS249	104101
Multilateral		04 Jun 54	Customs	276UNTS191	103992
France	UNESCO (Educ/Cult)	02 Jul 54	IGO Status/Immunit	357UNTS3	105103
Saudi Arabia	UK Great Britain	30 Jul 54	Dispute Settlement	201UNTS317	102722
Norway	USA (United States)	06 Aug 54	Air Transport	222UNTS269	103034
Netherlands	UK Great Britain	11 Aug 54	Non-ILO Labor	248UNTS235	103497
Multilateral		28 Sep 54	Refugees	360UNTS117	105158
Germany, West	USA (United States)	29 Oct 54	General Amity	273UNTS3	103943
Burma	Japan	05 Nov 54	Peace/Disarmament	251UNTS201	103542
Brazil	Italy	24 Nov 54	Dispute Settlement	284UNTS325	104146
Ecuador	Netherlands	14 Dec 54	Air Transport	232UNTS115	103233
Greece	UK Great Britain	24 Feb 55	Specif Claim/Waive	209UNTS187	102827
France	Sweden	05 Mar 55	Consul/Citizenship	427UNTS133	106150
WMO (Meteorology)	Switzerland	10 Mar 55	IGO Status/Immunit	211UNTS277	200524
Ecuador	USA (United States)	29 Mar 55	Claims and Debts	261UNTS343	103732
Pakistan	USA (United States)	26 May 55	General Economic	257UNTS93	103652
Norway	Sweden	28 May 55	Scientific Project	262UNTS151	103743
Korea, South	USA (United States)	29 May 55	Milit Installation	256UNTS263	103636
ICJ Option Clause	UK Great Britain	02 Jun 55	ICJ Option Clause	211UNTS109	102849
Honduras	USA (United States)	10 Jun 55	Claims and Debts	258UNTS51	103669

International Court of Justice (Cont.)

PARTY ONE	PARTY TWO	DATE	TOPIC	CITATION	NUMBER
CERN (Nuc Resrch)	Switzerland	11 Jun 55	IGO Status/Immunit	249UNTS405	200544
Denmark	WHO (World Health)	29 Jun 55	IGO Status/Immunit	247UNTS168	103467
Syria	United Arab Rep	03 Jul 55	Air Transport	393UNTS67	105652
Germany, West	USA (United States)	07 Jul 55	Air Transport	275UNTS3	103973
ICJ Option Clause	South Africa	12 Sep 55	ICJ Option Clause	216UNTS115	102935
Italy	Switzerland	17 Sep 55	Specific Resources	291UNTS213	104257
France	Germany, West	04 Oct 55	Air Transport	353UNTS203	105044
Iceland	USA (United States)	05 Oct 55	Claims and Debts	256UNTS285	103638
Denmark	Lebanon	21 Oct 55	Air Transport	248UNTS17	103482
ICJ Option Clause	UK Great Britain	31 Oct 55	ICJ Option Clause	219UNTS179	102973
India	Japan	26 Nov 55	Air Transport	311UNTS243	104506
Multilateral		13 Dec 55	IGO Operations	529UNTS141	107660
ICJ Option Clause	Portugal	19 Dec 55	ICJ Option Clause	224UNTS275	103079
ICJ Option Clause	India	07 Jan 56	ICJ Option Clause	226UNTS235	103116
France	Japan	17 Jan 56	Air Transport	255UNTS275	103614
Australia	Japan	19 Jan 56	Air Transport	311UNTS291	104507
Nicaragua	USA (United States)	21 Jan 56	General Amity	367UNTS3	105224
India	USA (United States)	03 Feb 56	Air Transport	272UNTS75	103932
Belgium	France	01 Mar 56	Admin Cooperation	337UNTS53	104815
Germany, West	Sweden	22 Mar 56	Claims and Debts	262UNTS361	103761
Netherlands	USA (United States)	27 Mar 56	General Amity	285UNTS231	104154
Belgium	Germany, West	14 Apr 56	Air Transport	344UNTS103	104945
Indonesia	United Nations	17 Apr 56	Non-IBRD Project	233UNTS267	103266
Multilateral		30 Apr 56	Air Transport	310UNTS229	104494
Brazil	France	04 May 56	Finance	323UNTS339	104675
Japan	Philippines	09 May 56	Reparations	285UNTS3	104148
Multilateral		19 May 56	Land Transport	399UNTS189	105742
India	Thailand	12 Jun 56	Air Transport	255UNTS341	103617
France	UK Great Britain	10 Jul 56	Non-ILO Labor	326UNTS23	104708
Germany, West	UK Great Britain	30 Jul 56	Consul/Citizenship	330UNTS233	104748
ICJ Option Clause	Netherlands	01 Aug 56	ICJ Option Clause	248UNTS33	103483
Philippines	Switzerland	30 Aug 56	General Amity	293UNTS43	104284
IBRD (World Bank)	Switzerland	17 Sep 56	Loans and Credits	340UNTS311	200560
ICJ Option Clause	Israel	03 Oct 56	ICJ Option Clause	252UNTS301	103571
Colombia	USA (United States)	24 Oct 56	Air Transport	476UNTS77	106905
Multilateral		26 Oct 56	IGO Establishment	276UNTS3	103988
Korea, South	USA (United States)	28 Nov 56	General Amity	302UNTS281	104367
ICJ Option Clause	Denmark	10 Dec 56	ICJ Option Clause	257UNTS35	103646
Greece	Sweden	11 Dec 56	Dispute Settlement	299UNTS247	104316
ICJ Option Clause	Norway	17 Dec 56	ICJ Option Clause	256UNTS315	103642
Mexico	ICAO (Civil Aviat)	20 Dec 56	IGO Operations	497UNTS3	107259
Italy	UK Great Britain	29 Jan 57	Non-ILO Labor	326UNTS119	104710
Multilateral		20 Feb 57	Consul/Citizenship	309UNTS65	104468
Japan	Norway	28 Feb 57	General Economic	280UNTS87	104054
Belgium	Netherlands	07 Mar 57	Dispute Settlement	282UNTS241	104100
Dominican Republic	USA (United States)	09 Mar 57	Gen Communications	279UNTS249	104044
Netherlands	Yugoslavia	13 Mar 57	Air Transport	327UNTS227	104723
Netherlands	USA (United States)	03 Apr 57	Air Transport	410UNTS193	105904
ICJ Option Clause	Sweden	06 Apr 57	ICJ Option Clause	264UNTS221	103794
Germany, West	Yugoslavia	10 Apr 57	Air Transport	463UNTS269	106708
Denmark	Pakistan	10 Apr 57	Air Transport	302UNTS53	104353
ICJ Option Clause	UK Great Britain	18 Apr 57	ICJ Option Clause	265UNTS221	103814
Korea, South	USA (United States)	24 Apr 57	Air Transport	288UNTS219	104207
Other Unilat Decla	United Arab Rep	24 Apr 57	General Ad Hoc	265UNTS299	103821
Multilateral		29 Apr 57	Dispute Settlement	320UNTS243	104646
Australia	Germany, West	22 May 57	Air Transport	357UNTS45	105105
ICJ Option Clause	Pakistan	23 May 57	ICJ Option Clause	269UNTS77	103875
Afghanistan	Pakistan	13 Jun 57	Air Transport	327UNTS51	104717
Special Decla ICJ	United Arab Rep	18 Jun 57	ICJ Option Clause	272UNTS225	103940
Honduras	Nicaragua	22 Jun 57	Specif Claim/Waive	277UNTS159	104005
Finland	United Nations	27 Jun 57	Status of Forces	271UNTS135	103913
United Nations	Sweden	01 Jul 57	Status of Forces	271UNTS187	103914
Norway	United Nations	09 Jul 57	Status of Forces	271UNTS223	103917
Denmark	United Nations	16 Jul 57	Milit Assistance	274UNTS81	103959
Canada	United Nations	29 Jul 57	Milit Assistance	274UNTS47	103957

International Court of Justice (Cont.)

PARTY ONE	PARTY TWO	DATE	TOPIC	CITATION	NUMBER
India	United Nations	14 Aug 57	Milit Assistance	274UNTS233	103968
ICJ Option Clause	Cambodia	09 Sep 57	ICJ Option Clause	277UNTS77	103998
United Nations	Yugoslavia	01 Oct 57	Milit Assistance	277UNTS191	104006
Italy	Pakistan	05 Oct 57	Air Transport	353UNTS91	105039
IAEA (Atom Energy)	United Nations	23 Oct 57	IGO Operations	281UNTS369	200548
USA (United States)	Vietnam, South	05 Nov 57	Finance	300UNTS23	104328
Multilateral		23 Nov 57	Refugees	506UNTS125	107384
Austria	IAEA (Atom Energy)	11 Dec 57	Atomic Energy	339UNTS110	104849
ICJ Option Clause	Sudan	30 Dec 57	ICJ Option Clause	284UNTS215	104139
Indonesia	Japan	20 Jan 58	Peace/Disarmament	324UNTS227	104688
Indonesia	Japan	20 Jan 58	Reparations	324UNTS247	104689
Multilateral		03 Feb 58	IGO Establishment	381UNTS165	105471
Australia	UK Great Britain	07 Feb 58	Air Transport	335UNTS23	104776
Norway	Pakistan	05 Mar 58	Air Transport	334UNTS199	104769
Pakistan	Sweden	06 Mar 58	Air Transport	393UNTS181	105656
Netherlands	Switzerland	28 Mar 58	Non-ILO Labor	318UNTS175	104614
Multilateral		03 Apr 58	Commodity Trade	336UNTS177	104806
ICJ Option Clause	Belgium	03 Apr 58	ICJ Option Ciause	302UNTS251	104364
Belgium	Iran	14 Apr 58	Air Transport	381UNTS309	105473
Sweden	Yugoslavia	18 Apr 58	Air Transport	393UNTS225	105658
Multilateral		29 Apr 58	Specific Resources	559UNTS285	108164
Multilateral		29 Apr 58	Dispute Settlement	450UNTS169	106466
Pakistan	Portugal	07 Jun 58	Air Transport	320UNTS225	104645
Ethiopia	United Nations	18 Jun 58	IGO Operations	317UNTS101	104597
ICJ Option Clause	Finland	25 Jun 58	ICJ Option Clause	303UNTS137	104376
Belgium	Pakistan	04 Jul 58	Air Transport	387UNTS305	105569
ICJ Option Clause	Japan	15 Sep 58	ICJ Option Clause	312UNTS155	104517
Ghana	USA (United States)	30 Sep 58	Admin Cooperation	336UNTS169	104805
ICJ Option Clause	UK Great Britain	26 Nov 58	ICJ Option Clause	316UNTS59	104577
Liberia	Netherlands	28 Nov 58	Air Transport	393UNTS55	105651
IMCO (Maritime Org)	United Nations	13 Jan 59	IGO Operations	324UNTS273	200553
UK Great Britain	Yugoslavia	03 Feb 59	Air Transport	359UNTS339	105151
Japan	Yugoslavia	28 Feb 59	General Economic	341UNTS179	104883
Sudan	USA (United States)	17 Mar 59	Admin Cooperation	342UNTS13	104896
Tunisia	USA (United States)	18 Mar 59	Admin Cooperation	344UNTS179	104948
Canada	IAEA (Atom Energy)	24 Mar 59	Atomic Energy	339UNTS315	104851
Japan	IAEA (Atom Energy)	24 Mar 59	Atomic Energy	339UNTS327	104852
Morocco	UN Special Fund	04 Apr 59	Direct Aid	354UNTS347	105069
Nicaragua	USA (United States)	14 Apr 59	Admin Cooperation	343UNTS119	104922
Fed of Malaya	USA (United States)	21 Apr 59	Admin Cooperation	343UNTS3	104916
Japan	Vietnam, South	13 May 59	Reparations	373UNTS101	105317
Greece	Yugoslavia	18 Jun 59	Admin Cooperation	368UNTS69	105235
Belgium	Japan	20 Jun 59	Air Transport	411UNTS3	105911
Multilateral		01 Jul 59	IGO Status/Immunit	374UNTS147	105334
ICJ Option Clause	France	10 Jul 59	ICJ Option Clause	337UNTS65	104816
Finland	USA (United States)	22 Jul 59	Admin Cooperation	354UNTS39	105051
Ghana	UN Special Fund	12 Aug 59	Direct Aid	338UNTS203	104836
Turkey	UK Great Britain	09 Sep 59	Non-ILO Labor	424UNTS267	106113
ICJ Option Clause	India	14 Sep 59	ICJ Option Clause	340UNTS289	104871
Iran	UN Special Fund	06 Oct 59	Direct Aid	342UNTS89	104902
Poland	UN Special Fund	15 Oct 59	Direct Aid	344UNTS29	104941
India	UN Special Fund	20 Oct 59	Direct Aid	344UNTS143	104946
UN Special Fund	Yugoslavia	27 Oct 59	Direct Aid	344UNTS159	104947
Korea, South	United Nations	06 Nov 59	Other Military	346UNTS289	200565
Ecuador	UN Special Fund	10 Nov 59	Direct Aid	345UNTS3	104955
Greece	UN Special Fund	13 Nov 59	Direct Aid	345UNTS171	104966
Multilateral		19 Nov 59	IGO Operations	410UNTS156	105902
UN Special Fund	Turkey	20 Nov 59	Direct Aid	345UNTS105	104963
Germany, West	Pakistan	25 Nov 59	General Economic	457UNTS22	106575
UN Special Fund	United Arab Rep	25 Nov 59	Direct Aid	345UNTS125	104964
Israel	UN Special Fund	01 Dec 59	Direct Aid	345UNTS197	104968
Guinea	UN Special Fund	02 Dec 59	Direct Aid	345UNTS215	104969
Argentina	UN Special Fund	04 Dec 59	Direct Aid	345UNTS263	104972
Liberia	Sweden	09 Dec 59	Air Transport	464UNTS219	106716
Jordan	UN Special Fund	15 Dec 59	Direct Aid	346UNTS3	104974

International Court of Justice (Cont.)

PARTY ONE	PARTY TWO	DATE	TOPIC	CITATION	NUMBER
UN Special Fund	UK Great Britain	07 Jan 60	Direct Aid	348UNTS177	105000
Peru	UN Special Fund	19 Jan 60	Direct Aid	349UNTS83	105010
Chile	UN Special Fund	22 Jan 60	Direct Aid	351UNTS115	105020
El Salvador	USA (United States)	29 Jan 60	Claims and Debts	372UNTS3	105283
Colombia	UN Special Fund	04 Feb 60	Direct Aid	355UNTS257	105080
Bolivia	UN Special Fund	09 Feb 60	Direct Aid	351UNTS203	105024
Korea, South	USA (United States)	19 Feb 60	Claims and Debts	372UNTS109	105291
Afghanistan	UN Special Fund	21 Feb 60	Direct Aid	351UNTS93	105019
Pakistan	UN Special Fund	25 Feb 60	Direct Aid	351UNTS141	105021
Guinea	Netherlands	09 Mar 60	Air Transport	392UNTS243	105646
France	UN Special Fund	17 Mar 60	Direct Aid	354UNTS119	105059
Belgium	Switzerland	24 Mar 60	Air Transport	416UNTS81	105996
Italy	UN Special Fund	01 Apr 60	Direct Aid	354UNTS261	105066
Germany, West	Netherlands	08 Apr 60	Territory Boundary	508UNTS14	107404
UN Special Fund	Tunisia	12 Apr 60	Direct Aid	355UNTS289	105082
Libya	UN Special Fund	19 Apr 60	Direct Aid	356UNTS11	105090
Germany, West	UK Great Britain	20 Apr 60	Non-ILO Labor	449UNTS77	106453
Germany, West	UK Great Britain	20 Apr 60	Non-ILO Labor	413UNTS236	105958
UN Special Fund	Sudan	21 Apr 60	Direct Aid	356UNTS213	105097
UN Special Fund	Vietnam, South	29 Apr 60	Direct Aid	357UNTS311	200567
Laos	UN Special Fund	30 Apr 60	Tech Assistance	361UNTS171	105179
Lebanon	UN Special Fund	07 May 60	Tech Assistance	360UNTS225	105160
Nepal	USA (United States)	17 May 60	Claims and Debts	372UNTS313	105307
UN Special Fund	Thailand	04 Jun 60	Tech Assistance	360UNTS97	105157
UN Special Fund	Togo	08 Jun 60	Tech Assistance	369UNTS401	200574
Austria	UK Great Britain	24 Jun 60	Consul/Citizenship	502UNTS79	107327
Kuwait	UN Special Fund	29 Jun 60	Tech Assistance	369UNTS419	200575
Guatemala	USA (United States)	09 Aug 60	Finance	461UNTS15	106648
Netherlands	UN Special Fund	12 Aug 60	Tech Assistance	372UNTS331	105309
Mexico	USA (United States)	15 Aug 60	Air Transport	402UNTS177	105786
Multilateral		16 Aug 60	Recognition	382UNTS8	105476
ICJ Option Clause	Pakistan	12 Sep 60	ICJ Option Clause	374UNTS127	105332
Brazil	UN Special Fund	16 Sep 60	Tech Assistance	375UNTS3	105351
Pakistan	IBRD (World Bank)	19 Sep 60	IBRD Project	444UNTS207	106370
Taiwan	UN Special Fund	20 Sep 60	Tech Assistance	375UNTS29	105352
Belgium	Jordan	19 Oct 60	Air Transport	479UNTS277	106959
El Salvador	UN Special Fund	24 Oct 60	Direct Aid	377UNTS171	105400
Belgium	Congo (Zaire)	15 Nov 60	Finance	394UNTS79	105670
Nepal	UN Special Fund	17 Nov 60	Direct Aid	380UNTS289	105461
Guatemala	UN Special Fund	17 Nov 60	Direct Aid	383UNTS67	105495
Cambodia	UN Special Fund	24 Nov 60	Direct Aid	382UNTS255	105487
Multilateral		14 Dec 60	Education	429UNTS93	106193
Japan	Pakistan	18 Dec 60	General Amity	423UNTS197	106093
Honduras	UN Special Fund	20 Dec 60	Direct Aid	383UNTS103	105497
Multilateral		30 Dec 60	Atomic Energy	395UNTS241	105689
Burma	UN Special Fund	03 Jan 61	Direct Aid	387UNTS219	105564
Costa Rica	UN Special Fund	10 Jan 61	Direct Aid	389UNTS253	105597
Sudan	UK Great Britain	16 Jan 61	Air Transport	424UNTS233	106112
Canada	USA (United States)	17 Jan 61	Specific Resources	542UNTS224	107894
UN Special Fund	Saudi Arabia	19 Jan 61	Direct Aid	396UNTS27	105692
Nicaragua	UN Special Fund	20 Jan 61	Direct Aid	387UNTS15	105555
Chad	UN Special Fund	23 Jan 61	Direct Aid	390UNTS69	105603
UN Special Fund	Somalia	28 Jan 61	Direct Aid	388UNTS75	105573
Gabon	UN Special Fund	02 Feb 61	Direct Aid	387UNTS289	105568
Nigeria	UN Special Fund	10 Feb 61	Direct Aid	390UNTS85	105604
Belgium	USA (United States)	21 Feb 61	General Amity	480UNTS149	106967
Mexico	UN Special Fund	23 Feb 61	Direct Aid	388UNTS151	105576
Cyprus	UN Special Fund	24 Feb 61	Direct Aid	389UNTS3	105588
Multilateral		08 Mar 61	Scientific Project	396UNTS255	200584
Belgium	UK Great Britain	08 Mar 61	Consul/Citizenship	523UNTS17	107554
Panama	UN Special Fund	09 Mar 61	Direct Aid	396UNTS3	105691
Cuba	UN Special Fund	10 Mar 61	Direct Aid	390UNTS35	105601
Multilateral		30 Mar 61	Sanitation	520UNTS151	107515
USA (United States)	Vietnam, South	03 Apr 61	General Amity	424UNTS137	106106
Multilateral		10 Apr 61	Atomic Energy	402UNTS281	105791

International Court of Justice (Cont.)

PARTY ONE	PARTY TWO	DATE	TOPIC	CITATION	NUMBER
Norway	IAEA (Atom Energy)	10 Apr 61	Scientific Project	402UNTS255	105790
Multilateral		18 Apr 61	Dispute Settlement	500UNTS243	107312
Ceylon (Sri Lanka)	UN Special Fund	03 May 61	Direct Aid	395UNTS217	105687
Honduras	IDA (Devel Assoc)	12 May 61	Loans and Credits	414UNTS180	105973
Sierra Leone	USA (United States)	19 May 61	Admin Cooperation	409UNTS251	105890
Cameroon	UN Special Fund	13 Jun 61	Direct Aid	397UNTS297	105713
Guinea	Sweden	17 Jun 61	Air Transport	465UNTS236	106729
Paraguay	UN Special Fund	22 Jun 61	Direct Aid	399UNTS117	105738
UN Special Fund	Upper Volta	26 Jun 61	Direct Aid	400UNTS3	105744
Haiti	UN Special Fund	28 Jun 61	Direct Aid	399UNTS171	105741
Philippines	UN Special Fund	28 Jun 61	Direct Aid	399UNTS141	105739
Mali	UN Special Fund	21 Jul 61	Direct Aid	401UNTS141	105768
Fed of Malaya	UN Special Fund	25 Jul 61	Direct Aid	401UNTS159	105769
UN Special Fund	Yemen	02 Aug 61	Direct Aid	402UNTS43	105777
Jordan	Netherlands	24 Aug 61	Air Transport	466UNTS3	106733
Ivory Coast	UN Special Fund	29 Aug 61	Direct Aid	406UNTS129	105844
Liberia	Switzerland	31 Aug 61	Air Transport	559UNTS215	108160
UN Special Fund	Sierra Leone	02 Oct 61	Direct Aid	422UNTS131	106073
Multilateral		04 Oct 61	Scientific Project	412UNTS210	105934
IAEA (Atom Energy)	Yugoslavia	04 Oct 61	Scientific Project	412UNTS226	105935
Multilateral		26 Oct 61	Patents/Copyrights	496UNTS43	107247
Mauritania	UN Special Fund	07 Nov 61	Direct Aid	412UNTS240	105936
Congo (Brazzaville)	UN Special Fund	09 Nov 61	Direct Aid	413UNTS58	105940
Congo (Zaire)	United Nations	27 Nov 61	IGO Status/Immunit	414UNTS229	105975
Ivory Coast	USA (United States)	01 Dec 61	Claims and Debts	462UNTS221	106681
Germany, West	Thailand	13 Dec 61	Claims and Debts	541UNTS181	107870
UN Special Fund	Senegal	16 Dec 61	Direct Aid	425UNTS97	106121
Malagasy	UN Special Fund	05 Jan 62	Direct Aid	419UNTS29	106028
Luxembourg	USA (United States)	23 Feb 62	General Amity	474UNTS3	106868
Pakistan	IAEA (Atom Energy)	05 Mar 62	Scientific Project	425UNTS17	106115
Multilateral		05 Mar 62	Scientific Project	425UNTS3	106114
Dahomey	UN Special Fund	28 Mar 62	Tech Assistance	424UNTS55	106099
IAEA (Atom Energy)	USA (United States)	30 Mar 62	Specific Property	442UNTS49	106338
Taiwan	Malagasy	04 Apr 62	General Amity	463UNTS195	106703
UN Special Fund	Uruguay	04 May 62	Direct Aid	429UNTS143	106196
Japan	United Arab Rep	10 May 62	Air Transport	498UNTS69	107278
Dominican Republic	UN Special Fund	06 Jun 62	Direct Aid	429UNTS169	106197
Multilateral		14 Jun 62	IGO Establishment	528UNTS33	107634
Guinea	Norway	21 Jun 62	Air Transport	466UNTS81	106738
Multilateral		27 Jun 62	Atomic Energy	463UNTS17	106690
Liberia	Norway	29 Jun 62	Air Transport	466UNTS95	106739
UN Special Fund	Syria	07 Jul 62	Direct Aid	443UNTS3	106355
UN Special Fund	Tanganyika	17 Jul 62	Direct Aid	435UNTS237	106281
Congo (Brazzaville)	USA (United States)	01 Sep 62	Claims and Debts	459UNTS117	106616
Multilateral		14 Sep 62	IGO Status/Immunit	494UNTS219	107236
Japan	Kuwait	06 Oct 62	Air Transport	498UNTS235	107284
Japan	UN Special Fund	31 Oct 62	Tech Assistance	444UNTS171	106368
Japan	UK Great Britain	14 Nov 62	General Trade	478UNTS29	106934
Algeria	UN Special Fund	15 Nov 62	Tech Assistance	452UNTS243	106512
Ivory Coast	Switzerland	17 Nov 62	Air Transport	499UNTS3	107289
Multilateral		10 Dec 62	Culture	521UNTS231	107525
Austria	Yugoslavia	11 Dec 62	Land Transport	546UNTS3	107938
Korea, South	USA (United States)	08 Jan 63	Consul/Citizenship	493UNTS105	107211
Trinidad/Tobago	USA (United States)	15 Jan 63	Finance	471UNTS141	106829
France	USA (United States)	22 Jan 63	Dispute Settlement	473UNTS3	106849
Sudan	Switzerland	18 Feb 63	Air Transport	563UNTS281	108215
UN Special Fund	Uganda	22 Mar 63	Direct Aid	456UNTS466	106572
ICJ Option Clause	Somalia	25 Mar 63	ICJ Option Clause	458UNTS143	106597
Burma	Japan	29 Mar 63	General Aid	518UNTS3	107490
Multilateral		20 Apr 63	IGO Establishment	495UNTS3	107239
Multilateral		24 Apr 63	Consul/Citizenship	596UNTS261	108638
Multilateral		24 Apr 63	Consul/Citizenship	596UNTS469	108639
Multilateral		24 Apr 63	Consul/Citizenship	596UNTS487	108640
UN Special Fund	Trinidad/Tobago	06 May 63	Direct Aid	463UNTS93	106695
Jamaica	UN Special Fund	22 May 63	Direct Aid	489UNTS191	107140

International Court of Justice (Cont.)

PARTY ONE	PARTY TWO	DATE	TOPIC	CITATION	NUMBER
Netherlands	Tunisia	23 May 63	Finance	523UNTS237	107558
Netherlands	UN Special Fund	24 May 63	Direct Aid	466UNTS289	106750
UN Special Fund	Western Samoa	05 Jun 63	Direct Aid	467UNTS463	200601
New Zealand	UN Special Fund	28 Jun 63	Non-IBRD Project	470UNTS3	106792
Finland	IAEA (Atom Energy)	02 Jul 63	Atomic Energy	490UNTS403	107167
Congo (Zaire)	UN Special Fund	26 Jul 63	Direct Aid	474UNTS137	106878
Cameroon	UK Great Britain	29 Jul 63	General Economic	478UNTS148	106935
Burundi	UN Special Fund	22 Aug 63	Direct Aid	476UNTS49	106903
Multilateral		23 Sep 63	Atomic Energy	488UNTS99	107122
ICJ Option Clause	Uganda	03 Oct 63	ICJ Option Clause	479UNTS35	106946
Italy	IAEA (Atom Energy)	11 Oct 63	IGO Establishment	639UNTS25	109142
Multilateral		26 Oct 63	Water Transport	587UNTS9	108506
Central Afri Rep	UN Special Fund	30 Oct 63	Direct Aid	481UNTS247	106985
ICJ Option Clause	UK Great Britain	27 Nov 63	ICJ Option Clause	482UNTS187	106995
Multilateral		03 Dec 63	IGO Establishment	529UNTS217	107663
IAEA (Atom Energy)	Yugoslavia	07 Dec 63	Scientific Project	501UNTS273	107322
Multilateral		18 Dec 63	Atomic Energy	490UNTS383	107166
Somalia	USA (United States)	08 Jan 64	Claims and Debts	505UNTS165	107372
Denmark	Yugoslavia	11 Feb 64	Air Transport	511UNTS241	107437
Rwanda	UN Special Fund	18 Mar 64	Direct Aid	491UNTS3	107170
Cyprus	United Nations	31 Mar 64	IGO Status/Immunit	492UNTS57	107187
Norway	Yugoslavia	15 Apr 64	Air Transport	602UNTS177	108712
United Arab Rep	USA (United States)	05 May 64	Air Transport	531UNTS229	107706
Multilateral		06 May 64	IGO Operations	514UNTS71	107442
Ireland	UN Special Fund	03 Jun 64	Direct Aid	496UNTS205	107253
Mali	USA (United States)	09 Jun 64	Claims and Debts	530UNTS133	107678
Multilateral		11 Jun 64	Atomic Energy	525UNTS61	107584
Multilateral		15 Jun 64	Atomic Energy	573UNTS85	108324
New Zealand	USA (United States)	24 Jun 64	Air Transport	524UNTS101	107568
Mauritania	USA (United States)	03 Jul 64	Finance	532UNTS307	107724
Belgium	Tunisia	15 Jul 64	General Economic	561UNTS297	108190
Multilateral		28 Jul 64	IGO Operations	555UNTS183	108113
Eur Space Research	Sweden	29 Jul 64	IGO Operations	528UNTS81	107636
France	Eur Space Research	10 Aug 64	IGO Operations	528UNTS135	107637
IAEA (Atom Energy)	United Arab Rep	17 Sep 64	Atomic Energy	525UNTS19	107581
Multilateral		18 Sep 64	IGO Operations	556UNTS25	108117
Multilateral		18 Sep 64	IGO Operations	555UNTS205	108114
Multilateral		21 Sep 64	IGO Operations	555UNTS227	108115
Multilateral		30 Sep 64	IGO Operations	556UNTS3	108116
Australia	UN Special Fund	30 Sep 64	Scientific Project	510UNTS277	107419
Kenya	UN Special Fund	01 Oct 64	IGO Operations	511UNTS181	107433
Malawi	UN Special Fund	24 Oct 64	Direct Aid	514UNTS235	200609
Italy	ILO (Labor Org)	24 Oct 64	IGO Establishment	541UNTS217	107871
Romania	UN Special Fund	24 Oct 64	IGO Operations	519UNTS29	107500
Argentina	IAEA (Atom Energy)	02 Dec 64	Atomic Energy	525UNTS29	107582
Multilateral		02 Dec 64	Atomic Energy	525UNTS51	107583
Ethiopia	ILO (Labor Org)	10 Dec 64	IGO Establishment	521UNTS217	107524
UN Special Fund	Zambia	15 Dec 64	Direct Aid	522UNTS3	107532
Laos	USA (United States)	29 Dec 64	Claims and Debts	542UNTS23	107876
IAEA (Atom Energy)	United Arab Rep	14 Jan 65	Atomic Energy	603UNTS45	108723
Malta	Switzerland	20 Jan 65	General Trade	548UNTS193	107978
Belgium	Congo (Zaire)	06 Feb 65	Claims and Debts	540UNTS227	107852
Multilateral		24 Feb 65	IGO Operations	556UNTS47	108118
Multilateral		26 Feb 65	IGO Operations	556UNTS69	108119
Multilateral		09 Mar 65	Water Transport	591UNTS265	108564
ICJ Option Clause	Kenya	12 Apr 65	ICJ Option Clause	531UNTS113	107697
UK Great Britain	Yugoslavia	21 Apr 65	Consul/Citizenship	595UNTS189	108620
Ivory Coast	Netherlands	26 Apr 65	General Economic	634UNTS81	109053
Uganda	USA (United States)	29 May 65	Claims and Debts	546UNTS209	107948
British Guiana	USA (United States)	29 May 65	Loans and Credits	605UNTS87	108761
USA (United States)	Upper Volta	18 Jun 65	Finance	549UNTS133	107996
Multilateral		18 Jun 65	Atomic Energy	573UNTS3	108320
Multilateral		23 Jun 65	Atomic Energy	548UNTS241	107981
Austria	Petrol Export Org	24 Jun 65	IGO Operations	589UNTS135	108540
UN Special Fund	Spain	30 Jun 65	Direct Aid	544UNTS159	107918

PARTY ONE	PARTY TWO	DATE	TOPIC	CITATION	NUMBER
International Court of Justice (Cont.)					
Multilateral		02 Jul 65	Sanitation	592UNTS215	108575
Cameroon	Netherlands	06 Jul 65	Tech Assistance	571UNTS63	108299
Switzerland	UK Great Britain	07 Jul 65	Dispute Settlement	605UNTS205	108765
Multilateral		08 Jul 65	General Trade	597UNTS3	108641
Australia	Eur Space Vehicle	13 Jul 65	IGO Operations	543UNTS183	107902
Multilateral		24 Sep 65	Atomic Energy	556UNTS141	108124
Afghanistan	IAEA (Atom Energy)	24 Sep 65	Atomic Energy	556UNTS101	108121
Morocco	IAEA (Atom Energy)	24 Sep 65	Atomic Energy	556UNTS109	108122
Multilateral		04 Dec 65	IGO Establishment	571UNTS123	108303
Mongolia	UN Special Fund	26 Jan 66	Direct Aid	552UNTS201	108055
IAEA (Atom Energy)	Turkey	08 Feb 66	Atomic Energy	573UNTS75	108323
Canada	United Nations	21 Feb 66	IGO Operations	555UNTS119	108107
Austria	United Nations	24 Feb 66	IGO Operations	557UNTS129	108131
Pakistan	IAEA (Atom Energy)	15 Mar 66	Claims and Debts	588UNTS261	108530
Romania	IAEA (Atom Energy)	22 Apr 66	Atomic Energy	603UNTS23	108721
ICJ Option Clause	France	16 May 66	ICJ Option Clause	562UNTS299	108196
Bulgaria	UN Special Fund	26 May 66	General Aid	563UNTS71	108205
ICJ Option Clause	Gambia	14 Jun 66	ICJ Option Clause	565UNTS21	108232
IAEA (Atom Energy)	UK Great Britain	20 Jun 66	IGO Operations	588UNTS269	108531
Multilateral		20 Jun 66	Atomic Energy	573UNTS41	108322
Brazil	Denmark	08 Jul 66	Loans and Credits	581UNTS95	108435
Denmark	Malawi	01 Sep 66	Loans and Credits	586UNTS3	108493
UN Special Fund	Singapore	23 Sep 66	General Aid	573UNTS115	108326
IAEA (Atom Energy)	USA (United States)	26 Sep 66	Atomic Energy	589UNTS3	108532
Multilateral		28 Sep 66	Specif Goods/Equip	589UNTS41	108534
IAEA (Atom Energy)	USA (United States)	09 Dec 66	Atomic Energy	589UNTS55	108535
India	IAEA (Atom Energy)	09 Dec 66	Atomic Energy	603UNTS35	108722
Asian Devel Bank	Philippines	22 Dec 66	IGO Establishment	615UNTS375	108887
Australia	UN Special Fund	06 Feb 67	IGO Operations	590UNTS3	108543
Multilateral		14 Feb 67	General Military	634UNTS281	109068
Hungary	UN Special Fund	28 Apr 67	General Aid	595UNTS171	108619
IAEA (Atom Energy)	USA (United States)	07 Jun 67	IGO Operations	614UNTS109	108866
Denmark	Peru	20 Jun 67	Loans and Credits	0UNTS0	109446
Multilateral		23 Jun 67	IGO Operations	614UNTS185	108871
Malta	UK Great Britain	10 Jul 67	Air Transport	619UNTS11	108936
Multilateral		26 Jul 67	IGO Operations	614UNTS217	108872
Mexico	IAEA (Atom Energy)	18 Aug 67	IGO Operations	614UNTS123	108867
Multilateral		23 Aug 67	IGO Operations	614UNTS145	108869
Botswana	UN Special Fund	12 Oct 67	Direct Aid	607UNTS37	108794
Multilateral		12 Oct 67	Direct Aid	607UNTS2	108792
Denmark	Iran	02 Nov 67	Loans and Credits	638UNTS217	109138
ICJ Option Clause	Mauritius	23 Sep 68	ICJ Option Clause	0UNTS0	109251
ICJ Option Clause	UK Great Britain	01 Jan 69	ICJ Option Clause	0UNTS0	109370
International Development Association					
Multilateral		26 Jan 60	IGO Establishment	439UNTS249	106333
Colombia	IBRD (World Bank)	28 Aug 61	IBRD Project	416UNTS23	105993
IBRD (World Bank)	Tunisia	03 Jul 63	IBRD Project	480UNTS209	106970
Ecuador	IBRD (World Bank)	26 May 64	IBRD Project	534UNTS113	107758
Paraguay	IBRD (World Bank)	16 Dec 64	IBRD Project	549UNTS173	107999
Taiwan	IBRD (World Bank)	28 Apr 65	IBRD Project	549UNTS145	107998
Multilateral		22 Jul 65	IBRD Project	561UNTS333	200618
IBRD (World Bank)	Thailand	19 Oct 66	IBRD Project	594UNTS347	108609
International Emergency Food Organization					
Argentina	USA (United States)	19 Sep 46	Commodity Trade	7UNTS131	100095
Netherlands	Thailand	30 Jan 47	General Amity	247UNTS353	103480
Czechoslovakia	Greece	30 Jul 47	Finance	185UNTS115	102463
International Exhibition Bureau					
Multilateral		10 May 48	Culture	289UNTS111	104215
International Finance Corporation					
Multilateral		10 Feb 47	Peace/Disarmament	49UNTS3	100747
Multilateral		25 May 55	IGO Establishment	264UNTS117	103791
IBRD (World Bank)	United Nations	20 Feb 57	IGO Operations	265UNTS312	200546
Israel	USA (United States)	06 Nov 58	US Agri Commod Aid	336UNTS275	104810

PARTY ONE	PARTY TWO	DATE	TOPIC	CITATION	NUMBER
International Fisheries Commission					
Canada	USA (United States)	02 Mar 53	Specific Resources	222UNTS77	103024
International Halibut Commission					
Canada	USA (United States)	02 Mar 53	Specific Resources	222UNTS77	103024
International Labour Organization					
Multilateral		28 Nov 19	ILO Labor	38UNTS67	100587
Multilateral		28 Nov 19	ILO Labor	38UNTS81	100588
Multilateral		28 Nov 19	ILO Labor	38UNTS93	100589
Multilateral		28 Nov 19	ILO Labor	38UNTS41	100585
Multilateral		28 Nov 19	ILO Labor	38UNTS17	100584
Multilateral		29 Nov 19	ILO Labor	38UNTS53	100586
Multilateral		09 Jul 20	ILO Labor	38UNTS109	100590
Multilateral		09 Jul 20	ILO Labor	38UNTS119	100591
Multilateral		10 Jul 20	ILO Labor	38UNTS129	100592
Multilateral		11 Nov 21	ILO Labor	38UNTS203	100598
Multilateral		11 Nov 21	ILO Labor	38UNTS217	100599
Multilateral		12 Nov 21	ILO Labor	38UNTS165	100595
Multilateral		12 Nov 21	ILO Labor	38UNTS153	100594
Multilateral		16 Nov 21	ILO Labor	38UNTS143	100593
Multilateral		17 Nov 21	ILO Labor	38UNTS187	100597
Multilateral		19 Nov 21	ILO Labor	38UNTS175	100596
Multilateral		05 Jun 25	ILO Labor	38UNTS257	100602
Multilateral		08 Jun 25	ILO Labor	38UNTS269	100603
Multilateral		10 Jun 25	ILO Labor	38UNTS229	100600
Multilateral		10 Jun 25	ILO Labor	38UNTS243	100601
Multilateral		05 Jun 26	ILO Labor	38UNTS281	100604
Multilateral		23 Jun 26	ILO Labor	38UNTS315	100606
Multilateral		24 Jun 26	ILO Labor	38UNTS295	100605
Multilateral		15 Jun 27	ILO Labor	38UNTS327	100607
Multilateral		15 Jun 27	ILO Labor	38UNTS343	100608
Multilateral		16 Jun 28	ILO Labor	39UNTS3	100609
Multilateral		26 Jun 28	ILO Labor	39UNTS15	100610
Multilateral		21 Jun 29	ILO Labor	39UNTS27	100611
Multilateral		28 Jun 30	ILO Labor	39UNTS85	100613
Multilateral		28 Jun 30	ILO Labor	39UNTS55	100612
Multilateral		27 Apr 32	ILO Labor	39UNTS103	100614
Multilateral		30 Apr 32	ILO Labor	39UNTS133	100615
Multilateral		29 Jun 33	ILO Labor	39UNTS211	100619
Multilateral		29 Jun 33	ILO Labor	39UNTS285	100622
Multilateral		29 Jun 33	ILO Labor	39UNTS189	100618
Multilateral		29 Jun 33	ILO Labor	39UNTS165	100617
Multilateral		29 Jun 33	ILO Labor	39UNTS259	100621
Multilateral		29 Jun 33	ILO Labor	39UNTS235	100620
Multilateral		29 Jun 33	ILO Labor	39UNTS151	100616
Multilateral		19 Jun 34	ILO Labor	40UNTS3	100623
Multilateral		21 Jun 34	ILO Labor	40UNTS33	100625
Multilateral		21 Jun 34	ILO Labor	40UNTS19	100624
Multilateral		23 Jun 34	ILO Labor	40UNTS45	100626
Multilateral		21 Jun 35	ILO Labor	40UNTS63	100627
Multilateral		22 Jun 35	ILO Labor	271UNTS199	103915
Multilateral		22 Jun 35	ILO Labor	40UNTS73	100628
Multilateral		25 Jun 35	ILO Labor	40UNTS97	100629
Multilateral		20 Jun 36	ILO Labor	40UNTS109	100630
Multilateral		24 Jun 36	ILO Labor	40UNTS137	100631
Multilateral		24 Oct 36	ILO Labor	40UNTS169	100633
Multilateral		24 Oct 36	ILO Labor	40UNTS187	100634
Multilateral		24 Oct 36	ILO Labor	40UNTS205	100635
Multilateral		24 Oct 36	ILO Labor	40UNTS153	100632
Multilateral		22 Jun 37	ILO Labor	40UNTS217	100636
Multilateral		23 Jun 37	ILO Labor	40UNTS233	100637
Multilateral		20 Jun 38	ILO Labor	40UNTS255	100638
Multilateral		27 Jun 39	ILO Labor	40UNTS311	100640
Multilateral		27 Jun 39	ILO Labor	40UNTS281	100639
Multilateral		28 Jun 39	ILO Labor	209UNTS39	102820

PARTY ONE	PARTY TWO	DATE	TOPIC	CITATION	NUMBER
International Labour Organization (Cont.)					
Multilateral		07 Nov 45	IGO Establishment	2UNTS17	100018
Multilateral		27 Jun 46	ILO Labor	264UNTS163	103792
Multilateral		27 Jun 46	ILO Labor	164UNTS37	102157
Multilateral		29 Jun 46	ILO Labor	214UNTS233	102901
Multilateral		29 Jun 46	ILO Labor	94UNTS11	101303
League of Nations	United Nations	19 Jul 46	Specific Property	1UNTS109	200002
Multilateral		09 Oct 46	IGO Establishment	15UNTS35	100229
Multilateral		09 Oct 46	ILO Labor	38UNTS3	100583
Multilateral		19 Jun 47	ILO Labor	171UNTS329	102235
Multilateral		11 Jul 47	ILO Labor	161UNTS113	102125
Multilateral		11 Jul 47	ILO Labor	218UNTS345	102961
Multilateral		11 Jul 47	ILO Labor	214UNTS33	102898
Multilateral		09 Jul 48	ILO Labor	81UNTS147	101070
Multilateral		18 Jun 49	ILO Labor	160UNTS223	102109
Multilateral		29 Jun 49	ILO Labor	138UNTS207	101870
Multilateral		01 Jul 49	ILO Labor	138UNTS225	101871
Multilateral		01 Jul 49	ILO Labor	96UNTS237	101340
Multilateral		01 Jul 49	ILO Labor	96UNTS257	101341
Multilateral		01 Jul 49	Non-ILO Labor	120UNTS71	101616
United Nations	WHO (World Health)	10 Feb 50	IGO Operations	46UNTS327	200188
Multilateral		27 Jul 50	Non-ILO Labor	166UNTS73	102186
Jordan	United Nations	29 Mar 51	Tech Assistance	137UNTS267	200448
Multilateral		28 Jun 51	ILO Labor	172UNTS159	102244
Multilateral		29 Jun 51	ILO Labor	165UNTS303	102181
Bolivia	United Nations	01 Oct 51	Tech Assistance	104UNTS263	101447
Multilateral		28 Jun 52	ILO Labor	214UNTS321	102907
Multilateral		28 Jun 52	ILO Labor	210UNTS132	102838
Multilateral		11 Dec 53	Non-ILO Labor	218UNTS211	102957
Multilateral		21 May 54	Non-ILO Labor	345UNTS285	104973
Multilateral		21 Jun 55	ILO Labor	305UNTS265	104423
Multilateral		20 Jun 56	Admin Cooperation	268UNTS3	103850
Multilateral		09 Jul 56	Non-ILO Labor	314UNTS3	104539
Multilateral		07 Sep 56	Humanitarian	266UNTS3	103822
Multilateral		01 Mar 57	Tech Assistance	264UNTS94	103790
Multilateral		24 May 57	Tech Assistance	268UNTS270	103861
Multilateral		26 Jun 57	ILO Labor	328UNTS247	104738
Multilateral		26 Jun 57	ILO Labor	325UNTS279	104704
Multilateral		29 Apr 58	Water Transport	450UNTS11	106465
Multilateral		13 May 58	ILO Labor	389UNTS277	105598
Multilateral		25 Jun 58	ILO Labor	362UNTS31	105181
Multilateral		19 Jun 59	ILO Labor	413UNTS148	105949
Multilateral		19 Jun 59	ILO Labor	413UNTS168	105951
Multilateral		19 Jun 59	ILO Labor	413UNTS158	105950
Multilateral		26 Jun 61	ILO Labor	423UNTS11	106083
Multilateral		18 Oct 61	IGO Establishment	529UNTS89	107659
Multilateral		26 Oct 61	Patents/Copyrights	496UNTS43	107247
Multilateral		22 Jun 62	IGO Establishment	466UNTS323	106752
Multilateral		25 Jun 63	ILO Labor	532UNTS159	107717
Multilateral		01 Dec 64	Water Transport	550UNTS133	108012
International Monetary Fund					
UK Great Britain	USA (United States)	06 Dec 45	Finance	126UNTS13	101679
Multilateral		27 Dec 45	IGO Establishment	2UNTS39	100020
Canada	UK Great Britain	06 Mar 46	Finance	20UNTS13	100312
Greece	USA (United States)	16 May 46	Direct Aid	184UNTS230	102451
France	USA (United States)	28 May 46	Milit Assistance	84UNTS59	101119
Belgium	USA (United States)	24 Sep 46	Claims and Debts	132UNTS80	101753
Taiwan	USA (United States)	04 Nov 46	General Amity	25UNTS69	100359
South Africa	UK Great Britain	09 Oct 47	Finance	17UNTS239	100278
Multilateral		30 Oct 47	General Economic	55UNTS188	100814
Belgium	UK Great Britain	14 Nov 47	Finance	25UNTS269	100367
France	Lebanon	24 Jan 48	Finance	173UNTS99	102263
India	UK Great Britain	15 Feb 48	Finance	134UNTS70	101796
IBRD (World Bank)	United Nations	15 Apr 48	IGO Operations	16UNTS341	200109
France	UK Great Britain	19 Apr 48	Status of Forces	83UNTS201	101109

PARTY ONE	PARTY TWO	DATE	TOPIC	CITATION	NUMBER
International Monetary Fund (Cont.)					
Ceylon (Sri Lanka)	UK Great Britain	30 Apr 48	Finance	182UNTS2	102421
Italy	USA (United States)	28 Jun 48	Direct Aid	20UNTS43	100314
Denmark	USA (United States)	29 Jun 48	Direct Aid	22UNTS217	100338
India	Pakistan	30 Jun 48	Finance	29UNTS199	100441
Austria	USA (United States)	02 Jul 48	Direct Aid	21UNTS29	100323
Netherlands	USA (United States)	02 Jul 48	Direct Aid	20UNTS91	100315
Norway	USA (United States)	03 Jul 48	Direct Aid	20UNTS185	100317
Iceland	USA (United States)	03 Jul 48	Direct Aid	20UNTS141	100316
UK Great Britain	USA (United States)	06 Jul 48	Direct Aid	22UNTS263	100339
United Arab Rep	UK Great Britain	31 Mar 49	Finance	83UNTS139	101106
Belgium	Bolivia	26 Apr 49	Finance	34UNTS103	100530
Ethiopia	USA (United States)	20 May 49	Milit Assistance	89UNTS99	101211
Multilateral		05 Aug 49	Finance	88UNTS229	101195
Multilateral		10 Aug 49	Finance	45UNTS3	100689
Czechoslovakia	UK Great Britain	18 Aug 49	Finance	86UNTS129	101155
Argentina	Norway	09 Sep 49	Finance	42UNTS125	100646
Denmark	Germany, West	15 Dec 49	Finance	51UNTS11	100749
Sweden	UK Great Britain	30 Dec 49	Finance	87UNTS59	101166
Norway	UK Great Britain	06 Nov 50	Finance	88UNTS257	101197
Sweden	UK Great Britain	10 Nov 50	Finance	88UNTS265	101198
Germany, West	UK Great Britain	09 Dec 50	Finance	88UNTS247	101196
Italy	UK Great Britain	21 Dec 50	Finance	175UNTS187	102301
Austria	UK Great Britain	31 Jan 51	Finance	88UNTS107	101187
United Arab Rep	UK Great Britain	01 Jul 51	Finance	249UNTS143	103504
Canada	France	04 Jul 51	Reparations	233UNTS101	103253
Portugal	UK Great Britain	20 Jul 51	Finance	105UNTS61	101453
Greece	USA (United States)	03 Aug 51	General Amity	224UNTS279	103080
France	UK Great Britain	20 Aug 51	Finance	108UNTS263	101479
Israel	USA (United States)	23 Aug 51	General Amity	219UNTS237	102979
Japan	USA (United States)	28 Aug 51	Education	147UNTS81	101930
Japan	UK Great Britain	31 Aug 51	Finance	149UNTS227	101955
Pakistan	UK Great Britain	29 Sep 51	Finance	134UNTS183	101798
Bolivia	United Nations	01 Oct 51	Tech Assistance	104UNTS263	101447
Jordan	USA (United States)	12 Feb 52	Tech Assistance	168UNTS25	102211
Israel	USA (United States)	27 Feb 52	Direct Aid	177UNTS123	102314
Japan	USA (United States)	28 Feb 52	Milit Assistance	208UNTS255	102817
South Africa	USA (United States)	26 Mar 52	Education	165UNTS187	102176
Israel	USA (United States)	09 May 52	Tech Assistance	177UNTS63	102309
Finland	USA (United States)	02 Jul 52	Education	165UNTS203	102177
Germany, West	USA (United States)	18 Jul 52	Education	165UNTS167	102175
UK Great Britain	Yugoslavia	20 Aug 52	Finance	158UNTS439	102077
Greece	Italy	04 Feb 53	Finance	189UNTS295	102552
Germany, West	USA (United States)	27 Feb 53	Claims and Debts	205UNTS103	102771
United Arab Rep	USA (United States)	19 Mar 53	Tech Assistance	215UNTS17	102909
Japan	USA (United States)	02 Apr 53	General Amity	206UNTS143	102788
Germany, West	UK Great Britain	22 May 53	Finance	172UNTS179	102246
India	UK Great Britain	20 Jul 53	Finance	196UNTS251	102628
Spain	USA (United States)	26 Sep 53	Direct Aid	207UNTS93	102802
Multilateral		01 Oct 53	Commodity Trade	258UNTS153	103677
Brazil	UK Great Britain	01 Oct 53	Claims and Debts	183UNTS207	102430
ECSC (Coal/Steel)	USA (United States)	23 Apr 54	Loans and Credits	229UNTS229	103170
Ethiopia	USA (United States)	01 Jun 54	Direct Aid	232UNTS311	103245
Germany, West	USA (United States)	29 Oct 54	General Amity	273UNTS3	103943
Pakistan	USA (United States)	11 Jan 55	Milit Assistance	251UNTS111	103537
Finland	USA (United States)	06 May 55	US Agri Commod Aid	251UNTS3	103529
Laos	USA (United States)	08 Jul 55	Direct Aid	278UNTS59	104021
Japan	USA (United States)	10 Feb 56	Direct Aid	275UNTS105	103979
Netherlands	USA (United States)	27 Mar 56	General Amity	285UNTS231	104154
Austria	Italy	07 May 56	Finance	284UNTS351	104147
Multilateral		25 Sep 56	Air Transport	334UNTS89	104767
Multilateral		25 Sep 56	Air Transport	334UNTS13	104766
Argentina	UK Great Britain	31 Oct 56	Finance	269UNTS229	103883
Finland	USA (United States)	10 May 57	US Agri Commod Aid	283UNTS43	104105
Iran	Italy	29 Jan 58	Finance	302UNTS181	104358
Belgium	Japan	30 Apr 58	Finance	303UNTS109	104373

PARTY ONE	PARTY TWO	DATE	TOPIC	CITATION	NUMBER
International Monetary Fund (Cont.)					
Philippines	USA (United States)	03 Jun 58	US Agri Commod Aid	316UNTS3	104573
Multilateral		01 Dec 58	Commodity Trade	385UNTS137	105534
Multilateral		06 Apr 59	Commodity Trade	349UNTS167	105013
Multilateral		11 May 59	Claims and Debts	527UNTS145	107623
Ethiopia	France	12 Nov 59	Specific Property	381UNTS3	105465
Germany, West	Pakistan	25 Nov 59	General Economic	457UNTS22	106575
Multilateral		04 Jan 60	IGO Establishment	370UNTS3	105266
Multilateral		26 Jan 60	IGO Establishment	439UNTS249	106333
Cuba	Japan	22 Apr 60	General Trade	442UNTS261	106354
Fed of Malaya	Japan	10 May 60	General Trade	383UNTS293	105506
Pakistan	IBRD (World Bank)	19 Sep 60	IBRD Project	444UNTS207	106370
Japan	Pakistan	18 Dec 60	General Amity	423UNTS197	106093
USA (United States)	Vietnam, South	03 Apr 61	General Amity	424UNTS137	106106
Indonesia	Japan	01 Jul 61	General Amity	517UNTS107	107484
Switzerland	UK Great Britain	20 Oct 61	Loans and Credits	431UNTS29	106206
Germany, West	Thailand	13 Dec 61	Claims and Debts	541UNTS181	107870
Argentina	Japan	20 Dec 61	General Amity	613UNTS323	108859
Multilateral		15 May 62	Commodity Trade	444UNTS3	106367
Japan	UK Great Britain	14 Nov 62	General Trade	478UNTS29	106934
France	Japan	14 May 63	General Economic	518UNTS111	107493
El Salvador	Japan	19 Jul 63	General Economic	518UNTS135	107494
Multilateral		04 Dec 65	IGO Establishment	571UNTS123	108303
International North Pacific Fisheries Commission					
Multilateral		09 May 52	Specific Resources	205UNTS65	102770
Japan	USA (United States)	25 Nov 64	Specific Property	533UNTS31	107730
International Office of Epizootics					
Italy	Switzerland	02 Feb 56	Sanitation	291UNTS113	104247
Belgium	Yugoslavia	31 Oct 61	Sanitation	426UNTS165	106136
International Olive Oil Council					
Multilateral		03 Apr 58	Commodity Trade	336UNTS177	104806
Multilateral		20 Apr 63	IGO Establishment	495UNTS3	107239
International Patent Institute					
Multilateral		06 Jun 47	Patents/Copyrights	46UNTS249	100714
International Poplar Commission					
Multilateral		19 Nov 59	IGO Operations	410UNTS156	105902
International Red Locust Control Service					
Multilateral		22 Feb 49	Sanitation	93UNTS129	101296
Multilateral		25 May 62	IGO Establishment	486UNTS103	107075
International Refugees Organization					
Multilateral		14 Jan 46	Reparations	555UNTS69	108105
Multilateral		15 Dec 46	IGO Establishment	18UNTS3	100283
Czechoslovakia	Norway	20 Mar 47	General Trade	30UNTS223	100460
France	UK Great Britain	13 Aug 47	Non-ILO Labor	91UNTS169	101249
France	USA (United States)	28 Jun 48	Direct Aid	19UNTS9	100302
Sweden	USA (United States)	03 Jul 48	Direct Aid	23UNTS101	100343
Turkey	USA (United States)	04 Jul 48	Direct Aid	24UNTS67	100351
France	USA (United States)	09 Jul 48	Direct Aid	24UNTS103	100352
Portugal	USA (United States)	28 Sep 48	Direct Aid	29UNTS213	100442
Germany, West	Netherlands	29 Mar 51	Non-ILO Labor	149UNTS71	101952
Italy	USA (United States)	16 May 51	Reparations	206UNTS325	102795
Multilateral		02 Jul 51	Refugees	189UNTS137	102545
Multilateral		06 Jun 55	IGO Establishment	219UNTS79	102968
International Rice Commission					
Multilateral		29 Nov 48	IGO Establishment	120UNTS13	101613
International Secretariat for the Unification of Pharmacopoeias					
Multilateral		20 May 52	Sanitation	219UNTS55	102966
International Sugar Council					
Multilateral		01 Oct 53	Commodity Trade	258UNTS153	103677
Multilateral		01 Dec 58	Commodity Trade	385UNTS137	105534

PARTY ONE	PARTY TWO	DATE	TOPIC	CITATION	NUMBER
International Telecommunication Union					
Anglo-Egypt Sudan	Fr Equatorial Afri	02 Nov 39	Telecommunications	2UNTS209	200012
Brazil	Paraguay	08 Oct 42	Telecommunications	65UNTS191	200211
Multilateral		04 Dec 45	Telecommunications	9UNTS101	100128
Multilateral		02 Oct 47	Telecommunications	193UNTS188	102616
Multilateral		17 Sep 48	Telecommunications	97UNTS31	101345
Multilateral		09 Jul 49	Telecommunications	168UNTS143	102218
Afghanistan	India	14 Dec 49	Telecommunications	53UNTS95	100774
Pakistan	UK Great Britain	26 Sep 51	Postal Service	118UNTS221	101608
Denmark	USA (United States)	04 Apr 52	Telecommunications	177UNTS13	102305
Multilateral		11 Jul 52	Postal Service	170UNTS269	102223
Iceland	USA (United States)	20 Jul 55	General Military	256UNTS245	103634
Mexico	USA (United States)	29 Jan 57	Telecommunications	418UNTS253	106025
United Nations	United Arab Rep	08 Feb 57	Status of Forces	260UNTS61	103704
Ethiopia	United Nations	18 Jun 58	IGO Operations	317UNTS101	104597
Congo (Zaire)	United Nations	27 Nov 61	IGO Status/Immunit	414UNTS229	105975
Canada	USA (United States)	24 Oct 62	Telecommunications	462UNTS67	106672
Niger	United Nations	20 Nov 63	IGO Establishment	536UNTS3	107793
Multilateral		22 Jan 65	Gen Communications	634UNTS239	109066
Spain	USA (United States)	14 Apr 66	Specific Property	579UNTS173	108406
International Tin Council					
Multilateral		01 Mar 54	Commodity Trade	256UNTS31	103622
Multilateral		01 Sep 60	Commodity Trade	403UNTS3	105792
International Union for the Protection of Industrial Property					
Multilateral		06 Jun 47	Patents/Copyrights	46UNTS249	100714
Multilateral		11 Dec 53	Patents/Copyrights	218UNTS27	102952
Multilateral		19 Dec 54	Patents/Copyrights	218UNTS51	102953
Multilateral		15 Jun 57	General Trade	550UNTS45	108008
Czechoslovakia	Germany, East	26 Jun 58	Patents/Copyrights	504UNTS221	107359
International Union for the Protection of Literary and Artistic Works					
Multilateral		26 Jun 48	Culture	331UNTS217	104757
Multilateral		06 Sep 52	Patents/Copyrights	216UNTS132	102937
Multilateral		15 Dec 58	Mass Media	546UNTS235	107950
Multilateral		22 Jun 60	Mass Media	546UNTS247	107951
International Union for the Publication of Customs Tariffs					
Multilateral		16 Dec 49	Admin Cooperation	72UNTS3	100924
International Whaling Commission					
Multilateral		02 Dec 46	Specific Resources	161UNTS72	102124
International Wheat Council					
Multilateral		23 Mar 49	Commodity Trade	203UNTS179	102746
Multilateral		25 Apr 56	Commodity Trade	270UNTS103	103896
Multilateral		06 Apr 59	Commodity Trade	349UNTS167	105013
Multilateral		15 May 62	Commodity Trade	444UNTS3	106367
Joint Institute for Nuclear Research					
Multilateral		26 Mar 56	IGO Establishment	259UNTS125	103686
Latin America Forestry Institute					
Multilateral		18 Nov 59	IGO Establishment	390UNTS227	105610
Latin American Free Trade Association					
Argentina	Paraguay	23 Jan 67	General Trade	634UNTS193	109061
Argentina	Uruguay	12 Feb 67	Water Transport	635UNTS125	109076
League of Nations					
ILO (Labor Org)	Switzerland	11 Mar 46	IGO Status/Immunit	15UNTS377	200103
Multilateral		22 Jul 46	IGO Establishment	9UNTS3	100125
Multilateral		09 Oct 46	ILO Labor	38UNTS3	100583
Multilateral		13 Dec 46	Trusteeship	8UNTS181	100122
Multilateral		13 Dec 46	Trusteeship	8UNTS151	100120
Multilateral		13 Dec 46	Trusteeship	8UNTS119	100118
Multilateral		13 Dec 46	Trusteeship	8UNTS71	100115
Multilateral		13 Dec 46	Trusteeship	8UNTS105	100117
Multilateral		13 Dec 46	Trusteeship	8UNTS91	100116
Multilateral		10 Feb 47	Peace/Disarmament	49UNTS3	100747

PARTY ONE	PARTY TWO	DATE	TOPIC	CITATION	NUMBER
League of Nations (Cont.)					
Multilateral		10 Feb 47	Peace/Disarmament	42UNTS3	100645
Multilateral		10 Feb 47	Peace/Disarmament	41UNTS135	100644
Multilateral		10 Feb 47	Peace/Disarmament	41UNTS21	100643
Multilateral		10 Feb 47	Peace/Disarmament	48UNTS203	100746
Multilateral		02 Apr 47	Trusteeship	8UNTS189	100123
Multilateral		10 Jun 47	Water Transport	208UNTS3	102814
Multilateral		12 Nov 47	Admin Cooperation	53UNTS13	100770
Multilateral		12 Nov 47	Admin Cooperation	53UNTS49	100772
Multilateral		12 Nov 47	Admin Cooperation	46UNTS201	100710
Multilateral		12 Nov 47	Admin Cooperation	46UNTS169	100709
Multilateral		09 Dec 48	Scientific Project	73UNTS39	100942
Multilateral		20 Jun 49	IGO Establishment	128UNTS141	101718
Germany, West	UK Great Britain	20 Apr 60	Non-ILO Labor	413UNTS236	105958
Austria	Hungary	31 Oct 64	Visas	545UNTS241	107937
Mekong Commission					
Multilateral		19 Oct 63	Direct Aid	523UNTS249	107559
Nauru Administrative Authority					
Australia	USA (United States)	25 Feb 58	Tech Assistance	317UNTS153	104601
Niger River Commission					
Multilateral		25 Nov 64	Water Transport	587UNTS19	108507
Nordic Council					
Norway	Sweden	09 Jun 58	Water Transport	427UNTS221	106156
Multilateral		23 Mar 62	General Amity	434UNTS145	106262
North Atlantic Treaty Organization					
Netherlands	USA (United States)	17 Jan 33	Status of Forces	474UNTS119	106877
Iraq	USA (United States)	31 Jul 45	Milit Assistance	121UNTS239	200402
Multilateral		04 Apr 49	General Military	34UNTS243	100541
France	USA (United States)	27 Jan 50	Milit Assistance	80UNTS171	101051
Denmark	USA (United States)	27 Jan 50	Milit Assistance	48UNTS115	100740
Italy	USA (United States)	27 Jan 50	Milit Assistance	80UNTS145	101050
Luxembourg	USA (United States)	27 Jan 50	Milit Assistance	80UNTS187	101052
Norway	USA (United States)	27 Jan 50	Milit Assistance	80UNTS241	101055
UK Great Britain	USA (United States)	27 Jan 50	Milit Assistance	80UNTS261	101056
Belgium	USA (United States)	27 Jan 50	Milit Assistance	51UNTS213	100767
Netherlands	USA (United States)	27 Jan 50	Milit Assistance	80UNTS219	101054
Portugal	USA (United States)	05 Jan 51	Milit Assistance	133UNTS75	101782
Denmark	USA (United States)	27 Apr 51	General Military	94UNTS35	101305
Iceland	USA (United States)	05 May 51	Milit Assistance	205UNTS173	102776
Portugal	USA (United States)	06 Sep 51	Milit Assistance	237UNTS217	103348
Jordan	USA (United States)	12 Feb 52	Tech Assistance	168UNTS25	102211
Japan	USA (United States)	28 Feb 52	Milit Assistance	208UNTS255	102817
Netherlands	USA (United States)	07 Mar 52	Taxation	135UNTS199	101821
Luxembourg	USA (United States)	13 Mar 52	Taxation	168UNTS57	102212
Canada	USA (United States)	30 Apr 52	Milit Installation	235UNTS269	103308
Canada	USA (United States)	08 Nov 52	Gen Communications	207UNTS3	102796
Belgium	UK Great Britain	12 Nov 52	Status of Forces	180UNTS15	102372
Portugal	USA (United States)	01 Apr 53	Taxation	205UNTS41	102769
Belgium	USA (United States)	18 Jun 53	Milit Assistance	222UNTS3	103019
Luxembourg	USA (United States)	17 Aug 53	Mass Media	234UNTS219	103284
Greece	USA (United States)	12 Oct 53	Milit Installation	191UNTS319	102589
Luxembourg	USA (United States)	17 Apr 54	Milit Assistance	257UNTS255	103661
Netherlands	USA (United States)	07 May 54	Milit Assistance	213UNTS325	102895
Denmark	USA (United States)	08 Jun 54	Milit Assistance	307UNTS133	104448
Turkey	USA (United States)	23 Jun 54	Taxation	222UNTS161	103027
Multilateral		09 Aug 54	General Amity	211UNTS237	102855
Multilateral		23 Oct 54	Status of Forces	334UNTS3	104765
Multilateral		23 Oct 54	Milit Occupation	332UNTS157	104761
Netherlands	USA (United States)	14 Dec 54	Milit Assistance	262UNTS35	103737
Multilateral		14 May 55	General Amity	219UNTS3	102962
Multilateral		22 Jun 55	Atomic Energy	249UNTS3	103498
Germany, West	USA (United States)	30 Jun 55	Milit Assistance	240UNTS47	103393
Greece	USA (United States)	07 Sep 56	Status of Forces	278UNTS141	104030
Iceland	USA (United States)	06 Dec 56	General Military	265UNTS261	103818
North Atlantic Treaty Organization (Cont.)					
Canada	Germany, West	10 Dec 56	Milit Assistance	392UNTS3	105633
Canada	Netherlands	13 Apr 57	Milit Assistance	316UNTS223	104588
Canada	Norway	17 Apr 57	Milit Assistance	316UNTS215	104587
Canada	Denmark	17 Apr 57	Milit Assistance	316UNTS207	104586
Germany, West	UK Great Britain	07 Jun 57	Milit Assistance	398UNTS275	105730
Germany, West	USA (United States)	07 Jun 57	Milit Assistance	346UNTS241	104984
Germany, West	Netherlands	10 Jul 57	Status of Forces	339UNTS97	104848
Greece	USA (United States)	05 Aug 57	Milit Assistance	290UNTS167	104235
Germany, West	UK Great Britain	03 Oct 58	Milit Assistance	398UNTS293	105731
Denmark	USA (United States)	08 May 59	Milit Assistance	344UNTS185	104949
Turkey	UK Great Britain	13 Jun 59	Claims and Debts	551UNTS59	108033
Multilateral		03 Aug 59	Status of Forces	481UNTS262	106986
Turkey	USA (United States)	28 Oct 59	Milit Assistance	360UNTS265	105162
Turkey	USA (United States)	13 Nov 59	Milit Assistance	361UNTS3	105168
Norway	USA (United States)	13 Feb 60	Milit Assistance	388UNTS255	105583
Greece	USA (United States)	15 Feb 60	Milit Assistance	377UNTS95	105397
Turkey	USA (United States)	02 Mar 60	Milit Assistance	372UNTS37	105286
Netherlands	USA (United States)	24 Mar 60	Milit Assistance	406UNTS165	105847
Denmark	USA (United States)	12 Apr 60	Milit Assistance	373UNTS9	105311
Belgium	USA (United States)	22 Apr 60	Milit Assistance	372UNTS277	105304
Canada	Norway	25 Apr 60	Milit Installation	470UNTS109	106801
Germany, West	USA (United States)	27 May 60	Milit Assistance	377UNTS45	105395
Argentina	USA (United States)	02 Aug 60	Military Mission	384UNTS105	105514
Canada	UK Great Britain	05 Aug 60	Milit Installation	470UNTS133	106804
Canada	USA (United States)	31 Aug 60	Milit Assistance	393UNTS247	105659
France	USA (United States)	19 Sep 60	Milit Assistance	400UNTS21	105745
Multilateral		21 Sep 60	Patents/Copyrights	394UNTS3	105664
Portugal	USA (United States)	26 Sep 60	Milit Assistance	393UNTS257	105660
Canada	USA (United States)	12 Jun 61	Milit Assistance	410UNTS21	105894
Germany, West	UK Great Britain	12 Jul 61	Status of Forces	424UNTS211	106109
Germany, West	UK Great Britain	26 Sep 61	Milit Assistance	424UNTS201	106108
Germany, West	UK Great Britain	06 Jun 62	Status of Forces	437UNTS39	106298
Italy	Netherlands	29 May 64	Other Military	541UNTS147	107867
Multilateral		18 Jun 64	Atomic Energy	542UNTS145	107886
Italy	USA (United States)	04 Aug 64	General Military	529UNTS205	107662
Germany, West	USA (United States)	18 Dec 65	Status of Forces	579UNTS193	108407
Northeast Atlantic Fisheries Commission					
Multilateral		24 Jan 59	IGO Establishment	486UNTS157	107078
Northern Pacific Fur Seal Commission					
Multilateral		09 Feb 57	Specific Resources	314UNTS105	104546
Northwest Atlantic Fisheries Commission					
Multilateral		08 Feb 49	Specific Resources	157UNTS157	102053
Office of the United Nations High Commissioner for Refugees					
Multilateral		23 Nov 57	Refugees	506UNTS125	107384
Austria	USA (United States)	03 Oct 61	Direct Aid	426UNTS187	106137
Organization for Economic Co-operation and Development					
France	Ireland	06 May 48	General Trade	558UNTS170	108141
Italy	USA (United States)	28 Jun 48	Direct Aid	20UNTS43	100314
France	USA (United States)	28 Jun 48	Direct Aid	19UNTS9	100302
Denmark	USA (United States)	29 Jun 48	Direct Aid	22UNTS217	100338
Netherlands	USA (United States)	02 Jul 48	Direct Aid	20UNTS91	100315
Belgium	USA (United States)	02 Jul 48	Direct Aid	19UNTS127	100309
Greece	USA (United States)	02 Jul 48	Direct Aid	23UNTS43	100342
Austria	USA (United States)	02 Jul 48	Direct Aid	21UNTS29	100323
Iceland	USA (United States)	03 Jul 48	Direct Aid	20UNTS141	100316
Sweden	USA (United States)	03 Jul 48	Direct Aid	23UNTS101	100343
Norway	USA (United States)	03 Jul 48	Direct Aid	20UNTS185	100317
Turkey	USA (United States)	04 Jul 48	Direct Aid	24UNTS67	100351
UK Great Britain	USA (United States)	06 Jul 48	Direct Aid	22UNTS263	100339
France	USA (United States)	09 Jul 48	Direct Aid	24UNTS103	100352
Multilateral		14 Jul 48	Direct Aid	23UNTS3	100340
Ireland	Netherlands	02 Sep 48	General Trade	558UNTS249	108145
Portugal	USA (United States)	28 Sep 48	Direct Aid	29UNTS213	100442

PARTY ONE	PARTY TWO	DATE	TOPIC	CITATION	NUMBER
Organization for Economic Co-operation and Development (Cont.)					
UK Great Britain	USA (United States)	30 Sep 48	Specific Resources	71UNTS241	100922
Trieste	USA (United States)	15 Oct 48	Direct Aid	29UNTS249	100443
Turkey	UK Great Britain	16 Oct 48	Finance	83UNTS85	101103
Belgium	Luxembourg	14 Jan 49	Direct Aid	36UNTS339	100572
France	Norway	09 Feb 49	General Economic	29UNTS13	100431
Multilateral		08 Apr 49	Milit Occupation	140UNTS196	101889
Ireland	Sweden	25 Jun 49	General Trade	558UNTS299	108148
Greece	UK Great Britain	29 Jun 49	Finance	86UNTS203	101160
Belgium	UK Great Britain	07 Sep 49	Loans and Credits	106UNTS61	101457
Belgium	France	07 Sep 49	Loans and Credits	123UNTS13	101651
Belgium	Netherlands	07 Sep 49	Loans and Credits	117UNTS3	101581
Multilateral		22 Nov 49	Recognition	185UNTS307	102477
Ireland	Netherlands	25 Nov 49	General Trade	558UNTS256	108146
Germany, West	USA (United States)	15 Dec 49	Direct Aid	92UNTS269	101277
Austria	Denmark	23 Feb 50	General Trade	74UNTS269	100969
Indonesia	USA (United States)	24 Mar 50	Direct Aid	92UNTS387	101281
India	Norway	29 Aug 50	General Trade	73UNTS179	100952
Iceland	Ireland	02 Dec 50	General Trade	558UNTS231	108143
Multilateral		15 Dec 50	IGO Operations	160UNTS267	102111
Germany, West	Greece	12 Feb 51	General Trade	198UNTS193	102665
Multilateral		18 Apr 51	IGO Establishment	261UNTS140	103729
Norway	Pakistan	21 May 51	General Trade	318UNTS163	104613
Denmark	Portugal	05 Jun 51	General Trade	101UNTS61	101402
Ireland	Norway	02 Jul 51	General Trade	100UNTS53	101387
Denmark	Italy	24 Oct 51	General Trade	118UNTS91	101598
Ireland	Switzerland	26 Dec 51	General Trade	558UNTS305	108149
Ireland	Portugal	06 Feb 52	General Trade	558UNTS289	108147
Norway	USA (United States)	27 Jun 52	Tech Assistance	184UNTS271	102452
France	Greece	31 Jul 52	General Trade	187UNTS169	102510
Denmark	Italy	28 Oct 52	General Trade	167UNTS125	102202
Greece	Italy	04 Feb 53	General Trade	189UNTS269	102551
Greece	Netherlands	05 Feb 53	General Trade	263UNTS361	103783
UK Great Britain	USA (United States)	25 Feb 53	Direct Aid	212UNTS157	102868
Ireland	Italy	27 Jul 53	General Trade	558UNTS237	108144
Multilateral		17 Oct 53	General Transport	184UNTS42	102438
Greece	Turkey	07 Nov 53	General Trade	225UNTS163	103098
Denmark	Italy	10 Apr 54	General Trade	196UNTS175	102623
Netherlands	Norway	09 Jun 54	Finance	287UNTS179	104184
Germany, West	Italy	28 Jun 54	Loans and Credits	288UNTS83	104199
Netherlands	UK Great Britain	09 Jul 54	Finance	199UNTS157	102682
Belgium	UK Great Britain	09 Jul 54	Finance	201UNTS299	102721
France	Netherlands	09 Jul 54	Finance	287UNTS169	104183
Austria	UK Great Britain	09 Jul 54	Finance	201UNTS277	102720
Portugal	UK Great Britain	10 Jul 54	Finance	199UNTS169	102683
Germany, West	UK Great Britain	10 Jul 54	Finance	199UNTS135	102680
Belgium	Italy	12 Jul 54	Finance	288UNTS59	104198
Switzerland	UK Great Britain	16 Jul 54	Claims and Debts	199UNTS197	102685
France	Greece	22 Jul 54	General Trade	225UNTS199	103099
Sweden	UK Great Britain	28 Jul 54	Finance	199UNTS181	102684
Greece	Netherlands	01 Nov 54	General Trade	223UNTS79	103057
Greece	Italy	10 Nov 54	General Trade	227UNTS9	103128
Iceland	Netherlands	28 Dec 54	Finance	287UNTS159	104182
Ceylon (Sri Lanka)	Germany, West	01 Apr 55	General Trade	369UNTS57	105251
France	Greece	28 Jun 55	General Trade	225UNTS219	103100
Greece	Netherlands	14 Jul 55	General Trade	227UNTS27	103129
Denmark	Netherlands	31 Jan 56	Finance	286UNTS255	104172
Germany, West	Italy	19 Apr 56	General Trade	281UNTS195	104080
Austria	Italy	07 May 56	Finance	284UNTS351	104147
France	Greece	25 Jun 56	General Trade	251UNTS167	103540
Italy	Netherlands	29 Jun 56	Finance	287UNTS193	104185
Italy	Switzerland	29 Jun 56	Finance	284UNTS299	104144
Austria	UK Great Britain	27 Oct 56	Air Transport	264UNTS67	103789
Multilateral		25 Mar 57	IGO Establishment	294UNTS259	104301
Ceylon (Sri Lanka)	Italy	23 Apr 57	General Trade	337UNTS115	104820
Denmark	Italy	12 Jul 57	General Trade	291UNTS169	104251

PARTY ONE	PARTY TWO	DATE	TOPIC	CITATION	NUMBER
Organization for Economic Co-operation and Development (Cont.)					
Germany, West	Italy	12 Jul 57	Finance	291UNTS181	104252
Italy	Tunisia	08 Apr 58	General Trade	378UNTS327	105430
Multilateral		18 Jun 58	General Trade	386UNTS345	105552
Portugal	UK Great Britain	18 Jul 58	Atomic Energy	313UNTS109	104532
Netherlands	Turkey	29 Nov 58	Direct Aid	335UNTS229	104790
France	UK Great Britain	05 Mar 59	Finance	343UNTS277	104932
Austria	UK Great Britain	14 Mar 59	Claims and Debts	343UNTS263	104930
Germany, West	UK Great Britain	10 Apr 59	Claims and Debts	343UNTS295	104935
Netherlands	Switzerland	14 Apr 59	Finance	486UNTS367	107086
Italy	UK Great Britain	14 Apr 59	Claims and Debts	343UNTS289	104934
Sweden	UK Great Britain	18 Apr 59	Claims and Debts	360UNTS89	105156
Belgium	UK Great Britain	23 Apr 59	Finance	343UNTS271	104931
Norway	UK Great Britain	23 Apr 59	Finance	343UNTS283	104933
Belgium	Netherlands	28 Apr 59	Finance	485UNTS123	107049
Denmark	UK Great Britain	28 Apr 59	Finance	343UNTS257	104929
Italy	Netherlands	29 Apr 59	Finance	486UNTS387	107089
Austria	Netherlands	29 Apr 59	Finance	486UNTS373	107087
France	Netherlands	29 Apr 59	Finance	486UNTS379	107088
Denmark	Netherlands	30 Apr 59	Finance	487UNTS23	107092
Netherlands	UK Great Britain	30 Apr 59	Claims and Debts	343UNTS307	104937
Iceland	Netherlands	30 Apr 59	Finance	487UNTS13	107091
Germany, West	Netherlands	30 Apr 59	Finance	485UNTS141	107052
Netherlands	Portugal	30 Apr 59	Finance	485UNTS129	107050
Netherlands	Norway	30 Apr 59	Finance	487UNTS3	107090
Greece	Netherlands	30 Apr 59	Finance	485UNTS135	107051
Netherlands	Sweden	30 Apr 59	Finance	485UNTS147	107053
Switzerland	UK Great Britain	06 May 59	Claims and Debts	343UNTS315	104938
Multilateral		11 May 59	Claims and Debts	527UNTS145	107623
Iceland	UK Great Britain	14 May 59	Finance	343UNTS301	104936
Greece	UK Great Britain	21 May 59	Claims and Debts	344UNTS3	104939
Guinea	UK Great Britain	22 Oct 59	General Trade	351UNTS341	105033
Italy	Tunisia	31 Oct 59	General Trade	378UNTS349	105431
Tunisia	UK Great Britain	16 Nov 59	General Trade	354UNTS367	105070
Multilateral		04 Jan 60	IGO Establishment	370UNTS3	105266
Greece	Tunisia	02 Mar 60	General Trade	483UNTS89	107008
Denmark	UK Great Britain	20 May 60	Atomic Energy	374UNTS245	105338
Austria	Spain	17 Jun 60	General Trade	390UNTS17	105600
Germany, West	UK Great Britain	20 Jun 60	Visas	385UNTS55	105528
France	UK Great Britain	14 Feb 61	Visas	398UNTS267	105729
Denmark	UK Great Britain	10 May 61	Visas	414UNTS17	105961
Norway	UK Great Britain	10 May 61	Visas	414UNTS9	105960
Turkey	UK Great Britain	28 Jun 61	Visas	414UNTS93	105968
Greece	Morocco	01 Nov 61	General Trade	483UNTS113	107009
Brazil	USA (United States)	13 Apr 62	Non-IBRD Project	445UNTS227	106391
Multilateral		14 May 64	Refugees	528UNTS23	107633
Organization of African Unity					
Multilateral		25 May 63	IGO Establishment	479UNTS39	106947
Multilateral		26 Oct 63	Water Transport	587UNTS9	108506
Multilateral		25 Nov 64	Water Transport	587UNTS19	108507
Multilateral		28 May 65	IGO Establishment	559UNTS273	108163
Multilateral		27 May 66	IGO Establishment	637UNTS0	109121
Morocco	Senegal	15 Sep 66	General Amity	634UNTS105	109055
Gambia	Senegal	19 Apr 67	General Amity	640UNTS101	109156
Organization of American States					
Multilateral		25 Jun 36	Privil/Immunities	161UNTS217	200486
Multilateral		17 Feb 40	Privil/Immunities	161UNTS229	200487
Multilateral		30 Jul 40	Admin Cooperation	161UNTS253	200488
Multilateral		12 Oct 40	Specific Resources	161UNTS193	200485
Multilateral		28 Nov 40	Commodity Trade	139UNTS159	200452
Multilateral		15 Jan 44	IGO Establishment	161UNTS281	200489
Multilateral		03 Sep 46	Commodity Trade	139UNTS3	101872
Multilateral		02 Sep 47	General Military	21UNTS77	100324
Multilateral		30 Apr 48	IGO Establishment	119UNTS3	101609
Multilateral		30 Apr 48	Dispute Settlement	30UNTS55	100449

PARTY ONE	PARTY TWO	DATE	TOPIC	CITATION	NUMBER
Organization of American States (Cont.)					
Costa Rica	USA (United States)	17 Jan 51	Land Transport	134UNTS215	101801
Panama	USA (United States)	26 Jan 51	Land Transport	137UNTS69	101849
El Salvador	USA (United States)	19 Mar 51	Land Transport	134UNTS245	101803
Mexico	United Nations	20 May 51	IGO Operations	102UNTS103	101413
Multilateral		14 Oct 51	IGO Establishment	122UNTS3	101631
Multilateral		01 May 57	Admin Cooperation	284UNTS201	104138
Honduras	Nicaragua	22 Jun 57	Specif Claim/Waive	277UNTS159	104005
Multilateral		08 Apr 59	IGO Establishment	389UNTS69	105593
Inter-Am Devel Bnk	USA (United States)	19 Jun 61	Direct Aid	410UNTS34	105895
Peru	USA (United States)	20 Dec 62	Milit Installation	471UNTS75	106822
Colombia	United Nations	27 Aug 63	Education	481UNTS3	106975
Argentina	USA (United States)	10 May 64	Milit Assistance	527UNTS77	107618
Organization of Central American States					
Multilateral		14 Oct 51	IGO Establishment	122UNTS3	101631
Multilateral		08 Nov 56	Commodity Trade	470UNTS171	106809
Multilateral		10 Jun 58	General Economic	454UNTS47	106539
Multilateral		10 Jun 58	Land Transport	454UNTS115	106540
Multilateral		10 Jun 58	Land Transport	454UNTS211	106541
Multilateral		01 Sep 59	Customs	454UNTS289	106542
Multilateral		26 Feb 60	Air Transport	418UNTS171	106022
Multilateral		13 Dec 60	IGO Establishment	455UNTS204	106544
Multilateral		13 Dec 60	General Economic	455UNTS3	106543
Multilateral		14 Dec 63	IGO Establishment	507UNTS149	107399
Organization of Petroleum Exporting Countries					
Multilateral		14 Sep 60	IGO Establishment	443UNTS247	106363
Other United Nations Organizations					
United Nations	United Arab Rep	26 Nov 65	IGO Operations	551UNTS253	108046
Pacific Salmon Commission					
Canada	USA (United States)	05 Aug 44	Specific Resources	121UNTS299	200408
Pan-American Health Organization					
Haiti	WHO (World Health)	21 Jun 50	Sanitation	103UNTS61	101424
Peru	WHO (World Health)	26 Sep 50	Sanitation	104UNTS233	101444
Guatemala	WHO (World Health)	28 Nov 50	Sanitation	103UNTS51	101423
Nicaragua	WHO (World Health)	02 Jan 51	Sanitation	103UNTS107	101428
El Salvador	WHO (World Health)	02 Jan 51	Sanitation	103UNTS29	101421
Colombia	WHO (World Health)	05 Jan 51	Sanitation	102UNTS139	101417
Bolivia	WHO (World Health)	07 Feb 51	Sanitation	104UNTS167	101438
Costa Rica	WHO (World Health)	13 Apr 51	Sanitation	103UNTS3	101419
Costa Rica	WHO (World Health)	14 Jun 51	Sanitation	102UNTS151	101418
Pan-American Institute of Geography and History					
Dominican Republic	USA (United States)	28 Aug 64	Scientific Project	531UNTS35	107691
Permanent Court of Arbitration					
League of Nations	United Nations	19 Jul 46	Specific Property	1UNTS109	200002
Taiwan	Spain	19 Feb 53	General Amity	181UNTS81	102400
Brazil	Italy	24 Nov 54	Dispute Settlement	284UNTS325	104146
United Arab Rep	Yugoslavia	20 Feb 55	Air Transport	255UNTS199	103611
Fed of Malaya	United Nations	29 May 58	Tech Assistance	330UNTS109	104742
Nepal	United Nations	18 Aug 58	Admin Cooperation	508UNTS3	107403
Burma	United Nations	15 Dec 58	Tech Assistance	319UNTS3	104629
United Nations	Tunisia	23 Dec 58	Tech Assistance	321UNTS23	104651
Ghana	United Nations	27 Feb 59	Tech Assistance	324UNTS133	104682
United Nations	Sudan	28 Mar 59	Tech Assistance	327UNTS95	104719
Denmark	Sudan	11 May 59	Air Transport	445UNTS105	106380
United Nations	Vietnam, South	03 Jun 59	IGO Status/Immunit	337UNTS361	200557
Panama	United Nations	24 Jun 59	IGO Operations	507UNTS245	107402
Libya	United Nations	27 Jun 59	Tech Assistance	336UNTS291	104811
Laos	United Nations	06 Jul 59	Tech Assistance	337UNTS41	104814
Paraguay	United Nations	01 Aug 59	Tech Assistance	341UNTS319	104894
Guinea	United Nations	15 Oct 59	Tech Assistance	344UNTS47	104942
Afghanistan	United Nations	24 Nov 59	Tech Assistance	397UNTS187	105705
United Nations	Togo	06 May 60	Tech Assistance	388UNTS53	105571
Ethiopia	United Nations	13 Jul 60	Tech Assistance	368UNTS143	105239

PARTY ONE	PARTY TWO	DATE	TOPIC	CITATION	NUMBER
Permanent Court of Arbitration (Cont.)					
Multilateral		19 Sep 60	IBRD Project	419UNTS125	106032
Kuwait	United Nations	31 Oct 60	Tech Assistance	391UNTS295	200581
Pakistan	United Nations	17 Nov 60	Tech Assistance	380UNTS277	105460
Cambodia	United Nations	30 Nov 60	Tech Assistance	383UNTS147	105500
Bolivia	United Nations	14 Dec 60	Tech Assistance	382UNTS283	105489
Iraq	United Nations	05 Mar 61	Tech Assistance	409UNTS56	105878
Cyprus	United Nations	15 Jun 61	Tech Assistance	398UNTS39	105716
Haiti	United Nations	28 Jun 61	Tech Assistance	399UNTS159	105740
Lebanon	United Nations	26 Aug 61	Tech Assistance	406UNTS105	105842
Jordan	United Nations	11 Sep 61	Tech Assistance	406UNTS255	105855
Ceylon (Sri Lanka)	United Nations	04 Dec 61	Tech Assistance	415UNTS236	105987
Greece	United Nations	18 May 62	Tech Assistance	429UNTS61	106190
United Nations	Tanganyika	01 Jun 62	Tech Assistance	479UNTS3	106944
Nigeria	United Nations	07 Aug 62	Tech Assistance	435UNTS167	106278
Cameroon	United Nations	29 Aug 62	Tech Assistance	442UNTS3	106334
Niger	United Nations	01 Oct 62	Tech Assistance	439UNTS181	106329
Multilateral		05 Oct 62	IGO Establishment	502UNTS225	107333
United Nations	Western Samoa	05 Nov 62	Tech Assistance	443UNTS297	200599
Ecuador	United Nations	26 Nov 62	Tech Assistance	445UNTS3	106372
Rwanda	United Nations	28 Nov 62	Tech Assistance	450UNTS267	106473
Ivory Coast	United Nations	10 Dec 62	Tech Assistance	451UNTS269	106498
Burundi	United Nations	29 Dec 62	Tech Assistance	450UNTS279	106474
Israel	United Nations	07 Jan 63	Tech Assistance	450UNTS229	106470
Mali	United Nations	09 May 63	Tech Assistance	463UNTS147	106699
Jamaica	United Nations	22 May 63	IGO Status/Immunit	479UNTS19	106945
Dominican Republic	United Nations	05 Aug 63	IGO Status/Immunit	472UNTS353	106847
United Nations	United Arab Rep	27 Aug 63	Tech Assistance	474UNTS221	106884
Burundi	WHO (World Health)	30 Aug 63	IGO Operations	490UNTS423	107169
WHO (World Health)	Somalia	08 Nov 63	IGO Operations	493UNTS243	107218
WHO (World Health)	Sierra Leone	22 Nov 63	IGO Operations	493UNTS255	107219
Nicaragua	United Nations	03 Dec 63	IGO Status/Immunit	482UNTS329	107002
United Nations	Sierra Leone	19 Feb 64	IGO Status/Immunit	489UNTS91	107136
United Nations	Upper Volta	26 Feb 64	IGO Status/Immunit	489UNTS179	107139
Morocco	United Nations	03 Mar 64	IGO Status/Immunit	490UNTS187	107154
Algeria	United Nations	23 Sep 64	IGO Operations	510UNTS217	107416
Kenya	United Nations	01 Oct 64	IGO Operations	511UNTS199	107434
Ethiopia	WHO (World Health)	27 Jan 65	IGO Operations	541UNTS135	107866
Multilateral		23 Feb 65	IGO Operations	527UNTS120	107622
Multilateral		26 Feb 65	IGO Operations	556UNTS69	108119
Multilateral		05 Mar 65	IGO Operations	527UNTS221	107627
Multilateral		08 Apr 65	IGO Operations	533UNTS66	107733
Multilateral		26 Apr 65	IGO Operations	533UNTS50	107732
Multilateral		12 May 65	IGO Operations	534UNTS390	107769
Multilateral		14 May 65	IGO Operations	550UNTS310	108026
Multilateral		25 May 65	IGO Operations	535UNTS374	107791
Multilateral		13 Sep 65	IGO Operations	547UNTS248	107961
Multilateral		21 Sep 65	IGO Operations	547UNTS280	107963
Multilateral		12 Nov 65	IGO Operations	550UNTS160	108013
Multilateral		23 Sep 66	General Aid	573UNTS148	108328
Czechoslovakia	UN Special Fund	13 Jul 67	Non-IBRD Project	606UNTS71	108776
Permanent Court of International Justice					
Canada	France	12 May 33	Admin Cooperation	253UNTS285	200545
Brazil	Venezuela	30 Mar 40	Dispute Settlement	51UNTS291	200195
Multilateral		10 Feb 47	Peace/Disarmament	49UNTS3	100747
Multilateral		10 Feb 47	Peace/Disarmament	48UNTS203	100746
Finland	Sweden	09 Apr 53	Dispute Settlement	198UNTS61	102657
Denmark	Finland	24 Sep 53	Dispute Settlement	188UNTS283	102532
Scandinavian Korea Mediation					
Multilateral		21 Dec 56	Humanitarian	427UNTS81	106147
South Pacific Health Service					
Multilateral		06 Feb 47	IGO Establishment	97UNTS227	101352
Nicaragua	UK Great Britain	25 May 51	Sanitation	101UNTS77	101404
New Zealand	UK Great Britain	20 Sep 57	Sanitation	287UNTS105	104180
Multilateral		07 Nov 64	Sanitation	548UNTS3	107965

PARTY ONE	PARTY TWO	DATE	TOPIC	CITATION	NUMBER
Southeast Asia Treaty Organization					
Philippines	USA (United States)	01 Nov 57	Status of Forces	307UNTS39	104440
Thailand	USA (United States)	23 Dec 60	IGO Establishment	405UNTS135	105830
Multilateral		23 Jul 62	Recognition	456UNTS302	106564
Thailand	USA (United States)	25 Apr 63	Sanitation	476UNTS115	106906
Special Commission					
Bolivia	Brazil	25 Feb 38	Land Transport	88UNTS379	200254
Bolivia	Brazil	25 Feb 38	Specific Resources	51UNTS245	200192
Brazil	Paraguay	14 Jun 41	IGO Establishment	54UNTS303	200202
Brazil	Paraguay	14 Jun 41	IGO Establishment	54UNTS323	200204
Canada	USA (United States)	27 Jun 41	IGO Establishment	103UNTS205	200315
Argentina	USA (United States)	14 Oct 41	General Trade	119UNTS193	200384
Canada	USA (United States)	27 Nov 41	Specific Resources	103UNTS193	200314
Peru	USA (United States)	21 Apr 42	Scientific Project	89UNTS317	200260
USA (United States)	Uruguay	21 Jul 42	General Trade	120UNTS211	200393
Brazil	USA (United States)	03 Sep 42	Non-IBRD Project	13UNTS109	200073
Nicaragua	USA (United States)	27 Oct 42	Scientific Project	99UNTS287	200283
UK Great Britain	USA (United States)	19 Aug 43	Atomic Energy	214UNTS341	200527
Liberia	USA (United States)	31 Dec 43	Non-IBRD Project	106UNTS199	200341
Mexico	USA (United States)	27 Jan 44	IGO Establishment	106UNTS275	200346
Mexico	USA (United States)	03 Feb 44	Specific Resources	3UNTS313	200025
Canada	USA (United States)	03 Mar 44	Specific Resources	109UNTS191	200359
Guatemala	USA (United States)	15 Jul 44	Scientific Project	106UNTS285	200347
Hungary	Yugoslavia	13 Aug 44	Dispute Settlement	113UNTS233	101553
Netherlands	UK Great Britain	02 Oct 44	Claims and Debts	231UNTS317	200535
Brazil	UNRRA (Relief)	12 Oct 44	IGO Establishment	67UNTS321	200228
Multilateral		07 Dec 44	Air Transport	171UNTS387	200502
Multilateral		20 Mar 45	General Economic	2UNTS299	200022
Poland	USSR (Soviet Union)	16 Aug 45	Territory Boundary	10UNTS193	200061
Multilateral		15 Nov 45	Atomic Energy	3UNTS123	100026
Czechoslovakia	France	08 Dec 45	Education	46UNTS77	100701
UK Great Britain	USA (United States)	10 Dec 45	Refugees	3UNTS177	100030
Multilateral		26 Dec 45	Peace/Disarmament	20UNTS259	100319
Multilateral		01 Jan 46	Peace/Disarmament	99UNTS131	101375
Poland	Yugoslavia	02 Jan 46	Visas	115UNTS21	101556
Belgium	Norway	21 Feb 46	General Trade	31UNTS435	100485
Belgium	France	22 Feb 46	Culture	68UNTS157	100892
France	UK Great Britain	28 Feb 46	Air Transport	27UNTS173	100407
ILO (Labor Org)	Switzerland	11 Mar 46	IGO Status/Immunit	15UNTS377	200103
Poland	Yugoslavia	16 Mar 46	Culture	10UNTS11	100139
France	Norway	26 Mar 46	General Trade	31UNTS69	100468
UK Great Britain	USA (United States)	27 Mar 46	Patents/Copyrights	4UNTS101	100040
Greece	United Arab Rep	30 Mar 46	Reparations	187UNTS263	102518
Denmark	Norway	30 Mar 46	General Trade	29UNTS163	100438
Multilateral		05 Apr 46	Specific Resources	231UNTS199	103221
Belgium	UK Great Britain	17 Apr 46	Health/Educ/Welfare	6UNTS177	100075
Thailand	UK Great Britain	01 May 46	Commodity Trade	99UNTS169	101377
Multilateral		06 May 46	Commodity Trade	99UNTS181	101379
UK Great Britain	USA (United States)	06 May 46	Admin Cooperation	99UNTS199	101381
Belgium	Netherlands	16 May 46	Culture	17UNTS13	100266
Afghanistan	USSR (Soviet Union)	13 Jun 46	Territory Boundary	31UNTS147	100476
Chile	UK Great Britain	25 Jun 46	General Trade	91UNTS137	101246
Albania	Yugoslavia	01 Jul 46	General Economic	111UNTS3	101517
Multilateral		19 Jul 46	IGO Operations	1UNTS97	200001
Norway	Yugoslavia	30 Aug 46	General Trade	30UNTS187	100457
Philippines	USA (United States)	17 Sep 46	IGO Establishment	15UNTS249	100240
Albania	Yugoslavia	03 Oct 46	General Trade	111UNTS227	101537
Multilateral		15 Oct 46	Refugees	11UNTS73	100150
Denmark	Sweden	18 Nov 46	Non-ILO Labor	7UNTS251	100104
France	Netherlands	19 Nov 46	Culture	32UNTS101	100493
Albania	Yugoslavia	28 Nov 46	Finance	111UNTS143	101527
Albania	Yugoslavia	28 Nov 46	Non-IBRD Project	111UNTS93	101520
Albania	Yugoslavia	28 Nov 46	Non-IBRD Project	111UNTS113	101523
Albania	Yugoslavia	28 Nov 46	Non-IBRD Project	111UNTS151	101528

PARTY ONE	PARTY TWO	DATE	TOPIC	CITATION	NUMBER
Special Commission (Cont.)					
Albania	Yugoslavia	28 Nov 46	Non-IBRD Project	111UNTS127	101525
UK Great Britain	USA (United States)	02 Dec 46	Milit Occupation	7UNTS163	100098
Norway	Poland	03 Dec 46	Finance	15UNTS203	100234
Canada	USA (United States)	06 Dec 46	Milit Assistance	149UNTS3	101945
United Arab Rep	UK Great Britain	10 Dec 46	Specif Claim/Waive	105UNTS15	101451
Hungary	Yugoslavia	01 Jan 47	General Trade	113UNTS63	101548
Multilateral		20 Jan 47	Water Transport	87UNTS247	101176
Finland	USSR (Soviet Union)	03 Feb 47	Territory Boundary	216UNTS231	102939
Multilateral		10 Feb 47	Peace/Disarmament	42UNTS3	100645
Multilateral		10 Feb 47	Peace/Disarmament	41UNTS135	100644
Multilateral		10 Feb 47	Peace/Disarmament	41UNTS21	100643
Burma	USA (United States)	28 Feb 47	Direct Aid	25UNTS27	100355
Belgium	Czechoslovakia	06 Mar 47	Culture	34UNTS77	100528
Belgium	Turkey	12 Mar 47	General Trade	37UNTS215	100578
Mexico	USA (United States)	17 Mar 47	Sanitation	167UNTS30	102200
Poland	Sweden	18 Mar 47	General Economic	12UNTS295	100190
Czechoslovakia	Norway	20 Mar 47	General Trade	30UNTS223	100460
Czechoslovakia	Poland	04 Apr 47	General Economic	85UNTS62	101146
Austria	Norway	14 Apr 47	General Trade	31UNTS21	100466
Czechoslovakia	Yugoslavia	27 Apr 47	Culture	33UNTS49	100514
Bulgaria	Denmark	09 May 47	General Trade	74UNTS131	100959
Hungary	Yugoslavia	11 May 47	Direct Aid	130UNTS171	101730
Poland	Yugoslavia	24 May 47	General Trade	115UNTS89	101560
Poland	Yugoslavia	24 May 47	General Trade	115UNTS37	101557
Albania	Yugoslavia	12 Jun 47	IGO Establishment	111UNTS201	101535
Czechoslovakia	UK Great Britain	16 Jun 47	Education	46UNTS61	100700
Bulgaria	Czechoslovakia	20 Jun 47	Education	46UNTS15	100698
Romania	Yugoslavia	26 Jun 47	Culture	116UNTS39	101568
Denmark	Yugoslavia	28 Jun 47	General Economic	78UNTS242	101020
Bulgaria	Poland	28 Jun 47	Culture	15UNTS123	100230
Czechoslovakia	Poland	04 Jul 47	Culture	25UNTS249	100366
Albania	Yugoslavia	09 Jul 47	Culture	33UNTS91	100516
Norway	Switzerland	15 Jul 47	Finance	12UNTS351	100192
Hungary	Yugoslavia	24 Jul 47	General Trade	114UNTS3	101554
Czechoslovakia	Greece	30 Jul 47	Finance	185UNTS115	102463
Multilateral		14 Aug 47	Reparations	138UNTS111	101863
Czechoslovakia	Romania	05 Sep 47	Education	46UNTS37	100699
Hungary	Yugoslavia	15 Oct 47	Culture	33UNTS73	100515
Multilateral		01 Nov 47	Trusteeship	10UNTS3	100138
Norway	USSR (Soviet Union)	18 Dec 47	Territory Boundary	52UNTS3	100768
France	Netherlands	02 Jan 48	Visas	70UNTS105	100899
France	Lebanon	24 Jan 48	Finance	173UNTS99	102263
Hungary	Poland	31 Jan 48	Culture	25UNTS283	100368
Brazil	USA (United States)	02 Feb 48	Status of Forces	67UNTS109	100870
Norway	Poland	04 Feb 48	General Trade	30UNTS205	100458
Belgium	Italy	09 Feb 48	Non-ILO Labor	71UNTS143	100915
Norway	UK Great Britain	19 Feb 48	Culture	34UNTS33	100526
Belgium	Norway	20 Feb 48	Culture	32UNTS39	100487
Poland	Romania	27 Feb 48	Culture	46UNTS143	100707
France	UK Great Britain	02 Mar 48	Culture	77UNTS33	100990
Multilateral		17 Mar 48	General Military	19UNTS51	100304
Hungary	Yugoslavia	18 Mar 48	Finance	113UNTS201	101551
Hungary	Yugoslavia	18 Mar 48	General Trade	113UNTS141	101550
Hungary	Yugoslavia	18 Mar 48	Finance	113UNTS219	101552
Belgium	Luxembourg	27 Mar 48	Culture	178UNTS265	102343
Czechoslovakia	Poland	05 Apr 48	Admin Cooperation	31UNTS325	100481
Poland	Yugoslavia	12 Apr 48	General Trade	115UNTS167	101563
Multilateral		30 Apr 48	Dispute Settlement	30UNTS55	100449
Hungary	Poland	13 May 48	General Economic	25UNTS301	100369
Ecuador	USA (United States)	14 May 48	Scientific Project	89UNTS71	101210
Czechoslovakia	Yugoslavia	24 May 48	Specif Goods/Equip	112UNTS215	101544
Czechoslovakia	Yugoslavia	24 May 48	General Trade	112UNTS111	101542
Bulgaria	Poland	30 May 48	General Trade	37UNTS3	100574
France	Netherlands	02 Jun 48	Non-ILO Labor	204UNTS275	102762
France	Norway	11 Jun 48	General Trade	31UNTS83	100469

Special Commission (Cont.)

PARTY ONE	PARTY TWO	DATE	TOPIC	CITATION	NUMBER
Greece	Sweden	25 Jun 48	General Trade	267UNTS337	103849
Taiwan	USA (United States)	03 Jul 48	Direct Aid	17UNTS119	100273
Netherlands	UK Great Britain	07 Jul 48	Culture	82UNTS259	101099
Poland	USSR (Soviet Union)	08 Jul 48	Territory Boundary	37UNTS25	100575
UNESCO (Educ/Cult)	WHO (World Health)	15 Jul 48	IGO Operations	44UNTS323	200184
Taiwan	USA (United States)	05 Aug 48	IGO Establishment	82UNTS109	101087
UK Great Britain	USA (United States)	30 Sep 48	Specific Resources	71UNTS241	100922
Greece	Lebanon	06 Oct 48	Consul/Citizenship	87UNTS351	101179
Austria	Denmark	29 Nov 48	General Trade	74UNTS243	100967
Belgium	Italy	29 Nov 48	Culture	41UNTS3	100641
Italy	Netherlands	04 Dec 48	Non-ILO Labor	46UNTS271	100716
South Africa	UK Great Britain	06 Dec 48	Customs	118UNTS183	101607
Finland	USSR (Soviet Union)	09 Dec 48	Territory Boundary	217UNTS135	102947
Italy	USA (United States)	18 Dec 48	Education	79UNTS133	101037
Belgium	Greece	27 Dec 48	General Trade	77UNTS265	101004
Norway	Poland	31 Dec 48	General Trade	29UNTS3	100430
Belgium	France	08 Jan 49	Non-ILO Labor	36UNTS151	100569
Poland	Yugoslavia	16 Jan 49	General Trade	115UNTS241	101564
Mexico	USA (United States)	25 Jan 49	IGO Establishment	99UNTS3	101367
Austria	Norway	28 Jan 49	General Trade	30UNTS145	100452
FAO (Food Agri)	UNESCO (Educ/Cult)	09 Feb 49	IGO Operations	43UNTS315	200182
France	Norway	09 Feb 49	General Economic	29UNTS13	100431
Israel	United Arab Rep	24 Feb 49	Peace/Disarmament	42UNTS251	100654
Denmark	Greece	25 Feb 49	General Trade	78UNTS325	101022
Netherlands	Norway	26 Feb 49	General Economic	29UNTS33	100432
Czechoslovakia	Yugoslavia	01 Mar 49	General Trade	113UNTS3	101547
Belgium	Norway	08 Mar 49	General Trade	29UNTS83	100435
Greece	Norway	12 Mar 49	General Trade	30UNTS161	100454
Multilateral		23 Mar 49	Commodity Trade	203UNTS179	102746
Israel	Lebanon	23 Mar 49	Peace/Disarmament	42UNTS287	100655
Finland	Greece	24 Mar 49	General Trade	78UNTS3	101008
Israel	Jordan	03 Apr 49	Peace/Disarmament	42UNTS303	100656
Canada	USA (United States)	12 Apr 49	Milit Assistance	206UNTS241	102789
India	Pakistan	23 Apr 49	Finance	54UNTS51	100795
Luxembourg	Netherlands	26 Apr 49	Culture	182UNTS187	102425
Denmark	Poland	12 May 49	Claims and Debts	87UNTS179	101172
Italy	Yugoslavia	23 May 49	Reparations	150UNTS179	101972
Costa Rica	USA (United States)	31 May 49	IGO Establishment	80UNTS3	101041
Canada	USA (United States)	04 Jun 49	Air Transport	122UNTS237	101649
Argentina	UK Great Britain	27 Jun 49	General Economic	83UNTS217	101110
Israel	Syria	20 Jul 49	Peace/Disarmament	42UNTS327	100657
Greece	Turkey	21 Jul 49	General Trade	78UNTS55	101011
France	Greece	06 Aug 49	General Trade	91UNTS95	101244
Mexico	USA (United States)	30 Aug 49	IGO Establishment	98UNTS183	101364
Greece	Italy	31 Aug 49	Reparations	78UNTS89	101014
Argentina	Norway	09 Sep 49	Finance	42UNTS125	100646
Multilateral		15 Sep 49	Air Transport	53UNTS235	100783
Bulgaria	Poland	26 Sep 49	Sanitation	260UNTS249	103712
Czechoslovakia	UK Great Britain	28 Sep 49	General Economic	86UNTS141	101156
Multilateral		27 Oct 49	Air Transport	53UNTS241	100784
Hungary	Poland	29 Oct 49	Sanitation	260UNTS113	103706
Italy	Norway	19 Nov 49	General Trade	47UNTS75	100723
Australia	New Zealand	26 Nov 49	Territory Boundary	198UNTS161	102662
Belgium	United Arab Rep	28 Nov 49	Culture	76UNTS91	100982
Denmark	Germany, West	15 Dec 49	Finance	51UNTS11	100749
Czechoslovakia	Denmark	17 Dec 49	General Trade	74UNTS147	100961
Norway	Poland	21 Dec 49	Finance	47UNTS107	100725
Norway	USSR (Soviet Union)	29 Dec 49	Territory Boundary	83UNTS291	101112
Greece	Portugal	31 Dec 49	General Trade	92UNTS71	101262
Panama	USA (United States)	26 Jan 50	Claims and Debts	132UNTS233	101763
Nicaragua	USA (United States)	01 Feb 50	Tech Assistance	99UNTS25	101368
India	USA (United States)	02 Feb 50	Education	89UNTS127	101214
China People's Rep	USSR (Soviet Union)	14 Feb 50	Privil/Immunities	226UNTS31	103105
Austria	Denmark	23 Feb 50	General Trade	74UNTS269	100969
Canada	USA (United States)	27 Feb 50	Specific Resources	132UNTS223	101762

Special Commission (Cont.)

PARTY ONE	PARTY TWO	DATE	TOPIC	CITATION	NUMBER
Italy	UK Great Britain	21 Mar 50	Territory Boundary	128UNTS225	101722
Italy	Turkey	24 Mar 50	General Amity	96UNTS207	101338
Multilateral		06 Apr 50	Admin Cooperation	119UNTS99	101610
Multilateral		08 Apr 50	IGO Establishment	66UNTS285	100860
Multilateral		08 Apr 50	Specif Goods/Equip	68UNTS99	100889
Austria	Greece	11 May 50	General Trade	184UNTS217	102450
Multilateral		13 May 50	Land Transport	128UNTS171	101719
Multilateral		31 May 50	General Trade	74UNTS95	100957
Luxembourg	UK Great Britain	27 Jun 50	Culture	183UNTS217	102431
Germany, East	Poland	06 Jul 50	Territory Boundary	319UNTS93	104631
Denmark	Spain	12 Jul 50	General Trade	71UNTS135	100914
Spain	Switzerland	03 Aug 50	Air Transport	254UNTS365	103600
Brazil	UK Great Britain	18 Sep 50	General Trade	88UNTS115	101188
Bulgaria	Romania	29 Sep 50	Scientific Project	342UNTS141	104905
Denmark	Italy	04 Oct 50	General Trade	78UNTS341	101024
Iran	USA (United States)	19 Oct 50	Tech Assistance	92UNTS135	101266
Canada	USA (United States)	26 Oct 50	Direct Aid	132UNTS247	101764
Czechoslovakia	Poland	17 Nov 50	Sanitation	530UNTS195	107682
Paraguay	USA (United States)	27 Nov 50	Direct Aid	122UNTS147	101644
Multilateral		02 Dec 50	Trusteeship	118UNTS255	200381
Albania	Poland	02 Dec 50	Culture	260UNTS131	103707
Multilateral		15 Dec 50	Customs	347UNTS127	104994
Multilateral		15 Dec 50	Customs	171UNTS305	102234
Brazil	Netherlands	15 Dec 50	Non-ILO Labor	123UNTS101	101657
Brazil	USA (United States)	19 Dec 50	Direct Aid	140UNTS365	101899
Liberia	USA (United States)	22 Dec 50	Direct Aid	133UNTS69	101781
Italy	Yugoslavia	23 Dec 50	Admin Cooperation	171UNTS291	102233
UK Great Britain	Yemen	20 Jan 51	General Amity	101UNTS39	101400
Albania	Poland	25 Jan 51	Scientific Project	260UNTS217	103710
Poland	USSR (Soviet Union)	15 Feb 51	Territory Boundary	432UNTS199	106222
Belgium	Netherlands	15 Mar 51	Reparations	93UNTS97	101294
China People's Rep	Poland	03 Apr 51	Culture	304UNTS187	104396
Greece	Turkey	20 Apr 51	Culture	178UNTS17	102333
Multilateral		25 Apr 51	Reparations	91UNTS21	101240
Denmark	Portugal	05 Jun 51	General Trade	101UNTS61	101402
Multilateral		15 Jun 51	Tech Assistance	148UNTS67	101936
UK Great Britain	USA (United States)	15 Jun 51	Tech Assistance	141UNTS79	101907
Finland	Sweden	15 Jun 51	Visas	198UNTS3	102651
Denmark	Spain	03 Jul 51	General Trade	101UNTS51	101401
Multilateral		10 Jul 51	Other Military	108UNTS287	101481
Brazil	USA (United States)	24 Jul 51	Direct Aid	134UNTS195,	101799
Australia	Belgium	25 Jul 51	Visas	108UNTS303	101482
Multilateral		29 Jul 51	Other Military	117UNTS85	101585
Canada	USA (United States)	01 Aug 51	Milit Installation	233UNTS109	103254
France	Italy	23 Aug 51	Consul/Citizenship	291UNTS143	104249
Japan	USA (United States)	28 Aug 51	Education	147UNTS81	101930
Multilateral		01 Sep 51	General Military	131UNTS83	101736
Greece	UK Great Britain	29 Sep 51	Culture	190UNTS260	102570
Pakistan	WHO (World Health)	07 Oct 51	Tech Assistance	126UNTS101	101684
Denmark	Italy	24 Oct 51	General Trade	118UNTS91	101598
Multilateral		31 Oct 51	Other Military	172UNTS193	102247
Italy	UK Great Britain	28 Nov 51	Culture	172UNTS27	102238
Denmark	WHO (World Health)	30 Nov 51	Scientific Project	118UNTS3	101592
El Salvador	Guatemala	14 Dec 51	General Economic	131UNTS131	101740
India	WHO (World Health)	20 Dec 51	Tech Assistance	124UNTS109	101669
India	USA (United States)	05 Jan 52	Tech Assistance	157UNTS39	102045
Germany, East	Poland	08 Jan 52	Culture	304UNTS113	104394
Denmark	Norway	14 Jan 52	Claims and Debts	120UNTS119	101618
Libya	USA (United States)	21 Jan 52	Tech Assistance	183UNTS177	102427
Germany, East	Poland	06 Feb 52	Water Transport	304UNTS131	104395
Multilateral		07 Mar 52	Specific Resources	175UNTS205	102302
Belgium	Pakistan	15 Mar 52	General Trade	316UNTS65	104578
Finland	Norway	18 Mar 52	Specific Resources	188UNTS187	102527
Belgium	France	21 Mar 52	Land Transport	137UNTS249	101856
Austria	Greece	22 Mar 52	General Economic	187UNTS255	102517

Special Commission (Cont.)

PARTY ONE	PARTY TWO	DATE	TOPIC	CITATION	NUMBER
South Africa	USA (United States)	26 Mar 52	Education	165UNTS187	102176
Multilateral		11 Apr 52	Tech Assistance	173UNTS2	102255
France	Israel	29 Apr 52	Air Transport	189UNTS55	102542
Canada	USA (United States)	30 Apr 52	Milit Installation	235UNTS269	103308
Israel	USA (United States)	09 May 52	Tech Assistance	177UNTS63	102309
Libya	USA (United States)	20 May 52	Tech Assistance	178UNTS155	102339
Libya	USA (United States)	20 May 52	Direct Aid	178UNTS307	102346
Brazil	USA (United States)	02 Jun 52	Scientific Project	181UNTS109	102403
Greece	Syria	02 Jun 52	General Trade	183UNTS251	102434
Denmark	Poland	09 Jun 52	General Trade	135UNTS209	101822
Denmark	Poland	09 Jun 52	Finance	135UNTS221	101823
Multilateral		12 Jun 52	Dispute Settlement	138UNTS183	101869
Ethiopia	USA (United States)	18 Jun 52	Tech Assistance	181UNTS207	102410
Ethiopia	USA (United States)	24 Jun 52	Tech Assistance	181UNTS215	102411
Canada	USA (United States)	30 Jun 52	Water Transport	234UNTS199	103283
Finland	USA (United States)	02 Jul 52	Education	165UNTS203	102177
Germany, West	USA (United States)	18 Jul 52	Education	165UNTS167	102175
Greece	Sweden	19 Aug 52	General Trade	189UNTS117	102544
Multilateral		21 Aug 52	Tech Assistance	141UNTS129	101912
Mexico	USA (United States)	26 Aug 52	IGO Establishment	264UNTS269	103797
Germany, West	Israel	10 Sep 52	Reparations	162UNTS205	102137
Austria	Greece	20 Sep 52	General Trade	187UNTS191	102512
Austria	Belgium	17 Oct 52	Culture	162UNTS183	102135
Denmark	Italy	28 Oct 52	General Trade	167UNTS125	102202
Austria	UK Great Britain	12 Dec 52	Culture	172UNTS9	102237
Liberia	USA (United States)	15 Dec 52	Tech Assistance	185UNTS45	102457
France	Greece	23 Dec 52	General Trade	187UNTS175	102511
Bolivia	Italy	31 Jan 53	Culture	281UNTS181	104079
Greece	Italy	04 Feb 53	Finance	189UNTS295	102552
Greece	Italy	04 Feb 53	General Trade	189UNTS269	102551
Greece	Netherlands	05 Feb 53	General Trade	263UNTS361	103783
Multilateral		07 Feb 53	Territory Boundary	173UNTS143	102264
Albania	Romania	14 Feb 53	Culture	342UNTS107	104903
Turkey	Yugoslavia	26 Feb 53	General Trade	247UNTS54	103460
Multilateral		27 Feb 53	Claims and Debts	333UNTS3	104764
Germany, West	USA (United States)	27 Feb 53	Claims and Debts	223UNTS167	103065
Greece	Yugoslavia	28 Feb 53	General Economic	252UNTS27	103557
United Arab Rep	USA (United States)	12 Mar 53	Tech Assistance	204UNTS3	102747
France	Italy	14 Mar 53	Land Transport	284UNTS221	104140
Austria	Yugoslavia	19 Mar 53	Visas	467UNTS293	106767
Czechoslovakia	Denmark	23 Apr 53	General Trade	174UNTS95	102280
Brazil	Ecuador	04 May 53	General Trade	369UNTS37	105249
Multilateral		11 May 53	Sanitation	456UNTS3	106555
Greece	United Arab Rep	21 May 53	General Trade	256UNTS17	103620
United Arab Rep	USA (United States)	21 May 53	Tech Assistance	204UNTS29	102748
Jordan	Syria	04 Jun 53	Specific Resources	184UNTS15	102437
United Arab Rep	USA (United States)	18 Jun 53	Education	204UNTS55	102749
Liberia	USA (United States)	23 Jun 53	Tech Assistance	213UNTS37	102879
Liberia	USA (United States)	23 Jun 53	Education	213UNTS57	102880
Brazil	USA (United States)	26 Jun 53	Direct Aid	336UNTS241	104808
UK Great Britain	USA (United States)	26 Jun 53	Loans and Credits	183UNTS225	102432
Pakistan	Turkey	29 Jun 53	Culture	211UNTS225	102854
Italy	Switzerland	02 Jul 53	Customs	257UNTS99	103653
Argentina	USSR (Soviet Union)	05 Aug 53	General Economic	221UNTS99	103004
UN Relief Palestin	United Arab Rep	14 Oct 53	Tech Assistance	190UNTS13	102555
Greece	Turkey	07 Nov 53	General Trade	225UNTS163	103098
Canada	USA (United States)	12 Nov 53	General Economic	223UNTS139	103062
Canada	USA (United States)	12 Nov 53	IGO Establishment	234UNTS97	103274
Bulgaria	Greece	05 Dec 53	General Trade	225UNTS135	103095
Chile	USA (United States)	30 Dec 53	Tech Assistance	236UNTS41	103315
Multilateral		18 Jan 54	IGO Establishment	330UNTS121	104743
Czechoslovakia	Greece	01 Feb 54	General Trade	225UNTS77	103091
Multilateral		19 Feb 54	Status of Forces	214UNTS51	102899
Bulgaria	Yugoslavia	20 Feb 54	Territory Boundary	397UNTS13	105700
Denmark	Italy	10 Apr 54	General Trade	196UNTS175	102623

Special Commission (Cont.)

PARTY ONE	PARTY TWO	DATE	TOPIC	CITATION	NUMBER
Peru	USA (United States)	13 Apr 54	Tech Assistance	236UNTS87	103318
Czechoslovakia	Hungary	16 Apr 54	Specific Resources	504UNTS231	107360
Bulgaria	Yugoslavia	22 Apr 54	Dispute Settlement	397UNTS43	105701
Panama	USA (United States)	11 May 54	Direct Aid	236UNTS107	103319
France	Greece	13 May 54	Non-ILO Labor	222UNTS299	103036
Greece	Spain	15 May 54	General Trade	299UNTS261	104318
Greece	Romania	19 May 54	General Trade	225UNTS17	103083
Multilateral		21 May 54	Non-ILO Labor	345UNTS285	104973
Multilateral		22 May 54	Non-ILO Labor	199UNTS3	102674
Greece	Hungary	05 Jun 54	General Trade	299UNTS285	104320
Italy	USA (United States)	28 Jun 54	Tech Assistance	237UNTS121	103340
Ecuador	USA (United States)	30 Jun 54	Tech Assistance	236UNTS163	103323
Brazil	USA (United States)	30 Jun 54	Non-IBRD Project	237UNTS137	103341
El Salvador	USA (United States)	16 Jul 54	Non-IBRD Project	237UNTS237	103350
France	Greece	22 Jul 54	General Trade	225UNTS199	103099
Multilateral		29 Jul 54	Sanitation	249UNTS45	103500
Mexico	USA (United States)	30 Jul 54	Sanitation	269UNTS39	103871
Multilateral		09 Aug 54	General Amity	211UNTS237	102855
Multilateral		24 Aug 54	Other Military	247UNTS213	103471
El Salvador	USA (United States)	31 Aug 54	Non-IBRD Project	237UNTS49	103336
Multilateral		08 Sep 54	Milit Assistance	209UNTS23	102819
Canada	USA (United States)	10 Sep 54	Specific Resources	238UNTS97	103355
Greece	Italy	11 Sep 54	Culture	284UNTS313	104145
Multilateral		05 Oct 54	Territory Boundary	235UNTS99	103297
China People's Rep	USSR (Soviet Union)	12 Oct 54	Milit Installation	226UNTS51	103107
Belgium	USA (United States)	12 Oct 54	Patents/Copyrights	202UNTS289	102735
Multilateral		23 Oct 54	Status of Forces	332UNTS3	104760
Multilateral		23 Oct 54	Reparations	332UNTS219	104762
Multilateral		23 Oct 54	Milit Occupation	332UNTS157	104761
Greece	Italy	10 Nov 54	General Trade	227UNTS9	103128
Portugal	UK Great Britain	18 Nov 54	Territory Boundary	210UNTS265	102841
Portugal	UK Great Britain	19 Nov 54	Culture	226UNTS305	103125
Austria	Yugoslavia	27 Nov 54	Specific Resources	396UNTS75	105694
Multilateral		29 Nov 54	General Trade	287UNTS209	104187
Multilateral		01 Dec 54	Admin Cooperation	210UNTS197	102839
Iran	USSR (Soviet Union)	02 Dec 54	Territory Boundary	451UNTS227	106497
Belgium	Greece	09 Dec 54	Culture	257UNTS243	103660
Italy	Yugoslavia	18 Dec 54	Peace/Disarmament	284UNTS239	104141
Multilateral		21 Dec 54	General Amity	258UNTS322	103678
USSR (Soviet Union)	Yugoslavia	05 Jan 55	General Trade	240UNTS207	103404
Austria	Yugoslavia	18 Jan 55	Mass Media	378UNTS31	105416
Iraq	USA (United States)	02 Mar 55	Non-IBRD Project	250UNTS229	103526
Greece	Japan	12 Mar 55	General Trade	227UNTS33	103130
Italy	Yugoslavia	31 Mar 55	General Trade	386UNTS317	105551
Italy	Yugoslavia	31 Mar 55	Visas	386UNTS307	105550
Chile	USA (United States)	31 Mar 55	Education	262UNTS19	103736
Argentina	UK Great Britain	31 Mar 55	General Economic	210UNTS223	102840
Haiti	USA (United States)	27 Apr 55	IGO Establishment	240UNTS17	103391
Netherlands	USA (United States)	29 Apr 55	Milit Installation	219UNTS105	102969
Iraq	UK Great Britain	30 Apr 55	Claims and Debts	226UNTS319	103126
Multilateral		14 May 55	General Amity	219UNTS3	102962
Netherlands	Norway	18 May 55	Culture	252UNTS269	103569
Italy	Norway	14 Jun 55	Culture	260UNTS307	103713
Belgium	USA (United States)	15 Jun 55	Atomic Energy	235UNTS133	103299
Greece	USA (United States)	16 Jun 55	Patents/Copyrights	262UNTS137	103742
France	Greece	28 Jun 55	General Trade	225UNTS219	103100
Germany, West	USA (United States)	07 Jul 55	Air Transport	275UNTS3	103973
Japan	Thailand	09 Jul 55	Finance	230UNTS13	103172
Greece	Netherlands	14 Jul 55	General Trade	227UNTS27	103129
Bolivia	USA (United States)	03 Aug 55	Non-IBRD Project	264UNTS225	103795
Italy	Spain	11 Aug 55	Culture	267UNTS125	103839
Italy	Switzerland	17 Sep 55	Specific Resources	291UNTS213	104257
Brazil	USA (United States)	20 Sep 55	Military Mission	257UNTS349	103665
Multilateral		21 Sep 55	Other Military	269UNTS241	103885
Liberia	USA (United States)	06 Oct 55	Direct Aid	275UNTS87	103977

Special Commission (Cont.)

PARTY ONE	PARTY TWO	DATE	TOPIC	CITATION	NUMBER
Austria	Italy	22 Oct 55	Specific Property	260UNTS327	103716
Italy	Lebanon	04 Nov 55	Tech Assistance	267UNTS147	103840
Italy	Syria	10 Nov 55	General Trade	267UNTS157	103841
Multilateral		13 Dec 55	IGO Operations	529UNTS141	107660
USSR (Soviet Union)	Yugoslavia	19 Dec 55	Scientific Project	378UNTS127	105423
Costa Rica	Guatemala	20 Dec 55	General Economic	280UNTS121	104056
Germany, West	USA (United States)	04 Jan 56	General Military	268UNTS143	103856
Bulgaria	Yugoslavia	10 Feb 56	Scientific Project	349UNTS21	105007
Multilateral		05 Mar 56	Other Military	326UNTS181	104712
Multilateral		05 Mar 56	Other Military	326UNTS169	104711
Burma	Yugoslavia	07 Mar 56	Tech Assistance	386UNTS235	105543
Iran	Pakistan	09 Mar 56	Culture	449UNTS183	106460
Turkey	UK Great Britain	12 Mar 56	Culture	313UNTS73	104530
Ceylon (Sri Lanka)	Romania	16 Mar 56	General Trade	315UNTS41	104558
Japan	USA (United States)	22 Mar 56	Patents/Copyrights	275UNTS195	103983
Romania	USSR (Soviet Union)	07 Apr 56	Culture	259UNTS377	103698
Austria	Hungary	09 Apr 56	Specific Resources	438UNTS123	106315
Germany, West	Italy	19 Apr 56	General Trade	281UNTS195	104080
Mongolia	USSR (Soviet Union)	24 Apr 56	Culture	259UNTS297	103693
Germany, East	USSR (Soviet Union)	26 Apr 56	Health/Educ/Welfare	259UNTS279	103692
Bulgaria	USSR (Soviet Union)	28 Apr 56	Culture	259UNTS363	103697
Peru	USA (United States)	03 May 56	Direct Aid	272UNTS59	103931
Albania	USSR (Soviet Union)	03 May 56	Culture	259UNTS391	103699
Mongolia	Romania	08 May 56	Culture	342UNTS291	104913
Japan	Philippines	09 May 56	Reparations	285UNTS3	104148
Denmark	Italy	12 May 56	General Trade	260UNTS357	103720
Turkey	USA (United States)	18 May 56	Patents/Copyrights	283UNTS167	104115
Czechoslovakia	USSR (Soviet Union)	01 Jun 56	Culture	259UNTS341	103696
Italy	Switzerland	04 Jun 56	Air Transport	378UNTS311	105429
Ceylon (Sri Lanka)	Hungary	04 Jun 56	General Trade	315UNTS13	104555
Multilateral		07 Jun 56	Non-ILO Labor	381UNTS145	105470
Bulgaria	Yugoslavia	16 Jun 56	Territory Boundary	375UNTS235	105368
Bulgaria	Yugoslavia	16 Jun 56	Territory Boundary	391UNTS3	105613
Bulgaria	Ceylon (Sri Lanka)	19 Jun 56	General Trade	315UNTS23	104556
Bulgaria	Ceylon (Sri Lanka)	19 Jun 56	Finance	315UNTS33	104557
France	Greece	25 Jun 56	General Trade	251UNTS167	103540
Hungary	USSR (Soviet Union)	28 Jun 56	Health/Educ/Welfare	259UNTS405	103700
Poland	USSR (Soviet Union)	30 Jun 56	Culture	259UNTS311	103694
Czechoslovakia	Yugoslavia	03 Jul 56	General Economic	397UNTS165	105704
Multilateral		06 Jul 56	Admin Cooperation	312UNTS109	104514
Multilateral		13 Jul 56	Dispute Settlement	281UNTS3	104066
Guatemala	Honduras	22 Aug 56	General Economic	263UNTS49	103767
Korea, North	USSR (Soviet Union)	05 Sep 56	Culture	259UNTS329	103695
Belgium	Germany, West	24 Sep 56	Territory Boundary	314UNTS195	104549
Belgium	Germany, West	24 Sep 56	Culture	263UNTS31	103766
Romania	Yugoslavia	25 Sep 56	Sanitation	395UNTS147	105683
Czechoslovakia	Hungary	13 Oct 56	Territory Boundary	300UNTS125	104336
Denmark	Italy	26 Oct 56	Culture	267UNTS261	103847
Romania	Yugoslavia	27 Oct 56	Scientific Project	389UNTS55	105592
India	Japan	29 Oct 56	Culture	318UNTS289	104622
Germany, West	Netherlands	31 Oct 56	Admin Cooperation	287UNTS21	104177
Ecuador	USA (United States)	31 Oct 56	Education	283UNTS151	104114
Argentina	USA (United States)	05 Nov 56	Education	277UNTS143	104004
Iceland	USA (United States)	06 Dec 56	General Military	265UNTS261	103818
Indonesia	Yugoslavia	14 Dec 56	General Trade	378UNTS117	105422
Canada	USA (United States)	28 Dec 56	Specific Resources	290UNTS103	104229
Belgium	Yugoslavia	05 Feb 57	Culture	276UNTS143	103990
Germany, West	Japan	14 Feb 57	Culture	318UNTS361	104626
Norway	USSR (Soviet Union)	15 Feb 57	Territory Boundary	312UNTS289	104523
France	Netherlands	15 Feb 57	Refugees	286UNTS243	104170
Iceland	USA (United States)	23 Feb 57	Education	283UNTS73	104107
Poland	USSR (Soviet Union)	05 Mar 57	Territory Boundary	274UNTS133	103963
Dominican Republic	USA (United States)	09 Mar 57	Gen Communications	279UNTS249	104044
Germany, East	USSR (Soviet Union)	12 Mar 57	Status of Forces	285UNTS105	104150
France	USA (United States)	12 Mar 57	Patents/Copyrights	279UNTS275	104045

Special Commission (Cont.)

PARTY ONE	PARTY TWO	DATE	TOPIC	CITATION	NUMBER
India	Poland	27 Mar 57	Culture	319UNTS263	104635
Paraguay	USA (United States)	04 Apr 57	Education	284UNTS161	104135
Poland	Vietnam, North	06 Apr 57	Culture	432UNTS255	106224
Romania	USSR (Soviet Union)	15 Apr 57	Status of Forces	274UNTS143	103964
Iran	USSR (Soviet Union)	14 May 57	Dispute Settlement	457UNTS161	106586
Czechoslovakia	Yugoslavia	22 May 57	Non-ILO Labor	391UNTS33	105615
Bulgaria	Yugoslavia	04 Jun 57	Sanitation	349UNTS35	105008
Bulgaria	Yugoslavia	17 Jun 57	Territory Boundary	375UNTS249	105369
Italy	United Arab Rep	06 Jul 57	Finance	302UNTS147	104357
Australia	FAO (Food Agri)	08 Jul 57	Tech Assistance	277UNTS315	104015
Multilateral		12 Jul 57	Visas	322UNTS245	104660
Denmark	Italy	12 Jul 57	General Trade	291UNTS169	104251
Multilateral		26 Jul 57	Land Transport	386UNTS3	105535
France	Italy	01 Aug 57	Non-ILO Labor	302UNTS221	104360
Poland	USSR (Soviet Union)	26 Oct 57	Status of Forces	432UNTS221	106223
France	Italy	08 Nov 57	Mass Media	305UNTS393	104427
Norway	USSR (Soviet Union)	22 Nov 57	Specific Resources	309UNTS269	104476
Argentina	Italy	25 Nov 57	General Economic	305UNTS275	104424
Italy	Monaco	06 Dec 57	Non-ILO Labor	363UNTS45	105198
Italy	Yugoslavia	12 Dec 57	Mass Media	386UNTS293	105549
Belgium	Denmark	31 Dec 57	Culture	305UNTS247	104422
Norway	Turkey	10 Jan 58	Culture	351UNTS229	105025
Ceylon (Sri Lanka)	USSR (Soviet Union)	15 Jan 58	Culture	305UNTS235	104421
Poland	Yugoslavia	16 Jan 58	Non-ILO Labor	340UNTS181	104864
Indonesia	Japan	20 Jan 58	Reparations	324UNTS247	104689
Australia	USA (United States)	24 Jan 58	Patents/Copyrights	307UNTS105	104446
Ceylon (Sri Lanka)	USSR (Soviet Union)	08 Feb 58	General Trade	348UNTS159	104999
Bulgaria	Italy	25 Feb 58	General Trade	362UNTS291	105194
Brazil	Ecuador	05 Mar 58	General Economic	369UNTS43	105250
Poland	USSR (Soviet Union)	18 Mar 58	Territory Boundary	340UNTS89	104861
Bulgaria	Yugoslavia	21 Mar 58	Land Transport	386UNTS119	105541
Italy	Tunisia	08 Apr 58	General Trade	378UNTS327	105430
Germany, West	UK Great Britain	18 Apr 58	Culture	343UNTS241	104928
Hungary	USSR (Soviet Union)	24 Apr 58	Status of Forces	408UNTS118	105868
Belgium	Sweden	08 May 58	Land Transport	312UNTS145	104516
Philippines	USA (United States)	15 May 58	Milit Assistance	316UNTS163	104583
Italy	Switzerland	23 May 58	Land Transport	363UNTS81	105201
Brazil	Colombia	28 May 58	Tech Assistance	369UNTS141	105255
Czechoslovakia	Poland	13 Jun 58	Territory Boundary	354UNTS221	105064
Multilateral		18 Jun 58	General Trade	386UNTS345	105552
Romania	Vietnam, North	30 Jun 58	Scientific Project	389UNTS43	105591
Cuba	USA (United States)	15 Aug 58	Specific Resources	358UNTS63	105124
United Arab Rep	USSR (Soviet Union)	18 Sep 58	Water Transport	338UNTS29	104831
Argentina	Brazil	19 Sep 58	Tech Assistance	374UNTS57	105329
Japan	Laos	15 Oct 58	General Aid	341UNTS25	104875
Spain	USA (United States)	16 Oct 58	Education	336UNTS153	104804
Canada	UK Great Britain	18 Oct 58	General Aid	392UNTS61	105639
Belgium	Spain	27 Oct 58	Culture	327UNTS107	104720
France	Italy	30 Oct 58	Visas	363UNTS3	105196
Israel	Yugoslavia	11 Dec 58	General Trade	386UNTS271	105547
Iraq	Romania	24 Dec 58	General Trade	405UNTS243	105836
Belgium	Turkey	29 Dec 58	Culture	357UNTS195	105118
Cambodia	Japan	02 Mar 59	General Economic	341UNTS163	104882
Iraq	Poland	02 Apr 59	Culture	432UNTS147	106218
Hungary	Iraq	11 Apr 59	Culture	439UNTS25	106323
Italy	United Arab Rep	29 Apr 59	Tech Assistance	363UNTS91	105202
Multilateral		29 Apr 59	Specific Property	346UNTS167	104980
Iran	UK Great Britain	06 May 59	Culture	398UNTS51	105717
Japan	Vietnam, South	13 May 59	Reparations	373UNTS101	105317
Finland	Hungary	10 Jun 59	Culture	439UNTS3	106321
Greece	Yugoslavia	18 Jun 59	Visas	388UNTS3	105570
Greece	Yugoslavia	18 Jun 59	Admin Cooperation	368UNTS125	105237
Greece	Yugoslavia	18 Jun 59	Culture	368UNTS137	105238
Greece	Yugoslavia	18 Jun 59	IGO Establishment	368UNTS17	105233
Greece	Yugoslavia	18 Jun 59	Land Transport	368UNTS27	105234

PARTY ONE	PARTY TWO	DATE	TOPIC	CITATION	NUMBER
Special Commission (Cont.)					
Greece	Yugoslavia	18 Jun 59	Specific Resources	363UNTS133	105205
Czechoslovakia	India	07 Jul 59	Culture	359UNTS259	105145
Multilateral		07 Jul 59	Specific Resources	377UNTS203	105402
Japan	Paraguay	22 Jul 59	Visas	373UNTS85	105316
Multilateral		03 Aug 59	Status of Forces	481UNTS262	106986
Norway	Spain	19 Aug 59	Culture	376UNTS145	105379
United Arab Rep	USA (United States)	28 Sep 59	Education	358UNTS97	105128
India	Italy	06 Oct 59	General Trade	378UNTS267	105427
Guinea	UK Great Britain	22 Oct 59	General Trade	351UNTS341	105033
India	Pakistan	23 Oct 59	Territory Boundary	362UNTS3	105180
Italy	Tunisia	31 Oct 59	General Trade	378UNTS349	105431
Sudan	United Arab Rep	08 Nov 59	Specific Resources	453UNTS51	106519
Tunisia	UK Great Britain	16 Nov 59	General Trade	354UNTS367	105070
France	Israel	30 Nov 59	Culture	377UNTS237	105404
Multilateral		14 Dec 59	Land Transport	422UNTS75	106069
Iraq	UK Great Britain	14 Dec 59	Culture	374UNTS253	105339
Multilateral		14 Dec 59	Sanitation	422UNTS33	106067
Multilateral		14 Dec 59	Sanitation	422UNTS57	106068
Australia	Indonesia	17 Dec 59	General Trade	354UNTS109	105058
India	Pakistan	11 Jan 60	Territory Boundary	375UNTS119	105364
Japan	USA (United States)	19 Jan 60	Status of Forces	373UNTS207	105321
Austria	Czechoslovakia	23 Jan 60	Specific Resources	495UNTS125	107242
Italy	USSR (Soviet Union)	09 Feb 60	Culture	399UNTS75	105735
India	USSR (Soviet Union)	12 Feb 60	Culture	392UNTS153	105642
Cuba	USSR (Soviet Union)	13 Feb 60	General Economic	369UNTS17	105248
Denmark	USA (United States)	19 Feb 60	Patents/Copyrights	354UNTS151	105061
Multilateral		26 Feb 60	Air Transport	418UNTS171	106022
Portugal	USA (United States)	19 Mar 60	Education	371UNTS131	105275
Multilateral		11 Apr 60	Visas	374UNTS3	105323
Mexico	USA (United States)	12 Apr 60	Scientific Project	372UNTS47	105287
Finland	Sweden	13 Apr 60	Culture	428UNTS131	106172
Cuba	Czechoslovakia	10 Jun 60	General Trade	447UNTS75	106412
Czechoslovakia	Germany, East	16 Jun 60	General Economic	415UNTS248	105988
Austria	Spain	17 Jun 60	General Trade	390UNTS17	105600
Spain	UK Great Britain	12 Jul 60	Culture	414UNTS123	105971
USA (United States)	Uruguay	22 Jul 60	Education	388UNTS315	105587
France	Greece	25 Jul 60	General Aid	533UNTS227	107745
Cyprus	UK Great Britain	16 Aug 60	Dispute Settlement	382UNTS183	105478
Austria	Czechoslovakia	14 Sep 60	Commodity Trade	495UNTS143	107243
Multilateral		19 Sep 60	IBRD Project	444UNTS259	106371
Pakistan	IBRD (World Bank)	19 Sep 60	IBRD Project	444UNTS207	106370
Portugal	USA (United States)	31 Oct 60	Patents/Copyrights	394UNTS127	105673
Greece	Poland	08 Nov 60	General Trade	483UNTS127	107010
Brazil	Japan	14 Nov 60	Consul/Citizenship	518UNTS29	107491
Belgium	Congo (Zaire)	15 Nov 60	Finance	394UNTS79	105670
Multilateral		01 Dec 60	Scientific Project	414UNTS110	105970
Denmark	USA (United States)	02 Dec 60	Milit Installation	402UNTS245	105789
Japan	UK Great Britain	03 Dec 60	Culture	414UNTS61	105966
Burma	UN Special Fund	03 Jan 61	Direct Aid	387UNTS219	105564
Nicaragua	UN Special Fund	20 Jan 61	Direct Aid	387UNTS15	105555
Gabon	UN Special Fund	02 Feb 61	Direct Aid	387UNTS289	105568
UK Great Britain	USA (United States)	10 Feb 61	Milit Installation	409UNTS68	105879
Multilateral		08 Mar 61	Scientific Project	396UNTS255	200584
Multilateral		27 Mar 61	IGO Establishment	420UNTS109	106043
IDA (Devel Assoc)	United Nations	10 Apr 61	IGO Operations	394UNTS221	200582
Germany, West	Netherlands	27 Apr 61	Culture	487UNTS77	107095
Somalia	USSR (Soviet Union)	02 Jun 61	General Trade	493UNTS173	107214
Japan	USA (United States)	22 Jun 61	General Economic	410UNTS53	105896
Indonesia	UK Great Britain	29 Jun 61	General Economic	443UNTS255	106364
Netherlands	Euratom	25 Jul 61	Scientific Project	462UNTS263	106686
Albania	Austria	27 Jul 61	General Economic	407UNTS37	105858
Multilateral		18 Oct 61	IGO Establishment	529UNTS89	107659
Belgium	Yugoslavia	31 Oct 61	Sanitation	426UNTS165	106136
Greece	Morocco	01 Nov 61	General Trade	483UNTS113	107009
Ethiopia	USA (United States)	06 Dec 61	Education	433UNTS231	106246

PARTY ONE	PARTY TWO	DATE	TOPIC	CITATION	NUMBER
Special Commission (Cont.)					
Cyprus	USA (United States)	18 Jan 62	Education	435UNTS3	106266
Ghana	USA (United States)	24 Jan 62	Education	435UNTS23	106268
Multilateral		28 Jul 62	Specific Resources	460UNTS219	106642
Multilateral		10 Sep 62	Other Military	502UNTS3	107323
Finland	USSR (Soviet Union)	27 Sep 62	Territory Boundary	479UNTS99	106949
Belgium	Romania	12 Oct 62	Sanitation	502UNTS31	107325
Belgium	Rwanda	13 Oct 62	Tech Assistance	456UNTS431	106569
Germany, West	USA (United States)	20 Nov 62	Education	505UNTS263	107377
Multilateral		15 Jan 63	Tech Assistance	456UNTS409	106567
Malaysia	USA (United States)	28 Jan 63	Education	473UNTS15	106850
United Nations	United Arab Rep	08 Feb 63	Direct Aid	453UNTS79	106520
Burma	Japan	29 Mar 63	General Aid	518UNTS3	107490
Austria	Bulgaria	05 Apr 63	General Trade	480UNTS3	106963
Burma	Thailand	17 May 63	Visas	468UNTS319	106779
Multilateral		09 Jun 63	General Economic	538UNTS309	107818
Austria	USA (United States)	25 Jun 63	Education	479UNTS223	106956
Dahomey	USSR (Soviet Union)	10 Jul 63	General Trade	528UNTS167	107640
Cameroon	UK Great Britain	29 Jul 63	General Economic	478UNTS148	106935
Paraguay	USA (United States)	20 Aug 63	Education	531UNTS197	107704
Mexico	USA (United States)	29 Aug 63	Territory Boundary	505UNTS185	107374
Greece	Poland	30 Sep 63	General Trade	534UNTS23	107751
Czechoslovakia	Yugoslavia	05 Oct 63	Sanitation	504UNTS151	107356
Canada	France	11 Oct 63	Mass Media	529UNTS71	107657
Belgium	Romania	13 Nov 63	Culture	520UNTS119	107513
Netherlands	Portugal	22 Nov 63	Non-ILO Labor	492UNTS31	107185
Romania	Yugoslavia	30 Nov 63	Specific Property	512UNTS2	107438
Multilateral		03 Dec 63	IGO Establishment	529UNTS217	107663
Belgium	Poland	09 Dec 63	Culture	514UNTS195	107448
Romania	Yugoslavia	20 Dec 63	Visas	527UNTS245	107629
Australia	Laos	24 Dec 63	Finance	503UNTS315	107350
Laos	UK Great Britain	24 Dec 63	Finance	502UNTS189	107330
Canada	USA (United States)	22 Jan 64	Specific Property	530UNTS89	107674
Iceland	USA (United States)	13 Feb 64	Education	524UNTS235	107576
Multilateral		28 Feb 64	Atomic Energy	501UNTS245	107321
Belgium	United Nations	20 Mar 64	Milit Installation	533UNTS83	107734
Kenya	USA (United States)	20 Apr 64	Claims and Debts	524UNTS165	107571
Finland	USSR (Soviet Union)	24 Apr 64	Territory Boundary	537UNTS231	107804
Japan	USA (United States)	25 Apr 64	General Economic	530UNTS61	107672
Liberia	USA (United States)	08 May 64	Education	526UNTS239	107608
Korea, South	USA (United States)	12 May 64	Commodity Trade	529UNTS299	107667
Austria	Turkey	15 May 64	Non-ILO Labor	515UNTS109	107457
Ecuador	IBRD (World Bank)	26 May 64	IBRD Project	534UNTS113	107758
France	UK Great Britain	03 Jun 64	Scientific Project	539UNTS253	107836
Multilateral		20 Jun 64	General Economic	539UNTS3	107819
Pakistan	IDA (Devel Assoc)	21 Jul 64	Non-IBRD Project	534UNTS373	107768
Germany, West	UK Great Britain	27 Jul 64	Status of Forces	539UNTS243	107835
Eur Space Research	Sweden	29 Jul 64	IGO Operations	528UNTS81	107636
Netherlands	Turkey	19 Aug 64	Non-ILO Labor	521UNTS197	107523
Australia	USA (United States)	28 Aug 64	Education	510UNTS201	107415
Ceylon (Sri Lanka)	USA (United States)	29 Aug 64	Education	531UNTS93	107695
USA (United States)	Yugoslavia	09 Nov 64	Education	533UNTS39	107731
Denmark	Thailand	25 Jan 65	Tech Assistance	530UNTS173	107680
The Hague Conference on Private International Law					
Multilateral		09 Oct 51	IGO Establishment	220UNTS121	102997
United Nations					
Multilateral		22 Jun 33	ILO Labor	78UNTS181	101016
Netherlands	USA (United States)	14 Jun 43	General Military	28UNTS397	200163
Australia	New Zealand	21 Jan 44	General Amity	18UNTS357	200113
Albania	Yugoslavia	23 Mar 44	General Military	1UNTS81	100015
Multilateral		07 Dec 44	IGO Establishment	15UNTS295	200102
Ethiopia	UK Great Britain	19 Dec 44	General Amity	93UNTS303	200272
Multilateral		20 Jan 45	Peace/Disarmament	140UNTS397	200471
Belgium	USA (United States)	19 Apr 45	Milit Installation	139UNTS179	200455
Netherlands	USA (United States)	30 Apr 45	Milit Installation	139UNTS319	200459

PARTY ONE	PARTY TWO	DATE	TOPIC	CITATION	NUMBER
United Nations (Cont.)					
Chile	USA (United States)	30 Jul 45	General Trade	6UNTS409	200042
Iraq	USA (United States)	31 Jul 45	Milit Assistance	121UNTS239	200402
Multilateral		27 Sep 45	IGO Establishment	5UNTS327	200035
Multilateral		07 Nov 45	IGO Establishment	2UNTS17	100018
France	USA (United States)	08 Nov 45	General Trade	76UNTS151	100986
Multilateral		15 Nov 45	Atomic Energy	3UNTS123	100026
Multilateral		16 Nov 45	IGO Establishment	4UNTS275	100052
Multilateral		26 Dec 45	Peace/Disarmament	20UNTS259	100319
Multilateral		01 Jan 46	Peace/Disarmament	99UNTS131	101375
Multilateral		04 Jan 46	IGO Establishment	6UNTS35	100066
Multilateral		14 Jan 46	Reparations	555UNTS69	108105
Netherlands	USA (United States)	11 Feb 46	Claims and Debts	3UNTS37	100023
Multilateral		13 Feb 46	IGO Status/Immunit	1UNTS15	100004
Poland	Yugoslavia	18 Mar 46	General Military	1UNTS53	100013
Jordan	UK Great Britain	22 Mar 46	General Amity	6UNTS143	100074
Iraq	Turkey	29 Mar 46	General Amity	37UNTS226	100580
Czechoslovakia	Yugoslavia	09 May 46	General Military	1UNTS67	100014
India	USA (United States)	16 May 46	Milit Assistance	4UNTS183	100045
France	USA (United States)	28 May 46	General Economic	84UNTS167	101127
Netherlands	ICJ (Int Court)	26 Jun 46	IGO Status/Immunit	8UNTS61	100114
Multilateral		27 Jun 46	ILO Labor	164UNTS37	102157
Multilateral		28 Jun 46	ILO Labor	442UNTS235	106352
Multilateral		28 Jun 46	Milit Occupation	138UNTS85	101862
Multilateral		29 Jun 46	ILO Labor	214UNTS233	102901
Multilateral		29 Jun 46	ILO Labor	94UNTS11	101303
Multilateral		22 Jul 46	IGO Establishment	9UNTS3	100125
Hungary	USA (United States)	09 Aug 46	Other Military	148UNTS313	101941
Multilateral		03 Sep 46	Commodity Trade	139UNTS3	101872
Multilateral		09 Oct 46	ILO Labor	78UNTS213	101018
Multilateral		09 Oct 46	ILO Labor	38UNTS3	100583
Multilateral		09 Oct 46	ILO Labor	78UNTS198	101017
Multilateral		09 Oct 46	ILO Labor	78UNTS227	101019
Multilateral		30 Oct 46	IGO Establishment	27UNTS77	100401
Multilateral		30 Oct 46	IGO Establishment	11UNTS107	100151
France	Thailand	17 Nov 46	Reparations	344UNTS59	104943
Accept UN Charter	Sweden	19 Nov 46	UN Charter	1UNTS43	100009
Accept UN Charter	Iceland	19 Nov 46	UN Charter	1UNTS41	100008
Accept UN Charter	Afghanistan	19 Nov 46	UN Charter	1UNTS39	100007
Multilateral		02 Dec 46	Specific Resources	161UNTS72	102124
Multilateral		15 Dec 46	IGO Establishment	18UNTS3	100283
Accept UN Charter	Thailand	16 Dec 46	UN Charter	1UNTS47	100011
Netherlands	Thailand	30 Jan 47	General Amity	247UNTS353	103480
Multilateral		06 Feb 47	IGO Establishment	97UNTS227	101352
Multilateral		10 Feb 47	Peace/Disarmament	49UNTS3	100747
Multilateral		10 Feb 47	Peace/Disarmament	41UNTS135	100644
Multilateral		10 Feb 47	Peace/Disarmament	41UNTS21	100643
Multilateral		10 Feb 47	Peace/Disarmament	48UNTS203	100746
Multilateral		10 Feb 47	Peace/Disarmament	42UNTS3	100645
France	UK Great Britain	04 Mar 47	General Amity	9UNTS187	100132
Czechoslovakia	Poland	10 Mar 47	General Military	25UNTS231	100365
Philippines	USA (United States)	14 Mar 47	Milit Installation	43UNTS271	100673
Philippines	USA (United States)	21 Mar 47	Milit Assistance	45UNTS47	100691
Nepal	USA (United States)	25 Apr 47	Consul/Citizenship	16UNTS97	100251
Multilateral		27 May 47	Air Transport	418UNTS161	106021
Netherlands	USA (United States)	28 May 47	General Military	17UNTS29	100267
Greece	USA (United States)	20 Jun 47	Direct Aid	7UNTS267	100105
Multilateral		11 Jul 47	ILO Labor	54UNTS3	100792
Multilateral		11 Jul 47	ILO Labor	214UNTS33	102898
Multilateral		11 Jul 47	ILO Labor	161UNTS113	102125
Turkey	USA (United States)	12 Jul 47	Direct Aid	7UNTS299	100106
Poland	UNICEF (Children)	23 Aug 47	Tech Assistance	65UNTS22	100815
Finland	UNICEF (Children)	23 Aug 47	IGO Operations	68UNTS224	200233
Bulgaria	UNICEF (Children)	23 Aug 47	IGO Operations	68UNTS223	200232
Romania	UNICEF (Children)	28 Aug 47	IGO Operations	68UNTS228	200235
Hungary	UNICEF (Children)	28 Aug 47	IGO Operations	68UNTS226	200234

PARTY ONE	PARTY TWO	DATE	TOPIC	CITATION	NUMBER
United Nations (Cont.)					
Guatemala	USA (United States)	29 Aug 47	Status of Forces	27UNTS11	100393
Multilateral		02 Sep 47	General Military	21UNTS77	100324
Taiwan	USA (United States)	03 Sep 47	Status of Forces	9UNTS91	100126
FAO (Food Agri)	ILO (Labor Org)	11 Sep 47	IGO Operations	18UNTS335	200111
Accept UN Charter	Yemen	30 Sep 47	UN Charter	8UNTS59	100113
Accept UN Charter	Pakistan	30 Sep 47	UN Charter	8UNTS57	100112
Multilateral		02 Oct 47	Telecommunications	193UNTS188	102616
Czechoslovakia	UNICEF (Children)	03 Oct 47	Tech Assistance	65UNTS26	100816
Multilateral		11 Oct 47	IGO Establishment	77UNTS143	100998
Greece	UNICEF (Children)	14 Oct 47	Humanitarian	102UNTS39	101409
Hungary	Yugoslavia	15 Oct 47	Culture	33UNTS73	100515
Netherlands	USA (United States)	30 Oct 47	General Economic	76UNTS47	100978
Canada	USA (United States)	30 Oct 47	General Economic	27UNTS19	100394
UK Great Britain	USA (United States)	30 Oct 47	General Economic	126UNTS39	101680
Multilateral		30 Oct 47	General Economic	55UNTS188	100814
Cuba	USA (United States)	30 Oct 47	General Economic	119UNTS163	101611
France	USA (United States)	30 Oct 47	General Economic	125UNTS171	101676
Multilateral		01 Nov 47	Trusteeship	10UNTS3	100138
Italy	UNICEF (Children)	06 Nov 47	IGO Operations	68UNTS240	200236
Austria	UNICEF (Children)	07 Nov 47	IGO Operations	68UNTS252	200237
Multilateral		12 Nov 47	Admin Cooperation	46UNTS169	100709
Multilateral		12 Nov 47	Admin Cooperation	53UNTS49	100772
Multilateral		12 Nov 47	Admin Cooperation	53UNTS13	100770
Multilateral		12 Nov 47	Admin Cooperation	53UNTS39	100771
Multilateral		12 Nov 47	Admin Cooperation	46UNTS201	100710
Albania	UNICEF (Children)	20 Nov 47	IGO Operations	65UNTS163	200208
UNICEF (Children)	Yugoslavia	20 Nov 47	Tech Assistance	65UNTS28	100817
Multilateral		21 Nov 47	IGO Status/Immunit	33UNTS261	100521
Italy	USA (United States)	02 Feb 48	General Amity	79UNTS171	101040
Brazil	USA (United States)	02 Feb 48	Status of Forces	67UNTS109	100870
France	UNICEF (Children)	19 Feb 48	IGO Operations	68UNTS75	100885
Romania	USA (United States)	26 Feb 48	Admin Cooperation	48UNTS9	100738
Multilateral		06 Mar 48	Water Transport	289UNTS3	104214
Finland	UK Great Britain	12 Mar 48	Admin Cooperation	104UNTS29	101433
Hungary	UK Great Britain	12 Mar 48	Admin Cooperation	104UNTS35	101434
Italy	UK Great Britain	13 Mar 48	Admin Cooperation	104UNTS41	101435
Bulgaria	UK Great Britain	13 Mar 48	Postal Service	104UNTS25	101432
Romania	UK Great Britain	13 Mar 48	Admin Cooperation	104UNTS117	101436
Jordan	UK Great Britain	15 Mar 48	General Military	77UNTS77	100994
Multilateral		17 Mar 48	General Military	19UNTS51	100304
Accept UN Charter	Burma	17 Mar 48	UN Charter	15UNTS3	100225
Finland	USSR (Soviet Union)	06 Apr 48	General Military	48UNTS149	100742
Multilateral		30 Apr 48	IGO Establishment	119UNTS3	101609
Multilateral		30 Apr 48	Dispute Settlement	30UNTS55	100449
Italy	South Africa	01 May 48	Admin Cooperation	225UNTS53	103087
Taiwan	UNICEF (Children)	21 May 48	Tech Assistance	65UNTS38	100818
Bulgaria	Poland	29 May 48	General Military	26UNTS213	100389
Multilateral		10 Jun 48	Humanitarian	164UNTS113	102163
Accept UN Charter	Ceylon (Sri Lanka)	16 Jun 48	UN Charter	223UNTS39	103047
Hungary	Poland	18 Jun 48	Culture	25UNTS319	100370
Multilateral		19 Jun 48	Air Transport	310UNTS151	104492
France	USA (United States)	28 Jun 48	Direct Aid	19UNTS9	100302
Ireland	USA (United States)	28 Jun 48	Direct Aid	24UNTS3	100349
Italy	USA (United States)	28 Jun 48	Direct Aid	20UNTS43	100314
Brazil	USA (United States)	30 Jun 48	General Trade	125UNTS111	101673
Greece	USA (United States)	02 Jul 48	Direct Aid	23UNTS43	100342
Netherlands	USA (United States)	02 Jul 48	Direct Aid	20UNTS91	100315
Luxembourg	USA (United States)	03 Jul 48	Direct Aid	24UNTS35	100350
Sweden	USA (United States)	03 Jul 48	Direct Aid	23UNTS101	100343
Norway	USA (United States)	03 Jul 48	Direct Aid	20UNTS185	100317
Iceland	USA (United States)	03 Jul 48	Direct Aid	20UNTS141	100316
Turkey	USA (United States)	04 Jul 48	Direct Aid	24UNTS67	100351
ICJ Option Clause	Switzerland	06 Jul 48	ICJ Option Clause	17UNTS111	100271
Multilateral		09 Jul 48	ILO Labor	70UNTS85	100898
France	USA (United States)	09 Jul 48	Direct Aid	24UNTS103	100352

PARTY ONE	PARTY TWO	DATE	TOPIC	CITATION	NUMBER
United Nations (Cont.)					
Multilateral		09 Jul 48	ILO Labor	81UNTS147	101070
Multilateral		09 Jul 48	ILO Labor	68UNTS17	100881
Multilateral		10 Jul 48	ILO Labor	91UNTS3	101239
UNESCO (Educ/Cult)	WHO (World Health)	15 Jul 48	IGO Operations	44UNTS323	200184
FAO (Food Agri)	WHO (World Health)	17 Jul 48	IGO Operations	76UNTS171	200244
FAO (Food Agri)	UNESCO (Educ/Cult)	23 Aug 48	IGO Operations	18UNTS345	200112
Korea, South	USA (United States)	24 Aug 48	General Military	79UNTS57	101031
Multilateral		14 Sep 48	Milit Occupation	18UNTS267	100296
Iceland	ICAO (Civil Aviat)	16 Sep 48	Air Transport	28UNTS267	100429
Israel	UNICEF (Children)	20 Sep 48	Direct Aid	71UNTS17	100907
Portugal	USA (United States)	28 Sep 48	Direct Aid	29UNTS213	100442
Accept UN Charter	Bulgaria	09 Oct 48	UN Charter	223UNTS31	103045
Trieste	USA (United States)	15 Oct 48	Direct Aid	29UNTS249	100443
Finland	South Africa	15 Nov 48	Admin Cooperation	225UNTS59	103088
Multilateral		15 Nov 48	IGO Establishment	120UNTS59	101615
Romania	South Africa	16 Nov 48	Admin Cooperation	225UNTS71	103090
Hungary	South Africa	16 Nov 48	Admin Cooperation	225UNTS65	103089
Multilateral		19 Nov 48	Sanitation	44UNTS277	100688
Philippines	UNICEF (Children)	20 Nov 48	Tech Assistance	65UNTS48	100819
Multilateral		29 Nov 48	IGO Establishment	120UNTS13	101613
Accept UN Charter	Israel	29 Nov 48	UN Charter	30UNTS53	100448
UNICEF (Children)	Thailand	01 Dec 48	IGO Operations	68UNTS94	100886
Accept UN Charter	Albania	02 Dec 48	UN Charter	223UNTS23	103043
Multilateral		09 Dec 48	Humanitarian	78UNTS277	101021
Multilateral		09 Dec 48	Scientific Project	73UNTS39	100942
Multilateral		09 Dec 48	Scientific Project	20UNTS229	100318
Korea, South	USA (United States)	10 Dec 48	Direct Aid	55UNTS157	100813
Australia	Hungary	07 Jan 49	Admin Cooperation	189UNTS233	102548
Australia	Finland	07 Jan 49	Admin Cooperation	189UNTS227	102547
Australia	Romania	07 Jan 49	Admin Cooperation	189UNTS263	102550
Australia	Italy	07 Jan 49	Admin Cooperation	189UNTS239	102549
Poland	Romania	26 Jan 49	General Military	85UNTS21	101143
IRO (Refugee Org)	United Nations	07 Feb 49	IGO Operations	26UNTS299	200153
Multilateral		08 Feb 49	Specific Resources	157UNTS157	102053
FAO (Food Agri)	UNESCO (Educ/Cult)	09 Feb 49	IGO Operations	43UNTS315	200182
Israel	United Arab Rep	24 Feb 49	Peace/Disarmament	42UNTS251	100654
Accept UN Charter	Hungary	10 Mar 49	UN Charter	223UNTS55	103051
Israel	Lebanon	23 Mar 49	Peace/Disarmament	42UNTS287	100655
Multilateral		23 Mar 49	Commodity Trade	203UNTS179	102746
Israel	Jordan	03 Apr 49	Peace/Disarmament	42UNTS303	100656
Multilateral		04 Apr 49	General Military	34UNTS243	100541
Multilateral		28 Apr 49	IGO Establishment	83UNTS105	101105
Multilateral		04 May 49	Admin Cooperation	47UNTS159	100728
Multilateral		04 May 49	Admin Cooperation	30UNTS23	100446
Multilateral		04 May 49	Admin Cooperation	98UNTS101	101358
Multilateral		04 May 49	Admin Cooperation	92UNTS19	101257
Multilateral		04 May 49	Admin Cooperation	30UNTS3	100445
Multilateral		05 May 49	IGO Establishment	87UNTS103	101168
India	UNICEF (Children)	10 May 49	IGO Operations	68UNTS96	100887
UNICEF (Children)	UK Great Britain	13 Jun 49	Tech Assistance	65UNTS58	100825
Multilateral		16 Jun 49	Land Transport	45UNTS149	100696
UNICEF (Children)	UK Great Britain	17 Jun 49	Tech Assistance	65UNTS54	100821
UNICEF (Children)	UK Great Britain	17 Jun 49	Tech Assistance	65UNTS56	100823
UNICEF (Children)	UK Great Britain	17 Jun 49	Tech Assistance	65UNTS56	100824
UNICEF (Children)	UK Great Britain	17 Jun 49	Tech Assistance	65UNTS54	100822
UNICEF (Children)	UK Great Britain	17 Jun 49	Tech Assistance	65UNTS50	100820
Multilateral		18 Jun 49	ILO Labor	160UNTS223	102109
Multilateral		20 Jun 49	IGO Establishment	128UNTS141	101718
Pakistan	UNICEF (Children)	20 Jun 49	Tech Assistance	65UNTS60	100826
Multilateral		29 Jun 49	ILO Labor	138UNTS207	101870
Multilateral		01 Jul 49	ILO Labor	138UNTS225	101871
Multilateral		01 Jul 49	ILO Labor	96UNTS237	101340
Multilateral		01 Jul 49	ILO Labor	96UNTS257	101341
Multilateral		15 Jul 49	Health/Educ/Welfare	197UNTS3	102631
Israel	Syria	20 Jul 49	Peace/Disarmament	42UNTS327	100657

PARTY ONE	PARTY TWO	DATE	TOPIC	CITATION	NUMBER
United Nations (Cont.)					
India	Pakistan	27 Jul 49	Peace/Disarmament	81UNTS273	101076
Multilateral		12 Aug 49	General Military	75UNTS135	100972
Multilateral		12 Aug 49	Humanitarian	75UNTS85	100971
Multilateral		12 Aug 49	Humanitarian	75UNTS31	100970
Multilateral		12 Aug 49	Humanitarian	75UNTS287	100973
Multilateral		19 Sep 49	Land Transport	125UNTS3	101671
Ecuador	UNICEF (Children)	12 Oct 49	Tech Assistance	65UNTS62	100827
Indonesia	Netherlands	02 Nov 49	Recognition	69UNTS3	100894
India	WHO (World Health)	09 Nov 49	IGO Status/Immunit	67UNTS43	100865
Germany, West	USA (United States)	15 Dec 49	Direct Aid	92UNTS269	101277
UNICEF (Children)	UK Great Britain	19 Dec 49	Tech Assistance	65UNTS64	100828
Haiti	UNICEF (Children)	20 Dec 49	Tech Assistance	65UNTS68	100829
Costa Rica	UNICEF (Children)	14 Jan 50	Tech Assistance	65UNTS70	100830
Nicaragua	UNICEF (Children)	17 Jan 50	Tech Assistance	65UNTS76	100832
Honduras	UNICEF (Children)	17 Jan 50	Tech Assistance	65UNTS74	100831
El Salvador	UNICEF (Children)	18 Jan 50	Tech Assistance	65UNTS78	100833
Korea, South	USA (United States)	26 Jan 50	Military Mission	178UNTS97	102337
Korea, South	USA (United States)	26 Jan 50	Milit Assistance	80UNTS205	101053
Belgium	USA (United States)	27 Jan 50	Milit Assistance	51UNTS213	100767
Denmark	USA (United States)	27 Jan 50	Milit Assistance	48UNTS115	100740
Peru	UNICEF (Children)	31 Jan 50	Tech Assistance	65UNTS80	100834
Bolivia	UNICEF (Children)	03 Feb 50	Tech Assistance	65UNTS82	100835
Guatemala	UNICEF (Children)	09 Feb 50	Tech Assistance	65UNTS84	100836
UNICEF (Children)	UK Great Britain	10 Feb 50	Direct Aid	65UNTS86	100837
Chile	UNICEF (Children)	03 Mar 50	Direct Aid	126UNTS119	101685
ICJ Option Clause	Liechtenstein	10 Mar 50	ICJ Option Clause	51UNTS115	100758
Colombia	UNICEF (Children)	15 Mar 50	Tech Assistance	65UNTS104	100838
Italy	UK Great Britain	20 Mar 50	Territory Boundary	128UNTS201	101721
Multilateral		21 Mar 50	Admin Cooperation	96UNTS271	101342
Korea, South	UNICEF (Children)	25 Mar 50	IGO Operations	65UNTS171	200209
Indonesia	UNICEF (Children)	06 Apr 50	IGO Operations	68UNTS254	200238
Multilateral		06 Apr 50	Admin Cooperation	119UNTS99	101610
Burma	UNICEF (Children)	22 Apr 50	IGO Operations	68UNTS96	100888
Ceylon (Sri Lanka)	UNICEF (Children)	07 Jun 50	IGO Operations	68UNTS256	200239
Brazil	UNICEF (Children)	09 Jun 50	IGO Operations	66UNTS75	100848
Netherlands	IRO (Refugee Org)	20 Jun 50	Refugees	76UNTS55	100979
Afghanistan	UNICEF (Children)	04 Jul 50	IGO Operations	71UNTS3	100906
Taiwan	UNICEF (Children)	19 Jul 50	IGO Operations	94UNTS21	101304
Multilateral		27 Jul 50	Non-ILO Labor	166UNTS73	102186
Korea, South	USA (United States)	28 Jul 50	Finance	140UNTS57	101883
FAO (Food Agri)	United Nations	02 Aug 50	IGO Operations	139UNTS407	200467
WHO (World Health)	United Arab Rep	25 Aug 50	IGO Operations	92UNTS39	101259
UN Relief Palestin	United Arab Rep	12 Sep 50	Refugees	121UNTS107	101630
Burma	USA (United States)	13 Sep 50	Direct Aid	92UNTS361	101280
Multilateral		16 Sep 50	General Transport	92UNTS91	101264
Thailand	USA (United States)	19 Sep 50	Tech Assistance	132UNTS199	101761
UN Relief Palestin	WHO (World Health)	23 Sep 50	Sanitation	103UNTS129	200310
Accept UN Charter	Indonesia	25 Sep 50	UN Charter	71UNTS153	100916
Indonesia	USA (United States)	16 Oct 50	Direct Aid	281UNTS105	104074
Thailand	USA (United States)	17 Oct 50	Milit Assistance	79UNTS41	101030
Burma	USA (United States)	06 Nov 50	Milit Assistance	122UNTS81	101638
Multilateral		22 Nov 50	Culture	131UNTS25	101734
Multilateral		02 Dec 50	Trusteeship	118UNTS255	200381
Multilateral		07 Dec 50	Admin Cooperation	212UNTS17	102861
Multilateral		15 Dec 50	Customs	157UNTS129	102052
Pakistan	USA (United States)	15 Dec 50	Milit Assistance	122UNTS89	101639
Multilateral		23 Dec 50	Tech Assistance	185UNTS3	102456
Portugal	USA (United States)	05 Jan 51	Milit Assistance	133UNTS75	101782
Netherlands	USA (United States)	19 Jan 51	Reparations	141UNTS221	101917
UK Great Britain	Yemen	20 Jan 51	General Amity	101UNTS39	101400
Ceylon (Sri Lanka)	ILO (Labor Org)	24 Jan 51	Tech Assistance	117UNTS355	200380
Paraguay	UNICEF (Children)	25 Jan 51	IGO Operations	79UNTS9	101027
Netherlands	IRO (Refugee Org)	13 Feb 51	IGO Operations	87UNTS239	101175
Israel	ILO (Labor Org)	19 Feb 51	Tech Assistance	100UNTS105	101391
ICAO (Civil Aviat)	United Nations	28 Feb 51	IGO Operations	139UNTS429	200469

PARTY ONE	PARTY TWO	DATE	TOPIC	CITATION	NUMBER
United Nations (Cont.)					
Indonesia	Pakistan	03 Mar 51	General Amity	188UNTS333	102537
ILO (Labor Org)	Syria	03 Mar 51	Tech Assistance	110UNTS69	101502
UNESCO (Educ/Cult)	United Nations	07 Mar 51	IGO Operations	139UNTS417	200468
India	USA (United States)	16 Mar 51	Milit Assistance	141UNTS47	101904
Multilateral		20 Mar 51	IGO Operations	82UNTS172	101091
WHO (World Health)	United Arab Rep	25 Mar 51	IGO Status/Immunit	223UNTS87	103058
Multilateral		28 Mar 51	Tech Assistance	181UNTS61	102399
Jordan	ILO (Labor Org)	29 Mar 51	Tech Assistance	100UNTS247	200287
Liberia	ILO (Labor Org)	02 Apr 51	Tech Assistance	100UNTS117	101392
Multilateral		05 Apr 51	Tech Assistance	84UNTS299	101139
Ceylon (Sri Lanka)	ILO (Labor Org)	06 Apr 51	Tech Assistance	100UNTS235	200286
Mexico	ILO (Labor Org)	06 Apr 51	Tech Assistance	100UNTS131	101393
Iraq	USA (United States)	10 Apr 51	Tech Assistance	151UNTS179	101993
Guatemala	ILO (Labor Org)	13 Apr 51	Tech Assistance	126UNTS249	101692
Peru	ILO (Labor Org)	13 Apr 51	Tech Assistance	100UNTS31	101385
Canada	ICAO (Civil Aviat)	14 Apr 51	IGO Status/Immunit	96UNTS155	101335
Multilateral		18 Apr 51	IGO Establishment	261UNTS140	103729
Ecuador	ILO (Labor Org)	19 Apr 51	Tech Assistance	100UNTS77	101389
Cuba	ILO (Labor Org)	21 Apr 51	Tech Assistance	99UNTS205	101382
Greece	ILO (Labor Org)	25 Apr 51	Tech Assistance	100UNTS93	101390
India	ILO (Labor Org)	26 Apr 51	Tech Assistance	100UNTS19	101384
Mexico	WHO (World Health)	30 Apr 51	Tech Assistance	103UNTS95	101427
WHO (World Health)	Yugoslavia	02 May 51	Tech Assistance	103UNTS117	101429
United Arab Rep	USA (United States)	05 May 51	Tech Assistance	198UNTS265	102670
Pakistan	ILO (Labor Org)	16 May 51	Tech Assistance	100UNTS147	101394
Multilateral		25 May 51	Status of Forces	175UNTS215	102303
Lebanon	USA (United States)	29 May 51	Tech Assistance	160UNTS49	102101
Multilateral		01 Jun 51	Tech Assistance	118UNTS57	101596
Lebanon	WHO (World Health)	07 Jun 51	Tech Assistance	126UNTS221	101690
Panama	UNICEF (Children)	14 Jun 51	IGO Operations	97UNTS3	101343
Saudi Arabia	USA (United States)	18 Jun 51	Milit Assistance	141UNTS67	101906
Dominican Republic	ILO (Labor Org)	18 Jun 51	Tech Assistance	100UNTS3	101383
ILO (Labor Org)	Vietnam, South	26 Jun 51	Tech Assistance	100UNTS223	200285
Sweden	USA (United States)	27 Jun 51	Milit Assistance	148UNTS77	101937
Italy	UK Great Britain	28 Jun 51	Claims and Debts	118UNTS115	101600
Multilateral		29 Jun 51	ILO Labor	165UNTS303	102181
Multilateral		02 Jul 51	Refugees	189UNTS137	102545
Burma	WHO (World Health)	09 Jul 51	Sanitation	107UNTS9	101463
ILO (Labor Org)	Thailand	11 Jul 51	Tech Assistance	100UNTS159	101395
Paraguay	ILO (Labor Org)	12 Jul 51	Tech Assistance	117UNTS155	101591
Burma	WHO (World Health)	17 Jul 51	Tech Assistance	102UNTS127	101415
Multilateral		18 Jul 51	Direct Aid	102UNTS291	200308
Philippines	WHO (World Health)	22 Jul 51	IGO Status/Immunit	149UNTS197	101953
Pakistan	Turkey	26 Jul 51	General Amity	188UNTS323	102536
Multilateral		27 Jul 51	Tech Assistance	97UNTS291	200273
Iran	UNICEF (Children)	02 Aug 51	Direct Aid	247UNTS11	103457
Israel	WHO (World Health)	07 Aug 51	Tech Assistance	104UNTS213	101442
Pakistan	United Arab Rep	28 Aug 51	General Amity	214UNTS247	102902
WHO (World Health)	Saudi Arabia	29 Aug 51	Tech Assistance	110UNTS277	101516
Philippines	USA (United States)	30 Aug 51	Milit Assistance	177UNTS133	102315
Multilateral		01 Sep 51	General Military	131UNTS83	101736
Multilateral		08 Sep 51	Peace/Disarmament	136UNTS45	101832
Japan	USA (United States)	08 Sep 51	General Military	136UNTS211	101835
Japan	USA (United States)	08 Sep 51	Milit Assistance	136UNTS203	101834
Norway	USA (United States)	17 Sep 51	Milit Assistance	140UNTS313	101895
Colombia	WHO (World Health)	18 Sep 51	Tech Assistance	109UNTS45	101489
Iraq	ICAO (Civil Aviat)	18 Sep 51	Tech Assistance	108UNTS219	101475
Korea, South	WHO (World Health)	19 Sep 51	Sanitation	109UNTS297	200366
WHO (World Health)	Vietnam, South	21 Sep 51	Tech Assistance	107UNTS63	200352
Multilateral		01 Oct 51	Tech Assistance	104UNTS249	101446
Pakistan	WHO (World Health)	07 Oct 51	Tech Assistance	126UNTS101	101684
India	WHO (World Health)	11 Oct 51	Non-IBRD Project	118UNTS27	101594
Multilateral		14 Oct 51	IGO Establishment	122UNTS3	101631
Ecuador	WHO (World Health)	16 Oct 51	Tech Assistance	110UNTS263	101515
ILO (Labor Org)	Venezuela	22 Oct 51	Tech Assistance	117UNTS139	101590

PARTY ONE	PARTY TWO	DATE	TOPIC	CITATION	NUMBER
United Nations (Cont.)					
Taiwan	WHO (World Health)	25 Oct 51	Sanitation	126UNTS77	101683
India	WHO (World Health)	01 Nov 51	Scientific Project	118UNTS13	101593
Denmark	WHO (World Health)	05 Nov 51	Sanitation	110UNTS253	101514
Panama	WHO (World Health)	09 Nov 51	Sanitation	118UNTS43	101595
South Africa	USA (United States)	09 Nov 51	Milit Assistance	160UNTS41	102100
Panama	ILO (Labor Org)	10 Nov 51	Tech Assistance	126UNTS269	101693
Liberia	USA (United States)	19 Nov 51	Milit Assistance	167UNTS141	102204
Council of Europe	ILO (Labor Org)	23 Nov 51	IGO Operations	126UNTS331	200435
ICJ Option Clause	Japan	24 Nov 51	ICJ Option Clause	137UNTS3	101842
Denmark	WHO (World Health)	30 Nov 51	Scientific Project	118UNTS3	101592
Multilateral		06 Dec 51	IGO Establishment	425UNTS61	106119
Iraq	UNICEF (Children)	10 Dec 51	Direct Aid	126UNTS57	101682
Mexico	WHO (World Health)	17 Dec 51	Tech Assistance	124UNTS121	101670
Guatemala	WHO (World Health)	17 Dec 51	Sanitation	120UNTS133	101619
Australia	Italy	20 Dec 51	Peace/Disarmament	190UNTS223	102566
Italy	New Zealand	20 Dec 51	Peace/Disarmament	150UNTS157	101970
India	WHO (World Health)	20 Dec 51	Tech Assistance	124UNTS109	101669
Italy	UK Great Britain	21 Dec 51	Peace/Disarmament	121UNTS89	101628
Italy	USA (United States)	21 Dec 51	Peace/Disarmament	167UNTS163	102206
Accept UN Charter	Libya	24 Dec 51	UN Charter	223UNTS51	103050
Guatemala	WHO (World Health)	29 Dec 51	Sanitation	124UNTS89	101668
France	USA (United States)	05 Jan 52	Milit Assistance	181UNTS177	102408
Lebanon	USA (United States)	05 Jan 52	Tech Assistance	180UNTS199	102385
Italy	USA (United States)	07 Jan 52	Milit Assistance	179UNTS165	102365
Portugal	USA (United States)	08 Jan 52	General Military	207UNTS51	102799
Norway	USA (United States)	08 Jan 52	Milit Assistance	179UNTS185	102367
UK Great Britain	USA (United States)	08 Jan 52	Milit Assistance	179UNTS201	102369
Luxembourg	USA (United States)	08 Jan 52	Milit Assistance	180UNTS191	102384
USA (United States)	Yugoslavia	08 Jan 52	Direct Aid	152UNTS61	102011
Iceland	USA (United States)	08 Jan 52	Milit Assistance	180UNTS183	102383
Netherlands	USA (United States)	08 Jan 52	Milit Assistance	179UNTS175	102366
Multilateral		10 Jan 52	Visas	163UNTS27	102139
Austria	WHO (World Health)	10 Jan 52	Tech Assistance	131UNTS295	200438
Multilateral		10 Jan 52	Visas	163UNTS3	102138
Costa Rica	WHO (World Health)	23 Jan 52	Sanitation	135UNTS265	101826
ICAO (Civil Aviat)	Yugoslavia	06 Feb 52	Tech Assistance	128UNTS97	101715
WHO (World Health)	UK Great Britain	07 Feb 52	Tech Assistance	121UNTS75	101627
Burma	USA (United States)	09 Feb 52	Milit Assistance	179UNTS91	102357
Italy	UK Great Britain	12 Feb 52	Claims and Debts	126UNTS297	101695
Lebanon	ICAO (Civil Aviat)	14 Feb 52	Tech Assistance	128UNTS83	101714
Dominican Republic	UNICEF (Children)	15 Feb 52	Humanitarian	121UNTS43	101625
UNICEF (Children)	UK Great Britain	15 Feb 52	Direct Aid	121UNTS63	101626
Multilateral		15 Feb 52	Scientific Project	132UNTS51	101751
Dominican Republic	WHO (World Health)	15 Feb 52	Sanitation	134UNTS291	101808
Ecuador	USA (United States)	20 Feb 52	Milit Assistance	177UNTS43	102308
Peru	USA (United States)	22 Feb 52	Milit Assistance	165UNTS31	102166
ICAO (Civil Aviat)	United Arab Rep	06 Mar 52	Tech Assistance	151UNTS111	101986
Finland	WHO (World Health)	07 Mar 52	Tech Assistance	128UNTS269	200436
Cuba	USA (United States)	07 Mar 52	Milit Assistance	165UNTS11	102165
Libya	UNICEF (Children)	05 Apr 52	Direct Aid	133UNTS287	200441
Chile	USA (United States)	09 Apr 52	Milit Assistance	186UNTS53	102482
Colombia	USA (United States)	17 Apr 52	Milit Assistance	174UNTS215	102287
Liberia	UNICEF (Children)	17 Apr 52	Direct Aid	133UNTS3	101773
Taiwan	Japan	28 Apr 52	Peace/Disarmament	138UNTS3	101858
India	ICAO (Civil Aviat)	29 Apr 52	Tech Assistance	151UNTS123	101987
UNICEF (Children)	United Arab Rep	18 May 52	Direct Aid	324UNTS161	104684
Multilateral		20 May 52	Sanitation	219UNTS55	102966
Australia	Italy	24 May 52	Reparations	161UNTS65	102123
Korea, South	USA (United States)	24 May 52	Direct Aid	179UNTS23	102353
Mexico	WHO (World Health)	28 May 52	Sanitation	134UNTS319	101810
India	WHO (World Health)	04 Jun 52	Sanitation	135UNTS279	101827
Brazil	WHO (World Health)	12 Jun 52	Scientific Project	151UNTS333	102003
Ethiopia	USA (United States)	13 Jun 52	Milit Assistance	205UNTS17	102766
Accept UN Charter	Cambodia	15 Jun 52	UN Charter	223UNTS35	103046
Accept UN Charter	Japan	16 Jun 52	UN Charter	256UNTS167	103626

PARTY ONE	PARTY TWO	DATE	TOPIC	CITATION	NUMBER
United Nations (Cont.)					
Belgium	UNICEF (Children)	17 Jun 52	Direct Aid	171UNTS249	102228
New Zealand	USA (United States)	19 Jun 52	Milit Assistance	178UNTS315	102347
WHO (World Health)	Syria	20 Jun 52	Tech Assistance	165UNTS219	102178
Multilateral		26 Jun 52	ILO Labor	196UNTS183	102624
Multilateral		28 Jun 52	ILO Labor	210UNTS132	102838
Multilateral		28 Jun 52	ILO Labor	214UNTS321	102907
Accept UN Charter	Laos	30 Jun 52	UN Charter	223UNTS47	103049
USA (United States)	Uruguay	30 Jun 52	Milit Assistance	207UNTS139	102804
Sweden	USA (United States)	01 Jul 52	Milit Assistance	187UNTS3	102497
Australia	FAO (Food Agri)	07 Jul 52	Tech Assistance	184UNTS209	102449
Jordan	UNICEF (Children)	08 Jul 52	Direct Aid	173UNTS353	200503
UNICEF (Children)	Syria	10 Jul 52	Direct Aid	136UNTS17	101830
Multilateral		11 Jul 52	IGO Establishment	169UNTS3	102220
Chile	WHO (World Health)	11 Jul 52	Tech Assistance	137UNTS27	101846
India	WHO (World Health)	16 Jul 52	Tech Assistance	135UNTS291	101828
France	WHO (World Health)	23 Jul 52	IGO Status/Immunit	209UNTS231	102829
Chile	ILO (Labor Org)	23 Jul 52	Tech Assistance	178UNTS323	102348
UNICEF (Children)	UK Great Britain	25 Jul 52	Direct Aid	135UNTS37	101812
Accept UN Charter	Austria	06 Aug 52	UN Charter	223UNTS27	103044
Laos	UNICEF (Children)	15 Aug 52	Direct Aid	161UNTS323	200491
UNICEF (Children)	Vietnam, South	29 Aug 52	Direct Aid	161UNTS335	200492
Ethiopia	UK Great Britain	29 Aug 52	Trusteeship	190UNTS329	102573
Italy	ILO (Labor Org)	04 Sep 52	Tech Assistance	178UNTS371	200505
Germany, West	Israel	10 Sep 52	Reparations	162UNTS205	102137
Dominican Republic	WHO (World Health)	10 Oct 52	Sanitation	150UNTS133	101967
Chile	WHO (World Health)	24 Oct 52	Sanitation	151UNTS339	102004
Chile	WHO (World Health)	04 Nov 52	Sanitation	150UNTS119	101966
Multilateral		07 Nov 52	General Trade	221UNTS255	103010
Mexico	ICAO (Civil Aviat)	28 Nov 52	Tech Assistance	164UNTS15	102156
India	WHO (World Health)	11 Dec 52	Sanitation	158UNTS391	102073
UNICEF (Children)	UK Great Britain	16 Dec 52	Direct Aid	151UNTS359	102005
Multilateral		16 Dec 52	Tech Assistance	158UNTS407	102074
ILO (Labor Org)	UN Relief Palestin	31 Dec 52	Tech Assistance	182UNTS201	200506
UK Great Britain	USA (United States)	19 Jan 53	General Military	161UNTS71	102117
Taiwan	ILO (Labor Org)	13 Feb 53	Tech Assistance	178UNTS337	102349
Multilateral		28 Feb 53	General Amity	167UNTS21	102199
Lebanon	USA (United States)	23 Mar 53	Milit Assistance	239UNTS45	103370
Libya	UK Great Britain	25 Mar 53	Finance	172UNTS281	102252
United Nations	WMO (Meteorology)	27 Mar 53	IGO Operations	178UNTS361	200504
Jordan	UN Relief Palestin	30 Mar 53	Direct Aid	165UNTS317	200495
Multilateral		31 Mar 53	Mass Media	435UNTS191	106280
Multilateral		31 Mar 53	Privil/Immunities	193UNTS136	102613
France	WHO (World Health)	02 Apr 53	Tech Assistance	174UNTS83	102279
Japan	Pakistan	24 Apr 53	Admin Cooperation	221UNTS325	103013
Ethiopia	UNICEF (Children)	27 Apr 53	Direct Aid	213UNTS169	102885
France	WHO (World Health)	30 Apr 53	Tech Assistance	174UNTS71	102278
Multilateral		11 May 53	Sanitation	456UNTS3	106555
Ethiopia	USA (United States)	22 May 53	Milit Assistance	207UNTS127	102803
ICAO (Civil Aviat)	Syria	28 May 53	Tech Assistance	173UNTS199	102267
Ethiopia	United Nations	22 Jun 53	Tech Assistance	172UNTS93	102241
Multilateral		25 Jun 53	ILO Labor	191UNTS143	102581
Philippines	USA (United States)	26 Jun 53	Milit Assistance	213UNTS77	102881
Pakistan	Turkey	29 Jun 53	Culture	211UNTS225	102854
Afghanistan	USA (United States)	30 Jun 53	Tech Assistance	215UNTS3	102908
Libya	UK Great Britain	29 Jul 53	General Amity	186UNTS185	102491
ICAO (Civil Aviat)	United Arab Rep	27 Aug 53	IGO Status/Immunit	215UNTS371	102925
Denmark	Finland	24 Sep 53	Dispute Settlement	188UNTS283	102532
Spain	USA (United States)	26 Sep 53	Milit Assistance	207UNTS61	102800
Korea, South	USA (United States)	01 Oct 53	General Military	238UNTS199	103363
UNICEF (Children)	UK Great Britain	07 Oct 53	Tech Assistance	180UNTS59	102375
Multilateral		09 Oct 53	Tech Assistance	190UNTS49	102557
Multilateral		26 Oct 53	Status of Forces	207UNTS237	102809
Japan	UNICEF (Children)	21 Nov 53	Direct Aid	183UNTS297	200507
Multilateral		07 Dec 53	Admin Cooperation	182UNTS51	102422
Multilateral		11 Dec 53	Sanitation	191UNTS285	102588

PARTY ONE	PARTY TWO	DATE	TOPIC	CITATION	NUMBER
United Nations (Cont.)					
Belgium	Lebanon	24 Dec 53	Air Transport	219UNTS153	102972
ICJ Option Clause	San Marino	11 Jan 54	ICJ Option Clause	186UNTS295	102495
Pakistan	Turkey	04 Feb 54	General Amity	211UNTS263	102858
Brazil	WHO (World Health)	04 Feb 54	Tech Assistance	233UNTS49	103250
Germany, West	USA (United States)	12 Feb 54	Milit Assistance	223UNTS153	103064
Multilateral		19 Feb 54	Status of Forces	214UNTS51	102899
ICJ Option Clause	Finland	26 Feb 54	Dispute Settlement	189UNTS223	102546
ICJ Option Clause	Japan	25 Mar 54	ICJ Option Clause	188UNTS137	102524
Iraq	USA (United States)	21 Apr 54	Milit Assistance	222UNTS251	103032
Nicaragua	USA (United States)	23 Apr 54	Milit Assistance	229UNTS37	103159
UNICEF (Children)	Spain	07 May 54	Direct Aid	190UNTS357	200515
Multilateral		12 May 54	Admin Cooperation	327UNTS3	104714
Pakistan	USA (United States)	19 May 54	Milit Assistance	202UNTS301	102736
Honduras	USA (United States)	20 May 54	Milit Assistance	222UNTS87	103025
Mexico	UNICEF (Children)	20 May 54	Direct Aid	192UNTS3	102591
Multilateral		21 May 54	Non-ILO Labor	345UNTS285	104973
Colombia	USA (United States)	22 May 54	Visas	354UNTS21	105050
Austria	Yugoslavia	25 May 54	Specific Resources	227UNTS111	103135
Multilateral		31 May 54	Tech Assistance	192UNTS20	102592
Multilateral		04 Jun 54	Customs	282UNTS249	104101
Multilateral		04 Jun 54	Customs	276UNTS191	103992
France	UNESCO (Educ/Cult)	02 Jul 54	IGO Status/Immunit	357UNTS3	105103
Multilateral		09 Aug 54	General Amity	211UNTS237	102855
New Zealand	UNICEF (Children)	26 Aug 54	Direct Aid	198UNTS173	102663
Multilateral		08 Sep 54	Milit Assistance	209UNTS23	102819
Libya	USA (United States)	09 Sep 54	Milit Installation	224UNTS217	103078
Multilateral		28 Sep 54	Refugees	360UNTS117	105158
UNESCO (Educ/Cult)	UN Special Fund	29 Sep 54	IGO Operations	363UNTS367	200572
Multilateral		05 Oct 54	Territory Boundary	235UNTS99	103297
China People's Rep	USSR (Soviet Union)	12 Oct 54	General Amity	226UNTS57	103108
Multilateral		23 Oct 54	Milit Occupation	331UNTS327	104759
Korea, South	USA (United States)	17 Nov 54	Milit Assistance	256UNTS251	103635
Austria	Yugoslavia	27 Nov 54	Specific Resources	396UNTS75	105694
Taiwan	USA (United States)	10 Dec 54	General Military	248UNTS213	103496
Haiti	USA (United States)	28 Jan 55	Milit Assistance	270UNTS83	103894
United Arab Rep	Yugoslavia	20 Feb 55	Air Transport	255UNTS199	103611
WMO (Meteorology)	Switzerland	10 Mar 55	IGO Status/Immunit	211UNTS277	200524
Multilateral		10 May 55	Claims and Debts	273UNTS121	103948
Multilateral		14 May 55	General Amity	219UNTS3	102962
Multilateral		15 May 55	Recognition	217UNTS223	102949
Pakistan	Sweden	04 Jun 55	Tech Assistance	228UNTS121	103146
Multilateral		06 Jun 55	IGO Establishment	219UNTS79	102968
Guatemala	USA (United States)	18 Jun 55	Milit Assistance	262UNTS105	103740
Denmark	WHO (World Health)	29 Jun 55	IGO Status/Immunit	247UNTS168	103467
Germany, West	USA (United States)	30 Jun 55	Milit Assistance	240UNTS47	103393
Libya	WHO (World Health)	05 Jul 55	Tech Assistance	219UNTS305	200530
Belgium	USA (United States)	15 Jul 55	Milit Assistance	223UNTS3	103040
Accept UN Charter	Spain	23 Sep 55	UN Charter	223UNTS63	103053
Accept UN Charter	Jordan	11 Oct 55	UN Charter	223UNTS43	103048
Multilateral		20 Oct 55	IGO Establishment	378UNTS159	105425
Guatemala	UNICEF (Children)	22 Nov 55	Direct Aid	221UNTS305	103012
Accept UN Charter	Romania	14 Dec 55	UN Charter	223UNTS59	103052
Accept UN Charter	Romania	15 Dec 55	UN Charter	223UNTS69	103055
Accept UN Charter	Nepal	15 Dec 55	UN Charter	223UNTS65	103054
ICJ Option Clause	Portugal	19 Dec 55	ICJ Option Clause	224UNTS275	103079
Accept UN Charter	Sudan	12 Jan 56	UN Charter	253UNTS81	103576
Accept UN Charter	Portugal	04 Feb 56	UN Charter	229UNTS3	103155
Ethiopia	WHO (World Health)	17 Feb 56	Tech Assistance	243UNTS91	103448
Accept UN Charter	Italy	22 Feb 56	UN Charter	231UNTS175	103217
Burma	Yugoslavia	07 Mar 56	Direct Aid	378UNTS99	105420
Multilateral		13 Mar 56	Humanitarian	427UNTS245	106158
Cambodia	UNICEF (Children)	28 Apr 56	Direct Aid	136UNTS341	200446
Multilateral		18 May 56	Customs	338UNTS103	104834
Multilateral		18 May 56	Land Transport	339UNTS3	104844
Multilateral		18 May 56	Customs	327UNTS123	104721

PARTY ONE	PARTY TWO	DATE	TOPIC	CITATION	NUMBER
United Nations (Cont.)					
Multilateral		18 May 56	Customs	319UNTS21	104630
Multilateral		19 May 56	Land Transport	399UNTS189	105742
Italy	UNICEF (Children)	28 May 56	Direct Aid	243UNTS43	103445
Multilateral		20 Jun 56	Admin Cooperation	268UNTS3	103850
Lebanon	UNICEF (Children)	03 Jul 56	Direct Aid	324UNTS145	104683
Accept UN Charter	Tunisia	14 Jul 56	UN Charter	253UNTS85	103577
Accept UN Charter	Morocco	17 Jul 56	UN Charter	253UNTS77	103575
UNICEF (Children)	Sudan	07 Aug 56	Direct Aid	248UNTS307	200542
Multilateral		25 Sep 56	Air Transport	334UNTS89	104767
Multilateral		25 Sep 56	Air Transport	334UNTS13	104766
ICJ Option Clause	Israel	03 Oct 56	ICJ Option Clause	252UNTS301	103571
UN Hi Com Refugees	Sweden	08 Oct 56	Refugees	428UNTS307	106182
Japan	USSR (Soviet Union)	19 Oct 56	General Amity	263UNTS99	103768
Multilateral		26 Oct 56	IGO Establishment	276UNTS3	103988
Accept UN Charter	Ireland	06 Nov 56	UN Charter	254UNTS223	103594
Multilateral		14 Dec 56	Taxation	436UNTS115	106292
Multilateral		14 Dec 56	Taxation	436UNTS131	106293
Mexico	ICAO (Civil Aviat)	20 Dec 56	IGO Operations	497UNTS3	107259
Japan	Poland	08 Feb 57	General Amity	318UNTS251	104620
Czechoslovakia	Japan	13 Feb 57	General Amity	300UNTS119	104335
Multilateral		20 Feb 57	Consul/Citizenship	309UNTS65	104468
Multilateral		22 Feb 57	Tech Assistance	274UNTS93	103960
Multilateral		01 Mar 57	Tech Assistance	264UNTS94	103790
Accept UN Charter	Ghana	01 Mar 57	IGO Establishment	261UNTS113	103727
Burma	USA (United States)	21 Mar 57	Direct Aid	300UNTS11	104327
Multilateral		25 Mar 57	IGO Establishment	294UNTS2	104300
Multilateral		25 Mar 57	IGO Establishment	294UNTS259	104301
Other Unilat Decla	United Arab Rep	24 Apr 57	General Ad Hoc	265UNTS299	103821
Multilateral		01 May 57	Admin Cooperation	284UNTS201	104138
Multilateral		24 May 57	Tech Assistance	268UNTS270	103861
Honduras	Nicaragua	22 Jun 57	Specif Claim/Waive	277UNTS159	104005
Multilateral		25 Jun 57	ILO Labor	320UNTS291	104648
Multilateral		26 Jun 57	ILO Labor	328UNTS247	104738
Multilateral		26 Jun 57	ILO Labor	325UNTS279	104704
Libya	USA (United States)	30 Jun 57	Milit Assistance	284UNTS177	104136
Morocco	UNICEF (Children)	31 Jul 57	Direct Aid	282UNTS99	104095
Accept UN Charter	Fed of Malaya	31 Aug 57	UN Charter	277UNTS3	103995
Japan	USA (United States)	14 Sep 57	Admin Cooperation	293UNTS247	104293
Multilateral		03 Oct 57	Postal Service	364UNTS3	105211
Netherlands	Sweden	23 Oct 57	Land Transport	306UNTS75	104433
Argentina	UNICEF (Children)	19 Nov 57	Direct Aid	300UNTS229	104338
Austria	IAEA (Atom Energy)	11 Dec 57	Atomic Energy	339UNTS110	104849
Multilateral		13 Dec 57	Land Transport	372UNTS159	105296
Multilateral		15 Jan 58	Customs	383UNTS229	105503
Ghana	WHO (World Health)	21 Jan 58	Tech Assistance	307UNTS3	104437
Multilateral		29 Jan 58	Specific Resources	339UNTS23	104845
Indonesia	WHO (World Health)	05 Feb 58	Tech Assistance	307UNTS15	104438
Ghana	USA (United States)	12 Feb 58	Admin Cooperation	442UNTS175	106348
Multilateral		20 Mar 58	Admin Cooperation	335UNTS211	104789
Multilateral		03 Apr 58	Commodity Trade	302UNTS121	104355
Multilateral		03 Apr 58	Commodity Trade	336UNTS177	104806
Israel	WHO (World Health)	11 Apr 58	Tech Assistance	307UNTS27	104439
Multilateral		29 Apr 58	Water Transport	450UNTS11	106465
Multilateral		29 Apr 58	Dispute Settlement	450UNTS169	106466
Multilateral		29 Apr 58	Territory Boundary	516UNTS205	107477
Multilateral		29 Apr 58	Territory Boundary	499UNTS311	107302
New Zealand	USA (United States)	05 May 58	Visas	317UNTS59	104594
Arab League	ILO (Labor Org)	26 May 58	IGO Operations	302UNTS343	200549
Multilateral		10 Jun 58	General Economic	454UNTS47	106539
Multilateral		10 Jun 58	Land Transport	454UNTS115	106540
Multilateral		10 Jun 58	Land Transport	454UNTS211	106541
Multilateral		10 Jun 58	Admin Cooperation	330UNTS3	104739
WHO (World Health)	Sudan	21 Jun 58	Tech Assistance	307UNTS235	104453
Multilateral		24 Jun 58	ILO Labor	348UNTS275	105005
Multilateral		25 Jun 58	ILO Labor	362UNTS31	105181

PARTY ONE	PARTY TWO	DATE	TOPIC	CITATION	NUMBER
United Nations (Cont.)					
EEC (Econ Commnty)	ILO (Labor Org)	07 Jul 58	IGO Operations	312UNTS387	200551
Ghana	UNICEF (Children)	12 Aug 58	Direct Aid	309UNTS103	104469
Indonesia	USA (United States)	13 Aug 58	Milit Assistance	335UNTS187	104785
Pakistan	Thailand	28 Aug 58	General Amity	394UNTS53	105668
FAO (Food Agri)	IAEA (Atom Energy)	01 Oct 58	IGO Operations	361UNTS211	200571
IAEA (Atom Energy)	UNESCO (Educ/Cult)	01 Oct 58	IGO Operations	339UNTS373	200558
Multilateral		01 Dec 58	Commodity Trade	385UNTS137	105534
Multilateral		03 Dec 58	Admin Cooperation	398UNTS9	105715
Accept UN Charter	Guinea	03 Dec 58	UN Charter	317UNTS77	104595
Korea, South	USA (United States)	18 Dec 58	Reparations	325UNTS233	104702
Afghanistan	WHO (World Health)	18 Dec 58	Tech Assistance	324UNTS121	104681
IMCO (Maritime Org)	United Nations	13 Jan 59	IGO Operations	324UNTS273	200553
ILO (Labor Org)	UK Great Britain	14 Jan 59	IGO Operations	355UNTS283	105081
Multilateral		15 Jan 59	Customs	348UNTS13	104996
ILO (Labor Org)	IMCO (Maritime Org)	16 Jan 59	IGO Operations	327UNTS309	200554
Japan	Yugoslavia	28 Feb 59	General Economic	341UNTS179	104883
IAEA (Atom Energy)	Thailand	18 Mar 59	Tech Assistance	339UNTS307	104850
Morocco	UN Special Fund	04 Apr 59	Direct Aid	354UNTS347	105069
Multilateral		06 Apr 59	Commodity Trade	349UNTS167	105013
Denmark	Sudan	11 May 59	Air Transport	445UNTS105	106380
IAEA (Atom Energy)	WHO (World Health)	28 May 59	IGO Operations	339UNTS387	200559
Guinea	UNICEF (Children)	08 Jun 59	Direct Aid	334UNTS277	104772
Multilateral		19 Jun 59	ILO Labor	413UNTS148	105949
Multilateral		19 Jun 59	ILO Labor	413UNTS168	105951
Multilateral		19 Jun 59	ILO Labor	413UNTS158	105950
Multilateral		01 Jul 59	IGO Status/Immunit	374UNTS147	105334
Multilateral		07 Jul 59	Specific Resources	377UNTS203	105402
Iraq	USA (United States)	07 Jul 59	Milit Assistance	357UNTS153	105114
Liberia	USA (United States)	08 Jul 59	Milit Assistance	357UNTS93	105108
Subsahara Tech Com	ILO (Labor Org)	25 Jul 59	IGO Operations	409UNTS290	200590
IAEA (Atom Energy)	WMO (Meteorology)	12 Aug 59	IGO Operations	341UNTS341	200561
Ghana	UN Special Fund	12 Aug 59	Direct Aid	338UNTS203	104836
ICJ Option Clause	India	14 Sep 59	ICJ Option Clause	340UNTS289	104871
FAO (Food Agri)	UN Special Fund	28 Sep 59	IGO Operations	341UNTS353	200562
IAEA (Atom Energy)	ICAO (Civil Aviat)	01 Oct 59	IGO Operations	361UNTS193	200570
Iran	UN Special Fund	06 Oct 59	Direct Aid	342UNTS89	104902
ILO (Labor Org)	UN Special Fund	12 Oct 59	IGO Operations	343UNTS325	200563
Poland	UN Special Fund	15 Oct 59	Direct Aid	344UNTS29	104941
India	UN Special Fund	20 Oct 59	Direct Aid	344UNTS143	104946
UN Special Fund	Yugoslavia	27 Oct 59	Direct Aid	344UNTS159	104947
Ecuador	UN Special Fund	10 Nov 59	Direct Aid	345UNTS3	104955
Greece	UN Special Fund	13 Nov 59	Direct Aid	345UNTS171	104966
UN Special Fund	WMO (Meteorology)	17 Nov 59	IGO Operations	345UNTS311	200564
Multilateral		18 Nov 59	IGO Establishment	390UNTS227	105610
Multilateral		19 Nov 59	IGO Operations	410UNTS156	105902
UN Special Fund	Turkey	20 Nov 59	Direct Aid	345UNTS105	104963
UN Special Fund	United Arab Rep	25 Nov 59	Direct Aid	345UNTS125	104964
Israel	UN Special Fund	01 Dec 59	Direct Aid	345UNTS197	104968
Guinea	UN Special Fund	02 Dec 59	Direct Aid	345UNTS215	104969
Argentina	UN Special Fund	04 Dec 59	Direct Aid	345UNTS263	104972
Italy	Netherlands	08 Dec 59	Land Transport	484UNTS309	107039
Jordan	UN Special Fund	15 Dec 59	Direct Aid	346UNTS3	104974
Ceylon (Sri Lanka)	WHO (World Health)	21 Dec 59	Tech Assistance	349UNTS109	105011
UN Special Fund	UK Great Britain	07 Jan 60	Direct Aid	348UNTS177	105000
Accept UN Charter	Cameroon	13 Jan 60	UN Charter	375UNTS79	105354
Peru	UN Special Fund	19 Jan 60	Direct Aid	349UNTS83	105010
Japan	USA (United States)	19 Jan 60	General Military	373UNTS179	105320
Pakistan	WHO (World Health)	20 Jan 60	Tech Assistance	351UNTS355	105034
Chile	UN Special Fund	22 Jan 60	Direct Aid	351UNTS115	105020
Multilateral		26 Jan 60	IGO Establishment	439UNTS249	106333
Colombia	UN Special Fund	04 Feb 60	Direct Aid	355UNTS257	105080
Bolivia	UN Special Fund	09 Feb 60	Direct Aid	351UNTS203	105024
Cuba	UNICEF (Children)	11 Feb 60	Direct Aid	349UNTS277	105014
Afghanistan	UN Special Fund	21 Feb 60	Direct Aid	351UNTS93	105019
Germany, West	UK Great Britain	23 Feb 60	Extradition	385UNTS39	105527

PARTY ONE	PARTY TWO	DATE	TOPIC	CITATION	NUMBER
United Nations (Cont.)					
Pakistan	UN Special Fund	25 Feb 60	Direct Aid	351UNTS141	105021
Multilateral		26 Feb 60	Air Transport	418UNTS171	106022
France	UN Special Fund	17 Mar 60	Direct Aid	354UNTS119	105059
Italy	UN Special Fund	01 Apr 60	Direct Aid	354UNTS261	105066
UN Special Fund	Tunisia	12 Apr 60	Direct Aid	355UNTS289	105082
Libya	UN Special Fund	19 Apr 60	Direct Aid	356UNTS11	105090
ICAO (Civil Aviat)	UN Special Fund	21 Apr 60	IGO Operations	360UNTS367	200569
UN Special Fund	Sudan	21 Apr 60	Direct Aid	356UNTS213	105097
UN Special Fund	Vietnam, South	29 Apr 60	Direct Aid	357UNTS311	200567
Laos	UN Special Fund	30 Apr 60	Tech Assistance	361UNTS171	105179
Lebanon	UN Special Fund	07 May 60	Tech Assistance	360UNTS225	105160
Accept UN Charter	Togo	21 May 60	UN Charter	375UNTS83	105355
UN Special Fund	WHO (World Health)	25 May 60	IGO Operations	359UNTS375	200568
UN Special Fund	Thailand	04 Jun 60	Tech Assistance	360UNTS97	105157
UN Special Fund	Togo	08 Jun 60	Tech Assistance	369UNTS401	200574
Multilateral		17 Jun 60	Humanitarian	536UNTS27	107794
Iraq	UN Special Fund	19 Jun 60	Direct Aid	376UNTS357	105389
Multilateral		22 Jun 60	Sanitation	431UNTS41	106208
Accept UN Charter	Malagasy	26 Jun 60	UN Charter	375UNTS87	105356
IAEA (Atom Energy)	USA (United States)	28 Jun 60	Direct Aid	374UNTS133	105333
Kuwait	UN Special Fund	29 Jun 60	Tech Assistance	369UNTS419	200575
ITU (Telecommun)	UN Special Fund	13 Jul 60	IGO Operations	368UNTS329	200573
Ethiopia	UN Special Fund	13 Jul 60	Tech Assistance	368UNTS159	105240
Multilateral		28 Jul 60	IGO Establishment	485UNTS3	107042
Accept UN Charter	Dahomey	02 Aug 60	UN Charter	375UNTS91	105357
WHO (World Health)	United Arab Rep	03 Aug 60	Tech Assistance	385UNTS3	105524
Accept UN Charter	Niger	07 Aug 60	UN Charter	375UNTS95	105358
Accept UN Charter	Upper Volta	07 Aug 60	UN Charter	375UNTS99	105359
Accept UN Charter	Ivory Coast	07 Aug 60	UN Charter	375UNTS103	105360
Accept UN Charter	Congo (Brazzaville)	12 Aug 60	UN Charter	375UNTS111	105362
Accept UN Charter	Chad	12 Aug 60	UN Charter	375UNTS107	105361
Netherlands	UN Special Fund	12 Aug 60	Tech Assistance	372UNTS331	105309
Accept UN Charter	Central Afri Rep	13 Aug 60	UN Charter	375UNTS115	105363
Multilateral		16 Aug 60	General Amity	397UNTS287	105712
Multilateral		16 Aug 60	Recognition	382UNTS3	105475
WHO (World Health)	Saudi Arabia	06 Sep 60	Tech Assistance	395UNTS169	105684
Lebanon	WHO (World Health)	08 Sep 60	Tech Assistance	387UNTS49	105557
Brazil	UN Special Fund	16 Sep 60	Tech Assistance	375UNTS3	105351
Pakistan	IBRD (World Bank)	19 Sep 60	IBRD Project	444UNTS207	106370
Multilateral		19 Sep 60	IBRD Project	419UNTS125	106032
Multilateral		19 Sep 60	IBRD Project	444UNTS259	106371
Taiwan	UN Special Fund	20 Sep 60	Tech Assistance	375UNTS29	105352
Accept UN Charter	Senegal	20 Sep 60	UN Charter	376UNTS79	105374
Guinea	USA (United States)	30 Sep 60	General Aid	394UNTS103	105671
Multilateral		06 Oct 60	Customs	473UNTS131	106861
Indonesia	UN Special Fund	07 Oct 60	Direct Aid	378UNTS141	105424
Liberia	UN Special Fund	11 Oct 60	Direct Aid	376UNTS341	105388
Accept UN Charter	Mali	22 Oct 60	UN Charter	377UNTS361	105412
El Salvador	UN Special Fund	24 Oct 60	Direct Aid	377UNTS171	105400
Accept UN Charter	Gabon	02 Nov 60	UN Charter	379UNTS99	105436
WHO (World Health)	Upper Volta	15 Nov 60	Tech Assistance	383UNTS91	105496
Norway	UK Great Britain	17 Nov 60	Specific Resources	398UNTS189	105723
Guatemala	UN Special Fund	17 Nov 60	Direct Aid	383UNTS67	105495
Nepal	UN Special Fund	17 Nov 60	Direct Aid	380UNTS289	105461
IAEA (Atom Energy)	OECD (Econ Coop)	24 Nov 60	IGO Operations	396UNTS273	200585
Cambodia	UN Special Fund	24 Nov 60	Direct Aid	382UNTS255	105487
Fed of Malaya	WHO (World Health)	25 Nov 60	Tech Assistance	387UNTS37	105556
WHO (World Health)	Yemen	03 Dec 60	Tech Assistance	395UNTS187	105685
Dahomey	WHO (World Health)	07 Dec 60	Tech Assistance	387UNTS277	105567
Multilateral		09 Dec 60	Customs	429UNTS211	106200
Congo (Brazzaville)	WHO (World Health)	12 Dec 60	Tech Assistance	399UNTS105	105737
Nepal	UNICEF (Children)	12 Dec 60	Direct Aid	382UNTS273	105488
Multilateral		14 Dec 60	Education	429UNTS93	106193
Cambodia	Thailand	15 Dec 60	Extradition	382UNTS321	105493
Cambodia	Thailand	15 Dec 60	Admin Cooperation	382UNTS307	105491

PARTY ONE	PARTY TWO	DATE	TOPIC	CITATION	NUMBER
United Nations (Cont.)					
Cambodia	Thailand	15 Dec 60	Extradition	382UNTS315	105492
Honduras	UN Special Fund	20 Dec 60	Direct Aid	383UNTS103	105497
Inter-Am Nuc Energ	IAEA (Atom Energy)	22 Dec 60	IGO Operations	396UNTS285	200586
Niger	WHO (World Health)	28 Dec 60	Tech Assistance	394UNTS195	105679
Burma	UN Special Fund	03 Jan 61	Direct Aid	387UNTS219	105564
UN Special Fund	Saudi Arabia	19 Jan 61	Direct Aid	396UNTS27	105692
Nicaragua	UN Special Fund	20 Jan 61	Direct Aid	387UNTS15	105555
Multilateral		23 Jan 61	Postal Service	530UNTS141	107679
Ivory Coast	WHO (World Health)	30 Jan 61	Tech Assistance	395UNTS205	105686
Gabon	UN Special Fund	02 Feb 61	Direct Aid	387UNTS289	105568
WHO (World Health)	Togo	03 Feb 61	Tech Assistance	394UNTS207	105680
Chad	WHO (World Health)	03 Feb 61	Tech Assistance	394UNTS161	105676
UK Great Britain	USA (United States)	10 Feb 61	Milit Installation	409UNTS68	105879
Guinea	WHO (World Health)	11 Feb 61	Tech Assistance	394UNTS173	105677
Accept UN Charter	Somalia	11 Feb 61	UN Charter	388UNTS179	105577
Central Afri Rep	WHO (World Health)	13 Feb 61	Tech Assistance	394UNTS149	105675
Korea, South	Philippines	24 Feb 61	General Trade	423UNTS217	106094
Denmark	Greece	04 Mar 61	Taxation	534UNTS157	107760
Multilateral		08 Mar 61	Scientific Project	396UNTS255	200584
Panama	UN Special Fund	09 Mar 61	Direct Aid	396UNTS3	105691
Iceland	UK Great Britain	11 Mar 61	Dispute Settlement	397UNTS275	105710
Kuwait	WHO (World Health)	16 Mar 61	Tech Assistance	397UNTS315	200588
Accept UN Charter	Nigeria	21 Mar 61	UN Charter	395UNTS237	105688
Multilateral		30 Mar 61	Sanitation	520UNTS151	107515
IAEA (Atom Energy)	IMCO (Maritime Org)	13 Apr 61	IGO Operations	425UNTS281	200595
Multilateral		14 Apr 61	IGO Establishment	422UNTS101	106071
Mauritania	WHO (World Health)	17 Apr 61	Tech Assistance	396UNTS301	200587
Multilateral		18 Apr 61	Consul/Citizenship	500UNTS223	107311
Multilateral		18 Apr 61	Dispute Settlement	500UNTS243	107312
Multilateral		18 Apr 61	Consul/Citizenship	500UNTS95	107310
Cyprus	UNICEF (Children)	19 Apr 61	Direct Aid	394UNTS185	105678
Multilateral		21 Apr 61	IGO Establishment	484UNTS349	107041
Taiwan	Nicaragua	25 Apr 61	Culture	423UNTS139	106090
Gabon	WHO (World Health)	27 Apr 61	Tech Assistance	397UNTS215	105707
Mali	WHO (World Health)	27 Apr 61	Tech Assistance	407UNTS66	105860
Accept UN Charter	Sierra Leone	27 Apr 61	UN Charter	409UNTS44	105876
Ceylon (Sri Lanka)	UN Special Fund	03 May 61	Direct Aid	395UNTS217	105687
Honduras	IDA (Devel Assoc)	12 May 61	Loans and Credits	414UNTS180	105973
Accept UN Charter	Cyprus	29 May 61	UN Charter	397UNTS283	105711
Multilateral		08 Jun 61	Customs	473UNTS187	106863
Multilateral		08 Jun 61	Customs	473UNTS153	106862
Cameroon	UN Special Fund	13 Jun 61	Direct Aid	397UNTS297	105713
Liberia	USA (United States)	17 Jun 61	Milit Assistance	410UNTS233	105907
Paraguay	UN Special Fund	22 Jun 61	Direct Aid	399UNTS117	105738
Multilateral		26 Jun 61	ILO Labor	423UNTS11	106083
Haiti	UN Special Fund	28 Jun 61	Direct Aid	399UNTS171	105741
Philippines	UN Special Fund	28 Jun 61	Direct Aid	399UNTS141	105739
UNICEF (Children)	Saudi Arabia	04 Jul 61	Direct Aid	413UNTS122	105947
Morocco	WHO (World Health)	09 Aug 61	Tech Assistance	412UNTS192	105932
Central Afri Rep	UNICEF (Children)	21 Aug 61	Direct Aid	413UNTS48	105939
Chad	UNICEF (Children)	26 Aug 61	Direct Aid	422UNTS231	106077
ILO (Labor Org)	Thailand	30 Aug 61	IGO Operations	422UNTS125	106072
Iraq	WHO (World Health)	13 Sep 61	Tech Assistance	419UNTS69	106030
Korea, South	Thailand	15 Sep 61	General Trade	413UNTS137	105948
Multilateral		18 Sep 61	Air Transport	500UNTS31	107305
UN Special Fund	Sierra Leone	02 Oct 61	Direct Aid	422UNTS131	106073
Brazil	Poland	19 Oct 61	Culture	552UNTS75	108050
Multilateral		26 Oct 61	Patents/Copyrights	496UNTS43	107247
Accept UN Charter	Congo (Zaire)	31 Oct 61	UN Charter	418UNTS157	106020
Gabon	UNICEF (Children)	02 Nov 61	Direct Aid	422UNTS241	106078
Mauritania	UN Special Fund	07 Nov 61	Direct Aid	412UNTS240	105936
Congo (Brazzaville)	UN Special Fund	09 Nov 61	Direct Aid	413UNTS58	105940
Malagasy	UNICEF (Children)	16 Nov 61	Direct Aid	422UNTS251	106079
IAEA (Atom Energy)	UN Special Fund	29 Nov 61	IGO Operations	415UNTS408	200593
Accept UN Charter	Mongolia	04 Dec 61	UN Charter	434UNTS141	106261

PARTY ONE	PARTY TWO	DATE	TOPIC	CITATION	NUMBER
United Nations (Cont.)					
Multilateral		06 Dec 61	Customs	473UNTS219	106864
Accept UN Charter	Tanganyika	09 Dec 61	UN Charter	416UNTS147	106000
UN Special Fund	Venezuela	11 Dec 61	Direct Aid	422UNTS149	106074
UN Special Fund	Senegal	16 Dec 61	Direct Aid	425UNTS97	106121
Malagasy	UN Special Fund	05 Jan 62	Direct Aid	419UNTS29	106028
Ivory Coast	UNICEF (Children)	10 Jan 62	Direct Aid	422UNTS261	106080
UNICEF (Children)	Yemen	31 Jan 62	Direct Aid	422UNTS271	106081
Dominican Republic	USA (United States)	08 Mar 62	Milit Assistance	527UNTS29	107615
WHO (World Health)	Sudan	11 Mar 62	Tech Assistance	432UNTS325	106226
Dahomey	UN Special Fund	28 Mar 62	Tech Assistance	424UNTS55	106099
Multilateral		29 Mar 62	IGO Establishment	507UNTS177	107401
FAO (Food Agri)	USA (United States)	29 Mar 62	IGO Operations	454UNTS13	106536
UNICEF (Children)	Somalia	01 Apr 62	Direct Aid	431UNTS75	106211
Congo (Brazzaville)	UNICEF (Children)	09 Apr 62	Direct Aid	431UNTS65	106210
UNICEF (Children)	Sierra Leone	11 Apr 62	Direct Aid	431UNTS55	106209
ILO (Labor Org)	Tanganyika	03 May 62	IGO Operations	429UNTS73	106191
UN Special Fund	Uruguay	04 May 62	Direct Aid	429UNTS143	106196
Multilateral		15 May 62	Commodity Trade	444UNTS3	106367
Multilateral		25 May 62	IGO Establishment	486UNTS103	107075
Dominican Republic	UN Special Fund	06 Jun 62	Direct Aid	429UNTS169	106197
Dahomey	USA (United States)	13 Jun 62	Milit Assistance	458UNTS219	106603
Multilateral		14 Jun 62	IGO Establishment	528UNTS33	107634
Niger	USA (United States)	14 Jun 62	Milit Assistance	458UNTS233	106605
Multilateral		22 Jun 62	ILO Labor	494UNTS249	107237
Multilateral		28 Jun 62	ILO Labor	494UNTS271	107238
Accept UN Charter	Rwanda	01 Jul 62	UN Charter	437UNTS145	106302
Accept UN Charter	Burundi	04 Jul 62	UN Charter	437UNTS149	106303
UN Special Fund	Syria	07 Jul 62	Direct Aid	443UNTS3	106355
UN Special Fund	Tanganyika	17 Jul 62	Direct Aid	435UNTS237	106281
Senegal	USA (United States)	20 Jul 62	Milit Assistance	458UNTS137	106596
Accept UN Charter	Jamaica	06 Aug 62	UN Charter	437UNTS153	106304
Indonesia	Netherlands	15 Aug 62	Territory Boundary	437UNTS273	106311
Syria	USSR (Soviet Union)	19 Aug 62	Culture	457UNTS285	106588
IAEA (Atom Energy)	USA (United States)	20 Aug 62	Commodity Trade	456UNTS447	106570
Accept UN Charter	Trinidad/Tobago	06 Sep 62	UN Charter	437UNTS157	106305
Multilateral		11 Sep 62	Tech Assistance	455UNTS402	106553
Multilateral		28 Sep 62	IGO Establishment	469UNTS169	106791
Accept UN Charter	Algeria	30 Sep 62	UN Charter	442UNTS37	106336
Multilateral		05 Oct 62	IGO Establishment	502UNTS225	107333
Accept UN Charter	Uganda	09 Oct 62	UN Charter	443UNTS47	106357
Japan	UN Special Fund	31 Oct 62	Tech Assistance	444UNTS171	106368
Algeria	UN Special Fund	15 Nov 62	Tech Assistance	452UNTS243	106512
Algeria	UNICEF (Children)	20 Nov 62	Direct Aid	453UNTS151	106522
Ceylon (Sri Lanka)	ILO (Labor Org)	21 Nov 62	IGO Operations	449UNTS263	106463
Niger	UNICEF (Children)	05 Dec 62	IGO Operations	503UNTS195	107344
Multilateral		10 Dec 62	Culture	521UNTS231	107525
Multilateral		12 Dec 62	IGO Establishment	552UNTS15	108048
Algeria	WHO (World Health)	20 Dec 62	Tech Assistance	463UNTS135	106698
Multilateral		15 Jan 63	Tech Assistance	456UNTS409	106567
Mauritania	UNICEF (Children)	19 Jan 63	Direct Aid	452UNTS271	106514
UNICEF (Children)	Tanganyika	25 Jan 63	Direct Aid	453UNTS249	106528
Congo (Zaire)	USA (United States)	23 Feb 63	US Agri Commod Aid	493UNTS17	107204
Congo (Zaire)	USA (United States)	23 Feb 63	US Agri Commod Aid	493UNTS3	107203
Multilateral		06 Mar 63	Tech Assistance	455UNTS386	106552
Accept UN Charter	Mauritania	20 Mar 63	UN Charter	457UNTS59	106576
UN Special Fund	Uganda	22 Mar 63	Direct Aid	456UNTS466	106572
ICJ Option Clause	Somalia	25 Mar 63	ICJ Option Clause	458UNTS143	106597
Multilateral		20 Apr 63	IGO Establishment	495UNTS3	107239
Accept UN Charter	Kuwait	20 Apr 63	UN Charter	463UNTS213	106705
Multilateral		24 Apr 63	Consul/Citizenship	596UNTS487	108640
Multilateral		24 Apr 63	Consul/Citizenship	596UNTS469	108639
Multilateral		24 Apr 63	Consul/Citizenship	596UNTS261	108638
Greece	Hungary	27 Apr 63	Air Transport	534UNTS3	107750
UN Special Fund	Trinidad/Tobago	06 May 63	Direct Aid	463UNTS93	106695
Jamaica	UN Special Fund	22 May 63	Direct Aid	489UNTS191	107140

PARTY ONE	PARTY TWO	DATE	TOPIC	CITATION	NUMBER
United Nations (Cont.)					
Netherlands	UN Special Fund	24 May 63	Direct Aid	466UNTS289	106750
Multilateral		25 May 63	IGO Establishment	479UNTS39	106947
Afromalagasy Org	ILO (Labor Org)	30 May 63	IGO Operations	467UNTS482	200602
UN Special Fund	Western Samoa	05 Jun 63	Direct Aid	467UNTS463	200601
Multilateral		25 Jun 63	ILO Labor	532UNTS159	107717
UNICEF (Children)	Togo	27 Jun 63	IGO Operations	540UNTS135	107847
New Zealand	UN Special Fund	28 Jun 63	Non-IBRD Project	470UNTS3	106792
Congo (Zaire)	UN Special Fund	26 Jul 63	Direct Aid	474UNTS137	106878
Multilateral		31 Jul 63	General Amity	550UNTS343	108029
UNICEF (Children)	Trinidad/Tobago	08 Aug 63	IGO Operations	473UNTS281	106865
Burundi	UN Special Fund	22 Aug 63	Direct Aid	476UNTS49	106903
Multilateral		26 Oct 63	Water Transport	587UNTS9	108506
Central Afri Rep	UN Special Fund	30 Oct 63	Direct Aid	481UNTS247	106985
Multilateral		09 Nov 63	Direct Aid	489UNTS209	107141
Iran	UNICEF (Children)	21 Nov 63	IGO Operations	485UNTS35	107044
ICJ Option Clause	UK Great Britain	27 Nov 63	ICJ Option Clause	482UNTS187	106995
Iraq	UNICEF (Children)	03 Dec 63	IGO Operations	482UNTS319	107001
Accept UN Charter	Zanzibar	10 Dec 63	UN Charter	483UNTS237	107016
Accept UN Charter	Kenya	12 Dec 63	UN Charter	483UNTS233	107015
Multilateral		14 Dec 63	IGO Establishment	507UNTS149	107399
Burundi	UNICEF (Children)	08 Jan 64	IGO Operations	485UNTS45	107045
UNICEF (Children)	Senegal	22 Jan 64	IGO Operations	486UNTS91	107074
Subsahara Tech Com	IAEA (Atom Energy)	06 Feb 64	IGO Operations	501UNTS285	200606
Rwanda	UN Special Fund	18 Mar 64	Direct Aid	491UNTS3	107170
USSR (Soviet Union)	Yemen	21 Mar 64	General Amity	553UNTS267	108094
Multilateral		06 May 64	IGO Operations	514UNTS71	107442
Ireland	UN Special Fund	03 Jun 64	Direct Aid	496UNTS205	107253
Germany, East	USSR (Soviet Union)	12 Jun 64	General Amity	553UNTS249	108093
Malaysia	UNICEF (Children)	01 Jul 64	IGO Operations	503UNTS229	107346
Iceland	UN Special Fund	10 Jul 64	IGO Operations	502UNTS343	107337
Denmark	Tanganyika	04 Aug 64	Dispute Settlement	544UNTS123	107915
Denmark	Tanganyika	04 Aug 64	Taxation	544UNTS117	107914
Accept UN Charter	Malawi	04 Aug 64	UN Charter	519UNTS3	107496
Multilateral		20 Aug 64	Telecommunications	514UNTS25	107441
Accept UN Charter	Malta	29 Sep 64	UN Charter	519UNTS7	107497
Australia	UN Special Fund	30 Sep 64	Scientific Project	510UNTS277	107419
Kenya	UN Special Fund	01 Oct 64	IGO Operations	511UNTS181	107433
Chad	Israel	07 Oct 64	Tech Assistance	630UNTS175	108969
Malawi	UN Special Fund	24 Oct 64	Direct Aid	514UNTS235	200609
Romania	UN Special Fund	24 Oct 64	IGO Operations	519UNTS29	107500
Accept UN Charter	Zambia	26 Oct 64	UN Charter	519UNTS11	107498
Multilateral		25 Nov 64	Water Transport	587UNTS19	108507
Multilateral		01 Dec 64	Water Transport	550UNTS133	108012
Ethiopia	ILO (Labor Org)	10 Dec 64	IGO Establishment	521UNTS217	107524
UN Special Fund	Zambia	15 Dec 64	Direct Aid	522UNTS3	107532
Denmark	Peru	30 Dec 64	Tech Assistance	595UNTS47	108611
Ecuador	Netherlands	14 Jan 65	Health/Educ/Welfare	551UNTS129	108038
Accept UN Charter	Gambia	18 Feb 65	UN Charter	545UNTS143	107928
Multilateral		09 Mar 65	Water Transport	591UNTS265	108564
Poland	USSR (Soviet Union)	08 Apr 65	General Amity	540UNTS97	107845
ICJ Option Clause	Kenya	12 Apr 65	ICJ Option Clause	531UNTS113	107697
Malta	UNICEF (Children)	22 Apr 65	IGO Operations	533UNTS107	107737
Iran	IBRD (World Bank)	28 Apr 65	IBRD Project	555UNTS45	108104
Australia	Philippines	16 Jun 65	General Trade	541UNTS31	107858
Multilateral		23 Jun 65	General IGO	614UNTS239	108873
UN Special Fund	Spain	30 Jun 65	Direct Aid	544UNTS159	107918
India	Pakistan	30 Jun 65	Territory Boundary	548UNTS277	107983
Multilateral		02 Jul 65	Sanitation	592UNTS215	108575
Multilateral		08 Jul 65	General Trade	597UNTS3	108641
Kenya	USA (United States)	19 Aug 65	Extradition	574UNTS153	108348
Accept UN Charter	Maldive Islands	26 Aug 65	UN Charter	545UNTS147	107929
Accept UN Charter	Singapore	04 Sep 65	UN Charter	545UNTS151	107930
Australia	Korea, South	21 Sep 65	General Trade	548UNTS163	107977
United Nations	Zambia	23 Oct 65	IGO Operations	549UNTS101	107993
OAU (Afri Unity)	United Nations	15 Nov 65	IGO Operations	548UNTS315	200614

PARTY ONE	PARTY TWO	DATE	TOPIC	CITATION	NUMBER
United Nations (Cont.)					
Multilateral		17 Jan 66	IGO Establishment	592UNTS101	108573
Mongolia	UN Special Fund	26 Jan 66	Direct Aid	552UNTS201	108055
UK Great Britain	Venezuela	17 Feb 66	Territory Boundary	561UNTS321	108192
WHO (World Health)	Singapore	28 Mar 66	Tech Assistance	562UNTS59	108195
Multilateral		05 Apr 66	Water Transport	640UNTS133	109159
Bulgaria	Turkey	18 Apr 66	Air Transport	631UNTS263	108999
Bulgaria	UN Special Fund	26 May 66	General Aid	563UNTS71	108205
Multilateral		27 May 66	IGO Establishment	637UNTS0	109121
Liberia	UNICEF (Children)	08 Jun 66	General Amity	570UNTS31	108286
FAO (Food Agri)	IMCO (Maritime Org)	11 Jul 66	IGO Operations	575UNTS238	200627
Morocco	Senegal	15 Sep 66	General Amity	634UNTS105	109055
Accept UN Charter	Botswana	30 Sep 66	UN Charter	575UNTS151	108357
Accept UN Charter	Lesotho	04 Oct 66	UN Charter	575UNTS155	108358
Indonesia	UNICEF (Children)	17 Nov 66	IGO Operations	578UNTS47	108386
ICJ Option Clause	Malta	29 Nov 66	ICJ Option Clause	580UNTS205	108423
Asian Devel Bank	Philippines	22 Dec 66	IGO Establishment	615UNTS375	108887
UNICEF (Children)	Zambia	02 Feb 67	IGO Operations	589UNTS89	108536
Australia	UN Special Fund	06 Feb 67	IGO Operations	590UNTS3	108543
Multilateral		14 Feb 67	General Military	634UNTS281	109068
Czechoslovakia	Poland	01 Mar 67	General Amity	632UNTS255	109027
Greece	Yugoslavia	15 Apr 67	Taxation	633UNTS373	109046
Gambia	Senegal	19 Apr 67	General Amity	640UNTS101	109156
Hungary	UN Special Fund	28 Apr 67	General Aid	595UNTS171	108619
Bulgaria	USSR (Soviet Union)	12 May 67	General Amity	631UNTS239	108997
Bulgaria	Germany, East	07 Sep 67	General Amity	631UNTS81	108988
Australia	UNICEF (Children)	21 Dec 67	IGO Operations	614UNTS83	108864
Multilateral		18 Mar 68	Commodity Trade	0UNTS0	109262
UN Special Fund	Syria	22 Apr 68	IGO Operations	634UNTS207	109063
State/IGO Group	IBRD (World Bank)	02 May 68	Direct Aid	637UNTS0	109110
Austria	United Nations	25 May 68	IGO Operations	637UNTS0	109117
Botswana	UNICEF (Children)	25 Jun 68	IGO Operations	639UNTS61	109144
ICJ Option Clause	Swaziland	06 Sep 68	UN Charter	0UNTS0	109252
ICJ Option Clause	UK Great Britain	01 Jan 69	ICJ Option Clause	0UNTS0	109370
State/IGO Group	Southern Yemen	04 Apr 69	Direct Aid	0UNTS0	109455
UN Special Fund	Southern Yemen	04 Apr 69	Direct Aid	0UNTS0	109456
State/IGO Group	Southern Yemen	04 Apr 69	Direct Aid	0UNTS0	109454
State/IGO Group	Yemen	23 Apr 69	Direct Aid	0UNTS0	109514
United Nations Administrative Tribunal					
IMCO (Maritime Org)	United Nations	11 Feb 64	IGO Operations	489UNTS357	200605
United Nations Children's Fund					
UNRRA (Relief)	United Nations	27 Sep 48	IGO Operations	27UNTS349	200158
United Nations	UK Great Britain	18 Mar 49	Humanitarian	47UNTS305	100736
Haiti	WHO (World Health)	21 Jun 50	Sanitation	103UNTS61	101424
Peru	WHO (World Health)	26 Sep 50	Sanitation	104UNTS233	101444
Guatemala	WHO (World Health)	28 Nov 50	Sanitation	103UNTS51	101423
Nicaragua	WHO (World Health)	02 Jan 51	Sanitation	103UNTS107	101428
El Salvador	WHO (World Health)	02 Jan 51	Sanitation	103UNTS29	101421
Colombia	WHO (World Health)	05 Jan 51	Sanitation	102UNTS139	101417
Bolivia	WHO (World Health)	07 Feb 51	Sanitation	104UNTS167	101438
Costa Rica	WHO (World Health)	13 Apr 51	Sanitation	103UNTS3	101419
Burma	WHO (World Health)	09 Jul 51	Sanitation	104UNTS187	101440
Burma	WHO (World Health)	09 Jul 51	Sanitation	104UNTS175	101439
Pakistan	WHO (World Health)	21 Feb 52	IGO Operations	131UNTS221	101742
Chile	WHO (World Health)	31 May 52	Sanitation	136UNTS323	101841
Chile	WHO (World Health)	11 Jul 52	Tech Assistance	137UNTS27	101846
Denmark	India	15 May 63	Tech Assistance	616UNTS49	108891
Afghanistan	IDA (Devel Assoc)	23 Nov 64	Non-IBRD Project	567UNTS155	108255
United Nations Commission for Korean Reconstruction					
Japan	United Nations	25 Jul 52	IGO Status/Immunit	135UNTS305	200443
Multilateral		21 Dec 56	Humanitarian	427UNTS81	106147
United Nations Economic Commission for Europe					
Austria	Sweden	18 Feb 58	Land Transport	427UNTS349	106166

PARTY ONE	PARTY TWO	DATE	TOPIC	CITATION	NUMBER
United Nations Educational, Scientific and Cultural Organization					
Multilateral		16 Nov 45	IGO Establishment	4UNTS275	100052
Multilateral		15 Jul 49	Health/Educ/Welfare	197UNTS3	102631
Multilateral		22 Nov 50	Culture	131UNTS25	101734
Jordan	United Nations	29 Mar 51	Tech Assistance	137UNTS267	200448
Multilateral		24 Dec 51	Tech Assistance	118UNTS290	200383
Ceylon (Sri Lanka)	United Nations	21 Jan 52	Tech Assistance	118UNTS281	200382
Multilateral		15 Feb 52	Scientific Project	132UNTS51	101751
Multilateral		06 Sep 52	Patents/Copyrights	216UNTS132	102937
Multilateral		17 Oct 52	Direct Aid	141UNTS121	101911
Pakistan	Turkey	29 Jun 53	Culture	211UNTS225	102854
Multilateral		01 Jul 53	IGO Establishment	200UNTS149	102701
Multilateral		01 Mar 57	Tech Assistance	264UNTS94	103790
Multilateral		24 May 57	Tech Assistance	268UNTS270	103861
Multilateral		26 Jun 57	ILO Labor	328UNTS247	104738
USA (United States)	USSR (Soviet Union)	27 Jan 58	Health/Educ/Welfare	301UNTS405	104350
Multilateral		29 Apr 58	Water Transport	450UNTS11	106465
Multilateral		03 Dec 58	Admin Cooperation	416UNTS51	105995
Czechoslovakia	United Arab Rep	07 Feb 59	General Economic	372UNTS243	105301
Taiwan	Nicaragua	25 Apr 61	Culture	423UNTS139	106090
Multilateral		08 Jun 61	Customs	473UNTS187	106863
Multilateral		08 Jun 61	Customs	473UNTS153	106862
Multilateral		26 Oct 61	Patents/Copyrights	496UNTS43	107247
Multilateral		06 Dec 61	Customs	473UNTS219	106864
Multilateral		26 Mar 62	IGO Establishment	539UNTS67	107825
Japan	UN Special Fund	31 Oct 62	Tech Assistance	444UNTS171	106368
Multilateral		09 Nov 63	Direct Aid	489UNTS209	107141
Taiwan	UNICEF (Children)	08 Apr 64	IGO Operations	500UNTS49	107306
Afghanistan	IDA (Devel Assoc)	23 Nov 64	Non-IBRD Project	567UNTS155	108255
Canada	United Nations	21 Feb 66	IGO Operations	555UNTS119	108107
Austria	United Nations	24 Feb 66	IGO Operations	557UNTS129	108131
United Nations Forces on Cyprus					
Denmark	United Nations	21 Feb 66	IGO Operations	555UNTS151	108108
United Nations	UK Great Britain	21 Feb 66	General Economic	555UNTS177	108112
Finland	United Nations	21 Feb 66	IGO Operations	555UNTS157	108109
Canada	United Nations	21 Feb 66	IGO Operations	555UNTS119	108107
New Zealand	United Nations	21 Feb 66	IGO Operations	555UNTS163	108110
United Nations	Sweden	21 Feb 66	IGO Operations	555UNTS169	108111
United Nations Mission to the Congo					
Multilateral		15 Feb 64	Milit Installation	533UNTS98	107736
Congo (Zaire)	United Nations	02 Mar 64	Milit Installation	533UNTS93	107735
United Nations Palestine Refugees Relief and Works Agency					
Jordan	WHO (World Health)	16 Jun 52	Direct Aid	135UNTS323	200445
Jordan	WHO (World Health)	21 Aug 52	Direct Aid	141UNTS341	200472
United Nations Refugee Fund					
UN Hi Com Refugees	Sweden	08 Oct 56	Refugees	428UNTS307	106182
United Nations Relief and Rehabilitation Administration					
Australia	New Zealand	21 Jan 44	General Amity	18UNTS357	200113
Multilateral		15 Dec 44	Sanitation	17UNTS305	200110
Multilateral		15 Dec 44	Sanitation	16UNTS247	200106
Belgium	Netherlands	02 Jan 45	Refugees	19UNTS259	200120
Belgium	Luxembourg	14 May 45	Refugees	19UNTS243	200118
Belgium	Czechoslovakia	16 May 45	Refugees	19UNTS251	200119
Greece	UK Great Britain	24 Jan 46	Finance	6UNTS45	100067
Multilateral		23 Apr 46	Sanitation	17UNTS3	100265
Multilateral		23 Apr 46	Sanitation	16UNTS179	100257
France	USA (United States)	28 May 46	Milit Assistance	84UNTS79	101120
Multilateral		22 Jul 46	IGO Establishment	9UNTS3	100125
Austria	UK Great Britain	23 Dec 46	General Aid	88UNTS93	101186
Netherlands	USA (United States)	28 May 47	General Military	17UNTS29	100267
United Nations	WHO (World Health)	15 Nov 47	IGO Operations	19UNTS193	200115
Australia	Poland	03 Jun 48	Direct Aid	16UNTS189	100258
Multilateral		06 Jun 55	IGO Establishment	219UNTS79	102968

PARTY ONE	PARTY TWO	DATE	TOPIC	CITATION	NUMBER
United Nations Special Fund					
IDA (Devel Assoc)	United Nations	10 Apr 61	IGO Operations	394UNTS221	200582
Malagasy	UN Special Fund	05 Jan 62	Direct Aid	419UNTS29	106028
ILO (Labor Org)	Tanganyika	03 May 62	IGO Operations	429UNTS73	106191
Ceylon (Sri Lanka)	ILO (Labor Org)	21 Nov 62	IGO Operations	449UNTS263	106463
Botswana	United Nations	30 Sep 66	Tech Assistance	576UNTS17	108362
Lesotho	United Nations	17 Nov 66	IGO Operations	580UNTS29	108418
Multilateral		03 Mar 67	Tech Assistance	594UNTS96	108597
State/IGO Group	Australia	21 May 68	Tech Assistance	636UNTS326	109108
United Nations Technical Assistance Board					
Pakistan	WHO (World Health)	21 Feb 52	IGO Operations	131UNTS221	101742
Pakistan	Sweden	04 Jun 55	Tech Assistance	228UNTS121	103146
Multilateral		20 Jan 62	Tech Assistance	429UNTS230	200596
Multilateral		10 Apr 62	Tech Assistance	429UNTS78	106192
Multilateral		17 May 62	Tech Assistance	429UNTS46	106189
Multilateral		12 Aug 62	Tech Assistance	443UNTS266	106365
Multilateral		29 Aug 62	Tech Assistance	443UNTS280	106366
Multilateral		15 Nov 62	Tech Assistance	448UNTS50	106424
Multilateral		06 Dec 62	Tech Assistance	450UNTS240	106471
Multilateral		21 Jan 63	Tech Assistance	453UNTS20	106517
Multilateral		05 Feb 63	Tech Assistance	453UNTS36	106518
United Nations	United Arab Rep	08 Feb 63	Direct Aid	453UNTS79	106520
Multilateral		14 Feb 63	Tech Assistance	453UNTS168	106524
Multilateral		28 Jan 64	Tech Assistance	502UNTS321	107336
Multilateral		23 Feb 65	IGO Operations	527UNTS120	107622
Multilateral		05 Mar 65	IGO Operations	527UNTS221	107627
Multilateral		08 Apr 65	IGO Operations	533UNTS66	107733
Multilateral		26 Apr 65	IGO Operations	533UNTS50	107732
Multilateral		12 May 65	IGO Operations	534UNTS390	107769
United Nations Temporary Executive Authority					
Indonesia	Netherlands	15 Aug 62	Territory Boundary	437UNTS273	106311
Multilateral		15 Aug 62	Territory Boundary	437UNTS292	106312
United Nations Unified Command in Korea					
Korea, South	USA (United States)	24 May 52	Direct Aid	179UNTS23	102353
United States-Canadian Defense Organization					
Canada	USA (United States)	18 Mar 42	Land Transport	101UNTS205	200294
Canada	USA (United States)	09 May 42	Land Transport	101UNTS215	200295
Canada	USA (United States)	27 Jun 42	Other Military	99UNTS223	200276
Canada	USA (United States)	15 Aug 42	Other Military	99UNTS233	200277
Canada	USA (United States)	27 Jan 43	Milit Installation	101UNTS257	200300
Canada	USA (United States)	27 Jun 44	Milit Installation	101UNTS273	200301
Canada	USA (United States)	03 Mar 46	Specific Property	6UNTS279	100081
Canada	USA (United States)	30 Mar 46	Milit Installation	7UNTS15	100089
Canada	USA (United States)	19 Mar 52	Status of Forces	174UNTS267	102291
Canada	USA (United States)	20 Jun 58	Milit Assistance	317UNTS37	104592
Canada	USA (United States)	17 Jan 61	Specific Resources	542UNTS224	107894
Universal Postal Union					
Brazil	Portugal	30 Apr 42	Postal Service	65UNTS183	200210
UK Great Britain	USA (United States)	10 May 43	Postal Service	147UNTS109	200473
Burma	Pakistan	22 Jun 48	Postal Service	91UNTS197	101252
New Zealand	Pakistan	28 Jun 48	Postal Service	91UNTS235	101253
Ceylon (Sri Lanka)	Pakistan	15 Dec 48	Postal Service	91UNTS303	101255
Greece	USA (United States)	09 Feb 49	Direct Aid	79UNTS95	101034
Trieste	USA (United States)	11 Feb 49	Direct Aid	79UNTS123	101036
USA (United States)	Yugoslavia	14 Aug 50	Postal Service	137UNTS131	101851
Czechoslovakia	USA (United States)	29 Sep 50	Postal Service	290UNTS3	104227
UK Great Britain	USA (United States)	03 Jun 51	Postal Service	137UNTS81	101850
Australia	Pakistan	16 Jan 52	Postal Service	151UNTS281	102001
Multilateral		16 Apr 52	General Economic	139UNTS35	101874
Australia	USA (United States)	27 May 52	Postal Service	178UNTS113	102338
Multilateral		11 Jul 52	IGO Establishment	169UNTS3	102220
Multilateral		11 Jul 52	Postal Service	171UNTS191	102227
Multilateral		11 Jul 52	Postal Service	170UNTS63	102222
Universal Postal Union (Cont.)					
Multilateral		11 Jul 52	Postal Service	171UNTS3	102224
Australia	Netherlands	22 Oct 53	Postal Service	184UNTS193	102448
Australia	Greece	24 May 54	Postal Service	191UNTS255	102586
Australia	Israel	18 Jun 54	Postal Service	220UNTS29	102985
India	USA (United States)	29 Jul 54	Postal Service	239UNTS69	103373
Australia	Poland	25 Nov 54	Postal Service	521UNTS281	107526
Australia	Austria	20 Dec 54	Postal Service	205UNTS157	102775
Australia	Hungary	10 Feb 55	Postal Service	207UNTS173	102806
Australia	Taiwan	22 Mar 55	Postal Service	209UNTS3	102818
Australia	Czechoslovakia	01 Apr 55	Postal Service	213UNTS199	102888
Spain	USA (United States)	16 Jul 55	Postal Service	270UNTS211	103899
Pakistan	USA (United States)	20 Jul 55	Postal Service	241UNTS255	103436
Australia	Yugoslavia	28 Feb 56	Postal Service	243UNTS53	103446
Canada	Japan	20 Mar 56	Postal Service	517UNTS33	107482
Liberia	USA (United States)	16 Mar 57	Postal Service	290UNTS59	104228
Taiwan	USA (United States)	30 Jul 57	Postal Service	300UNTS61	104331
Multilateral		03 Oct 57	Postal Service	366UNTS193	105218
Multilateral		03 Oct 57	Postal Service	364UNTS3	105211
Multilateral		03 Oct 57	Postal Service	366UNTS87	105216
Multilateral		03 Oct 57	Postal Service	365UNTS3	105213
Multilateral		03 Oct 57	Postal Service	366UNTS141	105217
Multilateral		03 Oct 57	Postal Service	366UNTS3	105215
Multilateral		03 Oct 57	Postal Service	366UNTS255	105219
Lebanon	United Nations	20 Jan 58	Postal Service	286UNTS199	104167
Czechoslovakia	Poland	31 Jan 58	Land Transport	431UNTS99	106214
Australia	USA (United States)	20 Jun 58	Postal Service	336UNTS97	104802
Portugal	USA (United States)	12 Jan 59	Postal Service	343UNTS49	104921
United Arab Rep	USA (United States)	13 Jan 59	Postal Service	358UNTS3	105122
Australia	USSR (Soviet Union)	29 Jun 60	Postal Service	392UNTS131	105641
Canada	USA (United States)	13 Jan 61	Postal Service	410UNTS62	105897
Multilateral		23 Jan 61	Postal Service	530UNTS141	107679
Korea, South	UN Special Fund	21 Apr 61	Direct Aid	394UNTS231	200583
Australia	Japan	01 Mar 62	Postal Service	517UNTS81	107483
Israel	Netherlands	28 May 62	Postal Service	448UNTS219	106434
Israel	Liberia	18 Sep 62	Postal Service	484UNTS209	107031
Japan	New Zealand	15 Mar 63	Postal Service	517UNTS229	107487
Japan	South Africa	06 Apr 63	Postal Service	484UNTS319	107040
Kuwait	USA (United States)	21 Oct 63	Postal Service	530UNTS281	107688
Western European Union					
Multilateral		07 Nov 49	Sanitation	132UNTS3	101748
Multilateral		07 Nov 49	Non-ILO Labor	132UNTS31	101749
Multilateral		17 Apr 50	Non-ILO Labor	126UNTS285	101694
Multilateral		17 Apr 50	Visas	131UNTS99	101738
Multilateral		02 Dec 54	General Amity	226UNTS153	103112
Multilateral		06 Jun 55	IGO Establishment	219UNTS79	102968
Germany, West	UK Great Britain	06 Jun 62	Status of Forces	437UNTS39	106298
World Health Organization					
Multilateral		23 Apr 46	Sanitation	16UNTS179	100257
Multilateral		22 Jul 46	IGO Establishment	14UNTS185	100221
Multilateral		22 Jul 46	IGO Establishment	9UNTS3	100125
Multilateral		11 Dec 46	Sanitation	12UNTS179	100186
League of Nations	United Nations	27 Jun 47	Specific Property	5UNTS389	200036
League of Nations	United Nations	27 Jun 47	Specific Property	5UNTS395	200037
Ireland	USA (United States)	28 Jun 48	Direct Aid	24UNTS3	100349
Luxembourg	USA (United States)	03 Jul 48	Direct Aid	24UNTS35	100350
Multilateral		19 Nov 48	Sanitation	44UNTS277	100688
IBRD (World Bank)	Turkey	07 Jul 50	IBRD Project	156UNTS75	102040
Jordan	United Nations	29 Mar 51	Tech Assistance	137UNTS267	200448
Multilateral		20 May 52	Sanitation	219UNTS55	102966
United Arab Rep	USA (United States)	18 Jun 53	Sanitation	215UNTS45	102910
Saudi Arabia	USA (United States)	29 Jun 53	Sanitation	206UNTS23	102784
New Zealand	UK Great Britain	20 Sep 57	Sanitation	287UNTS105	104180
USA (United States)	USSR (Soviet Union)	21 Nov 59	Culture	361UNTS35	105172
Multilateral		30 Mar 61	Sanitation	520UNTS151	107515

PARTY ONE	PARTY TWO	DATE	TOPIC	CITATION	NUMBER
World Health Organization (Cont.)					
Japan	Peru	15 May 61	General Trade	451UNTS3	106482
Denmark	India	15 May 63	Tech Assistance	616UNTS49	108891
Multilateral		07 Nov 64	Sanitation	548UNTS3	107965
Netherlands	Norway	17 Nov 64	Sanitation	579UNTS243	108412
Congo (Zaire)	Denmark	25 May 68	Tech Assistance	0UNTS0	109289
World Meteorological Organization					
Multilateral		12 May 40	Scientific Project	101UNTS91	101405
Multilateral		11 Oct 47	IGO Establishment	77UNTS143	100998
Japan	USA (United States)	28 Feb 52	Milit Assistance	208UNTS255	102817
Multilateral		25 Feb 54	Air Transport	215UNTS249	102922
Israel	USA (United States)	22 May 68	Scientific Project	0UNTS0	109356

UNTS SELF-INDEX SECTION

User's Guide

This is one of the five specialized sections of the INDEX. Each specialized section lists treaties in a different order: (1) by date of signature, (2) by party, (3) by international organizations mentioned in the treaty text, (4) by the topical categories of the UNTS Index and (5) by the topical categories of this INDEX.

Within each section there is a standard set of information per treaty: (1) parties, (2) date of signature, (3) topic, (4) citation and (5) treaty number.

In many cases a user will satisfy a query within one of the five specialized sections and will not need to go to the Main Entry Section (Volumes 1–3). It is for limited use of this kind that the present USER'S GUIDE has been designed. However, if the user is unfamiliar with the general format and search techniques of this INDEX, or if the search involves more than one specialized section, it is advisable to consult the Introduction in Volume 1.

Sample of UNTS Self-Index Section

PARTY ONE	PARTY TWO	DATE	TOPIC	CITATION	NUMBER
Administration					
Multilateral		30 Jul 40	Admin Cooperation	161UNTS253	200488
Netherlands	USA (United States)	16 May 44	Milit Occupation	132UNTS355	200440
Belgium	UK Great Britain	16 May 44	Admin Cooperation	90UNTS283	200266
Administration, Military					
Taiwan	USSR (Soviet Union)	14 Aug 45	General Amity	10UNTS300	200068
Greece	UK Great Britain	07 Apr 47	Territory Boundary	11UNTS201	100158
Adoption					
Multilateral		23 Mar 53	Admin Cooperation	202UNTS241	102732
Agricultural Commodities					
Brazil	USA (United States)	26 Jun 53	Direct Aid	336UNTS241	104808
USA (United States)	Yugoslavia	05 Jan 55	US Agri Commod Aid	251UNTS29	103531

Key Item. This section is ordered alphabetically according to the topical categories of the Cumulative Index to the United Nations Treaty Series (UNTS). In the above sample there are three treaties under Administration, two under Administration, Military, one under Adoption, and so forth. Each of these treaties is listed under that particular category in the UNTS Cumulative Index and is so reproduced here regardless of whether or not the category coincides with the topic of this INDEX (Column 4). For instance, the second treaty shown above involves civil administration in Netherlands territory liberated by the Allied Expeditionary Force in World War II. The UNTS Cumulative Index lists it under the topic of Administration; this INDEX, under Military Occupation.

Party One. In case of a bilateral treaty this column identifies one of the two parties. In case of a multilateral treaty it shows the word "Multilateral."

Party Two. In case of a bilateral treaty this column identifies the other of the two parties. In a multilateral treaty it remains blank.

Date. This column identifies the date of signature. Other dates (ratification, force, registration, accession, etc.) can be found in the Main Entry Section. Multiple dates of signature are represented only by the most recent date.

Topic. This column identifies the single dominant theme of each treaty. For a full list of INDEX topics see Volume 1, Introduction, Thesaurus, Topic List. The same information is reproduced also in the beginning of Volume 5.

Citation. This column identifies the printed source where the full text of the treaty can be found. For details on abbreviations see Volume 1, Introduction, Thesaurus, Sources and Citations.

Treaty Number. This column identifies the serial number of each treaty under which it is listed in the Main Entry Section. See that location for all further information on any treaty.

United Nations Treaty Series

PARTY ONE	PARTY TWO	DATE	TOPIC	CITATION	NUMBER
Administration					
Multilateral		30 Jul 40	Admin Cooperation	161UNTS253	200488
Netherlands	USA (United States)	16 May 44	Milit Occupation	132UNTS355	200440
Belgium	UK Great Britain	16 May 44	Admin Cooperation	90UNTS283	200266
Norway	USA (United States)	16 May 44	Privil/Immunities	67UNTS253	200223
France	USA (United States)	25 Aug 44	Milit Occupation	138UNTS247	200449
Multilateral		12 Sep 44	Milit Occupation	227UNTS279	200532
Multilateral		14 Nov 44	Milit Occupation	236UNTS359	200539
Ethiopia	UK Great Britain	19 Dec 44	General Amity	93UNTS303	200272
Multilateral		09 Jun 45	Milit Occupation	139UNTS381	200464
Multilateral		09 Jul 45	Milit Occupation	160UNTS359	200484
Multilateral		26 Jul 45	Milit Occupation	227UNTS297	200533
France	UK Great Britain	31 Aug 45	IGO Establishment	98UNTS249	200275
South Africa	UK Great Britain	22 Feb 49	Territory Boundary	93UNTS75	101291
Italy	UK Great Britain	20 Mar 50	Territory Boundary	128UNTS201	101721
Italy	UK Great Britain	21 Mar 50	Territory Boundary	128UNTS225	101722
Multilateral		15 Dec 50	Tech Assistance	76UNTS120	100985
Australia	UK Great Britain	19 Dec 50	Territory Boundary	93UNTS81	101292
Multilateral		09 May 52	Milit Occupation	168UNTS65	102213
France	UK Great Britain	10 Nov 52	Admin Cooperation	214UNTS255	102903
Japan	USA (United States)	24 Dec 53	Territory Boundary	222UNTS193	103028
Belgium	Netherlands	28 Jun 54	Territory Boundary	272UNTS235	103942
Multilateral		05 Oct 54	Territory Boundary	235UNTS99	103297
Ethiopia	UK Great Britain	29 Nov 54	Status of Forces	207UNTS283	102811
Ethiopia	UK Great Britain	12 Aug 55	Territory Boundary	227UNTS3	103127
Multilateral		29 Oct 56	Territory Boundary	263UNTS165	103772
Administration, Military					
Taiwan	USSR (Soviet Union)	14 Aug 45	General Amity	10UNTS300	200068
Greece	UK Great Britain	07 Apr 47	Territory Boundary	11UNTS201	100158
Administrative Assistance					
Norway	USA (United States)	16 May 44	Privil/Immunities	67UNTS253	200223
Belgium	UK Great Britain	16 May 44	Admin Cooperation	90UNTS283	200266
Multilateral		05 Jun 45	Milit Occupation	68UNTS189	200230
Iraq	Turkey	29 Mar 46	General Amity	37UNTS226	100580
Czechoslovakia	Romania	01 Mar 48	Admin Cooperation	26UNTS109	100381
Czechoslovakia	Poland	05 Apr 48	Non-ILO Labor	31UNTS355	100482
Adoption					
Multilateral		23 Mar 53	Admin Cooperation	202UNTS241	102732
Aerial Mapping					
France	USA (United States)	27 Nov 48	Scientific Project	168UNTS119	102217
Saudi Arabia	USA (United States)	10 Nov 51	Scientific Project	180UNTS263	102390
Brazil	USA (United States)	02 Jun 52	Scientific Project	181UNTS109	102403
Liberia	USA (United States)	15 Dec 52	Tech Assistance	185UNTS45	102457
Thailand	USA (United States)	03 Dec 53	Tech Assistance	213UNTS91	102882
USA (United States)	Venezuela	24 Sep 57	Tech Assistance	293UNTS307	104298

PARTY ONE	PARTY TWO	DATE	TOPIC	CITATION	NUMBER
Aerial Mapping (Cont.)					
New Zealand	USA (United States)	30 Oct 59	Tech Assistance	361UNTS21	105170
India	Netherlands	11 Dec 64	Scientific Project	570UNTS165	108292
Agricultural Commodities					
Brazil	USA (United States)	26 Jun 53	Direct Aid	336UNTS241	104808
USA (United States)	Yugoslavia	05 Jan 55	US Agri Commod Aid	251UNTS29	103531
Turkey	USA (United States)	10 Jun 55	Atomic Energy	238UNTS149	103359
Colombia	USA (United States)	23 Jun 55	US Agri Commod Aid	263UNTS337	103781
USA (United States)	Yugoslavia	03 Nov 56	US Agri Commod Aid	277UNTS119	104002
Colombia	USA (United States)	16 Apr 57	US Agri Commod Aid	283UNTS245	104121
Mexico	USA (United States)	23 Oct 57	US Agri Commod Aid	300UNTS35	104330
Colombia	USA (United States)	14 Mar 58	US Agri Commod Aid	308UNTS115	104459
Taiwan	USA (United States)	18 Apr 58	US Agri Commod Aid	308UNTS179	104461
Iceland	USA (United States)	03 May 58	US Agri Commod Aid	316UNTS137	104581
Pakistan	USA (United States)	26 Nov 58	US Agri Commod Aid	337UNTS3	104812
USA (United States)	Yugoslavia	22 Dec 58	US Agri Commod Aid	338UNTS243	104839
Taiwan	USA (United States)	09 Jun 59	US Agri Commod Aid	353UNTS257	105046
Colombia	USA (United States)	06 Oct 59	US Agri Commod Aid	358UNTS145	105132
Peru	USA (United States)	12 Feb 60	US Agri Commod Aid	372UNTS83	105290
Pakistan	USA (United States)	11 Apr 60	US Agri Commod Aid	372UNTS251	105302
Taiwan	USA (United States)	30 Aug 60	US Agri Commod Aid	388UNTS191	105579
USA (United States)	Yugoslavia	28 Apr 61	US Agri Commod Aid	409UNTS172	105884
USA (United States)	Vietnam, South	14 Jul 61	US Agri Commod Aid	416UNTS133	105999
Taiwan	USA (United States)	21 Jul 61	US Agri Commod Aid	416UNTS101	105998
Turkey	USA (United States)	29 Jul 61	US Agri Commod Aid	416UNTS151	106001
Austria	USA (United States)	03 Oct 61	Direct Aid	426UNTS187	106137
Pakistan	USA (United States)	14 Oct 61	US Agri Commod Aid	426UNTS237	106141
Sudan	USA (United States)	14 Nov 61	US Agri Commod Aid	434UNTS51	106255
Bolivia	USA (United States)	15 Nov 61	US Agri Commod Aid	456UNTS192	106557
Congo (Zaire)	USA (United States)	18 Nov 61	US Agri Commod Aid	433UNTS207	106244
Philippines	USA (United States)	24 Nov 61	US Agri Commod Aid	433UNTS315	106251
Portugal	USA (United States)	28 Nov 61	US Agri Commod Aid	434UNTS31	106253
USA (United States)	Yugoslavia	28 Dec 61	US Agri Commod Aid	434UNTS111	106259
United Arab Rep	USA (United States)	19 Jan 62	US Agri Commod Aid	435UNTS107	106273
Iran	USA (United States)	29 Jan 62	US Agri Commod Aid	435UNTS53	106270
Guinea	USA (United States)	02 Feb 62	US Agri Commod Aid	435UNTS35	106269
Bolivia	USA (United States)	12 Feb 62	US Agri Commod Aid	451UNTS281	106499
Indonesia	USA (United States)	19 Feb 62	US Agri Commod Aid	435UNTS137	106276
Korea, South	USA (United States)	02 Mar 62	US Agri Commod Aid	442UNTS185	106349
Brazil	USA (United States)	15 Mar 62	US Agri Commod Aid	456UNTS209	106558
USA (United States)	Yugoslavia	21 Apr 62	US Agri Commod Aid	442UNTS123	106344
Taiwan	USA (United States)	27 Apr 62	US Agri Commod Aid	436UNTS25	106287
USA (United States)	Uruguay	27 Apr 62	US Agri Commod Aid	452UNTS25	106502
Israel	USA (United States)	03 May 62	US Agri Commod Aid	442UNTS83	106340
USA (United States)	Venezuela	17 May 62	US Agri Commod Aid	456UNTS275	106562
Chile	USA (United States)	07 Aug 62	US Agri Commod Aid	461UNTS61	106652
Ethiopia	USA (United States)	13 Aug 62	US Agri Commod Aid	459UNTS31	106611

Agricultural Commodities (Cont.)

PARTY ONE	PARTY TWO	DATE	TOPIC	CITATION	NUMBER
Taiwan	USA (United States)	31 Aug 62	US Agri Commod Aid	460UNTS247	106644
Tunisia	USA (United States)	14 Sep 62	US Agri Commod Aid	461UNTS31	106649
United Arab Rep	USA (United States)	08 Oct 62	US Agri Commod Aid	462UNTS39	106670
Iran	USA (United States)	15 Oct 62	US Agri Commod Aid	473UNTS291	106866
Greece	USA (United States)	22 Oct 62	US Agri Commod Aid	462UNTS187	106678
Burma	USA (United States)	09 Nov 62	US Agri Commod Aid	461UNTS113	106655
Taiwan	USA (United States)	19 Nov 62	US Agri Commod Aid	459UNTS263	106629
USA (United States)	Vietnam, South	21 Nov 62	US Agri Commod Aid	469UNTS101	106786
Paraguay	USA (United States)	24 Nov 62	US Agri Commod Aid	471UNTS49	106821
India	USA (United States)	26 Nov 62	US Agri Commod Aid	460UNTS203	106641
USA (United States)	Yugoslavia	28 Nov 62	US Agri Commod Aid	460UNTS185	106640
Dominican Republic	USA (United States)	30 Nov 62	US Agri Commod Aid	471UNTS25	106819
India	USA (United States)	30 Nov 62	US Agri Commod Aid	459UNTS231	106626
Israel	USA (United States)	06 Dec 62	US Agri Commod Aid	460UNTS151	106638
Bolivia	USA (United States)	17 Dec 62	US Agri Commod Aid	469UNTS121	106788
Sudan	USA (United States)	31 Jan 63	US Agri Commod Aid	494UNTS119	107230
Poland	USA (United States)	01 Feb 63	US Agri Commod Aid	487UNTS143	107100
Bolivia	USA (United States)	04 Feb 63	US Agri Commod Aid	473UNTS65	106856
Turkey	USA (United States)	21 Feb 63	US Agri Commod Aid	473UNTS311	106867
Congo (Zaire)	USA (United States)	23 Feb 63	US Agri Commod Aid	493UNTS17	107204
Congo (Zaire)	USA (United States)	23 Feb 63	US Agri Commod Aid	493UNTS3	107203
Colombia	USA (United States)	27 Mar 63	US Agri Commod Aid	489UNTS289	107145
Ecuador	USA (United States)	05 Apr 63	US Agri Commod Aid	477UNTS135	106919
El Salvador	USA (United States)	07 May 63	US Agri Commod Aid	476UNTS35	106901
India	USA (United States)	09 May 63	US Agri Commod Aid	476UNTS43	106902
Guinea	USA (United States)	22 May 63	US Agri Commod Aid	487UNTS251	107108
Ethiopia	USA (United States)	11 Jun 63	US Agri Commod Aid	487UNTS269	107109
Japan	USA (United States)	14 Jun 63	Finance	479UNTS165	106951
Cyprus	USA (United States)	18 Jun 63	US Agri Commod Aid	479UNTS191	106953
India	USA (United States)	27 Jun 63	US Agri Commod Aid	479UNTS215	106955
Senegal	USA (United States)	03 Jul 63	US Agri Commod Aid	527UNTS95	107620
Dominican Republic	USA (United States)	13 Aug 63	US Agri Commod Aid	492UNTS327	107202
Iraq	USA (United States)	27 Aug 63	US Agri Commod Aid	489UNTS271	107144
Brazil	USA (United States)	11 Sep 63	US Agri Commod Aid	493UNTS267	107220
Paraguay	USA (United States)	16 Sep 63	US Agri Commod Aid	494UNTS101	107229
Peru	USA (United States)	23 Sep 63	US Agri Commod Aid	488UNTS91	107121
Greece	USA (United States)	30 Oct 63	US Agri Commod Aid	493UNTS29	107205
Paraguay	USA (United States)	14 Nov 63	US Agri Commod Aid	505UNTS87	107366
Iran	USA (United States)	17 Nov 63	US Agri Commod Aid	530UNTS41	107671
Syria	USA (United States)	18 Nov 63	US Agri Commod Aid	494UNTS169	107232
USA (United States)	Vietnam, South	09 Jan 64	US Agri Commod Aid	505UNTS173	107373
Poland	USA (United States)	03 Feb 64	US Agri Commod Aid	505UNTS245	107376
Poland	USA (United States)	03 Feb 64	US Agri Commod Aid	505UNTS215	107375
Jordan	USA (United States)	11 Feb 64	US Agri Commod Aid	511UNTS85	107429
Iceland	USA (United States)	13 Feb 64	US Agri Commod Aid	511UNTS3	107421
Iceland	USA (United States)	13 Feb 64	US Agri Commod Aid	510UNTS295	107420
Peru	USA (United States)	13 Feb 64	US Agri Commod Aid	511UNTS119	107431
Sudan	USA (United States)	02 Mar 64	US Agri Commod Aid	524UNTS217	107575
Korea, South	USA (United States)	18 Mar 64	US Agri Commod Aid	524UNTS263	107578
Bolivia	USA (United States)	25 Mar 64	US Agri Commod Aid	532UNTS3	107710
Tunisia	USA (United States)	07 Apr 64	US Agri Commod Aid	527UNTS3	107613
Australia	UK Great Britain	15 Apr 64	Commodity Trade	515UNTS23	107451
Canada	UK Great Britain	15 Apr 64	Commodity Trade	515UNTS39	107452
Argentina	UK Great Britain	15 Apr 64	Commodity Trade	515UNTS3	107450
UK Great Britain	USA (United States)	15 Apr 64	Commodity Trade	515UNTS55	107453
USA (United States)	Yugoslavia	27 Apr 64	US Agri Commod Aid	526UNTS89	107602
Congo (Zaire)	USA (United States)	28 Apr 64	US Agri Commod Aid	526UNTS55	107600
USA (United States)	Yugoslavia	28 Apr 64	US Agri Commod Aid	526UNTS103	107603
Philippines	USA (United States)	14 May 64	US Agri Commod Aid	526UNTS113	107604
Taiwan	USA (United States)	03 Jun 64	US Agri Commod Aid	526UNTS257	107610
Guinea	USA (United States)	13 Jun 64	US Agri Commod Aid	531UNTS263	107708
South Africa	UK Great Britain	22 Jun 64	Commodity Trade	515UNTS71	107454
Ireland	UK Great Britain	30 Jun 64	Commodity Trade	522UNTS141	107541
Sweden	UK Great Britain	30 Jun 64	Commodity Trade	515UNTS83	107455
Cyprus	UK Great Britain	02 Jul 64	Commodity Trade	522UNTS129	107540

Agricultural Commodities (Cont.)

PARTY ONE	PARTY TWO	DATE	TOPIC	CITATION	NUMBER
India	UK Great Britain	31 Jul 64	Commodity Trade	522UNTS153	107542
Kenya	UK Great Britain	25 Aug 64	Commodity Trade	522UNTS165	107543
Syria	UK Great Britain	31 Aug 64	Commodity Trade	539UNTS259	107837
Malawi	UK Great Britain	01 Sep 64	Commodity Trade	522UNTS117	107539
Tanganyika	UK Great Britain	02 Sep 64	Commodity Trade	522UNTS177	107544
Paraguay	USA (United States)	05 Sep 64	US Agri Commod Aid	530UNTS225	107685
Finland	UK Great Britain	12 Sep 64	Commodity Trade	535UNTS13	107773
Denmark	UK Great Britain	16 Sep 64	Commodity Trade	534UNTS427	107771
USA (United States)	Vietnam, South	29 Sep 64	US Agri Commod Aid	531UNTS183	107703
Iran	USA (United States)	29 Sep 64	US Agri Commod Aid	531UNTS163	107702
India	USA (United States)	30 Sep 64	US Agri Commod Aid	532UNTS321	107726
Colombia	USA (United States)	08 Oct 64	US Agri Commod Aid	579UNTS3	108395
USA (United States)	Yugoslavia	28 Oct 64	US Agri Commod Aid	533UNTS3	107728
USA (United States)	Yugoslavia	29 Oct 64	US Agri Commod Aid	533UNTS17	107729
Iran	USA (United States)	16 Nov 64	US Agri Commod Aid	532UNTS213	107719
Greece	USA (United States)	17 Nov 64	US Agri Commod Aid	532UNTS107	107714
Kenya	USA (United States)	07 Dec 64	US Agri Commod Aid	532UNTS263	107722
Congo (Zaire)	USA (United States)	09 Dec 64	US Agri Commod Aid	531UNTS249	107707
Israel	USA (United States)	22 Dec 64	US Agri Commod Aid	532UNTS231	107720
Morocco	USA (United States)	29 Dec 64	Commodity Trade	593UNTS185	108584
Iceland	USA (United States)	30 Dec 64	US Agri Commod Aid	542UNTS37	107878
Iceland	USA (United States)	30 Dec 64	US Agri Commod Aid	531UNTS287	107709
Taiwan	USA (United States)	31 Dec 64	US Agri Commod Aid	532UNTS29	107711
Korea, South	USA (United States)	31 Dec 64	US Agri Commod Aid	535UNTS315	107787
Dahomey	USA (United States)	31 Dec 64	US Agri Commod Aid	541UNTS117	107865
Taiwan	USA (United States)	31 Dec 64	US Agri Commod Aid	532UNTS59	107712
Sierra Leone	USA (United States)	29 Jan 65	US Agri Commod Aid	542UNTS87	107882
Tunisia	USA (United States)	17 Feb 65	US Agri Commod Aid	542UNTS125	107885
USA (United States)	Yugoslavia	16 Mar 65	US Agri Commod Aid	542UNTS161	107887
Dominican Republic	USA (United States)	18 Mar 65	US Agri Commod Aid	542UNTS215	107892
Ivory Coast	USA (United States)	05 Apr 65	US Agri Commod Aid	546UNTS143	107941
Morocco	USA (United States)	23 Apr 65	US Agri Commod Aid	594UNTS3	108591
Philippines	USA (United States)	23 Apr 65	US Agri Commod Aid	546UNTS157	107942
Bolivia	USA (United States)	12 May 65	US Agri Commod Aid	564UNTS143	108226
Afghanistan	USA (United States)	22 May 65	US Agri Commod Aid	579UNTS29	108396
USA (United States)	Vietnam, South	26 May 65	US Agri Commod Aid	550UNTS3	108005
Ecuador	USA (United States)	25 Jun 65	US Agri Commod Aid	549UNTS23	107986
Mali	USA (United States)	14 Jul 65	US Agri Commod Aid	564UNTS101	108223
USA (United States)	Yugoslavia	16 Jul 65	US Agri Commod Aid	549UNTS111	107994
Congo (Zaire)	USA (United States)	19 Jul 65	Direct Aid	593UNTS215	108586
Chile	USA (United States)	27 Jul 65	US Agri Commod Aid	574UNTS83	108342
Bolivia	USA (United States)	17 Aug 65	US Agri Commod Aid	587UNTS289	108514
Ethiopia	USA (United States)	17 Aug 65	US Agri Commod Aid	564UNTS119	108224
USA (United States)	Yugoslavia	22 Nov 65	US Agri Commod Aid	574UNTS211	108351
Ethiopia	USA (United States)	14 Dec 65	US Agri Commod Aid	574UNTS115	108344
United Arab Rep	USA (United States)	03 Jan 66	US Agri Commod Aid	579UNTS83	108400
United Arab Rep	USA (United States)	03 Jan 66	US Agri Commod Aid	579UNTS63	108399
Liberia	USA (United States)	06 Jan 66	US Agri Commod Aid	592UNTS101	108570
Guinea	USA (United States)	04 Feb 66	US Agri Commod Aid	579UNTS213	108409
Algeria	USA (United States)	23 Feb 66	Direct Aid	592UNTS117	108571
Multilateral		04 Mar 66	US Agri Commod Aid	578UNTS57	108387
Korea, South	USA (United States)	07 Mar 66	US Agri Commod Aid	579UNTS137	108404
Ceylon (Sri Lanka)	USA (United States)	12 Mar 66	US Agri Commod Aid	579UNTS117	108403
USA (United States)	Vietnam, South	21 Mar 66	US Agri Commod Aid	578UNTS165	108394
Romania	UK Great Britain	22 Mar 66	Commodity Trade	571UNTS281	108307
Ghana	USA (United States)	01 Apr 66	US Agri Commod Aid	579UNTS157	108405
Jordan	USA (United States)	05 Apr 66	Direct Aid	593UNTS239	108587
USA (United States)	Yugoslavia	11 Apr 66	US Agri Commod Aid	580UNTS239	108427
Sudan	USA (United States)	13 Apr 66	US Agri Commod Aid	586UNTS39	108495
Indonesia	USA (United States)	18 Apr 66	US Agri Commod Aid	578UNTS106	108390
Bolivia	USA (United States)	22 Apr 66	US Agri Commod Aid	578UNTS73	108388
Paraguay	USA (United States)	27 Apr 66	US Agri Commod Aid	578UNTS121	108391
Pakistan	USA (United States)	26 May 66	US Agri Commod Aid	594UNTS27	108592
Israel	USA (United States)	06 Jun 66	US Agri Commod Aid	578UNTS143	108392
Israel	USA (United States)	06 Jun 66	US Agri Commod Aid	593UNTS165	108583

PARTY ONE	PARTY TWO	DATE	TOPIC	CITATION	NUMBER
Agricultural Commodities (Cont.)					
Indonesia	USA (United States)	28 Jun 66	US Agri Commod Aid	593UNTS201	108585
Philippines	USA (United States)	22 Dec 66	US Agri Commod Aid	591UNTS219	108559
Agriculture					
Multilateral		12 Nov 21	ILO Labor	38UNTS153	100594
Multilateral		12 Nov 21	ILO Labor	38UNTS165	100595
Multilateral		16 Nov 21	ILO Labor	38UNTS143	100593
Multilateral		15 Jun 27	ILO Labor	38UNTS343	100608
Multilateral		29 Jun 33	ILO Labor	39UNTS285	100622
Multilateral		29 Jun 33	ILO Labor	39UNTS189	100618
Multilateral		29 Jun 33	ILO Labor	39UNTS235	100620
Peru	USA (United States)	21 Apr 42	Scientific Project	89UNTS317	200260
Nicaragua	USA (United States)	27 Oct 42	Scientific Project	99UNTS287	200283
Ecuador	USA (United States)	29 Oct 42	Scientific Project	89UNTS301	200259
El Salvador	USA (United States)	02 Dec 42	Scientific Project	122UNTS277	200410
Mexico	USA (United States)	26 Apr 43	Non-ILO Labor	21UNTS245	200127
Peru	USA (United States)	20 May 43	Non-IBRD Project	100UNTS259	200288
Mexico	USA (United States)	27 Jan 44	IGO Establishment	106UNTS275	200346
Guatemala	USA (United States)	15 Jul 44	Scientific Project	106UNTS285	200347
Peru	USA (United States)	22 Nov 46	Non-IBRD Project	100UNTS170	101396
Multilateral		06 Feb 47	IGO Establishment	97UNTS227	101352
Paraguay	USA (United States)	03 Mar 47	Tech Assistance	135UNTS156	101819
Czechoslovakia	Poland	04 Apr 47	General Economic	85UNTS62	101146
Bolivia	USA (United States)	16 May 47	Tech Assistance	168UNTS89	102215
Canada	USA (United States)	19 May 47	Non-ILO Labor	43UNTS97	100663
Czechoslovakia	USSR (Soviet Union)	28 Nov 47	Sanitation	216UNTS285	102941
Haiti	USA (United States)	19 Dec 47	Direct Aid	135UNTS130	101818
Paraguay	USA (United States)	01 Jan 48	Scientific Project	89UNTS191	101217
Costa Rica	USA (United States)	27 Feb 48	Direct Aid	135UNTS74	101816
Poland	USSR (Soviet Union)	08 Apr 48	Sanitation	26UNTS191	100388
Ecuador	USA (United States)	14 May 48	Scientific Project	89UNTS71	101210
Taiwan	USA (United States)	05 Aug 48	IGO Establishment	82UNTS109	101087
Canada	USA (United States)	23 Nov 48	Commodity Trade	81UNTS295	101078
Czechoslovakia	Poland	22 Jan 49	Sanitation	85UNTS3	101142
Multilateral		22 Feb 49	Sanitation	93UNTS129	101296
Chile	IBRD (World Bank)	23 Mar 49	IBRD Project	153UNTS141	102019
France	Netherlands	20 Jul 49	Mostfavored Nation	204UNTS287	102763
Colombia	IBRD (World Bank)	19 Aug 49	IBRD Project	154UNTS329	102032
Bulgaria	Poland	26 Sep 49	Sanitation	260UNTS227	103711
India	IBRD (World Bank)	29 Sep 49	IBRD Project	154UNTS393	102033
Hungary	Poland	29 Oct 49	Sanitation	260UNTS91	103705
Nicaragua	USA (United States)	01 Feb 50	Tech Assistance	99UNTS25	101368
Romania	USSR (Soviet Union)	27 May 50	Sanitation	221UNTS13	103000
Hungary	USSR (Soviet Union)	13 Jul 50	Sanitation	221UNTS35	103001
Bulgaria	USSR (Soviet Union)	25 Aug 50	Sanitation	221UNTS57	103002
Luxembourg	Netherlands	25 Aug 50	Non-ILO Labor	81UNTS13	101058
Iran	USA (United States)	19 Oct 50	Tech Assistance	92UNTS135	101266
IBRD (World Bank)	Thailand	27 Oct 50	IBRD Project	158UNTS25	102060
Chile	USA (United States)	16 Jan 51	Direct Aid	157UNTS3	102043
Honduras	USA (United States)	30 Jan 51	Direct Aid	124UNTS63	101667
El Salvador	USA (United States)	11 May 51	Direct Aid	141UNTS191	101915
Nicaragua	IBRD (World Bank)	07 Jun 51	IBRD Project	158UNTS215	102067
Brazil	USA (United States)	29 Jun 51	Tech Assistance	184UNTS303	102455
Panama	USA (United States)	30 Jul 51	Direct Aid	140UNTS321	101896
Mexico	USA (United States)	11 Aug 51	Non-ILO Labor	162UNTS103	102133
Italy	IBRD (World Bank)	10 Oct 51	IBRD Project	159UNTS383	200482
Chile	IBRD (World Bank)	10 Oct 51	IBRD Project	158UNTS369	102072
Iceland	IBRD (World Bank)	01 Nov 51	IBRD Project	159UNTS55	102083
Paraguay	IBRD (World Bank)	07 Dec 51	IBRD Project	159UNTS103	102085
Dominican Republic	USA (United States)	07 Jan 52	Direct Aid	174UNTS243	102289
Colombia	USA (United States)	12 Jan 52	Education	168UNTS109	102216
Iraq	USA (United States)	18 Mar 52	Tech Assistance	223UNTS131	103061
Peru	USA (United States)	09 Apr 52	Tech Assistance	184UNTS295	102454
Finland	IBRD (World Bank)	30 Apr 52	IBRD Project	159UNTS408	200483
Ethiopia	USA (United States)	15 May 52	Education	180UNTS227	102388

PARTY ONE	PARTY TWO	DATE	TOPIC	CITATION	NUMBER
Agriculture (Cont.)					
Ecuador	USA (United States)	29 May 52	Tech Assistance	185UNTS203	102471
Pakistan	IBRD (World Bank)	13 Jun 52	IBRD Project	191UNTS85	102578
Bolivia	USA (United States)	18 Jun 52	Tech Assistance	199UNTS211	102686
IBRD (World Bank)	Turkey	18 Jun 52	IBRD Project	159UNTS269	102091
Panama	USA (United States)	30 Jun 52	Tech Assistance	181UNTS121	102404
Australia	IBRD (World Bank)	08 Jul 52	IBRD Project	159UNTS295	102092
Peru	IBRD (World Bank)	08 Jul 52	IBRD Project	159UNTS321	102093
Iceland	IBRD (World Bank)	26 Aug 52	IBRD Project	159UNTS363	102095
Saudi Arabia	USA (United States)	10 Nov 52	Direct Aid	181UNTS295	102418
Saudi Arabia	USA (United States)	15 Dec 52	Tech Assistance	185UNTS67	102459
India	IBRD (World Bank)	23 Jan 53	IBRD Project	201UNTS145	102715
United Arab Rep	USA (United States)	21 May 53	Tech Assistance	204UNTS29	102748
Colombia	USA (United States)	09 Jun 53	Tech Assistance	213UNTS3	102877
Liberia	USA (United States)	23 Jun 53	Tech Assistance	213UNTS37	102879
Brazil	USA (United States)	26 Jun 53	Direct Aid	336UNTS241	104808
Chile	USA (United States)	27 Jun 53	Tech Assistance	229UNTS193	103167
Chile	USA (United States)	27 Jun 53	Tech Assistance	229UNTS53	103160
Nicaragua	USA (United States)	30 Jun 53	Tech Assistance	215UNTS133	102917
Ethiopia	USA (United States)	30 Jun 53	Direct Aid	212UNTS135	102865
Iceland	IBRD (World Bank)	04 Sep 53	IBRD Project	178UNTS275	102344
Panama	IBRD (World Bank)	25 Sep 53	IBRD Project	188UNTS95	102522
Panama	IBRD (World Bank)	25 Sep 53	IBRD Project	188UNTS71	102521
Japan	USA (United States)	08 Mar 54	Direct Aid	232UNTS243	103239
Japan	USA (United States)	08 Mar 54	Direct Aid	232UNTS227	103238
Peru	IBRD (World Bank)	12 Apr 54	IBRD Project	190UNTS231	102567
Ireland	USA (United States)	17 Jun 54	Direct Aid	241UNTS173	103432
Mexico	USA (United States)	17 Jun 54	Non-IBRD Project	237UNTS275	103352
Costa Rica	USA (United States)	30 Jun 54	Tech Assistance	235UNTS35	103294
El Salvador	USA (United States)	16 Jul 54	Non-IBRD Project	237UNTS237	103350
Peru	IBRD (World Bank)	12 Nov 54	IBRD Project	209UNTS287	102831
Turkey	USA (United States)	15 Nov 54	Commodity Trade	238UNTS135	103358
Colombia	IBRD (World Bank)	29 Dec 54	IBRD Project	211UNTS135	102851
USA (United States)	Yugoslavia	05 Jan 55	US Agri Commod Aid	251UNTS29	103531
El Salvador	USA (United States)	21 Mar 55	Non-IBRD Project	250UNTS261	103528
Peru	IBRD (World Bank)	05 Apr 55	IBRD Project	211UNTS115	102850
Spain	USA (United States)	20 Apr 55	US Agri Commod Aid	239UNTS117	103374
Argentina	USA (United States)	25 Apr 55	US Agri Commod Aid	251UNTS283	103546
Israel	USA (United States)	29 Apr 55	US Agri Commod Aid	261UNTS331	103731
Peru	USA (United States)	30 Apr 55	General Aid	263UNTS309	103780
Finland	USA (United States)	06 May 55	US Agri Commod Aid	251UNTS3	103529
Italy	USA (United States)	23 May 55	US Agri Commod Aid	251UNTS303	103547
Austria	USA (United States)	14 Jun 55	US Agri Commod Aid	258UNTS37	103668
Greece	USA (United States)	24 Jun 55	US Agri Commod Aid	270UNTS351	103905
Greece	USA (United States)	24 Jun 55	US Agri Commod Aid	270UNTS361	103906
Dominican Republic	USA (United States)	30 Jun 55	Non-IBRD Project	257UNTS313	103664
Libya	USA (United States)	28 Jul 55	Non-IBRD Project	270UNTS317	103903
France	USA (United States)	11 Aug 55	US Agri Commod Aid	251UNTS15	103530
Lebanon	IBRD (World Bank)	25 Aug 55	IBRD Project	230UNTS233	103188
Nicaragua	IBRD (World Bank)	26 Aug 55	IBRD Project	229UNTS145	103164
Israel	USA (United States)	10 Nov 55	US Agri Commod Aid	240UNTS3	103390
Multilateral		21 Dec 55	General Trade	292UNTS63	104267
Argentina	USA (United States)	21 Dec 55	Commodity Trade	240UNTS329	103411
Germany, West	USA (United States)	23 Dec 55	US Agri Commod Aid	240UNTS79	103395
Austria	USA (United States)	07 Feb 56	US Agri Commod Aid	272UNTS117	103933
Iran	USA (United States)	20 Feb 56	US Agri Commod Aid	272UNTS135	103934
Italy	USA (United States)	27 Feb 56	Direct Aid	291UNTS287	104260
Indonesia	USA (United States)	02 Mar 56	US Agri Commod Aid	271UNTS345	103925
France	Italy	03 Mar 56	Non-ILO Labor	267UNTS181	103843
Turkey	USA (United States)	12 Mar 56	US Agri Commod Aid	272UNTS21	103929
Chile	USA (United States)	13 Mar 56	US Agri Commod Aid	275UNTS49	103975
Germany, East	USSR (Soviet Union)	30 May 56	Sanitation	263UNTS143	103771
Pakistan	USA (United States)	07 Aug 56	US Agri Commod Aid	281UNTS75	104071
Greece	USA (United States)	08 Aug 56	US Agri Commod Aid	277UNTS203	104007
India	USA (United States)	29 Aug 56	US Agri Commod Aid	278UNTS25	104019
Israel	USA (United States)	11 Sep 56	US Agri Commod Aid	277UNTS215	104008

Agriculture (Cont.)

PARTY ONE	PARTY TWO	DATE	TOPIC	CITATION	NUMBER
Spain	USA (United States)	23 Oct 56	US Agri Commod Aid	277UNTS105	104001
Italy	USA (United States)	30 Oct 56	US Agri Commod Aid	263UNTS221	103775
USA (United States)	Yugoslavia	03 Nov 56	US Agri Commod Aid	277UNTS119	104002
France	USA (United States)	08 Nov 56	Direct Aid	280UNTS189	104058
Turkey	USA (United States)	12 Nov 56	US Agri Commod Aid	282UNTS77	104093
Australia	IBRD (World Bank)	03 Dec 56	IBRD Project	288UNTS99	104200
Japan	IBRD (World Bank)	19 Dec 56	IBRD Project	268UNTS203	103859
Brazil	USA (United States)	31 Dec 56	US Agri Commod Aid	266UNTS151	103829
Thailand	USA (United States)	04 Mar 57	US Agri Commod Aid	279UNTS235	104043
Peru	IBRD (World Bank)	13 Mar 57	IBRD Project	274UNTS59	103958
Iceland	USA (United States)	11 Apr 57	US Agri Commod Aid	283UNTS107	104110
Colombia	USA (United States)	16 Apr 57	US Agri Commod Aid	283UNTS245	104121
Peru	USA (United States)	02 May 57	US Agri Commod Aid	283UNTS55	104106
Austria	USA (United States)	10 May 57	US Agri Commod Aid	283UNTS15	104103
Finland	USA (United States)	10 May 57	US Agri Commod Aid	283UNTS43	104105
Poland	USA (United States)	07 Jun 57	Direct Aid	291UNTS41	104243
France	Italy	01 Aug 57	Non-ILO Labor	302UNTS221	104360
Japan	IBRD (World Bank)	09 Aug 57	IBRD Project	293UNTS59	104286
France	Italy	19 Sep 57	Non-ILO Labor	302UNTS225	104361
Mexico	USA (United States)	23 Oct 57	US Agri Commod Aid	300UNTS35	104330
Germany, East	Hungary	25 Oct 57	Sanitation	408UNTS156	105869
Israel	USA (United States)	07 Nov 57	US Agri Commod Aid	302UNTS255	104365
Pakistan	USA (United States)	15 Nov 57	US Agri Commod Aid	303UNTS173	104380
Greece	USA (United States)	18 Dec 57	US Agri Commod Aid	303UNTS159	104379
France	USA (United States)	27 Dec 57	US Agri Commod Aid	307UNTS79	104444
Turkey	USA (United States)	20 Jan 58	US Agri Commod Aid	304UNTS15	104389
Spain	USA (United States)	27 Jan 58	US Agri Commod Aid	303UNTS247	104384
USA (United States)	Yugoslavia	03 Feb 58	US Agri Commod Aid	304UNTS293	104404
UK Great Britain	USA (United States)	03 Feb 58	US Agri Commod Aid	307UNTS199	104450
Korea, South	USA (United States)	05 Feb 58	US Agri Commod Aid	307UNTS121	104447
Poland	USA (United States)	15 Feb 58	US Agri Commod Aid	307UNTS217	104452
Finland	USA (United States)	21 Feb 58	US Agri Commod Aid	304UNTS253	104401
France	USA (United States)	28 Feb 58	US Agri Commod Aid	366UNTS343	105222
Italy	USA (United States)	07 Mar 58	US Agri Commod Aid	303UNTS205	104381
Colombia	USA (United States)	14 Mar 58	US Agri Commod Aid	308UNTS115	104459
Multilateral		03 Apr 58	Commodity Trade	336UNTS177	104806
Multilateral		03 Apr 58	Commodity Trade	302UNTS121	104355
Peru	USA (United States)	09 Apr 58	US Agri Commod Aid	316UNTS37	104576
Taiwan	USA (United States)	18 Apr 58	US Agri Commod Aid	308UNTS179	104461
Iceland	USA (United States)	03 May 58	US Agri Commod Aid	316UNTS137	104581
Burma	USA (United States)	27 May 58	US Agri Commod Aid	315UNTS197	104569
Philippines	USA (United States)	03 Jun 58	US Agri Commod Aid	316UNTS3	104573
USA (United States)	Vietnam, South	17 Jun 58	Atomic Energy	321UNTS35	104652
Ceylon (Sri Lanka)	USA (United States)	18 Jun 58	US Agri Commod Aid	316UNTS15	104574
India	USA (United States)	23 Jun 58	US Agri Commod Aid	317UNTS181	104603
Ecuador	USA (United States)	30 Jun 58	US Agri Commod Aid	336UNTS11	104796
India	USA (United States)	26 Sep 58	US Agri Commod Aid	336UNTS59	104798
Israel	USA (United States)	06 Nov 58	US Agri Commod Aid	336UNTS275	104810
Pakistan	USA (United States)	26 Nov 58	US Agri Commod Aid	337UNTS3	104812
USA (United States)	Yugoslavia	22 Dec 58	US Agri Commod Aid	338UNTS243	104839
United Arab Rep	USA (United States)	24 Dec 58	US Agri Commod Aid	338UNTS221	104837
Finland	USA (United States)	30 Dec 58	US Agri Commod Aid	340UNTS259	104869
Spain	USA (United States)	13 Jan 59	US Agri Commod Aid	341UNTS241	104887
Turkey	USA (United States)	13 Feb 59	US Agri Commod Aid	340UNTS235	104867
USA (United States)	Uruguay	20 Feb 59	US Agri Commod Aid	341UNTS201	104884
Iceland	USA (United States)	03 Mar 59	US Agri Commod Aid	341UNTS261	104889
India	USA (United States)	03 Mar 59	US Agri Commod Aid	341UNTS235	104886
Ceylon (Sri Lanka)	USA (United States)	13 Mar 59	US Agri Commod Aid	342UNTS51	104900
France	USA (United States)	21 Mar 59	US Agri Commod Aid	342UNTS71	104901
Indonesia	USA (United States)	29 May 59	US Agri Commod Aid	347UNTS85	104992
Taiwan	USA (United States)	09 Jun 59	US Agri Commod Aid	353UNTS257	105046
Poland	USA (United States)	10 Jun 59	US Agri Commod Aid	347UNTS41	104989
Argentina	USA (United States)	12 Jun 59	US Agri Commod Aid	347UNTS59	104990
Korea, South	USA (United States)	30 Jun 59	US Agri Commod Aid	353UNTS297	105047
United Arab Rep	USA (United States)	29 Jul 59	US Agri Commod Aid	357UNTS121	105111

Agriculture (Cont.)

PARTY ONE	PARTY TWO	DATE	TOPIC	CITATION	NUMBER
Colombia	USA (United States)	06 Oct 59	US Agri Commod Aid	358UNTS145	105132
USA (United States)	Vietnam, South	16 Oct 59	US Agri Commod Aid	360UNTS271	105163
India	USA (United States)	13 Nov 59	US Agri Commod Aid	360UNTS287	105164
United Arab Rep	USA (United States)	14 Nov 59	US Agri Commod Aid	360UNTS311	105165
Multilateral		14 Dec 59	Sanitation	422UNTS33	106067
Turkey	USA (United States)	22 Dec 59	US Agri Commod Aid	367UNTS57	105225
IBRD (World Bank)	Uruguay	30 Dec 59	IBRD Project	384UNTS275	105523
Greece	USA (United States)	07 Jan 60	US Agri Commod Aid	368UNTS221	105243
Israel	USA (United States)	07 Jan 60	US Agri Commod Aid	368UNTS181	105241
Peru	USA (United States)	12 Feb 60	US Agri Commod Aid	372UNTS83	105290
Japan	USA (United States)	18 Feb 60	Direct Aid	372UNTS117	105292
Belgium	IBRD (World Bank)	30 Mar 60	IBRD Project	379UNTS103	105437
IBRD (World Bank)	UK Great Britain	01 Apr 60	IBRD Project	379UNTS397	105446
Iceland	USA (United States)	06 Apr 60	US Agri Commod Aid	372UNTS71	105289
Denmark	UK Great Britain	08 Apr 60	Customs	374UNTS233	105337
Pakistan	USA (United States)	11 Apr 60	US Agri Commod Aid	372UNTS251	105302
India	USA (United States)	04 May 60	US Agri Commod Aid	376UNTS279	105384
IBRD (World Bank)	UK Great Britain	27 May 60	IBRD Project	375UNTS201	105367
Peru	IBRD (World Bank)	01 Jun 60	IBRD Project	380UNTS15	105448
Chile	USA (United States)	02 Jun 60	US Agri Commod Aid	377UNTS11	105393
USA (United States)	Yugoslavia	03 Jun 60	US Agri Commod Aid	376UNTS243	105382
India	USA (United States)	13 Jun 60	Atomic Energy	377UNTS37	105394
IBRD (World Bank)	Sudan	17 Jun 60	IBRD Project	379UNTS253	105442
Spain	USA (United States)	22 Jun 60	US Agri Commod Aid	378UNTS3	105414
Poland	USA (United States)	21 Jul 60	US Agri Commod Aid	380UNTS157	105456
Iran	USA (United States)	26 Jul 60	US Agri Commod Aid	384UNTS141	105516
Japan	Pakistan	30 Jul 60	Education	384UNTS63	105511
United Arab Rep	USA (United States)	01 Aug 60	US Agri Commod Aid	384UNTS189	105519
United Arab Rep	USA (United States)	09 Aug 60	US Agri Commod Aid	388UNTS271	105584
Taiwan	USA (United States)	30 Aug 60	US Agri Commod Aid	388UNTS191	105579
Ecuador	USA (United States)	27 Sep 60	US Agri Commod Aid	401UNTS115	105766
USA (United States)	Vietnam, South	28 Oct 60	US Agri Commod Aid	401UNTS3	105758
Indonesia	USA (United States)	05 Nov 60	US Agri Commod Aid	400UNTS35	105746
Greece	USA (United States)	07 Nov 60	US Agri Commod Aid	400UNTS57	105748
Chile	USA (United States)	08 Nov 60	US Agri Commod Aid	405UNTS85	105825
Cyprus	USA (United States)	08 Dec 60	Direct Aid	405UNTS145	105831
Libya	USA (United States)	11 Dec 60	Health/Educ/Welfare	445UNTS125	106381
Korea, South	USA (United States)	28 Dec 60	US Agri Commod Aid	402UNTS3	105773
Turkey	USA (United States)	11 Jan 61	US Agri Commod Aid	405UNTS173	105833
Mexico	IBRD (World Bank)	16 Jan 61	IBRD Project	422UNTS203	106076
USA (United States)	Vietnam, South	25 Mar 61	US Agri Commod Aid	406UNTS187	105849
Ecuador	USA (United States)	03 Apr 61	US Agri Commod Aid	409UNTS140	105882
Bolivia	USA (United States)	07 Apr 61	US Agri Commod Aid	433UNTS3	106227
Iceland	USA (United States)	07 Apr 61	US Agri Commod Aid	406UNTS203	105850
USA (United States)	Yugoslavia	28 Apr 61	US Agri Commod Aid	409UNTS172	105884
Brazil	USA (United States)	04 May 61	US Agri Commod Aid	433UNTS91	106233
Israel	USA (United States)	10 May 61	US Agri Commod Aid	409UNTS213	105887
Spain	USA (United States)	22 May 61	US Agri Commod Aid	409UNTS260	105891
IBRD (World Bank)	Sudan	14 Jun 61	IBRD Project	415UNTS26	105980
IDA (Devel Assoc)	Sudan	14 Jun 61	Loans and Credits	415UNTS50	105981
Multilateral		14 Jun 61	IBRD Project	415UNTS4	105979
Finland	USA (United States)	16 Jun 61	Claims and Debts	413UNTS211	105955
IBRD (World Bank)	UK Great Britain	23 Jun 61	IBRD Project	415UNTS358	105991
Tunisia	USA (United States)	30 Jun 61	US Agri Commod Aid	434UNTS85	106257
Paraguay	USA (United States)	07 Jul 61	US Agri Commod Aid	433UNTS53	106231
Taiwan	USA (United States)	21 Jul 61	US Agri Commod Aid	416UNTS101	105998
Turkey	USA (United States)	29 Jul 61	US Agri Commod Aid	416UNTS151	106001
Finland	USA (United States)	04 Aug 61	US Agri Commod Aid	418UNTS19	106014
El Salvador	USA (United States)	21 Aug 61	US Agri Commod Aid	418UNTS35	106015
UK Great Britain	USA (United States)	28 Aug 61	Finance	434UNTS103	106258
Taiwan	IDA (Devel Assoc)	30 Aug 61	Loans and Credits	417UNTS227	106008
United Arab Rep	USA (United States)	02 Sep 61	US Agri Commod Aid	421UNTS251	106063
Taiwan	IDA (Devel Assoc)	06 Sep 61	Loans and Credits	417UNTS253	106009
India	IDA (Devel Assoc)	06 Sep 61	Loans and Credits	418UNTS81	106018
Austria	USA (United States)	03 Oct 61	Direct Aid	426UNTS187	106137

PARTY ONE	PARTY TWO	DATE	TOPIC	CITATION	NUMBER
Agriculture (Cont.)					
Pakistan	USA (United States)	14 Oct 61	US Agri Commod Aid	426UNTS237	106141
Greece	USA (United States)	18 Oct 61	US Agri Commod Aid	426UNTS209	106139
Pakistan	IDA (Devel Assoc)	19 Oct 61	Non-IBRD Project	447UNTS161	106415
Indonesia	USA (United States)	26 Oct 61	US Agri Commod Aid	433UNTS249	106248
Iceland	USA (United States)	06 Nov 61	US Agri Commod Aid	426UNTS225	106140
Syria	USA (United States)	09 Nov 61	US Agri Commod Aid	435UNTS75	106271
Sudan	USA (United States)	14 Nov 61	US Agri Commod Aid	434UNTS51	106255
Congo (Zaire)	USA (United States)	18 Nov 61	US Agri Commod Aid	433UNTS207	106244
India	IDA (Devel Assoc)	22 Nov 61	Loans and Credits	427UNTS55	106146
Philippines	USA (United States)	24 Nov 61	US Agri Commod Aid	433UNTS315	106251
Portugal	USA (United States)	28 Nov 61	US Agri Commod Aid	434UNTS31	106253
IBRD (World Bank)	UK Great Britain	29 Nov 61	IBRD Project	426UNTS49	106130
Poland	USA (United States)	15 Dec 61	US Agri Commod Aid	434UNTS3	106252
USA (United States)	Vietnam, South	27 Dec 61	US Agri Commod Aid	433UNTS185	106242
USA (United States)	Yugoslavia	28 Dec 61	US Agri Commod Aid	434UNTS111	106259
United Arab Rep	USA (United States)	19 Jan 62	US Agri Commod Aid	435UNTS107	106273
Iran	USA (United States)	29 Jan 62	US Agri Commod Aid	435UNTS53	106270
Guinea	USA (United States)	02 Feb 62	US Agri Commod Aid	435UNTS35	106269
Morocco	USA (United States)	09 Feb 62	Direct Aid	442UNTS135	106345
Tunisia	USA (United States)	16 Feb 62	US Agri Commod Aid	442UNTS161	106347
Indonesia	USA (United States)	19 Feb 62	US Agri Commod Aid	435UNTS137	106276
Korea, South	USA (United States)	02 Mar 62	US Agri Commod Aid	442UNTS185	106349
Cyprus	USA (United States)	02 Mar 62	Direct Aid	445UNTS189	106386
Multilateral		07 Mar 62	Commodity Trade	445UNTS199	106388
Peru	USA (United States)	20 Mar 62	US Agri Commod Aid	445UNTS61	106377
Liberia	USA (United States)	12 Apr 62	US Agri Commod Aid	445UNTS213	106390
Taiwan	USA (United States)	16 Apr 62	General Trade	445UNTS249	106392
Brazil	USA (United States)	19 Apr 62	General Trade	456UNTS255	106560
USA (United States)	Yugoslavia	21 Apr 62	US Agri Commod Aid	442UNTS123	106344
India	Japan	23 Apr 62	Education	451UNTS155	106491
UK Great Britain	USA (United States)	26 Apr 62	General Trade	445UNTS273	106395
Taiwan	USA (United States)	27 Apr 62	US Agri Commod Aid	436UNTS25	106287
Israel	USA (United States)	03 May 62	US Agri Commod Aid	442UNTS83	106340
Ireland	USA (United States)	03 May 62	General Trade	442UNTS117	106343
El Salvador	USA (United States)	15 May 62	General Trade	452UNTS49	106503
Colombia	USA (United States)	15 May 62	General Trade	445UNTS279	106396
Guatemala	USA (United States)	21 May 62	General Trade	451UNTS205	106495
Germany, West	Syria	25 Jun 62	Tech Assistance	489UNTS71	107135
India	IDA (Devel Assoc)	29 Jun 62	Non-IBRD Project	447UNTS221	106417
Pakistan	IDA (Devel Assoc)	29 Jun 62	Non-IBRD Project	447UNTS325	106421
India	IDA (Devel Assoc)	18 Jul 62	Non-IBRD Project	447UNTS191	106416
Israel	USA (United States)	28 Aug 62	US Agri Commod Aid	448UNTS317	106445
Mali	USSR (Soviet Union)	10 Oct 62	Tech Assistance	493UNTS219	107216
IBRD (World Bank)	Thailand	21 Dec 62	IBRD Project	467UNTS63	106758
IBRD (World Bank)	Thailand	21 Dec 62	IBRD Project	467UNTS43	106757
Belgium	Luxembourg	29 Jan 63	IGO Establishment	547UNTS39	107955
Nicaragua	IBRD (World Bank)	01 Mar 63	IBRD Project	481UNTS15	106976
Mexico	IBRD (World Bank)	29 Apr 63	IBRD Project	489UNTS151	107138
IDA (Devel Assoc)	Turkey	31 May 63	Non-IBRD Project	480UNTS127	106966
Pakistan	IDA (Devel Assoc)	26 Jul 63	Non-IBRD Project	492UNTS143	107190
Jordan	IDA (Devel Assoc)	12 Dec 63	Non-IBRD Project	492UNTS3	107184
Chile	IBRD (World Bank)	18 Dec 63	IBRD Project	504UNTS3	107351
Chile	IBRD (World Bank)	18 Dec 63	IBRD Project	504UNTS29	107352
Paraguay	IDA (Devel Assoc)	26 Dec 63	Non-IBRD Project	507UNTS3	107394
Multilateral		30 Dec 63	IBRD Project	568UNTS243	108272
Morocco	IBRD (World Bank)	26 Aug 64	IBRD Project	537UNTS193	107802
Jordan	UK Great Britain	31 Aug 64	Loans and Credits	541UNTS3	107856
Ghana	Israel	30 Nov 64	Tech Assistance	550UNTS231	108019
UK Great Britain	USSR (Soviet Union)	06 Jan 65	Scientific Project	543UNTS77	107897
Ecuador	Netherlands	14 Jan 65	Health/Educ/Welfare	551UNTS129	108038
France	UK Great Britain	25 Feb 65	Non-ILO Labor	543UNTS157	107899
IBRD (World Bank)	Uruguay	30 Mar 65	IBRD Project	567UNTS45	108251
Peru	IBRD (World Bank)	03 Jun 65	IBRD Project	551UNTS227	108045
Peru	IBRD (World Bank)	18 Jun 65	IBRD Project	568UNTS191	108269
Pakistan	IDA (Devel Assoc)	30 Jun 65	Non-IBRD Project	554UNTS111	108099

PARTY ONE	PARTY TWO	DATE	TOPIC	CITATION	NUMBER
Agriculture (Cont.)					
Cameroon	Netherlands	06 Jul 65	Tech Assistance	571UNTS75	108300
Mexico	IBRD (World Bank)	01 Oct 65	IBRD Project	589UNTS339	108542
Philippines	IBRD (World Bank)	02 Nov 65	IBRD Project	567UNTS3	108249
Morocco	IBRD (World Bank)	08 Nov 65	Claims and Debts	566UNTS279	108247
Malaysia	IBRD (World Bank)	17 Nov 65	IBRD Project	568UNTS23	108263
Denmark	Syria	28 Dec 65	Tech Assistance	588UNTS163	108523
Austria	Tunisia	30 Dec 65	Tech Assistance	589UNTS119	108539
IDA (Devel Assoc)	Tanzania	13 Jan 66	Non-IBRD Project	567UNTS177	108256
Pakistan	IDA (Devel Assoc)	10 Feb 66	Non-IBRD Project	575UNTS89	108355
Multilateral		10 Feb 66	Loans and Credits	575UNTS129	108356
Paraguay	IDA (Devel Assoc)	04 Apr 66	Non-IBRD Project	582UNTS331	108469
Mexico	IBRD (World Bank)	25 May 66	IBRD Project	596UNTS3	108627
Denmark	Iran	14 Jun 66	Tech Assistance	597UNTS283	108652
New Zealand	Western Samoa	29 Jul 66	Direct Aid	598UNTS115	108657
IBRD (World Bank)	Trinidad/Tobago	10 Mar 67	IBRD Project	599UNTS3	108662
Aid and Assistance					
USA (United States)	USSR (Soviet Union)	18 Apr 42	Milit Assistance	105UNTS285	200339
Taiwan	USA (United States)	02 Jun 42	Milit Assistance	14UNTS343	200092
Belgium	USA (United States)	16 Jun 42	Milit Assistance	105UNTS159	200329
Poland	USA (United States)	01 Jul 42	Milit Assistance	103UNTS267	200317
Netherlands	USA (United States)	08 Jul 42	Milit Assistance	103UNTS277	200318
Greece	USA (United States)	10 Jul 42	Milit Assistance	103UNTS289	200319
Czechoslovakia	USA (United States)	11 Jul 42	Milit Assistance	90UNTS257	200263
USA (United States)	Yugoslavia	24 Jul 42	Milit Assistance	34UNTS361	200179
New Zealand	USA (United States)	03 Sep 42	Milit Assistance	24UNTS185	200142
France	USA (United States)	03 Sep 42	Milit Assistance	24UNTS177	200141
Australia	USA (United States)	03 Sep 42	Milit Assistance	24UNTS195	200143
Multilateral		04 Dec 42	Direct Aid	24UNTS247	200150
Belgium	USA (United States)	30 Jan 43	Milit Assistance	13UNTS371	200084
Liberia	USA (United States)	08 Jun 43	Milit Assistance	117UNTS242	200373
Netherlands	USA (United States)	14 Jun 43	General Military	28UNTS397	200163
Ethiopia	USA (United States)	09 Aug 43	Milit Installation	29UNTS303	200169
France	USA (United States)	25 Sep 43	Direct Aid	76UNTS183	200245
Canada	Taiwan	22 Mar 44	Milit Assistance	14UNTS397	200096
Albania	Yugoslavia	23 Mar 44	General Military	1UNTS81	100015
Belgium	UK Great Britain	22 Aug 44	Direct Aid	90UNTS295	200267
Brazil	UNRRA (Relief)	12 Oct 44	IGO Establishment	67UNTS321	200228
France	USA (United States)	20 Feb 45	Direct Aid	76UNTS193	200246
France	USA (United States)	20 Feb 45	IGO Status/Immunit	76UNTS223	200248
Turkey	USA (United States)	23 Feb 45	Direct Aid	121UNTS165	200398
France	USA (United States)	28 Feb 45	IGO Status/Immunit	76UNTS213	200247
South Africa	USA (United States)	17 Apr 45	Direct Aid	90UNTS267	200264
Belgium	USA (United States)	19 Apr 45	Milit Installation	139UNTS179	200455
Poland	USSR (Soviet Union)	21 Apr 45	General Military	12UNTS391	200070
Netherlands	USA (United States)	30 Apr 45	Milit Installation	139UNTS319	200459
Iraq	USA (United States)	31 Jul 45	Milit Assistance	121UNTS239	200402
Denmark	UK Great Britain	24 Oct 45	Milit Assistance	93UNTS143	101297
France	USA (United States)	08 Nov 45	General Trade	76UNTS151	100986
Netherlands	UK Great Britain	20 Dec 45	Milit Assistance	4UNTS303	100053
Poland	Yugoslavia	18 Mar 46	General Military	1UNTS53	100013
UK Great Britain	USA (United States)	27 Mar 46	Milit Assistance	4UNTS2	100039
Czechoslovakia	Yugoslavia	09 May 46	General Military	1UNTS67	100014
India	USA (United States)	16 May 46	Milit Assistance	4UNTS183	100045
France	USA (United States)	28 May 46	Milit Assistance	84UNTS59	101119
France	USA (United States)	28 May 46	Milit Assistance	84UNTS79	101120
Australia	USA (United States)	07 Jun 46	Milit Assistance	4UNTS237	100048
Taiwan	USA (United States)	28 Jun 46	Milit Assistance	34UNTS121	100532
New Zealand	USA (United States)	10 Jul 46	Milit Assistance	6UNTS341	100087
Belgium	USA (United States)	24 Sep 46	Claims and Debts	132UNTS80	101753
France	UK Great Britain	04 Mar 47	General Amity	9UNTS187	100132
South Africa	USA (United States)	21 Mar 47	Milit Assistance	16UNTS47	100248
Czechoslovakia	Yugoslavia	27 Apr 47	Culture	33UNTS49	100514
Netherlands	USA (United States)	28 May 47	General Military	17UNTS29	100267
Greece	USA (United States)	20 Jun 47	Direct Aid	7UNTS267	100105

Aid and Assistance (Cont.)

PARTY ONE	PARTY TWO	DATE	TOPIC	CITATION	NUMBER
Austria	USA (United States)	25 Jun 47	Direct Aid	22UNTS141	100334
Italy	USA (United States)	04 Jul 47	Direct Aid	22UNTS173	100336
Greece	USA (United States)	08 Jul 47	Direct Aid	16UNTS157	100256
Albania	Yugoslavia	09 Jul 47	Culture	33UNTS91	100516
Turkey	USA (United States)	12 Jul 47	Direct Aid	7UNTS299	100106
Multilateral		02 Sep 47	General Military	21UNTS77	100324
Taiwan	USA (United States)	27 Oct 47	Direct Aid	12UNTS11	100178
Greece	USA (United States)	03 Dec 47	Milit Assistance	89UNTS119	101213
Taiwan	USA (United States)	08 Dec 47	Milit Installation	70UNTS3	100895
Romania	Yugoslavia	19 Dec 47	General Amity	116UNTS89	101571
Austria	USA (United States)	02 Jan 48	Direct Aid	34UNTS141	100534
France	USA (United States)	02 Jan 48	Direct Aid	31UNTS97	100470
Italy	USA (United States)	03 Jan 48	Direct Aid	31UNTS105	100471
Romania	USSR (Soviet Union)	04 Feb 48	General Military	48UNTS189	100745
Hungary	USSR (Soviet Union)	18 Feb 48	General Military	48UNTS163	100743
Norway	USA (United States)	24 Feb 48	Milit Assistance	34UNTS155	100535
France	USA (United States)	27 Feb 48	Reparations	84UNTS207	101131
Bulgaria	Czechoslovakia	05 Mar 48	Admin Cooperation	26UNTS115	100382
Finland	USSR (Soviet Union)	06 Apr 48	General Military	48UNTS149	100742
Greece	USA (United States)	23 Apr 48	Education	74UNTS107	100958
Bulgaria	Poland	29 May 48	General Military	26UNTS213	100389
Australia	Poland	03 Jun 48	Direct Aid	16UNTS189	100258
Hungary	Poland	18 Jun 48	Culture	25UNTS319	100370
Australia	Hungary	01 Jul 48	Direct Aid	22UNTS3	100325
Australia	Greece	01 Jul 48	Direct Aid	22UNTS33	100329
Greece	USA (United States)	02 Jul 48	Direct Aid	23UNTS43	100342
Taiwan	USA (United States)	03 Jul 48	Direct Aid	17UNTS119	100273
Australia	Italy	08 Jul 48	Direct Aid	22UNTS11	100326
Australia	Yugoslavia	09 Jul 48	Direct Aid	22UNTS17	100327
USA (United States)	Yugoslavia	19 Jul 48	Milit Assistance	34UNTS195	100537
Australia	Austria	19 Jul 48	Direct Aid	22UNTS25	100328
Korea, South	USA (United States)	11 Sep 48	Milit Assistance	89UNTS155	101216
New Zealand	USA (United States)	14 Sep 48	General Military	18UNTS251	100295
Czechoslovakia	USA (United States)	16 Sep 48	Milit Assistance	90UNTS35	101224
UK Great Britain	USA (United States)	22 Sep 48	Milit Assistance	71UNTS64	100910
UNRRA (Relief)	United Nations	27 Sep 48	IGO Operations	27UNTS349	200158
France	USA (United States)	22 Oct 48	Education	84UNTS173	101128
Monaco	UK Great Britain	10 Nov 48	Visas	81UNTS85	101065
Taiwan	USA (United States)	18 Nov 48	Direct Aid	198UNTS287	102672
Philippines	UNICEF (Children)	20 Nov 48	Tech Assistance	65UNTS48	100819
Italy	USA (United States)	26 Nov 48	Direct Aid	79UNTS71	101032
UK Great Britain	USA (United States)	01 Dec 48	Direct Aid	81UNTS93	101066
Korea, South	USA (United States)	10 Dec 48	Direct Aid	55UNTS157	100813
Multilateral		16 Dec 48	Direct Aid	79UNTS85	101033
France	USA (United States)	23 Dec 48	Direct Aid	67UNTS171	100876
Belgium	Luxembourg	14 Jan 49	Direct Aid	36UNTS339	100572
Netherlands	USA (United States)	17 Jan 49	Direct Aid	32UNTS241	100502
Poland	Romania	26 Jan 49	General Military	85UNTS21	101143
France	USA (United States)	07 Feb 49	Direct Aid	67UNTS189	100877
Greece	USA (United States)	09 Feb 49	Direct Aid	79UNTS95	101034
Trieste	USA (United States)	11 Feb 49	Direct Aid	79UNTS123	101036
Austria	USA (United States)	11 Feb 49	Direct Aid	79UNTS113	101035
France	USA (United States)	14 Mar 49	Claims and Debts	84UNTS237	101133
Multilateral		05 May 49	IGO Establishment	87UNTS103	101168
Netherlands	USA (United States)	17 May 49	Milit Assistance	46UNTS291	100717
Ethiopia	USA (United States)	20 May 49	Milit Assistance	89UNTS99	101211
Philippines	USA (United States)	07 Jun 49	Direct Aid	45UNTS63	100692
Norway	USA (United States)	31 Oct 49	Direct Aid	68UNTS3	100879
Australia	USA (United States)	26 Nov 49	Reparations	45UNTS133	100695
Korea, South	USA (United States)	26 Jan 50	Milit Assistance	80UNTS205	101053
France	USA (United States)	27 Jan 50	Milit Assistance	80UNTS171	101051
Italy	USA (United States)	27 Jan 50	Milit Assistance	80UNTS145	101050
Norway	USA (United States)	27 Jan 50	Milit Assistance	80UNTS241	101055
UK Great Britain	USA (United States)	27 Jan 50	Milit Assistance	80UNTS261	101056
Denmark	USA (United States)	27 Jan 50	Milit Assistance	48UNTS115	100740

Aid and Assistance (Cont.)

PARTY ONE	PARTY TWO	DATE	TOPIC	CITATION	NUMBER
Netherlands	USA (United States)	27 Jan 50	Milit Assistance	80UNTS219	101054
Luxembourg	USA (United States)	27 Jan 50	Milit Assistance	80UNTS187	101052
Belgium	USA (United States)	27 Jan 50	Milit Assistance	51UNTS213	100767
India	USA (United States)	02 Feb 50	Education	89UNTS127	101214
Iran	USA (United States)	23 May 50	Milit Assistance	81UNTS3	101057
Netherlands	IRO (Refugee Org)	20 Jun 50	Refugees	76UNTS55	100979
Indonesia	USA (United States)	15 Aug 50	Milit Assistance	134UNTS255	101804
Pakistan	USA (United States)	23 Sep 50	Education	82UNTS131	101088
Burma	USA (United States)	06 Nov 50	Milit Assistance	122UNTS81	101638
USA (United States)	Yugoslavia	21 Nov 50	Milit Assistance	93UNTS45	101286
USA (United States)	Yugoslavia	21 Nov 50	Direct Aid	93UNTS39	101285
Pakistan	USA (United States)	15 Dec 50	Milit Assistance	122UNTS89	101639
Portugal	USA (United States)	05 Jan 51	Milit Assistance	133UNTS75	101782
USA (United States)	Yugoslavia	06 Jan 51	Direct Aid	122UNTS137	101643
Argentina	USA (United States)	08 Jan 51	Milit Assistance	165UNTS89	102170
Multilateral		09 Jan 51	Humanitarian	197UNTS341	102647
Taiwan	USA (United States)	09 Feb 51	Milit Assistance	132UNTS273	101767
Pakistan	USA (United States)	09 Feb 51	Tech Assistance	100UNTS67	101388
Netherlands	IRO (Refugee Org)	13 Feb 51	IGO Operations	87UNTS239	101175
Australia	USA (United States)	20 Feb 51	Milit Assistance	132UNTS297	101769
India	USA (United States)	16 Mar 51	Milit Assistance	141UNTS47	101904
USA (United States)	Yugoslavia	17 Apr 51	Milit Assistance	162UNTS173	102134
Germany, West	USA (United States)	07 Jun 51	Direct Aid	238UNTS161	103360
United Nations	Thailand	11 Jun 51	Tech Assistance	90UNTS45	101225
Saudi Arabia	USA (United States)	18 Jun 51	Milit Assistance	141UNTS67	101906
India	USA (United States)	09 Jul 51	Customs	147UNTS43	101927
Japan	USA (United States)	08 Sep 51	General Military	136UNTS211	101835
Japan	USA (United States)	08 Sep 51	Milit Assistance	136UNTS203	101834
Canada	India	10 Sep 51	General Aid	391UNTS237	105629
South Africa	USA (United States)	09 Nov 51	Milit Assistance	160UNTS41	102100
USA (United States)	Yugoslavia	14 Nov 51	Milit Assistance	174UNTS201	102286
Denmark	USA (United States)	16 Nov 51	Milit Assistance	180UNTS275	102391
Liberia	USA (United States)	19 Nov 51	Milit Assistance	167UNTS141	102204
Jordan	USA (United States)	20 Dec 51	Tech Assistance	157UNTS69	102048
Taiwan	USA (United States)	02 Jan 52	Milit Assistance	181UNTS161	102407
Portugal	USA (United States)	08 Jan 52	General Military	207UNTS51	102799
UK Great Britain	USA (United States)	08 Jan 52	Direct Aid	126UNTS307	101696
UK Great Britain	USA (United States)	18 Jan 52	Commodity Trade	184UNTS79	102440
Netherlands	USA (United States)	07 Mar 52	Taxation	135UNTS199	101821
Luxembourg	USA (United States)	13 Mar 52	Taxation	168UNTS57	102212
Brazil	USA (United States)	15 Mar 52	Milit Assistance	199UNTS221	102687
Belgium	USA (United States)	07 Apr 52	Taxation	205UNTS3	102765
Chile	USA (United States)	09 Apr 52	Milit Assistance	186UNTS53	102482
Colombia	USA (United States)	17 Apr 52	Milit Assistance	174UNTS215	102287
Israel	USA (United States)	01 May 52	Direct Aid	177UNTS89	102311
Israel	USA (United States)	09 May 52	Tech Assistance	177UNTS269	102326
Ethiopia	USA (United States)	13 Jun 52	Milit Assistance	205UNTS17	102766
New Zealand	USA (United States)	19 Jun 52	Milit Assistance	178UNTS315	102347
USA (United States)	Uruguay	30 Jun 52	Milit Assistance	207UNTS139	102804
Portugal	USA (United States)	09 Jul 52	Milit Assistance	180UNTS251	102389
Canada	Ceylon (Sri Lanka)	11 Jul 52	General Aid	391UNTS245	105630
Panama	USA (United States)	21 Jul 52	Tech Assistance	181UNTS285	102417
Israel	USA (United States)	23 Jul 52	Milit Assistance	179UNTS139	102363
Pakistan	USA (United States)	17 Sep 52	Loans and Credits	227UNTS77	103132
USA (United States)	Yugoslavia	11 Oct 52	Direct Aid	235UNTS277	103309
USA (United States)	Yugoslavia	03 Dec 52	Direct Aid	185UNTS183	102469
Greece	USA (United States)	04 Feb 53	Milit Assistance	189UNTS3	102538
Germany, West	USA (United States)	27 Feb 53	Claims and Debts	224UNTS13	103067
Dominican Republic	USA (United States)	06 Mar 53	Milit Assistance	199UNTS267	102689
Lebanon	USA (United States)	23 Mar 53	Milit Assistance	239UNTS45	103370
Portugal	USA (United States)	01 Apr 53	Taxation	205UNTS41	102769
Ethiopia	USA (United States)	22 May 53	Milit Assistance	207UNTS127	102803
Pakistan	USA (United States)	25 Jun 53	Direct Aid	205UNTS139	102773
Philippines	USA (United States)	26 Jun 53	Milit Assistance	213UNTS77	102881
Spain	USA (United States)	26 Sep 53	Direct Aid	207UNTS93	102802

PARTY ONE	PARTY TWO	DATE	TOPIC	CITATION	NUMBER
Aid and Assistance (Cont.)					
UNICEF (Children)	UK Great Britain	07 Oct 53	Tech Assistance	180UNTS59	102375
Iran	USA (United States)	13 Oct 53	Customs	222UNTS67	103023
Jordan	USA (United States)	21 Oct 53	Direct Aid	222UNTS31	103020
Bolivia	USA (United States)	06 Nov 53	Direct Aid	222UNTS41	103021
Israel	USA (United States)	25 Nov 53	Direct Aid	219UNTS205	102976
USA (United States)	Yugoslavia	05 Jan 54	Direct Aid	234UNTS267	103289
Libya	USA (United States)	11 Jan 54	Direct Aid	229UNTS15	103157
Pakistan	Turkey	04 Feb 54	General Amity	211UNTS263	102858
Japan	USA (United States)	08 Mar 54	Milit Assistance	232UNTS215	103237
Japan	USA (United States)	08 Mar 54	Milit Assistance	232UNTS169	103236
USA (United States)	Yugoslavia	16 Apr 54	Direct Aid	237UNTS77	103337
Italy	USA (United States)	27 Apr 54	Milit Assistance	234UNTS103	103275
Jordan	USA (United States)	13 May 54	Direct Aid	234UNTS225	103285
Pakistan	USA (United States)	19 May 54	Milit Assistance	202UNTS301	102736
Belgium	Germany, West	28 May 54	Non-ILO Labor	249UNTS387	103512
Afghanistan	USA (United States)	29 May 54	Direct Aid	234UNTS3	103268
Bolivia	USA (United States)	16 Jun 54	Direct Aid	234UNTS35	103271
Jordan	USA (United States)	17 Jun 54	Direct Aid	266UNTS137	103828
Ireland	USA (United States)	17 Jun 54	Direct Aid	241UNTS173	103432
Lebanon	USA (United States)	18 Jun 54	Direct Aid	233UNTS177	103262
Jordan	USA (United States)	29 Jun 54	Direct Aid	237UNTS111	103339
Luxembourg	USA (United States)	07 Jul 54	Milit Assistance	233UNTS23	103247
Multilateral		09 Aug 54	General Amity	211UNTS237	102855
Pakistan	USA (United States)	23 Aug 54	Direct Aid	234UNTS243	103287
USA (United States)	Vietnam, South	26 Aug 54	Direct Aid	234UNTS111	103276
New Zealand	UNICEF (Children)	26 Aug 54	Direct Aid	198UNTS173	102663
Libya	USA (United States)	09 Sep 54	Direct Aid	238UNTS217	103365
Pakistan	USA (United States)	02 Oct 54	Direct Aid	236UNTS187	103324
Peru	USA (United States)	25 Oct 54	Direct Aid	238UNTS247	103368
United Arab Rep	USA (United States)	30 Oct 54	Direct Aid	234UNTS139	103279
Libya	USA (United States)	03 Nov 54	Direct Aid	238UNTS227	103366
Korea, South	USA (United States)	17 Nov 54	Milit Assistance	256UNTS251	103635
Guatemala	USA (United States)	13 Dec 54	Direct Aid	237UNTS169	103343
USA (United States)	Yugoslavia	05 Jan 55	US Agri Commod Aid	251UNTS29	103531
Pakistan	USA (United States)	11 Jan 55	Milit Assistance	251UNTS111	103537
Pakistan	USA (United States)	18 Jan 55	Direct Aid	241UNTS53	103423
Pakistan	USA (United States)	18 Jan 55	US Agri Commod Aid	239UNTS61	103372
Chile	USA (United States)	27 Jan 55	US Agri Commod Aid	262UNTS3	103735
Haiti	USA (United States)	28 Jan 55	Milit Assistance	270UNTS83	103894
Peru	USA (United States)	07 Feb 55	Direct Aid	241UNTS63	103424
USA (United States)	Yugoslavia	09 Feb 55	Direct Aid	241UNTS13	103419
Italy	USA (United States)	11 Feb 55	Milit Assistance	240UNTS87	103396
USA (United States)	Vietnam, South	07 Mar 55	Direct Aid	277UNTS285	104013
Honduras	USA (United States)	21 Mar 55	Direct Aid	253UNTS3	103572
Haiti	USA (United States)	01 Apr 55	Direct Aid	261UNTS361	103734
Chile	USA (United States)	05 Apr 55	Direct Aid	250UNTS253	103527
Spain	USA (United States)	20 Apr 55	US Agri Commod Aid	239UNTS117	103374
USA (United States)	Vietnam, South	23 Apr 55	Milit Assistance	277UNTS279	104012
Argentina	USA (United States)	25 Apr 55	US Agri Commod Aid	251UNTS283	103546
Philippines	USA (United States)	27 Apr 55	Direct Aid	261UNTS351	103733
Haiti	USA (United States)	27 Apr 55	IGO Establishment	240UNTS17	103391
Israel	USA (United States)	29 Apr 55	US Agri Commod Aid	261UNTS331	103731
Korea, South	USA (United States)	02 May 55	Direct Aid	258UNTS3	103666
Finland	USA (United States)	06 May 55	US Agri Commod Aid	251UNTS3	103529
USA (United States)	Yugoslavia	12 May 55	Direct Aid	251UNTS331	103549
USA (United States)	Yugoslavia	12 May 55	Direct Aid	251UNTS337	103550
USA (United States)	Yugoslavia	12 May 55	Direct Aid	251UNTS343	103551
Cambodia	USA (United States)	16 May 55	Milit Assistance	263UNTS273	103777
Italy	USA (United States)	19 May 55	Direct Aid	269UNTS83	103876
Italy	USA (United States)	23 May 55	US Agri Commod Aid	251UNTS303	103547
Libya	USA (United States)	30 May 55	Direct Aid	270UNTS43	103890
Japan	USA (United States)	31 May 55	Direct Aid	241UNTS197	103434
Korea, South	USA (United States)	31 May 55	US Agri Commod Aid	251UNTS321	103548
Japan	USA (United States)	31 May 55	Direct Aid	241UNTS243	103435
UK Great Britain	USA (United States)	07 Jun 55	General Military	265UNTS27	103804

PARTY ONE	PARTY TWO	DATE	TOPIC	CITATION	NUMBER
Aid and Assistance (Cont.)					
Austria	USA (United States)	14 Jun 55	US Agri Commod Aid	258UNTS37	103668
Thailand	USA (United States)	21 Jun 55	US Agri Commod Aid	262UNTS87	103738
Colombia	USA (United States)	23 Jun 55	US Agri Commod Aid	263UNTS337	103781
Greece	USA (United States)	24 Jun 55	US Agri Commod Aid	270UNTS361	103906
Greece	USA (United States)	24 Jun 55	US Agri Commod Aid	270UNTS351	103905
Italy	USA (United States)	30 Jun 55	US Agri Commod Aid	258UNTS15	103667
Laos	USA (United States)	08 Jul 55	Direct Aid	278UNTS59	104021
Libya	USA (United States)	18 Jul 55	Direct Aid	241UNTS305	103437
Germany, West	USA (United States)	02 Aug 55	Specif Goods/Equip	268UNTS121	103854
France	USA (United States)	11 Aug 55	US Agri Commod Aid	251UNTS15	103530
Ecuador	USA (United States)	24 Aug 55	Military Mission	256UNTS299	103640
Ecuador	USA (United States)	06 Sep 55	Direct Aid	256UNTS187	103628
Colombia	USA (United States)	16 Sep 55	Military Mission	256UNTS221	103631
India	USA (United States)	04 Oct 55	Direct Aid	268UNTS115	103853
Ecuador	USA (United States)	07 Oct 55	US Agri Commod Aid	256UNTS197	103629
Israel	USA (United States)	10 Nov 55	US Agri Commod Aid	240UNTS3	103390
United Arab Rep	USA (United States)	14 Dec 55	US Agri Commod Aid	240UNTS37	103392
Canada	Norway	20 Dec 55	Milit Assistance	305UNTS17	104408
Colombia	USA (United States)	20 Dec 55	US Agri Commod Aid	241UNTS25	103421
Argentina	USA (United States)	21 Dec 55	Commodity Trade	240UNTS329	103411
Libya	USA (United States)	22 Dec 55	Direct Aid	240UNTS111	103399
Germany, West	USA (United States)	23 Dec 55	US Agri Commod Aid	240UNTS79	103395
Haiti	USA (United States)	28 Dec 55	Non-IBRD Project	240UNTS95	103397
Austria	USA (United States)	07 Feb 56	US Agri Commod Aid	272UNTS117	103933
Japan	USA (United States)	10 Feb 56	Direct Aid	275UNTS105	103979
Japan	USA (United States)	10 Feb 56	Direct Aid	275UNTS181	103981
Japan	USA (United States)	10 Feb 56	Direct Aid	275UNTS157	103980
Iran	USA (United States)	20 Feb 56	US Agri Commod Aid	272UNTS135	103934
Italy	USA (United States)	27 Feb 56	Direct Aid	291UNTS287	104260
Indonesia	USA (United States)	02 Mar 56	US Agri Commod Aid	271UNTS345	103925
Pakistan	USA (United States)	02 Mar 56	US Agri Commod Aid	271UNTS371	103927
Spain	USA (United States)	05 Mar 56	US Agri Commod Aid	271UNTS329	103924
Turkey	USA (United States)	12 Mar 56	US Agri Commod Aid	272UNTS21	103929
Korea, South	USA (United States)	13 Mar 56	US Agri Commod Aid	272UNTS3	103928
Chile	USA (United States)	13 Mar 56	US Agri Commod Aid	275UNTS49	103975
Italy	USA (United States)	27 Apr 56	Direct Aid	273UNTS149	103949
Ceylon (Sri Lanka)	USA (United States)	28 Apr 56	Direct Aid	274UNTS35	103956
Paraguay	USA (United States)	02 May 56	US Agri Commod Aid	268UNTS299	103863
Peru	USA (United States)	07 May 56	US Agri Commod Aid	268UNTS285	103862
Peru	USA (United States)	08 May 56	Direct Aid	278UNTS117	104028
Portugal	USA (United States)	24 May 56	US Agri Commod Aid	268UNTS323	103865
Pakistan	USA (United States)	28 May 56	Milit Assistance	269UNTS15	103868
Pakistan	USA (United States)	07 Aug 56	US Agri Commod Aid	281UNTS75	104071
Netherlands	USA (United States)	07 Aug 56	US Agri Commod Aid	281UNTS57	104069
Greece	USA (United States)	08 Aug 56	US Agri Commod Aid	277UNTS203	104007
UNESCO (Educ/Cult)	UK Great Britain	09 Aug 56	Direct Aid	256UNTS139	103624
Taiwan	USA (United States)	14 Aug 56	US Agri Commod Aid	281UNTS257	104083
India	USA (United States)	29 Aug 56	US Agri Commod Aid	278UNTS25	104019
Israel	USA (United States)	11 Sep 56	US Agri Commod Aid	277UNTS215	104008
Liberia	USA (United States)	22 Sep 56	Specific Property	278UNTS109	104027
Jordan	USA (United States)	24 Sep 56	Milit Assistance	278UNTS51	104020
India	USA (United States)	27 Sep 56	Direct Aid	281UNTS289	104085
Czechoslovakia	Germany, East	06 Oct 56	Humanitarian	501UNTS109	107315
Philippines	USA (United States)	18 Oct 56	Taxation	280UNTS55	104050
Norway	USSR (Soviet Union)	19 Oct 56	Humanitarian	257UNTS3	103644
Spain	USA (United States)	23 Oct 56	US Agri Commod Aid	277UNTS105	104001
Italy	USA (United States)	30 Oct 56	US Agri Commod Aid	263UNTS221	103775
USA (United States)	Yugoslavia	03 Nov 56	US Agri Commod Aid	277UNTS119	104002
France	USA (United States)	08 Nov 56	Direct Aid	280UNTS189	104058
Israel	UN Relief Palestin	09 Nov 56	Direct Aid	280UNTS261	104063
Turkey	USA (United States)	12 Nov 56	US Agri Commod Aid	282UNTS77	104093
Turkey	USA (United States)	23 Nov 56	Direct Aid	290UNTS273	104239
Burma	USA (United States)	04 Dec 56	US Agri Commod Aid	268UNTS189	103858
Denmark	USA (United States)	12 Dec 56	Status of Forces	304UNTS311	104405
Haiti	USA (United States)	28 Dec 56	Direct Aid	279UNTS107	104035

PARTY ONE	PARTY TWO	DATE	TOPIC	CITATION	NUMBER
Aid and Assistance (Cont.)					
Brazil	USA (United States)	31 Dec 56	US Agri Commod Aid	266UNTS151	103829
Australia	USA (United States)	31 Dec 56	Milit Assistance	266UNTS89	103823
Korea, South	USA (United States)	30 Jan 57	US Agri Commod Aid	278UNTS85	104024
Ecuador	USA (United States)	15 Feb 57	US Agri Commod Aid	279UNTS155	104037
Denmark	Netherlands	20 Feb 57	Taxation	287UNTS41	104179
France	Italy	28 Feb 57	Visas	291UNTS191	104253
Thailand	USA (United States)	04 Mar 57	US Agri Commod Aid	279UNTS235	104043
Tunisia	USA (United States)	26 Mar 57	General Aid	283UNTS117	104111
Morocco	USA (United States)	02 Apr 57	General Aid	288UNTS157	104203
Paraguay	USA (United States)	04 Apr 57	Taxation	283UNTS193	104117
Iceland	USA (United States)	11 Apr 57	US Agri Commod Aid	283UNTS107	104110
Colombia	USA (United States)	16 Apr 57	US Agri Commod Aid	283UNTS245	104121
Ethiopia	USA (United States)	25 Apr 57	Direct Aid	283UNTS205	104118
Jordan	USA (United States)	29 Apr 57	Direct Aid	290UNTS111	104230
Peru	USA (United States)	02 May 57	US Agri Commod Aid	283UNTS55	104106
Austria	USA (United States)	10 May 57	Direct Aid	283UNTS33	104104
Austria	USA (United States)	10 May 57	US Agri Commod Aid	283UNTS15	104103
Finland	USA (United States)	10 May 57	US Agri Commod Aid	283UNTS43	104105
Iraq	USA (United States)	22 May 57	Direct Aid	284UNTS13	104125
Lebanon	USA (United States)	06 Jun 57	Tech Assistance	284UNTS155	104134
Germany, West	UK Great Britain	07 Jun 57	Milit Assistance	398UNTS275	105730
Bolivia	USA (United States)	07 Jun 57	US Agri Commod Aid	291UNTS77	104245
Poland	USA (United States)	07 Jun 57	Direct Aid	291UNTS41	104243
Philippines	USA (United States)	25 Jun 57	US Agri Commod Aid	289UNTS279	104224
Jordan	USA (United States)	27 Jun 57	General Aid	288UNTS269	104209
Tunisia	USA (United States)	28 Jun 57	Direct Aid	289UNTS301	104226
Jordan	USA (United States)	29 Jun 57	Direct Aid	288UNTS263	104208
Libya	USA (United States)	30 Jun 57	Milit Assistance	284UNTS177	104136
Peru	USA (United States)	19 Jul 57	Direct Aid	289UNTS271	104223
Ceylon (Sri Lanka)	China People's Rep	19 Sep 57	Direct Aid	337UNTS169	104822
Fed of Malaya	UK Great Britain	12 Oct 57	Milit Assistance	285UNTS59	104149
Mexico	USA (United States)	23 Oct 57	US Agri Commod Aid	300UNTS35	104330
Brazil	USA (United States)	05 Nov 57	Education	303UNTS3	104368
Israel	USA (United States)	07 Nov 57	US Agri Commod Aid	302UNTS255	104365
Pakistan	USA (United States)	15 Nov 57	US Agri Commod Aid	303UNTS173	104380
Germany, West	USA (United States)	10 Dec 57	Milit Assistance	307UNTS59	104442
Greece	USA (United States)	18 Dec 57	US Agri Commod Aid	303UNTS159	104379
France	USA (United States)	27 Dec 57	US Agri Commod Aid	307UNTS79	104444
Turkey	USA (United States)	20 Jan 58	US Agri Commod Aid	304UNTS15	104389
Japan	USA (United States)	25 Jan 58	Milit Assistance	304UNTS81	104392
Spain	USA (United States)	27 Jan 58	US Agri Commod Aid	303UNTS247	104384
UK Great Britain	USA (United States)	03 Feb 58	US Agri Commod Aid	307UNTS199	104450
USA (United States)	Yugoslavia	03 Feb 58	US Agri Commod Aid	304UNTS293	104404
Korea, South	USA (United States)	05 Feb 58	US Agri Commod Aid	307UNTS121	104447
Poland	USA (United States)	15 Feb 58	US Agri Commod Aid	307UNTS217	104452
Finland	USA (United States)	21 Feb 58	US Agri Commod Aid	304UNTS253	104401
UK Great Britain	USA (United States)	22 Feb 58	Milit Assistance	307UNTS207	104451
France	USA (United States)	28 Feb 58	US Agri Commod Aid	366UNTS343	105222
Italy	USA (United States)	07 Mar 58	US Agri Commod Aid	303UNTS205	104381
Colombia	USA (United States)	14 Mar 58	US Agri Commod Aid	308UNTS115	104459
Peru	USA (United States)	09 Apr 58	US Agri Commod Aid	316UNTS37	104576
Taiwan	USA (United States)	18 Apr 58	US Agri Commod Aid	308UNTS179	104461
Saudi Arabia	USA (United States)	01 May 58	Direct Aid	315UNTS221	104571
Iceland	USA (United States)	03 May 58	US Agri Commod Aid	316UNTS137	104581
Burma	USA (United States)	27 May 58	US Agri Commod Aid	315UNTS197	104569
Philippines	USA (United States)	03 Jun 58	US Agri Commod Aid	316UNTS3	104573
USA (United States)	Vietnam, South	17 Jun 58	Atomic Energy	321UNTS35	104652
Ceylon (Sri Lanka)	USA (United States)	18 Jun 58	US Agri Commod Aid	316UNTS15	104574
India	USA (United States)	23 Jun 58	US Agri Commod Aid	317UNTS181	104603
Philippines	USA (United States)	30 Jun 58	Direct Aid	321UNTS51	104653
Ecuador	USA (United States)	30 Jun 58	US Agri Commod Aid	336UNTS11	104796
Lebanon	USA (United States)	03 Sep 58	Direct Aid	336UNTS91	104801
Haiti	USA (United States)	09 Sep 58	Direct Aid	335UNTS257	104793
India	USA (United States)	26 Sep 58	US Agri Commod Aid	336UNTS59	104798
Israel	USA (United States)	06 Nov 58	US Agri Commod Aid	336UNTS275	104810

PARTY ONE	PARTY TWO	DATE	TOPIC	CITATION	NUMBER
Aid and Assistance (Cont.)					
Pakistan	USA (United States)	26 Nov 58	US Agri Commod Aid	337UNTS3	104812
Netherlands	Turkey	29 Nov 58	Direct Aid	335UNTS229	104790
India	USA (United States)	17 Dec 58	Milit Assistance	358UNTS77	105125
USA (United States)	Yugoslavia	22 Dec 58	US Agri Commod Aid	338UNTS243	104839
United Arab Rep	USA (United States)	24 Dec 58	US Agri Commod Aid	338UNTS221	104837
Finland	USA (United States)	30 Dec 58	US Agri Commod Aid	340UNTS259	104869
Spain	USA (United States)	13 Jan 59	US Agri Commod Aid	341UNTS241	104887
India	Netherlands	16 Jan 59	Tech Assistance	506UNTS153	107386
Turkey	USA (United States)	13 Feb 59	US Agri Commod Aid	340UNTS235	104867
USA (United States)	Uruguay	20 Feb 59	US Agri Commod Aid	341UNTS201	104884
Iceland	USA (United States)	03 Mar 59	US Agri Commod Aid	341UNTS261	104889
India	USA (United States)	03 Mar 59	US Agri Commod Aid	341UNTS235	104886
Ceylon (Sri Lanka)	USA (United States)	13 Mar 59	US Agri Commod Aid	342UNTS51	104900
France	USA (United States)	21 Mar 59	US Agri Commod Aid	342UNTS71	104901
India	Netherlands	27 Apr 59	Tech Assistance	506UNTS141	107385
Libya	USA (United States)	21 May 59	Tech Assistance	361UNTS123	105176
Indonesia	USA (United States)	29 May 59	US Agri Commod Aid	347UNTS85	104992
Taiwan	USA (United States)	09 Jun 59	US Agri Commod Aid	353UNTS257	105046
Poland	USA (United States)	10 Jun 59	US Agri Commod Aid	347UNTS41	104989
Argentina	USA (United States)	12 Jun 59	US Agri Commod Aid	347UNTS59	104990
Iceland	USA (United States)	23 Jun 59	Direct Aid	354UNTS3	105048
Burma	USA (United States)	24 Jun 59	Direct Aid	358UNTS91	105127
Korea, South	USA (United States)	30 Jun 59	US Agri Commod Aid	353UNTS297	105047
Iraq	USA (United States)	07 Jul 59	Milit Assistance	357UNTS153	105114
United Arab Rep	USA (United States)	29 Jul 59	US Agri Commod Aid	357UNTS121	105111
Peru	USA (United States)	22 Aug 59	Atomic Energy	357UNTS99	105109
USA (United States)	Yugoslavia	25 Aug 59	Milit Assistance	357UNTS77	105106
New Zealand	UK Great Britain	21 Sep 59	Milit Assistance	401UNTS51	105762
Colombia	USA (United States)	06 Oct 59	US Agri Commod Aid	358UNTS145	105132
USA (United States)	Vietnam, South	16 Oct 59	US Agri Commod Aid	360UNTS271	105163
UN Special Fund	Yugoslavia	27 Oct 59	Direct Aid	344UNTS159	104947
Ecuador	UN Special Fund	10 Nov 59	Direct Aid	345UNTS3	104955
India	USA (United States)	13 Nov 59	US Agri Commod Aid	360UNTS287	105164
United Arab Rep	USA (United States)	14 Nov 59	US Agri Commod Aid	360UNTS311	105165
UN Special Fund	Turkey	20 Nov 59	Direct Aid	345UNTS105	104963
UN Special Fund	United Arab Rep	25 Nov 59	Direct Aid	345UNTS125	104964
Argentina	UN Special Fund	04 Dec 59	Direct Aid	345UNTS263	104972
Turkey	USA (United States)	22 Dec 59	US Agri Commod Aid	367UNTS57	105225
Israel	USA (United States)	07 Jan 60	US Agri Commod Aid	368UNTS181	105241
Greece	USA (United States)	07 Jan 60	US Agri Commod Aid	368UNTS221	105243
UN Special Fund	UK Great Britain	07 Jan 60	Direct Aid	348UNTS177	105000
Chile	UN Special Fund	22 Jan 60	Direct Aid	351UNTS115	105020
Colombia	UN Special Fund	04 Feb 60	Direct Aid	355UNTS257	105080
Bolivia	UN Special Fund	09 Feb 60	Direct Aid	351UNTS203	105024
Peru	USA (United States)	12 Feb 60	US Agri Commod Aid	372UNTS83	105290
Japan	USA (United States)	18 Feb 60	Direct Aid	372UNTS117	105292
Afghanistan	UN Special Fund	21 Feb 60	Direct Aid	351UNTS93	105019
France	UN Special Fund	17 Mar 60	Direct Aid	354UNTS119	105059
Iceland	USA (United States)	06 Apr 60	US Agri Commod Aid	372UNTS71	105289
Pakistan	USA (United States)	11 Apr 60	US Agri Commod Aid	372UNTS251	105302
UN Special Fund	Tunisia	12 Apr 60	Direct Aid	355UNTS289	105082
UN Special Fund	Sudan	21 Apr 60	Direct Aid	356UNTS213	105097
India	USA (United States)	04 May 60	US Agri Commod Aid	376UNTS279	105384
Japan	USA (United States)	31 May 60	Direct Aid	376UNTS301	105385
Chile	USA (United States)	02 Jun 60	US Agri Commod Aid	377UNTS11	105393
USA (United States)	Yugoslavia	03 Jun 60	US Agri Commod Aid	376UNTS243	105382
UN Special Fund	Thailand	04 Jun 60	Tech Assistance	360UNTS97	105157
UN Special Fund	Togo	08 Jun 60	Tech Assistance	369UNTS401	200574
Spain	USA (United States)	22 Jun 60	US Agri Commod Aid	378UNTS3	105414
Chile	USA (United States)	29 Jun 60	Direct Aid	377UNTS355	105411
Ethiopia	UN Special Fund	13 Jul 60	Tech Assistance	368UNTS159	105240
Poland	USA (United States)	21 Jul 60	US Agri Commod Aid	380UNTS157	105456
Iran	USA (United States)	26 Jul 60	US Agri Commod Aid	384UNTS141	105516
United Arab Rep	USA (United States)	01 Aug 60	US Agri Commod Aid	384UNTS189	105519
United Arab Rep	USA (United States)	09 Aug 60	US Agri Commod Aid	388UNTS271	105584

Aid and Assistance (Cont.)

PARTY ONE	PARTY TWO	DATE	TOPIC	CITATION	NUMBER
Netherlands	UN Special Fund	12 Aug 60	Tech Assistance	372UNTS331	105309
Cyprus	UK Great Britain	16 Aug 60	Direct Aid	382UNTS231	105484
Congo (Zaire)	United Nations	23 Aug 60	Direct Aid	373UNTS327	200576
United Arab Rep	USSR (Soviet Union)	27 Aug 60	Tech Assistance	399UNTS37	105733
Taiwan	USA (United States)	30 Aug 60	US Agri Commod Aid	388UNTS191	105579
Brazil	UN Special Fund	16 Sep 60	Tech Assistance	375UNTS3	105351
Taiwan	UN Special Fund	20 Sep 60	Tech Assistance	375UNTS29	105352
Ecuador	USA (United States)	27 Sep 60	US Agri Commod Aid	401UNTS115	105766
Guinea	USA (United States)	30 Sep 60	General Aid	394UNTS103	105671
Ceylon (Sri Lanka)	USA (United States)	30 Sep 60	US Agri Commod Aid	389UNTS221	105594
Indonesia	UN Special Fund	07 Oct 60	Direct Aid	378UNTS141	105424
El Salvador	UN Special Fund	24 Oct 60	Direct Aid	377UNTS171	105400
Chile	USA (United States)	28 Oct 60	Direct Aid	401UNTS177	105770
USA (United States)	Vietnam, South	28 Oct 60	US Agri Commod Aid	401UNTS3	105758
Indonesia	USA (United States)	05 Nov 60	US Agri Commod Aid	400UNTS35	105746
Greece	USA (United States)	07 Nov 60	US Agri Commod Aid	400UNTS57	105748
Chile	USA (United States)	08 Nov 60	US Agri Commod Aid	405UNTS85	105825
Guatemala	UN Special Fund	17 Nov 60	Direct Aid	383UNTS67	105495
Cambodia	UN Special Fund	24 Nov 60	Direct Aid	382UNTS255	105487
Cyprus	USA (United States)	08 Dec 60	Direct Aid	405UNTS145	105831
Israel	USA (United States)	19 Dec 60	Direct Aid	401UNTS195	105772
Togo	USA (United States)	22 Dec 60	Direct Aid	401UNTS33	105760
Korea, South	USA (United States)	28 Dec 60	US Agri Commod Aid	402UNTS3	105773
Iceland	USA (United States)	30 Dec 60	Direct Aid	401UNTS43	105761
Burma	UN Special Fund	03 Jan 61	Direct Aid	387UNTS219	105564
Mali	USA (United States)	04 Jan 61	General Aid	405UNTS165	105832
Costa Rica	UN Special Fund	10 Jan 61	Direct Aid	389UNTS253	105597
Turkey	USA (United States)	11 Jan 61	US Agri Commod Aid	405UNTS173	105833
USA (United States)	Yugoslavia	19 Jan 61	General Aid	402UNTS163	105784
UN Special Fund	Saudi Arabia	19 Jan 61	Direct Aid	396UNTS27	105692
Chad	UN Special Fund	23 Jan 61	Direct Aid	390UNTS69	105603
Gabon	UN Special Fund	02 Feb 61	Direct Aid	387UNTS289	105568
Korea, South	USA (United States)	08 Feb 61	General Aid	405UNTS37	105821
Cyprus	UN Special Fund	24 Feb 61	Direct Aid	389UNTS3	105588
Cuba	UN Special Fund	10 Mar 61	Direct Aid	390UNTS35	105601
USA (United States)	Vietnam, South	25 Mar 61	US Agri Commod Aid	406UNTS187	105849
Colombia	USA (United States)	04 Apr 61	Direct Aid	405UNTS55	105822
Bolivia	USA (United States)	07 Apr 61	US Agri Commod Aid	433UNTS3	106227
Iceland	USA (United States)	07 Apr 61	US Agri Commod Aid	406UNTS203	105850
Cyprus	UNICEF (Children)	19 Apr 61	Direct Aid	394UNTS185	105678
USA (United States)	Yugoslavia	28 Apr 61	US Agri Commod Aid	409UNTS172	105884
Ceylon (Sri Lanka)	UN Special Fund	03 May 61	Direct Aid	395UNTS217	105687
Brazil	USA (United States)	04 May 61	US Agri Commod Aid	433UNTS91	106233
Israel	USA (United States)	10 May 61	US Agri Commod Aid	409UNTS213	105887
Spain	USA (United States)	22 May 61	US Agri Commod Aid	409UNTS260	105891
Niger	USA (United States)	26 May 61	General Aid	410UNTS213	105905
USA (United States)	Upper Volta	01 Jun 61	General Aid	410UNTS223	105906
Congo (Zaire)	United Nations	12 Jun 61	General Aid	494UNTS205	107234
Cameroon	UN Special Fund	13 Jun 61	Direct Aid	397UNTS297	105713
Finland	USA (United States)	16 Jun 61	Claims and Debts	413UNTS211	105955
Ecuador	USA (United States)	17 Jun 61	Direct Aid	411UNTS49	105913
UN Special Fund	Upper Volta	26 Jun 61	Direct Aid	400UNTS3	105744
Tunisia	USA (United States)	30 Jun 61	US Agri Commod Aid	434UNTS85	106257
Paraguay	USA (United States)	07 Jul 61	US Agri Commod Aid	433UNTS53	106231
USA (United States)	Vietnam, South	14 Jul 61	US Agri Commod Aid	416UNTS133	105999
Taiwan	USA (United States)	21 Jul 61	US Agri Commod Aid	416UNTS101	105998
Mali	UN Special Fund	21 Jul 61	Direct Aid	401UNTS141	105768
Fed of Malaya	UN Special Fund	25 Jul 61	Direct Aid	401UNTS159	105769
Turkey	USA (United States)	29 Jul 61	US Agri Commod Aid	416UNTS151	106001
UN Special Fund	Yemen	02 Aug 61	Direct Aid	402UNTS43	105777
Chile	USA (United States)	03 Aug 61	Direct Aid	433UNTS21	106228
Finland	USA (United States)	04 Aug 61	US Agri Commod Aid	418UNTS19	106014
El Salvador	USA (United States)	21 Aug 61	US Agri Commod Aid	418UNTS35	106015
Ivory Coast	UN Special Fund	29 Aug 61	Direct Aid	406UNTS129	105844
United Arab Rep	USA (United States)	02 Sep 61	US Agri Commod Aid	421UNTS251	106063

Aid and Assistance (Cont.)

PARTY ONE	PARTY TWO	DATE	TOPIC	CITATION	NUMBER
Paraguay	USA (United States)	26 Sep 61	General Aid	461UNTS91	106653
UN Special Fund	Sierra Leone	02 Oct 61	Direct Aid	422UNTS131	106073
Austria	USA (United States)	03 Oct 61	Direct Aid	426UNTS187	106137
Pakistan	USA (United States)	14 Oct 61	US Agri Commod Aid	426UNTS237	106141
Greece	USA (United States)	18 Oct 61	US Agri Commod Aid	426UNTS209	106139
Indonesia	USA (United States)	26 Oct 61	US Agri Commod Aid	433UNTS249	106248
Iceland	USA (United States)	06 Nov 61	US Agri Commod Aid	426UNTS225	106140
Mauritania	UN Special Fund	07 Nov 61	Direct Aid	412UNTS240	105936
Syria	USA (United States)	09 Nov 61	US Agri Commod Aid	435UNTS75	106271
Sudan	USA (United States)	14 Nov 61	US Agri Commod Aid	434UNTS51	106255
Bolivia	USA (United States)	15 Nov 61	US Agri Commod Aid	456UNTS192	106557
Congo (Zaire)	USA (United States)	18 Nov 61	US Agri Commod Aid	433UNTS207	106244
Philippines	USA (United States)	24 Nov 61	US Agri Commod Aid	433UNTS315	106251
Portugal	USA (United States)	28 Nov 61	US Agri Commod Aid	434UNTS31	106253
IAEA (Atom Energy)	UN Special Fund	29 Nov 61	IGO Operations	415UNTS408	200593
UN Special Fund	Venezuela	11 Dec 61	Direct Aid	422UNTS149	106074
Poland	USA (United States)	15 Dec 61	US Agri Commod Aid	434UNTS3	106252
UN Special Fund	Senegal	16 Dec 61	Direct Aid	425UNTS97	106121
Costa Rica	USA (United States)	22 Dec 61	General Aid	460UNTS277	106646
USA (United States)	Vietnam, South	27 Dec 61	US Agri Commod Aid	433UNTS185	106242
USA (United States)	Yugoslavia	28 Dec 61	US Agri Commod Aid	434UNTS111	106259
Malagasy	UN Special Fund	05 Jan 62	Direct Aid	419UNTS29	106028
United Arab Rep	USA (United States)	19 Jan 62	US Agri Commod Aid	435UNTS107	106273
Iran	USA (United States)	29 Jan 62	US Agri Commod Aid	435UNTS53	106270
Guinea	USA (United States)	02 Feb 62	US Agri Commod Aid	435UNTS35	106269
Morocco	USA (United States)	09 Feb 62	Direct Aid	442UNTS135	106345
Bolivia	USA (United States)	12 Feb 62	US Agri Commod Aid	451UNTS281	106499
Tunisia	USA (United States)	16 Feb 62	US Agri Commod Aid	442UNTS161	106347
Indonesia	USA (United States)	19 Feb 62	US Agri Commod Aid	435UNTS137	106276
Niger	UN Special Fund	26 Feb 62	Direct Aid	423UNTS83	106086
Korea, South	USA (United States)	02 Mar 62	US Agri Commod Aid	442UNTS185	106349
Cyprus	USA (United States)	02 Mar 62	Direct Aid	445UNTS189	106386
Brazil	USA (United States)	15 Mar 62	US Agri Commod Aid	456UNTS209	106558
Iceland	USA (United States)	16 Mar 62	US Agri Commod Aid	445UNTS49	106376
Peru	USA (United States)	20 Mar 62	US Agri Commod Aid	445UNTS61	106377
Dahomey	UN Special Fund	28 Mar 62	Tech Assistance	424UNTS55	106099
Nicaragua	USA (United States)	30 Mar 62	Tech Assistance	456UNTS241	106559
El Salvador	USA (United States)	13 Apr 62	Milit Assistance	451UNTS307	106500
USA (United States)	Yugoslavia	21 Apr 62	US Agri Commod Aid	442UNTS123	106344
USA (United States)	Uruguay	27 Apr 62	US Agri Commod Aid	452UNTS25	106502
Taiwan	USA (United States)	27 Apr 62	US Agri Commod Aid	436UNTS25	106287
India	USA (United States)	01 May 62	US Agri Commod Aid	451UNTS179	106493
Israel	USA (United States)	03 May 62	US Agri Commod Aid	442UNTS83	106340
UN Special Fund	Uruguay	04 May 62	Direct Aid	429UNTS143	106196
USA (United States)	Venezuela	17 May 62	US Agri Commod Aid	456UNTS275	106562
Dominican Republic	UN Special Fund	06 Jun 62	Direct Aid	429UNTS169	106197
UN Special Fund	Syria	07 Jul 62	Direct Aid	443UNTS3	106355
UN Special Fund	Tanganyika	17 Jul 62	Direct Aid	435UNTS237	106281
Ceylon (Sri Lanka)	USA (United States)	19 Jul 62	US Agri Commod Aid	454UNTS31	106538
Colombia	USA (United States)	23 Jul 62	General Aid	458UNTS123	106595
Chile	USA (United States)	07 Aug 62	US Agri Commod Aid	461UNTS61	106652
Ethiopia	USA (United States)	13 Aug 62	US Agri Commod Aid	459UNTS31	106611
Paraguay	USA (United States)	25 Aug 62	Milit Assistance	461UNTS207	106665
Israel	USA (United States)	28 Aug 62	US Agri Commod Aid	448UNTS317	106445
Taiwan	USA (United States)	31 Aug 62	US Agri Commod Aid	460UNTS247	106644
Morocco	USA (United States)	11 Sep 62	US Agri Commod Aid	462UNTS207	106680
Tunisia	USA (United States)	14 Sep 62	US Agri Commod Aid	461UNTS31	106649
United Arab Rep	USA (United States)	08 Oct 62	US Agri Commod Aid	462UNTS39	106670
Mali	USSR (Soviet Union)	10 Oct 62	Tech Assistance	493UNTS219	107216
Iran	USA (United States)	15 Oct 62	US Agri Commod Aid	473UNTS291	106866
Japan	UN Special Fund	31 Oct 62	Tech Assistance	444UNTS171	106368
Korea, South	USA (United States)	07 Nov 62	US Agri Commod Aid	462UNTS129	106674
Burma	USA (United States)	09 Nov 62	US Agri Commod Aid	461UNTS113	106655
Algeria	UN Special Fund	15 Nov 62	Tech Assistance	452UNTS243	106512
Taiwan	USA (United States)	19 Nov 62	US Agri Commod Aid	459UNTS263	106629

PARTY ONE	PARTY TWO	DATE	TOPIC	CITATION	NUMBER
Aid and Assistance (Cont.)					
USA (United States)	Vietnam, South	21 Nov 62	US Agri Commod Aid	469UNTS101	106786
Paraguay	USA (United States)	24 Nov 62	US Agri Commod Aid	471UNTS49	106821
India	USA (United States)	26 Nov 62	US Agri Commod Aid	460UNTS203	106641
USA (United States)	Yugoslavia	28 Nov 62	US Agri Commod Aid	460UNTS185	106640
Dominican Republic	USA (United States)	30 Nov 62	US Agri Commod Aid	471UNTS25	106819
Israel	USA (United States)	06 Dec 62	US Agri Commod Aid	460UNTS151	106638
Bolivia	USA (United States)	17 Dec 62	US Agri Commod Aid	469UNTS121	106788
UN Special Fund	Uganda	19 Dec 62	Admin Cooperation	449UNTS41	106451
Sudan	USA (United States)	31 Jan 63	US Agri Commod Aid	494UNTS119	107230
Poland	USA (United States)	01 Feb 63	US Agri Commod Aid	487UNTS143	107100
Bolivia	USA (United States)	04 Feb 63	US Agri Commod Aid	473UNTS65	106856
Iceland	USA (United States)	06 Feb 63	US Agri Commod Aid	473UNTS93	106858
Central Afri Rep	USA (United States)	10 Feb 63	Direct Aid	473UNTS83	106857
Turkey	USA (United States)	21 Feb 63	US Agri Commod Aid	473UNTS311	106867
Congo (Zaire)	USA (United States)	23 Feb 63	US Agri Commod Aid	493UNTS3	107203
Congo (Zaire)	USA (United States)	23 Feb 63	US Agri Commod Aid	493UNTS17	107204
UN Special Fund	Uganda	22 Mar 63	Direct Aid	456UNTS466	106572
Colombia	USA (United States)	27 Mar 63	US Agri Commod Aid	489UNTS289	107145
Ecuador	USA (United States)	05 Apr 63	US Agri Commod Aid	477UNTS135	106919
Laos	UK Great Britain	17 May 63	Direct Aid	475UNTS155	106891
Guinea	USA (United States)	22 May 63	US Agri Commod Aid	487UNTS251	107108
Jamaica	UN Special Fund	22 May 63	Direct Aid	489UNTS191	107140
Netherlands	UN Special Fund	24 May 63	Direct Aid	466UNTS289	106750
UN Special Fund	Western Samoa	05 Jun 63	Direct Aid	467UNTS463	200601
Ethiopia	USA (United States)	11 Jun 63	US Agri Commod Aid	487UNTS269	107109
Cyprus	USA (United States)	18 Jun 63	US Agri Commod Aid	479UNTS191	106953
India	USA (United States)	27 Jun 63	US Agri Commod Aid	479UNTS215	106955
New Zealand	UN Special Fund	28 Jun 63	Non-IBRD Project	470UNTS3	106792
Congo (Zaire)	UN Special Fund	26 Jul 63	Direct Aid	474UNTS137	106878
Burundi	UN Special Fund	22 Aug 63	Direct Aid	476UNTS49	106903
Iraq	USA (United States)	27 Aug 63	US Agri Commod Aid	489UNTS271	107144
Brazil	USA (United States)	11 Sep 63	US Agri Commod Aid	493UNTS267	107220
Paraguay	USA (United States)	16 Sep 63	US Agri Commod Aid	494UNTS101	107229
Belgium	Turkey	23 Sep 63	Direct Aid	566UNTS195	108244
Peru	USA (United States)	23 Sep 63	US Agri Commod Aid	488UNTS91	107121
Jamaica	USA (United States)	24 Oct 63	General Aid	489UNTS337	107148
Greece	USA (United States)	30 Oct 63	US Agri Commod Aid	493UNTS29	107205
Central Afri Rep	UN Special Fund	30 Oct 63	Direct Aid	481UNTS247	106985
Syria	USA (United States)	18 Nov 63	US Agri Commod Aid	494UNTS169	107232
Australia	India	03 Dec 63	Milit Assistance	486UNTS279	107082
Rwanda	UN Special Fund	18 Mar 64	Direct Aid	491UNTS3	107170
Ireland	UN Special Fund	03 Jun 64	Direct Aid	496UNTS205	107253
Iceland	UN Special Fund	10 Jul 64	IGO Operations	502UNTS343	107337
Kenya	UN Special Fund	01 Oct 64	IGO Operations	511UNTS181	107433
Malawi	UN Special Fund	24 Oct 64	Direct Aid	514UNTS235	200609
Romania	UN Special Fund	24 Oct 64	IGO Operations	519UNTS29	107500
UN Special Fund	Zambia	15 Dec 64	Direct Aid	522UNTS3	107532
UN Special Fund	Zambia	04 Feb 65	Admin Cooperation	527UNTS115	107621
Gambia	UN Special Fund	09 Jun 65	IGO Operations	538UNTS321	200612
UN Special Fund	Spain	30 Jun 65	Direct Aid	544UNTS159	107918
UN Special Fund	Singapore	31 Dec 65	Admin Cooperation	552UNTS299	108061
Mongolia	UN Special Fund	26 Jan 66	Direct Aid	552UNTS201	108055
Multilateral		04 May 66	IBRD Project	575UNTS49	108354
Italy	United Nations	23 May 66	IGO Operations	565UNTS11	108231
Bulgaria	UN Special Fund	26 May 66	General Aid	563UNTS71	108205
Guyana	UN Special Fund	11 Jun 66	Non-IBRD Project	564UNTS201	200622
New Zealand	Western Samoa	29 Jul 66	Direct Aid	598UNTS115	108657
UN Special Fund	UPU (Postal Union)	21 Sep 66	Non-IBRD Project	573UNTS259	200626
UN Special Fund	Singapore	23 Sep 66	General Aid	573UNTS115	108326
Botswana	UN Special Fund	30 Sep 66	IGO Operations	576UNTS3	108360
Lesotho	UN Special Fund	17 Nov 66	Recognition	580UNTS17	108416
Australia	UN Special Fund	06 Feb 67	IGO Operations	590UNTS3	108543
Barbados	UN Special Fund	03 Mar 67	Tech Assistance	594UNTS91	108596
Hungary	UN Special Fund	28 Apr 67	General Aid	595UNTS171	108619

PARTY ONE	PARTY TWO	DATE	TOPIC	CITATION	NUMBER
Airports					
United Arab Rep	USA (United States)	05 Jan 46	Status of Forces	160UNTS27	102098
Multilateral		31 Mar 46	Milit Installation	17UNTS159	100274
United Arab Rep	USA (United States)	15 Jun 46	Air Transport	151UNTS135	101988
Iceland	UK Great Britain	04 Jul 46	Specific Property	6UNTS223	100077
Canada	Newfoundland	29 Jul 46	Air Transport	17UNTS169	100275
Denmark	USA (United States)	01 Oct 46	Air Transport	42UNTS219	100650
Iceland	USA (United States)	07 Oct 46	Milit Installation	12UNTS163	100184
Norway	USA (United States)	12 Nov 46	Air Transport	42UNTS227	100651
Australia	USA (United States)	10 Mar 47	Air Transport	10UNTS89	100145
Switzerland	USA (United States)	30 Apr 47	Specif Goods/Equip	42UNTS235	100652
Thailand	USA (United States)	08 May 47	Air Transport	42UNTS241	100653
UK Great Britain	USA (United States)	23 May 47	Specific Property	11UNTS211	100159
Greece	UK Great Britain	05 Jun 47	Status of Forces	9UNTS197	100133
Portugal	UK Great Britain	25 May 48	Milit Installation	34UNTS311	100544
UK Great Britain	Uruguay	12 Jul 48	Finance	71UNTS199	100919
Australia	Italy	02 Aug 48	Air Transport	28UNTS165	100424
France	USA (United States)	19 Oct 48	Air Transport	98UNTS3	101355
UK Great Britain	USA (United States)	25 Apr 51	Specific Property	99UNTS97	101373
Saudi Arabia	USA (United States)	18 Jun 51	Specific Property	102UNTS73	101412
Saudi Arabia	USA (United States)	02 Apr 57	Milit Installation	283UNTS97	104109
Alcoholic Beverages					
India	United Nations	12 Jan 52	Tech Assistance	118UNTS175	101606
Alien Property					
Netherlands	UK Great Britain	02 Oct 44	Claims and Debts	231UNTS317	200535
Belgium	Norway	23 Oct 45	Claims and Debts	183UNTS337	200510
Denmark	UK Great Britain	06 Dec 45	Finance	5UNTS3	100061
Italy	USA (United States)	06 Dec 45	General Trade	3UNTS131	100027
Netherlands	USA (United States)	11 Feb 46	Claims and Debts	3UNTS37	100023
Czechoslovakia	Poland	12 Feb 46	Reparations	25UNTS207	100364
Greece	UK Great Britain	21 Mar 46	Claims and Debts	91UNTS149	101247
Canada	France	22 Mar 46	Reparations	230UNTS165	103182
Greece	United Arab Rep	30 Mar 46	Reparations	187UNTS263	102518
Belgium	Denmark	08 Apr 46	Claims and Debts	4UNTS429	100059
New Zealand	Norway	03 May 46	Claims and Debts	16UNTS211	100262
Denmark	Luxembourg	21 May 46	Claims and Debts	4UNTS435	100060
France	USA (United States)	18 Jul 46	Reparations	125UNTS165	101675
Multilateral		18 Jul 46	Reparations	125UNTS119	101674
Multilateral		27 Jul 46	Patents/Copyrights	90UNTS229	101238
Denmark	New Zealand	18 Sep 46	Claims and Debts	10UNTS39	100141
Greece	USA (United States)	08 Oct 46	Claims and Debts	180UNTS119	102379
Belgium	Netherlands	12 Oct 46	Claims and Debts	23UNTS179	100347
Denmark	South Africa	14 Oct 46	Claims and Debts	10UNTS29	100140
Luxembourg	UK Great Britain	11 Dec 46	Claims and Debts	11UNTS167	100155
Denmark	India	20 Dec 46	Reparations	7UNTS309	100107
Belgium	Sweden	30 Dec 46	Claims and Debts	23UNTS197	100348
Belgium	Denmark	28 Jan 47	Visas	18UNTS221	100291
Philippines	USA (United States)	14 Mar 47	Non-IBRD Project	16UNTS31	100247
Belgium	Czechoslovakia	19 Mar 47	Claims and Debts	23UNTS35	100341
Australia	Norway	24 Mar 47	Claims and Debts	18UNTS185	100288
Italy	UK Great Britain	17 Apr 47	Claims and Debts	54UNTS169	100802
France	South Africa	18 Apr 47	Reparations	225UNTS35	103085
Thailand	UK Great Britain	08 May 47	Claims and Debts	100UNTS47	101386
United Arab Rep	UK Great Britain	30 Jun 47	Finance	93UNTS165	101299
Belgium	United Arab Rep	01 Jul 47	Claims and Debts	34UNTS93	100529
Belgium	South Africa	04 Jul 47	Claims and Debts	47UNTS9	100720
Greece	South Africa	28 Jul 47	Reparations	185UNTS161	102467
Australia	France	28 Jul 47	Reparations	97UNTS271	101353
Belgium	India	04 Aug 47	Reparations	76UNTS23	100976
Czechoslovakia	New Zealand	08 Aug 47	Claims and Debts	18UNTS161	100285
Multilateral		14 Aug 47	Reparations	138UNTS111	101863
Italy	USA (United States)	14 Aug 47	Claims and Debts	36UNTS105	100567
Poland	UK Great Britain	24 Jan 48	Claims and Debts	87UNTS3	101163
Multilateral		10 May 48	Reparations	140UNTS129	101887

PARTY ONE	PARTY TWO	DATE	TOPIC	CITATION	NUMBER
Alien Property (Cont.)					
Multilateral		13 May 48	Reparations	140UNTS187	101888
Australia	Greece	16 Jun 48	Claims and Debts	18UNTS211	100290
France	UK Great Britain	15 Jul 48	Claims and Debts	71UNTS215	100920
Australia	Denmark	08 Oct 48	Claims and Debts	22UNTS43	100330
Australia	Belgium	09 Dec 48	Claims and Debts	25UNTS159	100361
UK Great Britain	Yugoslavia	23 Dec 48	Reparations	81UNTS121	101068
UK Great Britain	Yugoslavia	23 Dec 48	Reparations	81UNTS103	101067
Poland	UK Great Britain	14 Jan 49	Reparations	83UNTS51	101101
Netherlands	UK Great Britain	17 Jan 49	Reparations	83UNTS67	101102
Denmark	Poland	12 May 49	Claims and Debts	87UNTS179	101172
Italy	Yugoslavia	23 May 49	Reparations	150UNTS179	101972
Greece	Italy	31 Aug 49	Reparations	78UNTS89	101014
Czechoslovakia	UK Great Britain	28 Sep 49	Reparations	86UNTS161	101157
Australia	Yugoslavia	22 Feb 50	Claims and Debts	51UNTS201	100766
Israel	UK Great Britain	30 Mar 50	Claims and Debts	86UNTS231	101162
Italy	New Zealand	19 Apr 50	Claims and Debts	67UNTS81	100867
Australia	Netherlands	26 Apr 50	Claims and Debts	54UNTS83	100796
Belgium	Iraq	05 Jul 50	Claims and Debts	68UNTS165	100893
Multilateral		29 Nov 50	Patents/Copyrights	88UNTS221	101194
Switzerland	UK Great Britain	08 Dec 50	Claims and Debts	175UNTS55	102295
Italy	Yugoslavia	23 Dec 50	Admin Cooperation	150UNTS199	101974
Italy	Yugoslavia	23 Dec 50	Finance	150UNTS191	101973
Australia	Finland	04 Jan 51	Claims and Debts	80UNTS27	101042
New Zealand	Yugoslavia	27 Feb 51	Reparations	150UNTS165	101971
Greece	India	18 Apr 51	Reparations	166UNTS305	102195
Italy	UK Great Britain	28 Jun 51	Claims and Debts	118UNTS115	101600
Canada	Italy	20 Sep 51	Reparations	236UNTS251	103328
Italy	UK Great Britain	07 Nov 51	Claims and Debts	118UNTS133	101601
Italy	UK Great Britain	12 Feb 52	Claims and Debts	126UNTS297	101695
Australia	Italy	24 May 52	Reparations	161UNTS65	102123
Germany, West	Netherlands	20 Jun 52	Reparations	136UNTS221	101836
Norway	USA (United States)	21 Jun 52	Reparations	236UNTS9	103313
Austria	UK Great Britain	30 Jun 52	Reparations	138UNTS153	101867
Multilateral		28 Aug 52	Claims and Debts	175UNTS69	102296
Denmark	Poland	26 Feb 53	Claims and Debts	186UNTS301	102496
Austria	Yugoslavia	19 Mar 53	Visas	467UNTS293	106767
Multilateral		30 Apr 53	Admin Cooperation	175UNTS89	102297
India	Netherlands	04 Dec 54	Reparations	289UNTS221	104219
Germany, West	Sweden	22 Mar 56	Claims and Debts	262UNTS361	103761
Argentina	Italy	23 May 56	Claims and Debts	267UNTS255	103846
Multilateral		31 Jan 57	Claims and Debts	278UNTS105	104026
Multilateral		29 Mar 57	Claims and Debts	283UNTS137	104113
Australia	Netherlands	09 Oct 57	Dispute Settlement	312UNTS225	104520
Netherlands	Norway	30 Jun 58	Reparations	348UNTS3	104995
Multilateral		27 Oct 58	Reparations	351UNTS303	105031
United Arab Rep	UK Great Britain	28 Feb 59	Finance	343UNTS159	104925
Austria	Netherlands	30 Sep 59	Specific Property	507UNTS111	107397
Australia	Austria	18 Dec 59	Reparations	348UNTS201	105001
Cyprus	UK Great Britain	16 Aug 60	Consul/Citizenship	382UNTS247	105486
Japan	UK Great Britain	14 Nov 62	General Trade	478UNTS29	106934
Israel	USSR (Soviet Union)	07 Oct 64	Specific Property	516UNTS59	107471
Alliance and Mutual Guarantee					
Netherlands	USA (United States)	17 Jan 33	Status of Forces	474UNTS119	106877
Multilateral		29 Jan 42	General Military	93UNTS279	200271
Taiwan	USA (United States)	02 Jun 42	Milit Assistance	14UNTS343	200092
Czechoslovakia	USA (United States)	11 Jul 42	Milit Assistance	90UNTS257	200263
USA (United States)	Yugoslavia	24 Jul 42	Milit Assistance	34UNTS361	200179
Australia	USA (United States)	03 Sep 42	Milit Assistance	24UNTS195	200143
New Zealand	USA (United States)	03 Sep 42	Milit Assistance	24UNTS185	200142
France	USA (United States)	03 Sep 42	Milit Assistance	24UNTS177	200141
Netherlands	USA (United States)	14 Jun 43	General Military	28UNTS397	200163
Ethiopia	USA (United States)	09 Aug 43	Milit Installation	29UNTS303	200169
Australia	New Zealand	21 Jan 44	General Amity	18UNTS357	200113
Belgium	UK Great Britain	22 Aug 44	Direct Aid	90UNTS295	200267

PARTY ONE	PARTY TWO	DATE	TOPIC	CITATION	NUMBER
Alliance and Mutual Guarantee (Cont.)					
Ethiopia	UK Great Britain	19 Dec 44	General Amity	93UNTS303	200272
France	USA (United States)	20 Feb 45	Direct Aid	76UNTS193	200246
France	USA (United States)	20 Feb 45	IGO Status/Immunit	76UNTS223	200248
France	USA (United States)	28 Feb 45	IGO Status/Immunit	76UNTS213	200247
Multilateral		22 Mar 45	General Amity	70UNTS237	200241
South Africa	USA (United States)	17 Apr 45	Direct Aid	90UNTS267	200264
Taiwan	USSR (Soviet Union)	14 Aug 45	General Amity	10UNTS300	200068
Denmark	UK Great Britain	24 Oct 45	Milit Assistance	93UNTS143	101297
France	USA (United States)	08 Nov 45	General Trade	76UNTS151	100986
Mongolia	USSR (Soviet Union)	27 Feb 46	General Military	48UNTS177	100744
Jordan	UK Great Britain	22 Mar 46	General Amity	6UNTS143	100074
Multilateral		31 Mar 46	Milit Installation	17UNTS159	100274
France	USA (United States)	28 May 46	Milit Assistance	84UNTS59	101119
Taiwan	USA (United States)	28 Jun 46	Milit Assistance	34UNTS121	100532
France	UK Great Britain	04 Mar 47	General Amity	9UNTS187	100132
Czechoslovakia	Poland	10 Mar 47	General Military	25UNTS231	100365
Multilateral		02 Sep 47	General Military	21UNTS77	100324
Burma	UK Great Britain	17 Oct 47	Recognition	70UNTS183	100904
Ceylon (Sri Lanka)	UK Great Britain	11 Nov 47	Milit Assistance	86UNTS19	101148
Taiwan	USA (United States)	08 Dec 47	Milit Installation	70UNTS3	100895
Hungary	Romania	24 Jan 48	General Amity	477UNTS155	106920
Romania	USSR (Soviet Union)	04 Feb 48	General Military	48UNTS189	100745
Hungary	USSR (Soviet Union)	18 Feb 48	General Military	48UNTS163	100743
Norway	USA (United States)	24 Feb 48	Milit Assistance	34UNTS155	100535
Jordan	UK Great Britain	15 Mar 48	General Military	77UNTS77	100994
Multilateral		17 Mar 48	General Military	19UNTS51	100304
Bulgaria	USSR (Soviet Union)	18 Mar 48	General Military	48UNTS135	100741
Finland	USSR (Soviet Union)	06 Apr 48	General Military	48UNTS149	100742
Multilateral		30 Apr 48	Dispute Settlement	30UNTS55	100449
Bulgaria	Poland	29 May 48	General Military	26UNTS213	100389
Hungary	Poland	18 Jun 48	Culture	25UNTS319	100370
Bulgaria	Hungary	16 Jul 48	General Amity	477UNTS169	106921
USA (United States)	Yugoslavia	19 Jul 48	Milit Assistance	34UNTS195	100537
Czechoslovakia	USA (United States)	16 Sep 48	Milit Assistance	90UNTS35	101224
New Zealand	UK Great Britain	12 Nov 48	Milit Assistance	162UNTS197	102136
Poland	Romania	26 Jan 49	General Military	85UNTS21	101143
Multilateral		04 Apr 49	General Military	34UNTS243	100541
Czechoslovakia	Hungary	16 Apr 49	General Amity	477UNTS183	106922
Ethiopia	USA (United States)	20 May 49	Milit Assistance	89UNTS99	101211
Ecuador	Italy	24 Aug 49	General Amity	72UNTS35	100926
Korea, South	USA (United States)	26 Jan 50	Milit Assistance	80UNTS205	101053
Italy	USA (United States)	27 Jan 50	Milit Assistance	80UNTS145	101050
Luxembourg	USA (United States)	27 Jan 50	Milit Assistance	80UNTS187	101052
France	USA (United States)	27 Jan 50	Milit Assistance	80UNTS171	101051
Norway	USA (United States)	27 Jan 50	Milit Assistance	80UNTS241	101055
UK Great Britain	USA (United States)	27 Jan 50	Milit Assistance	80UNTS261	101056
Belgium	USA (United States)	27 Jan 50	Milit Assistance	51UNTS213	100767
Netherlands	USA (United States)	27 Jan 50	Milit Assistance	80UNTS219	101054
Denmark	USA (United States)	27 Jan 50	Milit Assistance	48UNTS115	100740
China People's Rep	USSR (Soviet Union)	14 Feb 50	General Amity	226UNTS3	103103
Iran	USA (United States)	23 May 50	Milit Assistance	81UNTS3	101057
USA (United States)	Yugoslavia	21 Nov 50	Milit Assistance	93UNTS45	101286
Multilateral		23 Dec 50	Tech Assistance	185UNTS3	102456
Taiwan	USA (United States)	09 Feb 51	Milit Assistance	132UNTS273	101767
India	USA (United States)	16 Mar 51	Milit Assistance	141UNTS47	101904
Denmark	USA (United States)	27 Apr 51	General Military	94UNTS35	101305
Philippines	USA (United States)	30 Aug 51	Milit Assistance	177UNTS133	102315
Multilateral		01 Sep 51	General Military	131UNTS83	101736
Portugal	USA (United States)	06 Sep 51	Milit Assistance	237UNTS217	103348
South Africa	USA (United States)	09 Nov 51	Milit Assistance	160UNTS41	102100
Liberia	USA (United States)	19 Nov 51	Milit Assistance	167UNTS141	102204
Cambodia	USA (United States)	28 Dec 51	Milit Assistance	179UNTS97	102358
Germany, West	USA (United States)	28 Dec 51	Milit Assistance	181UNTS45	102397
Thailand	USA (United States)	29 Dec 51	Milit Assistance	179UNTS113	102360
France	USA (United States)	05 Jan 52	Milit Assistance	181UNTS177	102408

PARTY ONE	PARTY TWO	DATE	TOPIC	CITATION	NUMBER
Alliance and Mutual Guarantee (Cont.)					
Austria	USA (United States)	05 Jan 52	Milit Assistance	179UNTS73	102355
Turkey	USA (United States)	07 Jan 52	Milit Assistance	179UNTS121	102361
Philippines	USA (United States)	07 Jan 52	Milit Assistance	179UNTS193	102368
Korea, South	USA (United States)	07 Jan 52	Milit Assistance	179UNTS105	102359
Italy	USA (United States)	07 Jan 52	Milit Assistance	179UNTS165	102365
Greece	USA (United States)	07 Jan 52	Milit Assistance	180UNTS171	102382
Belgium	USA (United States)	07 Jan 52	Milit Assistance	179UNTS81	102356
UK Great Britain	USA (United States)	08 Jan 52	Milit Assistance	179UNTS201	102369
Denmark	USA (United States)	08 Jan 52	Milit Assistance	179UNTS65	102354
Luxembourg	USA (United States)	08 Jan 52	Milit Assistance	180UNTS191	102384
Iceland	USA (United States)	08 Jan 52	Milit Assistance	180UNTS183	102383
Netherlands	USA (United States)	08 Jan 52	Milit Assistance	179UNTS175	102366
Norway	USA (United States)	08 Jan 52	Milit Assistance	179UNTS185	102367
USA (United States)	Vietnam, South	19 Jan 52	Milit Assistance	205UNTS127	102772
Burma	USA (United States)	09 Feb 52	Milit Assistance	179UNTS91	102357
Ecuador	USA (United States)	20 Feb 52	Milit Assistance	177UNTS43	102308
Peru	USA (United States)	22 Feb 52	Milit Assistance	165UNTS31	102166
Japan	USA (United States)	28 Feb 52	Milit Assistance	208UNTS255	102817
Ethiopia	USA (United States)	13 Jun 52	Milit Assistance	205UNTS17	102766
New Zealand	USA (United States)	19 Jun 52	Milit Assistance	178UNTS315	102347
USA (United States)	Uruguay	30 Jun 52	Milit Assistance	207UNTS139	102804
Ethiopia	USA (United States)	22 May 53	Milit Assistance	207UNTS127	102803
Libya	UK Great Britain	29 Jul 53	General Amity	186UNTS185	102491
Libya	UK Great Britain	29 Jul 53	Status of Forces	186UNTS201	102492
Spain	USA (United States)	26 Sep 53	Milit Assistance	207UNTS61	102800
Spain	USA (United States)	26 Sep 53	Milit Assistance	207UNTS83	102801
Korea, South	USA (United States)	01 Oct 53	General Military	238UNTS199	103363
Japan	USA (United States)	08 Mar 54	Milit Assistance	232UNTS169	103236
Norway	USA (United States)	13 Apr 54	Status of Forces	229UNTS223	103169
Nicaragua	USA (United States)	23 Apr 54	Milit Assistance	229UNTS37	103159
Pakistan	USA (United States)	19 May 54	Milit Assistance	202UNTS301	102736
Honduras	USA (United States)	20 May 54	Milit Assistance	222UNTS87	103025
Multilateral		09 Aug 54	General Amity	211UNTS237	102855
Netherlands	USA (United States)	13 Aug 54	Milit Installation	251UNTS91	103535
Multilateral		08 Sep 54	Milit Assistance	209UNTS23	102819
Libya	USA (United States)	09 Sep 54	Milit Installation	224UNTS217	103078
China People's Rep	USSR (Soviet Union)	12 Oct 54	General Amity	226UNTS57	103108
Multilateral		02 Dec 54	General Amity	226UNTS153	103112
Taiwan	USA (United States)	10 Dec 54	General Military	248UNTS213	103496
Netherlands	USA (United States)	14 Dec 54	Milit Assistance	262UNTS35	103737
Iraq	Turkey	24 Feb 55	General Military	233UNTS199	103264
Iraq	UK Great Britain	04 Apr 55	General Military	233UNTS118	103265
Multilateral		14 May 55	General Amity	219UNTS3	102962
Guatemala	USA (United States)	18 Jun 55	Milit Assistance	262UNTS105	103740
South Africa	UK Great Britain	30 Jun 55	General Military	248UNTS191	103495
Germany, West	USA (United States)	30 Jun 55	Milit Assistance	240UNTS47	103393
Brazil	USA (United States)	20 Sep 55	Military Mission	257UNTS349	103665
Syria	United Arab Rep	20 Oct 55	General Military	247UNTS117	103461
Afghanistan	USSR (Soviet Union)	18 Dec 55	Admin Cooperation	259UNTS101	103684
Taiwan	USA (United States)	03 Apr 56	Milit Assistance	268UNTS315	103864
Jordan	USA (United States)	24 Sep 56	Milit Assistance	278UNTS51	104020
Germany, West	Netherlands	10 Jul 57	Status of Forces	339UNTS97	104848
Japan	USA (United States)	14 Sep 57	Admin Cooperation	293UNTS247	104293
Fed of Malaya	UK Great Britain	12 Oct 57	Milit Assistance	285UNTS59	104149
Ethiopia	USA (United States)	26 Dec 57	Milit Assistance	307UNTS71	104443
Japan	USA (United States)	25 Jan 58	Milit Assistance	304UNTS81	104392
Bolivia	USA (United States)	22 Apr 58	Milit Assistance	317UNTS209	104605
Philippines	USA (United States)	15 May 58	Milit Assistance	316UNTS163	104583
Multilateral		10 Jun 58	Admin Cooperation	330UNTS3	104739
UK Great Britain	USA (United States)	03 Jul 58	Atomic Energy	326UNTS3	104707
Multilateral		28 Jul 58	General Military	335UNTS205	104788
Canada	USA (United States)	02 Sep 58	General Military	335UNTS249	104792
Iran	USA (United States)	05 Mar 59	General Military	327UNTS277	104725
Pakistan	USA (United States)	05 Mar 59	General Military	327UNTS285	104726
Turkey	USA (United States)	05 Mar 59	General Military	327UNTS293	104727

PARTY ONE	PARTY TWO	DATE	TOPIC	CITATION	NUMBER
Alliance and Mutual Guarantee (Cont.)					
Liberia	USA (United States)	08 Jul 59	Milit Assistance	357UNTS93	105108
Japan	USA (United States)	19 Jan 60	General Military	373UNTS179	105320
Multilateral		16 Aug 60	General Amity	397UNTS287	105712
Multilateral		16 Aug 60	Recognition	382UNTS3	105475
Multilateral		21 Apr 61	IGO Establishment	484UNTS349	107041
IBRD (World Bank)	Thailand	28 Apr 61	IBRD Project	415UNTS121	105983
France	USA (United States)	27 Jul 61	Milit Assistance	433UNTS29	106229
Belgium	USA (United States)	17 May 62	Milit Assistance	461UNTS3	106647
Australia	USA (United States)	09 May 63	Milit Installation	475UNTS331	106897
Czechoslovakia	USSR (Soviet Union)	27 Nov 63	General Amity	496UNTS161	107250
Malta	UK Great Britain	21 Sep 64	Military Mission	588UNTS55	108518
Malaysia	Singapore	07 Aug 65	Recognition	563UNTS89	108206
Mongolia	USSR (Soviet Union)	15 Jan 66	General Amity	562UNTS43	108194
Aluminum Industry					
Hungary	Yugoslavia	11 May 47	Direct Aid	130UNTS171	101730
Animal Industry					
New Zealand	USA (United States)	17 Feb 64	Commodity Trade	511UNTS37	107424
Australia	USA (United States)	17 Feb 64	Commodity Trade	511UNTS17	107422
Ireland	USA (United States)	25 Feb 64	Commodity Trade	511UNTS27	107423
Netherlands	Tunisia	03 Mar 64	Tech Assistance	533UNTS133	107739
Mexico	USA (United States)	14 May 64	Commodity Trade	526UNTS228	107607
Germany, West	Thailand	23 Dec 64	Sanitation	525UNTS201	107592
Anthropology					
Peru	USA (United States)	04 Apr 44	Scientific Project	89UNTS291	200258
Multilateral		19 Apr 44	Scientific Project	89UNTS279	200257
Peru	USA (United States)	25 Mar 49	Scientific Project	89UNTS15	101205
Mexico	USA (United States)	21 Jun 49	Scientific Project	89UNTS3	101204
Colombia	USA (United States)	24 Nov 50	Scientific Project	133UNTS49	101779
Apartheid					
Brazil	United Nations	24 Mar 66	IGO Establishment	560UNTS47	108167
United Nations	Zambia	06 Jul 67	IGO Operations	600UNTS81	108678
Arbitration and Conciliation					
Brazil	Venezuela	30 Mar 40	Dispute Settlement	51UNTS291	200195
Multilateral		22 Mar 45	General Amity	70UNTS237	200241
Czechoslovakia	Poland	04 Apr 47	General Economic	85UNTS62	101146
Albania	Yugoslavia	12 Jun 47	Dispute Settlement	111UNTS183	101532
Italy	USA (United States)	06 Feb 48	Air Transport	73UNTS113	100950
Romania	USA (United States)	26 Feb 48	Admin Cooperation	48UNTS9	100738
Bulgaria	USA (United States)	08 Mar 48	Admin Cooperation	29UNTS101	100437
Multilateral		30 Apr 48	Dispute Settlement	30UNTS55	100449
Multilateral		28 Apr 49	Dispute Settlement	71UNTS101	100912
Italy	Netherlands	16 Aug 49	Admin Cooperation	98UNTS21	101357
Italy	Turkey	24 Mar 50	General Amity	96UNTS207	101338
France	UK Great Britain	29 Dec 50	Dispute Settlement	118UNTS149	101603
Italy	USA (United States)	13 Feb 51	IGO Establishment	148UNTS57	101935
Multilateral		25 Apr 51	Reparations	91UNTS21	101240
Greece	UK Great Britain	05 Oct 53	Reparations	243UNTS73	103447
Belgium	Germany, West	30 Mar 54	Admin Cooperation	190UNTS63	102558
Saudi Arabia	UK Great Britain	30 Jul 54	Dispute Settlement	201UNTS317	102722
Brazil	Italy	24 Nov 54	Dispute Settlement	284UNTS325	104146
Greece	UK Great Britain	24 Feb 55	Specif Claim/Waive	209UNTS187	102827
Germany, West	USA (United States)	27 Jul 56	Admin Cooperation	278UNTS3	104017
Greece	Sweden	11 Dec 56	Dispute Settlement	299UNTS247	104316
Belgium	Netherlands	07 Mar 57	Dispute Settlement	282UNTS241	104100
Honduras	Nicaragua	22 Jun 57	Specif Claim/Waive	277UNTS159	104005
UK Great Britain	USA (United States)	01 Nov 57	Scientific Project	299UNTS167	104312
Multilateral		10 Jun 58	Admin Cooperation	330UNTS3	104739
Belgium	Germany, West	30 Jun 58	Admin Cooperation	387UNTS245	105566
Belgium	Switzerland	29 Apr 59	Admin Cooperation	443UNTS35	106356
Greece	Yugoslavia	18 Jun 59	Admin Cooperation	368UNTS69	105235
Germany, West	UK Great Britain	03 Aug 59	Dispute Settlement	502UNTS197	107331
Germany, West	Netherlands	08 Apr 60	Territory Boundary	508UNTS14	107404
Multilateral		21 Apr 61	IGO Establishment	484UNTS349	107041

PARTY ONE	PARTY TWO	DATE	TOPIC	CITATION	NUMBER
Arbitration and Conciliation (Cont.)					
Multilateral		17 Dec 62	General Economic	523UNTS93	107555
Multilateral		18 Mar 65	Dispute Settlement	575UNTS159	108359
Czechoslovakia	Poland	29 Jul 65	Dispute Settlement	572UNTS203	108313
Archives					
Italy	Yugoslavia	23 Dec 50	Admin Cooperation	171UNTS291	102233
Multilateral		30 Jun 54	Admin Cooperation	204UNTS99	102752
Germany, West	USA (United States)	18 Apr 56	Admin Cooperation	271UNTS319	103923
Denmark	Germany, West	10 Jun 63	Admin Cooperation	477UNTS405	106930
Arms and Ammunition					
Poland	Yugoslavia	21 Jan 48	Non-IBRD Project	115UNTS155	101562
UK Great Britain	USA (United States)	27 Jan 50	Milit Assistance	80UNTS261	101056
Italy	USA (United States)	27 Jan 50	Milit Assistance	80UNTS145	101050
UK Great Britain	USA (United States)	21 Jul 50	Milit Installation	97UNTS193	101351
Nepal	UK Great Britain	30 Oct 50	General Amity	97UNTS121	101346
Denmark	USA (United States)	16 Nov 51	Milit Assistance	180UNTS275	102391
Liberia	USA (United States)	19 Nov 51	Milit Assistance	167UNTS141	102204
Dominican Republic	UK Great Britain	26 Nov 51	Milit Installation	133UNTS205	101791
Dominican Republic	USA (United States)	26 Nov 51	Milit Installation	150UNTS227	101976
UK Great Britain	USA (United States)	15 Jan 52	Milit Installation	127UNTS3	101697
United Arab Rep	USA (United States)	29 Apr 52	Milit Assistance	241UNTS3	103418
Portugal	USA (United States)	09 Jul 52	Milit Assistance	180UNTS251	102389
Haiti	USA (United States)	29 Aug 52	Direct Aid	186UNTS35	102480
UK Great Britain	USA (United States)	02 Mar 53	Milit Installation	172UNTS257	102249
Canada	India	12 Jun 53	Admin Cooperation	248UNTS113	103490
Germany, West	USA (United States)	23 Nov 53	Milit Installation	224UNTS107	103071
Japan	USA (United States)	21 Jan 54	Tech Assistance	223UNTS145	103063
Japan	USA (United States)	08 Mar 54	Milit Assistance	232UNTS169	103236
Norway	USA (United States)	07 May 54	Milit Assistance	231UNTS157	103215
Spain	USA (United States)	19 May 54	Tech Assistance	235UNTS87	103296
France	USA (United States)	31 May 54	Milit Assistance	236UNTS141	103321
UK Great Britain	USA (United States)	15 Jun 54	Milit Assistance	236UNTS133	103320
Italy	USA (United States)	24 Jun 54	Tech Assistance	235UNTS3	103290
Luxembourg	USA (United States)	07 Jul 54	Milit Assistance	233UNTS23	103247
Belgium	USA (United States)	23 Nov 54	Tech Assistance	235UNTS19	103292
Iceland	USA (United States)	10 Dec 54	Milit Assistance	237UNTS191	103345
Turkey	USA (United States)	25 Apr 55	Milit Assistance	263UNTS299	103779
Netherlands	USA (United States)	29 Apr 55	Milit Assistance	251UNTS357	103553
Turkey	USA (United States)	26 May 55	Milit Assistance	262UNTS97	103739
Greece	USA (United States)	27 May 55	Milit Assistance	251UNTS349	103552
Korea, South	USA (United States)	29 May 55	Milit Installation	256UNTS263	103636
Guatemala	USA (United States)	18 Jun 55	Milit Assistance	262UNTS105	103740
USA (United States)	Yugoslavia	30 Sep 55	General Military	269UNTS89	103877
UK Great Britain	USA (United States)	25 Jun 56	Milit Installation	249UNTS59	103501
UK Great Britain	USA (United States)	25 Jun 56	Milit Installation	249UNTS91	103502
Ecuador	USA (United States)	19 Jul 56	Milit Assistance	372UNTS149	105295
Germany, West	USA (United States)	08 Oct 56	Milit Assistance	278UNTS9	104018
Australia	USA (United States)	31 Dec 56	Milit Assistance	266UNTS89	103823
Brazil	USA (United States)	21 Jan 57	Milit Installation	278UNTS97	104025
Iraq	USA (United States)	16 Jun 57	Tech Assistance	284UNTS39	104127
France	USA (United States)	23 Sep 57	Tech Assistance	293UNTS297	104297
Bolivia	USA (United States)	22 Apr 58	Milit Assistance	317UNTS209	104605
Lebanon	UK Great Britain	19 May 58	Milit Assistance	327UNTS43	104716
Burma	USA (United States)	24 Jun 58	Milit Assistance	335UNTS193	104786
Fed of Malaya	USA (United States)	09 Jul 58	Milit Assistance	336UNTS79	104799
Indonesia	USA (United States)	13 Aug 58	Milit Assistance	335UNTS187	104785
Panama	USA (United States)	20 May 59	Milit Assistance	346UNTS235	104983
Taiwan	USA (United States)	22 Jul 59	Milit Assistance	357UNTS293	105121
USA (United States)	Yugoslavia	25 Aug 59	Milit Assistance	357UNTS87	105107
Korea, South	USA (United States)	01 Oct 59	Direct Aid	358UNTS115	105129
Turkey	USA (United States)	28 Oct 59	Milit Assistance	360UNTS265	105162
Norway	USA (United States)	13 Feb 60	Milit Assistance	388UNTS255	105583
Greece	USA (United States)	15 Feb 60	Milit Assistance	377UNTS95	105397
Turkey	USA (United States)	02 Mar 60	Milit Assistance	372UNTS37	105286
Denmark	USA (United States)	12 Apr 60	Milit Assistance	373UNTS9	105311

PARTY ONE	PARTY TWO	DATE	TOPIC	CITATION	NUMBER
Arms and Ammunition (Cont.)					
Japan	USA (United States)	15 Apr 60	Milit Assistance	372UNTS267	105303
Belgium	USA (United States)	22 Apr 60	Milit Assistance	372UNTS277	105304
Germany, West	USA (United States)	27 May 60	Milit Assistance	377UNTS45	105395
Italy	USA (United States)	07 Jul 60	Milit Assistance	380UNTS143	105455
Australia	USA (United States)	23 Aug 60	General Military	388UNTS237	105581
Haiti	USA (United States)	01 Sep 60	Milit Assistance	388UNTS249	105582
France	USA (United States)	19 Sep 60	Milit Assistance	400UNTS21	105745
Portugal	USA (United States)	26 Sep 60	Milit Assistance	393UNTS257	105660
Canada	Italy	18 Dec 61	Specific Resources	470UNTS153	106807
Bolivia	USA (United States)	26 Apr 62	Milit Assistance	461UNTS105	106654
Panama	USA (United States)	23 May 62	Milit Assistance	458UNTS225	106604
Germany, West	USA (United States)	25 May 62	Milit Assistance	458UNTS259	106608
Dahomey	USA (United States)	13 Jun 62	Milit Assistance	458UNTS219	106603
Niger	USA (United States)	14 Jun 62	Milit Assistance	458UNTS233	106605
Senegal	USA (United States)	20 Jul 62	Milit Assistance	458UNTS137	106596
Honduras	USA (United States)	24 Oct 62	Milit Assistance	459UNTS211	106624
India	UK Great Britain	27 Nov 62	Milit Installation	466UNTS189	106744
Peru	USA (United States)	20 Dec 62	Milit Installation	471UNTS75	106822
UK Great Britain	USA (United States)	06 Apr 63	Milit Installation	474UNTS49	106871
Japan	USA (United States)	26 Apr 63	Milit Installation	477UNTS37	106914
Jamaica	USA (United States)	06 Jun 63	Milit Assistance	477UNTS29	106913
Netherlands	USA (United States)	26 Nov 63	Milit Assistance	388UNTS303	105586
Astronomy					
Multilateral		05 Oct 62	IGO Establishment	502UNTS225	107333
Atomic Energy					
Multilateral		15 Nov 45	Atomic Energy	3UNTS123	100026
Multilateral		26 Dec 45	Peace/Disarmament	20UNTS259	100319
Belgium	Canada	30 Mar 53	Status of Forces	181UNTS95	102401
Turkey	USA (United States)	10 Jun 55	Atomic Energy	238UNTS149	103359
Canada	USA (United States)	15 Jun 55	Atomic Energy	235UNTS176	103301
Belgium	USA (United States)	15 Jun 55	Atomic Energy	235UNTS133	103299
UK Great Britain	USA (United States)	15 Jun 55	Atomic Energy	229UNTS73	103161
Multilateral		22 Jun 55	Atomic Energy	249UNTS3	103498
Israel	USA (United States)	12 Jul 55	Atomic Energy	219UNTS185	102974
Switzerland	USA (United States)	18 Jul 55	Atomic Energy	239UNTS311	103388
Lebanon	USA (United States)	18 Jul 55	Atomic Energy	239UNTS247	103383
Netherlands	USA (United States)	18 Jul 55	Atomic Energy	240UNTS347	103412
Taiwan	USA (United States)	18 Jul 55	Atomic Energy	235UNTS221	103304
Spain	USA (United States)	19 Jul 55	Atomic Energy	239UNTS299	103387
Colombia	USA (United States)	19 Jul 55	Atomic Energy	235UNTS233	103305
Portugal	USA (United States)	21 Jul 55	Atomic Energy	239UNTS283	103386
USA (United States)	Venezuela	21 Jul 55	Atomic Energy	238UNTS121	103357
Denmark	USA (United States)	25 Jul 55	Atomic Energy	235UNTS245	103306
Philippines	USA (United States)	27 Jul 55	Atomic Energy	239UNTS271	103385
Italy	USA (United States)	28 Jul 55	Atomic Energy	239UNTS235	103382
Argentina	USA (United States)	29 Jul 55	Atomic Energy	235UNTS121	103298
Brazil	USA (United States)	03 Aug 55	Atomic Energy	235UNTS159	103300
Greece	USA (United States)	04 Aug 55	Atomic Energy	235UNTS257	103307
Chile	USA (United States)	08 Aug 55	Atomic Energy	235UNTS209	103303
Pakistan	USA (United States)	11 Aug 55	Atomic Energy	239UNTS259	103384
Belgium	UK Great Britain	18 Nov 55	Atomic Energy	222UNTS327	103038
USA (United States)	Uruguay	13 Jan 56	Atomic Energy	240UNTS401	103415
Sweden	USA (United States)	18 Jan 56	Atomic Energy	240UNTS413	103416
Netherlands	USA (United States)	22 Jan 56	Atomic Energy	287UNTS121	104181
Peru	USA (United States)	25 Jan 56	Atomic Energy	240UNTS425	103417
Korea, South	USA (United States)	03 Feb 56	Atomic Energy	240UNTS129	103401
Germany, West	USA (United States)	13 Feb 56	Atomic Energy	253UNTS119	103580
Thailand	USA (United States)	13 Mar 56	Atomic Energy	253UNTS105	103579
Ireland	USA (United States)	16 Mar 56	Atomic Energy	317UNTS195	104604
Costa Rica	USA (United States)	18 May 56	Atomic Energy	404UNTS237	105814
Austria	USA (United States)	08 Jun 56	Atomic Energy	253UNTS139	103581
New Zealand	USA (United States)	13 Jun 56	Atomic Energy	253UNTS155	103582
Dominican Republic	USA (United States)	15 Jun 56	Atomic Energy	265UNTS227	103815
France	USA (United States)	19 Jun 56	Atomic Energy	281UNTS341	104087

PARTY ONE	PARTY TWO	DATE	TOPIC	CITATION	NUMBER
Atomic Energy (Cont.)					
Switzerland	USA (United States)	21 Jun 56	Atomic Energy	279UNTS41	104033
Australia	USA (United States)	22 Jun 56	Atomic Energy	283UNTS275	104123
Cuba	USA (United States)	26 Jun 56	Atomic Energy	293UNTS257	104294
Germany, West	UK Great Britain	31 Jul 56	Atomic Energy	252UNTS93	103559
Guatemala	USA (United States)	15 Aug 56	Atomic Energy	288UNTS181	104205
Multilateral		26 Oct 56	IGO Establishment	276UNTS3	103988
Netherlands	USA (United States)	15 Feb 57	Atomic Energy	287UNTS239	104190
Norway	USA (United States)	25 Feb 57	Atomic Energy	284UNTS19	104126
Iran	USA (United States)	05 Mar 57	Atomic Energy	342UNTS29	104898
Multilateral		25 Mar 57	IGO Status/Immunit	294UNTS411	104302
Multilateral		25 Mar 57	IGO Establishment	294UNTS259	104301
Multilateral		25 Mar 57	IGO Establishment	294UNTS2	104300
Ecuador	USA (United States)	31 May 57	Atomic Energy	304UNTS61	104391
Nicaragua	USA (United States)	11 Jun 57	Atomic Energy	304UNTS267	104402
Germany, West	USA (United States)	28 Jun 57	Atomic Energy	288UNTS339	104213
Italy	USA (United States)	03 Jul 57	Atomic Energy	308UNTS195	104462
Germany, West	USA (United States)	03 Jul 57	Atomic Energy	288UNTS305	104212
South Africa	USA (United States)	08 Jul 57	Atomic Energy	290UNTS147	104234
Norway	UK Great Britain	12 Jul 57	Atomic Energy	310UNTS41	104485
Spain	USA (United States)	16 Aug 57	Atomic Energy	307UNTS169	104449
Sweden	UK Great Britain	20 Sep 57	Atomic Energy	310UNTS49	104486
Cambodia	USA (United States)	17 Oct 57	Scientific Project	299UNTS203	104313
Austria	IAEA (Atom Energy)	11 Dec 57	Atomic Energy	339UNTS110	104849
Italy	UK Great Britain	28 Dec 57	Atomic Energy	305UNTS357	104425
Euratom	USA (United States)	29 May 58	Atomic Energy	335UNTS161	104783
Japan	UK Great Britain	16 Jun 58	Atomic Energy	325UNTS185	104700
Japan	USA (United States)	19 Jun 58	Atomic Energy	325UNTS143	104699
UK Great Britain	USA (United States)	03 Jul 58	Atomic Energy	326UNTS3	104707
Portugal	UK Great Britain	18 Jul 58	Atomic Energy	313UNTS109	104532
USA (United States)	Venezuela	08 Oct 58	Atomic Energy	371UNTS69	105271
Euratom	USA (United States)	08 Nov 58	Atomic Energy	338UNTS135	104835
Euratom	UK Great Britain	04 Feb 59	Atomic Energy	331UNTS125	104752
USA (United States)	Vietnam, South	22 Apr 59	Atomic Energy	347UNTS113	104993
Germany, West	USA (United States)	05 May 59	Atomic Energy	355UNTS307	105083
Turkey	USA (United States)	05 May 59	Milit Assistance	355UNTS341	105085
Greece	USA (United States)	06 May 59	Milit Assistance	357UNTS163	105115
Netherlands	USA (United States)	06 May 59	Milit Installation	355UNTS327	105084
France	USA (United States)	07 May 59	Milit Assistance	354UNTS83	105055
IAEA (Atom Energy)	USSR (Soviet Union)	11 May 59	Atomic Energy	339UNTS341	104853
IAEA (Atom Energy)	USA (United States)	11 May 59	Atomic Energy	339UNTS359	104855
IAEA (Atom Energy)	UK Great Britain	11 May 59	Atomic Energy	339UNTS351	104854
Canada	Pakistan	14 May 59	Atomic Energy	426UNTS129	106133
Canada	USA (United States)	22 May 59	Milit Assistance	354UNTS63	105054
Canada	Japan	02 Jul 59	Atomic Energy	383UNTS243	105504
Austria	USA (United States)	22 Jul 59	Atomic Energy	368UNTS199	105242
Australia	Canada	04 Aug 59	Atomic Energy	391UNTS191	105623
Italy	IBRD (World Bank)	16 Sep 59	IBRD Project	375UNTS159	105366
Canada	Euratom	06 Oct 59	Scientific Project	475UNTS187	106894
Spain	UK Great Britain	19 Jan 60	Atomic Energy	404UNTS41	105804
Denmark	UK Great Britain	20 May 60	Atomic Energy	374UNTS245	105338
Indonesia	USA (United States)	08 Jun 60	Atomic Energy	388UNTS287	105585
Belgium	Burma	17 Aug 60	Air Transport	540UNTS185	107850
IBRD (World Bank)	Thailand	28 Apr 61	IBRD Project	415UNTS121	105983
France	USA (United States)	27 Jul 61	Milit Assistance	433UNTS29	106229
IAEA (Atom Energy)	UN Special Fund	29 Nov 61	IGO Operations	415UNTS408	200593
IAEA (Atom Energy)	USA (United States)	30 Mar 62	Specific Property	442UNTS49	106338
Colombia	USA (United States)	09 Apr 62	Scientific Project	476UNTS9	106899
Belgium	USA (United States)	17 May 62	Milit Assistance	461UNTS3	106647
Argentina	USA (United States)	22 Jun 62	Atomic Energy	458UNTS97	106594
Australia	Japan	07 Aug 62	Atomic Energy	435UNTS261	106283
Canada	Sweden	11 Sep 62	Atomic Energy	529UNTS9	107651
Multilateral		14 Sep 62	IGO Status/Immunit	494UNTS219	107236
Israel	Philippines	10 Jan 63	Atomic Energy	588UNTS205	108526
India	USA (United States)	01 Feb 63	Scientific Project	473UNTS37	106852
Multilateral		05 Aug 63	Sanitation	480UNTS43	106964

PARTY ONE	PARTY TWO	DATE	TOPIC	CITATION	NUMBER
Atomic Energy (Cont.)					
India	USA (United States)	08 Aug 63	Scientific Project	488UNTS21	107117
Multilateral		23 Sep 63	Atomic Energy	488UNTS99	107122
Canada	India	16 Dec 63	Atomic Energy	529UNTS45	107655
Multilateral		15 Jun 64	Atomic Energy	573UNTS85	108324
IAEA (Atom Energy)	USA (United States)	15 Jun 64	Atomic Energy	525UNTS3	107580
Multilateral		18 Jun 64	Atomic Energy	542UNTS145	107886
Multilateral		28 Jul 64	IGO Operations	555UNTS183	108113
Switzerland	UK Great Britain	11 Aug 64	Atomic Energy	552UNTS271	108059
IAEA (Atom Energy)	United Arab Rep	17 Sep 64	Atomic Energy	525UNTS19	107581
Multilateral		18 Sep 64	IGO Operations	556UNTS25	108117
Multilateral		18 Sep 64	IGO Operations	555UNTS205	108114
Multilateral		21 Sep 64	IGO Operations	555UNTS227	108115
Multilateral		30 Sep 64	IGO Operations	556UNTS3	108116
Pakistan	UK Great Britain	13 Oct 64	Atomic Energy	534UNTS71	107754
USA (United States)	USSR (Soviet Union)	18 Nov 64	Atomic Energy	535UNTS307	107786
Multilateral		02 Dec 64	Scientific Project	572UNTS229	108317
Argentina	IAEA (Atom Energy)	02 Dec 64	Atomic Energy	525UNTS29	107582
Multilateral		02 Dec 64	Atomic Energy	525UNTS51	107583
Switzerland	USA (United States)	30 Jan 65	Atomic Energy	594UNTS55	108594
Multilateral		24 Feb 65	IGO Operations	556UNTS47	108118
Multilateral		26 Feb 65	IGO Operations	556UNTS69	108119
Multilateral		18 Jun 65	Atomic Energy	573UNTS3	108320
Multilateral		23 Jun 65	Atomic Energy	548UNTS241	107981
Canada	USA (United States)	29 Jun 65	Scientific Project	549UNTS273	108003
Multilateral		24 Sep 65	Atomic Energy	556UNTS141	108124
IAEA (Atom Energy)	Uruguay	24 Sep 65	Atomic Energy	556UNTS117	108123
Afghanistan	IAEA (Atom Energy)	24 Sep 65	Atomic Energy	556UNTS101	108121
Morocco	IAEA (Atom Energy)	24 Sep 65	Atomic Energy	556UNTS109	108122
IAEA (Atom Energy)	Turkey	08 Feb 66	Atomic Energy	573UNTS75	108323
Pakistan	IAEA (Atom Energy)	15 Mar 66	Claims and Debts	588UNTS261	108530
UK Great Britain	USA (United States)	02 Jun 66	Atomic Energy	573UNTS229	108336
IAEA (Atom Energy)	UK Great Britain	20 Jun 66	IGO Operations	588UNTS269	108531
Multilateral		20 Jun 66	Scientific Project	572UNTS263	108318
Mexico	IAEA (Atom Energy)	20 Jun 66	Atomic Energy	573UNTS25	108321
Belgium	France	23 Sep 66	Atomic Energy	588UNTS227	108528
IAEA (Atom Energy)	USA (United States)	26 Sep 66	Atomic Energy	589UNTS3	108532
Multilateral		28 Sep 66	Specif Goods/Equip	589UNTS41	108534
Philippines	IAEA (Atom Energy)	28 Sep 66	Atomic Energy	589UNTS25	108533
IAEA (Atom Energy)	USA (United States)	09 Dec 66	Atomic Energy	589UNTS55	108535
Israel	Philippines	20 Feb 67	Atomic Energy	597UNTS139	108642
Malaysia	IBRD (World Bank)	09 Jan 69	IBRD Project	0UNTS0	109594
Automobile Driver's License					
Germany, West	Sweden	05 Aug 55	Land Transport	262UNTS265	103754
Finland	Sweden	15 Sep 56	Admin Cooperation	254UNTS31	103591
Multilateral		15 Sep 56	Admin Cooperation	254UNTS45	103592
Denmark	Norway	15 Sep 56	General Transport	259UNTS3	103680
Finland	Norway	15 Sep 56	Admin Cooperation	254UNTS17	103590
Denmark	Sweden	15 Sep 56	General Transport	263UNTS3	103764
Norway	Sweden	15 Sep 56	Admin Cooperation	263UNTS17	103765
Denmark	Finland	15 Sep 56	General Transport	254UNTS3	103589
Germany, West	Sweden	13 Feb 57	Admin Cooperation	428UNTS149	106174
Luxembourg	Sweden	06 Apr 57	Admin Cooperation	427UNTS173	106152
Austria	Sweden	10 Apr 57	Admin Cooperation	427UNTS343	106165
France	Sweden	10 May 57	Admin Cooperation	427UNTS127	106149
Netherlands	Sweden	21 May 57	Land Transport	286UNTS237	104169
Luxembourg	Sweden	12 Mar 58	Admin Cooperation	427UNTS179	106153
Italy	Sweden	14 Apr 58	Admin Cooperation	427UNTS167	106151
Sweden	Switzerland	30 Apr 58	Land Transport	427UNTS295	106161
Aviation					
Brazil	France	27 Jan 40	Air Transport	72UNTS77	100929
UK Great Britain	USSR (Soviet Union)	22 Jun 42	Finance	91UNTS355	200270
Canada	USA (United States)	04 Mar 43	Air Transport	13UNTS411	200087
Paraguay	USA (United States)	27 Oct 43	Military Mission	29UNTS391	200174
Australia	New Zealand	21 Jan 44	General Amity	18UNTS357	200113

PARTY ONE	PARTY TWO	DATE	TOPIC	CITATION	NUMBER
Aviation (Cont.)					
Spain	USA (United States)	02 Dec 44	Air Transport	89UNTS345	200262
Multilateral		07 Dec 44	Air Transport	171UNTS387	200502
Multilateral		07 Dec 44	Air Transport	171UNTS345	200501
Multilateral		07 Dec 44	IGO Establishment	15UNTS295	200102
Multilateral		07 Dec 44	Air Transport	84UNTS389	200252
Multilateral		15 Dec 44	Sanitation	16UNTS247	200106
Denmark	USA (United States)	16 Dec 44	Air Transport	10UNTS213	200063
Sweden	USA (United States)	16 Dec 44	Air Transport	6UNTS397	200041
Iceland	USA (United States)	27 Jan 45	Air Transport	122UNTS293	200411
Ireland	USA (United States)	03 Feb 45	Air Transport	122UNTS305	200412
Canada	USA (United States)	17 Feb 45	Air Transport	122UNTS261	200409
Iceland	USA (United States)	11 Apr 45	Air Transport	16UNTS241	200105
Switzerland	USA (United States)	03 Aug 45	Air Transport	51UNTS233	200191
Norway	USA (United States)	06 Oct 45	Air Transport	122UNTS319	200413
South Africa	UK Great Britain	26 Oct 45	Air Transport	72UNTS41	100927
France	UK Great Britain	04 Dec 45	Milit Installation	9UNTS121	100129
Sweden	USA (United States)	04 Dec 45	Air Transport	6UNTS273	100080
Portugal	UK Great Britain	06 Dec 45	Air Transport	6UNTS3	100065
Portugal	UK Great Britain	06 Dec 45	Air Transport	5UNTS37	100064
Portugal	USA (United States)	06 Dec 45	Air Transport	3UNTS139	100028
Canada	UK Great Britain	21 Dec 45	Air Transport	27UNTS155	100405
France	USA (United States)	29 Dec 45	Air Transport	139UNTS105	101878
Multilateral		01 Jan 46	Peace/Disarmament	99UNTS131	101375
Czechoslovakia	USA (United States)	03 Jan 46	Air Transport	6UNTS309	100084
Denmark	France	04 Jan 46	Air Transport	27UNTS169	100406
Spain	USA (United States)	15 Jan 46	Air Transport	89UNTS241	101221
Czechoslovakia	Poland	24 Jan 46	Air Transport	25UNTS181	100363
UK Great Britain	USA (United States)	11 Feb 46	Air Transport	3UNTS253	100036
Turkey	USA (United States)	12 Feb 46	Air Transport	13UNTS3	100196
Turkey	UK Great Britain	12 Feb 46	Air Transport	6UNTS79	100069
France	UK Great Britain	28 Feb 46	Air Transport	27UNTS173	100407
Denmark	USA (United States)	21 Mar 46	Air Transport	3UNTS301	100038
France	USA (United States)	27 Mar 46	Air Transport	139UNTS114	101879
Greece	USA (United States)	27 Mar 46	Air Transport	15UNTS233	100239
Multilateral		31 Mar 46	Milit Installation	17UNTS159	100274
Ireland	UK Great Britain	05 Apr 46	Air Transport	72UNTS57	100928
Belgium	USA (United States)	05 Apr 46	Air Transport	4UNTS125	100041
Netherlands	Portugal	12 Apr 46	Air Transport	4UNTS317	100054
Argentina	UK Great Britain	17 Apr 46	Air Transport	164UNTS53	102159
Multilateral		23 Apr 46	Sanitation	16UNTS179	100257
France	Portugal	30 Apr 46	Air Transport	35UNTS197	100556
France	Ireland	16 May 46	Air Transport	44UNTS105	100681
France	USA (United States)	28 May 46	Milit Assistance	84UNTS79	101120
Ireland	Sweden	29 May 46	Air Transport	35UNTS231	100557
Portugal	USA (United States)	30 May 46	Air Transport	174UNTS187	102285
Australia	Canada	11 Jun 46	Air Transport	10UNTS47	100142
United Arab Rep	USA (United States)	15 Jun 46	Air Transport	151UNTS135	101988
United Arab Rep	USA (United States)	15 Jun 46	Air Transport	71UNTS157	100917
France	USA (United States)	18 Jun 46	Air Transport	42UNTS183	100647
Sweden	Turkey	26 Jun 46	Air Transport	14UNTS21	100208
Iceland	UK Great Britain	04 Jul 46	Specific Property	6UNTS223	100077
Albania	Yugoslavia	11 Jul 46	Air Transport	4UNTS407	100058
Netherlands	Spain	13 Jul 46	Air Transport	4UNTS351	100055
Czechoslovakia	USSR (Soviet Union)	25 Jul 46	Air Transport	27UNTS231	100409
Canada	Newfoundland	29 Jul 46	Air Transport	17UNTS169	100275
UK Great Britain	USA (United States)	31 Jul 46	Air Transport	42UNTS199	100648
France	Sweden	02 Aug 46	Air Transport	27UNTS251	100410
Lebanon	USA (United States)	11 Aug 46	Air Transport	66UNTS211	100856
Netherlands	UK Great Britain	13 Aug 46	Air Transport	4UNTS367	100056
Denmark	UK Great Britain	16 Aug 46	Milit Installation	9UNTS163	100130
Norway	UK Great Britain	31 Aug 46	Air Transport	6UNTS235	100078
Brazil	USA (United States)	06 Sep 46	Air Transport	54UNTS197	100805
Norway	UK Great Britain	27 Sep 46	Milit Installation	6UNTS259	100079
Sweden	USA (United States)	30 Sep 46	Air Transport	42UNTS213	100649
Denmark	USA (United States)	01 Oct 46	Air Transport	42UNTS219	100650

PARTY ONE	PARTY TWO	DATE	TOPIC	CITATION	NUMBER
Aviation (Cont.)					
Iceland	USA (United States)	07 Oct 46	Milit Installation	12UNTS163	100184
France	Turkey	12 Oct 46	Air Transport	14UNTS33	100209
Belgium	Portugal	22 Oct 46	Air Transport	34UNTS49	100527
Brazil	UK Great Britain	31 Oct 46	Air Transport	11UNTS115	100152
Norway	USA (United States)	12 Nov 46	Air Transport	42UNTS227	100651
India	USA (United States)	14 Nov 46	Air Transport	22UNTS55	100331
Philippines	USA (United States)	16 Nov 46	Air Transport	7UNTS151	100097
Sweden	UK Great Britain	27 Nov 46	Air Transport	11UNTS229	100162
Australia	USA (United States)	03 Dec 46	Air Transport	7UNTS201	100100
New Zealand	USA (United States)	03 Dec 46	Air Transport	7UNTS175	100099
Netherlands	UK Great Britain	04 Dec 46	Milit Installation	12UNTS241	100187
Portugal	Switzerland	09 Dec 46	Air Transport	310UNTS251	104495
Brazil	Portugal	10 Dec 46	Air Transport	200UNTS67	102695
USA (United States)	Uruguay	14 Dec 46	Air Transport	532UNTS87	107713
Taiwan	USA (United States)	20 Dec 46	Air Transport	22UNTS87	100332
Peru	USA (United States)	27 Dec 46	Air Transport	152UNTS93	102013
Peru	USA (United States)	27 Dec 46	Air Transport	26UNTS227	100390
Ecuador	USA (United States)	08 Jan 47	Air Transport	22UNTS119	100333
Belgium	UK Great Britain	16 Jan 47	Milit Installation	54UNTS97	100797
Czechoslovakia	Ireland	29 Jan 47	Air Transport	27UNTS267	100411
USSR (Soviet Union)	Yugoslavia	04 Feb 47	Air Transport	130UNTS235	101731
Czechoslovakia	UK Great Britain	19 Feb 47	Milit Installation	9UNTS173	100131
Greece	UK Great Britain	21 Feb 47	Air Transport	70UNTS215	100905
Thailand	USA (United States)	26 Feb 47	Air Transport	16UNTS17	100246
Paraguay	USA (United States)	28 Feb 47	Air Transport	44UNTS25	100676
Czechoslovakia	Turkey	05 Mar 47	Air Transport	14UNTS101	100214
Portugal	Sweden	06 Mar 47	Air Transport	35UNTS243	100558
Australia	USA (United States)	10 Mar 47	Air Transport	10UNTS89	100145
Netherlands	Turkey	19 Mar 47	Air Transport	14UNTS59	100211
Muscat and Oman	UK Great Britain	05 Apr 47	Air Transport	27UNTS287	100412
Greece	Sweden	08 Apr 47	Air Transport	94UNTS73	101307
Canada	USA (United States)	12 Apr 47	Air Transport	122UNTS229	101648
Greece	Netherlands	17 Apr 47	Air Transport	32UNTS115	100494
Canada	Portugal	25 Apr 47	Air Transport	94UNTS87	101308
Syria	USA (United States)	28 Apr 47	Air Transport	262UNTS121	103741
Switzerland	USA (United States)	30 Apr 47	Specif Goods/Equip	42UNTS235	100652
France	Greece	05 May 47	Air Transport	76UNTS61	100980
Chile	USA (United States)	10 May 47	Air Transport	55UNTS21	100807
Philippines	USA (United States)	12 May 47	Scientific Project	16UNTS137	100254
Czechoslovakia	Denmark	14 May 47	Air Transport	27UNTS297	100413
South Africa	USA (United States)	23 May 47	Air Transport	66UNTS233	100857
UK Great Britain	USA (United States)	23 May 47	Specific Property	11UNTS211	100159
Multilateral		27 May 47	Air Transport	418UNTS161	106021
India	Netherlands	31 May 47	Air Transport	17UNTS65	100268
Ireland	USA (United States)	03 Jun 47	Air Transport	16UNTS151	100255
Greece	UK Great Britain	05 Jun 47	Status of Forces	9UNTS197	100133
Italy	USA (United States)	09 Jun 47	Air Transport	104UNTS157	101437
France	UK Great Britain	18 Jun 47	Air Transport	9UNTS203	100134
Norway	Sweden	21 Jun 47	Taxation	94UNTS107	101309
Canada	Sweden	27 Jun 47	Air Transport	27UNTS313	100414
Romania	Yugoslavia	30 Jun 47	Air Transport	116UNTS57	101569
Iraq	Turkey	30 Jun 47	Air Transport	72UNTS107	100930
Denmark	Turkey	30 Jun 47	Air Transport	32UNTS301	100504
France	India	16 Jul 47	Air Transport	27UNTS325	100415
Netherlands	Thailand	18 Jul 47	Air Transport	28UNTS27	100417
Greece	Turkey	22 Jul 47	Air Transport	72UNTS131	100931
Netherlands	South Africa	22 Jul 47	Air Transport	12UNTS257	100188
Taiwan	UK Great Britain	23 Jul 47	Air Transport	9UNTS207	100135
Multilateral		04 Aug 47	Air Transport	28UNTS41	100418
Canada	Ireland	08 Aug 47	Air Transport	28UNTS47	100419
Poland	Romania	09 Aug 47	Air Transport	12UNTS363	100193
Hungary	Poland	28 Aug 47	Air Transport	15UNTS145	100231
Czechoslovakia	Netherlands	01 Sep 47	Air Transport	32UNTS129	100495
Czechoslovakia	Switzerland	10 Sep 47	Air Transport	35UNTS275	100559
Chile	UK Great Britain	16 Sep 47	Air Transport	133UNTS143	101786

Aviation (Cont.)

PARTY ONE	PARTY TWO	DATE	TOPIC	CITATION	NUMBER
Lebanon	Turkey	16 Sep 47	Air Transport	44UNTS123	100682
ICAO (Civil Aviat)	United Nations	01 Oct 47	IGO Operations	8UNTS315	200045
Sweden	Yugoslavia	06 Oct 47	Air Transport	53UNTS107	100775
Austria	USA (United States)	08 Oct 47	Air Transport	25UNTS3	100354
UK Great Britain	USA (United States)	13 Oct 47	Air Transport	66UNTS269	100858
Czechoslovakia	Sweden	15 Oct 47	Air Transport	44UNTS149	100683
Colombia	UK Great Britain	16 Oct 47	Air Transport	160UNTS297	102115
Brazil	Netherlands	06 Nov 47	Air Transport	53UNTS59	100773
Norway	Portugal	11 Nov 47	Air Transport	34UNTS257	100542
Brazil	Sweden	14 Nov 47	Air Transport	94UNTS139	101310
Denmark	Greece	14 Nov 47	Air Transport	35UNTS295	100560
Brazil	Norway	14 Nov 47	Air Transport	44UNTS163	100684
Brazil	Denmark	14 Nov 47	Air Transport	47UNTS39	100722
Denmark	Ireland	18 Nov 47	Air Transport	35UNTS309	100561
Ireland	Italy	21 Nov 47	Air Transport	353UNTS73	105038
Taiwan	Netherlands	06 Dec 47	Air Transport	43UNTS185	100669
Denmark	Portugal	15 Dec 47	Air Transport	35UNTS329	100563
Peru	UK Great Britain	22 Dec 47	Air Transport	72UNTS143	100932
Ethiopia	Pakistan	01 Jan 48	Air Transport	35UNTS3	100547
Philippines	UK Great Britain	07 Jan 48	Air Transport	28UNTS63	100420
Austria	Netherlands	22 Jan 48	Air Transport	17UNTS99	100270
Italy	USA (United States)	06 Feb 48	Air Transport	73UNTS113	100950
UK Great Britain	USA (United States)	24 Feb 48	Milit Installation	73UNTS143	100951
Denmark	UK Great Britain	04 Mar 48	Milit Assistance	77UNTS57	100992
Czechoslovakia	Yugoslavia	14 Mar 48	Air Transport	28UNTS81	100421
Argentina	Denmark	18 Mar 48	Air Transport	94UNTS175	101311
Cuba	UK Great Britain	19 Mar 48	Air Transport	175UNTS23	102294
France	UK Great Britain	19 Apr 48	Status of Forces	83UNTS201	101109
Ireland	Switzerland	06 May 48	Air Transport	334UNTS187	104768
Pakistan	Sweden	06 May 48	Air Transport	36UNTS3	100564
Jordan	Turkey	07 May 48	Air Transport	32UNTS313	100505
Ireland	Netherlands	10 May 48	Air Transport	28UNTS121	100422
Norway	Turkey	20 May 48	Air Transport	26UNTS137	100384
India	Sweden	21 May 48	Air Transport	34UNTS285	100543
Portugal	UK Great Britain	25 May 48	Milit Installation	34UNTS311	100544
Greece	Switzerland	26 May 48	Air Transport	94UNTS217	101312
Luxembourg	UK Great Britain	27 May 48	Air Transport	53UNTS115	100776
Canada	Netherlands	02 Jun 48	Air Transport	32UNTS215	100499
Pakistan	USA (United States)	16 Jun 48	Air Transport	235UNTS29	103293
Multilateral		19 Jun 48	Air Transport	310UNTS151	104492
Ireland	Norway	21 Jun 48	Air Transport	34UNTS317	100545
Luxembourg	Netherlands	23 Jun 48	Air Transport	32UNTS229	100500
India	Pakistan	23 Jun 48	Air Transport	28UNTS143	100423
Italy	UK Great Britain	25 Jun 48	Air Transport	94UNTS239	101313
Australia	Italy	02 Aug 48	Air Transport	28UNTS165	100424
Brazil	Switzerland	10 Aug 48	Air Transport	94UNTS269	101314
France	Spain	23 Aug 48	Air Transport	28UNTS173	100425
Belgium	Switzerland	01 Sep 48	Visas	23UNTS139	100344
Greece	Lebanon	06 Sep 48	Air Transport	178UNTS37	102335
Iceland	ICAO (Civil Aviat)	16 Sep 48	Air Transport	28UNTS267	100429
Bolivia	USA (United States)	29 Sep 48	Air Transport	505UNTS139	107370
Netherlands	Spain	08 Oct 48	Air Transport	28UNTS209	100426
Netherlands	UK Great Britain	15 Oct 48	Taxation	74UNTS3	100955
France	USA (United States)	19 Oct 48	Air Transport	98UNTS3	101355
Mexico	Portugal	22 Oct 48	Air Transport	34UNTS329	100546
Belgium	France	28 Oct 48	Visas	25UNTS151	100360
Argentina	Netherlands	29 Oct 48	Air Transport	95UNTS21	101316
Argentina	Denmark	15 Dec 48	Taxation	67UNTS71	100866
Belgium	Sweden	16 Dec 48	Visas	26UNTS3	100372
Ceylon (Sri Lanka)	India	21 Dec 48	Air Transport	28UNTS223	100427
Belgium	Italy	01 Jan 49	Visas	26UNTS151	100385
Ceylon (Sri Lanka)	Pakistan	03 Jan 49	Air Transport	28UNTS247	100428
Argentina	Netherlands	15 Jan 49	Taxation	46UNTS241	100713
Italy	Lebanon	24 Jan 49	Air Transport	231UNTS241	103223
Canada	USA (United States)	31 Jan 49	Humanitarian	43UNTS119	100666

Aviation (Cont.)

PARTY ONE	PARTY TWO	DATE	TOPIC	CITATION	NUMBER
Switzerland	Turkey	16 Feb 49	Air Transport	72UNTS175	100933
Belgium	Sweden	21 Feb 49	Air Transport	95UNTS73	101317
Finland	Netherlands	25 Feb 49	Air Transport	53UNTS123	100777
Netherlands	Switzerland	07 Mar 49	Air Transport	35UNTS69	100551
Argentina	UK Great Britain	14 Mar 49	Taxation	83UNTS193	101108
Finland	USA (United States)	29 Mar 49	Air Transport	55UNTS59	100808
Panama	USA (United States)	31 Mar 49	Air Transport	55UNTS141	100812
Panama	USA (United States)	31 Mar 49	Air Transport	55UNTS87	100810
Finland	Sweden	26 Apr 49	Air Transport	95UNTS83	101318
Switzerland	USA (United States)	13 May 49	Air Transport	51UNTS129	100761
Bulgaria	Poland	16 May 49	Air Transport	84UNTS313	101140
Italy	Spain	31 May 49	Air Transport	231UNTS251	103224
Belgium	Denmark	31 May 49	Visas	32UNTS337	100506
Australia	Pakistan	03 Jun 49	Air Transport	35UNTS23	100549
Canada	USA (United States)	04 Jun 49	Air Transport	200UNTS201	102704
Canada	USA (United States)	04 Jun 49	Air Transport	122UNTS237	101649
Ethiopia	India	07 Jun 49	Air Transport	35UNTS13	100548
Peru	USA (United States)	20 Jun 49	Military Mission	92UNTS249	101276
Belgium	Greece	21 Jun 49	Air Transport	137UNTS215	101854
Norway	Pakistan	23 Jun 49	Air Transport	35UNTS49	100550
India	Switzerland	24 Jun 49	Air Transport	95UNTS109	101319
Korea, South	USA (United States)	29 Jun 49	Air Transport	55UNTS79	100809
Greece	Syria	05 Jul 49	Air Transport	78UNTS71	101013
Mexico	USA (United States)	05 Jul 49	Military Mission	68UNTS55	100884
Australia	India	11 Jul 49	Air Transport	35UNTS83	100552
Czechoslovakia	Finland	13 Jul 49	Air Transport	53UNTS153	100779
Pakistan	Philippines	16 Jul 49	Air Transport	35UNTS111	100553
Dominican Republic	USA (United States)	19 Jul 49	Air Transport	51UNTS145	100762
Pakistan	UK Great Britain	27 Jul 49	Air Transport	44UNTS199	100685
Ceylon (Sri Lanka)	UK Great Britain	05 Aug 49	Air Transport	35UNTS137	100554
Multilateral		12 Aug 49	Humanitarian	75UNTS85	100971
Italy	Netherlands	16 Aug 49	Admin Cooperation	98UNTS21	101357
Canada	UK Great Britain	19 Aug 49	Air Transport	44UNTS223	100686
Finland	Norway	24 Aug 49	Air Transport	53UNTS167	100780
Denmark	Finland	26 Aug 49	Air Transport	53UNTS191	100781
Belgium	Canada	30 Aug 49	Air Transport	53UNTS221	100782
USSR (Soviet Union)	Yugoslavia	31 Aug 49	Admin Cooperation	116UNTS345	101580
Denmark	ICAO (Civil Aviat)	09 Sep 49	Air Transport	53UNTS341	100791
Multilateral		15 Sep 49	Air Transport	53UNTS235	100783
Belgium	United Arab Rep	19 Sep 49	Air Transport	137UNTS189	101853
UK Great Britain	USA (United States)	19 Sep 49	Milit Installation	68UNTS31	100882
Lebanon	Netherlands	20 Sep 49	Air Transport	108UNTS205	101474
Burma	USA (United States)	28 Sep 49	Air Transport	55UNTS3	100806
Greece	Philippines	08 Oct 49	Air Transport	187UNTS221	102515
India	Philippines	20 Oct 49	Air Transport	72UNTS191	100934
Multilateral		27 Oct 49	Air Transport	53UNTS241	100784
Iran	Netherlands	31 Oct 49	Air Transport	254UNTS257	103596
Denmark	Pakistan	09 Nov 49	Air Transport	44UNTS255	100687
Belgium	Czechoslovakia	14 Nov 49	Visas	46UNTS319	100718
France	New Zealand	15 Nov 49	Air Transport	53UNTS247	100785
Sweden	Thailand	23 Nov 49	Air Transport	72UNTS217	100935
Denmark	Thailand	23 Nov 49	Air Transport	53UNTS255	100786
Italy	Turkey	25 Nov 49	Air Transport	192UNTS39	102594
Norway	Thailand	26 Nov 49	Air Transport	53UNTS269	100787
Brazil	Spain	28 Nov 49	Air Transport	215UNTS303	102923
Austria	Sweden	02 Dec 49	Air Transport	108UNTS3	101465
Austria	Denmark	02 Dec 49	Air Transport	53UNTS281	100788
Netherlands	United Arab Rep	08 Dec 49	Air Transport	95UNTS123	101320
Sweden	United Arab Rep	12 Dec 49	Air Transport	108UNTS15	101466
Canada	Denmark	13 Dec 49	Air Transport	72UNTS247	100937
Austria	Switzerland	19 Dec 49	Air Transport	254UNTS287	103597
Guatemala	USA (United States)	20 Dec 49	Status of Forces	70UNTS71	100897
USA (United States)	Yugoslavia	24 Dec 49	Air Transport	89UNTS209	101219
Australia	Ceylon (Sri Lanka)	12 Jan 50	Air Transport	53UNTS295	100789
Netherlands	Syria	13 Feb 50	Air Transport	108UNTS53	101467

PARTY ONE	PARTY TWO	DATE	TOPIC	CITATION	NUMBER
Aviation (Cont.)					
Canada	Norway	14 Feb 50	Air Transport	53UNTS329	100790
Spain	Sweden	18 Feb 50	Air Transport	166UNTS15	102184
Switzerland	USA (United States)	24 Feb 50	Admin Cooperation	93UNTS3	101282
Ceylon (Sri Lanka)	Thailand	24 Feb 50	Air Transport	72UNTS261	100938
Italy	Netherlands	04 Mar 50	Air Transport	254UNTS305	103598
Norway	United Arab Rep	11 Mar 50	Air Transport	95UNTS157	101321
Denmark	United Arab Rep	14 Mar 50	Air Transport	95UNTS197	101322
Philippines	USA (United States)	16 Mar 50	Air Transport	89UNTS199	101218
Iceland	Netherlands	22 Mar 50	Air Transport	95UNTS237	101323
Denmark	Iceland	22 Mar 50	Air Transport	72UNTS273	100939
Italy	Portugal	05 Apr 50	Air Transport	254UNTS329	103599
Sweden	UK Great Britain	05 Apr 50	Air Transport	99UNTS107	101374
Turkey	United Arab Rep	12 Apr 50	Air Transport	128UNTS3	101711
Australia	Philippines	14 Apr 50	Air Transport	127UNTS281	101709
Greece	United Arab Rep	24 Apr 50	Air Transport	163UNTS229	102149
Australia	UK Great Britain	28 Apr 50	Air Transport	95UNTS249	101324
Switzerland	United Arab Rep	15 May 50	Air Transport	95UNTS255	101325
Iceland	UK Great Britain	26 May 50	Air Transport	95UNTS277	101326
Israel	USA (United States)	13 Jun 50	Air Transport	212UNTS93	102863
Netherlands	Spain	20 Jun 50	Air Transport	95UNTS303	101327
Iraq	Pakistan	20 Jun 50	Air Transport	77UNTS215	101001
Denmark	Switzerland	22 Jun 50	Air Transport	96UNTS3	101328
Burma	Ceylon (Sri Lanka)	29 Jun 50	Air Transport	73UNTS3	100940
Spain	UK Great Britain	20 Jul 50	Air Transport	398UNTS101	105719
Argentina	USA (United States)	20 Jul 50	Taxation	89UNTS63	101209
UK Great Britain	USA (United States)	21 Jul 50	Milit Installation	97UNTS193	101351
France	Pakistan	31 Jul 50	Air Transport	96UNTS23	101329
Canada	France	01 Aug 50	Air Transport	73UNTS21	100941
Spain	Switzerland	03 Aug 50	Air Transport	254UNTS365	103600
France	United Arab Rep	08 Aug 50	Air Transport	127UNTS293	101710
Dominican Republic	USA (United States)	11 Aug 50	Status of Forces	92UNTS329	101278
Canada	New Zealand	16 Aug 50	Air Transport	77UNTS239	101002
Burma	Sweden	14 Sep 50	Air Transport	96UNTS45	101330
Brazil	Turkey	21 Sep 50	Air Transport	150UNTS299	101981
Ceylon (Sri Lanka)	United Arab Rep	26 Sep 50	Air Transport	192UNTS53	102595
France	UK Great Britain	06 Oct 50	Air Transport	96UNTS63	101331
Sweden	Switzerland	18 Oct 50	Air Transport	166UNTS49	102185
Luxembourg	Portugal	21 Oct 50	Air Transport	108UNTS67	101468
Taiwan	Philippines	23 Oct 50	Air Transport	215UNTS159	102918
Israel	Netherlands	23 Oct 50	Air Transport	189UNTS89	102543
Thailand	UK Great Britain	10 Nov 50	Air Transport	96UNTS77	101332
Greece	UK Great Britain	16 Nov 50	Taxation	166UNTS281	102193
Denmark	South Africa	30 Nov 50	Taxation	84UNTS51	101118
Israel	UK Great Britain	06 Dec 50	Air Transport	151UNTS33	101983
France	Greece	09 Dec 50	Taxation	166UNTS315	102196
Ethiopia	ICAO (Civil Aviat)	02 Feb 51	Tech Assistance	96UNTS123	101333
Israel	Turkey	05 Feb 51	Air Transport	193UNTS3	102607
Israel	ICAO (Civil Aviat)	19 Feb 51	Tech Assistance	96UNTS141	101334
Israel	USA (United States)	28 Feb 51	Taxation	220UNTS79	102991
Colombia	Portugal	09 Mar 51	Air Transport	108UNTS87	101469
Greece	Yugoslavia	15 Mar 51	Air Transport	187UNTS237	102516
Luxembourg	Switzerland	09 Apr 51	Air Transport	254UNTS389	103601
Canada	ICAO (Civil Aviat)	14 Apr 51	IGO Status/Immunit	96UNTS155	101335
Iraq	UK Great Britain	19 Apr 51	Air Transport	108UNTS121	101470
ICAO (Civil Aviat)	Thailand	19 Apr 51	Tech Assistance	96UNTS181	101336
France	UK Great Britain	20 Apr 51	Air Transport	106UNTS81	101458
UK Great Britain	USA (United States)	25 Apr 51	Specific Property	99UNTS97	101373
Belgium	UK Great Britain	08 May 51	Air Transport	158UNTS451	102079
Netherlands	UK Great Britain	17 May 51	Air Transport	118UNTS103	101599
India	Netherlands	24 May 51	Air Transport	108UNTS151	101471
Greece	Norway	28 May 51	Air Transport	187UNTS141	102507
Israel	USA (United States)	01 Jun 51	Visas	212UNTS129	102864
Iceland	ICAO (Civil Aviat)	07 Jun 51	Tech Assistance	96UNTS193	101337
Denmark	Iran	18 Jun 51	Air Transport	255UNTS3	103602
Cuba	Portugal	26 Jun 51	Air Transport	192UNTS115	102598

PARTY ONE	PARTY TWO	DATE	TOPIC	CITATION	NUMBER
Aviation (Cont.)					
Iceland	Norway	14 Jul 51	Air Transport	163UNTS265	102150
Greece	Netherlands	26 Jul 51	Taxation	109UNTS103	101495
Burma	Denmark	30 Jul 51	Air Transport	108UNTS167	101472
Israel	Philippines	07 Aug 51	Air Transport	192UNTS81	102596
Lebanon	UK Great Britain	15 Aug 51	Air Transport	160UNTS327	102116
Burma	Netherlands	06 Sep 51	Air Transport	108UNTS187	101473
Costa Rica	USA (United States)	11 Sep 51	Air Transport	234UNTS255	103288
Panama	UK Great Britain	15 Sep 51	Air Transport	560UNTS143	108172
Australia	Netherlands	25 Sep 51	Air Transport	128UNTS63	101713
Taiwan	Thailand	29 Sep 51	Air Transport	215UNTS166	102919
Philippines	Spain	06 Oct 51	Air Transport	215UNTS193	102920
Greece	Luxembourg	22 Oct 51	Air Transport	187UNTS119	102506
Italy	UK Great Britain	24 Oct 51	Air Transport	118UNTS143	101602
Denmark	Iraq	18 Nov 51	Air Transport	232UNTS25	103227
India	UK Great Britain	01 Dec 51	Air Transport	128UNTS39	101712
Colombia	Spain	11 Dec 51	Air Transport	216UNTS73	102933
Multilateral		20 Dec 51	Air Transport	163UNTS309	102152
Multilateral		20 Dec 51	Air Transport	163UNTS293	102151
Jordan	United Arab Rep	02 Jan 52	Air Transport	192UNTS157	102599
Costa Rica	USA (United States)	25 Feb 52	Status of Forces	174UNTS233	102288
Taiwan	Korea, South	01 Mar 52	Air Transport	255UNTS35	103603
Honduras	USA (United States)	07 Mar 52	Tech Assistance	233UNTS151	103260
Philippines	Switzerland	08 Mar 52	Air Transport	231UNTS301	103225
Belgium	Spain	10 Mar 52	Air Transport	178UNTS243	102342
Pakistan	Switzerland	17 Mar 52	Air Transport	192UNTS237	102603
Sweden	Uruguay	20 Mar 52	Air Transport	311UNTS3	104497
Norway	Uruguay	20 Mar 52	Air Transport	310UNTS279	104496
Netherlands	IBRD (World Bank)	20 Mar 52	IBRD Project	159UNTS207	102089
Iraq	Switzerland	31 Mar 52	Air Transport	311UNTS43	104498
Libya	UK Great Britain	31 Mar 52	Air Transport	151UNTS69	101984
France	Mexico	17 Apr 52	Air Transport	163UNTS321	102153
Belgium	Sweden	21 Apr 52	Air Transport	166UNTS9	102183
Denmark	Japan	28 Apr 52	Air Transport	166UNTS3	102182
France	Israel	29 Apr 52	Air Transport	189UNTS55	102542
Switzerland	UK Great Britain	13 May 52	Air Transport	164UNTS91	102160
Iceland	Sweden	03 Jun 52	Air Transport	215UNTS223	102921
India	United Arab Rep	14 Jun 52	Air Transport	173UNTS209	102268
Australia	United Arab Rep	14 Jun 52	Air Transport	173UNTS241	102269
Norway	UK Great Britain	23 Jun 52	Air Transport	151UNTS81	101985
Denmark	UK Great Britain	23 Jun 52	Air Transport	151UNTS3	101982
Greece	USA (United States)	25 Jun 52	Air Transport	181UNTS53	102398
Belgium	Israel	30 Jun 52	Air Transport	183UNTS263	102435
Mexico	USA (United States)	15 Jul 52	Air Transport	181UNTS263	102416
Netherlands	Pakistan	17 Jul 52	Air Transport	150UNTS277	101980
Panama	USA (United States)	08 Aug 52	Air Transport	181UNTS257	102415
Japan	USA (United States)	11 Aug 52	Air Transport	212UNTS27	102862
Burma	Philippines	15 Aug 52	Air Transport	200UNTS97	102696
Ethiopia	Pakistan	29 Aug 52	Air Transport	150UNTS257	101979
Netherlands	Peru	22 Sep 52	Air Transport	255UNTS49	103604
Multilateral		07 Oct 52	Admin Cooperation	310UNTS181	104493
Austria	Luxembourg	13 Oct 52	Air Transport	192UNTS291	102606
Mexico	Netherlands	13 Oct 52	Air Transport	163UNTS341	102154
Iceland	Luxembourg	23 Oct 52	Air Transport	193UNTS39	102609
Burma	UK Great Britain	25 Oct 52	Air Transport	150UNTS237	101978
Chile	Sweden	27 Oct 52	Air Transport	311UNTS63	104499
Chile	Denmark	27 Oct 52	Air Transport	271UNTS93	103911
Luxembourg	Norway	17 Nov 52	Air Transport	311UNTS95	104500
Luxembourg	Sweden	17 Nov 52	Air Transport	173UNTS277	102270
Israel	Switzerland	19 Nov 52	Air Transport	232UNTS3	103226
Japan	UK Great Britain	29 Dec 52	Air Transport	175UNTS129	102299
South Africa	Sweden	09 Jan 53	Air Transport	173UNTS299	102271
Netherlands	Philippines	05 Feb 53	Air Transport	216UNTS99	102934
Japan	Netherlands	17 Feb 53	Air Transport	192UNTS215	102602
Japan	Sweden	20 Feb 53	Air Transport	173UNTS307	102272
India	Pakistan	20 Feb 53	Air Transport	164UNTS3	102155

PARTY ONE	PARTY TWO	DATE	TOPIC	CITATION	NUMBER
Aviation (Cont.)					
Libya	UK Great Britain	21 Feb 53	Air Transport	311UNTS115	104501
Japan	Norway	23 Feb 53	Air Transport	192UNTS191	102601
Denmark	Japan	26 Feb 53	Air Transport	173UNTS329	102273
Lebanon	Sweden	23 Mar 53	Air Transport	255UNTS83	103605
Turkey	Yugoslavia	16 Apr 53	Air Transport	255UNTS99	103606
Philippines	Thailand	27 Apr 53	Air Transport	174UNTS3	102274
Denmark	South Africa	30 Apr 53	Air Transport	174UNTS19	102275
Israel	South Africa	05 May 53	Air Transport	192UNTS183	102600
Israel	UK Great Britain	13 May 53	Finance	175UNTS179	102300
Belgium	Germany, West	20 May 53	Admin Cooperation	180UNTS3	102370
Cuba	USA (United States)	26 May 53	Air Transport	224UNTS75	103070
Switzerland	Yugoslavia	28 May 53	Air Transport	232UNTS45	103228
Netherlands	USA (United States)	19 Jun 53	Admin Cooperation	212UNTS249	102875
Japan	Thailand	19 Jun 53	Air Transport	174UNTS29	102276
Burma	Norway	22 Jun 53	Air Transport	174UNTS49	102277
Canada	Mexico	27 Jul 53	Air Transport	192UNTS255	102604
Sweden	Switzerland	12 Aug 53	Customs	232UNTS59	103229
USA (United States)	Venezuela	14 Aug 53	Air Transport	213UNTS99	102883
Belgium	New Zealand	01 Sep 53	Air Transport	192UNTS283	102605
Ceylon (Sri Lanka)	Netherlands	14 Sep 53	Air Transport	193UNTS21	102608
Norway	South Africa	21 Sep 53	Air Transport	192UNTS105	102597
Australia	Thailand	26 Oct 53	Air Transport	255UNTS117	103607
Korea, South	Netherlands	26 Oct 53	Air Transport	200UNTS103	102697
Netherlands	Switzerland	03 Nov 53	Customs	293UNTS53	104285
Austria	Yugoslavia	11 Nov 53	Air Transport	363UNTS149	105206
Cuba	USA (United States)	26 Nov 53	Air Transport	205UNTS213	102777
Italy	Netherlands	21 Dec 53	Visas	189UNTS25	102540
Belgium	Lebanon	24 Dec 53	Air Transport	219UNTS153	102972
Ethiopia	Greece	20 Jan 54	Air Transport	222UNTS281	103035
Syria	UK Great Britain	30 Jan 54	Air Transport	449UNTS47	106452
France	Greece	08 Feb 54	Status of Forces	225UNTS121	103094
France	Greece	08 Feb 54	Status of Forces	225UNTS107	103093
Canada	Peru	18 Feb 54	Air Transport	411UNTS64	105915
Multilateral		25 Feb 54	Air Transport	215UNTS249	102922
Lebanon	Switzerland	03 Mar 54	Air Transport	255UNTS127	103608
Peru	Spain	31 Mar 54	Air Transport	232UNTS65	103230
France	South Africa	05 May 54	Air Transport	215UNTS401	102926
Switzerland	Syria	26 May 54	Air Transport	255UNTS145	103609
Iran	Switzerland	27 May 54	Air Transport	496UNTS273	107257
Multilateral		14 Jun 54	Air Transport	320UNTS209	104643
Multilateral		14 Jun 54	Air Transport	320UNTS217	104644
Belgium	Ireland	30 Jun 54	Air Transport	212UNTS255	102876
Laos	Thailand	07 Jul 54	Air Transport	200UNTS115	102698
Germany, West	USA (United States)	22 Jul 54	Taxation	221UNTS351	103016
Ireland	Luxembourg	27 Jul 54	Air Transport	232UNTS91	103231
Norway	USA (United States)	06 Aug 54	Air Transport	222UNTS269	103034
Denmark	USA (United States)	06 Aug 54	Air Transport	222UNTS235	103030
Norway	USA (United States)	06 Aug 54	Air Transport	222UNTS261	103033
Sweden	USA (United States)	06 Aug 54	Air Transport	221UNTS331	103014
Philippines	Sweden	20 Aug 54	Air Transport	200UNTS121	102699
South Africa	Switzerland	26 Aug 54	Air Transport	216UNTS19	102929
Belgium	South Africa	13 Sep 54	Air Transport	201UNTS15	102707
France	South Africa	17 Sep 54	Air Transport	216UNTS29	102930
Norway	Philippines	20 Oct 54	Air Transport	216UNTS11	102928
Denmark	Philippines	20 Oct 54	Air Transport	216UNTS3	102927
Netherlands	Venezuela	26 Oct 54	Air Transport	232UNTS103	103232
Sweden	UK Great Britain	29 Oct 54	Visas	209UNTS75	102823
Belgium	UK Great Britain	05 Nov 54	Visas	209UNTS69	102822
Pakistan	United Arab Rep	13 Dec 54	Air Transport	255UNTS167	103610
Ecuador	Netherlands	14 Dec 54	Air Transport	232UNTS115	103233
Denmark	USA (United States)	15 Dec 54	Air Transport	213UNTS273	102890
Sweden	USA (United States)	22 Dec 54	Air Transport	228UNTS85	103143
Norway	Switzerland	30 Dec 54	Air Transport	311UNTS147	104502
Austria	Belgium	07 Jan 55	Air Transport	380UNTS219	105458
Canada	Japan	12 Jan 55	Air Transport	311UNTS167	104503

PARTY ONE	PARTY TWO	DATE	TOPIC	CITATION	NUMBER
Aviation (Cont.)					
Italy	USA (United States)	26 Jan 55	Air Transport	238UNTS179	103361
Philippines	UK Great Britain	31 Jan 55	Air Transport	216UNTS51	102932
United Arab Rep	Yugoslavia	20 Feb 55	Air Transport	255UNTS199	103611
South Africa	USA (United States)	22 Feb 55	Air Transport	247UNTS247	103473
Iraq	United Arab Rep	23 Mar 55	Air Transport	311UNTS199	104504
Denmark	Israel	04 Apr 55	Taxation	213UNTS283	102891
Greece	Norway	25 May 55	Taxation	423UNTS77	106085
Japan	USA (United States)	03 Jun 55	Milit Assistance	270UNTS51	103891
Syria	United Arab Rep	03 Jul 55	Air Transport	393UNTS67	105652
Germany, West	USA (United States)	07 Jul 55	Air Transport	275UNTS3	103973
Italy	USA (United States)	08 Jul 55	Milit Installation	270UNTS29	103889
Germany, West	UK Great Britain	22 Jul 55	Air Transport	269UNTS189	103881
Germany, West	UK Great Britain	22 Jul 55	Air Transport	269UNTS223	103882
Germany, East	Romania	28 Jul 55	Air Transport	342UNTS207	104909
Germany, West	USA (United States)	02 Aug 55	Specif Goods/Equip	268UNTS121	103854
USSR (Soviet Union)	Yugoslavia	03 Sep 55	Air Transport	240UNTS267	103408
Germany, East	Hungary	10 Sep 55	Air Transport	407UNTS132	105863
Belgium	Ireland	10 Sep 55	Air Transport	255UNTS235	103612
Iceland	Sweden	17 Sep 55	Taxation	262UNTS273	103755
Multilateral		28 Sep 55	Air Transport	478UNTS371	106943
Multilateral		29 Sep 55	Air Transport	222UNTS313	103037
Bulgaria	Yugoslavia	01 Oct 55	Air Transport	396UNTS223	105698
France	Germany, West	04 Oct 55	Air Transport	353UNTS203	105044
Finland	USSR (Soviet Union)	19 Oct 55	Air Transport	353UNTS185	105043
Denmark	Syria	20 Oct 55	Air Transport	250UNTS61	103518
Denmark	Lebanon	21 Oct 55	Air Transport	248UNTS17	103482
Pakistan	Turkey	02 Nov 55	Air Transport	311UNTS217	104505
Netherlands	USA (United States)	04 Nov 55	Air Transport	269UNTS3	103867
Australia	South Africa	04 Nov 55	Air Transport	232UNTS143	103234
Burma	China People's Rep	08 Nov 55	Air Transport	306UNTS11	104430
Austria	USSR (Soviet Union)	09 Nov 55	Air Transport	255UNTS247	103613
Austria	Israel	17 Nov 55	Air Transport	232UNTS153	103235
India	Japan	26 Nov 55	Air Transport	311UNTS243	104506
Belgium	France	10 Dec 55	Taxation	231UNTS101	103211
France	Japan	17 Jan 56	Air Transport	255UNTS275	103614
Australia	Japan	19 Jan 56	Air Transport	311UNTS291	104507
Austria	Italy	23 Jan 56	Air Transport	393UNTS97	105653
Argentina	Switzerland	25 Jan 56	Air Transport	559UNTS121	108157
Romania	Yugoslavia	01 Feb 56	Air Transport	362UNTS203	105189
Hungary	Romania	03 Feb 56	Air Transport	362UNTS233	105190
India	USA (United States)	03 Feb 56	Air Transport	272UNTS75	103932
Austria	Poland	08 Feb 56	Air Transport	334UNTS221	104770
Netherlands	Sudan	12 Feb 56	Air Transport	311UNTS319	104508
Norway	Syria	25 Feb 56	Air Transport	463UNTS217	106706
Colombia	USA (United States)	27 Mar 56	Air Transport	273UNTS235	103954
Sweden	USSR (Soviet Union)	31 Mar 56	Air Transport	259UNTS239	103691
Denmark	USSR (Soviet Union)	31 Mar 56	Air Transport	259UNTS169	103689
Norway	USSR (Soviet Union)	31 Mar 56	Air Transport	259UNTS205	103690
Japan	USA (United States)	13 Apr 56	Milit Assistance	273UNTS223	103953
Belgium	Germany, West	14 Apr 56	Air Transport	344UNTS103	104945
Multilateral		30 Apr 56	Air Transport	310UNTS229	104494
Germany, West	Switzerland	02 May 56	Air Transport	559UNTS157	108158
Portugal	Venezuela	16 May 56	Air Transport	463UNTS239	106707
Italy	South Africa	21 May 56	Air Transport	255UNTS323	103616
Japan	Switzerland	24 May 56	Air Transport	312UNTS3	104509
Greece	Italy	26 May 56	Air Transport	496UNTS301	107258
Fed Rhod/Nyasaland	South Africa	30 May 56	Air Transport	255UNTS317	103615
Italy	Switzerland	04 Jun 56	Air Transport	378UNTS311	105429
Poland	Sweden	08 Jun 56	Air Transport	334UNTS257	104771
Germany, West	Ireland	12 Jun 56	Air Transport	353UNTS121	105040
India	Thailand	12 Jun 56	Air Transport	255UNTS341	103617
Israel	Sweden	17 Jun 56	Taxation	257UNTS47	103648
Multilateral		11 Sep 56	Humanitarian	266UNTS221	103832
Multilateral		25 Sep 56	Air Transport	334UNTS89	104767
Multilateral		25 Sep 56	Air Transport	334UNTS13	104766

PARTY ONE	PARTY TWO	DATE	TOPIC	CITATION	NUMBER
Aviation (Cont.)					
Germany, West	Netherlands	28 Sep 56	Air Transport	327UNTS185	104722
Switzerland	Thailand	13 Oct 56	Air Transport	312UNTS43	104510
Belgium	Poland	17 Oct 56	Air Transport	356UNTS279	105100
Colombia	USA (United States)	24 Oct 56	Air Transport	476UNTS77	106905
Belgium	Turkey	25 Oct 56	Air Transport	380UNTS3	105447
Austria	UK Great Britain	27 Oct 56	Air Transport	264UNTS67	103789
Belgium	United Arab Rep	31 Oct 56	Taxation	257UNTS235	103659
Australia	IBRD (World Bank)	15 Nov 56	IBRD Project	288UNTS117	104201
Albania	Yugoslavia	23 Nov 56	Air Transport	363UNTS123	105204
Peru	Switzerland	23 Nov 56	Air Transport	411UNTS97	105916
Albania	Yugoslavia	23 Nov 56	Air Transport	386UNTS73	105539
Belgium	Romania	04 Dec 56	Air Transport	317UNTS161	104602
France	USA (United States)	14 Dec 56	Air Transport	266UNTS117	103826
Iran	USA (United States)	16 Jan 57	Air Transport	308UNTS147	104460
Iceland	Thailand	22 Jan 57	Air Transport	312UNTS63	104511
Sweden	USSR (Soviet Union)	28 Jan 57	Finance	428UNTS315	106183
Denmark	Germany, West	29 Jan 57	Air Transport	302UNTS75	104354
Germany, West	Sweden	29 Jan 57	Air Transport	393UNTS113	105654
Germany, West	Norway	29 Jan 57	Air Transport	353UNTS39	105037
Norway	USA (United States)	05 Feb 57	Air Transport	279UNTS169	104038
India	IBRD (World Bank)	05 Mar 57	IBRD Project	272UNTS201	103939
Mexico	USA (United States)	07 Mar 57	Air Transport	279UNTS205	104042
Belgium	Czechoslovakia	12 Mar 57	Air Transport	312UNTS75	104512
Netherlands	Yugoslavia	13 Mar 57	Air Transport	327UNTS227	104723
Netherlands	USA (United States)	03 Apr 57	Air Transport	410UNTS193	105904
Germany, West	Yugoslavia	10 Apr 57	Air Transport	463UNTS269	106708
Denmark	Pakistan	10 Apr 57	Air Transport	302UNTS53	104353
Romania	Sweden	15 Apr 57	Air Transport	342UNTS325	104915
Bulgaria	Sweden	17 Apr 57	Air Transport	464UNTS3	106709
Korea, South	USA (United States)	24 Apr 57	Air Transport	288UNTS219	104207
Belgium	Bulgaria	14 May 57	Air Transport	317UNTS81	104596
Netherlands	United Arab Rep	15 May 57	Taxation	288UNTS29	104194
Australia	Germany, West	22 May 57	Air Transport	357UNTS45	105105
Hungary	Netherlands	28 May 57	Air Transport	334UNTS291	104773
Belgium	Hungary	01 Jun 57	Air Transport	291UNTS17	104242
Afghanistan	Pakistan	13 Jun 57	Air Transport	327UNTS51	104717
Czechoslovakia	United Arab Rep	30 Jun 57	Air Transport	411UNTS126	105917
Greece	Italy	02 Aug 57	Air Transport	533UNTS217	107744
Hungary	Sweden	02 Aug 57	Air Transport	334UNTS307	104774
Netherlands	Romania	27 Aug 57	Air Transport	342UNTS309	104914
Spain	USA (United States)	23 Sep 57	Air Transport	290UNTS261	104238
Italy	Pakistan	05 Oct 57	Air Transport	353UNTS91	105039
Fed of Malaya	UK Great Britain	18 Oct 57	Air Transport	335UNTS3	104775
Netherlands	UK Great Britain	22 Oct 57	Air Transport	313UNTS309	104538
France	Morocco	25 Oct 57	Air Transport	559UNTS95	108156
Belgium	USA (United States)	03 Dec 57	Air Transport	303UNTS45	104370
UK Great Britain	USSR (Soviet Union)	19 Dec 57	Air Transport	351UNTS235	105026
Australia	Ireland	30 Dec 57	Air Transport	497UNTS29	107260
Canada	Switzerland	10 Jan 58	Air Transport	464UNTS21	106710
Belgium	Morocco	20 Jan 58	Air Transport	288UNTS3	104192
Australia	UK Great Britain	07 Feb 58	Air Transport	335UNTS23	104776
Bulgaria	Netherlands	07 Feb 58	Air Transport	335UNTS45	104777
Afghanistan	Turkey	08 Feb 58	Air Transport	464UNTS39	106711
Sudan	Sweden	17 Feb 58	Air Transport	393UNTS161	105655
Norway	Pakistan	05 Mar 58	Air Transport	334UNTS199	104769
Pakistan	Sweden	06 Mar 58	Air Transport	393UNTS181	105656
Germany, West	Portugal	21 Mar 58	Air Transport	464UNTS71	106712
Norway	South Africa	28 Mar 58	Air Transport	300UNTS83	104332
South Africa	Sweden	28 Mar 58	Air Transport	300UNTS95	104333
Denmark	South Africa	28 Mar 58	Air Transport	300UNTS107	104334
Morocco	Portugal	03 Apr 58	Air Transport	393UNTS203	105657
Belgium	Iran	14 Apr 58	Air Transport	381UNTS309	105473
Sweden	Yugoslavia	18 Apr 58	Air Transport	393UNTS225	105658
Bulgaria	Denmark	28 May 58	Air Transport	312UNTS235	104521
India	USSR (Soviet Union)	02 Jun 58	Air Transport	393UNTS3	105650
Aviation (Cont.)					
Belgium	USSR (Soviet Union)	05 Jun 58	Air Transport	345UNTS145	104965
Pakistan	Portugal	07 Jun 58	Air Transport	320UNTS225	104645
Denmark	Luxembourg	10 Jun 58	Air Transport	356UNTS193	105096
Belgium	South Africa	11 Jun 58	Air Transport	335UNTS63	104778
Norway	Romania	16 Jun 58	Air Transport	405UNTS223	105835
Netherlands	USSR (Soviet Union)	17 Jun 58	Air Transport	335UNTS77	104779
Ireland	Switzerland	18 Jun 58	Taxation	553UNTS183	108086
Denmark	Romania	25 Jun 58	Air Transport	345UNTS231	104970
Belgium	Pakistan	04 Jul 58	Air Transport	387UNTS305	105569
Ethiopia	UK Great Britain	07 Jul 58	Air Transport	331UNTS3	104749
Austria	Romania	10 Jul 58	Air Transport	353UNTS155	105041
Denmark	Hungary	17 Jul 58	Air Transport	344UNTS281	104954
Sweden	United Arab Rep	21 Jul 58	Mostfavored Nation	427UNTS285	106160
Romania	United Arab Rep	14 Aug 58	Air Transport	405UNTS189	105834
Austria	Bulgaria	12 Sep 58	Air Transport	353UNTS3	105036
Ghana	UK Great Britain	24 Sep 58	Air Transport	411UNTS146	105918
Australia	South Africa	26 Sep 58	Air Transport	335UNTS121	104780
Liberia	Netherlands	28 Nov 58	Air Transport	393UNTS55	105651
Germany, West	USA (United States)	11 Dec 58	Air Transport	337UNTS31	104813
Finland	Switzerland	07 Jan 59	Air Transport	353UNTS173	105042
UK Great Britain	Yugoslavia	03 Feb 59	Air Transport	359UNTS339	105151
Indonesia	USA (United States)	02 Mar 59	Air Transport	357UNTS145	105113
Japan	Philippines	02 Mar 59	Air Transport	341UNTS49	104877
Netherlands	Tunisia	19 Mar 59	Air Transport	497UNTS61	107262
Sweden	Tunisia	19 Mar 59	Air Transport	497UNTS43	107261
Norway	Tunisia	28 Mar 59	Air Transport	497UNTS77	107263
Denmark	Tunisia	14 Apr 59	Air Transport	340UNTS273	104870
Ghana	UK Great Britain	17 Apr 59	Status of Forces	337UNTS353	104829
Austria	USA (United States)	30 Apr 59	Air Transport	343UNTS41	104920
Denmark	Sudan	11 May 59	Air Transport	445UNTS105	106380
Ceylon (Sri Lanka)	Sweden	29 May 59	Air Transport	464UNTS109	106713
Ceylon (Sri Lanka)	Norway	29 May 59	Air Transport	411UNTS165	105919
Ceylon (Sri Lanka)	Denmark	29 May 59	Air Transport	348UNTS225	105002
Belgium	Japan	20 Jun 59	Air Transport	411UNTS3	105911
Bulgaria	United Arab Rep	09 Jul 59	Air Transport	411UNTS187	105920
India	Italy	16 Jul 59	Air Transport	464UNTS129	106714
Afghanistan	Germany, West	22 Jul 59	Air Transport	464UNTS177	106715
UK Great Britain	Yugoslavia	22 Jul 59	Admin Cooperation	374UNTS319	105345
Germany, West	Iceland	12 Aug 59	Air Transport	411UNTS224	105921
Multilateral		20 Aug 59	Air Transport	376UNTS99	105376
Canada	Germany, West	04 Sep 59	Air Transport	411UNTS260	105922
Denmark	Pakistan	05 Sep 59	Admin Cooperation	354UNTS377	105071
Australia	Fed of Malaya	29 Sep 59	Air Transport	357UNTS29	105104
Germany, West	USA (United States)	01 Oct 59	Air Transport	358UNTS129	105130
Nicaragua	Peru	14 Oct 59	Air Transport	392UNTS303	105649
South Africa	Switzerland	19 Oct 59	Air Transport	559UNTS257	108162
Australia	USA (United States)	20 Nov 59	Air Transport	349UNTS293	105015
Liberia	Sweden	09 Dec 59	Air Transport	464UNTS219	106716
Czechoslovakia	UK Great Britain	15 Jan 60	Air Transport	374UNTS207	105336
Colombia	UN Special Fund	04 Feb 60	Direct Aid	355UNTS257	105080
Germany, West	United Arab Rep	16 Feb 60	Air Transport	464UNTS233	106717
France	Thailand	26 Feb 60	Air Transport	392UNTS279	105648
Multilateral		26 Feb 60	Air Transport	418UNTS171	106022
Australia	Thailand	26 Feb 60	Air Transport	392UNTS255	105647
Guinea	Netherlands	09 Mar 60	Air Transport	392UNTS243	105646
Finland	Iceland	10 Mar 60	Air Transport	497UNTS95	107264
Czechoslovakia	Iraq	11 Mar 60	Air Transport	464UNTS267	106718
Belgium	Switzerland	24 Mar 60	Air Transport	416UNTS81	105996
Luxembourg	Yugoslavia	09 Apr 60	Air Transport	464UNTS293	106719
Multilateral		22 Apr 60	Air Transport	418UNTS211	106023
Germany, West	Spain	28 Apr 60	Air Transport	465UNTS3	106720
Iran	UK Great Britain	02 May 60	Air Transport	566UNTS129	108241
Greece	Romania	02 May 60	Air Transport	485UNTS17	107043
Morocco	United Arab Rep	19 May 60	Air Transport	563UNTS121	108208
Switzerland	Tunisia	21 May 60	Air Transport	497UNTS109	107265

PARTY ONE	PARTY TWO	DATE	TOPIC	CITATION	NUMBER
Aviation (Cont.)					
Kuwait	UK Great Britain	24 May 60	Air Transport	412UNTS4	105923
Afghanistan	Czechoslovakia	28 May 60	Air Transport	497UNTS129	107266
Luxembourg	Tunisia	13 Jun 60	Air Transport	497UNTS143	107267
Denmark	Peru	22 Jun 60	Air Transport	439UNTS113	106326
Ireland	Portugal	24 Jun 60	Air Transport	412UNTS30	105924
Poland	UK Great Britain	02 Jul 60	Air Transport	385UNTS87	105532
Denmark	USA (United States)	07 Jul 60	Air Transport	380UNTS39	105449
Switzerland	United Arab Rep	14 Jul 60	Air Transport	497UNTS161	107268
Germany, West	Pakistan	20 Jul 60	Air Transport	465UNTS41	106721
Netherlands	Poland	21 Jul 60	Air Transport	497UNTS189	107269
Ghana	Netherlands	30 Jul 60	Air Transport	412UNTS51	105925
Mexico	USA (United States)	15 Aug 60	Air Transport	402UNTS177	105786
Belgium	Burma	17 Aug 60	Air Transport	540UNTS185	107850
Ghana	United Arab Rep	29 Aug 60	Air Transport	412UNTS71	105926
Czechoslovakia	India	19 Sep 60	Air Transport	465UNTS67	106722
Belgium	Jordan	19 Oct 60	Air Transport	479UNTS277	106959
Hungary	UK Great Britain	25 Oct 60	Air Transport	419UNTS309	106034
Burma	Switzerland	31 Oct 60	Air Transport	465UNTS97	106723
Norway	Peru	02 Nov 60	Air Transport	497UNTS207	107270
Australia	Italy	10 Nov 60	Air Transport	497UNTS247	107271
Indonesia	UK Great Britain	23 Nov 60	Air Transport	398UNTS71	105718
Canada	Pakistan	21 Dec 60	Air Transport	465UNTS115	106724
Luxembourg	Thailand	29 Dec 60	Air Transport	465UNTS131	106725
Jordan	Sweden	09 Jan 61	Air Transport	465UNTS155	106726
Sudan	UK Great Britain	16 Jan 61	Air Transport	424UNTS233	106112
Denmark	Poland	17 Jan 61	Air Transport	412UNTS111	105927
Norway	Poland	17 Jan 61	Air Transport	412UNTS130	105928
Germany, West	Japan	18 Jan 61	Air Transport	465UNTS173	106727
Cuba	Czechoslovakia	04 Mar 61	Air Transport	465UNTS209	106728
Ghana	Switzerland	17 May 61	Air Transport	559UNTS193	108159
Poland	Switzerland	18 May 61	Air Transport	559UNTS233	108161
Czechoslovakia	Morocco	08 Jun 61	Air Transport	497UNTS275	107272
New Zealand	UK Great Britain	13 Jun 61	Air Transport	497UNTS293	107273
Cameroon	France	16 Jun 61	Air Transport	412UNTS148	105929
Guinea	Sweden	17 Jun 61	Air Transport	465UNTS236	106729
Mexico	USA (United States)	19 Jul 61	Air Transport	433UNTS43	106230
Australia	New Zealand	25 Jul 61	Air Transport	523UNTS271	107561
Czechoslovakia	Ghana	02 Aug 61	Air Transport	465UNTS249	106730
Finland	Luxembourg	15 Aug 61	Air Transport	541UNTS45	107859
Jordan	Norway	21 Aug 61	Air Transport	465UNTS275	106731
Mexico	Netherlands	24 Aug 61	Air Transport	465UNTS291	106732
Jordan	Netherlands	24 Aug 61	Air Transport	466UNTS3	106733
Liberia	Switzerland	31 Aug 61	Air Transport	559UNTS215	108160
Multilateral		18 Sep 61	Air Transport	500UNTS31	107305
Ghana	Romania	30 Sep 61	Air Transport	467UNTS443	106769
Germany, West	Morocco	12 Oct 61	Air Transport	523UNTS289	107562
Switzerland	USA (United States)	13 Oct 61	Air Transport	459UNTS219	106625
Japan	Pakistan	17 Oct 61	Air Transport	466UNTS17	106734
Australia	UK Great Britain	14 Nov 61	Air Transport	466UNTS35	106735
Cyprus	Greece	23 Nov 61	Air Transport	497UNTS311	107274
Czechoslovakia	Mali	27 Nov 61	Air Transport	466UNTS41	106736
Czechoslovakia	Guinea	16 Dec 61	Air Transport	559UNTS49	108154
Netherlands	Sweden	08 Jan 62	Air Transport	466UNTS65	106737
Austria	Greece	15 Jan 62	Air Transport	498UNTS3	107275
Indonesia	Japan	23 Jan 62	Air Transport	559UNTS77	108155
Luxembourg	South Africa	31 Jan 62	Air Transport	563UNTS153	108209
Italy	Japan	31 Jan 62	Air Transport	498UNTS23	107276
Finland	Hungary	13 Feb 62	Air Transport	463UNTS61	106693
Germany, West	Thailand	05 Mar 62	Air Transport	563UNTS165	108210
Luxembourg	Spain	26 Mar 62	Air Transport	563UNTS205	108211
France	Luxembourg	29 Mar 62	Air Transport	563UNTS227	108212
Sierra Leone	UK Great Britain	05 Apr 62	Air Transport	434UNTS227	106265
Ghana	USSR (Soviet Union)	06 Apr 62	Air Transport	498UNTS41	107277
Netherlands	USA (United States)	24 Apr 62	Specific Property	436UNTS93	106289
Japan	United Arab Rep	10 May 62	Air Transport	498UNTS69	107278

PARTY ONE	PARTY TWO	DATE	TOPIC	CITATION	NUMBER
Aviation (Cont.)					
France	Romania	18 May 62	Air Transport	498UNTS115	107279
France	Senegal	15 Jun 62	Air Transport	524UNTS3	107563
Czechoslovakia	Senegal	20 Jun 62	Air Transport	498UNTS145	107280
Guinea	Norway	21 Jun 62	Air Transport	466UNTS81	106738
Liberia	Norway	29 Jun 62	Air Transport	466UNTS95	106739
Morocco	Switzerland	05 Jul 62	Air Transport	498UNTS189	107282
Morocco	Switzerland	05 Jul 62	Air Transport	498UNTS171	107281
Chile	Netherlands	13 Jul 62	Air Transport	466UNTS109	106740
Ecuador	Germany, West	20 Sep 62	Air Transport	498UNTS199	107283
Japan	Kuwait	06 Oct 62	Air Transport	498UNTS235	107284
Trinidad/Tobago	USA (United States)	08 Oct 62	Air Transport	462UNTS145	106675
Finland	France	12 Oct 62	Air Transport	498UNTS299	107285
Hungary	Syria	18 Oct 62	Air Transport	491UNTS209	107178
Netherlands	Norway	18 Oct 62	Air Transport	466UNTS145	106741
France	Ivory Coast	19 Oct 62	Air Transport	498UNTS317	107286
Poland	Syria	10 Nov 62	Air Transport	491UNTS228	107179
Ivory Coast	Switzerland	17 Nov 62	Air Transport	499UNTS3	107289
Jamaica	USA (United States)	29 Nov 62	Air Transport	462UNTS229	106682
France	UK Great Britain	29 Nov 62	Scientific Project	453UNTS325	106534
Ghana	Tunisia	11 Dec 62	Air Transport	563UNTS243	108213
Syria	United Arab Rep	27 Dec 62	Air Transport	491UNTS245	107180
Ghana	Mali	09 Jan 63	Air Transport	466UNTS165	106742
France	USA (United States)	22 Jan 63	Dispute Settlement	473UNTS3	106849
Senegal	Switzerland	23 Jan 63	Air Transport	524UNTS23	107564
New Zealand	Western Samoa	24 Jan 63	Air Transport	499UNTS21	107290
Guinea	Switzerland	01 Feb 63	Air Transport	499UNTS35	107291
Japan	USA (United States)	01 Feb 63	Air Transport	473UNTS49	106854
Mali	Senegal	07 Feb 63	Air Transport	524UNTS41	107565
UK Great Britain	Yugoslavia	16 Feb 63	Air Transport	507UNTS171	107400
Algeria	France	18 Feb 63	Air Transport	563UNTS263	108214
Sudan	Switzerland	18 Feb 63	Air Transport	563UNTS281	108215
Cyprus	Norway	05 Mar 63	Air Transport	563UNTS305	108216
Greece	Hungary	27 Apr 63	Air Transport	534UNTS3	107750
Cyprus	Denmark	27 Apr 63	Air Transport	529UNTS255	107664
Algeria	Morocco	30 Apr 63	Air Transport	564UNTS3	108217
Portugal	South Africa	07 May 63	Air Transport	499UNTS49	107292
Germany, West	Greece	07 Jun 63	Air Transport	544UNTS193	107919
Finland	Poland	10 Jun 63	Air Transport	503UNTS179	107343
Guinea	Ivory Coast	26 Jun 63	Air Transport	499UNTS71	107293
Austria	France	12 Jul 63	Air Transport	499UNTS91	107294
Taiwan	Luxembourg	19 Jul 63	Air Transport	564UNTS23	108218
Algeria	Mali	22 Jul 63	Air Transport	564UNTS29	108219
Cameroon	Israel	09 Aug 63	Air Transport	499UNTS121	107295
Pakistan	USSR (Soviet Union)	07 Oct 63	Air Transport	499UNTS161	107297
Ivory Coast	Netherlands	09 Oct 63	Air Transport	499UNTS141	107296
Canada	Denmark	28 Nov 63	Air Transport	496UNTS223	107254
Greece	Poland	21 Dec 63	Air Transport	538UNTS155	107813
Canada	USA (United States)	27 Dec 63	Air Transport	494UNTS21	107223
Mali	Niger	15 Jan 64	Air Transport	499UNTS197	107299
Denmark	Yugoslavia	11 Feb 64	Air Transport	511UNTS241	107437
France	New Zealand	27 Feb 64	Air Transport	499UNTS191	107298
Cameroon	Mali	17 Mar 64	Air Transport	524UNTS61	107566
Malaysia	Netherlands	07 Apr 64	Air Transport	524UNTS81	107567
United Arab Rep	USA (United States)	05 May 64	Air Transport	531UNTS229	107706
New Zealand	USA (United States)	24 Jun 64	Air Transport	524UNTS101	107568
Ivory Coast	Mali	09 Jul 64	Air Transport	524UNTS121	107569
UK Great Britain	USA (United States)	20 Aug 64	Specific Property	531UNTS85	107694
Malta	UK Great Britain	21 Sep 64	Military Mission	588UNTS55	108518
Germany, West	Jamaica	07 Oct 64	Air Transport	514UNTS187	107447
France	Trinidad/Tobago	12 Oct 64	Air Transport	535UNTS25	107774
Argentina	UK Great Britain	12 Jan 65	Air Transport	597UNTS177	108645
Finland	UK Great Britain	25 Mar 65	Air Transport	539UNTS103	107826
Denmark	Malaysia	26 Mar 65	Air Transport	540UNTS205	107851
Ghana	Malawi	04 May 65	Air Transport	541UNTS163	107869
Denmark	Spain	05 May 65	Air Transport	543UNTS255	107905

PARTY ONE	PARTY TWO	DATE	TOPIC	CITATION	NUMBER
Aviation (Cont.)					
Poland	USA (United States)	27 Sep 65	Air Transport	564UNTS169	108227
Finland	USA (United States)	03 Nov 65	Air Transport	573UNTS175	108330
Canada	USA (United States)	17 Jan 66	Air Transport	586UNTS151	108502
Portugal	UK Great Britain	17 Apr 66	Air Transport	573UNTS223	108335
Denmark	Ivory Coast	07 Jun 66	Air Transport	595UNTS313	108626
Fed Rhod/Nyasaland	Norway	18 Jun 66	Taxation	580UNTS9	108415
Denmark	Nigeria	08 Sep 66	Air Transport	591UNTS177	108557
Denmark	Singapore	20 Dec 66	Air Transport	593UNTS125	108580
Congo (Brazzaville)	Denmark	27 Feb 67	Air Transport	600UNTS189	108681
Bakeries					
Multilateral		08 Jun 25	ILO Labor	38UNTS269	100603
Bankruptcy					
Czechoslovakia	Poland	21 Jan 49	Admin Cooperation	31UNTS205	100480
Boundaries					
Finland	USSR (Soviet Union)	28 Oct 22	Specific Resources	67UNTS157	100874
Argentina	Brazil	27 Dec 27	Territory Boundary	51UNTS271	200193
Bolivia	Brazil	25 Feb 38	Land Transport	88UNTS379	200254
Brazil	UK Great Britain	15 Mar 40	Territory Boundary	5UNTS71	200029
Taiwan	UK Great Britain	18 Jun 41	Territory Boundary	10UNTS227	200064
Canada	USA (United States)	10 Nov 41	Specific Resources	23UNTS275	200134
Canada	USA (United States)	13 Mar 43	Other Military	99UNTS249	200279
Mexico	USA (United States)	03 Feb 44	Specific Resources	3UNTS313	200025
Hungary	Yugoslavia	13 Aug 44	Dispute Settlement	113UNTS233	101553
Brazil	Uruguay	22 Nov 44	Specif Goods/Equip	65UNTS289	200217
Belgium	Luxembourg	28 Apr 45	Visas	41UNTS265	200181
Belgium	France	21 May 45	Visas	23UNTS215	200133
Poland	USSR (Soviet Union)	16 Aug 45	Territory Boundary	10UNTS193	200061
USA (United States)	USSR (Soviet Union)	17 Sep 45	Milit Occupation	235UNTS346	200538
ICJ Option Clause	UK Great Britain	13 Feb 46	ICJ Option Clause	1UNTS3	100001
Iraq	Turkey	29 Mar 46	General Amity	37UNTS226	100580
Afghanistan	USSR (Soviet Union)	13 Jun 46	Territory Boundary	31UNTS147	100476
Denmark	Norway	08 Jul 46	Territory Boundary	7UNTS247	100103
Finland	USSR (Soviet Union)	03 Feb 47	Territory Boundary	216UNTS231	102939
Multilateral		10 Feb 47	Peace/Disarmament	48UNTS203	100746
Multilateral		10 Feb 47	Peace/Disarmament	49UNTS3	100747
Multilateral		10 Feb 47	Peace/Disarmament	41UNTS21	100643
Multilateral		10 Feb 47	Peace/Disarmament	42UNTS3	100645
Multilateral		10 Feb 47	Peace/Disarmament	41UNTS135	100644
Panama	USA (United States)	26 May 47	Territory Boundary	138UNTS137	101866
Denmark	Norway	09 Jul 47	Territory Boundary	7UNTS321	100108
Ethiopia	UK Great Britain	29 Sep 47	Territory Boundary	82UNTS191	101092
Canada	USA (United States)	15 Oct 47	Telecommunications	82UNTS53	101085
Norway	USSR (Soviet Union)	18 Dec 47	Territory Boundary	52UNTS3	100768
Belgium	France	23 Apr 48	Territory Boundary	19UNTS95	100307
Poland	USSR (Soviet Union)	08 Jul 48	Territory Boundary	37UNTS25	100575
Poland	USSR (Soviet Union)	08 Jul 48	Dispute Settlement	37UNTS107	100576
Czechoslovakia	Poland	12 Nov 48	Land Transport	84UNTS347	101141
Finland	USSR (Soviet Union)	09 Dec 48	Territory Boundary	217UNTS135	102947
Belgium	UK Great Britain	29 Dec 48	Visas	27UNTS135	100404
Romania	Yugoslavia	31 Dec 48	Visas	116UNTS103	101572
Canada	USA (United States)	31 Jan 49	Humanitarian	43UNTS119	100666
Czechoslovakia	Hungary	27 Feb 49	Admin Cooperation	26UNTS119	100383
India	Pakistan	27 Jul 49	Peace/Disarmament	81UNTS273	101076
Norway	USSR (Soviet Union)	29 Dec 49	Territory Boundary	83UNTS291	101112
Belgium	Netherlands	17 Feb 50	Water Transport	51UNTS101	100756
Multilateral		08 Apr 50	Specif Goods/Equip	68UNTS99	100889
Panama	USA (United States)	24 May 50	Territory Boundary	241UNTS139	103430
Germany, East	Poland	06 Jul 50	Territory Boundary	319UNTS93	104631
Belgium	Netherlands	23 Oct 50	Territory Boundary	136UNTS31	101831
Poland	USSR (Soviet Union)	15 Feb 51	Territory Boundary	432UNTS199	106222
Finland	Sweden	15 Jun 51	Visas	198UNTS3	102651
Mexico	USA (United States)	10 Aug 51	Telecommunications	152UNTS27	102009
Germany, West	Netherlands	18 Jan 52	Specific Property	179UNTS147	102364
Germany, East	Poland	06 Feb 52	Water Transport	304UNTS131	104395

PARTY ONE	PARTY TWO	DATE	TOPIC	CITATION	NUMBER
Boundaries (Cont.)					
Belgium	Pakistan	15 Mar 52	General Trade	316UNTS65	104578
Canada	USA (United States)	23 Jun 52	Telecommunications	207UNTS25	102798
India	Pakistan	21 Aug 52	Territory Boundary	207UNTS161	102805
Portugal	UK Great Britain	21 Jan 53	Non-IBRD Project	175UNTS13	102293
Belgium	France	30 Jan 53	Visas	188UNTS141	102525
Multilateral		07 Feb 53	Territory Boundary	173UNTS143	102264
Austria	Yugoslavia	19 Mar 53	Visas	467UNTS323	106768
Bulgaria	Yugoslavia	20 Feb 54	Territory Boundary	397UNTS13	105700
Bulgaria	Yugoslavia	22 Apr 54	Dispute Settlement	397UNTS43	105701
Norway	Sweden	12 May 54	Visas	198UNTS157	102661
Portugal	UK Great Britain	18 Nov 54	Territory Boundary	325UNTS307	104706
Portugal	UK Great Britain	18 Nov 54	Territory Boundary	210UNTS265	102841
Iran	USSR (Soviet Union)	02 Dec 54	Territory Boundary	451UNTS227	106497
USA (United States)	USSR (Soviet Union)	25 Jun 55	Territory Boundary	270UNTS15	103887
Bulgaria	Yugoslavia	04 Apr 56	Air Transport	391UNTS47	105616
Bulgaria	Yugoslavia	22 May 56	Visas	367UNTS119	105229
Bulgaria	Yugoslavia	16 Jun 56	Territory Boundary	391UNTS3	105613
Bulgaria	Yugoslavia	16 Jun 56	Territory Boundary	375UNTS235	105368
Belgium	Germany, West	24 Sep 56	Territory Boundary	314UNTS195	104549
Czechoslovakia	Hungary	13 Oct 56	Territory Boundary	300UNTS125	104336
Czechoslovakia	Hungary	13 Oct 56	Territory Boundary	300UNTS177	104337
Albania	Yugoslavia	23 Nov 56	Air Transport	363UNTS123	105204
Czechoslovakia	USSR (Soviet Union)	30 Nov 56	Territory Boundary	266UNTS243	103833
France	Libya	26 Dec 56	Territory Boundary	300UNTS263	104340
Norway	USSR (Soviet Union)	15 Feb 57	Territory Boundary	312UNTS289	104523
Poland	USSR (Soviet Union)	05 Mar 57	Territory Boundary	274UNTS133	103963
Belgium	Netherlands	07 Mar 57	Dispute Settlement	282UNTS241	104100
Iran	USSR (Soviet Union)	14 May 57	Dispute Settlement	457UNTS161	106586
Bulgaria	Yugoslavia	17 Jun 57	Territory Boundary	375UNTS249	105369
Norway	Sweden	16 Sep 57	Territory Boundary	428UNTS263	106178
China People's Rep	USSR (Soviet Union)	21 Dec 57	Visas	305UNTS213	104420
Afghanistan	USSR (Soviet Union)	18 Jan 58	Visas	321UNTS77	104655
Poland	USSR (Soviet Union)	18 Mar 58	Territory Boundary	340UNTS89	104861
Czechoslovakia	Poland	21 Mar 58	Specific Resources	538UNTS89	107811
Czechoslovakia	Poland	13 Jun 58	Territory Boundary	354UNTS221	105064
India	Pakistan	10 Sep 58	Territory Boundary	369UNTS81	105252
France	Italy	30 Oct 58	Visas	363UNTS3	105196
Czechoslovakia	Poland	04 Jul 59	Visas	363UNTS333	105210
Mexico	USA (United States)	05 Aug 59	Customs	356UNTS3	105089
India	Pakistan	23 Oct 59	Territory Boundary	362UNTS3	105180
India	Pakistan	11 Jan 60	Territory Boundary	375UNTS119	105364
Germany, West	Netherlands	08 Apr 60	Territory Boundary	508UNTS14	107404
Finland	USSR (Soviet Union)	23 Jun 60	Territory Boundary	379UNTS277	105443
Cyprus	UK Great Britain	16 Aug 60	Dispute Settlement	382UNTS183	105478
Cyprus	UK Great Britain	16 Aug 60	Specific Property	382UNTS207	105481
Cyprus	UK Great Britain	16 Aug 60	Specific Property	382UNTS201	105480
Cyprus	UK Great Britain	16 Aug 60	Specific Property	382UNTS189	105479
Poland	USSR (Soviet Union)	05 Feb 61	Territory Boundary	420UNTS161	106046
Finland	Sweden	18 Feb 61	Visas	428UNTS145	106173
Belgium	France	30 Mar 62	Visas	502UNTS297	107335
Austria	Yugoslavia	11 Dec 62	Land Transport	546UNTS3	107938
Burma	Thailand	17 May 63	Visas	468UNTS319	106779
Hungary	Romania	13 Jun 63	Territory Boundary	576UNTS275	108369
Mexico	USA (United States)	29 Aug 63	Territory Boundary	505UNTS185	107374
Austria	Switzerland	02 Sep 63	Visas	548UNTS91	107973
Multilateral		02 Sep 63	General Transport	548UNTS129	107974
Romania	Yugoslavia	30 Nov 63	Specific Property	512UNTS2	107438
Romania	Yugoslavia	20 Dec 63	Visas	527UNTS245	107629
Finland	USSR (Soviet Union)	24 Apr 64	Territory Boundary	537UNTS231	107804
Poland	USSR (Soviet Union)	17 Jul 64	Specific Resources	552UNTS175	108054
Austria	Hungary	31 Oct 64	Visas	545UNTS223	107936
Austria	Hungary	31 Oct 64	Visas	545UNTS241	107937
Greece	Yugoslavia	05 Nov 64	Territory Boundary	539UNTS13	107820
Hungary	Yugoslavia	08 Apr 65	Territory Boundary	587UNTS169	108511
Belgium	Netherlands	27 Apr 65	Specific Resources	596UNTS235	108636

PARTY ONE	PARTY TWO	DATE	TOPIC	CITATION	NUMBER
Boundaries (Cont.)					
Finland	USSR (Soviet Union)	20 May 65	Territory Boundary	566UNTS31	108238
India	Pakistan	30 Jun 65	Territory Boundary	548UNTS277	107983
UK Great Britain	Venezuela	17 Feb 66	Territory Boundary	561UNTS321	108192
Bounties					
Belgium	Netherlands	03 Feb 58	Territory Boundary	381UNTS305	105472
Bridges					
Canada	USA (United States)	24 Oct 56	Specif Goods/Equip	281UNTS281	104084
Finland	Norway	28 Jun 57	Non-IBRD Project	272UNTS191	103938
Finland	Sweden	29 Jun 63	Land Transport	477UNTS21	106912
Canal Project					
Belgium	Netherlands	24 Feb 61	Water Transport	474UNTS167	106881
Belgium	Netherlands	24 Feb 61	Admin Cooperation	474UNTS161	106880
Belgium	Netherlands	13 May 63	Territory Boundary	540UNTS3	107843
Panama	USA (United States)	15 Feb 66	Scientific Project	586UNTS27	108494
Cartography					
Brazil	USA (United States)	02 Jun 52	Scientific Project	181UNTS109	102403
Cambodia	USA (United States)	17 Oct 57	Scientific Project	299UNTS203	104313
Paraguay	USA (United States)	16 Jan 62	Scientific Project	433UNTS169	106240
Germany, West	United Nations	28 Jun 62	IGO Operations	434UNTS249	200597
Dominican Republic	USA (United States)	28 Aug 64	Scientific Project	531UNTS35	107691
United Nations	Tunisia	04 Aug 66	IGO Operations	576UNTS23	108363
United Nations	Sudan	08 Nov 66	Scientific Project	576UNTS85	108365
Cattle					
Brazil	Paraguay	14 Apr 41	Commodity Trade	54UNTS269	200199
Certificates of Origin					
Bulgaria	USA (United States)	08 Mar 48	Admin Cooperation	29UNTS101	100437
Child Labor					
Multilateral		28 Nov 19	ILO Labor	38UNTS81	100588
Multilateral		09 Jul 20	ILO Labor	38UNTS109	100590
Multilateral		11 Nov 21	ILO Labor	38UNTS217	100599
Multilateral		16 Nov 21	ILO Labor	38UNTS143	100593
Multilateral		30 Apr 32	ILO Labor	39UNTS133	100615
Multilateral		22 Jun 33	ILO Labor	78UNTS181	101016
Multilateral		24 Oct 36	ILO Labor	40UNTS205	100635
Multilateral		22 Jun 37	ILO Labor	40UNTS217	100636
Multilateral		09 Oct 46	ILO Labor	78UNTS198	101017
Multilateral		09 Oct 46	ILO Labor	78UNTS227	101019
Multilateral		09 Oct 46	ILO Labor	78UNTS213	101018
Multilateral		10 Jul 48	ILO Labor	91UNTS3	101239
Child Welfare					
Bulgaria	UNICEF (Children)	23 Aug 47	IGO Operations	68UNTS223	200232
Taiwan	UNICEF (Children)	19 Jul 50	IGO Operations	94UNTS21	101304
Iran	UNICEF (Children)	02 Aug 51	Direct Aid	247UNTS11	103457
Liberia	UNICEF (Children)	17 Apr 52	Direct Aid	133UNTS3	101773
Italy	USA (United States)	30 Jun 55	US Agri Commod Aid	258UNTS15	103667
Japan	USA (United States)	10 Feb 56	Direct Aid	275UNTS181	103981
Tunisia	USA (United States)	28 Jun 57	Direct Aid	289UNTS301	104226
Italy	USA (United States)	08 May 58	Direct Aid	316UNTS177	104584
Guinea	UNICEF (Children)	08 Jun 59	Direct Aid	334UNTS277	104772
Italy	USA (United States)	19 Jul 60	Direct Aid	389UNTS237	105595
Mali	UNICEF (Children)	17 Nov 60	Direct Aid	402UNTS23	105775
Italy	USA (United States)	28 Aug 62	Sanitation	461UNTS137	106657
Algeria	UNICEF (Children)	20 Nov 62	Direct Aid	453UNTS151	106522
Niger	UNICEF (Children)	05 Dec 62	IGO Operations	503UNTS195	107344
Mauritania	UNICEF (Children)	19 Jan 63	Direct Aid	452UNTS271	106514
UNICEF (Children)	Tanganyika	25 Jan 63	Direct Aid	453UNTS249	106528
Israel	USA (United States)	21 Mar 63	Education	476UNTS131	106907
Ethiopia	UNICEF (Children)	01 Apr 63	IGO Operations	457UNTS103	106579
UNICEF (Children)	Togo	27 Jun 63	IGO Operations	540UNTS135	107847
Poland	United Nations	16 Jul 63	IGO Operations	471UNTS3	106817
UNICEF (Children)	Trinidad/Tobago	08 Aug 63	IGO Operations	473UNTS281	106865
Dahomey	UNICEF (Children)	28 Aug 63	IGO Operations	507UNTS101	107396

PARTY ONE	PARTY TWO	DATE	TOPIC	CITATION	NUMBER
Child Welfare (Cont.)					
Iran	UNICEF (Children)	21 Nov 63	IGO Operations	485UNTS35	107044
Iraq	UNICEF (Children)	03 Dec 63	IGO Operations	482UNTS319	107001
Burundi	UNICEF (Children)	08 Jan 64	IGO Operations	485UNTS45	107045
Taiwan	UNICEF (Children)	08 Apr 64	IGO Operations	500UNTS49	107306
Jamaica	UNICEF (Children)	19 May 64	IGO Operations	500UNTS75	107308
Malaysia	UNICEF (Children)	01 Jul 64	IGO Operations	503UNTS229	107346
Rwanda	UNICEF (Children)	11 Sep 64	IGO Operations	510UNTS127	107409
Malta	UNICEF (Children)	22 Apr 65	IGO Operations	533UNTS107	107737
Gambia	UNICEF (Children)	29 May 65	IGO Operations	547UNTS29	107954
Mongolia	UNICEF (Children)	23 Jun 65	IGO Operations	540UNTS83	107844
Bulgaria	UNICEF (Children)	10 Mar 66	IGO Operations	559UNTS13	108152
Liberia	UNICEF (Children)	08 Jun 66	General Amity	570UNTS31	108286
Indonesia	UNICEF (Children)	17 Nov 66	IGO Operations	578UNTS47	108386
Guinea	UNICEF (Children)	22 Dec 66	IGO Operations	585UNTS137	108486
UNICEF (Children)	Zambia	02 Feb 67	IGO Operations	589UNTS89	108536
Cholera					
India	WHO (World Health)	01 Nov 51	Scientific Project	118UNTS13	101593
SEATO (SE Asia)	USA (United States)	29 May 59	Sanitation	347UNTS77	104991
Cinematography					
France	USA (United States)	28 May 46	Mass Media	84UNTS161	101126
France	USA (United States)	16 Sep 48	Culture	84UNTS185	101129
Citizenship					
Multilateral		03 Mar 56	Milit Servic/Citiz	243UNTS169	103452
USSR (Soviet Union)	Yugoslavia	22 May 56	Consul/Citizenship	259UNTS155	103688
Multilateral		20 Feb 57	Consul/Citizenship	309UNTS65	104468
Hungary	USSR (Soviet Union)	24 Aug 57	Consul/Citizenship	318UNTS35	104608
Romania	USSR (Soviet Union)	04 Sep 57	Consul/Citizenship	318UNTS89	104610
Albania	USSR (Soviet Union)	18 Sep 57	Consul/Citizenship	307UNTS251	104454
Czechoslovakia	USSR (Soviet Union)	05 Oct 57	Consul/Citizenship	320UNTS111	104640
Bulgaria	USSR (Soviet Union)	12 Dec 57	Consul/Citizenship	302UNTS3	104351
Korea, North	USSR (Soviet Union)	16 Dec 57	Consul/Citizenship	292UNTS107	104269
Poland	USSR (Soviet Union)	21 Jan 58	Consul/Citizenship	319UNTS277	104636
Czechoslovakia	Hungary	27 Jun 58	Consul/Citizenship	477UNTS321	106927
Mongolia	USSR (Soviet Union)	25 Aug 58	Consul/Citizenship	322UNTS201	104658
France	Israel	30 Jun 59	Milit Servic/Citiz	448UNTS107	106428
Bulgaria	Romania	21 Sep 59	Consul/Citizenship	387UNTS61	105558
Germany, West	Netherlands	08 Apr 60	Territory Boundary	508UNTS14	107404
Czechoslovakia	Hungary	04 Nov 60	Consul/Citizenship	397UNTS227	105708
Denmark	Germany, West	10 Nov 60	Consul/Citizenship	431UNTS21	106205
Italy	Netherlands	24 Jan 61	Milit Servic/Citiz	450UNTS207	106468
Multilateral		18 Apr 61	Consul/Citizenship	500UNTS223	107311
Hungary	Poland	05 Jul 61	Consul/Citizenship	437UNTS3	106296
Hungary	USSR (Soviet Union)	21 Jan 63	Consul/Citizenship	577UNTS201	108378
Multilateral		24 Apr 63	Consul/Citizenship	596UNTS469	108639
Argentina	Finland	08 May 63	Milit Servic/Citiz	482UNTS309	107000
Denmark	France	06 Jun 63	Milit Servic/Citiz	600UNTS213	108682
Austria	Denmark	17 Jul 63	Consul/Citizenship	479UNTS263	106958
Poland	USSR (Soviet Union)	31 Mar 65	Consul/Citizenship	571UNTS217	108304
Czechoslovakia	Poland	17 May 65	Consul/Citizenship	572UNTS181	108312
Bulgaria	USSR (Soviet Union)	06 Jul 66	Consul/Citizenship	596UNTS177	108632
Civil Defense					
Canada	USA (United States)	27 Mar 51	Milit Assistance	132UNTS333	101772
Canada	USA (United States)	15 Nov 63	Other Military	493UNTS67	107207
Civil Status Records					
Czechoslovakia	Italy	25 Feb 48	Admin Cooperation	26UNTS103	100380
Belgium	Monaco	05 Jun 48	Admin Cooperation	18UNTS245	100294
Belgium	Luxembourg	25 Feb 49	Admin Cooperation	47UNTS3	100719
Belgium	Switzerland	21 Mar 49	Admin Cooperation	34UNTS17	100524
France	UK Great Britain	23 Jan 50	Reparations	97UNTS149	101348
Belgium	Italy	24 Oct 50	Admin Cooperation	110UNTS39	101499
Belgium	Netherlands	29 Apr 53	Admin Cooperation	173UNTS61	102261
Luxembourg	Netherlands	06 Nov 53	Admin Cooperation	198UNTS187	102664
Germany, West	Japan	27 Jun 57	Admin Cooperation	318UNTS335	104624

PARTY ONE	PARTY TWO	DATE	TOPIC	CITATION	NUMBER
Civil Status Records (Cont.)					
Multilateral		27 Sep 57	Admin Cooperation	299UNTS211	104314
Belgium	Sweden	18 May 59	Admin Cooperation	341UNTS277	104890
Civilian Persons					
Multilateral		12 Aug 49	Humanitarian	75UNTS287	100973
Belgium	UK Great Britain	03 Oct 57	Reparations	394UNTS69	105669
Belgium	France	20 Sep 58	Reparations	376UNTS331	105387
Claims and Debts					
Norway	USA (United States)	28 Mar 40	Specif Claim/Waive	88UNTS365	200253
Mexico	USA (United States)	19 Nov 41	Claims and Debts	125UNTS287	200430
Mexico	USA (United States)	19 Nov 41	Claims and Debts	148UNTS367	200474
Canada	USA (United States)	26 May 43	Privil/Immunities	7UNTS345	200043
Mexico	USA (United States)	29 Sep 43	Claims and Debts	106UNTS265	200345
Turkey	UK Great Britain	23 Mar 44	Specif Claim/Waive	2UNTS227	200015
UK Great Britain	USA (United States)	28 Mar 44	Status of Forces	15UNTS413	200104
Belgium	UK Great Britain	22 Aug 44	Direct Aid	90UNTS295	200267
Norway	USA (United States)	29 May 45	Water Transport	34UNTS371	200180
Belgium	UK Great Britain	25 Jun 45	Reparations	90UNTS307	200268
Belgium	France	30 Oct 45	Reparations	19UNTS87	100306
Canada	UK Great Britain	06 Mar 46	Reparations	20UNTS3	100311
UK Great Britain	USA (United States)	27 Mar 46	Milit Assistance	4UNTS2	100039
Turkey	USA (United States)	07 May 46	Milit Assistance	6UNTS293	100083
India	USA (United States)	16 May 46	Milit Assistance	4UNTS183	100045
France	USA (United States)	28 May 46	Reparations	84UNTS93	101121
France	USA (United States)	28 May 46	Milit Assistance	84UNTS59	101119
France	USA (United States)	28 May 46	Reparations	84UNTS113	101122
Australia	USA (United States)	07 Jun 46	Milit Assistance	4UNTS237	100048
New Zealand	USA (United States)	10 Jul 46	Milit Assistance	6UNTS341	100087
Belgium	Canada	13 Jul 46	Reparations	230UNTS159	103181
UK Great Britain	USA (United States)	31 Jul 46	Air Transport	42UNTS199	100648
Luxembourg	USA (United States)	29 Aug 46	Reparations	140UNTS101	101885
Luxembourg	USA (United States)	12 Sep 46	Reparations	149UNTS19	101947
Belgium	USA (United States)	24 Sep 46	Claims and Debts	132UNTS80	101753
Canada	USA (United States)	15 Nov 46	Specif Claim/Waive	7UNTS141	100096
France	UK Great Britain	03 Dec 46	Reparations	54UNTS127	100799
Netherlands	UK Great Britain	04 Dec 46	Milit Installation	12UNTS241	100187
Thailand	UK Great Britain	06 Jan 47	Reparations	99UNTS149	101376
UK Great Britain	USA (United States)	23 Jan 47	Status of Forces	15UNTS281	100244
Multilateral		10 Feb 47	Peace/Disarmament	49UNTS3	100747
South Africa	USA (United States)	21 Mar 47	Milit Assistance	16UNTS47	100248
Italy	UK Great Britain	17 Apr 47	Claims and Debts	54UNTS169	100802
Italy	UK Great Britain	17 Apr 47	Finance	54UNTS149	100801
Austria	UK Great Britain	28 Apr 47	Reparations	93UNTS53	101287
Netherlands	USA (United States)	28 May 47	General Military	17UNTS29	100267
Austria	USA (United States)	21 Jun 47	Reparations	67UNTS89	100868
Austria	USA (United States)	21 Jun 47	Milit Occupation	67UNTS99	100869
Czechoslovakia	USA (United States)	25 Jul 47	Reparations	90UNTS19	101223
Czechoslovakia	Greece	30 Jul 47	Reparations	185UNTS149	102466
Taiwan	Italy	30 Jul 47	Reparations	12UNTS377	100194
Italy	USA (United States)	14 Aug 47	Claims and Debts	36UNTS105	100567
Italy	USA (United States)	14 Aug 47	Reparations	36UNTS53	100566
Haiti	USA (United States)	01 Oct 47	Other Ad Hoc	102UNTS67	101411
Greece	UNICEF (Children)	14 Oct 47	Humanitarian	102UNTS39	101409
Ecuador	USA (United States)	29 Oct 47	Admin Cooperation	21UNTS21	100322
Austria	UNICEF (Children)	07 Nov 47	IGO Operations	68UNTS252	200237
UNICEF (Children)	Yugoslavia	20 Nov 47	Tech Assistance	65UNTS28	100817
Denmark	UK Great Britain	01 Dec 47	Reparations	93UNTS151	101298
Italy	UK Great Britain	21 Jan 48	Milit Installation	77UNTS23	100989
Poland	UK Great Britain	24 Jan 48	Claims and Debts	87UNTS3	101163
Italy	USA (United States)	14 Feb 48	Reparations	67UNTS115	100871
Norway	USA (United States)	24 Feb 48	Milit Assistance	34UNTS155	100535
Romania	USA (United States)	26 Feb 48	Admin Cooperation	48UNTS9	100738
France	USA (United States)	27 Feb 48	Reparations	84UNTS207	101131
Hungary	USA (United States)	09 Mar 48	Admin Cooperation	183UNTS3	102426
Netherlands	UK Great Britain	11 Mar 48	Reparations	77UNTS69	100993

PARTY ONE	PARTY TWO	DATE	TOPIC	CITATION	NUMBER
Claims and Debts (Cont.)					
Taiwan	USA (United States)	17 Mar 48	Reparations	76UNTS157	100987
Multilateral		10 May 48	Reparations	140UNTS129	101887
Taiwan	UK Great Britain	18 May 48	Milit Assistance	66UNTS113	100850
Belgium	UK Great Britain	07 Jun 48	Reparations	20UNTS33	100313
UK Great Britain	Uruguay	12 Jul 48	Finance	71UNTS199	100919
USA (United States)	Yugoslavia	19 Jul 48	Claims and Debts	89UNTS43	101208
USA (United States)	Yugoslavia	19 Jul 48	Milit Assistance	34UNTS195	100537
Philippines	USA (United States)	27 Aug 48	Reparations	44UNTS13	100675
Korea, South	USA (United States)	11 Sep 48	Milit Assistance	89UNTS155	101216
New Zealand	USA (United States)	14 Sep 48	General Military	18UNTS251	100295
Israel	UNICEF (Children)	20 Sep 48	Direct Aid	71UNTS17	100907
UK Great Britain	USA (United States)	22 Sep 48	Milit Assistance	71UNTS64	100910
Multilateral		08 Oct 48	Education	19UNTS113	100308
Multilateral		19 Oct 48	Specif Claim/Waive	84UNTS201	101130
France	USA (United States)	22 Oct 48	Education	84UNTS173	101128
Canada	Netherlands	28 Oct 48	Reparations	231UNTS95	103210
Philippines	UNICEF (Children)	20 Nov 48	Tech Assistance	65UNTS48	100819
UNICEF (Children)	Thailand	01 Dec 48	IGO Operations	68UNTS94	100886
UK Great Britain	Yugoslavia	23 Dec 48	Reparations	81UNTS121	101068
Belgium	France	18 Feb 49	Claims and Debts	31UNTS173	100478
Czechoslovakia	Hungary	27 Feb 49	Admin Cooperation	26UNTS119	100383
France	USA (United States)	14 Mar 49	Claims and Debts	84UNTS225	101132
France	USA (United States)	14 Mar 49	Claims and Debts	84UNTS237	101133
Canada	USA (United States)	14 Mar 49	Reparations	82UNTS3	101079
Japan	USA (United States)	14 Apr 49	Specif Claim/Waive	89UNTS141	101215
United Arab Rep	UK Great Britain	17 Apr 49	Reparations	83UNTS183	101107
Canada	Netherlands	09 May 49	Reparations	46UNTS263	100715
India	UNICEF (Children)	10 May 49	IGO Operations	68UNTS96	100887
Denmark	Poland	12 May 49	Claims and Debts	87UNTS179	101172
Netherlands	USA (United States)	17 May 49	Milit Assistance	46UNTS291	100717
Pakistan	UNICEF (Children)	20 Jun 49	Tech Assistance	65UNTS60	100826
Greece	Turkey	21 Jul 49	Claims and Debts	78UNTS65	101012
Portugal	USA (United States)	04 Aug 49	Reparations	181UNTS15	102394
Australia	Netherlands	12 Aug 49	Reparations	34UNTS213	100539
Czechoslovakia	UK Great Britain	28 Sep 49	Claims and Debts	86UNTS175	101158
Czechoslovakia	UK Great Britain	28 Sep 49	Reparations	86UNTS161	101157
Switzerland	USA (United States)	21 Oct 49	Reparations	132UNTS163	101757
Finland	USA (United States)	01 Nov 49	Claims and Debts	68UNTS11	100880
Belgium	Canada	16 Nov 49	Reparations	51UNTS3	100748
Australia	USA (United States)	26 Nov 49	Reparations	45UNTS133	100695
Haiti	UNICEF (Children)	20 Dec 49	Tech Assistance	65UNTS68	100829
Costa Rica	UNICEF (Children)	14 Jan 50	Tech Assistance	65UNTS70	100830
Honduras	UNICEF (Children)	17 Jan 50	Tech Assistance	65UNTS74	100831
El Salvador	UNICEF (Children)	18 Jan 50	Tech Assistance	65UNTS78	100833
Canada	USA (United States)	24 Jan 50	Specif Claim/Waive	151UNTS171	101992
Panama	USA (United States)	26 Jan 50	Claims and Debts	132UNTS233	101763
Peru	UNICEF (Children)	31 Jan 50	Tech Assistance	65UNTS80	100834
India	USA (United States)	02 Feb 50	Education	89UNTS127	101214
Bolivia	UNICEF (Children)	03 Feb 50	Tech Assistance	65UNTS82	100835
Colombia	UNICEF (Children)	15 Mar 50	Tech Assistance	65UNTS104	100838
Canada	Norway	18 Mar 50	Reparations	230UNTS349	103194
Canada	Denmark	25 Mar 50	Reparations	230UNTS343	103193
Canada	Yugoslavia	29 Mar 50	Reparations	230UNTS357	103195
Burma	UNICEF (Children)	22 Apr 50	IGO Operations	68UNTS96	100888
Afghanistan	UNICEF (Children)	04 Jul 50	IGO Operations	71UNTS3	100906
Pakistan	USA (United States)	23 Sep 50	Education	82UNTS131	101088
Switzerland	UK Great Britain	08 Dec 50	Claims and Debts	175UNTS55	102295
Australia	Finland	04 Jan 51	Claims and Debts	80UNTS27	101042
Netherlands	USA (United States)	19 Jan 51	Reparations	141UNTS221	101917
Paraguay	UNICEF (Children)	25 Jan 51	IGO Operations	79UNTS9	101027
Multilateral		06 Mar 51	Claims and Debts	106UNTS141	101461
Belgium	Netherlands	15 Mar 51	Reparations	93UNTS97	101294
Germany, West	Netherlands	29 Mar 51	Non-ILO Labor	149UNTS71	101952
Multilateral		25 Apr 51	Reparations	91UNTS21	101240
Germany, West	Norway	07 May 51	Claims and Debts	92UNTS51	101260

Claims and Debts (Cont.)

PARTY ONE	PARTY TWO	DATE	TOPIC	CITATION	NUMBER
Panama	UNICEF (Children)	14 Jun 51	IGO Operations	97UNTS3	101343
Italy	Netherlands	15 Jun 51	Reparations	150UNTS103	101964
Canada	France	04 Jul 51	Reparations	233UNTS101	103253
Iran	UNICEF (Children)	02 Aug 51	Direct Aid	247UNTS11	103457
Canada	Italy	20 Sep 51	Reparations	236UNTS251	103328
Iraq	UNICEF (Children)	10 Dec 51	Direct Aid	126UNTS57	101682
Denmark	Norway	14 Jan 52	Claims and Debts	120UNTS119	101618
Canada	Spain	29 Jan 52	Claims and Debts	233UNTS117	103255
France	USA (United States)	02 Feb 52	Reparations	247UNTS223	103472
Libya	UNICEF (Children)	05 Apr 52	Direct Aid	133UNTS287	200441
UNICEF (Children)	United Arab Rep	18 May 52	Direct Aid	324UNTS161	104684
Australia	Italy	24 May 52	Reparations	161UNTS65	102123
Norway	USA (United States)	21 Jun 52	Reparations	236UNTS9	103313
Belgium	UK Great Britain	30 Jun 52	Milit Assistance	199UNTS113	102679
UNICEF (Children)	Vietnam, South	29 Aug 52	Direct Aid	161UNTS335	200492
Multilateral		05 Sep 52	Taxation	256UNTS3	103619
Japan	UK Great Britain	21 Nov 52	Reparations	172UNTS303	102254
Belgium	Germany, West	23 Dec 52	Claims and Debts	186UNTS69	102483
Germany, West	UK Great Britain	27 Feb 53	Claims and Debts	330UNTS217	104747
Germany, West	USA (United States)	27 Feb 53	Claims and Debts	224UNTS31	103068
Germany, West	USA (United States)	27 Feb 53	Claims and Debts	224UNTS13	103067
Multilateral		27 Feb 53	Claims and Debts	333UNTS3	104764
Germany, West	USA (United States)	27 Feb 53	Claims and Debts	223UNTS167	103065
Germany, West	USA (United States)	27 Feb 53	Claims and Debts	205UNTS103	102771
Japan	USA (United States)	23 Mar 53	Direct Aid	185UNTS93	102461
Germany, West	USA (United States)	30 Mar 53	Reparations	235UNTS285	103310
Germany, West	USA (United States)	01 Apr 53	Claims and Debts	224UNTS3	103066
Netherlands	Thailand	30 May 53	Reparations	293UNTS17	104282
Brazil	UK Great Britain	01 Oct 53	Claims and Debts	183UNTS207	102430
Czechoslovakia	Greece	01 Feb 54	General Trade	225UNTS77	103091
UNICEF (Children)	Spain	07 May 54	Direct Aid	190UNTS357	200515
Mexico	UNICEF (Children)	20 May 54	Direct Aid	192UNTS3	102591
Chile	USA (United States)	28 Jun 54	Tech Assistance	233UNTS3	103246
Belgium	UK Great Britain	09 Jul 54	Finance	201UNTS299	102721
Germany, West	UK Great Britain	10 Jul 54	Finance	199UNTS135	102680
Indonesia	Netherlands	11 Aug 54	Claims and Debts	241UNTS129	103429
Brazil	USA (United States)	20 Aug 54	Commodity Trade	410UNTS79	105898
Belgium	France	12 Nov 54	Reparations	306UNTS85	104434
Multilateral		01 Dec 54	Admin Cooperation	210UNTS197	102839
Iran	USSR (Soviet Union)	02 Dec 54	Territory Boundary	451UNTS227	106497
Japan	USA (United States)	04 Jan 55	Specif Claim/Waive	237UNTS197	103346
Greece	UK Great Britain	24 Feb 55	Specif Claim/Waive	209UNTS187	102827
Greece	UK Great Britain	07 Mar 55	General Military	211UNTS249	102856
Bulgaria	Yugoslavia	16 Mar 55	General Economic	397UNTS83	105702
Germany, West	USA (United States)	14 Apr 55	General Military	263UNTS351	103782
Iraq	UK Great Britain	30 Apr 55	Claims and Debts	226UNTS319	103126
Austria	UK Great Britain	15 May 55	Claims and Debts	344UNTS9	104940
India	Pakistan	12 Jun 55	Finance	228UNTS211	103153
Luxembourg	USA (United States)	15 Jun 55	Reparations	264UNTS279	103798
Indonesia	UNICEF (Children)	04 Jul 55	Admin Cooperation	212UNTS13	102860
Japan	Thailand	09 Jul 55	Finance	230UNTS13	103172
Sweden	UK Great Britain	22 Dec 55	Claims and Debts	231UNTS179	103218
Germany, West	Sweden	17 Jan 56	Reparations	262UNTS301	103758
Czechoslovakia	Yugoslavia	11 Feb 56	Admin Cooperation	397UNTS135	105703
Germany, West	USA (United States)	02 Mar 56	Claims and Debts	273UNTS209	103952
Japan	Netherlands	13 Mar 56	Claims and Debts	252UNTS3	103554
Germany, West	Sweden	22 Mar 56	Claims and Debts	262UNTS361	103761
Germany, West	Sweden	22 Mar 56	Reparations	262UNTS401	103762
Brazil	France	04 May 56	Finance	323UNTS339	104675
Italy	UNICEF (Children)	28 May 56	Direct Aid	243UNTS43	103445
Cambodia	UNICEF (Children)	25 Jun 56	Direct Aid	249UNTS153	103505
Poland	USA (United States)	28 Jun 56	Claims and Debts	273UNTS79	103944
Iceland	USA (United States)	23 Nov 56	Specif Claim/Waive	281UNTS361	104088
Sweden	UK Great Britain	08 Dec 56	Claims and Debts	264UNTS61	103788
Japan	Spain	08 Jan 57	Claims and Debts	318UNTS221	104615

Claims and Debts (Cont.)

PARTY ONE	PARTY TWO	DATE	TOPIC	CITATION	NUMBER
Germany, West	Netherlands	29 Jan 57	Status of Forces	314UNTS173	104548
Philippines	USA (United States)	06 Feb 57	Status of Forces	303UNTS237	104383
Italy	UK Great Britain	29 Mar 57	Reparations	310UNTS11	104481
Italy	USA (United States)	29 Mar 57	Reparations	299UNTS157	104311
Philippines	USA (United States)	01 Nov 57	Status of Forces	307UNTS39	104440
Argentina	UK Great Britain	25 Nov 57	Claims and Debts	313UNTS95	104531
Laos	UNICEF (Children)	11 Jan 58	Claims and Debts	287UNTS255	104191
Indonesia	Japan	20 Jan 58	Claims and Debts	325UNTS3	104690
Philippines	USA (United States)	20 Feb 58	Status of Forces	303UNTS261	104385
Czechoslovakia	Poland	29 Mar 58	Reparations	340UNTS199	104865
Netherlands	Yugoslavia	22 Jul 58	Claims and Debts	386UNTS263	105546
Jordan	UNICEF (Children)	09 Aug 58	Direct Aid	309UNTS297	104478
Denmark	USA (United States)	28 Aug 58	Reparations	335UNTS133	104781
Multilateral		27 Oct 58	Reparations	351UNTS303	105031
Korea, South	USA (United States)	18 Dec 58	Reparations	325UNTS233	104702
Philippines	USA (United States)	21 Jan 59	Specif Claim/Waive	341UNTS255	104888
Austria	UK Great Britain	14 Mar 59	Claims and Debts	343UNTS263	104930
Germany, West	USA (United States)	20 Mar 59	Claims and Debts	341UNTS15	104874
Germany, West	UK Great Britain	10 Apr 59	Claims and Debts	343UNTS295	104935
Italy	UK Great Britain	14 Apr 59	Claims and Debts	343UNTS289	104934
Denmark	UK Great Britain	28 Apr 59	Finance	343UNTS257	104929
Netherlands	UK Great Britain	30 Apr 59	Claims and Debts	343UNTS307	104937
Switzerland	UK Great Britain	06 May 59	Claims and Debts	343UNTS315	104938
Multilateral		11 May 59	Claims and Debts	527UNTS145	107623
Greece	UK Great Britain	14 May 59	Specif Claim/Waive	360UNTS69	105154
Greece	UK Great Britain	21 May 59	Claims and Debts	344UNTS3	104939
Austria	USA (United States)	22 May 59	Reparations	347UNTS3	104988
Turkey	UK Great Britain	13 Jun 59	Claims and Debts	551UNTS59	108033
Greece	Yugoslavia	18 Jun 59	Claims and Debts	368UNTS9	105232
Denmark	Yugoslavia	13 Jul 59	Specif Claim/Waive	386UNTS251	105545
Netherlands	Turkey	12 Aug 59	Admin Cooperation	527UNTS181	107624
Spain	USA (United States)	13 Feb 60	Milit Installation	371UNTS185	105279
Multilateral		15 Apr 60	Finance	470UNTS239	106811
Poland	USA (United States)	16 Jul 60	Specif Claim/Waive	384UNTS169	105518
Germany, West	USA (United States)	16 Aug 60	Claims and Debts	418UNTS235	106024
Japan	UK Great Britain	07 Oct 60	Reparations	384UNTS89	105513
United Nations	United Arab Rep	17 Oct 60	Specif Claim/Waive	388UNTS143	105575
Netherlands	Yugoslavia	09 Feb 61	Claims and Debts	453UNTS221	106526
Japan	USA (United States)	08 Jun 61	Reparations	410UNTS183	105903
Bulgaria	Netherlands	07 Jul 61	Finance	489UNTS21	107133
Canada	Japan	05 Sep 61	Reparations	451UNTS47	106483
Germany, West	Israel	01 Jun 62	Specific Property	448UNTS227	106435
Multilateral		08 Dec 62	Finance	510UNTS235	107418
Netherlands	USA (United States)	06 Feb 63	Status of Forces	487UNTS113	107098
Germany, West	USA (United States)	14 Mar 63	Status of Forces	474UNTS71	106872
Greece	Hungary	27 Apr 63	Finance	550UNTS197	108016
Bulgaria	USA (United States)	02 Jul 63	Claims and Debts	479UNTS245	106957
Austria	Romania	03 Jul 63	Claims and Debts	588UNTS3	108516
Austria	Belgium	14 Nov 63	Specific Property	544UNTS97	107912
Netherlands	Poland	20 Dec 63	Claims and Debts	514UNTS169	107446
Australia	USA (United States)	05 Feb 64	Status of Forces	511UNTS103	107430
Denmark	USSR (Soviet Union)	27 Feb 64	Specif Claim/Waive	509UNTS285	107407
Norway	Romania	21 May 64	Claims and Debts	563UNTS45	108203
Czechoslovakia	Netherlands	11 Jun 64	Claims and Debts	556UNTS89	108120
USA (United States)	Yugoslavia	05 Nov 64	Claims and Debts	550UNTS31	108007
Belgium	Congo (Zaire)	06 Feb 65	Claims and Debts	540UNTS227	107852
USA (United States)	Vietnam, South	09 Feb 65	Claims and Debts	542UNTS175	107888
Belgium	United Nations	20 Feb 65	Claims and Debts	535UNTS197	107780
Israel	UK Great Britain	15 Apr 65	Finance	551UNTS19	108031
Australia	Germany, West	21 Apr 65	Claims and Debts	598UNTS25	108654
Japan	Korea, South	22 Jun 65	Specific Resources	583UNTS51	108472
Hungary	Netherlands	02 Jul 65	Finance	564UNTS49	108220
Austria	Finland	21 Feb 66	Claims and Debts	597UNTS273	108651
United Nations	Switzerland	03 Jun 66	Claims and Debts	564UNTS193	200621
Greece	United Nations	20 Jun 66	Claims and Debts	565UNTS3	108230

PARTY ONE	PARTY TWO	DATE	TOPIC	CITATION	NUMBER
Claims and Debts (Cont.)					
Luxembourg	United Nations	28 Dec 66	Claims and Debts	585UNTS147	108487
Italy	United Nations	18 Jan 67	Specif Claim/Waive	588UNTS197	108525
Clearing Agreements					
Bulgaria	Yugoslavia	22 Aug 47	Finance	111UNTS241	101538
Multilateral		18 Nov 47	Finance	17UNTS89	100269
Belgium	Netherlands	11 Oct 48	Finance	26UNTS95	100379
Czechoslovakia	Hungary	27 Feb 49	Admin Cooperation	26UNTS119	100383
Belgium	Norway	21 Jan 52	Claims and Debts	123UNTS39	101653
Coal					
Taiwan	UK Great Britain	18 Jun 41	Territory Boundary	10UNTS227	200064
Multilateral		04 Jan 46	IGO Establishment	6UNTS35	100066
France	USA (United States)	28 May 46	Reparations	84UNTS93	101121
Poland	Sweden	18 Mar 47	General Economic	12UNTS295	100190
Czechoslovakia	Poland	04 Apr 47	General Economic	85UNTS62	101146
France	USA (United States)	19 Apr 47	General Trade	132UNTS135	101754
Multilateral		28 Apr 49	IGO Establishment	83UNTS105	101105
Multilateral		18 Apr 51	IGO Establishment	261UNTS140	103729
Germany, West	Netherlands	31 Oct 56	Admin Cooperation	287UNTS21	104177
Multilateral		26 Jul 57	Land Transport	386UNTS3	105535
Coffee					
Multilateral		28 Nov 40	Commodity Trade	139UNTS159	200452
Multilateral		03 Sep 46	Commodity Trade	139UNTS3	101872
Multilateral		28 Sep 62	IGO Establishment	469UNTS169	106791
Collisions at Sea					
Multilateral		10 Jun 48	Humanitarian	191UNTS3	102576
Multilateral		10 May 52	Taxation	439UNTS233	106332
Multilateral		10 May 52	Admin Cooperation	439UNTS217	106331
Colonialism					
United Nations	Zambia	06 Jul 67	IGO Operations	600UNTS81	108678
Commerce					
Multilateral		15 Jun 27	ILO Labor	38UNTS327	100607
Multilateral		28 Jun 30	ILO Labor	39UNTS85	100613
Multilateral		30 Apr 32	ILO Labor	39UNTS133	100615
Canada	France	12 May 33	Admin Cooperation	253UNTS285	200545
Argentina	Brazil	23 Jan 40	Admin Cooperation	51UNTS281	200194
Thailand	UK Great Britain	22 Mar 40	General Economic	2UNTS215	200013
Brazil	Paraguay	14 Apr 41	Commodity Trade	54UNTS269	200199
Brazil	Paraguay	14 Jun 41	IGO Establishment	54UNTS303	200202
Brazil	Paraguay	14 Jun 41	Finance	54UNTS313	200203
Brazil	Paraguay	14 Jun 41	Specific Property	54UNTS259	200198
USA (United States)	USSR (Soviet Union)	02 Aug 41	General Trade	102UNTS269	200306
UK Great Britain	USSR (Soviet Union)	16 Aug 41	Finance	91UNTS341	200269
Brazil	Canada	17 Oct 41	General Trade	67UNTS263	200224
Brazil	Uruguay	08 Jan 42	Admin Cooperation	54UNTS359	200206
Saudi Arabia	UK Great Britain	20 Apr 42	General Trade	10UNTS151	200058
UK Great Britain	USSR (Soviet Union)	22 Jun 42	Finance	91UNTS355	200270
Dominican Republic	USA (United States)	14 Nov 42	Customs	24UNTS233	200148
Mexico	USA (United States)	23 Dec 42	Finance	13UNTS231	200081
Iceland	USA (United States)	27 Sep 43	General Trade	29UNTS317	200170
El Salvador	UK Great Britain	16 Dec 43	General Trade	2UNTS221	200014
Chile	UK Great Britain	01 Jul 44	General Trade	2UNTS243	200017
Chile	USA (United States)	30 Jul 45	General Trade	6UNTS409	200042
France	USA (United States)	08 Nov 45	General Trade	76UNTS151	100986
Italy	USA (United States)	06 Dec 45	General Trade	3UNTS131	100027
Multilateral		01 Jan 46	Peace/Disarmament	99UNTS131	101375
Greece	USA (United States)	11 Jan 46	General Trade	3UNTS203	100032
Belgium	Norway	21 Feb 46	General Trade	31UNTS435	100485
UK Great Britain	USA (United States)	21 Feb 46	General Trade	6UNTS137	100073
Taiwan	France	28 Feb 46	General Amity	14UNTS137	100216
France	Norway	26 Mar 46	General Trade	31UNTS69	100468
Iraq	Turkey	29 Mar 46	Admin Cooperation	37UNTS333	100581
Denmark	Norway	30 Mar 46	General Trade	29UNTS163	100438

PARTY ONE	PARTY TWO	DATE	TOPIC	CITATION	NUMBER
Commerce (Cont.)					
Thailand	UK Great Britain	01 May 46	Commodity Trade	99UNTS175	101378
Thailand	UK Great Britain	01 May 46	Commodity Trade	99UNTS169	101377
USA (United States)	Yemen	04 May 46	General Economic	4UNTS165	100043
UK Great Britain	USA (United States)	06 May 46	Admin Cooperation	99UNTS199	101381
Thailand	UK Great Britain	06 May 46	Commodity Trade	99UNTS193	101380
Multilateral		06 May 46	Commodity Trade	99UNTS181	101379
France	USA (United States)	28 May 46	General Trade	84UNTS151	101125
Bolivia	USA (United States)	10 Jun 46	Mostfavored Nation	13UNTS19	100197
Chile	UK Great Britain	25 Jun 46	General Trade	91UNTS137	101246
Luxembourg	USA (United States)	03 Jul 46	Mostfavored Nation	32UNTS85	100491
Philippines	USA (United States)	04 Jul 46	General Trade	43UNTS135	100668
Ethiopia	USA (United States)	04 Jul 46	Mostfavored Nation	13UNTS27	100198
Norway	USA (United States)	08 Jul 46	Mostfavored Nation	13UNTS35	100199
Spain	USA (United States)	11 Jul 46	Mostfavored Nation	13UNTS51	100201
Belgium	USA (United States)	11 Jul 46	Mostfavored Nation	13UNTS43	100200
Italy	Norway	20 Jul 46	General Trade	30UNTS177	100456
Chile	USA (United States)	30 Jul 46	General Trade	7UNTS41	100090
United Arab Rep	USA (United States)	15 Aug 46	Mostfavored Nation	13UNTS59	100202
Norway	Portugal	16 Aug 46	Commodity Trade	30UNTS215	100459
Denmark	USSR (Soviet Union)	17 Aug 46	General Economic	8UNTS201	100124
Portugal	USA (United States)	26 Aug 46	Mostfavored Nation	13UNTS67	100203
Hungary	Norway	27 Aug 46	General Trade	31UNTS3	100465
Norway	Yugoslavia	30 Aug 46	General Trade	30UNTS187	100457
Denmark	USA (United States)	10 Sep 46	Mostfavored Nation	13UNTS75	100204
Australia	Sweden	16 Sep 46	General Trade	10UNTS63	100143
Argentina	UK Great Britain	17 Sep 46	General Economic	88UNTS47	101185
Canada	Taiwan	26 Sep 46	General Trade	14UNTS167	100219
USA (United States)	Yugoslavia	03 Oct 46	Mostfavored Nation	13UNTS83	100205
Dominican Republic	USA (United States)	07 Oct 46	Mostfavored Nation	13UNTS91	100206
Taiwan	USA (United States)	04 Nov 46	General Amity	25UNTS69	100359
Czechoslovakia	USA (United States)	14 Nov 46	General Trade	7UNTS119	100094
Netherlands	USA (United States)	21 Nov 46	General Trade	12UNTS173	100185
El Salvador	UK Great Britain	16 Dec 46	General Trade	6UNTS131	100072
Norway	USSR (Soviet Union)	27 Dec 46	Finance	17UNTS283	100282
Netherlands	Norway	28 Jan 47	General Trade	31UNTS29	100467
Belgium	Chile	11 Feb 47	Patents/Copyrights	76UNTS107	100983
Norway	USSR (Soviet Union)	19 Feb 47	General Trade	30UNTS293	100464
Belgium	Turkey	12 Mar 47	General Trade	37UNTS215	100578
Poland	Sweden	18 Mar 47	General Economic	12UNTS295	100190
Argentina	UK Great Britain	19 Mar 47	General Trade	11UNTS195	100157
Czechoslovakia	Norway	20 Mar 47	General Trade	30UNTS223	100460
Czechoslovakia	Poland	04 Apr 47	General Economic	85UNTS62	101146
Austria	Norway	14 Apr 47	General Trade	31UNTS21	100466
Jordan	United Arab Rep	21 Apr 47	General Trade	11UNTS3	100146
Nepal	USA (United States)	25 Apr 47	Consul/Citizenship	16UNTS97	100251
Thailand	UK Great Britain	08 May 47	Claims and Debts	100UNTS47	101386
Bulgaria	Denmark	09 May 47	General Trade	74UNTS131	100959
Sweden	USA (United States)	24 Jun 47	General Economic	36UNTS25	100565
Multilateral		11 Jul 47	ILO Labor	54UNTS3	100792
Canada	Switzerland	14 Jul 47	Admin Cooperation	43UNTS103	100664
Hungary	USSR (Soviet Union)	15 Jul 47	General Economic	216UNTS247	102940
Canada	Greece	28 Jul 47	Customs	43UNTS111	100665
Italy	USA (United States)	14 Aug 47	Claims and Debts	36UNTS105	100567
Multilateral		19 Sep 47	Finance	30UNTS269	100462
Multilateral		19 Sep 47	General Trade	30UNTS249	100461
Multilateral		05 Oct 47	Finance	34UNTS23	100525
Netherlands	USA (United States)	30 Oct 47	General Economic	76UNTS47	100978
Canada	USA (United States)	30 Oct 47	General Economic	27UNTS19	100394
Netherlands	New Zealand	30 Oct 47	General Economic	76UNTS41	100977
Multilateral		30 Oct 47	General Economic	55UNTS188	100814
Belgium	USSR (Soviet Union)	10 Nov 47	Finance	18UNTS299	100298
Finland	Norway	15 Nov 47	General Trade	29UNTS179	100439
Finland	USSR (Soviet Union)	01 Dec 47	General Trade	217UNTS3	102942
Czechoslovakia	USSR (Soviet Union)	11 Dec 47	General Economic	217UNTS35	102943
UK Great Britain	USSR (Soviet Union)	27 Dec 47	General Economic	91UNTS113	101245

PARTY ONE	PARTY TWO	DATE	TOPIC	CITATION	NUMBER
Commerce (Cont.)					
Italy	USA (United States)	02 Feb 48	General Amity	79UNTS171	101040
Norway	Poland	04 Feb 48	General Trade	30UNTS205	100458
Czechoslovakia	Italy	25 Feb 48	Admin Cooperation	26UNTS103	100380
Romania	USA (United States)	26 Feb 48	Admin Cooperation	48UNTS9	100738
Czechoslovakia	Romania	01 Mar 48	Admin Cooperation	26UNTS109	100381
Denmark	Guatemala	04 Mar 48	General Economic	96UNTS223	101339
Bulgaria	Czechoslovakia	05 Mar 48	Admin Cooperation	26UNTS115	100382
Bulgaria	USA (United States)	08 Mar 48	Admin Cooperation	29UNTS101	100437
Canada	Turkey	15 Mar 48	General Economic	231UNTS63	103205
Switzerland	USSR (Soviet Union)	17 Mar 48	General Trade	217UNTS73	102944
Bulgaria	USSR (Soviet Union)	01 Apr 48	General Economic	217UNTS97	102946
Canada	Italy	28 Apr 48	General Economic	231UNTS69	103206
Norway	Sweden	29 Apr 48	Commodity Trade	26UNTS33	100375
Canada	USA (United States)	30 Apr 48	Sanitation	77UNTS191	100999
Brazil	UK Great Britain	21 May 48	Finance	66UNTS121	100851
Bulgaria	Poland	30 May 48	General Trade	37UNTS3	100574
Netherlands	UK Great Britain	11 Jun 48	General Economic	66UNTS183	100853
France	Norway	11 Jun 48	General Trade	31UNTS83	100469
Spain	UK Great Britain	23 Jun 48	General Economic	66UNTS193	100854
Norway	Switzerland	26 Jun 48	General Trade	29UNTS193	100440
Italy	USA (United States)	28 Jun 48	Milit Occupation	25UNTS45	100356
Ireland	USA (United States)	28 Jun 48	Mostfavored Nation	32UNTS69	100489
France	USA (United States)	28 Jun 48	Mostfavored Nation	31UNTS115	100472
Denmark	USA (United States)	29 Jun 48	Mostfavored Nation	27UNTS35	100396
Austria	USA (United States)	02 Jul 48	Milit Occupation	25UNTS53	100357
Belgium	USA (United States)	02 Jul 48	Mostfavored Nation	27UNTS43	100397
Netherlands	USA (United States)	02 Jul 48	Mostfavored Nation	32UNTS77	100490
Greece	USA (United States)	02 Jul 48	Mostfavored Nation	31UNTS131	100474
Sweden	USA (United States)	03 Jul 48	Milit Occupation	27UNTS69	100400
Norway	USA (United States)	03 Jul 48	Milit Occupation	27UNTS59	100399
Belgium	Czechoslovakia	03 Jul 48	General Trade	77UNTS137	100997
Iceland	USA (United States)	03 Jul 48	Milit Occupation	27UNTS49	100398
Turkey	USA (United States)	04 Jul 48	Mostfavored Nation	34UNTS185	100536
France	Norway	05 Jul 48	General Trade	30UNTS281	100463
UK Great Britain	USA (United States)	06 Jul 48	Milit Occupation	25UNTS61	100358
France	USA (United States)	09 Jul 48	Mostfavored Nation	32UNTS93	100492
Multilateral		14 Jul 48	Mostfavored Nation	31UNTS123	100473
Ireland	UK Great Britain	31 Jul 48	General Trade	86UNTS37	101151
Portugal	USA (United States)	28 Sep 48	Mostfavored Nation	31UNTS139	100475
UK Great Britain	USA (United States)	30 Sep 48	Specific Resources	71UNTS241	100922
Greece	Lebanon	06 Oct 48	Consul/Citizenship	87UNTS351	101179
Canada	USA (United States)	23 Nov 48	Commodity Trade	81UNTS295	101078
Austria	Denmark	29 Nov 48	General Trade	74UNTS243	100967
Italy	USSR (Soviet Union)	11 Dec 48	General Economic	217UNTS181	102948
Argentina	Denmark	14 Dec 48	General Economic	74UNTS41	100956
Denmark	Turkey	15 Dec 48	General Trade	76UNTS17	100975
UK Great Britain	Yugoslavia	23 Dec 48	General Trade	81UNTS133	101069
Belgium	Greece	27 Dec 48	General Trade	77UNTS265	101004
Norway	Poland	31 Dec 48	General Trade	29UNTS3	100430
Poland	UK Great Britain	14 Jan 49	General Economic	83UNTS3	101100
Argentina	Netherlands	15 Jan 49	Taxation	46UNTS241	100713
Austria	Norway	28 Jan 49	General Trade	30UNTS145	100452
France	Norway	09 Feb 49	General Economic	29UNTS13	100431
Allied Milit Occup	Norway	17 Feb 49	Milit Occupation	30UNTS137	100451
Norway	Turkey	24 Feb 49	General Trade	29UNTS47	100433
Denmark	Greece	25 Feb 49	General Trade	78UNTS325	101022
Netherlands	Norway	26 Feb 49	General Economic	29UNTS33	100432
Belgium	Norway	08 Mar 49	General Trade	29UNTS83	100435
Greece	Norway	12 Mar 49	General Trade	30UNTS161	100454
Germany, West	Greece	16 Mar 49	General Trade	77UNTS307	101006
Multilateral		16 Mar 49	Finance	29UNTS95	100436
Finland	Greece	24 Mar 49	General Trade	78UNTS3	101008
Denmark	Portugal	08 Apr 49	General Trade	74UNTS209	100964
Argentina	UK Great Britain	27 Jun 49	General Economic	83UNTS217	101110
Greece	Turkey	21 Jul 49	General Trade	78UNTS55	101011

PARTY ONE	PARTY TWO	DATE	TOPIC	CITATION	NUMBER
Commerce (Cont.)					
Brazil	UK Great Britain	03 Aug 49	General Trade	86UNTS113	101154
France	Greece	06 Aug 49	General Trade	91UNTS95	101244
Multilateral		10 Aug 49	Finance	45UNTS3	100689
Multilateral		12 Aug 49	IGO Establishment	87UNTS131	101169
Denmark	UK Great Britain	13 Aug 49	General Trade	68UNTS105	100890
Italy	Netherlands	16 Aug 49	Admin Cooperation	98UNTS21	101357
Belgium	Chile	23 Aug 49	General Economic	46UNTS163	100708
Greece	Italy	31 Aug 49	Reparations	78UNTS89	101014
Argentina	Norway	09 Sep 49	Finance	42UNTS125	100646
Allied Milit Occup	Norway	16 Sep 49	General Trade	53UNTS3	100769
Czechoslovakia	UK Great Britain	28 Sep 49	General Economic	86UNTS141	101156
Indonesia	Netherlands	02 Nov 49	Recognition	69UNTS3	100894
Italy	Norway	19 Nov 49	General Trade	47UNTS75	100723
Denmark	Poland	07 Dec 49	Commodity Trade	81UNTS21	101059
Denmark	Germany, West	15 Dec 49	Finance	51UNTS11	100749
Czechoslovakia	Denmark	17 Dec 49	General Trade	74UNTS147	100961
Austria	Belgium	22 Dec 49	Admin Cooperation	46UNTS233	100712
UK Great Britain	Yugoslavia	26 Dec 49	General Trade	87UNTS71	101167
Greece	Portugal	31 Dec 49	General Trade	92UNTS71	101262
Finland	USA (United States)	18 Jan 50	General Economic	92UNTS197	101272
Austria	Denmark	23 Feb 50	General Trade	74UNTS269	100969
Belgium	UK Great Britain	15 Mar 50	Patents/Copyrights	76UNTS85	100981
Paraguay	UK Great Britain	03 Apr 50	General Economic	99UNTS81	101372
Denmark	Switzerland	06 Apr 50	General Trade	87UNTS197	101173
Sweden	USA (United States)	25 May 50	General Trade	88UNTS43	101184
Multilateral		31 May 50	General Trade	74UNTS95	100957
Denmark	Portugal	02 Jun 50	General Trade	74UNTS229	100966
South Africa	UK Great Britain	12 Jun 50	Customs	93UNTS67	101290
Denmark	Finland	08 Jul 50	General Trade	73UNTS191	100953
Denmark	Spain	12 Jul 50	General Trade	71UNTS135	100914
India	Norway	29 Aug 50	General Trade	73UNTS179	100952
Belgium	Japan	29 Aug 50	General Trade	82UNTS147	101089
Belgium	Japan	29 Aug 50	General Trade	76UNTS113	100984
Brazil	UK Great Britain	18 Sep 50	General Trade	88UNTS115	101188
Denmark	Poland	01 Oct 50	General Economic	81UNTS43	101061
Denmark	Italy	04 Oct 50	General Trade	78UNTS341	101024
Canada	Venezuela	11 Oct 50	General Economic	231UNTS3	103198
Canada	Ecuador	10 Nov 50	General Economic	231UNTS15	103199
Canada	Costa Rica	18 Nov 50	General Economic	231UNTS25	103200
Denmark	Hungary	10 Feb 51	General Trade	85UNTS49	101145
Greece	UK Great Britain	21 Feb 51	General Economic	88UNTS205	101192
Ireland	Norway	02 Jul 51	General Trade	100UNTS53	101387
El Salvador	USA (United States)	23 Jul 51	Direct Aid	138UNTS127	101865
Greece	USA (United States)	03 Aug 51	General Amity	224UNTS279	103080
Canada	Spain	29 Jan 52	Claims and Debts	233UNTS117	103255
Thailand	UK Great Britain	29 Sep 52	General Economic	173UNTS31	102257
Multilateral		07 Nov 52	General Trade	221UNTS255	103010
Denmark	Uruguay	04 Mar 53	General Economic	250UNTS51	103517
Germany, West	USA (United States)	02 Jun 53	General Amity	231UNTS151	103214
Germany, West	USA (United States)	03 Jun 53	General Amity	253UNTS89	103578
Brazil	UK Great Britain	01 Oct 53	Claims and Debts	183UNTS207	102430
Multilateral		09 Dec 53	General Economic	249UNTS197	103509
Cuba	UK Great Britain	18 Dec 53	General Trade	186UNTS157	102490
Canada	Japan	31 Mar 54	General Trade	236UNTS329	103334
Haiti	Italy	14 Jun 54	General Economic	267UNTS97	103837
Germany, West	USA (United States)	29 Oct 54	General Amity	273UNTS3	103943
Canada	Ethiopia	03 Jun 55	General Economic	247UNTS157	103465
Philippines	USA (United States)	06 Sep 55	Visas	238UNTS109	103356
Netherlands	USA (United States)	27 Mar 56	General Amity	285UNTS231	104154
Japan	Norway	28 Feb 57	General Economic	280UNTS87	104054
Netherlands	IBRD (World Bank)	15 May 57	IBRD Project	274UNTS211	103967
Communications					
Bolivia	Brazil	25 Feb 38	Land Transport	88UNTS379	200254
Multilateral		22 Mar 45	General Amity	70UNTS237	200241

PARTY ONE	PARTY TWO	DATE	TOPIC	CITATION	NUMBER
Communications (Cont.)					
Multilateral		04 May 49	Milit Occupation	138UNTS123	101864
Multilateral		16 Sep 50	General Transport	92UNTS91	101264
Belgium	IBRD (World Bank)	13 Sep 51	IBRD Project	158UNTS349	102071
Belgium	IBRD (World Bank)	13 Sep 51	IBRD Project	158UNTS323	102070
Canada	USA (United States)	08 Nov 52	Gen Communications	207UNTS3	102796
Saudi Arabia	USA (United States)	10 Nov 52	Tech Assistance	181UNTS235	102413
Czechoslovakia	Poland	13 Jan 56	Gen Communications	265UNTS157	103811
Companies					
Multilateral		25 Jun 36	Privil/Immunities	161UNTS217	200486
Computers					
Multilateral		06 Dec 51	IGO Establishment	425UNTS61	106119
Conferences and Meetings					
Netherlands	United Nations	27 May 64	IGO Status/Immunit	548UNTS79	107971
Mexico	United Nations	17 Jul 64	IGO Operations	533UNTS117	107738
Multilateral		11 Dec 64	IGO Operations	547UNTS297	107964
Iran	United Nations	16 Feb 65	Admin Cooperation	525UNTS211	107593
United Nations	Sweden	16 Jun 65	Admin Cooperation	539UNTS45	107823
United Nations	Zambia	23 Oct 65	IGO Operations	549UNTS101	107993
Monaco	United Nations	17 Dec 65	IGO Operations	550UNTS365	200615
Continental Shelf					
Multilateral		29 Apr 58	Territory Boundary	499UNTS311	107302
Norway	UK Great Britain	10 Mar 65	Territory Boundary	551UNTS213	108043
Denmark	Germany, West	09 Jun 65	Territory Boundary	570UNTS91	108289
Netherlands	UK Great Britain	06 Oct 65	Territory Boundary	595UNTS113	108616
Netherlands	UK Great Britain	06 Oct 65	Territory Boundary	595UNTS105	108615
Denmark	UK Great Britain	03 Mar 66	Territory Boundary	592UNTS207	108574
Contracts					
Multilateral		08 Sep 51	General Military	136UNTS165	101833
Italy	UK Great Britain	01 Jun 54	Admin Cooperation	312UNTS353	104525
Multilateral		06 Jul 56	Admin Cooperation	312UNTS109	104514
Austria	UK Great Britain	09 Jul 56	Non-ILO Labor	310UNTS61	104487
Germany, West	UK Great Britain	28 Jan 60	Reparations	420UNTS29	106038
Copyrights					
UK Great Britain	USA (United States)	10 Mar 44	Patents/Copyrights	5UNTS205	200030
France	UK Great Britain	29 Aug 45	Patents/Copyrights	11UNTS397	200069
Multilateral		10 Feb 47	Peace/Disarmament	48UNTS203	100746
Multilateral		10 Feb 47	Peace/Disarmament	42UNTS3	100645
Multilateral		10 Feb 47	Peace/Disarmament	41UNTS135	100644
Multilateral		10 Feb 47	Peace/Disarmament	49UNTS3	100747
Multilateral		10 Feb 47	Peace/Disarmament	41UNTS21	100643
France	USA (United States)	27 Mar 47	Patents/Copyrights	16UNTS65	100249
New Zealand	USA (United States)	24 Apr 47	Patents/Copyrights	16UNTS79	100250
Hungary	USA (United States)	09 Mar 48	Admin Cooperation	183UNTS3	102426
Multilateral		26 Jun 48	Culture	331UNTS217	104757
Philippines	USA (United States)	21 Oct 48	Patents/Copyrights	77UNTS197	101000
Australia	USA (United States)	29 Dec 49	Patents/Copyrights	71UNTS45	100909
Israel	USA (United States)	04 May 50	Patents/Copyrights	132UNTS189	101760
Finland	USA (United States)	16 Nov 51	Patents/Copyrights	140UNTS273	101893
Italy	USA (United States)	12 Dec 51	Patents/Copyrights	137UNTS175	101852
Denmark	USA (United States)	04 Feb 52	Patents/Copyrights	157UNTS25	102044
Multilateral		06 Sep 52	Patents/Copyrights	216UNTS132	102937
Monaco	USA (United States)	24 Sep 52	Patents/Copyrights	186UNTS43	102481
Japan	USA (United States)	10 Nov 53	Patents/Copyrights	224UNTS161	103076
India	USA (United States)	21 Oct 54	Patents/Copyrights	234UNTS119	103277
Italy	Norway	16 Dec 56	Patents/Copyrights	291UNTS207	104256
Brazil	USA (United States)	02 Apr 57	Patents/Copyrights	290UNTS119	104231
France	Italy	29 Jul 57	Patents/Copyrights	291UNTS163	104250
Italy	Spain	12 Oct 57	Patents/Copyrights	291UNTS229	104258
Austria	USA (United States)	15 Jun 60	Patents/Copyrights	376UNTS267	105383
Multilateral		26 Oct 61	Patents/Copyrights	496UNTS43	107247
France	Norway	16 Jul 64	Patents/Copyrights	510UNTS229	107417
Austria	Brazil	21 Dec 65	Admin Cooperation	595UNTS299	108624

PARTY ONE	PARTY TWO	DATE	TOPIC	CITATION	NUMBER
Cotton					
Multilateral		30 Oct 47	General Economic	55UNTS188	100814
Burma	UK Great Britain	18 Jun 56	Commodity Trade	256UNTS125	103623
Indonesia	UK Great Britain	02 Jul 56	Commodity Trade	265UNTS285	103820
Indonesia	UK Great Britain	02 Jul 56	Commodity Trade	265UNTS271	103819
Burma	UK Great Britain	20 Jan 59	Commodity Trade	343UNTS201	104926
Burma	UK Great Britain	06 Feb 59	Commodity Trade	343UNTS223	104927
Cuba	Korea, North	29 Aug 60	Consul/Citizenship	469UNTS163	106790
Japan	USA (United States)	16 Oct 61	General Trade	433UNTS287	106250
Italy	USA (United States)	06 Jul 62	Commodity Trade	459UNTS123	106617
Multilateral		02 Apr 63	Commodity Trade	475UNTS121	106889
Spain	USA (United States)	16 Jul 63	Commodity Trade	488UNTS77	107120
Japan	USA (United States)	27 Aug 63	Commodity Trade	487UNTS197	107105
Jamaica	USA (United States)	01 Oct 63	Commodity Trade	488UNTS133	107124
Taiwan	USA (United States)	19 Oct 63	Commodity Trade	494UNTS27	107224
Israel	USA (United States)	22 Nov 63	Commodity Trade	494UNTS89	107228
United Arab Rep	USA (United States)	04 Dec 63	Commodity Trade	505UNTS117	107368
Philippines	USA (United States)	24 Feb 64	Commodity Trade	505UNTS283	107378
Portugal	USA (United States)	12 Mar 64	Commodity Trade	542UNTS3	107875
India	USA (United States)	15 Apr 64	Commodity Trade	527UNTS19	107614
Turkey	USA (United States)	17 Jul 64	Commodity Trade	530UNTS25	107670
Greece	USA (United States)	17 Jul 64	Commodity Trade	530UNTS13	107669
Israel	UK Great Britain	15 Sep 64	Taxation	539UNTS283	107839
USA (United States)	Yugoslavia	05 Oct 64	Commodity Trade	531UNTS63	107693
Korea, South	USA (United States)	26 Jan 65	Commodity Trade	541UNTS77	107862
Pakistan	USA (United States)	26 Feb 65	Commodity Trade	542UNTS103	107883
Colombia	USA (United States)	09 Jun 65	Commodity Trade	549UNTS3	107985
Poland	USA (United States)	24 Jun 65	Commodity Trade	593UNTS147	108581
Multilateral		17 Jan 66	IGO Establishment	592UNTS101	108573
Credits					
Brazil	Paraguay	14 Apr 41	Commodity Trade	54UNTS269	200199
Brazil	Paraguay	14 Jun 41	Finance	54UNTS313	200203
UK Great Britain	USSR (Soviet Union)	16 Aug 41	Finance	91UNTS341	200269
UK Great Britain	USSR (Soviet Union)	22 Jun 42	Finance	91UNTS355	200270
Belgium	UK Great Britain	22 Aug 44	Direct Aid	90UNTS295	200267
Albania	Yugoslavia	01 Jul 46	Loans and Credits	111UNTS81	101518
Albania	Yugoslavia	03 Oct 46	Loans and Credits	111UNTS87	101519
Austria	UK Great Britain	23 Dec 46	General Aid	88UNTS93	101186
Australia	Netherlands	24 Jan 47	Finance	10UNTS77	100144
Albania	Yugoslavia	12 Jun 47	Loans and Credits	111UNTS189	101533
Albania	Yugoslavia	12 Jun 47	Direct Aid	111UNTS177	101531
France	New Zealand	02 Jul 47	Commodity Trade	16UNTS219	100263
USSR (Soviet Union)	Yugoslavia	25 Jul 47	Tech Assistance	130UNTS315	101732
Greece	Norway	08 Dec 47	Loans and Credits	30UNTS171	100455
Czechoslovakia	New Zealand	22 Jan 48	Commodity Trade	16UNTS229	100264
Greece	USA (United States)	23 Apr 48	Education	74UNTS107	100958
Italy	USA (United States)	18 Dec 48	Education	79UNTS133	101037
Norway	USA (United States)	25 May 49	Education	32UNTS345	100507
Australia	Netherlands	12 Aug 49	Reparations	34UNTS213	100539
Turkey	USA (United States)	27 Dec 49	Direct Aid	98UNTS141	101361
France	New Zealand	13 Jan 50	Reparations	150UNTS151	101969
China People's Rep	USSR (Soviet Union)	14 Feb 50	Loans and Credits	226UNTS21	103104
Austria	USA (United States)	06 Jun 50	Education	92UNTS201	101273
Netherlands	USA (United States)	07 Oct 50	Loans and Credits	79UNTS33	101029
UK Great Britain	Yugoslavia	28 Dec 50	Loans and Credits	88UNTS329	101201
UK Great Britain	Yugoslavia	10 May 51	Loans and Credits	102UNTS29	101408
Belgium	Sweden	18 Sep 51	Non-ILO Labor	133UNTS187	101789
Turkey	UK Great Britain	11 Feb 54	Milit Assistance	190UNTS343	102575
Belgium	UK Great Britain	09 Jul 54	Finance	201UNTS299	102721
Peru	IBRD (World Bank)	12 Nov 54	IBRD Project	209UNTS287	102831
India	IBRD (World Bank)	14 Mar 55	IBRD Project	309UNTS129	104472
Costa Rica	IBRD (World Bank)	18 Sep 56	IBRD Project	260UNTS369	103721
Peru	IBRD (World Bank)	13 Mar 57	IBRD Project	274UNTS59	103958
Argentina	Italy	25 Nov 57	General Economic	305UNTS275	104424

PARTY ONE	PARTY TWO	DATE	TOPIC	CITATION	NUMBER
Credits (Cont.)					
Pakistan	IBRD (World Bank)	17 Dec 57	IBRD Project	299UNTS321	104323
Austria	IBRD (World Bank)	28 Apr 58	IBRD Project	359UNTS145	105142
Finland	Sweden	16 Oct 58	Culture	428UNTS125	106171
Costa Rica	IBRD (World Bank)	11 Feb 59	IBRD Project	337UNTS245	104825
Ethiopia	Yugoslavia	06 Jun 59	Loans and Credits	386UNTS243	105544
India	IBRD (World Bank)	15 Jul 59	IBRD Project	355UNTS95	105075
Pakistan	IBRD (World Bank)	25 Sep 59	IBRD Project	355UNTS169	105077
Austria	IBRD (World Bank)	25 Sep 59	IBRD Project	355UNTS223	105079
Cuba	USSR (Soviet Union)	13 Feb 60	Claims and Debts	369UNTS3	105247
Peru	IBRD (World Bank)	01 Jun 60	IBRD Project	380UNTS15	105448
India	IBRD (World Bank)	28 Oct 60	IBRD Project	406UNTS27	105838
IDA (Devel Assoc)	Sudan	14 Jun 61	Loans and Credits	415UNTS50	105981
India	IDA (Devel Assoc)	21 Jun 61	Loans and Credits	418UNTS61	106017
IBRD (World Bank)	UK Great Britain	23 Jun 61	IBRD Project	415UNTS358	105991
Pakistan	IBRD (World Bank)	27 Jun 61	IBRD Project	425UNTS241	106127
Chile	IDA (Devel Assoc)	28 Jun 61	Loans and Credits	426UNTS89	106131
UK Great Britain	Yugoslavia	21 Jul 61	Loans and Credits	420UNTS61	106040
Colombia	IDA (Devel Assoc)	28 Aug 61	Loans and Credits	416UNTS3	105992
Taiwan	IDA (Devel Assoc)	30 Aug 61	Loans and Credits	417UNTS227	106008
Taiwan	IDA (Devel Assoc)	30 Aug 61	Loans and Credits	416UNTS175	106003
Taiwan	IDA (Devel Assoc)	06 Sep 61	Loans and Credits	417UNTS253	106009
India	IDA (Devel Assoc)	06 Sep 61	Loans and Credits	418UNTS81	106018
Costa Rica	IDA (Devel Assoc)	13 Oct 61	Non-IBRD Project	431UNTS3	106204
Pakistan	IDA (Devel Assoc)	19 Oct 61	Non-IBRD Project	447UNTS161	106415
Paraguay	IDA (Devel Assoc)	26 Oct 61	Non-IBRD Project	447UNTS277	106419
Pakistan	IDA (Devel Assoc)	22 Nov 61	Non-IBRD Project	447UNTS295	106420
India	IDA (Devel Assoc)	22 Nov 61	Loans and Credits	427UNTS55	106146
India	IDA (Devel Assoc)	22 Nov 61	Loans and Credits	427UNTS29	106145
India	IDA (Devel Assoc)	22 Nov 61	Loans and Credits	427UNTS3	106144
Taiwan	IDA (Devel Assoc)	01 Dec 61	Loans and Credits	426UNTS105	106132
Jordan	IDA (Devel Assoc)	22 Dec 61	Non-IBRD Project	448UNTS21	106423
India	IDA (Devel Assoc)	14 Feb 62	Non-IBRD Project	468UNTS177	106773
India	IBRD (World Bank)	28 Feb 62	IBRD Project	447UNTS3	106410
IDA (Devel Assoc)	UK Great Britain	13 Mar 62	Direct Aid	466UNTS331	106753
Pakistan	IDA (Devel Assoc)	29 Jun 62	Non-IBRD Project	447UNTS325	106421
India	IDA (Devel Assoc)	29 Jun 62	Non-IBRD Project	447UNTS221	106417
India	IDA (Devel Assoc)	18 Jul 62	Non-IBRD Project	447UNTS191	106416
India	IDA (Devel Assoc)	08 Aug 62	Non-IBRD Project	478UNTS335	106941
Korea, South	IDA (Devel Assoc)	17 Aug 62	Non-IBRD Project	468UNTS387	200603
Nicaragua	IDA (Devel Assoc)	07 Sep 62	Non-IBRD Project	478UNTS313	106940
India	IDA (Devel Assoc)	14 Sep 62	IBRD Project	467UNTS265	106766
India	IDA (Devel Assoc)	14 Sep 62	Non-IBRD Project	448UNTS3	106422
IDA (Devel Assoc)	Tunisia	17 Sep 62	Non-IBRD Project	469UNTS33	106783
Haiti	IDA (Devel Assoc)	02 Nov 62	Non-IBRD Project	468UNTS205	106774
El Salvador	IDA (Devel Assoc)	02 Nov 62	Non-IBRD Project	468UNTS331	106780
Pakistan	IDA (Devel Assoc)	02 Nov 62	Non-IBRD Project	468UNTS351	106781
IDA (Devel Assoc)	Turkey	23 Nov 62	Non-IBRD Project	469UNTS3	106782
IDA (Devel Assoc)	Turkey	01 Feb 63	Non-IBRD Project	468UNTS223	106775
Pakistan	IBRD (World Bank)	13 Feb 63	IBRD Project	467UNTS3	106756
India	New Zealand	22 Feb 63	Loans and Credits	486UNTS19	107069
Ethiopia	IDA (Devel Assoc)	27 Feb 63	Non-IBRD Project	478UNTS289	106939
India	IDA (Devel Assoc)	22 Mar 63	Non-IBRD Project	477UNTS3	106911
India	IDA (Devel Assoc)	24 May 63	Non-IBRD Project	483UNTS205	107014
IDA (Devel Assoc)	Turkey	31 May 63	Non-IBRD Project	480UNTS127	106966
India	IBRD (World Bank)	05 Jun 63	IBRD Project	481UNTS191	106983
Pakistan	IDA (Devel Assoc)	26 Jul 63	Non-IBRD Project	492UNTS143	107190
Pakistan	IDA (Devel Assoc)	16 Aug 63	Non-IBRD Project	492UNTS205	107192
Pakistan	IDA (Devel Assoc)	16 Aug 63	Non-IBRD Project	492UNTS171	107191
Jordan	IDA (Devel Assoc)	12 Dec 63	Non-IBRD Project	492UNTS3	107184
Jordan	IDA (Devel Assoc)	12 Dec 63	Non-IBRD Project	506UNTS51	107381
IDA (Devel Assoc)	Tanganyika	19 Dec 63	Non-IBRD Project	492UNTS241	107193
IDA (Devel Assoc)	Syria	24 Dec 63	Non-IBRD Project	534UNTS253	107764
Paraguay	IDA (Devel Assoc)	26 Dec 63	Non-IBRD Project	507UNTS3	107394
IDA (Devel Assoc)	Tanganyika	05 Feb 64	Non-IBRD Project	506UNTS91	107382
Pakistan	IDA (Devel Assoc)	25 Mar 64	Non-IBRD Project	534UNTS275	107765

PARTY ONE	PARTY TWO	DATE	TOPIC	CITATION	NUMBER
Credits (Cont.)					
Pakistan	IDA (Devel Assoc)	25 Mar 64	Non-IBRD Project	535UNTS43	107775
Ecuador	IDA (Devel Assoc)	26 May 64	Non-IBRD Project	534UNTS93	107757
IBRD (World Bank)	Tunisia	05 Jun 64	IBRD Project	539UNTS129	107827
India	IDA (Devel Assoc)	09 Jun 64	Non-IBRD Project	506UNTS31	107380
Pakistan	IDA (Devel Assoc)	11 Jun 64	Non-IBRD Project	534UNTS309	107766
Pakistan	IDA (Devel Assoc)	11 Jun 64	Non-IBRD Project	506UNTS3	107379
Niger	IDA (Devel Assoc)	24 Jun 64	Non-IBRD Project	554UNTS93	108098
Pakistan	IDA (Devel Assoc)	24 Jun 64	Non-IBRD Project	533UNTS191	107743
India	IDA (Devel Assoc)	06 Jul 64	Non-IBRD Project	534UNTS49	107753
IDA (Devel Assoc)	Turkey	14 Jul 64	Non-IBRD Project	534UNTS339	107767
Pakistan	IDA (Devel Assoc)	21 Jul 64	Non-IBRD Project	534UNTS373	107768
Bolivia	IDA (Devel Assoc)	24 Jul 64	Non-IBRD Project	534UNTS203	107763
Bolivia	IDA (Devel Assoc)	24 Jul 64	Non-IBRD Project	534UNTS171	107762
IDA (Devel Assoc)	UK Great Britain	31 Jul 64	Non-IBRD Project	535UNTS205	107781
Kenya	IDA (Devel Assoc)	17 Aug 64	Non-IBRD Project	535UNTS79	107776
Pakistan	IDA (Devel Assoc)	26 Aug 64	Non-IBRD Project	535UNTS263	107784
IDA (Devel Assoc)	Turkey	31 Aug 64	Non-IBRD Project	535UNTS111	107777
Pakistan	IDA (Devel Assoc)	22 Sep 64	Non-IBRD Project	594UNTS225	108605
Mali	IDA (Devel Assoc)	29 Sep 64	Non-IBRD Project	594UNTS187	108604
India	IDA (Devel Assoc)	26 Oct 64	Non-IBRD Project	535UNTS245	107783
India	UK Great Britain	20 Nov 64	Milit Assistance	534UNTS85	107756
Afghanistan	IDA (Devel Assoc)	23 Nov 64	Non-IBRD Project	567UNTS155	108255
Kenya	IDA (Devel Assoc)	29 Dec 64	Non-IBRD Project	535UNTS225	107782
Honduras	IDA (Devel Assoc)	02 Feb 65	Non-IBRD Project	561UNTS279	108189
Nigeria	IDA (Devel Assoc)	01 Mar 65	Non-IBRD Project	563UNTS3	108201
Nigeria	IDA (Devel Assoc)	01 Mar 65	Non-IBRD Project	571UNTS3	108297
IDA (Devel Assoc)	Somalia	29 Mar 65	Non-IBRD Project	586UNTS101	108499
Multilateral		29 Mar 65	Non-IBRD Project	540UNTS145	107848
IDA (Devel Assoc)	Turkey	01 Apr 65	Non-IBRD Project	554UNTS137	108100
Multilateral		29 Apr 65	Non-IBRD Project	586UNTS123	108500
India	IBRD (World Bank)	28 May 65	Loans and Credits	552UNTS39	108049
Kenya	IDA (Devel Assoc)	30 Jun 65	Non-IBRD Project	554UNTS75	108097
Pakistan	IDA (Devel Assoc)	30 Jun 65	Non-IBRD Project	554UNTS111	108099
Pakistan	IBRD (World Bank)	09 Jul 65	IBRD Project	554UNTS39	108096
India	IDA (Devel Assoc)	11 Aug 65	Non-IBRD Project	562UNTS277	108199
Mexico	IBRD (World Bank)	01 Oct 65	IBRD Project	589UNTS339	108542
Morocco	IDA (Devel Assoc)	11 Oct 65	Non-IBRD Project	562UNTS299	108200
Philippines	IBRD (World Bank)	02 Nov 65	IBRD Project	567UNTS3	108249
Morocco	IBRD (World Bank)	08 Nov 65	Claims and Debts	566UNTS279	108247
IDA (Devel Assoc)	Tanzania	13 Jan 66	Non-IBRD Project	567UNTS177	108256
Pakistan	IDA (Devel Assoc)	13 Jan 66	Non-IBRD Project	567UNTS67	108252
IDA (Devel Assoc)	UK Great Britain	08 Feb 66	Non-IBRD Project	567UNTS207	108257
Pakistan	IDA (Devel Assoc)	10 Feb 66	Non-IBRD Project	575UNTS89	108355
Multilateral		10 Feb 66	Loans and Credits	575UNTS129	108356
Ethiopia	IDA (Devel Assoc)	16 Feb 66	Loans and Credits	569UNTS43	108278
Burundi	IDA (Devel Assoc)	31 Mar 66	Loans and Credits	569UNTS3	108277
Paraguay	IDA (Devel Assoc)	04 Apr 66	Non-IBRD Project	582UNTS331	108469
Pakistan	IDA (Devel Assoc)	17 Jun 66	Non-IBRD Project	582UNTS297	108468
India	IDA (Devel Assoc)	29 Jun 66	Non-IBRD Project	582UNTS277	108467
India	IDA (Devel Assoc)	29 Jun 66	Non-IBRD Project	585UNTS101	108484
IDA (Devel Assoc)	Siam	02 Aug 66	Non-IBRD Project	585UNTS271	108492
IDA (Devel Assoc)	Turkey	10 Aug 66	Non-IBRD Project	585UNTS237	108491
India	IDA (Devel Assoc)	19 Aug 66	Non-IBRD Project	584UNTS193	108478
Kenya	IDA (Devel Assoc)	19 Aug 66	Non-IBRD Project	585UNTS119	108485
IDA (Devel Assoc)	Senegal	29 Sep 66	Non-IBRD Project	594UNTS277	108607
Malawi	IDA (Devel Assoc)	04 Oct 66	Non-IBRD Project	584UNTS215	108479
Pakistan	IDA (Devel Assoc)	23 Dec 66	Non-IBRD Project	594UNTS255	108606
India	IDA (Devel Assoc)	23 Dec 66	Non-IBRD Project	594UNTS165	108603
Crime Prevention					
Brazil	United Nations	04 Aug 52	Tech Assistance	135UNTS185	101820
Crime Prevention					
Japan	United Nations	15 Mar 61	IGO Operations	397UNTS199	105706

PARTY ONE	PARTY TWO	DATE	TOPIC	CITATION	NUMBER
Crime Prevention					
United Nations	Sweden	16 Jun 65	Admin Cooperation	539UNTS45	107823
Cultural Cooperation					
Belgium	France	22 Feb 46	Culture	68UNTS157	100892
Mongolia	USSR (Soviet Union)	27 Feb 46	General Economic	216UNTS221	102938
Belgium	Netherlands	16 May 46	Culture	17UNTS13	100266
Romania	Yugoslavia	26 Jun 47	Culture	116UNTS39	101568
Norway	UK Great Britain	19 Feb 48	Culture	34UNTS33	100526
Belgium	Luxembourg	27 Mar 48	Culture	178UNTS265	102343
Netherlands	UK Great Britain	07 Jul 48	Culture	82UNTS259	101099
Korea, North	USSR (Soviet Union)	17 Mar 49	General Economic	221UNTS3	102999
Luxembourg	Netherlands	26 Apr 49	Culture	182UNTS187	102425
Greece	Lebanon	10 Jun 49	Culture	178UNTS29	102334
Iran	USA (United States)	01 Sep 49	Direct Aid	79UNTS155	101039
Luxembourg	UK Great Britain	27 Jun 50	Culture	183UNTS217	102431
Albania	Poland	02 Dec 50	Culture	260UNTS131	103707
China People's Rep	Poland	03 Apr 51	Culture	304UNTS187	104396
Greece	Turkey	20 Apr 51	Culture	178UNTS17	102333
Netherlands	South Africa	31 May 51	Culture	188UNTS289	102533
India	Turkey	29 Jun 51	Culture	213UNTS183	102886
Greece	UK Great Britain	29 Sep 51	Culture	190UNTS260	102570
Italy	UK Great Britain	28 Nov 51	Culture	172UNTS27	102238
Germany, East	Poland	08 Jan 52	Culture	304UNTS113	104394
Austria	Belgium	17 Oct 52	Culture	162UNTS183	102135
Austria	UK Great Britain	12 Dec 52	Culture	172UNTS9	102237
Bolivia	Italy	31 Jan 53	Culture	281UNTS181	104079
Albania	Romania	14 Feb 53	Culture	342UNTS107	104903
Germany, West	USA (United States)	09 Apr 53	Culture	204UNTS79	102750
Greece	Netherlands	29 Apr 53	Culture	191UNTS235	102583
Israel	Uruguay	30 Apr 53	Culture	280UNTS269	104064
Pakistan	Turkey	29 Jun 53	Culture	211UNTS225	102854
Pakistan	United Arab Rep	14 Nov 53	Culture	485UNTS55	107046
UK Great Britain	Yugoslavia	31 Dec 53	Education	190UNTS335	102574
Belgium	South Africa	01 Jun 54	Culture	201UNTS25	102708
Ethiopia	Greece	31 Jul 54	Culture	241UNTS319	103439
Greece	Italy	11 Sep 54	Culture	284UNTS313	104145
Portugal	UK Great Britain	19 Nov 54	Culture	226UNTS305	103125
Belgium	Greece	09 Dec 54	Culture	257UNTS243	103660
Multilateral		19 Dec 54	Culture	218UNTS139	102955
UK Great Britain	Yugoslavia	31 Dec 54	Education	209UNTS81	102824
Belgium	Netherlands	13 Jan 55	Visas	210UNTS63	102834
Japan	Thailand	06 Apr 55	Culture	230UNTS219	103187
Netherlands	Norway	18 May 55	Culture	252UNTS269	103569
Italy	Norway	14 Jun 55	Culture	260UNTS307	103713
Belgium	Portugal	30 Jul 55	Culture	250UNTS213	103525
Italy	Spain	11 Aug 55	Culture	267UNTS125	103839
Iran	Pakistan	09 Mar 56	Culture	449UNTS183	106460
Turkey	UK Great Britain	12 Mar 56	Culture	313UNTS73	104530
Romania	USSR (Soviet Union)	07 Apr 56	Culture	259UNTS377	103698
Mongolia	USSR (Soviet Union)	24 Apr 56	Culture	259UNTS297	103693
Germany, East	USSR (Soviet Union)	26 Apr 56	Health/Educ/Welfare	259UNTS279	103692
Bulgaria	USSR (Soviet Union)	28 Apr 56	Culture	259UNTS363	103697
Albania	USSR (Soviet Union)	03 May 56	Culture	259UNTS391	103699
Mongolia	Romania	08 May 56	Culture	342UNTS291	104913
Korea, North	Poland	11 May 56	Culture	432UNTS161	106219
Korea, North	Romania	12 May 56	Culture	342UNTS189	104908
USSR (Soviet Union)	Yugoslavia	17 May 56	Culture	259UNTS145	103687
Czechoslovakia	USSR (Soviet Union)	01 Jun 56	Culture	259UNTS341	103696
Hungary	USSR (Soviet Union)	28 Jun 56	Health/Educ/Welfare	259UNTS405	103700
Poland	USSR (Soviet Union)	30 Jun 56	Culture	259UNTS311	103694
China People's Rep	USSR (Soviet Union)	05 Jul 56	Culture	263UNTS129	103770
Poland	Yugoslavia	06 Jul 56	Culture	281UNTS143	104076
Syria	USSR (Soviet Union)	20 Aug 56	Culture	274UNTS105	103961
Greece	United Arab Rep	04 Sep 56	Culture	299UNTS253	104317

PARTY ONE	PARTY TWO	DATE	TOPIC	CITATION	NUMBER
Cultural Cooperation (Cont.)					
Korea, North	USSR (Soviet Union)	05 Sep 56	Culture	259UNTS329	103695
Belgium	Germany, West	24 Sep 56	Culture	263UNTS31	103766
Romania	Vietnam, North	12 Oct 56	Culture	342UNTS173	104907
Norway	USSR (Soviet Union)	12 Oct 56	Culture	308UNTS95	104457
Denmark	Italy	26 Oct 56	Culture	267UNTS261	103847
Romania	Yugoslavia	27 Oct 56	Culture	389UNTS33	105590
India	Japan	29 Oct 56	Culture	318UNTS289	104622
Bulgaria	Yugoslavia	24 Dec 56	Culture	397UNTS3	105699
Czechoslovakia	Yugoslavia	29 Jan 57	Culture	300UNTS249	104339
Poland	United Arab Rep	02 Feb 57	Culture	319UNTS221	104633
Belgium	Yugoslavia	05 Feb 57	Culture	276UNTS143	103990
Taiwan	Spain	07 Feb 57	Culture	314UNTS161	104547
Taiwan	Turkey	12 Feb 57	Culture	282UNTS125	104097
Germany, West	Japan	14 Feb 57	Culture	318UNTS361	104626
USSR (Soviet Union)	Vietnam, North	15 Feb 57	Culture	274UNTS115	103962
Japan	United Arab Rep	20 Mar 57	Culture	318UNTS345	104625
India	Poland	27 Mar 57	Culture	319UNTS263	104635
Poland	Vietnam, North	06 Apr 57	Culture	432UNTS255	106224
Romania	United Arab Rep	15 Apr 57	Culture	389UNTS21	105589
Iran	Japan	16 Apr 57	Culture	325UNTS113	104697
India	Romania	30 Apr 57	Culture	342UNTS251	104911
Argentina	Israel	23 May 57	Culture	280UNTS199	104059
Japan	Pakistan	27 May 57	Culture	325UNTS21	104692
Czechoslovakia	Syria	18 Jun 57	Culture	303UNTS119	104374
Czechoslovakia	United Arab Rep	19 Oct 57	Culture	530UNTS181	107681
United Arab Rep	USSR (Soviet Union)	19 Oct 57	Culture	292UNTS151	104271
Taiwan	Iran	11 Nov 57	Culture	563UNTS31	108202
Israel	Norway	26 Nov 57	Culture	345UNTS99	104962
Belgium	Denmark	31 Dec 57	Culture	305UNTS247	104422
Norway	Turkey	10 Jan 58	Culture	351UNTS229	105025
Ceylon (Sri Lanka)	USSR (Soviet Union)	15 Jan 58	Culture	305UNTS235	104421
USA (United States)	USSR (Soviet Union)	27 Jan 58	Health/Educ/Welfare	301UNTS405	104350
Taiwan	Costa Rica	10 Apr 58	Culture	315UNTS165	104567
Germany, West	UK Great Britain	18 Apr 58	Culture	343UNTS241	104928
Poland	USA (United States)	30 May 58	Mass Media	315UNTS231	104572
Afghanistan	USA (United States)	26 Jun 58	Culture	321UNTS67	104654
Germany, East	Romania	15 Jul 58	Health/Educ/Welfare	387UNTS115	105560
Finland	Sweden	16 Oct 58	Culture	428UNTS125	106171
Czechoslovakia	Romania	25 Oct 58	Culture	338UNTS301	104843
Belgium	Spain	27 Oct 58	Culture	327UNTS107	104720
El Salvador	Israel	14 Nov 58	Culture	345UNTS67	104959
Multilateral		15 Dec 58	Mass Media	546UNTS235	107950
Norway	Poland	17 Dec 58	Culture	432UNTS193	106221
Mongolia	Poland	23 Dec 58	Culture	432UNTS177	106220
Belgium	Turkey	29 Dec 58	Culture	357UNTS195	105118
Iraq	Poland	02 Apr 59	Culture	432UNTS147	106218
Hungary	Iraq	11 Apr 59	Culture	439UNTS25	106323
Iraq	USSR (Soviet Union)	05 May 59	Culture	356UNTS179	105095
Iran	UK Great Britain	06 May 59	Culture	398UNTS51	105717
Iran	Netherlands	22 May 59	Culture	474UNTS195	106882
Finland	Hungary	10 Jun 59	Culture	439UNTS3	106321
Taiwan	Ecuador	12 Jun 59	Culture	387UNTS3	105554
Israel	Mexico	15 Jun 59	Culture	377UNTS267	105406
Greece	Yugoslavia	18 Jun 59	Culture	368UNTS137	105238
Brazil	Israel	24 Jun 59	Culture	515UNTS151	107458
Czechoslovakia	India	07 Jul 59	Culture	359UNTS259	105145
Iraq	Romania	04 Aug 59	Culture	502UNTS17	107324
Norway	Spain	19 Aug 59	Culture	376UNTS145	105379
Guinea	USA (United States)	28 Oct 59	Culture	358UNTS169	105134
USA (United States)	USSR (Soviet Union)	21 Nov 59	Culture	361UNTS35	105172
Czechoslovakia	Guinea	30 Nov 59	Culture	386UNTS63	105538
France	Israel	30 Nov 59	Culture	377UNTS237	105404
UK Great Britain	USSR (Soviet Union)	01 Dec 59	Health/Educ/Welfare	351UNTS313	105032
Czechoslovakia	Ethiopia	11 Dec 59	Culture	399UNTS93	105736
Iraq	UK Great Britain	14 Dec 59	Culture	374UNTS253	105339

PARTY ONE	PARTY TWO	DATE	TOPIC	CITATION	NUMBER
Cultural Cooperation (Cont.)					
Germany, East	Hungary	19 Dec 59	Health/Educ/Welfare	409UNTS4	105874
Belgium	Brazil	06 Jan 60	Culture	531UNTS149	107701
Guinea	Hungary	12 Jan 60	Culture	519UNTS131	107505
Italy	USSR (Soviet Union)	09 Feb 60	Culture	399UNTS75	105735
Argentina	Philippines	12 Feb 60	General Amity	535UNTS293	107785
India	USSR (Soviet Union)	12 Feb 60	Culture	392UNTS153	105642
Taiwan	Panama	26 Feb 60	Culture	435UNTS281	106285
Indonesia	USSR (Soviet Union)	28 Feb 60	Culture	392UNTS191	105644
UK Great Britain	Yugoslavia	12 Apr 60	Culture	360UNTS79	105155
Finland	Sweden	13 Apr 60	Culture	428UNTS131	106172
Netherlands	Turkey	12 May 60	Culture	463UNTS207	106704
Belgium	Iran	14 May 60	Culture	522UNTS249	107551
Finland	USSR (Soviet Union)	27 May 60	Culture	379UNTS381	105444
Denmark	Poland	08 Jun 60	Culture	424UNTS37	106097
Czechoslovakia	Germany, East	16 Jun 60	General Economic	415UNTS248	105988
Spain	UK Great Britain	12 Jul 60	Culture	414UNTS123	105971
Cuba	Korea, North	29 Aug 60	Culture	473UNTS117	106860
Israel	UK Great Britain	31 Aug 60	Culture	385UNTS71	105530
Cuba	Romania	28 Oct 60	Culture	457UNTS9	106574
Czechoslovakia	Ghana	23 Nov 60	Culture	431UNTS91	106213
Israel	Mali	24 Nov 60	Culture	413UNTS104	105945
Cambodia	Czechoslovakia	27 Nov 60	Culture	410UNTS263	105910
Japan	UK Great Britain	03 Dec 60	Culture	414UNTS61	105966
Netherlands	United Arab Rep	08 Dec 60	Culture	455UNTS276	106547
Romania	USA (United States)	09 Dec 60	Culture	401UNTS19	105759
Cuba	USSR (Soviet Union)	12 Dec 60	Culture	421UNTS3	106048
Cuba	Czechoslovakia	22 Dec 60	Culture	426UNTS145	106134
UK Great Britain	USSR (Soviet Union)	09 Jan 61	Health/Educ/Welfare	404UNTS175	105810
UK Great Britain	USSR (Soviet Union)	12 Jan 61	Culture	398UNTS157	105720
Ethiopia	USSR (Soviet Union)	13 Jan 61	Culture	421UNTS13	106049
Ghana	Poland	17 Jan 61	Culture	572UNTS209	108314
Brazil	Japan	23 Jan 61	Culture	569UNTS81	108281
Czechoslovakia	Hungary	24 Feb 61	Culture	422UNTS15	106066
Cuba	Poland	06 Mar 61	Culture	484UNTS123	107020
Cuba	Germany, East	29 Mar 61	Culture	448UNTS81	106426
India	Norway	19 Apr 61	Culture	404UNTS307	105818
Afghanistan	Czechoslovakia	23 Apr 61	Culture	437UNTS25	106297
Taiwan	Nicaragua	25 Apr 61	Culture	423UNTS139	106090
Germany, West	Netherlands	27 Apr 61	Culture	487UNTS77	107095
Ghana	Hungary	27 Apr 61	Culture	439UNTS17	106322
Taiwan	Uruguay	03 May 61	Culture	596UNTS121	108630
Somalia	USSR (Soviet Union)	02 Jun 61	Culture	528UNTS147	107638
Czechoslovakia	Somalia	04 Jun 61	Culture	479UNTS291	106960
Argentina	UK Great Britain	19 Jun 61	Culture	470UNTS71	106797
Pakistan	Philippines	15 Aug 61	Culture	522UNTS35	107534
Taiwan	Paraguay	18 Aug 61	Culture	438UNTS109	106314
Ghana	Romania	30 Sep 61	Culture	457UNTS3	106573
Hungary	Iraq	11 Oct 61	Gen Communications	577UNTS231	108380
Taiwan	Jordan	17 Oct 61	Culture	435UNTS267	106284
Brazil	Poland	19 Oct 61	Culture	552UNTS75	108050
United Arab Rep	UK Great Britain	14 Nov 61	Education	449UNTS129	106455
Guatemala	Israel	27 Nov 61	Culture	448UNTS191	106431
Taiwan	El Salvador	27 Nov 61	Culture	437UNTS161	106306
UK Great Britain	Yugoslavia	13 Feb 62	Culture	431UNTS35	106207
USA (United States)	USSR (Soviet Union)	08 Mar 62	Health/Educ/Welfare	460UNTS3	106630
Hungary	India	30 Mar 62	Culture	519UNTS119	107504
United Arab Rep	USA (United States)	21 May 62	Culture	458UNTS197	106601
Senegal	USSR (Soviet Union)	14 Jun 62	Culture	437UNTS233	106309
Israel	Peru	25 Jun 62	Culture	515UNTS263	107464
Israel	Liberia	25 Jun 62	Culture	448UNTS295	106442
Costa Rica	Israel	31 Jul 62	Education	484UNTS155	107024
Syria	USSR (Soviet Union)	19 Aug 62	Culture	457UNTS285	106588
Denmark	USSR (Soviet Union)	11 Sep 62	Culture	458UNTS3	106589
Cameroon	Israel	24 Oct 62	Culture	449UNTS15	106447
Mali	Poland	02 Nov 62	Culture	572UNTS219	108315

PARTY ONE	PARTY TWO	DATE	TOPIC	CITATION	NUMBER
Cultural Cooperation (Cont.)					
UK Great Britain	Yugoslavia	28 Nov 62	Commodity Trade	470UNTS65	106796
Belgium	Tunisia	21 Dec 62	Culture	482UNTS3	106987
UK Great Britain	USSR (Soviet Union)	21 Jan 63	Health/Educ/Welfare	475UNTS3	106887
Iraq	USA (United States)	23 Jan 63	Culture	488UNTS163	107126
Dahomey	USSR (Soviet Union)	20 Mar 63	Culture	528UNTS181	107641
Romania	USA (United States)	02 Apr 63	Culture	474UNTS95	106874
Czechoslovakia	Tunisia	06 Apr 63	Culture	555UNTS111	108106
Belgium	Venezuela	15 May 63	Culture	470UNTS259	106812
Taiwan	Liberia	15 Jun 63	Culture	521UNTS361	107531
Austria	USA (United States)	25 Jun 63	Education	479UNTS223	106956
Cameroon	UK Great Britain	20 Aug 63	Culture	539UNTS233	107834
Mali	Romania	26 Sep 63	Culture	528UNTS193	107642
Hungary	Yugoslavia	15 Oct 63	Health/Educ/Welfare	577UNTS49	108372
Tanganyika	USSR (Soviet Union)	06 Nov 63	Culture	528UNTS157	107639
Belgium	Romania	13 Nov 63	Culture	520UNTS119	107513
Belgium	Pakistan	14 Nov 63	Culture	535UNTS393	107792
Belgium	Poland	09 Dec 63	Culture	514UNTS195	107448
UK Great Britain	Yugoslavia	18 Dec 63	Commodity Trade	502UNTS177	107328
Netherlands	Tunisia	11 Feb 64	Culture	570UNTS173	108293
USA (United States)	USSR (Soviet Union)	22 Feb 64	Health/Educ/Welfare	526UNTS131	107605
Spain	USA (United States)	18 Mar 64	Culture	535UNTS343	107789
Ireland	Norway	02 Apr 64	Culture	553UNTS129	108078
Mexico	Netherlands	08 Apr 64	Culture	575UNTS35	108353
Algeria	Czechoslovakia	14 May 64	Culture	538UNTS301	107817
Germany, East	Poland	06 Oct 64	Culture	552UNTS89	108051
Czechoslovakia	Germany, East	06 Oct 64	Culture	545UNTS113	107927
Belgium	Mexico	19 Nov 64	Culture	546UNTS217	107949
Poland	Romania	26 Nov 64	Health/Educ/Welfare	552UNTS157	108053
Romania	USA (United States)	23 Dec 64	Health/Educ/Welfare	535UNTS359	107790
Belgium	Sweden	11 Jan 65	Education	533UNTS157	107741
Belgium	Hungary	11 Feb 65	Culture	544UNTS3	107908
UK Great Britain	USSR (Soviet Union)	13 Feb 65	Health/Educ/Welfare	543UNTS43	107896
UK Great Britain	Yugoslavia	01 Mar 65	General Trade	548UNTS85	107972
France	USA (United States)	07 May 65	Education	573UNTS183	108331
UK Great Britain	USA (United States)	10 May 65	Education	545UNTS181	107934
Bulgaria	Czechoslovakia	22 May 65	Culture	545UNTS65	107925
Ethiopia	Hungary	25 May 65	Health/Educ/Welfare	577UNTS193	108377
China People's Rep	Romania	27 May 65	Culture	592UNTS3	108566
Pakistan	USSR (Soviet Union)	05 Jun 65	Culture	593UNTS115	108579
Japan	Korea, South	22 Jun 65	Culture	584UNTS49	108475
Uganda	USSR (Soviet Union)	24 Jul 65	Culture	596UNTS199	108633
Bulgaria	Hungary	19 Aug 65	Culture	577UNTS67	108373
Israel	Sierra Leone	22 Aug 65	Culture	550UNTS275	108022
Czechoslovakia	Poland	22 Jan 66	Culture	588UNTS175	108524
UK Great Britain	Yugoslavia	27 Jan 66	Culture	573UNTS243	108337
UK Great Britain	Yugoslavia	02 Feb 66	Commodity Trade	571UNTS275	108306
Czechoslovakia	USSR (Soviet Union)	23 Apr 66	Culture	566UNTS159	108242
Cultural Property					
Multilateral		14 May 54	Culture	249UNTS215	103511
Customs					
Cuba	USA (United States)	16 May 32	Consul/Citizenship	234UNTS283	200537
Panama	USA (United States)	31 Jan 35	Consul/Citizenship	234UNTS277	200536
Brazil	Paraguay	14 Jun 41	Specific Property	54UNTS259	200198
Canada	USA (United States)	09 Nov 42	General Trade	101UNTS233	200298
Dominican Republic	USA (United States)	14 Nov 42	Customs	24UNTS233	200148
Iceland	USA (United States)	27 Sep 43	General Trade	29UNTS317	200170
Haiti	USA (United States)	24 Aug 45	Visas	139UNTS311	200458
United Arab Rep	USA (United States)	05 Jan 46	Status of Forces	160UNTS27	102098
UK Great Britain	USA (United States)	21 Feb 46	General Trade	6UNTS137	100073
Philippines	USA (United States)	04 Jul 46	General Trade	43UNTS135	100668
Czechoslovakia	Poland	04 Apr 47	General Economic	85UNTS62	101146
Canada	Switzerland	14 Jul 47	Admin Cooperation	43UNTS103	100664
Netherlands	New Zealand	30 Oct 47	General Economic	76UNTS41	100977
Canada	USA (United States)	30 Oct 47	General Economic	27UNTS19	100394

PARTY ONE	PARTY TWO	DATE	TOPIC	CITATION	NUMBER
Customs (Cont.)					
Netherlands	USA (United States)	30 Oct 47	General Economic	76UNTS47	100978
Multilateral		30 Oct 47	General Economic	55UNTS188	100814
Multilateral		22 Dec 47	Customs	32UNTS143	100496
Canada	Turkey	15 Mar 48	General Economic	231UNTS63	103205
Belgium	France	13 Apr 48	Territory Boundary	31UNTS409	100483
Belgium	Netherlands	13 Apr 48	Customs	32UNTS153	100497
Canada	Italy	28 Apr 48	General Economic	231UNTS69	103206
Italy	USA (United States)	28 Jun 48	Milit Occupation	25UNTS45	100356
Denmark	USA (United States)	29 Jun 48	Mostfavored Nation	27UNTS35	100396
Austria	USA (United States)	02 Jul 48	Milit Occupation	25UNTS53	100357
Belgium	USA (United States)	02 Jul 48	Mostfavored Nation	27UNTS43	100397
Iceland	USA (United States)	03 Jul 48	Milit Occupation	27UNTS49	100398
Sweden	USA (United States)	03 Jul 48	Milit Occupation	27UNTS69	100400
Norway	USA (United States)	03 Jul 48	Milit Occupation	27UNTS59	100399
UK Great Britain	USA (United States)	06 Jul 48	Milit Occupation	25UNTS61	100358
Liberia	USA (United States)	26 Jul 48	Customs	182UNTS73	102423
Multilateral		14 Sep 48	Milit Occupation	18UNTS267	100296
Poland	USA (United States)	30 Oct 48	Consul/Citizenship	15UNTS225	100238
Italy	USA (United States)	26 Nov 48	Direct Aid	79UNTS71	101032
UK Great Britain	USA (United States)	01 Dec 48	Direct Aid	81UNTS93	101066
South Africa	UK Great Britain	06 Dec 48	Customs	118UNTS183	101607
Korea, South	USA (United States)	10 Dec 48	Direct Aid	55UNTS157	100813
Multilateral		16 Dec 48	Direct Aid	79UNTS85	101033
France	USA (United States)	23 Dec 48	Direct Aid	67UNTS171	100876
France	USA (United States)	07 Feb 49	Direct Aid	67UNTS189	100877
Greece	USA (United States)	09 Feb 49	Direct Aid	79UNTS95	101034
Austria	USA (United States)	11 Feb 49	Direct Aid	79UNTS113	101035
Trieste	USA (United States)	11 Feb 49	Direct Aid	79UNTS123	101036
Chile	USA (United States)	09 Apr 49	Customs	122UNTS169	101646
Belgium	Netherlands	13 May 49	Customs	65UNTS133	100841
Multilateral		16 Jun 49	Land Transport	45UNTS149	100696
Liberia	USA (United States)	22 Jul 49	Visas	232UNTS283	103242
Belgium	Chile	23 Aug 49	General Economic	46UNTS163	100708
Norway	USA (United States)	31 Oct 49	Direct Aid	68UNTS3	100879
Multilateral		16 Dec 49	Admin Cooperation	72UNTS3	100924
Finland	USA (United States)	18 Jan 50	General Economic	92UNTS197	101272
Dominican Republic	USA (United States)	23 Jan 50	Consul/Citizenship	236UNTS3	103312
Multilateral		18 Feb 50	Customs	123UNTS45	101654
Multilateral		06 Apr 50	Admin Cooperation	119UNTS99	101610
Chile	USA (United States)	12 May 50	Consul/Citizenship	177UNTS103	102312
South Africa	UK Great Britain	12 Jun 50	Customs	93UNTS67	101290
Israel	Turkey	04 Jul 50	Mostfavored Nation	220UNTS3	102982
Canada	Venezuela	11 Oct 50	General Economic	231UNTS3	103198
Canada	Ecuador	10 Nov 50	General Economic	231UNTS15	103199
Canada	Costa Rica	18 Nov 50	General Economic	231UNTS25	103200
Multilateral		22 Nov 50	Culture	131UNTS25	101734
Multilateral		15 Dec 50	Customs	347UNTS127	104994
Multilateral		15 Dec 50	Customs	157UNTS129	102052
Multilateral		15 Dec 50	IGO Operations	160UNTS267	102111
Multilateral		15 Dec 50	Customs	171UNTS305	102234
Greece	UK Great Britain	21 Feb 51	General Economic	88UNTS205	101192
Israel	USA (United States)	28 Feb 51	Taxation	220UNTS79	102991
Belgium	Brazil	08 May 51	Consul/Citizenship	91UNTS75	101242
India	USA (United States)	09 Jul 51	Customs	147UNTS43	101927
Israel	Yugoslavia	29 Jul 51	Mostfavored Nation	220UNTS7	102983
Iraq	USA (United States)	08 Aug 51	Visas	229UNTS185	103166
Belgium	Brazil	11 Aug 51	Consul/Citizenship	104UNTS17	101431
Cuba	USA (United States)	17 Dec 51	Visas	152UNTS87	102012
Multilateral		10 Jan 52	Visas	163UNTS3	102138
Multilateral		10 Jan 52	Visas	163UNTS27	102139
Multilateral		05 Sep 52	Customs	247UNTS329	103479
France	Israel	15 Sep 52	Customs	220UNTS65	102989
Belgium	Italy	22 Sep 52	Customs	157UNTS121	102051
Nicaragua	USA (United States)	09 Oct 52	Consul/Citizenship	184UNTS105	102442
Multilateral		07 Nov 52	General Trade	221UNTS255	103010

PARTY ONE	PARTY TWO	DATE	TOPIC	CITATION	NUMBER
Customs (Cont.)					
USA (United States)	Uruguay	12 Nov 52	Visas	231UNTS145	103213
Denmark	Israel	14 Nov 52	General Economic	160UNTS275	102112
USA (United States)	Yugoslavia	03 Dec 52	Direct Aid	185UNTS183	102469
Belgium	France	30 Jan 53	Visas	188UNTS141	102525
Sweden	Switzerland	12 Aug 53	Customs	232UNTS59	103229
Netherlands	UK Great Britain	19 Oct 53	Customs	306UNTS99	104435
Netherlands	Switzerland	03 Nov 53	Customs	293UNTS53	104285
Belgium	Germany, West	15 Apr 54	Admin Cooperation	190UNTS253	102569
Chile	USA (United States)	10 May 54	Customs	247UNTS299	103477
Afghanistan	USA (United States)	29 May 54	Direct Aid	234UNTS3	103268
Multilateral		04 Jun 54	Customs	276UNTS191	103992
Multilateral		04 Jun 54	Customs	282UNTS249	104101
Bolivia	USA (United States)	16 Jun 54	Direct Aid	234UNTS35	103271
Jordan	USA (United States)	29 Jun 54	Direct Aid	237UNTS111	103339
USA (United States)	Vietnam, South	26 Aug 54	Direct Aid	234UNTS111	103276
Pakistan	USA (United States)	02 Oct 54	Direct Aid	236UNTS187	103324
Canada	UK Great Britain	19 Oct 54	Milit Assistance	214UNTS309	102906
Peru	USA (United States)	25 Oct 54	Direct Aid	238UNTS247	103368
United Arab Rep	USA (United States)	30 Oct 54	Direct Aid	234UNTS139	103279
Chile	USA (United States)	05 Apr 55	Direct Aid	250UNTS253	103527
Korea, South	USA (United States)	02 May 55	Direct Aid	258UNTS3	103666
Canada	USA (United States)	08 Jun 55	Customs	247UNTS163	103466
Ecuador	USA (United States)	06 Sep 55	Direct Aid	256UNTS187	103628
Libya	USA (United States)	22 Dec 55	Direct Aid	240UNTS111	103399
Multilateral		01 Mar 56	Customs	343UNTS129	104923
Paraguay	USA (United States)	11 May 56	Visas	269UNTS33	103870
Multilateral		18 May 56	Land Transport	339UNTS3	104844
Multilateral		18 May 56	Customs	319UNTS21	104630
Multilateral		18 May 56	Customs	327UNTS123	104721
Multilateral		18 May 56	Customs	338UNTS103	104834
USA (United States)	Yugoslavia	21 May 56	Visas	281UNTS93	104072
Philippines	USA (United States)	18 Oct 56	Taxation	280UNTS55	104050
Multilateral		08 Nov 56	Commodity Trade	470UNTS171	106809
Australia	Netherlands	29 Nov 56	Air Transport	302UNTS141	104356
Paraguay	USA (United States)	04 Apr 57	Taxation	283UNTS193	104117
Thailand	UK Great Britain	25 Jul 57	Customs	277UNTS81	103999
Ecuador	USA (United States)	06 Nov 57	Consul/Citizenship	307UNTS49	104441
Multilateral		15 Jan 58	Customs	383UNTS229	105503
Bulgaria	Yugoslavia	21 Mar 58	Customs	376UNTS53	105373
Bulgaria	Yugoslavia	21 Mar 58	Land Transport	349UNTS61	105009
Czechoslovakia	Hungary	08 May 58	Customs	407UNTS92	105862
El Salvador	USA (United States)	09 May 58	Visas	316UNTS29	104575
Hungary	USSR (Soviet Union)	21 Jul 58	Customs	408UNTS194	105871
Multilateral		25 Jul 58	Customs	352UNTS3	105035
France	Italy	30 Oct 58	Visas	363UNTS3	105196
Czechoslovakia	Poland	25 Nov 58	Customs	372UNTS205	105299
Multilateral		15 Jan 59	Customs	348UNTS13	104996
Ghana	USA (United States)	09 Apr 59	Customs	342UNTS21	104897
USA (United States)	Venezuela	17 Apr 59	Visas	358UNTS83	105126
Australia	Thailand	28 Jul 59	Customs	339UNTS91	104847
Germany, West	USA (United States)	03 Aug 59	Status of Forces	490UNTS28	107153
Mexico	USA (United States)	05 Aug 59	Customs	356UNTS3	105089
Multilateral		01 Sep 59	Customs	454UNTS289	106542
Czechoslovakia	Germany, East	18 Sep 59	Customs	363UNTS287	105209
Norway	Sweden	28 Oct 59	Visas	427UNTS225	106157
New Zealand	Thailand	24 Dec 59	Customs	351UNTS197	105023
Denmark	UK Great Britain	08 Apr 60	Customs	374UNTS233	105337
Cyprus	UK Great Britain	16 Aug 60	Customs	382UNTS215	105482
Multilateral		06 Oct 60	Customs	473UNTS131	106861
Multilateral		09 Dec 60	Customs	429UNTS211	106200
Multilateral		08 Jun 61	Customs	473UNTS187	106863
Multilateral		08 Jun 61	Customs	473UNTS153	106862
Australia	UK Great Britain	14 Nov 61	Air Transport	466UNTS35	106735
Multilateral		06 Dec 61	Customs	473UNTS219	106864
Hungary	Yugoslavia	09 Feb 62	Land Transport	577UNTS3	108370

PARTY ONE	PARTY TWO	DATE	TOPIC	CITATION	NUMBER
Customs (Cont.)					
Finland	Sweden	05 Nov 62	Customs	455UNTS289	106548
India	UK Great Britain	20 Oct 64	Customs	534UNTS77	107755
Multilateral		01 Dec 64	Water Transport	550UNTS133	108012
Hungary	Yugoslavia	25 May 65	Customs	576UNTS145	108367
Philippines	USA (United States)	04 Jan 67	Customs	590UNTS51	108546
Damages					
Denmark	UK Great Britain	09 Jul 56	Non-ILO Labor	264UNTS45	103787
Romania	Yugoslavia	30 Nov 63	Specific Property	512UNTS2	107438
Demography					
India	United Nations	27 Dec 62	Scientific Project	450UNTS3	106464
United Nations	United Arab Rep	08 Feb 63	Direct Aid	453UNTS79	106520
UNESCO (Educ/Cult)	Yugoslavia	27 Feb 64	IGO Operations	489UNTS257	107143
India	United Nations	25 Nov 64	Scientific Project	519UNTS47	107501
Dentistry					
Monaco	Netherlands	04 May 54	Admin Cooperation	291UNTS3	104240
Deportation					
Germany, West	Sweden	31 May 54	Extradition	200UNTS39	102693
Denmark	Germany, West	31 May 54	Extradition	200UNTS53	102694
Desalination					
India	Netherlands	27 Apr 59	Tech Assistance	506UNTS141	107385
USA (United States)	USSR (Soviet Union)	18 Nov 64	Atomic Energy	535UNTS307	107786
Multilateral		07 Oct 65	Atomic Energy	556UNTS175	108125
Saudi Arabia	USA (United States)	19 Nov 65	Non-IBRD Project	580UNTS35	108419
Diamonds					
Multilateral		26 Mar 43	Specif Goods/Equip	13UNTS427	200089
Diplomatic and Consular Service					
Cuba	USA (United States)	16 May 32	Consul/Citizenship	234UNTS283	200537
Panama	USA (United States)	31 Jan 35	Consul/Citizenship	234UNTS277	200536
Argentina	Brazil	23 Jan 40	Admin Cooperation	51UNTS281	200194
Brazil	Uruguay	08 Jan 42	Admin Cooperation	54UNTS359	200206
Panama	USA (United States)	07 Jul 42	Military Mission	9UNTS289	200048
Mexico	USA (United States)	12 Aug 42	Consul/Citizenship	125UNTS301	200431
Haiti	USA (United States)	24 Aug 45	Visas	139UNTS311	200458
Philippines	USA (United States)	04 Jul 46	General Amity	7UNTS3	100088
Philippines	USA (United States)	04 Jul 46	General Amity	6UNTS335	100086
Norway	USA (United States)	08 Jul 46	Mostfavored Nation	13UNTS35	100199
Iraq	UK Great Britain	02 Aug 46	Consul/Citizenship	14UNTS93	100213
Taiwan	Saudi Arabia	15 Nov 46	General Amity	18UNTS197	100289
Lebanon	Turkey	24 Dec 46	Visas	4UNTS269	100051
Philippines	USA (United States)	14 Mar 47	Consul/Citizenship	45UNTS23	100690
Nepal	USA (United States)	25 Apr 47	Consul/Citizenship	16UNTS97	100251
Taiwan	Italy	30 Jul 47	Consul/Citizenship	12UNTS383	100195
Costa Rica	USA (United States)	12 Jan 48	Consul/Citizenship	70UNTS27	100896
Romania	USA (United States)	26 Feb 48	Admin Cooperation	48UNTS9	100738
Italy	UK Great Britain	13 Mar 48	Admin Cooperation	104UNTS41	101435
Philippines	Spain	20 May 48	Consul/Citizenship	70UNTS143	100903
Austria	USA (United States)	02 Jul 48	Milit Occupation	25UNTS53	100357
Greece	Lebanon	06 Oct 48	Consul/Citizenship	87UNTS351	101179
Poland	USA (United States)	30 Oct 48	Consul/Citizenship	15UNTS225	100238
Panama	USA (United States)	14 Jun 49	Visas	89UNTS37	101207
Liberia	USA (United States)	22 Jul 49	Visas	232UNTS283	103242
Italy	Netherlands	16 Aug 49	Admin Cooperation	98UNTS21	101357
Dominican Republic	USA (United States)	23 Jan 50	Consul/Citizenship	236UNTS3	103312
Ireland	USA (United States)	01 May 50	Consul/Citizenship	222UNTS107	103026
Chile	USA (United States)	12 May 50	Consul/Citizenship	177UNTS103	102312
Greece	Philippines	28 Aug 50	General Amity	225UNTS155	103097
Canada	Turkey	09 Feb 51	Visas	233UNTS95	103252
Norway	UK Great Britain	22 Feb 51	Consul/Citizenship	326UNTS209	104713
Austria	Belgium	16 Mar 51	Visas	88UNTS357	101203
Netherlands	UK Great Britain	30 Apr 51	Consul/Citizenship	91UNTS177	101250
Belgium	Brazil	08 May 51	Consul/Citizenship	91UNTS75	101242
UK Great Britain	USA (United States)	06 Jun 51	Consul/Citizenship	165UNTS121	102174
Diplomatic and Consular Service (Cont.)					
Iraq	USA (United States)	08 Aug 51	Visas	229UNTS185	103166
Belgium	Brazil	11 Aug 51	Consul/Citizenship	104UNTS17	101431
Netherlands	UK Great Britain	30 Nov 51	Postal Service	123UNTS177	101659
France	UK Great Britain	31 Dec 51	Consul/Citizenship	330UNTS145	104744
Sweden	UK Great Britain	14 Mar 52	Consul/Citizenship	202UNTS157	102731
Belgium	Italy	22 Sep 52	Customs	157UNTS121	102051
Nicaragua	USA (United States)	09 Oct 52	Consul/Citizenship	184UNTS105	102442
Canada	Italy	10 Oct 52	Visas	233UNTS137	103258
Japan	UK Great Britain	04 Nov 52	Specific Property	164UNTS107	102162
Japan	UK Great Britain	04 Nov 52	Specific Property	164UNTS101	102161
USA (United States)	Uruguay	12 Nov 52	Visas	231UNTS145	103213
Greece	UK Great Britain	17 Apr 53	Consul/Citizenship	191UNTS151	102582
Germany, West	USA (United States)	02 Jun 53	General Amity	231UNTS151	103214
Germany, West	USA (United States)	03 Jun 53	General Amity	253UNTS89	103578
Netherlands	UK Great Britain	19 Oct 53	Customs	306UNTS99	104435
Mexico	UK Great Britain	20 Mar 54	Consul/Citizenship	331UNTS21	104750
Italy	UK Great Britain	01 Jun 54	Consul/Citizenship	403UNTS275	105798
France	Sweden	05 Mar 55	Consul/Citizenship	427UNTS133	106150
Iran	USA (United States)	15 Aug 55	General Amity	284UNTS93	104132
Bulgaria	Yugoslavia	15 Nov 55	Consul/Citizenship	396UNTS179	105696
Italy	Vatican/Holy See	16 Dec 55	Taxation	260UNTS319	103715
Australia	Greece	15 Mar 56	Consul/Citizenship	241UNTS313	103438
Paraguay	USA (United States)	11 May 56	Visas	269UNTS33	103870
USA (United States)	Yugoslavia	21 May 56	Visas	281UNTS93	104072
Austria	Canada	19 Jun 56	Visas	305UNTS51	104412
Germany, West	UK Great Britain	30 Jul 56	Consul/Citizenship	330UNTS233	104748
Dominican Republic	UK Great Britain	09 Aug 56	Consul/Citizenship	252UNTS127	103561
Canada	Turkey	21 Aug 56	Visas	305UNTS89	104416
Germany, East	USSR (Soviet Union)	10 May 57	Consul/Citizenship	285UNTS135	104151
Czechoslovakia	Germany, East	24 May 57	Consul/Citizenship	292UNTS327	104279
Germany, West	Japan	27 Jun 57	Admin Cooperation	318UNTS335	104624
Canada	Greece	01 Jul 57	Visas	316UNTS201	104585
Germany, East	Hungary	03 Jul 57	Consul/Citizenship	407UNTS186	105865
Hungary	USSR (Soviet Union)	24 Aug 57	Consul/Citizenship	318UNTS3	104607
Romania	USSR (Soviet Union)	04 Sep 57	Consul/Citizenship	318UNTS55	104609
Albania	USSR (Soviet Union)	18 Sep 57	Consul/Citizenship	307UNTS265	104455
Japan	Netherlands	20 Sep 57	Visas	305UNTS105	104418
Czechoslovakia	USSR (Soviet Union)	05 Oct 57	Consul/Citizenship	320UNTS129	104641
Ecuador	USA (United States)	06 Nov 57	Consul/Citizenship	307UNTS49	104441
Germany, East	Poland	25 Nov 57	Consul/Citizenship	340UNTS99	104862
Austria	Israel	25 Nov 57	Visas	314UNTS81	104542
Bulgaria	USSR (Soviet Union)	12 Dec 57	Consul/Citizenship	302UNTS21	104352
Korea, North	USSR (Soviet Union)	16 Dec 57	Consul/Citizenship	292UNTS121	104270
Poland	USSR (Soviet Union)	21 Jan 58	Consul/Citizenship	319UNTS291	104637
France	Israel	01 Mar 58	Visas	314UNTS87	104543
Sweden	USSR (Soviet Union)	28 Mar 58	Privil/Immunities	428UNTS321	106184
Germany, West	USSR (Soviet Union)	25 Apr 58	Consul/Citizenship	338UNTS49	104832
Albania	Yugoslavia	28 Apr 58	Consul/Citizenship	386UNTS103	105540
El Salvador	USA (United States)	09 May 58	Visas	316UNTS29	104575
Bulgaria	Hungary	27 Jun 58	Culture	438UNTS235	106318
Germany, East	Romania	15 Jul 58	Consul/Citizenship	387UNTS133	105561
Mongolia	USSR (Soviet Union)	25 Aug 58	Consul/Citizenship	322UNTS215	104659
Iraq	USSR (Soviet Union)	11 Oct 58	General Trade	328UNTS117	104731
Poland	Yugoslavia	17 Nov 58	Consul/Citizenship	432UNTS267	106225
Muscat and Oman	USA (United States)	20 Dec 58	General Amity	380UNTS181	105457
Albania	Czechoslovakia	16 Jan 59	Consul/Citizenship	363UNTS165	105207
Austria	USSR (Soviet Union)	28 Feb 59	Consul/Citizenship	356UNTS39	105091
Hungary	Romania	18 Mar 59	Consul/Citizenship	417UNTS3	106005
Czechoslovakia	Hungary	27 Mar 59	Consul/Citizenship	351UNTS57	105017
USA (United States)	Venezuela	17 Apr 59	Visas	358UNTS83	105126
Bulgaria	Romania	23 Apr 59	Consul/Citizenship	387UNTS81	105559
Hungary	Poland	20 May 59	Consul/Citizenship	432UNTS115	106217
Bulgaria	Czechoslovakia	27 May 59	Consul/Citizenship	360UNTS335	105167
USSR (Soviet Union)	Vietnam, North	05 Jun 59	Consul/Citizenship	356UNTS111	105093
China People's Rep	USSR (Soviet Union)	23 Jun 59	Consul/Citizenship	356UNTS83	105092

PARTY ONE	PARTY TWO	DATE	TOPIC	CITATION	NUMBER
Diplomatic and Consular Service (Cont.)					
Argentina	Brazil	26 Nov 59	Visas	374UNTS51	105328
China People's Rep	Czechoslovakia	07 May 60	Consul/Citizenship	402UNTS209	105787
Czechoslovakia	Poland	17 May 60	Consul/Citizenship	424UNTS3	106096
Czechoslovakia	Romania	21 May 60	Consul/Citizenship	397UNTS245	105709
Austria	UK Great Britain	24 Jun 60	Consul/Citizenship	502UNTS79	107327
Israel	Thailand	07 Jul 60	Visas	377UNTS325	105409
Cuba	Korea, North	29 Aug 60	Consul/Citizenship	469UNTS163	106790
Peru	USA (United States)	13 Feb 61	Visas	406UNTS177	105848
Belgium	UK Great Britain	08 Mar 61	Consul/Citizenship	523UNTS17	107554
Indonesia	USA (United States)	31 Mar 61	Visas	405UNTS119	105828
Multilateral		18 Apr 61	Consul/Citizenship	500UNTS95	107310
Multilateral		18 Apr 61	Consul/Citizenship	500UNTS223	107311
Spain	UK Great Britain	30 May 61	Consul/Citizenship	562UNTS169	108198
Israel	Liberia	03 Aug 61	Visas	484UNTS203	107030
Israel	Italy	30 Aug 61	Visas	484UNTS197	107029
Bulgaria	Poland	19 Sep 61	Consul/Citizenship	483UNTS249	107018
Ivory Coast	Netherlands	12 Feb 62	Visas	485UNTS219	107057
Central Afri Rep	Israel	14 Feb 62	Visas	484UNTS143	107022
Denmark	UK Great Britain	27 Jun 62	Consul/Citizenship	562UNTS75	108197
Philippines	Spain	04 Jul 62	Visas	490UNTS243	107158
Poland	Romania	05 Oct 62	Consul/Citizenship	521UNTS3	107516
Honduras	Israel	10 Oct 62	Visas	484UNTS189	107028
Gabon	Israel	10 Oct 62	Visas	484UNTS175	107026
Romania	Yugoslavia	08 Nov 62	Consul/Citizenship	472UNTS305	106845
Colombia	Israel	21 Dec 62	Visas	484UNTS149	107023
Czechoslovakia	USA (United States)	21 Dec 62	Visas	469UNTS115	106787
Korea, South	USA (United States)	08 Jan 63	Consul/Citizenship	493UNTS105	107211
Czechoslovakia	Vietnam, North	14 Jan 63	Consul/Citizenship	501UNTS181	107318
Austria	United Nations	29 Jan 63	Consul/Citizenship	452UNTS261	106513
Bolivia	Philippines	22 Feb 63	Visas	490UNTS231	107156
Japan	USA (United States)	22 Mar 63	Consul/Citizenship	518UNTS179	107495
Multilateral		24 Apr 63	Consul/Citizenship	596UNTS261	108638
Israel	Malagasy	04 May 63	Visas	484UNTS225	107033
Czechoslovakia	Yugoslavia	24 Jun 63	Consul/Citizenship	496UNTS3	107246
Hungary	Mongolia	10 Jul 63	Consul/Citizenship	519UNTS173	107508
Czechoslovakia	Mongolia	08 Nov 63	Consul/Citizenship	503UNTS125	107341
Multilateral		03 Mar 64	Consul/Citizenship	516UNTS53	107470
Luxembourg	Netherlands	24 Mar 64	Consul/Citizenship	548UNTS137	107975
Japan	UK Great Britain	04 May 64	Consul/Citizenship	561UNTS25	108179
Mongolia	Poland	28 Oct 64	Consul/Citizenship	552UNTS115	108052
UK Great Britain	Yugoslavia	21 Apr 65	Consul/Citizenship	595UNTS189	108620
Australia	Netherlands	01 Jun 65	Consul/Citizenship	560UNTS85	108170
Belgium	Luxembourg	30 Sep 65	Consul/Citizenship	590UNTS35	108545
Tanzania	USA (United States)	06 Dec 65	Consul/Citizenship	592UNTS51	108568
Finland	USSR (Soviet Union)	24 Jan 66	Consul/Citizenship	576UNTS35	108364
New Zealand	UK Great Britain	13 Jul 66	Taxation	598UNTS121	108658
Diplomatic Correspondence					
Brazil	Uruguay	16 Dec 44	Admin Cooperation	65UNTS305	200218
Brazil	Venezuela	30 Jan 46	Consul/Citizenship	65UNTS107	100839
Mexico	UK Great Britain	27 Sep 46	Consul/Citizenship	91UNTS161	101248
Norway	UK Great Britain	15 Jan 47	Consul/Citizenship	11UNTS187	100156
Brazil	Ecuador	31 May 47	Consul/Citizenship	72UNTS25	100925
Diplomatic Relations					
Netherlands	USSR (Soviet Union)	10 Jul 42	Consul/Citizenship	241UNTS475	200540
Netherlands	Thailand	30 Jan 47	General Amity	247UNTS353	103480
Denmark	Japan	29 Feb 52	Consul/Citizenship	126UNTS139	101686
China People's Rep	Sweden	24 Jun 55	Consul/Citizenship	228UNTS153	103148
Japan	USSR (Soviet Union)	19 Oct 56	General Amity	263UNTS99	103768
Japan	Poland	08 Feb 57	General Amity	318UNTS251	104620
Czechoslovakia	Japan	13 Feb 57	General Amity	300UNTS119	104335
Taiwan	Jordan	19 Nov 57	General Amity	308UNTS227	104463
Multilateral		18 Apr 61	Consul/Citizenship	500UNTS95	107310

PARTY ONE	PARTY TWO	DATE	TOPIC	CITATION	NUMBER
Diptheria					
Colombia	WHO (World Health)	05 Jan 51	Sanitation	102UNTS139	101417
Chile	WHO (World Health)	31 May 52	Sanitation	136UNTS323	101841
Diseases					
Multilateral		24 Jul 48	Sanitation	66UNTS25	100847
Denmark	UK Great Britain	09 Jul 56	Non-ILO Labor	264UNTS45	103787
Dispute Settlements					
Brazil	Venezuela	30 Mar 40	Dispute Settlement	51UNTS291	200195
Multilateral		22 Mar 45	General Amity	70UNTS237	200241
Multilateral		10 Feb 47	Peace/Disarmament	49UNTS3	100747
Multilateral		02 Sep 47	General Military	21UNTS77	100324
Philippines	Spain	27 Sep 47	General Amity	70UNTS133	100902
Multilateral		30 Apr 48	Dispute Settlement	30UNTS55	100449
Poland	USSR (Soviet Union)	08 Jul 48	Dispute Settlement	37UNTS107	100576
Belgium	Denmark	30 Dec 48	Dispute Settlement	25UNTS173	100362
Multilateral		28 Apr 49	Dispute Settlement	71UNTS101	100912
Italy	Netherlands	16 Aug 49	Admin Cooperation	98UNTS21	101357
Norway	USSR (Soviet Union)	29 Dec 49	Territory Boundary	83UNTS291	101112
Multilateral		12 Jun 52	Dispute Settlement	138UNTS183	101869
Finland	Sweden	09 Apr 53	Dispute Settlement	198UNTS61	102657
Denmark	Finland	24 Sep 53	Dispute Settlement	188UNTS283	102532
Multilateral		29 Apr 57	Dispute Settlement	320UNTS243	104646
Multilateral		29 Apr 58	Dispute Settlement	450UNTS169	106466
Multilateral		18 Apr 61	Dispute Settlement	500UNTS243	107312
Multilateral		24 Apr 63	Consul/Citizenship	596UNTS487	108640
IBRD (World Bank)	UK Great Britain	23 Sep 63	IBRD Project	503UNTS247	107348
Japan	Korea, South	22 Jun 65	Dispute Settlement	584UNTS147	108476
Dockers					
Multilateral		26 Jun 28	ILO Labor	39UNTS15	100610
Multilateral		21 Jun 29	ILO Labor	39UNTS27	100611
Multilateral		27 Apr 32	ILO Labor	39UNTS103	100614
Domestic Workers					
Multilateral		29 Jun 33	ILO Labor	39UNTS211	100619
UK Great Britain	USA (United States)	16 Apr 45	Taxation	6UNTS359	200039
UK Great Britain	USA (United States)	16 Apr 45	Taxation	6UNTS189	100076
Canada	UK Great Britain	05 Jun 46	Taxation	86UNTS3	101147
Canada	UK Great Britain	05 Jun 46	Taxation	27UNTS207	100408
South Africa	UK Great Britain	14 Oct 46	Taxation	86UNTS77	101153
South Africa	UK Great Britain	14 Oct 46	Taxation	86UNTS51	101152
Australia	UK Great Britain	29 Oct 46	Taxation	17UNTS181	100276
Denmark	Norway	30 Dec 46	Taxation	8UNTS21	100111
Finland	USA (United States)	07 Jan 47	Taxation	15UNTS273	100243
New Zealand	UK Great Britain	27 May 47	Taxation	17UNTS211	100277
Norway	Sweden	21 Jun 47	Taxation	94UNTS107	101309
India	Pakistan	10 Dec 47	Taxation	51UNTS173	100764
Czechoslovakia	Romania	01 Mar 48	Admin Cooperation	26UNTS109	100381
Belgium	Luxembourg	25 Mar 48	Taxation	18UNTS323	100300
Netherlands	USA (United States)	29 Apr 48	Taxation	32UNTS167	100498
Denmark	USA (United States)	06 May 48	Taxation	26UNTS55	100377
Netherlands	UK Great Britain	15 Oct 48	Taxation	74UNTS3	100955
Netherlands	UK Great Britain	15 Oct 48	Taxation	73UNTS203	100954
Argentina	Netherlands	15 Jan 49	Taxation	46UNTS241	100713
Argentina	UK Great Britain	14 Mar 49	Taxation	83UNTS193	101108
Belgium	France	30 Dec 49	Taxation	46UNTS111	100704
Israel	UK Great Britain	10 Feb 50	Taxation	86UNTS211	101161
Denmark	UK Great Britain	27 Mar 50	Taxation	68UNTS117	100891
Argentina	USA (United States)	20 Jul 50	Taxation	89UNTS63	101209
Denmark	South Africa	30 Nov 50	Taxation	84UNTS51	101118
Double Taxation					
France	USA (United States)	25 Jul 39	Taxation	125UNTS259	200429
Panama	USA (United States)	28 Mar 41	Taxation	103UNTS163	200312
Canada	USA (United States)	04 Mar 42	Taxation	124UNTS271	200426
Canada	USA (United States)	08 Jun 44	Taxation	124UNTS297	200427

PARTY ONE	PARTY TWO	DATE	TOPIC	CITATION	NUMBER
Double Taxation (Cont.)					
UK Great Britain	USA (United States)	16 Apr 45	Taxation	6UNTS189	100076
Canada	UK Great Britain	05 Jun 46	Taxation	27UNTS207	100408
South Africa	UK Great Britain	14 Oct 46	Taxation	86UNTS77	101153
France	USA (United States)	18 Oct 46	Taxation	140UNTS23	101882
South Africa	USA (United States)	13 Dec 46	Taxation	167UNTS171	102207
France	UK Great Britain	14 Dec 46	Taxation	105UNTS27	101452
South Africa	USA (United States)	10 Apr 47	Taxation	167UNTS211	102208
Canada	New Zealand	12 Mar 48	Taxation	231UNTS219	103222
New Zealand	USA (United States)	16 Mar 48	Taxation	127UNTS133	101703
Belgium	Netherlands	25 Sep 48	Taxation	123UNTS81	101655
Belgium	Luxembourg	09 Oct 48	Taxation	123UNTS29	101652
Netherlands	UK Great Britain	15 Oct 48	Taxation	73UNTS203	100954
Netherlands	UK Great Britain	15 Oct 48	Taxation	74UNTS3	100955
Sweden	Switzerland	16 Oct 48	Taxation	197UNTS55	102634
Sweden	Switzerland	16 Oct 48	Taxation	197UNTS101	102635
Belgium	USA (United States)	28 Oct 48	Taxation	173UNTS67	102262
Argentina	Sweden	20 Nov 48	Taxation	197UNTS47	102633
Sweden	UK Great Britain	30 Mar 49	Taxation	209UNTS129	102826
France	Sweden	08 Apr 49	Taxation	197UNTS177	102637
France	Sweden	08 Apr 49	Taxation	197UNTS183	102638
Ireland	UK Great Britain	18 May 49	Taxation	553UNTS209	108089
Norway	USA (United States)	13 Jun 49	Taxation	127UNTS163	101704
Norway	USA (United States)	13 Jun 49	Taxation	127UNTS189	101705
Argentina	Canada	06 Aug 49	Taxation	231UNTS43	103202
Ireland	USA (United States)	13 Sep 49	Taxation	127UNTS119	101702
Ireland	USA (United States)	13 Sep 49	Taxation	127UNTS89	101701
Norway	Sweden	17 Dec 49	Taxation	197UNTS197	102640
Finland	Sweden	21 Dec 49	Taxation	197UNTS243	102642
France	Netherlands	30 Dec 49	Taxation	203UNTS85	102742
France	Netherlands	30 Dec 49	Taxation	203UNTS133	102743
Greece	USA (United States)	20 Feb 50	Taxation	196UNTS269	102629
Greece	USA (United States)	20 Feb 50	Taxation	196UNTS291	102630
Burma	UK Great Britain	13 Mar 50	Taxation	131UNTS53	101735
Denmark	UK Great Britain	27 Mar 50	Taxation	68UNTS117	100891
Finland	Sweden	31 Mar 50	Taxation	197UNTS285	102643
Canada	USA (United States)	12 Jun 50	Taxation	127UNTS57	101699
Canada	USA (United States)	12 Jun 50	Taxation	127UNTS67	101700
Ceylon (Sri Lanka)	UK Great Britain	26 Jul 50	Taxation	337UNTS77	104818
Greece	UK Great Britain	16 Nov 50	Taxation	166UNTS281	102193
France	Greece	09 Dec 50	Taxation	166UNTS315	102196
Netherlands	Norway	29 Dec 50	Taxation	134UNTS19	101795
Canada	France	16 Mar 51	Taxation	236UNTS267	103330
Canada	France	16 Mar 51	Taxation	236UNTS297	103331
Canada	Sweden	06 Apr 51	Taxation	197UNTS393	102648
Norway	UK Great Britain	02 May 51	Taxation	106UNTS101	101460
Switzerland	USA (United States)	24 May 51	Taxation	127UNTS227	101706
South Africa	Sweden	25 May 51	Taxation	197UNTS425	102649
Switzerland	USA (United States)	09 Jul 51	Taxation	165UNTS51	102167
Austria	Sweden	19 Jul 51	Taxation	198UNTS9	102652
Netherlands	Switzerland	12 Nov 51	Taxation	126UNTS157	101688
Netherlands	Switzerland	12 Nov 51	Taxation	126UNTS173	101689
Canada	South Africa	26 Nov 51	Taxation	248UNTS107	103489
Finland	UK Great Britain	12 Dec 51	Taxation	172UNTS45	102239
France	Israel	24 Jan 52	Taxation	220UNTS55	102988
Belgium	Luxembourg	07 Feb 52	Taxation	147UNTS3	101924
Finland	USA (United States)	03 Mar 52	Taxation	177UNTS163	102317
Finland	USA (United States)	03 Mar 52	Taxation	177UNTS141	102316
Netherlands	Sweden	25 Apr 52	Taxation	163UNTS195	102148
Netherlands	Sweden	25 Apr 52	Taxation	163UNTS131	102147
Greece	Israel	22 Jul 52	Taxation	215UNTS365	102924
Israel	South Africa	24 Dec 52	Taxation	207UNTS303	102813
Belgium	UK Great Britain	27 Mar 53	Taxation	188UNTS153	102526
Belgium	Sweden	01 Apr 53	Taxation	185UNTS225	102473
Australia	USA (United States)	14 May 53	Taxation	205UNTS253	102779
Australia	USA (United States)	14 May 53	Taxation	205UNTS237	102778

PARTY ONE	PARTY TWO	DATE	TOPIC	CITATION	NUMBER
Double Taxation (Cont.)					
Australia	USA (United States)	14 May 53	Taxation	205UNTS277	102780
Greece	UK Great Britain	25 Jun 53	Taxation	190UNTS281	102571
Italy	South Africa	26 Jun 53	Taxation	211UNTS255	102857
Belgium	USA (United States)	18 Jul 53	Taxation	180UNTS9	102371
Denmark	Sweden	27 Oct 53	Taxation	198UNTS111	102659
Denmark	Sweden	27 Oct 53	Taxation	198UNTS71	102658
Denmark	Sweden	27 Oct 53	Taxation	198UNTS129	102660
Belgium	Finland	11 Feb 54	Taxation	211UNTS63	102848
Finland	Netherlands	29 Mar 54	Taxation	252UNTS185	103567
Finland	Netherlands	29 Mar 54	Taxation	252UNTS239	103568
Japan	USA (United States)	16 Apr 54	Taxation	238UNTS39	103354
Japan	USA (United States)	16 Apr 54	Taxation	238UNTS3	103353
Netherlands	South Africa	22 Apr 54	Taxation	211UNTS215	102853
Germany, West	USA (United States)	22 Jul 54	Taxation	239UNTS3	103369
Switzerland	UK Great Britain	30 Sep 54	Taxation	209UNTS197	102828
Ireland	Norway	18 Oct 54	Taxation	553UNTS123	108077
Ireland	Sweden	18 Oct 54	Taxation	262UNTS259	103753
Denmark	Ireland	18 Oct 54	Taxation	218UNTS295	102959
Germany, West	UK Great Britain	18 Oct 54	Taxation	218UNTS301	102960
Canada	Ireland	28 Oct 54	Taxation	304UNTS317	104406
Canada	Ireland	28 Oct 54	Taxation	305UNTS3	104407
France	Sweden	05 Nov 54	Taxation	262UNTS229	103748
France	South Africa	22 Nov 54	Taxation	219UNTS35	102963
Switzerland	United Arab Rep	05 Jan 55	Taxation	216UNTS41	102931
Italy	USA (United States)	30 Mar 55	Taxation	257UNTS199	103655
Italy	USA (United States)	30 Mar 55	Taxation	257UNTS169	103654
Denmark	Israel	04 Apr 55	Taxation	213UNTS283	102891
Israel	Italy	10 Jun 55	Taxation	280UNTS219	104061
Pakistan	UK Great Britain	10 Jun 55	Taxation	243UNTS15	103444
Denmark	Finland	18 Jul 55	Taxation	250UNTS149	103521
South Africa	Sweden	28 Jul 55	Taxation	230UNTS287	103191
Canada	Denmark	30 Sep 55	Taxation	258UNTS115	103675
Denmark	Iceland	10 Oct 55	Taxation	230UNTS3	103171
Austria	Sweden	17 Oct 55	Taxation	262UNTS283	103756
South Africa	Switzerland	07 Nov 55	Taxation	230UNTS279	103190
Belgium	France	10 Dec 55	Taxation	231UNTS101	103211
Belgium	Sweden	18 Jan 56	Taxation	293UNTS23	104283
New Zealand	Sweden	16 Apr 56	Taxation	274UNTS259	103971
Fed Rhod/Nyasaland	South Africa	22 May 56	Taxation	254UNTS227	103595
Denmark	Norway	23 May 56	Taxation	271UNTS75	103910
Canada	Germany, West	04 Jun 56	Taxation	316UNTS231	104589
Switzerland	UK Great Britain	12 Jun 56	Taxation	269UNTS133	103879
France	USA (United States)	22 Jun 56	Taxation	291UNTS101	104246
Honduras	USA (United States)	25 Jun 56	Taxation	279UNTS113	104036
Austria	UK Great Britain	20 Jul 56	Taxation	269UNTS147	103880
Ceylon (Sri Lanka)	India	10 Sep 56	Taxation	315UNTS59	104560
Norway	Sweden	27 Sep 56	Taxation	261UNTS71	103726
Germany, West	South Africa	28 Sep 56	Taxation	327UNTS83	104718
Canada	South Africa	28 Sep 56	Taxation	299UNTS3	104303
Canada	South Africa	28 Sep 56	Taxation	299UNTS17	104304
Austria	USA (United States)	25 Oct 56	Taxation	299UNTS123	104310
Japan	Sweden	12 Dec 56	Taxation	318UNTS309	104623
Italy	Sweden	20 Dec 56	Taxation	369UNTS305	105263
Italy	Sweden	20 Dec 56	Taxation	369UNTS357	105265
Finland	Switzerland	27 Dec 56	Taxation	277UNTS59	103997
Finland	Switzerland	27 Dec 56	Taxation	277UNTS7	103996
Denmark	Switzerland	14 Jan 57	Taxation	286UNTS27	104160
Denmark	Switzerland	14 Jan 57	Taxation	286UNTS85	104161
Italy	Netherlands	24 Jan 57	Taxation	485UNTS67	107047
Denmark	Netherlands	20 Feb 57	Taxation	287UNTS41	104179
Denmark	Norway	22 Feb 57	Taxation	286UNTS127	104164
Canada	Netherlands	02 Apr 57	Taxation	285UNTS193	104153
Ceylon (Sri Lanka)	Sweden	18 May 57	Taxation	315UNTS85	104561
Belgium	South Africa	11 Jun 57	Taxation	292UNTS165	104272
Pakistan	USA (United States)	01 Jul 57	Taxation	344UNTS203	104951

PARTY ONE	PARTY TWO	DATE	TOPIC	CITATION	NUMBER
Double Taxation (Cont.)					
Australia	Canada	01 Oct 57	Taxation	392UNTS41	105638
Belgium	Switzerland	05 Dec 57	Taxation	293UNTS317	104299
Ireland	South Africa	01 May 58	Taxation	398UNTS3	105714
Canada	Switzerland	23 Jun 58	Admin Cooperation	391UNTS213	105625
Denmark	Sweden	21 Jul 58	Taxation	320UNTS163	104642
Sweden	United Arab Rep	29 Jul 58	Taxation	369UNTS323	105264
India	Sweden	30 Jul 58	Taxation	369UNTS211	105259
Pakistan	Sweden	25 Aug 58	Taxation	369UNTS183	105258
Germany, West	Norway	18 Nov 58	Taxation	357UNTS205	105119
Belgium	France	20 Jan 59	Taxation	361UNTS155	105178
Japan	Pakistan	17 Feb 59	Taxation	341UNTS127	104880
Japan	Norway	21 Feb 59	Taxation	356UNTS231	105098
Denmark	Japan	10 Mar 59	Taxation	341UNTS55	104878
Canada	Finland	28 Mar 59	Taxation	355UNTS3	105072
Germany, West	Sweden	17 Apr 59	Taxation	428UNTS155	106175
Austria	Sweden	14 May 59	Taxation	428UNTS3	106167
Germany, West	Netherlands	16 Jun 59	Taxation	593UNTS3	108576
South Africa	UK Great Britain	18 Jun 59	Taxation	380UNTS103	105452
South Africa	UK Great Britain	18 Jun 59	Taxation	380UNTS81	105451
South Africa	UK Great Britain	18 Jun 59	Taxation	380UNTS59	105450
India	Norway	20 Jul 59	Taxation	356UNTS257	105099
Denmark	India	16 Sep 59	Taxation	405UNTS13	105820
Canada	Switzerland	22 Sep 59	Taxation	470UNTS101	106800
Austria	France	08 Oct 59	Taxation	453UNTS95	106521
Ireland	Sweden	06 Nov 59	Taxation	428UNTS231	106177
Israel	Sweden	22 Dec 59	Taxation	377UNTS277	105407
India	Japan	05 Jan 60	Taxation	384UNTS3	105507
Austria	Norway	25 Feb 60	Taxation	376UNTS155	105380
Iran	UK Great Britain	09 Apr 60	Taxation	385UNTS63	105529
Australia	New Zealand	12 May 60	Taxation	369UNTS119	105254
Italy	UK Great Britain	04 Jul 60	Taxation	466UNTS195	106745
Sweden	UK Great Britain	28 Jul 60	Taxation	404UNTS85	105806
Sweden	UK Great Britain	28 Jul 60	Taxation	404UNTS113	105808
Sweden	Tunisia	06 Sep 60	Taxation	427UNTS301	106162
Canada	USA (United States)	17 Feb 61	Taxation	445UNTS143	106383
Morocco	Sweden	30 Mar 61	Taxation	427UNTS185	106154
Japan	UK Great Britain	11 Apr 61	Taxation	420UNTS75	106042
South Africa	Sweden	29 May 61	Taxation	442UNTS15	106335
Finland	India	23 Jun 61	Taxation	421UNTS49	106051
Belgium	France	07 Jul 61	Taxation	406UNTS157	105846
Portugal	UK Great Britain	31 Jul 61	Taxation	449UNTS119	106454
Colombia	USA (United States)	01 Aug 61	Taxation	433UNTS123	106235
Italy	Norway	25 Aug 61	Taxation	475UNTS269	106896
Denmark	Pakistan	04 Sep 61	Taxation	455UNTS305	106549
Greece	Sweden	06 Oct 61	Taxation	481UNTS137	106981
Sweden	Thailand	20 Oct 61	Taxation	428UNTS275	106180
Austria	Denmark	23 Oct 61	Taxation	425UNTS115	106122
Belgium	Denmark	23 Oct 61	Taxation	425UNTS181	106123
Austria	Japan	20 Dec 61	Taxation	517UNTS155	107485
Argentina	Japan	20 Dec 61	Taxation	451UNTS91	106487
Israel	Sweden	15 May 62	Taxation	484UNTS261	107036
South Africa	UK Great Britain	28 May 62	Taxation	443UNTS79	106361
Greece	Switzerland	12 Jun 62	Taxation	492UNTS47	107186
Belgium	Luxembourg	30 Aug 62	Taxation	485UNTS313	107062
Japan	UK Great Britain	04 Sep 62	Taxation	475UNTS31	106888
Israel	UK Great Britain	26 Sep 62	Taxation	474UNTS233	106885
Austria	United Arab Rep	16 Oct 62	Taxation	491UNTS63	107174
Austria	Luxembourg	18 Oct 62	Taxation	496UNTS97	107248
Iceland	USA (United States)	27 Dec 62	Taxation	469UNTS91	106785
Japan	New Zealand	30 Jan 63	Taxation	517UNTS183	107486
Ceylon (Sri Lanka)	Denmark	16 Feb 63	Taxation	486UNTS285	107083
Japan	Thailand	01 Mar 63	Taxation	475UNTS233	106895
Norway	Spain	25 Apr 63	Taxation	503UNTS41	107340
Japan	Malaysia	04 Jun 63	Taxation	517UNTS245	107488
France	UK Great Britain	21 Jun 63	Taxation	540UNTS311	107855

PARTY ONE	PARTY TWO	DATE	TOPIC	CITATION	NUMBER
Double Taxation (Cont.)					
France	Israel	20 Aug 63	Taxation	515UNTS173	107460
France	Greece	21 Aug 63	Taxation	533UNTS235	107746
Austria	India	24 Sep 63	Taxation	545UNTS199	107935
Austria	Finland	08 Oct 63	Taxation	490UNTS255	107160
Lebanon	UK Great Britain	24 Oct 63	Taxation	535UNTS3	107772
France	UK Great Britain	05 Nov 63	Taxation	539UNTS277	107838
Norway	Thailand	09 Jan 64	Taxation	522UNTS65	107537
Denmark	Ireland	04 Feb 64	Taxation	525UNTS233	107596
Belgium	France	10 Mar 64	Taxation	557UNTS13	108127
Denmark	Finland	07 Apr 64	Taxation	525UNTS89	107586
Ceylon (Sri Lanka)	Norway	11 Jun 64	Taxation	559UNTS23	108153
Austria	Belgium	11 Jun 64	Taxation	521UNTS157	107518
Denmark	Tanganyika	04 Aug 64	Taxation	544UNTS117	107914
Mexico	USA (United States)	07 Aug 64	Taxation	530UNTS123	107677
Canada	Japan	05 Sep 64	Taxation	569UNTS99	108282
Sweden	UK Great Britain	14 Oct 64	Taxation	543UNTS135	107898
Norway	United Arab Rep	20 Oct 64	Taxation	543UNTS3	107895
France	Japan	27 Nov 64	Taxation	569UNTS157	108283
Finland	Israel	21 Jan 65	Taxation	581UNTS275	108450
Belgium	Luxembourg	11 Mar 65	Taxation	540UNTS297	107854
Finland	United Arab Rep	01 Apr 65	Taxation	562UNTS3	108193
Jamaica	UK Great Britain	02 Apr 65	Taxation	552UNTS219	108056
Denmark	Thailand	01 Jun 65	Taxation	551UNTS157	108040
Canada	UK Great Britain	06 Dec 65	Taxation	572UNTS161	108311
Iceland	Norway	30 Mar 66	Taxation	566UNTS51	108240
Fed Rhod/Nyasaland	Norway	18 Jun 66	Taxation	580UNTS9	108415
Denmark	Israel	27 Jun 66	Taxation	581UNTS227	108448
New Zealand	UK Great Britain	13 Jul 66	Taxation	598UNTS121	108658
Netherlands	Norway	22 Sep 66	Taxation	600UNTS227	108683
Drugs					
Multilateral		20 May 52	Sanitation	219UNTS55	102966
Belgium	Luxembourg	28 Mar 58	General Trade	303UNTS101	104372
Earthquakes					
Japan	UN Special Fund	31 Oct 62	Tech Assistance	444UNTS171	106368
Canada	USA (United States)	29 Jun 65	Scientific Project	549UNTS273	108003
Economic and Social Cooperation					
Canada	USA (United States)	27 Jun 41	IGO Establishment	103UNTS205	200315
Brazil	USA (United States)	03 Mar 42	Tech Assistance	105UNTS99	200325
Canada	USA (United States)	30 Nov 42	Reparations	119UNTS305	200387
Canada	USA (United States)	15 May 45	Peace/Disarmament	125UNTS353	200433
Mongolia	USSR (Soviet Union)	27 Feb 46	General Economic	216UNTS221	102938
Multilateral		06 Feb 47	IGO Establishment	97UNTS227	101352
Hungary	Yugoslavia	11 May 47	Direct Aid	130UNTS171	101730
France	USA (United States)	28 Jun 48	Direct Aid	19UNTS9	100302
Italy	USA (United States)	28 Jun 48	Direct Aid	20UNTS43	100314
Ireland	USA (United States)	28 Jun 48	Direct Aid	24UNTS3	100349
Denmark	USA (United States)	29 Jun 48	Direct Aid	22UNTS217	100338
Belgium	USA (United States)	02 Jul 48	Direct Aid	19UNTS127	100309
Netherlands	USA (United States)	02 Jul 48	Direct Aid	20UNTS91	100315
Austria	USA (United States)	02 Jul 48	Direct Aid	21UNTS29	100323
Greece	USA (United States)	02 Jul 48	Direct Aid	23UNTS43	100342
Luxembourg	USA (United States)	03 Jul 48	Direct Aid	24UNTS35	100350
Iceland	USA (United States)	03 Jul 48	Direct Aid	20UNTS141	100316
Sweden	USA (United States)	03 Jul 48	Direct Aid	23UNTS101	100343
Norway	USA (United States)	03 Jul 48	Direct Aid	20UNTS185	100317
Turkey	USA (United States)	04 Jul 48	Direct Aid	24UNTS67	100351
UK Great Britain	USA (United States)	06 Jul 48	Direct Aid	22UNTS263	100339
Portugal	USA (United States)	28 Sep 48	Direct Aid	29UNTS213	100442
Trieste	USA (United States)	15 Oct 48	Direct Aid	29UNTS249	100443
Korea, North	USSR (Soviet Union)	17 Mar 49	General Economic	221UNTS3	102999
Greece	Italy	31 Aug 49	Reparations	78UNTS89	101014
Germany, West	USA (United States)	15 Dec 49	Direct Aid	92UNTS269	101277
UK Great Britain	USA (United States)	27 Jan 50	Milit Assistance	80UNTS261	101056
Thailand	USA (United States)	19 Sep 50	Tech Assistance	132UNTS199	101761

PARTY ONE	PARTY TWO	DATE	TOPIC	CITATION	NUMBER
Economic and Social Cooperation (Cont.)					
Indonesia	USA (United States)	16 Oct 50	Direct Aid	281UNTS105	104074
Canada	USA (United States)	26 Oct 50	Direct Aid	132UNTS247	101764
Paraguay	USA (United States)	27 Nov 50	Direct Aid	122UNTS147	101644
Liberia	USA (United States)	22 Dec 50	Direct Aid	133UNTS69	101781
Philippines	USA (United States)	27 Apr 51	Direct Aid	174UNTS251	102290
Austria	USA (United States)	15 May 51	Direct Aid	139UNTS79	101876
Brazil	USA (United States)	24 Jul 51	Direct Aid	134UNTS195	101799
USA (United States)	Vietnam, South	07 Sep 51	Direct Aid	174UNTS165	102284
Cambodia	USA (United States)	08 Sep 51	Direct Aid	174UNTS115	102282
Laos	USA (United States)	09 Sep 51	Direct Aid	174UNTS141	102283
Canada	Pakistan	10 Sep 51	Direct Aid	122UNTS21	101632
Turkey	USA (United States)	15 Nov 51	Direct Aid	177UNTS315	102331
Italy	USA (United States)	28 Dec 51	General Economic	157UNTS63	102047
Indonesia	USA (United States)	05 Jan 52	Tech Assistance	215UNTS121	102916
USA (United States)	Yugoslavia	08 Jan 52	Direct Aid	152UNTS61	102011
Multilateral		11 Feb 52	Direct Aid	165UNTS77	102169
Austria	USA (United States)	16 Feb 52	Direct Aid	177UNTS299	102329
Philippines	USA (United States)	19 Feb 52	Direct Aid	177UNTS307	102330
Norway	USA (United States)	01 Apr 52	Direct Aid	177UNTS291	102328
Greece	USA (United States)	23 Apr 52	Direct Aid	177UNTS283	102327
Belgium	USA (United States)	12 May 52	Finance	179UNTS15	102352
Korea, South	USA (United States)	24 May 52	Direct Aid	179UNTS23	102353
Taiwan	USA (United States)	25 Jun 52	Direct Aid	136UNTS229	101837
France	USA (United States)	22 Jul 52	Direct Aid	181UNTS319	102420
Denmark	USA (United States)	08 Aug 52	Direct Aid	181UNTS249	102414
Israel	USA (United States)	08 Aug 52	Direct Aid	181UNTS37	102396
USA (United States)	Yugoslavia	15 Aug 52	Direct Aid	184UNTS97	102441
Multilateral		17 Oct 52	Direct Aid	141UNTS121	101911
Greece	Yugoslavia	28 Feb 53	General Economic	252UNTS27	103557
Haiti	USA (United States)	13 Mar 53	Direct Aid	212UNTS143	102866
UK Great Britain	USA (United States)	24 Jun 53	Tech Assistance	224UNTS141	103074
Ethiopia	Yugoslavia	21 Aug 53	General Economic	378UNTS105	105421
Canada	USA (United States)	12 Nov 53	General Economic	223UNTS139	103062
Panama	USA (United States)	11 May 54	Direct Aid	236UNTS107	103319
Burma	Japan	05 Nov 54	Reparations	251UNTS215	103543
Japan	USA (United States)	07 Apr 55	Tech Assistance	263UNTS285	103778
Burma	Yugoslavia	14 Jun 55	Direct Aid	378UNTS93	105419
Italy	Lebanon	04 Nov 55	Tech Assistance	267UNTS147	103840
Burma	Israel	05 Mar 56	Direct Aid	280UNTS209	104060
Ethiopia	Italy	05 Mar 56	Reparations	267UNTS189	103844
Multilateral		06 Jul 56	Admin Cooperation	312UNTS109	104514
Germany, West	Thailand	09 Oct 56	Direct Aid	258UNTS143	103676
Turkey	USA (United States)	15 Jan 57	Claims and Debts	280UNTS79	104053
Burma	USA (United States)	21 Mar 57	Direct Aid	300UNTS11	104327
Multilateral		25 Mar 57	IGO Establishment	294UNTS2	104300
Multilateral		25 Mar 57	IGO Status/Immunit	294UNTS411	104302
Multilateral		03 Feb 58	IGO Establishment	381UNTS165	105471
Brazil	Ecuador	05 Mar 58	General Economic	369UNTS43	105250
Sudan	USA (United States)	31 Mar 58	General Aid	308UNTS105	104458
Brazil	Colombia	28 May 58	Tech Assistance	369UNTS141	105255
EEC (Econ Commnty)	ILO (Labor Org)	07 Jul 58	IGO Operations	312UNTS387	200551
Japan	Laos	15 Oct 58	General Aid	341UNTS25	104875
Iran	Japan	09 Dec 58	General Aid	325UNTS221	104701
Cambodia	Japan	02 Mar 59	General Economic	341UNTS163	104882
Iraq	USSR (Soviet Union)	16 Mar 59	General Aid	346UNTS107	104979
Italy	United Arab Rep	29 Apr 59	Tech Assistance	363UNTS91	105202
Greece	Yugoslavia	18 Jun 59	Admin Cooperation	368UNTS125	105237
Multilateral		14 Dec 59	IGO Status/Immunit	368UNTS237	105244
Multilateral		14 Dec 59	IGO Establishment	368UNTS253	105245
Multilateral		06 Feb 60	General Economic	383UNTS3	105494
Indonesia	USSR (Soviet Union)	28 Feb 60	General Aid	392UNTS173	105643
Ghana	USSR (Soviet Union)	04 Aug 60	General Aid	399UNTS61	105734
Honduras	USA (United States)	12 Apr 61	Direct Aid	413UNTS182	105952
Sierra Leone	USA (United States)	05 May 61	General Aid	409UNTS194	105885
Senegal	USA (United States)	13 May 61	General Aid	409UNTS232	105888

PARTY ONE	PARTY TWO	DATE	TOPIC	CITATION	NUMBER
Economic and Social Cooperation (Cont.)					
Ivory Coast	USA (United States)	17 May 61	General Aid	409UNTS241	105889
Cameroon	USA (United States)	26 May 61	General Aid	413UNTS195	105953
Dahomey	USA (United States)	27 May 61	General Aid	445UNTS23	106373
Somalia	USSR (Soviet Union)	02 Jun 61	Tech Assistance	457UNTS263	106587
Madagascar	USA (United States)	22 Jun 61	General Aid	413UNTS219	105956
Tunisia	USSR (Soviet Union)	30 Aug 61	General Aid	437UNTS243	106310
Iraq	Syria	03 Nov 61	General Trade	489UNTS45	107134
Saudi Arabia	Syria	16 Nov 61	General Economic	491UNTS163	107177
COMECON (Econ Aid)	USSR (Soviet Union)	07 Dec 61	IGO Operations	506UNTS325	107392
Panama	USA (United States)	11 Dec 61	General Aid	445UNTS161	106384
El Salvador	USA (United States)	19 Dec 61	General Aid	445UNTS175	106385
Iran	USA (United States)	21 Dec 61	Direct Aid	433UNTS269	106249
Ecuador	USA (United States)	17 Apr 62	General Aid	442UNTS69	106339
Greece	Tunisia	26 May 62	General Aid	534UNTS163	107761
Taiwan	Paraguay	11 Jul 62	General Trade	458UNTS41	106591
Czechoslovakia	COMECON (Econ Aid)	20 Jul 62	IGO Operations	506UNTS345	107393
Cameroon	Israel	24 Oct 62	General Aid	449UNTS3	106446
Belgium	Luxembourg	29 Jan 63	IGO Establishment	547UNTS39	107955
Poland	COMECON (Econ Aid)	22 Feb 63	IGO Operations	506UNTS303	107391
Hungary	COMECON (Econ Aid)	28 Feb 63	IGO Operations	506UNTS281	107390
Burma	Japan	29 Mar 63	General Aid	518UNTS3	107490
Bulgaria	COMECON (Econ Aid)	30 Mar 63	IGO Operations	506UNTS257	107389
Cameroon	UK Great Britain	29 Jul 63	General Economic	478UNTS148	106935
Multilateral		04 Aug 63	IGO Establishment	510UNTS3	107408
Multilateral		23 Oct 63	IGO Establishment	506UNTS197	107388
Multilateral		26 Oct 63	Water Transport	587UNTS9	108506
Benelux Econ Union	Poland	17 Feb 65	General Economic	547UNTS165	107956
Multilateral		28 May 65	IGO Establishment	559UNTS273	108163
Japan	Korea, South	22 Jun 65	Claims and Debts	583UNTS173	108473
Italy	IBRD (World Bank)	28 Jun 65	IBRD Project	567UNTS127	108254
Cameroon	Netherlands	06 Jul 65	Tech Assistance	571UNTS63	108299
Iran	IBRD (World Bank)	12 Jul 65	IBRD Project	554UNTS3	108095
United Nations	Zambia	23 Oct 65	IGO Operations	549UNTS101	107993
United Nations	United Arab Rep	26 Nov 65	IGO Operations	551UNTS253	108046
Mongolia	USSR (Soviet Union)	15 Jan 66	General Amity	562UNTS43	108194
Guinea	IBRD (World Bank)	30 Mar 66	IBRD Project	568UNTS3	108262
IBRD (World Bank)	UK Great Britain	18 Apr 66	IGO Operations	573UNTS209	108334
IBRD (World Bank)	Tunisia	16 May 66	IBRD Project	584UNTS155	108477
Denmark	Jordan	28 Jun 66	Loans and Credits	574UNTS3	108338
France	USSR (Soviet Union)	30 Jun 66	Culture	589UNTS109	108538
Brazil	Denmark	08 Jul 66	Loans and Credits	581UNTS95	108435
Iran	IBRD (World Bank)	26 Jul 66	IBRD Project	582UNTS107	108461
Multilateral		02 Aug 66	Tech Assistance	582UNTS59	108457
Denmark	Malawi	01 Sep 66	Loans and Credits	586UNTS3	108493
Philippines	IBRD (World Bank)	23 Sep 66	IBRD Project	596UNTS71	108629
Ghana	United Nations	08 Apr 67	IGO Operations	594UNTS149	108601
Greece	United Nations	14 Apr 67	IGO Operations	595UNTS83	108613
Multilateral		04 May 67	IGO Establishment	595UNTS287	108623
Economic Development					
Switzerland	USSR (Soviet Union)	17 Mar 48	General Trade	217UNTS87	102945
Brazil	USA (United States)	19 Dec 50	Direct Aid	140UNTS365	101899
Canada	India	10 Sep 51	General Aid	391UNTS237	105629
Canada	Ceylon (Sri Lanka)	11 Jul 52	General Aid	391UNTS245	105630
Iraq	USA (United States)	23 Oct 52	Tech Assistance	212UNTS201	102872
Burma	USA (United States)	24 Oct 52	Tech Assistance	222UNTS55	103022
Italy	IBRD (World Bank)	06 Oct 53	IBRD Project	301UNTS135	104344
United Arab Rep	USA (United States)	06 Nov 54	Tech Assistance	237UNTS183	103344
Liberia	USA (United States)	06 Oct 55	Direct Aid	275UNTS87	103977
Burma	Yugoslavia	07 Mar 56	Direct Aid	378UNTS99	105420
Afghanistan	USA (United States)	23 Jun 56	Direct Aid	271UNTS295	103921
Iran	IBRD (World Bank)	22 Jan 57	IBRD Project	317UNTS129	104600
Libya	USA (United States)	04 Apr 57	Tech Assistance	283UNTS181	104116
Muscat and Oman	UK Great Britain	25 Jul 58	General Military	312UNTS347	104524
Canada	UK Great Britain	18 Oct 58	General Aid	392UNTS61	105639

PARTY ONE	PARTY TWO	DATE	TOPIC	CITATION	NUMBER
Economic Development (Cont.)					
Inter-Am Devel Bnk	USA (United States)	19 Jun 61	Direct Aid	410UNTS34	105895
Dominican Republic	USA (United States)	11 Jan 62	General Aid	433UNTS133	106236
Brazil	USA (United States)	13 Apr 62	Non-IBRD Project	445UNTS227	106391
Pakistan	USA (United States)	25 Jul 62	Direct Aid	459UNTS87	106614
Tunisia	USA (United States)	29 Oct 62	Direct Aid	462UNTS201	106679
Morocco	IBRD (World Bank)	21 Dec 62	IBRD Project	478UNTS205	106937
Philippines	IBRD (World Bank)	15 Feb 63	IBRD Project	478UNTS161	106936
Malaysia	IBRD (World Bank)	15 Jul 63	IBRD Project	482UNTS123	106993
Finland	IBRD (World Bank)	18 Sep 63	IBRD Project	491UNTS345	107183
Japan	USA (United States)	25 Apr 64	General Economic	530UNTS61	107672
Israel	Turkey	13 Nov 64	Tech Assistance	550UNTS303	108025
Taiwan	USA (United States)	09 Apr 65	General Economic	546UNTS81	107939
United Nations	Zambia	23 Oct 65	IGO Operations	549UNTS101	107993
Economic Integration					
El Salvador	Guatemala	14 Dec 51	General Economic	131UNTS131	101740
Costa Rica	Guatemala	20 Dec 55	General Economic	280UNTS121	104056
Guatemala	Honduras	22 Aug 56	General Economic	263UNTS49	103767
Economic Relations					
Bolivia	Brazil	25 Feb 38	Specific Resources	51UNTS245	200192
Brazil	Paraguay	14 Jun 41	Admin Cooperation	54UNTS279	200200
Peru	USA (United States)	20 May 43	Non-IBRD Project	100UNTS259	200288
Australia	New Zealand	21 Jan 44	General Amity	18UNTS357	200113
Multilateral		20 Mar 45	General Economic	2UNTS299	200022
Multilateral		22 Mar 45	General Amity	70UNTS237	200241
South Africa	USA (United States)	17 Apr 45	Reparations	90UNTS275	200265
Poland	Yugoslavia	23 Nov 45	General Economic	115UNTS3	101555
Multilateral		01 Jan 46	Peace/Disarmament	99UNTS131	101375
Greece	UK Great Britain	24 Jan 46	Finance	6UNTS45	100067
Iraq	Turkey	29 Mar 46	General Amity	37UNTS226	100580
Poland	USA (United States)	24 Apr 46	General Economic	4UNTS155	100042
France	USA (United States)	28 May 46	General Economic	84UNTS167	101127
Argentina	UK Great Britain	17 Sep 46	General Economic	88UNTS47	101185
Peru	USA (United States)	22 Nov 46	Non-IBRD Project	100UNTS170	101396
UK Great Britain	USA (United States)	02 Dec 46	Milit Occupation	7UNTS163	100098
Austria	UK Great Britain	23 Dec 46	General Aid	88UNTS93	101186
Multilateral		10 Feb 47	Peace/Disarmament	48UNTS203	100746
Multilateral		10 Feb 47	Peace/Disarmament	49UNTS3	100747
Multilateral		10 Feb 47	Peace/Disarmament	41UNTS21	100643
Multilateral		10 Feb 47	Peace/Disarmament	41UNTS135	100644
Multilateral		10 Feb 47	Peace/Disarmament	42UNTS3	100645
Poland	Sweden	18 Mar 47	General Economic	12UNTS295	100190
Czechoslovakia	Poland	04 Apr 47	General Economic	85UNTS62	101146
Poland	Yugoslavia	24 May 47	General Trade	115UNTS89	101560
Albania	Yugoslavia	12 Jun 47	IGO Establishment	111UNTS201	101535
Romania	USSR (Soviet Union)	04 Feb 48	General Military	48UNTS189	100745
Hungary	USSR (Soviet Union)	18 Feb 48	General Military	48UNTS163	100743
Multilateral		17 Mar 48	General Military	19UNTS51	100304
Bulgaria	USSR (Soviet Union)	18 Mar 48	General Military	48UNTS135	100741
Finland	USSR (Soviet Union)	06 Apr 48	General Military	48UNTS149	100742
Hungary	Poland	13 May 48	General Economic	25UNTS301	100369
Bulgaria	Poland	29 May 48	General Military	26UNTS213	100389
Bulgaria	Poland	30 May 48	General Trade	37UNTS3	100574
France	USA (United States)	28 Jun 48	Direct Aid	19UNTS9	100302
Italy	USA (United States)	28 Jun 48	Direct Aid	20UNTS43	100314
Ireland	USA (United States)	28 Jun 48	Direct Aid	24UNTS3	100349
Denmark	USA (United States)	29 Jun 48	Direct Aid	22UNTS217	100338
Greece	USA (United States)	02 Jul 48	Direct Aid	23UNTS43	100342
Netherlands	USA (United States)	02 Jul 48	Direct Aid	20UNTS91	100315
Belgium	USA (United States)	02 Jul 48	Direct Aid	19UNTS127	100309
Austria	USA (United States)	02 Jul 48	Direct Aid	21UNTS29	100323
Sweden	USA (United States)	03 Jul 48	Direct Aid	23UNTS101	100343
Taiwan	USA (United States)	03 Jul 48	Direct Aid	17UNTS119	100273
Luxembourg	USA (United States)	03 Jul 48	Direct Aid	24UNTS35	100350
Norway	USA (United States)	03 Jul 48	Direct Aid	20UNTS185	100317

PARTY ONE	PARTY TWO	DATE	TOPIC	CITATION	NUMBER
Economic Relations (Cont.)					
Iceland	USA (United States)	03 Jul 48	Direct Aid	20UNTS141	100316
Turkey	USA (United States)	04 Jul 48	Direct Aid	24UNTS67	100351
UK Great Britain	USA (United States)	06 Jul 48	Direct Aid	22UNTS263	100339
France	USA (United States)	09 Jul 48	Direct Aid	24UNTS103	100352
Multilateral		14 Jul 48	Direct Aid	23UNTS3	100340
Taiwan	USA (United States)	05 Aug 48	IGO Establishment	82UNTS109	101087
Portugal	USA (United States)	28 Sep 48	Direct Aid	29UNTS213	100442
UK Great Britain	USA (United States)	30 Sep 48	Specific Resources	71UNTS241	100922
Trieste	USA (United States)	15 Oct 48	Direct Aid	29UNTS249	100443
Italy	USA (United States)	26 Nov 48	Direct Aid	79UNTS71	101032
UK Great Britain	USA (United States)	01 Dec 48	Direct Aid	81UNTS93	101066
Multilateral		09 Dec 48	Scientific Project	73UNTS39	100942
Multilateral		09 Dec 48	Scientific Project	20UNTS229	100318
Korea, South	USA (United States)	10 Dec 48	Direct Aid	55UNTS157	100813
Multilateral		16 Dec 48	Direct Aid	79UNTS85	101033
France	USA (United States)	23 Dec 48	Direct Aid	67UNTS171	100876
Belgium	Luxembourg	14 Jan 49	Direct Aid	36UNTS339	100572
France	USA (United States)	07 Feb 49	Direct Aid	67UNTS189	100877
Greece	USA (United States)	09 Feb 49	Direct Aid	79UNTS95	101034
Austria	USA (United States)	11 Feb 49	Direct Aid	79UNTS113	101035
Trieste	USA (United States)	11 Feb 49	Direct Aid	79UNTS123	101036
Czechoslovakia	Hungary	27 Feb 49	Admin Cooperation	26UNTS119	100383
Netherlands	USA (United States)	26 Apr 49	Finance	70UNTS123	100901
Multilateral		05 May 49	IGO Establishment	87UNTS103	101168
Multilateral		05 Aug 49	Finance	88UNTS229	101195
Ecuador	Italy	24 Aug 49	General Amity	72UNTS35	100926
Greece	Italy	31 Aug 49	Reparations	78UNTS89	101014
Norway	USA (United States)	31 Oct 49	Direct Aid	68UNTS3	100879
Indonesia	Netherlands	02 Nov 49	Recognition	69UNTS3	100894
Korea, South	USA (United States)	26 Jan 50	Milit Assistance	80UNTS205	101053
Netherlands	USA (United States)	27 Jan 50	Milit Assistance	80UNTS219	101054
UK Great Britain	USA (United States)	27 Jan 50	Milit Assistance	80UNTS261	101056
Italy	USA (United States)	27 Jan 50	Milit Assistance	80UNTS145	101050
Norway	USA (United States)	27 Jan 50	Milit Assistance	80UNTS241	101055
Indonesia	USA (United States)	24 Mar 50	Direct Aid	92UNTS387	101281
Multilateral		31 May 50	General Trade	74UNTS95	100957
Burma	USA (United States)	13 Sep 50	Direct Aid	92UNTS361	101280
Netherlands	USA (United States)	07 Oct 50	Loans and Credits	79UNTS33	101029
Paraguay	USA (United States)	27 Nov 50	Direct Aid	122UNTS147	101644
Brazil	USA (United States)	19 Dec 50	Direct Aid	140UNTS365	101899
Ethiopia	USA (United States)	07 Sep 51	General Amity	206UNTS41	102785
El Salvador	Guatemala	14 Dec 51	General Economic	131UNTS131	101740
Canada	USA (United States)	12 Nov 53	General Economic	223UNTS139	103062
Multilateral		09 Dec 53	General Economic	249UNTS197	103509
Japan	USA (United States)	08 Mar 54	General Economic	232UNTS267	103241
Iran	USA (United States)	15 Aug 55	General Amity	284UNTS93	104132
Greece	Romania	25 Aug 56	Reparations	299UNTS231	104315
Economic Statistics					
Multilateral		20 Jun 38	ILO Labor	40UNTS255	100638
Czechoslovakia	Poland	04 Apr 47	General Economic	85UNTS62	101146
Multilateral		09 Dec 48	Scientific Project	73UNTS39	100942
Multilateral		09 Dec 48	Scientific Project	20UNTS229	100318
Education					
Brazil	Paraguay	14 Jun 41	Culture	54UNTS235	200196
Peru	USA (United States)	24 Aug 42	Education	24UNTS153	200139
Honduras	USA (United States)	12 Apr 44	Education	138UNTS271	200450
Peru	USA (United States)	15 Apr 44	Education	150UNTS317	200479
Brazil	Ecuador	24 May 44	Culture	73UNTS223	200242
Bolivia	USA (United States)	07 Sep 44	Education	162UNTS315	200494
Guatemala	USA (United States)	16 Sep 44	Education	135UNTS315	200444
Panama	USA (United States)	14 Nov 44	Education	139UNTS367	200462
Ecuador	USA (United States)	22 Jan 45	Education	24UNTS273	200152
El Salvador	USA (United States)	09 Jun 45	Education	149UNTS379	200478
Dominican Republic	USA (United States)	13 Oct 45	Education	149UNTS361	200477

PARTY ONE	PARTY TWO	DATE	TOPIC	CITATION	NUMBER
Education (Cont.)					
Multilateral		16 Nov 45	IGO Establishment	4UNTS275	100052
Czechoslovakia	France	08 Dec 45	Education	46UNTS77	100701
Brazil	USA (United States)	15 Feb 46	Education	162UNTS21	102130
Iraq	Turkey	29 Mar 46	General Amity	37UNTS226	100580
Brazil	USA (United States)	05 Apr 46	Education	12UNTS131	100183
Taiwan	USA (United States)	30 Aug 46	Direct Aid	12UNTS39	100179
Burma	USA (United States)	28 Feb 47	Direct Aid	25UNTS27	100355
Philippines	USA (United States)	14 Mar 47	Non-IBRD Project	16UNTS31	100247
Philippines	USA (United States)	12 May 47	Scientific Project	16UNTS137	100254
Philippines	USA (United States)	12 May 47	Scientific Project	16UNTS123	100253
Philippines	USA (United States)	12 May 47	Scientific Project	16UNTS109	100252
Ecuador	USA (United States)	14 Nov 47	Education	149UNTS297	101959
USSR (Soviet Union)	Yugoslavia	15 Dec 47	Education	116UNTS313	101578
France	Netherlands	02 Jan 48	Visas	70UNTS105	100899
Guatemala	USA (United States)	05 Jan 48	Education	135UNTS104	101817
Denmark	Switzerland	21 Feb 48	Non-ILO Labor	14UNTS321	100224
Paraguay	USA (United States)	12 Mar 48	Education	162UNTS30	102131
Greece	USA (United States)	23 Apr 48	Education	74UNTS107	100958
Peru	USA (United States)	30 Jun 48	Education	150UNTS45	101962
Taiwan	USA (United States)	05 Aug 48	IGO Establishment	82UNTS109	101087
FAO (Food Agri)	UNESCO (Educ/Cult)	23 Aug 48	IGO Operations	18UNTS345	200112
UK Great Britain	USA (United States)	22 Sep 48	Milit Assistance	71UNTS64	100910
Panama	USA (United States)	24 Sep 48	Education	150UNTS25	101961
Multilateral		08 Oct 48	Education	19UNTS113	100308
France	USA (United States)	22 Oct 48	Education	84UNTS173	101128
Afghanistan	UNESCO (Educ/Cult)	08 Dec 48	Education	46UNTS3	100697
Italy	USA (United States)	18 Dec 48	Education	79UNTS133	101037
Greece	USA (United States)	21 Feb 49	Status of Forces	88UNTS29	101182
Netherlands	USA (United States)	17 May 49	Milit Assistance	46UNTS291	100717
Norway	USA (United States)	25 May 49	Education	32UNTS345	100507
Multilateral		15 Jul 49	Health/Educ/Welfare	197UNTS3	102631
Iran	USA (United States)	01 Sep 49	Direct Aid	79UNTS155	101039
United Arab Rep	USA (United States)	03 Nov 49	Education	71UNTS31	100908
Turkey	USA (United States)	27 Dec 49	Direct Aid	98UNTS141	101361
India	USA (United States)	02 Feb 50	Education	89UNTS127	101214
Iran	Pakistan	18 Feb 50	General Amity	161UNTS23	102119
Korea, South	USA (United States)	28 Apr 50	Education	93UNTS21	101284
Austria	USA (United States)	06 Jun 50	Education	92UNTS201	101273
Thailand	USA (United States)	01 Jul 50	Education	81UNTS61	101063
Pakistan	USA (United States)	23 Sep 50	Education	82UNTS131	101088
Bolivia	USA (United States)	22 Nov 50	Education	152UNTS17	102008
Multilateral		22 Nov 50	Culture	131UNTS25	101734
France	Turkey	22 Dec 50	Non-ILO Labor	98UNTS11	101356
United Nations	Yugoslavia	06 Jan 51	Direct Aid	78UNTS165	101015
Chile	USA (United States)	16 Jan 51	Education	147UNTS11	101925
Nicaragua	USA (United States)	31 Jan 51	Education	150UNTS3	101960
Israel	ICAO (Civil Aviat)	19 Feb 51	Tech Assistance	96UNTS141	101334
Dominican Republic	USA (United States)	16 Mar 51	Education	148UNTS15	101932
Honduras	USA (United States)	24 Apr 51	Education	140UNTS287	101894
Mexico	WHO (World Health)	30 Apr 51	Tech Assistance	103UNTS95	101427
Multilateral		01 Jun 51	Tech Assistance	118UNTS57	101596
USA (United States)	Venezuela	07 Jun 51	Tech Assistance	141UNTS273	101918
Iraq	USA (United States)	16 Aug 51	Education	147UNTS65	101929
Denmark	USA (United States)	23 Aug 51	Education	147UNTS49	101928
Japan	USA (United States)	28 Aug 51	Education	147UNTS81	101930
India	WHO (World Health)	16 Oct 51	Tech Assistance	109UNTS49	101490
Panama	USA (United States)	23 Oct 51	Direct Aid	140UNTS3	101880
El Salvador	USA (United States)	12 Dec 51	Education	132UNTS287	101768
Peru	USA (United States)	04 Feb 52	Education	121UNTS255	200403
Burma	WHO (World Health)	18 Feb 52	Scientific Project	127UNTS43	101698
Taiwan	WHO (World Health)	07 Mar 52	Sanitation	128UNTS233	101723
South Africa	USA (United States)	26 Mar 52	Education	165UNTS187	102176
Ethiopia	USA (United States)	15 May 52	Education	180UNTS227	102388
Libya	USA (United States)	20 May 52	Tech Assistance	177UNTS81	102310
Iraq	USA (United States)	21 May 52	Tech Assistance	205UNTS25	102767

PARTY ONE	PARTY TWO	DATE	TOPIC	CITATION	NUMBER
Education (Cont.)					
Israel	USA (United States)	09 Jun 52	Mass Media	178UNTS297	102345
Ethiopia	USA (United States)	18 Jun 52	Tech Assistance	181UNTS207	102410
Brazil	USA (United States)	30 Jun 52	Tech Assistance	185UNTS79	102460
Finland	USA (United States)	02 Jul 52	Education	165UNTS203	102177
Germany, West	USA (United States)	18 Jul 52	Education	165UNTS167	102175
Ethiopia	USA (United States)	07 Nov 52	Tech Assistance	184UNTS285	102453
Ceylon (Sri Lanka)	USA (United States)	17 Nov 52	Education	180UNTS207	102386
Sweden	USA (United States)	20 Nov 52	Education	177UNTS203	102319
Saudi Arabia	USA (United States)	25 Jan 53	Education	201UNTS3	102706
United Arab Rep	USA (United States)	18 Jun 53	Education	204UNTS55	102749
Liberia	USA (United States)	23 Jun 53	Education	213UNTS57	102880
Ethiopia	USA (United States)	25 Jun 53	Tech Assistance	212UNTS175	102869
Netherlands	USA (United States)	27 Oct 53	Tech Assistance	221UNTS357	103017
Multilateral		11 Dec 53	Education	218UNTS125	102954
UK Great Britain	Yugoslavia	31 Dec 53	Education	190UNTS335	102574
Mexico	USA (United States)	06 Apr 54	Tech Assistance	236UNTS69	103317
Pakistan	USA (United States)	01 May 54	Mass Media	237UNTS231	103349
Haiti	USA (United States)	28 May 54	Non-IBRD Project	233UNTS281	103267
Mexico	USA (United States)	07 Jun 54	Tech Assistance	234UNTS11	103269
Ethiopia	USA (United States)	12 Jun 54	Tech Assistance	234UNTS25	103270
Ireland	USA (United States)	17 Jun 54	Direct Aid	241UNTS173	103432
Brazil	USA (United States)	30 Jun 54	Non-IBRD Project	237UNTS137	103341
Ethiopia	Sweden	13 Oct 54	Tech Assistance	202UNTS273	102734
UK Great Britain	Yugoslavia	31 Dec 54	Education	209UNTS81	102824
Chile	USA (United States)	14 Jan 55	Mass Media	238UNTS191	103362
United Arab Rep	USA (United States)	07 Mar 55	Mass Media	252UNTS159	103565
Chile	USA (United States)	31 Mar 55	Education	262UNTS19	103736
Pakistan	Sweden	04 Jun 55	Tech Assistance	228UNTS121	103146
Libya	USA (United States)	28 Jul 55	Non-IBRD Project	270UNTS245	103900
Indonesia	USA (United States)	15 Sep 55	Mass Media	256UNTS293	103639
Philippines	USA (United States)	28 Oct 55	Milit Installation	239UNTS165	103376
USA (United States)	Vietnam, South	03 Nov 55	Mass Media	239UNTS195	103379
Japan	USA (United States)	10 Feb 56	Direct Aid	275UNTS181	103981
Japan	USA (United States)	10 Feb 56	Direct Aid	275UNTS157	103980
Bolivia	USA (United States)	10 Mar 56	Mass Media	270UNTS199	103897
Peru	USA (United States)	03 May 56	Direct Aid	272UNTS59	103931
Austria	Italy	09 May 56	Education	267UNTS227	103845
Israel	USA (United States)	26 Jun 56	Education	257UNTS55	103649
Burma	USA (United States)	23 Oct 56	Mass Media	282UNTS37	104091
Ecuador	USA (United States)	31 Oct 56	Education	283UNTS151	104114
Argentina	USA (United States)	05 Nov 56	Education	277UNTS143	104004
Multilateral		15 Dec 56	Education	278UNTS73	104023
Colombia	USA (United States)	09 Jan 57	Education	462UNTS151	106676
Czechoslovakia	Yugoslavia	29 Jan 57	Culture	300UNTS249	104339
Multilateral		22 Feb 57	Tech Assistance	274UNTS93	103960
Iceland	USA (United States)	23 Feb 57	Education	283UNTS73	104107
Paraguay	USA (United States)	04 Apr 57	Education	284UNTS161	104135
Multilateral		12 Apr 57	Education	443UNTS128	106362
Brazil	USA (United States)	05 Nov 57	Education	303UNTS3	104368
Japan	USA (United States)	11 Jan 58	Education	304UNTS35	104390
Spain	USA (United States)	16 Oct 58	Education	336UNTS153	104804
Turkey	USA (United States)	26 May 59	Direct Aid	354UNTS57	105053
United Arab Rep	USA (United States)	28 Sep 59	Education	358UNTS97	105128
UK Great Britain	USSR (Soviet Union)	01 Dec 59	Health/Educ/Welfare	351UNTS313	105032
Multilateral		14 Dec 59	Admin Cooperation	444UNTS193	106369
Portugal	USA (United States)	19 Mar 60	Education	371UNTS131	105275
USA (United States)	Uruguay	22 Jul 60	Education	388UNTS315	105587
Multilateral		28 Jul 60	IGO Establishment	485UNTS3	107042
Czechoslovakia	Germany, East	08 Nov 60	Admin Cooperation	424UNTS71	106100
Council of Europe	ILO (Labor Org)	08 Dec 60	IGO Operations	389UNTS291	200579
Libya	USA (United States)	11 Dec 60	Health/Educ/Welfare	445UNTS125	106381
Multilateral		14 Dec 60	Education	429UNTS93	106193
Afghanistan	USA (United States)	15 Feb 61	Mass Media	406UNTS235	105852
Nepal	USA (United States)	09 Jun 61	Education	421UNTS223	106061
Argentina	UK Great Britain	19 Jun 61	Culture	470UNTS71	106797

PARTY ONE	PARTY TWO	DATE	TOPIC	CITATION	NUMBER
Education (Cont.)					
China People's Rep	Denmark	23 Sep 61	Taxation	446UNTS3	106397
United Arab Rep	UK Great Britain	14 Nov 61	Education	449UNTS129	106455
Ethiopia	USA (United States)	06 Dec 61	Education	433UNTS231	106246
Cyprus	USA (United States)	18 Jan 62	Education	435UNTS3	106266
Ghana	USA (United States)	24 Jan 62	Education	435UNTS23	106268
Austria	Czechoslovakia	13 Feb 62	Education	455UNTS381	106551
USA (United States)	USSR (Soviet Union)	08 Mar 62	Health/Educ/Welfare	460UNTS3	106630
Denmark	USA (United States)	28 May 62	Education	450UNTS215	106469
IDA (Devel Assoc)	Tunisia	17 Sep 62	Non-IBRD Project	469UNTS33	106783
Israel	OAS (Am States)	11 Oct 62	Tech Assistance	484UNTS241	107035
Germany, West	USA (United States)	20 Nov 62	Education	505UNTS263	107377
UK Great Britain	USSR (Soviet Union)	21 Jan 63	Health/Educ/Welfare	475UNTS3	106887
Malaysia	USA (United States)	28 Jan 63	Education	473UNTS15	106850
Philippines	USA (United States)	23 Mar 63	Education	474UNTS80	106873
Thailand	USA (United States)	24 May 63	Education	477UNTS123	106918
Korea, South	USA (United States)	18 Jun 63	Education	487UNTS297	107112
India	USA (United States)	19 Jun 63	Education	479UNTS175	106952
Austria	USA (United States)	25 Jun 63	Education	479UNTS223	106956
IBRD (World Bank)	Tunisia	03 Jul 63	IBRD Project	480UNTS209	106970
Paraguay	USA (United States)	20 Aug 63	Education	531UNTS197	107704
Afghanistan	USA (United States)	20 Aug 63	Education	488UNTS41	107118
Argentina	USA (United States)	21 Aug 63	Education	488UNTS61	107119
Ecuador	USA (United States)	20 Sep 63	Education	488UNTS147	107125
Iran	USA (United States)	24 Oct 63	Culture	489UNTS303	107146
Tunisia	USA (United States)	18 Nov 63	Education	494UNTS193	107233
Greece	USA (United States)	13 Dec 63	Education	494UNTS55	107226
IDA (Devel Assoc)	Tanganyika	19 Dec 63	Non-IBRD Project	492UNTS241	107193
Iceland	USA (United States)	13 Feb 64	Education	524UNTS235	107576
Spain	USA (United States)	18 Mar 64	Culture	535UNTS343	107789
Pakistan	IDA (Devel Assoc)	25 Mar 64	Non-IBRD Project	535UNTS43	107775
Pakistan	IDA (Devel Assoc)	25 Mar 64	Non-IBRD Project	534UNTS275	107765
Taiwan	USA (United States)	23 Apr 64	Health/Educ/Welfare	524UNTS141	107570
Liberia	USA (United States)	08 May 64	Education	526UNTS239	107608
Denmark	Kenya	26 Jun 64	Education	573UNTS107	108325
Australia	USA (United States)	28 Aug 64	Education	510UNTS201	107415
Ceylon (Sri Lanka)	USA (United States)	29 Aug 64	Education	531UNTS93	107695
Philippines	IBRD (World Bank)	28 Oct 64	IBRD Project	537UNTS165	107801
USA (United States)	Yugoslavia	09 Nov 64	Education	533UNTS39	107731
Afghanistan	IDA (Devel Assoc)	23 Nov 64	Non-IBRD Project	567UNTS155	108255
Netherlands	Nigeria	04 Dec 64	Education	545UNTS155	107931
Romania	USA (United States)	23 Dec 64	Health/Educ/Welfare	535UNTS359	107790
Belgium	Sweden	11 Jan 65	Education	533UNTS157	107741
Peru	USA (United States)	28 Jan 65	Education	587UNTS273	108513
Nigeria	IDA (Devel Assoc)	01 Mar 65	Non-IBRD Project	571UNTS3	108297
France	USA (United States)	07 May 65	Education	573UNTS183	108331
UK Great Britain	USA (United States)	10 May 65	Education	545UNTS181	107934
USA (United States)	Uruguay	17 May 65	Education	564UNTS69	108221
Morocco	IDA (Devel Assoc)	11 Oct 65	Non-IBRD Project	562UNTS299	108200
Italy	USA (United States)	12 Jan 66	Reparations	587UNTS309	108515
Ethiopia	IDA (Devel Assoc)	16 Feb 66	Loans and Credits	569UNTS43	108278
Pakistan	IDA (Devel Assoc)	17 Jun 66	Non-IBRD Project	582UNTS297	108468
Kenya	IDA (Devel Assoc)	19 Aug 66	Non-IBRD Project	585UNTS119	108485
Jamaica	IBRD (World Bank)	30 Sep 66	IBRD Project	582UNTS179	108463
Electric Power					
Canada	USA (United States)	10 Nov 41	Specific Resources	23UNTS275	200134
Canada	USA (United States)	27 Nov 41	Specific Resources	103UNTS193	200314
Albania	Yugoslavia	28 Nov 46	Non-IBRD Project	111UNTS109	101522
Albania	Yugoslavia	28 Nov 46	Non-IBRD Project	111UNTS113	101523
Albania	Yugoslavia	28 Nov 46	Non-IBRD Project	111UNTS123	101524
Korea, South	USA (United States)	11 Sep 48	Milit Assistance	89UNTS155	101216
Mexico	IBRD (World Bank)	06 Jan 49	IBRD Project	154UNTS81	102028
Mexico	IBRD (World Bank)	06 Jan 49	IBRD Project	154UNTS3	102027
Brazil	IBRD (World Bank)	27 Jan 49	IBRD Project	153UNTS264	102026
Belgium	IBRD (World Bank)	01 Mar 49	IBRD Project	154UNTS133	102029

PARTY ONE	PARTY TWO	DATE	TOPIC	CITATION	NUMBER
Electric Power (Cont.)					
Chile	IBRD (World Bank)	23 Mar 49	IBRD Project	153UNTS61	102018
Finland	IBRD (World Bank)	01 Aug 49	IBRD Project	156UNTS289	200480
El Salvador	IBRD (World Bank)	14 Dec 49	IBRD Project	155UNTS43	102035
Canada	USA (United States)	27 Feb 50	Specific Resources	132UNTS223	101762
India	IBRD (World Bank)	18 Apr 50	IBRD Project	155UNTS117	102036
Mexico	IBRD (World Bank)	28 Apr 50	IBRD Project	155UNTS185	102037
Brazil	IBRD (World Bank)	26 May 50	IBRD Project	301UNTS165	104345
IBRD (World Bank)	Uruguay	25 Aug 50	IBRD Project	156UNTS203	102042
Colombia	IBRD (World Bank)	02 Nov 50	IBRD Project	158UNTS59	102062
Colombia	IBRD (World Bank)	28 Dec 50	IBRD Project	158UNTS87	102063
IBRD (World Bank)	South Africa	23 Jan 51	IBRD Project	158UNTS135	102065
Iceland	IBRD (World Bank)	20 Jun 51	IBRD Project	158UNTS301	102069
IBRD (World Bank)	Yugoslavia	11 Oct 51	IBRD Project	159UNTS3	102081
Colombia	IBRD (World Bank)	13 Oct 51	IBRD Project	159UNTS75	102084
Mexico	IBRD (World Bank)	11 Jan 52	IBRD Project	159UNTS129	102086
IBRD (World Bank)	UK Great Britain	27 Feb 52	IBRD Project	159UNTS181	102088
Finland	IBRD (World Bank)	30 Apr 52	IBRD Project	159UNTS408	200483
IBRD (World Bank)	Turkey	18 Jun 52	IBRD Project	159UNTS269	102091
Brazil	IBRD (World Bank)	27 Jun 52	IBRD Project	190UNTS115	102561
Brazil	IBRD (World Bank)	27 Jun 52	IBRD Project	190UNTS85	102560
Australia	IBRD (World Bank)	08 Jul 52	IBRD Project	159UNTS295	102092
India	IBRD (World Bank)	23 Jan 53	IBRD Project	201UNTS145	102715
IBRD (World Bank)	Yugoslavia	11 Feb 53	IBRD Project	165UNTS231	102179
Brazil	IBRD (World Bank)	17 Jul 53	IBRD Project	190UNTS149	102563
Multilateral		20 Jul 53	Non-ILO Labor	227UNTS217	103140
IBRD (World Bank)	South Africa	28 Aug 53	IBRD Project	180UNTS91	102377
Nicaragua	IBRD (World Bank)	04 Sep 53	IBRD Project	186UNTS137	102488
Japan	IBRD (World Bank)	15 Oct 53	IBRD Project	187UNTS321	200512
Japan	IBRD (World Bank)	15 Oct 53	IBRD Project	187UNTS367	200513
Japan	IBRD (World Bank)	15 Oct 53	IBRD Project	187UNTS271	200511
Brazil	IBRD (World Bank)	18 Dec 53	IBRD Project	190UNTS179	102564
Brazil	IBRD (World Bank)	24 Feb 54	IBRD Project	301UNTS249	104347
Ceylon (Sri Lanka)	IBRD (World Bank)	09 Jul 54	IBRD Project	198UNTS313	200517
Multilateral		02 Oct 54	IBRD Project	201UNTS171	102716
Austria	IBRD (World Bank)	08 Nov 54	IBRD Project	216UNTS305	200528
India	IBRD (World Bank)	19 Nov 54	IBRD Project	309UNTS159	104473
Finland	IBRD (World Bank)	24 Mar 55	IBRD Project	211UNTS305	200525
Colombia	IBRD (World Bank)	24 Mar 55	IBRD Project	212UNTS217	102874
Italy	IBRD (World Bank)	01 Jun 55	IBRD Project	358UNTS203	105137
Austria	IBRD (World Bank)	14 Jun 55	IBRD Project	221UNTS375	200531
Pakistan	IBRD (World Bank)	20 Jun 55	IBRD Project	230UNTS41	103176
Nicaragua	IBRD (World Bank)	08 Jul 55	IBRD Project	229UNTS123	103163
Nicaragua	IBRD (World Bank)	08 Jul 55	IBRD Project	229UNTS97	103162
Lebanon	IBRD (World Bank)	25 Aug 55	IBRD Project	230UNTS233	103188
France	IBRD (World Bank)	26 Aug 55	IBRD Project	247UNTS305	103478
IBRD (World Bank)	Uruguay	29 Aug 55	IBRD Project	243UNTS123	103450
Ecuador	IBRD (World Bank)	26 Mar 56	IBRD Project	292UNTS391	104277
Norway	IBRD (World Bank)	03 May 56	IBRD Project	243UNTS281	103455
Finland	IBRD (World Bank)	22 May 56	IBRD Project	248UNTS57	103485
IBRD (World Bank)	UK Great Britain	21 Jun 56	IBRD Project	285UNTS355	104157
Fed Rhod/Nyasaland	IBRD (World Bank)	21 Jun 56	IBRD Project	285UNTS317	104156
Austria	IBRD (World Bank)	21 Sep 56	IBRD Project	259UNTS43	103682
Austria	IBRD (World Bank)	21 Sep 56	IBRD Project	259UNTS17	103681
Italy	IBRD (World Bank)	11 Oct 56	IBRD Project	359UNTS3	105138
IBRD (World Bank)	Uruguay	25 Oct 56	IBRD Project	265UNTS59	103807
Chile	IBRD (World Bank)	01 Nov 56	IBRD Project	261UNTS27	103724
India	IBRD (World Bank)	29 May 57	IBRD Project	309UNTS201	104474
IBRD (World Bank)	Thailand	12 Sep 57	IBRD Project	299UNTS349	104324
Ecuador	IBRD (World Bank)	20 Sep 57	IBRD Project	293UNTS135	104291
Austria	IBRD (World Bank)	10 Oct 57	IBRD Project	301UNTS95	104343
Philippines	IBRD (World Bank)	22 Nov 57	IBRD Project	293UNTS83	104287
Norway	USSR (Soviet Union)	18 Dec 57	Specific Resources	312UNTS257	104522
Mexico	IBRD (World Bank)	14 Jan 58	IBRD Project	293UNTS167	104292
Brazil	IBRD (World Bank)	22 Jan 58	IBRD Project	323UNTS99	104666
Pakistan	IBRD (World Bank)	23 Apr 58	IBRD Project	323UNTS253	104672

PARTY ONE	PARTY TWO	DATE	TOPIC	CITATION	NUMBER
Electric Power (Cont.)					
Mexico	IBRD (World Bank)	05 May 58	IBRD Project	309UNTS3	104466
India	IBRD (World Bank)	23 Jul 58	IBRD Project	317UNTS3	104590
Japan	IBRD (World Bank)	10 Sep 58	IBRD Project	323UNTS297	104673
Ceylon (Sri Lanka)	IBRD (World Bank)	17 Sep 58	IBRD Project	323UNTS51	104664
Fed of Malaya	IBRD (World Bank)	22 Sep 58	IBRD Project	323UNTS71	104665
Brazil	IBRD (World Bank)	03 Oct 58	IBRD Project	337UNTS177	104823
Austria	IBRD (World Bank)	02 Dec 58	IBRD Project	340UNTS3	104856
Colombia	IBRD (World Bank)	15 Dec 58	IBRD Project	354UNTS233	105065
Colombia	IBRD (World Bank)	30 Jan 59	IBRD Project	337UNTS327	104828
Denmark	IBRD (World Bank)	04 Feb 59	IBRD Project	328UNTS143	104733
Japan	IBRD (World Bank)	17 Feb 59	IBRD Project	337UNTS205	104824
El Salvador	IBRD (World Bank)	20 Feb 59	IBRD Project	362UNTS75	105183
India	IBRD (World Bank)	08 Apr 59	IBRD Project	348UNTS131	104998
Honduras	IBRD (World Bank)	20 May 59	IBRD Project	359UNTS119	105141
Brazil	IBRD (World Bank)	17 Jun 59	IBRD Project	377UNTS111	105398
Norway	IBRD (World Bank)	08 Jul 59	IBRD Project	344UNTS229	104952
Pakistan	IBRD (World Bank)	13 Aug 59	IBRD Project	355UNTS129	105076
Colombia	IBRD (World Bank)	20 Jan 60	IBRD Project	375UNTS49	105353
Iran	IBRD (World Bank)	20 Feb 60	IBRD Project	384UNTS213	105521
Colombia	IBRD (World Bank)	10 May 60	IBRD Project	379UNTS218	105441
Nicaragua	IBRD (World Bank)	22 Jun 60	IBRD Project	384UNTS243	105522
Honduras	IBRD (World Bank)	29 Jun 60	IBRD Project	400UNTS137	105751
Peru	IBRD (World Bank)	29 Jun 60	IBRD Project	400UNTS99	105750
El Salvador	IBRD (World Bank)	29 Jul 60	IBRD Project	390UNTS101	105605
Mexico	USA (United States)	24 Oct 60	Specific Property	401UNTS137	105767
Norway	IBRD (World Bank)	02 Dec 60	IBRD Project	390UNTS131	105606
Canada	USA (United States)	17 Jan 61	Specific Resources	542UNTS224	107894
Costa Rica	IBRD (World Bank)	03 Feb 61	IBRD Project	414UNTS314	105977
IBRD (World Bank)	Yugoslavia	23 Feb 61	IBRD Project	415UNTS92	105982
Japan	IBRD (World Bank)	16 Mar 61	IBRD Project	400UNTS201	105753
IBRD (World Bank)	UK Great Britain	29 Mar 61	IBRD Project	415UNTS300	105990
Colombia	IBRD (World Bank)	12 May 61	IBRD Project	415UNTS172	105985
Ceylon (Sri Lanka)	IBRD (World Bank)	06 Jun 61	IBRD Project	414UNTS349	105978
IBRD (World Bank)	UK Great Britain	16 Aug 61	IBRD Project	426UNTS287	106143
Philippines	IBRD (World Bank)	13 Oct 61	IBRD Project	415UNTS269	105989
IBRD (World Bank)	South Africa	01 Dec 61	IBRD Project	425UNTS215	106126
Argentina	IBRD (World Bank)	19 Jan 62	IBRD Project	446UNTS305	106407
Australia	IBRD (World Bank)	23 Jan 62	IBRD Project	430UNTS3	106201
Ghana	IBRD (World Bank)	08 Feb 62	IBRD Project	449UNTS207	106462
India	IDA (Devel Assoc)	14 Feb 62	Non-IBRD Project	468UNTS177	106773
Colombia	IBRD (World Bank)	23 May 62	IBRD Project	447UNTS39	106411
Mexico	IBRD (World Bank)	20 Jun 62	IBRD Project	468UNTS109	106771
IBRD (World Bank)	Yugoslavia	11 Jul 62	IBRD Project	468UNTS143	106772
Multilateral		25 Jul 62	Specific Property	506UNTS177	107387
India	IDA (Devel Assoc)	08 Aug 62	Non-IBRD Project	478UNTS335	106941
Finland	IBRD (World Bank)	15 Aug 62	IBRD Project	467UNTS177	106763
Panama	IBRD (World Bank)	14 Sep 62	IBRD Project	476UNTS153	106908
Philippines	IBRD (World Bank)	07 Nov 62	Loans and Credits	468UNTS281	106777
IDA (Devel Assoc)	Turkey	01 Feb 63	Non-IBRD Project	468UNTS223	106775
IBRD (World Bank)	Thailand	07 Mar 63	IBRD Project	467UNTS83	106759
IBRD (World Bank)	UK Great Britain	16 May 63	IBRD Project	476UNTS211	106910
IBRD (World Bank)	UK Great Britain	16 May 63	IBRD Project	477UNTS361	106929
India	IDA (Devel Assoc)	24 May 63	Non-IBRD Project	483UNTS205	107014
Colombia	IBRD (World Bank)	03 Jun 63	IBRD Project	490UNTS199	107155
El Salvador	IBRD (World Bank)	19 Jun 63	IBRD Project	481UNTS59	106978
Costa Rica	IBRD (World Bank)	10 Jul 63	IBRD Project	482UNTS69	106991
Colombia	IBRD (World Bank)	16 Jul 63	IBRD Project	482UNTS256	106998
Denmark	IBRD (World Bank)	24 Jul 63	IBRD Project	481UNTS171	106982
Malaysia	IBRD (World Bank)	07 Aug 63	IBRD Project	485UNTS253	107060
IBRD (World Bank)	UK Great Britain	06 Sep 63	IBRD Project	483UNTS173	107013
IBRD (World Bank)	Venezuela	20 Sep 63	IBRD Project	482UNTS227	106997
IBRD (World Bank)	UK Great Britain	23 Sep 63	IBRD Project	503UNTS247	107348
Norway	IBRD (World Bank)	15 Oct 63	IBRD Project	482UNTS103	106992
Portugal	IBRD (World Bank)	06 Nov 63	IBRD Project	492UNTS89	107188
Portugal	IBRD (World Bank)	06 Nov 63	IBRD Project	491UNTS137	107176

PARTY ONE	PARTY TWO	DATE	TOPIC	CITATION	NUMBER
Electric Power (Cont.)					
Peru	IBRD (World Bank)	22 Nov 63	IBRD Project	491UNTS101	107175
Romania	Yugoslavia	30 Nov 63	Specific Property	512UNTS2	107438
Multilateral		30 Dec 63	IBRD Project	551UNTS119	108037
Multilateral		30 Dec 63	IBRD Project	551UNTS105	108036
Multilateral		30 Dec 63	IBRD Project	551UNTS75	108035
Colombia	IBRD (World Bank)	07 Feb 64	IBRD Project	516UNTS99	107473
New Zealand	IBRD (World Bank)	12 Mar 64	IBRD Project	505UNTS3	107362
Nigeria	IBRD (World Bank)	12 Mar 64	IBRD Project	516UNTS325	107480
Ethiopia	IBRD (World Bank)	08 May 64	IBRD Project	505UNTS51	107364
Nigeria	IBRD (World Bank)	07 Jul 64	IBRD Project	537UNTS3	107795
IDA (Devel Assoc)	Turkey	14 Jul 64	Non-IBRD Project	534UNTS339	107767
Bolivia	IDA (Devel Assoc)	24 Jul 64	Non-IBRD Project	534UNTS203	107763
Bolivia	IDA (Devel Assoc)	24 Jul 64	Non-IBRD Project	534UNTS171	107762
IBRD (World Bank)	Sierra Leone	18 Aug 64	IBRD Project	516UNTS295	107479
IBRD (World Bank)	Venezuela	28 Aug 64	IBRD Project	537UNTS135	107800
Germany, West	Thailand	28 Oct 64	Non-IBRD Project	521UNTS311	107528
Japan	IBRD (World Bank)	13 Jan 65	IBRD Project	537UNTS293	107806
Chile	IBRD (World Bank)	12 Feb 65	IBRD Project	537UNTS35	107796
Brazil	IBRD (World Bank)	26 Feb 65	IBRD Project	567UNTS91	108253
Brazil	IBRD (World Bank)	26 Feb 65	IBRD Project	553UNTS3	108065
IBRD (World Bank)	Thailand	22 Mar 65	IBRD Project	538UNTS63	107810
Portugal	IBRD (World Bank)	29 Apr 65	IBRD Project	549UNTS69	107991
India	IBRD (World Bank)	11 Jun 65	IBRD Project	557UNTS101	108130
India	IBRD (World Bank)	11 Jun 65	IBRD Project	557UNTS59	108128
Laos	Thailand	12 Aug 65	Specific Property	547UNTS209	107958
Multilateral		07 Oct 65	Atomic Energy	556UNTS175	108125
Saudi Arabia	USA (United States)	19 Nov 65	Non-IBRD Project	580UNTS35	108419
Mexico	IBRD (World Bank)	15 Dec 65	IBRD Project	568UNTS125	108267
New Zealand	IBRD (World Bank)	17 Dec 65	IBRD Project	567UNTS255	108259
Brazil	IBRD (World Bank)	15 Mar 66	IBRD Project	599UNTS52	108664
Multilateral		04 May 66	IBRD Project	575UNTS49	108354
Portugal	IBRD (World Bank)	14 Jun 66	IBRD Project	581UNTS3	108430
Portugal	IBRD (World Bank)	14 Jun 66	IBRD Project	581UNTS29	108431
Jamaica	IBRD (World Bank)	20 Jun 66	IBRD Project	582UNTS145	108462
India	IDA (Devel Assoc)	29 Jun 66	Non-IBRD Project	585UNTS101	108484
Malaysia	IBRD (World Bank)	26 Jul 66	IBRD Project	586UNTS195	108504
Peru	IBRD (World Bank)	07 Sep 66	IBRD Project	585UNTS3	108481
IBRD (World Bank)	South Africa	08 Sep 66	IBRD Project	585UNTS71	108483
Iceland	IBRD (World Bank)	14 Sep 66	IBRD Project	598UNTS223	108660
Nicaragua	IBRD (World Bank)	05 Oct 66	IBRD Project	582UNTS231	108465
IBRD (World Bank)	Singapore	04 Nov 66	IBRD Project	585UNTS155	108488
Brazil	IBRD (World Bank)	19 Dec 66	IBRD Project	599UNTS177	108667
Brazil	IBRD (World Bank)	19 Dec 66	IBRD Project	599UNTS149	108666
Brazil	IBRD (World Bank)	19 Dec 66	IBRD Project	599UNTS205	108668
Brazil	IBRD (World Bank)	19 Dec 66	IBRD Project	599UNTS107	108665
Chile	IBRD (World Bank)	23 Dec 66	IBRD Project	595UNTS141	108618
IBRD (World Bank)	Venezuela	26 Jan 67	IBRD Project	596UNTS35	108628
Pakistan	IBRD (World Bank)	15 Mar 67	IBRD Project	599UNTS245	108670
IBRD (World Bank)	Thailand	24 Mar 67	IBRD Project	599UNTS299	108672
Philippines	IBRD (World Bank)	05 Apr 67	IBRD Project	598UNTS261	108661
IBRD (World Bank)	UK Great Britain	24 Apr 67	IBRD Project	600UNTS3	108674
Employment Service					
Multilateral		10 Jul 20	ILO Labor	38UNTS129	100592
Multilateral		29 Jun 33	ILO Labor	39UNTS151	100616
Multilateral		09 Jul 48	ILO Labor	70UNTS85	100898
Multilateral		01 Jul 49	ILO Labor	96UNTS237	101340
Peru	USA (United States)	31 Dec 54	Non-ILO Labor	251UNTS51	103533
Energy					
Italy	United Nations	23 Aug 61	IGO Operations	405UNTS3	105819
Equality of Treatment					
Multilateral		05 Jun 25	ILO Labor	38UNTS257	100602
Multilateral		10 Feb 47	Peace/Disarmament	49UNTS3	100747
Belgium	Netherlands	29 Aug 47	Non-ILO Labor	36UNTS349	100573

PARTY ONE	PARTY TWO	DATE	TOPIC	CITATION	NUMBER
Establishment					
Canada	Switzerland	14 Jul 47	Admin Cooperation	43UNTS103	100664
India	Switzerland	14 Aug 48	General Amity	33UNTS3	100509
Greece	Lebanon	06 Oct 48	Consul/Citizenship	87UNTS351	101179
Greece	Turkey	21 Jul 49	General Trade	78UNTS55	101011
Exchange of Information					
UK Great Britain	USA (United States)	01 Dec 43	Scientific Project	3UNTS209	100033
UK Great Britain	USA (United States)	27 Mar 46	Patents/Copyrights	4UNTS101	100040
Romania	USA (United States)	26 Feb 48	Admin Cooperation	48UNTS9	100738
Philippines	USA (United States)	07 Jun 48	Admin Cooperation	73UNTS89	100947
UK Great Britain	USA (United States)	19 Jan 53	General Military	161UNTS3	102117
Multilateral		31 Mar 53	Mass Media	435UNTS191	106280
Belgium	USA (United States)	12 Oct 54	Patents/Copyrights	202UNTS289	102735
Norway	USA (United States)	06 Apr 55	General Military	269UNTS65	103874
Netherlands	USA (United States)	29 Apr 55	Milit Installation	219UNTS105	102969
Canada	USA (United States)	15 Jun 55	Milit Assistance	235UNTS201	103302
UK Great Britain	USA (United States)	15 Jun 55	Atomic Energy	214UNTS301	102905
Greece	USA (United States)	16 Jun 55	Patents/Copyrights	262UNTS137	103742
Multilateral		22 Jun 55	Atomic Energy	249UNTS3	103498
Germany, West	USA (United States)	04 Jan 56	General Military	268UNTS143	103856
Germany, West	USA (United States)	07 Mar 56	Sanitation	271UNTS361	103926
Japan	USA (United States)	22 Mar 56	Patents/Copyrights	275UNTS195	103983
Turkey	USA (United States)	18 May 56	Patents/Copyrights	283UNTS167	104115
France	USA (United States)	12 Mar 57	Patents/Copyrights	279UNTS275	104045
Australia	USA (United States)	12 Jul 57	Milit Assistance	290UNTS139	104233
Australia	USA (United States)	24 Jan 58	Patents/Copyrights	307UNTS105	104446
Poland	USA (United States)	12 Feb 58	Mass Media	304UNTS287	104403
EEC (Econ Commnty)	ILO (Labor Org)	07 Jul 58	IGO Operations	312UNTS387	200551
Multilateral		03 Dec 58	Admin Cooperation	416UNTS51	105995
Multilateral		03 Dec 58	Admin Cooperation	398UNTS9	105715
Korea, South	USA (United States)	25 Sep 59	Mass Media	358UNTS163	105133
Denmark	USA (United States)	19 Feb 60	Patents/Copyrights	354UNTS151	105061
Belgium	USA (United States)	18 May 60	Patents/Copyrights	373UNTS31	105313
Canada	Norway	24 May 60	Milit Installation	470UNTS125	106803
Spain	USA (United States)	21 Jul 60	Milit Assistance	393UNTS289	105663
Portugal	USA (United States)	31 Oct 60	Patents/Copyrights	394UNTS127	105673
UK Great Britain	Yugoslavia	08 Jun 61	Mass Media	437UNTS111	106300
Canada	France	25 May 62	Other Military	470UNTS163	106808
Germany, West	UK Great Britain	20 Sep 62	Admin Cooperation	453UNTS317	106533
Sweden	USA (United States)	04 Oct 62	Milit Assistance	462UNTS31	106669
Guinea	USA (United States)	03 Nov 62	Mass Media	459UNTS259	106628
UK Great Britain	Vietnam, South	30 Nov 62	Admin Cooperation	470UNTS51	106794
Thailand	UK Great Britain	09 Jan 63	Admin Cooperation	470UNTS59	106795
Multilateral		18 Jun 64	Atomic Energy	542UNTS145	107886
Germany, West	Israel	12 Sep 66	Education	582UNTS17	108454
Exchange of Official Publications					
Brazil	Paraguay	14 Jun 41	Culture	54UNTS249	200197
Iceland	USA (United States)	17 Aug 42	Admin Cooperation	24UNTS163	200140
Dominican Republic	USA (United States)	10 Dec 42	Admin Cooperation	24UNTS257	200151
Brazil	Dominican Republic	09 Apr 45	Culture	67UNTS293	200226
France	USA (United States)	14 Aug 45	Admin Cooperation	73UNTS237	200243
Thailand	USA (United States)	05 Sep 47	Admin Cooperation	73UNTS57	100943
Ecuador	USA (United States)	29 Oct 47	Admin Cooperation	21UNTS21	100322
Sweden	USA (United States)	16 Dec 47	Admin Cooperation	73UNTS65	100944
Norway	USA (United States)	15 Mar 48	Admin Cooperation	73UNTS81	100946
Burma	USA (United States)	05 Apr 48	Admin Cooperation	73UNTS73	100945
Philippines	USA (United States)	07 Jun 48	Admin Cooperation	73UNTS89	100947
Ceylon (Sri Lanka)	USA (United States)	31 Jan 49	Admin Cooperation	88UNTS21	101181
Austria	USA (United States)	23 Mar 49	Admin Cooperation	43UNTS127	100667
Denmark	USA (United States)	01 Aug 49	Admin Cooperation	79UNTS147	101038
South Africa	USA (United States)	16 Nov 49	Admin Cooperation	73UNTS97	100948
Multilateral		16 Dec 49	Admin Cooperation	72UNTS3	100924
Switzerland	USA (United States)	24 Feb 50	Admin Cooperation	93UNTS3	101282
Honduras	USA (United States)	24 Mar 50	Admin Cooperation	93UNTS11	101283

PARTY ONE	PARTY TWO	DATE	TOPIC	CITATION	NUMBER
Exchange of Official Publications (Cont.)					
Spain	USA (United States)	08 May 50	Admin Cooperation	98UNTS175	101363
Indonesia	USA (United States)	07 Jun 50	Admin Cooperation	98UNTS167	101362
Excise Duties					
Multilateral		18 Feb 50	Customs	123UNTS45	101654
Belgium	Luxembourg	12 Sep 50	Customs	110UNTS21	101497
Israel	USA (United States)	28 Feb 51	Taxation	220UNTS79	102991
Multilateral		05 Sep 52	Customs	247UNTS329	103479
Exhibitions					
Multilateral		10 May 48	Culture	289UNTS111	104215
Expeditions					
New Zealand	USA (United States)	24 Dec 58	Scientific Project	324UNTS111	104680
Norway	South Africa	30 Oct 59	Specific Property	346UNTS21	104975
Explosives					
Canada	USA (United States)	27 Sep 46	Patents/Copyrights	21UNTS3	100320
Multilateral		08 Apr 50	Specif Goods/Equip	68UNTS99	100889
Expropriation					
Mexico	USA (United States)	19 Nov 41	Claims and Debts	148UNTS367	200474
Mexico	USA (United States)	29 Sep 43	Claims and Debts	106UNTS265	200345
Mexico	UK Great Britain	07 Feb 46	Claims and Debts	6UNTS55	100068
Mexico	Netherlands	07 Feb 46	Specif Claim/Waive	3UNTS13	100022
Greece	UK Great Britain	21 Mar 46	Claims and Debts	91UNTS149	101247
France	USA (United States)	28 May 46	Reparations	84UNTS113	101122
Belgium	Czechoslovakia	19 Mar 47	Claims and Debts	23UNTS35	100341
Czechoslovakia	Yugoslavia	04 Sep 47	Claims and Debts	112UNTS91	101540
Poland	UK Great Britain	24 Jan 48	Claims and Debts	87UNTS3	101163
Multilateral		10 May 48	Reparations	140UNTS129	101887
Multilateral		19 Oct 48	Specif Claim/Waive	84UNTS201	101130
UK Great Britain	Yugoslavia	23 Dec 48	Reparations	81UNTS103	101067
UK Great Britain	Yugoslavia	23 Dec 48	Reparations	81UNTS121	101068
Belgium	France	18 Feb 49	Claims and Debts	31UNTS173	100478
Denmark	Poland	12 May 49	Claims and Debts	87UNTS179	101172
Italy	Yugoslavia	23 May 49	Reparations	150UNTS179	101972
Czechoslovakia	UK Great Britain	28 Sep 49	Reparations	86UNTS161	101157
Finland	USA (United States)	01 Nov 49	Claims and Debts	68UNTS11	100880
Canada	France	26 Jan 51	Claims and Debts	233UNTS65	103251
France	UK Great Britain	11 Apr 51	Claims and Debts	106UNTS3	101456
Extra-territorial Application					
Taiwan	USA (United States)	11 Jan 43	Privil/Immunities	10UNTS261	200066
Taiwan	Netherlands	29 May 45	Privil/Immunities	2UNTS307	200023
Taiwan	France	28 Feb 46	Privil/Immunities	14UNTS113	100215
Taiwan	Switzerland	13 Mar 46	Consul/Citizenship	14UNTS159	100218
Taiwan	Denmark	20 May 46	Privil/Immunities	12UNTS59	100180
Taiwan	USA (United States)	04 Nov 46	General Amity	25UNTS69	100359
Taiwan	Portugal	01 Apr 47	Privil/Immunities	14UNTS177	100220
Extradition					
Bolivia	Brazil	25 Feb 38	Extradition	54UNTS333	200205
Luxembourg	UK Great Britain	29 May 39	Extradition	99UNTS301	200284
Colombia	USA (United States)	09 Sep 40	Extradition	125UNTS239	200428
Belgium	Brazil	14 Jun 41	Extradition	272UNTS157	103936
Saudi Arabia	UK Great Britain	20 Apr 42	Extradition	10UNTS99	200056
Multilateral		22 Mar 45	General Amity	70UNTS237	200241
Iraq	Turkey	29 Mar 46	Extradition	37UNTS369	100582
Italy	USA (United States)	17 Apr 46	Extradition	206UNTS263	102791
Belgium	Spain	24 Jan 47	Admin Cooperation	19UNTS3	100301
South Africa	USA (United States)	18 Dec 47	Extradition	148UNTS85	101938
Czechoslovakia	Italy	25 Feb 48	Admin Cooperation	26UNTS103	100380
Romania	USA (United States)	26 Feb 48	Admin Cooperation	48UNTS9	100738
Czechoslovakia	Romania	01 Mar 48	Admin Cooperation	26UNTS109	100381
Bulgaria	Czechoslovakia	05 Mar 48	Admin Cooperation	26UNTS115	100382
Bulgaria	USA (United States)	08 Mar 48	Admin Cooperation	29UNTS101	100437
Hungary	USA (United States)	09 Mar 48	Admin Cooperation	183UNTS3	102426
Italy	UK Great Britain	13 Mar 48	Admin Cooperation	104UNTS41	101435

PARTY ONE	PARTY TWO	DATE	TOPIC	CITATION	NUMBER
Extradition (Cont.)					
Romania	UK Great Britain	13 Mar 48	Admin Cooperation	104UNTS117	101436
Belgium	Luxembourg	24 Aug 48	Extradition	117UNTS131	101589
Italy	Netherlands	16 Aug 49	Admin Cooperation	98UNTS21	101357
Austria	Belgium	05 Nov 49	Extradition	48UNTS107	100739
France	Israel	03 Jun 51	Extradition	219UNTS215	102977
Canada	USA (United States)	26 Oct 51	Extradition	206UNTS319	102794
Belgium	Pakistan	20 Feb 52	Extradition	133UNTS199	101790
Japan	USA (United States)	22 Apr 53	Admin Cooperation	178UNTS169	102341
Belgium	Lebanon	24 Dec 53	Extradition	539UNTS321	107842
Belgium	Israel	08 Feb 54	Extradition	188UNTS251	102528
Israel	Italy	24 Feb 56	Extradition	316UNTS97	104580
Belgium	Israel	26 Mar 56	Extradition	260UNTS3	103702
Israel	Luxembourg	26 Jul 56	Extradition	550UNTS239	108020
Germany, West	Netherlands	01 Dec 56	Extradition	276UNTS127	103989
Israel	Netherlands	18 Dec 56	Extradition	276UNTS153	103991
Multilateral		13 Dec 57	Extradition	359UNTS273	105146
Belgium	Germany, West	17 Jan 58	Extradition	328UNTS173	104735
Belgium	Netherlands	04 Feb 58	Extradition	330UNTS83	104740
Germany, West	Netherlands	10 Oct 58	Visas	486UNTS345	107085
Israel	Switzerland	31 Dec 58	Extradition	377UNTS305	105408
Belgium	Morocco	27 Feb 59	Extradition	390UNTS275	105611
Hungary	Poland	06 Mar 59	Admin Cooperation	432UNTS3	106216
Austria	Belgium	22 Apr 59	Extradition	356UNTS309	105102
Israel	South Africa	18 Sep 59	Extradition	373UNTS47	105314
Germany, West	UK Great Britain	23 Feb 60	Extradition	385UNTS39	105527
Israel	UK Great Britain	04 Apr 60	Extradition	377UNTS331	105410
Brazil	USA (United States)	13 Jan 61	Extradition	532UNTS177	107718
Czechoslovakia	Poland	04 Jul 61	Admin Cooperation	436UNTS189	106295
Austria	Germany, West	19 Jul 61	Visas	414UNTS211	105974
Austria	Israel	10 Oct 61	Extradition	448UNTS161	106430
Sweden	USA (United States)	24 Oct 61	Extradition	494UNTS141	107231
Czechoslovakia	Hungary	02 Nov 61	Admin Cooperation	438UNTS3	106313
Fed Rhod/Nyasaland	South Africa	19 Nov 62	Extradition	458UNTS59	106592
Austria	France	30 Nov 62	Visas	463UNTS173	106701
Israel	USA (United States)	10 Dec 62	Extradition	484UNTS283	107038
Sweden	UK Great Britain	26 Apr 63	Extradition	590UNTS117	108551
Israel	Sweden	10 Sep 63	Extradition	516UNTS3	107467
Belgium	USA (United States)	14 Nov 63	Extradition	522UNTS237	107549
Multilateral		15 Feb 65	Visas	547UNTS3	107953
Kenya	USA (United States)	19 Aug 65	Extradition	574UNTS153	108348
Multilateral		03 Dec 65	Admin Cooperation	572UNTS105	108309
Multilateral		17 May 66	Visas	571UNTS89	108302
UK Great Britain	USA (United States)	06 Jul 66	Extradition	588UNTS137	108520
Family Allowances					
Multilateral		28 Aug 51	Non-ILO Labor	198UNTS17	102654
Belgium	San Marino	22 Apr 55	Non-ILO Labor	253UNTS41	103574
France	Italy	27 Mar 58	Non-ILO Labor	305UNTS409	104428
France	UK Great Britain	25 Feb 65	Non-ILO Labor	543UNTS157	107899
France	UK Great Britain	19 Nov 65	Non-ILO Labor	561UNTS19	108178
Family Planning					
Ceylon (Sri Lanka)	Sweden	22 May 58	Tech Assistance	428UNTS65	106168
Films					
France	USA (United States)	28 May 46	Mass Media	84UNTS161	101126
France	USA (United States)	16 Sep 48	Culture	84UNTS185	101129
Lebanon	WHO (World Health)	05 Jun 51	Scientific Project	104UNTS225	101443
Austria	Yugoslavia	18 Jan 55	Mass Media	378UNTS31	105416
USA (United States)	USSR (Soviet Union)	05 Sep 55	Sanitation	256UNTS307	103641
Germany, West	USA (United States)	26 Apr 56	Culture	283UNTS267	104122
Italy	Spain	05 Sep 56	Mass Media	302UNTS195	104359
France	Italy	08 Nov 57	Mass Media	305UNTS393	104427
Italy	Yugoslavia	12 Dec 57	Mass Media	386UNTS293	105549
Argentina	Sweden	12 Jun 59	Culture	427UNTS337	106164
Austria	Czechoslovakia	14 Sep 60	Commodity Trade	495UNTS143	107243
Belgium	Italy	28 Oct 61	Culture	429UNTS199	106199

PARTY ONE	PARTY TWO	DATE	TOPIC	CITATION	NUMBER
Films (Cont.)					
Canada	France	11 Oct 63	Mass Media	529UNTS71	107657
France	UK Great Britain	21 Sep 65	Culture	561UNTS3	108177
Financial Questions					
Netherlands	UK Great Britain	14 Jun 40	Finance	2UNTS251	200018
France	Netherlands	14 Jun 40	Finance	2UNTS263	200019
Netherlands	UK Great Britain	25 Jul 40	Finance	2UNTS275	200020
Brazil	Paraguay	14 Jun 41	IGO Establishment	54UNTS323	200204
Brazil	Paraguay	14 Jun 41	Finance	54UNTS313	200203
Haiti	USA (United States)	13 Sep 41	Other Ad Hoc	103UNTS141	200311
UK Great Britain	USSR (Soviet Union)	22 Jun 42	Finance	91UNTS355	200270
Haiti	USA (United States)	21 Sep 42	Other Ad Hoc	120UNTS177	200391
Haiti	USA (United States)	30 Sep 42	Other Ad Hoc	24UNTS205	200144
Multilateral		21 Oct 43	Finance	2UNTS281	200021
Canada	Czechoslovakia	01 Mar 45	Finance	45UNTS283	200185
France	UK Great Britain	27 Mar 45	Finance	98UNTS227	200274
South Africa	USA (United States)	17 Apr 45	Direct Aid	90UNTS267	200264
South Africa	USA (United States)	17 Apr 45	Reparations	90UNTS275	200265
Belgium	UK Great Britain	25 Jun 45	Reparations	90UNTS307	200268
Canada	Norway	25 Jun 45	Finance	45UNTS297	200186
Belgium	Canada	25 Oct 45	Finance	230UNTS127	103180
UK Great Britain	USA (United States)	06 Dec 45	Finance	126UNTS13	101679
Denmark	UK Great Britain	06 Dec 45	Finance	5UNTS3	100061
Netherlands	UK Great Britain	20 Dec 45	Milit Assistance	4UNTS303	100053
Multilateral		27 Dec 45	IGO Establishment	2UNTS39	100020
Greece	UK Great Britain	24 Jan 46	Finance	6UNTS45	100067
Canada	Netherlands	05 Feb 46	Finance	43UNTS3	100658
Canada	Taiwan	07 Feb 46	Finance	43UNTS23	100659
Mexico	UK Great Britain	07 Feb 46	Claims and Debts	6UNTS55	100068
Mexico	Netherlands	07 Feb 46	Specif Claim/Waive	3UNTS13	100022
Netherlands	USA (United States)	11 Feb 46	Claims and Debts	3UNTS37	100023
Colombia	USA (United States)	19 Feb 46	Sanitation	166UNTS104	102187
Canada	UK Great Britain	06 Mar 46	Finance	20UNTS13	100312
UK Great Britain	USA (United States)	27 Mar 46	Milit Assistance	4UNTS2	100039
Brazil	USA (United States)	05 Apr 46	Education	12UNTS131	100183
Belgium	Denmark	08 Apr 46	Claims and Debts	4UNTS429	100059
Canada	France	09 Apr 46	Finance	43UNTS43	100660
Poland	USA (United States)	24 Apr 46	General Economic	4UNTS155	100042
France	UK Great Britain	29 Apr 46	Finance	98UNTS123	101360
Haiti	USA (United States)	14 May 46	Finance	4UNTS179	100044
India	USA (United States)	16 May 46	Milit Assistance	4UNTS183	100045
Denmark	Luxembourg	21 May 46	Claims and Debts	4UNTS435	100060
France	USA (United States)	28 May 46	Milit Assistance	84UNTS59	101119
France	USA (United States)	28 May 46	General Economic	84UNTS167	101127
France	USA (United States)	28 May 46	Status of Forces	84UNTS141	101124
France	USA (United States)	28 May 46	Reparations	84UNTS93	101121
Canada	Norway	06 Jun 46	Finance	43UNTS57	100661
Australia	USA (United States)	07 Jun 46	Milit Assistance	4UNTS237	100048
Poland	UK Great Britain	24 Jun 46	Claims and Debts	11UNTS59	100149
Canada	Czechoslovakia	28 Jun 46	Finance	43UNTS81	100662
New Zealand	USA (United States)	10 Jul 46	Milit Assistance	6UNTS341	100087
Taiwan	USA (United States)	30 Aug 46	Direct Aid	12UNTS39	100179
Philippines	USA (United States)	11 Sep 46	Milit Assistance	43UNTS231	100670
Philippines	USA (United States)	17 Sep 46	IGO Establishment	15UNTS249	100240
Denmark	New Zealand	18 Sep 46	Claims and Debts	10UNTS39	100141
Haiti	USA (United States)	30 Sep 46	Other Ad Hoc	15UNTS257	100241
Belgium	Netherlands	12 Oct 46	Claims and Debts	23UNTS179	100347
Denmark	South Africa	14 Oct 46	Claims and Debts	10UNTS29	100140
Peru	USA (United States)	22 Nov 46	Non-IBRD Project	100UNTS170	101396
Albania	Yugoslavia	28 Nov 46	Finance	111UNTS171	101530
Albania	Yugoslavia	28 Nov 46	Finance	111UNTS143	101527
France	UK Great Britain	03 Dec 46	Finance	54UNTS117	100798
Luxembourg	UK Great Britain	11 Dec 46	Claims and Debts	11UNTS167	100155
Austria	UK Great Britain	23 Dec 46	General Aid	88UNTS93	101186
Belgium	Sweden	30 Dec 46	Claims and Debts	23UNTS197	100348

Financial Questions (Cont.)

PARTY ONE	PARTY TWO	DATE	TOPIC	CITATION	NUMBER
Australia	Netherlands	24 Jan 47	Finance	10UNTS77	100144
Netherlands	Norway	28 Jan 47	General Trade	31UNTS29	100467
Multilateral		10 Feb 47	Peace/Disarmament	49UNTS3	100747
Burma	USA (United States)	28 Feb 47	Direct Aid	25UNTS27	100355
Paraguay	USA (United States)	03 Mar 47	Tech Assistance	135UNTS156	101819
Philippines	USA (United States)	14 Mar 47	Non-IBRD Project	16UNTS31	100247
Belgium	Czechoslovakia	19 Mar 47	Claims and Debts	23UNTS35	100341
Australia	Norway	24 Mar 47	Claims and Debts	18UNTS185	100288
Czechoslovakia	Poland	04 Apr 47	General Economic	85UNTS62	101146
League of Nations	United Nations	11 Apr 47	Specific Property	4UNTS443	200026
League of Nations	United Nations	14 Apr 47	Specific Property	4UNTS449	200027
Italy	UK Great Britain	17 Apr 47	Claims and Debts	54UNTS169	100802
Italy	UK Great Britain	17 Apr 47	Finance	54UNTS149	100801
Peru	USA (United States)	19 Apr 47	Sanitation	136UNTS284	101840
Thailand	UK Great Britain	08 May 47	Claims and Debts	100UNTS47	101386
France	IBRD (World Bank)	09 May 47	IBRD Project	152UNTS111	102014
Netherlands	USA (United States)	28 May 47	General Military	17UNTS29	100267
Greece	USA (United States)	20 Jun 47	Direct Aid	7UNTS267	100105
Ecuador	USA (United States)	21 Jun 47	Sanitation	26UNTS275	100391
Sweden	USA (United States)	24 Jun 47	General Economic	36UNTS25	100565
League of Nations	United Nations	27 Jun 47	Specific Property	5UNTS395	200037
League of Nations	United Nations	27 Jun 47	Specific Property	5UNTS389	200036
USA (United States)	Venezuela	30 Jun 47	Sanitation	166UNTS198	102190
United Arab Rep	UK Great Britain	30 Jun 47	Finance	93UNTS165	101299
Belgium	United Arab Rep	01 Jul 47	Claims and Debts	34UNTS93	100529
France	New Zealand	02 Jul 47	Commodity Trade	16UNTS219	100263
Belgium	South Africa	04 Jul 47	Claims and Debts	47UNTS9	100720
Haiti	USA (United States)	04 Jul 47	Other Ad Hoc	22UNTS165	100335
Turkey	USA (United States)	12 Jul 47	Direct Aid	7UNTS299	100106
Czechoslovakia	USA (United States)	25 Jul 47	Reparations	90UNTS19	101223
Netherlands	IBRD (World Bank)	07 Aug 47	IBRD Project	152UNTS165	102015
Iraq	UK Great Britain	13 Aug 47	Finance	9UNTS259	100136
Italy	USA (United States)	14 Aug 47	Reparations	36UNTS53	100566
India	UK Great Britain	14 Aug 47	Finance	11UNTS371	100176
Denmark	IBRD (World Bank)	22 Aug 47	IBRD Project	152UNTS223	102016
Luxembourg	IBRD (World Bank)	28 Aug 47	IBRD Project	153UNTS3	102017
Haiti	USA (United States)	27 Sep 47	Sanitation	136UNTS258	101839
Haiti	USA (United States)	01 Oct 47	Other Ad Hoc	102UNTS67	101411
South Africa	UK Great Britain	09 Oct 47	Finance	17UNTS239	100278
Multilateral		10 Oct 47	Claims and Debts	54UNTS193	100804
Burma	UK Great Britain	17 Oct 47	Recognition	70UNTS183	100904
Taiwan	USA (United States)	27 Oct 47	Direct Aid	12UNTS11	100178
Multilateral		30 Oct 47	General Economic	55UNTS188	100814
Ecuador	USA (United States)	14 Nov 47	Education	149UNTS297	101959
Multilateral		18 Nov 47	Finance	17UNTS89	100269
Greece	Norway	08 Dec 47	Loans and Credits	30UNTS171	100455
Multilateral		16 Dec 47	Reparations	82UNTS237	101096
Haiti	USA (United States)	19 Dec 47	Direct Aid	135UNTS130	101818
UK Great Britain	USSR (Soviet Union)	27 Dec 47	General Economic	91UNTS113	101245
United Arab Rep	UK Great Britain	05 Jan 48	Finance	77UNTS3	100988
Italy	UK Great Britain	21 Jan 48	Milit Installation	77UNTS23	100989
Czechoslovakia	New Zealand	22 Jan 48	Commodity Trade	16UNTS229	100264
France	Lebanon	24 Jan 48	Finance	173UNTS99	102263
Italy	USA (United States)	14 Feb 48	Reparations	67UNTS115	100871
India	UK Great Britain	15 Feb 48	Finance	134UNTS70	101796
Pakistan	UK Great Britain	21 Feb 48	Finance	134UNTS128	101797
Norway	USA (United States)	24 Feb 48	Milit Assistance	34UNTS155	100535
Costa Rica	USA (United States)	27 Feb 48	Direct Aid	135UNTS74	101816
France	USA (United States)	27 Feb 48	Reparations	84UNTS207	101131
Netherlands	UK Great Britain	11 Mar 48	Reparations	77UNTS69	100993
Paraguay	USA (United States)	12 Mar 48	Education	162UNTS30	102131
Philippines	USA (United States)	23 Mar 48	Education	43UNTS247	100671
United Nations	USA (United States)	23 Mar 48	Loans and Credits	19UNTS43	100303
India	Pakistan	31 Mar 48	Finance	54UNTS33	100793
Greece	USA (United States)	23 Apr 48	Education	74UNTS107	100958

Financial Questions (Cont.)

PARTY ONE	PARTY TWO	DATE	TOPIC	CITATION	NUMBER
Ceylon (Sri Lanka)	UK Great Britain	30 Apr 48	Finance	182UNTS2	102421
Australia	Greece	16 Jun 48	Claims and Debts	18UNTS211	100290
India	Pakistan	30 Jun 48	Finance	29UNTS199	100441
Peru	USA (United States)	30 Jun 48	Education	150UNTS45	101962
Paraguay	USA (United States)	30 Jun 48	Sanitation	124UNTS34	101665
Taiwan	USA (United States)	03 Jul 48	Direct Aid	17UNTS119	100273
France	Norway	05 Jul 48	General Trade	30UNTS281	100463
UK Great Britain	Uruguay	12 Jul 48	Finance	71UNTS199	100919
Bolivia	USA (United States)	14 Jul 48	Sanitation	136UNTS238	101838
Netherlands	IBRD (World Bank)	15 Jul 48	IBRD Project	153UNTS259	102023
Netherlands	IBRD (World Bank)	15 Jul 48	IBRD Project	153UNTS259	102022
Netherlands	IBRD (World Bank)	15 Jul 48	IBRD Project	153UNTS259	102024
Netherlands	IBRD (World Bank)	15 Jul 48	IBRD Project	153UNTS259	102025
Netherlands	IBRD (World Bank)	15 Jul 48	IBRD Project	153UNTS211	102020
Netherlands	IBRD (World Bank)	15 Jul 48	IBRD Project	153UNTS259	102021
France	UK Great Britain	15 Jul 48	Claims and Debts	71UNTS215	100920
USA (United States)	Yugoslavia	19 Jul 48	Milit Assistance	34UNTS195	100537
Greece	UK Great Britain	07 Sep 48	Status of Forces	180UNTS144	102380
Korea, South	USA (United States)	11 Sep 48	Milit Assistance	89UNTS155	101216
New Zealand	USA (United States)	14 Sep 48	General Military	18UNTS251	100295
Czechoslovakia	USA (United States)	16 Sep 48	Milit Assistance	90UNTS35	101224
UK Great Britain	USA (United States)	22 Sep 48	Milit Assistance	71UNTS64	100910
Panama	USA (United States)	24 Sep 48	Education	150UNTS25	101961
Multilateral		08 Oct 48	Education	19UNTS113	100308
Australia	Denmark	08 Oct 48	Claims and Debts	22UNTS43	100330
Belgium	Netherlands	11 Oct 48	Finance	26UNTS95	100379
Burma	UK Great Britain	12 Oct 48	Finance	71UNTS255	100923
Turkey	UK Great Britain	16 Oct 48	Finance	83UNTS85	101103
France	USA (United States)	22 Oct 48	Education	84UNTS173	101128
Greece	USA (United States)	01 Nov 48	Direct Aid	185UNTS169	102468
Australia	Belgium	09 Dec 48	Claims and Debts	25UNTS159	100361
Italy	USA (United States)	18 Dec 48	Education	79UNTS133	101037
UK Great Britain	Yugoslavia	23 Dec 48	Reparations	81UNTS121	101068
UK Great Britain	Yugoslavia	23 Dec 48	Reparations	81UNTS103	101067
Mexico	IBRD (World Bank)	06 Jan 49	IBRD Project	154UNTS81	102028
Mexico	IBRD (World Bank)	06 Jan 49	IBRD Project	154UNTS3	102027
Poland	UK Great Britain	14 Jan 49	Reparations	83UNTS51	101101
Poland	UK Great Britain	14 Jan 49	General Economic	83UNTS3	101100
Netherlands	UK Great Britain	17 Jan 49	Reparations	83UNTS67	101102
Chile	USA (United States)	21 Jan 49	Sanitation	160UNTS185	102107
Brazil	IBRD (World Bank)	27 Jan 49	IBRD Project	153UNTS264	102026
France	Norway	09 Feb 49	General Economic	29UNTS13	100431
Mexico	USA (United States)	14 Feb 49	Sanitation	160UNTS75	102103
Belgium	France	18 Feb 49	Claims and Debts	31UNTS173	100478
Netherlands	Norway	26 Feb 49	General Economic	29UNTS33	100432
Czechoslovakia	Hungary	27 Feb 49	Admin Cooperation	26UNTS119	100383
Belgium	IBRD (World Bank)	01 Mar 49	IBRD Project	154UNTS133	102029
Belgium	Portugal	01 Mar 49	Finance	32UNTS49	100488
France	USA (United States)	14 Mar 49	Claims and Debts	84UNTS237	101133
Canada	USA (United States)	14 Mar 49	Reparations	82UNTS3	101079
Chile	IBRD (World Bank)	23 Mar 49	IBRD Project	153UNTS141	102019
Chile	IBRD (World Bank)	23 Mar 49	IBRD Project	153UNTS61	102018
United Arab Rep	UK Great Britain	31 Mar 49	Finance	83UNTS139	101106
Japan	USA (United States)	14 Apr 49	Specif Claim/Waive	89UNTS141	101215
India	Pakistan	23 Apr 49	Finance	54UNTS51	100795
Netherlands	USA (United States)	26 Apr 49	Finance	70UNTS123	100901
Canada	Netherlands	09 May 49	Reparations	46UNTS263	100715
Denmark	Poland	12 May 49	Claims and Debts	87UNTS179	101172
Netherlands	USA (United States)	17 May 49	Milit Assistance	46UNTS291	100717
Ethiopia	USA (United States)	20 May 49	Milit Assistance	89UNTS99	101211
Norway	USA (United States)	25 May 49	Education	32UNTS345	100507
Greece	UK Great Britain	29 Jun 49	Finance	86UNTS203	101160
Greece	Turkey	21 Jul 49	Claims and Debts	78UNTS65	101012
Netherlands	IBRD (World Bank)	26 Jul 49	IBRD Project	154UNTS178	102030
Finland	IBRD (World Bank)	01 Aug 49	IBRD Project	156UNTS289	200480

Financial Questions (Cont.)

PARTY ONE	PARTY TWO	DATE	TOPIC	CITATION	NUMBER
Australia	Netherlands	12 Aug 49	Reparations	34UNTS213	100539
Italy	Netherlands	16 Aug 49	Admin Cooperation	98UNTS21	101357
India	IBRD (World Bank)	18 Aug 49	IBRD Project	154UNTS269	102031
Colombia	IBRD (World Bank)	19 Aug 49	IBRD Project	154UNTS329	102032
Greece	Italy	31 Aug 49	Reparations	78UNTS89	101014
Iran	USA (United States)	01 Sep 49	Direct Aid	79UNTS155	101039
Argentina	Norway	09 Sep 49	Finance	42UNTS125	100646
IBRD (World Bank)	Yugoslavia	17 Sep 49	IBRD Project	155UNTS3	102034
Czechoslovakia	UK Great Britain	28 Sep 49	General Economic	86UNTS141	101156
Czechoslovakia	UK Great Britain	28 Sep 49	Claims and Debts	86UNTS175	101158
India	IBRD (World Bank)	29 Sep 49	IBRD Project	154UNTS393	102033
Finland	IBRD (World Bank)	17 Oct 49	IBRD Project	156UNTS355	200481
Indonesia	Netherlands	02 Nov 49	Recognition	69UNTS3	100894
United Arab Rep	USA (United States)	03 Nov 49	Education	71UNTS31	100908
Belgium	Canada	16 Nov 49	Reparations	51UNTS3	100748
Australia	USA (United States)	26 Nov 49	Reparations	45UNTS133	100695
El Salvador	IBRD (World Bank)	14 Dec 49	IBRD Project	155UNTS43	102035
UK Great Britain	Yugoslavia	26 Dec 49	General Trade	87UNTS71	101167
Turkey	USA (United States)	27 Dec 49	Direct Aid	98UNTS141	101361
Belgium	France	30 Dec 49	Taxation	46UNTS111	100704
India	USA (United States)	02 Feb 50	Education	89UNTS127	101214
Australia	Yugoslavia	22 Feb 50	Claims and Debts	51UNTS201	100766
Israel	UK Great Britain	30 Mar 50	Claims and Debts	86UNTS231	101162
India	IBRD (World Bank)	18 Apr 50	IBRD Project	155UNTS117	102036
Italy	New Zealand	19 Apr 50	Claims and Debts	67UNTS81	100867
Australia	Netherlands	26 Apr 50	Claims and Debts	54UNTS83	100796
Mexico	IBRD (World Bank)	28 Apr 50	IBRD Project	155UNTS185	102037
Korea, South	USA (United States)	28 Apr 50	Education	93UNTS21	101284
Brazil	IBRD (World Bank)	26 May 50	IBRD Project	301UNTS165	104345
Multilateral		31 May 50	General Trade	74UNTS95	100957
Austria	USA (United States)	06 Jun 50	Education	92UNTS201	101273
Iraq	IBRD (World Bank)	15 Jun 50	IBRD Project	155UNTS267	102038
Multilateral		28 Jun 50	Loans and Credits	87UNTS153	101170
Thailand	USA (United States)	01 Jul 50	Education	81UNTS61	101063
Belgium	Iraq	05 Jul 50	Claims and Debts	68UNTS165	100893
IBRD (World Bank)	Turkey	07 Jul 50	IBRD Project	156UNTS3	102039
IBRD (World Bank)	Turkey	07 Jul 50	IBRD Project	156UNTS75	102040
Korea, South	USA (United States)	28 Jul 50	Finance	140UNTS57	101883
IBRD (World Bank)	Uruguay	25 Aug 50	IBRD Project	156UNTS203	102042
Belgium	Japan	29 Aug 50	General Trade	76UNTS113	100984
Ethiopia	IBRD (World Bank)	13 Sep 50	IBRD Project	157UNTS233	102056
Ethiopia	IBRD (World Bank)	13 Sep 50	IBRD Project	157UNTS213	102055
Pakistan	USA (United States)	23 Sep 50	Education	82UNTS131	101088
Haiti	USA (United States)	28 Sep 50	Sanitation	162UNTS85	102132
Netherlands	USA (United States)	07 Oct 50	Loans and Credits	79UNTS33	101029
Mexico	IBRD (World Bank)	18 Oct 50	IBRD Project	157UNTS259	102057
IBRD (World Bank)	Turkey	19 Oct 50	IBRD Project	157UNTS333	102058
IBRD (World Bank)	Thailand	27 Oct 50	IBRD Project	158UNTS43	102061
IBRD (World Bank)	Thailand	27 Oct 50	IBRD Project	158UNTS3	102059
IBRD (World Bank)	Thailand	27 Oct 50	IBRD Project	158UNTS25	102060
Colombia	IBRD (World Bank)	02 Nov 50	IBRD Project	158UNTS59	102062
Australia	IBRD (World Bank)	14 Nov 50	IBRD Project	156UNTS147	102041
Bolivia	USA (United States)	22 Nov 50	Education	152UNTS17	102008
El Salvador	USA (United States)	13 Dec 50	Sanitation	166UNTS149	102188
Italy	Yugoslavia	23 Dec 50	Finance	150UNTS191	101973
Brazil	USA (United States)	27 Dec 50	Sanitation	147UNTS33	101926
UK Great Britain	Yugoslavia	28 Dec 50	Loans and Credits	88UNTS329	101201
Australia	Finland	04 Jan 51	Claims and Debts	80UNTS27	101042
Chile	USA (United States)	16 Jan 51	Direct Aid	157UNTS3	102043
IBRD (World Bank)	South Africa	23 Jan 51	IBRD Project	158UNTS115	102064
IBRD (World Bank)	South Africa	23 Jan 51	IBRD Project	158UNTS135	102065
Honduras	USA (United States)	30 Jan 51	Direct Aid	124UNTS63	101667
Nicaragua	USA (United States)	31 Jan 51	Education	150UNTS3	101960
Nicaragua	USA (United States)	31 Jan 51	Sanitation	160UNTS121	102105
Austria	UK Great Britain	31 Jan 51	Finance	88UNTS107	101187

Financial Questions (Cont.)

PARTY ONE	PARTY TWO	DATE	TOPIC	CITATION	NUMBER
Costa Rica	USA (United States)	13 Feb 51	Sanitation	141UNTS169	101914
France	UK Great Britain	17 Feb 51	Finance	88UNTS199	101191
Ethiopia	IBRD (World Bank)	19 Feb 51	IBRD Project	186UNTS101	102486
Panama	USA (United States)	26 Feb 51	Sanitation	160UNTS153	102106
USA (United States)	Uruguay	07 Mar 51	Sanitation	165UNTS113	102173
Dominican Republic	USA (United States)	16 Mar 51	Education	148UNTS15	101932
Colombia	IBRD (World Bank)	10 Apr 51	IBRD Project	158UNTS155	102066
Honduras	USA (United States)	24 Apr 51	Education	140UNTS287	101894
Jordan	UK Great Britain	01 May 51	Finance	117UNTS19	101582
Nicaragua	IBRD (World Bank)	07 Jun 51	IBRD Project	158UNTS215	102067
Nicaragua	IBRD (World Bank)	07 Jun 51	IBRD Project	158UNTS277	102068
Ethiopia	USA (United States)	16 Jun 51	Tech Assistance	148UNTS39	101933
Iceland	IBRD (World Bank)	20 Jun 51	IBRD Project	158UNTS301	102069
United Arab Rep	UK Great Britain	01 Jul 51	Finance	249UNTS125	103503
Iraq	USA (United States)	16 Aug 51	Education	147UNTS65	101929
Denmark	USA (United States)	23 Aug 51	Education	147UNTS49	101928
Japan	USA (United States)	08 Sep 51	General Military	136UNTS211	101835
Belgium	IBRD (World Bank)	13 Sep 51	IBRD Project	158UNTS349	102071
Belgium	IBRD (World Bank)	13 Sep 51	IBRD Project	158UNTS323	102070
UK Great Britain	Yugoslavia	28 Sep 51	Finance	117UNTS107	101587
Pakistan	UK Great Britain	29 Sep 51	Finance	134UNTS183	101798
Italy	IBRD (World Bank)	10 Oct 51	IBRD Project	159UNTS383	200482
Chile	IBRD (World Bank)	10 Oct 51	IBRD Project	158UNTS369	102072
IBRD (World Bank)	Yugoslavia	11 Oct 51	IBRD Project	159UNTS3	102081
Colombia	IBRD (World Bank)	13 Oct 51	IBRD Project	159UNTS75	102084
Nicaragua	IBRD (World Bank)	29 Oct 51	IBRD Project	159UNTS35	102082
Iceland	IBRD (World Bank)	01 Nov 51	IBRD Project	159UNTS55	102083
Paraguay	IBRD (World Bank)	07 Dec 51	IBRD Project	159UNTS103	102085
Libya	UK Great Britain	13 Dec 51	Direct Aid	123UNTS167	101658
Multilateral		20 Dec 51	Air Transport	163UNTS309	102152
Mexico	IBRD (World Bank)	11 Jan 52	IBRD Project	159UNTS129	102086
Peru	IBRD (World Bank)	23 Jan 52	IBRD Project	159UNTS163	102087
Multilateral		04 Feb 52	General Economic	124UNTS3	101662
IBRD (World Bank)	UK Great Britain	27 Feb 52	IBRD Project	159UNTS181	102088
Japan	USA (United States)	28 Feb 52	Milit Assistance	208UNTS255	102817
Netherlands	IBRD (World Bank)	20 Mar 52	IBRD Project	159UNTS207	102089
South Africa	USA (United States)	26 Mar 52	Education	165UNTS187	102176
Pakistan	IBRD (World Bank)	27 Mar 52	IBRD Project	159UNTS251	102090
Multilateral		16 Apr 52	General Economic	139UNTS35	101874
Finland	IBRD (World Bank)	30 Apr 52	IBRD Project	159UNTS408	200483
Iraq	UK Great Britain	22 May 52	Claims and Debts	175UNTS97	102298
Pakistan	IBRD (World Bank)	13 Jun 52	IBRD Project	191UNTS85	102578
IBRD (World Bank)	Turkey	18 Jun 52	IBRD Project	159UNTS269	102091
Brazil	IBRD (World Bank)	27 Jun 52	IBRD Project	190UNTS85	102560
Brazil	IBRD (World Bank)	27 Jun 52	IBRD Project	190UNTS115	102561
Finland	USA (United States)	02 Jul 52	Education	165UNTS203	102177
Australia	IBRD (World Bank)	08 Jul 52	IBRD Project	159UNTS295	102092
Peru	IBRD (World Bank)	08 Jul 52	IBRD Project	159UNTS321	102093
Iraq	UK Great Britain	10 Jul 52	Finance	151UNTS227	101998
Germany, West	USA (United States)	18 Jul 52	Education	165UNTS167	102175
UK Great Britain	Yugoslavia	20 Aug 52	Finance	158UNTS439	102077
Iceland	IBRD (World Bank)	26 Aug 52	IBRD Project	159UNTS363	102095
Colombia	IBRD (World Bank)	26 Aug 52	IBRD Project	159UNTS339	102094
Ethiopia	UK Great Britain	06 Sep 52	Finance	149UNTS57	101951
Japan	IBRD (World Bank)	12 Nov 52	IBRD Project	354UNTS313	105068
Ceylon (Sri Lanka)	USA (United States)	17 Nov 52	Education	180UNTS207	102386
Sweden	USA (United States)	20 Nov 52	Education	177UNTS203	102319
India	IBRD (World Bank)	18 Dec 52	IBRD Project	201UNTS241	102719
India	IBRD (World Bank)	23 Jan 53	IBRD Project	201UNTS145	102715
IBRD (World Bank)	Yugoslavia	11 Feb 53	IBRD Project	165UNTS231	102179
IBRD (World Bank)	UK Great Britain	11 Mar 53	IBRD Project	172UNTS115	102243
Libya	UK Great Britain	21 Mar 53	General Military	172UNTS85	102240
Libya	UK Great Britain	25 Mar 53	Finance	172UNTS281	102252
Brazil	IBRD (World Bank)	30 Apr 53	IBRD Project	190UNTS133	102562
Brazil	IBRD (World Bank)	17 Jul 53	IBRD Project	190UNTS149	102563

PARTY ONE	PARTY TWO	DATE	TOPIC	CITATION	NUMBER
Financial Questions (Cont.)					
Multilateral		20 Jul 53	Non-ILO Labor	227UNTS217	103140
India	UK Great Britain	20 Jul 53	Finance	196UNTS251	102628
Multilateral		24 Jul 53	General Amity	250UNTS108	103520
Libya	UK Great Britain	29 Jul 53	Finance	186UNTS277	102493
Libya	UK Great Britain	29 Jul 53	General Amity	186UNTS185	102491
Multilateral		30 Jul 53	Reparations	215UNTS97	102913
IBRD (World Bank)	South Africa	28 Aug 53	IBRD Project	180UNTS91	102377
IBRD (World Bank)	South Africa	28 Aug 53	IBRD Project	180UNTS73	102376
Nicaragua	IBRD (World Bank)	04 Sep 53	IBRD Project	186UNTS137	102488
Nicaragua	IBRD (World Bank)	04 Sep 53	IBRD Project	186UNTS117	102487
Iceland	IBRD (World Bank)	04 Sep 53	IBRD Project	188UNTS3	102519
Iceland	IBRD (World Bank)	04 Sep 53	IBRD Project	178UNTS275	102344
Colombia	IBRD (World Bank)	10 Sep 53	IBRD Project	203UNTS3	102738
IBRD (World Bank)	Turkey	10 Sep 53	IBRD Project	187UNTS71	102502
Chile	IBRD (World Bank)	10 Sep 53	IBRD Project	188UNTS25	102520
Panama	IBRD (World Bank)	25 Sep 53	IBRD Project	188UNTS71	102521
Panama	IBRD (World Bank)	25 Sep 53	IBRD Project	188UNTS95	102522
Italy	IBRD (World Bank)	06 Oct 53	IBRD Project	301UNTS135	104344
Japan	IBRD (World Bank)	15 Oct 53	IBRD Project	187UNTS271	200511
Japan	IBRD (World Bank)	15 Oct 53	IBRD Project	187UNTS321	200512
Japan	IBRD (World Bank)	15 Oct 53	IBRD Project	187UNTS367	200513
Libya	UK Great Britain	19 Oct 53	Admin Cooperation	186UNTS285	102494
Brazil	IBRD (World Bank)	18 Dec 53	IBRD Project	301UNTS229	104346
Brazil	IBRD (World Bank)	18 Dec 53	IBRD Project	190UNTS179	102564
Ecuador	IBRD (World Bank)	10 Feb 54	IBRD Project	209UNTS261	102830
Brazil	IBRD (World Bank)	24 Feb 54	IBRD Project	301UNTS249	104347
Japan	USA (United States)	08 Mar 54	Claims and Debts	232UNTS251	103240
Japan	USA (United States)	08 Mar 54	Milit Assistance	232UNTS169	103236
Japan	USA (United States)	08 Mar 54	General Economic	232UNTS267	103241
Japan	USA (United States)	08 Mar 54	Direct Aid	232UNTS227	103238
Norway	IBRD (World Bank)	08 Apr 54	IBRD Project	201UNTS131	102714
Peru	IBRD (World Bank)	12 Apr 54	IBRD Project	190UNTS231	102567
USA (United States)	Yugoslavia	16 Apr 54	Direct Aid	237UNTS77	103337
France	Netherlands	30 Apr 54	Reparations	202UNTS115	102727
Pakistan	IBRD (World Bank)	02 Jun 54	IBRD Project	324UNTS59	104678
France	IBRD (World Bank)	10 Jun 54	IBRD Project	210UNTS89	102836
Italy	USA (United States)	16 Jun 54	Loans and Credits	236UNTS149	103322
Ireland	USA (United States)	17 Jun 54	Direct Aid	241UNTS173	103432
Belgium	Israel	22 Jun 54	Visas	196UNTS245	102627
Multilateral		08 Jul 54	Finance	287UNTS27	104178
Ceylon (Sri Lanka)	IBRD (World Bank)	09 Jul 54	IBRD Project	198UNTS313	200517
Netherlands	UK Great Britain	09 Jul 54	Finance	199UNTS157	102682
Portugal	UK Great Britain	10 Jul 54	Finance	199UNTS169	102683
Germany, West	UK Great Britain	10 Jul 54	Finance	199UNTS135	102680
Switzerland	UK Great Britain	16 Jul 54	Claims and Debts	199UNTS197	102685
Sweden	UK Great Britain	28 Jul 54	Finance	199UNTS181	102684
Mexico	USA (United States)	30 Jul 54	Sanitation	269UNTS39	103871
Hungary	UK Great Britain	19 Aug 54	Finance	199UNTS149	102681
Mexico	IBRD (World Bank)	24 Aug 54	IBRD Project	286UNTS211	104168
El Salvador	USA (United States)	31 Aug 54	Non-IBRD Project	237UNTS49	103336
Thailand	USA (United States)	01 Sep 54	Claims and Debts	237UNTS209	103347
Multilateral		28 Sep 54	Reparations	207UNTS293	102812
Multilateral		02 Oct 54	IBRD Project	201UNTS171	102716
Multilateral		02 Oct 54	IBRD Project	201UNTS179	102717
El Salvador	IBRD (World Bank)	12 Oct 54	IBRD Project	203UNTS37	102739
Austria	UK Great Britain	14 Oct 54	Claims and Debts	204UNTS87	102751
Austria	IBRD (World Bank)	08 Nov 54	IBRD Project	216UNTS305	200528
Poland	UK Great Britain	11 Nov 54	Finance	204UNTS137	102755
Peru	IBRD (World Bank)	12 Nov 54	IBRD Project	209UNTS287	102831
India	IBRD (World Bank)	19 Nov 54	IBRD Project	309UNTS159	104473
Lebanon	UN Relief Palestin	26 Nov 54	Direct Aid	202UNTS123	102728
Belgium	IBRD (World Bank)	14 Dec 54	IBRD Project	210UNTS113	102837
Italy	Yugoslavia	18 Dec 54	Peace/Disarmament	284UNTS239	104141
UK Great Britain	Yugoslavia	22 Dec 54	Claims and Debts	207UNTS227	102808
Colombia	IBRD (World Bank)	29 Dec 54	IBRD Project	211UNTS135	102851

PARTY ONE	PARTY TWO	DATE	TOPIC	CITATION	NUMBER
Financial Questions (Cont.)					
Peru	USA (United States)	07 Jan 55	Milit Assistance	261UNTS321	103730
Italy	USA (United States)	11 Feb 55	Direct Aid	241UNTS91	103426
Germany, West	USA (United States)	18 Feb 55	Milit Assistance	247UNTS257	103474
Costa Rica	USA (United States)	26 Feb 55	Claims and Debts	252UNTS129	103562
India	IBRD (World Bank)	14 Mar 55	IBRD Project	309UNTS129	104472
IBRD (World Bank)	UK Great Britain	15 Mar 55	IBRD Project	265UNTS85	103808
Peru	USA (United States)	16 Mar 55	Claims and Debts	252UNTS151	103564
Australia	IBRD (World Bank)	18 Mar 55	IBRD Project	220UNTS131	102998
Guatemala	USA (United States)	23 Mar 55	Claims and Debts	252UNTS143	103563
Finland	IBRD (World Bank)	24 Mar 55	IBRD Project	211UNTS305	200525
Colombia	IBRD (World Bank)	24 Mar 55	IBRD Project	212UNTS217	102874
Chile	USA (United States)	31 Mar 55	Education	262UNTS19	103736
Iraq	UK Great Britain	04 Apr 55	General Military	233UNTS118	103265
Peru	IBRD (World Bank)	05 Apr 55	IBRD Project	211UNTS115	102850
Peru	IBRD (World Bank)	19 Apr 55	IBRD Project	221UNTS153	103007
Norway	IBRD (World Bank)	19 Apr 55	IBRD Project	211UNTS159	102852
USA (United States)	Vietnam, South	23 Apr 55	Milit Assistance	277UNTS279	104012
Iraq	UK Great Britain	30 Apr 55	Claims and Debts	226UNTS319	103126
Netherlands	USA (United States)	25 May 55	Claims and Debts	289UNTS227	104220
Italy	IBRD (World Bank)	01 Jun 55	IBRD Project	358UNTS203	105137
India	Pakistan	12 Jun 55	Finance	228UNTS211	103153
Austria	IBRD (World Bank)	14 Jun 55	IBRD Project	221UNTS375	200531
Colombia	IBRD (World Bank)	15 Jun 55	IBRD Project	248UNTS161	103494
Pakistan	IBRD (World Bank)	20 Jun 55	IBRD Project	230UNTS41	103176
Ecuador	USA (United States)	08 Jul 55	Milit Assistance	265UNTS49	103806
Nicaragua	IBRD (World Bank)	08 Jul 55	IBRD Project	229UNTS123	103163
Nicaragua	IBRD (World Bank)	08 Jul 55	IBRD Project	229UNTS97	103162
Japan	Thailand	09 Jul 55	Finance	230UNTS13	103172
Panama	IBRD (World Bank)	12 Jul 55	IBRD Project	219UNTS127	102970
Canada	USA (United States)	21 Jul 55	Milit Assistance	269UNTS53	103873
Guatemala	IBRD (World Bank)	29 Jul 55	IBRD Project	229UNTS167	103165
Pakistan	IBRD (World Bank)	04 Aug 55	IBRD Project	230UNTS79	103177
Peru	IBRD (World Bank)	05 Aug 55	IBRD Project	218UNTS3	102950
Pakistan	IBRD (World Bank)	06 Aug 55	IBRD Project	236UNTS195	103325
IBRD (World Bank)	Thailand	09 Aug 55	IBRD Project	221UNTS283	103011
Lebanon	IBRD (World Bank)	25 Aug 55	IBRD Project	230UNTS233	103188
France	IBRD (World Bank)	26 Aug 55	IBRD Project	247UNTS305	103478
Nicaragua	IBRD (World Bank)	26 Aug 55	IBRD Project	229UNTS145	103164
IBRD (World Bank)	Uruguay	29 Aug 55	IBRD Project	243UNTS123	103450
Belgium	USA (United States)	31 Aug 55	Milit Assistance	223UNTS111	103041
Bulgaria	UK Great Britain	22 Sep 55	Finance	222UNTS349	103039
Bolivia	USA (United States)	23 Sep 55	Claims and Debts	256UNTS275	103637
Multilateral		29 Sep 55	Air Transport	222UNTS313	103037
Iceland	USA (United States)	05 Oct 55	Claims and Debts	256UNTS285	103638
Japan	IBRD (World Bank)	25 Oct 55	IBRD Project	230UNTS379	200534
Colombia	USA (United States)	18 Nov 55	Claims and Debts	239UNTS173	103377
IBRD (World Bank)	South Africa	28 Nov 55	IBRD Project	230UNTS101	103178
Honduras	IBRD (World Bank)	22 Dec 55	IBRD Project	230UNTS262	103189
Germany, West	USA (United States)	23 Dec 55	US Agri Commod Aid	240UNTS79	103395
Haiti	USA (United States)	28 Dec 55	Non-IBRD Project	240UNTS95	103397
Cuba	USA (United States)	10 Jan 56	Milit Assistance	240UNTS101	103398
Japan	IBRD (World Bank)	21 Feb 56	IBRD Project	248UNTS321	200543
Ethiopia	Italy	05 Mar 56	Reparations	267UNTS189	103844
Ecuador	IBRD (World Bank)	26 Mar 56	IBRD Project	292UNTS391	104277
Peru	USA (United States)	03 May 56	Direct Aid	272UNTS59	103931
Norway	IBRD (World Bank)	03 May 56	IBRD Project	243UNTS281	103455
Brazil	France	04 May 56	Finance	323UNTS339	104675
Burma	IBRD (World Bank)	04 May 56	IBRD Project	253UNTS179	103584
Burma	IBRD (World Bank)	04 May 56	IBRD Project	253UNTS209	103585
Haiti	IBRD (World Bank)	07 May 56	IBRD Project	252UNTS279	103570
Nicaragua	IBRD (World Bank)	22 May 56	IBRD Project	253UNTS233	103586
Finland	IBRD (World Bank)	22 May 56	IBRD Project	248UNTS57	103485
UK Great Britain	USA (United States)	05 Jun 56	Milit Installation	247UNTS205	103470
Colombia	IBRD (World Bank)	06 Jun 56	IBRD Project	248UNTS139	103493
Fed Rhod/Nyasaland	IBRD (World Bank)	21 Jun 56	IBRD Project	285UNTS317	104156

Financial Questions (Cont.)

PARTY ONE	PARTY TWO	DATE	TOPIC	CITATION	NUMBER
IBRD (World Bank)	UK Great Britain	21 Jun 56	IBRD Project	285UNTS355	104157
India	IBRD (World Bank)	26 Jun 56	IBRD Project	301UNTS3	104341
Israel	USA (United States)	26 Jun 56	Education	257UNTS55	103649
Hungary	UK Great Britain	27 Jun 56	Claims and Debts	249UNTS19	103499
Burma	USA (United States)	30 Jun 56	Tech Assistance	281UNTS65	104070
Pakistan	USA (United States)	10 Sep 56	Milit Assistance	277UNTS259	104010
Costa Rica	IBRD (World Bank)	18 Sep 56	IBRD Project	260UNTS369	103721
Austria	IBRD (World Bank)	21 Sep 56	IBRD Project	259UNTS43	103682
Austria	IBRD (World Bank)	21 Sep 56	IBRD Project	259UNTS17	103681
Jordan	USA (United States)	24 Sep 56	Milit Assistance	278UNTS51	104020
Italy	IBRD (World Bank)	11 Oct 56	IBRD Project	359UNTS3	105138
IBRD (World Bank)	Thailand	12 Oct 56	IBRD Project	261UNTS117	103728
IBRD (World Bank)	Uruguay	25 Oct 56	IBRD Project	265UNTS59	103807
Ecuador	USA (United States)	31 Oct 56	Education	283UNTS151	104114
Chile	IBRD (World Bank)	01 Nov 56	IBRD Project	261UNTS27	103724
Argentina	USA (United States)	05 Nov 56	Education	277UNTS143	104004
Australia	IBRD (World Bank)	15 Nov 56	IBRD Project	288UNTS117	104201
Japan	IBRD (World Bank)	19 Dec 56	IBRD Project	268UNTS203	103859
India	IBRD (World Bank)	19 Dec 56	IBRD Project	310UNTS75	104489
Japan	IBRD (World Bank)	19 Dec 56	IBRD Project	264UNTS179	103793
France	Italy	28 Dec 56	Non-ILO Labor	291UNTS203	104255
Greece	USA (United States)	19 Jan 57	Milit Installation	280UNTS45	104049
Iran	IBRD (World Bank)	22 Jan 57	IBRD Project	317UNTS129	104600
Sweden	USSR (Soviet Union)	28 Jan 57	Finance	428UNTS315	106183
Ethiopia	IBRD (World Bank)	28 Jan 57	IBRD Project	286UNTS307	104175
Iceland	USA (United States)	23 Feb 57	Education	283UNTS73	104107
India	IBRD (World Bank)	05 Mar 57	IBRD Project	272UNTS201	103939
Burma	India	12 Mar 57	Finance	312UNTS131	104515
Peru	IBRD (World Bank)	13 Mar 57	IBRD Project	274UNTS59	103958
France	Japan	27 Mar 57	Specif Claim/Waive	318UNTS233	104617
Paraguay	USA (United States)	04 Apr 57	Education	284UNTS161	104135
Netherlands	IBRD (World Bank)	15 May 57	IBRD Project	274UNTS211	103967
India	IBRD (World Bank)	29 May 57	IBRD Project	309UNTS201	104474
Belgium	IBRD (World Bank)	26 Jun 57	IBRD Project	322UNTS301	104661
South Africa	USA (United States)	08 Jul 57	Atomic Energy	290UNTS147	104234
India	IBRD (World Bank)	12 Jul 57	IBRD Project	288UNTS135	104202
Chile	IBRD (World Bank)	24 Jul 57	IBRD Project	282UNTS189	104099
Chile	IBRD (World Bank)	24 Jul 57	IBRD Project	282UNTS139	104098
Japan	IBRD (World Bank)	09 Aug 57	IBRD Project	293UNTS59	104286
Belgium	IBRD (World Bank)	10 Sep 57	IBRD Project	286UNTS291	104174
IBRD (World Bank)	Thailand	12 Sep 57	IBRD Project	299UNTS349	104324
Ecuador	IBRD (World Bank)	20 Sep 57	IBRD Project	289UNTS237	104221
Ecuador	IBRD (World Bank)	20 Sep 57	IBRD Project	293UNTS135	104291
IBRD (World Bank)	South Africa	01 Oct 57	IBRD Project	280UNTS285	104065
Multilateral		03 Oct 57	Postal Service	366UNTS193	105218
Austria	IBRD (World Bank)	10 Oct 57	IBRD Project	301UNTS95	104343
Pakistan	IBRD (World Bank)	18 Oct 57	IBRD Project	299UNTS303	104322
India	IBRD (World Bank)	20 Nov 57	IBRD Project	301UNTS47	104342
Philippines	IBRD (World Bank)	22 Nov 57	IBRD Project	293UNTS83	104287
Belgium	IBRD (World Bank)	27 Nov 57	IBRD Project	292UNTS175	104273
Pakistan	IBRD (World Bank)	17 Dec 57	IBRD Project	299UNTS321	104323
Mexico	IBRD (World Bank)	14 Jan 58	IBRD Project	293UNTS167	104292
Brazil	IBRD (World Bank)	22 Jan 58	IBRD Project	323UNTS99	104666
Japan	IBRD (World Bank)	29 Jan 58	IBRD Project	310UNTS111	104490
Italy	IBRD (World Bank)	28 Feb 58	IBRD Project	359UNTS47	105139
Pakistan	IBRD (World Bank)	23 Apr 58	IBRD Project	323UNTS253	104672
Austria	IBRD (World Bank)	28 Apr 58	IBRD Project	359UNTS145	105142
IBRD (World Bank)	UK Great Britain	02 May 58	IBRD Project	324UNTS25	104677
Mexico	IBRD (World Bank)	05 May 58	IBRD Project	309UNTS3	104466
Honduras	IBRD (World Bank)	09 May 58	IBRD Project	323UNTS4	104662
Japan	IBRD (World Bank)	13 Jun 58	IBRD Project	312UNTS159	104518
IBRD (World Bank)	UK Great Britain	16 Jun 58	IBRD Project	309UNTS35	104467
India	IBRD (World Bank)	25 Jun 58	IBRD Project	323UNTS157	104668
India	IBRD (World Bank)	25 Jun 58	IBRD Project	323UNTS131	104667
Japan	IBRD (World Bank)	27 Jun 58	IBRD Project	312UNTS193	104519

Financial Questions (Cont.)

PARTY ONE	PARTY TWO	DATE	TOPIC	CITATION	NUMBER
Japan	IBRD (World Bank)	11 Jul 58	IBRD Project	318UNTS103	104611
IBRD (World Bank)	Sudan	21 Jul 58	IBRD Project	323UNTS183	104669
India	IBRD (World Bank)	23 Jul 58	IBRD Project	317UNTS3	104590
Japan	IBRD (World Bank)	18 Aug 58	IBRD Project	323UNTS205	104670
Japan	IBRD (World Bank)	10 Sep 58	IBRD Project	318UNTS133	104612
Japan	IBRD (World Bank)	10 Sep 58	IBRD Project	323UNTS297	104673
India	IBRD (World Bank)	16 Sep 58	IBRD Project	323UNTS235	104671
Ceylon (Sri Lanka)	IBRD (World Bank)	17 Sep 58	IBRD Project	323UNTS51	104664
Peru	IBRD (World Bank)	17 Sep 58	IBRD Project	323UNTS27	104663
Fed of Malaya	IBRD (World Bank)	22 Sep 58	IBRD Project	323UNTS71	104665
Brazil	IBRD (World Bank)	03 Oct 58	IBRD Project	337UNTS177	104823
Ecuador	IBRD (World Bank)	09 Oct 58	IBRD Project	337UNTS299	104827
Austria	IBRD (World Bank)	02 Dec 58	IBRD Project	340UNTS3	104856
IBRD (World Bank)	South Africa	02 Dec 58	IBRD Project	324UNTS3	104676
Colombia	IBRD (World Bank)	15 Dec 58	IBRD Project	354UNTS233	105065
El Salvador	IBRD (World Bank)	07 Jan 59	IBRD Project	346UNTS51	104977
Colombia	IBRD (World Bank)	30 Jan 59	IBRD Project	337UNTS327	104828
Denmark	IBRD (World Bank)	04 Feb 59	IBRD Project	328UNTS143	104733
Costa Rica	IBRD (World Bank)	11 Feb 59	IBRD Project	337UNTS245	104825
Japan	IBRD (World Bank)	17 Feb 59	IBRD Project	337UNTS205	104824
El Salvador	IBRD (World Bank)	20 Feb 59	IBRD Project	362UNTS75	105183
United Arab Rep	UK Great Britain	28 Feb 59	Finance	343UNTS159	104925
Finland	IBRD (World Bank)	16 Mar 59	IBRD Project	337UNTS269	104826
Multilateral		08 Apr 59	IGO Establishment	389UNTS69	105593
Italy	IBRD (World Bank)	21 Apr 59	IBRD Project	359UNTS191	105143
Honduras	IBRD (World Bank)	20 May 59	IBRD Project	359UNTS119	105141
Colombia	IBRD (World Bank)	20 May 59	IBRD Project	344UNTS251	104953
Iran	IBRD (World Bank)	29 May 59	IBRD Project	348UNTS103	104997
IBRD (World Bank)	South Africa	10 Jun 59	IBRD Project	340UNTS33	104857
Brazil	IBRD (World Bank)	17 Jun 59	IBRD Project	377UNTS111	105398
Norway	IBRD (World Bank)	08 Jul 59	IBRD Project	344UNTS229	104952
India	IBRD (World Bank)	15 Jul 59	IBRD Project	346UNTS33	104976
India	IBRD (World Bank)	15 Jul 59	IBRD Project	355UNTS95	105075
Pakistan	IBRD (World Bank)	13 Aug 59	IBRD Project	355UNTS129	105076
Multilateral		20 Aug 59	Air Transport	376UNTS99	105376
Italy	IBRD (World Bank)	16 Sep 59	IBRD Project	375UNTS159	105366
Pakistan	IBRD (World Bank)	25 Sep 59	IBRD Project	355UNTS169	105077
Austria	IBRD (World Bank)	25 Sep 59	IBRD Project	355UNTS223	105079
Japan	IBRD (World Bank)	12 Nov 59	IBRD Project	354UNTS279	105067
Iran	IBRD (World Bank)	23 Nov 59	IBRD Project	380UNTS245	105459
Pakistan	IBRD (World Bank)	30 Nov 59	IBRD Project	355UNTS203	105078
France	IBRD (World Bank)	10 Dec 59	IBRD Project	380UNTS319	105464
IBRD (World Bank)	United Arab Rep	22 Dec 59	IBRD Project	354UNTS197	105063
IBRD (World Bank)	Uruguay	30 Dec 59	IBRD Project	384UNTS275	105523
Colombia	IBRD (World Bank)	20 Jan 60	IBRD Project	375UNTS49	105353
Iran	IBRD (World Bank)	20 Feb 60	IBRD Project	384UNTS213	105521
Japan	IBRD (World Bank)	17 Mar 60	IBRD Project	362UNTS43	105182
Romania	USA (United States)	30 Mar 60	Claims and Debts	371UNTS163	105278
Belgium	IBRD (World Bank)	30 Mar 60	IBRD Project	379UNTS103	105437
Belgium	IBRD (World Bank)	30 Mar 60	IBRD Project	379UNTS161	105439
Belgium	IBRD (World Bank)	30 Mar 60	IBRD Project	379UNTS129	105438
IBRD (World Bank)	UK Great Britain	01 Apr 60	IBRD Project	379UNTS397	105446
Germany, West	Netherlands	08 Apr 60	Territory Boundary	508UNTS14	107404
Costa Rica	IBRD (World Bank)	04 May 60	IBRD Project	390UNTS201	105609
Colombia	IBRD (World Bank)	10 May 60	IBRD Project	379UNTS218	105441
IBRD (World Bank)	UK Great Britain	27 May 60	IBRD Project	375UNTS201	105367
Peru	IBRD (World Bank)	01 Jun 60	IBRD Project	380UNTS15	105448
IBRD (World Bank)	Sudan	17 Jun 60	IBRD Project	379UNTS253	105442
Nicaragua	IBRD (World Bank)	22 Jun 60	IBRD Project	384UNTS243	105522
IAEA (Atom Energy)	USA (United States)	28 Jun 60	Direct Aid	374UNTS133	105333
Peru	IBRD (World Bank)	29 Jun 60	IBRD Project	400UNTS99	105750
Honduras	IBRD (World Bank)	29 Jun 60	IBRD Project	400UNTS137	105751
El Salvador	IBRD (World Bank)	29 Jul 60	IBRD Project	390UNTS101	105605
India	IBRD (World Bank)	29 Jul 60	IBRD Project	377UNTS153	105399
Cyprus	UK Great Britain	16 Aug 60	Claims and Debts	382UNTS239	105485

PARTY ONE	PARTY TWO	DATE	TOPIC	CITATION	NUMBER
Financial Questions (Cont.)					
Panama	IBRD (World Bank)	19 Aug 60	IBRD Project	390UNTS153	105607
Colombia	IBRD (World Bank)	20 Sep 60	IBRD Project	390UNTS173	105608
Netherlands	Romania	30 Sep 60	General Economic	479UNTS91	106948
Belgium	Congo (Zaire)	15 Nov 60	Finance	394UNTS79	105670
Norway	IBRD (World Bank)	02 Dec 60	IBRD Project	390UNTS131	105606
Multilateral		13 Dec 60	IGO Establishment	455UNTS204	106544
Japan	IBRD (World Bank)	20 Dec 60	IBRD Project	400UNTS279	105754
Japan	IBRD (World Bank)	20 Dec 60	IBRD Project	400UNTS167	105752
Burma	IBRD (World Bank)	16 Jan 61	IBRD Project	400UNTS73	105749
Japan	IBRD (World Bank)	16 Mar 61	IBRD Project	400UNTS201	105753
Austria	USA (United States)	29 Mar 61	Direct Aid	459UNTS45	106612
Multilateral		14 Jun 61	IBRD Project	415UNTS4	105979
Multilateral		28 Aug 61	IBRD Project	416UNTS45	105994
OAS (Am States)	USA (United States)	29 Nov 61	Direct Aid	424UNTS119	106104
Israel	IBRD (World Bank)	01 Feb 62	IBRD Project	435UNTS155	106277
Denmark	USA (United States)	28 May 62	Education	450UNTS215	106469
Multilateral		15 Aug 62	Territory Boundary	437UNTS292	106312
IDA (Devel Assoc)	Turkey	23 Nov 62	Non-IBRD Project	469UNTS3	106782
Morocco	IBRD (World Bank)	21 Dec 62	IBRD Project	478UNTS205	106937
Austria	Bulgaria	02 May 63	Finance	535UNTS143	107778
Canada	India	14 May 63	Loans and Credits	529UNTS31	107653
Multilateral		04 Aug 63	IGO Establishment	510UNTS3	107408
Multilateral		19 Oct 63	Direct Aid	523UNTS249	107559
Romania	Yugoslavia	30 Nov 63	Specific Property	512UNTS2	107438
Belgium	Congo (Zaire)	06 Feb 65	Finance	540UNTS275	107853
Israel	IBRD (World Bank)	16 Sep 65	Claims and Debts	566UNTS212	108245
Philippines	USA (United States)	15 Nov 65	Milit Assistance	574UNTS205	108350
Multilateral		04 Dec 65	IGO Establishment	571UNTS123	108303
Fisheries					
Finland	USSR (Soviet Union)	28 Oct 22	Specific Resources	67UNTS157	100874
Mexico	USA (United States)	24 Oct 42	Non-IBRD Project	21UNTS189	200123
Mexico	USA (United States)	22 Oct 46	Non-IBRD Project	21UNTS13	100321
Multilateral		06 Feb 47	IGO Establishment	97UNTS227	101352
Philippines	USA (United States)	14 Mar 47	Non-IBRD Project	16UNTS31	100247
Norway	Sweden	29 Apr 48	Commodity Trade	26UNTS41	100376
Canada	USA (United States)	30 Apr 48	Sanitation	77UNTS191	100999
Belgium	Denmark	30 Dec 48	Dispute Settlement	25UNTS173	100362
Mexico	USA (United States)	25 Jan 49	IGO Establishment	99UNTS3	101367
Costa Rica	USA (United States)	31 May 49	IGO Establishment	80UNTS3	101041
Finland	Norway	13 Jun 49	Commodity Trade	34UNTS9	100523
Norway	Sweden	20 Dec 50	Specific Resources	92UNTS3	101256
Germany, West	Norway	07 May 51	Claims and Debts	92UNTS51	101260
India	Japan	31 Mar 62	Education	451UNTS143	106490
Japan	USA (United States)	24 Oct 62	Sanitation	462UNTS119	106673
Fishing					
Canada	USA (United States)	05 Aug 44	Specific Resources	121UNTS299	200408
Multilateral		05 Apr 46	Specific Resources	231UNTS199	103221
Multilateral		15 Nov 48	IGO Establishment	120UNTS59	101615
Norway	Sweden	28 Jan 49	Specific Resources	196UNTS3	102617
Multilateral		08 Feb 49	Specific Resources	157UNTS157	102053
Italy	Yugoslavia	13 Apr 49	Commodity Trade	171UNTS279	102232
Multilateral		24 Sep 49	IGO Establishment	126UNTS237	101691
Canada	USA (United States)	24 Mar 50	Customs	200UNTS211	102705
Norway	Sweden	20 Dec 50	Specific Resources	92UNTS3	101256
France	UK Great Britain	30 Jan 51	Privil/Immunities	121UNTS97	101629
El Salvador	USA (United States)	19 Jul 51	Tech Assistance	140UNTS259	101892
Denmark	Norway	14 Jan 52	Claims and Debts	120UNTS119	101618
Multilateral		07 Mar 52	Specific Resources	175UNTS205	102302
Multilateral		09 May 52	Specific Resources	205UNTS65	102770
Canada	USA (United States)	02 Mar 53	Specific Resources	222UNTS77	103024
Finland	Norway	20 May 53	Specific Resources	173UNTS163	102265
United Arab Rep	USA (United States)	21 May 53	Tech Assistance	204UNTS29	102748
Australia	Japan	24 May 54	Specif Claim/Waive	191UNTS125	102580
Denmark	UK Great Britain	23 Jul 54	Specific Resources	213UNTS313	102894
Fishing (Cont.)					
Canada	USA (United States)	10 Sep 54	Specific Resources	238UNTS97	103355
Multilateral		29 Nov 54	General Trade	287UNTS209	104187
Multilateral		03 Jun 55	Specific Resources	310UNTS145	104491
UK Great Britain	USSR (Soviet Union)	25 May 56	Specific Resources	266UNTS209	103831
Multilateral		16 Aug 56	General Trade	287UNTS223	104188
Canada	USA (United States)	28 Dec 56	Specific Resources	290UNTS103	104229
Australia	FAO (Food Agri)	08 Jul 57	Tech Assistance	277UNTS315	104015
Norway	USSR (Soviet Union)	22 Nov 57	Specific Resources	309UNTS269	104476
Multilateral		29 Jan 58	Specific Resources	339UNTS23	104845
Multilateral		29 Apr 58	Specific Resources	559UNTS285	108164
Cuba	USA (United States)	15 Aug 58	Specific Resources	358UNTS63	105124
Italy	Yugoslavia	20 Nov 58	Territory Boundary	379UNTS23	105433
Multilateral		24 Jan 59	IGO Establishment	486UNTS157	107078
Finland	USSR (Soviet Union)	21 Feb 59	Specific Resources	338UNTS3	104830
Multilateral		07 Jul 59	Specific Resources	377UNTS203	105402
Norway	USSR (Soviet Union)	09 Dec 59	Specif Claim/Waive	361UNTS93	105173
Fed of Malaya	UK Great Britain	07 Jun 60	Scientific Project	375UNTS141	105365
Finland	Norway	15 Nov 60	Specific Resources	383UNTS159	105501
Norway	UK Great Britain	17 Nov 60	Specific Resources	398UNTS189	105723
Iceland	UK Great Britain	11 Mar 61	Dispute Settlement	397UNTS275	105710
Ceylon (Sri Lanka)	Japan	20 Mar 61	Education	450UNTS385	106481
Germany, West	Iceland	19 Jul 61	Specific Resources	409UNTS47	105877
Denmark	Iceland	01 Aug 61	Specific Resources	425UNTS191	106124
Norway	USSR (Soviet Union)	16 Apr 62	Specific Resources	437UNTS175	106307
Multilateral		28 Jul 62	Specific Resources	460UNTS219	106642
Taiwan	IBRD (World Bank)	27 Sep 63	IBRD Project	483UNTS151	107012
Multilateral		09 Mar 64	Specific Resources	581UNTS57	108432
Multilateral		09 Mar 64	Specific Resources	581UNTS83	108433
Multilateral		09 Mar 64	Specific Resources	581UNTS89	108434
Finland	Norway	09 Jun 64	Specific Resources	503UNTS205	107345
Poland	UK Great Britain	26 Sep 64	Specific Property	539UNTS153	107828
Norway	UK Great Britain	28 Sep 64	Specific Property	548UNTS63	107970
UK Great Britain	USSR (Soviet Union)	30 Sep 64	Specific Property	539UNTS159	107829
Japan	USA (United States)	25 Nov 64	Specific Property	533UNTS31	107730
USA (United States)	USSR (Soviet Union)	14 Dec 64	Specific Property	531UNTS213	107705
USA (United States)	USSR (Soviet Union)	05 Feb 65	Specific Resources	541UNTS97	107863
Japan	Korea, South	22 Jun 65	Specific Resources	583UNTS51	108472
Multilateral		17 Mar 67	Non-IBRD Project	594UNTS105	108598
Flood Control					
Iraq	IBRD (World Bank)	15 Jun 50	IBRD Project	155UNTS267	102038
Pakistan	USA (United States)	23 Aug 54	Direct Aid	234UNTS243	103287
France	Netherlands	15 Dec 54	Reparations	288UNTS37	104195
India	USA (United States)	04 Oct 55	Direct Aid	268UNTS115	103853
Luxembourg	Netherlands	06 Feb 56	Reparations	261UNTS17	103723
India	USA (United States)	27 Sep 56	Direct Aid	281UNTS289	104085
Japan	USA (United States)	12 Nov 59	Direct Aid	361UNTS27	105171
India	IDA (Devel Assoc)	22 Nov 61	Loans and Credits	427UNTS3	106144
Pakistan	IDA (Devel Assoc)	26 Jun 63	Non-IBRD Project	492UNTS115	107189
Pakistan	IDA (Devel Assoc)	26 Jul 63	Non-IBRD Project	492UNTS143	107190
Food					
Multilateral		22 Apr 42	Commodity Trade	8UNTS237	200044
Brazil	USA (United States)	03 Sep 42	Non-IBRD Project	13UNTS109	200073
Multilateral		04 Dec 42	Direct Aid	24UNTS247	200150
USA (United States)	Venezuela	14 May 43	Non-IBRD Project	28UNTS359	200160
Peru	USA (United States)	20 May 43	Non-IBRD Project	100UNTS259	200288
Dominican Republic	USA (United States)	10 Jun 43	Specific Resources	21UNTS277	200129
Multilateral		21 Dec 43	Commodity Trade	65UNTS231	200214
Dominican Republic	USA (United States)	11 Feb 44	Milit Assistance	109UNTS251	200363
Argentina	USA (United States)	09 May 45	Commodity Trade	139UNTS227	200453
Thailand	UK Great Britain	01 May 46	Commodity Trade	99UNTS175	101378
Thailand	UK Great Britain	01 May 46	Commodity Trade	99UNTS169	101377
UK Great Britain	USA (United States)	06 May 46	Admin Cooperation	99UNTS199	101381
Multilateral		06 May 46	Commodity Trade	99UNTS181	101379
Thailand	UK Great Britain	06 May 46	Commodity Trade	99UNTS193	101380

PARTY ONE	PARTY TWO	DATE	TOPIC	CITATION	NUMBER
Food (Cont.)					
Multilateral		03 Jun 46	Commodity Trade	7UNTS331	100109
Multilateral		27 Jun 46	ILO Labor	264UNTS163	103792
Argentina	UK Great Britain	17 Sep 46	General Economic	88UNTS47	101185
Argentina	USA (United States)	19 Sep 46	Commodity Trade	7UNTS131	100095
Peru	USA (United States)	22 Nov 46	Non-IBRD Project	100UNTS170	101396
Czechoslovakia	Poland	04 Apr 47	General Economic	85UNTS62	101146
Austria	USA (United States)	25 Jun 47	Direct Aid	22UNTS141	100334
Greece	USA (United States)	08 Jul 47	Direct Aid	16UNTS157	100256
Haiti	USA (United States)	19 Dec 47	Direct Aid	135UNTS130	101818
Canada	USA (United States)	23 Nov 48	Commodity Trade	81UNTS295	101078
France	USA (United States)	23 Dec 48	Direct Aid	67UNTS171	100876
France	USA (United States)	07 Feb 49	Direct Aid	67UNTS189	100877
Norway	USA (United States)	31 Oct 49	Direct Aid	68UNTS3	100879
USA (United States)	Yugoslavia	21 Nov 50	Direct Aid	93UNTS39	101285
UK Great Britain	Yugoslavia	28 Dec 50	Loans and Credits	88UNTS329	101201
India	WHO (World Health)	11 Oct 51	Non-IBRD Project	118UNTS27	101594
Canada	USA (United States)	08 Jun 55	Customs	247UNTS163	103466
Italy	USA (United States)	30 Jun 55	US Agri Commod Aid	258UNTS15	103667
Japan	USA (United States)	10 Feb 56	Direct Aid	275UNTS157	103980
Multilateral		29 Apr 58	Specific Resources	559UNTS285	108164
Australia	Italy	12 Feb 59	Commodity Trade	328UNTS133	104732
Italy	USA (United States)	30 Jul 59	Direct Aid	355UNTS393	105088
Japan	USA (United States)	24 Oct 62	Sanitation	462UNTS119	106673
Israel	USA (United States)	21 Mar 63	Education	476UNTS131	106907
Kenya	IDA (Devel Assoc)	17 Aug 64	Non-IBRD Project	535UNTS79	107776
Foot and Mouth Disease					
Mexico	USA (United States)	17 Mar 47	Sanitation	167UNTS30	102200
Mexico	USA (United States)	26 Aug 52	IGO Establishment	264UNTS269	103797
United Arab Rep	USA (United States)	21 May 53	Tech Assistance	204UNTS29	102748
Multilateral		11 Dec 53	Sanitation	191UNTS285	102588
Chile	USA (United States)	30 Dec 53	Tech Assistance	236UNTS41	103315
Mexico	USA (United States)	30 Jul 54	Sanitation	269UNTS39	103871
Denmark	Sweden	28 Oct 54	Sanitation	262UNTS211	103747
Forced Labor					
Multilateral		28 Jun 30	ILO Labor	39UNTS55	100612
Multilateral		20 Jun 36	ILO Labor	40UNTS109	100630
Multilateral		27 Jun 39	ILO Labor	40UNTS311	100640
Multilateral		27 Jun 39	ILO Labor	40UNTS281	100639
Foreign Nationals					
Luxembourg	Netherlands	25 Aug 50	Non-ILO Labor	81UNTS13	101058
Forestry					
Australia	FAO (Food Agri)	07 Jul 52	Tech Assistance	184UNTS209	102449
IBRD (World Bank)	Yugoslavia	11 Feb 53	IBRD Project	165UNTS231	102179
Multilateral		18 Nov 59	IGO Establishment	390UNTS227	105610
Multilateral		19 Nov 59	IGO Operations	410UNTS156	105902
Cuba	UN Special Fund	10 Mar 61	Direct Aid	390UNTS35	105601
Denmark	Thailand	25 Jan 65	Tech Assistance	530UNTS173	107680
Friendship					
Greece	Iran	09 Jan 31	General Amity	166UNTS323	200496
Netherlands	Yemen	12 Apr 39	General Amity	79UNTS257	200249
Afghanistan	Netherlands	26 Jul 39	General Amity	32UNTS381	200177
Taiwan	Dominican Republic	11 May 40	General Amity	10UNTS285	200067
Afghanistan	Sweden	22 Oct 40	General Amity	191UNTS349	200516
Taiwan	Iraq	16 Mar 42	General Amity	14UNTS335	200091
Saudi Arabia	UK Great Britain	20 Apr 42	General Amity	10UNTS117	200057
Taiwan	Cuba	12 Nov 42	General Amity	10UNTS243	200065
Brazil	Taiwan	20 Aug 43	General Amity	14UNTS365	200094
Saudi Arabia	UK Great Britain	31 Oct 43	General Amity	10UNTS165	200059
Australia	New Zealand	21 Jan 44	General Amity	18UNTS357	200113
Albania	Yugoslavia	23 Mar 44	General Military	1UNTS81	100015
Taiwan	Costa Rica	05 May 44	General Amity	14UNTS427	200098
Taiwan	Mexico	01 Aug 44	General Amity	14UNTS441	200099
Multilateral		22 Mar 45	General Amity	70UNTS237	200241

PARTY ONE	PARTY TWO	DATE	TOPIC	CITATION	NUMBER
Friendship (Cont.)					
Poland	USSR (Soviet Union)	21 Apr 45	General Military	12UNTS391	200070
Taiwan	USSR (Soviet Union)	14 Aug 45	General Amity	10UNTS300	200068
United Arab Rep	Yemen	27 Sep 45	General Amity	9UNTS373	200053
Taiwan	Ecuador	06 Jan 46	General Amity	7UNTS233	100102
Taiwan	Thailand	23 Jan 46	General Amity	161UNTS127	102126
Mongolia	USSR (Soviet Union)	27 Feb 46	General Military	48UNTS177	100744
Taiwan	France	28 Feb 46	General Amity	14UNTS137	100216
Poland	Yugoslavia	18 Mar 46	General Military	1UNTS53	100013
Jordan	UK Great Britain	22 Mar 46	General Amity	6UNTS143	100074
Iraq	Turkey	29 Mar 46	General Amity	37UNTS226	100580
USA (United States)	Yemen	04 May 46	General Economic	4UNTS165	100043
Czechoslovakia	Yugoslavia	09 May 46	General Military	1UNTS67	100014
Bolivia	USA (United States)	10 Jun 46	Mostfavored Nation	13UNTS19	100197
Afghanistan	USSR (Soviet Union)	13 Jun 46	Territory Boundary	31UNTS147	100476
Philippines	USA (United States)	04 Jul 46	General Amity	7UNTS3	100088
Philippines	USA (United States)	04 Jul 46	General Amity	6UNTS335	100086
Norway	USA (United States)	08 Jul 46	Mostfavored Nation	13UNTS35	100199
Denmark	USA (United States)	10 Sep 46	Mostfavored Nation	13UNTS75	100204
Taiwan	USA (United States)	04 Nov 46	General Amity	25UNTS69	100359
Taiwan	Saudi Arabia	15 Nov 46	General Amity	18UNTS197	100289
Jordan	Turkey	11 Jan 47	General Amity	14UNTS49	100210
Argentina	Taiwan	10 Feb 47	General Amity	486UNTS143	107077
France	UK Great Britain	04 Mar 47	General Amity	9UNTS187	100132
Czechoslovakia	Poland	10 Mar 47	General Military	25UNTS231	100365
Taiwan	Philippines	18 Apr 47	General Amity	11UNTS361	100175
Czechoslovakia	Yugoslavia	27 Apr 47	Culture	33UNTS49	100514
Italy	Philippines	09 Jul 47	General Amity	44UNTS3	100674
Albania	Yugoslavia	09 Jul 47	Culture	33UNTS91	100516
Canada	Switzerland	14 Jul 47	Admin Cooperation	43UNTS103	100664
Philippines	Spain	27 Sep 47	General Amity	70UNTS133	100902
Hungary	Romania	24 Jan 48	General Amity	477UNTS155	106920
Italy	USA (United States)	02 Feb 48	General Amity	79UNTS171	101040
Romania	USSR (Soviet Union)	04 Feb 48	General Military	48UNTS189	100745
Hungary	USSR (Soviet Union)	18 Feb 48	General Military	48UNTS163	100743
Jordan	UK Great Britain	15 Mar 48	General Military	77UNTS77	100994
Bulgaria	USSR (Soviet Union)	18 Mar 48	General Military	48UNTS135	100741
Finland	USSR (Soviet Union)	06 Apr 48	General Military	48UNTS149	100742
Bulgaria	Poland	29 May 48	General Military	26UNTS213	100389
Hungary	Poland	18 Jun 48	Culture	25UNTS319	100370
Italy	USA (United States)	28 Jun 48	Milit Occupation	25UNTS45	100356
Denmark	USA (United States)	29 Jun 48	Mostfavored Nation	27UNTS35	100396
Austria	USA (United States)	02 Jul 48	Milit Occupation	25UNTS53	100357
Bulgaria	Hungary	16 Jul 48	General Amity	477UNTS169	106921
India	Switzerland	14 Aug 48	General Amity	33UNTS3	100509
Belgium	France	28 Oct 48	Visas	25UNTS151	100360
Poland	Romania	26 Jan 49	General Military	85UNTS21	101143
Czechoslovakia	Hungary	16 Apr 49	General Amity	477UNTS183	106922
Philippines	Thailand	14 Jun 49	General Amity	81UNTS53	101062
Ecuador	Italy	24 Aug 49	General Amity	72UNTS35	100926
Greece	Italy	31 Aug 49	Reparations	78UNTS89	101014
Afghanistan	India	04 Jan 50	General Amity	81UNTS75	101064
China People's Rep	USSR (Soviet Union)	14 Feb 50	General Amity	226UNTS3	103103
Iran	Pakistan	18 Feb 50	General Amity	161UNTS23	102119
Iraq	Pakistan	26 Feb 50	General Amity	214UNTS3	102896
India	Iran	15 Mar 50	General Amity	161UNTS15	102118
Italy	Turkey	24 Mar 50	General Amity	96UNTS207	101338
India	Nepal	31 Jul 50	General Amity	94UNTS3	101302
Greece	Philippines	28 Aug 50	General Amity	225UNTS155	103097
Pakistan	Syria	29 Aug 50	General Amity	109UNTS95	101494
Iran	Italy	24 Sep 50	General Amity	281UNTS157	104077
Nepal	UK Great Britain	30 Oct 50	General Amity	97UNTS121	101346
Indonesia	Pakistan	03 Mar 51	General Amity	188UNTS333	102537
India	Indonesia	03 Mar 51	General Amity	167UNTS3	102197
Burma	India	07 Jul 51	General Amity	149UNTS35	101949
Pakistan	Turkey	26 Jul 51	General Amity	188UNTS323	102536

PARTY ONE	PARTY TWO	DATE	TOPIC	CITATION	NUMBER
Friendship (Cont.)					
Greece	USA (United States)	03 Aug 51	General Amity	224UNTS279	103080
Pakistan	United Arab Rep	28 Aug 51	General Amity	214UNTS247	102902
Ethiopia	USA (United States)	07 Sep 51	General Amity	206UNTS41	102785
Denmark	USA (United States)	01 Oct 51	General Amity	421UNTS105	106056
Pakistan	Saudi Arabia	25 Nov 51	General Amity	177UNTS3	102304
India	Turkey	14 Dec 51	General Amity	137UNTS15	101845
Muscat and Oman	UK Great Britain	20 Dec 51	General Amity	149UNTS247	101956
India	Syria	25 Feb 52	General Amity	163UNTS55	102141
Italy	Jordan	24 Apr 52	General Amity	281UNTS167	104078
Burma	Pakistan	25 Jun 52	General Amity	173UNTS41	102259
India	Philippines	11 Jul 52	General Amity	203UNTS73	102741
Dominican Republic	Philippines	02 Nov 52	General Amity	543UNTS175	107901
India	Iraq	10 Nov 52	General Amity	172UNTS103	102242
Lebanon	Pakistan	16 Jan 53	General Amity	284UNTS193	104137
Taiwan	Spain	19 Feb 53	General Amity	181UNTS81	102400
Multilateral		28 Feb 53	General Amity	167UNTS21	102199
Germany, West	USA (United States)	02 Jun 53	General Amity	231UNTS151	103214
Germany, West	USA (United States)	03 Jun 53	General Amity	253UNTS89	103578
Libya	UK Great Britain	29 Jul 53	General Amity	186UNTS185	102491
Indonesia	Thailand	03 Mar 54	General Amity	213UNTS297	102893
Germany, West	USA (United States)	29 Oct 54	General Amity	273UNTS3	103943
Multilateral		06 Apr 55	General Amity	261UNTS55	103725
Iran	USA (United States)	15 Aug 55	General Amity	284UNTS93	104132
Nicaragua	USA (United States)	21 Jan 56	General Amity	367UNTS3	105224
Netherlands	USA (United States)	27 Mar 56	General Amity	285UNTS231	104154
Philippines	Switzerland	30 Aug 56	General Amity	293UNTS43	104284
Burma	Thailand	15 Oct 56	General Amity	277UNTS87	104000
Austria	USA (United States)	25 Oct 56	Taxation	299UNTS123	104310
Korea, South	USA (United States)	28 Nov 56	General Amity	302UNTS281	104367
Czechoslovakia	Mongolia	08 Apr 57	General Amity	501UNTS171	107317
Germany, East	Mongolia	22 Aug 57	General Amity	521UNTS351	107530
Taiwan	Jordan	19 Nov 57	General Amity	308UNTS227	104463
Ethiopia	Japan	19 Dec 57	General Amity	325UNTS91	104695
Israel	Philippines	26 Feb 58	General Amity	507UNTS135	107398
Pakistan	Thailand	28 Aug 58	General Amity	394UNTS53	105668
Muscat and Oman	USA (United States)	20 Dec 58	General Amity	380UNTS181	105457
Israel	Liberia	09 Apr 59	General Amity	448UNTS95	106427
Indonesia	Malaysia	17 Apr 59	General Amity	470UNTS273	106813
Pakistan	USA (United States)	12 Nov 59	General Amity	404UNTS259	105816
Czechoslovakia	Ethiopia	11 Dec 59	General Amity	386UNTS51	105537
Argentina	Philippines	12 Feb 60	General Amity	535UNTS293	107785
Cambodia	Czechoslovakia	27 Nov 60	General Amity	412UNTS179	105931
Japan	Pakistan	18 Dec 60	General Amity	423UNTS197	106093
Belgium	USA (United States)	21 Feb 61	General Amity	480UNTS149	106967
USA (United States)	Vietnam, South	03 Apr 61	General Amity	424UNTS137	106106
Czechoslovakia	Indonesia	29 May 61	General Amity	479UNTS337	106962
Indonesia	Japan	01 Jul 61	General Amity	517UNTS107	107484
Korea, North	USSR (Soviet Union)	06 Jul 61	General Amity	420UNTS145	106045
Hungary	Indonesia	23 Aug 61	General Amity	519UNTS163	107507
Israel	Malagasy	27 Aug 61	General Amity	484UNTS217	107032
Luxembourg	USA (United States)	23 Feb 62	General Amity	474UNTS3	106868
Taiwan	Malagasy	04 Apr 62	General Amity	463UNTS195	106703
Gabon	Israel	15 May 62	General Amity	484UNTS181	107027
New Zealand	Western Samoa	01 Aug 62	General Amity	453UNTS3	106515
Iraq	Kuwait	04 Oct 63	Visas	485UNTS321	107063
Czechoslovakia	USSR (Soviet Union)	27 Nov 63	General Amity	496UNTS161	107250
Mexico	United Nations	17 Jul 64	IGO Operations	533UNTS117	107738
Poland	USSR (Soviet Union)	08 Apr 65	General Amity	540UNTS97	107845
Frontier Traffic					
Belgium	Luxembourg	28 Apr 45	Visas	41UNTS265	200181
Belgium	France	21 May 45	Visas	23UNTS215	200133
Belgium	Netherlands	28 Apr 47	Visas	37UNTS199	100577
Belgium	France	13 Apr 48	Territory Boundary	31UNTS409	100483
Belgium	Netherlands	13 Apr 48	Customs	32UNTS153	100497

PARTY ONE	PARTY TWO	DATE	TOPIC	CITATION	NUMBER
Frontier Traffic (Cont.)					
Belgium	France	23 Apr 48	Territory Boundary	19UNTS95	100307
Poland	USSR (Soviet Union)	08 Jul 48	Dispute Settlement	37UNTS107	100576
Belgium	UK Great Britain	29 Dec 48	Visas	27UNTS135	100404
Italy	Yugoslavia	03 Feb 49	Visas	33UNTS105	100517
Belgium	France	12 Apr 49	Visas	30UNTS45	100447
Belgium	UK Great Britain	14 Apr 49	Visas	65UNTS117	100840
Belgium	Netherlands	13 May 49	Customs	65UNTS133	100841
Belgium	Luxembourg	15 Jul 49	Visas	41UNTS13	100642
Belgium	Netherlands	20 Aug 49	Visas	46UNTS133	100706
Belgium	France	14 Mar 50	Visas	65UNTS139	100842
Belgium	Luxembourg	06 Apr 50	Visas	65UNTS147	100843
Multilateral		10 Jan 52	Visas	163UNTS3	102138
Multilateral		10 Jan 52	Visas	163UNTS27	102139
Austria	Yugoslavia	19 Mar 53	Visas	467UNTS323	106768
Belgium	Netherlands	26 Mar 53	Visas	165UNTS297	102180
Italy	Switzerland	02 Jul 53	Customs	257UNTS99	103653
Denmark	Germany, West	30 Jun 56	Visas	258UNTS65	103671
Germany, West	Netherlands	30 May 58	Visas	570UNTS127	108291
Germany, West	Netherlands	10 Oct 58	Visas	486UNTS345	107085
Greece	Yugoslavia	18 Jun 59	Visas	388UNTS3	105570
Germany, West	Netherlands	03 Jun 60	Visas	487UNTS37	107094
Burma	Thailand	08 Jun 60	Visas	372UNTS321	105308
Cyprus	UK Great Britain	16 Aug 60	Specific Property	382UNTS177	105477
Belgium	Luxembourg	29 Nov 61	Visas	486UNTS37	107071
Austria	Czechoslovakia	22 Sep 62	Land Transport	495UNTS157	107244
Czechoslovakia	Hungary	16 Oct 62	Visas	479UNTS301	106961
Austria	France	30 Nov 62	Visas	463UNTS173	106701
Austria	Yugoslavia	11 Dec 62	Land Transport	546UNTS3	107938
Austria	Italy	22 Apr 63	Visas	491UNTS53	107173
Hungary	Romania	13 Jun 63	Territory Boundary	576UNTS275	108369
Multilateral		15 Feb 65	Visas	547UNTS3	107953
Hungary	Yugoslavia	09 Aug 65	Visas	577UNTS103	108375
Multilateral		17 May 66	Visas	571UNTS89	108302
Austria	Yugoslavia	10 Oct 66	Visas	595UNTS273	108622
Frontier Workers					
Belgium	France	17 Jan 48	Non-ILO Labor	36UNTS233	100570
Belgium	Luxembourg	25 Mar 48	Taxation	18UNTS323	100300
Belgium	France	08 Jan 49	Non-ILO Labor	36UNTS151	100569
Multilateral		17 Apr 50	Visas	131UNTS99	101738
Multilateral		10 Jan 52	Visas	163UNTS3	102138
Multilateral		10 Jan 52	Visas	163UNTS27	102139
Belgium	Germany, West	18 Jan 52	Visas	243UNTS3	103443
France	Italy	27 Mar 58	Visas	305UNTS387	104426
Fuel					
Argentina	USA (United States)	09 May 45	Commodity Trade	139UNTS227	200453
Gas Lines					
Pakistan	IBRD (World Bank)	02 Jun 54	IBRD Project	324UNTS59	104678
General Relations					
Greece	Iran	09 Jan 31	General Amity	166UNTS331	200497
Canada	France	12 May 33	Admin Cooperation	253UNTS285	200545
Panama	USA (United States)	18 May 42	General Amity	124UNTS221	200422
Syria	USA (United States)	08 Sep 44	Recognition	124UNTS251	200424
Lebanon	USA (United States)	08 Sep 44	Recognition	124UNTS187	200419
Ethiopia	UK Great Britain	19 Dec 44	General Amity	93UNTS303	200272
Taiwan	France	28 Feb 46	General Amity	14UNTS137	100216
Philippines	USA (United States)	04 Jul 46	General Amity	7UNTS3	100088
France	Thailand	17 Nov 46	Reparations	344UNTS59	104943
Netherlands	Thailand	30 Jan 47	General Amity	247UNTS353	103480
Italy	Philippines	09 Jul 47	General Amity	44UNTS3	100674
Burma	UK Great Britain	17 Oct 47	Recognition	70UNTS183	100904
Ceylon (Sri Lanka)	UK Great Britain	11 Nov 47	Consul/Citizenship	86UNTS25	101149
Romania	Yugoslavia	19 Dec 47	General Amity	116UNTS89	101571
Multilateral		17 Mar 48	General Military	19UNTS51	100304

PARTY ONE	PARTY TWO	DATE	TOPIC	CITATION	NUMBER
General Relations (Cont.)					
Multilateral		30 Apr 48	IGO Establishment	119UNTS3	101609
India	Switzerland	14 Aug 48	General Amity	33UNTS3	100509
Multilateral		05 May 49	IGO Establishment	87UNTS103	101168
Philippines	USA (United States)	16 May 49	Milit Installation	67UNTS199	100878
Guatemala	Italy	10 Sep 49	General Amity	102UNTS53	101410
Indonesia	Netherlands	02 Nov 49	Recognition	69UNTS3	100894
Multilateral		22 Nov 49	Recognition	185UNTS307	102477
Ireland	USA (United States)	21 Jan 50	General Amity	206UNTS269	102792
China People's Rep	USSR (Soviet Union)	14 Feb 50	General Amity	226UNTS3	103103
Czechoslovakia	Germany, East	23 Jun 50	General Amity	504UNTS163	107357
Greece	Philippines	28 Aug 50	General Amity	225UNTS155	103097
Panama	USA (United States)	14 Sep 50	Land Transport	124UNTS25	101664
UK Great Britain	Yemen	20 Jan 51	General Amity	101UNTS39	101400
Multilateral		18 Apr 51	IGO Establishment	261UNTS140	103729
Greece	USA (United States)	03 Aug 51	General Amity	224UNTS279	103080
France	Italy	23 Aug 51	Consul/Citizenship	291UNTS143	104249
Israel	USA (United States)	23 Aug 51	General Amity	219UNTS237	102979
Multilateral		14 Oct 51	IGO Establishment	122UNTS3	101631
Council of Europe	ILO (Labor Org)	23 Nov 51	IGO Operations	126UNTS331	200435
Muscat and Oman	UK Great Britain	20 Dec 51	General Amity	149UNTS247	101956
Finland	USA (United States)	04 Dec 52	General Amity	205UNTS149	102774
India	Muscat and Oman	15 Mar 53	General Amity	190UNTS69	102559
Japan	USA (United States)	02 Apr 53	General Amity	206UNTS143	102788
Germany, West	USA (United States)	02 Jun 53	General Amity	231UNTS151	103214
Libya	UK Great Britain	29 Jul 53	General Amity	186UNTS185	102491
China People's Rep	India	29 Apr 54	General Trade	299UNTS57	104307
China People's Rep	USSR (Soviet Union)	12 Oct 54	General Amity	226UNTS69	103109
China People's Rep	USSR (Soviet Union)	12 Oct 54	General Amity	226UNTS57	103108
United Arab Rep	UK Great Britain	19 Oct 54	General Amity	210UNTS3	102833
Germany, West	USA (United States)	29 Oct 54	General Amity	273UNTS3	103943
Multilateral		21 Dec 54	General Amity	258UNTS322	103678
Panama	USA (United States)	25 Jan 55	General Ad Hoc	243UNTS211	103454
Multilateral		02 Mar 55	IGO Establishment	225UNTS233	103101
Germany, East	USSR (Soviet Union)	20 Sep 55	General Amity	226UNTS201	103114
Multilateral		05 Nov 55	IGO Establishment	250UNTS201	103524
Japan	USSR (Soviet Union)	19 Oct 56	General Amity	263UNTS99	103768
Czechoslovakia	Japan	13 Feb 57	General Amity	300UNTS119	104335
IBRD (World Bank)	United Nations	20 Feb 57	IGO Operations	265UNTS312	200546
IAEA (Atom Energy)	United Nations	23 Oct 57	IGO Operations	281UNTS369	200548
Ghana	USA (United States)	12 Feb 58	Admin Cooperation	442UNTS175	106348
Arab League	ILO (Labor Org)	26 May 58	IGO Operations	302UNTS343	200549
Austria	Netherlands	16 Oct 59	Admin Cooperation	458UNTS173	106600
France	USA (United States)	25 Nov 59	Admin Cooperation	401UNTS75	105764
Czechoslovakia	Ethiopia	11 Dec 59	General Amity	386UNTS51	105537
UK Great Britain	Yugoslavia	08 Jun 61	Mass Media	437UNTS111	106300
Kuwait	UK Great Britain	19 Jun 61	General Amity	399UNTS239	105743
Austria	Yugoslavia	30 Jun 61	Admin Cooperation	443UNTS51	106358
Multilateral		23 Mar 62	General Amity	434UNTS145	106262
Algeria	France	03 Jul 62	Recognition	507UNTS25	107395
Belgium	Rwanda	13 Oct 62	Tech Assistance	456UNTS425	106568
Multilateral		31 Jul 63	General Amity	550UNTS343	108029
USSR (Soviet Union)	Yemen	21 Mar 64	General Amity	553UNTS267	108094
Hungary	Yemen	30 May 64	General Amity	577UNTS39	108371
Germany, East	USSR (Soviet Union)	12 Jun 64	General Amity	553UNTS249	108093
Mexico	United Nations	17 Jul 64	IGO Operations	533UNTS117	107738
Taiwan	Korea, South	27 Nov 64	General Amity	555UNTS3	108102
Japan	Korea, South	22 Jun 65	General Amity	583UNTS33	108471
ILO (Labor Org)	LAFTA (Free Trade)	02 Jul 65	IGO Operations	563UNTS327	200619
ILO (Labor Org)	Org Ctrl Am States	26 Jul 65	IGO Operations	563UNTS341	200620
Maldive Islands	UK Great Britain	26 Jul 65	General Amity	548UNTS223	107980
Malaysia	Singapore	07 Aug 65	Recognition	563UNTS89	108206
Hungary	Mongolia	02 Oct 65	General Amity	587UNTS35	108508
ILO (Labor Org)	OAU (Afri Unity)	25 Nov 65	General Amity	550UNTS389	200617
India	Pakistan	10 Jan 66	General Amity	560UNTS39	108166
Mongolia	USSR (Soviet Union)	15 Jan 66	General Amity	562UNTS43	108194

PARTY ONE	PARTY TWO	DATE	TOPIC	CITATION	NUMBER
Genocide					
Multilateral		09 Dec 48	Humanitarian	78UNTS277	101021
Geodesy					
Philippines	USA (United States)	12 May 47	Scientific Project	16UNTS109	100252
Geography					
New Zealand	Western Samoa	31 Dec 63	Scientific Project	521UNTS163	107519
Dominican Republic	USA (United States)	28 Aug 64	Scientific Project	531UNTS35	107691
Glass Workers					
Multilateral		21 Jun 34	ILO Labor	40UNTS33	100625
Multilateral		25 Jun 35	ILO Labor	40UNTS97	100629
Gold					
Multilateral		10 Oct 47	Claims and Debts	54UNTS193	100804
Multilateral		04 Nov 47	Reparations	93UNTS61	101288
Multilateral		16 Dec 47	Reparations	82UNTS237	101096
Multilateral		25 Apr 51	Reparations	91UNTS21	101240
Grain					
USSR (Soviet Union)	Yugoslavia	26 Apr 46	General Trade	116UNTS163	101575
Romania	Yugoslavia	23 Dec 46	Loans and Credits	116UNTS33	101567
IBRD (World Bank)	Turkey	07 Jul 50	IBRD Project	156UNTS3	102039
Nicaragua	IBRD (World Bank)	29 Oct 51	IBRD Project	159UNTS35	102082
Turkey	USA (United States)	15 Nov 54	Commodity Trade	238UNTS135	103358
Germany, West	USA (United States)	18 Feb 55	Milit Assistance	247UNTS257	103474
Guardianship					
Multilateral		23 Mar 53	Admin Cooperation	202UNTS241	102732
Headquarters					
United Nations	Switzerland	01 Jul 46	Specific Property	1UNTS153	200007
League of Nations	United Nations	19 Jul 46	Specific Property	1UNTS109	200002
United Nations	USA (United States)	18 Dec 47	IGO Status/Immunit	11UNTS347	100174
Council of Europe	France	02 Sep 49	IGO Status/Immunit	249UNTS207	103510
United Nations	WHO (World Health)	10 Feb 50	IGO Operations	46UNTS327	200188
Canada	ICAO (Civil Aviat)	14 Apr 51	IGO Status/Immunit	96UNTS155	101335
Chile	United Nations	16 Feb 53	IGO Operations	314UNTS49	104541
United Nations	Thailand	26 May 54	IGO Status/Immunit	260UNTS35	103703
France	UNESCO (Educ/Cult)	02 Jul 54	IGO Status/Immunit	357UNTS3	105103
NATO (North Atlan)	USA (United States)	22 Oct 54	IGO Establishment	249UNTS175	103507
Austria	IAEA (Atom Energy)	11 Dec 57	Atomic Energy	339UNTS110	104849
Ethiopia	United Nations	18 Jun 58	IGO Operations	317UNTS101	104597
UNICEF (Children)	Senegal	22 Jan 64	IGO Operations	486UNTS91	107074
Health					
Multilateral		11 Nov 21	ILO Labor	38UNTS217	100599
Multilateral		19 Nov 21	ILO Labor	38UNTS175	100596
Multilateral		10 Jun 25	ILO Labor	38UNTS243	100601
Multilateral		15 Jun 27	ILO Labor	38UNTS343	100608
Multilateral		15 Jun 27	ILO Labor	38UNTS327	100607
Multilateral		29 Jun 33	ILO Labor	39UNTS211	100619
Multilateral		29 Jun 33	ILO Labor	39UNTS235	100620
Multilateral		21 Jun 34	ILO Labor	40UNTS19	100624
Multilateral		22 Jun 35	ILO Labor	40UNTS73	100628
Multilateral		24 Oct 36	ILO Labor	40UNTS169	100633
Multilateral		24 Oct 36	ILO Labor	40UNTS187	100634
Netherlands	UK Great Britain	13 Jun 39	Sanitation	5UNTS65	200028
Ecuador	USA (United States)	24 Feb 42	Sanitation	26UNTS379	200157
Brazil	USA (United States)	14 Mar 42	Sanitation	102UNTS195	200302
Haiti	USA (United States)	07 Apr 42	Sanitation	106UNTS319	200349
El Salvador	USA (United States)	05 May 42	Sanitation	21UNTS215	200124
Honduras	USA (United States)	08 May 42	Sanitation	166UNTS351	200498
Peru	USA (United States)	11 May 42	Sanitation	136UNTS353	200447
Paraguay	USA (United States)	22 May 42	Sanitation	124UNTS243	200423
Nicaragua	USA (United States)	22 May 42	Sanitation	105UNTS141	200328
Bolivia	USA (United States)	16 Jul 42	Sanitation	13UNTS101	200072
Brazil	USA (United States)	17 Jul 42	Sanitation	102UNTS203	200303
Colombia	USA (United States)	23 Oct 42	Sanitation	105UNTS109	200326

PARTY ONE	PARTY TWO	DATE	TOPIC	CITATION	NUMBER
Health (Cont.)					
Brazil	USA (United States)	10 Feb 43	Sanitation	102UNTS217	200304
USA (United States)	Venezuela	18 Feb 43	Sanitation	21UNTS225	200125
Panama	USA (United States)	02 Mar 43	Sanitation	107UNTS55	200351
Chile	USA (United States)	11 May 43	Sanitation	139UNTS295	200456
Mexico	USA (United States)	01 Jul 43	Sanitation	28UNTS407	200164
Dominican Republic	USA (United States)	07 Jul 43	Sanitation	28UNTS419	200165
USA (United States)	Uruguay	01 Nov 43	Sanitation	106UNTS311	200348
Brazil	USA (United States)	25 Nov 43	Sanitation	102UNTS227	200305
Multilateral		15 Dec 44	Sanitation	17UNTS305	200110
Multilateral		15 Dec 44	Sanitation	16UNTS247	200106
Multilateral		22 Mar 45	General Amity	70UNTS237	200241
United Arab Rep	USA (United States)	05 Jan 46	Status of Forces	160UNTS27	102098
Colombia	USA (United States)	19 Feb 46	Sanitation	166UNTS104	102187
USA (United States)	Uruguay	23 Apr 46	Sanitation	160UNTS103	102104
Multilateral		23 Apr 46	Sanitation	16UNTS179	100257
Multilateral		23 Apr 46	Sanitation	17UNTS3	100265
Multilateral		22 Jul 46	IGO Establishment	14UNTS185	100221
Multilateral		22 Jul 46	IGO Establishment	9UNTS3	100125
Multilateral		09 Oct 46	ILO Labor	78UNTS213	101018
Multilateral		09 Oct 46	ILO Labor	78UNTS198	101017
Multilateral		06 Feb 47	IGO Establishment	97UNTS227	101352
Thailand	USA (United States)	26 Feb 47	Air Transport	16UNTS17	100246
Belgium	Poland	24 Mar 47	Non-ILO Labor	18UNTS279	100297
Peru	USA (United States)	19 Apr 47	Sanitation	136UNTS284	101840
Belgium	Netherlands	28 Apr 47	Visas	37UNTS199	100577
Honduras	USA (United States)	13 May 47	Sanitation	166UNTS159	102189
Ecuador	USA (United States)	21 Jun 47	Sanitation	26UNTS275	100391
League of Nations	United Nations	27 Jun 47	Specific Property	5UNTS389	200036
League of Nations	United Nations	27 Jun 47	Specific Property	5UNTS395	200037
USA (United States)	Venezuela	30 Jun 47	Sanitation	166UNTS198	102190
Haiti	USA (United States)	27 Sep 47	Sanitation	136UNTS258	101839
Portugal	UK Great Britain	16 Oct 47	Sanitation	82UNTS203	101093
Norway	Sweden	22 Dec 47	Non-ILO Labor	22UNTS203	100337
Denmark	Sweden	23 Dec 47	Non-ILO Labor	14UNTS3	100207
Denmark	Norway	21 Jan 48	Non-ILO Labor	14UNTS307	100223
Bulgaria	Czechoslovakia	05 Mar 48	Admin Cooperation	26UNTS115	100382
Canada	USA (United States)	30 Apr 48	Sanitation	77UNTS191	100999
Belgium	Italy	30 Apr 48	Non-ILO Labor	36UNTS305	100571
Denmark	Iceland	14 May 48	Non-ILO Labor	23UNTS163	100346
Multilateral		19 Jun 48	Air Transport	310UNTS151	104492
Paraguay	USA (United States)	30 Jun 48	Sanitation	124UNTS34	101665
Bolivia	USA (United States)	14 Jul 48	Sanitation	136UNTS238	101838
FAO (Food Agri)	WHO (World Health)	17 Jul 48	IGO Operations	76UNTS171	200244
Taiwan	USA (United States)	05 Aug 48	IGO Establishment	82UNTS109	101087
El Salvador	USA (United States)	23 Sep 48	Sanitation	181UNTS101	102402
Brazil	USA (United States)	30 Dec 48	Sanitation	102UNTS3	101406
Chile	USA (United States)	21 Jan 49	Sanitation	160UNTS185	102107
Mexico	USA (United States)	14 Feb 49	Sanitation	160UNTS75	102103
Philippines	USA (United States)	07 Jun 49	Direct Aid	45UNTS63	100692
El Salvador	USA (United States)	27 Jul 49	Sanitation	180UNTS219	102387
USA (United States)	Uruguay	27 Jul 49	Sanitation	151UNTS199	101995
Multilateral		12 Aug 49	General Military	75UNTS135	100972
Multilateral		12 Aug 49	Humanitarian	75UNTS287	100973
Multilateral		12 Aug 49	Humanitarian	75UNTS31	100970
Multilateral		12 Aug 49	Humanitarian	75UNTS85	100971
Italy	Netherlands	16 Aug 49	Admin Cooperation	98UNTS21	101357
Brazil	USA (United States)	31 Aug 49	Sanitation	102UNTS13	101407
Belgium	Luxembourg	03 Dec 49	Non-ILO Labor	91UNTS31	101241
Afghanistan	WHO (World Health)	04 Dec 49	Direct Aid	102UNTS117	101414
France	UK Great Britain	23 Jan 50	Reparations	97UNTS149	101348
France	UK Great Britain	28 Jan 50	Non-ILO Labor	97UNTS155	101349
Ceylon (Sri Lanka)	WHO (World Health)	17 Feb 50	Direct Aid	102UNTS309	200309
WHO (World Health)	United Arab Rep	25 Aug 50	IGO Operations	92UNTS39	101259
UN Relief Palestin	WHO (World Health)	23 Sep 50	Sanitation	103UNTS129	200310
Haiti	USA (United States)	28 Sep 50	Sanitation	162UNTS85	102132

PARTY ONE	PARTY TWO	DATE	TOPIC	CITATION	NUMBER
Health (Cont.)					
Austria	Sweden	31 Oct 50	Non-ILO Labor	197UNTS311	102645
Czechoslovakia	Poland	17 Nov 50	Sanitation	530UNTS195	107682
El Salvador	USA (United States)	13 Dec 50	Sanitation	166UNTS149	102188
Brazil	USA (United States)	27 Dec 50	Sanitation	147UNTS33	101926
Nicaragua	USA (United States)	31 Jan 51	Sanitation	160UNTS121	102105
Costa Rica	USA (United States)	13 Feb 51	Sanitation	141UNTS169	101914
Panama	USA (United States)	26 Feb 51	Sanitation	160UNTS153	102106
USA (United States)	Uruguay	07 Mar 51	Sanitation	165UNTS113	102173
Multilateral		25 May 51	Status of Forces	175UNTS215	102303
Nicaragua	UK Great Britain	25 May 51	Sanitation	101UNTS77	101404
Cambodia	WHO (World Health)	31 May 51	Tech Assistance	102UNTS279	200307
Multilateral		01 Jun 51	Tech Assistance	118UNTS57	101596
Sweden	USA (United States)	27 Jun 51	Milit Assistance	148UNTS77	101937
Burma	WHO (World Health)	17 Jul 51	Tech Assistance	102UNTS127	101415
Multilateral		01 Aug 51	Sanitation	107UNTS19	101464
Multilateral		04 Aug 51	Sanitation	104UNTS197	101441
Norway	USA (United States)	17 Sep 51	Milit Assistance	140UNTS313	101895
Korea, South	WHO (World Health)	19 Sep 51	Sanitation	109UNTS297	200366
WHO (World Health)	Thailand	04 Oct 51	Sanitation	109UNTS77	101492
India	WHO (World Health)	11 Oct 51	Non-IBRD Project	118UNTS27	101594
India	WHO (World Health)	16 Oct 51	Tech Assistance	109UNTS49	101490
Denmark	WHO (World Health)	05 Nov 51	Sanitation	110UNTS253	101514
Panama	WHO (World Health)	09 Nov 51	Sanitation	118UNTS43	101595
Guatemala	WHO (World Health)	17 Dec 51	Sanitation	120UNTS133	101619
India	WHO (World Health)	20 Dec 51	Tech Assistance	124UNTS109	101669
Costa Rica	WHO (World Health)	23 Jan 52	Sanitation	135UNTS265	101826
WHO (World Health)	UK Great Britain	07 Feb 52	Tech Assistance	121UNTS75	101627
Burma	WHO (World Health)	18 Feb 52	Scientific Project	127UNTS43	101698
Ceylon (Sri Lanka)	WHO (World Health)	26 Mar 52	Sanitation	134UNTS341	200442
India	WHO (World Health)	17 Apr 52	Tech Assistance	131UNTS241	101744
India	WHO (World Health)	19 Apr 52	Tech Assistance	131UNTS253	101745
Libya	USA (United States)	20 May 52	Tech Assistance	178UNTS155	102339
Iraq	USA (United States)	09 Jun 52	Tech Assistance	212UNTS193	102871
Brazil	WHO (World Health)	12 Jun 52	Scientific Project	151UNTS333	102003
Jordan	WHO (World Health)	16 Jun 52	Direct Aid	135UNTS323	200445
India	WHO (World Health)	16 Jul 52	Tech Assistance	135UNTS291	101828
Jordan	WHO (World Health)	21 Aug 52	Direct Aid	141UNTS341	200472
Dominican Republic	WHO (World Health)	10 Oct 52	Sanitation	150UNTS133	101967
Chile	WHO (World Health)	24 Oct 52	Sanitation	151UNTS339	102004
Chile	WHO (World Health)	04 Nov 52	Sanitation	150UNTS119	101966
Ceylon (Sri Lanka)	WHO (World Health)	21 Nov 52	Sanitation	161UNTS315	200490
Japan	WHO (World Health)	26 Nov 52	Tech Assistance	204UNTS301	200521
Saudi Arabia	USA (United States)	15 Dec 52	Direct Aid	185UNTS55	102458
Ethiopia	USA (United States)	29 Apr 53	Sanitation	224UNTS121	103073
United Arab Rep	USA (United States)	18 Jun 53	Sanitation	215UNTS45	102910
Saudi Arabia	USA (United States)	29 Jun 53	Sanitation	206UNTS23	102784
Multilateral		20 Jul 53	Non-ILO Labor	227UNTS217	103140
Belgium	UK Great Britain	04 Jan 54	Sanitation	247UNTS47	103459
Germany, West	USA (United States)	12 Feb 54	Milit Assistance	223UNTS153	103064
Belgium	Norway	24 Mar 54	Sanitation	219UNTS73	102967
Panama	USA (United States)	25 Mar 54	Specific Property	232UNTS289	103243
Mexico	USA (United States)	19 Nov 54	Non-ILO Labor	238UNTS237	103367
Multilateral		19 Mar 55	Sanitation	228UNTS95	103144
Czechoslovakia	Hungary	28 Apr 55	Sanitation	477UNTS197	106923
Colombia	USA (United States)	14 Jun 55	Non-IBRD Project	256UNTS211	103630
Iran	WHO (World Health)	04 Jul 55	Tech Assistance	227UNTS65	103131
Libya	USA (United States)	28 Jul 55	Non-IBRD Project	270UNTS269	103901
USA (United States)	USSR (Soviet Union)	05 Sep 55	Sanitation	256UNTS307	103641
Taiwan	USA (United States)	14 Oct 55	Milit Installation	268UNTS165	103857
Bulgaria	Yugoslavia	15 Nov 55	Consul/Citizenship	396UNTS179	105696
Bulgaria	Yugoslavia	11 Dec 55	Sanitation	378UNTS49	105417
Multilateral		13 Dec 55	Humanitarian	250UNTS3	103514
Multilateral		13 Mar 56	Humanitarian	427UNTS245	106158
Multilateral		21 Dec 56	Humanitarian	427UNTS81	106147
Ethiopia	Sweden	16 Mar 57	Tech Assistance	304UNTS214	104398

PARTY ONE	PARTY TWO	DATE	TOPIC	CITATION	NUMBER
Health (Cont.)					
Italy	UK Great Britain	12 Jun 57	Non-ILO Labor	310UNTS35	104484
Burma	WHO (World Health)	20 Sep 57	Tech Assistance	282UNTS113	104096
New Zealand	UK Great Britain	20 Sep 57	Sanitation	287UNTS105	104180
Hungary	Yugoslavia	20 Nov 57	Sanitation	477UNTS267	106925
Czechoslovakia	USSR (Soviet Union)	04 Dec 57	Sanitation	313UNTS291	104537
Hungary	Romania	17 Dec 57	Sanitation	477UNTS303	106926
Czechoslovakia	Romania	25 Mar 58	Sanitation	339UNTS77	104846
Albania	Yugoslavia	28 Apr 58	Consul/Citizenship	386UNTS103	105540
Hungary	Poland	08 May 58	Sanitation	408UNTS212	105872
Germany, East	Hungary	14 Jun 58	Sanitation	407UNTS78	105861
Philippines	USA (United States)	30 Jun 58	Direct Aid	321UNTS51	104653
Bulgaria	Hungary	03 Apr 59	Sanitation	438UNTS269	106319
Hungary	USSR (Soviet Union)	17 Apr 59	Sanitation	439UNTS41	106324
Czechoslovakia	Korea, North	04 Jun 59	Sanitation	338UNTS291	104842
Bulgaria	Czechoslovakia	19 Sep 59	Sanitation	355UNTS77	105074
Multilateral		26 Jan 60	IGO Establishment	439UNTS249	106333
Fed of Malaya	WHO (World Health)	25 Nov 60	Tech Assistance	387UNTS37	105556
Libya	USA (United States)	11 Dec 60	Health/Educ/Welfare	445UNTS125	106381
Korea, South	WHO (World Health)	20 Jan 61	Tech Assistance	406UNTS269	200589
Cuba	Czechoslovakia	05 Apr 61	Sanitation	442UNTS201	106350
Mali	WHO (World Health)	27 Apr 61	Tech Assistance	407UNTS66	105860
Morocco	WHO (World Health)	09 Aug 61	Tech Assistance	412UNTS192	105932
WHO (World Health)	Somalia	17 Aug 61	Tech Assistance	423UNTS111	106088
Iraq	WHO (World Health)	13 Sep 61	Tech Assistance	419UNTS69	106030
Malagasy	WHO (World Health)	13 Oct 61	Tech Assistance	421UNTS273	106064
Japan	Thailand	25 Nov 61	Sanitation	451UNTS55	106484
Ethiopia	WHO (World Health)	11 Jan 62	Tech Assistance	423UNTS99	106087
WHO (World Health)	Sudan	11 Mar 62	Tech Assistance	432UNTS325	106226
Nigeria	WHO (World Health)	27 Mar 62	Tech Assistance	429UNTS123	106194
Multilateral		14 May 62	Sanitation	544UNTS81	107911
Libya	WHO (World Health)	16 Jun 62	Tech Assistance	437UNTS127	106301
WHO (World Health)	Sierra Leone	19 Jun 62	Tech Assistance	439UNTS151	106327
WHO (World Health)	Senegal	06 Aug 62	Tech Assistance	435UNTS179	106279
WHO (World Health)	Western Samoa	14 Aug 62	Tech Assistance	437UNTS317	200598
Cameroon	WHO (World Health)	08 Dec 62	Tech Assistance	451UNTS215	106496
Multilateral		17 Dec 62	Sanitation	486UNTS119	107076
Algeria	WHO (World Health)	20 Dec 62	Tech Assistance	463UNTS135	106698
India	USA (United States)	01 Feb 63	Scientific Project	473UNTS37	106852
Hungary	Korea, North	29 Mar 63	Sanitation	577UNTS219	108379
Australia	UK Great Britain	06 Jun 63	Sanitation	472UNTS157	106838
Mongolia	WHO (World Health)	21 Jun 63	Tech Assistance	472UNTS373	106848
Burundi	WHO (World Health)	08 Aug 63	Tech Assistance	477UNTS346	106928
Burundi	WHO (World Health)	30 Aug 63	IGO Operations	490UNTS423	107169
Jamaica	WHO (World Health)	25 Sep 63	Tech Assistance	481UNTS125	106980
Czechoslovakia	Yugoslavia	05 Oct 63	Sanitation	504UNTS151	107356
WHO (World Health)	Tanganyika	05 Nov 63	Tech Assistance	496UNTS193	107252
WHO (World Health)	Somalia	08 Nov 63	IGO Operations	493UNTS243	107218
WHO (World Health)	Sierra Leone	22 Nov 63	IGO Operations	493UNTS255	107219
Rwanda	WHO (World Health)	22 Jun 64	Tech Assistance	514UNTS11	107440
WHO (World Health)	Trinidad/Tobago	23 Jun 64	Tech Assistance	503UNTS167	107342
Rwanda	WHO (World Health)	23 Jun 64	Tech Assistance	514UNTS157	107445
Ethiopia	Netherlands	28 Oct 64	Tech Assistance	541UNTS235	107872
Multilateral		07 Nov 64	Sanitation	548UNTS3	107965
Netherlands	Norway	17 Nov 64	Sanitation	579UNTS243	108412
Czechoslovakia	United Arab Rep	26 Nov 64	Sanitation	545UNTS11	107923
Malawi	WHO (World Health)	06 Jan 65	Tech Assistance	525UNTS165	107588
Malawi	WHO (World Health)	08 Jan 65	Tech Assistance	524UNTS281	107579
WHO (World Health)	Tunisia	27 Jan 65	IGO Operations	528UNTS209	107644
Ethiopia	WHO (World Health)	27 Jan 65	IGO Operations	541UNTS135	107866
Australia	Malaysia	21 Jun 65	Humanitarian	542UNTS75	107880
Poland	WHO (World Health)	26 Aug 65	Tech Assistance	552UNTS3	108047
Maldive Islands	WHO (World Health)	23 May 66	Tech Assistance	566UNTS19	108237
Canada	USA (United States)	09 Jun 66	Non-IBRD Project	580UNTS263	108429

PARTY ONE	PARTY TWO	DATE	TOPIC	CITATION	NUMBER
Hides and Skins					
Canada	USA (United States)	13 Dec 40	General Trade	117UNTS173	200368
Canada	USA (United States)	30 Oct 47	General Economic	27UNTS19	100394
Hours of Labor					
Multilateral		28 Nov 19	ILO Labor	38UNTS17	100584
Multilateral		28 Jun 30	ILO Labor	39UNTS85	100613
Multilateral		21 Jun 34	ILO Labor	40UNTS33	100625
Multilateral		25 Jun 35	ILO Labor	40UNTS97	100629
Housing					
Chile	USA (United States)	28 Jun 54	Tech Assistance	233UNTS3	103246
Colombia	USA (United States)	30 Jun 54	Non-IBRD Project	237UNTS263	103351
Canada	USA (United States)	19 Apr 56	Milit Installation	274UNTS3	103955
UK Great Britain	USA (United States)	05 Jun 56	Milit Installation	247UNTS205	103470
Austria	USA (United States)	03 Oct 61	Direct Aid	426UNTS187	106137
Human Rights					
Multilateral		02 Sep 49	IGO Status/Immunit	250UNTS12	103515
Multilateral		04 Nov 50	Humanitarian	213UNTS221	102889
Multilateral		31 Mar 53	Mass Media	435UNTS191	106280
New Zealand	United Nations	02 Feb 61	Humanitarian	391UNTS23	105614
Romania	United Nations	29 May 61	IGO Operations	406UNTS147	105845
Mexico	United Nations	18 Aug 61	Humanitarian	404UNTS297	105817
Multilateral		18 Oct 61	IGO Establishment	529UNTS89	107659
India	United Nations	19 Feb 62	Direct Aid	423UNTS3	106082
Japan	United Nations	11 Apr 62	IGO Operations	425UNTS45	106117
United Nations	Sweden	01 Jun 62	Admin Cooperation	429UNTS135	106195
Multilateral		10 Dec 62	Culture	521UNTS231	107525
Australia	United Nations	13 May 63	Education	463UNTS187	106702
Colombia	United Nations	27 Aug 63	Education	481UNTS3	106975
Italy	United Nations	18 Mar 64	Education	491UNTS21	107171
Afghanistan	United Nations	28 Apr 64	Education	494UNTS77	107227
United Nations	Togo	03 Jul 64	Education	502UNTS287	107334
Mongolia	United Nations	06 Jan 65	IGO Operations	522UNTS45	107535
United Nations	Yugoslavia	07 Jan 65	IGO Operations	522UNTS55	107536
Iran	United Nations	16 Feb 65	Admin Cooperation	525UNTS211	107593
United Nations	Senegal	12 Jan 66	Health/Educ/Welfare	551UNTS147	108039
Hungary	United Nations	04 Mar 66	IGO Operations	559UNTS3	108151
Philippines	United Nations	05 Apr 66	Health/Educ/Welfare	560UNTS191	108174
Finland	United Nations	16 Jan 67	Education	588UNTS153	108522
Poland	United Nations	20 Feb 67	IGO Operations	590UNTS71	108547
Hydro-electric Power					
Mexico	USA (United States)	03 Feb 44	Specific Resources	3UNTS313	200025
Iraq	Turkey	29 Mar 46	General Amity	37UNTS226	100580
Multilateral		10 Feb 47	Peace/Disarmament	49UNTS3	100747
Czechoslovakia	Poland	04 Apr 47	General Economic	85UNTS62	101146
France	Norway	15 Jul 47	Specific Property	15UNTS5	100226
India	Pakistan	04 May 48	Dispute Settlement	54UNTS45	100794
Belgium	France	18 Feb 49	Claims and Debts	31UNTS173	100478
Icebreakers					
Multilateral		20 Dec 61	Water Transport	419UNTS79	106031
Immigration					
Multilateral		05 Jun 26	ILO Labor	38UNTS281	100604
Multilateral		22 Jun 35	ILO Labor	40UNTS73	100628
Costa Rica	USA (United States)	29 May 44	Non-ILO Labor	124UNTS155	200417
Poland	Yugoslavia	02 Jan 46	Visas	115UNTS21	101556
France	Poland	09 Jun 48	Non-ILO Labor	32UNTS251	100503
Czechoslovakia	France	12 Oct 48	Non-ILO Labor	45UNTS81	100693
India	Pakistan	08 Apr 50	Visas	131UNTS3	101733
Netherlands	New Zealand	16 Oct 50	Non-ILO Labor	83UNTS269	101111
Brazil	Netherlands	15 Dec 50	Non-ILO Labor	123UNTS101	101657
Canada	India	26 Jan 51	Visas	248UNTS89	103486
Australia	Netherlands	22 Feb 51	Non-ILO Labor	128UNTS115	101717
Australia	Italy	29 Mar 51	Non-ILO Labor	131UNTS187	101741

PARTY ONE	PARTY TWO	DATE	TOPIC	CITATION	NUMBER
Immigration (Cont.)					
Canada	Ceylon (Sri Lanka)	24 Apr 51	Visas	248UNTS101	103488
Canada	Pakistan	23 Oct 51	Visas	248UNTS95	103487
Australia	Greece	23 May 52	Visas	223UNTS17	103042
Multilateral		14 Jul 52	Consul/Citizenship	198UNTS47	102656
Australia	Germany, West	29 Aug 52	Non-ILO Labor	184UNTS147	102446
Multilateral		19 Oct 53	IGO Establishment	207UNTS189	102807
India	Pakistan	08 May 54	Extradition	203UNTS167	102745
France	Greece	13 May 54	Non-ILO Labor	222UNTS299	103036
Germany, West	Norway	18 Mar 55	Extradition	209UNTS309	102832
Fed Rhod/Nyasaland	Netherlands	02 Nov 55	Non-ILO Labor	263UNTS381	103784
Multilateral		13 Dec 55	IGO Operations	529UNTS141	107660
Indonesia	Philippines	04 Jul 56	Admin Cooperation	401UNTS59	105763
Australia	Netherlands	01 Aug 56	Non-ILO Labor	280UNTS3	104047
Belgium	Spain	28 Nov 56	Non-ILO Labor	308UNTS285	104465
France	Italy	28 Dec 56	Non-ILO Labor	291UNTS203	104255
Australia	UK Great Britain	01 Apr 57	Non-ILO Labor	271UNTS235	103918
Australia	Germany, West	27 Aug 58	Non-ILO Labor	320UNTS303	104649
Japan	Paraguay	22 Jul 59	Visas	373UNTS85	105316
Multilateral		11 Apr 60	Visas	374UNTS3	105323
Brazil	Japan	14 Nov 60	Consul/Citizenship	518UNTS29	107491
Belgium	USA (United States)	21 Feb 61	General Amity	480UNTS149	106967
Netherlands	Spain	08 Apr 61	Non-ILO Labor	482UNTS193	106996
Luxembourg	USA (United States)	23 Feb 62	General Amity	474UNTS3	106868
Australia	UK Great Britain	28 May 62	Admin Cooperation	434UNTS219	106264
Japan	UK Great Britain	14 Nov 62	General Trade	478UNTS29	106934
Netherlands	Portugal	22 Nov 63	Non-ILO Labor	492UNTS31	107185
Australia	Italy	31 Jan 64	Non-ILO Labor	488UNTS197	107129
Australia	Malta	28 Apr 65	Non-ILO Labor	548UNTS203	107979
Australia	Netherlands	01 Jun 65	Consul/Citizenship	560UNTS85	108170
Australia	Germany, West	21 Jun 65	Visas	542UNTS53	107879
Japan	Korea, South	22 Jun 65	Consul/Citizenship	584UNTS3	108474
Industrial Accidents					
Multilateral		17 Oct 63	Atomic Energy	525UNTS75	107585
Benelux Econ Union	Poland	17 Feb 65	General Economic	547UNTS165	107956
Industrial Property					
France	UK Great Britain	29 Aug 45	Patents/Copyrights	11UNTS397	200069
UK Great Britain	USA (United States)	27 Mar 46	Patents/Copyrights	4UNTS101	100040
Multilateral		27 Jul 46	Patents/Copyrights	90UNTS229	101238
Canada	USA (United States)	27 Sep 46	Patents/Copyrights	21UNTS3	100320
Multilateral		08 Feb 47	Patents/Copyrights	14UNTS287	100222
Multilateral		10 Feb 47	Peace/Disarmament	42UNTS3	100645
Multilateral		10 Feb 47	Peace/Disarmament	41UNTS135	100644
Multilateral		10 Feb 47	Peace/Disarmament	41UNTS21	100643
Multilateral		10 Feb 47	Peace/Disarmament	48UNTS203	100746
Multilateral		10 Feb 47	Peace/Disarmament	49UNTS3	100747
France	USA (United States)	04 Apr 47	Patents/Copyrights	24UNTS133	100353
Multilateral		06 Jun 47	Patents/Copyrights	46UNTS249	100714
Italy	USA (United States)	14 Aug 47	Claims and Debts	36UNTS105	100567
Denmark	UK Great Britain	19 Aug 47	Reparations	9UNTS277	100137
Romania	USA (United States)	26 Feb 48	Admin Cooperation	48UNTS9	100738
Canada	France	05 May 48	Reparations	231UNTS87	103209
Philippines	USA (United States)	23 Aug 48	Patents/Copyrights	82UNTS11	101080
Greece	Lebanon	06 Oct 48	Consul/Citizenship	87UNTS351	101179
UK Great Britain	Yugoslavia	23 Dec 48	Reparations	81UNTS103	101067
Multilateral		29 Nov 50	Patents/Copyrights	88UNTS221	101194
Israel	UK Great Britain	10 Dec 50	Patents/Copyrights	88UNTS211	101193
Italy	Netherlands	22 Sep 52	Reparations	150UNTS113	101965
Japan	Sweden	31 Mar 54	Claims and Debts	262UNTS187	103744
Bulgaria	Yugoslavia	02 Nov 54	Patents/Copyrights	375UNTS333	105371
Germany, West	Sweden	22 Mar 56	Patents/Copyrights	262UNTS423	103763
Germany, East	Hungary	12 Jan 60	Patents/Copyrights	409UNTS22	105875
Industry					
Multilateral		28 Nov 19	ILO Labor	38UNTS93	100589
Multilateral		28 Nov 19	ILO Labor	38UNTS67	100587

PARTY ONE	PARTY TWO	DATE	TOPIC	CITATION	NUMBER
Industry (Cont.)					
Multilateral		28 Nov 19	ILO Labor	38UNTS17	100584
Multilateral		28 Nov 19	ILO Labor	38UNTS81	100588
Multilateral		29 Nov 19	ILO Labor	38UNTS53	100586
Multilateral		17 Nov 21	ILO Labor	38UNTS187	100597
Multilateral		19 Nov 21	ILO Labor	38UNTS175	100596
Multilateral		10 Jun 25	ILO Labor	38UNTS243	100601
Multilateral		15 Jun 27	ILO Labor	38UNTS327	100607
Multilateral		29 Jun 33	ILO Labor	39UNTS211	100619
Multilateral		29 Jun 33	ILO Labor	39UNTS165	100617
Multilateral		29 Jun 33	ILO Labor	39UNTS259	100621
Multilateral		19 Jun 34	ILO Labor	40UNTS3	100623
Multilateral		21 Jun 34	ILO Labor	40UNTS19	100624
Multilateral		22 Jun 37	ILO Labor	40UNTS217	100636
Brazil	USA (United States)	05 Apr 46	Education	12UNTS131	100183
Multilateral		09 Oct 46	ILO Labor	78UNTS198	101017
Czechoslovakia	Poland	04 Apr 47	General Economic	85UNTS62	101146
Italy	UK Great Britain	30 May 47	Non-ILO Labor	54UNTS131	100800
Multilateral		11 Jul 47	ILO Labor	54UNTS3	100792
USSR (Soviet Union)	Yugoslavia	25 Jul 47	Tech Assistance	130UNTS315	101732
Multilateral		09 Jul 48	ILO Labor	81UNTS147	101070
Multilateral		10 Jul 48	ILO Labor	91UNTS3	101239
Multilateral		31 Mar 49	Reparations	122UNTS57	101636
Canada	USA (United States)	12 Apr 49	Milit Assistance	206UNTS241	102789
Multilateral		14 Apr 49	Milit Occupation	141UNTS281	101919
Netherlands	IBRD (World Bank)	26 Jul 49	IBRD Project	154UNTS178	102030
Finland	IBRD (World Bank)	01 Aug 49	IBRD Project	156UNTS289	200480
IBRD (World Bank)	Turkey	19 Oct 50	IBRD Project	157UNTS333	102058
Multilateral		03 Apr 51	Milit Occupation	141UNTS303	101920
Multilateral		18 Apr 51	IGO Establishment	261UNTS140	103729
El Salvador	USA (United States)	23 Jul 51	Direct Aid	138UNTS127	101865
IBRD (World Bank)	Yugoslavia	11 Oct 51	IBRD Project	159UNTS3	102081
Iraq	USA (United States)	21 May 52	Tech Assistance	206UNTS3	102782
Chile	USA (United States)	30 Jun 52	Tech Assistance	199UNTS241	102688
Brazil	USA (United States)	30 Jun 52	Tech Assistance	185UNTS79	102460
Australia	IBRD (World Bank)	08 Jul 52	IBRD Project	159UNTS295	102092
Colombia	United Nations	17 Jul 52	Tech Assistance	135UNTS61	101815
India	IBRD (World Bank)	18 Dec 52	IBRD Project	201UNTS241	102719
IBRD (World Bank)	Yugoslavia	11 Feb 53	IBRD Project	165UNTS231	102179
IBRD (World Bank)	Turkey	10 Sep 53	IBRD Project	187UNTS71	102502
Denmark	UK Great Britain	15 Dec 53	Non-ILO Labor	196UNTS105	102620
Norway	USA (United States)	07 May 54	Milit Assistance	231UNTS157	103215
Spain	USA (United States)	19 May 54	Tech Assistance	235UNTS87	103296
France	USA (United States)	31 May 54	Milit Assistance	236UNTS141	103321
UK Great Britain	USA (United States)	15 Jun 54	Milit Assistance	236UNTS133	103320
Italy	USA (United States)	16 Jun 54	Loans and Credits	236UNTS149	103322
Ireland	USA (United States)	17 Jun 54	Direct Aid	241UNTS173	103432
Italy	USA (United States)	24 Jun 54	Tech Assistance	235UNTS3	103290
Ecuador	USA (United States)	30 Jun 54	Tech Assistance	236UNTS163	103323
Belgium	USA (United States)	23 Nov 54	Tech Assistance	235UNTS19	103292
Peru	IBRD (World Bank)	19 Apr 55	IBRD Project	221UNTS153	103007
Turkey	USA (United States)	25 Apr 55	Milit Assistance	263UNTS299	103779
Netherlands	USA (United States)	29 Apr 55	Milit Assistance	251UNTS357	103553
Peru	USA (United States)	30 Apr 55	General Aid	263UNTS309	103780
Greece	USA (United States)	27 May 55	Milit Assistance	251UNTS349	103552
Italy	IBRD (World Bank)	01 Jun 55	IBRD Project	358UNTS203	105137
USA (United States)	Yugoslavia	30 Sep 55	General Military	269UNTS89	103877
Japan	IBRD (World Bank)	25 Oct 55	IBRD Project	230UNTS379	200534
Colombia	Italy	20 Dec 55	Specif Goods/Equip	260UNTS315	103714
Japan	IBRD (World Bank)	21 Feb 56	IBRD Project	248UNTS321	200543
Costa Rica	IBRD (World Bank)	18 Sep 56	IBRD Project	260UNTS369	103721
Australia	IBRD (World Bank)	03 Dec 56	IBRD Project	288UNTS99	104200
India	IBRD (World Bank)	19 Dec 56	IBRD Project	310UNTS75	104489
Japan	IBRD (World Bank)	19 Dec 56	IBRD Project	264UNTS179	103793
Netherlands	IBRD (World Bank)	15 May 57	IBRD Project	274UNTS211	103967
Iraq	USA (United States)	16 Jun 57	Tech Assistance	284UNTS39	104127

PARTY ONE	PARTY TWO	DATE	TOPIC	CITATION	NUMBER
Industry (Cont.)					
France	USA (United States)	23 Sep 57	Tech Assistance	293UNTS297	104297
Pakistan	IBRD (World Bank)	17 Dec 57	IBRD Project	299UNTS321	104323
Japan	IBRD (World Bank)	29 Jan 58	IBRD Project	310UNTS111	104490
Japan	IBRD (World Bank)	13 Jun 58	IBRD Project	312UNTS159	104518
Japan	IBRD (World Bank)	27 Jun 58	IBRD Project	312UNTS193	104519
Japan	IBRD (World Bank)	11 Jul 58	IBRD Project	318UNTS103	104611
Argentina	Brazil	19 Sep 58	Tech Assistance	374UNTS57	105329
Iran	IBRD (World Bank)	23 Nov 59	IBRD Project	380UNTS245	105459
India	Japan	25 Jan 60	Tech Assistance	384UNTS31	105508
Costa Rica	IBRD (World Bank)	04 May 60	IBRD Project	390UNTS201	105609
Iran	Japan	12 Sep 60	Education	384UNTS43	105509
India	IBRD (World Bank)	28 Oct 60	IBRD Project	406UNTS27	105838
Japan	IBRD (World Bank)	20 Dec 60	IBRD Project	400UNTS279	105754
Japan	IBRD (World Bank)	20 Dec 60	IBRD Project	400UNTS167	105752
Afghanistan	Japan	15 Mar 61	Education	450UNTS373	106480
Pakistan	IBRD (World Bank)	27 Jun 61	IBRD Project	425UNTS241	106127
Israel	IBRD (World Bank)	11 Jul 61	IBRD Project	429UNTS3	106188
Finland	IBRD (World Bank)	09 Aug 61	IBRD Project	415UNTS204	105986
Costa Rica	IBRD (World Bank)	06 Sep 61	IBRD Project	446UNTS345	106408
Mexico	USA (United States)	15 Nov 61	Non-IBRD Project	460UNTS113	106634
Taiwan	IDA (Devel Assoc)	01 Dec 61	Loans and Credits	426UNTS105	106132
India	IBRD (World Bank)	28 Feb 62	IBRD Project	447UNTS3	106410
Austria	IBRD (World Bank)	15 Jun 62	IBRD Project	447UNTS127	106414
Pakistan	IDA (Devel Assoc)	02 Nov 62	Non-IBRD Project	468UNTS351	106781
Philippines	IBRD (World Bank)	15 Feb 63	IBRD Project	478UNTS161	106936
IBRD (World Bank)	Thailand	11 Mar 64	IBRD Project	504UNTS73	107354
Pakistan	IBRD (World Bank)	30 Jun 64	IBRD Project	519UNTS57	107502
IDA (Devel Assoc)	Turkey	31 Aug 64	Non-IBRD Project	535UNTS111	107777
Taiwan	IBRD (World Bank)	17 Dec 64	IBRD Project	538UNTS3	107808
IDA (Devel Assoc)	Turkey	01 Apr 65	Non-IBRD Project	554UNTS137	108100
Italy	IBRD (World Bank)	28 Jun 65	IBRD Project	567UNTS127	108254
Finland	IBRD (World Bank)	30 Jun 65	IBRD Project	550UNTS63	108009
India	IDA (Devel Assoc)	11 Aug 65	Non-IBRD Project	562UNTS277	108199
India	IBRD (World Bank)	07 Jul 66	IBRD Project	595UNTS3	108610
IDA (Devel Assoc)	Turkey	10 Aug 66	Non-IBRD Project	585UNTS237	108491
IBRD (World Bank)	Turkey	10 Aug 66	IBRD Project	585UNTS199	108490
India	IDA (Devel Assoc)	19 Aug 66	Non-IBRD Project	584UNTS193	108478
Pakistan	IDA (Devel Assoc)	23 Dec 66	Non-IBRD Project	594UNTS255	108606
India	IDA (Devel Assoc)	23 Dec 66	Non-IBRD Project	594UNTS165	108603
Inheritance					
UK Great Britain	USA (United States)	16 Apr 45	Taxation	6UNTS359	200039
Canada	UK Great Britain	05 Jun 46	Taxation	86UNTS3	101147
South Africa	UK Great Britain	14 Oct 46	Taxation	86UNTS51	101152
Czechoslovakia	Romania	01 Mar 48	Admin Cooperation	26UNTS109	100381
Netherlands	UK Great Britain	15 Oct 48	Taxation	73UNTS203	100954
Czechoslovakia	Poland	21 Jan 49	Admin Cooperation	31UNTS205	100480
Inland Navigation					
Finland	USSR (Soviet Union)	28 Oct 22	Specific Resources	67UNTS153	100873
Finland	USSR (Soviet Union)	28 Oct 22	Specific Resources	67UNTS157	100874
Brazil	Paraguay	14 Jun 41	IGO Establishment	54UNTS323	200204
Brazil	Paraguay	14 Jun 41	IGO Establishment	54UNTS303	200202
Canada	USA (United States)	10 Nov 41	Specific Resources	23UNTS275	200134
Mexico	USA (United States)	03 Feb 44	Specific Resources	3UNTS313	200025
Belgium	France	30 Mar 45	Water Transport	20UNTS297	200122
Multilateral		27 Sep 45	IGO Establishment	5UNTS327	200035
UK Great Britain	USA (United States)	05 Nov 45	IGO Establishment	138UNTS75	101861
Multilateral		20 Jan 47	Water Transport	87UNTS247	101176
USSR (Soviet Union)	Yugoslavia	04 Feb 47	Admin Cooperation	116UNTS171	101576
Multilateral		10 Feb 47	Peace/Disarmament	41UNTS21	100643
Multilateral		10 Feb 47	Peace/Disarmament	41UNTS135	100644
Multilateral		10 Feb 47	Peace/Disarmament	42UNTS3	100645
Belgium	Netherlands	13 Apr 48	Customs	32UNTS153	100497
Multilateral		18 Aug 48	Water Transport	33UNTS181	100518
Czechoslovakia	Hungary	27 Feb 49	Admin Cooperation	26UNTS119	100383

PARTY ONE	PARTY TWO	DATE	TOPIC	CITATION	NUMBER
Inland Navigation (Cont.)					
Belgium	Netherlands	13 May 49	Customs	65UNTS133	100841
USSR (Soviet Union)	Yugoslavia	31 Aug 49	Admin Cooperation	116UNTS345	101580
Belgium	Netherlands	17 Feb 50	Water Transport	51UNTS101	100756
Germany, West	Netherlands	14 Dec 50	Water Transport	87UNTS257	101177
Pakistan	USA (United States)	09 Feb 51	Tech Assistance	100UNTS67	101388
Belgium	Netherlands	14 Nov 51	Admin Cooperation	123UNTS91	101656
Germany, East	Poland	06 Feb 52	Water Transport	304UNTS131	104395
Czechoslovakia	Hungary	16 Apr 54	Specific Resources	504UNTS231	107360
Belgium	Germany, West	03 Nov 54	Admin Cooperation	201UNTS359	102724
Austria	Romania	11 May 55	Water Transport	342UNTS119	104904
Canada	USA (United States)	24 Oct 56	Specif Goods/Equip	281UNTS281	104084
Canada	USA (United States)	26 Feb 57	Water Transport	279UNTS179	104039
Canada	USA (United States)	09 Apr 57	Water Transport	283UNTS217	104119
Bulgaria	Yugoslavia	19 Apr 57	Water Transport	349UNTS3	105006
Austria	USSR (Soviet Union)	14 Jun 57	Water Transport	285UNTS169	104152
Belgium	IBRD (World Bank)	10 Sep 57	IBRD Project	286UNTS291	104174
Belgium	Netherlands	24 Oct 57	Water Transport	489UNTS3	107131
Belgium	Netherlands	24 Oct 57	Water Transport	292UNTS199	104274
China People's Rep	USSR (Soviet Union)	21 Dec 57	Visas	305UNTS213	104420
Canada	USA (United States)	27 Feb 59	Specific Resources	341UNTS3	104873
Canada	USA (United States)	09 Mar 59	Territory Boundary	340UNTS295	104872
Czechoslovakia	Germany, East	18 Sep 59	Customs	363UNTS287	105209
Multilateral		15 Mar 60	Water Transport	572UNTS133	108310
Germany, West	Netherlands	08 Apr 60	Territory Boundary	508UNTS14	107404
Belgium	Netherlands	20 Jun 60	Specific Property	423UNTS19	106084
Finland	Sweden	21 Nov 60	Territory Boundary	383UNTS125	105498
Canada	USA (United States)	05 May 61	Admin Cooperation	419UNTS9	106027
Canada	USA (United States)	17 Oct 61	Water Transport	424UNTS101	106102
Multilateral		26 Oct 63	Water Transport	587UNTS9	108506
Romania	Yugoslavia	30 Nov 63	Specific Property	512UNTS2	107438
Finland	USSR (Soviet Union)	24 Apr 64	Territory Boundary	537UNTS231	107804
Pakistan	IDA (Devel Assoc)	26 Aug 64	Non-IBRD Project	535UNTS263	107784
Multilateral		25 Nov 64	Water Transport	587UNTS19	108507
Denmark	Germany, West	09 Jun 65	Water Transport	581UNTS141	108439
Inland Transportation					
Italy	USA (United States)	26 Nov 48	Direct Aid	79UNTS71	101032
Multilateral		16 Dec 48	Direct Aid	79UNTS85	101033
France	USA (United States)	23 Dec 48	Direct Aid	67UNTS171	100876
France	USA (United States)	07 Feb 49	Direct Aid	67UNTS189	100877
Greece	USA (United States)	09 Feb 49	Direct Aid	79UNTS95	101034
Trieste	USA (United States)	11 Feb 49	Direct Aid	79UNTS123	101036
Austria	USA (United States)	11 Feb 49	Direct Aid	79UNTS113	101035
Norway	USA (United States)	31 Oct 49	Direct Aid	68UNTS3	100879
Insane Persons					
Germany, West	Netherlands	18 Jul 61	Sanitation	487UNTS95	107096
Insect Control					
Multilateral		22 Feb 49	Sanitation	93UNTS129	101296
Guatemala	WHO (World Health)	28 Nov 50	Sanitation	103UNTS51	101423
El Salvador	WHO (World Health)	02 Jan 51	Sanitation	103UNTS29	101421
Nicaragua	WHO (World Health)	02 Jan 51	Sanitation	103UNTS107	101428
Costa Rica	WHO (World Health)	13 Apr 51	Sanitation	103UNTS3	101419
Taiwan	WHO (World Health)	25 Oct 51	Sanitation	126UNTS77	101683
Dominican Republic	WHO (World Health)	15 Feb 52	Sanitation	134UNTS291	101808
Ethiopia	USA (United States)	05 Nov 52	Sanitation	184UNTS139	102445
Multilateral		25 May 62	IGO Establishment	486UNTS103	107075
Multilateral		03 Dec 63	IGO Establishment	529UNTS217	107663
Australia	UN Special Fund	30 Sep 64	Scientific Project	510UNTS277	107419
Multilateral		02 Jul 65	Sanitation	592UNTS215	108575
Intellectual Relations					
Brazil	Paraguay	14 Jun 41	Admin Cooperation	54UNTS279	200200
Brazil	Paraguay	14 Jun 41	Culture	54UNTS249	200197
Brazil	Paraguay	14 Jun 41	Culture	54UNTS235	200196
Brazil	Chile	18 Nov 41	Culture	67UNTS279	200225

PARTY ONE	PARTY TWO	DATE	TOPIC	CITATION	NUMBER
Intellectual Relations (Cont.)					
Peru	USA (United States)	21 Apr 42	Scientific Project	89UNTS317	200260
Peru	USA (United States)	24 Aug 42	Education	24UNTS153	200139
Brazil	Venezuela	22 Oct 42	Culture	65UNTS203	200212
Ecuador	USA (United States)	29 Oct 42	Scientific Project	89UNTS301	200259
Brazil	Dominican Republic	09 Dec 42	Culture	65UNTS217	200213
Albania	Yugoslavia	23 Mar 44	General Military	1UNTS81	100015
Peru	USA (United States)	04 Apr 44	Scientific Project	89UNTS291	200258
Multilateral		19 Apr 44	Scientific Project	89UNTS279	200257
Brazil	Ecuador	24 May 44	Culture	73UNTS223	200242
Brazil	Canada	24 May 44	Culture	65UNTS265	200215
Ecuador	USA (United States)	22 Jan 45	Education	24UNTS273	200152
Multilateral		22 Mar 45	General Amity	70UNTS237	200241
Brazil	Dominican Republic	09 Apr 45	Culture	67UNTS293	200226
Poland	USSR (Soviet Union)	21 Apr 45	General Military	12UNTS391	200070
Multilateral		16 Nov 45	IGO Establishment	4UNTS275	100052
Czechoslovakia	France	08 Dec 45	Education	46UNTS77	100701
Belgium	France	22 Feb 46	Culture	68UNTS157	100892
Poland	Yugoslavia	16 Mar 46	Culture	10UNTS11	100139
Iraq	Turkey	29 Mar 46	General Amity	37UNTS226	100580
Brazil	USA (United States)	05 Apr 46	Education	12UNTS131	100183
Belgium	UK Great Britain	17 Apr 46	Health/Educ/Welfare	6UNTS177	100075
Czechoslovakia	Yugoslavia	09 May 46	General Military	1UNTS67	100014
Belgium	Netherlands	16 May 46	Culture	17UNTS13	100266
Poland	UK Great Britain	24 Jun 46	Claims and Debts	11UNTS59	100149
Hungary	UK Great Britain	12 Aug 46	Finance	89UNTS219	101220
Taiwan	USA (United States)	30 Aug 46	Direct Aid	12UNTS39	100179
France	Netherlands	19 Nov 46	Culture	32UNTS101	100493
UNESCO (Educ/Cult)	United Nations	03 Feb 47	IGO Operations	1UNTS233	200011
Multilateral		06 Feb 47	IGO Establishment	97UNTS227	101352
Burma	USA (United States)	28 Feb 47	Direct Aid	25UNTS27	100355
Belgium	Czechoslovakia	06 Mar 47	Culture	34UNTS77	100528
Austria	France	15 Mar 47	Culture	12UNTS109	100182
Czechoslovakia	Poland	04 Apr 47	General Economic	85UNTS62	101146
League of Nations	United Nations	11 Apr 47	Specific Property	4UNTS443	200026
Czechoslovakia	Yugoslavia	27 Apr 47	Culture	33UNTS49	100514
France	Poland	19 May 47	Education	12UNTS95	100181
Czechoslovakia	UK Great Britain	16 Jun 47	Education	46UNTS61	100700
Bulgaria	Czechoslovakia	20 Jun 47	Education	46UNTS15	100698
Bulgaria	Poland	28 Jun 47	Culture	15UNTS123	100230
Czechoslovakia	Poland	04 Jul 47	Culture	25UNTS249	100366
Albania	Yugoslavia	09 Jul 47	Culture	33UNTS91	100516
Czechoslovakia	Romania	05 Sep 47	Education	46UNTS37	100699
Hungary	Yugoslavia	15 Oct 47	Culture	33UNTS73	100515
Ecuador	USA (United States)	27 Oct 47	Air Transport	44UNTS45	100677
Paraguay	USA (United States)	01 Jan 48	Scientific Project	89UNTS191	101217
France	Netherlands	02 Jan 48	Visas	70UNTS105	100899
Hungary	Poland	31 Jan 48	Culture	25UNTS283	100368
Norway	UK Great Britain	19 Feb 48	Culture	34UNTS33	100526
Belgium	Norway	20 Feb 48	Culture	32UNTS39	100487
Denmark	Switzerland	21 Feb 48	Non-ILO Labor	14UNTS321	100224
Poland	Romania	27 Feb 48	Culture	46UNTS143	100707
France	UK Great Britain	02 Mar 48	Culture	77UNTS33	100990
Multilateral		17 Mar 48	General Military	19UNTS51	100304
Philippines	USA (United States)	23 Mar 48	Education	43UNTS247	100671
Czechoslovakia	Poland	05 Apr 48	Admin Cooperation	31UNTS325	100481
Greece	USA (United States)	23 Apr 48	Education	74UNTS107	100958
Ecuador	USA (United States)	14 May 48	Scientific Project	89UNTS71	101210
Netherlands	UK Great Britain	07 Jul 48	Culture	82UNTS259	101099
New Zealand	USA (United States)	14 Sep 48	General Military	18UNTS251	100295
Greece	Italy	21 Sep 48	Culture	77UNTS259	101003
UK Great Britain	USA (United States)	22 Sep 48	Milit Assistance	71UNTS64	100910
Multilateral		08 Oct 48	Education	19UNTS113	100308
France	USA (United States)	22 Oct 48	Education	84UNTS173	101128
Belgium	Italy	29 Nov 48	Culture	41UNTS3	100641
Afghanistan	UNESCO (Educ/Cult)	08 Dec 48	Education	46UNTS3	100697

PARTY ONE	PARTY TWO	DATE	TOPIC	CITATION	NUMBER
Intellectual Relations (Cont.)					
Italy	USA (United States)	18 Dec 48	Education	79UNTS133	101037
Peru	USA (United States)	25 Mar 49	Scientific Project	89UNTS15	101205
Netherlands	USA (United States)	17 May 49	Milit Assistance	46UNTS291	100717
Norway	USA (United States)	25 May 49	Education	32UNTS345	100507
Mexico	USA (United States)	21 Jun 49	Scientific Project	89UNTS3	101204
Ecuador	Italy	24 Aug 49	General Amity	72UNTS35	100926
Mexico	USA (United States)	30 Aug 49	IGO Establishment	98UNTS183	101364
Iran	USA (United States)	01 Sep 49	Direct Aid	79UNTS155	101039
United Arab Rep	USA (United States)	03 Nov 49	Education	71UNTS31	100908
Australia	USA (United States)	26 Nov 49	Reparations	45UNTS133	100695
Belgium	United Arab Rep	28 Nov 49	Culture	76UNTS91	100982
Turkey	USA (United States)	27 Dec 49	Direct Aid	98UNTS141	101361
India	USA (United States)	02 Feb 50	Education	89UNTS127	101214
Korea, South	USA (United States)	28 Apr 50	Education	93UNTS21	101284
Austria	USA (United States)	06 Jun 50	Education	92UNTS201	101273
Thailand	USA (United States)	01 Jul 50	Education	81UNTS61	101063
Pakistan	USA (United States)	23 Sep 50	Education	82UNTS131	101088
France	Turkey	22 Dec 50	Non-ILO Labor	98UNTS11	101356
Internal Security					
Multilateral		01 May 57	Admin Cooperation	284UNTS201	104138
Mexico	USA (United States)	26 Jun 61	Direct Aid	413UNTS229	105957
Pakistan	United Nations	18 Apr 63	IGO Operations	503UNTS25	107339
International Law					
Mexico	United Nations	17 Jul 64	IGO Operations	533UNTS117	107738
Monaco	United Nations	17 Dec 65	IGO Operations	550UNTS365	200615
International Obligations					
Germany, West	Netherlands	31 Jan 52	Admin Cooperation	492UNTS295	107199
Somalia	USA (United States)	04 Feb 61	Tech Assistance	433UNTS179	106241
Germany, West	Netherlands	03 Aug 61	Admin Cooperation	492UNTS321	107201
Multilateral		07 Aug 62	Recognition	457UNTS117	106580
Multilateral		31 Aug 62	Recognition	457UNTS123	106581
New Zealand	Western Samoa	30 Nov 62	Recognition	476UNTS3	106898
Accept UN Charter	Mauritania	20 Mar 63	UN Charter	457UNTS59	106576
Accept UN Charter	Kuwait	20 Apr 63	UN Charter	463UNTS213	106705
Accept UN Charter	Zanzibar	10 Dec 63	UN Charter	483UNTS237	107016
Accept UN Charter	Kenya	12 Dec 63	UN Charter	483UNTS233	107015
Malta	UK Great Britain	31 Dec 64	Admin Cooperation	525UNTS221	107594
UN Special Fund	Zambia	04 Feb 65	Admin Cooperation	527UNTS115	107621
UN Special Fund	Singapore	31 Dec 65	Admin Cooperation	552UNTS299	108061
IDA (Devel Assoc)	UK Great Britain	08 Feb 66	Non-IBRD Project	567UNTS207	108257
Gambia	UK Great Britain	20 Jun 66	Recognition	573UNTS203	108333
Accept UN Charter	Lesotho	04 Oct 66	UN Charter	575UNTS155	108358
Accept UN Charter	United Arab Rep	30 Nov 66	UN Charter	581UNTS131	108437
International Organizations					
Somalia	UK Great Britain	26 Jun 60	Recognition	374UNTS357	105349
Nigeria	UK Great Britain	01 Oct 60	Recognition	384UNTS207	105520
Inventions					
Australia	Taiwan	29 Jul 55	Patents/Copyrights	213UNTS193	102887
Multilateral		24 Sep 56	Patents/Copyrights	253UNTS171	103583
Investments					
Turkey	USA (United States)	15 Nov 51	Direct Aid	177UNTS315	102331
Taiwan	USA (United States)	25 Jun 52	Direct Aid	136UNTS229	101837
Israel	USA (United States)	08 Aug 52	Direct Aid	181UNTS37	102396
Japan	USA (United States)	08 Mar 54	Claims and Debts	232UNTS251	103240
Thailand	USA (United States)	01 Sep 54	Claims and Debts	237UNTS209	103347
Costa Rica	USA (United States)	26 Feb 55	Claims and Debts	252UNTS129	103562
India	IBRD (World Bank)	14 Mar 55	IBRD Project	309UNTS129	104472
Peru	USA (United States)	16 Mar 55	Claims and Debts	252UNTS151	103564
Guatemala	USA (United States)	23 Mar 55	Claims and Debts	252UNTS143	103563
Ecuador	USA (United States)	29 Mar 55	Claims and Debts	261UNTS343	103732
Pakistan	USA (United States)	26 May 55	General Economic	257UNTS93	103652
Honduras	USA (United States)	10 Jun 55	Claims and Debts	258UNTS51	103669

PARTY ONE	PARTY TWO	DATE	TOPIC	CITATION	NUMBER
Investments (Cont.)					
Bolivia	USA (United States)	23 Sep 55	Claims and Debts	256UNTS275	103637
Paraguay	USA (United States)	28 Oct 55	Claims and Debts	273UNTS97	103946
Colombia	USA (United States)	18 Nov 55	Claims and Debts	239UNTS173	103377
Jordan	USA (United States)	24 Sep 56	Milit Assistance	278UNTS51	104020
Luxembourg	USA (United States)	07 Dec 56	General Military	265UNTS255	103817
Turkey	USA (United States)	15 Jan 57	Claims and Debts	280UNTS79	104053
Cuba	USA (United States)	04 Feb 57	Admin Cooperation	302UNTS273	104366
Afghanistan	USA (United States)	09 Jun 57	Admin Cooperation	307UNTS97	104445
India	USA (United States)	19 Sep 57	Claims and Debts	290UNTS175	104236
Iran	USA (United States)	21 Sep 57	Claims and Debts	293UNTS287	104296
USA (United States)	Vietnam, South	05 Nov 57	Finance	300UNTS23	104328
Pakistan	IBRD (World Bank)	17 Dec 57	IBRD Project	299UNTS321	104323
Indonesia	Japan	20 Jan 58	Loans and Credits	325UNTS13	104691
Ghana	USA (United States)	30 Sep 58	Admin Cooperation	336UNTS169	104805
Sudan	USA (United States)	17 Mar 59	Admin Cooperation	342UNTS13	104896
Tunisia	USA (United States)	18 Mar 59	Admin Cooperation	344UNTS179	104948
Nicaragua	USA (United States)	14 Apr 59	Admin Cooperation	343UNTS119	104922
Fed of Malaya	USA (United States)	21 Apr 59	Admin Cooperation	343UNTS3	104916
India	IBRD (World Bank)	15 Jul 59	IBRD Project	355UNTS95	105075
Finland	USA (United States)	22 Jul 59	Admin Cooperation	354UNTS39	105051
Pakistan	IBRD (World Bank)	25 Sep 59	IBRD Project	355UNTS169	105077
Germany, West	Pakistan	25 Nov 59	General Economic	457UNTS22	106575
Argentina	USA (United States)	22 Dec 59	Admin Cooperation	411UNTS42	105912
El Salvador	USA (United States)	29 Jan 60	Claims and Debts	372UNTS3	105283
Korea, South	USA (United States)	19 Feb 60	Claims and Debts	372UNTS109	105291
Nepal	USA (United States)	17 May 60	Claims and Debts	372UNTS313	105307
Chile	USA (United States)	29 Jul 60	Admin Cooperation	405UNTS127	105829
Guatemala	USA (United States)	09 Aug 60	Finance	461UNTS15	106648
Liberia	USA (United States)	06 Sep 60	Admin Cooperation	389UNTS245	105596
India	IBRD (World Bank)	28 Oct 60	IBRD Project	406UNTS27	105838
Panama	USA (United States)	23 Jan 61	Admin Cooperation	445UNTS135	106382
Morocco	USA (United States)	31 Mar 61	Admin Cooperation	406UNTS249	105854
Sierra Leone	USA (United States)	19 May 61	Admin Cooperation	409UNTS251	105890
Pakistan	IBRD (World Bank)	27 Jun 61	IBRD Project	425UNTS241	106127
Ivory Coast	USA (United States)	01 Dec 61	Claims and Debts	462UNTS221	106681
Germany, West	Thailand	13 Dec 61	Claims and Debts	541UNTS181	107870
India	IBRD (World Bank)	28 Feb 62	IBRD Project	447UNTS3	106410
Togo	USA (United States)	20 Mar 62	Admin Cooperation	445UNTS79	106378
Niger	USA (United States)	26 Apr 62	Claims and Debts	459UNTS129	106618
Dominican Republic	USA (United States)	02 May 62	Claims and Debts	442UNTS99	106341
Guinea	USA (United States)	09 May 62	Claims and Debts	451UNTS197	106494
Ethiopia	USA (United States)	03 Aug 62	Claims and Debts	459UNTS79	106613
Congo (Brazzaville)	USA (United States)	01 Sep 62	Claims and Debts	459UNTS117	106616
Colombia	USA (United States)	05 Oct 62	Finance	459UNTS191	106621
Congo (Zaire)	USA (United States)	17 Nov 62	Finance	474UNTS41	106870
USA (United States)	Venezuela	29 Nov 62	Finance	474UNTS107	106875
Nigeria	USA (United States)	24 Dec 62	Claims and Debts	462UNTS180	106677
Jamaica	USA (United States)	04 Jan 63	Finance	471UNTS119	106826
Trinidad/Tobago	USA (United States)	15 Jan 63	Finance	471UNTS141	106829
Pakistan	IBRD (World Bank)	13 Feb 63	IBRD Project	467UNTS3	106756
Gabon	USA (United States)	10 Apr 63	Finance	474UNTS113	106876
Netherlands	Tunisia	23 May 63	Finance	523UNTS237	107558
Cyprus	USA (United States)	29 May 63	Finance	487UNTS283	107110
India	IBRD (World Bank)	05 Jun 63	IBRD Project	481UNTS191	106983
United Arab Rep	USA (United States)	29 Jun 63	Finance	479UNTS207	106954
Malagasy	USA (United States)	26 Jul 63	Finance	487UNTS189	107104
Tanganyika	USA (United States)	14 Nov 63	Claims and Debts	493UNTS75	107208
Somalia	USA (United States)	08 Jan 64	Claims and Debts	505UNTS165	107372
Kenya	USA (United States)	20 Apr 64	Claims and Debts	524UNTS165	107571
Mali	USA (United States)	09 Jun 64	Claims and Debts	530UNTS133	107678
Mauritania	USA (United States)	03 Jul 64	Finance	532UNTS307	107724
Laos	USA (United States)	29 Dec 64	Claims and Debts	542UNTS23	107876
Central Afri Rep	USA (United States)	31 Dec 64	Claims and Debts	542UNTS29	107877
Malta	Switzerland	20 Jan 65	General Trade	548UNTS193	107978
SEATO (SE Asia)	UK Great Britain	12 Mar 65	IGO Status/Immunit	561UNTS313	108191

PARTY ONE	PARTY TWO	DATE	TOPIC	CITATION	NUMBER
Investments (Cont.)					
Dahomey	USA (United States)	13 Mar 65	Claims and Debts	549UNTS43	107987
Multilateral		18 Mar 65	Dispute Settlement	575UNTS159	108359
Chad	USA (United States)	12 May 65	Finance	546UNTS183	107944
USA (United States)	Upper Volta	18 Jun 65	Finance	549UNTS133	107996
Ceylon (Sri Lanka)	USA (United States)	23 Feb 66	Finance	586UNTS91	108498
Singapore	USA (United States)	25 Mar 66	Finance	580UNTS221	108425
Judicial Matters and Personnel					
Multilateral		25 Jun 36	Privil/Immunities	161UNTS217	200486
Multilateral		27 Jun 39	ILO Labor	40UNTS311	100640
Multilateral		17 Feb 40	Privil/Immunities	161UNTS229	200487
Norway	USA (United States)	28 Mar 40	Specif Claim/Waive	88UNTS365	200253
Brazil	Venezuela	30 Mar 40	Dispute Settlement	51UNTS291	200195
Multilateral		22 Mar 45	General Amity	70UNTS237	200241
Multilateral		08 Aug 45	General Military	82UNTS279	200251
Iraq	Turkey	29 Mar 46	Admin Cooperation	37UNTS333	100581
Multilateral		10 Feb 47	Peace/Disarmament	42UNTS3	100645
Multilateral		10 Feb 47	Peace/Disarmament	41UNTS135	100644
Multilateral		10 Feb 47	Peace/Disarmament	49UNTS3	100747
Multilateral		10 Feb 47	Peace/Disarmament	41UNTS21	100643
Multilateral		10 Feb 47	Peace/Disarmament	48UNTS203	100746
Greece	Lebanon	10 Sep 47	Dispute Settlement	187UNTS107	102504
Czechoslovakia	Italy	25 Feb 48	Admin Cooperation	26UNTS103	100380
Czechoslovakia	Romania	01 Mar 48	Admin Cooperation	26UNTS109	100381
Bulgaria	Czechoslovakia	05 Mar 48	Admin Cooperation	26UNTS115	100382
Multilateral		08 Mar 48	Admin Cooperation	27UNTS117	100403
India	Pakistan	04 May 48	Dispute Settlement	54UNTS45	100794
Multilateral		09 Dec 48	Humanitarian	78UNTS277	101021
Czechoslovakia	Poland	21 Jan 49	Admin Cooperation	31UNTS205	100480
France	USA (United States)	14 Mar 49	Claims and Debts	84UNTS225	101132
Multilateral		28 Apr 49	Dispute Settlement	71UNTS101	100912
Italy	Netherlands	16 Aug 49	Admin Cooperation	98UNTS21	101357
Austria	Belgium	05 Nov 49	Extradition	48UNTS107	100739
Austria	Belgium	22 Dec 49	Admin Cooperation	46UNTS233	100712
Italy	Turkey	24 Mar 50	General Amity	96UNTS207	101338
Austria	UK Great Britain	28 Jun 51	Admin Cooperation	117UNTS99	101586
Australia	Austria	17 Nov 51	Admin Cooperation	133UNTS137	101785
Austria	Canada	18 Jan 52	Admin Cooperation	236UNTS245	103327
Multilateral		10 May 52	Taxation	439UNTS233	106332
Multilateral		10 May 52	Admin Cooperation	439UNTS193	106330
Multilateral		10 May 52	Admin Cooperation	439UNTS217	106331
Austria	New Zealand	10 Jun 52	Admin Cooperation	171UNTS263	102229
Belgium	Germany, West	14 Aug 52	Admin Cooperation	139UNTS29	101873
Germany, West	USA (United States)	27 Feb 53	Claims and Debts	224UNTS31	103068
Belgium	Israel	29 May 53	Admin Cooperation	219UNTS197	102975
Canada	Germany, West	30 Oct 53	Admin Cooperation	236UNTS317	103332
Jordan	Syria	23 Dec 53	Admin Cooperation	204UNTS207	102759
Multilateral		01 Mar 54	Admin Cooperation	286UNTS265	104173
Belgium	Germany, West	30 Mar 54	Admin Cooperation	190UNTS63	102558
Bulgaria	Czechoslovakia	13 Apr 54	Admin Cooperation	501UNTS3	107314
Brazil	Italy	24 Nov 54	Dispute Settlement	284UNTS325	104146
Multilateral		01 Dec 54	Admin Cooperation	210UNTS197	102839
Belgium	Brazil	10 Jan 55	Admin Cooperation	272UNTS181	103937
Germany, West	New Zealand	30 Mar 55	Admin Cooperation	271UNTS207	103916
Multilateral		13 Jul 56	Dispute Settlement	281UNTS3	104066
Germany, West	USA (United States)	27 Jul 56	Admin Cooperation	278UNTS3	104017
Netherlands	Switzerland	23 Oct 56	Admin Cooperation	287UNTS203	104186
Greece	Sweden	11 Dec 56	Dispute Settlement	299UNTS247	104316
Germany, East	Poland	01 Feb 57	Admin Cooperation	319UNTS115	104632
Germany, East	Hungary	30 Oct 57	Admin Cooperation	408UNTS4	105867
Fed of Malaya	UK Great Britain	04 Mar 58	Admin Cooperation	314UNTS253	104550
Israel	Sweden	20 Mar 58	Admin Cooperation	314UNTS99	104545
Hungary	USSR (Soviet Union)	24 Apr 58	Status of Forces	408UNTS118	105868
Austria	Netherlands	03 May 58	Admin Cooperation	342UNTS3	104895
Multilateral		26 Jun 58	Admin Cooperation	324UNTS97	104679

PARTY ONE	PARTY TWO	DATE	TOPIC	CITATION	NUMBER
Judicial Matters and Personnel (Cont.)					
Belgium	Germany, West	30 Jun 58	Admin Cooperation	387UNTS245	105566
Hungary	Romania	07 Oct 58	Admin Cooperation	416UNTS199	106004
Czechoslovakia	Romania	25 Oct 58	Admin Cooperation	417UNTS37	106006
Bulgaria	Romania	03 Dec 58	Admin Cooperation	417UNTS133	106007
Hungary	Poland	06 Mar 59	Admin Cooperation	432UNTS3	106216
Brazil	Netherlands	16 Mar 59	Admin Cooperation	499UNTS219	107300
Italy	Netherlands	17 Apr 59	Admin Cooperation	474UNTS207	106883
Multilateral		20 Apr 59	Admin Cooperation	472UNTS185	106841
Belgium	Switzerland	29 Apr 59	Admin Cooperation	443UNTS35	106356
Austria	Belgium	16 Jun 59	Admin Cooperation	419UNTS45	106029
Greece	Yugoslavia	18 Jun 59	Admin Cooperation	368UNTS81	105236
Greece	Yugoslavia	18 Jun 59	Admin Cooperation	368UNTS69	105235
Albania	Hungary	12 Jan 60	Admin Cooperation	520UNTS3	107511
Belgium	Netherlands	20 Jan 60	Admin Cooperation	373UNTS3	105310
Poland	Yugoslavia	06 Feb 60	Admin Cooperation	521UNTS37	107517
Germany, West	UK Great Britain	09 Mar 60	Admin Cooperation	403UNTS253	105796
Germany, West	Netherlands	08 Apr 60	Territory Boundary	508UNTS14	107404
Hungary	Yugoslavia	07 May 60	Admin Cooperation	519UNTS237	107510
Ghana	UK Great Britain	04 Jun 60	Admin Cooperation	377UNTS197	105401
Germany, West	UK Great Britain	14 Jul 60	Admin Cooperation	414UNTS144	105972
Cambodia	Thailand	15 Dec 60	Admin Cooperation	382UNTS307	105491
Cambodia	Thailand	15 Dec 60	Extradition	382UNTS321	105493
Germany, West	USA (United States)	03 Jan 61	Admin Cooperation	416UNTS93	105997
Germany, West	UK Great Britain	02 May 61	Admin Cooperation	414UNTS3	105959
Norway	UK Great Britain	12 Jun 61	Admin Cooperation	424UNTS173	106107
Czechoslovakia	Poland	04 Jul 61	Admin Cooperation	436UNTS189	106295
Austria	UK Great Britain	14 Jul 61	Admin Cooperation	453UNTS267	106530
Multilateral		05 Oct 61	Patents/Copyrights	527UNTS181	107625
Multilateral		05 Oct 61	Dispute Settlement	510UNTS175	107413
Czechoslovakia	Hungary	02 Nov 61	Admin Cooperation	438UNTS3	106313
Austria	Czechoslovakia	10 Nov 61	Admin Cooperation	455UNTS337	106550
Denmark	UK Great Britain	15 Nov 61	Dispute Settlement	420UNTS67	106041
Bulgaria	Poland	04 Dec 61	Admin Cooperation	484UNTS3	107019
Poland	Romania	25 Jan 62	Admin Cooperation	468UNTS3	106770
USSR (Soviet Union)	Yugoslavia	24 Feb 62	Admin Cooperation	471UNTS195	106833
Belgium	Italy	06 Apr 62	Admin Cooperation	490UNTS317	107161
Belgium	India	16 Jul 62	Admin Cooperation	453UNTS259	106529
Germany, West	Netherlands	30 Aug 62	Admin Cooperation	547UNTS173	107957
Germany, West	Netherlands	30 Aug 62	Admin Cooperation	500UNTS3	107303
Austria	Netherlands	06 Feb 63	Admin Cooperation	570UNTS101	108290
Netherlands	USA (United States)	06 Feb 63	Status of Forces	487UNTS113	107098
Tanganyika	UK Great Britain	03 Apr 63	Admin Cooperation	478UNTS23	106933
Czechoslovakia	Yugoslavia	20 Jan 64	Admin Cooperation	538UNTS197	107816
Austria	Netherlands	23 Jul 64	Admin Cooperation	544UNTS265	107921
Denmark	Tanganyika	04 Aug 64	Dispute Settlement	544UNTS123	107915
Belgium	Luxembourg	30 Sep 65	Consul/Citizenship	590UNTS35	108545
Italy	USA (United States)	16 Dec 65	Specif Claim/Waive	574UNTS139	108346
New Zealand	United Nations	21 Feb 66	IGO Operations	555UNTS163	108110
United Nations	Sweden	21 Feb 66	IGO Operations	555UNTS169	108111
Denmark	United Nations	21 Feb 66	IGO Operations	555UNTS151	108108
Canada	United Nations	21 Feb 66	IGO Operations	555UNTS119	108107
Finland	United Nations	21 Feb 66	IGO Operations	555UNTS157	108109
United Nations	UK Great Britain	21 Feb 66	General Economic	555UNTS177	108112
Austria	United Nations	24 Feb 66	IGO Operations	557UNTS129	108131
Australia	United Nations	25 Feb 66	IGO Operations	557UNTS85	108129
Belgium	Israel	26 Apr 66	Admin Cooperation	566UNTS187	108243
Sierra Leone	USA (United States)	06 May 66	Admin Cooperation	594UNTS47	108593
Guyana	UK Great Britain	26 May 66	Status of Forces	595UNTS255	108621
UK Great Britain	USA (United States)	27 Oct 66	Claims and Debts	597UNTS265	108650
Peru	UK Great Britain	03 Dec 66	Loans and Credits	617UNTS231	108915
Jurisdiction					
Norway	USA (United States)	28 Mar 40	Specif Claim/Waive	88UNTS365	200253
UK Great Britain	USA (United States)	27 Jul 42	Status of Forces	117UNTS311	200378
India	USA (United States)	16 Oct 42	Status of Forces	109UNTS111	200353

PARTY ONE	PARTY TWO	DATE	TOPIC	CITATION	NUMBER
Jurisdiction (Cont.)					
UK Great Britain	USA (United States)	03 Nov 42	Admin Cooperation	109UNTS127	200354
New Zealand	USA (United States)	28 Jan 43	Admin Cooperation	121UNTS123	200395
Taiwan	USA (United States)	21 May 43	Status of Forces	14UNTS353	200093
Belgium	USA (United States)	04 Aug 43	Status of Forces	109UNTS149	200356
Canada	USA (United States)	13 Aug 43	Admin Cooperation	109UNTS135	200355
UK Great Britain	USA (United States)	24 Sep 43	Admin Cooperation	139UNTS373	200463
Turkey	UK Great Britain	23 Mar 44	Specif Claim/Waive	2UNTS227	200015
Australia	USA (United States)	10 May 44	Reparations	106UNTS237	200343
Belgium	UK Great Britain	16 May 44	Admin Cooperation	90UNTS283	200266
Netherlands	USA (United States)	16 May 44	Milit Occupation	132UNTS355	200440
Norway	USA (United States)	16 May 44	Privil/Immunities	67UNTS253	200223
France	USA (United States)	25 Aug 44	Milit Occupation	138UNTS247	200449
Taiwan	UK Great Britain	07 Jul 45	Status of Forces	14UNTS455	200100
ICJ Option Clause	UK Great Britain	13 Feb 46	ICJ Option Clause	1UNTS3	100001
ICJ Option Clause	Netherlands	05 Aug 46	ICJ Option Clause	1UNTS7	100002
ICJ Option Clause	USA (United States)	14 Aug 46	ICJ Option Clause	1UNTS9	100003
Poland	USA (United States)	29 Aug 46	Status of Forces	160UNTS11	102097
ICJ Option Clause	Taiwan	26 Oct 46	ICJ Option Clause	1UNTS35	100005
Syria	UK Great Britain	02 Nov 46	Dispute Settlement	11UNTS153	100153
ICJ Option Clause	Norway	16 Nov 46	ICJ Option Clause	1UNTS37	100006
ICJ Option Clause	Denmark	10 Dec 46	ICJ Option Clause	1UNTS45	100010
ICJ Option Clause	Guatemala	27 Jan 47	ICJ Option Clause	1UNTS49	100012
Multilateral		10 Feb 47	Peace/Disarmament	42UNTS3	100645
Multilateral		10 Feb 47	Peace/Disarmament	41UNTS135	100644
Multilateral		10 Feb 47	Peace/Disarmament	48UNTS203	100746
Multilateral		10 Feb 47	Peace/Disarmament	41UNTS21	100643
ICJ Option Clause	France	18 Feb 47	ICJ Option Clause	26UNTS91	100378
ICJ Option Clause	Sweden	05 Apr 47	ICJ Option Clause	2UNTS3	100016
Nepal	USA (United States)	25 Apr 47	Consul/Citizenship	16UNTS97	100251
ICJ Option Clause	Turkey	22 May 47	ICJ Option Clause	4UNTS265	100050
ICJ Option Clause	Philippines	12 Jul 47	ICJ Option Clause	7UNTS229	100101
ICJ Option Clause	Mexico	23 Oct 47	ICJ Option Clause	9UNTS97	100127
ICJ Option Clause	Honduras	02 Feb 48	ICJ Option Clause	15UNTS217	100236
ICJ Option Clause	Brazil	12 Feb 48	ICJ Option Clause	15UNTS221	100237
Czechoslovakia	Italy	25 Feb 48	Admin Cooperation	26UNTS103	100380
Multilateral		08 Mar 48	Admin Cooperation	27UNTS117	100403
ICJ Option Clause	Belgium	10 Jun 48	ICJ Option Clause	16UNTS203	100260
ICJ Option Clause	Pakistan	22 Jun 48	ICJ Option Clause	16UNTS197	100259
Greece	USA (United States)	02 Jul 48	Mostfavored Nation	31UNTS131	100474
ICJ Option Clause	Bolivia	05 Jul 48	ICJ Option Clause	16UNTS207	100261
ICJ Option Clause	Switzerland	06 Jul 48	ICJ Option Clause	17UNTS115	100272
ICJ Option Clause	Liechtenstein	10 Mar 50	ICJ Option Clause	51UNTS119	100759
ICJ Option Clause	Thailand	20 May 50	ICJ Option Clause	65UNTS157	100844
Korea, South	USA (United States)	12 Jul 50	Status of Forces	222UNTS229	103029
UK Great Britain	USA (United States)	01 Aug 50	Milit Installation	88UNTS273	101199
FAO (Food Agri)	United Nations	02 Aug 50	IGO Operations	139UNTS407	200467
ICJ Option Clause	Israel	04 Sep 50	ICJ Option Clause	108UNTS239	101477
ILO (Labor Org)	United Nations	12 Oct 50	IGO Operations	139UNTS395	200466
ICAO (Civil Aviat)	United Nations	28 Feb 51	IGO Operations	139UNTS429	200469
UNESCO (Educ/Cult)	United Nations	07 Mar 51	IGO Operations	139UNTS417	200468
ICJ Option Clause	Japan	24 Nov 51	ICJ Option Clause	137UNTS3	101842
ICJ Option Clause	Liberia	03 Mar 52	ICJ Option Clause	163UNTS117	102145
ICJ Option Clause	Ceylon (Sri Lanka)	23 Apr 52	UN Charter	137UNTS7	101843
ICJ Option Clause	Cambodia	17 Jul 52	UN Charter	137UNTS11	101844
ICJ Option Clause	Laos	24 Oct 52	UN Charter	149UNTS285	101957
ICJ Option Clause	Vietnam, South	05 Nov 52	ICJ Option Clause	150UNTS147	101968
Multilateral		10 Nov 52	Admin Cooperation	214UNTS265	102904
Netherlands	USA (United States)	19 Jun 53	Admin Cooperation	212UNTS249	102875
Multilateral		26 Oct 53	Status of Forces	207UNTS237	102809
ICJ Option Clause	Australia	06 Feb 54	ICJ Option Clause	186UNTS77	102484
ICJ Option Clause	Finland	26 Feb 54	Dispute Settlement	189UNTS223	102546
Libya	USA (United States)	09 Sep 54	Milit Installation	224UNTS217	103078
ICJ Option Clause	UK Great Britain	02 Jun 55	ICJ Option Clause	211UNTS109	102849
ICJ Option Clause	South Africa	12 Sep 55	ICJ Option Clause	216UNTS115	102935
ICJ Option Clause	UK Great Britain	31 Oct 55	ICJ Option Clause	219UNTS179	102973

PARTY ONE	PARTY TWO	DATE	TOPIC	CITATION	NUMBER
Jurisdiction (Cont.)					
ICJ Option Clause	Portugal	19 Dec 55	ICJ Option Clause	224UNTS275	103079
ICJ Option Clause	India	07 Jan 56	ICJ Option Clause	226UNTS235	103116
ICJ Option Clause	Israel	03 Oct 56	ICJ Option Clause	252UNTS301	103571
ICJ Option Clause	Denmark	10 Dec 56	ICJ Option Clause	257UNTS35	103646
ICJ Option Clause	Norway	17 Dec 56	ICJ Option Clause	256UNTS315	103642
ICJ Option Clause	Sweden	06 Apr 57	ICJ Option Clause	264UNTS221	103794
ICJ Option Clause	UK Great Britain	18 Apr 57	ICJ Option Clause	265UNTS221	103814
ICJ Option Clause	Pakistan	23 May 57	ICJ Option Clause	269UNTS77	103875
Special Decla ICJ	United Arab Rep	18 Jun 57	ICJ Option Clause	272UNTS225	103940
ICJ Option Clause	Cambodia	09 Sep 57	ICJ Option Clause	277UNTS77	103998
ICJ Option Clause	Sudan	30 Dec 57	ICJ Option Clause	284UNTS215	104139
ICJ Option Clause	Belgium	03 Apr 58	ICJ Option Clause	302UNTS251	104364
ICJ Option Clause	Finland	25 Jun 58	ICJ Option Clause	303UNTS137	104376
ICJ Option Clause	Japan	15 Sep 58	ICJ Option Clause	312UNTS155	104517
ICJ Option Clause	UK Great Britain	26 Nov 58	ICJ Option Clause	316UNTS59	104577
ICJ Option Clause	France	10 Jul 59	ICJ Option Clause	337UNTS65	104816
ICJ Option Clause	India	14 Sep 59	ICJ Option Clause	340UNTS289	104871
Germany, West	Netherlands	08 Apr 60	Territory Boundary	508UNTS14	107404
Somalia	UK Great Britain	26 Jun 60	Recognition	374UNTS357	105349
Ghana	UK Great Britain	05 Jul 60	Admin Cooperation	402UNTS17	105774
ICJ Option Clause	Pakistan	12 Sep 60	ICJ Option Clause	374UNTS127	105332
ICJ Option Clause	Somalia	25 Mar 63	ICJ Option Clause	458UNTS143	106597
ICJ Option Clause	UK Great Britain	27 Nov 63	ICJ Option Clause	482UNTS187	106995
ICJ Option Clause	Kenya	12 Apr 65	ICJ Option Clause	531UNTS113	107697
ICJ Option Clause	Nigeria	14 Aug 65	ICJ Option Clause	544UNTS113	107913
ICJ Option Clause	France	16 May 66	ICJ Option Clause	562UNTS299	108196
ICJ Option Clause	Gambia	14 Jun 66	ICJ Option Clause	565UNTS21	108232
ICJ Option Clause	Malawi	22 Nov 66	ICJ Option Clause	581UNTS135	108438
ICJ Option Clause	Malta	29 Nov 66	ICJ Option Clause	580UNTS205	108423
Juvenile Employment					
Multilateral		28 Nov 19	ILO Labor	38UNTS93	100589
Multilateral		11 Nov 21	ILO Labor	38UNTS203	100598
Multilateral		11 Nov 21	ILO Labor	38UNTS217	100599
Multilateral		09 Oct 46	ILO Labor	78UNTS198	101017
Multilateral		09 Oct 46	ILO Labor	78UNTS227	101019
Multilateral		09 Oct 46	ILO Labor	78UNTS213	101018
Multilateral		10 Jul 48	ILO Labor	91UNTS3	101239
Labor					
Canada	USA (United States)	04 Nov 42	Non-ILO Labor	24UNTS217	200146
Mexico	USA (United States)	26 Apr 43	Non-ILO Labor	21UNTS245	200127
Mexico	USA (United States)	29 Apr 43	Non-ILO Labor	105UNTS119	200327
Dominican Republic	USA (United States)	19 Oct 43	Non-ILO Labor	21UNTS295	200130
Multilateral		07 Nov 45	IGO Establishment	2UNTS17	100018
ILO (Labor Org)	Switzerland	11 Mar 46	IGO Status/Immunit	15UNTS377	200103
Greece	UK Great Britain	21 Mar 46	Claims and Debts	91UNTS149	101247
Belgium	Italy	23 Jun 46	Non-ILO Labor	19UNTS65	100305
Multilateral		09 Oct 46	ILO Labor	38UNTS3	100583
Multilateral		09 Oct 46	IGO Establishment	15UNTS35	100229
Denmark	Sweden	18 Nov 46	Non-ILO Labor	7UNTS251	100104
Albania	Yugoslavia	28 Nov 46	Non-ILO Labor	111UNTS163	101529
ILO (Labor Org)	United Nations	19 Dec 46	IGO Operations	1UNTS183	200009
Philippines	USA (United States)	16 May 47	Non-ILO Labor	280UNTS177	104057
Canada	USA (United States)	19 May 47	Non-ILO Labor	43UNTS97	100663
Italy	UK Great Britain	30 May 47	Non-ILO Labor	54UNTS131	100800
France	UK Great Britain	13 Aug 47	Non-ILO Labor	91UNTS169	101249
Belgium	Netherlands	29 Aug 47	Non-ILO Labor	36UNTS349	100573
France	USA (United States)	25 Oct 47	Non-ILO Labor	89UNTS111	101212
France	Netherlands	02 Jan 48	Visas	70UNTS105	100899
Belgium	France	17 Jan 48	Non-ILO Labor	36UNTS233	100570
Belgium	Italy	09 Feb 48	Non-ILO Labor	71UNTS143	100915
Denmark	Switzerland	21 Feb 48	Non-ILO Labor	14UNTS321	100224
Belgium	Luxembourg	25 Mar 48	Taxation	18UNTS323	100300
Belgium	France	23 Apr 48	Territory Boundary	19UNTS95	100307
Belgium	Italy	30 Apr 48	Non-ILO Labor	36UNTS305	100571

PARTY ONE	PARTY TWO	DATE	TOPIC	CITATION	NUMBER
Labor (Cont.)					
France	Netherlands	02 Jun 48	Non-ILO Labor	204UNTS275	102762
France	Poland	09 Jun 48	Non-ILO Labor	32UNTS251	100503
Czechoslovakia	France	12 Oct 48	Non-ILO Labor	45UNTS81	100693
Italy	Netherlands	04 Dec 48	Non-ILO Labor	46UNTS271	100716
Norway	Sweden	18 Dec 48	Non-ILO Labor	30UNTS117	100450
Italy	UK Great Britain	28 Jul 50	Non-ILO Labor	101UNTS25	101399
Luxembourg	Netherlands	25 Aug 50	Non-ILO Labor	81UNTS13	101058
Netherlands	New Zealand	16 Oct 50	Non-ILO Labor	83UNTS269	101111
France	Turkey	22 Dec 50	Non-ILO Labor	98UNTS11	101356
Mexico	USA (United States)	11 Aug 51	Non-ILO Labor	162UNTS103	102133
Belgium	France	29 Nov 52	Visas	160UNTS261	102110
Multilateral		22 May 54	Non-ILO Labor	199UNTS3	102674
El Salvador	USA (United States)	08 Aug 55	Non-IBRD Project	264UNTS301	103801
Philippines	UK Great Britain	29 Aug 55	Non-ILO Labor	221UNTS241	103009
Multilateral		07 Jun 56	Non-ILO Labor	381UNTS145	105470
Belgium	Spain	28 Nov 56	Non-ILO Labor	308UNTS285	104465
France	Italy	28 Dec 56	Non-ILO Labor	291UNTS203	104255
France	Italy	01 Aug 57	Non-ILO Labor	302UNTS221	104360
France	Italy	19 Sep 57	Non-ILO Labor	302UNTS225	104361
Belgium	France	12 Nov 57	Non-ILO Labor	328UNTS167	104734
Canada	USA (United States)	31 Oct 58	Non-ILO Labor	391UNTS219	105626
Italy	Netherlands	06 Aug 60	Non-ILO Labor	455UNTS259	106546
Austria	Turkey	15 May 64	Non-ILO Labor	515UNTS109	107457
Netherlands	Turkey	19 Aug 64	Non-ILO Labor	521UNTS197	107523
ILO (Labor Org)	LAFTA (Free Trade)	02 Jul 65	IGO Operations	563UNTS327	200619
ILO (Labor Org)	Org Ctrl Am States	26 Jul 65	IGO Operations	563UNTS341	200620
Austria	Yugoslavia	19 Nov 65	Non-ILO Labor	587UNTS239	108512
France	UK Great Britain	19 Nov 65	Non-ILO Labor	561UNTS19	108178
Land Reform					
Taiwan	USA (United States)	05 Aug 48	IGO Establishment	82UNTS109	101087
Law of the Sea					
Multilateral		29 Apr 58	Territory Boundary	516UNTS205	107477
Multilateral		29 Apr 58	Water Transport	450UNTS11	106465
Multilateral		29 Apr 58	Dispute Settlement	450UNTS169	106466
Lead Poisoning					
Multilateral		19 Nov 21	ILO Labor	38UNTS175	100596
Legal Aid					
Belgium	Brazil	10 Jan 55	Admin Cooperation	272UNTS181	103937
Israel	Italy	24 Feb 56	Extradition	316UNTS97	104580
Belgium	France	01 Mar 56	Admin Cooperation	337UNTS53	104815
France	Sweden	07 Mar 56	Admin Cooperation	369UNTS155	105256
France	Sweden	07 Mar 56	Admin Cooperation	369UNTS171	105257
Bulgaria	Yugoslavia	23 Mar 56	Admin Cooperation	367UNTS213	105230
Czechoslovakia	USSR (Soviet Union)	31 Aug 57	Admin Cooperation	308UNTS3	104456
Germany, East	USSR (Soviet Union)	28 Nov 57	Admin Cooperation	305UNTS113	104419
Bulgaria	USSR (Soviet Union)	12 Dec 57	Admin Cooperation	317UNTS217	104606
Korea, North	USSR (Soviet Union)	16 Dec 57	Admin Cooperation	301UNTS301	104349
Poland	USSR (Soviet Union)	28 Dec 57	Admin Cooperation	320UNTS3	104638
Belgium	Germany, West	17 Jan 58	Extradition	328UNTS173	104735
Romania	USSR (Soviet Union)	03 Apr 58	Admin Cooperation	313UNTS167	104535
Albania	USSR (Soviet Union)	30 Jun 58	Admin Cooperation	328UNTS3	104729
Germany, East	Romania	15 Jul 58	Admin Cooperation	395UNTS3	105681
Hungary	USSR (Soviet Union)	15 Jul 58	Admin Cooperation	322UNTS3	104656
Mongolia	USSR (Soviet Union)	25 Aug 58	Admin Cooperation	322UNTS105	104657
France	Israel	12 Nov 58	Admin Cooperation	345UNTS79	104960
Germany, West	Norway	18 Nov 58	Taxation	357UNTS205	105119
Albania	Czechoslovakia	16 Jan 59	Admin Cooperation	363UNTS195	105208
Belgium	Morocco	27 Feb 59	Extradition	390UNTS275	105611
Leisure Time					
Multilateral		17 Nov 21	ILO Labor	38UNTS187	100597
Lend-lease					
Iceland	USA (United States)	21 Nov 41	Milit Assistance	124UNTS179	200418

PARTY ONE	PARTY TWO	DATE	TOPIC	CITATION	NUMBER
Lend-lease (Cont.)					
Taiwan	USA (United States)	02 Jun 42	Milit Assistance	14UNTS343	200092
Czechoslovakia	USA (United States)	11 Jul 42	Milit Assistance	90UNTS257	200263
USA (United States)	Yugoslavia	24 Jul 42	Milit Assistance	34UNTS361	200179
Netherlands	USA (United States)	14 Jun 43	General Military	28UNTS397	200163
France	USA (United States)	25 Sep 43	Direct Aid	76UNTS183	200245
France	USA (United States)	20 Feb 45	IGO Status/Immunit	76UNTS223	200248
France	USA (United States)	20 Feb 45	Direct Aid	76UNTS193	200246
France	USA (United States)	28 Feb 45	IGO Status/Immunit	76UNTS213	200247
South Africa	USA (United States)	17 Apr 45	Direct Aid	90UNTS267	200264
Belgium	USA (United States)	17 Apr 45	Milit Assistance	139UNTS253	200454
Netherlands	USA (United States)	30 Apr 45	Milit Assistance	139UNTS341	200460
USA (United States)	USSR (Soviet Union)	15 Oct 45	Milit Assistance	278UNTS151	200547
France	USA (United States)	08 Nov 45	General Trade	76UNTS151	100986
UK Great Britain	USA (United States)	27 Mar 46	Milit Assistance	4UNTS2	100039
Turkey	USA (United States)	07 May 46	Milit Assistance	6UNTS293	100083
UK Great Britain	USA (United States)	07 May 46	Water Transport	6UNTS285	100082
India	USA (United States)	16 May 46	Milit Assistance	4UNTS183	100045
France	USA (United States)	28 May 46	Milit Assistance	84UNTS59	101119
France	USA (United States)	28 May 46	Reparations	84UNTS113	101122
France	USA (United States)	28 May 46	Reparations	84UNTS93	101121
Australia	USA (United States)	07 Jun 46	Milit Assistance	4UNTS237	100048
Taiwan	USA (United States)	14 Jun 46	Milit Assistance	4UNTS253	100049
Taiwan	USA (United States)	28 Jun 46	Milit Assistance	34UNTS121	100532
Brazil	USA (United States)	28 Jun 46	Milit Assistance	6UNTS327	100085
New Zealand	USA (United States)	10 Jul 46	Milit Assistance	6UNTS341	100087
UK Great Britain	USA (United States)	31 Jul 46	Air Transport	42UNTS199	100648
Belgium	USA (United States)	24 Sep 46	Claims and Debts	132UNTS80	101753
South Africa	USA (United States)	21 Mar 47	Milit Assistance	16UNTS47	100248
Netherlands	USA (United States)	28 May 47	General Military	17UNTS29	100267
Greece	USA (United States)	20 Jun 47	Direct Aid	7UNTS267	100105
Taiwan	USA (United States)	08 Dec 47	Milit Installation	70UNTS3	100895
Norway	USA (United States)	24 Feb 48	Milit Assistance	34UNTS155	100535
France	USA (United States)	27 Feb 48	Reparations	84UNTS207	101131
UK Great Britain	Uruguay	12 Jul 48	Finance	71UNTS199	100919
USA (United States)	Yugoslavia	19 Jul 48	Milit Assistance	34UNTS195	100537
New Zealand	USA (United States)	14 Sep 48	General Military	18UNTS251	100295
Czechoslovakia	USA (United States)	16 Sep 48	Milit Assistance	90UNTS35	101224
UK Great Britain	USA (United States)	22 Sep 48	Milit Assistance	71UNTS64	100910
Multilateral		08 Oct 48	Education	19UNTS113	100308
France	USA (United States)	14 Mar 49	Claims and Debts	84UNTS237	101133
Canada	USA (United States)	14 Mar 49	Reparations	82UNTS3	101079
Netherlands	USA (United States)	17 May 49	Milit Assistance	46UNTS291	100717
Ethiopia	USA (United States)	20 May 49	Milit Assistance	89UNTS99	101211
USA (United States)	USSR (Soviet Union)	27 Sep 49	Milit Assistance	149UNTS23	101948
Australia	USA (United States)	26 Nov 49	Reparations	45UNTS133	100695
India	USA (United States)	02 Feb 50	Education	89UNTS127	101214
Pakistan	USA (United States)	23 Sep 50	Education	82UNTS131	101088
Canada	USA (United States)	19 Mar 52	Status of Forces	174UNTS267	102291
USA (United States)	USSR (Soviet Union)	26 Mar 54	Milit Assistance	247UNTS263	103475
Netherlands	USA (United States)	25 May 55	Claims and Debts	289UNTS227	104220
USA (United States)	USSR (Soviet Union)	26 May 55	Milit Assistance	270UNTS61	103892
Poland	USA (United States)	28 Jun 56	Claims and Debts	273UNTS79	103944
Finland	Sweden	07 Jul 56	General Transport	258UNTS83	103672
Leprosy					
Burma	WHO (World Health)	09 Jul 51	Sanitation	107UNTS9	101463
Burma	WHO (World Health)	09 Jun 52	Sanitation	134UNTS273	101806
Libraries					
Poland	UK Great Britain	24 Jun 46	Claims and Debts	11UNTS59	100149
League of Nations	United Nations	19 Jul 46	Specific Property	1UNTS109	200002
League of Nations	United Nations	31 Jul 46	Specific Property	1UNTS119	200003
League of Nations	United Nations	01 Aug 46	Specific Property	1UNTS135	200005
League of Nations	United Nations	14 Apr 47	Specific Property	4UNTS449	200027
Multilateral		30 Apr 53	Admin Cooperation	175UNTS89	102297
Loans					
Haiti	USA (United States)	30 Sep 42	Other Ad Hoc	24UNTS205	200144
Haiti	USA (United States)	14 May 46	Finance	4UNTS179	100044
Haiti	USA (United States)	30 Sep 46	Other Ad Hoc	15UNTS257	100241
France	IBRD (World Bank)	09 May 47	IBRD Project	152UNTS111	102014
Haiti	USA (United States)	04 Jul 47	Other Ad Hoc	22UNTS165	100335
Netherlands	IBRD (World Bank)	07 Aug 47	IBRD Project	152UNTS165	102015
Denmark	IBRD (World Bank)	22 Aug 47	IBRD Project	152UNTS223	102016
Luxembourg	IBRD (World Bank)	28 Aug 47	IBRD Project	153UNTS3	102017
United Nations	USA (United States)	23 Mar 48	Loans and Credits	19UNTS43	100303
Netherlands	IBRD (World Bank)	15 Jul 48	IBRD Project	153UNTS211	102020
Netherlands	IBRD (World Bank)	15 Jul 48	IBRD Project	153UNTS259	102024
Netherlands	IBRD (World Bank)	15 Jul 48	IBRD Project	153UNTS259	102023
Netherlands	IBRD (World Bank)	15 Jul 48	IBRD Project	153UNTS259	102021
Netherlands	IBRD (World Bank)	15 Jul 48	IBRD Project	153UNTS259	102022
Netherlands	IBRD (World Bank)	15 Jul 48	IBRD Project	153UNTS259	102025
Mexico	IBRD (World Bank)	06 Jan 49	IBRD Project	154UNTS81	102028
Mexico	IBRD (World Bank)	06 Jan 49	IBRD Project	154UNTS3	102027
Brazil	IBRD (World Bank)	27 Jan 49	IBRD Project	153UNTS264	102026
Belgium	IBRD (World Bank)	01 Mar 49	IBRD Project	154UNTS133	102029
Chile	IBRD (World Bank)	23 Mar 49	IBRD Project	153UNTS141	102019
Chile	IBRD (World Bank)	23 Mar 49	IBRD Project	153UNTS61	102018
Netherlands	IBRD (World Bank)	26 Jul 49	IBRD Project	154UNTS178	102030
Finland	IBRD (World Bank)	01 Aug 49	IBRD Project	156UNTS289	200480
India	IBRD (World Bank)	18 Aug 49	IBRD Project	154UNTS269	102031
Colombia	IBRD (World Bank)	19 Aug 49	IBRD Project	154UNTS329	102032
Multilateral		02 Sep 49	IGO Status/Immunit	250UNTS12	103515
Belgium	Netherlands	07 Sep 49	Loans and Credits	117UNTS3	101581
Belgium	France	07 Sep 49	Loans and Credits	123UNTS13	101651
Belgium	UK Great Britain	07 Sep 49	Loans and Credits	106UNTS61	101457
IBRD (World Bank)	Yugoslavia	17 Sep 49	IBRD Project	155UNTS3	102034
India	IBRD (World Bank)	29 Sep 49	IBRD Project	154UNTS393	102033
Finland	IBRD (World Bank)	17 Oct 49	IBRD Project	156UNTS355	200481
El Salvador	IBRD (World Bank)	14 Dec 49	IBRD Project	155UNTS43	102035
India	IBRD (World Bank)	18 Apr 50	IBRD Project	155UNTS117	102036
Mexico	IBRD (World Bank)	28 Apr 50	IBRD Project	155UNTS185	102037
Brazil	IBRD (World Bank)	26 May 50	IBRD Project	301UNTS165	104345
Iraq	IBRD (World Bank)	15 Jun 50	IBRD Project	155UNTS267	102038
Multilateral		28 Jun 50	Loans and Credits	87UNTS153	101170
IBRD (World Bank)	Turkey	07 Jul 50	IBRD Project	156UNTS3	102039
IBRD (World Bank)	Turkey	07 Jul 50	IBRD Project	156UNTS75	102040
IBRD (World Bank)	Uruguay	25 Aug 50	IBRD Project	156UNTS203	102042
Ethiopia	IBRD (World Bank)	13 Sep 50	IBRD Project	157UNTS213	102055
Ethiopia	IBRD (World Bank)	13 Sep 50	IBRD Project	157UNTS233	102056
Mexico	IBRD (World Bank)	18 Oct 50	IBRD Project	157UNTS259	102057
IBRD (World Bank)	Turkey	19 Oct 50	IBRD Project	157UNTS333	102058
IBRD (World Bank)	Thailand	27 Oct 50	IBRD Project	158UNTS43	102061
IBRD (World Bank)	Thailand	27 Oct 50	IBRD Project	158UNTS3	102059
IBRD (World Bank)	Thailand	27 Oct 50	IBRD Project	158UNTS25	102060
Colombia	IBRD (World Bank)	02 Nov 50	IBRD Project	158UNTS59	102062
Australia	IBRD (World Bank)	14 Nov 50	IBRD Project	156UNTS147	102041
Colombia	IBRD (World Bank)	28 Dec 50	IBRD Project	158UNTS87	102063
IBRD (World Bank)	South Africa	23 Jan 51	IBRD Project	158UNTS135	102065
IBRD (World Bank)	South Africa	23 Jan 51	IBRD Project	158UNTS115	102064
Ethiopia	IBRD (World Bank)	19 Feb 51	IBRD Project	186UNTS101	102486
Colombia	IBRD (World Bank)	10 Apr 51	IBRD Project	158UNTS155	102066
Nicaragua	IBRD (World Bank)	07 Jun 51	IBRD Project	158UNTS215	102067
Nicaragua	IBRD (World Bank)	07 Jun 51	IBRD Project	158UNTS277	102068
Iceland	IBRD (World Bank)	20 Jun 51	IBRD Project	158UNTS301	102069
Belgium	IBRD (World Bank)	13 Sep 51	IBRD Project	158UNTS323	102070
Belgium	IBRD (World Bank)	13 Sep 51	IBRD Project	158UNTS349	102071
Italy	IBRD (World Bank)	10 Oct 51	IBRD Project	159UNTS383	200482
IBRD (World Bank)	Yugoslavia	11 Oct 51	IBRD Project	159UNTS3	102081
Colombia	IBRD (World Bank)	13 Oct 51	IBRD Project	159UNTS75	102084
Nicaragua	IBRD (World Bank)	29 Oct 51	IBRD Project	159UNTS35	102082

Loans (Cont.)

PARTY ONE	PARTY TWO	DATE	TOPIC	CITATION	NUMBER
Iceland	IBRD (World Bank)	01 Nov 51	IBRD Project	159UNTS55	102083
Paraguay	IBRD (World Bank)	07 Dec 51	IBRD Project	159UNTS103	102085
Mexico	IBRD (World Bank)	11 Jan 52	IBRD Project	159UNTS129	102086
Peru	IBRD (World Bank)	23 Jan 52	IBRD Project	159UNTS163	102087
IBRD (World Bank)	UK Great Britain	27 Feb 52	IBRD Project	159UNTS181	102088
Netherlands	IBRD (World Bank)	20 Mar 52	IBRD Project	159UNTS207	102089
Pakistan	IBRD (World Bank)	27 Mar 52	IBRD Project	159UNTS251	102090
Finland	IBRD (World Bank)	30 Apr 52	IBRD Project	159UNTS408	200483
Pakistan	IBRD (World Bank)	13 Jun 52	IBRD Project	191UNTS85	102578
IBRD (World Bank)	Turkey	18 Jun 52	IBRD Project	159UNTS269	102091
Brazil	IBRD (World Bank)	27 Jun 52	IBRD Project	190UNTS85	102560
Brazil	IBRD (World Bank)	27 Jun 52	IBRD Project	190UNTS115	102561
Peru	IBRD (World Bank)	08 Jul 52	IBRD Project	159UNTS321	102093
Iceland	IBRD (World Bank)	26 Aug 52	IBRD Project	159UNTS363	102095
Colombia	IBRD (World Bank)	26 Aug 52	IBRD Project	159UNTS339	102094
Pakistan	USA (United States)	17 Sep 52	Loans and Credits	227UNTS77	103132
Japan	IBRD (World Bank)	12 Nov 52	IBRD Project	354UNTS313	105068
India	IBRD (World Bank)	18 Dec 52	IBRD Project	201UNTS241	102719
India	IBRD (World Bank)	23 Jan 53	IBRD Project	201UNTS145	102715
IBRD (World Bank)	Yugoslavia	11 Feb 53	IBRD Project	165UNTS231	102179
IBRD (World Bank)	UK Great Britain	11 Mar 53	IBRD Project	172UNTS115	102243
Brazil	IBRD (World Bank)	30 Apr 53	IBRD Project	190UNTS133	102562
UK Great Britain	USA (United States)	26 Jun 53	Loans and Credits	183UNTS225	102432
Brazil	IBRD (World Bank)	17 Jul 53	IBRD Project	190UNTS149	102563
Multilateral		20 Jul 53	Non-ILO Labor	227UNTS217	103140
Multilateral		24 Jul 53	General Amity	250UNTS108	103520
IBRD (World Bank)	South Africa	28 Aug 53	IBRD Project	180UNTS91	102377
IBRD (World Bank)	South Africa	28 Aug 53	IBRD Project	180UNTS73	102376
Iceland	IBRD (World Bank)	04 Sep 53	IBRD Project	178UNTS275	102344
Nicaragua	IBRD (World Bank)	04 Sep 53	IBRD Project	186UNTS117	102487
Iceland	IBRD (World Bank)	04 Sep 53	IBRD Project	188UNTS3	102519
Nicaragua	IBRD (World Bank)	04 Sep 53	IBRD Project	186UNTS137	102488
IBRD (World Bank)	Turkey	10 Sep 53	IBRD Project	187UNTS71	102502
Colombia	IBRD (World Bank)	10 Sep 53	IBRD Project	203UNTS3	102738
Chile	IBRD (World Bank)	10 Sep 53	IBRD Project	188UNTS25	102520
Panama	IBRD (World Bank)	25 Sep 53	IBRD Project	188UNTS95	102522
Panama	IBRD (World Bank)	25 Sep 53	IBRD Project	188UNTS71	102521
Italy	IBRD (World Bank)	06 Oct 53	IBRD Project	301UNTS135	104344
Japan	IBRD (World Bank)	15 Oct 53	IBRD Project	187UNTS321	200512
Japan	IBRD (World Bank)	15 Oct 53	IBRD Project	187UNTS367	200513
Japan	IBRD (World Bank)	15 Oct 53	IBRD Project	187UNTS271	200511
Brazil	IBRD (World Bank)	18 Dec 53	IBRD Project	301UNTS229	104346
Brazil	IBRD (World Bank)	18 Dec 53	IBRD Project	190UNTS179	102564
Finland	USSR (Soviet Union)	06 Feb 54	Loans and Credits	221UNTS143	103006
Ecuador	IBRD (World Bank)	10 Feb 54	IBRD Project	209UNTS261	102830
Brazil	IBRD (World Bank)	24 Feb 54	IBRD Project	301UNTS249	104347
Australia	IBRD (World Bank)	02 Mar 54	IBRD Project	191UNTS103	102579
Norway	IBRD (World Bank)	08 Apr 54	IBRD Project	201UNTS131	102714
Peru	IBRD (World Bank)	12 Apr 54	IBRD Project	190UNTS231	102567
ECSC (Coal/Steel)	USA (United States)	23 Apr 54	Loans and Credits	229UNTS229	103170
Pakistan	IBRD (World Bank)	02 Jun 54	IBRD Project	324UNTS59	104678
France	IBRD (World Bank)	10 Jun 54	IBRD Project	210UNTS89	102836
Italy	USA (United States)	16 Jun 54	Loans and Credits	236UNTS149	103322
Ceylon (Sri Lanka)	IBRD (World Bank)	09 Jul 54	IBRD Project	198UNTS313	200517
Mexico	IBRD (World Bank)	24 Aug 54	IBRD Project	286UNTS211	104168
Multilateral		02 Oct 54	IBRD Project	201UNTS171	102716
Multilateral		02 Oct 54	IBRD Project	201UNTS179	102717
El Salvador	IBRD (World Bank)	12 Oct 54	IBRD Project	203UNTS37	102739
Austria	IBRD (World Bank)	08 Nov 54	IBRD Project	216UNTS305	200528
Peru	IBRD (World Bank)	12 Nov 54	IBRD Project	209UNTS287	102831
India	IBRD (World Bank)	19 Nov 54	IBRD Project	309UNTS159	104473
Belgium	IBRD (World Bank)	14 Dec 54	IBRD Project	210UNTS113	102837
Colombia	IBRD (World Bank)	29 Dec 54	IBRD Project	211UNTS135	102851
Finland	USSR (Soviet Union)	24 Jan 55	Loans and Credits	240UNTS243	103406
IBRD (World Bank)	UK Great Britain	15 Mar 55	IBRD Project	265UNTS85	103808

Loans (Cont.)

PARTY ONE	PARTY TWO	DATE	TOPIC	CITATION	NUMBER
Australia	IBRD (World Bank)	18 Mar 55	IBRD Project	220UNTS131	102998
Finland	IBRD (World Bank)	24 Mar 55	IBRD Project	211UNTS305	200525
Colombia	IBRD (World Bank)	24 Mar 55	IBRD Project	212UNTS217	102874
Peru	IBRD (World Bank)	05 Apr 55	IBRD Project	211UNTS115	102850
Peru	IBRD (World Bank)	19 Apr 55	IBRD Project	221UNTS153	103007
Norway	IBRD (World Bank)	19 Apr 55	IBRD Project	211UNTS159	102852
Italy	IBRD (World Bank)	01 Jun 55	IBRD Project	358UNTS203	105137
Austria	IBRD (World Bank)	14 Jun 55	IBRD Project	221UNTS375	200531
Colombia	IBRD (World Bank)	15 Jun 55	IBRD Project	248UNTS161	103494
Pakistan	IBRD (World Bank)	20 Jun 55	IBRD Project	230UNTS41	103176
Nicaragua	IBRD (World Bank)	08 Jul 55	IBRD Project	229UNTS123	103163
Nicaragua	IBRD (World Bank)	08 Jul 55	IBRD Project	229UNTS97	103162
Panama	IBRD (World Bank)	12 Jul 55	IBRD Project	219UNTS127	102970
Guatemala	IBRD (World Bank)	29 Jul 55	IBRD Project	229UNTS167	103165
Pakistan	IBRD (World Bank)	04 Aug 55	IBRD Project	230UNTS79	103177
Peru	IBRD (World Bank)	05 Aug 55	IBRD Project	218UNTS3	102950
Pakistan	IBRD (World Bank)	06 Aug 55	IBRD Project	236UNTS195	103325
IBRD (World Bank)	Thailand	09 Aug 55	IBRD Project	221UNTS283	103011
Lebanon	IBRD (World Bank)	25 Aug 55	IBRD Project	230UNTS233	103188
France	IBRD (World Bank)	26 Aug 55	IBRD Project	247UNTS305	103478
Nicaragua	IBRD (World Bank)	26 Aug 55	IBRD Project	229UNTS145	103164
IBRD (World Bank)	Uruguay	29 Aug 55	IBRD Project	243UNTS123	103450
Japan	IBRD (World Bank)	25 Oct 55	IBRD Project	230UNTS379	200534
IBRD (World Bank)	South Africa	28 Nov 55	IBRD Project	230UNTS101	103178
Honduras	IBRD (World Bank)	22 Dec 55	IBRD Project	230UNTS262	103189
USSR (Soviet Union)	Yugoslavia	02 Feb 56	Loans and Credits	259UNTS111	103685
Japan	IBRD (World Bank)	21 Feb 56	IBRD Project	248UNTS321	200543
Ecuador	IBRD (World Bank)	26 Mar 56	IBRD Project	292UNTS391	104277
Norway	IBRD (World Bank)	03 May 56	IBRD Project	243UNTS281	103455
Burma	IBRD (World Bank)	04 May 56	IBRD Project	253UNTS179	103584
Burma	IBRD (World Bank)	04 May 56	IBRD Project	253UNTS209	103585
Finland	IBRD (World Bank)	22 May 56	IBRD Project	248UNTS57	103485
Nicaragua	IBRD (World Bank)	22 May 56	IBRD Project	253UNTS233	103586
Colombia	IBRD (World Bank)	06 Jun 56	IBRD Project	248UNTS139	103493
Fed Rhod/Nyasaland	IBRD (World Bank)	21 Jun 56	IBRD Project	285UNTS317	104156
IBRD (World Bank)	UK Great Britain	21 Jun 56	IBRD Project	285UNTS355	104157
India	IBRD (World Bank)	26 Jun 56	IBRD Project	301UNTS3	104341
IBRD (World Bank)	Switzerland	17 Sep 56	Loans and Credits	340UNTS311	200560
Costa Rica	IBRD (World Bank)	18 Sep 56	IBRD Project	260UNTS369	103721
Austria	IBRD (World Bank)	21 Sep 56	IBRD Project	259UNTS17	103681
Austria	IBRD (World Bank)	21 Sep 56	IBRD Project	259UNTS43	103682
Italy	IBRD (World Bank)	11 Oct 56	IBRD Project	359UNTS3	105138
IBRD (World Bank)	Thailand	12 Oct 56	IBRD Project	261UNTS117	103728
IBRD (World Bank)	Uruguay	25 Oct 56	IBRD Project	265UNTS59	103807
Germany, West	Netherlands	31 Oct 56	Admin Cooperation	287UNTS21	104177
Chile	IBRD (World Bank)	01 Nov 56	IBRD Project	261UNTS27	103724
Australia	IBRD (World Bank)	15 Nov 56	IBRD Project	288UNTS117	104201
Japan	IBRD (World Bank)	19 Dec 56	IBRD Project	264UNTS179	103793
India	IBRD (World Bank)	19 Dec 56	IBRD Project	310UNTS75	104489
Japan	IBRD (World Bank)	19 Dec 56	IBRD Project	268UNTS203	103859
Iran	IBRD (World Bank)	22 Jan 57	IBRD Project	317UNTS129	104600
Ethiopia	IBRD (World Bank)	28 Jan 57	IBRD Project	286UNTS307	104175
India	IBRD (World Bank)	05 Mar 57	IBRD Project	272UNTS201	103939
Peru	IBRD (World Bank)	13 Mar 57	IBRD Project	274UNTS59	103958
Netherlands	IBRD (World Bank)	15 May 57	IBRD Project	274UNTS211	103967
India	IBRD (World Bank)	29 May 57	IBRD Project	309UNTS201	104474
Belgium	IBRD (World Bank)	26 Jun 57	IBRD Project	322UNTS301	104661
India	IBRD (World Bank)	12 Jul 57	IBRD Project	288UNTS135	104202
Chile	IBRD (World Bank)	24 Jul 57	IBRD Project	282UNTS189	104099
Chile	IBRD (World Bank)	24 Jul 57	IBRD Project	282UNTS139	104098
Japan	IBRD (World Bank)	09 Aug 57	IBRD Project	293UNTS59	104286
Belgium	IBRD (World Bank)	10 Sep 57	IBRD Project	286UNTS291	104174
IBRD (World Bank)	Thailand	12 Sep 57	IBRD Project	299UNTS349	104324
Ecuador	IBRD (World Bank)	20 Sep 57	IBRD Project	293UNTS135	104291
Ecuador	IBRD (World Bank)	20 Sep 57	IBRD Project	289UNTS237	104221

PARTY ONE	PARTY TWO	DATE	TOPIC	CITATION	NUMBER
Loans (Cont.)					
IBRD (World Bank)	South Africa	01 Oct 57	IBRD Project	280UNTS285	104065
Austria	IBRD (World Bank)	10 Oct 57	IBRD Project	301UNTS95	104343
India	IBRD (World Bank)	20 Nov 57	IBRD Project	301UNTS47	104342
Philippines	IBRD (World Bank)	22 Nov 57	IBRD Project	293UNTS83	104287
Belgium	IBRD (World Bank)	27 Nov 57	IBRD Project	292UNTS175	104273
Pakistan	IBRD (World Bank)	17 Dec 57	IBRD Project	299UNTS321	104323
Mexico	IBRD (World Bank)	14 Jan 58	IBRD Project	293UNTS167	104292
Indonesia	Japan	20 Jan 58	Loans and Credits	325UNTS13	104691
Brazil	IBRD (World Bank)	22 Jan 58	IBRD Project	323UNTS99	104666
Japan	IBRD (World Bank)	29 Jan 58	IBRD Project	310UNTS111	104490
Italy	IBRD (World Bank)	28 Feb 58	IBRD Project	359UNTS47	105139
Jordan	UK Great Britain	26 Mar 58	Loans and Credits	312UNTS373	104526
Pakistan	IBRD (World Bank)	23 Apr 58	IBRD Project	323UNTS253	104672
IBRD (World Bank)	UK Great Britain	02 May 58	IBRD Project	324UNTS25	104677
Mexico	IBRD (World Bank)	05 May 58	IBRD Project	309UNTS3	104466
Jordan	UK Great Britain	07 May 58	Loans and Credits	312UNTS379	104527
Honduras	IBRD (World Bank)	09 May 58	IBRD Project	323UNTS4	104662
Japan	IBRD (World Bank)	13 Jun 58	IBRD Project	312UNTS159	104518
IBRD (World Bank)	UK Great Britain	16 Jun 58	IBRD Project	309UNTS35	104467
India	IBRD (World Bank)	25 Jun 58	IBRD Project	323UNTS131	104667
India	IBRD (World Bank)	25 Jun 58	IBRD Project	323UNTS157	104668
Ecuador	USA (United States)	27 Jun 58	Direct Aid	317UNTS51	104593
Japan	IBRD (World Bank)	27 Jun 58	IBRD Project	312UNTS193	104519
Japan	IBRD (World Bank)	11 Jul 58	IBRD Project	318UNTS103	104611
IBRD (World Bank)	Sudan	21 Jul 58	IBRD Project	323UNTS183	104669
India	IBRD (World Bank)	23 Jul 58	IBRD Project	317UNTS3	104590
Japan	IBRD (World Bank)	18 Aug 58	IBRD Project	323UNTS205	104670
Japan	IBRD (World Bank)	10 Sep 58	IBRD Project	318UNTS133	104612
Japan	IBRD (World Bank)	10 Sep 58	IBRD Project	323UNTS297	104673
India	IBRD (World Bank)	16 Sep 58	IBRD Project	323UNTS235	104671
Ceylon (Sri Lanka)	IBRD (World Bank)	17 Sep 58	IBRD Project	323UNTS51	104664
Peru	IBRD (World Bank)	17 Sep 58	IBRD Project	323UNTS27	104663
Fed of Malaya	IBRD (World Bank)	22 Sep 58	IBRD Project	323UNTS71	104665
Brazil	IBRD (World Bank)	03 Oct 58	IBRD Project	337UNTS177	104823
Ecuador	IBRD (World Bank)	09 Oct 58	IBRD Project	337UNTS299	104827
Turkey	UK Great Britain	25 Nov 58	Loans and Credits	327UNTS35	104715
Austria	IBRD (World Bank)	02 Dec 58	IBRD Project	340UNTS3	104856
IBRD (World Bank)	South Africa	02 Dec 58	IBRD Project	324UNTS3	104676
Colombia	IBRD (World Bank)	15 Dec 58	IBRD Project	354UNTS233	105065
El Salvador	IBRD (World Bank)	07 Jan 59	IBRD Project	346UNTS51	104977
Colombia	IBRD (World Bank)	30 Jan 59	IBRD Project	337UNTS327	104828
Denmark	IBRD (World Bank)	04 Feb 59	IBRD Project	328UNTS143	104733
Japan	IBRD (World Bank)	17 Feb 59	IBRD Project	337UNTS205	104824
El Salvador	IBRD (World Bank)	20 Feb 59	IBRD Project	362UNTS75	105183
Finland	IBRD (World Bank)	16 Mar 59	IBRD Project	337UNTS269	104826
India	IBRD (World Bank)	08 Apr 59	IBRD Project	348UNTS131	104998
Italy	IBRD (World Bank)	21 Apr 59	IBRD Project	359UNTS191	105143
Fed of Malaya	UK Great Britain	01 May 59	Loans and Credits	345UNTS57	104958
Japan	Vietnam, South	13 May 59	Loans and Credits	373UNTS173	105319
Japan	Vietnam, South	13 May 59	Loans and Credits	373UNTS149	105318
Honduras	IBRD (World Bank)	20 May 59	IBRD Project	359UNTS119	105141
Colombia	IBRD (World Bank)	20 May 59	IBRD Project	344UNTS251	104953
Iran	IBRD (World Bank)	29 May 59	IBRD Project	348UNTS103	104997
IBRD (World Bank)	South Africa	10 Jun 59	IBRD Project	340UNTS33	104857
Jordan	UK Great Britain	11 Jun 59	Loans and Credits	351UNTS283	105028
Brazil	IBRD (World Bank)	17 Jun 59	IBRD Project	377UNTS111	105398
France	IBRD (World Bank)	30 Jun 59	IBRD Project	452UNTS67	106505
Congo (Brazzaville)	IBRD (World Bank)	30 Jun 59	IBRD Project	452UNTS123	106506
Gabon	IBRD (World Bank)	30 Jun 59	IBRD Project	452UNTS135	106507
Norway	IBRD (World Bank)	08 Jul 59	IBRD Project	344UNTS229	104952
India	IBRD (World Bank)	15 Jul 59	IBRD Project	346UNTS33	104976
Pakistan	IBRD (World Bank)	13 Aug 59	IBRD Project	355UNTS129	105076
Italy	IBRD (World Bank)	16 Sep 59	IBRD Project	375UNTS159	105366
Japan	IBRD (World Bank)	12 Nov 59	IBRD Project	354UNTS279	105067
Iran	IBRD (World Bank)	23 Nov 59	IBRD Project	380UNTS245	105459

PARTY ONE	PARTY TWO	DATE	TOPIC	CITATION	NUMBER
Loans (Cont.)					
Pakistan	IBRD (World Bank)	30 Nov 59	IBRD Project	355UNTS203	105078
France	IBRD (World Bank)	10 Dec 59	IBRD Project	380UNTS319	105464
IBRD (World Bank)	United Arab Rep	22 Dec 59	IBRD Project	354UNTS197	105063
IBRD (World Bank)	Uruguay	30 Dec 59	IBRD Project	384UNTS275	105523
Colombia	IBRD (World Bank)	20 Jan 60	IBRD Project	375UNTS49	105353
Iran	IBRD (World Bank)	20 Feb 60	IBRD Project	384UNTS213	105521
Mauritania	IBRD (World Bank)	17 Mar 60	IBRD Project	452UNTS211	106509
France	IBRD (World Bank)	17 Mar 60	IBRD Project	452UNTS147	106508
Japan	IBRD (World Bank)	17 Mar 60	IBRD Project	362UNTS43	105182
Belgium	IBRD (World Bank)	30 Mar 60	IBRD Project	379UNTS103	105437
Belgium	IBRD (World Bank)	30 Mar 60	IBRD Project	379UNTS129	105438
Belgium	IBRD (World Bank)	30 Mar 60	IBRD Project	379UNTS161	105439
IBRD (World Bank)	UK Great Britain	01 Apr 60	IBRD Project	379UNTS397	105446
Costa Rica	IBRD (World Bank)	04 May 60	IBRD Project	390UNTS201	105609
Jordan	UK Great Britain	04 May 60	Loans and Credits	385UNTS81	105531
Colombia	IBRD (World Bank)	10 May 60	IBRD Project	379UNTS218	105441
IBRD (World Bank)	UK Great Britain	27 May 60	IBRD Project	375UNTS201	105367
IBRD (World Bank)	Sudan	17 Jun 60	IBRD Project	379UNTS253	105442
Nicaragua	IBRD (World Bank)	22 Jun 60	IBRD Project	384UNTS243	105522
Honduras	IBRD (World Bank)	29 Jun 60	IBRD Project	400UNTS137	105751
Peru	IBRD (World Bank)	29 Jun 60	IBRD Project	400UNTS99	105750
El Salvador	IBRD (World Bank)	29 Jul 60	IBRD Project	390UNTS101	105605
India	IBRD (World Bank)	29 Jul 60	IBRD Project	377UNTS153	105399
Multilateral		16 Aug 60	Recognition	382UNTS8	105476
Panama	IBRD (World Bank)	19 Aug 60	IBRD Project	390UNTS153	105607
Israel	IBRD (World Bank)	09 Sep 60	IBRD Project	406UNTS3	105837
Pakistan	IBRD (World Bank)	19 Sep 60	IBRD Project	444UNTS207	106370
Colombia	IBRD (World Bank)	20 Sep 60	IBRD Project	390UNTS173	105608
Mexico	IBRD (World Bank)	18 Oct 60	IBRD Project	422UNTS177	106075
Chile	UK Great Britain	21 Oct 60	Loans and Credits	385UNTS15	105525
India	IBRD (World Bank)	28 Oct 60	IBRD Project	406UNTS27	105838
Norway	IBRD (World Bank)	02 Dec 60	IBRD Project	390UNTS131	105606
Italy	USA (United States)	03 Dec 60	Atomic Energy	410UNTS3	105893
Peru	IBRD (World Bank)	19 Dec 60	IBRD Project	417UNTS275	106010
Japan	IBRD (World Bank)	20 Dec 60	IBRD Project	400UNTS167	105752
Mexico	IBRD (World Bank)	16 Jan 61	IBRD Project	422UNTS203	106076
Burma	IBRD (World Bank)	16 Jan 61	IBRD Project	400UNTS73	105749
Costa Rica	IBRD (World Bank)	03 Feb 61	IBRD Project	414UNTS314	105977
IBRD (World Bank)	Yugoslavia	23 Feb 61	IBRD Project	415UNTS92	105982
Japan	IBRD (World Bank)	16 Mar 61	IBRD Project	400UNTS201	105753
IBRD (World Bank)	UK Great Britain	29 Mar 61	IBRD Project	415UNTS300	105990
Japan	IBRD (World Bank)	02 May 61	IBRD Project	415UNTS144	105984
Colombia	IBRD (World Bank)	12 May 61	IBRD Project	415UNTS172	105985
Ceylon (Sri Lanka)	IBRD (World Bank)	06 Jun 61	IBRD Project	414UNTS349	105978
IBRD (World Bank)	Sudan	14 Jun 61	IBRD Project	415UNTS26	105980
Multilateral		14 Jun 61	IBRD Project	415UNTS4	105979
Chile	IBRD (World Bank)	28 Jun 61	IBRD Project	426UNTS33	106129
Argentina	IBRD (World Bank)	30 Jun 61	IBRD Project	445UNTS85	106379
Jordan	UK Great Britain	17 Jul 61	Loans and Credits	420UNTS53	106039
Brazil	UK Great Britain	21 Jul 61	Loans and Credits	414UNTS26	105962
Philippines	IBRD (World Bank)	26 Jul 61	IBRD Project	414UNTS253	105976
Chile	USA (United States)	03 Aug 61	Direct Aid	433UNTS21	106228
Finland	IBRD (World Bank)	09 Aug 61	IBRD Project	415UNTS204	105986
India	IBRD (World Bank)	09 Aug 61	IBRD Project	417UNTS297	106011
IBRD (World Bank)	UK Great Britain	16 Aug 61	IBRD Project	426UNTS287	106143
India	IBRD (World Bank)	17 Aug 61	IBRD Project	417UNTS319	106012
Multilateral		28 Aug 61	IBRD Project	416UNTS45	105994
Colombia	IBRD (World Bank)	28 Aug 61	IBRD Project	416UNTS23	105993
Costa Rica	IBRD (World Bank)	06 Sep 61	IBRD Project	446UNTS345	106408
IBRD (World Bank)	Switzerland	11 Oct 61	IBRD Project	415UNTS396	200592
Costa Rica	IBRD (World Bank)	13 Oct 61	IBRD Project	430UNTS27	106202
Philippines	IBRD (World Bank)	13 Oct 61	IBRD Project	415UNTS269	105989
India	IBRD (World Bank)	13 Oct 61	IBRD Project	418UNTS3	106013
Switzerland	UK Great Britain	20 Oct 61	Loans and Credits	431UNTS29	106206
Peru	IBRD (World Bank)	03 Nov 61	IBRD Project	430UNTS47	106203

PARTY ONE	PARTY TWO	DATE	TOPIC	CITATION	NUMBER
Loans (Cont.)					
Ethiopia	IBRD (World Bank)	22 Nov 61	IBRD Project	426UNTS255	106142
Japan	IBRD (World Bank)	29 Nov 61	IBRD Project	426UNTS3	106128
IBRD (World Bank)	UK Great Britain	29 Nov 61	IBRD Project	426UNTS49	106130
IBRD (World Bank)	South Africa	01 Dec 61	IBRD Project	425UNTS215	106126
IBRD (World Bank)	South Africa	01 Dec 61	IBRD Project	425UNTS197	106125
IBRD (World Bank)	Venezuela	13 Dec 61	IBRD Project	446UNTS371	106409
India	IBRD (World Bank)	22 Dec 61	IBRD Project	481UNTS85	106979
Argentina	IBRD (World Bank)	19 Jan 62	IBRD Project	446UNTS305	106407
Australia	IBRD (World Bank)	23 Jan 62	IBRD Project	430UNTS3	106201
Israel	IBRD (World Bank)	01 Feb 62	IBRD Project	435UNTS155	106277
Ghana	IBRD (World Bank)	08 Feb 62	IBRD Project	449UNTS207	106462
Iceland	IBRD (World Bank)	14 Feb 62	IBRD Project	447UNTS95	106413
India	IBRD (World Bank)	28 Feb 62	IBRD Project	447UNTS3	106410
Colombia	IBRD (World Bank)	23 May 62	IBRD Project	447UNTS39	106411
Jordan	UK Great Britain	30 May 62	Loans and Credits	449UNTS167	106458
Ethiopia	IBRD (World Bank)	31 May 62	IBRD Project	467UNTS237	106765
Austria	IBRD (World Bank)	15 Jun 62	IBRD Project	447UNTS127	106414
Mexico	IBRD (World Bank)	20 Jun 62	IBRD Project	468UNTS109	106771
Mexico	IBRD (World Bank)	20 Jun 62	IBRD Project	467UNTS205	106764
IBRD (World Bank)	Yugoslavia	11 Jul 62	IBRD Project	468UNTS143	106772
Pakistan	USA (United States)	25 Jul 62	Direct Aid	459UNTS87	106614
Finland	IBRD (World Bank)	15 Aug 62	IBRD Project	467UNTS177	106763
Panama	IBRD (World Bank)	14 Sep 62	IBRD Project	476UNTS153	106908
Pakistan	IBRD (World Bank)	14 Sep 62	IBRD Project	467UNTS152	106762
Pakistan	IBRD (World Bank)	14 Sep 62	IBRD Project	467UNTS125	106761
Israel	IBRD (World Bank)	17 Oct 62	IBRD Project	467UNTS107	106760
IBRD (World Bank)	Uruguay	26 Oct 62	IBRD Project	481UNTS39	106977
Tunisia	USA (United States)	29 Oct 62	Direct Aid	462UNTS201	106679
Philippines	IBRD (World Bank)	07 Nov 62	Loans and Credits	468UNTS281	106777
Nigeria	IBRD (World Bank)	10 Dec 62	IBRD Project	468UNTS255	106776
Morocco	IBRD (World Bank)	21 Dec 62	IBRD Project	478UNTS205	106937
IBRD (World Bank)	Thailand	21 Dec 62	IBRD Project	467UNTS43	106757
IBRD (World Bank)	Thailand	21 Dec 62	IBRD Project	467UNTS63	106758
Pakistan	IBRD (World Bank)	13 Feb 63	IBRD Project	467UNTS3	106756
Philippines	IBRD (World Bank)	15 Feb 63	IBRD Project	478UNTS161	106936
Nicaragua	IBRD (World Bank)	01 Mar 63	IBRD Project	481UNTS15	106976
IBRD (World Bank)	Thailand	07 Mar 63	IBRD Project	467UNTS83	106759
Cyprus	IBRD (World Bank)	17 Apr 63	IBRD Project	476UNTS185	106909
Jordan	UK Great Britain	27 Apr 63	Loans and Credits	475UNTS169	106892
Mexico	IBRD (World Bank)	29 Apr 63	IBRD Project	489UNTS151	107138
IBRD (World Bank)	UK Great Britain	16 May 63	IBRD Project	477UNTS361	106929
IBRD (World Bank)	UK Great Britain	16 May 63	IBRD Project	476UNTS211	106910
Colombia	IBRD (World Bank)	03 Jun 63	IBRD Project	490UNTS199	107155
Argentina	UK Great Britain	05 Jun 63	Loans and Credits	482UNTS353	107004
India	IBRD (World Bank)	05 Jun 63	IBRD Project	481UNTS191	106983
IBRD (World Bank)	Thailand	11 Jun 63	IBRD Project	481UNTS227	106984
El Salvador	IBRD (World Bank)	19 Jun 63	IBRD Project	481UNTS59	106978
IBRD (World Bank)	Yugoslavia	21 Jun 63	IBRD Project	482UNTS43	106990
Colombia	IBRD (World Bank)	21 Jun 63	IBRD Project	482UNTS159	106994
Colombia	IBRD (World Bank)	28 Jun 63	IBRD Project	489UNTS113	107137
IBRD (World Bank)	Tunisia	03 Jul 63	IBRD Project	480UNTS209	106970
Costa Rica	IBRD (World Bank)	10 Jul 63	IBRD Project	482UNTS69	106991
Malaysia	IBRD (World Bank)	15 Jul 63	IBRD Project	482UNTS123	106993
Colombia	IBRD (World Bank)	16 Jul 63	IBRD Project	482UNTS256	106998
Denmark	IBRD (World Bank)	24 Jul 63	IBRD Project	481UNTS171	106982
Malaysia	IBRD (World Bank)	07 Aug 63	IBRD Project	485UNTS253	107060
IBRD (World Bank)	UK Great Britain	06 Sep 63	IBRD Project	483UNTS173	107013
Finland	IBRD (World Bank)	18 Sep 63	IBRD Project	491UNTS345	107183
Mexico	IBRD (World Bank)	20 Sep 63	IBRD Project	491UNTS317	107182
IBRD (World Bank)	Venezuela	20 Sep 63	IBRD Project	482UNTS227	106997
Belgium	Turkey	23 Sep 63	Direct Aid	566UNTS195	108244
IBRD (World Bank)	UK Great Britain	23 Sep 63	IBRD Project	503UNTS247	107348
Taiwan	IBRD (World Bank)	27 Sep 63	IBRD Project	483UNTS151	107012
Japan	IBRD (World Bank)	27 Sep 63	IBRD Project	485UNTS283	107061
El Salvador	IBRD (World Bank)	01 Oct 63	IBRD Project	517UNTS3	107481

PARTY ONE	PARTY TWO	DATE	TOPIC	CITATION	NUMBER
Loans (Cont.)					
Norway	IBRD (World Bank)	15 Oct 63	IBRD Project	482UNTS103	106992
IBRD (World Bank)	Spain	25 Oct 63	IBRD Project	491UNTS297	107181
IBRD (World Bank)	Yugoslavia	28 Oct 63	IBRD Project	503UNTS289	107349
Portugal	IBRD (World Bank)	06 Nov 63	IBRD Project	492UNTS89	107188
Portugal	IBRD (World Bank)	06 Nov 63	IBRD Project	491UNTS137	107176
New Zealand	IBRD (World Bank)	12 Nov 63	IBRD Project	485UNTS233	107059
Peru	IBRD (World Bank)	22 Nov 63	IBRD Project	491UNTS101	107175
Chile	IBRD (World Bank)	18 Dec 63	IBRD Project	504UNTS3	107351
Chile	IBRD (World Bank)	18 Dec 63	IBRD Project	504UNTS29	107352
Multilateral		30 Dec 63	IBRD Project	568UNTS233	108271
Multilateral		30 Dec 63	IBRD Project	568UNTS215	108270
Multilateral		30 Dec 63	IBRD Project	568UNTS243	108272
Multilateral		30 Dec 63	IBRD Project	551UNTS75	108035
Multilateral		30 Dec 63	IBRD Project	551UNTS119	108037
Multilateral		30 Dec 63	IBRD Project	551UNTS105	108036
Congo (Zaire)	UK Great Britain	03 Jan 64	Loans and Credits	534UNTS417	107770
Liberia	IBRD (World Bank)	08 Jan 64	IBRD Project	504UNTS53	107353
Colombia	IBRD (World Bank)	07 Feb 64	IBRD Project	516UNTS99	107473
IBRD (World Bank)	Thailand	11 Mar 64	IBRD Project	504UNTS73	107354
New Zealand	IBRD (World Bank)	12 Mar 64	IBRD Project	505UNTS3	107362
Nigeria	IBRD (World Bank)	12 Mar 64	IBRD Project	516UNTS325	107480
Japan	IBRD (World Bank)	22 Apr 64	IBRD Project	505UNTS21	107363
Peru	IBRD (World Bank)	22 Apr 64	IBRD Project	519UNTS95	107503
Ethiopia	IBRD (World Bank)	08 May 64	IBRD Project	505UNTS51	107364
Algeria	IBRD (World Bank)	14 May 64	IBRD Project	522UNTS265	107552
Pakistan	IBRD (World Bank)	14 May 64	IBRD Project	516UNTS145	107475
Ecuador	IBRD (World Bank)	26 May 64	IBRD Project	534UNTS113	107758
IBRD (World Bank)	Tunisia	05 Jun 64	IBRD Project	539UNTS129	107827
Iran	IBRD (World Bank)	10 Jun 64	IBRD Project	537UNTS111	107799
Pakistan	IBRD (World Bank)	30 Jun 64	IBRD Project	519UNTS57	107502
Nigeria	IBRD (World Bank)	07 Jul 64	IBRD Project	537UNTS3	107795
Gabon	IBRD (World Bank)	10 Jul 64	IBRD Project	537UNTS63	107797
Finland	IBRD (World Bank)	10 Jul 64	IBRD Project	516UNTS125	107474
Philippines	IBRD (World Bank)	22 Jul 64	IBRD Project	516UNTS171	107476
New Zealand	Western Samoa	23 Jul 64	Non-IBRD Project	521UNTS173	107520
IBRD (World Bank)	Spain	31 Jul 64	IBRD Project	537UNTS81	107798
IBRD (World Bank)	Sierra Leone	18 Aug 64	IBRD Project	516UNTS295	107479
Morocco	IBRD (World Bank)	26 Aug 64	IBRD Project	537UNTS193	107802
IBRD (World Bank)	Venezuela	28 Aug 64	IBRD Project	537UNTS135	107800
IBRD (World Bank)	Venezuela	28 Aug 64	IBRD Project	520UNTS97	107512
Jordan	UK Great Britain	31 Aug 64	Loans and Credits	541UNTS3	107856
Brazil	UK Great Britain	14 Oct 64	Loans and Credits	539UNTS289	107840
Philippines	IBRD (World Bank)	28 Oct 64	IBRD Project	537UNTS165	107801
Germany, West	Thailand	28 Oct 64	Loans and Credits	521UNTS333	107529
Germany, West	Thailand	28 Oct 64	Non-IBRD Project	521UNTS311	107528
IBRD (World Bank)	Thailand	25 Nov 64	IBRD Project	537UNTS273	107805
IBRD (World Bank)	Yugoslavia	11 Dec 64	IBRD Project	537UNTS321	107807
Paraguay	IBRD (World Bank)	16 Dec 64	IBRD Project	549UNTS173	107999
Taiwan	IBRD (World Bank)	17 Dec 64	IBRD Project	538UNTS3	107808
Japan	IBRD (World Bank)	23 Dec 64	IBRD Project	538UNTS37	107809
Japan	IBRD (World Bank)	13 Jan 65	IBRD Project	537UNTS293	107806
Honduras	IBRD (World Bank)	02 Feb 65	IBRD Project	561UNTS255	108188
Mexico	IBRD (World Bank)	04 Feb 65	IBRD Project	549UNTS189	108000
Chile	IBRD (World Bank)	12 Feb 65	IBRD Project	537UNTS35	107796
Brazil	IBRD (World Bank)	26 Feb 65	IBRD Project	567UNTS91	108253
Brazil	IBRD (World Bank)	26 Feb 65	IBRD Project	553UNTS3	108065
Malaysia	IBRD (World Bank)	26 Feb 65	IBRD Project	549UNTS239	108002
IBRD (World Bank)	Thailand	22 Mar 65	IBRD Project	538UNTS63	107810
IBRD (World Bank)	Uruguay	30 Mar 65	IBRD Project	567UNTS45	108251
Jamaica	IBRD (World Bank)	08 Apr 65	IBRD Project	539UNTS303	107841
Iran	IBRD (World Bank)	28 Apr 65	IBRD Project	555UNTS21	108103
Iran	IBRD (World Bank)	28 Apr 65	IBRD Project	555UNTS45	108104
Taiwan	IBRD (World Bank)	28 Apr 65	IBRD Project	549UNTS145	107998
Portugal	IBRD (World Bank)	29 Apr 65	IBRD Project	549UNTS69	107991
Japan	IBRD (World Bank)	26 May 65	IBRD Project	550UNTS95	108010

PARTY ONE	PARTY TWO	DATE	TOPIC	CITATION	NUMBER
Loans (Cont.)					
India	IBRD (World Bank)	28 May 65	Loans and Credits	552UNTS39	108049
Peru	IBRD (World Bank)	03 Jun 65	IBRD Project	551UNTS227	108045
Jordan	UK Great Britain	08 Jun 65	Loans and Credits	552UNTS251	108057
India	IBRD (World Bank)	11 Jun 65	IBRD Project	557UNTS59	108128
India	IBRD (World Bank)	11 Jun 65	IBRD Project	557UNTS101	108130
Peru	IBRD (World Bank)	18 Jun 65	IBRD Project	568UNTS191	108269
Japan	Korea, South	22 Jun 65	Claims and Debts	583UNTS173	108473
Italy	IBRD (World Bank)	28 Jun 65	IBRD Project	567UNTS127	108254
Finland	IBRD (World Bank)	30 Jun 65	IBRD Project	550UNTS63	108009
Pakistan	IBRD (World Bank)	09 Jul 65	IBRD Project	554UNTS39	108096
Iran	IBRD (World Bank)	12 Jul 65	IBRD Project	554UNTS3	108095
Multilateral		22 Jul 65	IBRD Project	561UNTS333	200618
Japan	IBRD (World Bank)	10 Sep 65	Claims and Debts	566UNTS249	108246
Israel	IBRD (World Bank)	16 Sep 65	Claims and Debts	566UNTS212	108245
Peru	IBRD (World Bank)	17 Sep 65	Loans and Credits	566UNTS311	108248
Nigeria	IBRD (World Bank)	26 Sep 65	IBRD Project	571UNTS39	108298
Nigeria	IBRD (World Bank)	26 Sep 65	IBRD Project	570UNTS233	108296
East Afri Service	IBRD (World Bank)	29 Sep 65	IBRD Project	568UNTS327	200623
IBRD (World Bank)	Uganda	29 Sep 65	IBRD Project	568UNTS317	108276
IBRD (World Bank)	Spain	29 Sep 65	IBRD Project	568UNTS49	108264
Kenya	IBRD (World Bank)	29 Sep 65	IBRD Project	568UNTS289	108274
IBRD (World Bank)	Tanzania	29 Sep 65	IBRD Project	568UNTS309	108275
Mexico	IBRD (World Bank)	01 Oct 65	IBRD Project	589UNTS339	108542
Chile	IBRD (World Bank)	06 Oct 65	IBRD Project	567UNTS293	108261
Turkey	UK Great Britain	21 Oct 65	Loans and Credits	561UNTS185	108180
Philippines	IBRD (World Bank)	02 Nov 65	IBRD Project	567UNTS3	108249
Morocco	IBRD (World Bank)	08 Nov 65	Claims and Debts	566UNTS279	108247
Malaysia	IBRD (World Bank)	17 Nov 65	IBRD Project	568UNTS23	108263
Chile	UK Great Britain	23 Nov 65	Loans and Credits	560UNTS215	108176
IBRD (World Bank)	Venezuela	13 Dec 65	IBRD Project	568UNTS77	108265
Mexico	IBRD (World Bank)	15 Dec 65	IBRD Project	568UNTS125	108267
Paraguay	IBRD (World Bank)	16 Dec 65	IBRD Project	568UNTS165	108268
New Zealand	IBRD (World Bank)	17 Dec 65	IBRD Project	567UNTS255	108259
New Zealand	IBRD (World Bank)	17 Dec 65	IBRD Project	567UNTS275	108260
IBRD (World Bank)	Sudan	27 Dec 65	IBRD Project	567UNTS27	108250
Ethiopia	IBRD (World Bank)	28 Dec 65	IBRD Project	567UNTS229	108258
Brazil	IBRD (World Bank)	15 Mar 66	IBRD Project	599UNTS52	108664
Guinea	IBRD (World Bank)	30 Mar 66	IBRD Project	568UNTS3	108262
Paraguay	IBRD (World Bank)	04 Apr 66	IBRD Project	570UNTS41	108287
IBRD (World Bank)	UK Great Britain	18 Apr 66	IGO Operations	573UNTS209	108334
IBRD (World Bank)	Venezuela	21 Apr 66	IBRD Project	568UNTS257	108273
Finland	IBRD (World Bank)	27 Apr 66	IBRD Project	568UNTS107	108266
Multilateral		04 May 66	IBRD Project	575UNTS49	108354
Peru	IBRD (World Bank)	13 May 66	IBRD Project	570UNTS61	108288
IBRD (World Bank)	Tunisia	16 May 66	IBRD Project	584UNTS155	108477
Mexico	IBRD (World Bank)	25 May 66	IBRD Project	596UNTS3	108627
Burma	USA (United States)	01 Jun 66	Loans and Credits	580UNTS253	108428
Portugal	IBRD (World Bank)	14 Jun 66	IBRD Project	581UNTS29	108431
Portugal	IBRD (World Bank)	14 Jun 66	IBRD Project	581UNTS3	108430
Jamaica	IBRD (World Bank)	20 Jun 66	IBRD Project	582UNTS145	108462
IBRD (World Bank)	Thailand	24 Jun 66	IBRD Project	582UNTS259	108466
Denmark	Jordan	28 Jun 66	Loans and Credits	574UNTS3	108338
India	IBRD (World Bank)	07 Jul 66	IBRD Project	595UNTS3	108610
Brazil	Denmark	08 Jul 66	Loans and Credits	581UNTS95	108435
Iraq	IBRD (World Bank)	22 Jul 66	IBRD Project	584UNTS233	108480
Jordan	UK Great Britain	26 Jul 66	Loans and Credits	597UNTS219	108647
Malaysia	IBRD (World Bank)	26 Jul 66	IBRD Project	586UNTS195	108504
Iran	IBRD (World Bank)	26 Jul 66	IBRD Project	582UNTS107	108461
Turkey	UK Great Britain	29 Jul 66	Loans and Credits	597UNTS241	108649
Japan	IBRD (World Bank)	29 Jul 66	IBRD Project	582UNTS209	108464
IBRD (World Bank)	Turkey	10 Aug 66	IBRD Project	585UNTS199	108490
IBRD (World Bank)	Singapore	11 Aug 66	IBRD Project	585UNTS39	108482
Honduras	IBRD (World Bank)	25 Aug 66	IBRD Project	582UNTS79	108460
Denmark	Malawi	01 Sep 66	Loans and Credits	586UNTS3	108493
Peru	IBRD (World Bank)	07 Sep 66	IBRD Project	585UNTS3	108481

PARTY ONE	PARTY TWO	DATE	TOPIC	CITATION	NUMBER
Loans (Cont.)					
IBRD (World Bank)	South Africa	08 Sep 66	IBRD Project	585UNTS71	108483
Iceland	IBRD (World Bank)	14 Sep 66	IBRD Project	598UNTS223	108660
Philippines	IBRD (World Bank)	23 Sep 66	IBRD Project	596UNTS71	108629
Jamaica	IBRD (World Bank)	30 Sep 66	IBRD Project	582UNTS179	108463
IBRD (World Bank)	Zambia	04 Oct 66	IBRD Project	585UNTS181	108489
Nicaragua	IBRD (World Bank)	05 Oct 66	IBRD Project	582UNTS231	108465
IBRD (World Bank)	Thailand	19 Oct 66	IBRD Project	594UNTS347	108609
IBRD (World Bank)	IFC (Finance Corp)	28 Oct 66	Loans and Credits	586UNTS225	200628
IBRD (World Bank)	Singapore	04 Nov 66	IBRD Project	585UNTS155	108488
Brazil	IBRD (World Bank)	19 Dec 66	IBRD Project	599UNTS107	108665
Brazil	IBRD (World Bank)	19 Dec 66	IBRD Project	599UNTS149	108666
Brazil	IBRD (World Bank)	19 Dec 66	IBRD Project	599UNTS177	108667
Brazil	IBRD (World Bank)	19 Dec 66	IBRD Project	599UNTS205	108668
Chile	IBRD (World Bank)	23 Dec 66	IBRD Project	595UNTS141	108618
Congo (Brazzaville)	IBRD (World Bank)	09 Jan 67	IBRD Project	598UNTS161	108659
Jamaica	IBRD (World Bank)	23 Jan 67	IBRD Project	594UNTS311	108608
IBRD (World Bank)	Venezuela	26 Jan 67	IBRD Project	596UNTS35	108628
IBRD (World Bank)	Tanzania	17 Feb 67	IBRD Project	599UNTS287	108671
East Afri Service	IBRD (World Bank)	17 Feb 67	IBRD Project	599UNTS335	200629
Kenya	IBRD (World Bank)	17 Feb 67	IBRD Project	599UNTS233	108669
IBRD (World Bank)	Yugoslavia	24 Feb 67	IBRD Project	599UNTS27	108663
IBRD (World Bank)	Trinidad/Tobago	10 Mar 67	IBRD Project	599UNTS3	108662
Pakistan	IBRD (World Bank)	15 Mar 67	IBRD Project	599UNTS245	108670
IBRD (World Bank)	Thailand	24 Mar 67	IBRD Project	599UNTS299	108672
Philippines	IBRD (World Bank)	05 Apr 67	IBRD Project	598UNTS261	108661
IBRD (World Bank)	UK Great Britain	24 Apr 67	IBRD Project	600UNTS3	108674
Locust Control					
Multilateral		22 Feb 49	Sanitation	93UNTS129	101296
Maintenance					
Multilateral		01 Apr 53	Non-ILO Labor	227UNTS169	103138
Multilateral		20 Jun 56	Admin Cooperation	268UNTS3	103850
Multilateral		24 Oct 56	Admin Cooperation	510UNTS161	107412
Austria	Belgium	25 Oct 57	Admin Cooperation	372UNTS177	105297
Multilateral		15 Apr 58	Health/Educ/Welfare	539UNTS27	107822
Germany, West	USA (United States)	03 Aug 59	Status of Forces	490UNTS28	107153
Multilateral		23 Mar 62	Admin Cooperation	470UNTS25	106793
Malaria					
Burma	WHO (World Health)	13 Jun 51	Sanitation	117UNTS115	101588
Taiwan	WHO (World Health)	25 Oct 51	Sanitation	126UNTS77	101683
Maritime Navigation					
Argentina	Brazil	23 Jan 40	Admin Cooperation	51UNTS281	200194
Brazil	Uruguay	08 Jan 42	Admin Cooperation	54UNTS359	200206
UK Great Britain	USSR (Soviet Union)	22 Jun 42	Finance	91UNTS355	200270
Canada	USA (United States)	26 May 43	Privil/Immunities	7UNTS345	200043
Brazil	USA (United States)	29 Sep 44	Military Mission	65UNTS271	200216
Norway	USA (United States)	29 May 45	Water Transport	34UNTS371	200180
UK Great Britain	USA (United States)	15 Jun 45	Reparations	89UNTS327	200261
Belgium	UK Great Britain	25 Jun 45	Reparations	90UNTS307	200268
Taiwan	USSR (Soviet Union)	14 Aug 45	General Amity	10UNTS300	200068
France	UK Great Britain	26 Jan 46	Reparations	91UNTS183	101251
UK Great Britain	USA (United States)	07 May 46	Water Transport	6UNTS285	100082
France	USA (United States)	28 May 46	General Economic	84UNTS167	101127
France	USA (United States)	28 May 46	Reparations	84UNTS113	101122
France	USA (United States)	28 May 46	Milit Assistance	84UNTS79	101120
Norway	Portugal	16 Aug 46	Commodity Trade	30UNTS215	100459
Multilateral		30 Oct 46	IGO Establishment	11UNTS107	100151
Taiwan	USA (United States)	04 Nov 46	General Amity	25UNTS69	100359
Canada	USA (United States)	15 Nov 46	Specif Claim/Waive	7UNTS141	100096
Philippines	USA (United States)	21 Mar 47	Milit Assistance	45UNTS47	100691
Nepal	USA (United States)	25 Apr 47	Consul/Citizenship	16UNTS97	100251
Italy	USA (United States)	14 Aug 47	Claims and Debts	36UNTS105	100567
Greece	USA (United States)	03 Dec 47	Milit Assistance	89UNTS119	101213
Taiwan	USA (United States)	08 Dec 47	Milit Installation	70UNTS3	100895

PARTY ONE	PARTY TWO	DATE	TOPIC	CITATION	NUMBER
Maritime Navigation (Cont.)					
Italy	USA (United States)	02 Feb 48	General Amity	79UNTS171	101040
Denmark	Guatemala	04 Mar 48	General Economic	96UNTS223	101339
Taiwan	UK Great Britain	18 May 48	Milit Assistance	66UNTS113	100850
Italy	USA (United States)	28 Jun 48	Milit Occupation	25UNTS45	100356
Denmark	USA (United States)	29 Jun 48	Mostfavored Nation	27UNTS35	100396
Greece	Lebanon	06 Oct 48	Consul/Citizenship	87UNTS351	101179
Netherlands	UK Great Britain	15 Oct 48	Taxation	74UNTS3	100955
Multilateral		19 Oct 48	Specif Claim/Waive	84UNTS201	101130
Argentina	Denmark	15 Dec 48	Taxation	67UNTS71	100866
Argentina	Netherlands	15 Jan 49	Taxation	46UNTS241	100713
Greece	USA (United States)	21 Feb 49	Status of Forces	88UNTS29	101182
Multilateral		28 Feb 49	Scientific Project	29UNTS53	100434
France	USA (United States)	14 Mar 49	Claims and Debts	84UNTS225	101132
Argentina	UK Great Britain	14 Mar 49	Taxation	83UNTS193	101108
Denmark	Portugal	08 Apr 49	General Trade	74UNTS209	100964
Japan	USA (United States)	14 Apr 49	Specif Claim/Waive	89UNTS141	101215
Argentina	Belgium	25 Jul 49	Taxation	46UNTS103	100703
Italy	Netherlands	16 Aug 49	Admin Cooperation	98UNTS21	101357
Greece	Italy	31 Aug 49	Reparations	78UNTS89	101014
Finland	USA (United States)	01 Nov 49	Claims and Debts	68UNTS11	100880
Czechoslovakia	Denmark	17 Dec 49	General Trade	74UNTS147	100961
Denmark	Portugal	02 Jun 50	General Trade	74UNTS229	100966
Canada	USA (United States)	22 Jun 50	Scientific Project	70UNTS115	100900
Argentina	USA (United States)	20 Jul 50	Taxation	89UNTS63	101209
Denmark	South Africa	30 Nov 50	Taxation	84UNTS51	101118
Greece	UK Great Britain	21 Feb 51	General Economic	88UNTS205	101192
UK Great Britain	USA (United States)	06 Mar 51	Status of Forces	97UNTS137	101347
Marriage					
Belgium	France	09 Jan 47	Admin Cooperation	36UNTS145	100568
Multilateral		23 Mar 53	Admin Cooperation	202UNTS241	102732
Multilateral		10 Dec 62	Culture	521UNTS231	107525
Austria	Denmark	09 Dec 63	Admin Cooperation	520UNTS133	107514
Maternity Welfare					
Multilateral		29 Nov 19	ILO Labor	38UNTS53	100586
Belgium	Luxembourg	03 Dec 49	Non-ILO Labor	91UNTS31	101241
Multilateral		20 Jul 53	Non-ILO Labor	228UNTS3	103141
Meat					
Argentina	UK Great Britain	17 Sep 46	General Economic	88UNTS47	101185
Medical Research					
Taiwan	USA (United States)	14 Oct 55	Milit Installation	268UNTS165	103857
Thailand	USA (United States)	23 Dec 60	IGO Establishment	405UNTS135	105830
Multilateral		14 May 62	Scientific Project	544UNTS39	107910
Thailand	USA (United States)	25 Apr 63	Sanitation	476UNTS115	106906
Ethiopia	USA (United States)	30 Dec 65	Milit Installation	574UNTS129	108345
Medical Study and Teaching					
Colombia	USA (United States)	14 Jun 55	Non-IBRD Project	256UNTS211	103630
Medical Supplies					
Italy	UK Great Britain	13 Mar 48	Admin Cooperation	104UNTS41	101435
Ceylon (Sri Lanka)	WHO (World Health)	04 Mar 52	Direct Aid	128UNTS281	200437
Chile	WHO (World Health)	11 Jul 52	Tech Assistance	137UNTS27	101846
Austria	Italy	19 Nov 56	Admin Cooperation	284UNTS293	104143
Multilateral		15 Dec 58	Sanitation	351UNTS159	105022
Multilateral		28 Apr 60	Health/Educ/Welfare	376UNTS111	105377
Meteorology					
Multilateral		12 May 40	Scientific Project	101UNTS91	101405
Mexico	USA (United States)	10 Nov 42	Scientific Project	66UNTS307	200219
Mexico	USA (United States)	14 Jun 43	Scientific Project	66UNTS331	200220
Multilateral		02 Aug 44	Scientific Project	67UNTS221	200221
Brazil	Uruguay	22 Nov 44	Specif Goods/Equip	65UNTS289	200217
Multilateral		31 Mar 46	Milit Installation	17UNTS159	100274
Mexico	USA (United States)	12 Apr 46	Scientific Project	66UNTS293	100861
France	USA (United States)	28 May 46	Milit Assistance	84UNTS79	101120

PARTY ONE	PARTY TWO	DATE	TOPIC	CITATION	NUMBER
Meteorology (Cont.)					
Philippines	USA (United States)	12 May 47	Scientific Project	16UNTS123	100253
Multilateral		11 Oct 47	IGO Establishment	77UNTS143	100998
Cuba	USA (United States)	27 Jan 48	Scientific Project	67UNTS3	100862
Multilateral		28 Feb 49	Scientific Project	29UNTS53	100434
Mexico	USA (United States)	15 Aug 49	Scientific Project	66UNTS13	100846
United Arab Rep	UK Great Britain	20 Mar 50	Tech Assistance	226UNTS287	103123
Ireland	Spain	11 May 50	Scientific Project	553UNTS147	108081
Canada	USA (United States)	22 Jun 50	Scientific Project	70UNTS115	100900
Spain	Sweden	12 Oct 50	Scientific Project	197UNTS305	102644
Multilateral		25 Feb 54	Air Transport	215UNTS249	102922
Belgium	Ireland	30 Jun 54	Air Transport	212UNTS255	102876
Netherlands	USA (United States)	21 Mar 55	Telecommunications	289UNTS129	104217
Norway	Sweden	28 May 55	Scientific Project	262UNTS151	103743
UK Great Britain	USA (United States)	15 Nov 55	Scientific Project	231UNTS185	103219
Colombia	USA (United States)	14 Mar 56	Scientific Project	271UNTS303	103922
France	USA (United States)	23 Mar 56	Specific Property	278UNTS131	104029
Dominican Republic	USA (United States)	11 Aug 56	Scientific Project	263UNTS181	103773
Netherlands	USA (United States)	16 Aug 56	Specific Property	279UNTS3	104031
UK Great Britain	USA (United States)	01 Nov 56	Scientific Project	264UNTS3	103785
UK Great Britain	USA (United States)	27 Nov 56	Scientific Project	282UNTS43	104092
Chile	USA (United States)	01 Mar 57	Non-ILO Labor	283UNTS127	104112
Peru	USA (United States)	17 Apr 57	Scientific Project	283UNTS3	104102
Ecuador	USA (United States)	24 Apr 57	Scientific Project	284UNTS3	104124
UK Great Britain	USA (United States)	01 Nov 57	Scientific Project	299UNTS167	104312
UK Great Britain	USA (United States)	20 Jan 58	Specific Property	304UNTS3	104387
Australia	USA (United States)	25 Feb 58	Tech Assistance	317UNTS153	104601
Argentina	USA (United States)	28 Apr 58	Status of Forces	315UNTS211	104570
UK Great Britain	USA (United States)	30 Dec 58	Specific Property	338UNTS281	104841
Colombia	USA (United States)	08 May 59	Direct Aid	344UNTS193	104950
Mexico	USA (United States)	04 Feb 60	Scientific Project	586UNTS57	108496
Canada	USA (United States)	14 Jun 60	Scientific Project	377UNTS365	105413
India	USA (United States)	07 Feb 61	Scientific Project	462UNTS57	106671
Multilateral		08 Mar 61	Scientific Project	396UNTS255	200584
Australia	USA (United States)	09 May 61	Scientific Project	409UNTS203	105886
Australia	USA (United States)	05 Jun 61	Scientific Project	409UNTS279	105892
Chile	USA (United States)	12 Aug 61	Scientific Project	421UNTS209	106059
UK Great Britain	USA (United States)	26 Sep 61	Scientific Project	421UNTS99	106055
India	USA (United States)	09 Oct 62	Scientific Project	471UNTS39	106820
Dominican Republic	USA (United States)	25 Oct 62	Scientific Project	459UNTS247	106627
Canada	USA (United States)	28 Dec 62	Scientific Project	471UNTS13	106818
UK Great Britain	USA (United States)	15 Jan 63	Scientific Project	466UNTS181	106743
New Zealand	Western Samoa	31 Dec 63	Scientific Project	521UNTS163	107519
Mexico	USA (United States)	14 Feb 64	Scientific Project	524UNTS197	107574
Colombia	USA (United States)	13 May 64	Scientific Project	530UNTS77	107673
Peru	USA (United States)	07 Jul 64	Scientific Project	530UNTS113	107676
USA (United States)	Western Samoa	03 Nov 64	Scientific Project	521UNTS181	107521
Canada	USA (United States)	11 Jun 65	Scientific Project	564UNTS83	108222
Multilateral		08 Dec 65	IGO Establishment	600UNTS161	108680
Migrant Employees					
Mexico	USA (United States)	19 Nov 54	Non-ILO Labor	238UNTS237	103367
Philippines	UK Great Britain	29 Aug 55	Non-ILO Labor	221UNTS241	103009
Military Missions					
Haiti	USA (United States)	23 May 41	Military Mission	117UNTS191	200370
Bolivia	USA (United States)	04 Sep 41	Military Mission	8UNTS345	200046
Colombia	USA (United States)	19 Feb 42	Military Mission	117UNTS185	200369
Brazil	USA (United States)	07 May 42	Military Mission	6UNTS377	200040
Colombia	USA (United States)	29 May 42	Military Mission	8UNTS365	200047
Panama	USA (United States)	07 Jul 42	Military Mission	9UNTS289	200048
Bolivia	USA (United States)	11 Aug 42	Military Mission	9UNTS309	200049
Colombia	USA (United States)	05 Nov 42	Military Mission	24UNTS227	200147
Chile	USA (United States)	14 Apr 43	Military Mission	9UNTS331	200050
Argentina	USA (United States)	02 Sep 43	Military Mission	9UNTS363	200052
Paraguay	USA (United States)	27 Oct 43	Military Mission	29UNTS391	200174
Iran	USA (United States)	27 Nov 43	Military Mission	31UNTS451	200176

PARTY ONE	PARTY TWO	DATE	TOPIC	CITATION	NUMBER
Military Missions (Cont.)					
Paraguay	USA (United States)	10 Dec 43	Military Mission	21UNTS305	200131
USA (United States)	Venezuela	13 Jan 44	Military Mission	109UNTS171	200358
Peru	USA (United States)	31 Mar 44	Military Mission	109UNTS165	200357
Peru	USA (United States)	02 May 44	Military Mission	109UNTS211	200361
Ecuador	USA (United States)	29 Jun 44	Military Mission	80UNTS283	200250
Peru	USA (United States)	10 Jul 44	Military Mission	117UNTS291	200377
Ethiopia	UK Great Britain	19 Dec 44	General Amity	93UNTS303	200272
Guatemala	USA (United States)	21 Feb 45	Military Mission	121UNTS133	200396
Guatemala	USA (United States)	21 May 45	Military Mission	121UNTS185	200399
Chile	USA (United States)	24 May 45	Military Mission	121UNTS219	200401
Colombia	USA (United States)	03 Dec 45	Military Mission	107UNTS3	101462
Costa Rica	USA (United States)	10 Dec 45	Military Mission	3UNTS157	100029
Honduras	USA (United States)	28 Dec 45	Military Mission	3UNTS185	100031
USA (United States)	Venezuela	03 Jun 46	Military Mission	4UNTS215	100047
Iran	USA (United States)	08 Aug 46	Military Mission	31UNTS423	100484
Peru	USA (United States)	19 Aug 46	Military Mission	109UNTS15	101485
Brazil	USA (United States)	17 Sep 46	Military Mission	7UNTS49	100091
Peru	USA (United States)	07 Oct 46	Military Mission	7UNTS71	100092
Colombia	USA (United States)	14 Oct 46	Military Mission	7UNTS97	100093
Philippines	USA (United States)	16 Nov 46	Air Transport	7UNTS151	100097
Peru	USA (United States)	27 Dec 46	Air Transport	152UNTS93	102013
Greece	UK Great Britain	05 Jun 47	Status of Forces	9UNTS197	100133
El Salvador	USA (United States)	19 Aug 47	Military Mission	51UNTS57	100752
Iran	USA (United States)	06 Oct 47	Military Mission	11UNTS303	100171
Burma	UK Great Britain	17 Oct 47	Recognition	70UNTS183	100904
Ecuador	USA (United States)	27 Oct 47	Air Transport	44UNTS45	100677
Bolivia	USA (United States)	03 Nov 47	Air Transport	51UNTS33	100750
Colombia	USA (United States)	22 Dec 47	Air Transport	51UNTS45	100751
USA (United States)	Venezuela	30 Jan 48	Military Mission	109UNTS25	101486
Peru	USA (United States)	02 Mar 48	Military Mission	109UNTS9	101484
USA (United States)	Venezuela	24 Mar 48	Air Transport	44UNTS57	100678
Brazil	USA (United States)	29 Jul 48	Military Mission	80UNTS111	101047
Greece	UK Great Britain	07 Sep 48	Status of Forces	180UNTS144	102380
Ecuador	USA (United States)	21 Sep 48	Military Mission	80UNTS127	101048
Argentina	USA (United States)	06 Oct 48	Military Mission	80UNTS91	101046
Guatemala	USA (United States)	08 Oct 48	Military Mission	121UNTS31	101623
Guatemala	USA (United States)	08 Oct 48	Military Mission	121UNTS37	101624
Haiti	USA (United States)	04 Jan 49	Military Mission	44UNTS69	100679
Ecuador	USA (United States)	04 Feb 49	Military Mission	80UNTS137	101049
Colombia	USA (United States)	21 Feb 49	Military Mission	92UNTS227	101275
Colombia	USA (United States)	21 Feb 49	Military Mission	44UNTS83	100680
Panama	USA (United States)	31 Mar 49	Air Transport	55UNTS141	100812
Haiti	USA (United States)	14 Apr 49	Military Mission	80UNTS37	101043
Ecuador	USA (United States)	17 May 49	Military Mission	66UNTS3	100845
Peru	USA (United States)	20 Jun 49	Military Mission	92UNTS249	101276
Italy	Netherlands	16 Aug 49	Admin Cooperation	98UNTS21	101357
Nicaragua	USA (United States)	01 Feb 50	Tech Assistance	99UNTS25	101368
Honduras	USA (United States)	06 Mar 50	Military Mission	80UNTS71	101045
Honduras	USA (United States)	06 Mar 50	Military Mission	80UNTS51	101044
Bolivia	USA (United States)	30 Mar 50	Military Mission	241UNTS77	103425
USA (United States)	Venezuela	23 Aug 50	Military Mission	92UNTS341	101279
Cuba	USA (United States)	22 Dec 50	Military Mission	122UNTS97	101640
Liberia	USA (United States)	11 Jan 51	Military Mission	122UNTS125	101642
Chile	USA (United States)	15 Feb 51	Military Mission	133UNTS95	101783
Chile	USA (United States)	15 Feb 51	Military Mission	133UNTS117	101784
Paraguay	USA (United States)	30 Jul 51	Military Mission	178UNTS163	102340
USA (United States)	Venezuela	10 Aug 51	Military Mission	140UNTS345	101898
Cuba	USA (United States)	28 Aug 51	Military Mission	134UNTS225	101802
Cuba	USA (United States)	28 Aug 51	Military Mission	140UNTS239	101891
Costa Rica	USA (United States)	11 Sep 51	Air Transport	234UNTS255	103288
USA (United States)	Uruguay	04 Dec 51	Military Mission	152UNTS41	102010
Honduras	USA (United States)	07 Mar 52	Tech Assistance	233UNTS151	103260
Nicaragua	USA (United States)	19 Nov 52	Military Mission	186UNTS3	102478
USA (United States)	Venezuela	16 Jan 53	Military Mission	199UNTS287	102690
El Salvador	USA (United States)	21 May 53	Military Mission	213UNTS15	102878

PARTY ONE	PARTY TWO	DATE	TOPIC	CITATION	NUMBER
Military Missions (Cont.)					
Nicaragua	USA (United States)	19 Nov 53	Military Mission	206UNTS117	102787
El Salvador	USA (United States)	23 Sep 54	Military Mission	237UNTS91	103338
Paraguay	USA (United States)	22 Jul 55	Military Mission	265UNTS3	103802
Paraguay	USA (United States)	22 Jul 55	Military Mission	265UNTS15	103803
Cuba	USA (United States)	03 Aug 55	Military Mission	265UNTS41	103805
Bolivia	USA (United States)	09 Sep 55	Military Mission	256UNTS239	103633
Brazil	USA (United States)	20 Sep 55	Military Mission	257UNTS349	103665
Colombia	USA (United States)	27 Mar 56	Air Transport	273UNTS235	103954
Bolivia	USA (United States)	30 Jun 56	Military Mission	271UNTS269	103920
Bolivia	USA (United States)	30 Jun 56	Military Mission	271UNTS243	103919
Peru	USA (United States)	06 Sep 56	Military Mission	277UNTS231	104009
Argentina	USA (United States)	03 Oct 56	Military Mission	279UNTS13	104032
Chile	USA (United States)	15 Nov 56	Military Mission	282UNTS3	104089
Dominican Republic	USA (United States)	07 Dec 56	Military Mission	263UNTS193	103774
El Salvador	USA (United States)	21 Nov 57	Military Mission	303UNTS19	104369
Peru	USA (United States)	15 Jul 60	Military Mission	384UNTS159	105517
Argentina	USA (United States)	02 Aug 60	Military Mission	384UNTS105	105514
Chile	USA (United States)	27 Oct 64	Military Mission	532UNTS347	107727
Guatemala	USA (United States)	04 May 65	Status of Forces	545UNTS163	107932
Military Occupation					
Norway	USA (United States)	16 May 44	Privil/Immunities	67UNTS253	200223
Belgium	UK Great Britain	16 May 44	Admin Cooperation	90UNTS283	200266
Multilateral		12 Sep 44	Milit Occupation	227UNTS279	200532
Multilateral		14 Nov 44	Milit Occupation	236UNTS359	200539
USA (United States)	USSR (Soviet Union)	11 Feb 45	Other Military	68UNTS175	200229
Multilateral		05 Jun 45	Milit Occupation	68UNTS189	200230
UK Great Britain	USA (United States)	15 Jun 45	Reparations	89UNTS327	200261
Belgium	UK Great Britain	25 Jun 45	Reparations	90UNTS307	200268
Multilateral		09 Jul 45	Milit Occupation	160UNTS359	200484
Multilateral		26 Jul 45	Milit Occupation	227UNTS297	200533
USA (United States)	USSR (Soviet Union)	17 Sep 45	Milit Occupation	235UNTS346	200538
Belgium	France	30 Oct 45	Reparations	19UNTS87	100306
Denmark	UK Great Britain	06 Dec 45	Finance	5UNTS3	100061
France	UK Great Britain	26 Jan 46	Reparations	91UNTS183	101251
Belgium	UK Great Britain	11 Mar 46	Status of Forces	26UNTS167	100387
Greece	UK Great Britain	21 Mar 46	Claims and Debts	91UNTS149	101247
Multilateral		28 Jun 46	Milit Occupation	138UNTS85	101862
Luxembourg	USA (United States)	03 Jul 46	Mostfavored Nation	32UNTS85	100491
UK Great Britain	USA (United States)	02 Dec 46	Milit Occupation	7UNTS163	100098
Luxembourg	UK Great Britain	11 Dec 46	Claims and Debts	11UNTS167	100155
Multilateral		20 Jan 47	Water Transport	87UNTS247	101176
Belgium	USA (United States)	23 Jan 47	Visas	47UNTS23	100721
Multilateral		10 Feb 47	Peace/Disarmament	49UNTS3	100747
Norway	USSR (Soviet Union)	19 Feb 47	General Trade	30UNTS293	100464
Denmark	UK Great Britain	22 Apr 47	Milit Occupation	8UNTS3	100110
Norway	UK Great Britain	05 Jun 47	Milit Occupation	54UNTS181	100803
Austria	USA (United States)	21 Jun 47	Milit Occupation	67UNTS99	100869
Austria	USA (United States)	21 Jun 47	Reparations	67UNTS89	100868
Czechoslovakia	USA (United States)	25 Jul 47	Reparations	90UNTS19	101223
Australia	France	28 Jul 47	Reparations	97UNTS271	101353
Italy	USA (United States)	03 Sep 47	Status of Forces	67UNTS15	100863
Multilateral		19 Sep 47	Finance	30UNTS269	100462
Multilateral		19 Sep 47	General Trade	30UNTS249	100461
Multilateral		05 Oct 47	Finance	34UNTS23	100525
France	USA (United States)	25 Oct 47	Non-ILO Labor	89UNTS111	101212
Belgium	USSR (Soviet Union)	10 Nov 47	Finance	18UNTS299	100298
Denmark	UK Great Britain	01 Dec 47	Reparations	93UNTS151	101298
Taiwan	USA (United States)	17 Mar 48	Reparations	76UNTS157	100987
Belgium	France	23 Apr 48	Territory Boundary	19UNTS95	100307
France	USA (United States)	28 Jun 48	Mostfavored Nation	31UNTS115	100472
Ireland	USA (United States)	28 Jun 48	Mostfavored Nation	32UNTS69	100489
Italy	USA (United States)	28 Jun 48	Milit Occupation	25UNTS45	100356
Denmark	USA (United States)	29 Jun 48	Mostfavored Nation	27UNTS35	100396
Austria	USA (United States)	02 Jul 48	Milit Occupation	25UNTS53	100357

PARTY ONE	PARTY TWO	DATE	TOPIC	CITATION	NUMBER
Military Occupation (Cont.)					
Greece	USA (United States)	02 Jul 48	Mostfavored Nation	31UNTS131	100474
Belgium	USA (United States)	02 Jul 48	Mostfavored Nation	27UNTS43	100397
Netherlands	USA (United States)	02 Jul 48	Mostfavored Nation	32UNTS77	100490
Norway	USA (United States)	03 Jul 48	Milit Occupation	27UNTS59	100399
Taiwan	USA (United States)	03 Jul 48	Direct Aid	17UNTS119	100273
Sweden	USA (United States)	03 Jul 48	Milit Occupation	27UNTS69	100400
Iceland	USA (United States)	03 Jul 48	Milit Occupation	27UNTS49	100398
Turkey	USA (United States)	04 Jul 48	Mostfavored Nation	34UNTS185	100536
France	Norway	05 Jul 48	General Trade	30UNTS281	100463
UK Great Britain	USA (United States)	06 Jul 48	Milit Occupation	25UNTS61	100358
France	USA (United States)	09 Jul 48	Direct Aid	24UNTS103	100352
France	USA (United States)	09 Jul 48	Mostfavored Nation	32UNTS93	100492
Multilateral		14 Jul 48	Mostfavored Nation	31UNTS123	100473
Multilateral		14 Jul 48	Direct Aid	23UNTS3	100340
Multilateral		14 Sep 48	Milit Occupation	18UNTS267	100296
Portugal	USA (United States)	28 Sep 48	Mostfavored Nation	31UNTS139	100475
UK Great Britain	USA (United States)	30 Sep 48	Specific Resources	71UNTS241	100922
Trieste	USA (United States)	15 Oct 48	Direct Aid	29UNTS249	100443
Multilateral		16 Dec 48	Direct Aid	79UNTS85	101033
UK Great Britain	Yugoslavia	23 Dec 48	Reparations	81UNTS103	101067
Belgium	UK Great Britain	29 Dec 48	Visas	27UNTS135	100404
France	USA (United States)	07 Feb 49	Direct Aid	67UNTS189	100877
Trieste	USA (United States)	11 Feb 49	Direct Aid	79UNTS123	101036
Allied Milit Occup	Norway	17 Feb 49	Milit Occupation	30UNTS137	100451
Germany, West	Greece	16 Mar 49	Finance	77UNTS327	101007
Germany, West	Greece	16 Mar 49	General Trade	77UNTS307	101006
Multilateral		16 Mar 49	Finance	29UNTS95	100436
Multilateral		08 Apr 49	Milit Occupation	140UNTS196	101889
Multilateral		14 Apr 49	Milit Occupation	141UNTS281	101919
Japan	USA (United States)	14 Apr 49	Specif Claim/Waive	89UNTS141	101215
Belgium	UK Great Britain	14 Apr 49	Visas	65UNTS117	100840
Multilateral		28 Apr 49	IGO Establishment	83UNTS105	101105
Multilateral		04 May 49	Milit Occupation	138UNTS123	101864
Multilateral		20 Jun 49	IGO Establishment	128UNTS141	101718
Multilateral		05 Aug 49	Finance	88UNTS229	101195
Multilateral		10 Aug 49	Finance	45UNTS3	100689
Multilateral		12 Aug 49	Humanitarian	75UNTS287	100973
Allied Milit Occup	Norway	16 Sep 49	General Trade	53UNTS3	100769
Multilateral		19 Sep 49	Land Transport	125UNTS3	101671
Denmark	Germany, West	15 Dec 49	Finance	51UNTS11	100749
Belgium	UK Great Britain	23 Dec 49	Status of Forces	99UNTS61	101371
Australia	Yugoslavia	22 Feb 50	Claims and Debts	51UNTS201	100766
Australia	Netherlands	26 Apr 50	Claims and Debts	54UNTS83	100796
Belgium	Japan	29 Aug 50	General Trade	82UNTS147	101089
Belgium	Japan	29 Aug 50	General Trade	76UNTS113	100984
Germany, West	Netherlands	14 Dec 50	Water Transport	87UNTS257	101177
New Zealand	Yugoslavia	27 Feb 51	Reparations	150UNTS165	101971
Multilateral		06 Mar 51	Milit Assistance	138UNTS67	101860
Belgium	Netherlands	15 Mar 51	Reparations	93UNTS97	101294
Multilateral		03 Apr 51	Milit Occupation	141UNTS303	101920
Germany, West	USA (United States)	30 Mar 53	Reparations	235UNTS285	103310
Multilateral		23 Oct 54	Milit Occupation	331UNTS253	104758
USA (United States)	USSR (Soviet Union)	25 Jun 55	Territory Boundary	270UNTS15	103887
Military Questions					
Netherlands	USA (United States)	17 Jan 33	Status of Forces	474UNTS119	106877
Canada	USA (United States)	10 Jun 39	Milit Assistance	149UNTS332	200476
Canada	USA (United States)	29 May 40	Status of Forces	119UNTS285	200385
Finland	USSR (Soviet Union)	11 Oct 40	Territory Boundary	67UNTS139	100872
Multilateral		27 Mar 41	Military Mission	67UNTS231	200222
Iceland	USA (United States)	01 Jul 41	Milit Assistance	12UNTS405	200071
Multilateral		29 Jan 42	General Military	93UNTS279	200271
Peru	USA (United States)	11 Mar 42	Military Mission	117UNTS266	200375
Canada	USA (United States)	20 Mar 42	Milit Servic/Citiz	105UNTS169	200330
USA (United States)	Yugoslavia	30 Mar 42	Milit Servic/Citiz	13UNTS199	200079
Military Questions (Cont.)					
Canada	USA (United States)	08 Apr 42	Milit Servic/Citiz	105UNTS179	200331
Taiwan	USA (United States)	02 Jun 42	Milit Assistance	14UNTS343	200092
Canada	USA (United States)	27 Jun 42	Other Military	99UNTS223	200276
Panama	USA (United States)	07 Jul 42	Military Mission	9UNTS289	200048
Czechoslovakia	USA (United States)	11 Jul 42	Milit Assistance	90UNTS257	200263
Guatemala	USA (United States)	21 Jul 42	Military Mission	103UNTS299	200320
USA (United States)	Yugoslavia	24 Jul 42	Milit Assistance	34UNTS361	200179
Norway	USA (United States)	28 Aug 42	Other Military	139UNTS361	200461
New Zealand	USA (United States)	03 Sep 42	Milit Assistance	24UNTS185	200142
Australia	USA (United States)	03 Sep 42	Milit Assistance	24UNTS195	200143
France	USA (United States)	03 Sep 42	Milit Assistance	24UNTS177	200141
Netherlands	USA (United States)	30 Sep 42	Milit Servic/Citiz	13UNTS151	200076
New Zealand	USA (United States)	30 Sep 42	Milit Servic/Citiz	13UNTS139	200075
India	USA (United States)	30 Sep 42	Milit Servic/Citiz	13UNTS185	200078
UK Great Britain	USA (United States)	30 Sep 42	Milit Servic/Citiz	13UNTS169	200077
Australia	USA (United States)	30 Sep 42	Milit Servic/Citiz	13UNTS125	200074
Belgium	USA (United States)	16 Oct 42	Milit Servic/Citiz	13UNTS211	200080
South Africa	USA (United States)	31 Oct 42	Milit Servic/Citiz	105UNTS269	200338
Canada	USA (United States)	04 Nov 42	Non-ILO Labor	24UNTS217	200146
El Salvador	USA (United States)	24 Nov 42	Military Mission	24UNTS241	200149
Norway	USA (United States)	16 Jan 43	Milit Servic/Citiz	13UNTS335	200082
Mexico	USA (United States)	22 Jan 43	Milit Servic/Citiz	105UNTS259	200337
Canada	USA (United States)	27 Jan 43	Milit Installation	101UNTS257	200300
Belgium	USA (United States)	30 Jan 43	Milit Assistance	13UNTS371	200084
Cuba	USA (United States)	01 Feb 43	Milit Servic/Citiz	13UNTS379	200085
Poland	USA (United States)	25 Feb 43	Milit Servic/Citiz	13UNTS395	200086
Greece	USA (United States)	16 Mar 43	Milit Servic/Citiz	105UNTS227	200335
El Salvador	USA (United States)	25 Mar 43	Military Mission	13UNTS419	200088
Multilateral		26 Mar 43	Specif Goods/Equip	13UNTS427	200089
Colombia	USA (United States)	29 Mar 43	Milit Installation	124UNTS139	200416
El Salvador	USA (United States)	21 May 43	Military Mission	9UNTS341	200051
Taiwan	USA (United States)	21 May 43	Status of Forces	14UNTS353	200093
Brazil	USA (United States)	24 May 43	Status of Forces	28UNTS385	200162
Canada	USA (United States)	26 May 43	Privil/Immunities	7UNTS345	200043
El Salvador	USA (United States)	31 May 43	Milit Servic/Citiz	105UNTS205	200333
Netherlands	USA (United States)	14 Jun 43	General Military	28UNTS397	200163
Guatemala	USA (United States)	17 Jul 43	Military Mission	28UNTS431	200166
Canada	USA (United States)	09 Aug 43	Milit Installation	29UNTS295	200168
Ethiopia	USA (United States)	09 Aug 43	Milit Installation	29UNTS303	200169
Ecuador	USA (United States)	13 Sep 43	Military Mission	29UNTS349	200171
Czechoslovakia	USA (United States)	21 Oct 43	Milit Servic/Citiz	29UNTS369	200172
Nicaragua	USA (United States)	25 Oct 43	Military Mission	29UNTS383	200173
Peru	USA (United States)	20 Dec 43	Military Mission	117UNTS285	200376
Colombia	USA (United States)	12 Feb 44	Milit Servic/Citiz	109UNTS287	200365
Canada	Taiwan	22 Mar 44	Milit Assistance	14UNTS397	200096
Canada	USA (United States)	23 Mar 44	Claims and Debts	125UNTS345	200432
UK Great Britain	USA (United States)	28 Mar 44	Status of Forces	15UNTS413	200104
Belgium	UK Great Britain	16 May 44	Admin Cooperation	90UNTS283	200266
Brazil	UK Great Britain	27 May 44	Milit Servic/Citiz	2UNTS235	200016
Taiwan	USA (United States)	13 Jun 44	Status of Forces	107UNTS43	200350
Canada	USA (United States)	27 Jun 44	Milit Installation	101UNTS273	200301
Belgium	UK Great Britain	22 Aug 44	Direct Aid	90UNTS295	200267
Brazil	USA (United States)	29 Sep 44	Military Mission	65UNTS271	200216
Portugal	USA (United States)	28 Nov 44	Milit Assistance	183UNTS311	200508
Ethiopia	UK Great Britain	19 Dec 44	General Amity	93UNTS303	200272
Canada	USA (United States)	13 Feb 45	Status of Forces	200UNTS219	200519
France	USA (United States)	20 Feb 45	IGO Status/Immunit	76UNTS223	200248
France	USA (United States)	20 Feb 45	Direct Aid	76UNTS193	200246
France	USA (United States)	28 Feb 45	IGO Status/Immunit	76UNTS213	200247
France	UK Great Britain	27 Mar 45	Finance	98UNTS227	200274
Ecuador	USA (United States)	05 Apr 45	Milit Servic/Citiz	121UNTS265	200404
USA (United States)	Venezuela	11 May 45	Milit Servic/Citiz	121UNTS273	200405
Multilateral		05 Jun 45	Milit Occupation	68UNTS189	200230
Chile	USA (United States)	11 Jun 45	Milit Servic/Citiz	121UNTS291	200407
Peru	USA (United States)	12 Jun 45	Milit Servic/Citiz	121UNTS283	200406

Military Questions (Cont.)

PARTY ONE	PARTY TWO	DATE	TOPIC	CITATION	NUMBER
UK Great Britain	USA (United States)	15 Jun 45	Reparations	89UNTS327	200261
Belgium	UK Great Britain	25 Jun 45	Reparations	90UNTS307	200268
Taiwan	UK Great Britain	07 Jul 45	Status of Forces	14UNTS455	200100
Denmark	UK Great Britain	24 Oct 45	Milit Assistance	93UNTS143	101297
Belgium	France	30 Oct 45	Reparations	19UNTS87	100306
France	USA (United States)	08 Nov 45	General Trade	76UNTS151	100986
Multilateral		01 Jan 46	Peace/Disarmament	99UNTS131	101375
France	UK Great Britain	26 Jan 46	Reparations	91UNTS183	101251
Czechoslovakia	Poland	12 Feb 46	Reparations	25UNTS207	100364
Taiwan	France	28 Feb 46	Milit Occupation	14UNTS151	100217
Canada	USA (United States)	03 Mar 46	Specific Property	6UNTS279	100081
Canada	UK Great Britain	06 Mar 46	Reparations	20UNTS3	100311
Belgium	UK Great Britain	11 Mar 46	Status of Forces	26UNTS167	100387
UK Great Britain	USA (United States)	27 Mar 46	Milit Assistance	4UNTS2	100039
Canada	USA (United States)	30 Mar 46	Milit Installation	7UNTS15	100089
Multilateral		31 Mar 46	Milit Installation	17UNTS159	100274
Thailand	UK Great Britain	06 May 46	Commodity Trade	99UNTS193	101380
France	USA (United States)	28 May 46	Reparations	84UNTS93	101121
France	USA (United States)	28 May 46	Milit Assistance	84UNTS79	101120
France	USA (United States)	28 May 46	Status of Forces	84UNTS141	101124
France	USA (United States)	28 May 46	Reparations	84UNTS113	101122
France	USA (United States)	28 May 46	Milit Assistance	84UNTS59	101119
France	USA (United States)	28 May 46	Status of Forces	84UNTS121	101123
Ecuador	USA (United States)	11 Jun 46	Status of Forces	167UNTS135	102203
Taiwan	USA (United States)	28 Jun 46	Milit Assistance	34UNTS121	100532
UK Great Britain	USA (United States)	31 Jul 46	Air Transport	42UNTS199	100648
Poland	USA (United States)	29 Aug 46	Status of Forces	160UNTS11	102097
Belgium	USA (United States)	24 Sep 46	Claims and Debts	132UNTS80	101753
Canada	USA (United States)	27 Sep 46	Patents/Copyrights	21UNTS3	100320
Iceland	USA (United States)	07 Oct 46	Milit Installation	12UNTS163	100184
Canada	USA (United States)	15 Nov 46	Specif Claim/Waive	7UNTS141	100096
UK Great Britain	USA (United States)	02 Dec 46	Milit Occupation	7UNTS163	100098
France	UK Great Britain	03 Dec 46	Reparations	54UNTS127	100799
Canada	USA (United States)	06 Dec 46	Milit Assistance	149UNTS3	101945
Thailand	UK Great Britain	06 Jan 47	Reparations	99UNTS149	101376
Canada	USA (United States)	09 Jan 47	Specific Property	11UNTS341	100173
UK Great Britain	USA (United States)	23 Jan 47	Status of Forces	15UNTS281	100244
Multilateral		10 Feb 47	Reparations	140UNTS111	101886
Multilateral		10 Feb 47	Peace/Disarmament	49UNTS3	100747
Multilateral		10 Feb 47	Peace/Disarmament	42UNTS3	100645
Multilateral		10 Feb 47	Peace/Disarmament	41UNTS135	100644
Multilateral		10 Feb 47	Peace/Disarmament	41UNTS21	100643
Multilateral		10 Feb 47	Peace/Disarmament	48UNTS203	100746
France	Poland	11 Feb 47	Reparations	12UNTS287	100189
Philippines	USA (United States)	14 Mar 47	Milit Installation	43UNTS271	100673
Philippines	USA (United States)	21 Mar 47	Milit Assistance	45UNTS47	100691
Greece	UK Great Britain	07 Apr 47	Territory Boundary	11UNTS201	100158
Italy	UK Great Britain	17 Apr 47	Finance	54UNTS149	100801
Denmark	UK Great Britain	22 Apr 47	Milit Occupation	8UNTS3	100110
Thailand	UK Great Britain	08 May 47	Claims and Debts	100UNTS47	101386
Netherlands	USA (United States)	28 May 47	General Military	17UNTS29	100267
Norway	UK Great Britain	05 Jun 47	Milit Occupation	54UNTS181	100803
Austria	USA (United States)	21 Jun 47	Milit Occupation	67UNTS99	100869
Austria	USA (United States)	21 Jun 47	Reparations	67UNTS89	100868
India	USA (United States)	05 Jul 47	Status of Forces	185UNTS293	102476
Belgium	USA (United States)	23 Jul 47	Other Military	33UNTS33	100512
Czechoslovakia	USA (United States)	25 Jul 47	Reparations	90UNTS19	101223
Taiwan	Italy	30 Jul 47	Reparations	12UNTS377	100194
Italy	USA (United States)	14 Aug 47	Reparations	36UNTS53	100566
Guatemala	USA (United States)	29 Aug 47	Status of Forces	27UNTS11	100393
Italy	USA (United States)	03 Sep 47	Status of Forces	67UNTS15	100863
Taiwan	USA (United States)	03 Sep 47	Status of Forces	9UNTS91	100126
Multilateral		10 Oct 47	Claims and Debts	54UNTS193	100804
Burma	UK Great Britain	17 Oct 47	Recognition	70UNTS183	100904
Chile	UK Great Britain	27 Oct 47	Milit Servic/Citiz	82UNTS209	101094

Military Questions (Cont.)

PARTY ONE	PARTY TWO	DATE	TOPIC	CITATION	NUMBER
Multilateral		04 Nov 47	Reparations	93UNTS61	101288
Ceylon (Sri Lanka)	UK Great Britain	11 Nov 47	Milit Assistance	86UNTS19	101148
Denmark	UK Great Britain	01 Dec 47	Reparations	93UNTS151	101298
Greece	USA (United States)	03 Dec 47	Milit Assistance	89UNTS119	101213
Taiwan	USA (United States)	08 Dec 47	Milit Installation	70UNTS3	100895
Multilateral		16 Dec 47	Reparations	82UNTS237	101096
Italy	UK Great Britain	21 Jan 48	Milit Installation	77UNTS23	100989
Brazil	USA (United States)	02 Feb 48	Status of Forces	67UNTS109	100870
Romania	USSR (Soviet Union)	04 Feb 48	General Military	48UNTS189	100745
Italy	USA (United States)	14 Feb 48	Reparations	67UNTS115	100871
India	UK Great Britain	15 Feb 48	Finance	134UNTS70	101796
Pakistan	UK Great Britain	21 Feb 48	Finance	134UNTS128	101797
UK Great Britain	USA (United States)	24 Feb 48	Milit Installation	73UNTS143	100951
Norway	USA (United States)	24 Feb 48	Milit Assistance	34UNTS155	100535
France	USA (United States)	25 Feb 48	Milit Servic/Citiz	67UNTS33	100864
Czechoslovakia	Italy	25 Feb 48	Admin Cooperation	26UNTS103	100380
France	USA (United States)	27 Feb 48	Reparations	84UNTS207	101131
Netherlands	UK Great Britain	11 Mar 48	Reparations	77UNTS69	100993
Taiwan	USA (United States)	17 Mar 48	Reparations	76UNTS157	100987
Multilateral		17 Mar 48	General Military	19UNTS51	100304
Canada	USA (United States)	31 Mar 48	Specific Property	81UNTS285	101077
France	UK Great Britain	19 Apr 48	Status of Forces	83UNTS201	101109
Portugal	UK Great Britain	25 May 48	Milit Installation	34UNTS311	100544
Belgium	UK Great Britain	07 Jun 48	Reparations	20UNTS33	100313
UK Great Britain	Uruguay	12 Jul 48	Finance	71UNTS199	100919
France	UK Great Britain	15 Jul 48	Claims and Debts	71UNTS215	100920
USA (United States)	Yugoslavia	19 Jul 48	Milit Assistance	34UNTS195	100537
Korea, South	USA (United States)	11 Sep 48	Milit Assistance	89UNTS155	101216
Czechoslovakia	USA (United States)	16 Sep 48	Milit Assistance	90UNTS35	101224
UK Great Britain	USA (United States)	22 Sep 48	Milit Assistance	71UNTS64	100910
UK Great Britain	USA (United States)	30 Sep 48	Specific Resources	71UNTS241	100922
Canada	Netherlands	28 Oct 48	Reparations	231UNTS95	103210
Cuba	USA (United States)	21 Feb 49	Status of Forces	231UNTS108	103212
Greece	USA (United States)	21 Feb 49	Status of Forces	88UNTS29	101182
Canada	USA (United States)	14 Mar 49	Reparations	82UNTS3	101079
France	USA (United States)	14 Mar 49	Claims and Debts	84UNTS237	101133
Multilateral		04 Apr 49	General Military	34UNTS243	100541
Japan	USA (United States)	14 Apr 49	Specif Claim/Waive	89UNTS141	101215
United Arab Rep	UK Great Britain	17 Apr 49	Reparations	83UNTS183	101107
Canada	Netherlands	09 May 49	Reparations	46UNTS263	100715
Philippines	USA (United States)	16 May 49	Milit Installation	67UNTS199	100878
Netherlands	USA (United States)	17 May 49	Milit Assistance	46UNTS291	100717
Ethiopia	USA (United States)	20 May 49	Milit Assistance	89UNTS99	101211
Philippines	USA (United States)	07 Jun 49	Direct Aid	45UNTS63	100692
Denmark	France	22 Jun 49	Milit Servic/Citiz	48UNTS3	100737
India	USA (United States)	04 Jul 49	Status of Forces	200UNTS181	102702
Mexico	USA (United States)	05 Jul 49	Military Mission	68UNTS55	100884
Multilateral		05 Aug 49	Finance	88UNTS229	101195
Philippines	USA (United States)	08 Aug 49	Milit Installation	163UNTS103	102144
Multilateral		12 Aug 49	Humanitarian	75UNTS85	100971
Multilateral		12 Aug 49	Humanitarian	75UNTS287	100973
Multilateral		12 Aug 49	General Military	75UNTS135	100972
Multilateral		12 Aug 49	Humanitarian	75UNTS31	100970
Italy	Netherlands	16 Aug 49	Admin Cooperation	98UNTS21	101357
Belgium	France	29 Aug 49	Milit Servic/Citiz	93UNTS87	101293
Finland	USA (United States)	01 Nov 49	Claims and Debts	68UNTS11	100880
Belgium	Canada	16 Nov 49	Reparations	51UNTS3	100748
Guatemala	USA (United States)	20 Dec 49	Status of Forces	70UNTS71	100897
France	UK Great Britain	21 Dec 49	Milit Servic/Citiz	264UNTS37	103786
Belgium	UK Great Britain	23 Dec 49	Status of Forces	99UNTS61	101371
France	UK Great Britain	23 Jan 50	Reparations	97UNTS149	101348
Korea, South	USA (United States)	26 Jan 50	Military Mission	178UNTS97	102337
Korea, South	USA (United States)	26 Jan 50	Milit Assistance	80UNTS205	101053
UK Great Britain	USA (United States)	27 Jan 50	Milit Assistance	80UNTS261	101056
Luxembourg	USA (United States)	27 Jan 50	Milit Assistance	80UNTS187	101052

Military Questions (Cont.)

PARTY ONE	PARTY TWO	DATE	TOPIC	CITATION	NUMBER
France	USA (United States)	27 Jan 50	Milit Assistance	80UNTS171	101051
Belgium	USA (United States)	27 Jan 50	Milit Assistance	51UNTS213	100767
Norway	USA (United States)	27 Jan 50	Milit Assistance	80UNTS241	101055
Italy	USA (United States)	27 Jan 50	Milit Assistance	80UNTS145	101050
Iran	USA (United States)	23 May 50	Milit Assistance	81UNTS3	101057
UK Great Britain	USA (United States)	21 Jul 50	Milit Installation	97UNTS193	101351
Dominican Republic	USA (United States)	11 Aug 50	Status of Forces	92UNTS329	101278
Thailand	USA (United States)	17 Oct 50	Milit Assistance	79UNTS41	101030
Philippines	USA (United States)	06 Nov 50	Finance	122UNTS63	101637
Norway	USA (United States)	28 Dec 50	Milit Assistance	240UNTS391	103414
Brazil	USA (United States)	04 Jan 51	Milit Assistance	165UNTS97	102171
Chile	USA (United States)	04 Jan 51	Milit Assistance	165UNTS105	102172
Australia	Finland	04 Jan 51	Claims and Debts	80UNTS27	101042
Argentina	USA (United States)	08 Jan 51	Milit Assistance	165UNTS89	102170
Multilateral		06 Mar 51	Milit Assistance	138UNTS67	101860
Belgium	Netherlands	15 Mar 51	Reparations	93UNTS97	101294
Belgium	USA (United States)	16 Mar 51	Reparations	93UNTS109	101295
Denmark	USA (United States)	27 Apr 51	General Military	94UNTS35	101305
Iceland	USA (United States)	05 May 51	Milit Assistance	205UNTS173	102776
Multilateral		19 Jun 51	Status of Forces	199UNTS67	102678
Canada	USA (United States)	01 Aug 51	Milit Installation	233UNTS109	103254
Japan	USA (United States)	08 Sep 51	General Military	136UNTS211	101835
Multilateral		20 Sep 51	IGO Status/Immunit	200UNTS3	102691
USA (United States)	Yugoslavia	14 Nov 51	Milit Assistance	174UNTS201	102286
Nicaragua	USA (United States)	12 Dec 51	Status of Forces	167UNTS151	102205
Cuba	USA (United States)	18 Dec 51	General Military	165UNTS3	102164
Greece	USA (United States)	07 Jan 52	Milit Assistance	180UNTS171	102382
Greece	USA (United States)	07 Jan 52	Milit Assistance	177UNTS249	102323
Peru	USA (United States)	22 Feb 52	Milit Assistance	165UNTS31	102166
Costa Rica	USA (United States)	25 Feb 52	Status of Forces	174UNTS233	102288
Japan	USA (United States)	28 Feb 52	Milit Assistance	208UNTS255	102817
Cuba	USA (United States)	07 Mar 52	Milit Assistance	165UNTS11	102165
Brazil	USA (United States)	15 Mar 52	Milit Assistance	199UNTS221	102687
Chile	USA (United States)	09 Apr 52	Milit Assistance	186UNTS53	102482
Colombia	USA (United States)	17 Apr 52	Milit Assistance	174UNTS215	102287
Honduras	USA (United States)	23 Apr 52	Status of Forces	198UNTS251	102669
United Arab Rep	USA (United States)	29 Apr 52	Milit Assistance	241UNTS3	103418
Canada	USA (United States)	30 Apr 52	Milit Installation	235UNTS269	103308
Netherlands	USA (United States)	15 May 52	Milit Assistance	177UNTS233	102321
Philippines	Vatican/Holy See	18 Jun 52	Status of Forces	543UNTS165	107900
South Africa	USA (United States)	24 Jun 52	Milit Assistance	177UNTS241	102322
USA (United States)	Uruguay	30 Jun 52	Milit Assistance	207UNTS139	102804
Sweden	USA (United States)	01 Jul 52	Milit Assistance	187UNTS3	102497
Ethiopia	UK Great Britain	03 Jul 52	Status of Forces	151UNTS207	101996
Germany, West	UK Great Britain	09 Sep 52	Milit Installation	151UNTS215	101997
China People's Rep	USSR (Soviet Union)	15 Sep 52	Milit Installation	226UNTS45	103106
Japan	USA (United States)	12 Nov 52	Milit Assistance	184UNTS111	102443
Portugal	UK Great Britain	21 Nov 52	Milit Assistance	404UNTS27	105802
Greece	USA (United States)	24 Dec 52	Milit Assistance	185UNTS193	102470
Dominican Republic	USA (United States)	06 Mar 53	Milit Assistance	199UNTS267	102689
Philippines	USA (United States)	09 Mar 53	Milit Servic/Citiz	227UNTS101	103134
Japan	USA (United States)	18 Mar 53	Tech Assistance	212UNTS149	102867
Libya	UK Great Britain	21 Mar 53	General Military	172UNTS85	102240
Belgium	Canada	30 Mar 53	Status of Forces	181UNTS95	102401
Ethiopia	USA (United States)	22 May 53	Milit Installation	191UNTS59	102577
Canada	India	12 Jun 53	Admin Cooperation	248UNTS113	103490
Belgium	USA (United States)	18 Jun 53	Milit Assistance	222UNTS3	103019
Philippines	USA (United States)	26 Jun 53	Milit Assistance	213UNTS77	102881
Canada	USA (United States)	30 Jun 53	Specific Property	206UNTS93	102786
USA (United States)	Yugoslavia	23 Jul 53	Taxation	221UNTS365	103018
Libya	UK Great Britain	29 Jul 53	Status of Forces	186UNTS201	102492
Germany, West	USA (United States)	20 Aug 53	Milit Assistance	224UNTS49	103069
France	USA (United States)	02 Sep 53	Milit Assistance	224UNTS153	103075
Belgium	USA (United States)	02 Sep 53	Milit Assistance	200UNTS127	102700
Finland	Norway	22 Sep 53	Milit Servic/Citiz	183UNTS245	102433

Military Questions (Cont.)

PARTY ONE	PARTY TWO	DATE	TOPIC	CITATION	NUMBER
Spain	USA (United States)	26 Sep 53	Milit Assistance	207UNTS61	102800
Greece	USA (United States)	12 Oct 53	Milit Installation	191UNTS319	102589
Chile	Denmark	22 Oct 53	Milit Servic/Citiz	348UNTS261	105004
Belgium	USA (United States)	17 Nov 53	Milit Assistance	251UNTS105	103536
Germany, West	USA (United States)	23 Nov 53	Milit Installation	224UNTS107	103071
France	Italy	28 Dec 53	Milit Servic/Citiz	267UNTS89	103836
Belgium	Taiwan	13 Jan 54	Milit Assistance	223UNTS111	103059
Japan	USA (United States)	21 Jan 54	Tech Assistance	223UNTS145	103063
Turkey	UK Great Britain	11 Feb 54	Milit Assistance	190UNTS343	102575
Multilateral		19 Feb 54	Status of Forces	214UNTS51	102899
Italy	USA (United States)	31 Mar 54	Milit Assistance	235UNTS293	103311
Norway	USA (United States)	13 Apr 54	Status of Forces	229UNTS223	103169
Luxembourg	USA (United States)	17 Apr 54	Milit Assistance	257UNTS255	103661
Iraq	USA (United States)	21 Apr 54	Milit Assistance	222UNTS251	103032
Nicaragua	USA (United States)	23 Apr 54	Milit Assistance	229UNTS37	103159
Italy	USA (United States)	27 Apr 54	Milit Assistance	234UNTS103	103275
Netherlands	USA (United States)	07 May 54	Milit Assistance	213UNTS325	102895
Japan	USA (United States)	14 May 54	Milit Assistance	247UNTS273	103476
Taiwan	USA (United States)	14 May 54	Milit Installation	231UNTS165	103216
Pakistan	USA (United States)	19 May 54	Milit Assistance	202UNTS301	102736
Honduras	USA (United States)	20 May 54	Milit Assistance	222UNTS87	103025
Honduras	USA (United States)	24 May 54	Milit Installation	433UNTS155	106238
Denmark	USA (United States)	08 Jun 54	Milit Assistance	307UNTS133	104448
Belgium	Netherlands	09 Jun 54	Milit Servic/Citiz	216UNTS121	102936
UK Great Britain	USA (United States)	15 Jun 54	Milit Assistance	236UNTS133	103320
Turkey	USA (United States)	23 Jun 54	Status of Forces	233UNTS189	103263
Turkey	USA (United States)	01 Jul 54	Milit Assistance	234UNTS147	103280
Denmark	Italy	15 Jul 54	Milit Servic/Citiz	250UNTS43	103516
UK Great Britain	USA (United States)	21 Jul 54	Status of Forces	222UNTS243	103031
Guatemala	USA (United States)	30 Jul 54	Milit Assistance	234UNTS235	103286
Greece	USA (United States)	30 Jul 54	Milit Assistance	234UNTS43	103272
Spain	USA (United States)	30 Jul 54	Milit Assistance	235UNTS45	103295
Netherlands	USA (United States)	13 Aug 54	Milit Installation	251UNTS91	103535
Germany, West	USA (United States)	28 Aug 54	Milit Installation	299UNTS377	104325
Libya	USA (United States)	09 Sep 54	Milit Installation	224UNTS217	103078
UK Great Britain	USA (United States)	24 Sep 54	Milit Installation	300UNTS3	104326
China People's Rep	USSR (Soviet Union)	12 Oct 54	Milit Installation	226UNTS51	103107
USA (United States)	Yugoslavia	18 Oct 54	Milit Assistance	273UNTS163	103951
Multilateral		23 Oct 54	Status of Forces	332UNTS387	104763
Multilateral		23 Oct 54	Milit Occupation	332UNTS157	104761
Multilateral		23 Oct 54	Milit Occupation	331UNTS327	104759
Multilateral		23 Oct 54	Status of Forces	332UNTS3	104760
Multilateral		23 Oct 54	Reparations	332UNTS219	104762
Multilateral		23 Oct 54	Status of Forces	334UNTS3	104765
Korea, South	USA (United States)	17 Nov 54	Milit Assistance	256UNTS251	103635
Japan	USA (United States)	19 Nov 54	Milit Installation	238UNTS207	103364
Multilateral		02 Dec 54	General Amity	226UNTS153	103112
France	Norway	06 Dec 54	Milit Servic/Citiz	202UNTS313	102737
Iceland	USA (United States)	10 Dec 54	Milit Assistance	237UNTS191	103345
Netherlands	USA (United States)	14 Dec 54	Milit Assistance	262UNTS35	103737
Pakistan	USA (United States)	11 Jan 55	Milit Assistance	251UNTS111	103537
Denmark	UK Great Britain	20 Jan 55	Milit Servic/Citiz	210UNTS303	102842
Haiti	USA (United States)	28 Jan 55	Milit Assistance	270UNTS83	103894
Korea, South	USA (United States)	29 Jan 55	Milit Assistance	239UNTS53	103371
Germany, West	USA (United States)	18 Feb 55	Milit Assistance	247UNTS257	103474
Germany, West	USA (United States)	04 Apr 55	Milit Assistance	279UNTS73	104034
Brazil	UK Great Britain	05 Apr 55	Milit Servic/Citiz	403UNTS139	105793
Haiti	USA (United States)	05 Apr 55	Milit Assistance	270UNTS97	103895
Dominican Republic	USA (United States)	22 Apr 55	Milit Assistance	239UNTS325	103389
Philippines	USA (United States)	27 Apr 55	Direct Aid	261UNTS351	103733
Canada	USA (United States)	05 May 55	Milit Installation	241UNTS179	103433
USA (United States)	Vietnam, South	10 May 55	Milit Assistance	273UNTS157	103950
Turkey	USA (United States)	26 May 55	Milit Assistance	262UNTS97	103739
Hungary	USSR (Soviet Union)	27 May 55	Status of Forces	407UNTS156	105864
Japan	USA (United States)	03 Jun 55	Milit Assistance	270UNTS51	103891

Military Questions (Cont.)

PARTY ONE	PARTY TWO	DATE	TOPIC	CITATION	NUMBER
Multilateral		22 Jun 55	Atomic Energy	249UNTS3	103498
Turkey	USA (United States)	29 Jun 55	Milit Assistance	269UNTS97	103878
Germany, West	USA (United States)	30 Jun 55	Milit Assistance	240UNTS69	103394
Belgium	USA (United States)	15 Jul 55	Milit Assistance	223UNTS3	103040
Cuba	USA (United States)	03 Aug 55	Military Mission	265UNTS41	103805
Ecuador	USA (United States)	24 Aug 55	Military Mission	256UNTS299	103640
Belgium	USA (United States)	31 Aug 55	Milit Assistance	223UNTS111	103041
Colombia	USA (United States)	16 Sep 55	Military Mission	256UNTS221	103631
Finland	USSR (Soviet Union)	19 Sep 55	Milit Installation	226UNTS187	103113
France	USA (United States)	23 Sep 55	Milit Assistance	270UNTS341	103904
Peru	USA (United States)	28 Oct 55	Military Mission	239UNTS181	103378
Belgium	UK Great Britain	10 Nov 55	Status of Forces	331UNTS209	104756
Iraq	USA (United States)	03 Dec 55	Milit Assistance	241UNTS19	103420
Canada	Norway	20 Dec 55	Milit Assistance	305UNTS17	104408
Germany, West	USA (United States)	04 Jan 56	General Military	268UNTS143	103856
Canada	UK Great Britain	09 Jan 56	Status of Forces	331UNTS192	104755
Canada	USA (United States)	26 Jan 56	Status of Forces	241UNTS115	103428
Multilateral		03 Mar 56	Milit Servic/Citiz	243UNTS169	103452
Taiwan	USA (United States)	03 Apr 56	Milit Assistance	268UNTS315	103864
Japan	USA (United States)	13 Apr 56	Milit Assistance	273UNTS223	103953
Honduras	USA (United States)	25 Apr 56	Military Mission	269UNTS25	103869
Pakistan	USA (United States)	28 May 56	Milit Assistance	269UNTS15	103868
Chile	Italy	04 Jun 56	Milit Servic/Citiz	362UNTS309	105195
Netherlands	UK Great Britain	11 Jun 56	Status of Forces	306UNTS107	104436
UK Great Britain	USA (United States)	25 Jun 56	Milit Installation	249UNTS91	103502
Korea, South	USA (United States)	02 Jul 56	Milit Assistance	281UNTS41	104067
Greece	USA (United States)	07 Sep 56	Status of Forces	278UNTS141	104030
Denmark	UK Great Britain	08 Oct 56	Consul/Citizenship	331UNTS181	104754
Germany, West	USA (United States)	08 Oct 56	Milit Assistance	278UNTS9	104018
Ceylon (Sri Lanka)	USA (United States)	02 Nov 56	Milit Assistance	282UNTS93	104094
Portugal	USA (United States)	07 Nov 56	Milit Assistance	277UNTS133	104003
Taiwan	USA (United States)	21 Nov 56	Milit Installation	265UNTS241	103816
Iceland	USA (United States)	06 Dec 56	General Military	265UNTS261	103818
Canada	Germany, West	10 Dec 56	Milit Assistance	392UNTS3	105633
Germany, West	USA (United States)	12 Dec 56	Milit Assistance	280UNTS71	104052
Germany, West	USA (United States)	12 Dec 56	Milit Assistance	280UNTS63	104051
Poland	USSR (Soviet Union)	17 Dec 56	Status of Forces	266UNTS179	103830
Brazil	USA (United States)	16 Jan 57	Milit Assistance	266UNTS99	103824
Germany, West	Netherlands	29 Jan 57	Status of Forces	314UNTS173	104548
Philippines	USA (United States)	06 Feb 57	Status of Forces	303UNTS237	104383
Nicaragua	USA (United States)	09 Feb 57	Milit Assistance	279UNTS191	104040
Spain	USA (United States)	09 Mar 57	Milit Assistance	283UNTS89	104108
Germany, East	USSR (Soviet Union)	12 Mar 57	Status of Forces	285UNTS105	104150
Germany, West	UK Great Britain	11 Apr 57	Status of Forces	331UNTS173	104753
Canada	Netherlands	13 Apr 57	Milit Assistance	316UNTS223	104588
Romania	USSR (Soviet Union)	15 Apr 57	Status of Forces	274UNTS143	103964
Canada	Norway	17 Apr 57	Milit Assistance	316UNTS215	104587
Canada	Denmark	17 Apr 57	Milit Assistance	316UNTS207	104586
Germany, West	USA (United States)	01 May 57	Milit Assistance	284UNTS85	104131
Lebanon	USA (United States)	06 Jun 57	Tech Assistance	284UNTS155	104134
Germany, West	UK Great Britain	07 Jun 57	Milit Assistance	398UNTS275	105730
Germany, West	USA (United States)	07 Jun 57	Milit Assistance	346UNTS241	104984
Finland	United Nations	27 Jun 57	Status of Forces	271UNTS135	103913
Libya	USA (United States)	30 Jun 57	Milit Assistance	284UNTS177	104136
United Nations	Sweden	01 Jul 57	Status of Forces	271UNTS187	103914
New Zealand	UK Great Britain	04 Jul 57	Milit Assistance	402UNTS109	105780
Norway	United Nations	09 Jul 57	Status of Forces	271UNTS223	103917
Germany, West	Netherlands	10 Jul 57	Status of Forces	339UNTS97	104848
Denmark	United Nations	16 Jul 57	Milit Assistance	274UNTS81	103959
Canada	United Nations	29 Jul 57	Milit Assistance	274UNTS47	103957
Panama	USA (United States)	05 Aug 57	Visas	299UNTS113	104309
Greece	USA (United States)	05 Aug 57	Milit Assistance	290UNTS167	104235
Austria	USA (United States)	09 Aug 57	Milit Assistance	288UNTS299	104211
Brazil	United Nations	13 Aug 57	Milit Assistance	274UNTS199	103966
India	United Nations	14 Aug 57	Milit Assistance	274UNTS233	103968
Turkey	UK Great Britain	16 Aug 57	Milit Assistance	310UNTS21	104482
United Nations	Yugoslavia	01 Oct 57	Milit Assistance	277UNTS191	104006
Poland	USSR (Soviet Union)	26 Oct 57	Status of Forces	432UNTS221	106223
Philippines	USA (United States)	01 Nov 57	Status of Forces	307UNTS39	104440
Ethiopia	USA (United States)	26 Dec 57	Milit Assistance	307UNTS71	104443
UK Great Britain	USA (United States)	22 Feb 58	Milit Assistance	307UNTS207	104451
Canada	USA (United States)	12 May 58	General Military	316UNTS151	104582
Philippines	USA (United States)	15 May 58	Milit Assistance	316UNTS163	104583
Philippines	USA (United States)	30 Jun 58	Direct Aid	321UNTS51	104653
Muscat and Oman	UK Great Britain	25 Jul 58	General Military	312UNTS347	104524
Lebanon	USA (United States)	06 Aug 58	Status of Forces	366UNTS361	105223
Turkey	USA (United States)	14 Oct 58	Milit Assistance	336UNTS145	104803
Haiti	USA (United States)	27 Oct 58	Military Mission	336UNTS235	104807
Greece	USA (United States)	15 Jan 59	Milit Assistance	357UNTS281	105120
Argentina	Sweden	16 Jan 59	Milit Servic/Citiz	427UNTS327	106163
Taiwan	USA (United States)	07 Feb 59	Milit Assistance	341UNTS225	104885
Denmark	USA (United States)	08 May 59	Milit Assistance	344UNTS185	104949
Thailand	USA (United States)	19 May 59	Milit Assistance	346UNTS271	104986
Peru	USA (United States)	15 Jun 59	Milit Assistance	346UNTS279	104987
Spain	USA (United States)	23 Jun 59	Milit Assistance	354UNTS11	105049
France	Israel	30 Jun 59	Milit Servic/Citiz	448UNTS107	106428
Taiwan	USA (United States)	08 Jul 59	Milit Assistance	354UNTS47	105052
Canada	USA (United States)	13 Jul 59	Milit Assistance	353UNTS237	105045
Japan	USA (United States)	31 Jul 59	Milit Assistance	357UNTS107	105110
Germany, West	UK Great Britain	03 Aug 59	Dispute Settlement	502UNTS197	107331
Multilateral		03 Aug 59	Status of Forces	481UNTS262	106986
Germany, West	USA (United States)	03 Aug 59	Status of Forces	490UNTS28	107153
Italy	USA (United States)	18 Aug 59	Milit Assistance	361UNTS11	105169
USA (United States)	Yugoslavia	25 Aug 59	Milit Assistance	357UNTS77	105106
New Zealand	UK Great Britain	21 Sep 59	Milit Assistance	401UNTS51	105762
Brazil	USA (United States)	19 Oct 59	Milit Assistance	372UNTS131	105293
Japan	USA (United States)	19 Jan 60	Status of Forces	373UNTS207	105321
Ecuador	USA (United States)	11 Feb 60	Milit Assistance	372UNTS141	105294
UK Great Britain	USA (United States)	15 Feb 60	Milit Assistance	371UNTS45	105269
Peru	USA (United States)	26 Feb 60	Milit Assistance	394UNTS141	105674
Netherlands	USA (United States)	24 Mar 60	Milit Assistance	406UNTS165	105847
Argentina	USA (United States)	01 Apr 60	Milit Assistance	371UNTS245	105281
Colombia	USA (United States)	07 Apr 60	Milit Assistance	372UNTS27	105285
Canada	Norway	25 Apr 60	Milit Installation	470UNTS109	106801
Canada	Norway	24 May 60	Milit Installation	470UNTS125	106803
Somalia	UK Great Britain	26 Jun 60	Non-ILO Labor	374UNTS347	105348
Haiti	USA (United States)	08 Jul 60	Milit Assistance	380UNTS135	105454
Chile	USA (United States)	16 Jul 60	Milit Assistance	393UNTS271	105661
Canada	UK Great Britain	05 Aug 60	Milit Installation	470UNTS133	106804
Canada	USA (United States)	31 Aug 60	Milit Assistance	393UNTS247	105659
Multilateral		21 Sep 60	Patents/Copyrights	394UNTS3	105664
Norway	USA (United States)	29 Nov 60	Milit Assistance	404UNTS251	105815
Denmark	USA (United States)	02 Dec 60	Milit Installation	402UNTS245	105789
Italy	Netherlands	24 Jan 61	Milit Servic/Citiz	450UNTS207	106468
Bolivia	USA (United States)	09 Feb 61	Milit Assistance	405UNTS113	105827
UK Great Britain	USA (United States)	10 Feb 61	Milit Installation	409UNTS68	105879
UK Great Britain	USA (United States)	10 Feb 61	Milit Installation	409UNTS129	105880
Colombia	USA (United States)	03 Apr 61	Milit Assistance	407UNTS3	105856
Mali	USA (United States)	20 May 61	Milit Assistance	413UNTS205	105954
Canada	USA (United States)	12 Jun 61	Milit Assistance	410UNTS21	105894
Liberia	USA (United States)	17 Jun 61	Milit Assistance	410UNTS233	105907
Germany, West	UK Great Britain	12 Jul 61	Status of Forces	424UNTS211	106109
UK Great Britain	USA (United States)	18 Jul 61	Milit Assistance	404UNTS227	105813
Canada	USA (United States)	23 Sep 61	Milit Installation	421UNTS79	106053
Germany, West	UK Great Britain	26 Sep 61	Milit Assistance	424UNTS201	106108
Canada	USA (United States)	27 Sep 61	Milit Assistance	421UNTS85	106054
Philippines	USA (United States)	04 Oct 61	Specif Goods/Equip	433UNTS83	106232
Canada	Ghana	08 Jan 62	Military Mission	528UNTS221	107645
Dominican Republic	USA (United States)	08 Mar 62	Milit Assistance	527UNTS29	107615
El Salvador	USA (United States)	13 Apr 62	Milit Assistance	451UNTS307	106500

PARTY ONE	PARTY TWO	DATE	TOPIC	CITATION	NUMBER
Military Questions (Cont.)					
Canada	France	25 May 62	Other Military	470UNTS163	106808
Germany, West	UK Great Britain	06 Jun 62	Status of Forces	437UNTS39	106298
New Zealand	USA (United States)	08 Jun 62	Loans and Credits	458UNTS209	106602
Canada	Greece	18 Jul 62	General Military	528UNTS265	107647
Taiwan	USA (United States)	15 Aug 62	Loans and Credits	460UNTS237	106643
Philippines	USA (United States)	21 Aug 62	Milit Assistance	461UNTS163	106660
Paraguay	USA (United States)	25 Aug 62	Milit Assistance	461UNTS207	106665
Japan	USA (United States)	28 Aug 62	Loans and Credits	460UNTS267	106645
UK Great Britain	USA (United States)	29 Aug 62	Milit Installation	449UNTS177	106459
Sweden	USA (United States)	04 Oct 62	Milit Assistance	462UNTS31	106669
Saudi Arabia	USA (United States)	13 Nov 62	Loans and Credits	488UNTS175	107127
Argentina	Denmark	28 Nov 62	Milit Servic/Citiz	455UNTS429	106554
Pakistan	USA (United States)	16 Jan 63	Milit Assistance	471UNTS133	106828
Netherlands	USA (United States)	06 Feb 63	Status of Forces	487UNTS113	107098
Belgium	USA (United States)	19 Apr 63	Water Transport	493UNTS83	107209
Argentina	Finland	08 May 63	Milit Servic/Citiz	482UNTS309	107000
Australia	USA (United States)	09 May 63	Status of Forces	469UNTS55	106784
New Zealand	USA (United States)	15 May 63	Military Mission	477UNTS55	106915
Netherlands	USA (United States)	20 May 63	Specif Goods/Equip	487UNTS123	107099
Pakistan	USA (United States)	29 Jun 63	Milit Assistance	487UNTS243	107107
Canada	Nigeria	03 Jul 63	Milit Assistance	529UNTS57	107656
Congo (Zaire)	USA (United States)	19 Jul 63	Milit Installation	511UNTS47	107425
UK Great Britain	USA (United States)	11 Oct 63	Scientific Project	483UNTS3	107005
Netherlands	UK Great Britain	30 Oct 63	Other Military	490UNTS11	107151
Australia	India	03 Dec 63	Milit Assistance	486UNTS279	107082
Multilateral		14 Dec 63	IGO Establishment	507UNTS149	107399
Taiwan	USA (United States)	19 Dec 63	Status of Forces	527UNTS69	107617
Brazil	USA (United States)	30 Jan 64	Milit Assistance	511UNTS77	107428
Australia	USA (United States)	05 Feb 64	Status of Forces	511UNTS103	107430
Paraguay	USA (United States)	10 Feb 64	Milit Assistance	511UNTS53	107426
Jamaica	UK Great Britain	20 Feb 64	Military Mission	496UNTS239	107256
Argentina	USA (United States)	10 May 64	Milit Assistance	527UNTS77	107618
Netherlands	NATO (North Atlan)	25 May 64	Status of Forces	544UNTS237	107920
Canada	USA (United States)	25 May 64	Milit Installation	526UNTS251	107609
Italy	Netherlands	29 May 64	Other Military	541UNTS147	107867
Multilateral		18 Jun 64	Atomic Energy	542UNTS145	107886
Germany, West	UK Great Britain	27 Jul 64	Status of Forces	539UNTS243	107835
Italy	USA (United States)	04 Aug 64	General Military	529UNTS205	107662
UK Great Britain	USA (United States)	20 Aug 64	Specific Property	531UNTS85	107694
Canada	UK Great Britain	11 Sep 64	Status of Forces	522UNTS99	107538
India	UK Great Britain	20 Nov 64	Milit Assistance	534UNTS85	107756
Japan	USA (United States)	04 Dec 64	Milit Installation	532UNTS249	107721
Trinidad/Tobago	USA (United States)	05 Dec 64	Milit Installation	535UNTS331	107788
Taiwan	USA (United States)	19 Dec 64	Status of Forces	532UNTS313	107725
India	USA (United States)	13 Jan 65	Milit Assistance	541UNTS107	107864
Philippines	USA (United States)	16 Mar 65	Status of Forces	542UNTS199	107890
Jamaica	UK Great Britain	31 Mar 65	Military Mission	539UNTS59	107824
Canada	USA (United States)	12 May 65	Milit Installation	545UNTS169	107933
Saudi Arabia	USA (United States)	05 Jun 65	Milit Installation	548UNTS285	107984
Guinea	USA (United States)	29 Jun 65	Milit Installation	549UNTS139	107997
India	Pakistan	30 Jun 65	Territory Boundary	548UNTS277	107983
Canada	Jamaica	16 Jul 65	Milit Assistance	548UNTS265	107982
Maldive Islands	UK Great Britain	26 Jul 65	General Amity	548UNTS223	107980
Philippines	USA (United States)	12 Aug 65	Milit Installation	579UNTS47	108397
China	USA (United States)	31 Aug 65	Status of Forces	572UNTS3	108308
Canada	USA (United States)	01 Dec 65	Milit Installation	574UNTS37	108340
Germany, West	USA (United States)	18 Dec 65	Status of Forces	579UNTS193	108407
Italy	USA (United States)	27 Dec 65	Specific Property	574UNTS145	108347
India	Pakistan	10 Jan 66	General Amity	560UNTS39	108166
Malta	USA (United States)	15 Jan 66	Specif Goods/Equip	579UNTS109	108402
Paraguay	USA (United States)	11 Apr 66	Milit Assistance	578UNTS99	108389
Spain	USA (United States)	21 Apr 66	Milit Assistance	580UNTS231	108426
Guyana	UK Great Britain	26 May 66	Status of Forces	595UNTS255	108621
Canada	USA (United States)	15 Jun 66	Milit Installation	594UNTS83	108595
Botswana	UK Great Britain	30 Sep 66	Status of Forces	597UNTS211	108646

PARTY ONE	PARTY TWO	DATE	TOPIC	CITATION	NUMBER
Military, Air and Naval Bases					
UK Great Britain	USA (United States)	11 Feb 46	Air Transport	3UNTS253	100036
UK Great Britain	USA (United States)	21 Feb 46	General Trade	6UNTS137	100073
Multilateral		31 Mar 46	Milit Installation	17UNTS159	100274
Philippines	USA (United States)	14 Mar 47	Milit Installation	43UNTS271	100673
Philippines	USA (United States)	21 Mar 47	Milit Assistance	45UNTS47	100691
UK Great Britain	USA (United States)	23 Oct 47	Territory Boundary	66UNTS277	100859
UK Great Britain	USA (United States)	24 Feb 48	Milit Installation	73UNTS143	100951
Philippines	USA (United States)	16 May 49	Milit Installation	67UNTS199	100878
Canada	USA (United States)	04 Jun 49	Air Transport	200UNTS201	102704
UK Great Britain	USA (United States)	19 Sep 49	Milit Installation	68UNTS31	100882
China People's Rep	USSR (Soviet Union)	14 Feb 50	Privil/Immunities	226UNTS31	103105
UK Great Britain	USA (United States)	21 Jul 50	Milit Installation	97UNTS193	101351
UK Great Britain	USA (United States)	01 Aug 50	Milit Installation	88UNTS273	101199
UK Great Britain	USA (United States)	06 Mar 51	Status of Forces	97UNTS137	101347
UK Great Britain	USA (United States)	25 Apr 51	Specific Property	99UNTS97	101373
Canada	USA (United States)	19 Mar 52	Status of Forces	174UNTS267	102291
Canada	USA (United States)	30 Apr 52	Milit Installation	235UNTS269	103308
UK Great Britain	USA (United States)	29 Jul 52	Status of Forces	179UNTS129	102362
China People's Rep	USSR (Soviet Union)	15 Sep 52	Milit Installation	226UNTS45	103106
Belgium	UK Great Britain	12 Nov 52	Status of Forces	180UNTS15	102372
Canada	USA (United States)	05 Dec 52	Milit Installation	206UNTS11	102783
China People's Rep	USSR (Soviet Union)	12 Oct 54	Milit Installation	226UNTS51	103107
Finland	USSR (Soviet Union)	19 Sep 55	Milit Installation	226UNTS187	103113
Philippines	USA (United States)	28 Oct 55	Milit Installation	239UNTS165	103376
Canada	USA (United States)	19 Apr 56	Milit Installation	274UNTS3	103955
UK Great Britain	USA (United States)	25 Jun 56	Milit Installation	249UNTS91	103502
Taiwan	USA (United States)	21 Nov 56	Milit Installation	265UNTS241	103816
Philippines	USA (United States)	06 Feb 57	Status of Forces	303UNTS237	104383
Saudi Arabia	USA (United States)	02 Apr 57	Milit Installation	283UNTS97	104109
Philippines	USA (United States)	08 Apr 57	Specific Resources	303UNTS227	104382
Ceylon (Sri Lanka)	UK Great Britain	07 Jun 57	Milit Installation	280UNTS107	104055
Philippines	USA (United States)	18 Jun 57	Milit Installation	289UNTS289	104225
Philippines	USA (United States)	01 Nov 57	Status of Forces	307UNTS39	104440
Germany, West	USA (United States)	10 Dec 57	Milit Assistance	307UNTS59	104442
Philippines	USA (United States)	20 Feb 58	Status of Forces	303UNTS261	104385
Canada	USA (United States)	20 Jun 58	Milit Assistance	317UNTS37	104592
Canada	USA (United States)	01 May 59	Specific Property	343UNTS27	104919
Philippines	USA (United States)	07 Dec 59	Milit Installation	359UNTS227	105144
Japan	USA (United States)	19 Jan 60	Status of Forces	373UNTS207	105321
Philippines	USA (United States)	11 Jan 63	Specific Resources	473UNTS43	106853
Multilateral		15 Feb 64	Milit Installation	533UNTS98	107736
Congo (Zaire)	United Nations	02 Mar 64	Milit Installation	533UNTS93	107735
Belgium	United Nations	20 Mar 64	Milit Installation	533UNTS83	107734
Belgium	United Nations	20 Feb 65	Finance	535UNTS191	107779
Minerals					
Brazil	USA (United States)	26 Nov 48	Scientific Project	88UNTS3	101180
Mines					
Multilateral		21 Jun 35	ILO Labor	40UNTS63	100627
Taiwan	UK Great Britain	18 Jun 41	Territory Boundary	10UNTS227	200064
Jordan	UK Great Britain	19 Jul 41	Extradition	9UNTS389	200055
Belgium	Italy	23 Jun 46	Non-ILO Labor	19UNTS65	100305
Albania	Yugoslavia	28 Nov 46	Non-IBRD Project	111UNTS151	101528
Multilateral		07 Dec 46	Commodity Trade	157UNTS103	102050
France	UK Great Britain	13 Aug 47	Non-ILO Labor	91UNTS169	101249
Belgium	Italy	09 Feb 48	Non-ILO Labor	71UNTS143	100915
France	Poland	09 Jun 48	Non-ILO Labor	32UNTS251	100503
Czechoslovakia	France	12 Oct 48	Non-ILO Labor	45UNTS81	100693
Italy	Netherlands	04 Dec 48	Non-ILO Labor	46UNTS271	100716
Belgium	Luxembourg	03 Dec 49	Non-ILO Labor	91UNTS31	101241
Belgium	Netherlands	23 Oct 50	Territory Boundary	136UNTS31	101831
Germany, West	Netherlands	18 Jan 52	Specific Property	179UNTS147	102364
Australia	IBRD (World Bank)	03 Dec 56	IBRD Project	288UNTS99	104200
Chile	IBRD (World Bank)	24 Jul 57	IBRD Project	282UNTS189	104099

PARTY ONE	PARTY TWO	DATE	TOPIC	CITATION	NUMBER
Mines (Cont.)					
Chile	IBRD (World Bank)	24 Jul 57	IBRD Project	282UNTS139	104098
Australia	New Zealand	30 Sep 58	Territory Boundary	340UNTS61	104859
France	UK Great Britain	26 Jan 59	Admin Cooperation	330UNTS213	104746
Czechoslovakia	Poland	16 Dec 59	Admin Cooperation	372UNTS223	105300
India	IBRD (World Bank)	09 Aug 61	IBRD Project	417UNTS297	106011
Belgium	Netherlands	27 Apr 65	Specific Resources	596UNTS235	108636
Minorities					
India	Pakistan	08 Apr 50	Visas	131UNTS3	101733
Missing Persons					
Multilateral		06 Apr 50	Admin Cooperation	119UNTS99	101610
Germany, West	USA (United States)	06 Jun 55	Humanitarian	315UNTS155	104566
Multilateral		06 Jun 55	IGO Establishment	219UNTS79	102968
Argentina	USA (United States)	03 Oct 56	Military Mission	279UNTS13	104032
Monetary Questions					
Multilateral		21 Oct 43	Finance	2UNTS281	200021
Belgium	UK Great Britain	05 Oct 44	Finance	5UNTS227	200031
Sweden	UK Great Britain	06 Mar 45	Finance	5UNTS241	200032
Sweden	UK Great Britain	06 Mar 45	Finance	82UNTS219	101095
UK Great Britain	USA (United States)	16 Apr 45	Taxation	6UNTS189	100076
Denmark	UK Great Britain	16 Aug 45	Finance	5UNTS251	200033
Netherlands	UK Great Britain	07 Sep 45	Finance	2UNTS325	200024
Denmark	UK Great Britain	24 Oct 45	Milit Assistance	93UNTS143	101297
Czechoslovakia	UK Great Britain	01 Nov 45	Finance	5UNTS15	100062
Netherlands	Norway	06 Nov 45	Finance	2UNTS5	100017
Norway	UK Great Britain	08 Nov 45	Finance	5UNTS27	100063
Netherlands	Sweden	30 Nov 45	Finance	2UNTS27	100019
Denmark	UK Great Britain	06 Dec 45	Finance	5UNTS3	100061
Czechoslovakia	Norway	13 Dec 45	Finance	17UNTS261	100280
Netherlands	UK Great Britain	20 Dec 45	Milit Assistance	4UNTS303	100053
Multilateral		27 Dec 45	IGO Establishment	2UNTS39	100020
Switzerland	UK Great Britain	12 Mar 46	Finance	6UNTS107	100070
Greece	UK Great Britain	21 Mar 46	Claims and Debts	91UNTS149	101247
France	Netherlands	09 Apr 46	Finance	3UNTS57	100024
Portugal	UK Great Britain	16 Apr 46	Finance	6UNTS119	100071
New Zealand	Norway	03 May 46	Claims and Debts	16UNTS211	100262
Belgium	Netherlands	24 May 46	Finance	31UNTS169	100477
Netherlands	UK Great Britain	16 Sep 46	Finance	4UNTS401	100057
Belgium	USA (United States)	24 Sep 46	Claims and Debts	132UNTS80	101753
Albania	Yugoslavia	03 Oct 46	Loans and Credits	111UNTS87	101519
Luxembourg	UK Great Britain	11 Dec 46	Claims and Debts	11UNTS167	100155
Denmark	India	20 Dec 46	Reparations	7UNTS309	100107
Netherlands	UK Great Britain	26 Feb 47	Finance	11UNTS279	100167
Spain	UK Great Britain	28 Mar 47	Finance	66UNTS91	100849
Albania	Yugoslavia	12 Jun 47	Finance	111UNTS195	101534
Sweden	USA (United States)	24 Jun 47	General Economic	36UNTS25	100565
Australia	France	28 Jul 47	Reparations	97UNTS271	101353
Belgium	India	04 Aug 47	Reparations	76UNTS23	100976
Czechoslovakia	New Zealand	08 Aug 47	Claims and Debts	18UNTS161	100285
Multilateral		30 Oct 47	General Economic	55UNTS188	100814
Multilateral		04 Nov 47	Reparations	93UNTS61	101288
Belgium	UK Great Britain	14 Nov 47	Finance	25UNTS269	100367
Multilateral		18 Nov 47	Finance	17UNTS89	100269
Multilateral		16 Dec 47	Reparations	82UNTS237	101096
France	Lebanon	24 Jan 48	Finance	173UNTS99	102263
India	Pakistan	31 Mar 48	Finance	54UNTS33	100793
India	Pakistan	30 Jun 48	Finance	29UNTS199	100441
USA (United States)	Yugoslavia	19 Jul 48	Claims and Debts	89UNTS43	101208
Netherlands	UK Great Britain	06 Sep 48	Finance	32UNTS235	100501
Belgium	Netherlands	11 Oct 48	Finance	26UNTS95	100379
Burma	UK Great Britain	12 Oct 48	Finance	71UNTS255	100923
Denmark	UK Great Britain	11 Nov 48	Finance	25UNTS333	100371
Korea, South	USA (United States)	10 Dec 48	Direct Aid	55UNTS157	100813
Spain	UK Great Britain	15 Dec 48	Finance	87UNTS49	101165
UK Great Britain	Yugoslavia	23 Dec 48	Reparations	81UNTS103	101067
Monetary Questions (Cont.)					
UK Great Britain	Yugoslavia	23 Dec 48	Reparations	81UNTS121	101068
Poland	UK Great Britain	14 Jan 49	Reparations	83UNTS51	101101
Netherlands	UK Great Britain	17 Jan 49	Reparations	83UNTS67	101102
United Arab Rep	UK Great Britain	31 Mar 49	Finance	83UNTS139	101106
Norway	Portugal	28 Nov 49	Finance	47UNTS117	100726
Sweden	UK Great Britain	30 Dec 49	Finance	87UNTS59	101166
Austria	UK Great Britain	26 Jan 50	Finance	97UNTS183	101350
Denmark	UK Great Britain	19 Oct 50	Finance	79UNTS25	101028
Norway	UK Great Britain	06 Nov 50	Finance	88UNTS257	101197
Sweden	UK Great Britain	10 Nov 50	Finance	88UNTS265	101198
Australia	Finland	04 Jan 51	Claims and Debts	80UNTS27	101042
Portugal	UK Great Britain	20 Jul 51	Finance	105UNTS61	101453
France	UK Great Britain	20 Aug 51	Finance	108UNTS263	101479
Austria	UK Great Britain	30 Jun 52	Reparations	138UNTS153	101867
United Arab Rep	UK Great Britain	30 Oct 52	Finance	172UNTS3	102236
Germany, West	USA (United States)	27 Feb 53	Claims and Debts	223UNTS167	103065
Germany, West	USA (United States)	01 Apr 53	Claims and Debts	224UNTS3	103066
Israel	UK Great Britain	13 May 53	Finance	175UNTS179	102300
Germany, West	UK Great Britain	22 May 53	Finance	172UNTS179	102246
Greece	UK Great Britain	05 Oct 53	Reparations	243UNTS73	103447
Belgium	Germany, West	03 Mar 54	Admin Cooperation	188UNTS259	102529
Austria	UK Great Britain	14 Oct 54	Claims and Debts	204UNTS87	102751
Argentina	UK Great Britain	31 Oct 56	Finance	269UNTS229	103883
Austria	USA (United States)	21 Nov 56	Claims and Debts	290UNTS181	104237
Turkey	USA (United States)	06 Sep 58	Loans and Credits	336UNTS85	104800
Taiwan	USA (United States)	24 Dec 58	Loans and Credits	340UNTS251	104868
Somalia	UK Great Britain	26 Jun 60	Finance	374UNTS363	105350
Cyprus	UK Great Britain	16 Aug 60	Privil/Immunities	382UNTS225	105483
Congo (Zaire)	United Nations	12 Jun 61	General Aid	494UNTS205	107234
United Nations	USA (United States)	18 Nov 61	US Agri Commod Aid	494UNTS213	107235
Belgium	Luxembourg	29 Jan 63	IGO Establishment	547UNTS39	107955
Multilateral		23 Oct 63	IGO Establishment	506UNTS197	107388
Australia	Laos	24 Dec 63	Finance	503UNTS315	107350
Laos	UK Great Britain	24 Dec 63	Finance	502UNTS189	107330
Money Orders					
Lebanon	USA (United States)	21 Jan 46	Postal Service	140UNTS73	101884
South Africa	UK Great Britain	24 Aug 46	Telecommunications	51UNTS187	100765
Romania	USA (United States)	26 Feb 48	Admin Cooperation	48UNTS9	100738
Bulgaria	USA (United States)	08 Mar 48	Admin Cooperation	29UNTS101	100437
Hungary	USA (United States)	09 Mar 48	Admin Cooperation	183UNTS3	102426
Bulgaria	UK Great Britain	13 Mar 48	Postal Service	104UNTS25	101432
France	UK Great Britain	12 Jul 48	Postal Service	90UNTS83	101230
New Zealand	Pakistan	17 Sep 48	Postal Service	91UNTS275	101254
Lebanon	UK Great Britain	20 Jun 49	Postal Service	90UNTS137	101232
Greece	UK Great Britain	17 Oct 49	Postal Service	93UNTS185	101300
India	UK Great Britain	07 Dec 49	Postal Service	281UNTS245	104082
Colombia	UK Great Britain	13 Dec 49	Finance	88UNTS133	101189
UK Great Britain	Yugoslavia	09 Feb 50	Finance	88UNTS287	101200
Sweden	UK Great Britain	17 Jan 51	Postal Service	93UNTS225	101301
France	UK Great Britain	24 Jan 51	Postal Service	90UNTS193	101237
India	UK Great Britain	05 Jun 51	Postal Service	135UNTS3	101811
Pakistan	United Arab Rep	08 Sep 51	Postal Service	133UNTS257	101793
Pakistan	UK Great Britain	26 Sep 51	Postal Service	118UNTS221	101608
Multilateral		11 Jul 52	Postal Service	170UNTS269	102223
Pakistan	UK Great Britain	22 Jul 52	Postal Service	157UNTS185	102054
Japan	USA (United States)	22 Apr 53	Admin Cooperation	178UNTS169	102341
Japan	UK Great Britain	27 Apr 53	Admin Cooperation	228UNTS227	103154
Canada	UK Great Britain	21 Jun 56	Postal Service	381UNTS111	105467
Canada	UK Great Britain	20 Oct 56	Postal Service	381UNTS99	105466
Canada	UK Great Britain	16 Nov 56	Postal Service	412UNTS166	105930
Multilateral		03 Oct 57	Postal Service	365UNTS207	105214
Taiwan	USA (United States)	08 Oct 57	Postal Service	304UNTS241	104400
Australia	Netherlands	23 Jul 58	Postal Service	328UNTS227	104736
United Arab Rep	USA (United States)	31 Oct 58	Postal Service	355UNTS355	105086

PARTY ONE	PARTY TWO	DATE	TOPIC	CITATION	NUMBER
Money Orders (Cont.)					
Australia	Japan	07 Feb 61	Postal Service	450UNTS343	106478
Japan	Pakistan	07 Mar 61	Postal Service	450UNTS359	106479
Philippines	USA (United States)	12 Mar 61	Postal Service	288UNTS285	104210
Morocco	USA (United States)	30 Nov 61	Postal Service	451UNTS167	106492
Thailand	USA (United States)	12 Jan 62	Postal Service	459UNTS95	106615
Jordan	UK Great Britain	28 Feb 62	Postal Service	466UNTS249	106748
Multilateral		16 Oct 62	Postal Service	470UNTS291	106814
Australia	UK Great Britain	06 Dec 62	Postal Service	457UNTS145	106584
Australia	UK Great Britain	23 Sep 63	Postal Service	483UNTS39	107006
Japan	UK Great Britain	22 Feb 65	Finance	560UNTS123	108171
India	Japan	24 Feb 65	Postal Service	570UNTS3	108284
Australia	Germany, West	08 Jul 65	Postal Service	543UNTS305	107907
Monuments					
UNESCO (Educ/Cult)	United Arab Rep	09 Nov 63	Culture	489UNTS233	107142
Multilateral		09 Nov 63	Direct Aid	489UNTS209	107141
UNESCO (Educ/Cult)	USA (United States)	16 Oct 64	Specific Property	550UNTS23	108006
Philippines	USA (United States)	22 Dec 66	Other Military	579UNTS203	108408
Most Favored Nation Treatment					
Haiti	USA (United States)	19 Feb 42	Customs	105UNTS238	200336
Dominican Republic	USA (United States)	14 Nov 42	Customs	24UNTS233	200148
Chile	UK Great Britain	01 Jul 44	General Trade	2UNTS243	200017
Taiwan	France	28 Feb 46	General Amity	14UNTS137	100216
Jordan	UK Great Britain	22 Mar 46	General Amity	6UNTS143	100074
USA (United States)	Yemen	04 May 46	General Economic	4UNTS165	100043
Bolivia	USA (United States)	10 Jun 46	Mostfavored Nation	13UNTS19	100197
Chile	UK Great Britain	25 Jun 46	General Trade	91UNTS137	101246
Luxembourg	USA (United States)	03 Jul 46	Mostfavored Nation	32UNTS85	100491
Ethiopia	USA (United States)	04 Jul 46	Mostfavored Nation	13UNTS27	100198
Norway	USA (United States)	08 Jul 46	Mostfavored Nation	13UNTS35	100199
Belgium	USA (United States)	11 Jul 46	Mostfavored Nation	13UNTS43	100200
Spain	USA (United States)	11 Jul 46	Mostfavored Nation	13UNTS51	100201
United Arab Rep	USA (United States)	15 Aug 46	Mostfavored Nation	13UNTS59	100202
Portugal	USA (United States)	26 Aug 46	Mostfavored Nation	13UNTS67	100203
Denmark	USA (United States)	10 Sep 46	Mostfavored Nation	13UNTS75	100204
Dominican Republic	USA (United States)	07 Oct 46	Mostfavored Nation	13UNTS91	100206
Taiwan	Saudi Arabia	15 Nov 46	General Amity	18UNTS197	100289
Belgium	Turkey	12 Mar 47	Mostfavored Nation	37UNTS221	100579
Greece	Switzerland	01 Apr 47	Mostfavored Nation	180UNTS115	102378
Nepal	USA (United States)	25 Apr 47	Consul/Citizenship	16UNTS97	100251
Bulgaria	Denmark	09 May 47	General Trade	74UNTS131	100959
Canada	Switzerland	14 Jul 47	Admin Cooperation	43UNTS103	100664
Multilateral		30 Oct 47	General Economic	55UNTS188	100814
Denmark	Guatemala	04 Mar 48	General Economic	96UNTS223	101339
Jordan	UK Great Britain	15 Mar 48	General Military	77UNTS77	100994
Canada	Italy	28 Apr 48	General Economic	231UNTS69	103206
France	USA (United States)	28 Jun 48	Mostfavored Nation	31UNTS115	100472
Italy	USA (United States)	28 Jun 48	Milit Occupation	25UNTS45	100356
Ireland	USA (United States)	28 Jun 48	Mostfavored Nation	32UNTS69	100489
Denmark	USA (United States)	29 Jun 48	Mostfavored Nation	27UNTS35	100396
Greece	USA (United States)	02 Jul 48	Mostfavored Nation	31UNTS131	100474
Belgium	USA (United States)	02 Jul 48	Mostfavored Nation	27UNTS43	100397
Netherlands	USA (United States)	02 Jul 48	Mostfavored Nation	32UNTS77	100490
Austria	USA (United States)	02 Jul 48	Milit Occupation	25UNTS53	100357
Norway	USA (United States)	03 Jul 48	Milit Occupation	27UNTS59	100399
Iceland	USA (United States)	03 Jul 48	Milit Occupation	27UNTS49	100398
Sweden	USA (United States)	03 Jul 48	Milit Occupation	27UNTS69	100400
Taiwan	USA (United States)	03 Jul 48	Direct Aid	17UNTS119	100273
Turkey	USA (United States)	04 Jul 48	Mostfavored Nation	34UNTS185	100536
UK Great Britain	USA (United States)	06 Jul 48	Milit Occupation	25UNTS61	100358
France	USA (United States)	09 Jul 48	Mostfavored Nation	32UNTS93	100492
Multilateral		14 Jul 48	Mostfavored Nation	31UNTS123	100473
Multilateral		14 Sep 48	Milit Occupation	18UNTS267	100296
Portugal	USA (United States)	28 Sep 48	Mostfavored Nation	31UNTS139	100475
Korea, South	USA (United States)	10 Dec 48	Direct Aid	55UNTS157	100813
Most Favored Nation Treatment (Cont.)					
Belgium	France	18 Feb 49	Claims and Debts	31UNTS173	100478
Finland	Greece	24 Mar 49	General Trade	78UNTS3	101008
France	Netherlands	20 Jul 49	Mostfavored Nation	204UNTS287	102763
Israel	Turkey	04 Jul 50	Mostfavored Nation	220UNTS3	102982
Canada	Venezuela	11 Oct 50	General Economic	231UNTS3	103198
Canada	Ecuador	10 Nov 50	General Economic	231UNTS15	103199
Canada	Costa Rica	18 Nov 50	General Economic	231UNTS25	103200
Israel	Yugoslavia	29 Jul 51	Mostfavored Nation	220UNTS7	102983
France	Greece	03 Sep 51	Mostfavored Nation	187UNTS113	102505
Australia	Israel	06 Sep 51	Mostfavored Nation	188UNTS303	102534
Israel	Italy	08 Nov 51	Mostfavored Nation	219UNTS293	102980
Ceylon (Sri Lanka)	Japan	06 Sep 52	General Economic	314UNTS279	104552
Denmark	Israel	14 Nov 52	General Economic	160UNTS275	102112
Canada	United Arab Rep	03 Dec 52	Mostfavored Nation	233UNTS145	103259
Greece	South Africa	27 Jan 53	Mostfavored Nation	533UNTS303	107748
Israel	Italy	22 May 53	Mostfavored Nation	219UNTS297	102981
France	Sweden	16 Feb 54	General Transport	228UNTS137	103147
Israel	USSR (Soviet Union)	15 Jul 55	Mostfavored Nation	226UNTS253	103119
Canada	Honduras	11 Jul 56	Mostfavored Nation	305UNTS39	104411
Japan	USSR (Soviet Union)	19 Oct 56	General Economic	263UNTS119	103769
Korea, South	USA (United States)	28 Nov 56	General Amity	302UNTS281	104367
Ireland	Portugal	11 Nov 57	Mostfavored Nation	553UNTS141	108080
Multilateral		16 Aug 60	Recognition	382UNTS8	105476
Saudi Arabia	Syria	16 Nov 61	General Economic	491UNTS163	107177
Israel	Vietnam, South	11 Apr 62	Mostfavored Nation	448UNTS205	106432
United Arab Rep	USSR (Soviet Union)	23 Jun 62	General Trade	472UNTS43	106836
South Africa	Spain	08 Feb 63	Mostfavored Nation	458UNTS79	106593
Austria	Czechoslovakia	08 Mar 63	General Economic	495UNTS219	107245
Motor Vehicles					
Netherlands	UK Great Britain	26 Feb 47	Finance	11UNTS279	100167
Chile	USA (United States)	09 Apr 49	Customs	122UNTS169	101646
Multilateral		16 Jun 49	Land Transport	45UNTS149	100696
Belgium	Czechoslovakia	02 May 51	Taxation	109UNTS3	101483
Austria	Sweden	01 Aug 51	Taxation	198UNTS13	102653
Belgium	France	30 Jun 52	General Transport	137UNTS259	101857
Chile	USA (United States)	10 May 54	Customs	247UNTS299	103477
Multilateral		04 Jun 54	Customs	282UNTS249	104101
Multilateral		04 Jun 54	Customs	276UNTS191	103992
Germany, West	Sweden	05 Aug 55	Land Transport	262UNTS265	103754
Austria	Sweden	17 Oct 55	Taxation	262UNTS283	103756
Multilateral		18 May 56	Land Transport	339UNTS3	104844
Multilateral		18 May 56	Customs	327UNTS123	104721
Norway	Sweden	15 Sep 56	Admin Cooperation	263UNTS17	103765
Denmark	Sweden	15 Sep 56	General Transport	263UNTS3	103764
Finland	Norway	15 Sep 56	Admin Cooperation	254UNTS17	103590
Denmark	Norway	15 Sep 56	General Transport	259UNTS3	103680
Finland	Sweden	15 Sep 56	Admin Cooperation	254UNTS31	103591
Denmark	Finland	15 Sep 56	General Transport	254UNTS3	103589
Multilateral		15 Sep 56	Admin Cooperation	254UNTS45	103592
Multilateral		08 Nov 56	Commodity Trade	470UNTS171	106809
Belgium	Sweden	20 Nov 56	Taxation	281UNTS239	104081
Multilateral		14 Dec 56	Taxation	436UNTS131	106293
Multilateral		14 Dec 56	Taxation	436UNTS115	106292
Austria	Sweden	19 Feb 58	Land Transport	427UNTS211	106155
Multilateral		20 Mar 58	Admin Cooperation	335UNTS211	104789
Bulgaria	Yugoslavia	21 Mar 58	Customs	376UNTS53	105373
Bulgaria	Yugoslavia	21 Mar 58	Land Transport	349UNTS61	105009
Multilateral		05 Nov 58	Land Transport	428UNTS73	106169
Greece	Yugoslavia	18 Jun 59	Land Transport	368UNTS27	105234
Panama	USA (United States)	31 Oct 60	Admin Cooperation	405UNTS63	105823
Italy	UK Great Britain	23 Oct 61	Admin Cooperation	424UNTS225	106111
Hungary	Netherlands	11 Jan 64	Taxation	522UNTS243	107550
Belgium	Denmark	20 Sep 65	Taxation	549UNTS63	107990
Pakistan	IDA (Devel Assoc)	13 Jan 66	Non-IBRD Project	567UNTS67	108252

PARTY ONE	PARTY TWO	DATE	TOPIC	CITATION	NUMBER
Motor Vehicles (Cont.)					
Belgium	Denmark	04 Feb 66	Land Transport	561UNTS233	108187
Narcotic Drugs					
Multilateral		11 Dec 46	Sanitation	12UNTS179	100186
Romania	USA (United States)	26 Feb 48	Admin Cooperation	48UNTS9	100738
Multilateral		19 Nov 48	Sanitation	44UNTS277	100688
Japan	USA (United States)	22 Apr 53	Admin Cooperation	178UNTS169	102341
Multilateral		11 May 53	Sanitation	456UNTS3	106555
Belgium	Germany, West	03 Apr 54	Admin Cooperation	190UNTS247	102568
Germany, West	USA (United States)	07 Mar 56	Sanitation	271UNTS361	103926
Multilateral		30 Mar 61	Sanitation	520UNTS151	107515
National Parks and Reserves					
Canada	USA (United States)	22 Jan 64	Specific Property	530UNTS89	107674
Nationality					
Multilateral		22 Mar 45	General Amity	70UNTS237	200241
Belgium	France	09 Jan 47	Admin Cooperation	36UNTS145	100568
Multilateral		10 Feb 47	Peace/Disarmament	49UNTS3	100747
France	USA (United States)	25 Feb 48	Milit Servic/Citiz	67UNTS33	100864
Philippines	Spain	20 May 48	Consul/Citizenship	70UNTS143	100903
Greece	Lebanon	06 Oct 48	Consul/Citizenship	87UNTS351	101179
Belgium	Luxembourg	25 Feb 49	Admin Cooperation	47UNTS3	100719
Multilateral		21 Dec 50	Admin Cooperation	90UNTS3	101222
Natural Resources					
Libya	USA (United States)	20 May 52	Direct Aid	178UNTS307	102346
Saudi Arabia	USA (United States)	10 Nov 52	Tech Assistance	181UNTS225	102412
Colombia	USA (United States)	09 Jun 53	Tech Assistance	213UNTS3	102877
Libya	USA (United States)	28 Jul 55	Non-IBRD Project	270UNTS293	103902
Brazil	USA (United States)	03 Aug 55	Scientific Project	270UNTS71	103893
Chile	USA (United States)	20 Apr 56	Atomic Energy	293UNTS277	104295
Philippines	USA (United States)	08 Apr 57	Specific Resources	303UNTS227	104382
Germany, West	Netherlands	28 Jan 58	Specif Goods/Equip	453UNTS183	106525
Congo (Brazzaville)	IBRD (World Bank)	30 Jun 59	IBRD Project	452UNTS123	106506
France	IBRD (World Bank)	30 Jun 59	IBRD Project	452UNTS67	106505
Gabon	IBRD (World Bank)	30 Jun 59	IBRD Project	452UNTS135	106507
Austria	Czechoslovakia	23 Jan 60	Scientific Project	495UNTS99	107241
Austria	Czechoslovakia	23 Jan 60	Specific Resources	495UNTS125	107242
France	IBRD (World Bank)	17 Mar 60	IBRD Project	452UNTS147	106508
Mauritania	IBRD (World Bank)	17 Mar 60	IBRD Project	452UNTS211	106509
Libya	USA (United States)	11 Dec 60	Health/Educ/Welfare	445UNTS125	106381
Algeria	IBRD (World Bank)	14 May 64	IBRD Project	522UNTS265	107552
Netherlands	UK Great Britain	06 Oct 65	Territory Boundary	595UNTS105	108615
Congo (Brazzaville)	IBRD (World Bank)	09 Jan 67	IBRD Project	598UNTS161	108659
Naturalization					
Bulgaria	USA (United States)	08 Mar 48	Admin Cooperation	29UNTS101	100437
Nature Protection					
Multilateral		12 Oct 40	Specific Resources	161UNTS193	200485
Austria	Czechoslovakia	30 Mar 50	Sanitation	495UNTS85	107240
Multilateral		06 Dec 51	Admin Cooperation	150UNTS67	101963
Czechoslovakia	Romania	31 Jul 52	Sanitation	362UNTS123	105185
Hungary	Romania	14 Dec 53	Sanitation	342UNTS151	104906
Bulgaria	Romania	22 Jul 54	Sanitation	362UNTS101	105184
Multilateral		29 Jul 54	Sanitation	249UNTS45	103500
Germany, East	Romania	05 Aug 55	Sanitation	342UNTS229	104910
Bulgaria	Greece	19 Apr 56	Sanitation	594UNTS131	108600
Czechoslovakia	Yugoslavia	16 Jun 56	Health/Educ/Welfare	552UNTS325	108064
Greece	Yugoslavia	11 Sep 56	Health/Educ/Welfare	552UNTS311	108063
Romania	Yugoslavia	25 Sep 56	Sanitation	395UNTS147	105683
Albania	Yugoslavia	20 May 57	Sanitation	363UNTS99	105203
Bulgaria	Yugoslavia	04 Jun 57	Sanitation	349UNTS35	105008
Hungary	Yugoslavia	06 Dec 57	Sanitation	519UNTS215	107509
Ecuador	USA (United States)	27 Jun 58	Direct Aid	317UNTS51	104593
Multilateral		14 Dec 59	Sanitation	422UNTS33	106067
Australia	Fed of Malaya	26 Nov 62	Specif Goods/Equip	453UNTS161	106523

PARTY ONE	PARTY TWO	DATE	TOPIC	CITATION	NUMBER
Nature Protection (Cont.)					
Austria	Hungary	09 Jul 63	Sanitation	482UNTS29	106989
Neutrality					
Afghanistan	USSR (Soviet Union)	18 Dec 55	Admin Cooperation	259UNTS101	103684
Multilateral		23 Jul 62	Recognition	456UNTS302	106564
Night Work					
Multilateral		28 Nov 19	ILO Labor	38UNTS93	100589
Multilateral		28 Nov 19	ILO Labor	38UNTS67	100587
Multilateral		08 Jun 25	ILO Labor	38UNTS269	100603
Multilateral		19 Jun 34	ILO Labor	40UNTS3	100623
Non-self-governing Territories					
Multilateral		06 Feb 47	IGO Establishment	97UNTS227	101352
UK Great Britain	USA (United States)	13 Jul 51	Tech Assistance	105UNTS71	101454
WHO (World Health)	UK Great Britain	07 Feb 52	Tech Assistance	121UNTS75	101627
Multilateral		31 May 54	Tech Assistance	192UNTS20	102592
UNESCO (Educ/Cult)	UK Great Britain	09 Aug 56	Direct Aid	256UNTS139	103624
Notification of Death					
Cuba	UK Great Britain	02 Dec 46	Admin Cooperation	11UNTS161	100154
Multilateral		06 Apr 50	Admin Cooperation	119UNTS99	101610
Nuclear Research					
Multilateral		15 Feb 52	Scientific Project	132UNTS51	101751
Multilateral		01 Jul 53	IGO Establishment	200UNTS149	102701
CERN (Nuc Resrch)	Switzerland	11 Jun 55	IGO Status/Immunit	249UNTS405	200544
Greece	USA (United States)	04 Aug 55	Atomic Energy	235UNTS257	103307
Multilateral		26 Mar 56	IGO Establishment	259UNTS125	103686
Peru	USA (United States)	22 Aug 59	Atomic Energy	357UNTS99	105109
Lebanon	USA (United States)	16 Sep 59	Scientific Project	358UNTS175	105135
Taiwan	USA (United States)	02 Dec 59	Atomic Energy	361UNTS115	105175
Colombia	USA (United States)	11 Jan 60	Tech Assistance	371UNTS37	105268
Chile	USA (United States)	19 Feb 60	Atomic Energy	371UNTS255	105282
Brazil	USA (United States)	27 Feb 60	Direct Aid	384UNTS131	105515
New Zealand	USA (United States)	23 Mar 60	Atomic Energy	371UNTS147	105276
Ireland	USA (United States)	24 Mar 60	Atomic Energy	371UNTS237	105280
Guatemala	USA (United States)	23 Apr 60	Atomic Energy	373UNTS23	105312
Argentina	USA (United States)	23 May 60	Atomic Energy	377UNTS3	105392
India	USA (United States)	13 Jun 60	Atomic Energy	377UNTS37	105394
IAEA (Atom Energy)	USA (United States)	28 Jun 60	Direct Aid	374UNTS133	105333
Korea, South	USA (United States)	18 Nov 60	Atomic Energy	400UNTS49	105747
Israel	USA (United States)	19 Dec 60	Direct Aid	401UNTS195	105772
Finland	IAEA (Atom Energy)	30 Dec 60	Atomic Energy	395UNTS257	105690
Brazil	USA (United States)	17 Mar 61	Atomic Energy	406UNTS241	105853
Norway	IAEA (Atom Energy)	10 Apr 61	Scientific Project	402UNTS255	105790
Multilateral		10 Apr 61	Atomic Energy	402UNTS281	105791
USA (United States)	Yugoslavia	19 Apr 61	Direct Aid	409UNTS163	105883
Netherlands	Euratom	25 Jul 61	Scientific Project	462UNTS263	106686
Multilateral		04 Oct 61	Scientific Project	412UNTS210	105934
IAEA (Atom Energy)	Yugoslavia	04 Oct 61	Scientific Project	412UNTS226	105935
Pakistan	IAEA (Atom Energy)	05 Mar 62	Scientific Project	425UNTS17	106115
Multilateral		05 Mar 62	Scientific Project	425UNTS3	106114
Congo (Zaire)	IAEA (Atom Energy)	27 Jun 62	Direct Aid	463UNTS31	106691
Multilateral		27 Jun 62	Atomic Energy	463UNTS11	106689
IAEA (Atom Energy)	USA (United States)	20 Aug 62	Commodity Trade	456UNTS447	106570
IAEA (Atom Energy)	Yugoslavia	04 Mar 63	Atomic Energy	490UNTS333	107162
IAEA (Atom Energy)	Yugoslavia	04 Jun 63	Atomic Energy	490UNTS343	107163
Austria	IAEA (Atom Energy)	21 Jun 63	Atomic Energy	490UNTS351	107164
Finland	IAEA (Atom Energy)	02 Jul 63	Atomic Energy	490UNTS403	107167
Finland	IAEA (Atom Energy)	30 Jul 63	Atomic Energy	490UNTS413	107168
Argentina	USA (United States)	30 Nov 63	Scientific Project	505UNTS131	107369
IAEA (Atom Energy)	Yugoslavia	07 Dec 63	Scientific Project	501UNTS273	107322
Mexico	IAEA (Atom Energy)	18 Dec 63	Atomic Energy	490UNTS361	107165
Finland	IAEA (Atom Energy)	27 Jan 64	Scientific Project	501UNTS213	107319
Multilateral		28 Feb 64	Atomic Energy	501UNTS245	107321
Multilateral		08 Apr 64	Loans and Credits	501UNTS221	107320
Multilateral		11 Jun 64	Atomic Energy	525UNTS61	107584

PARTY ONE	PARTY TWO	DATE	TOPIC	CITATION	NUMBER
Nuclear Research (Cont.)					
Italy	USA (United States)	23 Nov 64	Milit Assistance	532UNTS133	107716
Multilateral		24 Sep 65	Atomic Energy	556UNTS141	108124
Multilateral		30 Dec 65	Atomic Energy	557UNTS3	108126
Multilateral		20 Jun 66	Atomic Energy	573UNTS41	108322
Multilateral		08 Jul 66	Atomic Energy	572UNTS283	108319
Multilateral		28 Sep 66	Specif Goods/Equip	589UNTS41	108534
Nursing					
Multilateral		12 Nov 47	Admin Cooperation	46UNTS201	100710
Multilateral		12 Nov 47	Admin Cooperation	46UNTS169	100709
Multilateral		04 May 49	Admin Cooperation	47UNTS159	100728
Multilateral		04 May 49	Admin Cooperation	30UNTS3	100445
Costa Rica	WHO (World Health)	14 Jun 51	Sanitation	102UNTS151	101418
Burma	WHO (World Health)	09 Jul 51	Sanitation	104UNTS175	101439
Burma	WHO (World Health)	09 Jul 51	Sanitation	102UNTS131	101416
India	WHO (World Health)	23 Oct 51	Sanitation	109UNTS59	101491
Mexico	WHO (World Health)	17 Dec 51	Tech Assistance	124UNTS121	101670
Taiwan	WHO (World Health)	07 Mar 52	Sanitation	128UNTS233	101723
India	WHO (World Health)	04 Jun 52	Sanitation	135UNTS279	101827
India	WHO (World Health)	19 Jun 52	Sanitation	134UNTS307	101809
India	WHO (World Health)	11 Feb 53	Tech Assistance	163UNTS43	102140
Obscene Publications					
Multilateral		12 Nov 47	Admin Cooperation	46UNTS201	100710
Multilateral		12 Nov 47	Admin Cooperation	46UNTS169	100709
Multilateral		04 May 49	Admin Cooperation	47UNTS159	100728
Multilateral		04 May 49	Admin Cooperation	30UNTS3	100445
Oceanography					
Multilateral		08 Mar 61	Scientific Project	396UNTS255	200584
Official Publications					
Haiti	USA (United States)	05 Jun 41	Admin Cooperation	101UNTS125	200289
El Salvador	USA (United States)	27 Nov 41	Admin Cooperation	120UNTS161	200389
Liberia	USA (United States)	15 Jan 42	Admin Cooperation	117UNTS227	200372
Bolivia	USA (United States)	31 Jan 42	Admin Cooperation	101UNTS137	200290
Panama	USA (United States)	07 Mar 42	Admin Cooperation	101UNTS157	200291
Paraguay	USA (United States)	28 Nov 42	Admin Cooperation	101UNTS173	200292
Iran	USA (United States)	21 Aug 43	Admin Cooperation	101UNTS189	200293
Iraq	USA (United States)	16 Feb 44	Admin Cooperation	109UNTS223	200362
Afghanistan	USA (United States)	29 Feb 44	Admin Cooperation	106UNTS247	200344
Guatemala	USA (United States)	13 Apr 44	Admin Cooperation	106UNTS213	200342
Norway	USA (United States)	15 Mar 48	Admin Cooperation	73UNTS81	100946
Belgium	Denmark	13 Dec 49	Admin Cooperation	173UNTS193	102266
Israel	USA (United States)	19 Feb 50	Admin Cooperation	122UNTS117	101641
Brazil	USA (United States)	23 May 50	Admin Cooperation	151UNTS141	101989
USA (United States)	Yugoslavia	09 Oct 50	Admin Cooperation	133UNTS25	101776
Greece	USA (United States)	24 Oct 50	Admin Cooperation	133UNTS41	101778
Costa Rica	USA (United States)	02 Dec 50	Admin Cooperation	133UNTS61	101780
India	USA (United States)	11 Jan 51	Admin Cooperation	148UNTS49	101934
Pakistan	USA (United States)	23 May 51	Admin Cooperation	134UNTS265	101805
UK Great Britain	USA (United States)	30 Jul 51	Admin Cooperation	105UNTS81	101455
France	UK Great Britain	13 Apr 53	Admin Cooperation	172UNTS173	102245
Belgium	UK Great Britain	10 Sep 53	Admin Cooperation	183UNTS203	102429
Australia	Ceylon (Sri Lanka)	07 Nov 53	Admin Cooperation	191UNTS249	102585
Australia	Yugoslavia	19 Nov 53	Admin Cooperation	191UNTS241	102584
Denmark	Yugoslavia	27 Jan 54	Admin Cooperation	193UNTS181	102615
Australia	Vietnam, South	04 Oct 54	Admin Cooperation	201UNTS349	102723
Germany, West	USA (United States)	27 Oct 54	Admin Cooperation	234UNTS131	103278
Belgium	Israel	14 Dec 54	Admin Cooperation	220UNTS49	102987
Australia	France	27 Dec 55	Admin Cooperation	241UNTS325	103440
Japan	USA (United States)	05 Sep 56	Admin Cooperation	277UNTS267	104011
Australia	Thailand	20 Dec 56	Admin Cooperation	265UNTS149	103810
Belgium	Japan	18 Mar 58	Admin Cooperation	303UNTS149	104378
Multilateral		03 Dec 58	Admin Cooperation	398UNTS9	105715
Cambodia	USA (United States)	15 Jul 60	Admin Cooperation	380UNTS129	105453
USA (United States)	Vietnam, South	04 Apr 61	Admin Cooperation	405UNTS77	105824

PARTY ONE	PARTY TWO	DATE	TOPIC	CITATION	NUMBER
Official Publications (Cont.)					
Ethiopia	USA (United States)	25 Nov 64	Mass Media	532UNTS125	107715
Denmark	Germany, West	06 Jan 65	Admin Cooperation	528UNTS201	107643
Officials and Employees					
ICAO (Civil Aviat)	United Nations	28 Feb 51	IGO Operations	139UNTS429	200469
IAEA (Atom Energy)	United Nations	22 Sep 58	IGO Operations	313UNTS323	200552
Sierra Leone	UK Great Britain	05 May 61	Consul/Citizenship	420UNTS17	106037
Belgium	Rwanda	13 Oct 62	Tech Assistance	456UNTS431	106569
IMCO (Maritime Org)	United Nations	11 Feb 64	IGO Operations	489UNTS357	200605
Old Age Insurance					
Multilateral		29 Jun 33	ILO Labor	39UNTS165	100617
Multilateral		29 Jun 33	ILO Labor	39UNTS189	100618
Multilateral		22 Jun 35	ILO Labor	40UNTS73	100628
Belgium	France	17 Jan 48	Non-ILO Labor	36UNTS233	100570
France	UK Great Britain	11 Jun 48	Non-ILO Labor	66UNTS151	100852
Multilateral		27 Aug 49	Non-ILO Labor	47UNTS127	100727
Belgium	Luxembourg	03 Dec 49	Non-ILO Labor	91UNTS31	101241
France	UK Great Britain	28 Jan 50	Non-ILO Labor	97UNTS155	101349
Olive Oil					
Multilateral		03 Apr 58	Commodity Trade	336UNTS177	104806
Multilateral		03 Apr 58	Commodity Trade	302UNTS121	104355
Multilateral		20 Apr 63	IGO Establishment	495UNTS3	107239
Origin of Goods					
Romania	UK Great Britain	13 Mar 48	Admin Cooperation	104UNTS117	101436
France	Japan	25 Apr 53	Admin Cooperation	187UNTS41	102500
Japan	UK Great Britain	27 Apr 53	Admin Cooperation	228UNTS227	103154
Parcel Post					
UK Great Britain	USA (United States)	10 May 43	Postal Service	147UNTS109	200473
Portugal	UK Great Britain	01 Jul 45	Postal Service	5UNTS263	200034
Guatemala	USA (United States)	25 Oct 45	Postal Service	139UNTS45	101875
Ceylon (Sri Lanka)	India	12 Aug 46	Postal Service	196UNTS209	102626
Romania	USA (United States)	26 Feb 48	Admin Cooperation	48UNTS9	100738
Bulgaria	USA (United States)	08 Mar 48	Admin Cooperation	29UNTS101	100437
Hungary	USA (United States)	09 Mar 48	Admin Cooperation	183UNTS3	102426
Italy	UK Great Britain	13 Mar 48	Admin Cooperation	104UNTS41	101435
Burma	Pakistan	22 Jun 48	Postal Service	91UNTS197	101252
New Zealand	Pakistan	28 Jun 48	Postal Service	91UNTS235	101253
Ceylon (Sri Lanka)	Pakistan	15 Dec 48	Postal Service	91UNTS303	101255
Australia	Italy	07 Jan 49	Admin Cooperation	189UNTS239	102549
Korea, South	USA (United States)	17 Feb 49	Postal Service	74UNTS167	100963
Australia	Philippines	01 Sep 49	Postal Service	46UNTS215	100711
USA (United States)	Yugoslavia	14 Aug 50	Postal Service	137UNTS131	101851
Czechoslovakia	USA (United States)	29 Sep 50	Postal Service	290UNTS3	104227
UK Great Britain	USA (United States)	03 Jun 51	Postal Service	137UNTS81	101850
Australia	Pakistan	16 Jan 52	Postal Service	151UNTS281	102001
Australia	USA (United States)	27 May 52	Postal Service	178UNTS113	102338
Multilateral		11 Jul 52	Postal Service	170UNTS63	102222
Japan	UK Great Britain	27 Apr 53	Admin Cooperation	228UNTS227	103154
Australia	Japan	27 Apr 53	Admin Cooperation	193UNTS78	102612
Israel	Switzerland	01 Jul 53	Postal Service	220UNTS41	102986
Australia	Netherlands	22 Oct 53	Postal Service	184UNTS193	102448
Italy	South Africa	20 Dec 53	Postal Service	277UNTS293	104014
Australia	Greece	24 May 54	Postal Service	191UNTS255	102586
Australia	Israel	18 Jun 54	Postal Service	220UNTS29	102985
India	USA (United States)	29 Jul 54	Postal Service	239UNTS69	103373
Canada	South Africa	04 Aug 54	Postal Service	261UNTS3	103722
Australia	Poland	25 Nov 54	Postal Service	521UNTS281	107526
Australia	Austria	20 Dec 54	Postal Service	205UNTS157	102775
Israel	South Africa	31 Dec 54	Postal Service	220UNTS11	102984
Australia	Hungary	10 Feb 55	Postal Service	207UNTS173	102806
Australia	Taiwan	22 Mar 55	Postal Service	209UNTS3	102818
Australia	Czechoslovakia	01 Apr 55	Postal Service	213UNTS199	102888
Spain	USA (United States)	16 Jul 55	Postal Service	270UNTS211	103899
Ceylon (Sri Lanka)	USA (United States)	18 Jul 55	Postal Service	281UNTS295	104086

PARTY ONE	PARTY TWO	DATE	TOPIC	CITATION	NUMBER
Parcel Post (Cont.)					
Pakistan	USA (United States)	20 Jul 55	Postal Service	241UNTS255	103436
Australia	Yugoslavia	28 Feb 56	Postal Service	243UNTS53	103446
Nicaragua	USA (United States)	19 Mar 56	Postal Service	275UNTS231	103984
Canada	Japan	20 Mar 56	Postal Service	517UNTS33	107482
Liberia	USA (United States)	16 Mar 57	Postal Service	290UNTS59	104228
Taiwan	USA (United States)	30 Jul 57	Postal Service	300UNTS61	104331
Austria	South Africa	26 Sep 57	Postal Service	287UNTS3	104176
Multilateral		03 Oct 57	Postal Service	365UNTS3	105213
Japan	USA (United States)	03 Nov 58	Postal Service	341UNTS83	104879
Portugal	USA (United States)	12 Jan 59	Postal Service	343UNTS49	104921
United Arab Rep	USA (United States)	13 Jan 59	Postal Service	358UNTS3	105122
Ireland	South Africa	13 Apr 60	Postal Service	390UNTS307	105612
New Zealand	Philippines	09 May 60	Postal Service	486UNTS65	107073
Australia	USSR (Soviet Union)	29 Jun 60	Postal Service	392UNTS131	105641
Korea, South	USA (United States)	17 Aug 60	Postal Service	400UNTS339	105757
Australia	Japan	01 Mar 62	Postal Service	517UNTS81	107483
Australia	Germany, West	19 Mar 62	Postal Service	488UNTS203	107130
Israel	Netherlands	28 May 62	Postal Service	448UNTS219	106434
Thailand	USA (United States)	31 May 62	Postal Service	459UNTS135	106619
Israel	Liberia	18 Sep 62	Postal Service	484UNTS209	107031
Multilateral		16 Oct 62	Postal Service	470UNTS336	106816
Multilateral		16 Oct 62	Postal Service	470UNTS321	106815
Japan	Philippines	19 Jan 63	Postal Service	517UNTS281	107489
Japan	New Zealand	15 Mar 63	Postal Service	517UNTS229	107487
Japan	South Africa	06 Apr 63	Postal Service	484UNTS319	107040
Kuwait	USA (United States)	21 Oct 63	Postal Service	530UNTS281	107688
Philippines	USA (United States)	12 Nov 64	Postal Service	574UNTS159	108349
Passports					
Taiwan	Dominican Republic	11 May 40	General Amity	10UNTS285	200067
Argentina	USA (United States)	15 Apr 41	Visas	103UNTS307	200321
Belgium	France	30 Mar 45	Visas	21UNTS325	200132
Belgium	Luxembourg	28 Apr 45	Visas	41UNTS265	200181
Panama	USA (United States)	13 May 45	Visas	89UNTS273	200256
Belgium	France	21 May 45	Visas	23UNTS215	200133
Denmark	Norway	10 Oct 45	Visas	104UNTS335	200323
Netherlands	USA (United States)	13 Mar 46	Visas	84UNTS3	101113
France	Netherlands	27 Mar 46	Visas	247UNTS3	103456
Iraq	Turkey	29 Mar 46	General Amity	37UNTS226	100580
Belgium	Italy	23 Jun 46	Non-ILO Labor	19UNTS65	100305
Monaco	Netherlands	25 Sep 46	Visas	247UNTS199	103469
Multilateral		15 Oct 46	Refugees	11UNTS73	100150
France	USA (United States)	10 Dec 46	Visas	15UNTS265	100242
Lebanon	Turkey	24 Dec 46	Visas	4UNTS269	100051
France	UK Great Britain	27 Dec 46	Visas	11UNTS255	100163
Belgium	Denmark	28 Jan 47	Visas	18UNTS221	100291
Belgium	USA (United States)	03 Feb 47	Visas	84UNTS255	101134
Belgium	UK Great Britain	05 Feb 47	Visas	11UNTS261	100164
Luxembourg	UK Great Britain	14 Feb 47	Visas	11UNTS267	100165
Norway	UK Great Britain	26 Feb 47	Visas	11UNTS273	100166
Ireland	Sweden	19 Mar 47	Visas	553UNTS163	108083
Netherlands	Sweden	20 Mar 47	Visas	247UNTS145	103463
Belgium	Sweden	20 Mar 47	Visas	34UNTS3	100522
Sweden	UK Great Britain	20 Mar 47	Visas	11UNTS291	100169
Denmark	UK Great Britain	20 Mar 47	Visas	11UNTS285	100168
Netherlands	UK Great Britain	21 Mar 47	Visas	11UNTS297	100170
Belgium	Ireland	25 Mar 47	Visas	18UNTS227	100292
France	Ireland	22 Apr 47	Visas	553UNTS51	108068
Sweden	USA (United States)	30 Apr 47	Visas	84UNTS33	101116
Ireland	Netherlands	01 May 47	Visas	247UNTS193	103468
Denmark	Ireland	13 May 47	Visas	553UNTS37	108066
Ireland	Switzerland	09 Jun 47	Visas	553UNTS169	108084
Denmark	USA (United States)	09 Jun 47	Visas	132UNTS145	101755
Switzerland	UK Great Britain	10 Jun 47	Visas	11UNTS217	100160
Iceland	UK Great Britain	20 Jun 47	Visas	11UNTS223	100161

PARTY ONE	PARTY TWO	DATE	TOPIC	CITATION	NUMBER
Passports (Cont.)					
France	Norway	30 Jun 47	Visas	104UNTS313	101449
Belgium	Switzerland	03 Jul 47	Visas	29UNTS277	100444
Luxembourg	Norway	12 Jul 47	Visas	90UNTS59	101226
Belgium	Norway	15 Jul 47	Visas	33UNTS25	100511
Norway	USA (United States)	29 Jul 47	Visas	87UNTS343	101178
Norway	Switzerland	01 Aug 47	Visas	90UNTS65	101227
Netherlands	USA (United States)	20 Aug 47	Visas	84UNTS11	101114
France	USA (United States)	16 Sep 47	Visas	84UNTS19	101115
Liberia	USA (United States)	28 Oct 47	Visas	82UNTS23	101081
Multilateral		13 Nov 47	Visas	251UNTS79	103534
France	New Zealand	22 Nov 47	Visas	15UNTS29	100228
Italy	UK Great Britain	06 Dec 47	Visas	82UNTS243	101097
Iceland	USA (United States)	09 Dec 47	Visas	82UNTS31	101082
Ireland	Norway	17 Dec 47	Visas	90UNTS71	101228
Belgium	Italy	09 Feb 48	Non-ILO Labor	71UNTS143	100915
Belgium	Turkey	25 Feb 48	Visas	18UNTS237	100293
Romania	USA (United States)	26 Feb 48	Admin Cooperation	48UNTS9	100738
Bulgaria	USA (United States)	08 Mar 48	Admin Cooperation	29UNTS101	100437
Hungary	USA (United States)	09 Mar 48	Admin Cooperation	183UNTS3	102426
Belgium	Luxembourg	25 Mar 48	Taxation	18UNTS323	100300
Belgium	Ireland	16 Apr 48	Visas	26UNTS159	100386
Belgium	France	23 Apr 48	Territory Boundary	19UNTS95	100307
New Zealand	Sweden	04 Jun 48	Visas	18UNTS171	100286
France	Norway	11 Jun 48	General Trade	31UNTS83	100469
Monaco	Norway	16 Jul 48	Visas	90UNTS77	101229
New Zealand	Switzerland	30 Jul 48	Visas	18UNTS177	100287
India	USA (United States)	11 Aug 48	Visas	224UNTS115	103072
Belgium	Switzerland	01 Sep 48	Visas	23UNTS139	100344
Italy	USA (United States)	29 Sep 48	Visas	84UNTS43	101117
Belgium	USA (United States)	26 Oct 48	Visas	84UNTS265	101135
Italy	UK Great Britain	28 Oct 48	Visas	77UNTS129	100996
Greece	USA (United States)	01 Nov 48	Direct Aid	185UNTS169	102468
Panama	USA (United States)	05 Nov 48	Visas	89UNTS27	101206
Monaco	UK Great Britain	10 Nov 48	Visas	81UNTS85	101065
UK Great Britain	USA (United States)	12 Nov 48	Visas	84UNTS275	101136
Ireland	Luxembourg	01 Dec 48	Visas	553UNTS111	108075
Denmark	New Zealand	13 Dec 48	Visas	92UNTS65	101261
Belgium	Sweden	16 Dec 48	Visas	26UNTS3	100372
Belgium	UK Great Britain	29 Dec 48	Visas	27UNTS135	100404
Belgium	Italy	01 Jan 49	Visas	26UNTS151	100385
Belgium	France	08 Jan 49	Non-ILO Labor	36UNTS151	100569
Czechoslovakia	Poland	21 Jan 49	Admin Cooperation	31UNTS205	100480
Greece	USA (United States)	29 Jan 49	Visas	88UNTS35	101183
Italy	Yugoslavia	03 Feb 49	Visas	33UNTS105	100517
Canada	Turkey	28 Feb 49	Visas	231UNTS57	103204
Iraq	Pakistan	02 Mar 49	Visas	141UNTS319	101921
Netherlands	New Zealand	03 Mar 49	Visas	34UNTS207	100538
New Zealand	USA (United States)	14 Mar 49	Visas	32UNTS369	100508
France	USA (United States)	31 Mar 49	Visas	84UNTS283	101137
Belgium	France	12 Apr 49	Visas	30UNTS45	100447
Belgium	UK Great Britain	14 Apr 49	Visas	65UNTS117	100840
Iceland	Ireland	20 May 49	Visas	553UNTS99	108073
Pakistan	Turkey	27 May 49	Visas	141UNTS325	101922
Belgium	Denmark	31 May 49	Visas	32UNTS337	100506
Norway	Pakistan	08 Jun 49	Visas	90UNTS131	101231
Panama	USA (United States)	14 Jun 49	Visas	89UNTS37	101207
Canada	Sweden	30 Jun 49	Visas	231UNTS37	103201
Austria	USA (United States)	12 Jul 49	Visas	84UNTS291	101138
Belgium	Luxembourg	15 Jul 49	Visas	41UNTS13	100642
Ireland	USA (United States)	01 Aug 49	Visas	82UNTS37	101083
Italy	Netherlands	16 Aug 49	Admin Cooperation	98UNTS21	101357
San Marino	UK Great Britain	12 Sep 49	Visas	87UNTS37	101164
Netherlands	Switzerland	15 Sep 49	Visas	252UNTS13	103555
Canada	Denmark	14 Oct 49	Visas	46UNTS97	100702
Pakistan	USA (United States)	18 Oct 49	Visas	141UNTS333	101923

Passports (Cont.)

PARTY ONE	PARTY TWO	DATE	TOPIC	CITATION	NUMBER
USA (United States)	Uruguay	08 Nov 49	Visas	82UNTS45	101084
Belgium	Czechoslovakia	14 Nov 49	Visas	46UNTS319	100718
Belgium	Canada	19 Nov 49	Visas	150UNTS231	101977
New Zealand	Norway	22 Nov 49	Visas	51UNTS123	100760
Canada	Luxembourg	26 Nov 49	Visas	231UNTS51	103203
Ireland	Italy	28 Nov 49	Visas	553UNTS105	108074
UK Great Britain	USA (United States)	12 Dec 49	Visas	92UNTS191	101271
Canada	Netherlands	14 Dec 49	Visas	230UNTS337	103192
Belgium	San Marino	14 Dec 49	Visas	51UNTS107	100757
Denmark	Finland	21 Dec 49	Visas	46UNTS125	100705
Finland	Norway	30 Dec 49	Visas	90UNTS175	101234
Belgium	Italy	30 Dec 49	Visas	51UNTS83	100754
Belgium	Monaco	06 Feb 50	Visas	51UNTS93	100755
Belgium	Finland	09 Feb 50	Visas	51UNTS77	100753
Australia	USA (United States)	10 Feb 50	Visas	51UNTS167	100763
Portugal	USA (United States)	24 Feb 50	Visas	92UNTS219	101274
Canada	Norway	13 Mar 50	Visas	90UNTS181	101235
Belgium	France	14 Mar 50	Visas	65UNTS139	100842
USA (United States)	Yugoslavia	25 Mar 50	Visas	98UNTS195	101365
Belgium	Netherlands	29 Mar 50	Visas	68UNTS45	100883
Belgium	Luxembourg	06 Apr 50	Visas	65UNTS147	100843
Canada	France	17 Apr 50	Visas	230UNTS365	103196
Mexico	USA (United States)	03 May 50	Visas	98UNTS201	101366
Italy	Norway	24 Jul 50	Visas	90UNTS187	101236
Belgium	Switzerland	28 Jul 50	Visas	71UNTS91	100911
Chile	USA (United States)	29 Aug 50	Visas	122UNTS43	101634
UK Great Britain	USA (United States)	13 Sep 50	Visas	122UNTS51	101635
Belgium	France	26 Sep 50	Visas	79UNTS3	101026
Lebanon	Pakistan	03 Oct 50	Visas	219UNTS41	102964
Canada	Turkey	09 Feb 51	Visas	233UNTS95	103252
Australia	Netherlands	20 Feb 51	Visas	97UNTS283	101354
Cuba	UK Great Britain	02 Mar 51	Visas	88UNTS191	101190
Austria	Belgium	16 Mar 51	Visas	88UNTS357	101203
Israel	USA (United States)	01 Jun 51	Visas	212UNTS129	102864
Australia	Italy	19 Jun 51	Visas	184UNTS185	102447
Luxembourg	New Zealand	29 Jun 51	Visas	101UNTS71	101403
Belgium	Portugal	03 Jul 51	Visas	101UNTS17	101398
Australia	Belgium	25 Jul 51	Visas	108UNTS303	101482
Australia	Luxembourg	05 Sep 51	Visas	109UNTS31	101487
Australia	Sweden	26 Sep 51	Visas	109UNTS39	101488
Austria	Belgium	11 Oct 51	Visas	110UNTS45	101500
Australia	Norway	19 Oct 51	Visas	128UNTS109	101716
Pakistan	Turkey	22 Oct 51	Visas	219UNTS47	102965
Belgium	New Zealand	01 Nov 51	Visas	118UNTS169	101605
Belgium	Spain	04 Jan 52	Visas	121UNTS25	101622
Spain	USA (United States)	21 Jan 52	Visas	160UNTS63	102102
Netherlands	Portugal	14 Mar 52	Visas	309UNTS117	104470
Canada	Monaco	20 Mar 52	Visas	233UNTS123	103256
Monaco	USA (United States)	31 Mar 52	Visas	177UNTS195	102318
Belgium	Germany, West	01 Apr 52	Visas	132UNTS45	101750
Australia	Denmark	01 May 52	Visas	152UNTS3	102006
Monaco	New Zealand	13 Jun 52	Visas	171UNTS269	102230
Netherlands	South Africa	21 Jun 52	Visas	309UNTS123	104471
Belgium	Italy	25 Jun 52	Visas	137UNTS239	101855
Greece	Italy	05 Jul 52	Visas	187UNTS157	102508
Multilateral		14 Jul 52	Visas	198UNTS37	102655
Multilateral		14 Jul 52	Consul/Citizenship	198UNTS47	102656
Greece	Turkey	05 Aug 52	Visas	187UNTS163	102509
Japan	USA (United States)	18 Sep 52	Visas	227UNTS85	103133
Turkey	UK Great Britain	09 Oct 52	Visas	151UNTS233	101999
Canada	Italy	10 Oct 52	Visas	233UNTS137	103258
Belgium	Turkey	16 Oct 52	Visas	149UNTS289	101958
Belgium	Germany, West	14 Nov 52	Visas	160UNTS217	102108
Philippines	USA (United States)	24 Nov 52	Visas	181UNTS155	102406
Belgium	France	29 Nov 52	Visas	160UNTS261	102110

Passports (Cont.)

PARTY ONE	PARTY TWO	DATE	TOPIC	CITATION	NUMBER
Belgium	Germany, West	06 Dec 52	Visas	152UNTS11	102007
Australia	Germany, West	17 Dec 52	Visas	188UNTS267	102530
Germany, West	USA (United States)	09 Jan 53	Visas	212UNTS3	102859
Germany, West	Netherlands	13 Mar 53	Visas	293UNTS123	104289
Chile	Norway	16 Mar 53	Visas	167UNTS13	102198
Germany, West	Netherlands	17 Mar 53	Visas	293UNTS129	104290
Canada	Germany, West	15 Apr 53	Visas	236UNTS323	103333
Netherlands	Pakistan	01 May 53	Visas	293UNTS11	104281
Greece	UK Great Britain	01 Jun 53	Visas	172UNTS265	102250
Israel	Netherlands	16 Jun 53	Visas	220UNTS93	102993
Israel	Netherlands	18 Jun 53	Visas	220UNTS99	102994
Belgium	Greece	05 Aug 53	Visas	173UNTS53	102260
Greece	Netherlands	26 Sep 53	Visas	292UNTS23	104263
Germany, West	Netherlands	10 Oct 53	Visas	293UNTS115	104288
Netherlands	Turkey	04 Nov 53	Visas	293UNTS3	104280
Mexico	USA (United States)	12 Nov 53	Visas	224UNTS187	103077
El Salvador	USA (United States)	15 Dec 53	Visas	236UNTS25	103314
Belgium	Cuba	16 Dec 53	Visas	185UNTS285	102475
Belgium	Germany, West	19 Dec 53	Visas	185UNTS277	102474
Colombia	USA (United States)	22 May 54	Visas	354UNTS21	105050
Multilateral		22 May 54	Visas	199UNTS29	102675
Australia	Greece	24 May 54	Visas	193UNTS175	102614
Chile	Netherlands	18 Jun 54	Visas	292UNTS37	104265
Belgium	Israel	22 Jun 54	Visas	196UNTS245	102627
Ireland	Monaco	06 Jul 54	Visas	553UNTS117	108076
Denmark	Pakistan	30 Aug 54	Visas	203UNTS59	102740
Israel	Luxembourg	27 Oct 54	Visas	226UNTS241	103117
Sweden	UK Great Britain	29 Oct 54	Visas	209UNTS75	102823
Belgium	UK Great Britain	05 Nov 54	Visas	209UNTS69	102822
Finland	UK Great Britain	16 Nov 54	Visas	204UNTS177	102756
Portugal	UK Great Britain	23 Nov 54	Visas	204UNTS183	102757
Portugal	UK Great Britain	24 Nov 54	Visas	313UNTS125	104533
Guatemala	USA (United States)	01 Dec 54	Visas	237UNTS161	103342
Netherlands	Portugal	14 Dec 54	Visas	289UNTS121	104216
Belgium	Netherlands	13 Jan 55	Visas	210UNTS63	102834
Finland	Ireland	01 Feb 55	Visas	553UNTS45	108067
Israel	USA (United States)	02 Mar 55	Visas	220UNTS113	102996
Israel	Sweden	02 Mar 55	Visas	220UNTS105	102995
Israel	Luxembourg	30 Mar 55	Visas	226UNTS247	103118
Belgium	Israel	15 Apr 55	Visas	211UNTS43	102845
Denmark	Israel	29 Apr 55	Visas	220UNTS87	102992
Luxembourg	Netherlands	04 May 55	Refugees	292UNTS17	104262
Germany, West	New Zealand	10 Jun 55	Visas	380UNTS307	105462
Canada	Japan	13 Jun 55	Visas	247UNTS151	103464
Israel	Norway	26 Jul 55	Visas	226UNTS257	103120
Ireland	Portugal	29 Jul 55	Visas	553UNTS135	108079
Canada	Israel	02 Aug 55	Visas	226UNTS265	103121
Australia	USA (United States)	20 Aug 55	Visas	268UNTS133	103855
Israel	Netherlands	21 Aug 55	Visas	299UNTS51	104306
Philippines	USA (United States)	06 Sep 55	Visas	238UNTS109	103356
Ireland	Turkey	27 Sep 55	Visas	553UNTS193	108087
Turkey	USA (United States)	11 Oct 55	Visas	272UNTS145	103935
Nicaragua	USA (United States)	22 Oct 55	Visas	358UNTS51	105123
Finland	Israel	16 Nov 55	Visas	257UNTS39	103647
Greece	Netherlands	22 Nov 55	Visas	292UNTS31	104264
Finland	USA (United States)	14 Dec 55	Visas	335UNTS263	104794
Dominican Republic	USA (United States)	16 Dec 55	Visas	241UNTS101	103427
Austria	Italy	28 Dec 55	Visas	260UNTS345	103718
Iceland	Israel	29 Dec 55	Visas	227UNTS147	103136
Italy	Thailand	30 Dec 55	Visas	260UNTS351	103719
Belgium	Turkey	02 Jan 56	Visas	228UNTS203	103152
Canada	Finland	09 Jan 56	Visas	305UNTS33	104410
Italy	Japan	11 Jan 56	Visas	267UNTS175	103842
Netherlands	USA (United States)	22 Jan 56	Atomic Energy	287UNTS121	104181
Norway	South Africa	17 Feb 56	Visas	230UNTS213	103186

PARTY ONE	PARTY TWO	DATE	TOPIC	CITATION	NUMBER
Passports (Cont.)					
Taiwan	USA (United States)	20 Feb 56	Visas	275UNTS73	103976
Luxembourg	Netherlands	22 Feb 56	Visas	286UNTS249	104171
Australia	Austria	15 Mar 56	Visas	241UNTS331	103441
South Africa	USA (United States)	03 Apr 56	Visas	249UNTS395	103513
Australia	Turkey	10 Apr 56	Visas	247UNTS139	103462
Austria	Italy	09 May 56	Education	267UNTS227	103845
Japan	Netherlands	16 May 56	Visas	305UNTS97	104417
Panama	USA (United States)	25 May 56	Visas	268UNTS333	103866
Guatemala	USA (United States)	30 May 56	Visas	275UNTS271	103986
Iceland	USA (United States)	04 Jun 56	Visas	275UNTS189	103982
Greece	Ireland	05 Jun 56	Visas	553UNTS93	108072
Iraq	USA (United States)	06 Jun 56	Visas	275UNTS265	103985
Austria	Canada	19 Jun 56	Visas	305UNTS51	104412
Belgium	Japan	11 Jul 56	Visas	248UNTS129	103492
Belgium	Germany, West	26 Jul 56	Visas	249UNTS187	103508
Belgium	Czechoslovakia	08 Aug 56	Visas	257UNTS215	103656
Canada	Turkey	21 Aug 56	Visas	305UNTS89	104416
Israel	South Africa	01 Sep 56	Visas	251UNTS161	103539
Ceylon (Sri Lanka)	USA (United States)	07 Sep 56	Visas	280UNTS35	104048
Peru	USA (United States)	09 Oct 56	Visas	288UNTS165	104204
Belgium	Chile	09 Oct 56	Visas	257UNTS227	103658
Belgium	Pakistan	19 Oct 56	Visas	257UNTS221	103657
Finland	South Africa	05 Dec 56	Visas	258UNTS59	103670
Japan	Luxembourg	18 Dec 56	Visas	318UNTS227	104616
France	Netherlands	15 Feb 57	Refugees	286UNTS243	104170
Belgium	France	15 Feb 57	Refugees	267UNTS3	103834
Belgium	Brazil	27 Feb 57	Visas	265UNTS189	103812
France	Italy	28 Feb 57	Visas	291UNTS191	104253
Dominican Republic	Japan	20 Mar 57	Visas	318UNTS245	104619
Japan	USA (United States)	22 Mar 57	Visas	288UNTS201	104206
Japan	Switzerland	25 Mar 57	Visas	318UNTS239	104618
Netherlands	Portugal	26 Mar 57	Visas	288UNTS47	104196
Belgium	Peru	03 May 57	Visas	274UNTS251	103970
France	Netherlands	21 May 57	Visas	299UNTS43	104305
Belgium	Colombia	24 May 57	Visas	274UNTS245	103969
Italy	Monaco	01 Jun 57	Visas	291UNTS197	104254
Austria	South Africa	11 Jun 57	Visas	272UNTS229	103941
Canada	Greece	01 Jul 57	Visas	316UNTS201	104585
Austria	Pakistan	16 Aug 57	Visas	306UNTS3	104429
Japan	Netherlands	20 Sep 57	Visas	305UNTS105	104418
Japan	Turkey	05 Nov 57	Visas	318UNTS411	104628
Austria	Israel	25 Nov 57	Visas	314UNTS81	104542
Netherlands	Thailand	09 Dec 57	Visas	309UNTS291	104477
Multilateral		13 Dec 57	Visas	315UNTS139	104565
Canada	Portugal	24 Jan 58	Visas	392UNTS15	105634
France	Israel	01 Mar 58	Visas	314UNTS87	104543
Belgium	Mexico	18 Mar 58	Visas	301UNTS291	104348
Austria	Japan	20 Mar 58	Visas	324UNTS205	104686
Belgium	Ecuador	20 Mar 58	Visas	304UNTS207	104397
South Africa	Sweden	28 Mar 58	Air Transport	300UNTS95	104333
Netherlands	Switzerland	29 Mar 58	Visas	330UNTS101	104741
Germany, West	Netherlands	09 Apr 58	Visas	335UNTS237	104791
Belgium	Morocco	12 Apr 58	Visas	303UNTS141	104377
Belgium	South Africa	28 Apr 58	Visas	303UNTS131	104375
Israel	New Zealand	29 Apr 58	Visas	314UNTS93	104544
New Zealand	USA (United States)	05 May 58	Visas	317UNTS59	104594
Austria	New Zealand	14 May 58	Visas	317UNTS117	104598
Austria	Netherlands	30 May 58	Visas	458UNTS147	106598
New Zealand	Turkey	05 Jun 58	Visas	317UNTS123	104599
Japan	Philippines	24 Jul 58	Visas	325UNTS103	104696
Finland	USA (United States)	15 Aug 58	Visas	314UNTS43	104540
USA (United States)	USSR (Soviet Union)	20 Aug 58	Visas	336UNTS269	104809
Morocco	UK Great Britain	01 Oct 58	Visas	331UNTS119	104751
Canada	Finland	09 Dec 58	Visas	323UNTS331	104674
Finland	Japan	22 Dec 58	Visas	341UNTS41	104876

PARTY ONE	PARTY TWO	DATE	TOPIC	CITATION	NUMBER
Passports (Cont.)					
Malaysia	Netherlands	20 Jan 59	Visas	493UNTS147	107212
Norway	Philippines	18 Feb 59	Visas	359UNTS305	105147
Greece	Pakistan	05 Mar 59	Visas	338UNTS97	104833
Ireland	Spain	17 Apr 59	Visas	553UNTS157	108082
Multilateral		20 Apr 59	Visas	376UNTS85	105375
Argentina	Belgium	09 May 59	Visas	340UNTS53	104858
France	Israel	19 May 59	Admin Cooperation	377UNTS231	105403
Netherlands	Spain	27 May 59	Visas	458UNTS165	106599
Belgium	Spain	27 May 59	Visas	340UNTS81	104860
Australia	Monaco	07 Jul 59	Visas	354UNTS105	105057
Italy	Philippines	14 Jul 59	Visas	490UNTS237	107157
Pakistan	USA (United States)	28 Jul 59	Visas	360UNTS327	105166
Australia	USA (United States)	19 Aug 59	Visas	388UNTS183	105578
Belgium	Spain	11 Sep 59	Visas	345UNTS29	104956
Canada	Greece	30 Sep 59	Visas	470UNTS87	106798
Canada	Venezuela	08 Oct 59	Visas	470UNTS93	106799
Monaco	Netherlands	20 Oct 59	Visas	487UNTS29	107093
Mexico	UK Great Britain	13 Nov 59	Visas	360UNTS3	105152
Argentina	Brazil	26 Nov 59	Visas	374UNTS51	105328
Belgium	Thailand	02 Dec 59	Visas	351UNTS89	105018
Canada	Spain	18 Dec 59	Visas	470UNTS117	106802
Netherlands	Philippines	17 Feb 60	Visas	359UNTS317	105149
Belgium	Philippines	17 Feb 60	Visas	356UNTS303	105101
Luxembourg	Philippines	17 Feb 60	Visas	359UNTS311	105148
Australia	Philippines	23 Feb 60	Visas	358UNTS139	105131
Turkey	UK Great Britain	01 Mar 60	Visas	374UNTS295	105343
Bolivia	UK Great Britain	18 Mar 60	Visas	374UNTS199	105335
Luxembourg	UK Great Britain	01 Apr 60	Visas	374UNTS267	105340
Netherlands	UK Great Britain	01 Apr 60	Visas	374UNTS277	105341
Belgium	UK Great Britain	01 Apr 60	Visas	361UNTS135	105177
Spain	UK Great Britain	13 May 60	Visas	374UNTS287	105342
Accept UN Charter	Togo	21 May 60	UN Charter	375UNTS83	105355
Germany, West	UK Great Britain	20 Jun 60	Visas	385UNTS55	105528
France	Israel	07 Jul 60	Visas	413UNTS79	105942
Israel	Thailand	07 Jul 60	Visas	377UNTS325	105409
Belgium	Fed of Malaya	19 Jul 60	Visas	379UNTS391	105445
Japan	Luxembourg	21 Jul 60	Visas	384UNTS55	105510
El Salvador	Israel	05 Sep 60	Visas	413UNTS73	105941
Belgium	Tunisia	13 Oct 60	Visas	421UNTS71	106052
Korea, South	Philippines	11 Nov 60	Visas	490UNTS249	107159
Netherlands	Paraguay	21 Nov 60	Visas	450UNTS201	106467
Belgium	Paraguay	21 Nov 60	Visas	387UNTS237	105565
Japan	Pakistan	01 Dec 60	Visas	450UNTS337	106477
Israel	Philippines	14 Dec 60	Visas	449UNTS23	106448
Kuwait	USA (United States)	27 Dec 60	Visas	401UNTS185	105771
Italy	New Zealand	25 Jan 61	Visas	435UNTS255	106282
Iceland	UK Great Britain	09 Feb 61	Visas	398UNTS259	105728
France	UK Great Britain	14 Feb 61	Visas	398UNTS267	105729
Spain	UK Great Britain	15 Feb 61	Visas	404UNTS75	105805
Germany, West	UK Great Britain	20 Feb 61	Visas	398UNTS249	105727
Belgium	UK Great Britain	21 Feb 61	Visas	398UNTS229	105724
Netherlands	UK Great Britain	21 Feb 61	Visas	398UNTS235	105725
Luxembourg	UK Great Britain	21 Feb 61	Visas	398UNTS243	105726
Australia	Finland	21 Feb 61	Visas	390UNTS61	105602
Portugal	UK Great Britain	27 Feb 61	Visas	404UNTS33	105803
Switzerland	UK Great Britain	27 Feb 61	Visas	404UNTS167	105809
Italy	UK Great Britain	06 Mar 61	Visas	404UNTS3	105799
San Marino	UK Great Britain	08 Mar 61	Visas	414UNTS46	105964
Canada	Iran	10 Mar 61	Visas	470UNTS139	106805
Greece	UK Great Britain	06 Apr 61	Visas	403UNTS267	105797
Chile	Netherlands	07 Apr 61	Visas	453UNTS239	106527
Belgium	Chile	07 Apr 61	Visas	410UNTS255	105909
Monaco	UK Great Britain	11 Apr 61	Visas	404UNTS11	105800
Finland	UK Great Britain	05 May 61	Visas	414UNTS101	105969
Sweden	UK Great Britain	05 May 61	Visas	404UNTS105	105807

PARTY ONE	PARTY TWO	DATE	TOPIC	CITATION	NUMBER
Passports (Cont.)					
Chile	UK Great Britain	09 May 61	Visas	414UNTS37	105963
Norway	UK Great Britain	10 May 61	Visas	414UNTS9	105960
Denmark	UK Great Britain	10 May 61	Visas	414UNTS17	105961
Colombia	UK Great Britain	26 May 61	Visas	414UNTS85	105967
Luxembourg	South Africa	30 May 61	Visas	412UNTS203	105933
Finland	UK Great Britain	09 Jun 61	Visas	414UNTS53	105965
Turkey	UK Great Britain	28 Jun 61	Visas	414UNTS93	105968
Israel	Liberia	03 Aug 61	Visas	484UNTS203	107030
Cyprus	Israel	17 Aug 61	Visas	484UNTS169	107025
Israel	Italy	30 Aug 61	Visas	484UNTS197	107029
Costa Rica	Israel	01 Sep 61	Visas	448UNTS247	106436
France	USA (United States)	21 Sep 61	Visas	433UNTS243	106247
Australia	Spain	27 Sep 61	Visas	426UNTS159	106135
Bolivia	Netherlands	30 Sep 61	Visas	487UNTS105	107097
Belgium	Bolivia	30 Sep 61	Visas	425UNTS53	106118
New Zealand	Spain	02 Oct 61	Visas	453UNTS11	106516
El Salvador	Israel	04 Oct 61	Visas	448UNTS253	106437
IAEA (Atom Energy)	Yugoslavia	04 Oct 61	Scientific Project	412UNTS226	105935
Israel	Ivory Coast	26 Oct 61	Visas	515UNTS251	107462
Greece	New Zealand	06 Dec 61	Visas	486UNTS3	107067
Japan	Philippines	06 Dec 61	Visas	449UNTS29	106449
Multilateral		16 Dec 61	Visas	544UNTS19	107909
Dahomey	Israel	18 Dec 61	Visas	448UNTS259	106438
Argentina	Japan	20 Dec 61	Visas	451UNTS71	106485
Ivory Coast	Netherlands	12 Feb 62	Visas	485UNTS219	107057
Belgium	Ivory Coast	12 Feb 62	Visas	429UNTS193	106198
Central Afri Rep	Israel	14 Feb 62	Visas	484UNTS143	107022
Germany, West	Philippines	09 Mar 62	Visas	449UNTS35	106450
Honduras	UK Great Britain	30 Apr 62	Visas	449UNTS159	106457
Belgium	USA (United States)	23 May 62	Visas	434UNTS133	106260
Korea, South	USA (United States)	25 May 62	Visas	454UNTS25	106537
Romania	USA (United States)	26 May 62	Visas	456UNTS265	106561
Israel	Switzerland	29 Jun 62	Visas	448UNTS303	106443
Philippines	Spain	04 Jul 62	Visas	490UNTS243	107158
Tunisia	UK Great Britain	14 Jul 62	Visas	466UNTS235	106746
Malaysia	Philippines	31 Jul 62	Visas	452UNTS223	106510
Philippines	Thailand	31 Jul 62	Visas	452UNTS235	106511
Colombia	Netherlands	03 Aug 62	Visas	485UNTS225	107058
Multilateral		15 Aug 62	Territory Boundary	437UNTS292	106312
El Salvador	UK Great Britain	20 Aug 62	Visas	453UNTS309	106532
Belgium	Colombia	27 Aug 62	Visas	449UNTS199	106461
Israel	Sierra Leone	30 Aug 62	Visas	448UNTS309	106444
Austria	South Africa	31 Aug 62	Visas	443UNTS65	106359
Multilateral		14 Sep 62	Visas	443UNTS73	106360
Gabon	Israel	10 Oct 62	Visas	484UNTS175	107026
Honduras	Israel	10 Oct 62	Visas	484UNTS189	107028
Canada	San Marino	16 Oct 62	Visas	529UNTS3	107650
Canada	Iceland	17 Oct 62	Visas	528UNTS281	107649
Japan	UK Great Britain	02 Nov 62	Visas	466UNTS277	106749
Multilateral		29 Nov 62	Visas	457UNTS63	106577
Colombia	Israel	21 Dec 62	Visas	484UNTS149	107023
Czechoslovakia	USA (United States)	21 Dec 62	Visas	469UNTS115	106787
Ecuador	USA (United States)	07 Jan 63	Visas	477UNTS101	106917
Belgium	Ecuador	10 Jan 63	Visas	457UNTS153	106585
Cyprus	USA (United States)	11 Jan 63	Visas	471UNTS127	106827
Ecuador	Netherlands	21 Jan 63	Visas	514UNTS87	107443
Poland	USA (United States)	21 Jan 63	Visas	471UNTS151	106830
Bolivia	Philippines	22 Feb 63	Visas	490UNTS231	107156
France	Philippines	08 Mar 63	Visas	569UNTS77	108280
Australia	Portugal	29 Mar 63	Visas	468UNTS313	106778
Israel	Malagasy	04 May 63	Visas	484UNTS225	107033
Multilateral		19 Jun 63	Visas	482UNTS19	106988
Israel	Niger	23 Jul 63	Visas	515UNTS257	107463
United Arab Rep	USA (United States)	01 Aug 63	Visas	488UNTS189	107128
Switzerland	UK Great Britain	27 Aug 63	General Transport	486UNTS183	107079
Passports (Cont.)					
Ecuador	UK Great Britain	13 Sep 63	Visas	490UNTS19	107152
Israel	Tanganyika	17 Sep 63	Visas	516UNTS47	107469
Multilateral		10 Feb 64	Visas	496UNTS151	107249
USA (United States)	Yugoslavia	04 Apr 64	Visas	526UNTS47	107599
UK Great Britain	USSR (Soviet Union)	13 Apr 64	Visas	539UNTS197	107832
Congo (Zaire)	Israel	14 Apr 64	Visas	552UNTS305	108062
Australia	Israel	14 Apr 64	Visas	496UNTS233	107255
Multilateral		16 Apr 64	Visas	548UNTS27	107967
Multilateral		14 May 64	Visas	528UNTS3	107631
Netherlands	Yugoslavia	28 May 64	Visas	521UNTS191	107522
Israel	Yugoslavia	13 Jun 64	Visas	516UNTS91	107472
Czechoslovakia	Yugoslavia	08 Oct 64	Visas	544UNTS129	107916
Multilateral		19 Nov 64	Visas	523UNTS3	107553
Multilateral		27 Nov 64	Visas	548UNTS47	107968
Israel	Togo	09 Feb 65	Visas	550UNTS297	108024
Netherlands	Spain	10 Feb 65	Visas	545UNTS3	107922
Ivory Coast	UK Great Britain	29 Mar 65	Visas	551UNTS53	108032
Austria	Hungary	09 Apr 65	Visas	564UNTS179	108228
UK Great Britain	Yugoslavia	20 Apr 65	Visas	551UNTS69	108034
Brazil	USA (United States)	26 May 65	Visas	549UNTS125	107995
Greece	UK Great Britain	08 Jun 65	Visas	551UNTS205	108042
Austria	Bulgaria	12 Jul 65	Visas	587UNTS45	108509
Multilateral		08 Sep 65	Visas	578UNTS3	108382
Czechoslovakia	USSR (Soviet Union)	17 Sep 65	Visas	549UNTS221	108001
Greece	Malta	01 Oct 65	Visas	550UNTS329	108027
Italy	Malta	23 Oct 65	Visas	550UNTS337	108028
Austria	Romania	17 Nov 65	Visas	564UNTS185	108229
Israel	Paraguay	21 Nov 65	Visas	582UNTS65	108458
Hungary	Yugoslavia	23 Nov 65	Visas	577UNTS89	108374
Finland	Malta	08 Dec 65	Visas	561UNTS205	108183
Austria	Yugoslavia	20 Dec 65	Visas	573UNTS165	108329
Malta	Sweden	29 Dec 65	Visas	561UNTS217	108185
Malta	Norway	29 Dec 65	Visas	561UNTS211	108184
Denmark	Malta	30 Dec 65	Visas	561UNTS199	108182
Panama	UK Great Britain	07 Jan 66	Visas	565UNTS25	108233
Israel	Sweden	23 Feb 66	Visas	581UNTS195	108444
Israel	Norway	23 Feb 66	Visas	581UNTS203	108445
Denmark	Israel	23 Feb 66	Visas	581UNTS187	108443
Iceland	Israel	23 Feb 66	Visas	581UNTS211	108446
Finland	Israel	23 Feb 66	Visas	581UNTS219	108447
Romania	USSR (Soviet Union)	04 Mar 66	Visas	591UNTS327	108565
Israel	Uruguay	03 Apr 66	Visas	582UNTS73	108459
Malta	Turkey	06 Jun 66	Visas	579UNTS237	108411
Ecuador	Israel	20 Jun 66	Visas	581UNTS265	108449
Gambia	Israel	11 Jul 66	Visas	582UNTS11	108453
Colombia	Israel	12 Jul 66	Visas	581UNTS181	108442
Multilateral		12 Jul 66	Visas	578UNTS23	108384
Israel	Malawi	03 Aug 66	Visas	582UNTS53	108456
Malta	Portugal	01 Sep 66	Visas	579UNTS231	108410
Paraguay	UK Great Britain	27 Oct 66	Visas	597UNTS229	108648
Philippines	Sweden	11 Nov 66	Visas	587UNTS3	108505
Norway	Philippines	14 Dec 66	Visas	591UNTS253	108562
Denmark	Philippines	20 Dec 66	Visas	591UNTS259	108563
Austria	Malta	21 Dec 66	Visas	595UNTS307	108625
Patents					
UK Great Britain	USA (United States)	27 Mar 46	Patents/Copyrights	4UNTS101	100040
Multilateral		27 Jul 46	Patents/Copyrights	90UNTS229	101238
Canada	USA (United States)	27 Sep 46	Patents/Copyrights	21UNTS3	100320
Multilateral		06 Jun 47	Patents/Copyrights	46UNTS249	100714
Italy	USA (United States)	14 Aug 47	Claims and Debts	36UNTS105	100567
Philippines	USA (United States)	23 Aug 48	Patents/Copyrights	82UNTS11	101080
Denmark	Italy	01 Jul 50	Patents/Copyrights	133UNTS181	101788
Multilateral		29 Nov 50	Patents/Copyrights	88UNTS221	101194
Italy	UK Great Britain	16 Jun 51	Patents/Copyrights	172UNTS293	102253

PARTY ONE	PARTY TWO	DATE	TOPIC	CITATION	NUMBER
Patents (Cont.)					
UK Great Britain	USA (United States)	19 Jan 53	General Military	161UNTS3	102117
Multilateral		11 Dec 53	Patents/Copyrights	218UNTS27	102952
Belgium	USA (United States)	12 Oct 54	Patents/Copyrights	202UNTS289	102735
Multilateral		19 Dec 54	Patents/Copyrights	218UNTS51	102953
Norway	USA (United States)	06 Apr 55	General Military	269UNTS65	103874
Netherlands	USA (United States)	29 Apr 55	Milit Installation	219UNTS105	102969
Greece	USA (United States)	16 Jun 55	Patents/Copyrights	262UNTS137	103742
Germany, West	USA (United States)	04 Jan 56	General Military	268UNTS143	103856
Japan	USA (United States)	22 Mar 56	Patents/Copyrights	275UNTS195	103983
Turkey	USA (United States)	18 May 56	Patents/Copyrights	283UNTS167	104115
Canada	India	30 Aug 56	Patents/Copyrights	305UNTS59	104413
France	USA (United States)	12 Mar 57	Patents/Copyrights	279UNTS275	104045
Canada	Pakistan	15 Jan 58	Patents/Copyrights	392UNTS35	105637
Australia	USA (United States)	24 Jan 58	Patents/Copyrights	307UNTS105	104446
Czechoslovakia	Germany, East	26 Jun 58	Patents/Copyrights	504UNTS221	107359
Denmark	France	17 Sep 59	Taxation	410UNTS141	105901
Germany, East	Hungary	12 Jan 60	Patents/Copyrights	409UNTS22	105875
Denmark	USA (United States)	19 Feb 60	Patents/Copyrights	354UNTS151	105061
Greece	USA (United States)	26 Apr 60	Patents/Copyrights	372UNTS299	105306
Belgium	USA (United States)	18 May 60	Patents/Copyrights	373UNTS31	105313
Spain	USA (United States)	21 Jul 60	Milit Assistance	393UNTS289	105663
Multilateral		21 Sep 60	Patents/Copyrights	394UNTS3	105664
Portugal	USA (United States)	31 Oct 60	Patents/Copyrights	394UNTS127	105673
Sweden	USA (United States)	04 Oct 62	Milit Assistance	462UNTS31	106669
Australia	India	23 Jan 63	Patents/Copyrights	456UNTS185	106556
Denmark	Netherlands	06 Jun 63	Patents/Copyrights	484UNTS137	107021
Netherlands	UK Great Britain	30 Oct 63	Other Military	490UNTS11	107151
Italy	Netherlands	29 May 64	Other Military	541UNTS147	107867
Korea, South	Netherlands	08 Dec 65	Patents/Copyrights	571UNTS83	108301
Payments					
UK Great Britain	USSR (Soviet Union)	16 Aug 41	Finance	91UNTS341	200269
Canada	USA (United States)	27 Jun 44	Milit Installation	101UNTS273	200301
Belgium	UK Great Britain	22 Aug 44	Direct Aid	90UNTS295	200267
Belgium	Netherlands	02 Jan 45	Refugees	19UNTS259	200120
France	USA (United States)	20 Feb 45	IGO Status/Immunit	76UNTS223	200248
South Africa	USA (United States)	17 Apr 45	Direct Aid	90UNTS267	200264
Belgium	Norway	23 Oct 45	Finance	16UNTS311	200107
Netherlands	Switzerland	24 Oct 45	Finance	3UNTS73	100025
Romania	Yugoslavia	15 Dec 45	General Economic	116UNTS3	101565
Belgium	Portugal	07 Jan 46	Finance	19UNTS159	100310
Denmark	Netherlands	31 Jan 46	Finance	3UNTS3	100021
Belgium	Norway	21 Feb 46	Finance	31UNTS199	100479
France	Norway	06 Mar 46	Finance	15UNTS13	100227
UK Great Britain	USA (United States)	27 Mar 46	Milit Assistance	4UNTS2	100039
France	Greece	24 Apr 46	Finance	91UNTS83	101243
Greece	USA (United States)	16 May 46	Direct Aid	184UNTS230	102451
France	USA (United States)	28 May 46	Status of Forces	84UNTS121	101123
Poland	UK Great Britain	24 Jun 46	Claims and Debts	11UNTS59	100149
Romania	Yugoslavia	26 Jun 46	Finance	116UNTS21	101566
Albania	Yugoslavia	01 Jul 46	General Economic	111UNTS3	101517
Italy	Norway	20 Jul 46	Finance	17UNTS273	100281
Hungary	UK Great Britain	12 Aug 46	Finance	89UNTS219	101220
Norway	Yugoslavia	30 Aug 46	Finance	15UNTS163	100232
Argentina	UK Great Britain	17 Sep 46	General Economic	88UNTS47	101185
Belgium	USA (United States)	24 Sep 46	Claims and Debts	132UNTS80	101753
Norway	Sweden	22 Nov 46	Finance	15UNTS171	100233
Norway	Poland	03 Dec 46	Finance	15UNTS203	100234
Denmark	India	20 Dec 46	Reparations	7UNTS309	100107
Norway	USSR (Soviet Union)	27 Dec 46	Finance	17UNTS283	100282
Hungary	Yugoslavia	01 Jan 47	General Trade	113UNTS63	101548
Norway	USSR (Soviet Union)	19 Feb 47	General Trade	30UNTS293	100464
Belgium	Turkey	12 Mar 47	Finance	33UNTS43	100513
Poland	Sweden	18 Mar 47	General Economic	12UNTS295	100190
South Africa	USA (United States)	21 Mar 47	Milit Assistance	16UNTS47	100248

PARTY ONE	PARTY TWO	DATE	TOPIC	CITATION	NUMBER
Payments (Cont.)					
Czechoslovakia	Poland	04 Apr 47	General Economic	85UNTS62	101146
Denmark	Norway	15 Apr 47	Finance	12UNTS323	100191
Italy	UK Great Britain	17 Apr 47	Claims and Debts	54UNTS169	100802
Italy	UK Great Britain	17 Apr 47	Finance	54UNTS149	100801
Bulgaria	Denmark	09 May 47	Finance	74UNTS139	100960
Poland	Yugoslavia	24 May 47	Finance	115UNTS69	101558
Poland	Yugoslavia	24 May 47	General Trade	115UNTS37	101557
Netherlands	USA (United States)	28 May 47	General Military	17UNTS29	100267
Austria	USA (United States)	21 Jun 47	Reparations	67UNTS89	100868
Austria	USA (United States)	21 Jun 47	Milit Occupation	67UNTS99	100869
Denmark	Yugoslavia	28 Jun 47	General Economic	78UNTS242	101020
UK Great Britain	Uruguay	15 Jul 47	Finance	71UNTS179	100918
Norway	Switzerland	15 Jul 47	Finance	12UNTS351	100192
Czechoslovakia	USA (United States)	25 Jul 47	Reparations	90UNTS19	101223
Czechoslovakia	Greece	30 Jul 47	General Trade	185UNTS133	102464
Multilateral		19 Sep 47	General Trade	30UNTS249	100461
Multilateral		19 Sep 47	Finance	30UNTS269	100462
Romania	Yugoslavia	30 Sep 47	Finance	116UNTS71	101570
Multilateral		05 Oct 47	Finance	34UNTS23	100525
Poland	Yugoslavia	07 Nov 47	General Economic	115UNTS137	101561
Belgium	USSR (Soviet Union)	10 Nov 47	Finance	18UNTS299	100298
UK Great Britain	USSR (Soviet Union)	27 Dec 47	Finance	82UNTS251	101098
Italy	UK Great Britain	21 Jan 48	Milit Installation	77UNTS23	100989
Romania	USA (United States)	26 Feb 48	Admin Cooperation	48UNTS9	100738
Denmark	Hungary	28 Feb 48	Finance	85UNTS35	101144
Poland	UK Great Britain	02 Mar 48	Finance	77UNTS47	100991
Jordan	UK Great Britain	15 Mar 48	General Military	77UNTS77	100994
Hungary	Yugoslavia	18 Mar 48	Finance	113UNTS219	101552
Hungary	Yugoslavia	18 Mar 48	Finance	113UNTS201	101551
Hungary	Yugoslavia	18 Mar 48	General Trade	113UNTS141	101550
Poland	Yugoslavia	12 Apr 48	General Trade	115UNTS167	101563
Hungary	Yugoslavia	17 Apr 48	Reparations	130UNTS111	101728
Denmark	Norway	21 Apr 48	Finance	18UNTS139	100284
Norway	Sweden	29 Apr 48	Finance	26UNTS11	100374
Multilateral		10 May 48	Reparations	140UNTS129	101887
Brazil	UK Great Britain	21 May 48	Finance	66UNTS121	100851
Czechoslovakia	Yugoslavia	24 May 48	General Trade	112UNTS111	101542
Czechoslovakia	Yugoslavia	24 May 48	Finance	112UNTS225	101545
Czechoslovakia	Yugoslavia	24 May 48	Finance	112UNTS183	101543
Netherlands	UK Great Britain	11 Jun 48	General Economic	66UNTS183	100853
Spain	UK Great Britain	23 Jun 48	General Economic	66UNTS193	100854
Chile	UK Great Britain	24 Jun 48	Finance	77UNTS113	100995
Greece	Sweden	25 Jun 48	General Trade	267UNTS337	103849
UK Great Britain	Uruguay	12 Jul 48	Finance	71UNTS199	100919
Peru	UK Great Britain	20 Jul 48	Finance	66UNTS197	100855
Philippines	USA (United States)	27 Aug 48	Reparations	44UNTS13	100675
Turkey	UK Great Britain	16 Oct 48	Finance	83UNTS85	101103
Multilateral		19 Oct 48	Specif Claim/Waive	84UNTS201	101130
Austria	Denmark	29 Nov 48	Finance	74UNTS257	100968
Italy	Netherlands	04 Dec 48	Non-ILO Labor	46UNTS271	100716
Denmark	Poland	14 Dec 48	Finance	81UNTS33	101060
Argentina	Denmark	14 Dec 48	General Economic	74UNTS41	100956
Spain	UK Great Britain	15 Dec 48	Finance	87UNTS49	101165
Denmark	Turkey	15 Dec 48	Finance	76UNTS3	100974
UK Great Britain	Yugoslavia	23 Dec 48	Reparations	81UNTS121	101068
Belgium	Greece	27 Dec 48	Finance	77UNTS293	101005
Poland	Yugoslavia	16 Jan 49	General Trade	115UNTS241	101564
Austria	Norway	28 Jan 49	General Trade	30UNTS145	100452
Denmark	Sweden	08 Feb 49	Finance	33UNTS227	100519
Norway	Turkey	24 Feb 49	Finance	30UNTS151	100453
Denmark	Greece	25 Feb 49	Finance	78UNTS335	101023
Czechoslovakia	Yugoslavia	01 Mar 49	Finance	112UNTS241	101546
Czechoslovakia	Yugoslavia	01 Mar 49	General Trade	113UNTS3	101547
Belgium	Portugal	01 Mar 49	Finance	32UNTS49	100488
Greece	Norway	12 Mar 49	Finance	33UNTS13	100510

PARTY ONE	PARTY TWO	DATE	TOPIC	CITATION	NUMBER
Payments (Cont.)					
France	USA (United States)	14 Mar 49	Claims and Debts	84UNTS237	101133
Germany, West	Greece	16 Mar 49	Finance	77UNTS327	101007
Multilateral		16 Mar 49	Finance	29UNTS95	100436
Denmark	Finland	22 Mar 49	Finance	33UNTS247	100520
Finland	Greece	24 Mar 49	Finance	78UNTS13	101009
Greece	Turkey	02 Apr 49	Finance	78UNTS23	101010
Denmark	Portugal	08 Apr 49	Finance	74UNTS221	100965
Netherlands	USA (United States)	26 Apr 49	Finance	70UNTS123	100901
Belgium	Bolivia	26 Apr 49	Finance	34UNTS103	100530
Multilateral		04 May 49	Admin Cooperation	47UNTS159	100728
Argentina	UK Great Britain	27 Jun 49	General Economic	83UNTS217	101110
Greece	UK Great Britain	29 Jun 49	Finance	86UNTS203	101160
Multilateral		05 Aug 49	Finance	88UNTS229	101195
Multilateral		10 Aug 49	Finance	45UNTS3	100689
Czechoslovakia	UK Great Britain	18 Aug 49	Finance	86UNTS129	101155
Italy	Norway	19 Nov 49	Finance	47UNTS89	100724
Norway	Portugal	28 Nov 49	Finance	47UNTS117	100726
Denmark	Germany, West	15 Dec 49	Finance	51UNTS11	100749
Czechoslovakia	Denmark	17 Dec 49	Finance	74UNTS159	100962
Norway	Poland	21 Dec 49	Finance	47UNTS107	100725
UK Great Britain	Yugoslavia	26 Dec 49	General Trade	87UNTS71	101167
Turkey	USA (United States)	27 Dec 49	Direct Aid	98UNTS141	101361
Greece	Portugal	31 Dec 49	Finance	92UNTS83	101263
France	New Zealand	13 Jan 50	Reparations	150UNTS151	101969
Austria	UK Great Britain	26 Jan 50	Finance	97UNTS183	101350
Austria	Denmark	23 Feb 50	General Trade	74UNTS269	100969
Paraguay	UK Great Britain	03 Apr 50	General Economic	99UNTS81	101372
Denmark	Switzerland	06 Apr 50	General Trade	87UNTS197	101173
Multilateral		08 Apr 50	Specif Goods/Equip	68UNTS99	100889
Finland	UK Great Britain	07 Jul 50	Finance	138UNTS171	101868
Denmark	Spain	12 Jul 50	Finance	71UNTS129	100913
Canada	USSR (Soviet Union)	29 Sep 50	Claims and Debts	230UNTS371	103197
Denmark	Poland	01 Oct 50	General Economic	81UNTS43	101061
Denmark	Italy	04 Oct 50	Finance	78UNTS353	101025
Netherlands	USA (United States)	07 Oct 50	Loans and Credits	79UNTS33	101029
Philippines	USA (United States)	06 Nov 50	Finance	122UNTS63	101637
Norway	UK Great Britain	06 Nov 50	Finance	88UNTS257	101197
Germany, West	UK Great Britain	09 Dec 50	Finance	88UNTS247	101196
Italy	UK Great Britain	21 Dec 50	Finance	175UNTS187	102301
Italy	Norway	22 Jan 51	Finance	88UNTS339	101202
Colombia	Denmark	26 Jan 51	Finance	87UNTS161	101171
Austria	UK Great Britain	31 Jan 51	Finance	88UNTS107	101187
Belgium	USA (United States)	16 Mar 51	Reparations	93UNTS109	101295
Canada	USA (United States)	18 Apr 51	Milit Assistance	134UNTS205	101800
United Arab Rep	UK Great Britain	01 Jul 51	Finance	249UNTS143	103504
Japan	UK Great Britain	31 Aug 51	Finance	149UNTS227	101955
Japan	UK Great Britain	31 Aug 51	Finance	108UNTS273	101480
Spain	UK Great Britain	20 Dec 51	Finance	123UNTS187	101660
Japan	USA (United States)	28 Feb 52	Milit Assistance	208UNTS255	102817
Austria	Greece	22 Mar 52	General Economic	187UNTS255	102517
Greece	Switzerland	04 Apr 52	Finance	166UNTS271	102192
Greece	USA (United States)	23 Apr 52	Direct Aid	177UNTS283	102327
Belgium	Greece	24 Apr 52	Finance	166UNTS261	102191
Denmark	Poland	09 Jun 52	Finance	135UNTS221	101823
Denmark	Israel	14 Nov 52	Finance	160UNTS289	102114
Greece	Italy	04 Feb 53	Finance	189UNTS295	102552
Turkey	Yugoslavia	26 Feb 53	General Trade	247UNTS54	103460
Denmark	Germany, West	26 Feb 53	Claims and Debts	178UNTS3	102332
Greece	Yugoslavia	28 Feb 53	General Economic	252UNTS27	103557
Czechoslovakia	Denmark	23 Apr 53	Finance	174UNTS107	102281
Greece	United Arab Rep	21 May 53	Finance	256UNTS25	103621
Argentina	USSR (Soviet Union)	05 Aug 53	General Economic	221UNTS99	103004
Denmark	Uruguay	09 Sep 53	Finance	256UNTS149	103625
Greece	Turkey	07 Nov 53	General Trade	225UNTS163	103098
Bulgaria	Greece	05 Dec 53	Finance	225UNTS145	103096

PARTY ONE	PARTY TWO	DATE	TOPIC	CITATION	NUMBER
Payments (Cont.)					
Japan	UK Great Britain	29 Jan 54	Finance	190UNTS319	102572
Czechoslovakia	Greece	01 Feb 54	Finance	225UNTS95	103092
Turkey	UK Great Britain	11 Feb 54	Milit Assistance	190UNTS343	102575
Japan	USA (United States)	08 Mar 54	Milit Assistance	232UNTS169	103236
Lebanon	USSR (Soviet Union)	30 Apr 54	General Economic	226UNTS109	103111
Greece	Spain	15 May 54	Finance	299UNTS277	104319
Greece	Romania	19 May 54	Finance	225UNTS27	103084
Greece	Hungary	05 Jun 54	Finance	299UNTS295	104321
Netherlands	Norway	09 Jun 54	Finance	287UNTS179	104184
Germany, West	Italy	28 Jun 54	Loans and Credits	288UNTS83	104199
Belgium	UK Great Britain	09 Jul 54	Finance	201UNTS299	102721
Netherlands	UK Great Britain	09 Jul 54	Finance	199UNTS157	102682
France	Netherlands	09 Jul 54	Finance	287UNTS169	104183
Austria	UK Great Britain	09 Jul 54	Finance	201UNTS277	102720
Germany, West	UK Great Britain	10 Jul 54	Finance	199UNTS135	102680
Belgium	Italy	12 Jul 54	Finance	288UNTS59	104198
Switzerland	UK Great Britain	16 Jul 54	Claims and Debts	199UNTS197	102685
Multilateral		23 Oct 54	Milit Occupation	332UNTS157	104761
Iran	UK Great Britain	25 Oct 54	Finance	204UNTS131	102754
Belgium	Greece	16 Dec 54	Claims and Debts	223UNTS73	103056
Iceland	Netherlands	28 Dec 54	Finance	287UNTS159	104182
USSR (Soviet Union)	Yugoslavia	05 Jan 55	Finance	240UNTS225	103405
Turkey	UK Great Britain	17 Jan 55	Finance	204UNTS195	102758
Greece	Japan	12 Mar 55	General Trade	227UNTS33	103130
Bulgaria	Yugoslavia	16 Mar 55	General Economic	397UNTS83	105702
Argentina	UK Great Britain	31 Mar 55	General Economic	210UNTS223	102840
Syria	USSR (Soviet Union)	16 Nov 55	General Economic	259UNTS71	103683
Paraguay	UK Great Britain	21 Nov 55	General Economic	252UNTS107	103560
Italy	Switzerland	22 Dec 55	Finance	260UNTS339	103717
Sweden	UK Great Britain	22 Dec 55	Claims and Debts	231UNTS179	103218
Denmark	Netherlands	31 Jan 56	Finance	286UNTS255	104172
Ceylon (Sri Lanka)	Romania	16 Mar 56	Finance	315UNTS51	104559
Austria	Italy	07 May 56	Finance	284UNTS351	104147
Bulgaria	Ceylon (Sri Lanka)	19 Jun 56	Finance	315UNTS33	104557
Italy	Switzerland	29 Jun 56	Finance	284UNTS299	104144
Italy	Netherlands	29 Jun 56	Finance	287UNTS193	104185
Argentina	UK Great Britain	30 Jun 56	General Economic	269UNTS235	103884
Sweden	UK Great Britain	08 Dec 56	Claims and Debts	264UNTS61	103788
Netherlands	Paraguay	13 Apr 57	Finance	593UNTS85	108577
Denmark	Paraguay	18 May 57	Finance	286UNTS117	104163
Denmark	Uruguay	04 Jun 57	Finance	286UNTS107	104162
Germany, West	UK Great Britain	07 Jun 57	Milit Assistance	398UNTS275	105730
Germany, West	USA (United States)	07 Jun 57	Milit Assistance	346UNTS241	104984
Italy	United Arab Rep	06 Jul 57	Finance	302UNTS147	104357
Germany, West	Netherlands	10 Jul 57	Status of Forces	339UNTS97	104848
Germany, West	Italy	12 Jul 57	Finance	291UNTS181	104252
Ceylon (Sri Lanka)	China People's Rep	19 Sep 57	General Economic	337UNTS137	104821
Mexico	USA (United States)	23 Oct 57	US Agri Commod Aid	300UNTS35	104330
Argentina	UK Great Britain	25 Nov 57	Claims and Debts	313UNTS95	104531
Argentina	Denmark	25 Nov 57	General Economic	299UNTS83	104308
China People's Rep	Denmark	01 Dec 57	General Economic	309UNTS241	104475
Finland	Italy	17 Dec 57	Finance	291UNTS133	104248
Ethiopia	Japan	19 Dec 57	General Amity	325UNTS91	104695
Italy	Romania	28 Jan 58	Finance	302UNTS231	104362
Iran	Italy	29 Jan 58	Finance	302UNTS181	104358
France	USA (United States)	30 Jan 58	Specif Claim/Waive	304UNTS9	104388
Canada	India	20 Feb 58	Loans and Credits	391UNTS231	105628
Bulgaria	Italy	25 Feb 58	Finance	362UNTS279	105193
Belgium	Japan	30 Apr 58	Finance	303UNTS109	104373
Albania	Italy	26 May 58	Finance	362UNTS259	105191
Multilateral		18 Jun 58	Finance	386UNTS355	105553
Netherlands	Yugoslavia	22 Jul 58	Claims and Debts	386UNTS263	105546
Turkey	USA (United States)	06 Sep 58	Loans and Credits	336UNTS85	104800
Canada	India	22 Oct 58	Finance	392UNTS21	105635
Multilateral		27 Oct 58	Reparations	351UNTS303	105031

PARTY ONE	PARTY TWO	DATE	TOPIC	CITATION	NUMBER
Payments (Cont.)					
Canada	Ceylon (Sri Lanka)	05 Nov 58	Loans and Credits	391UNTS225	105627
Israel	Yugoslavia	11 Dec 58	Finance	386UNTS283	105548
Taiwan	USA (United States)	24 Dec 58	Loans and Credits	340UNTS251	104868
France	UK Great Britain	05 Mar 59	Finance	343UNTS277	104932
Austria	UK Great Britain	14 Mar 59	Claims and Debts	343UNTS263	104930
Germany, West	USA (United States)	20 Mar 59	Claims and Debts	341UNTS15	104874
Germany, West	UK Great Britain	10 Apr 59	Claims and Debts	343UNTS295	104935
Netherlands	Switzerland	14 Apr 59	Finance	486UNTS367	107086
Italy	UK Great Britain	14 Apr 59	Claims and Debts	343UNTS289	104934
Sweden	UK Great Britain	18 Apr 59	Claims and Debts	360UNTS89	105156
Belgium	UK Great Britain	23 Apr 59	Finance	343UNTS271	104931
Norway	UK Great Britain	23 Apr 59	Finance	343UNTS283	104933
Belgium	Netherlands	28 Apr 59	Finance	485UNTS123	107049
Denmark	UK Great Britain	28 Apr 59	Finance	343UNTS257	104929
Italy	Netherlands	29 Apr 59	Finance	486UNTS387	107089
France	Netherlands	29 Apr 59	Finance	486UNTS379	107088
Austria	Netherlands	29 Apr 59	Finance	486UNTS373	107087
Finland	USSR (Soviet Union)	29 Apr 59	Specif Claim/Waive	346UNTS209	104981
Netherlands	Norway	30 Apr 59	Finance	487UNTS3	107090
Iceland	Netherlands	30 Apr 59	Finance	487UNTS13	107091
Denmark	Netherlands	30 Apr 59	Finance	487UNTS23	107092
Greece	Netherlands	30 Apr 59	Finance	485UNTS135	107051
Germany, West	Netherlands	30 Apr 59	Finance	485UNTS141	107052
Netherlands	Sweden	30 Apr 59	Finance	485UNTS147	107053
Netherlands	Portugal	30 Apr 59	Finance	485UNTS129	107050
Netherlands	UK Great Britain	30 Apr 59	Claims and Debts	343UNTS307	104937
Switzerland	UK Great Britain	06 May 59	Claims and Debts	343UNTS315	104938
Iceland	UK Great Britain	14 May 59	Finance	343UNTS301	104936
Greece	UK Great Britain	14 May 59	Specif Claim/Waive	360UNTS69	105154
Greece	UK Great Britain	21 May 59	Claims and Debts	344UNTS3	104939
Denmark	Japan	25 May 59	Reparations	341UNTS157	104881
Greece	Yugoslavia	18 Jun 59	Claims and Debts	368UNTS3	105231
Denmark	Yugoslavia	13 Jul 59	Specif Claim/Waive	386UNTS251	105545
Norway	Yugoslavia	18 Nov 59	Finance	383UNTS131	105499
Cuba	USSR (Soviet Union)	13 Feb 60	General Economic	369UNTS17	105248
Germany, West	USA (United States)	16 Aug 60	Claims and Debts	418UNTS235	106024
Greece	Poland	08 Nov 60	Finance	483UNTS141	107011
Romania	UK Great Britain	10 Nov 60	Finance	385UNTS113	105533
Somalia	USSR (Soviet Union)	02 Jun 61	General Trade	493UNTS173	107214
Albania	Austria	27 Jul 61	General Economic	407UNTS37	105858
UK Great Britain	USA (United States)	28 Aug 61	Finance	434UNTS103	106258
Japan	USA (United States)	09 Jan 62	Direct Aid	451UNTS97	106488
United Arab Rep	USSR (Soviet Union)	23 Jun 62	Finance	472UNTS19	106835
Laos	USSR (Soviet Union)	01 Dec 62	Finance	471UNTS181	106832
Japan	USA (United States)	19 Feb 63	Direct Aid	473UNTS107	106859
Greece	UK Great Britain	09 May 63	Specific Property	398UNTS179	105722
Japan	USA (United States)	14 Jun 63	Finance	479UNTS165	106951
Austria	Mongolia	15 Jul 63	General Trade	496UNTS171	107251
Australia	USA (United States)	05 Feb 64	Status of Forces	511UNTS103	107430
Germany, West	UK Great Britain	27 Jul 64	Status of Forces	539UNTS243	107835
Israel	USA (United States)	20 Jul 65	Milit Assistance	549UNTS55	107989
Israel	USA (United States)	26 Jul 65	Status of Forces	549UNTS49	107988
Peace					
Finland	USSR (Soviet Union)	28 Oct 22	Specific Resources	67UNTS157	100874
Finland	USSR (Soviet Union)	28 Oct 22	Specific Resources	67UNTS153	100873
Finland	USSR (Soviet Union)	11 Oct 40	Territory Boundary	67UNTS139	100872
Multilateral		08 Oct 44	Reparations	45UNTS311	200187
Multilateral		28 Oct 44	Peace/Disarmament	123UNTS223	200414
Multilateral		20 Jan 45	Peace/Disarmament	140UNTS397	200471
Multilateral		05 Jun 45	Milit Occupation	68UNTS189	200230
Multilateral		02 Sep 45	Peace/Disarmament	139UNTS387	200465
Multilateral		26 Dec 45	Peace/Disarmament	20UNTS259	100319
Multilateral		01 Jan 46	Peace/Disarmament	99UNTS131	101375
Norway	USA (United States)	12 Nov 46	Air Transport	42UNTS227	100651

PARTY ONE	PARTY TWO	DATE	TOPIC	CITATION	NUMBER
Peace (Cont.)					
France	Thailand	17 Nov 46	Reparations	344UNTS59	104943
Multilateral		10 Feb 47	Peace/Disarmament	41UNTS21	100643
Multilateral		10 Feb 47	Peace/Disarmament	42UNTS3	100645
Multilateral		10 Feb 47	Peace/Disarmament	41UNTS135	100644
Multilateral		10 Feb 47	Peace/Disarmament	48UNTS203	100746
Multilateral		10 Feb 47	Peace/Disarmament	49UNTS3	100747
Italy	UK Great Britain	17 Apr 47	Finance	54UNTS149	100801
Italy	USA (United States)	14 Aug 47	Reparations	36UNTS53	100566
Italy	USA (United States)	14 Aug 47	Claims and Debts	36UNTS105	100567
Italy	USA (United States)	03 Sep 47	Status of Forces	67UNTS15	100863
Multilateral		29 Sep 47	Peace/Disarmament	45UNTS125	100694
Multilateral		10 Oct 47	Claims and Debts	54UNTS193	100804
Multilateral		16 Dec 47	Reparations	82UNTS237	101096
Hungary	Romania	24 Jan 48	General Amity	477UNTS155	106920
Czechoslovakia	Italy	25 Feb 48	Admin Cooperation	26UNTS103	100380
Romania	USA (United States)	26 Feb 48	Admin Cooperation	48UNTS9	100738
Czechoslovakia	Romania	01 Mar 48	Admin Cooperation	26UNTS109	100381
Bulgaria	Czechoslovakia	05 Mar 48	Admin Cooperation	26UNTS115	100382
Bulgaria	USA (United States)	08 Mar 48	Admin Cooperation	29UNTS101	100437
Bulgaria	Hungary	16 Jul 48	General Amity	477UNTS169	106921
Israel	United Arab Rep	24 Feb 49	Peace/Disarmament	42UNTS251	100654
Czechoslovakia	Hungary	27 Feb 49	Admin Cooperation	26UNTS119	100383
Israel	Lebanon	23 Mar 49	Peace/Disarmament	42UNTS287	100655
Israel	Jordan	03 Apr 49	Peace/Disarmament	42UNTS303	100656
Czechoslovakia	Hungary	16 Apr 49	General Amity	477UNTS183	106922
Israel	Syria	20 Jul 49	Peace/Disarmament	42UNTS327	100657
India	Pakistan	27 Jul 49	Peace/Disarmament	81UNTS273	101076
Italy	Netherlands	16 Aug 49	Admin Cooperation	98UNTS21	101357
Greece	Italy	31 Aug 49	Reparations	78UNTS89	101014
India	Nepal	31 Jul 50	General Amity	94UNTS3	101302
Nepal	UK Great Britain	30 Oct 50	General Amity	97UNTS121	101346
Multilateral		08 Sep 51	Peace/Disarmament	136UNTS45	101832
Australia	Italy	20 Dec 51	Peace/Disarmament	190UNTS223	102566
Italy	New Zealand	20 Dec 51	Peace/Disarmament	150UNTS157	101970
Italy	USA (United States)	21 Dec 51	Peace/Disarmament	167UNTS163	102206
Taiwan	Japan	28 Apr 52	Peace/Disarmament	138UNTS3	101858
Multilateral		12 Jun 52	Dispute Settlement	138UNTS183	101869
Burma	Japan	05 Nov 54	Peace/Disarmament	251UNTS201	103542
Italy	Yugoslavia	18 Dec 54	Peace/Disarmament	284UNTS239	104141
Multilateral		15 May 55	Recognition	217UNTS223	102949
Ethiopia	Italy	05 Mar 56	Reparations	267UNTS189	103844
Indonesia	Japan	20 Jan 58	Peace/Disarmament	324UNTS227	104688
Peace Corps Volunteers					
Peru	USA (United States)	25 Jan 62	Tech Assistance	473UNTS57	106855
FAO (Food Agri)	USA (United States)	29 Mar 62	IGO Operations	454UNTS13	106536
Ethiopia	USA (United States)	23 May 62	General Aid	456UNTS293	106563
USA (United States)	Venezuela	28 May 62	Tech Assistance	458UNTS249	106607
Pakistan	USA (United States)	31 May 62	General Aid	460UNTS75	106631
Bolivia	USA (United States)	19 Jun 62	General Aid	458UNTS239	106606
Honduras	USA (United States)	20 Jul 62	General Aid	460UNTS125	106635
Niger	USA (United States)	23 Jul 62	Tech Assistance	487UNTS325	107114
Ecuador	USA (United States)	03 Aug 62	General Aid	460UNTS133	106636
Cyprus	USA (United States)	23 Aug 62	General Aid	461UNTS147	106658
Nepal	USA (United States)	24 Aug 62	General Aid	460UNTS143	106637
Turkey	USA (United States)	27 Aug 62	General Aid	461UNTS55	106651
Togo	USA (United States)	05 Sep 62	General Aid	461UNTS47	106650
Cameroon	USA (United States)	10 Sep 62	Tech Assistance	461UNTS177	106662
Afghanistan	USA (United States)	11 Sep 62	General Aid	461UNTS169	106661
Chile	USA (United States)	04 Oct 62	Tech Assistance	461UNTS129	106656
Gabon	USA (United States)	04 Oct 62	General Aid	459UNTS185	106620
Multilateral		25 Oct 62	Tech Assistance	457UNTS129	106582
Multilateral		25 Oct 62	General Aid	457UNTS137	106583
Ceylon (Sri Lanka)	USA (United States)	21 Nov 62	General Aid	462UNTS237	106683
India	USA (United States)	21 Nov 62	General Aid	462UNTS255	106685

PARTY ONE	PARTY TWO	DATE	TOPIC	CITATION	NUMBER
Peace Corps Volunteers (Cont.)					
Guinea	USA (United States)	14 Dec 62	General Aid	462UNTS247	106684
Guatemala	USA (United States)	29 Dec 62	Tech Assistance	474UNTS31	106869
Senegal	USA (United States)	17 Jan 63	General Aid	493UNTS97	107210
ILO (Labor Org)	USA (United States)	22 Feb 63	IGO Operations	489UNTS347	107149
USA (United States)	Uruguay	31 Jul 63	Tech Assistance	488UNTS3	107115
Penicillin					
UK Great Britain	USA (United States)	01 Dec 43	Scientific Project	3UNTS209	100033
Pensions					
Belgium	France	17 Jan 48	Non-ILO Labor	36UNTS233	100570
India	UK Great Britain	15 Feb 48	Finance	134UNTS70	101796
Pakistan	UK Great Britain	21 Feb 48	Finance	134UNTS128	101797
United Nations	WHO (World Health)	20 Apr 50	IGO Operations	139UNTS445	200470
FAO (Food Agri)	United Nations	02 Aug 50	IGO Operations	139UNTS407	200467
ILO (Labor Org)	United Nations	12 Oct 50	IGO Operations	139UNTS395	200466
ICAO (Civil Aviat)	United Nations	28 Feb 51	IGO Operations	139UNTS429	200469
UNESCO (Educ/Cult)	United Nations	07 Mar 51	IGO Operations	139UNTS417	200468
Germany, West	Netherlands	29 Mar 51	Non-ILO Labor	149UNTS71	101952
United Nations	WMO (Meteorology)	27 Mar 53	IGO Operations	178UNTS361	200504
Belgium	France	18 Jul 56	Non-ILO Labor	248UNTS121	103491
Austria	IAEA (Atom Energy)	11 Dec 57	Atomic Energy	339UNTS110	104849
IAEA (Atom Energy)	United Nations	22 Sep 58	IGO Operations	313UNTS323	200552
IMCO (Maritime Org)	United Nations	23 Jun 59	IGO Operations	336UNTS317	200556
ITU (Telecommun)	United Nations	14 Jan 60	IGO Operations	348UNTS331	200566
USA (United States)	Uruguay	22 Jul 60	Education	388UNTS315	105587
IMF (Fund)	United Nations	22 Dec 60	IGO Operations	384UNTS315	200578
IBRD (World Bank)	United Nations	05 Jan 61	IGO Operations	384UNTS303	200577
Germany, West	Netherlands	09 Mar 61	Admin Cooperation	485UNTS185	107056
Israel	Netherlands	25 Apr 63	Admin Cooperation	484UNTS231	107034
Petroleum					
Bolivia	Brazil	25 Feb 38	Specific Resources	51UNTS245	200192
Jordan	UK Great Britain	19 Jul 41	Extradition	9UNTS389	200055
Mexico	USA (United States)	19 Nov 41	Claims and Debts	148UNTS367	200474
Mexico	USA (United States)	29 Sep 43	Claims and Debts	106UNTS265	200345
USSR (Soviet Union)	Yugoslavia	30 Nov 45	General Trade	116UNTS153	101574
Mexico	UK Great Britain	07 Feb 46	Claims and Debts	6UNTS55	100068
Mexico	Netherlands	07 Feb 46	Specif Claim/Waive	3UNTS13	100022
UK Great Britain	USA (United States)	27 Mar 46	Milit Assistance	4UNTS2	100039
France	USA (United States)	28 May 46	Reparations	84UNTS93	101121
Albania	Yugoslavia	28 Nov 46	Non-IBRD Project	111UNTS105	101521
Albania	Yugoslavia	28 Nov 46	Non-IBRD Project	111UNTS93	101520
Italy	USA (United States)	14 Aug 47	Reparations	36UNTS53	100566
UK Great Britain	Uruguay	12 Jul 48	Finance	71UNTS199	100919
Brazil	USA (United States)	16 Aug 50	Tech Assistance	140UNTS223	101890
India	WHO (World Health)	02 Apr 52	Sanitation	131UNTS227	101743
Canada	USA (United States)	30 Jun 53	Specific Property	206UNTS93	102786
United Arab Rep	UK Great Britain	19 Oct 54	Milit Installation	221UNTS227	103008
Canada	USA (United States)	22 Sep 55	Specif Goods/Equip	256UNTS227	103632
Canada	USA (United States)	17 Jan 57	Specif Goods/Equip	266UNTS109	103825
France	IBRD (World Bank)	10 Dec 59	IBRD Project	380UNTS319	105464
Multilateral		14 Sep 60	IGO Establishment	443UNTS247	106363
Canada	USA (United States)	19 Apr 62	Specific Property	445UNTS265	106394
Iran	United Nations	05 Sep 62	Specific Resources	442UNTS249	106353
Korea, South	USA (United States)	12 May 64	Commodity Trade	529UNTS299	107667
Physically Handicapped Persons					
United Nations	Yugoslavia	10 Apr 52	Tech Assistance	141UNTS89	101908
Multilateral		26 Feb 53	Tech Assistance	161UNTS31	102120
Multilateral		20 Jul 53	Non-ILO Labor	228UNTS41	103142
Multilateral		13 Dec 55	Humanitarian	250UNTS3	103514
Physics					
Multilateral		26 Mar 62	IGO Establishment	539UNTS67	107825
Pilgrims					
Netherlands	UK Great Britain	13 Jun 39	Sanitation	5UNTS65	200028
Police and Gendarmerie					
Iran	USA (United States)	27 Nov 43	Military Mission	31UNTS451	200176
Iran	USA (United States)	08 Aug 46	Military Mission	31UNTS423	100484
Belgium	France	13 Apr 48	Territory Boundary	31UNTS409	100483
Political Rights					
Liberia	USA (United States)	31 Dec 43	Non-IBRD Project	106UNTS199	200341
Liberia	USA (United States)	26 Jul 48	Customs	182UNTS73	102423
IBRD (World Bank)	Turkey	07 Jul 50	IBRD Project	156UNTS75	102040
IBRD (World Bank)	Thailand	27 Oct 50	IBRD Project	158UNTS43	102061
Belgium	UK Great Britain	06 Apr 51	Specific Property	110UNTS3	101496
Peru	IBRD (World Bank)	23 Jan 52	IBRD Project	159UNTS163	102087
Iraq	UK Great Britain	22 May 52	Claims and Debts	175UNTS97	102298
Multilateral		31 Mar 53	Privil/Immunities	193UNTS136	102613
UK Great Britain	USA (United States)	26 Jun 53	Loans and Credits	183UNTS225	102432
Jamaica	United Nations	06 Dec 66	IGO Operations	580UNTS211	108424
Pollution of the Seas					
Multilateral		12 May 54	Admin Cooperation	327UNTS3	104714
Ports					
IBRD (World Bank)	Turkey	07 Jul 50	IBRD Project	156UNTS75	102040
Belgium	Germany, West	23 Nov 54	Admin Cooperation	202UNTS109	102726
Belgium	IBRD (World Bank)	14 Dec 54	IBRD Project	210UNTS113	102837
IBRD (World Bank)	UK Great Britain	15 Mar 55	IBRD Project	265UNTS85	103808
Pakistan	IBRD (World Bank)	04 Aug 55	IBRD Project	230UNTS79	103177
Austria	Italy	22 Oct 55	Specific Property	260UNTS327	103716
Burma	IBRD (World Bank)	04 May 56	IBRD Project	253UNTS209	103585
Nicaragua	IBRD (World Bank)	22 May 56	IBRD Project	253UNTS233	103586
IBRD (World Bank)	Thailand	12 Oct 56	IBRD Project	261UNTS117	103728
Belgium	IBRD (World Bank)	26 Jun 57	IBRD Project	322UNTS301	104661
India	IBRD (World Bank)	25 Jun 58	IBRD Project	323UNTS157	104668
India	IBRD (World Bank)	25 Jun 58	IBRD Project	323UNTS131	104667
Peru	IBRD (World Bank)	17 Sep 58	IBRD Project	323UNTS27	104663
Ecuador	IBRD (World Bank)	09 Oct 58	IBRD Project	337UNTS299	104827
Israel	IBRD (World Bank)	09 Sep 60	IBRD Project	406UNTS3	105837
Philippines	IBRD (World Bank)	26 Jul 61	IBRD Project	414UNTS253	105976
India	IBRD (World Bank)	17 Aug 61	IBRD Project	417UNTS319	106012
Taiwan	IDA (Devel Assoc)	30 Aug 61	Loans and Credits	416UNTS175	106003
Pakistan	IDA (Devel Assoc)	22 Nov 61	Non-IBRD Project	447UNTS295	106420
India	IDA (Devel Assoc)	14 Sep 62	IBRD Project	467UNTS265	106766
Nigeria	IBRD (World Bank)	10 Dec 62	IBRD Project	468UNTS255	106776
New Zealand	IBRD (World Bank)	12 Nov 63	IBRD Project	485UNTS233	107059
Liberia	USA (United States)	14 Apr 64	Specific Property	526UNTS221	107606
Peru	IBRD (World Bank)	22 Apr 64	IBRD Project	519UNTS95	107503
Pakistan	IBRD (World Bank)	14 May 64	IBRD Project	516UNTS145	107475
IBRD (World Bank)	Tunisia	05 Jun 64	IBRD Project	539UNTS129	107827
New Zealand	Western Samoa	23 Jul 64	Non-IBRD Project	521UNTS173	107520
Malta	UK Great Britain	21 Sep 64	Military Mission	588UNTS55	108518
East Afri Service	IBRD (World Bank)	29 Sep 65	IBRD Project	568UNTS327	200623
IBRD (World Bank)	Tanzania	29 Sep 65	IBRD Project	568UNTS309	108275
Kenya	IBRD (World Bank)	29 Sep 65	IBRD Project	568UNTS289	108274
IBRD (World Bank)	Spain	29 Sep 65	IBRD Project	568UNTS49	108264
IBRD (World Bank)	Uganda	29 Sep 65	IBRD Project	568UNTS317	108276
Paraguay	IBRD (World Bank)	16 Dec 65	IBRD Project	568UNTS165	108268
Peru	IBRD (World Bank)	13 May 66	IBRD Project	570UNTS61	108288
IBRD (World Bank)	Singapore	11 Aug 66	IBRD Project	585UNTS39	108482
Honduras	IBRD (World Bank)	25 Aug 66	IBRD Project	582UNTS79	108460
Postal Service					
Brazil	Portugal	30 Apr 42	Postal Service	65UNTS183	200210
Brazil	Uruguay	16 Dec 44	Admin Cooperation	65UNTS305	200218
Iceland	USA (United States)	11 Apr 45	Air Transport	16UNTS241	200105
Brazil	Venezuela	30 Jan 46	Consul/Citizenship	65UNTS107	100839
Iraq	Turkey	29 Mar 46	General Amity	37UNTS226	100580
South Africa	UK Great Britain	24 Aug 46	Telecommunications	51UNTS187	100765
Norway	UK Great Britain	15 Jan 47	Consul/Citizenship	11UNTS187	100156

PARTY ONE	PARTY TWO	DATE	TOPIC	CITATION	NUMBER
Postal Service (Cont.)					
Belgium	Netherlands	25 Mar 47	Postal Service	18UNTS309	100299
Brazil	Ecuador	31 May 47	Consul/Citizenship	72UNTS25	100925
Philippines	USA (United States)	17 Sep 47	Postal Service	206UNTS249	102790
France	UK Great Britain	12 Jul 48	Postal Service	90UNTS83	101230
Belgium	Luxembourg	07 Jun 49	Postal Service	34UNTS117	100531
United Nations	Switzerland	14 Sep 49	IGO Operations	43UNTS327	200183
Greece	UK Great Britain	17 Oct 49	Postal Service	93UNTS185	101300
United Nations	USA (United States)	28 Mar 51	Postal Service	108UNTS231	101476
Ceylon (Sri Lanka)	India	30 Apr 51	General Trade	196UNTS199	102625
Multilateral		11 Jul 52	Postal Service	170UNTS63	102222
Multilateral		11 Jul 52	Postal Service	170UNTS3	102221
Multilateral		11 Jul 52	Postal Service	170UNTS269	102223
Multilateral		11 Jul 52	Postal Service	171UNTS3	102224
Multilateral		11 Jul 52	IGO Establishment	169UNTS3	102220
Multilateral		11 Jul 52	Postal Service	171UNTS191	102227
Multilateral		11 Jul 52	Postal Service	171UNTS89	102225
Multilateral		11 Jul 52	Postal Service	171UNTS143	102226
Bulgaria	Yugoslavia	15 Nov 55	General Transport	396UNTS191	105697
Korea, North	Romania	05 Dec 55	Postal Service	362UNTS163	105187
Romania	Yugoslavia	13 Jan 56	Postal Service	342UNTS265	104912
Dominican Republic	UK Great Britain	09 Aug 56	Consul/Citizenship	252UNTS127	103561
Greece	Yugoslavia	22 Apr 57	Postal Service	391UNTS109	105619
Albania	Yugoslavia	29 Aug 57	Postal Service	391UNTS127	105621
Albania	Yugoslavia	29 Aug 57	Postal Service	391UNTS167	105622
Multilateral		03 Oct 57	Postal Service	365UNTS3	105213
Multilateral		03 Oct 57	Postal Service	366UNTS87	105216
Multilateral		03 Oct 57	Postal Service	366UNTS3	105215
Multilateral		03 Oct 57	Postal Service	364UNTS3	105211
Multilateral		03 Oct 57	Postal Service	366UNTS193	105218
Multilateral		03 Oct 57	Postal Service	366UNTS255	105219
Multilateral		03 Oct 57	Postal Service	366UNTS141	105217
Lebanon	United Nations	20 Jan 58	Postal Service	286UNTS199	104167
Australia	USA (United States)	20 Jun 58	Postal Service	336UNTS97	104802
Philippines	USA (United States)	17 Jul 58	Specific Property	335UNTS199	104787
Canada	USA (United States)	13 Jan 61	Postal Service	410UNTS62	105897
Multilateral		23 Jan 61	Postal Service	530UNTS141	107679
Multilateral		16 Dec 65	Postal Service	570UNTS201	108295
Potatoes					
Canada	USA (United States)	23 Nov 48	Commodity Trade	81UNTS295	101078
Prisoners					
Cuba	UK Great Britain	02 Dec 46	Admin Cooperation	11UNTS161	100154
France	UK Great Britain	26 Jan 59	Admin Cooperation	330UNTS207	104745
Prisoners of War					
Germany, West	USA (United States)	30 Mar 42	Humanitarian	105UNTS219	200334
USA (United States)	USSR (Soviet Union)	11 Feb 45	Other Military	68UNTS175	200229
Thailand	UK Great Britain	06 Jan 47	Reparations	99UNTS149	101376
Multilateral		10 Feb 47	Peace/Disarmament	41UNTS21	100643
Multilateral		10 Feb 47	Peace/Disarmament	41UNTS135	100644
Multilateral		10 Feb 47	Peace/Disarmament	42UNTS3	100645
Multilateral		10 Feb 47	Peace/Disarmament	49UNTS3	100747
France	USA (United States)	11 Mar 47	Humanitarian	151UNTS159	101991
Italy	USA (United States)	14 Aug 47	Reparations	36UNTS53	100566
Italy	USA (United States)	14 Feb 48	Reparations	67UNTS115	100871
Israel	United Arab Rep	24 Feb 49	Peace/Disarmament	42UNTS251	100654
Israel	Lebanon	23 Mar 49	Peace/Disarmament	42UNTS287	100655
Israel	Syria	20 Jul 49	Peace/Disarmament	42UNTS327	100657
Multilateral		12 Aug 49	General Military	75UNTS135	100972
France	USA (United States)	02 Feb 52	Reparations	247UNTS223	103472
Privileges and Immunities					
Multilateral		13 Feb 46	IGO Status/Immunit	1UNTS15	100004
Netherlands	ICJ (Int Court)	26 Jun 46	IGO Status/Immunit	8UNTS61	100114
United Nations	Switzerland	01 Jul 46	IGO Status/Immunit	1UNTS163	200008
France	ICAO (Civil Aviat)	14 Mar 47	IGO Status/Immunit	94UNTS59	101306

PARTY ONE	PARTY TWO	DATE	TOPIC	CITATION	NUMBER
Privileges and Immunities (Cont.)					
Nepal	USA (United States)	25 Apr 47	Consul/Citizenship	16UNTS97	100251
United Nations	USA (United States)	26 Jun 47	IGO Establishment	11UNTS11	100147
United Nations	WHO (World Health)	15 Nov 47	IGO Operations	19UNTS193	200115
Multilateral		21 Nov 47	IGO Status/Immunit	33UNTS261	100521
Paraguay	USA (United States)	01 Jan 48	Scientific Project	89UNTS191	101217
Czechoslovakia	USA (United States)	16 Sep 48	Milit Assistance	90UNTS35	101224
Peru	ICAO (Civil Aviat)	22 Oct 48	IGO Status/Immunit	95UNTS3	101315
Poland	USA (United States)	30 Oct 48	Consul/Citizenship	15UNTS225	100238
WHO (World Health)	Switzerland	12 Jan 49	IGO Status/Immunit	26UNTS331	200155
IRO (Refugee Org)	United Nations	07 Feb 49	IGO Operations	26UNTS299	200153
Multilateral		02 Sep 49	IGO Status/Immunit	250UNTS12	103515
India	WHO (World Health)	09 Nov 49	IGO Status/Immunit	67UNTS43	100865
ILO (Labor Org)	United Nations	07 Jun 50	Visas	68UNTS213	200231
WHO (World Health)	United Arab Rep	25 Aug 50	IGO Operations	92UNTS39	101259
UN Relief Palestin	United Arab Rep	12 Sep 50	Refugees	121UNTS107	101630
Multilateral		15 Dec 50	Tech Assistance	76UNTS120	100985
United Nations	Yugoslavia	06 Jan 51	Direct Aid	78UNTS165	101015
Ethiopia	ICAO (Civil Aviat)	02 Feb 51	Tech Assistance	96UNTS123	101333
Multilateral		15 Feb 51	Tech Assistance	81UNTS245	101074
Israel	ICAO (Civil Aviat)	19 Feb 51	Tech Assistance	96UNTS141	101334
Israel	ILO (Labor Org)	19 Feb 51	Tech Assistance	100UNTS105	101391
Multilateral		05 Mar 51	Tech Assistance	81UNTS261	101075
WHO (World Health)	United Arab Rep	25 Mar 51	IGO Status/Immunit	223UNTS87	103058
Jordan	ILO (Labor Org)	29 Mar 51	Tech Assistance	100UNTS247	200287
Liberia	ILO (Labor Org)	02 Apr 51	Tech Assistance	100UNTS117	101392
Ceylon (Sri Lanka)	ILO (Labor Org)	06 Apr 51	Tech Assistance	100UNTS235	200286
Mexico	ILO (Labor Org)	06 Apr 51	Tech Assistance	100UNTS131	101393
Peru	ILO (Labor Org)	13 Apr 51	Tech Assistance	100UNTS31	101385
Canada	ICAO (Civil Aviat)	14 Apr 51	IGO Status/Immunit	96UNTS155	101335
Multilateral		18 Apr 51	IGO Establishment	261UNTS140	103729
Ecuador	ILO (Labor Org)	19 Apr 51	Tech Assistance	100UNTS77	101389
ICAO (Civil Aviat)	Thailand	19 Apr 51	Tech Assistance	96UNTS181	101336
Cuba	ILO (Labor Org)	21 Apr 51	Tech Assistance	99UNTS205	101382
Greece	ILO (Labor Org)	25 Apr 51	Tech Assistance	100UNTS93	101390
India	ILO (Labor Org)	26 Apr 51	Tech Assistance	100UNTS19	101384
Pakistan	ILO (Labor Org)	16 May 51	Tech Assistance	100UNTS147	101394
Iceland	ICAO (Civil Aviat)	07 Jun 51	Tech Assistance	96UNTS193	101337
United Nations	Thailand	11 Jun 51	Tech Assistance	90UNTS45	101225
Dominican Republic	ILO (Labor Org)	18 Jun 51	Tech Assistance	100UNTS3	101383
Multilateral		19 Jun 51	Status of Forces	199UNTS67	102678
Israel	United Nations	25 Jun 51	Tech Assistance	97UNTS21	101344
Multilateral		25 Jun 51	Tech Assistance	92UNTS27	101258
ILO (Labor Org)	Vietnam, South	26 Jun 51	Tech Assistance	100UNTS223	200285
IBRD (World Bank)	Switzerland	29 Jun 51	IGO Status/Immunit	216UNTS347	200529
ILO (Labor Org)	Thailand	11 Jul 51	Tech Assistance	100UNTS159	101395
Philippines	WHO (World Health)	22 Jul 51	IGO Status/Immunit	149UNTS197	101953
Multilateral		27 Jul 51	Tech Assistance	97UNTS291	200273
India	United Nations	14 Aug 51	Tech Assistance	98UNTS115	101359
Jordan	UN Relief Palestin	20 Aug 51	Refugees	120UNTS277	200394
Multilateral		20 Sep 51	IGO Status/Immunit	200UNTS3	102691
Korea, South	United Nations	21 Sep 51	IGO Status/Immunit	104UNTS323	200322
Netherlands	Portugal	14 Mar 52	Visas	309UNTS117	104470
Australia	Greece	23 May 52	Visas	223UNTS17	103042
OAS (Am States)	USA (United States)	22 Jun 52	IGO Status/Immunit	181UNTS147	102405
France	WHO (World Health)	23 Jul 52	IGO Status/Immunit	209UNTS231	102829
Japan	United Nations	25 Jul 52	IGO Status/Immunit	135UNTS305	200443
Chile	United Nations	16 Feb 53	IGO Operations	314UNTS49	104541
ICAO (Civil Aviat)	United Arab Rep	27 Aug 53	IGO Status/Immunit	215UNTS371	102925
Netherlands	UK Great Britain	19 Oct 53	Customs	306UNTS99	104435
Multilateral		19 Feb 54	Status of Forces	214UNTS51	102899
Multilateral		12 May 54	Admin Cooperation	327UNTS3	104714
United Nations	Thailand	26 May 54	IGO Status/Immunit	260UNTS35	103703
France	UNESCO (Educ/Cult)	02 Jul 54	IGO Status/Immunit	357UNTS3	105103
Lebanon	UN Relief Palestin	26 Nov 54	Direct Aid	202UNTS123	102728
Mexico	ILO (Labor Org)	05 Jan 55	IGO Status/Immunit	208UNTS225	102815

PARTY ONE	PARTY TWO	DATE	TOPIC	CITATION	NUMBER
Privileges and Immunities (Cont.)					
WMO (Meteorology)	Switzerland	10 Mar 55	IGO Status/Immunit	211UNTS277	200524
CERN (Nuc Resrch)	Switzerland	11 Jun 55	IGO Status/Immunit	249UNTS405	200544
Denmark	WHO (World Health)	29 Jun 55	IGO Status/Immunit	247UNTS168	103467
Australia	Greece	15 Mar 56	Consul/Citizenship	241UNTS313	103438
Austria	Canada	19 Jun 56	Visas	305UNTS51	104412
Germany, West	USA (United States)	27 Jul 56	Admin Cooperation	278UNTS3	104017
Canada	Turkey	21 Aug 56	Visas	305UNTS89	104416
Denmark	USA (United States)	12 Dec 56	Status of Forces	304UNTS311	104405
Mexico	ICAO (Civil Aviat)	20 Dec 56	IGO Operations	497UNTS3	107259
United Nations	United Arab Rep	08 Feb 57	Status of Forces	260UNTS61	103704
Japan	Netherlands	20 Sep 57	Visas	305UNTS105	104418
Ecuador	USA (United States)	06 Nov 57	Consul/Citizenship	307UNTS49	104441
Netherlands	Thailand	09 Dec 57	Visas	309UNTS291	104477
Austria	IAEA (Atom Energy)	11 Dec 57	Atomic Energy	339UNTS110	104849
Bulgaria	USSR (Soviet Union)	12 Dec 57	Consul/Citizenship	302UNTS21	104352
Lebanon	United Nations	13 Jun 58	IGO Status/Immunit	303UNTS271	104386
Ethiopia	United Nations	18 Jun 58	IGO Operations	317UNTS101	104597
Germany, East	Romania	15 Jul 58	Consul/Citizenship	387UNTS133	105561
Lebanon	USA (United States)	06 Aug 58	Status of Forces	366UNTS361	105223
Jordan	United Nations	18 Nov 58	IGO Operations	315UNTS125	104564
ILO (Labor Org)	UK Great Britain	14 Jan 59	IGO Operations	355UNTS283	105081
Mexico	United Nations	07 Apr 59	IGO Operations	381UNTS123	105468
Bulgaria	Romania	23 Apr 59	Consul/Citizenship	387UNTS81	105559
Multilateral		01 Jul 59	IGO Status/Immunit	374UNTS147	105334
Multilateral		14 Dec 59	IGO Status/Immunit	368UNTS237	105244
Peru	ILO (Labor Org)	22 Jun 60	IGO Status/Immunit	423UNTS165	106092
Multilateral		28 Jul 60	IGO Status/Immunit	394UNTS37	105667
Multilateral		26 Nov 60	Taxation	500UNTS25	107304
Peru	USA (United States)	13 Feb 61	Visas	406UNTS177	105848
Austria	United Nations	27 Feb 61	IGO Status/Immunit	394UNTS27	105666
Indonesia	USA (United States)	31 Mar 61	Visas	405UNTS119	105828
Multilateral		18 Apr 61	Consul/Citizenship	500UNTS95	107310
Netherlands	Euratom	25 Jul 61	IGO Status/Immunit	462UNTS313	106687
UNESCO (Educ/Cult)	Thailand	25 Aug 61	IGO Operations	410UNTS125	105899
ILO (Labor Org)	Thailand	30 Aug 61	IGO Operations	422UNTS125	106072
Congo (Zaire)	United Nations	27 Nov 61	IGO Status/Immunit	414UNTS229	105975
COMECON (Econ Aid)	USSR (Soviet Union)	07 Dec 61	IGO Operations	506UNTS325	107392
Czechoslovakia	COMECON (Econ Aid)	20 Jul 62	IGO Operations	506UNTS345	107393
Thailand	UK Great Britain	20 Nov 62	Tech Assistance	466UNTS243	106747
Ceylon (Sri Lanka)	ILO (Labor Org)	21 Nov 62	IGO Operations	449UNTS263	106463
Korea, South	USA (United States)	08 Jan 63	Consul/Citizenship	493UNTS105	107211
Poland	COMECON (Econ Aid)	22 Feb 63	IGO Operations	506UNTS303	107391
Hungary	COMECON (Econ Aid)	28 Feb 63	IGO Operations	506UNTS281	107390
Japan	USA (United States)	22 Mar 63	Consul/Citizenship	518UNTS179	107495
Bulgaria	COMECON (Econ Aid)	30 Mar 63	IGO Operations	506UNTS257	107389
Multilateral		24 Apr 63	Consul/Citizenship	596UNTS261	108638
United Nations	Saudi Arabia	23 Aug 63	IGO Status/Immunit	474UNTS155	106879
Niger	United Nations	20 Nov 63	IGO Establishment	536UNTS3	107793
UNESCO (Educ/Cult)	Yugoslavia	27 Feb 64	IGO Operations	489UNTS257	107143
Cyprus	United Nations	30 Mar 64	IGO Status/Immunit	492UNTS261	107194
Greece	United Nations	31 Mar 64	IGO Status/Immunit	492UNTS267	107195
United Nations	Turkey	31 Mar 64	IGO Status/Immunit	492UNTS273	107196
Cyprus	United Nations	31 Mar 64	IGO Status/Immunit	492UNTS57	107187
United Nations	UK Great Britain	02 Apr 64	IGO Status/Immunit	492UNTS279	107197
Afghanistan	United Nations	28 Apr 64	Education	494UNTS77	107227
Netherlands	NATO (North Atlan)	25 May 64	Status of Forces	544UNTS237	107920
Netherlands	United Nations	27 May 64	IGO Status/Immunit	548UNTS79	107971
Austria	United Nations	11 Jun 64	IGO Status/Immunit	500UNTS85	107309
Ethiopia	ILO (Labor Org)	10 Dec 64	IGO Establishment	521UNTS217	107524
SEATO (SE Asia)	UK Great Britain	12 Mar 65	IGO Status/Immunit	561UNTS313	108191
Austria	Petrol Export Org	24 Jun 65	IGO Operations	589UNTS135	108540
Chile	UNICEF (Children)	30 Nov 65	IGO Operations	596UNTS215	108635
United Nations	UK Great Britain	21 Feb 66	General Economic	555UNTS177	108112
Finland	United Nations	21 Feb 66	IGO Operations	555UNTS157	108109
United Nations	Sweden	21 Feb 66	IGO Operations	555UNTS169	108111

PARTY ONE	PARTY TWO	DATE	TOPIC	CITATION	NUMBER
Privileges and Immunities (Cont.)					
Canada	United Nations	21 Feb 66	IGO Operations	555UNTS119	108107
New Zealand	United Nations	21 Feb 66	IGO Operations	555UNTS163	108110
Denmark	United Nations	21 Feb 66	IGO Operations	555UNTS151	108108
Austria	United Nations	24 Feb 66	IGO Operations	557UNTS129	108131
Australia	United Nations	25 Feb 66	IGO Operations	557UNTS85	108129
Lebanon	ILO (Labor Org)	14 May 66	IGO Establishment	600UNTS69	108676
ILO (Labor Org)	Senegal	09 Feb 67	IGO Establishment	600UNTS75	108677
Algeria	ILO (Labor Org)	06 Apr 67	IGO Establishment	595UNTS99	108614
Romania	United Nations	08 Apr 67	Privil/Immunities	594UNTS159	108602
Austria	United Nations	13 Apr 67	IGO Establishment	600UNTS93	108679
Cameroon	ILO (Labor Org)	07 May 67	IGO Operations	596UNTS209	108634
Productivity					
El Salvador	USA (United States)	14 May 53	Direct Aid	234UNTS71	103273
El Salvador	USA (United States)	31 Aug 54	Non-IBRD Project	237UNTS49	103336
Mexico	USA (United States)	09 Mar 55	Tech Assistance	263UNTS247	103776
Japan	USA (United States)	07 Apr 55	Tech Assistance	263UNTS285	103778
Multilateral		14 Apr 61	IGO Establishment	422UNTS101	106071
Asian Productivity	ILO (Labor Org)	27 Oct 64	IGO Operations	516UNTS367	200610
Professions					
Belgium	France	15 Oct 54	Admin Cooperation	218UNTS19	102951
Property					
Haiti	USA (United States)	19 Oct 42	Territory Boundary	120UNTS171	200390
Czechoslovakia	Poland	12 Feb 46	Reparations	25UNTS207	100364
Greece	UK Great Britain	21 Mar 46	Claims and Debts	91UNTS149	101247
League of Nations	ILO (Labor Org)	04 May 46	IGO Operations	19UNTS187	200114
Thailand	UK Great Britain	06 Jan 47	Reparations	99UNTS149	101376
Multilateral		10 Feb 47	Peace/Disarmament	41UNTS135	100644
Multilateral		10 Feb 47	Peace/Disarmament	48UNTS203	100746
Multilateral		10 Feb 47	Peace/Disarmament	41UNTS21	100643
Multilateral		10 Feb 47	Peace/Disarmament	42UNTS3	100645
Multilateral		10 Feb 47	Peace/Disarmament	49UNTS3	100747
Italy	UK Great Britain	17 Apr 47	Claims and Debts	54UNTS169	100802
Norway	Sweden	21 Jun 47	Taxation	94UNTS107	101309
Multilateral		10 Oct 47	Claims and Debts	54UNTS193	100804
France	UK Great Britain	15 Jul 48	Claims and Debts	71UNTS215	100920
Korea, South	USA (United States)	11 Sep 48	Milit Assistance	89UNTS155	101216
Poland	UK Great Britain	14 Jan 49	Reparations	83UNTS51	101101
Netherlands	UK Great Britain	17 Jan 49	Reparations	83UNTS67	101102
Belgium	Canada	16 Nov 49	Reparations	51UNTS3	100748
Finland	Sweden	21 Dec 49	Taxation	197UNTS243	102642
Israel	UK Great Britain	30 Mar 50	Claims and Debts	86UNTS231	101162
Belgium	USA (United States)	16 Mar 51	Reparations	93UNTS109	101295
Italy	USA (United States)	16 May 51	Reparations	206UNTS325	102795
Belgium	Netherlands	14 Jun 51	Reparations	101UNTS3	101397
Australia	France	28 Sep 51	Reparations	161UNTS185	102128
Iraq	UK Great Britain	22 May 52	Claims and Debts	175UNTS97	102298
Germany, West	Israel	10 Sep 52	Consul/Citizenship	345UNTS91	104961
Belgium	Luxembourg	26 Sep 52	Reparations	141UNTS111	101910
Greece	Spain	03 Feb 53	Claims and Debts	225UNTS3	103081
Belgium	Sweden	01 Apr 53	Taxation	185UNTS225	102473
France	Japan	25 Apr 53	Admin Cooperation	187UNTS41	102500
Denmark	Sweden	27 Oct 53	Taxation	198UNTS71	102658
Finland	Netherlands	29 Mar 54	Taxation	252UNTS185	103567
Japan	USA (United States)	04 Jan 55	Specif Claim/Waive	237UNTS197	103346
Multilateral		10 May 55	Claims and Debts	273UNTS121	103948
Luxembourg	USA (United States)	15 Jun 55	Reparations	264UNTS279	103798
Japan	USA (United States)	24 Aug 55	Specif Claim/Waive	257UNTS297	103662
Austria	USA (United States)	26 Sep 55	Specific Property	272UNTS31	103930
Liberia	USA (United States)	22 Sep 56	Specific Property	278UNTS109	104027
Finland	Switzerland	27 Dec 56	Taxation	277UNTS7	103996
Denmark	Switzerland	14 Jan 57	Taxation	286UNTS27	104160
Denmark	Norway	22 Feb 57	Taxation	286UNTS127	104164
Czechoslovakia	Poland	29 Mar 58	Reparations	340UNTS199	104865
Greece	Yugoslavia	18 Jun 59	Claims and Debts	368UNTS3	105231

PARTY ONE	PARTY TWO	DATE	TOPIC	CITATION	NUMBER
Property (Cont.)					
Germany, West	Netherlands	08 Apr 60	Territory Boundary	508UNTS14	107404
Greece	UK Great Britain	09 May 63	Specific Property	398UNTS179	105722
Belgium	Tunisia	15 Jul 64	General Economic	561UNTS297	108190
Greece	Yugoslavia	05 Nov 64	Territory Boundary	539UNTS13	107820
Public Officers					
Multilateral		21 Jun 34	ILO Labor	40UNTS33	100625
Ceylon (Sri Lanka)	UK Great Britain	11 Nov 47	Admin Cooperation	86UNTS31	101150
Multilateral		22 Feb 57	Tech Assistance	274UNTS93	103960
Fed of Malaya	United Nations	29 May 58	Tech Assistance	330UNTS109	104742
Nepal	United Nations	18 Aug 58	Admin Cooperation	508UNTS3	107403
Fed of Malaya	UK Great Britain	08 Nov 58	Recognition	327UNTS301	104728
Burma	United Nations	15 Dec 58	Tech Assistance	319UNTS3	104629
United Nations	Tunisia	23 Dec 58	Tech Assistance	321UNTS23	104651
Ghana	United Nations	27 Feb 59	Tech Assistance	324UNTS133	104682
United Nations	Sudan	28 Mar 59	Tech Assistance	327UNTS95	104719
United Nations	Vietnam, South	03 Jun 59	IGO Status/Immunit	337UNTS361	200557
Panama	United Nations	24 Jun 59	IGO Operations	507UNTS245	107402
Libya	United Nations	27 Jun 59	Tech Assistance	336UNTS291	104811
Laos	United Nations	06 Jul 59	Tech Assistance	337UNTS41	104814
Fed of Malaya	UK Great Britain	27 Jul 59	Non-ILO Labor	374UNTS21	105324
Paraguay	United Nations	01 Aug 59	Tech Assistance	341UNTS319	104894
Guinea	United Nations	15 Oct 59	Tech Assistance	344UNTS47	104942
Afghanistan	United Nations	24 Nov 59	Tech Assistance	397UNTS187	105705
United Nations	Togo	06 May 60	Tech Assistance	388UNTS53	105571
Somalia	UK Great Britain	26 Jun 60	Direct Aid	374UNTS331	105346
Somalia	UK Great Britain	26 Jun 60	Non-ILO Labor	374UNTS339	105347
Ethiopia	United Nations	13 Jul 60	Tech Assistance	368UNTS143	105239
Kuwait	United Nations	31 Oct 60	Tech Assistance	391UNTS295	200581
Pakistan	United Nations	17 Nov 60	Tech Assistance	380UNTS277	105460
Cambodia	United Nations	30 Nov 60	Tech Assistance	383UNTS147	105500
Bolivia	United Nations	14 Dec 60	Tech Assistance	382UNTS283	105489
Iraq	United Nations	05 Mar 61	Tech Assistance	409UNTS56	105878
Jamaica	UK Great Britain	01 Jun 61	Recognition	478UNTS9	106932
Cyprus	United Nations	15 Jun 61	Tech Assistance	398UNTS39	105716
Haiti	United Nations	28 Jun 61	Tech Assistance	399UNTS159	105740
Lebanon	United Nations	26 Aug 61	Tech Assistance	406UNTS105	105842
Jordan	United Nations	11 Sep 61	Tech Assistance	406UNTS255	105855
Ceylon (Sri Lanka)	United Nations	04 Dec 61	Tech Assistance	415UNTS236	105987
United Nations	Somalia	20 Jan 62	Tech Assistance	420UNTS133	106044
UK Great Britain	Zambia	30 Jan 62	Non-ILO Labor	590UNTS173	108553
Tanganyika	UK Great Britain	14 Mar 62	Admin Cooperation	449UNTS147	106456
United Nations	Saudi Arabia	16 Mar 62	Tech Assistance	456UNTS379	106566
Greece	United Nations	18 May 62	Tech Assistance	429UNTS61	106190
United Nations	Tanganyika	01 Jun 62	Tech Assistance	479UNTS3	106944
Nigeria	United Nations	07 Aug 62	Tech Assistance	435UNTS167	106278
Cameroon	United Nations	29 Aug 62	Tech Assistance	442UNTS3	106334
Niger	United Nations	01 Oct 62	Tech Assistance	439UNTS181	106329
Uganda	UK Great Britain	10 Oct 62	Admin Cooperation	475UNTS177	106893
United Nations	Western Samoa	05 Nov 62	Tech Assistance	443UNTS297	200599
United Nations	Syria	17 Nov 62	IGO Status/Immunit	456UNTS359	106565
Ecuador	United Nations	26 Nov 62	Tech Assistance	445UNTS3	106372
Rwanda	United Nations	28 Nov 62	Tech Assistance	450UNTS267	106473
Ivory Coast	United Nations	10 Dec 62	Tech Assistance	451UNTS269	106498
Burundi	United Nations	29 Dec 62	Tech Assistance	450UNTS279	106474
Israel	United Nations	07 Jan 63	Tech Assistance	450UNTS229	106470
United Nations	Trinidad/Tobago	06 May 63	IGO Status/Immunit	463UNTS109	106696
Mali	United Nations	09 May 63	Tech Assistance	463UNTS147	106699
Jamaica	United Nations	22 May 63	IGO Status/Immunit	479UNTS19	106945
United Nations	Uganda	29 May 63	IGO Status/Immunit	466UNTS311	106751
United Nations	UK Great Britain	27 Jun 63	Trusteeship	469UNTS145	106789
Dominican Republic	United Nations	05 Aug 63	IGO Status/Immunit	472UNTS353	106847
United Nations	United Arab Rep	27 Aug 63	Tech Assistance	474UNTS221	106884
Burundi	WHO (World Health)	30 Aug 63	IGO Operations	490UNTS423	107169
Multilateral		21 Oct 63	Tech Assistance	480UNTS197	106969
Public Officers (Cont.)					
WHO (World Health)	Somalia	08 Nov 63	IGO Operations	493UNTS243	107218
WHO (World Health)	Sierra Leone	22 Nov 63	IGO Operations	493UNTS255	107219
Nicaragua	United Nations	03 Dec 63	IGO Status/Immunit	482UNTS329	107002
United Nations	Sierra Leone	19 Feb 64	IGO Status/Immunit	489UNTS91	107136
United Nations	Upper Volta	26 Feb 64	IGO Status/Immunit	489UNTS179	107139
Morocco	United Nations	03 Mar 64	IGO Status/Immunit	490UNTS187	107154
Malaysia	UK Great Britain	09 Jul 64	Consul/Citizenship	522UNTS213	107547
Malaysia	UK Great Britain	09 Jul 64	Consul/Citizenship	522UNTS189	107545
Malaysia	UK Great Britain	09 Jul 64	Consul/Citizenship	522UNTS201	107546
Malawi	UK Great Britain	28 Aug 64	Consul/Citizenship	522UNTS223	107548
Algeria	United Nations	23 Sep 64	IGO Operations	510UNTS217	107416
Kenya	United Nations	01 Oct 64	IGO Operations	511UNTS199	107434
WMO (Meteorology)	UK Great Britain	16 Dec 64	Tech Assistance	548UNTS57	107969
Ethiopia	WHO (World Health)	27 Jan 65	IGO Operations	541UNTS135	107866
Multilateral		23 Feb 65	IGO Operations	527UNTS120	107622
Multilateral		05 Mar 65	IGO Operations	527UNTS221	107627
Multilateral		08 Apr 65	IGO Operations	533UNTS66	107733
Multilateral		26 Apr 65	IGO Operations	533UNTS50	107732
Malaysia	UK Great Britain	07 May 65	Admin Cooperation	552UNTS259	108058
Multilateral		12 May 65	IGO Operations	534UNTS390	107769
Multilateral		14 May 65	IGO Operations	550UNTS310	108026
Multilateral		25 May 65	IGO Operations	535UNTS374	107791
Multilateral		02 Jun 65	Tech Assistance	551UNTS2	108030
Gambia	UK Great Britain	05 Jun 65	Admin Cooperation	551UNTS193	108041
Multilateral		05 Jul 65	General Aid	563UNTS104	108207
Multilateral		20 Jul 65	IGO Operations	541UNTS12	107857
Multilateral		13 Sep 65	IGO Operations	547UNTS248	107961
Multilateral		21 Sep 65	IGO Operations	547UNTS280	107963
Multilateral		12 Nov 65	IGO Operations	550UNTS160	108013
Multilateral		31 Dec 65	Recognition	552UNTS292	108060
Multilateral		12 May 66	General Aid	563UNTS54	108204
Guyana	UK Great Britain	26 May 66	Admin Cooperation	588UNTS143	108521
UK Great Britain	Zambia	28 Jul 66	Non-ILO Labor	590UNTS191	108554
Multilateral		23 Sep 66	General Aid	573UNTS148	108328
Botswana	United Nations	30 Sep 66	Tech Assistance	576UNTS17	108362
Lesotho	United Nations	17 Nov 66	IGO Operations	580UNTS29	108418
Multilateral		27 Feb 67	IGO Operations	590UNTS156	108552
Multilateral		13 Apr 67	IGO Operations	595UNTS60	108612
Multilateral		21 Jun 67	Tech Assistance	598UNTS2	108653
Quarantine					
Poland	USSR (Soviet Union)	08 Apr 48	Sanitation	26UNTS191	100388
Czechoslovakia	Poland	22 Jan 49	Sanitation	85UNTS3	101142
Rabies					
Mexico	WHO (World Health)	28 May 52	Sanitation	134UNTS319	101810
Radar					
Canada	USA (United States)	13 Jun 55	Specif Goods/Equip	268UNTS87	103851
Canada	USA (United States)	15 Jun 55	Specif Goods/Equip	268UNTS101	103852
Radioactive Contamination					
Australia	USA (United States)	09 May 61	Scientific Project	409UNTS203	105886
Radiobiology					
Brazil	USA (United States)	29 Mar 63	Scientific Project	476UNTS67	106904
Railways					
Bolivia	Brazil	25 Feb 38	Land Transport	88UNTS379	200254
Brazil	Paraguay	14 Jun 41	Land Transport	54UNTS289	200201
Mexico	USA (United States)	18 Nov 42	Claims and Debts	120UNTS183	200392
Canada	USA (United States)	23 Feb 43	Land Transport	101UNTS243	200299
Brazil	Paraguay	11 Aug 44	Land Transport	67UNTS303	200227
Taiwan	USSR (Soviet Union)	14 Aug 45	General Amity	10UNTS300	200068
Multilateral		27 Sep 45	IGO Establishment	5UNTS327	200035
Taiwan	France	28 Feb 46	General Amity	14UNTS137	100216
Mexico	USA (United States)	05 Mar 46	Claims and Debts	120UNTS3	101612
Multilateral		17 Apr 46	Land Transport	27UNTS103	100402

PARTY ONE	PARTY TWO	DATE	TOPIC	CITATION	NUMBER
Railways (Cont.)					
Argentina	UK Great Britain	17 Sep 46	General Economic	88UNTS47	101185
Albania	Yugoslavia	28 Nov 46	Land Transport	111UNTS139	101526
Albania	Yugoslavia	28 Nov 46	Non-IBRD Project	111UNTS127	101525
Czechoslovakia	Poland	04 Apr 47	General Economic	85UNTS62	101146
UK Great Britain	Uruguay	15 Jul 47	Finance	71UNTS179	100918
USSR (Soviet Union)	Yugoslavia	23 Aug 47	Reparations	116UNTS281	101577
Belgium	France	13 Apr 48	Territory Boundary	31UNTS409	100483
Belgium	Netherlands	13 Apr 48	Customs	32UNTS153	100497
Czechoslovakia	Poland	12 Nov 48	Land Transport	84UNTS347	101141
Belgium	Netherlands	13 May 49	Customs	65UNTS133	100841
Czechoslovakia	Poland	02 Jul 49	Land Transport	260UNTS149	103708
India	IBRD (World Bank)	18 Aug 49	IBRD Project	154UNTS269	102031
China People's Rep	USSR (Soviet Union)	14 Feb 50	Privil/Immunities	226UNTS31	103105
Multilateral		13 May 50	Land Transport	128UNTS171	101719
IBRD (World Bank)	Thailand	27 Oct 50	IBRD Project	158UNTS3	102059
Italy	Yugoslavia	23 Dec 50	Reparations	150UNTS213	101975
UK Great Britain	USA (United States)	18 Jul 51	Land Transport	117UNTS49	101583
Belgium	IBRD (World Bank)	13 Sep 51	IBRD Project	158UNTS323	102070
Belgium	IBRD (World Bank)	13 Sep 51	IBRD Project	158UNTS349	102071
Multilateral		10 Jan 52	Visas	163UNTS3	102138
Multilateral		10 Jan 52	Visas	163UNTS27	102139
Pakistan	IBRD (World Bank)	27 Mar 52	IBRD Project	159UNTS251	102090
Iraq	UK Great Britain	21 Jun 52	Admin Cooperation	149UNTS221	101954
Colombia	IBRD (World Bank)	26 Aug 52	IBRD Project	159UNTS339	102094
Multilateral		25 Oct 52	Land Transport	241UNTS336	103442
Saudi Arabia	USA (United States)	10 Nov 52	Direct Aid	181UNTS307	102419
IBRD (World Bank)	UK Great Britain	11 Mar 53	IBRD Project	172UNTS115	102243
Pakistan	United Nations	25 Jan 54	Tech Assistance	185UNTS213	102472
France	IBRD (World Bank)	10 Jun 54	IBRD Project	210UNTS89	102836
Mexico	IBRD (World Bank)	24 Aug 54	IBRD Project	286UNTS211	104168
Multilateral		02 Oct 54	IBRD Project	201UNTS179	102717
IBRD (World Bank)	UK Great Britain	15 Mar 55	IBRD Project	265UNTS85	103808
Bulgaria	Yugoslavia	16 Mar 55	General Economic	397UNTS83	105702
India	Pakistan	15 Apr 55	Land Transport	247UNTS25	103458
Colombia	IBRD (World Bank)	15 Jun 55	IBRD Project	248UNTS161	103494
Italy	Switzerland	23 Jul 55	Land Transport	284UNTS279	104142
IBRD (World Bank)	Thailand	09 Aug 55	IBRD Project	221UNTS283	103011
Multilateral		20 Oct 55	IGO Establishment	378UNTS159	105425
Czechoslovakia	Germany, East	24 Oct 55	Land Transport	504UNTS173	107358
Burma	IBRD (World Bank)	04 May 56	IBRD Project	253UNTS179	103584
Bulgaria	Yugoslavia	22 May 56	Visas	367UNTS119	105229
Finland	Sweden	07 Jul 56	General Transport	258UNTS83	103672
Finland	USSR (Soviet Union)	14 Sep 56	Land Transport	255UNTS365	103618
Australia	Netherlands	29 Nov 56	Air Transport	302UNTS141	104356
Australia	IBRD (World Bank)	03 Dec 56	IBRD Project	288UNTS99	104200
India	IBRD (World Bank)	12 Jul 57	IBRD Project	288UNTS135	104202
Multilateral		26 Jul 57	Land Transport	386UNTS3	105535
Pakistan	IBRD (World Bank)	18 Oct 57	IBRD Project	299UNTS303	104322
Multilateral		15 Jan 58	Customs	383UNTS229	105503
Czechoslovakia	Poland	31 Jan 58	Land Transport	431UNTS99	106214
IBRD (World Bank)	UK Great Britain	02 May 58	IBRD Project	324UNTS25	104677
IBRD (World Bank)	UK Great Britain	16 Jun 58	IBRD Project	309UNTS35	104467
IBRD (World Bank)	Sudan	21 Jul 58	IBRD Project	323UNTS183	104669
India	IBRD (World Bank)	16 Sep 58	IBRD Project	323UNTS235	104671
India	IBRD (World Bank)	15 Jul 59	IBRD Project	346UNTS33	104976
Ethiopia	France	12 Nov 59	Specific Property	381UNTS3	105465
Pakistan	IBRD (World Bank)	30 Nov 59	IBRD Project	355UNTS203	105078
India	IBRD (World Bank)	29 Jul 60	IBRD Project	377UNTS153	105399
Colombia	IBRD (World Bank)	20 Sep 60	IBRD Project	390UNTS173	105608
Italy	USA (United States)	03 Dec 60	Atomic Energy	410UNTS3	105893
Burma	IBRD (World Bank)	16 Jan 61	IBRD Project	400UNTS73	105749
Turkey	USSR (Soviet Union)	27 Apr 61	Land Transport	420UNTS307	106047
Japan	IBRD (World Bank)	02 May 61	IBRD Project	415UNTS144	105984
India	IBRD (World Bank)	13 Oct 61	IBRD Project	418UNTS3	106013
Korea, South	IDA (Devel Assoc)	17 Aug 62	Non-IBRD Project	468UNTS387	200603

PARTY ONE	PARTY TWO	DATE	TOPIC	CITATION	NUMBER
Railways (Cont.)					
Pakistan	IBRD (World Bank)	14 Sep 62	IBRD Project	467UNTS125	106761
Pakistan	IBRD (World Bank)	14 Sep 62	IBRD Project	467UNTS152	106762
Austria	Czechoslovakia	22 Sep 62	Land Transport	495UNTS157	107244
Czechoslovakia	Poland	16 Nov 62	Land Transport	526UNTS3	107597
Austria	Yugoslavia	11 Dec 62	Land Transport	546UNTS3	107938
Peru	IBRD (World Bank)	13 Mar 63	IBRD Project	478UNTS245	106938
India	IDA (Devel Assoc)	22 Mar 63	Non-IBRD Project	477UNTS3	106911
Poland	USSR (Soviet Union)	22 Apr 63	Land Transport	493UNTS229	107217
Colombia	IBRD (World Bank)	21 Jun 63	IBRD Project	482UNTS159	106994
Czechoslovakia	Hungary	22 Oct 63	Land Transport	514UNTS95	107444
IBRD (World Bank)	Yugoslavia	28 Oct 63	IBRD Project	503UNTS289	107349
Multilateral		30 Dec 63	IBRD Project	568UNTS233	108271
Multilateral		30 Dec 63	IBRD Project	568UNTS215	108270
Portugal	UK Great Britain	07 Apr 64	Land Transport	539UNTS167	107830
Pakistan	IDA (Devel Assoc)	24 Jun 64	Non-IBRD Project	533UNTS165	107742
Pakistan	IDA (Devel Assoc)	24 Jun 64	Non-IBRD Project	533UNTS191	107743
IBRD (World Bank)	Spain	31 Jul 64	IBRD Project	537UNTS81	107798
Mali	IDA (Devel Assoc)	29 Sep 64	Non-IBRD Project	594UNTS187	108604
India	IDA (Devel Assoc)	26 Oct 64	Non-IBRD Project	535UNTS245	107783
IBRD (World Bank)	Yugoslavia	11 Dec 64	IBRD Project	537UNTS321	107807
Taiwan	IBRD (World Bank)	28 Apr 65	IBRD Project	549UNTS145	107998
East Afri Service	IBRD (World Bank)	29 Sep 65	IBRD Project	568UNTS327	200623
IBRD (World Bank)	Tanzania	29 Sep 65	IBRD Project	568UNTS309	108275
IBRD (World Bank)	Uganda	29 Sep 65	IBRD Project	568UNTS317	108276
Kenya	IBRD (World Bank)	29 Sep 65	IBRD Project	568UNTS289	108274
New Zealand	IBRD (World Bank)	17 Dec 65	IBRD Project	567UNTS275	108260
IBRD (World Bank)	Sudan	27 Dec 65	IBRD Project	567UNTS27	108250
India	IDA (Devel Assoc)	29 Jun 66	Non-IBRD Project	582UNTS277	108467
IDA (Devel Assoc)	Senegal	29 Sep 66	Non-IBRD Project	594UNTS277	108607
Raw Materials					
UK Great Britain	USA (United States)	18 Jan 52	Commodity Trade	184UNTS79	102440
Canada	UK Great Britain	19 Oct 54	Milit Assistance	214UNTS309	102906
Argentina	Brazil	26 Nov 59	General Trade	374UNTS39	105326
Recreation					
UK Great Britain	USA (United States)	19 Jul 54	Territory Boundary	250UNTS193	103523
Refugees					
Multilateral		15 Oct 46	Refugees	11UNTS73	100150
Belgium	USA (United States)	23 Jan 47	Visas	47UNTS23	100721
Multilateral		02 Sep 49	IGO Status/Immunit	250UNTS12	103515
Netherlands	IRO (Refugee Org)	20 Jun 50	Refugees	76UNTS55	100979
UN Relief Palestin	WHO (World Health)	23 Sep 50	Sanitation	103UNTS129	200310
Netherlands	IRO (Refugee Org)	13 Feb 51	IGO Operations	87UNTS239	101175
Multilateral		02 Jul 51	Refugees	189UNTS137	102545
Israel	USA (United States)	07 Dec 51	Tech Assistance	157UNTS53	102046
Israel	USA (United States)	27 Feb 52	Direct Aid	177UNTS123	102314
Finland	Norway	18 Mar 52	Specific Resources	188UNTS187	102527
Multilateral		06 Sep 52	Patents/Copyrights	216UNTS132	102937
Germany, West	Israel	10 Sep 52	Reparations	162UNTS205	102137
Denmark	Germany, West	26 Feb 53	Claims and Debts	178UNTS3	102332
Jordan	UN Relief Palestin	30 Mar 53	Direct Aid	165UNTS317	200495
UN Relief Palestin	United Arab Rep	30 Jun 53	Tech Assistance	190UNTS3	102554
UN Relief Palestin	United Arab Rep	14 Oct 53	Tech Assistance	190UNTS13	102555
Multilateral		28 Sep 54	Refugees	360UNTS117	105158
Lebanon	UN Relief Palestin	26 Nov 54	Direct Aid	202UNTS123	102728
Belgium	Netherlands	16 Feb 55	Refugees	211UNTS49	102846
Belgium	Luxembourg	04 Apr 55	Refugees	211UNTS57	102847
Luxembourg	Netherlands	04 May 55	Refugees	292UNTS17	104262
UN Hi Com Refugees	Sweden	08 Oct 56	Refugees	428UNTS307	106182
Israel	UN Relief Palestin	09 Nov 56	Direct Aid	280UNTS261	104063
France	Netherlands	15 Feb 57	Refugees	286UNTS243	104170
Belgium	France	15 Feb 57	Refugees	267UNTS3	103834
Austria	USA (United States)	10 May 57	Direct Aid	283UNTS33	104104
Multilateral		23 Nov 57	Refugees	506UNTS125	107384
Multilateral		20 Apr 59	Visas	376UNTS85	105375

PARTY ONE	PARTY TWO	DATE	TOPIC	CITATION	NUMBER
Refugees (Cont.)					
Cambodia	Thailand	15 Dec 60	Extradition	382UNTS315	105492
Multilateral		14 May 64	Refugees	528UNTS23	107633
Multilateral		14 May 64	Refugees	528UNTS13	107632
Multilateral		15 Feb 65	Refugees	546UNTS277	107952
Reindeer					
Finland	Norway	10 Sep 48	Specific Resources	32UNTS3	100486
Norway	Sweden	14 Dec 49	Specific Resources	196UNTS19	102618
Finland	Norway	18 Mar 52	Specific Resources	188UNTS187	102527
Norway	Sweden	29 Jun 56	Specific Resources	262UNTS335	103759
Finland	USSR (Soviet Union)	04 Jun 65	Specific Resources	560UNTS169	108173
Reparations and Restitutions					
Multilateral		14 Jan 46	Reparations	555UNTS69	108105
Hungary	Yugoslavia	11 May 46	Reparations	129UNTS3	101725
Multilateral		20 Jan 47	Water Transport	87UNTS247	101176
Hungary	Yugoslavia	25 Jan 47	Reparations	130UNTS3	101726
Multilateral		10 Feb 47	Reparations	140UNTS111	101886
Multilateral		10 Feb 47	Peace/Disarmament	42UNTS3	100645
Multilateral		10 Feb 47	Peace/Disarmament	41UNTS135	100644
Multilateral		10 Feb 47	Peace/Disarmament	41UNTS21	100643
Multilateral		10 Feb 47	Peace/Disarmament	49UNTS3	100747
Multilateral		10 Feb 47	Peace/Disarmament	48UNTS203	100746
Multilateral		10 Oct 47	Claims and Debts	54UNTS193	100804
Multilateral		04 Nov 47	Reparations	93UNTS61	101288
Multilateral		16 Dec 47	Reparations	82UNTS237	101096
Hungary	Yugoslavia	17 Apr 48	Reparations	130UNTS111	101728
Hungary	Yugoslavia	17 Apr 48	Reparations	130UNTS121	101729
Hungary	Yugoslavia	17 Apr 48	Reparations	130UNTS101	101727
Spain	USA (United States)	03 May 48	Finance	132UNTS155	101756
France	UK Great Britain	15 Jul 48	Claims and Debts	71UNTS215	100920
Multilateral		31 Mar 49	Reparations	122UNTS57	101636
United Arab Rep	UK Great Britain	17 Apr 49	Reparations	83UNTS183	101107
Germany, West	Netherlands	14 Dec 50	Water Transport	87UNTS257	101177
Netherlands	USA (United States)	19 Jan 51	Reparations	141UNTS221	101917
New Zealand	Yugoslavia	27 Feb 51	Reparations	150UNTS165	101971
Belgium	Netherlands	14 Jun 51	Reparations	101UNTS3	101397
Canada	Netherlands	10 Apr 52	Reparations	233UNTS129	103257
Germany, West	Netherlands	19 May 52	Reparations	134UNTS3	101794
Germany, West	Israel	10 Sep 52	Consul/Citizenship	345UNTS91	104961
Germany, West	Israel	10 Sep 52	Reparations	162UNTS205	102137
Belgium	Luxembourg	26 Sep 52	Reparations	141UNTS111	101910
Japan	UK Great Britain	04 Nov 52	Specific Property	164UNTS101	102161
Japan	UK Great Britain	04 Nov 52	Specific Property	164UNTS107	102162
Germany, East	USSR (Soviet Union)	22 Aug 53	Reparations	221UNTS129	103005
France	Netherlands	27 Nov 53	Reparations	302UNTS245	104363
Burma	Japan	05 Nov 54	Reparations	251UNTS215	103543
Belgium	Switzerland	05 Jan 56	Reparations	228UNTS159	103149
Germany, West	Sweden	22 Mar 56	Reparations	262UNTS401	103762
Japan	Philippines	09 May 56	Reparations	285UNTS3	104148
Japan	Spain	08 Jan 57	Claims and Debts	318UNTS221	104615
Italy	USA (United States)	29 Mar 57	Reparations	299UNTS157	104311
Belgium	UK Great Britain	03 Oct 57	Reparations	394UNTS69	105669
Ethiopia	Japan	19 Dec 57	General Amity	325UNTS91	104695
Brazil	Italy	08 Jan 58	Reparations	362UNTS273	105192
Indonesia	Japan	20 Jan 58	Reparations	324UNTS247	104689
Indonesia	Japan	20 Jan 58	Peace/Disarmament	324UNTS227	104688
Netherlands	Norway	30 Jun 58	Reparations	346UNTS217	104982
Austria	USA (United States)	30 Jan 59	Claims and Debts	511UNTS145	107432
Japan	Vietnam, South	13 May 59	Reparations	373UNTS101	105317
Austria	USA (United States)	22 May 59	Reparations	347UNTS3	104988
Denmark	Japan	25 May 59	Reparations	341UNTS157	104881
Germany, West	Norway	07 Aug 59	Reparations	358UNTS185	105136
Germany, West	Netherlands	08 Apr 60	Territory Boundary	508UNTS14	107404
San Marino	UK Great Britain	22 Jul 61	Reparations	420UNTS3	106035
Belgium	Germany, West	21 Sep 62	Reparations	502UNTS63	107326

PARTY ONE	PARTY TWO	DATE	TOPIC	CITATION	NUMBER
Reparations and Restitutions (Cont.)					
Belgium	Netherlands	06 Jan 64	Reparations	531UNTS119	107698
Germany, West	UK Great Britain	09 Jun 64	Reparations	539UNTS187	107831
Repatriation					
Multilateral		23 Jun 26	ILO Labor	38UNTS315	100606
Belgium	Netherlands	02 Jan 45	Refugees	19UNTS259	200120
USA (United States)	USSR (Soviet Union)	11 Feb 45	Other Military	68UNTS175	200229
Belgium	Luxembourg	14 May 45	Refugees	19UNTS243	200118
Belgium	Czechoslovakia	16 May 45	Refugees	19UNTS251	200119
Belgium	Greece	16 Dec 54	Claims and Debts	223UNTS73	103056
Poland	USSR (Soviet Union)	25 Mar 57	Extradition	281UNTS121	104075
Austria	Yugoslavia	20 May 64	Extradition	514UNTS3	107439
Reunion					
Multilateral		29 Nov 19	ILO Labor	38UNTS53	100586
Multilateral		16 Nov 21	ILO Labor	38UNTS143	100593
Multilateral		10 Jun 25	ILO Labor	38UNTS229	100600
Multilateral		15 Jun 27	ILO Labor	38UNTS327	100607
Multilateral		21 Jun 34	ILO Labor	40UNTS19	100624
Multilateral		23 Jun 34	ILO Labor	40UNTS45	100626
Multilateral		24 Oct 36	ILO Labor	40UNTS153	100632
Multilateral		24 Oct 36	ILO Labor	40UNTS205	100635
Multilateral		24 Oct 36	ILO Labor	40UNTS169	100633
Multilateral		24 Oct 36	ILO Labor	40UNTS187	100634
Multilateral		23 Jun 37	ILO Labor	40UNTS233	100637
Multilateral		20 Jun 38	ILO Labor	40UNTS255	100638
Multilateral		27 Jun 46	ILO Labor	164UNTS37	102157
Multilateral		29 Jun 46	ILO Labor	94UNTS11	101303
Multilateral		09 Oct 46	ILO Labor	78UNTS198	101017
Multilateral		09 Oct 46	ILO Labor	78UNTS213	101018
Multilateral		11 Jul 47	ILO Labor	54UNTS3	100792
Multilateral		30 Oct 47	General Economic	55UNTS188	100814
Multilateral		09 Jul 48	ILO Labor	70UNTS85	100898
Multilateral		09 Jul 48	ILO Labor	81UNTS147	101070
Multilateral		09 Jul 48	ILO Labor	68UNTS17	100881
Multilateral		29 Nov 48	IGO Establishment	120UNTS13	101613
Multilateral		18 Jun 49	ILO Labor	160UNTS223	102109
Multilateral		29 Jun 49	ILO Labor	138UNTS207	101870
Multilateral		01 Jul 49	Non-ILO Labor	120UNTS71	101616
Multilateral		01 Jul 49	ILO Labor	138UNTS225	101871
Multilateral		01 Jul 49	ILO Labor	96UNTS237	101340
Multilateral		01 Jul 49	ILO Labor	96UNTS257	101341
Multilateral		28 Jun 51	ILO Labor	172UNTS159	102244
Multilateral		29 Jun 51	ILO Labor	165UNTS303	102181
Multilateral		26 Jun 52	ILO Labor	196UNTS183	102624
Multilateral		06 Sep 52	Patents/Copyrights	216UNTS132	102937
Multilateral		01 Mar 54	Admin Cooperation	286UNTS265	104173
Rice					
Multilateral		22 Mar 45	General Amity	70UNTS237	200241
Multilateral		01 Jan 46	Peace/Disarmament	99UNTS131	101375
Thailand	UK Great Britain	01 May 46	Commodity Trade	99UNTS169	101377
Thailand	UK Great Britain	01 May 46	Commodity Trade	99UNTS175	101378
Multilateral		06 May 46	Commodity Trade	157UNTS85	102049
Multilateral		06 May 46	Commodity Trade	99UNTS181	101379
UK Great Britain	USA (United States)	06 May 46	Admin Cooperation	99UNTS199	101381
Thailand	UK Great Britain	06 May 46	Commodity Trade	99UNTS193	101380
Multilateral		23 Dec 46	Commodity Trade	126UNTS47	101681
Multilateral		29 Nov 48	IGO Establishment	120UNTS13	101613
Burma	Yugoslavia	07 Mar 56	Commodity Trade	386UNTS207	105542
Rights of Association					
Multilateral		12 Nov 21	ILO Labor	38UNTS153	100594
Multilateral		09 Jul 48	ILO Labor	68UNTS17	100881
Rights of Correction					
Multilateral		31 Mar 53	Mass Media	435UNTS191	106280

PARTY ONE	PARTY TWO	DATE	TOPIC	CITATION	NUMBER
Road Traffic					
Multilateral		19 Sep 49	Land Transport	125UNTS3	101671
Multilateral		19 Mar 55	Sanitation	228UNTS95	103144
Multilateral		13 Dec 57	Land Transport	372UNTS159	105296
Multilateral		10 Jun 58	Land Transport	454UNTS115	106540
Multilateral		10 Jun 58	Land Transport	454UNTS211	106541
Austria	Netherlands	19 Mar 59	Admin Cooperation	485UNTS117	107048
Germany, West	Netherlands	08 Apr 60	Territory Boundary	508UNTS14	107404
Roads					
Panama	USA (United States)	23 Mar 40	Land Transport	124UNTS195	200420
Panama	USA (United States)	06 Sep 40	Land Transport	124UNTS209	200421
Jordan	UK Great Britain	19 Jul 41	Territory Boundary	9UNTS381	200054
Costa Rica	USA (United States)	16 Jan 42	Land Transport	23UNTS285	200135
El Salvador	USA (United States)	13 Feb 42	Land Transport	23UNTS293	200136
Canada	USA (United States)	18 Mar 42	Land Transport	101UNTS205	200294
Nicaragua	USA (United States)	08 Apr 42	Milit Installation	132UNTS343	200439
Nicaragua	USA (United States)	08 Apr 42	Land Transport	24UNTS145	200138
Canada	USA (United States)	09 May 42	Land Transport	101UNTS215	200295
Canada	USA (United States)	10 Sep 42	Land Transport	101UNTS221	200296
Honduras	USA (United States)	26 Oct 42	Land Transport	24UNTS209	200145
Canada	USA (United States)	04 Nov 42	Non-ILO Labor	24UNTS217	200146
Canada	USA (United States)	07 Dec 42	Land Transport	101UNTS227	200297
Canada	USA (United States)	10 Apr 43	Territory Boundary	21UNTS237	200126
Guatemala	USA (United States)	19 May 43	Land Transport	28UNTS377	200161
Panama	USA (United States)	07 Jun 43	Specific Property	21UNTS269	200128
Canada	USA (United States)	19 Jul 43	Land Transport	29UNTS289	200167
Canada	USA (United States)	27 Jun 44	Milit Installation	101UNTS273	200301
Brazil	Uruguay	22 Nov 44	Specif Goods/Equip	65UNTS289	200217
Multilateral		27 Sep 45	IGO Establishment	5UNTS327	200035
Philippines	USA (United States)	14 Feb 47	Non-IBRD Project	16UNTS3	100245
Panama	USA (United States)	26 May 47	Territory Boundary	138UNTS137	101866
Canada	USA (United States)	31 Mar 48	Specific Property	81UNTS285	101077
Guatemala	USA (United States)	18 May 48	Land Transport	67UNTS161	100875
Belgium	Netherlands	13 May 49	Customs	65UNTS133	100841
Multilateral		16 Jun 49	Land Transport	45UNTS149	100696
Norway	Sweden	28 Jan 50	Land Transport	202UNTS151	102730
Panama	USA (United States)	24 May 50	Territory Boundary	241UNTS139	103430
Ethiopia	IBRD (World Bank)	13 Sep 50	IBRD Project	157UNTS213	102055
Panama	USA (United States)	14 Sep 50	Land Transport	241UNTS159	103431
Panama	USA (United States)	14 Sep 50	Land Transport	124UNTS25	101664
Multilateral		16 Sep 50	General Transport	92UNTS91	101264
Costa Rica	USA (United States)	17 Jan 51	Land Transport	134UNTS215	101801
Panama	USA (United States)	26 Jan 51	Land Transport	137UNTS69	101849
El Salvador	USA (United States)	19 Mar 51	Land Transport	134UNTS245	101803
Colombia	IBRD (World Bank)	10 Apr 51	IBRD Project	158UNTS155	102066
Nicaragua	USA (United States)	20 Apr 51	Land Transport	138UNTS57	101859
Ethiopia	USA (United States)	02 May 51	Direct Aid	139UNTS85	101877
Nicaragua	IBRD (World Bank)	07 Jun 51	IBRD Project	158UNTS277	102068
France	Italy	14 Mar 53	Land Transport	284UNTS221	104140
Brazil	IBRD (World Bank)	30 Apr 53	IBRD Project	190UNTS133	102562
Nicaragua	USA (United States)	02 Sep 53	Land Transport	215UNTS69	102911
Nicaragua	IBRD (World Bank)	04 Sep 53	IBRD Project	186UNTS117	102487
Colombia	IBRD (World Bank)	10 Sep 53	IBRD Project	203UNTS3	102738
El Salvador	IBRD (World Bank)	12 Oct 54	IBRD Project	203UNTS37	102739
Honduras	USA (United States)	12 May 55	Direct Aid	270UNTS3	103886
Panama	IBRD (World Bank)	12 Jul 55	IBRD Project	219UNTS127	102970
Guatemala	IBRD (World Bank)	29 Jul 55	IBRD Project	229UNTS167	103165
Bolivia	USA (United States)	03 Aug 55	Non-IBRD Project	264UNTS225	103795
Peru	IBRD (World Bank)	05 Aug 55	IBRD Project	218UNTS3	102950
Honduras	IBRD (World Bank)	22 Dec 55	IBRD Project	230UNTS262	103189
Haiti	IBRD (World Bank)	07 May 56	IBRD Project	252UNTS279	103570
Colombia	IBRD (World Bank)	06 Jun 56	IBRD Project	248UNTS139	103493
Nicaragua	USA (United States)	02 Aug 56	Land Transport	281UNTS99	104073
Australia	IBRD (World Bank)	03 Dec 56	IBRD Project	288UNTS99	104200

PARTY ONE	PARTY TWO	DATE	TOPIC	CITATION	NUMBER
Roads (Cont.)					
Canada	USA (United States)	17 Jan 57	Specif Goods/Equip	266UNTS109	103825
Ethiopia	IBRD (World Bank)	28 Jan 57	IBRD Project	286UNTS307	104175
Belgium	IBRD (World Bank)	26 Jun 57	IBRD Project	322UNTS301	104661
Finland	Norway	28 Jun 57	Non-IBRD Project	272UNTS191	103938
Italy	Switzerland	19 Sep 57	Land Transport	363UNTS69	105200
Ecuador	IBRD (World Bank)	20 Sep 57	IBRD Project	289UNTS237	104221
Belgium	IBRD (World Bank)	27 Nov 57	IBRD Project	292UNTS175	104273
Honduras	IBRD (World Bank)	09 May 58	IBRD Project	323UNTS4	104662
El Salvador	IBRD (World Bank)	07 Jan 59	IBRD Project	346UNTS51	104977
Iran	IBRD (World Bank)	29 May 59	IBRD Project	348UNTS103	104997
Japan	IBRD (World Bank)	17 Mar 60	IBRD Project	362UNTS43	105182
Panama	IBRD (World Bank)	19 Aug 60	IBRD Project	390UNTS153	105607
Mexico	IBRD (World Bank)	18 Oct 60	IBRD Project	422UNTS177	106075
Peru	IBRD (World Bank)	19 Dec 60	IBRD Project	417UNTS275	106010
Honduras	IDA (Devel Assoc)	12 May 61	Loans and Credits	414UNTS180	105973
India	IDA (Devel Assoc)	21 Jun 61	Loans and Credits	418UNTS61	106017
Chile	IDA (Devel Assoc)	28 Jun 61	Loans and Credits	426UNTS89	106131
Chile	IBRD (World Bank)	28 Jun 61	IBRD Project	426UNTS33	106129
Argentina	IBRD (World Bank)	30 Jun 61	IBRD Project	445UNTS85	106379
Colombia	IBRD (World Bank)	28 Aug 61	IBRD Project	416UNTS23	105993
Colombia	IDA (Devel Assoc)	28 Aug 61	Loans and Credits	416UNTS3	105992
Costa Rica	IBRD (World Bank)	13 Oct 61	IBRD Project	430UNTS27	106202
Costa Rica	IDA (Devel Assoc)	13 Oct 61	Non-IBRD Project	431UNTS3	106204
Paraguay	IDA (Devel Assoc)	26 Oct 61	Non-IBRD Project	447UNTS277	106419
Peru	IBRD (World Bank)	03 Nov 61	IBRD Project	430UNTS47	106203
Japan	IBRD (World Bank)	29 Nov 61	IBRD Project	426UNTS3	106128
IBRD (World Bank)	Venezuela	13 Dec 61	IBRD Project	446UNTS371	106409
IDA (Devel Assoc)	UK Great Britain	13 Mar 62	Direct Aid	466UNTS331	106753
Mexico	IBRD (World Bank)	20 Jun 62	IBRD Project	467UNTS205	106764
Israel	IBRD (World Bank)	17 Oct 62	IBRD Project	467UNTS107	106760
IBRD (World Bank)	Uruguay	26 Oct 62	IBRD Project	481UNTS39	106977
El Salvador	IDA (Devel Assoc)	02 Nov 62	Non-IBRD Project	468UNTS331	106780
Haiti	IDA (Devel Assoc)	02 Nov 62	Non-IBRD Project	468UNTS205	106774
Ethiopia	IDA (Devel Assoc)	27 Feb 63	Non-IBRD Project	478UNTS289	106939
IBRD (World Bank)	Thailand	11 Jun 63	IBRD Project	481UNTS227	106984
IBRD (World Bank)	Yugoslavia	21 Jun 63	IBRD Project	482UNTS43	106990
Mexico	IBRD (World Bank)	20 Sep 63	IBRD Project	491UNTS317	107182
Japan	IBRD (World Bank)	27 Sep 63	IBRD Project	485UNTS283	107061
Guatemala	USA (United States)	03 Oct 63	Direct Aid	493UNTS45	107206
IBRD (World Bank)	Spain	25 Oct 63	IBRD Project	491UNTS297	107181
IDA (Devel Assoc)	Syria	24 Dec 63	Non-IBRD Project	534UNTS253	107764
Liberia	IBRD (World Bank)	08 Jan 64	IBRD Project	504UNTS53	107353
IDA (Devel Assoc)	Tanganyika	05 Feb 64	Non-IBRD Project	506UNTS91	107382
Paraguay	USA (United States)	10 Feb 64	Milit Assistance	511UNTS53	107426
Canada	USA (United States)	06 Mar 64	Specific Property	524UNTS255	107577
Ecuador	IBRD (World Bank)	26 May 64	IBRD Project	534UNTS113	107758
Multilateral		26 May 64	IBRD Project	541UNTS271	200613
Ecuador	IDA (Devel Assoc)	26 May 64	Non-IBRD Project	534UNTS93	107757
Iran	IBRD (World Bank)	10 Jun 64	IBRD Project	537UNTS111	107799
Pakistan	IDA (Devel Assoc)	11 Jun 64	Non-IBRD Project	534UNTS309	107766
Pakistan	IDA (Devel Assoc)	11 Jun 64	Non-IBRD Project	506UNTS3	107379
Niger	IDA (Devel Assoc)	24 Jun 64	Non-IBRD Project	554UNTS93	108098
Gabon	IBRD (World Bank)	10 Jul 64	IBRD Project	537UNTS63	107797
Finland	IBRD (World Bank)	10 Jul 64	IBRD Project	516UNTS125	107474
IDA (Devel Assoc)	UK Great Britain	31 Jul 64	Non-IBRD Project	535UNTS205	107781
IBRD (World Bank)	Venezuela	28 Aug 64	IBRD Project	520UNTS97	107512
Pakistan	IDA (Devel Assoc)	22 Sep 64	Non-IBRD Project	594UNTS225	108605
Paraguay	IBRD (World Bank)	16 Dec 64	IBRD Project	549UNTS173	107999
Japan	IBRD (World Bank)	23 Dec 64	IBRD Project	538UNTS37	107809
Mauritania	IDA (Devel Assoc)	28 Dec 64	Non-IBRD Project	540UNTS163	107849
Kenya	IDA (Devel Assoc)	29 Dec 64	Non-IBRD Project	535UNTS225	107782
Honduras	IDA (Devel Assoc)	02 Feb 65	Non-IBRD Project	561UNTS279	108189
Honduras	IBRD (World Bank)	02 Feb 65	IBRD Project	561UNTS255	108188
Mexico	IBRD (World Bank)	04 Feb 65	IBRD Project	549UNTS189	108000
Nigeria	IDA (Devel Assoc)	01 Mar 65	Non-IBRD Project	563UNTS3	108201

PARTY ONE	PARTY TWO	DATE	TOPIC	CITATION	NUMBER
Roads (Cont.)					
IDA (Devel Assoc)	Somalia	29 Mar 65	Non-IBRD Project	586UNTS101	108499
Multilateral		29 Mar 65	Non-IBRD Project	540UNTS145	107848
Jamaica	IBRD (World Bank)	08 Apr 65	IBRD Project	539UNTS303	107841
Iran	IBRD (World Bank)	28 Apr 65	IBRD Project	555UNTS21	108103
Iran	IBRD (World Bank)	28 Apr 65	IBRD Project	555UNTS45	108104
Multilateral		29 Apr 65	Non-IBRD Project	586UNTS123	108500
Japan	IBRD (World Bank)	26 May 65	IBRD Project	550UNTS95	108010
Australia	Germany, West	21 Jun 65	Visas	542UNTS53	107879
Kenya	IDA (Devel Assoc)	30 Jun 65	Non-IBRD Project	554UNTS75	108097
Multilateral		22 Jul 65	IBRD Project	561UNTS333	200618
Japan	IBRD (World Bank)	10 Sep 65	Claims and Debts	566UNTS249	108246
Peru	IBRD (World Bank)	17 Sep 65	Loans and Credits	566UNTS311	108248
Nigeria	IBRD (World Bank)	26 Sep 65	IBRD Project	570UNTS233	108296
Nigeria	IBRD (World Bank)	26 Sep 65	IBRD Project	571UNTS39	108298
IDA (Devel Assoc)	UK Great Britain	08 Feb 66	Non-IBRD Project	567UNTS207	108257
Paraguay	IBRD (World Bank)	04 Apr 66	IBRD Project	570UNTS41	108287
Finland	IBRD (World Bank)	27 Apr 66	IBRD Project	568UNTS107	108266
IBRD (World Bank)	Thailand	24 Jun 66	IBRD Project	582UNTS259	108466
Iraq	IBRD (World Bank)	22 Jul 66	IBRD Project	584UNTS233	108480
Japan	IBRD (World Bank)	29 Jul 66	IBRD Project	582UNTS209	108464
IDA (Devel Assoc)	Siam	02 Aug 66	Non-IBRD Project	585UNTS271	108492
Malawi	IDA (Devel Assoc)	04 Oct 66	Non-IBRD Project	584UNTS215	108479
IBRD (World Bank)	Zambia	04 Oct 66	IBRD Project	585UNTS181	108489
IBRD (World Bank)	Yugoslavia	24 Feb 67	IBRD Project	599UNTS27	108663
Rubber					
Nicaragua	USA (United States)	11 Jan 41	Specific Resources	117UNTS253	200374
Honduras	USA (United States)	28 Feb 41	Specific Resources	117UNTS205	200371
Mexico	USA (United States)	11 Apr 41	Non-IBRD Project	117UNTS323	200379
Costa Rica	USA (United States)	18 Jun 41	Specific Resources	103UNTS173	200313
Brazil	USA (United States)	03 Mar 42	Tech Assistance	105UNTS91	200324
USA (United States)	Venezuela	13 Oct 42	Commodity Trade	138UNTS282	200451
Costa Rica	USA (United States)	03 Apr 43	Specif Goods/Equip	13UNTS463	200090
Haiti	USA (United States)	08 Jan 45	Specific Resources	121UNTS153	200397
France	USA (United States)	07 Feb 46	Commodity Trade	3UNTS239	100034
Netherlands	USA (United States)	09 Feb 46	Commodity Trade	3UNTS247	100035
UK Great Britain	USA (United States)	01 Mar 46	Commodity Trade	3UNTS293	100037
USA (United States)	Venezuela	29 Mar 46	Specific Resources	124UNTS57	101666
Multilateral		06 May 46	Commodity Trade	99UNTS181	101379
Thailand	UK Great Britain	06 May 46	Commodity Trade	99UNTS193	101380
Haiti	USA (United States)	11 Feb 48	Specific Resources	149UNTS11	101946
Safety at Sea					
Multilateral		10 Jun 48	Humanitarian	191UNTS3	102576
Multilateral		10 Jun 48	Humanitarian	164UNTS113	102163
Canada	USA (United States)	21 Feb 52	Humanitarian	205UNTS293	102781
Sweden	USSR (Soviet Union)	29 Sep 54	Humanitarian	202UNTS259	102733
Canada	USA (United States)	15 Jun 55	Specif Goods/Equip	268UNTS101	103852
Multilateral		04 Jan 56	Scientific Project	256UNTS171	103627
Germany, West	Netherlands	20 Sep 56	Specific Property	509UNTS269	107405
Norway	USSR (Soviet Union)	19 Oct 56	Humanitarian	257UNTS3	103644
Finland	USSR (Soviet Union)	07 Dec 56	Humanitarian	258UNTS89	103673
Multilateral		31 Mar 58	Specific Property	320UNTS103	104639
Japan	IBRD (World Bank)	10 Sep 58	IBRD Project	323UNTS297	104673
Multilateral		17 Jun 60	Humanitarian	536UNTS27	107794
Mexico	USA (United States)	08 Jan 62	Humanitarian	433UNTS163	106239
Multilateral		20 Feb 62	Water Transport	597UNTS159	108644
Greece	USA (United States)	24 Apr 62	Water Transport	459UNTS3	106609
Germany, West	USA (United States)	29 Nov 62	Water Transport	460UNTS169	106639
Netherlands	USA (United States)	06 Feb 63	Status of Forces	487UNTS113	107098
Norway	USA (United States)	01 Mar 63	Water Transport	524UNTS185	107573
Belgium	USA (United States)	19 Apr 63	Water Transport	493UNTS83	107209
Ireland	USA (United States)	18 Jun 64	Water Transport	530UNTS217	107684
UK Great Britain	USA (United States)	19 Jun 64	Water Transport	530UNTS99	107675
Denmark	UK Great Britain	30 Jun 64	Water Transport	539UNTS203	107833
Denmark	USA (United States)	02 Jul 64	Water Transport	529UNTS277	107665

PARTY ONE	PARTY TWO	DATE	TOPIC	CITATION	NUMBER
Safety at Sea (Cont.)					
Sweden	USA (United States)	06 Jul 64	Water Transport	529UNTS287	107666
Spain	USA (United States)	16 Jul 64	Water Transport	529UNTS187	107661
Portugal	USA (United States)	12 Nov 64	Specific Property	541UNTS251	107874
Italy	USA (United States)	23 Nov 64	Milit Assistance	532UNTS133	107716
Italy	USA (United States)	16 Dec 65	Specif Claim/Waive	574UNTS139	108346
Safety Measures					
Multilateral		26 Jun 28	ILO Labor	39UNTS15	100610
Multilateral		21 Jun 29	ILO Labor	39UNTS27	100611
Multilateral		27 Apr 32	ILO Labor	39UNTS103	100614
Multilateral		23 Jun 37	ILO Labor	40UNTS233	100637
Scientific Cooperation					
Bulgaria	Romania	29 Sep 50	Scientific Project	342UNTS141	104905
Albania	Poland	25 Jan 51	Scientific Project	260UNTS217	103710
USSR (Soviet Union)	Yugoslavia	19 Dec 55	Scientific Project	378UNTS127	105423
Bulgaria	Yugoslavia	10 Feb 56	Scientific Project	349UNTS21	105007
Germany, East	USSR (Soviet Union)	26 Apr 56	Health/Educ/Welfare	259UNTS279	103692
Hungary	USSR (Soviet Union)	28 Jun 56	Health/Educ/Welfare	259UNTS405	103700
Czechoslovakia	Yugoslavia	03 Jul 56	General Economic	397UNTS165	105704
Romania	Yugoslavia	27 Oct 56	Scientific Project	389UNTS55	105592
Czechoslovakia	Yugoslavia	29 Jan 57	Culture	300UNTS249	104339
Czechoslovakia	United Arab Rep	06 May 57	Tech Assistance	292UNTS317	104278
Romania	Vietnam, North	30 Jun 58	Scientific Project	389UNTS43	105591
Germany, East	Romania	15 Jul 58	Health/Educ/Welfare	387UNTS115	105560
Ceylon (Sri Lanka)	Yugoslavia	05 May 59	Scientific Project	391UNTS101	105618
Greece	Yugoslavia	18 Jun 59	Culture	368UNTS137	105238
USA (United States)	USSR (Soviet Union)	21 Nov 59	Culture	361UNTS35	105172
UK Great Britain	USSR (Soviet Union)	01 Dec 59	Health/Educ/Welfare	351UNTS313	105032
Czechoslovakia	Ethiopia	11 Dec 59	Scientific Project	386UNTS45	105536
Germany, East	Hungary	19 Dec 59	Health/Educ/Welfare	409UNTS4	105874
India	USSR (Soviet Union)	12 Feb 60	Culture	392UNTS153	105642
Czechoslovakia	Germany, East	16 Jun 60	General Economic	415UNTS248	105988
France	Greece	25 Jul 60	General Aid	533UNTS227	107745
Czechoslovakia	Ghana	23 Nov 60	Tech Assistance	431UNTS85	106212
UK Great Britain	USSR (Soviet Union)	09 Jan 61	Health/Educ/Welfare	404UNTS175	105810
Cuba	Germany, East	29 Mar 61	Culture	448UNTS81	106426
Czechoslovakia	Somalia	04 Jun 61	Tech Assistance	480UNTS261	106973
United Arab Rep	UK Great Britain	14 Nov 61	Education	449UNTS129	106455
Ghana	USA (United States)	03 Jan 62	Scientific Project	433UNTS147	106237
USA (United States)	USSR (Soviet Union)	08 Mar 62	Health/Educ/Welfare	460UNTS3	106630
Italy	USA (United States)	05 Sep 62	Scientific Project	461UNTS185	106663
UK Great Britain	USSR (Soviet Union)	21 Jan 63	Health/Educ/Welfare	475UNTS3	106887
Dahomey	USSR (Soviet Union)	20 Mar 63	Culture	528UNTS181	107641
Mali	Romania	26 Sep 63	Culture	528UNTS193	107642
Hungary	Yugoslavia	15 Oct 63	Health/Educ/Welfare	577UNTS49	108372
USA (United States)	USSR (Soviet Union)	22 Feb 64	Health/Educ/Welfare	526UNTS131	107605
Australia	USA (United States)	17 Aug 64	Scientific Project	530UNTS209	107683
Poland	Romania	26 Nov 64	Health/Educ/Welfare	552UNTS157	108053
Romania	USA (United States)	23 Dec 64	Health/Educ/Welfare	535UNTS359	107790
Denmark	Peru	30 Dec 64	Tech Assistance	595UNTS47	108611
Belgium	Sweden	11 Jan 65	Education	533UNTS157	107741
UK Great Britain	USSR (Soviet Union)	13 Feb 65	Health/Educ/Welfare	543UNTS43	107896
Ethiopia	Hungary	25 May 65	Health/Educ/Welfare	577UNTS193	108377
Pakistan	USSR (Soviet Union)	05 Jun 65	Culture	593UNTS115	108579
Uganda	USSR (Soviet Union)	24 Jul 65	Culture	596UNTS199	108633
Bulgaria	Hungary	19 Aug 65	Culture	577UNTS67	108373
Czechoslovakia	USSR (Soviet Union)	23 Apr 66	Culture	566UNTS159	108242
France	USSR (Soviet Union)	30 Jun 66	Culture	589UNTS109	108538
Scrap Metal					
UK Great Britain	USA (United States)	02 Dec 46	Milit Occupation	7UNTS163	100098
UK Great Britain	USA (United States)	30 Sep 48	Specific Resources	71UNTS241	100922
Germany, West	USA (United States)	19 Sep 51	General Trade	180UNTS161	102381
Belgium	Germany, West	28 May 54	Non-ILO Labor	249UNTS387	103512
Italy	USA (United States)	22 Jun 57	Milit Assistance	284UNTS51	104128

PARTY ONE	PARTY TWO	DATE	TOPIC	CITATION	NUMBER
Seals					
Canada	USA (United States)	19 Dec 42	Commodity Trade	26UNTS363	200156
Canada	USA (United States)	26 Dec 47	Commodity Trade	27UNTS29	100395
Multilateral		01 Mar 52	Specific Resources	168UNTS9	102210
Multilateral		09 Feb 57	Specific Resources	314UNTS105	104546
Finland	USSR (Soviet Union)	21 Feb 59	Specific Resources	338UNTS3	104830
Seamen					
Multilateral		09 Jul 20	ILO Labor	38UNTS119	100591
Multilateral		09 Jul 20	ILO Labor	38UNTS109	100590
Multilateral		10 Jul 20	ILO Labor	38UNTS129	100592
Multilateral		11 Nov 21	ILO Labor	38UNTS217	100599
Multilateral		11 Nov 21	ILO Labor	38UNTS203	100598
Multilateral		23 Jun 26	ILO Labor	38UNTS315	100606
Multilateral		24 Jun 26	ILO Labor	38UNTS295	100605
Multilateral		24 Oct 36	ILO Labor	40UNTS205	100635
Multilateral		24 Oct 36	ILO Labor	40UNTS153	100632
Multilateral		24 Oct 36	ILO Labor	40UNTS187	100634
Multilateral		24 Oct 36	ILO Labor	40UNTS169	100633
Multilateral		29 Jun 46	ILO Labor	94UNTS11	101303
Italy	UK Great Britain	13 Mar 48	Admin Cooperation	104UNTS41	101435
Greece	USA (United States)	21 Feb 49	Status of Forces	88UNTS29	101182
Belgium	Italy	30 Dec 49	Visas	51UNTS83	100754
Belgium	Germany, West	14 Nov 52	Visas	160UNTS217	102108
France	UK Great Britain	14 Oct 53	Admin Cooperation	186UNTS151	102489
Multilateral		23 Nov 57	Refugees	506UNTS125	107384
France	Israel	19 May 59	Admin Cooperation	377UNTS231	105403
Spain	UK Great Britain	30 May 61	Consul/Citizenship	562UNTS169	108198
Multilateral		19 Jun 63	Visas	482UNTS19	106988
Multilateral		10 Feb 64	Visas	496UNTS151	107249
Netherlands	Norway	17 Nov 64	Sanitation	579UNTS243	108412
Multilateral		01 Dec 64	Water Transport	550UNTS133	108012
Netherlands	Spain	10 Feb 65	Visas	545UNTS3	107922
Multilateral		08 Sep 65	Visas	578UNTS3	108382
Sewerage					
Pakistan	IDA (Devel Assoc)	16 Aug 63	Non-IBRD Project	492UNTS205	107192
Pakistan	IDA (Devel Assoc)	16 Aug 63	Non-IBRD Project	492UNTS171	107191
Ships and Shipping					
Canada	France	12 May 33	Admin Cooperation	253UNTS285	200545
Argentina	Brazil	23 Jan 40	Admin Cooperation	51UNTS281	200194
Panama	USA (United States)	28 Mar 41	Taxation	103UNTS163	200312
Brazil	Uruguay	08 Jan 42	Admin Cooperation	54UNTS359	200206
UK Great Britain	USSR (Soviet Union)	22 Jun 42	Finance	91UNTS355	200270
UK Great Britain	USA (United States)	15 Jun 45	Reparations	89UNTS327	200261
Greece	UK Great Britain	11 Oct 45	Reparations	183UNTS329	200509
Greece	UK Great Britain	30 Nov 45	Reparations	183UNTS197	102428
France	UK Great Britain	26 Jan 46	Reparations	91UNTS183	101251
France	USA (United States)	28 May 46	Reparations	84UNTS113	101122
Finland	USA (United States)	07 Jan 47	Taxation	15UNTS273	100243
Multilateral		10 Feb 47	Reparations	140UNTS111	101886
Romania	USSR (Soviet Union)	20 Feb 47	General Economic	226UNTS79	103110
Philippines	USA (United States)	21 Mar 47	Milit Assistance	45UNTS47	100691
Multilateral		10 Jun 47	Water Transport	208UNTS3	102814
Greece	USA (United States)	03 Dec 47	Milit Assistance	89UNTS119	101213
Taiwan	USA (United States)	08 Dec 47	Milit Installation	70UNTS3	100895
Italy	USA (United States)	06 Feb 48	Air Transport	73UNTS113	100950
Multilateral		06 Mar 48	Water Transport	289UNTS3	104214
Netherlands	USA (United States)	29 Apr 48	Taxation	32UNTS167	100498
Taiwan	UK Great Britain	18 May 48	Milit Assistance	66UNTS113	100850
Multilateral		09 Jul 48	ILO Labor	68UNTS17	100881
Netherlands	IBRD (World Bank)	15 Jul 48	IBRD Project	153UNTS259	102021
Netherlands	IBRD (World Bank)	15 Jul 48	IBRD Project	153UNTS259	102022
Netherlands	IBRD (World Bank)	15 Jul 48	IBRD Project	153UNTS259	102023
Netherlands	IBRD (World Bank)	15 Jul 48	IBRD Project	153UNTS211	102020
Netherlands	IBRD (World Bank)	15 Jul 48	IBRD Project	153UNTS259	102025

PARTY ONE	PARTY TWO	DATE	TOPIC	CITATION	NUMBER
Ships and Shipping (Cont.)					
Netherlands	IBRD (World Bank)	15 Jul 48	IBRD Project	153UNTS259	102024
Argentina	Denmark	15 Dec 48	Taxation	67UNTS71	100866
Argentina	Netherlands	15 Jan 49	Taxation	46UNTS241	100713
Cuba	USA (United States)	21 Feb 49	Status of Forces	231UNTS108	103212
Argentina	UK Great Britain	14 Mar 49	Taxation	83UNTS193	101108
Greece	Turkey	02 Apr 49	Finance	78UNTS23	101010
Argentina	Belgium	25 Jul 49	Taxation	46UNTS103	100703
Italy	Netherlands	16 Aug 49	Admin Cooperation	98UNTS21	101357
Argentina	Greece	21 Mar 50	Taxation	187UNTS213	102514
Denmark	UK Great Britain	27 Mar 50	Taxation	68UNTS117	100891
Argentina	USA (United States)	20 Jul 50	Taxation	89UNTS63	101209
Burma	USA (United States)	06 Nov 50	Milit Assistance	122UNTS81	101638
Denmark	South Africa	30 Nov 50	Taxation	84UNTS51	101118
Brazil	USA (United States)	04 Jan 51	Milit Assistance	165UNTS97	102171
Chile	USA (United States)	04 Jan 51	Milit Assistance	165UNTS105	102172
Argentina	USA (United States)	08 Jan 51	Milit Assistance	165UNTS89	102170
Israel	Yugoslavia	29 Jul 51	Mostfavored Nation	220UNTS7	102983
Cuba	USA (United States)	17 Dec 51	Visas	152UNTS87	102012
Multilateral		10 May 52	Admin Cooperation	439UNTS193	106330
Italy	UK Great Britain	06 Nov 52	Specif Claim/Waive	158UNTS431	102076
Japan	USA (United States)	12 Nov 52	Milit Assistance	184UNTS111	102443
Greece	South Africa	27 Jan 53	Mostfavored Nation	533UNTS303	107748
Denmark	Uruguay	04 Mar 53	General Economic	250UNTS51	103517
Japan	South Africa	27 Mar 53	Admin Cooperation	173UNTS37	102258
France	Japan	25 Apr 53	Admin Cooperation	187UNTS41	102500
Japan	UK Great Britain	27 Apr 53	Admin Cooperation	228UNTS227	103154
Australia	Japan	27 Apr 53	Admin Cooperation	193UNTS78	102612
Israel	Italy	22 May 53	Mostfavored Nation	219UNTS297	102981
Canada	USA (United States)	30 Jun 53	General Military	215UNTS103	102914
Germany, West	USA (United States)	20 Aug 53	Milit Assistance	224UNTS49	103069
France	USA (United States)	02 Sep 53	Milit Assistance	224UNTS153	103075
Belgium	Taiwan	13 Jan 54	Milit Assistance	223UNTS111	103059
France	Sweden	16 Feb 54	General Transport	228UNTS137	103147
Finland	South Africa	24 Mar 54	Admin Cooperation	230UNTS121	103179
Belgium	Germany, West	01 Apr 54	Admin Cooperation	190UNTS43	102556
Canada	USA (United States)	03 May 54	Milit Assistance	221UNTS339	103015
Taiwan	USA (United States)	14 May 54	Milit Installation	231UNTS165	103216
Haiti	Italy	14 Jun 54	General Economic	267UNTS97	103837
Germany, West	USA (United States)	29 Oct 54	General Amity	273UNTS3	103943
India	Iran	15 Dec 54	General Economic	327UNTS245	104724
Peru	USA (United States)	07 Jan 55	Milit Assistance	261UNTS321	103730
Korea, South	USA (United States)	29 Jan 55	Milit Assistance	239UNTS53	103371
Denmark	Israel	04 Apr 55	Taxation	213UNTS283	102891
Ecuador	USA (United States)	08 Jul 55	Milit Assistance	265UNTS49	103806
Canada	USA (United States)	21 Jul 55	Milit Assistance	269UNTS53	103873
Iceland	Sweden	17 Sep 55	Taxation	262UNTS273	103755
Iceland	Sweden	23 Sep 55	Admin Cooperation	262UNTS241	103750
Norway	Sweden	07 Oct 55	Admin Cooperation	262UNTS253	103752
Austria	USSR (Soviet Union)	17 Oct 55	General Economic	240UNTS289	103409
Netherlands	Sweden	23 Nov 55	Admin Cooperation	262UNTS247	103751
Denmark	Sweden	07 Dec 55	Admin Cooperation	262UNTS235	103749
Cuba	USA (United States)	10 Jan 56	Milit Assistance	240UNTS101	103398
Sweden	UK Great Britain	18 Jan 56	Admin Cooperation	428UNTS301	106181
Nicaragua	USA (United States)	21 Jan 56	General Amity	367UNTS3	105224
Norway	Sweden	09 Mar 56	Land Transport	369UNTS285	105262
Netherlands	USA (United States)	27 Mar 56	General Amity	285UNTS231	104154
Israel	Sweden	17 Jun 56	Taxation	257UNTS47	103648
Burma	Japan	20 Jun 56	Admin Cooperation	306UNTS61	104431
Finland	Sweden	07 Jul 56	General Transport	258UNTS83	103672
UK Great Britain	Venezuela	20 Jul 56	Admin Cooperation	351UNTS289	105029
Pakistan	USA (United States)	10 Sep 56	Milit Assistance	277UNTS259	104010
Multilateral		11 Sep 56	Humanitarian	266UNTS221	103832
Costa Rica	Denmark	26 Sep 56	General Economic	341UNTS305	104893
Portugal	USA (United States)	07 Nov 56	Milit Assistance	277UNTS133	104003
Australia	USA (United States)	31 Dec 56	Milit Assistance	266UNTS89	103823

PARTY ONE	PARTY TWO	DATE	TOPIC	CITATION	NUMBER
Ships and Shipping (Cont.)					
Brazil	USA (United States)	16 Jan 57	Milit Assistance	266UNTS99	103824
Greece	USA (United States)	19 Jan 57	Milit Installation	280UNTS45	104049
USA (United States)	Venezuela	21 Feb 57	Water Transport	279UNTS199	104041
Japan	Norway	28 Feb 57	General Economic	280UNTS87	104054
Morocco	UK Great Britain	01 Mar 57	General Economic	310UNTS3	104480
Dominican Republic	USA (United States)	09 Mar 57	Gen Communications	279UNTS249	104044
Sweden	Venezuela	13 Mar 57	Admin Cooperation	428UNTS351	106185
Netherlands	Venezuela	11 Apr 57	Admin Cooperation	288UNTS23	104193
Germany, West	USA (United States)	01 May 57	Milit Assistance	284UNTS85	104131
Greece	USA (United States)	05 Aug 57	Milit Assistance	290UNTS167	104235
Panama	USA (United States)	05 Aug 57	Visas	299UNTS113	104309
Germany, East	USSR (Soviet Union)	27 Sep 57	General Economic	292UNTS75	104268
Ireland	Portugal	11 Nov 57	Mostfavored Nation	553UNTS141	108080
USSR (Soviet Union)	Vietnam, North	12 Mar 58	General Economic	356UNTS149	105094
Germany, West	USSR (Soviet Union)	25 Apr 58	General Economic	346UNTS71	104978
Sweden	Yugoslavia	31 May 58	Admin Cooperation	428UNTS357	106186
Norway	Sweden	09 Jun 58	Water Transport	427UNTS221	106156
USA (United States)	Yugoslavia	16 Jun 58	Admin Cooperation	317UNTS31	104591
Ireland	Switzerland	18 Jun 58	Taxation	553UNTS183	108086
Denmark	El Salvador	09 Jul 58	General Economic	341UNTS289	104892
United Arab Rep	USSR (Soviet Union)	18 Sep 58	Water Transport	338UNTS29	104831
Japan	Yugoslavia	28 Feb 59	General Economic	341UNTS179	104883
Denmark	USA (United States)	08 May 59	Milit Assistance	344UNTS185	104949
Czechoslovakia	Germany, East	25 Nov 59	General Economic	374UNTS101	105331
Korea, North	USSR (Soviet Union)	22 Jun 60	General Economic	399UNTS3	105732
Norway	USA (United States)	06 Jul 60	Milit Assistance	378UNTS25	105415
Multilateral		29 Jul 60	Water Transport	392UNTS69	105640
Norway	USA (United States)	29 Nov 60	Milit Assistance	404UNTS251	105815
Belgium	USA (United States)	21 Feb 61	General Amity	480UNTS149	106967
Canada	USA (United States)	17 Oct 61	Specific Property	426UNTS201	106138
Finland	UK Great Britain	05 Dec 61	Admin Cooperation	424UNTS217	106110
Multilateral		15 Dec 61	Admin Cooperation	424UNTS43	106098
Multilateral		20 Dec 61	Water Transport	419UNTS79	106031
Luxembourg	USA (United States)	23 Feb 62	General Amity	474UNTS3	106868
Multilateral		18 Sep 62	Water Transport	442UNTS215	106351
Finland	USSR (Soviet Union)	27 Sep 62	Territory Boundary	479UNTS99	106949
Finland	New Zealand	12 Nov 62	Water Transport	485UNTS331	107064
Japan	UK Great Britain	14 Nov 62	General Trade	478UNTS29	106934
Austria	Czechoslovakia	08 Mar 63	General Economic	495UNTS219	107245
Canada	Finland	05 Jun 63	Water Transport	472UNTS345	106846
Multilateral		07 Jun 63	Water Transport	472UNTS95	106837
Australia	Finland	31 Jul 63	Admin Cooperation	478UNTS363	106942
Ceylon (Sri Lanka)	Finland	08 Jan 64	Water Transport	492UNTS285	107198
Finland	South Africa	12 Jun 64	Water Transport	505UNTS107	107367
Canada	Denmark	15 Oct 64	Water Transport	525UNTS227	107595
Denmark	India	06 Feb 65	Water Transport	531UNTS23	107690
Multilateral		09 Mar 65	Water Transport	591UNTS265	108564
Denmark	Germany, West	09 Jun 65	Water Transport	581UNTS141	108439
Fed Rhod/Nyasaland	Norway	18 Jun 66	Taxation	580UNTS9	108415
Slavery					
Multilateral		07 Dec 50	Admin Cooperation	212UNTS17	102861
Multilateral		07 Dec 53	Admin Cooperation	182UNTS51	102422
Multilateral		07 Sep 56	Humanitarian	266UNTS3	103822
Smuggling					
Saudi Arabia	UK Great Britain	20 Apr 42	Extradition	10UNTS99	200056
Saudi Arabia	UK Great Britain	20 Apr 42	General Amity	10UNTS117	200057
Social Development					
Brazil	USA (United States)	13 Apr 62	Non-IBRD Project	445UNTS227	106391
Social Insurance					
Multilateral		28 Nov 19	ILO Labor	38UNTS41	100585
Multilateral		09 Jul 20	ILO Labor	38UNTS119	100591
Multilateral		12 Nov 21	ILO Labor	38UNTS165	100595
Multilateral		05 Jun 25	ILO Labor	38UNTS257	100602

PARTY ONE	PARTY TWO	DATE	TOPIC	CITATION	NUMBER
Social Insurance (Cont.)					
Multilateral		10 Jun 25	ILO Labor	38UNTS243	100601
Multilateral		10 Jun 25	ILO Labor	38UNTS229	100600
Multilateral		15 Jun 27	ILO Labor	38UNTS327	100607
Multilateral		15 Jun 27	ILO Labor	38UNTS343	100608
Multilateral		29 Jun 33	ILO Labor	39UNTS211	100619
Multilateral		29 Jun 33	ILO Labor	39UNTS285	100622
Multilateral		29 Jun 33	ILO Labor	39UNTS259	100621
Multilateral		29 Jun 33	ILO Labor	39UNTS189	100618
Multilateral		29 Jun 33	ILO Labor	39UNTS235	100620
Multilateral		29 Jun 33	ILO Labor	39UNTS165	100617
Multilateral		21 Jun 34	ILO Labor	40UNTS19	100624
Multilateral		23 Jun 34	ILO Labor	40UNTS45	100626
Multilateral		24 Oct 36	ILO Labor	40UNTS187	100634
Canada	USA (United States)	04 Nov 42	Non-ILO Labor	24UNTS217	200146
Dominican Republic	USA (United States)	19 Oct 43	Non-ILO Labor	21UNTS295	200130
Belgium	Poland	24 Mar 47	Non-ILO Labor	18UNTS279	100297
Social Insurance					
Belgium	Netherlands	29 Aug 47	Non-ILO Labor	36UNTS349	100573
Social Insurance					
Belgium	Netherlands	29 Aug 47	Non-ILO Labor	36UNTS349	100573
Norway	Sweden	22 Dec 47	Non-ILO Labor	22UNTS203	100337
Denmark	Sweden	23 Dec 47	Non-ILO Labor	14UNTS3	100207
Belgium	France	17 Jan 48	Non-ILO Labor	36UNTS233	100570
Denmark	Norway	21 Jan 48	Non-ILO Labor	14UNTS307	100223
Social Insurance					
Czechoslovakia	Poland	05 Apr 48	Non-ILO Labor	31UNTS355	100482
Social Insurance					
Czechoslovakia	Poland	05 Apr 48	Non-ILO Labor	31UNTS355	100482
Social Insurance					
Belgium	Italy	30 Apr 48	Non-ILO Labor	36UNTS305	100571
Social Insurance					
Belgium	Italy	30 Apr 48	Non-ILO Labor	36UNTS305	100571
Denmark	Iceland	14 May 48	Non-ILO Labor	23UNTS163	100346
France	Poland	09 Jun 48	Non-ILO Labor	32UNTS251	100503
France	UK Great Britain	11 Jun 48	Non-ILO Labor	66UNTS151	100852
Czechoslovakia	France	12 Oct 48	Non-ILO Labor	45UNTS81	100693
Social Insurance					
Greece	USA (United States)	25 Oct 48	General Trade	185UNTS103	102462
Social Insurance					
Norway	Sweden	18 Dec 48	Non-ILO Labor	30UNTS117	100450
Australia	New Zealand	15 Apr 49	Non-ILO Labor	34UNTS225	100540
Social Insurance					
Poland	UK Great Britain	22 Aug 49	Admin Cooperation	404UNTS17	105801
Social Insurance					
Multilateral		27 Aug 49	Non-ILO Labor	47UNTS127	100727
Belgium	Luxembourg	03 Dec 49	Non-ILO Labor	91UNTS31	101241
Finland	UK Great Britain	28 Dec 49	Peace/Disarmament	86UNTS191	101159
France	UK Great Britain	28 Jan 50	Non-ILO Labor	97UNTS155	101349
Denmark	Norway	18 Jan 51	Non-ILO Labor	82UNTS153	101090
Social Insurance					
Germany, West	Netherlands	29 Mar 51	Non-ILO Labor	149UNTS71	101952
Italy	UK Great Britain	28 Nov 51	Non-ILO Labor	172UNTS205	102248
Belgium	Switzerland	17 Jun 52	Non-ILO Labor	180UNTS23	102373
Italy	Netherlands	28 Oct 52	Non-ILO Labor	289UNTS144	104218
Switzerland	UK Great Britain	16 Jan 53	Non-ILO Labor	196UNTS119	102621
Multilateral		20 Jul 53	Non-ILO Labor	227UNTS217	103140
Denmark	UK Great Britain	15 Dec 53	Non-ILO Labor	196UNTS105	102620
Mexico	USA (United States)	19 Nov 54	Non-ILO Labor	238UNTS237	103367
Sweden	Switzerland	17 Dec 54	Non-ILO Labor	369UNTS233	105260
France	Italy	03 Mar 56	Non-ILO Labor	267UNTS181	103843
France	UK Great Britain	10 Jul 56	Non-ILO Labor	326UNTS23	104708

PARTY ONE	PARTY TWO	DATE	TOPIC	CITATION	NUMBER
Social Insurance (Cont.)					
Belgium	Spain	28 Nov 56	Non-ILO Labor	308UNTS239	104464
Multilateral		19 Dec 56	Non-ILO Labor	427UNTS93	106148
Italy	UK Great Britain	29 Jan 57	Non-ILO Labor	326UNTS119	104710
Czechoslovakia	Yugoslavia	22 May 57	Non-ILO Labor	391UNTS57	105617
Italy	Monaco	06 Dec 57	Non-ILO Labor	363UNTS45	105198
Poland	Yugoslavia	16 Jan 58	Non-ILO Labor	340UNTS137	104863
Netherlands	Switzerland	28 Mar 58	Non-ILO Labor	318UNTS175	104614
Fed Rhod/Nyasaland	South Africa	11 Oct 58	Non-ILO Labor	373UNTS75	105315
Hungary	Poland	14 Feb 59	Non-ILO Labor	431UNTS157	106215
Turkey	UK Great Britain	09 Sep 59	Non-ILO Labor	424UNTS267	106113
Social Insurance					
Germany, West	UK Great Britain	28 Jan 60	Reparations	420UNTS29	106038
Social Insurance					
Germany, East	Hungary	30 Jan 60	Health/Educ/Welfare	408UNTS230	105873
Bulgaria	Hungary	30 Jun 61	Admin Cooperation	438UNTS287	106320
Social Insurance					
Germany, West	USA (United States)	14 Mar 63	Status of Forces	474UNTS71	106872
Social Security					
Belgium	France	17 Jan 48	Non-ILO Labor	36UNTS233	100570
France	Poland	09 Jun 48	Non-ILO Labor	32UNTS251	100503
France	UK Great Britain	11 Jun 48	Non-ILO Labor	66UNTS151	100852
Multilateral		07 Nov 49	Non-ILO Labor	132UNTS31	101749
Belgium	Luxembourg	03 Dec 49	Non-ILO Labor	91UNTS31	101241
France	Netherlands	07 Jan 50	Non-ILO Labor	120UNTS25	101614
France	UK Great Britain	28 Jan 50	Non-ILO Labor	97UNTS155	101349
Luxembourg	Netherlands	08 Jul 50	Non-ILO Labor	135UNTS229	101824
Multilateral		27 Jul 50	Non-ILO Labor	166UNTS73	102186
Denmark	France	30 Jun 51	Non-ILO Labor	151UNTS241	102000
Multilateral		28 Jun 52	ILO Labor	210UNTS132	102838
Belgium	France	27 Feb 53	Non-ILO Labor	164UNTS49	102158
Germany, West	Italy	05 May 53	Non-ILO Labor	267UNTS9	103835
Australia	UK Great Britain	08 Jun 53	Non-ILO Labor	201UNTS187	102718
Denmark	Germany, West	14 Aug 53	Non-ILO Labor	202UNTS3	102725
Luxembourg	UK Great Britain	13 Oct 53	Non-ILO Labor	209UNTS87	102825
Multilateral		11 Dec 53	Non-ILO Labor	218UNTS153	102956
Multilateral		11 Dec 53	Non-ILO Labor	218UNTS211	102957
Netherlands	UK Great Britain	11 Aug 54	Non-ILO Labor	248UNTS235	103497
Belgium	Yugoslavia	01 Nov 54	Non-ILO Labor	251UNTS123	103538
Belgium	San Marino	22 Apr 55	Non-ILO Labor	253UNTS41	103574
Italy	Sweden	25 May 55	Non-ILO Labor	291UNTS235	104259
Multilateral		15 Sep 55	Non-ILO Labor	254UNTS55	103593
New Zealand	UK Great Britain	20 Dec 55	Non-ILO Labor	268UNTS243	103860
Netherlands	Yugoslavia	01 Jun 56	Non-ILO Labor	276UNTS319	103994
Sweden	UK Great Britain	09 Jun 56	Non-ILO Labor	309UNTS301	104479
Netherlands	UK Great Britain	12 Jun 56	Non-ILO Labor	250UNTS81	103519
Multilateral		09 Jul 56	Non-ILO Labor	314UNTS3	104539
France	UK Great Britain	10 Jul 56	Non-ILO Labor	326UNTS23	104708
Belgium	France	18 Jul 56	Non-ILO Labor	248UNTS121	103491
Belgium	Spain	28 Nov 56	Non-ILO Labor	308UNTS239	104464
Israel	UK Great Britain	29 Apr 57	Non-ILO Labor	280UNTS227	104062
Belgium	UK Great Britain	20 May 57	Non-ILO Labor	303UNTS53	104371
Norway	UK Great Britain	25 Jul 57	Non-ILO Labor	313UNTS3	104528
Hungary	Yugoslavia	07 Oct 57	Non-ILO Labor	439UNTS61	106325
Italy	Monaco	06 Dec 57	Non-ILO Labor	363UNTS59	105199
Bulgaria	Yugoslavia	18 Dec 57	Non-ILO Labor	376UNTS3	105372
Australia	UK Great Britain	29 Jan 58	Non-ILO Labor	292UNTS233	104275
France	Italy	27 Mar 58	Non-ILO Labor	305UNTS409	104428
Belgium	Greece	01 Apr 58	Non-ILO Labor	388UNTS93	105574
UK Great Britain	Yugoslavia	24 May 58	Non-ILO Labor	326UNTS69	104709
Czechoslovakia	Switzerland	04 Jun 59	Non-ILO Labor	349UNTS121	105012
Italy	Norway	12 Jun 59	Non-ILO Labor	428UNTS363	106187
Finland	UK Great Britain	28 Jul 59	Non-ILO Labor	355UNTS31	105073
Denmark	UK Great Britain	27 Aug 59	Non-ILO Labor	360UNTS11	105153

PARTY ONE	PARTY TWO	DATE	TOPIC	CITATION	NUMBER
Social Security (Cont.)					
Czechoslovakia	USSR (Soviet Union)	02 Dec 59	Non-ILO Labor	374UNTS63	105330
Canada	UK Great Britain	10 Dec 59	Non-ILO Labor	379UNTS201	105440
Bulgaria	USSR (Soviet Union)	11 Dec 59	Non-ILO Labor	368UNTS287	105246
Ireland	UK Great Britain	29 Mar 60	Non-ILO Labor	371UNTS3	105267
Germany, West	UK Great Britain	20 Apr 60	Non-ILO Labor	413UNTS236	105958
Germany, East	USSR (Soviet Union)	24 May 60	Non-ILO Labor	392UNTS205	105645
Romania	USSR (Soviet Union)	24 Dec 60	Admin Cooperation	472UNTS245	106843
Albania	Romania	03 May 61	Non-ILO Labor	592UNTS21	108567
Australia	UK Great Britain	16 Aug 62	Non-ILO Labor	439UNTS163	106328
Netherlands	Spain	17 Dec 62	Health/Educ/Welfare	499UNTS227	107301
Hungary	USSR (Soviet Union)	20 Dec 62	Non-ILO Labor	577UNTS245	108381
Philippines	USA (United States)	30 Aug 63	Non-ILO Labor	489UNTS323	107147
Austria	Spain	15 Jul 64	Non-ILO Labor	589UNTS169	108541
Luxembourg	Portugal	12 Feb 65	Non-ILO Labor	571UNTS239	108305
France	UK Great Britain	25 Feb 65	Non-ILO Labor	543UNTS157	107899
Austria	Yugoslavia	19 Nov 65	Non-ILO Labor	591UNTS3	108556
France	Israel	17 Dec 65	Non-ILO Labor	581UNTS311	108451
Ireland	UK Great Britain	28 Feb 66	Health/Educ/Welfare	565UNTS33	108234
IAEA (Atom Energy)	UK Great Britain	20 Jun 66	IGO Operations	588UNTS269	108531
Greece	Netherlands	13 Sep 66	Non-ILO Labor	596UNTS245	108637
Multilateral		24 Feb 67	Health/Educ/Welfare	596UNTS133	108631
Social Welfare					
Multilateral		22 Mar 45	General Amity	70UNTS237	200241
Hungary	USSR (Soviet Union)	18 Feb 48	General Military	48UNTS163	100743
Czechoslovakia	Poland	05 Apr 48	Admin Cooperation	31UNTS325	100481
Finland	USSR (Soviet Union)	06 Apr 48	General Military	48UNTS149	100742
France	Poland	09 Jun 48	Non-ILO Labor	32UNTS251	100503
Australia	New Zealand	15 Apr 49	Non-ILO Labor	34UNTS225	100540
Multilateral		07 Nov 49	Sanitation	132UNTS3	101748
Multilateral		09 Jan 51	Humanitarian	197UNTS341	102647
Germany, West	Netherlands	29 Mar 51	Non-ILO Labor	149UNTS71	101952
Iraq	USA (United States)	18 Aug 52	Direct Aid	184UNTS131	102444
Multilateral		20 Jul 53	Non-ILO Labor	228UNTS41	103142
Multilateral		11 Dec 53	Non-ILO Labor	218UNTS255	102958
Iraq	USA (United States)	02 Mar 55	Non-IBRD Project	250UNTS229	103526
Bulgaria	Czechoslovakia	25 Jan 57	Non-ILO Labor	501UNTS149	107316
Czechoslovakia	Romania	02 May 57	Health/Educ/Welfare	387UNTS167	105562
Czechoslovakia	Yugoslavia	22 May 57	Non-ILO Labor	391UNTS33	105615
Germany, East	Poland	13 Jul 57	Health/Educ/Welfare	319UNTS229	104634
Poland	Yugoslavia	16 Jan 58	Non-ILO Labor	340UNTS181	104864
Czechoslovakia	Hungary	30 Jan 59	Non-ILO Labor	351UNTS3	105016
Bulgaria	Romania	14 Mar 60	Admin Cooperation	472UNTS279	106844
Albania	Romania	03 May 61	Non-ILO Labor	592UNTS21	108567
Bulgaria	Hungary	30 Jun 61	Admin Cooperation	438UNTS287	106320
Bulgaria	Poland	12 Jul 61	Admin Cooperation	436UNTS147	106294
Hungary	Romania	07 Sep 61	Non-ILO Labor	519UNTS141	107506
Multilateral		18 Oct 61	IGO Establishment	529UNTS89	107659
Romania	Yugoslavia	20 Dec 63	Visas	527UNTS245	107629
Multilateral		01 Dec 64	Water Transport	550UNTS133	108012
France	Israel	17 Dec 65	Non-ILO Labor	582UNTS3	108452
Space Flight					
Chile	USA (United States)	19 Feb 59	Specific Property	343UNTS17	104918
UK Great Britain	USA (United States)	16 Apr 59	IGO Status/Immunit	343UNTS11	104917
Ecuador	USA (United States)	24 Feb 60	Tech Assistance	371UNTS55	105270
Australia	USA (United States)	26 Feb 60	Specific Property	354UNTS95	105056
Spain	USA (United States)	18 Mar 60	Scientific Project	372UNTS13	105284
Chile	USA (United States)	28 Mar 60	Scientific Project	401UNTS105	105765
Mexico	USA (United States)	12 Apr 60	Scientific Project	372UNTS47	105287
Canada	USA (United States)	24 Aug 60	Scientific Project	388UNTS225	105580
South Africa	USA (United States)	13 Sep 60	Specific Property	388UNTS65	105572
UK Great Britain	USA (United States)	14 Oct 60	Scientific Project	398UNTS165	105721
Nigeria	USA (United States)	19 Oct 60	Scientific Project	394UNTS113	105672
Multilateral		01 Dec 60	Scientific Project	414UNTS110	105970
UK Great Britain	USA (United States)	20 Jan 61	Scientific Project	402UNTS153	105783

PARTY ONE	PARTY TWO	DATE	TOPIC	CITATION	NUMBER
Space Flight (Cont.)					
UK Great Britain	USA (United States)	15 Mar 61	Scientific Project	404UNTS207	105811
UK Great Britain	USA (United States)	06 Apr 61	Scientific Project	404UNTS215	105812
Australia	USA (United States)	22 May 61	Scientific Project	419UNTS3	106026
UK Great Britain	USA (United States)	08 Sep 61	Scientific Project	418UNTS53	106016
Argentina	USA (United States)	16 Mar 62	Scientific Project	454UNTS3	106535
Multilateral		29 Mar 62	IGO Establishment	507UNTS177	107401
Multilateral		09 May 62	IGO Establishment	453UNTS299	106531
Multilateral		14 Jun 62	IGO Establishment	528UNTS33	107634
Italy	USA (United States)	05 Sep 62	Scientific Project	461UNTS185	106663
Japan	USA (United States)	06 Nov 62	Telecommunications	459UNTS203	106623
Italy	USA (United States)	14 Nov 62	Telecommunications	459UNTS197	106622
Canada	USA (United States)	23 Aug 63	Telecommunications	494UNTS13	107222
Multilateral		14 Sep 63	Telecommunications	488UNTS121	107123
Malagasy	USA (United States)	07 Oct 63	Scientific Project	494UNTS3	107221
Spain	USA (United States)	29 Jan 64	Specific Property	511UNTS61	107427
Canada	USA (United States)	06 May 64	Scientific Project	524UNTS173	107572
Multilateral		06 May 64	IGO Operations	514UNTS71	107442
Italy	Eur Space Research	23 May 64	IGO Operations	528UNTS75	107635
Eur Space Research	Sweden	29 Jul 64	IGO Operations	528UNTS81	107636
France	Eur Space Research	10 Aug 64	IGO Operations	528UNTS135	107637
Spain	USA (United States)	26 Jan 65	Scientific Project	542UNTS81	107881
Mexico	USA (United States)	27 Feb 65	Scientific Project	542UNTS181	107889
Mexico	USA (United States)	27 Feb 65	Scientific Project	546UNTS135	107940
UK Great Britain	USA (United States)	07 Jul 65	Specific Property	551UNTS221	108044
Australia	Eur Space Vehicle	13 Jul 65	IGO Operations	543UNTS183	107902
Norway	Eur Space Research	21 Sep 65	IGO Operations	579UNTS251	108413
Norway	Eur Space Research	31 Jan 66	Specific Property	580UNTS3	108414
Multilateral		30 Mar 66	Scientific Project	593UNTS261	108588
Spain	USA (United States)	14 Apr 66	Scientific Project	586UNTS79	108497
Spain	USA (United States)	14 Apr 66	Specific Property	579UNTS173	108406
France	USSR (Soviet Union)	30 Jun 66	Scientific Project	589UNTS99	108537
Stateless Persons					
Multilateral		02 Jul 51	Refugees	189UNTS137	102545
Multilateral		06 Sep 52	Patents/Copyrights	216UNTS132	102937
Multilateral		28 Sep 54	Refugees	360UNTS117	105158
Steel and Steel Industry					
Multilateral		28 Apr 49	IGO Establishment	83UNTS105	101105
Japan	IBRD (World Bank)	12 Nov 52	IBRD Project	354UNTS313	105068
India	IBRD (World Bank)	26 Jun 56	IBRD Project	301UNTS3	104341
India	IBRD (World Bank)	19 Dec 56	IBRD Project	310UNTS75	104489
Multilateral		26 Jul 57	Land Transport	386UNTS3	105535
India	IBRD (World Bank)	20 Nov 57	IBRD Project	301UNTS47	104342
Japan	IBRD (World Bank)	18 Aug 58	IBRD Project	323UNTS205	104670
Japan	IBRD (World Bank)	10 Sep 58	IBRD Project	318UNTS133	104612
Japan	IBRD (World Bank)	12 Nov 59	IBRD Project	354UNTS279	105067
India	IBRD (World Bank)	22 Dec 61	IBRD Project	481UNTS85	106979
Colombia	IBRD (World Bank)	28 Jun 63	IBRD Project	489UNTS113	107137
Straits Settlements					
Japan	UK Great Britain	27 Apr 53	Admin Cooperation	228UNTS227	103154
Strategic Materials					
Colombia	USA (United States)	29 Mar 43	Milit Installation	124UNTS139	200416
Student Employees					
Sweden	Switzerland	16 Mar 48	Non-ILO Labor	197UNTS39	102632
Ireland	Switzerland	14 Mar 49	Non-ILO Labor	553UNTS175	108085
Netherlands	Sweden	06 Jul 49	Non-ILO Labor	197UNTS189	102639
France	Ireland	21 Nov 49	Non-ILO Labor	553UNTS59	108069
Multilateral		17 Apr 50	Non-ILO Labor	126UNTS285	101694
Belgium	Finland	20 Mar 51	Non-ILO Labor	110UNTS27	101498
Belgium	Sweden	18 Sep 51	Non-ILO Labor	133UNTS187	101789
Belgium	Germany, West	18 Jan 52	Education	124UNTS9	101663
Netherlands	Switzerland	20 Nov 52	Non-ILO Labor	163UNTS121	102146
Austria	Italy	12 Jul 56	Non-ILO Labor	378UNTS249	105426
Canada	France	04 Oct 56	Non-ILO Labor	305UNTS65	104414

PARTY ONE	PARTY TWO	DATE	TOPIC	CITATION	NUMBER
Student Employees (Cont.)					
Italy	Spain	25 Nov 57	Non-ILO Labor	378UNTS289	105428
Ireland	Sweden	05 Dec 57	Non-ILO Labor	428UNTS221	106176
Germany, West	Netherlands	30 Jun 58	Non-ILO Labor	315UNTS179	104568
Ireland	Netherlands	28 May 59	Non-ILO Labor	344UNTS95	104944
Germany, West	Ireland	11 May 60	Non-ILO Labor	553UNTS69	108070
Finland	Italy	18 Feb 61	Non-ILO Labor	434UNTS199	106263
Denmark	Germany, West	12 Sep 61	Non-ILO Labor	516UNTS283	107478
Austria	Finland	01 Feb 62	Non-ILO Labor	425UNTS33	106116
Finland	Poland	18 Dec 63	Non-ILO Labor	486UNTS57	107072
Sugar					
New Zealand	UK Great Britain	28 Nov 51	General Trade	127UNTS263	101707
Multilateral		01 Oct 53	Commodity Trade	258UNTS153	103677
Multilateral		26 Jul 57	Land Transport	386UNTS3	105535
Multilateral		01 Dec 58	Commodity Trade	385UNTS137	105534
El Salvador	USA (United States)	07 May 63	US Agri Commod Aid	476UNTS35	106901
India	USA (United States)	09 May 63	US Agri Commod Aid	476UNTS43	106902
Ireland	UK Great Britain	25 Jun 64	Commodity Trade	553UNTS221	108090
Surplus War Property					
UK Great Britain	USA (United States)	27 Mar 46	Milit Assistance	4UNTS2	100039
Canada	USA (United States)	30 Mar 46	Milit Installation	7UNTS15	100089
Poland	USA (United States)	22 Apr 46	Loans and Credits	406UNTS215	105851
India	USA (United States)	16 May 46	Milit Assistance	4UNTS183	100045
France	USA (United States)	28 May 46	Milit Assistance	84UNTS59	101119
France	USA (United States)	28 May 46	Milit Assistance	84UNTS79	101120
France	USA (United States)	28 May 46	Reparations	84UNTS113	101122
Australia	USA (United States)	07 Jun 46	Milit Assistance	4UNTS237	100048
New Zealand	USA (United States)	10 Jul 46	Milit Assistance	6UNTS341	100087
UK Great Britain	USA (United States)	31 Jul 46	Air Transport	42UNTS199	100648
Taiwan	USA (United States)	30 Aug 46	Direct Aid	12UNTS39	100179
Philippines	USA (United States)	11 Sep 46	Milit Assistance	43UNTS231	100670
Canada	USA (United States)	09 Jan 47	Specific Property	11UNTS341	100173
Burma	USA (United States)	28 Feb 47	Direct Aid	25UNTS27	100355
South Africa	USA (United States)	21 Mar 47	Milit Assistance	16UNTS47	100248
Netherlands	USA (United States)	28 May 47	General Military	17UNTS29	100267
Italy	UK Great Britain	21 Jan 48	Milit Installation	77UNTS23	100989
France	USA (United States)	27 Feb 48	Reparations	84UNTS207	101131
Philippines	USA (United States)	23 Mar 48	Education	43UNTS247	100671
Greece	USA (United States)	23 Apr 48	Education	74UNTS107	100958
UK Great Britain	Uruguay	12 Jul 48	Finance	71UNTS199	100919
UK Great Britain	USA (United States)	22 Sep 48	Milit Assistance	71UNTS64	100910
Multilateral		08 Oct 48	Education	19UNTS113	100308
France	USA (United States)	22 Oct 48	Education	84UNTS173	101128
Netherlands	USA (United States)	17 May 49	Milit Assistance	46UNTS291	100717
Iran	USA (United States)	01 Sep 49	Direct Aid	79UNTS155	101039
United Arab Rep	USA (United States)	03 Nov 49	Education	71UNTS31	100908
Australia	USA (United States)	26 Nov 49	Reparations	45UNTS133	100695
Turkey	USA (United States)	27 Dec 49	Direct Aid	98UNTS141	101361
India	USA (United States)	02 Feb 50	Education	89UNTS127	101214
Korea, South	USA (United States)	28 Apr 50	Education	93UNTS21	101284
Austria	USA (United States)	06 Jun 50	Education	92UNTS201	101273
Thailand	USA (United States)	01 Jul 50	Education	81UNTS61	101063
Pakistan	USA (United States)	23 Sep 50	Education	82UNTS131	101088
Germany, West	USA (United States)	27 Feb 53	Claims and Debts	205UNTS103	102771
Germany, West	USA (United States)	17 Aug 54	Direct Aid	233UNTS31	103248
Germany, West	USA (United States)	14 Apr 55	General Military	263UNTS351	103782
Italy	USA (United States)	22 Jun 57	Milit Assistance	284UNTS51	104128
Canada	USA (United States)	01 Sep 61	Claims and Debts	421UNTS199	106058
Tariffs					
Turkey	USA (United States)	22 Apr 44	Customs	109UNTS279	200364
France	USA (United States)	30 Oct 47	General Economic	125UNTS171	101676
Belgium	USA (United States)	30 Oct 47	General Economic	125UNTS103	101672
UK Great Britain	USA (United States)	30 Oct 47	General Economic	126UNTS39	101680
Cuba	USA (United States)	30 Oct 47	General Economic	119UNTS163	101611
Multilateral		30 Oct 47	General Economic	55UNTS188	100814

PARTY ONE	PARTY TWO	DATE	TOPIC	CITATION	NUMBER
Tariffs (Cont.)					
Multilateral		12 Feb 49	Customs	189UNTS33	102541
Ceylon (Sri Lanka)	Germany, West	01 Apr 55	General Trade	369UNTS57	105251
Australia	Fed Rhod/Nyasaland	30 Jun 55	General Trade	226UNTS215	103115
Multilateral		27 Jun 57	General Economic	284UNTS139	104133
UK Great Britain	USA (United States)	27 Jun 57	General Economic	284UNTS75	104130
Multilateral		10 Jun 58	General Economic	454UNTS47	106539
Multilateral		01 Sep 59	Customs	454UNTS289	106542
Multilateral		13 Dec 60	General Economic	455UNTS3	106543
Japan	New Zealand	09 Mar 62	General Trade	485UNTS351	107066
Australia	New Zealand	29 Apr 63	Customs	483UNTS241	107017
New Zealand	UK Great Britain	15 May 63	Commodity Trade	486UNTS11	107068
Taxation					
France	USA (United States)	25 Jul 39	Taxation	125UNTS259	200429
Finland	Sweden	10 Mar 43	Taxation	198UNTS333	200518
Canada	USA (United States)	09 Aug 43	Milit Installation	29UNTS295	200168
Canada	UK Great Britain	05 Jun 46	Taxation	86UNTS3	101147
South Africa	UK Great Britain	14 Oct 46	Taxation	86UNTS51	101152
South Africa	UK Great Britain	14 Oct 46	Taxation	86UNTS77	101153
Norway	Sweden	21 Jun 47	Taxation	94UNTS107	101309
Canada	France	08 Sep 47	Taxation	253UNTS259	103587
Czechoslovakia	Romania	01 Mar 48	Admin Cooperation	26UNTS109	100381
Netherlands	USA (United States)	29 Apr 48	Taxation	32UNTS167	100498
Belgium	Netherlands	25 Sep 48	Taxation	123UNTS81	101655
Belgium	Luxembourg	09 Oct 48	Taxation	123UNTS29	101652
Netherlands	UK Great Britain	15 Oct 48	Taxation	74UNTS3	100955
Argentina	Denmark	15 Dec 48	Taxation	67UNTS71	100866
France	Sweden	08 Apr 49	Taxation	197UNTS177	102637
Argentina	Belgium	25 Jul 49	Taxation	46UNTS103	100703
Norway	Sweden	17 Dec 49	Taxation	197UNTS215	102641
Israel	UK Great Britain	10 Feb 50	Taxation	86UNTS211	101161
Greece	USA (United States)	20 Feb 50	Taxation	196UNTS291	102630
Argentina	Greece	21 Mar 50	Taxation	187UNTS213	102514
Denmark	UK Great Britain	27 Mar 50	Taxation	68UNTS117	100891
Chile	USA (United States)	12 May 50	Consul/Citizenship	177UNTS103	102312
Denmark	South Africa	30 Nov 50	Taxation	84UNTS51	101118
Finland	Sweden	29 Dec 50	Taxation	197UNTS333	102646
Netherlands	UK Great Britain	30 Apr 51	Consul/Citizenship	91UNTS177	101250
Belgium	Czechoslovakia	02 May 51	Taxation	109UNTS3	101483
Greece	Netherlands	26 Jul 51	Taxation	109UNTS103	101495
Austria	Sweden	01 Aug 51	Taxation	198UNTS13	102653
Italy	USA (United States)	05 Mar 52	Taxation	179UNTS3	102351
Netherlands	USA (United States)	07 Mar 52	Taxation	135UNTS199	101821
France	USA (United States)	13 Mar 52	Milit Assistance	177UNTS21	102306
Luxembourg	USA (United States)	13 Mar 52	Taxation	168UNTS57	102212
UK Great Britain	USA (United States)	18 Mar 52	Milit Assistance	177UNTS33	102307
Iceland	USA (United States)	18 Mar 52	Taxation	177UNTS263	102325
Belgium	USA (United States)	07 Apr 52	Taxation	205UNTS3	102765
Denmark	USA (United States)	07 Apr 52	Milit Assistance	177UNTS257	102324
France	USA (United States)	13 Jun 52	Taxation	181UNTS3	102393
Norway	USA (United States)	27 Jun 52	Tech Assistance	184UNTS271	102452
Belgium	France	30 Jun 52	General Transport	137UNTS259	101857
Japan	USA (United States)	25 Jul 52	Milit Assistance	198UNTS281	102671
Multilateral		05 Sep 52	Taxation	256UNTS3	103619
Portugal	USA (United States)	01 Apr 53	Taxation	205UNTS41	102769
France	Japan	25 Apr 53	Admin Cooperation	187UNTS41	102500
Israel	UK Great Britain	13 May 53	Finance	175UNTS179	102300
USA (United States)	Yugoslavia	23 Jul 53	Taxation	221UNTS365	103018
Multilateral		27 Aug 53	Other Military	213UNTS137	102884
Spain	USA (United States)	26 Sep 53	Milit Assistance	207UNTS61	102800
Denmark	Sweden	27 Oct 53	Taxation	198UNTS129	102660
Greece	Sweden	27 May 54	Taxation	219UNTS147	102971
Afghanistan	USA (United States)	29 May 54	Direct Aid	234UNTS3	103268
Bolivia	USA (United States)	16 Jun 54	Direct Aid	234UNTS35	103271
Turkey	USA (United States)	23 Jun 54	Taxation	222UNTS161	103027

PARTY ONE	PARTY TWO	DATE	TOPIC	CITATION	NUMBER
Taxation (Cont.)					
Belgium	Greece	23 Jun 54	Taxation	199UNTS43	102676
Germany, West	USA (United States)	22 Jul 54	Taxation	221UNTS351	103016
Pakistan	USA (United States)	02 Oct 54	Direct Aid	236UNTS187	103324
Germany, West	USA (United States)	15 Oct 54	Milit Assistance	239UNTS135	103375
Multilateral		23 Oct 54	Status of Forces	332UNTS387	104763
Peru	USA (United States)	25 Oct 54	Direct Aid	238UNTS247	103368
Denmark	Israel	04 Apr 55	Taxation	213UNTS283	102891
Chile	USA (United States)	05 Apr 55	Direct Aid	250UNTS253	103527
Korea, South	USA (United States)	02 May 55	Direct Aid	258UNTS3	103666
Israel	Norway	24 May 55	Taxation	220UNTS71	102990
Greece	Norway	25 May 55	Taxation	423UNTS77	106085
Denmark	Finland	18 Jul 55	Taxation	250UNTS167	103522
South Africa	Sweden	28 Jul 55	Taxation	230UNTS287	103191
Ecuador	USA (United States)	06 Sep 55	Direct Aid	256UNTS187	103628
Iceland	Sweden	17 Sep 55	Taxation	262UNTS273	103755
Multilateral		13 Dec 55	IGO Operations	529UNTS141	107660
Italy	Vatican/Holy See	16 Dec 55	Taxation	260UNTS319	103715
Libya	USA (United States)	22 Dec 55	Direct Aid	240UNTS111	103399
Multilateral		18 May 56	Land Transport	339UNTS3	104844
Denmark	Norway	23 May 56	Taxation	271UNTS49	103909
Israel	Sweden	17 Jun 56	Taxation	257UNTS47	103648
Austria	Sweden	14 Aug 56	Taxation	262UNTS355	103760
Philippines	USA (United States)	18 Oct 56	Taxation	280UNTS55	104050
Belgium	United Arab Rep	31 Oct 56	Taxation	257UNTS235	103659
Belgium	Sweden	20 Nov 56	Taxation	281UNTS239	104081
Multilateral		14 Dec 56	Taxation	436UNTS131	106293
Multilateral		14 Dec 56	Taxation	436UNTS115	106292
Denmark	Netherlands	20 Feb 57	Taxation	287UNTS41	104179
Paraguay	USA (United States)	04 Apr 57	Taxation	283UNTS193	104117
Netherlands	United Arab Rep	15 May 57	Taxation	288UNTS29	104194
Ireland	Switzerland	18 Jun 58	Taxation	553UNTS183	108086
Sweden	United Arab Rep	21 Jul 58	Mostfavored Nation	427UNTS285	106160
France	UK Great Britain	28 Nov 58	Taxation	351UNTS263	105027
Denmark	United Arab Rep	01 Dec 58	Taxation	337UNTS69	104817
New Zealand	Switzerland	30 Dec 58	Taxation	380UNTS313	105463
Japan	Pakistan	17 Feb 59	Taxation	341UNTS127	104880
Australia	Switzerland	21 May 59	Taxation	341UNTS283	104891
Denmark	France	17 Sep 59	Taxation	410UNTS141	105901
Germany, West	Netherlands	08 Apr 60	Territory Boundary	508UNTS14	107404
Sweden	Tunisia	06 Sep 60	Taxation	427UNTS301	106162
Multilateral		26 Nov 60	Taxation	500UNTS25	107304
Korea, South	USA (United States)	08 Feb 61	General Aid	405UNTS37	105821
Canada	USA (United States)	17 Feb 61	Taxation	445UNTS143	106383
Denmark	Greece	04 Mar 61	Taxation	534UNTS157	107760
Morocco	Sweden	30 Mar 61	Taxation	427UNTS185	106154
China People's Rep	Denmark	23 Sep 61	Taxation	446UNTS3	106397
Czechoslovakia	Norway	25 Oct 62	Taxation	498UNTS335	107287
Czechoslovakia	Sweden	25 Oct 62	Air Transport	498UNTS343	107288
Czechoslovakia	Denmark	25 Oct 62	Taxation	456UNTS457	106571
Norway	Sweden	31 Oct 62	Claims and Debts	466UNTS361	106755
Ethiopia	Greece	07 Nov 62	Taxation	550UNTS179	108014
Ethiopia	Greece	07 Nov 62	Taxation	550UNTS189	108015
Luxembourg	USA (United States)	18 Dec 62	Taxation	532UNTS277	107723
France	USA (United States)	01 Aug 63	Taxation	527UNTS89	107619
Panama	USA (United States)	30 Aug 63	Taxation	488UNTS11	107116
Sweden	USA (United States)	22 Oct 63	Taxation	530UNTS247	107686
France	Israel	20 Dec 63	Customs	515UNTS165	107459
Hungary	Netherlands	11 Jan 64	Taxation	522UNTS243	107550
Greece	Poland	21 Jan 64	Taxation	533UNTS309	107749
Czechoslovakia	Poland	29 Jul 65	Dispute Settlement	572UNTS203	108313
Belgium	Denmark	20 Sep 65	Taxation	549UNTS63	107990
Technical Assistance					
Brazil	Paraguay	14 Jun 41	Admin Cooperation	54UNTS279	200200
Nicaragua	USA (United States)	27 Oct 42	Scientific Project	99UNTS287	200283

Technical Assistance (Cont.)

PARTY ONE	PARTY TWO	DATE	TOPIC	CITATION	NUMBER
Brazil	USA (United States)	29 Sep 44	Military Mission	65UNTS271	200216
Argentina	USA (United States)	06 Oct 48	Military Mission	80UNTS91	101046
Brazil	USA (United States)	26 Nov 48	Scientific Project	88UNTS3	101180
Panama	USA (United States)	31 Mar 49	Air Transport	55UNTS141	100812
WHO (World Health)	Thailand	12 Aug 49	Sanitation	178UNTS347	102350
Nicaragua	USA (United States)	01 Feb 50	Tech Assistance	99UNTS25	101368
Ceylon (Sri Lanka)	WHO (World Health)	17 Feb 50	Direct Aid	102UNTS309	200309
Haiti	WHO (World Health)	27 Jun 50	Tech Assistance	110UNTS99	101504
Brazil	USA (United States)	16 Aug 50	Tech Assistance	140UNTS223	101890
WHO (World Health)	United Arab Rep	25 Aug 50	IGO Operations	92UNTS39	101259
WHO (World Health)	Venezuela	11 Sep 50	Tech Assistance	110UNTS237	101513
Iceland	WHO (World Health)	06 Oct 50	Tech Assistance	110UNTS127	101506
WHO (World Health)	Turkey	19 Oct 50	Tech Assistance	110UNTS215	101512
Iran	USA (United States)	19 Oct 50	Tech Assistance	92UNTS135	101266
Multilateral		02 Nov 50	Tech Assistance	81UNTS160	101071
Ceylon (Sri Lanka)	USA (United States)	07 Nov 50	Tech Assistance	92UNTS125	101265
Nicaragua	WHO (World Health)	10 Nov 50	Tech Assistance	110UNTS155	101508
Peru	WHO (World Health)	10 Nov 50	Tech Assistance	110UNTS187	101510
Multilateral		24 Nov 50	Tech Assistance	81UNTS188	101072
Multilateral		15 Dec 50	Tech Assistance	76UNTS120	100985
Panama	USA (United States)	20 Dec 50	Tech Assistance	92UNTS167	101269
Liberia	USA (United States)	22 Dec 50	Tech Assistance	92UNTS145	101267
Nicaragua	USA (United States)	23 Dec 50	Tech Assistance	92UNTS155	101268
Philippines	WHO (World Health)	28 Dec 50	Tech Assistance	110UNTS203	101511
India	USA (United States)	28 Dec 50	Tech Assistance	99UNTS39	101369
United Nations	Yugoslavia	06 Jan 51	Direct Aid	78UNTS165	101015
Costa Rica	USA (United States)	11 Jan 51	Tech Assistance	92UNTS179	101270
Multilateral		18 Jan 51	Tech Assistance	81UNTS233	101073
Ceylon (Sri Lanka)	ILO (Labor Org)	24 Jan 51	Tech Assistance	117UNTS355	200380
Honduras	USA (United States)	26 Jan 51	Tech Assistance	99UNTS49	101370
Ethiopia	ICAO (Civil Aviat)	02 Feb 51	Tech Assistance	96UNTS123	101333
Pakistan	USA (United States)	09 Feb 51	Tech Assistance	100UNTS67	101388
Paraguay	WHO (World Health)	15 Feb 51	Tech Assistance	110UNTS171	101509
Multilateral		15 Feb 51	Tech Assistance	81UNTS245	101074
Israel	ILO (Labor Org)	19 Feb 51	Tech Assistance	100UNTS105	101391
Israel	ICAO (Civil Aviat)	19 Feb 51	Tech Assistance	96UNTS141	101334
ILO (Labor Org)	Syria	03 Mar 51	Tech Assistance	110UNTS69	101502
Multilateral		05 Mar 51	Tech Assistance	81UNTS261	101075
Multilateral		20 Mar 51	IGO Operations	82UNTS172	101091
Multilateral		28 Mar 51	Tech Assistance	181UNTS61	102399
Indonesia	WHO (World Health)	28 Mar 51	Tech Assistance	103UNTS71	101425
Jordan	ILO (Labor Org)	29 Mar 51	Tech Assistance	100UNTS247	200287
Jordan	United Nations	29 Mar 51	Tech Assistance	137UNTS267	200448
Liberia	ILO (Labor Org)	02 Apr 51	Tech Assistance	100UNTS117	101392
Jordan	WHO (World Health)	03 Apr 51	Tech Assistance	110UNTS297	200367
Multilateral		05 Apr 51	Tech Assistance	84UNTS299	101139
Ceylon (Sri Lanka)	ILO (Labor Org)	06 Apr 51	Tech Assistance	100UNTS235	200286
Mexico	ILO (Labor Org)	06 Apr 51	Tech Assistance	100UNTS131	101393
Guatemala	ILO (Labor Org)	13 Apr 51	Tech Assistance	126UNTS249	101692
Peru	ILO (Labor Org)	13 Apr 51	Tech Assistance	100UNTS31	101385
Ecuador	ILO (Labor Org)	19 Apr 51	Tech Assistance	100UNTS77	101389
ICAO (Civil Aviat)	Thailand	19 Apr 51	Tech Assistance	96UNTS181	101336
Honduras	WHO (World Health)	20 Apr 51	Tech Assistance	110UNTS111	101505
Cuba	ILO (Labor Org)	21 Apr 51	Tech Assistance	99UNTS205	101382
Greece	ILO (Labor Org)	25 Apr 51	Tech Assistance	100UNTS93	101390
India	ILO (Labor Org)	26 Apr 51	Tech Assistance	100UNTS19	101384
Mexico	WHO (World Health)	30 Apr 51	Tech Assistance	103UNTS95	101427
WHO (World Health)	Yugoslavia	02 May 51	Tech Assistance	103UNTS117	101429
Colombia	WHO (World Health)	04 May 51	Tech Assistance	110UNTS83	101503
Pakistan	ILO (Labor Org)	16 May 51	Tech Assistance	100UNTS147	101394
Cambodia	WHO (World Health)	31 May 51	Tech Assistance	102UNTS279	200307
Multilateral		01 Jun 51	Tech Assistance	118UNTS57	101596
Lebanon	WHO (World Health)	07 Jun 51	Tech Assistance	126UNTS221	101690
Iceland	ICAO (Civil Aviat)	07 Jun 51	Tech Assistance	96UNTS193	101337
United Nations	Thailand	11 Jun 51	Tech Assistance	90UNTS45	101225

Technical Assistance (Cont.)

PARTY ONE	PARTY TWO	DATE	TOPIC	CITATION	NUMBER
WHO (World Health)	Uruguay	11 Jun 51	Tech Assistance	128UNTS251	101724
Liberia	WHO (World Health)	11 Jun 51	Tech Assistance	103UNTS83	101426
Costa Rica	WHO (World Health)	14 Jun 51	Sanitation	102UNTS151	101418
Multilateral		15 Jun 51	Tech Assistance	148UNTS67	101936
UK Great Britain	USA (United States)	15 Jun 51	Tech Assistance	141UNTS79	101907
Dominican Republic	ILO (Labor Org)	18 Jun 51	Tech Assistance	100UNTS3	101383
Israel	United Nations	25 Jun 51	Tech Assistance	97UNTS21	101344
Multilateral		25 Jun 51	Tech Assistance	92UNTS27	101258
ILO (Labor Org)	Vietnam, South	26 Jun 51	Tech Assistance	100UNTS223	200285
Multilateral		28 Jun 51	Tech Assistance	118UNTS154	101604
Iraq	WHO (World Health)	01 Jul 51	Tech Assistance	110UNTS139	101507
Ethiopia	WHO (World Health)	02 Jul 51	Tech Assistance	103UNTS39	101422
Burma	WHO (World Health)	09 Jul 51	Sanitation	104UNTS187	101440
ILO (Labor Org)	Thailand	11 Jul 51	Tech Assistance	100UNTS159	101395
Paraguay	ILO (Labor Org)	12 Jul 51	Tech Assistance	117UNTS155	101591
Burma	WHO (World Health)	17 Jul 51	Tech Assistance	102UNTS127	101415
Multilateral		27 Jul 51	Tech Assistance	97UNTS291	200273
Israel	WHO (World Health)	07 Aug 51	Tech Assistance	104UNTS213	101442
India	United Nations	14 Aug 51	Tech Assistance	98UNTS115	101359
WHO (World Health)	Saudi Arabia	29 Aug 51	Tech Assistance	110UNTS277	101516
Multilateral		05 Sep 51	Tech Assistance	173UNTS15	102256
Iraq	ICAO (Civil Aviat)	18 Sep 51	Tech Assistance	108UNTS219	101475
Colombia	WHO (World Health)	18 Sep 51	Tech Assistance	109UNTS45	101489
WHO (World Health)	Vietnam, South	21 Sep 51	Tech Assistance	107UNTS63	200352
Paraguay	United Nations	27 Sep 51	Tech Assistance	120UNTS105	101617
Multilateral		01 Oct 51	Tech Assistance	104UNTS249	101446
Bolivia	United Nations	01 Oct 51	Tech Assistance	104UNTS263	101447
Pakistan	WHO (World Health)	07 Oct 51	Tech Assistance	126UNTS101	101684
Ecuador	WHO (World Health)	16 Oct 51	Tech Assistance	110UNTS263	101515
India	WHO (World Health)	16 Oct 51	Tech Assistance	109UNTS49	101490
United Nations	Uruguay	17 Oct 51	Tech Assistance	122UNTS29	101633
ILO (Labor Org)	Venezuela	22 Oct 51	Tech Assistance	117UNTS139	101590
Panama	ILO (Labor Org)	10 Nov 51	Tech Assistance	126UNTS269	101693
Australia	USA (United States)	16 Nov 51	Tech Assistance	168UNTS75	102214
Mexico	WHO (World Health)	17 Dec 51	Tech Assistance	124UNTS121	101670
India	WHO (World Health)	20 Dec 51	Tech Assistance	124UNTS109	101669
Multilateral		24 Dec 51	Tech Assistance	118UNTS290	200383
Austria	WHO (World Health)	10 Jan 52	Tech Assistance	131UNTS295	200438
Ceylon (Sri Lanka)	United Nations	21 Jan 52	Tech Assistance	118UNTS281	200382
Multilateral		23 Jan 52	Tech Assistance	127UNTS269	101708
WHO (World Health)	Spain	30 Jan 52	Tech Assistance	124UNTS259	200425
ICAO (Civil Aviat)	Yugoslavia	06 Feb 52	Tech Assistance	128UNTS97	101715
Indonesia	United Nations	06 Feb 52	Tech Assistance	121UNTS3	101621
WHO (World Health)	UK Great Britain	07 Feb 52	Tech Assistance	121UNTS75	101627
Lebanon	ICAO (Civil Aviat)	14 Feb 52	Tech Assistance	128UNTS83	101714
Multilateral		18 Feb 52	Tech Assistance	126UNTS319	200434
Pakistan	WHO (World Health)	21 Feb 52	IGO Operations	131UNTS221	101742
Greece	United Nations	05 Mar 52	Tech Assistance	123UNTS3	101650
ICAO (Civil Aviat)	United Arab Rep	06 Mar 52	Tech Assistance	151UNTS111	101986
Finland	WHO (World Health)	07 Mar 52	Tech Assistance	128UNTS269	200436
India	United Nations	02 Apr 52	Tech Assistance	126UNTS145	101687
United Nations	Yugoslavia	10 Apr 52	Tech Assistance	141UNTS89	101908
Multilateral		11 Apr 52	Tech Assistance	173UNTS2	102255
India	WHO (World Health)	14 Apr 52	Tech Assistance	131UNTS265	101746
India	WHO (World Health)	17 Apr 52	Tech Assistance	131UNTS241	101744
India	WHO (World Health)	19 Apr 52	Tech Assistance	131UNTS253	101745
Pakistan	United Nations	28 Apr 52	Tech Assistance	128UNTS191	101720
India	ICAO (Civil Aviat)	29 Apr 52	Tech Assistance	151UNTS123	101987
Norway	WHO (World Health)	09 May 52	Tech Assistance	131UNTS281	101747
Multilateral		22 May 52	Tech Assistance	131UNTS115	101739
Multilateral		19 Jun 52	Tech Assistance	133UNTS165	101787
WHO (World Health)	Syria	20 Jun 52	Tech Assistance	165UNTS219	102178
Chile	USA (United States)	30 Jun 52	Tech Assistance	199UNTS241	102688
Australia	FAO (Food Agri)	07 Jul 52	Tech Assistance	184UNTS209	102449
Chile	WHO (World Health)	11 Jul 52	Tech Assistance	137UNTS27	101846

Technical Assistance (Cont.)

PARTY ONE	PARTY TWO	DATE	TOPIC	CITATION	NUMBER
India	WHO (World Health)	16 Jul 52	Tech Assistance	135UNTS291	101828
Chile	ILO (Labor Org)	23 Jul 52	Tech Assistance	178UNTS323	102348
Panama	United Nations	20 Aug 52	Tech Assistance	136UNTS3	101829
Multilateral		21 Aug 52	Tech Assistance	141UNTS129	101912
Italy	ILO (Labor Org)	04 Sep 52	Tech Assistance	178UNTS371	200505
ILO (Labor Org)	Uruguay	20 Sep 52	Tech Assistance	187UNTS25	102499
United Nations	Trieste	30 Sep 52	Tech Assistance	140UNTS11	101881
Multilateral		15 Oct 52	Tech Assistance	141UNTS96	101909
Multilateral		17 Oct 52	Direct Aid	141UNTS121	101911
Mexico	ICAO (Civil Aviat)	28 Nov 52	Tech Assistance	164UNTS15	102156
Multilateral		16 Dec 52	Tech Assistance	158UNTS407	102074
Multilateral		29 Dec 52	Tech Assistance	151UNTS317	102002
ILO (Labor Org)	UN Relief Palestin	31 Dec 52	Tech Assistance	182UNTS201	200506
India	WHO (World Health)	11 Feb 53	Tech Assistance	163UNTS43	102140
United Nations	Sweden	11 Feb 53	Tech Assistance	160UNTS3	102096
Taiwan	ILO (Labor Org)	13 Feb 53	Tech Assistance	178UNTS337	102349
Multilateral		26 Feb 53	Tech Assistance	161UNTS31	102120
Costa Rica	United Nations	27 Feb 53	Tech Assistance	161UNTS45	102121
Nepal	United Nations	02 Mar 53	Tech Assistance	161UNTS347	200493
France	WHO (World Health)	02 Apr 53	Tech Assistance	174UNTS83	102279
United Nations	Yemen	07 Apr 53	Tech Assistance	163UNTS73	102142
France	WHO (World Health)	30 Apr 53	Tech Assistance	174UNTS71	102278
ICAO (Civil Aviat)	Syria	28 May 53	Tech Assistance	173UNTS199	102267
Ecuador	United Nations	16 Jun 53	Tech Assistance	166UNTS289	102194
Ethiopia	United Nations	22 Jun 53	Tech Assistance	172UNTS93	102241
Japan	United Nations	24 Jun 53	Tech Assistance	167UNTS249	200499
Cambodia	United Nations	24 Jun 53	Tech Assistance	168UNTS309	200500
Panama	USA (United States)	26 Jun 53	Tech Assistance	215UNTS77	102912
Multilateral		09 Oct 53	Tech Assistance	190UNTS49	102557
Dominican Republic	United Nations	19 Nov 53	Tech Assistance	180UNTS45	102374
Multilateral		18 Jan 54	IGO Establishment	330UNTS121	104743
UK Great Britain	USA (United States)	20 Jan 54	Tech Assistance	196UNTS95	102619
Brazil	WHO (World Health)	04 Feb 54	Tech Assistance	233UNTS49	103250
Taiwan	United Nations	05 Feb 54	Tech Assistance	186UNTS85	102485
United Nations	Venezuela	05 Mar 54	Tech Assistance	187UNTS9	102498
Liberia	United Nations	09 Mar 54	Tech Assistance	187UNTS61	102501
Guatemala	United Nations	10 Mar 54	Tech Assistance	191UNTS271	102587
United Nations	Vietnam, South	24 Mar 54	Tech Assistance	188UNTS345	200514
Multilateral		20 Apr 54	Tech Assistance	189UNTS11	102539
Nepal	WHO (World Health)	13 May 54	Tech Assistance	204UNTS311	200522
Multilateral		31 May 54	Tech Assistance	192UNTS20	102592
Multilateral		01 Jun 54	Tech Assistance	200UNTS235	200520
UK Great Britain	USA (United States)	12 Jul 54	Tech Assistance	204UNTS123	102753
Multilateral		19 Aug 54	Tech Assistance	201UNTS51	102710
Multilateral		06 Oct 54	Tech Assistance	201UNTS75	102711
Ethiopia	Sweden	13 Oct 54	Tech Assistance	202UNTS273	102734
Multilateral		27 Oct 54	Tech Assistance	201UNTS95	102712
Multilateral		29 Oct 54	Tech Assistance	201UNTS115	102713
Multilateral		16 Dec 54	Tech Assistance	204UNTS323	200523
Multilateral		04 Apr 55	Tech Assistance	208UNTS239	102816
Taiwan	WHO (World Health)	21 Apr 55	Tech Assistance	210UNTS71	102835
Pakistan	Sweden	04 Jun 55	Tech Assistance	228UNTS121	103146
Multilateral		14 Jun 55	Tech Assistance	212UNTS263	200526
Iran	WHO (World Health)	04 Jul 55	Tech Assistance	227UNTS65	103131
Multilateral		04 Jul 55	Tech Assistance	214UNTS10	102897
Libya	WHO (World Health)	05 Jul 55	Tech Assistance	219UNTS305	200530
Liberia	USA (United States)	06 Oct 55	Tech Assistance	275UNTS93	103978
Multilateral		13 Dec 55	Tech Assistance	407UNTS8	105857
Multilateral		02 Feb 56	Tech Assistance	227UNTS153	103137
Multilateral		10 Feb 56	Tech Assistance	228UNTS167	103150
Multilateral		10 Feb 56	Tech Assistance	228UNTS189	103151
Ethiopia	WHO (World Health)	17 Feb 56	Tech Assistance	243UNTS91	103448
Indonesia	United Nations	17 Apr 56	Non-IBRD Project	233UNTS267	103266
Multilateral		10 May 56	Tech Assistance	243UNTS103	103449
Multilateral		31 May 56	Tech Assistance	251UNTS181	103541

Technical Assistance (Cont.)

PARTY ONE	PARTY TWO	DATE	TOPIC	CITATION	NUMBER
Multilateral		08 Jun 56	Tech Assistance	247UNTS366	200541
Multilateral		12 Jun 56	Tech Assistance	243UNTS187	103453
Multilateral		14 Jun 56	Tech Assistance	265UNTS125	103809
Multilateral		26 Jun 56	Tech Assistance	321UNTS2	104650
Multilateral		26 Jun 56	Tech Assistance	253UNTS12	103573
Burma	USA (United States)	30 Jun 56	Tech Assistance	281UNTS65	104070
Multilateral		02 Jul 56	Tech Assistance	540UNTS110	107846
Multilateral		02 Jul 56	Tech Assistance	248UNTS37	103484
Multilateral		31 Aug 56	Tech Assistance	249UNTS158	103506
Multilateral		05 Oct 56	Tech Assistance	251UNTS245	103544
Multilateral		05 Oct 56	Tech Assistance	251UNTS267	103545
Multilateral		21 Nov 56	Tech Assistance	253UNTS266	103588
Multilateral		15 Jan 57	Tech Assistance	376UNTS122	105378
Multilateral		23 Jan 57	Tech Assistance	259UNTS426	103701
Multilateral		17 Feb 57	Tech Assistance	271UNTS2	103907
Multilateral		22 Feb 57	Tech Assistance	274UNTS93	103960
Multilateral		01 Mar 57	Tech Assistance	264UNTS94	103790
Ethiopia	Sweden	16 Mar 57	Tech Assistance	304UNTS214	104398
Tunisia	USA (United States)	26 Mar 57	General Aid	283UNTS117	104111
Multilateral		09 Apr 57	Tech Assistance	274UNTS172	103965
Albania	Yugoslavia	20 May 57	Sanitation	363UNTS99	105203
Multilateral		24 May 57	Tech Assistance	268UNTS270	103861
Finland	India	14 Jun 57	Tech Assistance	277UNTS327	104016
Germany, West	Japan	27 Jun 57	Admin Cooperation	318UNTS335	104624
Jordan	USA (United States)	27 Jun 57	General Aid	288UNTS269	104209
Multilateral		30 Jun 57	Tech Assistance	286UNTS171	104165
Australia	FAO (Food Agri)	08 Jul 57	Tech Assistance	277UNTS315	104015
Multilateral		09 Jul 57	Tech Assistance	274UNTS300	103972
Burma	WHO (World Health)	20 Sep 57	Tech Assistance	282UNTS113	104096
Multilateral		05 Nov 57	Tech Assistance	285UNTS301	104155
Ghana	WHO (World Health)	21 Jan 58	Tech Assistance	307UNTS3	104437
Indonesia	WHO (World Health)	05 Feb 58	Tech Assistance	307UNTS15	104438
Multilateral		15 Mar 58	Tech Assistance	292UNTS273	104276
Sudan	USA (United States)	31 Mar 58	General Aid	308UNTS105	104458
USA (United States)	Yugoslavia	05 Apr 58	Tech Assistance	338UNTS233	104838
Israel	WHO (World Health)	11 Apr 58	Tech Assistance	307UNTS27	104439
Ceylon (Sri Lanka)	Sweden	22 May 58	Tech Assistance	428UNTS65	106168
Multilateral		19 Jun 58	Tech Assistance	306UNTS236	200550
WHO (World Health)	Sudan	21 Jun 58	Tech Assistance	307UNTS235	104453
Afghanistan	WHO (World Health)	18 Dec 58	Tech Assistance	324UNTS121	104681
United Nations	Tunisia	23 Dec 58	Tech Assistance	321UNTS23	104651
India	Netherlands	16 Jan 59	Tech Assistance	506UNTS153	107386
Ghana	United Nations	27 Feb 59	Tech Assistance	324UNTS133	104682
IAEA (Atom Energy)	Thailand	18 Mar 59	Tech Assistance	339UNTS307	104850
Japan	IAEA (Atom Energy)	24 Mar 59	Atomic Energy	339UNTS327	104852
United Nations	Sudan	28 Mar 59	Tech Assistance	327UNTS95	104719
India	Netherlands	27 Apr 59	Tech Assistance	506UNTS141	107385
Fed of Malaya	USA (United States)	22 May 59	Tech Assistance	346UNTS263	104985
Greece	Yugoslavia	18 Jun 59	Admin Cooperation	368UNTS125	105237
Libya	United Nations	27 Jun 59	Tech Assistance	336UNTS291	104811
Multilateral		09 Oct 59	Tech Assistance	376UNTS382	105391
USA (United States)	Yugoslavia	22 Oct 59	Tech Assistance	360UNTS259	105161
Multilateral		03 Dec 59	Tech Assistance	348UNTS246	105003
Multilateral		03 Dec 59	Tech Assistance	345UNTS251	104971
Ceylon (Sri Lanka)	WHO (World Health)	21 Dec 59	Tech Assistance	349UNTS109	105011
Pakistan	WHO (World Health)	20 Jan 60	Tech Assistance	351UNTS355	105034
Japan	USA (United States)	23 Mar 60	Tech Assistance	372UNTS289	105305
Multilateral		12 Apr 60	Tech Assistance	359UNTS323	105150
Cambodia	WHO (World Health)	19 May 60	Tech Assistance	372UNTS193	105298
Multilateral		04 Jun 60	Tech Assistance	360UNTS208	105159
Multilateral		19 Jun 60	IGO Operations	537UNTS214	107803
Multilateral		08 Jul 60	Tech Assistance	366UNTS310	105220
Jordan	WHO (World Health)	03 Aug 60	Tech Assistance	381UNTS133	105469
WHO (World Health)	United Arab Rep	03 Aug 60	Tech Assistance	385UNTS3	105524
WHO (World Health)	Tunisia	04 Aug 60	Tech Assistance	381UNTS335	105474

Technical Assistance (Cont.)

PARTY ONE	PARTY TWO	DATE	TOPIC	CITATION	NUMBER
Laos	WHO (World Health)	04 Aug 60	Tech Assistance	373UNTS313	105322
WHO (World Health)	Saudi Arabia	06 Sep 60	Tech Assistance	395UNTS169	105684
Lebanon	WHO (World Health)	08 Sep 60	Tech Assistance	387UNTS49	105557
Guinea	USA (United States)	30 Sep 60	General Aid	394UNTS103	105671
WHO (World Health)	Upper Volta	15 Nov 60	Tech Assistance	383UNTS91	105496
Israel	Mali	24 Nov 60	Tech Assistance	413UNTS95	105944
Fed of Malaya	WHO (World Health)	25 Nov 60	Tech Assistance	387UNTS37	105556
Cambodia	United Nations	30 Nov 60	Tech Assistance	383UNTS147	105500
WHO (World Health)	Yemen	03 Dec 60	Tech Assistance	395UNTS187	105685
Dahomey	WHO (World Health)	07 Dec 60	Tech Assistance	387UNTS277	105567
Congo (Brazzaville)	WHO (World Health)	12 Dec 60	Tech Assistance	399UNTS105	105737
Niger	WHO (World Health)	28 Dec 60	Tech Assistance	394UNTS195	105679
Mali	USA (United States)	04 Jan 61	General Aid	405UNTS165	105832
Korea, South	WHO (World Health)	20 Jan 61	Tech Assistance	406UNTS269	200589
Multilateral		28 Jan 61	Tech Assistance	387UNTS202	105563
Ivory Coast	WHO (World Health)	30 Jan 61	Tech Assistance	395UNTS205	105686
WHO (World Health)	Togo	03 Feb 61	Tech Assistance	394UNTS207	105680
Chad	WHO (World Health)	03 Feb 61	Tech Assistance	394UNTS161	105676
Korea, South	USA (United States)	08 Feb 61	General Aid	405UNTS37	105821
Guinea	WHO (World Health)	11 Feb 61	Tech Assistance	394UNTS173	105677
Central Afri Rep	WHO (World Health)	13 Feb 61	Tech Assistance	394UNTS149	105675
Afghanistan	Japan	15 Mar 61	Education	450UNTS373	106480
Kuwait	WHO (World Health)	16 Mar 61	Tech Assistance	397UNTS315	200588
Ceylon (Sri Lanka)	Japan	20 Mar 61	Education	450UNTS385	106481
Mali	WHO (World Health)	27 Apr 61	Tech Assistance	407UNTS66	105860
Gabon	WHO (World Health)	27 Apr 61	Tech Assistance	397UNTS215	105707
Sierra Leone	USA (United States)	05 May 61	General Aid	409UNTS194	105885
Senegal	USA (United States)	13 May 61	General Aid	409UNTS232	105888
Ivory Coast	USA (United States)	17 May 61	General Aid	409UNTS241	105889
Cameroon	USA (United States)	26 May 61	General Aid	413UNTS195	105953
Niger	USA (United States)	26 May 61	General Aid	410UNTS213	105905
Dahomey	USA (United States)	27 May 61	General Aid	445UNTS23	106373
USA (United States)	Upper Volta	01 Jun 61	General Aid	410UNTS223	105906
Israel	Upper Volta	11 Jun 61	Tech Assistance	413UNTS113	105946
Ethiopia	United Nations	14 Jun 61	Direct Aid	406UNTS81	105840
Madagascar	USA (United States)	22 Jun 61	General Aid	413UNTS219	105956
Ghana	USA (United States)	19 Jul 61	Direct Aid	416UNTS167	106002
Tanganyika	USA (United States)	21 Jul 61	Direct Aid	445UNTS33	106374
Morocco	WHO (World Health)	09 Aug 61	Tech Assistance	412UNTS192	105932
WHO (World Health)	Somalia	17 Aug 61	Tech Assistance	423UNTS111	106088
Israel	Malagasy	27 Aug 61	Direct Aid	413UNTS86	105943
Ghana	United Nations	29 Aug 61	Tech Assistance	406UNTS117	105843
Fed of Malaya	USA (United States)	04 Sep 61	Direct Aid	421UNTS215	106060
Iraq	WHO (World Health)	13 Sep 61	Tech Assistance	419UNTS69	106030
Multilateral		20 Sep 61	Tech Assistance	407UNTS52	105859
Paraguay	USA (United States)	26 Sep 61	General Aid	461UNTS91	106653
Japan	United Nations	04 Oct 61	Education	410UNTS133	105900
Malagasy	WHO (World Health)	13 Oct 61	Tech Assistance	421UNTS273	106064
Multilateral		16 Oct 61	Tech Assistance	410UNTS242	105908
Philippines	USA (United States)	31 Oct 61	Direct Aid	424UNTS129	106105
Multilateral		07 Nov 61	Tech Assistance	412UNTS258	105937
Brazil	USA (United States)	11 Nov 61	Direct Aid	433UNTS199	106243
El Salvador	USA (United States)	20 Nov 61	Direct Aid	433UNTS221	106245
Thailand	USA (United States)	28 Nov 61	Direct Aid	434UNTS77	106256
OAS (Am States)	USA (United States)	29 Nov 61	Direct Aid	424UNTS119	106104
El Salvador	USA (United States)	19 Dec 61	General Aid	445UNTS175	106385
Costa Rica	USA (United States)	22 Dec 61	General Aid	460UNTS277	106646
Multilateral		27 Dec 61	Tech Assistance	425UNTS83	106120
Sierra Leone	USA (United States)	29 Dec 61	Direct Aid	434UNTS43	106254
Dominican Republic	USA (United States)	11 Jan 62	General Aid	433UNTS133	106236
Ethiopia	WHO (World Health)	11 Jan 62	Tech Assistance	423UNTS99	106087
Multilateral		17 Jan 62	Tech Assistance	419UNTS294	106033
Multilateral		20 Jan 62	Tech Assistance	429UNTS230	200596
Multilateral		13 Feb 62	Tech Assistance	422UNTS288	200594
Tunisia	USA (United States)	13 Feb 62	Direct Aid	442UNTS155	106346

Technical Assistance (Cont.)

PARTY ONE	PARTY TWO	DATE	TOPIC	CITATION	NUMBER
Multilateral		21 Feb 62	Tech Assistance	423UNTS151	106091
UK Great Britain	USA (United States)	22 Feb 62	Direct Aid	435UNTS127	106275
Multilateral		01 Mar 62	Tech Assistance	423UNTS122	106089
Liberia	USA (United States)	08 Mar 62	Direct Aid	445UNTS41	106375
WHO (World Health)	Sudan	11 Mar 62	Tech Assistance	432UNTS325	106226
United Nations	Saudi Arabia	16 Mar 62	Tech Assistance	456UNTS379	106566
Nigeria	WHO (World Health)	27 Mar 62	Tech Assistance	429UNTS123	106194
Nicaragua	USA (United States)	30 Mar 62	Tech Assistance	456UNTS241	106559
Multilateral		10 Apr 62	Tech Assistance	429UNTS78	106192
Somalia	USA (United States)	17 Apr 62	Direct Aid	436UNTS107	106291
Ecuador	USA (United States)	17 Apr 62	General Aid	442UNTS69	106339
Multilateral		18 Apr 62	Tech Assistance	463UNTS44	106692
Ivory Coast	USA (United States)	21 Apr 62	General Aid	526UNTS39	107598
Dominican Republic	USA (United States)	02 May 62	Direct Aid	442UNTS107	106342
ILO (Labor Org)	Tanganyika	03 May 62	IGO Operations	429UNTS73	106191
Multilateral		17 May 62	Tech Assistance	429UNTS46	106189
United Nations	Tanganyika	01 Jun 62	Tech Assistance	479UNTS3	106944
WHO (World Health)	Sierra Leone	19 Jun 62	Tech Assistance	439UNTS151	106327
Germany, West	Syria	25 Jun 62	Tech Assistance	489UNTS71	107135
Colombia	USA (United States)	23 Jul 62	General Aid	458UNTS123	106595
WHO (World Health)	Senegal	06 Aug 62	Tech Assistance	435UNTS179	106279
Multilateral		12 Aug 62	Tech Assistance	443UNTS266	106365
WHO (World Health)	Western Samoa	14 Aug 62	Tech Assistance	437UNTS317	200598
UK Great Britain	USA (United States)	15 Aug 62	General Aid	580UNTS189	108421
Multilateral		29 Aug 62	Tech Assistance	443UNTS280	106366
Multilateral		11 Sep 62	Tech Assistance	455UNTS402	106553
Mali	USSR (Soviet Union)	10 Oct 62	Tech Assistance	493UNTS219	107216
Belgium	Rwanda	13 Oct 62	Tech Assistance	456UNTS425	106568
Belgium	Rwanda	13 Oct 62	Tech Assistance	456UNTS431	106569
WHO (World Health)	Syria	18 Nov 62	Tech Assistance	480UNTS249	106972
Ceylon (Sri Lanka)	ILO (Labor Org)	21 Nov 62	IGO Operations	449UNTS263	106463
Costa Rica	USA (United States)	23 Nov 62	General Aid	541UNTS67	107861
Laos	USSR (Soviet Union)	01 Dec 62	Direct Aid	472UNTS3	106834
Multilateral		06 Dec 62	Tech Assistance	450UNTS240	106471
Cameroon	WHO (World Health)	08 Dec 62	Tech Assistance	451UNTS215	106496
Ivory Coast	United Nations	10 Dec 62	Tech Assistance	451UNTS269	106498
Multilateral		12 Dec 62	Tech Assistance	457UNTS72	106578
Algeria	WHO (World Health)	20 Dec 62	Tech Assistance	463UNTS135	106698
Multilateral		21 Jan 63	Tech Assistance	453UNTS20	106517
United Nations	South Pacific Com	24 Jan 63	Tech Assistance	470UNTS361	200604
Central Afri Rep	USA (United States)	10 Feb 63	Direct Aid	473UNTS83	106857
Multilateral		14 Feb 63	Tech Assistance	453UNTS168	106524
United Nations	South Pacific Com	20 Feb 63	Tech Assistance	453UNTS333	200600
IAEA (Atom Energy)	Yugoslavia	04 Mar 63	Atomic Energy	490UNTS333	107162
Multilateral		06 Mar 63	Tech Assistance	455UNTS386	106552
Indonesia	USA (United States)	14 Mar 63	General Aid	505UNTS79	107365
Multilateral		18 Apr 63	Tech Assistance	463UNTS121	106697
Multilateral		06 May 63	Tech Assistance	463UNTS78	106694
United Nations	Trinidad/Tobago	06 May 63	IGO Status/Immunit	463UNTS109	106696
Multilateral		09 May 63	Tech Assistance	463UNTS159	106700
Mali	United Nations	09 May 63	Tech Assistance	463UNTS147	106699
Jamaica	United Nations	22 May 63	IGO Status/Immunit	479UNTS19	106945
Multilateral		22 May 63	Tech Assistance	483UNTS72	107007
Multilateral		24 May 63	Tech Assistance	470UNTS208	106810
Multilateral		24 May 63	Tech Assistance	466UNTS346	106754
United Nations	Uganda	29 May 63	IGO Status/Immunit	466UNTS311	106751
IAEA (Atom Energy)	Yugoslavia	04 Jun 63	Atomic Energy	490UNTS343	107163
Austria	IAEA (Atom Energy)	21 Jun 63	Atomic Energy	490UNTS351	107164
Mongolia	WHO (World Health)	21 Jun 63	Tech Assistance	472UNTS373	106848
United Nations	UK Great Britain	27 Jun 63	Trusteeship	469UNTS145	106789
Finland	IAEA (Atom Energy)	02 Jul 63	Atomic Energy	490UNTS403	107167
Multilateral		23 Jul 63	Tech Assistance	471UNTS158	106831
Finland	IAEA (Atom Energy)	30 Jul 63	Atomic Energy	490UNTS413	107168
Multilateral		31 Jul 63	Tech Assistance	472UNTS220	106842
Dominican Republic	United Nations	05 Aug 63	IGO Status/Immunit	472UNTS353	106847

PARTY ONE	PARTY TWO	DATE	TOPIC	CITATION	NUMBER
Technical Assistance (Cont.)					
Burundi	WHO (World Health)	08 Aug 63	Tech Assistance	477UNTS346	106928
Multilateral		27 Aug 63	Tech Assistance	511UNTS210	107435
United Nations	United Arab Rep	27 Aug 63	Tech Assistance	474UNTS221	106884
Burundi	WHO (World Health)	30 Aug 63	IGO Operations	490UNTS423	107169
Multilateral		10 Sep 63	Tech Assistance	480UNTS100	106965
Jamaica	WHO (World Health)	25 Sep 63	Tech Assistance	481UNTS125	106980
Multilateral		21 Oct 63	Tech Assistance	480UNTS197	106969
Jamaica	USA (United States)	24 Oct 63	General Aid	489UNTS337	107148
Panama	USA (United States)	30 Oct 63	General Aid	530UNTS3	107668
Multilateral		30 Oct 63	Tech Assistance	480UNTS180	106968
WHO (World Health)	Tanganyika	05 Nov 63	Tech Assistance	496UNTS193	107252
Multilateral		08 Nov 63	Tech Assistance	482UNTS286	106999
WHO (World Health)	Somalia	08 Nov 63	IGO Operations	493UNTS243	107218
WHO (World Health)	Sierra Leone	22 Nov 63	IGO Operations	493UNTS255	107219
Nicaragua	United Nations	03 Dec 63	IGO Status/Immunit	482UNTS329	107002
Cameroon	Netherlands	18 Dec 63	General Aid	521UNTS303	107527
Mexico	IAEA (Atom Energy)	18 Dec 63	Atomic Energy	490UNTS361	107165
Multilateral		28 Jan 64	Tech Assistance	502UNTS321	107336
United Nations	Sierra Leone	19 Feb 64	IGO Status/Immunit	489UNTS91	107136
Multilateral		20 Feb 64	Tech Assistance	491UNTS30	107172
United Nations	Upper Volta	26 Feb 64	IGO Status/Immunit	489UNTS179	107139
Israel	Philippines	16 Mar 64	Tech Assistance	550UNTS269	108021
Rwanda	WHO (World Health)	22 Jun 64	Tech Assistance	514UNTS11	107440
Rwanda	WHO (World Health)	23 Jun 64	Tech Assistance	514UNTS157	107445
Multilateral		23 Jun 64	Tech Assistance	506UNTS108	107383
WHO (World Health)	Trinidad/Tobago	23 Jun 64	Tech Assistance	503UNTS167	107342
Denmark	Kenya	26 Jun 64	Education	573UNTS107	108325
Multilateral		28 Jun 64	Tech Assistance	519UNTS14	107499
Colombia	Netherlands	06 Jul 64	General Aid	543UNTS289	107906
Multilateral		03 Aug 64	Tech Assistance	503UNTS239	107347
Kenya	USA (United States)	26 Aug 64	General Aid	531UNTS51	107692
Multilateral		24 Oct 64	Tech Assistance	514UNTS220	200608
Multilateral		11 Nov 64	Tech Assistance	515UNTS94	107456
Uganda	USA (United States)	16 Nov 64	General Aid	586UNTS143	108501
Netherlands	Nigeria	04 Dec 64	Education	545UNTS155	107931
Multilateral		15 Dec 64	Tech Assistance	522UNTS20	107533
Germany, West	Thailand	23 Dec 64	Non-IBRD Project	525UNTS193	107591
Germany, West	Thailand	23 Dec 64	Sanitation	525UNTS201	107592
Malawi	WHO (World Health)	06 Jan 65	Tech Assistance	525UNTS165	107588
Malawi	WHO (World Health)	08 Jan 65	Tech Assistance	524UNTS281	107579
WHO (World Health)	Tunisia	27 Jan 65	IGO Operations	528UNTS209	107644
Multilateral		27 Jan 65	Tech Assistance	523UNTS102	107556
Multilateral		02 Feb 65	Tech Assistance	523UNTS256	107560
Germany, West	Jamaica	03 Feb 65	Scientific Project	531UNTS143	107700
Multilateral		12 Feb 65	Tech Assistance	525UNTS148	107587
Malawi	USA (United States)	20 Apr 65	General Aid	546UNTS175	107943
Multilateral		02 Jun 65	Tech Assistance	537UNTS348	200611
UK Great Britain	USA (United States)	09 Aug 65	General Aid	580UNTS181	108420
Poland	WHO (World Health)	26 Aug 65	Tech Assistance	552UNTS3	108047
Multilateral		13 Sep 65	Tech Assistance	547UNTS264	107962
Multilateral		21 Oct 65	Tech Assistance	547UNTS216	107959
UK Great Britain	USA (United States)	10 Nov 65	General Aid	580UNTS197	108422
Saudi Arabia	USA (United States)	19 Nov 65	Non-IBRD Project	580UNTS35	108419
WHO (World Health)	Singapore	28 Mar 66	Tech Assistance	562UNTS59	108195
Maldive Islands	WHO (World Health)	23 May 66	Tech Assistance	566UNTS19	108237
Ivory Coast	Netherlands	01 Aug 66	Education	591UNTS245	108561
Multilateral		06 Aug 66	Tech Assistance	570UNTS178	108294
Multilateral		22 Aug 66	Tech Assistance	571UNTS298	200624
Multilateral		23 Sep 66	IGO Operations	573UNTS132	108327
Multilateral		30 Sep 66	IGO Operations	576UNTS8	108361
Multilateral		17 Nov 66	IGO Operations	580UNTS22	108417
Multilateral		25 Jan 67	IGO Operations	588UNTS212	108527
Multilateral		03 Mar 67	Tech Assistance	594UNTS96	108597
Multilateral		19 Apr 67	Tech Assistance	595UNTS120	108617

PARTY ONE	PARTY TWO	DATE	TOPIC	CITATION	NUMBER
Technical Cooperation					
USSR (Soviet Union)	Yugoslavia	13 Nov 45	Scientific Project	116UNTS139	101573
Albania	Yugoslavia	28 Nov 46	Non-ILO Labor	111UNTS163	101529
Thailand	USA (United States)	19 Sep 50	Tech Assistance	132UNTS199	101761
Bulgaria	Romania	29 Sep 50	Scientific Project	342UNTS141	104905
Brazil	USA (United States)	19 Dec 50	Tech Assistance	141UNTS3	101900
Panama	USA (United States)	20 Dec 50	Tech Assistance	92UNTS167	101269
Liberia	USA (United States)	22 Dec 50	Direct Aid	133UNTS69	101781
Liberia	USA (United States)	22 Dec 50	Tech Assistance	92UNTS145	101267
Nicaragua	USA (United States)	23 Dec 50	Tech Assistance	92UNTS155	101268
Paraguay	USA (United States)	29 Dec 50	Tech Assistance	122UNTS157	101645
Costa Rica	USA (United States)	11 Jan 51	Tech Assistance	92UNTS179	101270
Chile	USA (United States)	16 Jan 51	Tech Assistance	151UNTS147	101990
Saudi Arabia	USA (United States)	17 Jan 51	Direct Aid	140UNTS335	101897
Nepal	USA (United States)	23 Jan 51	Tech Assistance	184UNTS65	102439
Albania	Poland	25 Jan 51	Scientific Project	260UNTS217	103710
Honduras	USA (United States)	26 Jan 51	Tech Assistance	99UNTS49	101370
Afghanistan	USA (United States)	07 Feb 51	Tech Assistance	132UNTS265	101766
Pakistan	USA (United States)	09 Feb 51	Tech Assistance	100UNTS67	101388
Dominican Republic	USA (United States)	20 Feb 51	Tech Assistance	132UNTS305	101770
Lebanon	USA (United States)	24 Feb 51	Tech Assistance	223UNTS121	103060
Israel	USA (United States)	26 Feb 51	Tech Assistance	137UNTS57	101848
Jordan	USA (United States)	27 Feb 51	Tech Assistance	141UNTS55	101905
Colombia	USA (United States)	09 Mar 51	Tech Assistance	141UNTS15	101901
Bolivia	USA (United States)	14 Mar 51	Tech Assistance	132UNTS319	101771
Iraq	USA (United States)	10 Apr 51	Tech Assistance	151UNTS179	101993
El Salvador	USA (United States)	18 Apr 51	Tech Assistance	141UNTS37	101903
Philippines	USA (United States)	27 Apr 51	Direct Aid	174UNTS251	102290
Haiti	USA (United States)	02 May 51	Tech Assistance	151UNTS191	101994
Ecuador	USA (United States)	03 May 51	Tech Assistance	141UNTS27	101902
United Arab Rep	USA (United States)	05 May 51	Tech Assistance	198UNTS265	102670
Lebanon	USA (United States)	29 May 51	Tech Assistance	160UNTS49	102101
USA (United States)	Venezuela	07 Jun 51	Tech Assistance	141UNTS273	101918
Ethiopia	USA (United States)	16 Jun 51	Tech Assistance	148UNTS39	101933
Cuba	USA (United States)	20 Jun 51	Tech Assistance	148UNTS3	101931
Mexico	USA (United States)	27 Jun 51	Tech Assistance	141UNTS211	101916
Brazil	USA (United States)	29 Jun 51	Tech Assistance	184UNTS303	102455
UK Great Britain	USA (United States)	13 Jul 51	Tech Assistance	105UNTS71	101454
El Salvador	USA (United States)	23 Jul 51	Direct Aid	138UNTS127	101865
El Salvador	USA (United States)	23 Oct 51	Direct Aid	137UNTS43	101847
Israel	USA (United States)	07 Dec 51	Tech Assistance	157UNTS53	102046
Laos	USA (United States)	31 Dec 51	Tech Assistance	198UNTS243	102668
Indonesia	USA (United States)	05 Jan 52	Tech Assistance	215UNTS121	102916
Lebanon	USA (United States)	05 Jan 52	Tech Assistance	180UNTS199	102385
India	USA (United States)	05 Jan 52	Tech Assistance	157UNTS39	102045
El Salvador	USA (United States)	07 Jan 52	Tech Assistance	198UNTS231	102667
Guatemala	USA (United States)	08 Jan 52	Tech Assistance	181UNTS31	102395
Iran	USA (United States)	20 Jan 52	Tech Assistance	200UNTS191	102703
Libya	USA (United States)	21 Jan 52	Tech Assistance	183UNTS177	102427
Jordan	USA (United States)	12 Feb 52	Tech Assistance	168UNTS25	102211
Iraq	USA (United States)	21 Feb 52	Tech Assistance	198UNTS225	102666
OAS (Am States)	USA (United States)	03 Mar 52	Tech Assistance	165UNTS67	102168
Iraq	USA (United States)	18 Mar 52	Tech Assistance	223UNTS131	103061
El Salvador	USA (United States)	04 Apr 52	Tech Assistance	177UNTS219	102320
Israel	USA (United States)	09 May 52	Tech Assistance	177UNTS63	102309
Iraq	USA (United States)	21 May 52	Tech Assistance	212UNTS183	102870
Iraq	USA (United States)	21 May 52	Tech Assistance	205UNTS25	102767
Iraq	USA (United States)	21 May 52	Tech Assistance	206UNTS3	102782
Iraq	USA (United States)	21 May 52	Tech Assistance	205UNTS33	102768
Iraq	USA (United States)	09 Jun 52	Tech Assistance	212UNTS193	102871
Ethiopia	USA (United States)	24 Jun 52	Tech Assistance	181UNTS215	102411
Lebanon	USA (United States)	26 Jun 52	Tech Assistance	181UNTS187	102409
Brazil	USA (United States)	30 Jun 52	Tech Assistance	185UNTS79	102460
Panama	USA (United States)	08 Aug 52	Air Transport	181UNTS257	102415
Austria	Greece	20 Sep 52	General Trade	187UNTS191	102512

PARTY ONE	PARTY TWO	DATE	TOPIC	CITATION	NUMBER
Technical Cooperation (Cont.)					
USA (United States)	Venezuela	29 Sep 52	Tech Assistance	186UNTS23	102479
Iraq	USA (United States)	23 Oct 52	Tech Assistance	212UNTS201	102872
Burma	USA (United States)	24 Oct 52	Tech Assistance	222UNTS55	103022
Saudi Arabia	USA (United States)	10 Nov 52	Tech Assistance	181UNTS235	102413
Saudi Arabia	USA (United States)	10 Nov 52	Direct Aid	181UNTS295	102418
Liberia	USA (United States)	15 Dec 52	Tech Assistance	185UNTS45	102457
Saudi Arabia	USA (United States)	15 Dec 52	Direct Aid	185UNTS55	102458
Saudi Arabia	USA (United States)	15 Dec 52	Tech Assistance	185UNTS67	102459
Saudi Arabia	USA (United States)	25 Jan 53	Education	201UNTS3	102706
United Arab Rep	USA (United States)	12 Mar 53	Tech Assistance	204UNTS3	102747
United Arab Rep	USA (United States)	19 Mar 53	Tech Assistance	215UNTS17	102909
Brazil	USA (United States)	30 May 53	Tech Assistance	460UNTS89	106633
Ethiopia	USA (United States)	25 Jun 53	Tech Assistance	212UNTS175	102869
Brazil	USA (United States)	26 Jun 53	Direct Aid	336UNTS241	104808
Saudi Arabia	USA (United States)	29 Jun 53	Sanitation	206UNTS23	102784
Afghanistan	USA (United States)	30 Jun 53	Tech Assistance	215UNTS3	102908
Ethiopia	USA (United States)	30 Jun 53	Direct Aid	212UNTS135	102865
Netherlands	USA (United States)	27 Oct 53	Tech Assistance	221UNTS357	103017
Bolivia	USA (United States)	15 Jan 54	Tech Assistance	229UNTS213	103168
Multilateral		18 Jan 54	IGO Establishment	330UNTS121	104743
Netherlands	USA (United States)	22 Jan 54	Tech Assistance	190UNTS207	102565
United Arab Rep	USA (United States)	24 Feb 54	Tech Assistance	236UNTS61	103316
Mexico	USA (United States)	06 Apr 54	Tech Assistance	236UNTS69	103317
Mexico	USA (United States)	06 Apr 54	Non-IBRD Project	233UNTS163	103261
Peru	USA (United States)	13 Apr 54	Tech Assistance	236UNTS87	103318
Ethiopia	USA (United States)	21 Apr 54	Tech Assistance	232UNTS299	103244
Haiti	USA (United States)	28 May 54	Non-IBRD Project	233UNTS281	103267
Mexico	USA (United States)	07 Jun 54	Tech Assistance	234UNTS11	103269
Ethiopia	USA (United States)	12 Jun 54	Tech Assistance	234UNTS25	103270
Mexico	USA (United States)	17 Jun 54	Non-IBRD Project	237UNTS275	103352
Italy	USA (United States)	28 Jun 54	Tech Assistance	237UNTS121	103340
Costa Rica	USA (United States)	30 Jun 54	Tech Assistance	235UNTS35	103294
Colombia	USA (United States)	30 Jun 54	Non-IBRD Project	237UNTS263	103351
Brazil	USA (United States)	30 Jun 54	Non-IBRD Project	237UNTS137	103341
Guatemala	USA (United States)	01 Sep 54	Tech Assistance	199UNTS51	102677
United Arab Rep	USA (United States)	06 Nov 54	Tech Assistance	237UNTS183	103344
Mexico	USA (United States)	09 Mar 55	Tech Assistance	263UNTS247	103776
Colombia	USA (United States)	14 Jun 55	Non-IBRD Project	256UNTS211	103630
Haiti	USA (United States)	24 Jun 55	Non-IBRD Project	264UNTS291	103800
Libya	USA (United States)	21 Jul 55	Tech Assistance	264UNTS247	103796
Greece	USA (United States)	04 Aug 55	Atomic Energy	235UNTS257	103307
Liberia	USA (United States)	06 Oct 55	Tech Assistance	275UNTS93	103978
Italy	Lebanon	04 Nov 55	Tech Assistance	267UNTS147	103840
Colombia	USA (United States)	28 Nov 55	Non-IBRD Project	241UNTS39	103422
USSR (Soviet Union)	Yugoslavia	19 Dec 55	Scientific Project	378UNTS127	105423
Bulgaria	Yugoslavia	10 Feb 56	Scientific Project	349UNTS21	105007
Burma	Yugoslavia	07 Mar 56	Tech Assistance	386UNTS235	105543
USA (United States)	Uruguay	23 Mar 56	Tech Assistance	376UNTS311	105386
Czechoslovakia	Yugoslavia	03 Jul 56	General Economic	397UNTS165	105704
Germany, West	Thailand	09 Oct 56	Direct Aid	258UNTS143	103676
Romania	Yugoslavia	27 Oct 56	Scientific Project	389UNTS55	105592
Czechoslovakia	United Arab Rep	06 May 57	Tech Assistance	292UNTS317	104278
Argentina	USA (United States)	03 Jun 57	Tech Assistance	291UNTS61	104244
Ghana	USA (United States)	03 Jun 57	Tech Assistance	284UNTS63	104129
Thailand	UK Great Britain	25 Jul 57	Customs	277UNTS81	103999
USA (United States)	USSR (Soviet Union)	27 Jan 58	Health/Educ/Welfare	301UNTS405	104350
Brazil	Ecuador	05 Mar 58	General Economic	369UNTS43	105250
Brazil	Colombia	28 May 58	Tech Assistance	369UNTS141	105255
Romania	Vietnam, North	30 Jun 58	Scientific Project	389UNTS43	105591
Japan	Laos	15 Oct 58	General Aid	341UNTS25	104875
Cambodia	Japan	02 Mar 59	General Economic	341UNTS163	104882
Iraq	USSR (Soviet Union)	16 Mar 59	General Aid	346UNTS107	104979
Italy	United Arab Rep	29 Apr 59	Tech Assistance	363UNTS91	105202
Ceylon (Sri Lanka)	Yugoslavia	05 May 59	Scientific Project	391UNTS101	105618
Sudan	United Arab Rep	08 Nov 59	Specific Resources	453UNTS51	106519

PARTY ONE	PARTY TWO	DATE	TOPIC	CITATION	NUMBER
Technical Cooperation (Cont.)					
USA (United States)	USSR (Soviet Union)	21 Nov 59	Culture	361UNTS35	105172
UK Great Britain	USSR (Soviet Union)	01 Dec 59	Health/Educ/Welfare	351UNTS313	105032
Czechoslovakia	Ethiopia	11 Dec 59	Scientific Project	386UNTS45	105536
India	USSR (Soviet Union)	12 Feb 60	Culture	392UNTS153	105642
Indonesia	USSR (Soviet Union)	28 Feb 60	General Aid	392UNTS173	105643
USA (United States)	Uruguay	22 Jul 60	Education	388UNTS315	105587
France	Greece	25 Jul 60	General Aid	533UNTS227	107745
Ghana	USSR (Soviet Union)	04 Aug 60	General Aid	399UNTS61	105734
Czechoslovakia	Ghana	23 Nov 60	Tech Assistance	431UNTS85	106212
Libya	USA (United States)	11 Dec 60	Health/Educ/Welfare	445UNTS125	106381
Somalia	USA (United States)	04 Feb 61	Tech Assistance	433UNTS179	106241
Somalia	USSR (Soviet Union)	02 Jun 61	Tech Assistance	457UNTS263	106587
Czechoslovakia	Somalia	04 Jun 61	Tech Assistance	480UNTS261	106973
Cyprus	USA (United States)	29 Jun 61	General Aid	411UNTS56	105914
Tunisia	USSR (Soviet Union)	30 Aug 61	General Aid	437UNTS243	106310
Dahomey	Israel	28 Sep 61	Tech Assistance	448UNTS151	106429
Mexico	USA (United States)	15 Nov 61	Non-IBRD Project	460UNTS113	106634
Panama	USA (United States)	11 Dec 61	General Aid	445UNTS161	106384
Gabon	Israel	15 May 62	Tech Assistance	448UNTS211	106433
Ghana	Israel	25 May 62	Tech Assistance	515UNTS237	107461
Greece	Tunisia	26 May 62	General Aid	534UNTS163	107761
Central Afri Rep	Israel	13 Jun 62	Tech Assistance	448UNTS265	106439
Israel	Liberia	25 Jun 62	Tech Assistance	448UNTS287	106441
Israel	OAS (Am States)	11 Oct 62	Tech Assistance	484UNTS241	107035
Israel	Rwanda	23 Oct 62	Tech Assistance	515UNTS291	107466
Cameroon	Israel	24 Oct 62	General Aid	449UNTS3	106446
Multilateral		15 Jan 63	Tech Assistance	456UNTS409	106567
Israel	Tanganyika	28 Jan 63	Tech Assistance	516UNTS39	107468
Israel	Uganda	04 Feb 63	Tech Assistance	484UNTS273	107037
Burma	Japan	29 Mar 63	General Aid	518UNTS3	107490
Israel	Peru	02 Apr 63	Tech Assistance	515UNTS279	107465
Tanganyika	USA (United States)	09 Dec 63	Tech Assistance	526UNTS301	107612
Dominican Republic	Israel	25 Dec 63	Tech Assistance	550UNTS221	108018
Subsahara Tech Com	IAEA (Atom Energy)	06 Feb 64	IGO Operations	501UNTS285	200606
Germany, West	Thailand	02 Apr 64	Tech Assistance	503UNTS3	107338
Indonesia	Netherlands	03 Apr 64	Tech Assistance	566UNTS45	108239
Italy	Romania	16 Jun 64	Scientific Project	558UNTS313	108150
Belgium	Tunisia	15 Jul 64	Tech Assistance	560UNTS57	108168
Belgium	Tunisia	15 Jul 64	Tech Assistance	560UNTS65	108169
Multilateral		20 Aug 64	Telecommunications	514UNTS25	107441
Taiwan	Philippines	25 Aug 64	Tech Assistance	511UNTS233	107436
Ethiopia	Netherlands	28 Oct 64	Tech Assistance	541UNTS235	107872
Israel	Turkey	13 Nov 64	Tech Assistance	550UNTS303	108025
Germany, West	Jamaica	16 Dec 64	Tech Assistance	531UNTS129	107699
Germany, West	Thailand	23 Dec 64	Tech Assistance	525UNTS185	107590
Germany, West	Thailand	23 Dec 64	Scientific Project	525UNTS177	107589
Denmark	Peru	30 Dec 64	Tech Assistance	595UNTS47	108611
Colombia	Israel	15 Jan 65	Tech Assistance	581UNTS173	108441
Malta	Switzerland	20 Jan 65	General Trade	548UNTS193	107978
Denmark	Thailand	25 Jan 65	Tech Assistance	530UNTS173	107680
UK Great Britain	USSR (Soviet Union)	13 Feb 65	Health/Educ/Welfare	543UNTS43	107896
Benelux Econ Union	Poland	17 Feb 65	General Economic	547UNTS165	107956
Netherlands	Tanzania	27 Apr 65	Tech Assistance	594UNTS123	108599
Cameroon	Netherlands	06 Jul 65	Tech Assistance	571UNTS63	108299
Israel	Sierra Leone	22 Aug 65	Tech Assistance	550UNTS285	108023
Denmark	Zambia	12 Dec 65	Tech Assistance	574UNTS21	108339
Austria	Tunisia	30 Dec 65	Tech Assistance	589UNTS119	108539
Israel	Kenya	25 Feb 66	Tech Assistance	582UNTS23	108455
Brazil	Denmark	25 Feb 66	Tech Assistance	590UNTS95	108549
Denmark	Iran	14 Jun 66	Tech Assistance	597UNTS283	108652
Netherlands	Tunisia	08 Jul 66	Tech Assistance	591UNTS235	108560
Colombia	Netherlands	19 Jul 66	Tech Assistance	591UNTS201	108558
Telecommunications					
Anglo-Egypt Sudan	Fr Equatorial Afri	02 Nov 39	Telecommunications	2UNTS209	200012

Telecommunications (Cont.)

PARTY ONE	PARTY TWO	DATE	TOPIC	CITATION	NUMBER
Brazil	Uruguay	18 May 42	Telecommunications	54UNTS369	200207
Brazil	Paraguay	08 Oct 42	Telecommunications	65UNTS191	200211
Canada	USA (United States)	17 Jan 44	Mass Media	109UNTS199	200360
UK Great Britain	USSR (Soviet Union)	23 Sep 44	Telecommunications	10UNTS171	200060
Multilateral		22 Mar 45	General Amity	70UNTS237	200241
Denmark	Norway	07 Aug 45	Telecommunications	10UNTS203	200062
Multilateral		04 Dec 45	Telecommunications	9UNTS101	100128
Iraq	Turkey	29 Mar 46	General Amity	37UNTS226	100580
USA (United States)	USSR (Soviet Union)	24 May 46	Telecommunications	4UNTS201	100046
UK Great Britain	USA (United States)	31 Jul 46	Air Transport	42UNTS199	100648
South Africa	UK Great Britain	24 Aug 46	Telecommunications	51UNTS187	100765
Philippines	USA (United States)	19 Oct 46	Telecommunications	43UNTS263	100672
Norway	USA (United States)	12 Nov 46	Air Transport	42UNTS227	100651
Multilateral		07 Dec 46	Commodity Trade	157UNTS103	102050
Denmark	UK Great Britain	20 Jan 47	Telecommunications	118UNTS73	101597
Switzerland	USA (United States)	30 Apr 47	Specif Goods/Equip	42UNTS235	100652
Canada	USA (United States)	20 Aug 47	Telecommunications	27UNTS3	100392
Multilateral		02 Oct 47	Telecommunications	193UNTS188	102616
UK Great Britain	USA (United States)	13 Oct 47	Air Transport	66UNTS269	100858
Canada	USA (United States)	15 Oct 47	Telecommunications	82UNTS53	101085
Canada	USA (United States)	31 Mar 48	Specific Property	81UNTS285	101077
Canada	USA (United States)	01 Apr 48	Telecommunications	82UNTS99	101086
Multilateral		11 May 48	Telecommunications	500UNTS267	107313
France	UK Great Britain	12 Jul 48	Postal Service	90UNTS83	101230
Multilateral		17 Sep 48	Telecommunications	97UNTS31	101345
Brazil	IBRD (World Bank)	27 Jan 49	IBRD Project	153UNTS264	102026
Finland	Sweden	17 Feb 49	Specific Resources	197UNTS123	102636
Ceylon (Sri Lanka)	UK Great Britain	28 Feb 49	Gen Communications	314UNTS269	104551
Panama	USA (United States)	31 Mar 49	Telecommunications	55UNTS125	100811
Italy	UK Great Britain	14 Jun 49	Specific Property	135UNTS49	101813
Multilateral		09 Jul 49	Telecommunications	168UNTS143	102218
Multilateral		12 Aug 49	IGO Establishment	87UNTS131	101169
IBRD (World Bank)	Yugoslavia	17 Sep 49	IBRD Project	155UNTS3	102034
Finland	IBRD (World Bank)	17 Oct 49	IBRD Project	156UNTS355	200481
Greece	UK Great Britain	17 Oct 49	Postal Service	93UNTS185	101300
Afghanistan	India	14 Dec 49	Telecommunications	53UNTS95	100774
IBRD (World Bank)	Uruguay	25 Aug 50	IBRD Project	156UNTS203	102042
Liberia	USA (United States)	10 Jan 51	Gen Communications	132UNTS255	101765
Sweden	UK Great Britain	17 Jan 51	Postal Service	93UNTS225	101301
France	UK Great Britain	24 Jan 51	Postal Service	90UNTS193	101237
Canada	USA (United States)	08 Feb 51	Telecommunications	207UNTS17	102797
Ethiopia	IBRD (World Bank)	19 Feb 51	IBRD Project	186UNTS101	102486
Ceylon (Sri Lanka)	USA (United States)	14 May 51	Gen Communications	141UNTS159	101913
Mexico	USA (United States)	10 Aug 51	Telecommunications	152UNTS27	102009
Italy	UK Great Britain	12 Nov 51	Specif Claim/Waive	135UNTS55	101814
Canada	USA (United States)	21 Feb 52	Humanitarian	205UNTS293	102781
Cuba	USA (United States)	27 Feb 52	Gen Communications	168UNTS3	102209
Ecuador	USA (United States)	17 Mar 52	Telecommunications	177UNTS115	102313
Denmark	USA (United States)	04 Apr 52	Telecommunications	177UNTS13	102305
Germany, West	USA (United States)	11 Jun 52	Mass Media	273UNTS105	103947
Mexico	UK Great Britain	12 Jun 52	Telecommunications	196UNTS149	102622
Canada	USA (United States)	23 Jun 52	Telecommunications	207UNTS25	102798
Canada	USA (United States)	08 Nov 52	Gen Communications	207UNTS3	102796
Canada	USA (United States)	17 Mar 53	Telecommunications	236UNTS259	103329
Syria	Turkey	28 Apr 53	Telecommunications	204UNTS255	102760
Canada	USA (United States)	30 Jun 53	General Military	215UNTS103	102914
Luxembourg	USA (United States)	17 Aug 53	Mass Media	234UNTS219	103284
Iceland	IBRD (World Bank)	04 Sep 53	IBRD Project	188UNTS3	102519
Syria	UK Great Britain	05 Feb 54	Telecommunications	204UNTS267	102761
Canada	USA (United States)	03 May 54	Milit Assistance	221UNTS339	103015
Greece	USA (United States)	18 Aug 54	Telecommunications	234UNTS161	103282
Ceylon (Sri Lanka)	USA (United States)	23 Aug 54	Mass Media	314UNTS297	104553
Netherlands	USA (United States)	21 Mar 55	Telecommunications	289UNTS129	104217
Iceland	USA (United States)	20 Jul 55	General Military	256UNTS245	103634
Bulgaria	Yugoslavia	15 Nov 55	General Transport	396UNTS191	105697

Telecommunications (Cont.)

PARTY ONE	PARTY TWO	DATE	TOPIC	CITATION	NUMBER
Korea, North	Romania	05 Dec 55	Telecommunications	362UNTS141	105186
Panama	USA (United States)	01 Aug 56	Telecommunications	281UNTS49	104068
France	USA (United States)	06 Sep 56	Milit Installation	335UNTS173	104784
India	Poland	29 Sep 56	Telecommunications	276UNTS305	103993
Nicaragua	USA (United States)	16 Oct 56	Gen Communications	282UNTS29	104090
Costa Rica	USA (United States)	19 Oct 56	Gen Communications	278UNTS65	104022
Mexico	USA (United States)	29 Jan 57	Telecommunications	418UNTS253	106025
Dominican Republic	USA (United States)	09 Mar 57	Gen Communications	279UNTS249	104044
Albania	Yugoslavia	29 Aug 57	Postal Service	391UNTS167	105622
Mexico	USA (United States)	16 Jul 58	Telecommunications	335UNTS139	104782
Taiwan	USA (United States)	06 Aug 58	Milit Installation	462UNTS3	106666
Nicaragua	USA (United States)	05 Sep 58	Milit Installation	336UNTS33	104797
Multilateral		15 Dec 58	Mass Media	546UNTS235	107950
Canada	USA (United States)	07 Jan 59	Specific Property	391UNTS207	105624
Canada	USA (United States)	13 Apr 59	Specific Property	342UNTS43	104899
Pakistan	USA (United States)	18 Jul 59	Gen Communications	355UNTS367	105087
Mexico	USA (United States)	31 Jul 59	Gen Communications	357UNTS187	105117
Liberia	USA (United States)	13 Aug 59	Telecommunications	357UNTS181	105116
USA (United States)	Venezuela	12 Nov 59	Gen Communications	367UNTS81	105227
Haiti	USA (United States)	06 Jan 60	Gen Communications	367UNTS75	105226
Honduras	USA (United States)	19 Feb 60	Gen Communications	371UNTS109	105273
Germany, West	USA (United States)	16 Mar 60	Specific Property	371UNTS101	105272
Taiwan	USA (United States)	15 Apr 60	Milit Installation	462UNTS19	106667
Multilateral		22 Jun 60	Mass Media	546UNTS247	107951
UK Great Britain	USA (United States)	24 Jun 60	Gen Communications	377UNTS63	105396
Japan	Thailand	24 Aug 60	Education	384UNTS73	105512
Paraguay	USA (United States)	06 Oct 60	Gen Communications	393UNTS281	105662
UK Great Britain	USA (United States)	29 Mar 61	Scientific Project	405UNTS107	105826
France	USA (United States)	31 Mar 61	Scientific Project	409UNTS136	105881
Germany, West	USA (United States)	29 Sep 61	Scientific Project	424UNTS113	106103
Hungary	Iraq	11 Oct 61	Gen Communications	577UNTS231	108380
Bolivia	USA (United States)	23 Oct 61	Telecommunications	424UNTS93	106101
Brazil	USA (United States)	27 Oct 61	Telecommunications	433UNTS113	106234
Canada	Venezuela	22 Nov 61	Telecommunications	470UNTS148	106806
Taiwan	USA (United States)	28 Feb 62	Milit Installation	462UNTS25	106668
El Salvador	USA (United States)	05 Apr 62	Telecommunications	442UNTS41	106337
Mexico	USA (United States)	18 Apr 62	Telecommunications	452UNTS3	106501
Ethiopia	IBRD (World Bank)	31 May 62	IBRD Project	467UNTS237	106765
Turkey	USSR (Soviet Union)	09 Jun 62	Telecommunications	493UNTS155	107213
Canada	Mexico	30 Jul 62	Gen Communications	528UNTS257	107646
India	IDA (Devel Assoc)	14 Sep 62	Non-IBRD Project	448UNTS3	106422
Canada	Chile	14 Oct 62	Gen Communications	528UNTS273	107648
Canada	USA (United States)	24 Oct 62	Telecommunications	462UNTS67	106672
Canada	El Salvador	11 Mar 63	Gen Communications	529UNTS25	107652
Belgium	USA (United States)	19 Apr 63	Gen Communications	476UNTS29	106900
Dominican Republic	USA (United States)	22 Apr 63	Telecommunications	487UNTS169	107101
Cyprus	USA (United States)	23 Apr 63	Telecommunications	487UNTS291	107111
Philippines	USA (United States)	06 May 63	Telecommunications	477UNTS67	106916
Australia	USA (United States)	09 May 63	Milit Installation	475UNTS331	106897
Israel	USA (United States)	21 May 63	Telecommunications	487UNTS319	107113
Bolivia	Canada	31 May 63	Gen Communications	529UNTS37	107654
USA (United States)	USSR (Soviet Union)	20 Jun 63	Specif Goods/Equip	472UNTS163	106839
Costa Rica	IBRD (World Bank)	10 Jul 63	IBRD Project	482UNTS69	106991
El Salvador	IBRD (World Bank)	01 Oct 63	IBRD Project	517UNTS3	107481
Colombia	USA (United States)	29 Nov 63	Gen Communications	494UNTS49	107225
Australia	USA (United States)	03 Jan 64	Gen Communications	505UNTS159	107371
Saudi Arabia	USA (United States)	06 Jan 64	Telecommunications	531UNTS3	107689
India	IDA (Devel Assoc)	06 Jul 64	Non-IBRD Project	534UNTS49	107753
Multilateral		20 Aug 64	Telecommunications	514UNTS25	107441
Costa Rica	USA (United States)	24 Aug 64	Gen Communications	531UNTS107	107696
Canada	USA (United States)	16 Sep 64	Gen Communications	530UNTS267	107687
Germany, West	Thailand	28 Oct 64	Loans and Credits	521UNTS333	107529
Dominican Republic	USA (United States)	02 Feb 65	Gen Communications	542UNTS117	107884
Philippines	USA (United States)	16 Mar 65	Status of Forces	542UNTS199	107890
Bolivia	USA (United States)	16 Mar 65	Gen Communications	542UNTS209	107891

PARTY ONE	PARTY TWO	DATE	TOPIC	CITATION	NUMBER
Telecommunications (Cont.)					
Ecuador	USA (United States)	26 Mar 65	Gen Communications	542UNTS237	107893
Portugal	USA (United States)	26 May 65	Gen Communications	546UNTS189	107945
Brazil	USA (United States)	01 Jun 65	Gen Communications	546UNTS195	107946
Canada	USA (United States)	08 Jun 65	Gen Communications	546UNTS201	107947
Belgium	USA (United States)	18 Jun 65	Gen Communications	549UNTS95	107992
Australia	USA (United States)	25 Jun 65	Gen Communications	541UNTS155	107868
Israel	USA (United States)	07 Jul 65	Gen Communications	549UNTS281	108004
Luxembourg	USA (United States)	29 Jul 65	Gen Communications	573UNTS197	108332
Peru	USA (United States)	11 Aug 65	Gen Communications	564UNTS135	108225
Sierra Leone	USA (United States)	16 Aug 65	Telecommunications	579UNTS55	108398
Netherlands	Nigeria	28 Oct 65	Scientific Project	578UNTS15	108383
Colombia	USA (United States)	28 Oct 65	Telecommunications	574UNTS109	108343
UK Great Britain	USA (United States)	26 Nov 65	Gen Communications	561UNTS193	108181
IBRD (World Bank)	Venezuela	13 Dec 65	IBRD Project	568UNTS77	108265
Ethiopia	IBRD (World Bank)	28 Dec 65	IBRD Project	567UNTS229	108258
USA (United States)	Vietnam, South	03 Jan 66	Mass Media	579UNTS99	108401
Paraguay	USA (United States)	18 Apr 66	Gen Communications	586UNTS189	108503
France	USA (United States)	05 May 66	Admin Cooperation	593UNTS279	108589
India	USA (United States)	25 May 66	Gen Communications	593UNTS157	108582
Israel	USA (United States)	15 Jun 66	Telecommunications	578UNTS159	108393
Netherlands	USA (United States)	22 Jun 66	Gen Communications	590UNTS109	108550
Kuwait	USA (United States)	24 Jul 66	Gen Communications	593UNTS289	108590
Canada	Israel	12 Sep 66	Telecommunications	581UNTS167	108440
Jamaica	IBRD (World Bank)	23 Jan 67	IBRD Project	594UNTS311	108608
IBRD (World Bank)	Tanzania	17 Feb 67	IBRD Project	599UNTS287	108671
Kenya	IBRD (World Bank)	17 Feb 67	IBRD Project	599UNTS233	108669
East Afri Service	IBRD (World Bank)	17 Feb 67	IBRD Project	599UNTS335	200629
IBRD (World Bank)	Uganda	17 Feb 67	IBRD Project	599UNTS321	108673
Indonesia	Philippines	21 Feb 67	Gen Communications	593UNTS109	108578
Textile Industry					
Brazil	Japan	28 Mar 62	Education	451UNTS125	106489
Timber and Timber Floating					
Finland	USSR (Soviet Union)	28 Oct 22	Specific Resources	67UNTS153	100873
Multilateral		10 Feb 47	Peace/Disarmament	48UNTS203	100746
Finland	Sweden	17 Feb 49	Specific Resources	197UNTS123	102636
Tin					
Multilateral		01 Mar 54	Commodity Trade	256UNTS31	103622
Thailand	USA (United States)	11 Aug 54	Commodity Trade	234UNTS155	103281
Thailand	USA (United States)	09 Sep 55	Commodity Trade	264UNTS285	103799
Multilateral		01 Sep 60	Commodity Trade	403UNTS3	105792
Tobacco					
Ceylon (Sri Lanka)	India	13 Jan 58	Commodity Trade	315UNTS107	104562
Tolls					
Belgium	Netherlands	24 Oct 57	Water Transport	489UNTS3	107131
Belgium	Netherlands	24 Oct 57	Water Transport	489UNTS11	107132
Canada	USA (United States)	13 Jul 62	Water Transport	460UNTS83	106632
Touring					
Multilateral		16 Jun 49	Land Transport	45UNTS149	100696
Multilateral		04 Jun 54	Customs	276UNTS191	103992
Greece	Yugoslavia	11 Sep 56	Admin Cooperation	391UNTS117	105620
Greece	Yugoslavia	18 Jun 59	IGO Establishment	368UNTS17	105233
Netherlands	UK Great Britain	01 Apr 60	Visas	374UNTS277	105341
Multilateral		16 Dec 61	Visas	544UNTS19	107909
Italy	United Nations	26 Jul 63	IGO Operations	472UNTS173	106840
Czechoslovakia	Yugoslavia	14 Mar 64	Visas	544UNTS147	107917
Czechoslovakia	USSR (Soviet Union)	17 Sep 65	Visas	549UNTS221	108001
Trade					
Multilateral		12 May 40	Scientific Project	101UNTS91	101405
Canada	USA (United States)	13 Dec 40	General Trade	117UNTS173	200368
USA (United States)	USSR (Soviet Union)	02 Aug 41	General Trade	102UNTS269	200306
Argentina	USA (United States)	14 Oct 41	General Trade	119UNTS193	200384
Cuba	USA (United States)	23 Dec 41	General Trade	119UNTS313	200388

PARTY ONE	PARTY TWO	DATE	TOPIC	CITATION	NUMBER
Trade (Cont.)					
Haiti	USA (United States)	19 Feb 42	Customs	105UNTS238	200336
Ecuador	USA (United States)	02 Mar 42	General Trade	105UNTS195	200332
Peru	USA (United States)	07 May 42	General Trade	103UNTS219	200316
USA (United States)	Uruguay	21 Jul 42	General Trade	120UNTS211	200393
Iran	USA (United States)	08 Apr 43	General Trade	106UNTS155	200340
Colombia	USA (United States)	17 Apr 45	Customs	139UNTS303	200457
Romania	Yugoslavia	15 Dec 45	General Economic	116UNTS3	101565
Poland	Yugoslavia	18 Jan 46	General Trade	115UNTS83	101559
Canada	Netherlands	05 Feb 46	General Trade	230UNTS199	103184
Canada	Mexico	08 Feb 46	General Trade	230UNTS183	103183
Albania	Yugoslavia	01 Jul 46	General Economic	111UNTS3	101517
Philippines	USA (United States)	04 Jul 46	General Trade	43UNTS135	100668
Paraguay	USA (United States)	12 Sep 46	General Trade	125UNTS179	101677
Albania	Yugoslavia	03 Oct 46	General Trade	111UNTS227	101537
Canada	Nicaragua	19 Dec 46	General Trade	236UNTS229	103326
Hungary	Yugoslavia	01 Jan 47	General Trade	113UNTS63	101548
Romania	USSR (Soviet Union)	20 Feb 47	General Economic	226UNTS79	103110
Czechoslovakia	Yugoslavia	25 Feb 47	General Trade	112UNTS3	101539
Canada	USA (United States)	18 Mar 47	Commodity Trade	117UNTS79	101584
Poland	Yugoslavia	24 May 47	General Trade	115UNTS37	101557
Poland	Yugoslavia	24 May 47	General Trade	115UNTS89	101560
Albania	Yugoslavia	12 Jun 47	Loans and Credits	111UNTS189	101533
Albania	Yugoslavia	22 Jun 47	General Trade	111UNTS207	101536
Denmark	Yugoslavia	28 Jun 47	General Economic	78UNTS242	101020
Hungary	Yugoslavia	24 Jul 47	General Trade	114UNTS3	101554
USSR (Soviet Union)	Yugoslavia	25 Jul 47	Tech Assistance	130UNTS315	101732
Czechoslovakia	Greece	30 Jul 47	Claims and Debts	185UNTS143	102465
Czechoslovakia	Greece	30 Jul 47	Finance	185UNTS115	102463
USSR (Soviet Union)	Yugoslavia	23 Aug 47	Reparations	116UNTS281	101577
Multilateral		30 Oct 47	General Economic	55UNTS188	100814
Cuba	USA (United States)	30 Oct 47	General Economic	119UNTS163	101611
Belgium	USA (United States)	30 Oct 47	General Economic	125UNTS103	101672
UK Great Britain	USA (United States)	30 Oct 47	General Economic	126UNTS39	101680
France	USA (United States)	30 Oct 47	General Economic	125UNTS171	101676
Poland	Yugoslavia	07 Nov 47	General Economic	115UNTS137	101561
Italy	USA (United States)	02 Feb 48	General Amity	79UNTS171	101040
Romania	USA (United States)	26 Feb 48	Admin Cooperation	48UNTS9	100738
Italy	UK Great Britain	13 Mar 48	Admin Cooperation	104UNTS41	101435
Romania	UK Great Britain	13 Mar 48	Admin Cooperation	104UNTS117	101436
Canada	Turkey	15 Mar 48	General Economic	231UNTS63	103205
Switzerland	USSR (Soviet Union)	17 Mar 48	General Trade	217UNTS87	102945
Hungary	Yugoslavia	18 Mar 48	General Trade	113UNTS141	101550
Czechoslovakia	Yugoslavia	10 Apr 48	General Economic	112UNTS101	101541
Poland	Yugoslavia	12 Apr 48	General Trade	115UNTS167	101563
France	Ireland	06 May 48	General Trade	558UNTS170	108141
Brazil	UK Great Britain	21 May 48	Finance	66UNTS121	100851
Czechoslovakia	Yugoslavia	24 May 48	General Trade	112UNTS111	101542
Czechoslovakia	Yugoslavia	24 May 48	Specif Goods/Equip	112UNTS215	101544
Spain	UK Great Britain	23 Jun 48	General Economic	66UNTS193	100854
Greece	Sweden	25 Jun 48	General Trade	267UNTS337	103849
Brazil	USA (United States)	30 Jun 48	General Trade	125UNTS111	101673
UK Great Britain	USA (United States)	06 Jul 48	Milit Occupation	25UNTS61	100358
Ireland	UK Great Britain	31 Jul 48	General Trade	86UNTS37	101151
Ireland	Netherlands	02 Sep 48	General Trade	558UNTS249	108145
Canada	Finland	17 Nov 48	General Trade	231UNTS75	103207
Austria	Denmark	29 Nov 48	General Trade	74UNTS243	100967
USSR (Soviet Union)	Yugoslavia	27 Dec 48	General Trade	116UNTS327	101579
Poland	Yugoslavia	16 Jan 49	General Trade	115UNTS241	101564
Czechoslovakia	Yugoslavia	01 Mar 49	General Trade	113UNTS3	101547
Greece	Norway	12 Mar 49	General Trade	30UNTS161	100454
Finland	Greece	24 Mar 49	General Trade	78UNTS3	101008
Multilateral		04 May 49	Milit Occupation	138UNTS123	101864
Ireland	Sweden	25 Jun 49	General Trade	558UNTS299	108148
Argentina	UK Great Britain	27 Jun 49	General Economic	83UNTS217	101110
Colombia	USA (United States)	12 Oct 49	General Trade	133UNTS15	101774

Trade (Cont.)

PARTY ONE	PARTY TWO	DATE	TOPIC	CITATION	NUMBER
Ireland	Netherlands	25 Nov 49	General Trade	558UNTS256	108146
UK Great Britain	Yugoslavia	26 Dec 49	General Trade	87UNTS71	101167
Haiti	USA (United States)	29 Dec 49	General Trade	133UNTS21	101775
Mexico	Netherlands	27 Jan 50	General Trade	123UNTS197	101661
Nicaragua	USA (United States)	28 Feb 50	General Trade	132UNTS169	101758
Paraguay	UK Great Britain	03 Apr 50	General Economic	99UNTS81	101372
Afghanistan	India	04 Apr 50	General Trade	167UNTS105	102201
Costa Rica	USA (United States)	04 Apr 50	General Trade	132UNTS177	101759
Austria	Greece	11 May 50	General Trade	184UNTS217	102450
Germany, West	Ireland	12 Jul 50	General Trade	557UNTS221	108136
India	Nepal	31 Jul 50	General Economic	104UNTS3	101430
Belgium	Japan	29 Aug 50	General Trade	76UNTS113	100984
Belgium	Mexico	16 Sep 50	General Trade	188UNTS119	102523
Austria	Ireland	06 Oct 50	General Trade	557UNTS173	108133
Canada	Venezuela	11 Oct 50	General Economic	231UNTS3	103198
Switzerland	USA (United States)	13 Oct 50	General Trade	133UNTS33	101777
Iceland	Ireland	02 Dec 50	General Trade	558UNTS231	108143
Multilateral		15 Dec 50	Customs	171UNTS305	102234
Norway	UK Great Britain	15 Dec 50	General Trade	106UNTS87	101459
Finland	Ireland	06 Jan 51	General Trade	558UNTS120	108140
Denmark	Hungary	10 Feb 51	General Trade	85UNTS49	101145
Germany, West	Greece	12 Feb 51	General Trade	198UNTS193	102665
Pakistan	UK Great Britain	02 Apr 51	General Trade	168UNTS281	102219
Norway	Pakistan	21 May 51	General Trade	318UNTS163	104613
Denmark	Portugal	05 Jun 51	General Trade	101UNTS61	101402
Denmark	Spain	03 Jul 51	General Trade	101UNTS51	101401
Germany, West	Ireland	23 Jul 51	General Trade	558UNTS3	108137
Cuba	UK Great Britain	10 Aug 51	General Trade	108UNTS243	101478
France	USSR (Soviet Union)	03 Sep 51	General Trade	221UNTS79	103003
Denmark	Switzerland	15 Sep 51	General Trade	110UNTS55	101501
Peru	USA (United States)	28 Sep 51	General Trade	160UNTS35	102099
Burma	India	29 Sep 51	General Trade	132UNTS71	101752
Denmark	Italy	24 Oct 51	General Trade	118UNTS91	101598
El Salvador	Guatemala	14 Dec 51	General Economic	131UNTS131	101740
Ireland	Switzerland	26 Dec 51	General Trade	558UNTS305	108149
Multilateral		04 Feb 52	General Economic	124UNTS3	101662
Ireland	Portugal	06 Feb 52	General Trade	558UNTS289	108147
India	Syria	25 Feb 52	General Amity	163UNTS55	102141
Belgium	Pakistan	15 Mar 52	General Trade	316UNTS65	104578
Austria	Greece	22 Mar 52	General Economic	187UNTS255	102517
Czechoslovakia	Denmark	04 Apr 52	General Trade	133UNTS245	101792
Multilateral		16 Apr 52	General Economic	139UNTS35	101874
Greece	Syria	02 Jun 52	General Trade	183UNTS251	102434
Denmark	Poland	09 Jun 52	General Trade	135UNTS209	101822
Greece	Israel	22 Jul 52	General Economic	219UNTS231	102978
Germany, West	Greece	28 Jul 52	General Trade	182UNTS85	102424
Denmark	Spain	28 Jul 52	Commodity Trade	135UNTS255	101825
France	Greece	31 Jul 52	General Trade	187UNTS169	102510
Greece	Sweden	19 Aug 52	General Trade	189UNTS117	102544
USA (United States)	Venezuela	28 Aug 52	General Trade	178UNTS51	102336
Denmark	Portugal	29 Aug 52	General Trade	149UNTS49	101950
Ceylon (Sri Lanka)	Japan	06 Sep 52	General Economic	314UNTS279	104552
Denmark	Greece	15 Sep 52	General Trade	187UNTS207	102513
Austria	Greece	20 Sep 52	General Trade	187UNTS191	102512
Germany, West	Ireland	26 Sep 52	General Trade	558UNTS27	108138
New Zealand	Switzerland	09 Oct 52	General Trade	171UNTS275	102231
United Arab Rep	UK Great Britain	19 Oct 52	General Trade	158UNTS423	102075
Denmark	Italy	28 Oct 52	General Trade	167UNTS125	102202
Multilateral		07 Nov 52	General Trade	221UNTS255	103010
Australia	Iceland	13 Nov 52	General Trade	161UNTS59	102122
Denmark	Israel	14 Nov 52	General Trade	160UNTS279	102113
Denmark	Israel	14 Nov 52	General Economic	160UNTS275	102112
Canada	United Arab Rep	03 Dec 52	Mostfavored Nation	233UNTS145	103259
France	Greece	23 Dec 52	General Trade	187UNTS175	102511
Greece	Italy	04 Feb 53	General Trade	189UNTS269	102551

Trade (Cont.)

PARTY ONE	PARTY TWO	DATE	TOPIC	CITATION	NUMBER
Greece	Netherlands	05 Feb 53	General Trade	263UNTS361	103783
Turkey	Yugoslavia	26 Feb 53	General Trade	247UNTS54	103460
Greece	Yugoslavia	28 Feb 53	General Economic	252UNTS27	103557
Czechoslovakia	Denmark	23 Apr 53	General Trade	174UNTS95	102280
France	Japan	25 Apr 53	Admin Cooperation	187UNTS41	102500
Brazil	Ecuador	04 May 53	General Trade	369UNTS37	105249
Greece	United Arab Rep	21 May 53	General Trade	256UNTS17	103620
Japan	Syria	08 Jun 53	General Trade	184UNTS3	102436
Fed Rhod/Nyasaland	South Africa	28 Jun 53	General Trade	267UNTS270	103848
Burma	Yugoslavia	29 Jun 53	General Trade	378UNTS83	105418
Denmark	USSR (Soviet Union)	17 Jul 53	General Trade	175UNTS3	102292
India	Yugoslavia	24 Jul 53	General Trade	394UNTS13	105665
Greece	Sweden	24 Jul 53	General Trade	189UNTS309	102553
Ireland	Italy	27 Jul 53	General Trade	558UNTS237	108144
Ceylon (Sri Lanka)	Yugoslavia	30 Jul 53	General Trade	337UNTS103	104819
Argentina	USSR (Soviet Union)	05 Aug 53	General Economic	221UNTS99	103004
Ethiopia	Yugoslavia	21 Aug 53	General Economic	378UNTS105	105421
Denmark	Greece	19 Oct 53	General Trade	225UNTS9	103082
Greece	Turkey	07 Nov 53	General Trade	225UNTS163	103098
Canada	USA (United States)	12 Nov 53	General Economic	223UNTS139	103062
Ceylon (Sri Lanka)	Ireland	20 Nov 53	General Economic	345UNTS189	104967
USA (United States)	Uruguay	30 Nov 53	General Trade	229UNTS25	103158
Germany, West	Ireland	02 Dec 53	General Trade	558UNTS38	108139
India	USSR (Soviet Union)	02 Dec 53	General Trade	240UNTS143	103402
Bulgaria	Greece	05 Dec 53	General Trade	225UNTS135	103095
Cuba	UK Great Britain	18 Dec 53	General Trade	186UNTS157	102490
Czechoslovakia	Greece	01 Feb 54	General Trade	225UNTS77	103091
Australia	Belgium	26 Mar 54	General Trade	198UNTS305	102673
Denmark	Italy	10 Apr 54	General Trade	196UNTS175	102623
China People's Rep	India	29 Apr 54	General Trade	299UNTS57	104307
Lebanon	USSR (Soviet Union)	30 Apr 54	General Economic	226UNTS109	103111
Pakistan	Yugoslavia	15 May 54	General Trade	286UNTS3	104158
Greece	Spain	15 May 54	General Trade	299UNTS261	104318
Greece	Romania	19 May 54	General Trade	225UNTS17	103083
Canada	Spain	26 May 54	General Trade	391UNTS273	105632
Canada	Portugal	28 May 54	General Trade	391UNTS253	105631
Greece	Hungary	05 Jun 54	General Trade	299UNTS285	104320
Greece	Portugal	13 Jul 54	General Trade	230UNTS19	103173
Finland	USSR (Soviet Union)	17 Jul 54	General Trade	240UNTS173	103403
France	Greece	22 Jul 54	General Trade	225UNTS199	103099
Thailand	USA (United States)	11 Aug 54	Commodity Trade	234UNTS155	103281
Greece	USSR (Soviet Union)	02 Sep 54	General Trade	230UNTS33	103175
Greece	Netherlands	01 Nov 54	General Trade	223UNTS79	103057
Greece	Italy	10 Nov 54	General Trade	227UNTS9	103128
Turkey	USA (United States)	15 Nov 54	Commodity Trade	238UNTS135	103358
Ceylon (Sri Lanka)	United Arab Rep	17 Nov 54	General Trade	315UNTS3	104554
Multilateral		29 Nov 54	General Trade	287UNTS209	104187
India	Iran	15 Dec 54	General Economic	327UNTS245	104724
USSR (Soviet Union)	Yugoslavia	05 Jan 55	General Trade	240UNTS207	103404
Austria	Yugoslavia	18 Jan 55	Mass Media	378UNTS31	105416
Greece	Japan	12 Mar 55	General Trade	227UNTS33	103130
Bulgaria	Yugoslavia	16 Mar 55	General Economic	397UNTS83	105702
Canada	South Africa	21 Mar 55	Commodity Trade	213UNTS291	102892
Italy	Yugoslavia	31 Mar 55	General Trade	386UNTS317	105551
Argentina	UK Great Britain	31 Mar 55	General Economic	210UNTS223	102840
Ceylon (Sri Lanka)	Germany, West	01 Apr 55	General Trade	369UNTS57	105251
Argentina	USA (United States)	25 Apr 55	US Agri Commod Aid	251UNTS283	103546
Ceylon (Sri Lanka)	Pakistan	23 May 55	General Trade	286UNTS15	104159
France	Ireland	07 Jun 55	General Trade	558UNTS217	108142
France	Greece	28 Jun 55	General Trade	225UNTS219	103100
Australia	Fed Rhod/Nyasaland	30 Jun 55	General Trade	226UNTS215	103115
Greece	Netherlands	14 Jul 55	General Trade	227UNTS27	103129
Greece	Sweden	30 Jul 55	General Trade	225UNTS243	103102
Greece	USSR (Soviet Union)	23 Aug 55	General Trade	233UNTS39	103249
Denmark	Greece	29 Aug 55	General Trade	230UNTS25	103174

PARTY ONE	PARTY TWO	DATE	TOPIC	CITATION	NUMBER
Trade (Cont.)					
Thailand	USA (United States)	09 Sep 55	Commodity Trade	264UNTS285	103799
Guatemala	USA (United States)	28 Sep 55	General Trade	257UNTS307	103663
Austria	USSR (Soviet Union)	17 Oct 55	General Economic	240UNTS289	103409
Italy	Lebanon	04 Nov 55	General Trade	267UNTS113	103838
Italy	Syria	10 Nov 55	General Trade	267UNTS157	103841
Thailand	USA (United States)	14 Nov 55	Commodity Trade	239UNTS201	103380
Syria	USSR (Soviet Union)	16 Nov 55	General Economic	259UNTS71	103683
Paraguay	UK Great Britain	21 Nov 55	General Economic	252UNTS107	103560
Pakistan	Syria	18 Dec 55	General Trade	320UNTS269	104647
Costa Rica	Guatemala	20 Dec 55	General Economic	280UNTS121	104056
Argentina	USA (United States)	21 Dec 55	Commodity Trade	240UNTS329	103411
Nicaragua	USA (United States)	21 Jan 56	General Amity	367UNTS3	105224
Denmark	UK Great Britain	27 Feb 56	Commodity Trade	252UNTS83	103558
Canada	USSR (Soviet Union)	29 Feb 56	General Trade	252UNTS165	103566
Burma	Sweden	06 Mar 56	General Trade	369UNTS275	105261
Iceland	USA (United States)	06 Mar 56	General Trade	270UNTS205	103898
Burma	Yugoslavia	07 Mar 56	Commodity Trade	386UNTS207	105542
Ceylon (Sri Lanka)	Romania	16 Mar 56	General Trade	315UNTS41	104558
Germany, West	Italy	19 Apr 56	General Trade	281UNTS195	104080
Denmark	Italy	12 May 56	General Trade	260UNTS357	103720
Denmark	USSR (Soviet Union)	14 May 56	General Trade	271UNTS125	103912
Ceylon (Sri Lanka)	Hungary	04 Jun 56	General Trade	315UNTS13	104555
Burma	UK Great Britain	18 Jun 56	Commodity Trade	256UNTS125	103623
Bulgaria	Ceylon (Sri Lanka)	19 Jun 56	General Trade	315UNTS23	104556
France	Greece	25 Jun 56	General Trade	251UNTS167	103540
Argentina	UK Great Britain	30 Jun 56	General Economic	269UNTS235	103884
Indonesia	UK Great Britain	02 Jul 56	Commodity Trade	265UNTS285	103820
Indonesia	UK Great Britain	02 Jul 56	Commodity Trade	265UNTS271	103819
Multilateral		16 Aug 56	General Trade	287UNTS223	104188
Guatemala	Honduras	22 Aug 56	General Economic	263UNTS49	103767
Denmark	Greece	04 Sep 56	General Trade	256UNTS319	103643
Costa Rica	Denmark	26 Sep 56	General Economic	341UNTS305	104893
Taiwan	Philippines	18 Oct 56	General Trade	541UNTS57	107860
Japan	USSR (Soviet Union)	19 Oct 56	General Economic	263UNTS119	103769
Korea, South	USA (United States)	28 Nov 56	General Amity	302UNTS281	104367
Indonesia	Yugoslavia	14 Dec 56	General Trade	378UNTS117	105422
Austria	Pakistan	24 Dec 56	General Trade	316UNTS83	104579
Australia	UK Great Britain	26 Feb 57	General Trade	265UNTS197	103813
Turkey	UK Great Britain	28 Feb 57	General Economic	310UNTS69	104488
Morocco	UK Great Britain	01 Mar 57	General Economic	310UNTS3	104480
Japan	Switzerland	25 Mar 57	Visas	318UNTS239	104618
Ceylon (Sri Lanka)	Italy	23 Apr 57	General Trade	337UNTS115	104820
Denmark	Peru	10 Jun 57	General Economic	406UNTS63	105839
UK Great Britain	USA (United States)	27 Jun 57	General Economic	284UNTS75	104130
Multilateral		27 Jun 57	General Economic	284UNTS139	104133
Australia	Japan	06 Jul 57	General Trade	318UNTS381	104627
Denmark	Italy	12 Jul 57	General Trade	291UNTS169	104251
Ceylon (Sri Lanka)	China People's Rep	19 Sep 57	General Economic	337UNTS137	104821
Germany, East	USSR (Soviet Union)	27 Sep 57	General Economic	292UNTS75	104268
Denmark	UK Great Britain	18 Nov 57	General Trade	403UNTS153	105794
Argentina	Denmark	25 Nov 57	General Economic	299UNTS83	104308
Multilateral		25 Nov 57	General Trade	403UNTS169	105795
Argentina	Italy	25 Nov 57	General Economic	305UNTS275	104424
China People's Rep	Denmark	01 Dec 57	General Economic	309UNTS241	104475
Japan	USSR (Soviet Union)	06 Dec 57	General Economic	325UNTS35	104694
India	Japan	04 Feb 58	General Trade	324UNTS215	104687
Canada	Fed Rhod/Nyasaland	06 Feb 58	General Trade	392UNTS27	105636
Ceylon (Sri Lanka)	USSR (Soviet Union)	08 Feb 58	General Trade	348UNTS159	104999
Albania	USSR (Soviet Union)	15 Feb 58	General Economic	313UNTS261	104536
Bulgaria	Italy	25 Feb 58	General Trade	362UNTS291	105194
USSR (Soviet Union)	Vietnam, North	12 Mar 58	General Economic	356UNTS149	105094
Belgium	Luxembourg	28 Mar 58	General Trade	303UNTS101	104372
Italy	Tunisia	08 Apr 58	General Trade	378UNTS327	105430
China People's Rep	USSR (Soviet Union)	23 Apr 58	General Economic	313UNTS135	104534
Germany, West	USSR (Soviet Union)	25 Apr 58	General Economic	346UNTS71	104978

PARTY ONE	PARTY TWO	DATE	TOPIC	CITATION	NUMBER
Trade (Cont.)					
Japan	Poland	26 Apr 58	General Economic	340UNTS221	104866
Multilateral		10 Jun 58	General Economic	454UNTS47	106539
Multilateral		18 Jun 58	General Trade	386UNTS345	105552
Italy	Morocco	24 Jun 58	General Trade	363UNTS23	105197
Denmark	El Salvador	09 Jul 58	General Economic	341UNTS289	104892
Burma	USA (United States)	25 Aug 58	Commodity Trade	336UNTS3	104795
Australia	Fed of Malaya	26 Aug 58	General Trade	325UNTS253	104703
Japan	New Zealand	09 Sep 58	General Trade	325UNTS119	104698
Iraq	USSR (Soviet Union)	11 Oct 58	General Trade	328UNTS95	104730
Iraq	USSR (Soviet Union)	11 Oct 58	General Trade	328UNTS117	104731
Fed Rhod/Nyasaland	Portugal	29 Nov 58	General Trade	354UNTS137	105060
Israel	Yugoslavia	11 Dec 58	General Trade	386UNTS271	105547
Haiti	Japan	17 Dec 58	General Economic	518UNTS91	107492
Iraq	Romania	24 Dec 58	General Trade	405UNTS243	105836
Burma	UK Great Britain	20 Jan 59	Commodity Trade	343UNTS201	104926
Burma	UK Great Britain	06 Feb 59	Commodity Trade	343UNTS223	104927
Czechoslovakia	United Arab Rep	07 Feb 59	General Economic	372UNTS243	105301
Costa Rica	IBRD (World Bank)	11 Feb 59	IBRD Project	337UNTS245	104825
Japan	Yugoslavia	28 Feb 59	General Economic	341UNTS179	104883
Germany, West	New Zealand	20 Apr 59	General Trade	402UNTS125	105782
UK Great Britain	USSR (Soviet Union)	24 May 59	General Trade	374UNTS305	105344
Ethiopia	Greece	22 Jun 59	General Economic	534UNTS147	107759
New Zealand	UK Great Britain	12 Aug 59	General Trade	354UNTS161	105062
Multilateral		01 Sep 59	Customs	454UNTS289	106542
India	Italy	06 Oct 59	General Trade	378UNTS267	105427
Australia	Germany, West	14 Oct 59	General Trade	345UNTS35	104957
Guinea	UK Great Britain	22 Oct 59	General Trade	351UNTS341	105033
Italy	Tunisia	31 Oct 59	General Trade	378UNTS349	105431
Pakistan	USA (United States)	12 Nov 59	General Amity	404UNTS259	105816
Tunisia	UK Great Britain	16 Nov 59	General Trade	354UNTS367	105070
Czechoslovakia	Germany, East	25 Nov 59	General Economic	374UNTS101	105331
Argentina	Brazil	26 Nov 59	General Trade	374UNTS31	105325
Argentina	Brazil	26 Nov 59	General Trade	374UNTS45	105327
Argentina	Brazil	26 Nov 59	General Trade	374UNTS39	105326
Czechoslovakia	Japan	15 Dec 59	General Trade	383UNTS277	105505
Australia	Indonesia	17 Dec 59	General Trade	354UNTS109	105058
Albania	Yugoslavia	29 Dec 59	General Trade	396UNTS63	105693
Denmark	Sweden	04 Jan 60	General Trade	376UNTS375	105390
Multilateral		04 Jan 60	IGO Establishment	370UNTS3	105266
Australia	Canada	12 Feb 60	General Trade	369UNTS89	105253
Cuba	USSR (Soviet Union)	13 Feb 60	General Economic	369UNTS17	105248
Greece	Tunisia	02 Mar 60	General Trade	483UNTS89	107008
Austria	Guatemala	18 Mar 60	General Trade	379UNTS89	105435
Austria	El Salvador	23 Mar 60	General Trade	390UNTS3	105599
Switzerland	USA (United States)	29 Mar 60	General Trade	371UNTS155	105277
Iran	USA (United States)	12 Apr 60	General Trade	372UNTS63	105288
Cuba	Japan	22 Apr 60	General Trade	442UNTS261	106354
Fed of Malaya	Japan	10 May 60	General Trade	383UNTS293	105506
Fed Rhod/Nyasaland	South Africa	16 May 60	General Trade	376UNTS217	105381
Cuba	Czechoslovakia	10 Jun 60	General Trade	447UNTS75	106412
Austria	Spain	17 Jun 60	General Trade	390UNTS17	105600
Korea, North	USSR (Soviet Union)	22 Jun 60	General Economic	399UNTS3	105732
Multilateral		28 Jul 60	IGO Status/Immunit	394UNTS37	105667
Ghana	USSR (Soviet Union)	04 Aug 60	General Trade	421UNTS27	106050
Cuba	Korea, North	29 Aug 60	Consul/Citizenship	469UNTS163	106790
New Zealand	Yugoslavia	09 Sep 60	General Trade	402UNTS119	105781
Belgium	Ireland	23 Sep 60	Commodity Trade	557UNTS180	108134
Multilateral		08 Oct 60	General Trade	450UNTS309	106476
Greece	Poland	08 Nov 60	General Trade	483UNTS127	107010
Multilateral		13 Dec 60	General Economic	455UNTS3	106543
Japan	Pakistan	18 Dec 60	General Amity	423UNTS197	106093
Albania	Cuba	16 Jan 61	General Trade	448UNTS67	106425
Honduras	USA (United States)	18 Jan 61	General Trade	402UNTS169	105785
Malaysia	New Zealand	03 Feb 61	General Trade	447UNTS251	106418
Korea, South	Philippines	24 Feb 61	General Trade	423UNTS217	106094

PARTY ONE	PARTY TWO	DATE	TOPIC	CITATION	NUMBER
Trade (Cont.)					
Multilateral		27 Mar 61	IGO Establishment	420UNTS109	106043
USA (United States)	Vietnam, South	03 Apr 61	General Amity	424UNTS137	106106
Japan	Peru	15 May 61	General Trade	451UNTS3	106482
Somalia	USSR (Soviet Union)	02 Jun 61	General Trade	493UNTS173	107214
Japan	USA (United States)	22 Jun 61	General Economic	410UNTS53	105896
Indonesia	UK Great Britain	29 Jun 61	General Economic	443UNTS255	106364
Indonesia	Japan	01 Jul 61	General Amity	517UNTS107	107484
Austria	Romania	21 Jul 61	General Trade	421UNTS161	106057
Albania	Austria	27 Jul 61	General Economic	407UNTS37	105858
Sweden	USA (United States)	05 Sep 61	General Economic	421UNTS241	106062
Korea, South	Thailand	15 Sep 61	General Trade	413UNTS137	105948
Pakistan	Philippines	29 Sep 61	General Trade	422UNTS3	106065
Greece	Morocco	01 Nov 61	General Trade	483UNTS113	107009
Ghana	USSR (Soviet Union)	04 Nov 61	General Trade	437UNTS213	106308
Saudi Arabia	Syria	16 Nov 61	General Economic	491UNTS163	107177
Argentina	Thailand	10 Dec 61	General Trade	422UNTS87	106070
Peru	USA (United States)	05 Mar 62	General Economic	446UNTS65	106404
Finland	USA (United States)	05 Mar 62	General Economic	446UNTS19	106399
Sweden	USA (United States)	05 Mar 62	Commodity Trade	459UNTS17	106610
Denmark	USA (United States)	05 Mar 62	General Economic	446UNTS9	106398
Pakistan	USA (United States)	05 Mar 62	General Trade	446UNTS57	106403
Portugal	USA (United States)	05 Mar 62	General Trade	436UNTS101	106290
New Zealand	USA (United States)	05 Mar 62	General Economic	446UNTS39	106401
Norway	USA (United States)	05 Mar 62	General Economic	446UNTS47	106402
Israel	USA (United States)	05 Mar 62	General Economic	446UNTS29	106400
Canada	USA (United States)	07 Mar 62	General Trade	436UNTS3	106286
UK Great Britain	USA (United States)	07 Mar 62	General Economic	446UNTS231	106406
EEC (Econ Commnty)	USA (United States)	07 Mar 62	General Trade	445UNTS195	106387
EEC (Econ Commnty)	USA (United States)	07 Mar 62	General Trade	436UNTS49	106288
EEC (Econ Commnty)	USA (United States)	07 Mar 62	General Economic	446UNTS81	106405
Japan	New Zealand	09 Mar 62	General Trade	485UNTS339	107065
Brazil	USA (United States)	19 Apr 62	General Trade	456UNTS255	106560
El Salvador	USA (United States)	15 May 62	General Trade	452UNTS49	106503
Guatemala	USA (United States)	21 May 62	General Trade	451UNTS205	106495
Haiti	USA (United States)	06 Jun 62	General Trade	452UNTS59	106504
United Arab Rep	USSR (Soviet Union)	23 Jun 62	General Trade	472UNTS43	106836
Italy	USA (United States)	06 Jul 62	Commodity Trade	459UNTS123	106617
Taiwan	Paraguay	11 Jul 62	General Trade	458UNTS41	106591
Cameroon	Greece	29 Oct 62	General Trade	538UNTS185	107815
Japan	UK Great Britain	14 Nov 62	General Trade	478UNTS29	106934
Laos	USSR (Soviet Union)	01 Dec 62	General Trade	458UNTS21	106590
UK Great Britain	USA (United States)	10 Dec 62	Mostfavored Nation	471UNTS91	106824
Brazil	Taiwan	28 Dec 62	General Trade	500UNTS61	107307
Spain	USA (United States)	31 Dec 62	Commodity Trade	471UNTS99	106825
Japan	USA (United States)	31 Dec 62	Mostfavored Nation	471UNTS83	106823
Greece	Pakistan	17 Jan 63	General Trade	538UNTS175	107814
Belgium	Luxembourg	29 Jan 63	IGO Establishment	547UNTS39	107955
Austria	Czechoslovakia	08 Mar 63	General Economic	495UNTS219	107245
Multilateral		02 Apr 63	Commodity Trade	475UNTS121	106889
Austria	Bulgaria	05 Apr 63	General Trade	480UNTS3	106963
Multilateral		30 Apr 63	General Trade	570UNTS23	108285
France	Japan	14 May 63	General Economic	518UNTS111	107493
Multilateral		09 Jun 63	General Economic	538UNTS309	107818
Dahomey	USSR (Soviet Union)	10 Jul 63	General Trade	528UNTS167	107640
Switzerland	USA (United States)	11 Jul 63	General Trade	487UNTS177	107102
Iceland	USA (United States)	15 Jul 63	General Trade	527UNTS45	107616
Austria	Mongolia	15 Jul 63	General Trade	496UNTS171	107251
Spain	USA (United States)	16 Jul 63	Commodity Trade	488UNTS77	107120
El Salvador	Japan	19 Jul 63	General Economic	518UNTS135	107494
Argentina	USA (United States)	24 Jul 63	General Trade	487UNTS183	107103
Cameroon	UK Great Britain	29 Jul 63	General Economic	478UNTS148	106935
New Zealand	USSR (Soviet Union)	01 Aug 63	General Trade	486UNTS27	107070
Multilateral		13 Aug 63	General Trade	592UNTS139	108572
Tanganyika	USSR (Soviet Union)	14 Aug 63	General Trade	493UNTS195	107215
Japan	USA (United States)	27 Aug 63	Commodity Trade	487UNTS197	107105

PARTY ONE	PARTY TWO	DATE	TOPIC	CITATION	NUMBER
Trade (Cont.)					
Japan	USA (United States)	28 Aug 63	Commodity Trade	487UNTS237	107106
Denmark	Greece	26 Sep 63	General Trade	534UNTS43	107752
Greece	Poland	30 Sep 63	General Trade	534UNTS23	107751
Jamaica	USA (United States)	01 Oct 63	Commodity Trade	488UNTS133	107124
Taiwan	USA (United States)	19 Oct 63	Commodity Trade	494UNTS27	107224
Israel	USA (United States)	22 Nov 63	Commodity Trade	494UNTS89	107228
Czechoslovakia	Romania	16 Dec 63	General Trade	527UNTS285	107630
Czechoslovakia	Hungary	20 Dec 63	General Economic	538UNTS127	107812
Philippines	USA (United States)	24 Feb 64	Commodity Trade	505UNTS283	107378
Taiwan	Peru	08 Jun 64	General Trade	548UNTS151	107976
India	IDA (Devel Assoc)	09 Jun 64	Non-IBRD Project	506UNTS31	107380
Taiwan	Ecuador	17 Jun 64	General Trade	533UNTS141	107740
Multilateral		20 Jun 64	General Economic	539UNTS3	107819
Multilateral		15 Sep 64	General Trade	510UNTS147	107411
Taiwan	Mexico	25 Sep 64	General Trade	547UNTS233	107960
Austria	Thailand	30 Sep 64	General Trade	527UNTS239	107628
Taiwan	Ecuador	23 Oct 64	General Trade	543UNTS241	107904
Taiwan	Guatemala	08 Nov 64	General Trade	543UNTS227	107903
Ireland	Vietnam, South	01 Dec 64	General Trade	553UNTS233	108091
Malta	Switzerland	20 Jan 65	General Trade	548UNTS193	107978
Australia	Philippines	16 Jun 65	General Trade	541UNTS31	107858
New Zealand	Poland	07 Jul 65	General Trade	548UNTS19	107966
Multilateral		08 Jul 65	General Trade	597UNTS3	108641
Malta	Yugoslavia	15 Jul 65	General Trade	561UNTS223	108186
Multilateral		16 Jul 65	General Trade	600UNTS49	108675
Australia	New Zealand	31 Aug 65	General Trade	554UNTS169	108101
Australia	Korea, South	21 Sep 65	General Trade	548UNTS163	107977
Australia	USSR (Soviet Union)	15 Oct 65	General Trade	553UNTS239	108092
Ireland	UK Great Britain	14 Dec 65	General Trade	565UNTS58	108235
Canada	USA (United States)	17 Dec 65	General Trade	574UNTS49	108341
UK Great Britain	USA (United States)	05 Apr 66	General Trade	592UNTS61	108569
Taiwan	Thailand	23 Nov 66	General Trade	581UNTS125	108436
Korea, South	New Zealand	31 Jan 67	General Trade	598UNTS91	108656
Trade Marks					
Belgium	Chile	11 Feb 47	Patents/Copyrights	76UNTS107	100983
Romania	USA (United States)	26 Feb 48	Admin Cooperation	48UNTS9	100738
Belgium	UK Great Britain	15 Mar 50	Patents/Copyrights	76UNTS85	100981
Belgium	Iceland	10 Dec 52	Patents/Copyrights	158UNTS445	102078
Denmark	USA (United States)	15 Oct 53	Patents/Copyrights	215UNTS111	102915
Sweden	Switzerland	25 Sep 54	Patents/Copyrights	262UNTS205	103746
Denmark	Sweden	30 Sep 54	Patents/Copyrights	262UNTS199	103745
Bulgaria	Yugoslavia	02 Nov 54	Patents/Copyrights	375UNTS333	105371
USA (United States)	Vietnam, South	22 Nov 54	Patents/Copyrights	235UNTS11	103291
Norway	Sweden	10 Jan 55	Patents/Copyrights	204UNTS293	102764
Netherlands	Vietnam, South	05 Mar 55	Patents/Copyrights	288UNTS53	104197
Brazil	Sweden	29 Apr 55	Patents/Copyrights	228UNTS115	103145
Australia	Taiwan	29 Jul 55	Patents/Copyrights	213UNTS193	102887
UK Great Britain	Vietnam, South	14 Oct 55	Patents/Copyrights	231UNTS193	103220
Multilateral		05 Jul 56	Patents/Copyrights	258UNTS371	103679
Belgium	Philippines	05 Feb 57	Patents/Copyrights	269UNTS49	103872
China People's Rep	Sweden	08 Apr 57	Patents/Copyrights	428UNTS267	106179
Multilateral		15 Jun 57	Patents/Copyrights	583UNTS3	108470
Multilateral		15 Jun 57	General Trade	550UNTS45	108008
Czechoslovakia	Germany, East	26 Jun 58	Patents/Copyrights	504UNTS221	107359
Germany, East	Hungary	12 Jan 60	Patents/Copyrights	409UNTS22	105875
Iceland	Israel	15 Jun 60	Patents/Copyrights	377UNTS261	105405
Korea, South	Netherlands	08 Dec 65	Patents/Copyrights	571UNTS83	108301
Traffic in Persons					
Multilateral		12 Nov 47	Admin Cooperation	53UNTS49	100772
Multilateral		12 Nov 47	Admin Cooperation	53UNTS13	100770
Multilateral		12 Nov 47	Admin Cooperation	53UNTS39	100771
Multilateral		04 May 49	Admin Cooperation	30UNTS23	100446
Multilateral		04 May 49	Admin Cooperation	98UNTS101	101358
Multilateral		04 May 49	Admin Cooperation	92UNTS19	101257

PARTY ONE	PARTY TWO	DATE	TOPIC	CITATION	NUMBER
Traffic in Persons (Cont.)					
Multilateral		21 Mar 50	Admin Cooperation	96UNTS271	101342
Trainees					
France	Netherlands	02 Jan 48	Visas	70UNTS105	100899
Denmark	Switzerland	21 Feb 48	Non-ILO Labor	14UNTS321	100224
France	Turkey	22 Dec 50	Non-ILO Labor	98UNTS11	101356
Transit					
Multilateral		07 Dec 44	Air Transport	84UNTS389	200252
Czechoslovakia	Poland	04 Apr 47	General Economic	85UNTS62	101146
Czechoslovakia	Poland	12 Nov 48	Land Transport	84UNTS347	101141
Multilateral		16 Jun 49	Land Transport	45UNTS149	100696
Afghanistan	USSR (Soviet Union)	28 Jun 55	General Transport	240UNTS253	103407
Multilateral		08 Jul 65	General Trade	597UNTS3	108641
Multilateral		03 Dec 65	Admin Cooperation	572UNTS105	108309
Transport					
Australia	USA (United States)	08 Mar 45	Claims and Debts	121UNTS205	200400
Poland	Yugoslavia	24 May 47	General Trade	115UNTS37	101557
Multilateral		04 May 49	Milit Occupation	138UNTS123	101864
Multilateral		16 Jun 49	Land Transport	45UNTS149	100696
Multilateral		19 Sep 49	Land Transport	125UNTS3	101671
Multilateral		13 May 50	Land Transport	128UNTS171	101719
IBRD (World Bank)	South Africa	23 Jan 51	IBRD Project	158UNTS115	102064
Netherlands	UK Great Britain	17 May 51	Air Transport	118UNTS103	101599
Multilateral		25 May 51	Status of Forces	175UNTS215	102303
Italy	UK Great Britain	24 Oct 51	Air Transport	118UNTS143	101602
Multilateral		10 Jan 52	Visas	163UNTS3	102138
Multilateral		10 Jan 52	Visas	163UNTS27	102139
Belgium	France	21 Mar 52	Land Transport	137UNTS249	101856
Australia	IBRD (World Bank)	08 Jul 52	IBRD Project	159UNTS295	102092
Multilateral		25 Oct 52	Land Transport	241UNTS336	103442
Saudi Arabia	USA (United States)	10 Nov 52	Tech Assistance	181UNTS235	102413
IBRD (World Bank)	Yugoslavia	11 Feb 53	IBRD Project	165UNTS231	102179
IBRD (World Bank)	South Africa	28 Aug 53	IBRD Project	180UNTS73	102376
Multilateral		17 Oct 53	General Transport	184UNTS42	102438
Jordan	USA (United States)	29 Jun 54	Direct Aid	237UNTS111	103339
Multilateral		12 Mar 55	Land Transport	211UNTS3	102844
Italy	Yugoslavia	31 Mar 55	Visas	386UNTS307	105550
Peru	USA (United States)	30 Apr 55	General Aid	263UNTS309	103780
IBRD (World Bank)	South Africa	28 Nov 55	IBRD Project	230UNTS101	103178
Multilateral		19 May 56	Land Transport	399UNTS189	105742
Belgium	Sweden	20 Nov 56	Taxation	281UNTS239	104081
Australia	IBRD (World Bank)	03 Dec 56	IBRD Project	288UNTS99	104200
Multilateral		14 Dec 56	Taxation	436UNTS115	106292
Multilateral		14 Dec 56	Taxation	436UNTS131	106293
Netherlands	IBRD (World Bank)	15 May 57	IBRD Project	274UNTS211	103967
Multilateral		26 Jul 57	Land Transport	386UNTS3	105535
Italy	Switzerland	19 Sep 57	Land Transport	363UNTS69	105200
IBRD (World Bank)	South Africa	01 Oct 57	IBRD Project	280UNTS285	104065
Netherlands	Sweden	23 Oct 57	Land Transport	306UNTS75	104433
Denmark	Netherlands	13 Nov 57	Land Transport	306UNTS67	104432
Multilateral		06 Jan 58	General Transport	304UNTS227	104399
Austria	Sweden	18 Feb 58	Land Transport	427UNTS349	106166
Austria	Sweden	19 Feb 58	Land Transport	427UNTS211	106155
Bulgaria	Yugoslavia	21 Mar 58	Land Transport	386UNTS119	105541
Belgium	Sweden	08 May 58	Land Transport	312UNTS145	104516
Austria	Belgium	20 Jun 58	Land Transport	312UNTS95	104513
Finland	Sweden	22 Sep 58	Water Transport	428UNTS119	106170
Multilateral		05 Nov 58	Land Transport	428UNTS73	106169
IBRD (World Bank)	South Africa	02 Dec 58	IBRD Project	324UNTS3	104676
Multilateral		15 Jan 59	Customs	348UNTS13	104996
Austria	Netherlands	06 May 59	Land Transport	485UNTS175	107055
Austria	Netherlands	06 May 59	Land Transport	485UNTS153	107054
IBRD (World Bank)	South Africa	10 Jun 59	IBRD Project	340UNTS33	104857
Greece	Yugoslavia	18 Jun 59	Land Transport	368UNTS27	105234
Italy	Netherlands	08 Dec 59	Land Transport	484UNTS309	107039

PARTY ONE	PARTY TWO	DATE	TOPIC	CITATION	NUMBER
Transport (Cont.)					
Multilateral		14 Dec 59	Land Transport	422UNTS75	106069
Belgium	IBRD (World Bank)	30 Mar 60	IBRD Project	379UNTS161	105439
Belgium	IBRD (World Bank)	30 Mar 60	IBRD Project	379UNTS129	105438
Multilateral		09 Dec 60	Customs	429UNTS211	106200
IBRD (World Bank)	South Africa	01 Dec 61	IBRD Project	425UNTS197	106125
Hungary	Yugoslavia	09 Feb 62	Land Transport	577UNTS3	108370
Germany, West	Greece	08 Mar 62	Land Transport	533UNTS269	107747
Czechoslovakia	Yugoslavia	22 Oct 62	Land Transport	480UNTS267	106974
Romania	Yugoslavia	25 Dec 63	Land Transport	576UNTS95	108366
Austria	Belgium	20 Jan 64	Land Transport	509UNTS275	107406
Austria	Romania	27 May 64	Land Transport	588UNTS29	108517
Czechoslovakia	Hungary	17 Oct 64	Land Transport	545UNTS21	107924
Greece	Yugoslavia	05 Nov 64	Land Transport	539UNTS19	107821
Multilateral		25 Nov 64	Water Transport	587UNTS19	108507
Hungary	Poland	18 Jul 65	Land Transport	577UNTS161	108376
Belgium	Denmark	04 Feb 66	Land Transport	561UNTS233	108187
Austria	Spain	24 Mar 66	Land Transport	590UNTS203	108555
Belgium	Spain	19 Jul 66	Land Transport	575UNTS3	108352
Netherlands	Yugoslavia	08 Sep 66	Land Transport	597UNTS147	108643
Treaties					
Finland	USSR (Soviet Union)	28 Oct 22	Specific Resources	67UNTS157	100874
Finland	USSR (Soviet Union)	28 Oct 22	Specific Resources	67UNTS153	100873
Finland	USSR (Soviet Union)	11 Oct 40	Territory Boundary	67UNTS139	100872
Multilateral		09 Oct 46	ILO Labor	38UNTS3	100583
Czechoslovakia	Sweden	22 Oct 46	Admin Cooperation	200UNTS31	102692
Multilateral		10 Feb 47	Peace/Disarmament	41UNTS135	100644
Multilateral		10 Feb 47	Peace/Disarmament	49UNTS3	100747
Multilateral		10 Feb 47	Peace/Disarmament	42UNTS3	100645
Multilateral		10 Feb 47	Peace/Disarmament	48UNTS203	100746
Multilateral		10 Feb 47	Peace/Disarmament	41UNTS21	100643
Czechoslovakia	Italy	25 Feb 48	Admin Cooperation	26UNTS103	100380
Romania	USA (United States)	26 Feb 48	Admin Cooperation	48UNTS9	100738
Czechoslovakia	Romania	01 Mar 48	Admin Cooperation	26UNTS109	100381
Bulgaria	Czechoslovakia	05 Mar 48	Admin Cooperation	26UNTS115	100382
Bulgaria	USA (United States)	08 Mar 48	Admin Cooperation	29UNTS101	100437
Hungary	USA (United States)	09 Mar 48	Admin Cooperation	183UNTS3	102426
Finland	UK Great Britain	12 Mar 48	Admin Cooperation	104UNTS29	101433
Hungary	UK Great Britain	12 Mar 48	Admin Cooperation	104UNTS35	101434
Romania	UK Great Britain	13 Mar 48	Admin Cooperation	104UNTS117	101436
Italy	UK Great Britain	13 Mar 48	Admin Cooperation	104UNTS41	101435
Multilateral		30 Apr 48	Dispute Settlement	30UNTS55	100449
Italy	South Africa	01 May 48	Admin Cooperation	225UNTS53	103087
Finland	South Africa	15 Nov 48	Admin Cooperation	225UNTS59	103088
Romania	South Africa	16 Nov 48	Admin Cooperation	225UNTS71	103090
Hungary	South Africa	16 Nov 48	Admin Cooperation	225UNTS65	103089
Australia	Hungary	07 Jan 49	Admin Cooperation	189UNTS233	102548
Australia	Italy	07 Jan 49	Admin Cooperation	189UNTS239	102549
Australia	Finland	07 Jan 49	Admin Cooperation	189UNTS227	102547
Australia	Romania	07 Jan 49	Admin Cooperation	189UNTS263	102550
Czechoslovakia	Hungary	27 Feb 49	Admin Cooperation	26UNTS119	100383
Italy	Netherlands	16 Aug 49	Admin Cooperation	98UNTS21	101357
Austria	Sweden	29 May 51	General Amity	197UNTS431	102650
Italy	New Zealand	20 Dec 51	Peace/Disarmament	150UNTS157	101970
Italy	UK Great Britain	21 Dec 51	Peace/Disarmament	121UNTS89	101628
Japan	USA (United States)	22 Apr 53	Admin Cooperation	178UNTS169	102341
Japan	Pakistan	24 Apr 53	Admin Cooperation	221UNTS325	103013
France	Japan	25 Apr 53	Admin Cooperation	187UNTS41	102500
Japan	UK Great Britain	27 Apr 53	Admin Cooperation	228UNTS227	103154
Australia	Japan	27 Apr 53	Admin Cooperation	193UNTS78	102612
Japan	USA (United States)	14 Sep 57	Admin Cooperation	293UNTS247	104293
Treatment of Offenders					
Brazil	United Nations	04 Aug 52	Tech Assistance	135UNTS185	101820

PARTY ONE	PARTY TWO	DATE	TOPIC	CITATION	NUMBER
Trust Territories					
Multilateral		13 Dec 46	Trusteeship	8UNTS91	100116
Multilateral		13 Dec 46	Trusteeship	8UNTS71	100115
Multilateral		13 Dec 46	Trusteeship	8UNTS119	100118
Multilateral		13 Dec 46	Trusteeship	8UNTS105	100117
Multilateral		13 Dec 46	Trusteeship	8UNTS151	100120
Multilateral		13 Dec 46	Trusteeship	8UNTS135	100119
Multilateral		13 Dec 46	Trusteeship	8UNTS181	100122
Multilateral		13 Dec 46	Trusteeship	8UNTS165	100121
Multilateral		06 Feb 47	IGO Establishment	97UNTS227	101352
Multilateral		02 Apr 47	Trusteeship	8UNTS189	100123
Multilateral		19 Jun 47	ILO Labor	171UNTS329	102235
Multilateral		01 Nov 47	Trusteeship	10UNTS3	100138
Multilateral		02 Dec 50	Trusteeship	118UNTS255	200381
Multilateral		25 Jun 51	Tech Assistance	92UNTS27	101258
UK Great Britain	USA (United States)	13 Jul 51	Tech Assistance	105UNTS71	101454
WHO (World Health)	UK Great Britain	07 Feb 52	Tech Assistance	121UNTS75	101627
Multilateral		31 May 54	Tech Assistance	192UNTS20	102592
UNESCO (Educ/Cult)	UK Great Britain	09 Aug 56	Direct Aid	256UNTS139	103624
Tuberculosis					
El Salvador	WHO (World Health)	21 Apr 50	Sanitation	103UNTS13	101420
Burma	WHO (World Health)	09 Jul 51	Sanitation	104UNTS187	101440
Denmark	WHO (World Health)	30 Nov 51	Scientific Project	118UNTS3	101592
India	WHO (World Health)	11 Dec 52	Sanitation	158UNTS391	102073
Denmark	WHO (World Health)	03 Sep 56	Sanitation	258UNTS103	103674
Tunnels					
France	Italy	14 Mar 53	Land Transport	284UNTS221	104140
Italy	Switzerland	23 May 58	Land Transport	363UNTS81	105201
France	UK Great Britain	03 Jun 64	Scientific Project	539UNTS253	107836
Unemployment Insurance					
Multilateral		28 Nov 19	ILO Labor	38UNTS41	100585
Multilateral		09 Jul 20	ILO Labor	38UNTS119	100591
Multilateral		23 Jun 34	ILO Labor	40UNTS45	100626
Canada	USA (United States)	12 Mar 42	Non-ILO Labor	119UNTS295	200386
Belgium	France	17 Jan 48	Non-ILO Labor	36UNTS233	100570
Belgium	Luxembourg	03 Dec 49	Non-ILO Labor	91UNTS31	101241
Denmark	Norway	18 Jan 51	Non-ILO Labor	82UNTS153	101090
Canada	USA (United States)	11 Sep 51	Non-ILO Labor	206UNTS311	102793
Germany, West	Netherlands	29 Oct 54	Non-ILO Labor	237UNTS3	103335
Canada	USA (United States)	23 Apr 56	Non-ILO Labor	300UNTS29	104329
Finland	Norway	21 Jan 59	Non-ILO Labor	325UNTS295	104705
Multilateral		08 Sep 59	Non-ILO Labor	383UNTS203	105502
Universal Postal Union					
South Africa	UK Great Britain	24 Aug 46	Telecommunications	51UNTS187	100765
United Nations	UPU (Postal Union)	15 Nov 47	IGO Operations	19UNTS219	200116
Multilateral		21 Nov 47	IGO Status/Immunit	33UNTS261	100521
Multilateral		11 Jul 52	Postal Service	171UNTS89	102225
Multilateral		11 Jul 52	Postal Service	170UNTS269	102223
Multilateral		11 Jul 52	IGO Establishment	169UNTS3	102220
Multilateral		11 Jul 52	Postal Service	170UNTS63	102222
Multilateral		11 Jul 52	Postal Service	170UNTS3	102221
Multilateral		11 Jul 52	Postal Service	171UNTS3	102224
Multilateral		11 Jul 52	Postal Service	171UNTS191	102227
Multilateral		11 Jul 52	Postal Service	171UNTS143	102226
Multilateral		08 Jun 56	Tech Assistance	247UNTS366	200541
Multilateral		12 Jun 56	Tech Assistance	243UNTS187	103453
Multilateral		31 Aug 56	Tech Assistance	249UNTS158	103506
Multilateral		01 Mar 57	Tech Assistance	264UNTS94	103790
Multilateral		09 Apr 57	Tech Assistance	274UNTS172	103965
Multilateral		24 May 57	Tech Assistance	268UNTS270	103861
Multilateral		30 Jun 57	Tech Assistance	286UNTS171	104165
Multilateral		09 Jul 57	Tech Assistance	274UNTS300	103972
Multilateral		03 Oct 57	Postal Service	366UNTS141	105217
Universal Postal Union (Cont.)					
Multilateral		03 Oct 57	Postal Service	366UNTS3	105215
Multilateral		03 Oct 57	Postal Service	365UNTS207	105214
Multilateral		03 Oct 57	Postal Service	366UNTS193	105218
Multilateral		03 Oct 57	Postal Service	366UNTS87	105216
Multilateral		03 Oct 57	Postal Service	366UNTS255	105219
Multilateral		03 Oct 57	Postal Service	364UNTS3	105211
Multilateral		03 Oct 57	Postal Service	364UNTS331	105212
Multilateral		03 Oct 57	Postal Service	365UNTS3	105213
Multilateral		19 Jun 58	Tech Assistance	306UNTS236	200550
Multilateral		04 Jun 60	Tech Assistance	360UNTS208	105159
Multilateral		19 Jun 60	IGO Operations	537UNTS214	107803
Multilateral		28 Jan 61	Tech Assistance	387UNTS202	105563
Multilateral		18 Apr 62	Tech Assistance	463UNTS44	106692
Multilateral		29 Aug 62	Tech Assistance	443UNTS280	106366
Multilateral		15 Nov 62	Tech Assistance	448UNTS50	106424
Multilateral		06 Dec 62	Tech Assistance	450UNTS240	106471
Multilateral		12 Dec 62	Tech Assistance	457UNTS72	106578
Multilateral		05 Feb 63	Tech Assistance	453UNTS36	106518
Multilateral		14 Feb 63	Tech Assistance	453UNTS168	106524
Multilateral		06 Mar 63	Tech Assistance	455UNTS386	106552
Multilateral		18 Apr 63	Tech Assistance	463UNTS121	106697
Multilateral		06 May 63	Tech Assistance	463UNTS78	106694
Multilateral		09 May 63	Tech Assistance	463UNTS159	106700
Multilateral		22 May 63	Tech Assistance	483UNTS72	107007
Multilateral		24 May 63	Tech Assistance	466UNTS346	106754
Multilateral		24 May 63	Tech Assistance	470UNTS208	106810
Multilateral		23 Jul 63	Tech Assistance	471UNTS158	106831
Multilateral		31 Jul 63	Tech Assistance	472UNTS220	106842
Multilateral		27 Aug 63	Tech Assistance	511UNTS210	107435
Multilateral		10 Sep 63	Tech Assistance	480UNTS100	106965
Multilateral		30 Oct 63	Tech Assistance	480UNTS180	106968
Multilateral		07 Nov 63	Tech Assistance	480UNTS232	106971
Multilateral		08 Nov 63	Tech Assistance	482UNTS286	106999
Multilateral		28 Jan 64	Tech Assistance	502UNTS321	107336
Multilateral		20 Feb 64	Tech Assistance	491UNTS30	107172
Multilateral		23 Jun 64	Tech Assistance	506UNTS108	107383
Multilateral		28 Jun 64	Tech Assistance	519UNTS14	107499
Multilateral		03 Aug 64	Tech Assistance	503UNTS239	107347
Multilateral		24 Oct 64	Tech Assistance	514UNTS220	200608
Multilateral		11 Nov 64	Tech Assistance	515UNTS94	107456
Multilateral		15 Dec 64	Tech Assistance	522UNTS20	107533
Multilateral		02 Feb 65	Tech Assistance	523UNTS256	107560
Multilateral		23 Feb 65	IGO Operations	527UNTS120	107622
Multilateral		05 Mar 65	IGO Operations	527UNTS221	107627
Multilateral		08 Apr 65	IGO Operations	533UNTS66	107733
Multilateral		26 Apr 65	IGO Operations	533UNTS50	107732
Multilateral		12 May 65	IGO Operations	534UNTS390	107769
Multilateral		14 May 65	IGO Operations	550UNTS310	108026
Multilateral		25 May 65	IGO Operations	535UNTS374	107791
Multilateral		02 Jun 65	Tech Assistance	537UNTS348	200611
Multilateral		02 Jun 65	Tech Assistance	551UNTS2	108030
Multilateral		05 Jul 65	General Aid	563UNTS104	108207
Multilateral		20 Jul 65	IGO Operations	541UNTS12	107857
Multilateral		13 Sep 65	IGO Operations	547UNTS248	107961
Multilateral		13 Sep 65	Tech Assistance	547UNTS264	107962
Multilateral		21 Sep 65	IGO Operations	547UNTS280	107963
Multilateral		21 Oct 65	Tech Assistance	547UNTS216	107959
Multilateral		12 Nov 65	IGO Operations	550UNTS160	108013
Multilateral		31 Dec 65	Recognition	552UNTS292	108060
Multilateral		12 May 66	General Aid	563UNTS54	108204
Multilateral		06 Aug 66	Tech Assistance	570UNTS178	108294
Multilateral		22 Aug 66	Tech Assistance	571UNTS298	200624
UN Special Fund	UPU (Postal Union)	21 Sep 66	Non-IBRD Project	573UNTS259	200626
Multilateral		23 Sep 66	General Aid	573UNTS148	108328
Multilateral		23 Sep 66	IGO Operations	573UNTS132	108327

PARTY ONE	PARTY TWO	DATE	TOPIC	CITATION	NUMBER
Universal Postal Union (Cont.)					
Multilateral		30 Sep 66	IGO Operations	576UNTS8	108361
Multilateral		17 Nov 66	IGO Operations	580UNTS22	108417
Multilateral		25 Jan 67	IGO Operations	588UNTS212	108527
Multilateral		27 Feb 67	IGO Operations	590UNTS156	108552
Multilateral		03 Mar 67	Tech Assistance	594UNTS96	108597
Multilateral		13 Apr 67	IGO Operations	595UNTS60	108612
Multilateral		19 Apr 67	Tech Assistance	595UNTS120	108617
Multilateral		21 Jun 67	Tech Assistance	598UNTS2	108653
Uranium					
Norway	IAEA (Atom Energy)	10 Apr 61	Scientific Project	402UNTS255	105790
Multilateral		10 Apr 61	Atomic Energy	402UNTS281	105791
IAEA (Atom Energy)	Yugoslavia	04 Oct 61	Scientific Project	412UNTS226	105935
Multilateral		04 Oct 61	Scientific Project	412UNTS210	105934
Multilateral		05 Mar 62	Scientific Project	425UNTS3	106114
Multilateral		27 Jun 62	Atomic Energy	463UNTS17	106690
Japan	UK Great Britain	04 Sep 62	Taxation	475UNTS31	106888
Pakistan	UK Great Britain	13 Mar 63	Atomic Energy	482UNTS347	107003
Multilateral		18 Dec 63	Atomic Energy	490UNTS383	107166
Multilateral		08 Apr 64	Loans and Credits	501UNTS221	107320
Venereal Disease					
Guatemala	WHO (World Health)	29 Dec 51	Sanitation	124UNTS89	101668
India	WHO (World Health)	14 Apr 52	Tech Assistance	131UNTS265	101746
Veterinary Matters					
Belgium	Netherlands	20 Aug 49	Visas	46UNTS133	100706
Bulgaria	Poland	26 Sep 49	Sanitation	260UNTS249	103712
Hungary	Poland	29 Oct 49	Sanitation	260UNTS113	103706
Italy	Switzerland	02 Jul 53	Customs	257UNTS99	103653
Ireland	UK Great Britain	06 Apr 54	Sanitation	553UNTS197	108088
Ireland	USA (United States)	17 Jun 54	Direct Aid	241UNTS173	103432
Italy	Yugoslavia	26 Mar 55	Sanitation	379UNTS3	105432
Bulgaria	Yugoslavia	17 Jun 55	Sanitation	375UNTS287	105370
Czechoslovakia	Germany, East	30 Aug 55	Sanitation	504UNTS279	107361
Italy	Switzerland	02 Feb 56	Sanitation	291UNTS113	104247
Austria	Yugoslavia	15 Jun 56	Sanitation	396UNTS117	105695
Romania	Yugoslavia	04 Aug 56	Sanitation	395UNTS99	105682
Germany, East	Romania	08 Dec 56	Sanitation	362UNTS189	105188
Hungary	Yugoslavia	25 May 57	Sanitation	477UNTS219	106924
Bulgaria	Czechoslovakia	03 Jun 57	Sanitation	292UNTS3	104261
Czechoslovakia	Yugoslavia	11 Jun 57	Sanitation	504UNTS107	107355
Germany, East	Hungary	13 Nov 57	Sanitation	407UNTS216	105866
Czechoslovakia	Hungary	12 Mar 58	Sanitation	408UNTS178	105870
Bulgaria	Hungary	13 Mar 58	Sanitation	438UNTS173	106316
Bulgaria	Hungary	13 Mar 58	Sanitation	438UNTS191	106317
Germany, West	Netherlands	16 Apr 58	Sanitation	486UNTS331	107084
Italy	Netherlands	01 Dec 59	Sanitation	455UNTS241	106545
Multilateral		14 Dec 59	Sanitation	422UNTS57	106068
Poland	Yugoslavia	05 May 60	Sanitation	423UNTS229	106095
Czechoslovakia	Poland	14 Nov 60	Sanitation	413UNTS4	105938
Belgium	Yugoslavia	31 Oct 61	Sanitation	426UNTS165	106136
Argentina	Japan	20 Dec 61	Sanitation	451UNTS77	106486
Belgium	Romania	12 Oct 62	Sanitation	502UNTS31	107325
Cuba	Czechoslovakia	03 Jun 64	Sanitation	527UNTS205	107626
Czechoslovakia	Mongolia	21 Oct 64	Sanitation	545UNTS91	107926
Austria	Hungary	11 Nov 64	Sanitation	576UNTS163	108368
Ecuador	Netherlands	14 Jan 65	Health/Educ/Welfare	551UNTS129	108038
Austria	Bulgaria	12 Jul 65	Sanitation	587UNTS51	108510
Netherlands	Nigeria	28 Oct 65	Scientific Project	578UNTS15	108383
Vital Statistics					
Multilateral		24 Jul 48	Sanitation	66UNTS25	100847
Multilateral		18 Jul 51	Direct Aid	102UNTS291	200308
Multilateral		21 Aug 52	Tech Assistance	141UNTS129	101912
Ethiopia	United Nations	14 Jun 61	Direct Aid	406UNTS81	105840
Ghana	United Nations	29 Aug 61	Tech Assistance	406UNTS117	105843

PARTY ONE	PARTY TWO	DATE	TOPIC	CITATION	NUMBER
Vital Statistics (Cont.)					
East Afri Service	United Nations	27 Nov 65	Health/Educ/Welfare	550UNTS375	200616
Vocational Education					
Brazil	USA (United States)	05 Apr 46	Education	12UNTS131	100183
India	Netherlands	16 Jan 59	Tech Assistance	506UNTS153	107386
Brazil	Japan	28 Mar 62	Education	451UNTS125	106489
United Nations	South Pacific Com	24 Jan 63	Tech Assistance	470UNTS361	200604
United Nations	South Pacific Com	20 Feb 63	Tech Assistance	453UNTS333	200600
Italy	ILO (Labor Org)	24 Oct 64	IGO Establishment	541UNTS217	107871
Netherlands	Pakistan	30 Oct 64	Tech Assistance	541UNTS243	107873
Chile	IBRD (World Bank)	06 Oct 65	IBRD Project	567UNTS293	108261
IBRD (World Bank)	Thailand	19 Oct 66	IBRD Project	594UNTS347	108609
Wages					
Multilateral		16 Jun 28	ILO Labor	39UNTS3	100609
Multilateral		20 Jun 38	ILO Labor	40UNTS255	100638
War Cemetaries and Graves					
Multilateral		01 Jan 46	Peace/Disarmament	99UNTS131	101375
Romania	USA (United States)	28 Jun 46	Other Military	148UNTS355	101944
Hungary	USA (United States)	09 Aug 46	Other Military	148UNTS313	101941
Italy	USA (United States)	24 Sep 46	Other Military	148UNTS323	101942
Netherlands	USA (United States)	11 Apr 47	Other Military	148UNTS343	101943
Belgium	USA (United States)	23 Jul 47	Other Military	33UNTS33	100512
France	USA (United States)	01 Oct 47	Other Military	148UNTS303	101940
Burma	UK Great Britain	17 Oct 47	Recognition	70UNTS183	100904
Czechoslovakia	UK Great Britain	03 Mar 49	Other Military	83UNTS95	101104
Luxembourg	USA (United States)	20 Mar 51	Other Military	180UNTS283	102392
Multilateral		10 Jul 51	Other Military	108UNTS287	101481
Multilateral		29 Jul 51	Other Military	117UNTS85	101585
Netherlands	USA (United States)	26 Sep 51	Milit Installation	158UNTS469	102080
Multilateral		31 Oct 51	Other Military	172UNTS193	102247
Multilateral		08 Jun 52	Other Military	210UNTS317	102843
India	Italy	27 Aug 53	Other Military	275UNTS279	103987
Multilateral		27 Aug 53	Other Military	213UNTS137	102884
Australia	Italy	27 Aug 53	Other Military	225UNTS47	103086
Italy	South Africa	27 Aug 53	Other Military	212UNTS211	102873
Multilateral		18 Feb 54	Other Military	226UNTS297	103124
Multilateral		22 Feb 54	Other Military	188UNTS273	102531
UK Great Britain	USA (United States)	21 Jun 54	Other Military	209UNTS61	102821
Multilateral		24 Aug 54	Other Military	247UNTS213	103471
Germany, West	Netherlands	11 Oct 54	Other Military	291UNTS9	104241
France	USA (United States)	01 Jul 55	Other Military	270UNTS19	103888
Multilateral		21 Sep 55	Other Military	269UNTS241	103885
Germany, West	New Zealand	05 Mar 56	Other Military	402UNTS103	105779
Multilateral		05 Mar 56	Other Military	326UNTS169	104711
Multilateral		05 Mar 56	Other Military	326UNTS181	104712
France	USA (United States)	19 Mar 56	Other Military	275UNTS37	103974
Canada	France	04 Sep 56	Other Military	305UNTS79	104415
Multilateral		26 Jun 57	ILO Labor	328UNTS247	104738
Germany, West	UK Great Britain	16 Oct 59	Other Military	385UNTS21	105526
Korea, South	United Nations	06 Nov 59	Other Military	346UNTS289	200565
Belgium	USA (United States)	27 Nov 59	Other Military	366UNTS331	105221
Italy	Yugoslavia	12 Feb 60	Other Military	379UNTS77	105434
Germany, West	Netherlands	08 Apr 60	Territory Boundary	508UNTS14	107404
Multilateral		10 Sep 62	Other Military	502UNTS3	107323
Denmark	Germany, West	03 Oct 62	Other Military	450UNTS291	106475
Netherlands	UK Great Britain	27 Aug 63	Other Military	490UNTS3	107150
Germany, West	Greece	26 Sep 63	Other Military	550UNTS203	108017
Germany, West	Ireland	13 May 64	Other Military	553UNTS87	108071
Greece	UK Great Britain	12 Oct 66	Other Military	578UNTS33	108385
War Damages					
Canada	USA (United States)	26 May 43	Privil/Immunities	7UNTS345	200043
UK Great Britain	USA (United States)	28 Mar 44	Status of Forces	15UNTS413	200104
Belgium	UK Great Britain	25 Jun 45	Reparations	90UNTS307	200268
Belgium	France	30 Oct 45	Reparations	19UNTS87	100306

PARTY ONE	PARTY TWO	DATE	TOPIC	CITATION	NUMBER
War Damages (Cont.)					
Czechoslovakia	Poland	12 Feb 46	Reparations	25UNTS207	100364
Canada	UK Great Britain	06 Mar 46	Reparations	20UNTS3	100311
Hungary	Yugoslavia	11 May 46	Reparations	129UNTS3	101725
France	USA (United States)	28 May 46	General Trade	84UNTS151	101125
Canada	USA (United States)	15 Nov 46	Specif Claim/Waive	7UNTS141	100096
France	UK Great Britain	03 Dec 46	Reparations	54UNTS127	100799
Canada	Netherlands	30 Dec 46	Reparations	230UNTS205	103185
UK Great Britain	USA (United States)	23 Jan 47	Status of Forces	15UNTS281	100244
Belgium	Czechoslovakia	19 Mar 47	Claims and Debts	23UNTS35	100341
Canada	France	05 May 47	Reparations	231UNTS81	103208
Austria	USA (United States)	21 Jun 47	Milit Occupation	67UNTS99	100869
Austria	USA (United States)	21 Jun 47	Reparations	67UNTS89	100868
Czechoslovakia	USA (United States)	25 Jul 47	Reparations	90UNTS19	101223
Taiwan	Italy	30 Jul 47	Reparations	12UNTS377	100194
Italy	USA (United States)	14 Aug 47	Reparations	36UNTS53	100566
Netherlands	UK Great Britain	08 Oct 47	Reparations	252UNTS19	103556
Italy	USA (United States)	14 Feb 48	Reparations	67UNTS115	100871
Belgium	UK Great Britain	07 Jun 48	Reparations	20UNTS33	100313
USA (United States)	Yugoslavia	19 Jul 48	Claims and Debts	89UNTS43	101208
Philippines	USA (United States)	27 Aug 48	Reparations	44UNTS13	100675
Japan	USA (United States)	14 Apr 49	Specif Claim/Waive	89UNTS141	101215
United Arab Rep	UK Great Britain	17 Apr 49	Reparations	83UNTS183	101107
Canada	Netherlands	09 May 49	Reparations	46UNTS263	100715
Finland	USA (United States)	01 Nov 49	Claims and Debts	68UNTS11	100880
Belgium	Canada	16 Nov 49	Reparations	51UNTS3	100748
France	UK Great Britain	23 Jan 50	Reparations	97UNTS149	101348
Belgium	USA (United States)	16 Mar 51	Reparations	93UNTS109	101295
Belgium	Netherlands	14 Jun 51	Reparations	101UNTS3	101397
Australia	France	28 Sep 51	Reparations	161UNTS185	102128
Denmark	Netherlands	08 May 52	Reparations	131UNTS91	101737
Belgium	Luxembourg	26 Sep 52	Reparations	141UNTS111	101910
Belgium	France	11 Mar 53	Reparations	191UNTS329	102590
Germany, West	USA (United States)	30 Mar 53	Reparations	235UNTS285	103310
Italy	UK Great Britain	13 Apr 53	Reparations	172UNTS271	102251
France	Netherlands	27 Nov 53	Reparations	302UNTS245	104363
Luxembourg	UK Great Britain	18 Jun 54	Reparations	192UNTS33	102593
France	Netherlands	15 Dec 54	Reparations	288UNTS37	104195
Luxembourg	USA (United States)	15 Jun 55	Reparations	264UNTS279	103798
Belgium	Switzerland	05 Jan 56	Reparations	228UNTS159	103149
Luxembourg	Netherlands	06 Feb 56	Reparations	261UNTS17	103723
Japan	Spain	08 Jan 57	Claims and Debts	318UNTS221	104615
Italy	USA (United States)	29 Mar 57	Reparations	299UNTS157	104311
Netherlands	Norway	30 Jun 58	Reparations	346UNTS217	104982
San Marino	UK Great Britain	22 Jul 61	Reparations	420UNTS3	106035
War Pensions					
France	Poland	11 Feb 47	Reparations	12UNTS287	100189
War Victims					
Multilateral		12 Aug 49	General Military	75UNTS135	100972
Multilateral		12 Aug 49	Humanitarian	75UNTS85	100971
Multilateral		12 Aug 49	Humanitarian	75UNTS31	100970
Multilateral		12 Aug 49	Humanitarian	75UNTS287	100973
Multilateral		17 Dec 62	Sanitation	486UNTS119	107076
War Wounded					
Multilateral		12 Aug 49	Humanitarian	75UNTS85	100971
Multilateral		12 Aug 49	Humanitarian	75UNTS31	100970
Multilateral		13 Dec 55	Humanitarian	250UNTS3	103514
Water Resources					
Canada	USA (United States)	10 Nov 41	Specific Resources	23UNTS275	200134
Canada	USA (United States)	27 Nov 41	Specific Resources	103UNTS193	200314
Canada	USA (United States)	03 Mar 44	Specific Resources	109UNTS191	200359
United Arab Rep	UK Great Britain	10 Dec 46	Specif Claim/Waive	105UNTS15	101451
United Arab Rep	UK Great Britain	31 May 49	Specific Resources	226UNTS273	103122
Canada	USA (United States)	27 Feb 50	Specific Resources	132UNTS223	101762

PARTY ONE	PARTY TWO	DATE	TOPIC	CITATION	NUMBER
Water Resources (Cont.)					
United Arab Rep	UK Great Britain	20 Mar 50	Tech Assistance	226UNTS287	103123
Lebanon	USA (United States)	24 Feb 51	Tech Assistance	223UNTS121	103060
Iraq	USA (United States)	21 May 52	Tech Assistance	212UNTS183	102870
Ethiopia	USA (United States)	24 Jun 52	Tech Assistance	181UNTS215	102411
Canada	USA (United States)	30 Jun 52	Water Transport	234UNTS199	103283
United Arab Rep	UK Great Britain	05 Jan 53	Specific Property	207UNTS277	102810
Portugal	UK Great Britain	21 Jan 53	Non-IBRD Project	175UNTS13	102293
Jordan	Syria	04 Jun 53	Specific Resources	184UNTS15	102437
Chile	USA (United States)	27 Jun 53	Tech Assistance	229UNTS193	103167
Chile	USA (United States)	27 Jun 53	Tech Assistance	229UNTS53	103160
Canada	USA (United States)	12 Nov 53	IGO Establishment	234UNTS97	103274
Czechoslovakia	Hungary	16 Apr 54	Specific Resources	504UNTS231	107360
Austria	Yugoslavia	25 May 54	Specific Resources	227UNTS111	103135
Austria	Yugoslavia	27 Nov 54	Specific Resources	396UNTS75	105694
Italy	Switzerland	17 Sep 55	Specific Resources	291UNTS213	104257
Multilateral		24 Feb 56	Specific Resources	243UNTS147	103451
Austria	Hungary	09 Apr 56	Specific Resources	438UNTS123	106315
Norway	IBRD (World Bank)	03 May 56	IBRD Project	243UNTS281	103455
Norway	USSR (Soviet Union)	18 Dec 57	Specific Resources	312UNTS257	104522
Czechoslovakia	Poland	21 Mar 58	Specific Resources	538UNTS89	107811
Bulgaria	Yugoslavia	04 Apr 58	Water Transport	367UNTS89	105228
Multilateral		29 Apr 59	Specific Property	346UNTS167	104980
Finland	USSR (Soviet Union)	29 Apr 59	Specif Claim/Waive	346UNTS209	104981
Colombia	IBRD (World Bank)	20 May 59	IBRD Project	344UNTS251	104953
Greece	Yugoslavia	18 Jun 59	Specific Resources	363UNTS133	105205
Sudan	United Arab Rep	08 Nov 59	Specific Resources	453UNTS51	106519
United Arab Rep	USSR (Soviet Union)	27 Aug 60	Tech Assistance	399UNTS37	105733
Multilateral		19 Sep 60	IBRD Project	444UNTS259	106371
Pakistan	IBRD (World Bank)	19 Sep 60	IBRD Project	444UNTS207	106370
Multilateral		19 Sep 60	IBRD Project	419UNTS125	106032
Canada	USA (United States)	17 Jan 61	Specific Resources	542UNTS224	107894
Jordan	IDA (Devel Assoc)	22 Dec 61	Non-IBRD Project	448UNTS21	106423
Iceland	IBRD (World Bank)	14 Feb 62	IBRD Project	447UNTS95	106413
Nicaragua	IDA (Devel Assoc)	07 Sep 62	Non-IBRD Project	478UNTS313	106940
Pakistan	IDA (Devel Assoc)	16 Aug 63	Non-IBRD Project	492UNTS205	107192
Pakistan	IDA (Devel Assoc)	16 Aug 63	Non-IBRD Project	492UNTS171	107191
Romania	Yugoslavia	30 Nov 63	Specific Property	512UNTS2	107438
Jordan	IDA (Devel Assoc)	12 Dec 63	Non-IBRD Project	506UNTS51	107381
Poland	USSR (Soviet Union)	17 Jul 64	Specific Resources	552UNTS175	108054
Pakistan	IDA (Devel Assoc)	21 Jul 64	Non-IBRD Project	534UNTS373	107768
Philippines	IBRD (World Bank)	22 Jul 64	IBRD Project	516UNTS171	107476
Malaysia	IBRD (World Bank)	26 Feb 65	IBRD Project	549UNTS239	108002
Burundi	IDA (Devel Assoc)	31 Mar 66	Loans and Credits	569UNTS3	108277
IBRD (World Bank)	Venezuela	21 Apr 66	IBRD Project	568UNTS257	108273
Water Rights					
Canada	USA (United States)	10 Nov 41	Specific Resources	23UNTS275	200134
Mexico	USA (United States)	03 Feb 44	Specific Resources	3UNTS313	200025
Iraq	Turkey	29 Mar 46	General Amity	37UNTS226	100580
Afghanistan	USSR (Soviet Union)	13 Jun 46	Territory Boundary	31UNTS147	100476
Multilateral		10 Feb 47	Peace/Disarmament	49UNTS3	100747
UK Great Britain	USA (United States)	23 Oct 47	Territory Boundary	66UNTS277	100859
India	Pakistan	04 May 48	Dispute Settlement	54UNTS45	100794
Finland	Norway	13 Jun 49	Commodity Trade	34UNTS9	100523
Belgium	Netherlands	17 Feb 50	Water Transport	51UNTS101	100756
Multilateral		08 Apr 50	IGO Establishment	66UNTS285	100860
Norway	Sweden	20 Dec 50	Specific Resources	92UNTS3	101256
Ethiopia	USA (United States)	24 Jun 52	Tech Assistance	181UNTS215	102411
Weights and Measures					
Multilateral		12 Oct 55	IGO Establishment	560UNTS3	108165
Whaling					
Multilateral		02 Dec 46	Specific Resources	161UNTS72	102124
Netherlands	Norway	28 Jan 47	General Trade	31UNTS29	100467
Multilateral		03 Mar 47	Humanitarian	11UNTS43	100148
Multilateral		23 Mar 49	Commodity Trade	203UNTS179	102746

PARTY ONE	PARTY TWO	DATE	TOPIC	CITATION	NUMBER
Whaling (Cont.)					
Multilateral		25 Apr 56	Commodity Trade	270UNTS103	103896
Multilateral		06 Jun 62	Privil/Immunities	486UNTS271	107081
Multilateral		06 Jun 62	Privil/Immunities	486UNTS263	107080
Japan	UK Great Britain	06 Jan 64	Specific Resources	502UNTS183	107329
Wheat					
Multilateral		22 Apr 42	Commodity Trade	8UNTS237	200044
Multilateral		03 Jun 46	Commodity Trade	7UNTS331	100109
Canada	Hungary	08 Mar 56	Commodity Trade	305UNTS27	104409
Multilateral		25 Apr 56	Commodity Trade	270UNTS103	103896
Multilateral		06 Apr 59	Commodity Trade	349UNTS167	105013
USA (United States)	Yemen	30 Jun 59	Direct Aid	357UNTS137	105112
Cyprus	USA (United States)	08 Dec 60	Direct Aid	405UNTS145	105831
Cyprus	USA (United States)	15 Jan 62	Commodity Trade	435UNTS15	106267
Multilateral		07 Mar 62	Commodity Trade	445UNTS205	106389
Multilateral		15 May 62	Commodity Trade	444UNTS3	106367
Canada	Poland	05 Nov 63	Commodity Trade	529UNTS81	107658
Whooping Cough					
Colombia	WHO (World Health)	05 Jan 51	Sanitation	102UNTS139	101417
Chile	WHO (World Health)	31 May 52	Sanitation	136UNTS323	101841
Wine					
Germany, West	Greece	16 Mar 49	General Trade	77UNTS307	101006
Women					
Multilateral		29 Nov 19	ILO Labor	38UNTS53	100586
Multilateral		19 Jun 34	ILO Labor	40UNTS3	100623
Multilateral		21 Jun 35	ILO Labor	40UNTS63	100627

PARTY ONE	PARTY TWO	DATE	TOPIC	CITATION	NUMBER
Women (Cont.)					
Belgium	France	09 Jan 47	Admin Cooperation	36UNTS145	100568
Multilateral		09 Jul 48	ILO Labor	81UNTS147	101070
Wool					
Canada	UK Great Britain	06 Mar 46	Reparations	20UNTS3	100311
Austria	UK Great Britain	23 Dec 46	General Aid	88UNTS93	101186
France	New Zealand	02 Jul 47	Commodity Trade	16UNTS219	100263
Czechoslovakia	New Zealand	22 Jan 48	Commodity Trade	16UNTS229	100264
Australia	Poland	03 Jun 48	Direct Aid	16UNTS189	100258
Australia	Greece	01 Jul 48	Direct Aid	22UNTS33	100329
Australia	Hungary	01 Jul 48	Direct Aid	22UNTS3	100325
Australia	Yugoslavia	09 Jul 48	Direct Aid	22UNTS17	100327
Australia	Austria	19 Jul 48	Direct Aid	22UNTS25	100328
Workmen's Compensation					
Multilateral		12 Nov 21	ILO Labor	38UNTS165	100595
Multilateral		05 Jun 25	ILO Labor	38UNTS257	100602
Multilateral		10 Jun 25	ILO Labor	38UNTS229	100600
Multilateral		10 Jun 25	ILO Labor	38UNTS243	100601
Multilateral		21 Jun 34	ILO Labor	40UNTS19	100624
Belgium	Luxembourg	03 Dec 49	Non-ILO Labor	91UNTS31	101241
France	UK Great Britain	28 Jan 50	Non-ILO Labor	97UNTS155	101349
Yaws					
Haiti	WHO (World Health)	21 Jun 50	Sanitation	103UNTS61	101424
Zinc					
Czechoslovakia	Poland	04 Apr 47	General Economic	85UNTS62	101146